BBC
English
Dictionary

BBC English

HarperCollins Publishers

BBC English
Bush House
The Strand
London WC2B 4PH

HarperCollins Publishers
77-85 Fulham Palace Road
Hammersmith
London W6 8JB

10   9   8   7   6   5   4   3   2   1

ISBN (HarperCollins)   0 00 370554 4
ISBN (BBC English)   1 85497 269 3

Computer typeset by
Morton Word Processing Ltd, Scarborough
Printed and bound in Great Britain by
Clays Ltd, St Ives plc

Note: Entered words that we have reason to believe constitute
trademarks have been designated as such. However, neither the
presence nor absence of such designation should be regarded as
affecting the legal status of any trademark.

The encyclopedic entries have been monitored and updated until
immediately prior to publication, May 1992. Whilst every effort has
been made to make them as accurate as possible, no warranty of
accuracy is made or implied by the publishers. The publishers shall
have neither liability nor responsibility to any person or entity with
respect to loss or damages in connection with or arising from the
information contained in this dictionary.

輸入　日本総代理店
株式会社　秀文インターナショナル
東京都豊島区駒込 4 −12− 7
◆原著作権者の書面による許諾なく，無断引用，転載，複製などは禁じます．

Contents

BBC World Service

From BBC English
Julian Amey (Executive Director)
Douglas Cooksey (Head of Product Development)
Hamish Norbrook (Editorial Co-ordinator)
Adrian Stenton (Editorial Consultant)

Katie Elvin (Secretarial support)

The encyclopedic entries for the dictionary were monitored with the help of BBC World Service Staff:

From World Service News
Bob Jobbins (Editor), Peter Brooks, Susannah Ross, James Morgan

Newsroom validation by Anthony Rudolf

From English Services
Elizabeth Smith (Controller), Anthony Rendell, Ernest Warburton, Alastair Lack, Mary Raine; Religion, Drama and Sports Units, Topical Tapes and Caribbean Service

From Current Affairs Research and Information Section
Stephen Dalziel (Organiser)

From World Service Information Services
Maggie Smales (Manager)

From European Services
Andrew Taussig (Controller), Benny Ammar, Chris Pszenicki; Central European Service (Czechoslovak, Finnish, Hungarian and Polish Sections), French and Portuguese Language Service, German Language Service, Italian and Spanish Units, South East European Service (Bulgarian, Greek, Romanian and Turkish Sections), South Slavonic Section (Croatian, Serbian and Slovene Units), Russian Service, Ukrainian Section

From Overseas Services
Peter Udell and Sam Younger (Controllers), Basil Clarke; African Service (Hausa, Somali and Swahili Sections and Topical Unit), Arabic Service, Eastern Service (Bengali, Burmese, Hindi, Pashto, Persian, Tamil and Urdu Sections and Topical Unit), Far Eastern Service (Chinese, Indonesian, Thai and Vietnamese Sections and Topical Unit), Latin American Service (Spanish American and Brazilian Sections, and Topical Unit)

From World Service Training
Gwynneth Henderson (Head of Training)

From Monitoring (Research and Information Unit)
Hilary Whalley (Manager)

Data was supplied by World Service Engineering
Roger Powell (Head of Computer Services), Howard Stone (Technical Services Manager), Val O'Connor (Operations Support Manager)

The pronunciations for the encyclopedic entries were provided by Graham Pointon, Pronunciation Adviser, Pronunciation Research Unit, BBC Library and Information Research Services

Editorial Team

Editor in Chief	John Sinclair
Editorial Director	Gwyneth Fox
Editorial Manager	Stephen Bullon
Editors	Jane Bradbury
	Helen Bruce
	Alice Deignan
	Keith Harvey
	Ramesh Krishnamurthy
	Michael Murphy
	Jenny Watson
	Deborah Yuill
Pronunciation Editor	Jonathan Payne
Encyclopedic Editor	Martha Ross
Computer Staff	Zoe James
	Tim Lane
Secretary	Sue Crawley
Data Processing	John Lowe
	Robert Weaver
	Byte & Type Ltd, Birmingham

For HarperCollins Publishers
Annette Capel, Lorna Heaslip, Richard Thomas,
Douglas Williamson

The publishers and editorial team would like to thank the
following people who have contributed significantly to the
project: John Williams for editorial advice and assistance with
American vocabulary; Edwin Carpenter and Andrew
Delahunty for editorial advice; Gerlinde Hardt-Mautner for
advice on Business English; and Carole Murphy for her
assistance with the encyclopedic entries.

International Advisory Panel

AUSTRALIA	Emeritus Professor Arthur Delbridge Macquarie University
CHILE	Professor Alfredo Matus O Universidad Catolica de Chile Santiago
GERMANY	Professor Dieter Götz Universität Augsburg
HONG KONG	Professor Jack C Richards City Polytechnic of Hong Kong
JAPAN	Professor Ikuo Koike Keio University Yokohama
SAUDI ARABIA	Dr Ezzat Al Khattab King Saud University Riyadh
SINGAPORE	Professor Edwin Thumboo National University of Singapore
USA	Professor Robert Kaplan University of Southern California Los Angeles

Foreword

In the second half of the twentieth century English has emerged as the lingua franca of trade, commerce and communications. Five of the leading world broadcasters on radio, TV and satellite reach hundreds of millions of people every day through English. The BBC World Service alone has upwards of a hundred and twenty million listeners as well as the yet uncounted millions watching BBC World Service Television on satellite.

English today is a spoken language and radio and television are speaking media. That is why I welcome this co-venture between BBC English and the COBUILD unit to produce a dictionary of spoken English which reflects the way the language is used in broadcasting.

In the sixty years of its existence the BBC World Service has prided itself on the accuracy and impartiality of its reporting and on the standard of English of its presenters and newsreaders. Our aim, and that of our English Language teaching section, BBC English, is to reflect the quality of standard educated spoken English used in Britain today. Our colleagues in National Public Radio in Washington reflect the same standards.

English is the international language of broadcasting and the BBC English Dictionary is the essential companion. Listeners and viewers will welcome this dictionary, as I do.

John Tusa
Managing Director
BBC World Service

Introduction

This dictionary features the English used by the BBC World Service. It is a new kind of dictionary which uses modern computer technology to achieve new standards of accuracy and relevance.

Where does a dictionary get its words from? The starting point of any dictionary is the source of the words. For this dictionary, the words have come from the broadcasts made by the BBC World Service in the last four years. These are the words in use at the present time in broadcast English.

The dictionary has been compiled by COBUILD, a team of specialized lexicographers who have years of experience of working with large amounts of computer-stored language. For this project, thousands of broadcast programmes were transcribed and entered into a computer. Special computer programs tracked down the vocabulary and the lexicographers examined the usage and wrote the dictionary entries. We were particularly interested in new words and meanings, special meanings, and the names of people and places.

Many new words come into being as new gadgets and inventions become available to a wider public. In the last few years, shops have filled up with 'personal stereos', 'camcorders', 'flat-screen' televisions, and virtually 'fat-free' foods, while more and more people fill their cars with 'unleaded' instead of 'leaded' petrol and drive away with their 'catalytic converters' further reducing pollution.

Other new words emerge as a result of political developments or changing social trends. In recent years, ships and tankers have been 'reflagged', that is, they begin to carry the flag of a powerful nation in order to be entitled to protection from that country's navy in case of attack.

Many of these words have never before been recorded in a general dictionary.

We also came across words which we already knew about, but which our previous studies had not judged to be important enough for inclusion in a general dictionary.

Words such as 'repatriation', 'sustainable', and 'confrontational' all occur much more frequently in the BBC data than in a corpus of general English, and needed to be included in this dictionary.

Equally important are the meanings of old words. Words are constantly being revived with new meanings – for example, anyone who goes horse-riding knows how to 'saddle' a horse, but what does it mean when a sports reporter says: 'Lee saddled three winners at Haydock Park yesterday'? Did Francis Lee actually put the saddle on three horses? Probably not, though he trained three horses which won races at Haydock Park.

Journalists often seek to find different ways of saying the same thing, and you are quite likely to hear on the radio that two sides have agreed to a 'calendar' for talks. This means the same as a timetable, but it provides a variation, and can help to avoid repetition in a short news item.

In a corpus of general English, the word 'hardware' most typically refers to the shop that sells nails, hammers, drills, screwdrivers and the other things you use for those jobs around the house. In recent years, the word has gained currency meaning computer equipment. But in the BBC data, 'hardware' is most typically military equipment: guns, fighter planes, and so on.

Idiomatic spoken English is also evolving, and the BBC data provides ample evidence for many new expressions and metaphorical uses. For example, 'goalposts' are traditionally associated with football, rugby, or hockey, but these days people are often accused of trying to 'move the goalposts' – though not physically. When someone tries to 'move the goalposts', they want to change the rules or conditions of something in order to make things easier for themselves or more difficult for others.

Among the new meanings are some specialized meanings, associated with the BBC, radio, and the kinds of programmes that are commonly broadcast.

For most of us, a 'hike' is a refreshing walk in the country, but for journalists it is more likely to mean a steep rise in prices. This usage is especially found in our American data, but there is evidence that it is spreading all over the English-speaking world. Similarly, we imagine that a 'plank' is a piece of wood longer than it is wide, but in the BBC data the word is typically used to refer to the most important element of an idea or policy, as in 'The main plank of his election campaign had been trade policy.'

Finally, the dictionary includes hundreds of entries about people, places and events. Strictly speaking, entries of this kind might be reserved for encyclopedias, but we decided to include some basic information to help listeners follow a news or current affairs programme.

The design of the dictionary was carried out in co-operation with experts in language and current affairs from the BBC. The BBC is a very prominent user of English, setting international standards for spoken English. The constant reference to actual BBC usage ensures that the record of usage in the dictionary is reliable.

The layout of entries was carefully worked out, and is rather different from other dictionaries. Headwords are on a separate line, with their pronunciations and with a full list of inflected forms. This makes it easy to find the exact word that you want. The grammatical word class, such as ADJ, for adjective, or an indication of grammatical structure, such as V O A (verb followed by object followed by adjunct), is given at the beginning of each explanation. If you are not interested in the grammar, you can just ignore these notes.

In addition to pioneering the concept of dictionaries being based on text corpora, COBUILD has experimented with a number of changes to conventional lexicography. The BBC decided to adopt several of these novel features.

The most obvious feature is the style of the explanations, which are written in ordinary English sentences.

'If a race ends in a photo finish...'
'Someone who is phoney is ...'
'A pick-up or a pick-up truck is ...'
'When you perspire...'

The phrasing of the explanations tells you a lot about the meanings. Everyone perspires, hence 'When you perspire ...' but only a few races end in a photo finish, hence 'If a race ...'. The word 'phoney' has a special meaning when used of people ('someone who is...'); there is another paragraph beginning 'Something that is phoney...'. The word 'pick-up' can either be used to modify 'truck', or it can be used on its own as a subject or object.

The defining style also distinguishes between fact and opinion; for example:

'A pig is a farm animal...'
'If you call someone a pig, you mean...'

The first explanation is objective – there is no doubt about what is or is not a pig. But the word is also used in insults, or in talking rudely about someone, hence the phrasing 'If you call someone...'.

The natural English of these explanations makes the dictionary easy to read, and provides a great deal of support to the description of the meanings.

The examples in this dictionary are particularly helpful, and they are quite different from those in most one-volume dictionaries. They are all chosen directly from real English in use, and are not invented or heavily edited.

Serious academic dictionaries in the great tradition of Dr Johnson give actual quotations – called citations – to illustrate words and phrases in use. The reader can see a genuine context and an actual instance of the word in a communication. By contrast, most modern one-volume dictionaries print examples that are invented by the compilers to show what they mean by the definition. There is a huge difference between these two sources of examples, and the BBC dictionary, in company with COBUILD, has decided firmly to follow the policy of using actual citations.

Of course, not every real example is ideal for a dictionary. It is no more than a guarantee that the context is genuine. To get appropriate examples, the compilers need a huge number of examples to choose from. Here is where the Bank of English comes in.

The Bank of English is a very large collection of documents and conversations which are typical of contemporary English. At the time of writing it contains over 150 million words, and it is growing fast. Books, newspapers, journals, magazines, and correspondence pour in daily, and tape recordings of many kinds of conversations are transcribed. Everything is entered into computer stores. About 70 million words of BBC English and 10 million words from National Public Radio in Washington make up a component of the Bank of English, and our attention was focused very closely on this component in the course of compiling the dictionary. I believe this is by far the largest organized corpus currently available to lexicographers, and it ensures that the examples are relevant and reliable.

There are over 1000 entries about people, places and events in this dictionary, to help with the understanding of current affairs. Every country in the world has an entry, and there is also an entry for its capital city and one or more prominent public figures. This is a new feature for the international market, but it is increasingly popular in dictionaries sold in the UK. For this dictionary, lists were drawn up in consultation with the BBC, and short explanations were written, paying particular attention to present positions and recent events. The draft entries were read by BBC experts and special arrangements were made for late developments so that the dictionary is really up to date. For example, between now, when I write this Introduction, and June, when this book is published, there will be elections in a number of countries. We hope to be able to provide the most up-to-date political information, incorporating the results of these elections.

Pronunciation is particularly important for broadcasters, and in a world-wide service the pronunciation of foreign words is an extra concern. COBUILD has developed, with Dr David Brazil, a leading expert on speech, a notation for pronunciation which is simple to learn and helpful to use. A special version of Dr Brazil's system is used in this dictionary.

It has been helpful, in compiling the book, to think of a regular listener to the BBC World Service as the kind of user for whom the dictionary is specially intended. He or she will be someone with a reasonable standard of English and a developed skill in listening comprehension, interested in world affairs and in the perspectives given by people from different cultures – something of a citizen of the world. Anyone who answers to this description should find the dictionary a help and support to their listening, and to their language activities.

How do dictionaries improve? One way is that users write in, pointing out errors and omissions, disagreeing with our explanations, and offering all kinds of suggestions for improvement. I have been delighted at the response I have received from users over the years, and I hope that BBC users will be no exception. Future editions of this book will largely improve because of the recommendations of users, and I urge you to write to me with any queries or comments.

John Sinclair
Editor in Chief
Professor of Modern English Language
University of Birmingham

Main Features of the Dictionary Entries

Order of entries: in alphabetical order, taking no notice of capital letters, hyphens, apostrophes, accents, or spaces between words.

> air brake
> airbrick
> Airbus
> air-conditioned
> air-conditioner

Headwords: the main form of the headword appears in large bold face letters, starting in the left hand margin.

> **blast-off**
> NU **Blast-off** is the moment when a rocket or space shuttle leaves the ground and rises into the air. *The exact time of blast-off is being kept secret.*

Variant forms of a headword are given after the headword, in smaller bold face letters.

Alternative spellings are given at the end of the information about the headword.

> **cardamom** /kɑːdəməm/ or **cardamon** /kɑːdəmən/
> NU **Cardamom** is a spice that comes from the seeds of a plant that grows in Asia.

> **dramatize** /dræmətaɪz/ **dramatizes, dramatizing, dramatized;** also spelt **dramatise.**

> **encyclopedia** /ɪnsaɪkləpiːdɪə/ **encyclopedias;** also spelt **encyclopaedia.**

Inflected forms: given in smaller bold face letters, for noun forms, verb forms, and adjective forms.

Notes about inflected forms.

> **flame** /fleɪm/ **flames**

> **grip** /grɪp/ **grips, gripping, gripped**

> **happy** /hæpi/ **happier, happiest**

> **instil** /ɪnstɪl/ **instils, instilling, instilled;** spelt **instill, instills** in American English.

> **knife** /naɪf/ **knives; knifes, knifing, knifed.** The form **knives** is the plural of the noun. The form **knifes** is the third person singular, present tense, of the verb.

Pronunciations: using IPA symbols - see p. xxix for details.

Notes about pronunciations.

> **loath** /ləʊθ/; also spelt **loth.**

> **loathe** /ləʊð/ **loathes, loathing, loathed**

> **minute, minutes;** pronounced /mɪnɪt/ when it is a noun and /maɪnjuːt/ when it is an adjective.

Paragraph numbers: for words with more than one meaning or use.

> **nightcap** /naɪtkæp/ **nightcaps**
> 1 NC A **nightcap** is a drink that you have just before you go to bed. *What about a nightcap?*
> 2 NC A **nightcap** is also a kind of hat that people used to wear in bed. *He pulled his nightcap well over his ears.*

Grammar: in small capital letters - see p. xviii for details.

Changes in word class which do not involve any change in meaning are introduced by a triangle symbol.

Explanations: given in full sentences, showing the commonest ways in which the headword is used.

Examples: in italics, taken from radio broadcasts, newspapers, books, and conversations.

Derived words: formed with common suffixes such as '-ly' or '-ness' and not involving a change in meaning are given after a diamond symbol.

obvious /ɒbviəs/
ADJ If something is **obvious**, you can easily see it or understand it.

outsider /aʊtsaɪdə/ **outsiders**
NC An **outsider** is someone who is not involved in a particular group, or is not accepted by that group.

outsmart /aʊtsmɑːt/ **outsmarts, outsmarting, outsmarted**
VO If you **outsmart** someone, you cleverly defeat them or gain an advantage over them.

patter /pætə/ **patters, pattering, pattered**
1 VA If something **patters** on a surface, it makes light tapping sounds as it hits it. *Spots of rain pattered on the window... I heard her feet pattering about upstairs.*
▶ Also N SING *They heard a patter of paws as the dog came to meet them.*

pet /pet/ **pets, petting, petted**
1 NCorN+N A **pet** is an animal that you keep in your home to give you company and pleasure. *It is against the rules to keep pets. ...his pet dog. ...importing meat for pet food.*
2 ADJ ATTRIB Someone's **pet** theory or subject is one that they particularly support or like. *We were listening to a gardener with his pet theories.*
3 VO If you **pet** a person or animal, you pat or stroke them affectionately. *...being cuddled and petted and getting attention... He spends his time relaxing by the pool or petting his horse, Rising Sun.*

quieten /kwaɪətn/ **quietens, quietening, quietened**
V-ERG If you **quieten** a person or situation or if they **quieten**, they become less noisy or less tense. *Can you do anything to quieten those children a bit?... All efforts should be made now to open negotiations and quieten the tension... The mayhem has continued for over an hour, although in the last few minutes it has quietened slightly.*

rapid /ræpɪd/ **rapids**
1 ADJ Something that is **rapid** happens or moves very quickly. *...a time of rapid economic growth... He took a few rapid steps towards the beach.* ◆ **rapidly** ADV *The situation had rapidly deteriorated.* ◆ **rapidity** /rəpɪdəti/ NU *The film shows the rapidity of the changes in this area of medicine.*

reasonable /riːzəⁿnəbl/
1 ADJ If someone is being **reasonable**, they are behaving in a fair and sensible way. *I can't do that, Morris. Be reasonable... The rally leaders have appealed to people to be calm and reasonable.*
◆ **reasonableness** NU *The landlords responded with great reasonableness.*

Phrases: if the headword is used in several phrases, they are grouped together after any numbered paragraphs and before any phrasal verbs.

If the phrase is closely connected with another use or meaning of the headword, it may be included within the same paragraph.

If there is only one phrase, and it is not closely connected with any other use or meaning of the headword, it is explained in a paragraph by itself.

Phrasal verbs: in alphabetical order at the end of an entry, after any numbered paragraphs or phrases.

Style: stylistic information about a word or use; for example who uses it, in what situation, and whether it expresses their attitude.

Cross-references: indicating that relevant information can be found at another entry.

---

saddle /sædl/ saddles, saddling, saddled

4 VO In horse racing, you can say that someone **saddles** a horse when he or she is the trainer of that horse and decides when it should race. *Pipe became the first trainer to saddle one hundred winners before the New Year... Owen O'Neill saddles Mole Board for the Sun Alliance Hurdles on Wednesday.*
● **Saddle** is used in these phrases. ● To be **in the saddle** means to be riding a horse or bicycle, usually in a race. *He will be in the saddle for next month's Tour of the Americas.* ● To be **in the saddle** also means to be in a position of power or control. *The reformist leader is back in the saddle and looking a great deal stronger... The same commanders remained in the saddle.*
saddle up PHRASAL VERB If you **saddle up**, you put a saddle on a horse or pony. *I saddled up and rode off...*

smell /smel/ smells, smelling, smelled or smelt

6 VO If you **smell** something such as danger, you feel instinctively that it is likely to happen. *He's shrewd and can smell a successful project.* ● If you **smell a rat**, you become suspicious that there is something wrong; an informal expression. *Old Genco would never have fallen for it, he would have smelled a rat.*

sour /sauə/ sours, souring, soured

5 If a situation or relationship **turns sour**, it is not pleasant or satisfactory anymore. *By spring, the relationship had turned sour, and both manager and artist had resorted to law...*

think /θɪŋk/ thinks, thinking, thought

think back PHRASAL VERB If you **think back**, you remember things that happened in the past. *I'm thinking back to my own experience as a teacher.*
think out PHRASAL VERB If you **think out** a plan or a piece of writing, you prepare it fully and consider all the details of it before doing it. *She needed time to think out a strategy to deal with Gareth...*

uncritical /ʌnkrɪtɪkl/

ADJ If you are **uncritical**, you accept or approve of something without being able or willing to judge whether it is good or bad; used showing disapproval.

unsolicited /ʌnsəlɪsɪtɪd/

ADJ Something that is **unsolicited** is given without being asked for, and may not be wanted; a formal word.

uptown /ʌptaʊn/

ADV or ADJ If you go **uptown**, you go away from the centre of a city towards an outer part; used in American English.

valve /vælv/ valves

3 See also safety-valve.

vapor /veɪpə/. See vapour.

view /vjuː/ views, viewing, viewed

into view. ● If something is **on view**, it is being exhibited in public. *The Turner exhibition is on view at the Tate Gallery.* ● to take a dim view: see dim.

working /wɜːkɪŋ/ workings

8 in working order: see order.

Encyclopedic Entries

Countries:

Entries for countries include an account of historically significant events, and information about current developments.

A diamond symbol introduces information about adjectives and about nouns that can refer to inhabitants.

Entries also include a block of information about per capita GNP, religion, languages, and so on.

Australia /ɒstreɪliə/
The **Commonwealth of Australia** is a country in the Pacific. In 1788 Britain established the first of several colonies. During the 19th century they became self-governing and formed a federation in 1901. It is a member of the Commonwealth and ANZUS. Paul Keating, of the Australian Labor Party (ALP), became Prime Minister in 1991. Australia exports minerals, foodstuffs, wool and oil. ◆ **Australian** /ɒstreɪliən/ N, ADJ
▪ *per capita GNP:* US$12,390 ▪ *religion:* Christianity ▪ *language:* English ▪ *currency:* dollar ▪ *capital:* Canberra ▪ *largest city:* Sydney ▪ *population:* 17 million (1989) ▪ *size:* 7,682,300 square kilometres.

Major cities:

There is an entry for the capital city of each country. If the capital is not the largest city in a country, there is a separate entry for the largest city.

Canberra /kænbərə/
Canberra is the capital of Australia. Population: 274,000 (1985).

Sydney /sɪdni/
Sydney is the largest city in Australia and capital city of New South Wales. Population: 3,431,000 (1987).

Political leaders:

There are entries for the political leaders of each country, including information about their party affiliations, important positions held, and their date of birth.

Keating, Paul /pɔːl kiːtɪŋ/
Paul Keating became Prime Minister of Australia in 1991 after the resignation of Bob Hawke. He was first elected to the House of Representatives in 1969. He was Minister for Northern Australia in 1975, and Treasurer from 1983 to 1991. He also served as Deputy Prime Minister from 1990 to 1991. He is a member of the Australian Labor Party (ALP). Born: 1944.

World organizations:

Entries include information about the purpose of the organization, the location of its headquarters, and a list of its member states.

Arab League /ærəb liːg/
The **League of Arab States**, more commonly known as the **Arab League**, was founded in 1945 to promote the common good of all Arab countries. Egypt was suspended from the Arab League from 1979 to 1989, and during this period the headquarters were transfered from Cairo to Tunis. The members of the Arab League are: Algeria, Bahrain, Djibouti, Egypt, Iraq, Jordan, Kuwait, Lebanon, Libya, Mauritania, Morocco, Oman, Palestine, Qatar, Saudi Arabia, Somalia, Sudan, Syria, Tunisia, United Arab Emirates, and Yemen.

Grammar

The grammar labels in this dictionary indicate the typical way in which a word is used. A detailed explanation of the labels is provided in the glossary which begins on the following page.

The first part of the label is always the word class, for example N for noun, V for verb, ADJ for adjective, and so on. If there is a sub-class, that will be the next element, for example PRED (= predicative) for adjectives that come after a verb, REPORT for verbs that are used with a reporting structure, or C (= countable) for count nouns. Then there may be some further information about the typical grammatical behaviour of the word. When the label consists of only one element, it always indicates the word class.

For verbs, the basic label is V. The typical structures for a verb are shown by labels indicating the clause element that usually follows it, such as O for object, C for complement, and A for adjunct. There are a few common sub-classes for verbs, such as V-ERG, V-PASS, and V-REPORT. Further information is given after a plus sign, for example when a verb is followed by a particular preposition as in V+to, by an '-ing' form as in V O+ING, or by a 'to-infinitive' as in V-PASS+to-INF.

Four types of verb have special labels: auxiliary verbs (AUX); phrasal verbs (PHRASAL VERB); modals (MODAL); and semi-modals (SEMI-MODAL).

For the other word classes, a similar system is used. For example, N is the basic label for nouns; common sub-classes include count nouns (N C), uncount nouns (N U), and singular nouns (N SING), and further information is given after a plus sign, as in N C+SUPP, N U+to-INF, and N SING+of.

Two types of noun uses have a special label: TITLE and VOCATIVE. Nouns which are frequently used in front of another noun are labelled N+N.

The basic label for adjectives is ADJ. There are three sub-classes of adjective: ADJ ATTRIB, ADJ PRED, and ADJ after N, and further information is given after a plus sign, as in ADJ PRED+to.

If a word or meaning can be used in two different word classes or patterns, they are linked by 'or', for example PREP or ADV, N C or N U, V O or V, and so on. If there is likely to be any doubt or confusion, the elements are repeated, for example N C+SUPP or N U+SUPP.

In a few cases, usually verbs, more than two patterns can be used and commas separate all but the last pattern, which is again linked by 'or'. For example, verbs which are used to report what someone has said can often be used with an object, a 'that'-clause, or the actual words used, and are therefore labelled V O, V-REPORT, or V-QUOTE. For example at **assert**:

The protesters asserted their right to be heard. (V O)
He asserted that China would never enter into an alliance with either superpower. (V-REPORT)
'People in the West,' he asserted, 'are no better than us.' (V-QUOTE)

Note that when more than one label is used, the examples show the patterns in the same order as the labels.

In this dictionary, we thought it was not appropriate to give a grammar label for some items, for example for idiomatic expressions such as 'Oh dear' and 'an end in itself'.

Main word classes

ADJECTIVES

Adjectives are words such as 'old', 'red', 'big', or 'ugly', which give more information about things or people, such as their age, colour, size, or other qualities.

ADJ   ADJ means 'adjective'. It is used when the adjective can come either in front of a noun or after a verb.

beautiful 1 *...a very beautiful girl.*
beautiful 1 *The table looked beautiful.*

ADJ ATTRIB   ADJ ATTRIB means 'attributive adjective'. It is used when the adjective comes in front of a noun rather than after a verb.

daily 2 *Daily wage rates were around two dollars.*

ADJ PRED   ADJ PRED means 'predicative adjective'. It is used when the adjective comes after a verb rather than in front of a noun.

alive 1 *I think his father is still alive.*

ADJ PRED+*to*, ADJ PRED+*with*, and so on mean that the predicative adjective is usually followed by a particular preposition such as 'to' or 'with'.

equal 8 *He was confident that the two people would be equal to the task ahead of them.*
bursting 2 *Claud was bursting with pride and excitement.*

ADJ PRED+*to*-INF means that the predicative adjective is usually followed by a verb in the 'to-infinitive' form.

likely 2 *They were not likely to forget it.*

ADJ after N   ADJ after N means 'adjective after noun'. It is used when the adjective comes immediately after a noun, not in front of a noun or after a verb.

alone 5 *Simon alone knew the truth.*

ADVERBS

Adverbs are words which give more information about the time, place, or manner of an action.

ADV   ADV means 'adverb'. It is used when the adverb usually comments on a verb, but sometimes comments on an adjective or another adverb.

distantly 1 *From the other end of the street, he could distantly see a figure waiting.*
distantly 1 *The sound of a recorder was distantly audible.*

ADV SEN   ADV SEN means 'sentence adverb'. It is used when the adverb comments on a whole clause or sentence rather than on a single word. Sentence adverbs usually express the speaker's or writer's personal opinion.

thankfully 2 *Thankfully, the memory of it soon faded.*
strangely 2 *It has, strangely, only recently been discovered.*

SUBMOD SUBMOD means 'submodifier'. Submodifiers are adverbs which comment on another adverb or an adjective, in order to strengthen, weaken, or restrict its meaning.

very 1 *Think very carefully.*
faintly 1 *It was faintly possible.*
singularly *Then we did some singularly boring experiments.*

NOUNS

Nouns are words that refer to people, things, or abstract ideas such as feelings and qualities.

N C N C means 'count noun'. Count nouns have both a singular and a plural form, and are always used with a determiner when they are singular.

house 1 *He has a house in Pimlico.*
nation 1 *...the leaders of the seven main industrialised nations.*
village *She was born in a small Norfolk village.*

N C+*of*, N C+*for*, and so on mean that the count noun is usually followed by a particular preposition, such as 'of' or 'for'.

succession 1 *My life is a succession of failures.*
glutton 2 *He was a glutton for work.*

N C+POSS means that the count noun is usually used with a possessive or an 'of' phrase indicating possession.

birthplace 1 *Cruz returned to his birthplace, Hong Kong, and became champion jockey.*
namesake *Smith's namesake and fellow-Scot, John Smith MP, is the Shadow Chancellor of the Exchequer.*
blessing 2 *She did it with the full blessing of her parents.*

N C+SUPP means that the count noun is usually used with a supporting word or phrase, rather than being used on its own.

factor 1 *Confidence is the key factor in any successful career.*
progression *The progression from one extreme to the other is gradual.*

N COLL N COLL means 'collective noun'. It is used when the noun refers to a group of people or things. The singular form takes a determiner and can be used with either the singular or plural forms of verbs and pronouns.

committee *A parliamentary committee has to approve his list of candidates.*
team 1 *The Turkish football team have been beaten by five goals to nil.*

N MASS N MASS means 'mass noun'. Mass nouns normally behave like uncount nouns, but they can sometimes have a plural form when they refer to quantities or amounts of something.

fabric *...a bit of fabric.*
fabric *...silks and other soft fabrics.*

N PL N PL means 'plural noun'. It is used when the noun is used only in the plural.

alms *They are refusing to go there to collect alms.*

N PL+POSS means that the plural noun is usually used with a possessive or an 'of' phrase indicating possession.

affair 3 *What had induced her to meddle in his affairs?*
fortune 2 *In the following years, Victor's fortunes improved considerably.*
whereabouts 1 *We have discovered the whereabouts of one of the paintings.*

N PL+SUPP means that the plural noun is usually used with a supporting word or phrase, rather than being used on its own.

strait 2 *The company was now in dire financial straits.*
depth 5 *...his home in the depths of the English countryside.*

N PROP   N PROP means 'proper noun'. It is used when the noun refers to a particular place, person, or institution. Proper nouns begin with a capital letter.

earth 1 *...the Earth and other planets in the solar system.*
Home Secretary *The Home Secretary, Mr Hurd, acknowledged that the prison population was continuing to grow.*
NASA *Recently NASA has announced plans to make a return to Mars in the next few years.*

N SING   N SING means 'singular noun'. It is used when the noun is used only in the singular, and needs a determiner in front of it.

shame 5 *It's a shame to waste all this food.*
crackling 1 *The crackling became louder and louder.*

N SING+*of*, N SING+*for*, and so on mean that the singular noun is usually followed by a particular preposition such as 'of' or 'for'.

wealth 3 *...ordinary people, who have a tremendous wealth of experience.*
eye 2 *The artist has a marvellous eye for detail.*

N SING+POSS means that the singular noun is usually used with a possessive or an 'of' phrase indicating possession.

birthright *He felt that a decent standard of education and health care was his birthright.*
bounty 1 *They must accept the colonel's bounty.*
brainchild *Building a luxurious new opera house had been the brainchild of François Mitterrand.*

N SING+SUPP means that the singular noun is usually used with a supporting word or phrase, rather than being used on its own.

atmosphere 3 *It's got such a friendly atmosphere.*
jungle 2 *...the jungle of real politics.*

N U   N U means 'uncount noun'. Uncount nouns refer to things that you do not normally count or consider as individual items, and they only have one form. Uncount nouns do not need a determiner when used on their own. They are not used with numbers, and always take a singular verb.

life 7 *His book is well written and full of life.*
banking *...foreign earnings from services such as banking and insurance.*
coal *...a lump of coal.*

N U+*of*, N U+*to*, and so on mean that the the uncount noun is usually followed by a particular preposition such as 'of' or 'to'.

pursuit 1 *How far should any of us go in pursuit of what we want?*
testimony 2 *This is spectacular testimony to the computer's creative powers.*

N U+POSS means that the uncount noun is usually used with a possessive or an 'of' phrase indicating possession.

handiwork *He stood back and surveyed his handiwork.*
welfare 1 *I would devote my life to the child's welfare.*
presence 1 *He had to cope with the presence of her family.*

N U+SUPP means that the uncount noun is usually used with a supporting word or phrase, rather than being used on its own.

lettering *Underneath it, in smaller lettering, was a name.*
celebration 2 *...a festival held for the celebration of music and dance.*

N U+*to*-INF means that the uncount noun is usually followed by a verb in the 'to-infinitive' form.

inability *She despises her husband for his inability to work.*

N+N   N+N means that the noun often comes in front of another noun, and provides more information about the second noun. Nearly all nouns can come in this position, but those which typically come in front of another noun are labelled N+N.

host 2 *The host country won more than half the gold medals in the Games.*
standby 4 *...a standby loan from the International Monetary Fund.*

TITLE   TITLE means that the noun is used to address or refer to someone who has a particular role or position.

Excellency *I shall do my best, Your Excellency.*
lady 4 *...Lady Diana Cooper.*

VOCATIVE   VOCATIVE means that the noun is used when speaking directly to someone or writing to them.

madam *Good evening, Madam.*
sweetheart 1 *I'm sorry sweetheart, I couldn't make it.*

VERBS

Verbs are words that describe actions, thought, speech, or other activities. They tell you what someone or something does, or what happens to them.

V   V means 'verb'. It is used when the verb is intransitive, that is, when it does not have a direct object, and it can be used without any other structural element, such as an adjunct or a complement.

convene 2 *The grand jury did not convene until February.*
tauten *The rope tautened.*

V+*to*, V+*in*, and so on mean that the intransitive verb is usually followed by a particular preposition, such as 'to' or 'in'.

refer 1 *In his letters he rarely referred to political events.*
culminate *The struggle between King and Parliament had culminated in the Civil War.*

V+ING means that the intransitive verb is usually followed by the '-ing' form of another verb.

keep 3 *I keep making the same mistake.*

V+*to*-INF means that the intransitive verb is usually followed by another verb in the 'to-infinitive' form.

tend 1 *I tend to wake up early in the morning.*

V A V A means that the verb is intransitive and is used with an adjunct of some sort.

go 6 *There's a little road that goes off to the right.*
step 3 *Step over the wire.*

V C V C means that the verb is intransitive and is followed by a complement.

be 5 *It was terribly hot and airless in the car.*
sound 6 *The rustling of the woman's dress sounded alarmingly loud.*

V O V O means 'verb with object'. It is used when the verb is transitive, that is, when it has a direct object, and can be used without any other structural element, such as an adjunct or a complement.

borrow *Could I borrow your car?*

V O+*to*, V O+*with*, and so on mean that the transitive verb is usually followed by a particular preposition, such as 'to' or 'with'.

charge 2 *Please charge the bill to my account.*
trust 3 *Next year I hope the company will trust me with a bigger budget.*

V O+ING means that the transitive verb is usually followed by the '-ing' form of another verb.

send 3 *The noise sent them racing towards the bush.*

V O+*to*-INF means that the transitive verb is usually followed by a 'to-infinitive'.

defy 2 *I defy anyone to disprove it.*

V O A V O A means that the transitive verb is used with an adjunct.

put 1 *I put her suitcase on the table.*

V O C V O C means that the transitive verb is used with a complement.

call 2 *President Nixon called his opponents traitors.*

V O O V O O means that the transitive verb is used with two objects: a direct object and an indirect object. In most cases, the verb can also be used with the direct object and a prepositional phrase beginning with either 'to' or 'for' instead of the indirect object.

hand 4 *Could you hand me that piece of wood?*
hand 4 *He scribbled four lines and handed the note to the Field Marshal.*

V-ERG V-ERG means 'ergative verb'. It is used when the verb can be transitive or intransitive in the same meaning, and the object of the transitive use can be the subject of the intransitive use.

budge 2 *She could not budge the wheel.*
budge 2 *The screw just will not budge.*

V-ERG A means that the ergative verb is usually followed by an adjunct.

flick 1 *...flicking its tail backwards and forwards.*
flick 1 *Its tongue flicks in and out of its tiny mouth.*

V-ERG+*to*, V-ERG+*from*, and so on mean that the ergative verb is usually followed by a particular preposition such as 'to' or 'from'.

turn 6 *I wonder if we can turn our attention to something you mentioned earlier.*
turn 6 *His thoughts turned to Calcutta.*

V-PASS V-PASS means 'passive verb'. It is used when a transitive verb is only used in the passive. Passive verbs consist of a form of the auxiliary verb 'be' followed by the past participle of the verb.

orphan 2 *We adopted the twins when they were orphaned.*

V-PASS A means that the passive verb is usually followed by an adjunct.

entangle 1 *Suddenly she was entangled in the seaweed.*

V-PASS+*with*, V-PASS+*to*, and so on mean that the passive verb is usually followed by a particular preposition such as 'with' or 'to'.

smother 4 *One board in their classroom is smothered with photographs of mothers, fathers and other relatives.*

V-PASS+*to*-INF means that the passive verb is usually followed by a 'to-infinitive'.

calculate 3 *...a cool dignified attitude that was calculated to discourage familiarity.*

V-QUOTE V-QUOTE means that an intransitive verb is accompanied by the exact words that someone said.

demand 2 *'What have I done?' he demanded.*

V O-QUOTE means that a transitive verb is accompanied by the exact words that someone said. The object is the person that the words are said to.

tell 1 *She told a crowd of ten thousand, 'Let's have clean, peaceful and orderly elections.'*

V-RECIP V-RECIP means 'reciprocal verb'. It is used when the verb describes an action that involves two people or groups. There are three common types of reciprocal verb:

1. The verb can be intransitive, with both people or both groups as the subject, or with one person or group as the subject and one after a preposition.

argue 1 *They were arguing about who should sit in front.*
argue 1 *Don't argue with me, George, just do as you're told.*

2. The verb can be transitive, with one person or group as the subject and the other as the object, or intransitive, with both people or groups as the subject.

marry 1 *I want to marry you.*
marry 1 *They are in love with each other and wish to marry.*

3. The verb can be transitive, with both people or both groups as the object, or with one as the object and the other after a preposition.

separate 4 *Racial prejudice separates the two main ethnic groups.*
separate 4 *A fence at the back of the garden separated us from the neighbours.*

V-REFL   V-REFL means 'reflexive verb'. It is used when the subject and the object of the transitive verb are the same person or thing, so the object is a reflexive pronoun.

disguise 2 *I disguised myself as a French priest.*

V-REFL A means that the reflexive verb is usually followed by an adjunct.

drag 3 *I was able to drag myself shakily to my feet.*

V-REFL+*to*, V-REFL+*with*, and so on mean that the reflexive verb is usually followed by a particular preposition such as 'to' or 'with'.

dedicate 1 *...a man who had dedicated himself to his work.*

V-REPORT   V-REPORT means that an intransitive verb is followed by a report structure which is introduced by 'that' or a 'wh' word such as 'how' or 'whether'. This structure is often called indirect speech or reported speech. Note that 'that' is often omitted.

allege *It has been alleged that he was tortured by police.*
describe 1 *He described how he was kidnapped.*
say 1 *He said it was an accident.*

V O-REPORT means that a transitive verb is followed by a report structure. The object is the person who is being spoken to or who is receiving the information.

reassure *I was trying to reassure her that things weren't as bad as she thought.*
ask 1 *Janet Cochrane asked Gill whether there were still things we don't know about AIDS.*
tell 1 *Six Swedish hostages have been told they can leave the country tonight.*

PHRASAL VERB   Phrasal verbs are combinations of a verb and an adverb or preposition, used together to have a particular meaning. 'Give up' and 'set out' are phrasal verbs.

put off 1 *Don't put it off till tomorrow.*
lumber with *Women are still lumbered with the cooking and cleaning.*
put up with *I can't think why I put up with it.*

AUXILIARY VERBS

The auxiliary verbs are 'be', 'have', and 'do'. They are used with main verbs to form tenses, negatives, and questions.

AUX   AUX means 'auxiliary verb'.

be 1 *The Government is considering the introduction of student loans.*
do 2 *What did he say?*
do 4 *She made a lot of mistakes, didn't she?*

MODAL   MODAL means 'modal verb'. The modal verbs are words such as 'can' or 'would', which are used in a verb group and which express ideas such as possibility, intention, or necessity. Modal verbs do not inflect and are followed by the base form of another verb.

might 1 *I might go to a concert tonight.*
must 1 *These standards must apply at all times.*
should 1 *We should be there by dinner time.*
will 1 *Inflation is rising and will continue to rise.*

SEMI-MODAL   The semi-modals are the verbs 'dare', 'need', and 'used to'. They can be used like modal verbs, especially in negative sentences and questions, when they are followed by the base form of another verb. Note that 'dare' and 'need' can also be used as ordinary verbs.

dare 1 *He dared not show that he was pleased.*
need 2 *You needn't worry.*
used 1 *The situation is much better today than it used to be.*

Other word classes

CONJ   CONJ means 'conjunction'. Conjunctions are words which join together words, groups, or clauses.

and 1 *...my mother and father.*
but 1 *...a cheap but incredibly effective carpet cleaner.*
if 2 *I asked her if I could help her.*

DET   DET means 'determiner'. Determiners are words that are used in front of nouns to indicate which particular thing or person is being referred to.

a 1 *She wanted to be an actress.*
the 1 *The sea was really rough.*
some 1 *I've got some friends coming over.*
your 1 *Where's your father?*

PREDET   PREDET means 'predeterminer'. Predeterminers are words that are used in front of determiners and give more information about the noun in the noun group.

all 1 *All the girls think it's great.*
twice 2 *He's twice my size.*
what 5 *What a pity.*

PREFIX   A prefix is a letter or group of letters that are added to the beginning of a word in order to make a new word with a different meaning.

anti- 1 *...the anti-apartheid movement.*
post- *...a post-election survey.*

PREP   PREP means 'preposition'. Prepositions are words such as 'by', 'for', 'into', or 'with', which are always followed by a noun group or a clause built around the '-ing' form of a verb.

along 1 *She glanced along the corridor.*
from 5 *The men had not yet come back from fishing.*

PRON   PRON means 'pronoun'. Pronouns are words which are used instead of a noun group to refer to someone or something.

you 1 *What do you think?*
him 1 *There's no need for him to worry.*
it 1 *...a tray with glasses on it.*
mine 1 *Margaret was a very old friend of mine.*

PRON INDEF   PRON INDEF means 'indefinite pronoun'. Indefinite pronouns are pronouns which are used to refer to people or things in a general way. They are used with a singular verb.

anyone 1 *There wasn't anyone there.*
something 1 *Something terrible has happened.*

PRON REFL   PRON REFL means 'reflexive pronoun'. Reflexive pronouns are pronouns which are used as the direct or indirect object of a verb, or after a preposition, when referring to the same person as the subject of the clause. Reflexive pronouns are also used for emphasis.

herself 1 *She groaned and stretched herself out flat on the sofa.*
herself 1 *On the way home Rose bought herself a piece of cheese for lunch.*
herself 1 *Barbara stared at herself in the mirror.*
yourself 2 *You yourself said it's only a routine check.*
yourself 3 *Did you make these cakes yourself?*

QUANT   QUANT means 'quantifier'. Quantifiers are words such as 'half', 'few', and 'many' which are used in front of 'of' and a noun group, and which express ideas of quantity or amount.

dozen 2 *There had been dozens of attempts at reform.*
lot 1 *We owed a lot of money.*
many 1 *Many of the old people were blind.*

SUFFIX   A suffix is a letter or group of letters that are added to the end of a word in order to make a new word with a different meaning.

-able *They are both immediately recognizable.*
-ing *...the dazzling sun.*
-y *...her inky, chalky hand.*

Secondary elements

A   A means 'adjunct'. An adjunct is one of the main parts of a clause or sentence. It gives information about time, place, or manner. It is sometimes called an adverbial group. In the sentences 'They dived into the water' and 'Mr Shamir will visit Washington next month', 'into the water' and 'next month' are adjuncts. See V A, V O A, V-PASS A, V-REFL A, V-ERG A.

ATTRIB   See ADJ ATTRIB.

C   In verb labels, C means 'complement'. A complement is one of the elements of clause structure which gives information about the subject or the object of the verb. See V C, V O C.

In noun labels, C means 'count'. See N C.

COLL   See N COLL.

ERG   See V-ERG.

INDEF   See PRON INDEF.

ING   See V+ING, V O+ING.

MASS   See N MASS.

O	O means 'object'. The object of a verb is the person or thing that is affected by the action that the verb describes, rather than the person or thing that is doing the action. See V O, V O A, V O O, V O-QUOTE, V O-REPORT.
PASS	See V-PASS.
PL	See N PL.
POSS	POSS means 'possessive'. It is used to indicate that a noun is used with a possessive or an 'of' phrase indicating possession. A possessive is a form of a noun or pronoun used to indicate possession, for example 'John's', 'the doctor's', or 'his'. See N C+POSS, N PL+POSS, N SING+POSS, N U+POSS.
PRED	See ADJ PRED.
PROP	See N PROP.
QUOTE	See V-QUOTE.
RECIP	See V-RECIP.
REFL	See V-REFL, PRON REFL.
REPORT	See V-REPORT.
SEN	See ADV SEN.
SING	See N SING.
SUPP	See N C+SUPP, N PL+SUPP, N SING+SUPP, N U+SUPP.
_to_-INF	See ADJ PRED+_to_-INF, N U+_to_-INF, V+_to_-INF, V O+_to_-INF, V-PASS+_to_-INF.
U	See N U.

Pronunciation

The pronunciations in the BBC English Dictionary represent the standard accent of British English that is used by World Service newsreaders: 'Received Pronunciation' or 'RP'. This accent, familiarly known as 'BBC English', is also used as a standard in the teaching of English as a Foreign Language throughout the world.

The system of transcription is a modified version of that developed for the COBUILD English Language Dictionary by Dr David Brazil. The transcriptions themselves are the result of a programme of monitoring the BBC World Service and consulting leading reference works on RP. We are particularly indebted to the following books: the Collins COBUILD English Language Dictionary (Edited by JM Sinclair et al. 1987), the English Pronouncing Dictionary by Daniel Jones (14th. Edition revised by AC Gimson and SM Ramsaran 1988) and the Longman Pronunciation Dictionary by JC Wells (1990).

For this dictionary, the aim has been to provide a pronunciation key that is accurate, clear and simple. Alternative pronunciations are only provided when there is no single pronunciation which predominates.

Symbols

The symbols used in the dictionary are those of the International Phonetic Alphabet (IPA), as standardized in AC Gimson's 14th Edition of the English Pronouncing Dictionary:

ɑː	heart, start, calm	b	bed, rub
æ	act, mass, lap	d	done, red
aɪ	dive, cry, mind	f	fit, if
aɪə	fire, tyre, buyer	g	good, dog
aʊ	out, down, loud	h	hat
aʊə	flour, tower, sour	j	yellow
e	met, lend, pen	k	king, pick
eɪ	say, main, weight	l	lip, bill
eə	fair, care, wear	m	mat, ram
ɪ	fit, win, list	n	not, tin
iː	feed, me, beat	p	pay, lip
ɪə	near, beard, clear	r	run
ɒ	lot, lost, spot	s	soon, bus
əʊ	note, phone, coat	t	talk, bet
ɔː	more, cord, claw	v	van, love
ɔɪ	boy, coin, joint	w	win
ʊ	could, stood, hood	x	loch
uː	you, use, choose	z	zoo, bus
ʊə	lure, pure, cure	ʃ	ship, wish
ɜː	turn, third, word	ʒ	measure
ʌ	but, fund, must	ŋ	sing
ə	the weak vowel in butter, about, forgotten	tʃ	cheap, witch
		θ	thin, myth
i	the weak vowel in very, create	ð	then, loathe
u	the first weak vowel in tuition	dʒ	joy, bridge

Four of the above symbols are not used by Gimson, but are widely used in other standard works:

/i/ and /u/ are short vowels which only occur in unstressed syllables

/i/ has a sound like /iː/, but is short like /ɪ/ 'very' /veri/, 'create' /krieɪt/

/u/ has a sound like /uː/, but is short like /ʊ/ tuition /tjuɪʃn/

/aɪə/ and /aʊə/ are triphthongs. These are complex vowel sounds which may be pronounced as two syllables when a word is spoken in isolation, but are usually pronounced as a single syllable when the word is used in context, as in 'fire' /faɪə/ and 'shower' /ʃaʊə/.

/iə/, /uə/ and other combinations of vowel symbols which are not included above show that there is more than one syllable:

Compare: 'India' /ɪndiə/ (3 syllables) with 'reindeer' /reɪndɪə/ (2 syllables) 'lawyer' /lɔɪə/ (2 syllables) with 'shower' /ʃaʊə/ (1 or 2 syllables).

Words in isolation

Stress is shown by underlining the vowel in the stressed syllable:

'two' /tu:/ 'result' /rɪzʌlt/ 'disappointing' /dɪsəpɔɪntɪŋ/

When a word is spoken in isolation, stress falls on all the syllables that have vowels which are underlined. If there is one syllable marked in this way, it will have primary stress:

'TWO' 'reSULT'

If two syllables are marked in this way, the first will have secondary stress, and the second will have primary stress:

'DISapPOINTing'

Words in context

STRESSED SYLLABLES

When words are used in context, the way in which they are pronounced depends upon the information units that are constructed by the speaker. For example, a speaker could say:

1) 'the reSULT was disapPOINTing'
2) 'a DISappointing reSULT'
3) 'VERy disappointing inDEED'

In (3), neither of the two marked syllables in 'disappointing' /dɪsəpɔɪntɪŋ/ receives either primary or secondary stress. This shows that it is not posssible for a dictionary to predict whether a particular syllable will be stressed in context.

Two things *can* be stated about the marked syllables:

1) They have a *potential* for stress that is not shared by the other syllables.

2) Whether they are stressed or not, the vowel must be pronounced distinctly: it is *protected*.

These features are shared by most of the one syllable words in English, which are therefore transcribed with an underlined vowel:

'two' /tu:/ 'inn' /ɪn/ 'tree' /tri:/.

UNSTRESSED SYLLABLES

It is an important characteristic of English that vowels in unstressed syllables tend to be pronounced indistinctly. Many unstressed syllables contain the vowel /ə/, a neutral vowel which is not found in stressed syllables. The vowels /ɪ/ and /ʊ/, which are relatively neutral in quality, are also common in unstressed syllables. /ɪ/ and /ʊ/ become /i/ and /u/ before a vowel sound or at the end of a word.

While there are some unstressed syllables which always have a distinct quality, there are more which are sometimes pronounced with a distinct vowel but are usually pronounced with /ə/, /ɪ/ or /ʊ/. This means that vowel quality can vary in these syllables. We show only the most probable quality in this dictionary.

Grammatical words such as 'shall' and 'to', which consist of only one syllable, require a different approach. Although such words are often pronounced with /ə/, /ɪ/ or /ʊ/, under certain circumstances some of them must be pronounced with a more distinct vowel, for example when they occur at the end of an utterance. In these cases, both pronunciations are given: 'shall' /ʃəl, ʃæl/ 'to' /tə, tuː/.

Furthermore, a number of these words are typically stressed under certain circumstances, for example when they occur as the first word in a question. In these cases, both possibilities are shown in the transcription: how /haʊ, haʊ/.

DISAPPEARING SOUNDS

In rapid speech there is often considerable simplification of sounds, so that consonants, vowels and even syllables can disappear. For example, when there are three consonants together, it is frequently the case that the middle consonant is not pronounced. As it is not necessary for the non-native speaker to leave out sounds in this way, the only disappearing sounds that are indicated in this dictionary are:

/ə⁰/, which indicates a /ə/ which may disappear with resulting loss of a syllable: for 'blackberry', /blækbə⁰ri/ means /blækbəri/ or /blækbri/

/jᵒuː/, which indicates a long 'u' sound which is pronounced /juː/ by some speakers and /uː/ by others, as in 'voluminous' /vəljᵒuːmɪnəs/

/n⁰/, which indicates, in a French word, that some English speakers will pronounce an /n/ while others will not pronounce the /n/, although the vowel will have a 'nasal' quality. This occurs in words such as 'entrée', which is transcribed /ɒn⁰treɪ/. In some words, the optional sound is /m⁰/.

LINKING 'R'

When a word ends in /ə, ɑː, ɔː, ɜː, ɪə, eə, ʊə, aɪə/ or /aʊə/, and is spoken before a word which begins with a vowel sound, speakers of RP often link the two words with an /r/. Some people think that this is only correct when the first word is spelt with a silent 'r'. Linking 'r' is not shown explicitly in this dictionary.

Syllabic consonants

In the transcriptions, when an /l/ occurs after another consonant at the end of a word, or between two consonants it is always spoken as a syllable in its own right: 'battle' /bætl̩/ has two syllables, and 'battlefield' /bætl̩fiːld/ has three. This type of /l/ is called a syllabic consonant. The same is true of /n/, except when it is preceded by /l/: 'hidden' /hɪdn̩/ has two syllables, but 'kiln' /kɪln̩/ has one. Syllabic /l/ and /n/ are often alternative pronunciations where /əl/ and /ən/ are shown in the transcriptions, but as syllable loss is not involved, this potential has not been shown explicitly.

Corpus Acknowledgements

The dictionary has been compiled with special reference to a corpus of 70 million words of broadcast English provided by the BBC World Service. This corpus consists of broadcasts made over the years 1988-1992. We would also like to acknowledge with thanks the contribution of National Public Radio of Washington, who provided us with a further 10 million words of American English, broadcast in the course of 1991.

This extensive corpus of broadcast English is a component of the Bank of English, which is a large computerized corpus of texts currently amounting to over 150 million words. The editors had most of this corpus at their disposal during the editing of this dictionary.

We would like to thank the following people and organizations who have given their permission for the use of copyright material.

Times Newspapers Ltd for machine-readable copies of The Times and The Sunday Times.

Associated Business Programmes Ltd for: *The Next 200 Years* by Herman Kahn with William Brown and Leon Martel first published in Great Britain by Associated Business Programmes Ltd 1977 © Hudson Institute 1976. David Attenborough and William Collins Sons & Co Ltd for: *Life on Earth* by David Attenborough first published by William Collins Sons & Co Ltd 1979 © David Attenborough Productions Ltd 1979. James Baldwin for: *The Fire Next Time* by James Baldwin published in Great Britain by Michael Joseph Ltd 1963 © James Baldwin 1963. B T Batsford Ltd for: *Witchcraft in England* by Christina Hole first published by B T Batsford Ltd 1945 © Christina Hole 1945. Michael Billington for: 'Lust at First Sight' by Michael Billington in the *Illustrated London News* July 1981 and 'Truffaut's Tolerance' by Michael Billington in the *Illustrated London News* August 1981. Birmingham International Council For Overseas Students' Aid for: BICOSA Information Leaflets 1981. Basil Blackwell Publishers Ltd for: *Breaking the Mould? The Birth and Prospects of the Social Democratic Party* by Ian Bradley first published by Martin Robertson & Co Ltd 1981 © Ian Bradley 1981. *Seeing Green (The Politics of Ecology Explained)* by Jonathon Porritt first published by Basil Blackwell Publisher Ltd 1984 © Jonathon Porritt 1984. Blond & Briggs Ltd for: *Small is Beautiful* by E F Schumacher first published in Great Britain by Blond & Briggs Ltd 1973 © E F Schumacher 1973. The Bodley Head Ltd for: *The Americans (Letters from America 1969-1979)* by Alistair Cooke first published by Bodley Head Ltd 1979 © Alistair Cooke 1979. *Baby and Child Care* by Dr Benjamin Spock published in Great Britain by The Bodley Head Ltd 1955 © Benjamin Spock MD 1945, 1946, 1957, 1968, 1976, 1979. *What's Wrong With The Modern World?* by Michael Shanks first published by The Bodley Head Ltd 1978 © Michael Shanks 1978. *Future Shock* by Alvin Toffler first published in Great Britain by The Bodley Head Ltd 1970 © Alvin Toffler 1970. *Zen and the Art of Motorcycle Maintenance* by Robert M Pirsig first published in Great Britain by The Bodley Head Ltd 1974 © Robert M Pirsig 1974. *Marnie* by Winston Graham first published by the Bodley Head Ltd 1961 © Winston Graham 1961. *You Can Get There From Here* by Shirley MacLaine first published in Great Britain by The Bodley Head Ltd 1975 © Shirley MacLaine 1975. *It's An Odd Thing, But ...* by Paul Jennings first published by Max Reinhardt Ltd 1971 © Paul Jennings 1971. *King of the Castle (Choice and Responsibility in the Modern World)* by Gai Eaton first published by the Bodley Head Ltd 1977 © Gai Eaton 1977. *Revolutionaries in Modern Britain* by Peter Shipley first published by The Bodley Head Ltd 1976 © Peter Shipley 1976. *The Prerogative of the Harlot (Press Barons and Power)* by Hugh Cudlipp first published by The Bodley Head Ltd 1980 © Hugh Cudlipp 1980. *But What About The Children (A Working Parents' Guide to Child Care)* by Judith Hann first published by The Bodley Head Ltd 1976 © Judith Hann 1976. *Learning to Read* by Margaret Meek first published by The Bodley Head Ltd 1982 © Margaret Meek 1982. Bolt & Watson for: *Two is Lonely* by Lynne Reid Banks first published by Chatto & Windus 1974 © Lynne Reid Banks 1974. The British and Foreign Bible Society with William Collins Sons & Co Ltd for: *Good News Bible (with Deuterocanonical Books/Apocrypha)* first published by The British and Foreign Bible Society with William Collins Sons & Co Ltd 1979 © American Bible Society: Old Testament 1976, Deuterocanonical Books/Apocrypha 1979, New Testament 1966, 1971, 1976 © Maps, British and Foreign Bible Society 1976, 1979. The British Council for: *How to Live in Britain (The British Council's Guide for Overseas Students and Visitors)* first published by The British Council 1952 © The British Council 1984. Mrs R Bronowski for: *The Ascent of Man* by J Bronowski published by Book Club Associates by arrangement with The British Broadcasting Corporation 1977 © J Bronowski 1973. Alison Busby for: *The Death of Trees* by Nigel Dudley first published by Pluto Press Ltd 1985 © Nigel Dudley 1985. Tony Buzan for: *Make The Most of your Mind* by Tony Buzan first published by Colt Books Ltd 1977 © Tony Buzan 1977. Campbell Thomson & McLaughlin Ltd for: *Ring of Bright Water* by Gavin Maxwell first published by Longmans Green & Co 1960, published in Penguin Books Ltd 1976 © The Estate of Gavin Maxwell 1960. Jonathan Cape Ltd for: *Manwatching (A Field Guide to Human Behaviour)* by Desmond Morris first published in Great Britain by Jonathan Cape Ltd 1977 © Text, Desmond Morris 1977 © Compilation, Elsevier Publishing Projects SA, Lausanne, and Jonathan Cape Ltd, London 1977. *Tracks* by Robyn Davidson first published by Jonathan Cape Ltd 1980 © Robyn Davidson 1980. *In the Name of Love* by Jill Tweedie first published by Jonathan Cape Ltd 1979 © Jill Tweedie 1979. *The Use of Lateral Thinking* by Edward de Bono first published by Jonathan Cape 1967 © Edward de Bono 1967. *Trout Fishing in America* by Richard Brautigan first published in Great Britain by Jonathan Cape Ltd 1970 © Richard Brautigan 1967. *The Pendulum Years: Britain and the Sixties* by Bernard Levin first published by Jonathan Cape Ltd 1970 © Bernard Levin 1970. *The Summer Before The Dark* by Doris Lessing first published in Great Britain by Jonathan Cape Ltd 1973 © Doris Lessing 1973. *The Boston Strangler* by Gerold Frank first published in Great Britain by Jonathan Cape Ltd 1967 © Gerold Frank 1966. *I'm OK - You're OK* by Thomas A Harris MD first published in Great Britain as The Book of Choice by Jonathan Cape Ltd 1970 © Thomas A Harris MD, 1967, 1968, 1969. *The Vivisector* by Patrick White first published by Jonathan Cape Ltd 1970 © Patrick White 1970. *The Future of Socialism* by Anthony Crosland first published by Jonathan Cape Ltd 1956 © C A R Crosland 1963. *Funeral in Berlin* by Len Deighton first published by Jonathan Cape Ltd 1964 © Len Deighton 1964. Chatto & Windus Ltd for: *A Postillion Struck by Lightning* by Dirk Bogarde first published by Chatto & Windus Ltd 1977 © Dirk Bogarde 1977. *Nuns and Soldiers* by Iris Murdoch published by Chatto & Windus Ltd 1980 © Iris Murdoch 1980. *Wounded Knee (An Indian History of the American West)* by Dee Brown published by Chatto & Windus Ltd 1978 © Dee Brown 1970. *The Virgin in the Garden* by A S Byatt published by Chatto & Windus Ltd 1978 © A S Byatt 1978. *A Story Like The Wind* by Laurens van der Post published by Clarke Irwin & Co Ltd in association with The Hogarth Press Ltd 1972 © Laurens van der Post 1972. *Brave New World* by Aldous Huxley published by Chatto & Windus Ltd 1932 © Aldous Huxley and Mrs Laura Huxley 1932, 1960. *The Reivers* By William Faulkner first published by Chatto & Windus Ltd 1962 © William Faulkner 1962. *Cider With Rosie* by Laurie Lee published by The Hogarth Press 1959 © Laurie Lee 1959 *The Tenants* by Bernard Malamud first published in Great Britain by Chatto & Windus Ltd 1972 © Bernard Malamud 1971. *Kinflicks* by Lisa Alther first published in Great Britain by Chatto & Windus Ltd 1976 © Lisa Alther 1975. William Collins Sons & Co Ltd for: *The Companion Guide to London* by David Piper published by William Collins Sons & Co Ltd 1964 © David Piper 1964. *The Bedside Guardian 29* edited by W L Webb published by William Collins & Sons Ltd 1980 © Guardian Newspapers Ltd 1980. *Bear Island* by Alistair MacLean first published by William Collins Sons & Co Ltd 1971 © Alistair MacLean 1971. *Inequality in Britain: Freedom, Welfare and the State* by Frank Field first published by Fontana Paperbacks 1981 © Frank Field 1981. *Social Mobility* by Anthony Heath first published by Fontana Paperbacks 1981©Anthony Heath 1981. *Yours Faithfully* by Gerald Priestland first published by Fount Paperbacks 1979 © British Broadcasting Corporation 1977, 1978. *Power Without Responsibility: The Press and Broadcasting in Britain* by James Curran and Jean Seaton first published by Fontana Paperbacks 1981 © James Curran and Jean Seaton 1981. *The Times Cookery Book* by Katie Stewart first published by William Collins Sons & Co Ltd 1972 © Times Newspapers Ltd. *Friends from the Forest* by Joy Adamson by Collins and Harvill Press 1981 © Elsa Limited 1981. *The Media Mob* by Barry Fantoni and George Melly first published by William Collins Sons & Co Ltd 1980 © Text, George Melly 1980 © Illustrations, Barry Fantoni 1980. *Shalom (a collection of Australian and Jewish Stories)* compiled by Nancy Keesing first published by William Collins Publishers Pty Ltd 1978 © William Collins Sons &Co Ltd 1978. *The Bedside Guardian 31* edited by W L Webb first published by William Collins Sons & Co Ltd 1982 © Guardian Newspapers Ltd 1982. *The Bedside Guardian 32* edited by W L Webb first published by William Collins Sons & Co Ltd 1983 © Guardian Newspapers Ltd 1983. *Design for the Real World* by Victor Papanek first published in Great Britain by Thames & Hudson Ltd 1972 © Victor Papanek 1971. *Food For Free* by Richard Mabey first published by William Collins Sons & Co Ltd 1972 © Richard Mabey 1972. *Unended Quest* by Karl Popper (first published as Autobiography of Karl Popper in The Philosophy of Karl Popper in The Library of Philosophers edited by Paul Arthur Schlipp by the Open Court Publishing Co 1974) published by Fontana Paperbacks 1976 © The Library of Living Philosophers Inc 1974 © Karl R Popper 1976. *My Mother My Self* by Nancy Friday first published in Great Britain by Fontana Paperbacks 1979 © Nancy Friday 1977. *The Captain's Diary* by Bob Willis first published by Willow Books/William Collins Sons & Co Ltd 1984 © Bob Willis and Alan Lee 1984 © New Zealand Scorecards, Bill Frindall 1984. *The Bodywork Book* by Esme Newton-Dunn first published in Great Britain by Willow Books/William Collins Sons & Co Ltd 1982 © TVS Ltd/Esme Newton-Dunn 1982. *Collins' Encyclopaedia of Fishing in The British Isles* edited by Michael Prichard first published by William Collins Sons & Co Ltd 1976 © William Collins Sons & Co Ltd 1976. *The AAA Runner's Guide* edited by Heather Thomas first published by William Collins Sons & Co Ltd 1983 © Sackville Design Group Ltd 1983. *Heroes and Contemporaries* by David Gower with Derek Hodgson first published by William Collins Sons & Co Ltd 1983 © David Gower Promotions Ltd 1983. *The Berlin Memorandum* by Adam Hall first published by William Collins Sons & Co Ltd 1965 © Jonquil Trevor 1965. *Arlott on Cricket: His Writings on the Game* edited by David Rayvern Allen first published by William Collins (Willow Books) 1984 © John Arlott 1984. *A Woman in Custody* by Audrey Peckham first published by Fontana Paperbacks 1985 © Audrey Peckham 1985. *Play Golf with Peter Alliss* by Peter Alliss published by the British Broadcasting Corporation 1977 © Peter Alliss and Renton Laidlaw 1977. Curtis Brown Ltd for: *The Pearl* by John Steinbeck first published by William Heinemann Ltd 1948 © John Steinbeck 1948. *An Unfinished History of the World* by Hugh Thomas first published in Great Britain by Hamish Hamilton Ltd 1979 © Hugh Thomas 1979, 1981. *The Winter of our Discontent* by John Steinbeck first published in Great Britain by William Heinemann Ltd 1961 © John Steinbeck 1961. *Burr* by Gore Vidal first published in Great Britain by William Heinemann Ltd 1974 © Gore Vidal 1974. *Doctor on the Job* by Richard Gordon first published by William Heinemann Ltd 1976 © Richard Gordon Ltd 1976. Andre Deutsch Ltd for: *How to be an Alien* by George Mikes first published by Andre Deutsch Ltd 1946 © George Mikes and Nicholas Bentley 1946. *Jaws* by Peter Benchley first published in Great Britain by Andre Deutsch Ltd 1974 © Peter Benchley 1974. *A Bend in the River* by V S Naipaul first published by Andre Deutsch Ltd 1979 © V S Naipaul 1979. *Couples* by John Updike first published by Andre Deutsch Ltd 1968 © John Updike 1968. *Games People Play* by Eric Berne published in Great Britain by Andre Deutsch Ltd 1966 © Eric Berne 1964. *The Age of Uncertainty* by John Kenneth Galbraith first published by The British Broadcasting Corporation and Andre Deutsch Ltd 1977 © John Kenneth Galbraith 1977. The Economist Newspaper Ltd for: *The Economist* (9-15 May 1981 and 22-28 August 1981) © published by The Economist Newspaper Ltd 1981. Faber & Faber Ltd for: *Lord of the Flies* by William Golding first published by Faber & Faber Ltd 1954 © William Golding 1954. *The Complete Book of Self-Sufficiency* by John Seymour first published in Great Britain by Faber & Faber Ltd 1976 © Text, John Seymour 1976, 1977 © Dorling Kindersley Ltd 1976, 1977. *Conversations with Igor Stravinsky* by Igor Stravinsky and Robert Craft first published by Faber & Faber Ltd 1959 © Igor Stravinsky 1958,1959. John Farquharson Ltd for: *The Moon's A Balloon* by David Niven published in Great Britain by Hamish Hamilton Ltd 1971 © David Niven 1971. John Gaselee for: 'Going it Alone' by John Gaselee in the *Illustrated London News* July 1981 and 'The Other Car's Fault' by John Gaselee in the *Illustrated London News* August 1981. Glidrose Publications Ltd for: *The Man with the Golden Gun* by Ian Fleming first published by Jonathan Cape Ltd © Glidrose Productions Ltd 1965. Victor Gollancz Ltd for: *The Next Horizon* by Chris Bonnington published by Victor Gollancz Ltd 1976 © Chris Bonnington 1973. *Summerhill: A Radical Approach to Education* by A S Neill first published by Victor Gollancz Ltd 1962 © A S Neill 1926, 1932, 1937, 1953, 1961 (US permission by Hart Publishing Inc). *Lucky Jim* by Kingsley Amis first published by Victor Gollancz Ltd 1954 © Kingsley Amis 1953. *The Mighty Micro (The Impact of the Computer Revolution)* by Christopher Evans first published by Victor Gollancz Ltd 1979 © Christopher Evans 1979. *The Longest Day* by Cornelius Ryan published by Victor Gollancz Ltd 1960 © Cornelius Ryan 1959. *Asking for Trouble (Autobiography of a Banned Journalist)* by Donald Woods published by Victor Gollancz Ltd 1980 © Donald Woods 1980. *The Turin Shroud* by Ian Wilson first published in Great Britain by Victor Gollancz Ltd 1978 © Ian Wilson 1978. *Murdo and Other Stories* by Iain Crichton Smith published by Victor Gollancz Ltd 1981 © Iain Crichton Smith 1981. *The Class Struggle in Parliament* by Eric S Heffer published by Victor Gollancz Ltd 1973 © Eric S Heffer 1973. *A Presumption of Innocence (The Amazing Case of Patrick Meehan)* by Ludovic Kennedy published by Victor Gollancz Ltd 1976 © Ludovic Kennedy 1976. *The Treasure of Sainte Foy* by MacDonald Harris published by Victor Gollancz Ltd 1980 © MacDonald Harris 1980. *A Long Way to Shiloh* by Lionel Davidson first published by Victor Gollancz Ltd 1966 © Lionel Davidson 1966. *Education After School* by Tyrrell Burgess first published by Victor Gollancz Ltd 1977 © Tyrrell Burgess 1977. *The View From Serendip* by Arthur C Clarke published by Victor Gollancz Ltd 1978 © Arthur C Clarke 1967, 1968, 1970, 1972, 1974, 1976, 1977. *On Wings of Song* by Thomas M Disch published by Victor Gollancz Ltd 1979 © Thomas M Disch 1979. *The World of Violence* by Colin Wilson published by Victor Gollancz Ltd 1963 © Colin Wilson 1963. *The Lightning Tree* by Joan Aiken published by Victor Gollancz Ltd 1980 © Joan Aiken Enterprises 1980. *Russia's Political Hospitals* by Sidney Bloch and Peter Reddaway published by Victor Gollancz Ltd 1977 © Sidney Bloch and Peter Reddaway 1977. *Unholy Loves* by Joyce Carol Oates first published in Great Britain by Victor Gollancz Ltd 1980 © Joyce Carol Oates 1979. *Consenting Adults (or The Duchess will be Furious)* by Peter De Vries published by Victor Gollancz Ltd 1981 © Peter De Vries 1980. *The Passion of New Eve* by Angela Carter published by Victor Gollancz Ltd 1977 © Angela Carter 1977. Gower Publishing Co Ltd for: *Solar Prospects (The Potential for Renewable Energy)* by Michael Flood first published in Great Britain by Wildwood House Ltd in association with Friends of the Earth Ltd 1983 © Michael Flood. *Voiceless Victims* by Rebecca Hall first published in Great Britain by Wildwood House Ltd 1984 © Rebecca Hall 1984. Graham Greene and Laurence Pollinger Ltd for: *The Human Factor* by Graham Greene first published by The Bodley Head Ltd 1978 © Graham Greene 1978. Syndication Manager, The Guardian, for: *The Guardian* (12 May 1981, 7 September 1981 and 15 September 1981) © published by Guardian Newspapers Ltd 1981. Hamlyn for: *How to Play Rugby* by David Norrie published by The Hamlyn Publishing Group Ltd 1981 © The Hamlyn Publishing Group Ltd 1981. *How to Play Badminton* by Pat Davies first published by The Hamlyn Publishing Group Ltd 1979 © The Hamlyn Publishing Group Ltd 1979. Margaret Hanbury for: *Crisis and Conservation: Conflict in the British Countryside* by Charlie Pye-Smith and Chris Rose first published by Pelican/Penguin Books Ltd 1984 © Charlie Pye-Smith and Chris Rose 1984. Paul Harrison for: *Inside the Third World* by Paul Harrison first published in Great Britain by The Harvester Press Ltd 1980 © Paul Harrison 1979. A M Heath & Co Ltd for: *Rembrandt's Hat* by Bernard Malamud published by Chatto & Windus Ltd 1982 © Bernard Malamud 1968, 1972, 1973. William Heinemann Ltd for: *It's an Old Country* by J B Priestley first published in Great Britain by William Heinemann Ltd 1967 © J B Priestley 1967. Heinemann Educational Books Ltd and Gower Publishing Co Ltd for: *The Environmental Crisis (A Handbook for all Friends of the Earth)* edited by Des Wilson first published by Heinemann Educational Books Ltd 1984 © Foreword, David Bellamy 1984 © Individual Chapters, the Author of the Chapter 1984 © In the selection and all other matters Des Wilson 1984. The Controller, Her Majesty's Stationery Office, for: Department of Health and Social Security leaflets published by Her Majesty's Stationery Office 1981 © The Crown. David Higham Associates Ltd for: 'Two Peruvian Projects' by E R Chamberlain in the *Illustrated London News* September 1981. *Akenfield: Portrait of an English Village* by Ronald Blythe first published by Allen Lane, Penguin Books Ltd 1969 © Ronald Blythe 1969. *The Far Pavillions* by M M Kaye first published by Allen Lane/Penguin Books Ltd 1978 © M M Kaye 1978. *Staying On* by Paul Scott first published by William Heinemann Ltd 1977 © Paul Scott 1977. *Let Sleeping Vets Lie* by James Herriot first published by Michael Joseph Ltd 1973 © James Herriot 1973. *The Midwich Cuckoos* by John Wyndham first published in Great Britain by Michael Joseph Ltd 1957 © The Estate of John Wyndham 1957. *The Girl in a Swing* by Richard Adams first published in Great Britain by Allen Lane in Penguin Books Ltd 1980 © Richard Adams 1980. Dr K B Hindley for: 'Hot Spots of the Deep' by Dr K B Hindley in the *Illustrated London News July* 1981. Hodder and Stoughton Ltd for: *Supernature* by Lyall Watson first published by Hodder & Stoughton Ltd 1973 © Lyall Watson 1973. *Tinker Tailor Soldier Spy* by John Le Carre first published by Hodder & Stoughton Ltd 1974 © Le Carre Productions 1974. The Editor, Homes and Gardens, for: *Homes and Gardens* (October 1981) (Number 4 Volume 63) © published by IPC Magazines Ltd 1981. Hughes Massie Ltd for: *Elephants Can Remember* by Agatha Christie first published by William Collins Sons & Co Ltd 1972 © Agatha Christie Mallowan. Hutchinson Publishing Group Ltd for: *An Autobiography* by Angela Davis published in Great Britain by Hutchinson & Co Publishers Ltd by arrangement with Bantam Books Inc 1975 © Angela Davis 1974. *The Day of the Jackal* by Frederick Forsyth published in Great Britian by Hutchinson & Co Publishers Ltd 1971 © Frederick Forsyth 1971. *Roots* by Alex Haley first published in Great Britain by Hutchinson & Co Publishers Ltd 1977 © Alex Haley 1976. *The Climate of Treason* by Andrew Boyle first published by Hutchinson & Co Publishers Ltd 1979 © Andrew Boyle 1979. *The Collapsing Universe: The Story of Black Holes* by Isaac Asimov first published by Hutchinson & Co Publishers Ltd 1977 © Isaac Asimov. *XPD* by Len Deighton published by Book Club Associates by arrangement with Hutchinson & Co Publishers Ltd 1981 © Len Deighton 1981. *Show Jumping with Harvey Smith* by Harvey Smith first published by Stanley Paul & Co Ltd 1979 © Tyne-Tees Television Ltd, A Member of the Trident Group 1979. *2001: A Space Odyssey by* Arthur C Clarke first published by Hutchinson & Co Publishers Ltd 1968 © Arthur C Clarke and Polaris Productions Inc 1968 © Epilogue material, Serendip BV 1982, 1983. The Illustrated London News and Sketch Ltd for: *The Illustrated London News* (July 1981, August 1981 and September 1981) © published by the Illustrated London News and Sketch Ltd 1981. The Editor, International Herald Tribune, for: *International Herald Tribune* (25-26 July 1981) © published by International Herald Tribune with The New York Times and The Washington Post 1981. Michael Joseph Ltd for: *Chronicles of Fairacre: Village School* by Miss Read first published in Great Britain by Michael Joseph Ltd 1964 © Miss Read 1955, 1964. *Fire Fox* by Craig Thomas first published in Great Britain by Michael Joseph Ltd 1977 © Craig Thomas 1977. William Kimber & Co Ltd for: *Exodus* by Leon Uris originally published in Great Britain by Alan Wingate Ltd 1959 © Leon Uris 1958. Kogan Page Ltd for: *How to Save the World (Strategy for World Conservation)* by Robert Allen first published by Kogan Page Ltd 1980 © IUCN-UNEP-WWF 1980. Marketing Department, Lloyds Bank PLC, for: *Lloyds Bank Leaflets* (1981) © published by Lloyds Bank PLC 1981. Macmillan Publishers Ltd for: *Appropriate Technology: Technology with a Human Face* by P D Dunn first published by the Macmillan Press Ltd 1978 © P D Dunn 1978. John Murray Publishers Ltd for: *A Backward Place* by Ruth Prawer Jhabvala first published by John Murray Publishers Ltd 1965 © R Prawer Jhabvala 1965. *Food For All The Family* by Magnus Pyke first published by John Murray Publishers Ltd 1980 © Magnus Pyke 1980. *Simple Movement* by Laura Mitchell and Barbara Dale first published by John Murray Publishers Ltd 1980 © Laura Mitchell and Barbara Dale 1980. *Civilisation: A Personal View* by Kenneth Clark first published by the British Broadcasting Corporation and John Murray Publishers Ltd 1969 © Kenneth Clark 1969. The Editor, National Geographic, for: *National Geographic* January, February and March (1980) © published by The National Geographic Society 1979, 1980. The National Magazine Co Ltd for: *Cosmopolitan* (May 1981 and July 1981) © published by the National Magazine Co Ltd 1981. Neilson Leisure Group Ltd for: *NAT Holidays' 'Caravans and Tents in the Sun'* (Summer 1983) holiday brochure. Newsweek Inc for: *Newsweek* (11 May 1981, 27 July 1981 and August 1981) © published by Newsweek Inc 1981. The Associate Editor, Now!, for: *Now!* (14-20 November 1980) © published by Cavenham Communications Ltd 1980. Harold Ober Associates Inc for: *The Boys from Brazil* by Ira Levin first published by Michael Joseph Ltd 1976 © Ira Levin 1976. Edna O'Brien and A M Heath & Co Ltd for: *August is a Wicked Month* by Edna O'Brien first published by Jonathan Cape Ltd 1965 © Edna O'Brien 1965. Pan Books Ltd for: *Dispatches* by Michael Herr first published in Great Britain by Pan Books Ltd 1978 © Michael Herr 1968, 1969, 1970, 1977. *Health and Safety at Work* by Dave Eva and Ron Oswald first published by Pan Books Ltd 1981 © Dave Eva, Ron Oswald and the Workers' Educational Association 1981. *Democracy at Work* by Patrick Burns and Mel Doyle first published by Pan Books Ltd 1981 © Patrick Burns,Mel Doyle and the Workers' Educational Association 1981. *Diet for Life (A Cookbook for Arthritics)* by Mary Laver and Margaret Smith first published by Pan Books Ltd 1981 © Mary Laver and Margaret Smith 1981. Penguin Books Ltd for: *Inside the Company: CIA Diary* by Philip Agee first published in Allen Lane/Penguin Books Ltd 1975 © Philip Agee 1975. Penguin Books Ltd and Spare Ribs Ltd for: *Spare Rib Reader* edited by Marsha Rowe first published in Penguin Books Ltd 1982 © Spare Ribs Ltd 1982. A D Peters & Co Ltd for: 'The Dark Side of Israel' by Norman Moss in Illustrated London News July 1981, 'Aftermath of Osirak' by Norman Moss in the *Illustrated London News* August 1981 and 'Turning Point for Poland' by Norman Moss in the *Illustrated London News* September 1981. 'Recent Fiction' by Sally Emerson in the *Illustrated London News* July 1981, August 1981 and September 1981. *The Complete Upmanship* by Stephen Potter first published in Great Britain by Rupert Hart-Davis Ltd 1970 © Stephen Potter. Elaine Pollard for: Personal Letters 1981 donated by Elaine Pollard. Laurence Pollinger Ltd for: *A Glastonbury Romance* by John Cowper Powys first published by MacDonald & Co Ltd 1933. Murray Pollinger for: *Kiss Kiss* by Roald Dahl published in Great Britain by Michael Joseph Ltd 1960 © Roald Dahl 1962. *Can You Avoid Cancer?* by Peter Goodwin first published by the British Broadcasting Corporation 1984 © Peter Goodwin 1984. Preston Travel Ltd for: Preston Sunroutes 'Camping and Self-Catering' (April to October 1983) holiday brochure. Punch Publications Ltd for: *Punch* (6 May 1981, 29 July 1981, 12 August 1981, 26 August 1981 and 9 September 1981) © published by Punch Publications Ltd 1981. Radala and associates for: *The Naked Civil Servant* by Quentin Crisp first published by Jonathan Cape Ltd 1968 © Quentin Crisp 1968. The Rainbird Publishing Group Ltd for: *The Making of Mankind* by Richard E Leakey first published in Great Britain by Michael Joseph Ltd 1981 © Sherma BV 1981. Robson Books Ltd for: *The Punch Book of Short Stories 3* selected by Alan Coren first published in Great Britain by Robson Books Ltd in association with Punch Publications Ltd 1981 © Robson Books Ltd 1981.*The Best of Robert Morley* by Robert Morley first published in Great Britain by Robson Books Ltd 1981 © Robert Morley 1981. Deborah Rogers Ltd for: 'Picasso's Late Works' by Edward Lucie-Smith in the *Illustrated London News* July 1981, 'David Jones at the Tate' by Edward Lucie-Smith in the *Illustrated London News* August 1981 and 'Further Light on Spanish Painting' by Edward Lucie-Smith in the *Illustrated London News* September 1981. *The Godfather* by Mario Puzo first published in Great Britain by William Heinemann Ltd 1969 © Mario Puzo 1969. Routledge & Kegan Paul Ltd for: *How To Pass*

Examinations by John Erasmus first published by Oriel Press Ltd 1967 ©Oriel Press Ltd 1980. *Daisy, Daisy* by Christian Miller first published by Routledge & Kegan Paul Ltd 1980 © Christian Miller 1980. *The National Front* by Nigel Fielding first published by Routledge & Kegan Paul Ltd 1981 © Nigel Fielding 1981. *The Myth of Home Ownership* by Jim Kemeny first published by Routledge & Kegan Paul Ltd 1980 © J Kemeny 1981. *Absent With Cause (Lessons of Truancy)* by Roger White first published by Routledge & Kegan Paul Ltd 1980 © Roger White 1980. *The Powers of Evil (in Western Religion, Magic and Folk Belief)* by Richard Cavendish first published by Routledge & Kegan Paul Ltd 1975 © Richard Cavendish 1975. *Crime and Personality* by H J Eysenck first published by Routledge & Kegan Paul Ltd 1964 © H J Eysenck 1964, 1977. Martin Secker & Warburg Ltd for: *Changing Places* by David Lodge first published in England by Martin Secker & Warburg Ltd 1975 © David Lodge 1975. *The History Man* by Malcolm Bradbury first published by Martin Secker & Warburg 1975 © Malcolm Bradbury 1975. *Humboldt's Gift* by Saul Bellow first published in England by The Alison Press/Martin Secker & Warburg Ltd 1975 © Saul Bellow 1973, 1974, 1975. *Wilt* by Tom Sharpe first published in England by Martin Secker & Warburg Ltd 1976 © Tom Sharpe 1976. *The Last Days of America* by Paul E Erdman first published in England by Martin Secker & Warburg Ltd 1981 © Paul E Erdman 1981. *Autumn Manoeuvres* by Melvyn Bragg first published in England by Martin Secker & Warburg Ltd 1978 © Melvyn Bragg 1978. *The Act of Being* by Charles Marowitz first published in England by Martin Secker & Warburg Ltd 1978 © Charles Marowitz 1978. *As If By Magic* by Angus Wilson first published in England by Martin Secker & Warburg Ltd 1973 © Angus Wilson 1973. *All the President's Men* by Carl Bernstein and Bob Woodward first published in England by Martin Secker & Warburg Ltd 1974 © Carl Bernstein and Bob Woodward 1974. *The Myth of the Nation and the Vision of Revolution* by J L Talmon first published by Martin Secker & Warburg Ltd 1981 © J L Talmon 1980. *Animal Farm* by George Orwell first published by Martin Secker & Warburg 1945 © Eric Blair 1945. Anthony Sheil Associates Ltd for: *Daniel Martin* by John Fowles first published in Great Britain by Jonathan Cape Ltd 1977 © J R Fowles Ltd 1977. *Love Story* by Erich Segal published by Hodder & Stoughton Ltd 1970 © Erich Segal 1970. Sidgwick & Jackson Ltd for: *The Third World War* by General Sir John Hackett and others first published in Great Britain by Sidgwick & Jackson Ltd 1978 © General Sir John Hackett 1978. *Superwoman* by Shirley Conran first published by Sidgwick & Jackson Ltd 1975 © Shirley Conran 1975, 1977. *An Actor and His Time* by John Gielgud first published in Great Britain by Sidgwick & Jackson Ltd 1979 © John Gielgud, John Miller and John Powell 1979 © Biographical Notes, John Miller 1979. Simon & Schuster for: *Our Bodies Ourselves (A Health Book by and for Women)* by the Boston Women's Health Book Collective (British Edition by Angela Phillips and Jill Rakusen) published in Allen Lane and Penguin Books Ltd 1978 © The Boston Women's Health Collective Inc 1971, 1973, 1976 © Material for British Edition, Angela Phillips and Jill Rakusen 1978. Souvenir Press Ltd for: *The Bermuda Triangle* by Charles Berlitz (An Incredible Saga of Unexplained Disappearances) first published in Great Britain by Souvenir Press Ltd 1975 © Charles Berlitz 1974. Souvenir Press Ltd and Michael Joseph Ltd for: *Airport* by Arthur Hailey first published in Great Britain by Michael Joseph Ltd in association with Souvenir Press Ltd 1968 © Arthur Hailey Ltd 1968. Sunmed Holidays Ltd for: 'Go Greek' (Summer 1983) holiday brochure. Maurice Temple Smith Ltd for: *Friends of the Earth Pollution Guide* by Brian Price published by Maurice Temple Smith Ltd 1983 © Brian Price 1983. Maurice Temple Smith and Gower Publishing Co Ltd for: *Working the Land (A New Plan for a Healthy Agriculture)* by Charlie Pye-Smith and Richard North first published by Maurice Temple Smith Ltd 1984 © Charlie Pye-Smith and Richard North 1984. Times Newspapers Ltd for: *The Sunday Times Magazine* (13 January 1980, 20 January 1980 and 11 May 1980) © published by Times Newspapers Ltd 1981. *The Times* (7 September 1981) © published by Times Newspapers Ltd 1981. Twenty's Holidays for: 'The Best 18-33 Holidays' (Winter 1982/83) holiday brochure. University of Birmingham for: *Living in Birmingham* (1984) © published by The University of Birmingham 1984. Birmingham University Overseas Student Guide © The University of Birmingham. Working with Industry and Commerce © published by The University of Birmingham 1984. University of Birmingham Prospectus (June 1985) © published by The University of Birmingham 1985. University of Birmingham Library Guide © published by The University of Birmingham. University of Birmingham Institute of Research and Development (1984) © published by the University of Birmingham 1984. Biological Sciences at The University of Birmingham (1985) © published by The University of Birmingham 1985. History at the University of Birmingham (1985) © published by the University of Birmingham 1985. Faculty of Arts Handbook (1984-85) © published by The University of Birmingham 1984. Virago Press Ltd for: *Benefits* by Zoe Fairbairns published by Virago Press Ltd 1979 © Zoe Fairbairns 1979. *Simple Steps to Public Life* by Pamela Anderson, Mary Stott and Fay Weldon published in Great Britain by Virago Press Ltd 1980 © Action Opportunities 1980. *Tell Me A Riddle* by Tillie Olsen published by Virago Press Ltd 1980 © this edition Tillie Olsen 1980. A P Watt (& Sons) Ltd for: *The Glittering Prizes* by Frederic Raphael first published in Great Britain by Penguin Books Ltd 1976 © Volatic Ltd 1976. *Then and Now* by W Somerset Maugham first published by William Heinemann Ltd 1946 © W Somerset Maugham 1946. *The Language of Clothes* by Alison Lurie published by William Heinemann Ltd 1981 © Alison Lurie 1981. 'Herschel Commemorative'

by Patrick Moore in the *Illustrated London News* July 1981. 'The Outermost Giant' by Patrick Moore in the *Illustrated London News* August 1981. 'Cosmic Bombardment' by Patrick Moore in the *Illustrated London News* September 1981. Weidenfeld & Nicolson Ltd for: 'The Miraculous Toy' by Susan Briggs in the *Illustrated London News* August 1981. *The Needle's Eye* by Margaret Drabble first published by Weidenfeld & Nicolson Ltd 1972 © Margaret Drabble 1972. *Success Without Tears: A Woman's Guide to the Top* by Rachel Nelson first published in Great Britain by Weidenfeld & Nicolson Ltd 1979 © Rachel Nelson 1979. *Education in the Modern World* by John Vaizey published by Weidenfeld & Nicolson Ltd 1967 © John Vaizey 1967. *Rich Man, Poor Man* by Irwin Shaw first published in Great Britain by Weidenfeld & Nicolson Ltd 1970 © Irwin Shaw 1969, 1970. *Lolita* by Vladimir Nabokov first published in Great Britain by Weidenfeld & Nicolson Ltd 1959 © Vladimir Nabokov 1955, 1959, 1968, © G P Putnam's Sons 1963 © McGraw-Hill International Inc 1971. *The Third World* by Peter Worsley first published by Weidenfeld & Nicolson Ltd 1964 © Peter Worsley 1964, 1967. *Portrait of a Marriage* by Nigel Nicolson published by Weidenfeld & Nicolson Ltd 1973 © Nigel Nicolson 1973. *The Dogs Bark: Public People and Private Places* by Truman Capote first published in Great Britain by Weidenfeld & Nicolson Ltd 1974 © Truman Capote 1974. *Great Planning Disasters* by Peter Hall first published in Great Britain by George Weidenfeld & Nicolson Ltd 1980 © Peter Hall 1980. The Writers and Readers Publishing Co-operative Ltd for: *Working with Words, Literacy Beyond School* by Jane Mace published by The Writers and Readers Publishing Co-operative Ltd 1979 © Jane Mace 1979. *The Alienated: Growing Old Today* by Gladys Elder OAP published by The Writers and Readers Publishing Co-operative Ltd 1977 © Text, The Estate of Gladys Elder 1977 © Photographs, Mike Abrahams 1977. *Beyond the Crisis in Art* by Peter Fuller published by The Writers and Readers Publishing Cooperative Ltd 1980 © Peter Fuller 1980. *The War and Peace Book* by Dave Noble published by The Writers and Readers Publishing Co-operative Ltd 1977 © Dave Noble 1977. *Tony Benn: A Political Biography* by Robert Jenkins first published by The Writers and Readers Publishing Co-operative Ltd 1980 © Robert Jenkins 1980. *Nuclear Power for Beginners* by Stephen Croall and Kaianders Sempler first published by The Writers and Readers Publishing Co-operative Ltd 1978 © Text, Stephen Croall 1978, 1980 © Illustrations Kaianders Sempler 1978, 1980. Yale University Press for: *Life in the English Country House: A Social and Architectural History* by Mark Girouard published by Yale University Press Ltd, London 1978 © Yale University 1978. The British Broadcasting Corporation for transcripts of radio transmissions of 'Kaleidoscope', 'Any Questions', 'Money Box' and 'Arts and Africa' 1981 and 1982. The British Broadcasting Corporation and Mrs Shirley Williams for transcripts of television interviews with Mrs Shirley Williams 1979. Dr B L Smith, School of Mathematics and Physical Sciences, University of Sussex for programmes on Current Affairs, Science and The Arts originally broadcast on Radio Sussex 1979 and 1980 © B L Smith. The following people in the University of Birmingham: Professor J McH Sinclair, Department of English, for his tapes of informal conversation (personal collection). Mr R Wallace, formerly Department of Accounting and Finance, and Ms D Houghton, Department of English, for transcripts of his accountancy lectures. Dr B K Gazey, Department of Electrical Engineering and Dr M Montgomery, University of Strathclyde, Department of English, for a transcript of Dr Gazey's lecture. Dr L W Poel, Department of Plant Biology, and Dr M Montgomery, University of Strathclyde, Department of English, for a transcript of Dr Poel's lecture. Professor J G Hawkes, formerly Department of Plant Biology, for recordings of his lectures. Dr M S Snaith, Department of Transportation for recordings of his lectures. Dr M P Hoey, Department of English, and Dr M Cooper, The British Council, for a recording of their discussion on discourse analysis. Ms A Renouf, Department of English, for recordings of job and academic interviews 1977. Mr R H Hubbard, formerly a B Phil (Ed) student, Faculty of Education, for his research recordings of expressions of uncertainty 1978-79. Mr A E Hare, formerly a B Phil (Ed) student, Faculty of Education, for his transcripts of telephone conversations 1978. Dr A Tsui, formerly Department of English, for her recordings of informal conversation. Mr J Couperthwaite, formerly Department of English, for a recording of informal conversation 1981. Ms C Emmott, M Litt student, Department of English, for a recording of informal conversation 1981. Mrs B T Atkins for the transcript of an account of a dream 1981. The British Council for 'Authentic Materials Numbers 1-28' 1981. Professor M Hammerton and Mr K Coghill, Department of Psychology, University of Newcastle-upon-Tyne, for tape recordings of their lectures 1981. Mr G P Graveson, formerly research student, University of Newcastle, for his recordings of teacher discussion 1977. Mr W R Jones, formerly research student, University of Southampton, for his recordings of classroom talk. Mr Ian Fisher, formerly BA student, Newcastle Polytechnic, for his transcripts of interviews on local history 1981. Dr N Coupland, formerly PhD student, Department of English, UWIST, for his transcripts of travel agency talk 1981. Professor D B Bromley, Department of Psychology, University of Liverpool, for his transcript of a research recording. Mr Brian Lawrence, formerly of Saffron Walden County High School, for a tape of his talk on 'The British Education System' 1979.

Every effort has been made to trace the copyright holders, but if any have been inadvertently overlooked the publishers will be pleased to make the necessary acknowledgments at the first opportunity.

A a

A, a /eɪ/ **A's, a's**
NC **A** is the first letter of the English alphabet.

a or **an**. The form **a** is usually pronounced /ə/, but it is pronounced /eɪ/ when you are emphasizing it. The form **an** is used in front of words that begin with vowel sounds. It is usually pronounced /ən/, but it is pronounced /æn/ when you are emphasizing it.
1 DET You use **a** or **an** when you are referring to someone or something for the first time, or when you do not want to be specific. *Tom could see a hallway... She wanted to be an actress.*
2 DET You can use **a** or **an** instead of the number 'one'. *...in an hour's time. ...a year or two ago.*
3 DET When you express rates, prices, and measurements, you can use **a** or **an** to say how many units apply to each of the items being measured. *He charges 100 dollars an hour. ...once a year. ...five pounds a metre.*
4 DET You can use **a** or **an** in front of uncount nouns when they come after adjectives or in front of words that describe the uncount noun more fully. *...a happiness that he couldn't quite hide... A general education is more important than an exact knowledge of some particular theory.*

AA /eɪ eɪ/
1 N PROP The **AA** is a British motoring organization that helps members when their cars break down; an abbreviation for 'Automobile Association'.
2 N PROP **AA** is an organization that helps people who are suffering from alcoholism or who have given up alcoholic drinks for medical reasons; an abbreviation for 'Alcoholics Anonymous'.

aback /əbæk/. See take aback.

abacus /æbəkəs/ **abacuses**
NC An **abacus** is a frame that is used for counting. It has rods with sliding beads on them. *Many banks still use an abacus for counting.*

abandon /əbændən/ **abandons, abandoning, abandoned**
1 VO If you **abandon** a place, thing, or person, you leave them permanently or for a long time. *You're not supposed to abandon your car on the motorway. ...women who had been raped and abandoned.*
♦ **abandoned** ADJ *The getaway vehicle was later found abandoned in a nearby street. ...a charity organisation concerned with the plight of abandoned and starving children.*
2 VO To **abandon** an activity or idea means to stop doing it or thinking about it before it is finished. *He has abandoned his dream of returning to Jaffa... To abandon this view would be a breathtaking U-turn, and one which his critics would use against him... The ferry returned to Harwich, after abandoning the search for the missing man.*
3 When people **abandon ship**, they leave it because it is sinking. *The crew was forced to abandon ship when it caught fire.*
4 V-REFL+to If you **abandon** yourself to an emotion, you feel it strongly and do not try to control it; a literary use. *She abandoned herself to grief.*
5 NU If you do something with **abandon**, you do it in a carefree way. *...dancing with abandon... The security*

forces wouldn't engage again in such a tactic with such wild abandon because they know who the activists are now.

abandonment /əbændənmənt/
1 NU The **abandonment** of a place, person, or thing is the act of leaving them permanently or for a long time. *The abandonment of many farms will pose special problems for the returning refugees.*
2 NU The **abandonment** of a piece of work, plan, or activity is the act of stopping doing it, especially before it is finished. *She disagreed with the abandonment of the project... There was considerable outrage at the abandonment of the elections.*

abase /əbeɪs/ **abases, abasing, abased**
V-REFL If you **abase** yourself, you behave in a way which shows that you accept that something or someone else is much more important than you are. *So the Vikings decided to abase themselves before the High King of Ireland, and give him his tribute of gold.*

abashed /əbæʃt/
ADJ PRED If you are **abashed**, you feel embarrassed and ashamed. *The students looked guilty and abashed.*

abate /əbeɪt/ **abates, abating, abated**
V When an unpleasant situation or feeling **abates**, it becomes much less strong or widespread; a formal word. *My terror abated a little.*

abatement /əbeɪtmənt/
NU **Abatement** is a reduction in the strength or power of something; a formal word. *...the Noise Abatement Society.*

abattoir /æbətwɑː/ **abattoirs**
NC An **abattoir** is a place where animals are killed for meat. *The sheep were driven to the local abattoir, where the staff were obliged to slaughter them.*

abbess /æbes/ **abbesses**
NC An **abbess** is the senior nun who is in charge of the other nuns in a convent. *She is now an abbess in an English Orthodox Monastery.*

abbey /æbi/ **abbeys**
NC An **abbey** is a church with buildings attached to it in which monks or nuns live. *...an abbey he built at St Denis, just outside Paris.*

abbot /æbət/ **abbots**
NC An **abbot** is the senior monk who is in charge of the other monks in a monastery or abbey. *...the learned hermit and abbot Joachim of Fiore.*

abbr. or **abbrev.**
abbr. and **abbrev.** are written abbreviations for 'abbreviation' or 'abbreviated'.

abbreviate /əbriːvieɪt/ **abbreviates, abbreviating, abbreviated**
1 VO or V If you **abbreviate** a piece of writing or speech, you make it shorter. *The comet Grigg-Skjellerup, or G-S, as we shall surely abbreviate it as we become more familiar with it... Don't be afraid to abbreviate, to cut a paragraph here and there.*
2 VO A word or phrase that is **abbreviated** is made shorter by leaving out some of the letters or by using only the first letters of each word. *'Vehicle General Purpose' was abbreviated to GP, and that gave us the word 'jeep'.*

abbreviation /əbriːvieɪʃn/ **abbreviations**
NC An **abbreviation** is a short form of a word or phrase, made by leaving out some of the letters or by using only the first letters of each word. For example, 'Dr' is an abbreviation for 'Doctor'. *We've got this very efficient system of indexing, using abbreviations.*

ABC /eɪbiːsiː/
1 N SING+*of* The **ABC** of a subject or activity consists of the parts of it that you have to learn and understand first because they are the most important and basic. *...good training grounds in which to learn the ABC of committee work.*
2 N SING Children who have learned their **ABC** have learned to recognize, write, or say the alphabet. *She already knows her ABC.*

abdicate /æbdɪkeɪt/ **abdicates, abdicating, abdicated**
1 V or VO If a monarch **abdicates** or **abdicates** the throne, they formally announce that they are giving up their position as monarch. *...the day Edward VIII abdicated... When King Constantine was forced to abdicate the Greek throne, Xenia's parents moved to England.* ◆ **abdication** /æbdɪkeɪʃn/ NU *The officers took over and forced his abdication in 1952. ...the abdication crisis of 1936.*
2 VO If you **abdicate** responsibility for something, you refuse to accept responsibility for it any longer. *We would be abdicating our responsibility to the local community.* ◆ **abdication** NU *...an abdication of political responsibility.*

abdomen /æbdəmən/ **abdomens**
NC Your **abdomen** is the part of your body below your chest where your stomach and intestines are; a medical term. *She was admitted to hospital with a pain in her abdomen.*

abdominal /æbdɒmɪnl/
ADJ **Abdominal** means relating to or affecting the abdomen; a medical term. *...a patient suffering from abdominal pains.*

abduct /əbdʌkt/ **abducts, abducting, abducted**
VO If someone **abducts** another person, they take them away illegally, usually by force. *He was afraid of being abducted by a rival gang.* ◆ **abduction** /əbdʌkʃn/ **abductions** NU or NC *Detectives are questioning a woman about the child's abduction... Amnesty have expressed concern over reports of abductions and the killing of prisoners.*

abductor /əbdʌktə/ **abductors**
NC **Abductors** are people who take a person away illegally, usually by force. *His wife has appealed to his abductors to release him.*

abed /əbed/
ADJ PRED If you are **abed**, you are in bed; an old-fashioned word.

aberrant /æberənt/
ADJ **Aberrant** means unusual and not normal. *...aberrant behaviour. ...these aberrant ideas.*

aberration /æbəreɪʃn/ **aberrations**
NC An **aberration** is an action or way of behaving that is not normal. *Napoli staged such a stylish win that their previous losses must surely have been temporary aberrations.*

abet /əbet/ **abets, abetting, abetted**
VO If you **abet** someone, you help or encourage them to do something wrong. *If the international community did not make a concerted effort to fight the drugs menace, it would be abetting the problem, and the violence which grew from it. ...aiding and abetting the enemy.*

abeyance /əbeɪəns/
Something that is **in abeyance** is not operating or being used at the present time. *The extradition process has been in abeyance for the last six months... The title shall be deemed to be in abeyance.*

abhor /əbhɔː/ **abhors, abhorring, abhorred**
VO If you **abhor** something, you hate it very much; a formal word. *They say they abhor all violence.*

abhorrence /əbhɒrəns/
N U If you have an **abhorrence** of something, you hate it very much; a formal word. *...an abhorrence of war... These new measures are regarded with suspicion and abhorrence by the majority of teachers.*

abhorrent /əbhɒrənt/
ADJ If something is **abhorrent** to you, you hate it and find it unacceptable; a formal word. *...a ruthless and utterly abhorrent system.*

abide /əbaɪd/ **abides, abiding, abided**
1 If you **can't abide** someone or something, you dislike them very much. *He likes you but he can't abide Dennis.*
2 V If something **abides**, it continues to happen or exist for a long time. *Men come and go, but Earth abides.*
abide by PHRASAL VERB If you **abide by** a law, agreement, or decision, you do what it says. *Both parties must agree to abide by the court's decision.*

abiding /əbaɪdɪŋ/
ADJ ATTRIB An **abiding** quality or impression is one that continues for a long time, even after the thing that produced it is no longer there. *This gave him an abiding hatred of militarism and imperialism... The abiding impression from Rome is of a lady all alone.*

Abidjan /æbɪdʒɑːn/
Abidjan is the capital of Côte d'Ivoire and its largest city. Population: 1,850,000 (1982).

ability /əbɪləti/ **abilities**
N C or N U Your **ability** to do something is the quality or skill that makes it possible for you to do it. *...a dramatic decline in the reading abilities of seven-year-olds. ...the government's ability to hold down inflation.*

-ability /-əbɪləti/
SUFFIX **-ability** is added in place of '-able' at the end of adjectives to form nouns referring to a quality or state. These nouns are often not defined in this dictionary but are treated with the related adjectives. *...the suitability of particular courses. ...their vulnerability to criticism.*

abject /æbdʒekt/; a formal word.
1 ADJ ATTRIB **Abject** is used to emphasize how shameful or depressing a situation, state, or quality is. *A third of the total population of the world are living in abject poverty... Mr Mellor saw the abject squalor and overcrowding of the refugee camp... They are accused of pursuing a policy of abject surrender.*
2 ADJ Someone who is **abject** shows no self-respect, courage, or pride. *Even the most abject slaves joined in the revolt.*

abjure /əbdʒʊə/ **abjures, abjuring, abjured**
VO If you **abjure** something such as a belief or way of life, you state publicly that you will give it up; a formal word. *The Government had abjured such a disreputable way of proceeding.*

ablaze /əbleɪz/
1 ADJ PRED Something that is **ablaze** is burning fiercely. *The police say two houses were set ablaze.*
2 ADJ PRED+*with* If a place is **ablaze** with lights or colours, it is very bright. *The sky was ablaze with stars shining brightly.*

able /eɪbl/ **abler, ablest**
1 ADJ PRED+*to*-INF If you are **able** to do something, you have the skill, knowledge, means, or opportunity to do it. *The rebels were able to drive a convoy of tanks and troops from one army base to another... Mr Heath was able to bring messages and mail from relatives... I wasn't able to do these quizzes... The strong winds were the only thing the organizers of the Games were not able to control.*
2 ADJ An **able** person is clever or good at doing something. *He was an unusually able detective.*

-able /-əbl/
SUFFIX **-able** is added to some verbs to form adjectives which describe someone or something as being able to have something done to them. For example, something that is identifiable can be identified. *They are both immediately recognizable. ...an immediately likeable young man.*

able-bodied /eɪblbɒdid/
ADJ An **able-bodied** person is physically strong and healthy. *Only able-bodied men should stay behind to help.*

ablutions /əbluːʃnz/
N PL You can refer to the activity of washing yourself as your **ablutions**; a literary word, often used

humorously. *...watching his father's ablutions.*

ably /ˈeɪbli/
ADV **Ably** means skilfully and successfully. *They were ably supported by the Party members.*

abnegation /ˌæbnɪˈgeɪʃn/
NU **Abnegation** means giving up something that you want, even though you would like to do it or have it; a formal word. *I gave up smoking just to please you, and that's as far as abnegation goes.*

abnormal /æbˈnɔːml/
ADJ Someone or something that is **abnormal** is unusual or exceptional, especially in a worrying way. *Maybe my child is abnormal. ...an abnormal interest in food.*

abnormality /ˌæbnɔːˈmælɪti/ **abnormalities**
NCorNU An **abnormality** in something such as a person's body or behaviour is an unusual part or feature of it that is worrying or dangerous. *It is caused by an abnormality in the blood. ...psychological abnormalities... I cannot express a view as to your normality or abnormality.*

abnormally /æbˈnɔːməli/
1 SUBMOD **Abnormally** means to a much greater extent than usual. *...the abnormally warm day. ...an abnormally high number of penguin deaths.*
2 ADV **Abnormally** also means in an unusual, worrying way. *...people who are behaving abnormally... Blood vessels develop abnormally in cancer tumours.*

aboard /əˈbɔːd/
PREPorADJ If you are **aboard** a ship or plane, you are on or in it. *After days drifting at sea, the refugees aboard the two boats were rescued... We don't think we saw any of the royal family members who were aboard... The plane crashed, killing all 271 aboard.*

abode /əˈbəʊd/ **abodes**
NC Your **abode** is the place where you live; a formal word. *At his new abode in France he was able to receive other opposition leaders.* ● If you have the **right of abode** in a country, you are legally entitled to live there. *...Britain's refusal to allow all Hong Kong citizens the right of abode in Britain.*

abolish /əˈbɒlɪʃ/ **abolishes, abolishing, abolished**
VO If you **abolish** a system or practice, you put an end to it. *They believed the death penalty should be abolished. ...the widespread demand to abolish university examinations.*

abolition /ˌæbəˈlɪʃn/
NU+SUPP The **abolition** of a system or practice is the formal ending of it. *...the abolition of slavery... He's in favour of the abolition both of the monarchy and the House of Lords.*

A-bomb /ˈeɪbɒm/ **A-bombs**
NC An **A-bomb** is an atom bomb. *He compared the situation there to that in Japan after the A-bomb was dropped.*

abominable /əˈbɒmɪnəbl/
ADJ Something that is **abominable** is very unpleasant or very bad. *The crime was denounced as an abominable attack against Italian democracy... He described the political struggle as abominable.*

abominate /əˈbɒmɪneɪt/ **abominates, abominating, abominated**
VO If you **abominate** something, you dislike it very much; a literary word. *He signed a document which abominates such practices as arbitrary arrest and torture.*

abomination /əˌbɒmɪˈneɪʃn/ **abominations**
1 NC An **abomination** is something bad that is completely unacceptable to you; a formal use. *They had committed every abomination from which civilised men recoiled. ...the psychological consequences of one of the worst abominations this century.*
2 NU **Abomination** is great dislike and disgust; an old-fashioned use. *...their abomination of centralized power.*

aboriginal /ˌæbəˈrɪdʒənl/ **aboriginals**
1 NC An **Aboriginal** is a member of one of the tribes which were living in Australia when Europeans arrived. *Aboriginals have inhabited the country for at least five thousand years.* ► Also ADJ *For many Aboriginal people such measures don't go far enough.*
2 ADJ **Aboriginal** also means relating to or affecting

Aboriginals. *...respect for Aboriginal rights and customs. ...the conflict between Aboriginal and Western culture.*
3 ADJ The **aboriginal** people or animals of a place are ones that have been there from the earliest known times or that were there before Europeans arrived. *In another thirty years, no trace of aboriginal life anywhere will have survived.*

Aborigine /ˌæbəˈrɪdʒəni/ **Aborigines**
NC An **Aborigine** is an Australian aboriginal; some people find this word offensive. *...pituri, a tobacco-like plant that Aborigines chew.*

abort /əˈbɔːt/ **aborts, aborting, aborted**
1 V If a pregnant woman **aborts**, her pregnancy ends before the foetus has formed properly, and the foetus dies. *The pill causes women to abort, and is not approved by the Food and Drug Administration.*
2 VO If a foetus **is aborted**, a woman's pregnancy is deliberately ended before the foetus has formed properly, and it dies. *The foetus cannot be aborted after 28 weeks.*
3 VO If you **abort** a process, plan, or activity, you stop it before it is finished. *A passenger jet had to abort its landing when the pilot saw another plane on the runway.*

abortion /əˈbɔːʃn/ **abortions**
NCorNU If a woman has an abortion, her pregnancy is deliberately ended before the foetus has formed properly, and it dies. *...the right to decide whether to have an abortion... As a Catholic he is opposed to abortion.*

abortionist /əˈbɔːʃənɪst/ **abortionists**
NC An **abortionist** is someone who performs abortions, usually illegally. *A strong anti-abortion law would push up fees paid to back-street abortionists.*

abortive /əˈbɔːtɪv/
ADJ ATTRIB An **abortive** attempt or action is unsuccessful. *He is said to have been involved in an abortive coup in January 1987.*

abound /əˈbaʊnd/ **abounds, abounding, abounded**
V, V+with, or V+in If things **abound** or if a place **abounds** with them, there are very large numbers of them; a formal word. *Allegations and rumours abound... These waters abound with salmon... The Mediterranean was one of the most explosive regions in the world, abounding in huge military arsenals.*

about /əˈbaʊt/
1 PREP The thing that you talk, write, or think **about** is the subject of what you are saying, writing, or thinking. *I'll have to think about that... This is a book about India... They have expressed concern about the sea-based nuclear missiles.*
2 PREP If you do something **about** a problem, you take action to solve it. *They knew they had to do something about their mother's unhappiness... There is an increasing awareness that something ought to be done about debt relief.*
3 PREP When you say that there is a particular quality **about** someone or something, you mean that they have this quality. *There's something peculiar about him... There is a strong feel about it of the West Coast of America.*
4 ADV **About** in front of a number means approximately. *We went about forty miles... The new station will cost about £50 million... About fifty people were killed, and one hundred injured.*
5 ADV If someone or something moves **about**, they keep moving in different directions. *We saw them walking about... I'm waving my arms about.*
6 ADJ PRED If someone or something is **about**, they are present or available. *There was no money about... His lung has been drained, and he's now up and about.*
7 If you **are about to** do something, you are going to do it soon. *Her father is about to retire... May Day is about to be abolished as a national holiday here.*

about-face, about-faces
NC An **about-face** is the same as an about-turn; used in American English. *The Prime Minister's about-face on this issue is costing him a great deal of press support.*

about-turn, about-turns
NC If someone does an **about-turn**, they change their

attitude or opinion about something completely. *Is this a rather abrupt about-turn by the United Nations?... The about-turn is seen as a symptom of Romania's attempts to forge a new democratic order.*

above /əbˈʌv/
1 PREP or ADV If one thing is **above** another one, it is directly over it or higher than it. *...the branches above their heads... A noise was coming from the bedroom above.*
2 ADJ or N SING You use **above** in writing to refer to something that has already been mentioned. *All the above items can be obtained from Selfridges... The above is a fair description of teaching machines.*
3 PREP or ADV If an amount or measurement is **above** a particular level, it is greater than that level. *...a fraction of a degree above absolute zero. ...children aged 15 and above.*
4 PREP If someone is **above** you, they are in a position of authority over you. *He will have an executive above him to whom he reports.*
5 PREP If someone thinks that they are **above** a particular activity, they do not approve of it and refuse to become involved in it. *They consider themselves above such mercenary transactions.*
6 PREP If someone is **above** criticism or suspicion, they cannot be criticized or suspected because of their good qualities or their position. *...those whose loyalty and morals were above reproach.*
7 **above all:** see all.

above board
ADJ PRED If an arrangement or deal is **above board**, it is completely honest. *The Electoral Commission has ruled that the procedure was above board.*

abracadabra /ˌæbrəkəˈdæbrə/
Someone who is performing a magic trick says **'abracadabra'** in order to indicate that the magic is about to happen. *He waved his hands in front of him like a pantomime conjurer, and said 'Abracadabra, arise'.*

abrasion /əˈbreɪʒn/ **abrasions**
NC An **abrasion** is an area of scraped or damaged skin; a formal word. *The bacteria get into humans through abrasions in the skin.*

abrasive /əˈbreɪsɪv/ **abrasives**
1 ADJ An **abrasive** person is unkind and rude. *He could be abrasive and insensitive.*
2 ADJ An **abrasive** substance is rough and can be used to clean hard surfaces. *...specially designed abrasive granules.* ▸ Also NC *Abrasives are a useful aid to cleaning.*

abreast /əˈbrɛst/
1 ADV If people or things walk or move **abreast**, they are side by side. *...carts pulled by donkeys three abreast.*
2 PREP If you keep **abreast of** a subject, you know all the most recent facts about it. *The press kept abreast of each development.*

abridged /əˈbrɪdʒd/
ADJ An **abridged** version of a book, article, or play has been made shorter by removing some parts of the original text. *...an abridged version of the novel.*

abroad /əˈbrɔːd/
ADV If you go **abroad**, you go to a country that is not the one you normally live in. *He is keen to recruit more teachers from abroad... He's still not free to travel abroad... Cheap package holidays abroad have made Britons desert their own beaches.*

abrogate /ˈæbrəɡeɪt/ **abrogates, abrogating, abrogated**
VO To **abrogate** something such as a law or agreement means to put an end to it; a formal word. *No future government can or will abrogate the accord.*
◆ **abrogation** /ˌæbrəˈɡeɪʃn/ NU+of *...the abrogation of emergency laws.*

abrupt /əˈbrʌpt/
1 ADJ An **abrupt** action is very sudden and often unpleasant. *It came to an abrupt end.* ◆ **abruptly** ADV *I had to apply the brakes abruptly.*
2 ADJ Someone who is **abrupt** is rather rude and unfriendly. *...David's abrupt and bullying manner.*
◆ **abruptly** ADV *I wouldn't have spoken so abruptly if I'd realized you were ill.*

abscess /ˈæbses/ **abscesses**
NC An **abscess** is a painful swelling on the skin or in the body, containing a thick yellowish-white liquid. *The captain Viv Richards has an abscess and will miss the remaining four games.*

abscond /əbˈskɒnd/ **absconds, absconding, absconded**
1 V If someone **absconds** from somewhere such as a prison, they escape and run away from it. *Three men have absconded from Ashwell open prison in Leicestershire.*
2 V+with If someone **absconds** with something that does not belong to them, they steal it and run away with it; a formal use. *He absconded with everyone's wages.*

abseil /ˈæbseɪl/ **abseils, abseiling, abseiled**
V If you **abseil** down a cliff or rock face, you go down it by sliding in a controlled way down a rope, with your feet against the cliff or rock. *The stretcher is easy to carry and enables the rescuer to climb or abseil without hindrance.*

absence /ˈæbsəns/ **absences**
1 NU or NC Someone's **absence** from a place is the fact that they are not there. *He was twice sentenced to death in his absence for war crimes. ...frequent absences from school.*
2 NU The **absence** of something is the fact that it is not there. *The absence of electricity made matters worse... Rumours and speculation have been widespread in the absence of concrete information.*

absent /ˈæbsənt/
1 ADJ If someone or something is **absent** from a place or situation, they are not there. *You have been absent twenty minutes.*
2 ADJ If someone appears **absent**, they are not paying attention to what is happening because they are thinking about something else. *...an absent stare.*
◆ **absently** ADV *'Did you?' Boylan said absently.*

absentee /ˌæbsənˈtiː/ **absentees**
NC An **absentee** is a person who should be in a particular place but who is not there. *...absentees from school.*

absenteeism /ˌæbsənˈtiːɪzəm/
NU **Absenteeism** is the fact or habit of frequently being away from work or school, without a good reason. *Absenteeism from work had gone down by a third... The Commission says high absenteeism leads to poorer public services.*

absentia /æbˈsentiə/
If an action or event that concerns a particular person is done **in absentia**, it is done or happens when that person is not there; a formal expression. *...if he or she wishes to have the degree conferred in absentia... He was sentenced to death in absentia late last year.*

absent-minded
ADJ An **absent-minded** person is very forgetful. *She is so absent-minded and careless.* ◆ **absent-mindedly** ADV *...if you absent-mindedly drop a ring down the sink.*

absolute /ˈæbsəluːt/ **absolutes**
1 ADJ ATTRIB **Absolute** means total and complete. *...the necessity for absolute secrecy... It is far easier to enforce absolute bans.*
2 ADJ ATTRIB You use **absolute** to emphasize what you are saying. *The script is an absolute mess... The lights went out, and there was absolute chaos.*
3 ADJ ATTRIB An **absolute** ruler has complete power and authority over his or her country. *An uprising in 1932 ended the system of absolute monarchy in Thailand.*
4 ADJ ATTRIB **Absolute** rules and principles are believed to be true or right for all situations. *The government has insisted that all civil servants are bound by an absolute duty of confidentiality.* ▸ Also NC *...rigid absolutes, such as 'divorce is always wrong'.*

absolutely; pronounced /ˈæbsəluːtli/ for the meaning in paragraph 1 and /ˌæbsəˈluːtli/ for the meaning in paragraph 2.
1 ADV or SUBMOD **Absolutely** means totally and completely. *People will absolutely hate it... That's an absolutely fascinating piece of work.*
2 You say **absolutely** as an emphatic way of agreeing with someone. *'She's excellent, though.'—'Absolutely.'*

absolute majority
N SING If a political party wins an **absolute majority**, they obtain more seats or votes than the total number of seats or votes gained by their opponents in an election. *He may even fail to win an absolute majority. ...an absolute majority of those entitled to vote.*

absolution /æbsəluːʃn/
NU If someone is given **absolution**, they are forgiven for something wrong that they have done; a formal word. *There were incongruities about her sins that made him hesitate before he granted her absolution.*

absolutism /æbsəluːtɪzəm/
NU **Absolutism** is a political system in which one ruler or leader has complete power and authority over a country. *...the fight against absolutism.*

absolve /əbzɒlv/ **absolves, absolving, absolved**
VO If someone **is absolved** of blame or responsibility, a formal statement is made that they are not guilty or are not to blame. *He has been absolved of the charge of murdering the husband of his mistress... That does not absolve the authorities from their share of guilt.*

absorb /əbsɔːb/ **absorbs, absorbing, absorbed**
1 VO To **absorb** a substance means to soak it up or take it in. *These gases can be absorbed directly through the skin, and so gas masks are ineffective as protection... They claim that the artificial ivory is indistinguishable from the real thing, especially in its ability to absorb water.*
2 VO If a group **is absorbed** into a larger group, it becomes part of the larger group. *After twenty years of occupation, they are gradually being absorbed into the larger state... West Germany has absorbed almost one million refugees in the last year and a half.*
3 VO If a system or society **absorbs** changes or effects, it is able to cope with them. *The Soviet Union has to absorb the political consequences of its reforms.*
4 VO If you **absorb** information, you learn it and understand it. *Businessmen on both sides of the Atlantic had more immediate economic news to absorb. ...the Marxist ideology which he absorbed as a youth.*
5 VO If something **absorbs** you, it interests you and gets all your attention. *Games like this absorb old members of the school even years after they have left.*
♦ **absorbed** ADJ *I was utterly absorbed in what I was doing... The parade brings to a close four days of revelry in which the entire nation becomes absorbed.*
♦ **absorbing** ADJ *I haven't read such an amusing, lively, and absorbing book for ages.*

absorbent /əbsɔːbənt/
ADJ **Absorbent** material soaks up liquid easily. *Dry it inside with an absorbent cloth.*

absorption /əbsɔːpʃn/
1 NU+SUPP The **absorption** of something is the action of absorbing it. *Because they contain fibre, they have a beneficial effect on digestion and absorption... Deforestation in the hills makes the absorption of snow and rain water more difficult.*
2 NU+SUPP **Absorption** is also used to refer to the process by which people who come to live in a foreign country begin to get used to living there. *He's been given special responsibility for the absorption of Soviet Jews... Recently-arrived immigrants are taken straight to absorption centres.*
3 N SING+SUPP If you have an **absorption** in something, you are very interested in it. *...her growing absorption in the study of natural history.*

abstain /əbsteɪn/ **abstains, abstaining, abstained**
1 V+from If you **abstain** from doing something, you deliberately do not do it. *The Royal Family should abstain from being controversial... The Rowntrees, like all Quakers, abstained from alcohol.*
2 V If you **abstain** during a vote or election, you do not vote. *During the last vote in January Britain abstained, but today it voted in favour.*

abstemious /əbstiːmiəs/
ADJ An **abstemious** person avoids doing too much of something enjoyable such as eating or drinking; a formal word. *They lead an abstemious and careful existence.*

abstention /əbstenʃn/ **abstentions**
N C or NU An **abstention** is a formal act of not voting. *There were 4 abstentions... We have the right of abstention.*

abstinence /æbstɪnəns/
NU **Abstinence** is the practice of not having something you enjoy, such as alcoholic drinks. *The feast of St Patrick was regarded as a holiday from the rigours of fasting and abstinence.*

abstract /æbstrækt/ **abstracts, abstracting, abstracted**
1 ADJ An **abstract** idea or argument is based on general ideas rather than on particular things and events. *...our capacity for abstract reasoning.*
2 ADJ ATTRIB **Abstract** works of art use shapes and colours rather than representing people or things. *...abstract sculptures.*
3 ADJ ATTRIB An **abstract** noun describes a quality or idea rather than a physical object.
4 NC An **abstract** of an article or speech is a short piece of writing that summarizes the main points of it. *They can choose which abstract they want, and in what language.*
5 VO If you **abstract** information from an article or other piece of writing, you make a summary of the main points in it.

abstracted /əbstræktɪd/
ADJ Someone whose behaviour is **abstracted** does not notice what is happening around them. *...a dreamy, abstracted stare.*

abstraction /əbstrækʃn/ **abstractions**
NC An **abstraction** is a general idea rather than one relating to a specific thing. *...abstractions of philosophy and religion.*

abstruse /əbstruːs/
ADJ Something that is **abstruse** is difficult to understand; a formal word. *...abstruse scientific information.*

absurd /əbsɜːd/
ADJ Something that is **absurd** is ridiculous because it seems completely wrong, or because it is not sensible or appropriate. *It seemed absurd to try to carry a twenty-five-pound camera about... They want twelve thousand dollars in compensation—a claim which the company describe as absurd.* ♦ **absurdity** /əbsɜːdəti/ **absurdities** N C or NU *...the oddities and absurdities of the language. ...a feeling of absurdity.* ♦ **absurdly** ADV or SUBMOD *They were laughing absurdly. ...an absurdly low rent.*

Abu Dhabi /æbu daːbi/
Abu Dhabi is the capital of the United Arab Emirates and its largest city. Population: 722,000 (1988).

Abuja /əbuːdʒə/
Abuja was chosen as the site for the new capital of Nigeria in 1976. Many government offices remain in Lagos.

abundance /əbʌndəns/
1 N SING An **abundance** of something is a large quantity of it. *These photographic images suggest that Mars once had an abundance of water on its surface.*
2 If something is **in abundance**, there is a lot of it. *There was grass in abundance.*

abundant /əbʌndənt/
ADJ Something that is **abundant** is present in large quantities. *Nigeria has abundant oil which can be produced at very low cost... a country where food was abundant and where economic reforms were creating greater efficiency.*

abundantly /əbʌndəntli/
SUBMOD If something is **abundantly** obvious, it is extremely obvious. *It has become abundantly clear that there is no time to lose.*

abuse, abuses, abusing, abused; pronounced /əbjuːs/ when it is a noun and /əbjuːz/ when it is a verb.
1 NU or NC If someone suffers **abuse**, they are treated cruelly and violently. *...cases of alleged child abuse... They have been subjected to physical and verbal abuse. ...reports of continuing human rights abuses.*
2 VO If someone is **abused**, they are treated cruelly and violently. *The patients were often physically abused... Sixteen per cent of the children had been sexually abused.*

3 NUorNC **Abuse** of something is the use of it in a wrong way or for a bad purpose. ...*the growing problem of drug, alcohol and solvent abuse.* ...*official corruption and other abuses of power.*
4 VO If you **abuse** something, you use it in a wrong way or for a bad purpose. *He admitted that he had abused his position as a minister.*
5 NU **Abuse** is also rude and unkind things that people say when they are angry. *The girls shrieked abuse at the lawyers.*
6 VO To **abuse** someone also means to say rude or unkind things to them. *She gave an example of how a woman abused her one day in a shop.*

abuser /əbjuːzə/ **abusers**
1 NC+SUPP A drug **abuser** is someone who takes drugs that they should not take, for example in order to experience a pleasant effect on their senses. ...*drug abusers who are at risk from sharing needles.*
2 NC+SUPP You also use **abuser** to refer to someone who treats a person cruelly and violently. ...*a convicted child abuser.* ...*alleged human rights abusers.*

abusive /əbjuːsɪv/
ADJ Someone who is **abusive** says rude or unkind things. *The captain complained that the marines had been abusive...* *An angry crowd of about two-thousand people gathered and chanted abusive slogans against the government.*

abut /əbʌt/ **abuts, abutting, abutted**
V+onto, V+on, or VO If land or a building **abuts** on something, it is directly next to it; a formal word. *Eritrea is the only province of Ethiopia that abuts directly onto the sea...* *John's house also abutted the creek, and his three children used to play there too.*

abysmal /əbɪzməl/
ADJ **Abysmal** means very bad or poor in quality. *The policy was based on fantasy and was an abysmal failure...* *She described the government's response to the crisis as abysmal.* ♦ **abysmally** ADV *He failed abysmally.*

abyss /əbɪs/ **abysses**
1 NC An **abyss** is a very deep hole in the ground. *We looked down into the abyss.*
2 NC+SUPP A very frightening or threatening situation can be referred to as an **abyss**; a literary use. *The world was teetering on the edge of the abyss of World War III.*

AC /eɪsiː/
AC is used to refer to an electric current that continually changes direction as it flows; an abbreviation for 'alternating current'. *When the AC recycles, I hear a metallic sound in the car.*

acacia /əkeɪʃə/ **acacias.** The plural form can be either **acacias** or **acacia**.
NC An **acacia** is a tree with small yellow or white flowers which grows in warm countries. *If there's any one species that characterises East Africa, it's the acacia tree.*

academic /ækədemɪk/ **academics**
1 ADJ **Academic** work is work done in schools, colleges, and universities. *I didn't really want to do anything academic at school...* *It's an academic course, for which you get a diploma.* ...*the academic system.* ♦ **academically** ADV ...*people who are well qualified academically.*
2 ADJ Someone who is **academic** is good at studying. ...*children of high academic ability.*
3 NC An **academic** is a member of a university or college who teaches or does research. *Professor Xavier Ponce is a French academic specialising in the Pacific.*
4 ADJ You also use **academic** to say that you think a particular point has no real effect on or relevance to what is happening. *It was all academic, because there were never any profits to share out.*

academy /əkædəmi/ **academies**
NC A school or college specializing in a particular subject is sometimes called an **academy**. ...*the Royal Academy of Dramatic Art.*

accede /əksiːd/ **accedes, acceding, acceded**
1 V+toor V If you **accede** to someone's request, opinion, or demand, you agree to do what they want; a formal

word. *It is thought unlikely that the government will accede to Mr Wade's demands... This will cause him to accede before the election.*
2 V+to To **accede** to a position as the ruler of a country means to take up that position. *King Hassan II acceded to the throne on the death of his father in February 1961.*

accelerate /əkseləreɪt/ **accelerates, accelerating, accelerated**
1 V-ERG When a rate of change or a process **accelerates**, things begin to change or happen more and more quickly. *Inflation rates began to accelerate...* *The report says the pace of wildlife destruction is accelerating...* *These events persuaded the government to accelerate the pace of change.*
2 V When a vehicle or an object that is moving **accelerates**, its speed increases. *The bus pulled out on to the highway and accelerated out of sight.*

acceleration /əkseləreɪʃn/
1 NU **Acceleration** is the rate at which something increases more and more quickly. ...*the acceleration of economic growth.*
2 NU The **acceleration** of a car or other vehicle is the rate at which it can increase its speed. *The acceleration and performance are very impressive.*

accelerator /əkseləreɪtə/ **accelerators**
NC The **accelerator** in a vehicle is the pedal which is pressed to make the vehicle go faster. *The bus driver put his foot down on the accelerator and zoomed past.*

accent, accents, accenting, accented; pronounced /æksənt/ when it is a noun and /æksent/ when it is a verb.
1 NC Someone who speaks with a particular **accent** pronounces the words of a language in a way that indicates their country, region, or social class. *She has a strong Irish accent.*
2 NC An **accent** is also a mark written above or below certain letters in some languages to show how they are pronounced. *He changed a word or two and put in an accent he had missed.*
3 N SING If the **accent** is on a particular feature of something, that feature is its most important part. *The accent is on presentation in this contest.*
4 VO If you **accent** a word or a musical note, you emphasize it. *The choir claps and taps to accent the swing of the music.*

accented /æksentɪd/
ADJ Language or speech that is **accented** is spoken with a particular accent. *'Don't let me disturb your lunch,' Liebermann said in his heavily accented English.*

accentuate /əksentʃueɪt/ **accentuates, accentuating, accentuated**
VO To **accentuate** something means to emphasize it. *These laws accentuate inequality and exploitation.*

accept /əksept/ **accepts, accepting, accepted**
1 VOor V If you **accept** something that you have been offered, you agree to take it. *He accepted our invitation... I thanked him and accepted... The offer is being considered, but it's unlikely to be accepted... The banks were all closed, and no-one would accept cheques.*
2 VOor V-REPORT If you **accept** someone's advice or suggestion, you agree to do what they say. *I knew that they would accept my proposal... But Mr Newton, while agreeing that the threat exists, only accepts part of the advice... The Council accepts that women who wish or need to work should be entitled to keep their jobs in spite of pregnancy and childbirth.*
3 VOor V-REPORT If you **accept** a story or statement, you believe it. *The panel accepted her version of the story... The majority do not accept that there has been any discrimination.*
4 VO To **accept** a difficult or unpleasant situation means to recognize that it cannot be changed. ...*unwillingness to accept bad working conditions... The rehabilitation unit is independent, and is the creation of a group of parents who simply refuse to accept the status quo.*
5 VO If you **accept** the blame or responsibility for something, you admit that you are responsible for it. *The minister has resigned, saying he accepted moral*

responsibility for the killing of a police officer... If the government offers compensation to the victims, people might think it was accepting the blame.
6 vo When an institution or organization **accepts** someone, they give them a job or allow them to join. *I was accepted by the Open University... In the thirties, many colleges limited the number of Jewish students they would accept... The breed has now been accepted by the American Kennel Club.*
7 vo If a group **accepts** you, they begin to think of you as part of the group. *The children gradually begin to accept her... For craftsmen who want to be accepted as artists, gaining recognition can be difficult.*
8 See also **acceptance, accepted.**

acceptable /əksɛptəbl/
1 ADJ If a situation or action is **acceptable**, people generally approve of it or allow it to happen. *The report says that although competition in schools is acceptable, teachers should not criticize other schools and colleges... However, premarital sex is now slightly more acceptable.* ◆ **acceptably** SUBMOD *...an acceptably low heat loss.* ◆ **acceptability** /əksɛptəbɪləti/ NU *The proof of the doctrine is its acceptability to the man in the street.*
2 ADJ If you think that something such as an action, a plan, or a piece of work is **acceptable**, you consider it to be good enough. *To my relief he found the article acceptable. ...a strategy acceptable to all classes and interests... The incident ruined their attempts to give the party a new, acceptable image.*

acceptance /əksɛptəns/ **acceptances**
1 NU **Acceptance** of something that you have been offered is the act of taking it or agreeing to use it. *The rejection of the offer comes despite a union recommendation for acceptance... The acceptance of foreign aid does not inevitably involve political domination by the donor.*
2 NU **Acceptance** of an idea is a general belief or agreement that it is true. *...their acceptance of his right to rule... There is now a general acceptance that the war will eventually have to end through negotiations... Alternative medicine has begun to gain acceptance as a way of treating physical ailments.*
3 NU Your **acceptance** of an unpleasant or difficult situation is the fact that you recognize that you cannot change it. *...our ancestors' cheerful acceptance of their plight.*
4 NCorNU If you receive an **acceptance** for a job or membership that you have applied for, you are offered the job or membership. *The number of direct acceptances depends on each country's performance in previous games... Within two days I had a letter of acceptance from the manager.*
5 NU **Acceptance** of someone into a group is the act of beginning to think of them as part of the group. *Feeling the warm glow of acceptance, I enjoyed my first cigarette of the day.*

accepted /əksɛptɪd/
ADJ ATTRIB **Accepted** ideas are generally agreed to be correct. *...the accepted wisdom about old age.* ● See also **accept.**

access /æksɛs/ **accesses, accessing, accessed**
1 NU If you gain **access** to a building or other place, you succeed in getting into it; a formal use. *They attempted to gain access through a side entrance... The entrance door gives access to a living room.*
2 NU **Access** is also the opportunity or right to use or see something or someone. *I demanded access to a telephone... Has Donald got access to the child?*
3 vo If you **access** information from a computer, you get it. *You are already limited by someone else's ideas of how that information is accessed.*

accessible /əksɛsəbl/
1 ADJ If a place is **accessible**, you are able to reach it. *The hidden room was accessible only through a secret back entrance.* ◆ **accessibility** /əksɛsəbɪləti/ NU *London's new orbital road gave easy accessibility to farms and farm buildings.*
2 ADJ PRED+*to* If something is **accessible** to people, they are able to use it or understand it easily. *...computers cheap enough to be accessible to virtually everyone.* ◆ **accessibility** NU *The co-director Gunther*

Schuller says the accessibility of the concerts is crucial.

accession /əksɛʃn/
NU **Accession** is the act of taking up a position as the ruler of a country. *...Queen Victoria's accession in 1837.*

accessory /əksɛsəⁿri/ **accessories**
1 NC **Accessories** are extra parts added to a machine or tool to make it more efficient or useful. *...an attractive range of accessories such as built-in tape decks and radios.*
2 NC **Accessories** are also articles such as belts or handbags which you wear or carry but which are not part of your main clothing. *He owns the Nobidadez Department Store which sells women's clothing, lingerie, and accessories.*
3 NC An **accessory** to a crime is a person who knows who committed the crime but does not tell the police; a legal use. *They are all accessories to murder.*

accident /æksɪdənt/ **accidents**
1 NC An **accident** is an event which happens completely by chance. *The fact that there is a university here is due to a historic accident.* ● If something happens **by accident**, it happens completely by chance. *I only came to Liverpool by accident.*
2 NC An **accident** is also something unpleasant and unfortunate that happens and that often leads to injury or death. *She was killed in a motor accident.*

accidental /æksɪdɛntl/
ADJ Something that is **accidental** happens by chance. *The evidence doesn't suggest accidental death.* ◆ **accidentally** ADV *We accidentally found an ideal solution.*

accident-prone
ADJ Someone who is **accident-prone** often has accidents. *Tom played the trendy but accident-prone producer.*

acclaim /əkleɪm/ **acclaims, acclaiming, acclaimed**
vo If someone or something is **acclaimed**, they are praised enthusiastically. *He has been widely acclaimed for his paintings.* ▶ Also NU *When her book was published two years ago, it received the kind of critical acclaim rarely granted a first novel... He's earned international acclaim for his rough-edged guitar playing.*

acclamation /ækləmeɪʃn/
NU **Acclamation** is a noisy or enthusiastic expression of approval. *All her remarks were greeted with acclamation.*

acclimate /æklɪmeɪt/ **acclimates, acclimating, acclimated**
v, V-REFL, or VO **Acclimate** means the same as **acclimatize**; used in American English. *We need to see how much time they need to acclimate... She listened to briefings and watched American troops arrive and acclimate themselves to desert conditions... The officers would prefer to get all their troops in place and acclimated.*

acclimatize /əklaɪmətaɪz/ **acclimatizes, acclimatizing, acclimatized;** also spelt **acclimatise.**
v, V-REFL, or VO When you **acclimatize** to something, or **acclimatize** yourself to it, you become used to it. *Once you've acclimatized to the heat you won't feel so tired... He's been to India before, but he wants to spend a month acclimatizing himself again... They may place a crew on board for the next flight, to acclimatize them to shuttle flights.*

accolade /ækəleɪd/ **accolades**
NC+SUPP An **accolade** is praise or an award given publicly to someone who is greatly admired; a formal word. *This was the highest accolade he could receive.*

accommodate /əkɒmədeɪt/ **accommodates, accommodating, accommodated**
1 vo If you **accommodate** someone, you provide them with a place where they can stay, live, or work. *She can't accommodate guests at the moment.*
2 vo If a building can **accommodate** a number of people or things, it has enough room for them. *Several jails house twice as many prisoners as they were originally built to accommodate.*
3 vo If you **accommodate** someone's opinion or demands when planning or deciding something, you

take their opinion or demands into account so that the plan or decision is acceptable to them. *Sir Crispen produced a draft which he said aimed to accommodate all points of view. ...the need to accommodate legitimate Palestinian political rights.*
4 VO To **accommodate** someone in your dealings with them means to be helpful to them. *The bank is accommodating its customers more than it used to.*

accommodating /əkɒmədeɪtɪŋ/
ADJ Someone who is **accommodating** is very willing to help you. *The warder was always accommodating in allowing visitors in.*

accommodation /əkɒmədeɪʃn/ **accommodations**
1 NU **Accommodation** is a room or building to stay, work, or live in. *There is a shortage of accommodation.*
2 N PL **Accommodations** are places that are provided for people to stay, especially for a short period of time; used in American English. *He spent the whole time complaining about the quality of the accommodations... They will be transported to hotels until they can be found accommodations elsewhere.*

accompaniment /əkʌmpəˈnɪmənt/ **accompaniments**
1 NCorNU The **accompaniment** to a song or tune is the music that is played at the same time to form a background. *...a guitar accompaniment. ...a series of vocal quartets, some with tape accompaniment.*
2 NC An **accompaniment** to something is another thing that happens or exists at the same time. *He entered to the accompaniment of loud cheers.*

accompanist /əkʌmpənɪst/ **accompanists**
NC An **accompanist** is a musician who plays one part of a piece of music while someone else sings or plays the main tune. *James Galway talks about the conductors and accompanists he enjoys playing with.*

accompany /əkʌmpəni/ **accompanies, accompanying, accompanied**
1 VO If you **accompany** someone, you go somewhere with them. *She asked me to accompany her to the church.*
2 VO If one thing **accompanies** another, the two things happen or exist at the same time. *A high fever often accompanies a mild infection.*
3 VO If you **accompany** a singer or a musician, you play one part of a piece of music while they sing or play the main tune. *Rostropovich also accompanied his wife, the soprano Galina Vishnevskaya.*

accomplice /əkʌmplɪs/ **accomplices**
NC An **accomplice** is a person who helps to commit a crime. *He then jumped out of the car and ran back inside the flats to warn his accomplice.*

accomplish /əkʌmplɪʃ/ **accomplishes, accomplishing, accomplished**
VO If you **accomplish** something, you succeed in doing it. *I never seem to accomplish anything.*

accomplished /əkʌmplɪʃt/
ADJ If someone is **accomplished**, they are very good at something. *...an accomplished cook.*

accomplishment /əkʌmplɪʃmənt/ **accomplishments**
1 NU+SUPP The **accomplishment** of a task or plan is the fact of achieving it; a formal use. *The accomplishment of this task filled him with satisfaction.*
2 NC+SUPP An **accomplishment** is something remarkable that has been done or achieved. *The statement spoke of 'significant accomplishments'.*
3 NC Your **accomplishments** are the things you do well. *One of her few accomplishments was the ability to do cartwheels.*

accord /əkɔːd/ **accords, according, accorded**
1 NC An **accord** is a formal agreement between countries or organizations. *Under the terms of the peace accord the rebels agreed to defer their declaration of independence... Any fresh help to the rebels would violate the accords.*
2 VOOorVO+to To **accord** someone a particular kind of treatment means to treat them in that way. *Newsmen accorded her the kind of coverage normally reserved for film stars... They are given more importance than we would accord to them if left to ourselves.*
● **Accord** is used in these phrases. ● When you do something **of** your **own accord**, you do it freely and

because you want to. *She knew they would leave of their own accord.* ● If people are **in accord**, they agree about something. *The two factions are not in accord about what the next move should be... There are few issues on which the two are in perfect accord.*
● Something that is **in accord with** a particular view or method of doing something follows that view or method exactly. *His remarks were in accord with views already expressed by Sir Geoffrey. ...in accord with international air safety rules.*

accordance /əkɔːdəns/
If something is done **in accordance with** a rule or system, it is done in the way that the rule or system says it should be done. *His case is being dealt with in accordance with Islamic law.*

accordingly /əkɔːdɪŋli/
ADV You use **accordingly** to say that one thing happens as the result of another thing. *He wanted to be treated like any other star entertainer, and to be paid accordingly.*

according to
1 PREP If something is true **according to** a particular person or book, that person or book claims that it is true. *According to Dr Santos, the cause of death was drowning... The targets, according to the army, were completely destroyed... According to your book, the President ordered the CIA to begin a covert operation designed to destabilize the government.*
2 PREP If something is done **according to** a particular principle or plan, this principle or plan is used as the basis for the way it is done. *Each person was given tasks according to their skills... There are six classes organized according to age.*

accordion /əkɔːdiən/ **accordions**
NC An **accordion** is a box-shaped musical instrument which is played by pressing keys or buttons on either side and moving the two sides together and apart. *...the characteristic piercing sound of the Cajun accordion.*

accost /əkɒst/ **accosts, accosting, accosted**
VO If you **accost** someone, you stop them and speak to them, especially in a way they do not like. *In the hall he was accosted by two men.*

account /əkaʊnt/ **accounts, accounting, accounted**
1 NC An **account** is a written or spoken report of something that has happened. *A Soviet newspaper has given a detailed account of a disaster at a Moscow football stadium.*
2 NC **Accounts** are detailed records of all the money that a person or business receives and spends. *He had to submit accounts of his expenditure.*
3 NC If you have an **account** with a bank, you leave money with the bank and withdraw it when you need it. *He has never opened a bank account.*
4 NC If you have an **account** with a shop or company, you can get goods or services from there and pay at a later time. *...stores which offer credit if you open an account.*
● **Account** is used in these phrases. ● If you take **account of** something, or **take** it **into account**, you consider it when you are thinking about a situation. *One has to take account of all the different factors... He asked the jury to take into account the fact that none of the passengers had been injured.* ● If you do something **on account of** something or someone, you do it because of that thing or person. *'Auntie told me not to run,' he explained, 'on account of my asthma.'* ● If you say that something should **on no account** be done, you mean that it should never be done at all. *On no account must strangers be let in.* ● If something is of **no account**, it does not matter at all.

account for PHRASAL VERB 1 If you **account for** something, you explain how it happened. *How do you account for the dent in the car?* 2 If something **accounts for** a particular part or proportion of a whole thing, it is what that part or proportion consists of. *Computer software accounts for some 70 per cent of our range of products.*

accountable /əkaʊntəbl/
1 ADJ PRED If you are **accountable** for something that you do, you are responsible for it. *They cannot be held accountable for what they did.*

2 ADJ PRED If you are **accountable** to someone, especially someone in authority, you are controlled by them and must be prepared to explain and justify your actions to them. *Each agency will remain accountable to a minister... The Party must be accountable to the people at large.* ♦ **accountability** /əkaʊntəbɪləti/ NU *...the need for greater accountability of the police.*

accountancy /əkaʊntənsi/
NU **Accountancy** is the work of keeping financial accounts. *The school will run courses in all aspects of business including marketing and accountancy.*

accountant /əkaʊntənt/ **accountants**
NC An **accountant** is a person whose job is to keep or check financial accounts. *Government accountants are scrutinising the terms of the deal.*

accounting /əkaʊntɪŋ/
NU **Accounting** is the same as accountancy; used in American English. *Meanwhile, business professors at Pepperdine University are teaching Russian officials accounting and banking procedures. ...the nation's biggest accounting firms.*

accoutrements /əku:trəmənts/
N PL **Accoutrements** are all the things you have with you when you travel or when you take part in a particular activity; a formal word. *She is surrounded by all the expensive accoutrements of an ordered family life.*

Accra /əkrɑ:/
Accra is the capital of Ghana and its largest city. Population: 866,000 (1984).

accredit /əkrɛdɪt/ **accredits, accrediting, accredited**
VO If someone is **accredited** in a particular position or job, their position or job is officially recognized. *The Foreign Minister said the decision to accredit new American diplomats was intended to show goodwill.*
▶ Also ADJ ATTRIB *...an accredited shop steward.*
♦ **accreditation** /əkrɛdɪteɪʃn/ NU *She has had her accreditation withdrawn by the authorities.*

accretion /əkri:ʃn/ **accretions**; a formal word.
1 NC+SUPP An **accretion** is a layer of material which gradually forms on top of something. *...accretions of mud.*
2 NU **Accretion** is the process of new layers or parts being added to something so that it increases in size. *Coral is formed by a process of accretion.*

accrue /əkru:/ **accrues, accruing, accrued**
1 V-ERG If money or interest **accrues** or is **accrued**, it gradually increases in amount over a period of time. *...tax benefits accruing to owner-occupiers... The plan will allow investors a longer time in which to accrue profits.*
2 V-ERG If you **accrue** things or if they **accrue**, you collect them or allow them to accumulate over a period of time; a formal use. *We had accrued a fine collection of Chinese porcelain... Certain advantages accrue to a man or woman when they reach adult status... Although the President has steadily accrued new powers since his appointment, his decrees are largely ignored.*

accumulate /əkju:mjʊleɪt/ **accumulates, accumulating, accumulated**
V-ERG When you **accumulate** things or when they **accumulate**, they collect or gather over a period of time. *...the things I had accumulated over the last four years... So evidence of this sort is beginning to accumulate... Social and economic problems are accumulating rapidly.*

accumulation /əkju:mjʊleɪʃn/ **accumulations**
1 NC+SUPP An **accumulation** of things is a large number of them which have been gathered together over a period of time. *...an accumulation of facts... With this accumulation of evidence, the Prime Minister is under pressure to relax his policy.*
2 NU+SUPP **Accumulation** is the collecting together of things over a period of time. *...the accumulation of wealth. ...an increase in snow accumulation.*

accumulative /əkju:mjʊlətɪv/
ADJ If something is **accumulative**, it becomes increasingly great in amount, number, or intensity over a period of time. *...the eventual accumulative effect of these substances.*

accuracy /ækjərəsi/
1 NU **Accuracy** is the ability to perform a task without making a mistake. *...the speed and accuracy with which she typed.*
2 NU **Accuracy** is also the quality of being true or correct. *...the reputation of The Times for accuracy.*

accurate /ækjərət/
1 ADJ An **accurate** account or description gives a true idea of what someone or something is like. *...an accurate picture of social history.* ♦ **accurately** ADV *The story is accurately told.*
2 ADJ A person, device, or machine that is **accurate** is able to perform a task without making a mistake. *She is accurate in punctuation and spelling... Missiles are becoming more accurate.* ♦ **accurately** ADV *Some guards couldn't shoot accurately, and didn't know how to arrest intruders.*

accursed /əkɜ:sɪd/; an old-fashioned word.
1 ADJ ATTRIB You can use **accursed** to describe something or someone that you find very annoying or tiresome. *They begged me to take them to see that accursed film. ...this accursed pain.*
2 ADJ If a person is **accursed**, someone has put a curse on them. *...a being who was by God's own law accursed.*

accusation /ækju:zeɪʃn/ **accusations**
1 NC An **accusation** is a statement that someone has done something wrong. *The government has denied accusations of torture... None of the letters made accusations against the Chairman himself.*
2 NU **Accusation** is the quality of showing by your behaviour that you think someone has done something wrong. *Her eyes were full of accusation.*

accusative /əkju:zətɪv/
ADJ In the grammar of some languages, for example Latin, the **accusative** case is a particular form of a noun that is used when that noun is the object of a verb, or the object of certain prepositions. ▶ Also N SING *It's in the accusative.*

accusatory /əkju:zətə°ri/
ADJ An **accusatory** remark or tone of voice suggests blame or criticism. *Internal, accusatory dialogues are commonplace.*

accuse /əkju:z/ **accuses, accusing, accused**
1 VO+of If you **accuse** someone of something, you say they have done something wrong. *He was accused of incompetence... The staff accuse him of running the paper in an over-ambitious and authoritarian manner.*
2 VO If someone is **accused** of a crime, they have been charged with the crime and are on trial for it. *He is accused of killing ten young women... No-one has yet been accused of Kirov's murder.*
3 See also accusing.

accused /əkju:zd/; **accused** is both the singular and the plural form.
NC The **accused** refers to the person or people being tried in a court for a crime. *Will the accused please stand?*

accuser /əkju:zə/ **accusers**
NC Your **accusers** are people who say that you have done something wrong. *I had to prepare to face my accusers.*

accusing /əkju:zɪŋ/
ADJ If your expression or tone of voice is **accusing**, it indicates that you think someone has done something wrong. *She gave him an accusing look.* ♦ **accusingly** ADV *'You liked him,' he said accusingly.* ● See also accuse.

accustom /əkʌstəm/ **accustoms, accustoming, accustomed**
V-REFL or VO If you **accustom** yourself to something different, you make yourself get used to it. *He sat very still, trying to accustom himself to the darkness... I think it is preferable to accustom babies to sleeping on the stomach.*

accustomed /əkʌstəmd/
1 ADJ PRED+to If you are **accustomed** to something, you are used to it or familiar with it. *I am not accustomed to being interrupted... My eyes became accustomed to the dim lighting.*
2 ADJ ATTRIB **Accustomed** also means usual. *He drove with his accustomed, casual ease.*

ace /eɪs/ **aces**
1 NC An **ace** is a playing card with a single symbol on it. *...the ace of spades.*
2 NC An **ace** is also a fact or action that someone suddenly uses to their advantage, for example in an argument. *They saw acceptance of Israel as their ace, the only card they could play in the final stages of negotiation.*
3 ADJ **Ace** is also used to describe someone who is extremely good at something; an informal use. *We've got all the ace players in our team... Everyone in the room instantly felt the urge to act the ace reporter.*
▶ Also NC+SUPP *He plays a teacher who turns into a dance ace overnight to earn the respect of his pupils.*
4 If you are **within an ace of** something, you very nearly do it or experience it. *He came within an ace of being run over.*
5 NC In tennis, an **ace** is a serve that is so fast that the player receiving the serve cannot reach the ball. *Mecir served ten double faults and just one ace.*

acerbity /əsɜːbəti/
NU **Acerbity** is sharpness or bitterness in a remark, or in your voice or manner; a formal word. *No doubt much acerbity he showed was due to nerves.*

acetate /æsəteɪt/
NU **Acetate** is a smooth man-made cloth that is used for making clothes. *He developed a process to turn the waste into acetate.*

acetic acid /əsiːtɪk æsɪd/
NU **Acetic acid** is a colourless weak acid, and is the main substance in vinegar. *Acetic acid, which is another solvent sometimes used, will get extremely hot in a microwave oven.*

acetylene /əsetəliːn/
NU **Acetylene** is a colourless gas which burns with a very hot bright flame. It is often used in lamps and for cutting and welding metal. *The gang worked for up to ten hours with acetylene torches to open the vault.*

ache /eɪk/ **aches, aching, ached**
1 V If you **ache** or if a part of your body **aches**, you feel a dull steady pain. *I was tired, aching, and miserable... His leg ached.*
2 V+for or V+to-INF If you **ache** for something or **ache** to do something, you want it very much. *She was aching for a cigarette... I was aching to tell you all my news.*
3 NC An **ache** is a dull steady pain in a part of your body. *...my usual aches and pains.*

achieve /ətʃiːv/ **achieves, achieving, achieved**
VO If you **achieve** a particular aim or effect, you succeed in obtaining it. *The riots achieved nothing... Should an agreement on aid be achieved, the other difficulties will be swept aside.*

achievement /ətʃiːvmənt/ **achievements**
1 NC An **achievement** is something which someone has succeeded in doing, especially after a lot of effort. *It was an astonishing achievement.*
2 NU **Achievement** is the fact of achieving something. *This did not lessen her sense of achievement.*

Achilles heel /əkɪliːz hiːl/ **Achilles heels**
NC Someone's **Achilles heel** is the weakest point in their character, where it is easiest for other people to attack or criticize them. *Status is the businessman's Achilles heel.*

Achilles tendon /əkɪliːz tendən/ **Achilles tendons**
NC Your **Achilles tendon** is the cord inside the back of your leg just above your heel. *She is to have an operation on her right Achilles tendon.*

acid /æsɪd/ **acids**
1 N MASS An **acid** is a chemical liquid that turns litmus paper red. Strong acids can damage substances such as metals, cloth, and skin. *Dab it with a solution of weak acid.*
2 ADJ An **acid** fruit or drink has a sour or sharp taste.
3 ADJ An **acid** remark is unkind or critical. *...her acid wit.*
4 NU **Acid** is also the drug LSD; an informal use. *One speaker was high on acid.*

acid house
NU **Acid house** is a style of dance music that uses new technology to produce a loud, hypnotic beat. It is often considered to be associated with the use of hallucinogenic drugs. *Acid house is a development of the 'house' music of Chicago.*

acid house party, acid house parties
NC An **acid house party** is a secretly organized event at which acid house music is played. *Huge acid house parties were being held in aircraft hangars and disused warehouses.*

acidic /əsɪdɪk/
ADJ Something that is **acidic** contains acid or has a pH value of less than 7. *The city's soft, mildly acidic water dissolves lead from old pipes and taps.*

acidity /əsɪdəti/
1 NU **Acidity** is the quality of having a pH value lower than 7. *...the acidity of the wine.*
2 NU **Acidity** is also the making of unkind or critical remarks. *I noticed a certain acidity in his comments.*

acid rain
NU **Acid rain** is rain that is polluted by acid which has been released into the atmosphere from factories and industrial processes. The rain then destroys or damages the environment, especially trees. *Measures to curb the level of acid rain are proving successful.*

acid test
N SING An **acid test** is a sure way of proving whether something is true or not, or of good quality or not. *This venture is seen as an acid test of the alliance.*

acknowledge /əknɒlɪdʒ/ **acknowledges, acknowledging, acknowledged**
1 VO, VO+as, or V-REPORT If a fact or situation is **acknowledged**, it is accepted that it is true or that it exists. *It doesn't acknowledge the existence of the Nationalist Party... He was acknowledged as America's finest writer... Most people will now acknowledge that there is a crisis.*
2 VO If you **acknowledge** someone, you show that you have seen and recognized them. *I took care not to acknowledge Janet with more than a nod... He never even bothered to acknowledge her presence.*
3 VO If you **acknowledge** a message, letter, or parcel, you tell the person who sent it that you have received it. *You have to sign here and acknowledge receipt.*
4 VO or VO+as If people or their status, qualities, or achievements **are acknowledged**, they are known about by other people and are admired by them. *Reverend Jackson's skills as an orator are widely acknowledged... Johnson's virtues and accomplishments are tacitly acknowledged, but swiftly passed over... Once regarded as a clever but lightweight creator of domestic comedies, he's now acknowledged as a serious talent.*

acknowledgement /əknɒlɪdʒmənt/ **acknowledgements**; also spelt **acknowledgment**.
1 NU or NC **Acknowledgement** of something is admitting or accepting that it is true. *It would seem to amount to official acknowledgement of some brutality on the part of the police... This is the first public acknowledgement of the depth of the differences between the two governments.*
2 NU **Acknowledgement** is the expression of gratitude for something that someone has done or said. *...her acknowledgement of their offerings.*
3 NU **Acknowledgement** of someone is showing that you have seen and recognized them. *One of the men raised an arm in acknowledgement.*
4 NU or NC **Acknowledgement** of a message, letter, or parcel is telling the sender that it has arrived. *...in acknowledgement of telephone orders... He refused to sign the acknowledgement.*
5 N PL The **acknowledgements** in a book is the section in which the author thanks the people who have helped.

acme /ækmi/
N SING The **acme** of something is its highest point of achievement or excellence; a formal word. *Sir Robin is the acme of Whitehall tradition... Many people consider Blenheim to be the acme of ostentation.*

acne /ækni/
NU Someone who has **acne** has a lot of spots on their face and neck. *...medications to treat everything from acne to dandruff.*

acolyte /ækəlaɪt/ **acolytes**
1 NC The **acolytes** of an important person are people who agree with their views and support them fully,

often without being critical of anything that they do.
*Her acolytes are continuing to fight her battles, mainly
over Europe... Today, many of his self-appointed
acolytes regard the free market as an object of
veneration.*
2 NC An **acolyte** is also someone who assists a priest
in performing certain religious services. *The priests
and their two sallow-faced acolytes obviously intended
us to take part in the ceremony.*

acorn /eɪkɔːn/ **acorns**
NC **Acorns** are pale oval nuts that grow on oak trees.
*Last summer was wet, and there were plenty of
acorns in the wood.*

acoustic /əkuːstɪk/ **acoustics**
1 ADJ ATTRIB **Acoustic** means relating to sound or
hearing. *Acoustic contact had been made.*
2 N PL The **acoustics** of a room are the structural
features which determine how well you can hear
music or speeches in it. *The theatre was large, with
good acoustics.*

acquaint /əkweɪnt/ **acquaints, acquainting,
acquainted**
V O+with If you **acquaint** someone with something, you
tell them about it; a formal word. *I will acquaint you
with the facts.*

acquaintance /əkweɪntəns/ **acquaintances**
1 NC An **acquaintance** is someone who you have met
but do not know well. *My cousin is an acquaintance of
Lord Northcliffe.*
2 N SING+SUPP Your **acquaintance** with a subject is
your knowledge or experience of it. *...her
acquaintance with modern art.*
● **Acquaintance** is used in these phrases. ● When you
make someone's **acquaintance**, you meet them for the
first time. *One can easily imagine making his
acquaintance, and inviting him to drop by for dinner.*
● If you have a **nodding** or **passing acquaintance** with
someone, you know them slightly but not very well.
*I've been too busy studying to make more than a
passing acquaintance with anyone my own age... Apart
from a nodding acquaintance in night clubs, I didn't
meet Ellington alone.*

acquainted /əkweɪntɪd/
ADJ PRED If you are **acquainted** with someone, you
know them slightly but they are not a close friend.
*Mrs Oliver is acquainted with my mother... The
families were acquainted.*

acquiesce /ækwiɛs/ **acquiesces, acquiescing,
acquiesced**
V+in or to If you **acquiesce** in an activity, plan, or
decision, you agree to it or accept it, even though you
may not want to; a formal word. *He would have to
acquiesce in any deal on military aid... He acquiesced
to the demand.*

acquiescence /ækwiɛsns/
NU **Acquiescence** is agreement to do what someone
wants or acceptance of what they do. *Greece's
acquiescence in the project has prompted a diplomatic
row. ...Pakistan's sudden acquiescence to
Delhi's request signals a change in its official position.*

acquiescent /ækwiɛsnt/
ADJ Someone who is **acquiescent** is ready to agree to
do what someone wants or to accept what they do.
*Having believed they had an acquiescent workforce,
they were frightened by the strike.*

acquire /əkwaɪə/ **acquires, acquiring, acquired**
1 VO If you **acquire** something, you obtain it. *I tried
to acquire the information I needed.*
2 VO If you **acquire** a skill or habit, you learn it or
develop it. *It is a habit well worth acquiring.*
◆ **acquired** ADJ *...hereditary and acquired
characteristics.*

acquisition /ækwɪzɪʃn/ **acquisitions**
1 NC An **acquisition** is something that you have
obtained. *He invited me to inspect his latest
acquisition.*
2 NU+SUPP The **acquisition** of something is the process
of getting it or being given it. *...the acquisition of
land.*
3 NU+SUPP The **acquisition** of a skill or habit is the
process of learning it or developing it. *...the
acquisition of knowledge.*

acquisitive /əkwɪzətɪv/
ADJ Someone who is **acquisitive** likes getting new
possessions; used showing disapproval. *Part of the
answer to the continued extravagance lies in the
passionate and acquisitive nature of the Sheikh.*

acquit /əkwɪt/ **acquits, acquitting, acquitted**
1 V O or V O+of If someone **is acquitted** of a crime, it is
formally declared at the end of a trial that they did
not commit it. *Campbell was acquitted on all
charges... The jury acquitted her of theft.*
2 V-REFL If you **have acquitted** yourself in a particular
way, you have carried out a task or behaved in that
way; a formal use. *The general feeling is that Mr
Major acquitted himself well in Rome.*

acquittal /əkwɪtl/ **acquittals**
NU or NC **Acquittal** is a formal declaration at the end of
a trial that someone who has been accused of a crime
is innocent. *This does not mean that the cases are
dropped or that acquittal is certain... His attorney is
now optimistic that he can win an eventual acquittal.*

acre /eɪkə/ **acres**
NC An **acre** is a unit of area equal to 4840 square
yards or approximately 4047 square metres. *More
than half a million acres of farmland have been
affected.*

acreage /eɪkərɪdʒ/
NU The **acreage** of a piece of land is its area
measured in acres. *The financial value of its immense
acreage was enormous.*

acrid /ækrɪd/
ADJ An **acrid** smell or taste is strong, sharp, and
unpleasant. *The room was filling with acrid smoke.*

acrimonious /ækrɪməʊniəs/
ADJ **Acrimonious** words or quarrels are bitter and
angry; a formal word. *An acrimonious dispute broke
out.*

acrimony /ækrɪməni/
NU **Acrimony** is bitterness and anger about
something; a formal word. *...acrimony over the
involvement of the police.*

acrobat /ækrəbæt/ **acrobats**
NC An **acrobat** is an entertainer who performs difficult
jumps, somersaults, and balancing acts. *His father
was a circus acrobat.*

acrobatic /ækrəbætɪk/ **acrobatics**
1 ADJ An **acrobatic** movement or display involves
difficult jumps, somersaults, and balancing acts. *Hugo
Sanchez executed an acrobatic scissor kick for the first
goal.*
2 N PL **Acrobatics** are acrobatic movements. *...master
classes in clowning, acrobatics and dance.*

acronym /ækrənɪm/ **acronyms**
NC An **acronym** is a word made of the initial letters of
the words in a phrase, especially when this is the
name of something. An example of an acronym is
NATO which is made up of the initial letters of 'North
Atlantic Treaty Organization'.

across /əkrɒs/
1 PREP or ADV If you go or look **across** somewhere, you
go or look from one side of it to the other. *We ran
across the bridge... He turned his head and looked
across at me.*
2 PREP Something that is situated or stretched **across**
something else is situated or stretches from one side
to the other. *...a banner stretched across the street...
A straight line was ruled across the map.*
3 PREP Something that is situated **across** a street or
river is on the other side of it. *He stared at the houses
across the street.*
4 ADV **Across** is used to indicate the width of
something. *The bomb blasted a hole 200 kilometres
across.*

acrylic /əkrɪlɪk/
NU **Acrylic** is a material manufactured by a chemical
process. *...synthetic upholstery materials such as
nylon and acrylic. ...acrylic blankets.*

act /ækt/ **acts, acting, acted**
1 V When you **act**, you do something for a particular
purpose. *We have to act quickly... He acted alone in
the shooting... He described the accusations as
groundless, saying the police had acted according to
the law.*

2 VA If someone **acts** in a particular way, they behave in that way. *We acted as if we had never seen each other before... The suggestion is that the children were acting abnormally in some way.*

3 VA If someone or something **acts** in a particular role or with a particular function, they have that role or function. *The shark can twist its fins to act as brakes... He acted as a mediator during the peace talks.*

4 V or VO If you **act** in a play or film, you have a part in it. *Pinter spent three years acting in English provincial theatres... I only ever acted small parts.*

5 NC+SUPP An **act** is a single action or thing that someone does. *Sometimes the act of writing down the problems straightens out your thinking.* ● If you are in **the act of** doing something, you are doing it. *He saw Jones in the act of snatching a gun.*

6 N SING If you say that someone's behaviour is an **act**, you mean that it does not express their real feelings. *She appeared calm and confident but it was just an act.*

7 NC An **Act** is a law passed by the government. *...the 1944 Education Act... He is charged under Section 7 of the Official Secrets Act.*

8 NC An **act** in a play, opera, or ballet is one of the main parts into which it is divided. *This is an excerpt from act three.*

9 NC An **act** in a show is one of the short performances in the show. *...comedy acts.*

act up PHRASAL VERB If someone or something is **acting up**, they are not working or behaving properly. *Her car has started acting up again.*

acting /ˈæktɪŋ/

1 NU **Acting** is the activity or profession of performing in plays or films. *...the brilliant acting of Hawtrey.*

2 ADJ ATTRIB You use **acting** in front of the title of a job to indicate that someone is only doing that job temporarily. *The Vietnamese authorities have appointed Mr Vo Van Kiet as acting Prime Minister.*

action /ˈækʃn/ **actions**

1 NU **Action** is doing something for a particular purpose. *She said she wanted international action against the illegal dumping of oil at sea... The helicopters took evasive action and did not return the fire.*

2 NC An **action** is a movement or act that you do on a particular occasion. *The graceful action of the King was matched by the restraint shown by the crowd... Surely resigning was rather a rash action?*

3 NC A legal **action** is a process in which a court orders someone to stop doing something or to pay compensation for damage they have caused; a legal term. *Sometimes outraged patients bring actions against dentists... Mr Parns has decided not to contest the action.*

4 NU The **action** of a chemical is the way in which it works, or the effects that it has. *This drug inhibits the action of an enzyme.*

5 N SING You can refer to the important, exciting, or significant things that are happening as the **action**. *They want to be where the action is... The whole action of the book takes place in one day.*

6 NU **Action** is also fighting in a war. *...reports of military action.* ● **Action** is used in these phrases. ● If soldiers are in **action** or go **into action**, they are fighting in a war. *Most of them were listed as missing in action, believed killed... He said he would order Honduran forces into action against them.* ● If you put an idea or policy **into action**, you begin to use it. *The peace plan will be put into action to end eleven years of civil war.* ● If something or someone is **out of action**, they are not able to be used, or unable to work normally. *11 ambulances have been put out of action by vandals... Viv Richards has been out of action since having an operation in March.*

actionable /ˈækʃ(ə)nəbl/

ADJ PRED If a remark or act is **actionable**, it gives someone a valid reason for bringing a legal case against the person responsible; a legal term. *Lawyers believe the new ruling is actionable on six counts.*

action replay, action replays

NC An **action replay** is a slow, repeated showing of an event that has just been on television. *Let's just see an action replay of that incredible goal.*

activate /ˈæktɪveɪt/ **activates, activating, activated**

VO If a device or process is **activated**, something causes it to start working. *The gates will open automatically when the detection equipment is activated.*

active /ˈæktɪv/

1 ADJ An **active** person is energetic and always busy or moving about. *...active and noisy children.*

2 ADJ If someone is **active** in an organization or cause, they are involved in it and work hard for it. *He was active in drawing public attention to our problems. ...more active involvement in a Gulf war settlement.* ◆ **actively** ADV *He had not actively participated in politics.*

3 ADJ ATTRIB You use **active** to say that something is done with energy or enthusiasm. *The proposal is under active discussion.* ◆ **actively** ADV *Such qualities were actively discouraged.*

4 ADJ To become **active** means to start doing things again after a period of rest. *The bees won't become active again until the spring. ...spectacular photographs of active volcanos.*

active service

NU If you are on **active service**, you are fighting as a member of the armed forces. *Another son was killed on active service... After active service in France, he had received a commission.*

activist /ˈæktɪvɪst/ **activists**

NC An **activist** is someone who does things to bring about political or social changes. *Last year, human rights activists attempted to hold an illegal protest.*

activity /ækˈtɪvəti/ **activities**

1 NU **Activity** is a situation in which a lot of things are happening or being done. *...new laws regulating economic activity... He has found himself caught up in a flurry of diplomatic activity.*

2 NC An **activity** is something that you spend time doing. *I find tennis a very enjoyable activity.*

3 N PL+SUPP The **activities** of a group are the things they do to achieve their aims. *...the activities of trade unions.*

act of God, acts of God

NC An **act of God** is an event that is beyond human control, especially one in which some damage or harm is done. *...some act of God—a typhoon, perhaps.*

Act of Parliament, Acts of Parliament

NC An **Act of Parliament** is a law passed by the government. *...a profit-making industry licensed by Act of Parliament.*

actor /ˈæktə/ **actors**

NC An **actor** is someone whose job is acting in plays or films. *...a company of nine actors playing thirty-three parts.*

actress /ˈæktrəs/ **actresses**

NC An **actress** is a woman whose job is acting in plays or films. *This encouraged her to leave the shop and become a professional film actress.*

actual /ˈæktʃuəl/

1 ADJ ATTRIB **Actual** is used to emphasize that someone or something is real and not imaginary. *The predicted results and the actual results are very different.*

2 ADJ ATTRIB **Actual** is also used to refer to the most significant part of an event, rather than to other things that are associated with it. *The actual wedding procession starts at 10 a.m.*

actuality /ˌæktʃuˈæləti/

You use **in actuality** to emphasize that what you are saying is true or accurate. *The party in actuality contains only a small minority of extremists.*

actually /ˈæktʃuəli/

1 ADV You use **actually** to indicate that a situation exists in real life or to emphasize that it is true or correct. *No one actually saw this shark... He actually died in exile, didn't he?*

2 ADV SEN You can also use **actually** as a way of being more polite, especially when you are correcting or contradicting someone, advising them, or introducing a new topic of conversation. *Actually, it was more*

complicated than that... Actually it might be a good idea to stop recording now... I think that's pretty cheap, actually.

actuary /ˈæktʃuəri/ **actuaries**
NC An **actuary** is someone who is employed by a life insurance company to calculate how much the company should charge their clients. He is an actuary with the firm of Milliman and Robertson.

acumen /ˈækjumən/
NU **Acumen** is the ability to make good judgements and quick decisions. ...a man with big ideas and keen business acumen.

acupuncture /ˈækjupʌŋktʃə/
NU **Acupuncture** is the treatment of illness or pain by sticking small needles into the patient's body. ...the ancient principles of Chinese acupuncture.

acute /əˈkjuːt/
1 ADJ If an unpleasant situation or feeling is **acute**, it is very intense or severe. ...acute staff shortages... The tension throughout the occupied territories is acute.
2 ADJ ATTRIB An **acute** illness is a particularly serious one, which often begins suddenly. The post mortem revealed acute pneumonia and damage to the intestines.
3 ADJ If your sight, hearing, or sense of smell is **acute**, it is sensitive and powerful. The fish's sense of smell is most acute.
4 ADJ An **acute** angle is less than 90°; a technical term in mathematics.

acutely /əˈkjuːtli/
1 ADV If you feel something **acutely**, you feel it very strongly. They were acutely aware of the difficulties.
2 ADV If a feeling or quality is **acutely** unpleasant, it is very unpleasant indeed. It was acutely embarrassing.

ad /æd/ **ads**
NC An **ad** is an advertisement; an informal word. Some ads are spectacularly unsuccessful.

AD /ˌeɪˈdiː/
You use **AD** in dates to indicate the number of years or centuries since the year in which Jesus Christ is believed to have been born. ...the year 2000 AD. ...as early as AD 1200.

adage /ˈædɪdʒ/
N SING An **adage** is a saying which people use to express a general truth about life. She reminded me of the old adage: where there's love there's understanding.

Adam /ˈædəm/
If you say that you **don't know** someone **from Adam** or **wouldn't know** them **from Adam**, you mean that you do not know them at all; an informal expression.

adamant /ˈædəmənt/
ADJ If you are **adamant** about something, you are determined not to change your mind. He is adamant that we must put less emphasis on nationalism.
♦ **adamantly** ADV He adamantly refused to be moved to a hospital.

Adam's apple /ˌædəmz ˈæpl/ **Adam's apples**
NC Your **Adam's apple** is the lump that sticks out at the front of your neck.

adapt /əˈdæpt/ **adapts, adapting, adapted**
1 V or V-REFL If you **adapt** to a new situation or adapt yourself to it, you change in order to be able to deal with it. They set up a clinic to help these children to adapt physically and educationally... He cannot adapt himself to being free.
2 VO If you **adapt** something, you change it to make it suitable for a new purpose or situation. Reformers attempted to adapt traditional religion... Mortimer is adapting the novel for television.
3 See also **adapted**.

adaptable /əˈdæptəbl/
ADJ Someone or something that is **adaptable** is able to change or be changed in order to deal with new situations. The rural areas are losing their brightest, most educated and adaptable members to the cities. ...a new harvester which is adaptable for a number of crops... The flu virus is amazingly adaptable.
♦ **adaptability** /əˌdæptəˈbɪləti/ NU ...adaptability to his environment.

adaptation /ˌædæpˈteɪʃn/ **adaptations**
1 NC An **adaptation** of a story or novel is a play or film based on it. ...a new television adaptation of 'A Tale of Two Cities'.
2 NU **Adaptation** is the process of changing in order to deal with a new situation. We used a monkey to study the period of adaptation to weightlessness.

adapted /əˈdæptɪd/
ADJ PRED Something that is **adapted** for a particular purpose is made so that it is especially suitable for that purpose. The cleaner is well adapted for use in the home and car. ...a Regency period residence, skilfully adapted to the needs of a modern hotel. ● See also **adapt**.

adaptor /əˈdæptə/ **adaptors**; also spelt **adapter**.
1 NC An **adaptor** is a device that connects two or more electrical plugs to the same socket. If you use a multiple plug adaptor, make sure that the pieces of equipment used do not overload the circuit.
2 NC An **adaptor** is also a kind of electrical plug which enables you to use a device whose plug does not match the socket.
3 NC A mains **adaptor** is a kind of electrical lead which enables you to use mains electricity to power equipment which is usually battery operated It runs off either standard batteries or a mains adaptor.

add /æd/ **adds, adding, added**
1 VO If you **add** one thing to another, you put the first thing with the second. Grind the soap and add a bit of perfume to the mixture... The formulation can be added to soil as a dry powder, granule, or pellets.
2 VO or V If you **add** numbers or amounts, you calculate their total. Add three and fourteen... I am very slow at adding and subtracting.
3 V+to or VO+to If one thing **adds** to another, it makes the other thing greater in degree or amount. He is given answers that only add to his confusion... This process adds an extra £3 to the cost. ♦ **added** ADJ ATTRIB There are added complications.
4 V-REPORT or V-QUOTE If you **add** something when you are speaking, you say something more. He added that the fee would be £100... 'I felt sorry for them' he added.

add up PHRASAL VERB 1 If you **add up** several numbers or amounts, you calculate their total. The answers each carry a score which is added up at the end. 2 If something that someone has said or done **adds up**, it is consistent, reasonable, and believable. It is already clear that his electoral commitments do not add up. 3 If facts or events **add up**, they make you understand the true nature of the situation. It all added up. I became aware that Halliday was the thief.

add up to PHRASAL VERB If numbers **add up to** a particular total, you get that total when they are put together. They estimate that duties on gambling add up to around a billion pounds.

addendum /əˈdendəm/ **addenda** /əˈdendə/
NC An **addendum** is a section at the end of a book or document, containing extra information. In an unusual addendum to the communiqué, the state news agency says it asked for more details about the session but failed to get them.

adder /ˈædə/ **adders**
NC An **adder** is a small poisonous snake. Adders are found in Europe and Asia.

addict /ˈædɪkt/ **addicts**
1 NC An **addict** is someone who cannot stop taking harmful drugs. The President has blamed the disturbances on hooligans and drug addicts.
2 NC+SUPP An **addict** is also someone who is very keen about something. They're usually solved with ease by crossword addicts.

addicted /əˈdɪktɪd/
1 ADJ PRED Someone who is **addicted** to a harmful drug cannot stop taking it. Many were already addicted to alcohol or drugs.
2 ADJ PRED If you are **addicted** to something, you like it a lot. Viewers are also quite critical of what they see on screen, even if they are addicted to watching each episode of a soap opera.

addiction /əˈdɪkʃn/
1 NU **Addiction** is the condition of taking harmful

drugs and being unable to stop. ...*heroin addiction.*
2 N SING An **addiction** to something is a very strong
desire for it. *The addiction is in the excitement of
gambling.*
addictive /ədɪktɪv/
1 ADJ If a drug is **addictive**, people who start taking it
find that they cannot stop. ...*an addictive cocaine
derivative.*
2 ADJ You can also describe something as **addictive**
when people enjoy it very much, or are unable to give
it up. ...*going deeper into debt to continue with their
addictive lifestyles... Small payouts don't make the
fruit machines any less addictive.*
Addis Ababa /ædɪs æbəbə/
Addis Ababa is the capital of Ethiopia and its largest
city. It is the headquarters of the Organization of
African Unity. Population: 1,413,000 (1984).
addition /ədɪʃn/ **additions**
1 You say '**in addition**' to introduce some more
information that you add to something you have
already said. *In addition, there were meetings with
trade unionists.*
2 NC+SUPP An **addition** to something is a thing or
amount which is added to it. *They can also award a
weekly addition for extra heating.*
3 NU+SUPP The **addition** of something is the fact or
process of adding it as an extra. *These houses have
been improved by the addition of bathrooms.*
4 NU **Addition** is the process of calculating the total of
two or more numbers. *Researchers say that 33 per
cent had trouble with simple addition.*
additional /ədɪʃəⁿəl/
ADJ **Additional** means extra or more than the ones
mentioned or already there. *Britain is sending
additional forces... No additional details are being
released at the moment.*
additionally /ədɪʃəⁿəli/
1 ADV SEN You use **additionally** to introduce an extra
fact. *Additionally, there was a substantial bill... His
own hands were tied and he was additionally
manacled to a police officer.*
2 ADV If something happens **additionally**, it happens to
a greater extent than before. *There was no point in
additionally burdening her with this news.*
additive /ædɪtɪv/ **additives**
NC An **additive** is a substance which manufacturers
add to a product such as food or petrol for a particular
purpose. *We must also urge the use of detectable
additives to explosives. ...foods labelled additive-free.*
add-on, add-ons
NC An **add-on** is a piece of equipment that is attached
to a computer to make it better or more efficient; a
technical term in computing. *The price depends on
the sophistication required and the number of add-ons.*
address /ədres/ **addresses, addressing, addressed**
1 NC Your **address** is the number of the house, the
name of the street, and the town where you live. *The
address is 70 Brompton Road, London SW1.*
2 VO If a letter is **addressed** to you, your name and
address are written on it. *The parcel, which contained
explosives, was addressed to the ambassador.*
3 VO or V-REFL+to If you **address** a problem or **address**
yourself to it, you deal with it. *He has not addressed
the issue of the strike... The Chancellor addressed
himself to the problem of economic and monetary
union.*
4 VO If you **address** a group of people, you give a
speech to them. *He addressed a meeting in Bristol.*
► Also NC *Mr Bush is expected to deliver a short
inaugural address.*
address book, address books
NC An **address book** is a book in which you write
people's names and addresses. ...*a diary, notepad and
address book.*
addressee /ædresiː/ **addressees**
NC The **addressee** of a letter or parcel is the person or
company that it is addressed to.
adduce /ədjuːs/ **adduces, adducing, adduced**
VO If you **adduce** a fact, a reason, or evidence, you
use it to support an argument; a formal word. *Darwin
adduced the fossil record as support for his theory.*

adenoidal /ædɪnɔɪdl/
ADJ Someone who is **adenoidal** speaks nasally because
their adenoids are swollen.
adenoids /ædɪnɔɪdz/
N PL Your **adenoids** are two soft lumps of flesh at the
back of your throat.
adept /ədept/
ADJ Someone who is **adept** at doing something does it
well. *They have become adept at filling in forms... He
has proved to be an adept diplomat.*
adequacy /ædɪkwəsi/
NU The **adequacy** of something is the fact that it is
large or effective enough for its purposes. ...*the
adequacy of resources. ...proof of the adequacy of the
principles.*
adequate /ædɪkwət/
1 ADJ If an amount is **adequate**, there is just enough
of it. *The pay was adequate. ...a country with
adequate rainfall.* ◆ **adequately** ADV *The children are
not adequately fed.*
2 ADJ If something is **adequate**, it is good enough to be
used or accepted. *She could not think of an adequate
answer.* ◆ **adequately** ADV *This has never been
adequately explained.*
adhere /ədhɪə/ **adheres, adhering, adhered**
1 V+to If a substance **adheres** to a surface or object, it
sticks to it. *This helps the plaster to adhere to the
wall.*
2 V+to If you **adhere** to a rule or agreement, you act in
the way that it says you should. *All of us will be
adhering very closely to the guidelines... The fire
regulations have been adhered to.*
3 V+to If you **adhere** to an opinion or belief, you
support it. *She has adhered to the view that it is my
responsibility.*
adherence /ədhɪərəns/
1 NU+to **Adherence** to a rule or agreement is obeying
it exactly. *Do they question our adherence to the
treaty?*
2 NU Your **adherence** to a particular belief or opinion
is the fact that you support it. ...*their adherence to
democratic or totalitarian systems.*
adherent /ədhɪərənt/ **adherents**
NC An **adherent** is someone who holds a particular
belief or supports a particular person or group. *The
cult gained adherents at an alarming rate. ...a victory
for the adherents of economic reform.*
adhesion /ədhiːʒn/
NU **Adhesion** is the state or fact of one thing sticking
firmly to another. ...*the snow's adhesion to the rock.*
adhesive /ədhiːsɪv/ **adhesives**
1 N MASS An **adhesive** is a substance which is used to
make things stick together. *Make sure you stick them
on with the correct adhesive.*
2 ADJ Something that is **adhesive** sticks firmly to
something else. ...*adhesive plasters.*
ad hoc /æd hɒk/
ADJ ATTRIB An **ad hoc** arrangement is one which is
unplanned and which takes place only because a
situation has made it necessary. *Rescue work
continued on an ad hoc basis... The men agreed to set
up an ad hoc committee.*
adieu /ədjuː/ **adieux** or **adieus**
People sometimes say **adieu** instead of goodbye if they
are never going to see each other again; an old-
fashioned word.
ad infinitum /æd ɪnfɪnaɪtəm/
If something happens **ad infinitum**, it happens
repeatedly in the same way. *But a Bill going through
the House can't just go on and on ad infinitum.*
adjacent /ədʒeɪsnt/
ADJ If one thing is **adjacent** to another or if two things
are **adjacent**, they are next to each other. *The
contested area is immediately adjacent to the combat
zone... The two cathedrals stand on adjacent hills.*
adjectival /ædʒɪktaɪvl/
ADJ In grammar, **adjectival** means consisting of or
relating to adjectives.
adjective /ædʒɪktɪv/ **adjectives**
NC In grammar, an **adjective** is a word which gives
you more information about a noun. In the sentences
'He had a beautiful smile' and 'The house was quiet',

'beautiful' and 'quiet' are adjectives.

adjoin /ədʒɔɪn/ adjoins, adjoining, adjoined
vo If one room, place, or object **adjoins** another, the two are next to each other; a formal word. *Her bedroom adjoined Guy's room.* ◆ **adjoining** ADJ ATTRIB *The adjoining room is Professor Marvin's office.*

adjourn /ədʒɜːn/ adjourns, adjourning, adjourned
v-ERG If a meeting or trial **is adjourned** or if it **adjourns**, it is stopped for a short time. *The formal talks have now been adjourned for the weekend... He refused to answer questions and the court adjourned.*

adjournment /ədʒɜːnmənt/ adjournments
NC An **adjournment** is a temporary stopping of a trial, enquiry, or other meeting. *A ten-minute adjournment allowed time for tempers to cool.*

adjudge /ədʒʌdʒ/ adjudges, adjudging, adjudged
VO+to-INF or VOC If someone or something **is adjudged** to be something or to have done something, they are considered to be that thing or to have done that thing; a formal word. *All religious and mystical experiences were then adjudged to be counter-revolutionary... Pallister was adjudged to have tripped him up before scoring the goal... I was adjudged an extremist.*

adjudicate /ədʒuːdɪkeɪt/ adjudicates, adjudicating, adjudicated
Vor VO To **adjudicate** on a dispute or problem means to make an official decision about it; a formal word. *The boards adjudicate on the punishment of prisoners... The International Court of Justice might be a suitable place to adjudicate claims and counter-claims.* ◆ **adjudication** /ədʒuːdɪkeɪʃn/ adjudications NC *The dispute was being made the subject of international adjudication. ...severe criticisms of their handling of the Council's adjudications.*

adjudicator /ədʒuːdɪkeɪtə/ adjudicators
NC An **adjudicator** is someone who makes an official decision about a dispute or problem. *Each refugee claim will be assessed by an adjudicator.*

adjunct /ædʒʌŋkt/ adjuncts
1 NC An **adjunct** is something that is connected with a larger or more important thing. *Duncan's survey was an adjunct to the current population survey.*
2 NC or N+N An **adjunct** is also a person who is hired to work for an organization for a short period of time, usually only for a few hours each week; used in American English. *Camilia Sadat is the adjunct professor of Middle East studies at Bentley College.*
3 NC In grammar, an **adjunct** is one of the main parts of a clause or sentence. It gives information about time, place, or manner, and is sometimes called an **adverbial group**. In the sentences 'They dived into the water' and 'Mr Shamir will visit Washington next month', 'into the water' and 'next month' are adjuncts.

adjust /ədʒʌst/ adjusts, adjusting, adjusted
1 V+to or v When you **adjust** to a new situation, you get used to it by changing your behaviour or your ideas. *Couples do not give themselves time to adjust to marriage before a baby arrives... The tariffs are to be cut more slowly to give industry time to adjust.*
2 vo If you **adjust** something, you change it to make it more effective or appropriate. *The normal policy is to adjust interest rates when it is sensible to do so... Dosages may have to be adjusted from baby to baby.*
3 vo If you **adjust** a machine, you change its setting in order to make it work properly or more efficiently. *I went to adjust the television set.*
4 vo If you **adjust** a piece of clothing, you change its position so that it looks right. *He spent several minutes adjusting his tie.*

adjustable /ədʒʌstəbl/
ADJ If something is **adjustable**, it can be changed to different positions. *...an adjustable spanner.*

adjusted /ədʒʌstɪd/
ADJ A well **adjusted** person can control their behaviour and deal with the problems of life. A badly **adjusted** person cannot. *They grow up happy and well adjusted.*

adjustment /ədʒʌstmənt/ adjustments
1 NC or NU An **adjustment** is an alteration or correction to a machine or a method of doing things. *He spent weeks making repairs and adjustments... Major economic adjustment can be difficult to undertake in the short term.*
2 NU **Adjustment** is also the process of changing your behaviour in order to cope with a new situation. *Foreign students have problems of adjustment to living in Britain... Thousands of young marines have made the adjustment from combat.*

adjutant /ædʒʊtənt/ adjutants
NC An **adjutant** is an army officer who deals with administrative work. *...a chief adjutant, three sergeants and three privates.*

ad-lib /ædlɪb/ ad-libs, ad-libbing, ad-libbed
Vor VO If you **ad-lib** in a play or a speech, you say something which has not been prepared beforehand. *They ad-libbed so much and broke down in chuckles so often... I tried to ad-lib a joke I'd heard but my timing was completely wrong.*

admin /ædmɪn/
NU **Admin** is the paperwork and other routine tasks involved in running an organization or business; an informal word. *I help him do some of his admin. ...the new admin block.*

administer /ədmɪnɪstə/ administers, administering, administered
1 vo To **administer** a country, company, or institution means to be responsible for managing it. *She had a huge department to administer.*
2 vo To **administer** something also means to ensure that it is done or carried out correctly. *Experts administer the tests and publish the results.*
3 vo To **administer** a drug to someone means to give it to them to swallow or to inject it into them. *The prison officers helped to administer a sedative to him.*

administration /ədmɪnɪstreɪʃn/ administrations
1 NC The **administration** of a country or area is its government. *He said his administration was standing by its demands... The amendment has been strongly opposed by the Bush administration... He was right to blame the mistakes of past administrations for the present situation.*
2 N SING+SUPP The **administration** of a company or institution is the group of people who organize and supervise it. *...negotiations between the University administration and the Students' Union.*
3 NU **Administration** is the range of activities connected with the organization or supervision of a company, institution, or country. *They need to spend less on administration.*

administrative /ədmɪnɪstrətɪv/
ADJ **Administrative** work involves organizing and supervising a country, company, or institution. *...an attempt to preserve the old administrative bureaucratic system.*

administrator /ədmɪnɪstreɪtə/ administrators
NC An **administrator** is someone who manages and organizes a country, company, or institution. *The scheme has been condemned by football administrators.*

admirable /ædmərəbl/
ADJ An **admirable** quality or action deserves to be praised and admired. *The trains ran with admirable precision.* ◆ **admirably** ADV *It fulfills its purpose admirably.*

admiral /ædmərəl/ admirals
NC or TITLE An **admiral** is a naval officer of the highest rank. *The new interior minister is a former admiral in the navy. ...the former National Security Adviser, Admiral John Poindexter.*

Admiralty /ædmərəlti/
N PROP The **Admiralty** is the part of the government that is responsible for the Royal Navy. *The British Admiralty has announced an eight year programme of research into propulsion systems for torpedoes.*

admiration /ædməreɪʃn/
NU **Admiration** is a feeling of great liking and respect. *Benson had enormous admiration for them all... He referred with admiration to Mrs Thatcher's restructuring of the economy.*

admire /ədmaɪə/ admires, admiring, admired
1 vo If you **admire** someone or something, you like and respect them. *John admires Robert Browning's work... They had been admired for their discipline.*
2 vo If someone **admires** something, they look at it

with great pleasure. *He went along the lane admiring the crocuses.*

admirer /ədmaɪərə/ **admirers**
NC+SUPP An **admirer** of a particular person is someone who likes and respects that person. *He claims to be an admirer of Lenin and a supporter of Mikhail Gorbachev's perestroika... He has political admirers outside the Socialist party.*

admiring /ədmaɪərɪŋ/
ADJ ATTRIB You can use **admiring** to describe someone's behaviour or expression when they indicate their liking or respect for someone or something. *She gave me one of her rare admiring looks. ...signing autographs for admiring deputies.* ♦ **admiringly** ADV *Ralph glanced at them admiringly.*

admissible /ədmɪsəbl/
ADJ If evidence is **admissible**, it can be considered during a trial in a court of law; a legal term. *The society wants video-recorded interviews to be admissible as evidence in court.*

admission /ədmɪʃn/ **admissions**
1 NUorNC **Admission** to a place or organization is the fact of allowing someone to enter it or join it. *Everyone attending a match needs an identity card to gain admission... Alcohol intoxication is a common cause of admissions to hospital.*
2 NUorN+N **Admission** or an **admission** fee is the amount of money you pay to enter a place such as a museum or park. *The exhibition runs until June and admission is free... The admission charge doesn't help increase attendance.*
3 NC An **admission** is a statement that something bad, unpleasant, or embarrassing is true. *He submitted his resignation, together with an admission of his guilt. ...an admission of defeat.*

admit /ədmɪt/ **admits, admitting, admitted**
1 VO, V-QUOTE, V-REPORT, V+ING, or V+to If you **admit** something that is embarrassing, bad, or unpleasant, you say that it is true. *No group has yet admitted responsibility for the attack... 'I don't know,' he admitted... He admitted he couldn't prove his identity on the telephone... He admitted driving at more than a hundred miles an hour... He did admit to some possible errors in the way he'd responded.*
2 VO If someone **is admitted** to a place, organization, or agreement, they are allowed to enter it or join it. *Junior members of staff are not admitted. ...doubts about admitting Libya to the Treaty.*
3 VO If someone **is admitted** to hospital, they are kept there as a patient. *She has been admitted to hospital with ninety-five percent burns.*
● **Admit** is used in these phrases. ● If you **admit defeat**, you finally accept that you cannot do something that you have been trying to do. *His opponent admitted defeat even before all the votes had been counted.* ● If you **admit responsibility** or **admit liability**, you say that you are responsible for something that has happened. *No group has yet admitted responsibility for the explosion... British Rail admitted liability for the accident.*

admittance /ədmɪtns/
NU **Admittance** is the act of entering a place or the right to enter it. *An increasing number of emigrés were being refused admittance as refugees.*

admittedly /ədmɪtɪdli/
ADV SEN You use **admittedly** when you say something which weakens your previous statement. *Admittedly, economists often disagree among themselves.*

admonish /ədmɒnɪʃ/ **admonishes, admonishing, admonished**
VO If you **admonish** someone, you tell them firmly that they have done something wrong; a formal word. *They are frequently admonished for their failure to act quickly.*

admonition /ædmənɪʃn/ **admonitions**
NCorNU An **admonition** is a warning or rebuke about someone's behaviour; a formal word. *Mr Li's stern admonition came at a meeting of representatives of China's judiciary... He wagged his finger in mild admonition.*

ad nauseam /æd nɔːziæm/
If someone does something **ad nauseam**, they do it repeatedly for a long time, so that it becomes annoying or boring. *She went on ad nauseam about how well her children were doing at school.*

ado /əduː/
Something that is done **without further ado** is done immediately. *I felt that I ought to hand over the material without further ado.*

adolescence /ædəlesns/
NU **Adolescence** is the period of your life during which you develop from being a child into an adult. *She spent her adolescence in England.*

adolescent /ædəlesnt/ **adolescents**
NC An **adolescent** is a young person who is no longer a child but who is not yet an adult. *Adolescents participate in designing their own course materials in Denmark.* ▶ Also ADJ ATTRIB *...a father with an adolescent son.*

adopt /ədɒpt/ **adopts, adopting, adopted**
1 VO If you **adopt** an attitude, plan, or course of action, you begin to have it or carry it out. *The United Nations have adopted a resolution condemning the killings... All this suggests that they are capable of adopting a more flexible approach... It remains important for everyone to adopt a healthy lifestyle.* ♦ **adoption** /ədɒpʃn/ NU+of *The Council have called for the adoption of major reforms.*
2 VO If you **adopt** someone else's child, you take it into your own family and make it legally your own. *According to the law, anyone over 21 can apply to adopt a child.* ♦ **adopted** ADJ *...parents of adopted children.* ♦ **adoption, adoptions** NUorNC *...the shortage of children available for adoption. ...proposals dealing with adoptions from overseas.*
3 VO If you **adopt** a country or name, you choose it to be your own. *...the right of any person to adopt the nationality of the country in which he or she was born... This party has adopted the name of 'Citizens' Movement Democratic Action'.* ♦ **adopted** ADJ *She is very keen to play for her adopted country.*

adoptive /ədɒptɪv/
ADJ ATTRIB Someone's **adoptive** parents are the people who have adopted them. *At six weeks he was given to his adoptive family.*

adorable /ədɔːrəbl/
ADJ An **adorable** child or animal is delightful, lovable, and attractive. *...an adorable kitten.*

adoration /ædəreɪʃn/
NU **Adoration** is a feeling of great admiration and love. *This has in no way diminished the people's adoration of their leaders... He did not tell anyone of his adoration for her.*

adore /ədɔː/ **adores, adoring, adored**
1 VO If you **adore** someone, you love and admire them. *He clearly adores his wife... Garbo was adored by thousands, but she shunned publicity.* ♦ **adoring** ADJ ATTRIB *He was mobbed by adoring crowds.*
2 VO If you **adore** something, you like it very much. *People will adore this film... They adore winning.*

adorn /ədɔːn/ **adorns, adorning, adorned**
VO If a place is **adorned** with things, or if things **adorn** it, those things make it look more attractive or noticeable; a literary word. *Peking has been adorned with flags, banners, and flowers... Oil paintings adorned the walls.*

adornment /ədɔːnmənt/ **adornments**
1 NU **Adornment** is the act of making something more beautiful by adding something to it. *Styles of adornment have changed over the centuries.*
2 NC An **adornment** is something that is intended to make someone or something more attractive. *...adornments such as make-up and jewellery.*

adrenalin /ədrenəlɪn/; also spelt **adrenaline**.
NU **Adrenalin** is a substance produced by your body in response to stress. It makes your heart beat faster and gives you more energy. *...the adrenalin released while at the roulette table.*

adrift /ədrɪft/
1 ADJ PRED If a boat goes **adrift**, it floats on the water without being controlled. *The tanker went adrift in sixty mile an hour winds but is now under tow.*
2 ADJ after N In sport, if you are a particular number of points **adrift**, you are behind your opponent by that

number of points. *Sampdoria moved into third place, three points adrift of Napoli... Faldo finished on 68, leaving him one shot adrift.*

adroit /ədrɔɪt/
ADJ An **adroit** person is quick and skilful in their thoughts or actions; a formal word. *Jamie was adroit at flattering others... He is known as an adroit bureaucrat.* ◆ **adroitly** ADV *The young men picked up the papers adroitly.*

adulation /ædjʊleɪʃn/
NU **Adulation** is very great and uncritical admiration and praise; used showing disapproval. *He basked in the adulation of the Egyptian people... The President's birthday has become an occasion for extravagant adulation in the public and the press.*

adult /ædʌlt, ədʌlt/ **adults**
1 NC An **adult** is a mature, fully developed person or animal. *A happy home is one in which children and adults have equal rights. ...locusts which hatch from eggs and develop into adults.* ► Also ADJ ATTRIB *...adult insects.*
2 ADJ Something that is **adult** is suitable or intended for adult people. *Children can assist in adult work at an early age. ...universal adult franchise.*

adult education
NU **Adult education** is education for people who are no longer at school or college, but who wish to study or learn a new skill, usually in their spare time. *They have responded by putting more resources into adult education.*

adulterate /ədʌltəreɪt/ **adulterates, adulterating, adulterated**
VO If you **adulterate** drink or food, you weaken or contaminate it by adding something to it. *...a scandal over wine which had been adulterated with anti-freeze.*

adultery /ədʌltəri/
NU If a married person commits **adultery**, they have sex with someone that they are not married to. *They confronted the former senator about his admitted adultery with a young model last year.*

adulthood /ædʌlthʊd/
NU **Adulthood** is the state of being an adult. *There is no reason why she shouldn't survive into healthy adulthood.*

advance /ədvɑːns/ **advances, advancing, advanced**
1 V When people **advance**, they move forward, often in a threatening way. *Troops are still advancing rapidly through the city's eastern suburbs... She advanced on him, shouting and waving her ticket.* ◆ **advancing** ADJ *...rows of advancing enemy tanks.*
2 V If someone or something **advances**, they make progress in something, especially by increasing knowledge, understanding, or efficiency. *I know we have advanced socially a great deal... Technology is advancing faster than workers' skills... She advanced to the second round with a convincing victory.*
3 VO If you **advance** a particular situation or process, you help it to make progress. *He said he would only go if it would advance the search for a settlement... There's nothing to advance a courtship better than a poem.*
4 VO If you **advance** a cause, interest, or claim, you support it and help to make it successful. *There'll be little opportunity to advance Spain's claims to sovereignty... They feel that television helps advance the cause of terrorism... Their political aim can no longer be advanced by violence.*
5 VO If you **advance** a theory or argument, you put it forward for discussion. *It had been assumed that V.P. Singh would defuse the tension by advancing a compromise solution... Father Barbaric advances a different argument in favour of the miracle.*
6 NCorNU **Advance** in a particular field, subject, or industry is progress in understanding it or in improving ideas and techniques. *...radical advances in computer design... Technological advance has produced even more lethal weapons.*
7 N SING An **advance** is a sum of money which you give to someone earlier than arranged. *...a twenty pound advance.* ► Also VOO *Axel advanced him the money for a suit.*
8 ADJ ATTRIB **Advance** booking, warning, or notice is

done or given before an event happens. *There was no advance warning of the President's departure... This visit had received almost no advance publicity.*
● **Advance** is used in these phrases. ● If you do something **in advance**, you do it before a particular date or event. *You should book well in advance, preferably six weeks before.* ● If one thing happens or is done **in advance of** another, it happens or is done before the other thing. *He is holding a series of meetings in advance of his talks with Mrs Thatcher... Violence is continuing in advance of the forthcoming election.*

advanced /ədvɑːnst/
1 ADJ An **advanced** system, method, or design is modern and has been developed from an earlier version of the same thing. *Last year they chose to buy an advanced radar warning system. ...more advanced forms of music... The radar system is much more advanced than anything used before.*
2 ADJ A country that is **advanced** has reached a high level of industrial or technological development. *An advanced industrial nation might take certain skills for granted... He said that Zambia is already more advanced than many countries in Eastern Europe.*
3 ADJ Something that is at an **advanced** stage or level is at a late stage of development. *...patients at an advanced stage of the disease... The Turkish government says that negotiations are in an advanced state... The Northern economy was more advanced than that of the South.*

advancement /ədvɑːnsmənt/
1 NU **Advancement** is promotion or increased status, for example in your job. *...opportunity for personal advancement... They have little prospect of social or economic advancement.*
2 NU+SUPP The **advancement** of something is the process of helping it to progress or succeed. *...the advancement of knowledge... Its objectives are the advancement of the Christian religion.*

advantage /ədvɑːntɪdʒ/ **advantages**
1 NC An **advantage** is something that puts you in a better position than other people. *As a scientist I have a slight advantage over him... The subsidies have been seen as giving farmers an unfair advantage over small-holders.*
2 NC An **advantage** is also a benefit that is likely to result from something. *The advantages of electricity are the lack of fumes and the ease of distribution.*
● **Advantage** is used in these phrases. ● If something is **to your advantage**, it will be useful for you or will benefit you. *The party are now trying to use the issue to his advantage.* ● If you **take advantage of** a situation, you use it while you can for your own benefit, sometimes unfairly. *Visitors come here to take advantage of the low prices. ...delinquents who took advantage of the large crowd to rob and loot stores in the city centre.*

advantaged /ədvɑːntɪdʒd/
ADJ Someone who is **advantaged** is in a better social or financial position than other people. *He said there was a growing gap between the advantaged and disadvantaged elderly.*

advantageous /ædvənt10ɪdʒəs/
ADJ Something that is **advantageous** to you is likely to benefit you. *Economic growth is inevitable and advantageous.*

advent /ædvent/
N SING+*of* The **advent** of something is the fact of it starting or coming into existence; a formal word. *...the advent of a multi-party system in the Soviet Union.*

adventure /ədventʃə/ **adventures**
NCorNU An **adventure** is a series of events that you become involved in and that are unusual, exciting, and perhaps dangerous. *...my Arctic adventures... They were bored, and looking for adventure.*

adventure playground, adventure playgrounds
NC An **adventure playground** is a rough area of land where children can play on special equipment such as climbing frames, ropes, nets, and rubber tyres.

adventurer /ədventʃərə/ **adventurers**
1 NC An **adventurer** is someone who tries to become

rich, powerful, and influential by using dishonest methods. *...a bitter attack on political adventurers.*
2 NC An **adventurer** is also someone who enjoys adventure. *John Ridgway is a real adventurer—he's sailed twice round the world and canoed down the Amazon.*

adventurism /ədvˈentʃərɪzəm/
NU **Adventurism** is willingness to take risks, especially in order to obtain an unfair advantage from a bad situation. *The Polish people are on their guard against adventurism and irresponsibility... They had warned against military adventurism in the Gulf.*

adventurist /ədvˈentʃərɪst/ **adventurists**
1 NC An **adventurist** is someone who is willing to take risks or act illegally in order to gain an advantage. *Fears were being stirred up by political adventurists who sought power for themselves... President Aquino described the rebels as adventurists.*
2 ADJ **Adventurist** policies, methods, or ideas are risky, and are designed to take advantage of a bad situation. *He described the proposal as unconstitutional and adventurist. ...American adventurist and expansionist policies.*

adventurous /ədvˈentʃərəs/
1 ADJ An **adventurous** person is willing to take risks and eager to have new experiences. *...a warning of the possible pitfalls for adventurous travellers.*
2 ADJ You can describe things as **adventurous** when they are daring and exciting. *Mr Steel agreed that the document had been adventurous and hard to accept... Science is creative, adventurous, even mystical.*

adverb /ˈædvɜːb/ **adverbs**
NC In grammar, an **adverb** is a word which gives you more information about the time, place, or manner of the action. In the sentences 'The operation had gone very well' and 'I greatly enjoyed working with him', 'well' and 'greatly' are adverbs.

adverbial group /ædvˈɜːbiəl gruːp/ **adverbial groups**
NC In grammar, an **adverbial group** is a group of words which give you more information about the time, place, or manner of the action. In the sentences 'I used to go in three mornings a week' and 'He takes his job very seriously indeed', 'three mornings a week' and 'very seriously indeed' are adverbial groups.

adversarial /ædvəsˈeəriəl/
ADJ An **adversarial** method, system, or attitude is based on conflict or disagreement between two people or groups of people. *Sir Peter criticised the adversarial nature of criminal trials... According to one official, discussions with the Soviet Union were no longer adversarial.*

adversary /ˈædvəsəri/ **adversaries**
NC Your **adversary** is someone you are competing with, or arguing or fighting against. *She had two potential political adversaries.*

adverse /ˈædvɜːs/
ADJ ATTRIB **Adverse** decisions, conditions, or effects are unfavourable to you. *Falling prices had an adverse effect on business. ...adverse weather conditions... The organisers will surely avoid any further adverse publicity.* ♦ **adversely** ADV *The majority of children are adversely affected.*

adversity /ədvˈɜːsəti/
NU **Adversity** is a very difficult or unfavourable situation. *The papers say she thrives on adversity... They continue to fight in the face of adversity.*

advert /ˈædvɜːt/ **adverts**
NC An **advert** is the same as an **advertisement**; an informal word. *He placed adverts in a number of newspapers.*

advertise /ˈædvətaɪz/ **advertises, advertising, advertised**
1 VO If you **advertise** a product, event, or job, you tell people about it publicly, for example in newspapers or on television, in order to encourage them to buy that product, go to that event, or apply for that job. *...deodorants she had seen advertised on television. ...a leaflet advertising a fishing competition. ...application forms for jobs advertised in the papers.*
2 V If you **advertise** for something that you want, you announce in a newspaper, on television, or on a notice board that you want that thing. *The Council has*

advertised for accountants... *Should charities like Oxfam advertise on television?*

advertisement /ədvˈɜːtɪsmənt/ **advertisements**
NC An **advertisement** is a public announcement, for example in a newspaper or on television, that tells people about a product, event, or job vacancy. *...an advertisement for Adler shoes.*

advertiser /ˈædvətaɪzə/ **advertisers**
NC An **advertiser** is a person or company that pays for something to be advertised on television, in a newspaper, or on posters. *...special effects that advertisers use to sell their products.*

advertising /ˈædvətaɪzɪŋ/
NU **Advertising** is the activity of telling people about products or events in order to make them want to buy the products or go to the events. *...a new law regulating television advertising.*

advice /ədvˈaɪs/
NU If you give someone **advice**, you tell them what you think they should do. *She promised to follow his advice... All this could be avoided if people would take proper advice... They want advice on how to do it.*

advisable /ədvˈaɪzəbl/
ADJ If a course of action is **advisable**, it is sensible or is likely to achieve the result you want. *It's advisable to ring up first to make an appointment. ...drinking more than the medically advisable limit.*

advise /ədvˈaɪz/ **advises, advising, advised**
1 VO+to-INF, VO-REPORT, or VO+against If you **advise** someone, you tell them what you think they should do. *British citizens were advised not to travel... Their job involves advising people how to avoid this disease... Earlier the International Amateur Athletics Federation had advised the British authorities that she should be suspended... I would strongly advise you against it.*
2 VOor V If you **advise** people on a particular subject, you give them help and information on it. *They will advise me on which policies work and which will not... A panel of bishops has been appointed to advise on matters of religious policy.*
3 VO+of, VO-REPORT, or V-REPORT If you **advise** someone of something, or **advise** them that it is the case, you tell them about it; a formal use. *He said he had written to the King to advise him of the judge's concern... She has been advised that a guilty plea will shorten her trial... Its lawyers have advised that a court would be unlikely to overturn a ban.*

advisedly /ədvˈaɪzɪdli/
ADV If you use a word or expression **advisedly**, you deliberately use it, although it may sound odd, because it draws attention to what you are saying. *It's a crazy scheme, and I use that term advisedly.*

adviser /ədvˈaɪzə/ **advisers**; also spelt **advisor**.
NC An **adviser** is someone who gives help and information on a particular subject. *...an independent legal adviser. ...the President's advisers.*

advisory /ədvˈaɪzəᵊri/
ADJ An **advisory** group, or a group or person with an **advisory** role gives suggestions, help, and information on a particular subject. *...the National Women's Advisory Committee. ...an advisory body of four retired generals... Most of the advisory work is carried out over the phone.*

advocacy /ˈædvəkəsi/
NU **Advocacy** of a particular action or plan is the act of supporting it publicly. *...their advocacy of a strong state and a single party.*

advocate, advocates, advocating, advocated; pronounced /ˈædvəkeɪt/ when it is a verb and /ˈædvəkət/ when it is a noun.
1 VOor V-REPORT If you **advocate** a particular action or plan, you support it publicly; a formal use. *He had continued to advocate Tibetan independence while in jail... He advocated that Britain should join the alliance.*
2 NC+of An **advocate** of a particular action or plan is someone who supports it publicly. *...the advocates of women's rights. ...a strong advocate of nuclear power.*
3 NC An **advocate** is a lawyer who speaks in favour of someone or defends them in a court of law; a legal use. *Barristers are particularly critical of proposals for licensing advocates.*

adze /ædz/ **adzes**; also spelt **adz** in American English.
NC An **adze** is a heavy tool with a blade that is used for cutting and shaping wood.

aegis /iːdʒɪs/
Something that is done **under the aegis of** a particular organization is done with the support and backing of that organization; a formal expression. *The students spearhead a campaign under the aegis of Amnesty International.*

aeon /iːən, iːɒn/ **aeons**; also spelt **eon** in American English.
NC An **aeon** is an extremely long period of time. *...a dread that reaches back over the aeons to primitive man.*

aerate /eəreɪt/ **aerates, aerating, aerated**
VO If a substance is **aerated**, air is passed through it to make it fizzy. ◆ **aerated** ADJ *...some ghastly aerated chemical confection.*

aerial /eərɪəl/ **aerials**
1 ADJ ATTRIB You use **aerial** to describe things that are above the ground or that happen in the air. *An aerial railway had been erected. ...aerial warfare.*
2 ADJ ATTRIB **Aerial** photographs are photographs of things on the ground that are taken from the air. *All the papers carry large aerial photographs of a devastated army checkpoint.*
3 NC An **aerial** is a piece of wire that receives television or radio signals. *Connect the aerial to the radio and adjust its position for the best reception.*

aerobatics /eərəbætɪks/
N PL **Aerobatics** are spectacular and skilful movements made by aeroplanes, usually to entertain people watching from the ground. *They executed a series of aerobatics—criss-crossing, diving and soaring over our heads.*

aerobic /eərəʊbɪk/ **aerobics**
1 ADJ ATTRIB Something that is **aerobic** uses oxygen; a technical use in biology. *During the aerobic or oxygen-consuming process, heat is given off. ...aerobic exercise.*
2 NU **Aerobics** is a type of exercise which increases the amount of oxygen in your blood and strengthens your heart and lungs. *In aerobics, people exercise as vigorously as possible.*

aerodrome /eərədrəʊm/ **aerodromes**
NC An **aerodrome** is a place where small aeroplanes can land and take off. *He circled over the aerodrome.*

aerodynamic /eərəʊdaɪnæmɪk/ **aerodynamics**
1 ADJ ATTRIB **Aerodynamic** effects and principles are concerned with the way in which objects move in or through the air. *...aerodynamic improvements in design.* ◆ **aerodynamically** SUBMOD *...an aerodynamically designed wind and sun shelter.*
2 NC **Aerodynamics** is the study of the way in which objects move through the air. *According to the laws of aerodynamics, bumble bees shouldn't be able to fly.*

aeronautical /eərənɔːtɪkl/
ADJ **Aeronautical** engineering involves or relates to the design and construction of aeroplanes. *...aeronautical research.*

aeronautics /eərənɔːtɪks/
NU **Aeronautics** is the science of designing and constructing aeroplanes. *...his extensive knowledge of aeronautics.*

aeroplane /eərəpleɪn/ **aeroplanes**
NC An **aeroplane** is a vehicle with wings and engines that can fly through the air. *...the roar of military aeroplanes.*

aerosol /eərəsɒl/ **aerosols**
NC An **aerosol** is a pressurized container containing a liquid which is forced out as a fine spray when you press a button on the top. *Environmental groups have warned that aerosols may deplete the ozone layer... It's currently sold in aerosol form.*

aerospace /eərəʊspeɪs/
ADJ ATTRIB The **aerospace** industry is involved in developing and manufacturing rockets, missiles, and space vehicles. *...aerospace engineers.*

aesthete /iːsθiːt/ **aesthetes**; spelt **esthete** in American English.
NC An **aesthete** is someone who loves and appreciates works of art and beautiful things.

aesthetic /iːsθetɪk/ **aesthetics**; spelt **esthetic** in American English.
1 ADJ **Aesthetic** means involving beauty or art, and people's appreciation of beautiful things. *I'm cautious about any book that prescribes aesthetic responses.* ◆ **aesthetically** SUBMOD *...aesthetically appealing products.*
2 NU **Aesthetics** is the study of beauty in areas such as art, literature, and music. *His work ranges from poetry to philosophy, aesthetics, and criticism.*

afar /əfɑː/
From **afar** means from a long way away; a literary expression. *...visitors from afar... It's wrong for the government to interfere from afar.*

affable /æfəbl/
ADJ An **affable** person is pleasant and friendly. *He's known as a fairly affable chap, who takes life philosophically.*

affair /əfeə/ **affairs**
1 NC+SUPP You refer to an event as an **affair** when you are talking about it generally. *The wedding was a quiet affair. ...President Nixon's downfall in the Watergate affair.*
2 N PL+SUPP You can use **affairs** to refer to the important facts or activities connected with a particular subject. *Investigation of the BCCI affairs may have been blocked by a number of government departments over the last three years. ...a specialist in Eastern European affairs. ...affairs of state.* ● See also **current affairs, state of affairs.**
3 N PL+POSS Your **affairs** are your private and personal concerns. *What had induced her to meddle in his affairs?*
4 N SING+POSS If you say that something is your **affair**, you mean that it concerns only you and does not involve anyone else. *That's up to them, that's their affair... What went on behind that door was your own affair.*
5 NC If two people who are not married to each other are having an **affair**, they have a sexual relationship. *She was recruited by a secret agent, with whom she later had an affair.*

affect /əfekt/ **affects, affecting, affected**
1 VO When one thing **affects** another, it influences it or causes it to change. *...the ways in which computers can affect our lives. ...the crisis now affecting Hungarian society... Rural areas were barely affected.* ◆ **affected** ADJ *The worst affected township was Tembisa.*
2 VO If a disease **affects** you, it causes you to become ill. *The disease primarily affected Jane's lungs.* ◆ **affected** ADJ *It's more difficult to remove affected arteries.*
3 VOor V+to-INF If you **affect** a particular characteristic, you pretend that it is natural for you when it is not. *She affected a lisp... He affected to despise every Briton he met.*

affectation /æfekteɪʃn/ **affectations**
NCor NU An **affectation** is an attitude or type of behaviour that is false and intended to impress other people. *His film star affectations had disappeared. ...elegance without affectation.*

affected /əfektɪd/
ADJ Someone who is **affected** behaves in a false, unnatural way that is intended to impress other people. *He was affected and conceited.*

affection /əfekʃn/
N U **Affection** is a feeling of fondness and caring that you have for another person. *She gazed with deep affection at him... The king is known to inspire a lot of respect and affection among the refugees.*

affectionate /əfekʃənət/
ADJ An **affectionate** person shows their fondness for another person in their behaviour. *They were an affectionate couple. ...an affectionate tribute to President Reagan.* ◆ **affectionately** ADV *He stroked her affectionately.*

affidavit /æfɪdeɪvɪt/ **affidavits**
NC An **affidavit** is a written statement which you swear is true and which may be used as evidence in a court of law. *The authors submit a dozen sworn affidavits.*

affiliate, affiliates, affiliating, affiliated; pronounced /əˈfɪlieɪt/ when it is a verb and /əˈfɪliət/ when it is a noun.

1 V-REFL or V If an organization **affiliates** itself or is **affiliated** to another organization, it forms a close official link with it or becomes a member of it. *Such a group had already affiliated itself to them. ...an experimental group affiliated with the Royal Shakespeare Company.* ♦ **affiliated** ADJ ATTRIB *Questionnaires were sent to all affiliated trade unions.* 2 NC An **affiliate** is an organization which has a close official link with another, larger organization. *The organization has exercised a decisive influence over its British affiliates. ...the United Women's Front, an affiliate of the United Democratic Front.*

affiliation /əˌfɪliˈeɪʃn/ **affiliations**
1 NU If one group has **affiliation** with another group, it has a close official link with it. *In 1986, Solidarity was granted affiliation with the ICFTU.* 2 NC or NU Your religious or political **affiliation** is your support for a particular set of beliefs. *...ordinary people who don't have any strong political affiliations either way. ...discrimination on the grounds of political, religious, or cultural affiliation.*

affinity /əˈfɪnəti/ **affinities**
1 NU+SUPP If you have an **affinity** with someone or something, you feel that you belong with them and understand them. *Many Poles have an affinity with Afghans... I had this tremendous sense of affinity with the place... There is a natural affinity between Asian and British women.* 2 NC If people or things have an **affinity** with each other, they are similar in some ways. *In anatomical structure, Prehistoric Man has close affinities with modern humans.*

affirm /əˈfɜːm/ **affirms, affirming, affirmed**; a formal word.
1 V O or V-REPORT If you **affirm** a fact, you state that it is definitely true. *I affirmed my innocence... The commission affirmed that freedom of religious belief was a human right.* 2 V O If you **affirm** an idea or belief, you indicate clearly that you have this idea or belief. *It appealed to the authorities to affirm the full equality of women before the law.*

affirmation /ˌæfəˈmeɪʃn/ **affirmations**; a formal word.
1 NC An **affirmation** is a statement that something is true. *...affirmations that the retired businessman had made illegal profits.* 2 NC The **affirmation** of ideas, intentions, rights, or actions is a statement of your belief in and support for them. *...an affirmation of the ANC's policy.*

affirmative /əˈfɜːmətɪv/
ADJ ATTRIB An **affirmative** word or action indicates agreement, approval, or a positive attitude; a formal word. *Party leaders believe that a final affirmative vote can be taken before the summit is over... There's a generous, affirmative side to Yeats' imagination.*

affix, affixes, affixing, affixed; pronounced /əˈfɪks/ when it is a verb and /ˈæfɪks/ when it is a noun.
1 V O If you **affix** something somewhere, you stick, fasten, or attach it there; a formal use. *A page of a magazine was affixed to the wall.* 2 NC An **affix** is a letter or syllable which is added to the beginning or end of a word to make a different word, to change the tense of a verb, and so on.

afflict /əˈflɪkt/ **afflicts, afflicting, afflicted**
V O If you **are afflicted** by pain, illness, or a disaster, it affects you badly and makes you suffer; a formal word. *The continent was now afflicted by a drought... High mortality rates still afflict children of the Third World.*

affliction /əˈflɪkʃn/ **afflictions**
NC An **affliction** is something which causes suffering; a formal word. *...the horrors and afflictions of his time in prison.*

affluence /ˈæfluəns/
NU **Affluence** is the state of having a lot of money or a high standard of living; a formal word. *...a widening gap between poverty and affluence.*

affluent /ˈæfluənt/
ADJ If you are **affluent**, you have a lot of money; a

formal word. *...affluent young professionals... An affluent society can sow the seeds of its own downfall.*

afford /əˈfɔːd/ **affords, affording, afforded**
1 V O or V+to-INF If you can **afford** something, you have enough money to be able to pay for it. *...families who can afford cars... I can't afford to rent this flat.* 2 V O or V+to-INF If you say that you cannot **afford** to allow something to happen, you mean that it would be harmful or embarrassing to you if it did happen. *We can't afford another scandal... He could not afford to be associated with them.*

affordable /əˈfɔːdəbl/
ADJ If something is **affordable**, you have enough money to be able to pay for it. *This meant that pop records became more affordable for youngsters. ...a range of up-market and affordable clothing.*

afforestation /əˌfɒrɪˈsteɪʃn/
NU **Afforestation** is the practice of planting large numbers of trees on bare land. *...the afforestation of the uplands.*

affront /əˈfrʌnt/ **affronts, affronting, affronted**
1 V O If you **are affronted** by something, you feel insulted and hurt by it. *They were deeply affronted by their abrupt dismissal... He pointed out the buildings that affronted him, and those that he liked.* 2 NC If something is an **affront** to you, it is an obvious insult to you. *He condemned it as an act of terrorism and an affront to civilized values.*

Afghanistan /æfˈɡænɪstaːn/
The **Republic of Afghanistan** is a country in south-western Asia, between Iran and Pakistan. The main ethnic groups are Pashtun, Tadjik, and Uzbek. The monarchy was abolished in a coup in 1973. A second coup in 1979 established a one-party state, ruled by the People's Democratic Party of Afghanistan (PDPA). The coup was supported by the Soviet invasion of Afghanistan and opposed by the Mujaheddin rebels. In the resulting war over 5.5 million refugees fled into Pakistan or Iran. The Soviet Union withdrew their troops in 1989, but fighting continued between the Mujaheddin and government forces. Political parties were legalized in 1987. Dr Najibullah Ahmadzai of the Homeland Party (formerly the PDPA) became President in 1987. Fazl Haq Khaleqiar became Prime Minister in 1990. Afghanistan exports natural gas, fruit and nuts, textiles, carpets, wool, cotton, and hides. ♦ **Afghan** /ˈæfɡæn/ N, ADJ
▪ *religion:* Islam (mainly Sunni) ▪ *language:* Pashtu, Dari ▪ *currency:* afghani ▪ *capital:* Kabul ▪ *population:* 15 million (1989) ▪ *size:* 652,225 square kilometres.

afield /əˈfiːld/
1 You say that someone has come **from as far afield as** a place in order to emphasize that they have come a very long way. *Groups from as far afield as Scotland have sent deputations.* 2 ADV **Further afield** means in places or areas other than the nearest or most obvious one. *Some artillery shells have landed further afield... The pragmatism behind Tokyo's decision has spread further afield.*

aflame /əˈfleɪm/; a literary word.
1 ADJ PRED If your face is **aflame**, it is bright red and feels hot. *There she stood and blinked, cheeks aflame, hair awry... He was aflame with pride.* 2 ADJ PRED If something is on fire, you can say it is **aflame**. *Its wreckage was bent and the tyres aflame.*

afloat /əˈfləʊt/
1 ADJ PRED When someone or something is **afloat**, they remain partly above the surface of water and do not sink. *By kicking constantly he could stay afloat.* 2 ADJ PRED If you keep a business or industry **afloat**, you have only just enough money to run it. *Unprofitable companies cannot be kept afloat any longer. ...keeping the economy afloat.*

afoot /əˈfʊt/
ADJ PRED If a plan or scheme is **afoot**, it is already happening or being planned, often secretly; used showing disapproval. *They deny that there is anything sinister afoot.*

aforementioned /əˈfɔːmenʃnd/
ADJ ATTRIB When you refer to the **aforementioned** person or subject, you mean the person or subject that

has already been mentioned; a formal word. ...*the works of all the aforementioned writers.*

aforesaid /əfɔːsed/
ADJ ATTRIB **Aforesaid** means the same as **aforementioned**; a formal word. ...*a gay extrovert who sounds remarkably like the aforesaid Alison.*

afraid /əfreɪd/
1 ADJ PRED If you are **afraid** of someone or **afraid** to do something, you are frightened because you think that something horrible is going to happen. *They were afraid of you... He was afraid even to turn his head.*
2 ADJ PRED If you are **afraid** that something unpleasant will happen, you are worried that it may happen. *She was afraid that I might be embarrassed... He was terribly afraid of offending anyone... Don't be afraid to ask questions.*
3 ADJ PRED+*for* If you are **afraid** for someone or something, you are worried because you think that something horrible is going to happen to them. *As the crisis deepens, many are afraid for their lives.*
4 When you want to apologize to someone or to disagree with them in a polite way, you can begin by saying I'm **afraid**. *I'm afraid I can't agree.*

afresh /əfreʃ/
ADV If you do something **afresh**, you do it again in a different way. *I'm too old to start afresh... It's time to look afresh at England's rural inheritance.*

Africa /æfrɪkə/
Africa is the world's second largest continent, occupying over 30 million square kilometres. The four longest rivers are the Nile, Zaïre, Niger, and Zambezi. Mount Kilimanjaro (5,895 metres) is the highest point. Africa's population is approximately 568 million.

African /æfrɪkən/ **Africans**
1 ADJ **African** means belonging or relating to Africa. *The international community could help by guaranteeing access to markets for African exports.*
2 NC An **African** is a person who comes from Africa. ...*hundreds of students, most of them Africans.*

Afrikaans /æfrɪkɑːns/
1 NU **Afrikaans** is one of the official languages of South Africa. *We ran articles in Afrikaans.*
2 ADJ **Afrikaans** means belonging or relating to the white people living in South Africa who have Dutch ancestry. *An Afrikaans couple live in one of the houses opposite.*

Afrikaner /æfrɪkɑːnə/ **Afrikaners**
NC An **Afrikaner** is a white person who lives in South Africa and who has Dutch ancestry. *The Afrikaners are 60% of the white population.* ▶ Also ADJ ATTRIB *They had consolidated Afrikaner support.*

Afro- /æfrəʊ-/
PREFIX **Afro-** combines with adjectives to form new adjectives that describe something that is connected with Africa and another continent or country. ...*Afro-American music.*

after /ɑːftə/
1 PREP, ADV, or CONJ If something happens **after** a particular date or event, it happens later than that date or event. *He resigned after allegations that he was involved in drug-trafficking... Soon after, Faraday began his research into electricity... He was ill after eating the meal.*
2 PREP If you go **after** someone, or if you are **after** them, you follow or chase them. *She ran after him into the courtyard... The Germans were after him.*
3 PREP If you are **after** something, you are trying to get it for yourself. *Those youngsters are after my job.*
4 PREP To be named **after** someone means to be given the same name as them. ...*a street named after my grandfather.*
5 PREP Americans use **after** to tell the time. For example, if they say it is ten **after** six, the time is ten minutes past six.
6 If something happens **day after day** or **year after year**, it happens every day or every year. *Some jokes go round school year after year.*
7 **after all**: see **all**.

afterbirth /ɑːftəbɜːθ/
N SING The **afterbirth** is the material which comes out of a woman or female animal's womb soon after they have given birth. It consists of substances that

protected the young baby or animal while it was in the womb.

aftercare /ɑːftəkeə/
NU **Aftercare** is the nursing and care of people who have been ill in hospital and who are now recovering. *Exercise programmes should be central to aftercare.*

after-effect, after-effects
NC **After-effects** are the bad or harmful conditions which result from something. *Weather remained bad as an after-effect of the cyclone... The Financial Times says industry could be dealing with the after-effects of this recession well into the middle of the decade.*

afterlife /ɑːftəlaɪf/
N SING The **afterlife** is a life that some people believe begins when you die, for example a life in heaven or as another person or animal. *Do you think belief in an afterlife comes with old age?*

aftermath /ɑːftəmæθ/
N SING+SUPP The **aftermath** of an important, usually harmful, event is the situation that results from it. *In the immediate aftermath of the accident, no one knew who had been hurt... The aftermath to the killings also commands attention.*

afternoon /ɑːftənuːn/ **afternoons**
NC or NU The **afternoon** is the part of each day which begins at lunchtime and ends at about six o'clock. *The telephone lines are open all afternoon. ...five o'clock in the afternoon.*

after-shave /ɑːftəʃeɪv/
NU **After-shave** is a scented liquid that men sometimes put on their faces after they have shaved.

aftertaste /ɑːftəteɪst/ **aftertastes**
NC+SUPP An **aftertaste** is a taste that remains in your mouth after you have finished eating or drinking something. *It has a metallic or bitter aftertaste.*

afterthought /ɑːftəθɔːt/ **afterthoughts**
NC An **afterthought** is a remark or action which you say or do in addition to something else, but perhaps without careful thought. *After a while she said as an afterthought, 'I could do that.'... Mr Ghozali's remarks appear to be more of an afterthought than a serious preoccupation.*

afterwards /ɑːftəwədz/; the form **afterward** /ɑːftəwəd/ is also used.
ADV SEN If something is done or happens **afterwards**, it is done or happens later than a particular event or time that has already been described. *Afterwards we all helped with the washing up... She died soon afterwards.*

again /əgen, əgeɪn/
1 ADV If you do something **again**, you do it once more. *Try again in half an hour... Let's do it, I may never have the chance again.*
2 If you do something **again and again**, you do it many times or on many occasions. *The dangers of smoking will be repeated again and again.*
3 ADV When something is in a particular state or place **again**, it has returned to the state or place that it was before. *At last the assembly was silent again.*
4 ADV SEN When you are asking someone to repeat something that they have already told you, you can add **again** to the end of your question. *What's his name again?*
5 ADV SEN You can use **again** to emphasize a similarity between the subject you are talking about now and a previous subject. *My last question is again a personal one.*

against /əgenst, əgeɪnst/
1 PREP If something is leaning or pressing **against** something else, it is touching it. *Ralph leaned against a tree... She was pressing her nose against the window.*
2 PREP or ADV If you are **against** an idea, policy, or system, you are opposed to it. *He was fanatically against American intervention in the war... Mr Ligachov is not against perestroika... Are you voting for or against?*
3 PREP If you compete **against** someone in a game, you try to beat them. *He played in the first Test Match against Australia.*
4 PREP If you do something **against** someone or something, you do something that might harm them.

They were not allowed to use arms against their enemies... They launched a new attack against Angolan army positions.
5 PREP If you appeal **against** a decision that has been made in a court of law, you ask officially for the case to be reconsidered. *He's planning to appeal against the ban... The government will now start appealing against the court's decisions.*
6 PREP Something that is **against** the law is forbidden by law. *A judge will decide whether mass picketing is against the law.*
7 PREP If you take action **against** a possible future event, you try to prevent it. *He has taken certain precautions against burglary... The armed forces have been put on full alert to guard against the possibility of an attempted coup.*
8 PREP If you are moving **against** a current, tide, or wind, you are moving in the opposite direction to it. *We had to row against the pull of the stream... I turned against the wind.*
9 PREP If something happens or is considered **against** a particular background of events, it happens or is considered in relation to those events. *The celebrations are taking place against a background of continuing shortages.*
10 PREP If something is measured or valued **against** something else, it is measured or valued by comparing it with the other thing. *The dollar was little changed against other currencies.*
11 PREP or ADV The chances or odds **against** something happening are the chances or odds that it will not happen. *The odds against another attack were astronomical... The more handicaps the gambler accepts, the higher the odds against.*
Agaña /əgɑːnjə/
Agaña is the capital of Guam. Population: 880 (1980).
agape /əgeɪp/
ADJ after N If you stand with your mouth **agape**, your mouth is open very wide, often because you are very surprised by something. *The shark swam up under the woman, jaws agape.*
agate /ægət/ agates
N or NU An **agate** is a very hard stone which is used for making jewellery. *The griffin was supposed to have laid eggs of agate.*
age /eɪdʒ/ ages, ageing or aging, aged
1 NU+SUPP Your **age** is the number of years that you have lived. *He is eighty years of age... He died at the age of forty.*
2 NU **Age** is the state of being old. *Her age and frailty are giving him cause for concern. ...medals stained with age.*
3 V-ERG When someone **ages** or when something **ages** them, they become or seem much older. *She was dismayed to see how much he had aged... The strain of looking after her had aged him.*
4 NC An **age** is a period in history. *...the great age of Greek sport. ...a detailed study of woman's role throughout the ages.*
5 N SING or N PL An **age** or **ages** means a very long time; an informal use. *She took an age to dress... I've known him for ages.*
6 See also **ageing**.
● **Age** is used in these phrases. ● Someone who is **under age** is not legally old enough to do something, for example to buy an alcoholic drink. *Boys are getting drinks under age.* ● When someone **comes of age**, they become legally an adult. In Britain, young people come of age when they are 18. *When he came of age he made a will.*
aged; pronounced /eɪdʒd/ for the meaning in paragraph 1 and /eɪdʒɪd/ for the meanings in paragraphs 2 and 3.
1 ADJ PRED You use **aged** followed by a number to say how old someone is. *...men aged 60 and over.* ● See also **middle-aged**.
2 ADJ Someone or something that is **aged** is very old. *...his aged aunt.*
3 N PL You can refer to all people who are very old as **the aged**. *...voluntary help for the aged.*
age group, age groups
NC An **age group** is all the people in a place or organization who were born during a particular period

of time, for example all the people aged between 18 and 25. *There is now more competition for jobs in this age group... Children spend more time with their own age group.*
ageing /eɪdʒɪŋ/; also spelt **aging**.
1 ADJ **Ageing** means becoming older and less attractive or efficient. *...an ageing film star.*
2 NU **Ageing** is the process of becoming old. *...the less desirable aspects of ageing.*
3 See also **age**.
ageless /eɪdʒləs/
ADJ If you describe someone or something as **ageless**, you mean that it is impossible to tell how old they are. *...an ageless ritual.*
age limit, age limits
NC An **age limit** is the oldest or youngest age at which you are allowed to do a particular thing. *They introduced an age limit... The age limit was 21.*
agency /eɪdʒənsi/ agencies
1 NC An **agency** is a business which provides services for another business. *...an advertising agency.*
2 NC In the United States, an **agency** is an administrative organization run by a government. *...the Central Intelligence Agency.*
agenda /ədʒendə/ agendas
1 NC An **agenda** is a list of items to be discussed at a meeting. *What is on the agenda today?... A Government spokesman made it clear that no agenda had been set for the next meeting.*
2 NC+SUPP **Agenda** is also used to refer to political issues which are considered to be important at a particular time. *The Green Party's speaker claimed that her party was setting the political agenda on the environment... The issue of the Palestinians is back near the top of the international agenda... Mr Takeshita has put political reform high on his agenda for 1989.* ● See also **hidden agenda**.
agent /eɪdʒənt/ agents
1 NC An **agent** is someone who arranges work or business for other people, especially actors or musicians. *I phoned my agent in London about the job.*
2 NC An **agent** is also someone who works for a country's secret service. *...an enemy agent.*
3 NC+SUPP You can refer to the cause of a particular effect as its **agent**; a formal use. *...the agent of change.*
agent provocateur /æʒɒn⁰ prəvɒkətɜː/ agents provocateurs
NC An **agent provocateur** is someone who is employed by the government or the police to encourage people who are causing trouble to break the law so that they can then be arrested. *They were perhaps aided by agents provocateurs sent into our midst to disrupt the protest.*
age of consent
N SING The **age of consent** is the age at which a person can legally marry or have a sexual relationship with someone. *The Swiss Parliament has brought down the age of consent to fourteen.*
age-old
ADJ ATTRIB An **age-old** story, tradition, or connection has existed for a very long time. *...the difficulties of changing this age-old custom.*
aggrandizement /əgrændɪzmənt/; also spelt **aggrandisement**.
NU If you do something for **aggrandizement**, you do it in order to get power, wealth, and importance for yourself. *He may have sided with the masses for personal gain and aggrandizement.*
aggravate /ægrəveɪt/ aggravates, aggravating, aggravated
1 VO If you **aggravate** a situation, you make it worse. *National poverty was aggravated by rapid population growth.*
2 VO To **aggravate** someone means to make them annoyed; an informal use which some people believe is incorrect. *Thomas had a great deal to aggravate him at present.*
aggregate /ægrɪgət/ aggregates
1 NC An **aggregate** is the total of several figures added together. *He had spent an aggregate of fifteen years*

in various jails.
2 When two football teams play two matches against each other in a cup competition, the goals from the two games are added together, and the team with more goals wins **on aggregate**. *In the Rumbelows League Cup First Round, Southend win 4-3 on aggregate.*

aggression /əgreʃn/
1 NU If a country or group shows **aggression** in its political or military activities, it frequently makes attacks on other countries or groups. *Delegates issued a statement condemning aggression against the Arab nation.*
2 NU If someone behaves with **aggression**, they behave in an angry and forceful way that makes other people feel threatened. *Barbara defended herself with a sudden new aggression.*

aggressive /əgresɪv/
1 ADJ An **aggressive** person behaves in an angry and forceful way that makes other people feel threatened. *She was in a highly aggressive mood.* ◆ **aggressively** ADV *She strode aggressively into the office.*
2 ADJ If you are **aggressive** in your work or other activities, you behave in a forceful way because you are eager to succeed. *...aggressive businessmen... Gatting was the most aggressive of the England batsmen.*

aggressor /əgresə/ **aggressors**
NC The **aggressor** is the person or country that starts a fight. *He has maintained his belief that Japan was not an aggressor during the war.*

aggrieved /əgriːvd/
ADJ If you feel **aggrieved**, you feel upset and angry because of the way you have been treated. *...an opportunity for many aggrieved groups to protest against the Government.*

aggro /ægrəʊ/
NU **Aggro** is aggressive or violent behaviour; an informal word. *There wasn't a hint of aggro.*

aghast /əgɑːst/
ADJ PRED If you are **aghast**, you are filled with horror and surprise. *Reporters are aghast at the enormity of what they've seen.*

agile /ædʒaɪl/
1 ADJ An **agile** person can move very easily and quickly. *He was as agile as a monkey.* ◆ **agility** /ədʒɪləti/ NU *He leaped out of the car with surprising agility.*
2 ADJ If you have an **agile** mind, you can think quickly and intelligently. *Exercising the mind keeps it agile— the old adage 'Use it or lose it' applies.* ◆ **agility** NU *...tests of mental agility.*

aging /eɪdʒɪŋ/. See age, ageing.

agitate /ædʒɪteɪt/ **agitates, agitating, agitated**
1 V If you **agitate** for something, you talk and campaign enthusiastically in order to get it. *...a group agitating against the use of chemical fertilizers.* ◆ **agitation** /ædʒɪteɪʃn/ NU *...anti-imperialist agitation.*
2 VO If something **agitates** you, it worries you and makes you unable to think clearly. *I don't want to agitate him unduly.* ◆ **agitation** NU *I saw Peter glancing at his watch in some agitation.*

agitated /ædʒɪteɪtɪd/
ADJ Someone who is **agitated** is so worried about something that they are unable to think clearly or act calmly. *He looked dishevelled and agitated... She heard his agitated voice calling after them... I sent agitated messages to Miss Gray.* ◆ **agitatedly** ADV *Alexander wondered agitatedly what he should do.*

agitator /ædʒɪteɪtə/ **agitators**
NC An **agitator** is someone who campaigns to bring about political or social change, often in a way that causes trouble. *Police suspect political agitators of setting fire to a British-owned lorry.*

aglow /əgləʊ/; a literary word.
1 ADJ PRED If something is **aglow**, it is shining and bright with a soft, warm light. *...long green grass, all aglow in the evening sunlight.*
2 ADJ PRED If someone is **aglow** or if their face or expression is **aglow**, they look excited. *...Daniel, still aglow with a sense of his victory.*

AGM /eɪdʒiːem/ **AGMs**
NC An **AGM** is a meeting that a company or organization holds once a year in order to discuss the previous year's activities and accounts. **AGM** is an abbreviation for 'Annual General Meeting'. *...elected at an AGM attended by no more than 500 members. ...AGM resolutions.*

agnostic /ægnɒstɪk/ **agnostics**
NC An **agnostic** believes that it is not possible to know whether God exists or not. *...a self-proclaimed agnostic.* ▶ Also ADJ *I'm really rather agnostic at the moment.*

ago /əgəʊ/
ADV You use **ago** to refer to past time. For example, if something happened one year **ago**, it is one year since it happened. *Five years ago, I went to the tropics... How long ago was that?*

agog /əgɒg/
ADJ PRED or ADV If you are **agog**, you are excited by something and eager to know more about it. *The city was agog last night with rumours that the two had been executed... While the rest of the world stared agog at the men on the moon, Moscow television broadcast a musical variety programme.*

agonize /ægənaɪz/ **agonizes, agonizing, agonized**; also spelt **agonise**.
V or V+over If you **agonize** over something, you feel anxious and spend a long time thinking about it. *This company agonised as to whether they should move into electronic calculations... The leadership is agonizing over what attitude to adopt.*

agonized /ægənaɪzd/; also spelt **agonised**.
ADJ **Agonized** describes something that you say or do when you are in great physical or mental pain. *He could hear the prisoner's agonized moans... She spoke with agonized emphasis.*

agonizing /ægənaɪzɪŋ/; also spelt **agonising**.
1 ADJ Something that is **agonizing** causes you to feel great physical or mental pain. *...agonizing feelings of shame and guilt.* ◆ **agonizingly** SUBMOD *The sound was agonizingly painful.*
2 ADJ **Agonizing** decisions and choices are very difficult to make. *He asked the Senate whether it was ready to give the President a blank cheque to make war. For some, it was an agonizing choice, for others, it was a clear, moral decision.*

agony /ægəni/ **agonies**
NU or N PL **Agony** is great physical or mental pain. *The blow made him scream in agony... His family have now suffered the agonies of uncertainty for a year.*

agony aunt, agony aunts
NC An **agony aunt** is someone who writes a column in a newspaper or magazine in which they reply to readers who have written to them for advice on their personal problems. *Agony aunt Claire Rayner explains how expectations of married life have changed.*

agony column, agony columns
NC An **agony column** in a newspaper or magazine is the part where letters from readers about their personal problems are printed and where advice about these problems is given.

agoraphobia /ægərəfəʊbiə/
NU **Agoraphobia** is the fear of open spaces or of going outside your home; a technical term in psychology. *...children who had bouts of panic, anxiety or agoraphobia.*

agoraphobic /ægərəfəʊbɪk/ **agoraphobics**
NC An **agoraphobic** is someone who suffers from agoraphobia.

agree /əgriː/ **agrees, agreeing, agreed**
1 V-RECIP or V-REPORT If you **agree** with someone, you have the same opinion as they do about something. *Do you agree with him about this?... But, as all economists agree, he really has no alternative to the present economic programme... People agree that the law is behind the times.*
2 V+to or V+to-INF If you **agree** to do something, you say that you will do it. *She agreed to let us use her flat while she was away... He has agreed to the use of force.*
3 V+with If you **agree with** an action or a suggestion,

you approve of it. *I agree with what they are doing.*
4 V-RECIP If two stories, accounts, or totals **agree**, they
are the same as each other. *This bill doesn't agree
with my calculations.*
agreeable /əgriːəbl/
1 ADJ If something is **agreeable**, it is pleasant. *...an
agreeable sensation... The meeting had been agreeable
and each leader had expressed himself in a calm and
forceful manner... If the weather is agreeable, sources
say the shuttle will take off sometime around 6:45.*
2 ADJ If someone is **agreeable**, they are pleasant and
friendly. *She always made a point of being agreeable
to them... He said that the Greek Cypriot leader Mr
George Vassiliou was a moderate and agreeable man,
who could help bring about a lasting solution.*
3 ADJ PRED If you are **agreeable** to something or if it
is **agreeable** to you, you are willing to do it or to allow
it. *He was agreeable to the idea of a visit by Mr
Khieu Samphan... He has become an outspoken
Member of Parliament but has so far stuck his neck
out largely on issues agreeable to the military.*
agreed /əgriːd/
ADJ PRED If people are **agreed** about something, they
have reached a decision about it. *Are we agreed,
gentlemen?*
agreement /əgriːmənt/ **agreements**
1 NC An **agreement** is a formal decision or document
that two or more people have reached together about
something of importance. *Half of the land was given
away under the same agreement... Although these
talks have yielded no formal agreements, Lee Jong
Koo says they're an important first step... An
agreement in agriculture is considered crucial to the
talks if a full scale trade war is to be avoided.*
2 NU **Agreement** is the act of reaching a decision, or
of indicating that you will accept something. *There
was no general agreement on the timing.* ● If you are
in agreement with someone, you have the same
opinion as they have. *In expressing such views, he
finds himself in agreement with Muslim groups.*
agricultural /ægrɪkʌltʃərəl/
1 ADJ **Agricultural** means involving or relating to
agriculture. *...the agricultural problems of Third
World countries. ...modern agricultural methods.*
2 ADJ An **agricultural** place or society is one in which
agriculture is important or highly developed. *...a
villager in an agricultural society.*
agriculture /ægrɪkʌltʃə/
NU **Agriculture** is farming and the methods used to
look after crops and animals. *...the mechanisation of
agriculture.*
aground /əgraʊnd/
ADV If a ship runs **aground**, it touches the ground in a
shallow part of a river, lake, or the sea. *Their ship
ran aground and capsized off the north-east coast of
Japan.*
ah /ɑː/
When you want to express agreement, surprise,
pleasure, or sympathy, you can say 'ah'. *Ah, you poor
fellow... Ah, Howard. Come in.*
aha /ɑːhɑː/
When you want to indicate that you understand, know,
or have found something, you can say 'aha', especially
when you are pleased about it. *I had a report here
somewhere. Aha, here we are.*
ahead /əhed/
1 ADV If something is **ahead**, it is in front of you. *The
road ahead is foggy... She stared ahead... Up ahead I
see the lights of a town.*
2 ADV If you are **ahead** of someone in your work or
achievements, you have made more progress than
they have. *He is a good ten years ahead of the field.*
3 ADJ PRED If a person or a team is **ahead** in a
competition, they are winning. *The Irish team are
ahead in two of the second round matches... Both
India and Pakistan have come through the tournament
on maximum points, but Pakistan is ahead on goal
difference.*
4 ADV If something happens **ahead** of another thing, it
happens some time before the other thing. *Most of the
French African leaders arrived here a day ahead of
President Mitterrand... His comments come three days*

*ahead of the resumption of negotiations... The
tunnelling project has now been completed three
months ahead of schedule.* ● If someone goes **on ahead**
or is sent **on ahead**, they leave for a place before other
people. *Our parents had gone on ahead in father's
car.*
5 ADV **Ahead** also means in the future. *I haven't had
time to think far ahead.*
6 See also **go-ahead**.
Ahmeti, Vilson /vɪlsɒn æxmeti/
Vilson Ahmeti became Prime Minister of Albania in
1991 after holding the posts of Minister of Industry and
Minister of the Food Industry. Born: 1951.
Aho, Esko /ɛskəʊ ɡhəʊ/
Esko Aho became Prime Minister of Finland and
Chairman of the Centre Party (KESK or KP) in 1991.
Born: 1954.
ahoy /əhɔɪ/
Ahoy is a shout that people in boats use in order to
attract attention. *Ahoy there... Land ahoy!*
AI /eɪ aɪ/
AI is an abbreviation for 'artificial intelligence'.
aid /eɪd/ **aids, aiding, aided**
1 NU+SUPP **Aid** is money, equipment, or services that
are provided for people in need. *The aid can include
temporary housing grants, low-cost loans and funds to
rebuild bridges... The organization expects its food aid
programme to become the largest relief effort it's
undertaken since World War II.*
2 NC An **aid** is something that makes things easier to
do. *...a valuable aid to digestion.*
3 VO If you **aid** a person or an organization, you help
them. *He crossed the border aided by a priest... Mr.
Bush is under some criticism for refusing to aid the
Kurds in their fight against Saddam Hussein.*
4 See also **first aid, legal aid**.
● **Aid** is used in these phrases. ● If an activity or
event is **in aid of** a particular cause, it raises money
for that cause. *...a cricket match in aid of cancer
relief.* ● If you do something **with the aid of** a
particular person or thing, they help you to do it. *The
programmes had been prepared with the aid of
various broadcasters.* ● If you go **to the aid of**
someone, you try to help them. *They had rushed to
her aid.*
aide /eɪd/ **aides**
NC An **aide** is an assistant to a person who has an
important job, especially in government or in the
armed forces. *...a senior aide to the Prime Minister.*
aide-de-camp /eɪddəkɒmᵖ/ **aides-de-camp**
NC An **aide-de-camp** is an officer in the armed forces
who helps an officer of higher rank.
AIDS /eɪdz/
NU **AIDS** is an illness which destroys the natural
system of protection that the body has against disease.
AIDS is an abbreviation for 'acquired immune
deficiency syndrome'. *Why is it proving so difficult to
develop a vaccine against AIDS?*
ail /eɪl/ **ails, ailing, ailed**
1 V-ERG If someone **ails**, or if something **ails** them,
they are ill; an old-fashioned use. *He's ailed ever
since he went up to the council house... I cannot decide
what ails her: it's not a heat rash.*
2 VO If something **ails** a group or area of activity, it is
a problem or source of trouble for that group or
activity. *It's all too easy to itemize what ails soccer
off the field: hooliganism and violence.*
aileron /eɪlərɒn/ **ailerons**
NC An **aileron** is a flap on the back edge of the wing of
an aeroplane that can be raised or lowered in order to
control the plane's movement.
ailing /eɪlɪŋ/
1 ADJ If someone is **ailing**, they are ill and not getting
better. *Doctors attending the ailing Emperor say that
his condition is worsening.*
2 ADJ If an organization is **ailing**, it is in difficulty and
is becoming weaker. *...the ailing American defence
industry.*
ailment /eɪlmənt/ **ailments**
NC An **ailment** is an illness, especially one that is not
very serious. *Children who smoke are more likely to
be absent from school because of minor ailments.*

aim /eɪm/ **aims, aiming, aimed**

1 V OorV If you **aim** a weapon or object at someone or something, you judge the place where you want it to hit them, and point it in that direction. *Roger picked up a stone, aimed it, and threw it at Henry... He aimed at the far wall and squeezed the trigger.* ▸ Also NU+SUPP *He leaned against a tree to steady his aim.*

2 V+at, V+for, or V+to-INF If you **aim** at something or **aim** to do it, you plan or hope to achieve it. *We are aiming at a higher production level... A good solid job is the thing to aim for... The authorities have in the past accused Chinese dissidents abroad of aiming to overthrow the government.*

3 V-PASS+at If an action or plan **is aimed** at achieving something, it is intended to achieve it. *The measures were aimed at cutting government expenditure. ...policies aimed at securing mass support.*

4 VO+at If your action **is aimed** at a particular person, you intend it to affect and influence them. *The particular point was that they aimed the brochure not at the farmer but at the extension worker... This anti-smoking campaign is mainly aimed at young teenagers.*

5 NC+SUPP An **aim** is the thing that an action or plan is intended to achieve. *It is our aim to set up a workshop... This strategy has two main aims.*

6 If you **take aim** at someone or something, you point a weapon or object at them, ready to shoot or throw. *I took careful aim at his head and fired.*

aimless /eɪmləs/

ADJ A person or activity that is **aimless** has no clear purpose or plan. *About twenty soldiers, dishevelled and aimless but quite friendly, guarded the bridge. ...drawing aimless doodles in the sand.* ♦ **aimlessly** ADV *She wandered aimlessly along the beach.*

ain't /eɪnt/

Ain't is used in some dialects of English instead of 'am not', 'aren't', or 'isn't'. *'Don't worry about the bridge. We ain't even come to the bridge yet.'*

air /eə/ **airs, airing, aired**

1 NU **Air** is the mixture of gases which forms the earth's atmosphere and which we breathe. *She took a gulp of air... Warm air can hold more moisture than cold air.*

2 N SING The **air** is the space around things that is above the ground. *The police fired warning shots in the air... The smell of cooking filled the air.*

3 NU **Air** is also used to refer to travel in aircraft. *The fare by air from London to Luxembourg is £145 return... The worst part of air travel is the time you spend in airports.*

4 N SING+SUPP If someone or something has a particular **air**, they give this general impression. *He has a faintly old-fashioned air.*

5 VO If you **air** your opinions, you make them known to people. *He spoke on the radio, airing his views to the nation.*

6 V-ERG If a broadcasting company **airs** a television or radio programme or when the programme is **aired**, it is shown on television or played on the radio; used in American English. *CNN agreed to stop airing the tapes until the Supreme Court ruled on the issue... 'The Jesse Jackson Show' is a weekly syndicated talk show that's been airing in cities around the country since September.*

7 VO To **air** a room means to let fresh air into it. *The big windows had been opened to air the room.*

8 V-ERG When you **air** clothing or when it **airs**, you put it somewhere warm so that it becomes completely dry. *She hung her clothes up to air before she put them away.*

9 See also **airing**.

● **Air** is used in these phrases. ● To disappear **into thin air** means to disappear completely. *The truth is these people didn't disappear, didn't vanish into thin air. They have been kidnapped.* ● To appear **out of thin air** means to appear suddenly and mysteriously. *I can't simply conjure up the money out of thin air.* ● If someone is **on the air**, they are broadcasting on radio or television. *While we've been on the air, President Saddam Hussein has issued his latest statement on the Gulf crisis.*

air base, air bases

NC An **air base** is a centre where military aircraft take off or land and are serviced, and where many of the centre's staff live. *Asmara is an important military air base.*

airbed /eəbed/ **airbeds**

NC An **airbed** is a plastic or rubber mattress which can be folded or stored flat and which you fill with air before you use it.

airborne /eəbɔːn/

1 ADJ **Airborne** means flying in the air or coming from the air. *They mounted airborne assaults on suitable targets, especially airfields... Such air conditioning systems allow high levels of airborne pollutants to build up in the air.*

2 ADJ PRED If an aircraft is **airborne**, it is in the air and flying. *The planes are due to be airborne any time now but we have not had confirmation yet from Falmouth coastguards.*

3 ADJ ATTRIB **Airborne** troops are trained to fight on the ground after using parachutes to get into enemy territory. *...a task force consisting of two battalions of the Eighty-Second Airborne Division.*

air brake, air brakes

NC An **air brake** is a brake which is used on heavy vehicles such as buses and trains and which is operated by means of compressed air. *It's got all-round suspension and air disc brakes on each wheel.*

airbrick /eəbrɪk/ **airbricks**

NC An **airbrick** is a brick with holes in it which is put into the wall of a building so that air can get in.

Airbus /eəbʌs/ **Airbuses**

NC An **Airbus** is an aeroplane which is designed to carry a large number of passengers for fairly short distances; Airbus is a trademark. *The jet narrowly missed a mid-air collision with an Airbus over Washington.*

air-conditioned

ADJ If a room is **air-conditioned**, the air in it is kept cool and dry by an air-conditioner. *...air-conditioned first-class compartments.*

air-conditioner, air-conditioners

NC An **air-conditioner** is a machine which keeps the air cool and dry in a building.

air-conditioning

NU **Air-conditioning** is a method of providing buildings and vehicles with cool dry air. *Conditions on the plane would be appalling if the air-conditioning wasn't working.*

aircraft /eəkrɑːft/; **aircraft** is both the singular and the plural form.

NC An **aircraft** is a vehicle which can fly, for example an aeroplane or a helicopter. *The West German government has eased its ban on low flying by military aircraft.*

aircraft carrier, aircraft carriers

NC An **aircraft carrier** is a warship with a long, flat deck where aircraft can take off and land. *The incident involved two fighter planes from an American aircraft carrier.*

aircrew /eəkruː/ **aircrews**

N COLL The **aircrew** on a plane are the pilot and other people who are responsible for flying it and for looking after the passengers. *New restrictions will severely affect aircrew training.*

airfield /eəfiːld/ **airfields**

NC An **airfield** is a small area of ground where aircraft take off and land. *The aircraft had started to descend towards the airfield.*

air force, air forces

NC An **air force** is the part of a country's military organization that is concerned with fighting in the air. *The bomb was dropped by the German Air Force during raids on the capital in 1941... The Air Force had sent helicopters to rescue people stranded by the floods.*

airgun /eəgʌn/ **airguns**

NC An **airgun** is a gun which is fired by means of air pressure.

air hostess, air hostesses

NC An **air hostess** is a woman whose job is to look after the passengers in an aircraft. *An air hostess* *announced that the plane had been hijacked.*

airing /ˈeərɪŋ/
1 N SING If you give your ideas or opinions an **airing**, you make them known to other people. *He gave a wide airing to his strong views on the permissive society... There is no reason why these proposals shouldn't receive a widespread public airing.*
2 N SING If you give a room an **airing**, you let fresh air into it. *Give the room an airing by opening the window for a couple of minutes.*
3 N SING If you give clothing an **airing**, you put it somewhere warm so that it becomes completely dry.
4 See also **air**.

airing cupboard, airing cupboards
NC An **airing cupboard** is a warm cupboard where you put clothes and other things that have been washed and partly dried, to make sure they are completely dry.

airless /ˈeələs/
ADJ If a room is **airless**, there is no fresh air in it. *...a small airless theatre crammed with children.*

airletter /ˈeəletə/ **airletters**
NC An **airletter** is a letter which is sent by air, especially one written on a very thin sheet of paper that is then folded and does not need an envelope. *Many thanks for your airletter. We were glad to hear your news.*

airlift /ˈeəlɪft/ **airlifts, airlifting, airlifted**
1 NC An **airlift** is an operation to move people, troops, or goods by air, especially in a war or when land routes are closed. *...the Berlin airlift back in the late nineteen forties.*
2 VO To **airlift** people, troops, or goods means to carry them by air, especially in a war or when land routes are closed. *Two of the boys were airlifted to hospital after the accident in the Brecon Beacons... Emergency food supplies were being airlifted to Juba.*

airline /ˈeəlaɪn/ **airlines**
NC An **airline** is a company which provides regular services carrying people or goods in aeroplanes. *The American airline, Pan-Am, has decided to end its flights to and from Heathrow airport.*

airliner /ˈeəlaɪnə/ **airliners**
NC An **airliner** is a large aeroplane used for carrying passengers. *The airliner flew to Algiers from Cyprus after twelve hostages had been released.*

airlock /ˈeəlɒk/ **airlocks**
1 NC An **airlock** is a compartment between places which do not have the same air pressure, for example in a spacecraft or submarine. *We do not know yet whether the closure has sealed the airlock properly.*
2 NC An **airlock** is also a blockage in a pipe which is caused by a bubble of air that prevents liquid from flowing through.

airmail /ˈeəmeɪl/
NU **Airmail** is the system of sending letters, parcels, and goods by air. *She gave him a letter to post by airmail.*

airman /ˈeəmən/ **airmen** /ˈeəmən/
1 NC An **airman** is a man who serves in his country's air force. *The plane burst into flames, killing two of the airmen on board.*
2 NC or TITLE In the United States, an **airman** is a person in one of the four lowest ranks in the air force. *The US Air Force lost two airmen today in the Persian Gulf region when their jet went down... Senior Airman G.H. Fullerton.*

air miss, air misses
NC When two planes nearly crash into each other in the air, some people refer to the incident as an **air miss**. *An investigation has started into an air miss over the Midlands yesterday.*

airplane /ˈeəpleɪn/ **airplanes**
NC An **airplane** is the same as an **aeroplane**; used in American English. *The airplane landed safely in New Orleans.*

air pocket, air pockets
NC An **air pocket** is a downward flowing current of air which causes an aircraft suddenly to lose height when it flies into it.

airport /ˈeəpɔːt/ **airports**
NC An **airport** is a place with buildings, facilities, and

runways, where aircraft take off and land. The plane left Gatwick airport a short time ago.

air raid, air raids
NC An **air raid** is an attack by military aircraft in which bombs are dropped. *His plane was shot down during an air raid in Angola.*

air rifle, air rifles
NC An **air rifle** is a rifle which is fired by means of air pressure.

air-sea rescue
NU **Air-sea rescue** is the use of helicopters, other aircraft, and boats to rescue people who are in danger of drowning in the sea. *An air-sea rescue operation is underway in the North Sea.*

airship /ˈeəʃɪp/ **airships**
NC An **airship** is an aircraft that is supported in the air by a large balloon filled with gas. Passengers sit in a compartment underneath the balloon. *...the construction of an airship at a French research base.*

airshow /ˈeəʃəʊ/ **airshows**
NC An **airshow** is an event that is held for entertainment or for publicity, at which people can look at planes on the ground and watch them flying in the air. *Dick Oliver reports on the highlights of this year's airshow.*

airsick /ˈeəsɪk/
ADJ If you are **airsick**, the effects of flying in an aeroplane make you sick.

airspace /ˈeəspeɪs/
NU A country's **airspace** is the part of the sky that is over that country and is considered to belong to the country. *The plane crashed just after entering British airspace.*

airspeed /ˈeəspiːd/ **airspeeds**
NU or NC An aircraft's **airspeed** is the speed at which it travels through the air. *The two flight recorders will reveal the airspeed to the crash investigators.*

airstrike /ˈeəstraɪk/ **airstrikes**
NC An **airstrike** is the same as an **air raid**; used in American English. *Airstrikes on civilians became a matter of routine.*

airstrip /ˈeəstrɪp/ **airstrips**
NC An **airstrip** is a stretch of land which has been cleared so that aircraft can take off and land. *The plane landed on a grass airstrip.*

air terminal, air terminals
NC An **air terminal** is a building at an airport where you check in and wait for your flight, or arrive after your flight. *Gatwick is now the world's second busiest air terminal.*

airtight /ˈeətaɪt/
ADJ If a container is **airtight**, its lid fits so tightly that no air can get in or out. *Scientists observed the contents of a 4,600 year old Egyptian tomb without breaking its airtight seal.*

air time
NU **Air time** is a period of time on radio or television during which a particular item is broadcast. *The BBC has said that it will consider applications from charities for air time.*

air-to-air
ADJ ATTRIB **Air-to-air** combat is a battle between military aeroplanes where rockets or bullets are fired at one aeroplane from another. *He said eight Iraqi planes have been shot down in air-to-air combat... The planes were armed with air-to-air missiles.*

air-traffic control
NU **Air-traffic control** is the group of people who organize routes for aircraft and who give instructions to pilots by radio about their routes. *Air-traffic controllers need to know not only the grid reference of aeroplanes, but also the altitude.*

airwaves /ˈeəweɪvz/
N PL **Airwaves** are the radio waves used in radio and television broadcasting. *...debates were broadcast over the airwaves.*

airway /ˈeəweɪ/ **airways**
1 NC An **airway** is a route through the air which aircraft regularly use. *...the giant jets that increasingly dominate the world's airways.*
2 N PL **Airways** is used in the name of some airlines. *...British Airways.*

airworthy /ɛəwɜ:ði/
ADJ If an aircraft is **airworthy**, it is safe to fly. *They certified the plane as completely airworthy.*
◆ **airworthiness** NU *All the helicopters received certificates of airworthiness.*

airy /ɛəri/
1 ADJ An **airy** building is large and has plenty of fresh air inside. *The church was light and airy inside.*
2 ADJ You can use **airy** to describe someone who is light-hearted and casual about things which should be taken seriously. *He applied in an airy way for the job of assistant manager.* ◆ **airily** ADV *...talking airily of this and that.*

airy-fairy /ɛərifɛəri/
ADJ **Airy-fairy** means vague and fanciful, with no basis in fact or common sense. *...airy-fairy nonsense.*

aisle /aɪl/ **aisles**
1 NC An **aisle** is a long narrow gap that separates blocks of seats in a public building, or rows of shelves in a supermarket. *Late-comers were standing in the aisles because every seat was taken.*
2 You can use **the aisle** in expressions like 'walking down the aisle' or 'leading someone down the aisle' to refer to the activity of getting married. *She walked down the aisle to marry the father of her child.*

ajar /ədʒɑ:/
ADJ PRED If a door is **ajar**, it is slightly open. *She left the door ajar.*

Akayev, Askar /æsgɑ: əkɑɪəf/
Askar Akayev became the President of Kyrgyzstan in 1990. He is a member of the Kyrgyz Communist Party and was formerly President of the Academy of Sciences.

Akihito, Tsegu no Miya /ɑki:hi:təʊ/
Tsegu no Miya Akihito became Emperor of Japan in 1989, succeeding his father, the Emperor Hirohito. He became Crown Prince in 1952. Born: 1933.

akimbo /əkɪmbəʊ/
If you stand **arms akimbo** or **with arms akimbo** you stand with your hands on your hips and your elbows pointing outwards; an old-fashioned expression. *She stood, arms akimbo, looking round... Then she posed with arms akimbo.*

akin /əkɪn/
ADJ PRED+to If one thing is **akin** to another, it is similar to it in some way; a formal word. *She had answered with something akin to anger.*

-al /-l, əl/
SUFFIX **-al** is added to nouns to form adjectives that indicate what something relates to or what kind of thing something is. For example, 'agricultural' means related to agriculture and 'departmental' means related to the work of a department.

alabaster /æləbɑ:stə/
NU **Alabaster** is a white stone that is used for making statues, vases, and other ornaments.

à la carte /æ lɑ: kɑ:t/
ADV If you eat **à la carte** in a restaurant, you choose individual dishes on the menu rather than paying a fixed price for a complete meal. *It's normally more expensive to eat à la carte.* ▶ Also ADJ ATTRIB *...the à la carte menu.*

alacrity /əlækrəti/
NU If you do something with **alacrity**, you do it quickly and eagerly; a formal word. *The sort of book that travellers pounce on with alacrity.*

à la mode /æ lɑ: məʊd/
ADJ PRED If something, especially a style of clothing, is **à la mode**, it is the latest fashion; a literary expression. *It became not only à la mode but required wear.* ▶ Also ADV *She knew just how far to go in dressing à la mode.*

Åland Islands /ɔ:lənd aɪləndz/
The **Åland Islands** are a territory of Finland. The archipelago is comprised of 6,500 islands in the Gulf of Bothnia between Finland and Sweden. Fishing, tourism, shipping, and banking are important industries. ◆ **Åland Islander** /ɔ:lənd aɪləndə/ N
■ *religion:* Christianity (mainly Evangelical Lutheran) ■ *language:* Swedish ■ *currency:* markka ■ *capital:* Mariehamn ■ *population:* 24,000 (1989) ■ *size:* 1,552 square kilometres.

alarm /əlɑ:m/ **alarms, alarming, alarmed**
1 NU **Alarm** is a sudden feeling of fear or anxiety. *She looked round in alarm.*
2 NC An **alarm** is an automatic device that warns you of danger. *The alarm went off. ...a burglar alarm.*
● If you **sound** or **raise the alarm**, you warn people of danger. *A sentry raised the alarm when he spotted the fire.*
3 VO If something **alarms** you, it makes you suddenly afraid or anxious. *It alarms new parents when their baby first vomits a large amount of milk.*

alarm clock, alarm clocks
NC An **alarm clock** is a clock that you can set so that it wakes you up at a particular time. *She arrived late because her alarm clock failed to go off.*

alarmed /əlɑ:md/
ADJ If someone is **alarmed**, they feel fear or anxiety that something unpleasant or dangerous might happen. *Please don't be alarmed... She appeared alarmed and upset by the chaos around her.*

alarming /əlɑ:mɪŋ/
ADJ Something that is **alarming** makes you worried or concerned. *The world's forests are shrinking at an alarming rate.* ◆ **alarmingly** ADV *Her sight had begun to deteriorate alarmingly.*

alarmist /əlɑ:mɪst/
ADJ **Alarmist** means causing unnecessary alarm. *Soviet sources have made no direct comment on the alarmist press stories.*

alas /əlæs/
ADV SEN You use **alas** to say that you think that the facts you are talking about are sad, unfortunate, or regrettable; a formal word. *There was, alas, no shortage of assassinations.*

Albania /ælbeɪniə/
The **Republic of Albania** is a country in south-eastern Europe. It was occupied by Germany from 1943 to 1944. Enver Hoxha established a Communist state in 1946 and ruled until 1985. The Albanian Party of Labour (PLA) was the sole party from 1946 until 1991. Free elections were held in 1991 and the PLA, renamed the Socialist Party, remained in power. Ramiz Alia became President in 1982 but was forced by industrial unrest to share his powers with other parties. After a series of government crises Vilson Ahmeti was named Prime Minister in 1991. In 1992, Ramiz Alia resigned and Sali Berisha, of the Democratic Party, became President. Albania exports oil, coal, and agricultural products. ◆ **Albanian** /ælbeɪniən/ N, ADJ
■ *per capita GNP:* approximately US$930 ■ *religion:* Islam, Christianity ■ *language:* Albanian ■ *currency:* lek ■ *capital:* Tirana ■ *population:* 3 million (1988) ■ *size:* 28,748 square kilometres.

albatross /ælbətrɒs/ **albatrosses**
1 NC An **albatross** is a very large white sea bird.
2 N SING If you refer to something as an **albatross**, you are saying that it is a burden and causes you great problems, or prevents you from doing what you want to do. *The Observer described Mrs. Thatcher as 'an electoral albatross around the party's neck'.*

albeit /ɔ:lbi:ɪt/
CONJ You can use **albeit** to introduce a fact or comment which contrasts in some way with what you have just said; a formal word. *It continues to publish, albeit irregularly, two journals.*

albino /ælbi:nəʊ/ **albinos**
NC An **albino** is a person or animal with very white skin, white hair, and pink eyes.

album /ælbəm/ **albums**
1 NC An **album** is a record with about 25 minutes of music or speech on each side. *This track comes from their new album, 'Idlewild'.*
2 NC+SUPP An **album** is also a book in which you put photographs, stamps, or other things that you have collected. *He was looking through the family photograph album.*

albumen /ælbjumɪn/ **albumens**
1 NU or NC **Albumen** is the white or transparent part of the inside of an egg; a technical term in biology. *...a mixture of albumen from newly laid eggs.*
2 See also **albumin**.

albumin /ˈælbjʊmɪn/; also spelt **albumen**.
NU **Albumin** is a protein that is found in blood plasma, egg white, and some other substances. *In the experiment, rats were injected with egg albumin.*

alchemist /ˈælkəmɪst/ **alchemists**
NC An **alchemist** was a scientist in the Middle Ages who tried to discover how to change ordinary metals into gold.

alchemy /ˈælkəmi/
1 NU **Alchemy** is the form of chemistry studied in the Middle Ages, which was especially concerned with trying to discover ways to change ordinary metals into gold. *...people who studied the mysteries of Nature through equally mysterious experiments, including alchemy.*
2 NU **Alchemy** is also the power to do something so well that it seems mysterious and magical; a literary use. *...the alchemy of his performance.*

alcohol /ˈælkəhɒl/
1 NU **Alcohol** is drink such as beer, wine, and whisky that can make people drunk. *People who drink a moderate amount of alcohol tend to live healthy lives.*
2 NU **Alcohol** is also a colourless liquid which is found in drinks such as beer, wine, and whisky and which can be used as a solvent. *...an enormous quantity of waste which can be converted into industrial alcohol.*

alcoholic /ˌælkəˈhɒlɪk/ **alcoholics**
1 NC An **alcoholic** is someone who is addicted to alcohol. *Jim is an alcoholic whose health has been shattered by his drinking.*
2 ADJ An **alcoholic** drink contains alcohol. *...a ban on the sale of alcoholic drinks.*

alcoholism /ˈælkəhɒlɪzəm/
NU **Alcoholism** is the condition of being addicted to alcohol. *A senior police officer has called for improved measures to combat alcoholism.*

alcove /ˈælkəʊv/ **alcoves**
NC An **alcove** is a small area of a room which is formed when one part of a wall is built farther back than the rest of it. *His desk was in an alcove to one side of the chimney.*

alder /ˈɔːldə/ **alders**. The plural form can be either **alders** or **alder**.
NC An **alder** is a tree that grows in northern temperate areas, often in damp places. It has cones and leaves with small points along the edges.

alderman /ˈɔːldəmən/ **aldermen** /ˈɔːldəmən/
1 NCorTITLE Until 1974 in England and Wales, an **alderman** was a senior member of a local council who was elected by other councillors. *He was a councillor and an alderman in Grantham.*
2 NCorTITLE In the United States and Canada, an **alderman** is a member of the governing body of a city. *Alderman Guy Zimas asked the city council to amend the minutes of the last meeting.*

ale /eɪl/
N MASS **Ale** is a kind of beer. ● See also **ginger ale**.

alert /əˈlɜːt/ **alerts, alerting, alerted**
1 ADJ If you are **alert**, you are paying full attention to what is happening. *We have to be alert all the time and look for our opportunity.* ◆ **alertness** NU *The job requires constant alertness and vigilance.*
2 ADJ PRED+to If you are **alert** to something, you are fully aware of it. *They were both alert to the dangers.*
3 NC An **alert** is a situation in which people prepare themselves for danger. *The city centre was on a nuclear alert.* ● If you are **on the alert**, you are ready to deal with anything that might happen. *The country's police and defence forces were on the alert.*
4 VO If you **alert** someone, you warn them of danger or trouble. *He pressed the horn of the vehicle to alert the squadron.*

Alesana, Tofilau Eti /tɒfiːlaʊ eti æliːsɑːnə/
Tofilau Eti Alesana was the Prime Minister of Western Samoa from 1982 until 1985. He became Prime Minister again in 1988. He is a member of the Human Rights Protection Party.

A level /eɪ levl/ **A levels**
NC An **A level** is a British educational qualification which people take when they are seventeen or eighteen years old. *Pupils can now do an A level in sports studies.*

alfalfa /ælˈfælfə/
NU **Alfalfa** is a plant that is used for feeding farm animals. The shoots that develop from its seeds are sometimes eaten as a vegetable.

alfresco /ælˈfreskəʊ/
ADJ ATTRIB An **alfresco** meal is one that is eaten in the open air. *...an alfresco lunch of prawns and brown bread.* ► Also ADV *They often dined alfresco in the warm summer evenings.*

algae /ˈældʒiː/ **ælgaɪ/**
NUorN PL **Algae** is a type of plant with no stems or leaves. Seaweed is a type of algae; other types grow on damp surfaces, and are green and slimy. *Algae can be a source of important dietary supplements... The algae were thought to have been caused by nitrogen and phosphorus nutrients in sewage.*

algebra /ˈældʒɪbrə/
NU **Algebra** is a branch of mathematics in which letters are used to represent possible quantities.

Algeria /ælˈdʒɪəriə/
The **Democratic and Popular Republic of Algeria** is a country in northern Africa. It was a colony of France from 1848 until 1962, when it became independent after eight years of war. From 1963 until 1989, the National Liberation Front (FLN) was the only legal party. Colonel Chadli Bendjedid became President in 1979, and resigned in 1992 when a Council of State led by Mohamed Boudiaf took power. Sid Ahmed Ghozali was appointed Prime Minister in 1991. Algeria exports oil. It is a member of OPEC, the Arab League, and the Organization of African Unity. ◆ **Algerian** /ælˈdʒɪəriən/ N, ADJ
▪ *per capita GNP:* US$2,450 ▪ *religion:* Islam
▪ *language:* Arabic (official), French, Berber
▪ *currency:* dinar ▪ *capital:* Algiers ▪ *population:* 25 million (1990) ▪ *size:* 2,381,741 square kilometres.

Algiers /ælˈdʒɪəz/
Algiers is the capital of Algeria and its largest city. Population: 1,722,000 (1983).

algorithm /ˈælgərɪðəm/ **algorithms**
NC An **algorithm** is a special series of instructions that are carried out in a particular order, for example as part of a computer program. *We take the input signal and apply a series of algorithms to it.*

Ali, Zine al-Abidine ben /zeɪn əl æbɪdiːn ben æli/
General Zine al-Abidine ben Ali became President of Tunisia in 1987. He is a member of the Democratic Constitutional Assembly (RCD). He served as Secretary of State for National Security from 1984 to 1985, and as Minister of the Interior from 1986 to 1987. Born: 1936.

Alia, Ramiz /ræmiːz ɑːliːə/
Ramiz Alia was the President of the Presidium of the People's Assembly of Albania from 1982 to 1991, and was President of Albania from 1991 to 1992. He was First Secretary of the Central Committee of the Albanian Party of Labour (now known as the Socialist Party) from 1985 to 1991.

alias /ˈeɪliəs/ **aliases**
1 NC An **alias** is a false name, especially one used by a criminal. *A policeman and a customs officer infiltrated the gang using the aliases Dick and Eddie.*
2 PREP You use **alias** when you mention someone's false name. *...Dr Christopher Pallis, alias Martin Grainger.*

alibi /ˈæləbaɪ/ **alibis**
NC If you have an **alibi**, you can prove that you were somewhere else when a crime was committed. *They alleged that she gave false alibis to the police about her husband's movements.*

alien /ˈeɪliən/ **aliens**
1 ADJ If you describe something as **alien**, you mean that it seems strange and perhaps frightening, because you are not familiar with it. *...a totally alien and threatening environment... Their ideology is quite alien.*
2 ADJ If something is **alien** to your normal feelings or behaviour, it is not the way you would normally feel or behave. *Malice towards an enemy was completely alien to the man's nature.*
3 NC An **alien** is someone who is not a legal citizen of the country in which they live; a formal use. *The*

authorities have begun deporting alleged illegal aliens.
4 NC An **alien** is also a creature from outer space. *I suppose reactions to the sudden appearance of an alien would vary.*

alienate /ˈeɪliəneɪt/ **alienates, alienating, alienated**
1 VO If you **alienate** someone, you make them become unfriendly or unsympathetic towards you. *I managed to alienate Dennis, who earlier on had been so friendly.* ◆ **alienation** /ˌeɪliəˈneɪʃn/ NU *The government regretted the alienation of yet more of its former supporters.*
2 VO If someone **is alienated** from something, they are emotionally or intellectually separated from it. *People have been alienated from their roots.* ◆ **alienation** NU *...a growing feeling of despair and alienation.*

alight /əˈlaɪt/ **alights, alighting, alighted**
1 ADJ PRED If something is **alight**, it is burning. *The boats were set alight.*
2 ADJ PRED If you describe someone's face or expression as **alight**, you mean that they look excited. *She was looking at him, her eyes alight.*
3 V or VA If a bird or insect **alights** somewhere, it lands there. *It flew across to the tree and alighted on a branch.*
4 V or VA When you **alight** from a train, bus, or plane, you get out of it after a journey; a formal use. *Nobody met me at the station when I alighted... An hour and a half later after an uneventful flight they alighted in Amman.*

align /əˈlaɪn/ **aligns, aligning, aligned**
1 V-PASS or V-REFL If you **are aligned** with a particular group, you support them in the same political aim. *Mongolia has long been closely aligned with the Soviet Union... They have avoided aligning themselves with any one political party.*
2 VO If you **align** two objects, you place them in a particular position in relation to each other, usually parallel. *He aligned his papers in geometrical patterns on his desk... They drilled a narrow hole through 100 yards of rock between the two tunnels to ensure they are correctly aligned.*

alignment /əˈlaɪnmənt/ **alignments**
1 NC An **alignment** is support for a particular group, especially in politics, or for a side in a quarrel or a struggle. *...political alignments with foreign powers.*
2 NU The **alignment** of something is its position in relation to something else or its correct position. *Something had slipped out of alignment.*

alike /əˈlaɪk/
1 ADJ PRED If two or more things are **alike**, they are similar. *They all look alike to me... The Vanbrugh sisters were remarkably alike in appearance... Well, chimpanzees and humans are very alike, we share 98% of our DNA, of our genetic material.*
2 ADV **Alike** also means in a similar way. *The children are all treated alike... They did everything alike.*
3 ADV **Alike** is used after mentioning two or more people, groups, or things in order to emphasize that you are referring to both or all of them. *The strike is damaging to managers and workers alike... Mr. Tembo is a popular figure among the armed forces and civilians alike... The Uzbeks and Kirghiz alike are Sunni Muslims.*

alimentary /ˌælɪˈmentəri/
ADJ ATTRIB **Alimentary** is used to refer to the processes of eating or digestion; a medical term. *Alcohol is very easily absorbed from the stomach and from the alimentary tract.*

alimentary canal, alimentary canals
NC The **alimentary canal** in a person or animal is the passage in their body through which food passes from their mouth to their anus; a medical term.

alimony /ˈælɪməni/
NU **Alimony** is money that someone has to pay regularly to their former wife or husband after they have been divorced. *He was convicted on a charge of failing to pay alimony to his ex-wife.*

alive /əˈlaɪv/
1 ADJ PRED If people or animals are **alive**, they are not dead. *I think his father is still alive... As long as President Tito was alive Yugoslavia's foreign policy*

was dominated by his personality... Seventeen people were found alive, twenty-four days after the disaster.
2 ADJ PRED If you describe an activity or situation as **alive**, you mean that it exists or is functioning well. *Theatre outside London is very much alive... Oxford United needed a win to keep alive their hopes of First Division survival.*
3 ADJ PRED+*with* If you say that a place is **alive** with people, things, or emotions of a particular kind, you mean that it is full of them. *The ditches beside the fields were alive with frogs... The streets were alive with tension as the people waited for Prime Minister Lukanov's announcement... One critic wrote: 'Her face is alive with youthful spirit'.*
4 ADJ PRED+*to* If you are **alive** to a problem or situation, you are aware of it and realize its importance. *As you can see, I am fully alive to the problems facing the industry... In her psychological portrait of Gorbachev, she sees him as alive to the dark currents that flow through the history of his country.*
5 ADJ PRED If you describe someone as **alive**, you mean that they are lively and enjoy everything that they do. *Young people are so alive and exciting.*
● **Alive** is used in these phrases. ● If a story or description comes **alive**, it becomes interesting, lively, or realistic. *The descriptions of people and their circumstances in these stories come alive and are unforgettable.* ● If people or places come **alive**, they start to be active or lively again. *Today, thanks to a government-sponsored corporation, the dockland has come alive again.* ● If you say that someone or something is **alive and well**, you are emphasizing that they continue to survive and do very well. *Mr. Pastrana, who was kidnapped on Monday, has been found alive and well... The British class system is alive and well and living in British minds.* ● If you say that someone or something is **alive and kicking**, you mean that they are not only still living or existing, but are very active and lively. *Vice-President Bush's campaign for the White House is still very much alive and kicking... The group is still alive and kicking and is now capable of taking its challenge to the government onto the streets.*

alkali /ˈælkəlaɪ/ **alkalis**
N MASS An **alkali** is a chemical substance that turns litmus paper blue. *The bacterium produces an alkali which neutralises and so protects it against acidity.*

alkaline /ˈælkəlaɪn/
ADJ Something that is **alkaline** contains an alkali. *...alkaline soils derived from chalk or limestone.*

all /ɔːl/
1 PREDET, DET, or PRON You use **all** to indicate that you are referring to the whole of a group or thing. *All the girls think it's great... All of the defendants were proved guilty... Spending on all aspects of health care has risen rapidly... They all live together... All was quiet in the gaol.*
2 ADV You also use **all** to emphasize the extent to which something happens or is true. *He spilled coffee all over himself... I'm all alone... We start to see a lot of people who are homeless, stacked all along the street...*
3 PRON You can use **all** when you are emphasizing that something is the only thing that is important. *All you do is add water... All I know is that a man's dying while we're talking.*
4 ADV You also use **all** when you are talking about an equal score in a game. For example, if the score is three all, both players or teams have three points. *They were thirty all in the last game when it started to rain.*
● **All** is used in these phrases. ● You say **above all** to emphasize that a particular thing is more important than others. *Relax, and above all don't panic... Above all, the terrible economic situation will confront anyone brave enough to be Prime Minister... The poor, the sick, the old, and, above all, the women of Ireland are still struggling in the long march to equality.*
● You say **after all** to draw attention to something that other people might have forgotten or that you had not previously realized. *Could it be true, after all, that*

money did not bring happiness?... I mean, after all,
consumers are more aware than ever of the potential
problem of fat in their diet... The Prime Minister has,
after all, been in office eleven years. ● You use **all in
all** to introduce a summary or generalization. *All in
all, I'm not in favour... But all in all, it wasn't as
nasty as some people thought... All in all, the
opposition to the military option has been too limited.*
● If you say that something is not **all that** good or not
all that important, you mean that it is not very good
or not very important; an informal expression. *Their
political leadership is not all that good at this kind of
thing. ...an area where economic reform isn't all that
important.* ● **All the** more or **all the** better mean even
more or even better than before. *You must work all
the more quickly now... The 'playing down' technique
makes the agreement seem all the better when it
comes.* ● You use **at all** to emphasize a negative or a
question. *We didn't go there at all... Are you under
any restrictions at all?* ● You use **for all** to say that a
particular fact does not affect or contradict what you
are saying, although you know that it may seem to do
so. *For all her sensitivity, she's extremely tough...
For all their reforming zeal, the Young Turks were
ultimately unsuccessful... For all their differences,
both leaders need each other.* ● **In all** means in total.
There were nine in all. ● You say **in all** seriousness or
in all honesty to emphasize that you are being
completely serious or honest. *I say this in all
seriousness... Sir Geoffrey says that he cannot in all
honesty share her approach.* ● You use **of all** to
emphasize the words 'first' or 'last', or a superlative
adjective or adverb. *I asked them first of all if they
were Welsh... This view is the best of all.*

all- /ɔːl-/
1 PREFIX **All-** can be added to nouns or adjectives to
form adjectives which describe something as
consisting only of the thing mentioned or as having
only the quality indicated. *...all-wool jumpers.
...Nigeria's first all-female football championships.
...new all-electronic digital exchanges.*
2 PREFIX **All-** can also be added to present participles
in order to form adjectives which describe something
as including or affecting everything or everyone.
*...the belief that Christ was divine and all-knowing.
...his all-encompassing love... An all-pervading
dishonesty hung over our enterprise.*
3 PREFIX **All-** can also be added to nouns in order to
form adjectives which describe something that is
suitable for or includes all types of a particular thing.
*...an all-weather football pitch. ...all-party support for
the cause.*

Allah /ælə/
N PROP **Allah** is the name of God in Islam. *He spoke
of a war between right and wrong, between Allah and
the Devil.*

allay /əleɪ/ **allays, allaying, allayed**
VO If you **allay** someone's fears or doubts, you stop
them feeling afraid or doubtful; a formal word. *Mr
Poehl also allayed fears of a rise in inflation.*

all clear
N SING The **all clear** is a signal that a dangerous
situation has ended. *They eventually went back in
after the all clear was sounded.*

all-comers /ɔːlkʌməz/
N PL **All-comers** refers to people, especially people
taking part in a contest, regardless of their age,
qualifications, or experience. *The champion was
relaxing after an afternoon beating all-comers.*

allegation /æləgeɪʃn/ **allegations**
NC An **allegation** is a statement suggesting that
someone has done something wrong. *Pakistan has
denied an indirect Indian allegation that it is helping
to arm Sikh extremists in the Punjab. ...allegations of
improper business dealings... Libya has rejected an
allegation by Chad that it is massing troops along
their mutual border.*

allege /əledʒ/ **alleges, alleging, alleged**
V-REPORT or V-PASS+*to*-INF If you **allege** that something is
true, you say it but do not prove it. *The reports
alleged that the motive was financial... It has been
alleged that he was tortured by police... It is alleged*

that a number of troops had been drinking and
brandishing weapons... Members of the security forces
were alleged to have shot at least eleven people.

alleged /əledʒd/
ADJ ATTRIB An **alleged** fact has been stated but not
proved to be true. *...investigations into alleged abuses
of government power. ...the trial of an alleged
terrorist... Mr Parkinson said he treated all alleged
breaches of security very seriously.* ◆ **allegedly** ADV
...the crimes he had allegedly committed.

allegiance /əliːdʒəns/ **allegiances**
N U or N C Your **allegiance** to a group, person, or belief
is your support for and loyalty to them. *The Chinese
Catholic Church isn't permitted to give allegiance to
the Pope. ...their traditional allegiances.*

allegorical /æləgɒrɪkl/
ADJ An **allegorical** story, poem, or painting uses
allegory. *His plays are brutal allegorical fables which
are often too ambiguous for those who like their
drama clear cut.*

allegory /æləgəri/ **allegories**
N C or N U An **allegory** is a story, poem, or painting in
which the characters and events are symbols of
something else. *The film is an allegory on the
morality of the prison system.*

alleluia /æləluːjə/. See **hallelujah.**

all-embracing
ADJ Something that is **all-embracing** includes or
affects everyone or everything. *Political control was
equally all-embracing and bureaucratic.*

allergic /əlɜːdʒɪk/
ADJ If you are **allergic** to something, you become ill or
get a rash when you eat it, smell it, or touch it. *A lot
of people, including me, are allergic to house-dust...
Glass fibre can cause allergic reactions and coughs.*

allergy /ælədʒi/ **allergies**
N C or N U An **allergy** is an illness that you have when
you eat, smell, or touch a substance which does not
normally make people ill. *He had an allergy to milk...
Allergy to cats is one of the commonest causes of
asthma.*

alleviate /əliːvieɪt/ **alleviates, alleviating, alleviated**
VO If you **alleviate** pain, suffering, or an unpleasant
condition, you make it less severe. *Aid workers are
doing their best to alleviate the situation... Healthy
lifestyles can do a lot to alleviate suffering.*
◆ **alleviation** /əliːvieɪʃn/ N U *...the alleviation of
poverty.*

alley /æli/ **alleys**
NC An **alley** or **alleyway** is a narrow path or street.
*The route unfolded through the narrow winding alleys
and spacious boulevards... The man was dragged into
an alleyway by four men.* ● See also **blind alley.**

alley cat, alley cats
NC An **alley cat** is a cat that lives in the streets of a
town, is rather fierce, and is not owned by anyone.

alleyway /æliweɪ/ **alleyways**. See **alley.**

alliance /əlaɪəns/ **alliances**
1 NC An **alliance** is a group of countries or political
parties which are formally united and work together
for the same aims. *...the formation of an alliance to
campaign for multi-party democracy... The talks
involved members of the two great military alliances.
...the failure of the alliance between students and
workers.*
2 If two or more countries or groups of people are **in
alliance** with each other, they are working together for
the same purposes. *The Khmer Rouge currently
operates in alliance with the former monarch... The
two parties have settled their differences and will
remain in alliance.*

allied /ælaɪd/
1 ADJ ATTRIB **Allied** countries, political parties, or
other groups are united by a political or military
agreement. *They claimed that the invasion was
necessary to help an allied country.*
2 ADJ ATTRIB **Allied** describes things that are related to
other things because they have particular qualities or
characteristics in common. *The aircraft and allied
industries were nationalized.*
3 See also **ally.**

alligator /ˈælɪgeɪtə/ **alligators**
NC An **alligator** is a large animal, similar to a crocodile. *Alligators and snakes have been seen in flooded areas.*

alliteration /əˌlɪtəˈreɪʃn/
NU **Alliteration** is the use in speech or writing of several words close together which all begin with the same letter or sound. *Strong rhymes and alliteration make the verses enjoyable to chant.*

allocate /ˈæləkeɪt/ **allocates, allocating, allocated**
VO A, VO O, or VO+to-INF If something is **allocated** to a particular person or for a particular purpose, it is given to that person or used for that purpose. *The land is to be allocated to farmers... Money is also allocated for maintenance and repair programmes... She said Pakistan had not been allocated any money from the 1991 budget... Half the money in the fund has been allocated to help Poland... He wrote an article accusing the President of showing favouritism in allocating government posts.*

allocation /ˌæləˈkeɪʃn/ **allocations**
1 NC An **allocation** is a particular amount of something such as money that will be given to a particular person or used for a particular purpose. *The armed forces have by far the largest allocation from this budget... Britain's biggest aid allocations are to India and Kenya.*
2 NU The **allocation** of something is the decision that it should be given to a particular person or saved for them. *...the allocation of responsibilities... Students have objected to the new arrangement for the allocation of university places.*

allot /əˈlɒt/ **allots, allotting, allotted**
VO or VO+to If something is **allotted** to someone, it is given to them as their share. *All seats in the Public Gallery are allotted in advance by ticket... The bill allots $288 billion for the 1991 military budget... They were not being given the food allotted to them by the government.* ♦ **allotted** ADJ *...our allotted sum of money.*

allotment /əˈlɒtmənt/ **allotments**
1 NC An **allotment** is a small area of land which a person rents to grow vegetables on. *They often use this fertiliser on their gardens and allotments.*
2 N SING+of An **allotment** of something is an amount of it that is given to someone or is saved for them. *He is accused of having accepted an allotment of the shares.*

all-out
1 ADJ ATTRIB **All-out** actions are carried out in a very energetic and determined way, usually using all the resources available. *The army is preparing an all-out assault against the rebel forces.*
2 ADJ ATTRIB An **all-out** strike is one in which all the employees refuse to work. *...an all-out strike in support of pay demands.*

allow /əˈlaʊ/ **allows, allowing, allowed**
1 VO+to-INF or VO+ING If someone in authority **allows** you to do something, they say that it is all right for you to do it. *The new constitution will allow Hong Kong to maintain its capitalist system for fifty years after the changeover... He agreed to allow me to take the course... Mrs. Thatcher still refuses to allow sterling to join the exchange rate mechanism... Henry doesn't allow smoking in his office.*
2 VOO If you **are allowed** something, you are given permission to have it or are given it. *Sometimes, we were allowed a special treat... Inmates were allowed personal computers in their cells.*
3 VO+to-INF If you **allow** something to happen, you do not prevent it. *The further this process is allowed to go, the more difficult it will be to reverse it... The Nicaraguan government is allowing a number of private radio stations to resume broadcasting news programmes.*
4 VO+to-INF If something **allows** a particular thing to happen, it makes it possible. *The creatures had warm blood, which allowed them to be active at night... Holes in the ship allowed water to rush in the side when the vessel started to list... The schedule that had been set up allowed people to leave at 6:00 or 7:00.*
5 V-REPORT If you **allow** that something is true, you admit that it is true; a formal use. *He allowed that*

even world leaders could make mistakes.
6 V-REFL or VO If you **allow** a particular period of time or amount of something, you set aside that particular period of time or amount for a particular purpose. *How long did you allow yourself?... Allow 4 metres.*
7 VO or VO A If you **allow** someone to join a particular organization or **allow** them to be in a particular place, you let them belong to that organization or to go to that place. *The union would not allow women members... No one is allowed here after dark.*
8 If you say '**allow me**', you are politely offering to do something for someone, or politely introducing something you want to say. *Mr Smith jumped up and said, 'Allow me'... Please allow me to introduce myself.*

allow for PHRASAL VERB If you **allow for** something, you consider its effect on the plans you are making. *Expenditure is expected to rise by about 2.5% a year, after allowing for inflation... Even allowing for foreign earnings from services such as banking and insurance, the deficit was still some £900 million.*

allowable /əˈlaʊəbl/
ADJ If something is **allowable**, it is all right for you to do it. *...allowable departures from normal behaviour.*

allowance /əˈlaʊəns/ **allowances**
1 NC+SUPP An **allowance** is money that is given regularly to someone to help them pay for things they need. *...the weekly allowance paid to all parents.*
2 NC A child's **allowance** is the amount of money they are given each week by his or her parents; used in American English.
3 If you **make allowances** for something, you take it into account in your plans, judgements, or actions. *The researchers made allowances for differences in age.*

alloy /ˈælɔɪ/ **alloys**
N MASS An **alloy** is a metal that is made by mixing two or more types of metal together. *...an alloy of copper and tin.*

all-powerful
ADJ Someone or something that is **all-powerful** has a very great deal of power or influence. *...the country's all-powerful drugs barons.*

all right; also spelt **alright**.
1 ADJ PRED or ADV If something is **all right**, it is satisfactory or acceptable. *My house is all right, but I'd like to make the kitchen a lot bigger... He's getting on all right.*
2 ADJ PRED If someone is **all right**, they are well or safe. *Someone should see if she's all right... I'm all right, feeling good, doing good... Mr. Bush told reporters that he feels all right.*
3 You say '**all right**' when you are agreeing to a suggestion or a request. *'Can you help?'—'All right. What do you want me to do?'*
4 You also say '**all right?**' to someone when you are checking that they have understood what you have just said. *If you feel dizzy again put your head in your hands, all right?*

all-rounder, all-rounders
NC An **all-rounder** is someone who has a lot of different skills or is good at many sports. *...the Indian cricket all-rounder Manoj Prabhakar... The Swiss all-rounder Pirmin Zurbriggen has stretched his overall lead in the World Cup Giant Slalom.*

allspice /ˈɔːlspaɪs/
NU **Allspice** is a powder used as a spice in cooking, which is made from the berries of an allspice tree.

all-star
ADJ ATTRIB An **all-star** cast or performance is one which contains only famous or extremely good players or performers. *The all-star line-up contains many Caribbean artists.*

all-time
ADJ ATTRIB If something is the **all-time** best, at an all-time low, and so on, it is the best or lowest that there has ever been. *Prices are at an all-time high.*

allude /əˈluːd/ **alludes, alluding, alluded**
V+to If you **allude** to something, you mention it in an indirect way; a formal word. *I have already alluded to the energy problem.*

allure /əlʊə/
N SING The **allure** of something is a pleasing or exciting quality that attracts people to it. *...the allure of foreign travel.*

alluring /əlʊərɪŋ/
ADJ Someone or something that is **alluring** is very attractive. *Some people may have been persuaded by alluring television and radio advertisements. ...the alluring melodies of Brazil's best-known songwriter.*

allusion /əluːʒn/
N C or N U An **allusion** to something is an indirect or vague reference to it. *...allusions to Latin and Greek authors... You made an allusion to the events in Los Angeles: could you elaborate?*

alluvial /əluːviəl/
ADJ **Alluvial** soils are soils which consist of earth and sand left behind on land which has been flooded or where a river once flowed; a technical term. *The three cities that were affected are all on alluvial basins.*

ally, allies, allying, allied; pronounced /ælaɪ/ when it is a noun and /əlaɪ/ when it is a verb.
1 N C An **ally** is a country, organization, or person that helps and supports another. *...our European allies... The Foreign Minister said China regarded Thailand as an important ally in Asia.*
2 V-REFL+*with* If you **ally** yourself with someone, you support them. *Syria has allied itself with the United States in joining the anti-Iraqi camp in the Gulf crisis... They only managed to scrape into the Bundestag because they allied themselves with the Citizens' Rights movement.*
3 See also **allied**.

Alma Ata /ælmɑ: ətɑ:/
Alma Ata is the capital of Kazakhstan and its largest city. Population: 1,151,000 (1990).

alma mater /ælmə mɑːtə/
N SING Your **alma mater** is the college or school that you attended; used in American English. *News reports say Mr. Bush is headed to his alma mater, Yale, tomorrow for an honorary degree.*

almanac /ɔːlmənæk/ **almanacs**; also spelt **almanack**.
N C+SUPP An **almanac** is a book that is published every year, containing facts, figures, and other information about a particular subject. *...Wisden's Almanac, the bible of cricket. ...the annual astrological guide Old Moore's Almanack.*

almighty /ɔːlmaɪti/
1 N PROP The **Almighty** is another name for God. *...the mercy of the Almighty.* ▶ Also ADJ ATTRIB *...Almighty God.*
2 ADJ ATTRIB An **almighty** row, problem, or mistake is a very great or serious one; an informal use. *She made the most almighty fuss.*

almond /ɑːmənd/ **almonds**
N C An **almond** is a kind of pale oval nut.

almost /ɔːlməʊst/
ADV **Almost** means very nearly, but not completely. *I spent almost a month in China... He is almost blind... I had almost forgotten about the trip... In Oxford Street, you can buy almost anything.*

alms /ɑːmz/
N PL **Alms** are gifts of money, clothes, or food to poor people; an old-fashioned word. *They are refusing to go there to collect alms.*

almshouse /ɑːmzhaʊs/ **almshouses** /ɑːmzhaʊzɪz/
N C **Almshouses** were houses that were built and run by charities for poor or old people to live in without paying rent.

Alofi /ɑːlɔʊfi/
Alofi is the capital of Niue and its largest town. Population: 900 (1987).

aloft /əlɒft/
ADV Something that is **aloft** is in the air or off the ground; a literary word. *The flag was held aloft.*

alone /ələʊn/
1 ADJ PRED When you are **alone**, you are not with any other people. *I wanted to be alone... Barbara spent most of her time alone in the flat... Friends had invited Alvelita to spend the holiday with them so she wouldn't be alone.*
2 ADJ PRED A person who is **alone** is also someone who

has no family or friends. *I had never felt so alone and without hope in my life... What if something should happen to us and our kids were left alone?... We felt terribly alone, very much orphaned.*
3 ADJ PRED If one person is **alone** with another, they are together, and nobody else is present. *I was alone with the attendant... We'd never spent such a long time alone together.*
4 ADV If you do something **alone**, you do it without help from other people. *I was left to bring up my two children alone... The situation as it stands now is one that the President has had to face alone, without Congress.*
5 ADJ after N If you **alone** do something, you are the only person who does it. *Simon alone knew the truth.*
6 ADJ after N If something consists of one idea or feature **alone**, nothing else is involved. *Pride alone prevented her from giving up... Army leaders say air attacks alone cannot dislodge Iraqi forces from Kuwait.*

along /əlɒŋ/
1 PREP If you move or look **along** something, you move or look towards one end of it. *He was driving along a lane... She glanced along the corridor.*
2 PREP or ADV If something is situated **along** a road, river, or corridor, it is situated in it or beside it. *...an old house along the Lanark Road... Room 64 was half way along on the right.*
3 ADV When someone or something moves **along**, they keep moving steadily. *I put my arm around him as we walked along... The procession crawled along the ninety-mile route into the capital... Two hundred youths marched along the streets shouting neo-Nazi slogans.*
4 ADV If something is going **along** in a particular way, it is progressing in that way. *It was going along nicely... Everything was going along as normal.*
5 ADV If you take someone **along** when you go somewhere, you take them with you. *Why don't you come along too?*
● **Along** is used in these phrases. ● You use **all along** to say that something has existed or been the case throughout a period of time. *Perhaps they had been mistaken all along... Many people believe that Mr Gorbachev has all along wanted to extricate himself from Afghanistan with as much honour as possible.*
● If you do something **along with** someone else, you both do it. If you take one thing **along with** another, you take both things. *Along with thousands of others, he fled the country... The eggs were delivered along with the milk.*

alongside; pronounced /əlɒŋsaɪd/ when it is a preposition and /əlɒŋsaɪd/ when it is an adverb.
1 PREP or ADV If one thing is **alongside** another, it is next to it. *There was a butcher's shop alongside the theatre... A car drew up alongside.*
2 PREP If you work **alongside** other people, you are working in the same place and are co-operating with them. *The idea is to get them working on simple things alongside other people.*
3 PREP If one thing exists **alongside** another, the two things are both present in a situation. *I cannot imagine two political systems less likely to live at peace alongside each other.*

aloof /əluːf/
1 ADJ Someone who is **aloof** likes to be alone and does not talk much. *He was an aloof loner with no sense of humour.*
2 ADJ PRED If you stay **aloof** from something, you do not become involved with it. *The Royal Family must remain aloof from party politics.*

aloud /əlaʊd/
ADV When you speak or read **aloud**, you speak so that other people can hear you. *She read aloud to us from the newspaper.*

alpaca /ælpækə/
N U or N+N **Alpaca** is a kind of wool which is used for making clothes. *...an alpaca cardigan.*

alpha /ælfə/ **alphas**
N C or N U **Alpha** is the first letter of the Greek alphabet, sometimes used as a mark or grade given for a student's work.

alphabet /ˈælfəbet/ **alphabets**
N C The **alphabet** is the set of letters in a fixed order which is used for writing the words of a language. *...methods used by schools to teach youngsters the letters of the alphabet.*

alphabetical /ˌælfəˈbetɪkl/
ADJ ATTRIB **Alphabetical** means arranged according to the normal order of the letters in the alphabet. *From now on, names of candidates will be in alphabetical order.*

alpine /ˈælpaɪn/
ADJ ATTRIB **Alpine** means existing in or relating to mountains. *...alpine meadows.*

already /ɔːlˈredi/
1 ADV If something has **already** happened, it has happened before the present time. *The ceasefire had already been violated... I've had tea already, thank you... Relations between the two countries are already strained by the conflict in Kampuchea.*
2 ADV You also use **already** to indicate that something happened earlier than expected. *By the time he got home, Julie was already in bed... I'm half an hour late already.*

alright /ɔːlˈraɪt/. See **all right**.

Alsatian /ælˈseɪʃn/ **Alsatians**
N C An **Alsatian** is a large dog that is often used to guard buildings or by the police to help them find criminals. *Large dogs like Alsatians suffer from hip displacements and go lame.*

also /ˈɔːlsəʊ/
1 ADV You use **also** when you are giving more information about a person or thing. *Tony Nuttall is Vice-Chancellor and also a Professor of English at Sussex. ...also available in blue and green.*
2 ADV You can use **also** to say that the same fact applies to someone or something else. *His first wife was also called Margaret.*

also-ran, also-rans
N C If you refer to someone as an **also-ran**, you mean that they have been or are likely to be unsuccessful in a contest because they do not have much skill or ability; an informal word.

altar /ˈɔːltə/ **altars**
1 N C An **altar** is a holy table in a Christian church which the priest uses during a service. *She was driven to the Cathedral where she went to the main altar to give thanks.*
2 N C An **altar** is also a table or raised platform in temples of other religions where religious ceremonies or sacrifices are carried out. *Workers had built an altar of sandalwood logs upon which the mourners placed the body.*

alter /ˈɔːltə/ **alters, altering, altered**
V-ERG If something **alters** or if you **alter** it, it changes. *The weather could alter violently... America must radically alter its economic policy.* ♦ **alteration** /ˌɔːltəˈreɪʃn/ **alterations** N C *It is not possible to make major alterations to existing arrangements.*

altercation /ˌɔːltəˈkeɪʃn/ **altercations**
N C An **altercation** is a noisy argument; a formal word. *She had been threatened after an altercation with a taxi driver.*

alter ego /ˌæltər ˈiːɡəʊ/ **alter egos**
1 N C Your **alter ego** is the other side of your personality from the one which people normally see.
2 N C An **alter ego** is a very close and intimate friend. *Mrs Reagan regards herself as the President's alter ego.*

alternate, alternates, alternating, alternated; pronounced /ˈɔːltəneɪt/ when it is a verb and /ɔːlˈtɜːnət/ when it is an adjective.
1 V+*between* When you **alternate** between two things, you regularly do or use one thing and then the other. *They alternated between patronising us and ignoring us... In his songs, John alternated between an extrovert mood, and a more lyrical, inward looking approach.*
2 V+*with* When one thing **alternates** with another, the two things regularly occur in turn. *The Third World suffers from an annual cycle of drought alternating with flood... Union Square was filled with the sound of peace songs, alternated with moments of silence for*

the dead soldiers. ♦ **alternation** /ˌɔːltəˈneɪʃn/ N U *...an alternation of right-wing and left-wing governments.*
3 ADJ ATTRIB **Alternate** actions, events, or processes regularly occur after each other. *...the alternate contraction and relaxation of muscles... The equipment gives the baby normal air, and then air with reduced oxygen every alternate breath.* ♦ **alternately** ADV *Each piece of material is washed alternately in soft water and coconut oil.*
4 ADJ ATTRIB If something happens on **alternate** days, it happens on one day, then does not happen on the next day, then happens again on the day after it, and so on. In the same way, something can happen in **alternate** weeks, months, or years. *We saw each other on alternate Sunday nights... In Athens, cars are only allowed in on alternate days, depending on their number plates.*

alternating current
N U An **alternating current** is a continuous electric current that changes direction as it flows. *...a modern train using alternating current.*

alternative /ɔːlˈtɜːnətɪv/ **alternatives**
1 N C An **alternative** is one thing that can exist or that you can do instead of another. *Are there alternatives to prison?* ▸ Also ADJ ATTRIB *But still people try to find alternative explanations.*
2 ADJ ATTRIB **Alternative** is also used to describe something that is different from the usual things of its kind, especially when it is simpler or more natural, or not part of the establishment. *Alternative medicine has begun to gain acceptance as a way of treating physical ailments.*

alternatively /ɔːlˈtɜːnətɪvli/
ADV SEN You use **alternatively** to suggest or mention something different from what has just been mentioned. *Alternatively, you can use household bleach.*

alternative medicine
N U **Alternative medicine** is the treatment of illnesses using methods such as acupuncture and homeopathy rather than conventional drugs or surgery. *Alternative medicine has often been shown to be effective in cases where other treatments have failed... People are also resorting to alternative medicine like homeopathy, osteopathy, and natural remedies to cure their illnesses.*

alternator /ˈɔːltəneɪtə/ **alternators**
N C An **alternator** is a device, used especially in a car, that creates an electrical current that changes direction as it flows.

although /ɔːlˈðəʊ/
1 CONJ You use **although** to introduce a subordinate clause which contains a statement that makes the main clause seem surprising or contradictory. *Although he was late he stopped to buy a sandwich... Gretchen kept her coat on, although it was warm in the room.*
2 CONJ **Although** also introduces a subordinate clause, often containing 'not', that modifies the main clause and corrects a wrong impression that someone might get from it. *I have a lot of my grandfather's features, although I'm not so tall as he was.*

altimeter /ˈæltɪmiːtə/ **altimeters**
N C An **altimeter** is an instrument in an aircraft that measures height. *A radar altimeter will measure sea level and wave-height.*

altitude /ˈæltɪtjuːd/ **altitudes**
N U or N C If something is at a particular **altitude**, it is at that height above sea level. *The plane lost altitude, and its right wing began to detach itself at about the same time... Some of the larger aircraft are designed to fly for hours at very high altitudes.*

alto /ˈæltəʊ/ **altos**
1 N C An **alto** is a singer whose voice is higher than that of a tenor but lower than that of a soprano. *In the recording I have today, it is sung by a male alto... There are certain groups in the choir, you know, the altos, the tenors, the sopranos.*
2 ADJ ATTRIB An **alto** musical instrument has a range of musical notes of medium pitch. *...the alto saxophone.*

altogether /ɔːltəgeðə/
1 ADV **Altogether** is used to say that something has been done or stopped completely. *The second missile fired at the ship missed it altogether... He abandoned his work altogether.*
2 ADV If one thing is **altogether** different from another, the two things are completely different. *...an altogether different kind of support.*
3 ADV SEN You can use **altogether** to summarize something you have been talking about. *Yes, it's quite a pleasant place altogether... Altogether, I think Alan has written a remarkable biography.*
4 ADV You also use **altogether** to indicate that the amount you are mentioning is a total. *Altogether, he played in 44 matches.*

altruism /æltruɪzəm/
NU **Altruism** is unselfish concern for other people's happiness and welfare. *Altruism is often the motive for accepting the refugees.*

altruistic /æltruɪstɪk/
ADJ An **altruistic** person is unselfish and shows concern for other people's happiness and welfare. *My invitation was not completely altruistic. ...an altruistic desire for peace and goodwill.*

aluminium /æləmɪniəm/.
NU **Aluminium** is a silver-coloured, lightweight metal. *And being aluminium means it's very light, presumably?*

aluminum /əluːmɪnəm/
NU **Aluminum** is the same as **aluminium**; used in American English.

always /ɔːlweɪz/
1 ADV You use **always** to say that something is done all the time, or is the case all the time. *I had always been poor... He has always advocated a more moderate approach... It was always carefully checked before being used.*
2 ADV You can also use **always** to say that something will continue to be done, or will continue to be the case at all times in the future. *I shall always love you... The manufacturers say air defence will always be needed... Such decisions will always be taken by national governments and parliaments.*
3 ADV If you say that someone can **always** take a particular course of action, you mean that they will have the opportunity to try it later if other methods are unsuccessful. *Oh well, I can always come back later.*

am /m, əm, æm/
Am is the first person singular of the present tense of **be**.

a.m. /eɪ em/
a.m. after a number indicates that the number refers to a particular time between midnight and noon. *I try to get up around 7 a.m.*

amalgam /əmælgəm/ **amalgams**
NC An **amalgam** of two or more things is a mixture of them. *...a simple amalgam of previous doctrines.*

amalgamate /əmælgəmeɪt/ **amalgamates, amalgamating, amalgamated**
V-RECIP or V-ERG When two or more organizations **amalgamate** or **are amalgamated**, they become one large organization. *He admitted that there had been pressure to amalgamate. ...the Variety Artists Federation, which has since amalgamated with Equity... The north and east parts of the island are to be amalgamated under one council.* ♦ **amalgamation** /əmælgəmeɪʃn/ **amalgamations** NU or NC *...the amalgamation of several large businesses... He thinks that these amalgamations are a good thing.*

amass /əmæs/ **amasses, amassing, amassed**
1 V-ERG If you **amass** something such as money, or if it **amasses**, you gradually get a lot of it. *So far, 1.6 billion has been amassed... The combined loot of the army amassed as it advanced through South East Asia... You won't get anywhere if you don't amass a network of sympathetic, influential supporters.*
2 V If people **amass** somewhere, they gather there in large numbers. *There are reports of Turkish troops amassing near the border... More than fifty thousand demonstrators have now amassed in the square.*

amateur /æmətə/ **amateurs**
1 NC An **amateur** is someone who does something such as acting or playing sport for pleasure, and is not paid for doing it. *The tournament, for professionals and amateurs, is being played on four different courses. ...a good amateur viola player.*
2 ADJ **Amateur** can also mean the same as **amateurish**. *...amateur literature produced on duplicating machines.*

amateurish /æmətərɪʃ/
ADJ If you describe something as **amateurish**, you mean it is not skilfully made or done. *Some journalists believe that the polls are amateurish and biased.*

amaze /əmeɪz/ **amazes, amazing, amazed**
VO If something **amazes** you, it surprises you very much. *Her energy and capacity for hard work amazed everyone.*

amazed /əmeɪzd/
ADJ If you are **amazed**, you are very surprised indeed. *They were amazed at the way the heroin had been concealed in milk containers... She was amazed that I was only twenty.*

amazement /əmeɪzmənt/
NU **Amazement** is what you feel if you are very surprised by something. *Her eyes were wide with amazement.*

amazing /əmeɪzɪŋ/
ADJ If something is **amazing**, it is very surprising and makes you feel pleasure, admiration or excitement. *New York is an amazing city... The results were amazing... It's amazing how many couples look alike.* ♦ **amazingly** SUBMOD *Our holiday was amazingly cheap.*

ambassador /æmbæsədə/ **ambassadors**
NC An **ambassador** is someone who is sent to a foreign country as the chief representative of his or her government. *...the ambassador to Pakistan, Mr Robert Oakley.*

ambassadorial /æmbæsədɔːriəl/
ADJ ATTRIB **Ambassadorial** means belonging or relating to an ambassador. *...the ambassadorial residence.*

amber /æmbə/
1 NU **Amber** is a hard yellowish-brown substance used for making jewellery. *...a necklace of silver, glass, and amber. ...a huge amber ring.*
2 ADJ Something that is **amber** in colour is orange or yellowish-brown. *...a photograph of a crucifix floating in an amber haze.*

ambiance /æmbiəns/. See **ambience**.

ambidextrous /æmbɪdekstrəs/
ADJ Someone who is **ambidextrous** can use their right and left hand with the same amount of skill. *Some babies stay ambidextrous for the first year or so.*

ambience /æmbiəns/; also spelt **ambiance**.
N SING The **ambience** of a place is its character and atmosphere; a literary word. *The aim is to produce an ambience conducive to healing.*

ambient /æmbiənt/
ADJ The **ambient** temperature is the temperature of the air above the ground in a particular place; a technical term. *Incoming air has to be heated or cooled to the ambient temperature of the air in the building.*

ambiguity /æmbɪgjuːəti/ **ambiguities**
NU or NC You say that there is **ambiguity** when something can be understood in more than one way. *...a speech which was a masterpiece of ambiguity. ...contradictions and ambiguities.*

ambiguous /æmbɪgjuəs/
ADJ Something that is **ambiguous** can be understood in more than one way. *There was nothing ambiguous in the message... The treaty gave an ambiguous definition of the border.* ♦ **ambiguously** ADV *The announcement was ambiguously worded.*

ambit /æmbɪt/
N SING The **ambit** of something is its range or extent; a formal word. *These documents fell outside the ambit of the rule.*

ambition /æmbɪʃn/ **ambitions**
1 NC If you have an **ambition** to achieve something, you want very much to achieve it. *Her ambition was*

to be a teacher.

2 NU or N PL If someone has **ambition** or **ambitions**, they want to be successful, rich, or powerful. *...women of energy and ambition... He claims to have no political ambitions.*

ambitious /æmbɪʃəs/

1 ADJ An **ambitious** person wants to be successful, rich, or powerful. *Mr Mellor is an ambitious and outspoken politician.*

2 ADJ An **ambitious** idea or plan is on a large scale and needs a lot of work to be successful. *The government is taking its most ambitious and controversial step yet.*

ambivalence /æmbɪvələns/

NU **Ambivalence** is the state of feeling uncertain or undecided about something, because you can see advantages and disadvantages in it. *She was in a state of ambivalence about having children. ...his country's ambivalence to being a member of NATO.*

ambivalent /æmbɪvələnt/

ADJ If you are **ambivalent** about something, you are uncertain and cannot decide what you think about it. *Americans are ambivalent about the whole business of royalty... He has always had a strangely ambivalent, love-hate relationship with his home country.*

amble /æmbl/ **ambles, ambling, ambled**

V If you **amble** somewhere, you walk there slowly and in a relaxed manner. *I ambled home through the village.*

ambulance /æmbjʊləns/ **ambulances**

NC An **ambulance** is a vehicle which is used for taking people to and from hospital. *They shouted for someone to go and phone for an ambulance. ...the London ambulance service.*

ambulanceman /æmbjʊlənsmæn/ **ambulancemen** /æmbjʊlənsmen/

NC An **ambulanceman** is someone whose job is to drive an ambulance or take care of people in an ambulance until they get to hospital. *The man was already dead by the time ambulancemen arrived on the scene.*

ambush /æmbʊʃ/ **ambushes, ambushing, ambushed**

VO If people **ambush** their enemies, they attack them after hiding and waiting for them. *Weyler's troops successfully ambushed a rebel force... Three soldiers are said to have been ambushed and killed in the southern district.* ► Also NC *A whole battalion got caught in an ambush.*

ameba /əmiːbə/. See **amoeba**.

ameliorate /əmiːliəreɪt/ **ameliorates, ameliorating, ameliorated**

VO To **ameliorate** a situation means to make it better or easier in some way; a formal word. *They advocated increased intervention in the economy to ameliorate the worst effects of capitalism... Tissue transplants will only ameliorate Alzheimer's disease, not cure it.* ◆ **amelioration** /əmiːliəreɪʃn/ NU+SUPP *...an amelioration of the relationship between Turkey and Greece.*

amen /ɑːmen, eɪmen/

Amen is said or sung by Christians at the end of a prayer. *Mother Teresa describes her philosophy in the following prayer: Give all of us joy and peace and compassion for each other, Amen.*

amenable /əmiːnəbl/

ADJ If you are **amenable** to something, you are willing to do or accept it. *The coalition government is more amenable to compromise... The leadership might be more amenable towards the proposed resolution.*

amend /əmend/ **amends, amending, amended**

1 VO If you **amend** something that has been written or said, you change it. *...two important bills which will amend India's electoral laws... Last year the regulations were amended to allow other awards to be made.*

2 If you **make amends** when you have harmed someone, you try to make things better by doing something to please them. *They are trying to make amends by restoring and rebuilding some of the buildings.*

amendment /əmendmənt/ **amendments**

1 NC An **amendment** is a section that is added to a

law or rule in order to change it. *...amendments to the Industrial Relations Bill.*

2 NC An **amendment** is also a correction to a piece of writing. *She made a few amendments to the letter.*

amenity /əmiːnəti/ **amenities**

NC **Amenities** are facilities such as shopping centres or sports centres that are provided for people's convenience or enjoyment. *...Canary Wharf—a complex of offices, shops, restaurants and leisure amenities on derelict dockland.*

America /əmerɪkə/ See **North America, South America, United States of America.**

American /əmerɪkən/ **Americans**

1 ADJ **American** means belonging or relating to the United States of America. *...a discotheque frequented by American servicemen. ...doubts over the American proposals.*

2 NC An **American** is a person who comes from the United States of America. *For most Americans, buying a handgun is easy.*

3 ADJ **American** also means belonging or relating to North, Central, or South America. *...the white man's treatment of the American Indian. ...the livelihoods of several Central American and South American states.*

Americanism /əmerɪkənɪzəm/ **Americanisms**

NC An **Americanism** is an expression or custom that is typical of people living in the United States of America. *He was—to adopt a current Americanism—an 'empty suit'.*

Americanize /əmerɪkənaɪz/ **Americanizes, Americanizing, Americanized**; also spelt **Americanise.**

VO To **Americanize** something means to make it follow American customs and practice. *They say you are Americanizing the department in every possible way.*

American Samoa /əmerɪkən sɑːməʊə/ See **Samoa**

amethyst /æməθɪst/ **amethysts**

1 NC An **amethyst** is a purple stone which is used in making jewellery. *...a little wreath of intermingled amethysts and diamonds.*

2 ADJ Something that is **amethyst** is purple or violet in colour. *...shimmering embroideries in pink, green, rose, amethyst, yellow, gold, silver, and white.*

amiability /eɪmiəbɪləti/

NU **Amiability** is the quality in people of being friendly and pleasant. *He strove to retain a degree of amiability.*

amiable /eɪmiəbl/

ADJ Someone who is **amiable** is friendly and pleasant. *Mr Brooke, once considered amiable but uninspired, has surprised and impressed everyone.* ◆ **amiably** ADV *He chatted amiably with Dorothy.*

amicable /æmɪkəbl/

ADJ An **amicable** agreement or relationship is one that is pleasant and in which problems are solved without quarrelling. *We hope to settle the dispute in an amicable way. ...an amicable settlement.* ◆ **amicably** ADV *They parted amicably.*

amid /əmɪd/

1 PREP If something happens **amid** noises or events of some kind, it happens while they are occurring. *Suddenly, amid the cries, I heard some words... Nicholas Ridley has returned to London, amid growing speculation that he will have to resign.*

2 PREP If something is **amid** other things, it is surrounded by them; a literary use. *Tombstones stood amid the swaying grass.*

amidst /əmɪdst/

PREP **Amidst** means the same as **amid**.

amiss /əmɪs/

ADJ PRED If you say that there is something **amiss**, you mean there is something wrong. *The rioting indicated that there was something amiss with the country's democracy... The flight data recorder showed nothing amiss.*

● **Amiss** is used in these phrases. ● If you **take** something **amiss**, you feel offended and upset by it. *Colleagues were sometimes on the receiving end of his acerbic wit, but few took it amiss.* ● If you say that something would **not come amiss**, you mean it would be welcome and useful. *A little calm wouldn't come amiss.*

amity /ˈæməti/
NU **Amity** is peaceful, friendly relations between people or countries; a formal word. *...a treaty of amity and co-operation.*

Amman /əˈmɑːn/
Amman is the capital of Jordan and its largest city. Population: 972,000 (1986).

ammo /ˈæməʊ/
NU **Ammo** is an abbreviation for 'ammunition'; an informal word. *The Marines were always running out of things, even food, ammo and medicine.*

ammonia /əˈməʊnɪə/
NU **Ammonia** is a colourless liquid or gas with a strong, sharp smell. It is used for making cleaning substances, explosives, and fertilizer. *The ship is on fire, and ammonia is leaking from the tank.*

ammunition /ˌæmjʊˈnɪʃn/
1 NU **Ammunition** is bullets and rockets that are made to be fired from guns. *Both sides are short of arms and ammunition and fighting is only likely to start again when new supplies arrive.*
2 NU You can also use **ammunition** to refer to information that can be used against someone. *The letters might be used as ammunition by reactionary groups.*

amnesia /æmˈniːzɪə/
NU If someone is suffering from **amnesia**, they have lost their memory. *She blamed the episode on amnesia.*

amnesty /ˈæmnəsti/ **amnesties**
1 NC An **amnesty** is a period of time during which people can confess to a crime or give up weapons without being punished. *Many dissidents have already surrendered as part of the two-week amnesty.*
2 NC An **amnesty** is also an official pardon granted to a prisoner by the state. *Those set free, as part of the Christmas amnesty, are all members of the Civic Crusade.*

amoeba /əˈmiːbə/ **amoebas** or **amoebae** /əˈmiːbiː/; also spelt **ameba** in American English.
NC An **amoeba** is a tiny living creature which consists of only one cell and which lives in water or soil. *The bacteria can infect other micro-organisms known as amoebae.*

amok /əˈmɒk/ or **amuck** /əˈmʌk/
A person or animal that **runs amok** behaves in a violent and uncontrolled way. *The elephants had a tendency to panic and run amok.*

among /əˈmʌŋ/ or **amongst** /əˈmʌŋst/
1 PREP A person or thing that is **among** a group of people or things is surrounded by them. *We stood there among piles of wooden boxes... Police said they found thirty bodies among the wreckage.*
2 PREP If you are **among** people of a particular kind, you are with them. *I was among friends... The diplomats and 25 other Americans were among 94 foreigners who left later on a flight to Frankfurt.*
3 PREP If you move **among** a group of people or things, you move about through them in no particular direction. *I wandered amongst the ruins... He walked the dingy brick streets among factories and immigrants.*
4 PREP If something applies to a particular person or thing **among** others, it also applies to other people or things. *Bluestone, among other union leaders, argued against a strike... This can result in skin cancer, amongst other things.*
5 PREP If an opinion or state exists **among** a group of people, they have it or experience it. *The previous ruling has already caused unease among the clergy... Persian cats are very popular amongst Western cat lovers.*
6 PREP If something is divided **among** a number of people, they all get a part of it. *He expected power to be divided among several parties after the election. ...resources fragmented amongst countries.*
7 PREP If people talk, fight, or agree **among** themselves, they do it together, without involving anyone else. *Many stood in small groups talking among themselves, trying to sort out their feelings... They will decide to take civil action amongst themselves.*

amongst /əˈmʌŋst/
PREP **Amongst** means the same as **among**.

amoral /ˌeɪˈmɒrəl/
ADJ Someone who is **amoral** does not care whether what they do is right or wrong. *...the impeccably moral son of an infamously amoral father... They were clever amoral politicans.*

amorous /ˈæmərəs/
ADJ **Amorous** feelings and behaviour involve sexual desire. *...February the 29th, the day when amorous ladies are entitled to make marriage proposals.*

amorphous /əˈmɔːfəs/
ADJ Something that is **amorphous** has no clear shape or structure. *...the amorphous entity known as the general public.*

amount /əˈmaʊnt/ **amounts, amounting, amounted**
1 NC An **amount** of something is how much of it you have, need, or get. *...the amount of potatoes that people buy... I was horrified by the amount of work I had to do.*
2 V+to If something **amounts** to a particular total, all the parts of it add up to that total. *Losses in tanks and armoured vehicles amounted to 426 vehicles captured and 380 destroyed. ...very high fees which amount to £2,000.*

amp /æmp/ **amps**
1 NC An **amp** is the unit used for measuring electric current. **Amp** is an abbreviation for 'ampère'. *...electrical currents of a million amps.*
2 NC An **amp** is also the same as an **amplifier**; an informal use. *...a small practice amp.*

ampère /ˈæmpeə/ **ampères**
NC An **ampère** is a unit which is used for measuring electric current; a technical term in physics. *A nano-ampère is a billionth of an ampère.*

amphetamine /æmˈfetəmiːn/ **amphetamines**
N PL or NU **Amphetamines** are a group of drugs which increase people's energy and make them excited. *There's been a sharp rise in illegal amphetamines... Cannabis is the most popular drug of abuse and amphetamine is second. ...amphetamine derivatives.*

amphibian /æmˈfɪbɪən/ **amphibians**
NC An **amphibian** is an animal such as a frog that can live both on land and in water. *There may be a link between fish and the early amphibians that crawled onto land.*

amphibious /æmˈfɪbɪəs/
ADJ Something that is **amphibious** can live or function on land and in water. *...species such as the amphibious phytosaur. ...the amphibious Volkswagen car.*

amphitheatre /ˈæmfɪθɪətə/ **amphitheatres**; spelt **amphitheater** in American English.
NC An **amphitheatre** is a large, circular, open area with sloping sides which is used for theatrical performances. *Archaeologists have finally discovered the site of the city's Roman amphitheatre.*

ample /ˈæmpl/
1 ADJ If there is an **ample** amount of something, there is more than enough of it. *This leaves her ample time to prepare... They keep tabs on supplies and demand, and say supplies right now are ample.* ♦ **amply** ADV *This has been amply demonstrated over the past few years.*
2 ADJ ATTRIB **Ample** also means large. *There was provision for an ample lawn... The first unofficial returns had by then indicated an ample margin of victory for him.*

amplifier /ˈæmplɪfaɪə/ **amplifiers**
NC An **amplifier** is an electronic device in a radio or stereo system, which causes sounds or signals to become louder. *Mick Jagger used a guitar and amplifier to illustrate the way he composes songs.*

amplify /ˈæmplɪfaɪ/ **amplifies, amplifying, amplified**
1 VO If you **amplify** a sound, you make it louder. *These signals are then amplified... Ordinary hearing aids work by amplifying all the sounds that the microphone picks up.*
2 VO If you **amplify** an idea, statement, or account of an event, you add more to it, or emphasize what you have already said about it. *He did not amplify his remarks beyond saying things could get much worse...*

Many theoretical scenarios get amplified here because reporters have very little to report. ◆ **amplification** /æmplɪfɪkeɪʃn/ NU His story needed confirmation and amplification.

ampoule /æmpuːl/ **ampoules**; spelt **ampule** in American English.
NC An **ampoule** is a small container, usually made of glass, that contains a medicine. Ampoules of vaccines are sold in thousands and hundreds of doses... It's a cheap and simple device to stop doctors and nurses cutting themselves on broken ampoules.

amputate /æmpjʊteɪt/ **amputates, amputating, amputated**
VO or V If surgeons **amputate** a part of someone's body, they cut it off. There was still a danger the arm would have to be amputated... They tried to amputate, but it was trapped so tightly, they couldn't get to it. ◆ **amputation** /æmpjʊteɪʃn/ **amputations** NC or NU One of the surgeons performed 25 amputations in 15 days. ...punishments such as amputation and flogging.

amputee /æmpjʊtiː/ **amputees**
NC An **amputee** is someone who has had a limb removed surgically. The workshop could be used in the future to help other amputees adjust.

Amsterdam /æmstədæm/
Amsterdam is the capital of the Netherlands (the seat of government is The Hague) and its largest city. Population: 695,000 (1989).

amuck /əmʌk/. See amok.

amulet /æmjʊlət/ **amulets**
NC An **amulet** is a small object that you wear because you believe it will protect you from evil or injury. The men wore bead necklaces and amulets to protect them.

amuse /əmjuːz/ **amuses, amusing, amused**
1 VO If something **amuses** you, it makes you want to laugh or smile. He laughed as if the idea amused him... The remark particularly amused the Chinese delegation. ● See also **amusing**.
2 V-REFL or VO If you **amuse** yourself, or if someone **amuses** you, you do something in order to pass the time and not become bored. Sam amused himself by throwing branches into the fire. ...holding the dog as if it was a baby she was trying to amuse.

amused /əmjuːzd/
ADJ If you are **amused** at or by something, it makes you want to laugh or smile. I was highly amused by a comment Shaw made. ...an amused stare.

amusement /əmjuːzmənt/ **amusements**
1 NU **Amusement** is the feeling of pleasure that you have when you think that something is funny or when something entertains or interests you. She smiled in amusement... All the papers have been following with great amusement the antics of the charity event, Comic Relief... Every kind of facility was laid on for their amusement.
2 NC **Amusements** are ways of passing the time pleasantly. I tried to teach her tennis so we would have more amusements in common. ...a dozen coin-in-the-slot amusements.

amusement arcade, amusement arcades
NC An **amusement arcade** is a large room containing electronic machines that you can play games on, and sometimes win money. Computer games are already common in amusement arcades and pubs.

amusement park, amusement parks
NC An **amusement park** is a large outdoor area containing games, fairground rides, and other forms of entertainment. Plans to turn it into a Disney-style amusement park have been rejected.

amusing /əmjuːzɪŋ/
ADJ Someone or something that is **amusing** makes you laugh or smile. There was an amusing story in the paper. ...a light-hearted and amusing ballet set to the music of Scott Joplin. ◆ **amusingly** ADV He talked lightly and amusingly. ● See also **amuse**.

an /ən, æn/
DET **An** is used instead of 'a', the indefinite article, when the word that follows begins with a vowel sound: see a.

anachronism /ənækrənɪzəm/ **anachronisms**
1 NC An **anachronism** is something that you think is old-fashioned and no longer useful or significant. The English public schools are an anachronism... America's strict travel requirements have become something of an anachronism.
2 NU or NC **Anachronism** is the representation of something in a book, film, or play, in a historical period in which it could not have existed. The costumes are simply effective, not distracting in their anachronism... If errors and anachronisms do occur in this work, I take full responsibility for them.

anachronistic /ənækrənɪstɪk/
1 ADJ Something that is **anachronistic** is out of date or old-fashioned. ...a peculiarly anachronistic view of communism.
2 ADJ You can describe something as **anachronistic** when it is wrong because it could not have happened or existed in the historical period stated. His performances of Scarlatti's sonatas infuriate the historically-minded by their anachronistic expressive devices.

anaemia /əniːmiə/; also spelt **anemia**.
NU If you have **anaemia**, you do not have enough red cells in your blood, so that you feel tired and look pale. Two children are desperately ill with malaria-induced anaemia.

anaemic /əniːmɪk/; also spelt **anemic**.
ADJ Someone who is **anaemic** is suffering from anaemia. Patients on long-term dialysis become anaemic.

anaesthesia /ænəsθiːziə/; also spelt **anesthesia**.
NU **Anaesthesia** is the use of anaesthetics in medicine and surgery. The operation can only be carried out under anaesthesia. ...a specialist in anaesthesia.

anaesthetic /ænəsθetɪk/ **anaesthetics**; also spelt **anesthetic**.
NC or NU An **anaesthetic** is a drug that stops you feeling pain, particularly during an operation. When dentists administer anaesthetics, they use a disposable needle... Most abortions are carried out without anaesthetic.

anaesthetist /əniːsθətɪst/ **anaesthetists**; also spelt **anesthetist**.
NC An **anaesthetist** is a doctor who specializes in giving anaesthetics. Both anaesthetists are accused of tampering with the equipment.

anaesthetize /əniːsθətaɪz/ **anaesthetizes, anaesthetizing, anaesthetized**; also spelt **anaesthetise** or **anesthetize**.
VO If a doctor **anaesthetizes** someone, they make them unconscious by giving them an anaesthetic. He had to anaesthetize patients suffering from heart attacks, broken limbs and cancer.

anagram /ænəgræm/ **anagrams**
NC An **anagram** is a word or phrase that has been formed by changing the order of the letters in another word or phrase. For example, 'triangle' is an anagram of 'integral'. Crossword clues became inscrutably devious, packed with puns and anagrams.

anal /eɪnl/
ADJ ATTRIB **Anal** means relating to the anus.

analgesic /ænældʒiːzɪk/ **analgesics**
NC An **analgesic** is a drug that lessens the effect of pain. 20 per cent of women needed a mild analgesic during childbirth. ▶ Also ADJ ATTRIB This has very good analgesic properties and will help to reduce pain.

analogous /ənæləgəs/
ADJ If one thing is **analogous** to another, the two things are similar in some way. They discard the eggs in a process analogous to abortion.

analogue /ænəlɒg/ **analogues**; also spelt **analog**, especially for the meaning in paragraph 3.
1 NC If one thing is an **analogue** of another, the two things are similar in some way. Beta-carotene is an analogue of Vitamin A... Researchers have been keen to find analogues on earth for the sulphur lakes found on Jupiter.
2 ADJ ATTRIB An **analogue** watch or clock indicates the time by means of a pointer that moves round a dial. ...a conventional analogue watch.
3 ADJ ATTRIB An **analogue** device measures information using a variable voltage, rather than one which is fixed; a technical term in physics.

...thousands of different operations which analogue circuits can perform.

analogy /ənǽlədʒi/ **analogies**
NC If you make or draw an **analogy** between two things, you show that they are similar. *So, to use a military analogy, cells come along like soldiers and engage in combat with the parasite.*

analyse /ǽnəlaɪz/ **analyses, analysing, analysed**; also spelt **analyze**.
1 vo If you **analyse** something, you consider it or examine it in order to understand it or to find out what it consists of. *...a five-hour meeting to analyse the country's worsening economic problem... A supercomputer of vast capacity helps to analyze the data from the radio-telescope... Adrian Porter in Washington analyses what appears to be a new development in United States policy.*
2 vo When a psychiatrist **analyses** a patient, he or she gets them to talk about their feelings and their past in order to discover feelings or experiences which may be causing problems for the patient. *She's now being analysed by her ex-husband.*

analysis /ənǽləsɪs/ **analyses** /ənǽləsiːz/
1 NUorNC **Analysis** is the process of considering something in order to understand it or explain what it consists of. *The device will take up to ten samples for analysis. ...a historical analysis of World War Two.*
2 NU **Analysis** is also the process of analysing someone who is mentally ill or emotionally disturbed in order to cure them. *...adults broke through their emotional hang-ups in analysis.*
3 You say **in the final analysis** or **in the last analysis** to indicate that your statement is a summary of the basic facts of a situation. *He describes Mrs Currie as ambitious, talented, headstrong and in the last analysis, too indiscreet... In the final analysis, power rested in the hands of one man.*

analyst /ǽnəlɪst/ **analysts**
1 NC An **analyst** is someone who is a specialist in a particular subject and gives opinions about it. *Analysts estimate that sixteen thousand jobs have now been lost. ...an interview with the political analyst Leon Onikov... Military analysts say the new administration will have to go a lot further than that.*
2 NC An **analyst** is also a doctor who examines and treats people who are emotionally disturbed. *An analyst can only help a patient who tries to help themselves.*

analytic /ǽnəlɪtɪk/
ADJ **Analytic** means the same as **analytical**.

analytical /ǽnəlɪtɪkl/
ADJ **Analytical** refers to the use of logical reasoning to discuss or solve problems. *Certain newspapers were asked to reduce the analytical content of their editorials.* ◆ **analytically** SUBMOD *You can be analytically intelligent but uncreative.*

analyze /ǽnəlaɪz/. See **analyse**.

anarchic /ənɑːkɪk/
ADJ **Anarchic** means paying no attention to rules or laws that everyone else obeys and believes in. *The situation was anarchic, and dangerous for the country. ...a uniquely anarchic style of comedy.*

anarchism /ǽnəkɪzəm/
NU **Anarchism** is the political belief that people should not be controlled by laws or the power of government, but should work together freely. *Anarchism was the vogue among students and intellectuals until it was replaced by Marxism... Victorian England contained squalor, poverty, anarchism, and terror.* ◆ **anarchist** /ǽnəkɪst/ **anarchists** NC *Anarchists oppose the organised violence of war.*

anarchy /ǽnəki/
NU **Anarchy** is a situation where nobody obeys rules or laws. *...his will to reverse the drift into anarchy and economic chaos.*

anathema /ənǽθəmə/
NU If something is **anathema** to you, you disapprove of it very strongly. *Such thoughts are anathema to the Romanian leader... The idea of separate armies is a complete anathema to Mr Gorbachov.*

anatomical /ǽnətɒmɪkl/
ADJ ATTRIB **Anatomical** means relating to the structure of the bodies of people and animals. *...the development of male and female anatomical features.*

anatomy /ənǽtəmi/ **anatomies**
1 NCorNU Someone's **anatomy** is the structure of their body. *If we think about how animals survive and the way they live, their anatomy reflects what they are doing... His studies of human and animal anatomy are included in the exhibition.*
2 NU **Anatomy** is the study of the structure of the bodies of people or animals. *Some scientists have applied the principles of physics, anatomy, and evolution to find out why.*
3 NC An **anatomy** of a particular subject or idea is an examination or investigation of it. *...a fascinating anatomy of the political system.*

-ance /-əns/
SUFFIX **-ance** and **-ancy** replace '-ant' at the end of adjectives to form nouns that refer to the state or quality that is described by the adjective. *...his academic brilliance. ...the buoyancy of the economy.*

ancestor /ǽnsestə/ **ancestors**
1 NC Your **ancestors** are the people you are descended from. *...the religious and philosophical wisdom of our ancestors.*
2 NC An **ancestor** of something modern is an earlier thing from which it developed. *The hot-water dwelling eocytes are the common ancestors of all life today.*

ancestral /ænsestrəl/
ADJ ATTRIB **Ancestral** means relating to your family in former times. *The relics were unexpectedly discovered at the Caernarvon ancestral home, Highclere Castle.*

ancestry /ǽnsestri/ **ancestries**
NC Your **ancestry** is the people from whom you are descended. *Mr Fujimori's Japanese ancestry has ensured him a sympathetic hearing.*

anchor /ǽŋkə/ **anchors, anchoring, anchored**
1 NC An **anchor** is a heavy hooked object attached to a chain that is dropped from a boat into the water to make the boat stay in one place. *A fifteen thousand ton cargo ship is being towed back towards Falmouth after losing her anchor in heavy seas off the Cornish coast.* ● When a boat **drops anchor**, it lowers its anchor over the side because it is going to stay in one place for a while. *They dropped anchor a few hours ago.*
2 V-ERG When a boat **anchors** or when you **anchor** it, its anchor is dropped into the water to make it stay in one place. *The light must be switched on whenever the boat anchors... They anchored their boat about a mile and a half away from Sellafield.*
3 vo If you **anchor** an object, you prevent it from moving by fixing it firmly to something that is stationary. *Wind breaks and sun shelters have to be anchored to the ground or else you spend all day grimly hanging on to them. ...whether airliner seats are anchored strongly enough to the floor to resist the impact of a crash landing.*
4 NC An **anchor** of a radio or television broadcast is a person, usually based in a studio, who acts as a link between different parts of a programme. *He worked in the news division of ABC and was the anchor of its 15 minute evening newscast. ...men and women grouped round three workstations where they're writing the anchors' news scripts.* ▶ Also vo *In 1946 he came back to New York to anchor the 'World News Roundup' on radio... From 1962 until 1981, Mr Cronkite anchored the 'CBS Evening News'.*

anchorage /ǽŋkərɪdʒ/ **anchorages**
NC An **anchorage** is a place where a boat can remain stationary. *A North Sea oil storage vessel broke from its anchorage... The Soviets have to rely on temporary anchorages off the North African coast.*

anchor man, anchor men; also spelt **anchorman**.
NC An **anchor man** of a radio or television broadcast is a person, usually based in a studio, who acts as a link between different parts of a programme and, for example, maintains contact with people and reporters who are outside the studio. *At the moment he is an anchor man without any television programme to anchor... Why do you think they chose him to be the first television anchorman?*

anchovy /ˈæntʃəvi/ **anchovies**
NC An **anchovy** is a very small fish with a strong, salty taste. *...anchovies on toast. ...anchovy paste.*

ancient /ˈeɪnʃənt/
1 ADJ **Ancient** things belong to the distant past. *...a hoard of ancient Egyptian relics. ...ancient Greece and Rome.*
2 ADJ You also use **ancient** to describe things that are very old or that have a long history. *He came from an ancient Catholic family. ...the country's ancient capital, Sucre.*

ancillary /ˈænsɪləri/
ADJ ATTRIB **Ancillary** workers in an institution or company are people whose work supports the main work of the institution. *The pay increases will not provide more money for porters, cleaners, and other ancillary health service staff.*

-ancy /-ənsi/. See **-ance.**

and /ən, ənd, ænd/
1 CONJ You use **and** to link two or more words, groups, or clauses. *...my mother and father... I came here in 1972 and have lived here ever since... It was lovely and warm outside.*
2 CONJ You also use **and** to link two identical words or phrases to emphasize their degree or to suggest that something continues or increases over a period of time. *He became more and more annoyed... We talked for hours and hours... Her marks are getting worse and worse.*
3 CONJ **And** indicates that two numbers are to be added together. *Two and two is four... What's six and eight?*
4 CONJ **And** links two statements about events which follow each other. *He opened the car door and got out... She finished her Coke and put the bottle down under the bench.*
5 CONJ **And** also links two statements that contrast with each other. *I meant to buy some tea yesterday and I forgot... It can be difficult when you do not think something is important and someone else does.*
6 CONJ You use **and** to link two clauses when the second clause is the result of the first one. *Do as you're told and you'll be all right... Expect everything to go wrong and you won't feel quite so bad when it does.*
7 CONJ You also use **and** to interrupt yourself in order to make a comment on what you are saying. *Finally—and I really ought to stop in a minute—I wish to tell a little story... Some people, and I make no criticisms at all, have not been around much lately.*
8 CONJ **And** also introduces a question which relates directly to what someone else has just said. *'I was born at our house in Norfolk.'—'And did you like it there?'... 'I don't think he felt well.'—'And Sam Potter?'—'Same thing.'*
9 CONJ **And** is used by broadcasters and people making announcements when they start talking about a topic they have just mentioned, or when they are telling you what is happening. *And now it's time for 'Any Questions'... Football—and Manchester City are in the final of the European Cup.*
10 CONJ **And** is also used before a fraction that comes after a whole number. *Two and a half years... Eleven and three sixteenths.*
11 CONJ You use **and** in numbers larger than one hundred. **And** comes after the word 'hundred', 'thousand', and so on, and before a number between 1 and 99. *...three hundred and fifty people. ...a thousand and one. ...sixteen thousand five hundred and thirty-one.*

andante /ænˈdænti/ **andantes**
ADV **Andante** written above a piece of music means it should be played quite slowly. *...playing Strauss andante.* ► Also N SING *I think he played the andante much too fast, don't you?* ► Also ADJ ATTRIB *...a long andante section.*

Andorra /ænˈdɔːrə/
The **Principality of Andorra** is a country in southern Europe, on the border between France and Spain. It was formed as a co-principality in 1278. The co-princes are the President of France and the Bishop of Urgel. Oscar Ribas Reig became President in 1990. There are no political parties. Andorra is a neutral country. Tourism and banking are the main industries.
♦ **Andorran** /ænˈdɔːrən/ N, ADJ
▪ *per capita GDP:* US$9,834 ▪ *religion:* Christianity (mainly Roman Catholic) ▪ *language:* Catalan (official), French, Castillian Spanish ▪ *currency:* French franc, Spanish peseta ▪ *capital:* Andorra la Vella ▪ *population:* 50,528 (1989) (70% of the population are foreign residents) ▪ *size:* 467 square kilometres.

Andorra La Vella /ænˈdɔːrə lɑː ˈvɛljə/
Andorra La Vella is the capital of Andorra and its largest city. Population: 20,000 (1990).

Andreotti, Giulio /dʒuːliəʊ ænˈdreɪɒti/
Giulio Andreotti became Prime Minister of Italy in 1989. He previously served as Prime Minister from 1972 to 1973, and from 1976 to 1979. He was Minister of Foreign Affairs from 1983 to 1989. He has held numerous Cabinet posts since 1954, when he became Minister of the Interior. He is a member of the Christian Democrats (DC). Born: 1919.

androgynous /ænˈdrɒdʒənəs/
ADJ An **androgynous** person, animal, or plant has both male and female characteristics; a formal word. *It is all held together by her mesmerising, androgynous performance.*

anecdotal /ˌænɪkˈdəʊtl/
ADJ **Anecdotal** evidence or observations are not supported by definite facts, but are based on accounts which are not completely accurate or reliable. *Much of the evidence is patchy and anecdotal... Lintner's approach throughout the book is anecdotal rather than analytical.*

anecdote /ˈænɪkdəʊt/ **anecdotes**
1 NCorNU An **anecdote** is a short, entertaining account of something that has happened. *Every Londoner has a joke or anecdote based on that inescapable theme, 'the delay'... Travelling is always a rich source of anecdote.*
2 NCorNU An **anecdote** is also an account that is not completely accurate or reliable because it is not based on definite facts. *He claimed to have kept a copy of the film, but this anecdote was soon shown to be nonsense... It would be possible to say that this has been the case, at least on the basis of gossip and anecdote.*

anemia /əˈniːmiə/. See **anaemia.**
anemic /əˈniːmɪk/. See **anaemic.**
anemone /əˈnɛməni/ **anemones**
NC An **anemone** is a garden plant with red, purple, or white flowers.

anesthesia /ˌænəsˈθiːziə/. See **anaesthesia.**
anesthetic /ˌænəsˈθɛtɪk/. See **anaesthetic.**
anesthetist /əˈniːsθətɪst/. See **anaesthetist.**
anesthetize /əˈniːsθətaɪz/. See **anaesthetize.**
anew /əˈnjuː/
ADV If you do something **anew**, you do it again, often in a different way; a literary word. *...starting life anew in a fresh place.*

angel /ˈeɪndʒəl/ **angels**
1 NC **Angels** are spiritual beings that some people believe are God's messengers and servants in heaven. *One of the paintings depicts swirling figures, a winged angel and a band of musicians in heaven.*
2 NC If you call someone an **angel**, you mean that they are very good, kind, and considerate. *The nurses resent being called angels, they are ordinary human beings.* ● See also **guardian angel.**

angelic /ænˈdʒɛlɪk/
ADJ You can describe someone as **angelic** when they are very good, kind, and gentle. *McEnroe's behaviour was close to angelic against the former world number one.*

anger /ˈæŋɡə/ **angers, angering, angered**
1 NU **Anger** is the strong emotion that you feel when you think someone has behaved in such an unfair, cruel, and insulting way that you want to express your feelings towards them in a forceful or violent way. *'You're a fool.'—'Am I?' he said, red with anger. ...an explosive sense of injustice and anger... Unionist politicians have expressed anger at the decision.*
2 VO If someone or something **angers** you, they make you angry. *His hostile attitude angered her.*

angina /ændʒaɪnə/
NU **Angina** is severe pain in a person's chest and left arm, caused by heart disease. ...*waiting for cardiac surgery for angina.*

angle /æŋgl/ **angles, angling, angled**
1 NC An **angle** is the difference in direction between two lines or surfaces. Angles are measured in degrees. ...*an angle of 45 degrees.* ● If something is at **an angle**, it is not straight, horizontal, or vertical. *Will it cut the wood at an angle, or do you have to hold it perfectly horizontal?... The water butts were leaning at a crazy angle.* ● See also **right angle**.
2 NC An **angle** is also the shape that is created where two lines or surfaces join together. *In some of his best known paintings, the variation in angle and composition are almost non-existent.*
3 NC A particular **angle** is the position or direction from which you look at something. *He held the vase close to his face, peering at it from all angles.*
4 NC+SUPP You can refer to a way of presenting something, for example in a newspaper, as a particular **angle**. *The play's pacifist angle had a great appeal... I would state the problem as I see it from the political angle.*
5 V+*for* If you **angle** for something, you try to make someone offer it to you without asking for it directly. *He got the invitation to Washington he had been angling for.*
6 See also **angling**.

angler /æŋglə/ **anglers**
NC An **angler** is someone who fishes with a fishing rod as a hobby. *The missiles were discovered by anglers fishing off the southern coast.*

Anglican /æŋglɪkən/ **Anglicans**
NC An **Anglican** is a Christian who is a member of the Church of England. *There are sixty thousand Anglicans in Japan.* ► Also ADJ ...*an Anglican bishop.*

anglicize /æŋglɪsaɪz/ **anglicizes, anglicizing, anglicized**; also spelt **anglicise**.
VO To **anglicize** something means to make it follow English customs and practice. *He was the one who anglicized the family name. ...governed by an anglicized elite.*

angling /æŋglɪŋ/
NU **Angling** is the activity of fishing with a fishing rod. *I have recently taken up sea angling.*

Anglo- /æŋgləʊ-/
PREFIX **Anglo-** is added to adjectives indicating nationality to form adjectives which describe something which involves relations between Britain or England and another country. ...*the 1921 Anglo-Irish treaty.*

Angola /æŋgəʊlə/
The **People's Republic of Angola** is a country in south-western Africa. It was a Portuguese colony from the 15th century until it became independent in 1975. The Popular Movement for the Liberation of Angola—Workers' Party (MPLA-PT) was the sole legal party from 1975 until 1991. José Eduardo dos Santos became President in 1979. The MPLA-PT was supported by the USSR and Cuba in the war against UNITA (National Union for Total Independence of Angola). UNITA was led by Dr Jonas Savimbi and was supported by the USA and South Africa. In 1991 a ceasefire ended the civil war and political parties were legalized. Angola exports oil, diamonds, and coffee. It is a member of the Organization of African Unity. ◆ **Angolan** /æŋgəʊlən/ N, ADJ
▪ *per capita GDP:* approximately US$531 ▪ *religion:* animism, Christianity ▪ *language:* Portuguese (official) ▪ *currency:* kwanza ▪ *capital:* Luanda ▪ *population:* 10 million (1989) ▪ *size:* 1,246,700 square kilometres.

angora /æŋgɔːrə/ **angoras**
1 NC An **angora** goat, rabbit, or cat is a particular breed with long silky hair. ...*a fluffy Turkish angora.*
2 N+N **Angora** cloth or clothing is made from the hair of the angora goat or rabbit.

angry /æŋgri/ **angrier, angriest**
ADJ When you are **angry**, you feel strong emotion about something that you consider unfair, cruel, or insulting. *The mayor was murdered by an angry mob... The move is certain to provoke an angry*

response... There was also opposition from Republicans who were angry at proposed tax increases.* ◆ **angrily** ADV *The story was angrily denied by the dead man's family.*

Anguilla /æŋgwɪlə/
Anguilla is a territory of the United Kingdom in the Caribbean. It was a British colony from 1650 until 1967, when St Christopher-Nevis-Anguilla were granted internal self-government. Anguilla withdrew from the federation and became a dependent territory of the UK in 1980. Lobsters and fish are exported. Tourism and banking are important industries. ◆ **Anguillan** /æŋgwɪlən/ N, ADJ
▪ *Religion:* Christianity ▪ *language:* English (official) ▪ *currency:* East Caribbean dollar ▪ *capital:* The Valley ▪ *population:* 7,500 (1990) ▪ *size:* 96 square kilometres.

anguish /æŋgwɪʃ/
NU **Anguish** is great mental or physical suffering. ...*a quarrel which caused her intense unhappiness and anguish... The Foreign Office said that it understood the anguish of relatives of the hostages.*

anguished /æŋgwɪʃt/
ADJ **Anguished** means feeling or showing great mental or physical suffering. *The anguished cries continued.*

angular /æŋgjʊlə/
ADJ ATTRIB **Angular** things have shapes that seem to contain a lot of straight lines and sharp points. *Hooper listened, his angular face placid. ...the angular church steeple in the town square.*

animal /ænɪml/ **animals**
1 NC An **animal** is a living creature such as a dog, or horse, rather than a bird, fish, insect, or human. *They used to hunt wild animals.*
2 NC An **animal** is also any living thing that is not a plant. ...*the complex social hierarchies observed in all animals, including humans. ...the animal kingdom.*
3 ADJ ATTRIB **Animal** qualities or feelings relate to your physical nature and instincts rather than your mind. *Animal instinct warned me to tread carefully.*
4 NC If you refer to someone as an **animal**, you mean that you think their behaviour is unpleasant or disgusting. *Her husband was an animal.*

animate, animates, animating, animated; pronounced /ænɪmət/ when it is an adjective and /ænɪmeɪt/ when it is a verb.
1 ADJ Something that is **animate** has life, in contrast to things like stones and machines which do not. ...*an animate, living organism.*
2 VO To **animate** something means to make it lively or more cheerful. *An identical expression of amusement animated their faces... Society is not merely a passive mass, to be animated by the Communist Party.*

animated /ænɪmeɪtɪd/
1 ADJ Someone or something that is **animated** is lively and interesting. *Mr Martens described the meeting as animated... Kenneth was well-known to World Service listeners for his animated performance in the quiz show 'Just a Minute'.*
2 ADJ An **animated** film is one in which puppets or drawings appear to move around. ...*an animated cartoon.*

animation /ænɪmeɪʃn/ **animations**
1 NU **Animation** is the process of making films in which drawings or puppets appear to move. ...*a highly acclaimed video that blended animation and pictures together.*
2 NU Someone with **animation** behaves in a lively way. *This normally gloomy street is tonight alive with animation and excitement.*
3 NC An **animation** is a film in which drawings or puppets appear to move. *The animation was startlingly original, surreal in places, and magical overall. ...another in the series of animations from one of Britain's leading studios.*
4 See also **suspended animation**.

animator /ænɪmeɪtə/ **animators**
NC An **animator** is a person who makes films using puppets and drawings rather than real people. *The cartoon character Mickey Mouse gave the famous animator his first success.*

animism /ˈænɪmɪzəm/
NU **Animism** is the belief that everything in the universe is alive and has feelings and emotions, including objects such as stones or trees. *...a region where Islam co-exists with Christianity and animism. ...this natural animism that we experience as children.*

animosity /ˌænɪˈmɒsəti/
NU **Animosity** is a feeling of strong dislike and anger. *There is a long history of animosity between the two nations... Troop movements along the frontier have continued to fuel animosity.*

animus /ˈænɪməs/
N SING An **animus** is a feeling of strong dislike for someone. *He may have some kind of animus against you.*

aniseed /ˈænɪsiːd/
NU **Aniseed** is a substance made from the liquorice-flavoured seeds of a plant. It is used as a flavouring in sweets, drinks, and medicines.

Ankara /ˈæŋkərə/
Ankara is the capital of Turkey and its second largest city. Population: 3,236,626 (1990).

ankle /ˈæŋkl/ **ankles**
NC Your **ankle** is the joint where your foot joins your leg. *Edberg injured his ankle in practice last week.*

annals /ˈænlz/
N PL+SUPP The **annals** of a nation or society are the recorded events of its past; a formal word. *...the most improbable soldiers in the annals of military history.*

annex, annexes, annexing, annexed; pronounced /əˈnɛks/ when it is a verb and /ˈænɛks/ when it is a noun.
1 VO If a country **annexes** another country or an area of land, it seizes it and takes control of it. *The Soviet Union annexed the islands from Japan at the end of the Second World War.* ♦ **annexation** /ˌænɛkˈseɪʃn/ NU *...the annexation of Hawaii.*
2 NC An **annex** is the same as an **annexe**.

annexe /ˈænɛks/ **annexes**; also spelt **annex**.
NC An **annexe** is a building which is joined to or is next to a larger main building. *The paintings will be housed in an annexe of the Prado Museum.*

annihilate /əˈnaɪəleɪt/ **annihilates, annihilating, annihilated**
VO If something is **annihilated**, it is destroyed completely. *What would happen if the human race should be annihilated?* ♦ **annihilation** /əˌnaɪəˈleɪʃn/ NU *...threatening the total annihilation of the planet.*

anniversary /ˌænɪˈvɜːsərɪ/ **anniversaries**
NC An **anniversary** is a date which is remembered or celebrated because a special event happened on that date in a previous year. *...his wedding anniversary.*

annotate /ˈænəteɪt/ **annotates, annotating, annotated**
VO If a piece of writing is **annotated**, extra notes are added to it, for example to explain it more fully. *Researchers started annotating King's student papers.* ♦ **annotated** ADJ *...an annotated chronology of Christian history. ...an annotated reading list for those who want to pursue the subject further.*

annotation /ˌænəˈteɪʃn/ **annotations**
1 NC An **annotation** is a note that is added to a piece of writing, often in order to explain it. *...a cryptic pencil annotation.*
2 NU **Annotation** is the activity of adding notes to a piece of writing.

announce /əˈnaʊns/ **announces, announcing, announced**
1 VO or V-REPORT If you **announce** something, you tell people about it publicly or officially. *Mr Heath announced his decision... Mr Chirac interrupted a rally to announce that the hostages are free... The short-list for the Booker prize for literature has just been announced.*
2 VO, V-REPORT, or V-QUOTE If you **announce** something, you say it in a deliberate and often aggressive way. *I phoned the Major to announce my plans... His wife announced she was having contractions... 'I am Mrs Jones,' she announced.*
3 VO, V-REPORT, or V-QUOTE If you **announce** something in a public place, you tell people about it by means of a loudspeaker or Tannoy system. *As soon as the train to Hong Kong was announced, people poured onto the platform... They announced his plane was delayed...*

The cabin speaker announced, 'Preparing to separate from lower stage.'

announcement /əˈnaʊnsmənt/ **announcements**
1 NC An **announcement** is a public statement which gives information about something that has or will happen. *The Government announcement gave details of small increases in taxes... They were told to leave on Friday, but no public announcement was made.*
2 N SING The **announcement** of something is the act of telling people about it. *...the events which follow the announcement of your resignation.*

announcer /əˈnaʊnsə/ **announcers**
NC An **announcer** is someone who introduces programmes on radio or television. *The announcer's script had an addition signed by Wu Xiaoyong.*

annoy /əˈnɔɪ/ **annoys, annoying, annoyed**
VO If someone **annoys** you, they make you fairly angry and impatient. *You're just saying that to annoy me... The move has annoyed French soldiers already annoyed by bans on alcohol and pin-ups.* ● See also **annoying**.

annoyance /əˈnɔɪəns/
NU **Annoyance** is the feeling that you get when someone makes you feel fairly angry or impatient. *Sir Geoffrey has expressed annoyance at the delay... To the annoyance of his enemies, he's displaying considerable confidence.*

annoyed /əˈnɔɪd/
ADJ PRED If you are **annoyed**, you are fairly angry about something. *She shook her head, annoyed with herself for forgetting... Diplomats are annoyed at Mr Cordovez's more outspoken comments.*

annoying /əˈnɔɪɪŋ/
ADJ An **annoying** person or action makes you feel fairly angry and impatient. *It was annoying to be corrected by him all the time... It's the sort of annoying noise that people are used to hearing.*

annual /ˈænjuəl/ **annuals**
1 ADJ ATTRIB **Annual** means happening or done once every year. *He was speaking at the annual conference of the Police Federation. ...her annual holiday... The National Weather Service has produced its annual 90-day winter forecast.* ♦ **annually** ADV *Independence day is celebrated annually... Japanese defence reports are released annually.*
2 ADJ ATTRIB **Annual** also means calculated over a period of one year. *The perfume now produces annual profits of seventy million dollars. ...an annual income of twelve thousand dollars... There's been a sharp fall in the annual rate of inflation.* ♦ **annually** ADV *They import 500 million tonnes of crude oil annually... Around twelve million people visit the area annually.*
3 NC An **annual** is a book or magazine that is published once a year. *His work has been included in two out of three official Hayward Annuals.*
4 NC If a plant is an **annual**, it grows, flowers, and produces seeds, then dies within one year. *Some tropical species will grow there, but only as annuals... After flowering, annuals start to concentrate their food supplies into the seeds.*

annuity /əˈnjuːəti/ **annuities**
NC An **annuity** is a financial investment that pays out a fixed sum of money each year. *...to ensure a guaranteed income by the purchase of an annuity.*

annul /əˈnʌl/ **annuls, annulling, annulled**
VO If a contract or result is **annulled**, it is declared invalid, so that legally it is considered never to have existed. *The government announced that last Sunday's election results had been annulled... Such a move would have annulled a court ruling under which the party was outlawed.*

annulment /əˈnʌlmənt/ **annulments**
NU or NC **Annulment** of a contract or result is an official declaration that it is invalid, so that legally it is considered never to have existed. *This applies whether your marriage has ended by death, divorce, or annulment... Opposition parties called the ballot a farce and asked for an annulment.*

annum /ˈænəm/. See **per annum**.

Annunciation /əˌnʌnsiˈeɪʃn/
N PROP In Christian belief, the **Annunciation** is the announcement described in the Bible when Mary is

told that she will give birth to the Son of God. ...*two versions of 'The Annunciation of Christ' by El Greco.*

anode /ǽnəʊd/ **anodes**
NC An **anode** is the positive electrode in a cell such as a battery; a technical term in physics.

anodyne /ǽnədaɪn/ **anodynes**; a formal word.
1 ADJ Something that is **anodyne** is neutral, not dangerous or distressing. *We kept the talk on a safely anodyne level.*
2 N SING An **anodyne** is something that lessens or prevents the effects of distress or unhappiness. *He used to speak of work as 'the great anodyne'.*

anoint /ənɔ́ɪnt/ **anoints, anointing, anointed**
VO To **anoint** someone means to pour oil or another liquid on them as part of a religious ceremony. *They saved their most precious oils to anoint his feet.*

anomalous /ənɒ́mələs/
ADJ Something that is **anomalous** is different from what is normal or expected; a formal word. *These calculations have given anomalous results... His position as minister in charge of restructuring the economy was always rather anomalous.*

anomaly /ənɒ́məli/ **anomalies**
NC If something is an **anomaly**, it is different from what is normal or expected. *There was an anomaly making the theory unsatisfactory... It is easy to criticize the elections as being undemocratic when such anomalies occur.*

anon. /ənɒ́n/
Anon. is often written after poems or music to indicate that the author is not known. **Anon.** is an abbreviation for 'anonymous'. *'Star Peeps O'er the Hill' (Anon.), Salvationist Publishers Ltd.*

anonymity /ǽnənɪ́məti/
1 NU **Anonymity** is the state of not having your name or identity known. *...a benefactor who insisted on anonymity.*
2 NU+SUPP The **anonymity** of something is the fact that it hides your identity. *...the anonymity of life in big cities.*
3 NU+SUPP The **anonymity** of a place is its lack of interesting features. *...the anonymity of a hotel room.*

anonymous /ənɒ́nɪməs/
1 ADJ If you remain **anonymous** when you do something, you do not let people know that you were the person who did it. *An anonymous caller who spoke in English claimed that the plane would be sabotaged. ...anonymous death threats.* ♦ **anonymously** ADV *Anyone who wanted to make a complaint could do so anonymously.*
2 ADJ Something that is **anonymous** does not reveal who you are. *A taxi is anonymous. Nobody knows who's inside.*
3 ADJ You can say that something is **anonymous** when it has no interesting features. *...an anonymous little town.*

anorak /ǽnəræk/ **anoraks**
NC An **anorak** is a waterproof jacket, usually with a hood. *He sat silently in the dock, dressed in an anorak and blue jeans.*

anorexia /ǽnəréksiə/
NU People who have **anorexia** have a very strong fear of becoming fat, and refuse to eat so that they become ill. *6% of women have had anorexia, often called the slimmer's disease.*

anorexic /ǽnəréksɪk/
ADJ If someone is **anorexic**, they are suffering from anorexia and so are very thin.

another /ənʌ́ðə/
1 DET or PRON **Another** means additional to or similar to a particular thing or person. *We walked another hundred metres... The first rice ship which came into Monrovia just over a week ago has been followed by another... When they had dealt with the fire another crisis arose... Another bomb exploded in a hotel but there were no casualties in the two incidents.*
2 DET or PRON **Another** can also be used to mean a different thing or person from the one just mentioned. *The argument can be put another way... Parents say one thing and do another... Another approach to treating AIDS is to boost the body's immune defences.*
3 You use **one another** to indicate that each member

of a group does something to or for the other members. *We both have a very high admiration for one another... Despite the chaos, people were orderly—getting one another out and trying to save one another... The government and rebel delegations had begun to build up some trust in one another.*
4 If you say that **one** thing **after another** happens or is done, you mean that the same sort of thing happens continuously or repeatedly. *She found one excuse after another to postpone it... This has resulted in one disaster after another... He hired one team of production executives after another.*

answer /ɑ́ːnsə/ **answers, answering, answered**
1 VO, V-QUOTE, V-REPORT, or V When you **answer** someone who has asked you something, you say something back to them. *He refused to answer reporters' questions... 'Did he win?'—'No,' I answered... He answered that the price would be three pounds... Asked point blank whether Australia would walk out, Dr Blewitt refused to answer.*
2 VO or V If you **answer** a letter or advertisement, you write to the person who wrote it. *The office has been inundated with calls from people answering the job advertisements... I'm sure that Dr Vane-Wright would answer any letters.*
3 NC An **answer** is something that you say or write when you answer someone. *The answer to your question is no!... He said that he asked for a meeting on the twenty-fifth of May, but has not yet had an answer... They make sure an answer is sent, often with a small gift enclosed.*
4 VO or V When you **answer** the telephone, you pick it up and speak into it when it rings. When you **answer** the door, you open it when you hear a knock or the bell. *We all take turns to make the coffee and answer the phone... I phoned, and Alec answered... When our friend opened the door, he seemed surprised, but not pleased to see us.* ► Also NC *I rang the doorbell, but there was no answer.*
5 NC An **answer** to a problem is a possible solution to it. *He had no intention of giving easy answers to complex moral questions... She does not accept that money is an answer... They may even consider re-unification as an answer to their problems.*
6 VO When you **answer** a question in a test, you give the answer to it. *You have to answer four questions.* ► Also NC *...answers to a questionnaire.*
7 VO If you **answer** a criticism or accusation, you say or write something in your own defence against it. *He failed to appear before a Senate Commission to answer allegations that he took bribes from BCCI... Mr Yeltsin is going to Kuzbass on Monday to answer criticisms from striking miners... He was summoned to the camp to answer charges of murder and corruption.* ► Also N SING or NU *What would your answer be to the accusation that you are old-fashioned?... In answer to your criticism, I would say that you have completely misunderstood the nature of my work.*
8 VO If you **answer** something such as an appeal or request for something, you respond to it in a positive way. *Mr Ansari is confident that 60 to 70 percent of British Muslims will answer the appeal... About seven hundred answered a call today for volunteers with medical skills... He answered a request from the government.* ► Also N SING or NU *Correspondents say this can be seen as Mr Ashdown's answer to an appeal by Dr David Owen... The American servicemen were diverted to Bangladesh in answer to an appeal for international help.*

answer back PHRASAL VERB If someone, especially a child, **answers** you **back** or **answers back**, they speak rudely to you when you speak to them. *She was beaten up by her husband—punishment for answering him back... We didn't answer back—we were afraid.*
answer for PHRASAL VERB 1 When someone **answers for** a crime, they are punished for it. *They have requested his extradition to answer for his crimes against his country's people.* 2 If you say that you are able to **answer for** someone or able to **answer for** their qualities, you mean that you are sure that they will do what is wanted. *I can answer for his loyalty.* 3 If you

say that someone or something has a lot to **answer for**, you mean that they are responsible for something very bad or wrong. *Your diet of yams has a lot to answer for.*

answerable /ɑːnsəᵊrəbl/
1 ADJ PRED+*to* If you are **answerable** to someone, you have to report and explain your actions to them. *The Communist party is answerable to its members... We are alone in having a security system that is not answerable to any parliamentary committee.*
2 ADJ PRED+*for* If you are **answerable** for your actions or for someone else's actions, you are considered to be responsible for them. *They should be brought before a court and be answerable for their terrible deeds.*

answering /ɑːnsərɪŋ/
ADJ ATTRIB An **answering** action or remark is one that is done or said in response to something. *He looked around for answering smiles... 'Forward with the revolution' came the answering cry from 5000 people.*

answering machine, answering machines
NC An **answering machine** is a device which you connect to your telephone so that it will record telephone calls while you are out. *The shop proprietor recorded the threat on his answering machine.*

ant /ænt/ **ants**
NC **Ants** are small crawling insects that live in large groups. *...plants with hollow spines containing colonies of ants.*

antagonise /æntægənaɪz/. See **antagonize**.

antagonism /æntægənɪzəm/
NU **Antagonism** is hatred or hostility. *...the growing antagonism between church and state... They failed to convince observers that their mutual antagonism was past.*

antagonist /æntægənɪst/ **antagonists**
NC Your **antagonist** is your opponent or enemy. *...allegations concerning his arch political antagonist.*

antagonistic /æntægənɪstɪk/
ADJ Someone who is **antagonistic** shows hostility towards you. *Many of them are antagonistic towards the President. ...the resurgence of antagonistic national movements.*

antagonize /æntægənaɪz/ **antagonizes, antagonizing, antagonized;** also spelt **antagonise**.
VO If you **antagonize** someone, you make them feel angry or hostile towards you. *They must avoid antagonising Mr Jackson, who has ninety per cent of the vote... State intervention tends to antagonize the population.*

Antall, József /jɒuzef ɒntɒl/
József Antall became Prime Minister of Hungary in 1990. He was elected President of the Hungarian Democratic Forum (MDF) in 1989 and became a member of Parliament in 1990. Born: 1932.

Antananarivo /ʌntʌnənæriːvuː/
Antananarivo, formerly known as Tananarive, is the capital of Madagascar and its largest city. Population: 663,000 (1985).

Antarctic /æntɑːktɪk/
N PROP The **Antarctic** is the region around the South Pole. *...their final expedition to the Antarctic. ...the killing cold of the Antarctic nights.*

Antarctica /æntɑːktɪkə/
Antarctica is the world's fifth largest continent, occupying approximately 14 million square kilometres. It is almost entirely covered by the ice sheet, which is on average 2,000 metres thick and represents 90 per cent of the world's glacial ice. Antarctica is uninhabited. The Antarctic Treaty of 1959 reserved the continent for non-military, scientific research.

ante /ænti/ **antes, anteing, anted**
ante up PHRASAL VERB To **ante up** means to pay an amount of money or to provide money for something. *If Japan antes up the cash, as many in Congress want, does Japan also get some say in the policy?... Seidman rejects that, saying banks will have to ante up to replenish the fund.*
● to **up the ante**: see **up**.

anteater /æntiːtə/ **anteaters**
NC An **anteater** is an animal with a long snout which it uses for eating termites or ants.

antecedent /æntɪsiːdnt/ **antecedents**
1 NC An **antecedent** of something is a similar thing that happened or existed before it did. *...the prehistoric antecedents of the horse.*
2 N PL Your **antecedents** are your ancestors. *They rode back to the shore where their antecedents had become the first Europeans to make contact with the tribesmen.*

antechamber /æntitʃeɪmbə/ **antechambers**
NC An **antechamber** is a small room leading into a larger room. *Those wonderful relics were in the antechamber—more was to come in the other three rooms.*

antedate /æntideɪt/ **antedates, antedating, antedated**
VO Something that **antedates** something else happened or existed before it; a formal word. *The Egyptians' written records antedated those of the Greeks by thousands of years.*

antediluvian /æntɪdɪluːviən/
ADJ Something that is **antediluvian** is extremely old or old-fashioned; a literary word, often used humorously. *Old women with antediluvian ideas still ruled the roost... The idea of Britain setting a compelling example to the world was an antediluvian one.*

antelope /æntɪləup/ **antelopes**. The plural form can be either **antelopes** or antelope.
NC An **antelope** is an animal like a deer with long legs and horns, which can run very fast. *The antelope and other animals feed on acacia leaves.*

antenatal /æntineɪtl/ **antenatals**
1 ADJ ATTRIB **Antenatal** means relating to the medical care of pregnant women. *Much of the antenatal care is being undertaken in hospital. ...an antenatal clinic.*
2 NC An **antenatal** is a medical examination of a pregnant woman. *I'm going for my antenatal this morning.*

antenna /æntɛnə/ **antennae** /æntɛniː/ or **antennas**. For the meaning in paragraph 2 the plural form is usually **antennas**.
1 NC The **antennae** of an insect are the two long, thin parts attached to its head that it feels things with. *They pass the substances onto the antennae of other bees.*
2 NC An **antenna** is also an aerial. *It looks like a telephone handset, but it's got an antenna sticking out of it.*

anteroom /æntiruːm, æntirʊm/ **anterooms**; also spelt **ante-room**.
NC An **anteroom** is a small room where people can wait before going into a larger room; an old-fashioned word. *They were waiting in an anteroom for interrogation.*

anthem /ænθəm/ **anthems**
NC An **anthem** is a song which is used to represent a particular nation, society, or organized group, and which is sung on special occasions. *The European Community already has a flag, an anthem, and a parliament... They began singing their team anthem.*
● See also **national anthem**.

ant hill, ant hills
NC An **ant hill** is a mound of earth formed by ants when they are making a nest. *It's like trying to destroy an ant hill by stepping on it.*

anthology /ænθɒlədʒi/ **anthologies**
NC An **anthology** is a collection of writings by different writers published together in one book. *...an anthology of women's crime fiction.*

anthracite /ænθrəsaɪt/
NU **Anthracite** is a type of very hard coal which burns slowly, with a small flame and very little smoke, producing a lot of heat.

anthrax /ænθræks/
NU **Anthrax** is a serious disease of cattle and sheep, in which they get painful sores and a fever. *Twenty-five pigs have been slaughtered after anthrax had been discovered.*

anthropoid /ænθrəpɔɪd/ **anthropoids**
1 ADJ An **anthropoid** creature is one that is very like a human being. *...nothing more than a terrestrial anthropoid ape.*
2 NC **Anthropoids** are the apes that are most closely related to humans. *...man and the anthropoids.*

anthropology /ˌænθrəpɒlədʒi/
NU **Anthropology** is the study of people, society, and culture. ...*a historian with an interest in social anthropology*. ♦ **anthropologist, anthropologists** NC ...*an English anthropologist, Colin Turnbull*.

anthropomorphic /ˌænθrəpəmɔːfɪk/
ADJ **Anthropomorphic** means resulting from the belief that animals and things resemble human beings in actions, thoughts, or behaviour. ...*our anthropomorphic image of God... We are being anthropomorphic, attributing human feelings to animals*.

anthropomorphism /ˌænθrəpəmɔːfɪzəm/
NU **Anthropomorphism** is the belief that animals and things have human feelings.

anti- /ˌænti-/
1 PREFIX **Anti-** combines with nouns to form adjectives that describe people who are opposed to something such as a particular practice or group of people. ...*the anti-apartheid movement... An anti-EEC resolution was passed*.
2 PREFIX **Anti-** is also used to form words that describe or refer to something that is intended to prevent or destroy something. ...*anti-freeze. ...an anti-cholesterol drug*.

anti-aircraft
ADJ ATTRIB An **anti-aircraft** weapon or system of defence is intended to destroy enemy aircraft. ...*anti-aircraft missiles*.

antibiotic /ˌæntibaɪɒtɪk/ **antibiotics**
NC **Antibiotics** are drugs that are used in medicine to kill bacteria and to cure infections. *Sub-standard medicines including anti-malaria tablets and antibiotics, were still being sold. ...antibiotic therapy*.

antibody /ˈæntibɒdi/ **antibodies**
NC **Antibodies** are special proteins produced in your blood which are able to kill the harmful bacteria that cause disease and illness; a medical term. *The company claim that their artificial antibodies are just as effective as natural ones*.

anticipate /ænˈtɪsəpeɪt/ **anticipates, anticipating, anticipated**
1 VOor V-REPORT If you **anticipate** an event, you realize in advance that it may happen and you are prepared for it. *The Secretary had anticipated the question... In his speech, Mr Ashdown anticipated that the idea might receive a cool reception*. ♦ **anticipation** /ænˌtɪsəpeɪʃn/ NU *Petrol coupons were issued in anticipation of rationing*.
2 VOor V-REPORT If you **anticipate** something, you expect that it will happen. *The inflow of foreign investment has been far less than the government anticipated... The United Nations anticipate that these tasks will be complete by November*.
3 VO If you **anticipate** something that you know is going to happen or that you know you are going to receive, you act as though it has already happened or as though you have already received it. *They were anticipating the decision by several hours*.
4 VO If you **anticipate** something pleasant or exciting that is going to happen, you look forward to it with pleasure. *She had often pleasurably anticipated the moment when she would hand in her resignation*. ♦ **anticipation** NU *'Please!' the children cried, jumping up and down in anticipation. ...an atmosphere of excited anticipation*.

anticipatory /ænˌtɪsəpeɪtəri/
ADJ ATTRIB An **anticipatory** feeling or action is one that you have or do because you are expecting something to happen soon; a formal word. ...*anticipatory delight. ...anticipatory actions*.

anticlimax /ˌæntiklaɪmæks/ **anticlimaxes**
NCor NU An **anticlimax** is something that is disappointing because it is not as exciting as you expected, or because it happens after something that was very exciting. *Polling day was a bit of an anticlimax. ...a sense of anticlimax*.

anti-clockwise /ˌæntiklɒkwaɪz/
ADVor ADJ ATTRIB When something moves **anti-clockwise**, it moves in a circle in the opposite direction to the hands of a clock. *Triton has a retrograde orbit—it goes anti-clockwise, around Neptune*.

...*the slow circulation of the water in an anti-clockwise direction*.

antics /ˈæntɪks/
N PL **Antics** are funny, silly or unusual ways of behaving. *Their antics are greeted with gusts of laughter from the audience. ...the loutish antics of Members of Parliament*.

anticyclone /ˌæntiˈsaɪkləʊn/ **anticyclones**.
NC An **anticyclone** is an area of high atmospheric pressure which causes settled weather conditions and, in summer, clear skies and high temperatures. *The anticyclone is effectively diverting rain to keep Britain moist and cool*.

antidote /ˈæntɪdəʊt/ **antidotes**
1 NC An **antidote** is a chemical substance that stops or controls the effect of a poison. *Soldiers are equipped with a syringe so that they can inject themselves with the antidote*.
2 NC The **antidote** to something which is harmful, difficult, or unpleasant is something that helps to make it better or easier to deal with. *They regard their new album as the antidote to much 'regressive' pop music... Stricter central control is the antidote to corruption, disorder and inflation*.

anti-freeze
NU **Anti-freeze** is a liquid which is added to water to stop it freezing. It is used in the radiator of a car in cold weather. *Methyl alcohol is used as a solvent and as an anti-freeze*.

antigen /ˈæntɪdʒən/ **antigens**
NC **Antigens** are substances in your body which cause illness or allergies and which are attacked by the antibodies in your blood; a medical term. *Research is identifying which antigens stimulate the immune response*.

Antigua and Barbuda /ænˈtiːɡə, bɑːˈbjuːdə/
The **State of Antigua and Barbuda** is a country in the Caribbean. Antigua was a British colony from 1667 until it became independent in 1981. It is a member of the Commonwealth and the Organization of American States. Vere C. Bird, of the Antigua Labour Party (ALP), became Prime Minister in 1981. Tourism is the major industry. ♦ **Antiguan** /ænˈtiːɡən/ N, ADJ
▪ *per capita GNP:* US$2,800 ▪ *religion:* Christianity
▪ *language:* English ▪ *currency:* East Caribbean dollar
▪ *capital:* St John's ▪ *population:* 84,000 (1988) ▪ *size:* 442 square kilometres.

anti-hero, anti-heroes
NC An **anti-hero** is a main character in a novel, play, or film who behaves in a completely different way from the way that people expect a hero to behave. *The portrayal of the pilot as first hero, then anti-hero, had been wholly discreditable*.

anti-histamine /ˌæntiˈhɪstəmiːn/ **anti-histamines**; also spelt **antihistamine**.
NC **Anti-histamines** are drugs that are used to treat allergies. *They would act in the same way as anti-histamines do in combating hay fever*.

antimacassar /ˌæntiməˈkæsə/ **antimacassars**
NC An **antimacassar** is a decorative cloth that is used to protect the back of a chair.

antimatter
NU **Antimatter** is a form of matter whose particles have characteristics and properties opposite to those of ordinary matter; a technical term in physics. *When antimatter meets matter, they annihilate each other*.

antipathetic /ˌæntipəˈθetɪk/
ADJ If you are **antipathetic** to someone or something, you have a strong feeling of dislike or hostility towards them. *He is completely antipathetic to the aims of our organisation. ...a white establishment that is antipathetic to blacks and their achievements*.

antipathy /ænˈtɪpəθi/
NU **Antipathy** is a strong feeling of dislike or hostility. ...*artists towards whom Cezanne felt antipathy or even scorn. ...the strong personal antipathy between the two men*.

Antipodes /ænˈtɪpədiːz/
N PROP The **Antipodes** is used by people in the northern hemisphere to refer, often humorously, to Australia and New Zealand. ...*an island in the Antipodes*.

anti-pollutant, anti-pollutants
NC An **anti-pollutant** is a substance that is used to reduce the harmful effects of pollution.

antiquarian /æntɪkwɛəriən/
ADJ ATTRIB **Antiquarian** means concerned with old and rare objects. ...*antiquarian bookshops.*

antiquary /æntɪkwəri/ **antiquaries**
NC An **antiquary** is a person who studies the past, or who collects or buys and sells old and valuable objects. *Standing alongside the famous burial mound, he recalled how a local antiquary discovered it fifty-one years ago.*

antiquated /æntɪkweɪtɪd/
ADJ **Antiquated** things seem very old or old-fashioned. *The American shuttle technology is antiquated by contemporary standards. ...an authoritarian and antiquated régime.*

antique /æntiːk/ **antiques**
NC An **antique** is an old object which is valuable because of its beauty or rarity. *A million-pounds' worth of antiques have been stolen from the ancestral home of George Washington. ...a retired antiques dealer.*

antique shop, antique shops
NC An **antique shop** is a shop where antiques are sold. *She had been given them by a friend who bought them in an antique shop.*

antiquity /æntɪkwəti/ **antiquities**
1 NU **Antiquity** is the distant past, especially the time of the ancient Egyptians, Greeks, and Romans. ...*the great lost paintings of antiquity... How far back in antiquity can we go?*
2 NC **Antiquities** are interesting old things, such as buildings and statues, that you can go and see. *She was in Melbourne to open an exhibition of Macedonian antiquities.*

anti-Semite /æntisiːmaɪt/ **anti-Semites**
NC An **anti-Semite** is someone who strongly dislikes and is prejudiced against Jewish people.

anti-Semitic /æntisəmɪtɪk/
ADJ Someone or something that is **anti-Semitic** is hostile to and prejudiced against Jewish people. *Two anti-Semitic letters appeared in the paper... He has been criticized for his anti-semitic views.*

anti-Semitism /æntisɛmətɪzəm/
NU **Anti-Semitism** is prejudice against Jewish people. *During these 40 years, a lot was done to fight anti-semitism... Anti-Semitism was quite common in Europe when Hitler was growing up.*

antiseptic /æntiseptɪk/ **antiseptics**
N MASS **Antiseptic** is a substance that kills harmful bacteria. *Joseph Lister developed a new approach to surgery, introducing antiseptics and sterile equipment.*

anti-social
1 ADJ Someone who is **anti-social** is unwilling to meet and be friendly with other people. *Some have blamed the régime for making them more aggressive and more anti-social.*
2 ADJ **Anti-social** behaviour is annoying or upsetting to other people. *Youngsters between 16 and 20, without higher education, were inclined towards anti-social activities.*

anti-tank
ADJ ATTRIB An **anti-tank** weapon is designed for destroying military tanks. ...*an anti-tank rocket launcher.*

anti-theft
ADJ An **anti-theft** device prevents or discourages a thief from stealing something. *There are anti-theft alarms on all new models.*

antithesis /æntɪθəsɪs/ **antitheses** /æntɪθəsiːz/
NC The **antithesis** of something is its exact opposite; a formal word. *The vampire is the antithesis of everything that is ordered, normal and respectable.*

antler /æntlə/ **antlers**
NC A male deer's **antlers** are the branched horns on its head. *With their big antlers, their chances of injury are high.*

antonym /æntənɪm/ **antonyms**
NC The **antonym** of a word is another word which means the opposite. *'Good' is the antonym of 'bad'.*

antonymous /æntɒnəməs/
ADJ Words that are **antonymous** are opposite in meaning. *'Hard' and 'soft' are antonymous.*

anus /eɪnəs/ **anuses**
NC A person's **anus** is the hole between their buttocks, from which faeces leave their body; a medical term. *It's a kind of worm, but it doesn't have a gut, a mouth, or an anus.*

anvil /ænvɪl/ **anvils**
NC An **anvil** is a heavy iron block on which hot metals are beaten into shape.

anxiety /æŋzaɪəti/ **anxieties**
1 NU **Anxiety** is a feeling of nervousness or worry. *'What do you think?' asked the Belgian with a touch of anxiety.*
2 NC An **anxiety** is something which causes you to feel nervous or worried. ...*major financial anxieties.*

anxious /æŋkʃəs/
1 ADJ If you are **anxious**, you are nervous or worried about something. *She was anxious about her job.*
♦ **anxiously** ADV *'I'm not boring you?' she asked anxiously.*
2 ADJ ATTRIB An **anxious** time or situation is one during which you feel nervous and worried. *You must have had an anxious day. ...months of anxious anticipation.*
3 ADJ PRED If you are **anxious** to do something or **anxious** that something should happen, you very much want to do it or want it to happen. *Some sectors of government seem anxious to improve Japan's image abroad... Relatives of the dead men are anxious that the three policemen involved should give evidence in court.*

any /eni, əni/
1 DET or PRON You use **any** in negative statements, for example with 'not' or 'never', to mean none of a particular thing. *Morris hasn't made any public statements yet... I don't like any of this.*
2 DET or PRON You use **any** in questions and conditional clauses to ask if there is some of a particular thing or to suggest that there might be. *Were you in any danger?... They will retaliate if any of their ships are attacked.*
3 DET or PRON You use **any** in positive statements when you are referring to something or someone without saying exactly what, who, or which kind you mean. *Any big tin container will do... The meeting was different from any that had gone before.*
4 ADV You can also use **any** to emphasize a comparative adjective or adverb in a negative statement. *I couldn't stand it any longer... His paper has not yet been published, so we don't know any more about it.*

anybody /enibɒdi, enibədi/. See **anyone**.

anyhow /enihaʊ/
1 ADV **Anyhow** means the same as **anyway**.
2 ADV If you do something **anyhow**, you do it in a careless or untidy way. *They were all shoved in anyhow.*

anymore /enimɔː/
Anymore means the same as 'any more': see **more**.

anyone /eniwʌn, eniwən/ or **anybody** /enibədi/
1 PRON INDEF You use **anyone** or **anybody** in negative statements, for example with 'not' or 'never', to say that nobody is present or involved in an action. *There wasn't anyone there... There really wasn't much room for anybody else... He said that the Ivory Coast had never closed its borders to anybody.*
2 PRON INDEF You use **anyone** or **anybody** in questions and conditional clauses to ask or talk about whether someone is present or doing something. *Was there anyone behind you?... If anyone asks where you are I'll say you've just gone out... Does anybody else have a ship like this one?*
3 PRON INDEF You also use **anyone** or **anybody** to refer to a person or to people in general, when you do not want to say which particular person or people you are referring to. *Anyone who dared challenge them was arrested... He took longer than anybody else.*

anything /eniθɪŋ/
1 PRON INDEF You use **anything** in negative statements, for example with 'not' or 'never', to say

that nothing is present or an action or event does not happen. *I did not say anything... There isn't anything of that nature in this area... He never seemed to do anything at all.*
2 PRON INDEF You use **anything** in questions and conditional clauses to ask or talk about whether something is present or happening. *Has anything improved?... I've told her to come to you if she wants anything... Is there anything you can do about that?*
3 PRON INDEF You can use **anything** to refer to a thing, an event, or an idea without saying exactly which one you mean. *Lemon gives a fresh flavour to almost anything... To me, it's more important than anything else... We are ready to withstand anything.*
4 ADV You can use **anything** for emphasis, when you are saying that something is not at all like something else. *It didn't taste anything like soup... The total wasn't anything near what we'd expected... The economic slowdown will not be anything like as deep or severe as the recession in the early 1980s.*

anyway /ɛniweɪ/ or **anyhow** /ɛnihaʊ/
1 ADV SEN You use **anyway** or **anyhow** to indicate that a statement explains or supports a previous point. *We ought to spend less on the defence missiles, which I reckon are pretty useless anyway... They didn't much mind because they didn't believe it anyway.*
2 ADV SEN You use **anyway** or **anyhow** to suggest that a statement is true or relevant in spite of other things that have been said. *'I can give you a lift.'—'No, I'll walk. Thanks, anyway.'... We found a way to do it anyhow.*
3 ADV SEN You use **anyway** or **anyhow** to correct or modify a statement, for example to limit it to what you definitely know to be true. *'All of them?' I asked. 'Some, anyway.'... In Britain in recent years there has been hardly any snow at Christmas time, anyhow not in south-east England.*
4 ADV SEN You use **anyway** to change the topic or return to a previous topic. *What are you phoning for, anyway?... Anyway, I'll see you later.*

anywhere /ɛniweə/
1 ADV You can use **anywhere** in negative statements, questions, and conditional clauses to refer to a place without saying exactly where you mean. *Is there an ashtray anywhere?... I decided not to go anywhere.*
2 ADV You can use **anywhere** in positive statements to emphasize an expression that refers to a place or area. *They are the oldest rock paintings anywhere in North America... It's better to have it in the kitchen than anywhere else.*

ANZUS /ænzəs/
ANZUS was formed in 1951 by Australia, New Zealand, and the United States of America, for the collective defence of the Pacific. In 1984 New Zealand refused to permit United States ships carrying nuclear weapons to use its ports, and subsequently, in 1986, the United States suspended its commitment to New Zealand under the ANZUS Treaty.

aorta /eɪɔːtə/ **aortas**
NC Your **aorta** is the main artery through which blood leaves your heart before it flows through the rest of your body. *Sir Len has suffered a rupture of the aorta.*

apace /əpeɪs/
ADV If something is happening or growing **apace**, it happens or grows quickly; a literary word. *Darkness was coming on apace... Suspicion of learning grew apace.*

apart /əpɑːt/
1 ADV+*from* When something is **apart** from something else, there is a space between them. *I was sitting apart from the rest. ...a small shed set well apart from the main building... Their tactics were to try and keep the prisoners as far as possible apart from each other.*
2 ADJ after N If two things are a particular distance **apart**, they are that distance away from each other. *Their faces were a couple of inches apart... The machines should be positioned in different locations, at least one kilometre apart.*
3 ADJ after N If two events happen a certain amount of time **apart**, there is that amount of time between their

occurrence. *Motherwell beat Dunfermline with goals from Arnott and Cooper just four minutes apart... The frigate carried out two attacks some forty minutes apart.*
4 ADV If two things move **apart** or are pulled **apart**, they move away from each other. *The aircraft blew apart at thirty thousand feet... When molecules are expanding or moving apart, they cool down... Mr Berecz says the conflicts will ultimately pull the society apart.*
5 ADJ PRED If two people or groups of people grow **apart**, they no longer have very much in common with each other. *So often older people find themselves apart from the younger members... They felt it was better for them to be together than apart.*
6 ADV If you take something **apart**, you separate it into the pieces that it is made of. If it comes or falls **apart**, its parts separate from each other. *If you break one thread in the seam, you can pull the two pieces of cloth apart... Wire reinforcement prevents the glass from breaking apart.*
7 ADV If something such as an organization or relationship falls **apart**, it can no longer continue because it has serious difficulties. *The National Health Service, already on the brink of collapse, will simply fall apart... The country's political fabric is being torn apart... Do you think the alliance against Hussein is starting to come apart?*
● **Apart** is used in these phrases. ● You use **apart from** to say that you want to ignore one aspect of a situation so that you can talk about another aspect. *Quite apart from the expense, I don't think I would want to fly anyway.* ● You also use **apart from** when you are giving an exception to a general statement. *Apart from Ann, the car was empty... The refugees have no source of food, apart from Red Cross supplies.* ● If you **can't tell** two people or things **apart**, they look exactly the same to you. *He couldn't tell the boys apart.*

apartheid /əpɑːtheɪt, əpɑːthaɪt/
NU **Apartheid** is a political system in which people of different races are kept apart by law. *It could herald a new political era and the final collapse of apartheid.*

apartment /əpɑːtmənt/ **apartments**
1 NC An **apartment** is a flat; used in American English. *Christina set up home in a small Moscow apartment... His mother has secured a better life and has managed to move into an apartment.*
2 NC An **apartment** is also one of a set of large rooms used by an important person such as a king, queen, or president. *...splendid apartments of state.*

apartment house, apartment houses
NC In the United States, an **apartment house** is a tall building containing many different apartments on different floors. *There are many thousands of apartment houses in this city.*

apathetic /æpəθetɪk/
ADJ Someone who is **apathetic** is not interested in anything. *There was no serious opposition to worry about, because the public were too apathetic to bother.*

apathy /æpəθi/
NU **Apathy** is a state of mind in which you are not interested in or enthusiastic about anything. *It's a good thing that people are waking up from their political apathy... Electoral apathy was running high.*

ape /eɪp/ **apes, aping, aped**
1 NC **Apes** are animals such as chimpanzees or gorillas which look similar to monkeys but do not have tails. *...a common ancestor of humans and the great African apes.*
2 VO If you **ape** someone's speech or behaviour, you imitate it. *He indicated that he does not intend to ape the policies of Ronald Reagan.*

APEC /eɪpek/
APEC is an organization set up in 1989 between Australia, New Zealand, the United States, Canada, South Korea, Japan, and other countries from south-east Asia which tries to encourage economic co-operation between those countries.

apéritif /əperətiːf/ **apéritifs**
NC An **apéritif** is an alcoholic drink that you have before a meal.

aperture /ˈæpətʃə/ **apertures**
NC An **aperture** is a very narrow hole or gap. *The aperture of the camera is blocked, and we can't get any pictures. ...its ability to get through the tiniest aperture.*

apex /ˈeɪpeks/ **apexes**
1 NC The **apex** of something is its pointed top or end. *...looking here at the apex of this curve.*
2 NC The **apex** of an organization or system is the highest and most important position in it. *Four months ago, he would have found the Chinese leader at the apex of his power.*

APEX /ˈeɪpeks/
N+N An **APEX** ticket is a ticket for a journey by air which costs less than the standard ticket, but which you have to book a specified period in advance. *Fares range upwards from £220 for an Apex return in the low season.*

aphid /ˈeɪfɪd/ **aphids**
NC **Aphids** are very small insects which live on plants and suck their juices. *Aphids are an important pest in agriculture, destroying crops and spreading disease.*

aphorism /ˈæfərɪzəm/ **aphorisms**
NC An **aphorism** is a short, clever sentence which expresses a general truth. *I quoted Lord Acton's clever aphorism about how 'power corrupts, and absolute power corrupts absolutely'.*

aphrodisiac /ˌæfrəˈdɪziæk/ **aphrodisiacs**
NC An **aphrodisiac** is a food, drink, or drug which makes people want to have sex. *Pulverised rhino horn is in demand as an aphrodisiac.*

Apia /ɑːˈpiːə/
Apia is the capital of Western Samoa and its largest city. Population: 33,000 (1981).

apiece /əˈpiːs/
ADV If people have a particular number of things **apiece**, they have that number each. *He gave his daughters £200 apiece... Mike, Phil, and Paul all scored two points apiece.*

aplomb /əˈplɒm/
NU If you do something with **aplomb**, you do it with great confidence. *Gorbachev has responded with his customary aplomb by saying no.*

apocalypse /əˈpɒkəlɪps/
1 N PROP The **Apocalypse** is the total destruction and end of the world. *...a far from comforting vision of the Apocalypse.*
2 N SING The **apocalypse** of something such as a civilization is its total destruction. *They were pulled together from the wreckage which had survived the apocalypse.*

apocalyptic /əˌpɒkəˈlɪptɪk/
1 ADJ ATTRIB Something that is **apocalyptic** involves the total destruction of something, especially of the world. *...an apocalyptic nuclear exchange. ...the apocalyptic confrontation between capitalism and socialism.*
2 ADJ **Apocalyptic** also means relating to or involving prophecy about future disasters and the destruction of the world. *There is something apocalyptic about the tone of his writings. ...a sudden apocalyptic vision.*

apocryphal /əˈpɒkrəfl/
ADJ An **apocryphal** story or joke is one that is generally thought not to be true or not to have happened. *...the apocryphal story of Columbus and the egg.*

apolitical /ˌeɪpəˈlɪtɪkl/
ADJ Someone who is **apolitical** is not interested in politics. *Tomas, apolitical and non-committed, finds himself caught up with protesters on the streets.*

apologetic /əˌpɒləˈdʒetɪk/
ADJ If you are **apologetic**, you say or show that you are sorry that you have hurt someone or caused trouble for them. *He had been apologetic about his behaviour at dinner.* ◆ **apologetically** ADV *He smiled apologetically.*

apologia /ˌæpəˈləʊdʒiə/ **apologias**
NC An **apologia** is a statement in which you defend something that you strongly believe in, for example a way of life, an institution, or a philosophy; a formal word. *...a magnificent apologia for the House of Lords.*

apologise /əˈpɒlədʒaɪz/. See apologize.

apologist /əˈpɒlədʒɪst/ **apologists**
NC+for An **apologist** for an idea, cause, or belief is a person who writes or speaks in defence of it; a formal word. *Mr Strauss said that he was not an apologist for South Africa's apartheid laws.*

apologize /əˈpɒlədʒaɪz/ **apologizes, apologizing, apologized;** also spelt **apologise.**
V, V+for, V+to, or V-QUOTE When you **apologize** to someone for something, you say that you are sorry that you have hurt them or caused them trouble. *Reports suggest he apologized at the executive meeting last Friday... I apologise for my late arrival... The Finance Minister apologised to parliament for his Ministry's lack of supervision... 'Sorry I haven't called you yet,' Beynon apologized.*

apology /əˈpɒlədʒi/ **apologies**
NCorNU An **apology** is something that you say or write in order to tell someone that you are sorry that you have hurt them or caused trouble for them. *Few people here seem convinced of the sincerity of the apology... The President and Prime Minister have offered public apologies. ...a letter of apology.*

apoplexy /ˈæpəpleksi/
NU If someone has **apoplexy**, they have a stroke; an old-fashioned word. *He was so furious I thought he would have apoplexy.*

apostasy /əˈpɒstəsi/
NU Someone's **apostasy** is the abandoning of their religious faith, political loyalties, or principles; a formal word. *...his only punishment for his apostasy.*

apostate /əˈpɒsteɪt/ **apostates**
NC An **apostate** is someone who abandons their religious faith, political loyalties, or principles; a formal word. *...a family of apostates.* ▶ Also ADJ ATTRIB *He was an apostate Catholic.*

a posteriori /eɪ pɒstɪəriˈɔːraɪ/
ADJ A **posteriori** reasoning is based on observation or experience, so that you work out a general principle or theory from particular examples or evidence. The sentence: 'There is smoke coming from the chimney, therefore somebody must be at home' is an example of a posteriori reasoning.

apostle /əˈpɒsl/ **apostles**
1 NC The **Apostles** were the followers of Jesus Christ who went from place to place telling people about him and trying to persuade them to become Christians. *...the preaching of the Apostles. ...the Apostle Paul.*
2 NC An **apostle** of a particular philosophy, policy, or cause is someone who strongly believes in it and works hard to promote it. *...an apostle of change. ...the apostle of democracy.*

apostolic /ˌæpəˈstɒlɪk/
1 ADJ ATTRIB **Apostolic** means belonging or relating to a Christian religious leader, especially the Pope. *...the apostolic succession... The Pope's Apostolic Letter had been conveyed to the head of the Russian Orthodox Church.*
2 ADJ ATTRIB **Apostolic** also means belonging or relating to the early followers of Christ and to their teaching.

apostrophe /əˈpɒstrəfi/ **apostrophes**
NC An **apostrophe** is a mark written to indicate that one or more letters have been omitted from a word, as in 'can't' and 'he'll'. An apostrophe is also written before or after an 's' at the end of a word to indicate that what follows belongs or relates to the word, as in 'the cat's whiskers' and 'the players' entrance'.

apothecary /əˈpɒθəkəˈri/ **apothecaries**
NC An **apothecary** was a person who prepared medicines for people; an old-fashioned word.

apotheosis /əˌpɒθiˈəʊsɪs/ **apotheoses**; a formal word.
1 N SING+of If a particular thing is the **apotheosis** of something, it is an ideal or perfect example of it. *He seemed the apotheosis of generosity.*
2 NC+POSS When a person's **apotheosis** happens, they become, or are declared to be, a god or a goddess. *This scene may represent the apotheosis of the dead princess.*

appal /əˈpɔːl/ **appals, appalling, appalled;** spelt **appall, appalls** in American English.
VO If something **appals** you, it shocks and disgusts you

because it is so bad. *The levels of ignorance appalled me.*

appalled /əpɔːld/
ADJ PRED If you are **appalled** at something, or **appalled** by it, you feel disgust or dismay because it seems so bad or unpleasant. *I was absolutely appalled at the quality of the reporting... Both the Queen and the Prime Minister said they were shocked and appalled by the disaster.*

appalling /əpɔːlɪŋ/
ADJ Something that is **appalling** is so bad that it shocks you. *These people live in appalling conditions.*
♦ **appallingly** ADV *The situation has deteriorated appallingly since 1951.*

apparatus /æpəreɪtəs/
1 NU **Apparatus** is the equipment which is used to do a particular job or activity. *Firemen wearing breathing apparatus later neutralized the gas.*
2 NU+SUPP The **apparatus** of an organization is its structure and method of operation. *...the whole apparatus of the welfare state.*

apparel /əpærəl/
1 NU+SUPP Someone's **apparel** is the clothes that they are wearing, especially on an important occasion; a formal word. *...photographs of local brides in full wedding apparel.*
2 NU In American English, **apparel** means the same as **clothing**. *Their apparel consists of dark narrow-lapelled suits and skinny ties. ...a women's apparel firm.*

apparent /əpærənt/
1 ADJ ATTRIB An **apparent** situation, quality, or feeling seems to exist, although you cannot be certain that it exists. *...the apparent success of their marriage.*
2 ADJ PRED If something is **apparent** to you, it is clear and obvious to you. *It was becoming increasingly apparent to me that he disliked me.*

apparently /əpærəntli/
ADV SEN You use **apparently** to refer to something that seems to be the case although it may not be. *She was standing by the window, apparently quite calm and relaxed.*

apparition /æpərɪʃn/ **apparitions**
NC An **apparition** is something that you think you see but that is not really there. *Not all the visionaries continue to see the apparitions every day.*

appeal /əpiːl/ **appeals, appealing, appealed**
1 V+to, V+for, or V-QUOTE If you **appeal** to someone for something that you need, you make a serious and urgent request for it. *The authorities appealed to those taking part not to inflame the situation... The government of Sudan has appealed for emergency food aid... 'Ladies,' the Chairman appealed. 'Could we possibly begin?'*
2 NC An **appeal** is a serious and urgent request. *A radio appeal asking for money for cancer research raised £75,000.*
3 V+to If you **appeal** to someone's reason or feelings, you suggest that they should do what you ask if they want to seem reasonable or compassionate. *We went into the Professor's office confident we could appeal to his reason... They are confident they can appeal to her sense of duty.* ▶ Also NC *...an appeal to her maternal feelings.*
4 V If you **appeal** to someone in authority against a decision, you formally ask them to change it. *The President was confronted by a group of Chinese women who appealed to him against deportation... The RCD victims and their families appealed against the leniency of the sentences.*
5 NC An **appeal** is a formal request for a decision to be changed. *Officials upheld their appeal against disqualification in the final event... The Supreme Court turned down our appeal.*
6 V+to If something **appeals** to you, you find it attractive or interesting. *The idea appealed to him.*
♦ **appealing** ADJ *She had an appealing sense of humour.*
7 NU+SUPP The **appeal** of something is a quality that it has which people find attractive or interesting. *The myth of the small individual winning out over the powerful will never lose its appeal.*

appear /əpɪə/ **appears, appearing, appeared**
1 V When something **appears**, it moves into a position where you can see it. *A glow of light appeared over the sea... Two men suddenly appeared from nowhere... Placards appeared on streets in several parts of the city today.*
2 V When something new **appears**, it begins to exist or becomes available. *His second novel appeared under the title 'Getting By'... Pro-independence newspapers continued to appear in Lithuania today.*
3 V+in When someone **appears** in a play or show, they take part in it. *They appeared together in a Broadway production of Noel Coward's 'Private Lives'.*
4 V When someone **appears** before a court of law, they go there to answer charges or to give information. *An art dealer from North London is to appear before Bow Street magistrates court charged under the Official Secrets Act.*
5 V C, V+to-INF, or V-REPORT If someone or something **appears** to have a particular quality or appears to do something, they give the impression of having that quality or of doing that thing. *Miss Bhutto appeared alarmed and upset by the chaos around her... Their offer appears to be the most attractive... Margaret Thatcher appeared to rule out the idea of state aid... President Bush said there appeared to be grounds for hope... It does not appear that there will be the tough clamp-down which some expected.*

appearance /əpɪərəns/ **appearances**
1 N SING+SUPP The **appearance** of someone or something in a place is their arrival there, especially when it is unexpected. *The fight was soon stopped, thanks to the prompt appearance of the police... People get immensely excited about the appearance of a new object in the night sky.*
2 N SING+SUPP The **appearance** of something new is its coming into existence or into use. *With the appearance of credit cards more people got into debt... Today sees the appearance of The European, a new weekly broadsheet.*
3 N SING+SUPP Someone or something's **appearance** is the way that they look to people. *I had ceased to worry about my appearance... She walked slowly, conscious of both her gait and her appearance.*
4 NC When someone makes an **appearance** in a play or show, they take part in it. *She has made several television appearances recently.*
● **Appearance** is used in these phrases. ● If you **put in an appearance** at an event, you go to it for a short time but do not stay. *The family and their guests put in an appearance at all or most of these festivities.*
● If something is true **to all appearances** or **by all appearances**, it seems from what you know about it that it is true. *To all appearances he doesn't work hard.*

appearance money
NU **Appearance money** is money paid to a famous person such as a film or sports star for taking part in a public event. *The PGA has announced an end to appearance money to entice the big names to European tour events.*

appease /əpiːz/ **appeases, appeasing, appeased**
VO If you try to **appease** someone, you try to stop them being angry or aggressive by giving them what they want; a formal word. *They accused the central government of appeasing militants and fundamentalists.*

appeasement /əpiːzmənt/
NU **Appeasement** is the act or practice of trying to prevent someone from harming you or being angry with you by giving them what they want; a formal word. *...a policy of appeasement towards foreign dictatorships.*

appellation /æpəleɪʃn/ **appellations**
NC An **appellation** is a name or title; a formal word. *Few other bold experimenters would shudder at the appellation 'architect'.*

append /əpend/ **appends, appending, appended**
VO When you **append** something to something else, especially a piece of writing, you add it or join it on to the end of it; a formal word. *He appends a brief note on this subject to his report.*

appendage /əpɛndɪdʒ/ **appendages**
NC An **appendage** is something that is joined to
something larger or more important; a formal word.
*...a pair of feathery appendages... The House of
Commons must not be only an appendage of the
Executive.*

appendices /əpɛndɪsiːz/
Appendices is a plural of appendix.

appendicitis /əpɛndɪsaɪtɪs/
NU **Appendicitis** is an illness in which your appendix is
infected and painful. *The President has been
discharged from hospital where he was admitted
suffering from acute appendicitis.*

appendix /əpɛndɪks/ **appendixes** or **appendices**
/əpɛndɪsiːz/. The plural form for the meaning in
paragraph 1 is **appendixes**; for the meaning in
paragraph 2 it is **appendices**.
1 NC Your **appendix** is a small closed tube inside your
body at the end of your digestive system. *...a
grumbling appendix in an otherwise healthy body.*
2 NC An **appendix** to a book is extra information that
is placed at the end of it. *The result was a
compromise contained in a hastily written appendix.*

appertain /æpətɛɪn/ **appertains, appertaining,
appertained**
V+to If something **appertains** to something else, it
relates to it or belongs to it; a formal word. *...duties
appertaining to Members of Parliament.*

appetite /æpɪtaɪt/ **appetites**
1 NCorNU Your **appetite** is your desire to eat. *All that
work has given me an appetite. ...his loss of appetite.*
2 NC If you have an **appetite** for something, you have
a strong desire for it. *He had an insatiable appetite
for publicity. ...the appetite for power.*

appetizer /æpɪtaɪzə/ **appetizers**; also spelt **appetiser**.
NC An **appetizer** is a small amount of food or drink
that you eat before a meal in order to give you an
appetite. *There are places where chick-pea and
sesame butter mix is the favorite appetizer.*

appetizing /æpɪtaɪzɪŋ/; also spelt **appetising**.
ADJ Food that is **appetizing** looks and smells nice, so
that you want to eat it. *...a most appetizing breakfast
dish.*

applaud /əplɔːd/ **applauds, applauding, applauded**
1 VorVO When a group of people **applaud**, they clap
their hands in order to show approval, for example
when they have enjoyed a play. *The United States
ambassador to the UN did not applaud, and the
Americans remained unmoved... Spectators in the
court room applauded the verdict.*
2 VO When an action or attitude is **applauded**, people
praise it. *The new bill is loudly applauded by anti-
abortion groups... We applaud the changes that have
taken place.*

applause /əplɔːz/
NU **Applause** is an expression of praise or appreciation
by a group of people, in which they clap their hands.
*The conference greeted the speech with rapturous
applause.*

apple /æpl/ **apples**
NCorNU An **apple** is a round fruit with a smooth green,
yellow, or red skin and firm white flesh. *Heaped on
the same pile are some common fruits: an apple, a
pear and some strawberries. ...his ongoing search for
the finest variety of apple. ...a new kind of apple tree.*

applecart /æplkɑːt/
If you upset the **applecart**, or upset someone's
applecart, you do something which causes a plan,
arrangement, or system to go wrong.

appliance /əplaɪəns/ **appliances**
NC An **appliance** is a device or machine that does a
particular job in your home, for example a vacuum
cleaner or a washing machine. *GEC produces
everything from kitchen appliances to generators for
power stations.*

applicable /əplɪkəbl, æplɪkəbl/
ADJ PRED Something that is **applicable** to a particular
situation is relevant to it. *The following special
regulations are applicable to overseas students.*

applicant /æplɪkənt/ **applicants**
NC An **applicant** for a job or a place at a college is
someone who formally asks to be given the job or the

place. *An applicant has to have at least five O levels
before he or she can be considered as a trainee nurse.*

application /æplɪkeɪʃn/ **applications**
1 NCorNU An **application** for a job or a place at a
college is a formal written request to be given the job
or the place. *Applications may be accepted or refused
on grounds which are kept private... The archives are
open to scholars on application.*
2 NUorNC The **application** of a rule, piece of
knowledge, or piece of equipment is the use of it in a
particular situation. *Do the results have any practical
application?... That's one application, painting and
decorating, but it can do other things as well.*
3 NU **Application** is hard work and concentration on
what you are doing. *...evidence of enthusiasm,
application, team spirit and initiative.*
4 NU The **application** of something, for example a coat
of paint or skin cream, is the act or process of putting
it on to a surface. *The application of a cold wet cloth
will stop the swelling.*

applied /əplaɪd/
ADJ ATTRIB An **applied** subject of study is practical
rather than theoretical. *...applied psychology.*

apply /əplaɪ/ **applies, applying, applied**
1 V+to-INF, V+for, or V If you **apply** to have something or
to do something, you write asking formally to be
allowed to have it or do it. *...protesters calling on the
government to apply to rejoin the United Nations...
I've applied for another job... He applied last
December.*
2 V-REFLorVO If you **apply** yourself to something, you
concentrate hard on it. *...a thoughtful, quiet man who
applied himself to his work with vigour... He tried to
apply his mind to Rose's problems.*
3 V+toorV If something **applies** to a person or a
situation, it is relevant to the person or situation.
*Researchers wanted to find out if this also applied to
breast cancer... This chart no longer applies.*
4 VO If you **apply** a rule, system, or skill, you use it in
a situation or activity. *...the capacity to develop and
apply technology... British expertise can be applied to
improve Soviet food distribution.*
5 V-PASS If a name or phrase is **applied** to someone or
something, they are referred to by that name or
phrase. *'Sustainable Development' is a phrase we
hear a lot, especially applied to agriculture...
Journalists have expressed concern that this definition
is being applied too broadly.*
6 VO If you **apply** something to a surface, you put it
onto the surface or rub it into it; a formal use. *Apply
a little liquid wax polish.*

appoint /əpɔɪnt/ **appoints, appointing, appointed**
VO+to, VO+to-INF, VO+as, or VOC If you **appoint** someone to
a job or post, or if you **appoint** them to do something,
you formally choose them for that job or post or to do
that thing. *The President is expected to appoint a new
cabinet shortly... He was appointed by President
Gorbachev to take temporary charge of the Soviet
economy... The Archbishop of Canterbury appointed
him as a special envoy overseas... Ramsay MacDonald
appointed him Secretary of State for India.*

appointed
1 ADJ ATTRIB An **appointed** person or group has been
chosen rather than elected to occupy a post of
responsibility. *...a mixture of democratically elected
and appointed leaders... They will be outnumbered on
the council by appointed representatives and members
elected by the business community.*
2 ADJ ATTRIB The **appointed** time or place for
something to happen is when or where it has been
decided that it will happen. *I arrived at the appointed
time. ...the appointed place for foreign ambassadors to
Moscow to present their credentials.*

appointee /əpɔɪntiː/ **appointees**
NC An **appointee** is a person who is formally chosen to
do a particular job. *The names of the three new
appointees have not been disclosed.*

appointment /əpɔɪntmənt/ **appointments**
1 NC The **appointment** of a person to do a particular
job is the choice of that person to do it. *Conservative
businessmen have been clearly delighted by the
appointment.*

2 NC An **appointment** is a job or position of responsibility. *His latest appointment as Foreign Minister seems to indicate that he has fully returned to grace.*
3 NC If you have an **appointment** with someone, you have arranged to see them at a particular time. *The doctor's appointment was for 11 am.*

apportion /əpɔːʃn/ **apportions, apportioning, apportioned**
VO When you **apportion** something, especially praise or blame, you decide how much of it different people or groups deserve or should be given. *It is not the institute's responsibility to apportion blame.*

apposite /æpəzɪt/
ADJ Something that is **apposite** is very suitable or appropriate to what is happening or being discussed; a formal word. *...apposite questions... The image of the tomb seemed particularly apposite in this case.*

apposition /æpəzɪʃn/
If a noun or group of words is in **apposition** to another, they refer to the same person or thing and are placed next to each other but without being joined by a conjunction; a technical term in grammar.

appraisal /əpreɪzl/ **appraisals**
NCorNU If you make an **appraisal** of something, you consider it carefully and form an opinion about it. *...a frank appraisal of the relief operation. ...topics that deserve great public attention and critical appraisal.*

appraise /əpreɪz/ **appraises, appraising, appraised**
VO If you **appraise** something, you consider it carefully and form an opinion about it. *...projects that are appraised by the bank as being viable.*

appreciable /əpriːʃəbl/
ADJ ATTRIB An **appreciable** amount or effect is large enough to be important or clearly noticed. *There had been appreciable progress recently.* ◆ **appreciably** SUBMOD *The following week it was appreciably colder.*

appreciate /əpriːʃieɪt/ **appreciates, appreciating, appreciated**
1 VOorV-REPORT If you **appreciate** a situation or problem, you understand it and know what it involves. *They are beginning to appreciate the full cost... He told the American audience that he appreciated that they had similar problems.*
2 VOorV-REPORT If you say that you **appreciate** what someone has done for you, you mean that you are grateful to them for it. *I for one appreciate and value the sacrifices of the security forces... The President said he appreciated that he had been described as the great communicator.*
3 VO If you **appreciate** something, you like it because you recognize its good qualities. *...a better society which could appreciate and enjoy a full artistic life.*
4 V If something **appreciates** in value over a period of time, its value increases. *These diamonds should appreciate in value.*

appreciation /əpriːʃieɪʃn/ **appreciations**
1 NU **Appreciation** of something is recognition and enjoyment of its good qualities. *He had little appreciation of great plays... 'This trout is delicious,' he added, with appreciation.*
2 NU If you show your **appreciation** for something that someone has done for you, you express your gratitude for it. *There were mutual expressions of appreciation and gratitude.*
3 NC An **appreciation** of a situation, problem, or difficulty, is an understanding of it or of what it involves. *Graduates will leave the institutions with a better appreciation of agro-forestry... The subcommittee had been assured that Treasury appreciations were available.*
4 NC An **appreciation** of someone such as an artist is a discussion and evaluation of their work. *...an appreciation of Professor Corey's achievements.*
5 NUorNC **Appreciation** in the value of something is the increase in its value over a period of time. *The appreciation of its currency has dampened demand for exports... There has been an appreciation of 31.2 per cent in these shares.*

appreciative /əpriːʃətɪv/
ADJ An **appreciative** reaction or expression shows pleasure or gratitude. *...appreciative laughter... 'Thank you,' I said, flashing him an appreciative smile.* ◆ **appreciatively** ADV *'Want a lift?' she asked. I nodded appreciatively.*

apprehend /æprɪhend/ **apprehends, apprehending, apprehended**
1 VO If someone, especially a policeman, **apprehends** someone, they catch and arrest them; a formal use. *The police are anxious to apprehend a middle-aged man believed to be armed with a shot gun.*
2 VO If you **apprehend** something, you understand it fully. *We often fail to apprehend the real nature of change.*

apprehension /æprɪhenʃn/ **apprehensions**
NUorNC **Apprehension** is a feeling of fear that something terrible may happen. *The months of uncertainty and apprehension were at last ended... The rumours heightened the apprehension of Conservative MPs... The threat gave rise to deep apprehensions.*

apprehensive /æprɪhensɪv/
ADJ Someone who is **apprehensive** is afraid that something terrible may happen. *Many Ethiopians are apprehensive about what faces them if the rebels take over... I felt a bit apprehensive at first.*
◆ **apprehensively** ADV *She looked up apprehensively.*

apprentice /əprentɪs/ **apprentices**
NC An **apprentice** is a young person who works for someone in order to learn their skills. *He has started training his own apprentices with the help of the RT Training School... He left school at the age of 14 to become an apprentice signwriter.*

apprenticeship /əprentɪsʃɪp/ **apprenticeships**
1 NCorNU A person's **apprenticeship** is the period of time they spend learning the skills they need to do their job properly. *In Britain you have to go through a long Parliamentary apprenticeship. ...a desperately short period of apprenticeship.*
2 NCorNU An **apprenticeship** is also the fixed period of time that someone spends working as an apprentice. *He did an apprenticeship as a machinist, and progressed to a quite senior engineering job. ...new groups for their apprenticeship scheme.*

apprise /əpraɪz/ **apprises, apprising, apprised**
VO+of When you **apprise** someone of a fact or situation, you tell them about it; a formal word. *I apprised him of the political situation in Washington.*

approach /əprəʊtʃ/ **approaches, approaching, approached**
1 VorVO When someone or something **approaches** you, they come nearer to you. *He opened the car door for her as she approached... A major column of tanks was approaching the parliament.* ► Also NC+SUPP *The dogs began to bark as if aware of our approach.*
2 VOA When you **approach** a situation or problem in a particular way, you think about it or deal with it in that way. *Governments must approach the subject of disarmament in a new spirit... There were various ways of approaching the issue.*
3 NC An **approach** to a situation or problem is a way of thinking about it or of dealing with it. *The UN approach should take account of the specific conditions of each province... Mr Major's approach was very different from that of Mr Mitterrand.*
4 VO If you **approach** someone about something, you speak to them about it for the first time. *He was approached by the Head of the Security Service and offered a job... They had approached us about working with their party.*
5 NC An **approach** from someone about something is an informal request that you do something for them, or an informal inquiry to establish whether you would be interested in having something, especially a job. *Following approaches from the Department of Health, the drug was withdrawn... I had had an approach to join the staff of the Daily Mail.*
6 NC An **approach** to a place is a road or path that leads to it. *The track was not intended as an approach to the palace... Government forces were successfully beating off attacks on the approaches to Jalalabad.*
7 V-ERG When a future event or date **approaches** or when you **approach** it, it gradually becomes nearer.

*They are being drawn together as the 1990s
approach... We are approaching the day of the race.*
▶ Also N SING+SUPP *...the approach of winter.*
8 VO If something **approaches** a particular level or
state, it almost reaches that level or state. *These
rocket planes approached speeds of 4000 mph... The
system was approaching collapse.*

approachable /əprˈəʊtʃəbl/
1 ADJ Someone who is **approachable** is friendly and
easy to talk to. *...a hotel with approachable staff...
Relaxed and approachable, he refuses to wear the
general's uniform that was standard for all previous
ministers of the interior.*
2 ADJ PRED A place which is **approachable** by a
particular route can be reached by that route. *The
statue is approachable by steps inside the column.*

approbation /æprəbˈeɪʃn/
NU **Approbation** is approval of something or
agreement to it; a formal word. *He surveyed the
document with approbation.*

**appropriate, appropriates, appropriating,
appropriated**; pronounced /əprˈəʊprɪət/ when it is an
adjective and /əprˈəʊprɪeɪt/ when it is a verb.
1 ADJ Something that is **appropriate** is suitable or
acceptable for a particular situation. *It seemed
appropriate to end with a joke... The visit could not
have come at a more appropriate time.*
◆ **appropriately** ADV *He reminded himself to thank
Louis appropriately.*
2 VO If you **appropriate** something which does not
belong to you, you take it for yourself; a formal use.
*The materials are exported and other countries
appropriate the profits.*

approval /əprˈuːvl/
1 NU If a plan or request gets **approval**, someone
agrees to allow it. *I was given McPherson's approval
for the plan.*
2 NU **Approval** also means liking and admiration.
Oliver looked at Simon with approval.

approve /əprˈuːv/ **approves, approving, approved**
1 VO If someone in authority **approves** a plan or idea,
they formally agree to it. *Parliament in Argentina
has approved a bill to increase taxes... Appointments
and promotions had to be approved by the party.*
2 V+of If you **approve** of an action, event, or
suggestion, you are pleased about it. *My grandfather
did not approve of my father's marriage... He also
approves of the suggestion that these states could seek
individual membership of the UN.*
3 V+of If you **approve** of someone or something, you
like and admire them. *He doesn't approve of me... He
did not approve of my pictures.*

approved /əprˈuːvd/
1 ADJ An **approved** method or course of action is
generally or officially accepted as appropriate. *They
cannot work without a work permit or a place on an
approved work scheme.*
2 ADJ Someone who is **approved** in a particular
position has been formally accepted by people in
authority. *...lists of approved candidates.*

approving /əprˈuːvɪŋ/
ADJ An **approving** reaction or expression shows
support for something, or satisfaction with it. *There
were a few approving nods and smiles.* ◆ **approvingly**
ADV *His wife watched approvingly.*

approx.
approx. is an abbreviation for 'approximately'. *He
was kidnapped at approx. 0915 GMT.*

**approximate, approximates, approximating,
approximated**; pronounced /əprˈɒksɪmət/ when it is an
adjective and /əprˈɒksɪmeɪt/ when it is a verb.
1 ADJ An **approximate** number, time, or position is
close to the correct number, time, or position, but is
not exact. *She gave me some approximate figures...
The official estimate of how many people have died is
described as very approximate.* ◆ **approximately** ADV
We have approximately 40 pupils.
2 VOorV+to If something **approximates** to something
else, it is similar to it but not exactly the same.
*...social conditions approximate those of the early
thirties. ...stories which vaguely approximated to the
truth.*

approximation /əprˌɒksɪmˈeɪʃn/ **approximations**
1 NC An **approximation** is a fact, object, or description
which is similar to something else but not exactly the
same. *...an approximation to the truth.*
2 NC An **approximation** is also a number, calculation,
or position that is not exact. *The figure we have is
only an approximation of the actual cost involved.*

appurtenances /əpˈɜːtɪnənsɪz/
N PL+SUPP **Appurtenances** are minor or additional
features or possessions; a formal word. *...the
appurtenances of modern civilisation.*

Apr.
Apr. is a written abbreviation for 'April'. *...5 Apr.
1940.*

après-ski /ˌæpreɪskˈiː/
N SING **après-ski** is evening entertainment and social
activities which take place in ski resorts. *Come just
for the après-ski if you like.*

apricot /ˈeɪprɪkɒt/ **apricots**
NCorNU An **apricot** is a small, soft, round fruit with
yellowish-orange flesh and a stone inside. *...a couple
of pounds of dried apricots... She was still smelling of
apricot.*

April /ˈeɪprəl/
NU **April** is the fourth month of the year in the
Western calendar. *Provincial elections will be held in
March or April.*

a priori /ˌeɪ praɪˈɔːraɪ/
ADJ ATTRIBorADV SEN **A priori** reasoning involves using
a general principle to work out the expected facts or
effects in a particular situation. The sentence: 'You've
been rushing around all day, you must be tired,' is an
example of a priori reasoning. *A priori arguments are
no substitute for evidence... This is a deliberate
decision to exclude, a priori, an entire segment of the
homeless poor.*

apron /ˈeɪprən/ **aprons**
1 NC An **apron** is a piece of clothing that you put on
over the front of your normal clothes to prevent them
from getting dirty. *...gold dust which has fallen from
the apron of a jeweller.*
2 NC The **apron** at an airport is the area near the
runways where aircraft are parked. *An Algerian
Presidential jet landed and stood on the apron nearby
for more than an hour.*

apropos /ˈæprəpəʊ/; a formal word.
1 PREP Something that is **apropos** a subject or event,
or **apropos** of it, is connected with or relevant to it.
*...apropos some doings at Cardiff... And apropos of
space medicine, I would like to mention a new
development.*
2 ADV SEN **Apropos** is also used to introduce something
that is related to the subject you have just been
talking about. *I was at school with his sister. Apropos,
I have often wondered what became of my old
schoolfriends.*

apt /æpt/
1 ADJ **Apt** means suitable. *...a very apt description.
...words which I think are really very apt at the
moment.* ◆ **aptly** ADV *...the aptly named village of
Cold Weston.*
2 ADJ PRED+to-INF If someone is **apt** to behave in a
particular way, they often behave in that way. *I was
apt to fidget during a long performance.*

aptitude /ˈæptɪtjuːd/ **aptitudes**
NCorNU If you have an **aptitude** for something, you
are able to learn it quickly and do it well. *He says all
his work is based on a love and an aptitude for
drawing. ...a role for which they have neither
experience nor aptitude.*

aptitude test, aptitude tests
NC An **aptitude test** is a test that is specially designed
to find out how easily and well you can do something.
*They are hoping to complete the job in eight hours as
part of an aptitude test.*

aqualung /ˈækwəlʌŋ/ **aqualungs**
NC An **aqualung** is a piece of equipment that divers
use to breathe underwater. It consists of a container of
air which is connected by tubes to the diver's face
mask. *Some of them even bring aqualungs and
snorkel tubes.*

aquamarine /ˈækwəməriːn/ **aquamarines**
1 NCorNU An **aquamarine** is a clear, greenish-blue stone used especially for making jewellery.
2 ADJ Something that is **aquamarine** in colour is greenish-blue. ...*the aquamarine water of the Indian Ocean.*

aquarium /əˈkweəriəm/ **aquariums** or **aquaria** /əˈkweəriə/
1 NC An **aquarium** is a glass tank filled with water, usually used to keep fish in. *If you put sea-snakes in an aquarium, they just bump against the sides.*
2 NC An **aquarium** is also a building, often in a zoo, where fish and underwater animals are kept. ...*a consignment of goldfish to be shipped to an aquarium in San Francisco.*

aquatic /əˈkwætɪk/
ADJ ATTRIB **Aquatic** means existing or happening in water. *One visible impact of acid rain has been in aquatic life in rivers and lakes.* ...*aquatic sports.*

aqueduct /ˈækwɪdʌkt/ **aqueducts**
NC An **aqueduct** is a long bridge with many arches, which carries a water supply or a canal over a valley. *The aqueduct spans the valley for almost half a mile.*

aquiline /ˈækwɪlaɪn/
ADJ An **aquiline** nose curves round into a point like the beak of an eagle. ...*a large, aquiline nose, and sharp, powerful eyes.*

Aquino, Corazon /kɒrəsɒn əkiːnəʊ/
Corazon Aquino became President of the Philippines in 1986, when Ferdinand Marcos was overthrown. She is the widow of Benigno Aquino, who was assassinated in 1983. She is a member of the United Nationalist Democratic Organization (UNIDO). Born: 1933.

Arab /ˈærəb/ **Arabs**
NC An **Arab** is a member of a people who live in the Middle East and North Africa. *The majority of Arabs employed in Israel stayed away from work.* ► Also ADJ *The Ambassadors of several Arab countries were invited.*

Arabian /əreɪbiən/
ADJ ATTRIB **Arabian** means belonging or relating to Arabia, especially to Saudi Arabia.

Arabic /ˈærəbɪk/
1 NU **Arabic** is a language spoken in the Middle East and in parts of North Africa. ...*a list of nineteen languages—including Arabic, Chinese and Asian languages.*
2 ADJ Something that is **Arabic** belongs or relates to the language, writing, or culture of the Arabs. *The themes of his Arabic poems include love songs and history.*
3 ADJ ATTRIB An **Arabic** numeral is one of the written figures, such as 1, 2, 3, or 4. *Even Arabic numbers don't make for effortless calculating.*

arable /ˈærəbl/
ADJ **Arable** is used to describe things that relate to growing crops. *In Asia most of the good arable land is in production.* ...*arable farming.*

Arab League /ˈærəb liːg/
The **League of Arab States**, more commonly known as the **Arab League**, was founded in 1945 to promote the common good of all Arab countries. Egypt was suspended from the Arab League from 1979 to 1989, and during this period the headquarters were transferred from Cairo to Tunis. The members of the Arab League are: Algeria, Bahrain, Djibouti, Egypt, Iraq, Jordan, Kuwait, Lebanon, Libya, Mauritania, Morocco, Oman, Palestine, Qatar, Saudi Arabia, Somalia, Sudan, Syria, Tunisia, United Arab Emirates, and Yemen.

arbiter /ˈɑːbɪtə/ **arbiters**
NC An **arbiter** is a person or institution that judges and settles a quarrel between people or groups; a formal word. *The Council of Guardians is no longer the final arbiter of the country's legislation.*

arbitrary /ˈɑːbɪtrəri/
ADJ An **arbitrary** decision or action is not taken or carried out for any particular reason. ...*the brutal and arbitrary expulsion of immigrants.* ♦ **arbitrarily** ADV *The victim has almost always been arbitrarily arrested.*

arbitrate /ˈɑːbɪtreɪt/ **arbitrates, arbitrating, arbitrated**
V When someone **arbitrates** between two people who are in dispute, they consider all the facts and try to decide who is right. *Egypt has become involved in efforts to arbitrate between the sides.*

arbitration /ˌɑːbɪˈtreɪʃn/
NU **Arbitration** is the judging of a dispute between people or groups by someone who is not involved. ...*arbitration between employers and unions.*

arbitrator /ˈɑːbɪtreɪtə/ **arbitrators**
NC An **arbitrator** is someone who judges and settles a quarrel between other people or groups. *They would turn to the President as final arbitrator.*

arboreal /ɑːˈbɔːriəl/
ADJ An animal that is **arboreal** lives mainly in the tops of trees. *All these species are arboreal and occur only in Africa... These apes are excellently adapted for the arboreal life.*

arbour /ˈɑːbə/ **arbours**; spelt **arbor** in American English.
NC An **arbour** is a shelter in a garden, which is formed by leaves and stems of plants growing close together over a light framework. *The arbour was furnished only with a wooden seat.*

arc /ɑːk/ **arcs**
1 NC An **arc** is a smoothly curving shape or line of movement. *The crew flew the plane in a wide arc back to Dar es Salaam.*
2 NC An **arc** is a section of the circumference of a circle; a technical term in mathematics.

arcade /ɑːˈkeɪd/ **arcades**
NC An **arcade** is a covered passageway, leading off a street, that has shops along it. ...*a building containing army offices and a shopping arcade.*

arcane /ɑːˈkeɪn/
ADJ Something that is **arcane** is very secret or mysterious; a formal word. ...*arcane and unwanted emotions.* ► Also N SING *She was fascinated by the forbidden, the arcane.*

arch /ɑːtʃ/ **arches, arching, arched**
1 NC An **arch** is a structure with a roof or top that curves upwards and is supported on either side by a pillar or wall. ...*a house beneath the railway arches.*
2 V-ERG When someone **arches** a part of their body, or when something **arches**, it forms a shape or line that curves upwards in the middle. *He arched his back... Trees arched over the sidewalks.*
3 See also **arched**.

arch- /ɑːtʃ-/
PREFIX **Arch-** combines with nouns that refer to people. The nouns formed in this way refer to people who are extreme representatives of whatever the original nouns refer to. ...*Liverpool once more inflicting misery on their arch-rivals Manchester United.* ...*a meeting with a man who is his arch-enemy... He is regarded as one of the arch-villains of the Middle-East.*

archaeology /ˌɑːkiˈɒlədʒi/; also spelt **archeology**.
NU **Archaeology** is the study of the past by examining the remains of things such as buildings and tools. ...*archaeology's race against the bulldozers to unearth and record a number of Roman and Mediaeval sites.* ♦ **archaeological** /ˌɑːkiəˈlɒdʒɪkl/ ADJ ...*the most dramatic archaeological discovery of this century.* ♦ **archaeologist, archaeologists** NC *Archaeologists date the fragment between 4650 and 4500 BC.*

archaic /ɑːˈkeɪɪk/
ADJ Things that are **archaic** are very old or very old-fashioned. ...*one of the most archaic Slavonic languages.* ...*the twin problems of serious overcrowding and archaic conditions.*

archangel /ˈɑːkeɪndʒl/ **archangels**
NC An **archangel** is an angel of the highest rank. ...*the Archangel Gabriel.*

archbishop /ˌɑːtʃˈbɪʃəp/ **archbishops**
NC An **archbishop** is a bishop of the highest rank, who is in charge of all the bishops and priests in a region. ...*the Archbishop's call for a peaceful solution to the power struggle.* ...*leading churchmen, including the Archbishop of Canterbury.*

archdeacon /ɑːtʃdiːkən/ **archdeacons**
NC An **archdeacon** is a clergyman of high rank who works as an assistant to a bishop, especially in the Anglican church. *The move was made by the Archdeacon of Colchester, the Venerable Ernest Stroud.*

arched /ɑːtʃt/
ADJ An **arched** roof, window, or doorway has a curved top. *Under the house, Pope had a special arched tunnel constructed.* ● See arch.

archeology /ɑːkiɒlədʒi/. See archaeology.

archer /ɑːtʃə/ **archers**
NC An **archer** is someone who shoots with a bow and arrow. *It turns out that the boy is a descendant of Arjuna, the great archer and conqueror.*

archery /ɑːtʃəri/
NU **Archery** is a sport in which people shoot at a target with a bow and arrow. *...five events including archery, table tennis, cycling and some football.*

archetypal /ɑːkɪtaɪpl/
ADJ Someone or something that is **archetypal** has all the most typical characteristics of a particular kind of person or thing and is a perfect example of them; a formal word. *...archetypal Romantic heroes.*
◆ **archetypally** SUBMOD *Stratford is so archetypally English, isn't it?*

archetype /ɑːkɪtaɪp/ **archetypes**
NC+SUPP The **archetype** of a kind of person or thing is a perfect and typical example of it. *He is said to be the archetype of the modern journalist.*

archipelago /ɑːkɪpɛləgəʊ/ **archipelagos**
NC An **archipelago** is a group of small islands. *...the main island of the Maldives archipelago, Male.*

architect /ɑːkɪtekt/ **architects**
1 NC An **architect** is a person who designs buildings. *...the architect's plans for an extension to the National Gallery.*
2 NC+SUPP The **architect** of an idea or event is the person who invented it or made it happen. *He was the real architect of the country's independence.*

architectural /ɑːkɪtektʃəʳrəl/
ADJ ATTRIB **Architectural** means relating to the design and construction of buildings. *...the architectural style suitable for government buildings.*

architecture /ɑːkɪtektʃə/
1 NU **Architecture** is the art of designing and constructing buildings. *The Prince often launches attacks on the state of British architecture, voicing concern for dwellers of badly designed houses.*
2 NU+SUPP The **architecture** of a building is the style in which it is constructed. *It was a marvel of Gothic architecture.*

archive /ɑːkaɪv/ **archives**
N PL or NC **Archives** are collections of documents and records that contain information about the history of an organization or group of people. *I looked up some of those old radio talks in the BBC archives... The Berlin Document Centre is the world's biggest Nazi archive.*

archivist /ɑːkɪvɪst/ **archivists**
NC An **archivist** is a person whose job is to collect, sort, and preserve historical documents and records. *The team was composed of historians and archivists.*

archway /ɑːtʃweɪ/ **archways**
NC An **archway** is a passage or entrance that has a curved roof and leads between two walls, pillars, or trees. *A big archway leads through into a courtyard. ...an archway of huge trees.*

arctic /ɑːktɪk/
1 N PROP The **Arctic** is the area of the world around the North Pole, where it is extremely cold and where there is very little light in winter and very little darkness in summer. *This is the most isolated island in the Arctic. ...an Arctic explorer.*
2 ADJ ATTRIB **Arctic** clothing or equipment is designed to be used in very cold conditions. *...an Arctic sleeping bag.*
3 ADJ A room or building that is **arctic** feels extremely cold. *...the arctic chill of the bathroom.*

Arctic Circle
N PROP The **Arctic Circle** is an imaginary line drawn around the northern part of the world at approximately 66° North. *We were based three hundred miles north of the Arctic Circle.*

ardent /ɑːdnt/
ADJ ATTRIB An **ardent** supporter or opponent of something feels very strongly about it. *Bernstein was an ardent supporter of human rights. ...an ardent advocate of Canadian unity. ...ardent opponents of Communism.* ◆ **ardently** ADV *No woman desired more ardently to educate her sons.*

ardour /ɑːdə/; spelt **ardor** in American English.
NU **Ardour** is an intense and passionate feeling of love or enthusiasm. *...a cooling of revolutionary ardour.*

arduous /ɑːdjuəs/
ADJ Something that is **arduous** is tiring and involves a lot of effort. *...a long and arduous journey.*

are /ə, ɑː/
Are is the second person (singular and plural), and the first and third person plural of the present tense of **be**.

area /eəriə/ **areas**
1 NC An **area** is a particular part of a city, a country, or the world. *...a dry area that gets only a few months of rain a year. ...the Brighton area.*
2 NC+SUPP A particular **area** of a room or other place is a part that is used for a particular activity. *...an outdoor play area. ...a communal washing area.*
3 NC The **area** of a shape or piece of land is the amount that it covers, expressed in a measurement such as square metres or hectares. *The search has now been extended to an area of a hundred-and-fifty square miles.*
4 NC+SUPP An **area** of knowledge or activity is a particular subject or kind of activity. *His special interest lies in the area of literature.*

area code, area codes
NC In the USA and Canada, the **area code** is a three-number code that you dial before a telephone number when you are making a long-distance call. *To reach the Morning Edition listener comment line, call area code 202 775-8686.*

arena /əriːnə/ **arenas**
NC An **arena** is a place where sports and other public events take place. It has seats around it where people sit and watch. *Birmingham has just built a new sports arena, a concert hall and a convention centre.*

aren't /ɑːnt/
1 **Aren't** is the usual spoken form of 'are not'. *We aren't ready... They are coming, aren't they?*
2 **Aren't** is used instead of 'am not' in negative questions. *I'm right, aren't I?*

Argentina /ɑːdʒəntiːnə/
The **Argentine Republic** is a country in southern South America. It was a Spanish colony from the 16th century to 1816. Juan Perón was the President from 1946 to 1955 and from 1973 to 1974. From 1976 to 1983 the military were in power. The unsuccessful invasion of the Falkland Islands in 1982 led to the restoration of democracy. Dr Carlos Saúl Menem, of the Justicialist Party (the Peronist party), became President in 1989. Argentina exports wheat, beef, and wool. High inflation and large foreign debts have often been major economic problems. Argentina is a member of the Organization of American States. ◆ **Argentine, Argentinian** /ɑːdʒəntaɪn, ɑːdʒəntɪniən/ N, ADJ
■ *per capita GNP:* US$2,160 ■ *religion:* Christianity (mainly Roman Catholic) ■ *language:* Spanish ■ *currency:* peso ■ *capital:* Buenos Aires ■ *population:* 32 million (1989) ■ *size:* 2,766,889 square kilometres.

argot /ɑːgəʊ/ **argots**
NC+SUPP An **argot** is a special vocabulary used by a particular group of people, which other people find difficult to understand; a formal word. *...modern street argot. ...the argot of the sixties.*

arguable /ɑːgjuəbl/
1 ADJ An idea, point, or comment that is **arguable** is not obviously true or correct and should be questioned. *Whether he was right or not is arguable.*
2 ADJ If you say that it is **arguable** that something is true, you mean that there are good reasons for thinking that it is true. *It is arguable that western civilisation was saved by his actions.* ◆ **arguably** ADV SEN *Deforestation is arguably the most serious*

environmental issue of our time.

argue /ɑːgjuː/ **argues, arguing, argued**
1 V-RECIP If you **argue** with someone, you say things which show that you disagree with them, sometimes speaking angrily. *They were arguing about who should sit in front... Don't argue with me, George, just do as you're told.*
2 V-REPORT If you **argue** that something is the case, you say that you think it is the case and give reasons why. *The Guardian argues that Moscow is unwilling to antagonize Tehran... The INF treaty was only concluded, Mr Reagan argues, because the United States built up its defences.*
3 V A If you **argue** for or **argue** against something, you give reasons why it should or should not happen. *Chief Buthelezi argues for non-violent change in South Africa... Mr Mohammed often argued against apartheid legislation.*

argument /ɑːgjʊmənt/ **arguments**
1 N COR N U An **argument** is a disagreement between two or more people, sometimes resulting in them shouting at each other. *He and David had been drawn into a ferocious argument... Wrangling, argument, and lawsuits followed.*
2 N C An **argument** is also a set of reasons or statements that you use to try to convince people that your opinion is correct. *There are strong arguments against these measures.*

argumentative /ɑːgjʊmɛntətɪv/
ADJ Someone who is **argumentative** is always ready to disagree. *She was described as unreasonable, excitable and argumentative. ...the rapidly improving relationship between the two often argumentative neighbours.*

aria /ɑːriə/ **arias**
N C An **aria** is a song for one of the leading singers in an opera or choral work. *...the many memorable arias in the Matthew Passion.*

arid /ærɪd/
ADJ Land that is **arid** is so dry that very few plants can grow on it. *...the key to a sustainable way of life in the desert and other arid areas.*

aright /əraɪt/: an old-fashioned word.
1 ADV If you hear or understand something **aright**, you hear or understand it correctly, even though you find it difficult to believe. *Morris wondered if he had heard aright.*
2 If you **set** or **put** an affair or situation **aright**, you deal with any problems that have arisen and arrange things in a satisfactory manner. *We are setting the fundamentals aright so that government and people together can rise up to the challenge.*

arise /əraɪz/ **arises, arising, arose, arisen**
V When something such as an opportunity, problem, or new state of affairs **arises**, it begins to exist. *A serious problem has arisen.*

aristocracy /ærɪstɒkrəsi/ **aristocracies**
N COLL The **aristocracy** is a class of people in some countries who have a high social rank and special titles. *...Royalty and the aristocracy.*

aristocrat /ærɪstəkræt, ərɪstəkræt/ **aristocrats**
N C An **aristocrat** is someone whose family has a high social rank, especially someone with a title. *He's the second son of a minor aristocrat.*

aristocratic /ærɪstəkrætɪk/
ADJ **Aristocratic** means belonging to the aristocracy, or typical of them. *...Prince Carl Swarzenberg, from one of Central Europe's oldest aristocratic families.*

arithmetic /ərɪθmətɪk/
N U **Arithmetic** is the part of mathematics that deals with the addition, subtraction, multiplication, and division of numbers. *Millions of British adults have difficulty with basic arithmetic.*

arithmetical /ærɪθmɛtɪkl/
ADJ **Arithmetical** means relating to or involving the addition, subtraction, multiplication, or division of numbers. *...arithmetical solutions to the problem.*

ark /ɑːk/
1 N PROP In the Bible, the **Ark** was a large wooden boat which Noah built in order to save his family and two of every kind of animal from the Flood. *...Mount Ararat, where Noah's Ark is supposed to have come to*

rest after the Flood.
2 If you say that something has come **out of the ark**, you mean that it is extremely old or old-fashioned; an informal expression, often used humorously. *This cash register must have come out of the ark.*

arm /ɑːm/ **arms, arming, armed**
1 N C Your **arms** are the two long parts of your body that are attached to your shoulders and that have your hands at the end. *...an operation to re-set his broken arm.*
2 N C+SUPP An **arm** of an organization is a section of it. *...the political arm of a trade union movement. ...the international trading arm of Britain's main telephone company.*
3 N C The **arms** of a chair are the parts on which you rest your arms. *Hers is the only chair that has arms.*
4 N PL **Arms** are weapons that are used in a war. *China has so far restricted its military support to small arms, anti-tank weapons, mortars and ammunition.*
5 V O If you **arm** someone, you provide them with a weapon, especially a gun. *The government continued arming these groups to ensure their continued loyalty... We must know how to arm ourselves.*
● **Arm** is used in these phrases. ● If you are walking **arm in arm** with someone, your arm is linked through their arm. *...President Fidel Castro and other Cuban leaders walking arm in arm across Revolution Square.*
● If you welcome something such as a situation, event, or change **with open arms**, you are very pleased about it and accept it gladly. *A teaching degree is welcomed with open arms.* ● If you hold something **at arm's length**, you hold it as far as possible from your body.
● If you **keep** someone **at arm's length**, you avoid becoming too friendly or involved with them. *Mr Chirac's supporters do not in fact keep the National Front at arms length when its suits them.* ● If someone is **up in arms** about something, they are protesting strongly about it. *Feminists are now up in arms over the new laws.*

armada /ɑːmɑːdə/ **armadas**
N C An **armada** is a large fleet of warships. *...the US Navy's 50-ship armada in the Gulf, the Indian Ocean, and Red Sea.*

armadillo /ɑːmədɪləʊ/ **armadillos**
N C An **armadillo** is a small animal from South America whose body is covered with large bony scales. Armadillos eat insects and live in burrows. *...the Indian children with whom I had played, fished, and hunted armadillos.*

armament /ɑːməmənt/ **armaments**
1 N PL **Armaments** are weapons and military equipment belonging to an army or country. *International action is essential to control the world traffic in armaments.*
2 N U **Armament** is the process of increasing the number and efficiency of a country's weapons. *...whatever armament or disarmament strategy the Soviet leader proposes.*

armband /ɑːmbænd/ **armbands**
N C An **armband** is a band of fabric that you wear round your arm at an event in order to show that you have an official position. Some people also wear a black armband to show that a friend or relation has died. *...stewards wearing official armbands... Employees in some government offices went to work wearing black armbands.*

armchair /ɑːmtʃeə/ **armchairs**
N C An **armchair** is a comfortable chair with a support on each side for your arms. *...upholstered furniture— sofas, armchairs, and so on.*

armed /ɑːmd/
1 ADJ Someone who is **armed** is carrying a weapon. *It is recognised that more and more criminals are armed... He was seized by armed men.*
2 ADJ ATTRIB An **armed** attack or conflict involves people fighting with guns. *The Red Army faction was held responsible for killings and armed attacks.*
3 ADJ PRED+with If you are **armed** with something useful such as information or a skill, you have it. *Armed with secretarial skills, she will easily find a job.*

armed forces
N PL The **armed forces** of a country are its army, navy, and air force. *The government of Surinam has placed the country's armed forces on alert.*

Armenia /ɑːˈmiːnɪə/
The **Republic of Armenia** became independent of the USSR in 1991. It is located in the extreme south of the former USSR, between the Black and Caspian Seas. Levon Ter-Petrosian, a nationalist, became President in 1990. Armenia exports wine, other agricultural products, chemicals, and machinery. It claims the Nagorny-Karabakh area of Azerbaijan. In 1991 Armenia joined the Commonwealth of Independent States. ◆ **Armenian** /ɑːˈmiːnɪən/ N, ADJ
■ *per capita GNP:* US$4,710 ■ *religion:* Christianity (Armenian Orthodox, Armenian Catholic) ■ *language:* Armenian ■ *currency:* dram ■ *capital:* Yerevan ■ *population:* 4 million (1991) ■ *size:* 29,800 square kilometres.

armful /ˈɑːmfʊl/ armfuls
NC An **armful** of something is the amount that you can carry in one or both of your arms. *...a big chunky armful of books.*

armhole /ˈɑːmhəʊl/ armholes
NC An **armhole** is an opening in an item of clothing such as a shirt or coat, through which you put your arm and where the sleeve is attached if there is one. *Make sure that the armholes are not too tight for you.*

armistice /ˈɑːmɪstɪs/ armistices
NCorNU An **armistice** is an agreement between countries who are at war to stop fighting for a time in order to discuss ways of making a peaceful settlement. *A just and lasting peace was obtained instead of a temporary armistice. ...a declaration of armistice.*

armour /ˈɑːmə/; spelt armor in American English.
1 NU **Armour** is a group of armoured vehicles, especially tanks. *...amphibious landings of troops and armour onto a series of beaches.*
2 N SING+SUPP **Armour** is also a hard covering that protects something from attack. *...advanced types of armour for tanks and other fighting vehicles. ...equipped for civil disturbance with body armour and riot shields... The animal has an armour of horny scales.*
3 NU The metal clothing that soldiers used to wear for protection in battle is also referred to as **armour**. *...suits of armour.*

armoured /ˈɑːməd/; spelt armored in American English.
ADJ ATTRIB An **armoured** vehicle has a hard metal covering that protects it from gunfire and other missiles. *An armoured vehicle was struck by artillery and rifle fire.*

armour-plated; spelt armor-plated in American English.
ADJ Something, especially a vehicle, that is **armour-plated** has a hard metal covering to protect it from attack. *He drove from Bonn to Cologne airport in an armour-plated car. ...cars that were not only armour-plated but also equipped with rocket launchers.*

armoury /ˈɑːmərɪ/ armouries; spelt armory in American English.
1 NC An **armoury** is a place where weapons, bombs, and other military equipment are stored. *They stole guns from the armoury and freed nearly thirty prisoners.*
2 NC A country's **armoury** is all the military equipment and weapons that it has. *They did not want to use any of their considerable nuclear armoury.*
3 NC+SUPP An **armoury** is also a collection of different things that you keep for a particular purpose. *...the housewife's armoury of medicines... This trick is one more part of her political armoury.*

armpit /ˈɑːmpɪt/ armpits
NC Your **armpit** is the area under your arm where your arm joins your shoulder. *...a tiny hidden scar within the armpit.*

arms race
N SING The **arms race** is the attempt by powerful countries always to have more and better weapons than their rivals. *They wanted an international agreement on ending the nuclear arms race.*

arm wrestling
NU **Arm wrestling** is an informal contest between two people. They both put one elbow on a flat surface, keeping the forearm vertical. They then clasp each other's hand and try to force it down until it touches the surface.

army /ˈɑːmɪ/ armies
1 N COLL An **army** is a large organized group of people who are armed and trained to fight. Most armies are organized and controlled by governments. *...an officer in the German army.*
2 NC+SUPP An **army** of people, animals, or things is a large number of them together. *...a vast army of poorly paid people across the world.*

aroma /əˈrəʊmə/ aromas
NC An **aroma** is a strong, pleasant smell. *The flavour and aroma of many fruits is better when salt water is used.*

aromatherapist /əˌrəʊməˈθerəpɪst/ aromatherapists
NC An **aromatherapist** is someone who is qualified to practise aromatherapy. *Aromatherapists do not generally make extravagant claims for success.*

aromatherapy /əˌrəʊməˈθerəpi/
NU **Aromatherapy** is a type of treatment, used especially to relieve tension, which involves massaging the body with special fragrant oils. *In some National Health Service hospitals, nurses have begun to use aromatherapy in the wards... Aromatherapy, homeopathy, and acupuncture are just a few of the alternative treatments available.*

aromatic /ˌærəˈmætɪk/
ADJ A plant or food that is **aromatic** has a strong, pleasant smell. *Ancient Egyptian medicine is based, almost entirely, on aromatic substances.*

arose /əˈrəʊz/
Arose is the past tense of **arise**.

around /əˈraʊnd/
1 ADVorPREP **Around** can be an adverb or preposition, and is often used instead of **round** as the second part of a phrasal verb. Examples of these uses of **around** are explained at **round**.
2 If someone or something is **around**, they are present or available. *It's a gadget which has been around for years... He went back down again to see who was around.*
3 ADV **Around** also means approximately. *He owns around 200 acres.*

arousal /əˈraʊzl/
NU+SUPP If something causes the **arousal** of a feeling, it causes people to have this feeling. *...the arousal of interest.*

arouse /əˈraʊz/ arouses, arousing, aroused
1 VO If something **arouses** a feeling or reaction in you, it causes you to have this feeling or reaction. *It may arouse his interest in the subject... The case has aroused tremendous controversy.*
2 VO If something **arouses** people, it makes them angry. *Yesterday's incident could well arouse the settlers to even greater violence.*
3 VO If something **arouses** you from sleep, it wakes you up; a literary use. *Diana had aroused them just before dawn.*

arr.
arr. is an abbreviation for 'arrives'. It is used on timetables to indicate what time a bus, train, or plane will reach a place.

arrange /əˈreɪndʒ/ arranges, arranging, arranged
1 VO If you **arrange** an event or meeting, you make plans for it to happen. *The date and venue for the talks still had to be arranged... Could you come up here and I'll arrange a meeting.*
2 V+with, V+to-INF, or V-REPORT If you **arrange** with someone to do something, you make plans together to do it. *I've arranged with somebody else to go there... We had arranged to meet in the street outside... It had been arranged that it would start on June the twenty-seventh.*
3 VO If you **arrange** something for someone, you make it possible for them to have it or to do it. *We can arrange loans... A possible deal may be arranged to allow him to resign.*

4 VOA If you **arrange** a number of objects, you put them in a particular position or order. *He began arranging his things. ...four chairs arranged around the table.*

arranged marriage, arranged marriages
NC In an **arranged marriage**, the parents choose the person who their son or daughter will marry. *...the traditional values which push them into arranged marriages.*

arrangement /ərɛɪndʒmənt/ **arrangements**
1 N PL **Arrangements** are plans and preparations which you make so that something will happen or be possible. *I've made all the arrangements for the conference.*
2 NC+SUPP An **arrangement** of things, for example flowers or furniture, is a group of them displayed in a particular way. *There was an arrangement of books in the window.*

arrant /ærənt/
ADJ ATTRIB You use **arrant** to emphasize that someone or something is very bad in some way. *...an arrant coward... That was probably the most arrant piece of folly you have committed in your life.*

array /ərɛɪ/ **arrays**
1 NC+of An **array** of things is a large number of different things. *...a vast array of fine furniture, porcelain, silver, clocks and books. ...an impressive array of weapons.*
2 NC An **array** is also a large number of things of a particular type that are connected so that they can work together; a technical term in physics. *Power could have been supplied by a solar cell array.*

arrears /ərɪəz/
N PL **Arrears** are amounts of money that someone owes. *There's been a big increase in rent arrears by council tenants. ...the deadline for the arrears to be paid.*
● **Arrears** is used in these phrases. ● If someone is **in arrears**, they have not paid the regular amounts of money that they should have paid. *Zambia is in arrears in its repayments to the IMF and World Bank.*
● If you are paid **in arrears**, your wages are paid to you at the end of the period of time in which you earned them. *She was paid every four weeks in arrears.*

arrest /ərɛst/ **arrests, arresting, arrested**
1 VO When the police **arrest** someone, they catch them and take them somewhere in order to decide whether they should be charged with an offence. *The authorities continue to arrest and harass members of the opposition movement... A friend had been arrested for possession of explosives.*
2 NUorNC When the police make an **arrest**, they arrest someone. *A number of arrests were made. ...opposition leaders had gone underground to escape arrest.*
3 If someone is **under arrest**, they have been caught by the police and are not allowed to go free. *The president and most of his ministers are under arrest.*
4 VO To **arrest** something means to stop it happening; a formal use. *He tried to arrest the course of destruction.*

arrest warrant, arrest warrants
NC An **arrest warrant** is an official document that has been signed by an officer of the court ordering the arrest of a named individual. *A US magistrate has issued an arrest warrant for a fourth person.*

arrival /ərɑɪvl/ **arrivals**
1 NU Your **arrival** at a place is the act of arriving there. *I apologise for my late arrival... British Airways announce the arrival of flight BA072 from New York... He made no reference on his arrival to the latest developments in South Africa.*
2 N SING+SUPP If you talk about the **arrival** of something new, you are referring to the fact that it has begun to exist or happen. *Industry has been revolutionized by the arrival of the computer... Housing was meant to improve with the arrival of the bright new communist future.*
3 N SING The **arrival** of a baby is its birth. *And how's the latest arrival, then?*
4 NC An **arrival** is someone who has just arrived at a

place. *One of the new arrivals at the college was an old friend.*

arrive /ərɑɪv/ **arrives, arriving, arrived**
1 VorVA When you **arrive** at a place, you reach it at the end of a journey, or you come to it for the first time in order to stay or live there. *I sent a Telegram to my mother saying I had arrived safely... He arrived back at his hotel... Since arriving in England in 1979, she has established herself as a major writer.*
2 VorVA When something **arrives** at a place, it reaches that place or is delivered there. *Relief supplies for flood victims are continuing to arrive... Letters which arrived last October were only opened in December... He was arrested by police after his plane arrived at Heathrow.*
3 V+at When you **arrive** at an idea, decision, or conclusion, you reach it or decide on it. *It was not possible to arrive at a conclusive result... Each side can present its own arguments and arrive at a decision.*
4 V When a baby **arrives**, it is born. *My baby arrived at a quarter to midnight.*
5 V When a time or event that you have been waiting for **arrives**, it happens. *The next round of talks has now arrived... The moment for action has arrived.*

arrogance /ærəgəns/
NU **Arrogance** is excessively proud and unpleasant attitudes or behaviour. *This was answered with arrogance and disrespect.*

arrogant /ærəgənt/
ADJ Someone who is **arrogant** behaves in a proud, unpleasant way because they believe they are more important than other people. *They are arrogant and aggressive people.* ◆ **arrogantly** ADV *They regarded me arrogantly.*

arrow /ærəʊ/ **arrows**
1 NC An **arrow** is a long thin weapon with a sharp point at one end which is shot from a bow. *...a full range of weaponry, from bows and arrows to cannons and muskets.*
2 NC An **arrow** is also a written sign which points in a particular direction to indicate where something is. *They are marked out with directional arrows.*

arrowhead /ærəʊhed/ **arrowheads**
NC An **arrowhead** is the sharp, pointed end of an arrow. *I was trying to think what animal I would kill with the arrowhead.*

arrowroot /ærəʊruːt/
NU **Arrowroot** is a starch obtained from a West Indian plant that is used in cooking, for example for thickening sauces or in making biscuits. *...the sweet potato, arrowroot, cassava and other root crops.*

arse /ɑːs/ **arses, arsing, arsed**
NC Your **arse** is your bottom; an informal and rude word which some people find offensive.
● **Arse** is used in these informal phrases. ● If someone tells you to **move your arse** or **shift** your **arse**, they are telling you very impolitely to make a space for them to sit down. ● If someone tells you to **get off** your **arse**, they are telling you very impolitely that you should hurry up and do something or get on with what you are supposed to be doing.

arse about or **arse around** PHRASAL VERB If you say that someone **is arsing about**, you mean that they are behaving in a silly and irritating way instead of getting something done; an informal and rude expression which some people find offensive.

arsenal /ɑːsənəl/ **arsenals**
1 NC An **arsenal** of weapons and equipment is all the weapons and military equipment which a country or group has. *...an agreement to cut the Soviet and US nuclear arsenals by fifty percent... Their arsenal totalled 36 pistols and a few rifles.*
2 NC An **arsenal** is a building where weapons and pieces of military equipment are stored and made. *They raided a British arsenal and ambushed several convoys.*
3 NC+SUPP An **arsenal** of ideas or objects is a large number or collection of ideas or objects, especially when they can be used to hurt people or to deal with a difficult problem. *...mankind's arsenal of horrors... He told Parliament that a whole arsenal of measures*

was needed to curb inflation.

arsenic /ɑːsəⁿnɪk/

NU **Arsenic** is a very strong poison which can kill people. *Arsenic poisoning causes burning pain in the mouth and throat.*

arson /ɑːsn/

NU **Arson** is the crime of deliberately setting fire to a building. *Sporadic outbreaks of arson have occurred in other parts of the city... Bombing and arson attacks destroyed more than a million dollars' worth of property.*

art /ɑːt/ **arts**

1 NU **Art** is the making of paintings, drawings, and sculpture which are beautiful or which express an artist's ideas. *...an incredible impulse that came to art in the middle of the twentieth century. ...the development of post-war American art.*

2 NU **Art** is also used to refer to the paintings, drawings, and sculpture produced by artists. *...one of the world's priceless works of art. ...a great art collection.*

3 N PL The **arts** refers to the creation or performance of drama, music, poetry, or painting. *...Europe's largest arts extravaganza, the Edinburgh International Festival... How much will they spend on sport, how much on the arts?*

4 N PL The **arts** are subjects such as languages, literature, or history, rather than science. *The proportion of students in arts is fairly high. ...an arts degree.*

5 N SING+SUPP The **art** of something, or the **art** of doing something is the skills you need in order to do it. *...the art of camouflage... The real art of coping with disaster is to avoid it!*

artefact /ɑːtɪfækt/ **artefacts**; also spelt **artifact**.

NC An **artefact** is an ornament, tool, or other object made by a human being. *...gold jewellery and artefacts excavated from the site of Troy.*

arterial /ɑːtɪəriəl/

1 ADJ ATTRIB **Arterial** means involving or relating to your arteries and the movement of blood through your body. *...arterial and heart disease.*

2 ADJ ATTRIB An **arterial** road or railway is a road or railway that is the main route from one place to another. *...an ambitious system of new arterial highways.*

artery /ɑːtəri/ **arteries**

NC Your **arteries** are the tubes that carry blood from your heart to the rest of your body. *...the aorta, the main artery leading from the heart.*

artesian well /ɑːtiːziən wel/ **artesian wells**

NC An **artesian well** is a well in which the water is continuously forced up out of the ground as a result of pressure from water flowing into the well from a higher level. *They have to rely on rationed supplies of water from artesian wells.*

artful /ɑːtfl/

ADJ Someone who is **artful** is clever and skilful, often in a cunning way. *They became the most artful of all the hunters.* ◆ **artfully** ADV *The lighting was artfully arranged to flatter people's faces.*

arthritic /ɑːθrɪtɪk/

ADJ An **arthritic** person or joint is affected by arthritis. *It's the progressive loss of bone material that causes the arthritic joint to become unstable.*

arthritis /ɑːθraɪtɪs/

NU **Arthritis** is a condition in which the joints in someone's body are swollen and painful. *Anti-inflammatory drugs have been very successful in giving sufferers relief from the crippling pain of arthritis.*

artichoke /ɑːtɪtʃəuk/ **artichokes**

1 NC An **artichoke** or a **globe artichoke** is a round, green vegetable with fleshy leaves, of which you eat the bottom part. *The famous Toulouse chef prepared compôte of pigeons, duck with artichokes and oxtail fondue.*

2 NC An **artichoke** or a **Jerusalem artichoke** is a small, yellowish-white vegetable that grows underground and looks like a potato.

article /ɑːtɪkl/ **articles**

1 NC An **article** is a piece of writing in a newspaper or magazine. *...a front page article in the US newspaper The New York Times.*

2 NC You can use **article** to refer generally to an object. *He was ordered to pay for the articles he had stolen.*

3 NC An **article** of a formal document is a section dealing with a particular point. *The invasion contravened article 51 of the UN charter.*

4 In grammar, **articles** are the words 'a', 'an', and 'the'. In this dictionary, articles are called **determiners**. ● See also **definite article, indefinite article**.

articled /ɑːtɪkld/

ADJ Someone who is **articled**, for example to a firm of lawyers or accountants, is employed by the firm and is training to become qualified. *I had been articled for three years. ...an articled clerk.*

article of faith, articles of faith

NC An **article of faith** is something that you believe very strongly in, even though there might not be very much evidence to support your belief. *Nationalism was a deep-rooted article of faith.*

articulate, articulates, articulating, articulated; pronounced /ɑːtɪkjʊlət/ when it is an adjective and /ɑːtɪkjʊleɪt/ when it is a verb.

1 ADJ If you are **articulate**, you are able to express yourself well. *...a small but very articulate, very vocal and very influential minority.*

2 VO When you **articulate** your ideas or feelings, you say in words what you think or feel; a formal use. *General Chatichai was quick to articulate a new policy towards Indo-China.*

articulated /ɑːtɪkjʊleɪtɪd/

ADJ ATTRIB An **articulated** vehicle is made in two sections which are joined so that the vehicle can turn corners more easily. *The drivers have parked their big articulated trucks across ferry-loading ramps.*

articulation /ɑːtɪkjʊleɪʃn/

1 NU The **articulation** of an idea or feeling is its expression in words; a formal use. *...the articulation of an alternative housing policy.*

2 NU The **articulation** of a sound or word is the way it is spoken.

artifact /ɑːtɪfækt/. See **artefact**.

artifice /ɑːtɪfɪs/ **artifices**

1 NC An **artifice** is a clever trick or deception; a formal use. *...small and subtle artifices... They saw through the artifice.*

2 NU **Artifice** is the clever use of tricks and devices. *...the audience's awareness of the play's artifice.*

artificial /ɑːtɪfɪʃl/

1 ADJ An **artificial** state or situation is not natural and exists because people have created it. *These results appear only in very artificial conditions... The artificial scarcity of his product increases its value... These national distinctions were fairly artificial.* ◆ **artificially** SUBMOD *The government keeps prices artificially high.* ◆ **artificiality** /ɑːtɪfɪʃiælətɪ/ NU *There was a strong element of artificiality in this movement.*

2 ADJ **Artificial** objects or materials do not occur naturally and are made by people. *...some of the most popular crisp flavours use artifical sweeteners. ...artificial fibres.* ◆ **artificially** ADV *It might be possible to manufacture petrol artificially from coal or gas.*

3 ADJ ATTRIB An **artificial** arm or leg is made of metal or plastic and is fitted to someone's body when their own arm or leg has been removed. *...new developments in the design of artificial arms and legs.*

4 ADJ If someone's behaviour is **artificial**, they are pretending to have attitudes and feelings which they do not really have. *They jumped at the suggestion with artificial enthusiasm.*

artificial intelligence

NU **Artificial intelligence** is the study of how to make computers work in an intelligent way to do things that humans do, especially in the areas of language, vision, and movement. *...the fascinating world of robots and artificial intelligence.*

artificial light

NU **Artificial light** is light that is created, for example, by gas or electricity rather than being produced by the sun. ...*a room without windows, lit by artificial light.*

artificial respiration
NU **Artificial respiration** is the forcing of air into the lungs of someone who has stopped breathing, in order to keep them alive and to help them to start breathing again. *He was given artificial respiration but died a few hours later in hospital.*

artillery /ɑːtɪləri/
NU **Artillery** consists of large, powerful guns which are transported on wheels and used by an army. *Heavy fighting ensued with each side using artillery, mortar and heavy machine-guns.*

artisan /ɑːtɪzæn/ **artisans**
NC An **artisan** is a person who has a job which requires skill with their hands. *Industry has destroyed the livelihood of village artisans.*

artist /ɑːtɪst/ **artists**
1 NC An **artist** is someone who draws, paints, or produces other works of art. *...England's most famous landscape artist, John Constable.*
2 NC You can refer to a musician, actor, dancer, or other performer as an **artist**. *She has acted with great artists like Edith Evans.*

artiste /ɑːtiːst/ **artistes**
NC An **artiste** is a professional entertainer, for example a singer or dancer. *...she was soon established as a popular artiste in her own right.*

artistic /ɑːtɪstɪk/
1 ADJ Someone who is **artistic** is good at drawing and painting or at arranging things in an attractive way. *Artistic people are in a tiny minority in this country... She is very artistic.* ♦ **artistically** ADV *She was artistically gifted.*
2 ADJ **Artistic** also means relating to art or artists. *The preview was a social rather than an artistic occasion. ...calls for more artistic freedom.*
3 ADJ A design or arrangement that is **artistic** is attractive. *...a very artistic design.* ♦ **artistically** ADV *The flowers were artistically arranged.*

artistry /ɑːtɪstri/
NU **Artistry** is the great skill with which something is done. *He acted the final scenes with superb artistry.*

artless /ɑːtləs/
ADJ Someone who is **artless** is simple and honest, and does not think of deceiving other people. *Jonathan was innocent and artless. ...Willie's artless simplicity.* ♦ **artlessly** ADV *Betty artlessly divulged where they had been.* ♦ **artlessness** NU *The sincerity and artlessness with which she discussed the problem was disarming.*

Art Nouveau /ɑːt nuːvəʊ/
NU **Art Nouveau** is a style of art that was common in the 1890s and that has flowing lines and patterns of flowers and leaves. *...art nouveau tiles.*

artwork /ɑːtwɜːk/
NU **Artwork** is drawings and photographs that are prepared in order to be included in a book or an advertisement. *The computer graphic design system produces complex artwork in a fraction of the normal time.*

arty /ɑːti/
ADJ Someone who is **arty** seems to be very interested in painting, sculpture, and other works of art. *My grandmother cooked spaghetti for her arty friends.*

Aruba /əruːbə/
Aruba is a territory of the Netherlands in the Caribbean. It became a Dutch colony in 1636. In 1986 it became independent of the Netherlands Antilles.Tourism and banking are important industries. ♦ **Aruban** /əruːbən/ N, ADJ
▪ *per capita GNP:* US$6,000 ▪ *religion:* Christianity (mainly Roman Catholic) ▪ *language:* Dutch (official), Papiamento ▪ *currency:* guilder or florin ▪ *capital:* Oranjestad ▪ *population:* 62,000 (1989) ▪ *size:* 193 square kilometres.

as /əz, æz/
1 CONJ If something happens **as** something else happens, it happens at the same time. *She wept bitterly as she told her story... As men retire they are replaced on the board.*
2 PREP You use **as** to introduce a prepositional phrase referring to something's appearance or function. *You*

regard the whole thing as a joke... Hydrogen gas can be used as a fuel... Over the summer she worked as a waitress.*
3 CONJ You use **as** when you are saying how something is done. *I like the freedom to organize my day as I want to... They were people who spoke and thought as he did.*
4 CONJ You can also use **as** to mean 'because'. *She bought herself an iron, as she felt she couldn't keep borrowing Anne's... As he had been up since 4 a.m. he was no doubt very tired.*
5 PREP or CONJ You use **as** to introduce a comment that you are making. *As usual at the weekend, the club was almost empty... As you can see, we've got a problem with the engine.*
● **As** is used in these phrases. ● You use the structure **as...as** when you are comparing things. *You've never been as late as this without telephoning... I'm as good a cook as she is.* ● You use **as if** and **as though** when you are comparing one situation to another. *The furniture looked as though it had come out of somebody's attic... He looked at me as if I were mad.* ● You use **as for** to introduce a slightly different subject. *That's the answer. As for the cause, how do I know?* ● If you say that something will happen **as of** or **as from** a particular date or time, you mean that it will happen from that time onwards. *As of next week I'll be working at home.* ● You use **as to** to indicate what something refers to. *John had been given no directions as to what to write.* ● You say **as it were** in order to make what you are saying sound less definite. *That was, as it were, part of the job.*

asbestos /æsbɛstəs/
NU **Asbestos** is a grey material which does not burn, and is used in making some fireproof materials. *Thick black soot containing asbestos dust has spread over a wide area.*

ascend /əsɛnd/ **ascends, ascending, ascended**; a literary word.
1 V If something **ascends**, it goes upwards. *The blossoms are like flames ascending to the heavens.*
2 VO If you **ascend** a hill or a staircase, you go up it. *The television cameras gather to shoot a British Prime Minister ascending the steps of the White House.*

ascendancy /əsɛndənsi/
NU If one group or organization has **ascendancy** over another, it has more power or influence than the second group; a formal word. *German ascendancy in the monetary sphere means it can willingly back monetary union.* ● If a group is in the **ascendancy**, it is becoming more powerful than other groups. *It is the moderate opinion which will have triumphed, and will be in the ascendancy over the extremists.*

ascendant /əsɛndənt/
If someone or something is **in the ascendant**, they are increasing in power, influence, or popularity. *Democratic trends are now in the ascendant in many countries.*

ascending /əsɛndɪŋ/
ADJ ATTRIB If a group of things is arranged in **ascending** order, each thing is bigger or more important than the thing before it. *Arrange the four digits in ascending order. ...little houses built on ascending levels on the slopes of the hills.*

ascent /əsɛnt/ **ascents**
NC An **ascent** is a steep upward slope, or a journey up a steep slope. *The final ascent took an hour.*

ascertain /æsəteɪn/ **ascertains, ascertaining, ascertained**
V-REPORT or VO If you **ascertain** that something is the case, you find out that it is the case; a formal word. *I ascertained that Lo was still sound asleep... The embassy was still trying to ascertain the truth of reports that mass killings occurred in the north-east of the country.*

ascetic /əsɛtɪk/ **ascetics**
ADJ People who are **ascetic** have a way of life that is simple and strict, often because of their religious beliefs. *...the ascetic world of scientific journals.* ▶ Also NC *...a Christian ascetic.*

ascribe /əskraɪb/ **ascribes, ascribing, ascribed**
1 VO+to If you **ascribe** an event or state of affairs to a particular factor, you think that it is caused by that factor. *...headaches which may be ascribed to stress.*
2 VO+to If you **ascribe** a quality to someone, you consider that they have it. *Husbands are often mistaken in the virtues they ascribe to their wives.*

ASEAN /æsiæn/ See **Association of South East Asian Nations**

aseptic /eɪsɛptɪk/
ADJ Something such as a wound or a dressing that is **aseptic** is clean and free from germs; a medical term.

asexual /eɪsɛkʃuəl/
ADJ Something that is **asexual** has no sex or involves no sexual activity. *...two methods of reproduction, sexual and asexual.*

ash /æʃ/ **ashes**
1 NUorN PL **Ash** is the grey powder that is left after something is burnt. *...cigarette ash... Ashes blew into Ralph's face from the dead fire.*
2 NCorNU An **ash** is a tree. It produces small green flowers and winged seeds. The wood that is obtained from this tree is also called **ash**. *The area will be planted with broad leaf trees, such as ash, oak, and sycamore.*

ashamed /əʃeɪmd/
1 ADJ PRED If you are **ashamed** of something you have done, you feel embarrassed or guilty because of it. *He should be ashamed of himself... There is no reason to be ashamed because you've been diagnosed HIV positive... She was ashamed of her tears... They do things which they are desperately ashamed of.*
2 ADJ PRED+to-INF If you are **ashamed** to do something, you do not want to do it, or do not like doing it, because you feel embarrassed about it. *I bet that's what happened, and you're ashamed to admit it... The General in charge said he was ashamed to show his face in public... He was almost ashamed to see the boxes of charity food arriving in his country.*
3 ADJ PRED+of If you are **ashamed** of someone, you disapprove of something they have done and feel embarrassed to be connected with them. *He was ashamed of her for writing such lies... I always tried to behave in such a way that my people would not be ashamed of me.*

ashcan /æʃkæn/ **ashcans**
NC An **ashcan** is the same as a **dustbin**; used in American English. *He threw them in the ashcan.*

Ashdown, Paddy /pædi æʃdaʊn/
Paddy Ashdown became the leader of the Liberal Democrat party in the United Kingdom in 1988. He entered Parliament in 1983 as the MP for Yeovil. Born: 1941.

ashen /æʃn/
ADJ Someone who is **ashen** looks very pale, especially because they are shocked or afraid. *Joan collapsed, pale and trembling, her face ashen.*

Ashkhabad /æʃxəbæd/
Ashkhabad is the capital of Turkmenistan and its largest city. Population: 402,000 (1989).

ashore /əʃɔː/
ADV Something that comes **ashore** comes from the sea onto the shore. *He managed to swim ashore.*

ashtray /æʃtreɪ/ **ashtrays**
NC An **ashtray** is a small dish in which people put the ash from their cigarettes and cigars. *...a table with empty beer cans serving as ashtrays.*

Asia /eɪʃə, eɪʒə/
Asia is the world's largest and most populous continent. It comprises about one third of the world's landmass and 60 per cent of the world's population. It is about 45 million square kilometres. The estimated population for 1989 was 3 billion. The highest point in Asia, and the world, is Mount Everest (8,848 metres).

Asian /eɪʃn, eɪʒn/ **Asians**
1 ADJ **Asian** means belonging or relating to Asia. *At these games, the hosts have been trying to introduce a distinctive Asian flavour.*
2 NC An **Asian** is a person who comes from India, Pakistan, or some other part of Asia. *Blacks and Asians are still dramatically under-represented in Parliament... The tribunal ruled that the Asian police*

officer had suffered racial discrimination.

aside /əsaɪd/ **asides**
1 ADV If you move something **aside**, you move it to one side of you. *He threw the manuscript aside... He put the bottle aside without taking any himself... He put his pencil aside when I spoke to him.*
2 ADV If you move **aside**, you get out of someone's way. *They moved aside when the crowds pressed around them, chanting 'Let them through'... Police are reported to have stepped aside and allowed the opposition figures to enter.*
3 ADV If you put a problem, feeling, or suggestion **aside**, you reject it or ignore it because you do not think that it is important. *This possibility cannot be put aside completely... They have for the moment put aside their differences over the UN peace plan... They brushed aside an appeal by the President to discuss their demands.*
4 ADV If you set something such as money **aside**, for a particular purpose, you save it and do not use it for any other purpose. *The Senate set aside $150m to rebuild the embassy... They have now got permission from the state to have areas of the Amazon rainforest set aside for them to farm... The bonus would have to be put aside for college for our two children.*
5 ADV If you take someone **aside**, you take them away from a group of people in order to deal with them in private. *According to the youths, they were taken aside and beaten by four or five soldiers... One health worker takes the village women aside to teach them about hygiene.*
6 NC An **aside** is a remark or comment that is not directly connected with what you are saying or writing. *It was a brisk aside, which will not have gone unnoticed in the developing world... We learn almost nothing about these events from the book, except through editorial asides.*
7 PREP **Aside from** means the same as **apart from**. *Aside from some minor military activity in the provinces, the country remains calm.*

asinine /æsɪnaɪn/
ADJ Someone or something that is **asinine** is very foolish; a literary word.

ask /ɑːsk/ **asks, asking, asked**
1 VO, VO-REPORT, V-QUOTE, or VOO If you **ask** someone something, you say something in the form of a question because you want some information. *Nobody's really asked this question before... I asked him what he wanted... Janet Cochrane asked Gill whether there were still things we don't know about AIDS... 'Why?' he asked... He started asking Diana a lot of questions.*
2 VO If you **ask** someone to do something, you say to them that you want them to do it. *He asked her to marry him... The American consulate asked him to return later this week... I asked John Marshall to describe the kind of disabilities that such patients experience.*
3 VO If you **ask** someone's permission or forgiveness, you try to obtain it. *I asked permission to leave... He asked the crowd's forgiveness for failing, as President, to prevent the men from dying in defence of the parliament.*
4 VOA If you **ask** someone somewhere, you invite them there. *She asked me in... I asked her to the party.*
● **Ask** is used in these phrases. ● If someone says that something is yours **for the asking**, they mean that it is very easy for you to get or achieve. *If they truly wanted peace, it was there for the asking.* ● You can say **'if you ask me'** to emphasize that you are stating your personal opinion. *The whole thing's stupid if you ask me.*

ask after PHRASAL VERB If you **ask after** someone, you ask how or where they are. *Two lawyers who went to the police offices asking after Mr Rubia were told not to leave the building.*

ask for PHRASAL VERB 1 If you **ask for** someone, you say that you would like to speak to them. *He rang the office and asked for Cynthia.* 2 If you **ask for** something, you say that you would like it. *They have asked for a boycott of the elections... The Americans*

have asked for thirty billion dollars in compensation.
3 If you say that someone is **asking for** something, you mean that they are behaving in a way that makes it likely that something unpleasant will happen to them; an informal expression. *You're really asking for trouble speaking to me like that.*

askance /əskǽns/
If you **look askance** at someone, you view them in a doubtful or suspicious way. *The far right looks askance at the flood of new immigrants to Germany.*

askew /əskjúː/
ADJ PRED Something that is **askew** is not straight or level. *...a dustbin with its lid knocked askew.*

asking price
N SING The **asking price** for something is the price which the person who is selling it says they want for it. *They reduced their asking price by almost a half.*

asleep /əslíːp/
ADJ PRED Someone who is **asleep** is sleeping. *For no apparent reason, the babies simply stop breathing while asleep.* ● **Asleep** is used in these phrases. ● When you **fall asleep**, you start sleeping. *I'd better get up before I fall asleep.* ● Someone who is **fast asleep** or **sound asleep** is sleeping deeply. *Many were slumped over their desks, fast asleep.*

asparagus /əspǽrəgəs/
NU **Asparagus** is a vegetable with green shoots that you cook and eat. *...a two-hour banquet of veal fillets and asparagus.*

aspect /ǽspekt/ **aspects**
1 NC+SUPP An **aspect** of something is one of the parts of its character or nature. *The most terrifying aspect of nuclear bombing is radiation... There's a women's point of view on each and every aspect of government... I have maybe five hundred books on my shelves covering every aspect of American history.*
2 NC+SUPP A room or a window with a particular **aspect** faces in that direction; a formal use. *...an office with a south-west aspect.*

asperity /æspérəti/
NU **Asperity** is impatience and sternness that you express in your voice; a formal word. *I said, with some asperity, that it was no concern of mine.*

aspersions /əspɜ́ːʃnz/
If you **cast aspersions** on someone or something, you suggest that they are not very good in some way; a formal expression. *...casting aspersions on the Association's management and reputation.*

asphalt /ǽsfælt/
NU **Asphalt** is a black substance used to make the surfaces of things such as roads and playgrounds. *On top was a layer of cement, and this was covered with asphalt.*

asphyxia /æsfíksiə/
NU **Asphyxia** is death or loss of consciousness caused by being unable to breathe properly. *One child was rescued alive, though suffering from asphyxia.*

asphyxiate /æsfíksieɪt/ **asphyxiates, asphyxiating, asphyxiated**
VO If someone is **asphyxiated**, they die because they are unable to breathe properly. *One report says the pilgrims were crushed or asphyxiated during a stampede.* ◆ **asphyxiation** /æsfíksieɪʃn/ NU *Heavy doses of mustard gas caused asphyxiation of the victim.*

aspic /ǽspɪk/
NU **Aspic** is a clear shiny jelly made from meat juices and used in cold savoury dishes. *...chicken in aspic.*

aspirant /əspáɪrənt, ǽspərənt/ **aspirants**
NC An **aspirant** is someone who has a strong desire to achieve power or an important position; a formal word. *Joseph Momoh had not been seen as a political aspirant, despite his long association with the government.*

aspirate, aspirates, aspirating, aspirated;
pronounced /ǽspərət/ when it is a noun and /ǽspəreɪt/ when it is a verb.
1 NC An **aspirate** is the sound represented in English by the letter 'h'; a technical term in linguistics.
2 VO To **aspirate** a letter in a word means to pronounce it with the sound of a letter 'h'. *The 'h' in*

honour isn't aspirated.

aspiration /æspəreɪʃn/ **aspirations**
N C or NU Someone's **aspirations** are their ambitions to achieve something. *His sympathies with the culture and political aspirations of his new home were strong... The agreement was a compromise between popular aspiration and the Communists' wish to remain in power.*

aspire /əspáɪə/ **aspires, aspiring, aspired**
V+to or V+to-INF If you **aspire** to something such as an important job, you have a strong desire to have it. *Edward has always aspired to leadership... Those canvassed said they valued education highly and aspired to be responsible adults.* ◆ **aspiring** ADJ ATTRIB *...an aspiring concert pianist.*

aspirin /ǽsprɪn/ **aspirins**
NU or NC **Aspirin** is a mild drug which reduces pain and fever. It is sold in the form of tablets called **aspirins**. *Aspirin is believed to inhibit the formation of blood clots... If they took an aspirin a day, it would reduce the risk of having a second heart attack.*

ass /æs/ **asses**
1 NC An **ass** is an animal similar to a horse but smaller and with long ears. *...women in sun-veils, trying to look dignified on an ass.*
2 NC You can call someone an **ass** when you think they have done something foolish. *He has made something of an ass of himself, trying to put forward this view.*
3 NC Your **ass** is your bottom; used in informal American English. *She had gone to work in a night-club, wiggling her ass and showing her legs as high up as the law allowed... She said, 'I can't bear to see his ass on my sofa, his feet on my rug.'*

Assad, Hafiz al- /háːfɪz əl ʌsəd, æsæd/
Lieutenant-General Hafiz al-Assad became President of Syria in 1971. He was Minister of Defence and Commander of the Air Force from 1966 to 1970. He became Secretary of the Arab Socialist Renaissance (Baath) Party in 1970 and served as Prime Minister from 1970 to 1971. Born: 1928.

assail /əseɪl/ **assails, assailing, assailed**; a literary word.
1 VO If you **are assailed** by unpleasant thoughts or problems, you are greatly troubled by a lot of them. *They are assailed by doubts... Teachers in the eastern part of Germany are assailed by fears of mass unemployment.*
2 V-PASS If someone **is assailed**, they are criticized strongly or threatened. *He was assailed in the press... He has been assailed with death threats and obscene phone calls.*

assailant /əseɪlənt/ **assailants**
NC Someone's **assailant** is a person who physically attacks them; a formal word. *The soldiers opened fire on their assailants, killing two of them.*

assassin /əsǽsɪn/ **assassins**
NC An **assassin** is a person who assassinates someone. *One of them has given himself up as the assassin, but no-one believes that he really is the murderer.*

assassinate /əsǽsɪneɪt/ **assassinates, assassinating, assassinated**
VO When someone important is **assassinated**, they are murdered as a political act. *The president was assassinated as he left the building.* ◆ **assassination** /əsæsɪneɪʃn/ **assassinations** NU or NC *...the assassination of Martin Luther King... They used threats, car bombs and assassinations to disrupt the voting.*

assault /əsɔ́ːlt/ **assaults, assaulting, assaulted**
1 NC An **assault** by an army is a strong attack made against an enemy. *The guerrillas say they will continue to press on with their assault.*
2 NC or NU An **assault** on a person is a physical attack. *There have been several assaults recently... They arrested him for assault.*
3 VO To **assault** someone means to attack them physically. *She was found guilty of assaulting a police officer.*
4 NC+SUPP An **assault** on someone's beliefs is a strong criticism of them. *...an all-out assault on racism.*

assault and battery

NU **Assault and battery** is the crime of threatening to attack someone physically and then actually attacking them; a legal term. *You're being charged with assault and battery.*

assault course, assault courses

NC An **assault course** is an area of land covered with obstacles which soldiers run over as an exercise.

assay /əseɪ/ **assays, assaying, assayed**

NC An **assay** is a test or analysis done on a substance, especially in order to find out how pure it is; a technical term in chemistry. *We developed an assay that could be used for analysing normal bone marrow.*

assemblage /əsɛmblɪdʒ/ **assemblages**; a formal word.

1 NC+SUPP An **assemblage** is a collection of people, animals, or things. *The greatest assemblage of marsupials today live in Australia.*

2 NU **Assemblage** is the process of putting things together, for example in order to construct something. *...the assemblage of ideas.*

assemble /əsɛmbl/ **assembles, assembling, assembled**

1 V When people **assemble**, they gather together in a group, usually for a particular purpose. *The witnesses would assemble in the Detective Sergeant's room.* ◆ **assembled** ADJ *She announced to the assembled relatives that she intended to move abroad.*

2 VO If you **assemble** a number of objects or facts, you bring them together. *She began to assemble her belongings... His job was to assemble the facts.*

3 VO If you **assemble** something, you fit its parts together. *The engines are assembled in a factory in Derby.*

assembly /əsɛmbli/ **assemblies**

1 NC An **assembly** is a large number of people gathered together, especially a group of people who meet regularly to make laws. *The assembly was shocked into silence... He asked the newly-elected National Assembly (which meets next Tuesday) to accept his resignation.*

2 NU **Assembly** is the gathering together of people for a particular purpose. *Citizens enjoy freedom of assembly, procession, and demonstration... They are demanding rights of assembly.*

3 NU The **assembly** of a machine or device is the process of fitting its parts together. *The assembly of the machine is being completed while it digs into the rock.*

assembly line, assembly lines

NC An **assembly line** is an arrangement of workers and machines in a factory where the product passes from one worker to another until it is finished. *...the latest jumbo jet to roll off the assembly line.*

assemblyman /əsɛmblɪmən/ **assemblymen** /əsɛmblɪmən/

TITLE or NC In the United States, an **assemblyman** is a man who is in an assembly of people who make laws. *Assemblyman Dove Heikend, who serves the Borough Park community, blames Yakov's death on the negligence of welfare authorities... Tom Hayden is an assemblyman from Los Angeles.*

assemblywoman /əsɛmbliwʊmən/ **assemblywomen**

TITLE or NC In the United States, an **assemblywoman** is a woman who is in an assembly of people who make laws. *...state Assemblywoman Marguerite Archie Hutchinson.*

assent /əsɛnt/ **assents, assenting, assented**

1 NU If someone gives their **assent** to something that has been suggested, they agree to it. *16 and 17 year-olds do not need parental assent to get married... The Iraqis have given their formal written assent to the arrangement.*

2 V+to or V-QUOTE To **assent** to something means to agree to it; a formal use. *Our Ministers do not necessarily assent to everything the government says... 'Perfectly true,' assented Lebel. 'Providing a single police officer can stop this man.'*

assert /əsɜːt/ **asserts, asserting, asserted**

1 VO, V-REPORT, or V-QUOTE If you **assert** a fact or belief, you state it firmly. *The protesters asserted their right to be heard... He asserted that China would never enter into an alliance with either superpower... 'People*

in the West' he asserted 'are no better than us'. ◆ **assertion** /əsɜːʃn/ **assertions** NC or NU *...evidence to support government assertions that the attack was the work of activists... The essence of the speech was the assertion of democracy.*

2 VO If you **assert** your authority, you make it clear that you have it. *He wished to assert his authority in his own house... This is another area where the government finds it difficult to assert its authority.* ◆ **assertion** NU *Jack had meant to leave him in doubt, as an assertion of power.*

3 V-REFL If you **assert** yourself, you speak and act in a forceful way so that people take notice of you. *His close rival had rapidly asserted himself, and within months had taken the key post of First Secretary.*

assertive /əsɜːtɪv/

ADJ Someone who is **assertive** speaks and acts in a forceful way so that people take notice of them. *Children are being more assertive in the classroom and less deferential... They're willing to see the European Parliament play a much more assertive role.* ◆ **assertiveness** NU *...the revival of national assertiveness in the three Baltic republics.*

assess /əsɛs/ **assesses, assessing, assessed**

1 VO or V-REPORT When you **assess** a person, feeling, or situation, you consider them and make a judgement about them. *They meet monthly to assess the current political situation... Two officials arrived to assess whether it is safe to bring in emergency food supplies.*

2 VO When you **assess** the amount of money that something is worth or that should be paid, you calculate or estimate it. *She looked the house over and assessed its rough market value.*

assessment /əsɛsmənt/ **assessments**

1 NC+SUPP An **assessment** is the consideration and judgement of someone or something. *There has to be a clear assessment of the country's social needs. ...the assessment of his academic progress.*

2 NC An **assessment** of the amount of something is a calculation or estimate of that amount. *There is a very large margin of error in whale stock assessment.*

asset /æset/ **assets**

1 NC An **asset** is someone or something that is considered to be useful or helpful to a person or group. *He was a great asset to the committee.*

2 N PL The **assets** of a company or a person are all the things that they own. *One idea is to use frozen assets to make the payments. ...the sale of public assets.*

assiduous /əsɪdjuəs/

ADJ Someone who is **assiduous** works hard; a formal word. *...an assiduous student... Assiduous research might have produced contradictions in their previously expressed opinions.* ◆ **assiduously** ADV *He kept on painting assiduously.*

assign /əsaɪn/ **assigns, assigning, assigned**

1 V+to-INF, VO, or VOO If you **assign** a task or function to someone, you give it to them. *Two journalists, a man and a woman, have been assigned to interview her... He says they were not adequately trained to handle some of the cases they were assigned... Women are not specifically assigned combat jobs.*

2 VO+to If you **are assigned** to a place or group, you are sent to work in the place or with the group. *She was assigned to the men's wards... Hundreds of these youngsters had no social worker assigned to their case.*

assignation /æsɪɡneɪʃn/ **assignations**

NC An **assignation** is a secret meeting with someone, especially a lover; a literary word. *His first step in this direction was to cancel an assignation he had made with her for the following day... The dark room was in constant use for assignations of all sorts.*

assignment /əsaɪnmənt/ **assignments**

1 NC An **assignment** is a piece of work that you are given to do, as part of your job or studies. *Four ministers who left the government to join Mr Shekar have been given senior assignments ... ...writing an assignment for the UN Relief and Works agency.*

2 NU+POSS You can refer to someone being given a task or job as their **assignment** to that task or job. *The aim is to abolish the centralised assignment of graduates to jobs.*

assimilate /əsɪməleɪt/ **assimilates, assimilating, assimilated**

1 VO If you **assimilate** ideas, customs, or methods, you learn them and make use of them. *He was quick to assimilate new ideas.* ◆ **assimilation** /əsɪməleɪʃn/ NU *...the rapid assimilation of new techniques in industry.*

2 V-ERG When immigrants **assimilate** or are **assimilated** into a community, they become a part of it and often lose some of their own traditions and culture. *Bulgaria has been accused of mounting a campaign about four years ago to force those 800,000 ethnic Turks to assimilate... Many Chakmas have left the refugee areas and have been assimilated into the local population. ...concern over Romania's policy of assimilating minorities.* ◆ **assimilation** NU *...the assimilation of the new arrivals.*

assist /əsɪst/ **assists, assisting, assisted**

1 VOorV If you **assist** someone, you help them. *He took pride in having assisted them... We may be able to assist with the tuition fees... He was asked to assist in keeping the hotel under surveillance.*

2 VOorV If something **assists** with a task, it makes it easier. *The aid operation has been assisted by a long lull in the civil war... We believe the result will assist in the election of a Labour government.*

assistance /əsɪstəns/

NU If you give someone **assistance**, you help them. *He thanked me for my assistance... Financial assistance is being provided by the European Community.* ● If something is **of assistance**, it is helpful or useful to you. *The packs are designed to be of assistance to journalists, researchers, and businessmen.*

assistant /əsɪstənt/ **assistants**

1 NC+POSS Someone's **assistant** is a person who helps them in their work. *...a twenty-seven year old research assistant.*

2 ADJ ATTRIB **Assistant** is used in front of titles or jobs to indicate a slightly lower rank. For example, an **assistant** director is one rank lower than a director. *...Assistant Chief Fire Officer David Williams.*

3 NC An **assistant** or a **shop assistant** is a person who sells things in a shop. *It's a frequent comment that shop assistants, taxi-drivers and switchboard operators are all able to speak English.*

assizes /əsaɪzɪz/

N PL **Assizes** are court sessions which used to take place regularly in all English and Welsh counties; a legal term. *She was committed for trial at the Guildford assizes.*

associate, associates, associating, associated; pronounced /əsəʊʃieɪt/ when it is a verb and /əsəʊʃiət/ when it is a noun.

1 VO+*with* If you **associate** one thing with another, the two things are connected in your mind. *Dignity is the quality which I associate mostly with her... Zuse worked on problems associated with aircraft design... It's the first time that brandy, a drink usually associated with France, has been made from English wine.*

2 VO If one thing is **associated** with another, the two things are connected because they often happen or exist together. *The season is traditionally associated with giving donations to charities... Escalating violence on the streets has been associated with the cocaine derivative 'crack'.* ◆ **associated** ADJ *...warrants and associated documents.*

3 VO+*with* If you are **associated** with an organization, cause, or point of view, or if you **associate** yourself with it, you support it publicly. *But a small band of left-wing Labour MPs—by no means all associated with Militant—ostentatiously supported a campaign of non-payment... Mr Pilger has been widely associated with Cambodia since 1979.*

4 V+*with* If you **associate** with a group of people, you spend a lot of time with them; a formal use. *His poetry was never understood by the establishment writers with whom he associated... They kept track of what he wrote, said and signed, who he associated with and where he lived.*

5 NC Your **associates** are your business colleagues. *Close associates of Mr Hamed say that police raided his house yesterday... These rules clearly apply between business associates and distant friends.*

Associated /əsəʊʃieɪtɪd/

ADJ ATTRIB **Associated** is used in the name of a company to indicate that it is made up of a number of smaller companies. *...Associated Industrial Consultants. ...Associated Newspapers.*

association /əsəʊsieɪʃn/ **associations**

1 NC An **association** is an official group of people with a common occupation, aim, or interest. *Several hundred places will be provided by housing associations, in shared flats and houses... Like all clubs, societies and other associations, they have to apply for official recognition. ...the British Medical Association.*

2 NU+SUPP Your **association** with a person, group, or organization is the connection that you have with them. *There has been widespread comment about her association with British M.P.s... a sign of his recent association with terrorism.* ● If someone does something **in association with** someone else, they do it together. *...a production made in association with the National Theatre Company.*

3 NC+SUPP If something has a particular **association** for you, it is connected in your mind with a particular memory or feeling. *The term 'reconciliation' has particular associations for the Sudanese... Her image has undoubtedly suffered by association with such issues.*

Association of South East Asian Nations (ASEAN) The **Association of South East Asian Nations** was founded in 1967 to encourage economic progress and stability in South East Asia. The headquarters are in Jakarta. The members of ASEAN are: Brunei, Indonesia, Malaysia, Philippines, Singapore, and Thailand.

assorted /əsɔːtɪd/

ADJ ATTRIB A group of **assorted** things of a particular kind have different sizes, colours, or qualities. *...a bunch of assorted wild flowers.*

assortment /əsɔːtmənt/ **assortments**

NC An **assortment** is a group of similar things that have different sizes, colours, or qualities. *...an assortment of plastic bags.*

asst.

Asst. is a written abbreviation for 'assistant'. *...Asst. Chief Constable Phillips.*

assuage /əsweɪdʒ/ **assuages, assuaging, assuaged;** a literary word.

1 VO To **assuage** an unpleasant feeling that someone has means to make them feel it less strongly. *He tried to calm the woman but could not assuage her terror.*

2 VO If you **assuage** a need or desire for something, you satisfy it. *Her thirst for knowledge could never be assuaged.*

assume /əsjuːm/ **assumes, assuming, assumed**

1 V-REPORTorVO+*to*-INF If you **assume** that something is true, you suppose that it is true, sometimes wrongly. *I assume you don't drive... I was mistakenly assumed to be a Welshman.*

2 VO If someone **assumes** power or responsibility, they begin to have power or responsibility. *Their position has not changed since the army assumed control... After assuming office, the President offered an amnesty to the militants.*

3 VO To **assume** a particular expression, quality, or way of behaving means to begin to look, behave, or be that way. *...the kind of posture that President Reagan assumed at certain times... The dispute has assumed an increasingly bitter and personal character.*

assumed name, assumed names

NC If you do something under an **assumed name**, you do it using a name that is not your real name. *He lived and worked there under an assumed name... She wrote an anti-Nazi novel under an assumed name.*

assuming /əsjuːmɪŋ/

CONJ You use **assuming** or **assuming that** when you are supposing that something is true, so that you can think about what the consequences would be. *They are willing to end their support for the regime, assuming its conditions are met... Keep your goods* *(assuming that you have any) separate from his.*

assumption /əsʌmpʃn/ **assumptions**

1 NC If you make an **assumption,** you suppose that something is true, sometimes wrongly. *His suggestions are based on an assumption that the system is out of date... Both societies make this assumption fairly confidently despite warnings from the Chancellor... The assumption is that the rest of the world will follow.*

2 NU+of Someone's **assumption** of power or responsibility is their taking of it. *...the thirtieth anniversary of Castro's assumption of power... He will organise democratic elections within ninety days of assumption of office.*

assurance /əʃɔːrəns/ **assurances**

1 NC or NU If you give someone an **assurance** about something, you say that it is definitely true or will definitely happen, in order to make them less worried. *The prisoners were given assurances that they would not be physically harmed... Despite assurances that they want to maintain good relations, neither side is prepared to move on the issue... They couldn't give me that same level of assurance.*

2 NU If you do something with **assurance,** you do it with confidence and certainty. *'She'll like that,' said Lally with assurance... I can say with assurance, 'I know this works.'*

3 NU **Assurance** is also insurance that provides for events which are certain to happen, such as death. *They get a discount on insurance and life assurance, and cut-price mortgages. ...Britain's largest life assurance company.*

assure /əʃɔː/ **assures, assuring, assured**

1 VO-REPORT or VO-QUOTE If you **assure** someone that something is true or will happen, you tell them that it is definitely true or will definitely happen, in order to make them less worried. *Kurt assured me that he was an excellent climber... 'I want a vibrant and mutually beneficial relationship' he assured her.*

2 VO+of or VOO If you **are assured** of something, you will definitely get it. *Mr Quayle assured him of his continued support... This film had assured him a place in movie history.*

assured /əʃɔːd/

ADJ Someone who is **assured** is very confident and feels at ease. *Mr Channon gave an assured and confident account in the face of hostile questioning.*

assuredly /əʃɔːrɪdli/

ADV or ADV SEN If something is **assuredly** true, it is definitely true. *There could, assuredly, be a reaction the other way if the violence gets worse.*

asterisk /æstərɪsk/ **asterisks**

NC An **asterisk** is the sign *. It is used, for example, to indicate that there is a comment at the bottom of the page.

astern /əstɜːn/; a technical term.

1 ADJ PRED Something that is **astern** is at the back of a ship or behind it. *The captain was astern, talking to one of the passengers... Just before nightfall, with Italy far astern, we spotted a sail on the horizon.*

2 ADV A ship that is moving **astern** is moving backwards. *The steamer is capable of some forty knots retreating astern.*

asteroid /æstərɔɪd/ **asteroids**

NC An **asteroid** is one of the very small planets that move around the sun. *This object, which we call Phaeton, seems to resemble an asteroid.*

asthma /æsmə/

NU **Asthma** is an illness which affects the chest and makes breathing difficult. *The drug could also help sufferers of hay fever, asthma, and sinusitis.*

asthmatic /æsmætɪk/ **asthmatics**

1 NC An **asthmatic** is someone who suffers from asthma. *Mr Kapoor, an asthmatic, collapsed a week ago at a ceremony.*

2 ADJ **Asthmatic** means relating to asthma. *Parents of asthmatic children were not fully informed of the dangers. ...the wheezing and breathlessness which characterize an asthmatic attack.*

astonish /əstɒnɪʃ/ **astonishes, astonishing, astonished**

VO If something **astonishes** you, it surprises you very much. *Recent visitors to the country have been astonished by the degree of criticism of the government... I'm now going to say something that will astonish you... He astonished medical staff by being able to go home three days later.*

astonished /əstɒnɪʃt/

ADJ If you are **astonished,** you are very surprised about something. *They were astonished at the extraordinary beauty of the pictures... I was as astonished as you.*

astonishing /əstɒnɪʃɪŋ/

ADJ Something that is **astonishing** is very surprising. *The shape of their bodies changes with astonishing speed... His tutor says he has an astonishing talent... She said that it was astonishing that nurses should go on strike while their pay levels were under review.* ♦ **astonishingly** SUBMOD or ADV SEN *Birth rates there are astonishingly high.*

astonishment /əstɒnɪʃmənt/

NU **Astonishment** is a feeling of great surprise. *John stared at him in astonishment... His request will nevertheless be viewed with astonishment and outrage in many parts of the Arab world... The judgement was greeted with gasps of astonishment.*

astound /əstaʊnd/ **astounds, astounding, astounded**

VO If something **astounds** you, you are amazed by it. *The sheer volume of work astounds us... His decision to leave the Cabinet has astounded Members of Parliament of all parties... What I saw on television astounded me.* ♦ **astounding** ADJ *...the most astounding discoveries of the 20th century.* ♦ **astounded** ADJ *The words rang through the astounded court-room.*

astrakhan /æstrəkæn/

N+N An **astrakhan** coat or hat is made from lamb skins and is curly, and black or grey in colour. *...a man in a grey astrakhan hat.*

astral /æstrəl/

ADJ **Astral** means relating to the stars; a technical term. *...astral bodies.*

astray /əstreɪ/

● **Astray** is used in these phrases. ● If you **lead** someone **astray,** you make them behave in a bad or foolish way. *He'd been led astray by counter-revolutionaries.* ● If something **goes astray,** it gets lost. *In these circumstances, it's hardly surprising that funds go astray.*

astride /əstraɪd/

PREP If you sit or stand **astride** something, you sit or stand with one leg on each side of it. *Karen sat astride a large white horse.*

astringent /əstrɪndʒənt/

1 ADJ **Astringent** substances make your skin less greasy or stop it bleeding. *...an astringent lotion.*

2 ADJ **Astringent** comments are forceful and critical. *...Clive James, the funniest and most astringent TV critic to date.*

astrologer /əstrɒlədʒə/ **astrologers**

NC An **astrologer** is a person who uses astrology to tell you things about your character and future. *His wife often consults an astrologer.*

astrology /əstrɒlədʒi/

NU **Astrology** is the study of the movements of the planets, sun, moon, and stars in the belief that they can influence people's lives. *1988 was the year of the dragon in Chinese astrology.* ♦ **astrological** /æstrəlɒdʒɪkl/ ADJ *But do astrological beliefs have any foundation in fact?*

astronaut /æstrənɔːt/ **astronauts**

NC An **astronaut** is a person who travels in a spacecraft. *The space shuttle blew up shortly after its launch, killing seven astronauts.*

astronomer /əstrɒnəmə/ **astronomers**

NC An **astronomer** is a scientist who studies the stars, planets, and other natural objects in space. *Galileo was probably far greater as a physicist than as an astronomer.*

astronomical /æstrənɒmɪkl/

1 ADJ **Astronomical** means relating to astronomy. *There's no particular optical or astronomical evidence that black holes exist.*

2 ADJ If you describe a value, price, or amount as **astronomical,** you mean that it is very large indeed.

But the B52 bomber's costs are astronomical, at over $500 million per aircraft.

astronomy /əstrɒnəmi/
NU **Astronomy** is the scientific study of the stars, planets, and other natural objects in space. *Over the past quarter of a century, the study of astronomy has changed fundamentally.*

astrophysics /æstrəʊfɪzɪks/
NU **Astrophysics** is the study of the physical and chemical structure of the stars, planets, and other natural objects in space. *...the Harvard-Smithsonian Center for Astrophysics in Cambridge, Massachusetts.*

astute /əstjuːt/
ADJ Someone who is **astute** is clever and skilful at understanding behaviour and situations. *She was described by colleagues as diligent, able, and astute... He is too astute a politician to be unaware of the shocked reaction this would cause.*

Asunción /æsuːnsjɒn/
Asunción is the capital of Paraguay and its largest city. Population: 455,000 (1982).

asunder /əsʌndə/
ADV If something is torn **asunder**, it is separated violently into two or more parts; a literary word. *They have sufficient destructive power to blow a battleship asunder... The Party would be torn asunder.*

asylum /əsaɪləm/ **asylums**
1 NU **Asylum** is protection given to foreigners who have left their own country for political reasons. *Three Burmese diplomats in Australia have applied for political asylum... A spokesman said the asylum seekers had visas valid for six months.*
2 NC An **asylum** is a mental hospital; an old-fashioned use. *Van Gogh later voluntarily committed himself to an asylum.*

asymmetric /eɪsɪmɛtrɪk/
ADJ **Asymmetric** means the same as **asymmetrical**. *...an asymmetric skull.*

asymmetrical /eɪsɪmɛtrɪkl/
ADJ Something that is **asymmetrical** has two sides or halves that are different. *His films all seem to be very asymmetrical.*

asymmetry /eɪsɪmətri/
NU **Asymmetry** is the appearance that something has when its two sides or halves are different in shape, size, or style. *...the asymmetry of the view... If there's any assymetry in the shape of this compact neutron star then it will emit gravitational waves.*

at /ət, æt/
1 PREP You use **at** to say where something happens or is situated. *The play takes place at a beach club... Relatives have been waiting for them at Gatwick airport... They want to use it at exhibitions and open air rock concerts... There was a knock at his door... His two teenage children were at home.*
2 PREP If you look **at** something or someone, you look towards them. If you direct something **at** someone, you direct it towards them. *He looked at me and laughed... An old man with cuts across his face sat staring at what was once his home... They suggest that a quick glance at a patient's hands could allow a doctor to dispense with costly blood tests... Supporters threw petals at his car... They were throwing stones over the wall at soldiers.*
3 PREP You use **at** to say when something happens. *She leaves her house every day at 11 a.m... Decent meat can be obtained at the moment but only on the black market... At breakfast, Mark greeted me coldly... The talks come at a time when prices have reached a new low level.*
4 PREP You use **at** to say how quickly or regularly something happens. *He hurtles through the air at 600 miles per hour... It is now travelling at a speed of 18,000 miles an hour... They use the latest Stealth technology to avoid radar while flying at high speed... The high technology companies have grown at an astonishing rate.*
5 PREP If you buy, sell, or value something **at** a particular price, you buy it or sell it for that price, or estimate its value as being that price. *The book is published at £7.95... Fifty-four thirty second advertising slots have been sold at $700,000 a time...*

The cost of restoring the railway links across the centre of the country has been put at $100,000.
6 PREP If you are working **at** something, you are dealing with it. If you are aiming **at** something, you are trying to achieve it. *It means working harder at your thesis... The charter is aimed at improving the quality of public services... There are projects aimed at stopping young people coming to London from other parts of Britain.*
7 PREP If something is done **at** someone's command or invitation, it is done as a result of it. *At the director's command, some thirty or forty people left... She went at the invitation of an unknown man... Mrs Thatcher has arrived in the Soviet Union for a four day visit at the invitation of President Gorbachev.*
8 PREP You use **at** to say that someone or something is in a particular state or condition. *He remains at liberty... The two nations are at war... India needs a strong leader of vision who can keep the country united and at peace.*
9 PREP You use **at** to say how something is done. *Guardsmen herded them back at gunpoint... He seemed to read at random.*
10 PREP If you are good **at** something, you do it well. If you are bad **at** something, you do it badly. *They seemed to be very good at reading... Parking is something we're very bad at... She is an expert at it.*
11 PREP If you are delighted, pleased, or appalled **at** something, that is the effect it has on you. *The FA naturally are delighted at the outcome... Afterwards, relatives of the men said they were disgusted at the decision... I was appalled at the quality of some of the reporting.*
12 PREP You use **at** after a verb to indicate that something is being done in a tentative way. *Rudolph sipped at his drink.*

atavistic /ætəvɪstɪk/
ADJ **Atavistic** feelings or behaviour remind you of the feelings or behaviour of your primitive ancestors; a formal word. *Many of those present felt this atavistic fear.*

ate /ɛt, eɪt/
Ate is the past tense of **eat**.

atheism /eɪθiːɪzəm/
NU **Atheism** is the belief that there is no God. *A Party dedicated to atheism is likely to lose out in the fight for votes.* ◆ **atheist, atheists** NC *Hobbes was regarded as a terrible atheist and a champion of despotism.*

atheistic /eɪθiːɪstɪk/
ADJ ATTRIB **Atheistic** beliefs, systems, or ideas are based on atheism. *...a campaign of atheistic education... Czechoslovakia is not an atheistic state, but a socialist one.*

Athens /æθənz/
Athens is the capital of Greece and its largest city. Population: 3,027,000 (1981).

athlete /æθliːt/ **athletes**
NC An **athlete** is a person who takes part in athletics competitions. *You have to train for it like an athlete preparing for a race.*

athletic /æθlɛtɪk/ **athletics**
1 NU **Athletics** consists of sports such as running, the high jump, and the javelin. *Clark was a promising rugby player until he chose athletics at the age of 14.*
2 ADJ ATTRIB **Athletic** means relating to athletes and athletics. *The IAFF could ban the British team from all athletic events.*
3 ADJ An **athletic** person looks fit, healthy, and active. *His athletic figure, rugged face and gravelly voice epitomised the English officer... He danced with an athletic ease.*

-ation /-eɪʃn/ **-ations**
SUFFIX **-ation**, **-tion**, and **-ion** are added to verbs to form nouns referring to an action or the result of an action. In this dictionary, nouns of this kind are often not defined but are treated with the related verbs. *We will make such alterations as we consider necessary. ...upon completion of their studies.*

atishoo /ətɪʃuː/
Atishoo is used in writing to represent the sound that you make when you sneeze.

atlas /ætləs/ **atlases**
NC An **atlas** is a book of maps. ...*bulky reference books such as encyclopaedias and atlases.*

atmosphere /ætməsfɪə/ **atmospheres**
1 NC A planet's **atmosphere** is the layer of air or other gas around it. *Mars was once a warm, wet planet with huge oceans and an atmosphere rich in carbon dioxide. ...ozone depletion in the atmosphere... To a large extent the chemistry of the earth's atmosphere is determined by the fact that there is life on Earth.*
2 N SING The **atmosphere** of a place is the air that you breathe there. *...the polluted atmosphere of towns and cities... He is afflicted by insect bites, back pains and the stifling atmosphere of the poorly ventilated and dimly lit room.*
3 N SING+SUPP You can also refer to the general impression that you get of a place as its **atmosphere**. *It's got such a friendly atmosphere... There is an atmosphere of cautious optimism.*

atmospheric /ætməsfɛrɪk/
ADJ ATTRIB **Atmospheric** is used to describe something which relates to the earth's atmosphere. *...atmospheric pollution... But why couldn't divers live and work in a sealed chamber breathing air at atmospheric pressure?*

atoll /ætɒl/ **atolls**
NC An **atoll** is a circular arrangement of coral rocks surrounding a lagoon. *Sea levels rose, thereby flooding coastal areas, atolls, and islands.*

atom /ætəm/ **atoms**
NC An **atom** is the smallest amount of a substance that can take part in a chemical reaction. *All the electrons have been stripped off the atoms.*

atom bomb, atom bombs
NC An **atom bomb** or an **atomic bomb** causes an explosion by the sudden release of energy that results from splitting atoms. *...the atom bomb which destroyed the Japanese city of Hiroshima... He described the first atomic bomb explosion.*

atomic /ətɒmɪk/
1 ADJ ATTRIB **Atomic** means relating to the power produced by splitting atoms. *Plutonium is used almost exclusively in atomic weapons. ...atomic energy.*
2 ADJ ATTRIB **Atomic** also means relating to the atoms that substances consist of. *The process starts with carbon atoms implanted into the top few atomic layers of a thin copper sheet. ...the mysteries of atomic nuclei.*

atomize /ætəmaɪz/ **atomizes, atomizing, atomized;** also spelt **atomise.**
1 VO If a structure or system is **atomized**, it is divided up into a lot of very small parts and so loses its unity; a formal use. *In Latin America the pre-colonial society was totally atomized... This would be healthier than seeing society atomised with as many parties as there were individuals.*
2 VO If people or things are **atomized**, they are destroyed completely by nuclear weapons; an informal use. *The skyscrapers would still be there long after the human race had been atomized.*

atomizer /ætəmaɪzə/ **atomizers;** also spelt **atomiser.**
NC An **atomizer** is a device which turns a liquid such as perfume into a very fine spray.

atone /ətəʊn/ **atones, atoning, atoned**
V+*for* If you **atone** for something wrong or bad that you have done, you do something to show that you are sorry; a formal word. *In cash terms, West Germany has tried to atone for the past.*

atonement /ətəʊnmənt/
NU **Atonement** is something that you do to show that you are sorry for having done something wrong; a formal word. *They're still trying to make some sort of atonement and reparation.*

atop /ətɒp/
PREP If something is **atop** something else, it is on top of it; a literary word. *They perched atop the sheds... She let her hands rest, one atop the other, on her stomach.*

A to Z /eɪ tə zɛd/ **A to Zs**
NC An **A to Z** is a map or book of maps showing the roads in a particular city or area; **A to Z** is a trademark.

atrocious /ətrəʊʃəs/
ADJ Something that is **atrocious** is extremely bad. *...speaking French with an atrocious accent.*
◆ **atrociously** ADV *The farm animals are treated atrociously.*

atrocity /ətrɒsəti/ **atrocities**
NCorNU An **atrocity** is a very cruel, shocking action. *They accused the army of committing atrocities against civilians. ...a repetition of last year's atrocity... They killed people, they did unbelievable acts of atrocity.*

atrophy /ætrəfi/ **atrophies, atrophying, atrophied;** a formal word.
1 V-ERG If a muscle or other part of the body **atrophies** or is **atrophied**, it decreases in size or strength, often as a result of an illness. *Muscles only weaken and atrophy when they are not used.* ▶ Also NU *...physical atrophy of the optic nerves.*
2 V-ERG If something **atrophies** or is **atrophied**, it decreases in size or strength. *If the economy is not to atrophy, immediate steps must be taken... Many rural communities have atrophied... His personality was increasingly more stunted and atrophied.* ▶ Also NU *Their society is in a state of atrophy.*

attach /ətætʃ/ **attaches, attaching, attached**
1 VO If you **attach** something to an object, you join it or fasten it to the object. *They have attached cables to the damaged section of the bridge to stop it falling... This new nylon rope ladder is very firmly attached and fits neatly above any window.*
2 V-PASS If someone is **attached** to an organization, they are working for it, usually for a short time. *Hospital officers would be temporarily attached to NHS hospitals... The new force would be attached to the republic's Interior Ministry.*
3 VO+*to* If you **attach** a quality to something or someone, you consider that they have that quality. *Don't attach too much importance to what he said... There is far less social stigma attached to illegitimate births these days.*

attaché /ætæʃeɪ/ **attachés**
NC An **attaché** is a member of the staff in an embassy. *President Doe expelled the United States Military Attaché.*

attaché case, attaché cases
NC An **attaché case** is a briefcase. *He wore a shirt and a pair of black torn trousers, and he carried an attaché case.*

attached /ətætʃt/
ADJ PRED+*to* If you are **attached** to someone or something, you are very fond of them. *Professional users of the machine are very attached to Samuel Morse's invention.*

attachment /ətætʃmənt/ **attachments**
1 NC An **attachment** to someone or something is a fondness for them. *...a romantic attachment. ...a land where the attachment to monarchy has deep historic roots.*
2 NC An **attachment** is a device that can be fixed onto a machine in order to enable it to do different jobs. *...a special attachment for cleaning upholstery.*

attack /ətæk/ **attacks, attacking, attacked**
1 VOorV If you **attack** a person or building, you try to hurt or damage them using physical violence. *The court decided that he was insane when he attacked the women... They attacked at dawn under cover of heavy artillery fire... One of the main hotels was burned and public buildings were attacked.* ▶ Also NCorNU *...a worrying increase in attacks on old people... He said that the army had been given strict instructions to fire only if it came under attack.*
2 VO If you **attack** a person, belief, or idea, you criticize them strongly. *The senator attacked the press for misleading the public... The judge attacked the callous attitude of some officers... The Labour Party has attacked what it claims to be an outrageous decision by a London hospital.* ▶ Also NCorNU *...attacks on various aspects of apartheid... Burt's work came under violent attack.*
3 VO If you **attack** a job or a problem, you start to deal with it in an energetic way. *...a tough new programme aims to attack the country's worsening*

*economic problems... He attacked his task with
determination.*
4 v When players **attack** in a game such as football,
they try to score a goal. *After half-time the players
began to attack in earnest.* ◆ **attacking** ADJ ATTRIB
*The offside rule has also been changed to give
attacking players a better chance of scoring.*
5 NC+SUPP An **attack** of an illness is a short period in
which you suffer badly from it. *She had been left
totally deaf by an attack of smallpox... His condition
was being treated with drugs but there was no
indication he'd suffered a heart attack.*

attacker /ətǽkə/ **attackers**
NC Someone's **attacker** is a person who attacks them.
He described his attacker to the police.

attain /ətéɪn/ **attains, attaining, attained**
vo If you **attain** something, you achieve it, often after
a lot of effort. *...the qualities which enabled him to
attain his ambitions... If a child fails an exam at the
age of eleven, and is put into a school for the less
able, he or she will be discouraged from ever attaining
a high academic standard.*

attainable /ətéɪnəbl/
ADJ Something that is **attainable** can be achieved.
*This kind of accuracy is attainable by modern
techniques... This, I believe, is a much more realistic
and attainable goal.*

attainment /ətéɪnmənt/ **attainments**; a formal word.
1 NU+SUPP The **attainment** of something is the
achieving of it. *Before World War II, the attainment
of independence seemed a very remote possibility.
...areas of high unemployment and low educational
attainment.*
2 NC An **attainment** is a skill you have learned, or
something you have achieved. *Earning power is
significantly improved with the attainment of a
degree... Mr Baker wanted the group to give him a list
of attainments that could easily be tested.*

Attas, Haydar Abu Bakr al- /ǽbuː bǽkə æl ɑːtɑːs/
Haydar Abu Bakr al-Attas became Prime Minister of
the newly united Yemen in 1990. He was Prime
Minister of the People's Democratic Republic of
Yemen (also known as South Yemen) from 1985 to
1986, and President of South Yemen from 1986 to 1990.
Born: 1939.

attempt /ətémpt/ **attempts, attempting, attempted**
Vo or V+to-INF If you **attempt** something or **attempt** to
do something, you try to do it. *A long time had
elapsed since I had attempted any serious study...
Johnson will attempt to qualify for the 100 metres at
the Canadian championships in Montreal next week...
The police attempted to turn back protesters marching
towards the offices of the president.* ▶ Also NC *The
young birds manage to fly several kilometres at their
first attempt... They are retaining coffee stocks in an
attempt to push up prices.*

attempted /ətémptɪd/
ADJ ATTRIB An **attempted** crime is an unsuccessful
effort to commit a crime. *He was charged with
attempted murder... Earlier this year he survived an
attempted assassination by a right-wing extremist.*

attend /əténd/ **attends, attending, attended**
1 vo If you **attend** a meeting or other event, you are
present at it. *I stopped off in London to attend a
conference... He was speaking after hundreds of
people attended a special memorial service in
Timisoara... The funeral was attended by senior
politicians from both Britain and Ireland.*
2 Vo or V If you **attend** an institution such as a school
or church, you go to it regularly. *I attended a high
school in Atlanta... When people arrive at the clinic,
we ask them to attend for five days.*
3 V+to If you **attend** to something, you deal with it.
*The requirements in law must be attended to first.
...the pain of having a badly decayed tooth attended
to... Doctors attended to Chavez's wounds inside the
jail.*

attendance /əténdəns/ **attendances**
1 NCorNU The **attendance** at an event is the number of
people who are present there. *The attendance for the
game was just nine thousand. ...a drop in attendance.*
● If you are **in attendance** at a place, you are present

*there. An ambulance team was in attendance at the
ground and took him to the local hospital... Nearly
2,000 deputies were in attendance.*
2 NU Someone's **attendance** at an event or place is the
fact that they were present at the event or that they
go to the place regularly. *He cut short his attendance
at a dinner hosted by the Institute for International
Studies... The poor attendance at schools reflected a
loss of confidence in him as a teacher.*
3 If you are **in attendance**, you are present in a place,
or accompanying another person; a formal use. *There
was no longer any reason to keep Gerald in attendance
on him.*

attendant /əténdənt/ **attendants**
NC An **attendant** is someone whose job is to serve
people in a place such as a petrol station or a
museum. *A flight attendant was killed, but the plane
landed safely.*

attender /əténdə/ **attenders**
NC The **attenders** at a particular place or event are
the people who go there. *Women do, after all, form
the majority of church attenders... The military
governor, Colonel Ahmed Daku, is a regular attender.*

attention /əténʃn/ **attentions**
1 NU If you give something your **attention**, you look at
it, listen to it, or think about it carefully. *When he felt
he had their attention, he began... Even if the
television set is on, there is no guarantee that viewers
are giving it their full attention... Much attention will
also be focused on pay and conditions.*
2 NU If something is getting **attention**, it is being dealt
with. *They needed medical attention... The ministers
recommended that this should receive urgent attention
at next week's meeting of the EC heads of government
in Dublin.*
3 NU **Attention** is great interest that is shown in
someone or something, particularly by the general
public when they want to find out more about them.
*At the time, the proposals received relatively little
attention... Inevitably, the incident has attracted a
great deal of media attention.*
4 N PL You can refer to someone's unwelcome help or
interference as their **attentions**. *But the attentions of
the United States are not universally welcome... The
meeting was held away from the attentions of the
media.*
● **Attention** is used in these phrases. ● If someone
brings something **to your attention** or **draws** your
attention to it, they point it out to you. *Our excuse for
bringing this matter to your attention is that it is the
250th anniversary of Herschel's birth... He has praised
the French leader for drawing world attention to
Bangladesh's problems.* ● If something **attracts** your
attention or **catches** your **attention**, you notice it. *The
case has attracted attention mainly because of the
youth of those condemned to die.* ● If you **pay
attention** to something, you watch it, listen to it, or
take notice of it. *There's far too much attention being
paid to these hooligans.* ● When soldiers **stand to
attention**, they stand up straight with their feet
together and their arms by their sides. *It happened
all through the National Anthem when everyone was
standing to attention.*

attentive /əténtɪv/
1 ADJ If you are **attentive**, you are paying close
attention to what is being said or done. *...an attentive
audience... Most MPs have quickly come to adapt to
television, choosing the best spot to speak from and
getting friends to gather round and look attentive.*
◆ **attentively** ADV *He was listening attentively.*
2 ADJ To be **attentive** also means to be helpful and
polite. *He was unfailingly attentive. ...one of
Budapest's many elegant new restaurants, with
attentive waiters and the obligatory pianist.*

attenuate /əténjueɪt/ **attenuates, attenuating,
attenuated**
vo To **attenuate** something means to reduce it or
weaken it; a formal word. *We're also interested to
know whether this could somehow attenuate the stress
and reduce the anxiety.*

attenuated /əténjueɪtɪd/ a formal word.
1 ADJ Something that is **attenuated** is reduced in size

or strength, often deliberately. *The attenuated vaccine is actually made from three different strains of the polio virus.*
2 ADJ An **attenuated** object is unusually thin and long. *They have thin, attenuated bodies.*

attest /ətest/ **attests, attesting, attested**
V0or V+*to* To **attest** something or to attest to it means to show that it is true; a formal word. *The perfection of their design is attested by the fact that they survived for thousands of years... Historic documents attest to the truth of this.*

attic /ætik/ **attics**
NC An **attic** is a room at the top of a house just below the roof. *He had amassed a fortune, which he hoarded in the attic of his house in Liverpool.*

attire /ətaɪə/
NU Your **attire** is the clothes you are wearing; a formal word. *All government employees are required to wear mourning attire.*

attired /ətaɪəd/
ADJ Someone who is **attired** in a particular way is dressed that way; a formal word. *He was elegantly attired in a cashmere coat... She was attired simply, her hair bedecked with flowers.*

attitude /ætɪtjuːd/ **attitudes**
1 NC+SUPP Your **attitude** to something is the way you think and feel about it. *...a more tolerant attitude to Tibetan culture and religion... They tend to develop a negative attitude towards conservation... He criticized what he called the 'stupid attitude of the police'.*
2 NC+POSS Your **attitude** to someone is the way you behave when you are dealing with them. *I resented his attitude... Her attitude became much more placatory.*
3 NC+SUPP An **attitude** is also a position in which you hold your body. *...with her arms flung out in an attitude of surrender.*

Attlee, /ætli/ **Clement**
Clement Attlee was Prime Minister of the United Kingdom from 1945 to 1951. He was born in 1883. He was MP for Limehouse from 1922 to 1950, and for West Walthamstow from 1950 to 1955. He was the leader of the Labour Party from 1935 to 1955. On his retirement in 1955, he was created Earl Attlee. He died in 1967.

attorney /ətɜːni/ **attorneys**
NC In the United States, an **attorney** is a lawyer. *The prosecuting attorney asked the judges to give the death penalty to seven of them.* ● See also **power of attorney.**

Attorney General, Attorneys General
NC A country's **Attorney General** is its chief law officer who advises the monarch or the government. *...John Mitchell, the former U.S. Attorney General.*

attract /ətrækt/ **attracts, attracting, attracted**
1 VO If something **attracts** people or animals, it has features that cause them to come to it. *The show attracted large crowds this year... Under the new funding method, a school's income depends on the number of pupils it attracts... Moths are attracted to lights.*
2 VO If someone or something **attracts** you, they have qualities which cause you to like or admire them. You can also say that their qualities **attract** you to them. *She didn't attract me physically... What attracted me to Valeria was her sense of humour.*
3 VO If something **attracts** support or publicity, its qualities or features are interesting enough to make people want to support it or know more about it. *The tree, known as the Major Oak, attracts hundreds of visitors a year... His books attracted a large and loyal readership.*
4 VO If something magnetic **attracts** an object, it causes the object to move towards it. *Electromagnets in the bottom of the train are attracted towards the coils underneath the track.*
5 to **attract** someone's **attention**: see **attention.**

attracted /ətræktɪd/
ADJ PRED+*to* If you are **attracted** to someone or something, you like them and are interested in them. *I was becoming attracted to a girl from the next office... I'm not attracted to sociology.*

attraction /ətrækʃn/ **attractions**
1 NU **Attraction** is a feeling of liking someone, and often of being sexually interested in them. *...the attraction between the sexes.*
2 NC+SUPP **Attraction** is also the quality of being interesting or desirable. *The attraction of the house lay in its simplicity... This sums up the economic attractions of the cocaine trade.*
3 NC An **attraction** is a feature which makes something interesting or desirable. *One of the main attractions of the city was its superb transport system... The scheme had one big attraction; it was cheap.*
4 NC An **attraction** is also something that people can go to for interest or enjoyment, for example a famous building. *The famous tower, which is 55 metres tall, is one of Italy's greatest tourist attractions... Tourists flock to the ancient city of Petra, Jordan's biggest attraction.*

attractive /ətræktɪv/
1 ADJ A person who is **attractive** is pretty or handsome. *One night he meets an attractive young woman called Sharon... The photos made him look quite attractive.* ♦ **attractiveness** NU *...youthful attractiveness.*
2 ADJ Something that is **attractive** has a pleasant appearance or sound. *...attractive illustrations... The sets are attractive in their simplicity and the colourful costumes are in the style of the 18th century.*
3 ADJ You also say that something is **attractive** when it seems desirable. *The company offers more time off and attractive pay... It's also an attractive location for businesses... By making the deutschmark more attractive, the bond issue could push up interest rates.*

attributable /ətrɪbjʊtəbl/
ADJ PRED+*to* If something is **attributable** to an event or situation, it is likely that the event or situation caused it. *These hardships are directly attributable to changes in the country's benefits system.*

attribute, attributes, attributing, attributed;
pronounced /ətrɪbjuːt/ when it is a verb and /ætrɪbjuːt/ when it is a noun.
1 VO+*to* If you **attribute** something to an event or situation, you think that it was caused by that event or situation. *Economists attributed the lack of progress to poor cooperation... Their poverty can be attributed to the country's trade policies... Dealers attributed the rise to continued demand for property shares.*
2 V-PASS If a remark, a piece of writing, or a work of art is **attributed** to one person, someone else says that that person said it, wrote it, or produced it. *A speech attributed to Mr Wan on Saturday appeared to back martial law. ...some of the lesser plays attributed to Shakespeare.*
3 VO+*to* If you **attribute** a particular quality or feature to someone or something, you think they have it. *Here we are attributing human feelings to animals... I shrink from attributing mean motives to anyone.* ♦ **attribution** /ætrɪbjuːʃn/ NU *...the attribution of mysterious powers to these men.*
4 NC An **attribute** is a quality or feature. *...her physical attributes... Neil Kinnock said the Queen Mother possessed attributes of greatness: kindness, dignity, intuition and an ability to make everyone feel special.*

attributive /ətrɪbjutɪv/
ADJ When an adjective is used in **attributive** position it comes in front of a noun; a technical term in linguistics. Compare **predicative.**

attrition /ətrɪʃn/
1 NU **Attrition** is a process in which you steadily reduce the strength of an enemy by continually attacking them; a formal word. *...attrition of the enemy forces. ...a war of attrition.*
2 NU **Attrition** is the reduction in a company's workforce that is caused by not replacing people when they leave or retire. *The group will be eliminating 1500 jobs through attrition and lay-offs.*

attuned /ətjuːnd/
1 ADJ PRED+*to* If you are **attuned** to something, you can understand and appreciate it. *The public is not quite attuned to this kind of art.*

2 ADJ PRED+*to* If your ears are **attuned** to a sound, you can hear it and recognize it quickly. *We're so attuned to that alarm, you know, as soon as you hear it, it's just a reflex action, you're moving.*

atypical /eɪtɪpɪkl/
ADJ Something that is **atypical** is not a typical thing of its kind. *I soon tumbled to the fact that my weekends were atypical.* ◆ **atypically** ADV *He was well-informed and atypically open to new information.*

aubergine /əʊbəʒiːn/ **aubergines**
NCorNU An **aubergine** is a vegetable with a smooth purple skin. *They can also be engaged in horticulture, like growing tomatoes, aubergine, and okra.*

auburn /ɔːbən/
ADJ **Auburn** hair is reddish brown. *Her neat cap of auburn hair was graying here and there.*

Auckland /ɔːklənd/
Auckland is the largest city in New Zealand. Population: 865,000 (1990).

auction /ɔːkʃn/ **auctions, auctioning, auctioned**
1 NCorNU An **auction** is a public sale where goods are sold to the person who offers the highest price. *Van Gogh's paintings have recently fetched record prices at auctions... The big house was sold by auction.*
2 VO If you **auction** something, you sell it in an auction. *They are going to auction the pictures at the end of the month.*
auction off PHRASAL VERB If you **auction off** something, you sell it to the person who offers the most money for it, often at an auction. *The IBA say they're opposed to the idea of auctioning off the franchise.*

auctioneer /ɔːkʃənɪə/ **auctioneers**
NC An **auctioneer** is a person who organizes or is in charge of an auction. *The auctioneer opened the bidding... They've been described by Christie's, the auctioneers, as very valuable.*

auction house, auction houses
NC An **auction house** is a company which arranges and holds auctions. They also provide the service of telling people how much things are worth. *The prestigious international auction house, Sotheby's, is to put up for sale two previously unknown manuscripts by Beethoven.*

audacious /ɔːdeɪʃəs/
ADJ **Audacious** behaviour is behaviour in which you take risks in order to achieve something. *He made an audacious escape from a London prison. ...a highly audacious move. ...a series of audacious adventures.*

audacity /ɔːdæsəti/
NU **Audacity** is audacious behaviour. *It was remarkable what you could accomplish with audacity... He had the audacity to blame Baldwin for their failure... Judy was amazed at her own audacity.*

audible /ɔːdəbl/
ADJ An **audible** sound is one that can be heard easily. *...sounds too high pitched to be audible.* ◆ **audibly** ADV *The clock ticked audibly.*

audience /ɔːdiəns/ **audiences**
1 N COLL The **audience** is all the people who are watching or listening to something such as a play, concert, film, or television programme. *The television audience were able to hear some of the comments... She spoke before an audience of schoolchildren... 'The Doors' has already attracted huge audiences.*
2 N COLL You can also use **audience** to refer to the people who read someone's books or hear about their ideas. *The authorities gave a different account of the visit to the nation's domestic audience... It's the second film version of the book, this time aimed at a wider, more commercial audience... The report also deals with radio, its audiences, and its future.*
3 NC If you have an **audience** with someone important, you have a formal meeting with them. *The Prime Minister will seek an audience with the Queen later this morning... Mr Ganesh Man Singh had an audience with the King.*

audio /ɔːdiəʊ/
ADJ ATTRIB **Audio** equipment is used for recording and reproducing sound. *...a library of audio cassettes on various health problems.*

audio-typist, audio-typists
NC An **audio-typist** is a typist who types letters and reports that have been dictated into a tape-recorder. *We have a vacancy for an audio-typist.*

audio-visual
ADJ ATTRIB **Audio-visual** teaching aids involve both recorded sound and pictures. *This is no ordinary audio-visual show.*

audit /ɔːdɪt/ **audits, auditing, audited**
VO When accountants **audit** an organization's accounts, they examine them officially to make sure that they are correct. *He complained that the government accounts were not properly audited.* ▶ Also NC *We're going to conduct a full audit.*

audition /ɔːdɪʃn/ **auditions, auditioning, auditioned**
1 NC An **audition** is a short performance that someone gives so that a director can decide if they are good enough to be in a play, film, or orchestra. *He qualified for an audition, which in turn led to a job as a singer.*
2 V-ERG If you **audition** or if someone **auditions** you, you perform an audition. *I was so lucky, I never had to audition... Mr Maxwell was auditioned for the part of Uncle Vanya.*

auditor /ɔːdɪtə/ **auditors**
NC An **auditor** is an accountant who officially examines the accounts of organizations. *Once a year an auditor came to audit the accounts. ...a report from the official auditors.*

auditorium /ɔːdɪtɔːriəm/ **auditoriums** or **auditoria** /ɔːdɪtɔːriə/.
NC In a theatre or concert hall, the **auditorium** is the part of the building where the audience sits. *We sat in the auditorium while the Russian company rehearsed.*

auditory /ɔːdɪtəʳri/
ADJ **Auditory** means relating to hearing; a technical or formal word. *...conflict between visual and auditory information.*

au fait /əʊ feɪ/
ADJ PRED If you are **au fait** with something, you are familiar with it and know about it. *I'm not exactly au fait with the rules of cricket.*

Aug.
Aug. is a written abbreviation for 'August'. *...an all Johann-Strauss programme on Aug. 18.*

augment /ɔːgmɛnt/ **augments, augmenting, augmented**
VO To **augment** something means to make it larger by adding something to it; a formal word. *They hit upon another idea to augment their income... Many American firms, not just banks, sought to expand by buying others, rather than by augmenting their own operations.*

augur /ɔːgə/ **augurs, auguring, augured**
VA If something **augurs** well or badly, it is a sign that things will go well or badly; a formal word. *If the surveys augur well, the work on the tunnel will start at the end of this week... This doesn't augur well for the future... This augurs poorly for the new international order we hear so much about.*

augury /ɔːgjʊri/ **auguries**
NC An **augury** is a sign of what will happen in the future; a literary word. *What happened yesterday could be an augury of even worse to come.*

august; pronounced /ɔːgəst/ when it is a noun and /ɔːgʌst/ when it is an adjective.
1 NU **August** is the eighth month of the year in the Western calendar. *War broke out on August 4th... You start your new job in August.*
2 ADJ Someone or something that is **august** is dignified and impressive; a literary use. *He was probably the most august figure in the House of Lords.*

auk /ɔːk/ **auks**
NC An **auk** is a bird with a heavy body and short tail that dives into the sea for its food. *It is estimated that up to one thousand auks drown each day during stormy weather.*

aunt /ɑːnt/ **aunts**
NC Your **aunt** is the sister of your mother or father, or the wife of your uncle. *My aunt lived in that village until her death... Aunt Alice is coming to stay for the weekend.*

auntie /ˈɑːnti/ **aunties**; also spelt **aunty**.
NC Your **auntie** is your aunt; an informal word. *I used to go to an old lady there, an auntie of my mother and she used to tell me stories.*

au pair /əʊ ˈpeə/ **au pairs**
NC An **au pair** is a young woman who lives for a time with a family in a different country from her own so that she can learn the language. Au pairs help with housework and looking after small children, and receive a small wage. *One of the au pairs bankrupted them. ...a teenage au pair girl who comes to New York to take care of a couple's children.*

aura /ˈɔːrə/ **auras**
NC An **aura** is a quality or feeling that seems to surround a person or place. *...an aura of glamour and prestige.*

aural /ˈɔːrəl, ˈaʊrəl/
ADJ **Aural** means related to the sense of hearing. *I have used written and aural material.*

aurora borealis /ərɔːrə bɔːriˈeɪlɪs/
N SING The **aurora borealis** consists of moving bands of coloured light sometimes seen in the sky in Arctic regions. *The Aurora Borealis is one of the most strikingly beautiful natural wonders of the world.*

auspices /ˈɔːspɪsɪz/
If something is done **under the auspices of** a particular person or organization, it is done with their support and approval; a formal expression. *...a big international peace conference under the auspices of the United Nations.*

auspicious /ɔːˈspɪʃəs/
ADJ Something that is **auspicious** indicates that success is likely; a formal word. *The newly sworn in government got off to an auspicious start. ...the Year of the Dragon, traditionally the most auspicious in the Chinese calendar.*

Aussie /ˈɒzi/ **Aussies**
NC An **Aussie** is an Australian; an informal word. *Meninga converted to put the Aussies 10-6 up. ...the stereotyped image of the Aussie male.*

austere /ɔːˈstɪə/
1 ADJ Something that is **austere** is plain and not decorated. *The interior of the church is sober and austere... The new housing blocks are in themselves austere and grim.*
2 ADJ An **austere** person is strict and serious. *He certainly appears as an austere man... The minister faced his critics with an austere but brisk determination.*
3 ADJ An **austere** way of life is simple and has no luxuries. *...the austere life of the mountain people.*

austerity /ɔːˈstɛrəti/
1 NU **Austerity** is a situation in which only things that are essential to life are available. Austerity is often caused by government policies designed to help the country's economy in the long term. *The country is now facing real austerity, with the particular problem of unemployment... Oil prices are low, and austerity is biting hard... The government must continue its policies of economic austerity.* ▸ Also ADJ *New austerity measures have been announced in Peru.*
2 NUorN PL **Austerity** is also the quality of being simple, plain, and undecorated. *...the austerity of these surroundings... It's been a day of celebrations, despite the austerities of Ramadan.*

Australia /ɒsˈtreɪliə/
The **Commonwealth of Australia** is a country in the Pacific. In 1788 Britain established the first of several colonies. During the 19th century they became self-governing and formed a federation in 1901. It is a member of the Commonwealth and ANZUS. Paul Keating, of the Australian Labor Party (ALP), became Prime Minister in 1991. Australia exports minerals, foodstuffs, wool and oil. ◆ **Australian** /ɒsˈtreɪliən/ N, ADJ
▪ *per capita GNP:* US$12,390 ▪ *religion:* Christianity ▪ *language:* English ▪ *currency:* dollar ▪ *capital:* Canberra ▪ *largest city:* Sydney ▪ *population:* 17 million (1989) ▪ *size:* 7,682,300 square kilometres.

Austria /ˈɒstriə/
The **Republic of Austria** is a country in central Europe. German forces entered Austria unopposed in the Anschluss of 1938 and Austria was made part of Nazi Germany. In 1945 Austria was divided into four zones, which were occupied by the forces of the United States, United Kingdom, the Soviet Union, and France. The occupation forces left in 1955. Austria applied for membership in the European Community in 1989. In 1986 Dr Kurt Waldheim, of the Austrian People's Party (OVP), became President and Dr Franz Vranitzky, of the Socialist Party of Austria (SPO), became Chancellor. Austria exports machinery and equipment, iron, steel, lumber, and textiles. Tourism is an important industry. ◆ **Austrian** /ˈɒstriən/ N, ADJ
▪ *per capita GNP:* US$15,560 ▪ *religion:* Christianity (mainly Roman Catholic) ▪ *language:* German ▪ *currency:* Schilling ▪ *capital:* Vienna ▪ *population:* 8 million (1988) ▪ *size:* 83,856 square kilometres.

authentic /ɔːˈθentɪk/
1 ADJ If a letter or painting is **authentic**, it is genuine rather than a forgery or an imitation. *...the authentic writings of the period... As yet, no-one knows whether this bizarre new version is authentic. ...music played on authentic medieval instruments.*
2 ADJ If information or an account is **authentic**, it is reliable and accurate. *The book gives an authentic account of that awful war.*

authenticate /ɔːˈθentɪkeɪt/ **authenticates, authenticating, authenticated**
VO If you **authenticate** something, you officially state that it is genuine after examining it. *A federal judge wants her to authenticate that document in testimony... These stories seem to be well authenticated.* ◆ **authentication** /ɔːˈθentɪkeɪʃn/ NU *For authentication, the statement was accompanied by photocopies of the identity cards.*

authenticity /ˌɔːθenˈtɪsəti/
1 NU **Authenticity** is the fact of something having been genuinely made, painted, or written by the person who is thought to have done it. *He challenged the authenticity of the letter... The painting is of doubtful authenticity.*
2 NU The **authenticity** of a story or a piece of information is the fact that it is reliable, accurate, and able to be believed. *No historian has ever doubted the authenticity of Haldane's account.*

author /ˈɔːθə/ **authors**
1 NC The **author** of a piece of writing is the person who wrote it. *...the author of a recent report on discrimination... According to the authors, wage inflation fell from fifteen to less that four percent.*
2 NC An **author** is a person whose occupation is writing books. *The British author Graham Greene lived in the neighbouring village... The Edinburgh Book Festival attracts authors from around the world.*

authorise /ˈɔːθəraɪz/. See **authorize**.

authoritarian /ɔːˌθɒrɪˈteəriən/ **authoritarians**
ADJ A person or organization that is **authoritarian** wants to control other people rather than letting them decide things for themselves. *...the emergence of a more authoritarian leadership... Her attitude, he claimed, was authoritarian and dictatorial.* ▸ Also NC *The old rulers were essentially authoritarians.*

authoritarianism /ɔːˌθɒrɪˈteəriənɪzəm/
NU **Authoritarianism** is the belief that people with power, especially the State, have the right to control other people's thoughts and actions; a formal word. *Authoritarianism in government repelled him... He is intent on replacing one form of authoritarianism for another.*

authoritative /ɔːˈθɒrɪtətɪv/
1 ADJ If someone behaves in an **authoritative** way, they give an impression of power and importance. *...an authoritative display of discipline... She said in an authoritative tone, 'I've just been there'.* ◆ **authoritatively** ADV *'Don't do that,' he said authoritatively.*
2 ADJ An **authoritative** piece of writing is based on a lot of knowledge or facts. *...his authoritative study of the Commonwealth... They insisted that before any wider exchange becomes possible, they must receive authoritative information about their own prisoners.*

authority /ɔːˈθɒrəti/ **authorities**
1 NC An **authority** is an official organization or

government department that has the power to make decisions. *The authorities have got to clamp down on people like this... She sold the house to the local authority... The governor of the Airports Authority said the accident was unavoidable.*
2 NU If you have **authority** over someone, you have the power to control them. *He made efforts to reassert his authority over them... He would be reported to those in authority... Some observers worry that he may not be able to maintain his authority.*
3 NU **Authority** is a personal quality that some people have. If someone has authority, other people pay attention to what they say and usually obey them. *Her voice carried a note of authority... 'I'll make sure it's done,' he said with great authority.*
4 NU **Authority** is official permission to do something. *Have you been ordering taxis without signed authority?... A referendum yesterday gave the Parliament complete authority to declare independence.*
5 NC Someone who is an **authority** on a subject knows a lot about it. *He is an authority on India... He is an authority on international debt.*
6 If you **have it on good authority** that something is true, you are fairly sure that it is true because you trust the person who told you; a formal expression. *I have it on good authority that Frieda Maloney will be prosecuted.*

authorization /ɔːθəˈraɪzeɪʃn/ **authorizations**; also spelt **authorisation**.
NUorNC **Authorization** is official permission to do something, especially when it is written down. *You can't even send a cable without government authorization... Has the authorisation for my visa come through yet?*

authorize /ˈɔːθəraɪz/ **authorizes, authorizing, authorized**; also spelt **authorise**.
VOorVO+to-INF If someone **authorizes** something, they give their official permission for it to happen. *The President authorized the bombings... Today, he authorised the Bank of England to raise interest rates... Civilians were authorised to carry guns during the war.*

authorship /ˈɔːθəʃɪp/
1 NU The **authorship** of a piece of writing is the identity of the person who wrote it. *The letter's authorship could not be kept secret... The Bible is a work of collective authorship.*
2 NU **Authorship** is the activity or job of writing books or articles. *I depend upon authorship for my entire living.*

autism /ˈɔːtɪzəm/
NU **Autism** is a severe mental illness that affects children and makes them unable to respond to other people. *Music therapy can help with a variety of problems, ranging from autism to stress.*

autistic /ɔːˈtɪstɪk/
ADJ An **autistic** person suffers from autism. *...the story of an autistic man discovering the outside world.*

auto /ˈɔːtəʊ/ **autos**
NC In the United States, cars are sometimes called **autos**. *Overall, imports fell $2.7 billion to 43.3 billion as imports of autos, parts and other machinery fell along with oil. ...television sets, auto spares, and radios.*

autobiographical /ˌɔːtəbaɪəˈgræfɪkl/
ADJ A piece of writing that is **autobiographical** relates to events in the life of the person who has written it. *...an autobiographical novel... 'In My Life' is a tender autobiographical poem set to music.*

autobiography /ˌɔːtəbaɪˈɒɡrəfi/ **autobiographies**
NCorNU Your **autobiography** is an account of your life, which you write yourself. *He was speaking in London, where he's promoting his autobiography.*

autocracy /ɔːˈtɒkrəsi/
NU **Autocracy** is government or management by one person who has complete power. *They said they would rise against the forces of autocracy and dictatorship. ...leading the fight against military autocracy.*

autocrat /ˈɔːtəkræt/ **autocrats**
NC An **autocrat** is a person in authority who has complete power. *Voltaire believed that social progress could best be achieved under an enlightened autocrat.*

autocratic /ˌɔːtəˈkrætɪk/
ADJ Someone who is **autocratic** has complete power and makes decisions without asking anyone else's advice. *According to critics, he was an autocratic and domineering leader.* ♦ **autocratically** ADV *It had a self-appointed King, who ruled the country autocratically.*

Autocue /ˈɔːtəʊkjuː/ **Autocues**
NC An **Autocue** is a device used by people speaking on television, which displays words for them to read so that they can look straight at the camera when they are speaking. Autocue is a trademark. *An ability to read the autocue is essential.*

autograph /ˈɔːtəɡrɑːf/ **autographs, autographing, autographed**
1 NC If you ask someone famous for their **autograph**, you ask them to write their signature for you. *She shunned publicity, and would not even give autographs... There were babies in American flag T-shirts and teenage girls clutching autograph books.*
2 VO When a famous person **autographs** something, they put their signature on it. *He was shown moving among them, autographing banners and petitions.* ♦ **autographed** ADJ *He gave me an autographed copy of his book.*

auto-immune
ADJ An **auto-immune** disease or reaction is one in which your antibodies attack normal substances that are present in your body, rather than attacking harmful bacteria. *If he is successful, the drug may eventually be used to treat auto-immune diseases such as multiple sclerosis... Some researchers have suggested that arthritis is a kind of auto-immune response.*

automat /ˈɔːtəmæt/ **automats**
NC In the United States, an **automat** is a machine which sells food by releasing it after the right amount of money has been put into it. *During the Depression, there were hundreds of the automats, mostly in New York city, dispensing macaroni and cheese, baked beans and so on.*

automate /ˈɔːtəmeɪt/ **automates, automating, automated**
VO If a factory, office, or industrial process is **automated**, it operates using machinery rather than people. *Such an error is unlikely because the aircraft is so fully automated... Let's hope they don't automate radio presenters!* ♦ **automation** /ˌɔːtəˈmeɪʃn/ NU *This is an age of high technology and automation.*

automatic /ˌɔːtəˈmætɪk/ **automatics**
1 ADJ An **automatic** machine is one which has controls that enable it to perform a task without needing to be constantly operated by a person. *...automatic washing machines... They have introduced automatic cash machines... Police were alerted by automatic alarm systems.* ♦ **automatically** ADV *The lights come on automatically.*
2 NC An automatic gun, car, or washing machine can be called an **automatic**. *They are a collection of everything from single barrel shotguns to heavy automatics... The five-speed is about $600 more than the automatic.*
3 ADJ An **automatic** action is one that you do without thinking about it. *Most of our decisions in day-to-day life are automatic... It was an automatic gesture.* ♦ **automatically** ADV *Billy found himself automatically walking up to the house.*
4 ADJ If something such as an action or a punishment is **automatic**, it happens as the normal result of something else. *These offences carry automatic fines... The FA disciplinary hearing did not impose a ban beyond the automatic three-match suspension. ...automatic trading penalties.* ♦ **automatically** ADV *Once people retire they automatically cease to be union members.*

automatic pilot, automatic pilots
1 NC An **automatic pilot** is a device in an aircraft that controls its speed and direction automatically. *The plane is now on automatic pilot.*
2 If you are **on automatic pilot**, you are acting without thinking about what you are doing, usually because

you have done it many times before; an informal expression. *I had lost all interest in the game. I was on automatic pilot now.*

automaton /ɔːˈtɒmətən/ **automatons** or **automata** /ɔːˈtɒmətə/.

NC If you say that someone is an **automaton**, you mean that they act without thinking, usually because they are tired or bored. *Eventually, you become an automaton, saying the same dull things over and over again.*

automobile /ˈɔːtəməbiːl/ **automobiles**

NC In the United States, cars are sometimes called **automobiles**. *...a man driving a Mercedes automobile.*

autonomous /ɔːˈtɒnəməs/

ADJ An **autonomous** country, organization, or group governs or controls itself rather than being controlled by anyone else. *This would give Serbia more control over its troubled autonomous province, Kosova.*

autonomy /ɔːˈtɒnəmi/

NU **Autonomy** is the control of a country, organization, or group by itself, rather than by others. *People in the republics stepped up their campaigns for autonomy. ...demands for cultural and political autonomy.*

autopsy /ˈɔːtɒpsi/ **autopsies**

NCorNU An **autopsy** is an examination of a dead body by a doctor who cuts it open in order to try to discover the cause of death. *An independent autopsy by two doctors had found no evidence of torture... Some skulls had bullet holes in them, and others were sectioned for autopsy.*

autumn /ˈɔːtəm/ **autumns**

NUorNC **Autumn** is the season between summer and winter. In the autumn the weather becomes cooler and on some kinds of tree the leaves change colour and drop off. *...autumn leaves... The rain began in the late autumn.*

autumnal /ɔːˈtʌmnəl/

ADJ Something that is **autumnal** has features that are characteristic of autumn. *...a warm and sunny autumnal day in southern England.*

auxiliary /ɔːɡˈzɪliəri/ **auxiliaries**

1 NC An **auxiliary** is a person who is employed to help other people. Auxiliaries are often medical workers or members of the armed forces. *The new reforms could leave a gap in patient care between the fully-qualified nurse and the auxiliary. ...nursing auxiliaries.* ▶ Also ADJ ATTRIB *...six auxiliary squadrons.*

2 ADJ ATTRIB **Auxiliary** equipment is extra equipment that is used when necessary. *It depends if they have auxiliary electric power generators within their hospitals. ...auxiliary scaffolding.*

3 NC In grammar, the **auxiliary verbs** are 'be', 'have', and 'do'. They are used with a main verb to form tenses, negatives, and questions.

avail /əˈveɪl/

If an action is **of no avail** or is done **to no avail**, it does not achieve what you want. *Speeches and protests were of no avail... They were fighting to no avail.*

available /əˈveɪləbl/

1 ADJ If something is **available**, you can use it or obtain it. *...the amount of money available for spending.* ◆ **availability** /əˌveɪləˈbɪləti/ NU *...the availability of oil.*

2 ADJ Someone who is **available** is not busy and is therefore free to talk to you or to do a particular task. *It's not clear whether he'll be available for the first match.*

avalanche /ˈævəlɑːntʃ/ **avalanches**

1 NC An **avalanche** is a large mass of snow or rock that falls down the side of a mountain. *During the night, the camp was buried in an avalanche... Nineteen people have died in an avalanche following some of the worst snows in south-eastern Turkey for fifteen years.*

2 NC+SUPP You can refer to a large quantity of things that arrive or happen at the same time as an **avalanche** of them. *...an avalanche of tourists... This began the political avalanche that overwhelmed Eastern Europe's Communist regimes.*

avant-garde /ˌævɒŋˈɡɑːd/

ADJ **Avant-garde** art, theatre, and writing is modern and experimental. *Teatro del Sur, the avant-garde theatre company, make their British debut tonight.*

avarice /ˈævərɪs/

NU **Avarice** is extreme greed for money; a literary word. *...riches beyond the dreams of avarice.*

avaricious /ˌævəˈrɪʃəs/

ADJ Someone who is **avaricious** is very greedy for money. *...a combination of avaricious business interests, corrupt officials, and an authoritarian government.*

Avarua /ɑːˈvəruːə/

Avarua is the capital and largest town of the Cook Islands. It is on the island of Rarotonga. Population: 9,000 (1986).

ave.

Ave. is a written abbreviation for 'avenue', when it is part of the name of a road. *...184, Poplar Ave.*

avenge /əˈvendʒ/ **avenges, avenging, avenged**

VO If you **avenge** a wrong or harmful act, you hurt or punish the person who did it. *He was determined to avenge his father's death.*

avenue /ˈævənjuː/ **avenues**

1 **Avenue** is a name sometimes used for a street in a town. *...Belfast's main shopping thoroughfare, Royal Avenue.*

2 NC An **avenue** is a wide road with trees on either side. *The Princess was driven in a motorcade along the city's main avenue... The broad avenues of Peking are hung with banners and flags.*

3 NC+SUPP An **avenue** is also a way of getting something done. *There is another avenue of approach that we must pursue... The Americans seem to have blocked off his only avenue of escape... It does however open up new avenues of research.*

aver /əˈvɜː/ **avers, averring, averred**

VO, V-REPORT, or V-QUOTE If you **aver** something, you say very firmly that it is true; a formal word. *He averred his innocence... Certain critics scoffed, averring that nobody would pay to see it... 'I know he didn't steal it,' she averred.*

average /ˈævərɪdʒ/ **averages, averaging, averaged**

1 NC An **average** is the result you get when you add several amounts together and divide the total by the number of amounts. *These pupils were examined in 39 subjects, an average of 6.5 subjects for each pupil... Unemployment in the town is already well above the national average.* ▶ Also ADJ ATTRIB *The average age of the group was thirty-nine years... During the 1980s the average air temperatures across the globe have been the warmest ever recorded.*

2 VC To **average** a particular amount means to be that amount as an average over a period of time. *Price increases during these years averaged around 20%... He averaged over 146 kilometers per hour... World Cup matches in the 1950s averaged five goals each.*

3 ADJ ATTRIB **Average** is sometimes used to mean normal in size or quality. *...a sheet of paper of average thickness... Their language development is below average.*

4 You say **on average** to indicate that a number is the average of several numbers. *We can discover how many words, on average, a person reads in a minute.*

average out PHRASAL VERB When you **average out** a set of numbers, you work out the average. *We find that, averaging it out, only 8,000 chairs could have been purchased.*

averse /əˈvɜːs/

ADJ PRED+*to* If you are not **averse** to something, you quite like it or quite want to do it; a formal word. *The talks went well, and Mr Vorontsov was not averse to the idea of a transitional government.*

aversion /əˈvɜːʃn/ **aversions**

1 N SING If you have an **aversion** to someone or something, you dislike them very much. *She had a great aversion to children.*

2 NC Your **aversion** is something that you strongly dislike. *His current aversion is pop music.*

avert /əˈvɜːt/ **averts, averting, averted**

1 VO To **avert** something unpleasant means to prevent it from happening. *There must be immediate action if total chaos is to be averted... The Organisation is*

appealing to the international community to take
urgent action to avert serious food shortages.
2 VO If you **avert** your eyes from something, you look
away from it. *During the trial, people were averting
their eyes from one another. ...as you avert your eyes
from the mirror.*

aviary /ˈeɪvɪəri/ **aviaries**
NC An **aviary** is a large cage or covered area in which
birds are kept. *I was cleaning out my budgerigar
aviaries in the garden.*

aviation /eɪviˈeɪʃn/
NU **Aviation** is the operation, production, and use of
aircraft. *More than thirty British firms, representing
agriculture, aviation, and printing, are involved... This
was the worst aviation disaster in Canada.*

aviator /ˈeɪvɪeɪtə/ **aviators**
NC An **aviator** is someone who flies small aeroplanes;
an old-fashioned word. *With his moustache, he looked
every inch the aviator.*

avid /ˈævɪd/
ADJ ATTRIB You use **avid** to describe someone who is
very keen and enthusiastic about something. *...an
avid reader of movie magazines. ...voters who are
avid supporters of Jesse Jackson.* ◆ **avidly** ADV *They
listened avidly.*

avocado /ævəˈkɑːdəʊ/ **avocados**
NCorNU An **avocado** or **avocado pear** is a dark green,
tropical fruit. *We offer everything from oranges and
avocados, to coffee and cut flowers... You've got here
avocado, mango, pineapple and passion fruit.*

avoid /əˈvɔɪd/ **avoids, avoiding, avoided**
1 VO If you **avoid** something that might happen, you
take action in order to prevent it from happening. *...a
book on how to avoid a heart attack... He is not
optimistic that war can be avoided.*
2 V+ING If you **avoid** doing something, you deliberately
manage not to do it. *Thomas turned his head, trying
to avoid breathing in the smoke... They avoided paying
tax on their profits.*
3 VO If you **avoid** someone or something, you keep
away from them. If you avoid a subject, you keep the
conversation away from it. *For many centuries, the
islands were avoided by sailors as the currents made
them treacherous... John McCann stayed with friends
overnight, having avoided waiting journalists at Dublin
airport... He studiously avoided the subject of internal
Irish politics.*

avoidable /əˈvɔɪdəbl/
ADJ Something that is **avoidable** can be prevented
from happening. *He said the tragedy had been wholly
avoidable. ...avoidable risks.*

avoidance /əˈvɔɪdəns/
NU **Avoidance** of someone or something is the act of
avoiding them. *...the avoidance of responsibilities...
His reinstatement depends on his continued avoidance
of drugs. ...tax avoidance.*

avow /əˈvaʊ/ **avows, avowing, avowed**
VO, V-REPORT, or V+to-INF If you **avow** something, you
admit it or declare it; a formal word. *Both sides have
avowed their intention to achieve reunification... She
was obliged to avow openly that she had been there...
Hardline commanders avow to keep up the ambushes
to the bitter end.*

avowal /əˈvaʊəl/ **avowals**
NC An **avowal** of something is an admission or
declaration of it; a formal word. *He made a shy
avowal of love.*

avowed /əˈvaʊd/; a formal word.
1 ADJ ATTRIB If you are an **avowed** supporter or
opponent of something, you have declared that you
support it or oppose it. *...avowed enemies. ...a
Protestant clergyman who was an avowed
homosexual.*
2 ADJ ATTRIB An **avowed** belief or aim is one that you
hold very strongly. *Will they achieve their avowed
goal of removing Congress from power?*

avowedly /əˈvaʊɪdli/
SUBMOD **Avowedly** is used when mentioning a
characteristic which someone openly admits they
have. *The truth is that the Mauritian economy is
avowedly capitalist, and becoming more so... Many of
the speeches have an avowedly political message.*

avuncular /əˈvʌŋkjʊlə/
ADJ An **avuncular** man acts in a friendly and helpful
way towards someone younger; a literary word. *In
my best avuncular fashion I put my arm round her
shoulder.*

await /əˈweɪt/ **awaits, awaiting, awaited**
1 VO If you **await** someone or something, you wait for
them. *I returned to the States to find the FBI awaiting
me... Troops and ambulances awaited its arrival... The
result is eagerly awaited throughout India.* ◆ **awaited**
ADJ ATTRIB *This is the first single from his long
awaited new LP.*
2 VOorV Something that **awaits** you is going to happen
to you in the future. *...the adventures that awaited
him... Once through his trial, security and
respectability await.*

awake /əˈweɪk/ **awakes, awaking, awoke, awoken**
1 ADJ PRED Someone who is **awake** is not sleeping. *He
lay awake all night... It's keeping them awake all
night, he said, night after night... He played dominoes
before the game to stay awake.*
2 V-ERG When you **awake** or when something **awakes**
you, you wake up; a literary use. *She awoke to find a
fireman in her smoke-filled room... In a good-natured
joke, the flight controllers awoke the crew with the
theme tune of the film 'Star Wars'.*

awaken /əˈweɪkən/ **awakens, awakening, awakened**;
a literary word.
1 VO To **awaken** a feeling in a person means to cause
them to have this feeling. *My first visit to a theatre
awakened an interest which never left me... The
reforms awakened ancient ethnic rivalries in the
province.*
2 V-ERG+to When you **awaken** to a fact or when
someone **awakens** you to it, you become aware of it.
*Gradually people are awakening to their
responsibilities... He said France wanted to awaken
the world's conscience to the plight of the Lebanese.*
3 V-ERG When you **are awakened** or when you **awake**,
you wake up. *Southern England was awakened by the
unearthly red glow of a flying saucer early this
morning... Each time a dog barked, we awakened with
a start.*

awakening /əˈweɪkəⁿnɪŋ/
1 N SING+SUPP The **awakening** of a feeling in someone
is the start of it. *These political changes have
encouraged what he calls a social awakening in his
country... Only now are we beginning to see an
awakening of interest in the candidates.*
2 If you have a **rude awakening**, you are suddenly
made aware of an unpleasant fact. *For the Party
establishment, these results are beginning to add up to
a rude awakening.*

award /əˈwɔːd/ **awards, awarding, awarded**
1 NC An **award** is a prize or certificate that a person
is given for doing something well. *He won a
Hollywood 'Oscar' award for his role as a butler in the
American film 'Arthur'. ...award winners... Three
British soldiers have been given bravery awards.*
2 VOOorVO To **award** something to someone means to
give it to them as a prize or reward. *The Australasian
team were awarded the title... Of the 51,000 Military
Crosses awarded so far, over 40,000 were given during
the First World War.*
3 NC An **award** is also a sum of money that a court of
law decides should be given to someone as
compensation. *The award of fifty thousand dollars
was in French francs... He received an award of
£10,000 in compensation for his injuries.*
4 VOOorVO If a court of law **awards** someone a sum of
money, they say that the money must be paid to them
as compensation. *She has been awarded damages of
more than £8000... The jury awarded $1,000,000 in
damages.*

aware /əˈweə/
1 ADJ PRED If you are **aware** of a fact or situation, you
know about it. *He was aware that he had drunk too
much whisky... He added he was not aware of any
request for additional aid from the United States... I
was quite aware of this before we married.*
◆ **awareness** NU *...the public awareness of the need
for conservation.*

2 ADJ PRED If you are **aware** of something that is present or happening, you know that it is present or happening because you can hear it, see it, smell it, or feel it. *Ralph was aware of the heat for the first time... His story is that he became aware that he was dreaming.*
3 ADJ If you say that someone is **aware**, you mean that they notice what is happening around them. *Some people are more politically aware... Children should be creative and aware.*

awash /əwɒʃ/
1 ADJ PRED If a place is **awash**, it is covered in water. *In the monsoon the whole place is awash.*
2 ADJ PRED+*with* **Awash** is also used to say that a particular place or period of time contains a large number of people or things, especially when this is considered to be too much. *During the mid-1960s the world became awash with dollars... In London earlier the market was awash with news.*

away /əweɪ/
1 ADV If you move **away** from a place, you move so that you are no longer there. *He rose and walked away. ...children who run away from home... A man was led away in handcuffs... People began to run away in panic.*
2 ADV If you look or turn **away** from something, you move your head so that you are no longer looking at it. *Turn your head away from the cooker... I do not think I would be able to turn away... He looks away.*
3 ADV **Away** from a person or place means at a distance from that person or place. *...a pleasant picnic spot away from the city... It's away from the tourist routes... They have warned people living in Las Vegas, one hundred miles away, that there may be a small earth tremor.*
4 ADV If you put something **away**, you put it in a safe place. *Tom put the book away... The report is not yet ready to be filed away... Residents were told they could put away their gas-masks.*
5 ADV If someone is **away**, they are not in the place where people expect them to be. *Is he at home or has he gone away?... Bob Edwards is away... Many of them remain away from home today.*
6 ADV You also use **away** to talk about future events. For example, if an event is a week **away**, it will happen in a week. *The elections are only three weeks away now... With the start of the World Cup just days away, many countries have been completing their warm-up preparations... A final regulation is at least nine months away.*
7 ADV If you give something **away** or if someone takes it **away** from you, you no longer have it. *It's always a problem finding a present to give away to your customers... The police took the gun away for forensic tests... She gave a fortune away.*
8 ADJ ATTRIB or ADV When a sports team plays an **away** game, it plays on its opponents' ground. *We haven't won a single away game this season... They beat Toulon 3—1 away.*
9 ADV You can use **away** to say that something slowly disappears, or changes so that it is no longer the same. *Official Trade Union support has dropped away... The snow had all melted away.*
10 ADV **Away** is also used to emphasize that an action is continuous or repeated. *Howard was still working away in the university library... She was coughing away.*
11 **right away**: see **right**. **straight away**: see **straight**.

awe /ɔː/ **awed**
1 NU **Awe** is the respect and amazement that you feel when you are faced with something wonderful and rather frightening. *The child stared at him in silent awe... I don't want to lose that sense of awe and wonder.*
2 If you are **in awe** of someone, you have a lot of respect for them and are slightly afraid of them. *By the end, I had grown to be in awe of her.*
3 V-PASS If you **are awed** by someone or something, you are impressed by them and rather frightened of them. *Others have been awed by the effects of sunlight shining through the stained glass windows... One would look at the mountain peaks around and be*

awed by the grandeur of it. ◆ **awed** ADJ *...talking in an awed whisper.*

awe-inspiring
ADJ Something that is **awe-inspiring** is amazing and rather frightening. *The grandiose splendour of the Kremlin is awe-inspiring.*

awesome /ɔːsəm/
ADJ Something that is **awesome** is very impressive and frightening. *...the awesome complexity of the universe. ...an awesome weapon... Tackling pollution on that scale is an awesome task.*

awestruck /ɔːstrʌk/
ADJ If someone is **awestruck**, they are very impressed and amazed by something; a literary word. *...watching with awestruck interest... I am a little awestruck by what I heard.*

awful /ɔːfl/
1 ADJ If you say that something is **awful**, you mean that it is very unpleasant or bad. *Isn't the weather awful? ...that awful war... They were working in awful conditions.*
2 ADJ PRED If you look or feel **awful**, you look or feel ill. *Asked by reporters how he felt, the Prince smiled and replied 'Awful'... He looks awful.*
3 ADJ ATTRIB You can use **awful** to emphasize how large an amount is; an informal use. *It must have taken an awful lot of courage... It can tell you an awful lot about what has happened in the past.*

awfully /ɔːfəli/
SUBMOD You use **awfully** to emphasize how much of a quality someone or something has; an informal word. *She was awfully nice... I'm awfully sorry... I think it's an awfully ambitious programme.*

awhile /əwaɪl/
ADV **Awhile** means for a short time; a literary word. *He longed to be allowed to rest awhile.*

awkward /ɔːkwəd/
1 ADJ An **awkward** movement or position is uncomfortable or clumsy. *...an awkward gesture.* ◆ **awkwardly** ADV *He fell and lay awkwardly, covered in mud.*
2 ADJ Someone who is **awkward** behaves in a shy or embarrassed way. *I hated the big formal dances and felt very awkward... Initially a slightly awkward girl who bit her nails, she developed into a poised young woman.* ◆ **awkwardly** ADV *I said, 'How do you do?' awkwardly.* ◆ **awkwardness** NU *There was no awkwardness between them.*
3 ADJ You also say that someone is **awkward** when they are unreasonable and difficult to live with or deal with. *...awkward neighbours... He will have to leave early because his wife is so awkward.*
4 ADJ An **awkward** job is difficult to do. *Getting the wheel off can be awkward.*
5 ADJ An **awkward** situation is embarrassing and difficult to deal with. *McPherson started making things awkward for him... He asked a lot of awkward questions.*

awning /ɔːnɪŋ/ **awnings**
NC An **awning** is a piece of material attached to a caravan or building which provides shelter from the rain or sun. *The shop was freshly painted with a large green awning to protect the plate-glass window.*

awoke /əwəʊk/
Awoke is the past tense of **awake**.

awoken /əwəʊkən/
Awoken is the past participle of **awake**.

awry /əraɪ/
1 ADJ PRED If something is **awry**, it is not in its normal or proper position. *His tie was awry.*
2 ADJ PRED If something goes **awry**, it does not happen in the way it was planned and it goes wrong. *Plans for a massive swim across shark-infested waters have gone awry. ...improving airport security systems, which seem to have gone awry.*

axe /æks/ **axes, axing, axed**
1 NC An **axe** is a tool used for cutting wood. It consists of a blade attached to the end of a long handle. *The men, armed with pistols and an axe, forced their way into the van and tied up the driver.*
2 VO If the government or a company **axes** a project or plan, it suddenly ends it. *Wages were slashed,*

taxes raised, and jobs axed... The show is being axed after more than twenty-five years to make way for a new programme.

axes

1 Axes, pronounced /ˈæksɪz/, is the plural of **axe**.

2 Axes, pronounced /ˈæksiːz/, is the plural of **axis**.

axiom /ˈæksiəm/ **axioms**

NC An **axiom** is a statement or idea which people accept as true; a formal word. *It's an axiom of mountaineering that a good climber knows when to turn back.*

axiomatic /ˌæksiəˈmætɪk/

ADJ PRED Something that is **axiomatic** is obviously true; a formal word. *It has come to be regarded as axiomatic that good nutrition must always imply eating expensively.*

axis /ˈæksɪs/ **axes** /ˈæksiːz/

1 NC An **axis** is an imaginary line through the middle of something. *The earth's axis is tilted at an angle of about 23°.*

2 NC An **axis** of a graph is one of the two lines on which the scales of measurement are marked. *The horizontal axis is twice as long as the vertical one.*

3 N SING **Axis** is used to refer to the friendly relationship that exists between two countries. *A new Brazil-Argentina trade axis was launched eighteen months ago... They want to see an end to the Tehran-Damascus axis.*

axle /ˈæksl/ **axles**

NC An **axle** is a rod connecting a pair of wheels on a car or other vehicle. *I found three wheelbarrow*

wheels that had come off their axle.

aye /aɪ/

Aye means yes. *'Would there be any risks involved in this system?'—'Oh, aye. The danger would be quite real.'*

Aylwin Azócar, Patricio /pætriːsjəʊ eɪlwɪn æsəʊkɑː/

Patricio Aylwin Azócar became President of Chile in 1990, succeeding General Pinochet. He was President of the Christian Democrat Party (PDC) from 1987 to 1989 and is a member of the Alliance of Parties for Democracy, a coalition of 17 political parties. Born: 1919.

Azerbaijan /ˌæzəbaɪdʒɑːn/

The Republic of Azerbaijan became independent of the USSR in 1991. It is located in the extreme south of the former USSR, between the Black and Caspian Seas. Yagub Mammadov became President in 1992. Azerbaijan produces chemicals, machinery, cotton, tobacco, and oil. The Nagorny-Karabakh region, inhabited mainly by Armenians, is claimed by Armenia. The dispute has caused extensive civil disorder. In 1991 Azerbaijan joined the Commonwealth of Independent States. ◆ **Azeri, Azerbaijani** /əzɡərɪ, ˌæzəbaɪdʒɑːni/ N, ADJ

▪ *per capita GNP:* US$3,750 ▪ *religion:* Islam (mainly Shi'a) ▪ *language:* Azeri ▪ *currency:* rouble ▪ *capital:* Baku ▪ *population:* 7 million (1990) ▪ *size:* 86,600 square kilometres.

azure /ˈæʒə, ˈæzjʊə/

ADJ Something that is **azure** in colour is bright blue. *...under an azure sky.*

B b

B, b /biː/ **B's, b's**
NC **B** is the second letter of the English alphabet.
B.A. /biː eɪ/ **B.A.s**
A **B.A.** is a degree in an arts or social science subject. **B.A.** is an abbreviation for 'Bachelor of Arts'. *He went on to Yale University where he took a B.A. degree.*
Babangida, Ibrahim /ɪbrɑːhɪm baːbʌŋgɪdɑː/
Major-General Ibrahim Babangida became President of Nigeria after a coup in 1985. He was a member of the Supreme Military Council and Chief of Army Staff from 1983 to 1985. Born: 1941.
babble /bæbl/ **babbles, babbling, babbled**
V or V-QUOTE If you **babble**, you talk in a confused or excited way that makes it difficult for others to understand you. *He babbled on about old enemies... The war could last a year, babbled the defense experts... He is found lying in a street, delirious and babbling to phantoms.* ► Also N SING *...the babble of women's voices.*
babe /beɪb/ **babes**
1 NC A **babe** is the same as a **baby**; an old-fashioned use. *You were just a babe in arms when Stalinism descended on Czechoslovakia.*
2 VOCATIVE Some people use **babe** as an affectionate way of addressing someone; an informal use. *There's your change, babe, thank you... Oh, babe, you look good today.*
babel /beɪbl/
N SING If there is a **babel** of noise or of voices, you hear a lot of people talking at the same time, so that you cannot understand what they are saying. *The hall filled with a babel of voices demanding money.*
baboon /bəbuːn/ **baboons**
NC A **baboon** is a type of monkey that has a pointed face, large teeth, and a long tail. *People have been studying groups of baboons for years and years.*
baby /beɪbi/ **babies**
1 NC A **baby** is a very young child that cannot yet walk or talk. *There was a small baby wrapped up in shawls.*
2 VOCATIVE Some people use **baby** as an affectionate way of addressing someone; an informal use. *I hear him saying, 'Why, baby, why, why?'... Don't worry, baby, I'll think of something.*
baby buggy, baby buggies
NC A **baby buggy** is a small chair with wheels and handles, in which an infant can sit and be pushed around. *She attempts to wheel her baby buggy into a hotel bar.*
baby carriage, baby carriages
NC A **baby carriage** is the same as a **baby buggy**; used in American English. *They had a baby carriage with them.*
babyhood /beɪbihʊd/
NU Your **babyhood** is the period of your life when you were a baby. *Children should feel that they are being encouraged by their parents to grow out of babyhood.*
babyish /beɪbiɪʃ/
ADJ **Babyish** things are suitable for a baby, or typical of a baby. *Do not worry if your child likes books that you think are too babyish for him... His voice was soft*

and babyish.
baby-minder, baby-minders
NC A **baby-minder** is someone who takes babies or young children into his or her own home and looks after them while their parents are working. *We can't afford a proper baby-minder, so I don't go out.*
baby-sit, baby-sits, baby-sitting, baby-sat
V If you **baby-sit**, you look after someone's children while they are out. *The judge barred her from seeing her sons, and also banned her from baby-sitting for others.*
baby-sitter, baby-sitters
NC A **baby-sitter** is a person who goes to someone else's home to look after their children while they go out. *Can't you find a baby-sitter and come over for dinner?*
baby-talk
NU **Baby-talk** is the language used by babies when they are just learning to speak. It is also used to refer to the way in which some adults speak when they are talking to babies. *The songs and the baby-talk had been a secret between Andy and his foster-mother.*
bacchanalian /bækəneɪliən/
ADJ ATTRIB A **bacchanalian** party is one at which people drink a lot of alcohol and behave in an extremely uncontrolled way, often involving sexual activity; a literary word. *...a night of bacchanalian revelry.*
bachelor /bætʃələ/ **bachelors**
NC A **bachelor** is a man who is not married. *...a highly eligible bachelor... He was still a bachelor at the age of 46.*
Bachelor of Arts, Bachelors of Arts
NC A **Bachelor of Arts** is a person with a degree in an arts or social science subject. *...each candidate reading for the degree of Bachelor of Arts.*
Bachelor of Science, Bachelors of Science
NC A **Bachelor of Science** is a person with a degree in a science subject.
bachelor's degree, bachelor's degrees
NC A **bachelor's degree** is a first degree, such as a B.A. or a B.Sc. *He graduated from Cornell University with a bachelor's degree in mechanical engineering.*
back /bæk/ **backs, backing, backed**
1 ADV If someone moves **back**, they move in the opposite direction to the one in which they are facing. *The child stepped back nervously... She pushed back her chair.*
2 ADV You use **back** to say that someone or something returns to a particular place or state. *I went back to the kitchen... She put it back on the shelf... He went back to sleep.*
3 ADV If you get something **back**, you get it again after not having it for a while. *You'll get the money back.*
4 ADV If you do something **back**, you do to someone what they have done to you. *He looked at her, and the girl stared back... I shall make some enquiries and call you back.*
5 ADV If someone or something is kept or situated **back** from a place, they are at a distance from it. *Police struggled to keep the crowd back... The house*

is set back from the road.
6 ADV You use **back** to indicate that you are talking or thinking about something that happened in the past. *I invested in the company way back in 1971... Think back to what we've said.*
7 NC Your **back** is the part of your body from your neck to your waist that is on the opposite side to your chest, stomach, and face. *He had his hands tied behind his back.*
8 NC+SUPP The **back** of something is the part of it that is towards the rear or farthest from the front. *Sign on the back of the prescription form... He went to the small counter at the back of the store.* ► Also ADJ ATTRIB *The back wheels were spinning in the mud.*
9 NC+SUPP The **back** of a chair is the part that you lean against. *Then fold down the back of the chair and clip it into place.*
10 ADJ ATTRIB A **back** road is small and narrow with very little traffic on it. *I took a back road to get back to the centre of town.*
11 V-ERG or V When a motor vehicle **backs** or when you **back** it, it moves backwards. *The Chevrolet backed off the ramp with a roar of engine and a puff of smoke... They had backed the truck through the doors... She backed out of the driveway.*
12 VO If you **back** someone, you give them support or money. *The organization is backed by the U.N... Of the regional powers, only Egypt has backed the plan... Britain is backing Pakistan's return to democracy.* ● See also **-backed.**
13 VO If you **back** a particular person, team, or horse in a competition, you bet money that they will win. *He won eight thousand pounds from a one pound bet, backing horses.*
14 See also **backing.**
● **Back** is used in these phrases. ● If someone moves **back and forth,** they repeatedly move in one direction and then in the opposite one. *Someone was pacing back and forth behind the curtains.* ● If you are wearing something **back to front,** you are wearing it with the back of it on the front of your body. *You've got your jumper on back to front.* ● If you do something **behind** someone's **back,** you do it without them knowing about it. *Their purchase of missiles behind the Reagan Administration's back has alarmed many US politicians.* ● If you **turn** your **back on** someone or something, you ignore them or refuse to help them. *We have turned our backs on the very principles we were elected to uphold.*
back away PHRASAL VERB If you **back away,** you move away because you are nervous or frightened. *The Republic of Lithuania has backed away from a confrontation with the Kremlin.*
back down PHRASAL VERB If you **back down,** you withdraw a claim or demand that you made earlier, or you decide not to do something that you had threatened to do. *Washington was backing down on its original charges... The players have backed down after saying they'd take action.*
back off PHRASAL VERB **1** If you **back off,** you move away in order to avoid problems or a fight. *They backed off while the confusion was unravelled.* **2** To **back off** also means the same as to back down. *The union's executive were accused of displaying a lack of courage in backing off from secondary industrial action.*
back out PHRASAL VERB If you **back out,** you decide not to do something that you had previously agreed to do. *They backed out of their ambitious plans to invest in India... Those who were due to take part had backed out.*
back up PHRASAL VERB **1** If you **back up** a statement, you supply evidence to prove that it is true. *...overall guidelines backed up by proper research... The speculation, backed up by some suggestive evidence, came from an American scientist.* **2** If you **back** someone **up,** you help and support them. *He had no militia and no men or guns to back him up.* **3** See also **back-up.**
backache /bækeɪk/
NU **Backache** is a pain in your back. *...minor health*

problems like backache, headaches and stomach pains.
backbench /bækbentʃ/ **backbenches**
1 N PL In the British House of Commons, the **backbenches** are the seats that are occupied by Members of Parliament who are not ministers in the government and who do not hold an official position in an opposition party. *A rumble of discontent is spreading from the backbenches to the leadership of his party... He walked down from his place on the backbenches.*
2 N+N **Backbench** MPs are Members of Parliament who are not ministers in the government and who do not hold an official position in an opposition party. *The bill got the support of several Labour backbench MPs... A Conservative backbench MP asked how many such schemes had been delayed because of lack of money.* ● See also **bench, front bench.**
backbencher /bækbentʃə/ **backbenchers**
NC In Britain, a **backbencher** is an MP who does not hold an official position in the government or its opposition. *The Opposition parties and Conservative backbenchers have welcomed the decision... A senior Conservative backbencher, Mr John Biffen, called on the government to forego another tax cut in the budget.*
backbiting /bækbaɪtɪŋ/
NU **Backbiting** is the saying of unpleasant things about someone who is not there. *The result was that the bickering and backbiting in the centre of British politics continued.*
backbone /bækbəʊn/ **backbones**
1 NC The **backbone** of a person or animal is the column of small linked bones down the middle of their back. *...from a study of the skeleton, in particular the skull, the backbone and the foot.*
2 N SING+SUPP The **backbone** of an organization or system is the part that gives it its main strength or unity. *The centralised trading system has been the backbone of the national economy since the Communist state was founded in 1917... They are the backbone of a community.*
3 NU If someone has **backbone,** they have the courage to do things despite the danger or risk involved. *Until they recover that backbone they will not be taken seriously as an alternative government.*
back-breaking
ADJ **Back-breaking** work is very hard physical work. *There's not a great rush of applicants for back-breaking tasks like seeding or transplanting.*
backchat /bæktʃæt/
NU **Backchat** is a series of slightly rude or cheeky remarks that you make in reply to someone, especially someone in authority such as your teacher or employer; an informal word.
backcloth /bækklɒθ/ **backcloths**
1 NC A **backcloth** is a large piece of cloth, often with scenery or buildings painted on it, that is hung at the back of a stage while a play is being performed. *Against a backcloth depicting a red rose, they performed a dance full of vigour and joy.*
2 N SING+SUPP The **backcloth** to an event is the general situation in which it happens. *The events stood out against a backcloth of industrial unrest in Britain.*
back-comb, back-combs, back-combing, back-combed
VO If you **back-comb** your hair, you move a comb through it towards your scalp instead of away from it, so that your hair looks thicker.
back copy, back copies
NC A **back copy** of a magazine or newspaper is not the most recent edition, but one that was published some time ago. *He started to work his way through back copies of France's leading daily newspaper.*
backdate /bækdeɪt/ **backdates, backdating, backdated**
VO If an arrangement or document is **backdated,** it is put into effect from an agreed date that is earlier than the time when the contract or agreement is completed or signed. *...a 4% increase in basic pay backdated to last April.*

backdoor /bækdɔː/
ADJ ATTRIB **Backdoor** activities are done or achieved in a secret, indirect, or dishonest way. *...charges of backdoor nationalization... A lot of people will see his challenge as a backdoor way of getting at Neil Kinnock.*

backdrop /bækdrɒp/ **backdrops**
1 NC A **backdrop** is a large piece of cloth, often with scenery or buildings painted on it, that is hung at the back of a stage while a play is being performed. *...a backdrop depicting a Russian town.*
2 N SING You can use **backdrop** to refer to something such as a row of hills or trees that is seen behind a place. *...the steep hills that form a backdrop to the city.*

-backed /-bækt/
1 SUFFIX **-backed** is added to some nouns or adjectives to make an adjective that means supported or kept in power by that thing, group, or country. *...the military-backed government. ...a government-backed research organisation. ...the Soviet-backed régime in Afghanistan.*
2 SUFFIX **-backed** is added to some nouns or adjectives to make an adjective that describes the back of an object. *...a velvet-backed couch... They were wearing open-backed dresses.*

backer /bækə/ **backers**
NC+SUPP A **backer** is someone who gives support or financial help to a person or project. *Robert Maxwell is one of the backers of the union offer... Japan has emerged as one of the major backers of the South Korean initiative. ...a series of military successes by UNITA and their South African backers.*

backfire /bækfaɪə/ **backfires, backfiring, backfired**
1 V If a plan **backfires**, it has the opposite result to the one that was intended. *It looks as if his plan has backfired.*
2 V When a motor vehicle or its engine **backfires**, there is an explosion in the exhaust pipe. *The car was choking and backfiring.*

backgammon /bækgæmən, bækgæmən/
NU **Backgammon** is a game for two people. You throw dice and move pieces of wood or plastic around a board marked with long triangles. *He's learned to play backgammon.*

background /bækgraʊnd/ **backgrounds**
1 NC+SUPP Your **background** is the kind of family you come from and the kind of education you have had. *...people from working-class backgrounds.*
2 N SING+SUPP The **background** to an event or situation consists of the facts that explain what caused it. *The incident comes against a background of deteriorating relations between Warsaw Pact allies.*
3 N SING You can also use **background** to refer to the things, shapes, colours, or sounds that are present in a situation but are not as noticeable or important as the things you are paying attention to. *In the background is a tall cypress tree. ...blue flowers on a grey background. ...background music.*

backhand /bækhænd/ **backhands**
NC A **backhand** is a shot in tennis or squash which you make with your arm across your body. *The number one seed missed a backhand drop volley at 30-40.*

backhanded /bækhændɪd/
1 ADJ A **backhanded** shot or blow is one that you do with the back of your hand facing in the direction in which you are hitting. *...a backhanded slap.*
2 ADJ A **backhanded** compliment or remark is one that seems to express admiration but that could also be an insult. *The Prime Minister is paying the Soviet leader a backhanded compliment.*

backhander /bækhændə/ **backhanders**
1 NC A **backhander** is a small bribe; an informal use. *She had to pay the backhander which bank officials invariably demanded.*
2 NC A **backhander** is also a comment that is in fact an insult or criticism although it may appear not to be.

backing /bækɪŋ/ **backings**
1 NU+SUPP **Backing** is the money, resources, or support given to a person or organization. *Mr Yasser Arafat had received the full backing of the U.S...*

Security Council members have given the Secretary-General their full backing and support.
2 NU **Backing** is also a layer of strong material that is put onto the back of something in order to protect it. *The flat end, with its self-adhesive backing, sticks firmly to the skin.*
3 N SING The **backing** of a popular song is the music which is sung or played to accompany the main tune. *...the simple musical backing of her own acoustic guitar... The single incorporates a 'hip hop' style backing to the melody.*

back issue, back issues
NC A **back issue** is the same as a back copy. *He said, after examining back issues of the paper, that he found no hint of bigotry or prejudice.*

backlash /bæklæʃ/
N SING A **backlash** is a sudden, strong reaction against a tendency or development in society or politics. *Homosexuals fear an anti-gay backlash. ...a backlash against the Thatcher government.*

backless /bækləs/
ADJ A **backless** dress leaves most of a woman's back uncovered down to her waist. *Backless dresses should not plunge below the waist.*

backlog /bæklɒg/ **backlogs**
1 NC A **backlog** of vehicles or people is a queue that has developed somewhere such as a port or an airport because of a delay that prevents them from travelling any further. *The backlog of tourist cars and coaches waiting to cross the channel has now cleared.*
2 NC A **backlog** is a build-up of work which has not yet been done, but which needs to be done. *The backlog of work has meant passport delays.*

back number, back numbers
NC A **back number** is the same as a back copy. *...back numbers of the American Bee Journal.*

backpack /bækpæk/ **backpacks**
NC A **backpack** is the same as a rucksack; used in American English. *They looked a little out of place, despite their military backpacks and battle helmets.*

back passage, back passages
NC You can use **back passage** as a polite way of referring to your rectum. *A police surgeon found clear evidence of recent penetration of the back passage possibly with a penis.*

back pay
NU **Back pay** is money which an employer owes an employee for work that was done in the past. *Nurses will receive back pay owing to them since April.*

back-pedal, back-pedals, back-pedalling, back-pedalled; also spelt **back-pedaling, back-pedaled** in American English.
V If you **back-pedal**, you say or do something different from what you originally said or intended to do. *The General back-pedalled, saying that he had had no intention of offending the West Germans... President Blanco was forced to back-pedal, cancelling some of the price increases.*

backroom boy /bækrʊm bɔɪ/ **backroom boys**
NC The **backroom boys** in an organization are the workers who do a lot of the important work but who are not seen or known about by the public. *If the backroom boys want to be really disloyal, they can even blame President Reagan.*

back-seat driver, back-seat drivers
NC A **back-seat driver** is a passenger in a car who repeatedly gives advice to the driver without being asked for it.

backside /bæksaɪd/ **backsides**
NC Your **backside** is the part of your body that you sit on; an informal word. *The hip flask is designed to curve around one's backside, basically keeping the booze warm on frosty mornings.*

backsliding /bækslaɪdɪŋ/
NU **Backsliding** means doing something that you had agreed or promised not to do; used especially of people who take up bad habits again after they have given them up. *She had, despite the occasional backsliding in training, successfully competed in the Championships. ...no backsliding into nationalist tendencies.*

backstage /bæksteɪdʒ/
ADV In a theatre, **backstage** refers to the areas behind the stage. *Backstage, she met the stars.*

backstreet /bækstriːt/
ADJ ATTRIB **Backstreet** activities are unofficial, secret, and often illegal. *That would mean a return to backstreet abortions.*

backstroke /bækstrəʊk/
N SING **Backstroke** is a swimming stroke which you do lying on your back. *The 100 metres backstroke was won by China's Lin Lai Ju.*

backtrack /bæktræk/ **backtracks, backtracking, backtracked**
1 V If you **backtrack** on a statement or a decision you have made, you change your mind and no longer stand by it. *The strikers said the management had backtracked on its offer.*
2 V If you **backtrack**, you go back along a path or route you have just used, often to find something that you have lost. *I felt rather lightheaded as I backtracked to the club.*

back-up
1 NU **Back-up** is extra help from people or machines which you need in order to be able to achieve something. *...the computer back-up which each mission required... A back-up generator is now supplying a small amount of electricity to limited areas of the city.*
2 NU If you have something such as a second set of plans as **back-up**, you have arranged for them to be available for use in case the first one does not work. *There are back-up laws that would impede the freedom of the press, even though the state of emergency is lifted.*

backward /bækwəd/ **backwards.** In British English, **backwards** is an adverb and **backward** is an adjective. In formal British English and in American English, **backward** is both an adjective and an adverb.
1 ADV If you move or look **backwards**, you move or look in the direction that your back is facing. *She stepped backwards onto a coffee cup.* ▶ Also ADJ ATTRIB *...a backward jerk of her head.*
2 ADV If you do something **backwards**, you do it in the opposite way to the usual way. *Listen to the tape backwards.*
3 If you **know** something **backwards**, you know it very well. *He knew their history backwards.*
4 ADJ If you refer to a country or society as **backward**, you mean that it does not have a modern industrialized economy. *...a backward, agrarian society... It's a basic problem: a big population and a backward economy.*
5 ADJ A **backward** child has difficulty in learning. *We are sorry to tell you that your son is backward.*

backward-looking
ADJ **Backward-looking** attitudes, ideas, or actions are based on old-fashioned opinions or methods; used showing disapproval. *...their backward-looking suspicion of gadgets.*

backwash /bækwɒʃ/
1 N SING The **backwash** is the water from waves that are moving back into the sea. *Sand is picked up and stirred by the backwash.*
2 N SING The **backwash** of a boat is the wave that spreads behind it on either side as it moves through the water.
3 N SING+SUPP The **backwash** of an event or situation is an unpleasant situation that exists after it and as a result of it. *...food shortages in the backwash of the war.*

backwater /bækwɔːtə/ **backwaters**
NC A **backwater** is a place or an institution that is isolated from modern ideas or influences. *...a cultural backwater.*

backwoods /bækwʊdz/
N PL Someone who lives in the **backwoods** lives a long way from large towns, and is isolated from modern life and modern ideas. *...peasants in the backwoods. ...the smaller towns out in the backwoods.* ▶ Also ADJ ATTRIB *...this tiny backwoods community.*

back yard, back yards; also spelt **backyard.**
1 NC A **back yard** is a small garden behind a house;

used in American English. *...a lady who was installing a rectangular swimming pool in her back yard.*
2 NC In Britain, a **back yard** is a small area of land behind a house, usually paved and with no grass or plants. *...artisans who have a small piece of equipment in their back yard or in their front room.*
3 N SING+POSS If you refer to a country's own **back yard**, you are referring to somewhere that is very close and where that country wants to be able to influence events. *The success of the Arias plan in Nicaragua depends on what the United States is prepared to tolerate in its backyard... UK companies also see the European single market in 1992 as their own backyard.*

bacon /beɪkən/
NU **Bacon** is salted or smoked meat taken from the back or sides of a pig. *The traditional English breakfast includes cereal, bacon, eggs, sausage, tomatoes and tea or coffee.*

bacteria /bæktɪərɪə/
N PL **Bacteria** are very small organisms which can cause disease. *...food poisoning caused by salmonella bacteria. ...a virulent strain of bacteria.*

bacteriology /bæktɪərɪɒlədʒi/
NU **Bacteriology** is the science and study of bacteria. *In the early days of bacteriology, we were trying to pin bacteria down as disease organisms.*
♦ **bacteriological** /bæktɪərɪəlɒdʒɪkl/ ADJ ATTRIB *...chemical and bacteriological warfare. ...the Bacteriological Research Institute.*

bad /bæd/ **worse, worst** See also separate entries at **worse** and **worst.**
1 ADJ You describe something as **bad** if it is undesirable, unpleasant, or of poor quality. *I have some very bad news... Candy is bad for your teeth... Is the pain bad?*
2 ADJ Someone who is **bad** at doing something is not very skilful at it. *I was bad at sports. ...a bad actor.*
3 ADJ or ADV Food that has gone **bad** has started to decay. *There's that unmistakable whiff of bad eggs.*
4 ADJ If you have a **bad** leg, heart, or eye, there is something wrong with it. *We see a lot of kids with really bad feet.*
5 ADJ If you call a child **bad**, you mean that he or she is naughty and disobedient. *The children were very bad, especially towards me.*
6 ADJ If you are in a **bad** mood, you are cross and behave unpleasantly to people. *Hassan felt he was being mocked, and has been in a bad mood ever since.*
7 ADJ If someone uses **bad** language, they use offensive swear words. *...a survey on reactions to bad language on radio and television in Britain.*
● **Bad** is used in these phrases. ● If you say that something is **not bad**, you mean that it is quite good or acceptable. *It was an awful job, but the money wasn't bad.* ● If you **feel bad** about something, you feel rather sorry and sad about it. *I really feel bad about having to say he can't go.* ● If you say '**too bad**', you are indicating in a rather harsh way that nothing can be done to change the situation. *'I want to speak to the director.'—'Too bad,' Castle said. 'You can't.'* ● **bad blood**: see **blood.** ● **bad luck**: see **luck.**

bad cheque, bad cheques
NC A **bad cheque** is a bank cheque that will not be paid because there is a mistake on it or because there is not enough money in the account.

bad debt, bad debts
NC A **bad debt** is a debt that is owed to you but is not likely to be paid. *I wrote off six thousand dollars worth of bad debts.*

baddy /bædi/ **baddies**
NC A **baddy** is a person in a story, film, or play who is considered to be evil or wicked, or who is fighting on the wrong side; an informal word. *...the goodies and the baddies... You don't want him to win—he's a baddy!*

bade /bæd, beɪd/
Bade is the past tense of some senses of **bid.**

badge /bædʒ/ **badges**
1 NC A **badge** is a small piece of metal or cloth which you attach to your clothes and wear as a sign of rank, or as a symbol of merit or distinction, or for

decoration. *Submariners have their own distinctive hard-earned badge: two dolphins under a crown and anchor.*
2 NC+SUPP Any feature which is regarded as a sign of a particular quality can be referred to as a **badge** of that quality. *Wisdom is the badge of maturity.*

badger /ˈbædʒə/ **badgers, badgering, badgered**
1 NC A **badger** is a wild animal with a white head with two wide black stripes on it. Badgers live underground and are active mainly at night. *A bill to protect badgers and the sets in which they live comes before Parliament on Friday.*
2 VO If you **badger** someone, you repeatedly tell them to do something or repeatedly ask them questions. *She said it did not help for foreign leaders to badger the United States into action.*

badinage /ˈbædɪnɑːʒ/
NU **Badinage** is a series of remarks or a conversation that is humorous, not very serious, and often involves teasing someone; a literary word. *They exchanged ideas and badinage on subjects ranging from the tango to the nature of God.*

badly /ˈbædli/ **worse, worst** See also separate entries at **worse** and **worst**.
1 ADV If something is done **badly**, it is done with very little success or effect. *The party did badly in the election.*
2 ADV If someone or something is **badly** hurt or **badly** affected, they are severely hurt or affected. *The house was badly damaged.*
3 ADV If you need or want something **badly**, you need or want it very much. *We need the money badly.*
4 ADV You can use **badly** to say that something harms the reputation of someone or something, or affects them in a harmful way. *The story reflected badly on Amity... He got badly confused.*

badly off, worse off, worst off
ADJ PRED If you are **badly off**, you do not have much money. *In the cities, the poor are as badly off as they were in the villages.*

badminton /ˈbædmɪntən/
NU **Badminton** is a game played using rackets to hit a small feathered object called a shuttlecock over a net. *World class performances can be expected in badminton. ...the final of the men's badminton tournament.*

bad-tempered /bædˈtempəd/
1 ADJ **Bad-tempered** people become angry very easily. *Little John was not a jovial giant but a bad-tempered outlaw... Most people consider the camel an animal of curiosity, smelly and bad-tempered.*
2 ADJ A **bad-tempered** event or occasion is full of anger and bad feeling, and is likely to become violent. *Players were involved in the melée, which came during the second half of a bad-tempered game.*

baffle /ˈbæfl/ **baffles, baffling, baffled**
VO If you **are baffled** by something, you cannot understand it or explain it. *I was baffled by his refusal.* ◆ **baffling** ADJ *...the baffling array of new problems.*

bafflement /ˈbæflmənt/
NU **Bafflement** is the state of being baffled. *It was a weekend of bafflement and anger.*

bag /bæg/ **bags**
1 NC A **bag** is a container made of paper, plastic, or leather which is used to carry things. *...a paper bag... He packed his bags and drove to the airport.*
2 NC You can use **bag** to refer to a bag and its contents, or to the contents only. *He ate a whole bag of sweets.*
3 N PL **Bags** under your eyes are folds of skin, usually caused by not having enough sleep. *He was tall and painfully thin with black bags under his eyes.*
4 If you say that something is **in the bag**, you mean that you are certain to get it or achieve it; an informal expression. *The treaty, as he put it, is by no means in the bag.*

bagatelle /ˌbægəˈtel/ **bagatelles**
NC If you describe something as a **bagatelle**, you mean that you consider it unimportant or easy to achieve; a literary word. *A billion dollars is a mere bagatelle compared to the enormous wealth they have.*

baggage /ˈbægɪdʒ/
NU Your **baggage** consists of the suitcases and bags that you take with you when you travel. *They should have no more than one suitcase per person plus hand baggage.*

baggy /ˈbægi/ **baggier, baggiest**
ADJ If a piece of clothing is **baggy**, it hangs loosely on your body. *He wears baggy linen trousers and a matching jacket.*

Baghdad /ˈbægdæd/
Baghdad is the capital of Iraq and its largest city. Population: 4,649,000 (1985).

bagpipes /ˈbægpaɪps/
N PL **Bagpipes** are a musical wind instrument consisting of a leather bag and several pipes. *They play flutes, fiddles, bagpipes and drums, producing beautiful laments.*

Bahamas /bəˈhɑːməz/
The **Commonwealth of the Bahamas** is a country in the Caribbean, which consists of over 700 islands. The main islands include Grand Bahama, Andros, Eleuthera, Great Abaco, and New Providence. The first successful British colony began in 1656. In 1973 it became independent. The Bahamas are a member of the Commonwealth and the Organization of American States. Sir Lynden O. Pindling, of the Progressive Liberal Party (PLP), became Prime Minister in 1967. Tourism and banking are the main industries. In recent years illegal drug trafficking has become a serious problem. ◆ **Bahamian** /bəˈheɪmiən/ N, ADJ
■ *per capita GNP:* US$11,370 ■ *religion:* Christianity ■ *language:* English ■ *currency:* dollar ■ *capital:* Nassau ■ *population:* 247,000 (1988) ■ *size:* 13,939 square kilometres.

Bahrain /bɑːˈreɪn/
The **State of Bahrain** is a country in the Gulf. It was under British protection from 1816, and became independent in 1971. Sheikh Isa bin Sulman al-Khalifa became Amir in 1961. There are no political parties. Bahrain produces oil and is an important financial centre. It is a member of the Arab League and the Gulf Co-operation Council. ◆ **Bahraini** /bɑːˈreɪni/ N, ADJ
■ *per capita GNP:* US$6,610 ■ *religion:* Islam ■ *language:* Arabic (official) ■ *currency:* dinar ■ *capital:* Manama ■ *population:* 489,000 (1989) ■ *size:* 691 square kilometres.

bail /beɪl/ **bails, bailing, bailed**; also spelt **bale, bales, baling, baled** for the meanings in paragraphs 1, 3 and 4 of **bail out**.
NU If an arrested person is given **bail**, or if they are released on **bail**, they are freed after a required sum of money has been paid to a law court to make sure that they will return for trial at the necessary time. You can also refer to the sum of money as **bail**. *The judge refused to grant bail... She was released on $2,500 bail.*

bail out PHRASAL VERB 1 If you **bail** someone **out**, you pay bail on their behalf. *I had to borrow £1,000 to bail my friend out.* 2 You can also say that you **bail** someone **out** when you help them in a difficult situation. *The US will spend 50 thousand million dollars next year bailing out bankrupt savings and loan institutions. Their sole mission was to bail out Marines in trouble.* 3 If a pilot **bails out** of an aircraft that is crashing, he or she jumps to safety using a parachute. *The pilot was forced to bail out of his aircraft due to technical malfunction.* 4 If you **bail out** water from something that is flooded or sinking, you remove it, usually by using a pump or an instrument of some kind. *The papers showed unhappy locals bailing out their flooded homes.*

bailiff /ˈbeɪlɪf/ **bailiffs**
1 NC A **bailiff** is a law officer who makes sure that the decisions of a court are obeyed, especially by taking property as payment for money that is owed. *Demonstrators blocked police and bailiffs trying to impound the printing presses.*
2 NC A **bailiff** is also someone who is employed to look after someone's land or property. *Local water bailiffs began a detailed survey of the river.*

Bairiki /baɪˈriːki/
Bairiki , an island in Tarawa Atoll, is the capital of

Kiribati and its largest settlement. Population: 22,000 (1985).

bairn /bɛ_ə_n/ **bairns**
NC In some dialects of English, a **bairn** is a child.

bait /beɪt/ **baits, baiting, baited**
1 NU **Bait** is food which you put on a hook or in a trap in order to catch fish or animals. *I took a slice of white bread to use as bait.*
2 VO When you **bait** a hook or trap, you put bait on it. *Bait the hook with a raisin.*
3 N SING A person or thing that is used as **bait** is used to tempt or encourage someone to do something. *To persuade the South Africans to leave Angola, the bait on offer will be the withdrawal of Cuban troops.*
4 VO If you **bait** someone, you deliberately try to make them angry by teasing them. *Lucy seemed to take a positive delight in baiting him.*

baize /beɪz/
NU **Baize** is a thick green woollen material used for covering snooker tables and card tables. *...talking across the green baize table.*

bake /beɪk/ **bakes, baking, baked**
1 V-ERG or V When you **bake** food or when it **bakes**, you cook it in an oven without using extra liquid or fat. *She said she would bake a cake... I cleaned the kitchen while the bread was baking... Mrs Burns was baking.* ♦ **baked** ADJ *...baked potatoes.*
2 V-ERG When earth or clay **bakes**, or when you **bake** it, it becomes hard and dry because it has been heated very strongly. *The ground was baked hard... It involves coating it with a layer of silver and then baking it at high temperatures.*
3 See also **baking**.

baked beans
N PL **Baked beans** are beans cooked in tomato sauce. *Baked beans form the most popular snack meal in Britain.*

Bakelite /beɪkəlaɪt/
NU **Bakelite** is a type of hard plastic that was used in the past for making toys, telephones, and other objects; **Bakelite** is a trademark. *Leo Baekaland helped found the modern plastics industry through his invention of Bakelite.*

baker /beɪkə/ **bakers**
1 NC A **baker** is a person whose job is to bake and sell bread and cakes. *Customers can buy bread made by the baker on the shop's premises.*
2 NC A **baker** or a **baker's** is a shop where bread and cakes are sold. *The baker would be open but almost all other shops would be closed.*

baker's dozen
N SING A **baker's dozen** is a group of thirteen things; an old-fashioned expression. *I acquired a baker's dozen of small, brilliant tropical birds.*

bakery /beɪkəri/ **bakeries**
NC A **bakery** is a building where bread and cakes are baked or sold. *They promised to guarantee supplies of flour to bakeries.*

baking /beɪkɪŋ/
ADJ If you say that a place is **baking**, you mean that it is very hot indeed. *...the baking Jordanian desert.*

Baku /bɑːkuː/
Baku is the capital of Azerbaijan and its largest city. Population: 1,757,000 (1989).

balaclava /bæləklɑːvə/ **balaclavas**
NC A **balaclava** or a **balaclava helmet** is a close-fitting woollen hood that covers every part of your head except your face. *Two of the gunmen were wearing balaclavas.*

Balaguer Ricardo, Dr Joaquín /xəʊækiːn bælægeə riːkɑːdəʊ/
Dr Joaquín Balaguer Ricardo became President of the Dominican Republic in 1986. He served as Minister of Foreign Affairs from 1954 to 1955, and of Education and Arts from 1955 to 1957. He was Vice President from 1957 to 1960. He previously served as President in 1960, and from 1966 to 1978. He became the leader of the Social Christian Reformist Party (PRSC) in 1962. Born: 1907.

balalaika /bæləlaɪkə/ **balalaikas**
NC A **balalaika** is a musical instrument with a triangular body and three strings, which is mainly played in Russia.

balance /bæləns/ **balances, balancing, balanced**
1 V-ERG If someone or something **balances** or is **balanced**, they are steady and do not fall over. *Balancing on one leg is an excellent exercise... An ashtray was balanced on the arm of her chair.*
2 NU **Balance** is the stability that someone or something has when they are standing or sitting on something. *She lost her balance.*
3 N SING+SUPP **Balance** is a situation in which all the different things involved are equal or correct in size, strength, or importance. *...the ecological balance of the lake. ...the strategic balance in Europe... The best practicable option will mean striking a balance between what we can afford and what the environment needs.*
4 V-RECIP If you **balance** one thing with another or if several things **balance** each other, each of the things has the same weight, strength, or importance. *A settlement was sought that balanced the interests of all parties... Any escapism in the magazine is balanced by more practical items.*
5 N SING In a game or contest, if the **balance** swings in your favour, you start winning.
6 V-ERG If you **balance** a financial matter or if finances **balance**, the amount of money that is spent is not greater than the amount that is received. *...insistence that the US budget should be balanced... Hospital managers are becoming more concerned with balancing their budgets than providing proper health care.*
7 NC The **balance** in a bank account is the amount of money in it. *We have a large commercial balance of about ten billion dollars a year.*
● **Balance** is used in these phrases. ● If you are **off balance**, you are in an unsteady position and about to fall. *I pulled her off balance and she slipped down.*
● If something is **in the balance**, it is uncertain whether it will happen or continue. *The destiny of our race lies in the balance.* ● You can say **on balance** to indicate that you are stating your opinion only after you have considered all the relevant facts or arguments. *It seems, in that case, cash crops are a benefit on balance.*

balanced /bælənst/
1 ADJ A **balanced** account or report is a fair and reasonable one. *...a balanced summary of the debate.*
2 ADJ Something that is **balanced** is effective because its parts have been used or arranged skilfully and in the correct proportions. *...a beautifully balanced play. ...a balanced diet.*

balance of payments, balances of payments
NC A country's **balance of payments** is the difference between the payments it makes to other countries for imports, services, and investments, and the payments it receives from other countries for exports, services, and investments. A country's balance of payments is usually calculated over a period of one year. *The economy continued to expand and the balance of payments improved.*

balance sheet, balance sheets
NC A **balance sheet** is a written statement of the amount of money and property a company has, the amount of money it is owed, and the amount of money it owes to other people. *The figures show a deficit of 56 million dollars in the balance sheet for 1986.*

balancing act, balancing acts
NC If you do a **balancing act**, you try to please two or more people or groups who are in opposition to each other. *He kept up his balancing act by making promises to each side.*

balcony /bælkəni/ **balconies**
1 NC A **balcony** is a platform on the outside of a building with a wall or railing around it. *...Victorian terraced houses with ornate balconies... President Havel appeared on the balcony of Prague Castle.*
2 NC The **balcony** in a theatre or cinema is the area of seats on the upper floor of the building. There can be more than one **balcony** in a theatre or cinema. *He fell from the balcony of the Metropolitan Opera House.*

bald /bɔːld/ **balder, baldest**
1 ADJ Someone who is **bald** has little or no hair on the

top of their head. *You're going bald... He has a large bald patch.* ◆ **baldness** NU *I think you'll suffer from early baldness.*

2 ADJ A **bald** tyre has become very smooth and is no longer safe to use.

3 ADJ ATTRIB A **bald** statement, question, or account has no unnecessary words in it. *Those bald figures mask the size of the operation.* ◆ **baldly** ADV *Stated baldly like this, these comments seem rather obvious.*

bald eagle, bald eagles
NC A **bald eagle** is a type of large white-headed eagle that lives in North America. *Lots of bald eagles have been spotted here.*

balderdash /bɔːldədæʃ/
NU If you say that something that has been said or written is **balderdash**, you mean that you think it is completely untrue or very stupid; an old-fashioned word. *The Daily Mail ridicules as bureaucratic balderdash the notion that aligning VAT rates is the key to unity.*

balding /bɔːldɪŋ/
ADJ Someone who is **balding** is losing their hair. *...a trim, balding man in his early 60's.*

bale /beɪl/ **bales, baling, baled**
1 NC A **bale** is a large quantity of something such as cloth, paper, or hay, tied into a tight bundle. *Almost four million bales of wool remain unsold and farm incomes this year are expected to drop.*
2 See also **bail**.

baleful /beɪlfl/
ADJ Something that is **baleful** is likely to have harmful effects, or expresses someone's harmful intentions; a literary word. *We saw his baleful eye fixed on us.*

balk /bɔːk, bɔːlk/ **balks, balking, balked**; also spelt **baulk**.
V If you **balk** at something, you are very reluctant to do it. *They would have balked at the idea of a socialist society.*

ball /bɔːl/ **balls**
1 NC A **ball** is a round object used in games such as tennis, cricket, and football. *Players have been spending more time groaning in agony than kicking the ball.*
2 NC A **ball** is also something that has a round shape. *He rolled the socks into a ball.*
3 NC The **ball** of your foot is the rounded part where your toes join your foot. *You get the maximum load on the ball of the foot.*
4 NC A **ball** is also a large, formal, social event at which people dance. *...a gala ball at the city's Opera House.*
● **Ball** is used in these phrases. ● If you say that **the ball is** in someone's **court**, you mean that it is their responsibility to take the next decision or action in a particular situation. *Now the ball is in the UN Secretary General's court.* ● If someone is **on the ball**, they are very alert and aware of what is happening. *If you're sharp and if you're on the ball, you'll recognize it.* ● If you **start the ball rolling**, or **set the ball rolling**, you start something happening. *The banks set the ball rolling when they reduced their lending rates.*

ballad /bæləd/ **ballads**
1 NC A **ballad** is a long song or poem which tells a story. *His ballads told of Communist party privileges and of the humiliations suffered by ordinary people.*
2 NC A **ballad** is also a song in popular music with a slow tempo and a romantic theme. *Smooth, soul-searching ballads have been her hallmark.*

ballast /bæləst/
NU **Ballast** consists of a substance such as sand, iron, or water that is used in ships or balloons to make them heavier and more stable. *They want to see the filling of ballast compartments with buoyant material such as foam.*

ball bearing, ball bearings
NC **Ball bearings** are small metal balls used to make the moving parts of a machine run smoothly. *...hoists and gears, with ball bearings to minimise the effects of wear and friction.*

ballcock /bɔːlkɒk/ **ballcocks**
NC A **ballcock** is the part of the valve inside a water

tank or cistern that controls the flow of water going into and out of the tank. It consists of a floating ball that is attached to the hinged arm which opens and closes the valve.

ballerina /bæləriːnə/ **ballerinas**
NC A **ballerina** is a woman ballet dancer. *The company has several ballerinas that dance with distinction.*

ballet /bæleɪ/ **ballets** /bæleɪz/
1 NU **Ballet** is a type of skilled and artistic dancing with carefully planned movements. *She continued to learn ballet from emigré Russian teachers.*
2 NC A **ballet** is an artistic work performed by ballet dancers. *...Prokofiev's ballet 'Cinderella'.*

ball game, ball games
1 NC **Ball games** are games played with a ball, such as football, tennis, and hockey. *In Roman and Greek civilisations there were certainly ball games played, quite probably with leather balls.*
2 NC A **ball game** is a baseball match; used in American English. *Last week I took my kids to a ball game.*
3 If a situation is **a whole new ball game**, it is completely different from the previous situation. *The moment the Cubans go, he said, it will be a whole new ball game.*

ballistic /bəlɪstɪk/ **ballistics**
1 NU **Ballistics** is the study of the movement of objects that are shot or thrown through the air, for example bullets fired from a gun. *...a police ballistics expert.*
2 ADJ ATTRIB **Ballistic** means relating to ballistics. *At the scene of the shooting, extensive ballistic and forensic examinations have to be carried out.*

ballistic missile, ballistic missiles
NC A **ballistic missile** is one that is guided automatically in the first part of its flight, but which falls freely when it gets near its target. *...a defensive shield against incoming ballistic missiles.*

balloon /bəluːn/ **balloons, ballooning, ballooned**
1 NC A **balloon** is a small, thin rubber bag that you fill with air so that it stretches and becomes larger. Balloons are used as toys or decorations. *It was a good-natured rally with music and balloons.*
2 NC A **balloon** is also a large, strong bag filled with gas or hot air, which can carry passengers in a basket or compartment underneath it. *...a spectacular stunt like flying a hot-air balloon across the Atlantic.*
3 V When something **balloons**, it quickly becomes bigger and rounder in shape. *She crossed the park, her skirt ballooning in the wind.*

ballot /bælət/ **ballots, balloting, balloted**
1 NC A **ballot** is a vote in which people select a candidate in an election, or express their opinion about something. *The deal will now go to the workforce for them to vote in a secret ballot... George Bush has enough delegates to win the Republican nomination on the first ballot.*
2 VO If you **ballot** a group of people, you find out what they think about something by organizing a secret vote. *Workers are to be balloted on their pay offer.*
◆ **balloting** NU *The result of today's balloting will be known in about three weeks.*

ballot box, ballot boxes
NC A **ballot box** is the box into which ballot papers are put after people have voted. *Some people may have used strong arm tactics like seizing ballot boxes.*

ballot paper, ballot papers
NC A **ballot paper** is a piece of paper on which you mark your choice or opinion in a ballot. *Many polling stations opened late because ballot papers did not arrive... Voters had six ballot papers to mark for local and republican assemblies.*

ballot rigging
NU **Ballot rigging** is the act of illegally changing the result of an election by producing a false record of the number of votes. *The government has promised clean elections following evidence of ballot rigging in many earlier votes. ...opposition allegations of ballot rigging and fraud.*

ballpoint /bɔːlpɔɪnt/ **ballpoints**
NC A **ballpoint** or a **ballpoint pen** is a pen with a small

metal ball at the end which transfers the ink onto the paper. *The Biro brothers invented the ballpoint pen.*

ballroom /bɔːlrum/ **ballrooms**

NC A **ballroom** is a very large room used for dancing or for formal balls. *The Queen Mary was a floating hotel with 12 decks, a ballroom and three cinemas.*

ballroom dancing

NU **Ballroom dancing** is a type of dancing in which a man and a woman dance together, using fixed sequences of steps and movements. *His mother passed a ballroom dancing exam at the age of 89.*

balls /bɔːlz/ **ballses, ballsing, ballsed**

balls up PHRASAL VERB If you **balls up** a task or activity, you do it very badly, making a lot of mistakes or doing it without any skill; an informal expression that some people find offensive. *How did he manage to balls up such a simple job?*

balls-up, balls-ups

NC If you make a **balls-up** of a task or activity, you do it very badly, making a lot of mistakes or doing it without any skill; an informal word that some people find offensive. *You can rely on George to make a balls-up of everything.*

balm /bɑːm/ **balms**

1 NUorNC **Balm** is a sweet-smelling oil that is obtained from some tropical trees. It is used to make ointments that heal wounds or lessen pain.
2 NU **Balm** can also be used to refer to anything which is comforting or soothing. *Prayer had been balm to her spirit.*

balmy /bɑːmi/ **balmier, balmiest**

ADJ When the weather is **balmy**, it is mild and pleasant. *The air was warm and balmy.*

baloney /bələʊni/

NU If you say that something is **baloney**, you mean that it is nonsense; used in informal American English. *The plot of the film is pure baloney... That's a lot of baloney.*

balsa /bɔːlsə/

NU **Balsa** or **balsa wood** is a very light wood which is used to make things such as rafts and model aeroplanes. *...a consignment of balsa wood from Ecuador.*

balustrade /bæləstreɪd/ **balustrades**

NC A **balustrade** is a railing or wall on a balcony or staircase.

Bamako /bæməkəʊ/

Bamako is the capital of Mali and its largest city. Population: 478,000 (1980).

bamboo /bæmbuː/ **bamboos**

NUorNC **Bamboo** is a tall tropical plant with hard hollow stems. The young shoots of the plant can be eaten, and the stems are used to make furniture and fences. *Houses in the area were generally made of wood and bamboo... Slide the poles, which are saplings or bamboos, underneath the block of stone.*

bamboozle /bæmbuːzl/ **bamboozles, bamboozling, bamboozled**

VO If you **bamboozle** someone, you confuse them or trick them; an informal word. *Their sermons were intended to bamboozle the workers into obedience.*

ban /bæn/ **bans, banning, banned**

1 VO If something is **banned**, it is not allowed to be done, shown, or used. *His play was banned by the BBC... The movement was banned by the government.* ◆ **banning, bannings** NC *The banning of the newspaper was announced yesterday... Mr Mandela seemed taken aback by the scale of the bannings.*
2 NC A **ban** is an official statement showing that something is forbidden. *...a world wide chemical weapons ban.*
3 VO If you **are banned** from doing something, you are officially prevented from doing it. *Mr Walesa was banned from attending the meeting... She has been banned from driving for one month.*

banal /bənɑːl/

ADJ Something that is **banal** is so ordinary that it is not at all effective or interesting. *...the banal morality of soap operas.* ◆ **banality** /bənæləti/ NU *Throughout the film, there are moments of banality.*

banana /bənɑːnə/ **bananas**

NCorNU A **banana** is a long curved fruit with a yellow skin. *Bananas were their subsistence crop... Farmers working in Colombia's main banana growing district were abducted from a village.*

banana republic, banana republics

NC If you refer to a country as a **banana republic**, you mean that it is economically poor and politically unimportant or unstable. *Chancellor Kohl complained of the US treating his country like a banana republic.*

banana skin, banana skins

NC A remark or incident that accidentally makes someone look foolish can be referred to as a **banana skin**; an informal expression. *They urged ministers to beware of political banana skins that might trip them up.*

banana split, banana splits

NCorNU A **banana split** is a dessert made of a banana cut in half along its middle, with ice cream, nuts, and sauce, on top.

band /bænd/ **bands, banding, banded**

1 N COLL+SUPP A **band** of people is a group of people who have joined together because they share an interest or belief. *...a small band of revolutionaries.*
2 N COLL A **band** is a group of musicians who play jazz, rock, or pop music. It is also a group who play brass instruments together. *The Irish band U2 was judged outright winner for Best International Group... A brass band and a crowd waving coloured banners were on hand at Tunis Airport.*
3 NC A **band** is also a flat, narrow strip of cloth which you wear round your head or wrists, or round a piece of clothing. *...a panama hat with a red band.*
4 NC+SUPP A range of numbers or values within a system of measurement can also be referred to as a **band**. *...a very wide band of radio frequencies.*

band together PHRASAL VERB If people **band together**, they meet and act as a group in order to try and achieve something. *Everywhere women banded together to talk about liberation.*

Banda, Dr Hastings Kamuzu /heɪstɪŋz kəmuːzu bændə/

Dr Hastings Kamuzu Banda became the first President of Malawi in 1964. He previously served as Prime Minister of Nyasaland from 1963 to 1964. He was named President for Life in 1971. He became the leader of the Malawi Congress Party (MCP), the sole party, in 1958. Born: 1906.

bandage /bændɪdʒ/ **bandages, bandaging, bandaged**

1 NC A **bandage** is a long strip of cloth which is wrapped around a wounded part of someone's body to protect it. *She was wearing a bandage round her head.*
2 VO If you **bandage** a wound or part of someone's body, you tie a bandage around it. ◆ **bandaged** ADJ *...a man with a bandaged arm.*

bandage up PHRASAL VERB If you **bandage** someone up, or if you **bandage up** their wounds, you wrap their wounds up completely in a bandage. *I bandaged him up.*

Band-Aid, Band-Aids

NCorNU **Band-Aid** is a type of sticky plaster used to cover small cuts on your body; **Band-Aid** is a trademark. *I've tried using bandaging and I've tried using Band-Aid... Rather than go to the doctor and get stitches in it, I decided to just put a Band-Aid on it.*

bandanna /bændænə/ **bandannas**; also spelt **bandana**.

NC A **bandanna** is a large brightly-coloured handkerchief which is worn around a person's neck or head. *...Mohawk Indians wearing traditional warpaint and bandannas.*

Bandar Seri Begawan /bʌndə sriː bəgɑːwən/

Bandar Seri Begawan is the capital of Brunei and its largest city. It was formerly called Brunei Town. Population: 51,000 (1986).

b. and b. /biː ən biː/

b. and b. is a written abbreviation for 'bed and breakfast'. It is used especially in newspaper advertisements and outside houses. *Accommodation is offered at the rate of £25 per night for b. and b. and evening meal.*

bandit /bændɪt/ **bandits**

NC A **bandit** is an armed robber. *...a remote area frequented by armed gangs of bandits.*

banditry /bǽndɪtri/
NU **Banditry** is a term that is used to refer to acts of robbery and violence in places where civil order or the country's rule of law has broken down. *The main problem is distributing food in an area affected by civil war and banditry.*

bandsman /bǽndzmən/ **bandsmen**
NC A **bandsman** is a musician in a brass band or a military band. *Small crowds of people applauded the bandsmen warmly. ...the bandsmen of the Royal Anglian Regiment.*

bandstand /bǽndstænd/ **bandstands**
NC A **bandstand** is a platform with a roof where a military band or a brass band can play in the open air. *The Temperance Seven will perform from a specially designed bandstand.*

bandwagon /bǽndwægən/
If you say that someone has **jumped on the bandwagon**, you mean that they have become involved in an activity only because it is fashionable. *They have jumped on the Popular Front bandwagon.*

bandy /bǽndi/ **bandies, bandying, bandied**
1 VOA If you **bandy** ideas or arguments, you discuss them with other people in a casual way. *Many of the programmes started off as ideas just bandied to and fro between producer and writer.*
2 If you **bandy words with** someone, you argue with them. *I'm not going to bandy words with Jimmy.*
bandy about or **bandy around** PHRASAL VERB If ideas or words **are bandied about** or **are bandied around**, they are discussed or used by a lot of people, often casually or without paying too much attention to what they mean. *...just another label for journalists to bandy about... Various suggestions were bandied around by the younger members.*

bandy-legged
ADJ Someone who is **bandy-legged** has legs which curve outwards at the knees.

bane /beɪn/
1 N SING Someone or something that is the **bane** of a particular person or organization causes unhappiness or distress to that person or organization. *...a journalist regarded by some as the bane of Whitehall. ...a costly system of files and folders—the bane of hospital administration.*
2 Someone or something that is **the bane of** your life causes you constant unhappiness or distress. *That radio was the bane of my life.*

bang /bæŋ/ **bangs, banging, banged**
1 NC A **bang** is a loud noise such as the noise of an explosion. *She slammed the drawer shut with a bang.*
2 V-ERG If you **bang** a door or if it **bangs**, it closes violently with a loud noise. *Don't bang the door!... The big oak front door banged.*
3 V AorVOA If you **bang** on something or if you **bang** it, you hit it so that it makes a loud noise. *Pickets banged on the window. ...wagging his finger and banging his fists on the table.*
4 V-ERG If something **bangs** into you or if you **bang** against something, you accidentally knock into it and hurt yourself. *Ingham was manhandled and had a rifle butt banged into his stomach... I bang my head against it every time.* ► Also NC *Did you suffer any bangs or bumps?*
● **Bang** is used in these informal phrases. ● If something goes **with a bang**, it is very successful. *He is determined to go with a bang rather than a whimper.* ● **Bang** is used in expressions which emphasize an exact position or time. For example, if something is **bang in the middle**, it is exactly in the middle. *Emory University is bang in the middle of Atlanta... The consortium says that twelve months on from the project's launch it is bang on target to open the tunnel by May 1993.*
bang down PHRASAL VERB If you **bang** something **down**, you put it down violently so that it makes a loud noise. *He banged down the phone... I heard Marvin bang his files down hard on the desk.*

banger /bǽŋə/ **bangers**; an informal word.
1 NC A **banger** is a sausage. *He found that the British banger didn't have enough meat in it and wasn't very fresh.*

2 NC Old cars are sometimes called **bangers**.

Bangkok /bǽŋkɒk/
Bangkok is the capital of Thailand and its largest city. Population: 5,845,000 (1989).

Bangladesh /bǽŋglədeʃ/
The **People's Republic of Bangladesh** is a country in southern Asia, east of India. It is a member of the Commonwealth. Bangladesh was part of the British colony of India until 1947, when it became East Pakistan. It was renamed Bangladesh in 1971 when, after a civil war, it became independent from West Pakistan. The Bangladesh Nationalist Party (BNP) was elected in 1991. Abdur Rahman Biswas became President in 1991. Begum Khaleda Zia became Prime Minister in 1991. Bangladesh exports clothing and jute.
◆ **Bangladeshi** /bǽŋglədeʃi/ N, ADJ
▪ *per capita GNP:* US$170 ▪ *religion:* Islam ▪ *language:* Bengali ▪ *currency:* taka ▪ *capital:* Dhākā ▪ *population:* 115 million (1989) ▪ *size:* 143,998 square kilometres.

bangle /bǽŋgl/ **bangles**
NC A **bangle** is a bracelet or band that you wear round your wrist or ankle. *...bangles and earrings.*

bang on
ADJ PRED If you say that something is **bang on**, you mean that it is absolutely correct or perfect; an informal expression.

Bangui /bɒŋgiː/
Bangui is the capital of the Central African Republic and its largest city. Population: 474,000 (1985).

banish /bǽnɪʃ/ **banishes, banishing, banished**
VO If someone or something is **banished**, they are sent away from a place or got rid of altogether. *They were banished to the penal colony... Tobacco had been banished from polite society.*

banishment /bǽnɪʃmənt/
NU **Banishment** is the act of banishing someone, or the state of being banished; a literary word. *After his banishment, Trotsky's supporters were soon also expelled.*

banister /bǽnɪstə/ **banisters**; also spelt **bannister**.
NC A **banister** is a rail supported by posts which is fixed along the side of a staircase. *...carved oak banisters.*

banjo /bǽndʒəʊ/ **banjos** or **banjoes**
NC A **banjo** is a musical instrument with a circular body and four or more strings. *She remembers the moment she first saw T-Bone playing a banjo in a Fort Worth hotel.*

Banjul /bǽndʒuːl/
Banjul , formerly called Bathurst, is the capital of Gambia and its second largest city. Population: 44,000 (1983).

bank /bæŋk/ **banks, banking, banked**
1 NC A **bank** is an institution where people or businesses can keep their money. **Banks** also offer services such as lending, exchanging, or transferring money. *The World Bank has lent more money in the past year than ever before... The Chairman of the National Westminster Bank has resigned... The bank can see exactly how much money they've got.*
2 NC A **bank** is also a building where a bank offers its services. *The bank opens at nine thirty... Turn left at the bank.*
3 NC+SUPP You use **bank** to refer to a store of something. For example, a blood **bank** or a data **bank** is a store of blood or a store of data that is kept ready for use. *...the food and agricultural bank.*
4 NC A **bank** is also the raised ground along the edge of a river or lake. *...fishermen having a picnic on the river bank.*
5 NC+SUPP A **bank** of something is a long, high row or mass of it. *...a bank of fog.*
bank on PHRASAL VERB If you **bank on** something happening, you expect it to happen and rely on it happening; an informal expression. *He may come, but I'm not banking on it.*

bank account, bank accounts
NC A **bank account** is an arrangement with a bank which allows you to keep your money in the bank and to withdraw it when you need it. *...a Swiss bank account. ...transferring funds electronically between bank accounts.*

bank balance, bank balances
NC Someone's **bank balance** is the amount of money that they have in their bank account at a particular time. *A healthy bank balance removes worries about paying bills.*

banker /bæŋkə/ **bankers**
NC A **banker** is someone involved in banking at a senior level. *The bankers all agreed that non-payment of interest was no solution to the debt problem.*

banker's card, banker's cards
NC A **banker's card** is the same as a **cheque card**.

banker's order, banker's orders
NC A **banker's order** is the same as a **standing order**.

bank holiday, bank holidays
NC A **bank holiday** is a public holiday. *Thousands of holiday-makers set off for the Bank Holiday weekend.*

banking /bæŋkɪŋ/
NU **Banking** is the business activity of banks and similar institutions. *...foreign earnings from services such as banking and insurance... The state-owned banking system has collapsed.*

bank loan, bank loans
NC A **bank loan** is a sum of money that a bank lends you for a period of time and that you have to pay back with interest. *We got a bank loan to buy a car.*

bank manager, bank managers
NC A **bank manager** is a person who is in charge of a branch of a bank. *Cocoa shippers and their bank managers have been having sleepless nights.*

banknote /bæŋknəʊt/ **banknotes**
NC A **banknote** is a piece of paper money with a particular value. *Larger denomination banknotes in Britain still carry scenes depicting famous people.*

bank rate
N SING The **bank rate** is the rate of interest at which a bank lends money, especially the minimum rate of interest that banks are allowed to charge, which is decided from time to time by the country's central bank. *The bank rate was increased to 8 per cent.*

bankrupt /bæŋkrʌpt/ **bankrupts, bankrupting, bankrupted**
1 ADJ People or organizations that are **bankrupt** do not have enough money to pay their debts. *The company has gone bankrupt.*
2 VO To **bankrupt** a person or company means to make them go bankrupt. *The Khmer Rouge terrorised and bankrupted Cambodia when it was in power... They accused the government of bankrupting them with interest rates and taxes.*
3 NC A **bankrupt** is a person who has been legally declared bankrupt. *Undischarged bankrupts were on the list of those disbarred from the Inner Temple.*
4 ADJ Something that is **bankrupt** is completely lacking in a particular quality. *...the mindless, intellectually bankrupt leadership.*

bankruptcy /bæŋkrʌpsi/ **bankruptcies**
N U or NC **Bankruptcy** is the state of being bankrupt. *Economic sanctions have left the government close to bankruptcy... Inevitably that will mean bankruptcies, unemployment and lower living standards for many ordinary people.*

bank statement, bank statements
NC A **bank statement** is a printed document showing all the money paid into and taken out of a bank account. *...information on the tax returns and bank statements of suspected traffickers.*

banner /bænə/ **banners**
NC A **banner** is a long strip of cloth with a message or slogan on it. *Crowds filled the streets carrying banners.*

bannister /bænɪstə/. See **banister**.

banns /bænz/
N PL When a vicar reads or publishes the **banns**, he makes a public announcement in church that two people are going to be married.

banquet /bæŋkwɪt/ **banquets**
NC A **banquet** is a large-scale formal dinner consisting of several courses. **Banquets** are often followed by speeches. *The occasion was a state banquet in the capital, Nairobi.*

banshee /bænʃiː/ **banshees**
NC In Irish folklore, a **banshee** is a female spirit who warns you by her long, sad cry that someone in your family is going to die. *The kettle whistled like a banshee screaming.*

bantam /bæntəm/ **bantams**
NC A **bantam** is a small-sized breed of chicken.

banter /bæntə/
NU **Banter** is teasing or joking talk that is amusing and friendly. *There was some good-humoured banter about their differences.*

Bantu /bæntuː/
1 ADJ **Bantu** tribes live in central and southern Africa. *...the history of the Bantu peoples.*
2 ADJ **Bantu** languages are spoken in central and southern Africa. *She began to speak, not in a Bantu tongue but in broken English.*

banyan /bænjən/ **banyans**
NC A **banyan** is a tree that grows mainly in India and the East Indies. Its branches grow down into the ground to form additional trunks. *...the planting of a banyan tree in the main square.*

baptise /bæptaɪz/. See **baptize**.

baptism /bæptɪzəm/ **baptisms**
NC or NU A **baptism** is a Christian ceremony in which a person is baptized. *...family occasions such as births, baptisms, or marriages... In the Orthodox Church, anybody who comes forward for baptism must have his passport.*

Baptist /bæptɪst/ **Baptists**
NC A **Baptist** is a type of Christian. **Baptists** believe that it is not possible to be a true Christian unless you are baptized at an age when you are old enough to understand what you are doing. *They are strict Baptists. ...the son of a Baptist minister.*

baptize /bæptaɪz/ **baptizes, baptizing, baptized**; also spelt **baptise**.
VO When someone is **baptized**, water is sprinkled on them or they are immersed in water as a sign that they have become a member of a Christian Church. *A Catholic aunt persuaded him to be baptized.*

bar /bɑː/ **bars, barring, barred**
1 NC A **bar** is a place where alcoholic drinks are bought and drunk. *Norris was drinking at a bar in San Francisco... He called for the menu and ordered in the bar while they were finishing their drinks.*
2 NC A **bar** is also the counter on which alcoholic drinks are served. *Sally serves behind the bar.*
3 N PROP The **Bar** is used to refer to the profession of a barrister in England, or any kind of lawyer in other countries. *The Bar Association urged an end to all such abuses.*
4 NC A **bar** is also a long straight rigid piece of metal. *...an iron bar... We beat on the bars of our cells.*
5 NC+SUPP A **bar** of something is a piece of it which is more or less rectangular. *...a bar of soap... A standard chocolate bar has about 270 kilocalories of energy.*
6 VO If you **bar** someone from going somewhere or doing something, you prevent them from going there or doing it. *I turned to go. Stryker barred my way. ...restrictions barring the use of US-supplied weapons.*
7 PREP You can use **bar** to mean 'except'. For example, all the work **bar** the washing means all the work except the washing; a formal use. *German economic union is all over bar the haggling.*
8 NC In music, a **bar** is one of the several short parts of the same length into which a piece of music is divided; a technical term. *...the first few bars of Estonia's national anthem.*
9 See also **barring, crossbar, snack bar**.

barb /bɑːb/ **barbs**
1 NC A **barb** is a sharp curved point on the end of an arrow or fish-hook. *...the wire, straight and stiff, not curled as you'd expect, the barbs four inches apart.*
2 NC A **barb** is also an unkind remark. *The comment is a stinging barb at a western European government.*

Barbados /bɑːbeɪdɒs/
Barbados is a country in the Caribbean. It was a British colony from 1627 until its independence in 1966. It is a member of the Commonwealth and the Organization of American States. Erskine Sandiford, of the Democratic Labour Party (DLP), became Prime

Minister in 1987. Tourism and banking are important industries. The production and refining of sugar are also important. ◆ **Barbadian** /bɑːbeɪdiən/ N, ADJ ▪ *per capita GNP:* US$5,990 ▪ *religion:* Christianity (mainly Anglican) ▪ *language:* English ▪ *currency:* dollar ▪ *capital:* Bridgetown ▪ *population:* 255,000 (1988) ▪ *size:* 430 square kilometres.

barbarian /bɑːbeəriən/ **barbarians**
1 NC In former times, **barbarians** were members of wild and violent tribes in Europe. *...the economic relationship between the Graeco-Roman world and its barbarian neighbours.*
2 NC If you refer to an area or its people as **barbarian**, you think they act in a rough, violent or uncivilized way. *Mr Steel said Britain was becoming more violent and lawless and is being seen as the barbarian of Europe.*

barbaric /bɑːbærɪk/
ADJ **Barbaric** behaviour is extremely cruel. *...the barbaric sport of hunting.*

barbarism /bɑːbərɪzəm/
NU **Barbarism** is cruel or uncivilized behaviour. *War is barbarism.*

barbarity /bɑːbærəti/ **barbarities**
1 NU **Barbarity** is extremely cruel behaviour. *Both sides were guilty of barbarity. ...scenes of squalid barbarity.*
2 NC A **barbarity** is an extremely cruel and shocking act. *Many barbarities were mentioned, including the shooting of six hundred children.*

barbarous /bɑːbərəs/
ADJ Something that is **barbarous** is rough and uncivilized, or very cruel. *...the most barbarous atrocities.*

barbecue /bɑːbɪkjuː/ **barbecues**
1 NC A **barbecue** is a grill used to cook food outdoors. *...a place where the sun always shines and the barbecue is always on the go.*
2 NC A **barbecue** is also a meal cooked outside on a grill. *The crowds seem hungrier for the barbecue than for his speech.*

barbecue sauce
NU **Barbecue sauce** is a highly seasoned sauce used to flavour food, especially meat cooked on a barbecue.

barbed /bɑːbd/
ADJ A **barbed** remark or joke seems humorous or polite, but contains a cleverly hidden criticism. *His barbed wit sometimes comes over as a mean form of sarcasm... Spain and the United States were the main targets of Dr Castro's barbed remarks.*

barbed wire
NU **Barbed wire** is strong wire with sharp points sticking out of it, which is used to make fences. *...huge coils of razor-sharp barbed wire.*

barber /bɑːbə/ **barbers**
1 NC A **barber** is a man who cuts men's hair and shaves or trims their beard. *An Athens barber offered him free shaves for life.*
2 N SING A **barber's** is a shop where a barber works. *He went to the barber's to please his mother... She worked for a while as an assistant in a barber's shop.*

barbershop /bɑːbəʃɒp/
NU or N+N **Barbershop** is a type of singing in close harmony that is popular in the USA and is usually performed by four men. *...all time barbershop favourites by Mark Brayne. ...a barbershop quartet.*

barber's pole, barber's poles
NC A **barber's pole** is a red and white striped pole, which was the traditional sign outside barber's shops in Britain.

barbiturate /bɑːbɪtjʊrət/ **barbiturates**
NC A **barbiturate** is a drug which people take to make them calm or to put them to sleep. *She was also suffering from withdrawal from barbiturates.*

bar code, bar codes
NC A **bar code** is a set of thin and thick lines that are printed on the labels of things that are sold in shops. When you buy something, the bar code can be read into a computer and used to provide information for the shop about the number of items sold, the number in stock, and so on. *It's similar to the bar codes you might see on supermarket shelves.*

bard /bɑːd/ **bards**
1 NC A **bard** is a poet; an old-fashioned or literary word. *He's earned a reputation as a modern-day bard.*
2 N PROP Some people refer to William Shakespeare as the **Bard**. *...a new production of the Bard's early tragedy, Richard III.*

bare /beə/ **barer, barest; bares, baring, bared**
1 ADJ If a part of your body is **bare**, it is not covered by any clothing. *...her bare feet.* ● If someone does something with their **bare hands**, they do it without using weapons or tools. *He killed those two men with his bare hands.*
2 ADJ If an object is **bare**, it is not covered or decorated with anything. *The doctor stood uneasily on the bare floor... The trees were almost bare.*
3 ADJ If a room, cupboard, or shelf is **bare**, it is empty. *The shelves in every shop are bare.*
4 ADJ ATTRIB The **bare** minimum or the **bare** essentials are the smallest number of things that are necessary. *She packed the barest minimum of clothing.*
5 VO If you **bare** something, you uncover it. *She bared her teeth.*

bareback /beəbæk/
ADV If you ride **bareback**, you ride a horse without a saddle. *He managed to cling to the horse, riding virtually bareback.*

barefaced /beəfeɪst/
ADJ ATTRIB **Barefaced** means not caring about how wrongly you are behaving. *He's a barefaced liar... How she had the barefaced gall to do it, I don't know!*

barefoot /beəfʊt/
ADJ Someone who is **barefoot** or **barefooted** is not wearing anything on their feet. *Correspondents say some of the troops were barefoot and without uniforms... He was barefooted and wore only shorts and a sweater.* ▶ Also ADV *She ran barefoot through the field.*

barefooted /beəfʊtɪd/. See **barefoot**.

barely /beəli/
ADV If something is **barely** true or possible, it is only just true or possible. *He was so drunk that he could barely stand.*

bargain /bɑːgɪn/ **bargains, bargaining, bargained**
1 NC A **bargain** is a business agreement in which two people or groups agree what each of them will do, pay, or receive. *We shook hands on the bargain.*
2 V When people **bargain** with each other, they discuss what each of them will do, pay, or receive. *Trade unions bargain with employers for better conditions.* ◆ **bargaining** NU *...the kind of bargaining that goes on in industry.*
3 NC A **bargain** is also something which is sold at a lower price than it would be normally. *He couldn't resist a bargain.*

bargain for PHRASAL VERB If you say that someone had not **bargained for** something, you mean that they did not expect it to happen. *They had not bargained for such opposition.*

bargaining chip, bargaining chips
NC In discussions between people, a **bargaining chip** is something of value which is held by one of the people involved, and which can be exchanged in order to obtain something from the other party. *President Bush was not tempted to use the canal as a bargaining chip... Prisoners of war are being used as bargaining chips in the peace process.*

bargaining table
N SING If you say that people are at the **bargaining table**, you mean that they are having serious discussions about something on which they disagree, and that they are trying to reach an agreement. *He said Washington should use its maximum influence to persuade the countries concerned to go to the bargaining table... The West will want to see more details of the Soviet proposals on the bargaining table in Vienna.*

barge /bɑːdʒ/ **barges, barging, barged**
1 V A or V O A If you **barge** into a place or person, you rush into it or push past them in a rude or rough way. *Arthur barged into the garden. ...barging his way through the crowd.*
2 NC A **barge** is a boat with a flat bottom, used for

carrying heavy loads. *A tug is on its way to take up the tow of the barge, which is drifting. ...rail, road, and barge routes.*

barge in PHRASAL VERB If you **barge in**, you rudely interrupt what someone else is doing or saying; an informal expression. *I'm sorry to barge in on you.*

barge pole
If you say that you **wouldn't touch** someone or something **with a barge pole**, you mean that you do not want to have anything to do with them because they are untrustworthy or unreliable; an informal expression. *I wouldn't touch those cars with a barge pole—they're rubbish.*

baritone /bærɪtəʊn/ **baritones**
NC A **baritone** is a man with a fairly deep singing voice. *The poems should be sung by an English tenor and a German baritone.*

barium /beərɪəm/
NU **Barium** is a soft, silvery-white metal. *A research team has made a new material containing barium, potassium, and bismuth oxide.*

bark /bɑːk/ **barks, barking, barked**
1 V When a dog **barks**, it makes a short, loud noise, once or several times. *Each time a dog barks, we awaken with a start.* ▶ Also NC *His spaniel gave a sudden bark.*
2 VOorV-QUOTE If you **bark** an order or question at someone, you shout it at them in a loud, rough voice. *Senior officers barked orders to the young and well-armed troops... Another rather rudely barked 'Who are you?'*
3 NU **Bark** is the tough material that covers the outside of a tree. *...traditional medicines made from pepper bark or wild ginger.*
4 to **bark up the wrong tree**: see tree.

barley /bɑːli/
NU **Barley** is a tall grass-like plant, or the grain produced by it, that is grown for food and for making beer and whisky. *...people eating unrefined barley, rye, and oats would get lots of fibre. ...the annual barley crop.*

barley sugar
NU **Barley sugar** is a hard sweet made from boiled sugar.

barley water
NU **Barley water** is a non-alcoholic drink made from barley.

barmaid /bɑːmeɪd/ **barmaids**
NC A **barmaid** is a woman who serves drinks in a bar or pub. *Behind the bar was a genial landlord and a plump, attractive barmaid.*

barman /bɑːmən/ **barmen** /bɑːmən/
NC A **barman** is a man who serves drinks in a bar or pub. *...the apparently motiveless murder of a barman.*

bar mitzvah /bɑː mɪtsvə/ **bar mitzvahs**
NC A **bar mitzvah** is a Jewish ceremony in which a thirteen-year old boy is formally given the status, religious duties, and responsibilities of an adult. *He was preparing for his Bar Mitzvah.*

barmy /bɑːmi/ **barmier, barmiest**
ADJ Someone or something that is **barmy** is slightly mad or foolish; an informal word. *The old woman's very rich and quite barmy... The whole scheme seems barmy to me.*

barn /bɑːn/ **barns**
NC A **barn** is a large building on a farm in which crops or animal food can be kept. *The haul, including rifles and rocket warheads, was hidden in a barn... Thousands more barns will be converted without providing jobs.*

barnacle /bɑːnəkl/ **barnacles**
NC **Barnacles** are small shellfish that fix themselves tightly to rocks and the bottoms of boats. *I feel I shall spend all my life researching barnacles.*

barn dance, barn dances
NC A **barn dance** is an informal dance that people go to for country dancing. *The atmosphere of a modern barn dance, says Trim, is not much different from the village dances which Hardy describes.*

barn owl, barn owls
NC A **barn owl** is a type of owl with pale brown and white feathers and a heart-shaped face. *The two initial findings generated a lot of interest in barn owls.*

barnstorm /bɑːnstɔːm/ **barnstorms, barnstorming, barnstormed**
VO If a politician **barnstorms** a country, he or she travels to a lot of towns in order to make speeches as part of a campaign. *He has agonized over whether to challenge Walesa, who has already begun barnstorming the country.*

barnyard /bɑːnjɑːd/ **barnyards**
NC A **barnyard** is a yard next to or near a barn on a farm.

barometer /bərɒmɪtə/ **barometers**
1 NC A **barometer** is an instrument that measures air pressure and so shows when the weather is changing. *The barometer was falling.*
2 NC+SUPP You can also use **barometer** to refer to something that indicates the way in which a particular situation is likely to develop. *Commodity prices are a good barometer for inflationary trends... The early morning radio commentary is often a good barometer of government thinking.*

baron /bærən/ **barons**
1 NCorTITLE A **baron** is a man who is a member of the nobility. *In the last forty years, the baron has spent a considerable amount of time and money in buying back some of his father's collection... He inherited the aristocratic title of Baron Byron of Rochdale.*
2 NC+SUPP You use **baron** to refer to someone who controls a large amount of an industry and who is therefore extremely powerful. *Miss Bhutto has often accused unnamed drug barons of financing conspiracies against her government.*

baroness /bærənes/ **baronesses**
NCorTITLE A **baroness** is a woman who has the same rank as a baron, or who is the wife of a baron. *Two peers—one of them a baroness—are on the sick list... Baroness Warnock chaired a committee on human embryo experimentation.*

baronet /bærənɪt/ **baronets**
NC A **baronet** is a man who has the British title 'baronet'. The title is passed on from father to son. *Denis Thatcher was made a baronet.*

baronial /bərəʊnɪəl/
ADJ ATTRIB **Baronial** means belonging or relating to a baron or barons. *He lives in baronial splendour in a twelfth century castle.*

baroque /bərɒk/
1 ADJ ATTRIB **Baroque** architecture or art is an elaborate style of architecture or art that was built or painted in Europe from the late 16th to the early 18th century. *The set shows the ruins of a baroque palace, with the roof open to the sky.*
2 ADJ ATTRIB **Baroque** music is a style of European music that was written in the 18th century. *...a background of baroque music.*

barrack /bærək/ **barracks, barracking, barracked.**
The form **barracks** is both the singular and the plural of the noun.
1 NC A **barracks** is a building or group of buildings in which members of the armed forces live and work. *The hunt is still on for the bombers of the barracks... Troops and police units were confined to barracks.*
2 VOorV If you **barrack** someone, you shout loudly in order to interrupt them when they are making a speech. *The Prime Minister was barracked as she offered her sympathy to the relatives... She expressed sympathy with those supporters who had been barracking.* ◆ **barracking** NU *The barracking was led by a bearded man in jeans.*

barracuda /bærəkjuːdə/ **barracudas**
NC A **barracuda** is a large tropical sea fish with a protruding lower jaw and sharp teeth.

barrage /bærɑːʒ/ **barrages**
NC+SUPP A **barrage** of questions or complaints is a large amount of them. *...a barrage of criticism.*

barrage balloon, barrage balloons
NC **Barrage balloons** are large balloons which are fixed to the ground by steel cables. They are used in wartime, when the cables are intended to destroy low-flying enemy aircraft.

barred /bɑːd/
ADJ Windows or doors that are **barred** have bars across them to prevent people from getting in or out. *Markets and shops remained shuttered and barred.*

barrel /bærəl/ **barrels**
1 NC A **barrel** is a round container for liquids. Barrels are wider in the middle than at the top and bottom and are usually made of wood. *...a wine barrel.*
2 NC You can use **barrel** to refer to a barrel and its contents, or to the contents only. *...a barrel of beer.*
3 NC The **barrel** of a gun is the long cylindrical part through which the bullet moves when the gun is fired. *The Minister was jabbed in the face by the barrel of a policeman's rifle.*

barrel organ, barrel organs
NC A **barrel organ** is a large old-fashioned machine that plays music when you turn a handle on the side.

barren /bærən/
1 ADJ **Barren** land has soil of such poor quality that plants cannot grow on it. *The islands are barren and largely unpopulated. ...reclaiming barren land and deserts.*
2 ADJ A **barren** woman is unable to have babies; an old-fashioned use. *Barren women are rejected by the tribesmen.*

barricade /bærɪkeɪd/ **barricades, barricading, barricaded**
1 NC A **barricade** is a line of vehicles or other objects placed across a road or passage to stop people getting past. *The demonstrators set up barricades, burned tyres, and threw stones.*
2 VO If you **barricade** a road or passage, you put something across it to stop people reaching it. *Hours earlier, the police barricaded all roads leading to the capital... The two top floors of the prison were barricaded.*
3 VOA If you **barricade** yourself inside a room or building, you put something heavy against the door so that other people cannot get in. *We rushed into the bedroom and barricaded ourselves in... They were barricaded behind concrete slabs.*

barrier /bærɪə/ **barriers**
1 NC A **barrier** is a fence or wall that prevents people or things from moving from one area to another. *London Regional Transport are to modify their automatic ticket barriers... Reports say their car tried to ram the barriers on the border, but it crashed.*
2 NC+SUPP A **barrier** to the happening or achievement of something makes it difficult or impossible for the thing to happen or to be achieved. *Pollution is not a barrier to future economic growth... All remaining trade barriers between the two countries will be removed.*

barring /bɑːrɪŋ/
PREP You use **barring** to indicate that the person, thing, or event that you are mentioning is an exception to the point that you are making. *It is hard to imagine anyone, barring a lunatic, starting a war.*

barrister /bærɪstə/ **barristers**
NC A **barrister** is a lawyer who speaks in the higher courts of law on behalf of either the defence or the prosecution. *The union have hired a leading human rights barrister to fight the case.*

barrow /bærəʊ/ **barrows**
1 NC A **barrow** is the same as a **wheelbarrow**. *He wept with exhaustion as he tried to push four crates on a barrow up a hill.*
2 NC A **barrow** is also a cart from which fruit or other goods are sold in the street. *The President made an impromptu speech from a street vendor's barrow.*

bartender /bɑːtendə/ **bartenders**
NC A **bartender** is a person who serves drinks in a bar; used in American English. *...a man with the manner and look of a bartender.*

barter /bɑːtə/ **barters, bartering, bartered**
VOorV If you **barter** goods, you exchange them for other goods, rather than selling them for money. *They bring meat, grain, and vegetables to sell or barter... He learned to survive, searching for extra food and bartering on behalf of the other inmates.* ▶ Also NU *Metal discs and chains were used for barter.*

basalt /bæsɔːlt/
NU **Basalt** is a type of black rock that is produced by volcanoes.

base /beɪs/ **bases** /beɪsɪz/ **basing, based**
1 NC The **base** of something is its lowest edge or part, or the part at which it is attached to something else. *...at the base of a cliff. ...the scar at the base of his thumb.*
2 NC+SUPP A position or thing that is a **base** for something is one from which that thing can be developed or achieved. *This innovation was regarded as a sensible base for teaching and research... The League had no real power base on which it could build.*
3 VO+on or upon If one thing **is based** on another, the first thing is developed from the second one. *The new agreement is based on the original United Nations proposal. ...movies based on British life... The officials said that an aid plan could be based upon the methods used in Hungary and Poland.*
4 V-PASS If you **are based** in a particular place, that is the place where you live or do most of your work. *I was based in London.* ▶ Also NC *The company made Luxembourg their base.*
5 NCorNU A military **base** is a place which part of an army, navy, or air force works from. *...the new air base at Buzaruto... The submarines abandoned the chase and returned to base.*

baseball /beɪsbɔːl/
NU **Baseball** is a game played by two teams of nine players. Each player hits a ball with a bat and then tries to run round four points on the field before the other team can get the ball back. *In the United States, baseball is almost a religion... They set upon them with iron bars and baseball bats.*

-based /-beɪst/
1 SUFFIX **-based** is added to the names of places, or to adjectives describing nationality, to make adjectives which mean being positioned, controlled from, or existing mainly in that place. *...village-based post-offices... The eleven million pound contract will go to a Hampshire-based computer company. ...British-based car makers.*
2 SUFFIX **-based** is added to nouns to make adjectives which mean having that thing as a very important or central feature. *The new computer-based technology may mean fewer jobs... It is vital now for scientists to learn all they can about the new carbon-based semiconductors. ...a tourist-based economy.*

baseless /beɪsləs/
ADJ A **baseless** story or belief is not true and is not based on facts. *A spokesman said the rumours were baseless and irresponsible. ...baseless allegations.*

baseline /beɪslaɪn/ **baselines**
1 NC The **baseline** of a tennis or badminton court is one of the lines at each end of the court that mark the limits of play. *She played mainly from the baseline, but showed volleying promise.*
2 NC A **baseline** is a value or starting point on an imaginary scale with which other values can be compared. *It serves as a baseline from which you are able to improve... Our contention is that nobody should be using non-drinkers as a baseline.*

basement /beɪsmənt/ **basements**
NC The **basement** of a building is a floor built partly or wholly below ground level. *The papers were stored in an archive in the basement, which escaped the blaze.*

base metal, base metals
NC A **base metal** is a metal, such as copper, zinc, tin, or lead, that is not a precious metal.

base rate, base rates
NC The **base rate** is the rate of interest that banks use as a basis when they are calculating the rates that they charge on loans. *They cut their base rate by 1 per cent.*

bases
1 **Bases**, pronounced /beɪsɪz/, is the plural of **base**.
2 **Bases**, pronounced /beɪsiːz/, is the plural of **basis**.

bash /bæʃ/ **bashes, bashing, bashed;** an informal word.
1 VO If you **bash** someone or something, you deliberately hit them hard. *She was bashing him over*

the head with a saucepan.

2 VA If you **bash** into something or against something, you hit it or bump into it accidentally with a lot of force. *He bashed into a tree.* ▶ Also NC *...a bash on the nose.*

3 If you **have a bash** at something or if you **give it a bash**, you try to do it. *She was going to have a bash at swimming the Channel.*

4 NC A **bash** is also a very lively and enjoyable party. *They would like to attend the New Year's Eve bash in Time Square.*

bashful /ˈbæʃfl/
ADJ A **bashful** person is shy and easily embarrassed. *Most parents are bashful about asking questions.*
◆ **bashfully** ADV *He smiled bashfully.*

Bashir, Omar Hassan Ahmad al-
/ˈəʊmɑː hʌsn ɑɪxməd əlbəʃɪə/
Lieutenant-General Omar Hassan Ahmad al-Bashir became Chairman of the Revolutionary Council and Prime Minister of Sudan in a coup in 1989. Born: 1944.

basic /ˈbeɪsɪk/ **basics**
1 ADJ ATTRIB You use **basic** to describe a thing which is the most important or the simplest part of something. *The basic theme of these stories never varies. ...people with only a basic education.*

2 ADJ PRED An activity, situation, or plan that is **basic** to the achievement or success of something else is necessary for it. *There are certain things that are absolutely basic to a good relationship.*

3 ADJ You describe something as **basic** when it has only the most important features and no luxuries. *The facilities are terribly basic.*

4 N PL The **basics** of a subject or activity are the simplest and most important aspects of it. *For a year I learnt the basics of journalism.*

BASIC /ˈbeɪsɪk/
N PROP **BASIC** is a simple computer language which uses English words. **BASIC** is an abbreviation for 'Beginner's All-purpose Symbolic Instruction Code'.

basically /ˈbeɪsɪkli/
ADV SEN You use **basically** to indicate what the most important feature of something is or to give a general description of something complicated. *There are basically three types of vacuum cleaner... Basically, I think Britain shouldn't have gone into the Common Market.*

basil /ˈbæzl/
NU **Basil** is a strongly scented herb that is used to add flavour in cooking. *In this garden, there are chives, marjoram, and two kinds of basil.*

basilica /bəˈzɪlɪkə/ **basilicas**
NC A **basilica** is a rectangular Roman building which has a rounded end and two aisles. *Pope John Paul is to consecrate the world's largest basilica.*

basin /ˈbeɪsn/ **basins**
1 NC A **basin** is a deep bowl used for mixing or storing food. *...a jug of milk, a basin of butter, and some cheeses.*

2 NC A **basin** is also a washbasin.

3 NC+SUPP The **basin** of a large river is the area of land around it from which water and streams run down into it. *...the Amazon basin.*

basis /ˈbeɪsɪs/ **bases** /ˈbeɪsiːz/
1 NC+SUPP The **basis** of something is the central and most important part of it, from which it can be further developed. *This was the basis of the final design.*

2 NC+SUPP The **basis** for something is the thing that provides a reason for it. *...arguments which had no logical basis.*

3 If something happens or is done **on a** particular **basis**, it happens or is done in that way or using that method. *We run the service on a voluntary basis... The Chairman is paid on a part-time basis.*

bask /bɑːsk/ **basks, basking, basked**
1 V If you **bask** in the sunshine, you lie in it and enjoy its warmth. *Most of the prisoners seem happy to bask in the sun.*

2 V To **bask** in someone's approval, favour, or admiration means to enjoy the amount of attention you are getting. *Deng Yingchao has basked in the self-esteem and popularity enjoyed by her husband... Nasser's strength was his charisma, and he basked in*

the admiration of the Egyptian people.

basket /ˈbɑːskɪt/ **baskets**
1 NC A **basket** is a container that is made of thin strips of cane woven together, or of thin metal wire or plastic. You use baskets, for example, for carrying shopping or for laundry. *...a shopping basket... This poster shows a boy holding a basket full of green vegetables. ...a log basket.*

2 NC+of In economics, a **basket** of currencies is a group of currencies which are used as a measure of the strength or weakness of other currencies. *Sterling's value against a basket of currencies is down point five at ninety-three exactly.*

basketball /ˈbɑːskɪtbɔːl/
NU **Basketball** is a game in which two teams of five players each try to score goals by throwing a large ball through a circular net fixed to a metal ring at each end of the court. *He felt that basketball was too rough for those approaching middle age.*

basketweave /ˈbɑːskɪtwiːv/
NU **Basketweave** is a type of weaving found in wool or linen that makes a criss-cross pattern. *...an inter-leaving basketweave pattern.*

basmati rice /bɑːsməti raɪs/
NU **Basmati rice** is a type of rice that is produced in India. It has long grains and is used in savoury dishes. *Basmati rice has been available on the menu in Indian restaurants for twenty or thirty years. The failure of the monsoon affected winter crops, though there was a compensating spurt in basmati rice production.*

bas-relief /ˈbæsrɪliːf/ **bas-reliefs**
1 NU **Bas-relief** is a technique of sculpture in which shapes are carved so that they stand out from the background.

2 NC A **bas-relief** is a sculpture carved on a surface so that it stands out from the background.

bass /beɪs/ **basses**
1 NC A **bass** is a man with a deep singing voice. *...the legendary Russian bass, Chaliapin.*

2 ADJ ATTRIB A **bass** musical instrument has a range of notes of low pitch. *It features Gail Ann on bass guitar... Craig Logan, the bass player, has left the band.*

Basse-Terre /bɑːsteə/
Basse-Terre is the capital of Guadeloupe and its third largest town. Population: 14,000 (1990).

Basseterre /bæsteə/
Basseterre is the capital of St Christopher and Nevis and its largest city. Population: 14,000 (1980).

bassoon /bəsuːn/ **bassoons**
NC A **bassoon** is a woodwind musical instrument which can produce a very deep sound. *This charming duet for bassoon and cello by Mozart demonstrates the basic principles of playing chamber music.*

bastard /ˈbɑːstəd/ **bastards**
1 NC If you call someone a **bastard**, you are insulting them in a very offensive way. *Some of the mourners gave chase, shouting 'Kill the bastard'.*

2 NC A **bastard** is someone whose parents were not married to each other when he or she was born; an old-fashioned use. *...a dynasty riddled with wives, mistresses and bastards.*

baste /beɪst/ **bastes, basting, basted**
1 VO If you **baste** meat, you pour hot fat and the juices from the meat itself over it while it is cooking in an oven.

2 VO If you **baste** pieces of material, you sew them together with big, loose stitches before sewing them properly.

bastion /ˈbæstɪən/ **bastions**
NC+SUPP If a system or organization is described as a **bastion** of a particular way of life, it is seen as being important and effective in defending it; a literary word. *They regard the wealth-producing system as a bastion of capitalist privilege.*

bat /bæt/ **bats, batting, batted**
1 NC A **bat** is a specially shaped piece of wood that is used for hitting the ball in cricket, baseball, or table tennis. *...a cricket bat.*

2 V In cricket or baseball, when you **bat**, it is your turn to try and hit the ball with a bat to score runs.

The county side won the toss, and decided to bat.
3 NC A **bat** is also a small flying animal that looks like a mouse with leathery wings. Bats fly at night. *In Australia, there's a gradual change in the type of bats seen. ...very thin, rather like a bat wing.*
4 **to bat an eyelid**: see eyelid.

Bata /bɑːtə/
Bata is the largest town in Equatorial Guinea. Population: 24,000 (1983).

batch /bætʃ/ **batches**
NC+SUPP A **batch** of things or people is a group of them, especially one that is dealt with at the same time. *Another batch of letters came in. ...the next batch of trainees.*

bated /beɪtɪd/
If you wait for something **with bated breath**, you are very anxious about it; a literary expression. *Many people will wait with bated breath to hear what he has to say.*

bath /bɑːθ/ **baths, bathing, bathed**
1 NC A **bath** is a long rectangular container which you fill with water and sit in while you wash your body. *There's a danger of being scalded by the hot water taps of the bath.*
2 NC When you have a **bath** or take a **bath**, you wash your body while sitting in a bath filled with water. *The survey reveals everything from how much television they watch to how often they take a bath.*
3 VO When you **bath** a child or other person, you wash them in a bath. *She will show you how to bath the baby.*

bathe /beɪð/ **bathes, bathing, bathed**
1 V When you **bathe** in the sea, a river, or a lake, you swim or play there. *It is dangerous to bathe in the sea here... The water's 45 degrees centigrade, it's so nice to bathe in.* ▶ Also N SING *Let's go for a bathe.*
2 V When you **bathe**, you have a bath; used in American English. *During the winter, the prisoners weren't allowed to bathe for weeks on end.*
3 VO When you **bathe** a child or other person, you wash them in a bath; used in American English. *One morning I bathed the baby and did everything.*
4 VO When you **bathe** a wound, you wash it gently. *He bathed the cut in ice-cold water.*
5 VOA If a place is **bathed** in light, it is very bright. *The room was bathed in sunlight... The opera opens to a stage bathed in light.*
6 VOA If you **bathe** in the admiration or attention of other people, you receive lots of attention from them. *He will bathe in the publicity of a special UN session... Vladimir bathed in the full limelight when he was here three years ago for his first concert.*

bather /beɪðə/ **bathers**
NC A **bather** is a person who is swimming or playing in the sea, a river, or a lake. *The weed covers bathers in green slime... The beach was covered with weekend bathers.*

bathing cap, bathing caps
NC A **bathing cap** is a rubber cap which you wear to keep your hair dry when swimming.

bathing costume, bathing costumes
NC A **bathing costume** or **bathing suit** is the same as a **swimming costume**; used in old-fashioned English. *He wasn't sure if contestants would be allowed to wear bathing costumes.*

bathing trunks
N PL **Bathing trunks** are the same as **swimming trunks**; an old-fashioned expression.

bathmat /bɑːθmæt/ **bathmats**
NC A **bathmat** is a mat which you stand on while you dry yourself after getting out of the bath.

bath oil, bath oils
N MASS **Bath oil** is thick perfumed liquid that you use in the bath to make the water smell nice.

bathos /beɪθɒs/
NU **Bathos** is a sudden change in speech or writing from a serious or important subject to a ridiculous or very ordinary one. *The ascent into tragedy keeps slipping into bathos.*

bathrobe /bɑːθrəʊb/ **bathrobes**
NC A **bathrobe** is a loose piece of clothing which you wear before or after you have a bath or a swim.

bathroom /bɑːθruːm, bɑːθrʊm/ **bathrooms**
1 NC A **bathroom** is a room in a house that contains a bath or shower, a washbasin, and sometimes also a toilet. *He listens to the radio in the bathroom.*
2 N SING People sometimes refer to a toilet as the **bathroom**. *...running for the bathroom.*

bath salts
N PL **Bath salts** are mineral salts that you use in the bath to make the water smell nice.

bathtub /bɑːθtʌb/ **bathtubs**
NC A **bathtub** is the same as a **bath**; used in American English. *He was found dead in the bathtub in his apartment.*

batik /bətiːk/ **batiks**
1 NU **Batik** is a process for printing designs on cloth which uses wax on areas of the cloth that are not to be coloured by a dye. *Four of us are doing batik. ...Java's batik industry.*
2 NC A **batik** is a cloth which has been printed with a batik design. *Anne was most impressed with the batiks.*

batman /bætmən/ **batmen** /bætmən/
NC A **batman** is the personal servant of an officer in the army, navy, or air force.

baton /bætɒn/ **batons**
1 NC A **baton** is a thin lightweight stick used by a conductor when he or she is conducting an orchestra. *He has been told by his doctors to lay down his conductor's baton.*
2 NC A **baton** is also a short heavy stick used as a weapon by a policeman. *The Israeli army has issued stronger batons, made of fibreglass.*

baton charge, baton charges
NC A **baton charge** is an attacking forward movement made by a large group of policemen carrying batons. *The police retaliated with baton charges, tear-gas and water-cannons.*

batsman /bætsmən/ **batsmen** /bætsmən/
NC In a game of cricket, the **batsman** is the person who is batting. *...an experienced opening batsman.*

battalion /bətæliən/ **battalions**
NC A **battalion** is a large group of soldiers consisting of three or more companies. *One battalion already serves in Brunei.*

batten /bætn/ **battens, battening, battened**
NC A **batten** is a long strip of wood that is fixed to something to strengthen it or to hold it firm. *The lid of the crate was fixed down with battens.*
batten down PHRASAL VERB If you **batten** something **down**, you make it secure by fixing battens across it or by closing it firmly. *The hatches were battened down as the storm grew fiercer.*
batten on or **batten upon** PHRASAL VERB If someone **battens on** or **battens upon** another person, they live comfortably or become successful by using that person's money or position in society for their own benefit. *...the archetype of the predatory foreign nobleman battening on the people.*

batter /bætə/ **batters, battering, battered**
1 VO To **batter** someone means to hit them many times. *Such parents have been known to batter their children... Lora battered his opponent into submission.*
◆ **battered** ADJ *His horribly battered and mutilated body was dredged up from the lake... Lalonde was a battered child himself.*
2 VO When the wind, rain, or a storm **batters** something, it keeps striking it with great force. *The first cyclone of the season battered seven of the South Pacific's tiny islands... Coastal areas have been battered by high winds.*
3 N MASS **Batter** is a mixture of flour, eggs, and milk, often used to make pancakes. *...fish in batter... The flour is added, then the yeast to make a batter.*
4 See also **battered**.
batter down PHRASAL VERB If you **batter down** a door, you hit it so hard that it breaks and falls down. *There was no need to batter it down.*

battered /bætəd/
ADJ Something that is **battered** is old, worn, and damaged. *...a battered old hat.*

battering /bætərɪŋ/ **batterings**
NC A **battering** is an experience in which someone

suffers badly through being attacked. *The Eighth Army had taken the worst battering.*

battering ram, battering rams
NC A **battering ram** is a long heavy piece of wood that was used for breaking down the doors of fortified buildings. *Thousands of protesters are said to have used battering rams to break into the houses of party members.*

battery /bǽtəᵊri/ **batteries**
1 NC A **battery** is a device that produces the electricity in something such as a torch or radio. *...mercury-free batteries.*
2 NC+SUPP A **battery** of things, people, or events is a large number of them. *Batteries of cameras were set to record the event.*
3 ADJ ATTRIB **Battery** hens are kept in small cages and made to produce large numbers of eggs.

battle /bǽtl/ **battles, battling, battled**
1 NCorNU In a war, a **battle** is a fight between armies or between groups of ships, planes, or people. *...the Battle of Balaclava... Running street battles continued as rebel forces hunted down the President's diminishing supporters... The general was killed in battle.*
2 NC A **battle** is also a process in which two people or two groups compete for power or try to achieve opposite things. *...the battle between the sexes. ...his battle for control of the company.*
3 NC You can also use **battle** to refer to a joint attempt by a group of people to do something that is very difficult to achieve. *...the battle against inflation.*
4 VA When people **battle**, they fight very hard. *Dad was soon battling for his life... Anti-government guerrillas and troops battled for control.*

battle-axe, battle-axes
1 NC A **battle-axe** is a large axe that used to be used as a weapon.
2 NC If you call a middle-aged or older woman a **battle-axe**, you mean that you think she is very difficult and unpleasant. *When you get to my age, you're regarded as a battle-axe.*

battle cry, battle cries
1 NC A **battle cry** is a phrase that is used to urge people to take part in activities connected with a particular cause or campaign. *'One man, one vote' became our battle cry.*
2 NC A **battle cry** is also a shout that soldiers used to utter as they went into battle.

battlefield /bǽtlfiːld/ **battlefields**
NC A **battlefield** is a place where a battle is fought. *Success on the battlefield could be assured by the possession of the latest equipment. ...battlefield casualties.*

battleground /bǽtlɡraʊnd/ **battlegrounds**
1 NC A **battleground** is the same as a **battlefield**. *Foreign diplomats are worried that the capital city may be the next battleground, and they are urging their citizens to leave now.*
2 NC You can also refer to a subject over which people disagree or compete as a **battleground**. *The theory of evolution is no longer a battleground.*

battlements /bǽtlmənts/
N PL The **battlements** of a castle or fortress consist of a wall built round the top, with gaps through which guns or arrows can be fired. *The battlements gave the place the air of an intimidating fortress.*

battleship /bǽtlʃɪp/ **battleships**
NC A **battleship** is a very large, heavily armoured warship. *The US announced the withdrawal of the battleship 'Iowa' and two escort ships.*

battle zone, battle zones
NC A **battle zone** is the area in which a war is being fought. *For civilians caught in the middle of the battle zone it's hard to know what's going on.*

batty /bǽti/ **battier, battiest**
ADJ Someone or something that is **batty** is rather strange, foolish, or slightly mad; an informal word. *She must be going batty... He called the idea batty, half-baked, and politically mad.*

bauble /bɔ́ːbl/ **baubles**
NC A **bauble** is a small, cheap ornament or piece of jewellery. *...Christmas tree baubles.*

Baudouin, King of the Belgians /bɑ́udwænᵒ/
Baudouin I of Belgium succeeded his father, King Léopold III, in 1951. Born: 1930.

baulk /bɔːk, bɔːlk/. See **balk**.

bauxite /bɔ́ːksaɪt/
NU **Bauxite** is a substance from which aluminium is obtained. *...excavating bauxite from the Nimba mountains.*

bawdy /bɔ́ːdi/
ADJ A **bawdy** story or joke contains humorous references to sex; an old-fashioned word. *...bawdy songs.*

bawl /bɔːl/ **bawls, bawling, bawled**
1 V, VO, or V-QUOTE If you **bawl**, you shout or sing something loudly and harshly. *On Sunday mornings, the paper boys are allowed to bawl with all their might... Later, a Labour M.P. bawled abuse in the face of a minister.*
2 V If a child **bawls**, it cries loudly. *Josephine started bawling.*
bawl out PHRASAL VERB If someone **bawls** you **out**, they scold you angrily for doing something wrong; an informal expression. *I was regularly bawled out at school for not doing homework.*

Bawoyeu, Jean Alingue /ʒɑ́ːnᵒ ælǽŋ bɑːwɑːjʒɪ́/
Jean Alingue Bawoyeu was appointed Prime Minister of Chad in 1991. He was Speaker of the National Assembly and served as Acting Head of State in 1990. He is a member of the Patriotic Salvation Movement (MPS). Born: 1937.

bay /beɪ/ **bays, baying, bayed**
1 NC A **bay** is a part of a coastline where the land curves inwards. *Hearst sailed from San Francisco across the bay to Oakland. ...a therapist from Shelley Bay, Bermuda.*
2 NC+SUPP A **bay** is also a space or area used for a particular purpose. *...the loading bay.*
3 If you **keep** something frightening or upsetting at bay, you prevent it from reaching you. *...lighting a fire to keep dangerous animals at bay. ...methods of trying to keep the disease at bay.*
4 V When a dog or wolf **bays**, it howls.

bayonet, bayonets, bayonetting, bayonetted;
pronounced /béɪənət/ when it is a noun and /béɪənet/ when it is a verb.
1 NC A **bayonet** is a long, sharp blade that is fixed to the end of a rifle and used as a weapon. *Some, he says, are killed, more often with bayonets than bullets.*
2 VO To **bayonet** someone means to injure or kill them with a bayonet. *Armed men bayonetted a black farmer after questioning him.*

bay window, bay windows
NC A **bay window** is a window that sticks out from the outside wall of a house.

bazaar /bəzɑ́ː/ **bazaars**
1 NC A **bazaar** is an area with many small shops and stalls, especially in the Middle East and India. *...stallholders in the old bazaar... It was described by one aid worker as an arms bazaar.*
2 NC A **bazaar** is also a sale that is held to raise money for charity. *Our local church is having a Christmas bazaar.*

bazooka /bəzúːkə/ **bazookas**
NC A **bazooka** is a type of hand-held gun that fires rockets. *...gunmen armed with machine guns and bazookas.*

BBC /bìːbiːsíː/
1 N PROP The **BBC** is a British organization which broadcasts programmes on radio and television. **BBC** is an abbreviation for 'British Broadcasting Corporation'. *How should the BBC be financed?*
2 NU **BBC** is also used to refer to particular channels on television and radio. *It's on Monday evenings on BBC 2... Speaking on BBC Radio Cambridgeshire, he said that they would be released without delay.*

BC /bìːsíː/
You use **BC** in dates to indicate a number of years or centuries before the year in which Jesus Christ is believed to have been born. *...1600 BC. ...the fifth century BC.*

be /bi, biː/, **am, are, is, was, were; being, been**
1 AUX You use **be** in front of a present participle to

form the continuous tenses of the verb. *The Government is considering the introduction of student loans... I don't know where they were all going.*
2 V+*to*-INF You use **be** in front of an infinitive to talk about future events. *She is to appeal against the decision... Mr Sandy Saunders is to be chairman.*
3 AUX You use **be** in front of a past participle to form the passive voice. *Some milk products have been found to contain aluminium... Mr Harris was elected by the Council last month.*
4 VCorVA You use **be** in front of an adjective, a noun, or a prepositional phrase in order to give more information about the subject of a sentence. For example, you may want to name a person or place, or to give information about their qualities, features, age, and so on. *She was slightly disappointed with her Grade C pass... The head of the Corporation is Mr Paul Simpson... The iron was in her left hand... I'm from Dortmund originally.*
5 VC You use 'it' with **be** in order to describe something, or to mention one of its qualities. *It was terribly hot and airless in the car... It's a shame she didn't enjoy the film... It couldn't have been wrong.*
6 VC **Be** is also used with 'it' or 'what' as the subject in order to delay the final part of the sentence. For example, you can change the statement 'John bought the car' into 'It was John who bought the car' when you want to emphasize the person or thing that performs the action of the verb. *It was Ted who broke the news to me... What I'm talking about is the satellite that fell out of its orbit.*
7 VC **Be** is used with 'there' as the subject to say that something exists or happens. *There was a rustling of papers... There is no such thing as a happy marriage.*
8 **Be** is used on its own in co-ordinating structures where the subject of the second clause is different from the subject of the first. *She wasn't enjoying it, but the children were... He's exactly the same age as I am.*
9 **Be** can also be used on its own in a response to a question. *'Rose, are you interested in underdeveloped countries at all?'—'Yes, I am.'*
10 **Be** is also used in expressions such as 'isn't it?' and 'aren't you?' which are added to the end of a statement to change it into a question. *He was regarded as the most powerful man in the world, wasn't he?... She's Welsh, isn't she?... They weren't ready, were they?*

beach /biːtʃ/ **beaches, beaching, beached**
1 NC A **beach** is an area of sand or pebbles by the sea. *...a desolate beach. ...dealing with pollution on beaches.*
2 VO When you **beach** a boat, you bring it out of the water and leave it on dry land. *When the three suspects beached their boats, they were followed ashore by the Spaniards... They had to wait until the hovercraft had been beached.*

beach ball, beach balls
NC A **beach ball** is a large, lightweight air-filled ball that people play with.

beachcomber /biːtʃkəʊmə/ **beachcombers**
NC A **beachcomber** is someone who spends their time looking for things on the beach, especially for objects of value.

beachhead /biːtʃhed/ **beachheads**
NC A **beachhead** is an area of coastland where an attacking army has taken control and is preparing to advance. *The Allies established a firm beachhead in Normandy.*

beacon /biːkən/ **beacons**
1 NC A **beacon** is a light or a fire on a hill or tower, which acts as a signal or a warning. *They are exempt from fees which pay for the upkeep of lighthouses, buoys, and beacons around the coast.*
2 N SING+SUPP If you say that someone or something is a **beacon** of hope or light, you mean that they offer hope for the future; a literary use. *There is a feeling that the broadcasts act as a beacon of hope to people striving under dictatorships... The more liberal regime in Tirana serves as a beacon for separatists.*

bead /biːd/ **beads**
1 NC **Beads** are small pieces of coloured glass, wood,

or plastic with a hole through the middle which are strung together and used for jewellery or decoration. *...strings of beads.*
2 NC+SUPP A **bead** of liquid or moisture is a small drop of it. *Beads of perspiration began to form on his brow.*

beaded /biːdɪd/
1 ADJ A **beaded** dress, cushion, or other object is decorated with beads. *The women wore their traditional embroidered and beaded trousers.*
2 ADJ PRED+*with* If part of your body is **beaded** with sweat, it is covered in small drops of sweat. *His face was completely beaded with perspiration.*

beading /biːdɪŋ/ **beadings**
NUorNC **Beading** is a narrow strip of wood that is used to make a neat or decorative edge on a piece of furniture.

beady /biːdi/
ADJ **Beady** eyes are small, round, and bright. *Take your beady eyes off me!*

beagle /biːgl/ **beagles**
NC A **beagle** is a short-haired black and brown dog with long ears and short legs. *His only friend in the world is his beagle puppy, Snoopy.*

beak /biːk/ **beaks**
NC A bird's **beak** is the hard curved or pointed part of its mouth. *It has black and white feathers, and a long pointed orange beak.*

beaker /biːkə/ **beakers**
NC A **beaker** is a plastic cup used for drinking. *Many other things vary, like the size of the beaker available.*

be-all and end-all
If something is the **be-all and end-all** to you, it is the only important thing in your life, or the only important feature of a particular activity. *For some people, competing is the be-all and end-all of their running.*

beam /biːm/ **beams, beaming, beamed**
1 V If you **beam**, you smile because you are happy. *He beamed at Ralph.* ► Also NC *...a beam of satisfaction.*
2 NC+SUPP A **beam** of light is a line of light that shines from an object such as a torch or the sun. *I could see the beam of his flashlight... They used laser beams to burn tiny holes in the affected part.*
3 VOA If you **beam** a signal or information to a place, you send it by means of radio waves. *We were able to beam pictures of the riots out to Denmark... Their English language services are beamed throughout the world to carry advertising.*
4 NC A **beam** is also a long thick bar of wood, metal, or concrete, especially one which is used to support the roof of a building. *...the low oak beams.*

beam-ends
If someone is **on** their **beam-ends**, they have no money left to live on; an informal, old-fashioned expression.

bean /biːn/ **beans**
1 NC **Beans** are the pods of a climbing plant, or the seeds that the pods contain, which are eaten as a vegetable. *I'm rather partial to baked beans... Three thousand tons of beans, maize and corn are to be delivered to the villages.*
2 NC **Beans** are also the seeds of various plants which are used for different purposes, for example to make drinks such as coffee or cocoa, or to produce oil. *Brazil produces very high quality coffee beans.*
3 If someone is **full of beans**, they are very lively and full of energy and enthusiasm; an informal expression. *A spokeswoman denied the report, and said that Bani Sadr was 'full of beans'.*

bean feast, bean feasts
NC A **bean feast** is a party or lively social event where there is lots of food to eat; an informal expression.

beanpole /biːnpəʊl/ **beanpoles**
NC If you refer to someone as a **beanpole**, you mean that they are very tall and thin; an informal word.

beansprout /biːnspraʊt/ **beansprouts**
NC **Beansprouts** or **beanshoots** are small shoots grown from beans. They are eaten raw or lightly cooked, and are frequently used in Chinese cookery.

bear /beə/ **bears, bearing, bore, borne**
1 NC A **bear** is a large, strong wild animal with thick fur and sharp claws. *Two years ago, there was

nothing but the brown bear and the antelope in this area... The emblem features an appealing cuddly bear. ● See also **polar bear**.

2 VO If you **bear** something, you carry it; a formal use. *Camels and donkeys bear those goods inland... She arrived bearing a large bunch of grapes.*

3 VO If something **bears** the weight of something else, it supports the weight of that thing. *His ankle now felt strong enough to bear his weight.*

4 VO If something **bears** a particular mark or characteristic, it has that mark or characteristic. *The scene bore all the marks of a country wedding... His proposals bear a striking resemblance to those of his main opponents.*

5 VO If you **bear** something difficult, you accept it and are able to deal with it. *Their policies are putting a greater strain on the economic system than it can bear... It's clear that the delegates will bear a formidable responsibility.* ● **grin and bear it**: see grin.

6 VO To **bear** the cost of something means to pay for it. *It's unfair that some boroughs should bear all the cost.*

7 VO When a plant or tree **bears** flowers, fruit, or leaves, it produces them. *Even if the plants were attacked by insects, they usually recovered and bore fruit.*

8 VO When a woman **bears** a child, she gives birth to it. *Older, post-menopausal women can bear healthy babies.*

9 VOO If you **bear** someone a feeling such as love or hate, you feel that emotion towards them; a formal use. *He bore his children no malice.*

10 VA If you **bear** left or **bear** right when you are driving or walking along, you turn slightly in that direction. *Bear right down the south side of the church.*

● **Bear** is used in these phrases. ● If you **bring pressure** or influence **to bear** on someone, you use it to try and persuade them to do something. *The group's aim is to bring pressure to bear on Parliament to get the law changed.* ● **to bear the brunt** of something: see brunt. ● **to bear fruit**: see fruit. ● **to bear** something **in mind**: see mind. ● **to bear witness**: see witness. ● **teddy bear**: see teddy.

bear down PHRASAL VERB If something **bears down** on you, it moves quickly towards you in a threatening way. *We struggled to turn the boat as the wave bore down on us.*

bear out PHRASAL VERB If something **bears** someone **out** or **bears out** what they are saying, it supports what they are saying. *The claims are not borne out by the evidence.*

bear up PHRASAL VERB If you **bear up** when experiencing problems, you remain cheerful and show courage in spite of them. *You have to bear up under the strain.*

bear with PHRASAL VERB If you ask someone to **bear with** you, you are asking them to be patient. *I hope you'll bear with me as I explain.*

bearable /ˈbeərəbl/
ADJ If something is **bearable**, you can accept it, although it is fairly unpleasant. *The heat was just bearable.*

beard /bɪəd/ **beards**
NC A man's **beard** is the hair that grows on his chin and cheeks. *...a self-portrait, showing him with a bushy red beard.*

bearded /bɪədɪd/
ADJ ATTRIB A **bearded** man is a man who has a beard. *Bearded college students were no novelty in Cambridge.*

bearer /ˈbeərə/ **bearers**
1 NC A **bearer** is a person who carries a stretcher or coffin. *The four bearers lifted the coffin slowly.*

2 NC The **bearer** of something such as a letter, a document, or a piece of news is the person who has it in their possession, and who brings it to you. *...the bearer of the invitation... The document contains the bearer's fingerprints.*

3 NC The **bearer** of a name or title is the person who has it. *...the announcement of new party office bearers.*

bear hug, bear hugs
NC A **bear hug** is a rather rough, tight hug. *President Dos Santos was given a big bear hug by Fidel Castro.*

bearing /ˈbeərɪŋ/ **bearings**
1 If something **has a bearing on** a situation or event, it is relevant to it. *That is all in the past, it has no bearing on what is happening today.*

2 N SING+SUPP Someone's **bearing** is the way that they move or stand; a formal use. *He is straight-backed, with an imposing military bearing.*

3 If you **get** or **find** your **bearings**, you find out where you are or what you should do next. If you **lose** your **bearings**, you do not know where you are or what you should do next. *They stopped to get their bearings.*

bearskin /ˈbeəskɪn/ **bearskins**
1 NC A **bearskin** is a tall fur hat that is worn by some British soldiers on ceremonial occasions. *...dressed in red tunics and tall, black bearskin helmets.*

2 NC **Bearskin** is the skin and fur of a bear, used for example as a rug or a cover.

beast /biːst/ **beasts**
NC A **beast** is an animal, especially a large one. *They like to dress up as ghouls, ghosts, and supernatural beasts.*

beastly /ˈbiːstli/
ADJ **Beastly** means very unpleasant, unkind, or spiteful; an old-fashioned word. *He was so beastly, you've no idea... I think war is a beastly condition for anyone to be involved in.*

beat /biːt/ **beats, beating, beaten.** The form **beat** is used in the present tense and is also the past tense of the verb.

1 VO If you **beat** someone or something, you hit them very hard. *His stepfather used to beat him.*

2 VAorVO To **beat** on, at, or against something means to hit it repeatedly and forcefully. *Once you've actually stopped beating on the bars of the cage, there is freedom for negotiation... He beat the water with his hands.*

3 V-ERG When a bird or insect **beats** its wings or when its wings **beat**, its wings move up and down. *Some birds beat their wings as fast as 80 times a second.* ► Also NC *Flies can move their wings at 1000 beats per second.*

4 V When your heart or pulse **beats**, it is continually making movements with a regular rhythm. *They have confirmed that his heart did stop beating for several minutes.*

5 NC The **beat** of your heart or pulse is a single movement of it. *He could feel the beat of her heart.*

6 N SING The **beat** of a piece of music is the main rhythm that it has. *...music with a powerful, hypnotic beat.*

7 VO If you **beat** eggs, cream, or butter, you mix them thoroughly using a fork or whisk. *Beat two eggs and add them to the butter and sugar.*

8 VO If you **beat** someone in a competition or election, you defeat them or do better than them. *West Germany has won the World Cup, beating the defending champions, Argentina, by one goal to nil... The coalition won the elections, beating the mainly Fijian Government party.*

● **Beat** is used in these phrases. ● If you say 'It beats me', you are indicating that you cannot understand or explain something; an informal expression. *What beats me is where they get the money from.* ● A police officer **on the beat** is on duty, walking around the area for which they are responsible. *Crime on housing estates would be more effectively controlled by police officers on the beat.* ● If you **beat time** to a piece of music, you tap your hand or foot up and down in time with the rhythm. *You'd have this curious humming and his hand would go, beating time to the music.* ● **to beat about the bush**: see bush. ● See also **dead beat**.

beat down PHRASAL VERB 1 When the sun **beats down**, it is very hot and bright. *...superb sands, blue sky, the sun beating down.* 2 When the rain **beats down**, it rains very hard. *The soil absorbs only a fraction of the rain that beats down.* 3 When you **beat down** a person who is selling you something, you force them to accept a lower price for it. *I beat him down* *from £500 to £400.*

beat up PHRASAL VERB If someone beats a person **up**, they hit or kick the person many times so that they are badly hurt. *He told us that he had been beaten up by the police.* ● See also **beat-up**.

beaten-up
ADJ A **beaten-up** car or other object is old, battered, and in bad condition. *...a beaten-up yellow mini.*

beatific /bi:ətɪfɪk/
ADJ An idea or expression that is **beatific** shows or expresses great happiness or calmness; a literary word. *This beatific vision is that of the final stages of Communism... He swept aside the inquiry with a beatific smile.*

beatify /biætɪfaɪ/ **beatifies, beatifying, beatified**
VO To **beatify** a dead person means to declare formally in a church ceremony that they are a blessed person, usually as the first step in making them a saint. *...attempts to have the head of state beatified.*

beating /bi:tɪŋ/ **beatings**
1 NC If you are given a **beating**, you are hit hard many times. *They allege torture by beatings, electric shocks, and sexual abuse.*
2 N SING If a team or political party takes a **beating**, it is defeated by a large amount in a competition or election. *Pakistan's only national party has taken a severe beating.*

beating up, beatings up
NC A **beating up** is an attack on someone in which they are hit and kicked so that they are very badly hurt. *They gave him an awful beating up.*

beatnik /bi:tnɪk/ **beatniks**
NC Young people in the late 1950's who wore strange clothes and had unconventional beliefs were referred to as **beatniks**. *The beatniks admired, above all, the French poet Rimbaud.*

Beatrix, Queen of the Netherlands /bi:ətrɪks/
Queen Beatrix succeeded to the throne of the Netherlands in 1980, on the abdication of her mother, Queen Juliana. Born: 1938.

beat-up
ADJ ATTRIB A **beat-up** car, piece of equipment, or other object is old, battered, and in bad condition; an informal word. *...my beat-up 1958 Buick.*

beaut /bju:t/ **beauts**
NC You refer to something as a **beaut** when you think it is very good; an informal word. *That shot was a real beaut.*

beauteous /bju:tiəs/
ADJ **Beauteous** means the same as **beautiful**; a literary word.

beautician /bju:tɪʃn/ **beauticians**
NC A **beautician** is a person whose job is giving people beauty treatments such as cutting and polishing their nails or treating their skin. *The wife, a beautician aptly named Jewel, is trying to sue her husband.*

beautiful /bju:tɪfl/
1 ADJ You say that someone or something is **beautiful** when you find them very attractive or pleasant. *...a very beautiful girl... The table looked beautiful.*
◆ **beautifully** ADV *...beautifully dressed young men.*
2 ADJ You can describe something that someone does as **beautiful** when they do it very skilfully. *It was a beautiful shot.* ◆ **beautifully** ADV *Doesn't he play the piano beautifully?*

beautify /bju:tɪfaɪ/ **beautifies, beautifying, beautified**
VO If you **beautify** something, you make it look more beautiful. *The avenue has been beautified by a spectacular fountain.* ◆ **beautification** /bju:tɪfɪkeɪʃn/
NU *She said that the beautification was unnecessary because Kaduna is already a beautiful place.*

beauty /bju:ti/ **beauties**
1 NU **Beauty** is the state or quality of being beautiful. *Her beauty grew in her old age... She learned to appreciate beauty.*
2 NC A **beauty** is a beautiful woman. *Vita had turned into a beauty.*
3 NC+SUPP The **beauties** of something are its attractive qualities or features. *...the beauties of nature.*
4 N SING+SUPP If you say that a particular feature is the **beauty** of something, you mean that this feature is

what makes the thing so good. *That's the beauty of the plan—it's so simple.*
5 N+N **Beauty** is used to describe people, products, and activities that are concerned with making women look attractive. *...beauty products. ...the magazine's beauty editor.*

beauty contest, beauty contests
NC A **beauty contest** is a competition in which a panel of judges decides which of the entrants is the most beautiful. *...a former finalist in a Miss South Africa beauty contest... Maybe the next beauty contest will be for men?*

beauty parlour, beauty parlours
NC A **beauty parlour** is the same as a **beauty salon**; an old-fashioned expression.

beauty queen, beauty queens
NC A **beauty queen** is a woman who has won a beauty contest. *His resignation came after reports linking him with a former beauty queen.*

beauty salon, beauty salons
NC A **beauty salon** is a place where women can go for treatment to make them look more beautiful. *Women may visit one of the many Vietnamese-run beauty salons.*

beauty sleep
NU Your **beauty sleep** is sleep that you have when you go to bed early, which is considered to help you stay looking young and beautiful; an informal expression often used humorously. *You've had your beauty sleep?*

beauty spot, beauty spots
NC A **beauty spot** is a place that is popular because of its beautiful countryside. *Britain's tourist industry recorded another success story last year as visitors flocked to English beauty spots and the countryside.*

beaver /bi:və/ **beavers, beavering, beavered**
NC A **beaver** is a furry animal like a large rat with a big flat tail. *They exterminated the beaver and the buffalo without a thought for tomorrow.*

beaver away PHRASAL VERB If you **are beavering away** at something, you are working very hard at it; an informal expression. *We met a semi-retired motorcycle engineer beavering away in his garage at home.*

becalm /bɪkɑ:md/ **becalms, becalming, becalmed**
VO If a sailing ship is **becalmed**, it is unable to move because there is no wind. *Light winds virtually becalmed the leaders as they approached the finish.*

became /bɪkeɪm/
Became is the past tense of **become**.

because /bɪkəz, bɪkɒz/
1 CONJ You use **because** to introduce a subordinate clause which gives a reason. *I couldn't see Helen's expression, because her head was turned.*
2 PREP You also use **because of** at the beginning of a prepositional phrase which gives a reason. *He retired last month because of illness.*

beck /bek/
If you are **at someone's beck and call**, you are constantly available and ready to do what they ask; used showing disapproval. *China has never been completely at the beck and call of her socialist allies.*

beckon /bekən/ **beckons, beckoning, beckoned**
1 V+to, V, or VO If you **beckon** to someone, you signal to them to come to you. *Claus beckoned to him excitedly... The press officer beckoned, and I came into the office... He beckoned me to follow him.*
2 VO or V If something **beckons** you, it is so attractive that you feel you must become involved in it. *Restaurants beckoned late diners into the area... The world of Islam beckoned, and she went willingly.*

become /bɪkʌm/ **becomes, becoming, became** The form **become** is used in the present tense and is also the past participle.
1 VC If something **becomes** a particular thing, it starts being that thing. *The smell became stronger and stronger... It became clear that the Conservatives were not going to win... We became good friends at once.*
2 If you wonder **what has become of** someone or something, you notice that they have not been seen or heard of for a long time, and you wonder what has

happened to them. *Mr Hurd asked what had become of the former strong moral influence of the Church.*

becoming /bɪkʌmɪŋ/
ADJ A piece of clothing, a colour, or a hairstyle that is **becoming** makes the person who is wearing it look attractive; an old-fashioned word. *She was dressed in an extremely becoming trouser suit.*

becquerel /bɛkərel/ **becquerels**
NC A **becquerel** is a unit that is used for measuring the radioactivity of a substance. *Radioactivity in beef has doubled this year to around 3,000 becquerels per kilo.*

bed /bɛd/ **beds**
1 NCorNU A **bed** is a piece of furniture that you lie on when you sleep. *He sat down on the bed... Shamir was working normally from his hospital bed... He went to bed at ten.*
2 NC You can use **bed** to refer to the number of people a place such as a hospital or hotel is able to accommodate overnight. *The hospice has nine beds, and already there's a waiting list... Twenty thousand mental hospital beds have been closed in the last ten years.*
3 NU **Bed** is also used to refer to sexual activity. For example, if someone is in **bed** with someone else, they are having sex. *I like you, but I have no intention of going to bed with you... One in ten eighteen year olds admits to being bored in bed.*
4 NC+SUPP A flower **bed** is an area of earth in which you grow plants. *The fixed blade is difficult to manoeuvre around a flower bed... We grew the corn on raised beds.*
5 NC+SUPP The sea **bed** or a river **bed** is the ground at the bottom of the sea or of a river. *Record rains have flooded normally dry river beds over the last few weeks. ...a prepared trench on the estuary bed.*
bed down PHRASAL VERB If you **bed down** somewhere, you sleep there for the night, not in your own bed. *They live in illegal properties, or they bed down with friends.*

bed and breakfast
NU **Bed and breakfast** is a system of accommodation in a hotel or guest house in which you pay for a room for the night and for breakfast the following morning. *...£15.50 a night for bed and breakfast... Many of them will spend Christmas in the squalor of bed and breakfast hotels.*

bed-bath, bed-baths
NC A **bed-bath** is a thorough wash given to someone who is ill in bed. *Patients just see us as a source of medicines, giving them bed-baths and things.*

bedbug /bɛdbʌg/ **bedbugs**
NC A **bedbug** is a small, round insect which lives in dirty houses. **Bedbugs** bite people and suck their blood. *Infectious diseases spread quickly, and lice, fleas, and bedbugs are common.*

bedclothes /bɛdkləʊðz/
N PL **Bedclothes** are the sheets and covers which you put over you when you get into bed. *...hands pulling off the bedclothes.*

bedding /bɛdɪŋ/
NU **Bedding** is sheets, blankets, and other covers used on beds. *She changed the bedding. ...carrying bundles of bedding for the hunger strikers.*

bedding plant, bedding plants
NC A **bedding plant** is a flowering plant which is taken out of the flower bed when it has finished flowering. *They've been doing some more work on it as a bedding plant.*

bedeck /bɪdɛk/ **bedecks, bedecking, bedecked**
VO If a place is **bedecked** with things, those things are arranged all over it in a pretty, decorative way. *The streets were bedecked in the team's colours of blue and yellow... A few multi-coloured flags bedecked Moscow's lamp posts.*

bedevil /bɪdɛvl/ **bedevils, bedevilling, bedevilled;** spelt **bedeviling, bedeviled** in American English.
VO If you **are bedevilled** by something unpleasant, it causes you a lot of problems; a formal word. *He has been bedevilled by injuries... Constitutional problems bedevilled his five years in office.*

bedfellow /bɛdfeləʊ/ **bedfellows**
NC You refer to two people or things as **bedfellows** when they have become associated with each other, especially when you did not expect this. *The oddest of enemies might become bedfellows... The two parties were never natural bedfellows.*

bedlam /bɛdləm/
NU If you say that a place or situation is **bedlam**, you mean that it is very noisy and disorderly. *There are often scenes of bedlam filled with yelling and screaming brokers trying to buy or sell.*

bed linen
NU **Bed linen** is sheets and pillowcases. *White bed linen always looks crispest.*

Bedouin /bɛduɪn/ **Bedouins**. The plural form can be either **Bedouins** or **Bedouin**.
NC A **Bedouin** is a member of the nomadic tribes of the North African, Syrian, and Arabian deserts. *The Bedouin came with their dark muffled faces. ...the Bedouin tribes.*

bedpan /bɛdpæn/ **bedpans**
NC A **bedpan** is a shallow bowl which people use as a toilet when they are too ill to get out of bed.

bedraggled /bɪdrægld/
ADJ Someone or something that is **bedraggled** is untidy and disorderly, because they have got wet or dirty. *He described the soldiers as tired, bedraggled, and dejected.*

bedridden /bɛdrɪdn/
ADJ Someone who is **bedridden** is so ill or disabled that they cannot get out of bed. *She came via Hong Kong to visit her bedridden father.*

bedrock /bɛdrɒk/
N SING+SUPP The **bedrock** of something is all the principles, ideas, or facts on which it is based. *The Act reaffirmed family values as the moral bedrock of the nation.*

bedroom /bɛdruːm, bɛdrʊm/ **bedrooms**
NC A **bedroom** is a room which is used for sleeping in. *Upstairs, the children have their own bedrooms.*

bedside /bɛdsaɪd/
N SING Your **bedside** is the area beside your bed. *An excellent breakfast had been left on the tray by his bedside. ...a bedside light.*

bedside manner
N SING A doctor's **bedside manner** is the way in which he or she talks to a patient, and the extent to which this is friendly and reassuring. *She has a lovely bedside manner.*

bedsit /bɛdsɪt/ **bedsits**
NC A **bedsit** is a single furnished room in a house, which you rent and in which you live and sleep. *You could get a grant to pay a deposit on independent accommodation, for example, a bedsit.*

bedspread /bɛdspred/ **bedspreads**
NC A **bedspread** is a decorative cover which is put over a bed.

bedstead /bɛdsted/ **bedsteads**
NC A **bedstead** is the metal or wooden frame of an old-fashioned bed. *...bits of old iron bedsteads.*

bedtime /bɛdtaɪm/ **bedtimes**
NUorNC Your **bedtime** is the time when you usually go to bed. *They sometimes react by being frightened at bedtime... Bedtimes are getting later, with one in ten children staying up till 11.00 pm. ...bedtime stories.*

bee /biː/ **bees**
NC A **bee** is a yellow and black insect that makes a buzzing noise as it flies. Bees make honey, and live in large groups. *They stood waving their hands, as if chasing away a swarm of bees.* ● If you **have a bee in your bonnet**, you are so enthusiastic or worried about something that you keep talking about it. *I've the greatest respect and affection for Zoe, but that doesn't mean that she doesn't get bees in her bonnet.*

beech /biːtʃ/ **beeches**
NCorNU A **beech** is a tree which has dark green leaves and a smooth grey trunk. The wood obtained from this tree is also called **beech**. *A third of the country's native trees like oak, yew, and beech, were either sick or dying. ...alarm over damage to the deciduous beech trees.*

beef /biːf/ beefs, beefing, beefed
NU Beef is the meat of a cow, bull, or ox. ...*exports such as bananas, rum, and beef.* ...*a good joint of beef.*
beef up PHRASAL VERB If you **beef** something **up**, you strengthen it or make it more interesting, significant, or important. *They had beefed up the evening news programme.* ...*starting with something timid and vapid which had to be beefed up later.* ◆ **beefed up**
ADJ ATTRIB *The city attorney, James Hahn, announced a beefed up police presence.*

beefburger /biːfbɜːgə/ beefburgers
NC A **beefburger** is the same as a **hamburger**. *The best beefburgers are made from lean, minced steak.*

beef cattle
N PL **Beef cattle** are cattle which are bred to provide meat. ...*the practice of feeding or injecting beef cattle with growth hormones.*

Beefeater /biːfiːtə/ Beefeaters
NC A **Beefeater** is a guard at the Tower of London, with a uniform in the style of the sixteenth century.

beefsteak /biːfsteɪk/
NU **Beefsteak** is beef without very much fat on it.

beefy /biːfi/
ADJ A **beefy** man is strong and muscular; an informal word. *In the last few weeks we saw some very beefy bodyguards appearing wherever Duke was.*

beehive /biːhaɪv/ beehives
NC A **beehive** is a place where bees are kept so that someone can collect the honey that they produce. ...*how to make a low-cost, modern beehive using sticks and mud.*

bee-keeper, bee-keepers
NC A **bee-keeper** is someone who keeps bees in order to collect the honey that they produce. *They have a lot of information for experienced bee-keepers too.*

bee-keeping
NU **Bee-keeping** is the activity of keeping bees in order to collect the honey that they produce. ...*bee-keeping as a money-making project.*

beeline /biːlaɪn/
If you **make a beeline for** a place, you go to it as quickly and as directly as possible; an informal expression. *Three of them made a beeline for the pub.*

been /bɪn, biːn, bɪn/
1 **Been** is the past participle of **be**.
2 PAST PARTICIPLE You use **been** after the auxiliaries 'has', 'have', and 'had' to say that someone has gone to a place, or has visited it, when they are no longer there. *Has the milkman been yet?*... *I haven't been to Birmingham.*

beep /biːp/ beeps, beeping, beeped
NC A **beep** is a fairly short, harsh sound like that made by a car horn or the engaged tone of a telephone. *This could soon be replaced by an electronic beep.* ► Also V or VO *A computer screen behind his desk beeped intermittently...* *Thousands take to the streets to wave their flags and beep their horns.*

beer /bɪə/ beers
1 N MASS **Beer** is a bitter alcoholic drink made from grain. *We drank a few pints of beer.*
2 NC A **beer** is a glass, bottle, or can containing beer. *He'd had two beers.*

beer belly, beer bellies
NC If someone has a **beer belly** or a **beer gut**, they have a big fat stomach because they regularly drink a lot of beer; an informal expression.

beeswax /biːzwæks/
NU **Beeswax** is wax that is made by bees. It is used especially for making candles and furniture polish. ...*beeswax candles.*

beet /biːt/
1 NU **Beet** is a root vegetable used as food for animals. *They talked endlessly about beet and cattle feed...* *Heavy losses were expected in the production of grain, beet, rape and hay.*
2 NC A **beet** is the same as a **beetroot**; used in American English. *It comes with a garnish of red beets, white cottage cheese and blueberries.* ...*a plate of pickled beets.*
3 NU **Beet** is the same as sugar beet. *Prices cannot be allowed to fall, otherwise we'd have neither cane nor beet industries.*

beetle /biːtl/ beetles
NC A **beetle** is an insect with a hard covering to its body. *When the maize is eaten, the beetle moves into the woodwork of a store and sits and waits... Research workers have been trying out ways of poisoning caterpillars and beetles without harming other wildlife.*

beetroot /biːtruːt/ beetroots
NU or NC **Beetroot** is a dark red root vegetable which can be cooked or pickled, and eaten in salads.

beet sugar
NU **Beet sugar** is the sugar that is obtained from sugar beet. *The grape juice was fortified with beet sugar to produce a better wine... The EC decision to increase production of beet sugar.*

befall /bɪfɔːl/ befalls, befalling, befell, befallen
VO If something bad or unlucky **befalls** you, it happens to you; a literary word. *She knew no harm would ever befall her.*

befit /bɪfɪt/ befits, befitting, befitted
VO If something **befits** a person or thing, it is suitable for them or is expected of them; a formal word. *He was courteous, as befitted a young man speaking to an older man.*

befitting /bɪfɪtɪŋ/
ADJ or PREP Something that is **befitting** is appropriate or proper for someone or something. *He went on to say that the Indian Army would give a befitting reply to anyone who attacked it... The office was furnished in streamlined stainless steel and glass, as befitting the director's image.*

before /bɪfɔː/
1 PREP or CONJ If something happens **before** a time or event, it happens earlier than that time or event. *We arrived just before two o'clock... Can I see you before you go, Helen?... A dozen ideas were considered before he decided on this plan.*
2 ADJ after N If something happened the day **before**, it happened during the previous day. *It had rained the night before.*
3 ADV If someone has done something **before**, they have done it on a previous occasion. *Have you been to Greece before?*
4 PREP If someone is **before** something, they are in front of it; a formal use. *He stood before the door to the cellar... He will appear before the magistrate.*
5 PREP When you have a task or difficult situation **before** you, you have to deal with it. *Let's get started. I have a difficult job before me.*

beforehand /bɪfɔːhænd/
ADV If you do something **beforehand**, you do it earlier than a particular event. *Kathleen got married without telling anyone beforehand.*

befriend /bɪfrend/ befriends, befriending, befriended
VO If you **befriend** someone, you make friends with them. *I befriended a lonely little boy in the village.*

befuddle /bɪfʌdl/ befuddles, befuddling, befuddled
VO If something **befuddles** you, it confuses you. *His words were sufficient to befuddle the girls.*

beg /beg/ begs, begging, begged
1 VO+to-INF, V+for, or V-QUOTE If you **beg** someone to do something, you ask them anxiously or eagerly to do it. *I begged him to stay, but he wouldn't... He begged for help... 'Tell me all the news,' I begged.*
2 V or VO When someone **begs**, they ask people to give them food or money because they are poor. ...*children in the streets begging for money... Kids were begging milk from the governor.*
3 I **beg your pardon**: see **pardon**.

began /bɪgæn/
Began is the past tense of **begin**.

beget /bɪget/ begets, begetting, begot, begotten
VO To **beget** something means to cause it to happen or be created; a formal word. *Malnutrition begets disease.* ...*a vicious circle in which freedom begets unrest, which the leadership then feels it must quell.*

beggar /begə/ beggars
NC A **beggar** is someone who lives by asking people for money or food. *Beggars and homeless children appeared on the streets of the capital.*

beggarly /bɛgəli/
ADJ A sum of money that is **beggarly** is very small and not at all generous. *He only received a miserly, beggarly, begrudging pittance.*

begin /bɪgɪn/, begins, beginning, began, begun
1 V+to-INF or V+ING If you **begin** to do something, you start doing it. *The actors began to rehearse a scene... I began eating the grapes.*
2 V or V-ERG When something **begins** or when you **begin** it, it takes place from a particular time onwards. *The concerts begin at 8 pm... Malcolm began his speech... They began by looking at the problems.*
3 V A You say that a place or region **begins** somewhere when you are indicating where its edges are. *The ocean begins here.*
4 You use **to begin with** to talk about the first event or stage in a process, or to introduce the first thing you want to say. *To begin with, they just take your name and address.*

beginner /bɪgɪnə/ beginners
NC A **beginner** is someone who has just started learning to do something and cannot do it well yet. *This is the sort of thing that beginners write.*

beginning /bɪgɪnɪŋ/ beginnings
1 NC The **beginning** or the **beginnings** of something is the first part of it. *I say this at the beginning of my book. ...the beginnings of a new relationship.*
2 N SING The **beginning** of a period of time is when it starts. *I came back at the beginning of the term... The number had increased by the beginning of the following year.*

begot /bɪgɒt/
Begot is the past tense of **beget**.

begotten /bɪgɒtn/
Begotten is the past participle of **beget**.

begrudge /bɪgrʌdʒ/ begrudges, begrudging, begrudged
V OO If you say that you do not **begrudge** someone something, you mean that you do not feel angry, upset, or jealous that they have got it. *I do not begrudge her that happiness.*

beguile /bɪgaɪl/ beguiles, beguiling, beguiled
V O If someone or something **beguiles** you, they trick you into doing something stupid, especially by making it seem attractive. *He used his newspapers to beguile the readers into buying shares in his company.*

beguiling /bɪgaɪlɪŋ/
ADJ Something that is **beguiling** seems attractive, but may be dangerous or harmful. *It is beguiling to think this is the threshold of a new political order... She has a beguiling, haunting, doll's face.*

begun /bɪgʌn/
Begun is the past participle of **begin**.

behalf /bɪhɑːf/
If someone does something **on** your **behalf**, they do it as your representative. *Wilkins spoke on behalf of the Labour Party.*

behave /bɪheɪv/ behaves, behaving, behaved
1 V A If you **behave** in a particular way, you do things in that way. *In New York, he had behaved in a very strange way... You are behaving like a silly child.*
2 V-REFL or V If you **behave** yourself, you act in the way that people think is correct and proper. *He's old enough to behave himself... Their startled boyfriends got warnings to behave.*

behaviour /bɪheɪvjə/; spelt **behavior** in American English.
1 NU A person's **behaviour** is the way they behave. *I had been puzzled by his behaviour. ...the obstinate behaviour of a small child.*
2 NU The **behaviour** of something is the way in which it acts, functions, or changes. *...the behaviour of the metal as we heat it.*

behaviourism /bɪheɪvjərɪzəm/
NU **Behaviourism** is the belief that some psychologists have that the only valid way of understanding the psychology of people and animals is to observe how they behave.

behead /bɪhɛd/ beheads, beheading, beheaded
V O If someone is **beheaded**, their head is cut off. *A convicted murderer was beheaded after noon prayers yesterday.*

beheld /bɪhɛld/
Beheld is the past tense and past participle of **behold**.

behind /bɪhaɪnd/ behinds
1 PREP or ADV If you are **behind** a thing or person, you are facing the back of that thing or person. *There were two boys sitting behind me... Joe was limping along behind his wife... He followed a few paces behind.*
2 ADV If you stay **behind**, you remain in a place after other people have gone. *Orville stayed behind to do test flights for the U.S. military.*
3 ADV If you leave something **behind**, you do not take it with you when you go. *They'd been forced to leave behind their businesses and possessions.*
4 ADV or PREP When someone or something is **behind**, they are delayed or are making less progress than other people think they should. *I got more and more behind... The bus was badly behind schedule.*
5 PREP or ADV If an experience is **behind** you, it is finished. *...now that the war is behind us... We must leave adolescence behind and grow up.*
6 PREP The people, reasons, or events **behind** a situation are the causes of it or are responsible for it. *These were the reasons behind Macleod's statement. ...the man behind the modernizing of the station.*
7 PREP If you are **behind** someone, you support them. *The country was behind the President.*
8 NC Your **behind** is the part of your body that you sit on.

behindhand /bɪhaɪndhænd/
ADJ If someone is **behindhand**, they have been delayed or have made less progress in their work than they or other people think they should. *I'm a bit behindhand with my work.*

behold /bɪhəʊld/ beholds, beholding, beheld
V O If you **behold** someone or something, you look at them; a literary word. *She was a terrible sight to behold.*

beholden /bɪhəʊldən/
ADJ PRED If you are **beholden** to someone, you feel that you have a duty to them because they have helped you; a formal word. *I am beholden to you, John, for looking after us.*

beholder /bɪhəʊldə/ beholders
NC The **beholder** of something is the person looking at it; an old-fashioned word. *The picture was very pleasing to beholders.*

beige /beɪʒ/
ADJ Something that is **beige** is pale brown. *He's now more soberly dressed in a brown shirt and beige trousers.*

Beijing /beɪdʒɪŋ/ See **Peking**.

being, beings; pronounced /biːɪŋ, bɪŋ/ for the meaning in paragraph 1, and /biːɪŋ/ for the meanings in paragraphs 2, 3, and 4.
1 Being is the present participle of **be**.
2 Something that is **in being** exists. *...laws already in being... The Polytechnic came into being in 1971.*
3 NC You can refer to any real or imaginary creature as a **being**; a literary use. *...beings from outer space.*
● See also **human being**.
4 **for the time being**: see **time**.

Beirut /beɪruːt/
Beirut is the capital of Lebanon and its largest city. Population: 1,500,000 (1975).

Belarus /bɛlærʊs/ See **Byelorussia**.

belated /bɪleɪtɪd/
ADJ ATTRIB A **belated** action happens later than it should have done; a formal word. *Please accept my belated thanks for your kind gift.* ◆ **belatedly** ADV *Bill belatedly agreed to call in the police.*

Belau /bəlaʊ/
The **Republic of Belau**, also called Palau, is a United Nations trusteeship, administered by the United States, consisting of over 200 islands in the Caroline chain in the Pacific. The islands were occupied by Germany from 1899 until the First World War, and then governed by Japan until the Second World War. The islands were captured by US forces in 1944 and 1945. They became the Republic of Belau in 1981. In 1982 Belau signed a Compact of Free Association with the United States, but the treaty has not yet come into

effect. Belau exports tuna and copra. Tourism is an important industry. Large foreign debts are a serious economic problem. ◆ **Belauan** /bəlaʊən/ N, ADJ ▪ *religion:* Christianity (mainly Roman Catholic) ▪ *language:* Belauan (official), English ▪ *currency:* US dollar ▪ *capital:* Koror ▪ *population:* 15,000 (1990) ▪ *size:* 508 square kilometres.

belch /belt∫/ **belches, belching, belched**
1 v If someone **belches**, they make a sudden noise in their throat because air has risen up from their stomach. *The baby drank his milk and belched.* ▶ Also NC *'Amazing,' said Brody, stifling a belch.*
2 v Aor VO If something **belches** out smoke, steam, or other gases, it releases them into the air in large quantities. *...out-of-date factories belching out noxious gases, so bad that you can taste the pollution. ...the ship began taking on water and belching black smoke.*

beleaguered /bəliːgəd/
ADJ ATTRIB A **beleaguered** person is experiencing a lot of difficulties, problems, or criticism; a formal word. *The beleaguered prime minister explained this to an angry crowd.*

belfry /belfri/ **belfries**
NC The **belfry** of a church is the top part of the tower, where the bells are. *...an incident in which a vandal scaled the belfry of the local church.*

Belgium /beldʒəm/
The **Kingdom of Belgium** is a country in north-west Europe. It was occupied by Germany from 1940 to 1944. It is a member of the European Community and NATO. Dutch is spoken in the north of Belgium, called Flanders. French is spoken in the south of the country, called Wallonia. King Baudouin succeeded his father, King Léopold III, in 1951. Jean-Luc Dehaene, of the Flemish Christian Social Party (CVP), became Prime Minister in 1992. Belgium exports steel, chemicals, and textiles. ◆ **Belgian** /beldʒən/ N, ADJ
▪ *per capita GNP:* US$16,390 ▪ *religion:* Christianity (mainly Roman Catholic) ▪ *language:* Dutch, French ▪ *currency:* franc ▪ *capital:* Brussels ▪ *population:* 10 million (1988) ▪ *size:* 30,519 square kilometres.

Belgrade /belgreɪd/
Belgrade is the capital and largest city of Serbia, and was formerly the capital of Yugoslavia. Population: 1,470,000 (1981).

belie /bɪlaɪ/ **belies, belying, belied;** a formal word.
1 vo If one thing **belies** another, it makes the other thing seem very surprising. *The young face belied the grey hair above it.*
2 vo You can also say that something **belies** another when it proves that the other thing is not genuine or true. *Their social attitudes belie their words.*

belief /bɪliːf/ **beliefs**
NCor NU **Belief** is a feeling of certainty that something exists, is true, or is good. *...belief in God... It is my belief that more people could have been helped. ...religious beliefs.*

believable /bɪliːvəbl/
ADJ Something that is **believable** makes you think that it could be true or real. *...the only believable explanation for the disappearance of the plane.*

believe /bɪliːv/ **believes, believing, believed**
1 V-REPORT, V OC, or V O+to-INF If you **believe** that something is true, you think that it is true. *It is believed that two prisoners have escaped... I couldn't believe what I had heard... We believed him dead... I believed him to be right.*
2 vo If you **believe** someone, you accept that they are telling the truth. *I didn't believe him... Don't believe a word he says.*
3 v+in If you **believe** in things such as God, fairies, or miracles, you are sure that they exist or happen. *I don't believe in ghosts.*
4 v+in If you **believe** in something, you are in favour of it because you think it is good or right. *...all those who believe in democracy... He did not believe in educating women.*

believer /bɪliːvə/ **believers**
1 NC If you are a **believer** in something, you think that it is good or right. *...the true believer in democracy... Bob is a great believer in jogging.*
2 NC A **believer** is someone who is sure that their

religion is true. *Of course you, as a believer, try to convert others?*

Belisha beacon /bəliːʃə biːkən/ **Belisha beacons**
NC A **Belisha beacon** is a post with a round orange light on top which flashes on and off. Belisha beacons are used at zebra crossings, to warn motorists that people may be crossing the road there.

belittle /bɪlɪtl/ **belittles, belittling, belittled**
vo If you **belittle** someone or something, you make them seem unimportant or not very good. *The press gave the election no publicity and belittled its significance... Don't think I'm trying to belittle Turner. He was a genius.*

Belize /bəliːz/
Belize is a country in Central America, formerly known as British Honduras. It was a British colony from the 17th century until it became independent in 1981. Guatemala has laid claim to parts of Belize since 1821. Belize is a member of the Commonwealth and of the Organization of American States. George Price, of the People's United Party (PUP), became Prime Minister in 1989. Belize exports sugar, molasses, fruit, clothing, and wood. Cannabis is illegally exported. Tourism is a growing industry. ◆ **Belizean** /bəliːziən/ N, ADJ
▪ *per capita GNP:* US$1,460 ▪ *religion:* Christianity ▪ *language:* English (official), Spanish ▪ *currency:* dollar ▪ *capital:* Belmopan ▪ *largest city:* Belize City ▪ *population:* 182,000 (1988) ▪ *size:* 22,965 square kilometres.

Belize City /bəliːz sɪti/
Belize City is the largest city of Belize and its former capital. Population: 50,000 (1988).

bell /bel/ **bells**
1 NC A **bell** is a device that makes a ringing sound which is used to attract people's attention. *He approached the front door and rang the bell.*
2 NC A **bell** is also a hollow metal object shaped like a cup which has a piece hanging inside it that hits the sides and makes a sound. *In the distance a church bell was ringing.*
3 If you say that something **rings a bell**, you mean that it reminds you of something else, but you cannot remember exactly what; an informal expression. *The name rings a bell.*

belladonna /belədɒnə/
NU **Belladonna** is a drug obtained from the leaves and roots of the deadly nightshade.

bell-bottomed /belbɒtəmd/
ADJ **Bell-bottomed** trousers are very wide at the bottom of the leg, near your feet.

bellboy /belbɔɪ/ **bellboys**
NC A **bellboy** is a man or boy who works in a hotel, carrying bags or bringing things to the guests' rooms. *The bellboy and the head waiter still have their purple tunics on.*

belle /bel/ **belles**
NC A **belle** is a beautiful woman, especially the most beautiful woman at a party or in a group; an old-fashioned word. *She has become the reigning belle.*

bellhop /belhɒp/ **bellhops**
NC A **bellhop** is the same as a bellboy; used in American English.

bellicose /belɪkəʊs/
ADJ Someone who is **bellicose** is aggressive and likely to start an argument or a fight; a literary word. *...bellicose governments. ...bellicose pronouncements by public men.*

belligerence /bəlɪdʒərəns/
NU **Belligerence** is the quality of being hostile and aggressive. *They watched him, their eyes heavy with belligerence.*

belligerent /bəlɪdʒərənt/ **belligerents**
1 ADJ **Belligerent** people are eager to defend themselves and their opinions in an aggressive or forceful way. *Not even the belligerent Leggett was willing to face that mob.* ◆ **belligerently** ADV *Mr Kidley looked at him belligerently.*
2 NC A **belligerent** is a person or country that is fighting in a war; a formal use. *...the halting of arms supplies to all belligerents.*

bellow /bɛləʊ/ bellows, bellowing, bellowed
1 V, V-QUOTE, or V O If someone **bellows**, they shout in a loud, deep voice. *The president bellowed with laughter... 'Thirty-two!' bellowed Mrs Pringle... Lionel bellowed his contribution from across the room.* ▸ Also NC *He raised his voice to a bellow.*
2 V When an animal **bellows**, it makes a loud, deep sound. *The cow charged across the farmyard with the bull bellowing after it.*
3 NC A **bellows** is a device used for blowing air into a fire in order to make it burn more fiercely. The plural is also 'bellows'. *The bellows and the whole equipment to do the blacksmithing just wasn't there.*

bell push, bell pushes
NC A **bell push** is a button that you press to cause a bell to ring, usually on the front door of a building.

bell-ringing
NU **Bell-ringing** is the activity of ringing church bells. *...the dying art of bell-ringing.*

belly /bɛli/ bellies
1 NC Your **belly** is your stomach. *...a child with a swollen belly.*
2 NC The **belly** of an animal is the lower part of its body. *...lions creeping on their bellies.*

bellyache /bɛlieɪk/ bellyaches, bellyaching, bellyached; an informal word.
1 NCorNU A **bellyache** is a pain inside your abdomen, especially in your stomach. *He was moaning and groaning about his bellyache before he dropped off.*
2 V If you say that someone is **bellyaching**, you mean they are complaining loudly and frequently about something, often in an unreasonable or unfair way. *If only mother would stop bellyaching!*

belly button, belly buttons
NC Children sometimes refer to their navel as their **belly button**.

belly dance, belly dances
NC A **belly dance** is a Middle Eastern dance performed by women, in which the dancer moves her hips and abdomen vigorously.

belly dancer, belly dancers
NC A **belly dancer** is a woman who performs a belly dance.

belly flop, belly flops
NC A **belly flop** is an unskilful dive in which the whole of the front of your body hits the water at the same time; an informal expression.

bellyful /bɛlifʊl/
If you say that you have **had a bellyful of** something, you mean that you have had too much of it and don't want any more; an informal expression. *Their only function is killing and I've had a bellyful of that.*

belly laugh, belly laughs
NC A **belly laugh** is a very loud, deep laugh. *Belly laughs provide not only stress relief, but also benefit almost every muscle in the body.*

Belmopan /bɛlməʊpæn/
Belmopan is the capital of Belize and its fifth largest town. Population: 4,500 (1988).

belong /bɪlɒŋ/ belongs, belonging, belonged
1 V+to If something **belongs** to you, you own it or it is yours. *The land belongs to a big family. ...a myth belonging to some tribe in Western Australia.*
2 V+to If someone or something **belongs** to a particular group, they are a member of that group. *She belongs to the Labour Party.*
3 V A or V If a person or thing **belongs** in a particular place, that is where they should be. *...the feeling of being away from the battlefront, where they say they belong... The plates don't belong in that cupboard... Although from a prominent English family, Philby felt he didn't belong.*

belongings /bɪlɒŋɪŋz/
N PL Your **belongings** are the things that you own and that you have with you or have in your house. *She was tidying up her belongings.*

beloved /bɪlʌvɪd/; also pronounced /bɪlʌvd/ when used after a noun or after the verb 'be'.
ADJ A **beloved** person, thing, or place is one that you feel great affection for. *He withdrew to his beloved Kent.*

below /bɪləʊ/
1 PREP or ADV If something is **below** something else, it is in a lower position. *The sun had just sunk below the horizon... Their office is on the floor below... The fish attacked from below.*
2 PREP If something is **below** a particular amount, rate, or level, it is less than that amount, rate, or level. *The temperature was below freezing... Their reading ability is below average.*
3 ADV You use **below** in a piece of writing to refer to something that is mentioned later. *Get legal advice on how to do this (see below).*

belt /bɛlt/ belts, belting, belted
1 NC A **belt** is a strip of leather or cloth that you fasten round your waist. *The sensor is contained in the buckle of the belt.* ● See also **safety belt**, **seat-belt**.
2 NC A **belt** is also a circular strip of rubber used in machines to drive moving parts or to move objects along. *A belt snapped in the vacuum cleaner.* ● See also **conveyor belt**.
3 NC+SUPP A **belt** of land or sea is a long, narrow area of it that has some special feature. *...the cotton belt of the USA.*
4 If you have to **tighten your belt**, you have less money to spend than you are used to. *The Philippines is under pressure from the IMF and the World Bank to tighten its belt.* ● See also **belt-tightening**.
5 VO If someone **belts** you, they hit you very hard; an informal use.
6 VA If you **belt** somewhere, you move or travel there very fast; an informal use. *I came belting out of the woods.*

belt-tightening
NU If you need to do some **belt-tightening**, you must spend less money and manage without things, because you have less money than you used to have. *The Bangladeshi government has called for severe belt-tightening... To engineer a recovery will require further belt-tightening and austerity.*

bemoan /bɪməʊn/ bemoans, bemoaning, bemoaned
VO If you **bemoan** something, you express sorrow or dissatisfaction about it; a formal word. *The farmer bemoaned his loss.*

bemused /bɪmjuːzd/
ADJ If you are **bemused**, you are slightly puzzled or confused. *Many people seemed bemused at the choices facing them.*

bench /bɛntʃ/ benches
1 NC A **bench** is a long seat of wood or metal. *...sitting on a bench in the courtyard.*
2 N PL In the British Parliament, the government **benches**, the Labour **benches**, and so on are the seats used by the Members of Parliament who belong to the political party mentioned. *...the tradition of having the government benches facing the opposition benches.*
3 N PL You can also talk about the government **benches**, the Labour **benches**, and so on when you want to refer to the Members of Parliament who sit on particular seats. *Mr Cannon can expect some criticism from his own benches. ...the attack from the opposition benches.* ● See also **backbench**, **front bench**.
4 NC A **bench** is also a long, narrow table in a factory, laboratory, or workshop. *The tubes could be hooked onto the bench and simply bolted in place with a screw attachment.*

benchmark /bɛntʃmɑːk/ benchmarks
1 NC+SUPP A **benchmark** is something whose quality, quantity, or capability is known and which is used as a standard with which other things can be compared. *The document was a vital benchmark against which to test progress... Last year OPEC set a benchmark price of eighteen dollars a barrel.*
2 NC A **benchmark** is also a mark on a fixed object such as a stone post, stating the height above sea level, which is used as a reference point in surveying.

bend /bɛnd/ bends, bending, bent
1 V When someone **bends** or **bends** down, they move the top part of their body towards the ground. *He was bending over the basin... He bent down and undid his shoelaces.* ◆ **bent** ADJ PRED *Dan is bent over the fireplace.*

2 V-ERG When you bend a part of your body such as your arm or leg or when it bends, you change its position so that it is no longer straight. *Bend the arm at the elbow... Try to maintain a straight kicking leg, although the supporting leg may bend a little.* ◆ bent ADJ *Keep your knees bent.*
3 V-ERG When something that is flat or straight bends or when you bend it, it becomes curved or angular because force is used on it. *Aluminium tubing is just as strong and also retains its stiffness when it bends a little. ...pliers for bending wire.* ◆ bent ADJ *...two bent pipes.*
4 NC A bend in a road, river, or pipe is a curved part of it. *I was out of sight around the next bend.*
5 See also bent.
● Bend is used in these phrases. ● If you say that someone or something is driving you round the bend, you mean that they are annoying you or upsetting you very much; an informal expression. ● If you bend the rules, you interpret them in a way that allows you to do something that they really forbid. ● to bend double: see double.

bended /bɛndɪd/
1 On bended knee means kneeling; a formal expression. *On bended knee, he asked her to marry him.*
2 If you say that you ask someone on bended knees to do something, you mean that you want them to do it very much. *He said he was begging on his bended knees for the violence to end.*

bender /bɛndə/ benders
NC When someone goes on a bender, they drink a very large amount of alcohol; an informal word. *I'm going to go on a bender when the exams finish.*

bendy /bɛndi/ bendier, bendiest
1 ADJ Something that is bendy has many curves and angles. *...a very bendy road.*
2 ADJ A bendy object bends easily into a curved or angular shape. *...crinkle cut chips and bendy straws.*

beneath /bɪniːθ/
1 PREP Something that is beneath another thing is under the other thing. *She concealed the bottle beneath her mattress.*
2 PREP If you talk about what is beneath the surface of something, you are talking about the aspects of it which are hidden or not obvious. *Beneath the veneer of civilization, he was a very vulgar man.*

Benedictine, Benedictines; pronounced /bɛnɪdɪktɪn/ for the meaning in paragraph 1, and /bɛnɪdɪktiːn/ for the meaning in paragraph 2.
1 NC A Benedictine is a monk or nun who is a member of a Christian religious community that follows the rule of St Benedict. *...a huge Benedictine Abbey.*
2 NU Benedictine is a yellow liqueur.

benediction /bɛnɪdɪkʃn/ benedictions; a formal word.
1 NC A benediction is a prayer asking God to bless someone.
2 NU Benediction is the act of blessing someone. *I raised my hand in benediction.*

benefactor /bɛnɪfæktə/ benefactors
NC Your benefactor is a person who helps you by giving you money or something that you need. *The work was on loan to the museum from an anonymous benefactor.*

beneficent /bənɛfɪsənt/
ADJ Someone or something that is beneficent helps people or results in something good; a formal word. *...the most beneficent regime in history.*

beneficial /bɛnɪfɪʃl/
ADJ Something that is beneficial helps people or improves their lives. *Such a system will be beneficial to society.*

beneficiary /bɛnɪfɪʃəri/ beneficiaries
NC A beneficiary of something is a person who receives it or is helped by it. *Who are the main beneficiaries of the changes?*

benefit /bɛnɪfɪt/ benefits, benefiting, benefited
1 V-ERG If something benefits you or if you benefit from it, it helps you or improves your life. *...a medical service which will benefit rich and poor... The*

firm benefited from his ingenuity.
2 NC The benefits of something are the advantages that it brings to people. *...the benefits of modern technology.*
3 NU Benefit is money given by the government to people who are poor, ill, or unemployed. *You are entitled to child benefit.*
4 fringe benefits: see fringe.
● Benefit is used in these phrases. ● If something is to your benefit or is of benefit to you, it helps you or improves your life. *He said this would stabilize the oil market, to everyone's benefit... This will be of benefit to the country as a whole.* ● If you have the benefit of something, it gives you an advantage. *I had the benefit of a good education.* ● If you do something for the benefit of someone, you do it specially for them. *He smiled for the benefit of the reporters.* ● If you give someone the benefit of the doubt, you accept what they say as true, because you cannot prove that it is not true. *The West German authorities gave him the benefit of the doubt.*

benevolence /bənɛvələns/
NU Benevolence is the quality of being kind, helpful, and tolerant. *Grandma was looking on with amused benevolence.*

benevolent /bənɛvələnt/
ADJ A benevolent person is kind, helpful, and tolerant. *My aunt and uncle were looking benevolent and prepared to forgive me.* ◆ benevolently ADV *He smiled benevolently.*

benevolent fund, benevolent funds
NC A benevolent fund is an amount of money that is used to help members of a particular group of people when they are in need. *...a charity match for the Indian Players' Benevolent Fund.*

benighted /bɪnaɪtɪd/
ADJ ATTRIB Benighted describes someone whom you consider to be unfortunate or ignorant; a literary word. *A glimmer of hope for that benighted country has been the emergence of a United Nations peace plan.*

benign /bɪnaɪn/
1 ADJ Someone who is benign is kind, gentle, and harmless. *They are among the most benign people on earth... His face was calm and benign.* ◆ benignly ADV *He smiled benignly at his guest.*
2 ADJ A benign disease will not cause death or serious harm; a medical term. *...women with benign breast disease.*

Benin /bɛnɪn/
The Republic of Benin is a country in western Africa. It was part of French West Africa from the 19th century until it became independent in 1960 under the name Dahomey. Mathieu Kérékou came to power in 1972, and in 1975 established a one-party state ruled by the Benin People's Revolutionary Party (PRPB). In 1990 political parties were legalized, and Nicéphore Soglo was elected President at the head of a coalition of three parties. Benin exports oil, cotton, palm oil and kernels, and cocoa. It is a member of the Organization of African Unity. ◆ Beninese, Beninois /bɛniniːz, bɛninwɑː/ N, ADJ
▪ *per capita GNP:* US$390 ▪ *religion:* animism, Christianity, Islam ▪ *language:* French (official), Fon, Yoruba, Bariba, Fulani ▪ *currency:* CFA franc
▪ *capital:* Porto-Novo ▪ *largest city:* Cotonou
▪ *population:* 5 million (1989) ▪ *size:* 112,622 square kilometres.

bent /bɛnt/
1 Bent is the past tense and past participle of bend.
2 ADJ If a person or thing is bent, they are curved and no longer have their normal shape. *He was bent with arthritis. ...bent saucepans.*
3 ADJ PRED+on or upon If you are bent on or bent upon doing something, you are determined to do it. *That's something Mr Gorbachev is bent on changing... The Soviet Union is bent upon withdrawing its troops.*
4 N SING+SUPP If you have a bent for something, you like doing it or have a natural ability to do it. *The new bent for staying at home seems to be doing little for marriages in Britain. ...a boy with a mechanical bent.*

bequeath /bɪkwiːð/ **bequeaths, bequeathing, bequeathed**
VOOorVO+to If you **bequeath** money or property to someone, you legally state that they should have it when you die; a formal word. ...*the forty million dollars he bequeathed Phoebe... He bequeathed his collection to the nation.*

bequest /bɪkwest/ **bequests**
NC A **bequest** is money or property which you legally leave to someone when you die; a formal word. *Except for a few small bequests to relatives, he left all his property to charity.*

berate /bɪreɪt/ **berates, berating, berated**
VO If you **berate** someone, you scold them angrily; a formal word. *He continued to scream and berate me when I did something wrong.*

bereaved /bɪriːvd/
ADJ A **bereaved** person is one who had a relative or close friend who has recently died. *He could find few words to comfort the bereaved families.*

bereavement /bɪriːvmənt/ **bereavements**
NUorNC **Bereavement** is the experience you have or the state you are in when a relative or close friend dies. ...*bereavement in old age.* ...*planning for the future after a bereavement.*

bereft /bɪreft/
ADJ PRED+of If a person or thing is **bereft** of something, they no longer have it; a literary word. *Her cheeks were bereft of colour.* ...*crumbling slums bereft of basic amenities.*

Bérégovoy, Pierre /pieə beɪreɪgəvwaː/
Pierre Bérégovoy of the Socialist Party (PS), became Prime Minister of France in 1992. He was Minister of Social Affairs from 1982 to 1984, and Minister of Finance from 1984 to 1986, and from 1988 to 1992. Born: 1925.

beret /bereɪ/ **berets**
NC A **beret** is a circular flat hat that is made of soft material and has no brim.

Berlin /bɜːlɪn/
Berlin is the largest city in Germany. It became the capital of the re-united Germany in 1990, though most government functions remained in Bonn. Population: 3,409,000 (1987).

Bermuda /bəmjuːdə/
Bermuda is a territory of the United Kingdom in the Atlantic, off the east coast of the United States. It became a British colony in the 17th century. Tourism, banking, and insurance are important industries.
♦ **Bermudian, Bermudan** /bəmjuːdiən, bəmjuːdən/ N, ADJ
▪ *per capita GNP:* US$22,540 ▪ *religion:* Christianity ▪ *language:* English ▪ *currency:* dollar ▪ *capital:* Hamilton ▪ *population:* 58,000 (1989) ▪ *size:* 53 square kilometres.

Bern /beən/
Bern is the capital of Switzerland and its fourth largest city. Population: 135,000 (1988).

berry /beri/ **berries**
NC A **berry** is a small round fruit that grows on a bush or a tree. ...*exotic grewia berries, a fruit from a small African tree.*

berserk /bəzɜːk/
ADJ PRED If someone goes **berserk**, they lose control of themselves and become very violent. *One night she went berserk and wrecked her room.*

berth /bɜːθ/ **berths, berthing, berthed**
1 If you give someone or something **a wide berth**, you avoid them because they are unpleasant or dangerous. *The Mujahedin give government forces a wide berth.*
2 NC A **berth** is a space in a harbour where a ship stays for a period of time. *The Zanoobia has now been moved to a remote berth in Genoa harbour.*
3 V-ERG When a ship **berths** or when sailors **berth** it, it moves into a space in a harbour after a journey. *The Vishwa Sidhi had been allowed to berth and had begun discharging its cargo... The ADCP is to provide data on harbour currents to help pilots berth large vessels.*
4 NC A **berth** is also a bed in a boat, train, or caravan.

beseech /bɪsiːtʃ/ **beseeches, beseeching, beseeched** or **besought**
VO+to-INF or VO-QUOTE If you **beseech** someone to do something, you ask them very insistently and desperately to do it; a literary word. *I beseech you to tell me... Paul Wellstone of Minnesota beseeched his colleagues, 'We must not rush to war.'*

beseeching /bɪsiːtʃɪŋ/
ADJ A **beseeching** expression, gesture, or tone of voice conveys the idea that someone wants something very much. *She was staring at me with great beseeching eyes... Mary Stuart put a beseeching hand on my arm.*
♦ **beseechingly** ADV *Larsen looked beseechingly at Rudolph.*

beset /bɪset/ **besets, besetting.** The form **beset** is used in the present tense and is also the past tense and past participle.
VO If someone or something is **beset** by problems or fears, they have many of them; a formal word. *The policy is beset with problems... She had been beset by doubts.*

beside /bɪsaɪd/
1 PREP Something that is **beside** something else is at the side of it or next to it. *I sat down beside my wife.*
2 See also **besides**.
● **Beside** is used in these phrases. ● If you are **beside yourself** with anger or excitement, you are extremely angry or excited. ● **beside the point:** see **point**.

besides /bɪsaɪdz/. The form **beside** can be used for the meaning in paragraph 1 in American English.
1 PREP or ADV **Besides** or **beside** something means in addition to it. *What languages do you know besides English?... He needed so much else besides... Thomas was the only blond in the family, beside the mother... Another reason that it makes money, beside good management, is that it's stingy.*
2 ADV SEN You use **besides** to make an additional point or give an additional reason. *Would these figures prove anything? And besides, who keeps such statistics?*

besiege /bɪsiːdʒ/ **besieges, besieging, besieged**
1 VO If you **are besieged** by people, many people want something from you and continually bother you. *I am besieged with visitors from abroad.*
2 VO If soldiers **besiege** a place, they surround it and wait for the people in it to surrender. *It is understood that rebel troops which are now besieging Monrovia are likely to capture the city.*

besotted /bɪsɒtɪd/
ADJ If you are **besotted** with someone or something, you like them so much that you seem foolish or silly. *He was besotted with me.* ...*an age besotted with the concept of the unattainable.*

besought /bɪsɔːt/
Besought is a past tense and past participle of **beseech**.

bespectacled /bɪspektəkld/
ADJ Someone who is **bespectacled** is wearing spectacles. ...*a sallow, bespectacled young man.*

bespoke /bɪspəuk/; an old-fashioned word.
1 ADJ ATTRIB A **bespoke** tailor makes or sells clothes that are specially made to fit the customer who ordered them.
2 ADJ ATTRIB **Bespoke** clothes have been specially made by a tailor to fit a particular customer. ...*a bespoke suit.*

best /best/
1 ADJ **Best** is the superlative of **good**. *That was one of the best films I've seen. ...my best friend... It's best to be as clear as possible... I want her to have the very best.*
2 ADV **Best** is also the superlative of **well**. *I think mine would suit her best... It is they, after all, who should know their businesses best.*
3 N SING Your **best** is the greatest effort or the highest achievement that you are capable of. *They are trying their best to discourage them.*
4 ADV or ADJ If you like something **best** or like it the **best**, you prefer it. *Which did you like best—the Vivaldi or the Schumann?... Who did he love the best?*
5 You use **best** to form the superlative of compound adjectives beginning with 'good' and 'well'. ...*the*

best-looking women. ...the best-known author of books for children.
6 See also **second-best**.
● **Best** is used in these phrases. ● You use **at best** to indicate that even if you describe something as favourably as possible, it is still not very good. ● If you **make the best of** an unsatisfactory situation, you accept it and try to be cheerful about it. *There is nowhere else to go, so make the best of it.* ● to **know best**: see **know**. ● the **best part of** something: see **part**. ● the **best of both worlds**: see **world**.

bestial /bɛstɪəl/
ADJ **Bestial** behaviour is very unpleasant or disgusting; a literary word. *A statement spoke of bestial aggression and a horrible massacre. ...sado-masochistic and bestial fantasies.*

bestiality /bɛstɪælətɪ/
1 NU **Bestiality** is revolting or disgusting behaviour; a literary use. *...the depths of bestiality to which Man could sink... The poems vividly describe the horror and bestiality of war.*
2 NU Sexual activity in which a person has sex with an animal is called **bestiality**.

best man
N SING The **best man** at a wedding is the man who acts as an attendant to the bridegroom. *She remembered the speech the best man had made at their wedding.*

bestow /bɪstəʊ/ **bestows, bestowing, bestowed**
VO If you **bestow** something on someone, you give it to them; a formal word. *The Duke bestowed this property on him. ...the attention bestowed upon her son.*

bestowal /bɪstəʊəl/
N SING+SUPP The **bestowal** of something is the giving of it as a special gift or honour to someone or something; a formal word. *The bestowal of freedom is the bestowal of love. ...the responsibilities associated with the bestowal of unification... The general surely merits the bestowal of a knighthood.*

best-seller, best-sellers
NC A **best-seller** is a book of which a very large number of copies have been sold. *The book is now an international best-seller.*

bet /bɛt/ **bets, betting.** The form **bet** is used in the present tense and is also the past tense and past participle of the verb.
1 V,VO,or VOO If you **bet** on a future event, you make an agreement with someone which means that you receive money if you are right about what happens, and lose money if you are wrong. *The British love to bet, especially if it involves horses... The anonymous gambler bet £110 on seven victories... He bet me a hundred pounds that I wouldn't get through.* ► Also NC *I didn't put a bet on... But at this stage, no-one is willing to place bets. ...bookmakers who will take bets on just about anything.*
2 V-REPORT or V O-REPORT If you say 'I bet' that something is true or will happen, you mean that you are very sure that it is true or will happen. *I bet nobody's been here before... I bet you there'll be dozens of them.*
● **Bet** is used in these phrases. ● You say '**You bet**' as an emphatic way of saying 'yes', or to emphasize a statement; an informal expression. *'Are you coming?'—'You bet!'... You bet I'm getting out.* ● If you say '**Don't bet on**' something, or '**I wouldn't bet on**' something, you mean that you think it is unlikely to happen or be true. *Don't bet on the economists being right... You just might manage it. I wouldn't bet on it, though.* ● If you tell someone that something is a **good bet** or their **best bet**, you are advising them about what they should do or choose. *This seems like a good bet to increase yield... He believed fast-breeder reactors were the world's best bet for providing cheap electricity.* ● If you say that something is a **good bet** or a **safe bet**, you mean that you think it is very likely to happen or be true. *Mitterrand still appears a good bet to become the first president to be re-elected... It is a safe bet that most of them have already complied.*
● to **hedge** your **bets**: see **hedge**.

beta /biːtə/ **betas**
N C or NU **Beta** is the second letter of the Greek

alphabet, and is sometimes used as a mark given for a student's work. *I am confident that I would still, 14 years on, gain at very least a beta plus.*

betel /biːtl/
NU **Betel** is a plant that grows in Southeast Asia, where some people chew its leaves and red nuts as a type of drug.

bête noire /beɪt nwɑː/ **bêtes noires** /beɪt nwɑːz/
NC+POSS A person, thing, or situation that you describe as your **bête noire** is one that you especially hate or that annoys you a great deal. *The main speaker was Boris Yeltsin, the 'bête noire' of party conservatives... Two of those are believed to be Washington's 'bêtes noires': the Interior Minister and the Minister of Defence.*

betide /bɪtaɪd/
woe betide: see **woe**.

betray /bɪtreɪ/ **betrays, betraying, betrayed**
1 VO If you **betray** someone who thinks you support or love them, you do something which harms them, often by helping their enemies or opponents. *His best friend betrayed him.*
2 VO If you **betray** a secret, you tell it to people who you should not tell it to. *The charges range from plotting to overthrow the state to betraying defence secrets.*
3 VO If you **betray** your feelings or thoughts, you show them without intending to. *People learned never to betray their anger.*

betrayal /bɪtreɪəl/ **betrayals**
N C or NU A **betrayal** is an action that betrays someone or something. *It is being seen as a betrayal of what remains of Germany's far left... Many Iranians feel a deep sense of betrayal.*

betrothal /bɪtrəʊðl/ **betrothals**
NC A **betrothal** is an engagement to be married; an old-fashioned word. *...the betrothal of Catherine of Aragon to Prince Arthur.*

betrothed /bɪtrəʊðd/; an old-fashioned word.
1 ADJ If you are **betrothed** to someone, you are engaged to be married to them. *He is already betrothed to someone else.*
2 N SING Your **betrothed** is the person you are going to marry. *...seeing them in animated conversation with her betrothed.*

better /bɛtə/
1 ADJ **Better** is the comparative of **good**. *The results were better than expected... Milk is much better for you than lemonade.*
2 ADV **Better** is also the comparative of **well**. *Some people can ski better than others... There is no indication that they will be able to do any better.*
3 ADV If you like one thing **better** than another, you like it more. *I love this place better than anywhere else.*
4 ADJ PRED If you are **better** after an illness or injury, you are less ill or no longer ill. *Her cold was better.*
5 You use **better** to form the comparative of compound adjectives beginning with 'good' or 'well.' *My husband was better-looking than that... She's much better known in Europe.*
● **Better** is used in these phrases. ● If you say that someone **had better** do something, you mean that they ought to do it. *I'd better go.* ● If someone is **better off**, they have more money or are in a more pleasant situation than before. *They are much better off than they were two years ago... She will be better off in hospital.* ● If something changes **for the better**, it improves. *The weather had changed for the better.* ● If something gets **the better of** you, you are unable to resist it. *My curiosity got the better of me.* ● You use expressions like **the more the better** or **the sooner the better** to say that an action or situation will be more helpful or satisfactory if something is done by more people, done more often, or done more quickly. *The more nations that guarantee any compromise reached, the better... The more you practice, the better you become... The sooner they are joined by their families the better.* ● to **know better**: see **know**. ● the **better part of**: see **part**. ● to **think better of it**: see **think**.

betterment /bɛtəmənt/
NU The **betterment** of something is the act or process of improving its standard or status; a formal word. *We are working for the betterment of society.*

betting /bɛtɪŋ/
1 NU **Betting** involves making an agreement with someone about what you think will happen in the future. You give them a sum of money and either lose that money or gain more money according to whether you are right. *Ali and Gordon spent all their money on betting.*
2 N SING The **betting** is used in expressions like 'What's the betting?' and 'The betting is...' to suggest that something is very likely to happen or to be true. *What's the betting they'll be asleep when we get back?*
3 See also **bet**.

betting shop, betting shops
NC A **betting shop** is a place where people can go to bet on something such as a horse race. *They were shot while apparently robbing a betting shop. ...several betting shops where smoking is to be banned. ...the William Hill betting shop chain.*

between /bɪtwiːn/
1 PREP or ADV If something is **between** two things or is in between them, it has one of the things on one side of it and the other thing on the other side. *She put the cigarette between her lips and lit it. ...Penn Close, Court Road, and all the little side streets in between.*
2 PREP If people or things are moving **between** two places, they are moving regularly from one place to the other and back again. *I have spent a lifetime commuting between Britain and the United States.*
3 PREP A relationship, discussion, or difference **between** two people, groups, or things is one that involves them both or relates to them both. *...a clash between the two gangs... I asked whether there was much difference between British and European law.*
4 PREP If people have a particular amount of something **between** them, this is the total amount that they have. *They have both been married before and have five children between them.*
5 PREP When something is divided or shared **between** people, they each have a share of it. *The land was divided equally between them.*
6 PREP If something is **between** or in between two amounts or ages, it is greater or older than the first one and smaller or younger than the second one. *...at temperatures between 36 and 39°C... This region receives in between 350 and 550 mm of rainfall.*
7 PREP If someone stands **between** you and what you want, they prevent you from having it. If they stand **between** you and something you do not want, they help you to avoid it. *These men stand between you and the top jobs... Many ordinary people feel that the current military government has stood between them and chaos.*
8 PREP If something happens **between** or in between two times or events, it happens after the first time or event and before the second one. *The house was built between 1840 and 1852... Between sessions I spent my time with my husband.*
9 PREP If you must choose **between** two things, you must choose either one thing or the other. *The choice is between defeat or survival.*

bevelled /bɛvld/
ADJ A **bevelled** edge is the sloping edge of a piece of wood or metal, such as the edge on a picture frame. *You have to use a small, sharp knife and angle it just right to get a bevelled edge.*

beverage /bɛvərɪdʒ/ **beverages**
NC A **beverage** is a drink; a formal word. *...over-indulging in any form of alcoholic beverage.*

bevy /bɛvi/
N SING A **bevy** of people or things is a large group of them often found or occurring together. *...a bevy of village girls. ...a bevy of events throughout Britain.*

bewail /bɪweɪl/ **bewails, bewailing, bewailed**
VO If you **bewail** something, you express great sorrow about it; a formal word. *Frequently they bewail the ingratitude of their children.*

beware /bɪweə/
If you tell someone to **beware** of a person or thing, you

are warning them that the person or thing may harm them. *Beware of the dog!... I would beware of companies which depend on one product only.*

bewhiskered /bɪwɪskəd/
ADJ A man who is **bewhiskered** has a long beard or sideboards; a literary word, often used humorously.

bewilder /bɪwɪldə/ **bewilders, bewildering, bewildered**
VO If something **bewilders** you, it is so confusing or difficult that you cannot understand it. *A confession of this nature would bewilder and perhaps anger some of my Indian friends... You bewilder me.*

bewildered /bɪwɪldəd/
ADJ If you are **bewildered**, you are very confused and cannot understand something or decide what to do. *His wife watched him, bewildered... They looked tired and bewildered... The bewildered child was taken from his family's farm to Lhasa.*

bewildering /bɪwɪldərɪŋ/
ADJ Something that is **bewildering** is confusing and difficult to understand or make a decision about. *There is a bewildering variety of activities. ...a bewildering and upsetting experience.*

bewilderment /bɪwɪldəmənt/
NU **Bewilderment** is the feeling of being confused or unable to understand something. *To my complete bewilderment, she rang and offered to buy the place... 'But I just rented it,' Morris protested in bewilderment.*

bewitch /bɪwɪtʃ/ **bewitches, bewitching, bewitched**
VO If someone or something **bewitches** you, you find them so attractive that you cannot think about anything else. *'You've bewitched her,' Calderwood said. 'She's in tears five times a week about you.'... The splendour of the forest bewitched Margaret from the very beginning.* ♦ **bewitching** ADJ *...a bewitching smile... Its bewitching quality owes much to the subtle way in which colours overlap.*

beyond /bɪjɒnd/
1 PREP or ADV If something is **beyond** a place, it is on the other side of it. *...a farm beyond Barnham... He indicated the street beyond.*
2 PREP To extend, continue, or progress **beyond** a particular thing or point means to extend or continue further than that thing or point. *Few children remain in the school beyond the age of 16.*
3 PREP If someone or something is **beyond** belief, understanding, or control, it has become impossible to believe in, understand, or control it. *The situation has changed beyond recognition.*
4 PREP If you say that something is **beyond** you, you mean that you cannot understand it. *How he managed to find us is beyond me.*

BFPO /biːɛfpiːəʊ/
BFPO is used as part of addresses when sending letters or parcels by post to members of the British armed forces living abroad. **BFPO** is an abbreviation for 'British Forces Post Office'.

Bhumibol, King Adulyadej /əduːləjədɛd puːmɪpɒn/
King Adulyadej Bhumibol succeeded his brother, King Ananda Mahidol, on the throne of Thailand in 1946. Born: 1927.

Bhutan /buːtɑːn/
The **Kingdom of Bhutan** is a country in the Himalayas, in southern Asia. It was established as a Buddhist theocracy in the 17th century, and the Drukpa monasteries still hold considerable political power. The monarchy was established in 1907. King Jigme Singye Wangchuck succeeded in 1972. There are no political parties. Although independent, Bhutan accepts India's guidance in foreign affairs. Ethnic conflict between the majority Drukpa population and the minority Nepalese community has been a source of civil disorder. Bhutan exports cement, minerals, timber, cardamom, and ginger. ♦ **Bhutanese** /buːtəniːz/ N, ADJ
▪ *per capita GNP:* US$360 ▪ *religion:* Buddhism (Mahayana), Hinduism ▪ *language:* Dzongkha (official), Nepali ▪ *currency:* ngultrum ▪ *capital:* Thimphu ▪ *population:* 600,000 (1991) ▪ *size:* 46,500 square kilometres.

bi- /baɪ-/
1 PREFIX **bi-** is used at the beginning of nouns and

adjectives that have two as part of their meaning. ...*a biped. ...a biplane. ...bilingual children.*
2 PREFIX bi- is also used to say how often something happens or how often something is produced. For example, if something happens bi-weekly, it happens twice a week or once every two weeks. ...*a bi-monthly magazine.*

biannual /baɪ ænjuəl/
ADJ A **biannual** event happens or is done twice a year. ...*a biannual check-up.*

bias /baɪəs/ **biases**
NU or NC Someone who shows **bias** is unfair in their judgements or decisions, because they are only influenced by their own opinions, rather than considering the facts. *You're accusing me of bias in my marking... There's an intense bias against women.*

biased /baɪəst/
1 ADJ PRED Someone or something that is **biased** towards one thing is more concerned with it than with other things. *The university is biased towards the sciences.*
2 ADJ If someone is **biased**, they show favouritism towards a particular person or group, and so do not judge things fairly. *I am biased in favour of Eisenhower.*

bib /bɪb/ **bibs**
NC A **bib** is a piece of cloth or plastic worn by very young children while they are eating, to protect their clothes.

bible /baɪbl/ **bibles**
1 N PROP The **Bible** is the sacred book of the Christian religion. The first part of it, the Old Testament, is a sacred book for Jews. ...*a new translation of the Bible.*
2 NC A **bible** is a copy of the Bible. *They also gave the delegation rosaries, prayer books and bibles.*

biblical /bɪblɪkl/
ADJ ATTRIB **Biblical** means contained in, or relating to the Bible. ...*the Biblical account of creation... It is a way of life that one imagines hasn't changed much since biblical times.*

bibliography /bɪblɪɒgrəfi/ **bibliographies**
1 NC A **bibliography** is a list of books on a particular subject. ...*a helpful select bibliography of easily available works.*
2 NC A **bibliography** is also a list of the books and articles referred to in a particular book. *It has over 1200 textual notes, some excellent photographs, and a very full bibliography.*

bicarb /baɪkɑːb/
NU **Bicarb** is an abbreviation for 'bicarbonate of soda'; an informal word.

bicarbonate of soda /baɪkɑːbənət əv səudə/
NU **Bicarbonate of soda** is a white powder which is used in baking to make cakes rise. It is also used as a medicine to help your stomach when you have indigestion. ...*consisting of honey, bicarbonate of soda and salt.*

bicentenary /baɪsentiːnəri/ **bicentenaries**
NC A **bicentenary** is the year in which you celebrate something important that happened exactly two hundred years earlier. ...*bicentenary celebrations.*

bicentennial /baɪsentenɪəl/ **bicentennials**
ADJ ATTRIB **Bicentennial** celebrations are held to celebrate a bicentenary. ...*during the American bicentennial year.* ► Also NC *France has found a novel way of celebrating the bicentennial of the French Revolution.*

biceps /baɪseps/; **biceps** is both the singular and the plural form.
NC Your **biceps** are the large muscles at the front of the upper part of your arms.

bicker /bɪkə/ **bickers, bickering, bickered**
V When people **bicker**, they argue or quarrel about unimportant things. *Its 400 members have bickered, often over trivialities.* ♦ **bickering** NU *The American people, he said, wanted action not bickering... After months of bickering over alternative schemes, the feeling is that even an unsatisfactory plan is better than no plan at all.*

bicycle /baɪsɪkl/ **bicycles**
NC A **bicycle** is a vehicle with two wheels which you ride by sitting on it and pushing two pedals with your feet. *Some of their supporters rode to the square on bicycles.*

bid /bɪd/ **bids, bidding, bade, bidden.** The form **bid** is used in the present tense of all meanings of the verb, and is also the past tense and past participle for the meaning in paragraph 3.
1 NC A **bid** is an attempt to obtain or do something. *He's expected to make a bid for the leadership... Brandt failed in a bid to see Reagan.*
2 NC A **bid** is also an offer to pay a particular amount of money to buy something. *A bid has already been made on the house across the street... Stet submitted an unsuccessful bid for the telephone business. ...bids for other oil companies.* ● See also **takeover bid.**
3 V or VO If you **bid** for something that is being sold, you offer to pay a particular amount of money for it. *Mexico's creditors were encouraged to bid for the new securities... He bid a quarter of a million pounds for the portrait.*
4 V OO or VO+*to* If you **bid** someone good morning, you say good morning to them; a formal use. *I bid you good night, young man... The outgoing president today bade farewell to his staff.*
5 VO+INF If you **bid** someone do something, you ask or invite them to do it; an old-fashioned, literary use. *They sent letters to her, bidding her improve her mind with good books.*

bidden /bɪdn/
Bidden is a past participle of **bid.**

bidder /bɪdə/ **bidders**
NC A **bidder** is someone who tries to buy something at an auction; items are usually sold to the **highest bidder**, the person who offers the most amount of money. ...*the selling of independent television franchises to the highest bidder... Reports in Japan say the businessman who bought the Van Gogh was also the successful bidder for the Renoir.*

bidding /bɪdɪŋ/; a formal word.
1 If you do something at someone's **bidding**, you do it because they have asked you to do it. *At his mother's bidding, Mr Jones wrote a letter to our father.*
2 If you **do** someone's **bidding**, you do what they have asked you to do. *He assumes she is only there to do his bidding.*

bide /baɪd/ **bides, biding, bided**
If you **bide** your **time**, you wait for a good opportunity before doing something. *Mr Terzi made it clear that he was prepared to bide his time.*

bidet /biːdeɪ/ **bidets**
NC A **bidet** is a low basin in a bathroom which you wash your bottom in.

biennial /baɪenɪəl/ **biennials**
1 ADJ A **biennial** event happens or is done once every two years. *Every union has its own annual or biennial conference.*
2 NC A **biennial** is a plant that lives for two years. It flowers, produces seed, and dies in its second year.

bier /bɪə/ **biers**
NC A **bier** is a movable stand or frame on which a corpse or coffin is placed or carried at a funeral. *The bodies, on biers, were accompanied by an honour guard.*

biff /bɪf/ **biffs, biffing, biffed**
VO If you **biff** someone, you hit them with your fist; an old-fashioned word. *It is not uncommon for the porters to be sworn at, and some have even been biffed.* ► Also NC *I'll give you a biff on the nose if you don't shut up!*

bifocal /baɪfəukl/ **bifocals**
N PL **Bifocals** are glasses with lenses made in two halves. The top part is for looking at things some distance away, and the bottom part is for reading and looking at things nearby. ► Also ADJ ...*the first pair of bifocal spectacles.*

big /bɪg/ **bigger, biggest**
1 ADJ Something that is **big** is large in size or great in degree, extent, or importance. *He was holding a big black umbrella... The biggest problem at the moment is unemployment... You're making a big mistake.*
2 ADJ **Big** is used in questions about size, degree, extent, or importance. *'It's a shark.'—'How big?'*

3 ADJ ATTRIB You can refer to your older brother or sister as your **big** brother or sister; an informal use. *With his big brother away for three weeks, Chun must be feeling very lonely.*

bigamist /bɪɡəmɪst/ **bigamists**
NC A **bigamist** is a person who commits the crime of marrying someone when they are already legally married to someone else.

bigamous /bɪɡəməs/
ADJ A **bigamous** marriage is one in which one of the partners is already married to someone else.

bigamy /bɪɡəmi/
NU **Bigamy** is the crime of marrying a person when you are already legally married to someone else. *She accused him of bigamy in Taiwan courts.*

big bang theory
N SING The **big bang theory** is a theory in astronomy that suggests that the universe was created as a result of a massive explosion. *According to the Big Bang theory our universe is expanding.*

Big Brother
NU If you describe a government or person in authority as **Big Brother**, you mean that you think they have too much power over you and that they limit your freedom. *The last thing they need is Big Brother to watch over them. ...in the nineteen-fifties, when the Chinese say Moscow took on the role of Big Brother.*

big business
1 NU **Big business** is business or commerce which involves very large companies and very large sums of money. *...the great male-dominated world of industry and big business.*
2 NU Something that is **big business** is something which people spend a lot of money on, and which has become an important commercial activity. *English private coaching schools have become big business in Turkish cities... Elections are now big business.*

big deal
1 You say '**Big deal**' to express your opinion that something is unimportant, uninteresting, or not surprising; an informal expression. *Well, so what? So he's a poor fisherman, big deal!... 'So, big deal,' Tom said. 'She got a ride in a Buick.'*
2 You use **big deal** in informal expressions which indicate how important or unimportant someone thinks something is. *We can get fresh eggs, you know, and that's a big deal... He makes a big deal, for example, about pact contributions... You're not going to get fined or punished, so what's the big deal?... For us $50 is no big deal; he won't starve.*

big dipper, big dippers
1 NC A **big dipper** is a narrow railway track at a fairground which goes up and down steeply and round sharp bends. People ride in carriages which run on the track, for enjoyment and excitement. *...a teenage girl riding the big dipper at the funfair.*
2 N SING The **Big Dipper** is an American name for the group of stars also known as 'The Plough'.

big end, big ends
NC A car's **big end** is the end of a long rod in its engine where it joins the crank.

big fish; big fish is both the singular and the plural form.
NC Someone who is a **big fish** is powerful or important; an informal expression. *Little is known about eight of the ten suspects arrested in the past two weeks. But two of them are believed to be very big fish.*

big game
NU Large and sometimes dangerous wild animals such as lions or elephants are referred to as **big game**, especially when they are being hunted. *Today's poachers are armed with automatic weapons and go after big game for money.*

biggish /bɪɡɪʃ/
ADJ Something that is **biggish** is fairly big. *He was a biggish fellow. ...a biggish town.*

big hand, big hands
NC The **big hand** on a clock is the hand that points to the minutes; used by children.

big head, big heads
NC If you refer to someone as a **big head**, you mean that they think they are very clever and know everything about a subject; used in informal English, showing disapproval.

big-headed
ADJ Someone who is **big-headed** thinks that they are very clever or very good at something; used showing disapproval. *I'm selfish about what I write, or big-headed about it.*

big-hearted
ADJ Someone who is **big-hearted** is kind and generous to other people, and is always willing to help them. *...a country that is big-hearted.*

big mouth, big mouths
NC If you say that someone is a **big mouth** or that they have a **big mouth**, you mean that they tell people things that should have been kept secret; an informal expression, used showing disapproval. *Once again that boy's big mouth was going to get them all punished... Shut your big mouth!*

big name, big names
NC Someone who is a **big name** is successful and famous because of their work; an informal expression. *He had become a big name, a real pop hero.*

big noise
N SING Someone who is a **big noise** has an important position in a group or organization; an informal expression.

bigot /bɪɡət/ **bigots**
NC A **bigot** is someone who has strong and unreasonable opinions and refuses to change them, even when they are proved to be wrong.

bigoted /bɪɡətɪd/
ADJ Someone who is **bigoted** has strong and often unreasonable opinions and will not change them, even when they are proved to be wrong. *He was a bigoted, narrow-minded fanatic.*

bigotry /bɪɡətri/
NU **Bigotry** is the possession or expression of strong and often unreasonable opinions. *...campaigns against bigotry and racism.*

big shot, big shots
NC If you refer to someone as a **big shot**, you mean that he or she is an important and powerful person in an organization; an informal expression. *He is an Englishman, once a big shot in the BBC. ...people who maybe don't think you're such a big shot.*

big time
N SING The **big time** is used to refer to the highest level of an activity or career where you achieve the greatest amount of success, fame, or importance; an informal expression. *We've made the big time now... I became involved in 'big time' politics.*

big toe, big toes
NC Your **big toe** is the largest toe on your foot.

big top
N SING A **big top** is a large round tent that a circus uses for its performances.

bigwig /bɪɡwɪɡ/ **bigwigs**
NC You can refer to an important person as a **bigwig**; an informal word. *The bigwigs in Paris wanted to have a look at it.*

bijou /biːʒuː/
ADJ ATTRIB Very small houses are sometimes described as **bijou** in order to make them sound attractive or fashionable. *...a bijou residence.*

bike /baɪk/ **bikes**
NC A **bike** is a bicycle or a motorcycle; an informal word. *Although he was unhurt by the fall, his bike was too damaged for him to continue.*

bikini /bɪkiːni/ **bikinis**
NC A **bikini** is a two-piece swimming costume worn by women. *It was the 'swinging' sixties that finally made the bikini completely acceptable.*

bilateral /baɪlætərəl/
ADJ **Bilateral** negotiations, meetings, or agreements involve only the two groups or countries that are directly concerned; a formal word. *Mr Gorbachev and Mr Reagan will discuss bilateral relations between their two countries... Last year the volume of bilateral*

trade dropped by no less than nine per cent.
♦ **bilaterally** ADV *India sees the problem as one which should be resolved bilaterally.*

bilberry /bɪlbəᵊri/ **bilberries**
NC A **bilberry** is a small edible blue or blackish berry. It is also the bush on which it grows. *...that American national dish, bilberry pie.*

Bildt, Carl /kɑːl bɪlt/
Carl Bildt became Prime Minister of Sweden in 1991. He was elected Chairman of the Moderate Party (MS) in 1986. Born: 1949.

bile /baɪl/
NU **Bile** is a liquid produced by your liver which helps you to digest fat; a medical term. *After a meal, the bile duct releases the bile to help digestion.*

bilingual /baɪlɪŋgwəl/
1 ADJ **Bilingual** means involving or using two languages. *...bilingual dictionaries. ...the decision to ban bilingual signs in French and English outside stores.*
2 ADJ Someone who is **bilingual** can speak two languages fluently. *During that time he has also visited France where, despite being bilingual, he spoke only Arabic.*

bilious /bɪliəs/
1 ADJ **Bilious** means unpleasant and rather disgusting; an old-fashioned use. *...a great quantity of bilious yellow matter.*
2 ADJ If you feel **bilious**, you feel sick and have a headache; a medical use. *...bilious attacks.*

bill /bɪl/ **bills, billing, billed**
1 NC A **bill** is a written statement of money that you owe for goods or services. *...an enormous electricity bill... The bill for food imports could go up by 40 per cent this year. ...people who run up bills they just can't pay. ...a tendency to cut down on fuel bills.*
● to **foot the bill**: see **foot**.
2 NC A **bill** is also a piece of paper money; used in American English. *...a dollar bill.*
3 NC In systems of government, a **bill** is a formal statement of a proposed new law that is discussed and then voted on. *The Bill was defeated by 238 votes to 145... Since then, a tough U.S. trade bill has been passed by Congress.* ● See also **private member's bill**.
4 N SING The **bill** of a show or concert is the people who are going to appear in it, or the items of entertainment that a show or concert consists of. *There were some famous names on the bill... The Chamber Opera is offering a double bill of Mozart and Haydn.*
5 VO If a performer or show is **billed** as a particular thing, they are advertised as that thing. *...what was being billed as the greatest show on earth.* ♦ **billing** NU *It wasn't long before he was getting solo billing at big variety theatres and night clubs.*
6 NC A bird's **bill** is its beak.

billboard /bɪlbɔːd/ **billboards**
NC A **billboard** is a very large board, hung or standing outside, on which posters are displayed. *...billboards carrying the names of Alliance candidates... Last year a billboard went up in Washington, D.C., that attracted considerable attention. ...a billboard on the side of the store.*

billet /bɪlɪt/ **billets, billeting, billeted**
VO If members of the armed forces are **billeted** in a particular place, that place is provided for them to stay in for a period of time. *...the soldiers that were billeted in private houses in Sutton.*

billfold /bɪlfəʊld/ **billfolds**
NC A **billfold** is a wallet; used in American English.

billiards /bɪliədz/. The form **billiard** is used as a noun modifier.
NU **Billiards** is a game played on a large table, in which you use a long stick called a cue to hit balls against each other or into pockets around the sides of the table. *...a game of billiards. ...a billiard table.*

billion /bɪljən/ **billions**
1 A **billion** is a thousand million. *It was predicted that Britain's trade deficit would reach four billion pounds by the end of the year... Each year, the oceans absorb 105 billion tons of carbon dioxide.*
2 A **billion** can also mean one million million; an old-

fashioned British English use.
3 NC You can also use **billions** and **billion** to mean an extremely large amount. *They're really seeing the galaxies as they were billions of years ago... They printed the papers off by the billion.*

billionaire /bɪljəneə/ **billionaires**
NC A **billionaire** is an extremely rich person who has property worth at least a thousand million pounds or dollars. *Billionaires are usually fairly secretive about the exact amount that they're worth.*

billionth /bɪljənθ/ **billionths**
1 ADJ The **billionth** item in a series is the one you count as number one billion.
2 NC A **billionth** is one of a billion equal parts of something. *An atom landing on one side may weigh less than a billionth of a gram... Each pulse is a mere tenth of a billionth of a second long.*

bill of fare, bills of fare
NC The **bill of fare** at a restaurant is the menu; a list of the food for a meal from which you may choose what you want to eat; an old-fashioned expression.

bill of health
1 If you are given a **clean bill of health** after a medical examination, you are told that you are fit and that there is nothing wrong with you. *The President was given a clean bill of health after his latest six-monthly hospital check-up.*
2 If someone is suspected of doing something dishonest or improper, and is later given a **clean bill of health**, they are officially stated to have done nothing wrong. *...a statement in parliament giving him a clean bill of health.*

bill of rights; also written **Bill of Rights**.
N SING A **bill of rights** is a written list of citizens' rights, usually part of the constitution of a country. *Her government included a bill of rights in the new constitution.*

billow /bɪləʊ/ **billows, billowing, billowed**
1 V When something made of cloth **billows**, it swells out and flaps slowly in the wind. *...a teenage girl, her dress billowing in the breeze.*
2 V When smoke or cloud **billows**, it moves slowly upwards or across the sky. *They saw tourists jumping from the windows as smoke billowed from bedrooms.*

bill poster, bill posters
NC A **bill poster** or a **bill sticker** is a person who sticks notices or posters onto walls, often illegally. *Bill posters will be prosecuted.*

billy /bɪli/ **billies**
NC A **billy** or a **billy can** is a metal can or pot used for cooking over a camp fire or outdoor stove.

billy goat, billy goats
NC A **billy goat** is a male goat.

billy-o /bɪliəʊ/; also spelt **billy-oh**.
If you say that something is being done or is happening **like billy-o**, you mean that it is being done or is happening with great excitement, speed, or force; an informal expression. *It's raining like billy-o.*

bimonthly /baɪmʌnθli/
1 ADJ A **bimonthly** event or magazine is one that happens or appears every two months or twice per month. *The paper is starting as a bi-monthly publication but hopes to become a weekly... The camp inhabitants are completely dependent on bi-monthly handouts of rice.*
2 ADV If something happens **bimonthly**, it happens every two months or twice per month. *We review our progress bimonthly.*

bin /bɪn/ **bins**
NC A **bin** is a container that you use to put rubbish in, or to store things in. *She threw both letters in the bin. ...grain store bins.*

binary /baɪnəri/
1 ADJ ATTRIB The **binary** system expresses numbers using only the two digits 0 and 1. It is used especially in computing. *Each reading is recorded as a binary number... The way to do this was to use binary instead of decimal calculating units.* ▶ Also NU *Normal computing is based on counting in binary.*
2 ADJ ATTRIB **Binary** is used to describe something that consists of two things or parts. *The bomb, known as a binary weapon, contains two chemicals which become*

lethal when mixed. ...binary star systems.

bind /baɪnd/ **binds, binding, bound**

1 VO If you **bind** something, you tie string or rope tightly round it so that it is held firmly. *His hands were bound behind the post.*

2 VO If a duty or legal order **binds** you to a course of action, it forces you to do it. *This oath binds you to secrecy.*

3 VO When a book is **bound**, the pages are joined together and the cover is put on.

4 N SING If something is a **bind**, it is unpleasant and boring to do; an informal use. *It's a terrible bind to have to cook your own meals.*

5 See also **binding, bound**.

binder /baɪndə/ **binders**

NC A **binder** is a hard cover with metal rings inside, which is used to hold loose pieces of paper. *...a six-ring binder containing over two hundred pages of information.*

binding /baɪndɪŋ/ **bindings**

1 ADJ If a promise or agreement is **binding**, it must be obeyed or carried out. *...a Spanish law that is still binding in California... These would not have to be legally binding documents.*

2 NCorNU The **binding** of a book is its cover. *...books in ugly economy bindings. ...durable leather binding.*

binge /bɪndʒ/ **binges**; an informal word.

1 NC If you go on a **binge**, you drink a lot of alcohol or eat a lot of food that may not be good for you. *Barber had gone on a monumental binge the night before and was so drunk by midday that he could barely stand... When a hunter shoots an elephant, the village goes on a binge, eating meat every day for weeks.*

2 NC A **binge** is also a short period in which you spend far more money than you usually do or than is advisable. *He embarked on the most remarkable takeover binge... They're having one last spending binge.*

bingo /bɪŋgəʊ/

NU **Bingo** is a game in which each player has a card with numbers on. Someone calls out numbers and if you are the first person to have all your numbers called out, you win the game. *Bingo is more British—even though the game originated in Italy.*

binman /bɪnmæn/ **binmen**

NC A **binman** is the same as a **dustman**. *He was working as a council binman.*

binoculars /bɪnɒkjʊləz/

N PL **Binoculars** consist of two small telescopes joined together side by side, which you look through in order to see things that are a long way away. *The President was shown using binoculars, apparently looking across the border to Saudi Arabia.*

bio- /baɪəʊ-, baɪn-/

PREFIX **Bio-** is used at the beginning of nouns and adjectives that refer to life or to the study of living things. *...biography. ...biophysicist. ...biology. ...bio-medical.*

biochemist /baɪəʊkemɪst/ **biochemists**

NC A **biochemist** is a scientist or student who studies biochemistry. *...a team of biochemists from Cambridge University.*

biochemistry /baɪəʊkemɪstri/

NU **Biochemistry** is the science which is concerned with the chemistry of living things. *They are now employing the techniques of biochemistry and genetic engineering to make more deadly weapons.*

biodegradable /baɪəʊdɪgreɪdəbl/

ADJ Something that is **biodegradable** breaks down or decomposes naturally without any special treatment, and therefore does not cause pollution. *All British detergents were made biodegradable in 1964.*

biogas /baɪəʊgæs/ **biogases**

NUorNC **Biogas** is a gas produced by the action of bacteria on organic waste matter. It is used as a fuel. *They've installed an electric generator fueled by biogas... Biogases like methane are a 21st century fuel.*

biographer /baɪɒgrəfə/ **biographers**

NC Someone's **biographer** is a person who writes an account of their life. *...Blunt's latest biographer, John Costello.*

biographical /baɪəgræfɪkl/

ADJ You use **biographical** to describe something which gives information about a person's life. *...biographical sketches of the man who has assumed power.*

biography /baɪɒgrəfi/ **biographies**

NC A **biography** of a person is an account of their life, written by someone else. *...a biography of Dylan Thomas.*

Bioke Malabo, Cristino Seriche /kriːstiːnəʊ serɪtʃeɪ bjəʊkeɪ mæləbəʊ/

Lieutenant-Colonel Cristino Seriche Bioke Malabo became Prime Minister of Equatorial Guinea in 1982. He was Minister of Government Co-ordination, Planning, Economic Development and Finance from 1982 to 1986. He is a member of the Democratic Party of Equatorial Guinea (PDGE), the only legal party, although a multi-party system is to be introduced.

biological /baɪəlɒdʒɪkl/

1 ADJ A **biological** process, system, or product is connected with or produced by natural processes in plants, animals, and other living things. *...the effect of heat on biological activity.* ◆ **biologically** ADV *These beings were biologically different from man.*

2 ADJ ATTRIB **Biological** studies and discoveries are connected with research in biology. *...recent biological breakthroughs.*

3 ADJ ATTRIB **Biological** weapons and **biological** warfare involve the use of organisms which damage living things. *...the stockpiling of biological weapons.*

biological clock

N SING Your **biological clock** is your body's way of registering time. It does not depend on external events such as day or night. *When the biological clock says it's time to go to sleep, most animals go to sleep... When one crosses time zones, one has to re-synchronise one's biological clock to local time.*

biology /baɪɒlədʒi/

NU **Biology** is the science which is concerned with the study of living things. *...Fred Cooke, a professor of biology at Queen's University.* ◆ **biologist** /baɪɒlədʒɪst/ **biologists** NC *This has puzzled biologists for a long time.*

bionic /baɪɒnɪk/

ADJ **Bionic** technology or studies involve taking ideas from natural things such as plants or animals and using them in machines. *One example of bionic design investigation is a remarkably accurate speed indicator for aeroplanes that was developed using the same principle found in beetles' eyes. ...a so-called bionic ear, which helps deaf people hear.*

biophysics /baɪəʊfɪzɪks/

NU **Biophysics** is the science which explains biology by using the laws of physics. *...the Laboratory of Molecular Biophysics at Oxford.*

biosphere /baɪəsfɪə/

N SING The **biosphere** is the part of the earth's surface and atmosphere which is inhabited by living things; a technical term. *We are poisoning the biosphere with industrial pollution.*

biotechnology /baɪəʊteknɒlədʒi/

NU **Biotechnology** is the use of living parts, such as cells or bacteria, in industry and technology. *They will be using biotechnology to aid industrial research... Arguably, the most important benefits of biotechnology to the developing world will be in the field of medicine.*

bipartisan /baɪpɑːtɪzæn, baɪpɑːtɪzən/

ADJ **Bipartisan** means concerning or involving two different political parties or groups. *The Labour Party rejected Churchill's offer of a bipartisan reform... The President can expect bipartisan support for the bill.*

biped /baɪped/ **bipeds**

NC A **biped** is a creature with two feet; a technical term. *A biped exposes much less of its surface area to the sun than a quadruped.*

biplane /baɪpleɪn/ **biplanes**

NC A **biplane** is an old-fashioned aeroplane with two pairs of wings, one above the other. *The 34p stamp shows a large biplane operated by Imperial Airways.*

birch /bɜːtʃ/ **birches**

1 NCorNU A **birch** or a **birch tree** is a tall tree with thin branches. *Much of the forest is coniferous, but there are many birch trees too.*

2 N SING If someone is given the **birch**, they are punished by being hit with a wooden cane. *...its reluctance to banish the birch for punishing criminals.*

bird /bɜːd/ **birds**
NC A **bird** is a creature with feathers and wings. Most birds can fly. *Farmers seem to have pretty good ways of preventing their crops being eaten by birds.* ● **Bird** is used in these phrases. ● If you say that **a bird in the hand is worth two in the bush**, you mean that it is better to keep what you already have than to risk losing it by trying to achieve something else. ● If you say that something will **kill two birds with one stone**, you mean that two things are achieved rather than just one. *I think the army are trying to kill two birds with one stone; they want to try and open up trade and they are also trying to press hard against the rebel bases.* ● If you say that something is **for the birds**, you mean that it is silly; used in informal American English. *Sorry, people, this story was for the birds... Strictly for the birds.*

Bird, Vere C. /vɪə bɜːd/
Vere C. Bird became the first Prime Minister of Antigua and Barbuda in 1981. He was President of the Antigua Trades and Labour Union from 1943 to 1967. He served as Chief Minister of Antigua from 1960 to 1967, and as Premier from 1967 to 1971, and from 1976 to 1981. He is a member of the Antigua Labour Party (ALP). Born: 1909.

bird-brained
ADJ If you say that someone is **bird-brained**, you think they are stupid and always concerned with unimportant things; an informal word.

birdcage /bɜːdkeɪdʒ/ **birdcages**
NC A **birdcage** is a cage in which a bird is kept.

birdie /bɜːdi/ **birdies, birdying, birdied**
1 NC Children use the word **birdie** to refer to a bird. *Little birdie, why do you fly upside down?*
2 NC If you get a **birdie** in golf, you get the ball into a hole in one stroke fewer than the number that it is thought a good golfer should take. *He managed his seventh birdie on the final hole, making the new course record... Lee's round of 66 included six birdies.* ► Also VO *Dan Forsman birdied the last five holes.*

bird of paradise, birds of paradise
NC A **bird of paradise** is a songbird which is found mainly in New Guinea. The male birds have very brightly coloured feathers. *The noise of our walking startles a bird of paradise.*

bird of prey, birds of prey
NC A **bird of prey** is a bird, such as an eagle or a hawk, that kills and eats other birds and animals. *Many birds of prey fetch a high price from falconers who use them for sport.*

birdseed /bɜːdsiːd/
NU **Birdseed** is seed for feeding birds.

bird's eye view, bird's eye views
1 NC A **bird's eye view** is a view that you see from far above, so that things look very small. *From this tower you get a bird's eye view of the city, including the racecourse and the airport.*
2 NC If you have a **bird's eye view** of something, you have a general or overall impression of it. *...then we'll have a bird's eye view of what we've done so far.*

bird watcher, bird watchers
NC A **bird watcher** is someone whose hobby is watching and studying wild birds in their natural surroundings. *There are over 2 million serious bird watchers in the United States.*

Birendra Bir Bikram Shah Dev, King of Nepal /bɪrendrə bɪə bɪkrəm ʃɑː deɪv/
King **Birendra Bir Bikram Shah Dev** succeeded to the throne of Nepal in 1972. Born: 1945.

Birkirkara /bɪəkəkɑːrə/
Birkirkara is Malta's largest city. Population: 21,000 (1988).

Biro /baɪrəʊ/ **Biros**
NC A **Biro** is a ballpoint pen; **Biro** is a trademark.

birth /bɜːθ/ **births**
1 NU or NC When a baby is born, you refer to this event as its **birth**. *...a girl deaf from birth... She came back to the country of her birth... the birth of her first child.*

2 N SING+SUPP You can refer to the beginning or origin of something as its **birth**. *...the birth of television. ...the birth of popular democracy.*
● **Birth** is used in these phrases. ● When a woman **gives birth**, she produces a baby from her body. *Beth gave birth to our third child.* ● You use **by birth** after your nationality in order to indicate where you or your parents were born. *Dr Cort's father is a Russian by birth.* ● See also **date of birth**.

birth control
NU **Birth control** means planning when to have or not have children, and using natural or other methods of contraception to prevent having them when they are not wanted. *The Family Planning Association pioneered public education on birth control and sexual health in Britain and worldwide.*

birthday /bɜːθdeɪ, bɜːθdi/ **birthdays**
NC Your **birthday** is the anniversary of the date on which you were born. *Happy birthday!... Mr Mandela came home on his seventy-second birthday... The affair became public knowledge at her birthday party last month.*

birthmark /bɜːθmɑːk/ **birthmarks**
NC A **birthmark** is a mark on someone's skin that has been there since they were born. *...complaints from other parents about a large birthmark on his face.*

birthplace /bɜːθpleɪs/ **birthplaces**
1 NC+POSS Your **birthplace** is the place where you were born. *Cruz returned to his birthplace, Hong Kong, and became champion jockey.*
2 N SING+POSS The **birthplace** of something is the place where it began or originated. *...the birthplace of the Renaissance.*

birth rate, birth rates
NC The **birth rate** is the number of babies born for every 1000 people in a particular area during a particular period of time. *While the birth rate in the north declines, in the south the population is booming... Unemployment seems set to rise because of the country's high birth rate.*

birthright /bɜːθraɪt/
N SING+POSS Something that is your **birthright** is something that you feel you have a right to have, simply because you are a human being. *He felt that a decent standard of education and health care was his birthright.*

biscuit /bɪskɪt/ **biscuits**
NC A **biscuit** is a small, flat cake that is crisp and usually sweet. *Yorkshire residents apparently like sweet things like cake and biscuits.*

bisect /baɪsekt/ **bisects, bisecting, bisected**
VO If something **bisects** an area or line, it divides the area or line in half. *The main north-south road bisects the town.*

bisexual /baɪsekʃuəl/ **bisexuals**
ADJ Someone who is **bisexual** is sexually attracted to both men and women. *People can be heterosexual and then become bisexual.* ► Also NC *The girl told her father that she was a bisexual.*

Bishkek /bɪʃkek/
Bishkek, formerly called Frunze, is the capital of Kyrgyzstan and its largest city. Population: 626,000 (1989).

bishop /bɪʃəp/ **bishops**
1 NC A **bishop** is a Christian clergyman of high rank, especially in the Roman Catholic, Anglican, and Orthodox churches. *...a Roman Catholic bishop and three priests. ...the Bishop of Chester.*
2 NC In chess, a **bishop** is a piece which is moved diagonally across the board.

bison /baɪsn/ **bisons**. The plural form can be either **bisons** or **bison**.
NC A **bison** is a large hairy animal of the cattle family, which used to be common in North America and Europe. *Game wardens will join hunters to shoot bison that wander out of their Yellowstone National Park home.*

Bissau /bɪsaʊ/
Bissau is the capital of Guinea-Bissau and its largest city. Population: 109,000 (1979).

bistro /biːstrəʊ/ **bistros**
NC A **bistro** is a small restaurant or bar where food is

served. ...*luxury hotels with indoor swimming pools and built-in bars and bistros.*

Biswas, Abdur Rahman /ˈæbduə rəxmɑːn bɪswɑːs/
Abdur Rahman Biswas became President of Bangladesh in 1991. He was Minister of Jute from 1979 to 1980, and Minister of Health and Population Control from 1981 to 1982. Born: 1926.

bit /bɪt/ **bits**
1 NC A **bit** of something is a small amount or piece of it. ...*a little bit of cheese... I really enjoyed your letter, especially the bits about Dr O'Shea... People need a bit of help and encouragement.*
2 NC You also use **bit** to refer to an item or thing of a particular kind. ...*a bit of furniture.*
3 NC In computing, a **bit** is the smallest unit of information that is held in a computer's memory.
4 **Bit** is also the past tense of **bite**.
• **Bit** is used in these informal phrases. • **A bit** means to a small extent or degree. *He was a bit deaf... It's a little bit more complicated... Wait until the wind dies down a bit... The situation might calm down quite a bit.* • You can use **a bit of** to make a statement less extreme. For example, the statement 'It's a bit of a nuisance' is less extreme than 'It's a nuisance'. *The Ambassador has received a bit of a snub from the municipal authorities.* • You can say that someone's behaviour is **a bit much** when you are annoyed about it. *It's asking a bit much to expect a lift.* • You say that something is **every bit as** good or bad as something else to emphasize that they are just as good or bad as each other. *She wanted to prove to them that she was every bit as clever as they were... What was going on now, he said, was every bit as bad as 1915.* • If you do something **for a bit**, you do it for a short period of time. *Why can't we stay here for a bit?* • You use **not a bit** when you want to make a strong negative statement. *It was all very clean and tidy, not a bit like his back garden.* • **Quite a bit** of something is quite a lot of it. ...*a rich Irishman who's made quite a bit of money.*

bitch /bɪtʃ/ **bitches, bitching, bitched**
1 NC If you call a woman a **bitch**, you mean that she behaves in a very unpleasant way; an offensive use.
2 V If someone **bitches**, they complain about something in a nasty way; an informal use. *You haven't done a thing except bitch ever since we got here.*
3 NC A **bitch** is also a female dog. ...*a three-year-old biscuit-coloured bitch.*

bitchy /bɪtʃi/ **bitchier, bitchiest**
ADJ Someone who is **bitchy** says nasty things about other people. *Being bitchy was one of Cindy's failings.* ...*a bitchy remark.*

bite /baɪt/, **bites, biting, bit, bitten**
1 VOorVA When a person or animal **bites** something, they use their teeth to cut into it or through it. *My dog bit me... She bit into her rock cake.* ▶ Also NC *Madeleine took a bite. 'It's delicious.'*
2 VO When an insect or a snake **bites** you, it pierces your skin and causes that area of your skin to itch or be painful. ...*areas where the risk of being bitten by insects is high.* ▶ Also NC *My hands are covered with mosquito bites.*
3 V When an action or policy begins to **bite**, it begins to have a significant or harmful effect. *The sanctions are beginning to bite.*
4 N SING If you have a **bite** to eat, you have a small meal; an informal use. *Shall we have a bite to eat?... 'Stay and have a bite,' said Charlie.'We'll find something in the kitchen.'*

biting /baɪtɪŋ/
1 ADJ A **biting** wind is extremely cold. *Standing without a coat or hat in the biting January wind, President Bush began his inaugural address.*
2 ADJ **Biting** speech or writing is sharp and clever in a way that makes people feel uncomfortable. ...*a writer with a biting wit.*

bit part, bit parts
NC A **bit part** is a small and unimportant part for an actor in a film or play. *My writing was beginning to take over and I was making more money out of that than doing bit parts.*

bitten /bɪtn/
Bitten is the past participle of **bite**.

bitter /bɪtə/ **bitterest; bitters**
1 ADJ If someone is **bitter**, they feel angry and resentful. *He was a jealous, slightly bitter man.*
♦ **bitterly** ADV *'I'm glad somebody's happy,' he said bitterly... Those who had to be turned away complained bitterly.* ♦ **bitterness** NU *He remembers with bitterness how his father was cheated.*
2 ADJ ATTRIB If you have a **bitter** disappointment or experience, you feel angry or unhappy about it. *I have had long and bitter experience of dealing with people like that... The decision was a bitter blow for Mr Stephen Solarz.*
3 ADJ In a **bitter** argument, war, or struggle, people argue or fight fiercely and angrily. *There has been a bitter debate about when to move on to the next stage of the democratisation process... This was the scene of bitter fighting in 1969. ...an increasingly bitter war of words between the two authorities.* ♦ **bitterly** ADV *...the dam, which is bitterly opposed by environmentalists... He has bitterly attacked Mrs Thatcher over her recent statements. ...one of the government's most bitterly contested pieces of legislation.* • **to the bitter end**: see **end**.
4 ADJ A **bitter** wind or **bitter** weather is extremely cold. ...*hot food to keep the survivors and the rescue workers warm in the bitter winter weather.* ♦ **bitterly** SUBMOD ...*a bitterly cold New Year's Day.*
5 ADJ Something that tastes **bitter** has a sharp, unpleasant taste. *It has a very bitter taste, but it does wash off.* • **a bitter pill to swallow**: see **pill**.
6 N MASS **Bitter** is a kind of British beer. ...*two pints of bitter... Old Thumper is a strong bitter brewed in Hampshire.*

bitter lemon, bitter lemons
N MASS **Bitter lemon** is a fizzy drink that is made partly from the juice of lemons. It is drunk on its own or mixed with alcoholic drinks, such as gin or vodka.

bitterly /bɪtəli/
ADV **Bitterly** means strongly and intensely. You use it to describe strong emotions such as anger, hatred, or shame. *No man could have hated the old order more bitterly.* • See also **bitter**.

bitter-sweet
1 ADJ Something that tastes or smells **bitter-sweet** seems both bitter and sweet at the same time. ...*the bitter-sweet scent of blackcurrant leaves.*
2 ADJ An experience or a memory that is **bitter-sweet** has both happy and sad qualities or features. ...*the bitter-sweet memory of their first meeting.*

bitty /bɪti/
ADJ Something that is **bitty** seems to consist of a lot of different parts which do not fit together or go together well; an informal word. *The play was very bitty in the second act.*

bitumen /bɪtʃumɪn/
NU **Bitumen** is a black sticky substance which is obtained from tar or petrol. It is used in making roads. ...*producing, transporting and processing bitumen and heavy crude oil.*

bivouac /bɪvuæk/ **bivouacs, bivouacking, bivouacked**
1 NC A **bivouac** is a temporary camp made by soldiers or mountaineers.
2 VA If soldiers or mountaineers **bivouac** in a mountainous place, they stop there and stay in a rough temporary camp. ...*regiments that had bivouacked at places like Valley Forge.*

Biya, Paul /pɔːl biːjə/
Paul Biya became President of Cameroon in 1982. He was Prime Minister from 1975 to 1982. He is a member of the Cameroon People's Democratic Movement (RDPC). Born: 1933.

bizarre /bɪzɑː/
ADJ Something that is **bizarre** is very odd and strange. ...*bizarre gadgets. ...some of the more bizarre aspects of this case.*

blab /blæb/ **blabs, blabbing, blabbed**
V If you **blab**, you reveal a secret; an informal word. *I wonder who blabbed... He's been blabbing to the Press.*

blabber /blæbə/ blabbers, blabbering, blabbered
v If someone **blabbers**, they talk about something in a way that is considered to be boring, irritating, or foolish; an informal word. *He was blabbering on about human rights.*

blabbermouth /blæbəmauθ/ blabbermouths
NC A **blabbermouth** is a person who tells other people things that you did not want them to know; an informal word.

black /blæk/ blacker, blackest; blacks, blacking, blacked
1 ADJ Something that is **black** is of the darkest colour that there is, the colour of the sky at night when there is no light at all. *...a black leather coat... She turned up in a fairly traditional black evening gown.* ● See also **black and blue**, **black and white**.
2 NC Someone who is **black** belongs to a race of people with dark skins, especially a race from Africa. *...black musicians.* ▶ Also NC *He was the first black to be elected to the Congress.*
3 ADJ **Black** coffee or tea has no milk or cream added to it. *...a cup of very strong, black coffee.*
4 ADJ If you describe a situation as **black**, you mean that it is bad and not likely to improve. *I don't think the future is as black as that.*
5 ADJ ATTRIB **Black** magic involves communicating with evil spirits. *He was a pretty disreputable character—a practitioner of black arts.*
6 ADJ ATTRIB **Black** humour involves jokes about things that are sad or unpleasant. *...a black comedy.*
7 VO When a group such as a trade union **blacks** particular goods or people, it refuses to handle those goods or to have dealings with those people. *Their members had blacked these goods at the London Docks.*
black out PHRASAL VERB 1 If you **black out**, you lose consciousness for a short time. 2 If a town or city is **blacked out**, its electricity supply is cut off. *Other cities on the coast were blacked out for several hours... A guerilla attack blacked out much of Lima.* 3 If news or news programmes **are blacked out**, they are prevented from being printed or broadcast. *An interview he gave to the media was blacked out. ...a strike which has blacked out programmes for the past three weeks.* ● See also **blackout**.

black and blue; also spelt black-and-blue.
ADJ PRED Someone who is **black and blue** is badly bruised, usually because they have been hit by someone. *He used to beat me black-and-blue.*

black and white; also spelt black-and-white.
1 ADJ In a **black and white** photograph or film, everything is shown in black, white, and grey. *...black-and-white horror movies.*
2 You say that something is **in black and white** when it has been written or printed, and not just spoken. *He was surprised to see his conversation in black-and-white... The agreement sets out in black and white a clear role for his own country's government.*

blackball /blækbɔ:l/ blackballs, blackballing, blackballed
VO If you **blackball** someone, you prevent them from joining a club or other group by voting against their election. *Voters were entitled to blackball any candidate they did not like.*

black belt, black belts
1 NC A **black belt** is a belt worn by someone who has reached a particular high standard in judo, karate, or another martial art. *He's got a black belt in karate.*
2 NC A **black belt** is also a person who has reached a particular high standard in judo, karate, or another martial art. *She's a black belt now at judo.*

blackberry /blækbəⁱri/ blackberries
NC A **blackberry** is a small black or dark purple fruit that grows on wild bushes.

blackberrying /blækbəriiŋ/
NU If you go **blackberrying**, you go out and pick wild blackberries.

blackbird /blækbɜ:d/ blackbirds
NC A **blackbird** is a common European bird with black or brown feathers.

blackboard /blækbɔ:d/ blackboards
NC A **blackboard** is a dark-coloured board which teachers write on with chalk. *The teacher is writing on the blackboard, and some of the students are practising their writing.*

black box, black boxes
1 NC A **black box** is an electronic device in an aircraft which records information about its flights. It is often used to provide evidence about accidents. *As yet there is no indication as to the cause of the crash, but the plane's black box has been recovered. ...the black box flight recorder.*
2 NC You can refer to a part of an electronic or computer system as a **black box** when you know what it does, but do not know exactly how it works. *A small black box receives the infra-red data and passes it to the vehicle's computer.*

blackcurrant /blækkʌrənt/ blackcurrants
NC **Blackcurrants** are very small dark purple fruits that grow in bunches on bushes.

black economy
N SING The **black economy** of a country is the earning of money that goes on without the government being informed, in order to avoid paying tax on it. *The black economy, which makes life tolerable, is still dependent on the official one.*

blacken /blækən/ blackens, blackening, blackened
1 VO To **blacken** something means to make it black or very dark in colour. *His face was blackened with charcoal.*
2 VO If someone **blackens** your reputation or name, they try to make other people believe that you are a bad person. *...an embittered man who wanted to blacken the reputation of the police... He accused the Prime Minister of trying to blacken the party's name.*

black eye, black eyes
NC If someone has a **black eye**, they have a dark-coloured bruise around one of their eyes. *...following hospital treatment for a black eye he suffered on Tuesday.*

blackguard /blægɑ:d/ blackguards
NC If you describe someone as a **blackguard**, you mean that they are wicked and dishonourable; an old-fashioned word. *Now don't lie to me, you young blackguard!*

blackhead /blækhed/ blackheads
NC A **blackhead** is a small black spot on the skin, which is caused by a pore in the skin being blocked by dirt.

black hole, black holes
NC A **black hole** is an area in space that is believed to exist, where gravity is so strong that nothing, not even light, can move away from it. *If the centre of our galaxy does contain a black hole, then it's most likely to be a rotating black hole.*

black ice
NU **Black ice** is a thin transparent layer of ice on a road, which is difficult to see and therefore often causes accidents. *Thousands of motorists have been stranded in southern England by freezing fog and black ice.*

blacking /blækiŋ/
NU **Blacking** is a type of polish that was used in former times to make shoes or metal objects such as stoves blacker. *Their pallor was disguised with boot blacking.*

blackish /blækiʃ/
ADJ Something that is **blackish** is very dark in colour. *The water in the shallow well was blackish.*

blackjack /blækdʒæk/
NU **Blackjack** is a card game that is usually played for money; used in American English. *A year ago he started dealing blackjack and poker... You still have to get the cards at the blackjack table to win.*

blackleg /blækleg/ blacklegs
NC If you say that someone is a **blackleg**, you mean that they are continuing to work when the people they work with are on strike, or they are working instead of the people who are on strike; used showing disapproval.

blacklist /blæklɪst/ blacklists, blacklisting, blacklisted
1 NC A **blacklist** is a list made by a government, organization, or important person, which contains the

names of people who they think cannot be trusted or who have done something wrong. *Many of the teachers had been placed on a blacklist.*
2 vo If someone **blacklists** a person or organization, they put them on a blacklist. *So far this year the authorities have blacklisted seventeen firms.*

blackmail /blækmeɪl/ **blackmails, blackmailing, blackmailed**
vo If someone **blackmails** you, they try and force you to do what they want or to give them money, by threatening to harm you or your reputation. *Workers say they have been blackmailed by the employers into going back... Two of the men were charged with blackmailing him.* ▶ Also nu *The government accuses the rebels of using blackmail... He was found guilty of blackmail.*

blackmailer /blækmeɪlə/ **blackmailers**
nc A **blackmailer** is someone who blackmails someone else, usually in order to get money from them. *I could grab this blackmailer by the throat and strangle him.*

black Maria /blæk məraɪə/ **black Marias**
nc A **black Maria** is a black van that the police use to transport prisoners in. *Vehicles, including buses and a black Maria, were attacked and set ablaze.*

black mark, black marks
nc If someone has a **black mark** against them, they have done something or have a quality which causes people to disapprove of them. *My refusal to go would be a black mark against me.*

black market, black markets
nc If something is bought or sold on the **black market**, it is bought or sold illegally. *He whispered that he could change money on the black market.*

black marketeer /blæk mɑːkɪtɪə/ **black marketeers**
nc A **black marketeer** is someone who trades on the black market. *Seven policemen have been charged with taking bribes from black marketeers.*

black marketeering /blæk mɑːkɪtɪərɪŋ/
nu **Black marketeering** is the activity of trading on the black market. *The disturbance erupted following attempts by the authorities to crack down on black marketeering.*

blackout /blækaʊt/ **blackouts**
1 nc A **blackout** during a war is a period of time in which a place is made dark for safety reasons. *We couldn't get home before the blackout.*
2 nc A news **blackout** is a temporary stopping of news from being printed or broadcast, usually for political reasons. *The Home Office asked for a blackout on news reports of the incident... The government has decided to impose a news blackout on four countries.*
3 nc A power **blackout** is a temporary cutting off of the electricity supply to a place. *The government began restricting electricity supplies some weeks ago to avoid a total blackout. ...a power blackout after a transmission line was blown up.*
4 nc If you have a **blackout**, you temporarily lose consciousness. *Last year he suffered a series of blackouts which doctors were unable to explain.*

black pudding, black puddings
nuornc **Black pudding** is a thick sausage with a black skin. It is made from pork fat and pig's blood. *They consume too much fish and chips, black pudding and beer.*

black section, black sections
nc In Britain, a **black section** is an unofficial group within a political party which represents the interests of black members. *...the question of establishing black sections within the Labour Party.*

black sheep
n sing If you refer to someone as the **black sheep** of a family, you mean that everyone else in the family is good, but that person is bad.

blacksmith /blæksmɪθ/ **blacksmiths**
nc A **blacksmith** is someone whose job is making things out of metal, such as horseshoes or farm tools. *Only the point is made of steel, and this is made by blacksmiths.*

black spot, black spots
1 nc A **black spot** on a road is a place where accidents often happen. *These repair sections have been the worst accident black spots.*

2 nc A **black spot** is an area of a country where a particular situation is especially bad. *Government money should be diverted to unemployment black spots.*

black tie
adj A **black tie** event is a formal event such as a party at which the men wear formal clothes, including dinner jackets and bow ties. *Around forty people, mostly Oxford and Cambridge students, were at the black tie party.*

bladder /blædə/ **bladders**
nc Your **bladder** is the part of your body where urine is held until it leaves your body. *These stones form in the bladder and make it very painful to urinate.* ● See also **gall bladder**.

blade /bleɪd/ **blades**
1 nc The **blade** of a knife, axe, or saw is the sharp part. *...a formidable curved dagger with a 40 centimeter blade.*
2 nc The **blades** of a propeller or the **blades** in some engines are the parts that turn round. *A turbine blade broke free and sliced through the casing.*
3 nc The **blade** of an oar is the thin, flat part that you put into the water.
4 See also **razor blade, shoulder blade**.

blah /blɑː/
You use **blah, blah, blah** to refer to something that has been said or written without giving the actual words, because you think that they are boring or unimportant; used in informal speech. *He said they were marvellous, couldn't have been more helpful, blah, blah, blah.*

blame /bleɪm/ **blames, blaming, blamed**
1 vo If you **blame** a person for something bad, or you **blame** it on them, you think or say that they are responsible for it. *I was blamed for the theft... Police have blamed the bomb attacks on extremists.* ▶ Also nu *You haven't said a word of blame.*
2 nu The **blame** for something bad is the responsibility for causing it or letting it happen. *He had to take the blame for everything... British Rail put the blame on renovation work which was in progress... The management lays the blame on an inefficient workforce.*
3 vo If you say that you do not **blame** someone for doing something, you mean that it was a reasonable thing to do in the circumstances. *I can't really blame him for wanting to make me suffer.*

blameless /bleɪmləs/
adj Someone who is **blameless** has not done anything wrong. *Whilst the driver of the second train died in the crash, he is almost certainly blameless.*

blameworthy /bleɪmwɜːðɪ/
adj Someone who is **blameworthy** has done something bad or wrong. *I hardly feel I am blameworthy.*

blanch /blɑːntʃ/ **blanches, blanching, blanched**
v If you **blanch**, you suddenly become very pale, usually because you are shocked, embarrassed, or frightened. *I don't think anyone blanched about it.*

blancmange /bləmɒndʒ/ **blancmanges**
nuornc **Blancmange** is a cold jelly-like pudding made from milk, sugar, cornflour, and flavouring.

bland /blænd/ **blander, blandest**
1 adj Someone who is **bland** is calm and polite, and rarely shows or causes interest or excitement. *...bland, middle-of-the-road, evasive men... A former lawyer from the South, he has a bland public image.* ◆ **blandly** adv *Mr Jones blandly dismissed their arguments... They say blandly that, of course, they will take note of our wishes and opinions.*
2 adj **Bland** things are dull and uninteresting. *...bland cheeses... Some critics call his music bland. ...bland official statements.*

blandishments /blændɪʃmənts/
n pl **Blandishments** are pleasant things that you say to someone in order to persuade them to do something; a formal word. *He remained impervious to all Nell's blandishments.*

blank /blæŋk/ **blanker, blankest**
1 adj Something that is **blank** has nothing on it. *...a blank sheet of paper. ...a blank wall.*
2 adj If you look **blank**, your face shows no feeling,

understanding, or interest. *Her face went blank.*
♦ **blankly** ADV *I sat quietly, staring blankly ahead.*
3 ADJ or N SING If your mind or memory goes **blank** or is a **blank**, you cannot think of anything or remember anything. *The list helped to prompt the patient and prevent his mind going blank.*
4 If you **draw a blank** when you are looking for someone or something, you fail to find them; an informal expression. *So far however, efforts to trace the original document have drawn a blank.*
5 See also **blank verse, point-blank.**

blank cheque, blank cheques
1 NC A **blank cheque** is a cheque that you sign and give to someone for them to write in the amount of money that they want you to pay them. *It would be totally irresponsible to sign a blank cheque that could be cashed at any stage.*
2 If you **give** someone **a blank cheque**, you give them the authority to do what they think is best in a particular situation or to spend as much money as they think is necessary. *One might argue that the vote amounts to giving the President a blank cheque... He said that the NHS needed another £1000 million of investment, but the government didn't think it sensible to write blank cheques.*

blanket /blæŋkɪt/ **blankets, blanketing, blanketed**
1 NC A **blanket** is a large piece of thick cloth which you put on a bed to keep you warm. *She offered British help for the victims in the form of blankets, food and shelter.*
2 VO If something such as snow **blankets** an area, it covers it. *Snow has blanketed many areas—the Midlands has been worst hit.* ► Also N SING ...*a blanket of cloud.*
3 ADJ ATTRIB You use **blanket** to describe something which affects or refers to every person or thing in a group. ...*our blanket acceptance of everything they say.* ...*a blanket ban on both military and civilian flights... The search for the culprits is given blanket coverage on the front pages.*

blank verse
NU **Blank verse** is poetry that does not rhyme. In English literature it usually consists of lines with five unstressed and five stressed syllables. ...*'Paradise Lost', an epic in blank verse written by the seventeenth century poet John Milton.*

Blantyre /blæntaɪə/
Blantyre is the largest city in Malawi. Population: 332,000 (1987).

blare /bleə/ **blares, blaring, blared**
V When something such as a siren or radio **blares**, it makes a loud, unpleasant noise. *The TV set was blaring in the background.* ► Also N SING ...*the blare of conversation.*
blare out PHRASAL VERB When something such as a radio or record player **blares out** music or noise or when music or noise **blares out** of it, it produces a very loud unpleasant sound. *The music blared out continually from the loudspeakers.*

blarney /blɑːni/
NU **Blarney** consists of a lot of pleasant but perhaps untrue things that someone says to you, usually to try and make you like them or to persuade you to do something.

blasé /blɑːzeɪ/
ADJ If you are **blasé** about something which other people find exciting or alarming, you show no real interest in it, often because you have experienced it before. *You sound very blasé about it... I've worked in the tropics a lot myself, and you do get a bit blasé about mosquito bites.*

blaspheme /blæsfiːm/ **blasphemes, blaspheming, blasphemed**
V If someone **blasphemes**, they say rude or disrespectful things about God. ...*anyone who might blaspheme or defame their holy image of the Emperor... They believe that he has blasphemed against their religion.*

blasphemous /blæsfəməs/
ADJ Words or actions that are **blasphemous** show disrespect for God. ...*a blasphemous poem.*

blasphemy /blæsfəmi/ **blasphemies**
NU or NC If someone says or does something that shows disrespect for God, you can say that what they are saying or doing is **blasphemy**. *Any attempt to violate that image is blasphemy.* ...*blasphemy laws in Britain... It would be regarded as a blasphemy.*

blast /blɑːst/ **blasts, blasting, blasted**
1 NC A **blast** is a big violent explosion. *Nobody had been hurt in the blast... Six more died in a bomb blast at a charity event.*
2 VO If people or things **blast** something, they destroy or damage it with a bomb or an explosion. *Tunnels have been blasted through bedrock beneath the city... The rocket blasted its way through two walls.*
3 NC A **blast** is also a sudden strong rush of air or wind, or a short, loud sound carried by the wind. ...*icy blasts... Ralph blew a series of short blasts.*
4 If a machine is on at **full blast**, it is producing as much sound or heat as it is able to. *She insists on having the radio on at full blast.*
5 **Blast** is a mild swear word that people use when they are irritated or annoyed about something.
blast off PHRASAL VERB When a space rocket **blasts off**, it leaves the ground at the start of its journey. *The space shuttle Atlantis blasted off from Cape Canaveral last night.*

blasted /blɑːstɪd/
ADJ ATTRIB You can use **blasted** to indicate that you are annoyed or irritated with someone or something; an informal word. ...*that blasted bank manager... That's part of the confusion of the whole blasted thing.*

blast furnace, blast furnaces
NC A **blast furnace** is a furnace in which iron ore is heated under pressure until it melts and the pure iron separates out and can be collected. *An explosion damaged a blast furnace at the steel works.*

blast-off
NU **Blast-off** is the moment when a rocket or space shuttle leaves the ground and rises into the air. *The exact time of blast-off is being kept secret.*

blatant /bleɪtnt/
ADJ **Blatant** is used to describe something bad which is done in an open or obvious way. ...*blatant discrimination.* ...*blatant disregard for international law.* ...*a blatant violation of the basic rights of minorities.* ♦ **blatantly** ADV *They blatantly ignored the truce agreement.*

blaze /bleɪz/ **blazes, blazing, blazed**
1 V When a fire **blazes**, it burns strongly and brightly. *The fire in the top two storeys of the building was blazing out of control.*
2 NC A **blaze** is a large fire in which things are damaged. *You never saw such a blaze.*
3 V Something that **blazes** with light or colour is extremely bright. *The flower beds blazed with colour.*
4 NC+SUPP A **blaze** of light or colour is a large amount of it. ...*a blaze of sunlight.*
5 N SING+of A **blaze** of publicity or attention is a great amount of it. *She eventually retired in a blaze of glory.*

blazer /bleɪzə/ **blazers**
NC A **blazer** is a kind of jacket, especially one worn by schoolchildren or members of a sports team. *To the left was another man, who wore a blue blazer.*

blazing /bleɪzɪŋ/
1 ADJ ATTRIB You use **blazing** to describe the weather or a place when it is very hot and sunny. ...*the blazing beach.* ...*the blazing heat of the plain.*
2 ADJ ATTRIB When people have a **blazing** row, they quarrel in a noisy and excited way. *Surveys show that 2 out of 3 husbands and wives have a blazing row during the festive season.*

bleach /bliːtʃ/ **bleaches, bleaching, bleached**
1 V-ERG To **bleach** material or hair means to make it white or pale, by using a chemical or by leaving it in the sun. *He bleaches his hair... Their bones would have been bleached by the sun... I left the cloth in the sun to bleach.*
2 NU **Bleach** is a chemical that is used to make cloth white, or to clean things thoroughly. ...*a strong household bleach.*

bleak /bliːk/ **bleaker, bleakest**
1 ADJ If a situation is **bleak**, it is bad, and seems unlikely to improve. *The future looked bleak.* *...painted a bleak picture of the economic outlook... The prospects for the left-wing are bleak.* ♦ **bleakness** NU *...the bleakness of the post war years.*
2 ADJ If something is **bleak**, it looks cold and bare. *...the bleak coastline. ...the bleak winters.*
3 ADJ If someone looks or sounds **bleak**, they seem depressed, hopeless, or unfriendly. *...his bleak features.* ♦ **bleakly** ADV *He stared bleakly ahead.*
bleary /bliəri/
ADJ If your eyes are **bleary** or if you are **bleary-eyed**, your eyes are red and watery, usually because you are tired. *The Australian cricketers arrived five hours late, bleary-eyed.*
bleat /bliːt/ **bleats, bleating, bleated**
1 V When a sheep or goat **bleats**, it makes the high-pitched noise that sheep and goats typically make. ► Also NC *...the bleat of a goat.*
2 V When people **bleat**, they speak in a weak, high, complaining voice. *They bleat about how miserable they are.*
bled /bled/
Bled is the past tense and past participle of **bleed**.
bleed /bliːd/ **bleeds, bleeding, bled**
V When you **bleed**, you lose blood from your body as a result of an injury or illness. *He was bleeding heavily... His feet had begun to bleed.*
bleeder /bliːdə/ **bleeders**
NC+SUPP People sometimes refer to a man who they dislike or feel sorry for as a **bleeder**; an informal word which some people find offensive. *They didn't give the poor bleeder a chance.*
bleeding /bliːdɪŋ/
1 NU **Bleeding** is the state of losing blood from your body as a result of injury or illness. *Had the bleeding stopped? ...heavy internal bleeding caused by an abdominal tumour.*
2 ADJ ATTRIB or ADV **Bleeding** is also a swear word used to emphasize what you are saying, especially when you dislike something; an offensive use.
bleep /bliːp/ **bleeps, bleeping, bleeped**
1 NC A **bleep** is a short, high-pitched sound, usually one of a series, that is made by an electrical device. *If you hear long bleeps, the phone is engaged.* ► Also V *The alarm was bleeping... You clip it on to your pocket and it bleeps when someone wants to contact you.*
2 VO If you **bleep** someone, for example a doctor, you inform them that they are wanted by making an electrical device bleep.
bleeper /bliːpə/ **bleepers**
NC A **bleeper** is an electrical device which someone carries around with them and which bleeps to tell them that they are wanted, or to tell other people where they are. *...a bleeper which would wake up even the most dozy security guard. ...carrying bleepers to help locate them if they were buried by snow.*
blemish /blemɪʃ/ **blemishes, blemishing, blemished**
1 NC A **blemish** is a mark that spoils the appearance of something. *We don't send tomatoes with blemishes on.*
2 VO If something **blemishes** your reputation, it spoils it. *...people who could blemish its new reformist image.* ► Also NC *...the biggest blemish on the government's human rights record... We all have blemishes in our personal history.*
blench /blentʃ/ **blenches, blenching, blenched**
V If you **blench** at something, you are very frightened of it, and often move away in fear. *Even strong men blench at the thought of walking into their boss's office.*
blend /blend/ **blends, blending, blended**
1 V-RECIP When you **blend** substances together, you mix them together so that they become one substance. *Next, blend the tomatoes, garlic, and cream to form a paste... Blend the cornflour with a little cold water... It could be used to make sure perfumes are perfectly blended.*
2 V-RECIP When colours or sounds **blend**, they come

together or are combined in a pleasing way. *...their voices blending marvellously as they sing in harmony... Three young men from Luton who blend jazz, soul, and blues... If you're going to play in a group, you've got to make a sound that blends with the other instruments.*
3 V-RECIP If you **blend** ideas, policies, or styles, you use them together in order to achieve something. *...how to blend warmth and caution in the right proportions... The Gorbachov plan blends economic radicalism with political caution. ...new ways of building which just didn't blend with the traditional ones.*
4 NC A **blend** of things is a mixture or combination of them that is useful or pleasing. *Each drug requires its own special blend of polymers. ...gasoline-ethanol blends. ...a quite unrivalled blend of performance and economy for a family car. ...a candidate with an exceptional blend of intellect, humour, and political experience.*
blend into or **blend in** PHRASAL VERB If something **blends into** the background or **blends in**, it is so similar to the background in appearance or sound that it is difficult to see or hear it separately. *Tree snakes blend well into foliage... Because the community is predominantly Latino, outsiders can blend in more easily.*
blender /blendə/ **blenders**
NC A **blender** is a machine used in the kitchen for mixing liquids and soft foods together at high speed. *They put them in a blender and make a juice.*
bless /bles/ **blesses, blessing, blessed** /blest/
1 VO When a priest **blesses** people or things, he asks for God's favour and protection for them. *He blessed his supporters and then gave a thumbs up sign... The Pope blessed the foundation stones of six new parish churches.*
2 V-PASS+with If someone is **blessed** with a particular good quality or skill, they have it. *She is blessed with immense talent and boundless energy.*
● **Bless** is used in these phrases. ● When people say **God bless** or **bless you** to someone, they are expressing their affection, thanks, or good wishes. *Thanks for listening, and God bless you... Bless you, it's terribly good of you to come.* ● You can say **bless you** to someone who has just sneezed.
blessed /blesɪd/
ADJ ATTRIB You use **blessed** to describe something that you think is wonderful, and that you are thankful for or relieved about. *...blessed freedom.* ♦ **blessedly** SUBMOD *...the blessedly cool oasis of the airport.*
blessing /blesɪŋ/ **blessings**
1 NC A **blessing** is something good that you are thankful for. *Health is a blessing that money cannot buy.*
2 NC+POSS If something is done with someone's **blessing**, they approve of it. *She did it with the full blessing of her parents. ...to contact the North without the official blessing of the government.*
3 If you say that a situation is a **mixed blessing**, you mean that it has disadvantages as well as advantages. *The withdrawal is seen as something of a mixed blessing by Western governments.*
blether /bleðə/ **blethers, blethering, blethered**
V If you say that someone is **blethering**, you mean that they are talking stupidly and not making sense; an informal word. *What are you blethering about?*
blew /bluː/
Blew is the past tense of **blow**.
blight /blaɪt/ **blights, blighting, blighted**
1 NC You can refer to something as a **blight** when it causes great difficulties, and damages or spoils other things. *We think of pollution as a modern blight, but it is not. ...the blight of hooliganism and crime.*
2 VO If something **blights** your life or your hopes, it damages and spoils them. *Her career has been blighted by clashes with the authorities... Deprivation and poverty were blighting the lives of millions of people.*
blighter /blaɪtə/ **blighters**
NC People refer to someone they do not like, or who they think has done something wrong as a **blighter**.

People occasionally use **blighter** to express sympathy or mild envy; an informal word. *Let's make these blighters pay... Gosh, do you poor blighters have to put up with this?... You lucky blighter!*

blimey /ˈblaɪmi/
Some people say 'Blimey' or 'Cor blimey' to indicate how surprised they are or how strongly they feel about something; used in informal speech. *Blimey, you were asking for trouble... Caron listened in silence. 'Blimey!' he said at last.*

blind /blaɪnd/ **blinds, blinding, blinded**
1 ADJ Someone who is **blind** cannot see because their eyes are damaged. *The accident had left him almost totally blind.* ◆ **blindness** NU *Eye damage can result in temporary or permanent blindness.*
2 N PL You can refer to people who are blind as the **blind**. *One of the main problems for the blind is communication by writing.*
3 VO If something **blinds** you, you become unable to see, either for a short time or permanently. *My eyes were momentarily blinded by flash bulbs.*
4 ADJ PRED+*to* If you are **blind** to a fact or situation, you take no notice of it or are unaware of it. *He was blind to everything except his immediate needs.*
5 If you **turn a blind eye** to something wrong or bad that someone is doing, you pretend not to notice, and allow them to continue doing it. *...bribes paid to government ministers and policemen to turn a blind eye to smuggling... He blames the international community for turning a blind eye to human rights abuses.*
6 VO+*to* If something **blinds** you to the real situation, it prevents you from noticing or being aware of its reality. *We have to beware that missionary zeal doesn't blind us to the realities here.*
7 ADJ ATTRIB You describe someone's beliefs or actions as **blind** when they take no notice of the facts or behave in an unreasonable way. *...her blind faith in the wisdom of her Church... She had driven him into a blind rage.*
8 ADJ When you are driving along a road, a **blind** corner is one that curves very sharply so that you cannot see round it.
9 NC A **blind** is a roll of cloth or paper which you pull down over a window to keep out the light. *We've taken the normal standard blind that you find in offices... Four explosions echoed round the building, shaking the window blinds.*
10 See also **blinding, colour blind, Venetian blind.**

blind alley, blind alleys
1 NC A **blind alley** is a very narrow road which is blocked at one end so that there is no way out.
2 NC If you go up a **blind alley** when you are trying to achieve something, you end up in a situation in which no progress is possible, and have to start again. *The Opposition accuses the General of leading it up a blind alley during negotiations.*

blind date, blind dates
NC A **blind date** is an arrangement made for you to spend an evening with someone of the opposite sex who you have never met before. *We met on a blind date.*

blind drunk
ADJ PRED Someone who is **blind drunk** is very drunk indeed.

blinders /ˈblaɪndəz/
N PL If you say that someone is wearing **blinders**, you mean that they are considering only a narrow point of view and are ignoring other opinions or information; used in American English. *They'd worn racial blinders most of their lives... The government shouldn't operate with blinders on.*

blindfold /ˈblaɪndfəʊld/ **blindfolds, blindfolding, blindfolded**
1 NC A **blindfold** is a strip of cloth that is tied over someone's eyes so that they cannot see. *I had a blindfold put round my eyes... He and his colleague had to wear blindfolds during daily interrogations.*
2 VO If you **blindfold** someone, you tie a blindfold over their eyes. *I was blindfolded and taken away in an unmarked car.* ◆ **blindfolded** ADV *One man is said to have been held blindfolded for two days.*

blinding /ˈblaɪndɪŋ/
1 ADJ A **blinding** light is extremely bright. *There came a blinding flash.*
2 ADJ ATTRIB You use **blinding** to emphasize that something is very clear, but may stop you from seeing other things. *...the blinding obviousness of the advantage. ...a blinding revelation... They have a blinding faith in modern weaponry, which, I must admit, I don't share.* ◆ **blindingly** SUBMOD *Isn't it blindingly obvious?*
3 See also **blind.**

blindly /ˈblaɪndli/
1 ADV If you do something **blindly**, you do it when you cannot see properly. *He ran blindly across the clearing.*
2 ADV You can also use **blindly** to say that you do something without enough information, or without thinking much about it. *With the information we have now, we can only speculate blindly. ...to avoid criticism that it is blindly pursuing profits.*

blind man's buff
NU **Blind man's buff** is a children's game in which one child has a piece of cloth tied over their eyes so that they cannot see, and then has to catch the other children.

blind spot, blind spots
NC If you have a **blind spot** about something, you cannot understand it. *London Underground had 'a blind spot over the hazards of fire on escalators', the report says.*

blink /blɪŋk/ **blinks, blinking, blinked**
1 V or VO When you **blink** or when you **blink** your eyes, you shut your eyes and very quickly open them again. *They looked at him without blinking... The baby blinked and put her hand over her face... The girl blinked her eyes several times.* ▶ Also NC *It was his guilty blink that gave him away.*
2 V When a light **blinks**, it flashes on and off. *Dots and dashes blinked out from a signal light.*

blinkered /ˈblɪŋkəd/
ADJ A **blinkered** view, attitude, or approach considers only a narrow point of view and does not take into account other people's opinions. *...blinkered self-interest... Sir Geoffrey accused those who opposed private health care of having a blinkered approach... Wasn't he too blinkered and set in his ways to exercise effective political leadership in the modern world?*

blinkers /ˈblɪŋkəz/
1 N PL **Blinkers** are two pieces of leather which are placed at the side of a horse's eyes so that it can only see straight ahead.
2 N PL If you say that someone is wearing **blinkers**, you mean that they are considering only a narrow point of view and are ignoring other opinions or information. *He accused them of wearing moral blinkers. ...wearing intellectual blinkers.*

blinking /ˈblɪŋkɪŋ/
ADJ ATTRIB You can use **blinking** to describe someone or something which irritates or annoys you; an informal word.

blip /blɪp/ **blips**
1 NC A **blip** is a small spot of light, sometimes occurring with a short, high-pitched sound, which flashes on and off regularly on a piece of equipment such as a radar screen. *As the two radar blips converged, frantic radio warnings were sent out.*
2 NC A **blip** in a straight line is a point at which the line suddenly makes a sharp change in direction before returning to its original direction. *Towards the end of the 1970s, there seemed to be a blip on the graph and it got rapidly worse.*
3 NC A **blip** in a situation is a sudden but temporary interruption to it or difference in it. *According to the government this will be only a temporary blip in its otherwise clean record.*

bliss /blɪs/
NU **Bliss** is a state of complete happiness, or a time or situation in which you are very happy. *For a couple of months, weekends were bliss.*

blissful /ˈblɪsfl/
ADJ A **blissful** time or state is a very happy one. *They sat there together in blissful silence.* ◆ **blissfully** ADV

His eyes shut blissfully and he smiled.

blister /blɪstə/ **blisters, blistering, blistered**
1 NC A **blister** is a painful swelling containing clear liquid on the surface of your skin. *Mercury can also cause rashes and blisters on the skin.*
2 V-ERG When your skin **blisters**, blisters appear on it as a result of burning or rubbing. *...diseases where the skin blisters and peels off if it's touched... He could blister his hands grilling hamburgers... My face was blistered with a crimson rash.*
3 V-ERG When paint or rubber **blisters**, small bumps appear on its surface.

blistering /blɪstərɪŋ/
1 ADJ When the weather or the sun is **blistering**, it is extremely hot. *...the blistering days of midsummer.*
2 ADJ A **blistering** remark expresses great anger or sarcasm. *...had recently been exposed to a blistering attack.*
3 ADJ **Blistering** is used to describe actions in sports events which are done with great speed or force. *...winning the first 16 rallies at a blistering pace. ...setting a blistering world record of 9.83. ...a blistering boundary which brought the crowd to their feet.*

blithe /blaɪð/
ADJ You use **blithe** to indicate that something is done casually, without serious or careful thought. *I made a blithe comment about the fine weather.* ◆ **blithely** ADV *...the blessing of good health which we blithely take for granted.*

blithering /blɪðərɪŋ/
ADJ ATTRIB If you call someone a **blithering** idiot, you are emphasizing how stupid you think they are; an informal word.

blitz /blɪts/ **blitzes, blitzing, blitzed**
1 VO When a city or building is **blitzed** during a war, it is attacked by bombs dropped by enemy aircraft. ◆ **blitzing** NU *...the blitzing of Queen's Hall in Portland Place.*
2 N PROP The **Blitz** was the heavy bombing of British cities by German aircraft from 1940-41. *She was killed in the Blitz.*
3 NC When you have a **blitz** on something, you make a big effort to get it done; an informal use. *We're going to have a blitz on the house and get it all decorated by Christmas.*
4 NC+SUPP An advertising **blitz** is a sudden major effort to publicize something. *...its current advertising blitz for Diet-Coke... Senator Gore's massive television blitz of the last seventy-two hours obviously paid off.*

blizzard /blɪzəd/ **blizzards**
NC A **blizzard** is a storm in which snow falls heavily and there are strong winds. *Scotland and the North of England have been hit by blizzards... A climber is feared to have been buried in an avalanche as blizzards swept across the Scottish Highlands.*

bloated /bləʊtɪd/
1 ADJ Something that is **bloated** is much larger than normal because it has a lot of liquid, food, or gas inside it. *...bloated corpses... Their stomachs were unnaturally bloated.*
2 ADJ If you describe an organization or its budget as **bloated**, you mean that it has far more money than it needs; used showing disapproval. *Bloated government bureaucracy swallows up a big share of the budget... Bloated with subsidies from the Ministry of Central Planning, these state monopolies accounted for 90 percent of Polish industry.*

bloater /bləʊtə/ **bloaters**
NC A **bloater** is a herring that has been soaked in salted water and smoked.

blob /blɒb/ **blobs**
1 NC A **blob** of thick or sticky liquid is a small amount of it. *...a blob of melted wax.*
2 NC You describe something that you cannot see very clearly, for example because it is far away, as a **blob**. *...a blob of grey in the distance.*

bloc /blɒk/ **blocs**
NC+SUPP A **bloc** is a group of countries with similar political aims and interests acting together. *Since the Madrid conference, important changes have occurred in the Soviet bloc. ...any evidence that comes from*

Eastern Bloc countries... He reiterated his call for the formation of an Asia-Pacific trading bloc. ● See also **en bloc.**

block /blɒk/ **blocks, blocking, blocked**
1 NC A **block** of flats or offices is a large building containing them. *...a large office block. ...the basement of an apartment block... They escaped through a tunnel dug from a cell block, under the prison garden.* ● See also **tower block.**
2 NC A **block** in a town is an area of land with streets on all its sides. *The store was three blocks away.*
3 NC A **block** of a substance is a large rectangular piece of it. *...a block of ice.*
4 VO To **block** a road, channel, or pipe means to put something across or in it so that nothing can get past. *The Turks had blocked the land routes... Mounted police blocked the entrance to Westminster Bridge... Some streets were blocked for a time by protestors... The runways are blocked with trucks or tanks.* ◆ **blocked** ADJ *The road was completely blocked.*
5 VO If something **blocks** your view, it prevents you from seeing something by being between you and that thing. *The driver blocked his view.*
6 VO If you **block** something that is being arranged, you prevent it from being done. *The Council blocked his plans... The government has blocked an attempt by the company to sell fifty trainer jets. ...two main reasons why progress was being blocked.*
7 See also **building block, road block, stumbling block.**

block out PHRASAL VERB If you **block out** a thought, you try not to think about it. *They attempt to withdraw from the world, to block it out.*

block up PHRASAL VERB If you **block** something **up** or if it **blocks up**, it becomes completely blocked so that nothing can get through it. *Never block up ventilators... The sink keeps blocking up.*

blockade /blɒkeɪd/ **blockades, blockading, blockaded**
NC A **blockade** is an action that is taken to prevent goods from reaching a place. *...the blockade of Berlin... An air blockade against Iraq is being considered... He denied that his country had imposed an economic blockade on Nepal.* ► Also VO *The Atlantic Squadron promptly blockaded Santiago.*

blockage /blɒkɪdʒ/ **blockages**
N or NU A **blockage** in a pipe, tube, or tunnel is the state of being blocked or the thing that is blocking it. *Perhaps there was a blockage in the fuel line... Blockage of either or both tubes is the commonest cause of infertility in women.*

block and tackle
N SING A **block and tackle** is a device for lifting heavy things, consisting of a rope or chain that is passed around a pair of blocks containing pulleys.

blockbuster /blɒkbʌstə/ **blockbusters**
NC A new film or book that is described as a **blockbuster** is one that is extremely popular and successful. *'Total Recall' is the latest blockbuster starring Austrian-born muscleman Arnold Schwarzenegger.*

block capitals
N PL **Block capitals** or **block letters** are simple capital letters that are not decorated in any way. *Please answer all the questions in block capitals... A poster instructed us, in block letters, to 'Work Hard for the Continuing Revolution'.*

blockhead /blɒkhed/ **blockheads**
NC If you call someone a **blockhead**, you mean that they are stupid; an informal word. *Happy anniversary, blockhead! So where's the cake and ice-cream?*

block letters. See **block capitals.**

block vote, block votes
NC A **block vote** is a large number of votes that are all cast in the same way by one person on behalf of a group of people. *The union has decided to cast its block vote in favour of unilateralism. ...the system of large block votes wielded by trade union representatives at the party's annual conferences.*

Bloemfontein /bluːmfənteɪn/
Bloemfontein is the judicial capital of South Africa and the capital of the Orange Free State. Population: 233,000 (1985).

bloke /bləʊk/ **blokes**

NC A **bloke** is a man; an informal word. *The bloke just looked at it and waved me through... He was a nice bloke but he wasn't a tough enough leader.*

blonde /blɒnd/ **blondes**; also spelt **blond.**

1 ADJ **Blonde** hair is pale yellow-coloured hair. *...her long blonde hair.*

2 NC A **blonde** is a person, especially a woman, who has blonde hair. *...a former model, Miss Janie Allen, a blonde who's now a columnist for the local newspaper... Do blondes really have more fun?* ▶ Also ADJ *...a tall, blond Englishman.*

blood /blʌd/

1 NU **Blood** is the red liquid that flows inside your body. *We can measure the flow of blood to the brain... Blood samples are taken as part of routine medical examinations.*

2 NU+SUPP You can use **blood** to refer to the race or social class of someone's parents or ancestors. *There was eastern blood on her mother's side.*

● **Blood** is used in these phrases. ● **Bad blood** refers to feelings of hate and anger between groups of people. *The rebels hoped to create bad blood between Spain and the United States.* ● If you **give blood**, you allow doctors to take some of the blood from your body to be used for operations and transfusions. *Those involved are being advised not to give blood.* ● If something violent and cruel is done **in cold blood**, it is done deliberately and in an unemotional way. *His organisation says he was shot in cold blood.* ● If a quality or talent is **in your blood**, it is part of your nature, and other members of your family have it too. *Music is in her blood.* ● If something **makes** your **blood boil**, it makes you very angry. *The mention of one particular name is guaranteed to make the blood boil of even the most placid Israeli.* ● If something **makes** your **blood run cold**, it makes you feel very frightened or horrified. *My blood ran cold as he repeatedly referred to the soldiers as kids... He said the military knew things about politicians which would make the public's blood run cold.* ● New people who are introduced into an organization and whose fresh ideas are likely to improve it are referred to as **new blood, fresh blood,** or **young blood.** *The government urgently needs to bring in new blood before the younger generation becomes disenchanted... There is no encouragement for fresh blood within the party ranks.*

blood bank, blood banks

NC A **blood bank** is a place where blood is stored until it is needed for blood transfusions. *They say that the new public blood banks are not being properly monitored.*

bloodbath /blʌdbɑːθ/ **bloodbaths**

NC If you describe an event as a **bloodbath,** you mean that a lot of people were killed very violently. *Only American intervention could avert a bloodbath... Prison officers have warned of a possible bloodbath.*

blood brother, blood brothers

NC A man's **blood brother** is a man whom he has sworn to treat as a brother, often in a ceremony which involves mixing a small amount of their blood.

blood cell, blood cells

NC A **blood cell** is one of the small red or white cells which are found in your blood. *The body makes blood cells, and in fact billions of cells per day are produced in normal adults.*

blood count, blood counts

NC A **blood count** is a check on the number of red and white blood cells in someone's blood, to see how healthy they are. *They have low blood counts, which prevents us from treating them with drugs.*

bloodcurdling /blʌdkɜːdlɪŋ/

ADJ ATTRIB A **bloodcurdling** sound or story is very frightening and horrible. *...a bloodcurdling shriek. ...bloodcurdling allegations.*

blood donor, blood donors

NC **Blood donors** are people who give blood from their bodies so that it can be used for transfusions or operations. *Hundreds are injured and hospitals have appealed for blood donors to come forward.*

blood group, blood groups

NC A **blood group** is one of the different types of blood that is found in different people. The commonest blood groups are O and A. *What blood group are you? ...people with blood groups O and B.*

bloodhound /blʌdhaʊnd/ **bloodhounds**

NC A **bloodhound** is a large dog with a very good sense of smell, which is sometimes used to follow people or to find them if they are lost. *Bloodhounds should have diamond-shaped eyes.*

bloodless /blʌdləs/

1 ADJ If you describe someone's face or skin as **bloodless,** you mean that it is very pale.

2 ADJ A **bloodless** coup or victory is one in which nobody is killed. *...a very different man from his predecessor, whom he ousted in a bloodless coup in November... They came to power in 1986 through a bloodless revolution.*

blood-letting

NU **Blood-letting** is violence or killing of particular people for a particular reason, especially between rival gangs or families. *The violence began as they were returning to their hostels, and the blood-letting continued into the night.*

blood money

NU **Blood money** is money that is paid to the families of people who have been murdered. *Defence lawyers have still not agreed to terms for payment of blood money to the families of the murdered Sudanese. ...exacting blood money in compensation.*

blood poisoning

NU **Blood poisoning** is a serious illness resulting from an infection in your blood. *In severe cases Salmonella can lead to blood poisoning, causing kidney failure and death.*

blood pressure

NU Your **blood pressure** is a measure of the amount of force with which your blood flows around your body. *I have high blood pressure and heart trouble.*

blood relation, blood relations

NC A **blood relation** or **blood relative** is a relative who is part of your family by birth rather than by marriage. *Wives, in-laws, and step-children were six times more likely to be murdered than blood relatives.*

bloodshed /blʌdʃed/

NU **Bloodshed** is violence in which people are killed or wounded. *The Pope called for action to prevent further bloodshed. ...to try and end the siege without bloodshed.*

bloodshot /blʌdʃɒt/

ADJ If your eyes are **bloodshot,** the parts that are usually white are red or pink. *In the morning the side of my head was swollen, my eye was bloodshot and I felt pain in my knees. ...big bloodshot eyes.*

blood sport, blood sports

NC **Blood sports** are sports such as hunting in which animals are killed. *The problems in trying to stamp out these illegal blood sports are enormous... Not all blood sports are banned in Britain.*

bloodstained /blʌdsteɪnd/

ADJ Something that is **bloodstained** is covered with blood. *Their bloodstained bodies were shown to journalists this morning.*

bloodstock /blʌdstɒk/

NU Thoroughbred horses that have been specially bred for a particular purpose such as racing are referred to as **bloodstock.** *...bloodstock sales.*

bloodstream /blʌdstriːm/ **bloodstreams**

NC Your **bloodstream** is your blood as it flows around your body. *...a drug that dissolves in the bloodstream. ...into the bloodstreams of the volunteers.*

bloodthirsty /blʌdθɜːsti/

ADJ A **bloodthirsty** person is eager to use violence or to see other people use violence. *It was important to show that the ANC was not made up of bloodthirsty people.*

blood transfusion, blood transfusions

NC When a patient is given a **blood transfusion,** blood is put into his or her body. *...the need for blood transfusions after heart operations.*

blood type, blood types

NC A **blood type** is the same as a **blood group.**

Automated systems to determine different blood types are normally very expensive.

blood vessel, blood vessels
NC **Blood vessels** are the narrow tubes through which your blood flows. *This chemical affects nerves, blood vessels and other tissues in the body.*

bloody /blʌdi/ **bloodier, bloodiest**
1 **Bloody** is a swear word, used to emphasize how annoyed or angry you are. *I feel bloody angry at the way we are getting treated.*
2 ADJ A situation or event that is **bloody** is one in which there is a lot of violence and people are killed. *The effects will be violent, disruptive, and probably bloody. ...the prospect of a bloody civil war. ...since the bloody riots of 1981.*
3 ADJ Something that is **bloody** has a lot of blood on it. *Orest raises his bloody hands to heaven.*

bloody mary, bloody marys
NC A **bloody mary** is a drink that is made from vodka and tomato juice.

bloody-minded
ADJ Someone who is being **bloody-minded** is deliberately making difficulties instead of being helpful. *You're just being bloody-minded.* ◆ **bloody-mindedness** NU *It's sheer bloody-mindedness on their part.*

bloom /bluːm/ **blooms, blooming, bloomed**
1 NC A **bloom** is the flower on a plant. *...great scarlet hibiscus blooms.* ● A plant or tree that is **in bloom** has flowers on it.
2 V When a plant or tree **blooms**, it produces flowers. When a flower **blooms**, the flower bud opens. *This variety of rose blooms late into the autumn.*

bloomer /bluːmə/ **bloomers**
1 N PL **Bloomers** are an old-fashioned kind of women's underwear consisting of wide, loose trousers that are gathered at the knees. *...a pair of bloomers.*
2 NC A **bloomer** is a mistake; an old-fashioned use. *I made a bit of a bloomer.*

blooming /bluːmɪŋ/
1 ADJ ATTRIB **Blooming** is a mild swear word used to emphasize what you are saying, especially when you are annoyed. *It's a blooming nuisance.*
2 ADJ Someone who is **blooming** looks attractively healthy and full of energy. *Martha appeared, blooming and pretty... She was blooming with health.*

blossom /blɒsəm/ **blossoms, blossoming, blossomed**
1 NU or NC **Blossom** is the flowers that appear on a tree before the fruit. *The trees were heavy with yellow blossom... Spectators and those in the parade throw blossoms at one another.* ● A tree that is **in blossom** has blossom on it.
2 V When a tree **blossoms**, it produces blossom. *...the bare trees poised to blossom.*
3 V You say that a person **blossoms** when they develop attractive qualities or abilities. *She had blossomed into a real beauty.*

blot /blɒt/ **blots, blotting, blotted**
1 N SING If something is a **blot** on someone's reputation, it spoils their reputation and makes people think badly of them. *He has called the coup a shameful blot on Caribbean history... Child pornography and abuse are a blot on civilisation.*
2 NC A **blot** is a drop of liquid, especially ink, that has been spilled on a surface and has dried. *...ink blots on the paper.*
3 VO If you **blot** a surface, you remove liquid from it by pressing a piece of soft paper or cloth onto it. *Paint the surface of the potato, then blot it on newspaper.*

blot out PHRASAL VERB If one thing **blots out** another, it is in front of the other thing and prevents it from being seen. *The resulting dust cloud blotted out the sun.*

blotch /blɒtʃ/ **blotches**
NC A **blotch** is a small area of colour, for example on someone's skin. *There were purple blotches around her eyes.*

blotchy /blɒtʃi/
ADJ Something that is **blotchy** has blotches on it. *The fine blood vessels will have expanded, making the face blotchy and reddened.*

blotter /blɒtə/ **blotters**
1 NC A **blotter** is a sheet of blotting paper attached to cardboard. You use a blotter for drying ink on a piece of paper.
2 NC In American English, a **blotter** is also a notebook where information is written before it is copied and stored somewhere else. *...people whose names appear on the police blotter.*

blotting paper
NU **Blotting paper** is thick, soft paper that you use for drying ink on a piece of paper.

blotto /blɒtəʊ/
ADJ PRED Someone who is **blotto** is extremely drunk; an old-fashioned, informal word.

blouse /blaʊz/ **blouses**
NC You can refer to a shirt worn by a girl or a woman as a **blouse**. *...wearing a blue blouse and white trousers.*

blow /bləʊ/ **blows, blowing, blew, blown**
1 V When a wind or breeze **blows**, the air moves. *The winds had been blowing from the west... A fierce wind was blowing across the desert.*
2 V-ERG If something **blows** somewhere or if the wind **blows** it there, it is moved there by the wind. *...the dangers of inhaling radioactive dust that was blowing across the site... High winds had blown a sheet of corrugated iron onto the pitch.*
3 V or VOA If you **blow**, you send out a stream of air from your mouth. *Eric put his lips close to the hole and blew softly... He lit a cigarette and blew a cloud of smoke across the table.*
4 VO To **blow** bubbles means to make them by blowing air into a liquid. *It is more effective than conventional aerators which blow bubbles or stir up the slurry.*
5 V-ERG When you **blow** a whistle or a horn, or when it **blows**, it makes a sound because you send air into it using your lips. *The lips are tightly pursed when blowing a wind instrument... When the whistle blows after ten or twenty minutes, the Lakwenas cease firing.*
6 VO When you **blow** your nose, you force air out of it through your nostrils in order to clear it.
7 NC If you give someone a **blow**, you hit them. *He knocked Thomas unconscious with one blow of his fist.*
8 NC A **blow** is also something that happens which makes you very disappointed or unhappy. *It must have been a fearful blow to him... The attack was clearly a major blow.*
9 NC A **blow** for a particular cause or principle is an action that makes it more likely to succeed. A **blow** against it makes it less likely to succeed. *He struck a blow for liberty. ...the most devastating blow against the provisional IRA in modern times.*
10 VOA If something is **blown** off or is **blown** to pieces, it is violently removed or destroyed by an explosion. *He would have blown his hand off if he'd fired the gun... The vehicle was blown to pieces.* ● If an explosion **blows** a hole in something, it suddenly and violently causes a hole to appear in it. *It blew a hole in the roof.*
11 VO If you **blow** a large amount of money, you spend it quickly on things that you do not really need; an informal use. *We blew twenty-three bucks on a lobster dinner.*

blow out PHRASAL VERB If you **blow out** a flame or a candle, you blow at it so that it stops burning. *...wishing him a happy birthday and blowing out the candles.*

blow over PHRASAL VERB If something such as trouble or an argument **blows over**, it comes to an end. *Senior government ministers hope that the whole affair will now blow over.*

blow up PHRASAL VERB 1 If you **blow** something **up** or if it **blows up**, it is destroyed by an explosion. *The hijackers have threatened to blow the plane up if their demands are not met... Imagine the horror of an atomic power station blowing up.* 2 If you **blow up** something such as a balloon or a tyre, you fill it with air. *This isn't something you can blow up with a foot pump, you need compressed air.*

blow-by-blow
ADJ ATTRIB A **blow-by-blow** account of an event

describes every stage of it in detail. *The book gives us a blow-by-blow account of the most famous takeovers in recent history.*

blow-dry, blow-dries, blow-drying, blow-dried
N SING A **blow-dry** is a way of drying someone's hair using a hairdryer to give it a particular shape or style. *He is having a cut and blow-dry.* ▶ Also V O *I don't think you're going to get any man admitting he blow-dries his hair.*

blower /bləʊə/
N SING The **blower** is the telephone; an old-fashioned, informal word. *Miss Callaghan was on the blower to Atkinson.*

blowlamp /bləʊlæmp/ **blowlamps**
N C A **blowlamp** is the same as a **blowtorch**.

blown /bləʊn/
Blown is the past participle of **blow**.

blow-out, blow-outs
1 N C A **blow-out** is a sudden uncontrolled rush of oil or gas from a well. *They have suspended drilling until the alternative methods of controlling blow-outs are installed.*
2 N C In a vehicle, a **blow-out** happens when a tyre suddenly bursts. *If the bus had suffered a blow-out, it should still have been able to avoid falling on its side.*
3 N C A **blow-out** is also a meal that is larger than you normally have; an informal use. *Have a blow-out on your birthday.*

blowpipe /bləʊpaɪp/ **blowpipes**
N C A **blowpipe** is a long tube from which weapons such as arrows can be blown.

blowtorch /bləʊtɔːtʃ/ **blowtorches**
N C A **blowtorch** is a hand-held device which uses gas to produce a hot flame. It is used for removing old paint from wood or metal. *They instituted a crude test involving application of a blowtorch.*

blow-up, blow-ups
N C A **blow-up** is an enlargement of a photograph or picture. *...blow-ups of the best photographs on the wall.*

blowy /bləʊɪ/
ADJ If the weather is **blowy**, it is windy; an informal word.

blubber /blʌbə/ **blubbers, blubbering, blubbered**
1 N U **Blubber** is the fat of whales, seals, and similar sea animals. *Polar bears will gorge themselves on seal blubber.*
2 V, V-QUOTE, or V-REPORT If you **blubber**, you cry noisily and in an unattractive way. *I was blubbering helplessly.*

bludgeon /blʌdʒən/ **bludgeons, bludgeoning, bludgeoned**
V O+*into* If someone **bludgeons** you into doing something, they make you do it by bullying or threatening you. *The authorities' tactic seems to be to bludgeon the demonstrators into submission.*

blue /bluː/ **bluer, bluest; blues**
1 ADJ Something that is **blue** is the colour of the sky on a sunny day. *Huge blue and gold flags are now fluttering from outside the prime minister's office... He was seen driving a blue car.*
2 Something that happens **out of the blue** happens suddenly and unexpectedly. *Mr Kohl suggested quick monetary union, more or less out of the blue... Out of the blue, six soldiers jumped out of the police van and opened fire.*
3 N U The **blues** is a type of music which is similar to jazz, but is always slow and sad. *Other types of music, such as rhythm and blues, attract visitors to the Mardi Gras. ...a blues ballad.*
4 N PL If you have the **blues**, you are feeling very sad. *It is definitely not just a mild dose of the winter blues... I had the blues too.*
5 ADJ **Blue** films, stories, or jokes are mainly about sex. *...blue videos.*

bluebell /bluːbel/ **bluebells**
N C **Bluebells** are plants with thin upright stems and blue bell-shaped flowers.

blueberry /bluːbəⁱri/ **blueberries**
N C A **blueberry** is a small, dark blue North American fruit that is usually cooked before being eaten. *They cultivate a variety of fruits—grapes, peaches,*

watermelon, blueberries and others. ...organic blueberry yoghurt.

bluebird /bluːbɜːd/ **bluebirds**
N C A **bluebird** is a small North American bird that has blue feathers and can sing.

blue-black
ADJ Something that is **blue-black** is a very deep blue. *For days the blue-black smoke from these fires has been rising and forming huge clouds.*

blue-blooded
ADJ A **blue-blooded** person belongs to a royal or noble family. *The Reform Club's members are certainly not all blue-blooded aristocrats.*

bluebottle /bluːbɒtl/ **bluebottles**
N C A **bluebottle** is a large fly with a shiny dark-blue body. *The maggots are the larvae of the common bluebottle.*

blue-chip
ADJ A **blue-chip** investment or company is one in which it is considered to be profitable and safe to invest. *This followed a rally in bond prices, with most of the gains confined to blue-chip stocks.*

blue-collar
ADJ **Blue-collar** workers work in industry, doing physical work, rather than in offices. *The town's white population are mainly miners and blue-collar workers.*

blue-eyed boy, blue-eyed boys
N C+POSS If you refer to a boy or a man as someone's **blue-eyed boy**, you mean that they like them more than anyone else and therefore treat them especially well; an informal expression, used showing disapproval. *He is, again, the manager's blue-eyed boy.*

blueish /bluːɪʃ/
See **bluish**.

blue jeans
N PL **Blue jeans** are the same as **jeans**; used in American English. *He wears blue jeans, boots, and sunglasses.*

blue law, blue laws
N C In the United States, a **blue law** is a law to control activities which some people consider immoral, such as sexual behaviour, drinking alcohol, working on Sundays, and so on; an informal expression. *A repeal of the state's blue laws takes effect from today.*

blueprint /bluːprɪnt/ **blueprints**
N C A **blueprint** for something is an original plan or description of how it is expected to work. *The blueprint for economic reform has been approved... Visionaries are creating blueprints for the restoration of Berlin. ..the blueprints for submarines.*

bluestocking /bluːstɒkɪŋ/ **bluestockings**
N C A **bluestocking** is a clever, highly educated woman who is more interested in academic ideas than in behaving in a traditionally feminine way; an old-fashioned word, used showing disapproval.

blue tit blue tits
N C A **blue tit** is a small European bird with a blue head, wings, and tail, and a yellow breast. *Young blue tits are much yellower around the head than their parents.*

blue water
ADJ A **blue water** fleet or ship is capable of being used in the sea and over long distances. *It's a blue water navy which means it can protect India's power and strength in the Indian Ocean.*

bluff /blʌf/ **bluffs, bluffing, bluffed**
1 N Cor N U A **bluff** is an attempt to make someone believe that you will do something when you do not really intend to do it. *The boy was thinking up a clever bluff... His threats are merely bluff.*
2 If you **call** someone's **bluff**, you tell them to do what they have been threatening to do, because you are sure that they will not really do it. *Mr Shamir called his bluff, and he had to back down... Any attempt to call the hijacker's bluff could end in the massacre of the passengers.*
3 V or V O If you **bluff** someone, you make them believe that you will do something although you do not really intend to do it. *You're just bluffing... She wasn't bluffing him.*

bluish /ˈbluːɪʃ/

ADJ Something that is **bluish** is slightly blue. *Six grapefruit were found to contain a bluish substance.*

blunder /ˈblʌndə/ **blunders, blundering, blundered**

1 V If you **blunder**, you make a stupid or careless mistake. *The authorities blundered, and made their move too soon.* ▸ Also NC *I might have committed some dreadful blunder.*

2 V A If you **blunder** somewhere, you move there in a clumsy and careless way. *She blundered into a tree.*

blunt /blʌnt/ **blunter, bluntest; blunts, blunting, blunted**

1 ADJ If you are **blunt**, you say exactly what you think without trying to be polite. *The Minister of State was more blunt—he condemned the remarks as 'unprecedented, insulting, scandalous and incomprehensible'... Let me ask a blunt question.*
♦ **bluntly** ADV *He told them bluntly what was acceptable.* ♦ **bluntness** NU *Trueman is famous for his bluntness.*

2 ADJ A **blunt** object has a rounded or flat end rather than a sharp one. *...a wooden spoon or similar blunt instrument.*

3 ADJ A **blunt** knife is no longer sharp and does not cut well. *The operation is often carried out using blunt and dirty knives.*

4 VO If something **blunts** an emotion or feeling, it weakens it. *This side of his personality has been blunted by toil.*

blur /blɜː/ **blurs, blurring, blurred**

1 NC A **blur** is a shape or area which you cannot see clearly because it has no distinct outline or because it is moving very fast. *He discovered a faint, fuzzy blur in the sky near where the galaxy was supposed to be.*

2 V-ERG If something **blurs** a shape or picture, or if the shape or picture is **blurred**, you cannot see it clearly because its edges are no longer distinct. *A fault in the mirror of the telescope is blurring the image... Part of it is blurred because it is out of focus.* ♦ **blurred** ADJ *...a blurred snapshot.*

3 VO If something **blurs** an idea or a concept, the idea or concept no longer seems clear. *It blurred our essential message of racial reconciliation... The tabloid press tend to blur the line between what is real and what is not.* ♦ **blurred** ADJ *The distinction between reform and revolution had become blurred in his mind. ...the blurred outlines of a new policy.*

blurb /blɜːb/

N SING The **blurb** about a book, film, play, or exhibition is information about it that is intended to attract people's interest. *'Murder Mystery', as the blurb makes haste to assure us, contains no explicit violence... I noticed his name in the blurb that you let me have.*

blurry /ˈblɜːri/ **blurrier, blurriest**

ADJ A **blurry** shape or picture is one with an unclear outline. *The trees and hedges were just blurry shapes.*

blurt /blɜːt/ **blurts, blurting, blurted**

blurt out PHRASAL VERB If you **blurt** something **out**, you say it suddenly, after trying hard to keep quiet or to keep it secret. *There's no way I could just blurt out 'Actually, the sketch is of you, not Ted.'*

blush /blʌʃ/ **blushes, blushing, blushed**

V When you **blush**, your face becomes redder than usual because you are ashamed or embarrassed. *Philip blushed and laughed uneasily.* ▸ Also NC *'I made it myself,' Mr Solomon informed them with a modest blush.*

bluster /ˈblʌstə/ **blusters, blustering, blustered**

V When someone **blusters**, they speak angrily and aggressively because they are outraged or offended. *They blustered and swore the pictures were fakes.* ▸ Also NU *She simply ignored his bluster.*

blustery /ˈblʌstəri/

ADJ You say the weather is **blustery** when there are many gusts of strong wind. *The game, played in cold and blustery weather, was dull.*

boa /ˈbəʊə/ **boas**

NC A **boa** is a large snake that kills animals by squeezing them. *Thieves smashed the door of the reptile house and took the only female Blue-Ring boa in Europe.*

boa constrictor /ˈbəʊə kənstrɪktə/ **boa constrictors**

NC A **boa constrictor** is the same as a **boa**.

boar /bɔː/ **boars.** The plural form can be either **boars** or **boar**.

1 NC A **boar** is a male pig. *If you spray this chemical onto the sows or the boars, it actually increases the amount of mating that takes place.*

2 NC A **boar** or a **wild boar** is a wild pig. *The sign on the cage said 'pure bred wild boar'.*

board /bɔːd/ **boards, boarding, boarded**

1 NC A **board** is a flat piece of wood which is used for a particular purpose. *The television director held a board up in front of the audience. ...a chopping board. ...a drawing board... I'll write the sum up on the board.*

2 NC The **board** of a company or organization is the group of people who control it. *...members of the board. ...the International Rugby Board.*

3 VO If you **board** a train, ship, or aircraft, you get on it in order to travel somewhere; a formal use. *That same afternoon I boarded the plane at Kastrup... The police prevented them from boarding the train.*

4 NU **Board** is the food which is provided when you stay somewhere, for example in a hotel. *...the low price that my hostess was asking for board and bed.*
● See also **board and lodging, full board, half board**.
● **Board** is used in these phrases. ● When you are **on board** a train, ship, or aircraft, you are on it or in it. *He looked around at the other people on board.* ● An arrangement or deal that is **above board** is legal and is being carried out honestly and openly. *The General Secretary said the elections were above board, and he had received no complaints.* ● If a policy or a situation applies **across the board**, it affects everything or everyone in a particular group. *We're aiming for a 20% reduction across the board.* ● If an arrangement or plan **goes by the board**, it is not used or does not happen. *If they won't accept a UN presence there, the whole idea of getting agreement may go by the board.*

board up PHRASAL VERB If you **board up** a door or window, you fix pieces of wood over it so that it is covered up. *Many shopkeepers and businessmen could only board up wrecked and empty premises when the curfew was lifted... Muslim areas are deserted, with shops and houses boarded up.*

board and lodging

Board and lodging consists of food and a place to sleep, usually provided in a boarding house or sometimes offered as part of the conditions of a job. *The staff are paid £80 a month with board and lodging... These people are entitled to board and lodging while awaiting a decision.*

boarder /ˈbɔːdə/ **boarders**

NC A **boarder** is a pupil who lives at school during term time. *All the children in the school were boarders and the annual fee was £1200.*

board game, board games

NC A **board game** is a game such as chess or snakes and ladders, which people play by moving small objects around on a board. *...a new board game called 'Capital Adventure' in which players travel around a map of the world.*

boarding /ˈbɔːdɪŋ/

1 ADJ ATTRIB **Boarding** is used to refer to the system in which children live at school during the term. *Annual day fees stood at £1038, and average boarding fees at £2289.*

2 ADJ ATTRIB **Boarding** is also used to refer to the system of looking after people's pets in kennels for a short period of time. *League Kennels offer short term boarding facilities to all dog owners. ...boarding kennels.*

3 NU Wooden boards which are used for making fences or floors are also called **boarding**.

boarding card, boarding cards

NC A **boarding card** is a card which a passenger must have when boarding an aeroplane or a boat before a journey. *They have a system of boarding cards so they know exactly how many people are on board the ferry.*

boarding house, boarding houses

NC A **boarding house** is a house rather like a small

hotel where people pay to stay for a short time. *...the demise of the traditional boarding house.*

boarding party, boarding parties
1 NC A **boarding party** is a team of investigators who are sent to a ship to inspect it for a particular purpose, for example to look for weapons. *The vessel was eventually stopped and submitted to inspection by a boarding party... The boarding party reports that there is no cargo on board.*
2 NC A **boarding party** is also a group of people who board a ship or plane illegally or by force. *A boarding party made up of fifteen crewmen took control.*

boarding pass, boarding passes
NC A **boarding pass** is the same as a **boarding card**. *Ferry operators in Sweden refused boarding passes to English football supporters.*

boarding school, boarding schools
NC A **boarding school** is a school where the pupils live during the term. *His parents saved up money to send him to boarding school.*

board meeting, board meetings
NC A **board meeting** is a meeting for the group of people who own or run a company or other organization. *Members of the Commission walked out of a board meeting in protest... The other directors have to give their approval at a board meeting tomorrow.*

boardroom /bɔːdrʊm/ **boardrooms**
NC The **boardroom** is a room where the board of a company meets. *All the shareholders crowded into the bank's boardroom for the A.G.M. ...a vitriolic boardroom struggle.*

boardwalk /bɔːdwɔːk/ **boardwalks**
NC In the United States, a **boardwalk** is a footpath made of boards, usually beside the sea. *It got chilly on the boardwalk and the beach at night.*

boast /bəʊst/ **boasts, boasting, boasted**
1 VA,V,V-REPORT,or V-QUOTE If you **boast** about something that you have done or that you own, you talk about it in a way that shows that you are too proud of it; used showing disapproval. *The army was one of the things that they had boasted about... Williams boasted of his influence on the Prime Minister... We've gone quite a long way, and, if I may boast a little, I think largely thanks to British original thinking... President Ershad frequently boasts that he has done more for the army than his predecessors... 'I'll have him ready for a public appearance within a year,' she boasted.* ► Also NC *It is his boast that he has read the entire works of Trollope.*
2 VO If something or someone can **boast** a particular achievement or possession, they have achieved or possess that thing. *The Daily Mirror boasts a world exclusive interview with Mr Mandela... Canada can boast a much lower crime rate than the US.*

boastful /bəʊstfl/
ADJ If someone is **boastful**, they talk too proudly about something that they have done or something that they own. *They are rather boastful about their equipment.*
♦ **boastfully** ADV *His learning is worn lightly, not boastfully displayed.*

boat /bəʊt/ **boats**
1 NC A **boat** is a small vehicle that is used for travelling across water. *About forty men landed in small boats... Two men were rescued after the boat capsized.*
2 NC You can refer to a passenger ship as a **boat**; an informal use. *She was intending to take the boat to Stockholm... You can't reach it by plane in the winter, you have to go by boat.*
● **Boat** is used in these informal phrases. ● If you say that someone is **rocking the boat**, you mean that they are upsetting a calm situation and causing trouble. *Now isn't the time to be rocking the boat.* ● If two or more people are **in the same boat**, they are in the same unpleasant situation. *When the regulations come into force, more families will be in the same boat as the Goddens.*

boater /bəʊtə/ **boaters**
NC A **boater** is a hard straw hat with a flat top and a brim. *...Tony Greig, resplendent in boater, blazer and tie.*

boat-hook, boat-hooks
NC A **boat-hook** is a long pole with a hook at the end, which is used to pull a boat in to the bank or to push it away from other boats.

boathouse /bəʊthaʊs/ **boathouses**
NC A **boathouse** is a building near a river or lake where boats are stored.

boating /bəʊtɪŋ/
NU If you go **boating**, you go on a lake or river in a small boat for pleasure. *...near-perfect conditions for boating... Four British students are missing after a boating accident. ...fruit machines and a boating lake.*

boat people
N PL **Boat people** are refugees who leave their country by boat in the hope that they will be taken to another country in a passing ship. The term **boat people** is often used to refer to the refugees who left Vietnam in the 1970s. *Fifty-one boat people were sent home against their will... He has expressed his concern over the decision to turn away the boat people.*

boatswain /bəʊsn/ **boatswains**
NC A **boatswain** is the officer who is responsible for the maintenance of a ship and its equipment. *The accused are the first officer and the assistant boatswain.*

boat train, boat trains
NC A **boat train** is a train that takes you to or from a port. *We went straight from the boat train to Paddington.*

bob /bɒb/ **bobs, bobbing, bobbed**
1 V If something **bobs**, it moves up and down, like something does when it is floating on water. *The roofs of submerged houses bobbed like flotsam above a sea of brown mud... I saw his anxious face bobbing among a sea of delegates.*
2 NC In informal speech, people used to refer to a shilling as a **bob**. The plural form was also 'bob'. *They used to get four bob an hour.*
3 NC A **bob** is also a hair style in which a woman's hair is cut level with her chin. *...a stout lady with a raven-black bob.*

bobbed /bɒbd/
ADJ If a woman's hair is **bobbed**, it is cut in a bob.

bobbin /bɒbɪn/ **bobbins**
NC A **bobbin** is a small round object which holds the thread or wool on a sewing machine or spinning wheel.

bobble /bɒbl/ **bobbles**
NC A **bobble** is a small ball of material which is used for decorating clothes, lampshades, and so on. *...a cap with a bobble on top.*

bobby /bɒbi/ **bobbies**
NC A **bobby** is a British policeman; an informal word. *...the village bobby... The unpleasantness of an inner-city bobby's life is child's play compared to the South Bronx.*

bobsled /bɒbsled/ **bobsleds**
NC A **bobsled** is the same as a **bobsleigh**. *The Prince raced in a bobsled competition at Calgary.*

bobsleigh /bɒbsleɪ/ **bobsleighs**
NC A **bobsleigh** is a vehicle with long thin strips of metal fixed to the bottom, which is used for racing downhill on ice. *In another hair-raising event, the bobsleigh, there's a record entry of nearly 50 sleds this year.*

bod /bɒd/ **bods**
NC A **bod** is a person; an informal word. *He's a nice bod.*

bode /bəʊd/ **bodes, boding, boded**; a literary word.
If something **bodes ill**, it makes you think that something bad will happen in the future. If it **bodes well**, it makes you think that something good will happen. *He said the policy boded ill for the country's future... The fact that the Iranians walked out of the conference does not bode well, does it?... If there is agreement between Washington and Moscow, it bodes well for the rest of the world.*

bodge /bɒdʒ/ **bodges, bodging, bodged**; an informal word.
VO If you **bodge** something, you make it or mend it in a way that is not as good as it should be. *We'll have to bodge it.* ► Also NC *...a kind of bodge good carpenters strive to avoid.*

bodice /bɒdɪs/ **bodices**
NC The **bodice** of a dress is the part above the waist; an old-fashioned word. *She even specified the style— old-fashioned bodices for women, long woollen pants for men.*

bodily /bɒdɪli/
1 ADJ ATTRIB Your **bodily** needs and functions are the needs and functions of your body. *They have no interests beyond their bodily needs.*
2 ADV You use **bodily** to refer to actions that involve the whole of someone's body. *He hurled himself bodily at the Prince.*

body /bɒdi/ **bodies**
1 NC Your **body** is all your physical parts, including your head, arms, and legs. *His whole body felt as if it were on fire... The disease spread to other parts of the body.*
2 NC You can also refer to the main part of your body, excluding your head, arms, and legs, as your **body**. *They respond with slow movements of their arms, legs, and bodies.*
3 NC A **body** is the body of a dead person. *Police looking for a girl who vanished yesterday have found a child's body.*
4 NC+SUPP A **body** is also an organized group of people who deal with something officially. *They are members of a larger body called the Senate Committee... The society would be a profit-making body with shareholders.*
5 NC The **body** of a car or aeroplane is the main part of it, excluding its engine, wheels, and wings. *The headlights are not built into the body, but perched on stalks above the bonnet.*

body blow, body blows
NC If something is a **body blow**, it causes great disappointment and difficulty to someone who is trying to achieve something. *The news of his resignation was yet another body blow... This vote for independence is another body blow to the unity of the Soviet party.*

body-builder, body-builders
NC A **body-builder** is a person who does special exercises regularly in order to make his or her muscles grow bigger. *...an American model who has developed her muscles like a male body-builder.*

body-building
NU **Body-building** is the activity of doing special exercises regularly in order to make your muscles grow bigger. *Body-building is popular with both sexes.*

bodyguard /bɒdigaːd/ **bodyguards**
NCorNU Someone's **bodyguard** is the person or group of people employed to protect them. *He came striding into the room followed by his two bodyguards. ...one of the Rajah's personal bodyguard.*

body language
NU **Body language** is the way in which you show your feelings or thoughts to other people by means of the position or movements of your body rather than with words. *...displays of impatient body language.*

body odour
NU **Body odour** is the smell of a person's body; usually used to describe the unpleasant smell caused by someone sweating. *They had no body odour... Is their personal body odour attractive to you?*

body politic
N SING The **body politic** is all the people of a nation; a formal expression. *It was not in the interests of the body politic at the present moment.*

body search, body searches
NC A **body search** is a procedure in which the police or customs officials examine people's clothing and sometimes their bodies to make sure they are not carrying anything illegal, such as drugs or weapons. *They intend to have two hundred extra men on duty to carry out body searches.*

body stocking, body stockings
NC A **body stocking** is a piece of clothing that covers the whole of someone's body and fits tightly. Dancers often wear body stockings when they are performing. *These imaginative costumes certainly are a change from body stockings.*

bodywork /bɒdiwɜːk/
NU The **bodywork** of a motor vehicle or plane is the outside part of it. *By examining the bodywork, the investigators will be able to tell if the plane broke up as a result of metal fatigue.*

Boer /bɔː/ **Boers**
NC A **Boer** is a descendant of the Dutch people who went to live in South Africa. *Despite the carnival atmosphere, the Boers are divided amongst themselves.*

boffin /bɒfɪn/ **boffins**
NC A **boffin** is a scientist; an informal word. *Now the boffins at Imperial College, London, think they may have found a solution.*

bog /bɒg/ **bogs, bogging, bogged**
NC A **bog** is an area of land which is very wet and muddy. *The north of Scotland has one of the world's biggest bogs.*
bog down PHRASAL VERB If a plan or task **bogs down** or if something **bogs** it **down**, it is delayed and no progress is made. *The U.S. peace plan has bogged down and no date was set for the peace talks... An all-out confrontation could bog the Syrians down in military involvement... He has managed to push aside one of the obstacles that is bogging down the talks.* ● See also **bogged down.**

bogey /bəʊgi/ **bogeys**; also spelt **bogie** or **bogy**.
1 NC A **bogey** is something that people are worried about, perhaps without cause or reason. *We must put to rest the old bogey that military expenditure is vital for national security. ...the familiar bogies of foreign intervention and anti-apartheid activities.* ● See also **bogeyman.**
2 NC When a golfer gets a **bogey**, he or she finishes a hole by taking one more shot than the standard score. *Hulbert began his final round with a bogey... His bogey at the 16th was compensated for with a birdie at the last.*
3 NC A **bogey** is also a piece of dried mucus that comes from inside your nose; an informal use.

bogeyman /bəʊgimæn/ **bogeymen**
NC A **bogeyman** or a **bogey** is an imaginary frightening evil spirit. *You should never threaten her with bogeymen.*

bogged down
ADJ PRED If you are **bogged down** in something, it prevents you from making progress or getting something done; an informal expression. *Don't get bogged down in details... The Congress now appears to be bogged down because of internal squabbles.*

boggle /bɒgl/ **boggles, boggling, boggled**
If your **mind boggles** or if something **boggles** your **mind**, you find something difficult to imagine or understand; an informal expression. *My imagination boggled at the thought of her reaction... The questions raised by the new biology simply boggle the mind.*

boggy /bɒgi/
ADJ **Boggy** land is very wet and muddy. *...peat that has taken hundreds of years to build up under boggy and wet grassland.*

bogie /bəʊgi/. See bogey.

Bogotá /bɒgətaː/
Bogotá is the capital of Colombia and its largest city. In 1991, the government decreed that it should return to its traditional name of Santa Fé de Bogotá. Population: 4,236,000 (1985).

bogus /bəʊgəs/
ADJ You say that something is **bogus** when you know that it is not genuine. *The telegram turns out to have been bogus... Progress towards a settlement is being delayed by many thousands of bogus claims.*

bogy /bəʊgi/. See bogey.

bohemian /bəʊhiːmiən/ **bohemians**
NC Artistic people who live in an unconventional way are sometimes referred to as **bohemians**. *Brian saw Tim as a romantic bohemian.* ▶ Also ADJ *My parents disapproved of the bohemian life I led.*

boil /bɔɪl/ **boils, boiling, boiled**
1 V-ERG When a liquid **boils** or when you **boil** it, it becomes very hot, bubbles appear in it and, it starts to change into steam or vapour. *When the water has boiled, let it cool... Boil the solution in the pan for five minutes... Experts have told all households to boil their tap water.*

2 N SING When you bring a liquid to the **boil,** you heat it until it boils. *How long would it take you to bring a pot of water to the boil on a wood stove?*
3 V-ERG When you **boil** a kettle, you heat it until the water inside it boils. When a kettle **is boiling,** the water inside it is boiling. *It has just enough power to boil a kettle... When a kettle boils, the lid rises slightly to stop it boiling over.*
4 VO When you **boil** food, you cook it in boiling water. *She didn't know how to boil an egg.* ◆ **boiled** ADJ *The typical Czech evening meal is boiled potatoes, pickled vegetables, and cold meats.*
5 V If you **are boiling** with anger, you are very angry. *She had just witnessed an officer slapping a prisoner, and was boiling with rage.*
6 NC A **boil** is a red painful swelling on your skin. *...the bacteria which cause boils.*
7 See also **boiling.**
boil away PHRASAL VERB When a liquid **boils away,** all of it changes into steam or vapour. *He believes that the planet once had an ocean, but that it boiled away hundreds of years ago.*
boil down to PHRASAL VERB If you say that a situation or problem **boils down to** a particular thing, you mean that this is the most important aspect of it. *What it all seemed to boil down to was money.*
boil over PHRASAL VERB **1** When a liquid that is being heated **boils over,** it rises and flows over the edge of the container. *The milk is boiling over on the stove.*
2 If a difficult situation in which people are angry **boils over,** it gets out of control. *The row over copyright boiled over last week... The simmering frustration of the activists has boiled over into violence.*
boiler /ˈbɔɪlə/ **boilers**
NC A **boiler** is a device which burns gas, oil, electricity, or coal to provide hot water, especially for central heating. *They were shovelling coal so furiously that the boiler was threatening to burst from overpressure.*
boiler suit, boiler suits
NC A **boiler suit** is a piece of protective clothing consisting of trousers and a top that are joined together in one piece. *...an oil-stained denim boiler suit.*
boiling /ˈbɔɪlɪŋ/
ADJ If something is very hot, you can say that it is **boiling** or **boiling hot.** *I immersed my boiling body in a cool pool... The beetle defends itself by squirting a spray of boiling hot, irritating liquid from its abdomen.*
boiling point, boiling points
1 NCorNU The **boiling point** of a liquid is the temperature at which it starts to change into steam or vapour by heating. *The boiling point of water is 100°C... After the pan has reached boiling point, turn the gas as low as possible.*
2 NU If a situation reaches **boiling point,** the people involved have become so agitated or angry that they can no longer remain calm and in control of themselves. *This has brought the present situation to boiling point... Emotions are reaching boiling point.*
boisterous /ˈbɔɪstərəs/
ADJ Someone who is **boisterous** is noisy, lively, and full of energy. *The mood of the crowd was boisterous but good-humoured.*
bold /bəʊld/ **bolder, boldest**
1 ADJ A person who is **bold** is not afraid to do things which involve risk or danger. *Professor Salibi is a bold man. ...a bold action.* ◆ **boldly** ADV *He boldly seized the initiative from Mr Gorbachev with his calls for increased human rights and religious freedom.*
◆ **boldness** NU *For any success, boldness is required.*
2 ADJ You also say that someone is **bold** when they are not shy or embarrassed in the company of other people, and perhaps behave less respectfully than you would expect. *Mary was surprisingly bold for a girl who seemed so young.* ◆ **boldly** ADV *He returned her gaze boldly.*
3 ADJ **Bold** lines or designs are painted or drawn in a clear, strong way. *...bold handwriting.*

bold face
NU **Bold face** refers to letters printed in darker ink than the rest of the words in a book, in order to make them stand out. The headwords in this dictionary are printed in bold face.
bolero /bəˈleərəʊ/ **boleros;** also pronounced /bɒˈlɛərəʊ/ for the meaning in paragraph 1.
1 NC A **bolero** is a type of short jacket, worn especially by women.
2 NC A **bolero** is also a traditional Spanish dance. *The couple danced a romantic bolero together.*
Bolger, Jim /dʒɪm ˈbɒldʒə/
Jim Bolger was elected Prime Minister of New Zealand in 1990. He became an MP in 1972. He served as Minister of Fisheries and Associate Minister of Agriculture in 1977, Minister of Labour from 1978 to 1984, and Minister of Immigration from 1978 to 1981. He was the deputy leader of the National Party from 1984 to 1985, and became Leader in 1986. Born: 1935.
Bolivia /bəˈlɪviə/
The **Republic of Bolivia** is a country in central America. The main ethnic groups are Quechua and Aymará. It was a Spanish colony from the 16th century until independence in 1825, and was ruled by the military from 1964 until 1982. Jaime Paz Zamora, of the Movement of the Revolutionary Left (MIR), became President in 1989. Bolivia exports tin, natural gas, and coffee. Cocaine is illegally exported and drug trafficking is an increasing threat to public order. Large foreign debts have often been major economic problems. Bolivia is a member of the Organization of American States. ◆ **Bolivian** /bəˈlɪviən/ N, ADJ
■ *per capita GNP:* US$630 ■ *religion:* Christianity (mainly Roman Catholic) ■ *language:* Spanish, Quechua, Aymará ■ *currency:* boliviano ■ *capital:* La Paz (administrative), Sucre (judicial) ■ *population:* 7 million (1988) ■ *size:* 1,084,391 square kilometres.
Bolkiah, Sir Hassanal /ˈhʌsænəl ˈbɒlkɪə/
Sir Hassanal Bolkiah became Sultan of Brunei in 1967. He was named Crown Prince in 1961 and became Prime Minister of Brunei in 1984. Born: 1946.
bollard /ˈbɒlɑːd/ **bollards**
NC **Bollards** are short thick posts that are used to stop cars going on to someone's land or on to part of a road. *...concrete bollards that divide the lanes of the main roads.*
bollocks /ˈbɒləks/; an offensive word.
1 Bollocks is a rude swear word which is used in informal English to express disagreement, dislike, or defiance.
2 NU If you say that something someone has said, written, or done is **bollocks,** you are saying in a rude and offensive way that you think that it is completely wrong or foolish.
3 N PL A man's **bollocks** are his testicles; a rude and offensive use.
Bolshevik /ˈbɒlʃəvɪk/ **Bolsheviks**
1 ADJ ATTRIB **Bolshevik** is used to describe the political system and ideas that Lenin and his supporters introduced in Russia after the 1917 Russian Revolution. *International Socialists maintain the old Bolshevik slogans of arming the workers.*
2 NC A **Bolshevik** was a person who supported Lenin and his political ideas. *The death sentence on a leading Bolshevik, Rykov, was cancelled.*
bolshy /ˈbɒlʃi/; also spelt **bolshie.**
ADJ Someone who is **bolshy** behaves in a bad-tempered or difficult and rebellious way; an informal word. *The miners were getting bolshy.*
bolster /ˈbəʊlstə/ **bolsters, bolstering, bolstered**
1 VO If you **bolster** someone's confidence or courage, you make them more confident or more courageous. *The outcome of the strike should bolster trade union confidence.*
2 VO If people **bolster** a system or organization that is in danger of collapsing, they support it in order to make it stronger. *It was they who bolstered the Zia regime and kept the Pakistani economy afloat... He has appealed to Mr van den Broek to restore aid to bolster the democratic process.*
bolster up PHRASAL VERB If you **bolster** something **up,** you help or support it in order to make it stronger. *To*

bolster up their case, they quoted a speech by Ray Gunter.

bolt /bəʊlt/ **bolts, bolting, bolted**

1 NC A **bolt** is a long metal object which screws into a nut and is used to fasten things together. *They are recalling the model after discovering faults in the suspension bolts.*

2 VO When you **bolt** one thing to another, you fasten the two things together firmly using a bolt. *It's a bar that you bolt onto the shafts of the cart. ...an iron cot bolted to the floor.*

3 NC A **bolt** on a door or window is a metal bar that you slide across in order to fasten the door or window. *The bolts used to secure the windscreen were too small.*

4 VO When you **bolt** a door or window, you slide the bolt across to fasten it. *Visitors were ushered out of the church and its two massive wooden doors were closed and bolted.*

5 V If a person or animal **bolts**, they suddenly start to run very fast, often because something has frightened them. *Passengers clearly overheard his shouted warning to the control room and they all bolted into the next carriage.*

6 VO If you **bolt** your food or **bolt** it down, you eat it very quickly.

7 NC+SUPP A **bolt** of lightning is a flash of lightning that is seen as a white line in the sky. *The ancient cathedral was struck by a bolt of lightning and nearly burnt to the ground.*

● **Bolt** is used in these phrases. ● If someone is sitting or standing **bolt upright**, they are sitting or standing very straight. ● The **nuts and bolts** of a situation are the most important and basic things in it. *Should children be taught the nuts and bolts of spoken and written English?... They came to negotiate the nuts and bolts of procedures for stopping the fighting.*

bolt-hole, bolt-holes

NC If you have a **bolt-hole**, you have a place you can go to in order to get away from other people. *He used the garden shed as a bolt-hole for when the children got too noisy.*

bomb /bɒm/ **bombs, bombing, bombed**

1 NC A **bomb** is a device which explodes and damages or destroys a large area. *Nine people were injured when a bomb went off in the sleeping quarters of the barracks... Their car was hit by a petrol bomb and set on fire.*

2 N SING Nuclear weapons are sometimes referred to as the **bomb**. *Ban the bomb!*

3 VO When people **bomb** a place, they attack it with bombs. *They bombed the airports in three cities... The base is constantly being shelled and bombed.* ◆ **bombing, bombings** NUorNC *It replaced the building destroyed by bombing in 1940. ...the current wave of bombings.*

4 V In informal American English, to **bomb** also means to fail.

5 See also **car bomb, letter-bomb, parcel bomb, time bomb**.

bomb out PHRASAL VERB If a building is **bombed out**, it is destroyed by a bomb. If people are **bombed out**, their houses are destroyed by bombs. *Since Baghdad's water treatment plant was bombed out, doctors lack sufficient water to scrub properly before operations. ...refugees who had been bombed out of their small apartments.* ◆ **bombed out** ADJ *...refugees returning to bombed out homes.*

bombard /bɒmbɑːd/ **bombards, bombarding, bombarded**

1 VO When soldiers **bombard** a place, they attack it with continuous heavy gunfire or bombs. *The artillery has continued to bombard Laotian positions... Parts of the building had been heavily bombarded.*

2 VO If you **bombard** someone with questions or criticism, you keep asking questions or criticizing them. *The government was bombarded with calls for its resignation... The newspapers have been bombarding the population with information on how to vote.*

bombardment /bɒmbɑːdmənt/ **bombardments**

1 NUorNC A **bombardment** is a strong and continuous

attack of gunfire or bombing. *The naval and air bombardment had failed to knock out the coastal defences... There was heavy aerial bombardment by government planes.*

2 NUorNC A **bombardment** of questions, criticism, and so on is constant aggressive questioning or complaining. *Back in London, the daily bombardment of messages and complaints began again... The bombardments continued, and Mr Ozal was left with his credibility looking damaged.*

bombast /bɒmbæst/

NU **Bombast** is an attempt to impress other people, for example by using long words or behaving in a pompous way. *At the time, the threat was treated as little more than bombast.*

bombastic /bɒmbæstɪk/

ADJ **Bombastic** statements are intended to impress people because they contain long and important sounding words; used showing disapproval. *...bombastic threats of retaliation.*

bomb disposal

NU **Bomb disposal** is the job of removing unexploded bombs safely. *...an extensive research programme into mine detection and bomb disposal... The package—found in the basement of the London store—was made safe by bomb disposal experts.*

bomber /bɒmə/ **bombers**

1 NC A **bomber** is an aircraft which drops bombs. *The B-52 is America's chief long-range bomber... Their fighter bombers attacked several tankers moored off Kharg Island.*

2 NC A **bomber** is also a person who causes a bomb to explode in a public place. *An American woman and a convicted bomber have been married in prison.*

bomber jacket, bomber jackets

NC A **bomber jacket** is a short jacket which is gathered into a band at the waist or hips. *...young men with closely cropped hair, bomber jackets and high black boots.*

bomb factory, bomb factories

NC A **bomb factory** is a place where bombs are made illegally. *Police are hunting two men after the discovery of a bomb factory in south London.*

bombing raid, bombing raids

NC A **bombing raid** is an attack on a place using aircraft which drop bombs. *Their bombing raids are said to be causing extensive damage... On Wednesday, a family of four died in a bombing raid on a village.*

bomb scare, bomb scares

NC When there is a **bomb scare**, a telephone call is received from someone who claims to have placed a bomb in a particular place. *A bomb scare led to the temporary evacuation of the Australian embassy.*

bombshell /bɒmʃel/ **bombshells**

NC A **bombshell** is a sudden piece of bad or unexpected news. *She dropped her bombshell—'I'm pregnant.'... His resignation is a bit of a political bombshell.*

bombsite /bɒmsaɪt/ **bombsites**

NC A **bombsite** is an empty area where a bomb has destroyed all the buildings. *The place looks like a Second World War bombsite.*

bona fide /bəʊnə faɪdi/

ADJ ATTRIB **Bona fide** means genuine; a formal expression. *...bona fide applications... He's a bona fide contender for this year's most valuable player award.*

bonanza /bənænzə/ **bonanzas**

NC A **bonanza** is a time or situation when people suddenly become much richer. *The war provided a bonanza for arms manufacturers... The unexpected oil bonanza is a mixed blessing.*

bond /bɒnd/ **bonds, bonding, bonded**

1 NC A **bond** between people is a strong feeling of friendship, love, or shared beliefs that unites them. *...the bond between mother and child... Many see the ideal of marriage as a permanent bond.*

2 V-PASS When people or animals **are bonded**, they unite to help and protect each other; a formal use. *Societies have always been bonded together by a threat from outside.*

3 N PL+SUPP **Bonds** are feelings, duties, or customs

that force you to behave in a particular way. ...*the bonds of party discipline.*

4 vo When you **bond** two things, you stick them together using adhesive. *The glue used to bond these large glass windows into the vehicle is sensitive to light.*

5 NC A **bond** is also a certificate issued by a government or company which shows that you have lent them money and that they will pay you interest. ...*low risk government, municipal, and housing bonds... They repaid depositors in ten-year bonds.*

bondage /bɒndɪdʒ/
NU **Bondage** is the condition of belonging to someone as their slave; a literary word. ...*celebrating the Israelites' escape from bondage.*

bonded labour
NU **Bonded labour** is a system in which people are forced to repay a debt by working for the person who lent them the money. *Bonded labour and the use of children under 14 in industry are illegal in India... She pledged to abolish bonded labour.*

bone /bəʊn/ **bones, boning, boned**
1 NCorNU Your **bones** are the hard parts inside your body which together form your skeleton. ...*shoulder and hip bones... Its eye sockets are encircled by bone.*
2 vo If you **bone** a piece of meat or fish, you remove the bones from it before or after cooking it.
3 ADJ A **bone** tool or ornament is made of bone. *They fished with carefully carved bone harpoons.*
● **Bone** is used in these phrases. ● If you **feel** or **know** something in your **bones**, you are certain about it, although you cannot explain why; used in informal English. *I know in my bones that there is such a thing as a West Indian identity.* ● If you **make no bones** about doing something unpleasant or difficult, you do it without hesitation; an informal expression. *The Alliance is making no bones about its wish to be an independent political organisation.* ● If an amount of money or a service is **cut to the bone**, it is greatly reduced. *Overtime has been cut to the bone... Our grant is always cut to the bone, so we have to make do and mend.*

bone china
NU **Bone china** is very fine porcelain containing powdered bone. ...*fresh fruit, vegetables and meat served on bone china laid out on white linen.*

bone dry
ADJ PRED Something that is **bone dry** is very dry indeed. *A tumble drier gets things bone dry.*

bone marrow. See **marrow.**

bonemeal /bəʊnmiːl/
NU **Bonemeal** is a substance made from dried and ground animal bones. It is often used as a fertilizer or to feed animals. ...*a ban on using cattle remains in meat and bonemeal fed to animals.*

bone of contention, bones of contention
NC If an issue is a **bone of contention**, it is the subject of a disagreement or argument. *The Kurdish issue has always been a bone of contention.*

boneshaker /bəʊnʃeɪkə/ **boneshakers**
NC A **boneshaker** is an old, uncomfortable vehicle; an old-fashioned word.

bonfire /bɒnfaɪə/ **bonfires**
NC A **bonfire** is a fire that is made outdoors, usually to burn rubbish. Bonfires are also sometimes lit as part of a celebration. *The man's clothes were thrown on a bonfire... It's a good excuse for a big bonfire and fireworks.*

bonfire night, bonfire nights
NUorNC In Britain, **bonfire night** is the night of November 5 when people have bonfire parties and let off fireworks. *An even bigger attraction nowadays is firework displays held on bonfire night... A twelve year old boy has died in a bonfire night accident.*

bongo /bɒŋgəʊ/ **bongos**
NC A **bongo** is a small drum that you play with your hands. ...*banging on the hide of a bongo drum.*

Bongo, Omar /əʊmɑː bɒŋgəʊ/
Omar Bongo, formerly named Albert-Bernard Bongo, became President of Gabon in 1967. He had previously been Vice President. In 1968 he founded and became the leader of the Democratic Party of Gabon (PDG),

which was the sole legal party from 1969 to 1990. Born: 1935.

bonhomie /bɒnəmi/
NU **Bonhomie** is happy, jolly friendliness; a literary word. ...*the grin of bonhomie on his face.*

bonk /bɒŋk/ **bonks, bonking, bonked**
V-RECIP To **bonk** someone means to have sexual intercourse with them; an informal word.

bonkers /bɒŋkəz/
ADJ PRED If you say that someone is **bonkers**, you mean that they are silly or mad; an informal word. *Archbishop Tutu said the government had gone bonkers.*

Bonn /bɒn/
Bonn was the capital of West Germany from 1949 until 1990, when Berlin became the capital of the re-united Germany. Many government functions, however, remained in Bonn. Population: 287,000 (1987).

bonnet /bɒnɪt/ **bonnets**
1 NC The **bonnet** of a car is the metal cover over the engine at the front. *All we have to do is find the brake fluid reservoir, here under the bonnet. ...theft-resistant doors and bonnets.*
2 NC A baby's or woman's **bonnet** is a hat tied under their chin. ...*a small lace bonnet.*
3 to have a bee in your bonnet: see **bee**.

bonny /bɒni/; also spelt **bonnie**.
ADJ In some dialects of English, **bonny** means pretty or nice to look at. *She had a big bonny baby boy with fair hair.*

bonsai /bɒnsaɪ/ **bonsais**. The plural form can be either **bonsais** or **bonsai**.
NC A **bonsai** is a tree or shrub that has been kept very small by growing it in a little pot and trimming it in a special way. ...*trimmed dwarf Japanese bonsai trees.*

bonus /bəʊnəs/ **bonuses**
1 NC A **bonus** is an extra amount of money that is added to someone's pay, usually because they have worked very hard. *The wage increase is 8%, and the rest consists of quality and efficiency bonuses.*
2 NC A **bonus** is also something good that you get in addition to something else, and which you would not usually expect. *Any sort of party after work was a bonus... The prospect of a visit by the Chancellor is an added bonus.*

bony /bəʊni/
ADJ If you say that someone is **bony**, you think they are very thin. *He was tall, thin, and bony. ...his long bony fingers.*

boo /buː/ **boos, booing, booed**
VorVO If you **boo** a speaker or performer, you shout 'boo' to show that you do not like them, their opinions, or their performance. *Some of them booed when she appeared... Members boo and heckle speakers they do not agree with.* ▶ Also NC *There were loud boos.*

boob /buːb/ **boobs**; an informal word.
1 NC A woman's **boobs** are her breasts; some people find this use offensive.
2 NC A **boob** is also a mistake. *Moving him to a new job at such a delicate stage of the discussions is a diplomatic boob.*
3 NC In American English, you can refer to a foolish person as a **boob**. *Who are these boobs?*

booby prize /buːbi praɪz/ **booby prizes**
NC The **booby prize** is a prize given to the person who comes last in a competition. *Looks like you get the booby prize.*

booby-trap /buːbitræp/ **booby-traps, booby-trapping, booby-trapped**
1 NC A **booby-trap** is something such as a bomb which is hidden or disguised and which explodes when it is touched. *They approached the area cautiously in case there were any booby-traps... A guard was seriously injured by a booby-trap bomb.*
2 vo If something is **booby-trapped**, a booby-trap is placed in it or on it. *The external doors in this section of the plane are booby-trapped.*

boogie /buːgi/ **boogies, boogieing, boogied**
v When you **boogie**, you dance to fast pop music; an informal word. *We all boogied, either as couples or singly.*

boohoo /buːhuː/ boohoos, boohooing, boohooed
1 v If someone **boohoos**, they cry noisily like a child. *Don't just sit there boohooing like a baby.*
2 **Boohoo** is used in written English to represent the sound of noisy, childish crying. *'I ain't.'—'You are.'—'Boohoo.'*

book /buk/ books, booking, booked
1 NC A **book** consists of a number of pieces of paper, usually with words or pictures printed on them, which are fastened together and fixed inside a cover of stronger paper or cardboard. *He intends to publish a book of his findings... The book is a mixture of observation and analysis.*
2 NC A **book** of something such as stamps, matches, or tickets is a small number of them fastened together between thin cardboard or plastic covers. *Spectators will have to buy a book of tickets covering admission to all games.*
3 N PL A company's or organization's **books** are written records of money that has been spent and earned, or of the names of people who work for it. *He's going to help me go over my books and check the totals... His name is no longer on our books.*
4 VO When you **book** something such as a hotel room or a ticket, you arrange to have it or use it at a particular time. *I'd like to book a table for four for tomorrow night.*
5 VO In football, if a player is **booked**, the referee writes his or her name down in a book and reports him or her to the football authorities. *Mick Quinn was sent off, and manager Alan Ball was booked.*
6 See also **booking**.
● **Book** is used in these phrases. ● If a hotel, restaurant, or theatre is **booked up** or **fully booked**, it has no rooms, tables, or tickets left for a particular time or date. *Demand has been so strong that they are already booked up... He asked for a room for the night, and was told the hotel was fully booked.* ● If you are in someone's **bad books**, they are annoyed with you. If you are in their **good books**, they are pleased with you. *I was in his bad books, and there was talk that I might be dismissed... They have succeeded in fighting their way back into the good books of the Western powers.*
book into or **book in** PHRASAL VERB When you book into a hotel or book in, you officially state that you have arrived to stay there, usually by signing your name in a register. *Police say he booked into a cheap hotel earlier this week... It was too late to go shopping, so he booked in at the Hotel d'Angleterre.*

bookable /bukəbl/
ADJ A **bookable** theatre seat, plane ticket, and so on can be booked in advance.

bookbinding /bukbaindiŋ/
NU **Bookbinding** is the work of fastening books together and putting covers on them. *Some students take bookbinding as an option.*

bookcase /bukkeis/ bookcases
NC A **bookcase** is a piece of furniture with shelves for books. *He paid seven and a half million pounds for an eighteenth century American desk and bookcase.*

bookend /bukend/ bookends
NC **Bookends** are a pair of supports which are used to hold a row of books in an upright position by placing one at each end of the row.

bookie /buki/ bookies
NC A **bookie** is the same as a **bookmaker**; an informal word. *The bookies are now fancying Brown Windsor to take first prize.*

booking /bukiŋ/ bookings
NC A **booking** is the arrangement that you make when you book something such as a theatre seat or a hotel room. *Airlines and ferry companies have reported heavy bookings... Travellers were told not to come to the port unless they had a firm booking.*

booking office, booking offices
NC A **booking office** is a room where tickets are sold and booked, especially in a theatre or a railway station. *Parents besieged booking offices seeking plane, bus, or train tickets to take their children away from the town... Two of the buildings burnt were a telephone exchange and a railway booking office.*

bookish /bukiʃ/
ADJ Someone who is **bookish** spends a lot of time reading serious books. *He seems to have been bookish from childhood onwards.*

bookkeeping /bukkiːpiŋ/
NU **Bookkeeping** is the job of keeping an accurate record of the money spent and received by an organization. *The business studies course would include typing, bookkeeping and commercial law.*

booklet /buklət/ booklets
NC A **booklet** is a small book with a paper cover that gives you information. *I have a small booklet, and if people are interested, I'll pass it around.*

bookmaker /bukmeikə/ bookmakers
NC A **bookmaker** is a person whose job is to take your money when you bet and to pay you money if you win. *The bookmakers made Labour the favourite to win the next election.*

bookmark /bukmaːk/ bookmarks
NC A **bookmark** is a narrow piece of card or leather that you put between the pages of a book so that you can find a particular page easily.

book plate, book plates
NC A **book plate** is a piece of decorated paper which is stuck in the front of a book and on which the owner's name is printed or written.

bookseller /buksela/ booksellers
NC A **bookseller** is a person or company that sells books. *He'd already failed as a bookseller, and took up painting full-time... Britain's largest bookseller, W.H.Smith, has refused to stock the book.*

bookshelf /bukʃelf/ bookshelves
NC A **bookshelf** is a bookcase, or a shelf on which you keep books. *The problem with making things like bookshelves or window frames is the amount of wasted wood.*

bookshop /bukʃɒp/ bookshops
NC A **bookshop** is a shop where books are sold. *Mr Osunding runs the University bookshop in Ife, Nigeria.*

bookstall /bukstɔːl/ bookstalls
NC A **bookstall** is a small shop with an open front where books and magazines are sold. *Many bookstalls still stock magazines that fall within this definition of pornography.*

bookstore /bukstɔː/ bookstores
NC A **bookstore** is the same as a **bookshop**. *We have arts and crafts still being sold in our bookstore here.*

book token, book tokens
NC A **book token** is a card with a special piece of paper stuck inside that you buy and then use instead of money to buy books. *I've won a £10 book token!*

bookworm /bukwɜːm/ bookworms
1 NC A **bookworm** is a person who is very fond of reading.
2 NC A **bookworm** is also an insect that eats the bindings of books.

boom /buːm/ booms, booming, boomed
1 NC+SUPP If there is a **boom** in something, there is a fast increase or development in it. *...the population boom. ...the familiar pattern of a short-term economic boom... Attendance has fallen from the boom years of the 1950's.* ▶ Also v *The gardening industry is booming.*
2 NC A **boom** is also a large floating sponge that is used for soaking up large quantities of liquid such as water or oil. *Engineers are using huge booms and high powered pumps to contain the oil spillage.*
3 V, VO, or V-QUOTE When something such as a big drum, a cannon, or someone's voice **booms**, it makes a loud, deep, echoing sound. *The cannon boomed again... Outside in the square, the artillery boomed a 19-gun salute.* ▶ Also NC *The boom of the drum echoed along the street.*
boom out PHRASAL VERB You can say that something such as a big drum, a cannon, or someone's voice **booms out** when it is very loud and deep. *The loudspeaker booms out all the way to Admiralty Arch... Then the organ boomed out the two national anthems.*

boomerang /buːməræŋ/ boomerangs, boomeranging, boomeranged
1 NC A **boomerang** is a curved piece of wood which

comes back to you if you throw it correctly. Boomerangs were used by Australian natives as weapons. *The visitor can ponder over the boomerangs used by the aborigines at the time of Cook.*
2 v If a plan **boomerangs**, it has an unexpectedly bad effect on the person who is carrying it out. *If they use the hostages to ward off military action, it could well boomerang... He said the policy would boomerang on the government in Nepal.*

boom town, boom towns
NC A **boom town** is a town which has become very rich and full of people, usually because industry or business has developed there. *This used to be a boom town until they closed down all the car factories.*

boon /buːn/ **boons**
NC A **boon** is something that makes life better or easier for someone. *The bus service is a great boon to old people.*

boor /buə, bɔː/ **boors**
NC A **boor** is a boorish person; an old-fashioned word.

boorish /buərɪʃ, bɔːrɪʃ/
ADJ Someone who is **boorish** behaves in a rough, impolite, and clumsy way. *They've already been snubbed by the employer's boorish and arrogant attitude.*

boost /buːst/ **boosts, boosting, boosted**
1 VO If one thing **boosts** another, it causes it to increase. *This new technology will boost food production... Mr Mousavi said revenue would be boosted by further exports of oil and natural gas.* ▶ Also NC *This will be a great boost to the economy.*
2 VO If something **boosts** your confidence or morale, it improves it. *The Bill is intended to boost confidence in Hong Kong... She would have to boost morale among her own backbenchers.* ▶ Also NC *...a boost to self-confidence.*

booster /buːstə/ **boosters**
1 NC A **booster** is an extra injection which renews the effectiveness of a previous vaccine injection. *They have to be injected daily for 14 days, followed by booster shots.*
2 NC A **booster** is also something that makes you feel more confident or cheerful. *The capture of the camp would be a considerable morale booster for the rebels... The fact that the agreement has been signed is a major booster for the government.*

boot /buːt/ **boots, booting, booted**
1 NC **Boots** are shoes that cover your whole foot and your ankle. Some boots also cover the lower part of your leg. *He was wearing cowboy boots and a colourful shirt. ...overalls, protective gloves and boots.*
2 NC The **boot** of a car is a covered space at the back in which you carry things such as luggage and shopping. *The police discovered the man bound and gagged in the boot of a car.*
● **Boot** is used in these informal phrases. ● To **put the boot in** means to say something cruel to someone who is already upset. *He wasn't interested in Europe, he just wanted to put the boot in against the Prime Minister.* ● To **put the boot in** also means to repeatedly kick someone who has been knocked to the ground. ● If someone says that you are **getting too big for your boots**, they mean that you are becoming too proud and pleased with yourself. ● If you **get the boot** or **are given the boot**, you are dismissed from your job.

boot out PHRASAL VERB If you **are booted out** of a place or position that you hold, you are forced to leave it; an informal expression. *Both of them were booted out when price rises caused mass unrest.*

boot camp, boot camps
NCorNU In the United States, a **boot camp** is a camp where army, navy, or marine recruits are trained. *In boot camp they try to bring to the surface the killer instinct in you... We've just got out of boot camp and now we're going to war.*

bootee /buːtiː/ **bootees**
NC **Bootees** are soft, woollen boots that cover the foot and ankle. They are often worn by babies.

booth /buːð/ **booths**
1 NC A **booth** is a small area separated from a larger public area by screens or thin walls where you can do something privately, for example make a telephone call. *Vandals burnt cars and wrecked telephone booths. ...a new kind of mobile polling booth.*
2 NC A **booth** is also a small tent or stall, usually at a fair, in which you can buy goods or watch some entertainment. *Crowds of people stream past the beer stalls and hamburger booths.*

bootlace /buːtleɪs/ **bootlaces**
NC A **bootlace** is a long narrow cord that is used to fasten a boot.

bootleg /buːtleg/
ADJ ATTRIB You use **bootleg** to refer to alcohol, fuel, or recorded music that has been made or transported illegally. *...a sixteen year old carrying a hip flask of bootleg liquor... In the eighties, it was thought that bootleg CDs wouldn't be a problem.*

bootlegger /buːtlegə/ **bootleggers**
NC A **bootlegger** is someone who makes or transports things illegally, especially alcohol. *...a group of Italian bootleggers who smuggled alcohol and whiskey in from the States.*

bootstraps /buːtstræps/
If you **pull** yourself **up** by your **bootstraps**, you achieve something with very little help or support from anyone else. *What we're attempting to do is help other countries pull themselves up by their bootstraps.*

booty /buːti/
NU **Booty** consists of valuable things taken from a place, especially by soldiers after a battle; a literary word. *We are sure these weapons will eventually become Mujahedin booty... The war booty included three armoured vehicles.*

booze /buːz/ **boozes, boozing, boozed**; an informal word.
1 NU **Booze** is alcoholic drink. *Cut out the booze and concentrate on eating fresh vegetables.*
2 v When people **booze**, they drink alcohol. *'I used to booze a hell of a lot' he told me jokingly, 'but since 1981 I haven't touched a drop.'*

boozer /buːzə/ **boozers**; an informal word.
1 NC A **boozer** is a person who drinks a lot of alcohol. *I used to be a boozer for years during the war.*
2 NC The **boozer** is a public house, especially one that is near your home or workplace. *We're off to the boozer. Coming?*

booze-up, booze-ups
NC A **booze-up** is a party or similar occasion in which people drink a lot of alcohol, usually in order to get very drunk together; an informal word.

boozy /buːzi/ **boozier, booziest**
ADJ A **boozy** person drinks a lot of alcohol; an informal word. *...his boozy companions. ...boozy singing.*

bop /bɒp/ **bops, bopping, bopped**
1 NC A **bop** is a dance; an informal use. *Shall we go and have a bop?* ▶ Also v *There we were, bopping away till the small hours.*
2 NU **Bop** is also a type of music that is similar to jazz. *Bop makes few concessions to the casual listener. ...the hard bop school which added blues and gospel rhythms to the music.*

borax /bɔːræks/
NU **Borax** is a white powder used, for example, in the making of glass and as a cleaning chemical.

border /bɔːdə/ **borders, bordering, bordered**
1 NC The **border** between two countries is the dividing line between them. *They crossed the border into Mexico. ...disputed border territory... They tried to ambush a border patrol.*
2 NC A **border** is also a strip or band around the edge of something. *It's painted in white with a gold border.*
3 NC In a garden, a **border** is a strip of ground planted with flowers along the edge of a lawn or a path. *...unkempt flower borders.*
4 VO If one thing **borders** another, it forms a line along the edge of it. *Huge elm trees bordered the road.*

border on PHRASAL VERB When you say that something is **bordering on** a particular state, you mean that it has almost reached that state. *I was in a state of excitement bordering on insanity.*

borderland /bɔːdələænd/ **borderlands**
1 NCorNU A **borderland** is an area of land between two countries or regions. ...*communities from the old pre-war German borderlands*. ...*the flat, featureless stretch of borderland here between Saudi Arabia and Iraq.*
2 N SING The **borderland** between two things is an area which contains features from both things so that it is not possible to say that it belongs to one or the other. ...*that perplexing borderland between working-class anarchism and middle-class conformity.*

borderline /bɔːdəlaɪn/
1 ADJ You use **borderline** to say that something is only just acceptable as a member of a particular class or group. *He is a borderline candidate for a special school... Perhaps we have deficiencies, or are borderline in certain things.*
2 N SING The **borderline** between two conditions or qualities is the division between them. ...*the narrow borderline between laughter and tears.*

border post, border posts
NC A **border post** is a group of buildings that is used by an army unit who are guarding the border between two countries. *The bombs shattered windows in the military border post and left a crater two metres deep.* ...*smashing a heavy lorry through barriers on a border post.*

bore /bɔː/ **bores, boring, bored**
1 VO If something **bores** you, you find it dull and uninteresting. *Most of the book had bored him... I won't bore you with the details.* ● If something **bores** you **to tears**, **bores** you **to death**, or **bores** you **stiff**, it bores you very much indeed; used in informal English. *I like acting, but the film world bores me to tears... The subject bores them stiff.*
2 NC You describe someone as a **bore** when you think that they talk in a very uninteresting way. *He's fast becoming our greatest bore.*
3 N SING You can describe a situation as a **bore** when you find it annoying or a nuisance. ...*an audience which found the whole event a crashing bore.*
4 VO If you **bore** a hole in something, you make a deep round hole in it using a special tool. ...*a cavern bored into a hillside.*
5 **Bore** is also the past tense of **bear**.

bored /bɔːd/
ADJ When you are **bored**, you feel tired and impatient because you have lost interest in something or because you have nothing to do. *Tom was bored with the film... He had such a lot of work to do he never got bored.*

boredom /bɔːdəm/
NU **Boredom** is the state of being bored. *Many of the audience walked out through sheer boredom.*

borehole /bɔːhəʊl/ **boreholes**
NC A **borehole** is a deep round hole made by a special tool or machine, especially one that is made in the ground when searching for oil or water. *Samples from 8 metre-deep boreholes were examined.*

boring /bɔːrɪŋ/
1 ADJ Something that is **boring** is so dull and uninteresting that it makes people tired and impatient. ...*a boring journey... Are all your meetings so boring?*
2 ADJ A thing that is **boring** has been made in an uninteresting and unimaginative way. *The gardens were a bit boring... Their houses were so boring that they were glad to get to the pub.*

Borja Cevallos, Rodrigo /rɒdriːgəʊ bɔːrxə sevæljəʊs/
Rodrigo Borja Cevallos became President of Ecuador in 1988. He was a Deputy in the National Congress from 1962 to 1982. He is the founder and leader of the Democratic Left (ID). Born: 1937.

born /bɔːn/
1 V-PASS When a baby is **born**, it comes out of its mother's body. *Mary was born in Glasgow.*
2 V-PASS When an idea or organization is **born**, it starts to exist. ...*the Lenin shipyard where Solidarity was born eight years ago... In the explosion of a star, a new science was born—neutrino astronomy.*
3 ADJ ATTRIB You use **born** to talk about something

that someone can do well and easily. For example, a **born** cook has a natural ability to cook well. *This little boy was a born actor.*

-born /-bɔːn/
SUFFIX **-born** is added to the name of a place or nationality to indicate where a person was born. ...*Lennox Lewis of Canada, the British-born Olympic boxing champion.*

born-again
ADJ ATTRIB A **born-again** Christian is someone who has been converted to evangelical Christianity. *This year, a born-again faith healer is running for President.*

borne /bɔːn/
Borne is the past participle of **bear**.

borough /bʌrə/ **boroughs**
NC A **borough** is a town, or a district within a large town, which has its own council. ...*the London Borough of Lewisham.*

borrow /bɒrəʊ/ **borrows, borrowing, borrowed**
VO If you **borrow** something that belongs to someone else, you take it intending to return it, usually with their permission. *Could I borrow your car?... I need to borrow five thousand pounds... He flew from Honolulu in a private jet borrowed from friends.*
◆ **borrowing** NU *Lowering interest rates will make borrowing cheaper.* ...*years of high public spending financed by foreign borrowing.*

borrower /bɒrəʊə/ **borrowers**
NC A **borrower** is a person or organization that borrows money. *The country has been transformed from being the world's largest lender to the world's largest borrower... The cut in interest rates will be extended to existing borrowers.*

borstal /bɔːstl/ **borstals**
NCorNU In Britain, prisons for young criminals used to be known as **borstals**. *He has spent more than half his life in one institution or another, from borstals to Dartmoor... I believe the way we treat our juveniles, who we send to borstal or to prison, is totally wrong.*

Bosnia-Herzegovina /bɒzniə hɜːtsəgəviːnə/
Bosnia-Herzegovina is a country in south-east Europe. After a referendum held in 1992 it declared independence from Yugoslavia and was recognized by the European Community and other countries. Capital: Sarajevo.

bosom /bʊzəm/ **bosoms**
1 NUorNC A woman's **bosom** is her breasts; an old-fashioned use. *Women's dresses show much less bosom.* ...*bare bosoms on page three.*
2 N SING+SUPP If you are in the **bosom** of your family or of a community, you are among people who love and protect you; a literary use. *He returned to his birthplace, and the bosom of the party whose leadership he'd left in disgrace.*
3 NC+POSS Strong feelings are sometimes described as being in your **bosom**; a literary use. ...*some dark, sinful passion you're nursing in your bosom.*
4 N+N A **bosom** friend is a very close friend; an old-fashioned use. ...*the son of her bosom friend Klara.*

boss /bɒs/ **bosses, bossing, bossed**
1 NC Your **boss** is the person in charge of the company or department that you work for. *Her boss has been criticised for being naive and badly misjudging the situation... His boss at the finance ministry is Mr Shimon Peres.*
2 If you **are** your **own boss**, you work for yourself or do not have to ask other people for permission to do something. *After all, workers were supposed to be their own bosses. ...Mr Dole was himself his own boss as leader of the Republican Party.*
3 NC+SUPP In informal American English, the leader of a local political party is sometimes referred to as a **boss**. ...*long-time Chicago mayor and Democratic boss Richard J. Daley.*
4 VO If someone **bosses** you, they keep telling you what to do; used showing disapproval. *They were talking and bossing her continually... They've bossed us around enough.*

boss-eyed /bɒsaɪd/
ADJ If someone is **boss-eyed**, they have eyes that look inward towards each other; an informal word.

bossy /bɒsi/
ADJ A **bossy** person enjoys telling other people what to do; used showing disapproval. *The television profile showed her as determined, bossy, and possibly arrogant.* ◆ **bossiness** NU *His bossiness didn't worry her unduly.*

bosun /bəusn/ **bosuns**
NC A **bosun** is the same as a **boatswain**. *He was the ferry's assistant bosun on the night of the disaster.*

botanical /bətænɪkl/
ADJ ATTRIB **Botanical** books, research, and activities relate to the scientific study of plants. *...a botanical study of Amazonia. ...a botanical artist.*

botanic gardens
N PL **Botanic gardens** are large gardens where plants are grown and studied. *...the Royal Botanic Gardens at Kew.*

botanist /bɒtənɪst/ **botanists**
NC A **botanist** is a scientist who studies plants. *He praised her unique work as an artist and botanist.*

botany /bɒtəni/
NU **Botany** is the scientific study of plants. *He is professor of medicine and botany at the Swedish University of Uppsala.*

botch /bɒtʃ/ **botches, botching, botched**
VO If you **botch** a task or a piece of work, you do it badly or clumsily; an informal word. *Their side of the operation has been botched.* ◆ **botched** ADJ *The coup last month was a botched affair.*

both /bəυθ/
1 PREDET, DET, or QUANT You use **both** when you are referring to two people or things and saying something about each of them. *Both her parents were dead... Both policies made good sense.* ► Also PRON *He got angry with both of them... Most of them speak either English or German or both... We were both young.*
2 You use the structure **both...and** when you are giving two facts or alternatives and emphasizing that each of them is true or possible. *These are dangers that threaten both men and women... The prospects both excited and worried me.*

bother /bɒðə/ **bothers, bothering, bothered**
1 V If you do not **bother** to do something, you do not do it, because you think it is unnecessary or would involve too much effort. *I never bother to iron my shirts... Don't bother with the washing-up.*
2 If you say that you **can't be bothered** to do something, you mean that you are not going to do it because you think it is unnecessary or would involve too much effort. *It's too easy to say we can't be bothered to do any more about it.*
3 NU **Bother** is trouble, fuss, or difficulty. *We found the address without any bother.*
4 N SING If a task or a person is a **bother**, it is boring or irritating. *Sorry to be a bother, but could you sign this for me?*
5 V O or V+*about* If something **bothers** you or if you **bother** about it, you are worried, concerned, or upset about it. *Is something bothering you?... I didn't bother about what I looked like.* ◆ **bothered** ADJ PRED *She was bothered about Olive.*
6 VO If you **bother** someone, you talk to them or interrupt them when they are busy. *Don't bother me with little things like that.*

Botswana /bɒtswɑːnə/
The **Republic of Botswana** is a country in southern Africa. The area was settled by the British and was known as Bechuanaland from 1885. It became an independent country named Botswana in 1966. It is a member of the Commonwealth and the Organization of African Unity. Dr Quett Masire, of the Botswana Democratic Party (BDP), became President in 1980. Botswana exports diamonds, copper, nickel, and meat. ◆ **Botswanan** /bɒtswɑːnən/ N, ADJ
■ *per capita GNP:* US$1,010 ■ *religion:* animism, Christianity ■ *language:* English (official), Setswana ■ *currency:* pula ■ *capital:* Gaborone ■ *population:* 1 million (1988) ■ *size:* 582,000 square kilometres.

bottle /bɒtl/ **bottles, bottling, bottled**
1 NC A **bottle** is a glass or plastic container for keeping liquids in. *...a scent bottle... He injured his leg on a broken bottle.*

2 NC You can use **bottle** to refer to a bottle and its contents, or to the contents only. *She drank half a bottle of whisky a day.*
3 VO If you **bottle** wine, beer, or food, you put it into bottles in order to store it. *One project included a local woman bottling fruit and vegetables.*
4 NC A **bottle** is also a drinking container used by babies. It has a special rubber part called a teat through which the baby sucks. *...a teat from a feeding bottle.*

bottle up PHRASAL VERB If you **bottle up** strong feelings, you do not express them or show them. *...all the rage that had been bottled up in him for so long.*

bottle bank, bottle banks
NC A **bottle bank** is a large container in the street in which people can put their empty glass bottles. The bottles are then collected and used to make new bottles. *Fifty bottle banks are being set up in the city.*

bottled /bɒtld/
ADJ **Bottled** drinks are sold in bottles. *...bottled beer. ...Britain's bottled water industry.*

bottle-feed bottle-feeds, bottle-feeding, bottle-fed
V O or V A baby who is **bottle-fed** is given milk in a bottle rather than sucking milk from its mother's breasts. *They bottle-feed their babies, give them sweetened fizzy drinks and buy them tinned baby food... Bottle-fed babies fuss as much as breast-fed babies if their feed is late.*

bottle green
ADJ Something that is **bottle green** is dark green in colour. *...a bottle green jumper.*

bottleneck /bɒtlnek/ **bottlenecks**
1 NC A **bottleneck** is a narrow part of a road where the traffic often has to slow down or stop. *The bottlenecks at the bridges create tremendous traffic jams.*
2 NC A **bottleneck** is also a situation that stops a process or activity from progressing. *The shortage of skilled labour is often a serious industrial bottleneck.*

bottle-opener, bottle-openers
NC A **bottle-opener** is a metal device for removing lids from bottles.

bottom /bɒtəm/ **bottoms, bottoming, bottomed**
1 NC The **bottom** of something is the lowest part of it. *I stood there at the bottom of the steps... It sank to the bottom of the lake.*
2 ADJ ATTRIB The **bottom** thing in a series of things is the lowest one. *...the bottom button of my waistcoat.*
3 NC The **bottom** of a place such as a street or garden is the end farthest from the entrance. *...down at the bottom of the meadow.*
4 ADJ PRED If you are **bottom** of the class or come **bottom** in a test, you are the worst student in the class or get the lowest marks in the test. *I was sure I'd come bottom.*
5 ADJ PRED If a team comes **bottom** in a game or competition, all the other teams have done better than they have. *Glamorgan finished bottom of the championship last year.*
6 If you **get to the bottom of** something, you discover the real truth about it or the real cause of it. *He was interviewed by fraud squad detectives trying to get to the bottom of the dispute.*
7 NC Your **bottom** is the part of your body that you sit on. *He had broad shoulders and chest, a nice bottom, and was tall.*

bottom out PHRASAL VERB When something that has been getting worse **bottoms out**, it stops getting worse, and remains at a particular level. *Even if the recession has bottomed out, it will not help the unemployed.*

bottom drawer, bottom drawers
NC If a woman gets something for her **bottom drawer**, she keeps it to use until she is married; an old-fashioned expression.

bottomless /bɒtəmləs/
ADJ If you describe a supply of something as **bottomless**, you mean that it seems so large that it will never run out. *...American millionaires with bottomless purses.*

bottom line
N SING The **bottom line** of a situation or discussion is

the most important consideration in it, or the most important result that it will have. *You've got to remember, at the bottom line, Marx was a German... The bottom line is that we've now got rising prices, and the taxpayer has to subsidise the industry.*

botulism /bɒtjʊlɪzəm/
NU **Botulism** is a serious form of food poisoning caused by eating preserved food which has gone bad; a medical term. *...toxins responsible for causing cholera, botulism, and tetanus.*

Boudiaf, Mohamed /məʊhæmɪd buːdjɑːf/
Mohamed Boudiaf became head of the five-man Council of State which took control of Algeria after the resignation of President Chadli Benjedid in 1992. Born: 1919.

boudoir /buːdwɑː/ **boudoirs**
NC A woman's **boudoir** is her bedroom or private sitting room; an old-fashioned word. *While Marguerite celebrates sacred love in her boudoir, the fairies cast a spell on her.*

bougainvillea /buːgənvɪliə/ **bougainvilleas**
NUorNC **Bougainvillea** is a climbing plant with very thin red or purple leaves which look like flowers. Bougainvillea grows mainly in hot countries.

bough /baʊ/ **boughs**
NC A **bough** is a large branch of a tree; a literary word. *We lay on the soft moss under a roof of leafy boughs.*

bought /bɔːt/
Bought is the past tense and past participle of **buy**.

boulder /bəʊldə/ **boulders**
NC A **boulder** is a large rounded rock. *Efforts to move the boulder with bulldozers are underway.*

boulevard /buːləvɑːd, buːlvɑː/ **boulevards**
NC A **boulevard** is a wide street in a city, usually with trees along each side. *...Shanghai's famous boulevard, the Bund.*

bounce /baʊns/ **bounces, bouncing, bounced**
1 V-ERG When something such as a ball **bounces**, or when you **bounce** it, it moves upwards or away immediately after hitting a surface. *I managed to land, and my helmet came bouncing past me... Some countries allow the players to bounce the ball off the side-boards.*
2 VorVA You can say that something **bounces** when it swings or moves up and down. *The rucksack bounced and jingled on my shoulders... There's a tendency for the car to bounce up and down.*
3 VA If you **bounce** on something, you jump up and down on it repeatedly. *...bouncing on a trampoline.*
4 VA If someone **bounces** somewhere, they move in an energetic way, because they are feeling happy. *He came bouncing in, grinning.*
5 V If a cheque that you write **bounces**, the bank refuses to accept it and pay out the money, because there is not enough money in your account. *There is no money left—payroll cheques are bouncing.*
bounce back PHRASAL VERB If you **bounce back** after a bad experience, you quickly return to your previous level of activity, enthusiasm, or success. *Can she bounce back from this crushing election defeat?... The top seed Jimmy Connors bounced back after losing the first set.*
bounce off PHRASAL VERB 1 If one thing **bounces off** another, it hits it and moves outwards or upwards immediately afterwards. *If the field was planted with trees, the ball would bounce off the trunks and go in almost any direction... Several people were injured when the grenade bounced off the windscreen.* 2 If light or sound **bounces off** a surface, or if you **bounce** it **off**, it reaches the surface and is reflected back. *When light bounces off the mirror, it produces an image of an object... If you have a transmitter, you can bounce radio waves off what you're trying to detect.*

bouncer /baʊnsə/ **bouncers**
1 NC A **bouncer** is a man whose job is to prevent unwanted people from coming into a pub or a nightclub and to throw people out if they cause trouble. *I went, and there was this enormous bouncer on the door, and I hadn't got my ticket.*
2 NC In cricket, a **bouncer** is a ball that bounces very

high after it has been bowled. *He suffered a fractured cheekbone after being struck in the face by a bouncer from Ambrose.*

bouncing /baʊnsɪŋ/
ADJ If you say that someone is **bouncing** with health, or if you refer to a child as a **bouncing** baby, you mean that they are looking very healthy.

bouncy /baʊnsi/
ADJ Someone who is **bouncy** is very lively and enthusiastic. *...a bouncy little man.*

bound /baʊnd/ **bounds, bounding, bounded**
1 ADJ PRED+to-INF If something is **bound** to happen, it is certain to happen. *We are bound to win.*
2 ADJ PRED If you are **bound** by an agreement or law, you have a duty to obey it. *We are bound by the government's pay policy.*
3 N PL **Bounds** are limits which restrict what can be done. *It is not outside the bounds of possibility.*
4 VO If an area of land is **bounded** by something, that thing is situated around its edge. *The plantation was bounded by marsh.*
5 ADJ PRED+for If a vehicle is **bound** for a particular place, it is travelling towards it. *He put her aboard the steamer bound for New York.*
6 V When animals or people **bound**, they move quickly with large leaps. *He bounded up the stairs.*
7 **Bound** is also the past tense and past participle of **bind**.
● **Bound** is used in these phrases. ● You can say 'I am **bound to say**' or 'I am **bound to admit**' when mentioning a fact which you regret. *Sometimes, I'm bound to say, they are a hopeless muddle.* ● If one thing is **bound up with** another, it is closely connected with it. *All this was bound up with what was happening in Egypt.* ● If a place is **out of bounds**, people are forbidden to go there. *The areas have been ruled out of bounds to journalists.*

-bound /-baʊnd/
1 SUFFIX **-bound** combines with nouns to form adjectives. Adjectives formed in this way describe someone or something as being restricted or limited by the thing referred to by the original noun. For example, someone who is 'wheelchair bound' has to stay in their wheelchair because they are not able to move around without it. *The baby dinosaurs would have been nest-bound and helpless... For much of the night, the airport was fog-bound.*
2 SUFFIX **-bound** combines with nouns that refer to places, or with adverbs and adjectives that express direction, to form new adjectives. Adjectives formed in this way describe someone or something as travelling to that place or in that direction. For example, a 'southbound' train is heading towards the south. *They set two coaches of a Delhi-bound express on fire.*

boundary /baʊndə⁰ri/ **boundaries**
NC The **boundary** of an area of land is an imaginary line that separates it from other areas. *You have to stay within your county boundary.*

bounder /baʊndə/ **bounders**
NC If someone calls a man a **bounder**, they mean that he behaves in an unkind, deceitful, or selfish way; an old-fashioned word.

boundless /baʊndləs/
ADJ If you describe something as **boundless**, you mean that there seems to be no end or limit to it. *...her boundless energies.*

bountiful /baʊntɪfl/
ADJ Something that is **bountiful** is provided very generously or in large amounts; a literary word. *...a bountiful supply of Madame's favourite cigarettes.*

bounty /baʊnti/
1 N SING+POSS Someone's **bounty** is their generosity in giving something. *They must accept the colonel's bounty.*
2 NU **Bounty** is also something provided in large amounts. *...cashing in on the quarter of a million pound bounty offered to the finder.*

bouquet /bʊkeɪ, bəʊkeɪ/ **bouquets**
NC A **bouquet** is a bunch of flowers arranged in an attractive way, especially one given as a present. *...a bouquet of roses.*

bourbon /bɜːbən/ **bourbons**
N MASS **Bourbon** is a type of whisky that is made mainly in America. *Bourbon is the drink favoured by one of the characters in the novel.*

bourgeois /bʊəʒwɑː/
1 ADJ If you describe something such as an attitude as **bourgeois**, you mean it is typical of fairly rich middle-class people; used showing disapproval. *I found their ideas insufferably bourgeois. ...giving the bourgeois media a pretext to start an anti-Czechoslovak campaign.*
2 ADJ Communists use **bourgeois** when referring to the capitalist system and to the social class who own most of the wealth in that system. *She condemns modern bourgeois society... The document contained no reference to bourgeois liberalisation.*

bourgeoisie /bʊəʒwɑːziː/
N COLL In Marxist theory, the **bourgeoisie** are the middle-class people who own most of the wealth in a capitalist system. *In other words, the bourgeoisie are a product of the French Revolution.*

bout /baʊt/ **bouts**
1 NC+SUPP If you have a **bout** of something such as an illness, you have it for a short period. *...a bout of flu.*
2 NC+SUPP A **bout** of activity is a short time during which you put a lot of effort into doing something. *...frenzied bouts of writing.*

boutique /buːtiːk/ **boutiques**
NC A **boutique** is a small shop that sells fashionable clothes, shoes, or jewellery. *...an extravagant boutique in Manila.*

bovine /bəʊvaɪn/
1 ADJ ATTRIB **Bovine** means relating to cattle. *...bovine tuberculosis.*
2 ADJ If you say that someone's behaviour or appearance is **bovine**, you mean that you think they are slow-moving, stupid, or ugly; a literary use. *...the typical media woman's bovine leer. ...the bovine apathy of members.*

bow, **bows**, **bowing**, **bowed**; pronounced /baʊ/ for the meanings in paragraphs 1 to 4 and for the phrasal verbs, and /bəʊ/ for the meanings in paragraphs 5, 6, and 7.
1 V When you **bow** to someone, you briefly bend your body towards them as a formal way of greeting them or showing respect. *They bowed before a portrait of the emperor.* ▶ Also NC *He opened the door with a bow.*
2 VO If you **bow** your head, you bend it downwards so that you are looking towards the ground. *Alone in my room, I bowed my head and prayed.*
3 V+to If you **bow** to someone's wishes or **bow** to pressure, you agree to do what someone wants you to do; a formal use. *It wasn't until later that he bowed to pressure and resigned... The paper says that the government has finally bowed to the inevitable.*
4 NCor N PL The front part of a ship is called the **bow** or the **bows**. *A destroyer fired warning shots across its bow... The submarine suffered damage to its bows and navigational equipment.*
5 NC A **bow** is a knot with two loops and two loose ends that is used in tying shoelaces and ribbons. *...Easter baskets with big pink bows... In one town, they tied a giant bow around the Town Hall and let off fireworks.*
6 NC A **bow** is also a weapon for shooting arrows, consisting of a long piece of wood bent into a curve by a string attached to both its ends. *This is the first time that they have attacked using bows and arrows and spears... The sample is taken from a whale, using a specialised bow and arrow.*
7 NC The **bow** of a violin or other stringed instrument is a long, thin piece of wood with hair from a horse's tail stretched along it. You move the bow across the strings of the instrument in order to play it. *At the same auction, a record price was paid for a violin bow.*

bow down PHRASAL VERB 1 If you **bow down**, you bow very low to show great respect. *The angels were commanded to bow down.* 2 If you **bow down** to what someone says or does, you do as they tell you instead of what you want to do. *Zola is an outstanding example of intellectual bravery, and a refusal to bow down to conventional thinking.*

bow out PHRASAL VERB If you **bow out** of something, you stop taking part in it. *We may do one more performance before we bow out... He may have decided that this is the time to bow out from a long and unrewarding struggle.*

bowed; pronounced /bəʊd/ for the meaning in paragraph 1 and /baʊd/ for the meaning in paragraph 2.
1 ADJ Something that is **bowed** is curved. *He had slightly bowed legs.*
2 ADJ If someone is **bowed**, their body is bent forward, usually because they are very old. *I remember seeing an old man bent and bowed walking slowly along Queen Anne Street.*

bowel /baʊəl/ **bowels**
1 N PL Your **bowels** are the tubes in your body through which digested food passes from your stomach to your anus. *He could not be discharged from hospital until his bowels were functioning normally. ...genes involved in bowel cancer.*
2 N PL+SUPP You can refer to the parts deep inside something as its **bowels**. *...deep in the bowels of the earth... We're down now in the bowels of Bush House, in the heating plant.*

bower /baʊə/ **bowers**
NC A **bower** is a shady, leafy shelter in a garden or wood; a literary word.

bowl /bəʊl/ **bowls**, **bowling**, **bowled**
1 NC A **bowl** is a circular container with a wide, uncovered top. Bowls are used, for example, for serving food. *...a china bowl. ...a goldfish in a bowl.*
2 NC You can use **bowl** to refer to a bowl and its contents, or to the contents only. *I ate a big bowl of porridge.*
3 NC The **bowl** of something such as a lavatory or a tobacco pipe is the part of it that is shaped like a bowl. *The whole thing went down the toilet bowl.*
4 V When someone **bowls** in cricket, they throw the ball down the pitch towards the batsman. *He had bowled badly.*
5 NU **Bowls** is a game in which the players try to roll large wooden balls as near as possible to a small ball. *It was the best ever result for Botswana in international bowls.*
6 See also **bowling**.

bowl over PHRASAL VERB 1 If you **bowl** someone **over**, you knock them down by accidentally hitting them when you are moving very quickly. *They leapt aside to avoid being bowled over by three boys as they raced past.* 2 If you **are bowled over** by something, you are very impressed or surprised by it. *I was bowled over by the beauty of Malawi... It's pure emotion, and it just bowls people over.*

bow-legged /bəʊlegɪd/
ADJ Someone who is **bow-legged** has legs that curve apart. *People become bow-legged in their old age.*

bowler /bəʊlə/ **bowlers**
NC In a game of cricket, the **bowler** is the person who is bowling. *The new fast bowler, Curtley Ambrose, produced another good performance.*

bowler hat, **bowler hats**
NC A **bowler hat** or a **bowler** is a firm round black hat with a narrow curved brim, worn especially by some British businessmen. *...dressed as a city gent in a bowler hat and pin-striped suit.*

bowling /bəʊlɪŋ/
NU **Bowling** is a game in which you roll a heavy ball down a long, narrow track towards a group of wooden objects and try to knock them down. *They achieved one of the biggest winning margins since World bowling started 22 years ago.*

bowling alley, **bowling alleys**
NC A **bowling alley** is a building which contains several tracks for bowling. You can also refer to the tracks as **bowling alleys**. *They provide everything from bowling alleys to cinemas.*

bowling green, **bowling greens**
NC A **bowling green** is an area of very smooth, short grass on which the game of bowls is played.

bow tie /bəʊ taɪ/ **bow ties**
NC A **bow tie** is a man's tie in the form of a bow, worn especially for formal occasions. *With his bow tie and cigarette holder, the picture is instantly recognisable.*

bow window /bəʊ wɪndəʊ/ **bow windows**
NC A **bow window** is a curved window that sticks out further than the surface of the wall. *...the bow window on the ground floor.*

bow-wow /baʊwaʊ/ **bow-wows**
Small children often use **bow-wow** to refer to the sound that a dog makes.

box /bɒks/ **boxes, boxing, boxed**
1 NC A **box** is a container which has stiff sides and which sometimes has a lid. *...a cardboard box. ...a standard tool box.*
2 NC You can use **box** to refer to a box and its contents, or to the contents only. *...a box of chocolates.*
3 NC A **box** on a form that you fill in is a square or rectangular space in which you have to write something. *Put your age in the grey box.*
4 NC A **box** in a theatre is a separate area like a little room where a small number of people can sit to watch the performance. *Two tall Greek princes ran down from the royal box to join him.*
5 V To **box** means to fight someone according to the rules of the sport of boxing. *Wangila boxed in Seoul four times last year.*
box in PHRASAL VERB If you **are boxed in**, you are unable to move from a particular place because you are surrounded by other people or cars. *In the 800 metres, he was boxed in and came second.*

box camera, box cameras
NC A **box camera** is a simple type of camera, shaped like a box. *The photographs were shot by two young girls with a simple box camera.*

boxed /bɒkst/
ADJ Something that is **boxed** is sold in a box. *...a boxed set of Beethoven's symphonies. ...boxed cereals.*

boxer /bɒksə/ **boxers**
NC A **boxer** is a sportsman whose sport is boxing. *...the first British boxer to regain a world title.*

boxing /bɒksɪŋ/
NU **Boxing** is a sport in which two men wearing large padded gloves fight according to special rules, by punching each other. *...dangerous pastimes, like rock-climbing and boxing.*

Boxing Day
NU In Britain, **Boxing Day** is December 26th, the day after Christmas Day. *The film Moonwalker goes on general release on Boxing Day.*

box junction, box junctions
NC In Britain, a **box junction** is a road junction marked with yellow lines on the road. If the road beyond the junction is blocked you must not drive onto the marked area.

box number, box numbers
NC A **box number** is a number used as an address, especially one given by a newspaper for replies to a private advertisement. *The advert didn't give the address, just a box number.*

box office, box offices
1 NC The **box office** in a theatre, cinema, or concert hall is the place where the tickets are sold. *Tickets are available from the Wembley Arena box office.*
2 N SING or N+N You also use **box office** to say how successful a film, play, or actor is in terms of the number of tickets sold to go and see them. *She was a very hot box office attraction indeed.*

box pleat, box pleats
NC A **box pleat** is a type of pleat used especially in skirts, which consists of two large pleats that are folded away from each other.

boy /bɔɪ/ **boys**
1 NC A **boy** is a male child. *The baby boy has waited almost four months for a life-saving operation.*
2 You can express excitement or admiration by saying '**Boy**' or '**Oh boy**'; used in American English. *Boy, was that some party!*

boycott /bɔɪkɒt/ **boycotts, boycotting, boycotted**
VO When people **boycott** a country, organization, or event, they refuse to be involved with it, because they strongly disapprove of it. *He urged all citizens to boycott the polls... These proceedings were boycotted by the opposition.* ▶ Also NC *...an Olympic boycott.*

boyfriend /bɔɪfrend/ **boyfriends**
NC Someone's **boyfriend** is the man with whom they are having a romantic or sexual relationship. *The two women were on holiday with their boyfriends.*

boyhood /bɔɪhʊd/
NU A man's **boyhood** is the period of his life during which he is a boy. *He began to talk about his boyhood in London.*

boyish /bɔɪɪʃ/
ADJ If you say that someone is **boyish**, you mean that you think they are like a boy in their appearance or behaviour. *He still seemed boyish. ...her boyish clothes.* ◆ **boyishly** ADV *He grinned boyishly.*

boy scout, boy scouts
NC A **boy scout** is a member of the Scout Association. Boy scouts are encouraged to be disciplined and to learn practical skills. *I was a boy scout, so I was able to take care of myself.*

Br.
Br. is a written abbreviation for 'British'.

bra /brɑː/ **bras**
NC A **bra** is a piece of underwear that a woman wears to support her breasts. *This is an underwired bra, which gives more support.*

brace /breɪs/ **braces, bracing, braced.** The plural form for the noun in paragraph 7 is **brace**.
1 V-REFL If you **brace** yourself for something unpleasant or difficult, you prepare yourself for it. *She had braced herself to read the letter... The company managers are bracing themselves for the effects of the new law.*
2 VO+against If you **brace** a part of your body against something, you press the part of your body against it, to steady yourself or to avoid falling. *He braced a hand against a doorpost... I'm having to brace myself against the wind.*
3 VO If you **brace** your shoulders or legs, you keep them stiffly in a particular position. *He stood to attention, his shoulders braced.*
4 NC A **brace** is a metal device fastened to a child's teeth to help them grow straight. *I'm afraid she'll need braces, but prevention is better than cure.*
5 NC A **brace** is also a device attached to a person's leg to strengthen or support it. *Barnett has begun to learn to walk with the use of braces.*
6 N PL **Braces** are a pair of straps that people wear over their shoulders to prevent their trousers from falling down. *He wore scarlet braces.*
7 NC You can refer to two things of the same kind as a **brace**. *...a brace of pheasants... Her confident performance produced a brace of gold medals.*

brace and bit, braces and bits
NC A **brace and bit** is a hand tool that is used for boring holes in wood.

bracelet /breɪslət/ **bracelets**
NC A **bracelet** is a chain or band that you wear round your wrist. *...a traditional High Street jeweller where you can buy a wedding ring or a charm bracelet... The judge ordered him to wear an electronic bracelet so that his movements could be monitored.*

bracing /breɪsɪŋ/
ADJ If you describe a place, climate, or activity as **bracing**, you mean that it makes you feel fit and full of energy. *...splashing and wading in the bracing British seas.*

bracken /brækən/
NU **Bracken** is a plant like a large fern that grows on hills and in woods. *...removing the bracken and rhododendron that's choking the heather and gorse.*

bracket /brækɪt/ **brackets, bracketing, bracketed**
1 NC **Brackets** are a pair of written marks such as ( ) that you place round a word, expression, or sentence in order to indicate that you are giving extra information. *Qualifying matches are shown with the kick-off time in brackets.*
2 NC+SUPP If something is in a particular **bracket**, it is within a particular range, for example a range of prices or ages. *...the 14-16 age bracket. ...a quality car in the middle or upper bracket.*

3 VO+*together* or *with* When you **bracket** two or more things or people together, you consider them as being similar or related in some way. *They frequently bracket the Association with the IMF and World Bank.* 4 NC A **bracket** is also a piece of metal, wood, or plastic that is fastened to a wall to support something such as a shelf. *Alternatively, it can be fixed without the bracket by drilling a hole in the bodywork.*

bracketed /ˈbrækɪtɪd/
ADJ A **bracketed** word, expression, or sentence has brackets written around it. *Bracketed sentences may be omitted.*

brackish /ˈbrækɪʃ/
ADJ **Brackish** water is slightly salty. *These reeds grow best in brackish water.*

brag /bræg/ **brags, bragging, bragged**
VA, V, V-REPORT, or V-QUOTE If you **brag** about something, you say in a very proud way that you possess it or have done it; used showing disapproval. *He recorded him bragging about his police contacts... We were aware that she was not bragging... He bragged to two nurses that he had killed a man... Americans used to brag, 'We come from everywhere', although that was never quite so.*

braggart /ˈbrægət/ **braggarts**
NC A **braggart** is a person, usually a man, who brags about what he has done or will do or what he possesses; an old-fashioned word, used showing disapproval. *The force of events will reveal him for the braggart that he is.*

Brahmin /ˈbrɑːmɪn/ **Brahmins**; also spelt **Brahman.**
NC A **Brahmin** is a Hindu of the highest caste. *...an elegant young Brahmin.*

braid /breɪd/ **braids, braiding, braided**
1 NU **Braid** is a narrow piece of decorated cloth or twisted threads, which is used to decorate clothes or curtains. *...a cap with gold braid on it.* 2 VO If you **braid** hair, you plait it; used in American English. *They braid the hair of tourists, and this can earn them as much as 50 US dollars in two and a half hours.* 3 NC A **braid** is a length of hair which has been plaited and tied; used in American English. *Carole was plump, with long braids.*

Braille /breɪl/;
NU **Braille** is a system of printing for blind people. The letters are printed as groups of raised dots that blind people feel with their fingers. *...the trouble and expense of using Braille. ...sending teachers, braille equipment, and toys to help incurably blind children.*

brain /breɪn/ **brains**
1 NC Your **brain** is the organ inside your head that enables you to think and to feel things such as heat and pain. *The organism attacks nerve cells in the brain... The vaccine is prepared from the rabies virus found in the brains of sheep.* 2 NC You also use **brain** to refer to your mind and the way you think. *He had one clear wish in his confused brain.* 3 NC If you say that someone has **brains** or has a good **brain**, you mean that they have the ability to learn and understand things quickly, to solve problems, and to make good decisions. *He'd got brains but wouldn't use them... She has a very capable business brain.* 4 NC Very clever people are sometimes referred to as **brains**; an informal use. *Not even the great brains of Cambridge can solve his problem.* 5 N SING The person who plans the activities of an organization can be referred to as its **brains**; an informal use. *She was the brains of the company.* ● **Brain** is used in these informal phrases. ● If you **pick** someone's **brains**, you ask them to help you with a problem because they know a lot about the subject. *...picking the brains of colleagues for ideas.* ● If you **rack** your **brains**, you try very hard to think of something. *Racking his brains, he couldn't think of a single example.*

brainchild /ˈbreɪntʃaɪld/
N SING+POSS Someone's **brainchild** is an idea or invention that they have thought up or created. *Building a luxurious new opera house had been the brainchild of François Mitterrand.*

brain death
NU **Brain death** occurs when someone's brain stops functioning, even though their heart may be kept beating using a machine.

brain drain
N SING When people talk about a **brain drain**, they are referring to the movement of a large number of scientists or academics away from their own country to other countries where the conditions and salaries are better. *He said his own country was one of the worst culprits in the brain drain to South Africa.*

brainless /ˈbreɪnləs/
ADJ If you say that someone is **brainless**, you mean that they are very silly. *The generals were singularly brainless men.*

brainpower /ˈbreɪnpaʊə/
NU Your **brainpower** is your ability to think intelligently and logically. *Newton's sheer brainpower and total concentration gets him there.*

brainstorm /ˈbreɪnstɔːm/ **brainstorms**
NC If you have a **brainstorm**, you suddenly become unable to think sensibly. *I must have had a brainstorm.*

brainstorming /ˈbreɪnstɔːmɪŋ/
N+N A **brainstorming** session is a meeting of people in order to develop ideas together. *It was decided to call in the advertisers for a brainstorming session.*

brain teaser, brain teasers
NC A **brain teaser** is a question or problem that is difficult to answer or solve, but is not serious or important. *If you think you know the answer to that brain teaser, do send it to us.*

brainwash /ˈbreɪnwɒʃ/ **brainwashes, brainwashing, brainwashed**
VO If someone **is brainwashed**, they are forced to believe something by being continually told that it is true, and prevented from thinking about it properly. *The United Nations has accused them of brainwashing prisoners... They were taken to special camps and brainwashed.*

brainwave /ˈbreɪnweɪv/ **brainwaves**
NC If you have a **brainwave**, you suddenly think of a clever idea. *Then he had a brainwave. He could ask the librarian who the girl was.*

brainy /ˈbreɪni/ **brainier, brainiest**
ADJ Someone who is **brainy** is clever and good at learning; an informal word. *Did it make them feel unusually brainy, being at Cademuir school?*

braise /breɪz/ **braises, braising, braised**
VO When you **braise** meat or a vegetable, you fry it quickly and then cook it slowly in a covered dish with a small amount of liquid. *When meat is braised it should be cooked first by browning and then in the oven with a bed of flavouring vegetables under the meat.* ◆ **braised** ADJ ATTRIB *...braised beef.*

brake /breɪk/ **brakes, braking, braked**
1 NC A vehicle's **brakes** are devices that make it go slower or stop. *The driver of the bus sent a radio message saying his brakes had failed.* 2 V When the driver of a vehicle **brakes**, or when the vehicle **brakes**, the driver makes the vehicle slow down or stop by using the brakes. *I thought he was going to walk across in front of my path, so I braked very hard.*

brake light, brake lights
NC The **brake lights** of a motor vehicle are the red lights at the back which light up when the driver uses the brakes. *...the compulsory fitting of brake lights.*

bramble /ˈbræmbl/ **brambles**
NC **Brambles** are wild, thorny bushes that produce blackberries. *A handful of hikers, their faces smeared with dirt and their clothing torn by brambles, stumble up the trail.*

bran /bræn/
NU **Bran** is the small brown flakes that are left when wheat grains have been used to make white flour. *We hear so much about added bran, added fibre and fruit.*

branch /brɑːntʃ/ **branches, branching, branched**
1 NC The **branches** of a tree are the parts that grow out from its trunk and that have leaves, flowers, or fruit growing on them. *...trimming off branches with a chain saw.*

2 NC+SUPP A **branch** of a business or other organization is one of the offices, shops, or local groups which belong to it. *Managers at the bank's branches were warned yesterday to be vigilant. ...one of the founders of the Belgrade branch of the Association.*
3 NC+SUPP A **branch** of a subject is a part or type of it. *...specialists in particular branches of medicine.*
branch off PHRASAL VERB A road or path that **branches off** from another one starts from it and goes in a slightly different direction. *The road to Oxford branches off here.*
branch out PHRASAL VERB If you **branch out**, you do something different from your normal activities or work. *She decided to branch out alone and launch a campaign.*
branch line, branch lines
NC A **branch line** is a railway line that goes to small towns rather than one that goes between large cities. *...a foreign-owned branch line.*
brand /brænd/ **brands, branding, branded**
1 NC A **brand** of a product is the version made by one particular manufacturer. *...a preference for one brand of soft drink rather than another.*
2 NC+*of* You can refer to a kind of thought, behaviour, or writing as a particular **brand** of it. *...their brand of politics.*
3 VOCorVO+*as* If you **are branded** as something bad, people decide and say that you are that thing. *His political supporters had been branded traitors... Hamburgers have been branded as junk food.*
4 VO When an animal **is branded**, a permanent mark is burned on its skin, in order to indicate who it belongs to.
branded /brændɪd/
ADJ ATTRIB A **branded** product is one which is made by a well-known manufacturer and has the manufacturer's label on it. *They crave the money for luxurious branded goods.*
branding iron, branding irons
NC A **branding iron** is a long piece of metal with a design at one end which is used for branding animals.
brandish /brændɪʃ/ **brandishes, brandishing, brandished**
VO If you **brandish** something, especially a weapon, you wave it around vigorously. *They sprang high into the air brandishing their spears.*
brand name, brand names
NC The **brand name** of a product made by a particular manufacturer is the name that appears on it. *Everything that's got a famous brand name is faked.*
brand-new
ADJ Something that is **brand-new** is completely new. *...a brand-new Olympic stadium.*
brandy /brændi/ **brandies**
N MASS **Brandy** is a strong alcoholic drink, usually made from wine. *Churchill was known for his fondness for whisky and brandy.*
brandy butter
NU **Brandy butter** is a thick paste made from butter, sugar and brandy. It is usually eaten at Christmas with Christmas pudding or mince pies.
brandy snap, brandy snaps
NC A **brandy snap** is a very thin, crisp biscuit in the shape of a hollow cylinder, flavoured with ginger.
brash /bræʃ/ **brasher, brashest**
ADJ If someone's behaviour is **brash**, they are being too confident and aggressive. *Jenny was alarmed by these brash children.*
Brasília /brəzɪliə/
Brasília is the capital of Brazil and its fifth largest city. It replaced Rio de Janeiro as the capital in 1961. Population: 1,803,000 (1989).
brass /brɑːs/
1 NU **Brass** is a yellow metal made from copper and zinc. It is used especially for making ornaments and musical instruments. *...a plaque made of polished brass. ...toilets with porcelain handles and brass fittings.*
2 N PL The section of an orchestra which consists of brass wind instruments such as trumpets and horns is called the **brass**. *They had piano, brass and strings.*

...the Royal College of Music Brass Ensemble.
3 N COLL You can refer to the most senior members of an army as the **brass**; an informal use. *Speeches were cut to a minimum and there was no top brass from Moscow.*
brass band, brass bands
NC A **brass band** is a band that consists of people playing brass wind instruments. *Flag-waving girls and a brass band greeted the royal couple.*
brassed off
ADJ PRED If you are **brassed off**, you are bored and annoyed; an informal expression. *I'm really brassed off... I'm brassed off with this stupid essay.*
brass hat, brass hats
NC You can refer to a very high ranking military officer as a **brass hat**; an informal expression.
brassiere /bræziə/ **brassieres**
NC A **brassiere** is a bra; an old-fashioned word.
brass knuckles
N PL **Brass knuckles** are the same as a **knuckle-duster**; used in American English. *At the same moment he slipped onto his right hand a specially made set of brass knuckles studded with iron spikes.*
brass rubbing, brass rubbings
NC A **brass rubbing** is a picture made by placing a piece of paper over a block of brass that has writing or a picture on it, and rubbing it with a wax crayon to copy it onto the paper.
brass tacks
If you **get down to brass tacks**, you discuss the basic and most important facts, truths, or realities of a situation. *Now, let's get down to brass tacks: how much did we actually lose last year?*
brassy /brɑːsi/ **brassier, brassiest**
1 ADJ If you describe something as **brassy**, you mean that it has a yellowish metallic colour. *Your hair's looking a bit brassy—what have you been doing to it?*
2 ADJ A sound that is **brassy** is unpleasantly harsh and loud. *The music played incessantly; now soft and slow, now brassy and loud... Joanna gave a brassy laugh.*
3 ADJ If a person's appearance or behaviour is **brassy**, they have very poor taste and they dress or behave in a way that is too bright, daring, harsh, or lively.
brat /bræt/ **brats**
NC If you call a child a **brat**, you mean that they are badly behaved; an informal word. *...the spawning of a generation of spoiled brats.*
Brathwaite, Nicholas /nɪkələs bræθət/
Nicholas Brathwaite became Prime Minister of Grenada in 1990. He is a member of the National Democratic Congress (NDC).
bravado /brəvɑːdəʊ/
NU **Bravado** is an appearance of courage that someone shows in order to impress other people. *...a display of bravado.*
brave /breɪv/ **braver, bravest; braves, braving, braved**
1 ADJ Someone who is **brave** is willing to do things which are dangerous, and does not show fear in difficult or dangerous situations. *...the brave young men who have fallen in the struggle... I think you were very brave to defy convention.* ♦ **bravely** ADV *He fought bravely at the Battle of Waterloo.*
2 VO If you **brave** a difficult or dangerous situation, you deliberately experience it, in order to achieve something. *Farmers braved wintry conditions to rescue the sheep.*
● **Brave** is used in these phrases. ● If someone uses **brave words**, they try with difficulty to convince people that things are going well by sounding confident and optimistic. *The President's brave words are unlikely to convince the sceptics... Brave words, to be sure. But not all Argentinians will share his confidence.* ● If someone is **putting a brave face on** a difficult situation, they are pretending that the situation is not as bad as it really is. *You are obviously putting a brave face on things, but it must be a disappointment to you.*
bravery /breɪvəri/
NU **Bravery** is brave behaviour or the quality of being brave. *The Princess was clearly moved by the*

bravery and selflessness of those she met. ...bravery awards.

bravo /brɑːvəʊ/
You say 'Bravo' to express appreciation when someone has done something well.

bravura /brəvjʊərə/
NU **Bravura** is a way of doing something in which you add unnecessary extra actions that emphasize your skill or importance; a literary word. *There is no bravura, no show; everything is very precisely done. ...in between flashing smiles and bravura flourishes of the gold pen.*

brawl /brɔːl/ **brawls, brawling, brawled**
1 NC A **brawl** is a rough fight or struggle. *A wild brawl followed.*
2 V When people **brawl**, they take part in a brawl. *They were brawling in the street.*

brawn /brɔːn/
1 NU **Brawn** is physical strength. *Too little bone and brawn had isolated Bernard from his fellow men... It's a difference of mind and body, a difference of brain and brawn.*
2 NU **Brawn** is food made from pieces of pork and jelly pressed together so that it is solid and can be sliced.

brawny /brɔːni/
ADJ A **brawny** man is strong and muscular. *...a brawny worker.*

bray /breɪ/ **brays, braying, brayed**
V When a donkey **brays**, it makes the loud, harsh sound that donkeys make. ▶ Also NC *...the bray of a donkey.*

brazen /breɪzn/ **brazens, brazening, brazened**
ADJ If you describe someone as **brazen**, you mean that they are very bold and do not care if other people think that they are behaving wrongly. *...his brazen breaking of the law... The opposition City Affairs spokesman said the Minister's denials of government negligence were so brazen as to be laughable.*
♦ **brazenly** ADV *No industry is more brazenly orientated towards quick, easy profits.*
brazen out PHRASAL VERB If you have done something wrong and you **brazen** it **out**, you behave confidently in order not to appear ashamed. *The writer says the Socialists have decided to brazen it out.*

brazier /breɪzɪə/ **braziers**
NC A **brazier** is a large metal container in which people make a fire when they are outside in cold weather.

Brazil /brəzɪl/
The **Federative Republic of Brazil** is a country in South America. It was a Portuguese colony from the 16th century until it became independent in 1822. From 1822 to 1889 it was an empire. A republic was proclaimed in 1889. The military ruled from 1964 until 1985. In the 1970s and 1980s Brazil became unable to pay its foreign debts, which were the largest in the developing world. High inflation and large foreign debts remain major economic problems. Fernando Collor de Mello, of the National Reconstruction Party (PRN), became President in 1990. Brazil exports coffee, oil, soya, iron, and cocoa. It is a member of the Organization of American States. ♦ **Brazilian** /brəzɪliən/ N, ADJ
▪ *per capita GNP:* US$2,280 ▪ *religion:* Christianity (mainly Roman Catholic) ▪ *language:* Portuguese ▪ *currency:* cruzeiro ▪ *capital:* Brasília ▪ *largest city:* São Paulo ▪ *population:* 144 million (1988) ▪ *size:* 8,511,965 square kilometres.

Brazzaville /bræzəvɪl/
Brazzaville is the capital of Congo and its largest city. Population: 596,000 (1984).

breach /briːtʃ/ **breaches, breaching, breached;** a formal word.
1 NC A **breach** of a law, agreement, or promise is the act of breaking it. *Their treatment of prisoners is a serious breach of the Geneva Convention. ...breaches in security at the world's busiest airport.* ● If a company or individual is **in breach of contract**, they have failed to carry out the terms of a legally binding agreement. *The company will lose their assets for being in breach of contract.*

2 VO If you **breach** an agreement, law, or promise, you break it. *The union had repeatedly and flagrantly breached a court order against such disruption... The Committee will decide whether the Human Rights Convention has been breached.*
3 NC A **breach** in a relationship is a serious disagreement which often results in the relationship ending. *This was the most profound breach in our marriage... There have been diplomatic attempts to heal the breach.*
4 VO If you **breach** a barrier, you make a gap in it in order to get through it. *He breached the enemy barbed wire... The demonstrators were accused of trying to breach a police cordon.*
5 NC A **breach** in a barrier is a gap or crack in it. *They looked on helplessly as the water poured through a twenty-foot breach in the river bank.*
6 If someone **steps into the breach**, they help in a difficult situation by doing a job or task that another person was supposed to do. *In the meantime, the Karabakh Committee stepped into the breach, organising rescue work supplies.*

breach of the peace, breaches of the peace
NC A **breach of the peace** is noisy or violent behaviour in a public place which is illegal because it disturbs other people; a legal term. *They were arrested for causing a breach of the peace.*

bread /bred/
NU **Bread** is a very common food made from flour, water, and often yeast. The mixture is made into a soft dough and baked in an oven. *...some bread and cheese. ...a loaf of bread.*

bread and butter
1 NU+SUPP The **bread and butter** of a person or organization is the activity or work that provides their main source of income. *It's their living, it's their bread and butter... Comedies and pantomimes are the bread and butter of the local theatre... This was just bread-and-butter work for which he couldn't spare creative energy.*
2 ADJ ATTRIB The **bread-and-butter** issues, questions, or problems are the ones that are the most basic and important. *People vote only on immediate, bread-and-butter issues... He's a pragmatic man, a sort of bread-and-butter President when it comes to foreign policy.*

bread-bin, bread-bins
NC A **bread-bin** is a container for keeping bread in.

bread-board, bread-boards
NC A **bread-board** is a wooden board for cutting bread on.

breadcrumb /bredkrʌm/ **breadcrumbs**
NC **Breadcrumbs** are tiny pieces of bread.

breaded /bredɪd/
ADJ **Breaded** food has been covered in breadcrumbs before being cooked. *...breaded veal cutlets.*

breadfruit /bredfruːt/ **breadfruits**
NCorNU A **breadfruit** is a large, round, tropical fruit that grows on trees. When it is baked, it looks and feels like bread. *In this area there's mangoes, breadfruit and several other types of trees.*

breadline /bredlaɪn/
N SING Someone who is on or near the **breadline** is very poor indeed. *One family in four was on the breadline.*

breadth /bretθ/
1 NU The **breadth** of something is the distance between its two sides. *...six yards in breadth and fifty yards long.*
2 NU+SUPP **Breadth** is also the quality of consisting of or involving many different things. *The very breadth of the subject gives it an added interest. ...his breadth of vision.*
3 See also **hair's breadth**.

breadwinner /bredwɪnə/ **breadwinners**
NC In a family, the **breadwinner** is the person who earns the money that the family needs. *...assumptions that men are the breadwinners.*

break /breɪk/ **breaks, breaking, broke, broken**
1 V-ERG When an object **breaks** or when you **break** it, it suddenly separates into two or more pieces, often because it has been hit or dropped. *The string broke...*

He has broken a window... The tanker broke in two, spilling its cargo of oil onto the sea.
2 vo When you **break** a bone in your body, you damage it in an accident so that it breaks or cracks. *He broke his ankle after a fall... How do you know when someone has broken a bone?*
3 v-ERG When a tool or piece of machinery **breaks** or when you **break** it, it is damaged and no longer works. *The axle broke after only a few hundred yards... It's quite robust, and if you do break anything, it's easy to repair.*
4 vo If you **break** a rule, promise, or agreement, you do something that disobeys it. *The authorities had not told them of any conditions they might be breaking... He was wounded by troops when he broke a curfew in the city... She becomes vulnerable to attack if she breaks her word.*
5 vo To **break** a connection, contact, or relationship means to destroy or end it. *Telecommunications links were subsequently broken... This is the first time that diplomatic ties have been formally broken... Police believe they have broken a major South American crime syndicate.*
6 vo To **break** something such as a system or situation in which no progress can be made means to end that system or situation. *The agreement broke a three week stalemate in Irish politics, but there followed days of hard bargaining... There are no obvious signs that the deadlock has been broken.*
7 voorVO+of To **break** a habit, feeling, or way of doing something, or to **break** someone of it, means to stop them having that habit, feeling, or way of doing something. *The thumb-sucking habit in children can be broken... The production of Puccini's 'Turandot' also breaks conventions.*
8 vo If someone **breaks** their silence, they say something about a situation that they were previously refusing to talk about. *Sir David broke his silence on events when he told newsmen he was hoping for a peaceful settlement.*
9 vo If you **break** your journey, you stop at a place while you are on your way to somewhere else. *President Moi broke his journey home in Delhi, where he had talks with the Indian Prime Minister.*
10 vo If you **break** a record, you do better than the previous record for a particular achievement. *Oliver Barrett was out to break his New York-Boston speed record.*
11 vo If a river **breaks** a barrier such as its banks or a dam, the water in it flows over the top of the banks. *Many rivers broke their banks and emergency teams had to move people from their homes... The river Nile floodwaters have again broken the dykes erected to protect the city.*
12 vo To **break** someone means to destroy their success, career, or hopes. *Despite the efforts of the government security forces, the opposition was not broken... Her pride will not allow her to show that the execution of her father broke her and her family.*
13 v-ERG When you **break** a piece of news to someone, or when it **breaks**, the news is told to someone. *It was Ted who broke the news to me... He is the fourth minister to resign since the scandal broke.*
14 vo To **break** the force of something such as a blow means to reduce its impact. *Fortunately, the tree broke her fall.*
15 v+for If you **break** for a meal or for a pause in what you are doing, you stop what you are doing for a while. *We broke for tea... It was the last Cabinet reshuffle before the government breaks for the summer holidays.*
16 NC A **break** is also a short period of time when you have a rest or a change from what you are doing. *We all met in the pub during the lunch break... The doctors had worked without a break.*
17 NC A **break** is also a lucky opportunity; an informal use. *His big break came last spring in Australia.*
18 v When day or the dawn **breaks**, it starts to grow light after the night has ended. *As dawn broke in Peking, there were no further reports of unrest... Sergeant Hainey checked the damage as daylight*

broke.
19 v When a wave **breaks**, the highest part of it falls down. *...waves breaking on the sandy shoreline.*
20 v When a storm **breaks**, it begins. *Most of the missing are fishermen who were out at sea when the storm broke.*
21 vo If you **break** a secret code, you work out how to understand it. *He brought in a former aide to try to break a code the general was using in some of his conversations.*
22 v When a boy's voice **breaks**, it becomes permanently deeper. *Testosterone is the hormone that makes you have hair and makes your voice break.*
23 vo In tennis, if you **break** your opponent's serve, you win a game in which your opponent is serving. *Lendl broke Edberg's serve in the third game of the match.*
24 See also **broke**, **broken**.
● **Break** is used in these phrases. ● If you **break free** or **break** someone's **hold**, you free yourself by force from someone who is holding you. *He was trying to break free... He had my hands behind my back in a hold that was impossible to break.* ● When a company **breaks even**, it makes neither a profit nor a loss. *Last year, the Opera House broke even and cleared its deficit.* ● If you **break ranks** with someone that you have been helping in a joint effort or agreement, you stop supporting them. *The Irish Foreign Minister warned Britain against breaking ranks with the rest of the European Community by lifting the sanctions... They will stop supplying weapons if one side breaks ranks.*
break away PHRASAL VERB **1** When you **break away** from a group, you stop being a part of it. *Some of these hardliners are threatening to break away and form their own party.* **2** If part of something **breaks away**, it separates and moves away from another, larger thing. *Cells from the infected area break away and stray across the placenta.*
break down PHRASAL VERB **1** When a machine or a vehicle **breaks down**, it stops working. *The car broke down three miles outside Winchester... If a computer broke down the delays could make an otherwise good-tempered crowd turn hostile.* **2** When a system, plan, or discussion **breaks down**, it fails because of a problem or disagreement. *The talks broke down over differences on doctrine... The peace process has not broken down, although it has been thrown into uncertainty.* **3** When a substance **breaks down** or when something **breaks** it **down**, it changes into a different form because of a chemical process. *Enzymes break down proteins by chemical action... When the gene gets into the environment, it breaks down rapidly.* **4** When you **break down** an idea, information, or a task, you separate it into smaller parts so that it is easier to deal with. *The work was broken down into thousands of tiny, routine tasks... Sometimes, moral problems require political initiatives to start breaking the problem down.* **5** If someone **breaks down**, they start crying. *Some children broke down and wept while giving evidence.* **6** If you **break down** a door or barrier, you hit it so hard that it falls down. *They forced their way into his room by breaking down a door and he was escorted away.* **7** See also **breakdown**.
break in PHRASAL VERB **1** If someone **breaks in**, they get into a building by force. *The thieves stole five oil paintings and two frames after breaking in through a window.* **2** If you **break in** on someone's conversation or activity, you interrupt them. *Can I break in here for just a moment?... 'Don't look at me,' Etta broke in brusquely.* **3** See also **break-in**.
break into PHRASAL VERB **1** If someone **breaks into** a building, they get into it by force. *There was little chance of an intruder breaking into the Palace.* **2** If someone **breaks into** a computer system, they use it via another computer without the permission or knowledge of the owners. *A young West German has succeeded in breaking into military computer networks in the United States.* **3** If you **break into** a new area of activity, you become involved in it. *...women wanting to break into the labour market... This is Patrick's first attempt to break into the pop*

world. **4** You can also use **break into** to indicate that someone suddenly starts doing something. *Rudolph broke into a run... Ten thousand people watched the ceremony, breaking into patriotic hymns and chanting slogans.*

break off PHRASAL VERB **1** When part of something **breaks off** or when you **break** it **off**, it is snapped off or torn away. *...a moon which was part of the earth and broke off... Garroway broke off another piece of bread.* **2** If you **break off** when you are doing or saying something, you suddenly stop doing it or saying it. *Mrs Thatcher broke off one of her replies to the reporters to comment on the sweltering heat.* **3** If you **break off** a relationship or agreement with someone, you end it. *She broke off her engagement... Diplomatic relations were restored after being broken off during the war.*

break out PHRASAL VERB **1** If something such as a fight, disease, or fire **breaks out**, it begins suddenly. *The building was evacuated when a fire broke out on the top floor... A row broke out over the deportation of sixty Sierra Leoneans... The fighting is reported to have broken out a week ago.* **2** If you **break out** in a rash or a sweat or if it **breaks out**, it appears on your skin. *The doctors suspended treatment when the Emperor broke out in a rash... She felt the sweat break out on her forehead.*

break through PHRASAL VERB **1** If you **break through** a barrier, you succeed in forcing your way past it. *I broke through the bushes... Some of the demonstrators broke through a cordon of police vehicles.* **2** See also **breakthrough**.

break up PHRASAL VERB **1** When something **breaks up** or when you **break** it **up**, it separates or is divided into several smaller parts. *The wood broke up into a shower of fragments. ...bacteria that break up decaying vegetation.* **2** If you **break up** with your wife, husband, girlfriend, or boyfriend, or if your relationship with them **breaks up**, you end your relationship with them; an informal use. *The number of one-parent families is rising, and more marriages are breaking up.* **3** If an activity **breaks up** or if you **break** it **up**, it is brought to an end. *The party had just broken up... The talks have broken up in disarray... The policemen broke the fight up.* **4** When schools or their pupils **break up**, the term ends and the pupils start their holidays. *We're lucky, we break up quite early.* **5** See also **break-up.**

break with PHRASAL VERB **1** If you **break with** a group of people, you stop being involved with them. *He broke with the party because of their attitude to self-government for Scotland.* **2** If you **break with** a particular way of doing things, you stop doing things that way. *He broke with precedent by making his maiden speech on a controversial subject... In fact, they were the ones who broke with tradition.*

breakable /breɪkəbl/
ADJ **Breakable** objects are easy to break by accident. *Gramophone records were those breakable, crackly things that played for three minutes on each side.*

breakage /breɪkɪdʒ/ **breakages**
NUorNC **Breakage** is the act or result of breaking something; a formal word. *Accidental breakage of your household glass will be covered by the policy. ...the cost of breakages.*

breakaway /breɪkəweɪ/
ADJ ATTRIB A **breakaway** group is a group of people who have separated from a larger group. *A breakaway organization rapidly appeared. ...the breakaway Baltic republic of Lithuania.*

break-dancing
NU **Break-dancing** is a kind of dancing to pop music which involves quick, jerky movements, and where the dancers sometimes spin on their heads, their shoulders or their hips.

breakdown /breɪkdaʊn/ **breakdowns**
1 NC+SUPPorNU+SUPP The **breakdown** of a system, plan, or discussion is its failure or ending. *There was a serious breakdown of communications. ...industrial and social breakdown.* **2** NC If you suffer a **breakdown,** you become so depressed that you cannot cope with life. *Her*

biographers think she had some sort of nervous breakdown. **3** NC If a car or other vehicle has a **breakdown**, it stops working while it is travelling somewhere. *...investigations into the cause of the plane's mechanical breakdown.* **4** NC A **breakdown** of something is a list of its separate parts. *The paper published a breakdown of how the average Soviet woman spends her day... Even five days after the disaster, they have not given a breakdown of this figure.*

breaker /breɪkə/ **breakers**
1 NC **Breakers** are large sea waves. *...the sound of breakers on the beach.* **2** NC A **breaker** of a law, promise, or agreement is someone who breaks it. *The government has doubled fines on rule breakers... Police warned curfew breakers that they would be shot on sight.*

breakfast /brekfəst/ **breakfasts, breakfasting, breakfasted**
1 NUorNC **Breakfast** is the first meal of the day, which is usually eaten early in the morning. *...a two hour meeting over breakfast... The doctors, like everyone else, had had no breakfast.* **2** V When you **breakfast**, you have breakfast; a formal use. *Last night he went to a jazz club, and breakfasted next morning with a group of activists.*

breakfast television
NU **Breakfast television** refers to television programmes which are broadcast in the morning at the time when most people are having breakfast. *I never watch breakfast television.*

break-in, break-ins
NC When there is a **break-in,** someone gets into a building by force. *The first police knew of the break-in was the automatic alarm.*

breaking point
NU If someone or something is at **breaking point**, they have reached a crisis in a particular situation, and are unable to cope any more. *The prison service is under great stress, but not yet at breaking point... It was the dispute over land rights which stretched the two countries' relations to breaking point.*

breakneck /breɪknek/
ADJ ATTRIB Something that happens or travels at **breakneck** speed happens or travels very fast. *Camps are being erected at breakneck speed all over West Germany.*

breakthrough /breɪkθruː/ **breakthroughs**
NC A **breakthrough** is an important development or achievement. *Scientists are on the brink of a major breakthrough... There were optimistic reports of a breakthrough.*

break-up, break-ups
NUorNC When the **break-up** of a group, relationship, or system occurs, it comes to an end. *This caused the break-up of the coalition... All marriage break-ups are traumatic.*

breakwater /breɪkwɔːtə/ **breakwaters**
NC A **breakwater** is a wooden or stone wall that extends from the shore into the sea. It is built to protect a harbour or beach from the force of the waves. *If you build a breakwater, then the motion of the waves is blocked.*

breast /brest/ **breasts**
1 NC A woman's **breasts** are the two soft rounded fleshy parts on her chest that can produce milk to feed a baby. *...swollen breasts. ...breast cancer.* **2** NC A person's chest can be referred to as his or her **breast**; a literary use. *The bullet pierced Joel's breast.* **3** NC+SUPP When someone experiences an emotion, you can say that they feel it in their **breast**; a literary use. *...the creation of national pride in the breasts of Frenchmen.* **4** NC A bird's **breast** is the front part of its body. *The American robin has greyish-brown feathers and a brick-red breast.* **5** If you **make a clean breast of** something, you tell someone the truth about yourself or about something wrong that you have done. *The leadership need to make a clean breast of their involvement in*

administration and business.

breastbone /brestbəʊn/ **breastbones**

NC Your **breastbone** is the long vertical bone in the centre of your chest. *...a burning sensation behind the breastbone.*

breast-feed, breast-feeds, breast-feeding, breast-fed

VO When a woman **breast-feeds** her baby, she feeds it with milk from her breasts, rather than from a bottle. *...babies who cannot be breast-fed.* ◆ **breast-feeding** NU *A big advantage of breast-feeding is that the milk is always pure.*

breastplate /brestpleɪt/ **breastplates**

NC A **breastplate** is a piece of armour that covers and protects the chest. *...members of the Cavalry in red uniforms with gleaming breastplates.*

breast pocket, breast pockets

NC The **breast pocket** of a man's coat or jacket is a pocket, usually on the inside, next to his chest. *He reached into his breast pocket.*

breaststroke /breststrəʊk/

1 NU **Breaststroke** is a swimming stroke which you do lying on your front, moving your arms and legs horizontally in circles. *Breaststroke has continued unchanged since the early days of competitive swimming.*

2 ADV If you swim a particular distance **breaststroke**, you swim that distance using breaststroke. *No-one has managed to swim 100 metres breaststroke in less than a minute.*

breath /breθ/ **breaths**

1 NCorNU Your **breath** is the air which you take into and let out of your lungs when you breathe. *You could smell the whisky on his breath... Some gasped for breath and had to be given oxygen.*

2 NC When you take a **breath**, you breathe in. *Take a deep breath, and put your head under the water.*

● **Breath** is used in these phrases. ● If you are **out of breath**, you are breathing quickly and with difficulty because you have been doing something energetic. *They think he will run out of breath before then.* ● If you are **short of breath**, you have difficulty breathing because you cannot get enough air into your lungs. *Patients on long-term dialysis become short of breath and tire very easily.* ● When you **get your breath** back after doing something energetic, you start breathing normally again. ● If you **hold your breath**, you stop breathing for a short while. *Fear can cause babies to hold their breath for some time.* ● If you say something **under your breath**, you say it in a very quiet voice. *I was cursing him under my breath.* ● If you get a **breath of fresh air**, you go outside because it is stuffy indoors. ● You can describe something as a **breath of fresh air** when you think that it will help to change a bad situation that has been the same for a long time. *The arrival of the London Sinfonietta was a breath of fresh air... The election of Mr Clerides or Mr Vassiliou will come as a breath of fresh air.* ● If you say that something **takes your breath away**, you mean that it is extremely beautiful, amazing, or hard to believe. *The speed of events still takes the breath away.*

breathalyze /breθəlaɪz/ **breathalyzes, breathalyzing, breathalyzed**; also spelt **breathalyse**.

VO When a driver is **breathalyzed**, he or she is asked by the police to breathe into a special bag which measures the amount of alcohol that he or she has drunk. *They can be stopped at any time and be breathalysed by a police officer... Police forces in England and Wales breathalysed more than sixty-eight thousand motorists over the Christmas period.*

Breathalyzer /breθəlaɪzə/ **Breathalyzers**; also spelt **Breathalyser**.

NC A **Breathalyzer** is a device used in Britain to measure the amount of alcohol that someone has drunk by testing their breath; **Breathalyzer** is a trademark. *...forty per cent fewer positive Breathalyser tests.*

breathe /briːð/ **breathes, breathing, breathed**

1 VorVO When people or animals **breathe**, they take air into their lungs and let it out again. *I breathed deeply... When we breathed the air, it smelt sweet.* ◆ **breathing** NU *...her deep, regular breathing.*

2 VOA If you **breathe** smoke or fumes over someone, you send smoke or fumes out of your mouth towards them.

3 If you say that someone is **breathing down** your **neck**, you mean that they are paying such careful attention to everything you do that you feel uncomfortable and unable to act freely. *Relaxing seems a difficult prospect with Bernard breathing down your neck.*

4 V-QUOTEorVO If someone says something very quietly, you can say that they **breathe** it; a literary use. *'Frank,' she breathed. 'Help me, please.'... He breathed a quiet prayer of thanks.*

5 VO Someone who **breathes** life, confidence, or excitement into something gives this quality to it; a literary use. *They believe the President has breathed fresh life into black protest.*

breathe in PHRASAL VERB When you **breathe in**, you take some air into your lungs. *...smoke that is breathed in by non-smokers whilst in the company of smokers... No-one can speak at the same time as they are breathing in.*

breathe out PHRASAL VERB When you **breathe out**, you send air out of your lungs through your nose or mouth. *The sufferer's lungs are distended and full of air that can't be breathed out.*

breather /briːðə/ **breathers**

NC If you take or have a **breather**, you stop what you are doing for a short time and have a rest; an informal word. *There's time for a breather, whether you're changing your costume or not.*

breathing space

N SING A **breathing space** is a short period of time in which you can recover from one activity and prepare for a second one. *It's feared they will use the ceasefire as a breathing space before launching another offensive... His resignation allows a breathing space for the government to reconsider.*

breathless /breθləs/

ADJ If you are **breathless**, you have difficulty in breathing properly, for example because you have been running. *She opened the door, a little breathless from climbing the stairs.* ◆ **breathlessly** ADV *'Miss Crabbe's on the telephone,' I said breathlessly.* ◆ **breathlessness** NU *Obesity causes breathlessness.*

breathtaking /breθteɪkɪŋ/

ADJ If you say that something is **breathtaking**, you mean that it is extremely beautiful or amazing. *...a breathtaking view of snow-covered mountains and meadows dotted with small ice-covered lakes.* ◆ **breathtakingly** SUBMOD *...breathtakingly beautiful gowns.*

breath test, breath tests

NC When the police carry out a **breath test** on a driver, they use a Breathalyzer to find out how much alcohol he or she has drunk. *The government is opposed to introducing random breath tests for motorists. ...a seven per cent reduction in positive breath tests.*

bred /bred/

Bred is the past tense and past participle of **breed**.

breeches /brɪtʃɪz/

N PL **Breeches** are trousers which reach as far as your knees. *Some of them were stripped to their breeches.*

breed /briːd/ **breeds, breeding, bred**

1 NC A **breed** of animal is a particular type of it. For example, terriers are a breed of dog. *Different breeds of sheep give wool of varying lengths.*

2 VO If you **breed** animals or plants, you keep them for the purpose of producing more animals or plants with particular qualities, in a controlled way. *He originally took the monkeys from the wild, but he is breeding them and releasing many back into the jungle... Strains of the plant have been bred that resist more diseases.*

3 V When animals **breed**, they mate and produce offspring. *Seals are breeding in increasing numbers.*

4 VO If something **breeds** a situation or feeling, it causes it to develop; a literary use. *At home, the war has bred cynicism and despair.*

5 Someone who was **born and bred** in a particular place was born there and spent their childhood there.

He was, after all, an Austrian born and bred... He was born and bred in the years of the Depression.
6 NC+SUPP A particular **breed** of person is a type of person, with special qualities or skills. *This required a whole new breed of actors.*

breeding /briːdɪŋ/
1 NU Someone who has **breeding** has been taught how to behave correctly with good manners, and is often upper-class. *She certainly lacked breeding.*
2 NU or N+N **Breeding** is the process by which animals mate and produce offspring. *We retain a small proportion of bulls for breeding purposes... The breeding season is a very long one.*

breeding ground, breeding grounds
1 NC+SUPP A place that is a **breeding ground** for a particular situation or activity is a place where it is very likely to develop. *...breeding grounds for passport forgery... The waterlogged city is a potential breeding ground for spreading disease.*
2 NC The **breeding ground** of a particular type of animal is the place where this animal goes to breed. *Those cliffs are the finest bird breeding grounds in the Northern Hemisphere.*

breeze /briːz/ **breezes, breezing, breezed**
1 NC A **breeze** is a gentle wind. *...German flags waving in the breeze.*
2 VA If you **breeze** somewhere, you go there in a casual, confident way. *I just breezed into her room, flinging the door wide... Steffi Graf breezed through her match with ease.*

breeze-block, breeze-blocks
NC or NU A **breeze-block** is a large grey-coloured kind of brick made from ashes and cement which is used as a building material. *...the shattered sprawl of breeze-block and shanty towns. ...unpainted breeze-block walls.*

breezy /briːzi/
1 ADJ Someone who is **breezy** behaves in a brisk, casual, cheerful, and confident manner. *...his breezy self-confidence and insatiable curiosity.*
2 ADJ When the weather is **breezy**, there is a fairly strong but pleasant wind blowing. *...a warm, breezy day.*

brethren /brɛðrən/
Brethren is an old-fashioned plural of **brother**.

brevity /brɛvəti/
NU The **brevity** of something is the fact that it lasts for only a short time; a formal word. *...the brevity and frailty of human existence.*

brew /bruː/ **brews, brewing, brewed**
1 V If an unpleasant situation is **brewing**, it is starting to develop. *The row has been brewing for a while.*
2 V-ERG When you **brew** tea or coffee or when it **brews**, it is made by letting hot water absorb the flavour of tea leaves or ground coffee. *She set about brewing some hot herb tea for them... We were waiting for the coffee to brew.*
3 NC A **brew** is a drink made by mixing something such as tea with hot water. *...herbal brews.*
4 VO When people **brew** beer, they make it. *Twenty five years ago all beer was brewed in open tanks.*

brewer /bruːə/ **brewers**
NC A **brewer** is a person who makes beer or who owns a brewery. *The brewers want to attract more women to pubs.*

brewery /bruːəri/ **breweries**
NC A **brewery** is a company which makes beer, or a place where beer is made. *People are buying so much beer that the brewery has announced a shortage.*

briar /braɪə/ **briars**
NC A **briar** is a wild rose with long, thorny stems. *They came to a large house, all overgrown with briars and brambles.*

bribe /braɪb/ **bribes, bribing, bribed**
1 NC A **bribe** is a sum of money or something valuable given to an official in order to persuade the official to do something. *The Vice President admitted taking bribes.*
2 VO If someone **bribes** an official, they give them a sum of money or something valuable in order to persuade them to do something. *The attempt to bribe the clerk had failed.*

bribery /braɪbəri/
NU **Bribery** is the action of giving an official a sum of money or something valuable in order to persuade them to do something. *The court found Williams guilty of bribery. ...serious allegations of bribery and corruption.*

bric-a-brac /brɪkəbræk/
NU **Bric-a-brac** consists of small ornamental objects of no great value. *...a selection of period and contemporary bric-a-brac.*

brick /brɪk/ **bricks, bricking, bricked**
NC or NU **Bricks** are rectangular blocks of baked clay that are used for building walls. *Cheques had been given to the bank for the supply of timber, bricks, and other building materials. ...a massive old building of crumbling red brick.*
brick up PHRASAL VERB If you **brick up** a door or window, you close it with a wall of bricks. *The arches over the main gate have been bricked up.*

bricklayer /brɪkleɪə/ **bricklayers**
NC A **bricklayer** is a person whose job is to build walls using bricks. *He was working as a bricklayer in the Baka area.*

brickwork /brɪkwɜːk/
NU You can refer to the bricks in the walls of a building as the **brickwork**. *...about twenty-five tons of brickwork have collapsed.*

bridal /braɪdl/
ADJ ATTRIB **Bridal** means relating to a bride or a wedding. *...her bridal costume... The manager of a bridal shop says there are few orders for the months ahead.*

bride /braɪd/ **brides**
NC A **bride** is a woman who is getting married or who has just got married. *His bride was a young English woman.*

bridegroom /braɪdgruːm/ **bridegrooms**
NC A **bridegroom** is a man who is getting married. *When does my daughter leave with her bridegroom?*

bridesmaid /braɪdzmeɪd/ **bridesmaids**
NC A **bridesmaid** is a woman or a girl who helps and accompanies a bride on her wedding day. *Traditionally, the bride pays for her bridesmaids' dresses.*

bridge /brɪdʒ/ **bridges, bridging, bridged**
1 NC A **bridge** is a structure built over a river, road, or railway so that people or vehicles can cross from one side to the other. *...the little bridge over the stream.*
2 NC Something that is a **bridge** between two groups or things makes it easier for the differences between them to be overcome. *We need to build a bridge between East and West... He'll continue the process of building bridges with the Catholic community.*
3 VO If someone or something **bridges** the gap between people or things, they help to overcome the differences between them. *We can hardly expect him to make a contribution towards bridging the gap between the government and its opponents... Thousands of extra jobs are needed to bridge the gap in employment opportunities between black and white people.*
4 NC The **bridge** of a ship is the high part from which the ship is steered. *...the officer in command on the bridge.*
5 NU **Bridge** is a card game for four players. *He was my bridge partner, and that was how we used to pass the time.*

bridgehead /brɪdʒhed/ **bridgeheads**
NC A **bridgehead** is a good position which an army has taken in the enemy's territory and from which it can advance or attack. *Two brigades seized bridgeheads on the far side of the river.*

Bridgetown /brɪdʒtaʊn/
Bridgetown is the capital and principal town of Barbados. Population: 8,000 (1980).

bridging loan, bridging loans
NC A **bridging loan** is money that a financial institution lends to a person or another institution to cover the period until they get money from somewhere else. *The US government has offered the country a short-term bridging loan.*

bridle /braɪdl/ **bridles, bridling, bridled**
1 NC A **bridle** is a set of straps that is put around a horse's head and mouth so that the person riding or driving the horse can control it. *If his foot slips, let go of the bridle, lest he pulls you with him.*
2 VO When you **bridle** a horse, you put a bridle on it. *Her horse was already saddled and bridled.*
3 V If you **bridle**, you react in a way that shows that you are angry or displeased with something that someone has done or suggested. *She seems to bridle at the Western assumption that the traditions of Islam oppress modern women... The Cabinet have long bridled at the economic consequences of the Kampuchean conflict.*

bridle path, bridle paths
NC A **bridle path** is the same as a bridleway.

bridleway /braɪdlweɪ/ **bridleways**
NC A **bridleway** is a path which is intended to be used by people riding horses. *There are more than a hundred thousand miles of footpaths and bridleways in England and Wales.*

brief /briːf/ **briefer, briefest; briefs, briefing, briefed**
1 ADJ Something that is **brief** lasts for only a short time. *There was a brief scuffle... Last night's strike was small, brief, and limited to one hospital... A brief hearing was held for evidence of identification.*
2 ADJ PRED If you are **brief**, you say what you want to say in as few words as possible. *The suspect was brief when asked by the judge to identify himself.*
3 VO If you **brief** someone, you provide them with specific information that they have asked for about a particular subject. *Mr Dizdarevic briefed Mr Honecker on the reform programme in Yugoslavia... Mr. Primakov also briefed President Hussein on his recent diplomatic visit to Rome. ...a senior Pakistani official who briefed journalists in Islamabad.* ● See also **briefing.**
4 VO When soldiers or other military people **are briefed**, they are given precise instructions about a particular task that they have to carry out. *The Reservists have already been briefed and issued with kit and documents... A meeting is held in order to brief the new volunteer.*
5 NC If someone is given a **brief**, they are officially given instructions to do something or deal with something. *His brief was to exercise rigid government control over the operation of these institutions... He told members of his party that they'd kept their brief, and it was a deal he could accept.*
6 NC A **brief** is a document containing all the facts about a particular legal case which is used by a barrister when representing a client; a legal term. *...piles of dusty briefs.*
7 N PL **Briefs** are pants or knickers. *A sales assistant commented on the rapid turnover of briefs, saying they had taken over where socks and hankies left off.*

briefcase /briːfkeɪs/ **briefcases**
NC A **briefcase** is a case for carrying documents. *I kept my American passport hidden in my briefcase.*

briefing /briːfɪŋ/ **briefings**
1 NC At a press **briefing** or a news **briefing**, a politician or a spokesperson gives journalists information about a particular issue or situation. *He was speaking at a press briefing to publicise the proposal.*
2 NC A **briefing** is a meeting at which people are given information or instructions, usually just before they do something. *He was in the final stages of a briefing from the Commander in Chief.*

briefly /briːfli/
1 ADV Something that happens **briefly** happens for a very short period of time. *He smiled briefly... Traffic was halted briefly, but no arrests were made.*
2 ADV If you say something **briefly**, you use very few words or give very few details. *She told them briefly what had happened.*
3 ADV SEN You can say **briefly** to indicate that you are about to say something in as few words as possible. *The facts, briefly, are these.*

Brig.
Brig. is a written abbreviation for 'brigadier' when it is a person's title. *...Brig. Gerald Haywood.*

brigade /brɪgeɪd/ **brigades**
N COLL A **brigade** is one of the groups which an army is divided into. *...an armoured brigade of between six and eight thousand troops.* ● See also **fire brigade.**

brigadier /brɪgədɪə/ **brigadiers**
N Cor TITLE A **brigadier** is an army officer of high rank. *The two other men killed were brigadiers... Brigadier Cordingly said his soldiers had been told to expect a tour of duty of about six months.*

brigand /brɪgənd/ **brigands**
NC In former times, a **brigand** was someone who attacked people and stole their property, especially in mountainous areas or forests. *The Barnsdale road was a popular haunt for brigands.*

bright /braɪt/ **brighter, brightest**
1 ADJ A **bright** colour is strong and noticeable, and not dark. *Her eyes were bright blue. ...a large wall map, scattered with bright colours.* ◆ **brightly** ADV *...brightly coloured silk blouses.*
2 ADJ A **bright** light shines very strongly. *The sun was bright and hot... The young birds are attracted to bright artificial lighting.* ◆ **brightly** ADV *The sun shone brightly.* ◆ **brightness** NU *Already the stars were losing their brightness.*
3 ADJ A place or a day that is **bright** has a lot of light or sunshine. *Inside the house, it was warm and bright... It's a bright sunny day in New York.*
4 ADJ **Bright** people are quick at learning things. *...the brightest girls in the school... One of them, a bright, 11-year old boy, was asking questions about the curfew.*
5 ADJ ATTRIB A **bright** idea is clever and original. *They had hit on a bright idea to publicise their anti-drink campaign... All of a sudden, some kid gets a bright idea that might make the news.*
6 ADJ PRED If someone looks or sounds **bright**, they look or sound cheerful. *He was bright and cheerful... It is a disillusioned age, not a bright and cheerful one.* ◆ **brightly** ADV *'Fine!' I said brightly.*
7 ADJ If the future is **bright**, it is likely to be pleasant and successful. *The economic outlook is bright... We are back in business, and looking forward to a bright and prosperous future.*
8 **Bright and early** means very early in the morning. *I was up bright and early, eager to be off... Bright and early at 6.45, I was back at the airport.*

brighten /braɪtn/ **brightens, brightening, brightened**
1 V If you **brighten** or if your face **brightens**, you suddenly look happier. *Her face brightened. 'Oh, hi! It's you.'... 'Ah,' says Henry, brightening, 'that's what I call a really serious issue'.*
2 V-ERG If a situation **brightens** or if something **brightens** it, it becomes more pleasant or hopeful. *Prospects for a fresh start appeared to brighten... A strong dollar will brighten the economy by next summer.*
3 V-ERG When a light **brightens** a place, or when a place **brightens**, the place becomes brighter or lighter. *Stars brighten the night sky... The grey sky brightened with the flash of their guns... The sky began to brighten in the east.*

brighten up PHRASAL VERB 1 If something **brightens up** a situation, it makes it seem more pleasant or hopeful. *The announcement brightened up a grey January day in London.* 2 To **brighten up** a place means to make it more colourful and attractive. *Houseplants would brighten up your room.* 3 If you **brighten up**, you look happier. *From looking glum, she brightened up a little.*

bright lights
N PL If someone talks about the **bright lights**, they are referring to a big city where you can do a lot of enjoyable and interesting things. *...heading for the bright lights of Elysium, Ohio.*

brill /brɪl/
ADJ If someone says 'brill!' or says that something is **brill**, they are very pleased about it or think that it is very good; an informal word. *Oh brill, you remembered to bring the camera.*

brilliance /brɪliəns/
1 NU **Brilliance** is used to refer to someone's great cleverness or skill. *Dorothy Sayers was a writer of*

tremendous brilliance. ...an opening chapter of quite stunning brilliance.
2 NU The **brilliance** of a colour, light, or of a coloured or shiny thing is its great brightness. *The painting has been restored to its former brilliance. ...the brilliance of the lagoon under the burning sun.*

brilliant /brɪliənt/
1 ADJ If you describe people or ideas as **brilliant**, you mean that they are extremely clever. *...a brilliant young engineer... She had given us a brilliant idea to minimize the company's losses... His routine was a brilliant and witty exposé of the follies and foibles of the press.* ♦ **brilliantly** ADV *He acted brilliantly in a wide range of parts.*
2 ADJ People also say that something is **brilliant** when they are very pleased with it or think it is very good; an informal use. *We drew great crowds, it was brilliant.*
3 ADJ ATTRIB A **brilliant** career is very successful. *He predicted a brilliant future for the child... Jim took holy orders, and made a brilliant career in the Society of Jesus.*
4 ADJ ATTRIB A **brilliant** light or colour is extremely bright. *...a brilliant yellow flame... It's autumn, and the leaves are turning brilliant hues of orange, red, and gold.* ♦ **brilliantly** ADV *Many of them are brilliantly coloured.*

Brillo pad /brɪləʊ pæd/ **Brillo pads**
NC A **Brillo pad** is a square pad made of metal threads and soap which is used for cleaning metal pots and pans; **Brillo pad** is a trademark. *Clean the base of the iron with a damp Brillo pad.*

brim /brɪm/ **brims, brimming, brimmed**
1 NC The **brim** of a hat is the wide part that sticks outwards at the bottom. *Her hat had an up-turned brim to show her face.*
2 If a container is filled **to the brim** with something, it is filled right up to the top. *The pool was full to the brim with brown water.*
3 V+*with* If something **is brimming** with things of a particular kind, it is full of them. *...a group of youngsters, all brimming with ideas... Her eyes brimmed with tears.*

brim over PHRASAL VERB **1** When a container or the liquid in it **brims over**, the liquid spills out. *He poured wine into Daniel's glass until it brimmed over.* **2** If you **are brimming over** with a pleasant feeling, you behave in a way that shows how pleased you are. *She rushed to her mother, brimming over with joy and pride.*

brimful /brɪmfʊl/
1 ADJ PRED+*of* A container that is **brimful** of something is full right up to the top. *He was holding a bottle brimful of milk.*
2 ADJ PRED+*of* Someone or something that is **brimful** of something else has or contains a lot of it. *He joined up at once, brimful of patriotism... The letter is brimful of slangy, vivid expressions.*

brimstone /brɪmstəʊn/ **brimstones**
1 NU **Brimstone** is the same as **sulphur**; an old-fashioned use.
2 People use **fire and brimstone** as a way of referring to hell and of emphasizing how people are punished there after death; a literary expression. *The preacher warned us of the fire and brimstone that awaits sinners. ...Swaggart's style of fire and brimstone evangelism.*
3 NC A **brimstone** is a type of yellow butterfly. *I've seen a peacock, yes, and a brimstone too, which is very yellow... Brimstone butterflies can occasionally be found hibernating in clumps of ivy.*

brine /braɪn/
NU **Brine** is salty water that is used for preserving food. *When they get a glut of fruit, they store it in the form of pulp and then preserve it in brine.*

bring /brɪŋ/ **brings, bringing, brought**
1 VO If you **bring** someone or something with you when you come to a place, they come with you or you have them with you. *He would have to bring Judy with him... Please bring your calculator to every lesson.*
2 VOA If you **bring** something to a different place or

position, you move it there. *He opened the case and brought out a pair of glasses... Sheldon brought his right hand to his head.*
3 VOO or VOA If you **bring** something to someone, you fetch it for them or carry it to them. *Bring me a glass of wine... A servant would bring a chair for him.*
4 VOA When something causes people to come to a place, you can say that it **brings** them there. *The festival brings a great many people to Glastonbury... Mr Gorbachov's first engagement brings Congressional leaders to the Soviet Embassy for the first time.*
5 VOA To **bring** someone or something into a particular state or condition means to cause them to be in that state or condition. *These ideas had brought him into conflict with Stalin... The wind had brought several trees down... The Serbs bombed key railway lines, bringing train traffic to a halt.*
6 VOA To **bring** something such as a new product or a new fashion to a particular place means to introduce it to that place. *In bringing Chicano culture to a wider audience, they've revolutionized the American theatre... It's a way of bringing art closer to the people.*
7 VO If something **brings** a particular feeling, situation, or quality, it causes it. *Could it be true that money did not bring happiness?... The biting wind brought tears to her eyes... Liberation itself brings a host of new problems for the Church to tackle.*
8 V-REFL+*to*-INF If you cannot **bring** yourself to do something, you cannot make yourself do it. *I could not bring myself to touch him.*
9 VO If you **bring** a legal action against someone, you officially accuse them of doing something unlawful. *The ferry company brought the action against the union... What's the purpose of bringing criminal charges against the parent?*

bring about PHRASAL VERB To **bring** something **about** means to cause it to happen. *The Administration helped bring about a peaceful settlement... The Central Bank said the recovery had been brought about by the fall in oil prices.*

bring along PHRASAL VERB If you **bring** someone or something **along**, you bring them with you when you come to a place. *Bring your friends along... He brought along several examples of his work.*

bring around PHRASAL VERB See **bring round**.

bring back PHRASAL VERB **1** If something **brings** back a memory, it makes you start thinking about it. *Losing a husband can bring back memories of childhood loss... I've enjoyed it because its bringing back a lot of things about me when I was young.*
2 When people **bring back** a fashion or practice that existed at an earlier time, they introduce it again. *Many of the students appear to be trying to bring back the crew cut... Critic Bob Mondello is with us to talk about the film 'Spartacus'; Bob, why are they bringing this film back?*

bring down PHRASAL VERB To **bring down** a government or ruler means to cause them to lose power. *A national strike would bring the government down... This fragile coalition could be brought down at any time.*

bring forward PHRASAL VERB **1** If you **bring forward** a meeting or an event, you arrange for it to take place at an earlier time than had been planned. *The meeting has been brought forward to Tuesday... In response to the escape, he has brought forward the opening of a new prison in Woolwich in south London.*
2 If you **bring forward** an argument or proposal, you state it so that people can consider it. *A revised proposal was brought forward in August... He said that each side had brought forward to him the issues that mattered most.*

bring in PHRASAL VERB **1** When a government or organization **brings in** a new law or system, they introduce it. *The government intends to bring in legislation to control their activities... The country's second biggest city, Leningrad, brings in food rationing today.* **2** To **bring in** money or other resources means to earn or create them. *Tourism is a big industry, bringing in over £7 billion a year... Tobacco is a major cash crop which brings in money* *and jobs to fragile economies.*

bring off PHRASAL VERB If you **bring off** something difficult, you succeed in doing it; an informal expression. *The dilemma for the president is whether he can bring off the enormous coup of achieving peace... The Ghost is the hardest thing to bring off in 'Hamlet'.*

bring out PHRASAL VERB 1 When a person or company **brings out** a new product, they produce it and sell it. *I've just brought out a book on Dostoevski.* 2 If something **brings out** a particular kind of behaviour in you, it causes you to behave in that way. *These dreadful circumstances bring out the worst in everybody.*

bring round PHRASAL VERB 1 If someone is unconscious and you **bring** them **round,** you make them conscious again. *Nobody was making any attempt to bring her round.* 2 If someone disagrees with you and you **bring** them **round** or **bring** them **around,** you cause them to change their opinion and to agree with you. *He spent a lot of time trying to bring them around... They are not enthusiastic, although I think they can be brought around.*

bring to PHRASAL VERB If you **bring** someone **to,** you revive them and make them conscious again after they have been unconscious. *She was eventually brought to after several minutes of unconsciousness.*

bring up PHRASAL VERB 1 To **bring up** a child means to look after it until it is grown up. *Tony was brought up strictly... I was born and brought up in Britain... She was brought up as a Roman Catholic.* 2 If you **bring up** a particular subject, you introduce it into a discussion or conversation. *They had not expected him to bring up the problem in his initial speech... After several months, I could not resist bringing up the subject.* 3 If you **bring up** food, you vomit. *I had some toast but brought it up again soon after.*

brink /brɪŋk/
N SING If you are on the **brink** of something important, terrible, or exciting, you are just about to do it or experience it. *The country was on the brink of civil war... I was on the brink of losing my temper.*

brinkmanship /brɪŋkmənʃɪp/
NU **Brinkmanship** is a method of behaviour, especially in politics, in which you deliberately get into dangerous situations which could result in disaster but which could also bring success. *They have a tradition of political brinkmanship.*

briny /braɪni/
ADJ Something that is **briny,** for example sea water or a smell, is salty; a literary word. *The seaweed swayed in the briny water.*

brisk /brɪsk/ **brisker, briskest**
1 ADJ If trade or business is **brisk,** things are being sold very quickly and a lot of money is being made. *They are doing a brisk trade in cars... Sales of earthquake insurance and survival equipment have been brisk.* 2 ADJ A **brisk** action is done quickly and in an energetic way. *I went for a brisk swim... I established a brisk pace for my eight-block walk.* ◆ **briskly** ADV *He walked briskly down the street.* 3 ADJ Someone who is **brisk** behaves in a busy, confident way which shows that they want to get things done quickly. *Lynn's tone was brisk... He faces his critics with an austere but brisk determination.* ◆ **briskly** ADV *'We've been into that,' said Posy briskly.* 4 ADJ If the weather is **brisk,** it is cold and refreshing. *...a sunny but brisk autumn morning... The fog was aggravated by a brisk spring gale.*

bristle /brɪsl/ **bristles, bristling, bristled**
1 NCorNU **Bristles** are thick, strong animal hairs that are sometimes used to make brushes. *...hog's bristles. ...a bristle toothbrush.* 2 NPL The **bristles** of a brush are the thick hairs or hair-like pieces of plastic attached to the handle. *This paint brush is unusable because the bristles have stuck together.* 3 NPL The **bristles** on the chin of a man who has shaved recently are the short hairs growing there. *...a few days' growth of white bristles.*

4 V If the hair on your body **bristles,** it rises away from your skin because you are cold, frightened, or angry. *I felt the hairs bristle along the back of my neck.* 5 V If you **bristle** at something, you react to it angrily. *Eddie bristled at being called a 'girl'... Army officials bristle when asked about the report.*

bristle with PHRASAL VERB If a place **bristles with** objects or people, there are a lot of them there. *The hotel was bristling with policemen... The small town of Ventersdorp bristled with guns and reverberated to the chants of the protesters.*

bristling /brɪslɪŋ/
ADJ ATTRIB **Bristling** is used to describe beards, moustaches, or eyebrows that are thick, hairy, and rough. *...an old man with a bristling moustache.*

bristly /brɪsli/
1 ADJ **Bristly** hair is rough, coarse, and thick. *His bristly red hair was standing on end.* 2 ADJ If a man's chin is **bristly,** it is covered with bristles because he has not shaved recently.

Brit /brɪt/ **Brits**
NC British people are sometimes referred to as **Brits;** an informal word. *A lot of rich Brits have made it from selling food and drink.*

Britain /brɪtn/ See **United Kingdom.**

British /brɪtɪʃ/
1 ADJ **British** means belonging or relating to Great Britain. *...British textile companies.* 2 NPL The **British** are the people who come from Great Britain. *The British are very good at sympathy.*

Britisher /brɪtɪʃə/ **Britishers**
NC Americans sometimes refer to British people as **Britishers.** *The two Britishers were arrested in 1987.*

British Honduras /brɪtɪʃ hɒndjʊərəs/ See **Belize.**

British Summer Time. See **BST.**

British Virgin Islands. See **Virgin Islands, British.**

Briton /brɪtn/ **Britons**
NC A **Briton** is a person who comes from Great Britain. *Sources said one of the dead men was a Briton... The British government is advising Britons not to travel.*

brittle /brɪtl/
1 ADJ A **brittle** object or substance is hard but easily broken. *...dry sticks as brittle as candy.* 2 ADJ A **brittle** sound is short, loud, and sharp. *There was a sharp, brittle tinkling.*

broach /brəʊtʃ/ **broaches, broaching, broached**
V O When you **broach** a subject, you mention it in order to start a discussion on it. *Parliament has not yet dared broach the subject of private ownership of land.*

broad /brɔːd/ **broader, broadest**
1 ADJ Something that is **broad** is wide. *The streets of this town are broad... He was tall, with broad shoulders.* 2 ADJ You also use **broad** to describe something that involves many different things or people. *...a broad feeling that the West lacks direction... She had a broader range of interests than Jane... British officials said the ministers had reached broad agreement and had resolved a number of differences... There was greater demand for a broad range of goods.* 3 ADJ ATTRIB A **broad** description is general rather than detailed. *The book gives a broad introduction to linguistics.* 4 ADJ ATTRIB You use **broad** to describe a hint or sarcastic remark to indicate that its meaning is very obvious. *Broad hints were aired that the paper should be closed down.* 5 ADJ A **broad** accent is strong and noticeable. *He has a broad Wiltshire accent.* 6 If something such as a crime is committed in **broad daylight,** it is committed during the day when people can see it, rather than at night. *The attack was unusual, taking place in broad daylight.*

broad bean, broad beans
NC **Broad beans** are flat light green beans that can be cooked and eaten.

broadcast /brɔːdkɑːst/ **broadcasts, broadcasting.** The form **broadcast** is used in the present tense and is also the past tense and past participle of the verb.
1 NC A **broadcast** is something that you hear on the

radio or see on television. *...the Queen's Christmas Day broadcast to Britain and the Commonwealth... He was criticized for making these broadcasts.*
2 VOorV To **broadcast** a programme means to send it out by radio waves, so that it can be heard on the radio or seen on television. *There was strong pressure from the government not to broadcast the programme. ...a television channel which broadcasts exclusively in Welsh.* ♦ **broadcasting** NU *The day started with a debate on broadcasting... A new body was set up to watch over standards of taste and decency in broadcasting.*

broadcaster /brɔːdkɑːstə/ **broadcasters**
NC A **broadcaster** is someone who gives talks or takes part in discussions on radio or television. *...the writer and broadcaster Sir David Attenborough.*

broaden /brɔːdn/ **broadens, broadening, broadened**
1 V When something **broadens**, it becomes wider. *Her smile broadened a little.*
2 V-ERG If something **broadens**, or if you **broaden** it, it involves or affects more things or people. *The scope of the Salvation Army's work has broadened immensely... The force should be broadened to include troops from other countries.*
3 If an experience **broadens** your **mind**, it makes you more willing to accept other people's beliefs and customs. *The meetings don't help my work much, but they broaden my mind, and they are jolly good fun.*

broadly /brɔːdli/
1 ADV SEN You can use **broadly** or **broadly speaking** to indicate that although there may be a few exceptions to what you are saying, it is true in almost all cases. *You can see that, broadly speaking, it is really quite straightforward... Broadly, there are two wings to the party, as far as Europe is concerned.*
2 ADV You can also use **broadly** to say that something happens to a large extent and in all the ways that are important. *I was broadly in favour of it... The rebels have broadly accepted a nine-point peace plan.*
3 ADV If someone smiles **broadly**, their mouth is stretched very wide because they are very pleased or amused. *They were clutching their new red Albanian passports and smiling broadly.*

broadly-based
ADJ **Broadly-based** organizations involve many different kinds of things or people. *Both men are committed to forming a broadly-based government... He wants it to be a broadly-based movement.*

broadminded /brɔːdmaɪndɪd/
ADJ Someone who is **broadminded** is tolerant of different kinds of behaviour and opinions. *She assured me that her parents were broadminded... Now I'm a broad-minded sort of chap, and would be the last to say that science explained everything.*

broadsheet /brɔːdʃiːt/ **broadsheets**
1 NC A **broadsheet** is a newspaper that is printed on large sheets of paper measuring approximately 38 cm. by 61 cm. Broadsheets are generally considered to be more serious than other newspapers. See also **tabloid**. *This week sees the launch of a new weekly broadsheet from Maxwell's publishing house... Among the broadsheet newspapers, the Chancellor receives the support of the editors of The Times and The Financial Times.*
2 NC A **broadsheet** is also an advertisement or announcement that is printed on a single piece of paper. *The students pressed broadsheets into our hands, explaining their demands... They were passing out broadsheets with details of the alleged fraud in the recent elections.*

broadside /brɔːdsaɪd/ **broadsides**
1 NC A **broadside** is a strong written or spoken attack on someone. *He launched a broadside against the government's plans... His latest broadside comes in a lengthy article published by the People's Daily.*
2 NC A **broadside** is also the firing of all the guns on one side of a warship at the same time; an old-fashioned use. *The English fleet stayed close to the Armada and harried it with broadsides as it sailed eastwards.*
3 ADV If a ship is **broadside** to something, it has its longest side facing in the direction of that thing; a

technical use. *As the ship came close and turned broadside, we saw that there was only one man on it.*

brocade /brəkeɪd/
NU **Brocade** is a thick, expensive material, often made of silk, with a raised pattern on it. *...a mirror wrapped in purple and gold brocade.*

broccoli /brɒkəli/
NU **Broccoli** is a vegetable with green stalks and green or purple flower buds. *Eat lots of green leafy vegetables such as broccoli.*

brochure /brəʊʃə/ **brochures**
NC A **brochure** is a magazine or booklet with pictures that gives you information about a product or service. *A report claims that brochures are unlikely to give an accurate impression of hotels and resorts.*

brogue /brəʊg/ **brogues**
1 N SING+SUPP If someone has a **brogue**, they speak English with a strong accent, especially Irish or Scots. *Mrs Joyce spoke in a thick Galway brogue.*
2 NC **Brogues** are a kind of thick leather shoes made specifically for walking in. *Mud spattered his new brogues.*

broil /brɔɪl/ **broils, broiling, broiled**
VO When you **broil** food, you grill it; used in American English. *...trout broiled over charcoal.*

broke /brəʊk/
1 **Broke** is the past tense of **break**.
2 ADJ PRED If you are **broke**, you have no money; an informal use. *They say he's broke and can't afford the bail.*
3 If a company **goes broke**, it loses money and is unable to continue in business. *He went broke, and then no-one would lend him any money.*

broken /brəʊkən/
1 **Broken** is the past participle of **break**.
2 ADJ An object that is **broken** has split into pieces or has cracked, usually because it has been hit or dropped. *He sweeps away the broken glass under the window... There was a lot of broken furniture in the room... Part of the car roof was broken, but no-one was injured.*
3 ADJ A bone in your body that is **broken** has cracked or split as a result of an accident or a blow. *He fell eight hundred feet, but escaped with only a broken arm.*
4 ADJ A **broken** tool or piece of machinery is damaged and no longer works. *Andrea used to have running water, but the pump's broken and there's no money to fix it.*
5 ADJ A **broken** line, sound, or process is interrupted rather than continuous. *...a broken curve. ...angry crying with broken, irregular screaming.*
6 ADJ A **broken** promise or contract has not been kept or obeyed. *Many voters are tired of broken promises... A spokesman said Britain had broken an agreement signed at a United Nations session.*
7 ADJ ATTRIB A **broken** marriage has ended in divorce. *The steady rise in broken marriages means there are now over one million one-parent families in Britain.*
8 ADJ ATTRIB If someone talks, for example, in **broken** French, they speak slowly and make a lot of mistakes because they do not know French very well. *The hijackers read out a twenty-five minute statement in halting broken English.*

broken-down
ADJ A **broken-down** vehicle or machine no longer works because it has something wrong with it. *...two men pushing a broken-down car.*

broken-hearted
ADJ Someone who is **broken-hearted** is very sad and upset because they have had a serious disappointment. *This is where Mahler lived, and died, broken-hearted... I wrote to the editor of the Milwaukee Journal, saying I was a broken-hearted teenager.*

broken home, broken homes
NC If someone comes from a **broken home**, their family did not live together, because their parents were separated or divorced. *...the tragic consequences of a broken home... She has seen for herself the problem of broken homes, unmarried mother, abandoned children and the like.*

broker /brəʊkə/ **brokers, brokering, brokered**
1 NC A **broker** is a person whose job is to buy and sell shares, foreign money, or goods for other people. *...a leading British firm of brokers in London's financial centre.*
2 VO If someone **brokers** a deal or an agreement, they negotiate with the two sides to find an arrangement that is acceptable to both sides. *The United Nations brokered the Afghan peace agreement in Geneva last year... The deal has been brokered by Algeria.*
3 See also **honest broker.**

brolly /brɒli/ **brollies**
NC A **brolly** is an umbrella; an informal word. *There's no predicting the weather and you should always carry a brolly.*

bromide /brəʊmaɪd/ **bromides**
1 NCorNU A **bromide** is a drug which you take to calm you down quickly when you are unhappy or worried. *She thought it was a tablet of mild bromides... Pregnant women should not take bromides, atropine, ergot, or steroids... I added bromide to the protein, which cuts at the amino acid chains.*
2 NC A **bromide** is also a comment which is intended to calm someone down when they are angry, but which has been expressed so often that it has become boring and meaningless; a formal use. *I think some of the old bromides about television and the permissive society might have some validity.*

bronchial /brɒŋkiəl/
1 ADJ ATTRIB **Bronchial** means affecting or concerned with the bronchial tubes. *He had been ill for a number of weeks with bronchial pneumonia.*
2 ADJ ATTRIB You can also use **bronchial** to describe something which is caused by or which reminds you of bronchitis. *'I'll never see ninety-one,' he croaked, coughing his most bronchial cough... There was a chugging sound like a bronchial road drill.*

bronchial tubes
N PL Your **bronchial tubes** are the two tubes which connect your windpipe and your lungs. *The healing of the bronchial tubes was enhanced if the peritoneum was wrapped around the incision.*

bronchitis /brɒŋkaɪtɪs/
NU **Bronchitis** is an illness in which your bronchial tubes become sore and infected. *He had contracted bronchitis about three weeks ago.*

bronze /brɒnz/ **bronzes**
1 NU **Bronze** is a yellowish-brown metal made from copper and tin. *There is a bronze statue of the horse in the Windsor Castle museum.*
2 ADJ Something that is **bronze** is yellowish-brown. *...shoulder-length, brilliant bronze hair.*
3 NCorNU A **bronze** is also the same as a bronze medal. *Iran picked up a bronze in the Men's Discus... South Korea took bronze in the Men's 4 × 200 metres Freestyle Relay.*

bronzed /brɒnzd/
ADJ Someone who is **bronzed** is sun-tanned in an attractive way. *...the bronzed lifeguards on a beach.*

bronze medal, bronze medals
NC A **bronze medal** or a **bronze** is a medal made of bronze which is awarded as third prize in a contest or competition. *Canadian Karen Percy came third to win her second bronze medal.*

brooch /brəʊtʃ/ **brooches**
NC A **brooch** is a small piece of jewellery which you attach to your clothing. *They buried rings and brooches in the grave with their king.*

brood /bruːd/ **broods, brooding, brooded**
1 N COLL A **brood** is a group of baby birds belonging to the same mother. *Britain's only pair of Golden Eagles have been seen feeding a new brood.*
2 V If someone **broods** about something, they think about it a lot, seriously and often unhappily. *He brooded on his failure.*

brooding /bruːdɪŋ/
ADJ Something that is **brooding** is disturbing and threatening; a literary word. *Once or twice the grey, brooding sky rumbled and flashed.*

broody /bruːdi/
1 ADJ Someone who is **broody** is thinking a lot about something that makes them unhappy. *Frustrated*

workers become broody and resentful.
2 ADJ If a woman is **broody**, she wants to have children, and spends a lot of time thinking about it. *At this age, married women are either broody if not already stretched with a family.*
3 ADJ A **broody** hen is ready to lay or sit on eggs. *Chickens never seem to mind whose eggs they sit on when they are broody.*

brook /brʊk/ **brooks, brooking, brooked**
1 NC A **brook** is a small stream. *...summer, a lazy afternoon sitting by a brook with friends and family. ...a babbling brook*
2 VO If you will not **brook** something, you will not allow it or accept it. *He would brook no interference or disagreement from anybody. ...the bloody-minded determination to brook no opposition.*

broom /bruːm/ **brooms**
NC A **broom** is a long-handled brush which is used to sweep the floor. *With a broom, a sieve, and a brass bowl, they leave their slum dwellings to sweep the dingy streets. ...broom handles.*

broomstick /bruːmstɪk/ **broomsticks**
NC A **broomstick** is a broom with a bundle of twigs at the end. Witches are said to fly on broomsticks. *...hags in pointed black hats riding about on broomsticks.*

Bros. /brɒs/
N PL **Bros.** is a written abbreviation for 'brothers'; used especially in the name of a company. *...the glossy windows of Moss Bros.*

broth /brɒθ/
NU **Broth** is soup, often with meat or vegetables floating in it. *...a nutrient broth.*

brothel /brɒθl/ **brothels**
NC A **brothel** is a building where men pay to have sex with prostitutes. *Southwark was a district notorious for its brothels.*

brother /brʌðə/ **brothers.** The old-fashioned form **brethren** /breðrən/ is also used as the plural for the meanings in paragraphs 2 and 3.
1 NC Your **brother** is a boy or a man who has the same parents as you. *I have two brothers and one sister.* ● See also **half-brother.**
2 NC Some people describe a man as their **brother** when he belongs to the same nation, religion, or trade union as they do. *He hoped the issue could be resolved between trade union brothers.*
3 TITLE **Brother** is a title given to a man who belongs to a religious institution such as a monastery. *...Brother Michael.*

brotherhood /brʌðəhʊd/ **brotherhoods**
1 NU **Brotherhood** is the affection and loyalty that you feel for people who you have something in common with. *...Martin Luther King's dream of justice and brotherhood for all.*
2 NC A **brotherhood** is an organization whose members all have the same political aims and beliefs or the same job or profession. *...the largest opposition group, the Muslim Brotherhood.*

brother-in-law, brothers-in-law
NC Your **brother-in-law** is the brother of your husband or wife, or the man who is married to your sister or to your wife's or husband's sister. *An armed gang has kidnapped the president's brother-in-law.*

brotherly /brʌðəli/
ADJ ATTRIB **Brotherly** feelings are the feelings of affection and loyalty which you expect a brother to show. *They shared a strong sense of brotherly feeling. ...brotherly love.*

brougham /bruːəm/ **broughams**
NC A **brougham** was a type of light carriage pulled by one horse, used in Europe and America in the 19th century. *Enormous hailstones hit the roof of the brougham and bounced off the pavements.*

brought /brɔːt/
Brought is the past tense and past participle of **bring.**

brow /braʊ/ **brows**
1 NC Your **brow** is your forehead. *He mopped his sweating brow.*
2 NC Your **brows** are your eyebrows. *...deep-set eyes framed by dark, severe brows.* ● to knit your **brows**: see **knit.**

3 NC The **brow** of a hill is the top of it. *The car came over the brow of a hill.*

browbeat /braʊbiːt/ **browbeats, browbeating, browbeaten.** The form **browbeat** is used in the present tense and is also the past tense.

VO If you **browbeat** someone, you bully them and try to force them to do what you want. *She browbeat her parents into letting her go... He would not be browbeaten into submission by the party.*

browbeaten /braʊbiːtn/

ADJ Someone who is **browbeaten** has been bullied so much that they have become quiet, obedient, and depressed. *Cora is quite simply a browbeaten wife.*

brown /braʊn/ **browner, brownest; browns, browning, browned**

1 ADJ Something that is **brown** is the colour of earth or wood. *...long brown hair.*

2 ADJ You can say that someone is **brown** when their skin is darker than usual because they have been in the sun. *His body was golden brown... It was obvious to me that I wasn't black, I was brown.*

3 V-ERG When something **browns** or is **browned**, it becomes browner in colour. *Grass browned and trees drooped that summer... Her hands had been browned by the sun.*

browned-off

ADJ PRED If you are **browned-off** with something, you are bored and no longer feel any enthusiasm for it, and might even be slightly angry about it; an informal expression. *He was a bit browned-off with the job.*

brownie /braʊni/ **brownies**

1 NC A **brownie** or a **brownie guide** is a girl who is a member of the Brownie Guides, the junior branch of the Girl Guides Association. Brownies are encouraged to be disciplined and to learn practical skills. They are usually between seven and ten years old. *A group of twelve girls in the Brownies and Guides have been rescued by helicopter after they were stranded.*

2 If you earn yourself **brownie points**, you do something helpful or clever and you get praise or credit for it; an informal expression. *...scoring brownie points for showing concern for the environment.*

3 NC A **brownie** is also a small flat chocolate cake with nuts in it. *As part of your duties, you bake cookies and brownies. ...a packet of brownie mix.*

brownish /braʊnɪʃ/

ADJ Something that is **brownish** is slightly brown. *...a patch of brownish lawn.*

browse /braʊz/ **browses, browsing, browsed**

1 V+through If you **browse** through a book or magazine, you look through it in a casual way. *I was browsing through the report... There is much instruction and entertainment to be had from browsing through this enormous volume.*

2 V If you **browse** in a shop, you look at things in a casual way, without intending to buy anything. *She browsed for a while, then picked up a glossy magazine... Gone are the days when you asked for a pair of socks—nowadays, you just browse around the rack of socks, don't you?* ▶ Also NC+SUPP *I had a browse in the children's picture book section.*

3 VorVO When animals **browse** or **browse** on an area or particular plant, they feed on that area or plant. *Camels browse on trees... It has an ability to browse vegetation beyond the reach of other animals... Certain areas have been planted and are not grazed or browsed by livestock.*

bruise /bruːz/ **bruises, bruising, bruised**

1 NC A **bruise** is an injury produced when a part of your body is hit and a purple mark appears. *They struck him about the head leaving him with bruises and an injured eye.*

2 VO If you **bruise** a part of your body, you accidentally injure yourself so that a purple mark appears under your skin. *Smith bruised a finger during yesterday's practice match... They were jostled, bruised, and scratched.*

bruiser /bruːzə/ **bruisers**

NC A **bruiser** is a big strong man, especially one who enjoys fighting; an informal word. *That son of yours will be an incredible bruiser.*

brunch /brʌntʃ/ **brunches**

NUorNC **Brunch** is a meal that you eat in the late morning, instead of breakfast or lunch. *Sunday brunches are served at the Trade Winds restaurant.*

Brundtland, Gro Harlem /gruː haːləm brʊntlæn/

Gro Harlem Brundtland became Prime Minister of Norway in 1990. She was Minister of the Environment from 1974 to 1979, and was previously Prime Minister in 1981 and from 1986 to 1989. She was the deputy leader of the Norwegian Labour Party (DNA) from 1975 to 1981, and became Leader in 1981. Born: 1939.

Brunei /bruːnaɪ/

The **Sultanate of Brunei** is a country on the north-west coast of the island of Borneo (Kalimantan) in the Pacific. It became a British protectorate in 1888. Sir Hassanal Bolkiah became Sultan in 1967 and later became Prime Minister when Brunei became independent in 1984. Brunei was occupied by Japan from 1941 to 1945. It is a member of the Commonwealth and the Association of South East Asian Nations. Brunei exports oil and gas. ◆ **Bruneian** /bruːnaɪən/ N, ADJ

▪ *per capita GNP:* approximately US$15,390 ▪ *religion:* Islam (mainly Sunni) ▪ *language:* Malay, English, Chinese ▪ *currency:* dollar ▪ *capital:* Bandar Seri Begawan ▪ *population:* 243,000 (1988) ▪ *size:* 5,765 square kilometres.

brunette /bruːnet/ **brunettes**

NC A **brunette** is a white-skinned woman or girl with dark brown hair. *I met a man who got married to a beautiful brunette, a girl whom he loves and adores.*

Brunhart, Hans /hæns brʊnhaːt/

Hans Brunhart became the Head of Government of Liechtenstein in 1978. He was Deputy Head of Government from 1974 to 1978. He is a member of the Patriotic Union (VU). Born: 1945.

brunt /brʌnt/

If someone **bears the brunt** or **takes the brunt** of something unpleasant, they suffer most of the effects of it. *Ground troops would bear the brunt of any military action... Long distance commuters are bearing the brunt of the extra travel costs.*

brush /brʌʃ/ **brushes, brushing, brushed**

1 NC A **brush** is an object with a large number of bristles fixed to it. Different types of brushes are used for different jobs, such as sweeping, painting, or tidying your hair. *...dustpans and brushes with wooden handles. ...a new, thin paint brush.*

2 VO When you **brush** something, you clean it or tidy it using a brush. *I'm going to brush my teeth.* ▶ Also N SING *Give the carpet a hard brush.*

3 VOA If you **brush** something away, you remove it by pushing it lightly with your hand. *She brushed back the hair from her eyes.*

4 VOorVA To **brush** something or **brush** against it means to touch it lightly while passing it. *The girl's hair brushed his cheek... An arm brushed against hers.*

5 If you **give** someone **the brush off**, you refuse to talk to them or be pleasant to them, especially by ignoring them or by saying something rude; an informal expression. *They accused Ministers of giving them the brush off.*

brush aside PHRASAL VERB If you **brush aside** an idea, remark, or feeling, you refuse to consider it because you do not think it is important. *She brushed his protests aside.*

brush up PHRASAL VERB If you **brush up** a subject or **brush up on** it, you revise or improve your knowledge of it. *They need to brush up their French.*

brushed /brʌʃt/

ADJ ATTRIB **Brushed** fabrics have been treated in a special way so that they feel soft and furry. *Sheets are often made of cotton or brushed nylon.*

brushwood /brʌʃwʊd/

NU **Brushwood** consists of small branches and twigs that have broken off trees and bushes. *Typically, houses are made of brushwood, strung together with bits of timber.*

brushwork /brʌʃwɜːk/

NU **Brushwork** is the particular technique that an artist has of using his or her brush to put paint on a canvas and the effect that this has in the picture.

...the individualistic brushwork employed by Leonardo.

brusque /bruːsk, brʌsk/
ADJ Someone who is **brusque** wastes no time when dealing with things and does not show much consideration for other people. *She had a brusque manner.* ◆ **brusquely** ADV *'Sorry—no time to waste,' she said brusquely.*

Brussels /brʌsəlz/
Brussels is the capital of Belgium and its largest city. It is the headquarters of the European Commission, the European Council of Ministers, and NATO. Population: 971,000 (1988).

brussels sprout, brussels sprouts; also spelt **brussel sprout**.
NC **Brussels sprouts** are green vegetables which look like very small cabbages. *Spring vegetables, like brussel sprouts, kale, and chinese cabbage have just been put in the ground.*

brutal /bruːtl/
ADJ Someone or something that is **brutal** is cruel and violent. *...the government's brutal treatment of political prisoners.* ◆ **brutally** ADV *Richard II was brutally murdered.*

brutality /bruːtæləti/ **brutalities**
1 NU **Brutality** is cruel, violent treatment or behaviour. *There is so much brutality shown on the television screen.*
2 NC A **brutality** is an instance of cruel or violent treatment or behaviour. *...reports of brutalities by the Tamil Tigers.*

brutalize /bruːtəlaɪz/ **brutalizes, brutalizing, brutalized**; also spelt **brutalise**.
1 VO If someone is **brutalized** by an unpleasant experience, it makes them cruel or violent. *Many young offenders are brutalized by their experience in custody.*
2 VO If one person **brutalizes** another, they treat them in a cruel or violent way. *They were found guilty of brutalizing their prisoner.*

brute /bruːt/ **brutes**
1 NC If you call a man a **brute**, you mean that he is rough and insensitive. *The workers referred to him as 'the brute'.*
2 NC You can also call a large animal a **brute**. *...the poor half-starved brutes.*
3 ADJ ATTRIB When you refer to **brute** strength or **brute** force, you are contrasting it with gentler methods or qualities. *We will never yield to brute force... Climbing the pole required brute strength as well as technique.*

brutish /bruːtɪʃ/
ADJ If you describe human conditions or actions as **brutish**, you mean that they seem like an animal's; used showing disapproval. *...a picture of early man as a brutish savage. ...military dictatorships which have at times been brutish and short-lived.*

BS /biː es/
BS is an abbreviation for 'British Standard'; a standard that something must reach in a test to prove that it is satisfactory or safe. Each standard has a number for reference. *Manufactured to BS 9650.*

B.Sc. /biːessiː/ **B.Sc.s**
A **B.Sc.** is a science degree. **B.Sc.** is an abbreviation for 'Bachelor of Science'. *He's got a B.Sc. in Civil Engineering. ...B.Sc. students.*

BSE /biːesiː/
NU **BSE** is a serious disease which affects cattle. **BSE** is an abbreviation for 'Bovine Spongiform Encephalopathy'. *More than 4,000 cows with BSE have been slaughtered in the last 9 months.*

BST /biːestiː/
NU **BST** is an abbreviation for 'British Summer Time', the time used in Great Britain from late March to late October, when clocks are set one hour ahead of Greenwich Mean Time. *President Gorbachev arrives in Paris on Tuesday morning at 10.55 BST.*

bubble /bʌbl/ **bubbles, bubbling, bubbled**
1 NC A **bubble** is a ball of air in a liquid. *Tiny bubbles were rising from the dissolving tablets. ...gas bubbles which form under the ice.*
2 NC A **bubble** is also a delicate, hollow ball of soapy liquid floating in the air or standing on a surface.

Each one is like the bubble in the froth on a glass of beer. ...soap bubbles.
3 V When a liquid **bubbles**, bubbles form in it, because it is boiling, fizzy, or moving quickly. *The champagne bubbled in her glass. ...poisonous gases which bubble up from the ocean floor.*
4 V If you are **bubbling** with a feeling, you are full of it. *I was bubbling with excitement... Both sides have shown some flexibility, but acrimony bubbles beneath the surface.*
5 If you say that the **bubble has burst**, you mean that a feeling, plan, or success which seemed perfect at first has now been suddenly ruined. *I'm sorry to come down to earth and burst the romantic bubble... But the economic bubble burst, and the President was accused of indecision... If he fails, for whatever reason, the bubble of his popularity might burst.*

bubble and squeak
NU In Britain, **bubble and squeak** is a food made by mixing together cold cooked cabbage and potato, sometimes with meat, and then grilling or frying the mixture. *...bacon, served with bubble and squeak.*

bubble bath, bubble baths
N MASS **Bubble bath** is a pleasant smelling liquid soap that you pour into running bathwater to make a lot of foam.

bubble gum
NU **Bubble gum** is chewing gum that you can blow into the shape of a bubble. *The typical piece of bubblegum consists of sweeteners, flavours, and colours.*

bubbly /bʌbli/ **bubblier, bubbliest**
1 ADJ A **bubbly** liquid is full of bubbles. *...bubbly wines.*
2 ADJ Someone who is **bubbly** is very lively and cheerful. *...a bubbly little girl.*
3 NU You can refer to champagne as **bubbly**; an informal use. *Bubbly will become more pricey in the coming months, thanks to a jump in the price of champagne grapes.*

buccaneer /bʌkənɪə/ **buccaneers**
1 NC In the 17th and 18th centuries, a **buccaneer** was a pirate, especially one who attacked and stole from Spanish ships. *They had suffered at the hands of English buccaneers in the past.*
2 NC A **buccaneer** is also a person who is clever and successful, especially in business, but who you do not completely trust. *Selling cars is big business in which the buccaneers make huge profits.*

buccaneering /bʌkənɪərɪŋ/
ADJ A **buccaneering** person is eager to be involved in risky or adventurous activities, especially in order to make money. *The most dangerous mistake he made was to annoy the buccaneering British businessman, Tiny Rowland.*

Bucharest /bjuːkərest/
Bucharest is the capital of Romania and its largest city. Population: 10,728,000 (1985).

buck /bʌk/ **bucks, bucking, bucked**
1 NC A **buck** is a US or Australian dollar; an informal use. *It cost me four bucks... That's got to be worth a million bucks.*
2 NC A **buck** is also the male of various animals, including the deer and the rabbit. *They want enough excess males to be able to set up a buck breeding station.*
3 V If a horse **bucks**, it jumps into the air wildly with all four feet off the ground. *When they jump, they buck like a wild stallion stung by horseflies.*
● **Buck** is used in these informal phrases. ● When someone **makes a fast buck**, they make a lot of money quickly, usually by doing something dishonest. *They talk of opportunists who are out to make a fast buck... Rest assured, though, that no-one's just out to make a fast buck on it.* ● If you **pass the buck**, you refuse to accept responsibility for something, and say that someone else is responsible. *He accused the bosses of always trying to pass the buck... They've passed the buck to the British authorities, and I find that a fascinating bit of manipulation.* ● You say **the buck stops here** to say that it is your responsibility to deal with a problem, rather than people who are junior to you. *He will need to put a sign in his office reminding*

him that the buck stops here... In the end, the buck stops with the Secretary of State.

buck up PHRASAL VERB 1 If you **buck up** or if something **bucks** you **up**, you become more cheerful. *I need something to buck my spirits up today... She bucked up a bit after she started going out with Phillip.* 2 If you tell someone to **buck up**, you are telling them to hurry up; an informal expression. *Buck up, we haven't got all day!*

bucked /bʌkt/
ADJ PRED If you are **bucked**, you feel pleased because you have been praised or because something has gone well; an informal, old-fashioned word. *I was pretty bucked by her approval, I must admit.*

bucket /bʌkɪt/ **buckets**
1 NC A **bucket** is a round metal or plastic container with a handle. Buckets are often used for holding and carrying water. *The hotel cleaner entered carrying a bucket and mop. ...champagne in a bucket of ice.* 2 NC You can use **bucket** to refer to a bucket and its contents, or to the contents only. *...a bucket of warm water.*

bucketful /bʌkɪtfʊl/ **bucketfuls**
NC A **bucketful** of something is the amount contained in a bucket. *...a bucketful of cold water.*

bucket seat, bucket seats
NC A **bucket seat** is a seat for one person in a car or aeroplane which has rounded sides that partly enclose and support the body. *Wedged in the bucket seat, my first panic-stricken thought was 'I can't move'.*

bucket shop, bucket shops
NC In Britain, a **bucket shop** is a travel agency that sells airline tickets cheaply in order to fill seats which would otherwise be empty. *Bucket shops, once the purveyors of cut-price tickets of doubtful legality, were legitimized by the legalizing of fare discounting.*

buckle /bʌkl/ **buckles, buckling, buckled**
1 NC A **buckle** is a piece of metal or plastic attached to one end of a belt or strap and used to fasten it. *...shoes fastened with big metal buckles.* 2 VO If you **buckle** a belt or strap, you fasten it. *The cuffs of the raincoat are tightly buckled.* 3 V-ERG If an object **buckles** or if something **buckles** it, it becomes bent as a result of severe heat or force. *There was an explosion. The door buckled and swung inwards... The forces within the earth have buckled the strata.* 4 V If your legs or knees **buckle**, they bend because they have become very weak or tired. *His knees almost buckled under him.*

buckle down PHRASAL VERB If you **buckle down** to something, you start working seriously at it. *The new Prime Minister will have to buckle down to a host of tough decisions... The star of the New Zealand team buckled down to steady the side.*

buckle under PHRASAL VERB If you **buckle under** to a person or situation, you do what they require you to do, even though you do not want to. *Chesnokov refused to buckle under against Emilio Sanchez, and now he must be the favourite to win... He's not the sort of person to buckle under to rumours and reports.*

buckshot /bʌkʃɒt/
NU **Buckshot** consists of large pellets of lead shot used for shooting animals when they are being hunted. *Police opened fire with buckshot and rubber bullets.*

buckskin /bʌkskɪn/ **buckskins**
1 NU **Buckskin** is soft, strong leather made from the skin of a deer or a goat. *He had white buckskin shoes with rubber soles.* 2 N PL **Buckskins** are trousers made of buckskin. *They were dressed in buckskins and moccasins.*

buck-toothed /bʌktuːθt/
ADJ Someone who is **buck-toothed** has teeth that stick forwards out of their mouth. *Buck-toothed, bespectacled faces glared at us from around the room.*

buckwheat /bʌkwiːt/
NU **Buckwheat** is a type of small black grain used for feeding animals and making flour. **Buckwheat** is also used to refer to the flour itself. *They received white flour instead of buckwheat.*

bucolic /bjuːkɒlɪk/
ADJ **Bucolic** means relating to the countryside; a

literary word. *There was a charming bucolic print above the fireplace.*

bud /bʌd/ **buds, budding, budded**
1 NC A **bud** is a small pointed lump that appears on a tree or plant and develops into a leaf or flower. *Don't pick all the buds or the plant won't flower again... A weekend cold snap has damaged vine buds in the French Bordeaux region.* 2 V When a tree or plant **buds**, buds appear on it. *The branch had budded, blossomed, and produced ripe almonds.* 3 If you **nip** something **in the bud**, you put an end to it at an early stage; an informal expression. *This incident very nearly nipped his political career in the bud.* 4 See also **budding**.

Budapest /bjuːdəpest/
Budapest is the capital of Hungary and its largest city. Population: 2,114,000 (1989).

Buddha /bʊdə/ **Buddhas**
1 N PROP **Buddha** or the **Buddha** is the title given to Gautama Siddhartha, who was a religious teacher and the founder of Buddhism. *The South Koreans observe a national holiday marking Buddha's birthday.* 2 NC A **Buddha** is a statue or picture of the Buddha. *...a low table with a Buddha and lighted incense on it.*

Buddhism /bʊdɪzəm/
NU **Buddhism** is a religion which teaches that the way to end suffering is by overcoming your desires. *He went to India to follow up his interest in Buddhism.*

Buddhist /bʊdɪst/ **Buddhists**
1 NC A **Buddhist** is a person whose religion is Buddhism. *The new President is a devout Buddhist.* 2 ADJ **Buddhist** means relating to Buddhism. *...Buddhist philosophy.*

budding /bʌdɪŋ/
ADJ ATTRIB A **budding** poet, artist, or musician is one who is just beginning to develop and be successful. *...a budding writer.*

buddy /bʌdi/ **buddies**; an informal word.
1 NC A man's **buddy** is his close friend. *I'd been approached by a buddy of mine to buy one... He brought in his old college buddy as general manager.* 2 VOCATIVE In the United States, men sometimes address other men as **buddy**. *Keep going, buddy.*

budge /bʌdʒ/ **budges, budging, budged**
1 V If someone will not **budge** on a matter, they refuse to change their mind or to compromise. *He refuses to budge on his design principles.* 2 V-ERG If you cannot move something, you can say that it will not **budge** or that you cannot **budge** it. *The screw just will not budge... She could not budge the wheel.*

budgerigar /bʌdʒərɪgɑː/ **budgerigars**
NC **Budgerigars** are small, brightly-coloured birds that people keep in their houses as pets. *5% of households own a budgerigar.*

budget /bʌdʒɪt/ **budgets, budgeting, budgeted**
1 NC A **budget** is a plan showing how much money a person or organization has available and how it should be spent. *Work out a weekly budget... Education budgets have been cut.* 2 NC The **Budget** is the financial plan announced by a government, which states how much money they intend to get through taxation and how they intend to spend it. *The British Chancellor of the Exchequer has presented his Budget to Parliament.* 3 V or VO If you **budget**, you plan carefully how much will be spent on each thing you want. *Some holiday-makers had not budgeted properly and had run out of money to get themselves home... The Apple Commission has budgeted half a million dollars to promote Washington apples in Spain.* ♦ **budgeting** NU *Through careful budgeting they had equipped the entire school.* 4 ADJ ATTRIB **Budget** is used in advertising to suggest that something is being sold cheaply. *...budget prices.*

budget for PHRASAL VERB If you **budget for** something, you take account of it in your budget. *These expenses can all be budgeted for... The authorities had budgeted for some non-payment, but say they are now owed nearly 160 million pounds.*

budget account, budget accounts
NC A **budget account** is an account with a large shop or a bank into which you make regular payments either to pay for things that you buy at the shop or to pay household bills. *...plans to cut budget account deficit.*

budgetary /bʌdʒɪtəʰri/
ADJ ATTRIB A **budgetary** matter or policy is concerned with the amount of money that is available and how it is to be spent; a formal word. *...disagreements over budgetary policies.*

budgie /bʌdʒi/ **budgies**
NC A **budgie** is the same as a budgerigar; an informal word. *I bet the budgie can't say its own name, can it?*

Buenos Aires /bwenɒs aɪərəs/
Buenos Aires is the capital of Argentina and its largest city. Population: 10,728,000 (1985).

buff /bʌf/ **buffs**
1 ADJ Something that is **buff** is pale brown. *She was wearing a buff uniform.*
2 NC+SUPP You can use **buff** to talk about people who know a lot about a particular subject. For example, someone who is a film **buff** knows a lot about films; an informal use. *...a West German computer buff... This was definitely not an evening for the heavyweight opera buff.*

buffalo /bʌfələʊ/ **buffaloes**. The plural form can be either **buffaloes** or **buffalo**.
NC A **buffalo** is a wild animal like a large cow with long curved horns. *...the row over the future of the largest buffalo herd in the world.*

buffer /bʌfə/ **buffers**
1 NC+SUPP A **buffer** is something that prevents something else from being harmed. *The world lacks the buffer of large international grain reserves... He plans to settle them along the borders to serve as a buffer against the West Bank.*
2 NC The **buffers** on a train or at the end of a railway line are two metal discs on springs that reduce the shock when they are hit. *Two men were injured when a train collided with the buffers at a platform at Victoria Station.*

buffer zone, buffer zones
NC A **buffer zone** is an area of land which is between two rival countries or areas, and which serves to keep them apart. *The US forces are withdrawing to a narrow buffer zone. ...security schemes based on buffer zones.*

buffet, buffets, buffeting, buffeted; pronounced /bʊfeɪ/ for the meanings in paragraphs 1 and 2, and /bʌfɪt/ for the meanings in paragraphs 3 and 4.
1 NC A **buffet** is a meal of cold food at a party or public occasion. Guests usually help themselves to the food. *We found a huge buffet laid out.*
2 NC A **buffet** is also a café in a station or a carriage in a train where you can buy snacks and drinks. *He was cutting up a white plastic tray from the train buffet.*
3 VO If the wind or the sea **buffets** something, it pushes against it suddenly and violently. *The vessel was buffeted by huge waves.*
4 V-PASS If a person or thing has several bad experiences or suffers shocks or damage, and is shaken but not destroyed by them, you can say that they **are buffeted** by these experiences. *The stock market was buffeted by scandal. ...an economy buffeted by war and recession.* ◆ **buffeting, buffetings** NC *The pound sterling had taken another buffeting on the financial markets.*

buffet car /bʊfeɪ kɑː/ **buffet cars**
NC A **buffet car** is a carriage on a train where you can buy snacks and drinks. *The buffet car is situated in the centre of the train.*

buffoon /bəfuːn/ **buffoons**
NC You call someone a **buffoon** when they do silly things; an old-fashioned word. *He initially achieved a reputation as something of a buffoon.*

bug /bʌg/ **bugs, bugging, bugged**
1 NC A **bug** is a tiny insect, especially one that causes damage. *30,000 hectares have been devastated by rice bugs... He was bitten by bugs in his prison mattress.*
2 NC A **bug** is also a minor illness such as a cold that

people catch from each other; an informal use. *There must be a bug going around.*
3 VO If a place or a telephone is **bugged**, tiny microphones are hidden there to record secretly what people are saying. *He said that while he was in Bucharest his phone was bugged.*
4 VO If something or someone **bugs** you, they worry or annoy you; an informal use. *Something is bugging Alice, though she can't quite put her finger on what... It's kind of intentional when I bug him, you know.*
5 You can say that someone is **bitten by** a **bug** when they suddenly become very enthusiastic about something; an informal expression. *She's been bitten by the skiing bug.*

bugbear /bʌgbeə/ **bugbears**
NC A **bugbear** is something that worries or upsets people. *Noise from engines is a current bugbear... Wage costs are much the biggest bugbear.*

bugger /bʌgə/ **buggers, buggering, buggered**; an informal, rude word which some people find offensive.
1 NC People call someone a **bugger** or describe them as a **bugger** when they are angry with them, or when they think the other person has done something foolish. *You bugger! You had no right to tell him he could come. It's not your party!*
2 NC People also sometimes call someone a **bugger** when they are pretending to be rude to them as a joke, although they are actually fond of them or friendly with them. *'You old bugger,' she said, affectionately.*
3 VO To **bugger** someone means to have anal intercourse with them.
● **Bugger** is used in these informal phrases. ● People refer to someone as a **poor bugger** when they are sorry for them. ● **Bugger all** means very little or nothing at all. People use this expression when they are angry or annoyed about something. ● When people say that they **do not give a bugger** about something, they mean that they are not concerned about it.

bugger off PHRASAL VERB 1 If someone **buggers off**, they go away quickly or unexpectedly; an informal use that some people may find offensive. 2 If you tell someone to **bugger off**, you are telling them rudely to go away; a rude and offensive use.

bugger up PHRASAL VERB To **bugger** something **up** means to ruin it or spoil it; an informal, rude expression which some people find offensive. *If they come, they'll bugger everything up.*

buggered /bʌgəd/; an informal, rude word which some people find offensive.
1 ADJ PRED If someone says that they will be **buggered** if they will do something, they mean that they will definitely not do it.
2 ADJ PRED If someone says that they are **buggered**, they mean that they are exhausted.
3 ADJ PRED If someone says that something is **buggered**, they mean that it is completely ruined or broken.

buggy /bʌgi/ **buggies**
1 NC A **buggy** is a small lightweight carriage pulled by one horse. *I got back in the buggy.*
2 NC A **buggy** is also a lightweight folding pram. *This is a four-wheeled buggy.*
3 See also **baby buggy**.

bugle /bjuːgl/ **bugles**
NC A **bugle** is a simple brass instrument that looks like a small trumpet. *A wreath was laid and a bugle sounded in honour of those who died.*

build /bɪld/ **builds, building, built**
1 VO If you **build** something, you make it by joining things together. *John had built a house facing the river... They were building a bridge.*
2 VO If people **build** an organization or a society, they gradually form it. *They struggled to build a more democratic society.*
3 NU+SUPP Your **build** is the shape that your bones and muscles give to your body. *She was in her early thirties, with a lean, athletic build.*
4 See also **built**.

build into PHRASAL VERB 1 If you **build** something **into** a wall or object, you make it in such a way that it is in the wall or object, or is part of it. *There was a* *cupboard built into the whitewashed wall.* 2 If something is **built into** a policy, system, or product, it is made a part of it. *...the inequalities built into our system of financing... What sort of questions were built into the questionnaire?*

build on or **build upon** PHRASAL VERB 1 To **build** an organization, system, or product on something means to base it on it. *...the principles on which these organizations are built. ...an economy built upon manufacturing industry.* 2 If you **build on** or **build upon** the success of something, you take advantage of this success in order to make further progress. *We must try to build on the success of these growth industries.*

build up PHRASAL VERB 1 If an amount of something **builds up** or if you **build** it **up**, it gradually gets bigger as a result of more being added to it. *Mud builds up in the lake... We're trying to build up a collection of herbs and spices.* 2 If you **build up** someone's trust or confidence, you gradually make them more trusting or confident. *Being a cop means building up trust with the people on the streets.* 3 To **build** someone **up** means to cause them to be their normal weight again after they have been ill. *We must build him up before he goes home.* 4 See also **build-up, built-up**.

build upon PHRASAL VERB See **build on**.

builder /bɪldə/ **builders**
1 NC A **builder** is a person whose job is to build houses and other buildings. *Architects, builders and planning officials allowed sub-standard homes and factories to be built.*
2 NC+SUPP You can refer to someone who builds bridges, canals, ships, and so on as a bridge **builder**, canal **builder**, or ship **builder**. *The designers, engineers and engine builders are just so good. ...a spokesman for the submarine builders... The tunnel builders say the machine cost eight million pounds.*

building /bɪldɪŋ/ **buildings**
NC A **building** is a structure with a roof and walls such as a house or a factory. *They ran into a nearby building and came out with two sacks. ...shops, schools and other buildings. ...threatening to block roads and public buildings.*

building block, building blocks
NC+SUPP The **building blocks** of an organization or structure are the separate parts that combine to make something. *The basic building blocks of the computer have become smaller... Discord and harmony, rhythm and emotion—these are the building blocks of music. ...an essential building block in a new European security structure.*

building site, building sites
NC A **building site** is an area of land on which a building or group of buildings is in the process of being built. *He went looking for work on a building site. ...a building site on the outskirts of North Belfast... Strikes were continuing in factories and on building sites.*

building society, building societies
NC In Britain, a **building society** is a business which will lend you money to buy a house. You can also invest money in a building society. *Lower mortgage rates. ...away from the riskier shares and unit trusts and into the greater safety of a building society account.*

build-up, build-ups
1 NC+SUPP A **build-up** of something is a gradual increase in it. *...the build-up of traffic on approach roads to the capital. ...the build-up of industrial gases in the atmosphere. ...the military build-up in the Gulf... There were no reports of any massive troop build-ups.*
2 NC The **build-up** to an important event is the period of time immediately before the event and the preparations that take place during that time. *...a worthwhile part of England's build-up to the World Cup... There's a tense atmosphere in the build-up to presidential elections on Sunday.*

built /bɪlt/
1 **Built** is the past tense and past participle of **build**.
● See also **purpose-built**.

2 ADJ If you say that someone is **built** in a particular way, you are describing the kind of body they have. *He didn't look as if he was built for this kind of work.*
● See also **well-built**.

built-in
ADJ ATTRIB **Built-in** devices or features are included in something as an essential part of it. *...a dishwasher with a built-in waste disposal unit.*

built-up
ADJ A **built-up** area is an area where there are many buildings. *He ordered all ammunition dumps near built-up areas to be shifted to safer localities.*

Bujumbura /budʒumbuərə/
Bujumbura is the capital of Burundi and its largest city. Population: 215,000 (1987).

bulb /bʌlb/ **bulbs**
1 NC A **bulb** or **light bulb** is the glass part of an electric lamp. *The council is to start charging residents for the cost of bulbs for street lamps. ...an ordinary 100 watt bulb... It has two electric light bulbs, which give off a bit of heat.*
2 NC A **bulb** is also an onion-shaped root that grows into a plant. *The seeds and bulbs didn't seem to have very much dust on them. ...a tulip bulb.*

bulbous /bʌlbəs/
ADJ Something that is **bulbous** is round and fat in a rather ugly way. *...people with great bulbous noses.*

Bulgaria /bʌlgeəriə/
The **Republic of Bulgaria** is a country in south-eastern Europe. It was a member of the former Warsaw Pact. The monarchy was abolished in 1946 and a Communist state was established in 1947. Todor Zhivkov was General Secretary of the Bulgarian Communist Party (BCP) from 1954 until 1989. The BCP renounced its monopoly of power in 1989. Zhelyu Zhelev, an independent, became President in 1990. In 1991, in the country's second free elections since 1989, the UDF won a small majority and its leader, Philip Dimitrov, became Prime Minister. Tension between Bulgarians and the ethnic Turkish minority is a political factor. Bulgaria is the fourth largest exporter of wine in the world. Large foreign debts, inflation, and shortages of basic commodities are serious economic problems.
◆ **Bulgarian** /bʌlgeəriən/ N, ADJ
▪ *per capita GNP:* approximately US$5,676 ▪ *religion:* Christianity (mainly Bulgarian Orthodox), Islam ▪ *language:* Bulgarian (official), Turkish ▪ *currency:* lev ▪ *capital:* Sofia ▪ *population:* 9 million (1990) ▪ *size:* 110,994 square kilometres.

bulge /bʌldʒ/ **bulges, bulging, bulged**
1 V If something **bulges**, it sticks out from a surface. *Guns bulged on their hips... Her eyes bulged from their sockets.*
2 V If something **is bulging** with things, it is very full of them. *The shelves were bulging with knick-knacks... The shops now bulge with consumer goods, most of them imported.* ◆ **bulging** ADJ ATTRIB *He arrived in the office with a bulging briefcase.*
3 NC A **bulge** is a lump on a surface that is otherwise flat. *The old ice by contrast is covered in blisters and bulges... These are bulges in the hull which improve a ship's stability.*

bulk /bʌlk/ **bulks**
1 NU An object's **bulk** is its large size, weight, or volume. *...the dark bulk of the building... Despite its huge bulk, the plane amazed us with its short take-off run. ...products that have a high value, but low bulk, such as gold.*
2 If you refer to **the bulk of** something or a group of things, you mean most of it or most of them. *...the bulk of the population... The Community seems likely to occupy the bulk of his time. ...the west, which contains the bulk of Fiji's economic resources.*
3 If goods or products are handled, bought, or sold **in bulk**, they are handled, bought, or sold in large quantities, usually before they are put into packets or tins. *...packing foodstuffs in boxes and bags, instead of shipping them in bulk... They are sold in bulk to hospitals. ...a cheap effective process for making them in bulk.*
4 ADJ **Bulk** is used to describe things that are large in size or exist in large quantities. *...trying to find uses*

for these bulk wastes. ...sacks of grain, boxes of vegetables and bulk supplies of milk. ...a bulk order for ten thousand wooden clubs. ...a bulk terminal for liquid cargo.

bulk buy, bulk buys, bulk buying, bulk bought
v If you **bulk buy**, you buy goods in large quantities in order to save time and money. *We live in the city and don't often bulk buy... Large supermarket chains who bulk buy and are able to sell their goods more cheaply.*

bulk carrier, bulk carriers
NC A **bulk carrier** is a large cargo ship that carries solid substances, such as coal or grain. *The two-hundred-and-fifty metre long bulk carrier was lashed by fifteen metre high waves. ...a collision with a Swedish bulk carrier.*

bulkhead /bʌlkhed/ **bulkheads**
NC A **bulkhead** is a wall which divides the inside of a ship or aeroplane into separate sections; a technical term. *...bulkheads across the ship which are sealed by doors or shutters during a voyage. ...a bulkhead explosion at the rear of a 747.*

bulky /bʌlki/ **bulkier, bulkiest**
ADJ Something that is **bulky** is large and heavy. *They wear bulky green military winter coats... Because it's smaller, it's less bulky, leaving room for more instrumentation.*

bull /bʊl/ **bulls**
1 NC A **bull** is a male animal of the cow family. *...enabling any farmer to choose a first-class bull for his cows. ...a high quality beef bull.*
2 NC Some other male animals, such as male elephants and whales, are also called **bulls**. *...bull camels.*

bulldog /bʊldɒg/ **bulldogs**
NC A **bulldog** is a type of dog with a large square head and short hair.

bulldog clip, bulldog clips
NC A **bulldog clip** is a large metal clip used for holding bunches of paper together.

bulldoze /bʊldəʊz/ **bulldozes, bulldozing, bulldozed**
VO When people **bulldoze** something such as a small building, they knock it down with a bulldozer. *The authorities intend to bulldoze all damaged buildings... The ruins of the museum were bulldozed to build a car park... Flooding made it essential to bulldoze the area.*

bulldozer /bʊldəʊzə/ **bulldozers**
NC A **bulldozer** is a large, powerful tractor with a broad metal blade at the front, used for moving large amounts of earth or rubble. *...equipment like mobile cranes and bulldozers... Men were using bulldozers to clear the huge piles of snow.*

bullet /bʊlɪt/ **bullets**
NC A **bullet** is a small piece of metal which is fired from a gun. *One of them was hit by a bullet in the neck. ...a barrage of bombs and bullets.* ● See also plastic bullet, rubber bullet.

bulletin /bʊlətɪn/ **bulletins**
1 NC A news **bulletin** is a short news summary or programme on radio or television. *...radio bulletins... The debate will be screened nationwide after the main evening news bulletin... We'll be speaking to the Chancellor after this bulletin.*
2 NC+SUPP A **bulletin** on a particular situation or event is a short report of the latest developments or progress by the official or organization responsible for it. *The FAA issued a security bulletin warning about the possible hijacking of an aircraft... The latest medical bulletin says there has been a big fall in his blood pressure.*
3 NC A **bulletin** is also a regular newspaper or leaflet produced by an organization. *In its latest Quarterly Bulletin, the Bank of England says that there was a slowdown in the British economy. ...the latest issue of the TUC bulletin.*

bulletin board, bulletin boards
NC A **bulletin board** is the same as a **noticeboard**; used in American English. *...notices on embassy bulletin boards.*

bullet-proof
ADJ Something that is **bullet-proof** is made especially strong so that bullets cannot pass through it. *...bullet-*

proof glass... The paratroopers were armed with automatic weapons and some were wearing bullet-proof vests.

bullfight /bʊlfaɪt/ **bullfights**
NC A **bullfight** is a public entertainment in Spain and some other countries, in which a bull is made angry and then killed with a sword.

bullfighter /bʊlfaɪtə/ **bullfighters**
NC A **bullfighter** is the man who tries to kill the bull in a bullfight. *...gypsies, flamenco dancers, bullfighters... She enjoys it like a bullfighter enjoys fighting a bull.*

bullfighting /bʊlfaɪtɪŋ/
NU **Bullfighting** is the public entertainment in which men try to kill bulls in bullfights. *The apprentice matadors tried to learn the skills of bullfighting.*

bullfinch /bʊlfɪntʃ/ **bullfinches**
NC A **bullfinch** is a small bird with a pinkish breast and a black head, usually found in woodlands or gardens.

bullfrog /bʊlfrɒg/ **bullfrogs**
NC A **bullfrog** is a large frog that makes a loud croaking noise.

bullion /bʊliən/
NU **Bullion** is gold or silver in the form of lumps or bars. *Others have been jailed for conspiracy to handle the stolen bullion. ...one of the major gold bullion dealers in London. ...a bullion van.*

bullock /bʊlək/ **bullocks**
NC A **bullock** is a young bull that has been castrated. *It should be possible to produce more bullocks for meat production.*

bullring /bʊlrɪŋ/ **bullrings**
NC A **bullring** is a circular area of ground surrounded by rows of seats where bullfights take place.

bull's-eye, bull's-eyes
1 N SING The **bull's-eye** is the small circular area at the centre of a target such as a dartboard.
2 NC A **bull's-eye** is a shot or throw with something such as a dart that hits the bull's-eye.

bullshit /bʊlʃɪt/
NU Some people use **bullshit** to describe an idea or statement that they think is nonsense or completely untrue; an informal, rude word, which some people find offensive. *What they say is hypocrisy. It's bullshit.*

bull terrier, bull terriers
NC A **bull terrier** is a strong dog with a short, whitish-coloured coat and a long nose. *...the growing popularity of the particularly aggressive breeds such as Rottweilers, certain bull terriers, Dobermans and Alsatians.*

bully /bʊli/ **bullies, bullying, bullied**
1 NC A **bully** is someone who uses their strength or power to hurt or frighten people. *...bullies in Britain's schools... There will be an attempt to weed out potential bullies.*
2 VO If someone **bullies** you, they use their strength or power to hurt or frighten you. *For the first month at my new school I was bullied constantly.* ◆ **bullying** NU *All cases of bullying will be severely dealt with.*
3 VO If someone **bullies** you into doing something, they make you do it by using force or threats. *He had been bullied into driving her home.*

bully boy, bully boys
NC A **bully boy** is a rough, aggressive man, especially one who has been paid to injure another person. *...thugs and bully boys... Such bully-boy tactics should not be allowed to strangle freedom of speech.*

bulrush /bʊlrʌʃ/ **bulrushes**
NC **Bulrushes** are tall, stiff reeds that grow on the edges of rivers.

bulwark /bʊlwək/ **bulwarks**
NC A **bulwark** against an unpleasant or dangerous situation is a strong thing or person that protects you from it. *The fund is a bulwark against your benefits being cut... Pakistan suddenly became, in American eyes, an essential bulwark against potential Soviet expansion... They see him as a bulwark against a general uprising.*

bum /bʌm/ **bums, bumming, bummed**
1 NC A **bum** is a tramp; used in informal American English.

2 NC **Bum** is used to refer to someone who is considered to be worthless or irresponsible; used in informal American English. *'I heard you're a bum and you were evicted out of your apartment by people in the neighbourhood.'*
3 NC Your **bum** is the part of your body which you sit on; an informal, rude use, which some people find offensive. *He has a very nice figure, a nice bum.*
4 VO If you **bum** something from someone, you obtain it from them by asking them for it; used in informal American English. *Low-life prostitutes who used to be bumming cigarettes are now bumming condoms.*
5 ADJ ATTRIB You can use **bum** to refer to things that you think are false or invalid; used in informal American English. *I've expressed my support for Dan Quayle. I think he's getting a bum rap in the press... 'I forgot about taxes,' he said. 'I'm broke, and I wrote two bum checks. I ought to be in jail.'*
bumble /bʌmbl/ **bumbles, bumbling, bumbled**
V If you **bumble**, you behave in a confused way and make a lot of mistakes.
bumblebee /bʌmblbiː/ **bumblebees**
NC A **bumblebee** is a large hairy bee. *Scientists measured the energy requirements of the bumblebee in flight.*
bumbling /bʌmblɪŋ/
ADJ ATTRIB A **bumbling** person behaves in a very confused, disorganized way and often makes mistakes. *Michael Hordern plays the bumbling Englishman yet again. ...Jimmy, the old bumbling fool. ...his bumbling ineptitude.*
bumf /bʌmf/; also spelt **bumph**.
NU If you refer to documents as **bumf**, you mean that they contain information, instructions, or publicity material which you consider to be uninteresting or unimportant; an informal word. *I've had some bumf through the post from the trade department... I've just got as far as the educational bumph at the beginning.*
bummer /bʌmə/
NU If you describe something that happens to you as a **bummer**, you mean that you find that experience an extremely bad one; used in informal American English. *I was just sitting around waiting for it to happen, it was a bummer.*
bump /bʌmp/ **bumps, bumping, bumped**
1 V AorVO To **bump** into a thing or a person means to accidentally hit them while moving. *The canoe bumped against the bank... She bumped into Zola Budd... He kept bumping into things... He knocked himself out by bumping his head against a lamp.*
2 VA If a vehicle **bumps** over a surface, it travels in a rough, bouncing way because the surface is very uneven. *The buses had a long, hard journey, bumping along more than five-hundred miles of rough road.*
3 NC A **bump** is a collision involving two things hitting each other. It is also the injury or damage caused by the collision. *...the knocks and bumps suffered by fruit when they are harvested. ...without anyone getting so much as a bump on the head.*
4 NC A **bump** in a surface is a raised, uneven part in it. *...the bumps in the London streets... I presume from the bump it must be under the carpet... You get cells proliferating, growing into bumps in blood vessel walls.*
bump into PHRASAL VERB If you **bump into** someone, you meet them by chance; an informal expression. *The men bumped into each other at a buffet... We bumped into the leader of one of the committees.*
bump off PHRASAL VERB To **bump** someone **off** means to kill them; an informal expression. *...plans to bump off the leader.*
bumper /bʌmpə/ **bumpers**
1 NC **Bumpers** are the bars at the front and back of a vehicle which protect it if it bumps into something. *The mascot of the Games can be seen on posters, shop windows and car bumpers all over Beijing.*
2 ADJ ATTRIB A **bumper** crop or harvest is larger than usual. *Sudan is heading for a bumper harvest despite some damage from locusts. ...its largest grain harvest since the bumper crop of 1978.*
3 ADJ ATTRIB A **bumper** year is a very successful one. *Tourism in England had a bumper year in 1988.*

bumph /bʌmf/. See **bumf**.
bumpkin /bʌmpkɪn/ **bumpkins**
NC If you call someone a **bumpkin**, you mean that they come from a country area and that you think they are stupid or ignorant; an informal word. *...narrow-minded country bumpkins.*
bumptious /bʌmpʃəs/
ADJ You say that someone is **bumptious** when they are continually expressing their own opinions and ideas in a self-important way. *I disliked these noisy bumptious types.*
bumpy /bʌmpi/ **bumpier, bumpiest**
1 ADJ A **bumpy** surface, such as a road or path, has a lot of bumps on it. *They are driving on one of the bumpiest roads you can imagine... The edges fit together precisely, but the bits in between are bumpy.*
2 ADJ A **bumpy** journey or vehicle is uncomfortable, usually because you are travelling over an uneven surface. *She made a safe if bumpy landing at the second attempt... The car was plain-looking and rather bumpy to ride in... Few films have shown the sheer discomfort of flying in a noisy, bumpy, cramped bomber quite so vividly.*
3 ADJ You can use **bumpy** to describe situations and processes that are difficult and often change rapidly. *The road to economic recovery may be disagreeably bumpy... US-Israel relations could be in for a bumpy ride... The committee got off to a bumpy start... Shares on Wall Street had a bumpy session.*
bun /bʌn/ **buns**
1 NC A **bun** is a small cake or bread roll, often containing currants or spices. *...two loaves of bread, some buns, and a slice of sponge cake. ...a currant bun.*
2 NC If a woman has her hair in a **bun**, it is fastened into a round shape at the back of her head.
bunch /bʌntʃ/ **bunches, bunching, bunched**
1 NC+SUPP A **bunch** of people or similar things is a group of them. *They're a bunch of tired old men. ...a big bunch of keys... They're a completely different bunch altogether.*
2 NC+SUPP A **bunch** of flowers is a number of them held or tied together. *Mrs Thatcher held a bunch of daffodils someone had given her... He laid a bunch of flowers on the grave.*
3 NC+SUPP A **bunch** of bananas, grapes, or other fruit is a group of them growing on the same stem.
4 V If people **bunch** together or **bunch** up, they stay close together in a group. *The column of troops bunched up on the narrow streets of the Shiite village and made no attempt to patrol up ahead.*
bundle /bʌndl/ **bundles, bundling, bundled**
1 NC A **bundle** is a number of things tied together or wrapped in a cloth so that they can be carried or stored. *He tied the wood into a bundle.*
2 VOA If you **bundle** someone somewhere, you push them there in a rough and hurried way. *They bundled him into the ambulance.*
bundle off PHRASAL VERB If you **bundle** someone **off** somewhere, you send them there in a hurry. *Jack was bundled off to Ely to stay with friends.*
bundle up PHRASAL VERB If you **bundle up** a mass of things, you make them into a bundle by gathering or tying them together. *My mother bundled up all my comics and threw them out.*
bung /bʌŋ/ **bungs, bunging, bunged**
1 NC A **bung** is a round piece of wood, cork, or rubber which is used to close the hole in a barrel or flask. *...a very large glass jar with a rubber bung.*
2 VOA If you **bung** something somewhere, you put it there in a quick, careless way; an informal use. *I bunged the books on the shelf.*
bungalow /bʌŋgələu/ **bungalows**
NC A **bungalow** is a house with only one storey. *I was in the front bedroom of our bungalow... Her timber-framed bungalow was blown down by gale-force winds.*
bunged up
ADJ PRED If a hole is **bunged up**, it is blocked; an informal expression.
bungle /bʌŋgl/ **bungles, bungling, bungled**
V orV If you **bungle** something, you fail to do it properly, because you make mistakes or are clumsy.

They bungled the whole operation... The costs have been high in Britain only because the politicians bungled. ◆ **bungled** ADJ *...the bungled murder of Bernard Lustig.* ◆ **bungling** ADJ *...this bungling administration.*

bungler /bʌŋglə/ **bunglers**
NC A **bungler** is a person who often fails to do things properly, because they make mistakes or are clumsy. *His colleague was branded a bungler for not disclosing his business interests during a parliamentary debate.*

bunion /bʌnjən/ **bunions**
NC A **bunion** is a large painful lump on the first joint of a person's big toe.

bunk /bʌŋk/ **bunks**
1 NC A **bunk** is a bed fixed to a wall, especially in a ship or caravan. *Thomas was lying in the lower bunk... Climb into your bunk and draw the curtains.*
2 If you **do a bunk**, you suddenly leave a place without telling anyone; an informal expression.

bunk bed, bunk beds
NC A **bunk bed** consists of two beds, one above the other, held in a frame. *There were bunk beds for the children to sleep in. ...curtains hanging on bunk beds in the cell.*

bunker /bʌŋkə/ **bunkers**
1 NC A **bunker** is a place, usually underground, which is built with strong walls to protect it against heavy gunfire and bombing. *A shell hit the bunker he was sheltering in... The army is stationed in bunkers and trenches around the city.*
2 NC A **bunker** is also a container for coal or other fuel. *The plastic bags were found hidden in a fuel bunker.*
3 NC On a golf course, a **bunker** is a large hollow filled with sand, which is deliberately put there as an obstacle that golfers must try and avoid. *He missed two short putts, and had to get out of a bunker at the last hole... He hit his first drive into a bunker.*

bunny /bʌni/ **bunnies**
NC Small children often call a rabbit a **bunny** or a **bunny rabbit**.

bunny girl, bunny girls
NC A **bunny girl** is a young woman who serves drinks in a nightclub and who wears a costume that includes a pair of rabbit's ears and a rabbit's tail.

bunsen burner /bʌnsn bɜːnə/ **bunsen burners**
NC A **bunsen burner** is a small gas burner used for heating things in laboratories. *The flask was then heated with a bunsen burner and a colourless gas was given off... I was told to heat it gently over a bunsen burner.*

bunting /bʌntɪŋ/
NU **Bunting** consists of rows of small coloured flags that are used to decorate streets and buildings on special occasions. *Nairobi is already decked out in bunting. ...coloured bunting and flags draped at every road-side.*

buoy /bɔɪ/ **buoys, buoying, buoyed**
1 NC A **buoy** is a floating object that shows ships and boats where they can go and warns them of danger. *...lighthouses, buoys and beacons around the coast... Construction teams began placing buoys to mark the route of the bridge.*
2 V OorVO+up If someone in a difficult situation is **buoyed** or **buoyed up** by something, it makes them feel more cheerful and optimistic. *Still buoyed by the victory, Dr Kohl was confident that he would become Chancellor of a united Germany... He has been buoyed up by tremendous support since the controversy began... The economy has been buoyed up by a boom in consumer credit.*

buoyancy /bɔɪənsi/
1 NU **Buoyancy** is the ability that something has to float on a liquid or in the air. *New chambers were added to provide buoyancy... Each of the balloons has its own buoyancy and lift.*
2 NU **Buoyancy** is a person's ability to remain cheerful, even in sad or unpleasant situations. *His personal buoyancy and vigour were a tonic... We will miss her buoyancy and charm.*
3 NU **Buoyancy** is a feeling of cheerfulness. *...a sensation of buoyancy and freedom.*

buoyant /bɔɪənt/
1 ADJ If you are **buoyant**, you feel cheerful and behave in a lively way. *He suddenly smiled, feeling buoyant and at ease... The diplomats are in a buoyant mood.*
2 ADJ Something that is **buoyant** floats on a liquid or in the air. *...a row of buoyant cylinders.*
3 ADJ If you describe an economy, a market, or prices as **buoyant**, you mean that they are stable or increasing, and not likely to be affected by any crisis. *A buoyant economy makes it more likely that the Republicans will retain control... The market for books is relatively buoyant... Oil prices have been generally buoyant since the beginning of the year.*

burble /bɜːbl/ **burbles, burbling, burbled**
V If something **burbles**, it makes a low continuous bubbling sound. *Hot mud burbled down from a side valley... Lucy was making burbling noises.*

burden /bɜːdn/ **burdens**
1 NC Something that is a **burden** causes you a lot of worry, hard work, or financial problems. *Many observers doubt whether he should continue to shoulder the heavy burden of government responsibility... Concern was expressed about the greater burden of work being imposed on teachers... The country's foreign debt burden is a major obstacle to recovery.* ● **lighten** your **burden**: see **lighten**.
2 NC A **burden** is also a heavy load that is difficult to carry; a literary use. *Men and women came carrying heavy burdens of provisions.*
3 If you say that **the burden of proof** is on someone, you mean that they have the task of proving that they are correct, for example when they have accused someone else of a crime. *The burden of proof is on the Government to prove that he's a spy... The burden of proof of ill-treatment rests with the victim.*

burdened /bɜːdnd/
ADJ PRED If you are **burdened** by or with something, it causes you a lot of worry, hard work, or financial problems. *...a man burdened by private problems... These countries are all burdened by massive foreign debt... Britain continues to be burdened with the highest inflation in the European Community.*

burdensome /bɜːdnsəm/
ADJ Something that is **burdensome** is worrying or tiring; a formal word. *...a burdensome responsibility.*

bureau /bjʊərəʊ/ **bureaux** or **bureaus**
1 NC+SUPP A **bureau** is an office, organization, or government department that collects and distributes information. *....the first marriage bureau specifically aimed at young black professionals. ...the political bureau of the Israeli Labour Party. ...a new survey by the United States Census Bureau.*
2 NC A **bureau** is also a desk with drawers and a lid that opens to form a writing surface; an old-fashioned use. *The judge is seated behind a grand mahogany bureau.*

bureaucracy /bjʊɒrɒkrəsi/ **bureaucracies**
1 NC A **bureaucracy** is an administrative system operated by a large number of officials. *There has been an expansion in the bureaucracy of the Church. ...the provision of jobs in the bureaucracy in exchange for bribes.*
2 NU **Bureaucracy** is all the rules and procedures followed by government departments and similar organizations; used showing disapproval. *...part of the continuing campaign against bureaucracy... The work of rebuilding after last month's earthquake is being slowed down by bureaucracy.*

bureaucrat /bjʊərəkræt/ **bureaucrats**
NC A **bureaucrat** is an official who works in a large administrative system, especially one who seems to follow rules and procedures too strictly. *...endless paperwork dished out by bureaucrats... He was regarded as a tough, efficient bureaucrat.*

bureaucratic /bjʊərəkrætɪk/
ADJ **Bureaucratic** rules and procedures are complicated and can cause long delays. *...to overhaul the state planning system and make it less bureaucratic. ...a speeding up of bureaucratic procedures.*

bureaux /bjʊərəʊz/
Bureaux is a plural of **bureau**.

burgeon /bɜːdʒən/ burgeons, burgeoning, burgeoned
v If something **burgeons**, it develops or grows rapidly;
a literary word. *The spring came and the leaves
burgeoned... Life in the sea burgeoned into many
forms.* ◆ **burgeoning** ADJ ATTRIB *...a burgeoning
manufacturing industry. ...the country's burgeoning
pacifist movement.*

burger /bɜːɡə/ burgers
NC A **burger** is a flat round mass of minced food such
as beef or vegetables, which is fried and often eaten in
a bread roll. *...the burgers and fried chicken pieces
they buy as snacks.*

burgher /bɜːɡə/ burghers
NC A **burgher** is a person who lives in a city,
especially a middle-class person; an old-fashioned
word. *...the burghers of New York.*

burglar /bɜːɡlə/ burglars
NC A **burglar** is a thief who breaks into a house and
steals things. *Burglars yesterday ransacked the
offices of the Deputy Minister.*

burglar alarm, burglar alarms
NC A **burglar alarm** is a device that makes a bell ring
loudly if someone tries to break into a building. *The
wires of the burglar alarm had been cut. ...controls on
noisy burglar alarms.*

burglarize /bɜːɡləraɪz/ burglarizes, burglarizing,
burglarized
vo If a thief **burglarizes** a building, they burgle it;
used in American English. *Her home had been
burglarized... We had no intention of burglarizing any
store.*

burglary /bɜːɡləri/ burglaries
NCorNU If someone carries out a **burglary** or commits
burglary, they break into a building and steal things.
*Contact the police as soon as possible after a
burglary... He was found guilty of burglary.*

burgle /bɜːɡl/ burgles, burgling, burgled
vo If a house is **burgled**, someone breaks in and steals
things. *They worry that their house may be burgled
while they are away... Their offices were burgled over
the weekend.*

burial /beriəl/ burials
NCorNU A **burial** is the ceremony that takes place
when a dead body is put into a grave. *...the burial of
an important person... The bodies are brought home
for burial.*

burial ground, burial grounds
NC A **burial ground** is a place where bodies are
buried, especially an ancient site, or a site used to
bury large numbers of soldiers killed in a battle. *They
objected to plans to expand a golf course on what they
say is an ancient burial ground.*

Burkina Faso /buəkiːnə fæsəu/
The **Popular Republic of Burkina Faso** is a country in
western Africa. It was part of French West Africa
from the 19th century until 1960, when it became an
independent country called Upper Volta. In 1984 it was
renamed Burkina Faso, 'the land of incorruptible
men'. The constitution was suspended in 1980. Blaise
Compaoré became the Chairman of the Popular Front
(FP), the head of state, in 1987. In 1991 political
parties were legalized. Burkina Faso exports cotton. It
is a member of the Organization of African Unity.
◆ **Burkinabé** /buəkɪnəbeɪ/ N, ADJ
▪ *per capita GNP:* US$310 ▪ *religion:* animism, Islam,
Christianity ▪ *language:* French (official), Mossi
▪ *currency:* CFA franc ▪ *capital:* Ouagadougou
▪ *population:* 9 million (1989) ▪ *size:* 274,200 square
kilometres.

burlesque /bɜːlɛsk/ burlesques
1 NCorNU A **burlesque** is a piece of writing which
makes fun of a particular style by copying it in an
exaggerated way. *The poem is really a burlesque...
They make fun of them through ridicule, satire, or
burlesque.*
2 NUorNC **Burlesque** was a type of comedy show
which was popular in America in the late 19th and
early 20th centuries. *We could have joined any
burlesque show in the country.*

burly /bɜːli/
ADJ A **burly** man has a broad body and strong
muscles. *...the burly and avuncular Helmut Kohl.*

...burly men in white tee-shirts.

Burma /bɜːmə/
Burma, or the **Union of Myanmar**, is a country in
south-east Asia. It became a British colony in 1886 and
was occupied by Japan from 1942 to 1945. Burma
became independent from Britain in 1948 and was a
democracy until 1958 when General U Ne Win
introduced military rule for a limited period. He took
control permanently in 1962. In 1974 a new constitution
was introduced, under which the Burma Socialist
Programme Party became the only legal political
party. General U Ne Win resigned in 1988 after
nationwide protests, but the army once again took
control of the country, and General Saw Maung
became Prime Minister and Chairman of the State
Law and Order Restoration Council (SLORC). The
new military government organized a general election
in 1990. The election was won by the National League
for Democracy (NLD), but the government ignored
the result. The leader of the NLD, Aung San Suu Kyi,
had been placed under house arrest in 1989 and was
not allowed to form a government. Burma exports
teak, jade, and rubies. Cannabis and opium are
illegally exported. Large foreign debts and high
inflation are major economic problems. ◆ **Burmese,
Myanmar** /bɜːmiːz, mjænmɑː/ N,N PL, ADJ
▪ *per capita GNP:* approximately US$200 ▪ *religion:*
Theravada Buddhism ▪ *language:* Burmese
(Myanmar) ▪ *currency:* kyat ▪ *capital:* Rangoon
(Yangon) ▪ *population:* 40 million (1989) ▪ *size:* 676,552
square kilometres.

burn /bɜːn/ burns, burning, burned or burnt /bɜːnt/
1 v If something is **burning**, it is on fire. *The stubble
was burning in the fields.* ◆ **burning** NU *There was a
smell of burning.* ◆ **burnt** ADJ *...a charred bit of burnt
wood.*
2 vo If you **burn** something, you destroy it with fire.
We couldn't burn the rubbish because it was raining.
3 vo If you **burn** yourself or a part of your body, you
are injured by fire or by something very hot. *'What's
the matter with your hand?'—'I burned it on my
cigar.'*
4 v+with If you **are burning** with an emotion such as
anger, you feel it very strongly. *...letters burning with
indignation.*
5 v-ERG If the sun **burns** your skin, it makes it red or
brown and rather painful. *Because his albino skin
burnt easily, he couldn't work in the fields... High
levels of sunlight can burn the skin.*
6 vo If chemicals, electricity, or radiation **burn** your
skin, they cause serious damage to it. *...mustard gas,
which blisters and burns the skin and lungs... Human
beings who were careless enough to touch these
bacteria burned their skin.*
7 NC A **burn** is an injury caused to someone's body by
fire, chemicals, electricity, or radiation. *Many of
those hurt have suffered serious burns. ...evidence of
burns and skin conditions consistent with chemical
weapon attacks.*

burn down PHRASAL VERB If a building **burns down** or
is **burned down**, it is completely destroyed by fire.
*Twenty houses burned down before troops were called
in... Several government buildings were burned down.*

burn out PHRASAL VERB 1 If a fire **burns** itself **out**, it
stops burning because there is nothing left to burn.
All the fires had now burned themselves out. 2 If you
burn yourself **out**, you make yourself exhausted or ill
by working too hard; an informal use. *He could well
burn himself out.*

burn up PHRASAL VERB 1 If something **burns up**, it is
completely destroyed by fire or strong heat. *The
satellite had burned up on re-entering the atmosphere.*
2 If you say that an engine **burns up** fuel, you mean
that it uses a lot of fuel. *Because of a malfunction,
the craft has burnt up all of its fuel and will not
respond to control commands.*

burned out. See burnt-out.

burner /bɜːnə/ burners
1 NC A **burner** is a device which produces heat or a
flame, especially as part of a cooker or heater. *In
future, the heating may not have to be done over the
flame of a burner or on an electric hotplate.*

2 If an issue is placed **on the back burner**, it is left to be dealt with later, because it is considered to have become less urgent or important. *Nuclear reductions have been placed on the back burner by the Brussels compromise... Mansell's threat to retire from motor racing seems to be on the back burner.*

burning /bɜːnɪŋ/
1 ADJ If something is extremely hot, you can say that it is **burning** or **burning hot**. *They waited patiently under the burning sun.*
2 ADJ You can use **burning** to describe strong feelings, or situations that are causing strong feelings. *He does have a burning ambition to become President himself... The burning issue is the restoration of party-based democracy... The government had failed to answer a number of burning questions.* ● See also **burn**.

burnish /bɜːnɪʃ/ burnishes, burnishing, burnished
VO If you **burnish** metal, you polish it so that it shines.
burnished /bɜːnɪʃt/
ADJ **Burnished** means bright or smooth; a literary word. *...her burnished skin... Everything's burnished and bright and gleaming again.*

burnt /bɜːnt/
Burnt is a past tense and past participle of **burn**.

burnt offering, burnt offerings
1 NC You can refer to a meal as a **burnt offering** when it has accidentally been burnt; often used humorously.
2 NC A **burnt offering** is an animal that is burned as a sacrifice to a god or goddess.

burnt-out or **burned-out**
ADJ **Burnt-out** vehicles or buildings have been very badly damaged by fire. *...littered with glass and rubble and burnt-out cars... He said he saw burned-out tanks and wrecked army helicopters.*

burp /bɜːp/ burps, burping, burped
V When someone **burps**, they make a noise because air from their stomach has been forced up through their throat. ▶ Also NC *A slight burp interrupted her flowing speech.*

burr /bɜː/ burrs, burring, burred; also spelt **bur** for the meaning in paragraph 1.
1 NC On some plants, a **burr** is a small round part which contains seeds and has little hooks on it that stick to your clothes or to animals' fur. *...removing burrs from a dog's coat.*
2 NC If someone has a **burr**, they speak English with an accent in which 'r' sounds are pronounced in a very noticeable way. *He had a slight Irish burr.*
3 N SING A **burr** is also a whirring or humming sound. *He could hear the burr of a car in the distance.* ▶ Also V *The telephone burred.*

burro /bʊrəʊ/ burros
NC A **burro** is a donkey; used in American English. *One guy was on a burro with a huge ammunition crate.*

burrow /bʌrəʊ/ burrows, burrowing, burrowed
1 NC A **burrow** is a tunnel or hole in the ground, dug by an animal such as a rabbit. *The mother drops her young into a narrow burrow where they are protected from predators.*
2 V When an animal **burrows**, it digs a tunnel or hole in the ground. *...a worm that burrows down into the ground.*

bursar /bɜːsə/ bursars
NC The **bursar** of a school or college is the person who is in charge of its finance or general administration. *Some schools would need bursars to take over detailed financial management.*

bursary /bɜːsəri/ bursaries
NC A **bursary** is a sum of money given to someone to allow them to study in a college or university. *She's received a £2500 bursary from Britain's Arts Council. ...protests over non-payment of grants and bursaries.*

burst /bɜːst/ bursts, bursting. The form **burst** is used in the present tense and is also the past tense and past participle of the verb.
1 V-ERG When something **bursts** or when you **burst** it, it suddenly splits open, and air or some other substance comes out. *As he braked, a tyre burst... She burst the balloon.* ▶ Also ADJ ATTRIB *...a burst water pipe.*

2 V+*open* When something such as a door or lid **bursts** open, it opens very suddenly because of the pressure behind it. *The end of the hull burst open in flight, putting the plane out of control... The fire apparently began when a corroded underground gas pipe burst open.*
3 V A If you **burst** into or through something, you suddenly go into it or through it with a lot of energy. *Six masked men armed with automatic weapons burst into a bar and opened fire... O'Shea burst through the opposite door... Lee Atwater first burst onto the national political scene at the age of 28... The others burst from their tents.*
4 NC+*of* A **burst** of something is a sudden short period of it. *...a burst of automatic rifle fire.*

burst in on PHRASAL VERB If you **burst in on** someone, you suddenly enter the room that they are in. *Angry Belgian farmers burst in on the Prime Minister as he was having his hair cut and complained about the farm price freeze.*

burst into PHRASAL VERB If you **burst into** something such as tears or laughter, you suddenly begin to cry or laugh. *Many of them burst into tears... Delegates at the UN burst into spontaneous applause. ...standing on their seats and bursting into revolutionary song.* ● to **burst into flames**: see **flame**.

burst out PHRASAL VERB If you **burst out** laughing or crying, you suddenly begin laughing or crying loudly. *We'd probably burst out laughing and say, 'This is ridiculous.'... He looked afraid and then suddenly burst out crying.*

bursting /bɜːstɪŋ/; an informal word.
1 ADJ PRED+*with* If a place is **bursting** with people or things, it is full of them. *...parks bursting with flowers.*
2 ADJ PRED+*with* If you are **bursting** with a feeling, you are full of it. *Claud was bursting with pride and excitement.*
3 ADJ PRED+*to*-INF If you are **bursting** to do something, you are very eager to do it. *I was bursting to tell someone.*

burton /bɜːtn/; an old-fashioned, informal word.
1 If something **goes for a burton**, it is lost or damaged, or made useless. *Well, that's our pay rise gone for a burton.*
2 If someone **goes for a burton**, they fall down or fall off something.

Burundi /bʊrʊndɪ/
The **Republic of Burundi** is a country in central Africa. It was part of German East Africa from 1899 until the First World War. Belgium administered it until independence in 1962. Ethnic conflict, between the majority Hutu and politically dominant Tutsi, has been a source of civil disorder and widespread violence. The Union for National Progress (UPRONA) became the sole party in 1966. Major Pierre Buyoya became President in a coup in 1987. Burundi is a member of the Organization of African Unity. It exports coffee, tea, and cotton. ◆ **Burundian** /bʊrʊndɪən/ N, ADJ
▪ *per capita GNP:* US$220 ▪ *religion:* Christianity, animism ▪ *language:* Kirundi and French (official) ▪ *currency:* franc ▪ *capital:* Bujumbura ▪ *population:* 5 million (1989) (Hutu 85%, Tutsi 14%) ▪ *size:* 27,834 square kilometres.

bury /beri/ buries, burying, buried
1 VO When a dead person is **buried**, their body is put into a grave and covered with earth. *He is due to be buried tomorrow in a state funeral... Those executed were buried in unmarked graves.*
2 VO To **bury** something means to put it into a hole in the ground and cover it up, often in order to hide it. *Reptiles bury their eggs in holes.* ● to **bury the hatchet**: see **hatchet**.
3 VO If you **are buried** under something that falls on top of you, you are completely covered and may not be able to get out. *People were buried beneath mountains of rubble.*
4 VO A If you **bury** your face in something, you try to hide your face by pressing it against that thing. *She buried her face in her hands.*
5 V-REFL+*in* If you **bury** yourself in your work or an activity, you concentrate hard on it. *He buried*

himself in the wine list.

bury away PHRASAL VERB If something is buried away somewhere, you cannot easily find it or see it. *Some reports suggest there are heroin factories buried away in remote parts of the border regions.*

bus /bʌs/ **buses; busses, bussing, bussed.** The form **buses** is the plural of the noun. The form **busses** is the third person singular, present tense, of the verb. The verb is also spelt **buses, busing, bused** in American English.
1 NC A **bus** is a large motor vehicle which carries passengers from one place to another. *...waiting for a bus to take them on the long journey... The bus was on a routine trip transporting office workers to the mine site.*
2 V-ERG If someone **busses** to a particular place or when they are **bussed** there, they travel there on a bus. *One has the option of walking one way and bussing back... Workers were bussed in from Serbia to maintain the essential services... Hundreds of shanty town residents were bussed up to Brasilia overnight.*
3 VO In the United States, if children **are bussed** to school, they are transported to by bus to a school in a different area in order that children of different races can be educated together. *When she was bused in Oklahoma City, she was shunted aside into segregated classrooms... School board officials stopped busing schoolchildren because they felt they had achieved racial integration.* ♦ **busing** N SING *...a Supreme Court ruling on busing. ...the campaign against school busing.*

busboy /bʌsbɔɪ/ **busboys**
NC A **busboy** is someone who assists a waiter or waitress in a restaurant by setting tables and clearing away dirty dishes; used in American English. *They supply unskilled labor as busboys, dishwashers and maintenance workers.*

busby /bʌzbi/ **busbies**
NC A **busby** is a tall fur hat that is worn by some British soldiers on ceremonial occasions.

bus conductor, bus conductors
NC A **bus conductor** is an official on a bus who sells tickets.

bush /bʊʃ/ **bushes**
1 NC A **bush** is a plant which is like a very small tree. *...planting trees or bushes... I hid behind some bushes and waited for him.*
2 N SING The wild parts of some hot countries are referred to as the **bush**. *I went for a walk in the bush.*
3 If you say **'Don't beat about the bush'**, you mean that you want someone to tell you something immediately and directly rather than trying to avoid doing so. *Don't beat around the bush no matter how embarrassed you are.*

Bush, George /dʒɔːdʒ bʊʃ/
George Bush was elected President of the United States in 1989. He was Vice-President from 1981 to 1989. He is a member of the Republican Party. Born: 1924.

bushbaby /bʊʃbeɪbi/ **bushbabies**
NC A **bushbaby** is a small furry African animal that has very large eyes and a long tail and lives in trees.

bushed /bʊʃt/
ADJ PRED If you say that you are **bushed**, you mean that you are very tired; an informal word. *I'm pretty bushed after last night.*

bushel /bʊʃl/ **bushels**
1 NC A **bushel** is a unit of volume that is equal to eight gallons or 36.4 litres. *...five bushels of oats.*
2 If you **hide your light under a bushel** or **hide your** talents or abilities **under a bushel**, you keep your abilities or good qualities hidden from other people. *There were many lights hidden under his bushel... He was not a man much given to hiding his own brilliance under a bushel.*

bush fire, bush fires
NC A **bush fire** is a fire that starts, usually by itself, in the wild parts of some hot countries, and spreads rapidly, causing great damage. *...raging bush fires in central Brazil... A number of large bush fires are burning out of control near towns on the border between New South Wales and Victoria.*

Bushman /bʊʃmən/ **Bushmen** /bʊʃmən/
NC A **Bushman** is a member of a southern African tribe, especially from the Kalahari region. *It's a fruit which can be used as a staple food by the local Bushmen.*

bushy /bʊʃi/ **bushier, bushiest**
ADJ **Bushy** hair or fur grows very thickly. *...bushy eyebrows.*

busily /bɪzɪli/
ADV If you do something **busily**, you do it in a very active way. *I went on writing busily.*

business /bɪznəs/ **businesses**
1 NU **Business** is work relating to the production, buying, and selling of goods or services. *There are good profits to be made in the hotel business... Are you in San Francisco for business or pleasure?... The radio said that shops were open for business... The appeal was made by Mrs Chalker in a speech in London to members of the international business community.*
2 NC A **business** is an organization which produces and sells goods or provides a service. *He set up a small travel business... Until June, he ran a business in Nairobi.*
3 NU+SUPP You can use **business** to refer to any activity, situation, or series of events. *She got on with the business of clearing up... The whole business affected him profoundly... He has to deal with a mass of unfinished business. ...watching people going about their business.*
4 N SING+SUPP You can give a warning or a negative opinion about an event or situation by saying it is, for example, a difficult **business**, a dangerous **business**, or an expensive **business**. *The counting of the votes will be a complicated business, because there are 14 candidates... The replacement of existing plants at a large chemical works is a costly business.*
5 NU You can use **business** to refer to serious or important matters. *The two sides exchanged pleasantries before getting down to business... I don't know whether they work or not, but anyhow let us get back to business.*
6 N SING+POSS If you say that something is your **business**, you mean that it concerns you personally and that other people should not get involved in it. *That's his business and no one else's.*
● **Business** is used in these phrases. ● When people or companies **do business**, one of them sells goods or provides a service to the other. *This gives dealers the opportunity to meet their clients and to do business. ...companies intending to do business in Poland.* ● If one politician or government **does business** with another, they have discussions or make agreements. *He wanted to do business only with a freely-elected government... There's no doubt which side the Americans feel they can do business with.* ● If a shop or company is or stays **in business**, it is continuing to trade, often despite difficulties. *It cost taxpayers three thousand million pounds to keep the company in business... All the theatres in Paris stayed in business.* ● If you say that a person or organization is **in business**, you mean they have overcome some problems and are able to continue their activities. *For the time being, Mr Papandreou remains in business... Dr Owen has told its members that, politically speaking, they are still in business... The trade-union movement is back in business.* ● If a shop or company goes **out of business**, it has to stop trading because it is not making enough money. *Hairdressers say they're going out of business... Factories are being forced out of business.* ● If someone describes a situation by saying that it is **business as usual**, they mean that the situation is normal, especially after an emergency or crisis. *But in every other respect, said Mr Tusa, it was business as usual at the BBC.* ● If someone **means business**, they are serious and determined about what they are doing; an informal expression. *...measures to prove that America means business.* ● If you say that someone **has no business** to do something, you mean that they have no right to do it. *She had no business to publish his letters.* ● If you say to someone **'Mind your own business'** or **'It's none of your business'**, you are telling them not to ask

about something that does not concern them; an informal expression. *Anyone who does is told to mind his own business... It's none of our business, he said.*
● See also **big business, show business, small business.**

businesslike /bɪznəslaɪk/
ADJ Someone who is **businesslike** deals with things in an efficient way without wasting time. *He won a reputation among officials as a tough but businesslike negotiator... Both sides reported that the session was businesslike.*

businessman /bɪznəsmæn, bɪznəsmən / **businessmen** /bɪznəsmen, bɪznəsmən/
1 NC A **businessman** is a man who works in business, for example by running a firm. *Robert is a young American businessman. ...a gathering of leading businessmen.*
2 NC+SUPP If you describe a man as a good **businessman**, you mean that he knows how to deal with money and how to make good deals. *Any good businessman would immediately know that a stolen piece of art is a risky investment.* ● See also **small businessman.**

businesspeople /bɪznəspiːpl/
NPL **Businesspeople** are men or women who work in business. *...the concerns of businesspeople worried about his attitude to nationalisation.*

business school, business schools
NC A **business school** is a college where people go to learn about various aspects of managing a business, such as finance, marketing, and law. *...Eastern Europe's first international business school.*

businesswoman /bɪznəswʊmən/ **businesswomen**
NC A **businesswoman** is a woman who works in business, for example by running a firm. *... a British businesswoman who finally left Tibet last weekend.*

busk /bʌsk/ **busks, busking, busked**
V Someone who is **busking** is playing music or singing for money in a city street or station.

busker /bʌskə/ **buskers**
NC A **busker** is a person who plays music or sings for money in city streets or stations. *In the meantime, buskers keep the tourists entertained.*

busman's holiday /bʌsmənz hɒlɪdeɪ/
If you have a holiday, but spend it doing something similar to your usual work, you can refer to it as a **busman's holiday.**

bus-shelter, bus-shelters
NC A **bus-shelter** is a bus stop that has a roof and at least one open side, which protects you from the rain when you are waiting for a bus. *Two demonstrators climbed on a bus-shelter and waved placards.*

bus stop, bus stops
NC A **bus stop** is a place on a road where buses stop to let people get on and off. *Lack of information at the bus stops is not in the operator's interests.*

bust /bʌst/ **busts, busting, busted.** The past tense and past participle of the verb can be either **busted** or **bust.**
1 VO When you **bust** something, you damage it so badly that it cannot be used; an informal use. *She found out about Jack busting the double bass and was very annoyed.*
2 ADJ PRED If something is **bust**, it is broken or very badly damaged; an informal use. *The television's bust.*
3 If a company **goes bust**, it loses so much money that it is forced to close down; an informal expression. *A major accountancy firm predicts that 25,000 companies will go bust in 1990.*
4 VO If a country **busts** sanctions, it continues to export and import goods after it has been ordered not to by another country or by an international organization. *The statement has created concern in the West that Iran may help Iraq bust UN sanctions.*
▶ Also NU *...a clear case of sanctions busting.*
5 VO When the police **bust** someone, they arrest them; an informal use. *Officers busted him on half a dozen drug and money laundering charges... The state of Louisiana has busted an IRS agent for tax fraud.*
6 VO When the police **bust** a place, they raid it in order to arrest people who are doing illegal things; an informal use.

7 NC A drug **bust** is the finding of illegal drugs by the police or customs, and the arresting of the criminals involved. *...eight people arrested during a major cocaine bust. ...a number of drug busts over the last eighteen months.*
8 NC A **bust** is a statue of someone's head and shoulders. *...a bust of Karl Marx in London's Highgate Cemetery.*
9 NC A woman's **bust** is her breasts.

buster /bʌstə/
VOCATIVE **Buster** is used to address a man in an impolite, aggressive manner. *'That's enough, buster!'.*

bustle /bʌsl/ **bustles, bustling, bustled**
1 VA If someone **bustles** somewhere, they move there in a hurried, determined way. *I watched housewives bustle in and out of a supermarket.*
2 NU **Bustle** is busy, noisy activity. *...the bustle of the airport.*

bustling /bʌslɪŋ/
1 ADJ A **bustling** place is full of people and very busy and lively. *Grimsby is a bustling fishing town... The station was bustling with activity.*
2 ADJ A **bustling** person always seems to be very busy and active. *...the bustling curator of the Museum of the Holy Shrine.*

bust-up, bust-ups; an informal word.
1 NC A **bust-up** is a serious quarrel, especially one which ends a relationship. *They've had another bust-up.*
2 NC A **bust-up** is also a fight. *There was a bust-up down at the pub last night.*

busty /bʌsti/ **bustier, bustiest**
ADJ A woman who is **busty** has very large breasts; an informal word.

busy /bɪzi/ **busier, busiest; busies, busying, busied**
1 ADJ If you are **busy**, you are working hard or concentrating on a task, so that you are not free to do anything else. *She's going to be busy till Friday.*
2 ADJ PRED+ING If you are **busy** doing something, it is taking all your attention. *Jon has been busy acting and writing songs... Workmen have been busy clearing away the evidence of yesterday's bomb explosion.*
3 V-REFL If you **busy** yourself with something, you occupy yourself by dealing with it. *I decided to busy myself with our untidy lawn.*
4 ADJ A **busy** time is a time when you have a lot of things to do. *I've had a busy day... It's been a busy night for football... December is usually the busiest time of year.*
5 ADJ A **busy** place is full of people who are doing things or moving about. *...a busy office.*
6 ADJ A **busy** road, station, or airport is one that is used by large numbers of cars, trains, or planes. *...a busy road just outside Armagh city. ...Heathrow, at present the busiest international airport in the world.*
7 ADJ When a telephone is **busy**, it is engaged; used in American English. *Cuts in staff mean more busy signals when you call for help.*

busybody /bɪzibɒdi/ **busybodies**
NC If you call someone a **busybody**, you mean that they interfere in other people's affairs. *Mr Heath said that Britain should not be an interfering busybody.*

but /bət, bʌt/
1 CONJ You use **but** to introduce something which contrasts with what you have just said. *It was a long walk but it was worth it... We'll have a meeting. But not today. ...a cheap but incredibly effective carpet cleaner.*
2 CONJ You use **but** when you are adding something or changing the subject. *Later I'll be discussing this with Dr Peter Unsworth. But first let me remind you of some of the issues.*
3 CONJ You use **but** to link an excuse or apology with what you are about to say. *I'm sorry, but she's not in at the moment... Forgive my ignorance, but just what is Arista?*
4 PREP **But** also means 'except'. *It hurt nobody but himself... It could do everything but stop.*
5 ADV **But** can also mean 'only'; a formal use. *Low cost and high speed are but two of the advantages of electronic data handling.*
● **But** is used in these phrases. ● You use **but then**

before a remark which slightly contradicts what you have just said. *Iron would do the job better. But then you can't bend iron so easily.* ● You also use **but then** before indicating that what you have just said is not surprising. *They're very close. But then, they've known each other for years and years.* ● You use **but for** to introduce the only factor that causes a particular thing not to happen or not to be completely true. *But for his ice-blue eyes, he looked like a bearded, wiry Moor.*

butane /bjuːteɪn/
NU **Butane** is a gas that is obtained from petroleum and is used as a fuel. *They will supply them with butane to replace the wood which is traditionally used for fuel.*

butch /bʊtʃ/
ADJ If you describe a woman as **butch**, you mean that you think she behaves or dresses in a masculine way; an offensive word.

butcher /bʊtʃə/ butchers, butchering, butchered
1 NC A **butcher** is a shopkeeper who sells meat. *A butcher agreed to give him some meat in exchange for the yams.*
2 NC A **butcher** or a **butcher's** is a shop where meat is sold. *There's a family butcher at the end of our road.*
3 VO To **butcher** a lot of people means to kill them in a cruel way. *Men, women and children are being butchered... The squabbling erupted into a civil war, with the Yorks murdering and butchering their way to the throne.*

butchery /bʊtʃəri/
NU You can refer to the cruel killing of a lot of people as **butchery**. *...a little nation which had endured a terrible amount of butchery. ...this barbarous act of butchery.*

butler /bʌtlə/ butlers
NC A **butler** is the most important male servant in a house. *...a retired family butler... The butler opened a hidden cupboard.*

butt /bʌt/ butts, butting, butted
1 NC The **butt** of a weapon is the thick end of its handle. *...the padded butt of the rifle.*
2 NC The **butt** of a cigarette or cigar is the small part that is left when you have finished smoking it. *...a fire thought to be caused by a discarded cigarette butt. ...the butts in the ashtrays.*
3 NC A **butt** is a large barrel used for collecting or storing liquid. *...a water butt.*
4 N SING If you are the **butt** of teasing or criticism, people keep teasing you or criticizing you. *They made him the butt of endless practical jokes.*
5 VO If you **butt** something, you hit it with your head. *He butted Brian in the chest.*

butt in PHRASAL VERB If you **butt in**, you rudely join in a private conversation or activity without being asked to. *I was always butting in and saying the wrong thing.*

butter /bʌtə/ butters, buttering, buttered
1 NU **Butter** is a yellowish substance made from cream which you spread on bread or use in cooking. *...white bread and butter. ...imports of butter and lamb.* See also **peanut butter**.
2 VO When you **butter** bread or toast, you spread butter on it. *Rosamund went on buttering her potato pancake.*
3 If you say that **butter wouldn't melt in** someone's **mouth**, you mean that they look very innocent but you know that they have done something wrong or are intending to.
4 See also **bread and butter**.

butter up PHRASAL VERB If you **butter** someone **up**, you praise them or try to please them, because you want to ask them a favour; an informal expression. *I'm buttering him up for a pay rise.*

buttercup /bʌtəkʌp/ buttercups
NC A **buttercup** is a small wild plant with bright yellow flowers.

butterfingers /bʌtəfɪŋgəz/
You say '**butterfingers!**' when someone drops something they were holding, or fails to catch something that was thrown to them; often used humorously. *The coin rolled into the grass at my feet.*

'Butterfingers!' called Mr Ben.

butterfly /bʌtəflaɪ/ butterflies
1 N C or N U A **butterfly** is an insect with large colourful wings and a thin body. *...special measures to protect rare species of butterfly.*
2 If you have **butterflies in** your **stomach**, you are very nervous about something; an informal expression.
3 NU **Butterfly** is a swimming stroke which you do lying on your front, bringing your arms together over your head. *Japan's Kunio Sugimoto won the men's 200 metres butterfly.*

buttermilk /bʌtəmɪlk/
NU **Buttermilk** is the liquid that remains when fat is removed from cream to make butter. You can drink buttermilk or use it for making bread or cheesecake.

butterscotch /bʌtəskɒtʃ/ butterscotches
N U or N C **Butterscotch** is a hard yellowish-brown sweet substance made by boiling butter and sugar together.

buttery /bʌtəri/ butteries
1 ADJ Something that is **buttery** tastes of butter or contains a lot of butter. *...a buttery cake.*
2 NC In some universities, a **buttery** is a place where you can buy food and drinks; an old-fashioned use. *You could purchase tea and buns at the buttery.*

buttock /bʌtək/ buttocks
NC Your **buttocks** are the part of your body that you sit on. *Fat tends to build around the buttocks and thighs during pregnancy.*

button /bʌtn/ buttons, buttoning, buttoned
1 NC **Buttons** are small, hard objects sewn on to shirts, coats, or other pieces of clothing. You fasten the clothing by pushing the buttons through holes called buttonholes. *...a collarless shirt with the top button fastened.*
2 VO If you **button** a shirt, coat, or other piece of clothing, you fasten it by pushing its buttons through the buttonholes. *Sam stands up, buttoning his jacket.*
3 NC You can refer to a plastic or metal badge that expresses a message of some kind as a **button**; used in American English. *The newest button on blouses and jackets says, 'My sweetheart's in Saudi'. ...wearing Malcolm X T-shirts and buttons.*
4 NC A **button** is also a small object on a machine that you press in order to operate the machine. *I couldn't remember which button turns it off. ...access to information at the press of a button.*

button up PHRASAL VERB If you **button up** a shirt, coat, or other piece of clothing, you fasten it completely by pushing all its buttons through the buttonholes. *He began to gather his papers and button up his coat.*

buttonhole /bʌtnhəʊl/ buttonholes, buttonholing, buttonholed
1 NC A **buttonhole** is a hole in an item of clothing which you push a button through. *I tried to fumble buttons through buttonholes without touching her.*
2 NC+POSS Your **buttonhole** is a hole in the lapel of your jacket, in which you wear a flower on special occasions. *...a red rose in his buttonhole... People took sprigs of leaves and put them in their buttonholes.*
3 VO If you **buttonhole** someone, you stop them and make them listen to you. *I was just on my way out and he buttonholed me.*

buttress /bʌtrəs/ buttresses, buttressing, buttressed
1 NC **Buttresses** are supports, usually made of stone or brick, that support a wall.
2 VO If someone or something **buttresses** a system or argument, they give it support and strength. *The present system serves to buttress the social structure in Britain... He used the latest figures to buttress his view that action has to be taken immediately.* ► Also NC *...the armed forces, who are the main buttress for his government. ...one of the essential buttresses of democratic freedom.*

buxom /bʌksəm/
ADJ A **buxom** woman looks attractive and has big breasts; an old-fashioned word. *She was blonde and buxom.*

buy /baɪ/ buys, buying, bought
1 V O, V O O, or V O+for If you **buy** something, you obtain it by paying money for it. *She could not afford to buy*

it... Let me buy you a drink... Many people have their cars bought for them by their firm.
2 NC+SUPP If you say that something is a good **buy**, you mean that it is of good quality and can be bought cheaply. *Other good buys include cameras and toys.*
buy into PHRASAL VERB When someone **buys into** a business or organization, they buy part of it, often in order to gain some control over it. *He's been trying to buy into the printing industry.*
buy off PHRASAL VERB If you **buy** someone **off**, you give them money or something else to stop them acting against you. *They thought initially they could buy off some governments... The Government offered concessions amounting to millions of pounds to buy off the strikers.*
buy out PHRASAL VERB If you **buy** someone **out**, you buy their share of something that you previously owned together. *He sold off the shops to buy out his partner.*
buy up PHRASAL VERB If you **buy up** land or property, you buy large quantities of it, or all of it that is available. *The race is on for the major exporters to buy up oil refineries... Rising prices earlier this year caused people to buy up essential supplies... When land prices fall the barons can buy up large estates very cheaply.*
buyer /baɪə/ **buyers**
1 NC A **buyer** is a person who is buying something or who intends to buy it. *I have a buyer for the house.*
2 NC A **buyer** is also someone who works for a large store or organization, and whose job is to decide what goods to buy for sale in the store or for use by the organization. *The powder was shown to the major buyers for the soup industry... A buyer for their state television is in Britain at the moment.*
buy-out, buy-outs
NC A **buy-out** is the purchase of a company, especially by its managers or employees. *It's the second foreign buy-out of a Hollywood studio this month... There was talk of a management buy-out... The buy-out price is considered extremely generous.*
Buyoya, Pierre /pjeə buːjɔə/
Major Pierre Buyoya became President of Burundi in a coup in 1987. He was a member of the Central Committee of the Union for National Progress (UPRONA), the sole party, from 1982 to 1987. Born: 1949.
buzz /bʌz/ **buzzes, buzzing, buzzed**
1 N SING A **buzz** is a continuous sound, like the sound of a bee when it is flying. *You could hear the buzz of relief in the hall. ...the buzz of conversation.*
2 V When something **buzzes**, it makes a continuous sound, like the sound that bees make when they are flying. *Troops are patrolling the streets, helicopters buzz overhead.*
3 V A If thoughts **are buzzing** round your head, you are thinking about a lot of things. *Anne's head buzzed with angry, crazy thoughts.*
4 V If a place **buzzes**, there is a lot of excitement or activity there. *The narrow streets in the area buzzed with stories of the killers... The normally sleepy capital is buzzing with activity.* ▶ Also N SING *There was a buzz of discontent when he laid out his views on the party.*
buzz off PHRASAL VERB If you say '**buzz off**' to someone, you are telling them to go away; an informal, rude expression. *They told me to buzz off and stop bothering them.*
buzzard /bʌzəd/ **buzzards**
NC A **buzzard** is a large bird of prey.
buzzer /bʌzə/ **buzzers**
NC A **buzzer** is a device that makes a buzzing sound, for example in an alarm clock or an office telephone. *They pressed the buzzer at the gates of the embassy.*
buzz word, buzz words
NC A **buzz word** is a word, expression, or idea which has become fashionable in a particular field, and is being used a lot by the media. *'Community policing' is a buzz word at the moment... The buzz word these days is communication.*
BVI. See Virgin Islands, British.

by /baɪ/
1 PREP If something is done **by** a person or thing, that person or thing does it. *He was brought up by an aunt... I was startled by his anger. ...the use of pocket calculators by schoolchildren.*
2 PREP+ING If you achieve one thing **by** doing another thing, your action enables you to achieve the first thing. *By bribing a nurse I was able to see some files... They were making a living by selling souvenirs to the tourists.*
3 PREP **By** is used to say how something is done. *The money will be paid by cheque... We heard from them by phone... I always go by bus.*
4 PREP If you say that a book, a piece of music, or a painting is **by** someone, you mean that they wrote it or created it. *...three books by a great Australian writer.*
5 PREP Something that is **by** something else is beside it and close to it. *I sat by her bed.*
6 PREP or ADV If something passes **by** you, it moves past without stopping. *People rushed by us... They watched the cars whizzing by.*
7 PREP or ADV If you stop or come **by** someone's house, you visit them; used in informal American English. *You can stop by and you can see it... He came by to take us to Pittsburgh.*
8 PREP If something happens **by** a particular time, it happens at or before that time. *He can be out by seven... By 1940 the number had grown to 185 millions.*
9 PREP If you are **by** yourself, you are alone. If you do something **by** yourself, you do it without anyone helping you. *He was standing by himself in a corner of the room... She did not think she could manage by herself.*
10 PREP Things that are made or sold **by** the million or **by** the dozen are made or sold in those quantities. *Books can be mailed by the dozen.*
11 PREP You use **by** in expressions such as 'day by day' to say that something happens gradually. *The university gets bigger year by year... The children had one by one fallen asleep.*
12 PREP If something increases or decreases **by** a particular amount, that amount is gained or lost. *Its grant is to be cut by more than 40 per cent.*
13 PREP If you hold someone or something **by** a particular part of them, you hold that part. *My mother took me firmly by the hand.*
Byambasüren, Dashiyn /dæʃiːn bjæmbəsuərɛn/
Dashiyn Byambasüren became Prime Minister of Mongolia in 1990. He was Deputy Chairman of the Council of Ministers from 1989 to 1990. Born: 1942.
bye /baɪ/ **byes**
1 '**Bye**' and '**bye-bye**' are ways of saying goodbye; used in informal English. *'OK, see you soon then.'— 'Thanks very much.'—'Bye.'... From me Roberta Symes, bye for now... That's all for this week. Bye bye.*
2 NC In sports, a **bye** is automatic progress to the next stage of a competition, because there are not enough competitors, or because a competitor is not able to take part. *AC Milan received a bye into the second round.*
bye-law. See by-law.
by-election, by-elections
NC A **by-election** is an election that is held to choose a new member of parliament when a member has resigned or died. *...the Party's surprise win in the Eastbourne by-election. ...a parliamentary by-election.*
Byelorussia /bjɛləʊrʌʃə/
The Republic of Belarus became independent of the USSR in 1991. It is located in the west of the former USSR, bordering Poland. Stanislav Shushkevich became President in 1991. In 1991 it joined the Commonwealth of Independent States. Byelorussia produces manufactured goods, oil, and agricultural products. ◆ **Byelorussian** /bjɛləʊrʌʃn/ N, ADJ
■ *per capita GNP:* US$5,960 ■ *religion:* Christianity ■ *language:* Byelorussian ■ *currency:* rouble ■ *capital:* Minsk ■ *population:* 10 million (1990) ■ *size:* 207,600 square kilometres.
bygone /baɪɡɒn/
ADJ ATTRIB **Bygone** means happening or existing a very long time ago; a literary word. *...empires*

established in bygone centuries.

by-law, by-laws; also spelt **bye-law.**
NC A **by-law** is a law made by a local authority which applies only in that authority's area. *...the first city in the country to pass a by-law prohibiting public drinking.*

by-line, by-lines
NC In journalism, a **by-line** is a line after the headline in a newspaper or magazine article, which gives the author's name. *It appeared last week in the San Francisco Examiner under the by-line of Ed Montgomery.*

bypass /baɪpɑːs/ **bypasses, bypassing, bypassed**
1 VO If you **bypass** someone in authority, you avoid asking their permission to do something. *The company decided to bypass the Union and appeal directly to its employees.*
2 VO If you **bypass** a difficulty, you avoid dealing with it. *We can perhaps bypass any possible ethical or practical problems... These new methodologies allow you to bypass that very difficult step.*
3 NC A **bypass** is a main road which takes traffic round the edge of a town rather than through its centre. *...the Oxford bypass. ...building more motorways and bypasses.*
4 VO If you **bypass** a place, you go round it rather than through it. *Rebels appear to have bypassed the camp.*
5 N+N A **bypass** operation is one in which doctors redirect the flow of blood to avoid the heart, often because the heart is diseased or weak. *The former Premier underwent heart bypass surgery in London in September. ...his coronary bypass operation earlier this week.*

by-play
NU **By-play** is something that is happening at the same time as something else, but that is not as important. By-play is very common in drama.

by-product, by-products
1 NC A **by-product** is something which is made during the manufacture or processing of another product. *Oxygen is released as a by-product of the photosynthesis.*
2 NC A **by-product** of an event or situation is an unexpected or unplanned result of it. *A by-product of their meeting was the release of these fourteen men. ...by-products of its brilliantly successful foreign policy.*

byre /baɪə/ **byres**
NC A **byre** is a cowshed; an old-fashioned word.

bystander /baɪstændə/ **bystanders**
NC A **bystander** is a person who is present by chance when something happens, especially in a city street. *...curious bystanders watching from a distance... A number of innocent bystanders were beaten in the process.*

byte /baɪt/ **bytes**
NC A **byte** is a unit of storage in a computer. *...a megabyte of data, which is about the number of bytes in an average novel.*

byway /baɪweɪ/ **byways**
NC A **byway** is a small road which is not used by many cars or people.

byword /baɪwɜːd/ **bywords**
NC+*for* Something that is a **byword** for a particular quality is well known for having that quality. *The department had become a byword for obstinacy and brutality.*

C c

C, c /siː/ **C's, c's**
1 NC **C** is the third letter of the English alphabet.
2 **C** is a written abbreviation for 'century' or 'centuries'. You put 'C' before or after a number which refers to a particular century. ...*living in the C14. ...the 14th C.*
3 **c.** is written in front of a date or number to indicate that it is approximate. **c.** is an abbreviation for 'circa'. *He was born c.834 A.D.*
4 **C** is also a written abbreviation for 'centigrade'. *During the day, temperatures in the desert rise to over 50C.*

cab /kæb/ **cabs**
1 NC A **cab** is a taxi. *All new cabs operating in London will have to be able to accommodate wheelchairs.*
2 NC The **cab** of a lorry is the part in which the driver sits. *The soldier was sitting in the cab of a lorry... Many lorries had flat tyres, cab windows broken or brake and fuel lines cut.*

C.A.B. /siːeɪbiː/ **C.A.B.s**
C.A.B. is an abbreviation for 'Citizens Advice Bureau'. *It began last year when the CAB annual meeting voted to improve services to the 'gay' community.*

cabal /kəbæl/ **cabals**
N COLL A **cabal** is a small group of people who meet secretly, especially for political purposes. ...*a secret cabal of powerful 'insiders'.*

cabaret /kæbəreɪ/ **cabarets**
NCorNU A **cabaret** is a show of dancing, singing, or comedy acts. *The cabaret was just finishing. ...a cabaret artiste. ...a week of theatre, cabaret, music and film.*

cabbage /kæbɪdʒ/ **cabbages**
NCorNU A **cabbage** is a large green leafy vegetable. *Tomatoes and cabbages were still being imported from Miami a few years ago... It's carrots, onions and cabbage mixed together with vinegar, then a few spices.*

cabbie /kæbi/ **cabbies**; also spelt **cabby**.
NC A **cabbie** is a person who drives a taxi; an informal word.

cab driver, cab drivers
NC A **cab driver** is someone who drives a taxi for a living. *When a cab driver is working he's supposed to go anywhere his passenger wants to go... One of the main problems for London cab drivers is stress.*

cabin /kæbɪn/ **cabins**
1 NC A **cabin** is a small room in a boat or plane. ...*the First Class cabin.*
2 NC A **cabin** is also a small wooden house. *Many people are living in shacks or wooden cabins while new housing goes up... Guests stay in luxury log cabins.*

cabin cruiser, cabin cruisers
NC A **cabin cruiser** is a motorboat which has a cabin for people to live or sleep in. *Their cabin cruiser was found anchored about a mile and a half offshore.*

cabinet /kæbɪnət/ **cabinets**
1 N COLL The **Cabinet** is a group of the most senior ministers in a government. *Mr Majid is a member of*

the Iraqi cabinet... Malaysia's prime minister has announced his new cabinet.
2 NC A **cabinet** is a cupboard used for storing things such as medicines or alcoholic drinks. *This is for use in kitchens and to stop kids getting into medicine cabinets.* ● See also **filing cabinet**.

cabinet-maker, cabinet-makers
NC A **cabinet-maker** is a person who makes high-quality wooden furniture.

cable /keɪbl/ **cables, cabling, cabled**
1 NC A **cable** is a strong, thick rope. *Someone had forgotten to untie the ship's mooring cable.*
2 NCorNU A **cable** is also a bundle of electrical wires inside a rubber or plastic covering. *Trees weakened by the hurricane have brought down electricity cables. ...ten metres of electrical cable.*
3 NC A **cable** is also a message that is sent by means of electricity over a long distance, and is printed out when it arrives. *MacArthur sent a cable to Washington advising against the action.*
4 VO If you **cable** a message to someone, you send it to them by cable. ...*a New Year message cabled to all British ships.*

cable car, cable cars
NC A **cable car** is a vehicle for taking people up mountains. It is pulled by a moving cable. ...*holidaymakers trapped in cable cars thirty feet above the ground.*

cable railway, cable railways
NC A **cable railway** is a railway on which the cars are pulled up a steep slope by a moving cable.

cable television
NU **Cable television** is a television system in which signals are sent along wires, rather than by radio waves. *With the expansion of cable television, a Cable Authority was created to regulate that area of broadcasting.*

cache /kæʃ/ **caches**
NC A **cache** is a quantity of things that have been hidden. *Police are questioning a man after the discovery of an arms cache in Belfast.*

cachet /kæʃeɪ/
N SING+SUPP If someone or something has a certain **cachet**, they have a quality which makes people admire them or approve of them. *The visit to Hollywood had given me a certain cachet in her parents' eyes.*

cackle /kækl/ **cackles, cackling, cackled**
VorV-QUOTE If you **cackle**, you laugh in a loud unpleasant way. *She cackled with delight... 'Fools,' she cackled.* ► Also N SING *He gave a malicious cackle.*

cacophony /kəkɒfəni/
N SING You can describe a loud, unpleasant mixture of sounds as a **cacophony**; a literary word. ...*a cacophony of car horns.*

cactus /kæktəs/ **cactuses** or **cacti** /kæktaɪ/
NC A **cactus** is a thick, fleshy desert plant, often with spikes. ...*fields of dry grass and prickly pear cactus... Desert rocks, flowers and cacti are arranged here.*

cad /kæd/ **cads**
NC If you say that a man is a **cad**, you mean that he

deceives other people, especially women, or treats them badly or unfairly; an old-fashioned word. *I thought I could trust you not to behave like a cad.*

cadaver /kədǽvə/ **cadavers**
NC A **cadaver** is a corpse; used in American English.

cadaverous /kədǽvərəs/
ADJ Someone who is **cadaverous** is extremely thin and pale; a literary word. *He was tall and spare, with a cadaverous face.*

caddie /kǽdi/ **caddies, caddying, caddied;** also spelt **caddy.**
NC A **caddie** is a person who carries golf clubs and other equipment for a person playing golf. ► Also v *He was a member of the golf club and we used to caddy for him.*

cadence /kéɪdns/ **cadences**
NC The **cadence** of your voice is the way it goes up and down as you speak; a formal word. *Most of the people here have no difficulty detecting the difference between Noah's smooth deep Kentucky cadences and my own accent.*

cadenza /kədénzə/ **cadenzas**
NC A **cadenza** is a complex solo in a piece of classical music written for an orchestra and a soloist. *This virtuosity shows up particularly in the cadenza.*

cadet /kədét/ **cadets**
NC A **cadet** is a young person who is being trained in the armed forces or the police force. *...a group of young army cadets on a hill walking expedition in Wales.*

cadge /kædʒ/ **cadges, cadging, cadged**
V0 or VA If you **cadge** something from someone, or **cadge** off them, you ask them for food, money, or help, and succeed in getting it; an informal word, used showing disapproval. *He only came to cadge free drinks. ...living by cadging off relatives.*

cadre /kɑ́ːdə/ **cadres**
N COLL A **cadre** is a small group of people who have been specially chosen, trained, and organized for a particular purpose, especially by a political organization. *...the creation of revolutionary cadres in universities and colleges... A cadre of paid workers was recruited from both villages and cities.*

Caesarean /sɪzéəriən/ **Caesareans**
NC A **Caesarean** or a **Caesarean section** is an operation in which a baby is lifted out of a woman's womb through an opening cut in her abdomen. *He was delivered by Caesarean section.*

café /kǽfeɪ/ **cafés;** also written **cafe.**
NC A **café** is a place where you can buy light meals and drinks. *...cafes serving coffee and snacks all day.*

cafeteria /kæfətɪəriə/ **cafeterias**
NC A **cafeteria** is a self-service restaurant in a large shop or workplace. *Cafeterias and gift shops will also be built... I grabbed four oranges from the cafeteria.*

caffeine /kǽfiːn/; also spelt **caffein.**
NU **Caffeine** is a substance found in coffee and tea which makes you more active. *You would be well advised to cut down on drinks with caffeine in them.*

caftan /kǽftæn/ **caftans;** also spelt **kaftan.**
NC A **caftan** is a long loose garment with long sleeves, worn by men in Arab countries, and by women in America and Europe. *...society women in their silk caftans.*

cage /keɪdʒ/ **cages**
1 NC A **cage** is a structure of wire or metal bars in which birds or animals are kept. *They started breeding the parrots in cages and then returning the young ones gradually to the wild.*
2 NC A **cage** is also a structure of wire or metal bars which is used to carry or protect someone or something. *The sack is placed in the cage and lowered.*

caged /keɪdʒd/
ADJ A **caged** bird or animal is inside a cage. *He felt like a caged lion.*

cagey /kéɪdʒi/
ADJ If people are being **cagey**, they are careful not to reveal too much information; an informal word. *Governments are always cagey about policy on such things as currencies.*

cagoule /kəgúːl/ **cagoules**
NC A **cagoule** is a waterproof jacket that you wear over other clothes to prevent them getting wet.

cahoots /kəhúːts/
If someone is **in cahoots with** someone else, they are planning something with them; used showing disapproval. *Their rivals claim they've been in cahoots with the government for a long time.*

cairn /keən/ **cairns**
NC A **cairn** is a pile of stones in the countryside, which has been placed there to guide people or in memory of someone or something.

Cairo /káɪərəʊ/
Cairo is the capital of Egypt and the largest city in Africa. Population: 6,325,000 (1986).

cajole /kədʒə́ʊl/ **cajoles, cajoling, cajoled**
V0 If you **cajole** someone into doing something that they do not want to do, you persuade them to do it. *...tactics used by parents to cajole their children into eating all their food... Britain can do little more than cajole and encourage them to talk to each other.*

cake /keɪk/ **cakes**
1 NC or NU A **cake** is a sweet food made by baking a mixture of flour, eggs, sugar, and fat. *She cut the cake and gave me a piece. ...a slice of cake.*
2 NC A **cake** of soap is a small block of it.
● **Cake** is used in these phrases. ● If something is **a piece of cake**, it is very easy; an informal expression. *Wimbledon will be a piece of cake for me.* ● If things are **selling like hot cakes**, people are buying a lot of them; an informal expression. ● the **icing on the cake**: see **icing**.

caked /keɪkt/
1 ADJ If a substance is **caked**, it has changed into a dry layer or lump. *...dried blood caked in his hair.*
2 ADJ PRED If a surface is **caked** with a substance, it is covered with a solid layer of it. *...heavy farm shoes caked with mud.*

cake mix, cake mixes
NU or NC **Cake mix** is a powder that you can buy which contains all the dry ingredients you need to make a cake.

cake tin, cake tins
1 NC A **cake tin** is a metal container with a lid, which you put a cake into in order to keep it fresh.
2 NC A **cake tin** is also a metal container which you bake a cake in.

cal., cals.
cal. is a written abbreviation for **calorie;** often used on packets of food. *Marvel contains 355 cals (approx) per 100g.*

calamitous /kəlǽmɪtəs/
ADJ A **calamitous** event or situation is very unfortunate or serious; a formal word. *He has taken the chief blame for Bulgaria's calamitous foreign debt.*

calamity /kəlǽməti/ **calamities**
NC A **calamity** is an event that causes a great deal of damage or distress; a formal word. *The world is seeing a whole series of dreadful calamities.*

calcium /kǽlsiəm/
NU **Calcium** is a soft white element found in bones, teeth, and limestone. *Many older women suffer from loss of calcium from the bones.*

calculate /kǽlkjʊleɪt/ **calculates, calculating, calculated**
1 V0, V-REPORT, or V If you **calculate** a number or amount, you work it out by doing some arithmetic. *The number of votes cast will then be calculated... It has been calculated that to repair the Antarctic ozone hole might take between forty to four hundred years... He paused and calculated for a moment.*
2 V0 or V-REPORT If you **calculate** the effects of something, you consider what they will be. *...actions whose consequences can in no way be calculated... Perhaps those last words then were carefully calculated... She calculated that the risks were worth taking.*
3 V-PASS+to-INF If something is **calculated** to have a particular effect, it is done in order to have that effect. *...a cool dignified attitude that was calculated to discourage familiarity.*

calculated /kælkjʊleɪtɪd/
1 ADJ Bad or violent behaviour that is **calculated** is very carefully planned or arranged. *...the deliberate, calculated use of violence to achieve their objectives. ...a calculated act of political irresponsibility.*
2 ADJ ATTRIB A **calculated** risk is one where you are aware of the possible bad consequences but think that the risk is worth taking because of what you will gain if you are successful. *They took a calculated risk by deciding to delay any financial aid.*

calculating /kælkjʊleɪtɪŋ/
ADJ A **calculating** person arranges situations and controls people in order to get what he or she wants; used showing disapproval. *He called him a callous and calculating thug.*

calculation /kælkjʊleɪʃn/ **calculations**
1 NCorNU A **calculation** is something that you think about and work out mathematically. *I did a rapid calculation. ...a technique for quick calculation.*
2 NU **Calculation** is behaviour in which someone deliberately thinks only of themselves and not of other people. *His behaviour seems free of all calculation.*

calculator /kælkjʊleɪtə/ **calculators**
NC A **calculator** is a small electronic device used for doing mathematical calculations. *They were asked questions involving money, time, measurement and graphs and were allowed to use calculators.*

calculus /kælkjʊləs/
NU **Calculus** is a branch of advanced mathematics which deals with variable quantities.

Calcutta /kælkʌtə/
Calcutta is the largest city in India and the capital of West Bengal State. Population: 9,194,000 (1981).

Calderón Fournier, Rafael Angel
/ræfɑːel ænxel kælderɒn fuənjeə/
Rafael Angel Calderón Fournier became President of Costa Rica in 1990. He is the son of Rafael Calderón Guardia, President of Costa Rica from 1940 to 1944. He served as Foreign Minister from 1978 to 1980 and became President of the Social Christian Unity Party (PUSC) in 1983. Born: 1949.

caldron /kɔːldrən/ **caldrons**. See cauldron.

calendar /kæləndə/ **calendars**
1 NC A **calendar** is a chart showing the dates on which the days, weeks, and months of a year fall. *They issued a number of commemorative calendars.*
2 ADJ ATTRIB A **calendar** month is one of the twelve periods of time that a year is divided into. *It costs one hundred dollars per calendar month.*
3 NC A **calendar** is also a list of dates within a year that are important for a particular organization or activity. *...a major event in the theatrical calendar.*
4 N SING If you have a **calendar** for something you want to achieve, you have planned to complete various stages of it by particular dates. *The delegates discussed a calendar for the redeployment of troops.*

calf /kɑːf/ **calves** /kɑːvz/
1 NC A **calf** is a young cow. *...a very shaggy Highland cow and calf.*
2 NC Some other young animals, such as young elephants, giraffes, and whales, are also called calves... *a young calf elephant.*
3 NC Your **calves** are the backs of your legs between your ankles and knees. *A calf injury forced him to withdraw from several matches.*

Calfa, Marián /mærjæn tʃælfə/
Marián Calfa, of the Civic Democratic Union—Public Against Violence Party, became Prime Minister of Czechoslovakia in 1989.

caliber /kæləbə/. See calibre.

calibrate /kæləbreɪt/ **calibrates, calibrating, calibrated**; a technical term.
VO If you **calibrate** an instrument or tool, you adjust it or mark it so that you can use it to measure something accurately. *It's very easy to calibrate the machine so that you know what the tension should be.*
♦ **calibrated** ADJ *...a calibrated glass beaker.*

calibre /kæləbə/ **calibres**; spelt **caliber** in American English.
1 NU+SUPP The **calibre** of a person is their ability and intelligence, especially when these are of a high standard. *...directors of the right calibre.*

2 NC+SUPP The **calibre** of a gun is the width of the inside of its barrel. *...a medium calibre machine gun.*

calico /kælɪkəʊ/
NU **Calico** is plain white fabric made from cotton.

caliper /kælɪpə/. See calliper.

Caliph /keɪlɪf/ **Caliphs**; also spelt Calif.
NC A **Caliph** was a Muslim ruler. *...Omar, the second Caliph, third after Muhammad the Prophet.*

calisthenics /kælɪsθenɪks/. See callisthenics.

call /kɔːl/ **calls, calling, called**
1 VOC If someone or something is **called** a particular name, that is their name or title. *...an Austrian called Andreas Sommer... They hope to raise one hundred and twenty five thousand pounds for a charity called 'Homes for the Homeless'... Dietsky Mir, or Children's World, as it is called, is just a few steps from the Kremlin.*
2 VOC If you **call** people or situations something, you use a particular word or phrase to describe them. *President Nixon called his opponents traitors... He told them to resist what he called the IRA's terror campaign... He calls his book a personal report rather than a biography.*
3 VO If you **call** a meeting, you arrange for it to take place. *President Reagan has called a meeting of his senior foreign policy advisers... The 12 nation EC has called an emergency meeting of foreign ministers tomorrow... They forced President Gorbachev to call an emergency meeting to discuss the state of the nation.*
4 NCorNU A **call** for something is a demand or desire for it to be done or provided. *Representatives will today debate a call for strike action over pay... There is little call for his services.*
5 VO, V-QUOTE, orV A If you **call** someone's name, you say it loudly to get their attention. *I could hear a voice calling my name... 'Edward!' she called... Children are as likely to call for their father as for their mother.*
6 VOorV If you **call** someone, you telephone them. *He promised to call me soon... 'I want to speak to Mr Landy, please.'—'Who is calling?'*
7 VO To **call** someone also means to ask them to come to you by shouting to them or telephoning them. *When Margaret collapsed, I called the doctor.*
8 NC When you make a phone **call**, you phone someone. *Yesterday the BBC received a phone call from Basil Davidson.*
9 V A If you **call** somewhere, you make a short visit there. *We called at the Vicarage... In April, Mr Brown called at her flat in Sussex.*
10 NC If you pay a **call** on someone, you visit them briefly. *Doctors have no time these days to make regular calls.*
11 NC A bird's **call** is the sound that it makes. *The call is unique to each bird.*
12 to **call** it a day: see day.

call for PHRASAL VERB 1 If you **call for** someone or something, you go to collect them. *I'll call for you about eight... I called at the station for my luggage.*
2 If you **call for** an action, you demand that it should happen. *The declaration called for an immediate ceasefire.* 3 If something **calls for** a particular action or quality, it needs it in order to be successful. *Controlling a class calls for all your skill as a teacher.*

call in PHRASAL VERB If you **call** someone **in**, you ask them to come and do something for you. *We called in the police.*

call off PHRASAL VERB If you **call** something **off**, you cancel it. *We had to decide whether classes should be called off.*

call on PHRASAL VERB 1 If you **call on** someone to do something or **call upon** them to do it, you appeal to them to do it; a formal use. *The Opposition called on the Prime Minister to stop the arms deal.* 2 To **call on** someone also means to pay them a short visit.

call out PHRASAL VERB 1 If you **call** something **out**, you shout it. *'Where shall I put them?' I called out. ...calling out to the porter that she'd arrived.* 2 If you **call** someone **out**, you order them to come to help, especially in an emergency. *The National Guard has been called out.*

call up PHRASAL VERB **1** If you **call** someone **up**, you telephone them; used in American English. *I called them up and asked what it was like.* **2** If someone is **called up**, they are ordered to join the armed forces. *Retired officers have been called up.*

call upon PHRASAL VERB See **call on.**

Callaghan, James /dʒeɪmz kæləhən/
James Callaghan was Prime Minister of the United Kingdom from 1976 to 1979. He is a member of the Labour Party. He was the MP for South Cardiff from 1945 to 1950, for South East Cardiff from 1950 to 1983, and for Cardiff South and Penarth from 1983 to 1987. He served as Chancellor of the Exchequer from 1964 to 1967, Home Secretary from 1967 to 1970, and Foreign Secretary from 1974 to 1976. He was the leader of the Labour Party from 1976 to 1980. In 1987 he was created Baron Callaghan of the City of Cardiff. Born: 1912.

call box, call boxes
NC A **call box** is a telephone box. *They telephoned the West Berlin police from a call box.*

Callejas, Rafael Leonardo /ræfaːel leɪɒŋɡːdəʊ kæljexæs/
Rafael Leonardo Callejas became President of Honduras in 1990. He served as Minister of Agriculture and Natural Resources from 1978 to 1981. He was President of the National Party (PN) from 1987 to 1990. Born: 1943.

caller /kɔːlə/ **callers**
1 NC A **caller** is someone who telephones you. *The anonymous caller claimed to represent the 'Organisation of Jihad Brigades'.* **2** NC A **caller** is also a person who comes to see you for a short visit. *I had a lot of callers when I came home from hospital.*

call girl, call girls
NC A **call girl** is a prostitute who makes appointments by telephone. *She was lucratively rewarded for performing services as a high class call girl.*

calligraphy /kəlɪɡrəfi/
NU **Calligraphy** is the art of producing beautiful handwriting often using a brush or a special pen. *Other examples of fine calligraphy include anthologies of poetry and imperial documents. ...fine examples of Islamic calligraphy.*

calling /kɔːlɪŋ/ **callings**
NC A **calling** is a profession or career, especially one which involves helping other people. *Teaching is said to be a worthwhile calling.*

calliper /kælɪpə/ **callipers**; also spelt **caliper.**
1 N PL **Callipers** are instruments that are used to measure the size of things. They consist of two long thin pieces of metal joined together at one end by a hinge. **2** NC **Callipers** are also devices for supporting a person's leg when they cannot walk properly. They consist of metal rods that are held together by straps.

callisthenics /kælɪsθenɪks/; also spelt **calisthenics.**
N PL **Callisthenics** are simple light exercises that you do to keep fit and healthy. *After a few days of doing calisthenics together, we added some simple karate exercises.*

callous /kæləs/
ADJ A **callous** person or action is cruel and shows no concern for other people. *He called him a callous and calculating thug... The local priest described Mr McAnespie's killing as callous.*

calloused /kæləst/
ADJ A foot or hand that is **calloused** is covered in calluses. *My feet became blackened, tough, split and calloused.*

callow /kæləʊ/
ADJ A young person who is **callow** has very little experience or knowledge of the way they should behave as an adult. *...a very callow youth.*

call sign, call signs
NC A **call sign** is the letters and numbers which identify a person, vehicle, or organization that is broadcasting on the radio or sending messages by radio. *...a Soviet aircraft with the call sign Aeroflot 38000.*

call-up, call-ups
1 N+N If a person gets their **call-up** papers, they receive an official order to join the armed forces. *A large number of men have received call-up papers and reported for military duty.* **2** NC A **call-up** is a time when people are officially ordered to report for service in the armed forces. *...the annual call-up for the Soviet forces.*

callus /kæləs/ **calluses**
NC A **callus** is an area of unwanted, unnaturally thick skin, usually on the palms of your hands or the soles of your feet, which has been caused by rubbing.

calm /kɑːm/ **calmer, calmest; calms, calming, calmed**
1 ADJ A **calm** person does not show any worry or excitement. *Gary was a calm and reasonable man... Sit down and keep calm.* ◆ **calmly** ADV *She calmly wiped the blood away.* ◆ **calmness** *Mrs Thatcher won admiration for her calmness, courage and determination.* **2** NU **Calm** is a state of being quiet and peaceful. *...the calm of the vicarage.* **3** ADJ If the weather or sea is **calm**, there is no wind and so the trees are not moving or the water is not moving. *...a calm, sunny evening.* **4** VO If you **calm** someone or **calm** their fears, you do something to make them less upset, worried, or excited. *Mitchell tried to calm her, but she didn't hear him.*

calm down PHRASAL VERB If you **calm down** or if someone or something **calms** you **down**, you become less upset, excited, or lively. *'Calm down. Let me explain.'... He had been provided with drugs to calm him down.*

Calor Gas /kæləgæs/
NU **Calor Gas** is gas that is sold in portable metal containers. You can use it for cooking and heating; Calor Gas is a trademark. *...a little Calor Gas stove.*

calorie /kæləri/ **calories**
NC A **calorie** is a unit of measurement for the energy value of food. *...a diet of only 1,700 calories a day.*

calorific /kælərɪfɪk/
ADJ ATTRIB **Calorific** means relating to calories or heat; a technical term. *This process gives the fuel a better calorific value.*

calumny /kæləmni/ **calumnies**
N U or NC **Calumny** or a **calumny** is an untrue statement made about someone in order to reduce other people's respect and admiration for them; a formal word. *The Lord Chancellor became the target for further calumny... Mandela regarded this as an outrageous calumny.*

calve /kɑːv/ **calves, calving, calved**
1 V When a cow **calves**, it gives birth to a calf. **2** **Calves** is the plural of **calf.**

calypso /kəlɪpsəʊ/ **calypsos**
NC A **calypso** is a song about something topical or interesting, sung in a style which comes from the West Indies. *This year's calypso competition was won with a song about the government.*

cam /kæm/ **cams**
NC A **cam** is a device or part of an engine which is designed to change circular motion into up and down motion or side to side motion. *There's no cam to open the valve... When I checked it out, the cam wasn't turning.*

camaraderie /kæmərɑːdəri/
NU **Camaraderie** is a feeling of trust and friendship among a group of people; a formal word. *...scenes of much heavy drinking, camaraderie and also bitter rivalry. ...the camaraderie that exists among amateur astronomers.*

camber /kæmbə/ **cambers**
NC A **camber** is a gradual downward slope from the centre of a road to each side of it so that water flows off the road. *The road-builders dug out earth for the camber.*

Cambodia /kæmbəʊdiə/
The State of Cambodia is a country in south-east Asia. It became part of French Indochina in the 19th century and was occupied by Japan from 1940 until 1945. In 1953 Prince Norodom Sihanouk became the ruler of Cambodia, when it became independent from France. He was overthrown in 1970. The Khmer Rouge

established a Communist government in 1975. Pol Pot was Prime Minister from 1976 until 1978. Vietnam invaded Cambodia in 1978 and established the People's Republic of Kampuchea in 1979, which since 1989 has been called the State of Cambodia. The sole party from 1979 to 1991 was the Kampuchean People's Revolutionary Party (KPRP). In 1991 it was renamed the Cambodian People's Party (CPP). Heng Samrin became President in 1979 and General Secretary of the KPRP in 1981. Hun Sen became Prime Minister in 1985. Most UN members did not recognize the government established by Vietnam's invasion, but rather the rival National Government of Cambodia, led by Prince Sihanouk in alliance with the Khmers Rouges. A peace treaty was signed in 1991 in Paris, and Prince Sihanouk returned to Cambodia to head a new government, ruling with Heng Samrin and Hun Sen. Cambodia exports rubber and timber. The civil war has substantially destroyed its economy.
♦ **Cambodian** /kæmbˈɔ̌ðiən/ N, ADJ
▪ *per capita GDP:* approximately US$78 ▪ *religion:* Buddhism (mainly Theravada) ▪ *language:* Khmer (official) ▪ *currency:* riel ▪ *capital:* Phnom Penh ▪ *population:* 8 million (1989) ▪ *size:* 181,035 square kilometres.

camcorder /kæmkɔːdə/ **camcorders**
NC A **camcorder** is a small video camera and recorder that you can hold in one hand. *If there's ever a big tornado or an earthquake, somebody's always got that camcorder ready.*

came /keɪm/
Came is the past tense of come.

camel /kæml/ **camels**
NC A **camel** is a large animal which lives in the desert. It has a long neck and one or two humps on its back. *I met him on the farm where he keeps his herd of camels.*

camel hair
NU **Camel hair** is soft, thick woollen cloth, usually creamy brown in colour, which is used especially for making coats. *He wore a camel hair cape over one shoulder.*

camellia /kəmiːliə/ **camellias**
NC A **camellia** is a tall shrub that has shiny leaves and large white, pink, or red flowers similar to a rose. *You would not be able to propagate a camellia unless you'd got warmth for the roots.*

cameo /kæmiəʊ/ **cameos**
1 NC A **cameo** is a short descriptive piece of acting or writing. *He gave cameos of debates with exquisite touches of irony.*
2 NC A **cameo** is also a brooch with a raised stone design on a flat stone of another colour. *At the centre of the gems is a cameo of the Emperor Augustus... She was wearing a cameo brooch which had been their mother's.*

camera /kæmərə/ **cameras**
NC A **camera** is a piece of equipment used for taking photographs or for making a film. *...a picture of the hot spring taken by a highly sensitive camera.*

cameraman /kæmrəmæn/ **cameramen**
NC A **cameraman** is a person who operates a television or film camera. *...a unique film portrait of North Korea, made by cameraman Erik Durschmied.*

camera-shy
ADJ Someone who is **camera-shy** is nervous and uncomfortable about being filmed or about having their photograph taken.

Cameroon /kæmərʊːn/
The **Republic of Cameroon** is a country in western Africa. It was a German colony from 1884 until 1916, when it was divided into French and British Cameroon. French Cameroon became independent in 1960. In 1961 part of British Cameroon merged with Nigeria and the rest became part of the Republic of Cameroon. A one-party state was established in 1972, with the Cameroon People's Democratic Movement (RDPC) as the ruling party. Paul Biya became President in 1982. Political parties were legalized in 1990. Cameroon exports oil and gas, coffee, and cocoa. It is a member of the Organization of African Unity.
♦ **Cameroonian** /kæmərʊːniən/ N, ADJ

▪ *per capita GNP:* US$1,010 ▪ *religion:* Christianity, animism, Islam ▪ *language:* French and English (official) ▪ *currency:* CFA franc ▪ *capital:* Yaoundé ▪ *largest city:* Douala ▪ *population:* 12 million (1989) ▪ *size:* 475,442 square kilometres.

camomile /kæməmaɪl/; also spelt **chamomile**.
NU **Camomile** is a scented plant with flowers that look like daisies. It is often used to make herbal tea. *Camomile is a plant that is supposed to calm the nerves.*

camouflage /kæməflɑːʒ/ **camouflages, camouflaging, camouflaged**
1 NU **Camouflage** consists of things such as leaves, branches, or paint. It is used to make military forces and equipment look like their surroundings, so that it is difficult for the enemy to see them. *Troops piled out of the planes in full battledress and facial camouflage... As darkness fell, the crews draped camouflage nets over the tanks and dug trenches alongside.*
2 VO To **camouflage** military forces and equipment means to use camouflage to make them difficult to see. *To camouflage a large ship at sea is impossible.*
♦ **camouflaged** ADJ *The gun crews were in camouflaged bunkers.*
3 VO To **camouflage** something also means to hide it or make it appear to be something different. *A good accountant can camouflage troubles within his company... Some advertisers camouflage the fact that they've got something to sell.* ♦ **camouflaged** ADJ *...the camouflaged hot-water pipes.*
4 NU **Camouflage** is also the way in which some animals are coloured and shaped to blend in with their natural surroundings. *The snake's skin had the colours and patterns necessary for perfect camouflage.*

camp /kæmp/ **camps, camping, camped**
1 NCorNU A **camp** is a group of tents or temporary buildings for people to live in for a short time. *Large crowds took part in protests in the city centre and in refugee camps around the capital... We set up camp near the bay.*
2 V If you **camp** somewhere, you stay there in a tent or caravan. *I camped in the hills.*
3 NC+SUPP You can use **camp** to refer to a group of people with a particular idea or belief. *The realignment produced two clear-cut camps, reformists and reactionaries.*
4 See also **camping, concentration camp.**

camp out PHRASAL VERB If you **camp out**, you sleep outdoors, usually in a tent. *They were unprepared for camping out in the desert... Thousands of demonstrators again camped out overnight.*

campaign /kæmpeɪn/ **campaigns, campaigning, campaigned**
1 NC A **campaign** is a set of activities planned to achieve something such as social or political change. *...the campaign against world hunger... An election campaign for leader has started sooner than expected.*
2 VA To **campaign** means to carry out activities planned to achieve something such as social or political change. *He campaigned for political reform.*
3 NC In a war, a **campaign** is a series of planned movements by armed forces. *...a massive aerial campaign against Iraq.*

campaigner /kæmpeɪnə/ **campaigners**
NC A **campaigner** is a person who campaigns for social or political change. *Boaks is an energetic campaigner in the cause of road safety. ...anti-apartheid campaigners.* ● If you describe someone as an **old campaigner**, you mean that they have had a lot of experience in a particular activity.

camp bed, camp beds
NC A **camp bed** is a small folding bed. *The refugees spent the night on camp beds.*

camper /kæmpə/ **campers**
1 NC A **camper** is a person who goes camping.
2 NC A **camper** is also a van equipped with beds and cooking equipment.

camp follower, camp followers
1 NC A **camp follower** is someone who does not officially belong to a particular group or organization but who is interested in it and supports it, often

because it makes them feel important. *She wanted to be more than a hanger-on, a camp follower: she wanted to be a full member.*
2 NC A **camp follower** is also a person who obtains money by travelling with a group of people such as an army and doing jobs for them.

campground /ˈkæmpgraʊnd/ **campgrounds**
NC A **campground** is a campsite; used in American English. *The campgrounds he stopped at were filled with people.*

camping /ˈkæmpɪŋ/
NU If you go **camping** you go somewhere and stay in a tent there, usually as a holiday. *I don't like camping... We ask people not to light fires or use camping stoves.* ● See also **camp**.

campion /ˈkæmpɪən/ **campions**
NC A **campion** is a plant that grows wild in Europe and has red, pink, or white flowers.

campsite /ˈkæmpsaɪt/ **campsites**
NC A **campsite** is a place where people can stay in tents or caravans. *The Eastbourne area is popular with holidaymakers and there are hundreds of guesthouses, campsites and hotels in the vicinity.*

campus /ˈkæmpəs/ **campuses**
NCorNU A university or college **campus** is the area of land containing its main buildings. *...the university campus... How many students live on campus?*

camshaft /ˈkæmʃɑːft/ **camshafts**
NC A **camshaft** is a part of an engine consisting of a rod with one or more cams attached to it.

can, cans, canning, canned; pronounced /kən/ or /kæn/ for the meanings in paragraphs 1 to 5 and /kæn/ for the meanings in paragraphs 6 to 8. For the meanings in paragraphs 1 to 5, the form **cannot** is used in negative statements; the usual spoken form of **cannot** is **can't** /kɑːnt/. **Could** is sometimes considered to be the past tense of the modal **can**, but in this dictionary the two words are dealt with separately. The form **cans** is the plural of the noun, and the forms **cans, canning** and **canned** are used for the verb in paragraph 8.
1 MODAL If you **can** do something, it is possible for you to do it or you are allowed to do it. *You can borrow that pen if you want to... Many people cannot afford telephones... 'Will you stay for lunch?'—'I can't.'... There are only eight listed companies whose shares can be bought and sold.*
2 MODAL If you **can** do something, you have the skill or ability to do it. *Some people can ski better than others... My wife can't sew... Larger insects can maintain continuous flight for longer than smaller insects.*
3 MODAL You use **can** in questions as a polite way of asking someone to do something. *Can you tell me the time?... Can I have my book now please?*
4 MODAL If you say that something **cannot** be true or **cannot** happen, you mean that you feel sure that it is not true or will not happen. *This cannot be the whole story... He can't have said that... He can hardly have read the report with much care.*
5 MODAL You use **can't** and **can...not** in questions in order to ask people to do something, and sometimes to show you are annoyed or unhappy. *Can't we talk about it?... Can't you keep your voice down?... Can you not remember any other examples?*
6 NC A **can** is a sealed metal container for food, drink, or paint. *...rusty old beer cans... Storing these empty drinks cans might cause problems as they take up a considerable amount of space.*
7 NC You also use **can** to refer to a can and its contents, or to the contents only. *...cans of tuna... We are allowed three cans of beer each and half a bottle of wine... Baked beans form the most popular snack meal in Great Britain, which consumes over a million cans a day.*
8 VO When food or drink is **canned**, it is put into a metal container and sealed. *The asparagus is trimmed and peeled in the factory before it is canned.*
◆ **canned** ADJ *...canned beer... There is increased buying of canned food, batteries and candles.*
9 See also **canned**.

Canada /ˈkænədə/
Canada is a country in North America. It is the second

largest country in the world. It is a member of the Commonwealth, NATO, and the Organization of American States. Brian Mulroney, of the Progressive Conservative Party (PCP), became Prime Minister in 1984. Canada exports paper, timber, and grain.
◆ **Canadian** /kəˈneɪdɪən/ N, ADJ
■ *per capita GNP:* US\$16,760 ■ *religion:* Christianity ■ *language:* English, French ■ *currency:* dollar ■ *capital:* Ottawa ■ *largest city:* Toronto ■ *population:* 26 million (1989) ■ *size:* 9,215,430 square kilometres.

canal /kəˈnæl/ **canals**
1 NC A **canal** is a long, narrow man-made stretch of water. *The bus was crossing a bridge over the canal... It used to put huge sums of money into big irrigation schemes with massive canals and dams.*
2 See also **alimentary canal**.

canapé /ˈkænəpeɪ/ **canapés**
NC A **canapé** is a small piece of biscuit or toast with meat, cheese, or other savoury food on top. Canapés are often served with drinks at parties.

canard /kæˈnɑːd, kəˈnɑːd/ **canards**
NC A **canard** is an idea or a piece of information that is false. Canards are often made up and spread deliberately, sometimes in order to discredit someone or their work. *The resolutions contained innumerable canards and falsehoods.*

canary /kəˈneəri/ **canaries**
NC **Canaries** are small yellow birds that sing. They are often kept as pets.

Canberra /ˈkænbərə/
Canberra is the capital of Australia. Population: 274,000 (1985).

can-can /ˈkænkæn/
N SING The **can-can** is a dance in which women kick their legs in the air to fast music. *...the frilled skirts of a can-can dancer.*

cancel /ˈkænsl/ **cancels, cancelling, cancelled;** spelt **canceling, canceled** in American English.
1 VO If you **cancel** something that has been arranged, you stop it from happening. *The performances were cancelled because the leading man was ill.*
◆ **cancellation** /ˌkænsəˈleɪʃn/ **cancellations** NUorNC *The cancellation of his visit has disappointed many people... Cancellation of export contracts will have a serious impact on the economy.*
2 VO If you **cancel** something such as a hotel room or theatre seat, you tell the management that you no longer want it. *Any holidays already booked must be cancelled.* ◆ **cancellation, cancellations** NC *I've had two cancellations already this morning. ...a cancellation charge.*
3 VO If you **cancel** something such as a cheque or a business arrangement, you cause it to be no longer valid. *Military sales and ministerial contacts have already been cancelled... Their outstanding debts will be cancelled.*
cancel out PHRASAL VERB If two things **cancel** each other **out**, they have opposite effects which combine to produce no real effect. *These political factions cancelled each other out... Gary Bannister's goal was cancelled out by Chris Waddle's.*

cancer /ˈkænsə/ **cancers**
NUorNC **Cancer** is a serious illness in which abnormal body cells increase, producing growths. *Breast cancer in women this young is extremely uncommon. ...the body's ability to identify and destroy cancer cells... Most cancers are preventable.*

cancerous /ˈkænsərəs/
ADJ **Cancerous** growths are the result of cancer. *She refused to have an operation to remove a cancerous growth.*

candelabra /ˌkændəˈlɑːbrə/ **candelabrum** /ˌkændəˈlɑːbrəm/ **candelabras**. The singular form can be either **candelabra** or **candelabrum** and the plural form can be either **candelabra** or **candelabras**.
NC A **candelabra** is an ornamental holder for two or more candles. *...a splendid great brass candelabra. ...a heavy bronze candelabrum. ...two giant candelabra.*

candid /ˈkændɪd/
ADJ Speech or behaviour that is **candid** is honest and open. *She described the talks as friendly, businesslike*

and candid. ...candid comments.

candidacy /kǽndɪdəsi/
NU Someone's **candidacy** is their position of being a candidate in an election. *He is due to announce his candidacy for the presidency today.*

candidate /kǽndɪdət/ **candidates**
1 NC A **candidate** is someone who is being considered for a position, for example in an election or for a job. *There are eight candidates for president. ...a parliamentary candidate.*
2 NC A **candidate** is also someone taking an examination. *Sixty percent of the candidates failed.*
3 NC A **candidate** can also be a person or thing regarded as suitable for a particular purpose. *Small companies are likely candidates for take-over.*

candidature /kǽndɪdətʃə/
NU Someone's **candidature** is their candidacy; a formal word. ...the controversial tactics of people supporting his candidature.

candidly /kǽndɪdli/
1 ADV If you speak **candidly** to someone, you speak honestly and do not try to hide anything. *She answered his questions fully and candidly.*
2 ADV SEN You sometimes use **candidly** to make it clear that you are expressing your honest opinion, even though it may be slightly indiscreet. *Candidly, Daniel, I hoped I might manage to avoid going to her party this time.*

candied /kǽndid/
ADJ **Candied** fruit or other food has a covering of sugar or has been cooked in sugar syrup in order to preserve it. ...currants and candied peel.

candle /kǽndl/ **candles**
NC A **candle** is a stick of hard wax with a wick through the middle. The lighted wick gives a flame that provides light. *Next time you light a candle, have a look at the flame.*

candlelight /kǽndllaɪt/
NU **Candlelight** is the light from a candle. *She was reading a book by candlelight.*

candlelit /kǽndllɪt/
ADJ A room or table that is **candlelit** is lit by the light of candles. ...a little candlelit restaurant.

candlestick /kǽndlstɪk/ **candlesticks**
NC A **candlestick** is a holder for a candle.

candour /kǽndə/; spelt **candor** in American English.
NU **Candour** is the quality of speaking honestly and openly about things. *He covered a wide range of topics with unusual candour.*

candy /kǽndi/ **candies**
NCorNU A **candy** is a sweet; used in American English. *There was a bowl of candies on his desk... You eat too much candy.*

candy floss
NU **Candy floss** is a large soft mass of pink or white sugar threads which is put on a stick and eaten, usually out of doors.

candy-striped
ADJ **Candy-striped** cloth has narrow alternate white and coloured stripes, especially white and pink.

cane /keɪn/ **canes, caning, caned**
1 NU **Cane** is the long, hollow stems of a plant such as bamboo. ...fields of tall sugar cane.
2 NU **Cane** is also strips of cane used for weaving. *The rattan palm is widely used for making cane furniture.*
3 NC A **cane** is a long narrow stick. *They assaulted them with hockey sticks and bamboo canes... Attempts to escape are punished by strokes of a cane.*
4 N SING When schoolchildren used to be given the **cane**, they were hit with a cane as a punishment. *I got the cane for smoking.*
5 VO If someone **is caned,** he or she is hit with a cane as a punishment. *They have been told that unless they leave within two weeks, they will be caned, imprisoned and then deported.*

canine /keɪnaɪn/
ADJ ATTRIB **Canine** means relating to or resembling a dog. *Aggression is a normal and natural part of canine behaviour.*

canister /kǽnɪstə/ **canisters**
NC A **canister** is a metal container. ...a plant intended

to build canisters to carry poisonous gas.

canker /kǽŋkə/ **cankers**
1 NC+SUPP A **canker** is something evil that spreads and affects things or people; a formal use. *There is no time to lose in cutting out the Nazi canker... Hypocrisy is the canker in the soul of these people.*
2 NU **Canker** is a disease which affects the mouth and ears of animals and people, spreading quickly and making the skin sore.
3 NU **Canker** is also a disease which affects the wood of shrubs and trees, making the outer layer peel away to expose the inside of the stem.

cannabis /kǽnəbɪs/
NU **Cannabis** is a drug which some people smoke. It is illegal in many countries. *Customs officers seized about two tons of cannabis.*

canned /kǽnd/
1 ADJ **Canned** music, laughter, or applause on the television or radio has been recorded beforehand and is added to the programme to make it sound as if there is a live audience.
2 See also **can.**

cannery /kǽnəri/ **canneries**
NC A **cannery** is a factory where food is canned. *They will be able to carry out unannounced inspections of canneries around the world.*

cannibal /kǽnɪbl/ **cannibals**
NC A **cannibal** is a person who eats human flesh. ...spear-carrying primitive cannibals.

cannibalism /kǽnɪbəlɪzəm/
NU If a person eats human flesh, or an animal eats another animal of the same species as itself, this act is referred to as **cannibalism**. *He was charged with conspiracy, murder and cannibalism... They were forced to practise cannibalism in order to survive.*

cannibalize /kǽnɪbəlaɪz/ **cannibalizes, cannibalizing, cannibalized;** also spelt **cannibalise.**
VO If you **cannibalize** a machine or vehicle, you take parts from it in order to repair another machine or vehicle. *Parts are frequently cannibalised from one aircraft to put on another.*

cannon /kǽnən/ **cannons.** The plural form can be either **cannons** or **cannon.**
1 NC A **cannon** is a large gun on wheels, which used to be used in battles. ...a full range of the weaponry they used, from bows and arrows to cannons and muskets.
2 NC A **cannon** is also a heavy automatic gun, especially one fired from an aircraft. *The troops have dug themselves in with machine-guns, mortars and cannon.* ● See also **water cannon.**
3 **loose cannon:** see **loose.**

cannon ball, cannon balls
NC A **cannon ball** is a heavy metal ball that used to be fired from a cannon.

cannon fodder
NU Soldiers who were expected to fight in battles in which large numbers of people would be killed were sometimes referred to as **cannon fodder**, especially in the First World War. *These people are cannon fodder in rivalries with bordering states.*

cannot /kǽnɒt, kənɒt/
Cannot is the negative form of **can.**

canny /kǽni/ **cannier, canniest**
ADJ Someone who is **canny** is clever and able to think quickly. *He has again shown himself to be a canny politician.*

canoe /kənúː/ **canoes**
NC A **canoe** is a small, narrow boat which you move through the water by using a paddle. *He spent more than thirty years braving the dangers of the Amazon, travelling by canoe.*

canoeing /kənúːɪŋ/
NU **Canoeing** is the sport of racing and performing tests of skill in canoes. *The women's canoeing brought another 3 gold medals for China.*

canon /kǽnən/ **canons**
1 TITLEorNC A **canon** is one of the clergy on the staff of a cathedral. *Canon Moss said the cathedral was in one of the poorest areas of Britain... A number of women have already been made rural deans and canons.*
2 NC+SUPP A **canon** is also a basic rule or principle; a

formal use. *According to the canons of British constitutional practice, the Prime Minister is regarded as 'first among equals' in relation to the cabinet.*

canonize /kænənaɪz/ **canonizes, canonizing, canonized;** also spelt **canonise.**
vo If a dead person is **canonized**, it is officially announced that he or she is a saint; used especially in the Catholic Church. *Two years after his death the bishop was canonised.*

canon law
NU **Canon law** is the law of the Christian church. It has authority only over the church and its members. *Canon law decreed that adultery was as reprehensible for a husband as for a wife.*

canoodle /kənuːdl/ **canoodles, canoodling, canoodled**
v If two people are **canoodling**, they are kissing and cuddling each other a lot; an informal word. *Over in the corner a couple sat canoodling.*

can-opener, can-openers
NC A **can-opener** is a the same as a **tin-opener.** *...a hand operated can-opener.*

canopy /kænəpi/ **canopies**
1 NC A **canopy** is a decorated cover above something such as a bed or throne. *The Prince and Princess were taking their seats beneath a red and white canopy.*
2 NC+SUPP You can also use **canopy** to refer to a layer of something that covers an area, for example branches and leaves at the top of a forest. *The leaves created a dense canopy that cut out much of the light.*

can't /kɑːnt/
Can't is the usual spoken form of 'cannot'.

cantankerous /kæntæŋkərəs/
ADJ Someone who is **cantankerous** is always finding things to argue or complain about. *Their boredom made them quarrelsome and cantankerous.*

cantata /kæntɑːtə/ **cantatas**
NC A **cantata** is a fairly short musical work for singers and instruments. *He sang arias from Bach cantatas.*

canteen /kæntiːn/ **canteens**
NC A **canteen** is a place in a factory, office, or shop where the workers can have meals. *She works as a cook in a factory canteen... The survey found a wide variation in the prices charged for canteen food.*

canter /kæntə/ **canters, cantering, cantered**
v When a horse **canters**, it moves at a speed between a gallop and a trot. *She heard the sound of his horse cantering up the sandy path.* ▶ Also N SING *It broke into an easy canter.*

canticle /kæntɪkl/ **canticles**
NC A **canticle** is a short religious song, especially one that uses words taken from the Bible.

canto /kæntəu/ **cantos**
NC A **canto** is one of the main sections of a long poem. *Back in England, Byron published the first two cantos of what was to be one of his major works.*

canton /kænton/ **cantons**
NC A **canton** is a political or administrative region in some countries, for example Switzerland. *Which canton is Zurich in?*

canvas /kænvəs/ **canvases**
1 NU **Canvas** is strong, heavy cloth used for making tents, sails, and bags. *They were frantically filling their canvas hold-alls with bargains.*
2 If you are living and sleeping **under canvas**, you are living and sleeping in a tent. *They'll be living under canvas until they can find work and housing.*
3 NUorNC A **canvas** is also a piece of canvas on which an oil painting is done. It can also refer to the painting itself. *...oil paintings on canvas. ...the canvases of Hieronymus Bosch.*

canvass /kænvəs/ **canvasses, canvassing, canvassed**
1 v If you **canvass** for a particular person or political party, you try to persuade people to vote for them. *He had canvassed for Mr Foot in the leadership election.* ◆ **canvassing** NU *...house-to-house canvassing.*
2 vo If you **canvass** opinion, you find out how people feel about something. *King Hussein has already visited Iraq and Kuwait to canvass Arab opinion.*

canyon /kænjən/ **canyons**
NC A **canyon** is a long, narrow valley with very steep

sides. *...the Grand Canyon... We cross the river through a narrow canyon then climb onto a plateau of acacia trees.*

cap /kæp/ **caps, capping, capped**
1 NC A **cap** is a flat hat, usually with a peak at the front. Caps are often worn as part of a uniform. *The soldiers were wearing crisply pressed green suits, white shirts and peaked caps.*
2 NC When a sports person represents their country in a team game such as football, rugby, or cricket, you can say that they have been awarded a **cap**. *Goalkeeper Andy Goram will earn his sixth cap when he plays for Scotland tomorrow... John Bentley will win his first England cap against Ireland in Dublin.*
3 V-PASS When a sports person is **capped**, he or she is chosen to represent their country in a team game such as football, rugby, or cricket. *Sansom has been capped 86 times by England.* ◆ **capped** ADJ *...Australia's most capped rugby union player, Simon Poidevin.*
4 NC+SUPP You can refer to someone who is representing their country in a team game such as football, rugby, or cricket for the first time as a new **cap**. *...new Welsh cap Arthyr Emyr touched down near the posts... The team to play Ireland on Saturday includes nine new caps.*
5 NC The **cap** of a bottle is its lid. *To seal the canister again the cap is simply tightened by hand.*
6 VO If a local authority is **capped** by the government, the government limits the amount that the authority is allowed to spend. *Some councils have had their spending levels capped by the government... They opposed the government's threat to cap more councils next year.* ◆ **capped** ADJ ATTRIB *Some capped councils are considering setting their new poll tax higher than the government figure.* ◆ **capping** NU *Voluntary groups have also had their grants cut because of charge capping.*
7 NC A **cap** is also a contraceptive device placed inside a woman's vagina. *Marie Stopes pioneered the use of the cervical cap.*
8 NC **Caps** are very small explosives used in toy guns.
9 VO If you **cap** an action, you do something that is better immediately afterwards. *He capped his performance by telling the funniest joke I have ever heard.*

capability /keɪpəbɪləti/ **capabilities**
1 NUorNC If you have the **capability** to do something, you are able to do it. *The work may be beyond his capability... She may worry about her capabilities as a parent.*
2 NU A country's military **capability** is its ability to fight in a war. *He said Moscow still possessed a major military capability in the Asia-Pacific region.*

capable /keɪpəbl/
1 ADJ PRED+of If you are **capable** of doing something, you are able to do it. *...a man capable of killing. ...a mind capable of original ideas.*
2 ADJ Someone who is **capable** has the ability to do something well. *Basil proved a capable cricketer.* ◆ **capably** ADV *...a capably performed dance.*

capacious /kəpeɪʃəs/
ADJ Something that is **capacious** has a lot of room; a formal word. *She put her knitting into one of the capacious pockets of her apron.*

capacity /kəpæsəti/ **capacities**
1 NU+SUPP The **capacity** of something is the amount that it can hold or produce. *The pipeline has a capacity of 1.2m barrels a day.* ● If something is filled **to capacity**, it is as full as possible. *The government hospital in Khan Yunif was full to capacity.*
2 N+N A **capacity** crowd completely fills a theatre or stadium. *A capacity crowd of fifty thousand will watch the world heavyweight title fight.*
3 NC+SUPP Your **capacity** to do something is your ability to do it. *The country has the capacity to produce many times its daily fuel needs... People have different capacities for learning.*
4 NU+SUPP Someone's **capacity** for food or drink is the amount that they can eat or drink. *His capacity for brandy was phenomenal.*
5 If someone does something in a particular **capacity,**

they do it as part of their duties. *I was involved in an advisory capacity.*
6 NU In industry, **capacity** is the quantity that can be produced. *We need to raise productivity and expand capacity.*

cape /keɪp/ **capes**
1 NC A **cape** is a large piece of land that sticks out into the sea. *The ship was wrecked in storms near Cape Horn.*
2 NC A **cape** is also a short cloak. *...soldiers dressed in capes against the rain.*

caper /keɪpə/ **capers, capering, capered**
1 NC **Capers** are small pickled flower buds which are used to season food. *...wild duck in caper sauce.*
2 V If you **caper** about, you dance or leap about energetically; an old-fashioned use. *The little girl capered towards Bill.*
3 NC A **caper** is a light-hearted practical joke or trick; an old-fashioned use.

Cape Town /keɪptaʊn/
Cape Town is the legislative capital of South Africa and its largest city. It is the capital of Cape Province. Population: 1,912,000 (1985).

Cape Verde /keɪp vɜːd/
The **Republic of Cape Verde** is a country west of Africa in the Atlantic. There are ten main islands in two groups: the Ilhas do Barlavento and the Ilhas do Sotovento. Cape Verde was a Portugese colony from the 15th century until independence in 1975. From 1975 until 1990 it was a one-party state and the President was Arístides Maria Pereira. Antonio Mascarenhas Monteiro, an independent supported by the Movement for Democracy (MPD), became Cape Verde's first freely elected President in 1991. Carlos Veiga (MPD) became Prime Minister in 1991. Cape Verde is a member of the Organization of African Unity. It exports fish, bananas, and salt. ◆ **Cape Verdian, Cape Verdean** /keɪp vɜːdiən/ N, ADJ
▪ *per capita GNP:* US$680 ▪ *religion:* Christianity (mainly Roman Catholic) ▪ *language:* Portuguese (official) ▪ *currency:* escudo ▪ *capital:* Cidade de Praia ▪ *population:* 369,000 (1989) ▪ *size:* 4,033 square kilometres.

capillary /kəpɪləri/ **capillaries**
NC **Capillaries** are tiny blood vessels. *It dilates the blood capillaries and increases the blood flow.*

capital /kæpɪtl/ **capitals**
1 NC The **capital** of a country is the city where its government meets. *Mr Heath is flying in from Amman, the capital of Jordan. ...a report from the Malaysian capital Kuala Lumpur by Peter Nettleship.*
2 NU **Capital** is a large sum of money used in a business or invested to make more money. *Most Hungarian companies desperately lack capital... The Soviet Union is keen to attract foreign capital to help revitalise industry.*
3 N+N In industry, **capital** investment or expenditure is money spent on equipment and buildings. *There's a growing shortage of loans and capital investment for poor nations.*
4 If you **make capital out of** a situation, you use it for personal gain; a formal expression. *They could make capital out of the current crisis... He said they were trying to make political capital out of this murder.*
5 NC A **capital** or a **capital** letter is the large form of a letter used at the beginning of sentences and names. *...written in capitals.*
6 ADJ ATTRIB A **capital** offence is one that is punished by death. *They were warned that the harbouring of fugitives is a capital offence... He would again be tried for a capital crime.*

capital gains
N PL **Capital gains** are the profits that you make when you buy something and then sell it again. *There will not be a cut in the tax on capital gains.*

capitalise /kæpɪtəlaɪz/. See **capitalize**.

capitalism /kæpɪtəlɪzəm/
NU **Capitalism** is an economic and political system in which property, business, and industry are owned by private individuals and not by the state. *Some aspects of modern capitalism are not all that bad... He believes that capitalism can't work and that it has to*

be replaced by socialism.

capitalist /kæpɪtəlɪst/ **capitalists**
1 ADJ ATTRIB A **capitalist** country or system supports or is based on the principles of capitalism. *...a modern capitalist economy. ...the United States and other capitalist countries.*
2 NC A **capitalist** is someone who believes in and supports the principles of capitalism. *The measures made possible joint ventures with foreign capitalists.*

capitalistic /kæpɪtəlɪstɪk/
ADJ **Capitalistic** means supporting or based on the principles of capitalism; used showing disapproval. *He blames Western capitalistic imperialism for the fall in export prices.*

capitalize /kæpɪtəlaɪz/ **capitalizes, capitalizing, capitalized**; also spelt **capitalise**.
V If you **capitalize** on a situation, you use it to gain some advantage. *Mr Healey has been capitalizing on the anxiety expressed throughout the House.*

capital punishment
NU **Capital punishment** is punishment which involves the legal killing of a person who has committed a serious crime. *It's unlikely that MPs will vote for the return of capital punishment.*

Capitol /kæpɪtl/
N PROP The **Capitol** is the main building of the Congress of the United States of America. *The budget has dominated the news out of the Capitol for months.*

capitulate /kəpɪtʃʊleɪt/ **capitulates, capitulating, capitulated**
V If you **capitulate**, you stop resisting and do what someone else wants you to do. *Economic pressures finally forced the Government to capitulate to our demands.* ◆ **capitulation** /kəpɪtʃʊleɪʃn/ NU *...the capitulation of the city without a struggle.*

capon /keɪpən/ **capons**
NC A **capon** is a male chicken that has had its sex organs removed and has been specially fattened up to be eaten. *...plump, tender capons raised by a local farmer.*

caprice /kəpriːs/ **caprices**
NCorNU A **caprice** is an unexpected action or decision which has no good reason or purpose; a literary word. *Newspapers became subject to the whims and caprices of their owners... His drawings could be hideous or comical according to caprice.*

capricious /kəprɪʃəs/
ADJ A **capricious** person often changes their mind unexpectedly. *Authoritarian rulers are typically capricious.*

caps. /kæps/
caps. is an abbreviation for 'capital letters': see **capital**. *Write the title in caps.*

capsicum /kæpsɪkəm/ **capsicums**
NCorNU A **capsicum** is a vegetable that is a type of pepper.

capsize /kæpsaɪz/ **capsizes, capsizing, capsized**
V-ERG If a boat **capsizes**, or if you **capsize** it, it turns upside down in the water. *The boat sank so fast it may be difficult to determine exactly how it capsized... On several occasions the yacht was nearly capsized by mountainous seas.*

capsule /kæpsjuːl/ **capsules**
1 NC A **capsule** is a small container with powdered medicine inside which you swallow. *The capsules were found to contain less than a sixth of the required amount of the drug.*
2 NC A **capsule** is also a small, strong container used for storing or carrying things. *...a mass of electronic circuits compressed into a tiny capsule.*
3 NC The **capsule** of a spacecraft is the part in which the astronauts travel. *Millions watched with bated breath as the capsule splashed down in the sea.*

Capt.
Capt. is a written abbreviation for 'Captain'; often used as part of a person's military title. *...Capt. Paul Eckel, the group's head.*

captain /kæptɪn/ **captains, captaining, captained**
1 NC The **captain** of an aeroplane or ship is the officer in charge of it. *At least one hundred people survived the crash, including the plane's captain.*
2 NCorTITLE In the army, a **captain** is an officer of the

rank immediately above lieutenant; in the navy, a **captain** is an officer of the rank immediately above commander. *He was jailed for life in 1981 for the murder of a British army captain... Captain Sharpe says the surface fleet is hard-pressed to meet all its commitments.*
3 NC The **captain** of a sports team is its leader. *The top scorer was England's captain, Kelvin Tatum.*
4 VO If you **captain** a sports team, you are its leader. *Willis is probably the best player to have captained England.*

caption /ˈkæpʃn/ **captions**
NC The **caption** of a picture or cartoon is the words printed underneath. *The caption on the poster says simply 'They did not do their duty'.*

captivate /ˈkæptɪveɪt/ **captivates, captivating, captivated**
VO If you **are captivated** by someone or something, you find them fascinating and attractive. *At eighteen he had been captivated by a charming brunette.*

captive /ˈkæptɪv/ **captives**
1 NC A **captive** is a prisoner. *There's no doubt that all the British and American captives are still alive.*
2 If you **take** someone **captive**, you take them prisoner. *The two judges were taken captive by gunmen.*

captivity /kæpˈtɪvəti/
NU If a person or animal is in **captivity**, they are being held somewhere and are not free to move away from the place in which they are held. *...wild birds raised in captivity.*

captor /ˈkæptə/ **captors**
NC A **captor** is someone who has captured a person or animal. *Two of the UN staff have since been released by their captors.*

capture /ˈkæptʃə/ **captures, capturing, captured**
1 VO If you **capture** someone, you take them prisoner. *They had been captured and thrown in chains.* ▶ Also NU *...the night before his capture.*
2 VO When military forces **capture** an area, they take control of it by force. *The city took 24 days to capture.* ▶ Also NU *...the capture of the city.*
3 VO To **capture** something also means to gain control of it. *Overseas firms captured almost 41 per cent of the market.*
4 VO If someone **captures** the atmosphere or quality of something, they represent it successfully in pictures, music, or words. *The parade captured the spirit of the Canadian west.*

car /kɑː/ **cars**
1 NC A **car** is a motor vehicle with room for a small number of passengers. *He parked the car about a hundred yards from the gates... They usually go by car.*
2 NC In the United States, railway carriages are called **cars**.
3 NC+SUPP In Britain, railway carriages are called **cars** when they are used for a particular purpose. *...the dining car.*
4 See also **cable car, car chase**.

Caracas /kəˈrækəs/
Caracas is the capital of Venezuela and its largest city. Population: 3,373,000 (1989).

carafe /kəˈræf/ **carafes**
NC A **carafe** is a glass container for water or wine. *...a carafe of wine on the family table at mealtime.*

caramel /ˈkærəmel/ **caramels**
1 NC A **caramel** is a kind of toffee.
2 NU **Caramel** is burnt sugar used for colouring and flavouring food.

carat /ˈkærət/ **carats**
1 NC A **carat** is a unit equal to 0.2 grams used for measuring the weight of diamonds and other precious stones. *A labourer last week found a one hundred and fifty-eight carat diamond.*
2 NC A **carat** is also a unit for measuring the purity of gold. The purest gold is 24-carat gold. *...an 18 carat gold egg commissioned from famous jewellers Mappin & Webb.*

caravan /ˈkærəvæn/ **caravans**
1 NC A **caravan** is a vehicle with no engine in which people live or spend their holidays. It is usually pulled

by a car, but some caravans are parked in one place permanently. *He lived in a caravan on the outskirts of the town.*
2 NC A **caravan** is also a group of people and animals that travel together in deserts and other similar places. *...a caravan of twelve thousand camels.*

caravanning /ˈkærəvænɪŋ/
NU **Caravanning** is the activity of having a holiday in a caravan. *We went caravanning in North Wales.*

caraway /ˈkærəweɪ/
NU **Caraway** is a plant with seeds that are used in cooking.

carbine /ˈkɑːbaɪn/ **carbines**
NC A **carbine** is a light automatic rifle. *The carbines offered an advantage over existing weapons.*

carbohydrate /ˌkɑːbəʊˈhaɪdreɪt/ **carbohydrates**
NU or NC **Carbohydrate** is a substance that gives you energy. It is found in foods such as sugar and bread. *Most fish are free from carbohydrate... Vegetarians get protein from eggs and cheese and energy from carbohydrates.*

carbolic acid /kɑːˈbɒlɪk ˈæsɪd/
NU **Carbolic acid** is a liquid that is used as a disinfectant and antiseptic. *Antiseptics like carbolic acid do more harm to your body than they do to the germs.*

car bomb, car bombs
NC A **car bomb** is a bomb that is placed inside or underneath a car. *His wife and four children were killed by a car bomb... The latest car bomb attack was aimed at civilians.*

carbon /ˈkɑːbən/
NU **Carbon** is a chemical element. Diamonds and coal are made of **carbon**. *Graphite appears to be a naturally occurring type of carbon.*

carbonated /ˈkɑːbəneɪtɪd/
ADJ **Carbonated** drinks contain small bubbles of carbon dioxide to make them fizzy. *If no water is available, carbonated drinks such as Coca Cola will do.*

carbon copy, carbon copies
1 NC A **carbon copy** is a copy of a piece of writing that is made using carbon paper. *I kept a carbon copy of my letter.*
2 NC+SUPP A **carbon copy** of an event is one that is identical to a previous event. *It was almost a carbon copy of the assassination of the chairman five months ago.*

carbon dating
NU **Carbon dating** is a method of calculating the age of a very old object, such as a fossil, by measuring the amount of radioactive carbon in it. *Carbon dating is only accurate for samples up to 40,000 years old.*

carbon dioxide /ˈkɑːbən daɪˈɒksaɪd/
NU **Carbon dioxide** is a gas that animals and people breathe out. It is also produced as a result of some chemical reactions. *Japan has announced its plans to stabilize its emissions of carbon dioxide.*

carbon monoxide /ˈkɑːbən mɒˈnɒksaɪd/
NU **Carbon monoxide** is a poisonous gas produced for example by cars. *Dr Bennett died from carbon monoxide poisoning from the exhaust fumes of his car.*

carbon paper
NU **Carbon paper** is thin paper with a dark substance on one side. **Carbon paper** is used between two sheets of ordinary paper to make one or more copies. *I now use a little stationer's duplicate book with numbered pages and carbon paper.*

car boot sale, car boot sales
NC A **car boot sale** is a sale to which people bring small items to sell from the boots of their cars. The cars are parked in a car park which has been hired for the occasion. *It sounds like something out of a car boot sale.*

carbuncle /ˈkɑːbʌŋkl/ **carbuncles**
NC A **carbuncle** is a large swelling under the skin like a boil.

carburettor /ˌkɑːbəˈretə/ **carburettors**; spelt **carburetor** in American English.
NC The **carburettor** is the part of an engine where air and petrol are mixed together. *The bus burst into flames when the driver tried to start it by pouring*

petrol straight into the carburettor.

carcass /kɑːkəs/ **carcasses**; also spelt **carcase**.
NC A **carcass** is the body of a dead animal. *Hundreds of animal carcasses litter the countryside.*

car chase, car chases
NC When there is a **car chase**, one car chases another at high speed. *A motorist was killed after being caught up in a police car chase which reached speeds of up to one hundred miles per hour.*

carcinogen /kɑːsɪnədʒən/ **carcinogens**
NC A **carcinogen** is a substance which can cause cancer; a medical term. *...efforts to control industrial carcinogens.*

carcinogenic /kɑːsɪnədʒɛnɪk/
ADJ Something that is **carcinogenic** is likely to cause cancer; a medical term. *...the carcinogenic properties of cigarettes.*

card /kɑːd/ **cards**
1 NCorNU A **card** is a piece of stiff paper or plastic containing specific information. *Put all the details on the card... Make a second copy on card or paper.*
2 NC A **card** is also a piece of stiff paper with a picture and a message which you send to someone on a special occasion. *...a Christmas card.*
3 NC **Cards** are thin pieces of cardboard decorated with numbers or pictures that are used to play various games. *The General liked her because she played cards well.*
4 NC+SUPP You can also use **card** to refer to something that gives you an advantage in a particular situation. *Her chief card was her perfect memory.*
● **Card** is used in these phrases. ● If you **play your cards** right, you are skilful in the way you handle a situation and make use of all your advantages. *He should get in at the General Election if he plays his cards right... Robespierre had not played his cards well... If the British play their cards correctly, the man's life may be saved.* ● If you say that something is **on the cards**, you mean that it is very likely to happen. *Were it not for the fact that the US presidential election is now fast approaching, a renewal of Contra aid would be on the cards. ...a political breakthrough is on the cards.* ● **In the cards** means the same as 'on the cards'; used in American English. *A major expansion is not in the cards right now... Was that not in the cards?*

cardamom /kɑːdəməm/ or **cardamon** /kɑːdəmən/
NU **Cardamom** is a spice that comes from the seeds of a plant that grows in Asia.

cardboard /kɑːdbɔːd/
NU **Cardboard** is thick, stiff paper that is used to make boxes and other containers. *He has designed a bed which uses a relatively inexpensive base made of cardboard. ...cardboard boxes.*

card-carrying
ADJ ATTRIB A **card-carrying** member of a political organization is an official, fully committed member. *There are 30,000 card-carrying members in the capital.*

cardiac /kɑːdiæk/
ADJ ATTRIB **Cardiac** means relating to the heart; a medical term. *...death caused by cardiac failure.*

cardiac arrest, cardiac arrests
NCorNU A **cardiac arrest** is a heart attack; a medical term. *...a high risk of having a cardiac arrest... Mr Fernando suffered cardiac arrest and died on the operating table.*

cardigan /kɑːdɪgən/ **cardigans**
NC A **cardigan** is a knitted woollen garment that fastens at the front. *She is dressed in a cranberry cardigan and jade green pants.*

cardinal /kɑːdɪnl/ **cardinals**
1 NC A **cardinal** is a high-ranking priest in the Catholic church. *She also met the Polish church leader, Cardinal Glemp.*
2 ADJ ATTRIB **Cardinal** means extremely important; a formal use. *...a cardinal part of the scheme. ...a fact of cardinal importance.*

cardinal number, cardinal numbers
NC A **cardinal number** is a number that is used for counting, such as 1, 3, and 10; compare **ordinal number**.

cardinal sin, cardinal sins
NC If you refer to an action as a **cardinal sin**, you are indicating that some people strongly disapprove of it. *I had committed the cardinal sin of shutting the window.*

card-index, card-indexes
NC A **card-index** is a set of cards with information on them which are arranged alphabetically. *The students were just names in the card-index.*

card sharp, card sharps
NC A **card sharp** or **card sharper** is a professional card player who cheats in order to win and so make money.

card vote, card votes
NC A **card vote** is a method of voting in which one delegate votes on behalf of all the members of the organization that he or she represents. *The initial show of hands indicated the rejection, but it was eventually decided by a card vote.*

care /keə/ **cares, caring, cared**
1 V If you **care** about something, you are concerned about it or interested in it. *...people who care about the environment... Most Germans care about unification more than about green issues.*
2 V-REPORT If you do not **care** what you do or what happens, it does not matter to you at all. *I don't care what we do or where we go... He no longer cared if he lived or died.*
3 V If you **care** for someone or **care** about them, you like them a great deal and feel a lot of affection for them. *Do you think she still cares for him?*
4 NU **Care** is the act of providing what people need to keep them healthy, or to make them well after they have been ill. *...the care of mental patients. ...the children in her care.*
5 V+to-INF If you **care** to do something, you want or choose to do it; a formal use. *It's wrong whichever way you care to look at it... It's not a problem I'd care to face myself.*
6 NU If you do something with **care**, you do it with great attention in order to avoid mistakes or damage. *He chose every word with care.*
7 NC **Cares** are worries; a formal use. *These celebrations will only provide a brief respite from the cares besetting Canadians about the future of their country. ...without a care in the world.*
8 See also **caring**.
● **Care** is used in these phrases. ● If you say that someone **couldn't care less** about something, you are saying in an emphatic way that it does not matter to them at all. *She couldn't care less what they thought.* ● If you say **for all I care**, you are indicating in an emphatic way that it does not matter to you at all what someone does. *You can go with Roger for all I care.* ● Children who are **in care** are being looked after by the state. *A recent case in the British High Courts has highlighted the dilemma of black children in care being placed with white families for adoption.* ● If you **take care of** someone, you look after them. *...parents who traditionally want large numbers of children to take care of them in their old age... He takes good care of my goats.* ● If you **take care of** a problem or something that needs attention, you deal with it. *We have to take care of the civil problems, like medicine and education... Quebec was forced to call in the army to take care of the dispute.* ● If you **take care** to do something, you make absolutely certain that you do it. *Mr Kohl and Mrs Thatcher will take care to present an image of Western unity this weekend... Mr Bush should take care he doesn't damage America's reputation.* ● You can tell someone to **take care** when you think they are in danger, or when you are saying goodbye to them. *...a warning to motorists to take care in treacherous conditions... Well, Leonore, take care. Thanks very much for coming in.*

care for PHRASAL VERB 1 If you **care for** someone or something, you look after them. *You must learn how to care for children.* 2 If you say that you do not **care for** something, you mean that you do not like it; an old-fashioned use. *I didn't much care for the way he looked at me.*

career /kərɪə/ careers, careering, careered
1 NC A **career** is a type of job or profession that someone does for a long period of their life and in which they hope to gain advancement. *...a career in accountancy. ...careers like teaching and medicine. ...a political career.*
2 NC Your **career** is the part of your life that you spend working. *Her early career was not a great success... I did it for the sake of my husband's career.*
3 VA If a person or vehicle **careers** somewhere, they move fast and in an uncontrolled way. *He careered into a wall.*

careerist /kərɪərɪst/ careerists
NC A **careerist** is a person who values their career very highly, and who will therefore do anything to succeed in it; used showing disapproval. *...an ambitious young careerist who did what he thought would please his political bosses.*

career woman, career women
NC A **career woman** is a woman with a career who wishes to work and progress in her job rather than stay at home and bring up a family. *...the middle-class career women of the United States.*

carefree /keəfriː/
ADJ If someone is **carefree**, they have no problems or responsibilities which worry them. *...his normally carefree attitude.*

careful /keəfl/
1 If you say 'Be careful' to someone, you are warning them of a danger or a problem. *Be careful or you'll fall!... Please be careful with the washing machine.*
2 ADJ If you are **careful**, you do something with a lot of attention to make sure that you do it well or correctly. *This law will encourage more careful driving... He made a careful copy of the notes. ...careful preparation.* ◆ **carefully** ADV *He walked carefully around the broken glass.*

careless /keələs/
1 ADJ If you are **careless**, you do not pay enough attention to what you are doing, and so you make mistakes. *We are rather careless about the way we cook... I had been careless and let him wander off on his own.* ◆ **carelessly** ADV *...a gate left carelessly ajar.* ◆ **carelessness** NU *There seems to have been some carelessness recently at the office.*
2 ADJ You do something in a **careless** way when you are relaxed, unworried, or confident. *...a careless laugh. ...her simplicity and careless grace.* ◆ **carelessly** ADV *'I'll give him a ring later,' Rudolph said, carelessly.* ◆ **carelessness** NU *She handled it with the carelessness of an expert.*

carer /keərə/ carers
NC A **carer** is someone who looks after an ill or old person, particularly one who is a relative or a neighbour. *One of the principal aims is to enhance the professional skills of the carers.*

caress /kəres/ caresses, caressing, caressed
V-RECIP If you **caress** someone, you stroke them gently and affectionately. *I caressed her hair and we kissed... They caressed and looked into each other's eyes.* ▶ Also NC *...a loving caress.*

caretaker /keəteɪkə/ caretakers
1 NC A **caretaker** is a person who looks after a large building such as a school or a block of flats. *He was a labourer who later became a caretaker.*
2 ADJ ATTRIB You can use **caretaker** to refer to someone or something that is temporarily in charge of a situation. *They are calling for a caretaker administration to oversee the elections... He has been appointed caretaker manager for their next three games.*

careworn /keəwɔːn/
ADJ A person who looks **careworn** looks worried, tired, and unhappy. *He looked careworn and refused to talk... She detected in his face a careworn, grief-stricken expression.*

cargo /kɑːɡəʊ/ cargoes
NCorNU The **cargo** of a ship or plane is the goods that it is carrying. *...a cargo of wool... The port is still handling cargo... Officials had expected a cargo ferry.*

caribou /kærəbuː/ caribous. The plural form can be either **caribous** or **caribou**.

NC A **caribou** is a large North American deer. *The sanctuary is the breeding ground for the world's largest herd of caribou.*

caricature /kærɪkətʃʊə/ caricatures, caricaturing, caricatured
1 NCorNU A **caricature** is a drawing or description of someone that exaggerates their appearance or behaviour in order to make people laugh. *...a caricature of Max Beerbohm. ...a master of caricature.*
2 VO If you **caricature** someone, you portray them in a way that exaggerates their features or personality in order to make people laugh. *Lawson caricatured his boss in his cartoons.*
3 NC+SUPP A **caricature** of an event or situation is an exaggerated account of it which is intended to make people laugh. *...an outrageous caricature of the truth.*

caricaturist /kærɪkətʃʊərɪst/ caricaturists
NC A **caricaturist** is someone who portrays people in drawings or writing in an exaggerated way in order to make other people laugh. *It was home to the brilliant caricaturist, William Hogarth.*

caries /keəriz/
NU **Caries** is tooth decay; a medical term. *...the appallingly high incidence of dental caries.*

carillon /kərɪljən/ carillons
NC A **carillon** is a set of bells hung in a tower. It is also a tune played on these bells.

caring /keərɪŋ/
1 ADJ A **caring** person is affectionate, helpful, and sympathetic. *...a caring parent... We need a more caring society.*
2 NU **Caring** is affection, help, and sympathy. *...love and caring between a man and a woman.*

Carlot, Maxime /mæksiːm kɑːləʊ/
Maxime Carlot became Prime Minister of Vanuatu in 1991. He is a member of the Union of Moderate Parties. Born: 1941.

Carl XVI Gustav, King of Sweden /kɑːl ɡʊstɑːf/
King Carl XVI Gustav succeeded to the throne of Sweden in 1973, at the death of his grandfather, King Gustav VI Adolf. He became Crown Prince in 1950. Born: 1946.

carmine /kɑːmaɪn/
ADJ **Carmine** is a deep red colour. *The flowers may be anything from light carmine to crimson in colour.*

carnage /kɑːnɪdʒ/
NU When there is **carnage**, a lot of people are killed; a literary word. *Refugees crossed the border to escape the carnage.*

carnal /kɑːnl/
ADJ ATTRIB **Carnal** desires or activities are bodily and sexual ones; a literary word, used showing disapproval. *...the restriction of carnal relations to marriage.*

carnation /kɑːneɪʃn/ carnations
NC A **carnation** is a plant with sweet-smelling white, pink, red, or yellow flowers. *A thousand well-wishers threw red carnations as they walked into church.*

carnival /kɑːnɪvl/ carnivals
1 NC A **carnival** is a public festival with music, processions, and dancing. *...preparations for next week's carnival. ...intoxicating carnival music.*
2 NU **Carnival** is a period of time just before Lent which is celebrated in some Roman Catholic countries with processions, dancing, music and so on. *The Assembly is taking a week-long break for carnival in mid-February... Just a week ago, Rio was celebrating carnival.*

carnivore /kɑːnɪvɔː/ carnivores
NC A **carnivore** is an animal that eats meat rather than plants; a formal word. *...carnivores like the lion and the cheetah.*

carnivorous /kɑːnɪvərəs/
ADJ **Carnivorous** animals eat meat. *Snakes are carnivorous.*

carob /kærəb/ carobs
1 NC A **carob** is an evergreen Mediterranean tree with dark brown edible pods.
2 NU You also use **carob** to refer to the pods of the carob tree which are powdered and are used instead of cocoa in health foods. *...'diet' bars of chocolate made*

from carob powder.

carol /kǽrəl/ **carols**
NC **Carols** are Christian religious songs that are sung at Christmas. *The procession culminated in a service of carols and prayers at the City Hall.*

carotid artery /kərɒtɪd ɑːtəri/ **carotid arteries**
NC A **carotid artery** is one of the two arteries in the neck that supply blood to the head; a medical expression. *The drug only affects the blood vessels supplied by the carotid arteries.*

carouse /kərǽʊz/ **carouses, carousing, caroused**
V If people **carouse**, they enjoy themselves by drinking a lot of alcohol and making a lot of noise; an old-fashioned word, used showing disapproval. *...drunken soldiers carousing in the streets.*

carousel /kǽrəsɛl/ **carousels**
1 NC A **carousel** is a large rotating mechanical device with seats in the shape of animals or cars which children can sit on in a fairground; used in American English. *The Washington Merry-Go-Round is an actual carousel located on the mall.*
2 NC At an airport, a **carousel** is a wide moving belt from which passengers can collect their luggage. *When all the other passengers had left, a locked grey bag was still going round the carousel.*

carp /kɑːp/; **carp** is both the singular and the plural form.
NC A **carp** is a large fish that lives in lakes and rivers. *They plan to introduce fresh water carp to eat up the plants.*

car park, car parks
NC A **car park** is an area or building where people can leave their cars. *...the multi-storey car park... He was arrested in a pub car park a few miles away.*

carpenter /kɑːpɪntə/ **carpenters**
NC A **carpenter** is a person whose job is making and repairing wooden things, such as furniture. *Mauritania has lost most of its skilled carpenters.*

carpentry /kɑːpɪntri/
NU **Carpentry** is the skill or the work of a carpenter. *His favourite pastimes are carpentry, gardening, and watching television.*

carpet /kɑːpɪt/ **carpets**
1 NC A **carpet** is a thick covering for a floor, made of wool or a similar material. *He asked what the marks were on the stair carpet.*
2 NC+SUPP A **carpet** of something is a layer of it covering the ground. *There was a carpet of snow everywhere.*
3 If you **sweep** something **under the carpet**, you try to stop people hearing about it or finding out about it. *We haven't forgotten about our past, we haven't swept it under the carpet... The leaders are sweeping their differences under the carpet so that they can present a unified image.*
4 See also **carpeted, carpeting**.

carpetbagger /kɑːpɪtbægə/ **carpetbaggers**
NC You can describe a politician as a **carpetbagger** when they try to get elected in an area which is not their home, simply because they think they are more likely to succeed there; used in American English, showing disapproval. *His supporters were demonstrating against the victory of a Republican carpetbagger.*

carpeted /kɑːpɪtɪd/
1 ADJ A **carpeted** area is covered in carpet. *His house was carpeted and furnished show-room style.*
2 ADJ PRED If an area is **carpeted** in something, it is covered in it. *The ground was carpeted in flowers.*
3 See also **carpet**.

carpeting /kɑːpɪtɪŋ/
NU **Carpeting** is the carpets that are fitted in a room or building. **Carpeting** is also used to refer to the type of material that carpets are made from. *...wall-to-wall carpeting. ...a shabby house with worn carpeting on the stairs.*

carpet slipper, carpet slippers
NC **Carpet slippers** are comfortable plain slippers. *...workers shod in carpet slippers to avoid damaging the floor.*

carpet sweeper, carpet sweepers
NC A **carpet sweeper** is a device with a long handle

and rotating brushes which is used for cleaning carpets.

car port, car ports
NC A **car port** is a shelter for one or two cars which consists of a flat roof supported on pillars.

carriage /kærɪdʒ/ **carriages**
1 NC A **carriage** is one of the separate sections of a train that carries passengers. *A bomb on the line derailed the engine and six carriages.*
2 NC A **carriage** is also an old-fashioned vehicle which is pulled by horses. *...a procession of eight carriages led by the Queen.*

carriageway /kærɪdʒweɪ/ **carriageways**
NC A **carriageway** is one of the two sides of a motorway or dual carriageway, where traffic travels in one direction only, in two or three lanes. *...the southbound carriageway of the M1.*

carried away
ADJ PRED If you are **carried away**, you are so enthusiastic about something that you behave in a foolish way. *She can get so carried away that she forgets the time.*

carrier /kærɪə/ **carriers**
1 NC A **carrier** is a vehicle or device used for carrying things. *...a new luggage carrier for bicycles.*
2 NC A **carrier** is also a military vehicle or ship that is used for transporting soldiers, other vehicles, and weapons. *The carrier is making her way back to port. ...a large new armoured personnel carrier. ...an aircraft carrier.*
3 NC A **carrier** is also someone who is infected with a disease and so can make other people ill with that disease. *...mothers identified from blood tests as carriers.*
4 NC A **carrier** or a **carrier bag** is a paper or plastic bag with handles. *They were given pens and badges, and a special carrier bag to put it all in.*

carrier pigeon, carrier pigeons
NC A **carrier pigeon** is a pigeon that is used to carry written messages which are attached to its leg. *They were using carrier pigeons to talk to each other.*

carrion /kærɪən/
NU **Carrion** is the decaying flesh of dead animals. *These birds live by scavenging carrion.*

carrot /kærət/ **carrots**
1 NCorNU A **carrot** is a long, thin orange vegetable that grows under the ground. It can be used as a savoury or as a sweet food. *...drinking wine and eating carrots and peanuts... The wedding cake would not have been bean curd but carrot or pumpkin.*
2 NC You can use **carrot** to refer to something that is offered to people in order to persuade them to do something. The word 'stick' is often used to refer to the harsher methods of persuasion. *...the juicy carrot of high profits... So the Prime Minister has decided to use the carrot as well as the stick.*

carroty /kærəti/
ADJ **Carroty** hair is bright reddish-orange.

carry /kæri/ **carries, carrying, carried**
1 VO If you **carry** something, you take it with you, holding it so that it does not touch the ground. *The students carried banners saying that the union leader was the first victim of the new dictatorship... He picked up his suitcase and carried it into the bedroom.*
2 VO To **carry** something also means to have it with you wherever you go. *I always carry a gun... Not enough people were carrying kidney donor cards.*
3 VO If something **carries** a person or thing somewhere, it takes them there. *A gentle current carried him slowly to the shore. ...trucks that carried casualties.*
4 VO If someone or something **carries** a disease, they are infected with it and can pass it on to people or animals. *Rats carry very nasty diseases.*
5 VO If an action **carries** a particular quality or consequence, it involves it. *Any job carries with it periods of boredom... Adultery carried the death penalty.*
6 VOA If you **carry** an idea or a method to a particular extent, you use or develop it to that extent. *George carried this idea one step further.*
7 VO If a newspaper or poster **carries** a picture or an

article, it contains it. *A poster carried a portrait of Churchill.*
8 VO If a radio station **carries** a particular report or programme, it broadcasts it. *Soviet television has carried a ninety-minute documentary on the demonstrations and riots in the southern republics... The military communiqué was carried on Baghdad radio.*
9 V-PASS If a proposal or motion **is carried** in a debate, a majority of people vote in favour of it. *My proposal was not carried... The motion was carried by 259 votes to 162.*
10 V If a sound **carries**, it can be heard a long way away. *...a faint voice which carried no farther than the front row.*
11 VO If a woman is pregnant, you can say that she is **carrying** a child. *While I was carrying Mary her father left me.*
carry on PHRASAL VERB 1 If you **carry on** doing something, you continue to do it. *I carried on without their support... The man holding the gun carried on shooting.* 2 If you **carry on** an activity, you take part in it. *Our work is carried on in an informal atmosphere.*
carry out PHRASAL VERB If you **carry out** a task or order, you do it. *They also have to carry out many administrative duties... He was simply carrying out the instructions he had received.*
carry over PHRASAL VERB If you **carry** something **over** from one situation to another, you make it continue to exist in the new situation. *The habit of obedience is carried over from the war.*
carry through PHRASAL VERB If you **carry** a plan or decision **through**, you put it into practice. *...the task of carrying through the necessary reforms.*
carrycot /kærɪkɒt/ **carrycots**
NC A **carrycot** is a cot with handles which is used for small babies.
carry-on
1 N SING A **carry-on** is behaviour that you think is annoying and unnecessary; an informal use. *He'd thought his future was secure—nobody had imagined this carry-on.*
2 ADJ PRED **Carry-on** luggage can be taken onto a plane with you, instead of being stored in the luggage hold. *Airport staff will stop travellers at random and search their carry-on baggage and clothing.*
carsick /kɑːsɪk/
ADJ If you are **carsick**, you feel ill while travelling in a car. *They had to stop twice because Billy got carsick.*
cart /kɑːt/ **carts, carting, carted**
1 NC A **cart** is an old-fashioned wooden vehicle, usually pulled by an animal. *...a cart loaded with hay.*
2 VOA If you **cart** things or people somewhere, you carry or transport them there, often with difficulty; an informal use. *It took several trips to cart it all back up the stairs... He was carted off to hospital.*
carte blanche /kɑːt blɒnᵓʃ/
NU If someone gives you **carte blanche**, they give you the authority to do whatever you think is right. *They gave him carte blanche to publish his proposals.*
cartel /kɑːtel/ **cartels**
NC A **cartel** is an association of similar companies or businesses that have grouped together in order to prevent competition and to control prices. *...the setting up of an international cartel like the oil producers' OPEC. ...the man who is said to run the world's largest drugs cartel.*
Carter, Jimmy /dʒɪmi kɑːtə/
Jimmy Carter was President of the United States of America from 1977 to 1981. He was Governor of Georgia from 1971 to 1974. He is a member of the Democratic Party. Born: 1924.
carthorse /kɑːthɔːs/ **carthorses**
NC A **carthorse** is a big powerful horse that is used to pull carts or wagons. *You hitch the machine up behind a cart horse and it turns it into a tractor.*
cartilage /kɑːtᵊlɪdʒ/
NU **Cartilage** is a strong, flexible substance which surrounds the joints in your body. *Unlike bone, cartilage does not contain any blood vessels... He has just undergone a cartilage operation.*

cartographer /kɑːtɒgrəfə/ **cartographers**
NC A **cartographer** is a person whose job is drawing maps. *A committee of lawyers and cartographers studied the details of the land dispute.*
cartography /kɑːtɒgrəfi/
NU **Cartography** is the art of drawing maps. *...a feasibility study in the fields of energy, cartography, and transport.*
carton /kɑːtn/ **cartons**
1 NC A **carton** is a plastic or cardboard container in which food or drink is sold. *...a plastic carton filled with fried potatoes. ...a carton of milk.*
2 NC A **carton** is also a large, strong cardboard box. *Seventy bodies have been discovered in bags and cartons.*
cartoon /kɑːtuːn/ **cartoons**
1 NC A **cartoon** is a drawing in a newspaper or magazine, which is funny or makes a political point. *Mrs Thatcher's dilemma is summed up in a cartoon. ...the near-sighted cartoon character, Mr Magoo.*
2 NC A **cartoon** is also a film in which all the characters and scenes have been drawn rather than being real people or objects. *Mickey Mouse has appeared in more than a hundred cartoons on the big screen.*
cartoonist /kɑːtuːnɪst/ **cartoonists**
NC A **cartoonist** is a person whose job is to draw cartoons for newspapers and magazines. *I think this is the first time the prize has been given to a cartoonist.*
cartridge /kɑːtrɪdʒ/ **cartridges**
1 NC A **cartridge** is a tube containing a bullet and an explosive substance. It is inserted into a gun. *Police say the gunmen ran off, leaving behind spent cartridges from an AK-47 rifle.*
2 NC Ink **cartridges** are disposable plastic tubes that hold the ink for a fountain pen.
cartridge paper
NU **Cartridge paper** is a type of strong paper that is suitable for drawing on.
cartwheel /kɑːtwiːl/ **cartwheels, cartwheeling, cartwheeled**
1 NC If you turn a **cartwheel**, you do a fast, circular movement by falling sideways, supporting your body with one hand after the other until you are standing again. *The boxer, who'd dedicated the fight to his son, did cartwheels of joy.*
2 V If a vehicle or a plane **cartwheels**, it turns over several times very quickly. *The plane hit the runway and then cartwheeled before breaking up in flames... The weapon, armed with dummy warheads, cartwheeled out of control and exploded.*
carve /kɑːv/ **carves, carving, carved**
1 VO If you **carve** an object, you cut it out of stone or wood. *The statue was carved by John Gibson.*
◆ **carved** ADJ ATTRIB *Pat loved the carved Buddhas.*
2 VO If you **carve** a design on an object, you cut it into the surface. *He begins to carve his initials on the tree.* ◆ **carved** ADJ ATTRIB *...an intricately carved door.*
3 VO If you **carve** meat, you cut slices from it. *...sitting at a dinner table together, carving for themselves generous slices of roast beef.*
carve out PHRASAL VERB If you **carve out** something for yourself, you create or obtain it, often with difficulty. *The company is carving out a huge slice of the electronics market... However, Banda has carved out an important place for women in Indian society.*
carve up PHRASAL VERB If you **carve** something **up**, you divide it into smaller areas or pieces. *Stalin and Hitler effectively carved up Poland between them... When the old man died the estate was carved up and sold.*
carvery /kɑːvəri/ **carveries**
NC A **carvery** is a restaurant where roast meat is carved and served at a special counter in the room in which you are eating.
carving /kɑːvɪŋ/ **carvings**
NC A **carving** is an object that has been cut out of stone or wood. *He did a deal with the Turkish authorities and brought the marble carvings to London. ...a thousand-year old stone carving.*

carving knife, carving knives
NC A **carving knife** is a large knife that is used for cutting cooked meat. *She'd just cut herself with a carving knife.*

Casablanca /ˌkæsəˈblæŋkə/
Casablanca is the largest city in Morocco. Population: 2,904,000 (1987).

cascade /kæsˈkeɪd/ **cascades, cascading, cascaded**
1 NC A **cascade** is a waterfall; a literary use. *From there the river fell in a series of cascades down towards the Hudson.*
2 VA When water **cascades**, it pours downwards very fast and in large quantities. *The water is cascading through the air.*
3 N SING+SUPP A **cascade** of things is a large amount of them. *The lectures contain memories, witticisms, and a powerful cascade of ideas... A cascade of television commercials was released.*

case /keɪs/ **cases**
1 NC+SUPP A **case** of something is a particular situation or instance of it. *In Catherine's case, it led to divorce... These tribes are a classic case of people living in harmony with their environment... All cases of bullying will be severely dealt with.*
2 NC Doctors sometimes refer to a patient as a **case**. *...road accident cases.*
3 NC A crime, or a trial that takes place after a crime, can be called a **case**. *...one of Sherlock Holmes' cases... He had lost the case.*
4 NC In an argument, the **case** for or against something consists of the facts and reasons used to support or oppose it. *...a book arguing the case for better adult education... He stated his case.*
5 NC A **case** is also a container that is specially designed to hold or protect something. *...scissors in a leather case.*
6 NC A suitcase can be referred to as a **case**. *They unload their trunks and cases.*
● **Case** is used in these phrases. ● You say **in that case** or **in which case** to indicate that you are assuming that a previous statement is correct or true. *'The bar is closed,' the waiter said. 'In that case,' McFee said, 'I'll go to another hotel.'* ● When you say that a job or task **is a case of** doing a particular thing, you mean that the job or task consists of doing that thing. *There's very little work involved. It's just a case of drafting the summons.* ● If you say that something **is a case in point**, you mean that it is a good example of a general statement you have just made. *A case in point is the recent controversy sparked by an influx of refugees.* ● You say **in any case** when you are adding another reason for something you have said or done. *I couldn't ask him all the time, and in any case he wasn't always there.* ● You say **in case** to indicate that you have something or are doing something because a particular thing might happen or might have happened. *I've got the key in case we want to go inside... I have a phone number in case of emergency... Escape ropes had been tied to the balcony, just in case things got difficult.*

casebook /keɪsbʊk/ **casebooks**
NC A **casebook** is a written record of the cases dealt with by a doctor, social worker, police officer, and so on. *His sexual problem seems to come straight from Freud's casebook.*

case history, case histories
NC Someone's **case history** is the record of past events or problems that have affected them; a formal expression. *They had no case history of illness... She was making out a case history for each child.*

case law
NU **Case law** is law established by following decisions that have been made by judges in earlier cases; a legal term. *I frankly wish there were some case law on this point that would give us guidance.*

casement /keɪsmənt/ **casements**
NC A **casement** is a window that opens by means of hinges, usually at the side. *...a casement violently opened just over my head... I threw open the casement windows.*

case study, case studies
NC A **case study** is an account giving details about someone or something, and their development over a period of time. *...case studies of particular pieces of legislation.*

casework /keɪswɜːk/
NU **Casework** is social work that involves actually dealing or working with people who need help. *I really do a lot of casework.*

cash /kæʃ/ **cashes, cashing, cashed**
1 NU **Cash** is money in the form of notes and coins rather than cheques. *...four hundred dollars in cash.*
2 VO If you **cash** a cheque, you exchange it at a bank for the amount of money that it is worth. *Cheques up to 50 pounds may be cashed at any of our branches.*
cash in PHRASAL VERB If you **cash in** on a situation, you use it to gain an advantage for yourself; an informal expression. *They cashed in on the public's growing suspicion... The entrepreneur responsible for the demolition cashed in too.*

cash-and-carry, cash-and-carries
NC A **cash-and-carry** is a large shop where people who work for a business can buy goods more cheaply and in larger quantities than in ordinary shops. *I cannot go to the cash-and-carry supermarket to do my purchasing.*

cash book, cash books
NC A **cash book** is a book in which you can write down payments made and money received.

cash card, cash cards
NC A **cash card** is a plastic card that you use to withdraw money from a cash dispenser. *...machines that read your credit card, cash card, or ID card.*

cash crop, cash crops
NC A **cash crop** is a crop that is grown in order to be sold. *Bananas and citrus fruits are the only cash crops grown in the area.*

cash desk, cash desks; also spelt **cash-desk**.
NC A **cash desk** is the place in a large shop where you pay for your purchases.

cash dispenser, cash dispensers
NC A **cash dispenser** is a machine where you can take money out of your bank account at any time by using a special card and typing in your code number. *Automatic cash dispensers transmit transactions in electronic code.*

cashew /kæʃuː/ **cashews**
NC A **cashew** or a **cashew nut** is a curved nut that you can eat. *...a local beer made from cashews. ...cashew nut oil.*

cash flow
N SING The **cash flow** of a firm or business is the movement of money which goes into it and out of it. *Work out a projected cash flow for your first 12 months trading. ...cash flow problems.*

cashier /kæˈʃɪə/ **cashiers**
NC A **cashier** is the person that customers pay money to or get money from in a shop, bank, or garage. *He pointed a loaded gun at the cashier.*

cashmere /kæʃmɪə/
NU **Cashmere** is a kind of very fine, soft wool. *...her cashmere shawl.*

Cashpoint /kæʃpɔɪnt/ **Cashpoints**
NC A **Cashpoint** is the same as a cash dispenser. **Cashpoint** is a trademark. *...a different type of 'through the wall' Cashpoint machine... It's made of plastic and is about the same size as a Cashpoint card.*

cash register, cash registers
NC A **cash register** is a machine in a shop, pub, or restaurant that is used to register sales and to add up how much money people pay. Money is kept in a cash register. *Looters have carried away clothing, electrical goods, and even cash registers.*

casing /keɪsɪŋ/ **casings**
NC A **casing** is a substance or object that covers and protects something. *...the outer casing of a vacuum flask.*

casino /kəˈsiːnəʊ/ **casinos**
NC A **casino** is a place where people play gambling games. *Gambling and casinos are officially illegal in South Africa.*

cask /kɑːsk/ **casks**

NC A **cask** is a wooden barrel used for storing alcoholic drink. ...*the reactions that occur as a whisky matures in the cask.*

casket /kɑːskɪt/ **caskets**

1 NC A **casket** is a small box in which you keep valuable things. ...*a casket believed to contain the stone tablets.*

2 NC A **casket** is also a coffin; used in American English. *Thousands of mourners have been paying their last respects to Gandhi, filing past his casket at his family home in Delhi.*

cassava /kəsɑːvə/

1 NU **Cassava** is a tropical plant with thick roots that is grown for food. It is also called 'manioc'. ...*the use of cassava for cattle feed.*

2 NU **Cassava** is also flour that is obtained from the roots of the cassava plant. ...*bread made from cassava, sorghum, and millet.*

casserole /kæsərəʊl/ **casseroles**

1 NCorNU A **casserole** is a dish made by cooking food in liquid in an oven. *Use this stock in soups or casseroles... There's lamb casserole for dinner.*

2 NC A **casserole** is also a large, heavy container with a lid which is used for cooking.

cassette /kəsɛt/ **cassettes**

NCorNU A **cassette** is a small, flat rectangular plastic container with magnetic tape inside which is used for recording and playing back sounds. ...*extracts from romantic love stories on cassette.* ...*a storage rack for cassettes.*

cassette deck, cassette decks

NC A **cassette deck** is the part of a hi-fi system that you can play cassettes on.

cassette player, cassette players

NC A **cassette player** is a machine that is used for playing cassettes and sometimes also for recording them. ...*explosives hidden in a radio cassette player... This market sells the latest cassette players.*

cassette recorder, cassette recorders

NC A **cassette recorder** is a machine that is used for recording and listening to cassettes. *Many people today have cassette recorders of reasonable quality.*

cassette tape, cassette tapes

NC A **cassette tape** is the same as a **cassette**.

cassock /kæsək/ **cassocks**

NC A **cassock** is a long robe that is worn by the clergy of some churches. *He was wearing a black cassock and a dog collar.*

cast /kɑːst/ **casts, casting**. The form **cast** is used in the present tense and is also the past tense and past participle of the verb.

1 N COLL The **cast** of a play or film is all the people who act in it. *The whole cast worked wonderfully together.*

2 VO To **cast** an actor means to choose him or her to act a particular role. *I was cast as the husband, a man of about fifty.*

3 VOA If you **cast** your eyes somewhere, you look there. *He cast a quick glance at his friend.*

4 VOA If you **cast** doubt or suspicion on something, you make other people unsure about it. *He had cast doubt on our traditional beliefs.*

5 If you **cast** your **mind back**, you think about things in the past or try to remember them. *He cast his mind back over the day.*

6 VO When you **cast** your vote in an election, you vote. *On April 24th, voters in France will cast their votes in the first round of elections for a new President.*

7 VO When people **cast** an object, they make it by pouring hot, liquid metal into a mould and allowing it to cool and harden. *All the parts can be made locally except the furnace doors, which will have to be cast abroad.*

8 See also **casting**.

cast around PHRASAL VERB If you **cast around** or **cast about** for something, you try to find it; a literary expression. *I cast around for some place to hide.*

cast aside PHRASAL VERB If you **cast** someone or something **aside**, you get rid of them; a formal expression, used showing disapproval. *His country*

cast him aside and disgraced him.

cast off PHRASAL VERB 1 If you **cast** something **off**, you get rid of it or no longer use it; a formal use. *Organizations must cast off old-fashioned practices in order to survive.* ● See also **cast-off**. 2 If you are on a boat and you **cast off**, you untie the rope that fastens it to the shore. *We cast off as quietly as we could.*

castanet /kæstənɛt/ **castanets**

NC **Castanets** are a musical instrument made of two small round pieces of wood which are knocked together to make a clicking sound. Castanets are played in Spanish flamenco music. *I learned to play the castanets.*

castaway /kɑːstəweɪ/ **castaways**

NC A **castaway** is a person who has survived a shipwreck and has managed to reach an isolated island or shore. ...*castaways marooned on a desert island.*

caste /kɑːst/ **castes**

NCorNU A **caste** is one of the social classes into which people in a Hindu society are divided. *Sushma came from a lower caste.* ...*government jobs for the socially backward castes... Duties were determined by caste.*

castellated /kæstəleɪtɪd/

ADJ A **castellated** wall or building has turrets and battlements like a castle.

caster /kɑːstə/. See **castor**.

caster sugar; also spelt **castor sugar**.

NU **Caster sugar** is fine grained white sugar that is often used in baking.

castigate /kæstɪgeɪt/ **castigates, castigating, castigated**

VO If you **castigate** someone or something, you scold or criticize them severely; a formal word. *They castigated the report as inadequate.*

casting /kɑːstɪŋ/

NU **Casting** is the activity of choosing actors to play particular roles. ...*people doing the casting for films.*

casting vote, casting votes

NC When an equal number of votes have been given for and against a proposal, the **casting vote** is the vote that the chairperson gives which decides whether or not the proposal will be passed. *R A Butler used his casting vote as chairman to defeat the motion by 6 votes to 5.*

cast-iron

1 ADJ ATTRIB **Cast-iron** objects are made of a special type of iron containing carbon. ...*a cast-iron stove.*

2 ADJ ATTRIB A **cast-iron** guarantee, reason, or assurance is absolutely certain to be effective, real, or true. *They will go ahead with the plan provided the unions offer a cast-iron guarantee of co-operation... You have a very good cast-iron reason for not attacking now.* ...*cast-iron assurances that they would never again ignore police advice.*

castle /kɑːsl/ **castles**

1 NC A **castle** is a large building with thick, high walls, built by important people in former times, for protection during wars and battles. *The meeting would take place in a castle on the outskirts of the city.*

2 NC In chess, a **castle** is a piece which can move in a straight line, either forwards, backwards, or sideways. A **castle** is also called a rook.

cast-off, cast-offs

ADJ ATTRIB **Cast-off** things, especially clothes, are ones which you give to someone else or throw away because you no longer use them. *They were wearing cast-off jackets.* ▶ Also NC *They dressed up in Winifred's cast-offs.*

castor /kɑːstə/ **castors**; also spelt **caster**.

NC **Castors** are small wheels fitted to a piece of furniture. ...*a washing bin on castors.*

castor oil

NU **Castor oil** is thick yellow oil that is obtained from the seeds of the castor oil plant. ...*a mosquito trap made of polythene sheeting with castor oil smeared on it.*

castor sugar. See **caster sugar**.

castrate /kæstreɪt/ **castrates, castrating, castrated**

VO When a male animal is **castrated**, its testicles are removed. *The two bulls had to be castrated.*

♦ **castration** /kæsˈtreɪʃn/ NU *They used castration as a form of punishment.*

Castries /ˈkæstiːs/
Castries is the capital of St Lucia and its largest city. Population: 53,000 (1986).

Castro, Fidel /fiːˈdel kæˈstrəʊ/
Fidel Castro Ruz became Prime Minister of Cuba in 1959, when he overthrew the regime of General Batista. He later became the First Secretary of the Cuban Communist Party, and in 1976 he became President. Born: 1927.

casual /ˈkæʒuəl/
1 ADJ If you are **casual**, you are relaxed and do things without attention to formality. *He tried to appear casual as he asked her to dance. ...a casual glance.* ♦ **casually** ADV *...saying goodbye as casually as I could.* ♦ **casualness** NU *...working with apparent casualness.*
2 ADJ Something that is **casual** happens by chance or without planning. *...a casual friendship... It is not open to casual visitors.* ♦ **casually** ADV *...any casually assembled group of men.*
3 ADJ ATTRIB **Casual** clothes are ones that you normally wear at home or on holiday, and not on formal occasions. *She wears casual clothes in bright colours.* ♦ **casually** ADV *The students dress casually, in jeans and sweatshirts.*
4 ADJ ATTRIB **Casual** work is done for short periods, and not on a permanent or regular basis. *They tried to get casual work in pubs and garages. ...a casual labourer.*

casualty /ˈkæʒuəlti/ **casualties**
1 NC A **casualty** is a person who is injured or killed in a war or an accident. *No casualties were reported... There were heavy casualties on both sides. ...small inefficient casualty units.*
2 NC If a person is the **casualty** of an event or situation, they have suffered badly as a result of it. *She was one of the casualties of the system.*

casuistry /ˈkæzjuɪstri/
NU **Casuistry** is reasoning that is extremely subtle and designed to mislead other people; a formal word. *There is a feeling that his refusal may be a matter of casuistry rather than practical reality.*

cat /kæt/ **cats**
1 NC A **cat** is a small furry animal with a tail, whiskers, and sharp claws. Cats are often kept as pets. *One day, the lighthouse keeper's cat brought in a dead bird.*
2 NC A **cat** is also any larger animal that is a type of cat, such as a lion or tiger. *Footprints and unconfirmed sightings indicate that it may be a variety of large cat.*
3 If someone who has the advantage in a situation plays **cat and mouse** with someone else, they provoke them by pretending to fail to catch them before they actually catch them. If someone who is in a weak position plays **cat and mouse** with someone else, they provoke them by repeatedly avoiding being caught. *There followed a game of cat and mouse with my tormentor... Bus loads of women played cat and mouse with the peace-keeping forces.*

cataclysm /ˈkætəklɪzəm/ **cataclysms**
NC A **cataclysm** is a disaster or violent change; a formal word. *Europe is approaching a terrible cataclysm.*

cataclysmic /kætəˈklɪzmɪk/
ADJ A **cataclysmic** event is one that changes a situation or society very much; a formal word. *Death is simply the greatest and most cataclysmic of the 'rites of passage'.*

catacomb /ˈkætəkuːm/ **catacombs**
NC **Catacombs** are a series of underground rooms used for burials, especially in ancient Rome. *...a painting from the catacombs.*

catalogue /ˈkætəlɒg/ **catalogues, cataloguing, catalogued**; spelt **catalog** in American English.
1 NC A **catalogue** is a book containing a list of goods that are available from a company, or a list of objects that are in a museum. *...expensive illustrated catalogues. ...catalogues from publishers.*
2 VO To **catalogue** things means to make a list of

them. *Books are catalogued on white cards that are filed alphabetically.*
3 NC+*of* A **catalogue** of things is a number of them considered one after another. *Mrs Zapp recited a catalogue of her husband's sins.*
4 VO If you **catalogue** a series of similar events or qualities, you list them. *They had been cataloguing the many discomforts of life in India.*

catalysis /kəˈtælɪsɪs/
NU In chemistry, **catalysis** is a process by which the rate of a chemical reaction increases because of the presence of a catalyst; a technical term. *...inorganic materials that could be used in catalysis.*

catalyst /ˈkætəlɪst/ **catalysts**
1 NC A **catalyst** is something that causes a change or event to happen; a formal use. *Nuclear power served as a catalyst for the emergence of the Greens as a political force.*
2 NC In chemistry, a **catalyst** is a substance that increases the rate of a chemical reaction, but which does not change its own chemical composition; a technical use. *The drug inhibits the action of an enzyme which is a biological catalyst.*

catalytic converter /kætəlɪtɪk kənˈvɜːtə/ **catalytic converters**
NC A **catalytic converter** is a device that is fitted to a car's exhaust system in order to reduce the amount of poisonous gases that come from the engine. *Virtually all new petrol engine cars will need to be fitted with catalytic converters.*

catamaran /kætəməˈræn/ **catamarans**
NC A **catamaran** is a sailing boat with two parallel hulls that are held in place by a single deck. *The winner will compete against the Stars and Stripes catamaran.*

catapult /ˈkætəpʌlt/ **catapults, catapulting, catapulted**
1 NC A **catapult** is a device for shooting small objects such as stones over a short distance. *The government is planning to ban high-powered catapults and various types of knives... There are reports of monks using home-made catapults to fire stones at soldiers.*
2 NC A **catapult** is also a device that is used to launch aircraft from an aircraft carrier. *The display also shows the use of gliders, catapults, and rockets.*
3 V-ERG A When something **catapults** or is **catapulted** somewhere, it moves very suddenly, quickly, and violently through the air. *The rebels threw two car bombs which served to catapult other bombs over the wall of the base. ...a man catapulted into the water. ...the risk of a back-seat passenger being catapulted into the windscreen.*
4 VOA If something **catapults** you to a particular state or situation, you are suddenly in that state or situation. *He was catapulted to prominence by his first speech in Parliament... He claims credit for catapulting Madonna to stardom by producing her first single.*

cataract /ˈkætərækt/ **cataracts**
NC A **cataract** is a layer that has grown over a person's eye that prevents them from seeing properly. *Ultra-violet radiation will lead to an increase in skin cancers and cataracts... Labradors are prone to eye problems, including cataracts.*

catarrh /kəˈtɑː/
NU If you have **catarrh**, you have a lot of mucus in your nose and throat. *Someone with catarrh was sniffing loudly behind her.*

catastrophe /kəˈtæstrəfi/ **catastrophes**
NCorNU A **catastrophe** is an unexpected event that causes great suffering or damage. *Unemployment is a personal catastrophe. ...an overwhelming sense of catastrophe.*

catastrophic /kætəˈstrɒfɪk/
ADJ If something is **catastrophic**, it is extremely bad or serious, often causing great suffering or damage. *The impact on Belgium has already been catastrophic. ...catastrophic mistakes.*

catcall /ˈkætkɔːl/ **catcalls**
NC **Catcalls** are the loud noises and shouting that people make to show that they disapprove of something. *In the street, the whistles and catcalls began. ...a chorus of boos and catcalls.*

catch /kætʃ/ catches, catching, caught

1 VO If you **catch** an animal or person, you capture them. *I went fishing and caught a nice little trout. ...a wild otter caught in a trap... We can get six months in prison if they catch us.*

2 VO If you **catch** an object which is moving through the air, you take hold of it or collect it while it is moving. *I couldn't catch the ball because I was carrying my shoes... 'Catch,' said Howard. He threw the book over to her.*

3 VO If you **catch** someone doing something wrong, you discover them doing it. *A gardener was sacked if he was caught smoking... Don't let him catch you at it.*

4 VO If one object **catches** another one, it hits the other object with a lot of force. *The wave caught the trawler on her bow.*

5 VA If something **catches** on an object, it becomes attached to it. *There was a bit of rabbit's fur caught on the fence.*

6 VOA If you **catch** part of your body or part of your clothing in something, it becomes trapped in it. *I knew a baby once who caught his fingers in the spokes of the pram wheel.*

7 VO If you **catch** a bus, train, or plane, you get on it to travel somewhere. *She caught a train to Boston.*

8 VO If you cannot **catch** something that someone has said, you do not manage to hear it. *She whispered something he could not catch.*

9 VO If something **catches** your interest, imagination, or attention, you notice it or become interested in it. *A poster caught her attention.*

10 V-PASS A If you **are caught** in a storm or other unpleasant situation, it happens when you cannot avoid its effects. *They were caught in an earthquake.*

11 VO If you **catch** a cold or a disease, you become ill with it. *Can humans catch mad cow disease?... Doctors who checked them decided they hadn't caught a contagious disease.*

12 VO If something **catches** the light or if the light **catches** it, it reflects the light and looks bright or shiny. *His fine-featured face and crinkly brown hair caught the light... The grass is sparkling where the sunlight catches small drops from the rain.*

13 NC A **catch** on a window or door is also a device that fastens it. *He put his hand through the hole in the glass and released the catch.*

14 N SING A **catch** is also a hidden problem or difficulty in a plan or course of action. *'There's a catch in this.'—'There's no catch, Gordon. I swear it.'*

15 to **catch** someone's eye: see eye. to **catch** fire: see fire.

catch at PHRASAL VERB If you **catch at** something, you quickly take hold of it. *The children caught at my skirts and tugged me back.*

catch on PHRASAL VERB 1 If you **catch on** to something, you understand it, or realize that it is happening. *You were expected to catch on quick... They finally caught on to our game.* 2 If something **catches on**, it becomes popular. *Ballroom dancing caught on.*

catch out PHRASAL VERB If you **catch** someone **out**, you make them make a mistake, often by an unfair trick. *Are you trying to catch me out?*

catch up PHRASAL VERB 1 If you **catch up** with someone, you reach them by moving faster than them. *Tim had just reached the corner when Judy caught up with him... She stood still, allowing him to catch her up.* 2 To **catch up** with someone also means to reach the same standard or level that they have reached. *Most leaders were obsessed with catching up with the West.* 3 If you **are caught up** in something, you are involved in it, usually unwillingly. *He was determined not to get caught up in any publicity nonsense.*

catch up on If you **catch up on** an activity that you have not had much time to do, you spend time doing it. *They went to the office to catch up on correspondence... I was catching up on my sleep.*

catch up with PHRASAL VERB 1 When people **catch up with** someone who has done something wrong, they succeed in finding them. *When Birmingham authorities finally caught up with her, she had spent*

all the money. 2 If something **catches up with** you, you find yourself in an unpleasant situation which you have been able to avoid but which you are now forced to deal with. *I am sure that the truth will catch up with him.*

catching /kætʃɪŋ/

1 ADJ PRED If an illness or a disease is **catching**, it is easily passed on to someone else. *Measles is very catching.*

2 ADJ PRED If a feeling or emotion is **catching**, it has a strong influence on other people and spreads quickly, for example through a crowd. *Panic is catching.*

catchment area /kætʃmənt eərɪə/ catchment areas

NC The **catchment area** of a school or hospital is the area that it serves. *The catchment area includes about 70 million people.*

catch-phrase, catch-phrases

NC A **catch-phrase** is a sentence or phrase which becomes popular or well-known for a while because it is often used. *The catch-phrase of the Chinese legal system is 'Reform through labour'.*

catchy /kætʃi/ catchier, catchiest

ADJ A **catchy** tune is pleasant and easy to remember. *The songs are irresistibly catchy. ...a blend of soul, funk, and catchy choruses.*

catechism /kætəkɪzəm/ catechisms

NC A **catechism** is a series of questions and answers about the religious beliefs of a particular church which people learn before they become members.

categorical /kætəgɒrɪkl/

ADJ If you are **categorical** about something, you state your views with certainty and firmness. *On this point we can be clear and categorical.* ♦ **categorically** ADV *The proposals had been categorically rejected.*

categorize /kætəgəraɪz/ categorizes, categorizing, categorized; also spelt categorise.

VO If you **categorize** people or things, you divide them into sets. *Animals can be categorised according to the food they eat.* ♦ **categorization**, /kætəgəraɪzeɪʃn/ **categorizations** N II or NC *We don't think it's necessary to have such rigid categorization... The categorisation of the report ranges from illogical to totally unfounded.*

category /kætəgə⁰ri/ categories

NC If people or things are divided into **categories**, they are divided into groups according to their qualities and characteristics. *They divided the nation into six social categories... There are three categories of machine.*

cater /keɪtə/ caters, catering, catered

V+for or V+to To **cater** for people means to provide them with the things they need. *We can cater for all age groups. ...places of entertainment that cater to mixed black and white clientele.*

caterer /keɪtərə/ caterers

NC A **caterer** is a person or a company that provides food and drink in a particular place or on a special occasion. *...a hotel caterer.*

catering /keɪtərɪŋ/

NU **Catering** is the activity or business of providing food and drink for people. *'Who did the catering?'—'A firm in Arundel.'*

caterpillar /kætəpɪlə/ caterpillars

NC A **caterpillar** is a small worm-like animal that eventually develops into a butterfly or moth. *The main pest, a caterpillar, is killed by a virus.*

caterpillar tracks

N PL The **caterpillar tracks** of a heavy vehicle such as a tank are the ridged belts round the wheels which enable it to grip soft ground. *The so-called 'Sno-Cat' had caterpillar tracks that proved equal to the treacherous terrain.*

caterwaul /kætəwɔːl/ caterwauls, caterwauling, caterwauled

V If an animal or a person **caterwauls**, they make an unpleasant noise by wailing or howling loudly. ► Also N SING *We were woken by a high, snarling caterwaul, a sort of screaming wail.*

catfish /kætfɪʃ/; **catfish** is both the singular and the plural form.

NC A **catfish** is a fish with long thin spines around its mouth that look like whiskers. *He once caught a 40-pound catfish.*

catharsis /kəθɑːsɪs/
NU **Catharsis** is getting rid of strong emotions or unhappy memories by expressing them in some way; a formal word. *The catharsis of the confession had left her exhausted.*

cathartic /kəθɑːtɪk/
ADJ Something that is **cathartic** has the effect of catharsis; a formal word. *I felt the cathartic power of his speech.*

cathedral /kəθiːdrəl/ **cathedrals**
NC A **cathedral** is a large important church which has a bishop in charge of it. *A crowd gathered outside the main Catholic cathedral.*

catherine wheel /kæθrɪn wiːl/ **catherine wheels**
NC A **catherine wheel** is a firework in the shape of a circle which spins round and round when it is lit. *There are catherine wheels and roman candles giving out showers of coloured lights.*

cathode /kæθəʊd/ **cathodes**
NC A **cathode** is the negative electrode in a cell such as a battery; a technical term in physics. *The negative charge of the cathode attracted positive ions.*

cathode ray tube, cathode ray tubes; also spelt **cathode-ray tube.**
NC A **cathode ray tube** is a device used in televisions and computer terminals which sends an image onto the screen; a technical term in physics. *The crystals are much smaller than the ones you would get in a normal cathode ray tube.*

Catholic /kæθəlɪk/ **Catholics**
NC A **Catholic** is someone who belongs to the branch of the Christian church which accepts the Pope as its leader. *...four million Ukrainian Catholics. ...the Catholic Church.*

Catholicism /kəθɒləsɪzəm/
NU **Catholicism** is the set of Christian beliefs held by Catholics. *...a revival of Catholicism.*

catkin /kætkɪn/ **catkins**
NC **Catkins** are long thin soft flowers that hang from birch or hazel trees.

catnap /kætnæp/ **catnaps, catnapping, catnapped**
NC A **catnap** is a short sleep; an informal word. *...six hours' sleep plus a few daytime catnaps.* ► Also V *He catnapped in his seat.*

cat's cradle
NU **Cat's cradle** is a game using a loop of string that you hold and twist between your fingers.

cat's-eye, cat's-eyes
NC **Cat's-eyes** are small pieces of reflective glass fixed in the middle of a road that help drivers to see the road at night.

cat's paw, cat's paws
NC If one person uses another as a **cat's paw**, they use them unfairly in order to achieve something that is illegal or likely to cause trouble; an old-fashioned expression. *They are trying to incite a rebellion and are using Mr Pradhan as a cat's paw.*

catsuit /kætsuːt/ **catsuits**
NC A **catsuit** is a piece of women's clothing that is made in one piece and fits closely over the body and legs. *...one plastic wet-look catsuit.*

catsup /kætsəp/
NU **Catsup** is the same as ketchup; used in American English. *They poured catsup on their hamburgers.*

cattle /kætl/
N PL **Cattle** are cows and bulls. *The idea is to keep the cattle in stalls and bring the fodder to them. ...cattle raiders.*

cattle-grid, cattle-grids
NC A **cattle-grid** is a metal grid that is set into the road so that cattle and sheep cannot cross but people and vehicles can. *...rough tracks guarded at their junction with the tarmac by metal cattle-grids.*

cattle market, cattle markets
1 NC A **cattle market** is a market where cattle are bought and sold. *The future of one of the biggest cattle markets in England is under threat.*
2 NC You can also refer to an event such as a beauty contest where women are being considered only for their sexual attractiveness as a **cattle market**; used showing disapproval. *The Miss World contest is nothing more than a cattle market.*

catty /kæti/ **cattier, cattiest**
ADJ If a woman or girl is being **catty**, she is being unpleasant and spiteful. *Miss Haynes was capable of being catty and jealous.*

catwalk /kætwɔːk/ **catwalks**
1 NC A **catwalk** is a narrow bridge high in the air between two parts of a tall building or on the outside of a large structure. *...tiptoeing on the catwalk of a skyscraper in a high wind.*
2 NC In a fashion show, the **catwalk** is the narrow platform that models walk along to display clothes. *The new spring season's clothes were being paraded on the catwalk.*

caucus /kɔːkəs/ **caucuses**
NC A **caucus** is an influential group of people within an organization who share similar aims and interests; a formal word. *...the California caucus at the National Convention.*

caught /kɔːt/
Caught is the past tense and past participle of **catch.**

cauldron /kɔːldrən/ **cauldrons**; spelt **caldron** in American English.
1 NC A **cauldron** is a very large round metal pot used for cooking over a fire. *His shield, sword, drinking horn and cooking cauldron were buried with him.*
2 NC+SUPP You can also refer to a situation that is likely to become violent or dangerous as a **cauldron**. *It's a cauldron of spiritual emotions which frequently take on political connotations... The move has thrown her right into the cauldron of Polish politics.*

cauliflower /kɒlɪflaʊə/ **cauliflowers**
NCorNU A **cauliflower** is a large round white vegetable surrounded by green leaves. *The stamp shows a pile of vegetables such as a cabbage, a cauliflower, and a bundle of leeks. ...the nutritional value of cauliflower and young vegetables.*

causal /kɔːzl/
ADJ ATTRIB **Causal** means connected by a relationship of cause and effect. *There may be no causal link... It is hard to see how such a causal relationship could be proved.*

causality /kɔːzæləti/
NU **Causality** is the relationship of cause and effect; a formal word. *...simple models of causality.*

causation /kɔːzeɪʃn/
NU **Causation** is the same as causality; a formal word. *From what is our knowledge of causation received?*

cause /kɔːz/ **causes, causing, caused**
1 NC The **cause** of an event is the thing that makes it happen. *Nobody knew the cause of the explosion... The men died of natural causes.*
2 VOorVOO If someone or something **causes** a situation or an event, they make it happen. *She caused a sensation by winning more votes than Mr Heath on the first ballot. ...difficulties caused by price increases... What's causing you so much concern?... The sound caused her to step aside.*
3 NU+for orNU+to-INF If you have **cause** for a particular feeling or action, you have good reasons for it. *Years of training gave him every cause for confidence... I have no cause to go back.*
4 NC A **cause** is also an aim which a group of people supports or is fighting for. *...the cause of world peace.*

cause célèbre /kəʊz səlɛb/ **causes célèbres.** The singular and the plural are pronounced in the same way.
NC A **cause célèbre** is a controversial issue, person, or criminal trial that attracts a lot of public attention. *The strike has now exploded into a national cause célèbre. ...the Boy Scout leader from Bristol who became a cause célèbre of the Left.*

causeway /kɔːzweɪ/ **causeways**
NC A **causeway** is a raised path or road that crosses water or marshland. *...a truck carrying soldiers across the causeway.*

caustic /kɔːstɪk/
1 ADJ **Caustic** chemical substances can dissolve other substances. *Do not use a caustic cleaner on enamel.*
2 ADJ A **caustic** remark is extremely critical or bitter. *...her caustic sense of humour.*

caustic soda
NU **Caustic soda** is a powerful chemical substance that is used to make cleaning materials such as strong soaps. *The accused had put cyanide and caustic soda in baby foods.*

cauterize /kɔːtəraɪz/ **cauterizes, cauterizing, cauterized;** also spelt **cauterise.**
VO If you **cauterize** a wound, you burn it with heat in order to close it and to prevent infection; a medical term. *He cauterized the wound and the bleeding stopped.*

caution /kɔːʃn/ **cautions, cautioning, cautioned**
1 NU **Caution** is great care taken in order to avoid danger. *You must proceed with extreme caution.*
2 V-REPORT, VO-REPORT, VO+to-INF, or V-QUOTE If someone **cautions** you that something will happen, they warn you of it. *The doctor cautioned that any such state of tension could be highly dangerous... The report cautions him that Greece will need careful handling next year... I cautioned him not to reveal too much to anyone... 'However,' the President cautioned, 'Congress can approve one kind of aid today, and another tomorrow.'* ▶ Also NU *...a word of caution.*
3 VO+against or V+against If you **caution** someone against a particular action, you advise them not to do it. *He is cautioning the United States against a war... He cautioned against reading too much into one month's figures.*
4 VO If you **caution** patience or restraint, you tell someone to be patient or to restrain themselves. *The Foreign Secretary is anxious not to get into a slanging match, and is cautioning patience.*
5 VO When the police **caution** someone, they warn them that anything that they say may be used as evidence in a trial. *One man was cautioned, and charges against another were dismissed.*

cautionary /kɔːʃənˈri/
1 ADJ ATTRIB A **cautionary** story or tale is intended to give a warning or advice. *And now a cautionary tale for people who don't use banks.*
2 ADJ ATTRIB A **cautionary** remark, speech, or statement warns someone that they need to be careful. *The Foreign Minister struck a cautionary note about how much the government could be expected to achieve.*

cautious /kɔːʃəs/
ADJ A **cautious** person acts very carefully in order to avoid danger. *Her husband is reserved and cautious.* ◆ **cautiously** ADV *We moved cautiously forward.*

Cavaço Silva, Aníbal /ænɪbæl kævæsəʊ sɪlvə/
Aníbal Cavaço Silva became Prime Minister of Portugal in 1985. He was Minister of Finance and Planning from 1980 to 1981. He was elected leader of the Social Democratic Party (PSD) in 1985. Born: 1939.

cavalcade /kævlkeɪd/ **cavalcades**
NC A **cavalcade** is a procession of people on horses or in cars or carriages. *A great cavalcade swept dramatically into the castle courtyard.*

cavalier /kævəlɪə/
ADJ Someone who behaves in a **cavalier** way does not consider other people's feelings or the seriousness of a situation. *...the government's cavalier attitude to elections.*

cavalry /kævlri/
N SING In an army, the **cavalry** used to be the group of soldiers who rode horses. Nowadays, it is usually the part of the army that uses armoured vehicles. *...a cavalry charge.*

cave /keɪv/ **caves, caving, caved**
NC A **cave** is a large hole in the side of a cliff or hill, or under the ground. *...separatists holding a number of hostages in a remote cave.*
cave in PHRASAL VERB 1 When a roof or wall **caves in**, it collapses inwards. *One said they heard a terrible noise and the roof caved in.* 2 If you **cave in**, you suddenly stop arguing or resisting. *Under the frenzied and abusive attacks of the Chief Prosecutor, most of the defendants caved in.*

caveat /kæviæt/ **caveats**
1 NC A **caveat** is a warning that you have to allow for something before you act or carry out plans; a formal use. *That view can be put another way, but with inevitable caveats.*
2 NC A **caveat** is also a formal notice in a law court that a particular action should not be taken without telling the person who is giving this notice; a legal use. *They have filed a caveat before the chief election commissioner.*

cave-in, cave-ins
NC A **cave-in** is the sudden collapse of a roof into a building, room, or cave below it. *One man died in a cave-in at the Victorian mine.*

caveman /keɪvmæn/ **cavemen**
NC **Cavemen** were people in prehistoric times who lived in caves.

cavern /kævn/ **caverns**
NC A **cavern** is a large deep cave. *This would mean digging out a number of caverns five-hundred metres below ground.*

cavernous /kævənəs/
ADJ A **cavernous** building is very large inside. *They arrived at the cavernous Great Hall of the People.*

caviar /kæviɑː/; also spelt **caviare.**
NU **Caviar** is the salted eggs of a fish called the sturgeon.

cavil /kævl/ **cavils, cavilling, cavilled;** spelt **caviling, caviled** in American English.
V If someone **cavils**, they complain about things that are unimportant; a formal word. *Captain Paget could find nothing to cavil at.*

cavity /kævəti/ **cavities**
NC A **cavity** is a small space or hole in something solid. *...the filling of tooth cavities.*

cavity wall, cavity walls
NC A **cavity wall** is a wall consisting of two separate walls with a space between them. *...the inner wall of a cavity wall. ...cavity wall insulation.*

cavort /kəvɔːt/ **cavorts, cavorting, cavorted**
V When people or animals **cavort**, they leap about in a noisy and excited way. *...politicians cavorting in front of the camera.*

caw /kɔː/ **caws, cawing, cawed**
V When a bird such as a crow or a rook **caws**, it makes a loud harsh sound. *Rooks cawed in the great beeches all around.* ▶ Also NC *The crane let out a raucous caw.*

Cayenne /kaɪen/
Cayenne is the capital of French Guiana and its largest city. Population: 42,000 (1990).

cayenne pepper /keɪen pepə/
NU **Cayenne pepper** is a hot-tasting red powder made from dried peppers that is used to flavour food.

Cayman Islands /keɪmən aɪləndz/
The **Cayman Islands** is a territory of the United Kingdom in the Caribbean. The principal islands are Grand Cayman, Little Cayman, and Cayman Brac. They became a British colony in the 17th century and were administered by Jamaica until 1962, when Jamaica became independent. Tourism and banking are important industries. ◆ **Cayman Islander** /keɪmən aɪləndə/ NC **Caymanian** /keɪmæniən/ ADJ
▪ *per capita GDP:* US$17,400 ▪ *religion:* Christianity
▪ *language:* English (official) ▪ *currency:* dollar
▪ *capital:* George Town ▪ *population:* 25,000 (1989)
▪ *size:* 260 square kilometres.

CB /siːbiː/
CB is an abbreviation for Citizens' Band. *...CB radio equipment. ...his new CB rig.*

CBE /siːbiːiː/ **CBEs**
The **CBE** is an honour given to a person by the British monarch for an outstanding service or achievement. CBE is an abbreviation for 'Commander of the Order of the British Empire'. *She was made a CBE in 1981. ...Major-General David Mostyn CBE.*

CBI /siːbiːaɪ/
N PROP The **CBI** is an organization which a large number of companies belong to and which is concerned with all aspects of business and industry. CBI is an abbreviation for 'Confederation of British Industry'. *The CBI will be pressing for a limit on business rates.*

cc. /siːsiː/
cc. is an abbreviation for 'cubic centimetres'; used to

refer to the volume or capacity of something. *The dose for an adult cow is about 40 cc. ...a five-hundred cc. motorbike.*

CD /ˌsiːˈdiː/ **CDs**
NC A **CD** is a compact disc. *The biggest selling CD of all time in Britain is 'Brothers in Arms' by Dire Straits. ...a CD player.*

cease /siːs/ **ceases, ceasing, ceased;** a formal word.
1 v If something **ceases**, it stops happening. *Hostilities must cease at once... Most civil and commercial activity has ceased.*
2 V+to-INF or V+ING If you **cease** to do something, you stop doing it. *Once people retire they cease to be union members... The vicar sighed as he ceased speaking.*
3 vo To **cease** something that is being produced or provided means to stop producing or providing it. *They threatened to cease financial support to the university.*

ceasefire /ˈsiːsfaɪə/ **ceasefires**
NC A **ceasefire** is an agreement between countries or groups who are at war to stop fighting for a time. *Ever since the ceasefire in August, they have been supplying weapons to the enemy. ...a six week unilateral ceasefire.*

ceaseless /ˈsiːsləs/
ADJ ATTRIB **Ceaseless** means continuing for ever or for a long time; a formal word. *...the ceaseless traffic.*
♦ **ceaselessly** ADV *Clarissa talked ceaselessly.*

cedar /ˈsiːdə/ **cedars**
NC A **cedar** is a large evergreen tree. It has needle-like leaves and brown cones. The wood that is obtained from this tree is also called **cedar.** *...the fragrance of the cedar. ...a large area of cedar forest.*

cede /siːd/ **cedes, ceding, ceded**
vo If you **cede** something to someone, you formally allow them to have it; a formal word. *The colony was ceded to Spain in 1762.*

cedilla /səˈdɪlə/ **cedillas**
NC A **cedilla** is a symbol that is written under a letter 'c' in French, Portuguese, and Spanish to show that you pronounce it like a letter 's' rather than like a letter 'k'. It is written ç.

Cedras, Raoul /rɑːˈuːl sedrɑːs/
Brigadier-General Raoul Cedras took control of the government of Haiti in a coup in 1991. At the time of the coup, he was the Commander-in-Chief of the Army.

ceilidh /ˈkeɪli/ **ceilidhs**
NC A **ceilidh** is an informal Scottish or Irish entertainment, at which there is folk music, singing, and dancing. *The traditional ceilidh due to take place at a local pub has been cancelled.*

ceiling /ˈsiːlɪŋ/ **ceilings**
1 NC A **ceiling** is the top inside surface of a room. *...a large room with a high ceiling.*
2 NC+SUPP A **ceiling** is also an official upper limit on prices or wages. *...a ceiling on business rate increases.*

celebrant /ˈselɪbrənt/ **celebrants**
NC A **celebrant** is a person who performs or takes part in a religious ceremony; a technical term.

celebrate /ˈselɪbreɪt/ **celebrates, celebrating, celebrated**
1 V or VO If you **celebrate** an event or anniversary, you do something special and enjoyable because of it. *We ought to celebrate; let's have a bottle of champagne... His victory was celebrated with music and dancing... The company was celebrating its fiftieth birthday.*
2 vo When priests **celebrate** Holy Communion or Mass, they officially perform the actions and ceremonies that are involved. *Pope John Paul has celebrated an open-air Mass before thousands of miners and their families.*

celebrated /ˈselɪbreɪtɪd/
ADJ ATTRIB A **celebrated** person or thing is very famous. *...a celebrated actress... Richard Attenborough made celebrated films on the lives of Gandhi and Steve Biko.*

celebration /ˌselɪˈbreɪʃn/ **celebrations**
1 NC or NU A **celebration** is a special event that is organized so that people can enjoy themselves, for example on a birthday or anniversary. *We ought to have a little celebration of our own... The celebrations marking the 300th anniversary have been cancelled... It was a time of celebration.*
2 NU+SUPP The **celebration** of someone or something is praise and appreciation which is given to them; a formal use. *...a festival held for the celebration of music and dance.*

celebratory /ˈselɪbreɪtəri/
ADJ ATTRIB **Celebratory** means organized or happening in order to celebrate a special event such as a birthday or anniversary; a formal word. *...traditional celebratory dinners on special occasions.*

celebrity /səˈlebrəti/ **celebrities**
1 NC A **celebrity** is someone who is famous. *Members of Parliament and well-known celebrities were at the launch of the campaign.*
2 NU **Celebrity** is the fact or state of being famous. *Miss Doi had achieved celebrity in the 1970's for her appearance on quiz shows... The 1980's were a time when celebrity became more than an obsession.*

celery /ˈseləri/
NU **Celery** is a vegetable with long pale green stalks. *...a stick of celery.*

celestial /səˈlestiəl/
ADJ ATTRIB **Celestial** is used to describe things connected with heaven or with the sky. *...astronomy, the scientific study of celestial bodies... One picture shows swirling celestial figures, a winged angel and a band of musicians in heaven.*

celibacy /ˈseləbəsi/
NU **Celibacy** is the state of being celibate; a formal word. *...vows of poverty, celibacy and obedience.*

celibate /ˈseləbət/
ADJ Someone who is **celibate** does not marry or have sex; a formal word. *The celibate life was beginning to appeal to him.*

cell /sel/ **cells**
1 NC A **cell** is the smallest independent part of an animal or plant. Animals and plants are made up of millions of cells. *These chemicals are found on the surface of cancer cells, not normal blood cells.*
2 NC A **cell** is also a small room in which a prisoner is locked, or one in which a monk or nun lives. *Lawyers complained that their clients were held in police cells in cramped and unsanitary conditions.*

cellar /ˈselə/ **cellars**
NC A **cellar** is a room underneath a building, often used for storing things in. *...a uniquely decorated 15th century cellar.*

cellist /ˈtʃelɪst/ **cellists**
NC A **cellist** is a person who plays a cello. *The cellist Jacqueline du Pre died 2 years ago at the age of 42.*

cello /ˈtʃeləʊ/ **cellos**
NC A **cello** is a musical instrument that looks like a large violin. You hold it upright and play it sitting down. *...a piece for cello and strings.*

Cellophane /ˈseləfeɪn/
NU **Cellophane** is a thin transparent material that is used to wrap things such as food in order to keep them fresh; **Cellophane** is a trademark. *...drugs wrapped in cellophane.*

cell-phone, cell-phones
NC A **cell-phone** is a telephone that uses radio signals and a network of transmitters to send and receive messages across a distance. You can use it when you are on a train or in a car, because it does not have a cord attached to it. *The guerrillas are said to be using cell-phones to communicate with each other.*

cellular /ˈseljʊlə/
1 ADJ ATTRIB **Cellular** means relating to the cells of animals or plants. *...cellular structure.*
2 ADJ ATTRIB **Cellular** fabrics are loosely woven and keep you warm.

cellular telephone, cellular telephones
NC A **cellular phone** is the same as a **cell-phone**. *...the world's smallest pocket cellular telephone.*

celluloid /ˈseljʊlɔɪd/
1 NU **Celluloid** is a type of plastic. *Corks have been replaced with celluloid balls.*
2 NU You can use **celluloid** to refer to films and the cinema; a literary use. *...the celluloid world of Hollywood.*

cellulose /sɛljuləʊs/
NU **Cellulose** is a substance found in plants which is used to make paper, plastic, and various textiles and fibres. *Carbohydrates may be used as cellulose to form the structure of the plant. ...cellulose paint.*

Celsius /sɛlsiəs/
NU **Celsius** is a scale for measuring temperature, in which water freezes at 0° and boils at 100°. *Beyond about 3000 degrees Celsius, it becomes difficult to measure resistance.*

Celt /kɛlt/ **Celts**; pronounced /sɛlt/ in Scotland.
NC In ancient times, the **Celts** were a race of people who lived in Britain, Ireland and other parts of Europe. *The Celts had their own mythology about a divine child, which preceded the birth of Christ. ...the Celts in Scotland and Ireland.*

Celtic /kɛltɪk/; pronounced /sɛltɪk/ in Scotland.
ADJ If you describe something as **Celtic**, you mean that it is connected with the people, culture and traditions of Scotland, Wales, Ireland, and Brittany. *...the Celtic legends... Their faces are Celtic. ...the Celtic language.*

cement /səmɛnt/ **cements, cementing, cemented**
1 NU **Cement** is a grey powder which is mixed with sand and water in order to make concrete. *All over the city, young men armed with bags of cement and shovels are repairing potholes.*
2 VO If you **cement** something, you cover it with cement. *A recently introduced procedure is to cement fine porcelain to the surface.*
3 VO If things are **cemented** together, they are stuck or fastened together. *The lumps were cemented to the reef with coral.*
4 VO Something that **cements** a relationship or agreement makes it stronger. *State visits were necessary to cement relations between the countries concerned... These ties were cemented when the Indian government signed a treaty of peace and friendship.*

cement mixer, cement mixers
NC A **cement mixer** is a machine with a large revolving container which is used for mixing cement, sand, and water to make concrete. *The crash was like being in a cement mixer—I just spun round and round.*

cemetery /sɛmətri/ **cemeteries**
NC A **cemetery** is a place where dead people are buried. *A crowd of several thousand had gathered at the cemetery.*

cenotaph /sɛnətɑːf/ **cenotaphs**
NC A **cenotaph** is a monument that is built in honour of soldiers who died in a war. *All the men used to raise their hats when passing the cenotaph.*

censor /sɛnsə/ **censors, censoring, censored**
1 VO If someone **censors** something that has been printed, written, or broadcast, they officially examine it and cut out any parts that they consider unacceptable. *He was censoring his platoon's mail.*
2 NC A **censor** is a person who has been officially appointed to censor books, plays, and films, or public information. *This news has not been passed by the official censor.*

censorious /sɛnsɔːriəs/
ADJ When someone is **censorious**, they strongly criticize someone else's behaviour; a formal word. *There is no need to be censorious about such activities... She had had to put up with a number of censorious comments.*

censorship /sɛnsəʃɪp/
NU When there is **censorship**, books, plays, films, letters, or reports are censored. *...the censorship of bad news in wartime.*

censure /sɛnʃə/ **censures, censuring, censured**
VO If you **censure** someone, you tell them that you strongly disapprove of what they have done; a formal word. *He had been censured for showing cowardice in the battle.* ▶ Also NU *The result exposed him to official censure.*

census /sɛnsəs/ **censuses**
NC A **census** is an official survey of the population of a country. *The country conducted its first national census using modern scientific methods.*

cent /sɛnt/ **cents**
NC A **cent** is a small unit of money in many countries, worth one hundredth of the main unit. *A forty gram bar would be sixteen cents.* ● See also **per cent**.

cent- /sɛnt-/, sent-/
1 PREFIX **Cent-** or centi- is sometimes used at the beginning of nouns or adjectives that have 'one hundred' as part of their meaning. *...century. ...centipede. ...centennial.*
2 PREFIX **Cent-** is used at the beginning of nouns referring to measurements or units of money that are a one-hundredth part of other measurements or units of money. *...centimetre. ...centilitre.*

centaur /sɛntɔː/ **centaurs**
NC In classical mythology, a **centaur** is a creature that has the body and legs of a horse and the upper body and head of a man. *In Greek mythology, the centaur Chiron is known as the Wounded Healer.*

centenarian /sɛntɪnɛəriən/ **centenarians**
NC A **centenarian** is a person who is a hundred years old or older. *Parliamentary sessions have been distinguished by the presence of at least one centenarian.*

centenary /sɛntiːnəri/ **centenaries**
NC A **centenary** is a year when people celebrate something important that happened one hundred years earlier. *1928 was the centenary of Ibsen's birth. ...centenary celebrations.*

centennial /sɛntɛniəl/ **centennials**
NC A **centennial** is the same as a **centenary**; used in American English. *The student newspaper celebrates the centennial of its founding... The centennial Olympics will be held in Atlanta, Georgia.*

center /sɛntə/. See **centre**.
centi- /sɛnti-/. See **cent-**.

Centigrade /sɛntɪɡreɪd/
NU **Centigrade** is a scale for measuring temperature, in which water freezes at 0° and boils at 100°. *The water that comes out of the Mendip hills is about 45 degrees Centigrade.*

centimetre /sɛntɪmiːtə/ **centimetres**; spelt **centimeter** in American English.
NC A **centimetre** is a unit of length equal to ten millimetres or one-hundredth of a metre. *He reportedly used a forty centimetre knife on his victims.*

centipede /sɛntɪpiːd/ **centipedes**
NC A **centipede** is a long, thin insect with lots of legs. *...the class of animal which includes centipedes, scorpions, spiders and even ticks.*

central /sɛntrəl/
1 ADJ Something that is **central** is in the middle of a place or area. *The houses are arranged around a central courtyard. ...a film about central Poland.*
◆ **centrally** ADV *The pin is centrally positioned on the circle.*
2 ADJ A place that is **central** is easy to reach because it is in the centre of a city. *The cafe was near Oxford Street, very central for her.* ◆ **centrally** ADV *...a centrally located flat.*
3 ADJ ATTRIB A **central** group or organization makes all the important decisions for a larger organization or country. *Their activities are strictly controlled by a central committee. ...local and central government.*
◆ **centrally** ADV *France has a centrally organized system.*
4 ADJ The **central** person or thing in a particular situation is the most important one. *These statistics were central to the debate.*

Central African Republic /sɛntrəl æfrɪkən rɪpʌblɪk/
The **Central African Republic** is a country, which was part of French Equatorial Africa from 1911 until 1960, when it became independent. Colonel Jean-Bédel Bokassa seized power in 1966 and crowned himself emperor in 1977 in a ceremony costing approximately US$25 million. In 1979 he was overthrown. General André Kolingba became President in a coup in 1981. The Central African Democratic Assembly (RDC) became the sole legal party in 1987, but the transition to multi-party government was announced in 1991. The Central African Republic exports diamonds, coffee, cotton, and timber. It is a member of the Organization

of African Unity. ◆ **Central African** /sɛntrəl æfrɪkən/
N, ADJ
▪ *per capita GNP:* US$390 ▪ *religion:* animism,
Christianity ▪ *language:* French (official), Sango
▪ *currency:* CFA franc ▪ *capital:* Bangui ▪ *population:* 3
million (1989) ▪ *size:* 622,984 square kilometres.

central heating
NU **Central heating** is a heating system in which water
or air is heated and passed round a building through
pipes and radiators. *...a house equipped with central
heating and its own garden.*

centralise /sɛntrəlaɪz/. See **centralize**.

centralism /sɛntrəlɪzəm/
NU **Centralism** is a way of governing a country or
organizing something such as industry, education, or
politics, by having one central group of people who
give instructions to all the other regional groups. *The
opposition attacked its rigid centralism.*

centralist /sɛntrəlɪst/ **centralists**
1 ADJ **Centralist** policies or organizations govern a
country or organize things using one central group of
people who control and instruct other regional groups.
*He accused her of running a centralist and
authoritarian Cabinet... We know that some of the
centralist leaders will not accept this agreement.*
2 NC A **centralist** is someone who supports and agrees
with centralism. *The division between the democratic
socialists and the centralists has not been clear to the
voters.*

centrality /sɛntræləti/
NU+SUPP **Centrality** is the quality of being central; a
formal word. *Fine Art tradition was given cultural
centrality.*

centralization /sɛntrəlaɪzeɪʃn/; also spelt
centralisation.
NU **Centralization** is the process of changing a system
or organization so that it is controlled by one central
group. *Large-scale technology brings centralization.*

centralize /sɛntrəlaɪz/ **centralizes, centralizing,
centralized**; also spelt **centralise**.
VO To **centralize** a country or state means to create a
system of government in which one central group of
people gives instructions to regional groups. *Just
about everything is prescribed, standardised and
centralized.*

centralized /sɛntrəlaɪzd/; also spelt **centralised**.
ADJ If a country or system is **centralized**, it is
controlled by one central group. *We believe in a
strong centralized state.*

centrally heated
ADJ A building that is **centrally heated** has central
heating. *Whites had a better chance of getting a
centrally heated home.*

centre /sɛntə/ **centres, centring, centred**; spelt **center,
centers, centering, centered** in American English.
1 NC The **centre** of something is the middle of it. *He
moved the table over to the centre of the room... The
fighting spread to the city centre... It has a galvanised
iron centre column running through it.* ▶ Also
ADJ ATTRIB *...a black wig with a centre parting... The
centre section was coloured pink.*
2 NC A **centre** is a place where people have meetings,
get help of some kind, or take part in a particular
activity. *...a new arts centre. ...the university's
health centre.*
3 NC+SUPP If an area or town is a **centre** for a
particular industry or activity, that industry or
activity is very important there. *The region began as
a centre for sheep-farming... Moss Side is the biggest
centre for drug dealing in the north-west of England.*
4 NC+SUPP The **centre** of a situation is the most
important thing involved. *Smith was right in the
centre of the action... The future of the National
Health Service continues to be the centre of a fierce
row among the party leaders.*
5 NC+SUPP If something is the **centre** of attention or
interest, people are giving it a lot of attention. *She
was the centre of public admiration... At Wimbledon,
Andre Agassi is again the centre of attention.*
6 N SING In politics, the **centre** refers to political
groups and beliefs that are neither left-wing nor right-
wing. *In election year, a disunited nation would suit*

the centre more. *...a relatively small centre party
called the Free Democrats.*
7 V-PASS Someone or something that is **centred** in a
particular place has its base there. *They were now
centred in the new Royal Observatory at Greenwich...
Cuban affairs are centred in a special branch.*

centre around PHRASAL VERB If something **centres
around, centres round**, or **centres on** a person or thing,
that person or thing is the main feature or subject of
attention. *The workers' demands centred around pay
and conditions... His proposals centre on big
reductions in the prices paid to farmers for their
produce.*

centre on PHRASAL VERB See **centre around**.

centre round PHRASAL VERB See **centre around**.

centre of gravity, centres of gravity
1 NC The **centre of gravity** of an object is the point on
the object at which it balances perfectly. *In a canoe,
the centre of gravity is below the surface of the water.*
2 N SING The **centre of gravity** of an organization or
activity is that part of it which is considered to be
most important or influential. *The centre of gravity in
French politics has shifted rightwards paradoxically
under a left-wing President... The political centre of
gravity is more authentically social democrat than is
found anywhere in the two neighbouring continents.*

centrepiece /sɛntəpiːs/ **centrepieces**
1 N SING The **centrepiece** of a set of things that is
greatly admired is something that you show as the
best example of the set. *The centrepiece of the
modern navy is the nuclear submarine... This Bill is
the centrepiece of Labour's legislative programme.*
2 NC A **centrepiece** is an ornament which you put in a
noticeable place so that it can be admired. *...a
beautiful vase of orchids as a centrepiece.*

centre-stage
NU You use **centre-stage** to say that someone or
something has a very important or significant role in a
particular situation. *Egypt now occupies the centre-
stage in Middle East politics... This train of events has
put the PLO at centre-stage, diplomatically speaking.*

centrifugal force /sɛntrɪfjuːgl fɔːs, sɛntrɪfʊgl/
NU **Centrifugal force** is the force that makes objects
move outwards when they are spinning around
something or travelling in a curve; a technical term in
physics. *You can't hold the bike up because of
centrifugal force.*

centrifuge /sɛntrɪfjuːdʒ/ **centrifuges**
NC A **centrifuge** is a machine that uses centrifugal
force to separate different substances. *The only
expense at the moment is the centrifuge.*

centripetal force /sɛntrɪpiːtl fɔːs, sɛntrɪpɪtl/
NU **Centripetal force** is the force that makes objects
move inwards when they are spinning around
something or travelling in a curve; a technical term in
physics.

centrist /sɛntrɪst/ **centrists**
NC In politics, a **centrist** is someone with moderate
political views which are neither strongly right-wing
nor strongly left-wing. *He has made determined
efforts to portray himself as a party centrist... The
group intends to serve as the nucleus of a new centrist
group.*

centurion /sɛntjʊəriən/ **centurions**
NC A **centurion** was an officer in the Roman army.
...men dressed up as Roman centurions.

century /sɛntʃəˠri/ **centuries**
1 NC A **century** is the period of a hundred years that
is used when stating a date. For example, the 19th
century was the period from 1801 to 1900. *...calling for
harmful gas emissions to be halved by the end of this
century.*
2 NC A **century** is also any period of a hundred years.
Olivier's career spanned more than half a century.

ceramic /səræmɪk/ **ceramics**
1 ADJ ATTRIB **Ceramic** objects are made of clay that
has been heated to a very high temperature.
...ceramic tiles.
2 NC **Ceramics** are ceramic objects. *...Chinese
ceramics.*

cereal /sɪəriəl/ **cereals**
1 NCorNU A **cereal** is a plant such as wheat, maize, or

rice that produces grain. ...*chemicals used to control mildew and mould in cereals, fruit and vegetables*... *A senior Red Cross official took cereal, drugs and cooking oil to Aweil yesterday.* ...*cereal crops.*
2 NU or NC **Cereal** is also a food made from grain, usually mixed with milk and eaten for breakfast. *An English breakfast includes fruit juice, cereal, smoked fish or bacon.* ...*sugary breakfast cereals.*

cerebral /sɛrəbrəl/
1 ADJ **Cerebral** means relating to thought or reasoning rather than to emotions; a formal use. ...*the cerebral challenge of police work.*
2 ADJ ATTRIB **Cerebral** also means relating to the brain; a medical use. ...*a cerebral hemorrhage.*

cerebral palsy
NU **Cerebral palsy** is an illness caused by damage to a baby's brain before it is born, which makes its limbs and muscles permanently weak. *She has suffered cerebral palsy ever since staff at the hospital failed to detect complications before the birth.*

cerebrum /sɛriːbrəm/ **cerebrums** or **cerebra** /sɛriːbrə/
NC The **cerebrum** is the front part of the brain which is concerned with thought and perception; a medical term.

ceremonial /sɛrəməʊniəl/ **ceremonials**
1 ADJ Something that is **ceremonial** is used in a ceremony or relates to a ceremony. ...*a ceremonial robe from Africa.* ...*ceremonial dances.*
♦ **ceremonially** ADV *One of the helicopters was ceremonially handed over to the Indian High Commission*... *About a thousand protesters ceremonially burned the book at a demonstration last Saturday.*
2 ADJ PRED A position, function, or event that is **ceremonial** is considered to be representative of an institution, but has very little authority or influence. *Under the Ayatollah, the presidential post was largely ceremonial*... *An international conference must have a substantive role, and cannot be merely ceremonial.*
3 NU or NC **Ceremonial** consists of all the impressive things that are done, said, or worn on very formal occasions. *The drive is meticulously timed, like all royal ceremonial*... *He loved parades and ceremonials.*

ceremonious /sɛrəməʊniəs/
ADJ **Ceremonious** behaviour is excessively polite and formal. *He bid her an unusually ceremonious farewell.* ♦ **ceremoniously** ADV *He filled all their glasses ceremoniously.*

ceremony /sɛrəməni/ **ceremonies**
1 NC A **ceremony** is a formal event such as a wedding or a coronation. ...*a graduation ceremony.*
2 NU **Ceremony** consists of the special things that are said and done on very formal occasions. *The end of the war was remembered as always with honour and ceremony.*
3 NU **Ceremony** is also very formal and polite behaviour. *At the BBC she was received with respectful ceremony.*

certain /sɜːtn/
1 ADJ If you are **certain** about something, you have no doubt in your mind about it. *He felt certain that she would disapprove*... *I'm absolutely certain of that.*
2 ADJ If an event or situation is **certain**, you are sure that it will definitely happen or exist. *She's certain to be late*... *Such a vote would mean the certain defeat of the government.*
3 ADJ ATTRIB You use **certain** to indicate that you are referring to one particular thing, person, or group, although you are not saying exactly which it is. *She arranged to meet him at three o'clock on a certain afternoon*... *Certain areas in Sussex are better than others for keeping bees.* ▶ Also QUANT *Certain of our judges have claimed that this is the case.*
● **Certain** is used in these phrases. ● If you know something **for certain**, you have no doubt at all about it. *It is not known for certain where they are now.*
● When you **make certain** that something happens, you take action to ensure that it happens. *We want to make certain that we have the forces over there to deal with any contingency*... *This will make it almost certain that the High Court will seize their assets.* ● If something is done or achieved **to a certain extent**, it is

only partly done or achieved. *That takes care of my anxieties to a certain extent.*

certainly /sɜːtnli/
1 ADV You use **certainly** to emphasize what you are saying when you are making a statement. *If nothing is done there will certainly be an economic crisis*... *It certainly looks wonderful, doesn't it?*
2 You also use **certainly** when you are agreeing with what someone has said or suggested. *'Would you agree that it is still a difficult world for women to live in?'—'Oh certainly.'*
3 You say **certainly not** when you want to say 'no' in a strong way. *'Had you forgotten?'—'Certainly not.'*

certainty /sɜːtnti/ **certainties**
1 NU **Certainty** is the state of being definite or of having no doubts at all. *Answers to such questions would never be known with certainty.* ...*the certainty of death in battle.*
2 NC A **certainty** is something that nobody has any doubts about. *It's by no means a certainty that we'll win.* ...*probabilities rather than certainties.*

certifiable /sɜːtɪfaɪəbl/
ADJ Someone who is **certifiable** can be declared insane. ...*people who are certifiable under the Mental Health Act.*

certificate /sətɪfɪkət/ **certificates**
NC A **certificate** is an official document which states that particular facts are true. For example, certificates are given to people to say that they have successfully completed a course of study or training. ...*a medical certificate.* ...*your birth certificate.*

certify /sɜːtɪfaɪ/ **certifies, certifying, certified**
1 VO or V-REPORT To **certify** something means to declare formally that it is true. ...*a piece of paper certifying the payment of his taxes*... *The President must certify that these officials had nothing to do with terrorist attacks.*
2 VO To **certify** someone or something means to issue a certificate saying that they have completed a course of training, or that they are acceptable for a particular purpose. *The two stroke engine is the first to be certified for aircraft use.*
3 V-PASS or V-PASSC If someone is **certified** insane, they are officially declared to be insane. *Whether he was ever formally certified is not known*... *Morison's statement that Northfield was certified insane was not deleted.*
4 VOC or VO+as To **certify** someone as being in a particular condition means to declare officially that they are in that condition. ...*a medical form certifying him fit for infantry duties*... *A hospital spokesman said the woman was certified dead on arrival*... *On his release from hospital, he had been certified as 'an invalid of the second category'.*

certitude /sɜːtɪtjuːd/
NU **Certitude** is the same as certainty; a formal word. *They were certainly sceptical to the proposition that this represented a change—but sceptical without certitude.*

cervical /səvaɪkl, sɜːvɪkl/; a medical term.
1 ADJ ATTRIB **Cervical** means relating to the cervix. ...*cervical cancer.*
2 ADJ ATTRIB **Cervical** also means relating to the neck. *It severed the spinal column just above the first cervical vertebra.*

cervix /sɜːvɪks/ **cervixes** /sɜːvɪsiːz/ or **cervices** /səvaɪsiːz/
NC The **cervix** is the entrance to the womb; a medical term. *Stimulating the cervix can actually cause an increase in maternal behaviour.*

cessation /seseɪʃn/
NU+SUPP The **cessation** of something is the stopping of it; a formal word. ...*a cessation of hostilities.*

cesspit /sɛspɪt/ **cesspits**
NC A **cesspit** is a hole or tank in the ground into which waste water and sewage flow. *He saw the muddy lanes and the open sewers and cesspits.*

cf.
cf. is used in writing to introduce something that should be compared with the subject you are discussing. *Juniper-tree; cf. the Biblical story of Elijah.*

CFC /ˌsiːˈefsiː/ **CFCs**
NC **CFCs** are man-made chemicals that are used in aerosol sprays, refrigerators, and air-cooling systems. **CFC** is an abbreviation for 'chlorofluorocarbon'. *The widespread use of CFCs has serious environmental drawbacks. ...an agreement to cut the use of CFC chemicals.*

Chad /tʃæd/
The **Republic of Chad** is a country in central Africa. It was part of French Equatorial Africa from the 19th century until independence in 1960. Ethnic, political, and religious divisions have caused civil conflicts since 1963. Libya invaded northern Chad in 1973 and remained at war until a ceasefire in 1987. France has given military assistance to Chad against Libya. Hissène Habré was President from 1982 until 1990, when he was overthrown by Colonel Idriss Déby, a member of the Patriotic Salvation Movement (MPS). Jean Alingue Bawoyeu (MPS) was appointed Prime Minister in 1991. Chad is a member of the Organization of African Unity. It exports cotton. Civil war has seriously damaged its economy. ♦ **Chadian** /tʃædiən/ N, ADJ
■ *per capita GNP:* US$160 ■ *religion:* Islam, animism ■ *language:* French and Arabic (official) ■ *currency:* CFA franc ■ *capital:* N'Djaména ■ *population:* 6 million (1989) ■ *size:* 1,284,000 square kilometres.

chafe /tʃeɪf/ **chafes, chafing, chafed**
1 V-ERG or V If your skin **chafes** or if something **chafes** it, it becomes sore as a result of being rubbed. *Powder is helpful if the baby's skin chafes easily... His collar was chafing his neck as usual... There were sores on his legs where the chains chafed.*
2 V If you **chafe** at a restriction or delay, you feel annoyed and impatient about it; a formal use. *The young sergeant chafed at the thought that he would not be promoted into the officer corps.*

chaff /tʃɑːf/
NU **Chaff** consists of the outer parts of grain such as wheat that are removed before the grain is used to make food. *...sorting the wheat from the chaff.*

chaffinch /tʃæfɪntʃ/ **chaffinches**
NC A **chaffinch** is a small, reddish-brown and grey songbird that is found in Europe.

chagrin /ʃægrɪn/
NU **Chagrin** is a feeling of annoyance or disappointment; a formal word. *Thomas discovered to his great chagrin that he was too late.*

chain /tʃeɪn/ **chains, chaining, chained**
1 NC or NU A **chain** consists of metal rings connected together in a line. *She wore a silver chain. ...a length of chain.*
2 VO When you **chain** a person or thing to something, you fasten them to it with a chain. *I chained my bike to some railings... They chained themselves to the fence.*
3 NC+SUPP A **chain** of things is a group of them arranged in a line. *...the island chains of the Pacific.*
4 NC+SUPP A **chain** of shops or hotels is a number of them owned by the same company. *She is setting up a chain of hotels in Argentina... A supermarket chain has applied for planning permission to develop the site.* ● See also **chain store**.
5 NC+SUPP A **chain** of events is a series of them happening one after another. *...the brief chain of events that led up to her death.*
6 See also **food chain**.

chain letter, chain letters
NC If someone sends a **chain letter**, they send several copies of it to different people, who in turn send copies of it to different people. Chain letters usually ask for money, or offer to sell something. They are illegal in some countries.

chain mail
NU **Chain mail** is armour made from small metal rings that are joined together.

chain reaction, chain reactions
1 N SING A **chain reaction** is a chemical process in which each individual process causes the following one. *Sunlight starts off a chain reaction which converts the ALA into highly toxic chemicals.*
2 N SING You can also refer to a series of events in which one incident causes the next as a **chain reaction**. *The government's decision to pull out will start a chain reaction with the Italian Embassy being the next to go.*

chain saw, chain saws
NC A **chain saw** is a large motorized saw. *Drills, chain saws, even water pumps can all be used from this power source.*

chain-smoke, chain-smokes, chain-smoking, chain-smoked.
V Someone who **chain-smokes** smokes cigarettes continuously. *...the eighty-three year old Deng Xiaoping, who chain-smokes the top Panda brand.*

chain-smoker, chain-smokers
NC A **chain-smoker** is a person who smokes cigarettes continuously. *...a chain-smoker, who usually has a cigarette in his fingers.*

chain store, chain stores
NC A **chain store** is one of many similar shops owned by the same company. *Several large chain stores have already stopped selling the sprays.*

chair /tʃeə/ **chairs, chairing, chaired**
1 NC A **chair** is a piece of furniture for one person to sit on. **Chairs** have a back and four legs. *I sat in a low chair by the fire, reading.*
2 NC At a university, a **chair** is the post of professor. *The Association has asked for 1 million pounds to set up the first university chair in stroke medicine.*
3 VO If you **chair** a meeting, you are the chairperson. *He will have no executive function, but he would still chair the meetings of the central committee... They prevented her from chairing a debate on the right to free expression.*
4 NC The **chair** of a meeting is the chairperson. *...remarks made by the chair of the Tanzania's women's organisation.* ● If you are **in the chair** or **take the chair** at a meeting, you are the chairperson. *When the heads of government meet next week, Chancellor Kohl will be in the chair... The coalition want Prince Sihanouk to take the chair.*

chairlift /tʃeəlɪft/ **chairlifts**
NC A **chairlift** is a line of chairs attached to a moving cable which can carry people up or down a mountain. *The manager of a northern Arizona ski area said the main chairlift in the area was damaged in 1987.*

chairman /tʃeəmən/ **chairmen** /tʃeəmən/
NC The **chairman** of a meeting, committee, or organization is the person in charge of it. *...the former chairman of the Hong Kong stock exchange.*

chairmanship /tʃeəmənʃɪp/ **chairmanships**
NC Someone's **chairmanship** is the fact that they are the chairperson, or the period of time they spend holding the position of chairperson. *...the efforts of the Spartacus League, under the chairmanship of Peter Gowan... The League say their candidates won chairmanships in more than a quarter of the municipalities.*

chairperson /tʃeəpɜːsn/ **chairpersons**
NC The **chairperson** of a meeting, committee, or organization is the person in charge of it. *Their chairperson, Mr Paul Jones, is currently on a lecture tour.*

chairwoman /tʃeəwumən/ **chairwomen**
NC The **chairwoman** of a meeting, committee, or organization is the woman in charge of it. *Some members, including the chairwoman, have said that the bulletins were ineffective.*

chaise longue /ʃeɪz lɒŋ/ **chaises longues.** The singular and the plural are pronounced in the same way.
NC A **chaise longue** is a couch with only one arm and usually a back along half its length. *He described the car as a 'chaise longue on wheels covered by an umbrella'.*

chalet /ʃæleɪ/ **chalets**
NC A **chalet** is a small wooden house, especially in a mountain area or holiday camp. *They were not on the ski slopes—they were in their chalet at the time.*

chalice /tʃælɪs/ **chalices**
NC A **chalice** is a large metal cup which is used in the Christian service of Holy Communion. *He celebrated Mass every day, with a wineglass serving as a chalice.*

chalk /tʃɔːk/ chalks, chalking, chalked
1 NU **Chalk** is soft white rock. You can use small pieces of it for writing or drawing with. *He took a piece of chalk from his pocket. ...the chalk uplands of Wiltshire.*
2 NC **Chalks** are small pieces of chalk used for writing or drawing with. *They were drawing patterns on the board in coloured chalks.*
3 VOorVA If you **chalk** something, you draw or write it using a piece of chalk. *A line was chalked round the body. ...a young man chalking on the blackboard.*
chalk up PHRASAL VERB If you **chalk up** a success, you achieve it. *They chalked up several victories... The Daily Express has chalked up what it says is a world exclusive.*

chalky /tʃɔːki/
ADJ Something that is **chalky** contains chalk or is covered with chalk. *...the white, chalky road.*

challenge /tʃælɪndʒ/ challenges, challenging, challenged
1 NCorNU A **challenge** is something new and difficult which will require great effort and determination. *Mount Everest presented a challenge to Hillary... She thrives on feud and challenge.*
2 NCorNU A **challenge** to something is a questioning of its truth, value, or authority. *There will inevitably be challenges to the existing order... These ideas are open to challenge.*
3 VO If you **challenge** someone, you invite them to fight or compete with you. *They had challenged and beaten the best teams in the world.*
4 VO If you **challenge** ideas or people, you question their truth, value, or authority. *The idea has never been challenged... He challenged the minister to produce evidence.*

challenger /tʃælɪndʒə/ challengers
NC A **challenger** is someone who competes for a position or title, for example a sports championship. *...a challenger to Mitterrand's leadership.*

challenging /tʃælɪndʒɪŋ/
1 ADJ A **challenging** job or activity requires great effort and determination. *Life as a housewife does not seem very challenging to the highly educated girl.*
2 ADJ **Challenging** behaviour seems to be inviting people to argue or compete. *...a suspicious challenging look.*

chamber /tʃeɪmbə/ chambers
1 NC A **chamber** is a large room that is used for formal meetings, or that is designed and equipped for a particular purpose. *...the Council Chamber... He led the way to the torture chamber.*
2 NC+of A **Chamber** of Commerce or **Chamber** of Trade is a group of business people who work together to improve business in their town. *Two officials of the Swiss Chamber of Commerce were kidnapped. ...a panel discussion at the Ankara Chamber of Trade.*
3 N PL **Chambers** are offices used by judges and barristers. *Mr Roberts, who owns his own chambers, specialises in crime and common law.*

chamberlain /tʃeɪmbəlɪn/ chamberlains
NC A **chamberlain** is the person who is in charge of the household affairs of a monarch or noble. *Akihito was taken away from his parents at birth and raised by imperial chamberlains and tutors.*

chambermaid /tʃeɪmbəmeɪd/ chambermaids
NC A **chambermaid** is a woman who cleans and tidies the bedrooms in a hotel. *A chambermaid wandered into the room where the conference was being held.*

chamber music
NU **Chamber music** is classical music written for a small number of instruments. *The stage is best suited to the performance of contemporary drama and chamber music.*

chamber orchestra, chamber orchestras
NC A **chamber orchestra** is a small orchestra which plays classical music.

chamber pot, chamber pots
NC A **chamber pot** is a round china container that some people keep in their bedrooms so that they can urinate in them during the night. *...prisoners held three to a cell with only one chamber pot between them.*

chameleon /kəmiːliən/ chameleons
NC A **chameleon** is a lizard whose skin changes colour to match its surroundings. *Like a chameleon, they're able to change their colours.*

chamois; pronounced /ʃæmwɑː/ for the meaning in paragraph 1, and /ʃæmi/ for the meaning in paragraph 2. **Chamois** is both the singular and the plural form.
1 NC A **chamois** is a small antelope that lives in the mountains of Europe and South West Asia.
2 NCorN+N A **chamois** or a **chamois** leather is a piece of cloth made from the skin of a chamois. It is used for cleaning and polishing. *Dust furniture and occasionally wipe clean with a damp chamois leather.*

chamomile. See camomile.

Chamorro, Violeta Barrios de /viːɒleɪtə bæriəus deɪ tʃæmɒrəʊ/
Violeta Barrios de Chamorro became President of Nicaragua in 1990. She is the owner and director of La Prensa newspaper and the widow of Pedro Joaquín Chamorro, whose death in 1978 was a factor in the overthrow of the Somoza government. She is a member of the National Opposition Union (UNO), an alliance of 14 parties. Born: 1929.

champ /tʃæmp/ champs, champing, champed
1 VAorVO If a person or an animal **champs** something, they eat it noisily and with enjoyment. *They lived on the sea floor, champing their way through mud... A small boy stood champing gum.*
2 If you are **champing at the bit**, you are very eager to start or to continue doing something.
3 NC A **champ** is a champion; an informal use. *The Olympic downhill champ, Zurbriggen, has won the overall cup title.*

champagne /ʃæmpeɪn/
NU **Champagne** is a good quality fizzy white wine from France. *In the streets of Berlin, people drank champagne, let off fireworks, and tooted their car horns.*

champers /ʃæmpəz/
NU **Champers** is the same as champagne; an informal word. *Come and have some more champers.*

champion /tʃæmpiən/ champions, championing, championed
1 NC A **champion** is someone who has won the first prize in a competition. *...the school tennis champion.*
2 NC+SUPP A **champion** of a cause or principle is someone who supports or defends it. *...a champion of liberty.*
3 VO If you **champion** a cause or principle, you support or defend it. *He made an immense impact on English law, championing the rights of the individual against the state.*

championship /tʃæmpiənʃɪp/ championships
NC A **championship** is a competition to find the best player or team in a particular sport. A **championship** is also the title or status of the winner. *...the first round of the U.S. open golf championship. ...the heavyweight championship of the world.*

chance /tʃɑːns/ chances, chancing, chanced
1 NCorNU If there is a **chance** of something happening, it is possible that it will happen. *We've got a good chance of winning... What are her chances of getting the job?... There's little chance that the situation will improve... Bingo is a game of chance.*
2 NC When you take a **chance**, you try to do something although there is a risk of danger or failure. *It was doubtful that the disease had been passed on, but they couldn't take any chances.*
3 Something that happens by **chance** was not planned. *Almost by chance I found myself talking to him... It's a matter of chance which organ a particular tumour cell comes to rest in.* ▶ Also ADJ *...a chance meeting.*
4 V+to-INF If you **chance** to do something, you do it although you had not planned to; a formal use. *I chanced to overhear them.*

chancel /tʃɑːnsl/ chancels
NC A **chancel** is the part of a church containing the altar.

Chancellor /tʃɑːnsəlⁿlə/ Chancellors
1 NC The **Chancellor** is the name used to refer to the head of government in Germany and Austria. *...the West German Chancellor Helmut Kohl.*

2 NC In Britain, the **Chancellor** is the Chancellor of the Exchequer. *Harold Wilson chose Jim Callaghan as his Chancellor... The Chancellor bowed to City advice.*
3 NC The official head of a British university is called the **Chancellor.** *I think he's the Chancellor of the Open University now.*
4 See also **vice-chancellor.**

Chancellor of the Exchequer, Chancellors of the Exchequer
NC The **Chancellor of the Exchequer** is the minister in the British government who makes decisions about finance and taxes. *...a full statement by the Chancellor of the Exchequer.*

chancy /tʃɑːnsi/ **chancier, chanciest**
ADJ Something that is **chancy** involves a lot of risk or uncertainty; an informal word. *Taking a case to the High Court is a chancy matter... Many teachers think this is too chancy and they make lists to remind them.*

chandelier /ʃændəlɪə/ **chandeliers**
NC A **chandelier** is an ornamental light fitting which hangs from a ceiling. *...huge, sparkling chandeliers and marble columns.*

change /tʃeɪndʒ/ **changes, changing, changed**
1 NCorNU If there is a **change** in something, it becomes different. *...a radical change in attitudes. ...the changes that had taken place since he had left China... There have been little change.*
2 V-ERG When something **changes** or when you **change** it, it becomes different. *Her disdain changed to surprised respect... They can be used to change uranium into plutonium... A bird changes direction by dipping one wing and lifting the other... The situation in southern Africa has changed dramatically since the last summit meeting.* ♦ **changed** ADJ *He returned to parliament a changed man.* ♦ **changing** ADJ *...a report on changing fashions in food.*
3 VO To **change** something also means to replace it with something new or different. *The fuel filter was changed about two years ago... His doctor advised that he change his job.*
4 NC+SUPP If there is a **change** of something, it is replaced. *...a change of government... That motorcycle needs a change of oil.*
5 VOorV When you **change** your clothes, you take them off and put on different ones. *I want to change my socks... She changed into her street clothes.*
6 NC+*of* A **change** of clothes is an extra set of clothes that you take with you when you go away. *They were allowed one shower and one change of clothes per week... They'll be offered a jogging suit if they need a change of clothing.*
7 VO When you **change** a baby or **change** its nappy, you take off its dirty nappy and put on a clean one. *Some Soviet husbands are known to go shopping, to wash up occasionally, or even change and bath the baby... If it seems necessary, you can change nappies not only before and after feedings but also midway between feedings.*
8 VOorV When you **change** buses or trains, you get off one and get on another to continue your journey. *They were waiting to change trains... Don't forget to change at Crewe.*
9 NU Your **change** is the money that you receive when you pay for something with more money than it costs. *Morris handed Hooper his change.*
10 NU **Change** or loose **change** is money in the form of coins, rather than notes. *We only had 80p in change. ...East Germans spending their loose change before it became worthless.*
11 NU+*for* If you have **change** for a note or a large coin, you have the same amount of money in smaller notes or coins. *Have you got change for a fiver?*
12 VO When you **change** money, you exchange it for the same amount of money in different coins or notes. *Can anyone change a ten pound note?... Do you change foreign currency?*
● **Change** is used in these phrases. ● If you say that something is happening **for a change,** you mean that it is different from what usually happens. *They were glad to leave their cars and walk for a change.* ● If you say that an experience **makes a change,** you mean that it is enjoyable and different from what you are

used to. *Being out in the country made a refreshing change.* ● **to change hands:** see **hand.** ● **to change your mind:** see **mind.** ● **change of heart:** see **heart.**

change over PHRASAL VERB If you **change over** from one thing to another, you stop doing one thing and start doing the other. *They had been Liberal till several years ago, then they changed over to Conservative.*

changeable /tʃeɪndʒəbl/
ADJ If something is **changeable,** it is likely to change. *...as changeable as the weather.*

changeling /tʃeɪndʒlɪŋ/ **changelings**
NC In stories, a **changeling** is a baby who has been substituted for another baby by fairies.

change of life
N SING The **change of life** is the same as the **menopause.** *I wondered if it had anything to do with the change of life, which she was now passing through.*

changeover /tʃeɪndʒəʊvə/ **changeovers**
NC A **changeover** is a change from one activity or system to another. *The changeover had taken place in the Easter vacation.*

channel /tʃænl/ **channels, channelling, channelled;** spelt **channeling, channeled** in American English.
1 NC A **channel** is a wavelength on which television programmes are broadcast. *He switched to the other channel.*
2 NC+SUPP If you say that something has been done through particular **channels,** you are referring to the people who arranged for it to be done. *It is always done through diplomatic channels... I notified the authorities through the normal channels.*
3 VO If you **channel** money into something, you arrange for it to be used for that purpose. *...the need to channel North Sea oil revenues into industry.*
4 NC A **channel** is also a passage along which water flows, or a route used by boats. *...irrigation channels... The main channels had been closed by enemy submarines.*
5 N PROP The **Channel** or the **English Channel** is the narrow area of sea between England and France. *...a cargo ship that sank in the English Channel.*

Channel Islands /tʃænl aɪləndz/
The **Channel Islands** are dependencies of the British Crown in the English Channel, off the north-west coast of France. The four main islands are Jersey, Guernsey, Alderney, and Sark. They were occupied by Germany in the Second World War. Banking, tourism, and agriculture are important industries. ♦ **Channel Islander** /tʃænl aɪləndə/
■ *religion:* Christianity ■ *language:* English, French ■ *currency:* pound sterling ■ *capital:* St Helier (Jersey), St Peter Port (Guernsey) ■ *population:* 138,000 (1985) ■ *size:* 194 square kilometres.

Channel Tunnel
N PROP The **Channel Tunnel** is a railway tunnel under the English Channel between England and France. *The British and French teams building the Channel Tunnel are about to achieve a breakthrough. ...proposed rail links with the Channel Tunnel.*

chant /tʃɑːnt/ **chants, chanting, chanted**
1 NC A **chant** is a word or group of words that is repeated over and over again. *The assembly broke into a chant: 'What's your name? What's your name?'*
2 NC A **chant** is also a religious song or prayer that is sung on only a few notes. *...a variety of musical styles, from Gregorian chant to jazz and synthesized rock.*
3 V-QUOTE,VO,orV When you **chant,** you repeat the same words over and over again, or you sing a religious song or prayer. *Workers marched through the streets, chanting 'We want bread' and 'Down with the Dictator'... A small group waved flags and chanted slogans as Mr Genscher laid a wreath on the grave. ...a huge temple, around which thousands of pilgrims mingle, chanting and praying.*

chaos /keɪɒs/
NU **Chaos** is a state of complete disorder and confusion. *Gales swept across Britain, causing chaos on land and sea... Economic chaos is growing... Large numbers of unauthorised flights have brought chaos and a high risk of accidents.*

chaotic /keɪɒtɪk/
ADJ If a situation is **chaotic**, it is disordered and confused. ...*a chaotic jumble of motor vehicles.*

chap /tʃæp/ **chaps**
NC You can use **chap** to refer to a man or boy; an informal word. *He's not a bad chap, and we hope he's successful.*

chapel /tʃæpl/ **chapels**
1 NC A **chapel** is a part of a church which has its own altar and which is used for private prayer. *The entrance archway and chapel have been declared protected monuments.*
2 NC A **chapel** is also a small church in a school, hospital, or prison. *The funeral will be held in the memorial chapel of the Royal Military Academy at Sandhurst.*
3 NC A **chapel** is also a building used for worship by members of some Protestant churches. ...*a Methodist chapel.*

chaperone /ʃæpərəʊn/ **chaperones**; also spelt **chaperon.**
NC A **chaperone** is a person who accompanies another person somewhere in order to make sure that they do not come to any harm. *Patients are permitted occasional visits home, always accompanied by a chaperone.*

chaplain /tʃæplɪn/ **chaplains**
NC A **chaplain** is a member of the Christian clergy who works in a hospital, school, or prison, or in the armed forces. *The service was conducted by Father Raymond Murray, chaplain of the women's prison in Armagh.* ...*a naval chaplain.*

chaplaincy /tʃæplənsi/ **chaplaincies**
1 NC A **chaplaincy** is the building or office in which a chaplain works. *There's a barbecue at the Catholic Chaplaincy on Friday night.*
2 NU **Chaplaincy** is the position or work of a chaplain. *What is chaplaincy work like in a modern university?*

chapped /tʃæpt/
ADJ If your skin is **chapped**, it is dry, cracked, and sore.

chapter /tʃæptə/ **chapters**
1 NC A **chapter** is one of the parts that a book is divided into. ...*the subjects of the next two chapters... I'd nearly finished chapter 8.*
2 NC+SUPP You can refer to a part of your life or to a period in history as a **chapter**; a literary use. *A new chapter of my career as a journalist was about to commence.*
3 NC A **chapter** is also a local branch of a particular organization; used in American English. *A four-week inspection found a number of serious problems at the Portland chapter.* ...*local chapters of the NAACP, the Urban League, and other civil rights groups.* ...*Frank Ortez, president of the union's Miami chapter.*

char /tʃɑː/ **chars, charring, charred**; an old-fashioned word.
1 NU **Char** is tea.
2 NC A **char** is a woman who is employed to clean houses or offices.
3 V If a woman is **charring**, she is working as a cleaner in an office or private house.
4 See also **charred.**

charabanc /ʃærəbæŋ/ **charabancs**
NC A **charabanc** is a kind of large old-fashioned motor coach with many seats which was used for taking people on holiday. *Outside in the yard the charabanc waited.*

character /kærəktə/ **characters**
1 NC+SUPP The **character** of a person or place consists of all the qualities they have that make them distinct. *There was another side to his character.* ...*the character of New York.*
2 If someone behaves **in character**, they behave in the way you expect them to. If they behave **out of character**, they do not behave as you expect. *It's quite in character for Carey to use a word like that.*
3 NU+SUPP You use **character** when you are mentioning a particular quality that something has. ...*the radical character of our demands... But insanity is not always purely negative in character.*
4 NC The **characters** in a film, book, or play are the

people in it. *The book teems with colourful characters.*
5 NC You can refer to a person as a **character**, especially when describing their qualities; an informal use. *He's a strange character, Evans.*
6 NC A **character** is also a letter, number, or symbol that is written, printed, or displayed on a computer screen. *You can delete characters, words, or even blocks of text.*

character actor, character actors
NC A **character actor** is an actor who specializes in playing unusual or eccentric people. ...*one of the company's leading character actors, Bruce Alexander.*

character assassination, character assassinations
N Uor NC **Character assassination** is the deliberate attempt to destroy someone's reputation by criticizing them in an unfair and dishonest way. ...*hypocrisy, double-dealing, innuendo and character assassination... Allegations of an immoral relationship were described as 'a character assassination'.*

characteristic /kærəktərɪstɪk/ **characteristics**
1 NC A **characteristic** is a quality or feature that is typical of someone or something. *Ambition is a characteristic of all successful businessmen.*
2 ADJ If something is **characteristic** of a person, thing, or place, it is typical of them. ...*those large brick tiles so characteristic of East Anglia.* ♦ **characteristically**
ADV *He proposed a characteristically brilliant solution.*

characterize /kærəktəraɪz/ **characterizes, characterizing, characterized**; also spelt **characterise.**
V To **characterize** someone or something means to be typical of them. ...*the incessant demand for change that characterizes our time... The relationship between them was characterized by tension and rivalry from the first.*

charade /ʃərɑːd/
N SING A **charade** is a pretence which is so obvious that nobody is deceived. *He told newsmen that the whole appeals procedure was a charade.*

charcoal /tʃɑːkəʊl/
NU **Charcoal** is a black substance obtained by burning wood without much air. Charcoal is used as a fuel and also for drawing. *It collided with a lorry carrying sacks of charcoal.*

charge /tʃɑːdʒ/ **charges, charging, charged**
1 VOOor VO If you **charge** someone an amount of money, you ask them to pay that amount for something that you have provided or sold to them. *You can be sure he's going to charge you something for the service... 'How much do you charge?'—'£6 a night.'... One driver charged $35 extra.*
2 VO+to If you **charge** goods or services to a person or organization, you arrange for the bill to be sent to them. *Please charge the bill to my account.*
3 NC The **charge** for something is the price that you have to pay for it. ...*increases in postal and telephone charges... No charge is made for repairs.*
4 NC A **charge** is a formal accusation that someone has committed a crime. *He is wanted in Northern Ireland to answer charges of armed robbery.* ...*a murder charge... He was serving a twenty month sentence on smuggling charges.*
5 VO When the police **charge** someone, they formally accuse them of having committed a crime. *He was arrested and charged with a variety of offences... The men have not been charged and no reason was given for their arrest.*
6 NU If you have **charge** of something or someone, you have responsibility for them. *She intended to take charge of the boy herself... My first concern is for people under my charge.* ● If you are **in charge** of something or someone, you have responsibility for them. *You had left me in charge... He is to be in charge of Transport and Public Works.*
7 V If you **charge** towards someone or something, you move quickly and aggressively towards them. ...*pictures of policemen charging on horseback.*
8 VO When you **charge** a battery, you pass an electric current through it to make it more powerful. *They use solar panels to charge the batteries.*

charged /tʃɑːdʒd/
ADJ **Charged** means filled with emotion and therefore very tense or excited. *...a highly charged silence... His voice was charged with suppressed merriment.*
Chargé d'Affaires /ʃɑːʒeɪ dæfeə/ **Chargés d'Affaires.** The singular and the plural are pronounced in the same way.
NC A **Chargé d'Affaires** is a person appointed to act as the head of a diplomatic mission in a foreign country. *Pakistan's Chargé d'Affaires was summoned to the Foreign Office yesterday.*
charge hand, charge hands
NC A **charge hand** is a workman who is slightly less important than a foreman.
charge nurse, charge nurses
NC A **charge nurse** is a senior male nurse who is in charge of a hospital ward. *...the grading of ward sisters and charge nurses.*
charger /tʃɑːdʒə/ **chargers**
1 NC A **charger** is a device used for charging or recharging batteries. *How about a solar powered battery charger?*
2 NC A **charger** is also a strong horse that a knight in the Middle Ages used to ride in battle. *...a knight on a white charger.*
charge sheet, charge sheets
NC A **charge sheet** is the official form on which the police write down legal charges against a person. *According to the charge sheet, they were both in London at the end of 1983.*
chariot /tʃærɪət/ **chariots**
NC A **chariot** is a fast-moving vehicle with two wheels that is pulled by horses. Chariots were used in ancient times. *He's journeying across India in a model of a chariot.*
charioteer /tʃærɪətɪə/ **charioteers**
NC A **charioteer** was, in ancient times, someone who drove a chariot, for example in a race.
charisma /kərɪzmə/
NU If someone has **charisma**, they can attract, influence, and inspire people by their personal qualities. *Jesse Jackson promises radical change and oozes charisma... The leaders lack charisma.*
charismatic /kærɪzmætɪk/
1 ADJ Someone who is **charismatic** is able to attract, influence, and inspire people by their personal qualities. *...a charismatic leader of people. ...a charismatic figure and fiery orator.*
2 ADJ The **charismatic** church is the part of the Christian Church that believes that people can obtain special supernatural gifts from God. *...the charismatic movement in the Church. ...a new-style charismatic Christianity.*
charitable /tʃærɪtəbl/
1 ADJ Someone who is **charitable** is kind and tolerant. *She was being unusually charitable to me. ...a charitable remark.*
2 ADJ ATTRIB A **charitable** organization or activity helps and supports people who are ill, handicapped, or poor. *Governments and charitable organisations were responding to the appeals to help the needy... The hospice is run by a Christian charitable trust.*
charity /tʃærəti/ **charities**
1 NCorNU A **charity** is an organization which raises money to help people who are ill, handicapped, or poor. *The proceeds will go to local charities... According to the latest statistics, each American household donates two and a half per cent of its income to charity.*
2 NU **Charity** is money or gifts given to poor people. *He's too proud to accept charity.*
3 NU **Charity** is also a kind and generous attitude towards other people. *She found the charity in her heart to forgive them.*
charlady /tʃɑːleɪdi/ **charladies**
NC A **charlady** is the same as a **charwoman**; an old-fashioned word.
charlatan /ʃɑːlətən/ **charlatans**
NC A **charlatan** is someone who pretends to have skills or knowledge that they do not really have; an old-fashioned word. *The doctor was either a charlatan or a shrewd old rogue.*

Charles, Mary Eugenia /meəri tʃɑːlz/
Mary Eugenia Charles became Prime Minister of Dominica in 1980. She became an MP in 1975 and was Leader of the Opposition from 1975 to 1979. She was the co-founder and first leader of the Dominica Freedom Party (DFP). Born: 1919.
Charles, Prince of Wales /tʃɑːlz/
Prince Charles is the eldest son and heir of Queen Elizabeth II. He was created Prince of Wales in 1958. In 1981 he married Lady Diana Spencer. They have two sons, Prince William and Prince Henry. Born: 1948.
charleston /tʃɑːlstən/ **charlestons**
NC The **charleston** is a lively dance that was popular in the 1920s. *Twenty years ago, the old were shaking their heads in despair over the charleston.*
Charlotte Amalie /ʃɑːlət əmɑːljə/
Charlotte Amalie is the capital of the US Virgin Islands and its largest town. It is on the island of St Thomas. Population: 12,000 (1980).
charm /tʃɑːm/ **charms, charming, charmed**
1 NUorNC **Charm** is the quality of being attractive and pleasant. *He bowed with infinite grace and charm. ...the charms of the exotic.*
2 VO If you **charm** someone, you please them. *I was charmed by his courtesy.*
3 NC A **charm** is a small ornament that is fixed to a bracelet or necklace.
4 NC A **charm** is also an action, saying, or object that is believed to be lucky or to have magic powers. *Once he threatened to pull out of a performance because he'd mislaid his good luck charm. ...tiny icons, crosses and charms.*
charmer /tʃɑːmə/ **charmers**
NC You call someone a **charmer** when they appear to be very charming but are actually rather insincere. *They're both tremendous charmers in their different ways.*
charming /tʃɑːmɪŋ/
ADJ If someone or something is **charming**, they are very pleasant and attractive. *Celia is a charming girl. ...this charming duet for bassoon and cello.*
♦ **charmingly** ADV *...a charmingly medieval atmosphere.*
charred /tʃɑːd/
ADJ Something that is **charred** is partly burnt and made black by fire. *...surrounded by the charred and blackened remains of buildings.*
chart /tʃɑːt/ **charts, charting, charted**
1 NC A **chart** is a diagram or graph which makes information easy to understand. *...large charts illustrating world poverty.*
2 NC A **chart** is also a map of the sea or stars. *Look at the chart, and find the objects you've taken your bearings from.*
3 NPLorNC The **charts** are the official lists that show which pop records have sold the most copies each week. *The single is currently No.2 in the British charts... 'Blue Monday' reached No.9 in the singles chart.*
4 VO If you **chart** something, you observe and record it carefully. *We charted their movements... There are several articles charting the rise to power of Mr Premadasa.*
charter /tʃɑːtə/ **charters, chartering, chartered**
1 NC A **charter** is a document describing the rights or principles of an organization. *...the Working Women's Charter... It contravened article 51 of the UN charter.*
2 ADJ ATTRIB A **charter** plane or boat is hired for use by a particular person or group. *He is travelling on a charter flight.*
3 VO If you **charter** a vehicle, you hire it for your private use. *We plan to charter a special train for London.*
chartered /tʃɑːtəd/
ADJ ATTRIB **Chartered** is used to describe someone who has formally qualified in a profession such as accountancy or surveying. *...a chartered accountant. ...the Royal Institution of Chartered Surveyors.*
charwoman /tʃɑːwumən/ **charwomen**
NC A **charwoman** is a woman who is employed to clean houses or offices; an old-fashioned word.

chary /ˈtʃeəri/
ADJ If you are **chary** of doing something, you are careful and cautious about doing it. *Enterprises are becoming increasingly chary of taking on new workers... She started a chary descent of the stairs.*

chase /tʃeɪs/ chases, chasing, chased
1 V or VA If you **chase** someone, you run after them or follow them in order to catch them or drive them away. *Youngsters chase one another up trees... They were chased from the village... A dozen soldiers chased after the car.* ▶ Also NC *They abandoned the chase and returned home.* ● See also **car chase**.
2 V or V+after If you **chase** something such as work or money, you try hard to get it. *We are getting more and more applicants chasing fewer and fewer jobs. ...a debate over whether the Christian Democrats should go chasing after right-wing votes.*

chaser /ˈtʃeɪsə/ chasers
1 NC A **chaser** is an alcoholic drink that is drunk straight after an alcoholic drink of a different kind and of a different strength.
2 NC A **chaser** is also someone who is chasing you.

chasm /ˈkæzəm/ chasms
1 NC A **chasm** is a very deep crack in rock or ice. *He used his body as a human bridge to help people cross a water-filled chasm.*
2 NC If there is a **chasm** between two things or between two groups, there is a very large difference between them. *...the chasm between rich and poor... The differences between Moscow and Belgrade broadened into a yawning chasm.*

chassis /ˈʃæsi/; chassis is both the singular and the plural form. The plural is pronounced /ˈʃæsiz/.
NC A **chassis** is the framework that a vehicle is built on. *All these cars have a very strong, multi-tubular steel chassis.*

chaste /tʃeɪst/
ADJ A **chaste** person does not have sex with anyone, or only has sex with their husband or wife; an old-fashioned word, used showing approval. *She was a holy woman, innocent and chaste.*

chasten /ˈtʃeɪsn/ chastens, chastening, chastened
VO If you **are chastened** by something, it makes you regret your behaviour; a formal word. *The cheeky prince got a ticking off and looked suitably chastened... Now somewhat chastened by his experience, he is not keen to return.*

chastise /tʃæsˈtaɪz/ chastises, chastising, chastised
VO If you **chastise** someone, you scold or punish them; a formal word. *He chastised members at the conference for not taking things seriously enough.*

chastity /ˈtʃæstəti/
NU **Chastity** is the state of not having sex with anyone, or of only having sex with your husband or wife; an old-fashioned word, used showing approval. *A monk makes vows of poverty, chastity and obedience.*

chat /tʃæt/ chats, chatting, chatted
1 V When people **chat**, they talk in an informal and friendly way. *We sat by the fire and chatted all evening.*
2 NC or NU A **chat** is an informal, friendly talk. *We had a nice long chat about our schooldays. ...entertaining them with light chat.*
chat up PHRASAL VERB If you **chat** someone **up**, you talk to them in a friendly way because you are sexually attracted to them; an informal expression. *She was being chatted up by this bloke.*

château /ˈʃætəʊ/ châteaux /ˈʃætəʊz/
NC A **château** is a large country house in France. *The meeting was held in a converted château in Northern France.*

chatline /ˈtʃætlaɪn/ chatlines
NC A **chatline** is a commercial telephone service that enables you to have a conversation with several other callers at the same time. *Ruinous and impossible bills have been run up by addicted users of the chatlines... He recently set up the Caribbean Funline, a telephone chatline service, and it's getting 15,000 calls a week.*

chat show, chat shows
NC A **chat show** is a television or radio show in which an interviewer and his or her guests talk in a friendly, informal way about different topics. *From November,* the afternoon soap operas and chat shows will have a new rival in the ratings. ...a radio chat show host.

chattel /ˈtʃætl/ chattels
NC Your **chattels** are the things that belong to you; an old-fashioned word. *He left all his worldly goods and chattels to his daughter.*

chatter /ˈtʃætə/ chatters, chattering, chattered
1 V If you **chatter**, you talk quickly and continuously about unimportant things. *Off we set, with Bill chattering away all the time.* ▶ Also NU *At teatime there was much excited chatter.*
2 V When birds and small animals **chatter**, they make a series of short high-pitched noises. *The monkeys chattered and the parrots screeched above their heads.*
3 V If your teeth **chatter**, they rattle together because you are cold. *He started shivering spasmodically, and his teeth chattered.*

chatterbox /ˈtʃætəbɒks/ chatterboxes
NC A **chatterbox** is someone who talks a lot; an informal word. *One teenage chatterbox ran up a phone bill of over £2,000.*

chatterer /ˈtʃætərə/ chatterers
NC A **chatterer** is the same as a chatterbox. *The two chatterers were silenced.*

chatty /ˈtʃæti/
ADJ A **chatty** person or piece of writing sounds friendly and informal. *In the first few pages, he sounds disturbingly chatty and brash... His chatty style and wealth of knowledge make it an illuminating experience for the audience.*

chauffeur /ˈʃəʊfə, ʃəʊˈfɜː/ chauffeurs, chauffeuring, chauffeured
1 NC A **chauffeur** is a person whose job is to drive and look after another person's car. *He joined the household as chauffeur and handyman.*
2 VO If you **chauffeur** someone somewhere, you drive them there in a car, usually as part of your job. *The Soviet envoy was chauffeured by Iraqi officials in a white Mercedes.*

chauvinism /ˈʃəʊvɪnɪzəm/
NU **Chauvinism** is a strong and unreasonable belief that your own country is the best and most important. *...racism and national chauvinism.* ◆ **chauvinist** /ˈʃəʊvɪnɪst/ **chauvinists** NC or N+N *The worst fear is that the chauvinists will provoke violence. ...chauvinist pride.* ● See also **male chauvinism**.

chauvinistic /ˌʃəʊvɪˈnɪstɪk/
ADJ A **chauvinistic** person has an unreasonable belief that their own country is more important and morally better than other people's. *...chauvinistic nationalism and ethnic prejudice.*

cheap /tʃiːp/ cheaper, cheapest
1 ADJ **Cheap** goods or services do not cost very much money. *...cheap plastic buckets... A solid fuel cooker is cheap to run.* ◆ **cheaply** ADV *He decorated my home cheaply and efficiently.*
2 ADJ **Cheap** behaviour and remarks are unkind and unnecessary. *He could not resist making cheap jokes at their expense.*

cheapen /ˈtʃiːpən/ cheapens, cheapening, cheapened
1 VO or V-REFL If something **cheapens** you, it lowers your reputation or dignity. *He says the revolutionary black nationalist image has been sullied and cheapened by the award... I would not cheapen myself by doing such a thing.*
2 VO If you **cheapen** something, you reduce its price in order to sell it more easily. *The resulting increase in prices of imports could not be compensated for by a corresponding cheapening of their exports on hard currency markets.*

cheat /tʃiːt/ cheats, cheating, cheated
1 V When someone **cheats**, they lie or behave dishonestly in order to get or achieve something. *They want changes in this election which would make it harder to cheat.* ◆ **cheating** NU *Students have been disqualified from sitting examinations on charges of cheating.*
2 VO If someone **cheats** you out of something or **cheats** you of something, they get something from you by behaving dishonestly. *She cheated her sister out of some money... The opposition claims it was cheated of the governorship in the elections a fortnight ago.*

3 NC If you call someone a **cheat**, you mean that they behave dishonestly in order to get what they want. *You might say I am a cheat, but I am just trying to win a game.*

cheat on PHRASAL VERB **1** If you **cheat on** someone that you are having a sexual relationship with, you deceive them by secretly having a relationship with someone else; an informal expression. *There's a fascinating paper on what was called cuckoldry—that's cheating on marriage... It is the story of his son, who discovers that his father is cheating on his mother.* **2** To **cheat on** something means to lie or behave dishonestly about that particular thing; an informal expression. *The opposition says the government has cheated on its promises... Students have been cheating on their final exams... Corporations are far more likely to cheat on their taxes than individual citizens are.*

check /tʃɛk/ **checks, checking, checked**
1 VO, V-REPORT, or V If you **check** something, you make sure that it is satisfactory, safe, or correct. *Did you check the engine?... He checked that both rear doors were safely shut... Tony came in from time to time, to check on my progress... He needed a chance to check with Hooper to see if his theory was plausible.*
2 NC A **check** is an examination or inspection to make sure that everything is correct or safe. *Checks on cars and televisions are thorough. ...security checks.*
3 VO To **check** something also means to stop it from continuing or spreading. *The destruction of the bridge checked the enemy's advance.*
4 V-REFL or VO If you **check** yourself or if something **checks** you, you suddenly stop what you are doing or saying. *He began to saunter off, then checked himself and turned back... Sudhir held up his hand to check him.*
5 If you keep something **in check**, you keep it under control. *He had not conquered inflation but he had held it in check.*
6 In a game of chess, you say '**check**' when you have moved one of your pieces into a position where it could take your opponent's king. *...Bishop to King's knight five, check.*
7 NC In a restaurant in the United States, your **check** is your bill. *He waved to a waiter to get the check.*
8 NU or NC **Check** is a pattern consisting of squares. *...a green jacket with sky-blue checks. ...a tall man in a check suit.*
9 See also **cheque**.

check in PHRASAL VERB **1** When you **check in** at a hotel or **check into** it, you fill in the necessary forms before staying there. *I checked in at the Gordon Hotel... He checked into a small boarding house.* **2** When you **check in** at an airport, you arrive and show your ticket before going on a flight. *He had already checked in for his return flight.* ● See also **check-in**.

check into PHRASAL VERB See **check in**.

check out PHRASAL VERB **1** When you **check out** of the hotel where you have been staying, you pay the bill and leave. *Mr Leonard checked out this afternoon.* **2** If you **check** something **out**, you find out about it. *It might be difficult to transfer your money, so check it out with the manager.* **3** To **check** someone **out** means to obtain information about them in order to find out if they are suitable for something; an informal expression. *We'd better check him out before we let him join the group... You have to wait seven days so the cops can check you out... As much as Prince was checking me out, I was checking him out to see if this is something that musically I wanted to be involved in.* **4** See also **checkout**.

check up PHRASAL VERB If you **check up** on someone or something, you obtain information about them. *They are doing too little to check up on these people.* ● See also **check-up**.

checked /tʃɛkt/
ADJ Something that is **checked** has a check pattern. *...a checked blouse... He still wears baggy checked trousers.*

checker /tʃɛkə/ **checkers**
1 NU **Checkers** is the game of draughts; used in American English. *The men played checkers and*

listened to records.
2 NC A **checker** is a person or a machine that has the job of checking something. *Normally the labels are checked by eye but there's now an automated checker that can literally read the label.*

checkered /tʃɛkəd/. See **chequered**.

check-in, check-ins
NC A **check-in** is the place in an airport or a port where you check-in. *The report spoke of lax security at Pan Am check-ins at London and Frankfurt.* ▶ Also ADJ ATTRIB *The new rules will apply at all check-in facilities run by US airlines throughout the world.*

checking account, checking accounts
NC A **checking account** is a current account; used in American English. *There's $119 dollars missing from the checking account.*

checkmate /tʃɛkmeɪt/
1 NU In chess, **checkmate** is a situation in which you cannot stop your king being captured and so you lose the game.
2 NU You can refer to a situation in which all progress has stopped as **checkmate**. *It looks like checkmate for this particular scheme.*

checkout /tʃɛkaut/ **checkouts**
NC In a supermarket, a **checkout** is a counter where you pay for the things you have bought. *At the checkout the bill came to just over two hundred pounds.*

checkpoint /tʃɛkpɔɪnt/ **checkpoints**; also spelt **check-point**.
NC A **checkpoint** is a place where traffic has to stop and be checked. *A soldier was injured as the car crashed through an army checkpoint.*

check-up, check-ups
NC A **check-up** is a routine examination by a doctor or dentist. *All potential miners have to go through a medical check-up before recruitment.*

cheddar /tʃɛdə/ **cheddars**
N MASS **Cheddar** is a type of hard cheese. *...English cheddar.*

cheek /tʃiːk/ **cheeks**
1 NC Your **cheeks** are the soft parts of your face on either side of your nose. *His mother had tears streaming down her cheeks.*
2 NU You say that someone has **cheek** when you are annoyed about something unreasonable that they have done; an informal use. *You've got a cheek, coming in here.*

cheekbone /tʃiːkbəun/ **cheekbones**
NC Your **cheekbones** are the two bones in your face just below your eyes. *His cheekbone was broken in three places.*

cheeky /tʃiːki/
ADJ A child who is **cheeky** is rude or disrespectful. *They're such cheeky boys.*

cheer /tʃɪə/ **cheers, cheering, cheered**
1 V or VO When you **cheer**, you shout loudly to show approval or encouragement. *Mr Bickerstaffe's speech had the delegates on their feet cheering... The home crowd cheered their team enthusiastically.* ▶ Also NC *I heard a great cheer go up.*
2 VO If you **are cheered** by something, it makes you happier or less worried. *We were cheered by her warmth and affection.* ◆ **cheering** ADJ *It was very cheering to have her here.*
3 People say '**Cheers**' just before they drink an alcoholic drink.
4 People also say '**Cheers**' as an informal way of saying 'thank-you'. *'Nice to talk to you. Cheers, thank you.'*
5 You can also say '**cheers**' as an informal way of saying 'good-bye'. *'Cheers Paul. Bye bye mate.'*

cheer on PHRASAL VERB If you **cheer** someone **on**, you cheer loudly in order to encourage them. *The protesters were cheered on by a small group in the public gallery.*

cheer up PHRASAL VERB When you **cheer up**, you stop feeling depressed and become more cheerful. *She cheered up a little... Her friends tried to cheer her up.*

cheerful /tʃɪəfl/
1 ADJ Someone who is **cheerful** is happy and joyful. *She remained cheerful throughout the trip.*

◆ **cheerfully** ADV   *He smiled cheerfully at everybody.*
◆ **cheerfulness** NU   *They worked with great energy and cheerfulness.*
2 ADJ **Cheerful** things are pleasant and make you feel happy. *...literature of a more cheerful nature.*

cheerio /tʃɪəriˈəʊ/
Cheerio is an informal way of saying 'goodbye'.

cheerleader /ˈtʃɪəliːdə/ **cheerleaders**
NC A **cheerleader** is one of the people who leads the crowd in cheering at a large public event, especially a sports event. *They chanted and waved flags, urged on by cheerleaders.*

cheerless /ˈtʃɪələs/
ADJ Something that is **cheerless** is gloomy and depressing. *It was a cold, cheerless morning.*

cheery /ˈtʃɪəri/
ADJ **Cheery** means cheerful and happy; an old-fashioned word. *I wrote cheery letters home.*
◆ **cheerily** ADV   *'Hello!' I shouted cheerily.*

cheese /tʃiːz/ **cheeses**
N MASS **Cheese** is a solid food made from milk. There are many different kinds of cheese. *Foods rich in calcium are skimmed milk and dairy produce like hard cheese... The world-famous Stilton cheese comes from the Midlands.*

cheeseboard /ˈtʃiːzbɔːd/ **cheeseboards**
1 NC A **cheeseboard** is a board on which you put several kinds of cheese so that people can choose the ones that they want to eat.
2 N SING The **cheeseboard** is the course at the end of a meal when cheese is served on a cheeseboard. *Would you like a sweet, sir, or the cheeseboard?*

cheesecake /ˈtʃiːzkeɪk/ **cheesecakes**
NUorNC **Cheesecake** is a dessert that consists of biscuit covered with a soft mixture containing cream cheese. *Have some more cheesecake. ...a delicious creamy cheesecake.*

cheesecloth /ˈtʃiːzklɒθ/
NU **Cheesecloth** is a cotton cloth that is very light and loosely woven. *...a cheesecloth shirt.*

cheesed off /tʃiːzd ˈɒf/
ADJ PRED If you are **cheesed off**, you are annoyed, bored, or disappointed; an informal expression. *I was really cheesed off when he didn't turn up.*

cheese-paring
NU **Cheese-paring** is behaviour in which you are extremely careful with your money and spend as little as possible; used showing disapproval. *He thought of industrial accidents and the cheese-paring of employers when it came to safety precautions. ...cheese-paring economies.*

cheetah /ˈtʃiːtə/ **cheetahs**
NC A **cheetah** is a wild animal like a large cat with black spots. Cheetahs can run very fast. *The cheetah requires cover in order to be able to hunt.*

chef /ʃef/ **chefs**
NC A **chef** is a cook in a restaurant or hotel. *The famous chef Lucien Vanel prepared duck with artichokes and oxtail fondue.*

chef-d'oeuvre /ʃeɪdɜːvrə/ **chefs-d'oeuvre.** /ʃeɪdɜːvrə/
NC A writer's, artist's, or composer's **chef-d'oeuvre** is the best and most impressive piece of work that they produce in their career.

Cheffou, Amadou /æməduː ʃefuː/
Amadou Cheffou was appointed Prime Minister of Niger in 1991 by a conference on constitutional reform. Born: 1942.

chemical /ˈkemɪkl/ **chemicals**
1 ADJ ATTRIB **Chemical** means concerned with chemistry or made by a process in chemistry. *...the chemical composition of the atmosphere. ...chemical fertilizers.* ◆ **chemically** ADV   *Chemically, this substance is similar to cellulose.*
2 NC A **chemical** is a substance that is used in or made by a chemical process. *Aerosol chemicals are believed to destroy the earth's ozone layer.*
3 ADJ ATTRIB In **chemical** warfare, dangerous chemicals are used as weapons. *Chemical warfare dates from the First World War... More countries than ever before now have chemical weapons.*

⸱emist /ˈkemɪst/ **chemists**
NC In Britain, a **chemist** or a **chemist's** is a shop

where you can buy medicine, cosmetics, and some household goods. *...Britain's major high street chemist... He bought the perfume at the chemist's in St James's Arcade.*
2 NC In Britain, a **chemist** is also a person who is qualified to sell medicines prescribed by a doctor. *...a dispensing chemist.*
3 NC A **chemist** is also a scientist who does research in chemistry. *She was a research chemist in her thirties.*

chemistry /ˈkemɪstri/
NU **Chemistry** is the scientific study of the characteristics and composition of substances. *...Dr.Neil Ward, a lecturer in chemistry at the university.*

chemotherapy /kiːməʊˈθerəpi/
NU **Chemotherapy** is the treatment of disease using chemicals. It is often used in treating cancer. *It's common for patients undergoing chemotherapy to lose their hair.*

cheque /tʃek/ **cheques**; spelt **check** in American English.
NC A **cheque** is a printed form on which you write an amount of money and say who it is to be paid to. Your bank then pays the money to that person from your account. *The man mistakenly thought he'd be able to cash his pension cheque.* ● See also **blank cheque**.

chequebook /ˈtʃekbʊk/ **chequebooks**; spelt **checkbook** in American English.
NC A **chequebook** is a book of cheques.

cheque card, cheque cards
NC A **cheque card** is a small plastic card which your bank gives you and which you have to show when you are paying for something by cheque or when you are cashing a cheque at another bank. *We only accept cheques if you have a cheque card.*

chequered /ˈtʃekəd/; spelt **checkered** in American English.
ADJ ATTRIB If a person or organization has had a **chequered** career or history, they have had a varied past with both good and bad parts. *The Journal was a paper with a chequered history.*

cherish /ˈtʃerɪʃ/ **cherishes, cherishing, cherished**
1 VO If you **cherish** a hope or a memory, you keep it in your mind so that it gives you happy feelings. *I cherish a hope that one day we will be reunited.*
◆ **cherished** ADJ   *...cherished memories.*
2 VO If you **cherish** someone, you care for them in a loving way. *Comfort and cherish those you love.*
3 VO If you **cherish** a right or a privilege, you regard it as important and try hard to keep it. *Can he preserve the values he cherishes?* ◆ **cherished** ADJ *One of our cherished privileges is the right of free speech.*

cheroot /ʃəˈruːt/ **cheroots**
NC A **cheroot** is a cigar with both ends cut flat.

cherry /ˈtʃeri/ **cherries**
1 NC A **cherry** or a **cherry tree** is a tree which produces a small round fruit that is also called a **cherry**. *Forsythias are blooming here and the cherry trees peak next week... Here's another plum tree, and that one there is a cherry.*
2 NC **Cherries** are small round fruit with red or black skins and a hard round stone at the centre that grow on cherry trees. *They were put on a better diet, and given a bowl of cherries.*
3 ADJ Something that is **cherry** or **cherry red** is bright red in colour. *...her cherry lips. ...a cherry-red vinyl border.*

cherub /ˈtʃerəb/ **cherubs** or **cherubim** /ˈtʃerəbɪm/
1 NC A **cherub** is an angel that is represented in art as a plump, naked child with wings. *The coach is decorated on top with naked cherubs blowing trumpets.*
2 NC You can refer to a sweet, pretty child or young person as a **cherub**.

cherubic /tʃəˈruːbɪk/
ADJ If you say that someone looks **cherubic**, you mean that they look sweet and innocent like a cherub; a literary word. *...a cherubic child... The child had a round, cherubic face.*

chess /tʃɛs/
NU **Chess** is a game for two people, played on a
chessboard. Each player has 16 pieces, including a
king. You try to move your pieces so that your
opponent cannot prevent his or her king from being
taken. ...*more books are written on chess than all
other sports combined.*

chessboard /tʃɛsbɔːd/ **chessboards**
NC A **chessboard** is a square board on which you play
chess. It is divided into sixty-four squares of two
alternating colours, usually black and white.

chessman /tʃɛsmæn/ **chessmen**
NC A **chessman** is a playing piece used in chess,
usually coloured black or white. Each player has
sixteen chessmen at the start of the game.

chest /tʃɛst/ **chests**
1 NC Your **chest** is the top part of the front of your
body. *He folded his arms on his chest... She has
severe pains in her chest.*
2 If you **get** something **off** your **chest**, you say what
you have been worrying about; an informal
expression.
3 NC A **chest** is a large, heavy box. ...*an oak chest.*
4 See also **chest of drawers.**

chestnut /tʃɛsnʌt/ **chestnuts**
1 NC A **chestnut** or a **chestnut tree** is a tree that
produces nuts which can be eaten. ...*couples strolling
hand in hand under the blossoming chestnut trees.*
2 NC **Chestnuts** are the reddish-brown nuts that grow
on chestnut trees and which can be eaten. *At
Christmas people bring in the tree and roast chestnuts
on an open fire.*
3 ADJ Something that is **chestnut** is reddish-brown. *He
had dark chestnut curls and blue-grey eyes.*

chest of drawers, chests of drawers
NC A **chest of drawers** is a piece of furniture with
drawers which you keep clothes in. *There was no
dressing table, only a square mirror over an old oak
chest of drawers.*

chesty /tʃɛsti/
ADJ If you have a **chesty** cough, you have a lot of
catarrh in your lungs.

chevron /ʃɛvrən/ **chevrons**
1 NC A **chevron** is a V shape. *A road sign of black
and white chevrons indicates a sharp bend.*
2 NC A **chevron** is one of a number of V shapes worn
on the sleeve by a person in the armed forces or by
someone in the police force. It shows his or her rank.
*His action had got him the officer's chevrons he had
longed for.*

chew /tʃuː/ **chews, chewing, chewed**
1 VO or V When you **chew** food, you break it up with
your teeth and make it easier to swallow. *For
centuries people there have chewed the coca leaf as a
mild stimulant... A US firm have developed a chewing
gum that will retain its flavour for up to six hours of
continuous chewing.*
2 If you say that someone **has bitten off** more than
they **can chew**, you mean that they are trying to do
something which is too difficult for them. *The
Government now realise that financially they've bitten
off more than they can chew.*

chew over PHRASAL VERB If you **chew over** a problem
or an idea, you think carefully about it; an informal
expression. ...*scientific ideas chewed over and
sometimes rejected.*

chewing gum
NU **Chewing gum** is a kind of sweet which you chew
for a long time but do not swallow. *A new report has
suggested that chewing gum may be a health hazard.*

chewy /tʃuːi/ **chewier, chewiest**
ADJ Food that is **chewy** needs to be chewed a lot
before you can swallow it. *Oatmeal makes very
chewy bread.*

chic /ʃiːk/
ADJ **Chic** people and things are fashionable and
sophisticated. ...*a man with a chic set of clothes and a
stylish sports car.*

chicanery /ʃɪkeɪnəri/ **chicaneries**
NU or NC **Chicanery** is an act of verbal deception or
trickery of some kind; a formal word. *The
government was guilty of flagrant injustices, chicanery*

and corruption. ...political chicanery.

Chicano /tʃɪkɑːnəʊ/ **Chicanos**
NC A **Chicano** is a citizen of the United States whose
family originally came from Mexico. *While many now
prefer the term Hispanic or Latino, in the 1960s and
'70s, many Mexican-Americans called themselves
Chicano... Chicano artists also make use of images
that have become cultural icons such as the Virgin of
Guadelupe.*

chick /tʃɪk/ **chicks**
NC A **chick** is a baby bird. *It's not known how many
chicks have hatched.*

chicken /tʃɪkɪn/ **chickens, chickening, chickened**
1 NC A **chicken** is a type of bird which is kept for its
eggs and its meat. *Free range eggs are laid by
chickens that are allowed to roam around outside.*
2 NU **Chicken** is the meat of a chicken. *There was
fried chicken and mashed potatoes for dinner.*
3 If you say to someone '**Don't count your chickens**',
or '**Don't count your chickens before they hatch**', you
are warning them not to make plans according to what
they expect to happen before it has actually happened;
an informal expression. *Although I don't want to
count chickens before they are hatched, there have
been diplomatic moves which have led to the major
obstacles being removed.*

chicken out PHRASAL VERB If you **chicken out** of
something, you decide not to do it because you are
afraid; an informal expression. *He had chickened out
of going to fight for his country when he had a chance
to do so.*

chicken feed
NU **Chicken feed** is an amount of money which is so
small that it is hardly worth having or considering; an
informal expression. *He's earning chicken feed
compared to what you get.*

chickenpox /tʃɪkɪnpɒks/
NU **Chickenpox** is a disease which gives you a high
temperature and itchy red spots. *Rush has been
suffering from chickenpox, shingles and a liver
infection this summer.*

chickpea /tʃɪkpiː/ **chickpeas**
NC **Chickpeas** are hard round seeds that look like pale
brown peas. They can be cooked and eaten. *Some
farmers are planting chickpeas much earlier than
usual.*

chicory /tʃɪkəri/
NU **Chicory** is a vegetable with crunchy, sharp-tasting
leaves.

chide /tʃaɪd/ **chides, chiding, chided**
VO If you **chide** someone, you scold them; an old-
fashioned word. *Maurice chided him for his
carelessness.*

chief /tʃiːf/ **chiefs**
1 NC The **chief** of an organization is the person in
charge of it. ...*the current CIA chief. ...the chief of
the Presidential Security Corps.*
2 NC The **chief** of a tribe is its leader. *He was the last
of the Apache chiefs.*
3 ADJ ATTRIB **Chief** is used to describe the most
important worker of a particular kind in an
organization. ...*the chief cashier. ...the chief
American arms negotiator, Mr Max Kampelman.*
4 ADJ ATTRIB The **chief** cause, part, or member of
something is the main or most important one. *The
1902 Education Act was the chief cause of the
Progressives' downfall... I was his chief opponent.*

Chief Constable, Chief Constables
NC The **Chief Constable** in a particular county or area
in Britain is the officer who is in charge of the police
force there. ...*Greater Manchester's Chief Constable...
The Chief Constable was speaking at a news
conference in Belfast.*

Chief Justice, Chief Justices
NC A **Chief Justice** is the head judge of a court,
especially a supreme court. ...*Chief Justice Warren.*

chiefly /tʃiːfli/
1 ADV or ADV SEN You use **chiefly** to indicate the most
important cause or feature of something. *They were
chiefly interested in making money... The experiment
was not a success, chiefly because the machine tools
were of poor quality.*

2 ADV If something is done **chiefly** in a particular way or place, it is done mainly in that way or place. *They lived chiefly by hunting... Washington dealt chiefly with London and Paris during the Gulf crisis.*

Chief of Staff, Chiefs of Staff
NC The **Chiefs of Staff** are the highest-ranking officers of each service of the armed forces. *...the Israeli Army Chief of Staff, Major General Dan Shamron.*

chieftain /ˈtʃiːftən/ **chieftains**
NC A **chieftain** is the leader of a tribe. *...the legendary British chieftain, King Arthur.*

chiffon /ˈʃɪfɒn/
NU **Chiffon** is a kind of very thin silk or nylon cloth that you can see through. *...wispy, delicate garments in pink, yellow or sky blue silk and chiffon.*

chihuahua /tʃɪˈwɑːwə/ **chihuahuas**
NC A **chihuahua** is a very small short-haired dog.

chilblain /ˈtʃɪlbleɪn/ **chilblains**
NC **Chilblains** are painful red swellings which people get on their fingers or toes in cold weather. *...in stone cottages heated by coal fireplaces, the first nip of chilblains and the first hacking coughs of bronchitis.*

child /tʃaɪld/ **children** /ˈtʃɪldrən/
1 NC A **child** is a human being who is not yet an adult. *He left his native Guyana as a child of five... As a child she wanted to be a hairdresser.*
2 N PL Someone's **children** are their sons and daughters of any age. *Their children are all married... His wife was due to give birth to their first child.*

childbearing /ˈtʃaɪldbeərɪŋ/
1 NU **Childbearing** is the process of giving birth to babies. *...the dangers associated with childbearing.*
2 ADJ ATTRIB A woman of **childbearing** age is of an age when women are usually able to give birth to children. *Now these women are themselves reaching childbearing age... She must use birth-control for the rest of her childbearing years.*

childbirth /ˈtʃaɪldbɜːθ/
NU **Childbirth** is the act of giving birth to a child. *His mother died in childbirth.*

childhood /ˈtʃaɪldhʊd/
NU A person's **childhood** is the time when they are a child. *James Berry has been talking to Annemarie Grey about his childhood in Jamaica... He was living in London and dreaming of his childhood home in Ireland.*

childish /ˈtʃaɪldɪʃ/
ADJ You describe someone as **childish** when they behave in a silly and immature way. *I thought her nice but rather childish.* ♦ **childishly** ADV *'It's too hot here,' he complained childishly.*

childless /ˈtʃaɪldləs/
ADJ Someone who is **childless** has no children. *This method enabled many childless couples to have children.*

childlike /ˈtʃaɪldlaɪk/
ADJ You describe someone as **childlike** when they seem like a child in their appearance or behaviour. *He adored all the attention, in a rather childlike way.*

childminder /ˈtʃaɪldmaɪndə/ **childminders**
NC A **childminder** is someone who is paid to use their own home to look after other people's children. *Both children had been looked after by the same childminder.*

childminding /ˈtʃaɪldmaɪndɪŋ/
NU **Childminding** is the supervision and care given to children by a childminder or by a local government authority.

child prodigy, child prodigies
NC A **child prodigy** is a child with a very great talent, such as the ability to play a musical instrument. *...a child prodigy like Mozart... Dorothy Donegan was a child prodigy, giving concerts before she was a teenager.*

childproof /ˈtʃaɪldpruːf/
ADJ Something that is **childproof** is designed in a way which ensures that children cannot harm it or be harmed by it. *He is the official toy tester, with a mandate to check if toys are childproof... Medicines should be kept in childproof containers.*

children /ˈtʃɪldrən/
Children is the plural of **child**.

children's home, children's homes
NC A **children's home** is a place where children are sent to live if their parents cannot look after them properly. Children go to live in a children's home when their parents have treated them very badly or are ill. *She grew up in a children's home.*

child's play
NU If you say that something is **child's play**, you mean that it can be done very easily; an informal expression. *The test was real child's play.*

Chile /ˈtʃɪli/
The **Republic of Chile** is a country in western South America. It was a Spanish colony from the 16th century until 1818, when it became independent. General Augusto Pinochet overthrew the left-wing government of Salvador Allende in 1973 and ruled until the elections of 1990, when Patricio Aylwin Azócar became President. He is a member of the Christian Democrat Party and heads an alliance of Parties for Democracy (CPD), a coalition of 17 parties. Chile is the world's largest producer of copper. It is a member of the Organization of American States. ♦ **Chilean** /ˈtʃɪliən/ N, ADJ
■ *per capita GNP:* US$1,510 ■ *religion:* Christianity (mainly Roman Catholic) ■ *language:* Spanish ■ *currency:* peso ■ *capital:* Santiago ■ *population:* 13 million (1990) ■ *size:* 756,626 square kilometres.

chili /ˈtʃɪli/. See **chilli**.

chill /tʃɪl/ **chills, chilling, chilled**
1 VO When you **chill** something, you lower its temperature without freezing it. *White wine should be slightly chilled.*
2 VO When something **chills** you, it makes you feel very cold or frightened. *She was chilled by his callousness... A thin wail out of the darkness chilled them.* ♦ **chilling** ADJ *A chilling wind swept round them... The thought was chilling.*
3 NC A **chill** is a mild illness which can give you a slight fever. *The Chairman of the NPC has a serious chill, bordering on pneumonia.*

chilli /ˈtʃɪli/ **chillies**; also spelt **chili**.
NC or NU **Chillies** are small red or green seed pods with a hot, spicy taste. *...chilli peppers... Ceviche is a mouth-watering dish comprising uncooked fish marinated in a mixture of lemon juice, chilli and onion.*

chilli powder
NU **Chilli powder** is dark red powder made from dried chillies. It is used for flavouring food.

chilly /ˈtʃɪli/
1 ADJ **Chilly** means rather cold and unpleasant. *A draught of chilly air entered the room.*
2 ADJ PRED If you feel **chilly**, you feel cold. *Light the fire if you feel chilly.*
3 ADJ If a relationship between people or a response to something is **chilly**, it is not very friendly, welcoming, or enthusiastic. *Relations with Japan have remained chilly because Soviet soldiers still occupy islands to the north of the Japanese mainland... General Moiseyev's trip to Washington comes at the end of a comparatively chilly period in US-Soviet relations.*

Chiluba, Frederick /ˈfredrɪk tʃɪˈluːbə/
Frederick Chiluba became President of Zambia in 1991, when he defeated Kenneth Kaunda in elections. He was elected President of the Movement for Multi-Party Democracy (MMD) in 1991. He became Chairman of the Zambia Congress of Trade Unions in 1974. Born: 1943.

chime /tʃaɪm/ **chimes, chiming, chimed**
V When church bells or clocks **chime**, they make ringing sounds to show the time. *It was impossible to hear Big Ben chiming midnight, such was the noise of party-goers in the Square.* ► Also NC *...the silvery chime of the old stable clock.*
chime in PHRASAL VERB When someone **chimes in**, they say something just after someone else has spoken. *Bill chimed in with 'This is an emergency situation.'*

chimera /kaɪˈmɪərə/ **chimeras**
1 NC A **chimera** is a hope that is very unlikely to be

fulfilled, or an unrealistic idea that you have about something; a literary use. *I let myself be dazzled by the gilt chimeras of the career of writing.*
2 NC A **chimera** is a mythological monster with the head of a lion, the body of a goat, and the tail of a serpent.

chimney /tʃɪmni/ **chimneys**
NC A **chimney** is a pipe above a fireplace or furnace through which smoke can go up into the air. *Factory chimneys belch out soot and sulphur dioxide into the atmosphere.*

chimney breast, chimney breasts
NC A **chimney breast** is the part of a wall in a room which is built out round a chimney.

chimney pot, chimney pots
NC A **chimney pot** is a short pipe on top of a chimney stack. *They watched from between the TV aerials and chimney pots on the roofs of the terraced houses.*

chimney stack, chimney stacks
NC A **chimney stack** is the brick or stone part of a chimney on the roof of a building.

chimney sweep, chimney sweeps
NC A **chimney sweep** is a person whose job is to clean the soot out of chimneys.

chimp /tʃɪmp/ **chimps**
NC A **chimp** is a chimpanzee; an informal word. *The mother chimp sat hugging her baby.*

chimpanzee /tʃɪmpænziː/ **chimpanzees**
NC A **chimpanzee** is a kind of small African ape. *She has been studying the behaviour of chimpanzees.*

chin /tʃɪn/ **chins**
NC Your **chin** is the part of your face below your mouth and above your neck. *Although he got to his feet quickly, a left to the chin floored him a minute later... He's a fine-looking fellow who's got hair on his chin and on his head as well.*

china /tʃaɪnə/
1 NU or N+N **China** or **china clay** is a very thin clay from which cups, plates, and ornaments are made. *The freighter was on its way to Finland with a cargo of china clay. ...tea served in real china cups and saucers.*
2 NU Things such as cups, plates, and ornaments made of china clay are referred to as **china**. *She laid out a small tray with the best china.*

China /tʃaɪnə/
The **People's Republic of China** is a country in Asia. It is the most populous country in the world and the third largest in area. It was established in 1949, with Mao Zedong as its leader, and the Chinese Communist Party (CCP) as the ruling party. During the Cultural Revolution, which lasted from 1966 to 1976, young people banded together in groups of Red Guards, to eliminate reactionary thought and culture. In 1989 student pro-democracy demonstrations took place in Tiananmen Square in Beijing and were suppressed by the military. Deng Xiaoping, the dominant political figure since the death of Mao Zedong in 1976, resigned from his last official post, as Chairman of the CCP Central Military Commission, in 1989. He was succeeded by Jiang Zemin, who also became General Secretary of the CCP. In 1988 Yang Shangkun became President and Li Peng became Prime Minister. China produces one third of the world's rice. It is also the world's largest producer of coal, cotton, textiles, and cement. ◆ **Chinese** /tʃaɪniːz/ N, ADJ ▪ *per capita GNP:* US$330 ▪ *religion:* Buddhism, Christianity, Islam ▪ *language:* Mandarin (Putonghua) ▪ *currency:* yuan ▪ *capital:* Peking ▪ *largest city:* Shanghai ▪ *population:* 1,134 million (1990) ▪ *size:* 9,571,300 square kilometres.

China tea
NU **China tea** is tea made from large dark green or reddish-brown tea leaves. It is usually drunk without milk or sugar. *There was sweet and sour pork, rice and China tea.*

Chinese /tʃaɪniːz/.
1 ADJ **Chinese** means belonging or relating to China. *The Asian Games are due to begin in the Chinese capital next Saturday... The Prime Minister was presented with flowers by Chinese children.*
2 N PL The **Chinese** are the people who come from

China. *The Chinese have a completely different diet to us... So far the Chinese have given few details of the discussions.*
3 NU **Chinese** is the main language spoken by people who live in China. *They begin their courses in China by learning to speak Chinese.*

Chinese puzzle, Chinese puzzles
NC A **Chinese puzzle** is a puzzle consisting of several different boxes which you try to fit inside one another. *It was like the last piece in a Chinese puzzle.*

chink /tʃɪŋk/ **chinks, chinking, chinked**
1 NC A **chink** is a very narrow opening. *Through a chink she could see a bit of blue sky.*
2 V When objects **chink**, they touch each other, making a short, light ringing sound. *Empty bottles chinked as the milkman put them into his crate.*
▶ Also N SING+of *...the chink of money.*

chinless /tʃɪnləs/
ADJ If you describe someone as **chinless**, you mean that they are weak and rather cowardly.

chintz /tʃɪnts/
NU **Chintz** is a cotton fabric with bright patterns on it. *...chintz curtains.*

chinwag /tʃɪnwæg/
N SING If friends have a **chinwag**, they have a long enjoyable conversation; an informal word. *I had a good chinwag with my sister yesterday.*

chip /tʃɪp/ **chips, chipping, chipped**
1 NC In Britain, **chips** are long, thin pieces of fried potato. *They each had a meal of steak and chips.*
2 NC In the United States, **chips** or **potato chips** are very thin slices of potato that have been fried until they are hard and crunchy. *A report published today says that chips—crisps as they're called over in Britain—are rich in vitamin C and E and a good snack for kids.*
3 NC A **chip** or **silicon chip** is a very small piece of silicon with electric circuits on it which is part of a computer. *Today's computers are based on silicon chips.*
4 VO When you **chip** something, you accidentally damage it by breaking a small piece off it. *Graf chipped a bone in her thumb last February... He put down his glass of whisky so hard that he chipped the glass.* ◆ **chipped** ADJ *...a chipped mug.*
5 NC **Chips** are also small pieces which have been broken off something. *...granite chips.*
6 If someone has **a chip on** their **shoulder**, they behave rudely and aggressively because they feel they have been treated unfairly; an informal expression. *He struck me as a politician with a chip on his shoulder.*
chip away at PHRASAL VERB If you **chip away at** something such as an idea, a feeling, or a system, you make it weaker or less likely to succeed than it was before by a series of repeated efforts. *Mr Shultz has been trying to chip away at these apparently irreconcilable differences.*
chip in PHRASAL VERB 1 When a number of people **chip in**, each person gives some money so that they can pay for something together; an informal expression. *They all chipped in to pay the doctor's bill.* 2 When someone **chips in** during a conversation, they interrupt it; an informal expression.

chipboard /tʃɪpbɔːd/
NU **Chipboard** is a hard material made out of wood chips which have been pressed together. It is often used instead of wood for making doors and furniture because it is cheaper.

chipmunk /tʃɪpmʌŋk/ **chipmunks**
NC A **chipmunk** is a small animal which looks rather like a squirrel but which has a striped back.

chip shop, chip shops
NC In Britain, a **chip shop** is a shop which sells food such as fish, chips, meat pies, pieces of chicken, and so on. The food is cooked in the shop and people take it away to eat.

chiropodist /kɪrɒpədɪst/ **chiropodists**
NC A **chiropodist** is a person whose job is to treat people's feet.

chiropody /kɪrɒpədi/
NU **Chiropody** is the professional treatment and care of people's feet.

chirp /tʃɜːp/ chirps, chirping, chirped
v When a bird or insect **chirps**, it makes short high-pitched sounds. *...the sound of crickets chirping away in the background.*

chirpy /tʃɜːpɪ/ chirpier, chirpiest
ADJ Someone who is **chirpy** is very cheerful and lively; an informal word. *It was good to see her looking so bright and well and chirpy. ...his quick wit and chirpy humour.*

chirrup /tʃɪrəp/ chirrups, chirruping, chirruped
v When a bird or insect **chirrups**, it makes short high-pitched sounds. *A cricket chirruped tirelessly.* ▶ Also NC *With a frightened chirrup, the bird flew away.*

chisel /tʃɪzl/ chisels, chiselling, chiselled; spelt chiseling, chiseled in American English.
1 NC A **chisel** is a tool that has a long metal blade with a sharp edge at the end. It is used for cutting and shaping wood and stone. *They slowly began removing the soft sandstone with small chisels and brushes.*
2 VO If you **chisel** wood or stone, you cut and shape it using a chisel. *The men chisel the blocks out of solid rock.*

Chissano, Joaquim Alberto
/ʒuəkiːmˀ ælbeətuː ʃɪsænuː/
Joaquim Alberto Chissano became President of Mozambique in 1986, when Samora Machel was killed in a plane crash. He was Prime Minister from 1974 to 1975, and Minister of Foreign Affairs from 1975 to 1986. He is a member of the Front for the Liberation of Mozambique (Frelimo). Born: 1939.

chit /tʃɪt/ chits
1 NC A **chit** is a short official note, such as a receipt, an order, or a memo, usually signed by someone in authority. *This chit is signed Percival... A mother must have a chit from a health worker to get skimmed milk for her baby.*
2 NC People refer to a girl as a **chit** when they think that she behaves in a wild, silly, or childish way; an old-fashioned use. *He's thrown it all away on some silly chit. ...a spoilt, curly-haired chit called Elaine Somers.*

chit-chat
NU **Chit-chat** is informal talk about things that are not very important. *I felt unequal to any cosy chit-chat about the new publication.*

chitty /tʃɪtɪ/ chitties
NC A **chitty** is a short official note, such as a receipt, order, or memo, usually signed by someone in authority; an informal word.

chivalrous /ʃɪvəlrəs/
ADJ **Chivalrous** men are polite, kind, and unselfish, especially towards women. *They were treated with chivalrous consideration.*

chivalry /ʃɪvəlrɪ/
NU **Chivalry** is chivalrous behaviour. *...small acts of chivalry.*

chives /tʃaɪvz/
NU or N PL **Chives** is a plant with long thin hollow leaves that you cut into small pieces and add to food to give it a flavour similar to that of onions. *Snip the chives and mix these in with the potatoes.*

chivvy /tʃɪvɪ/ chivvies, chivvying, chivvied; also spelt chivy.
VO If you **chivvy** someone, you keep urging them to do something that they do not want to do. *I chivvied everyone up to make the place tidy... Gifford needed to chivvy us into our fielding practice this morning.*

chloride /klɔːraɪd/ chlorides
NC or NU A **chloride** is a chemical compound of chlorine and another substance; a technical term in chemistry. *The waxiness of the leaves will reduce the uptake of sodium chloride... Health authorities are distributing chloride to put in the water where it has been contaminated.*

chlorinate /klɔːrɪneɪt/ chlorinates, chlorinating, chlorinated
VO When people **chlorinate** water, for example in a swimming pool, they disinfect it by putting chlorine into it. *Monroe chlorinates the intake pipe constantly ...o kill zebra mussels before they hatch... A power ...ilure has put the plant out of action, and the water is ...t being properly chlorinated.* ◆ **chlorinated** ADJ

...swimming up and down the chlorinated Cowley baths.

chlorine /klɔːriːn/
NU **Chlorine** is a strong-smelling gas that is used to disinfect water and to make cleaning products. *The water is treated daily with chlorine.*

chloroform /klɒrəfɔːm/ chloroforms, chloroforming, chloroformed
1 NU **Chloroform** is a colourless liquid with a strong sweet smell, which makes you unconscious if you breathe its vapour. *He was given 'knock-out drops', which he said had the same effect as chloroform.*
2 VO To **chloroform** a person or an animal means to use chloroform in order to make them unconscious or kill them. *The victim had been chloroformed and then strangled.*

chlorophyll /klɒrəfɪl/
NU **Chlorophyll** is a green substance in plants which enables them to use the energy from sunlight in order to grow. *The green colour in the commonest algae is due to the presence of chlorophyll.*

choc-ice /tʃɒkaɪs/ choc-ices
NC A **choc-ice** is a small block of ice cream covered with chocolate.

chock-a-block /tʃɒkəblɒk/
ADJ PRED A place that is **chock-a-block** is very full of people, things, or vehicles; an informal expression. *The house was chock-a-block... London is chock-a-block with tourists at the moment.*

chocolate /tʃɒklət/ chocolates
1 NU **Chocolate** is a sweet hard brown food made from cocoa beans. *...a bar of chocolate. ...chocolate cake.*
2 NC A **chocolate** is a sweet or nut covered with a layer of chocolate. *...a box of chocolates.*
3 N MASS **Chocolate** is also a hot drink made from a powder containing chocolate. *Hercule Poirot drank his morning chocolate.*

chocolate-box
ADJ ATTRIB **Chocolate-box** scenery, pictures, and so on are very pretty, but often in a boring or conventional way. *We drove through chocolate-box countryside.*

choice /tʃɔɪs/ choices; choicer, choicest
1 NC If there is a **choice**, there are at least two things from which you can choose. *There's a choice of eleven sports. ...the choice between peace and war.*
2 NC Your **choice** is the person or thing that you choose. *Mr Lefever is President Reagan's choice as Assistant Secretary of State.*
3 ADJ ATTRIB You use **choice** to describe things that are of high quality. *...choice cuts of meat... I had put a vase of my choicest roses on the table.*
● **Choice** is used in these phrases. ● The thing or person **of** your **choice** is the one that you choose. *She was prevented from marrying the man of her choice.*
● If you **have no choice** but to do something, you cannot avoid doing it. *The President had no choice but to agree.*

choir /kwaɪə/ choirs
NC A **choir** is a group of people who sing together. *The choir sang a mixture of traditional hymns and African songs.*

choirboy /kwaɪəbɔɪ/ choirboys
NC A **choirboy** is a boy who sings in a church choir. *He came from Lincoln and as a boy became a choirboy in the city's famous cathedral.*

choke /tʃəʊk/ chokes, choking, choked
1 V-ERG When you **choke**, or when something **chokes** you, you cannot breathe properly because something is blocking your windpipe. *Philip choked on his drink... The pungent smell of sulphur choked him.* ◆ **choking** ADJ *They were enveloped in a cloud of choking dust.*
2 VO To **choke** someone means to squeeze their neck until they are dead. *An old woman was found choked to death.*
3 V-PASS If a place is **choked** with things or people, it is full of them and nothing can move. *The centre of the city was choked with cars.*
4 NC The **choke** in a car or other vehicle is a device that reduces the amount of air going into the engine and makes it easier to start.

choke back PHRASAL VERB If you **choke back** an emotion, you force yourself not to show it. *I choked* *back my anger... She choked back her sobs.*

choked /tʃəʊkt/
ADJ ATTRIB If you say something in a **choked** voice, your voice does not have its full sound, because you are upset or afraid. *He let out a choked scream.*

choker /tʃəʊkə/ **chokers**
NC A **choker** is a necklace that fits very closely round your neck. *She wore a choker of jet beads.*

cholera /kɒlərə/
NU **Cholera** is a serious disease that affects your digestive organs. *More than ninety people have died in an outbreak of cholera.*

cholesterol /kəlɛstɒⁿrəl/
NU **Cholesterol** is a substance that exists in the fat, tissues, and blood of all animals. Too much cholesterol in your blood can cause heart disease. *The fat from meat tends to raise the cholesterol level in the blood.*

chomp /tʃɒmp/ **chomps, chomping, chomped**
VOorV If a person or animal **chomps** their food, they chew it noisily; an informal word.

choose /tʃuːz/ **chooses, choosing, chose** /tʃəʊz/ **chosen** /tʃəʊzn/
1 VO If you **choose** something from all the things that are available, you decide to have that thing. *I chose a yellow dress... I had been chosen to be trained as editor.* ◆ **chosen** ADJ ATTRIB *They undergo training in their chosen professions.*
2 V If you **choose** to do something, you do it because you want to or because you feel that it is right. *Mr Mitterrand can choose to call an early general election if he so wishes... They could fire employees whenever they chose.*
3 If there is **little to choose** between things or **not much to choose** between them, it is difficult to decide which is better. *Politically, there is little to choose between them... There's nothing to choose between the two countries.*

choosy /tʃuːzi/
ADJ A **choosy** person will only accept something if it is exactly right or of very high quality. *I'm very choosy about my whisky.*

chop /tʃɒp/ **chops, chopping, chopped**
1 VO If you **chop** something, you cut it into pieces with an axe or a knife. *I don't like chopping wood... Peel, slice, and chop the apple.*
2 NC A **chop** is a small piece of meat cut from the ribs of a sheep or pig. *...a one hundred gramme lamb chop.*
3 When people **chop and change**, they keep changing their minds about what to do; an informal expression. *All this chopping and changing is very confusing.*

chop down PHRASAL VERB If you **chop down** a tree, you cut through its trunk with an axe so that it falls to the ground. *A fine has been imposed on a timber company which was illegally chopping down trees.*

chop up PHRASAL VERB If you **chop** something **up**, you chop it into small pieces. *Chop up some tomatoes and add them to the onion.*

chopper /tʃɒpə/ **choppers**; an informal word.
1 NC A **chopper** is a helicopter. *Investigators say it appears the chopper's rotors struck the wing of the plane moments before the crash... The chopper was carrying supplies to a remote camp on the Turkish-Iraqi border.*
2 NC A **chopper** is also an axe. *They dragged them out of the jeep and killed them with iron bars, choppers and spears.*

chopping board, chopping boards
NC A **chopping board** is a board that you cut meat and vegetables on.

choppy /tʃɒpi/
ADJ When water is **choppy**, there are a lot of small waves on it. *The sea suddenly turned from smooth to choppy.*

chopstick /tʃɒpstɪk/ **chopsticks**
NC **Chopsticks** are a pair of thin sticks used by people in the Far East for eating food. *At a luncheon he had difficulty handling his chopsticks.*

chop suey /tʃɒp suːi/
NU **Chop suey** is a Chinese-style meal made with chopped meat, bean sprouts, and other vegetables in a sauce.

choral /kɔːrəl/
ADJ ATTRIB **Choral** music is sung by a choir. *It will probably be very difficult to get any tickets for concerts of large choral works.*

chord /kɔːd/ **chords**
1 NC A **chord** is a number of musical notes played or sung together with a pleasing effect. *I was just learning how to play the piano, so I was learning about chords and things... He could play just three chords on this guitar.*
2 If something **strikes a chord** or **touches a chord**, it makes you feel a particular emotion, usually of sympathy or enthusiasm. *The Charter 77 appeal has obviously struck a chord... His calls for radical change have clearly touched a chord with young people in the cities.*

chore /tʃɔː/ **chores**
1 NC A **chore** is a task that you have to do, but that you do not enjoy because it is not very interesting. *This newly-designed musical instrument promises to make learning very much less of a chore.*
2 **Chores** are tasks such as cleaning, washing, and ironing that you have to do regularly at home. *Does your husband do his fair share of the household chores?*

choreograph /kɒriəgrɑːf/ **choreographs, choreographing, choreographed**
VO When someone **choreographs** a ballet or other dance, they invent the steps and movements and tell the dancers how to perform them. *The new ballet was choreographed by Christopher Bruce.*

choreographer /kɒriɒgrəfə/ **choreographers**
NC A **choreographer** is someone who invents the movements for a ballet and tells the dancers how to perform them. *He joined the company as a choreographer in 1975.*

choreography /kɒriɒgrəfi/
NU **Choreography** is the inventing of movements for ballets. *The choreography for their dance in the balcony scene expresses the wonder and joy of young love.*

chorister /kɒrɪstə/ **choristers**
NC A **chorister** is a singer in a church choir. *Britten's Requiem will be performed by the Choristers of St Paul's Cathedral.*

chortle /tʃɔːtl/ **chortles, chortling, chortled**
V When someone **chortles**, they laugh with pleasure or amusement. *She chortled with delight.*

chorus /kɔːrəs/ **choruses, chorusing, chorused**
1 NC A **chorus** is a large group of people who sing together. *...a performance of Verdi's Requiem with the BBC Symphony Chorus.*
2 NC The **chorus** of a song is the part which is repeated after each verse. *...the chorus of a popular patriotic hymn.*
3 N SING+SUPP When there is a **chorus** of disapproval or satisfaction, these attitudes are expressed by many people. *There has been a growing chorus demanding his resignation.*
4 V-QUOTE When people **chorus** something, they say or sing it together. *'Shall I tell you a story?'—'Please!' the children would chorus.*

chorus girl, chorus girls
NC A **chorus girl** is a young woman who sings and dances in the chorus of a show or film.

chose /tʃəʊz/
Chose is the past tense of **choose**.

chosen /tʃəʊzn/
Chosen is the past participle of **choose**.

chow /tʃaʊ/ **chows**
1 NC A **chow** is a dog with a thick coat and a curled tail, originally from China.
2 NU **Chow** is food; used in informal American English. *We lift weights, eat chow, and that's about it... I came out to go to the chow hall for breakfast.*

chowder /tʃaʊdə/
NU **Chowder** is a thick soup containing pieces of fish or shellfish.

chow mein /tʃaʊ meɪn/
NU **Chow mein** is a Chinese-style meal of fried noodl with cooked meat or vegetables. *...chicken chow mein.*

Christ /kraɪst/
1 N PROP **Christ** is one of the names of Jesus, whom Christians believe to be the son of God and whose teachings are the basis of Christianity. *...the teachings of Christ. ...a believer in God and a follower of Christ.*
2 Some people say **'Christ!'** when they are surprised, shocked, or annoyed, or in order to emphasize what they are saying; an informal and rude use which some people find offensive.

christen /krɪsn/ **christens, christening, christened**
1 V OR V OC When a baby is **christened**, he or she is given Christian names during a christening. *She was christened Victoria Mary... Charles II was christened in this church.*
2 VOC To **christen** a place or an object means to choose a name for it and to start calling it by that name; an informal use. *The crew christened the hot geysers the 'black smokers'.*

Christendom /krɪsndəm/
N PROP **Christendom** is all the Christian people and countries in the world; an old-fashioned word. *At the height of its power Christendom was mighty and unified.*

christening /krɪsənɪŋ/ **christenings**
NC A **christening** is a ceremony in which a baby is made a member of the Christian church and is officially given his or her Christian names. *The photo shows the Duchess of York cradling the baby Princess Beatrice at her christening yesterday. ...Mrs Moffat had made the christening gown.*

Christian /krɪstʃən/ **Christians**
NC A **Christian** is a person who believes in Jesus Christ and follows his teachings. *For Christians, Easter is the greatest celebration in the year.* ▶ Also ADJ *...Christian virtues.*

Christianity /krɪstiænəti/
NU **Christianity** is a religion based on the teachings of Jesus Christ and on the belief that he was the son of God. *....celebrations in Moscow and Kiev marking 1000 years of Christianity in Russia.*

Christian name, Christian names
NC A person's **Christian names** are the names given to them when they are born or when they are christened. *Do all your students call you by your Christian name?*

Christmas /krɪsməs/ **Christmases**
NU OR NC **Christmas** is the Christian festival on the 25th of December celebrating the birth of Jesus Christ. *Merry Christmas and a Happy New Year!... The past few Christmases had been very quiet.*

Christmas Day
NU **Christmas Day** is December 25th, when Christmas is celebrated. *The Royal Family will be spending Christmas Day at Sandringham... We expect snow on or near Christmas Day.*

Christmas Eve
NU **Christmas Eve** is December 24th, the day before Christmas Day. *Santa Claus makes his annual journey across the world on Christmas Eve.*

Christmas Island /krɪsməs aɪlənd/
Christmas Island is a territory of Australia, located in the Indian Ocean, south of Indonesia. It was annexed by the United Kingdom in 1888 and extensively mined for phosphates. Administration was transfered to Australia in 1958. ◆ **Christmas Islander** /krɪsməs aɪləndə/ N
▪ *religion:* Buddhism, Islam, Christianity ▪ *language:* English (official) ▪ *currency:* Australian dollar ▪ *capital:* Flying Fish Cove ▪ *population:* 1,230 (1989) ▪ *size:* 135 square kilometres. ▪

Christmas pudding, Christmas puddings
NC OR NU A **Christmas pudding** is a special pudding that is eaten at Christmas. It is made from dried fruit, spices, and suet. *The Christmas pudding was set on the table... They were eating turkey and Christmas pudding.*

Christmas tree, Christmas trees
NC A **Christmas tree** is a fir tree, or an artificial tree that looks like a fir tree. People put them in their houses at Christmas and decorate them with lights and balls. *Every year since 1946 the Norwegian*

government has donated a Christmas tree to Britain.

chrome /krəʊm/
NU **Chrome** is metal plated with chromium. *He was handed a bottle of wine and a chrome corkscrew.*

chromium /krəʊmiəm/
NU **Chromium** is a hard, shiny metallic element, used to make steel alloys and to coat other metals. *South African mines produce one third of the world's chromium.*

chromosome /krəʊməsəʊm/ **chromosomes**
NC A **chromosome** is a part of a cell in an animal or plant. It contains genes which determine what characteristics the animal or plant will have. *Each cell of our bodies contains 46 chromosomes.*

chronic /krɒnɪk/
1 ADJ A **chronic** illness lasts for a very long time. *Her father was dying of chronic asthma.*
2 ADJ ATTRIB You describe someone's bad habits or behaviour as **chronic** when they have behaved like that for a long time and do not seem able to stop themselves. *...chronic drunkenness.*
3 ADJ A **chronic** situation is very severe and unpleasant. *Some areas of the developing world continue to face chronic debt problems.*

chronically /krɒnɪkli/
1 SUBMOD Someone who is **chronically** ill has been ill for a very long time. *Air pollution makes many people chronically ill.*
2 SUBMOD You use **chronically** to indicate that a situation is very severe and unpleasant. *The country remains chronically short of cash.*

chronicle /krɒnɪkl/ **chronicles, chronicling, chronicled**; a formal word.
1 VO If you **chronicle** a series of events, you write about them in the order in which they happened. *Xenophon chronicled the Persian Wars.*
2 NC A **chronicle** is a formal account or record of a series of events. *Amnesty's latest document is a horrifying chronicle of imprisonment, torture, and death.*

chronological /krɒnəlɒdʒɪkl/
ADJ If you describe a series of events in **chronological** order, you describe them in the order in which they happened. *...a chronological account of the Arab-Israeli problems.* ◆ **chronologically** ADV *They proceeded to examine developments chronologically.*

chronology /krənɒlədʒi/
NU The **chronology** of a series of past events is the times at which they happened in the order in which they happened. *The chronology of subsequent events was as follows... My memories are sharp, but have no chronology.*

chrysalis /krɪsəlɪs/ **chrysalises**
NC A **chrysalis** is a butterfly or moth in the stage between being a larva and an adult. *...a butterfly that won't come out of its chrysalis.*

chrysanthemum /krɪsænθɪməm/ **chrysanthemums**
NC A **chrysanthemum** is a large garden flower with many long, thin petals. *We have the most superb range of autumn chrysanthemums.*

chubby /tʃʌbi/
ADJ Someone who is **chubby** is rather fat. *Seibou is big, chubby, jovial and talkative.*

chuck /tʃʌk/, **chucks, chucking, chucked**; an informal word.
VOA When you **chuck** something somewhere, you throw it there in a casual or careless way. *Chuck my tights across, please.*

chuck away or **chuck out** PHRASAL VERB If you **chuck** something **away** or **chuck** it **out**, you throw it away. *If there's no way of controlling a pest animal without killing it, doesn't it make sense to sell the skin instead of chucking it away?*

chuckle /tʃʌkl/ **chuckles, chuckling, chuckled**
VOR V-QUOTE When people **chuckle**, they laugh quietly. *They were chuckling over the photographs... 'She wanted to be in touch with eternal reality,' Mom said chuckling.* ▶ Also NC *He shook his head with a soft chuckle.*

chuck steak
NU **Chuck steak** is meat from the neck or shoulder of a cow.

chuffed /tʃʌft/
ADJ PRED If you are **chuffed** about something, you are very pleased about it; an informal word. *I'm absolutely chuffed to have been chosen.*

chug /tʃʌg/ chugs, chugging, chugged
V When a vehicle **chugs** somewhere, its engine makes short thudding sounds. *A small fishing boat comes chugging towards them.*

chum /tʃʌm/ chums, chumming, chummed; an old-fashioned, informal word.
1 NC Your **chum** is your friend. *In Dublin he met an old school chum.*
2 VOCATIVE Men sometimes address each other as **chum**, usually in a slightly aggressive or unfriendly way. *You've had it, chum.*
chum up PHRASAL VERB If you **chum up** with someone, you make friends with them. *We chummed up together when we were in Egypt.*

chummy /tʃʌmi/ chummier, chummiest
ADJ If someone is **chummy**, they are friendly; an old-fashioned, informal word. *She always wanted to be chummy.*

chump /tʃʌmp/ chumps
NC You call someone a **chump** when you want to tell them in a friendly way that they have done something silly; an informal word. *'You chump,' she said, smiling at me.*

Chung Won Shik /tʃʌŋ wɒn ʃɪk/
Chung Won Shik was appointed Prime Minister of South Korea in 1991. He was Minister of Education from 1988 to 1991. He is a member of the Democratic Liberal Party (DLP).

chunk /tʃʌŋk/ chunks
1 NC+SUPP A **chunk** of something is a piece of it. *...a great chunk of meat.*
2 NC+SUPP A **chunk** is also a large amount or part of something; an informal use. *Research and development now take up a sizeable chunk of the military budget.*

chunky /tʃʌŋki/
ADJ A **chunky** person or thing is large and heavy. *A chunky waitress came waddling towards him. ...great chunky cardigans.*

church /tʃɜːtʃ/ churches
1 NCorNU A **church** is a building in which Christians worship. *There were no services that day, and the church was empty... His parents go to church now and then.*
2 NC A **Church** is one of the groups of people within the Christian religion, for example Catholics or Methodists, that have their own beliefs, clergy, and form of worship. *Jane had been received into the Church a month previously.*

churchgoer /tʃɜːtʃgəʊə/ churchgoers
NC A **churchgoer** is a person who goes to church regularly. *He is an active churchgoer who once wanted to become a parson.*

Churchill, Sir Winston /wɪnstən tʃɜːtʃɪl/
Sir Winston Churchill was Prime Minister of the United Kingdom from 1940 to 1945, and from 1951 to 1955. He was born in 1874. His career in Parliament lasted from 1900 until 1964, and he represented five constituencies in that time. From 1904 to 1924 he was a Liberal, but before 1904 and after 1924 he was a member of the Conservative Party. He led the coalition government during the Second World War. He died in 1965 and was given a State Funeral.

churchman /tʃɜːtʃmən/ churchmen /tʃɜːtʃmən/
NC A **churchman** is the same as a clergyman; a formal word. *...the Anglican churchman, Canon John Collins.*

Church of England
N PROP The **Church of England** is the main church in England, which has the Queen as its head and which does not recognize the authority of the Pope. *On this issue he found himself in opposition to most of the Church of England... She had brought her children up in the Church of England.*

churchwarden /tʃɜːtʃwɔːdn/ churchwardens
NC A **churchwarden** is a person who is chosen by a church congregation to help the vicar of a parish with administration and other duties.

churchyard /tʃɜːtʃjɑːd/ churchyards
NC A **churchyard** is an area of land around a church where dead people are buried.

churlish /tʃɜːlɪʃ/
ADJ **Churlish** behaviour is unfriendly, bad-tempered, or impolite. *The paper calls the Government's attitude a churlish piece of hypocrisy.*

churn /tʃɜːn/ churns, churning, churned
1 NC A **churn** is a container used for making butter.
2 VO To **churn** milk or cream means to stir it vigorously in order to make butter.
churn out PHRASAL VERB To **churn** things **out** means to produce large numbers of them very quickly; an informal expression. *His organization began churning out tracts and posters.*
churn up PHRASAL VERB When something **churns up** mud or water, it moves it about violently. *The wind churned up the water into a swirling foam.*

chute /ʃuːt/ chutes
NC A **chute** is a steep, narrow slope down which people or things can slide. *There were no emergency chutes leading down to the ground but he jumped anyway.*

chutney /tʃʌtni/
NU **Chutney** is a strong-tasting mixture of fruit, vinegar, sugar, and spices. *We still make super jam and chutney.*

C.I.A. /siːaɪeɪ/
N PROP The **C.I.A.** is an agency in the United States that tries to obtain secret information about the political and military activities of individuals or governments in other countries. **C.I.A.** is an abbreviation for 'Central Intelligence Agency'. *They were each sentenced to eight years in jail by a Cuban court for spying for the C.I.A... The statement accused Colonel Higgins of being a C.I.A. agent.*

cicada /sɪkɑːdə/ cicadas
NC A **cicada** is a large insect that lives in hot countries and makes a loud high-pitched noise.

C.I.D. /siːaɪdiː/
N PROP The **C.I.D.** is a branch of the police force in Britain which is concerned with finding out who has committed crimes. **C.I.D.** is an abbreviation for 'Criminal Investigation Department'. *...Chief Superintendant Meadows of the C.I.D.*

Cidade de Praia /sɪdɑːdə də praɪə/
Cidade de Praia is the capital of Cape Verde and its largest city. Population: 58,000 (1980).

cider /saɪdə/
NU **Cider** is an alcoholic drink made from apples. *Beer and cider will go up by about a penny a pint.*

cigar /sɪgɑː/ cigars
NC **Cigars** are rolls of dried tobacco leaves which people smoke. *Realising he must not smoke, he pulled the cigar out of his mouth and threw it away.*

cigarette /sɪgəret/ cigarettes
NC **Cigarettes** are small tubes of paper containing tobacco which people smoke. *If someone smokes 20 cigarettes daily, they increase their risk of getting lung cancer ten times.*

cigarette holder, cigarette holders
NC A **cigarette holder** is a narrow tube that you can put a cigarette into in order to hold it while you smoke it. *She flourished an enormously long cigarette holder.*

cigarette lighter, cigarette lighters
NC A **cigarette lighter** is a device which produces a small flame when you flick a switch. You use it to light a cigarette or cigar. *...a plastic, disposable cigarette lighter.*

cigarette paper, cigarette papers
NC A **cigarette paper** is a small thin piece of paper which you put tobacco on and roll into a tube in order to make a cigarette.

cinch /sɪntʃ/
If you say that something **is a cinch**, you mean that it is very easy to do; an informal expression. *Beating Rangers should be a cinch.*

cinder /sɪndə/ cinders
NC **Cinders** are the pieces of material that are left after wood or coal has burned. *...an insulating layer of cinders that would allow a low transmission of hea*
● If something has been burned **to a cinder**, it has

been burned until it is black.

cinder track, cinder tracks
NC A **cinder track** is a running track that is covered with fine cinders.

cine camera /sɪni kæmərə/ **cine cameras**
NC A **cine camera** is a camera that takes a moving film rather than photographs.

cinema /sɪnəmə/ **cinemas**
1 NC A **cinema** is a place where people go to watch films. *There's been a big rise in the number of people going to the cinema.*
2 NU **Cinema** is the business and art of making films that are shown in cinemas. *...one of the classic works of Hollywood cinema... Sean Connery has received a special award for his achievements in cinema.*

cinematic /sɪnəmætɪk/
ADJ ATTRIB **Cinematic** means relating to films made for the cinema. *The cinematic effects are the work of the man who designed the sets for Madonna's last tour.*

cinematography /sɪnəmətɒgrəfi/
NU **Cinematography** is the technique of making films for the cinema. *The film only took one award for best cinematography.*

cinnamon /sɪnəmən/
NU **Cinnamon** is a spice used for flavouring sweet food and curries. *...cookies made out of pie dough and cinnamon and sugar.*

cipher /saɪfə/ **ciphers**; also spelt **cypher**.
NCorNU A **cipher** is a secret system of writing. *The necessary codes and ciphers will be included in your orders... They had been corresponding with one another in cipher.*

circa /sɜːkə/
PREP If you write **circa** in front of a year, you mean that the date is approximate. *...an old British newspaper, circa 1785.*

circle /sɜːkl/ **circles, circling, circled**
1 NC A **circle** is a round shape. Every part of its edge is the same distance from the centre. *The students sit in a circle on the floor... Stand the paint tin on a circle of aluminium foil.*
2 V If a bird or aircraft **circles**, it moves round in a circle. *Hawks circled overhead looking for prey.*
3 NC+SUPP You can refer to a group of people as a **circle**. *I have widened my circle of acquaintances... This proposal caused an uproar in parliamentary circles.*
4 N SING The **circle** in a theatre or cinema is an area of seats on the upper floor.
5 See also **vicious circle**.

circlet /sɜːklət/ **circlets**
NC A **circlet** is a decorated band of precious metal worn round a person's head, especially in former times. *...a circlet of pearls.*

circuit /sɜːkɪt/ **circuits**
1 NC An electrical **circuit** is a complete route which an electric current can flow around. *Engineers checked and tested every circuit.*
2 NC+SUPP A **circuit** is also a series of places that are visited regularly by a person or group. *...the American college lecture circuit.*
3 NC A racing **circuit** is a track on which cars or motorbikes race. *Senna took his McLaren round the circuit in one minute 24.12 seconds.*

circuit breaker, circuit breakers
NC A **circuit breaker** is a device which can stop the flow of electricity around a circuit by switching itself off if anything goes wrong. *You can have your house fitted with circuit breakers in place of fuses.*

circuitous /səkjuːɪtəs/
ADJ A **circuitous** route is long and complicated; a formal word. *...a long and circuitous journey by train and boat.*

circuitry /sɜːkɪtri/
NU **Circuitry** is a system of electric circuits. *Now he could see the electronic circuitry of the unit.*

circular /sɜːkjʊlə/ **circulars**
1 ADJ Something that is **circular** is shaped like a circle. *...a circular pond... The large circular saw blade is driven by hydraulic motors.*
2 ADJ If you make a **circular** journey, you go somewhere and then return by a different route.

3 ADJ A **circular** argument or theory is not valid because it uses a statement to prove the conclusion and the conclusion to prove the statement. *Groff and other young drivers face a circular problem because sponsors only want to invest in winning teams with proven drivers.*
4 NC A **circular** is a letter or advertisement which is sent to a large number of people at the same time. *Their aim is to deliver the circular to every household in the country.*

circulate /sɜːkjʊleɪt/ **circulates, circulating, circulated**
1 V-ERG When a piece of writing **circulates** or is **circulated**, copies of it are passed round among a group of people. *A union newspaper was circulating at the congress... The report was circulated to all the members... Dissidents have circulated leaflets calling for people to defy the authorities.* ◆ **circulation** /sɜːkjʊleɪʃn/ NU *...the circulation of illegal books.*
2 V-ERG When a joke or a rumour **circulates** or is **circulated**, people tell it to each other. *Stories about him circulated at his club... A wicked rumour had been circulated that she was a secret drinker.*
3 V When a substance **circulates**, it moves easily and freely within a closed place or system. *We are governed by the hormones that circulate around our bodies.* ◆ **circulation** NU *...the circulation of air.*
4 V If you **circulate** at a party, you move among the guests and talk to different people. *After John had circulated amongst his guests, dinner was announced.*

circulation /sɜːkjʊleɪʃn/ **circulations**
1 NC+SUPP The **circulation** of a newspaper or magazine is the number of copies sold each time it is produced. *The local paper had a circulation of only six thousand.*
2 N SING Your **circulation** is the movement of blood around your body. *He stamped his feet from time to time to keep the circulation going.*
3 NU Money that is in **circulation** is being used by the public. *The main aim will be to reduce the amount of money in circulation to prevent inflation.*

circulatory /sɜːkjʊleɪtəˀri/
ADJ ATTRIB **Circulatory** problems are problems related to the circulation of blood in the body; a medical term. *Mr Dean suffers from a circulatory disease which has left him barely able to walk.*

circumcise /sɜːkəmsaɪz/ **circumcises, circumcising, circumcised**
VO If a man or boy **has been circumcised**, the loose skin has been cut off the end of his penis for religious or medical reasons. ◆ **circumcision** /sɜːkəmsɪʒn/ NU *Of course, circumcision of the male has religious significance for many.*

circumference /səkʌmfərəns/ **circumferences**
NC+SUPP The **circumference** of a circle, place, or round object is the distance around its edge. *The area has a circumference of 54 miles.*

circumflex /sɜːkəmfleks/ **circumflexes**
NC A **circumflex** is a symbol written over a vowel in French and other languages, usually to indicate that it should be pronounced as a longer sound than usual. It is used for example in the word 'rôle'.

circumlocution /sɜːkəmləkjuːʃn/ **circumlocutions**
NCorNU A **circumlocution** is a way of saying or writing something using more words than necessary instead of being clear and direct; a formal word. *...the use of circumlocutions like 'concerted action'.*

circumscribe /sɜːkəmskraɪb/ **circumscribes, circumscribing, circumscribed**
VO If someone's power or freedom is **circumscribed**, it is limited; a formal word. *All political activity has been severely circumscribed... Their life was extremely circumscribed, with long hours of study and few of play.*

circumspect /sɜːkəmspekt/
ADJ If you are **circumspect**, you avoid taking risks; a formal word. *Physicians are now more circumspect about making recommendations for surgery.*

circumspection /sɜːkəmspekʃn/
NU **Circumspection** is cautious behaviour; a formal word. *They behaved with considerable sense and circumspection.*

circumstance /sɜːkəmstəns/ **circumstances**

1 N PL+SUPP **Circumstances** are the conditions which affect what happens in a particular situation. *In normal circumstances I would have resigned immediately... She died without ever learning the circumstances of her grandfather's death.* ● You can emphasize that something will not happen by saying that it will not happen under any **circumstances**. *The Baltic states and Georgia say they won't sign the Union treaty under any circumstance... Under no circumstances whatsoever will I support Mr Baldwin.*
2 N PL+POSS Your **circumstances** are the conditions of your life, especially the amount of money that you have. *...change in George's circumstances was abrupt ...continued ...about the financial circumstances and alleged luxurious lifestyle of the president.*

circumstantial /sɜːkəmstænʃl/
1 ADJ **Circumstantial** evidence makes it seem likely that something happened, but does not prove it. *The evidence presented to the court was largely circumstantial.*

circumvent /sɜːkəmvent/ **circumvents**, **circumventing**, **circumvented**, a formal word
1 VO If someone **circumvents** a rule or restriction, they avoid being prevented from doing something the rule of restriction in a clever and perhaps dishonest way. *Although charging interest in return if they loan, the landlords circumvent this by calling it a payment, or a 'gift'.*
2 VO If you **circumvent** someone, you cleverly prevent them from achieving something, especially when they are trying to harm you. *We all want and they are trying to do and we must try to circumvent them.*

circus /sɜːkəs/ **circuses**
1 N A circus is a travelling show performed in a large tent, with clowns, acrobats, and trained animals. *A number of local authorities have banned circuses with animals, claiming they consider them cruel.*
2 VO If someone describes an event as a circus, they mean that they think it is only being done for publicity, attention or to impress people, and will not achieve anything. *The trial had been an unnecessary circus at public expense.*

cirrhosis /sɪrəʊsɪs/
N-U Cirrhosis is a serious disease which destroys people's livers. It is often caused by drinking too much alcohol. *...suffering from cirrhosis of the liver... treatment for advanced cirrhosis of the liver.*

cirrus /sɪrəs/
N-U Cirrus is a type of thin cloud that occurs very high in the sky, a technical term. *...a high blanket of cirrus. ...cirrus clouds.*

CIS /siːaɪes/ See Commonwealth of Independent States.
cissy /sɪsi/ **cissies**. See sissy.

cistern /sɪstən/ **cisterns**
N-C A cistern is a container which holds water for example to flush a toilet or to store the water supply of a building. *A plumber was ordered to repair the main cistern. The ancient Greek cisterns were found in a garden under the mosque more than fifty years ago.*

citadel /sɪtədl/ **citadels**
N-C A citadel is a strongly fortified building in a city. *The citadel had not been stormed, but neither is it unscathed. ...the vast, walled citadel, and ancient soul of power ...the Mission Tower.*

citation /saɪteɪʃn/ **citations**, a formal term
1 N-C A citation is an official argument or speech which praises a person for something brave or special that they have done. *The policeman subsequently received citations for their action.*
2 N-C A citation from a book, or piece of writing is a quotation from it. *There are over 250 literature citations in the directory.*

cite /saɪt/ **cites**, **citing**, **cited**; a formal word
1 VO If you cite something, you quote it or mention it, especially as an example or proof of what you are saying. *The General cited intelligence reports which suggest a new coup attempt is planned... Low wages were cited as the main cause for dissatisfaction.*
2 VO In a legal case, to cite a person means to

officially name them, and to cite a reason or cause means to state it as the official justification for your case. *Legal experts say that if more than one person is cited as responsible, the public prosecutor will have a hard job... Most divorce cases are brought by wives who cite adultery or intolerable behaviour.*

citizen /sɪtɪzn/ **citizens**
1 N-C+SUPP If someone is a **citizen** of a country, they are legally accepted as belonging to that country. *...a Swedish citizen.*
2 N-C+SUPP The **citizens** of a town are the people who live there. *...the citizens of Bristol.*
3 See also senior citizen.

Citizens' Advice Bureau, Citizens' Advice Bureau
N-C or N PROP The **Citizens' Advice Bureau** is a voluntary organization in Britain which gives people free advice, often on legal or financial problems. *...nearly 900 specialist debt counsellors mostly working within Citizens Advice Bureaux, local authorities and the DHSS. The Citizens' Advice Bureau says its offices throughout the country handled a record number of enquiries last year.*

Citizens' Band
N PROP Citizens' Band is the range of radio waves which the general public is allowed to use in order to send messages to one another. It is used especially by lorry drivers and other motorists who use radio sets in their vehicles. *...Citizens' Band Radio... I'm not a citizens' band freak by any manner of means.*

citizenship /sɪtɪznʃɪp/
N-U+SUPP If you have **citizenship** of a country, you are legally accepted as belonging to it. *The constitution guarantees their citizenship. ...a campaign to give people more than a million immigrants to take up citizenship.*

citric /sɪtrɪk/
N-U Citric acid is a weak acid found in many fruits especially citrus fruits such as oranges and lemons. *...the juice of the fruit containing some citric acid.*

citrus fruit /sɪtrəs fruːt/ **citrus fruits**
N A citrus fruit is a juicy sharp-tasting such as an orange, lemon, or grapefruit. Citrus grow very well in those relatively dry conditions. *...export of citrus fruit and other agricultural produce.*

city /sɪti/ **cities**
1 N-C A city is a large town. *...the city of Birmingham. ...a modern city centre.*
2 N PROP The City is the part of London where banks and other financial institutions have their offices. *You can work in the City and make money... And we have the latest news where there are predictions of an oil crisis on some electricity shares.*

City Hall
N In the USA and many City Hall is the building in which the staff of the government or municipal administration have their offices. *They gather at City Hall... I go up to the City Hall. The city hall was packed with people.*
2 N City Hall is used to refer to the administration of a city; used in America. *They criticise what they see as City Hall. ...The Commission to independently from City Hall. ...important City Hall elections.*

civic /sɪvɪk/
ADJ ATTRIB Civic means having or relating to the town or city, or relating to the town centre, with pride.

civics /sɪvɪks/
N-U Civics is the study of the rights and duties of citizens and the working of government; used mainly in British English and US.

civil /sɪvl/
1 ADJ ATTRIB You use relate to the people or activities, often in

They have their own regional systems of military and civil administration. ...wars or civil disturbances. ...a supersonic civil airliner.
2 ADJ A **civil** person is polite. *He'd been careful to be civil to everyone.* ◆ **civilly** ADV *He was somewhat upset but he answered civilly enough.*

civil defence, civil defences
1 NU **Civil defence** is the organization and training of the ordinary people in a country so that they can help the armed forces, medical services, and police force, for example if the country is attacked by an enemy. *His job is to establish a centre of civil defence in every village.*
2 N PL A country's **civil defences** are the preparations that it makes to protect its people and buildings and to make sure that the government and police, medical and other essential services can continue to function, for example when an enemy attacks the country. *...the UK's civil defences against air attack. ...civil defence measures. ...the civil defence corps.*

civil disobedience
NU **Civil disobedience** is the refusal by ordinary people in a country to obey laws or pay taxes, usually in order to protest about something. *They achieved their ends through non-violent demonstrations and civil disobedience.*

civil divorce, civil divorces
NCorNU A **civil divorce** is one which is recognized by the state but not by the church. *Caroline is a Roman Catholic and though she obtained a civil divorce, she's still married in the eyes of the church.*

civil engineer, civil engineers
NC A **civil engineer** is a person whose job is concerned with planning, designing, and constructing roads, bridges, harbours, and public buildings. *Civil engineers have turned more and more to reinforced concrete to build their structures.*

civil engineering
NU **Civil engineering** is the planning, design, and construction of roads, bridges, harbours, and public buildings. *The Incas were capable of great feats of civil engineering. ...a four year course in civil engineering.*

civilian /səvɪliən/ civilians
NC A **civilian** is anyone who is not a member of the armed forces. *They tried to avoid bombing civilians. ...a heinous attack on innocent civilians... They entered into co-operation with the Italians in order to protect their civilian population.*

civilise /sɪvəlaɪz/. See civilize.

civility /səvɪləti/
NU **Civility** is behaviour which is polite but not very friendly. *She was treated with civility and consideration.*

civilization /sɪvəlaɪzeɪʃn/ civilizations; also spelt civilisation.
1 NCorNU A **civilization** is a human society with its own social organization and culture which makes it distinct from other societies. *...the earliest great civilizations: Egypt, Sumer, Assyria. ...the entire history of Western civilisation.*
2 NU **Civilization** is the state of having an advanced level of social organization and a comfortable way of life. *The Romans brought civilization to much of Europe.*

civilize /sɪvəlaɪz/ civilizes, civilizing, civilized; also spelt civilise.
VO To **civilize** a person or society means to educate them and improve their way of life. *...their mission of civilizing and modernizing that society.*

civilized /sɪvəlaɪzd/; also spelt civilised.
1 ADJ A **civilized** society has an advanced level of social organization. *They aim to create an orderly, just and civilised society.*
2 ADJ A **civilized** person or behaviour is polite and reasonable. *...a civilized discussion.*

civil law
NU **Civil law** is the part of a country's set of laws which is concerned with the private affairs of citizens, such as marriage and property ownership, rather than crime. *These debts, unlike all others, were not recoverable at civil law.*

civil liberty, civil liberties
NCorNU A person's **civil liberties** are the rights they have to say, think, and do what they want as long as they respect other people's rights. *Here too there has been a similar attack on civil liberties. ...the only party to truly support civil liberty in Britain.*

civil marriage, civil marriages
NCorNU A **civil marriage** is a marriage ceremony which is performed by a government official and not by a representative of a religion such as a priest. *Reforms proposed by the government could lead to more glamorous civil marriages... In Israel there is no civil marriage.*

civil rights
N PL **Civil rights** are the rights that people have in a society to equal treatment and equal opportunities, whatever their race, sex, or religion may be. *The American battle for civil rights helped the battle for women's liberation. ...the civil rights movement.*

civil servant, civil servants
NC A **civil servant** is a person who works in the Civil Service. *The government insisted that all civil servants are bound by an absolute duty of confidentiality.*

Civil Service
N COLL The **Civil Service** of a country consists of the government departments and the people who work in them. *...a series of austerity measures which attacked the perks of the civil service. ...a string of top civil service appointments.*

civil war, civil wars
NCorNU A **civil war** is a war which is fought between different groups of people living in the same country. *...the Spanish Civil War... There might be civil war again.*

cl
cl is a written abbreviation for 'centilitre'. *Many bottles these days, though, are 70 cl.*

clack /klæk/ clacks, clacking, clacked
1 NC A **clack** is a short loud noise made by two hard objects hitting against each other, for example objects made of wood. *...the clack of ball on bat. ...the clack of high heels as she crosses the yard.*
2 V-ERG If you **clack** something or if it **clacks**, it makes a short loud noise. *I picked up the shears and began to clack them menacingly in mid-air... We skied on, our tips clacking together, and the snow crunching under us.*

clad /klæd/
ADJ If you are **clad** in particular clothes, you are wearing them; a literary word. *...beggars clad in dirty white rags.*

cladding /klædɪŋ/
NU **Cladding** is a covering of tiles, wooden boards, or other material that is fixed to the outside of a building to protect it against bad weather or to make it look more attractive. *The roof cladding and kitchen shutters were made from corrugated iron.*

claim /kleɪm/ claims, claiming, claimed
1 V-REPORTorV+to-INF You use **claim** to report what someone says when you are not sure whether what they are saying is true. *He claimed that he found the money in the forest... They claimed to have shot down twenty-two planes.*
2 NC A **claim** is something which a person says but which cannot be proved and which may be false. *Forecasts do not support the government's claim that the economy is picking up.*
3 VO If someone **claims** responsibility or credit for something, they say that they are responsible for it. *The rebels claimed responsibility for the bombing.*
4 VOorVA If you **claim** something such as money or property, you ask for it because you have a right to it. *Voluntary workers can claim travelling expenses... Don't forget to claim for a first-class rail ticket to London.*
5 NC A **claim** is also a demand for something that you think you have a right to. *...a pay claim. ...a claim for compensation.*
6 VO If a fight or disaster **claims** someone's life, they are killed in it; a formal use. *The wave of bombings and street clashes is claiming new lives every day.*

were still fundamental differences which needed a clear-headed approach.

clearing /klɪərɪŋ/ **clearings**
NC A **clearing** is a small area of grass or bare ground in a wood. *...a clearing made by a forest fire.*

clearing bank, clearing banks
NC In Britain, a **clearing bank** is a bank that uses the central clearing house in London in all its dealings with other banks. *The other three major clearing banks followed suit and raised their interest rates.*

clearing house, clearing houses
1 NC A **clearing house** is an organization which collects, sorts, and distributes information. *Their national service committee, an information clearing house and resource centre... The less he knows the better. Let him be simply a clearing house for information.*
2 NC A **clearing house** is also a central bank which deals with all the transactions between the banks that use its services. *...the Bank for International Settlements in Switzerland, a clearing house for Western Central Banks.*

clear-out
N SING If you have a **clear-out**, you collect together and then throw away all the things you do not want, and tidy and clean the things that remain; an informal word. *This room is in a real mess! We'll have to have a good clear-out soon.*

clear-sighted
ADJ Someone who is **clear-sighted** is able to understand situations well and to make sensible judgements and decisions about them. *He was too clear-sighted not to see what problems would follow.*

clearway /klɪəweɪ/ **clearways**
NC In Britain, a **clearway** is a road on which you are not allowed to stop unless your vehicle breaks down or develops a fault. *...the development of clearways linking the tunnel with London.*

cleavage /kliːvɪdʒ/ **cleavages**
1 NC A woman's **cleavage** is the space between her breasts, especially the top part which you see when she is wearing a low-cut dress. *...the same conventionally sexy model, with the obligatory cleavage. ...a lipsticked blonde wearing little enough to disclose a deep cleavage.*
2 NC A **cleavage** between people is a division or disagreement between them; a formal use. *...a political cleavage between the classes.*

cleave /kliːv/ **cleaves, cleaving, cleaved, clove, cloven, cleft**. The past tense can be either **cleaved** or **clove**, and the past participle can be **cleaved, cloven,** or **cleft**; a literary word.
1 V-ERG When you **cleave** something or when it **cleaves**, it is split or divides into two separate parts, often violently. *His spade cleaved the firm sand with a satisfying crunch. ...a child's head cloven in half... The front of the palace is cleft by the grand flight of steps... Oak cleaves well too, but not as well as chestnut.*
2 V-ERG+to When one thing **cleaves** to another or when you **cleave** one thing to another, you cannot move them apart because they seem to be stuck together. *Without this weight their feet no longer cleave to the ground... My tongue clove to the roof of my mouth.*

cleaver /kliːvə/ **cleavers**
NC A **cleaver** is a knife with a large square blade, used for chopping meat or vegetables. *Split the carcass right down the backbone with a cleaver... With a cleaver, she chops bamboo twigs for firewood... Inmates armed with iron pipes, staves and a cleaver, were attacking other prisoners.*

clef /klef/ **clefs**
NC A **clef** is the symbol at the beginning of a line of music that indicates its pitch.

cleft /kleft/ **clefts**
1 NC A **cleft** in a rock or the ground is a narrow opening in it. *He could see the valley through a cleft in the rocks.*
2 If you are **in a cleft stick**, you are in a difficult situation that will give you problems or harm you whatever you decide to do.
3 **Cleft** is a form of the past participle of **cleave**.

cleft palate, cleft palates
N C or N U If someone has a **cleft palate**, they were born with a narrow opening along the roof of their mouth which makes it difficult for them to speak properly. *...babies who are born with cleft palates... If cleft palate could be treated in the embryo there would be no scarring.*

clematis /klemətɪs/
N U **Clematis** is a climbing plant that has large purple, pink, or white flowers. *...a cottage garden with lupins, roses, marigolds and clematis climbing over the doorways.*

clemency /klemənsi/
N U If someone is shown **clemency**, they receive kind and merciful treatment from a person who has the authority to punish them; a formal word. *...appeals for clemency.*

clench /klentʃ/ **clenches, clenching, clenched**
1 VO When you **clench** your fist, you curl your fingers up tightly. *Ralph clenched his fist and went very red.*
2 VO When you **clench** your teeth, you squeeze them together firmly. *She hissed through clenched teeth, 'Get out of here.'*
3 VO If you **clench** something in your hand or teeth, you hold it tightly. *There he sat, pipe clenched in his mouth, typing away.*

clergy /klɜːdʒi/
1 N PL The **clergy** are the religious leaders of a Christian church. *...Britain's two most senior Anglican clergy, the Archbishops of Canterbury and York. ...the clergy of all denominations.*
2 N PL The **clergy** are also religious leaders of non-Christian churches. *Buddhist clergy are refusing to conduct religious ceremonies with members of the army.*

clergyman /klɜːdʒimən/ **clergymen**
NC A **clergyman** is a male member of the clergy. *...clergymen and theological students.*

cleric /klerɪk/ **clerics**
1 NC A **cleric** is a member of the Christian clergy; an old-fashioned use. *The clerics have taken their mission from the church steps to the public.*
2 NC A **cleric** is also used to refer to religious leaders in other religions. *...one of the country's leading clerics, Ayatollah Abdul Karim Musavi. ...the influential Lebanese cleric Sheikh Mohammed Hussein Fadlallah.*

clerical /klerɪkl/
1 ADJ **Clerical** jobs and workers are concerned with work in offices. *...routine clerical work.*
2 ADJ **Clerical** also means relating to the clergy; a formal use. *...a priest in a clerical grey suit.*

clerk /klɑːk/ **clerks**
1 NC A **clerk** works in an office, bank, or law court and looks after the records or accounts. *...a humdrum, mild-mannered bank clerk. ...a junior clerk in the Peruvian foreign ministry.*
2 NC In American English, a **clerk** is also a person whose job is to sell things in a shop or large store. *He works as a clerk in a shoe store... The man bought a magazine and a bag of chips, then told the clerk he was robbing the store. ...grocery clerks.* ● See also **sales clerk.**

clever /klevə/ **cleverer, cleverest**
1 ADJ A **clever** person is intelligent and able to understand things easily or to plan things well. *My sister was very clever and passed all her exams at school... How clever of you to know that.* ♦ **cleverly** ADV *They had gone about the scheme cleverly.* ♦ **cleverness** N U *I admire cleverness—and courage too.*
2 ADJ An idea, book, or invention that is **clever** is extremely effective and skilful. *This is a very clever way of running a college. ...a clever gadget.*

cliché /kliːʃeɪ/ **clichés**; also spelt **cliche.**
NC A **cliché** is a phrase or idea which has been used so much that it no longer has any real effect. *It has almost become a cliché to say that he is redrawing the map of the world. ...like actors with their stock, dramatic cliches.*

clichéd /kliːʃeɪd/; also spelt **cliched.**
ADJ Something that is **clichéd** has become a cliché;

used showing disapproval. *'Behind every great man, there has to be a great woman', or so runs the clichéd phrase... Their dancing can be embarrassing but at least it's never cliched.*

click /klɪk/ **clicks, clicking, clicked**
1 V-ERG When something **clicks**, it makes a short, sharp sound. *His camera was clicking away... He clicked the switch on the radio.* ▶ Also NC *The lock opened with a click.*
2 V When you suddenly understand something, you can say that it **has clicked**; an informal use. *Straight away it clicked that that's what we had to do.*

client /klaɪənt/ **clients**
NC A **client** is someone for whom a professional person or organization is providing a service or doing some work. *...a solicitor and his client.*

clientele /kliːɒntɛl/
N COLL The **clientele** of a place or business are its customers or clients. *...a restaurant with a predominantly upper-class clientele.*

cliff /klɪf/ **cliffs**
NC A **cliff** is a high area of land with a very steep side, especially one next to the sea. *They lost their footing and plunged some one-hundred metres over a cliff.*

cliff-hanger, cliff-hangers
NC If you describe a situation as a **cliff-hanger**, you mean that it is very exciting or frightening, because you are left for a long time not knowing what will happen next. *There's a real cliff-hanger in the final scene.*

climactic /klaɪmæktɪk/
ADJ A **climactic** moment in a situation is one in which a very exciting or important event occurs; a formal word. *He keeps it secret from her until a climactic point in the story.*

climate /klaɪmət/ **climates**
1 NCorNU The **climate** of a place is the typical weather conditions that occur there. *...the English climate. ...changes in climate. ...very cold climates.*
2 NC+SUPP You can use **climate** to refer to a situation, usually when referring to the way it is changing people's attitudes or opinions. *...this changing climate of public opinion... The improving economic climate may be a contributing factor. ...last year's improvement in the political climate between East and West. ...the climate of reform in Eastern Europe.*

climatic /klaɪmætɪk/
ADJ ATTRIB **Climatic** conditions, changes, and effects are those that relate to the general weather conditions of a place. *We must stop burning fossil fuels in our current wasteful manner if we are to avoid undesirable climatic changes. ...favourable climatic conditions.*

climax /klaɪmæks/ **climaxes**
NC The **climax** of something is the most exciting or important moment in it, usually near the end. *This proved to be the climax of his political career.*

climb /klaɪm/ **climbs, climbing, climbed**
1 VAorVO If you **climb** something such as a tree, mountain, or ladder, you move towards the top of it. *We climbed to the top of the mountain... We started to climb the hill.* ▶ Also NC *We were still out of breath from the climb.*
2 VA If you **climb** somewhere, you move there carefully and sometimes awkwardly, because there is not much room to move. *She climbed into her car... Four men climbed down through the hatch.*
3 V To **climb** also means to move upwards or to increase in level or value. *The plane climbed steeply and banked... The cost has climbed to a staggering £35 billion.*

climb-down, climb-downs
NC A **climb-down** in an argument or dispute is the act of admitting that you are wrong or of agreeing to reduce the demands or conditions that you were previously insisting on. *A much higher proportion of strikes may culminate in a climb-down on the part of management.*

climber /klaɪmə/ **climbers**
1 NC A **climber** is someone who climbs rocks or mountains as a sport. *The Huaraz area is the site of*

Peru's highest mountains and a popular destination for climbers and walkers.
2 NC A **climber** is also a plant that grows upwards by attaching itself to other plants or objects. *...scented climbers, such as jasmine and honeysuckle.*

climbing /klaɪmɪŋ/
NU **Climbing** is the sport of climbing rocks or mountains. *...a book about climbing... One man has died after a climbing accident in north-west Scotland.*

climbing frame, climbing frames
NC A **climbing frame** is a structure that is made for children to climb and play on. It consists of metal or wooden bars that are joined together. *In their garden was a climbing frame and a swing, made entirely from local materials.*

clime /klaɪm/ **climes**
NC+SUPP You use **clime** to refer to a place that has a particular kind of climate; a literary word. *He retreats to sunny climes, leaving the winter behind.*

clinch /klɪntʃ/ **clinches, clinching, clinched**
1 VO To **clinch** something that is uncertain or doubtful means to settle it in a definite way; an informal use. *It was the arrival of the dark blue caravan that finally clinched matters... What had clinched her decision?... I had to be absolutely certain before I could speak. It was your voice that clinched it; it hasn't changed at all.*
2 VO To **clinch** something you are trying to achieve such as victory in a contest or agreement on a business deal, means to succeed in obtaining it. *They clinched victory over China in the doubles... It was Stein's second goal that clinched the match for Luton... Mr George Bush has clinched the Republican Party's Presidential nomination... They would only negotiate after a deal with the private banks had been clinched.*

clincher /klɪntʃə/ **clinchers**
NC A **clincher** is something that you use as a way of finally agreeing something or of settling an argument. *As a clincher, he made particular reference to previously negotiated agreements.*

cling /klɪŋ/ **clings, clinging, clung** /klʌŋ/
1 VA If you **cling** to someone or something, you hold onto them tightly. *I clung to the door to support myself.*
2 VA Clothes that **cling** stay pressed against your body when you move. *The dress clung tight to Etta's waist.*
3 V+to If you **cling** to someone, you do not allow them enough freedom or independence. *A working woman is not so likely to cling to her children when they leave home.*
4 V+to If you **cling** to an idea or way of behaving, you continue to believe in its value or importance, even though it may no longer be valid or useful. *They cling to all the old, inefficient methods of doing things.*

clinging /klɪŋɪŋ/
1 ADJ Someone who is **clinging** becomes very attached to people and too dependent on them; used showing disapproval. *...something weak and clinging in his nature.*
2 ADJ Clothing that is **clinging** fits tightly round your body. *She sat staring in horror at her own nipples, exposed by the clinging dress.*

clinic /klɪnɪk/ **clinics**
NC A **clinic** is a building where people receive medical advice or treatment.

clinical /klɪnɪkl/
1 ADJ ATTRIB **Clinical** refers to the direct medical treatment of patients, as opposed to theoretical research; a medical term. *Doctors are hoping to start clinical tests next month.* ◆ **clinically** ADV *On examination she looked well and was not clinically anaemic.*
2 ADJ **Clinical** thought or behaviour is very logical, detached, and unemotional; used showing disapproval. *She adopted an icy, impersonal, clinical attitude.*
3 ADJ A **clinical** room or building is very plain, or is too neat and clean, so that people do not enjoy being in it. *...tiny offices painted clinical white.*

clinician /klɪnɪʃn/ **clinicians**
NC A **clinician** is a doctor who treats patients directly as opposed to doing theoretical research. *The test*

guests immediately clustered around the table.
3 NC A **cluster bomb** is a type of bomb which is dropped from an aircraft and contains a large number of smaller bombs that spread out before they hit the ground and then explode where they land. *Reports speak of cluster bombs being dropped.*
...fragmentation weapons and cluster bombs.

clutch /klʌtʃ/ **clutches, clutching, clutched**
1 VOorVA If you **clutch** something, you hold it very tightly. *Myra came in, clutching her handbag... Children clutched at the sleeves of fathers, revealing nightmares now long past.*
2 N PL If you are in the **clutches** of another person, that person has power or control over you; an informal use. *He escaped the clutches of the law.*
3 NC In a car, the **clutch** is the pedal that you press before you change gear, and the mechanism that it operates. *...a gearbox with an automated clutch.*
clutch at PHRASAL VERB **1** If you **clutch at** someone or something, you move your hands quickly in order to hold the person or thing tightly. *Her pony stumbled, and she clutched at the reins.* **2** If you **clutch at** something, you desperately attempt to use it for a particular reason, especially as an excuse or in order to solve a problem. *She would have clutched at any excuse to miss school for the day.* • **to clutch at straws:** see **straw**.

clutch bag, clutch bags
NC A **clutch bag** is a handbag without a handle which a woman carries under her arm or in her hand.

clutter /klʌtə/ **clutters, cluttering, cluttered**
1 NU **Clutter** is a lot of unnecessary or useless things in an untidy state. *The rooms were full of clutter.*
2 VO If things **clutter** a place, they fill it in an untidy way. *Cluttering the table were papers, books, and ashtrays.* ◆ **cluttered** ADJ *He glanced around the small, cluttered room.*
clutter up PHRASAL VERB If things **clutter up** a place, they fill it in an untidy way so that it is difficult to move around. *...a model student who would never bother him by cluttering up his lab with experimental apparatus.*

cm.
cm. is a written abbreviation for 'centimetre'. *...two rolls of sterile bandage 5 cm. wide.*

CND /siːcndiː/
N PROP **CND** is a British organization which opposes the development and use of nuclear weapons. **CND** is an abbreviation for 'Campaign for Nuclear Disarmament'. *He was a member of CND... Don't forget to wear your CND badge.*

c/o
You write **c/o** before an address on an envelope when you are sending it to someone who is staying or working at that address, often for only a short time. **c/o** is an abbreviation for 'care of'. *Mr A D Bright, c/o Sherman Ltd, 62 Burton Road, Bristol 8.*

co- /kəʊ-/
PREFIX **Co-** is used to form words that refer to people sharing things or doing things together. *...the co-author of a cookery book... The two countries coexist peacefully.*

Co. /kəʊ/
Co. is used as an abbreviation for 'company' in the names of companies. *...Morris, Marshall, Faulkner & Co.*

C.O. /siː əʊ/
C.O. is an abbreviation for 'commanding officer'. *The C.O. sent out patrols three times.*

coach /kəʊtʃ/ **coaches, coaching, coached**
1 NC A **coach** is a bus that carries passengers on long journeys. *The coach leaves Cardiff at twenty to eight... We usually go there by coach.*
2 NC A **coach** on a train is one of the separate sections for passengers. *The track was obstructed by a wrecked coach that had been thrown sideways.*
3 NC A **coach** is also an enclosed four-wheeled vehicle pulled by horses. *Amid considerable splendour and pageantry, the Queen goes by horse-drawn coach to the House of Lords.*
4 VO If you **coach** someone, you help them to become better at a particular sport or subject. *She had been*

coached by a former Wimbledon champion.
5 NC A **coach** is also someone who coaches a person or sports team. *The British Lions' coach, Ian McGeechan, has said he's bitterly disappointed.*

coach-and-four, coach-and-fours
NC A **coach-and-four** is an old-fashioned coach that was pulled by four horses. *In 1825 a Mr Hunt drove a coach-and-four across the frozen Serpentine.*

coachload /kəʊtʃləʊd/ **coachloads**
NC A **coachload** of people is a group of people who travel somewhere together in a coach. *...coachloads of tourists.*

coachman /kəʊtʃmən/ **coachmen** /kəʊtʃmən/
NC A **coachman** was a man who drove a horse-drawn coach. *...a liveried coachman and groom.*

coach park, coach parks
NC A **coach park** is a place where coaches and buses are allowed to park.

coach station, coach stations
NC A **coach station** is a building where coaches arrive at or leave from on regular journeys.

coagulate /kəʊægjʊleɪt/ **coagulates, coagulating, coagulated**
V When paint or blood **coagulates**, it becomes very thick.

coal /kəʊl/ **coals**
NU **Coal** is a hard black substance that is taken from under the ground and burned as fuel. *...a lump of coal. ...the coal mining industry.*

coalesce /kəʊəles/ **coalesces, coalescing, coalesced**
V A If things or people **coalesce**, they join to form a larger system or group; a formal word. *There is a tendency for industrial systems to coalesce into large units. ...the radical grouping which has coalesced around Boris Yeltsin.*

coalface /kəʊlfeɪs/ **coalfaces**
NC In a coal mine, the **coalface** is the part where the coal is being cut out of the rock. *Miners commonly have to crawl as much as a kilometre to reach the coalface.*

coalfield /kəʊlfiːld/ **coalfields**
NC A **coalfield** is a region where there is coal under the ground. *Miners' leaders have recommended that a strike which has disrupted coal production in Britain's largest coalfield should be called off.*

coal gas
NU **Coal gas** is gas produced from coal. It is used especially for heating and cooking in people's homes. See also **natural gas**. *We used coal gas before natural gas came in... It might be necessary to convert the whole country back to coal gas.*

coalition /kəʊəlɪʃn/ **coalitions**
NC A **coalition** is a group consisting of people from different political or social groups who are co-operating to achieve a particular aim. *...the formation of an opposition coalition. ...a broad coalition of community groups in the area... Yitzak Shamir is still trying to put together a coalition government.*

coalman /kəʊlmæn/ **coalmen**
NC A **coalman** is a person who delivers coal to people's houses.

coalminer /kəʊlmaɪnə/ **coalminers**
NC A **coalminer** is a person whose job is mining coal. *Soviet coalminers at thirteen pits in the Vorkuta region are said to have ended their strike.*

coal scuttle, coal scuttles
NC A **coal scuttle** is a special kind of bucket for keeping coal in.

coal tar
NU **Coal tar** is a thick black liquid made from coal. It is used for making drugs and chemical products.

coarse /kɔːs/ **coarser, coarsest**
1 ADJ Something that is **coarse** has a rough texture. *...coarse white cloth. ...coarse black hair.*
2 ADJ A **coarse** person talks and behaves in a rude, offensive way. *He objected to her coarse remarks.*
◆ **coarsely** ADV *She speaks rather coarsely.*
◆ **coarseness** NU *With deliberate coarseness, he wiped his mouth with his hand.*

coarse fishing
NU **Coarse fishing** is the sport of catching fish, other than trout and salmon, that live in lakes or rivers. See

also **fly-fishing**. ...*the start of the coarse fishing season.*

coarsen /kɔːsn/ **coarsens, coarsening, coarsened**
 v If someone **coarsens**, they become less polite or caring. *My whole nature had coarsened in a way that horrified me.*

coast /kəʊst/ **coasts**
 1 NC The **coast** is an area of land next to the sea. ...*a trawler fishing off the coast of Portugal... We had made up our minds to stay on the East Coast.*
 2 If you say that **the coast is clear**, you mean that there is nobody around to see you or catch you. *When the coast was clear, the other four reappeared one by one from various directions.*

coastal /kəʊstl/
 ADJ ATTRIB **Coastal** means in the sea or on the land near a coast. ...*coastal waters... The Liberal Democratic Party holds its annual conference in the coastal resort of Bournemouth this week.*

coaster /kəʊstə/ **coasters**
 1 NC A **coaster** is a ship that sails along a coast taking goods to ports on the coast. *The men were part of the crew of the British registered coaster, the Union Jupiter. ...a Dutch coaster which is drifting in stormy seas off the coast of North Wales.*
 2 NC A **coaster** is also a small mat that you put underneath a glass or mug in order to protect the surface of a table. *The waitress put a paper coaster down.*
 3 See also **roller-coaster**.

coastguard /kəʊstgɑːd/ **coastguards**
 NC A **coastguard** is an official who watches the sea near a coast, in order to give help when it is needed. *The crew were picked up by the coastguard as first light broke.*

coastline /kəʊstlaɪn/ **coastlines**
 NC A country's **coastline** is the edge of its coast. ...*a rocky and treacherous coastline.*

coat /kəʊt/ **coats, coating, coated**
 1 NC A **coat** is a long piece of clothing with long sleeves that you wear over your other clothes in order to keep you warm or protect you from bad weather. *She wrapped herself in a warm coat and smart fur hat.*
 2 NC An animal's **coat** is its fur or hair. *He had never seen a bigger leopard, nor, indeed, one with so beautiful a coat.*
 3 VO If you **coat** something with a substance, you cover it with a thin layer of the substance. *The sweets are then coated with chocolate.*
 4 NC+SUPP A **coat** of paint or varnish is a thin layer of it. *Then go over it with a final coat of a resinous paint.*

coat hanger, coat hangers
 NC A **coat hanger** is a curved piece of wood, metal, or plastic for hanging clothes on. ...*a metal coat hanger.*

coating /kəʊtɪŋ/ **coatings**
 NC+SUPP A **coating** of a substance is a thin layer of it. ...*a coating of dust.*

coat of arms, coats of arms
 NC A **coat of arms** is a design in the form of a shield used as an emblem by a family, a town, or an organization. ...*the ancient Hungarian coat of arms with its crown of St Stephen.*

coat of mail, coats of mail
 NC A **coat of mail** is a piece of armour made of metal rings linked together. *Soldiers wore them in medieval times over the top part of their bodies.*

coat-tails
 1 N PL A man's **coat-tails** are the two long parts at the back of a formal coat. *My father once got his coat-tails stuck in a lift door.*
 2 If you **ride on the coat-tails** of someone or something, you take advantage of something that they have done, without making any real effort yourself. *The Europeans could ride on the coat-tails of US technology... He made his fortune riding on the coat-tails of a successful gimmick.*

co-author /kəʊ ɔːθə/ **co-authors**
 NC The **co-authors** of a book are the people who have written it together. ...*Ann Tusa, co-author of a book on the Berlin blockade.*

coax /kəʊks/ **coaxes, coaxing, coaxed**
 V Oor V-QUOTE If you **coax** someone to do something, you gently try to persuade them to do it. *She might be coaxed into giving their marriage another chance. ...the veteran Roger Milla was coaxed out of retirement at the age of 38... 'It won't hurt you,' Marsha coaxed.*

cob /kɒb/ **cobs**
 NC A **cob** is a round loaf of bread. ...*a crusty cob.*

cobalt /kəʊbɔːlt/
 1 NU **Cobalt** is a hard silvery-white metal. ...*the radioactive decay of cobalt and nickel into iron.*
 2 ADJ Something that is **cobalt** or **cobalt blue** in colour is greenish-blue. *The river below her was cobalt.*

cobber /kɒbə/
 VOCATIVE Some Australian men address each other as **cobber**; an informal word. *'Quite right, Cobber.'*

cobble /kɒbl/ **cobbles, cobbling, cobbled**
 NC **Cobbles** are the same as **cobblestones**. *The parade ended with young Soviet athletes dancing on the cobbles of Red Square.*
 cobble together PHRASAL VERB If you **cobble** something **together**, you make it roughly and without spending much time or effort on it; an informal expression. *Its author has cobbled together a guide to the islands... A compromise of sorts was cobbled together.*

cobbled /kɒbld/
 ADJ A **cobbled** street has a surface made of cobblestones. ...*its cobbled streets nestling round its great mediaeval cathedral.*

cobbler /kɒblə/ **cobblers**
 NC A **cobbler** is a person whose job is to make or mend shoes; an old-fashioned word. *They want to take their shoes to the cobbler to have them mended.*

cobblestone /kɒblstəʊn/ **cobblestones**
 NC **Cobblestones** are stones with a rounded upper surface which were once used for making streets. *They used cobblestones and tree branches to block roads.*

cobra /kəʊbrə/ **cobras**
 NC A **cobra** is a kind of poisonous snake. *The venom is ten times as harmful as that of the cobra.*

cobweb /kɒbweb/ **cobwebs**
 NC A **cobweb** is the fine net that a spider makes in order to catch insects. ...*the cobwebs which no-one has disturbed for years.*

cobwebbed /kɒbwebd/
 ADJ Something that is **cobwebbed** is covered with cobwebs. ...*the dusty cobwebbed bulb.*

Coca-Cola /kəʊkəkəʊlə/ **Coca-Colas**
 N MASS **Coca-Cola** is a non-alcoholic fizzy brown drink; **Coca-Cola** is a trademark. *Do you want a Coca-Cola?... She and Colin had coffee and Billy had a Coca-Cola.*

cocaine /kəʊkeɪn/
 NU **Cocaine** is an addictive drug which people take for pleasure. In most countries it is illegal to take cocaine. ...*trafficking in both heroin and cocaine. ...large scale drug smugglers who bring in cocaine.*

coccyx /kɒksɪks/ **coccyxes**
 NC The **coccyx** is the small triangular bone at the lower end of the spine in human beings and some apes.

cochineal /kɒtʃɪniːl/
 NU **Cochineal** is a red substance that is used for colouring food. It is obtained from an insect. *This is cochineal, you see, there's all this beautiful variety of reds.*

cock /kɒk/ **cocks, cocking, cocked**
 1 NC A **cock** is an adult male chicken. *When your business is poultry farming and you want laying hens, cocks are no good to you.*
 2 VO If you **cock** your head or your leg, you lift it sideways. *He stepped back, his head cocked to one side, to admire his work... A stray dog cocked his leg against a lamp-post.*
 cock up PHRASAL VERB If you **cock** something **up**, you ruin it by doing something wrong; an informal expression which some people find offensive. *We don't want to cock the whole thing up.* ● See also **cock-up**.

cock-a-hoop
ADJ PRED If you are **cock-a-hoop** about something, you are extremely pleased about it; an informal expression. *Their supporters here are cock-a-hoop.*

cock-and-bull story, cock-and-bull stories
NC A **cock-and-bull story** is an improbable or unbelievable story, especially one that is given as an excuse; an informal expression. *He gave me some cock-and-bull story about his brother being a film star.*

cockatoo /kɒkətuː/ **cockatoos**
NC A **cockatoo** is a kind of parrot with a crest on its head. *...a man carrying a cage with two peach-coloured cockatoos.*

Cockburn Town /kɒkbɜːn taʊn/
Cockburn Town, on Grand Cayman Island, is the capital of the Turks and Caicos Islands and its largest town. Population: 2,500 (1987).

cockcrow /kɒkkrəʊ/
NU **Cockcrow** is the dawn; a literary word. *We had to be up at cockcrow.*

cocked hat, cocked hats
1 NC A **cocked hat** is a hat with three corners that used to be worn with some uniforms.
2 If you say that one thing **knocks** or **beats** something else **into a cocked hat**, you mean that it is much better or much more interesting than the other thing; used in informal English. *This certainly knocks knitting into a cocked hat.*

cockerel /kɒkəⁿrəl/ **cockerels**
NC A **cockerel** is a young cock. *...roosters sitting on their perch crowing and doing what hens and cockerels do.*

cocker spaniel /kɒkə spænjəl/ **cocker spaniels**
NC A **cocker spaniel** is a small dog with silky hair and long ears. *The cocker spaniel growled deep in its throat and bared its teeth.*

cockeyed /kɒkaɪd/
ADJ If an idea or scheme is **cockeyed**, it is stupid and very unlikely to succeed; an informal word. *That sounds a cockeyed way of going about things.*

cockfight /kɒkfaɪt/ **cockfights**; also spelt **cock-fight**.
NC A **cockfight** is a fight between two cocks that have sharp pieces of metal fixed to their claws. People watch the fight for entertainment and in order to bet on it. *They gambled on the commodity markets as if they were at a casino or a cockfight.*

cockle /kɒkl/ **cockles**
NC **Cockles** are a kind of small shellfish. *...Goolwa, famous for its succulent cockles.*

cockleshell /kɒklʃel/ **cockleshells**
1 NC A **cockleshell** is the shell of a cockle.
2 NC A **cockleshell** is also a very small lightweight boat. *That little cockleshell was in difficulties from the moment I launched her.*

cockney /kɒkni/ **cockneys**
1 NC A **cockney** is a person who was born in the East End of London. *...the veteran cockney comedian Tommy Trinder.*
2 NU **Cockney** is the dialect and accent of the East End of London. *...the strident cockney language.*

cockpit /kɒkpɪt/ **cockpits**
NC The **cockpit** in a plane or racing car is the part where the pilot or driver sits. *The crew shut down an engine after experiencing vibration and smoke in the cockpit.*

cockroach /kɒkrəʊtʃ/ **cockroaches**
NC **Cockroaches** are large brown insects that are said to be found especially in dirty rooms and where food is kept. *There are many different insecticides available to kill cockroaches.*

cockscomb /kɒkskəʊm/ **cockscombs**
NC A **cockscomb** is the red growth that a cock has on its head.

cocksure /kɒkʃɔː/
ADJ If someone is **cocksure**, they are extremely confident; used showing disapproval. *These days the General is less cocksure than before.*

cocktail /kɒkteɪl/ **cocktails**
1 NC A **cocktail** is an alcoholic drink containing several ingredients. *...a champagne cocktail.*
2 NC+SUPP Something which is made by combining a number of different things can be called a **cocktail**.

...a shrimp cocktail.
3 See also **Molotov cocktail**.

cock-up, cock-ups
NC A **cock-up** is a mistake that prevents something from being done successfully; an informal word which some people find offensive. *There has been a series of cock-ups.*

cocky /kɒki/
ADJ A **cocky** person is very self-confident and pleased with himself or herself; an informal word, used showing disapproval. *Don't be too cocky, you were only third.*

cocoa /kəʊkəʊ/
1 NU **Cocoa** is a brown powder made from the seeds of a tropical tree, which is used in making chocolate. *The prices for their main exports, cocoa and coffee, are falling. ...trucks of cocoa beans waiting for buyers.*
2 N MASS **Cocoa** is also a hot drink made with cocoa powder and milk. *Make yourself a cup of cocoa.*

coconut /kəʊkənʌt/ **coconuts**
NC A **coconut** is a very large nut with a hairy shell which contains white flesh and milky juice. *He grows bananas, coconuts, fruit and vegetables. ...the site of a former coconut plantation.*

coconut matting
NU **Coconut matting** is a coarse, straw-coloured mat that is made from the fibre from the outer shell of coconuts.

coconut shy, coconut shies
NC A **coconut shy** is a stall at a fair where you throw balls at coconuts on stands. If you knock one off, you win a prize.

cocoon /kəkuːn/ **cocoons**
1 NC A **cocoon** is a covering of silky threads made by the larvae of moths and other insects before they grow into adults. *The cocoons of the silkworm have to be harvested by hand.*
2 NC+SUPP You can use **cocoon** to describe a safe and protective environment. *I lived in a cocoon of love and warmth... Police and security men formed a cocoon to escort the President inside the hotel.*

cocooned /kəkuːnd/
1 ADJ If someone is **cocooned** in blankets or clothes, they are completely wrapped in them.
2 ADJ If you say that someone is **cocooned**, you mean that they are isolated and protected from everyday life and problems. *...a cosy, almost cocooned, little world.*

Cocos Islands /kəʊkɒs aɪləndz/
The **Cocos Islands**, also known as the Keeling Islands, are a territory of Australia, in the Indian Ocean, south of Indonesia. They became a British possession in 1857. Administration was transfered to Australia in 1955. The Cocos Islands export coconuts and copra.
♦ **Cocos Islander** /kəʊkɒs aɪləndə/ N
▪ *religion:* Islam, Christianity ▪ *language:* English (official), Cocos Malay ▪ *currency:* Australian dollar ▪ *capital:* West Island ▪ *population:* 600 (1989) ▪ *size:* 14 square kilometres.

cod /kɒd/; **cod** is both the singular and the plural form.
NU **Cod** is a kind of fish. *Their diet centres upon cod and fried chicken.*

coda /kəʊdə/ **codas**; a technical term.
1 NC A **coda** is the final part of a fairly long piece of music which is added in order to finish it off.
2 NC A **coda** is also a separate passage at the end of a book or speech that finishes it of. *The book's coda is a wry conclusion quoted from Shakespeare.*

coddle /kɒdl/ **coddles, coddling, coddled**
VO If you **coddle** someone, you treat them too kindly or you protect them too much. *Teachers shouldn't coddle their pupils.*

code /kəʊd/ **codes, coding, coded**
1 NC A **code** is a set of rules about how people should behave. *...accepted codes of behaviour. ...the IBA's code of advertising standards and practice.* ● See also **criminal code, penal code**.
2 NCorNU A **code** is also a system of sending secret messages by replacing letters and words, usually with other letters or words. *It is a code that even I can crack... The messages were typed in code.* ● See also **morse code**.
3 VO If you **code** a message, you change it by

replacing the letters or symbols with different letters or symbols so that people who do not know the code cannot understand it. *These messages were different in that every word was coded.* ◆ **coded** ADJ *For several hours now coded messages had been going out by telephone.*
4 NC A group of numbers or letters used to identify something is also called a **code**. *My university course code is E5L21. ...similar to the bar code you might see on supermarket goods.*
5 VO To **code** something means to identify it by a short group of numbers or letters. *The data on fathers' occupation are not coded in the same way.*
6 NC A phone **code** is the same as a **dialling code**. *London's 01 code was being replaced by two new codes—071 for inner London, and 081 for outer London.*

code book, code books
1 NC A **code book** is a book with codes in it, which you use to write a message in code or to help you understand one. *The report said they had espionage tools like invisible ink and code books.*
2 NC A **code book** is also a book that contains a list of the codes that you need in order to make telephone calls to different areas.

codeine /kəʊdiːn/
NU **Codeine** is a drug which is used to relieve pain, especially headaches, and cold symptoms. *Narcotics include heroin, morphine and codeine.*

code name, code names; also spelt **code-name**.
NC A **code name** is a name used for someone or something in order to keep their identity secret. *He is listed in the files by his code-name, the Jackal.*

code-named
ADJ If a police or military operation is **code-named** a particular name, it is known by that name to the people involved in it. *It was code-named Operation Pegasus.*

code of practice, codes of practice
NC A **code of practice** is a set of written rules which explains how people working in a particular profession should behave. *The Law Society is currently drawing up a new code of practice for solicitors.*

code word, code words
NC A **code word** is a word or phrase that has a special meaning for the people who have agreed to use it in this way. *...'oyster'—an intelligence code word meaning 'my lips are sealed'.*

codger /kɒdʒə/ **codgers**
NC If you call a man an **old codger**, you are referring to him in a slightly disrespectful but also sometimes affectionate way. *I looked at this marvellous old codger laughing his head off.*

codicil /kəʊdɪsɪl/ **codicils**
NC A **codicil** is an instruction that is added to a will after the main part of it has been written; a legal term.

codify /kəʊdɪfaɪ/ **codifies, codifying, codified**
VO If you **codify** a set of rules, you present them in a clear and ordered way. *When were the rules of snooker codified?*

cod-liver oil
NU **Cod-liver oil** is a thick yellow oil which is given as a medicine, especially to children, because it is full of vitamins A and D. *Cod-liver oil used to be given as a source of fat soluble vitamins.*

codpiece /kɒdpiːs/ **codpieces**
NC A **codpiece** was a piece of material worn by men in the 15th and 16th centuries to cover their genitals.

codswallop /kɒdzwɒləp/
NU If you say that something someone has said is **codswallop**, you mean that you think it is nonsense; an informal word. *Quintin Hogg dismissed his ideas as 'a load of old codswallop'.*

co-ed /kəʊed/ **co-eds**
1 ADJ A **co-ed** school is the same as a **co-educational** school. *He talked about his two children, who were at a co-ed school.*
2 NC In informal American English, a **co-ed** is a female student at a co-educational college or university. *A 25-year-old co-ed was killed in a clash between students and police.*

co-educational /kəʊedʒʊkeɪʃᵊnəl/
ADJ A **co-educational** school is a school which is attended by both boys and girls. *Schools should be co-educational because life is co-educational.*

coefficient /kəʊɪfɪʃnt/ **coefficients**
NC+SUPP A **coefficient** is a number that expresses a measurement of a particular quality of a substance or object under specified conditions; a technical term in mathematics. *...a coefficient figure of 0.38.*

coerce /kəʊɜːs/ **coerces, coercing, coerced**
VO If you **coerce** someone into doing something, you force them to do it; a formal word. *They tried to coerce me into changing my appearance.*

coercion /kəʊɜːʃn/
NU **Coercion** is the act or process of persuading someone forcefully to do something that they did not want to do. *No one was using coercion.*

coercive /kəʊɜːsɪv/
ADJ Something that is **coercive** is used to persuade people forcefully to do something that they did not want to do; a formal word. *...the superior coercive power of the State.*

coexist /kəʊɪgzɪst/ **coexists, coexisting, coexisted**
V-RECIP If two or more things **coexist**, they exist at the same time or in the same place. *Large numbers of species coexist here... The forest peoples can coexist with the forest.*

coexistence /kəʊɪgzɪstəns/
NU **Coexistence** is the state of existing together, usually peacefully. *She changed her foreign policy from one of force to one of coexistence and cooperation. ...the need for peaceful coexistence.*

C. of E. /siː əv iː/
C. of E. is an abbreviation for 'Church of England'. *Ma was brought up C. of E.*

coffee /kɒfi/ **coffees**
1 N MASS **Coffee** is a hot brown drink made with boiling water and the roasted and ground seeds of a coffee tree. *...coffee and biscuits... He said that most of all he wanted to have a cup of coffee... 'Two more coffees, please, with cream.'*
2 NU **Coffee** is also the roasted seeds or powder from which the drink is made. *...Brazil, the world's largest producer of coffee.*

coffee bar, coffee bars
NC A **coffee bar** is a small café where drinks and snacks are sold. *...the coffee bars that were popular amongst young people at the time.*

coffee bean, coffee beans
NC **Coffee beans** are the seeds of a coffee tree. The roasted seeds are ground up and hot water is poured over them in order to make the drink coffee. *Tin ore and coffee beans are exported to the Soviet Union.*

coffee break, coffee breaks
NC A **coffee break** is a short time, usually in the morning and afternoon, when you stop working and have a cup of coffee. *...an extended coffee break.*

coffee grinder, coffee grinders
NC A **coffee grinder** is a machine for grinding coffee beans.

coffee mill, coffee mills
NC A **coffee mill** is the same as a **coffee grinder**.

coffee morning, coffee mornings
NC A **coffee morning** is a social event that takes place in the morning in someone's house. It is often intended to raise money for charity. *People are wondering whether they can go on with their charity coffee mornings.*

coffee pot, coffee pots
NC A **coffee pot** is a tall narrow jug in which coffee is made or served. *He went over to the table where the coffee pot was standing and poured himself a cup.*

coffee table, coffee tables
NC A **coffee table** is a small, low table in a living-room. *The Colonel put his cup and saucer on the coffee table.*

coffee-table book, coffee-table books
NC A **coffee-table book** is a large, expensive book with a lot of pictures. It is designed to be looked at rather than to be read in great detail. *The second, 'Planet Drum', will be a large coffee-table book.*

collaborative /kəlǽbərətɪv/
ADJ ATTRIB A **collaborative** piece of work is done by two or more people working together; a formal word. *The project is a collaborative one.*

collaborator /kəlǽbəreɪtə/ **collaborators**
1 NC A **collaborator** is someone that you work with on a particular project. *My collaborator Roy Lewis and I did a series of articles for Radio 4.*
2 NC A **collaborator** is also someone who helps the enemy; used showing disapproval. *...violence against alleged collaborators.*

collage /kɒlɑːʒ/ **collages**
NC A **collage** is a picture made by sticking pieces of paper and cloth onto paper. *...complicated, photographic collages.*

collapse /kəlǽps/ **collapses, collapsing, collapsed**
1 V If something **collapses**, it suddenly falls down or falls inwards. If a person **collapses**, they suddenly fall down because they are ill or tired. *These flimsy houses are liable to collapse in a heavy storm... As we walked into the hotel, Jane collapsed.* ▶ Also NU *The collapse of buildings trapped thousands of people... Upon her collapse she was rushed to hospital.*
2 V If a system or institution **collapses**, it fails completely and suddenly. *Their marriage had collapsed.* ▶ Also NU *...a company on the verge of collapse.*

collapsible /kəlǽpsəbl/
ADJ A **collapsible** object is designed to be folded flat when it is not being used. *...a collapsible bed.*

collar /kɒlə/ **collars**
1 NC The **collar** of a shirt or coat is the part which fits round the neck and is usually folded over. *...crisp, green, olive uniforms with white collars.*
2 NC A **collar** is also a band made out of leather or plastic which is put round the neck of a dog or cat. *The dog had a collar but it had no identification marks.*

collarbone /kɒləbəʊn/ **collarbones**
NC Your **collarbone** is one of the two long bones which run from the base of your neck to your shoulder. *Rosi fell and broke his collarbone in training.*

collate /kəleɪt/ **collates, collating, collated**
VO When you **collate** pieces of information, you gather them all together and examine them. *All the new evidence had been collated.*

collateral /kəlǽtəᵒrəl/
NU **Collateral** is money or property which is used as a guarantee that someone will repay a loan; a formal word. *They have nothing to offer as collateral. The banks demand land as collateral.*

collateral damage
NU **Collateral damage** is unintentional injury to civilians or damage to civilian buildings which occurs during a military operation. *As we all know, there are going to be instances of collateral damage. General Powell says that collateral damage has been kept very low.*

collation /kəleɪʃn/ **collations**
1 NU **Collation** is the act or process of collating something. *The figures are ready for tabulation and collation... After a day and a night of counting and collation they are still waiting for the results of yesterday's election.*
2 NC A **collation** is a light uncooked meal; a formal use. *We had a large cold collation at a lakeside restaurant.*

colleague /kɒliːg/ **colleagues**
NC Your **colleagues** are the people you work with, especially in a professional job. *The older workers were generally better salespeople than their younger colleagues.*

collect /kəlekt/ **collects, collecting, collected**
1 VO If you **collect** a number of things, you bring them together from several places. *The state government is determined to continue with its campaign to collect unlicensed weapons... The council tax will be simple and cheap to collect.*
2 VO If you **collect** things as a hobby, you get and keep a large number of them because you are interested in them. *Do you collect antiques?*
3 VO When you **collect** someone or something, you go

and fetch them from somewhere. *I have to collect the children from school... She had to collect water from the village pump... They're collecting wood for the fire.*
4 V A When things **collect** somewhere, they gather there over a period of time. *Damp leaves collect in gutters... There are certain places where a lot of dust collects.*
5 V A or VO If you **collect** for a charity or for a present, you ask people to give you money for it. *I'm collecting for a leaving present for Mary... Relief agencies have collected nearly half a million dollars... How much have you collected so far?*
6 V-REFL or VO If you **collect** yourself or **collect** your thoughts, you make an effort to calm or prepare yourself. *He collected himself enough to tell his friends about the accident... I had five minutes in which to collect my thoughts before the interview.*
collect up PHRASAL VERB If you **collect up** a number of things, you bring them together from different places. *They collected up their gear.*

collected /kəlektɪd/
ADJ Someone's **collected** works are all their works published together. *...the collected works of Proust.*

collecting /kəlektɪŋ/
1 NU **Collecting** is the hobby of collecting a particular type of thing. *...stamp collecting... art collecting.*
2 ADJ ATTRIB A **collecting** tin or box is one that is used to collect money for charity. *The collecting box grew heavier.*

collection /kəlekʃn/ **collections**
1 NC A **collection** of things is a group of similar or related things. *Davis had a large collection of pop records. ...a collection of Scott Fitzgerald's short stories.*
2 NU **Collection** is the act of collecting something from a place or from people. *...the collection of national taxes... Your curtains are ready for collection.*
3 NC A **collection** is also the organized collecting of money from people for charity, or the amount of money that is collected. *They organized dances and collections which raised £450.*

collective /kəlektɪv/
ADJ ATTRIB **Collective** means shared by or involving every member of a group of people. *It was a collective decision.*

collective bargaining
NU **Collective bargaining** is the talks that a trade union has with an employer which are intended to settle what the workers' pay or conditions should be. *The unions should concentrate on securing their demands through collective bargaining.*

collectively /kəlektɪvli/
1 ADV If people do something **collectively**, they do it together. *All key decisions had been taken collectively... They were collectively responsible.*
2 ADV You use **collectively** when you are referring to a group of things as a whole. *...a small group of marsupials called, collectively, rat-kangaroos.*

collector /kəlektə/ **collectors**
1 NC+SUPP A **collector** is a person who collects things as a hobby. *...an art collector... The thieves may try to smuggle the treasures out for sale to foreign collectors.*
2 NC+SUPP A **collector** is also someone whose job is to take something such as money or tickets from people. For example, a rent **collector** collects rent from tenants. *...a new design of overalls for refuse collectors. ...relying less on the efficiency and honesty of individual tax collectors.*

collector's item, collector's items
NC A **collector's item** is an object which is highly valued by collectors because it is very rare or beautiful. *I had a stack of Scrooge comic books, which were collector's items by now.*

college /kɒlɪdʒ/ **colleges**
1 NC or NU A **college** is an institution where students study after they have left school. *...the local technical college... What do you plan to do after college?*
2 NC A **college** in a university is one of the institutions which some British universities are divided into. *...Jesus College, Cambridge.*

collegiate /kəliːdʒiət/
1 ADJ ATTRIB A collegiate university is one that is divided into several colleges. *Some new universities have attempted to adopt a collegiate system.*
2 ADJ ATTRIB Collegiate means belonging or relating to a college. *I enjoy collegiate life.*

collide /kəlaɪd/ collides, colliding, collided
V-RECIP If people or vehicles collide, they bump into each other. *The two vehicles collided... He almost collided with me when I stopped.*

collie /kɒli/ collies
NC A collie is a kind of dog, often used for controlling sheep. *The black and white border collie was rescued by a team of forty searchers.*

colliery /kɒljəri/ collieries
NC A colliery is a coal mine. *British Coal is to close two of its loss-making collieries in South Wales.*

collision /kəlɪʒn/ collisions
1 NCorNU A collision occurs when a moving object hits something. *...a mid-air collision... Henry and a window came into chance collision.*
2 NCorNU A collision of cultures or ideas occurs when two very different cultures or people meet and conflict. *...a collision of egos. ...the collision of private and public interests.*

collision course, collision courses
1 N SING If two or more people or things are on a collision course, there is likely to be a sudden and violent disagreement between them. *Conservation and agriculture are set on an eventual collision course... The Government has turned aside from its collision course with the unions.*
2 NC You can also say that people or things are on a collision course when they are moving in a particular direction and are likely to meet and hit each other violently. *A meteor is on a collision course with the Earth... Both were on collision courses with the American planes.*

collocate, collocates, collocating, collocated;
pronounced /kɒləkət/ when it is a noun and /kɒləkeɪt/ when it is a verb; a technical term in linguistics.
1 NC A collocate of a particular word is another word which often occurs with that word.
2 V-RECIP If two or more words collocate, they often occur together.

collocation /kɒləkeɪʃn/
NU Collocation is the way that some words occur regularly whenever another word is used; a technical term in linguistics.

colloquial /kəlɔʊkwiəl/
ADJ Colloquial words and phrases are informal and are used mainly in conversation. *...the Stasi, the colloquial name for the secret police. ...a course in colloquial Greek.* ◆ colloquially ADV *This game is colloquially known as 'Buzz off, Buster'.*

colloquialism /kəlɔʊkwiəlɪzəm/ colloquialisms
NC A colloquialism is an informal word or phrase that is used mainly in conversation. *The aim is to encourage the use of set phraseology in company documentation, and to eliminate colloquialisms.*

colloquium /kəlɔʊkwiəm/ colloquia /kəlɔʊkwiə/
NC A colloquium is a large academic seminar; a formal word.

colloquy /kɒləkwi/ colloquies
NC A colloquy is a conversation or meeting; a formal word.

Collor de Mello, Fernando
/fənɛndu: kɒlʊə di mɛlu:/
Fernando Collor de Mello became President of Brazil in 1990. He was State Governor of Alagoas in 1986. He founded the National Reconstruction Party (PRN) in 1989. Born: 1949.

collude /kəluːd/ colludes, colluding, colluded
V-RECIP To collude with someone means to co-operate with them secretly; used showing disapproval. *Some groups have colluded with the unions in avoiding a ballot... They have begun investigating whether the oil companies have colluded on pricing... People are often forced to collude in their own dismissal.*

collusion /kəluːʒn/
NU Collusion is secret or illegal cooperation, especially between countries or organizations; a formal word.

...the council's collusion with the strikers... They act in collusion to control the market.

collywobbles /kɒliwɒblz/
N PL If you have the collywobbles, you are very nervous and worried; an informal word. *All this must have given the President the collywobbles.*

cologne /kəlɔʊn/ colognes
N MASS Cologne is a kind of weak perfume. *...a bottle of cologne... They are marketing a new cologne.*

Colombia /kəlɒmbiə/
The Republic of Colombia is a country in north-western South America. It was a Spanish colony from the 16th century until 1819. César Gaviria Trujillo, of the Liberal Party (PL), became President in 1990. Colombia is the second largest coffee producer in the world. Drug cartels based in Medellín and Cali are major suppliers of cocaine throughout the world. They pose a serious threat to public order in Colombia. Colombia is a member of the Organization of American States. ◆ Colombian /kəlɒmbiən/ N, ADJ
▪ *per capita GNP:* US$1,240 ▪ *religion:* Christianity (mainly Roman Catholic) ▪ *language:* Spanish ▪ *currency:* peso ▪ *capital:* Bogotá ▪ *population:* 32 million (1989) ▪ *size:* 1,141,748 square kilometres.

Colombo /kəlʌmbəʊ/
Colombo is the commercial capital of Sri Lanka. The new capital is nearby at Sri Jayawardenepura. Population: 609,000 (1988).

colon /kɔʊlən/ colons
1 NC A colon is the punctuation mark (:).
2 NC Your colon is the part of your intestine above your rectum. *...cancers of the stomach and colon.*

colonel /kɜːnl/ colonels
NCorTITLE A colonel is an army officer of fairly high rank. *...a colonel with the internal security troops. ...the armed forces commander, Colonel Rene Emilio Ponce.*

colonial /kəlɔʊniəl/
ADJ ATTRIB Colonial means relating to countries that are colonies, or to colonialism. *...the liberation of oppressed peoples from colonial rule.*

colonialism /kəlɔʊniəlɪzəm/
NU Colonialism is the practice by which a powerful country directly controls less powerful countries. *The politics of the Third World had their origins in colonialism.*

colonialist /kəlɔʊniəlɪst/
ADJ Colonialist means relating to colonialism. *Many people think of Northern Ireland as a colonialist situation.*

colonist /kɒlənɪst/ colonists
NC Colonists are people who start a colony. *...the Australian colonists.*

colonize /kɒlənaɪz/ colonizes, colonizing, colonized;
also spelt colonise.
VO When large numbers of people or animals colonize a place, they go to live there and make it their home. *...the Europeans who colonized North America... The plains were colonised by ant-eaters and other species.* ◆ colonization /kɒlənaɪzeɪʃn/ NU *...the period of Italian colonization which began before the First World war. ...large-scale colonisation by Sinhalese settlers in Tamil areas.*

colonnade /kɒləneɪd/ colonnades
NC A colonnade is a row of evenly spaced columns. *...Regency colonnades.*

colony /kɒləni/ colonies
1 NC A colony is a country which is controlled by a more powerful country. *Portugal was eager to give independence to its African colonies. ...France's reconciliation with its former colonies in Arab North Africa.*
2 NC A colony is also a group of people or animals of a particular sort living together. *The report says some bird colonies lost up to 70 per cent of their breeding population. ...a leper colony.*

color /kʌlə/. See colour.

coloration /kʌləreɪʃn/
NU The coloration of an animal or a plant is the colours and patterns on it. *...some kind of dye or coloration.*

coloratura /kɒlərətuərə/ **coloraturas**; a technical term in music.
1 NU **Coloratura** is very ornamental and complicated music for a solo singer, for example in an opera or oratorio. ...*the elaborate coloratura style.*
2 NC A **coloratura** is a singer, especially a woman, who is skilled at singing coloratura.

color line
N SING The **color line** was a social system in some parts of the United States in which black people were not allowed to mix freely with white people. *She was also instrumental in helping Althea Gibson break the color line in tennis.*

colossal /kəlɒsl/
ADJ Something that is **colossal** is very large. ...*colossal sums of money... It's such a colossal country.*

colossus /kəlɒsəs/ **colossuses**; a literary word.
1 NC You describe someone as a **colossus** when you admire them because you think they are extremely important and influential in a particular profession. ...*the great actor-producer, the colossus of the Bombay film world... He is a colossus; there is no denying his brilliance.*
2 NC A **colossus** is also an extremely large statue. ...*the stone colossus of the rain god.*

colour /kʌlə/ **colours, colouring, coloured**; spelt **color** in American English.
1 NCorNU The **colour** of something is the appearance that it has as a result of reflecting light. Red, blue, and green are colours. *All the rooms were painted different colours... His face was greyish in colour.*
2 NU Someone's **colour** is the normal colour of their skin. *It was illegal to discriminate on the grounds of colour.*
3 ADJ ATTRIB A **colour** television, film, or photograph is one that shows things in all their colours, and not just in black and white. ...*marvellous colour illustrations.*
4 NU **Colour** is also a quality that makes something interesting or exciting. *The audiences liked the romance and colour of 'The Lady's Not for Burning'.*
5 VO If something **colours** your opinion, it affects your opinion. *Anger had coloured her judgement.*
6 If you achieve something **with flying colours**, you achieve it in an extremely successful way. *Mr Chirac will have to pass that test with flying colours.*
colour in PHRASAL VERB If you **colour** something **in**, you give it different colours using crayons. *His little girl was busy colouring in her picture.*

colour bar
N SING A **colour bar** is a social system in which black people are not allowed to mix freely with white people. *They broke all the social taboos of their time in reaching across the colour bar.*

colour blind
ADJ Someone who is **colour blind** cannot distinguish clearly between some colours. *I'm colour blind so I don't have a full appreciation of flowers.*

colour blindness
NU **Colour blindness** is the inability to distinguish easily between colours, especially red and green, because you have something wrong with your eyes. *Colour blindness is a serious problem for pilots.*

colour-coded
ADJ Things that are **colour-coded** have different colours on them to indicate that they contain different things, belong to different groups, or have different functions. *On arrival, each member receives a colour-coded badge.*

coloured /kʌləd/ **coloureds**; spelt **colored** in American English.
1 ADJ Something that is **coloured** a particular colour has that colour. *The sky was mauve coloured... He was wearing a sandy coloured tropical army uniform.* ...*brilliantly coloured costumes.*
2 ADJ Something that is **coloured** has a colour such as red or blue rather than being just white or black. *He drew patterns on the floor in coloured chalks.*
3 ADJ A person who is **coloured** belongs to a race of people who do not have white or pale skins; an old-fashioned use, which some people now find offensive. *He told a rally that what had happened to him was happening all over the world to coloured people.*
4 NC In South Africa, a **coloured** is a person who has some ancestors who were white and some who were black or Asian. *His most immediate task will be to launch a drive to increase membership, particularly among whites, coloureds, and Indians.* ▶ Also ADJ *South Africa's best coloured sprinter is Winkler.*

colour fast
ADJ A fabric that is **colour fast** has a colour that does not change when the fabric is washed or worn. *Never soak fabrics which are not colour fast.*

colourful /kʌləfl/; spelt **colorful** in American English.
1 ADJ Something that is **colourful** has bright colours. ...*colourful posters of Paris and Venice.*
2 ADJ **Colourful** also means interesting and exciting. *Many colourful stories were told about him.*
3 ADJ If someone uses **colourful** language, they use words to describe things in an interesting but also sometimes rude or offensive way. ...*music with colourful or risqué lyrics... The stories are vivid: the language often colourful and sometimes coarse.*

colouring /kʌlərɪŋ/ **colourings**; spelt **coloring** in American English.
1 NU The **colouring** of something is the colours that it has. ...*its rounded fins and distinctive green colouring.*
2 N SING+POSS Someone's **colouring** is the colour of their hair, skin, and eyes. *Her colouring was the same as Mark's—olive skin, dark brown eyes, thick dark hair.*
3 N MASS **Colouring** is a substance that is used to give colour to food. *Alcoholic beverages contain flavouring, colouring and other chemicals... Colourings are used in the canning industry, as well as in many processed foods.*

colourless /kʌlələs/; spelt **colorless** in American English.
1 ADJ Something that is **colourless** is dull and uninteresting. *He spoke in the same colourless, plodding voice.*
2 ADJ **Colourless** things have no colour at all. ...*a colourless and tasteless liquid.*

colour scheme, colour schemes
NC A **colour scheme** is an arrangement of colours that you choose, for example for the walls, curtains, and carpet in a room. *At a later date you may want to change your kitchen colour scheme.*

colour supplement, colour supplements
NC In Britain, a **colour supplement** is a magazine that you get free when you buy a newspaper. *The paper carries more details in its colour supplement.*

colt /kəult/ **colts**
NC A **colt** is a young male horse. *Lester Piggott will ride the colt Royal Academy for Irish trainer Vincent O'Brien.*

coltish /kəultɪʃ/
ADJ A young person or animal that is **coltish** is full of energy, but is clumsy or awkward because they lack physical skill or control.

columbine /kɒləmbaɪn/ **columbines**
NC A **columbine** is a garden plant that has brightly coloured flowers with five petals.

column /kɒləm/ **columns**
1 NC A **column** is a tall solid cylinder, especially one supporting part of a building. *The canal itself is built on tall slender columns, across the river Dee.*
2 NC+SUPP Something that has a tall narrow shape can be called a **column**. ...*columns of smoke.* ...*the spinal column.*
3 NC+SUPP A **column** of people or animals is a group of them moving in a line. *Behind the brass band came a column of workers.* ...*the advance of large columns of troops.*
4 NC In a newspaper, magazine, or dictionary, a **column** is a vertical section of writing. *The headline ran across all six columns.*
5 NC A **column** is also a regular section or article in a newspaper or magazine that is written by the same person. *Bill used to write a column for the Bristol Evening News.*

columnist /kɒləmnɪst/ **columnists**
NC A **columnist** is a journalist who writes a regular

section or article in a newspaper or magazine.
...gossip columnists.
coma /ˈkəʊmə/ **comas**
  NC If someone is in a **coma**, they are deeply
  unconscious. *Mr Stevens has regained consciousness
  after four days in a coma.*
comatose /ˈkəʊmətəʊs/
  1 ADJ A person who is **comatose** is in a coma; a
  medical use. *Patients who are comatose or mentally
  deranged need careful nursing.*
  2 ADJ You can also say that someone is **comatose** if
  they are in a deep sleep because they are tired or
  have had too much to drink; an informal use. *Wilks
  was still comatose on the sofa at lunch time.*
comb /kəʊm/ **combs, combing, combed**
  1 NC A **comb** is a flat piece of plastic or metal with
  long thin pointed parts, which you use to tidy your
  hair. *Running a comb through his hair, he strode into
  the foyer.*
  2 VO When you **comb** your hair, you tidy it using a
  comb. *They could see Mr Baker busily combing his
  hair.*
  3 VO If you **comb** a place for something, you search
  thoroughly for it. *It might amuse her to comb the
  town for antiques.*
  comb out PHRASAL VERB If you **comb** something **out** of
  your hair, you remove it using a comb. *Head lice
  attach their eggs to the base of your hair, and you
  can't comb them out.*
combat, combats, combating, combated;
  pronounced /ˈkɒmbæt/ when it is a noun and /kɒmˈbæt/
  or /kəmˈbæt/ when it is a verb.
  1 NUorNC **Combat** is fighting that takes place in a
  war; a formal use. *He was awarded the Military
  Cross for gallantry in combat. ...the mighty combats
  between the West and the East. ...three squadrons of
  combat aircraft as well as reconnaissance planes.*
  2 VO If people in authority **combat** something, they try
  to stop it happening. *The police had a difficult task in
  combating the crime... The basic problem is that of
  combating poverty.*
combatant /ˈkɒmbətənt/ **combatants**
  NC A **combatant** is someone who takes part in a fight
  or a war. *A SWAPO spokesman said they had no
  armed combatants in the area.*
combative /ˈkɒmbətɪv/
  ADJ A person who is **combative** is aggressive and
  eager to fight or argue. *...a severely agitated,
  combative child.*
combination /ˌkɒmbɪˈneɪʃn/ **combinations**
  1 NC A **combination** is a mixture of things. *All actors
  use a combination of these techniques.*
  2 NC The **combination** of a lock is the series of letters
  or numbers used to open it. *I can't remember the
  combination.*
combination lock, combination locks
  NC A **combination lock** is a lock which can only be
  opened by turning a dial according to a particular
  series of letters or numbers. *...a military combination
  lock similar to the one protecting the Prime Minister's
  personal safe.*
combine, combines, combining, combined;
  pronounced /kəmˈbaɪn/ when it is a verb and /ˈkɒmbaɪn/
  when it is a noun.
  1 V-RECIP or V-ERG If you **combine** two or more things or
  if they **combine**, they exist or join together. *He's due
  to see rituals combining African and Catholic religious
  elements... We would all prefer to combine liberty
  with order... He talks of a 'new world order' in which
  strong nations combine to protect others against
  aggression... Recurring drought has combined with the
  civil war to cause terrible famine in the country.*
  2 NC A **combine** is a group of people or organizations
  that are working together. *...a newspaper combine.*
  3 V-RECIP If someone or something **combines** two or
  more qualities or features, they have them at the
  same time. *Carbon fibre combines flexibility with
  immense strength... Morality and national pride
  combine in his public statements.*
  4 V-RECIP If someone **combines** two or more activities,
  they do them at the same time. *One person combines
  the work of both District Nurse and Health Visitor...*

It's difficult to combine family life with a career.
combined /kəmˈbaɪnd/
  1 ADJ PRED+*with* or ADJ after N If someone or something
  has one quality or feature **combined** with another, they
  have both those qualities or features. *...a perfect
  example of professional expertise combined with
  personal charm... His eyes were wide with amazement
  and adoration combined.*
  2 ADJ ATTRIB A **combined** effort or attack is made by
  groups of people at the same time. *The combined
  efforts of police and military were at last successful.*
combine harvester /ˈkɒmbaɪn ˈhɑːvɪstə/ **combine
  harvesters**
  NC A **combine harvester** is a large machine which is
  used on farms to cut, sort, and clean grain.
  *Sergeyevich himself was driving a combine harvester
  at the age of 14.*
combo /ˈkɒmbəʊ/ **combos**
  NC A **combo** is a small group of jazz musicians. *...the
  night spot where John played guitar with his all-black
  combo.*
combustible /kəmˈbʌstəbl/
  ADJ Something that is **combustible** catches fire and
  burns easily; a formal word. *...combustible
  material... Everything combustible was destroyed.*
combustion /kəmˈbʌstʃən/
  NU **Combustion** is the act of burning something or the
  process of burning; a formal word. *...the combustion
  of fossil fuels.* ● See also **internal combustion engine.**
come /kʌm/ **comes, coming, came** /keɪm/. The form
  come is used in the present tense and is also the past
  participle of the verb.
  1 V You use **come** to say that someone or something
  arrives somewhere, or moves towards you. *She looked
  up when they came into the room... She eventually
  came to the town of Pickering... She came to Britain
  on many occasions.*
  2 VA If something **comes** to a particular point, it
  reaches it. *Her hair came right down to her waist...
  Mum doesn't even come up to my shoulder.*
  3 VA You use **come** in expressions which state what
  happens to someone or something. *It just came apart
  in my hands... They had come to power ten years
  earlier.*
  4 V When a particular time or event **comes**, it arrives
  or happens. *The time has come for a full campaign
  against the government's spending cuts.*
  5 VA If a reporter says that something **comes** at a
  particular time, it happens at that time. *The move
  came after public statements by both leaders... The
  trouble in the camp comes at a time of high tension...
  The attack came during a visit by the Dutch Foreign
  Minister.*
  6 VC If someone or something **comes** first, next, or
  last, they are first, next, or last in a series, list, or
  competition. *What comes next then?... I was never in
  any race in which I didn't come last... Manchester
  came eleventh out of the top one hundred places to
  live.*
  7 VA If a product **comes** in a particular range of
  colours, styles, or sizes, it is available in any of those
  colours, styles, or sizes. *The van came in two colours,
  medium brown or medium grey.*
  8 V+*to*-INF If someone **comes** to do something, they
  gradually start to do it. *I have come to like him quite
  a lot.*
  9 You say **'Come to think of it'** to indicate that you
  have suddenly realized something. *Come to think of it,
  why should I apologize?*
  10 See also **coming.**
  come about PHRASAL VERB The way that something
  comes about is how it happens. *The discovery of
  adrenalin came about through a mistake... Change has
  come about largely by peaceful means.*
  come across PHRASAL VERB 1 If you **come across**
  someone or something, you meet or find them by
  chance. *I came across a letter from Brunel the other
  day.* 2 The way that someone **comes across** is the
  impression they make on other people. *He wasn't
  coming across as the idiot I had expected him to be.*
  3 When an idea or meaning **comes across**, you
  understand exactly what is meant by it. *Do you think*

this idea comes across in the play?

come along PHRASAL VERB 1 When something **comes along**, it arrives or happens, perhaps by chance. *A new generation of planners came along who were much more scientifically based.* 2 See also **come on**.

come at PHRASAL VERB If a person or animal **comes at** you or **comes for** you, they move towards you in a threatening way. *The bear came at me... Jake was coming for me with a knife.*

come back PHRASAL VERB 1 If you **come back** to a topic or point, you return to it. *We'll come back to that question a little later.* 2 If something that you had forgotten **comes back** to you, you remember it. *During those Gettysburg conversations, when a lot came back to me, I reflected on that question.* 3 When something **comes back**, it becomes fashionable again. *She was pleased to see that mini skirts were coming back.* 4 See also **comeback**.

come by PHRASAL VERB To **come by** something means to find or obtain it. *He had not come by these things through his own labour... Full statistics are hard to come by.*

come down PHRASAL VERB 1 If the cost, level, or amount of something **comes down**, it becomes less than it was before. *Inflation is starting to come down.* 2 If a structure such as a building or a tree **comes down**, it falls to the ground. *In the storm a tree came down.*

come down on PHRASAL VERB To **come down on** someone means to criticize them. *Social workers like me come down harder on parents than on their children.*

come down to PHRASAL VERB If a problem or decision **comes down to** a particular thing, that thing is the most important factor involved. *Your final choice of kitchen may well come down to cost.*

come down with PHRASAL VERB If you **come down with** an illness, you get it. *She came down with pneumonia.*

come for PHRASAL VERB See **come at**.

come forward PHRASAL VERB If someone **comes forward**, they offer to do something. *Hundreds of men and women are expected to be called up because too few volunteers came forward... Four of them came forward to say that they had been pressured to vote guilty.*

come from PHRASAL VERB 1 To **come from** somewhere means to be born in a particular place or into a particular family, or to have a particular background. *'Where do you come from?'—'India.'... Many of them come from as far away as New Zealand... I don't come from the right background or the right school.* 2 If something **comes from** a particular place or thing, that is its source or starting point. *Did you know the word 'idea' comes from Greek?* 3 Something that **comes from** something else is the result of it. *...the warm glow that comes from working co-operatively.*

come in PHRASAL VERB 1 If information or a report **comes in**, you receive it. *Reports are coming in from Mexico of a major earthquake.* 2 If you have money **coming in**, you receive it, for example as your salary or other means of support. *The state has had less tax revenue coming in and more expenditures going out... Aid money is coming in from a variety of sources.* 3 If someone **comes in** on a discussion or an arrangement, they join in. *He should come in on the deal.* 4 If someone or someone **comes in**, they are involved in the situation you are discussing. *Where does your husband come in?*

come in for PHRASAL VERB If someone or something **comes in for** criticism or blame, they receive it. *The airline is now coming in for criticism for not making the threat public.*

come into PHRASAL VERB 1 If someone **comes into** money or property, they inherit it. *She was going to come into some more money on her mother's death.* 2 If something or someone **comes into** a situation, they are involved in it. *Prestige comes into it as much as other factors.*

come of PHRASAL VERB Something that **comes of** something is the result of it. *I'll let you know what comes of the meeting.*

come off PHRASAL VERB If something **comes off**, it is successful or effective. *Sotheby's publicity stunt came off brilliantly.*

come on PHRASAL VERB 1 You say 'Come on' or 'Come along' to someone to encourage them to do something or to make them hurry up. *Come on, Wendy, you say something... Come along, now, drink this.* 2 If you have got a cold or a headache **coming on**, it is just starting. *I felt a cold coming on.* 3 If something is **coming on** or **coming along**, it is developing or making progress. *My new book is coming on quite well... He's coming along pretty well.* 4 When a machine or appliance **comes on**, it starts working. *The lights came on.*

come on to PHRASAL VERB When you **come on to** a particular topic, you start discussing it. *I want to come on to the question of disease in a minute.*

come out PHRASAL VERB 1 If information **comes out**, it is revealed or made public. *All the facts came out after Seery's death.* 2 When something such as a book **comes out**, it is published or becomes available to the public. *When Ehren's book came out there was a storm of protest from anthropologists... She asked me to send her any new stamps which might come out.* 3 To **come out** in a particular way means to be in the position or state described at the end of a process or event. *Who do you think will come out on top?... The press was coming out of the affair very badly.* 4 If you **come out** for or against something, you declare that you do or do not support it. *He came out in support of the claim... She never came out publicly in favour of the presidential system... Most of them came out against the scheme.* 5 If someone **comes out**, they publicly declare that they are homosexual. *Only one has come out as gay... She was being harassed by the tabloid press about having come out as a gay woman.* 6 If a photograph **comes out**, it is developed successfully. *Did those photos come out that you took at Hilda's party?* 7 When the sun, moon, or stars **come out**, they appear in the sky. *The dust in the atmosphere slowly settled, the sun came out and everything seemed to be normal.*

come out in PHRASAL VERB If you **come out in** spots, you become covered with them.

come over PHRASAL VERB 1 If a feeling **comes over** you, it affects you. *She wondered what could have come over him all of a sudden.* 2 When someone **comes over**, they call at your house for a short time. *You can come over tomorrow at four.*

come round PHRASAL VERB 1 If you **come round** to an idea, you eventually change your mind and accept it. *If Mr Gorbachev can convince the West, the G7 members will very likely come round to the idea in the end... He knew I would have to come round to his way of thinking in the end.* 2 When something **comes round**, it happens as a regular or predictable event. *Don't wait for April to come round before planning your vegetable garden.* 3 When someone who is unconscious **comes round**, they become conscious again. 4 If someone **comes round** to a place, they visit it for a few minutes or hours. *Consultants come round once or twice a week.*

come through PHRASAL VERB 1 If you **come through** a dangerous or difficult situation, you survive it. *Most of the troops came through the fighting unharmed.* 2 If something that takes time to be dealt with **comes through**, it is ready and you receive it. *Has my visa come through yet?* 3 If a quality or impression **comes through**, you perceive it. *I think the teacher's own personality has got to come through.*

come to PHRASAL VERB 1 If a thought or idea **comes to** you, you suddenly realize it. *The answer came to him just before noon... It came to me suddenly that what was wrong was that I was tired.* 2 If something such as a sum **comes to** a particular number or amount, it adds up to it. *My income now comes to £65 a week.* 3 If someone who is unconscious **comes to**, they become conscious again. *That's about all I remember, until I came to in a life-raft.*

come under PHRASAL VERB 1 If something **comes under** a particular authority, it is managed by that authority. *Day Nurseries come under the Department of Health and Social Security.* 2 If something or someone **comes under** criticism or attack, they are criticized or attacked. *The plan has come under attack from the Japanese parliament... British produce came under pressure from foreign competition.* 3 If something **comes under** a particular heading, it is in the category mentioned. *Records and tapes come under published material.*

come up PHRASAL VERB 1 If a topic **comes up** in a conversation or meeting, or if you **come up with** it, that topic is mentioned or discussed. *His name came up at a buffet lunch... I hope to come up with some of the answers.* 2 If an event **is coming up**, it is about to happen or take place. *There's a royal wedding coming up.* 3 If something **comes up**, it happens unexpectedly. *I can't see you tonight. Something's come up.* 4 When someone **comes up** for election, it is time for them to take part in an election again. *A third of my colleagues will come up for election next May.* 5 When the sun or moon **comes up**, it rises. *The sun comes up in the east.*

come up against PHRASAL VERB If you **come up against** a problem or difficulty, you have to deal with it. *Everyone comes up against discrimination sooner or later.*

come upon PHRASAL VERB If you **come upon** someone or something, you meet or find them by chance. *They rounded a turn and came upon a family of lions.*

come up to PHRASAL VERB To be **coming up to** a time or state means to be getting near to it. *It was just coming up to ten o'clock... Some of them are coming up to retirement.*

come up with PHRASAL VERB If you **come up with** an idea or plan, you think of it and suggest it. *I hope to come up with some of the answers.*

comeback /kʌmbæk/ **comebacks**
NC If someone or something makes a **comeback**, they become popular or successful again. *She confounded critics by making a spectacular political comeback... Wigs and elaborate hairstyles made a comeback.*

comedian /kəmiːdiən/ **comedians**
NC A **comedian** is an entertainer whose job is to make people laugh by telling jokes. *After a career as a comedian, he turned to serious drama... The autobiography of the American comedian Bob Hope has recently been published.*

comedienne /kəmiːdien/ **comediennes**
NC A **comedienne** is a female comedian.

comedown /kʌmdaʊn/; also spelt **come-down**.
N SING You say that something is a **comedown** if you think that it is not as good, or does not have as high a status, as something else that you have just done or had. *Professionally it is considered a comedown to work in portrait classes... The Polytechnic seemed a bit of a come-down after Oxford... What a comedown!*

comedy /kɒmədi/ **comedies**
1 NC A **comedy** is an amusing play or film. *...a revival of Maugham's comedy Caroline.* 2 NU You can refer to amusing things in a play or film as **comedy**. *The play had plenty of excitement as well as comedy. ...her rare gift for comedy on the stage.*

comely /kʌmli/ **comelier, comeliest**
ADJ A **comely** woman is attractive; an old-fashioned word. *...a very well-looking, comely woman.*

come-on, come-ons
NC A **come-on** is something that is intended to make you want to do something or buy something; used showing disapproval. *Remarks like this are a tease, a come-on. ...the come-on bargains at the chain stores.*

comet /kɒmɪt/ **comets**
NC A **comet** is an object that travels around the sun leaving a bright trail behind it. *...analysing the content of the dust and gases in the comet's tail... Halley's Comet turns out to be much younger than expected.*

come-uppance /kʌmʌpəns/
N SING+POSS When someone gets their **come-uppance**, they are justly punished for something wrong that they have done. *It is difficult not to be pleased at his come-uppance.*

comfort /kʌmfət/ **comforts, comforting, comforted**
1 NU **Comfort** is the state of being physically or mentally relaxed. *She longed to stretch out in comfort. ...a hard narrow chair not made for comfort... I found comfort in his words.* 2 NU You can refer to a pleasant style of life in which you have everything you need as **comfort**. *She wanted a life of reasonable comfort.* 3 NC **Comforts** are things that make your life more pleasant or help you stop worrying. *I longed for the comforts of home... It will be a comfort to know that you are standing by.* 4 VO If you **comfort** someone, you make them feel less worried or unhappy. *Jeannie came to comfort him.* ♦ **comforting** ADJ *It's a comforting thought that we have a few days before it starts.*

comfortable /kʌmftəbl/
1 ADJ Something that is **comfortable** makes you feel physically relaxed. *That chair is quite comfortable.* 2 ADJ If you are **comfortable**, you are physically relaxed and at ease, and not worried, afraid, or embarrassed. *He did not feel comfortable with strangers.* ♦ **comfortably** ADV *They were too cold to sleep comfortably.* 3 ADJ PRED When an ill or injured person is said to be **comfortable**, they are in a stable physical condition and are not getting worse. *One of them is seriously ill in hospital; the other is said to be comfortable.* 4 ADJ A **comfortable** job or task is one which you can do without difficulty. *It's a comfortable two hours' walk from here.* ♦ **comfortably** ADV *I can manage the work comfortably.*

comforter /kʌmfətə/ **comforters**
1 NC A **comforter** is a person or thing that comforts you. *He rang up another comforter, seeking the same reassurances.* 2 NC A baby's **comforter** is a rubber or plastic object that you give to it to suck so that it feels comforted; used in American English. 3 NC A **comforter** is a long scarf that you wind around your neck in order to keep warm. *They spent their time knitting comforters.*

comfrey /kʌmfri/
NU **Comfrey** is a herb that is used to make drinks and medicines. *Comfrey has been used to treat arthritis and gout for some time.*

comfy /kʌmfi/ **comfier, comfiest**; an informal word.
1 ADJ If something such as a chair is **comfy**, it is soft and comfortable. *The first three women to arrive had the comfy chairs.* 2 ADJ PRED If you are **comfy**, you feel comfortable and relaxed. *'Comfy?' he enquired.*

comic /kɒmɪk/ **comics**
1 ADJ Someone or something that is **comic** makes you want to laugh. *...a story rich in comic and dramatic detail.* 2 ADJ ATTRIB A **comic** action or thing is intended to make people laugh. *She's well-known for her wry, comic poems... Is she a tragic or comic figure?* 3 NC A **comic** is a person who tells jokes to make people laugh. *When the comic comes on they'll all laugh.* 4 NC A **comic** is also a magazine that contains stories told in pictures. *She was based on a character called Tracey, from the adult comic, Viz.* 5 N PL The **comics** are the pages containing comic strips in a newspaper; used in American English. *By the time you get to the paper, you can go straight to the comics. ...the comics page of 16 American newspapers.*

comical /kɒmɪkl/
ADJ Someone or something that is **comical** makes you want to laugh. *There is something slightly comical about him... The tour ended on a comical note.* ♦ **comically** ADV *David looked comically astonished.*

comic book, comic books
NC A **comic book** is a magazine, usually for children, that contains stories told in pictures; used in American English. *He seemed to read a lot of comic books.*

comic strip, comic strips
NC A **comic strip** is a series of drawings that tell a

story. ...*Roy Lichtenstein's expanded comic strips.*

coming /kʌmɪŋ/
ADJ ATTRIB A **coming** event or time will happen soon. *The real struggle will take place in the coming weeks.*

comma /kɒmə/ **commas**
NC A **comma** is the punctuation mark (,). *There is a comma after that clause.* ● See also **inverted commas.**

command /kəmɑːnd/ **commands, commanding, commanded**
1 VO+*to*-INF or V-QUOTE If you **command** someone to do something, you order them to do it. *She commanded me to lie down and relax... 'Stay here!' he commanded.* ▸ Also NC *They waited for their master's command.*
2 VO If you **command** something, you order it. *The king had commanded his presence at court.*
3 VO If you **command** something such as obedience or attention, you obtain it as a result of being popular or important. *She was no longer in a position to command obedience or admiration.*
4 VO An officer who **commands** part of an army, navy, or air force is in charge of it. *He commanded a regiment of cavalry in Algiers.* ▸ Also NU *He had been in command of HMS Churchill for a year.*
5 N SING+SUPP The high **command** or the military **command** refers to the senior officers of a country's armed forces. *...a statement released by the High Command... The military command is continuing to give only the barest amount of information.*
6 NU **Command** is control over a particular situation. *Lady Sackville took command... He was looking more relaxed and in command than ever before.*
7 NU+SUPP Your **command** of something, especially a language, is your knowledge of it and ability to use it. *...a good command of spoken English... He had an excellent command of Latin and Greek but was self-educated... His critics say he lacks command of detail.*
8 See also **commanding.**

commandant /kɒməndænt/ **commandants**
NC A **commandant** is an army officer in charge of a particular place or group of people. *The local military commandant ordered that demonstrators should be searched for weapons and explosives.*

command economy, command economies
NC A **command economy** is the same as a **planned economy.** *...moving from a bureaucratic, regulated command economy to a free market.*

commandeer /kɒməndɪə/ **commandeers, commandeering, commandeered**
VO If someone uses their authority or power to **commandeer** a vehicle or building, they take it in order to use it. *The Sudanese army has commandeered a number of lorries supplied by the British government for food relief operations. ...a house in the city which had been commandeered by three masked men.*

commander /kəmɑːndə/ **commanders**
NC A **commander** is an officer in charge of a military operation. *A military commander said the rebels were being pushed back... Two guerrilla commanders were reported to have surrendered.*

commander-in-chief, commanders-in-chief
NC A **commander-in-chief** is an officer in charge of all the forces in a particular area. *General Bashir holds the positions of prime minister, defence minister and commander-in-chief.*

commanding /kəmɑːndɪŋ/
1 ADJ ATTRIB If you are in a **commanding** position, you are able to control people and events because you are in the most powerful position. *Britain had lost her commanding position in the world... The French vessel 'Corum Saphir' has a commanding lead as the Fastnet Race draws to a finish.*
2 ADJ If you have a **commanding** voice or manner, you seem powerful and confident. *She was a passionate woman, tall, commanding, capable of inciting people to rebellion.*
3 ADJ ATTRIB A building that has a **commanding** position is high up with good views of the surrounding area. *The University stands in a commanding position overlooking the bay.*
4 See also **command.**

commanding officer, commanding officers
NC A **commanding officer** is an officer who is in charge of a military unit. *The Colonel was a good commanding officer who stuck by his men.*

commandment /kəmɑːndmənt/ **commandments**
NC The Ten **Commandments** are the rules of behaviour which, according to the Old Testament of the Bible, people should obey. *Moses parted the waters of the Red Sea and delivered the Ten Commandments.*

commando /kəmɑːndəʊ/ **commandos**
NC **Commandos** are soldiers who have been specially trained to carry out raids. *Commandos using plastic explosives have taken command of the building... The commandos have rifles with telescopic sights and machine guns.*

command post, command posts
NC A **command post** is a place from which a commander in the army controls and organizes his forces. *...a divisional command post.*

commemorate /kəmɛməreɪt/ **commemorates, commemorating, commemorated**
1 VO An object that **commemorates** a person or an event is intended to remind people of that person or event. *...a monument commemorating a great soldier.*
2 VO If you **commemorate** an event, you do something special to show that you remember it. *...a Jewish holiday commemorating the destruction of the Temple.*

commemoration /kəmɛməreɪʃn/ **commemorations**
NCorNU The **commemoration** of an important event is something special that you do in order to show that you remember it. *...the commemorations of last year's pro-democracy demonstrations... The move was in commemoration of the twenty-ninth anniversary of the nation's independence from Britain.*

commemorative /kəmɛmərətɪv/
ADJ ATTRIB A **commemorative** object such as a stamp or a medal is one that commemorates a particular event or person. *...the issue of commemorative stamps. ...a commemorative plaque.*

commence /kəmɛns/ **commences, commencing, commenced**
V-ERG When something **commences** or when you **commence** something, it begins to take place from a particular time onwards; a formal word. *He had been in prison for nine months when his trial commenced... The officer commenced duty earlier than usual... I'm certain that a court action would be commenced immediately if they refused.*

commencement /kəmɛnsmənt/
1 NU The **commencement** of something is its beginning; a formal use. *...the commencement of the flight... Mr Brooke seeks to establish a date for the commencement of talks.*
2 NU In the United States, **Commencement** is a ceremony at a university in which graduates formally receive their degrees. *Seventeen thousand people jam into Harvard Yard on Commencement morning.*

commend /kəmɛnd/ **commends, commending, commended**; a formal word.
1 VO If you **commend** someone or something, you praise them formally to other people. *I was commended for my reports... Rothermere commended Baldwin to his readers as a great man.*
◆ **commendation** /kɒməndeɪʃn/ **commendations**
NUorNC *...a degree of duty and devotion which deserves commendation. ...a list of officers who were recommended for a commendation.*
2 V-REFL+*to* If something **commends** itself to you, you approve of it. *The defence would scarcely commend itself even to other lawyers.*

commendable /kəmɛndəbl/
ADJ **Commendable** behaviour is admired and praised. *The committee acted with commendable fairness.*

commensurate /kəmɛnʃərət/
ADJ PRED+*with* If the level of one thing is **commensurate** with the level of another, the first level is in proportion to the second; a formal word. *...action commensurate with the gravity of what has happened.*

comment /kɒmɛnt/ **comments, commenting, commented**
1 V+*on*, V-REPORT, V-QUOTE, or V If you **comment** on

something, you give your opinion of it. *Police have not commented on any possible links... The Guardian comments in an editorial that airport security has collapsed again... 'It needs washing,' she commented... Both companies declined to comment.*
2 NCorNU A **comment** is a statement which expresses your opinion of something. *People in the town started making rude comments... There's been no official comment on the explosion... He was not available for comment yesterday.* ● People say **'no comment'** as a way of refusing to answer a question during an interview. *'Do you intend to keep them in prison?'— 'No comment.'*

commentary /kɒməntri/ **commentaries**
1 NC A **commentary** is a description of an event that is broadcast on radio or television while the event is taking place. *We were gathered round a radio to hear the commentary.*
2 NCorNU A **commentary** is also a book or article which explains or discusses something. *...political commentaries... The programme linked commentary from the BBC correspondent with first-hand accounts.*

commentate /kɒmənteɪt/ **commentates, commentating, commentated**
v When someone **commentates**, they give a radio or television commentary on an event. *David Mercer, who was commentating on the match, now describes the deciding point.*

commentator /kɒmənteɪtə/ **commentators**
1 NC A **commentator** is a broadcaster who gives a commentary on an event. *Brian Moore is a famous television football commentator.*
2 NC A **commentator** is also someone who often writes or broadcasts about a particular subject. *...Peter Jenkins, an experienced commentator on political affairs.*

commerce /kɒmɜːs/
NU **Commerce** is the activity of buying and selling things on a large scale. *It's expected that industry and commerce will also be affected... They are working on a number of accords aimed at freeing international commerce in manufactured goods.*

commercial /kəmɜːʃl/ **commercials**
1 ADJ ATTRIB **Commercial** means relating to commerce and business. *...commercial and industrial organisations.*
2 ADJ ATTRIB A **commercial** activity involves producing goods to make a profit. *...commercial agriculture. ...a big commercial bakery.* ◆ **commercially** ADV *Slate was quarried commercially here.*
3 ADJ ATTRIB **Commercial** television and radio are paid for by the broadcasting of advertisements between programmes. *The film was shown on commercial television last night.*
4 NC A **commercial** is an advertisement broadcast on television or radio. *Selling air-time for commercials will finance programmes.*

commercial art
NU **Commercial art** is the activities, processes, and skills involved in producing advertisements and in designing the way that products look.

commercial artist, commercial artists
NC A **commercial artist** is a person whose job involves producing advertisements and designing the way that products look. *She began life training as a commercial artist.*

commercial bank, commercial banks
NC A **commercial bank** is a bank which makes short-term loans using money from current accounts. *The huge debts of many poor countries mean that commercial banks have been reluctant to issue new loans.*

commercialism /kəmɜːʃəlɪzəm/
NU **Commercialism** is the practice of making a lot of money by selling products, but without caring very much about their quality or how useful they are; used showing disapproval. *...the shoddy culture of mass commercialism.*

commercialization /kəmɜːʃəlaɪzeɪʃn/; also spelt **commercialisation**.
NU **Commercialization** is the process by which something becomes commercialized. *...the*

commercialization of sport.

commercialized /kəmɜːʃəlaɪzd/; also spelt **commercialised**.
ADJ If something such as an activity is **commercialized**, people use it as an opportunity for making money rather than for any other purpose. *The ceremonies have degenerated into vulgar, commercialized spectacles.*

commercial traveller, commercial travellers; spelt **commercial traveler** in American English.
NC A **commercial traveller** is a salesperson who travels to different places in order to sell goods or take orders for goods.

commercial vehicle, commercial vehicles
NC A **commercial vehicle** is a vehicle used for carrying goods or passengers along roads. *...the declining commercial vehicle market.*

commie /kɒmi/ **commies**
NC A **commie** is someone who believes in communism; used showing disapproval.

commiserate /kəmɪzəreɪt/ **commiserates, commiserating, commiserated**
v If you **commiserate** with someone when they have a small problem, you show pity or sympathy for them; a formal word. *I commiserated with him over the recent news.* ◆ **commiseration** /kəmɪzəreɪʃn/ NU *...a look of commiseration.*

commissariat /kɒmɪseərɪət/ **commissariats**
N COLL A **commissariat** is a military department that is in charge of food supplies.

commissary /kɒmɪsəri/ **commissaries**
NC A **commissary** is a shop that provides food and equipment in a place such as a military camp or a prison; used in American English. *The only available source of real milk was the commissary.*

commission /kəmɪʃn/ **commissions, commissioning, commissioned**
1 VOorVO+to-INF If you **commission** something, or **commission** someone to do something, you arrange to pay someone to do the thing for you. *The Times commissioned a Public Opinion Poll... I was immediately commissioned to write another book.* ▸ Also NC *Red House was Webb's first commission as an architect.*
2 NUorNC **Commission** is a sum of money paid to a person selling goods for every sale that he or she makes. *They get commission on top of their basic salary... No agents could be involved in the deal and so no commissions were payable.*
3 N COLL A **commission** is also a group of people appointed to find out about something or to control something. *A commission was appointed to investigate the assassination of the President.* ● See also **High Commission, European Commission.**

commissionaire /kəmɪʃəneə/ **commissionaires**
NC A **commissionaire** is a person employed by a hotel, theatre, or cinema to open doors and help customers. *The commissionaire refused to let him into the hall because he hadn't got a ticket.*

commissioned officer, commissioned officers
NC A **commissioned officer** is an officer in the armed forces who has a commission, usually one who was recruited as an officer. *Three junior commissioned officers were also retired following an argument involving a senior army officer in the frontier corps.*

commissioner /kəmɪʃənə/ **commissioners**
NC A **commissioner** is an important official in an organization. *...the Church Commissioners... The decision was taken by the commissioners responsible for ensuring that government aid does not distort free trade.* ● See also **High Commissioner.**

commit /kəmɪt/ **commits, committing, committed**
1 VO If someone **commits** a crime or a sin, they do something wrong. *He has committed a criminal offence... Research has shown that ordinary sane people can falsely confess to crimes they haven't committed.*
2 VO To **commit** money or resources to something means to use them for a particular purpose. *Rolls Royce must commit its entire resources to the project.*
3 V-REFLorVO If you **commit** yourself or someone else to a course of action, you definitely decide that you or

they will do it, and you inform other people of your decision. *I really wouldn't like to commit myself... President Bush is reluctant to commit himself to large scale financial aid... Mrs. Thatcher did indeed commit Britain to joining the ERM.*
4 VO If someone is **committed** to a hospital or prison, they are officially sent there. *She was committed to a mental hospital.*
5 If you **commit** something **to memory**, you memorize it. *You'll need these figures so often that you must commit them to memory.*

commitment /kəmɪtmənt/ **commitments**
1 NU **Commitment** is a strong belief in an idea or system. *The Thatcher government has renewed its commitment to nuclear energy... They appeared to be united only by a commitment to the principles of democracy and free speech.*
2 NC A **commitment** is a regular task which takes up some of your time. *She's got family commitments.*
3 NC If you give a **commitment** to something, you promise faithfully that you will do it; a formal use. *He gave a clear commitment to reopen disarmament talks.*

committal /kəmɪtl/
NU **Committal** is the process of officially sending someone to prison or to hospital. *Mr Chung sought to delay the committal on two grounds.*

committee /kəmɪti/ **committees**
N COLL A **committee** is a group of people who represent a larger group or organization and make decisions for them. *A parliamentary committee has to approve his list of candidates... No date was fixed for the central committee meeting.*

commode /kəməʊd/ **commodes**
NC A **commode** is a movable piece of furniture shaped like a chair or a stool, which contains a large pot. It is used as a toilet, especially by people who are ill. *It is a hoist for lifting severely disabled people between a wheelchair, bed or commode.*

commodious /kəməʊdiəs/
ADJ A **commodious** room or house is large and has plenty of space; a formal word. *...a commodious building suitable for conversion.*

commodity /kəmɒdəti/ **commodities**
NC A **commodity** is something that is sold for money; a formal word. *...customers queueing for long hours for basic commodities like sugar and oil. ...fluctuating commodity prices.*

commodore /kɒmədɔː/ **commodores**
TITLE or NC A **commodore** is an officer of senior rank in the navy or air force. *Commodore Haddacks said the Allied navies had been completely successful. ...the commodore of the Royal New Zealand Yacht Squadron.*

common /kɒmən/ **commoner, commonest; commons**
1 ADJ If something is **common**, it is found in large numbers or it happens often. *Durand is a common name there... It was quite common for dogs to be poisoned this way.* ◆ **commonly** ADV *The most commonly used argument is that clients do not like long delays.*
2 ADJ If something is **common** to several people, it is possessed, done, or used by them all. *We shared a common language... It suppressed the desire for freedom common to all people. ...a common European currency.*
3 ADJ ATTRIB **Common** is also used to indicate that something is ordinary and not special. *Sodium chloride is better known as common salt.*
4 ADJ A **common** person behaves in a way that shows lack of taste, education, and good manners. *She was often ill-behaved, sometimes even common and rude.*
5 NC A **common** is a public area of grassy land near a village. *...Clapham Common.*
6 N PL The **Commons** is the same as the **House of Commons**; used in speech. *When the issue comes up in the Commons this afternoon there will inevitably be stormy scenes... There's expected to be a Commons debate within the next two or three weeks.*
● **Common** is used in these phrases. ● Something that is done **for the common good** is done for the benefit of everyone. *He said he needs to impose stability and*

unity for the common good. ● If two or more things have something in common, they have the same characteristics or features. *In common with many other companies, we advertise in the local press.*

commonality /kɒmənæləti/ **commonalities**
NU or NC If two or more people or things have **commonality**, they share some of the same characteristics or features. *there is no commonality of interests between the two countries... Let's look at the differences, and also the commonalities.*

common cold, common colds
NC A **common cold** is a mild, very common illness which makes you sneeze a lot and gives you a sore throat or a cough. *As far as we know, they have not found a cure for the common cold.*

common denominator, common denominators
1 NC A **common denominator** is a characteristic that is shared by all the members of a group of people or things. *The shocking common denominator of the recent crime wave is its lack of any rational motivation... War has been a common denominator among all five countries.*
2 NC A **common denominator** is also a number that can be divided exactly by all the denominators in a group of fractions; a technical use in mathematics.

commoner /kɒmənə/ **commoners**
NC A **commoner** is a person who is not a member of the nobility. *He has defied tradition by marrying a commoner.*

common ground
N SING or NU If two opposing people or groups can find some things which they agree about and can use these as the basis for discussion, you can refer to these things as their **common ground**. *It is hoped that this might provide the common ground for closer ties between the two organisations... He said there were many areas of common ground between the government and the SPLA.*

common land
NU **Common land** is land which everyone is allowed to go on. *The authorities had exceeded their powers in enclosing common land within the security fence.*

common-law
ADJ ATTRIB A **common-law** relationship is regarded as a marriage because it has lasted a long time, although no official marriage contract has been signed. *...common-law marriage. ...his common-law wife.*

Common Market
N PROP The **Common Market** is an organization of European countries, including the UK, that make decisions together about their trade, agriculture, and other policies. The official name of the Common Market is the **European Community**. *Edward Heath took Britain into the Common Market in 1973.*

commonplace /kɒmənpleɪs/
ADJ Something that is **commonplace** happens often. *Air travel has now become commonplace... A few years ago it was quite rare to see women unaccompanied by men in a pub, now it's commonplace.*

common room, common rooms
NC A **common room** is a room in a university or school where people can sit, talk, and relax. *...the graduate common room at Christ Church College.*

common sense
NU **Common sense** is the natural ability to make good judgements and behave sensibly. *Use your common sense. ...a few common-sense steps to help the situation.*

commonwealth /kɒmənwelθ/ **commonwealths**
NC A **commonwealth** is a nation, a state, or a federation regarded as a unit composed of people who have similar political interests for many purposes; an old-fashioned use. *This would clear the way for admission to what he called the commonwealth of democratic countries.*

Commonwealth /kɒmənwelθ/
The **Commonwealth** is a voluntary association of independent sovereign states, including the United Kingdom and most of its former dependencies. Queen Elizabeth II is Head of the Commonwealth. It represents about one quarter of the world's population.

The headquarters are in London. Members of the Commonwealth are: Antigua and Barbuda, Australia, Bahamas, Bangladesh, Barbados, Belize, Botswana, Brunei, Canada, Cyprus, Dominica, Gambia, Ghana, Grenada, Guyana, India, Jamaica, Kenya, Kiribati, Lesotho, Malawi, Malaysia, Maldives, Malta, Mauritius, Namibia, Nauru, New Zealand, Nigeria, Pakistan, Papua New Guinea, St Christopher and Nevis, St Lucia, St Vincent and the Grenadines, Seychelles, Sierra Leone, Singapore, Solomon Islands, Sri Lanka, Swaziland, Tanzania, Tonga, Trinidad and Tobago, Tuvalu, Uganda, United Kingdom, Vanuatu, Western Samoa, Zambia, and Zimbabwe.

Commonwealth of Independent States
The Commonwealth of Independent States was founded in 1991 at the dissolution of the Union of Soviet Socialist Republics. Its headquarters are in Minsk. Former Soviet republics which founded the Commonwealth of Independent States are: Armenia, Azerbaijan, Byelorussia, Kazakhstan, Kyrgyzstan, Moldavia, Russia, Tadjikistan, Turkmenistan, Ukraine, and Uzbekistan.

commotion /kəmˈəʊʃn/
N SING or NU A **commotion** is a lot of noise and confusion. *Suddenly there was a commotion at the other end of the bar... We reached home, where there was much commotion.*

communal /kɒmjʊnl/
ADJ Something that is **communal** is shared by a group of people. *...a communal dining-room. ...a communal style of life.* ◆ **communally** ADV *The mills are owned communally.*

commune, communes, communing, communed;
pronounced /kɒmjuːn/ when it is a noun and /kəmjuːn/ when it is a verb.
1 N COLL A **commune** is a group of people who live together and share everything. *...caring responsible parents, frequently vegetarian, living in communes... I wanted to hitchhike to California and live on a commune.*
2 V+with If you **commune** with nature, God, or spirits, you spend time thinking about it, feeling that you are in close contact with it in some way. *Many ancient societies believed that sound and chant are the doorways through which people can commune with God and nature.*

communicant /kəmjuːnɪkənt/ **communicants**
NC A **communicant** is a person in the Christian church who receives communion. *The bell was to summon communicants.*

communicate /kəmjuːnɪkeɪt/ **communicates, communicating, communicated**
1 V-RECIP, V O, or V-REPORT If you **communicate** with someone, you give them information, for example by speaking, writing, or sending radio signals. *He communicates with Miami by radio... Anthony and I hadn't communicated for years... They communicated their offer to the Soviet Embassy about two weeks ago... Through signs she communicated that she wanted a drink.*
2 V O If you **communicate** an idea or a feeling to someone, you make them aware of it. *...the failure of intellectuals to communicate their ideas to a wider audience.*
3 V-RECIP or V If people can **communicate**, they understand each other's feelings or attitudes. *Cliff talked to me a few times but we couldn't really communicate... He described Mr Gorbachev as a great man who could communicate with the crowds. ...his tough background and ability to communicate.*

communicating /kəmjuːnɪkeɪtɪŋ/
ADJ ATTRIB **Communicating** doors link one room directly to another. *The two rooms were next to each other, with a communicating door.*

communication /kəmjuːnɪkeɪʃn/ **communications**
1 NU **Communication** is the activity or process of giving information to other people or living things. *Insects such as ants have a highly effective system of communication... There was poor communication between officers and crew.*
2 N PL **Communications** are the systems and processes that are used to communicate or broadcast

information. *Communications inside the country have also been seriously disrupted... Lack of communications, transport and bad weather are still holding up relief in many areas. ...large numbers of communications satellites.*
3 NC A **communication** is a letter or telephone call; a formal use. *...a secret communication from the Foreign Minister.*

communication cord, communication cords
NC The **communication cord** is a rope or chain on a train that passengers can pull to stop the train in an emergency. *Eye-witnesses said that the communication cord was pulled.*

communicative /kəmjuːnɪkətɪv/
ADJ Someone who is **communicative** is able to talk to people easily. *He was as friendly and communicative as taxi-drivers commonly are.*

communion /kəmjuːnjən/
NU **Communion** is the Christian ceremony in which people eat bread and drink wine as a symbol of Christ's death and resurrection. *A quiet Communion service was held at All Saint's Church for parents and pupils.*

communiqué /kəmjuːnɪkeɪ/ **communiqués**
NC A **communiqué** is an official statement. *A joint communiqué was issued at the end of their talks... A military communiqué said a second plane was missing.*

communism /kɒmjʊnɪzəm/
NU **Communism** is the political belief that the state should control the means of producing everything, and that there should be no private property. *He referred to Communism as a failed system.*

communist /kɒmjʊnɪst/ **communists**
1 NC A **communist** is someone who believes in communism. *...a young communist from Cleveland, Ohio.*
2 ADJ ATTRIB **Communist** is used to refer to people and things that are connected with communism. *...the South African communist party... People are certain that the present Communist government will fall. ...communist doctrine.*

community /kəmjuːnəti/ **communities**
1 N COLL A **community** is a group of people who live in a particular area or who are alike in some way. *Members are drawn from all sections of the local community... The Soviets want to be seen as good citizens of the international community.*
2 N SING The European Community is often referred to as the **Community**: see **European Community**. *The Community has made it clear that there is no question of any new members joining before the end of 1992.*

community centre, community centres
NC A **community centre** is a place where people, groups, and organizations in a particular area can hold meetings and run courses and other social activities. *They will support projects such as flats and community centres for the young... Sister Martin runs the small community centre.*

community charge
N SING or NU The **community charge** was introduced in Britain in 1989 and 1990 as a local tax which every adult should pay. It replaced the previous system of local taxation which was based on property values. *This would enable local authorities to set their bills for the community charge at under £400 per person per year... Central government can insist that councils reduce the level of community charge.*

community policing
NU **Community policing** is a system in which policemen work only in one particular area of the community, so that everyone knows them. *Recent outbreaks of violence in several British cities have underlined the need for a return to community policing... Supporters say that community policing can give residents a sense of control over their crime-prone streets.*

community service
NU **Community service** is unpaid work that is done to help other people. People who have been convicted of a minor crime sometimes do community service instead of being punished. *After release he will do one*

thousand hours of community service.

commute /kəmjuːt/ **commutes, commuting, commuted**

1 v If you **commute**, you travel a long distance every day between your home and your place of work. *...workers from Gaza who commute to jobs in Israel.*

2 N SING+SUPP You can refer to the journey that you make when you commute as a particular kind of commute; used in American English. *...drivers accustomed to a 12-mile commute. ...black workers making a long commute to rich white areas.*

3 vo To **commute** a death sentence or prison sentence means to change it to a less severe punishment. *Her sentence was later commuted to life imprisonment.*

commuter /kəmjuːtə/ **commuters**

NC A **commuter** is a person who commutes to work, especially by train. *The strike left thousands of commuters stranded. ...commuter trains.*

Comoros /kəmɔːrəuz/

The **Federal Islamic Republic of the Comoros** is a country in the Indian Ocean, off the east coast of Africa. It was a French colony from the 19th century until independence in 1975. The main islands are Njazidja, Nzwani, and Mwali, formerly known as Grande-Comore, Anjouan, and Mohéli. Ahmed Abdallah became President in 1978, established a one-party state in 1979, and ruled until his assassination in 1989. Saïd Mohammed Djohar, of the Comoran Union for Progress (Udzima), became President in 1989 and held multi-party elections in 1990. It is a member of the Organization of African Unity. The Comoros export cloves, vanilla, and perfume oils. ◆ **Comoran** /kəmɔːrən/ N, ADJ

▪ *per capita GNP:* US$440 ▪ *religion:* Islam (mainly Sunni) ▪ *language:* Arabic and French (official), Comoran ▪ *currency:* franc ▪ *capital:* Moroni ▪ *population:* 459,000 (1989) ▪ *size:* 1,862 square kilometres.

compact, compacts, compacting, compacted; pronounced /kəmpækt/ or /kɒmpækt/ when it is an adjective and /kəmpækt/ when it is a verb.

1 ADJ Something that is **compact** takes up very little space. *The kitchen was small, compact, and immaculately clean. ...smaller, more compact computers.*

2 ADJ A **compact** car is a small one; used in American English. *Ford Motor company plans to idle its compact car plant in Kansas City, Missouri... There are 10 separate models in all, from the compact Capri to the full-size Continental.*

3 vo To **compact** something means to press it so that it becomes more dense; a formal use. *The tractor wheels compact the soil to a damaging extent.*

compact disc /kɒmpækt dɪsk/ **compact discs**

NC **Compact discs** are played on special machines which use lasers to read their signals and convert the signals into sound of a very high quality. 'Compact disc' is often abbreviated to 'CD'. *There was a strong demand from music-lovers for compact discs of old performances by some of this century's great musicians.*

companion /kəmpænjən/ **companions**

NC A **companion** is someone who you spend time with or travel with. *Several shots were fired, killing the man and seriously injuring his companion.*

companionable /kəmpænjənəbl/

ADJ A person who is **companionable** is friendly and pleasant.

companionship /kəmpænjənʃɪp/

NU **Companionship** is the state of being with someone you know and like, rather than being on your own. *She missed her mother's companionship and love.*

companionway /kəmpænjənweɪ/ **companionways**

NC A **companionway** is a stairway or ladder that leads from one deck to another on a ship.

company /kʌmpəni/ **companies**

1 N COLL A **company** is a business organization that makes money by selling goods or services. *...light industrial projects in which Libyan and Algerian companies would each have a stake.*

2 N COLL A theatre or dance **company** is a group of performers who work together. *...the Royal*

Shakespeare Company.

3 N COLL A **company** of soldiers is a group of soldiers that is usually part of a battalion or regiment, and that is divided into two or more platoons. *About two hundred soldiers of the 551 Company of the Slovene Defence Force came to hand in their weapons at their headquarters in Brod.*

4 NU **Company** is the state of having someone with you, rather than being on your own. *Are you expecting company?... She preferred his company to that of most people.*

5 If you **keep** someone **company**, you spend time with them and stop them feeling lonely or bored. *He kept his mother company in the late afternoons.*

Compaoré, Blaise /blez kɒmpɑːɔreɪ/

Blaise Compaoré became Chairman of the Popular Front (FP) and President of Burkina Faso in 1987. He was Minister of State to the Presidency from 1983 to 1984 and Minister of Justice from 1984 to 1987.

comparable /kɒmpərəbl/

ADJ If two or more things are **comparable**, they are as good as each other, or they are similar in size or quality. *The sums of money involved were not, of course, comparable... They have much lower fuel consumption than comparable petrol-engined cars.*

◆ **comparability** /kɒmpərəbɪləti/ NU *There are problems over the comparability of data.*

comparative /kəmpærətɪv/ **comparatives**

1 ADJ ATTRIB You use **comparative** to indicate that something is true only when compared to what is normal. *He hoped they could spend the night in comparative safety... There was a period of comparative calm.*

2 ADJ ATTRIB A **comparative** study involves the comparison of similar things. *...a comparative study of Indian and Western food.*

3 NC In grammar, the **comparative** is the form of an adjective that indicates that the thing it describes is greater or smaller in size or quantity than another thing. Comparatives usually end in '-er' or have 'more' or 'less' in front of them. In the sentences 'My brother is younger than me' and 'Charlie was more honest than his predecessor', 'younger' and 'more honest' are comparatives.

comparatively /kəmpærətɪvli/

SUBMOD **Comparatively** few or little means fewer or less than usual or than you expect. *They lay comparatively few eggs... There was comparatively little pressure for change.*

compare /kəmpeə/ **compares, comparing, compared**

1 V-RECIP When you **compare** things, you consider them and discover their differences or similarities. *It's interesting to compare the two prospectuses. ...studies comparing Russian children with those in Britain... The fee is low, compared with that at many other independent schools.*

2 VO+to If you **compare** one person or thing to another, you say that they are similar. *As an essayist he is compared frequently to Paine and Hazlitt.*

comparison /kəmpærɪsən/ **comparisons**

NCorNU When you make a **comparison**, you consider two or more things and discover their differences and similarities. *We have to find out more before we can make a proper comparison... Here, for comparison, is the French version.*

compartment /kəmpɑːtmənt/ **compartments**

1 NC A **compartment** is one of the separate sections of a railway carriage. *The fire began in a steward's compartment.*

2 NC A **compartment** is also one of the separate parts of an object used for keeping things in. *He tucked the ticket into the inner compartment of his wallet.*

compartmentalize /kɒmpɑːtmentəlaɪz/ **compartmentalizes, compartmentalizing, compartmentalized**; also spelt **compartmentalise**.

vo To **compartmentalize** something means to divide it into separate sections. *I have found it best to compartmentalize my contracts... Different academic disciplines get compartmentalised, and there is virtually no communication between theologians and sociologists.*

compass /kʌmpəs/ **compasses**
1 NC A **compass** is an instrument with a magnetic needle which always points north. It is used for finding directions. *He never walked in the mountains again without a map and a compass... Equipped with a small compass and some charts, they worked their way down the waterway that separates Iraq and Iran.*
2 N PL **Compasses** are a hinged V-shaped instrument used for drawing circles.

compassion /kəmpæʃn/
NU **Compassion** is a strong feeling of pity and sympathy. *The suffering of the Cubans aroused their compassion... Whatever choice they make, they deserve our compassion and our full support.*

compassionate /kəmpæʃəⁿnət/
ADJ A **compassionate** person feels strong pity and sympathy. *She was among the most compassionate of women.* ◆ **compassionately** ADV *Liz looked at her compassionately.*

compassionate leave
NU **Compassionate leave** is time away from your work that your employer allows you for personal reasons, especially when a member of your family dies or is seriously ill.

compass point, compass points
NC A **compass point** is one of the 32 marks on the dial of a compass that show direction, for example north, south, east, and west.

compatible /kəmpætəbl/
1 ADJ If things or ideas are **compatible**, they work together well or are suited to each other. *There are doubts within the industry about whether strict quality control can be compatible with healthy profit margins... We assumed that all these objectives were compatible.* ◆ **compatibility** /kəmpætəbɪləti/ NU *They failed to achieve any compatibility of planning aims.*
2 ADJ If people, especially a couple, are **compatible**, they can live or spend time together happily. *We weren't really compatible... They are hoping for someone wonderful in every department, with enough money, very attractive and sexually compatible.*

compatriot /kəmpætriət/ **compatriots**
NC Your **compatriots** are people from your own country. *Li Lingwe beat her compatriot Han Aiping in the women's competition.*

compel /kəmpel/ **compels, compelling, compelled**
VO+to-INF If something **compels** you to act or behave in a particular way, it forces you to do it. *...illnesses which compel people to change their diet.*

compelling /kəmpelɪŋ/
ADJ A **compelling** argument or reason for something convinces you that it is true or right. *I had ended a man's life for no compelling reason.*

compensate /kɒmpənseɪt/ **compensates, compensating, compensated**
1 VO To **compensate** someone for something means to give them money to replace it. *The allowance should be paid to compensate people for loss of earnings.*
2 V To **compensate** for the bad effect of something means to do something that cancels out this effect. *Fish compensate for the current by moving their fins.*

compensation /kɒmpənseɪʃn/ **compensations**
1 NU **Compensation** is money that you claim from a person or organization to compensate you for something unpleasant that has happened to you. *If you were killed, your dependants could get compensation.*
2 NCorNU A **compensation** is something that cancels out another thing that has had a bad effect. *Look for some of the compensations your body has to make... Letters that began to arrive from Nell were some compensation.*

compensatory /kɒmpənseɪtəri/
ADJ ATTRIB Something that is **compensatory** involves helping people by giving them money or resources to compensate for something bad that has happened. *There must be compensatory payments to the farmers.*

compere /kɒmpeə/ **comperes, compering, compered;** also spelt **compère**
NC A **compere** is the person on a radio or television show who introduces the guests and performers. *Your compere tonight is Jimmy Tarbuck.* ▶ Also VO *Esther Rantzen agreed to compere the Miss World contest.*

compete /kəmpiːt/ **competes, competing, competed**
1 V-RECIP When people or organizations **compete** with each other for something, they each try to get it for themselves rather than letting another person or organization have it. *This would enable British shipbuilders to compete with foreign yards... Senior members of staff competed eagerly for the honour of representing the company.*
2 VA If a person or team **competes** in a contest or a game, they take part in it and try to win. *Dave Moorcroft has now competed in two Olympics.*
3 See also **competing**.

competence /kɒmpɪtəns/
NU **Competence** is the ability to do something well, effectively, and following professional standards. *Piero carried out his commission with his usual competence... He will be expected to show competence in the relevant methods of research.*

competent /kɒmpɪtənt/
ADJ Someone who is **competent** is efficient, effective, and follows professional standards. *He was a competent amateur pilot... It was a highly competent piece of work.* ◆ **competently** ADV *He carved the bird roughly, but competently.*

competing /kəmpiːtɪŋ/
1 ADJ ATTRIB Two **competing** statements or ideas cannot both be right. *The experts will consider the competing claims... Various competing theories are compared and discussed.*
2 See also **compete**.

competition /kɒmpətɪʃn/ **competitions**
1 NU **Competition** is a situation in which two or more people or groups are trying to get something which not everyone can have. *Competition for admission to the college is keen... They have often been in competition for western investment.*
2 NU **Competition** is also a situation involving two or more companies in which each company tries to get people to buy their products. *More competition will be better for the consumer... Part of the reason for the drop in sales is competition from overseas suppliers.*
3 NCorNU A **competition** is an event in which people take part in order to find out who is best at a particular activity. *The men's competition is expected to be a contest between two Soviet skaters... Mexico was banned from international competition for two years.*

competitive /kəmpetətɪv/
1 ADJ Something that is **competitive** involves people or firms competing with each other. *...a highly competitive society... On tour you play more competitive cricket than back at home.*
2 ADJ A **competitive** person is eager to be more successful than other people. *I realize how awfully competitive I am.* ◆ **competitiveness** NU *Why should we put such an emphasis on individualism and competitiveness?*
3 ADJ Goods that are **competitive** are cheaper than similar goods. *...a competitive car for the 1980s... The reforms are expected to make industry more competitive and attract more foreign investment.* ◆ **competitively** ADV *...competitively priced newspapers.*
4 ADJ If someone's salary is **competitive**, they are paid the same as, or more than, other people in equivalent jobs in other companies or countries. *The government agrees that top pay must be competitive.*

competitor /kəmpetɪtə/ **competitors**
1 NC Companies that are **competitors** sell similar kinds of goods. *...Austin-Rover's challenge to its foreign competitors.*
2 NC A **competitor** is a person who takes part in a competition. *Ten competitors were disqualified.*

compilation /kɒmpɪleɪʃn/ **compilations**
NC A **compilation** is a book, record, or programme containing many different things. *...a compilation of Victorian poetry.*

compile /kəmpaɪl/ **compiles, compiling, compiled**
VO When you **compile** a book, report, or film, you produce it by putting together different pieces of

information. *The programme was compiled and presented by Dr Brian Smith.*

complacency /kəmpleɪsnsi/
NU **Complacency** is the state of being complacent about a situation; used showing disapproval. *No one has any cause for complacency... There is far too much political complacency in this country.*

complacent /kəmpleɪsnt/
ADJ If you are **complacent** about a situation, you do not feel that you need to worry or do anything; used showing disapproval. *She's warned people that they shouldn't be complacent about the energy problem... She's warned people that they shouldn't be complacent.*
♦ **complacently** ADV *Her mother smiled complacently.*

complain /kəmpleɪn/ **complains, complaining, complained**
1 V A, V-REPORT, or V-QUOTE If you **complain** about something, you express the fact that you are not satisfied with it. *People had complained to Uncle Harold about his fights... Black students have often complained of racial harassment... She complained that the office was not 'businesslike'... 'He never told me, sir,' Watson complained.*
2 V+*of* If you **complain** of pain or illness, you say you have it. *He was taken to hospital after complaining of abdominal pains.*

complainant /kəmpleɪnənt/ **complainants**
NC A **complainant** is a person who starts a court case in a court of law; a legal term. *It's recommending that complainants be told about the outcome of police disciplinary action.*

complaint /kəmpleɪnt/ **complaints**
1 NC or NU A **complaint** is a statement of dissatisfaction or a reason for it. *There were the usual complaints of violence... There will be a tribunal to investigate complaints... She wrote a letter of complaint to the manufacturer.*
2 NC A **complaint** is also an illness. *...a minor complaint... They were suffering from stomach complaints.*

complaisance /kəmpleɪzəns/
NU **Complaisance** is willingness to accept what other people are doing without complaining; an old-fashioned word. *...the government's complaisance in the face of newspaper excesses.*

complaisant /kəmpleɪzənt/
ADJ If you are **complaisant**, you are willing to accept what other people are doing without complaining; an old-fashioned word. *It would be better to close our eyes like a complaisant husband whose wife has taken a lover.*

complement, complements, complementing, complemented; pronounced /kɒmplɪment/ when it is a verb and /kɒmplɪmənt/ when it is a noun.
1 V O If two people or things **complement** each other, they both have desirable qualities which make a good combination when they are put together. *Crisp pastry complements the juicy fruit of an apple pie... They've been doing experiments which complement some of ours... They complemented each other to perfection.*
► Also NC *The exercises are an ideal complement to my usual rehearsal methods.*
2 N SING+SUPP The full **complement** of a group, set, or amount is every item or person that it normally includes or should include. *A child has to come fourteen times to get a full complement of vaccine... The normal complement of seven officers at the service had been increased to fifteen.*
3 NC In grammar, a **complement** is a noun group or adjective which occurs after a verb such as 'be', 'seem', or 'become'. In the sentences 'He is a geologist' and 'Nobody seemed amused', 'a geologist' and 'amused' are complements.

complementary /kɒmplɪmentri/
ADJ If two different things are **complementary**, they form a complete unit when they are brought together, or fit well together. *These two approaches are complementary... The two ideas, she said, did not duplicate each other, but were complementary.*

complete /kəmpliːt/ **completes, completing, completed**
1 ADJ If something is **complete**, it contains all the

parts that it should contain. *This is not a complete list. ...an almost complete skeleton of a dinosaur.*
2 ADJ You use **complete** to indicate that something is as great in degree or amount as it possibly can be. *...a complete change of diet... They were in complete agreement.* ♦ **completely** ADV *He was completely bald.*
3 V O If you **complete** something, you finish doing, making, or producing it. *The cathedral was begun in 1240 and completed forty years later.*
4 ADJ PRED If a task is **complete**, it is finished. *The harvesting was complete... The withdrawal is by no means complete.*
5 V O If something **completes** a set, it is the last item needed to make it whole or finished. *A black silk tie completed the outfit.*
6 V O To **complete** a form means to write the necessary information on it. *Councils will canvass every household to ensure the forms are completed.*
7 Something that is **complete with** a particular thing includes that thing as an extra part. *...a lovely mansion, complete with swimming pool.*

completion /kəmpliːʃn/
NU **Completion** is the finishing of a piece of work. *The house was due for completion in 1983... The dam is nearing completion.*

complex /kɒmpleks/ **complexes**
1 ADJ **Complex** things have many different parts and are hard to understand. *...complex lace patterns... It is a complex problem.*
2 NC+SUPP A **complex** is a group of many things which are connected with each other in a complicated way. *...a complex of little roads... But that is only one aspect of a whole complex of problems which have marred relations between Czechoslovakia and its neighbours.*
3 NC A **complex** is also a group of buildings used for a particular purpose. *...a splendid new sports and leisure complex.*
4 NC If you have a **complex**, you have a mental or emotional problem caused by an unpleasant experience in the past. *I am developing a guilt complex about it.*

complexion /kəmplekʃn/ **complexions**
NC Your **complexion** is the natural quality of the skin on your face. *She said I had a good complexion.*

complexity /kəmpleksəti/ **complexities**
1 NU **Complexity** is the state of having many different parts related to each other in a complicated way. *...problems of varying complexity... Because of the complexity of the voting system in Slovenia, the final results of last Sunday's elections will probably not be known until the weekend.*
2 N PL The **complexities** of something are its connected parts, which make it difficult to understand. *...the complexities of tax law.*

compliance /kəmplaɪəns/
NU **Compliance** is doing what you have been asked to do; a formal word. *This film has been made with the compliance of the Korean authorities... These new measures are in compliance with the Central American peace agreement.*

compliant /kəmplaɪənt/
ADJ Someone who is **compliant** willingly does what they are asked to do. *He is eager, willing, and compliant to the demands of others.*

complicate /kɒmplɪkeɪt/ **complicates, complicating, complicated**
V O To **complicate** something means to make it more difficult to understand or deal with. *Just to complicate matters, I have to be back by the end of the month.*

complicated /kɒmplɪkeɪtɪd/
ADJ Something that is **complicated** has many parts and is difficult to understand. *I find the British legal system extremely complicated... The situation is much more complicated than that.*

complication /kɒmplɪkeɪʃn/ **complications**
NC A **complication** is a problem or difficulty. *Finally, there is the complication that wages help to determine the level of inflation.*

complicity /kəmplɪsəti/
NU **Complicity** is involvement in an illegal activity; a

formal word. *She suspected him of complicity in Ashok's escape.*

compliment, compliments, complimenting, complimented; pronounced /kɒmplɪment/ when it is a verb, and /kɒmplɪmənt/ when it is a noun.
1 NC If you pay someone a **compliment**, you say something nice about them. *He had just been paid a great compliment... Some of the warmest compliments came from the President.*
2 VO If you **compliment** someone, you praise them or tell them how much you like something that they own or that they have done. *He complimented Morris on his new car... A number of lorry drivers on board also complimented the crew.*
3 N PL If someone sends or presents their **compliments**, they express good wishes or respect; a formal use. *The Secretary of State presents his compliments.*

complimentary /kɒmplɪmentri/
1 ADJ If you are **complimentary** about something, you express admiration for it. *In Russia a rhythmic slow handclap can be highly complimentary... He was complimentary about the Prime Minister.*
2 ADJ ATTRIB A **complimentary** ticket, meal, or drink is free. *We picked up a couple of glasses from a tray of complimentary aperitifs.*

comply /kəmplaɪ/ **complies, complying, complied**
V If you **comply** with an order or rule, you do what you are required to do; a formal word. *Iceland has complied with the ban on commercial whaling... New vehicles must comply with certain standards.*

component /kəmpəʊnənt/ **components**
NC The **components** of something are its parts. *The factory makes components for cars. ...electronic components.*

comport /kəmpɔːt/ **comports, comporting, comported**
V-REFL If you **comport** yourself in a particular way, you behave in that way; a formal word. *The Colonel gave me advice on how to comport myself in the White House.*

compose /kəmpəʊz/ **composes, composing, composed**
1 V-PASS The things that something **is composed** of are its parts or members. *The book is composed of essays written over the last twenty years... The National Committee was composed of 22 manual workers and 6 white-collar workers.*
2 VOor V When someone **composes** a piece of music, they write it. *This work is written for the organ, for which he has composed some of his most outstanding music... He conducts and composes.*
3 VO If you **compose** a letter, poem, or speech, you write it, often using a great deal of concentration and skill; a formal use. *Mr Morris sat down to compose his letter of resignation.*
4 V-REFL If you **compose** yourself, you become calm after being angry or excited. *She lay on her bed and cried and then she composed herself and went downstairs.*

composed /kəmpəʊzd/
ADJ If someone is **composed**, they are calm and able to control their feelings. *I felt calmer and more composed than I had in a long time. We are shocked, but composed and determined.*

composer /kəmpəʊzə/ **composers**
NC A **composer** is a person who writes music. *He was a brilliant pianist, a teacher, and of course a prolific composer.*

composite /kɒmpəzɪt/
ADJ ATTRIB A **composite** object or item is made up of several different things or parts. *...the composite annual fee.*

composition /kɒmpəzɪʃn/ **compositions**
1 NU The **composition** of something is the things that it consists of and the way that they are arranged. *...the chemical composition of the atmosphere.*
2 NC A **composition** is a piece of work you write at school on a particular subject. *The composition had to be at least three pages long.*
3 NC A composer's **compositions** are the pieces of music he or she has written. *His compositions include chamber music, concertos and suites for strings and oboe... Paul McCartney's first classical composition*

has been performed in his home city of Liverpool.
4 NU **Composition** is also the act of composing something such as a piece of music or a poem. *...a poem of his own composition.*

compositor /kəmpɒzɪtə/ **compositors**
NC A **compositor** is a person whose occupation is setting up the text and illustrations of a book, magazine, or newspaper before it is printed.

compos mentis /kɒmpəs mentɪs/
ADJ PRED If you are **compos mentis**, you are able to think clearly and understand what you are doing because you are mentally normal and well; a formal expression, often used humorously. *By the time I was fully compos mentis again the worst was over.*

compost /kɒmpɒst/
NU **Compost** is a mixture of decaying plants and manure which is used to improve soil. *...a compost heap.*

composure /kəmpəʊʒə/
NU **Composure** is the ability to stay calm; a formal word. *He had recovered his composure.*

compote /kɒmpəʊt/ **compotes**
NU or NC **Compote** is fruit stewed with sugar or in syrup. *...compote of oranges with candied peel.*

compound, compounds, compounding, compounded; pronounced /kɒmpaʊnd/ when it is a noun or modifier and /kəmpaʊnd/ when it is a verb.
1 NC A **compound** is an enclosed area of land used for a particular purpose. *He led the men into the prison compound... Some of the protesters managed to get inside the Soviet embassy compound.*
2 NC In chemistry, a **compound** is a substance consisting of two or more elements. *The cells release histamine, a chemical compound which dilates blood vessels and contracts muscles.*
3 NC If something is a **compound** of different things, it consists of those things. *The new threat was a compound of nationalism and social revolution.*
4 VO To **compound** a problem means to make it worse by increasing it in some way; a formal use. *Her uncertainty was now compounded by fear.*

compound fracture, compound fractures
NC A **compound fracture** is a broken bone which has cut through the flesh or skin near it. *One of the British soldiers suffered a compound fracture of the jaw.*

compound interest
NU **Compound interest** is interest that is calculated not only on the original amount of money that has been invested, but also on the interest that is earned, which is added to the original amount. See also **simple interest.**

comprehend /kɒmprɪhend/ **comprehends, comprehending, comprehended**
V Oor V-REPORT If you cannot **comprehend** something, you cannot fully understand or appreciate it; a formal word. *...a failure to comprehend the huge power of computers... They did not comprehend how hard he had struggled.*

comprehensible /kɒmprɪhensəbl/
ADJ If something is **comprehensible**, it is easily understood. *The operas will not be immediately comprehensible to most Soviets, all of them being sung in English. ...clear, comprehensible directions.*

comprehension /kɒmprɪhenʃn/ **comprehensions**
1 NU **Comprehension** is the ability to understand or appreciate something fully. *The problems of solar navigation seem beyond comprehension.*
2 NC A **comprehension** is an exercise to find out how well you understand a piece of text. *Now we're going to do a listening comprehension.*

comprehensive /kɒmprɪhensɪv/
ADJ Something that is **comprehensive** includes everything necessary or relevant. *...a comprehensive list of all the items in stock. ...the need for a comprehensive settlement.*

comprehensive school, comprehensive schools
NC A **comprehensive school** is one where children of all abilities are taught. *The vast majority of children go to state comprehensive schools.*

compress /kəmpres/ **compresses, compressing, compressed**

V-ERG When you **compress** something, you squeeze it or make it smaller or shorter. *I soon finished a paper, which I compressed to minimum length... Once on the ground the snow is compressed by more snow falling on top... I could feel my lips compress into a white line.* ◆ **compressed** ADJ ATTRIB *...a high pressure hose running off compressed air.* ◆ **compression** /kəmprɛʃn/ NU *...the compression of air by the piston.*

compressor /kəmprɛsə/ **compressors**
NC A **compressor** is a machine or part of a machine that squeezes gas or air and makes it take up less space. *It has an air chamber, which accepts compressed air from the compressor on the sprayer and mixes it with the liquid.*

comprise /kəmpraɪz/ **comprises, comprising, comprised**; a formal word.
1 VO If an organization or group **comprises** a number of people or things, or is **comprised** of them, it has them as its members or parts. *The delegation comprised nine church leaders... The government itself is comprised of a multi-party coalition.*
2 VC If a number of people or things **comprise** a group or organization, they are its members or parts. Some speakers of English believe that it is not correct to use **comprise** with this meaning. *Aborigines comprise less than 2% of Australia's population.*

compromise /kɒmprəmaɪz/ **compromises, compromising, compromised**
1 NCorNU A **compromise** is an agreement in which people agree to accept less than they originally wanted. *It was necessary for members to make compromises to ensure party unity... Delegates predict that some compromise will be reached.*
2 V If you **compromise**, you reach an agreement with another person or group in which you both give up something that you originally wanted. *The best thing to do is to compromise.*
3 V-REFLorVO If you **compromise** yourself or your beliefs, you do something which makes people doubt your sincerity or honesty. *They claim he has already compromised himself... The Government had compromised its principles.* ◆ **compromising** ADJ ATTRIB *They released compromising photographs of him with a woman guide... The military police were destroying compromising files.*

Compton, John /dʒɒn kɒmptən/
John Compton became Prime Minister of St Lucia in 1982. He was Chief Minister in 1964, Premier from 1967 to 1979, and previously served as Prime Minister in 1979. He is a member of the United Workers' Party (UWP). Born: 1926.

compulsion /kəmpʌlʃn/ **compulsions**
1 NC A **compulsion** is a strong desire to do something. *She feels a compulsion to tidy up all the time.*
2 NU If someone uses **compulsion** to get you to do something, they force you to do it. *We are not entitled to use compulsion.*

compulsive /kəmpʌlsɪv/
1 ADJ You use **compulsive** to describe people who cannot stop doing something. *...a compulsive gambler... Compulsive shopping can result in both financial and psychological problems.* ◆ **compulsively** ADV *He steals compulsively.*
2 ADJ If a book or television programme is **compulsive**, it is so interesting that you do not want to stop reading or watching it. *It has become compulsive reading for professional people keenly following Soviet political developments. ...compulsive viewing.*

compulsory /kəmpʌlsəri/
ADJ If something is **compulsory**, you must do it. *In most schools, sports are compulsory. ...compulsory retirement.*

compunction /kəmpʌŋkʃn/
NU If you do something that is wrong without **compunction**, you do it without feeling ashamed or guilty; a formal word. *I could have shot him without any compunction... They had no compunction about taking the furniture.*

computation /kɒmpjuteɪʃn/ **computations**
NUorNC **Computation** is mathematical calculation, especially using a computer. *There had been a sudden advance in the field of automatic computation... He sat*

over his adding machine making rapid computations.

compute /kəmpjuːt/ **computes, computing, computed**
VO To **compute** a quantity or number means to calculate it. *It is difficult to compute the loss in revenue.*

computer /kəmpjuːtə/ **computers**
NC A **computer** is an electronic machine which makes quick calculations and deals with large amounts of information. *Portable computers can be plugged into TV sets... The entire process is done by computer. ...computer games.*

computerize /kəmpjuːtəraɪz/ **computerizes, computerizing, computerized**; also spelt **computerise**.
VO To **computerize** a system or type of work means to arrange for it to be done by computers. *We are currently computerizing the Inland Revenue.*
◆ **computerized** ADJ *The Department of Linguistics is now fully computerized.* ◆ **computerization** /kəmpjuːtəraɪzeɪʃn/ NU *...the economic benefits of computerization.*

computing /kəmpjuːtɪŋ/
NU **Computing** is the activity of using a computer and writing programs for it. *Developments in computing should soon overcome these problems.*

comrade /kɒmreɪd/ **comrades**
1 VOCATIVE Socialists or communists sometimes call each other **comrade**, especially in meetings. *This is what I propose, comrades.*
2 NC Someone's **comrades** are their friends or companions; an old-fashioned use. *Margaret was my only link to my comrades, my friends.*

comrade in arms, comrades in arms
NC A **comrade in arms** is someone who has worked for the same cause or purpose as you and has shared the same difficulties and dangers. *They were considered comrades in arms and joint founders of the new republic.*

comradely /kɒmreɪdli/
ADJ If you do something in a **comradely** way, you are being pleasant and friendly to other people. *We had a comradely chat... The debate was conducted in a comradely and constructive spirit.*

comradeship /kɒmreɪdʃɪp/
NU **Comradeship** is friendship between a number of people who are doing the same work or who share the same difficulties or dangers. *...the close comradeship of war... There was a spirit of comradeship.*

con /kɒn/ **cons, conning, conned**
VO If someone **cons** you, they trick you into doing or believing something by saying things that are not true; an informal word. *A lot of people are conned into thinking that they can't fight back.* ► Also NC *The whole thing was a big con.* ● **Pros and cons**: see **pro**.

Con.
Con. is a written abbreviation for 'constable'; used in Britain as part of a policeman's title. *Det. Con. Tucker.*

Conakry /kɒnəkri/
Conakry is the capital of Guinea and its largest city. Population: 626,000 (1982).

concave /kɒnkeɪv/
ADJ A surface that is **concave** curves inwards in the middle. *...a strong and heavy concave seat.*

conceal /kənsiːl/ **conceals, concealing, concealed**
VO If you **conceal** something, you hide it or keep it secret. *She concealed the bottle beneath her mattress... He might be concealing a secret from me.*

concealment /kənsiːlmənt/
NU **Concealment** is the state of being hidden or the act of hiding something. *The trees offered concealment and protection. ...the concealment of truth.*

concede /kənsiːd/ **concedes, conceding, conceded**
V-REPORTorVO If you **concede** that something is the case, you admit or accept that it is true. *The company conceded that an error had been made... The government was forced to concede defeat.*

conceit /kənsiːt/
NU **Conceit** is very great pride in your abilities or achievements; used showing disapproval. *His recent movies have shown signs of arrogance and conceit.*

conceited /kənsiːtɪd/
ADJ Someone who is **conceited** is very proud of their abilities or achievements; used showing disapproval. *His image was of a big-mouthed bully boy, opinionated and conceited. ...a conceited old fool.*

conceivable /kənsiːvəbl/
ADJ If something is **conceivable**, you can believe that it is possible. *It is conceivable that he drowned... A change of the party in power is almost conceivable at present... There is no conceivable reason why there should be any difficulty.* ◆ **conceivably** ADV SEN *It might conceivably be useful.*

conceive /kənsiːv/ **conceives, conceiving, conceived**
1 V+of or V-REPORT If you can **conceive** of something, you can imagine it or believe it. *He could never conceive of such a thing happening... I cannot conceive how a Christian who takes the gospel seriously could possibly not be political.*
2 V O A or V+of If you **conceive** something as a particular thing, you consider it to be that thing. *A politician conceives the world as a variety of conflicts... It's become fashionable to conceive of intelligence not as one attribute, but many.*
3 V O If you **conceive** a plan or idea, you think of it and work out how it can be done. *A Prices and Incomes policy was boldly conceived.*
4 V or V O When a woman **conceives**, she becomes pregnant. *The method enabled many childless women to conceive... If a woman drinks alcohol even before she conceives a baby, it can damage the unfertilized egg.*

concentrate /kɒnsntreɪt/ **concentrates, concentrating, concentrated**
1 V+on If you **concentrate** on something, you give all your attention to it. *Concentrate on your driving... The talks concentrated on the implementation of a bilateral economic agreement.*
2 V O When something is **concentrated** in one place, it is all there rather than being spread around. *Modern industry has been concentrated in a few large urban centres... The president has concentrated enormous powers in his own hands.*

concentrated /kɒnsntreɪtɪd/
1 ADJ A **concentrated** liquid has been increased in strength by having water removed from it. *...concentrated orange juice.*
2 ADJ ATTRIB A **concentrated** activity is directed with great intensity in one place or in a short space of time. *...a heavily concentrated attack. ...a week of concentrated political activity.*

concentration /kɒnsntreɪʃn/ **concentrations**
1 NU **Concentration** on something involves giving all your attention to it. *It requires considerable concentration. ...his concentration on civil rights.*
2 NC or NU A **concentration** of something is a large amount of it or large numbers of it in a small area. *...the densest concentrations of people in the Third World. ...concentration of power in the hands of a single person as head of state.*

concentration camp, concentration camps
NC A **concentration camp** is a prison for political prisoners, especially in Germany during the Second World War. *Many opponents of the regime had been put into prisons or concentration camps.*

concentric /kənsentrɪk/
ADJ ATTRIB **Concentric** circles are placed one inside the other and have the same centre. *...concentric circles of stones.*

concept /kɒnsept/ **concepts**
NC A **concept** is an idea or abstract principle. *...the concept of trade unionism... He welcomed Mr Gorbachev's support for the concept that the republics would be free to determine their own future.*

conception /kənsepʃn/ **conceptions**
1 NC or NU A **conception** is an idea or the forming of an idea in your mind. *He had a definite conception of how he wanted things arranged... The plan was very imaginative in conception.*
2 NU **Conception** is also the process in which a woman becomes pregnant. *...the nine months between conception and birth.*

conceptual /kənseptʃuəl/
ADJ ATTRIB **Conceptual** means related to ideas and concepts formed in the mind; a formal word. *Most people have little conceptual understanding of computers.*

concern /kənsɜːn/ **concerns, concerning, concerned**
1 NU or NC **Concern** is worry about a thing or situation. *...the growing public concern over Britain's poor economic performance... My concern is that many of these cases are going unnoticed... Soldiers in the vicinity of the camp were a concern.*
2 V O If something **concerns** you, it worries you. *One of the things that concerns me is the rise in vandalism.*
3 V-REFL or V-PASS+with If you **concern** yourself with something, you give attention to it because you think that it is important. *I don't want you to concern yourself with it... We are more concerned with efficiency than expansion.*
4 NC A **concern** is something that is important to you. *Full account is to be taken of all legitimate concerns... What are the concerns of ordinary people?*
5 N SING or NU Your **concern** for someone is a feeling that you want them to be happy, safe, and well. *She shows a true concern for others... I didn't doubt Mum and Dad's love and concern.*
6 V O If a situation, event, or activity **concerns** you, it affects or involves you. *These are matters which some of my colleagues think do not concern them.*
7 N SING+POSS If a situation or problem is your **concern**, it is your duty or responsibility. *Education in the 12 inner London boroughs is the concern of the ILEA... That's your concern, I'm afraid.*
8 V O or V-PASS+with If a book, discussion, or piece of information **concerns** a particular subject or is **concerned** with it, it is about that subject. *The story concerns a former girlfriend of the Duke of York... Much of the discussion concerned American servicemen missing in action in Vietnam... This chapter is concerned with changes that are likely to take place.* ● See also **concerning**.
9 NC A **concern** is also a company or business. *...the giant West German chemical concern, Hoechst.*

concerned /kənsɜːnd/
1 ADJ PRED If you are **concerned** about something, you are worried about it. *The Red Cross says it is deeply concerned about the gravity of the situation... He was concerned about the level of unemployment.*
2 ADJ after N The people **concerned** are the people who take part in something or are affected by it. *It was a perfect arrangement for all concerned.*
● **Concerned** is used in these phrases. ● You say as **far as** something is **concerned** to indicate the subject that you are talking about. *We have rather a poor record as far as regional studies are concerned.* ● You say '**as far as I'm concerned**' to indicate that you are giving your own opinion. *This is all rubbish as far as I'm concerned.*

concerning /kənsɜːnɪŋ/
PREP You use **concerning** to indicate what something is about. *He refused to answer questions concerning his private life.* ● See also **concern**.

concert /kɒnsət/ **concerts**
NC A **concert** is a performance of music. *He conducted his first concert at the age of eighteen... More than three hundred thousand people attended a fund-raising pop concert in Hong Kong.*

concerted /kənsɜːtɪd/
ADJ ATTRIB A **concerted** action is done by several people together. *Everyone makes a concerted effort to help.*

concert-goer /kɒnsətgəʊə/ **concert-goers**
NC A **concert-goer** is a person who goes to concerts regularly. *Concert-goers in Britain last year had an opportunity to hear a full range of Bulgarian music.*

concertina /kɒnsətiːnə/ **concertinas, concertinaing, concertinaed**
1 NC A **concertina** is a musical instrument consisting of two flat end pieces made of wood or other hard material, with stiff paper or cloth that folds up between them. *David the clown starts to play a concertina.*

2 v To **concertina** means to get smaller by folding up like a concertina. *In a head-on crash the front of the car concertinas to absorb the impact.*

concerto /kənt∫eətəʊ/ **concertos**
NC A **concerto** is a piece of music for a solo instrument and an orchestra. *Paul Tortelier was playing the Dvořák Cello Concerto with the Royal Philharmonic Orchestra.*

concession /kənse∫n/ **concessions**
NC A **concession** is something that you agree to let someone do or have, especially after a disagreement or as a special privilege. *The Prime Minister had been urged to make a concession by the government... They may yet be forced to make territorial concessions.*

conch /kɒnt∫/ **conches**
NC A **conch** is a shellfish with a large shell rather like a snail's. It is also used to refer to the shell. *They rang bells, blew conch shells and whistles and carried lighted candles.*

concierge /kɒnsieʒ/ **concierges**
NC A **concierge** is a person, especially in France, who looks after a block of flats and checks people entering and leaving the building. *The concierge sat in her doorway and knitted.*

conciliate /kənsɪlieɪt/ **conciliates, conciliating, conciliated**
V or VO If you **conciliate**, you try to end a disagreement with someone; a formal word. *She has been learning to conciliate and make compromises... His government tried at first to conciliate the opposition.*

conciliation /kənsɪlieɪ∫n/
NU **Conciliation** is the process of ending a disagreement, or the fact that it has ended. *Did you make any efforts at conciliation?... Lord Caradon worked hard for conciliation between Greeks and Turks.*

conciliatory /kənsɪliətəⁿri/
ADJ When you are **conciliatory**, you are willing to end a disagreement with someone. *The authorities were taking a conciliatory approach to the strikes. He was both conciliatory and humble.*

concise /kənsaɪs/
ADJ Something that is **concise** gives all the necessary information in a very brief form. *The text was concise and to the point. ...a concise survey of English literature.* ◆ **concisely** ADV *Write clearly and concisely.*

conclave /kɒnkleɪv/ **conclaves**
NC or NU A **conclave** is a meeting at which people keep what happens secret. The meeting of cardinals held to elect a new Pope is called a conclave. *Had their conclave been overheard?... The cardinals were in secret conclave.*

conclude /kənkluːd/ **concludes, concluding, concluded**
1 V-REPORT or V+*from* If you **conclude** that something is true, you decide that it is true because of other things that you know. *Darwin concluded that men were descended from apes... What do you conclude from all that?*
2 V-QUOTE or V When you **conclude**, you say the last thing that you are going to say. *The statement concluded, 'Our military campaign remains on schedule.'... Perhaps I ought to conclude with a slightly more light-hearted question.*
3 V-ERG When you **conclude** something or when it concludes, it finishes; a formal use. *I will conclude this chapter with a quotation... Her book concludes with an account of the death of her parents.* ◆ **concluding** ADJ ATTRIB *...his concluding remark.*
4 VO If you **conclude** a treaty or business deal, you arrange or settle it finally; a formal use. *The agreement was concluded during a four-day meeting in Moscow.*

conclusion /kənkluːʒn/ **conclusions**
1 NC A **conclusion** is something that you decide is true after careful thought. *I came to the conclusion that I didn't really like civil engineering... Experts had reached the conclusion that the telegram was not authentic.*
2 N SING The **conclusion** of something is its ending. *We*

tried an experiment which had an interesting conclusion... In Peking, life is returning to normal after the conclusion of the Asian Games.
3 N SING The **conclusion** of a treaty or business deal is its final settlement. *They had no objection to the conclusion of a trade agreement between the EC and Argentina.*
● **Conclusion** is used in the following phrases. ● **In conclusion** is used to indicate that you are about to say the last thing that you want to say. *In conclusion, running can only be beneficial to the general health of the individual.* ● **foregone conclusion**: see **foregone**.

conclusive /kənkluːsɪv/
ADJ **Conclusive** evidence or facts show that something is certainly true. *Investigators said they had found conclusive evidence of an explosion... The court demanded conclusive proof that she had died of natural causes... Investigators had found nothing conclusive so far.* ◆ **conclusively** ADV *This has been difficult to prove conclusively.*

concoct /kənkɒkt/ **concocts, concocting, concocted**
1 VO If you **concoct** an excuse, explanation, or account, you invent it. *He accused the Interior Minister of concocting false evidence against police officers.*
2 VO If you **concoct** something, you make it by mixing several things together. *Nancy had concocted a red wine sauce.*

concoction /kənkɒk∫n/ **concoctions**
NC A **concoction** is something that has been made out of several things mixed together. *Chutney is a concoction of almost any fruit or vegetable you like.*

concomitant /kənkɒmɪtənt/
ADJ Something that is **concomitant** with another thing happens at the same time and is connected with it; a formal word. *...the growth of bureaucracy, with its concomitant dangers of corruption.*

concord /kɒnkɔːd/
NU **Concord** is the state of being in agreement with others; a formal word. *One day we shall all live in peace, concord and union... He said the move would help bring about a new national concord.*

concordance /kənkɔːdns/ **concordances**
1 NU **Concordance** is the state of being similar to or consistent with something else; a formal use. *There is a marvellous concordance between our two proposals... They spoke of the two countries' 'concordance of views' on European issues.* ● If something is **in concordance with** another thing, it is similar to or consistent with the other thing; used especially of ideas or actions. *This move would not be in concordance with our original plan.*
2 NC A **concordance** is an alphabetical list of the words in a book or a set of books which also says where each word can be found and often how it is used. *...a concordance of Shakespeare. ...the analysis of concordance data.*

concourse /kɒnkɔːs/ **concourses**
1 NC A **concourse** is a wide hall in a building, where people walk about or gather together. *She was standing at a coffee bar in the main airport concourse.*
2 NC A **concourse** is also a large group of people gathered together; a formal use. *...an immense concourse of bishops and priests.*

concrete /kɒnkriːt/
1 NU **Concrete** is a substance used for building made from cement, sand, small stones, and water. *What sort of amounts of concrete will you need for a job like this?*
2 ADJ Something that is **concrete** is definite or real. *Both sides say they've failed to reach any concrete agreement... There was no concrete evidence to support the allegations.*

concubine /kɒnkjubaɪn/ **concubines**
NC In former times, a **concubine** was a woman who had a sexual relationship with a man who was not married to her and who may also have had a wife. The man usually gave the woman financial support and had some authority over her. *The palace housed the emperors with their many wives and concubines.*

concur /kənkɜː/ **concurs, concurring, concurred**
V or V-REPORT When you **concur**, you agree with an

opinion or statement; a formal word. *The judge concurred with earlier findings... The Chinese concurred that this plan is not enough to guarantee a settlement.*

concurrence /kənkʌrəns/
1 N SING+SUPP **Concurrence** is agreement; a formal use. *The French President gave his instant concurrence... The child was adopted by Jo and his wife, with the concurrence of Julie.*
2 N SING A **concurrence** is also the fact of two or more things happening at the same time. *...a bizarre concurrence of events.*

concurrent /kənkʌrənt/
ADJ If two things are **concurrent**, they happen at the same time. *Both factions aim to make their own choice of chief minister at concurrent meetings tomorrow.* ♦ **concurrently** ADV *Two subjects will be studied concurrently.*

concussed /kənkʌst/
ADJ PRED If you are **concussed** by a blow to your head, you lose consciousness or feel sick or confused. *He spent the night in hospital after being badly concussed.*

concussion /kənkʌʃn/
NU If you suffer **concussion** after a blow to your head, you lose consciousness or feel sick or confused. *She was in Newcastle Infirmary with concussion.*

condemn /kəndem/ **condemns, condemning, condemned**
1 VO If you **condemn** something, you say that it is bad and unacceptable. *He condemned the report as partial and inadequate. ...a government whose methods have been widely condemned.*
2 VO+to or VO+to-INF If someone is **condemned** to a particular type of punishment, they are given that punishment. *Susan was condemned to death... The six men are condemned to hang on Friday... So you'd condemn me to be shot at dawn?*
3 VO+to or VO+to-INF If you **are condemned** to something unpleasant, you have to suffer it. *Most of the applicants are condemned to spend all morning waiting to be seen... Unless there is urgent action, the people of the region will be condemned to further suffering... Lack of education condemns them to extreme poverty.*
4 VO If a building has been **condemned**, the authorities have decided that it is not safe and must be pulled down. *Why do you think the fire department hasn't condemned the place?*

condemnation /kɒndemneɪʃn/ **condemnations**
1 NU or NC **Condemnation** is the act of saying that something or someone is very bad and unacceptable. *This blatant act of oppression calls out for universal condemnation. ...their strong condemnation of her conduct. ...the Pope's strenuous condemnations of consumerism.*
2 N SING A **condemnation** of something or someone is a fact or situation that suggests how bad they are. *It's a great condemnation of the church that it's got caught up in all this.*

condemned /kəndemd/
ADJ ATTRIB A **condemned** prisoner is going to be executed. *At five o'clock the condemned men were executed by firing squad.*

condemned cell, condemned cells
NC A **condemned cell** is a prison cell for someone who is going to be executed. *The two men were taken from their condemned cells and led to the gallows.*

condensation /kɒndenseɪʃn/
NU **Condensation** is a coating of tiny drops of water which form on a cold surface. *Check the walls for condensation.*

condense /kəndens/ **condenses, condensing, condensed**
1 VO If you **condense** a piece of writing or speech, you make it shorter, by removing the less important parts. *I tried to condense every report into as few words as possible.*
2 V-ERG When a gas or vapour **condenses** or when you **condense** it, it changes into a liquid. *Some of the gases are cooled down so that they condense into liquid... The steam is then condensed and pumped back into the boiler tubes.*

condensed milk
NU **Condensed milk** is milk that has been thickened by removing some of the water in it and that has sugar added to it.

condescend /kɒndɪsend/ **condescends, condescending, condescended**
1 V or V+to If you **condescend** to people, you behave in a way which shows them that you think you are superior to them; a formal use. *He never condescended, never spoke down to me... He condescended to other people.* ♦ **condescending** ADJ *She addressed him with the same condescending tone.*
2 V+to-INF If you **condescend** to do something, you agree to do it in a way that shows that you think you are superior. *She did not condescend to have dinner with him.*

condescension /kɒndɪsenʃn/
NU **Condescension** is the quality of being condescending. *He spoke to the labourers with no condescension.*

condiment /kɒndɪmənt/ **condiments**
NC A **condiment** is a substance such as salt, pepper, or mustard that you add to food when you eat it in order to increase the flavour.

condition /kəndɪʃn/ **conditions, conditioning, conditioned**
1 N SING+SUPP The **condition** of someone or something is the state they are in. *You can't go home in that condition... Keep your car exterior in good condition.*
2 NC+SUPP You can refer to an illness or other medical problem as a particular **condition**. *He has a heart condition.*
3 N PL+SUPP The **conditions** in which people live or do things are the qualities or factors that affect their comfort, safety, or success. *...adverse weather conditions. ...appalling living conditions.*
4 NC A **condition** is something which must happen in order for something else to be possible. *They will not agree to the talks if this condition is maintained... You have to live there as a condition of your job.*
5 VO If someone is **conditioned** to think or do something in a particular way, they do it as a result of their upbringing or training. *Men had been conditioned to regard women as their inferiors... We have conditioned our minds to accept the fact that we might never see our loved ones again.* ♦ **conditioning** NU *It is very difficult to overcome your early conditioning.*
● **Condition** is used in these phrases. ● When you agree to do something **on condition that** something else happens, you mean that you will only do it if this other thing happens or is agreed to first. *He has agreed to come on condition that there won't be any publicity.*
● If someone is **out of condition**, they are unhealthy and unfit. *He admitted that Tyson was out of condition and not ready for the fight.*

conditional /kəndɪʃənl/ **conditionals**
1 ADJ If a situation or agreement is **conditional** on something, it will only happen if this thing happens. *Their support is conditional upon further reduction in public expenditure.* ♦ **conditionally** ADV *...the agreement of the Labour Party leader, Mr Shimon Peres, to accept conditionally the post of Finance Minister... She said yes, conditionally.*
2 ADJ ATTRIB In grammar, a **conditional** clause is used to talk about a possible or imaginary situation and its consequences. *In the sentence 'They would be rich if they had taken my advice', 'if they had taken my advice' is a conditional clause.*

conditioner /kəndɪʃənə/ **conditioners**
1 N MASS **Conditioner** is a substance which you can put on your hair after washing it in order to make it softer.
2 N MASS **Conditioner** is also a thick liquid which you can use when you wash clothes in order to make them feel softer.

condo /kɒndəʊ/ **condos**
NC A **condo** is the same as a **condominium**; used in informal American English. *They will be able to settle down in a little condo in the East 60s... He opposed a plan to build high-rise condo towers along Lake Champlain.*

condolence /kəndˈəʊləns/ **condolences**
N U or N PL **Condolence** is sympathy that you express for someone whose friend or relative has died. *...letters of condolence... She wished to offer her condolences.*

condom /ˈkɒndəm, ˈkɒndɒm/ **condoms**
N C A **condom** is a rubber covering which a man can wear on his penis during sexual intercourse. Condoms are worn as a contraceptive and as a protection against catching or spreading diseases such as AIDS. *...education about safe sexual practices and use of condoms.*

condominium /kɒndəˈmɪniəm/ **condominiums**
N C A **condominium** is a block of flats in which each flat is owned by the person who lives there. It is also used to refer to one of the flats; used in American English. *Federal authorities say they want the squatters out of the condominium so its 980 apartments can be sold to wealthier Brazilians.*

condone /kənˈdəʊn/ **condones, condoning, condoned**
V O If someone **condones** behaviour that is morally wrong, they accept it and allow it to happen. *We cannot condone the daily massacre of innocent people... You sound as though you condone the terrorists.*

condor /ˈkɒndɔː/ **condors**
N C A **condor** is a large South American bird that eats the meat of dead animals. *...in 1987, when the last wild condor was captured.*

conducive /kənˈdjuːsɪv/
ADJ PRED+to If one thing is **conducive** to another, it makes the other thing likely to happen. *Competition is not conducive to human happiness... We aim to create a business climate conducive to foreign and domestic investment.*

conduct, conducts, conducting, conducted;
pronounced /kənˈdʌkt/ when it is a verb and /ˈkɒndʌkt/ when it is a noun.
1 V O When you **conduct** an activity or task, you organize it and do it. *So far the negotiations have been conducted in separate meetings... We have been conducting a survey of the region.* ▶ Also N U *Secrets are essential to the conduct of a war.*
2 V-REFL The way you **conduct** yourself is the way you behave; a formal use. *He instructed them in how to conduct themselves inside the mosque.* ▶ Also N U *The minister had several good reasons for his conduct.*
3 V O or V When someone **conducts** an orchestra or choir, they stand in front of it and direct its performance. *Giuseppe Sinopoli conducts the Philharmonia Orchestra... I remember when I first conducted in London.*
4 V O If something **conducts** heat or electricity, it allows heat or electricity to pass through it. *Superconductors are materials that conduct electricity with total efficiency.*

conducted tour, conducted tours
N C A **conducted tour** is a visit around a building, town, or area during which someone goes with you and explains everything to you. *Moumouni took me on a conducted tour of his fields.*

conduction /kənˈdʌkʃn/
N U **Conduction** is the process by which heat or electricity passes through or along something; a technical term. *...the conduction of electricity through gases.*

conductor /kənˈdʌktə/ **conductors**
1 N C The **conductor** of an orchestra or choir is the person who conducts it. *...Pierre Boulez, the internationally renowned composer and conductor of modern music.*
2 N C A **conductor** is a substance that heat or electricity can pass through or along. *Aluminium is a good conductor of heat.*
3 See also **bus conductor**.

conductress /kənˈdʌktrəs/ **conductresses**
N C A **conductress** is a woman who sells tickets on buses. *...not even a waitress or a bus conductress wants to marry a soldier today.*

conduit /ˈkɒndjʊɪt, ˈkɒndɪt/ **conduits**
1 N C A **conduit** is a route which is used by governments or organisations to send things such as drugs or arms to other countries, or to illegal

organisations. *Pakistan is known to be an important conduit for arms supplies to the guerrillas.*
2 N C A **conduit** is also a small tunnel, pipe, or channel through which water or electrical wires go. *...the tubes, the pipes and so forth that are used in buildings for electrical conduits and for water supply.*

cone /kəʊn/ **cones**
1 N C A **cone** is a three-dimensional shape similar to a pyramid but with a circular base. *...build a big cone of wood over it.*
2 N C The **cones** of a pine or fir tree are its fruit. They consist of a cluster of woody scales containing seeds.

confection /kənˈfekʃn/ **confections**; an old-fashioned word.
1 N C A **confection** is an elaborately decorated cake or some other sweet food. *Cake-shops occasionally offer confections covered in blue icing.*
2 N C A **confection** is also something such as a piece of clothing that is elaborately made. *Her hat was a charming confection of net and feathers.*

confectioner /kənˈfekʃənə/ **confectioners**
N C A **confectioner** is a person or a company that makes and sells sweets and chocolates. *...a bitter struggle for the ownership of the leading British confectioner.*

confectionery /kənˈfekʃənəri/
N U You can refer to sweets and chocolates as **confectionery**. *...the company that makes some of Europe's best-known confectionery.*

confederacy /kənˈfedərəsi/ **confederacies**
N C A **confederacy** is a union of states or people who are trying to achieve the same thing. *They may have buried their differences and formed a confederacy.*

confederate /kənˈfedərət/ **confederates**
1 ADJ ATTRIB **Confederate** means belonging or related to a confederacy. *...the confederate constitution proposed by Croatia and Slovenia.*
2 N C Someone's **confederates** are the people they are working with in a secret activity. *The confederates had put land mines on the road.*

confederation /kənˌfedəˈreɪʃn/ **confederations**
N C A **confederation** is an organization of groups for political or business purposes. *We are in favour of a loose confederation of states.*

confer /kənˈfɜː/ **confers, conferring, conferred**
1 V-RECIP When you **confer** with someone, you discuss something with them in order to make a decision. *The jury conferred for only twelve minutes... The Secretary of State came here to Brussels to confer with the President.*
2 V O To **confer** something such as an honour, a gift, or an advantage on someone means to give it to them; a formal use. *Mr Mitterrand conferred the Legion of Honour on seven war veterans... The system had conferred great benefits.*

conference /ˈkɒnfərəns/ **conferences**
1 N C A **conference** is a meeting, often lasting several days, where people discuss a particular subject or a shared interest. *This theory was much discussed at a conference on heart disease... The Young Conservatives begin their annual conference at Eastbourne later today... The Managing Director has daily conferences with the other staff members.*
2 If someone is **in conference**, they are having a formal meeting. *They were in conference to examine the conflict in Mozambique.*
3 See also **press conference**.

confess /kənˈfes/ **confesses, confessing, confessed**
1 V-REPORT, V-QUOTE, V O, or V+to If you **confess** that you have done something that you are ashamed of, you admit it. *He confessed that his mother still makes his bed... 'We have not mastered it yet,' he confessed... Perhaps I shouldn't confess this, but I did on one occasion forge Tony's signature... I confess to a certain weakness for puddings.*
2 V+to, V-REPORT, V O, or V If you **confess** to a crime, you admit that you have committed it. *Bianchi had confessed to five of the murders... Hammadi has confessed that he and an accomplice hijacked a TWA airliner to Beirut in 1985... All had confessed their guilt... She was maltreated by her interrogators in order to make her confess.*

confessed /kənfɛst/
ADJ ATTRIB You use **confessed** to describe someone who openly admits that they have a particular fault or weakness. *He was self-indulgent and cynical, a confessed failure.*

confession /kənfɛʃn/ **confessions**
1 NC If you make a **confession**, you admit that you have committed a crime or done something wrong. *...a man's confession to the murder of a teenage boy... He said that his confession had been extracted by torture.*
2 NU **Confession** is also a religious act in which you tell a priest about your sins and ask for forgiveness. *He had gone to confession.*

confessional /kənfɛʃəºnəl/ **confessionals**
1 NC A **confessional** is the small room or area in a church where Christians, especially Roman Catholics, go to confess their sins. *...the secrets of the confessional. ...the confessional box.*
2 ADJ ATTRIB A **confessional** speech or letter is one in which you confess something. *His name was mentioned in a confessional statement.*

confessor /kənfɛsə/ **confessors**
NC A **confessor** is a priest who hears a person's confession.

confetti /kənfɛti/
NU **Confetti** consists of small pieces of coloured paper thrown over the bride and bridegroom at a wedding or over people during a celebration or a procession. *The vehicle was showered with tons of confetti from the skyscrapers around.*

confidant /kɒnfɪdænt, kɒnfɪdænt/ **confidants**; spelt **confidante** when referring to a woman.
NC Someone's **confidant** or **confidante** is a person who they discuss their private problems with; an old-fashioned word. *He is a close confidant of his country's leader.*

confide /kənfaɪd/ **confides, confiding, confided**
VO, V-REPORT, or V-QUOTE If you **confide** a secret to someone, you tell it to them. *I never confided my fear to anyone... He had confided to me that he wasn't an Irishman at all... She confided that the subjects did not interest her much... 'I feel sorry for Stein,' Max confided.*
confide in PHRASAL VERB If you **confide in** someone, you tell them about a private problem or some other secret matter. *While in prison Martin confided in me that he intended to escape.*

confidence /kɒnfɪdəns/ **confidences**
1 NU If you have **confidence** in someone or something, you feel you can trust them to do what they are supposed to do. *The voters have confidence in both Mr Barre and President Mitterrand... I have tremendous confidence in British industry... They had no confidence in the computer system.*
2 NU If you have **confidence**, you feel sure about your abilities, qualities, or ideas. *I was full of confidence... Working in a group gives you a bit more confidence.*
● See also **self-confidence**.
3 NU **Confidence** is also a situation in which you tell someone a secret that they should not tell to anyone else. *I'm telling you this in the strictest confidence.*
● If you **take** someone **into** your **confidence**, you tell them a secret. *Take her into your confidence as much as possible.*
4 NC A **confidence** is a secret that you tell someone. *Edith was used to receiving confidences.*
5 See also **vote of confidence**.

confidence trick, confidence tricks
NC A **confidence trick** is the same as a **con**; a formal expression. *One officer said this had all the hallmarks of a massive confidence trick.*

confident /kɒnfɪdənt/
1 ADJ If you are **confident** about something, you are certain that it will happen in the way you want it to. *I thought George Bush looked very calm and very confident... He said he was confident that the scheme would be successful.* ◆ **confidently** ADV *One could confidently rely on him.*
2 ADJ People who are **confident** feel sure of their own abilities, qualities, or ideas. *...a witty, young and confident lawyer.* ◆ **confidently** ADV *I strode*

confidently up the hall. ● See also **self-confident**.

confidential /kɒnfɪdɛnʃl/
1 ADJ Information that is **confidential** is meant to be kept secret. *There is evidence that some of the company's employees had stolen confidential documents... This arrangement is to be kept strictly confidential.* ◆ **confidentially** ADV *I wrote to you confidentially on 30th September 1987.*
2 ADJ If you talk to someone in a **confidential** way, you talk to them quietly because what you are saying is secret. *He became very confidential.* ◆ **confidentially** ADV *She leaned forward and whispered to him confidentially.*

confidentiality /kɒnfɪdɛnʃiælətɪ/
1 NU **Confidentiality** is the state or condition of being secret or private. *Please respect the confidentiality of this information.*
2 NU **Confidentiality** is also the ability to keep information secret or private when this is necessary. *Your discretion and confidentiality are being questioned.*

confiding /kənfaɪdɪŋ/
ADJ Someone who is **confiding** is willing to talk to you about personal matters. *At first she was suspicious, then she became confiding.* ◆ **confidingly** ADV *Frau Döring leaned forward confidingly.*

configuration /kənfɪgəreɪʃn/ **configurations**
NC A **configuration** is an arrangement of a group of things; a formal word. *...a new political configuration... Every species of animal has a unique configuration of DNA.*

confine, confines, confining, confined; the verb is pronounced /kənfaɪn/, and the plural noun is pronounced /kɒnfaɪnz/.
1 VOA If something is **confined** to only one place, situation, or person, it only exists there or only affects that person. *The problem appears to be confined to the tropics... The festivities will be confined to the ethnic Romanian population.*
2 V-REFL A or VOA If you **confine** yourself to something, you do only that thing. *They confine themselves to discussing the weather... Confine your messages to official business.*
3 VOA To **confine** someone means to keep them in a place which they cannot leave. *William was confined to an institution for some years... The remaining sixty percent would be confined to encampments supervised by the United Nations.*
4 VOA To **confine** something to a particular place or area means to stop it from spreading beyond that place or area. *It is very difficult to confine the disease to the farm where it has broken out.*
5 N PL The **confines** of an area are its boundaries; a formal use. *They have wider interests beyond the confines of their own country.*

confined /kənfaɪnd/
ADJ A **confined** space is small and enclosed by walls. *I hate being in a confined space.*

confinement /kənfaɪnmənt/
NU **Confinement** is the state of being forced to stay in a prison or another place which you cannot leave. *He's in poor health after a long confinement in the Western province of Qinghai.* ● See also **solitary confinement**.

confirm /kənfɜːm/ **confirms, confirming, confirmed**
1 VO or V-REPORT If something **confirms** what you believe, it shows that it is definitely true. *The survey confirms expectations of slower growth in the economy... My suspicions were confirmed... The report confirms that he was never involved in criminal activities.* ◆ **confirmation** /kɒnfəmeɪʃn/ **confirmations**
NU or NC *There was no immediate confirmation of the report... This discovery was a confirmation of Darwin's proposition.*
2 VO or V-REPORT If you **confirm** something, you say that it is true. *The Iranians have partially confirmed the Iraqi account... He is only confirming what observers already suspected... She asked me if it was my car and I confirmed that it was.* ◆ **confirmation**
NU *She turned to Jimmie for confirmation and he nodded.*
3 VO or V-REPORT If you **confirm** an arrangement or

appointment, you say that it is definite. *The Foreign Ministry in Ankara confirmed the June visit. ...a letter confirming that they expect you on the twelfth.*
◆ **confirmation** NUorNC *All times are approximate and subject to confirmation... Have we received the confirmation for this booking yet?*
4 VO When someone **is confirmed**, they are formally accepted as a member of a Christian church. *They were confirmed in Westminster Abbey.* ◆ **confirmation** NU *I went to my sister's confirmation last week.*

confirmed /kənfɜːmd/
ADJ ATTRIB You use **confirmed** to describe someone who has a particular habit or belief that they are unlikely to change. *I am a confirmed non-smoker.*

confiscate /kɒnfɪskeɪt/ **confiscates, confiscating, confiscated**
VO If you **confiscate** something from someone, you take it away from them, often as a punishment. *We had instructions to confiscate all their cameras... Some of their video material was confiscated.* ◆ **confiscation** /kɒnfɪskeɪʃn/ **confiscations** NC *I faced two years' jail plus the confiscation of the tapes. ...demonstrating against land confiscations.*

conflagration /kɒnfləɡreɪʃn/ **conflagrations**
1 NC A **conflagration** is a sudden outburst of violence involving a large number of people. *He warned that the crisis could burst into a tremendous conflagration.*
2 NC A **conflagration** is a large fire; an old-fashioned use. *...the conflagration that consumed 53 houses.*

conflate /kənfleɪt/ **conflates, conflating, conflated**
VO If you **conflate** two or more accounts, ideas, or pieces of writing, you combine them in order to produce a single one; a formal word. *Four of Shakespeare's history plays were conflated by John Barton.*

conflict, conflicts, conflicting, conflicted; pronounced /kɒnflɪkt/ when it is a noun and /kənflɪkt/ when it is a verb.
1 NUorNC **Conflict** is disagreement and argument. *...the familiar conflict between government and opposition. ...a number of conflicts in the engineering industry.*
2 NCorNU A **conflict** is a war or battle. *A conventional conflict might escalate to a nuclear confrontation... Europe was encircled by conflict.*
3 V-RECIP If ideas, interests, or accounts **conflict**, they are very different from each other and it seems impossible for them to exist together or for both to be true. *These criteria might undoubtedly conflict... There is some research that conflicts with this view.*
◆ **conflicting** /kənflɪktɪŋ/ ADJ *The evidence seems to be conflicting.*

confluence /kɒnfluəns/ **confluences**
1 NC The **confluence** of two rivers is the place where they join and become one larger river. *...the confluence of the rivers Darwen and Ribble.*
2 N SING A **confluence** is the point at which two or more things join together; a formal use. *...a confluence of social, economic, and intellectual change... I stared out at the grey confluence of sky and sea.*

conform /kənfɔːm/ **conforms, conforming, conformed**
1 V If you **conform**, you behave in the way that you are expected to behave. *School uniform encourages children to conform... He just refused to conform, and did things his own way, no matter what.*
2 V+to or with If something **conforms to** a law or someone's wishes, it is what is required or wanted. *Such a change would not conform to the wishes of the people... These activities do not conform with diplomatic rules and regulations.*

conformist /kənfɔːmɪst/ **conformists**
NC A **conformist** is someone who behaves like everyone else rather than doing original things. *Many members have tended to be conformists, anxious to please rather than to take initiatives.* ▶ Also ADJ *The school had grown more conformist and cautious.*

conformity /kənfɔːmɪti/
NU **Conformity** is behaviour, thought, or appearance that is the same as that of most other people. *All that seems to be required of us is conformity.*

confound /kənfaʊnd/ **confounds, confounding, confounded**
1 VO If someone **confounds** their critics, or **confounds** their critics' opinions, they succeed in doing something that other people thought they would fail in. *The Socialists managed to confound their critics by holding on to their share of the vote... His victory confounded the predictions of many political observers.*
2 VO If someone **confounds** their opponents, they succeed in doing something that other people had tried to stop them doing. *The Japanese have confounded every attempt to bring a complete halt to commercial whaling.*
3 VO If something **confounds** you, it makes you confused or surprised. *There are several reasons why trade confounded the experts in 1988.*

confounded /kənfaʊndɪd/
ADJ ATTRIB **Confounded** is used to express your annoyance or irritation with something or someone. *She is a confounded nuisance. ...those confounded breakfast cereal packets.*

confront /kənfrʌnt/ **confronts, confronting, confronted**
1 VO If you **are confronted** with a problem or task, you have to deal with it. *The EC will probably be confronted with a major dilemma in The Hague... The Sunday Times examines the domestic problems confronting President Gorbachev.*
2 VO If you **confront** an enemy, you meet them face to face. *The security forces confronted a group of armed terrorists.*
3 VO+with If you **confront** someone with facts or evidence, you present it to them in order to accuse them of something. *I decided to confront her with the charges of racism.*

confrontation /kɒnfrʌnteɪʃn/ **confrontations**
1 NCorNU A **confrontation** is a fight, battle, or war. *A Palestinian youth was shot during a confrontation with Israeli troops... They say they want to stabilise the country, and prevent confrontation and violence.*
2 NCorNU A **confrontation** is also a serious dispute between two groups of people who have opposing ideas or policies. *The government is facing a confrontation with school and university students... He hoped the agreement would end an era of confrontation.*

confrontational /kɒnfrʌnteɪʃənəl/
ADJ If the behaviour of a person or group of people is **confrontational**, they often provoke or get involved in disputes, fights, or battles. *He criticised Mr Suwar for his confrontational approach to ethnic problems... The French position on the crisis is less confrontational than the British stance... He resigned in protest at the confrontational politics of his chief minister.*

confuse /kənfjuːz/ **confuses, confusing, confused**
1 VO If you **confuse** two things, you get them mixed up, so that you think one is the other. *You must be confusing me with someone else... Children confuse fantasy with fact.*
2 VO To **confuse** someone means to make it difficult for them to know what to do. *You're trying to confuse me... This could be an elaborate ruse to confuse the enemy.*
3 VO To **confuse** a situation means to make it more complicated or difficult to understand. *This latest incident merely confuses the situation... To confuse matters further, her sister is married to her husband's uncle.*

confused /kənfjuːzd/
1 ADJ Something that is **confused** does not have any order or pattern and is difficult to understand. *My thoughts were confused... Reports from the area are confused.*
2 ADJ If you are **confused**, you do not understand what is happening or you do not know what to do. *She was bewildered and confused... Many young people are confused about the causes of cancer.*

confusing /kənfjuːzɪŋ/
ADJ Something that is **confusing** makes it difficult for people to know exactly what is happening or what is meant. *The evidence is confusing... The Government has described the agreement as confusing and ambiguous.*

confusion /kənfjuːʒn/ **confusions**
1 NU **Confusion** is making a mistake about a person or thing and thinking that they are another person or thing. *There is danger of confusion between them.*
2 NU **Confusion** is also a situation where it is not clear what is happening. *In all the confusion, both men managed to grab me.*
3 NU If your mind is in a state of **confusion**, you do not know what to believe or what you should do. *Her answers to his questions have only added to his confusion.*

congeal /kəndʒiːl/ **congeals, congealing, congealed**
v When a liquid **congeals**, it becomes very thick and sticky and almost solid. *The blood had already congealed in the cold.* ♦ **congealed** ADJ *The room smelled of congealed fat.*

congenial /kəndʒiːniəl/
ADJ Someone or something that is **congenial** is pleasant; a formal word. *He chose to live in Italy, where he found the atmosphere more congenial.*

congenital /kəndʒenɪtl/
ADJ A **congenital** illness is one that a person has had from birth, but is not inherited; a medical term. *The brain damage was congenital.*

congested /kəndʒestɪd/
ADJ A road or area that is **congested** is very crowded. *Britain's motorways are said to be the most congested in Europe.*

congestion /kəndʒestʃən/
NU If there is **congestion** in a place, the place is very crowded. *The Transport Minister intends to introduce new measures to ease traffic congestion.*

conglomerate /kənglɒmərət/ **conglomerates**
NC A **conglomerate** is a large business consisting of several different companies. *...the British food and drinks conglomerate, Cadbury-Schweppes.*

conglomeration /kənglɒməreɪʃn/ **conglomerations**
NC+SUPP A **conglomeration** is a group of many, often different things. *...a conglomeration of white buildings.*

Congo /kɒŋgəu/
The **People's Republic of the Congo** is a country in central Africa. It was part of French Equatorial Africa from the 19th century and became independent in 1960. In 1970 the Congolese Party of Labour (PCT) became the sole legal party. General Denis Sassou-Nguesso became President in 1979 but most of his powers were stripped in 1991. Political parties were legalized in 1990, and André Milongo became Prime Minister in 1991. Congo exports oil. Large foreign debts are a serious economic problem. It is a member of the Organization of African Unity. ♦ **Congolese** /kɒŋgəliːz/ N, ADJ
■ *per capita GNP:* US$930 ■ *religion:* animism, Christianity ■ *language:* French (official), Kongo, Lingala ■ *currency:* CFA franc ■ *capital:* Brazzaville ■ *population:* 2 million (1989) ■ *size:* 342,000 square kilometres.

congrats /kəngræts/
Congrats means congratulations; an informal word.

congratulate /kəngrætʃuleɪt/ **congratulates, congratulating, congratulated**
vo If you **congratulate** someone, you express pleasure for something good that has happened to them, or praise them for something they have achieved. *Friends came to congratulate the parents and to see the baby... I must congratulate you on a successful interview.* ♦ **congratulation** /kəngrætʃuleɪʃn/ NU *...lack of any official congratulation from the government. ...a letter of congratulation.*

congratulations /kəngrætʃuleɪʃnz/
1 You say '**congratulations**' to someone in order to congratulate them. *'Congratulations,' the doctor said. 'You have a son.'*
2 N PL If you offer someone your **congratulations**, you congratulate them. *The two leaders have gone to offer congratulations to Colonel Gaddafi... Chancellor Kohl telephoned Mr Bush with his congratulations.*

congratulatory /kəngrætʃuleɪtəri, kəngrætʃulətə⁰ri/
ADJ Something that is **congratulatory** expresses congratulations. *Among the congratulatory messages was a telegram from the Professor.*

congregate /kɒŋgrɪgeɪt/ **congregates, congregating, congregated**
v When people **congregate**, they gather together. *The crowds congregated around the pavilion.*

congregation /kɒŋgrɪgeɪʃn/ **congregations**
N COLL The people who attend a church service are the **congregation**. *There were only ten in the congregation.*

congress /kɒŋgres/ **congresses**
1 NC A **congress** is a large meeting held to discuss ideas and policies. *His remarks were made at the annual congress of his party. ...the second Congress of Writers and Artists.*
2 N PROP **Congress** is the elected group of politicians that is responsible for making the law in the USA. It consists of two parts: the House of Representatives and the Senate. *Such agreements have to be ratified by Congress before they can take effect... He told reporters that some members of the United States Congress were hypocritical in their approach to human rights.*

congressional /kəngreʃə⁰nəl/
ADJ ATTRIB **Congressional** means belonging to or relating to the U.S. Congress. *...a leading congressional Republican... Mr Reagan won congressional approval for his tax cuts.*

congressman /kɒŋgresmən/ **congressmen** /kɒŋgresmən/
TITLE or NC A **congressman** is a male member of the U.S. Congress, especially of the House of Representatives. *The delegation was led by Congressman Francis McCloskey... Senators and congressmen are urging caution.*

congresswoman /kɒŋgreswumən/ **congresswomen**
TITLE or NC A **congresswoman** is a female member of the U.S. Congress, especially of the House of Representatives. *...a bill sponsored by Californian Democrat Congresswoman Nancy Pelosi. ...a press conference of congresswomen.*

congruent /kɒŋgruənt/
ADJ If two things are **congruent**, there is a similarity or correspondence between them; a formal word. *The sentence was scarcely congruent with his crime.*

conical /kɒnɪkl/
ADJ A **conical** object is shaped like a cone. *...a small conical shell.*

conifer /kɒnɪfə/ **conifers**
NC A **conifer** is any type of evergreen tree that produces cones, such as a pine or a fir. *The area has been ploughed up and planted with conifers.*

coniferous /kənɪfə⁰rəs/
ADJ A forest or woodland that is **coniferous** is made up of conifers. *Much of the forest is coniferous.*

conjecture /kəndʒektʃə/
NU **Conjecture** is the formation of opinions from incomplete or doubtful information; a formal word. *The exact figure is a matter for conjecture.*

conjugal /kɒndʒugl/
ADJ ATTRIB **Conjugal** means relating to marriage and to the relationship between a husband and wife; a formal word. *...conjugal happiness... Women were in the cell on what were described as conjugal visits.*

conjunction /kəndʒʌŋkʃn/ **conjunctions**
1 NC A **conjunction** of things is a combination of them; a formal use. *The cause of suicide is a nasty conjunction of personal and social factors.* ● If a person or organization does something **in conjunction** with another person or organization, they do it together. If something is done **in conjunction with** another thing, both things are done together. *...a committee to run the ministries in conjunction with senior civil servants... This course can only be taken in conjunction with course 234.*
2 NC In grammar, a **conjunction** is a word that joins together words, groups, or clauses. In the sentences 'I was standing by the window when I heard her speak' and 'Someone may be killed or seriously injured', 'when' and 'or' are conjunctions.

conjunctivitis /kəndʒʌŋktɪvaɪtɪs/
NU **Conjunctivitis** is a painful eye disease which causes the thin skin that covers the eyeball and the eyelid to become inflamed. *There's already been a*

serious outbreak of conjunctivitis among the children.

conjure /kʌndʒə/ **conjures, conjuring, conjured**
VO A If you **conjure** something into existence, you make it appear as if by magic. *He appeared with a small bucket he'd apparently conjured from nowhere.*
conjure up PHRASAL VERB If you **conjure up** a memory, picture, or idea, you create it in your mind. *Dreams never cease to amaze us with the extraordinary images they conjure up.*

conjurer /kʌndʒərə/ **conjurers**; also spelt **conjuror.**
NC A **conjurer** is an entertainer who does magic tricks.

conjuring trick, conjuring tricks
NC A **conjuring trick** is a trick in which something is made to appear or disappear as if by magic. *He was being shown a simple conjuring trick... The US was accused of attempting a financial conjuring trick.*

conk /kɒŋk/ **conks, conking, conked**; an informal word.
NC Your **conk** is your nose.
conk out PHRASAL VERB If something such as a machine or vehicle **conks out**, it stops working or breaks down. *The washing machine has finally conked out.*

conker /kɒŋkə/ **conkers**
NC **Conkers** are round brown nuts which come from horse chestnut trees.

con man, con men
NC A **con man** is a man who persuades people to give him money or property by lying to them. *He repeatedly referred to him as a dangerous con man... They are experienced con men.*

connect /kənɛkt/ **connects, connecting, connected**
1 VO+to or VO To **connect** one thing to another means to join them together. *Connect the fishing line to the hook... The optic nerve connects the eye to the brain... A major highway connecting the north and south of the country was blocked.* ♦ **connecting** ADJ ATTRIB *The rooms had connecting doors between them.*
2 VO+with If you **connect** a person or thing with something, you realize that there is a link between them. *There is no evidence to connect Griffiths with the murder... The American public just doesn't connect the President with his own government.*
3 VO+to If a piece of equipment is **connected** to another piece of equipment, it is joined by a wire to an electricity supply to it. *The tiny microphone was connected to a tape recorder.*
4 VO If a telephone operator **connects** you, he or she enables you to speak to another person by telephone. *Telephone operators had been refusing to connect calls between the students.*
5 V+with If a train, plane, or bus **connects** with another form of transport, it arrives at a time which allows passengers to change to the other form of transport to continue their journey. *This train connects with a bus service to Worcester.*

connected /kənɛktɪd/
ADJ PRED If one thing is **connected** with another, there is a relationship or link between them. *There are serious questions connected with radioactive waste disposal... There's no suggestion from the police that the incidents are connected.*

connection /kənɛkʃn/ **connections**; also spelt **connexion.**
1 NC A **connection** is a relationship between two things. *I do not think there is any logical connection between the two halves of the question... Our correspondent says it is unlikely there is any connection between the two bombing incidents.*
2 If you talk to someone **in connection with** something, you talk to them about that thing. *The police wanted to interview him in connection with the murder.*
3 NC A **connection** is also the joint where two wires or pipes are joined together. *There must be a loose connection.*
4 NC If you get a **connection** at a station or airport, you continue your journey by catching another train, bus, or plane. *I missed my connection.*

connivance /kənaɪvns/
NU **Connivance** is a willingness to allow or assist something to happen which you know is wrong and

which you ought to prevent or report to someone. *The Prime Minister was accused of connivance in the coup attempt.*

connive /kənaɪv/ **connives, conniving, connived**
1 V+at If someone **connives** at something, they allow it to happen even though they know that it is wrong and that they ought to prevent it. *Peace should not be put at risk by the actions of others who connived at terrorism... He suggested that the government had connived at the violence.*
2 V+to-INF or V+in If you **connive** to do something, you secretly try to achieve it, or to cause it to happen because it is to your advantage. *The Party leadership connived to cover up a wave of killings. ...rumours that the regional military connived in the escape from China of fugitive dissidents and student leaders.*

connoisseur /kɒnəsɜː/ **connoisseurs**
NC A **connoisseur** is someone who knows a lot about the arts, food, or drink. *Charles was an enthusiastic connoisseur of art.*

connotation /kɒnəteɪʃn/ **connotations**
NC The **connotations** of a word are the ideas or qualities that it makes you think of. *Chatwin himself explains the title and its connotations... He noted the word socialism does not have a favorable connotation in much of the world today.*

connubial /kənjuːbɪəl/
ADJ ATTRIB **Connubial** means relating to marriage; a formal word. *We were well into our second spring of connubial delights.*

conquer /kɒŋkə/ **conquers, conquering, conquered**
1 VO If one country or group of people **conquers** another, the first group takes complete control of the other group's land. *...the white people who had conquered their land... Britain was conquered by the Romans.*
2 VO If you **conquer** something difficult or dangerous, you succeed in destroying it or getting control of it. *...a tremendous international effort to conquer cancer.*

conqueror /kɒŋkərə/ **conquerors**
NC A **conqueror** is a person who conquers a country or group of people. *...the European conquerors of Mexico.*

conquest /kɒŋkwest/ **conquests**
1 NU **Conquest** is the act of conquering a country or group of people. *The land was taken from the Aboriginals by conquest.*
2 NC A **conquest** is land that has been conquered in war. *He feels confident that he can hold on to his illegal conquest.*
3 N SING+SUPP The **conquest** of something difficult or dangerous is success in getting control of it. *...the conquest of space. ...the life and achievements of one of the last pioneers of air conquest.*

conscience /kɒnʃns/ **consciences**
1 NC Your **conscience** is the part of your mind that tells you what you should or should not do. *My conscience told me to vote against the others.* ● If you have a **guilty conscience**, you feel guilty because you have done something wrong. *He was gripped by his guilty conscience, as he saw his country and people sink into ruin and starvation.*
2 NU **Conscience** is doing what you believe is right even though it might be unpopular, difficult, or dangerous. *The exercise of conscience is an individual act... In all conscience, I couldn't make things difficult for him.*

conscience-stricken
ADJ Someone who is **conscience-stricken** feels very guilty about something wrong that they have done. *He said his people were conscience-stricken after the war and now devote themselves to world peace.*

conscientious /kɒnʃiˈenʃəs/
ADJ Someone who is **conscientious** always does their work properly. *He was a very conscientious minister.* ♦ **conscientiously** ADV *He'd been doing his job conscientiously.*

conscientious objector, conscientious objectors
NC A **conscientious objector** is a person who refuses to join the armed forces because he or she thinks that it is morally wrong to do so. *Conscientious objectors have never been popular with governments... Many of*

Poland's conscientious objectors are not so much pacifists as opposed to the new military oath.

conscious /kɒnʃəs/
1 ADJ PRED If you are **conscious** of something, you notice it or are aware of it. *She became conscious of Rudolph looking at her... I was conscious that he had changed his tactics.*
2 ADJ **Conscious** is used in expressions such as 'socially conscious' and 'politically conscious' to describe someone who believes that a particular aspect of life is important. *Hundreds of women had become politically conscious. ...environmentally conscious West Germans.*
3 ADJ ATTRIB A **conscious** action or effort is done deliberately. *He made a conscious effort to look pleased.* ♦ **consciously** ADV *She couldn't believe that Mr Foster would ever consciously torment her.*
4 ADJ PRED Someone who is **conscious** is awake rather than asleep or unconscious. *The patient was fully conscious during the operation.*
5 See also **self-conscious.**

consciousness /kɒnʃəsnəs/
1 N SING Your **consciousness** is your mind together with your thoughts, beliefs and attitudes. *Doubts were starting to enter into my consciousness. ...the awakening political consciousness of Africans.*
2 NU If you lose **consciousness**, you are unconscious rather than awake. If you have regained **consciousness**, you are awake again rather than unconscious. *A woman passenger made a successful landing after the pilot lost consciousness... He has regained consciousness after four days in a coma.*

conscript, conscripts, conscripting, conscripted; pronounced /kənskrɪpt/ when it is a verb and /kɒnskrɪpt/ when it is a noun.
1 VO If someone is **conscripted**, they are officially made to join the armed forces. *Nine countries decided to let women be conscripted.*
2 NC A **conscript** is a person who has been made to join the armed forces of a country. *Many European armies rely heavily on conscripts.*

conscription /kənskrɪpʃn/
NU **Conscription** is officially making people in a particular country join the armed forces. *The period of conscription had been extended to more than three years.*

consecrate /kɒnsɪkreɪt/ **consecrates, consecrating, consecrated**
VO When a building, place, or object is **consecrated**, it is officially declared to be holy. *King Edward consecrated the original church here in 1065.* ♦ **consecrated** ADJ *He was refused burial in consecrated ground.* ♦ **consecration** /kɒnsɪkreɪʃn/ NU *...the consecration of the church.*

consecutive /kənsekjʊtɪv/
ADJ **Consecutive** periods of time or events happen one after the other without interruption. *...two consecutive years of drought... Labour has lost three consecutive general elections.*

consensus /kənsensəs/
N SING or NU A **consensus** is general agreement amongst a group of people. *They reached a consensus in favour of economic sanctions... There was some consensus of opinion.*

consent /kənsent/ **consents, consenting, consented**
1 NU **Consent** is permission given to someone to do something. *It is against the law to test patients without their knowledge and consent.*
2 NU **Consent** is also agreement between people about something. *By common consent, he ran the White House rather well.*
3 V If you **consent** to something, you agree to do it or to allow it to be done. *The Minister consented to talks with the protesting farmers.*
4 See also **age of consent.**

consenting /kənsentɪŋ/
ADJ ATTRIB A **consenting** adult is a person who is considered to be responsible or old enough to make their own decisions about what they do, especially about who they have sex with. *It's twenty years since parliament legalised homosexual acts between consenting adults.*

consequence /kɒnsɪkwəns/ **consequences**
1 NC A **consequence** of something is a result or effect of it. *Three-hundred refugees are now without homes as a consequence of the army's action.*
2 NU Someone or something that is of **consequence** is important or valuable. Someone or something that is of little **consequence** is not important or valuable. *Mr Chowdhury is a politician of consequence... The relief planes are of little consequence for the towns of Malakal and Wau.*

consequent /kɒnsɪkwənt/
ADJ ATTRIB **Consequent** means happening as a direct result of something; a formal word. *...advances in medical care and consequent improved chances of survival for premature babies... Moves to liberalise the economy and consequent removals of subsidies have hit the poor hard.* ♦ **consequently** ADV SEN *Absolute secrecy is essential. Consequently, the fewer who are aware of the plan the better.*

consequential /kɒnsɪkwenʃl/; a formal word.
1 ADJ Something or someone that is **consequential** is important or significant. *The Europeans have really no consequential effect on the Americans. ...one of the most consequential leaders of the free world.*
2 ADJ ATTRIB **Consequential** means happening as a direct result of a particular event or situation. *...overcrowding and the consequential lack of privacy.*

conservation /kɒnsəveɪʃn/
NU **Conservation** is the preservation and protection of the environment. *One of our aims is to make people realise the importance of conservation.*

conservationist /kɒnsəveɪʃənɪst/ **conservationists**
NC A **conservationist** is someone who cares greatly about conservation. *Conservationists have won the battle to establish the area as a nature reserve.*

conservatism /kənsɜːvətɪzəm/
1 NU **Conservatism** is unwillingness to accept changes and new ideas. *Its report accuses the police of inefficiency and conservatism about new methods. ...the conservatism of older teachers.*
2 NU **Conservatism** is also the political philosophy of the Conservative Party in a country. *The Citizen's Charter is intended to become one of the hallmarks of Conservatism under John Major.*

conservative /kənsɜːvətɪv/ **conservatives**
1 NC A **Conservative** is a member or supporter of the Conservative Party. *Most of the MPs involved are right-wing Conservatives.* ▸ Also ADJ *The Conservative government recovered its popularity after the Falklands War.*
2 ADJ Someone who is **conservative** is unwilling to accept changes and new ideas. *Publishers in Britain are more conservative than their continental counterparts.* ♦ **conservatively** ADV *He dresses conservatively.*
3 ADJ A **conservative** estimate or guess is cautious. *How long will it last? Three hundred years at a fairly conservative estimate.* ♦ **conservatively** ADV *It is conservatively estimated that 500 are in jail.*

Conservative Party
N PROP The **Conservative Party** is the main right of centre party in the United Kingdom. It is committed to free enterprise, low personal taxation and the maintenance of the United Kingdom in its present form. *...the former chairman of the Conservative Party, Mr Norman Tebbit... He made a speech to Conservative Party supporters in Gloucester.*

conservatory /kənsɜːvətri/ **conservatories**
1 NC A **conservatory** is a glass room, attached to a house, in which plants are kept. *He gave her a white cyclamen from the conservatory.*
2 NC A **conservatory** is also an institution where musicians are trained. *He studied in Germany and at the Paris Conservatory.*

conserve /kənsɜːv/ **conserves, conserving, conserved**
1 VO If you **conserve** a supply of something, you use it carefully so that it lasts longer. *The government has appealed to householders to make greater efforts to conserve water.*
2 VO To **conserve** something means to protect it from harm, loss, or change. *Mr Saouma called for support for a global plan to conserve tropical forests.*

consider /kənsɪdə/ **considers, considering, considered**

1 VO+to-INF, VOC, or V-REPORT If you **consider** a person or thing to be something, this is your opinion of them. *They consider themselves to be very lucky... Some British generals considered the attack a mistake... I consider that one is enough.*
2 VO If you **consider** something, you think about it carefully. *He had no time to consider the matter... A request by Rwanda for military assistance from Belgium is being considered.*
3 VO If you **consider** a person's needs, wishes, or feelings, you pay attention to them. *The party leaders said they would consider the demands of the protestors.*
4 See also **considerate, consideration, considered, considering.**

considerable /kənsɪdəⁿrəbl/
ADJ **Considerable** means great in amount or degree. *The building suffered considerable damage... Latest opinion polls suggest considerable support for the President's policies.* ◆ **considerably** ADV *His work had improved considerably.*

considerate /kənsɪdəⁿrət/
ADJ A **considerate** person pays attention to the needs, wishes, or feelings of other people. *His family says he is a kind and considerate man, to friends and strangers alike.*

consideration /kənsɪdəreɪʃn/ **considerations**
1 NU **Consideration** is careful thought about something. *After careful consideration, her parents gave her permission.*
2 NU Someone who shows **consideration** pays attention to the needs, wishes, or feelings of other people. *He showed no consideration for his daughters.*
3 NC A **consideration** is something that should be thought about, when you are planning or deciding something. *An important consideration is the amount of time it will take.*
● **Consideration** is used in these phrases. ● If you **take** something **into consideration**, you think about it because it is relevant to what you are doing. *The first thing one has to take into consideration is the cost.*
● Something that is **under consideration** is being discussed. *The case was still under consideration.*

considered /kənsɪdəd/
ADJ ATTRIB A **considered** opinion or act is the result of careful thought. *He said that the Director General must be allowed enough time to make a considered response.*

considering /kənsɪdəⁿrɪŋ/
CONJ or PREP You use **considering** to indicate that you are taking a particular fact into account when giving an opinion. *Considering that he received no help, his results are very good... Considering her dislike of Martin, it was surprising that she invited him.*

consign /kənsaɪn/ **consigns, consigning, consigned**
VO+to If you **consign** something to a place, you put it there to get rid of it; a formal word. *I discovered some wheels that had been consigned to the loft... The Assembly has consigned the bi-partisan system to history... The Communist Party here had in effect already been consigned to the political dustbin.*

consignment /kənsaɪnmənt/ **consignments**
NC A **consignment** of goods is a load that is being delivered to a place or person. *A consignment of emergency food supplies is on its way to Liberia.*

consist /kənsɪst/ **consists, consisting, consisted**
V+of Something that **consists** of particular things is formed from them. *Their diet consisted mainly of dumplings and vegetables... The committee consists of scientists and engineers.*

consistency /kənsɪstənsi/
1 NU **Consistency** is the condition of being consistent. *Consistency and clarity were the essential features of the President's policies... Up to now these measures have not been pursued with great consistency.*
2 NU The **consistency** of a substance is its thickness, smoothness, and so on. *Small children dislike food with a sticky consistency.*

consistent /kənsɪstənt/
1 ADJ A **consistent** person always behaves or responds in the same way. *Mrs Thatcher is quite consistent in*

her attitude... Brook was Baldwin's most dangerous and consistent adversary. ◆ **consistently** ADV *Hearst consistently opposed Roosevelt's policies.*
2 ADJ If two facts or ideas are **consistent**, they do not contradict each other. *Their accounts were consistent and detailed... She said that her political policies were consistent with the teachings of the Bible.*
3 ADJ An idea or argument that is **consistent** is organized so that each part of it agrees with all the other parts. ...a set of ideas that is consistent... The idea is really to see whether this is a consistent theory.

consolation prize /kɒnsəleɪʃn praɪz/ **consolation prizes**
1 NC A **consolation prize** is a small prize which is given to a person who fails to win a competition.
2 NC A **consolation prize** is also something that is given to a person to make them feel happier when they have failed to achieve something better; often used humorously. *It would seem that these portfolios are in fact intended as consolation prizes for the sacked chief ministers.*

console, consoles, consoling, consoled; pronounced /kənsəʊl/ when it is a verb and /kɒnsəʊl/ when it is a noun.
1 VO If you **console** someone who is unhappy, you try to make them more cheerful. *She tried to console me by saying that I'd probably be happier in a new job.* ◆ **consoling** ADJ ATTRIB *Dad laid a consoling hand on his shoulder.* ◆ **consolation** /kɒnsəleɪʃn/ NU ...a few words of consolation.
2 NC A **console** is a panel with switches or knobs used to operate a machine. *This information is normally displayed on the switchboard console.*

consolidate /kənsɒlɪdeɪt/ **consolidates, consolidating, consolidated**
1 VO If you **consolidate** power or a plan, you strengthen it so that it becomes more effective or secure. *General Avril has been steadily consolidating his power since the September coup.* ◆ **consolidation** /kənsɒlɪdeɪʃn/ NU ...the long-term consolidation of party power.
2 VO To **consolidate** a number of small groups or firms means to make them into one large organization. *They consolidated the states of the north into a unified Northern region.* ◆ **consolidation** NU ...a dangerous trend toward consolidation that could destroy small businesses.

consommé /kɒnsɒmeɪ/ **consommés**
N MASS **Consommé** is a thin, clear soup, usually made from meat juices.

consonant /kɒnsənənt/ **consonants**
NC A **consonant** is a sound such as 'p', 'f', 'n', or 't' which you pronounce by stopping the air flowing freely through your mouth.

consort, consorts, consorting, consorted; pronounced /kənsɔːt/ when it is a verb and /kɒnsɔːt/ when it is a noun.
1 V+with If someone **consorts** with a particular person or group, they spend a lot of time with them; used in formal English, showing disapproval. *Daddy would never approve of her consorting with drug addicts.*
2 NC A **consort** is the wife or husband of the ruling monarch. ...Caroline of Brunswick, the eccentric and embarrassing consort of the repulsive George IV.

consortium /kənsɔːtiəm/ **consortia** /kənsɔːtiə/ or **consortiums**
N COLL A **consortium** is a group of people or firms who have agreed to work together. ...a consortium of Birmingham businessmen.

conspicuous /kənspɪkjuəs/
ADJ If something is **conspicuous**, people can see or notice it very easily. *If an insect eats a crop the damage is very conspicuous... The conspicuous police presence hasn't diminished.* ◆ **conspicuously** ADV *He had been conspicuously successful.*

conspiracy /kənspɪrəsi/ **conspiracies**
N U or NC **Conspiracy** is the secret planning by a group of people to do something illegal, often for political reasons. *Very few people knew the details of the conspiracy... The police arrested her on a charge of conspiracy to murder.*

conspirator /kənspɪrətə/ **conspirators**
NC A **conspirator** is a person who joins a conspiracy. *A Lieutenant-Colonel arrested earlier this month revealed the identity of the other conspirators.*

conspiratorial /kənspɪrətɔːriəl/
1 ADJ Something that is **conspiratorial** is secret and illegal, often with a political purpose. *A delegate has accused a close associate of Zhao of conspiratorial activities.*
2 ADJ If you are **conspiratorial**, you behave as if you are sharing a secret with someone. *He spoke in a conspiratorial whisper.*

conspire /kənspaɪə/ **conspires, conspiring, conspired**
1 V-RECIP If you **conspire**, you secretly agree with other people to do something illegal or harmful. *They'd conspired to overthrow the government... My enemies are conspiring against me... I disliked the feeling of conspiring with her father.*
2 V+to If events **conspire** to produce a particular result, they seem to cause this result; a literary use. *Everything had conspired to make him happy. Foreign debts conspired against efforts to ensure education for all.*

constable /kʌnstəbl/ **constables**
NCorTITLE A **constable** is a police officer of the lowest rank in Britain. *The constable was alone at a police station in north London when he disappeared... Constable Steven Hanson led passengers to safety.*

constabulary /kənstæbjʊləri/ **constabularies**
NC In Britain, a **constabulary** is the police force of a particular area. *...the Wiltshire Constabulary.*

constancy /kɒnstənsi/
1 NU **Constancy** is the quality of staying the same even though other things change. *...the constancy of family life... He had a constancy of will that impressed me. ...the constancy of the temperature.*
2 NU **Constancy** is also faithfulness and loyalty to a particular person or belief even when you are in difficulty or danger. *I might have known not to expect constancy from someone like you.*

constant /kɒnstənt/ **constants**
1 ADJ Something that is **constant** happens all the time or is always there. *He was in constant pain... There's going to be constant speculation about the date of the election.* ♦ **constantly** ADV *The world around us is constantly changing.*
2 ADJ An amount or level that is **constant** stays the same over a particular period of time. *...a constant voltage... We've put a constant current through this piece of aluminium.*
3 ADJ A **constant** person is always faithful to a particular person, organization, or belief.
4 NC A **constant** is a thing or a value that always stays the same, even though other things may change. *The family has been one of the constants of human existence.*

constellation /kɒnstəleɪʃn/ **constellations**
NC A **constellation** is a named group of stars. *The men spotted a new star shining brightly in the constellation of Doredus.*

consternation /kɒnstəneɪʃn/
NU **Consternation** is a feeling of anxiety or fear. *We looked at each other in consternation.*

constipated /kɒnstɪpeɪtɪd/
ADJ Someone who is **constipated** has difficulty in defecating. *Sometimes babies who are getting hungry will become constipated.*

constipation /kɒnstɪpeɪʃn/
NU **Constipation** is a medical condition which causes people to have difficulty defecating. *You should increase your roughage intake to prevent constipation.*

constituency /kənstɪtjuənsi/ **constituencies**
NC A **constituency** is an area for which someone is elected as the representative in parliament. *There were 14,000 voters in the constituency.*

constituent /kənstɪtjuənt/ **constituents**
1 NC A **constituent** is someone who lives in a particular constituency, especially someone who is eligible to vote in an election. *He is still a Member of Parliament with constituents to represent.*
2 NC+SUPP A **constituent** of something is one of the things that it is made from. *Nitrogen is one of the essential constituents of living matter.*

constitute /kɒnstɪtjuːt/ **constitutes, constituting, constituted**
1 VC If something **constitutes** a particular thing, it can be regarded as being that thing. *Conifers constitute about a third of the world's forests... Local campaigners say the factory constitutes a health risk.*
2 VO To **constitute** something also means to form it from a number of parts or elements; a formal use. *...the way in which the modern artist constitutes his images... The recently constituted board may do something to change the status quo.*

constitution /kɒnstɪtjuːʃn/ **constitutions**
1 NC The **constitution** of a country or organization is the system of laws which formally states people's rights and duties. *...the US constitution... It had been expected that the new constitution, fully guaranteeing democratic rights, would be proclaimed this week.*
2 NC Your **constitution** is your health. *He has a strong constitution.*
3 N SING The **constitution** of something is also what it is made of, and how its parts are arranged. *Questions were asked concerning the constitution and scope of the proposed commission.*

constitutional /kɒnstɪtjuːʃəⁿnəl/
ADJ **Constitutional** means relating to the constitution of a particular country or organization. *The last time the government attempted to bring in constitutional change, it was unable to get the required majority... The law was an infringement on Canadians' constitutional rights to freedom of expression.*

constitutional monarch, constitutional monarchs
NC A **constitutional monarch** has a title such as King, Queen, or Emperor, in a country which has a democratically elected government. The constitutional monarch is the head of state but does not take part in the process of government.

constitutional monarchy, constitutional monarchies
NC A **constitutional monarchy** is a country that has someone with a title such as a King, Queen, or Emperor as its head of state, but that has a democratically elected government. *Morocco is a constitutional monarchy, rich in history and tradition.*

constrain /kənstreɪn/ **constrains, constraining, constrained**
VO To **constrain** someone or something means to limit their development or force them to behave in a particular way; a formal word. *The US is unlikely to welcome ideas which would constrain its freedom of action... A painful duty constrains me.* ♦ **constrained** ADJ PRED *These restrictions could make political activity for the opposition very constrained... He felt constrained to apologize.*

constraint /kənstreɪnt/ **constraints;** a formal word.
1 NC A **constraint** is something that limits or controls the way you behave. *Benazir Bhutto still faces many constraints on her power... The Government is going to have to cut the defence budget because of financial constraints.*
2 NU **Constraint** is control over the way you behave which prevents you from doing what you want to do. *The list of instructions and guidelines brings with it a flavour of constraint.*

constrict /kənstrɪkt/ **constricts, constricting, constricted**
1 VO To **constrict** something means to squeeze it tightly. *He rubbed his ankles where the bindings had constricted him.*
2 VO If something **constricts** you, it limits your actions so that you cannot do what you want to do. *This frees him from many of the rules that constricted his predecessor. ...the constricting structure of schools.*

constriction /kənstrɪkʃn/ **constrictions**
1 NC A **constriction** is a fact or situation that limits what you can do and prevents you from doing what you want to do. *So, considering all these constrictions, what will the new leadership of Hungary do?... Eventually, unable to bear the constrictions of family life, he left home.*
2 NU **Constriction** is also the limitation of someone's actions so that they cannot do what they want to do.

The feeling of constriction was terrible.
3 N SING A **constriction** is also a feeling of tightness, especially in your chest or throat. *There was a certain constriction in his throat.*
4 NU **Constriction** is the act of tightly squeezing something. *The more advanced snakes kill, not by constriction, but by poison.*

construct, constructs, constructing, constructed; pronounced /kənstrʌkt/ when it is a verb and /kɒnstrʌkt/ when it is a noun.
1 V O If you **construct** something, you build, make, or create it. *We constructed a raft... The allies need to construct a new strategy based on mixed or balanced forces. ...a building constructed of brick.*
2 NC A **construct** is a complex idea; a formal use. *...a construct which has evolved to explain the basic forces of nature. ...theoretical constructs.*

construction /kənstrʌkʃn/ **constructions**
1 NU **Construction** is the building or creating of something. *The project involves the construction of a canal between the rivers Dnieper and Danube.*
2 NC A **construction** is an object that has been made or built. *These wigs are complicated constructions of real and false hair... Ants have produced the greatest animal constructions the world has seen.*
3 NU You use the word **construction** to talk about how things have been built. For example, if something is of simple construction, it is simply built. *The main walls of the building are of solid brick construction.*

constructive /kənstrʌktɪv/
ADJ **Constructive** advice or criticism is useful and helpful. *I did not have anything constructive to say... He admitted that even world leaders needed constructive criticism now and then.* ◆ **constructively** ADV *You must channel your anger constructively.*

construe /kənstruː/ **construes, construing, construed**
V-PASS+*as* If a situation, event, or statement is **construed** as a particular thing, it is interpreted as being that thing; a formal word. *They made a point not to do anything that might be construed as a hostile act.*

consul /kɒnsl/ **consuls**
NC A **consul** is a government official who lives in a foreign city and looks after all the people there who are from his or her own country. *The British consul, John Francis, is visiting both girls in prison today.*

consular /kɒnsjʊlə/
ADJ ATTRIB **Consular** means involving or relating to a consul or to the work of a consul. *...the British Consular authorities in Barcelona.*

consulate /kɒnsjʊlət/ **consulates**
NC A **consulate** is the place where a consul works. *Americans should check with the US Consulate in Jerusalem before going there.*

consult /kənsʌlt/ **consults, consulting, consulted**
1 V O or V+*with* If you **consult** someone, you ask them for their opinion and advice. *If your baby is losing weight, you should consult your doctor promptly... They would have to consult with their allies.*
2 V O If you **consult** a book or a map, you refer to it for information. *During the early 1920s libraries in the United States were besieged by people wanting to consult dictionaries.*

consultancy /kənsʌltənsi/ **consultancies**
NC A **consultancy** is a group of people who give professional advice on a particular subject. *...General Technology Systems Ltd, a British consultancy led by Dr. Geoffrey Pardoe.*

consultant /kənsʌltənt/ **consultants**
1 NC A **consultant** is an experienced doctor specializing in one area of medicine. *I was the first woman consultant on the staff of Charing Cross Hospital.*
2 NC A **consultant** is also a person who gives expert advice to people who need professional help. *...a firm of public relations consultants.*

consultation /kɒnsltèɪʃn/ **consultations**
1 NC A **consultation** is a meeting held to discuss something. *Heads of State on both sides have been brought into the consultation.*
2 NU **Consultation** is discussion between people, especially when advice is given. *This is a matter for*

the Prime Minister to decide in consultation with the Ministry of Defence.

consultative /kənsʌltətɪv/
ADJ ATTRIB A **consultative** committee or document is formed or written in order to give advice about something; a formal word. *He welcomed their idea of forming a consultative council to talk about a future government for the country.*

consulting room, consulting rooms
NC A **consulting room** is a room in which a doctor sees patients.

consume /kənsjuːm/ **consumes, consuming, consumed**
1 V O To **consume** an amount of fuel, energy, or time means to use it up. *The ship consumed a great deal of fuel... Whole days were consumed by exhausting discussions.*
2 V O If you **consume** something, you eat or drink it; a formal use. *They spend their evenings consuming vodka.*
3 V O If a feeling or desire **consumes** you, it affects you very strongly; a literary use. *His hatred of them consumed him.*
4 See also **consuming.**

consumer /kənsjuːmə/ **consumers**
NC A **consumer** is a person who buys goods or uses services. *...gas consumers... The consumer is entitled to products that give value for money.*

consumer goods
N PL **Consumer goods** are items other than basic food and clothes, which are not considered to be essential. *People have come to want more consumer goods, like tape-recorders, fridges and washing machines.*

consumerism /kənsjuːmərɪzəm/
1 NU **Consumerism** is the belief that a strong economy is based on a high rate of production and consumption of goods. *...the onslaught of Western-style consumerism in Eastern Europe.*
2 NU You can also use **consumerism** to refer to the consumption of goods. *Black consumerism in Britain represents a market force that has been steadily growing since the 1950s. ...the happy consumerism of a detergent commercial.*
3 NU **Consumerism** is also the protection of the rights and interests of consumers. *She has a very keen interest in consumerism.*

consuming /kənsjuːmɪŋ/
ADJ ATTRIB A **consuming** passion or interest is more important to you than anything else. *They were both still young schoolboys with a consuming interest in Rock 'n' Roll.*

consummate, consummates, consummating, consummated; pronounced /kɒnsəmeɪt/ when it is a verb and /kənsʌmət/ or /kɒnsəmət/ when it is an adjective. A formal word.
1 V O If two people **consummate** a marriage or relationship, they make it complete by having sex. *In a clearing in a forest they were able finally to consummate their love.* ◆ **consummation** /kɒnsəmeɪʃn/ NU *...the consummation of their marriage.*
2 V O To **consummate** something means to do something which makes it complete. *We need to consummate what we have so far achieved.*
◆ **consummation** NU *This expedition was the consummation of what he regarded as his life's work.*
3 ADJ ATTRIB You use **consummate** to describe someone who is extremely skilful. *He was a fighter of consummate skill... Stael and Bomberg were consummate craftsmen.*

consumption /kənsʌmpʃn/
1 NU+SUPP The **consumption** of fuel or energy is the amount of it that is used or the act of using it. *Conservationists want people to cut their consumption of electricity by a fifth... Oil prices had to be increased in the face of rising consumption.*
2 NU **Consumption** is the act of eating or drinking something; a formal use. *The water was unfit for consumption.*
3 NU **Consumption** is also the act of buying and using things. *...heavy restrictions on the sale and consumption of alcohol. ...new patterns of consumption.*

4 If something such as a piece of information, a book, or a film is **for** a particular person's or group's **consumption**, it is intended to be seen or heard by that person or group. *He believed the film should be available for public consumption.*
5 NU **Consumption** is also the same as tuberculosis; an old-fashioned use.

consumptive /kənsʌmptɪv/ **consumptives**
ADJ Someone who is **consumptive** suffers from tuberculosis; an old-fashioned word. ▶ Also NC *Watteau was a consumptive.*

contact /kɒntækt/ **contacts, contacting, contacted**
1 NU or NC **Contact** involves meeting or communicating with someone, especially regularly. *There is little contact between governors and parents... My first contact with him was about twenty-five years ago.*
2 VO If you **contact** someone, you get in touch with them, usually by telephoning or writing to them. *As soon as we find out, we'll contact you.*
3 NC A **contact** is someone you know, for example a person in an organization or profession, who helps you or gives you information. *He had contacts in America. ...business contacts.*
4 NU **Contact** also refers to the state of things touching each other. *Close physical contact is important for a baby... The main moment of greeting is when body contact is made.*
● **Contact** is used in these phrases. ● If you are **in contact** with someone, you regularly meet them or communicate with them. *I'm in contact with a number of schools.* ● When things are **in contact**, they are touching each other. *One foot must always be in contact with the ground.* ● If you **come into contact with** someone or something, you meet that person or thing in the course of your work or your other activities. *Everyone who came into contact with her liked her.* ● If one thing **comes into contact with** another, the first thing touches the second. *My hand came into contact with a small lump.* ● If you **make contact** with someone, you find out where they are and talk or write to them. *Pan-Am is trying to make contact with passengers arriving at JFK.* ● If you **lose contact** with someone, you no longer have any communication with them. *Ground control lost contact with the two probes.*

contact lens, contact lenses
NC **Contact lenses** are small lenses that you put on your eyes to help you to see better, instead of wearing glasses. *Opticians will tell you to get a pair of glasses or contact lenses.*

contagion /kənteɪdʒən/ **contagions**; a formal word.
1 NU **Contagion** is the spreading of disease, caused by someone touching another person who is already infected by the disease. *The doctor says there is no chance of contagion.*
2 NC A **contagion** is a disease that is spread through contact between people; an old-fashioned use. *Thousands fled the contagion.*
3 NU+SUPP You can also use **contagion** to refer to the spreading of bad or unacceptable ideas, attitudes, or feelings among a group of people. *Another problem is the swift contagion of uncertainty and fear... They attempted to isolate the population from ideological contagion.*

contagious /kənteɪdʒəs/
1 ADJ A **contagious** disease can be caught by contact with people or things that are infected with it. *Syphilis is a highly contagious disease.*
2 ADJ A **contagious** feeling or attitude spreads quickly among a group of people. *Quint's confidence was contagious.*

contain /kənteɪn/ **contains, containing, contained**
1 VO If something such as a box or a room **contains** particular things, those things are inside it. *...a basket containing groceries... The urban areas contain several million people.*
2 VO If something **contains** a particular substance, that substance is part of its ingredients. *...chemical compounds containing mercury.*
3 VO To **contain** something such as a feeling, problem, or activity means to control it and prevent it from increasing; a formal use. *He could hardly contain his*

eagerness to leave. ...measures to contain population growth.

container /kənteɪnə/ **containers**
1 NC A **container** is something such as a box or bottle that is used to hold, carry, or store things in. *A lot of the food is put into containers and sent abroad. ...ammunition hidden in a large plastic container.*
2 N+N **Container** ships and lorries transport goods in very large sealed metal boxes called containers. *...P&O's large fleet of container ships... A container lorry left Turkey carrying food and medical supplies.*

containment /kənteɪnmənt/
1 NU **Containment** is the action or policy of keeping another country's power or influence within acceptable limits. *The President had better start explaining how containment would work... It was a policy of containment which had led to the treaty.*
2 NU The **containment** of something dangerous or unpleasant is the act or process of keeping it within a particular area or place. *The conditions have made containment and cleaning up of the oil more difficult... There is no containment vessel to stop the release of radioactive material if an accident does occur.*

contaminant /kəntæmɪnənt/ **contaminants**
NC A **contaminant** is a substance that contaminates air, water, or food and makes them impure; a formal word. *Keep all contaminants out of your wine. ...microbes which are effective against contaminants such as DDT and dioxin.*

contaminate /kəntæmɪneɪt/ **contaminates, contaminating, contaminated**
VO When something is **contaminated** by dirt, chemicals, or radiation, it becomes polluted by them and is then impure or harmful. *Many wells have been contaminated by chemicals. ...foods that are easily contaminated with poisonous bacteria.* ♦ **contaminated** ADJ *...contaminated water.* ♦ **contamination** /kəntæmɪneɪʃn/ NU *...infections caused by the contamination of milk.*

contd.
contd. is a written abbreviation for 'continued'. It is used at the bottom of a page to indicate that a letter or story continues on another page.

Conté, Lansana /lɔːnsənə kɒnteɪ/
General Lansana Conté became President of Guinea in a coup in 1984.

contemplate /kɒntəmpleɪt/ **contemplates, contemplating, contemplated**
1 V+ING, VO, or V-REPORT If you **contemplate** doing something, you think about whether to do it or not. *Lawrence contemplated publishing the book... He is prepared to contemplate the use of force... He may contemplate whether harsh responses to the discontent can continue.*
2 VO If you **contemplate** an idea or subject, you think about it carefully for a long time. *...the worries of the people of Hong Kong as they contemplate their future.* ♦ **contemplation** /kɒntəmpleɪʃn/ NU *...religious contemplation.*
3 VO To **contemplate** something or someone means to look at them for a long time. *They contemplated each other in silence.*

contemplative /kəntɛmplətɪv/
ADJ **Contemplative** people think deeply in a serious and calm way. *Daniel Pinkwater is a contemplative type.*

contemporaneous /kəntɛmpəreɪnɪəs/
ADJ If two things are **contemporaneous**, they happen or exist during the same period of time; a formal word. *The mound of stones is probably not contemporaneous with the tomb... The theories were more or less contemporaneous.*

contemporary /kəntɛmpərəri/ **contemporaries**
1 ADJ ATTRIB **Contemporary** means happening or existing now or at the particular time you are referring to. *My studies were devoted almost entirely to contemporary literature. ...a contemporary account of the trial.*
2 NC A person's **contemporaries** are people who are approximately the same age as them, or who lived during approximately the same period of time as them. *...Darwin's contemporary, Sir James Simpson.*

contempt /kəntɛmpt/
1 NU If you have **contempt** for someone or something, you do not like or respect them at all. *The women would often look at us with contempt. ...his contempt for the truth.*
2 NU **Contempt** or **contempt of court** is the criminal offence of disobeying an instruction from a judge or a court of law; a legal use. *Private Eye has been fined for contempt over the articles... Contempt of court notices were issued for instigating hooliganism.*
3 If you **hold** someone or something **in contempt**, you feel contempt for them. *...madmen who hold the West in contempt.*

contemptible /kəntɛmptəbl/
ADJ If you feel that someone or something is **contemptible**, you feel a very strong dislike and disrespect for them. *Her attitude is contemptible... Gandhi described all terrorism and violence as contemptible... The Guardian newspaper accuses the Sun of contemptible hypocrisy.*

contemptuous /kəntɛmptjuəs/
ADJ If you are **contemptuous** of someone or something, you do not like or respect them at all. *Mr Barre is contemptuous of party politics... Hamilton gave me a contemptuous look.* ◆ **contemptuously** ADV *He tossed the paper contemptuously on to the table.*

contend /kəntɛnd/ **contends, contending, contended**
1 V+*with* If you have to **contend** with a problem or difficulty, you have to deal with it or overcome it. *The girls had problems of their own at home to contend with.*
2 V-RECIP To **contend** with someone for something such as power means to compete with them in order to get it. *Three parties are contending for power... He did not have the high profile of other ministers contending for the job.* ◆ **contending** ADJ ATTRIB *Those decisions were fought out between contending groups.*
3 V-REPORT or V-QUOTE If you **contend** that something is true, you state or argue that it is true; a formal use. *She contended that the report was deficient... 'At present,' he contends, 'there is no really effective international collaboration.'*

contender /kəntɛndə/ **contenders**
NC A **contender** in a competition is someone who takes part in it, usually someone who has a chance of winning. *...a contender in the Presidential election.*

content, contents, contenting, contented; pronounced /kɒntent/ for the meanings in paragraphs 1 to 5 and /kəntɛnt/ for the meanings in paragraphs 6 to 9.
1 N PL The **contents** of a container such as a bottle, box, or room are the things inside it. *He drank the contents of his glass in one gulp. ...the contents of the bag.*
2 N PL The **contents** of something such as a document or a tape are the things written or recorded on it. *He knew by heart the contents of the note... Peter Smith has more details of the report's contents.*
3 N PL The list of **contents** in a book is the list at the beginning which gives the title of every section and its page reference.
4 NU The **content** of a piece of writing, speech, or television programme is its subject matter and the ideas expressed in it. *I was disturbed by the content of some of the speeches. ...an agreement to regulate the content of broadcasts, especially by satellite.*
5 N SING+SUPP You can use **content** to refer to the amount or proportion of something that a substance contains. *No other food has such a high iron content.*
6 ADJ PRED If you are **content**, you are happy and satisfied. *However hard up they were, they stayed content.*
7 ADJ PRED If you are **content** with something or you are **content** to do something, you are willing to accept it or do it. *A few teachers were content to pay the fines... Children are not content with glib explanations.*
8 V-REFL+*with* If you **content** yourself with something, you accept it and do not try to do or have other things. *She didn't take part in the discussion, but contented herself with smoking cigarettes.*
9 **to your heart's content:** see heart.

contented /kəntɛntɪd/
ADJ If you are **contented**, you are happy and satisfied.

We are very contented here. ...firms with a loyal and contented labour force. ◆ **contentedly** ADV *She plays contentedly by herself.*

contention /kəntɛnʃn/ **contentions;** a formal word.
1 NC Someone's **contention** is the idea or opinion that they are expressing. *My contention is that we must offer all our children the same opportunities.*
2 NU **Contention** is disagreement or argument about something. *This is an issue of great contention at the moment.*
3 If you are **in contention** in a contest, you have a chance of winning it. *Beth Daniel is back in contention for the women's world championship.*
4 see also **bone of contention**.

contentious /kəntɛnʃəs/
ADJ A **contentious** subject or opinion causes disagreement and arguments. *...his contentious view that mental illness is a myth.*

contentment /kəntɛntmənt/
NU **Contentment** is a feeling of quiet happiness and satisfaction. *I sighed with contentment.*

contest, contests, contesting, contested; pronounced /kɒntest/ when it is a noun and /kəntɛst/ when it is a verb.
1 NC A **contest** is a competition or game in which people try to do better than others in order to win a prize. *We entered a fishing contest. ..the Eurovision Song Contest.*
2 NC A **contest** is also a struggle to win power or control. *He won the contest for the deputy leadership.*
3 VO To **contest** an election or competition means to take part in it in order to win. *There was an election contested by six candidates.*
4 VO If you **contest** something such as a statement or decision, you disagree with it and make a formal objection. *We hotly contest the idea that any of them were ours... The diagnoses were strongly contested by many parents.*

contestant /kəntɛstənt/ **contestants**
NC The **contestants** in an event such as a competition, election, or quiz, etc are the people taking part in it. *...the contestants in the world championship... A number of candidates filed objections against their fellow contestants.*

context /kɒntɛkst/ **contexts**
1 NC or NU The **context** of an idea or event is the general situation that relates to it and which helps it to be understood. *We need to place present events in some kind of historical context... The journal placed its comments in the context of constitutional reform.*
2 NC or NU The **context** of a word or sentence consists of the words or sentences before it and after it which help make its meaning clear. *Try and guess what it means from the context... Context is so important when you are translating.*
3 If something is seen **in context** or if it is put **into context**, it is considered with all the factors that relate to it. *The Libyan leaders actions must first be put in context.*
4 If a statement or remark is taken or quoted **out of context**, the circumstances in which it was said are not correctly reported so the statement or remark is misleading. *The Defence Minister's comments had been taken out of context and misconstrued.*

contextual /kəntɛkstjuəl/
ADJ Something that is **contextual** relates to a particular context.

contiguous /kəntɪgjuəs/
ADJ Things that are **contiguous** are next to each other or touch each other; a formal word. *There may be as many as seven houses contiguous with the property. ...large contiguous areas of the globe.*

continent /kɒntɪnənt/ **continents**
1 NC A **continent** is one of the world's seven large land masses, such as Africa or Asia. *...the North American continent.*
2 N PROP In Britain, the mainland of Europe is sometimes referred to as the **Continent**. *British artists are very well known on the Continent.*

continental /kɒntɪnɛntl/ **continentals**
1 ADJ ATTRIB **Continental** is used to refer to something that belongs to or relates to a continent. *Birds and*

reptiles from continental South America had reached the Galapagos. ...the continental shelf.
2 ADJ ATTRIB In Britain, **continental** is used to refer to things situated on or relating to the mainland of Europe, especially central and southern Europe. ...scientific co-operation between Britain and continental Europe. ...our continental neighbours.
3 NC In Britain, people sometimes refer to people who come from the mainland of Europe, especially from central or southern Europe, as **continentals**; an informal use. The British are deeper in debt than the continentals.
4 ADJ In the United States, **continental** is used to refer to things situated in or relating to the mainland of North America. They expect three flu viruses to affect the continental United States this winter.

continental breakfast, **continental breakfasts**
NCorNU A **continental breakfast** is a light breakfast that usually consists of bread or a sweet roll and a hot drink. More Britons have now taken to a continental breakfast.

contingency /kəntɪndʒənsi/ **contingencies**
NC A **contingency** is an event or situation that might happen in the future. He had anticipated all contingencies. ...contingency plans for nuclear attack.

contingent /kəntɪndʒənt/ **contingents**; a formal word.
1 NC A **contingent** is a group of people representing a country or organization. ...a contingent of European scientists.
2 NC+SUPP A **contingent** of police or soldiers is a group of them. Police contingents were ordered into the area.
3 ADJ PRED+on If an event is **contingent** on something, it can only happen if that thing happens or exists. Troop withdrawal was contingent on agreement being reached in Geneva.

continual /kəntɪnjuəl/
ADJ ATTRIB **Continual** means happening without stopping, or happening repeatedly. ...a continual movement of air... He ignored the continual warnings of his nurse. ◆ **continually** ADV Tom was continually asking me questions.

continuance /kəntɪnjuəns/
NU The **continuance** of something is its continuation; a formal word. ...the continuance of the war.

continuation /kəntɪnjueɪʃn/
1 NU The **continuation** of something is the fact that it continues to happen or exist. People take for granted the continuation of economic growth.
2 N SING A **continuation** of one thing is a continuation of another, it follows on from it and forms an extra part of it. The carpet seemed a continuation of the lawn.

continue /kəntɪnjuː/ **continues**, **continuing**, **continued**
1 V+to-INF or V+ING To **continue** to do something means to keep doing it without stopping. The orchestra continued to play... He continued talking.
2 V or V-ERG If something **continues** or if you **continue** it, it does not stop. The battle continued for an hour... They want to continue their education.
3 V or V-ERG You can also say that if something **continues** or if you **continue** it, it starts again after stopping for a period of time. The next day the performance continued... He arrived in Norway, where he continued his campaign.
4 V+with If you **continue** with something, you keep doing it or using it. The girls should continue with their mathematics.
5 V-QUOTE or V To **continue** also means to begin speaking again after a pause or interruption. 'I mean Phil,' she continued, 'It's for him.'
6 V A If someone or something **continues** in a particular direction, they keep going in that direction. I continued up the path.

continuing education
NU **Continuing education** is the same as **further education**; used in American English.

continuity /kɒntɪnjuːɪti/
NU The **continuity** of something is the smooth continuation and development of it. ...the importance of continuity in government policy.

continuous /kəntɪnjuəs/
1 ADJ A **continuous** event or process happens or exists

without stopping. ...the continuous increase in their military capacity. ◆ **continuously** ADV The volcano had been erupting continuously since March.
2 ADJ ATTRIB A **continuous** line or surface has no gaps in it.
3 ADJ In grammar, the **continuous** form of verbs contains a form of the verb 'be' and the '-ing' form of the main verb. It is sometimes called the progressive form. In the sentences 'She was laughing' and 'They had been playing badminton', the verbs 'laugh' and 'play' are in the continuous form.

continuum /kəntɪnjuəm/
N SING A **continuum** is a series of events that are considered as a single process; a formal word. ...the continuum of the seasons.

contort /kəntɔːt/ **contorts**, **contorting**, **contorted**
V-ERG When something **contorts** or when you **contort** it, it changes into an unnatural and unattractive shape. His upper lip had been contorted by so much trumpet playing. ...contorting his features into an expression of agony. ◆ **contorted** ADJ ...his mad contorted smile.

contortion /kəntɔːʃn/ **contortions**
NCorNU A **contortion** is a movement of your body into an unusual shape or position. Holding the bat this way requires some difficult contortions from the player, especially on the backhand.

contortionist /kəntɔːʃənɪst/ **contortionists**
NC A **contortionist** is someone who twists their body into strange and unnatural positions in order to entertain other people, for example in a circus. A contortionist did her act on top of a piano.

contour /kɒntʊə, kɒntɔː/ **contours**
1 NC The **contours** of something are its shape or outline. Pain altered the contours of his face... The jacket curves at the waist to follow the body's contours.
2 NC On a map, a **contour** is a line joining points of equal height. A map can be plotted as contours or displayed like a picture. ...a contour map showing two hills and a mountain in the middle.

contraband /kɒntrəbænd/
NU **Contraband** refers to goods which are brought into or taken out of a country illegally in order to avoid taxation. Flights were routinely checked for drugs and contraband.

contraception /kɒntrəsepʃn/
NU **Contraception** refers to methods of preventing pregnancy. The Pope has delivered a powerful attack on abortion and contraception.

contraceptive /kɒntrəseptɪv/ **contraceptives**
NCorN+N A **contraceptive** is a device or pill that prevents a woman from becoming pregnant. ...the absence of cheap and readily available contraceptives... Women have been using the contraceptive pill for 30 years.

contract, **contracts**, **contracting**, **contracted**; pronounced /kɒntrækt/ when it is a noun and /kəntrækt/ when it is a verb.
1 NC A **contract** is a written legal agreement, especially one connected with the sale of something or with the carrying out of a job. We won a contract to build fifty-eight planes.
2 V+to-INF If you **contract** with someone to do something, you agree to do it for a set fee or within a set period of time which is then legally binding. They contracted to supply us with horses.
3 V-ERG When something such as your muscles **contract** or when you **contract** them, they become smaller or shorter. Shivering produces body heat because it makes the body's muscles contract and relax very rapidly... He unbuttoned his shirt and contracted his stomach muscles.
4 V O If you **contract** an illness, you become ill with it; a formal use. Three quarters of the haemophiliacs in Rio have contracted AIDS.
5 **breach of contract**: see **breach**.

contraction /kəntrækʃn/ **contractions**
1 NC A **contraction** is a shortened form of a word or words. She used the surname Terson (a contraction of Terry and Neilson).
2 NCorNU A **contraction** of something makes that thing shorter or smaller. ...the contraction of the muscles.

contractor /kəntræktə/ **contractors**
NC A **contractor** is a person or a company that does work for other people or companies, especially in the building industry. *...houses built by private contractors.*

contractual /kəntræktʃuəl/
ADJ ATTRIB A **contractual** relationship involves a legal agreement between people; a formal word. *The union had a contractual agreement with the company.*

contradict /kɒntrədɪkt/ **contradicts, contradicting, contradicted**
1 V Oor V-QUOTE If you **contradict** someone, you say that what they have just said is untrue or incorrect. *I took care not to contradict her... 'No,' contradicted her sister, 'it's because he doesn't care.'*
2 VO If one statement **contradicts** another, the first statement puts forward an opposing opinion to the second. *Perfectly reputable books may contradict each other.*

contradiction /kɒntrədɪkʃn/ **contradictions**
1 NCor NU A **contradiction** exists when two facts or statements are inconsistent with each other. *There is a contradiction between the two laws... I hate to admit all these contradictions in myself... There is no contradiction in this approach.*
2 If you say that something is a **contradiction in terms**, you mean that it is described as having a quality that it cannot have. *A rational religion is almost a contradiction in terms.*

contradictory /kɒntrədɪktəºri/
ADJ If two ideas or statements are **contradictory**, they are opposite. *The government had made two contradictory promises.*

contralto /kəntræltəu/ **contraltos**
NC A **contralto** is a woman with a low singing voice.

contraption /kəntræpʃn/ **contraptions**
NC A **contraption** is a strange-looking device or machine. *Over his door was a contraption with a sliding shutter.*

contrary /kɒntrəri/
1 ADJ **Contrary** ideas or opinions are completely opposed to each other in such a way that both cannot be accepted as true by the same person. *They happily tolerated the existence of opinions contrary to their own.*
2 PREP If you say that something is true **contrary to** what someone else believes or says, you are saying that it is true and that they are wrong. *Contrary to what is generally assumed, the adjustment is easily made.*
● **Contrary** is used in these phrases. ● You say **on the contrary** when you are disputing what has just been said and stating that the opposite is true. *'You'll get tired of it.'—'On the contrary. I shall enjoy it.'*
● Evidence or statements **to the contrary** contradict what you are saying or what someone else has said. *This method, despite statements to the contrary, has no damaging effects.*

contrast, contrasts, contrasting, contrasted;
pronounced /kɒntrɑːst/ when it is a noun and /kəntrɑːst/ when it is a verb.
1 NC A **contrast** is a great difference between two or more things, which is very clear when they are compared with each other. *...the contrast between his public image and his private life... There's quite a contrast between findings in Antarctica and Greenland.*
2 NC If one thing is a **contrast** to another, it is very different from it. *The atmosphere of the Second War was a complete contrast to that of the First.*
3 You say **by contrast** or **in contrast** when you are mentioning something that is very different to what you have just said. *Its exotic setting is in sharp contrast with his last book... By contrast, our use of oil has increased enormously.*
4 V+*with* If one thing **contrasts** with another, it is very different from it. *The British position contrasts sharply with that taken by the United States.*
◆ **contrasting** ADJ ATTRIB *...their contrasting attitudes. ...contrasting colours.*
5 VO If you **contrast** things, you compare them to show the differences between them. *The book contrasts the methods used in America and Russia.*

contravene /kɒntrəviːn/ **contravenes, contravening, contravened**
VO To **contravene** a law or rule means to do something that is forbidden by it; a formal word. *They contravened the drug laws.* ◆ **contravention** /kɒntrəvenʃn/ **contraventions** NUor NC *The advert was in contravention of the Race Relations Act. ...contraventions of the ban.*

contretemps /kɒntrətɒmº/; **contretemps** is both the singular and the plural form. The plural is pronounced /kɒntrətɒmºz/ or /kɒntrətɒmº/.
NC A **contretemps** is a small disagreement that is rather embarrassing; a literary word. *He felt obliged to smooth over the awkwardness of this contretemps with Smith.*

contribute /kəntrɪbjuːt/ **contributes, contributing, contributed**
1 VOor V If you **contribute** to something, you say or do things which help to make it successful. *He contributed a great deal to the ANC's international profile.*
2 VOor V If you **contribute** money to something, you give money in order to help pay for something. *The US contributed about seven million dollars for development aid and about five million for drugs eradication... The ODA says it has contributed a million pounds to a disaster relief appeal.*
3 V If something **contributes** to a situation, it is one of its causes. *Soaring land prices contribute to the high cost of housing.*
4 Vor VO To **contribute** to a book, magazine, or newspaper means to write a piece of work that is published in it. *Distinguished writers had contributed to its pages... She contributed anonymous items to the Chronicle.*

contribution /kɒntrɪbjuːʃn/ **contributions**
1 NC If you make a **contribution** to something, you do, say, or give something to help make it successful. *...the BBC's contribution to the adult literacy campaign... A UNITA spokesman described the offer as a goodwill gesture and a contribution to the process of peace and national reconciliation in Angola.*
2 NC In Britain, your national insurance **contributions** are the amounts of money that you pay out of your salary to the government and which you receive back as social security payments or as a pension. *...an increase in the retirement age and a rise in national insurance contributions.*
3 NC A **contribution** is something that you write which is published in a book, magazine, or newspaper. *...pamphlets with contributions from trade unionists.*

contributor /kəntrɪbjutə/ **contributors**
1 NC A **contributor** is someone who donates money, resources, or help to something. *...contributors to a fund to save the house.*
2 NC A **contributor** is also someone who writes something that is published in a book, magazine, or newspaper. *...a contributor of short stories to a national weekly... Lenin was a regular contributor.*
3 NC+SUPP You can also use **contributor** to refer to one of the causes of an event or situation. *Drinking alcohol is another possible contributor to liver cancer.*

contributory /kəntrɪbjutəºri/
ADJ A **contributory** factor is one of the causes of something; a formal word. *The inefficient use of oil was a major contributory factor.*

contrite /kɒntraɪt/
ADJ If you are **contrite**, you are ashamed and apologetic because you have done something wrong; a formal word. *I tried to look contrite.* ◆ **contrition** /kəntrɪʃn/ NU *They tell lies and show no sign of contrition.*

contrivance /kəntraɪvəns/ **contrivances**
NC A **contrivance** is an unusual device, machine, or method, especially one that is being used for a particular purpose. *...a contrivance of wood and wire. ...a contrivance to raise prices.*

contrive /kəntraɪv/ **contrives, contriving, contrived**
1 V+*to*-INF If you **contrive** to do something difficult, you try hard to succeed in doing it; a literary use. *I shall contrive to see you again... Mike contrived to grin without taking his cigar out of his mouth.*

2 VO If you **contrive** an event or situation, you succeed in making it happen, often by deceiving other people in some way; a formal use. *Confidential talks with professors were contrived by reporters posing as students.*

contrived /kəntraɪvd/
ADJ Something that is **contrived** appears false and unnatural because it is so obviously deliberate or planned. *Do you think his dramatic resignation was in some way contrived? ...a photographic smile, contrived and a little artificial.*

control /kəntrəʊl/ **controls, controlling, controlled**
1 VO People who **control** a country or organization have the power to take all the important decisions about the way it is run. *The Australians controlled the island... They will control the National Development Council, which advises the government.* ♦ **controlling** ADJ ATTRIB *The family had a controlling interest in the firm.*
2 NU **Control** is the power or authority that someone has to make decisions about the way things are managed. *The rebels took control of a television station... They still retain some political control over their former colonies.*
3 VO To **control** a machine, process, or system means to make it work in the way that is required. *Computer systems control the lighting and heating.* ♦ **controlled** ADJ *...growing plants inside a controlled environment chamber. ...a programme of controlled reform.*
4 NU **Control** of a machine, process, or system is the fact of making it work in the way required. *You should have control of your vehicle at all times.*
5 V-REFL or VO If you **control** yourself or your feelings, you make yourself behave calmly when you are feeling angry, excited, or upset. *She cannot really control herself, as demonstrated by her tantrums in Rome.* ♦ **controlled** ADJ *Some of the survivors were deeply shocked but many were controlled and lucid.*
6 NU If you have **control** over yourself, you have the ability to make yourself behave calmly. *He told himself that he mustn't lose control.*
7 VO To **control** something dangerous means to prevent it from becoming worse or spreading. *...a way of controlling cancer.*
8 NC A **control** is a device such as a switch which is used to operate a machine. *Just turn the volume control.*
9 N PL **Controls** are the methods that are used by a government or official organization to make restrictions on wage increases, immigration, credit, and so on. *Germans had waited forty years for today's lifting of border controls... Tight import controls had prevailed since the 1930s.*
● **Control** is used in these phrases. ● If you are **in control** of something that is happening, you are able to decide how it develops. *Those who begin the revolution rarely stay in control to complete the process.* ● If something is **beyond** your **control** or **outside** your **control**, you do not have any power to affect or change it. *He blamed his problems on factors beyond his control... The service is being withdrawn for reasons outside anyone's control.* ● If something is **out of control**, no-one has the power to stop it causing damage or harm. *Inflation got out of control.* ● If something harmful is **under control**, it is being dealt with successfully and is unlikely to cause any more harm. *The fever was brought under control.*
● If something is **under** your **control**, you have the power to decide what will happen to it. *He said that the troops under his control would not surrender... One by one, the states came under Communist control.*

controlled /kəntrəʊld/
ADJ **Controlled** is used after an adjective or noun which refers to a country or to an organization such as the United Nations, to say that it controls something. *They will help augment security along the American controlled Panama Canal... Government controlled newspapers say thousands of volunteers have already come forward. ...the Conservative controlled Association of District Councils.*

controller /kəntrəʊlə/ **controllers**
NC+SUPP A **controller** in an organization is someone

who has the responsibility for a particular task or duty. *...the BBC's controller of editorial policy. ...the financial controller.*

control tower, control towers
NC A **control tower** is a building at an airport from which people give instructions to aircraft when they are taking off or landing. *The aircraft lost contact with the control tower before landing.*

controversial /kɒntrəvɜːʃl/
ADJ Someone or something that is **controversial** causes strong feelings of anger or disapproval and which often leads to a lot of discussion and disagreement. *Many of the new taxes are controversial... He is a controversial politician.*

controversy /kəntrɒvəsi, kɒntrəvɜːsi/ **controversies**
NU or NC **Controversy** is a disagreement about something that many people do not approve of which leads to a lot of discussion and argument. *The government tried to avoid controversy. ...a violent controversy over a commercial treaty.*

contusion /kəntjuːʒn/ **contusions**
NC or NU A **contusion** is an internal injury, such as a bruise, that leaves the skin unbroken; a medical term. *...a large contusion to the left knee.*

conundrum /kənʌndrəm/ **conundrums**
NC A **conundrum** is a difficult or confusing problem; a formal word. *The belief in reincarnation poses some conundrums.*

conurbation /kɒnəbeɪʃn/ **conurbations**
NC A **conurbation** is a large urban area which has been formed by several towns that have grown in size and merged together. *...the conurbation of Greater Manchester.*

convalesce /kɒnvəles/ **convalesces, convalescing, convalesced**
V If you **are convalescing**, you are resting and regaining your health after an illness or operation. *The fever is gone and the child is convalescing.*

convalescence /kɒnvəlesns/
NU **Convalescence** is the period of time during which you recover from an illness, or the process of recovery. *Clem wasn't allowed to visit me during my convalescence.*

convalescent /kɒnvəlesnt/
ADJ ATTRIB **Convalescent** means relating to regaining health. *...a convalescent home.*

convection /kənvekʃn/
NU **Convection** is the process by which heat travels through air, water, and other gases and liquids; a technical term in physics. *The vacuum eliminates conduction and convection losses. ...convection currents.*

convector /kənvektə/ **convectors**
NC A **convector** or a **convector heater** is a heater that heats a room by means of circulating hot air. *I have a convector in the spare room.*

convene /kənviːn/ **convenes, convening, convened**; a formal word.
1 VO If you **convene** a meeting or a conference, you arrange for it to take place. *The European Community might help to convene a Middle East peace conference.*
2 V If a group of people **convene**, they come together for a meeting. *The grand jury did not convene until February.*

convener /kənviːnə/ **conveners**. See **convenor**.

convenience /kənviːniəns/ **conveniences**
1 NU+POSS If something is done for your **convenience**, it is done in a way that is useful or suitable for you. *The entire event had been arranged for their convenience.*
2 NC A **convenience** is something that is useful. *...a house with every modern convenience.* ● See also **flag of convenience, marriage of convenience, public convenience.**

convenience food, convenience foods
N MASS **Convenience food** is frozen, dried, or tinned food that can be cooked quickly without any preparation. *Poorer people eat more of what you might call convenience food... Food stores report selling more and more convenience foods suited to vegetarians.*

convenience store, convenience stores
NC A **convenience store** is a small shop which is open
for long hours; used in American English. *His wife
Beatrice runs the convenience store they own.*
convenient /kənvi:niənt/
ADJ Something that is **convenient** is useful or suitable
for a particular purpose and often saves you time or
effort. *It will be more convenient to stick to a three-
hour timetable. ...a convenient place to live.*
♦ **conveniently** ADV *The amount of fuel is displayed
conveniently on a gauge.*
convenor /kənvi:nə/ **convenors**; also spelt **convener.**
1 NC In Britain, a **convenor** is a trade union official
who is responsible for organizing the shop stewards at
a particular place of work or in a particular area. *A
convenor from North West London said a growing
number of ambulance workers throughout the country
were saying they would reject the offer... The
convenor of the local district read out a message from
the President.*
2 NC A **convenor** is also an official representative of a
political organization or special interest group. *He is
the ANC's southern Natal convenor... Hashmi was the
convener of the Cultural Front of the Communist
Party of India.*
convent /kɒnvənt/ **convents**
NC A **convent** is a building where a community of nuns
live, or a school run by nuns. *She learned to cook at a
convent school.*
convention /kənvɛnʃn/ **conventions**
1 NCorNU A **convention** is an accepted way of
thinking, behaving, or doing something. *A lot of the
usual conventions are ignored when you go on holiday.
...his arrogance and rejection of convention.*
2 NC A **convention** is also an official agreement or
code of conduct between countries or organizations.
*The US called on Israel to apply the provisions of the
fourth Geneva convention.*
3 NC A **convention** is also a large meeting of an
organization or political group. *He left New York
before the convention ended.*
conventional /kənvɛnʃᵊnəl/
1 ADJ **Conventional** people, opinions, or behaviour
conform to what is considered ordinary and normal.
*...the conventional housewife... He sprang from a
conventional middle-class family background.*
♦ **conventionally** ADV *...a more conventionally
acceptable life.*
2 ADJ ATTRIB A **conventional** method or product is the
one that is usually used. *Conventional advice for the
overweight is not to worry too much about exercise,
but rather to cut food input... Conventional vaccines
are made from entire killed or weakened viruses.*
♦ **conventionally** ADV *...conventionally educated
students.*
3 ADJ ATTRIB **Conventional** wars and weapons do not
involve the use of nuclear or chemical weapons.
*...arms reductions in the conventional, chemical and
nuclear fields.*
converge /kənvɜ:dʒ/ **converges, converging,
converged**
1 V When roads, paths, or lines **converge**, they meet
or join. *The paths converge under the trees.*
2 V When people or vehicles **converge** on a place, they
move towards it from different directions. *Thousands
of Liverpool and Everton supporters are converging on
Wembley for today's FA Cup final match.*
3 V When ideas or societies **converge**, they stop being
different and gradually become similar to each other.
*Two radically different types of society were
converging.*
convergence /kənvɜ:dʒəns/ **convergences**
NU+SUPP The **convergence** of societies, tendencies, or
beliefs is the process by which they stop being
separate or different and become alike; a formal
word. *...the predicted convergence of the
industrialized societies.*
conversant /kənvɜ:snt/
ADJ PRED If you are **conversant** with something, you
are familiar with it; a formal word. *The designer
must be conversant with all the aspects of the
problem.*

conversation /kɒnvəseɪʃn/ **conversations**
1 NCorNU If you have a **conversation** with someone,
you talk to each other in an informal situation. *Roger
and I had a conversation about the risks... He spent
some hours in conversation with me.*
2 When you **make conversation**, you talk to someone
in order to be polite rather than because you want to.
He didn't like having to make conversation.
conversational /kɒnvəseɪʃᵊnəl/
ADJ ATTRIB **Conversational** describes something that
relates to conversation. *...their brilliant
conversational powers.* ♦ **conversationally** ADV *'Tell
me,' she said conversationally, 'does he bite?'*
conversationalist /kɒnvəseɪʃᵊnəlɪst/
conversationalists
NC+SUPP A good **conversationalist** is someone who is
able to talk well about interesting things when they
have conversations. *It's always interesting to meet
such a good conversationalist... I'm a poor
conversationalist, I'm afraid.*
converse, converses, conversing, conversed;
pronounced /kənvɜ:s/ when it is a verb and /kɒnvɜ:s/
when it is a noun or an adjective; a formal word.
1 V-RECIP If you **converse** with someone, you talk to
each other. *I consider it a privilege to have conversed
with you... After the meeting, members conversed in
small groups.*
2 N SING The **converse** of a statement or fact is the
opposite of it, or a reversed form of it. For example,
the converse of 'Investment stimulates growth' is
'Growth stimulates investment'. *Sometimes the
patient rejects the transplant, but we can have the
converse of that—the transplant itself can attack the
patient.* ▶ Also ADJ ATTRIB *Political power is used to
win economic power. But the converse process is just
as common.*
conversely /kɒnvɜ:sli/
ADV SEN You say **conversely** to indicate that the
statement you are about to make is the opposite of, or
an alternative to, the one you have just made. *You
can use beer yeast for bread-making. Conversely, you
can use bread yeast in beer-making.*
conversion /kənvɜ:ʃn/ **conversions**
1 NCorNU A **conversion** is the act or process of
changing something into a different state or form.
...the conversion of coal into oil and gas.
2 NUorNC Someone's **conversion** from one set of
religious or political beliefs to another is the process of
that change. *...his recent conversion to Christianity...
All they say is that 'many people go to Medjugorje,
there are many conversions, there are many prayers'.*
convert, converts, converting, converted;
pronounced /kənvɜ:t/ when it is a verb and /kɒnvɜ:t/
when it is a noun.
1 V-ERG When something **converts** from one thing into
another or when you **convert** it, it changes from the
first thing into the second. *A solar cell takes radiation
from the sun and converts it into electricity... The
house has been converted into two apartments. ...the
formula for converting kilometres to miles.*
♦ **converted** ADJ ATTRIB *The theatre is a converted
squash court.*
2 V-ERG If someone **converts** you, or if you **convert**,
you change your religious or political beliefs. *Not
surprisingly, he failed to convert her... Many members
of Congress have been converted to this view... He
converted to the Muslim religion after his highly
successful career as a pop singer.*
3 NC A **convert** is someone who has changed their
religious or political beliefs. *...a Catholic convert.*
convertible /kənvɜ:təbl/ **convertibles**
1 ADJ **Convertible** money can be easily exchanged for
other forms of money. *The loan is freely convertible
into dollars.*
2 NC A **convertible** is a car with a soft roof that can
be folded down or removed. *Jaguar today launches its
first convertible car since the E-type.*
convex /kɒnveks/
ADJ A **convex** object curves outwards at its centre.
...a convex lens.
convey /kənveɪ/ **conveys, conveying, conveyed**
1 VOorV-REPORT To **convey** information, ideas, or

feelings means to make them known or understood by others. *Newspapers convey the impression that the war is over. ...trying to convey that it did not really matter.*
2 VO To **convey** someone or something to a place means to transport them there; a formal use. *...the truck conveying Daniel and the work crew.*

conveyance /kənveɪəns/ **conveyances**
NC A **conveyance** is a vehicle; an old-fashioned word. *The conveyance had drawn up at her door.*

conveyancing /kənveɪənsɪŋ/
NU In Britain, **conveyancing** is the process of transferring the legal ownership of property. *Lawyers no longer have a monopoly of house conveyancing.*

conveyor belt /kənveɪə belt/ **conveyor belts**
NC A **conveyor belt** or a **conveyor** is a continuously moving strip or a series of rollers which is used in factories for moving objects from one place to another. *Rock then falls onto a conveyor belt which carries it through the machine.*

convict, convicts, convicting, convicted; pronounced /kənvɪkt/ when it is a verb and /kɒnvɪkt/ when it is a noun.
1 VO To **convict** someone of a crime means to find them guilty of it in a court of law. *He was convicted of spying.* ◆ **convicted** ADJ *...convicted criminals.*
2 NC A **convict** is someone who is serving a prison sentence; an old-fashioned use. *...an escaped convict.*

conviction /kənvɪkʃn/ **convictions**
1 NCorNU A **conviction** is a strong belief or opinion that someone holds. *...his conviction that he could run a newspaper... 'Yes,' I said without much conviction.*
2 NCorNU A **conviction** is also the act of finding someone guilty of a crime in a court of law. *...the trial and conviction of Ward. ...his record of previous convictions.*

convince /kənvɪns/ **convinces, convincing, convinced**
VOorVO-REPORT If you **convince** someone of something, you make them believe that it is true or that it exists. *This had convinced her of the problems... It took them a few days to convince me that it was possible.*

convinced /kənvɪnst/
ADJ PRED If you are **convinced** of something, you are sure that it is true or genuine. *I am convinced of your loyalty... He was convinced that her mother was innocent.*

convincing /kənvɪnsɪŋ/
1 ADJ If someone is **convincing**, you believe that what they say is true. *They found his story very convincing.* ◆ **convincingly** ADV *She must speak more convincingly.*
2 ADJ If something is **convincing**, it has qualities which make you believe that it is true, real, or beyond doubt. *Does the film add up to a convincing portrayal of Hirohito during the war?... Providing a convincing replica of the turtles' natural habitat is very difficult... He had been elected by a convincing majority.*

convivial /kənvɪvɪəl/
ADJ **Convivial** people or occasions are pleasant, friendly and relaxed; a formal word. *...a happy and convivial group... The meal was a convivial one.*
◆ **conviviality** NU *...the atmosphere of conviviality.*

convocation /kɒnvəkeɪʃn/ **convocations**
1 NC A **convocation** is a meeting of a large group of people such as church leaders or politicians. *The two day convocation ended with a service at the Regina Mundi Church in Soweto.*
2 N SING The **convocation** of a large assembly is the act of arranging for it to be held; a formal word. *He was trying to block the convocation of a conference.*

convoluted /kɒnvəluːtɪd/
ADJ A **convoluted** problem, structure, or sentence is complicated and difficult to understand. *Nobody expects quick solutions to a problem with so many convoluted ramifications. ...highly convoluted turns of phrase.*

convolution /kɒnvəluːʃn/ **convolutions**
NC A **convolution** is one of the curves in an object or a design that has many curves; a formal word. *The façade was startling in its baroque convolutions. ...the convolutions of the cortex.*

convoy /kɒnvɔɪ/ **convoys**
NC A **convoy** is a group of ships, people, or vehicles travelling together. *...a convoy of police cars... The rebels attacked a military convoy in the mountains... A famine relief convoy has reached northern Ethiopia.*
● If a group of vehicles or people are travelling **in convoy**, they are travelling together. *Women and children travelled in convoy from Kuwait to Baghdad.*

convulse /kənvʌls/ **convulses, convulsing, convulsed**
V If someone **convulses**, their body moves suddenly and violently in an uncontrolled way. *He convulsed in pain... A quiver convulsed his body.*

convulsion /kənvʌlʃn/ **convulsions**
NCorN PL If someone has a **convulsion** or has **convulsions**, they suffer sudden uncontrollable movements of their muscles. *The word 'epilepsy' conjures up an image of someone going into convulsions.*

convulsive /kənvʌlsɪv/
ADJ A **convulsive** movement or action is sudden and violent and cannot be controlled. ◆ **convulsively** ADV *He shivered convulsively.*

coo /kuː/ **coos, cooing, cooed**
V When a dove or pigeon **coos**, it makes soft sounds. *A pigeon was cooing in one of the elms.*

cook /kʊk/ **cooks, cooking, cooked**
1 V-ERGorV When food **cooks** or when you **cook** food, you prepare it and then heat it, for example in an oven or in a saucepan. *I could smell vegetables cooking in the kitchen... He returned to cook lunch the next day... Mildred cooks remarkably well.* ◆ **cooked** ADJ *...informal restaurants serving a wide range of cooked dishes. ...pre-packed cooked food.*
2 NC A **cook** is a person who prepares and cooks food as their job. *...a young woman who works as a cook in a factory canteen.*
3 NC+SUPP You say someone is a good **cook** when they cook well. You say that they are a bad **cook** when they cook badly. *Are you a good cook?*
4 See also **cooking**.
5 If someone **cooks the books**, they seek to deceive people by changing the economic figures or other written records of a country or organization; an informal expression. *The system allows him to cook the books.*
cook up PHRASAL VERB If someone **cooks up** a dishonest scheme, they plan it; an informal expression. *They cook up all sorts of little deals.*

cookbook /kʊkbʊk/ **cookbooks**
NC A **cookbook** is the same as a **cookery book**. *...The Working Wives' Cookbook.*

cooker /kʊkə/ **cookers**
NC A **cooker** is a large box-shaped object with an oven, grill and hob that cooks food by heating it. *The milk was warming in a saucepan on the cooker.* ● See also **pressure cooker**.

cookery /kʊkəri/
NU **Cookery** is the activity of preparing and cooking food. *...magazine columns that deal with cookery and television.*

cookery book, cookery books
NC A **cookery book** is a book that contains recipes for preparing food. *He could make a new dish without referring to any cookery book. ...the first vegetarian cookery book.*

cookie /kʊki/ **cookies**
NC A **cookie** is a biscuit. *You'll have the cookies and coffee ready? ...chocolate chip cookies.*

cooking /kʊkɪŋ/
1 NU **Cooking** is the activity of preparing and cooking food. *My mother was fond of cooking.*
2 NU+SUPP You can also use **cooking** to refer to cooked food of a particular type. *She loves your cooking... I like Portuguese cooking.*

cooking oil, cooking oils
N MASS **Cooking oil** is oil that you use for frying food. It is usually produced from vegetables. *The government has recently announced a rise in the prices of consumer necessities such as cooking oil and sugar.*

Cook Islands /kʊk aɪləndz/
The **Cook Islands** are a self-governing territory of New Zealand in the south Pacific, east of Australia. They

were claimed by the United Kingdom in 1888 and annexed by New Zealand in 1901. In 1965 they became self-governing in association with New Zealand, which retains responsibility for defence and foreign policy. The Cook Islands export clothing and papayas. Tourism and banking are important industries. ♦ **Cook Islander** /kʊk aɪləndʳ/ N
▪ *religion:* Christianity (mainly Congregational)
▪ *language:* English and Cook Islands Maori (official)
▪ *currency:* New Zealand dollar and Cook Islands dollar ▪ *capital:* Avarua ▪ *population:* 19,000 (1991)
▪ *size:* 237 square kilometres.

cool /kuːl/ **cooler, coolest; cools, cooling, cooled**
1 ADJ Something that is **cool** has a low temperature but is not cold. *The air was cool and fresh. ...a cool drink.* ♦ **coolness** NU *...the coolness of the room.*
2 ADJ **Cool** clothing is made of thin material that is comfortable to wear in hot weather. *I'll just change into a cooler frock.*
3 V-ERG When something **cools** or when you **cool** it, it becomes less hot. *The water began to cool... Cool your feet in the stream.*
4 ADJ If you stay **cool** in a difficult situation, you remain calm. *He asked his members to stay cool and wait for the report.* ♦ **coolly** ADV *He drove coolly and carefully.* ♦ **coolness** NU *...the coolness with which he dealt with a crisis.*
5 ADJ If someone is **cool** towards you, they are unfriendly. If they are **cool** towards an idea or suggestion, they are not enthusiastic about it. *Normally relations between them are cool to say the least... Response to these proposals has been cool.* ♦ **coolly** ADV *'I'm not asking you,' she informed him coolly.* ♦ **coolness** NU *Hagen was hurt by my coolness.*
6 If you **keep** your **cool**, you control your temper and remain calm in difficult situations. If you **lose** your **cool** about something, you become angry and excited about it. Used in informal English. *Frustrated they may be, but they have kept their cool.*
cool down PHRASAL VERB 1 If something **cools down**, it becomes cooler until it reaches the temperature you want. *The engine will take half an hour to cool down.*
2 If someone **cools down**, they become less angry. *He has had time to cool down and look at what has happened less objectively.*
cool off PHRASAL VERB If you **cool off**, you make yourself cooler after being too hot. *We cooled off with a refreshing swim.*

coolant /kuːlənt/ **coolants**
NCorNU A **coolant** is a liquid that keeps a machine such as an engine cool while it is operating.

cooler /kuːlə/ **coolers**
NC A **cooler** is a container for keeping something such as a drink cool. *He went below and took three cans from a cooler. ...a beer cooler.*

coolie /kuːli/ **coolies**
NC **Coolies** were unskilled native workers in China, India, and other parts of Asia; an old-fashioned, offensive word.

cooling-off period, cooling-off periods
NC A **cooling-off period** is a set period of time during which two groups with opposing views try to resolve a dispute before taking any serious action. *Our union is opposed to any cooling-off period... President Mubarak proposed a six month cooling-off period in the occupied territories.*

cooling tower, cooling towers
NC A **cooling tower** is a very large container in which water is stored for use in the cooling processes of large factories or power stations, or as part of an air-conditioning system. *Any power station has to have cooling towers... Bacteria have been identified in a water cooling tower.*

co-op /kəʊɒp/ **co-ops**
NC A **co-op** is a co-operative; an informal word. *I'm in the food co-op.*

cooped up /kuːpt ʌp/
ADJ PRED If someone is **cooped up**, they live or are kept in a place which is too small or which does not allow them much freedom. *I hate being cooped up in the flat every day.*

co-operate /kəʊɒpəreɪt/ **co-operates, co-operating, co-operated**
1 V-RECIP When people **co-operate**, they work or act together, often for a specific purpose. *Mrs Thatcher said the British and French were co-operating on various defence projects... The workers co-operated with the management and the police... Guatemala continued to cooperate fully with the US in combatting the drug trade.* ♦ **co-operation** /kəʊɒpəreɪʃn/ NU *...co-operation between staff and parents.*
2 V To **co-operate** also means to undertake willingly what someone has asked you to do. *General Quainoo has called on Mr Taylor to co-operate with his troops.* ♦ **co-operation** NU *Thank you for your co-operation.*

co-operative /kəʊɒpərətɪv/ **co-operatives**
1 NC A **co-operative** is a business or organization which is owned by the people who manage it. They then share its benefits and profits. *They will take over land themselves and work it as a co-operative.*
2 ADJ A **co-operative** activity is done by people working together. *The allies are involved in a co-operative effort to counter the Iranian mining threat.* ♦ **co-operatively** ADV *The work is carried on co-operatively.*
3 ADJ Someone who is **co-operative** does what you ask them to. *Her children are considerate and co-operative. How co-operative were the authorities in enabling you to help these people?* ♦ **co-operatively** ADV *'Okay,' she said co-operatively.*

co-operative society, co-operative societies
NC In Britain, a **co-operative society** is a commercial organization which customers can join and receive a share of its profits. *He was on the side of the little trader and against the co-operative society.*

co-opt /kəʊɒpt/ **co-opts, co-opting, co-opted**
1 VO If someone is **co-opted** onto a committee, they are asked by the committee to become a member of it without being elected by the other members of the organization. *Mr Dubcek was co-opted into the Federal Assembly.*
2 VO If you **co-opt** someone, you persuade them to help you or support you in what you are doing. *Monsieur Rocard tried to co-opt ministers from the centre-right as well as Socialists.*

co-ordinate /kəʊɔːdɪneɪt/ **co-ordinates, co-ordinating, co-ordinated**
1 VO To **co-ordinate** a project or activity means to organize the different aspects of it to make sure they all run efficiently. *They were asked to co-ordinate the election campaign.* ♦ **co-ordinated** ADJ *They launched a co-ordinated attack on the enemy trenches.* ♦ **co-ordination** /kəʊɔːdɪneɪʃn/ NU *...the co-ordination of public transport.*
2 VO If you **co-ordinate** the movements of your body, you make them work together smoothly. *The children could not co-ordinate their movements.* ♦ **co-ordination** NU *The symptoms of weakness and loss of co-ordination got worse.*

co-ordinating conjunction, co-ordinating conjunctions
NC In grammar, a **co-ordinating conjunction** is a type of conjunction that joins together words, groups, or clauses of the same type or quality. In the sentences 'My mother and father worked hard' and 'Call me if you feel lonely or depressed', 'and' and 'or' are co-ordinating conjunctions.

co-ordinator /kəʊɔːdɪneɪtə/ **co-ordinators**
NC The **co-ordinator** of a project or activity is the person who organizes the various aspects of it such as making sure that people work together properly or that things arrive at the right place on time. *The United Nations appointed a co-ordinator for economic assistance to Afghanistan.*

coot /kuːt/ **coots**
NC A **coot** is a water bird with black feathers and a white patch on its forehead.

cop /kɒp/ **cops**
NC A **cop** is a policeman or policewoman; an informal word. *The cops and robbers chase provoked a diplomatic incident.*

cope /kəʊp/ **copes, coping, coped**
V If you **cope** with a problem, task, or difficult

situation, you deal with it successfully. *John and Sally coped with all their problems cheerfully. ...a computer capable of coping with domestic requirements.*

Copenhagen /kəʊpənheɪɡən/
Copenhagen is the capital of Denmark and its largest city. Population: 1,337,000 (1990).

copier /kɒpɪə/ **copiers**
NC A **copier** is a machine which makes exact copies of writing or pictures on paper, usually by a photographic process. *We've got a small Xerox copier.*

co-pilot, co-pilots
NC The **co-pilot** of an aeroplane is a pilot who assists the chief pilot. *Two survivors, including the co-pilot, have been rescued.*

coping /kəʊpɪŋ/ **copings**
NCorNU A **coping** is a layer of sloping or rounded bricks on the top of a wall.

copious /kəʊpɪəs/
ADJ A **copious** amount of something is a large amount of it; a formal word. *Plants need copious sunshine... She made copious notes.* ◆ **copiously** ADV *He cried copiously.*

cop-out, cop-outs
NC You can refer to something as a **cop-out** when you think that it is a way for someone to avoid doing something that they should do; an informal word. *Such international co-operation is often merely a cop-out.*

copper /kɒpə/ **coppers**
1 NU **Copper** is a soft reddish-brown metal. *...a copper mine. ...copper wire.*
2 NC In Britain, a **copper** is a policeman or policewoman; an informal use.
3 NC A **copper** is also a brown metal coin of low value. *It only cost a few coppers.*

copper beech, copper beeches
NC A **copper beech** is a tree with reddish-brown leaves.

copperplate /kɒpəpleɪt/
NU **Copperplate** is a very neat and regular style of handwriting, in which letters are formed with a lot of loops. *It was written in her beautiful flowing copperplate hand.*

coppice /kɒpɪs/ **coppices**
NC A **coppice** is a small group of trees growing very close to each other. *...a neglected coppice. ...coppices of alders, aspens and birches.*

copse /kɒps/ **copses**
NC A **copse** is a small group of trees growing close together. *The two cars were parked about two weeks ago in a copse in a lane leading to a popular fishing spot.*

Coptic Church /kɒptɪk tʃɜːtʃ/
N PROP The **Coptic Church** is a part of the Christian Church which was founded in Egypt. *...denominations including representatives of the Egyptian Coptic Church.*

copula /kɒpjʊlə/ **copulas**
NC In grammar, a **copula** is a verb which takes a complement. In the sentences 'We were very happy' and 'You don't want them to become suspicious', 'were' and 'become' are copulas.

copulate /kɒpjʊleɪt/ **copulates, copulating, copulated**
V-RECIP When a female and a male animal **copulate**, their sex organs come together so that fertilization can take place; a formal word. *They copulate, and the male fertilizes the female's eggs.* ◆ **copulation** /kɒpjʊleɪʃn/ NU *For a female dinosaur with a male this weight on her back, copulation may well have been a bone-crushing experience.*

copy /kɒpɪ/ **copies, copying, copied**
1 NC A **copy** is something that has been made to look exactly the same as something else. *I will send you a copy of the letter.*
2 VO If you **copy** something that has already been written, you write down exactly the same thing. *...a comment she had copied from his notes.*
3 VO If you **copy** a person's style of dress, behaviour, or ideas, you try to be like them. *Our scheme has been copied by other universities.*
4 NC A **copy** is one book, newspaper, or record of

which there are many others exactly the same. *Sixty thousand copies of the record were sold.*

copy down PHRASAL VERB If you **copy down** what someone says or writes, you write it down yourself. *I shouldn't bother to copy these figures down.*

copy out PHRASAL VERB If you **copy out** a long piece of writing, you write it all down. *I remember copying out the whole play.*

copybook /kɒpɪbʊk/
1 ADJ ATTRIB A **copybook** action is done perfectly according to established rules. *The pilot made a copybook landing.*
2 If you **blot your copybook**, you spoil your good reputation by doing something wrong. *I'd blotted my copybook by marrying without my father's approval... I can't have you blotting your copybook having punch-ups with students.*

copycat /kɒpɪkæt/ **copycats**
NC If you call someone a **copycat**, you are accusing them of copying someone's behaviour, dress, or ideas; an informal word, used showing disapproval. *Resist the urge to be a creative copycat.*

copyright /kɒpɪraɪt/ **copyrights**
NCorNU If someone has the **copyright** on a piece of writing or music, it is illegal to reproduce or perform it without their permission. *Who holds the copyright of the song?*

copywriter /kɒpɪraɪtə/ **copywriters**
NC A **copywriter** is a person who writes the words for advertisements. *...the mediocrity of his work as an advertising copywriter.*

coquetry /kɒkɪtri/
NU **Coquetry** is used to refer to coquettish behaviour; a literary word.

coquette /kɒkɛt/ **coquettes**
NC A **coquette** is a woman who behaves in a coquettish way; a literary word.

coquettish /kɒkɛtɪʃ/
ADJ **Coquettish** behaviour is behaviour in which a woman acts in a playful way that is intended to make men find her attractive; a literary word. *She gave a coquettish smile... Whenever she talked to Peter, she became very coquettish and feminine.* ◆ **coquettishly** ADV *She looked at him coquettishly.*

coracle /kɒrəkl/ **coracles**
NC A **coracle** is a simple round rowing boat made of woven sticks covered with animal skins.

coral /kɒrəl/ **corals**
NU **Coral** is a hard substance which is found in certain ocean areas. It is formed from the skeletons of very small sea animals. *Coral can extract particles from sea water... Cone snails have become the number one killers in the world's coral reefs.*

cor anglais /kɔːr ɒŋɡleɪ/ **cors anglais**
NC A **cor anglais** is a woodwind instrument with a double reed. It is slightly lower in pitch than an oboe.

cord /kɔːd/ **cords**
1 NUorNC **Cord** is a type of strong, thick string. *...a piece of cord... She tied a cord around her box.*
2 NC A **cord** is also a piece of electrical wire covered in insulation material such as rubber or plastic which is attached to an electrical item in order to connect it to the electricity supply. *...a small electric heater on a long cord.*
3 N PL **Cords** are trousers made of corduroy.

cordial /kɔːdiəl/ **cordials**
1 ADJ **Cordial** behaviour is warm and friendly; a formal use. *Relations between the two men were far from cordial.* ◆ **cordially** ADV *She shook hands cordially with Charley.* ◆ **cordiality** /kɔːdiæləti/ NU *The talks had been held in an atmosphere of cordiality and friendship.*
2 N MASS **Cordial** is a sweet drink made from fruit juice. *...lime juice cordial.*

cordiale /kɔːdiɑːl/. See **entente**.

cordite /kɔːdaɪt/
NU **Cordite** is an explosive substance used in the production of explosive devices such as bombs. *...the acrid smell of cordite.*

cordon /kɔːdn/ **cordons, cordoning, cordoned**
NC A **cordon** is a line of police, soldiers, or vehicles arranged in a way that prevents people from entering

or leaving an area. *The crowd attempted to break through the police cordons. ...a cordon around the mosque was breached.*
cordon off PHRASAL VERB If police or soldiers **cordon off** an area, they prevent people from entering or leaving by forming a protective ring around it. *The area surrounding the office had been cordoned off.*
cordon bleu /ˌkɔːdɒn blɜː/
ADJ ATTRIB **Cordon bleu** is used to describe cooks or cookery of the highest standard. *...a cordon bleu cook.*
corduroy /ˈkɔːdərɔɪ/
NU **Corduroy** is thick cotton cloth with raised parallel lines on the outside. *...a corduroy jacket.*
core /kɔː/ **cores**
1 NC The **core** of a fruit is the hard central part containing seeds or pips. *...the core of an apple.*
2 NC The **core** of an object or a place is its central or most important part. *The planet probably has a molten core. ...the conditions found at the core of the Sun.*
3 N SING The **core** of something such as a problem or proposal is its most essential part. *He was also unyielding on the issue of land for peace at the core of any negotiations.*
4 See also **hard core**.
coriander /ˌkɒriˈændə/
NU **Coriander** is a plant. Its seeds are used as a spice and its leaves are used as a herb. *Coriander grows wild in a few scattered places. ...a dessert-spoonful of ground coriander.*
cork /kɔːk/ **corks**
1 NU **Cork** is the soft, light, spongy bark of a Mediterranean tree. It is used especially for making household goods such as table mats or notice boards. *...a floor covering such as cork.*
2 NC A **cork** is a type of stopper made from cork. It is pushed into the end of a bottle to close it. *He removed the cork from the wine bottle.*
corkscrew /ˈkɔːkskruː/ **corkscrews**
NC A **corkscrew** is a device for pulling corks out of bottles. *...a bottle complete with chrome corkscrew.*
cormorant /ˈkɔːmərənt/ **cormorants**
NC A **cormorant** is a dark-coloured bird with a long neck which nests near coastal areas. *...a Byzantine mosaic depicting cormorants and herons.*
corn /kɔːn/ **corns**
1 NU **Corn** refers to crops such as wheat and barley, or their seeds. *Their yields in corn, beans, and rice will be better than what they have been for the last 20 to 50 years. ...a field of corn.*
2 NU In American English, **corn** is maize. *Iowa grows more corn than anywhere else... He got his momma to make him corn bread.*
3 NC A **corn** is a small, painful area of hard skin which can form on your foot. *He had a bad corn on his left foot.*
cornea /ˈkɔːniə/ **corneas**
NC The **cornea** of someone's eye is the curved transparent layer of skin that covers its surface. *It is possible to transplant a new cornea into the eye, but it is an expensive operation.*
corned beef /ˌkɔːnd ˈbiːf/
NU **Corned beef** is beef which has been cooked and preserved in salt water. *...a consignment of tinned corned beef.*
corner /ˈkɔːnə/ **corners, cornering, cornered**
1 NC A **corner** is a place where two sides or edges of something meet. *...a television set in the corner of the room.*
2 NC A **corner** is also a place where a road bends sharply or meets another road. *There's a telephone box on the corner.*
3 VO If you **corner** a person or animal, you get them into a place or situation that they cannot escape from. *The police had cornered the wrong car.* ♦ **cornered** ADJ *She had me cornered between the front porch and her car.*
4 VO If you **corner** a market or other area of activity, you gain control of it so that nobody else can succeed in it. *Distributors, keen to corner the rich Japanese market, are filling shelves with Scotch.*
● **Corner** is used in these phrases. ● If you are **in a**

corner or if you have been pushed **into a corner**, you are in a difficult situation. *In such a corner, he has reverted to his old confrontational approach... There are fears that Mr Gandhi will be forced into a corner by the Chinese.* ● If you **cut corners**, you do something quickly by doing it less thoroughly than you should. *The state of emergency only encouraged policemen to cut corners and break rules.*
corner shop, corner shops
NC A **corner shop** is a small shop, usually on the corner of a street, that sells food and household goods. *How do corner shops survive in the face of competition from large supermarkets?*
cornerstone /ˈkɔːnəstəʊn/ **cornerstones**
NC+SUPP The **cornerstone** of something is the basis of its existence or success. *The cornerstone of the peace accord lies in negotiated ceasefires... NATO must remain the cornerstone of military cooperation between the United States and Europe.*
cornet /ˈkɔːnɪt/ **cornets**
1 NC A **cornet** is a musical instrument that looks like a small trumpet. *The British jazz cornet player, Ken Collier, has died at the age of fifty-nine.*
2 NC A **cornet** is also a cone-shaped wafer with ice cream in it.
cornflake /ˈkɔːnfleɪk/ **cornflakes**
NC **Cornflakes** are a breakfast cereal of flakes made from maize, eaten with milk and sometimes sugar. *...a bowl of cornflakes. ...cornflakes packets.*
cornflour /ˈkɔːnflaʊə/
NU **Cornflour** is a very fine white maize flour. *Bring the liquid to the boil and stir in the cornflour.*
cornflower /ˈkɔːnflaʊə/ **cornflowers**
NC A **cornflower** is a small plant with bright flowers, usually blue in colour. *...olive leaves interspersed with blue cornflowers.*
cornice /ˈkɔːnɪs/ **cornices**
NC A **cornice** is a strip of plaster, wood, or stone which goes along the top of a wall or building. *...a Queen Anne mansion of red brick, tile-roofed, with a deep, plastered cornice.*
Cornish /ˈkɔːnɪʃ/
ADJ Something that is **Cornish** comes from or is connected with the county of Cornwall. *...the Cornish countryside.*
Cornish pasty, Cornish pasties
NC A **Cornish pasty** is a flat semicircular pie with meat and vegetables inside it.
corn on the cob
N MASS **Corn on the cob** is the long round part of the maize plant that has sweet corn on it. It is eaten as a vegetable.
cornucopia /ˌkɔːnjʊˈkəʊpiə/
N SING A **cornucopia** of good things is a large number of them; a literary word. *There was a positive cornucopia of fish fingers on my plate.*
corny /ˈkɔːni/
ADJ Something that is **corny** is very obvious or sentimental. *Ben loves corny old jokes.*
corollary /kəˈrɒləri/ **corollaries**
NC A **corollary** of something is an idea or fact that results directly from it; a formal word. *...an imminent slowdown in the economy with its natural corollory of reduced demand.*
corona /kəˈrəʊnə/ **coronas**
1 NC A **corona** is the circle of light that you can sometimes see around the moon at night, or around the sun during an eclipse; a technical term in astronomy. *Scientists were analysing the light from the corona to identify the precise colours in it.*
2 NC A **corona** is a long cigar with flat ends. *...bull-neck producers chewing fat corona cigars.*
coronary /ˈkɒrənəri/ **coronaries**
NC A **coronary** is a serious and often fatal illness caused when blood cannot reach the heart because of a large blood clot. *He went into his cubicle to change, and a few minutes later was stricken with a massive coronary... Polyunsaturated fats are no longer regarded as being particularly good at helping people to avoid coronaries.*
coronary thrombosis, coronary thromboses
NU or NC A **coronary thrombosis** is the same as a

coronary; a medical term. *It stops the flow of oxygen-rich blood to the heart, and causes coronary thrombosis... They will try and bring forward the time at which a patient who has a coronary thrombosis can be treated.*

coronation /kɒrəneɪʃn/ **coronations**
NC A **coronation** is the ceremony at which a king or queen is crowned. *He attended Queen Elizabeth's coronation in London.*

coroner /kɒrənə/ **coroners**
NC A **coroner** is an official responsible for investigating sudden or unusual deaths. *The judge said he was not going to order the coroner to adjourn the inquest.*

coronet /kɒrənət/ **coronets**
NC A **coronet** is a small crown.

Corp.
Corp. is a written abbreviation for 'corporation' and 'corporal' in names and titles. *...chairman of Occidental Petroleum Corp.*

corpora /kɔːpərə/
Corpora is the plural of **corpus**. *...words which occur statistically more frequently in that corpus than in other corpora that we've got.*

corporal /kɔːprəl/ **corporals**
N or TITLE A **corporal** is a non-commissioned officer of low rank in the army or air force. *The court also demoted the soldier from corporal to private... Corporal Stephen Harvey received the Queen's Commendation for bravery.*

corporal punishment
NU **Corporal punishment** is the punishment of people by beating them. *Corporal punishment has been banned in state schools in Britain.*

corporate /kɔːpə⁰rət/
1 ADJ ATTRIB **Corporate** means owned by or relating to one or more large businesses or companies. *The company was the subject of several corporate takeovers. ...corporate headquarters. ...a big network of financial contributors, both individual and corporate.*
2 ADJ ATTRIB **Corporate** also means owned or shared by all the members of a group or organization. *'The Times' feels the Prison Service lacks a corporate identity.*

corporate hospitality
NU **Corporate hospitality** is an arrangement by which companies or organizations entertain their clients by providing them with free tickets for a sporting or theatrical event. *...an increase in corporate hospitality... As well as Henley and Wimbledon, top targets for corporate hospitality include the Ryder Cup and yachting at Cowes... They will be in the corporate hospitality area, where champagne and dinner is included.*

corporation /kɔːpəreɪʃn/ **corporations**
1 NC A **corporation** is a large business or company. *The Digital Equipment Corporation will unveil a new line of its personal computers today in New York. ...a goldmine administered by the Anglo-American Corporation.*
2 NC The **corporation** of a town or city is the authority responsible for running it. *A petition was sent from the mayor and corporation... 82 municipal bodies in West Bengal and Calcutta Corporation will go to the polls.*

corporation tax
NU **Corporation tax** is a tax that companies have to pay on the profits they make. *...a reduction in the basic rate of corporation tax.*

corporatism /kɔːpə⁰rətɪzəm/
NU **Corporatism** refers to the organization and control of a country by self-interest groups who share a common profession or outlook; used showing disapproval. *...the party's support for the enterprise economy and its opposition to corporatism.*

corporeal /kɔːpɔːrɪəl/
ADJ **Corporeal** means involving or relating to the physical world rather than the spiritual world; a formal word. *...corporeal existence.*

corps /kɔː/; corps is both the singular and the plural form. The plural is pronounced /kɔːz/.

1 NC A **corps** is a part of the army which has special duties. *...the Royal Army Ordnance Corps.*
2 NC+SUPP A **corps** is also a small group of people who do a special job. *...the diplomatic corps.*

corpse /kɔːps/ **corpses**
NC A **corpse** is a dead body. *In the narrow street lay the twitching corpse of a young guerilla.*

corpulent /kɔːpjʊlənt/
ADJ Someone who is **corpulent** is fat; a literary word. *...his corpulent figure.*

corpus /kɔːpəs/ **corpora** /kɔːpərə/ or **corpuses**.
1 NC A **corpus** is a large number of articles, books, magazines, and so on that have been deliberately collected together for some purpose; a technical use. *We have been trying to collect a corpus of listening comprehension materials. ...that classic corpus of law, the Code Napoleon.*
2 See also **habeas corpus**.

corpuscle /kɔːpʌsl/ **corpuscles**
NC A **corpuscle** is a red or white blood cell. *...a concentrate of oxygen-carrying red corpuscles.*

corral /kərɑːl/ **corrals, corralling, corralled**
1 NC A **corral** is a space surrounded by a fence where cattle or horses are kept, for example on a ranch or farm. *He pointed to his sheep shivering in a muddy corral. ...building wood for cattle corrals.*
2 VO To **corral** cattle or horses means to drive them into a corral and keep them there. *Three thousand ponies were corralled along the stream.*

correct /kərɛkt/ **corrects, correcting, corrected**
1 ADJ Something that is **correct** is accurate and has no mistakes. *That's the correct answer... There's now very good evidence that Darwin's explanation for evolution is correct.* ◆ **correctly** ADV *I hope I pronounced his name correctly.* ◆ **correctness** NU *This confirmed the correctness of my decision.*
2 ADJ PRED If you are **correct**, what you have said or thought is true. *Jenkins is correct. We've got to change our strategy... If Mr Vorontsov is correct, there was a serious threat of a coup attempt last March.*
3 ADJ ATTRIB The **correct** thing is the right or most suitable one. *Make sure you ask for the correct fuse... The government is doubling the fines on airlines which bring passengers into Britain without the correct visas and documents.* ◆ **correctly** ADV *Rice, correctly cooked and prepared, is delicious.*
4 VO If you **correct** a mistake, problem, or fault, you put it right. *I wish to correct a false impression which may have been created.*
5 VO or V-REFL If you **correct** someone, you say something which is more accurate or appropriate than what they have just said. *Correct me if I'm wrong, but I think it's only scheduled for a five or six hour meeting... 'I'm a fighter like your dad is—or was,' Mr Cupples corrected himself.*
6 VO When someone **corrects** a piece of writing, they mark the mistakes or change the errors in it. *Prior to its publication, he had actually previewed the piece, revising and correcting it.*
7 ADJ **Correct** behaviour is considered socially acceptable. *Charter's dealings with him have been wholly correct.* ◆ **correctly** ADV *We tried to behave correctly.* ◆ **correctness** NU *Such a person should be treated with polite correctness.*

correcting fluid
NU **Correcting fluid** is an opaque, usually white, liquid which is used to cover over errors in written or typed work.

correction /kərɛkʃn/ **corrections**
1 NC or NU A **correction** is something which puts right something that is wrong. *The Bill would force newspapers to print corrections as prominently as the original story... A couple of mistakes need correction.*
2 NU or NC **Correction** is the changing of something so that it is no longer faulty or unsatisfactory. *Deaf children need speech correction... Make the necessary corrections to get the spacecraft as close as possible to the next comet.*
3 NU **Correction** of someone's behaviour is the act of trying to improve their standard of conduct when they have done something wrong; used especially to refer

to the act or process of punishing criminal behaviour. *The system of labour camps had failed in its declared aim of correction and re-education.*

corrective /kərɛktɪv/ **correctives**
ADJ Corrective measures are intended to put right something that is wrong. *When we put the corrective optics on the camera, that will cure that problem.* ▶ Also NC *This analysis provides an important corrective to the traditional view.*

Correia, Carlos /kɑːləʊs kɒreɪjə/
Carlos Correia was appointed prime minister of Guinea-Bissau in 1991. He was Secretary of the Council of State and Minister for Rural Development and Agriculture from 1989 to 1991. He is a member of the African Party for the Independence of Guinea and Cape Verde (PAIGC).

correlate /kɒrəleɪt/ **correlates, correlating, correlated**
V-RECIP If one thing correlates with another, or if two things are correlated, they are closely connected or influence each other. *The position where they're turned on correlates with the order of the genes on the chromosome... In Britain, class and region are strongly correlated... It has become almost impossible to correlate conclusions and data...* ◆ **correlation** /kɒrəleɪʃn/ **correlations** NC *There was a definite correlation between rates of unemployment and wage stability.*

correlative /kɒrɛlətɪv/
ADJ Correlative is used to describe something which always exists or happens together with something else; a formal word. *...correlative ideas.*

correspond /kɒrəspɒnd/ **corresponds, corresponding, corresponded**
1 V-RECIP If one thing corresponds with another or if the two things correspond, they have a similar purpose, position or status. *This view corresponds less and less with reality... His job in Moscow corresponds to her position here.*
2 V-RECIP If two numbers or amounts correspond, they are the same. *Check the telephone numbers in case they don't correspond... The date of her birth corresponded with her father's visit.*
3 V-RECIP If two people correspond, they write letters to each other. *I've been corresponding with Tim.*

correspondence /kɒrəspɒndəns/ **correspondences**
1 NU Correspondence is the act of writing letters to someone. *The judges' decision is final and no correspondence will be entered into.*
2 NU Correspondence also refers to the letters that someone receives. *The letter had been among his correspondence that morning.*
3 NC If there is a correspondence between two things, there is a close relationship or similarity between them. *In African languages there is a close correspondence between sounds and letters.*

correspondence course, correspondence courses
NC A correspondence course is a course in which you study at home, receiving your work by post and sending it back by post.

correspondent /kɒrəspɒndənt/ **correspondents**
NC A correspondent is a television or newspaper reporter. *Graham Leach, the BBC's Southern Africa correspondent described for me South Africa's reaction... Our correspondent in Manila, Humphrey Hawkesley, reports.*

corresponding /kɒrəspɒndɪŋ/
ADJ ATTRIB You use corresponding to indicate that one thing is similar or related to another; a formal word. *In France they study to the same standard and take the corresponding examinations... Any increase in complexity brings with it a corresponding probability of error.* ◆ **correspondingly** ADV SEN *The new edition is bigger and correspondingly more expensive.*

corridor /kɒrɪdɔː/ **corridors**
1 NC A corridor is a long passage in a building or train.
2 NC A corridor is also a strip of land that connects one country to another or gives it a route to the sea through another country. *Mike Hall has just made the journey through the corridor from Malawi to Zimbabwe.*

corridors of power
N PL The corridors of power are the places where the most important decisions in government are made. *So much official money has been washing through the corridors of power that accusations of corruption can no longer be suppressed.*

corroborate /kərɒbəreɪt/ **corroborates, corroborating, corroborated**
VO If someone or something corroborates an idea, account, or argument, they provide evidence to support it; a formal word. *Abrams and Rose corroborated this view in their influential study of the subject.* ◆ **corroboration** /kərɒbəreɪʃn/ NU *Evangelina's story was later published without corroboration.*

corrode /kərəʊd/ **corrodes, corroding, corroded**
V-ERG When metal corrodes or when something corrodes it, it is gradually destroyed by rust or a chemical. *It has to be made of a metal that won't be corroded by anything... Vinegar will corrode metal.* ◆ **corroded** ADJ *The generator was badly corroded.*

corrosion /kərəʊʒn/
NU Corrosion is the damage that is caused when something is corroded. *Check that the terminals of the battery are free from dirt and corrosion.*

corrosive /kərəʊsɪv/
ADJ A corrosive substance can destroy solid materials as a result of a chemical reaction. *...a corrosive poison.*

corrugated /kɒrəgeɪtɪd/
ADJ ATTRIB Corrugated metal or cardboard has parallel folds in it to make it stronger. *...a corrugated iron roof.*

corrupt /kərʌpt/ **corrupts, corrupting, corrupted**
1 ADJ A corrupt person behaves dishonestly or illegally in return for money or power. *Some were greedy, some were corrupt. ...corrupt party officials. ...corrupt practices.*
2 VOorV To corrupt someone means to make them dishonest or immoral. *They believe western culture is corrupting Soviet youth... It is claimed that television corrupts... Young people in prison are corrupted by hardened criminals.*

corruption /kərʌpʃn/
1 NU Corruption is dishonesty and illegal behaviour by people in positions of authority or power. *Mr Churbanov is accused of bribery and corruption.*
2 NU The corruption of someone is the process of making them behave in a way that is morally wrong. *His whole life seemed dedicated to the corruption of the young.*

corsage /kɔːsɑːʒ/ **corsages**
NC A corsage is a very small bunch of flowers which is fastened to the front of a woman's dress below the shoulder. *...a corsage of orchids.*

corset /kɔːsɪt/ **corsets**
NC A corset is a stiff piece of underwear, worn by some women around their hips and waist to make them look slimmer. *Once upon a time you could tell a woman by her corsets and cleavage, and a man by his breeches and boots.*

cortege /kɔːteɪʒ/ **corteges**
N COLL A cortege is a procession of people who are walking or riding in cars to a funeral. *Thousands of people accompanied Ghaffar Khan's funeral cortege from Peshawar to Jalalabad.*

cortex /kɔːteks/ **cortices** /kɔːtɪsiːz/
NC The cortex of the brain or of another organ is its outer layer; a medical term. *...the cerebral cortex.*

cortisone /kɔːtɪzəʊn/
NU Cortisone is a hormone used in the treatment of arthritis, allergies, and some skin diseases. *He said he took only cortisone for an injury and an energy-building potion given him by his doctor.*

cos /kəz/
CONJ Cos is a very informal way of saying 'because'. *'You'd better make a note of that, cos I haven't'.*

cosh /kɒʃ/ **coshes, coshing, coshed**
1 NC A cosh is a weapon that is used to hit people with. It is a short piece of thick rubber or metal. *A man has been charged with possessing a teargas cannister and a metal cosh.*

2 VO To **cosh** someone means to hit them hard on the head with a cosh or some other blunt weapon. *The driver was dragged out of his van and coshed.*

cosine /kəʊsaɪn/ **cosines**

NC A **cosine** is the ratio of the length of the adjacent side of a right-angled triangle to that of the hypotenuse; a technical term in mathematics.

cosmetic /kɒzmɛtɪk/ **cosmetics**

1 NC **Cosmetics** are substances such as lipstick or face powder. *...protesting about the use of animals in testing cosmetics.*
2 ADJ **Cosmetic** measures or changes improve the appearance of something without changing its basic character or without solving a basic problem. *...some form of genuine, rather than cosmetic, economic cooperation among member states.*

cosmetic surgery

NU **Cosmetic surgery** is surgery which is done to people in order to make them look more attractive. *He has had his face remodelled by cosmetic surgery.*

cosmic /kɒzmɪk/

ADJ ATTRIB **Cosmic** means belonging or relating to the universe. *Sudden bursts of cosmic radiation from space have been detected since the 60s.*

cosmic ray, cosmic rays

NC **Cosmic rays** are rays that reach earth from outer space. They consist of atomic nuclei. *X-rays, particles, magnetic fields and incoming cosmic rays will be measured by nine instruments.*

cosmology /kɒzmɒlədʒi/ **cosmologies**

1 NCorNU A **cosmology** is a theory about the origin and nature of the universe. *Raymond Curswile believes they've altered our cosmology, our viewpoint of ourselves in the universe... Trying to describe Aboriginal cosmology briefly is just about impossible.*
2 NU **Cosmology** is the study of the origin and nature of the universe. *Particle physics is providing a test of the theory of cosmology... If you study cosmology, you realize that all humans are the same and should have equal status.*

cosmonaut /kɒzmənɔːt/ **cosmonauts**

NC A **cosmonaut** is an astronaut from the Commonwealth of Independent States. *The crew consists of two cosmonauts and the first British astronaut, Miss Helen Sharman, who is a scientist.*

cosmopolitan /kɒzməpɒlɪtən/

ADJ **Cosmopolitan** people or things have been influenced by many different countries and cultures. *Berlin was lively, cosmopolitan, cultured, daring, avant-garde.*

cosmos /kɒzmɒs/

N SING The **cosmos** is the universe; a literary word. *...large telescopes that peer into the cosmos.*

cosset /kɒsɪt/ **cossets, cosseting, cosseted**

VO If you **cosset** someone, you do everything for them and protect them too much. *...domesticated felines being cosseted by American owners.*

Cossiga, Francesco /frænt͡ʃɛskəʊ kɒsiːgə/

Francesco Cossiga became President of Italy in 1985. He became MP for Cagliari in 1963. He has served as Minister for Public Administration from 1974 to 1976, of the Interior from 1976 to 1978, Prime Minister from 1979 to 1980, and President of the Senate from 1983 to 1985. He is a Christian Democrat (DC). Born: 1928.

cost /kɒst/ **costs, costing.** The form **cost** is used in the present tense and is also the past tense and past participle of the verb.

1 NC The **cost** of something is the amount of money needed to buy, do, or make it. *The total cost of the holiday was £300... The building was restored at a cost of £500,000. ...the huge increases in fuel costs.*
2 VOorVOO You use **cost** to talk about the amount of money that you have to pay for things. *Those books cost £2.95 each... A two-day stay there cost me $125... A freezer doesn't cost much to run.*
3 N SING The **cost** of achieving something is the loss, damage, or injury involved in achieving it. *The cost in human life had been enormous... It will have been worthwhile, even though so many ordinary decent families have had to pay such a terrible cost.*
4 VOOorVO If an event or mistake **costs** you something, you lose that thing because of it. *A single*

error here could cost you your life... It was Mrs Thatcher's hostility to Europe that finally cost her her job.
5 You say that something must be done **at all costs** to emphasize the importance of doing it. *Confrontation and violence had to be avoided at all costs... He expressed fears that the government would be intent on clinging to power at all costs.*

co-star, co-stars

NC+SUPP An actor or actress who is a **co-star** of a film has one of the most important parts in it. *His co-star was Vivien Leigh.*

Costa Rica /kɒstə riːkə/

The **Republic of Costa Rica** is a country in Central America. It was a Spanish colony from the 16th century until it became independent in 1821. Rafael Angel Calderón Fournier, of the Social Christian Unity Party (PUSC), became President in 1990. Costa Rica exports coffee and bananas. Large foreign debts and high inflation are serious economic problems. It is a member of the Organization of American States.
♦ **Costa Rican** /kɒstə riːkən/ N, ADJ
▪ *per capita GNP:* US$1,760 ▪ *religion:* Christianity (mainly Roman Catholic) ▪ *language:* Spanish
▪ *currency:* colón ▪ *capital:* San José ▪ *population:* 3 million (1989) ▪ *size:* 51,060 square kilometres.

cost-effective

ADJ Something that is **cost-effective** saves or makes a lot of money in comparison with the costs involved. *...more cost-effective methods of production.*

costing /kɒstɪŋ/ **costings**

NCorNU A **costing** is the estimation of all the costs involved in something such as a project or business venture. *Magistrates would receive detailed costings of the whole range of possible sentences... You'll find it's very expensive when you do a proper accountant's costing of it.*

costly /kɒstli/ **costlier, costliest**

1 ADJ Something that is **costly** is very expensive. *...a costly mistake... The government is to embark on a costly advertising campaign.*
2 ADJ **Costly** also describes things that take a lot of time or effort. *That route will be too costly in time.*

cost of living

N SING The **cost of living** is the average amount of money that people need to spend on food, housing, and clothing. *The Retail Prices Index put the rise in the cost of living at 10·6 per cent... A minimum wage would be set based on the cost of living.*

cost price, cost prices

NC The **cost price** of a product is its price when it is sold without any profit but only for what it cost the manufacturer to produce it or the seller to buy it. *Even if we sell at cost price we might not clear the stock.*

costume /kɒstjuːm/ **costumes**

1 NC A **costume** is a set of clothes worn by an actor. *The cast makes its own costumes ...an Elizabethan costume of padded breeches, square shoes, and a ruff.*
2 NU **Costume** is also used to refer to the clothing worn in a particular place or during a particular period. *...portraits of people dressed in seventeenth century costume.*
3 ADJ ATTRIB A **costume** play or drama is one which is set in the past and in which the actors wear the type of clothes worn in that period.

costume jewellery

NU **Costume jewellery** is jewellery made from cheap materials. *...costume jewellery and handbags.*

costumier /kɒstjuːmɪə/ **costumiers**

NC A **costumier** is a person or firm that makes or supplies theatrical or fancy dress costumes.

cosy /kəʊzi/ **cosier, cosiest; cosies;** spelt **cozy** in American English.

1 ADJ **Cosy** means comfortable and warm. *The room was wonderfully warm and cosy... A hot water bottle will make you feel cosier.* ♦ **cosily** ADV *We were all sitting cosily in the recreation room.*
2 ADJ You use **cosy** to describe activities that are pleasant and friendly. *I had a cosy chat with him... They meet at private sessions which have been described as cosy, informal and useful.* ♦ **cosily** ADV

We spent the afternoon cosily gossiping.
3 NC⟩SUPP A tea **cosy** is a soft cover used to keep a teapot warm.
cot /kɒt/ **cots**
1 NC A **cot** is a baby's bed with bars or panels round it. *Neglect has left the homes bereft of facilities with toddlers often sleeping two or three to a cot.*
2 NC In American English, a **cot** is a small, narrow bed. *Some soldiers are sleeping on cots, others are playing cards. ...neat rows of metal cots.*
cot death, cot deaths
NUorNC **Cot death** is the sudden death of a baby while it is asleep, although the baby had not previously been ill. *Only about one baby in four thousand succumbs to cot death... The Netherlands have had a three fold increase in cot deaths between 1971 and 1978.*
Côte d'Ivoire (Ivory Coast) /kəʊtdiːvwɑː/
The Republic of Côte d'Ivoire is a country in western Africa. It was part of French West Africa until it became independent in 1960. Dr Félix Houphouët-Boigny became President in 1960 and established a one-party state, ruled by the Democratic Party of Côte d'Ivoire (PDCI). Political parties were legalized in 1990. Côte d'Ivoire is the world's largest producer of cocoa and the fifth largest producer of coffee. It is a member of the Organization of African Unity.
♦ **Ivorian** /aɪvɔːrɪən/ N, ADJ
▪ *per capita GNP:* US$740 ▪ *religion:* animism, Islam, Christianity ▪ *language:* French (official), Akan, Kru ▪ *currency:* CFA franc ▪ *capital:* Abidjan ▪ *population:* 12 million (1989) ▪ *size:* 322,462 square kilometres.
coterie /kəʊtəri/ **coteries**
N COLL A **coterie** is a small group of people who are close friends or have a common interest, and who do not want other people to join them; a literary word. *The name is known to only a small coterie of concert-goers.*
Cotonou /kɒtənuː/
Cotonou is the largest city in Benin. Population: 383,000 (1981).
cottage /kɒtɪdʒ/ **cottages**
NC A **cottage** is a small house in the country. *He's spending two weeks in a cottage in the Italian Alps. ...a quaint little cottage by the seashore.*
cottage cheese
NU **Cottage cheese** is soft white lumpy cheese made from sour milk. *This is terrific cottage cheese. ...a garnish of beetroot, white cottage cheese and blueberries.*
cottage industry, cottage industries
NC A **cottage industry** is a small business that is run from someone's home, especially one that involves a craft such as knitting or pottery. *It's no longer a small cottage industry among a few chums. It's now a huge international business... The apprentices would be trained to run their own cottage industry.*
cottage loaf, cottage loaves
NC A **cottage loaf** is a loaf of bread which has a smaller round part on top of a larger round part.
cottage pie, cottage pies
NUorNC **Cottage pie** is a dish which consists of minced meat in gravy with mashed potato on top.
cottager /kɒtɪdʒə/ **cottagers**
NC A **cottager** is a person who lives in a cottage. *...cottagers and farm labourers.*
cotton /kɒtn/ **cottons, cottoning, cottoned**
1 N MASS **Cotton** is cloth made from the soft fibres of a plant. *If it's white cotton or cotton polyester, it's safe for all types of bleaching. ...a cotton dress.*
2 NU The plant grown for these fibres is also called **cotton**. *They now earn much more money from cotton than any other crop. ...cotton fields.*
3 N MASS **Cotton** is also thread that is used for sewing. *Then you get a needle and cotton and carefully sew up the slit. ...reels of cotton.*
cotton on PHRASAL VERB If you **cotton on** to something, you understand it or come to realize it; an informal expression. *At long last he has cottoned on to the fact that I don't want him!*
cotton candy
NU **Cotton candy** is a large soft mass of pink or white sugar threads which is put on a stick and eaten,

usually out of doors; used in American English. *They went every Sunday to ride the rides and eat cotton candy and try to win prizes.*
cotton wool
NU **Cotton wool** is soft, fluffy cotton, often used for applying liquids or creams to your skin. *...scraps of gauze or cotton wool that they could find in their first aid kits.*
couch /kaʊtʃ/ **couches, couching, couched**
1 NC A **couch** is a long, soft piece of furniture for sitting or lying on. *...after spending the night on a couch in an immigration office in the capital.*
2 VO If a statement **is couched** in a particular style of language, it is expressed in that language; a formal use. *...a resolution couched in forthright terms.*
couchette /kuːʃet/ **couchettes**
NC A **couchette** is a bed in a railway carriage or ferry boat, which is either folded against the wall or used as an ordinary seat during the day.
couch grass /kaʊtʃ grɑːs, kʊtʃ grɑːs/
NU **Couch grass** is a type of grass that has long roots that make it spread quickly.
couch potato, couch potatoes
NC You can use **couch potato** to refer to someone who is very lazy and who spends a lot of their time sitting watching television; an informal expression. *It's cheaper than a video, so couch potatoes won't have to worry about that exhausting walk to the shop... I want my audience to participate, rather than just sit there like couch potatoes.*
cougar /kuːgə/ **cougars**
NC A **cougar** is a wild animal that is a member of the cat family. Cougars have brownish-grey fur and live in mountain regions of North and South America.
cough /kɒf/ **coughs, coughing, coughed**
1 V When you **cough**, air is forced out of your throat with a sudden, harsh noise. *Mr Willet coughed nervously.* ▶ Also NC *There was a muffled cough outside the study door.* ♦ **coughing** NU *They suffered abdominal pains and intense coughing.*
2 VO or VO+up If you **cough** blood or phlegm, you force it out of your throat with a sudden, harsh noise. *In the later stages of the disease the victim will start to cough up blood.*
3 NC A **cough** is also an illness in which you cough a lot and your chest or throat hurts. *Most coughs and colds will get better on their own.*
cough up PHRASAL VERB If you **cough up** money, you give someone money; an informal expression. *How can he persuade the authorities to cough up for the private education of his children?*
could /kəd, kʊd/. **Could** is sometimes considered to be the past tense of **can**, but in this dictionary the two words are dealt with separately.
1 MODAL If you **could** do something, you were able to do it. *They complained that they couldn't sleep... When I was young you could buy a packet for two shillings... It was difficult to find a house that he could afford.*
2 MODAL **Could** is used in indirect speech to indicate that someone has said that something is allowed or possible. *She said I could go... I asked if we could somehow get a car.*
3 MODAL If something **could** happen, it is possible that it will happen or it is possible to do it. If something **could** have happened, it was possible, but it did not actually happen. *The river could easily overflow, couldn't it?... We could do a great deal more in this country to educate people... If one could measure this sort of thing, one might understand it better... You were lucky. It could have been awful.*
4 MODAL If something **could** be the case, it is possibly the case. If something **could** have been the case, it was possibly the case in the past. *It could be a symbol, couldn't it?... It couldn't possibly be poison... He couldn't have rowed away.*
5 MODAL You use **could** when you are making suggestions. *You could phone her... Couldn't you just build more factories?... I could ask her, I suppose.*
6 MODAL You also use **could** when you are making polite requests. *Could you just switch the projector on?... Could I speak to Sue, please?*

couldn't /kʊdnt/
Couldn't is the usual spoken form of 'could not'. *'I visited the university and I felt I couldn't fit in'.*

could've /kʊdəv/
Could've is the usual spoken form of 'could have', especially when 'have' is an auxiliary verb. *'I'd have hoped they could've brought themselves to say explicitly that they are prepared to enter negotiations'.*

council /kaʊnsl/ councils
1 N COLL A **council** is a group of people elected to run a town or other area. *I served seventeen years on my local council ...Wiltshire County Council. ...council meetings.*
2 N COLL Some other advisory or administrative groups are also called **councils**. *...the Arts Council.*
3 N+N A **council** house or flat is accommodation that is owned by the local council and rented to people to live in. *...council estates. ...a council tenant.*
4 NC A **council** is also a specially organized meeting. *A council of ministers and generals was held at No. 10.*

councillor /kaʊnsələ/ councillors
NC A **councillor** is a member of a council. *In a low turnout Mr Eddie O'Hara, a local councillor, increased Labour's share of the vote.*

council of war, councils of war
NC A **council of war** is a meeting that is held in order to decide how a particular threat or emergency should be dealt with. *The President likened his approach to a military exercise—he called the meeting a council of war and laid out his 'battle plan'.*

counsel /kaʊnsl/ counsels, counselling, counselled; spelt counseling, counseled in American English. A formal word.
1 NU **Counsel** is careful advice. *...giving counsel in times of stress.*
2 VO, VO+to-INF, or V-QUOTE If you **counsel** someone to do something, you advise them to do it. *Some wanted to fight. Others counselled caution... He had earlier counselled Argentina not to sign any agreements... 'Ignore them,' Mrs Jones counselled.*
3 VO If you **counsel** people, you give them advice about their problems. *Part of her work is to counsel families when problems arise.*
4 NC or NU A **counsel** is a lawyer who gives advice on a legal case and fights the case in court. *That is one of the arguments that is used by defence counsels... In his opening remarks, Counsel to the inquiry referred to other tragedies at football grounds.*

counselling /kaʊnsəlɪŋ/; spelt counseling in American English.
NU **Counselling** is the activity of giving people advice as part of your job. *Do you see chaplaincy work as essentially counselling?... He had a period of psychiatric counselling.*

counsellor /kaʊnsələ/ counsellors; spelt counselor in American English.
NC A **counsellor** is a person whose job is to give advice to people who need it. *The hospital has trained counsellors who are used to dealing with depressed patients.*

count /kaʊnt/ counts, counting, counted
1 V or VO When you **count**, you say all the numbers in order up to a particular number. *I'm going to count up to three... After counting sixty the rest set off in pursuit.*
2 VO If you **count** all the things in a group, you add them up to see how many there are. *He withdrew to his office to count the money.*
3 NC A **count** is a number that you get by counting a particular set of things. *The official government count has now risen to eight million.*
4 V The thing that **counts** in a particular situation is the most important thing. *What counts is how you feel about yourself.*
5 V+for If a particular thing **counts** for something, it is valuable or important. *I felt that all my years there counted for nothing.*
6 V-ERG If you **count** something as another thing or if something **counts** as a particular thing, it is regarded as being that thing. *These benefits do not count as income for tax purposes... They can hardly be counted as friends.*

7 NC or TITLE A **count** is also a European nobleman with the same rank as a British earl. *Count Otto Lambsdorff is visiting East Berlin.*
● **Count** is used in these phrases. ● If you **keep count** of a number of things, you keep a record of how many have occurred or exist. If you **lose count** of a number of things, you cannot remember how many have occurred or exist. *I've lost count of how many theories have been proposed to account for that... There is no agreement yet on how to keep count of mobile missiles.* ● If something is wrong on a number **of counts**, it is wrong for that number of reasons. *The use of these tests is criticized on two counts... They are right on the first count but wrong on the second.*

count against PHRASAL VERB If something **counts against** you, it may cause you to be punished or rejected. *A non-nuclear defence strategy was one of the issues which counted against the Labour Party in its general election defeat... There are other factors which may count against him.*

count on PHRASAL VERB To **count on** or **count upon** someone or something means to rely on them. *Doctors could now count on a regular salary.*

count out PHRASAL VERB If you **count out** a sum of money, you count it as you put the notes or coins in a pile. *The girl could barely open the shop door or count out the correct money.*

count up PHRASAL VERB If you **count up** all the things of a particular kind, you count them. *I counted up my years of teaching experience.*

count upon. See count on. PHRASAL VERB

countable noun /kaʊntəbl naʊn/ countable nouns
NC A **countable noun** is the same as a count noun.

countdown /kaʊntdaʊn/ countdowns
NC A **countdown** is the counting aloud of numbers in reverse order before something happens. *NASA has decided to go ahead with the countdown for the launch of a shuttle space mission.*

countenance /kaʊntənəns/ countenances, countenancing, countenanced
1 NC Someone's **countenance** is their face; a literary use. *There were some harsh lines on his face—usually a grave and rather stern countenance.*
2 VO If you **countenance** something, you agree with it and allow it to happen; a formal use. *Shimon Peres has declared his willingness to countenance returning occupied territory in exchange for peace... He has refused to countenance any move towards multi-party politics.*

counter /kaʊntə/ counters, countering, countered
1 NC A **counter** in a shop is a long, flat surface where goods are displayed or sold. *Marks and Spencers does not have a sale but it does fill one or two counters with reduced goods.*
2 VO If you **counter** something that is being done, you take action to make it less effective. *To counter this the police will equip themselves with riot shields and tear gas... Mr Genscher said violations of those principles must be countered with sanctions.*
3 V If you **counter** something that has just been said, you say something in reaction to it or in opposition to it; a formal use. *I countered by enquiring whether she actually knew this man... He was immediately countered by his own chief judge saying exactly the opposite.*
4 NC If something is used as a bargaining **counter**, it is put forward as a potential item of exchange for something of equal value. *The Soviet Union may simply be using the issue as a bargaining counter... The foreigners may yet find themselves being used as bargaining counters in the crisis.*
5 NC A **counter** is also a small, flat round object used in board games.

counter- /kaʊntə-/
PREFIX **Counter-** is added to other words that refer to actions or activities to form words that put forward an opposite course of action or activity. *...counter-revolutionary. ...counter-culture. ...counter-demonstrations.*

counteract /kaʊntərækt/ counteracts, counteracting, counteracted
VO To **counteract** something means to reduce its effect

by doing something that has the opposite effect. *The move by the Bank of England is to try to counteract the current strength of the pound... Fusion pushes atoms apart, counteracting the inward pull of gravity.*

counter-attack, counter-attacks
N C or N U A **counter-attack** is an attack on a person or group that has already attacked you. *...counter-attacks against enemy civilians... The counter-attack is led by a group who include an Englishman called Colin.*

counterbalance /kaʊntəbælens/ **counterbalances, counterbalancing, counterbalanced**
V O To **counterbalance** something means to balance or correct it with something that has an equal but opposite effect. *...sufficient salt in the diet to counterbalance the amount of salt lost in sweat.*

counterclockwise /kaʊntəklɒkwaɪz/
ADV or ADJ ATTRIB **Counterclockwise** means the same as **anti-clockwise**; used in American English. *The management regularly saw fit to break up the free skating with a passage of counterclockwise skating.*

counter-espionage
N U **Counter-espionage** consists of the measures that a country takes in order to limit the effectiveness of another country's spying activities. *It's understood that military intelligence and counter-espionage will continue.*

counterfeit /kaʊntəfɪt/ **counterfeits, counterfeiting, counterfeited**
1 ADJ Something that is **counterfeit** is not genuine, but has been made to look genuine to deceive people. *...the Turkish police's test for detecting counterfeit money. ...heavy penalties for trading in counterfeit medicines.*
2 V O To **counterfeit** something means to make a version of it that is not genuine, but that has been made to look genuine to deceive people. *He said Iraqi forgers were counterfeiting dollars.*

counterfoil /kaʊntəfɔɪl/ **counterfoils**
N C A **counterfoil** is the part of a cheque or receipt that you keep as a record of the money you have spent. *...the counterfoil of his flight ticket.*

countermand /kaʊntəmɑːnd/ **countermands, countermanding, countermanded**
V O If you **countermand** an order, you cancel it, usually by giving a different order; a formal word. *...attempts by the government to countermand decisions of radical city councils.*

counter-measure, counter-measures
N C A **counter-measure** is an action that you take in order to weaken the effect of another action or a situation, or to make it harmless. *Unless specific counter-measures are taken, unemployment will continue to rise.*

counterpane /kaʊntəpeɪn/ **counterpanes**
N C A **counterpane** is a decorative cover on a bed; an old-fashioned word.

counterpart /kaʊntəpɑːt/ **counterparts**
N C+POSS The **counterpart** of someone or something is another person or thing with a similar function in a different place. *...talks between the American Secretary of State and his Soviet counterpart. ...the English merchant bank and its American counterpart, the Wall Street investment bank.*

counterpoint /kaʊntəpɔɪnt/
N U In music, **counterpoint** is a technique in which two different tunes are played together at the same time in order to produce a particular effect; a technical term. *He saw that the composer set himself his counterpoint of melodic lines one on top of the other.*

counter-productive
ADJ Something that is **counter-productive** has the opposite effect from what you intend. *The government appears to have accepted that censorship was counter-productive.*

counter-revolution, counter-revolutions
N C A **counter-revolution** is a revolution that is intended to reverse the effects of a previous revolution. *Castro felt that if he allowed economic counter-revolution, political counter-revolution would follow.*

counter-revolutionary, counter-revolutionaries
N C A **counter-revolutionary** is a person who is trying

to reverse the effects of a previous revolution. *They planned to overawe all counter-revolutionaries through sheer mass and armed might.* ▶ Also ADJ *...illicit counter-revolutionary activity.*

countersign /kaʊntəsaɪn/ **countersigns, countersigning, countersigned**
V O If you **countersign** a document, you sign it after someone else has signed it, in order to confirm that their signature is genuine. *Jaruzelski countersigned the parliamentary resolution yesterday.*

countertenor /kaʊntətenə/ **countertenors**
N C A **countertenor** is a man who sings with a high voice that is similar to a low female singing voice; a technical term in music. *Bill Zukof is a countertenor for the Western Wind Vocal Ensemble.*

counterweight, /kaʊntəweɪt/ **counterweights**
N C A **counterweight** is an action or proposal that is intended to balance or counter other actions or proposals. *The organization has been set up to act as a counterweight to the Latvian People's Front... Their victory would mean a welcome boost and a counterweight to years in the doldrums of opposition.*

countess /kaʊntɪs/ **countesses**
N C or TITLE A **countess** is a woman with the same rank as a count or earl. A countess is also the wife of a count or earl. *...an engagement party for the daughter of a countess. ...the Countess of Derby.*

countless /kaʊntləs/
ADJ ATTRIB **Countless** means very many. *The W.H.O. through its health campaigns has saved countless lives throughout the world... He's taken part in countless demonstrations.*

count noun, count nouns
N C A **count noun** is a noun that has a singular and a plural form and is always used after a determiner when singular.

country /kʌntri/ **countries**
1 N C A **country** is one of the areas the world is divided into which has its own government, language, and culture. *The level of unemployment in this country is too high... Forests cover about one third of the country.*
2 N SING You can also refer to the people who live in a particular country as the **country**. *The country was stunned.*
3 N SING The **country** is land away from towns and cities. *We live in the country. ...schools in country areas.* ▶ Also ADJ ATTRIB *...country roads.*
4 NU+SUPP **Country** is used to refer to an area with particular characteristics or connections. *...mountain country. ...an area which is generally known as bandit country.*
5 ADJ ATTRIB **Country** music is a style of popular music. *Country music singers kept the excitement high.*

country-and-western
N U **Country-and-western** is a style of popular music that originated in the USA. *The celebrations began with a female country-and-western band holding an open air concert.*

country club, country clubs
N C A **country club** is a club in the country where you can play sports and attend social events. *The Buick Open starts at the Warwick Hills Country Club in Michigan later today.*

country dancing
N U **Country dancing** is traditional dancing in which people dance in rows or circles. *They'd like to learn Scottish country dancing.*

country house, country houses
N C A **country house** is a large house in the country owned by a rich or titled family. *For people brought up in haunted country houses, ghosts aren't really a novelty.*

countryman /kʌntrɪmən/ **countrymen** /kʌntrɪmən/
N C Your **countrymen** are people from your own country. *Henri Leconte of France has defeated his countryman Jerome Potier to take the Nice Open title.*

country seat, country seats
N C A **country seat** is a large house and estate in the country, which is owned by someone who also owns a house in a town. *Alton Towers was once an English*

stately home, the country seat of the Earl of Shrewsbury.

countryside /kʌntrisaɪd/

N SING or NU The **countryside** is land that is away from towns and cities. *...the English countryside... It's very nice countryside around there.*

countrywide /kʌntriwaɪd/

ADJ ATTRIB or ADV Something that happens or exists **countrywide** happens or exists throughout the whole of a particular country. *Proportional representation, the report claims, would accurately reflect the countrywide support of each party... Mr Buyoya said that the charter details would be distributed countrywide. ...a forty-eight hour country-wide general strike.*

county /kaʊnti/ **counties**

NC A **county** is a region of Britain, Ireland, or the USA with its own local government. *...the English county of Yorkshire.*

county council, county councils

NC A **county council** is an organization which administers local government in a British county. *...Kent County Council... The county council's move to appoint the ten new teachers was heavily criticized.*

county town, county towns

NC A **county town** is the most important town in a county, from which the county is administered. *...the picturesque village of Milford, a few miles from the county town of Stafford.*

coup /kuː/ **coups**

1 NC A **coup** is a military action intended to seize power in a country by getting rid of its government or its president. *The Indian authorities say mercenaries and rebels were behind a coup attempt in the Maldives.*

2 NC A **coup** is also an achievement thought to be especially brilliant because of its difficulty. *Brooke went on to bigger things, his next notable coup being the case of Robert Scott.*

coup de grâce /kuː də grɑːs/

N SING A **coup de grâce** is an action or event which finally destroys something, for example an institution, which has been gradually growing weaker; a formal expression. *This trouble finally gave the coup de grâce to the crumbling edifice of empire.*

coup d'état /kuː deɪtɑː/ **coups d'état.** The singular and the plural are pronounced in the same way.

NC When there is a **coup d'état**, a group of people seize power in a country. *Right wing elements created havoc in the country's past and led to an eventual military coup d'état.*

coupé /kuːpeɪ/ **coupés**

NC A **coupé** is a car with a fixed roof, a sloping back, two doors, and seats for four people. *He had a fast '36 Ford coupé... The base price on Saturn's top model, a sporty coupé, will be under $12,000.*

couple /kʌpl/ **couples, coupling, coupled**

1 N COLL A **couple** is two people who are married, living together, or having a sexual or romantic relationship. *The party was to celebrate the couple's third wedding anniversary.*

2 N COLL You can also use **couple** to describe two people who you see together on a particular occasion. *...a couple on the dance floor.*

3 NC A **couple** of people or things means two people or things. *He met her a couple of years ago.*

4 VO+with If one thing is **coupled** with another, the two things are done or dealt with together. *Strong protests were made, coupled with demands for an international inquiry.*

couplet /kʌplət/ **couplets**

NC A **couplet** is two lines of poetry together, especially two lines that rhyme with each other and have the same number of syllables. *Pope's particular form of verse was the rhyming heroic couplet.*

coupon /kuːpɒn/ **coupons**

1 NC A **coupon** is a piece of printed paper issued by the maker or supplier of a product which allows you to pay less than usual for it. *...special coupons whereby they can apply for cheaper petrol.*

2 NC A **coupon** is also a small form which you fill in and send off to ask for information or to enter a

competition. *So far, five-million households have received lottery coupons.*

courage /kʌrɪdʒ/

NU **Courage** is the quality shown by someone who does something difficult or dangerous, even though they may be afraid. *She would never have had the courage to defy him.*

courageous /kəreɪdʒəs/

ADJ Someone who is **courageous** shows courage. *...his courageous attempt to get the facts published.*

♦ **courageously** ADV *She fought courageously for her principles.*

courgette /kɔːʒet/ **courgettes**

NC **Courgettes** are small marrows, eaten as a vegetable.

courier /kʊriə/ **couriers**

1 NC A **courier** is someone employed by a travel company to look after holidaymakers. *They've appealed for help from travel couriers on the island.*

2 NC A **courier** is also someone who is paid to take a special letter or a special goods from one place to another. *As soon as copies are available, couriers will be dashing round London to the financial houses... Children were being used as drug couriers in Pakistan.*

course /kɔːs/ **courses, coursing, coursed**

1 NC A **course** is a series of lessons or lectures. *Degrees will be awarded on the basis of exam performance and course work.*

2 NC+of A series of medical treatments is also called a **course**. *Another course of injections was prescribed.*

3 NC A **course** is also one part of a meal. *...a three-course dinner.*

4 NC The **course** of a ship or aircraft is its route. *The B-2's advanced radar will enable it to follow a highly accurate course.*

5 N SING You can refer to the way that events develop as the **course** of history, nature, or events. *This allowed Egypt a continuing influence on the course of events... President Bush is monitoring the course of events.*

6 V If a liquid **courses** somewhere, it flows quickly; a literary use. *Tears coursed down my face.*

7 See also **golf course, racecourse.**

● **Course** is used in these phrases. ● You say **of course** when you are saying something that you expect other people to realize or understand. *There is of course an element of truth in this argument.* ● You also use **of course** when you are talking about an event or situation that does not surprise you. *He never writes to me, of course.* ● **Of course** is also a polite way of giving permission or agreeing with someone. *'Could I make a telephone call?' he said. 'Of course,' Boylan said.* ● You use **of course** to emphasize what you are saying. *'Do you love him, Dolly?'—'Of course I do. He's wonderful.'... 'Do you think he was killed?'—'No, no, of course not.'* ● A **course of action** is one of the things you can do in a situation. *The German embassy is considering what course of action to take.* ● If you do something **as a matter of course**, you do it as part of your normal work or way of life. *We now expect to see TV from all over our globe as a matter of course, not a rare thrill.* ● If something happens **in the course of** a period of time, it happens during that time. *In the course of the day, Mr Bush gave several speeches.* ● If a ship or aircraft is **on course**, it is travelling along the correct route. If it is **off course**, it is no longer travelling along the correct route. *If the two jets had continued on course, they would have collided... The question is what the aircraft was doing so far off course.* ● If something **runs its course** or **takes its course**, it develops naturally and comes to a natural end. *The illness was allowed to run its course... Justice could now take its course.* ● **in due course**: see **due.**

court /kɔːt/ **courts, courting, courted**

1 NC A **court** is a place where legal matters are decided by a judge and jury or by a magistrate. *He could try to clear his name before a court of law.*

2 NC You can also refer to the judge and jury or magistrates as the **court**. *The court dismissed the charges.*

3 NC A **court** is also an area in which you play a game

such as tennis, badminton, or squash. *There are two squash courts and an indoor swimming pool.*
4 NC The **court** of a king, queen, or emperor is the place where he or she lives and carries out ceremonial or administrative duties. *Salieri was the court composer at the Viennese court of Emperor Joseph II.*
5 VO If one country **courts** another country, they make an effort to improve diplomatic relations between them. *Pretoria is now courting the outside world... China is in the position of being courted by both superpowers.*
6 VorVO If a man and a woman **are courting**, they are paying each other a lot of attention because they are planning to marry; an old-fashioned use. *...the girl he had previously courted.*
7 VO To **court** something such as danger, sympathy, or publicity, means to act in a way that makes it likely to happen. *She courted publicity by inviting newspaper photographers to be present.*
● **Court** is used in these phrases. ● If someone is **in court**, they are in a court while a trial is taking place. *Ferdinand Marcos has appeared in court in New York.*
● If you **go to court** or **take** someone **to court**, you take legal action against them. *We're prepared to go to court and prove it... He took me to court for libelling him.* ● When someone is **at court**, they are present at the king's or queen's residence. *...the gardens used by British royalty as a pleasurable escape from the formal duties at court.*

courteous /kɜːtiəs/
ADJ Someone who is **courteous** is polite, respectful, and considerate. *He was the kindest, most courteous gentleman to work for.* ◆ **courteously** ADV *The jailer received me courteously.*

courtesan /kɔːtɪzæn/ **courtesans**
NC A **courtesan** is a woman who was looked after financially by the rich and important men that she had sexual relationships with; an old-fashioned word. *Mata Hari, an exotic dancer and courtesan, was involved with both French and German Intelligence.*

courtesy /kɜːtəsi/ **courtesies**
1 NU **Courtesy** is polite, respectful, and considerate behaviour. *He replied with promptness and courtesy.*
2 N PL **Courtesies** are polite and respectful things that you say or do; a formal use. *The plaudits from all sides for Mr Major's chairing of the summit are more than just the customary courtesies to the host. ...a brief exchange of courtesies.*
3 If something is done **by courtesy of** someone, it is done with their permission. *...the pre-released recording supplied by courtesy of Nimbus Records.*
4 If something happens **by courtesy of** someone or something, they make it possible. *Rangers' three-nil win at Dunfermline came by courtesy of McCoist, Walters and Gough... The electronic book is just around the corner by courtesy of a machine based on the same technology as the compact disc player.*

courtesy title, courtesy titles
NC A **courtesy title** is a title that has no legal power, such as those held by the children of the English aristocracy. *The post of deputy Prime Minister is mainly a courtesy title.*

courthouse /kɔːthaʊs/ **courthouses**
NC A **courthouse** is a building in which a law court meets. *Gunmen murdered an Italian judge as he was on his way to work at the courthouse in Agrigento.*

courtier /kɔːtiə/ **courtiers**
NC **Courtiers** were noblemen and noblewomen at the court of a king or queen. *...the rich costumes of the courtiers.*

courtly /kɔːtli/ **courtlier, courtliest**
ADJ Someone who is **courtly** acts in the polite and dignified manner that is associated with the age of chivalry. *...a courtly old gentleman named John Jameson.*

court-martial, court-martials, court-martialling, court-martialled
VO To **court-martial** a member of the armed forces means to try them in a military court. *The colonel threatened to court-martial him.* ► Also NC *They arrested General Lee for disobedience, and ordered a court-martial.*

court of appeal, courts of appeal
NC A **court of appeal** is a court which deals with appeals against legal judgements. *The latest decision by the court of appeal has reversed a previous ruling by a lower court... The Court of Appeal is to re-examine the convictions of the so-called Guildford Four.*

court of inquiry, courts of inquiry
1 NC A **court of inquiry** is an official investigation into a serious accident or incident. *The government in Kashmir has instituted a court of inquiry into the allegations against the central reserve police force.*
2 You can also refer to a group of people who are officially appointed to investigate a serious accident or incident as a **court of inquiry**. *A court of inquiry sharply criticized the local authority.*

court of law, courts of law
NC When you refer to a **court of law**, you are referring to a legal court, especially when talking about the evidence that might be given in a trial. *...evidence which would stand up in a court of law.*

courtroom /kɔːtruːm, kɔːtrʊm/ **courtrooms**
NC A **courtroom** is a room in which a law court meets. *The courtroom swarmed with lawyers.*

courtship /kɔːtʃɪp/
1 NU **Courtship** is an activity in which a man and a woman spend a lot of time together, because they are intending to get married; an old-fashioned use. *There is nothing to advance a courtship better than a poem.*
2 NU The **courtship** of male and female animals is their behaviour before they mate. *Courtship will include displays in which the male fluffs up his feathers.*

court shoe, court shoes
NC **Court shoes** are ladies' shoes that have high heels and are made of plain leather with no design.

courtyard /kɔːtjɑːd/ **courtyards**
NC A **courtyard** is a flat open area of ground surrounded by buildings or walls. *...a rather quaint courtyard on the side of the Kabul River.*

cousin /kʌzn/ **cousins**
1 NC Your **cousin** is the child of your uncle or aunt. *Mr Waite's cousin, John, called for greater efforts to secure their release.*
2 NC You can use **cousins** to refer to people who come from a different place but who are like you or have similar interests and opinions. *Whereas West Germans drink wine, their Eastern cousins prefer Schnapps.*
3 See also **first cousin, second cousin**.

couture /kuːtjʊə/
NU **Couture** is high fashion designing and dressmaking. *Rome couture would be nowhere without Valentino. ...the big couture establishments.*

couturier /kuːtjʊəriei/ **couturiers**
NC A **couturier** is a person who designs, makes, and sells fashion clothes for women. *She is dressed by the famous couturiers Reville and Rossiter.*

cove /kəʊv/ **coves**
NC A **cove** is a small bay on the coast. *The coves and isolated beaches of West Wales have long been a target for drugs smugglers.*

covenant /kʌvənənt/ **covenants**
1 NC A **covenant** is a formal written agreement between two people or groups of people which is recognized in law. *...the Palestine National Covenant... Such practices violated the international covenant on civil and political rights.*
2 NC A **covenant** is also a formal written promise to pay a sum of money each year for a fixed period towards a charity or financial trust. *...the loss of tax relief on covenants... Many students receive parental contributions by covenant.*

Coventry /kɒvntri/
If you **send** someone **to Coventry**, you avoid speaking to them whenever you meet them, as a punishment for something that they have done. *They punished me by sending me to Coventry for the rest of the summer holiday.*

cover /kʌvə/ **covers, covering, covered**
1 VO If you **cover** something, you place something else over it to protect it or hide it. *She covered her face*

with her hands... Dug into the hillside and then covered by earth and plants are scores of stone shelters.
2 vo If one thing **covers** another, it forms a layer over that thing. *Her hand was covered with blood... The oil spill covered an area ten miles long and two miles wide.*
3 vo If you **cover** a particular distance, you travel that distance. *I covered approximately twenty miles a day.*
4 vo An insurance policy that **covers** a person or thing guarantees that money will be paid in relation to that person or thing. *The entire risk is covered to the full value and a policy is then issued.* ► Also NU *This policy gives unlimited cover for hospital charges.*
5 vo If a law **covers** a particular set of people, things, or situations, it applies to them. *Muslims want the government to change the blasphemy laws to cover all religions.*
6 vo If you **cover** a particular topic, you discuss it in a lecture, course, or book. *We've covered a wide range of subjects today.*
7 vo If reporters, newspapers, or television companies **cover** an event, they report on it. *The Presidential election is widely covered in today's press... Glenny has been asked by the BBC to cover all aspects of the events in Prague.*
8 vo If a sum of money **covers** something, it is enough to pay for it. *I'll give you a cheque to cover the cost of your journey.*
9 NC A **cover** is something which is put over an object, usually in order to protect it. *The cover clips on over the electrical connections, and is very neat.*
10 NC If respectable or normal behaviour is a **cover** for secret or illegal activities, it is intended to hide them. *...a cover for murder.*
11 N PL Bed **covers** are the sheet, blankets, and bedspread that you have on top of you when you are in bed. *He sneaks up to the bed, pulls back the covers and edges in.*
12 NC The **cover** of a book or a magazine is its outside. *His piercing blue eyes dominate the magazine's front cover.*
13 NU **Cover** is trees, rocks, or other places where you shelter from the weather or hide from someone. *They crossed to the other side of the stream in search of cover.*
14 NC A **cover** of a song is an alternative version that has been made by another singer or group. *The song is a cover of the 1964 hit for Gerry and the Pacemakers.*
● **Cover** is used in these phrases. ● If you **take cover**, you shelter from the weather or from gunfire. *They made it a few yards before taking cover on hearing a patrol approaching.* ● If you do something **under cover** of a particular condition, this enables you to do it without being noticed. *The attack usually takes place under cover of darkness.*
cover up PHRASAL VERB 1 If you **cover** something **up**, you put something else over it to protect it or hide it. *We'll cover the wound up with a clean dry bandage.*
2 If you **cover up** something that you do not want people to know about, you hide it from them. *She tried to cover up for Willie.* ● See also **cover-up**.
coverage /kʌvəʳrɪdʒ/
NU The **coverage** of something in the news is the reporting of it. *They put an immediate ban on all television coverage of their operations.*
cover charge, cover charges
NC A **cover charge** is a sum of money that you have to pay to enter most nightclubs and that you must pay at some restaurants in addition to the price of the food and drink.
cover girl, cover girls
NC A **cover girl** is an attractive woman whose photograph appears on the front of a magazine.
covering /kʌvəʳrɪŋ/ **coverings**
NCorNU A **covering** is a layer of something that goes over something else. *...fabric coverings for chairs... Kitchen floor covering should be non-slip.*
covering letter, covering letters
NC A **covering letter** is a letter that you send with a

parcel or with another document to give extra information.
coverlet /kʌvələt/ **coverlets**
NC A **coverlet** is a decorative cover which is put over a bed.
covert /kʌvət, kəʊvɜːt/
ADJ Something that is **covert** is secret or hidden; a formal word. *...a covert involvement in activist politics.* ◆ **covertly** ADV *She watched Marina covertly.*
cover-up, cover-ups
NC A **cover-up** is an attempt to hide a crime or mistake. *The government is investigating allegations of a high level cover-up over the air disaster.*
covet /kʌvɪt/ **covets, coveting, coveted**
VO If you **covet** something, you badly want it for yourself; a formal word. *It was an honour he had long coveted.*
covetous /kʌvɪtəs/
ADJ ATTRIB **Covetous** feelings and actions involve a strong desire to possess something; a formal word. *The United States Steel Corporation was casting covetous eyes at his company.*
cow /kaʊ/ **cows, cowing, cowed**
1 NC A **cow** is a large female animal kept on farms for its milk. *...baby feed made from cow's milk.*
2 NC A **cow** is also any animal of this species, either male or female. *...a herd of cows.*
3 vo If someone is **cowed**, they are frightened into behaving in a particular way; a formal use. *People shouldn't allow themselves to be cowed into this.* ◆ **cowed** ADJ *...his tragically cowed and battered wife.*
coward /kaʊəd/ **cowards**
NC A **coward** is someone who is easily frightened and avoids dangerous or difficult situations. *People will lose respect for him and call him a coward.*
cowardice /kaʊədɪs/
NU **Cowardice** is cowardly behaviour. *He despised them for their cowardice and ignorance.*
cowardly /kaʊədli/
ADJ Someone who is **cowardly** is easily frightened and so avoids doing dangerous or difficult things. *...a cowardly refusal to face reality.*
cowboy /kaʊbɔɪ/ **cowboys**
1 NC A **cowboy** is a man employed to look after cattle in America. *...Argentina, home of the gaucho, or South American cowboy.*
2 NC A **cowboy** is also a male character in a western. *Lots of deaths in cowboy films made them seem less real.*
3 NC If you refer to workmen or a firm of contractors as **cowboys**, you mean that their method of working or the work they produce is unsatisfactory. *By allowing unscrupulous cowboy operators to dump waste unchecked, Britain is facing a legacy of environmental disasters.*
Cowboys and Indians
NU **Cowboys and Indians** is a children's game in which one group pretends to be cowboys and another group pretends to be American Indians and the two groups pretend to fight each other.
cower /kaʊə/ **cowers, cowering, cowered**
v If you **cower**, you bend downwards or move back because you are afraid. *Bernadette cowered in her seat. ...a crowd in prison-like costumes cowering before the truncheons of cruel guards.*
cowhide /kaʊhaɪd/
NU **Cowhide** is leather made from the skin of a cow. *The upper part is made of cowhide, the soles are rubber.*
cowl /kaʊl/ **cowls**
1 NC A **cowl** is a large loose hood covering a person's head or their head and shoulders. Cowls are especially worn by monks.
2 NC A **cowl** is a metal cover that is put on top of a chimney in order to help the smoke come out and to prevent the wind coming down the chimney.
cowman /kaʊmən/ **cowmen** /kaʊmən/
NC A **cowman** is a person employed to look after cattle.
cowpat /kaʊpæt/ **cowpats**
NC A **cowpat** is a pool of dung from a cow.

cowrie /kaʊri/ cowries
1 NC A **cowrie** is a shellfish which has an oval shell with a long narrow opening.
2 NC A **cowrie** is also the oval shell of a cowrie. These shells are often used as items of jewellery. *...masks set with cowrie shells around the eyes.*
cowshed /kaʊʃed/ cowsheds
NC A **cowshed** is a building where cows are kept or milked.
cowslip /kaʊslɪp/ cowslips
NC A **cowslip** is a small wild plant with yellow sweet-smelling flowers. *...one species it believes is being harmed by the pollution is cowslips.*
coy /kɔɪ/
1 ADJ If someone is **coy**, they pretend to be shy and modest. *...a coy little smile.* ♦ **coyly** ADV *They were looking at us coyly through their elegant lashes.*
♦ **coyness** NU *There is no false modesty or coyness about her.*
2 ADJ **Coy** can also mean unwilling to say something, in a way that people find slightly irritating. *Let us not be coy about the identity of this great man.*
coyote /kɔɪəʊti/ coyotes
NC A **coyote** is a small wolf which lives in the plains of North America. *These scars are caused in many instances by animals, coyotes, jackrabbits and so on.*
cozy /kaʊzi/. See cosy.
Cpl.
Cpl. is the usual written abbreviation for 'corporal'.
crab /kræb/ crabs
NC A **crab** is a sea creature with a flat round body covered by a shell, and five pairs of legs with claws on the front pair. *Turtle soups, crabs or eels can be surprisingly tasty.*
crab apple, crab apples
NC A **crab apple** is a type of small sour apple. *He was lectured as a child on the dangers of eating crab apples.*
crabbed /kræbɪd/
1 ADJ **Crabbed** handwriting is handwriting that is squashed together and hard to read. *...the name of Duggan, written in a crabbed hand.*
2 ADJ **Crabbed** means the same as **crabby**; an old-fashioned use. *He met a crabbed, cantankerous director.*
crabby /kræbi/
ADJ Someone who is **crabby** is bad-tempered and unpleasant to people. *Our two year old was a bit crabby, having just been woken up from a nap.*
crabwise /kræbwaɪz/
ADV If you move **crabwise**, you move sideways. *I edged my way crabwise along the row to my allotted place.*
crack /kræk/ cracks, cracking, cracked
1 V-ERG If something **cracks** or if you **crack** it, it becomes slightly damaged, with lines appearing on its surface. *If you hold a glass under the hot tap, it may crack... He gave the piece of jewellery to his colleague who cracked it.*
2 V If someone **cracks**, they come close to having a nervous breakdown or they become mentally ill because of stress; an informal use. *I thought I might crack if I didn't get away soon.*
3 VO If you **crack** a problem or a code, you solve it, especially after a lot of thought. *They were eager to crack the codes.*
4 VO If you **crack** a joke, you tell it. *The two beaming leaders cracked jokes together at a surprise press conference.*
5 NC A **crack** is a very narrow gap between two things. *...the cracks between the boards of the ceiling.*
6 NC A **crack** is also a line appearing on the surface of something when it is slightly damaged or partly broken. *She found a crack in one of the tea-cups.*
7 NC A **crack** is also a sharp sound like the sound of something suddenly breaking. *He heard a crack of bones breaking. ...the crack of a whip.*
8 NC A **crack** is also a slightly rude or cruel joke.
9 ADJ ATTRIB A **crack** soldier or sportsman is highly trained and very skilful. *...the army's crack SAS Regiment... The crack French hurdler Marly River is to race at Auteuil in Paris.*

10 NU **Crack** is a form of the drug cocaine which has been purified and made into crystals. *The abuse of crack has reached epidemic proportions in the US.*
11 See also **cracked**.
● **Crack** is used in these phrases. ● If you do something **at the crack of dawn**, you do it very early in the morning. *The big game hunting season opens at the crack of dawn tomorrow.* ● If you **have a crack at** something, you make an attempt to do it; an informal expression. *Everyone in the government has had a crack at it.*
crack down PHRASAL VERB If people in authority **crack down** on someone or something, they enforce the rules or laws against it. *Her first reaction to the riots was to crack down hard. ...President Mubarak's determination to crack down on corruption.* ● See also **crackdown**.
crack up PHRASAL VERB If someone **cracks up**, they are under such a lot of emotional strain that they become mentally ill; an informal expression. *I'd crack up if there wasn't someone I could talk to... Of course, there are people who finish by cracking up.*
● See also **crack-up**.
crackdown /krækdaʊn/ crackdowns
NC A **crackdown** is strong official action taken to punish people who break laws. *The government enforced one of its biggest crackdowns on dissidents in ten years. ...a crackdown on criminals.*
cracked /krækt/
ADJ A **cracked** object has lines on its surface because it has been damaged or partly broken. *There's little worse than a badly scratched or cracked record.*
cracker /krækə/ crackers
1 NC A **cracker** is a thin, crisp biscuit often eaten with cheese. *...a plateful of water crackers and baguettes.*
2 NC A **cracker** is also a small paper-covered tube that is pulled apart with a bang to reveal a small toy and a paper hat.
cracking /krækɪŋ/
1 If you tell someone to **get cracking**, you are telling them to start doing something immediately; an informal expression. *Get cracking or we'll never finish in time.*
2 If you walk at a **cracking pace**, you walk very quickly; an informal expression. *Gillian used to go at a cracking pace.*
crackle /krækl/ crackles, crackling, crackled
V If something **crackles**, it makes a series of short, harsh noises. *The loudspeaker crackled... The lightbulb suddenly crackled overhead, and for a moment I thought it was laughter.* ► Also N SING *...the crackle of the fire... The coup began with the crackle of gunfire around the national palace.*
crackling /kræklɪŋ/; pronounced /krækəlɪŋ/ for the meaning in paragraph 1 and /kræklɪŋ/ for the meaning in paragraph 2.
1 N SING **Crackling** is a rapid series of short, harsh noises. *...the crackling of Mr Willet's bonfire... The crackling became louder and louder.*
2 NU **Crackling** is also the crisp, brown skin of pork when it has been roasted. *...scallops with ginger and deep-fried pork crackling.*
crackpot /krækpɒt/ crackpots
NC A **crackpot** is someone who has strange and crazy ideas; an informal word. *The Sun newspaper have denounced him as a crackpot... Nobody wants to take industrial action except a crackpot.*
crack-up
N SING If someone has a **crack-up**, they lose control of themselves and become mentally ill; an informal word. *People gossiped about his crack-up.*
cradle /kreɪdl/ cradles, cradling, cradled
1 NC A **cradle** is a small box-shaped bed for a baby. *The new baby was in a cradle in a bare room.*
2 N SING+SUPP The **cradle** of something is the place where it began; a literary use. *New England saw itself as the cradle of American technology... Mali is the cradle of some of Africa's richest civilizations.*
3 VO If you **cradle** something in your arms, you hold it carefully. *She cradled a child in her arms... I found him collapsed over the telephone, his head cradled in his arms.*

4 If something happens to you **from the cradle to the grave**, it happens throughout your life. *...a woman who, from the cradle to the grave, bore about her a grace and elegance... The government provides cradle-to-grave security, free education, and cheap housing.*

cradle-snatcher, cradle-snatchers
NC If you refer to someone as a **cradle-snatcher**, you mean that they have a sexual relationship or marriage with someone who is much younger than themselves; an informal word, used showing disapproval. *She would be with an older man, and I'd be seen as a cradle-snatcher.*

craft /krɑːft/ **crafts**. The plural form for the meaning in paragraph 1 is **craft**.
1 NC You can refer to a boat, a spacecraft, or an aircraft as a **craft**. *There were eight destroyers and fifty smaller craft.*
2 NC A **craft** is an activity such as weaving, carving, or pottery that involves making things skilfully with your hands. *...traditional crafts such as thatching and weaving. ...a craft festival.*
3 NC You can use **craft** to refer to any activity or job that involves doing something skilfully. *He was still learning his journalistic craft.*

craftsman /krɑːftsmən/ **craftsmen**
NC A **craftsman** is someone who makes things skilfully with their hands. *The violin was made in 1709 by the Italian craftsman, Antonio Stradivarius.*

craftsmanship /krɑːftsmənʃɪp/
1 NU **Craftsmanship** is the skill of making beautiful things with your hands. *East German artists had a reputation for good craftsmanship... They all have one thing in common—impeccable craftsmanship and an urgency to express themselves.*
2 NU **Craftsmanship** is also the quality that something has when it is beautiful and has been carefully made. *I bent down to examine the exquisite craftsmanship... The funereal longboat is nothing less than superb in its craftsmanship.*

craftswoman /krɑːftswumən/ **craftswomen**
NC A **craftswoman** is a woman who makes things skilfully with her hands. *The room was packed with talented craftswomen.*

crafty /krɑːfti/
ADJ If a person or their behaviour is **crafty**, they achieve things by deceiving people in a clever way. *...the crafty tactics of journalists.* ♦ **craftily** ADV *Several ploys are being craftily developed.*

crag /kræg/ **crags**
NC A **crag** is a steep, rocky cliff or part of a mountain. *...the crags and crevices of the moon's surface... The accident happened in an area at Bizzle Crags in Northumberland.*

craggy /krægi/
ADJ A **craggy** mountain is steep and rocky. *She's lived in this house, perched on a craggy hill, for over a year.*

cram /kræm/ **crams, cramming, crammed**
VOA If you **cram** people or things into a place, you push as many of them in it as possible. *Thirty of us were crammed into a small dark room... He crammed the bank notes into his pockets.*

crammed /kræmd/
ADJ PRED If a place is **crammed** with things or people, it is very full of them. *A helicopter whirrs upwards crammed with American marines. ...a concrete bunker crammed full of radio equipment.*

cramp /kræmp/ **cramps, cramping, cramped**
1 NU or N PL If you have **cramp** or **cramps**, you feel a strong pain caused by a muscle suddenly contracting. *I had the most excruciating cramp in my leg... She had severe stomach cramps.*
2 If you **cramp** someone's **style**, your presence restricts their behaviour in some way; an informal expression. *If the race to be elected is helping Mr Wilder, it is cramping the style of Mr Coleman, the former Attorney General.*

cramped /kræmpt/
ADJ A **cramped** room or building is not big enough for the people or things in it. *He lives with his harassed mother in a cramped apartment... The report*

describes many hostels as damp and cramped, with unsafe windows and electrical appliances.

cranberry /krænbəʳri/ **cranberries**
NC A **cranberry** is a red berry with a sour taste which is often used to make a sauce that you eat with poultry. *...turkey and cranberry sauce.*

crane /kreɪn/ **cranes, craning, craned**
1 NC A **crane** is a large machine that moves heavy things by lifting them in the air. *A crane was already unloading crates and pallets... The authorities are using helicopters and cranes to bring in the goods.*
2 NC A **crane** is also a kind of large bird with a long neck and long legs. *Her long, slender, bare legs were as delicate as a crane's.*
3 VO If you **crane** your neck, you stretch it to see or hear something better. *He craned his neck out of the window... Curious passengers craned their necks for a better view.*

crane fly, crane flies
NC A **crane fly** is a harmless flying insect with long legs. *Other insects, for example crane flies, don't feed as adults.*

cranial /kreɪniəl/
ADJ ATTRIB **Cranial** means relating to your cranium; a technical term in biology. *...the cranial cavity.*

cranium /kreɪniəm/ **crania** /kreɪniə/ or **craniums**
NC Your **cranium** is the round part of your skull that contains your brain; a technical term in biology. *The bottom part of the cranium is delicate and breaks easily.*

crank /kræŋk/ **cranks, cranking, cranked**
1 NC A **crank** is someone with peculiar ideas who behaves in a strange way; an informal use. *Police believe he is a mentally disturbed religious crank.*
2 VO If you **crank** a device or machine, you make it move by turning a handle. *This is a hands-on museum—you can ring the bell of the school house and crank the old telephones. ...crazy old women who can't even crank their cars.*

crank up PHRASAL VERB **1** If you **crank up a** machine, engine, or vehicle, you make it start or increase its output by turning a handle. *Mommy cranked up the car and drove Sarah to school... The warm weather caused some Americans to crank up their air-conditioning.* **2** To **crank up** a system or organization means to increase its activities. *In the past two weeks, they have been cranking up the civil defence routines they developed during the war... Florida is cranking up its resources in order to catch some of the drug runners.*

crankshaft /kræŋkʃɑːft/ **crankshafts**
NC A **crankshaft** is the main shaft of an internal combustion engine. *The up-and-down motion of the piston drives the crankshaft round.*

cranky /kræŋki/ **crankier, crankiest**
1 ADJ **Cranky** behaviour is strange behaviour which results from someone having unusual ideas; used showing disapproval. *...a bachelor of cranky habits... The Front has often been dismissed as a cranky fringe group. ...a cranky old woman.*
2 ADJ **Cranky** also means bad tempered; used in American English. *Worried lawyers and cranky reporters have been demanding that the public is kept informed. ...the long and cranky queues for customs.*

cranny /kræni/ **crannies**
every nook and cranny: see **nook**.

crap /kræp/ **craps, crapping, crapped**; Except for the meaning in paragraph 5, 'crap' is an informal, rude word which some people find offensive.
1 NU You describe something that someone says or writes as **crap** when you think that it is wrong or foolish.
2 NU You refer to objects as **crap** if they are unimportant, useless, or in your way.
3 NU **Crap** also means the same as **faeces**.
4 V When you **crap**, you get rid of faeces from your body.
5 NU **Craps** or **crap** is a gambling game, played mainly in the United States, in which you throw two dice and bet on the total score. *The boys gathered there to play a game of craps... He stopped for a moment to watch the crap game.*

crappy /krǽpi/ **crappier, crappiest**
ADJ You describe something as **crappy** when you think that it is of very poor quality; an informal, rude word which some people find offensive. *They watch those crappy old films on TV.*

crash /kræʃ/ **crashes, crashing, crashed**
1 NC A **crash** is an accident in which a moving vehicle hits something and is damaged or destroyed. *Her mother was killed in a car crash... Fifteen people died in an air crash earlier today.*
2 V-ERG If a moving vehicle **crashes** or if the driver **crashes** it, it hits something and is damaged or destroyed. *The plane crashed within seconds of taking off... Ms. Langley swerved to avoid a deer and crashed... He crashed his car into the bar.*
3 VA To **crash** also means to move or fall violently, making a loud noise. *The door crashed open... A glass crashed to the floor... When the raft plunges into a rapid, large waves come crashing over the sides.*
4 V If a business or organization **crashes**, it fails suddenly, often with serious financial effects on its customers. *In the old days, when a bank crashed, the depositors often lost much of their money... That's the largest decline in the index since the stock market crashed three years ago.* ▸ Also NC *Consumer spending and business investment have not been affected by last October's stock market crash. ...one of the most spectacular financial crashes of the decade.*
5 V If a computer or a computer program **crashes**, it fails suddenly. *The computer system crashed amid widespread accusations of fraud.*
6 N SING A **crash** is also a sudden, loud noise. *...a terrific crash of thunder.*

crash barrier, crash barriers
NC A **crash barrier** is a strong low fence built along the side of a road at a dangerous corner or between the two halves of a motorway in order to prevent accidents. *The lorry hit the crash barrier and overturned.*

crash course, crash courses
NC A **crash course** in a subject is a short course in which you are taught the most important things you need to know about it, for example before you start a new job. *Crash courses in Arabic were arranged.*

crash helmet, crash helmets
NC A **crash helmet** is a helmet worn by motor cyclists to protect their heads. *Two men, both wearing crash helmets, walked up to the bar.*

crashing /kræʃɪŋ/
ADJ ATTRIB **Crashing** is used to emphasize the great extent or degree of something; an old-fashioned, informal word, used showing disapproval. *I find him a crashing bore... She's just had a crashing row with a friend.* ◆ **crashingly** SUBMOD *His parents are crashingly orthodox.*

crash-land, crash-lands, crash-landing, crash-landed
V-ERG If a pilot **crash-lands** a plane or if it **crash-lands**, the pilot makes an emergency landing in an abnormal or dangerous way, for example when the plane has developed a fault and cannot land normally. *The captain of the jumbo has threatened to crash-land the plane into the sea if he cannot land properly... Three helicopters have been shot down or forced to crash-land in the last few weeks... The Chinook, which was said to be overloaded, dropped like a stone and crash-landed in the same area.* ◆ **crash-landing, crash-landings** NC *A crippled fighter plane came in for a crash-landing, following an engine failure... The passengers were told to prepare for a crash-landing.*

crass /kræs/
ADJ **Crass** behaviour is stupid and insensitive. *He has offended millions with his crass remarks about the poor... His criticism of Israel was crass, glib, unhelpful, and showed a lack of political wisdom.*

crate /kreɪt/ **crates**
NC A **crate** is a large box used for transporting or storing things. *...a crate of oranges.*

crater /kreɪtə/ **craters**
NC A **crater** is a large hole in the ground, caused by an explosion or by something large that hits it. *There are dozens of craters from artillery shells.*

cravat /krəvǽt/ **cravats**
NC A **cravat** is a piece of cloth which a man wears around his neck and tucked inside the collar of his shirt. *...a bearded figure in a grey suit and cravat.*

crave /kreɪv/ **craves, craving, craved**
V O or V+*for* If you **crave** something or **crave** for it, you want to have it very much. *She craved luxury... Baker was craving for a smoke.*

craven /kreɪvn/
ADJ **Craven** behaviour is behaviour in which you do not do something because you are afraid; an old-fashioned word, used showing disapproval. *It is indeed a craven House of Commons which is prepared to accept such a reduction of civil liberties.* ◆ **cravenly** ADV *With any luck, I thought cravenly, the dispute will be forgotten by then.*

craving /kreɪvɪŋ/ **cravings**
NC A **craving** for something is a very strong desire for it. *She was renowned for her beauty and her craving for privacy... Her lack of talent in no way diminished her insatiable craving to succeed.*

crawl /krɔːl/ **crawls, crawling, crawled**
1 V When you **crawl**, you move forward on your hands and knees. *Her baby is crawling about now.*
2 VA When an insect or vehicle **crawls** somewhere, it moves there slowly. *A spider was crawling up my leg... An open-topped bus crawled its way from Highbury to Islington Town Hall.*
3 V+*with* If you say that a place is **crawling** with people or things, you mean that it is full of them; an informal use. *The forecourt was crawling with security men.*
4 V If you **crawl** to someone, you try to please them in order to gain some advantage; used in informal English, showing disapproval. *Let's see who comes crawling to whom.*
5 N SING If traffic moves at a **crawl**, it moves very slowly. *Traffic on many motorways has been reduced to a crawl.*
6 N SING The **crawl** is a swimming stroke in which you lie on your front, swinging first one arm over your head, and then the other arm. *You use your arms as in the crawl, and kick with your legs.*

crawler /krɔːlə/ **crawlers**
NC If you call someone a **crawler**, you mean that they try hard to please someone in order to gain some advantage for themselves; an informal word, used showing disapproval. *He's a real crawler.*

crayfish /kreɪfɪʃ/ **crayfishes.** The plural form can be either **crayfishes** or **crayfish**.
NC A **crayfish** is a small shellfish with five pairs of legs which lives in rivers and ponds. *Australian freshwater crayfish can survive indefinitely out of water.*

crayon /kreɪɒn/ **crayons**
NC A **crayon** is a pencil containing coloured wax or clay. *...a box of crayons.*

craze /kreɪz/ **crazes**
NC A **craze** is something that is popular for a very short time. *...the latest dance craze from America.*

crazed /kreɪzd/
ADJ ATTRIB **Crazed** behaviour is wild and uncontrolled. *She fought with crazed ferocity.*

crazy /kreɪzi/ **crazier, craziest**; an informal word.
1 ADJ A **crazy** person or idea seems very strange or foolish. *My fellow students thought I was crazy... It's crazy to have a picnic in October.* ◆ **crazily** ADV *A man rushed past him shouting crazily.*
2 ADJ PRED or ADJ after N If you are **crazy** about something, you are very enthusiastic about it. *They are crazy about football... Everyone was jazz crazy.*
3 ADJ PRED If something makes or drives you **crazy**, it makes you extremely annoyed or upset. *You have to get used to the misery and dirt, or you'd go crazy... This business of wrapping the Christmas presents every year drives me crazy.*

crazy paving
N U **Crazy paving** consists of irregular pieces of flat stone that have been fitted together on the ground in order to make a path or terrace. *The previous owner's refinements had included a sun-dial, crazy paving, and wrought iron gates.*

creak /kriːk/ creaks, creaking, creaked
v If something **creaks**, it makes a harsh sound when it
moves or when you put weight on it. *The door
creaked and Castle turned quickly... The bed creaked
as he lay down on it.* ▶ Also NC *There were odd
creaks from the staircase... The creak of the mattress
did not wake her.*

creaking /kriːkɪŋ/
ADJ If something such as a system or the economy is
creaking, it is working very badly, and may soon
break down completely. *Successive LDP leaders have
attempted to change the country's creaking tax system
for more than a decade. ...Gorbachev's efforts to
improve his country's creaking economy.*

creaky /kriːki/ creakier, creakiest
ADJ Something that is **creaky** makes a harsh sound
when it moves. *He was careful on the creaky stairs.*

cream /kriːm/ creams, creaming, creamed
1 NU **Cream** is a thick liquid that is produced from
milk. You can use it in cooking or put it on fruit or
puddings. *...strawberries and cream... Have a cup of
coffee, put a little cream in it and stir it.*
2 NU **Cream** is also an artificial food that looks and
tastes rather like cream. *...chocolates with cream
fillings.*
3 N MASS **Cream** is also a thick substance that you rub
into your skin. *She wiped the cream off her face...
You can use the cream directly on the eczema.*
4 ADJ Something that is **cream** in colour is yellowish-
white. *The room was decorated in its original colours
of cream, gold, scarlet and green... The bridesmaids
wore cream silk dresses with lace collars and cuffs.*
5 N SING+SUPP You can refer to the best people or
things in a group as the **cream** of it. *They were the
cream of their generation... Will they be able to
persuade the cream of Hong Kong society to remain in
the colony?*
6 VO If you **cream** two or more substances, you mix
them together until they are smooth. *Cream the
margarine with the parsley and season with a little
salt.*
7 See also **clotted cream**, **ice cream**, **sour cream**.
cream off PHRASAL VERB 1 If you **cream off** part of a
group of people, you separate them and treat them
differently, because you think they are better or more
easy to deal with than the rest of the group. *The best
pupils would be creamed off and given a superior
training... They accused private practitioners of
creaming off the easy operations, leaving the NHS
with the chronically sick.* 2 If a government **creams
off** an amount of money from a firm or other business,
they take it in taxes. *The worker's collective will
decide what to do with the remainder of the revenue
after the state has creamed off a larger part of it...
The money which the government creamed off from
sales paid for an impressive network of roads.*

cream cheese
NU **Cream cheese** is a very rich, soft white cheese.
*Products such as matches, bread, detergent, and
cream cheese join the list of rationed items.*

cream cracker, cream crackers
NC A **cream cracker** is a crisp unsweetened biscuit
which is often eaten with cheese. *She held a cream
cracker between her thumb and forefinger before
taking a bite.*

cream tea, cream teas
NC In Britain, a **cream tea** is an afternoon meal
consisting of tea to drink and scones with jam and
clotted cream to eat.

creamy /kriːmi/
1 ADJ Something that is **creamy** in colour is yellowish-
white. *The female is creamy silver and she lays her
eggs on the leaf.*
2 ADJ Food or drink that is **creamy** is soft and
contains a lot of cream, or reminds you of cream.
*...all the deliciously creamy cakes you can eat... It's
essentially risotto, which is a creamy rice dish.*

crease /kriːs/ creases, creasing, creased
1 NC **Creases** are lines or folds that appear in cloth or
paper when it is crushed. *She smoothed down the
creases in her dress... The creases at the front are
really handy for picking up the hat.*

2 V-ERG If you **crease** something such as cloth or
paper or if it **creases**, lines or folds appear in it
because it has been crushed. *The parchment had been
creased over and over again... It's made of special
material that doesn't crease.* ◆ **creased** ADJ *His suit
had become creased... He brought out some creased
dollar bills.*
3 V-ERG If your face **creases** or is **creased**, lines
appear on it because you are frowning or smiling. *A
wrinkle of doubt creased her forehead. ...a broad and
easy smile that spreads across a face that is creased
like cracked earth.*
4 NC In cricket, the **crease** is a line on the pitch near
the wicket where the batsman stands. *He collapsed at
the crease during a match in the Gambia.*

create /kriˈeɪt/ creates, creating, created
1 VO To **create** something means to cause it to happen
or exist. *His work created enormous interest in
England... They opened windows and doors to create a
draught... He admitted that he did not have a clear
idea of the sort of society he wished to create.*
2 VO To **create** something also means to increase
something that already exists. *They feared that the
policy would create a bigger gap between the rich and
poor... He said forestry could create employment and
generate extra income in areas with few other
prospects... The decision is bound to create further
tension in the Kosovo region.*
3 VO If you **create** something that is new, useful, or
interesting, you invent, design, or manufacture it. *The
scientists hope to create full colour TV pictures five
metres across... Perhaps dairy cows can be used to
create insulin, interferon, and other human medical
products.*

creation /kriˈeɪʃn/ creations
1 NU The **creation** of something is the act of bringing
it into existence. *They proposed the creation of Welsh
and Scottish parliaments. ...a job creation scheme.*
2 N PROP In the Bible, the **Creation** is the making of
the universe, earth, and creatures by God. *...those
who believe in the biblical version of Creation.*
3 NU People sometimes refer to the entire universe as
creation. *They look upon everything in creation as
material for exploitation.*
4 NC A **creation** is something that has been made or
produced; a literary use. *...his ceramic creations.*

creative /kriˈeɪtɪv/
1 ADJ A **creative** person has the ability to invent and
develop original ideas, especially in art. *He has more
time to be creative... The chilling scene had been
caught beautifully, by a creative cameraman.*
◆ **creativity** /kriːeɪˈtɪvəti/ NU *...adults who want to
express their own creativity.*
2 ADJ If something that you do is **creative**, it is new,
unusual, and original. *Good science is creative,
adventurous, even mystical. ...creative writing... In
the future, we hope for more freedom in creative art.*
3 ADJ If you use something in a **creative** way, you use
it in a new way that produces interesting and unusual
results. *...the creative use of language... His creative
and original interpretation of Marxist-Leninism is what
led us to victory.*

creator /kriˈeɪtə/ creators
1 NC The **creator** of something is the person who
made it or invented it. *...Walt Disney, the creator of
Mickey Mouse and Donald Duck.*
2 N PROP God is sometimes referred to as the **Creator**.
He offered a few prayers to the Creator.

creature /kriːtʃə/ creatures
1 NC A **creature** is a living thing such as an animal,
bird, or insect. *Worms are very simple creatures.*
2 NC+SUPP You can refer to someone as a particular
kind of **creature** in order to emphasize a particular
quality that they have. *She was a weak and helpless
creature.*

creature comforts
N PL **Creature comforts** are the things that you need to
feel comfortable in your life, such as good food and
nice clothes. *They do very well for themselves when it
comes to creature comforts.*

crèche /kreʃ/ crèches
NC A **crèche** is a place where small children are left

and looked after while their parents are working. *Some organizations are organising 24-hour crèches to attract young mothers back to work... It has a very male atmosphere, and there are no crèche facilities.*

credence /ˈkriːdns/
NU If something gives **credence** to a theory or story, it makes it easier to believe. *These latest discoveries give credence to Burke's ideas... The recent findings lend credence to the age-old belief that lines on the hands indicate one's fortune and life-expectancy.*

credentials /krəˈdenʃlz/
1 N PL Your **credentials** are your previous achievements, training, and general background, which indicate that you are qualified to do something. *His credentials as a journalist were beyond dispute.*
2 N PL **Credentials** are also a letter or certificate that proves your identity or qualifications. *Didn't you ask for his credentials?*

credibility /ˌkredəˈbɪləti/
NU If someone or something has **credibility**, people believe in them and trust them. *He felt that he had lost credibility... The affair represents a serious blow to the credibility of the Japanese government.*

credibility gap
N SING A **credibility gap** is the difference between what a person says or promises and what they actually think or do. *There's rather a large credibility gap between their election pledges and the policies that they actually implemented... He has attacked what he calls Labour's yawning credibility gap.*

credible /ˈkredəbl/
1 ADJ Someone who is **credible** is able to convince you that they are telling the truth. *No politicians seem credible these days... The State Department has learned from credible sources that Doe died in a shootout yesterday.*
2 ADJ A plan, system, or method that is **credible** is possible, sensible, and people think that it will work. *Civil rights lawyers are trying to find new and credible ways to improve employment discrimination... They will certainly want to maintain a credible nuclear defence.*
3 ADJ A belief or theory that is **credible** can be believed. *The students weren't exposed to a very credible scientific theory... When we receive credible evidence of wrongdoing, we follow that evidence wherever it leads.*

credit /ˈkredɪt/ **credits, crediting, credited**
1 NU **Credit** is a system where you pay for goods or services several weeks or months after you have received them. *...the availability of cheap long-term credit.*
2 NC A **credit** or an export **credit** is an arrangement by which a financial organization or government guarantees that it will insure payment for exports to a particular country. This is so that firms will export important goods to that country without worrying that they will not be paid for them. *He believes the West has no real intention of granting Poland badly-needed credits... The project was financed by export credits from France and Japan.*
3 NU If you get the **credit** for something, people praise you for it. *Some of the credit should go to Nick... Environmentalists give Bush credit for providing the framework for the revision of the Clean Air Act.*
4 VO If you **are credited** with an achievement or if it **is credited** to you, people believe that you were responsible for it. *An Australian doctor is credited with exposing the dangers of the drug... She was credited with transforming modern dance from the formality and classicism of the 19th century... Now the film's success will be credited to Roberts... The policy of dialogue and consultation should not be entirely credited to the government.*
5 VO If you cannot **credit** something, you cannot believe it; a formal use. *There must be many of you who find this case hard to credit.*
6 N PL The list of people who helped to make a film, a record, or a television programme is called the **credits**. *The credits to 'Miller's Crossing' say 'directed by Joel Cohen and produced by Ethan Cohen'.*

● **Credit** is used in these phrases. ● If you buy goods **on credit**, you are allowed to have the goods a few months or weeks before you have to pay for them. *They sold grain on credit during times of famine... The worst hit are individuals who've bought heavily on credit and need the money to pay the next instalment.* ● If a person or organization is **in credit**, they have earned more money than they have spent. *The government said the country was in credit by more than £3.5 million... The company was one and three-quarter million dollars in credit.* ● If your bank account is **in credit**, it still has some money in it and you are not overdrawn. ● If something **does** you **credit**, you should be respected or admired for it. *Gorbachev's desire to withdraw troops from Afghanistan does him credit.* ● If something **is to your credit**, you deserve praise for it. *Price, to his credit, denounced in private the brutalities of the regime... To its credit, my family has always tried to do something special for Christmas.* ● If you have one or more achievements **to your credit**, you have achieved them. *This year he has four victories to his credit... McCorckle, with four novels to her credit, is one of the new voices of the South.*

creditable /ˈkredɪtəbl/
1 ADJ Something that is **creditable** is of a reasonably high standard. *He polled a creditable 44.8 per cent.*
2 ADJ If someone's behaviour is **creditable**, it should be respected or admired. *...some of the less creditable features of his past.*

credit account, credit accounts
NC A **credit account** is an account that you have with a shop which allows you to buy its goods on credit, especially by using a credit card which they give you. *...a shortage of money in the credit account.*

credit card, credit cards
NC A **credit card** is a plastic card that you use to buy goods on credit or to borrow money. *The report allows shops to charge higher prices to people who use credit cards. ...the lucrative credit card business.*

credit note, credit notes
NC A **credit note** is a piece of paper that a shop gives you when you return goods that you have bought from them, for example because they are faulty. It states that you are entitled to have goods of the same value without paying for them. *If you return the shoes in bad condition, you will not be able to obtain a credit note for them.*

creditor /ˈkredɪtə/ **creditors**
NC Your **creditors** are the people who you owe money to. *The government is said to owe hundreds of millions of dollars to foreign creditors.*

credit transfer, credit transfers
N Cor NU A **credit transfer** is a direct payment of money from one bank account to another. *We get paid monthly by credit transfer.*

creditworthy /ˈkredɪtwɜːði/
ADJ If someone is **creditworthy**, you can safely lend them money or allow them to have goods on credit, for example because in the past they have always paid back what they owe. *The problem had to be solved quickly if Nicaragua was to become creditworthy and attract loans from international institutions.*
♦ **creditworthiness** NU *The economic recession has made banks worry about the creditworthiness of their customers.*

credo /ˈkreɪdəʊ, ˈkriːdəʊ/ **credos**
NC A **credo** is a set of beliefs, principles, or opinions that strongly influence the way people live or work; a formal word. *This belief is fundamental to Raymond Barre's political credo.*

credulity /krəˈdjuːləti/
NU **Credulity** is willingness to believe that something is real or true; a formal word. *It would be straining the credulity of this Council to suggest that such an exercise could threaten anyone.*

credulous /ˈkredjʊləs/
ADJ If you are **credulous**, you are always ready to believe what people tell you, and are easily deceived. *He felt that they had been too credulous of the goodwill of their creditors... There were both credulous and sceptical reactions to the reports.*

creed /kriːd/ **creeds**
1 NC A **creed** is a set of beliefs or principles that influence the way people live or work. *They never embraced any particular creed.*
2 NC A **creed** is also a religion; a formal use. *...the Christian creed.*

creek /kriːk/ **creeks**
1 NC A **creek** is a narrow inlet where the sea comes a long way into the land. *...the muddy creeks of my home coast.*
2 NC A **creek** is also a small stream or river; used in American English. *By early summer the creek was almost dry.*

creel /kriːl/ **creels**
NC A **creel** is a basket in which you put fish that you have just caught. *He laid the fish with the others in the creel.*

creep /kriːp/ **creeps, creeping, crept**
1 VA If you **creep** somewhere, you move there quietly and slowly. *I heard my landlady creeping stealthily up to my door... The soldiers crept along quietly, careful not to wake the enemy.*
2 VA If something **creeps** somewhere, it moves slowly so that you hardly notice it. *Here and there, little breezes crept over the water... The giant oil spill is now creeping southwards... The budget process is still creeping along.*
3 VA If the rate of something **creeps** to a higher level, it gradually reaches that level. *The unemployment trend has crept up for the second month running... Temperatures are just beginning to creep above normal.*
4 NC You call someone a **creep** to show you dislike them, especially because they flatter people; an informal use. *He's a creep. He lies about everything.*
creep in PHRASAL VERB If a feeling, idea or custom **creeps in**, it gradually spreads among a lot of people. *The paper says that a sense of disillusion has crept in since the President was inaugurated.*
creep into PHRASAL VERB If an attitude or feeling **creeps into** something, it begins to be felt or expressed gradually. *It's a sign of the insecurity that's creeping into the Japanese economy... One thing I always find creeping into my music is our relationship with the planet.*
creep up on PHRASAL VERB 1 If you **creep up on** someone, you move slowly closer to them without being seen. *One child stands facing a wall while all the others creep up on him.* 2 If a feeling or situation **creeps up on** you, you hardly notice that it is happening to you or affecting you. *Fame has crept up on her almost by accident... The desire to be a mother can creep up on you unawares.*

creeper /kriːpə/ **creepers**
NC A **creeper** is a plant with long stems that wind themselves around things. *...an impenetrable tangle of creepers and trees. ...a long strand of the hanging creeper which grew upon the high place above.*

creepy /kriːpi/
ADJ Something that is **creepy** gives you a strange, unpleasant feeling of fear; an informal word. *Bats are widely regarded as rather creepy and even sinister as they wing their way through the air.*

creepy-crawly, creepy-crawlies
NC A **creepy-crawly** is a small insect which gives you a feeling of fear or disgust; an informal use. *There are lots of creepy-crawlies, slugs, and snails that tend to be one sex or the other at a time.*

cremate /krəmeɪt/ **cremates, cremating, cremated**
VO When someone is **cremated**, their dead body is burned. *He will be cremated tomorrow at his village home... He plans to have his favourite paintings cremated with him when he dies.*

cremation /krəmeɪʃn/ **cremations**
1 NC A **cremation** is a funeral service during which a dead body is cremated. *Afterwards there will be a private cremation. If the death occurs abroad, arrange a local burial or cremation to avoid the expense of bringing the body back.*
2 NU **Cremation** is the process of burning a dead body at a funeral. *More than forty bodies were brought in for cremation.*

crematorium /krɛmətɔːriəm/ **crematoria** /krɛmətɔːriə/ or **crematoriums**
NC A **crematorium** is a building in which bodies are cremated. *He addressed the congregation at a North London crematorium.*

crème de la crème /krɛmdələːkrɛm/
N SING When you talk about the **crème de la crème**, you mean the very best things or people of their kind; a literary word. *These trees are the crème de la crème in Britain's landscape.*

creole /kriːəʊl/ **creoles**
1 NCorNU A **creole** is a language that has developed from a mixture of different languages and has become the main language in a particular place; compare **pidgin**. *The address was broadcast to Haitians in their native creole... He spoke creole to the crowd.*
2 NC A **Creole** is also a person descended from the Europeans who first colonized the West Indies or the southern United States of America. *The new states became the property of the rich Creole elites.*
3 NC A **Creole** is also a person of mixed African and European race, who lives in the West Indies and speaks a Creole language. *He was a Creole, his parents a mixture of black and French.*
4 ADJ ATTRIB You can also use **creole** to refer to the traditions, culture, art, and so on, that belong to West Indian Creoles. *The folklorist Nick Spitzer looks at the roots of Creole music... The festival was starting to bring attention to the Creole traditions.*

creosote /kriːəsəʊt/ **creosotes, creosoting, creosoted**
1 NU **Creosote** is a thick dark liquid made from coal tar which is used to protect wood from the weather. *...wood impregnated with creosote.*
2 VO If you **creosote** something such as a wooden fence, you spread creosote over it in order to prevent it from rotting. *Wooden gates will last a long time if you creosote them every now and then.*

crepe /kreɪp/
NU **Crepe** is a thin fabric made of cotton, silk, or wool with an uneven, wrinkled surface. *I have a couple of crepe bandages in my first-aid box. ...the pink crepe dress which she used for all such occasions.*

crepe paper
NU **Crepe paper** is a kind of paper with an uneven, ridged surface. It is used for making decorations. *We put white and blue crepe paper round them so they looked rather pretty... Crepe paper streamers, balloons, and bouquets of yellow ribbon drape the podium.*

crept /krɛpt/
Crept is the past tense and past participle of **creep**.

crescendo /krəʃɛndəʊ/
1 N SING In music, a **crescendo** is a passage that gets louder and louder. *It's possible for the organist to reach a very quick crescendo by using all these stops.*
2 N SING **Crescendo** can also be used to refer to any noise that gets louder and louder, or to the time when a noise reaches its loudest point. *He was forced to endure taunts and a crescendo of boos... Their chants reached a crescendo as the plane taxied out for take-off.*
3 N SING You can also use **crescendo** to refer to a feeling or type of behaviour that becomes more and more intense, or to the time when it reaches its climax. *In the past ten days Zaire has published a mounting crescendo of attacks on Belgium... Resignation calls have reached a crescendo.*

crescent /krɛsnt/ **crescents**
1 NC A **crescent** is a curved shape that is wider in the middle than at its ends, like the moon in its first and last quarters. *The oil slick is about sixty miles long, stretching in a giant crescent.*
2 NC A **crescent** is also a street, especially one which is curved. *Police found the explosives under the kitchen floor of a house in Thornhill Crescent. ...23 Chestnut Crescent.*

cress /krɛs/
NU **Cress** is a plant with small, strong-tasting green leaves that are used in salads or as a garnish for food. *You don't need to eat carrots, you can eat red pepper, cress, spinach or broccoli.* ● See also **watercress**.

crest /krɛst/ crests, cresting, crested
1 NC The **crest** of a hill or a wave is the highest part of it. *We had reached the crest of the hill. ...the crests of gigantic waves.*
2 NC A **crest** is also a design that is the sign of a noble family, a town, or an organization. *The gown has scarlet shields and crests on the bosom. ...a casket emblazoned with the family crest.*
3 V If a river, lake, or floodwaters **crest** at a particular level, that is the highest level that they reach. *The river is expected to crest at 11.00 this morning at 57 feet... Huge waves, cresting at 24 feet, caused severe flooding.*
4 **the crest of a wave**: see **wave**.

crested /krɛstɪd/
ADJ ATTRIB A **crested** bird is a bird that has a tuft of feathers on its head. *...one of the loveliest European water birds, the great crested grebe.*

crestfallen /krɛstfɔːlən/
ADJ PRED Someone who looks **crestfallen** looks sad and disappointed. *Last night, a crestfallen Chancellor Kohl said there are times in history when people face too many demands... The five handcuffed men looked crestfallen as they were handed over to the police.*

cretin /krɛtɪn/ cretins
NC If you call someone a **cretin**, you mean that they are very stupid; an offensive word. *Save your explanations for that cretin Gerran.*

crevasse /krəvæs/ crevasses
NC A **crevasse** is a deep crack in thick ice, for example in a glacier. *...a little wooden bridge over one of the deeper crevasses.*

crevice /krɛvɪs/ crevices
NC A **crevice** is a narrow crack in a rock. *The insects are hidden in rock crevices.*

crew /kruː/ crews, crewing, crewed
1 N COLL The people who work on and operate a ship, aeroplane, or spacecraft are called the **crew**. *The 'Maine' carried a crew of three hundred and fifty.*
2 N COLL You also use **crew** to refer to people with special technical skills who work together on a task or project. *He was interviewed by an American television crew.*
3 VO The people who **crew** a ship, aeroplane, or spacecraft are the people who work on it or operate it. *The ferries are crewed by non-union sailors.*
♦ **crewed** ADJ *No British crewed ships are sailing into or out of the port.*

crew cut, crew cuts
NC A **crew cut** is a hairstyle where the hair is cut very short. *...a normal-looking man, with a big white face and a crew cut.*

crewman /kruːmən/ crewmen /kruːmən/
NC A **crewman** is a member of a crew. *One of the crewmen died. ...TV crewmen.*

crib /krɪb/ cribs, cribbing, cribbed
1 NC A **crib** is a baby's cot; used in American English. *She used to throw her toys out of her crib.*
2 V or VO If you **crib**, you copy something that someone else has written. *The teacher thought that we'd cribbed off each other... The story was cribbed.*

cribbage /krɪbɪdʒ/
NU **Cribbage** is a card game for two, three, or four players in which you record the score by putting pegs in a wooden board. *...an assortment of objects, including a brass whistle, a cribbage board, and some newspaper cuttings.*

crick /krɪk/
N SING If you have a **crick** in your neck, you have a pain caused by stiff muscles. *Swimming on your front just gives you a crick in your neck.*

cricket /krɪkɪt/ crickets
1 NU **Cricket** is an outdoor game played between two teams who try to score points, called runs, by hitting a ball with a wooden bat. *Now some sports news, beginning with cricket. ...a one-day international cricket match between England and India.*
2 NC A **cricket** is a small jumping insect that produces sharp sounds by rubbing its wings together. *I could hear crickets chirping away in the background.*

cricketer /krɪkɪtə/ cricketers
NC A **cricketer** is a person who plays cricket. *He's a*

keen cricketer. *...Sir Donald Bradman, the legendary cricketer.*

crikey /kraɪki/
Some people say **crikey** in order to express surprise, or to add emphasis to an opinion they are giving; an informal word. *Crikey, you were quick!*

crime /kraɪm/ crimes
1 NCorNU A **crime** is an illegal action for which a person can be punished by law. *The crimes were all committed in prosperous suburbs to the south of London... The number of serious crimes rose by sixty-five percent last year... Crime is a far greater problem in the US than it is in Britain.*
2 NC You can also refer to an action which seems morally wrong as a **crime**. *He said the use of chemical weapons was a crime against humanity.*

criminal /krɪmɪnl/ criminals
1 NC A **criminal** is a person who has committed a crime. *...one of the country's ten most wanted criminals.*
2 ADJ Something that is **criminal** is connected with crime. *He had done nothing criminal. ...a criminal offence.* ♦ **criminally** SUBMOD *He insisted that he had done nothing criminally wrong.*
3 ADJ **Criminal** also means morally wrong. *To refuse medical aid would be criminal.*

criminal code, criminal codes
NC A country's **criminal code** consists of all the laws that are concerned with crime and punishment. *The entire criminal code was being reviewed with a move towards lighter sentencing.*

criminology /krɪmɪnɒlədʒi/
NU **Criminology** is the scientific study of crime and criminals. *Our police commissioner, who happens to have a doctorate in criminology, is very knowledgeable about these things.* ♦ **criminologist** /krɪmɪnɒlədʒɪst/ criminologists NC *Death was caused by what the criminologists call a solid object.*

crimp /krɪmp/ crimps, crimping, crimped
1 VO If you **crimp** a piece of fabric or pastry, you make small folds along its edges. *She had crimped the edges with an iron.* ♦ **crimped** ADJ *The hills on either side of the river were crimped like a pie crust.*
2 VO If you **crimp** your hair, you style it into tight curls or waves, usually by using heated tongs. *Roman ladies used to bleach, dye, and crimp their hair.* ♦ **crimped** ADJ *She patted her crimped grey bun.*

crimson /krɪmzn/
ADJ Something that is **crimson** in colour is dark purplish-red. *They were dressed in their new uniform of khaki fatigues and crimson berets.*

cringe /krɪndʒ/ cringes, cringing, cringed
1 V A or V If you **cringe** from someone or something, you back away because of fear. *She cringed against the wall.*
2 V or V A You say that people **cringe** when they are very embarrassed. *Cringing under the stares of passers-by, I tried to read my newspaper.*

crinkle /krɪŋkl/ crinkles, crinkling, crinkled
1 V-ERG When something **crinkles** or is **crinkled**, it becomes slightly creased or folded. *His face crinkled into a smile... Carl crinkled his brow.* ♦ **crinkled** ADJ *...brown crinkled leaves.*
2 NC **Crinkles** are small creases or folds. *There were crinkles at the outer corners of his eyes.*

crinkly /krɪŋkli/
ADJ Something that is **crinkly** has many small creases or folds. *Her bodice was made of crinkly material.*

crinoline /krɪnəlɪn/ crinolines
NC A **crinoline** is a very stiff petticoat which was worn by women in the nineteenth century in order to make their skirts stand out away from their legs. *We wore taffeta, silk, and crinolines.*

cripple /krɪpl/ cripples, crippling, crippled
1 NC A **cripple** is someone who cannot move properly because of illness or injury. *He said the attack had been vicious, and on a cripple who could not defend himself.*
2 VO If something **cripples** you, you are seriously injured so that you cannot move properly. *The child's feet are being crippled by his shoes, which are too small... The toxic cooking oil killed six-hundred people*

and crippled thousands.

3 vo If something **cripples** an organization or system, it prevents it from working properly, especially by damaging it in some way. *The transport strike is crippling the country... The International Monetary Fund is vital to countries who are crippled by debt.*

crippled /krɪpld/

1 ADJ Someone who is **crippled** cannot move their body properly because it is weak, injured, or affected by disease. *...his crippled mother... They will be crippled for life.*

2 ADJ An organization or system that is **crippled** is very badly damaged and therefore cannot work properly. *They chose Ricardo Camero Cardiel to take charge of the crippled union's affairs.*

crippling /krɪpəºlɪŋ/

1 ADJ ATTRIB A **crippling** illness or disability severely damages your health or body. *...a crippling, incurable disease.*

2 ADJ **Crippling** prices, taxes, or restrictions are too high or too severe and have a damaging effect on people or organizations. *...the country's crippling twenty billion dollar foreign debt. ....crippling economic sanctions.*

crisis /kraɪsɪs/ **crises** /kraɪsiːz/

1 NCorNU A **crisis** is a serious or dangerous situation which could cause great hardship or death. *Sudan is in the midst of a major economic crisis... Peru is facing an agricultural crisis which may lead to serious food shortages... The economy is in crisis.*

2 NC A **crisis** is also a situation where a conflict has become so threatening or dangerous that people are afraid there will be fighting or a war. *...an emergency summit to discuss the crisis in the Gulf... He welcomed suggestions which could help to find a peaceful solution to the crisis.*

3 NCorNU A **crisis** in someone's life is a time when they have serious personal problems. *He had an emotional crisis... Who can you turn to in a time of crisis?*

crisp /krɪsp/ **crisper, crispest; crisps**

1 ADJ Something that is **crisp** is pleasantly stiff and fresh. *...crisp bacon. ...crisp new bank notes.*

2 NC **Crisps** are very thin slices of potato that have been fried until they are hard and crunchy. *...a packet of crisps... Crisps remain the most popular snack in Britain.*

3 ADJ **Crisp** air or weather is pleasantly fresh, cold, and dry. *...a crisp October morning... It was spring, and the air was crisp.*

4 ADJ A **crisp** remark or response is brief and perhaps unfriendly. *He sent off two crisp telegrams.* ◆ **crisply** ADV *'What did she want?' Etta said crisply. 'Money?'*

crispy /krɪspi/ **crispier, crispiest**

ADJ Food which is **crispy** has been fried or toasted until it becomes pleasantly hard and crunchy. *...crispy fried bacon.*

criss-cross /krɪskrɒs/ **criss-crosses, criss-crossing, criss-crossed**

1 vo If things **criss-cross** a place, they create a pattern of crossed lines in it or on it. *Coils of hose pipes criss-cross the roads and pavements.*

2 ADJ ATTRIB A **criss-cross** pattern or design has lines crossing each other. *...a criss-cross pattern of tree trunks.*

Cristiani Burkard, Alfredo Félix

/ælfreɪðəʊ feɪlɪks krɪstiːɑːni buəkɑːd/

Alfredo Félix Cristiani Burkard became President of El Salvador in 1989. He became the leader of the Nationalist Republican Alliance (ARENA) in 1985 and a member of the National Assembly in 1988. Born: 1948.

criterion /kraɪtɪəriən/ **criteria** /kraɪtɪəriə/

NC A **criterion** is a standard by which you judge or decide something. *My own criterion of success is the ability to work joyfully... The statement complied with the criteria set by the United States government.*

critic /krɪtɪk/ **critics**

1 NC A **critic** is a person who writes reviews and expresses opinions about books, films, music, and art. *His play has not been well received by critics.*

2 NC A **critic** of a person or system disapproves of them and criticizes them publicly. *The writer was an outspoken critic of apartheid... Critics say that the new system won't work.*

critical /krɪtɪkl/

1 ADJ A **critical** time or situation is extremely important. *This was a critical moment in his career... The withdrawal of Cuban troops from Angola is the critical issue.* ◆ **critically** ADV *The distribution of resources is critically important.*

2 ADJ A **critical** situation or illness is very serious or dangerous. *The problem is a critical shortage of vital equipment... He was taken to hospital in Brighton, where his condition is said to be critical.* ◆ **critically** ADV *He became critically ill.*

3 ADJ If you are **critical** of someone or something, you express severe judgements and opinions about them. *He had long been critical of Conservative policy... The judge was highly critical, saying both parties were using the case for maximum publicity.* ◆ **critically** ADV *She had mentioned the book critically to friends.*

4 ADJ ATTRIB A **critical** approach to something involves careful examination and judgement of it. *Each player regarded the other with critical interest... To be creative, then, is to cast a critical eye over your own work.* ◆ **critically** ADV *The problem should be analysed more critically.*

5 ADJ **Critical** also means relating to the work of a person who is a critic. *He wrote a biography of Prince Charles which received great critical acclaim... His work is receiving a lot of critical attention in the West.*

criticise /krɪtɪsaɪz/. See **criticize**.

criticism /krɪtɪsɪzm/ **criticisms**

1 NU **Criticism** is the expression of disapproval of someone or something. *Some fierce public criticism of the plan had been voiced.*

2 NC A **criticism** is a comment in which you say that something has a particular fault. *One of the main criticisms against him is that he is lazy.*

3 NU **Criticism** of a book, play, or other work of art is a serious examination and judgement of it. *He has written several volumes of literary criticism.*

criticize /krɪtɪsaɪz/ **criticizes, criticizing, criticized;** also spelt **criticise**.

1 vo If you **criticize** someone or something, you express your disapproval of them by saying what you think is wrong with them. *Please don't get angry if I criticize you... He was criticized for pursuing a policy of conciliation.*

2 vo If you **criticize** a work of art, literature, music, and so on, you form judgements and opinions about it after considering it carefully. *They're here to criticize, analyze, and to argue together... We read and criticize each others' poems.*

critique /krɪtiːk/ **critiques**

NC A **critique** of something is an examination and judgement of it, usually written; a formal word. *...a powerful and sophisticated critique of the military establishment.*

croak /krəʊk/ **croaks, croaking, croaked**

1 v When animals or birds **croak**, they utter harsh, low sounds. *A bullfrog was croaking in the distance.* ► Also N SING *...the croak of a raven.*

2 v-QUOTE When someone **croaks** something, they say it in a hoarse, rough voice. *'Brandy,' he croaked.* ► Also N SING *His voice was a weak croak.*

Croatia /krəʊeɪʃə/

The **Republic of Croatia** is a country in south-eastern Europe. It declared its independence from Yugoslavia in 1991 and, after several months of fighting, was recognized by the European Community and other countries in 1992. Dr Franjo Tudjman, of the Croatian Democratic Union (HDZ), became President after the first free elections in 1990. ◆ **Croat** /krəʊæt/ N **Croatian** /krəʊeɪʃən/ ADJ

▪ *religion:* Christianity (mainly Roman Catholic) ▪ *language:* Croatian ▪ *currency:* dinar ▪ *capital:* Zagreb ▪ *population:* 5 million (1981) ▪ *size:* 56,538 square kilometres.

crochet /krəʊʃeɪ/ **crochets, crocheting, crocheted**

NU **Crochet** is a way of making clothes and other

things out of thread by using a special needle with a small hook at the end. *She would also like to learn patchwork and crochet.* ► Also VO *I usually knit or crochet something, because this makes my job worthwhile.*

crock /krɒk/ **crocks**
NC A **crock** is an earthenware pot or jar; an old-fashioned word. *She returned with a loaf of warmed soda bread and a crock of sweet butter.*

crockery /krɒkəri/
NU **Crockery** is plates, cups, and saucers. *...a sink overflowing with dirty crockery.*

crocodile /krɒkədaɪl/ **crocodiles**
NC A **crocodile** is a large reptile with a long body. Crocodiles live in rivers and eat meat. *Crocodiles and snakes have been seen in flooded areas.*

crocodile tears
N PL **Crocodile tears** are tears or other expressions of grief that are not genuine or sincere. *I did not shed any crocodile tears over his death.*

crocus /krəʊkəs/ **crocuses**
NC **Crocuses** are small white, yellow, or purple flowers that are grown in gardens in the early spring. *Nearby, a large number of crocuses have been planted.*

croft /krɒft/ **crofts**
NC A **croft** is a small piece of land, especially in Scotland, which is owned and farmed by one family and which provides them with food. *He's spent the last 30 years on a croft.*

crofter /krɒftə/ **crofters**
NC A **crofter** is the owner or tenant of a croft or small farm, especially in Scotland. *The Shetland farmers and crofters are struggling to survive.*

croissant /kwæsɒn⁰/ **croissants** /kwæsɒn⁰z/
NC A **croissant** is a type of small bread-like cake that is eaten for breakfast. *...the traditional French breakfast of coffee and croissants.*

crone /krəʊn/ **crones**
NC A **crone** is an old woman; an offensive word. *...a hideous, cackling old crone.*

crony /krəʊni/ **cronies**
NC You can refer to someone's friends as their **cronies** when you do not like or approve of them. *He promoted his cronies to positions of influence.*

crook /krʊk/ **crooks, crooking, crooked**
1 NC A **crook** is a criminal or dishonest person; an informal use. *The accountants turned out to have been crooks.*
2 NC The **crook** of your arm or leg is the soft inside part where you bend your elbow or knee. *She buried her face in the crook of her arm.*
3 VO If you **crook** your arm or finger, you bend it. *He backed away, his arms crooked, his fingers outspread.*

crooked /krʊkɪd/
1 ADJ Something that is **crooked** is bent or twisted. *My back is so crooked and painful that I cannot stand upright.*
2 ADJ Someone who is **crooked** is dishonest or a criminal. *Most crooked businessmen rely on substantial tax evasion.*

croon /kruːn/ **croons, crooning, crooned**
VO,V,or V-QUOTE If you **croon** something, you sing or say it quietly and gently. *She crooned sentimental songs to visiting dignitaries... He sat there, crooning to himself... 'You little charmer,' he crooned.*

crooner /kruːnə/ **crooners**
NC A **crooner** is a male singer who sings sentimental ballads; an old-fashioned word. *The song was originally sung by the crooner Matt Munroe.*

crop /krɒp/ **crops, cropping, cropped**
1 NC **Crops** are plants such as wheat and potatoes that are grown in large quantities to be stored, processed, or sold. *Scientists have discovered a better way to irrigate crops... Coffee is one of the country's major export crops.*
2 NC The plants that are collected at harvest time are referred to as a **crop**. *Zimbabwe looks as if it will bring in a bumper crop of maize this year... They get two crops of rice a year.*
3 NC+SUPP You can also refer to a group of people or things that appear together as a **crop**; an informal

use. *What do you think of the current crop of school-leavers?*
4 VO When an animal **crops** grass or leaves, it eats them. *Our goat was cropping the hedge, her tail swishing.*
5 See also **cash crop**.

crop up PHRASAL VERB If something **crops up**, it happens or appears unexpectedly; an informal expression. *They were accompanied by officials to deal with any problems that might crop up.*

cropped /krɒpt/
ADJ **Cropped** hair has been cut very short. *...a boy with closely cropped hair... Tammam's hair was short and curly, cropped like a boy soldier's.*

cropper /krɒpə/
If you say that someone **has come a cropper**, you mean that they have had an unexpected and embarrassing failure; an informal expression. *Despite all his cheating, he came a cropper in the exams.*

croquet /krəʊkeɪ/
NU **Croquet** is a game in which the players use long-handled wooden sticks to hit balls through metal arches stuck in a lawn. *He was playing croquet on the lawn.*

croquette /krəkɛt/ **croquettes**
NC A **croquette** is a savoury item of food which is made using cheese or fish mixed with mashed potato, rolled in breadcrumbs, and fried. *He ate all the potato croquettes in sight. ...salmon croquettes.*

cross /krɒs/ **crosses, crossing, crossed; crosser, crossest**
1 VO If you **cross** a room, road, or area of land, you move or travel to the other side of it. *He crossed the room slowly... I wanted to prove that a woman could cross the desert.*
2 V or VA If you **cross** to a place, you go across an area of land or water to reach it. *He stood up at once and crossed to the door... Where and how did you cross into Swaziland?*
3 V-RECIP Lines or roads that **cross** meet and go across each other. *...a place where four canyons crossed... Brook Street runs west, crossing Bond Street... They blocked several of the roads that cross with France.*
4 VO If you **cross** your arms, legs, or fingers, you put one of them on top of the other. *She sat back and crossed her legs.*
5 VO If an expression **crosses** someone's face, it appears briefly on their face; a literary use. *A flicker of unconcealed distaste crossed his features.*
6 When a thought **crosses** your **mind**, you think of something or remember something. *It had not crossed my mind to tell them I was leaving.*
7 NC A Christian **cross** is a shape that consists of a vertical line with a shorter horizontal line that goes across it near the top. It is the most important symbol of the Christian faith. *....a huge dome topped by a copper cross. ...a stone slab roughly carved into the shape of a cross.*
8 N SING The **Cross** means the cross on which Jesus Christ died. *She had a vision of Christ on the Cross.*
9 NC A **cross** is also a written mark in the shape of an X. *The reader has to indicate the answer with a cross or a tick.*
10 ADJ Someone who is **cross** is angry. *We all get cross with our children.* ◆ **crossly** ADV *'Don't ask me,' the post office lady replied, crossly.*
11 NC Something that is a **cross** between two things is neither one thing nor the other, but a mixture of both. *A Barbary duck is a cross between a wild duck and an ordinary duck.*

cross off PHRASAL VERB If you **cross off** items on a list, you draw a line through them. *More than half the voters crossed his name off the ballot paper.*

cross out PHRASAL VERB If you **cross out** words, you draw a line through them. *She saw her name and crossed it out.*

crossbar /krɒsbɑː/ **crossbars**
1 NC A **crossbar** is a horizontal piece of wood attached to two upright pieces, for example the top part of the goal in the game of football. *Juanico's goal went in off the crossbar.*

2 NC The **crossbar** on a man's bicycle is the horizontal metal bar between the handlebars and the saddle. *She was lifted over the saddle and onto the crossbar.*

crossbones /krɒsbəʊnz/. See **skull and crossbones.**

crossbow /krɒsbəʊ/ **crossbows**
NC A **crossbow** is a weapon consisting of a small bow fixed across a piece of wood, which releases an arrow with great power when you press a trigger. *Later, police recovered a sawn-off shotgun and a crossbow from the car.*

cross-Channel
ADJ ATTRIB **Cross-Channel** is used to describe travel, communications, and so on across the English Channel between England and France, Belgium, or the Netherlands, especially when this involves travelling by boat. *...a cross-Channel trip. ...the cross-Channel ferry.*

cross-check, cross-checks, cross-checking, cross-checked
VO If you **cross-check** something such as results or data, you use a different method from the one originally used, in order to check that the results or data are correct. *Until the information has been carefully assembled, cross-checked and evaluated, none of it will be reliable.*

cross-country
1 ADV or ADJ ATTRIB If you go somewhere **cross-country**, you use paths or less important routes, rather than main roads. *He walked cross-country to the hospital. ...a cross-country bicycle trip.*
2 NU **Cross-country** is the sport of running across open countryside. *African runners dominated the famous Five Mills cross-country race at San Vittora Olano in Italy.*

cross-cultural
ADJ ATTRIB **Cross-cultural** means dealing with or involving two or more different cultures. *...Donnison's influential cross-cultural study of housing policy.*

cross-examination, cross-examinations
NU or NC **Cross-examination** is the questioning of someone such as a witness during a trial in a court of law about the evidence they have already given, often in order to prove that it is false, mistaken, or misleading. *Later today, she'll face cross-examination by lawyers representing Johnson. ...a gruelling 6 hour cross-examination.*

cross-examine, cross-examines, cross-examining, cross-examined
VO If you **are cross-examined**, for example during a trial in a court of law, you are questioned about evidence or information that you have already given. *One of three other men standing trial was also cross-examined... Mr Kelly was cross-examined about statements by prominent politicians... The special council will be cross-examining witnesses.*

cross-eyed
ADJ A person who is **cross-eyed** has eyes that seem to look towards each other. *A friend, a beautiful woman, fell in love with a short, dark, cross-eyed man.*

crossfire /krɒsfaɪə/
1 NU **Crossfire** is gunfire, for example in a battle, that comes from two or more different places but that is aimed at or passes through the same point. *Four civilians were killed in the crossfire.*
2 If you **are caught in the crossfire**, you become involved in an unpleasant situation in which people are arguing with each other, although you do not want to be involved or to say which of them is right. *Jordan has been caught in the crossfire of the region's conflicts.*

crossing /krɒsɪŋ/ **crossings**
1 NC A **crossing** is a journey by boat to the other side of a sea. *...the night ferry crossing to Esbjerg.*
2 NC A **crossing** is also the same as a pedestrian crossing. *The driver ignored a red light at the crossing.*

crossing point, crossing points
NC A **crossing point** is the part of a border between two countries where people and vehicles are allowed to go through. *There was tight security at the crossing points... Pickets blocked border crossing points with France and Portugal.*

cross-legged
ADJ If someone is sitting **cross-legged**, they are sitting with their legs bent close to their body, their knees pointing outwards, and their feet pointing inwards. *Amina was sitting cross-legged on the sofa beside the coffee table.*

cross-purposes
When people are **at cross-purposes**, they do not understand each other because they are thinking or talking about different things without realizing it. *They are bound to be at cross-purposes.*

cross-question, cross-questions, cross-questioning, cross-questioned
VO If you **cross-question** someone, you ask them a lot of questions about something. *I can't bring myself to cross-question the child about her activities... I heard them cross-questioning her thoroughly.*

cross-reference, cross-references
NC A **cross-reference** is a note in a book which tells you that there is relevant or more detailed information in another part of the book. *It contains a list of all the names of the artists on show, with extensive cross-references.*

crossroads /krɒsrəʊdz/; **crossroads** is both the singular and the plural form.
1 NC A **crossroads** is a place where two roads meet and cross each other. *The incident occurred at a busy crossroads in the centre of the city.*
2 If you say that someone or something is **at a crossroads**, you mean that they have reached a point in their development where they must decide what to do next. *China's leaders again find themselves at a crossroads... He said that his country is at a crossroads.*

cross-section, cross-sections
1 NC A **cross-section** of something such as a group of people is a typical or representative sample of it. *It attracts a remarkable cross-section of the public.*
2 NC+SUPP A **cross-section** of an object is what you would see if you cut straight through the middle of it. *...a cross-section of a human brain.*

crosswind /krɒswɪnd/ **crosswinds**
NC A **crosswind** is a strong wind that blows across the direction that vehicles or ships and aircraft are travelling in, and that makes it difficult for them to keep moving steadily forward. *The problem is strong crosswinds at Edwards Air Force Base.*

crosswise /krɒswaɪz/
ADV If something is **crosswise**, it goes from one corner of a thing to the opposite corner. *Her umbrella was clutched crosswise against her bosom.*

crossword /krɒswɜːd/ **crosswords**
NC A **crossword** or **crossword puzzle** is a word game in which you work out answers to clues, and write the answers in the white squares of a pattern of black and white squares. *Most of the world's national newspapers carry crosswords... Her husband settled down to do a crossword puzzle.*

crotch /krɒtʃ/ **crotches**
1 NC Your **crotch** is the part of your body between the tops of your legs. *Travis James swung his hips and thrust his crotch around as he sang.*
2 NC The **crotch** of a pair of trousers or pants is the part that covers the area between the tops of your legs. *I bought myself a pair of jeans, and I tell you, the crotch was damn tight.*

crotchet /krɒtʃɪt/ **crotchets**
NC A **crotchet** is a musical note that has a time value equal to two quavers or half a minim. It is often used to represent one beat. *Why do contemporary composers tend to use quaver beats instead of crotchets?*

crotchety /krɒtʃəti/
ADJ Someone who is **crotchety** is grumpy and easily irritated; an informal word. *...the most crotchety judge in Cape Town.*

crouch /kraʊtʃ/ **crouches, crouching, crouched**
1 V If you **are crouching**, your legs are bent under you so that you are close to the ground and leaning forward slightly. *He crouched down among the tangled foliage.*
2 VA If you **crouch** over something, you bend over it

so that you are very near to it. *Stephanie was crouched over a small table with a pile of exercise books.*

croup /kruːp/
N U or N SING **Croup** is a disease which makes it difficult for people to breathe and causes them to cough a lot. Children most frequently suffer from croup. *Most of the children are ill, with diarrhoea or croup.*

croupier /kruːpɪeɪ/ **croupiers**
N C A **croupier** is the person in charge of a particular gambling table in a casino, who collects the bets and pays money to the people who have won. *I agreed to play a croupier in the film.*

crouton /kruːton/ **croutons**
N C **Croutons** are small pieces of toasted or fried bread that are added to soup just before you eat it. *Crunchy croutons add interest to a smooth creamy soup.*

crow /krəʊ/ **crows, crowing, crowed**
1 N C A **crow** is a kind of large black bird which makes a loud, harsh noise. *Many thrushes are shot or trapped, while others are poisoned by pesticide-laced bait laid for foxes and crows.*
2 V When a cock **crows**, it utters a loud sound early in the morning. *The cocks crowed again.*
3 V+*about or over* If someone **crows** about or over something, they keep telling people proudly about it; used in informal English, showing disapproval. *I do wish he'd stop crowing over his success... Now perhaps that is something to crow about.*
4 If you say that a place is a certain distance away **as the crow flies**, you mean that the distance stated is correct if you travel there in a straight line. *The villages are about twelve miles from the Iranian front, as the crow flies.*

crowbar /krəʊbɑː/ **crowbars**
N C A **crowbar** is a heavy iron bar which is used for forcing things open. *Some of the crowd were armed with sticks and crowbars.*

crowd /kraʊd/ **crowds, crowding, crowded**
1 N C A **crowd** is a large group of people who have gathered together. *The crowd was silent. ...crowds of tourists.*
2 N C A **crowd** is also a group of friends, or people with the same interests or occupation; an informal use. *They were mostly women, the usual crowd.*
3 V A When people **crowd** round someone or something, they gather closely together around them. *They crowded round the television to see the football match.*
4 V O or V A If a group of people **crowd** a place or **crowd** into it, they fill it completely. *People have been crowding shops to buy food... Thousands of other people crowded into the town centre to welcome the Prime Minister.*

crowded /kraʊdɪd/
ADJ A **crowded** place is full of people or things. *The bar was very crowded... The centre of the city was crowded with people as usual... The refugees live on bunkbeds in crowded camps.*

crown /kraʊn/ **crowns, crowning, crowned**
1 N C A **crown** is a circular ornament for the head, usually made of gold and jewels, which kings and queens wear at official ceremonies. *The Queen, adorned in robes and crown, delivered her address to a throng of peers and MPs.*
2 N PROP The monarchy of a particular country is referred to as the **Crown** when it is regarded as an institution. *...a senior Minister of the Crown.*
3 V O or V OC When someone is **crowned**, a crown is placed on their head as part of a ceremony in which they are officially made king or queen. *...Prague Castle where the kings of Bohemia used to be crowned... In December, he will be crowned King Joseph of Asaba, ruler of 1 million Nigerians.*
4 V O If one thing **crowns** another, it is on the top of it; a literary use. *...the shattered rocks that crowned the hill.*
5 N C In sport, a **crown** is a title or championship. *It's the first defence for Chavez since winning the crown three months ago... Mike Tyson has retained his undisputed World Heavyweight crown.*
6 N C Your **crown** is the top part of your head, at the back. *She smoothed the hair on his crown.*

7 V O An achievement, event, or quality that **crowns** something is the best part of it. *The evening was crowned by a dazzling performance from Maria Ewing.* ◆ **crowning** ADJ ATTRIB *These major new discoveries are the crowning achievement of 16 years of research.*

crown court, crown courts
N C In England and Wales a **crown court** is a court in which criminal cases are tried by a judge and jury rather than by a magistrate. *He was committed for trial at Knightsbridge Crown Court.*

crowned head, crowned heads
N C A **crowned head** is a king or queen who is the ruler of their country. *The tiny building, through which passed many of the crowned heads of Europe, is to become a museum.*

crown jewels
N PL The **crown jewels** are the crown, sceptre, and other jewels which are used on important official occasions by the King or Queen. *The diamond is now part of the crown jewels.*

Crown Prince, Crown Princes
N C A **Crown Prince** is a prince who will be king of his country when the present king or queen dies. *...Crown Prince Hassan of Jordan.*

Crown Princess, Crown Princesses
1 N C A **Crown Princess** is the wife of a Crown Prince. *We spoke with the Crown Princess about preparing for the refugees.*
2 N C A **Crown Princess** is also a princess who will be queen of her country when the present king or queen dies. *It was felt that the Crown Princess of Thailand was the best possible role model for other royals as well as potential leaders in Asia.*

crow's feet
N PL **Crow's feet** are little lines of wrinkles on the skin at the outside corner of some people's eyes. *She had a maze of crow's feet when she smiled.*

crucial /kruːʃl/
ADJ Something that is **crucial** is extremely important. *Success or failure here would be crucial to his future prospects... The crucial question is whether these injuries could be prevented.* ◆ **crucially** ADV SEN or ADV *Crucially, however, it limits the right to vote... The answer will depend crucially on the kind of data collected.*

crucible /kruːsəbl/ **crucibles**
N C A **crucible** is a pot in which metals or other substances can be melted or heated up to very high temperatures. *...a crucible that had been used for melting metal.*

crucifix /kruːsɪfɪks/ **crucifixes**
N C A **crucifix** is a cross with a figure of Christ on it. *The man is wearing a crucifix around his neck.*

crucifixion /kruːsɪfɪkʃn/ **crucifixions**
N U or N SING In the Roman Empire, **crucifixion** was a way of executing people by crucifying them. The **Crucifixion** was the death of Christ by this method. *...injury to the wrists and feet consistent with crucifixion. ...the shroud in which Christ was laid to rest after the Crucifixion.*

crucify /kruːsɪfaɪ/ **crucifies, crucifying, crucified**
V O To **crucify** someone means to kill them by tying or nailing them to a cross and leaving them to die. *...the city of Jerusalem, where Christ was crucified.*

crude /kruːd/ **cruder, crudest**
1 ADJ Something such as a method or idea that is **crude** is simple and unsophisticated; used showing disapproval. *This is perhaps a crude method of administration. ...a barrage of crude propaganda.* ◆ **crudely** ADV *The situation can be expressed, crudely, by a mathematical equation.*
2 ADJ Something that is **crude** is made from simple parts and is put together in a very simple way. *...crude stone tools found at archaeological sites all over the world.* ◆ **crudely** ADV *...crudely sewn shorts and shirts.*
3 ADJ **Crude** language is rude and offensive. *Do you have to be so crude?*
4 NU **Crude** is also the same as **crude oil**. *The price of crude today rose to a new high.*

crude oil
NU **Crude oil** is oil in its natural state before it has been processed. *He attacked the current high price of crude oil.*

cruel /kruːəl/ **crueller, cruellest**
ADJ Someone who is **cruel** causes pain or distress, usually deliberately. *She had cruel parents... He thinks that it is cruel to keep turtles as pets.* ♦ **cruelly** ADV *They treated him cruelly.*

cruelty /kruːəlti/
NU **Cruelty** is behaviour that causes pain or distress to people or animals, usually deliberately. *He was jailed for eighteen months after being convicted of cruelty. ...the campaign against cruelty to animals.*

cruet /kruːɪt/ **cruets**
NC A **cruet** is a container that holds small pots for salt, pepper, and mustard. It is used at mealtimes.

cruise /kruːz/ **cruises, cruising, cruised**
1 NC A **cruise** is a holiday spent on a large ship which visits a number of places. *...a cruise in the South Pacific.*
2 V If a car or a ship **cruises**, it moves at a constant moderate speed. *The taxi cruised off down the Cromwell Road.*

cruise missile, cruise missiles
NC A **cruise missile** is a missile which can carry a nuclear warhead and which is guided by a computer. *...surface vessels equipped with cruise missiles. ...sea-launched cruise missiles.*

cruiser /kruːzə/ **cruisers**
1 NC A **cruiser** is a motor boat with a cabin for people to sleep in. *...a motor cruiser called the Maroulies.*
2 NC A **cruiser** is also a large, fast warship. *The first HMS Sheffield was a cruiser which fought in several battles of the Second World War.*
3 NC A **cruiser** is also a police car; used in American English. *The police installed cameras in a handful of cruisers... A guy stole a police cruiser from a shopping center.*

crumb /krʌm/ **crumbs**
1 NC **Crumbs** are very small pieces of bread or cake. *She dusted the biscuit crumbs from her fingers.*
2 NC+SUPP A **crumb** of something such as information, knowledge, or comfort is a very small amount of it. *The release of one more hostage this week is a crumb of comfort for President Assad.*

crumble /krʌmbl/ **crumbles, crumbling, crumbled**
1 V-ERG When something soft, brittle, or old **crumbles**, it breaks into a lot of little pieces. *The bread crumbled in my fingers... Factories lie flattened and houses have crumbled... The flakes can be crumbled into small pieces.*
2 V When a society, organization, or relationship **crumbles**, it fails and comes to an end. *As the government's authority crumbled, law and order appeared to be breaking down rapidly... His first Labour Government crumbled.* ♦ **crumbling** ADJ ATTRIB *...crumbling state industries... They are faced with an American trade embargo and crumbling links with Eastern Europe.*

crumbly /krʌmbli/
ADJ Something that is **crumbly** is easily broken into a lot of little pieces. *...crumbly rock rich in phosphates.*

crummy /krʌmi/ **crummier, crummiest**
ADJ If you say that something is **crummy**, you mean that it is of very poor quality; an informal word. *...a crummy little flat.*

crumpet /krʌmpɪt/ **crumpets**
NC A **crumpet** is a round, flat bread-like cake with holes in one side. You toast crumpets and eat them with butter and jam.

crumple /krʌmpl/ **crumples, crumpling, crumpled**
1 VO If you **crumple** paper or cloth, you squash it and it becomes full of creases and folds. *He took the letter and crumpled it in his hand.* ♦ **crumpled** ADJ *He was dressed in crumpled clothes.*
2 V If someone or something **crumples**, they collapse suddenly in an untidy and helpless way. *He crumpled into a heap.*

crumple up PHRASAL VERB If you **crumple up** a piece of paper, you crush it into a ball. *She crumpled it up and threw it into the wastebasket.*

crunch /krʌntʃ/ **crunches, crunching, crunched**
1 VO If you **crunch** something with your teeth or feet, you crush it noisily. *He put seven or eight pieces into his mouth and began crunching them... I crunched a wine glass underfoot.* ▶ Also NC+SUPP *...the crunch of footsteps on the gravel.*
2 N SING You can use **crunch** to refer to the moment when a situation becomes so serious that you are forced to decide something or to take action. *The crunch will come in December, which is when the two countries have agreed to resume negotiations... When it comes to the crunch, you're really on your own.*

crunchy /krʌntʃi/
ADJ **Crunchy** food is hard or crisp, and makes a noise when you eat it. *...that bread; crunchy outside, soothingly smooth inside. ...Its the nuts that make it so crunchy.*

crusade /kruːseɪd/ **crusades, crusading, crusaded**
1 NC+SUPP A **crusade** is a long and determined attempt to achieve something for a cause that you feel strongly about. *He vowed to continue his crusade against apartheid. ...a crusade to clean up Britain... Prince Charles launched his crusade with a speech delivered to an assembly of British architects.*
2 VO If you **crusade** for a particular cause, you make a long and determined effort to achieve something for it. *Throughout history people have banded together to crusade for equality, justice, and liberty.* ♦ **crusading** ADJ *Gunter Wallraff is a crusading radical journalist from Cologne.*

crusader /kruːseɪdə/ **crusaders**
NC+SUPP A **crusader** is someone who is involved in activities in support of a cause that they feel strongly about. *...an outspoken crusader against corruption.*

crush /krʌʃ/ **crushes, crushing, crushed**
1 VO If an object is **crushed**, it is pressed or squeezed very hard so that it is broken or its shape is destroyed. *His car was crushed by a falling tree... People who are frightened of lifts are often afraid of being caught and crushed between their closing doors.*
2 VO If you **crush** a substance, you make it into a powder by pressing and grinding it. *To get the oil out you will have to crush the seeds.*
3 VO If you **crush** an opponent or an enemy, you defeat them completely. *The government still think they can crush the unions... He fled to the West after the democracy movement was crushed... It is still not clear whether the army has managed to crush the revolt.* ♦ **crushing** ADJ ATTRIB *The Government had suffered a crushing defeat.*
4 V-PASS If you **are crushed** against other people or things, you are pushed or pressed against them. *Two people were crushed to death by the crowds... They were crushed up against a wire fence, like prisoners in a cage.*
5 NC A **crush** is a dense crowd of people. *A reporter made his way through the crush.*
6 NC If you have a **crush** on someone, you are strongly attracted to them for a short time; an informal use. *I had a crush on the violin master.*

crush barrier, crush barriers
NC A **crush barrier** is a fence in the middle of a large crowd, for example at a football match, which divides the crowd and helps to prevent people from being pressed too closely together. *Many of the crowd pushed their way through the crush barriers.*

crust /krʌst/ **crusts**
1 NCorNU The **crust** on a loaf of bread is the hard, crisp outside part of it.
2 NC A **crust** of bread is a small, hard piece of old bread. *...a society where people are fighting for a crust of bread.*
3 NC A **crust** is also the hard upper layer of something. *The snow had a fine crust on it.*
4 NC+SUPP The earth's **crust** is its outer layer. *Earthquakes happen because the earth's crust isn't static.*

crustacean /krʌsteɪʃn/ **crustaceans**
NC A **crustacean** is an animal with a hard outer shell and several pairs of legs, which usually lives in water. Crabs, lobsters, and shrimps are crustaceans. *Whelks are the country's commonest crustaceans.*

crusted /krʌstɪd/
ADJ PRED Something that is **crusted** with a substance is covered with a hard layer of it. *The lane was crusted with cow dung.*

crusty /krʌsti/
ADJ Something that is **crusty** has a hard, crisp outer layer. *Serve the soup with hot crusty bread.*

crutch /krʌtʃ/ **crutches**
1 NC A **crutch** is a support like a stick, which you lean on to help you to walk when you have injured your foot or leg. *...soldiers who have got one leg and are walking on crutches.*
2 NC A **crutch** is also a person or thing that gives you help or support. *...the economic crutch provided by the Soviet Union.*
3 NC Someone's **crutch** is the same as their **crotch**.

crux /krʌks/
N SING The **crux** of a problem or argument is the most important or difficult part, which affects everything else. *The crux of the issue is modernisation... This brings us to the crux of the dilemma; maintaining order without paralysing society.*

cry /kraɪ/ **cries, crying, cried**
1 V When you **cry**, you produce tears because you are unhappy or hurt. *Helen began to cry... He kept on crying... The baby became thirsty and was crying for a drink.* ► Also N SING *I think she had had a good cry.*
2 V-QUOTE or V If you **cry** something, you shout it or say it loudly. *'Come on!' he cried. ...wounded soldiers crying for help.* ► Also NC *I heard a cry for help... Claud let out a cry of horror.*
3 NC You can describe a loud sound made by a bird as a **cry**. *A sea bird flapped upwards with a hoarse cry.*
4 Something that is a **far cry** from something else is very different from it. *The tropical grasslands are a far cry from the lush green pastures of Ireland.*
5 to **cry wolf**: see **wolf**. See also **crying**.

cry off PHRASAL VERB If you **cry off**, you decide not to do something that you had arranged to do; an informal expression. *I'm afraid I cried off at the last moment.*

cry out PHRASAL VERB If you **cry out**, you call out or say something loudly, usually because you are anxious or frightened. *I heard Mary cry out in fright... 'Father! You must stop that!' he suddenly cried out.*

cry out for PHRASAL VERB If you say that one thing is **crying out for** another, you mean that it needs that thing very much. *There is a vast surplus of workers crying out for employment.*

crybaby /kraɪbeɪbi/ **crybabies**
NC If you say that someone, especially a young child, is a **crybaby**, you mean that they cry a lot for no good reason; an informal word. *You're a lot of crybabies and sissies.*

crying /kraɪɪŋ/
1 NU **Crying** is the sound that a baby makes when he or she is unhappy, hungry, or tired. *They worry about the baby's crying.*
2 ADJ ATTRIB If there is a **crying** need for something to be done, there is a very great need for it, especially for it to be done urgently. *We still haven't answered one crying need in education.*
3 If you say that something is a **crying shame**, you are emphasizing what a great pity or shame it is, often when you are annoyed about it.
4 See also **cry**.

crypt /krɪpt/ **crypts**
NC A **crypt** is an underground room beneath a church or cathedral. *The committee met in the crypt of a Warsaw church.*

cryptic /krɪptɪk/
ADJ A **cryptic** remark or message contains a hidden meaning. *I didn't ask what this cryptic remark was intended to convey.* ◆ **cryptically** ADV *'I have taken precautions,' she said cryptically.*

crystal /krɪstl/ **crystals**
1 NC A **crystal** is a mineral that has formed naturally into a regular symmetrical shape. *Pure copper is made up of layers of crystals. ...research into new ways of making large artificial diamond crystals.*
2 NU **Crystal** is a transparent rock used in jewellery

and ornaments. *The throne has a beautiful inlay of agate, onyx and crystal.*
3 NU **Crystal** is also very high quality glass, usually with its surface cut into patterns. *...a shimmering crystal chandelier. ...an engraved Waterford crystal bowl.*

crystal ball, crystal balls
1 NC A **crystal ball** is a ball made of clear glass which is used by fortune-tellers, who claim that they can see things that are going to happen in the future when they look into it. *I peered into my crystal ball.*
2 NC People sometimes say that they are gazing into their **crystal ball** when they are trying to imagine what the future will be like. *Can I get you to gaze into your crystal ball and give us some indication as to how this drug might be used?*

crystal clear
ADJ An explanation that is **crystal clear** is very easy to understand. *He challenged every point which he did not find crystal clear.*

crystalline /krɪstəlaɪn/
1 ADJ Something that is **crystalline** is clear, bright, and sparkling like crystal; a literary use. *The light here has a crystalline quality I have not seen in any other place.*
2 ADJ **Crystalline** also means in the form of crystals or containing crystals; a technical use in chemistry. *...a crust of hard crystalline rock.*

crystallize /krɪstəlaɪz/ **crystallizes, crystallizing, crystallized**; also spelt **crystallise**.
1 V-ERG When an opinion or idea **crystallizes**, it becomes fixed and definite in your mind. *My thoughts began to crystallize... This experience crystallized his attitude to democracy.*
2 V When a substance **crystallizes**, it turns into crystals. *When calcium carbonate is allowed to crystallize from solution, the crystals are shaped like lopsided cubes.*

crystallized /krɪstəlaɪzd/
ADJ ATTRIB **Crystallized** fruits and sweets are covered in sugar which has been melted and then allowed to go hard.

CSE /siːesiː/ **CSE's**
NC **CSE's** were examinations in various subjects which some children in Britain took at the age of fifteen or sixteen. CSE's were replaced by GCSE's in 1988. CSE is an abbreviation for 'Certificate of Secondary Education'. *Wendy'll only be doing CSE's. ...CSE certificates.*

CS gas /siːes gæs/
NU **CS gas** is a gas which causes you to cry and makes breathing painful. It is sometimes used by the army in war or to control a crowd which is rioting. *The trouble started when a CS gas canister was hurled into the crowd.*

cub /kʌb/ **cubs**
1 NC A **cub** is a young wild animal such as a lion, wolf, or bear. *...a two month-old leopard cub.*
2 NC A **cub** is also the same as a **cub scout**. *Britain's boy scouts and cubs are being asked if they want to change their traditional uniform.*

Cuba /kjuːbə/
The **Republic of Cuba** is a country in the Caribbean. It was a Spanish colony until 1898. Dr Fidel Castro Ruz became Prime Minister in 1959, when he overthrew the government of General Batista. The Cuban Communist Party (PCC) became the sole legal party. In 1961 an invasion of Cuba, backed by the USA, failed at the Bay of Pigs. In 1962 the presence of Soviet missile bases caused the Cuban Missile Crisis between the USA and the USSR. Cuba is the second largest producer of sugar in the world. ◆ **Cuban** /kjuːbən/ N, ADJ
■ *religion:* Christianity (mainly Roman Catholic) though officially atheist ■ *language:* Spanish ■ *currency:* peso ■ *capital:* Havana ■ *population:* 10 million (1988) ■ *size:* 110,860 square kilometres.

cubby-hole /kʌbihəʊl/ **cubby-holes**; also spelt **cubbyhole**.
NC A **cubby-hole** is a very small room or space for storing things. *This is my office, my cubby-hole... He was given a miserable little cubby-hole to work in.*

cube /kju:b/ cubes

1 NC A **cube** is a three-dimensional shape with six square surfaces which are all the same size. ...*a half-kilo cube of plastic.*
2 NC The **cube** of a number is another number that is produced by multiplying the first number by itself twice. For example, the cube of 2 is 2x2x2, or 8.

cube root, cube roots

NC If you multiply one number by itself twice to get a second number, the first number is the **cube root** of the second number. For example, 2 is the cube root of 8.

cubic /kju:bɪk/

ADJ ATTRIB **Cubic** is used in front of units of length to form units of volume such as 'cubic metre' and 'cubic foot'. *The new plant will increase the country's gas production by 34 million cubic metres per day.*

cubicle /kju:bɪkl/ cubicles

NC A **cubicle** is a small enclosed area in a public building which is used for a particular purpose, such as changing your clothes or talking to someone privately. *He went into his cubicle to change.*

cubism /kju:bɪzəm/

NU **Cubism** is a style of art, begun in the early twentieth century, in which objects are represented as if they could be seen from several different positions at the same time, using many lines and geometrical shapes. *Cubism is represented by Picasso and Braque.* ◆ **cubist, cubists** NC *The Cubists discovered a new way of representing reality.* ...*cubist paintings.*

cub reporter, cub reporters

NC A **cub reporter** is a young reporter for a newspaper who is still being trained in his or her job. *He started, at sixteen, as a ten-dollar-a-week cub reporter.*

cub scout, cub scouts

NC A **cub scout** is a boy who is a member of the Cub Scouts, the junior branch of the Scout Association. Cub scouts are encouraged to be disciplined and to learn practical skills. They are usually between eight and eleven yers old. *They stood in their Cub Scout uniforms.*

cuckold /kʌkəuld/ cuckolds, cuckolding, cuckolded; an old-fashioned word.

1 NC A **cuckold** is a man whose wife is deceiving him by having a sexual relationship with another man. *That girl is making him a cuckold.*
2 VO If a woman **cuckolds** her husband, she deceives him by having an affair with another man. *He had kicked her out for cuckolding him.*

cuckoo /kuku:/ cuckoos

NC A **cuckoo** is a grey bird with a call of two quick notes. Cuckoos lay their eggs in other birds' nests. *The sighting of the cuckoo has traditionally signified the arrival of spring in Britain.*

cuckoo clock, cuckoo clocks

NC A **cuckoo clock** is a pretty clock with a door. A toy cuckoo pops out of the door and makes a little noise each time the clock chimes.

cucumber /kju:kʌmbə/ cucumbers

NC A **cucumber** is a long vegetable with a dark green skin and white flesh, usually eaten uncooked in salad.

cud /kʌd/

When cows **chew the cud**, they chew their partly digested food over and over again.

cuddle /kʌdl/ cuddles, cuddling, cuddled

V-RECIP or VO If you **cuddle** someone, you put your arms round them and hold them close. *I cuddled her a bit but what can you say?... We kissed and cuddled... A baby must be cuddled a lot.* ▶ Also NC *Give them a few cuddles and talk nicely to them.*

cuddle up PHRASAL VERB When you **cuddle up** to someone, you sit or lie as near to them as possible and hold them. *He may want to cuddle up and get warm under the bedclothes.*

cuddly /kʌdəⁱli/

1 ADJ **Cuddly** animals or toys are soft and furry so that they are nice to cuddle. ...*a cuddly panda bear.*
2 ADJ If you describe someone as **cuddly**, you mean that you think they are nice and you would like to cuddle them. *He gave her a hug and said 'she's nice and cuddly'.*

cudgel /kʌdʒl/ cudgels

1 NC A **cudgel** is a thick, short stick used for hitting people; an old-fashioned use. *The couple were confronted with six masked men, two carrying guns and a third armed with a cudgel.*
2 If you **take up the cudgels** for someone or something, you speak or fight in support of them. *Brown took up the cudgels on his behalf.*

cue /kju:/ cues

1 NC+SUPP A **cue** is something said or done by a performer that is a signal for another performer to begin speaking or doing something. *The violinist was late for her cue.*
2 NC You can refer to something that is a signal for someone to do something as a **cue**. *They started yawning, and that was our cue to leave.*
3 NC A **cue** is also a long stick used in snooker, billiards, and pool. *They put down their pool cues.*
● **Cue** is used in these phrases. ● If you **take** your **cue** from someone, you use their behaviour as an indication of what you should do. *Michael took his cue from the Duke's tone.* ● If you say that something happened **on cue**, you mean that it happened just when it was expected to happen. *Then, right on cue, the coach broke down.*

cuff /kʌf/ cuffs, cuffing, cuffed

1 NC The **cuffs** of a piece of clothing are the end parts of the sleeves. *There was a button missing from his shirt cuff.*
2 If you are making a statement **off the cuff**, you have not prepared what you are saying. *I can't answer that question off the cuff... There's no telling whether Gorbachev's proposal for a referendum was serious or off the cuff.*
3 VO If you **cuff** someone, you hit them lightly with your hand. *Sally cuffed my head lightly.*

cufflink /kʌflɪŋk/ cufflinks

NC **Cufflinks** are small decorative objects used for holding together a shirt cuff.

cuisine /kwɪzi:n/

NU+SUPP The **cuisine** of a region is its characteristic style of cooking. *Good Western vegetarian food and traditional Eastern vegetarian cuisine all reduce heart disease risks.* ...*the delights of the Paris cuisine.*

cul-de-sac /kʌldəsæk/ cul-de-sacs

NC A **cul-de-sac** is a road which is closed at one end. *The men burst into a first floor flat in a cul-de-sac.*

culinary /kʌlɪnəʳri/

ADJ ATTRIB **Culinary** means concerned with cooking. ...*that most Scottish of culinary delights, the haggis.*

cull /kʌl/ culls, culling, culled

1 VO If you **cull** ideas or information, you gather them so that you can use them. ...*materials that I'd culled from all sorts of places.*
2 VO To **cull** a group of animals means to kill some of them in order to reduce their numbers. *They start to cull the herds in dry years.* ▶ Also NC ...*a big elephant cull in Zimbabwe.*

culminate /kʌlmɪneɪt/ culminates, culminating, culminated

V+in If a situation **culminates** in an event, this event is the end result of the situation. *The struggle between King and Parliament had culminated in the Civil War.*

culmination /kʌlmɪneɪʃn/

NU The **culmination** of a situation or process is what happens as its final result. *The protests were the culmination of a week of demonstrations... He says his appointment is the culmination of years of hard work.*

culottes /kju:lɒts/

N PL **Culottes** are women's trousers which have very wide legs so that they look rather like a skirt.

culpable /kʌlpəbl/

ADJ PRED You say that someone is **culpable** when they are responsible for something wrong or unpleasant that has happened; a formal word. *Their presence at the murder made them equally culpable.*

culprit /kʌlprɪt/ culprits

NC When some harm has been done, the **culprit** is the person who did it. *The main culprits were caught and heavily sentenced.*

cult /kʌlt/ cults

1 NC A **cult** is a religious group with special rituals,

which is regarded by many people as extreme or dangerous. *The 'Moonies' cult gained adherents at an alarming rate.*
2 NC When a person, object, or activity becomes a **cult**, they become very popular or fashionable. *The Beatles became the heroes of a world-wide cult... The Soviet leader has become something of a cult figure.*

cultivate /kʌltɪveɪt/ **cultivates, cultivating, cultivated**
1 VO To **cultivate** land means to prepare it and grow crops on it. *He retired to his estate near Bordeaux to cultivate his vineyard.* ◆ **cultivated** ADJ *Only 1 per cent of the cultivated area was under irrigation.* ◆ **cultivation** /kʌltɪveɪʃn/ NU *Some extra land is being brought under cultivation in Asia.*
2 VO If you **cultivate** an attitude, you deliberately develop it and make it stronger. *He was anxious to cultivate the trust of moderate Tories.* ◆ **cultivation** NU+of *...the cultivation of good taste.*
3 VO If you **cultivate** someone, you try to develop a friendship with them; a formal use. *Their cooperation is vital, so cultivate them assiduously... For some thirty years France has been cultivating their friendship.*

cultivated /kʌltɪveɪtɪd/
1 ADJ Someone who is **cultivated** has had a good education, and shows this in their behaviour. *She was a cultivated and beautiful girl.*
2 ADJ ATTRIB **Cultivated** plants have been developed for growing on farms or in gardens. *Cultivated sunflowers and wild sunflowers usually grow in close proximity.*

cultivator /kʌltɪveɪtə/ **cultivators**
1 NC A **cultivator** is a tool or machine which is used to break up the earth or to remove weeds in a garden or field. *The engine was used for pulling a cultivator backwards and forwards across the fields.*
2 NC A **cultivator** is also someone who prepares the ground and grows crops in it. *Falling sugar prices have hit the island's sugar cane cultivators hard.*

cultural /kʌltʃərəl/
1 ADJ ATTRIB **Cultural** means relating to the arts generally. *...cultural activities such as plays, concerts, and poetry readings... Athenian democracy gave birth to some of the finest cultural achievements of the ancient world.*
2 ADJ **Cultural** also means relating to a particular society and way of life. *Turkey and Azerbaijan have close cultural and historic links. ...children from different ethnic and cultural backgrounds.* ◆ **culturally** ADV *They have little in common culturally with us.*

cultural desert, cultural deserts
NC If you describe a place as a **cultural desert**, you mean that there is very little artistic or intellectual activity there; an informal expression. *The city is a great cultural desert.*

culture /kʌltʃə/ **cultures, culturing, cultured**
1 NUorNC **Culture** consists of the ideas, customs, and art produced by a particular society. *He was specially interested in culture and history. ...the great cultures of Japan and China.*
2 NC+SUPP A **culture** is a particular society or civilization. *We must respect the practices of cultures different from our own.*
3 NC In science, a **culture** is a group of bacteria or cells grown in a laboratory as part of an experiment. *They are to be inoculated with a bacterial culture.* ▶ Also VO *The infected cells were carefully cultured to make them grow into complete new plants.*

cultured /kʌltʃəd/
ADJ Someone who is **cultured** has good manners, is well educated, and knows a lot about the arts. *He is a highly cultured man.*

cultured pearl, cultured pearls
NC A **cultured pearl** is a pearl that is deliberately created by putting sand or grit into an oyster. *She wore the string of cultured pearls he had given her.*

culture shock
NU **Culture shock** is a feeling of anxiety, loneliness, and confusion that people sometimes experience when they first arrive in another country. *She was still suffering from culture shock after her arrival in Britain.*

culvert /kʌlvət/ **culverts**
NC A **culvert** is a water pipe or sewer that crosses under a road or railway. *The water poured through a culvert under the highway.*

-cum- /-kʌm-/
You put **-cum-** between two words to form a compound noun referring to something or someone that is partly one thing and partly another; used in old-fashioned English. *...a dining-cum-living room.*

cumbersome /kʌmbəsəm/
1 ADJ Something that is **cumbersome** is large and heavy and therefore difficult to carry, wear, or handle. *...a cumbersome piece of machinery.*
2 ADJ A **cumbersome** system or process is complicated and inefficient. *Its administration is cumbersome and excessively costly.*

cumin /kʌmɪn/; also spelt **cummin**.
NU **Cumin** is a sweet-smelling spice used in cooking, especially Indian cooking. *...black cumin seeds for sprinkling on bread.*

cummerbund /kʌməbʌnd/ **cummerbunds**
NC A **cummerbund** is a wide sash worn round the waist as part of a man's evening dress.

cumulative /kjuːmjʊlətɪv/
ADJ Something that is **cumulative** keeps increasing in quantity or degree. *He was concerned about the cumulative effect of the weather on China's crops.*

cumulus /kjuːmjʊləs/ **cumuli** /kjuːmjʊlaɪ/
NUorNC **Cumulus** is a type of thick, fluffy white cloud formed when hot air rises very quickly. *Around midday, the fog lifted and puffy cumulus clouds appeared across the sky.*

cunning /kʌnɪŋ/
1 ADJ A **cunning** person is clever and deceitful. *He knew nothing of the cunning means employed to get him out of his job.*
2 NU **Cunning** is the ability to plan things cleverly, often by deceiving people. *They achieved their aim by stealth and cunning.*

cunt /kʌnt/ **cunts**; a rude and offensive word which you should avoid using.
1 NC A **cunt** is a woman's vagina; an extremely offensive use.
2 NC If someone calls another person a **cunt**, they are being very offensive and showing how much they hate or despise that person.

cup /kʌp/ **cups, cupping, cupped**
1 NC A **cup** is a small round container with a handle, which you drink from. *John put his cup and saucer on the table.*
2 NC You can use **cup** to refer to a cup and its contents, or to the contents only. *I've just made some tea. Would you like a cup?... I had a cup of hot flavourless coffee.*
3 NC You can also use **cup** to refer to something which is small, round, and hollow. *....an egg cup... She tipped a pile of raisins into the cup of his hand.*
4 NC A **cup** is also a metal cup given as a prize to the winner of a game or competition. *The Czechs first won the Cup in 1975... Middlesex have won the Refuge Assurance Cup.*
5 VO If you **cup** something in your hands, you hold it with your hands touching all round it. *His hands were cupped around his lighter.*

cupboard /kʌbəd/ **cupboards**
NC A **cupboard** is a piece of furniture with doors at the front and usually shelves inside. *...a well-stocked kitchen cupboard.* ◆ **a skeleton in the cupboard**: see skeleton.

cupboard love
NU **Cupboard love** is the sudden or extremely friendly or loving behaviour of one person to another, especially of a child towards one of its parents, in order to get something that he or she wants.

Cup Final, Cup Finals
1 NC In sport, a **Cup Final** is the last match in a competition when the two winners from the previous rounds play against each other to see who will win the cup for that year. *They were angry at not being able to get tickets for a Cup Final match.*
2 NC In Britain, the **Cup Final** is the last match of the Football Association Cup soccer competition. It is held

every year in London. ...*the Cup Final at Wembley*.

cupful /kʌpful/ **cupfuls**

NC A **cupful** of something is the amount which one cup can hold. *Dissolve two cupfuls of sugar in half a cup of water*.

Cupid /kjuːpɪd/ **Cupids**

1 N PROP **Cupid** is the Roman god of love, the son of the goddess Venus. He is usually drawn as a baby boy with wings and a bow and arrow. *The stamp shows a picture of Cupid*.

2 NC A **cupid** is a picture or statue of a pretty little boy with wings, often holding a bow and arrow. ...*a big mirror with little carved cupids at each corner*.

cupidity /kjuːpɪdəti/

NU **Cupidity** is a greedy desire for money and possessions; a formal word. *Appeals to human cupidity reach their lowest point in TV give-away shows*.

cupola /kjuːpələ/ **cupolas**

NC A **cupola** is a roof or part of a roof that is shaped like a round bowl turned upside-down, usually with a pointed spire in the centre. ...*the golden cupolas of the Kremlin*.

cuppa /kʌpə/ **cuppas**

N SING A **cuppa** is a cup of tea; used in informal speech. *What about a cuppa? ...their morning cuppa*.

cup-tie, **cup-ties**; also spelt **cup tie**.

NC In sport, a **cup-tie** is a match between two teams who are playing in a competition in which the prize is a cup. The winner of one match plays the winner of another, and so on, until two teams reach the final. ...*Nottingham Forest's cup-tie victory over Queen's Park Rangers*.

curable /kjuərəbl/

ADJ A **curable** disease or illness can be cured. *Cervical cancer can be completely curable if it is diagnosed reasonably early*.

curacy /kjuərəsi/ **curacies**

NC A **curacy** is the position held by a curate, or the work that a curate has to do. ...*Somerset, where my father had his first curacy*.

curate /kjuərət/ **curates**

NC A **curate** is a clergyman who helps a vicar or priest. *Father Popieluszko was a young curate in a working class parish in Warsaw*.

curative /kjuərətɪv/

ADJ ATTRIB **Curative** is used to describe something that can cure people's illnesses or problems. ...*the curative power of herbal remedies*.

curator /kjuəreɪtə/ **curators**

NC The **curator** of a museum or art gallery is the person in charge of the exhibits. *Mr Volkov is curator of the Trotsky Museum in Mexico City*.

curb /kɜːb/ **curbs, curbing, curbed**

1 VO If you **curb** something, you control it and keep it within fixed limits. ...*proposals to curb the powers of the Home Secretary*. ▶ Also NC *This requires a curb on public spending*.

2 See also **kerb**.

curdle /kɜːdl/ **curdles, curdling, curdled**

V-ERG When milk **curdles** or when something **curdles** it, it becomes sour. *The acidity of some coffee can cause the milk to curdle*.

curds /kɜːdz/

N PL **Curds** are the thick white substance formed when milk turns sour.

cure /kjuə, kjɔː/ **cures, curing, cured**

1 VO To **cure** an illness means to make it end. *It's a disease that can't be cured... There are few diseases that these modern drugs cannot cure... The cancer can be cured without losing all the bone marrow*.

2 VO To **cure** a sick or injured person means to make them well again. *Her patients appear to be cured... Those people whose cancer is detected early will be cured through surgery or radiation... You're cured; go home*.

3 NC A **cure** is a medicine or other treatment that cures an illness. *There's no known cure for a cold. ...a possible cure for AIDS*.

4 VO To **cure** a problem means to deal with it successfully. *The bishop had done nothing to cure the widespread lack of faith*.

5 NC A **cure** for a problem is a way of dealing with it successfully. *The only cure for her unhappiness was to leave home... The trade deficit is going the wrong way, and the presidential election is unlikely to produce an instant cure*.

6 VO+*of* To **cure** someone of a habit or attitude means to make them give it up. *The shock of losing my purse cured me of my former carelessness*.

7 VO When food, tobacco, or animal skin **is cured**, it is treated by being dried, smoked, or salted so that it will last for a long time. *There are great quantities of white fish taken and cured*. ◆ **cured** ADJ ...*cured ham*.

curé /kjuəreɪ/ **curés**

NC A **curé** is a parish priest in France.

cure-all, **cure-alls**

NC A **cure-all** is something that people think will solve all their problems. *Lowering of interest rates has been presented by the media as a kind of universal cure-all*.

curfew /kɜːfjuː/ **curfews**

NC A **curfew** is a law stating that people must stay inside their houses after a particular time at night until a particular time the next morning. *An emergency curfew was enforced*.

curio /kjuəriəu/ **curios**

NC A **curio** is an object such as a small ornament which is unusual and fairly rare. ...*an auction of antiques, furniture and curios*.

curiosity /kjuərɪɒsəti/ **curiosities**

1 NU **Curiosity** is a desire to know about things. *She looked at me, eyes wide open and full of curiosity... I have very little curiosity about anything*.

2 NC **Curiosities** are things which are interesting and fairly rare. ...*old but natural curiosities like fossils*.

curious /kjuəriəs/

1 ADJ If you are **curious** about something, you are interested in it and want to know more about it. *He seemed awfully curious about Robertson's day-to-day routine... She was curious to see what would happen*. ◆ **curiously** ADV *They stopped and looked at her curiously*.

2 ADJ Something that is **curious** is unusual and interesting or surprising. *Not long after our arrival, a curious thing happened... It is curious how two such different problems can be solved so similarly*. ◆ **curiously** ADV or ADV SEN *She had a curiously husky voice... Curiously, Hearst worked energetically during his mental breakdown*.

curl /kɜːl/ **curls, curling, curled**

1 NC **Curls** are lengths of hair shaped in curves and circles. ...*a little girl with golden curls*.

2 V If something **curls**, it has tight curves or becomes tightly curved. *Her hair curled about her head like a child's... The bark was curling and falling away from the trunk*.

3 V A If something **curls** somewhere, it moves in circles or spirals. *Smoke was curling out of kitchen chimneys*. ▶ Also NC ...*curls of smoke*.

curl up PHRASAL VERB 1 When someone who is lying down **curls up**, they bring their arms, legs, and head in towards their stomach. *He was lying curled up with his back to us*. 2 When something such as a leaf or a piece of paper **curls up**, its edges bend up or towards its centre. *Her photographs curl up, yellowing, in some dusty drawer*.

curler /kɜːlə/ **curlers**

NC **Curlers** are small plastic or metal tubes that women roll their hair round in order to make it curly. *In her short, dark hair were rows of pink plastic curlers... When she took her curlers out she looked much younger*.

curlew /kɜːljuː/ **curlews**

NC A **curlew** is a large brown bird with long legs and a long curved beak. Curlews live near water and have a very distinctive cry. ...*the searing wail of the curlew*.

curling tongs

N PL **Curling tongs** are a cylindrical device for curling people's hair. The metal part of the device is heated, and then strands of hair are wound around it.

curly /kɜːli/ **curlier, curliest**

1 ADJ **Curly** hair is full of curls. *One of the men was*

five foot ten inches tall with long curly, blonde hair.
2 ADJ **Curly** objects are curved or spiral-shaped. *What are these curly bits of paper for?*

currant /kʌrənt/ **currants**
NC **Currants** are small dried grapes which are often put into cakes. *The buns are flavoured with spices and baked with currants.*

currency /kʌrənsi/ **currencies**
1 NCorNU The money used in a country is referred to as its **currency**. *Sterling has once again become one of the stronger currencies... Do you change foreign currency?*
2 NU If ideas, expressions, or customs have **currency** at a particular time, they are generally used and accepted by people at that time; a formal use. *They have seen many of their basic ideas gain wide currency.*

current /kʌrənt/ **currents**
1 NC A **current** is a steady, continuous, flowing movement of water or air. *The child had been swept out to sea by the current.*
2 NC An electric **current** is electricity flowing through a wire or circuit. *These new compounds can carry a strong electric current.*
3 ADJ Something that is **current** is happening, being done, or being used at the present time. *Our current methods of production are too expensive... The words 'light pollution' are in current use among astronomers.*
♦ **currently** ADV *...experiments currently in progress.*

current account, current accounts
1 NC A **current account** is a bank account which you can take money out of at any time using your cheque book or cheque card. *Banks made a great fanfare when they started paying interest on current accounts... His bank refuses to make automatic transfers between savings and current accounts.*
2 NC A country's **current account** is the difference between the payment that is made for imports and the payment that is received from exports over a particular period of time. *Japan says its current account surplus in July exceeded five thousand million dollars... The current account balance for August showed a deficit of £1,100 million.*

current affairs
N PL **Current affairs** are political and social events which are happening at the present time. *...the BBC's current affairs programmes. ...the personalization and over-simplification of current affairs.*

curriculum /kərɪkjʊləm/ **curriculums** or **curricula** /kərɪkjʊlə/
1 NC In a school, college, or university, the **curriculum** consists of all the different courses of study that are taught there. *Social studies have now been added to the curriculum.*
2 NC+SUPP A particular course of study can also be referred to as a **curriculum**. *...our English curriculum.*

curriculum vitae /kərɪkjʊləm viːtaɪ/
N SING Your **curriculum vitae** is a brief written account of your personal details, your education, and the jobs you have had. You are often asked to send your curriculum vitae when you are applying for a job. It is often abbreviated to CV.

curried /kʌrid/
ADJ ATTRIB **Curried** food has been flavoured with hot spices. *...huge dishes of curried chicken.*

curry /kʌri/ **curries, currying, curried**
1 N MASS **Curry** is an Asian way of cooking which uses hot spices. *I really like sultanas in curry... This is how I make a vegetable curry. ...salted or dried, in soups or curries.*
2 If you **curry favour** with someone, you try to please them by praising them or doing things to help them; used showing disapproval. *The whole plan had been designed to curry favour with the Arabs.*

curry powder, curry powders
NUorNC **Curry powder** is a powder made of a mixture of spices, which you add to food in order to make a curry.

curse /kɜːs/ **curses, cursing, cursed**
1 V If you **curse**, you swear or say rude words because you are angry about something. *He missed*

the ball and cursed violently. ► Also NC *With a curse he disentangled his head from the netting.*
2 VO If you **curse** someone, you say insulting things to them because you are angry with them. *I was cursing him under my breath for his carelessness.*
3 VO If you **curse** something, you complain angrily about it, usually using rude language as you do so. *I cursed the orders that brought me here... Cursing my plight, I tried to find shelter for the night.*
4 NC If you say that there is a **curse** on someone, you mean that a supernatural power is causing unpleasant things to happen to them. *There is a curse on this family.*
5 NC+SUPP You can also refer to something that causes a lot of trouble or unhappiness as a **curse**. *Loneliness in old age is the curse of modern society.*

cursed /kɜːst, kɜːsɪd/
1 ADJ Someone who is **cursed** is suffering as the result of a curse. *The descendants of Ham were cursed for ever.*
2 ADJ PRED+*with* If you are **cursed** with something, you are very unlucky in having it. *...a land cursed with almost continuous rainfall.*

cursor /kɜːsə/ **cursors**
NC The **cursor** is a marker on a computer screen which indicates where anything typed by the user will appear. *She moved the cursor to the start of the word.*

cursory /kɜːsəᵊri/
ADJ A **cursory** glance or examination is a brief one in which you do not pay much attention to detail. *Even a cursory reading of the ingredients may make you think twice before you open your next tin of soup.*

curt /kɜːt/
ADJ If someone is **curt**, they speak in a brief and rather rude way. *He had been curt with Gertrude.*
♦ **curtly** ADV *Marsha said curtly, 'You're supposed to be on watch.'*

curtail /kɜːteɪl/ **curtails, curtailing, curtailed**
VO If you **curtail** something, you reduce or restrict it; a formal word. *Countries are under pressure to curtail public expenditure. ...further legislation to curtail basic union rights.*

curtailment /kɜːteɪlmənt/
NU+SUPP The **curtailment** of something is the act of reducing or restricting it; a formal word. *...the curtailment of military aid from the US.*

curtain /kɜːtn/ **curtains, curtaining, curtained**
1 NC **Curtains** are hanging pieces of material which you can pull across a window to keep light out or prevent people from looking in. *He drew the curtains.*
2 N SING In a theatre, the **curtain** is a large piece of material that hangs in front of the stage until a performance begins. *There was a burst of applause as the curtain went up.*
3 See also **curtained**.

curtain off PHRASAL VERB If you **curtain off** part of a room, you separate it from the rest of the room by hanging a curtain across the room. *The other end of the room had been curtained off.*

curtain call, curtain calls
NC In a theatre, when actors take a **curtain call**, they come forward to the front of the stage after a performance in order to receive the applause of the audience. *Last night we took four curtain calls.*

curtained /kɜːtnd/
ADJ A **curtained** window, door, or other opening has a curtain hanging across it. *The curtained stage was empty.* ● See also **curtain**.

curtain-raiser, curtain-raisers
1 NC A **curtain-raiser** is a short play that is performed before a longer, more important one. *It should make a nice curtain-raiser.*
2 NC A **curtain-raiser** is also a relatively minor event that is like a major one that happens after it. *The Dieppe landing was a curtain-raiser to the invasion.*

curtsy /kɜːtsi/ **curtsies, curtsying, curtsied**; also spelt **curtsey**.
V When a woman **curtsies**, she lowers her body briefly, bending her knees and holding her skirt with both hands, as a way of showing respect. *The ladies curtsied to him.* ► Also NC *I bobbed him a curtsy.*

curvaceous /kɜːveɪʃəs/
ADJ You say that a woman's body is **curvaceous** when it has curves that make it pleasing to look at. *The next instant a long curvaceous body was leaning up against mine. ...a curvaceous blonde.*

curvature /kɜːvətʃə/
NU The **curvature** of something is its curved shape, especially when this shape is part of the circumference of a circle; a technical term. *...the curvature of the earth.*

curve /kɜːv/ **curves, curving, curved**
1 NC A **curve** is a smooth, gradually bending line, for example part of the edge of a circle. *The beach stretched away before them in a gentle curve.*
2 VA If something **curves**, it is shaped like a curve, or moves in a curve. *The lane curved round to the right... The missile curved gracefully towards its target.*

curved /kɜːvd/
ADJ A **curved** object has the shape of a curve. *...the curved tusks of a walrus.*

curvy /kɜːvi/
ADJ **Curvy** means the same as **curved**; an informal word. *...a settee with only one curvy end.*

cushion /kʊʃn/ **cushions, cushioning, cushioned**
1 NC A **cushion** is a fabric case filled with soft material, which you put on a seat to make it more comfortable. *He brought a cushion with him to sit on during the two hour show.*
2 VO To **cushion** an impact means to reduce its effect. *The pile of branches cushioned his fall... The bureaucracy was being cushioned from the worst effects of the cutting exercise.*

cushy /kʊʃi/ **cushier, cushiest**
ADJ A **cushy** job or task is very easy; an informal word. *...that nice cushy job in the bank.*

cuss /kʌs/ **cusses, cussing, cussed**
VorVO If someone **cusses**, they say rude or offensive words because they are angry; an informal, old-fashioned word. *They found her lying on her bed yelling and cussing.*

custard /kʌstəd/
NU **Custard** is a sweet yellow sauce made from milk and eggs or from milk and a powder. It is eaten with puddings. *Her mother passed round plates of jelly and custard. ...custard powder.*

custard pie, custard pies
NC A **custard pie** or a **custard tart** is a flat open pie filled with custard. Clowns and comedians sometimes throw custard pies at each other. *Students were pelting a double of the Australian actress Kylie Minogue with custard pies.*

custodial /kʌstəʊdiəl/
ADJ **Custodial** means relating to the custody of people in prison; a formal word. *...offences which called for custodial sentences.*

custodian /kʌstəʊdiən/ **custodians**
NC The **custodian** of a collection, art gallery, or museum is the person in charge of it. *...the custodian of the two holiest shrines of Islam.*

custody /kʌstədi/
1 NU **Custody** is the legal right to look after a child, especially the right given to the child's father or mother when they become divorced. *Divorce courts usually award custody to mothers.*
2 Someone who is in **custody** has been arrested and is being kept in prison until they can be tried. *...people who have been quite wrongly held in custody.*

custom /kʌstəm/ **customs**
1 NC A **custom** is a traditional activity or festivity. *My wife likes all the old English customs.*
2 N SING If something is the **custom**, it is usually done in particular circumstances. *It is the custom to take chocolates or fruit when visiting a patient in hospital... It is Howard's custom to take his class for coffee afterwards.*
3 NUorN PL **Customs** is the place where people arriving from a foreign country have to declare goods that they bring with them. **Customs** is also used to refer to the people who work there. *At Kennedy airport I went through the customs... Police and customs officers have seized cannabis with a street value of one and a*

half million pounds... *Customs are continuing their investigations to establish whether any offences have been committed.*
4 NU If a shop has your **custom**, you regularly buy things there; a formal use. *Many local services depend on the University's custom.*

customary /kʌstəməʳri/
ADJ **Customary** means usual; a formal word. *Peter had never seen her so shaken out of her customary calm... It was customary for our children to curtsy to the gentlemen.* ◆ **customarily** ADV *...the civil exchange of letters which customarily marks the departure of a minister.*

custom-built
ADJ Something that is **custom-built** is built according to someone's special requirements. *The Council provided them with custom-built homes.*

customer /kʌstəmə/ **customers**
NC A **customer** is someone who buys something. *She's one of our regular customers.*

customize /kʌstəmaɪz/ **customizes, customizing, customized**; also spelt **customise**.
VO If you **customize** something, especially a car, you adapt it to the individual customer's own needs or tastes, often by changing its appearance. *They were customizing some twelve vehicles a month. ...a Rolls Royce that he'd bought and then had customized... The plaque is designed to be easily customized for personal or promotional purposes.*

custom-made
ADJ Something that is **custom-made** is made according to people's special requirements. *...custom-made cars.*

Customs and Excise /kʌstəmz ənd eksaɪz/
N PROP **Customs and Excise** is a British government department which is responsible for collecting duty on imported goods and for collecting taxes on some goods produced in Britain. *The Customs and Excise must be notified. ...a retired Customs and Excise officer.*

cut /kʌt/ **cuts, cutting**. The form **cut** is used in the present tense and is also the past tense and past participle of the verb.
1 VO If you **cut** something, you push a knife or similar tool into it in order to remove a piece of it or to mark or damage it. *She cut the cake and gave me a piece... People were arrested for cutting the fence with hacksaws.* ► Also ADJ *...thinly cut rye bread.*
2 NC If you make a **cut** in something, you push a knife or similar tool into it in order to mark or damage it. *He made a deep cut in the wood.*
3 V-REFLorVO If you **cut** yourself, or **cut** part of your body, you accidentally injure yourself on a sharp object and you bleed. *I've quite often had accidents and cut myself... Robert cut his knee quite badly.*
4 NC A **cut** is also the injury caused when a sharp object makes you bleed. *I had some cuts and bruises but I'm OK.*
5 VA To **cut** through something means to move or pass through it easily. *The big canoe was cutting through the water.*
6 VA If you **cut** across or through a place, you go across or through it because it is the shortest route to another place. *I cut across country for the next hundred miles.*
7 VO To **cut** an amount means to reduce it. *Interest rates are to be cut from fifteen to fourteen percent... They are cutting the airline's staff by a third.*
8 NC A **cut** is also a reduction in an amount of money and resources. *The cuts in subsidies are to begin in November... National Health Service cuts have made facilities at the hospital inadequate.*
9 VO When a part of a piece of writing is **cut**, it is not printed or broadcast. *Her publishers insisted on cutting several stories out of her memoirs.* ► Also NC *He agreed to make a few minor changes and cuts in the play.*
10 VO If you **cut** someone's hair, you shorten it using scissors. *Tell him to get his hair cut.*
11 ADJ Well **cut** clothes have been well designed and well made. *He wears beautifully cut suits.*
12 NC A **cut** of meat is a large piece of it which has been cut so that it is ready to be sold and cooked. *Consumers are more aware than ever of the problem*

of fat in their diets and producers offer leaner cuts of meat.
13 If something is a **cut above** other things of the same kind, it is better than them. *The meals they serve are a cut above most pub food.*
14 See also **cutting**.

cut across PHRASAL VERB If an issue or problem **cuts across** the division between two groups of people, it affects the people in both groups. *These issues, however, tended to cut across party lines.*

cut back PHRASAL VERB If you **cut back** an amount of money or resources or **cut back** on it, you reduce it. *Congress cut back the funds... They have been forced to cut back on the number of pages they can publish.* ● See also **cutback**.

cut down PHRASAL VERB **1** If you **cut down** on an activity, you do it less often. *She had cut down on smoking.* **2** If you **cut** a tree **down**, you cut through its trunk so that it falls to the ground. *...a plan to cut down ancient trees on a road in South Carolina.*

cut in PHRASAL VERB If you **cut in** on someone, you interrupt them when they are speaking. *Mrs Travers began a reply, but Mrs Patel cut in again.*

cut off PHRASAL VERB **1** If you **cut** something **off**, you remove it by cutting it. *Lexington cut off a small piece of meat. ...egg sandwiches with the crusts cut off.* **2** To **cut off** a place or a person means to separate them from things they are normally connected with. *The town was cut off... We have cut ourselves off from the old ways of thinking.* ▶ Also ADJ PRED *She is completely cut off from friends.* **3** If a supply of something is **cut off**, it stops being provided. *Gas supplies had now been cut off... They are threatening to cut off funds.* **4** If you **cut** someone **off** when they are having a telephone conversation, you disconnect them. *They cut you off by mistake.* **5** See also **cut-off**.

cut out PHRASAL VERB **1** If you **cut out** part of something, you remove it using a tool with a sharp edge. *Badly decayed timber should be cut out and replaced.* **2** If you **cut out** something that you are doing or saying, you stop doing or saying it. *Cut out waste... He's cut out the drinking altogether.* **3** If an object **cuts out** the light, it prevents light from reaching a place. *Even if sunglasses cut out the bright light they may still allow ultraviolet radiation to pass through.* **4** When an engine **cuts out**, it suddenly stops working. *It keeps cutting out when I stop.* **5** If you are **cut out** for a particular type of work, you have the qualities needed to do it. *I'm not really cut out for this job.*

cut up PHRASAL VERB If you **cut** something **up**, you cut it into several pieces. *The plant can be cut up into individual buds.* ● See also **cut up**.

cut-and-dried
ADJ A **cut-and-dried** answer or solution is clear and obvious. *There is no cut-and-dried formula which can answer these questions.*

cutback /kʌtbæk/ **cutbacks**
NC A **cutback** is a reduction in an amount of money or resources. *The President has outlined a series of cutbacks in his new budget.*

cute /kjuːt/ **cuter, cutest**
ADJ Someone or something that is **cute** is pretty or attractive. *My parents thought I looked cute in the dress... Penguins are cute, although they smell.*

cut glass
N U or N+N **Cut glass** is glass with patterns cut into its surface. *Wash delicate china or cut glass by hand. ...a cut-glass bowl.*

cutlass /kʌtləs/ **cutlasses**
NC A **cutlass** is a curved sword with one sharp edge. Cutlasses used to be used by sailors. *The leader already had his cutlass in his hand.*

cutlery /kʌtləri/
NU The knives, forks, and spoons that you eat with are referred to as **cutlery**. *Sheffield is best known for the manufacture of stainless steel cutlery.*

cutlet /kʌtlət/ **cutlets**
NC A **cutlet** is a small piece of meat, or a mixture of vegetables and nuts pressed into a rounded shape. Cutlets are usually fried or grilled. *...veal cutlets. ...a nut cutlet.*

cut-off, cut-offs
1 N SING A **cut-off** or a **cut-off point** is the level or limit at which you decide that something should stop happening. *The cut-off to the savings limit is likely to be raised... We thought it was already past the cut-off point.*
2 NC You use **cut-off** to refer to the action of stopping a supply of money or resources. *...a cut-off in aid to the guerrillas.*

cut-out, cut-outs
1 NC A **cut-out** is an automatic device that turns off a motor, often because there is something wrong with it. *...a cut-out to prevent the battery from overcharging.*
2 NC A cardboard **cut-out** is a shape cut from card. *...cardboard cut-out policemen.*

cut-price
ADJ A **cut-price** item is for sale at a reduced price. *The Royal Navy says it is to stop selling cut-price cigarettes to sailors.*

cutter /kʌtə/ **cutters**
NC or N PL A **cutter** or a pair of **cutters** is a tool that you use for cutting something. *...a glass cutter. ...a pair of wire cutters.*

cut-throat
ADJ In a **cut-throat** situation, people all want the same thing and do not care if they harm each other in getting it. *...grain producers engaged in cut-throat competition to sell their surpluses.*

cutting /kʌtɪŋ/ **cuttings**
1 NC A **cutting** is a piece of writing cut from a newspaper or magazine. *...a collection of press cuttings.*
2 NC A **cutting** is also a piece of stalk that you cut from a plant and use to grow a new plant. *They are easy roses to grow from cuttings.*
3 ADJ A **cutting** remark is unkind and likely to hurt someone's feelings. *Does this sound cutting? It's not meant to be.*

cutting edge
1 N SING The **cutting edge** of something is the part of it which is most likely to change things or have a particular effect. *Mr Mokaba said the Youth League was the cutting edge of the revolution... The East German army was long considered to be the cutting edge of the Warsaw Pact.*
2 If you are **at the cutting edge** of something, you are involved in its most recent developments. *...the large cities at the cutting edge of the recent economic reforms.*

cuttlefish /kʌtlfɪʃ/ **cuttlefishes**. The plural form can be either **cuttlefishes** or **cuttlefish**.
1 NC A **cuttlefish** is an animal with a hard internal shell that lives close to the bottom of the sea near a coast. *The cod's staple diet includes Norway lobster, squid and cuttlefish.*
2 NC or NU A **cuttlefish** is also the shell of a cuttlefish. *...a cuttlefish stuck between the bars of the bird cage.*

cut up
ADJ PRED If you are **cut up** about something, you are very unhappy because of it; an informal expression. *She's still terribly cut up about his death.* ● See also **cut**.

CV /siːviː/ **CV's**
NC Your **CV** is a brief written account of your personal details, your education, and the jobs you have had. You are often asked to send your CV when you are applying for a job. CV is an abbreviation for 'curriculum vitae'.

cwt, cwts. The plural form can be either **cwts** or **cwt**. **cwt** is a written abbreviation for 'hundredweight'. *...75 cwt of wheat.*

cyanide /saɪənaɪd/
NU **Cyanide** is a substance which is highly poisonous. *He committed suicide by swallowing a cyanide capsule.*

cybernetics /saɪbənetɪks/
NU **Cybernetics** is a science in which control systems in electronic and mechanical devices are studied and compared to biological systems. *...the world of cybernetics. ...the Cybernetics Department.*

cyclamen /sɪkləmən/ **cyclamens**
NCorNU A **cyclamen** is a plant with white, pink, or red flowers.

cycle /saɪkl/ **cycles, cycling, cycled**
1 v If you **cycle**, you ride a bicycle. *I decided to cycle into town.* ◆ **cycling** NU *We recommend cycling as a good form of exercise.*
2 NC A **cycle** is a bicycle or a motorcycle. *...the Bremen six-day cycle race.*
3 NC+SUPP A **cycle** is also a series of events that is repeated again and again, always in the same order. *...the endless cycle of the seasons.*
4 NC In an electrical, electronic, or mechanical process, a **cycle** is a single complete series of movements. *...50 cycles per second.*
5 NC+SUPP A **cycle** of songs or poems is a series of them, intended to be performed or read one after the other. *...a cycle of seven Shakespeare plays.*

cyclic /saɪklɪk/
ADJ **Cyclic** means the same as **cyclical**. *...cyclic variations in the Sun's brightness.*

cyclical /sɪklɪkl, saɪklɪkl/
ADJ A **cyclical** process happens again and again in cycles. *...cyclical fluctuations in investment.*

cyclist /saɪklɪst/ **cyclists**
NC A **cyclist** is someone who rides a bicycle. *More than two thirds of injuries sustained by cyclists are head injuries.*

cyclone /saɪkləʊn/ **cyclones**
NC A **cyclone** is a violent storm in which air circulates rapidly in a clockwise direction. *Village after village had been destroyed by the cyclone.*

cygnet /sɪgnɪt/ **cygnets**
NC A **cygnet** is a young swan.

cylinder /sɪlɪndə/ **cylinders**
1 NC A **cylinder** is a shape or container with flat circular ends and long straight sides. *...two cylinders of the same diameter. ...the hot water cylinder.*
2 NC In an engine, a **cylinder** is a piece of machinery shaped like a cylinder, in which a piston moves backwards and forwards. *...a five cylinder engine.*

cylindrical /sɪlɪndrɪkl/
ADJ Something that is **cylindrical** has flat circular ends and long straight sides. *...two cylindrical tanks.*

cymbal /sɪmbl/ **cymbals**
NC A **cymbal** is a flat circular brass object used as a musical instrument. You hit it with a stick or hit two cymbals together. *They sang songs to the accompaniment of drums and cymbals.*

cynic /sɪnɪk/ **cynics**
NC A **cynic** is someone who always thinks the worst of people or things. *Cynics have described corruption as one of the country's growth industries.*

cynical /sɪnɪkl/
ADJ Someone who is **cynical** or who has a **cynical** attitude always thinks the worst of people or things. *You are taking a rather cynical view of marriage.* ◆ **cynically** /sɪnɪkli/ ADV *Grant smiled cynically.*

cynicism /sɪnɪsɪzəm/
NU **Cynicism** is an attitude in which you always think the worst of people or things. *The mood of political cynicism and despair deepened.*

cypher /saɪfə/. See **cipher**.

cypress /saɪprəs/ **cypresses**
NC A **cypress** is an evergreen tree. It has dark green leaves and rounded cones. The wood obtained from this tree is also called **cypress**. *The shadow of the cypress swayed across the lawn.*

Cyprus /saɪprəs/
Cyprus is an island in the eastern Mediterranean. It was a British colony until 1960, when it became a republic with Archbishop Makarios as its first president. After independence, conflict between the Greek Cypriot and Turkish Cypriot communities increased. In 1974 there was a military coup, instigated by the military junta of Greece, after which Turkey invaded the northern part of the island. Cyprus is now divided into two separate areas, the Republic of Cyprus which is controlled by Greek Cypriots, and the Turkish Republic of Northern Cyprus which declared itself independent in 1983 and is recognized only by Turkey. Georgios Vassiliou (Independent) became President of the Republic of Cyprus in 1988. Cyprus exports clothing, potatoes, and shoes. Tourism is an important industry. ◆ **Greek Cypriot, Turkish Cypriot** /griːk sɪpriət, tɜːkɪʃ sɪpriət/ N, ADJ
▪ *per capita GNP:* US$6,260 ▪ *religion:* Greek Orthodox, Islam ▪ *language:* Greek, Turkish ▪ *currency:* pound ▪ *capital:* Nicosia ▪ *population:* 686,000 (77% Greek, 18% Turkish) (1988) ▪ *size:* 9,251 square kilometres (including both areas).

cyst /sɪst/ **cysts**
NC A **cyst** is a growth containing liquid that appears inside your body or under your skin. *In the past, surgery was the only way to get rid of the cysts.*

cystitis /sɪstaɪtɪs/
NU **Cystitis** is an infection of your bladder. *Cystitis can be treated easily by antibiotics.*

czar /zɑː/. See **tsar**.

czarina /zɑːriːnə/. See **tsarina**.

czarist /zɑːrɪst/. See **tsarist**.

Czechoslovakia /tʃekəsləvɑːkiə/
The **Czech and Slovak Federative Republic** is a country in central Europe. It was a member of the former Warsaw Pact. Czechoslovakia was established in 1918. It was occupied by Germany from 1939 to 1945 and it became a Communist country in 1948. Alexander Dubček introduced a period of reform and liberalization in 1968 known as the Prague Spring, which was repressed the same year by Warsaw Pact troops. Throughout 1989 demonstrations against the government increased and at the end of the year the Communist Party renounced its monopoly of power. Václav Havel, of Civic Forum (a coalition of opposition groups), was elected President in 1989. Marián Calfa of the Civic Democratic Union—Public Against Violence (ODU-VPN) became Prime Minister in 1989. Czechoslovakia exports machinery and other manufactured goods, glass, and beer. ◆ **Czechoslovak** /tʃekəsləʊvæk/ N, ADJ
▪ *per capita GNP:* US$10,140 ▪ *religion:* Christianity (mainly Roman Catholic) ▪ *language:* Czech, Slovak ▪ *currency:* koruna ▪ *capital:* Prague ▪ *population:* 16 million (1989) ▪ *size:* 127,899 square kilometres.

D d

D, d /diː/ **D's, d's**
NC **D** is the fourth letter of the English alphabet.

-'d; pronounced /-d/ after a vowel sound, and /-əd/ after a consonant.
SUFFIX **-'d** is a short form of 'would' or 'had', especially when 'had' is an auxiliary verb. It is used in spoken English and informal written English *I knew there'd be trouble... I'd heard it many times.*

D.A. /diː eɪ/ **D.A.s**
NC A **D.A.** is the same as a **district attorney**. *If you want to understand the meaning of this law, go to the D.A.*

dab /dæb/ **dabs, dabbing, dabbed**
1 VOA If you **dab** a substance onto a surface, you put it there with quick, light strokes. If you **dab** a surface with something, you touch it quickly and lightly with that thing. *She dabbed some powder on her nose... He dabbed the cuts with disinfectant.*
2 NC A **dab** of something is a small amount of it. *She returned wearing a dab of rouge on each cheekbone.*
3 If you are a **dab hand** at something, you are good at doing it; an informal expression.

dabble /dæbl/ **dabbles, dabbling, dabbled**
V+*in* If you **dabble** in an activity, you take part in it but are not seriously involved. *They dabble in politics.*

dachshund /dækshʊnd/ **dachshunds**
NC A **dachshund** is a small dog that has very short legs, a long body, and long ears.

dad /dæd/ **dads**
NCorVOCATIVE Your **dad** is your father; an informal word. *My dad was raised in Manchester... Hey, Dad, what's for dinner?*

daddy /dædi/ **daddies**
NCorVOCATIVE Your **daddy** is your father; an informal word, used by children. *My daddy used to tell all kinds of wonderful stories... Daddy, why do we grow old?*

daddy-long-legs /dædilɒŋlegz/; **daddy-long-legs** is both the singular and the plural form.
NC A **daddy-long-legs** is a harmless flying insect with very long legs.

daffodil /dæfədɪl/ **daffodils**
NC A **daffodil** is a yellow bell-shaped flower that blooms in the spring. *...great splashes of colour from bank upon bank of daffodils.*

daft /dɑːft/ **dafter, daftest**
ADJ If you describe someone or something as **daft**, you mean that you think they are stupid or not sensible; an informal word. *Mr Kinnock has described the decision as daft and absurd.*

dagger /dægə/ **daggers**
NC A **dagger** is a weapon like a knife with two sharp edges. *They hacked them to death with daggers, bayonets and machetes.*

dahlia /deɪlɪə/ **dahlias**
NC A **dahlia** is a garden flower with a lot of brightly coloured petals.

Dahomey /dəhəʊmi/ See **Benin**.

daily /deɪli/
1 ADVorADJ ATTRIB Something that happens **daily** happens every day. *He wrote to her almost daily. ...Margaret's daily visits.*
2 ADJ ATTRIB **Daily** also means relating to a single day or to one day at a time. *Daily wage rates were around two dollars.*
3 ADJ ATTRIBorNC A **daily** newspaper or a **daily** is a newspaper that is published every day except Sunday. *Two of the four national daily papers are to become weeklies... An editorial that appeared in the Sydney-based national daily, The Australian... 'Thatcher's nice little earner', declares The Daily Mirror's headline.*

dainty /deɪnti/
ADJ A **dainty** movement, person, or object is small, neat, or pretty. *...walking with neat, dainty steps. ...a dainty little girl.* ◆ **daintily** ADV *She raised a plump arm, fingers daintily extended.*

Daio, Daniel Lima dos Santos
/dənjel liːmə dʊʃ sæntʊʃ daɪuː/
Major Daniel Lima dos Santos Daio became the Prime Minister of São Tomé and Príncipe in 1991. He was Minister of National Defence and Security from 1977 to 1982. He is a member of the Democratic Convergence Party - Reflexion Group (PDC-GR). Born: 1948.

dairy /deəri/ **dairies**
1 NC A **dairy** is a company that sells milk, butter, and cheese. *Pinhill Dairies also pack fruit juices and yoghurt.*
2 NC On a farm, a **dairy** is a building where milk is kept or cream, butter, and cheese are made. *On his 17 acre plot, he's got vegetables, fruit, sugar and a dairy.*
3 N+N **Dairy** products are foods made from milk, for example butter and cheese. *Meat and dairy products are in short supply.*
4 N+N **Dairy** also refers to the use of cattle to produce milk rather than meat. *...a dairy herd of 105 cattle.*

dairymaid /deərimeɪd/ **dairymaids**
NC A **dairymaid** was a girl or woman who milked cows and did other work on a farm.

dairyman /deərimən/ **dairymen** /deərimən/
NC A **dairyman** is a farm worker who looks after cows.

dais /deɪɪs/
N SING A **dais** is a raised platform in a hall that is designed to be used by people who are talking to an audience. *...the dais from which the Pope will lead Mass this weekend.*

daisy /deɪzi/ **daisies**
NC A **daisy** is a small wild flower with a yellow centre and white petals.

daisywheel /deɪziwiːl/ **daisywheels**
NC A **daisywheel** is a small flat disc with letters around its edge which is the part of an electric typewriter or word processor that prints the letters. It is also the name of printers or typewriters which have this kind of printing device.

Dakar /dækɑː/
Dakar is the capital of Senegal and its largest city. Population: 671,000 (1984).

dale /deɪl/ **dales**
1 NC A **dale** is a valley. In Northern England it is often used as part of an area's place-name. *...the Yorkshire Dales.*
2 If you say that you went **up hill and down dale**, you

mean that you went somewhere by a long, slow, or winding route; an informal expression.

dalliance /dæliəns/
1 NU You can use **dalliance** to refer to people's behaviour or their activities when they are wasting time in an idle and unnecessary manner; a literary use. *Their current dalliance is just a negotiating tactic.*
2 NU **Dalliance** is the behaviour shown by two people who are flirting with each other; an old-fashioned use.

dally /dæli/ **dallies, dallying, dallied**
1 V If you **dally**, you act or move very slowly, wasting time; an old-fashioned use. *The children dallied in the lane.*
2 V+with If you **dally** with an idea or plan, you think about it, but not in a serious way. *I'm dallying with the idea of giving up my job.*
3 V+with If someone **dallies** with you, they flirt with you; an old-fashioned use.

dam /dæm/ **dams, damming, dammed**
1 NC A **dam** is a wall built across a river to stop the flow of the water and make a lake. *The Aswan Dam holds back the Nile to form Lake Nasser.*
2 VO To **dam** a river means to build a dam across it. *The River Madford has been dammed in two places.*
dam up PHRASAL VERB To **dam up** a river means to dam it or block it completely. *Water board officials have dammed up a two-and-a-half mile stretch of river.*

damage /dæmidʒ/ **damages, damaging, damaged**
1 VO To **damage** something means to injure, harm, or weaken it in some way. *A fire had severely damaged part of the school... Unofficial strikes were damaging the British economy.* ♦ **damaging** ADJ *The incident was damaging to his career and reputation.*
2 NU **Damage** is injury or harm that is caused to something. *It can cause lethal damage to the liver... He could not repair the damage done to the party's credibility.* ● See also **collateral damage**.
3 N PL When a court of law awards **damages** to someone, it orders those who are responsible for harming them, or for harming their reputation or property, to pay them a set amount of money as compensation; a legal use. *He finally got £4,000 in damages.*

Damascus /dəmaːskəs/
Damascus is the capital of Syria and its largest city. Population: 1,292,000 (1987).

damask /dæməsk/
NU **Damask** is a type of heavy cloth with a pattern woven into it. *...the world's finest brocade and damask and lace.*

dame /deɪm/ **dames**
1 NC In informal American English, **dame** is a term that is used by some men to refer to women. *Remember, some of these dames are very powerful in movies.*
2 TITLE or NC In Britain, **Dame** is a title given to a woman as a special honour because of important service or work that she has done. *...Dame Flora Robson... Among the honours, P.D. James received a life peerage, and Barbara Cartland was made a dame.*

dammit /dæmɪt/. See **damn**.

damn /dæm/
Damn is a mild swear word which can be used to express anger, annoyance, or emphasis. *It's a damn nuisance!... By and large they do a damn good job.*

damnation /dæmneɪʃn/
NU According to some religions, if someone suffers **damnation**, they are condemned to stay in hell for ever after they have died because of their sins. *...eternal damnation.*

damned /dæmd/
1 N PL According to some religions, the **damned** are people condemned to stay in hell for ever after they have died. *The painting portrayed the damned burning in hell.*
2 ADJ PRED People who are **damned** have been condemned to stay in hell for ever after they have died. *The Devil will come and Faustus will be damned.*

damnedest /dæmdɪst/; an informal, old-fashioned word.
1 ADJ The **damnedest** means the most amazing and surprising in an agreeable way. *New York is full of the damnedest eccentrics.*
2 If you **do your damnedest**, you try as hard as you can to do something. *I'll have to do my damnedest to find out what really happened.*

damn-fool
ADJ ATTRIB **Damn-fool** is a mild swear word meaning very stupid. *Another one of his damn-fool ideas!*

damning /dæmɪŋ/
ADJ Something that is **damning** suggests strongly that someone is guilty of a crime or a serious error of some kind. *The investigation would produce damning evidence against the government... Historians provided a damning indictment of his character.*

damp /dæmp/ **damper, dampest; damps, damping, damped**
1 ADJ Something that is **damp** is slightly wet. *The building was cold and damp... She wiped the table with a damp cloth.* ♦ **dampness** NU *...the cold and dampness of winter.*
2 NU **Damp** refers to moisture that is found in the air or on the walls of a house. *Details such as whether the house is damp or mouldy will also be recorded.*
damp down PHRASAL VERB To **damp down** a difficult situation means to make it calmer or less intense. *Neighbouring countries had been of no help in damping down the crisis.*

damp course, damp courses
NC A building's **damp course** is a layer of waterproof material which is put into the brickwork near the bottom of a wall to prevent wetness from rising. *Virtually all the buildings have rising damp, and this is because of lack of knowledge about putting in a damp course.*

dampen /dæmpən/ **dampens, dampening, dampened**
1 VO To **dampen** something means to make it less lively or intense. *The prospect of an election in no way dampened his spirits... The flaps can be opened or closed so as to increase or dampen the sound... Serious attempts were made to dampen down the Gulf conflict.*
2 VO If you **dampen** something, you make it slightly wet. *Dampen some paper and paste it with glue.*

damper /dæmpə/ **dampers**
1 If someone or something **puts a damper on** something, they have an effect on it which stops it being as enjoyable or as successful as it should be; an informal expression. *Soviet forces have put a damper on suggestions of a compromise... Driving rain has put something of a damper on the picket line.*
2 NC A **damper** is a small sheet of metal in a fire, boiler, or furnace that can be moved to increase or reduce the amount of air that enters.
3 NC A **damper** is also a device in a piano or similar musical instrument which makes the sound less loud by restricting the movement of the strings.

damp-proof course, damp-proof courses
NC A **damp-proof course** is the same as a **damp course**.

damsel /dæmzl/ **damsels**
NC A **damsel** is a young, unmarried woman; an old-fashioned word.

damson /dæmzn/ **damsons**
NC A **damson** is a small, sour purple plum. The tree that it grows on is also called a **damson**.

dance /dɑːns/ **dances, dancing, danced**
1 V or VO When you **dance**, you move your body in time to music. *John danced with Julie. ...girls dancing the can-can.*
2 NC A **dance** is a series of steps and movements which you do to music. It is also a piece of music which people can dance to. *Madonna's show is full of acrobatic dance routines. ...dance music known as Bhangra.*
3 NC A **dance** is also a social event where people dance with each other. *Students took the Chinese girls to a university dance.*
4 NU **Dance** is the activity of performing dances as a public entertainment. *They are supreme artists of dance and theatre.*
5 V If someone **dances** around or from place to place,

they move about lightly and quickly, often because they are very happy. *Ralph danced out into the street.*

dance floor, dance floors
NC A **dance floor** is a part of the floor in a restaurant or club where guests can dance. *Lighting equipment fell onto the dance floor of a discotheque.*

dancer /dɑːnsə/ **dancers**
NC A **dancer** is a person who earns money by dancing, or a person who is dancing. *Tudor began as dancer and choreographer with the Ballet Rambert.*

dance studio, dance studios
NC A **dance studio** is a place where people pay to learn how to dance. *John owned a dance studio known as the Wardon School of Dancing.*

dancing /dɑːnsɪŋ/
NU **Dancing** is the performance of dances as a profession, an art, or an activity. *The music and dancing lasted for hours. ...a dancing teacher.*

dandelion /dændɪlaɪən/ **dandelions**
NC A **dandelion** is a wild plant that has yellow flowers with lots of thin petals. When the petals drop off, they leave fluffy balls of seeds.

dandruff /dændrʌf/
NU **Dandruff** refers to the small white pieces of dead skin in someone's hair. *There are various shampoos available for treating dandruff.*

dandy /dændi/ **dandies; dandier, dandiest**
1 NC A **dandy** is a man who thinks a great deal about his appearance and always dresses in smart clothes; an old-fashioned word, used showing disapproval. *...a yacht full of upper-class dandies drinking sherry.*
2 ADJ In informal American English, something that is **dandy** is very good. *The chocolate-coated cherries are dandy, Mrs Breslow.*

danger /deɪndʒə/ **dangers**
1 NU **Danger** is the possibility that someone may be harmed or killed. *The child is too young to understand danger... I was in no danger.*
2 NC A **danger** is something or someone that can hurt or harm you. *Cigarette smoking is a danger to health. ...the dangers of making assumptions.*
3 N SING+SUPP If there is a **danger** that something unpleasant will happen, it is possible that it will happen. *There was a danger that she might marry the wrong man... There is no danger of fire.*

danger money
NU **Danger money** is extra money that is paid to someone for doing dangerous work. *He deserves to get danger money for that job.*

dangerous /deɪndʒərəs/
ADJ If something is **dangerous**, it may hurt or harm you. *...a dangerous animal... It is dangerous to drive with a dirty windscreen.* ♦ **dangerously** ADV *She was dangerously close to the fire.*

dangle /dæŋgl/ **dangles, dangling, dangled**
V-ERG If something **dangles** or if you **dangle** it, it hangs or swings loosely. *Huge wooden earrings dangled from her ears... Charlie was leaning across my desk dangling the long roll of paper.*

dank /dæŋk/
ADJ A **dank** place, especially an underground place such as a cave or cellar, is damp, cold, and unpleasant. *I slept in the dank basement room.*

dapper /dæpə/
ADJ A **dapper** man is slim and neatly dressed. *Zhao Ziyang is a dapper figure, given to wearing Western suits.*

dappled /dæpld/
ADJ Something that is **dappled** has light and dark patches, or patches of light and shade; a literary word. *...dappled leafy sunlight.*

dare /deə/ **dares, daring, dared**
1 V+to-INF or SEMI-MODAL If you do not **dare** to do something, you lack the courage to do it. *She did not dare to look at him... He dared not show that he was pleased... I can't do that—I simply wouldn't dare.*
2 VO If you **dare** someone to do something, you challenge them to prove they are not frightened of doing it. *He looked round fiercely, daring them to contradict... She only started her writing career because her sister had dared her to.*
3 NC A **dare** is a challenge to do something dangerous

or frightening. *It was many years since James had accepted a dare.*
● **Dare** is used in these phrases. ● You say '**dare I say it**' when you know that what you are going to say will upset or disappoint someone. *I can see he's got, dare I say it, baggier eyes.* ● You say '**Don't you dare**' when you are angrily telling someone not to do something. *Don't you dare throw it away.* ● You say '**I dare say**' to show that you think something is probably true. The form **daresay** is also used in writing. *There would be, I dare say, a considerable variety in the scope of protection... I daresay you've spent all your money by now.*

daredevil /deədevl/ **daredevils**
NC A **daredevil** is someone who enjoys doing dangerous things. *...a daredevil motorcycle rider.*

daren't /deənt/
Daren't is the usual spoken form of 'dare not'. *You shot me yourself, and you daren't admit it.*

daresay /deəseɪ/
Daresay is a written form of 'dare say'. See **dare**.

Dar es Salaam /dɑːr es səlɑːm/
Dar es Salaam is the capital of Tanzania and its largest city. The new administrative capital is Dodoma. Population: 1,096,000 (1985).

daring /deərɪŋ/
1 ADJ Someone who is **daring** is prepared to do things which might be dangerous. *The rescue was a daring and complex operation.*
2 ADJ A **daring** person does or says things which might shock or anger other people because they challenge normal conventions. *He was the most daring of contemporary writers of fiction.*
3 NU **Daring** is the courage to take risks and do things which might be dangerous or shocking. *...the efficiency and daring shown by our armed forces.*

dark /dɑːk/ **darker, darkest**
1 ADJ When it is **dark**, there is not enough light to see clearly. *Luckily it was too dark for anyone to see me blushing... The room was dark and empty.* ♦ **darkness** NU *The lights went out and the hall was plunged into darkness.*
2 N SING The **dark** is the lack of light in a place. *He was sitting in the dark at the back of the theatre.*
3 ADJ Something that is **dark** has a lot of brown, blue, or black colours in it. *...long dark hair. ...dark red curtains.*
4 ADJ Someone who is **dark** has brown or black hair, brown eyes, and often brown skin. *He was a tall, dark, and undeniably handsome man... Other whites had taunted him because of his dark complexion.*
5 ADJ ATTRIB A **dark** period of time is unpleasant or frightening. *...the dark days of high unemployment... This is going to be a dark, bleak, winter in East Germany.*
6 ADJ ATTRIB **Dark** looks or remarks suggest that something horrible is going to happen. *...with lawyers becoming involved and dark hints of fraud.* ♦ **darkly** ADV *Another of the men hinted darkly that there would be violence.*
● **Dark** is used in these phrases. ● If you do something **before dark**, you do it before the sun sets. If you do something **after dark**, you do it when night has begun. *They had been travelling back before dark every night... You have to be very keen to go out after dark in sub-zero winter temperatures.* ● If you are **in the dark** about something, you do not know anything about it. *Many hostages are still in the dark about their future.*

dark age, dark ages
1 NC A **dark age** is a period in which there is a lack of culture and progress in a society and people are kept in ignorance. *The President warned of a new dark age in the Soviet Union.*
2 N PL The **Dark Ages** are the period of European history between about 500 A.D. and 1000 A.D. *Many weapons look like relics of the Dark Ages.*

darken /dɑːkən/ **darkens, darkening, darkened**
1 V-ERG If something such as the sky **darkens** or if something **darkens** it, it becomes darker in colour. *The sky darkened. ...the clouds that darken the sky... His hair was darkened by the rain.*

2 vo If someone's face **darkens**, they suddenly look angry. *Hugh's face darkened and became stormy and set.*

darkened /dɑːkənd/
ADJ A **darkened** building has no lights on inside it. *We sat in the darkened living room.*

dark glasses
N PL **Dark glasses** are glasses with dark lenses to protect your eyes in the sunshine. *He woke so dazzled by the sunshine that he had to put on dark glasses.*

dark horse, dark horses
NC If you say that someone is a **dark horse**, you mean that they lead a private life and do not tell others very much about themselves or what they are doing. *He is still something of a dark horse and an unknown quantity.*

darkish /dɑːkɪʃ/
ADJ **Darkish** means quite dark in colour. *Manfred was formally dressed as usual in a dark suit, white shirt, and darkish silk tie.*

darkroom /dɑːkruːm, dɑːkrʊm/ **darkrooms**
NC A **darkroom** is a room which has been sealed off from natural daylight and is lit only by red light. It is used for developing film.

darling /dɑːlɪŋ/ **darlings**
1 VOCATIVE You call someone **darling** if you love them or like them very much. *You're looking marvellous, darling.*
2 ADJ ATTRIB You can use **darling** to describe someone that you love or like very much. *...her darling baby brother.*
3 NC+POSS The **darling** of a group of people is someone who is especially liked by that group. *She quickly became the darling of the crowds.*

darn /dɑːn/ **darns, darning, darned**
1 VOorV When you **darn** something made of wool or cloth, you mend a hole in it by sewing stitches across the hole and then weaving stitches in and out of them. *I offered to darn Sean's socks... She started darning.*
2 NC A **darn** is the part of a piece of clothing that has been darned. *Her jumper had a darn at the bottom.*

dart /dɑːt/ **darts, darting, darted**
1 v If a person or animal **darts** somewhere, they move there suddenly and quickly. *...butterflies darting from one flower to another.*
2 VOA If you **dart** a glance at something, you look at it very quickly. *Kate darted a resentful glance at the new mistress.*
3 NC A **dart** is a small, narrow object with a sharp point which you can throw or shoot. *They killed the elephants with tiny poisoned darts.*
4 NU **Darts** is a game in which you throw darts at a round board with numbers on it. *They went to meet their friends for a pint of beer and a game of darts.*

dartboard /dɑːtbɔːd/ **dartboards**
NC A **dartboard** is a circular board with numbers on it which is used as the target in a game of darts.

dash /dæʃ/ **dashes, dashing, dashed**
1 VA If you **dash** somewhere, you go there quickly and suddenly. *People dashed out into the street to see what was happening.* ▶ Also N SING *He made a dash for the door.*
2 N SING+SUPP A **dash** of a liquid is a small quantity of it added to food or a drink. *Some soups are delicious served cold with a dash of cream.*
3 VOA If you **dash** something somewhere, you throw it or push it there violently. *She picked up his photograph and dashed it to the ground.*
4 vo If your hopes **are dashed**, something makes it impossible for you to get what you hope for. *Their hopes have been raised and dashed too many times.*
5 NC A **dash** is also a short horizontal line (—) used in writing.

dash off PHRASAL VERB **1** If you **dash off** somewhere, you make your way to that place very quickly. *They are dashing off to a committee meeting.* **2** If you **dash off** a letter or other piece of writing, you write it quickly without thinking much about it. *His essay seemed to have been dashed off in seconds.*

dashboard /dæʃbɔːd/ **dashboards**
NC The **dashboard** in a car is the panel facing the driver's seat where most of the instruments and switches are. *...a display fitted to the dashboard of their vehicle.*

dashing /dæʃɪŋ/
ADJ Someone who looks **dashing** is stylish and attractive. *She felt very dashing in her yellow suit.*

dastardly /dæstədli/
ADJ A **dastardly** action is wicked and planned to hurt someone; an old-fashioned word. *...a dastardly crime... He condemned the raid as a dastardly attack.*

data /deɪtə/
N U or N PL **Data** is information, usually in the form of facts or statistics that you can analyse. *The data was being processed at the Census Office... It isn't present in the data when they are received.*

data bank, data banks
NC A **data bank** is a collection of data that is stored in a computer. *Both machines hold information on some form of data bank.*

database /deɪtəbeɪs/ **databases**
1 NC A **database** is a collection of data that is stored in a computer in such a way that it can be retrieved quickly and efficiently. *...a list of users stored in the database.*
2 NC A **database** is also an item of software that enables you to retrieve data quickly and efficiently. *The new database provides a comprehensive range of search facilities.*

data processing
NU **Data processing** is the series of operations that are carried out on data, especially by computers, in order to present, interpret, or obtain information. *...the technology gap in such areas as data processing.*

date /deɪt/ **dates, dating, dated**
1 NC A **date** is a particular day, for example 7th June 1990, or year, for example 1066. *No date was announced for the talks.* ● To **date** means up until the present time. *Their effects to date have been limited.*
2 vo When you **date** something, you give the date when it began or was made. *How can we date these fossils?*
3 vo When you **date** a letter or a cheque, you write the day's date on it. *The letter was dated September 18 1952.*
4 N SING At a particular **date** means at a particular time or stage. *The matter may be worth pursuing at a later date.*
5 v If something **dates**, it goes out of fashion. *Her performance is in danger of becoming dated.*
6 NC A **date** is also an appointment to meet someone or go out with them, especially someone of the opposite sex. *Sorry I can't come—I have a date with Jill.*
7 NC Your **date** is someone of the opposite sex that you have a date with; used in American English. *Her date says that he doesn't know either.*
8 V-RECIP or V If you **are dating** someone of the opposite sex, you go out regularly with them; used in American English. *They didn't like the idea of me dating anybody... Even while they were dating, they felt and acted like a married couple... Do you think she should be dating?*
9 NC A **date** is also a small, sticky dark brown fruit. Dates grow on palm trees. *Dates have been planted in this area for 20 years.*
10 See also **out of date, up-to-date.**

date back PHRASAL VERB If something **dates back** to a particular time, it started or was made then. *The present city hall dates back to the 1880s... Much of this debt dated back many years.*

date from PHRASAL VERB If something **dates from** a particular time, it started or was made at that time. *...a manuscript dating from the eleventh century.*

dated /deɪtɪd/
ADJ **Dated** things seem old-fashioned, although they were once fashionable. *...dated clothes.*

date of birth, dates of birth
NC Your **date of birth** is the exact date on which you were born, including the year. *Give your name, age, and date of birth.*

dative /deɪtɪv/
ADJ In the grammar of some languages, for example Latin, the **dative** case is a case used for a noun when

it is the indirect object of the verb. It is also used with some prepositions. ► Also N SING *The next word is obviously a noun in the dative.*

daub /dɔːb/ **daubs, daubing, daubed**
V O A When you **daub** a substance on something, you carelessly spread it on that thing. *Police say that slogans were daubed on the wall in Arabic... Others carry cans of paint and brushes, daubing walls with the red and blue of the Haitian flag.*

daughter /dɔːtə/ **daughters**
N C Your **daughter** is your female child. *She is the daughter of a retired Army officer.*

daughter-in-law, daughters-in-law
N C Your **daughter-in-law** is the wife of your son. *Professor Lerner was accompanied by his son, daughter-in-law and their daughter.*

daunt /dɔːnt/ **daunts, daunting, daunted**
V O If something **daunts** you, it makes you feel afraid or worried about dealing with it. *They may be daunted by the size of the task.* ♦ **daunting** ADJ *It's a very daunting prospect to realise that the whole thing may have to be undergone again next year.*

dauntless /dɔːntləs/
ADJ Someone who is **dauntless** is brave and not easily frightened or discouraged; a literary word. *Alfred's mother was a dauntless woman.*

dawdle /dɔːdl/ **dawdles, dawdling, dawdled**
V If you **dawdle**, you spend more time than is necessary doing something or going somewhere. *Billy dawdled behind her, balancing on the cracks in the pavement.*

dawn /dɔːn/ **dawns, dawning, dawned**
1 N U or N C **Dawn** is the time of day when light first appears in the sky, before the sun rises. *Tom woke me at dawn.*
2 V When a day **dawns**, the sky grows light after the night. *The day dawned with people waiting to board the few ferries that were sailing.*
3 N SING+SUPP The **dawn** of a period of time or a situation is the beginning of it; a literary use. *This marked the dawn of a new era in human history.*
4 V If something **is dawning**, it is beginning to develop or appear; a literary use. *The age of the answering machine is just dawning. ...the dawning hopes of reconciliation in Western Europe.*

dawn on PHRASAL VERB If a fact or idea **dawns on** you or **dawns upon** you, you realize it. *Then it dawned on me that they were speaking Spanish... The awful truth dawned upon him.*

dawn chorus, dawn choruses
N C The **dawn chorus** is the singing of birds at dawn. *We walked through the woods to the sound of the dawn chorus.*

day /deɪ/ **days**
1 N C A **day** is one of the seven twenty-four hour periods of time in a week. *The attack occurred six days ago... Can you go any day of the week? What about Monday?*
2 N C or N U **Day** is the part of a day when it is light. *They had waited three days and nights for this opportunity... They hunt by day.*
3 N C+SUPP You can refer to a period in history as a particular **day**. *This is the main problem of the present day... Are students interested in religion these days?*
● **Day** is used in these phrases. ● If you **call it a day**, you stop what you are doing altogether or you leave it to be finished later. *He has decided to call it a day following a persistent knee injury.* ● If something happens **day and night** or **night and day**, it happens all the time without stopping. *They worked day and night.* ● If something **makes your day**, it makes you feel very happy; an informal expression. *Her smile somehow makes my day.* ● **One day, some day,** or **one of these days** means at some future time. *We're all going to be old one day... I'd like to go to China some day... You'll have an accident one of these days if you drive like that.* ● If it is a year **to the day** since something happened, it happened exactly a year ago. *It's a year to the day since she died... Four months to the day after he seized power, Burkina Faso's President has arrived in neighbouring Ivory Coast.*

daybreak /deɪbreɪk/
N U **Daybreak** is the time in the morning when light first appears. *They had to leave at daybreak.*

day care
N U **Day care** is care that is provided for small children during the day while their parents are at work. *Private nurseries provide day care for a quarter of the children under five. ...a day care centre. ...inadequate day-care facilities.*

daydream /deɪdriːm/ **daydreams, daydreaming, daydreamed**
1 N C A **daydream** is a series of pleasant thoughts, especially about things that you would like to happen. *He drifted off into another daydream.*
2 V When you **daydream**, you think about pleasant things that you would like to happen. *Boys and girls daydream about what they want to be.*

daylight /deɪlaɪt/
N U **Daylight** is the light during the day, or the time of day when it is light. *We've got at least two more hours of daylight... The ship sailed into harbour before daylight on 1 May.* ● **in broad daylight:** see **broad.**

daylight robbery
N U If you think that someone charges too much money for something, you can describe this action as **daylight robbery**; an informal expression.

daylights /deɪlaɪts/
1 If someone or something scares **the living daylights** out of you, they make you feel very scared indeed; an informal expression. *That scared the living daylights out of me. I hope I never see anything like that again... It terrified the living daylights out of the Russians.*
2 If you beat **the living daylights** out of someone or something, you hit them very hard and repeatedly; an informal expression. *Go on, lads. Beat the living daylights out of them... He threw me on the ground and just started pounding the living daylights out of me.*

daylight saving time
N U **Daylight saving time** is the same as **summer time**; used in American English.

day nursery, day nurseries
N C A **day nursery** is a place where children who are too young to go to school can be left all day while their parents are at work. *The union says most day nurseries will close.*

day off, days off
N C A **day off** is a day when you do not have to go to work even though it is usually a working day. *'Where's Cynthia?' — 'It's her day off.'*

day of reckoning
N SING The **day of reckoning** is a day or time in the future when people will be punished for what they have done wrong. *The day of reckoning had not yet come for him.*

day pupil, day pupils
N C A **day pupil** is a pupil who goes to a boarding school but lives at home.

day release
N U **Day release** is a system in which workers spend one day each week at a college, so that they can study a subject connected with their work. *I'd like to see a compulsory day release scheme brought in.*

day return, day returns
N C A **day return** is a train or bus ticket which allows you to go somewhere and come back on the same day for a lower price than an ordinary return ticket.

day school, day schools
N C A **day school** is a school where all the pupils go home in the evening and do not live at the school.

daytime /deɪtaɪm/
N U or N SING **Daytime** is the part of a day when it is light. *The forests were dark even in the daytime.*

day-to-day
ADJ ATTRIB **Day-to-day** means happening every day as part of ordinary life. *...the day-to-day life of the village.*

day trip, day trips
N C A **day trip** is a journey for pleasure to a place and back again on the same day. *...coaches returning from day trips to Boulogne.*

day-tripper, day-trippers
  NC A **day-tripper** is someone who makes a day trip. *Day-trippers and holidaymakers returning home will mean problems on the roads.*

daze /deɪz/ **dazed**
  1 If you are **in a daze**, you feel confused or upset. *The manager is still in a daze after his side's defeat of the cup winners.*
  2 V-PASS If you **are dazed** by a sudden injury or unexpected event, you are unable to think clearly. *She was dazed by the news.* ◆ **dazed** ADJ *He seemed dazed and bewildered.*

dazzle /dæzl/ **dazzles, dazzling, dazzled**
  1 VO If something **dazzles** you, you are extremely impressed by its quality or beauty. *She had clearly been dazzled by the evening's performance.* ◆ **dazzling** ADJ *She gave him a dazzling smile. ...his dazzling political career.*
  2 NU The **dazzle** of a light is its sudden brightness, so you cannot see properly. *They both blinked in the sudden dazzle.*
  3 VO If a bright light **dazzles** you, you cannot see properly. *They were interrupted by the cry 'Armed police!' and dazzled in the glare of powerful searchlights.* ◆ **dazzling** ADJ *...the dazzling sun.*

DC /diːsiː/
  DC is used to refer to an electric current that always flows in the same direction. **DC** is an abbreviation for 'direct current'. *It will run off 12 or 24 volts DC.*

DDT /diːdiːtiː/
  NU **DDT** is a poisonous substance used for killing insects. *Minute amounts of DDT paralyse the respiratory system of insects.*

de- /diː-/
  1 PREFIX **De-** is sometimes added to a verb, changing the meaning of the verb to its opposite. *The next step was to denationalize the steel industry.*
  2 PREFIX **De-** is sometimes added to a noun, making it a verb and giving it the meaning of removing the thing described by the noun. *Whole areas were deforested... You'll have to de-ice the windscreen.*

deacon /diːkən/ **deacons**
  1 NC A **deacon** is a member of the clergy, for example in the Church of England, who is lower in rank than a priest. *A Russian Orthodox deacon was sentenced to 12 years for anti-Soviet agitation... The Reverend Kathleen Young and the Reverend Eileen Templeton were among five deacons ordained by the Bishop of Connor during a service at St Ann's Cathedral in Belfast.*
  2 NC A **deacon** is also a man or woman who is not ordained but who assists the minister in some Protestant churches. *He's a deacon of the Methodist Church.*

deactivate /diːæktɪveɪt/ **deactivates, deactivating, deactivated**
  VO If you **deactivate** a bomb or other explosive device, you make it harmless by removing the active part of it. *The naval force have found and deactivated another mine.*

dead /ded/
  1 ADJ A **dead** person, animal, or plant is no longer living. *He was shot dead in a gunfight... Mary threw away the dead flowers.*
  2 N PL The **dead** are people who are dead, especially people who have been killed. *Among the dead was Captain Burroughs.*
  3 ADJ PRED If your arm or leg goes **dead**, you lose the sense of feeling in it for a short time.
  4 ADJ PRED If a telephone or other device is **dead**, it is not functioning. *The phone went dead.*
  5 ADJ ATTRIB **Dead** can mean complete or absolute, especially with the words 'silence', 'centre', and 'stop'. *There was dead silence... The table was placed in the dead centre of the room.* ▶ Also ADV or SUBMOD *I was staring dead ahead.*
  6 SUBMOD **Dead** also means very or very much; used in informal speech. *It's dead easy... They were dead against the idea.*
  ● **Dead** is used in these phrases. ● The **dead of night** is the middle part of it, when it is dark and quiet. *They came at dead of night.* ● If something **stops**

dead, it stops suddenly.

deadbeat /dedbiːt/ **deadbeats**
  NC A **deadbeat** is a person who is lazy or who does not want to be part of ordinary society; an informal word. *The usually sober New York Times denounces them as sideline soldiers or deadbeats... He says each month, an estimated 10,000 people lose their credit in California alone. About 3 per cent of them are deadbeats.*

dead beat
  ADJ If you are **dead beat**, you are very tired and have no energy left; an informal expression. *I knew I'd be dead beat in the morning.*

dead duck, dead ducks
  NC Something that is a **dead duck** has absolutely no chance of succeeding or surviving; an informal expression. *That plan's a dead duck.*

deaden /dedn/ **deadens, deadening, deadened**
  VO If something **deadens** a feeling or sound, it makes it less strong or loud. *Drugs deaden the pangs of hunger... The three main engines ignited in the last ten seconds of countdown, behind a spray of water to deaden their roar.*

dead end, dead ends
  1 NC If a street is a **dead end**, there is no way out at one end of it.
  2 NC A job or course of action that is a **dead end** does not progress anywhere. *The investigation has reached a dead end. ...a dead-end job.*

deadening /dedəⁿnɪŋ/
  ADJ Something that is **deadening** destroys people's enthusiasm and creativity. *In electing him, the delegates have chosen a man who can be expected to sweep away much of the deadening bureaucracy that is the legacy of the organisation's long years in exile. ...degrading, deadening tasks.*

dead heat, dead heats
  NC If a race ends in a **dead heat**, two or more competitors reach the finishing line first at exactly the same time. *The French St Leger ended in a dead heat between two English horses.*

deadline /dedlaɪn/ **deadlines**
  NC A **deadline** is a time or date before which a particular task must be finished. *We must meet the deadline.*

deadlock /dedlɒk/
  NU **Deadlock** is a state of affairs in an argument or dispute in which neither side is willing to give in, and so no agreement can be reached. *The meeting between management and unions ended in deadlock.*

deadlocked /dedlɒkt/
  ADJ If a situation is **deadlocked**, no agreement can be reached because neither side will give in at all. *The East-West meeting has been deadlocked for eight months.*

deadly /dedli/ **deadlier, deadliest**
  1 ADJ If something is **deadly**, it is likely or able to kill. *This is one of nature's deadliest poisons. ...deadly spiders.*
  2 SUBMOD You use **deadly** to emphasize an unpleasant or serious quality. *The air was deadly cold... He was deadly serious.*
  3 ADJ You can also use **deadly** to say that something is extremely effective, especially in the context of hurting someone. *...the deadliest insult he could think of. ...deadly accuracy.*

deadpan /dedpæn/
  ADV If you do something **deadpan**, you appear to be serious and are hiding the fact that you are joking or teasing. *She looked at me deadpan.* ▶ Also ADJ *He speaks in a deadpan way.*

dead weight, dead weights
  1 NC A **dead weight** is a load which is heavy and difficult to lift. *...the nine thousand three hundred ton dead weight vessel.*
  2 NC You can also refer to something which makes change or progress difficult as a **dead weight**. *His death may liberate the nation from the dead weight of its militaristic past.*

dead wood
  NU **Dead wood** refers to people or things that have been used for a very long time and are no longer

useful. *Low profits gave the company an excuse to clean out the dead wood.*

deaf /dɛf/ **deafer, deafest**
1 ADJ Someone who is **deaf** is unable to hear anything or unable to hear very well. *...a school for deaf children... He was very deaf.* ◆ **deafness** NU *They finally diagnosed her deafness when she was thirteen.*
2 N PL The **deaf** are people who are deaf. *Help for the deaf has lagged behind other medical services.*
3 ADJ PRED+to If you are **deaf** to something, you refuse to pay attention to it. *He was deaf to the public's complaints.*
4 If you **turn a deaf ear** to something that someone says, you refuse to pay attention to it. *President Ceauşescu has turned a deaf ear to Mr Gorbachov's criticisms.*

deaf-aid, deaf-aids
NC A **deaf-aid** is a hearing aid.

deafen /dɛfn/ **deafens, deafening, deafened**
VO If you **are deafened** by a noise, it is so loud that you cannot hear anything else. *She was momentarily deafened by the din.* ◆ **deafening** ADJ *The noise was deafening.*

deaf-mute, deaf-mutes
NC A **deaf-mute** is a person who is unable to hear or speak.

deal /diːl/ **deals, dealing, dealt**
1 A good **deal** or a great **deal** of something is a lot of it. *There was a great deal of concern about energy shortages... They talked a great deal... The teaching of the older children is a good deal better.*
2 NC A **deal** is an agreement or arrangement, especially in business. *He certainly hadn't done badly on the deal.*
3 NC If someone has had a bad **deal**, they have been unfortunate or have been treated unfairly. *He has had a lousy deal out of life.* ● **a raw deal**: see **raw**.
4 VOOorVO+to If you **deal** someone a blow, you hit them or harm them in some way. *This woman dealt him an alarming series of blows... The growth of modern industry had dealt a heavy blow to their way of life.*
5 VOorV When you **deal** cards, you give them out to the players in a game of cards. *Deal seven cards to each player... Whose turn is it to deal?*
deal in PHRASAL VERB To **deal in** a type of goods means to sell that type of goods. *The shop deals only in trousers.*
deal out PHRASAL VERB When you **deal out** cards, you give them out to the players in a game of cards. *He drank the last of his whisky, then swiftly dealt out the next hand.*
deal with PHRASAL VERB 1 When you **deal with** a situation or problem, you do what is necessary to achieve the result you want. *They learned to deal with any sort of emergency.* 2 If a book, speech, or film **deals with** a subject, it is concerned with it. *The film deals with a strange encounter between two soldiers.*

dealer /diːlə/ **dealers**
NC A **dealer** is a person whose business involves buying and selling things. *...a dealer in antique furniture.*

dealing /diːlɪŋ/ **dealings**
1 N PL Your **dealings** with a person or organization are the relations that you have with them or your business with them. *Ford insists that Carter's dealings with him have been totally correct... He was questioned about his past business dealings.*
2 NU+SUPP **Dealing** refers to the buying and selling of things as a business. For example, antique **dealing** involves buying and selling antiques. *The violence is directly connected with drug dealing. ...suspicious share dealing.*

dealt /dɛlt/
Dealt is the past tense and past participle of **deal**.

Dean /diːn/ **Deans**
1 N PROP A **Dean** in a university or college is an important administrator there. *...Dean of Trinity College, Cambridge.*
2 N PROP A **Dean** in a large church is a priest who is its main administrator. *...the Dean of Hereford, the*

Very Reverend Peter Haynes.

deanery /diːnəri/ **deaneries**
1 N+N **Deanery** means connected with the responsibilities of a dean. *...diocesan and deanery affairs.*
2 NC A **deanery** is the place where a dean lives.

dear /dɪə/ **dears; dearer, dearest**
1 VOCATIVE You can call someone **dear** as a sign of affection. *How are you, dear?... Now, my dears, come with me.*
2 ADJ ATTRIB **Dear** is written at the beginning of a letter, followed by the name or title of the person you are writing to. *Dear Mum, I was glad to get your letter... Dear Sir, I regret to inform you that I cannot accept your kind invitation.*
3 ADJ ATTRIB You use **dear** to describe someone or something that you feel affection for. *...dear old Aunt Elizabeth. ...a dear friend.*
4 ADJ PRED+to If something is **dear** to you, you care deeply about it. *Sussex was very dear to him. ...a cause that is very dear to her heart.*
5 You say **'Oh dear'** when you are sad or upset about something. *Oh dear, I'm late.*
6 ADJ PRED Something that is **dear** costs a lot of money. *Firewood is getting dearer.*

dearest /dɪərɪst/
1 VOCATIVE You can call someone **dearest** when you are very fond of them; an old-fashioned use. *It's too late now, my dearest.*
2 ADJ You can use **dearest** to describe something that is very important to you. *His dearest wish was to become a civil servant. ...my cherished dreams and dearest hopes.*

dearly /dɪəli/; a formal word.
1 ADV If you love someone **dearly**, you love them very much. *He was an affectionate father, who loved his children dearly.*
2 ADV If you would **dearly** like to do or have something, you would very much like to do it or have it. *I dearly wish I had more money.*
3 If you **pay dearly** for doing something, you suffer a lot as a result. *He paid dearly for his mistake.*

dearth /dɜːθ/
N SING If there is a **dearth** of something, there is not enough of it; a literary word. *There is a dearth of good children's plays.*

death /dɛθ/ **deaths**
NUorNC **Death** is the end of the life of a person or animal. *...after the death of her parents... He bled to death... The two deaths could have been prevented.* ● **Death** is used in these phrases. ● If something frightens or worries you **to death**, it frightens or worries you very much; used in informal English. *He was frightened to death of her.* ● If you are **sick to death** of a situation, you feel very angry about it and want it to stop; an informal expression. *We all get sick to death of having to come onto the radio, week after week, to say that one of these ghastly documents is the most dreadful nonsense.* ● If someone **is put to death**, they are executed. *Both men and women are thought to have been put to death.*

deathbed /dɛθbɛd/
N SING If someone is on their **deathbed**, they are in bed and are about to die. *On his deathbed he asked her forgiveness.*

deathblow /dɛθbləʊ/
N SING A **deathblow** is an event or action which puts an end to something, for example to a plan, an experiment, or someone's hopes. *The resignation of the two top people dealt a deathblow to the project.*

death certificate, death certificates
NC A **death certificate** is an official certificate signed by a doctor which states the cause of a person's death. *His hanging was witnessed by a doctor, who signed a death certificate.*

death duty, death duties
N PLorNU **Death duties** are a tax which has to be paid when someone inherits property from a person who has died. *Death duties had severely diminished the estate. ...a public debate on whether to abolish death duty.*

death knell

N SING When you say that the **death knell** of a particular thing is tolling or being sounded, you mean that it will end soon. *A diplomatic crisis would sound the death knell of any hopes of disarmament. ...the death knell of their way of life.*

deathly /dεθli/

ADJ ATTRIB **Deathly** is used to describe something that is as cold, pale, or quiet as a dead person. *A deathly hush lay in the streets.* ▸ Also SUBMOD *Her feet were deathly cold.*

death mask, death masks

NC Someone's **death mask** is a model of their facial features, which is made from a mould that has been taken of their face after they have died. *...the Pharaoh's golden death mask.*

death penalty

N SING The **death penalty** is the punishment of death, used in some countries for people who have committed very serious crimes. *Those convicted of treason face the death penalty.*

death row /dεθ rəʊ/

NU **Death row** is the part of a prison which contains the cells for criminals who have been sentenced to death. *The Sharpeville Six had been on death row for nearly three years.*

death sentence, death sentences

NC A **death sentence** is a punishment of death given by a judge to someone who has been found guilty of a serious crime such as murder. *He commuted two of the death sentences to life imprisonment.*

death squad, death squads

NC **Death squads** are groups of people who operate as vigilantes and carry out the execution of their political opponents without the approval of any official political organization. *The killings are the work of paramilitary death squads... Dozens of left wing activists have been murdered by death squads.*

death throes

1 N PL **Death throes** are violent, uncontrolled movements which people sometimes make while they are dying, especially if they are suffering great pain. *His death throes were watched by his family.*
2 N PL The **death throes** of something are its final stages, just before it fails or ends completely. *The project was in its death throes.*

death toll, death tolls

NC The **death toll** of an accident, disaster, or war is the number of people who die in it. *The death toll stood at 111 with nearly 200 more people still trapped.*

death trap, death traps

NC A place or vehicle that is a **death trap** is in such bad condition that it might cause someone's death. *These timber houses are an absolute death trap if they catch fire.*

death warrant, death warrants

1 NC A **death warrant** is an official document which orders that someone is to be executed as a punishment for a crime. *The sudden issue of death warrants has come as a terrible shock.*
2 If someone is **signing** their own **death warrant**, they are behaving in a way which might cause their ruin or death. *Using energy in this extravagant way is tantamount to signing our own death warrant.*

death-watch beetle, death-watch beetles

NC A **death-watch beetle** is a type of beetle that digs into wood, for example in old houses, and makes a tapping noise.

death wish

N SING A **death wish** is a conscious or unconscious desire to die or be killed. *I don't have a death wish but I'll die for what I believe in.*

debacle /deɪbɑːkl/ **debacles**; also spelt **débâcle**.

NC A **debacle** is an event or attempt that is a complete failure. *...the debacle of the TV series.*

debar /dɪbɑː/ **debars, debarring, debarred**

VO If you **are debarred** from doing something, you are prevented from doing it by a law or rule; a formal word. *He was debarred from attending the meetings.*

debase /dɪbeɪs/ **debases, debasing, debased**

VO If something **is debased**, its original value or quality is reduced or tainted; a formal word. *The*

quality of life can only be debased by such a system.

debatable /dɪbeɪtəbl/

ADJ Something that is **debatable** is not definitely true or not certain. *'They won't notice it's gone.'—'Well. That's debatable.'*

debate /dɪbeɪt/ **debates, debating, debated**

1 NCorNU A **debate** is a discussion in which people express different opinions about a subject. *...a debate on education... There was a great deal of debate about the National Health Service.*
2 VOorV-REPORT When people **debate** something, they discuss it fairly formally, putting forward different views. *These issues have been widely debated... The party will debate whether to set up a formal leadership team.*
3 V-REPORTorV+ING If you **debate** what to do, you think about possible courses of action before deciding what to do. *He turned round, debating whether to go back... He debated heating up the stew.*
4 If something is **open to debate**, it has not been proved to be true or has not been firmly decided upon. *Foreign policy could not be open to debate.*

debater /dɪbeɪtə/ **debaters**

NC A **debater** is someone who takes part in a debate. *He's a brilliant debater but has no strong principles.*

debauched /dɪbɔːtʃt/

ADJ Someone who is **debauched** behaves in a way that is socially unacceptable, for example because they drink a lot of alcohol or are sexually promiscuous; an old-fashioned word. *Americans find it difficult to accept the sort of debauched aristocratic society that Congreve draws.*

debauchery /dɪbɔːtʃəri/

NU **Debauchery** is excessive drunkenness or sexual activity; a formal word. *His reputation for debauchery and violence has been challenged.*

debilitated /dɪbɪləteɪtɪd/

ADJ A person, country, or organization that is **debilitated** has been made weak, a formal word. *...the shabby and debilitated economy.*

debilitating /dɪbɪleɪtɪŋ/

ADJ A **debilitating** illness, situation, or action makes you weak; a formal word. *...the debilitating effects of the fast. ...economically debilitating subsidies.*

debility /dɪbɪləti/

NU **Debility** is physical or mental weakness, especially weakness caused by illness; a formal word. *...the debility produced by old age.*

debit /debɪt/ **debits, debiting, debited**

1 VO When your bank **debits** your account, money is taken from it and paid to someone else. *...cards that debit your account direct from the shop.*
2 NC A **debit** is a record of the money taken from your bank account, for example when you write a cheque. *...a statement showing all the credits and debits.*

debonair /debənεə/

ADJ A man who is **debonair** is well-dressed, charming, and confident. *Jeremy Paxman is known for his debonair good looks and a flair for fancy ties.*

debrief /diːbriːf/ **debriefs, debriefing, debriefed**

VO If someone such as a soldier, diplomat, or astronaut **is debriefed**, they are asked to give a report on a mission or task that they have just completed. *When he returns to Mexico City he'll be debriefed by an officer from the Miami station.* ◆ **debriefing** NU *Prior arrangements are made for immediate debriefing at a safe site.*

debris /deɪbri/

NU **Debris** consists of pieces of things that have been destroyed, or rubbish that is lying around. *She began clearing up the debris.*

debt /det/ **debts**

1 NC A **debt** is a sum of money that you owe someone. *You must spend less until your debts are paid off.*
2 NU **Debt** is the state of owing money. *He began getting deeper and deeper into debt.*
3 If you are in someone's **debt**, you are grateful to them for something, and you feel that you ought to do something for them in return; a formal expression. *We are in your debt, Dr Marlowe.*

debtor /dɛtə/ **debtors**
NC A **debtor** is a person, institution, or country that owes money. *For some time now, both creditors and debtors have been searching for new solutions... Commercial banks should reduce the debt owed by debtor countries by thirty per cent.*

debug /diːbʌg/ **debugs, debugging, debugged**
VO When you **debug** a computer program, you look for the faults in it and correct them so that it will run properly. *Alan spent hours debugging the program.*

debunk /diːbʌŋk/ **debunks, debunking, debunked**
VO If you **debunk** an idea or belief, you show that it is false or not important. *Anthropologist Stephen Nugent went on a journey to find the 'invisible' city-dwellers of the Amazon, to debunk the myths and portray the region's intricate realities.*

debut /deɪbjuː/ **debuts**
NC The **debut** of a singer, musician, footballer, or other performer is his or her first public performance or recording. *She made her debut in this theatre.*

debutante /dɛbjuːtɑːnt/ **debutantes**
NC In Britain, a **debutante** is a young woman from the upper classes who has started going to social events with other young people; an old-fashioned word. *...rich playboys and debutantes.*

Déby, Idriss /ɪdriːs dəbiː/
Colonel Idriss Déby became President of Chad in a coup in 1990. He was Commander-in-Chief of the Armed Forces from 1982 to 1985, under the previous president, Hissène Habré, but was exiled after an attempted coup in 1989. He founded the Patriotic Salvation Movement (MPS) in 1990.

Dec.
Dec. is a written abbreviation for 'December'. *...Thursday Dec. 27.*

decade /dɛkeɪd, dɪkeɪd/ **decades**
NC A **decade** is a period of ten years, especially one that begins with a year ending in 0, for example 1980 to 1989. *By the end of the decade he had acquired international fame.*

decadence /dɛkədəns/
NU **Decadence** is the state of living or behaving in a way that shows lower standards, especially lower moral standards, than in a previous time. *...the indubitable decadence of the professional Fine Art tradition... The Eastern bloc tend to view AIDS as a problem of Western decadence.*

decadent /dɛkədənt/
ADJ If someone or something is **decadent**, they show low standards, especially low moral standards. *He spent 18 months in a Soviet labor camp during the Brezhnev regime, after his poems were denounced as decadent. ...decadent values.*

decaffeinated /diːkæfɪneɪtɪd/
ADJ **Decaffeinated** coffee has had most of the caffeine removed. *...a study into the relative effects of decaffeinated and ordinary coffee.*

decamp /dɪkæmp/ **decamps, decamping, decamped**
V If you **decamp**, you go away from somewhere secretly or suddenly. *I came home to find Nell and Caro had decamped to Wytham without warning.*

decant /dɪkænt/ **decants, decanting, decanted**
VO If you **decant** wine, you pour it slowly from its bottle into another container before serving it. *'Come again?' she inquired, as she decanted some vintage port.*

decanter /dɪkæntə/ **decanters**
NC A **decanter** is a glass container that you use for serving wine, sherry, and so on. *...a free case of champagne and a crystal decanter.*

decapitate /dɪkæpɪteɪt/ **decapitates, decapitating, decapitated**
VO To **decapitate** someone means to cut off their head; a formal word. *The four bodies, two of which had been decapitated, appeared in two locations in the city this morning... Elsewhere, a motorcyclist was decapitated during a freak storm when a gust of wind blew him into a tree.* ◆ **decapitated** ADJ *His tortured and decapitated body was found in a mailbag.* ◆ **decapitation** /dɪkæpɪteɪʃn/ NU *...an independent investigation into the decapitation of one of the General's outspoken critics.*

decathlon /dɪkæθlɒn/ **decathlons**
NC A **decathlon** is a competition in which athletes compete in ten different sporting events. *Daley Thompson will not be defending his decathlon title at the European Championships.*

decay /dɪkeɪ/ **decays, decaying, decayed**
1 V When something **decays**, it rots and starts to fall apart. *The body had already started to decay.* ◆ **decayed** ADJ *...a decayed tooth.* ◆ **decaying** ADJ *...a smell of decaying meat.*
2 NU **Decay** is the process of something rotting. *Dental decay in children has almost reached epidemic levels.*
3 V If buildings **decay**, their condition becomes worse because they have not been looked after and repaired. *The old palace decayed badly during Cromwell's time.* ▶ Also NU *...saving houses from falling into decay.* ◆ **decaying** ADJ *...decaying urban centres.*
4 V If a society, culture, or system **decays**, it gradually becomes weaker or more corrupt. *The Communist Party was decaying long before the coup that killed it.* ▶ Also NU *...a religion in the final stages of decay.* ◆ **decaying** ADJ *...a corrupt and decaying political system.*

decease /dɪsiːs/
N SING+POSS Someone's **decease** is their death; a legal term. *Upon your decease the capital will pass to your grandchildren.*

deceased /dɪsiːst/; a formal word.
1 N SING A person who has recently died can be referred to as the **deceased**. *...the property of the deceased.*
2 ADJ A **deceased** person is one who has recently died. *...the relatives of the deceased couple.*

deceit /dɪsiːt/ **deceits**
NU **Deceit** is lying, or behaviour that is intended to make people believe something which is not true. *They want the truth. They don't want the deceit and lies of the past. ...marriages in which deceit was commonplace.*

deceitful /dɪsiːtfl/
ADJ Someone who is **deceitful** tries to make people believe things that are not true. *The Conservative Party said it proved the government had been deceitful... The judge described the police reply as evasive and deceitful.*

deceive /dɪsiːv/ **deceives, deceiving, deceived**
1 VO To **deceive** someone means to cause them to believe something that is not true. *He tried to deceive me... His unkempt appearance deceived the staff into believing that he was a student.*
2 V-REFL If you **deceive** yourself, you do not admit to yourself something that you know is true. *They try to deceive themselves that everything is all right.*

decelerate /diːseləreɪt/ **decelerates, decelerating, decelerated**
V When a vehicle or machine **decelerates** or when someone in a vehicle **decelerates**, they begin gradually to go more slowly. *He decelerated as he came to the corner.* ◆ **deceleration** /diːseləreɪʃn/ NU *The jets begin their gentle but steady deceleration.*

December /dɪsembə/
NU **December** is the twelfth and last month of the year in the Western calendar. *...Friday 2nd December 1988.*

decency /diːsnsi/
1 NU **Decency** is behaviour which follows accepted moral standards. *They tried to restore some sense and decency to the Administration.*
2 NU **Decency** is also kind and considerate behaviour. *Why hadn't they had the decency to ask him if he'd like to join in?*

decent /diːsnt/
1 ADJ **Decent** means acceptable in standard or quality. *...decent wages. ...a decent night's rest.* ◆ **decently** ADV *The farm animals are decently treated.*
2 ADJ ATTRIB **Decent** also means morally correct or acceptable. *He would marry her as soon as a decent amount of time had elapsed.* ◆ **decently** ADV *They only want the chance to live their lives decently.*
3 ADJ ATTRIB **Decent** people are honest and respectable and behave morally. *...decent, hard-working citizens.*

decentralize /diːsentrəlaɪz/ **decentralizes, decentralizing, decentralized;** also spelt **decentralise.**
VO To **decentralize** a large organization means to move some of its departments away from the main administrative area, or to give more power to local departments. *He accused the Minister of seeking to decentralise the Commission.* ◆ **decentralized** ADJ *...a decentralized health service.* ◆ **decentralization** /diːsentrəlaɪzeɪʃn/ NU *...the decentralization of government.*

deception /dɪsepʃn/ **deceptions**
1 NC A **deception** is something that you say or do in order to deceive someone. *He would quickly have seen through Mary's deceptions.*
2 NU **Deception** is the act of deceiving someone. *...his part in the deception of the British public.*

deceptive /dɪseptɪv/
ADJ If something is **deceptive**, it might cause you to believe something which is not true. *Its fragile appearance was deceptive.* ◆ **deceptively** SUBMOD or ADV *It all looks deceptively simple... It was deceptively presented as a scientific study.*

deci- /desɪ-/
PREFIX **Deci-** is added to the beginning of nouns referring to measurements in order to form nouns meaning one-tenth as large. For example, a decilitre is one-tenth of a litre.

decibel /desɪbel/ **decibels**
NC A **decibel** is a unit of measurement that is used to record how loud something is. *He lowered his voice a few decibels.*

decide /dɪsaɪd/ **decides, deciding, decided**
1 V+to-INF, V A, or V-REPORT If you **decide** to do something, you choose to do it. *What made you decide to get married?... I'm glad you decided against a career as a waiter... She decided that she would leave... He has a month to decide whether he's going to stay.*
2 VO When something is **decided**, people choose what should be done. *The case is to be decided by the International Court.*
3 VO If an event or fact **decides** something, it makes a particular result definite or unavoidable. *It was this that decided the fate of the company.* ◆ **deciding** ADJ ATTRIB *I suppose cost shouldn't be a deciding factor.*
4 V-REPORT If you **decide** that something is the case, you form that opinion after considering the facts. *He decided that the doorbell was broken... I couldn't decide whether she was joking or not.*
decide on PHRASAL VERB If you **decide on** something or **decide upon** it, you choose it from two or more possibilities. *He decided on a career in the army... The men would be selected according to criteria which had to be decided upon.*

decided /dɪsaɪdɪd/
ADJ ATTRIB **Decided** means clear and definite. *This gave them a decided advantage over their opponents... He thought that their plan held very decided dangers.*

decidedly /dɪsaɪdɪdli/
1 SUBMOD **Decidedly** means to a great extent and in a way that is obvious. *The men looked decidedly uncomfortable.*
2 ADV If you say something **decidedly**, you say it in a way that suggests you are unlikely to change your mind. *'It's time things were altered,' said Mrs Moffat decidedly.*

deciduous /dɪsɪdjuəs/
ADJ A **deciduous** tree loses its leaves in autumn every year. *Deciduous trees grow mainly on the chalky soil of Southern England.*

decimal /desəml/ **decimals**
1 ADJ ATTRIB A **decimal** system involves counting in units of ten. *Most human calculating is done according to the principles of decimal arithmetic. ...the change to decimal currency.*
2 NC A **decimal** is a fraction written in the form of a dot followed by one or more numbers representing tenths, hundredths, and so on: for example .5, .51, .517. *Mr Baker has taught his daughter decimals and fractions.*

decimal point, decimal points
NC A **decimal point** is the dot in front of a decimal fraction.

decimate /desəmeɪt/ **decimates, decimating, decimated**
1 VO To **decimate** a group of people or animals means to destroy a very large number of them. *The soldiers would be decimated long before they reached the beaches... Last year's freezing weather decimated our bird population.*
2 VO To **decimate** a system or organization means to reduce greatly its size and effectiveness. *The Somali army has been decimated by defections in the last two years... In 1980 Britain fell into a recession which decimated the nation's manufacturing industry.*

decipher /dɪsaɪfə/ **deciphers, deciphering, deciphered**
VO If you **decipher** a piece of writing, speech, or coded information, you work out what it says, even though it is difficult to read or understand. *The genetic code of DNA was deciphered in 1961... It was the only code the Japanese were unable to ever decipher.*

decision /dɪsɪʒn/ **decisions**
1 NC When you make a **decision**, you choose what should be done or which is the best of various alternatives. *I think that I made the wrong decision... A decision on the issue might not be necessary.*
2 NU **Decision** is the act of deciding something. *Philip laced up his shoes slowly, delaying the moment of decision.*
3 NU **Decision** is also the ability to decide quickly and definitely what to do. *...a man of decision and action.*

decisive /dɪsaɪsɪv/
1 ADJ If a fact, action, or event is **decisive**, it makes it certain that there will be a particular result. *...a decisive battle... This promise was not a decisive factor in the election.* ◆ **decisively** ADV *Thornton was decisively defeated.*
2 ADJ If someone is **decisive**, they have the ability to make quick decisions. *...a decisive leader.* ◆ **decisively** ADV *'Can I see him?' Edgar shook his head decisively.* ◆ **decisiveness** NU *The real problem is lack of decisiveness.*

deck /dek/ **decks, decking, decked**
1 NC A **deck** on a bus or ship is a downstairs or upstairs area. *They got on the bus and sat on the top deck.*
2 N SING The **deck** of a ship is also a floor in the open air which you can walk on. *People and baggage were spread across the deck for the journey.*
3 NC A record **deck** is a piece of equipment on which you play records.
4 NC A **deck** of cards is a pack of playing cards. *He took out his deck of cards and shuffled them.*
5 NC In American English, a **deck** is also the same as a **patio**. *They have a lovely new home with a deck overlooking a golf course.*
6 VO+with If something is **decked** with attractive things, it is decorated with them; a literary use. *The graves are decked with flowers.*
7 See also **flight deck.**
deck out PHRASAL VERB If you **deck** someone or something **out**, you decorate them or make them look attractive. *I decked myself out in a suit and tie.*

deckchair /dektʃeə/ **deckchairs**
NC A **deckchair** is a simple folding chair which is used out of doors. *...500 deckchairs on Weymouth beach.*

deck hand, deck hands
NC A **deck hand** is a person who does the cleaning and other work on the deck of a ship. *He worked as a deck hand on the lake steamers.*

declaim /dɪkleɪm/ **declaims, declaiming, declaimed**
V-QUOTE, VO, or V If you **declaim**, you speak dramatically, as if you were acting in a theatre. *'I am a true patriot,' he declaimed... Instead of placing lone characters on stage declaiming grand principles, director Ken Kazan has broken with tradition by having secondary characters crowd the stage during solo arias.*

declamatory /dɪklæmətəᵘri/
ADJ Something that is **declamatory** is spoken dramatically, as if in a theatre. **Declamatory** is also used of a dramatic style of writing. *The style is often*

declamatory and repetitive.

declaration /dɛkləreɪʃn/ **declarations**

1 NC A **declaration** is a firm, emphatic statement. *He seemed embarrassed by her declaration of love. ...his earlier declarations that things were improving.*

2 NC A **declaration** is also an official announcement or statement. *...the day after the declaration was signed. ...formal declarations of war.*

declare /dɪkleə/ **declares, declaring, declared**

1 V-QUOTE or V-REPORT If you **declare** that something is the case, you say it in a firm, deliberate way. *'I like it,' she declared... They were heard to declare that they would never steal again.*

2 VO If you **declare** an attitude or intention, or if you **declare** yourself as having this attitude or intention, you make it known that you have it. *He declared his intention to fight... Mr Bell has declared his support... He declared himself strongly in favour of the project.* ♦ **declared** ADJ ATTRIB *...his declared intention to resign.*

3 VO If you **declare** something, you state it officially and formally. *The French declared war on England... At his trial he was declared innocent.*

4 VO When you **declare** goods that you have bought abroad or money that you have earned, you tell customs or tax officials about it so that you can pay tax on it. *'Have you anything to declare?'*

declassify /diːklæsɪfaɪ/ **declassifies, declassifying, declassified**

VO If information or documents **are declassified**, it has been officially stated that they are no longer secret. *Most cabinet papers are declassified after thirty years.*

decline /dɪklaɪn/ **declines, declining, declined**

1 V If something **declines**, it becomes smaller, weaker, or worse. *The number of congress members declined from 371 to 361... Since 1971 the party's influence has declined.* ♦ **declining** ADJ ATTRIB *...a steadily declining income. ...declining industries.*

2 NC or NU If there is a **decline** in something, it becomes smaller, weaker, or worse. *...a decline in standards. ...the decline of the motor industry.*

3 If something is **in decline** or **on the decline**, it is growing smaller, weaker or worse. *The city's population is in decline... Organized religion seems to be on the decline.*

4 VO or V+to-INF If you **decline** something or **decline** to do something, you politely refuse to accept it or do it; a formal use. *He has declined the invitation... Mr Santos declined to comment on the news.*

decode /diːkaʊd/ **decodes, decoding, decoded**

VO If you **decode** a message or signal that has been written or spoken in code, you change it into ordinary language. *Receiving signals and decoding them requires a radio telescope.*

décolleté /deɪkɒlteɪ/ **décolletés; also spelt décolletée.**

1 NC If you refer to a woman's **décolleté**, you are referring to the fact that she is wearing a dress or blouse with a very low neckline that does not cover her shoulders.

2 ADJ A **décolleté** dress or blouse is one that has a very low neckline and does not cover the shoulders. *...a yellowish décolleté lace blouse.*

decolonize /diːkɒlənaɪz/ **decolonizes, decolonizing, decolonized; also spelt decolonise.**

VO To **decolonize** a country that was formerly a colony means to give it political independence. *We believe that these countries should be decolonized.* ♦ **decolonization** /diːkɒlənaɪzeɪʃn/ NU *Some African leaders wanted radical decolonization.*

decompose /diːkəmpəʊz/ **decomposes, decomposing, decomposed**

V When something that has died **decomposes**, it changes chemically and begins to rot. *Shellfish decompose very quickly after death.*

decomposition /diːkɒmpəzɪʃn/

NU **Decomposition** is the process of rotting that takes place when living matter dies and changes chemically. *Organic matter is heaped onto raised beds to allow for decomposition.*

decompression /diːkəmpreʃn/

1 NU **Decompression** is the reduction of the force on something that is caused by the weight of the air.

After decompression, strong winds would have ripped the cabin apart.

2 NU **Decompression** is also the process of bringing someone back to the normal pressure of the air after they have been underwater and under greater pressure. *...a decompression chamber.*

decongestant /diːkəndʒestənt/ **decongestants**

NC A **decongestant** is a medicine which helps someone who has a cold to breathe more easily.

decontaminate /diːkəntæmɪneɪt/ **decontaminates, decontaminating, decontaminated**

VO To **decontaminate** something means to clean it by removing all radioactivity, germs, or dangerous substances. *The boat was decontaminated several times.* ♦ **decontamination** /diːkəntæmɪneɪʃn/ N+N or NU *...teams of observers and decontamination experts... A ban on visits to a Scottish island used for war-time biological experiments has been lifted after extensive decontamination there.*

decor /deɪkɔː/

NU The **decor** of a house or room is the style in which it is furnished and decorated. *...the pine decor of the kitchen.*

decorate /dekəreɪt/ **decorates, decorating, decorated**

1 VO If you **decorate** something, you make it look more attractive by adding things to it. *The walls were all decorated with posters.*

2 VO or V If you **decorate** a building or room, you paint it or wallpaper it. *He can't afford to decorate his flat... The plan was for its original interior to be covered over and decorated in an art-deco style.* ♦ **decorated** ADJ *The offices were crowded and badly decorated. ...a decorated ceiling.* ♦ **decorating** NU *We said we would do the decorating.*

3 VO If someone **is decorated**, they are given a medal or other honour. *He was decorated for valour in the Vietnam war.* ♦ **decorated** ADJ *...one of the most decorated pilots of the war.*

decoration /dekəreɪʃn/ **decorations**

1 NC or NU **Decorations** are features added to something to make it look more attractive. *...Christmas decorations. ...dresses that are free of all decoration.*

2 NU The **decoration** of a room or building is the furniture, wallpaper, and ornaments there. *...the style of decoration typical of the 1920s.*

3 NC A **decoration** is a medal given to someone as an official honour. *The George Cross is the highest decoration for bravery given to civilians.*

decorative /dekə⁰rətɪv/

ADJ Something that is **decorative** is intended to look pretty or attractive. *...decorative clothing. ...four highly decorative gold boxes.*

decorator /dekəreɪtə/ **decorators**

NC A **decorator** is a person whose job is to paint houses or put wallpaper on the walls. *...a painter and decorator.*

decorous /dekərəs/

ADJ **Decorous** behaviour is polite and correct and does not offend people; a formal word. *He gave his wife a decorous kiss.* ♦ **decorously** ADV *...teenage lovers strolling decorously.*

decorum /dɪkɔːrəm/

NU **Decorum** is behaviour that people consider to be correct and polite; a formal word. *They have behaved with utter decorum.*

decoy, **decoys, decoying, decoyed;** pronounced /diːkɔɪ/ when it is a noun and /dɪkɔɪ/ when it is a verb.

1 NC A **decoy** is a person or object that you use to lead someone away from where they intended to go, especially so that you can catch them. *The plane was acting as a decoy for other aircraft on spying missions.*

2 VOA If you **decoy** someone, you lead them away from where they intended to go, often by means of a trick. *Eight of the missiles were decoyed away from targets.*

decrease, **decreases, decreasing, decreased;** pronounced /diːkriːs/ when it is a verb and /diːkriːs/ when it is a noun.

1 V-ERG When something **decreases** or when you **decrease** it, it becomes smaller. *The number of*

marriages has decreased by forty per cent... To save money, decrease the temperature.
2 NC A **decrease** is a reduction in the quantity or size of something. *A decrease in exports had left the country short of foreign money.*

decreasing /diːkriːsɪŋ/
ADJ ATTRIB Something that is **decreasing** is growing less in quantity, size, or strength. *It was a life of increasing labour and decreasing leisure.*
♦ **decreasingly** SUBMOD *The parliamentary forum becomes a decreasingly effective democratic institution.*

decree /dɪkriː/ **decrees, decreeing, decreed**
1 NC A **decree** is an official order, especially one made by the ruler of a country. *President Gorbachev has issued a decree ordering big changes in the Soviet television and radio system.*
2 V-REPORT If someone in authority **decrees** that something must happen, they order this officially. *The Finance Ministry decreed that taxes must be paid either in cash or with government cheques.*

decree absolute, decrees absolute
NC A **decree absolute** is the final order made by a court in a divorce case which ends a marriage completely.

decree nisi /dɪkriː naɪsaɪ/ **decrees nisi**
NC A **decree nisi** is an order made by a court which states that a divorce must take place at a certain time in the future unless a good reason is produced to prevent this.

decrepit /dɪkrɛpɪt/
ADJ Something that is **decrepit** is very old and in bad condition. *The towns and villages are often sad and decrepit after forty years of neglect... The proceeds will finance restructuring and modernization of East Germany's decrepit industry.*

decry /dɪkraɪ/ **decries, decrying, decried**
VO If you **decry** something, you say that it is bad; a formal word. *She decried a recent wave of crimes involving police and soldiers.*

dedicate /dɛdɪkeɪt/ **dedicates, dedicating, dedicated**
1 V-REFL+*to* If you **dedicate** yourself to something, you give a lot of time and effort to it because you think it is important. *...a man who had dedicated himself to his work.*
2 VO+*to* If you **dedicate** something such as a book or a piece of music to someone, you say that the work is written for them, as a sign of affection or respect. *She dedicated her first book to her husband.*
3 VO When a monument, building, or church is **dedicated** to someone, a formal ceremony is held to show that the building will always be associated with them. *...a Museum dedicated to the memory of the British nurse, Florence Nightingale.*

dedicated /dɛdɪkeɪtɪd/
ADJ If you are **dedicated** to something, you give a lot of time and effort to it because you think it is important. *...people dedicated to social or political change. ...a dedicated surgeon.*

dedication /dɛdɪkeɪʃn/ **dedications**
1 NU If you show **dedication** to something, you give a lot of time and effort to it because you think it is important. *I admired her dedication to her family.*
2 NC A **dedication** is a message written at the beginning of a book or a statement made before a piece of music is played, as a sign of affection or respect for someone. *...a book complete with a table of contents, a dedication and a cover designed by the author.*
3 NC A **dedication** is also a ceremony during which a monument, church, or public building is dedicated to someone. *They were attending the dedication of a stained glass window in memory of members of the Royal Ulster Constabulary.*

deduce /dɪdjuːs/ **deduces, deducing, deduced**
V-REPORT or VO If you **deduce** that something is true, you reach that conclusion because of what you know to be true. *From this information, they deduced that in mammals some genes do differ... It should be possible to deduce the precise location of an impending earthquake... What do you deduce from all this?*

deduct /dɪdʌkt/ **deducts, deducting, deducted**
VO When you **deduct** an amount from a total, you reduce the total by that amount. *Tax will be deducted automatically from your wages.*

deduction /dɪdʌkʃn/ **deductions**
1 NCorNU A **deduction** is a conclusion that you reach because of what you know to be true. *What scientific deductions can you make from an observation of this eclipse?... If the battery is dead the horn will not work: that is deduction, not guesswork.*
2 NCorNU A **deduction** is also an amount subtracted from a total. *...national insurance deductions. ...automatic deduction from pay.*

deductive /dɪdʌktɪv/
ADJ **Deductive** is used to describe a method of reasoning where conclusions are reached logically from other things that are already known. *...the deductive procedure of testing statements in physics.*

deed /diːd/ **deeds**
1 NC A **deed** is something that is done, especially something very good or very bad; a literary use. *Their violent deeds aggravated the tragic situation... They exalted his great life and lauded his daring deeds... He said that what mattered were deeds, not words.*
2 NC+SUPP A **deed** is also a legal document containing an agreement or contract. *The land was simply taken by the Communists and the original title deeds have long since disappeared.*

deed box, deed boxes
NC A **deed box** is a strong case or box, often made of metal, in which deeds and other official, legal, or important papers are kept.

deed poll
If you change your name **by deed poll**, you change it officially and legally. *He moved to London to live as a woman, eventually changing name by deed poll and undergoing a sex-change operation.*

deem /diːm/ **deems, deeming, deemed**
VO If you **deem** something to be the case, you consider that it is the case; a formal word. *She was deemed by the judge to be in contempt of court... Force was deemed necessary.*

deep /diːp/ **deeper, deepest**
1 ADJ or ADV If something is **deep**, it extends a long way down from its surface. *The sea is not very deep there... They dug deep down into the earth.*
2 ADJ after N You use **deep** to talk about measurements. For example, if something is two metres **deep**, it measures two metres from top to bottom, or from front to back. *Some roads were flooded by water up to 15 inches deep. ...shallow trenches about thirty metres deep.*
3 ADJ or ADV **Deep** in an area means a long way inside it. *...deep in the forest... Guerrilla forces were advancing deep into enemy territory.*
4 ADJ ATTRIB You use **deep** to emphasise the seriousness, strength, importance, or degree of something. *This was a matter of deep concern. ...the deep mistrust between the two countries... Frank was still in deep financial trouble... Our hearts go out to you in deepest sympathy.* ♦ **deeply** SUBMOD *He has always been deeply opposed to EC membership.*
5 ADJ ATTRIB If you are in a **deep** sleep, you are sleeping and it is difficult to wake you. *About three in the morning I awoke from a deep sleep.*
6 ADJ ATTRIB A **deep** breath or sigh uses the whole of your lungs. *She took a deep breath and put her head under the water.* ♦ **deeply** ADV *She sighed deeply.*
7 ADJ A **deep** colour is strong and fairly dark. *The sky was a deep purple.*
8 ADJ A **deep** sound is a low one. *He sang in a deep voice.*
9 ADJ **Deep** thoughts are serious thoughts. *I have no deep thought, no profound philosophy.*
● **Deep** is used in these phrases. ● If you are **deep in thought**, you are thinking very hard about something. *He was soon so deep in thought that he forgot all about her.* ● If you say that something **goes** or **runs deep**, you mean that it is very serious and hard to change. *The crisis in the prisons goes deep.*

deepen /díːpən/ **deepens, deepening, deepened**
1 VO To **deepen** something means to make it deeper. *The authority wants to widen and deepen the River Soar.*
2 V Where a river or a sea **deepens**, the water gets deeper. *The sea deepens gradually.*
3 V-ERG If a situation or emotion **deepens** or if something **deepens** it, it becomes more intense. *The crisis deepened... The main impact on these families has been to deepen their love for each other.*
◆ **deepening** ADJ ATTRIB *...the country's deepening economic crisis... There was a deepening sense of fear, frustration and futility.*
4 VO If something **deepens** your knowledge of a subject, you learn more about it. *Their object was to deepen man's understanding of the universe... He has deepened his understanding of a broad range of the British people.*
5 V-ERG When a sound **deepens** or when you **deepen** it, it becomes lower in tone. *The engine sound deepened from a steady whine to a thunderous roar.*

deep freeze, deep freezes
NC A **deep freeze** is a very cold refrigerator in which food or other things which need to be kept frozen are stored. *He had an enormous deep freeze in which he stored his bagels... The cultures are kept in suspended animation in a deep freeze.*

deep-fried
ADJ **Deep-fried** food has been fried in a large amount of fat or oil. *...deep-fried chicken and chips.*

deep-rooted
ADJ An idea or feeling that is **deep-rooted** or **deeply rooted** is so firmly fixed in a person or a society that it is difficult to change or remove. *...a deep-rooted prejudice that runs through our society... A problem as deeply rooted as this is not going to be solved quickly.*

deep-sea
ADJ ATTRIB **Deep-sea** activities take place in areas of the sea that are a long way from the coast. *...deep-sea diving.*

deep-seated
ADJ Something such as a feeling or a problem that is **deep-seated** is caused by an attitude, condition, or idea that is very strong and unchanging. *The country is still suffering from deep-seated economic problems... There is a deep-seated resentment of their behaviour during the war.*

deep-set
ADJ **Deep-set** eyes have deep sockets. *...her deep-set grey eyes.*

deer /dɪə/; **deer** is both the singular and the plural form.
NC A **deer** is a large wild animal. Male deer usually have large, branching horns. *...a move to ban the hunting of deer on Church land.*

de-escalate /diː ɛskəleɪt/ **de-escalates, de-escalating, de-escalated**
V-ERG If an unpleasant situation or problem **de-escalates** or if something **de-escalates** it, it becomes less intense and less dangerous or harmful. *This fearsome battle that's being fought down in southern Angola may now de-escalate... These moves are aimed at de-escalating the present conflict.*

deface /dɪféɪs/ **defaces, defacing, defaced**
VO If someone **defaces** something such as a wall or a notice, they spoil it by writing or drawing on it. *Under Kenyan law it's illegal to deface banknotes... The graves of soldiers have been defaced.*

de facto /deɪ fæktəʊ/
De facto is used to say that something exists, even though it was not planned or is not legally recognized; a formal expression. *There is a de facto state of emergency here... They saw Tibet as de facto an independent state.*

defamation /dɛfəméɪʃn/
NU **Defamation** is the damaging of someone's reputation by saying something bad and untrue about them; a legal term. *He's begun legal proceedings against three newspapers for defamation.*

defamatory /dɪfǽmətəʳri/
ADJ Speech or writing that is **defamatory** is likely to damage someone's good reputation by saying something bad and untrue about them; a formal word. *They said the article was untruthful and defamatory.*

defame /dɪféɪm/ **defames, defaming, defamed**
VO If you **defame** someone or something, you say something bad and untrue about them; a formal word. *It took the jury just two hours to decide that the magazine had defamed the woman.*

default /dɪfɔːlt/ **defaults, defaulting, defaulted**
1 V If you **default**, you fail to do something that you are legally supposed to do, such as make a payment that you owe. *He said he had been right to default on that loan.* ▶ Also NU *Guarantors would have to undertake to repay the loan in cases of default.*
2 If something happens **by default**, it happens only because something else has not happened. *They gained a colony by default because no other European power wanted it.*

defaulter /dɪfɔːltəʳ/ **defaulters**
NC A **defaulter** is someone who does not do something that they are legally supposed to do, such as make a payment at a particular time, or appear in a court of law. *Police evicted rent defaulters.*

defeat /dɪfíːt/ **defeats, defeating, defeated**
1 VO If you **defeat** someone, you win a victory over them in a battle, game, or contest. *England have been narrowly defeated by West Germany in the semi-final of the World Cup... The Labour Party was defeated in the last three general elections... As soon as the Janata party had achieved the unthinkable by defeating Mrs Gandhi in the elections, its unity began to fall apart.*
2 VO If a proposal or a motion in a debate **is defeated**, more people vote against it than vote for it. *The motion was defeated by 221 votes to 152.*
3 VO If a task or a problem **defeats** you, it is so difficult that you cannot do it or solve it. *...a complex sum which defeats many adults as well as children.*
4 VO To **defeat** an action or plan means to cause it to fail. *He would like to see the strike defeated.*
5 NU **Defeat** is the state of being beaten in a battle or contest, or of failing to achieve what you wanted to. *The bad weather contributed to the defeat of the navy... Her friend finally gave up in defeat.*
6 NC A **defeat** is a contest in which you lose or fail to achieve what you wanted to. *These defeats came as a setback for Thorne.*

defeatism /dɪfíːtɪzəm/
NU **Defeatism** is a way of thinking or talking which suggests that you expect to be unsuccessful. *We were accused of defeatism.*

defeatist /dɪfíːtɪst/ **defeatists**
NC A **defeatist** is someone who thinks or talks in a way that suggests that they expect to be unsuccessful. *They dismissed him as a defeatist.* ▶ Also ADJ *I was in a defeatist mood when he told me the result.*

defecate /dɛfəkeɪt/ **defecates, defecating, defecated**
V To **defecate** means to get rid of waste matter from the body through the anus; a formal word.

defect, defects, defecting, defected; pronounced /díːfekt/ when it is a noun and /dɪfékt/ when it is a verb.
1 NC A **defect** is a fault or imperfection in a person or thing. *Several of the planes had wiring defects... His lawyer says there were serious defects in the government's handling of the hijack.*
2 V If you **defect**, you leave your own country, political party, or other group, and join an opposing one. *Several of the Labour MPs defected to the new party.* ◆ **defection** /dɪfékʃn/ **defections** NCorNU *The number of defections has increased in recent years. ...defection from the National Front.*

defective /dɪféktɪv/
ADJ If something is **defective**, it is imperfect and therefore does not work properly. *Engineers found some defective welding in a seal on one of the engines.*

defector /dɪféktəʳ/ **defectors**
NC A **defector** is someone who leaves their country, political party, or other group, and joins an opposing country, party, or group. *The party welcomed defectors from the Nationalists and other parties.*

defence /dɪfɛns/ **defences**; spelt **defense** in American English.
1 NU **Defence** is action taken to protect someone or something from attack. *Prince Sultan said the new missiles were purely for defence. ...the defence of civil liberties.* ● If you say something **in defence** or **in your defence**, you say it in order to support ideas or actions that have been criticized. *Brown, in defence, said that it was his boss who was violent.*
2 NU **Defence** is also used to refer to a country's armies and weapons, and their activities. *...the Ministry of Defence. ...defence spending.*
3 NC A **defence** is something that people or animals can use or do to protect themselves. *The jellyfish has had to develop this deadly poison as a defence... He had found coldness his only defence against despair.*
4 NC A **defence** is also something that you say in support of ideas or actions that have been criticized. *His economists have drawn up a defence of his policy.*
5 N PL The **defences** of a country or region are its armed forces and weapons. *The Government has not yet made any firm decisions about Britain's future defences... The city's defences are to be strengthened in anticipation of an attack.*
6 NC In a court of law, a person's **defence** is their denial of a charge against them. *He decided to conduct his own defence.*
7 N SING The **defence** is the case presented by a lawyer in a trial for the person who has been accused of a crime, or the lawyers for this person. *Those who took up the case for the defence are still certain that this is a case of mistaken identity.*
8 N COLL In a sports team, the **defence** is the group of players who try to stop the opposing team scoring a goal or a point. *Arsenal's defence is very strong this season.*

defenceless /dɪfɛnsləs/; spelt **defenseless** in American English.
ADJ If someone or something is **defenceless**, they are weak and cannot defend themselves. *The army opened fire on defenceless civilians... Baby mammals are born defenceless.*

defence mechanism, defence mechanisms
NC A **defence mechanism** is a way of behaving or thinking which is not conscious or deliberate, but is an automatic reaction to unpleasant actions or feelings such as anxiety or fear. *Surgeons have a sort of defence mechanism that puts a distance between themselves and their patients.*

defend /dɪfɛnd/ **defends, defending, defended**
1 V O or V-REFL If you **defend** someone or something, you take action to protect them. *The guard had been defending the building by firing warning shots into the air... He said Iran was strong enough to defend itself.*
2 V O or V-REFL If you **defend** someone or something when they have been criticized, you argue in support of them. *The bank has defended its actions in these cases... He used the speech to defend himself against charges of corruption.*
3 V O A lawyer who **defends** a person in court tries to show that the charges against the person are not true or that there was an excuse for the crime. *The authorities did not allow Mr Guillo's lawyer to defend him at his trial.*
4 V O If a sports champion **defends** his or her title, he or she plays a match or a game against someone who will become the new champion if they win. *Jeff Fenech of Australia will defend his featherweight title against Marcos Villasana of Mexico in February.* ● **defending** ADJ ATTRIB *The defending champion, Betsy King, finished third.*

defendant /dɪfɛndənt/ **defendants**
NC The **defendant** in a trial is the person accused of a crime. *One defendant was sentenced to life imprisonment.*

defender /dɪfɛndə/ **defenders**
1 NC If someone is a **defender** of a particular idea, belief, or person that has been criticized, they argue or act in support of that idea, belief, or person. *They were staunch defenders of social democracy. ...an outspoken defender of eccentric right-wing views.*
2 NC A **defender** in a game such as football or hockey

is a player whose main task is to try and stop the other side scoring. *He slipped past two defenders to score.*

defense /dɪfɛns/. See **defence**.

defensible /dɪfɛnsəbl/
1 ADJ An opinion, system, or action that is **defensible** is one that people can argue is right or good. *Our action was taken on fully justifiable and defensible grounds.*
2 ADJ A place that is **defensible** can be defended against attacks. *Roads have been rebuilt there, allegedly making the city more defensible.*

defensive /dɪfɛnsɪv/
1 ADJ ATTRIB You use **defensive** to describe things that are intended to protect someone or something. *The military build-up is a defensive measure.*
2 If you are **on the defensive**, you are trying to protect yourself or your interests because you feel unsure or threatened. *The paper says that Israel is now firmly on the defensive... The Party is now trying to put its rivals on the defensive.*
3 ADJ Someone who is **defensive** is behaving in a way that shows that they feel unsure or threatened. *The officials were defensive about their policies.*
● **defensively** ADV *'I'm in no hurry,' said Rudolph defensively.*

defer /dɪfɜː/ **defers, deferring, deferred**; a formal word.
1 V O or V+ING If you **defer** an event or action, you arrange for it to take place at a later date than was planned. *They offered to defer his appointment for a year... The UN Security Council has deferred taking any action in response to the report.*
2 V+to If you **defer** to someone, you accept their opinion or do what they want because you respect them. *He's a medical man and we'd be fools not to defer to him in medical matters.*

deference /dɛfərəns/
NU **Deference** is a polite, respectful attitude that you show towards someone or something. *She is treated with deference... He had reluctantly agreed to go to Japan in deference to the Thai Prime Minister... Out of deference to Syria, they did not attend the recent Arab League summit.*

deferential /dɛfərɛnʃl/
ADJ A **deferential** person is polite and respectful. *I made every effort to be pleasant and deferential to Mr Thomas.*

defiance /dɪfaɪəns/
1 NU **Defiance** is behaviour which shows that you are not willing to obey someone or are not worried about their disapproval. *In a gesture of defiance, I wore a black mini-skirt.*
2 If you do something **in defiance of** a rule, you do it even though it is forbidden. *The houses were erected in defiance of all building regulations.*

defiant /dɪfaɪənt/
ADJ If you are **defiant**, you refuse to obey someone or you ignore their disapproval of you. *The girl sat down with a defiant look at Judy.* ● **defiantly** ADV *She announced defiantly that she intended to stay.*

deficiency /dɪfɪʃnsi/ **deficiencies**
1 NC+SUPP or NU+SUPP A **deficiency** in something, especially something that your body needs, is a lack or shortage of it. *...deficiencies in personnel and equipment. ...vitamin deficiency... Deficiency of insulin causes wasting of the body and eventual death.*
2 NC+SUPP or NU+SUPP If someone or something has a **deficiency**, they have a weakness or imperfection in them. *They have complained of deficiencies in the electoral system... The deficiency of the answers was obvious to everybody.*

deficient /dɪfɪʃnt/
1 ADJ If someone or something is **deficient** in a particular thing, they do not have as much of it as they need. *...a poor diet, deficient in essential vitamins and minerals.*
2 ADJ Something that is **deficient** is not good enough; a formal use. *...deficient standards of hygiene and sanitation.*

deficit /dɛfəsɪt/ **deficits**
NC A **deficit** is the amount by which the money

received by a country or organization is less than the money it has spent. *The Post Office's deficit totalled 150 million pounds.*

defile /dɪfaɪl/ **defiles, defiling, defiled**
vo If you **defile** something precious or holy, you spoil it or damage it. *...secret thoughts which defiled her purity.*

definable /dɪfaɪnəbl/
ADJ Something that is **definable** can be described clearly. *The war has been through several clearly definable stages during the past eight years.*

define /dɪfaɪn/ **defines, defining, defined**
1 vo If you **define** something, you show, describe, or state what it is and what it is like. *Sharia law is the Islamic legal system which defines and codifies the way in which Muslims should live... There still remained a large number of risks which could not be clearly defined.*
2 vo If you **define** a word or expression, you explain its meaning. *My dictionary defines 'crisis' as a 'turning point'... A refugee is defined as someone who has been forced to leave their country through fear of persecution.*
3 vo If an object **is defined**, its visible outline is clearly shown. *The picture was sharp and clearly defined.*

definite /dɛfənət/
1 ADJ If something is **definite**, it is firm and clear, and unlikely to be changed. *There's a definite date for the wedding... Make sure that nobody sets off for Italy without tickets for the matches and definite accommodation arrangements.*
2 ADJ **Definite** also means true rather than being someone's opinion or guess. *There was no definite evidence... They may tell us that there is a definite answer that has come out of the study.*

definite article, definite articles
NC In grammar, the **definite article** is the word 'the'. In this dictionary the word 'the' is called a determiner.

definitely /dɛfənətli/
1 ADV SEN You use **definitely** to emphasize that something is certainly the case. *They were definitely not for sale.*
2 ADV If something has **definitely** been decided, the decision will not be changed. *I haven't definitely decided on going to law school.*

definition /dɛfənɪʃn/ **definitions**
1 NC A **definition** of a word or term is a statement giving its meaning, especially in a dictionary. *What is meant by 'combat aircraft'? The definition is not easy to pin down.*
2 If you say that something has a particular quality **by definition**, you mean that it has this quality simply because of what it is. *It is a compromise, and therefore by definition imperfect.*
3 NU **Definition** is the quality of being clear and distinct. *They lack definition and identity as a class.*

definitive /dəfɪnətɪv/
1 ADJ Something that is **definitive** provides a firm, unquestionable conclusion. *...a definitive verdict.*
◆ **definitively** ADV *'Hearts of Darkness' will definitively establish McCullin as a writer.*
2 ADJ A book or performance that is **definitive** is thought to be the best of its kind that has ever been done or that will ever be done. *...the definitive biography of Josef Stalin.*

deflate /diːfleɪt/ **deflates, deflating, deflated**
1 vo If you **deflate** someone, you take away their confidence or make them seem less important. *...a desire to deflate the reputation of some contemporary... In 'Vincent and Theo', Altman deflates the reverent historical biography.* ◆ **deflated** ADJ *If that left us feeling deflated, worse was to come.*
2 V-ERG When a tyre or balloon **deflates** or when you **deflate** it, all the air comes out of it. *There was a series of bubbling sounds as the balloon deflated... Stick-on labels warn the person at the garage to take extra care when deflating the tyre.*

deflation /diːfleɪʃn/
NU **Deflation** is a reduction in economic activity in a country that leads to lower industrial production and

lower prices. *...a worldwide deflation in real estate values.*

deflationary /diːfleɪʃənəri/
ADJ A **deflationary** economic policy or measure is one that is intended to, or is likely to, cause deflation. *...a mildly deflationary budget.*

deflect /dɪflɛkt/ **deflects, deflecting, deflected**
1 vo If you **deflect** something such as someone's attention or criticism, you cause them to turn their attention to something else or to do something different. *Their main purpose was to deflect attention from the Government's proposals.*
2 vo If you **deflect** something that is moving, you make it go in a slightly different direction, for example by hitting or pushing it. *Our goalie deflected their shot... The two streams of water are deflected.*

deflection /dɪflɛkʃn/ **deflections**
1 NCorNU A **deflection** is an action of making something go in a slightly different direction from the way in which it was going before. *Jose Bakero's shot took a deflection off Miguel Tendillo... Shilton's deflection led to the first goal.*
2 NC A **deflection** is also the amount by which something is turned away from its original course or moved from its original position; a technical use in physics. *This is the deflection with both forces acting... They are designed to follow the function of the human foot, allowing deflection at the heel and toe.*

deflower /diːflaʊə/ **deflowers, deflowering, deflowered**
vo When a woman **is deflowered**, she has sexual intercourse with a man for the first time; a literary word.

defoliant /diːfəʊliənt/ **defoliants**
NC A **defoliant** is a chemical that is used on trees and plants which makes all their leaves fall off. *One fifth of Vietnam's agricultural land had been destroyed by napalm and defoliants... The thickets will have to be sprayed with defoliants and herbicides to weaken them.*

defoliate /diːfəʊlieɪt/ **defoliates, defoliating, defoliated**
vo If you **defoliate** plants, you make all their leaves fall off, especially by using a defoliant. *The airforce used the chemical for defoliating the jungle.*

deforest /diːfɒrɪst/ **deforests, deforesting, deforested**
vo If an area is **deforested**, all the trees there are cut down or destroyed. *The Amazon Basin is quickly becoming deforested.* ◆ **deforestation** /diːfɒrɪsteɪʃn/
NU *Deforestation is by no means a new phenomenon.*

deform /dɪfɔːm/ **deforms, deforming, deformed**
vo If something **deforms** a person's body or an object, it causes it to have an unnatural shape or appearance. *Badly fitting shoes can deform the feet.* ◆ **deformed** ADJ *The drug may have caused deformed babies.*

deformity /dɪfɔːməti/ **deformities**
1 NC A **deformity** is a part of someone's body which is the wrong shape. *He was born with a severe deformity of the right foot... The home has been opened to cope with the growing numbers of children born with deformities.*
2 NU **Deformity** is the condition of having a deformity. *Many cases of deformity and death occurred in the villagers who ate the fish.*

defraud /dɪfrɔːd/ **defrauds, defrauding, defrauded**
VOorV If someone **defrauds** you, they take something away from you or stop you from getting something that belongs to you by means of tricks and lies. *... a plot to defraud an elderly heiress of her valuable art collection... He was charged with conspiracy to defraud.*

defray /dɪfreɪ/ **defrays, defraying, defrayed**
vo If you **defray** someone's costs or expenses, you give them money which represents an amount that they have spent, for example while they have been doing something for you or acting on your behalf; a formal word. *The bill would also provide emergency funds for Israel to defray war-related expenses... Mr Baker is hoping to raise funds to defray the cost of the American defence of Saudi Arabia.*

defrost /diːfrɒst/ **defrosts, defrosting, defrosted**
1 V-ERG When you **defrost** a fridge or freezer or when

it **defrosts**, you switch it off so that the ice inside it can melt. *Clean up after the weekend, defrost the fridge and clean the oven.*
2 v-ERG When you **defrost** frozen food or when it **defrosts**, you allow it to melt so that you can cook and eat it. *You must defrost a frozen chicken before you cook it... Destruction of vitamin C takes place as frozen vegetables are left to defrost.*

deft /dɛft/
ADJ A **deft** action is skilful and often quick. *The deft fingers massaged his scalp.* ◆ **deftly** ADV *He deftly slit open the envelope.*

defunct /dɪfʌŋkt/
ADJ If something is **defunct**, it no longer exists or it is no longer functioning. *Dr David Owen was one of the four main founders of the now defunct Social Democratic Party... The East German state and its ideology are defunct.*

defuse /diːfjuːz/ **defuses, defusing, defused**
1 VO If you **defuse** a dangerous or tense situation, you make it less dangerous or tense. *The immediate crisis may have been defused.*
2 VO If someone **defuses** a bomb, they remove the fuse from it so that it cannot explode. *A five-pound bomb found hidden behind a wall was safely defused.*

defy /dɪfaɪ/ **defies, defying, defied**
1 VO If you **defy** people or laws, you refuse to obey them. *A substantial number of opposition MPs defied their party's instructions... Residents defied a curfew to attend prayers.*
2 VO+to-INF If you **defy** someone to do something which you think is impossible, you challenge them to do it. *I defy anyone to disprove it.*
3 VO If something **defies** description or understanding, it is so strange or surprising that it is almost impossible to describe or understand. *...forces within the human character which defy rational analysis.*

degeneracy /dɪdʒɛnəⁿrəsi/
NU **Degeneracy** is behaviour which many people think is shocking or disgusting. *It's a part of the degeneracy of the age.*

degenerate, degenerates, degenerating, degenerated; pronounced /dɪdʒɛnəreɪt/ when it is a verb and /dɪdʒɛnəⁿrət/ when it is an adjective or a noun.
1 v To **degenerate** means to become worse in quality, behaviour, appearance, or intelligence. *The tapes degenerate with repeated use... The discussion degenerated into a row.* ◆ **degeneration** /dɪdʒɛnəreɪʃn/ NU *This disease causes physical and mental degeneration.*
2 ADJ If someone is **degenerate**, they show very low standards of morality. *It blamed degenerate elements for the disruption in the schools.*
3 NC A **degenerate** is someone who shows very low standards of morality. *The world is full of degenerates.*

degenerative /dɪdʒɛnəⁿrətɪv/
ADJ A **degenerative** disease or condition is one which is getting worse. *...degenerative arthritis.*

degradation /dɛgrədeɪʃn/
NU **Degradation** is a state of poverty and dirt. *They forgot the squalor and degradation around them.*

degrade /dɪgreɪd/ **degrades, degrading, degraded**
VO To **degrade** someone means to make them seem less respectable or important than they really are. *...films that degrade women.* ◆ **degrading** ADJ *...the vicious and degrading cult of violence.*

degree /dɪgriː/ **degrees**
1 NC+SUPP You use **degree** to indicate the extent to which something happens or is felt. *This has been tried with varying degrees of success... The number of police carrying guns has increased to an alarming degree.* ● If something happens **by degrees**, it happens gradually. *Only by degrees did it dawn on him.*
2 NC A **degree** is a unit of measurement for temperatures, angles, and longitude and latitude. It is often written as '°', for example 23°. *Sea water freezes at about minus two degrees Centigrade*
3 NC A **degree** at a university or polytechnic is a qualification gained after completing a course of study there. *He had taken a degree in music at Cambridge.*

Dehaene, Jean-Luc /ʒɒnⁿ luːk dəhaːnə/
Jean-Luc Dehaene became Prime Minister of Belgium in 1992. He was Minister of Social Affairs and Institutional Reforms from 1981 to 1988. From 1988 to 1992 he was Deputy Prime Minister and Minister of Communications and Institutional Reforms. He is a member of the Flemish Christian Social Party (CVP).

dehumanize /diːhjuːmənaɪz/ **dehumanizes, dehumanizing, dehumanized**; also spelt **dehumanise**.
1 VO Something that **dehumanizes** people takes away from them the qualities which are often thought of as being best in human beings, such as kindness and individuality. *It is said that science will dehumanise people... To impose on them a wretched life of deprivation and poverty is to dehumanize them.*
◆ **dehumanizing** ADJ *...the harmful and dehumanizing effect of retirement.* ◆ **dehumanization** /diːhjuːmənaɪzeɪʃn/ NU *It's a dehumanisation of sexuality, where it's looked at as a sort of battle.*
2 VO If an activity is **dehumanized**, it is made dull and mechanical, with no originality or variation.

dehydrated /diːhaɪdreɪtɪd, diːhaɪdreɪtɪd/
1 ADJ **Dehydrated** food has been through a process that removes all the water from it, often in order to preserve it. *There is a market for dehydrated asparagus powder in the soup industry. ...packets of dehydrated soup.*
2 ADJ If you **are dehydrated**, you feel ill because you have lost too much water from your body. *Many refugees arrive exhausted and dehydrated.*

dehydration /diːhaɪdreɪʃn/
NU If someone is suffering from **dehydration**, they are ill because they do not have enough water in their body. *A number of them are said to be suffering from dehydration... The biggest single killer of young children is dehydration caused by diarrhoea.*

deify /deɪɪfaɪ/ **deifies, deifying, deified**
VO If you **deify** someone or something, you consider them to be a god and treat them as an object of worship; a formal word. *The African wildcat was tamed and deified by the ancient Egyptians.*

deign /deɪn/ **deigns, deigning, deigned**
V+to-INF If you **deign** to do something, you do it even though you think you are too important to do it; a formal word. *They said there is little chance of Mr Kim deigning to talk to Mr Roh as an equal.*

deity /deɪəti/ **deities**
NC A **deity** is a god or goddess; a formal word. *...the birthplace of Rama, one of their main deities.*

déjà vu /deɪʒɑː vuː/
NU **Déjà vu** is the feeling that you have already experienced in the past exactly the same sequence of events as is happening at the present moment. *There is a strong sense of déjà vu amongst the audience.*

dejected /dɪdʒɛktɪd/
ADJ If you are **dejected**, you feel unhappy or disappointed. *He had a dejected, saddened look.*
◆ **dejectedly** ADV *'I can't,' said the girl dejectedly.*

dejection /dɪdʒɛkʃn/
NU **Dejection** is a feeling of unhappiness and disappointment. *A mood of dejection has now set in.*

de Klerk, F W /ɛf dʌblju: dəkleək/
Frederik Willem de Klerk became President of South Africa and the leader of the National Party in 1989. He was Minister of Mineral and Energy Affairs from 1980 to 1982, of Internal Affairs from 1982 to 1985, and of National Education and Planning from 1984 to 1989. Born: 1936.

delay /dɪleɪ/ **delays, delaying, delayed**
1 V+ING, VO, or V If you **delay** doing something, you do not do it until a later time. *The Security Council had delayed authorising the operation... Try and persuade them to delay some of the changes... They're delaying in the hope that they won't have to pay.*
2 VO To **delay** someone or something means to make them late or slow them down. *I'm afraid I was slightly delayed... The shock of the operation delayed his recovery.*
3 NCorNU If there is a **delay**, something does not happen until later than planned or expected. *Ferry services are still subject to delays because of the*

strike... If anything is paid in we shall inform you without delay.

delectable /dɪlɛktəbl/

ADJ Something that is **delectable** is very pleasant. *It will grow into a very delectable food.*

delectation /diːlekteɪʃn/

NU **Delectation** is very great pleasure and amusement; a literary word. *Some of our greatest music was written for the discerning delectation of a vast audience of musical amateurs.*

delegate, delegates, delegating, delegated;
pronounced /dɛləgət/ when it is a noun and /dɛlɪgeɪt/ when it is a verb.

1 NC A **delegate** is a person chosen to make decisions on behalf of a group of people, especially at a meeting. *Delegates are due to meet again later today to try to agree the resolution... The Swedish delegate said the draft was not well-balanced.*

2 VO If you **delegate** someone to do something, you formally ask them to do it on your behalf. *Officials have been delegated to start work on a draft of the settlement... The Bishop delegated me to approach the local press.*

3 VOorV If you **delegate** duties or responsibilities, you give them to someone else so that they can act on your behalf. *They agreed to delegate authority to the Executive Committee... He sees the President's ability to delegate as a strength.*

delegation /dɛlɪgeɪʃn/ **delegations**

NC A **delegation** is a group of people chosen to represent a larger group of people. *The Sudanese government sent a delegation to the Ethiopian capital to discuss a peace settlement.*

delete /dɪliːt/ **deletes, deleting, deleted**

VO If you **delete** information that has been written down or stored in a computer, you remove it. *Vietnam is expected to delete these clauses from the constitution. ...passages can be deleted or stored just as with an ordinary word processor.*

deleterious /dɛlɪtɪəriəs/

ADJ Something that is **deleterious** has a harmful effect on a person or thing; a formal word. *Many women breast-feed several babies with no deleterious effect.*

Delhi /dɛli/

Delhi is the capital of India. The metropolitan area of Delhi includes Old Delhi and New Delhi, and is the second largest city in India. Population: 273,000 (New Delhi) 4,884,000 (Delhi) (1981).

deli /dɛli/ **delis**

NC A **deli** is the same as a **delicatessen**; used in informal American English.

deliberate, deliberates, deliberating, deliberated;
pronounced /dɪlɪbərət/ when it is an adjective and /dɪlɪbəreɪt/ when it is a verb.

1 ADJ If something that you do is **deliberate**, you intended to do it. *He told his mother a deliberate lie... Opposition leaders say that government descriptions of an imminent crisis are deliberate scaremongering.*
♦ **deliberately** ADV *The terms of the agreement were left deliberately vague.*

2 ADJ A **deliberate** action or movement is slow and careful. *His manner was quiet, his speech deliberate.*
♦ **deliberately** ADV *He climbed the stairs slowly and deliberately.*

3 V If you **deliberate**, you think about something carefully before making a decision. *We had been waiting for two days while the jury deliberated.*

deliberation /dɪlɪbəreɪʃn/ **deliberations**

1 NU **Deliberation** is careful consideration of a subject. *After considerable deliberation, I decided to accept the job.*

2 If you do something **with deliberation,** you do it slowly and carefully. *'It's the vacation,' she repeated, speaking with deliberation, as if to a stupid child.*

3 N PL **Deliberations** are formal discussions; a formal use. *I left the committee to its deliberations.*

deliberative /dɪlɪbərətɪv/

ADJ ATTRIB A **deliberative** group or organization has the task of considering and discussing problems or important questions. *...a deliberative assembly such as Congress.*

delicacy /dɛlɪkəsi/ **delicacies**

1 NU If something has **delicacy**, it is graceful and attractive. *...the delicacy of their features. ...a country where the feminine ideal is delicacy, slimness and grace.*

2 NU If you do or say something with **delicacy**, you do or say it carefully and tactfully because you do not want to offend anyone. *West Germany needs to show great delicacy and understanding in its dealings with Eastern Europe.*

3 NC A **delicacy** is a rare or expensive food, considered especially nice to eat. *Tunisians consider locusts a great delicacy.*

delicate /dɛlɪkət/

1 ADJ Something that is **delicate** is narrow and graceful or attractive. *She had long delicate fingers.*
♦ **delicately** ADV *...delicately veined pale skin.*

2 ADJ A **delicate** colour, taste, or smell is pleasant and not intense. *...a delicate pale cream colour.*

3 ADJ A **delicate** object is fragile and needs to be handled carefully. *...delicate china... Even a mild frost can damage the delicate flowers... Martin Redfern of our Science Unit describes the deployment of the shuttle's delicate cargo.*

4 ADJ A **delicate** movement is gentle, controlled, and not at all clumsy. *...delicate ballet steps... The patient is only in hospital for three days, as it's a delicate operation, but not a traumatic one.*
♦ **delicately** ADV *The princess took the pot delicately from him.*

5 ADJ A **delicate** situation or problem needs very careful, tactful treatment. *The state of relations between the two countries is still considered to be delicate... He described his mission as difficult and delicate... The debate has arisen at a delicate moment.*
♦ **delicately** ADV *...highly sensitive and delicately balanced economic systems.*

6 ADJ A **delicate** sense or a **delicate** scientific instrument is capable of noticing very small changes or differences. *Bees have a delicate sense of smell.*

7 ADJ Someone who is **delicate** is often ill; an old-fashioned use. *She was a very delicate child.*

delicatessen /dɛlɪkətɛsn/ **delicatessens**

NC A **delicatessen** is a shop that sells high quality foods such as cheeses and cold meats that have been imported from other countries. *The crew stopped at a delicatessen and got out to buy coffee and sandwiches.*

delicious /dɪlɪʃəs/

1 ADJ Food that is **delicious** has an extremely pleasant taste. *...a delicious cake... I thought his new rice bread was delicious.*

2 ADJ A **delicious** sensation is extremely pleasant; an informal use. *...a delicious feeling.* ♦ **deliciously** SUBMOD *The sun felt deliciously warm.*

delight /dɪlaɪt/ **delights, delighting, delighted**

1 NU **Delight** is a feeling of very great pleasure. *There was delight on the faces of the children... South Korea won the final match to the huge delight of their supporters.*

2 If someone **takes a delight** or **takes delight** in doing something, they get a lot of pleasure from doing it. *They took great delight in pelting him with tomatoes and custard pies.*

3 NC You can refer to someone or something that gives you great joy or pleasure as a **delight**. *Mrs Travers was a delight to interview.*

4 VO If something **delights** you, it gives you a lot of pleasure. *The thought of divorce neither distressed nor delighted her.*

5 V+in If you **delight** in something, you get a lot of pleasure from it. *Morris delighted in hard manual work.*

delighted /dɪlaɪtɪd/

ADJ If you are **delighted**, you are extremely pleased and excited about something. *He was grinning, delighted with his achievement.* ♦ **delightedly** ADV *She laughed delightedly.*

delightful /dɪlaɪtfl/

ADJ Someone or something that is **delightful** is very pleasant. *...a delightful room... My fellow humans really, with all their faults, are very delightful people... The narration is crisp and sharp, with*

delightful touches of humour. ◆ **delightfully** SUBMOD
...a delightfully smooth soup.

delimit /diːlɪmɪt/ **delimits, delimiting, delimited**
VO If you **delimit** something, you fix or establish its limits; a formal word. *We need to delimit the scope of our discussion.*

delineate /dɪlɪnieɪt/ **delineates, delineating, delineated**
1 VO If an idea or argument is **delineated**, it is described or defined in great detail; a formal use. *The principal problems can be delineated... Liberty must be firmly and clearly delineated.* ◆ **delineation** /dɪlɪnieɪʃn/ NU *...a detailed delineation of the principles.*
2 VO If you **delineate** a border, you say exactly where it is going to be. *Markers will be fixed later today, delineating the border between Egypt and Israel.* ◆ **delineation** NU *Much progress has been made on delineation of the border.*

delinquency /dɪlɪŋkwənsi/
NU **Delinquency** is criminal behaviour, especially that of young people. *...children taken into care because of their delinquency.*

delinquent /dɪlɪŋkwənt/ **delinquents**
ADJ You use **delinquent** to describe young people who repeatedly commit minor crimes; a formal word. *They arrested a group of delinquent youngsters who had been trying to terrorise schools.* ► Also NC *A few months of this may deter some potential delinquents.* ● See also **juvenile delinquent.**

delirious /dɪlɪriəs, dɪlɪəriəs/
1 ADJ Someone who is **delirious** is unable to think or speak in a rational way, usually because they have a fever. *I fell ill with a virus and spent the weekend in bed, delirious.*
2 ADJ **Delirious** also means extremely excited and happy. *He announced, to delirious applause, that all three hostages were free.*

delirium /dɪlɪriəm, dɪlɪəriəm/
NU If someone is suffering from **delirium**, they cannot think or speak in a rational way, usually because they have a fever. *The disease's main effects are on the brain and spinal chord, causing delirium and aggressive behaviour.*

delirium tremens /dɪlɪriəm triːmenz/
NU **Delirium tremens** is the same as **DTs.**

deliver /dɪlɪvə/ **delivers, delivering, delivered**
1 VO If you **deliver** something, you take it to someone's house or office. *He delivered newspapers as a boy... The association delivered a cheque for four hundred pounds to the headquarters to cover the outstanding legal fees.*
2 VO If you **deliver** a lecture or speech, you give it. *He delivered an emotional speech on the horrors of war... He was heckled by deputies, who delivered a barrage of questions from the floor.*
3 VO When someone **delivers** a baby, they help the woman who is giving birth. *The co-pilot delivered a premature baby girl in mid-flight... The baby had to be delivered by Caesarian operation.*
4 VorVO When you **deliver** something that you have promised to do or make, you do it or make it. *If Yanayev cannot deliver, his tenure at the Kremlin may be shorter than he thinks... People feel that our politicians are incapable of delivering a solution.*
5 VOA To **deliver** something also means to give it to someone; a formal use. *Chance delivered his enemy into his hands.*

delivery /dɪlɪvəri/ **deliveries**
1 NU **Delivery** is the bringing of letters, parcels, or goods to someone's house or office. *All goods must be paid for before delivery... We had to wait fourteen days for delivery.*
2 NU Someone's **delivery** of a speech is the way in which they give it. *His delivery was slow and ponderous.*
3 NCorNU **Delivery** is also the process of giving birth to a baby. *It was a simple, routine delivery... If the mother has a period, she's very unlikely to become pregnant in the first six months after delivery.*
4 NC A **delivery** of something is an amount of it that is delivered. *...an extra delivery of coal.*

dell /del/ **dells**
NC A **dell** is a small valley which has trees growing in it; a literary word.

delouse /diːlaʊs/ **delouses, delousing, deloused**
VO If you **delouse** a person or an animal, you get rid of lice from their body, hair, or fur.

delphinium /delfɪniəm/ **delphiniums**
NC A **delphinium** is a large garden plant with a tall stem and blue flowers which grow up its stem.

delta /deltə/ **deltas**
NC A **delta** is an area of flat land where a river spreads out into several smaller rivers before entering the sea. *Egypt has reclaimed all the low-lying areas of the river and the delta.*

delude /dɪluːd/ **deludes, deluding, deluded**
1 V-REFL If you **delude** yourself about something, you let yourself believe it, even though you know that is probably not true. *Had he deluded himself into believing that he could keep this action quiet?*
2 VO If you **delude** someone, you make them believe something that is not true. *Simon had deluded the child into believing that he shared his interest.*

deluge /deljuːdʒ/ **deluges, deluging, deluged**
1 NC A **deluge** is a sudden, very heavy fall of rain. *The deluge ended weeks of drought.*
2 N SING A **deluge** of things is a very large number of them which arrive at the same time. *Western embassies in Amman have been facing a deluge of visa applications from Palestinians who have left Kuwait.*
3 VO If you **are deluged** with things, a very large number of them arrive at the same time. *They were deluged with requests to play the song.*

delusion /dɪluːʒn/ **delusions**
NCorNU A **delusion** is a false belief. *Had it really happened? Was it a delusion?... He was under no delusions about the dangers involved... His latest work is based on a Navajo myth about a great warrior who conquers his people's spiritual enemies: despair, fear and delusion.*

de luxe /dɪlʌks/
ADJ You use **de luxe** to describe things that are better and more expensive than other things of the same kind. *...a de luxe version of the Ford Escort.*

delve /delv/ **delves, delving, delved**
1 VA If you **delve** into a question or problem, you try to discover more information about it. *She couldn't delve too deeply into the past.*
2 VA If you **delve** inside something such as a cupboard or bag, you search inside it.

demagogue /deməgɒg/ **demagogues**
NC A **demagogue** is a political leader who tries to win support by appealing to people's emotions rather than by using rational arguments; used showing disapproval. *He was denounced as an extremist demagogue.*

demand /dɪmɑːnd/ **demands, demanding, demanded**
1 VO, V+*to*-INF, or V-REPORT If you **demand** something, you ask for it very forcefully. *The hijackers demanded more fuel so that they could fly on elsewhere... I demand to see a doctor... She had been demanding that he visit her.*
2 V-QUOTE To **demand** also means to ask a question in a forceful way. *'What have I done?' he demanded.*
3 VO If a job or situation **demands** something, that thing is necessary for it. *He has most of the qualities demanded of a leader.*
4 NC A **demand** is a firm request for something. *Mr Rafsanjani reiterated Iran's demand for an unconditional Iraqi withdrawal from Kuwait.*
5 NU If there is **demand** for something, a lot of people want to buy it or have it. *The demand for health care is unlimited.*
6 NC The **demands** of an activity, process, or situation are the things that have to be done or provided for it. *...the demands of family life... The body's fuel demands are very low.*
● **Demand** is used in these phrases. ● If someone or something **makes demands** on you, they require you to do things which need a lot of time, energy, or money. *The system has always made heavy demands on those working in it.* ● If something is **in demand**, a lot of

people want to buy it or have it. *Other goods in demand include running shoes, track suits, and assorted sports wear.* ● If something is available **on demand**, you can have it whenever you ask for it. *These measures would allow married couples to obtain a divorce on demand.*

demanding /dɪmɑːndɪŋ/
1 ADJ A **demanding** job or task requires a lot of time, energy, or attention. *It's been a very difficult and demanding task.*
2 ADJ Someone who is **demanding** always wants something and is not easily satisfied. *...an impatient and demanding public.*

demarcate /diːmɑːkeɪt/ **demarcates, demarcating, demarcated**
VO If you **demarcate** something, you establish its boundaries or limits in order to separate it from other things of the same type; a formal word. *...the Berlin line, drawn by the British in the nineteenth century to demarcate Afghanistan's borders.*

demarcation /diːmɑːkeɪʃn/
N+N or NU **Demarcation** refers to a boundary or limit which separates two areas, groups, or activities. *...the demarcation lines between ethnic groups... There is no identifiable area of demarcation.*

demean /dɪmiːn/ **demeans, demeaning, demeaned**
V-REFL or VO If you **demean** yourself or **demean** something, you behave in a way which makes people have less respect for you or for that thing; a formal word. *He will lose face with the boss by having to demean himself in this way... He persistently betrayed and publicly demeaned his wife.*

demeaning /dɪmiːnɪŋ/
ADJ An action that is **demeaning** is one which makes people lose some of the respect that they have for you. *Addressing women as 'dear', 'girls', or 'the ladies' is demeaning and patronising.*

demeanour /dɪmiːnə/; spelt **demeanor** in American English.
NU Your **demeanour** is the way you behave, which gives people an impression of your character and feelings; a formal word. *Stefan Edberg won the hearts of the public with his placid, well-mannered demeanour.*

demented /dɪmentɪd/
ADJ Someone who is **demented** behaves in a wild or violent way, often because they are mad. *He thought that the deaf old person was also mildly demented.*

dementia /dɪmenʃə/
NU **Dementia** is a serious illness of the mind; a medical term. *Dementia and depression are often confused.*

demerara sugar /demərɛərə ʃugə/
NU **Demerara sugar** is a crunchy, light brown sugar which usually comes from the West Indies.

demerit /diːmerɪt/ **demerits**
NC The **demerits** of something are its faults or disadvantages; a formal word. *...a discussion on the merits and demerits of the play.*

demijohn /demɪdʒɒn/ **demijohns**
NC A **demijohn** is a large bottle with a short narrow neck, which is used in making wine.

demilitarize /diːmɪlɪtəraɪz/ **demilitarizes, demilitarizing, demilitarized**; also spelt **demilitarise**.
VO When an area is **demilitarized**, all military forces are removed from it. *He said Moscow wanted to demilitarize the Sino-Soviet border.* ● **demilitarization** /diːmɪlɪtəraɪzeɪʃn/ NU *Demilitarization would be the most important step... A substantial demilitarization of Europe would reduce the need for the two alliances.*

Demirel, Süleyman /suleɪmɑːn demɪrel/
Süleyman Demirel became Prime Minister of Turkey in 1991. He was Chairman of the Justice Party from 1964 to 1971, 1974 to 1978, and 1979 to 1980. He was detained after the 1980 coup and banned from political activities. In 1987 he became the leader of the True Path Party (DYP). Born: 1924.

demise /dɪmaɪz/
N SING+SUPP The **demise** of something or someone is their end or death; a formal word. *He said that the demise of classical languages would undermine educational standards.*

demist /diːmɪst/ **demists, demisting, demisted**
VO If you **demist** a car windscreen, you remove the condensation from it, usually by blowing warm air over it.

demo /deməʊ/ **demos**
NC A **demo** is the same as a **demonstration**; an informal word. *He is always going on demos.*

demobilized /diːməʊbəlaɪzd/ also spelt **demobilised**.
V-PASS When people are **demobilized**, they are released from one of the armed forces. *The troops were stationed around the country before being demobilised... The army was demobilized.* ● **demobilized** ADJ ATTRIB *Special classes are being planned to help prepare demobilised soldiers for the national university entrance exams.* ● **demobilization** /diːməʊbəlaɪzeɪʃn/ NU *HQ are dealing with the complex problem of demobilization.*

democracy /dɪmɒkrəsi/ **democracies**
1 NU **Democracy** is a system of government or organization in which the citizens or members choose leaders or make other important decisions by voting. *...an untiring struggle for democracy... Democracy has to be built up through carefully thought out legislation.*
2 NC A **democracy** is a country in which the people choose their government by voting for it. *The country has nearly always been a democracy.*

democrat /deməkræt/ **democrats**
1 NC A **Democrat** is a member or supporter of a political party which has the word 'democrat' or 'democratic' as part of its title. *Both Republicans and Democrats in the House of Representatives opposed the budget plan.*
2 NC A **democrat** is also a person who believes in democracy. *Their leader insists he is a democrat.*

democratic /deməkrætɪk/
1 ADJ A **democratic** country, organization, or system is one in which leaders are chosen or decisions are made by voting. *They called again for a return to a democratic government... The opposition parties demanded democratic elections.* ● **democratically** ADV *...a democratically elected government.*
2 ADJ **Democratic** is also used in the titles of some political parties. *...the Christian Democratic Party. ...the People's Democratic Party of Afghanistan.*

demographic /deməgræfɪk/
ADJ **Demographic** means relating to or concerning demography. *Several western countries are all suffering the same sort of demographic trends.*

demography /dɪmɒgrəfi/
NU **Demography** is the study of the changes in numbers of births, deaths, marriages, and diseases in a community over a period of time. *...dramatic changes in demography.*

demolish /dɪmɒlɪʃ/ **demolishes, demolishing, demolished**
1 VO When a building is **demolished**, it is knocked down, often because it is old or dangerous. *The old prison was demolished in 1890.*
2 VO If you **demolish** someone's idea, argument, or belief, you prove that it is completely wrong. *He soon demolished Mr Stewart's suggestions.*

demolition /deməlɪʃn/ **demolitions**
1 NU or NC The **demolition** of a building is the act of knocking it down. *The Old Vic was closed down and threatened with demolition... They protested at the planned demolitions.*
2 NU or NC The **demolition** of an argument, idea, or belief is the act of proving that it is incorrect. *...the demolition of the myth of Stalin's greatness.*

demon /diːmən/ **demons**
NC A **demon** is an evil spirit. *Frederica seemed sometimes possessed by a demon.*

demonic /dɪmɒnɪk/
ADJ Something that is **demonic** is evil. *...drawings of a demonic figure chewing a human leg... Abu Jihad may have been a demonic figure to many Israelis, but in PLO terms he was a staunch moderate.*

demonstrable /dɪmɒnstrəbl, demɒnstrəbl/
ADJ Something that is **demonstrable** can be shown to exist or to be true. *The economic advantages are clearly demonstrable.* ● **demonstrably** ADV *Their*

vehicles are demonstrably more reliable than ours.
demonstrate /dɛmənstreɪt/ **demonstrates,**
demonstrating, demonstrated
1 V O or V-REPORT To **demonstrate** a fact or theory
means to make it clear to people. *The confusion in
guerrilla ranks demonstrates the chronic divisions in
their alliance... Harry Ritchie's recent book
demonstrates that these ideas were an invention of the
media.*
2 V O or V-REPORT If you **demonstrate** something to
someone, you show them how to do it or how it works.
*He recently had the opportunity of demonstrating one
of the machines in Kenya... She has been
demonstrating how you make bread.*
3 V O If you **demonstrate** a skill, quality, or feeling,
you show that you have it. *She has not demonstrated
much generosity.*
4 V When people **demonstrate**, they take part in a
march or a meeting to show that they oppose or
support something. *They were part of a crowd
demonstrating against rent increases.*
demonstration /dɛmənstreɪʃn/ **demonstrations**
1 N C A **demonstration** is a public meeting or march
held by people to show that they oppose or support
something. *Four policemen and ten students were
injured during the demonstration.*
2 N C A **demonstration** of something is a talk in which
someone shows you how to do it or how it works. *Phil
Rickman went to the College for the Blind for a
demonstration of the machine by student Adama
Bangura.*
3 N C or N U A **demonstration** is also a proof that
something exists or that something such as a theory is
true. *...a demonstration of the army's strength. ...a
demonstration of support for Soviet arms control... It
was an unforgettable demonstration of the power of
reason.*
4 N C+SUPP or N U+SUPP A **demonstration** of a quality or
feeling is an expression of it. *...spontaneous
demonstrations of affection... The actor had a
tendency to play the soliloquy as a demonstration of
indignation rather than as an expression of self-disgust.*
demonstrative /dɪmɒnstrətɪv/
ADJ A **demonstrative** person shows their feelings freely
and openly. *After yesterday's subdued speech Mr
Gorbachev today gave a more demonstrative and
energetic performance.*
demonstrator /dɛmənstreɪtə/ **demonstrators**
1 N C A **demonstrator** is a person taking part in a
public meeting or march to show their opposition to
something or their support for something. *There was
a battle between police and demonstrators lasting all
afternoon.*
2 N C A **demonstrator** is also a person, usually in a
shop, who shows people how a machine or device
works by operating it themselves and explaining what
they are doing. *...a demonstrator of appliances at
stores and showrooms.*
demoralize /dɪmɒrəlaɪz/ **demoralizes, demoralizing,
demoralized**; also spelt **demoralise**.
V O If something **demoralizes** you, it makes you lose
confidence and feel depressed. *They disrupt, divide,
and demoralize whole communities.* ♦ **demoralized**
ADJ *...the stream of desperate and demoralized
people seeking work.* ♦ **demoralization** /dɪmɒrəlaɪzeɪʃn/
N U *...the growing mood of doubt and demoralisation.*
demote /dɪməʊt/ **demotes, demoting, demoted**
V O If someone in authority **demotes** you, they reduce
your rank, often as a punishment. *He was demoted
after criticising the slow rate of reform.*
demotic /dɪmɒtɪk/
1 ADJ **Demotic** is used to describe something that is
typical of or used by ordinary people; a formal use.
...television, that most demotic of the arts.
2 N U **Demotic** is the spoken form of the modern Greek
language.
demur /dɪmɜː/ **demurs, demurring, demurred**
V If you **demur**, you say that you do not agree with
something, or do not want to do it; a formal word.
Morris invited her out for a meal. She demurred.
demure /dɪmjʊə/
ADJ A woman who is **demure** is quiet and rather shy,

and behaves very correctly. *The demure former
English Language student has endeared herself to the
people of her adopted country by learning to speak
Hindi.*
demystify /diːmɪstɪfaɪ/ **demystifies, demystifying,
demystified**
V O If you **demystify** something, you make it easier to
understand by giving a clear explanation of it. *I
began working to demystify some of our society's
myths.*
den /dɛn/ **dens**
1 N C A **den** is the home of certain types of wild
animals such as foxes or lions.
2 N C Your **den** is a quiet room in your house where
you can go to study or carry on with a hobby without
being disturbed; used in American English. *Our
degrees from college hung side by side on the wall in
the den.*
3 N C A **den** is also a secret place where people meet,
usually for dishonest purposes. *His home had been
turned into what was described as a den of drug abuse
and trafficking.*
denationalize /diːnæʃ°nəlaɪz/ **denationalizes,
denationalizing, denationalized**; also spelt
denationalise.
V O If people **denationalize** an industry or business,
they transfer it into private ownership so that it is no
longer owned and controlled by the state. *There were
plans to denationalize the steel industry.*
denial /dɪnaɪəl/ **denials**
1 N C or N U A **denial** of something such as an accusation
is a statement that it is not true. *He made a personal
denial of all the charges against him. ...the
government's policy of denial.*
2 N U If there is **denial** of something that people think
they have a right to, they are not allowed to have it.
*They protested against the continued denial of civil
liberties.*
denier /dɛniə/
N U **Denier** is a measure of the fineness of the nylon or
silk thread that is used, for example, in making
stockings and tights. *...a pair of 15 denier stockings.*
denigrate /dɛnɪɡreɪt/ **denigrates, denigrating,
denigrated**
V O If you **denigrate** someone or something, you
criticize them in order to damage their reputation; a
formal word. *They denounced his attempts to
denigrate his country.* ♦ **denigration** /dɛnɪɡreɪʃn/ N U
...a campaign of denigration against the government.
denim /dɛnɪm/ **denims**
1 N U or N+N **Denim** is a thick cotton cloth used to make
clothes. *He was dressed casually in denim. ...denim
jeans.*
2 N PL **Denims** are denim trousers. *They're paying
top dollar for old Levi denims with that lived-in look.*
denizen /dɛnɪzən/ **denizens**
N C A **denizen** of a particular place is a person, animal,
or plant that lives or grows in this place; a literary
word. *...that aged denizen of Dye's Hole... The red
spider mite is a harmless denizen of orchards.*
Denmark /dɛnmɑːk/
The **Kingdom of Denmark** is a country in northern
Europe. It was occupied by Germany from 1940 to
1945. It is a member of the European Community and
NATO. Queen Margrethe II succeeded in 1972. Poul
Schlüter, of the Conservative People's Party (KF),
became Prime Minister in 1982. Denmark exports
meat and dairy products, transport equipment, and
fish. ♦ **Dane** /deɪn/ N **Danish** /deɪnɪʃ/ ADJ
■ *per capita GNP:* US$18,470 ■ *religion:* Christianity
(mainly Evangelical Lutheran) ■ *language:* Danish
■ *currency:* krone ■ *capital:* Copenhagen ■ *population:* 5
million (1989) ■ *size:* 43,093 square kilometres.
denomination /dɪnɒmɪneɪʃn/ **denominations**
1 N C A **denomination** is a religious group within a
particular religion. *...Christians of denominations
other than the Church of England.*
2 N C The **denomination** of a bank note or coin is the
amount of money that it is worth. *In the past year
new bank notes appeared, first in denominations of five
thousand córdobas, then twenty thousand. ...an acute
shortage of small denomination coins.*

denominational /dɪnɒmɪneɪʃəʰnəl/
ADJ **Denominational** institutions, groups, or events belong to or are organized by a particular religious denomination. *...Jewish denominational schools.*

denominator /dɪnɒmɪneɪtə/ **denominators**
NC A **denominator** is the number which appears under the line in a fraction. It is the amount by which you should divide the top number. *In the fraction ⅜ 8 is the denominator.* ● See also **lowest common denominator.**

denote /dɪnəʊt/ **denotes, denoting, denoted**; a formal word.
1 VOor V-REPORT If one thing **denotes** another, it is a sign or indication of it. *The badges come in 20 different colours and shapes, denoting the status of the wearer... The soldiers stopped cars with blue license plates, denoting their occupants came from the West Bank.*
2 VO What a word or name **denotes** is what it means or refers to. *The 'retro' part of the name denotes that the virus has a slightly different structure.*

denouement /deɪnuːmɒnⁿ/ **denouements**; also spelt **dénouement.**
NC A **denouement** is the explanation of something that has previously been unclear or that has been kept secret, especially at the end of a book or a play. *It was the preparation for this denouement in the second act that impressed me most.*

denounce /dɪnaʊns/ **denounces, denouncing, denounced**
VO If you **denounce** someone or something, you criticize them severely and publicly. *He has denounced the action as illegal... Anti-apartheid groups denounced Mrs Mandela last year.*

dense /dens/ **denser, densest**
1 ADJ Something that is **dense** contains a lot of things or people in a small area. *...a dense forest inhabited by dangerous beasts... The seals leave the water and gather in dense herds on the shorelines.* ◆ **densely** ADV *...the most densely populated region in the country.*
2 ADJ **Dense** fog or smoke is thick and difficult to see through. *The aircraft came down in dense freezing fog.*
3 ADJ A **dense** substance is very heavy. *Meteors are made up of fairly dense material.*
4 ADJ PRED If you say that someone is **dense**, you mean they are stupid and take a long time to understand things; an informal use. *He is so dense that he never understands anything I say to him.*

density /densəti/ **densities**
1 NU+SUPPor NC+SUPP **Density** is the extent to which something is filled with people and things. *Traffic density was increasing... Rwanda has one of the highest population densities in the world.*
2 NUorNC The **density** of a substance or object is the relation of its mass to its volume; a technical use. *Heating air lessens its density. ...cells of different sizes and densities.*

dent /dent/ **dents, denting, dented**
1 VO If you **dent** something, you damage its surface by hitting it and making a hollow in it. *I drove into a post and dented the bumper slightly... Hailstones the size of dimes dented cars and sidings.* ◆ **dented** ADJ *...a dented green Cadillac.*
2 NC A **dent** is a hollow in the surface of something which has been caused by hitting it. *There is a dent in the side of the crown, probably from bumping against the packing case.*
3 VO If something **dents** your pride, ideas, or hopes, it makes you realize that you are not as good or successful as you thought. *His image as a hero has been seriously dented... The budget and other problems have dented his popularity... Their prestige in the Arab world has been dented by the war... The fighting has dented hopes for a sustained ceasefire.*
4 NC If one thing makes a **dent** in another, it reduces it considerably. *It proved a severe dent for their confidence and pride... We must help the world's poorer farmers to grow enough food to make a real dent in the international hunger problem.*

dental /dentl/
ADJ ATTRIB **Dental** is used to describe things relating to

teeth. *...free dental treatment.*

dentist /dentɪst/ **dentists**
NC A **dentist** is a person qualified to treat people's teeth. *One dentist has tried coating dentures to improve their ease of use.*

dentistry /dentɪstri/
NU **Dentistry** is the work done by a dentist. *Today dentistry concentrates more and more on retaining the original tooth.*

dentures /dentʃəz/
N PL **Dentures** are false teeth. *Full dentures today are usually made of acrylic plastic.*

denude /dɪnjuːd/ **denudes, denuding, denuded**
VO If something is **denuded**, everything is taken off it or from it; a formal word. *The Christmas tree was soon denuded of its parcels.*

denunciation /dɪnʌnsieɪʃn/ **denunciations**
NUorNC **Denunciation** of someone or something is severe public criticism of them. *There has been enough denunciation of Government proposals. ...repeating their denunciations of violence.*

deny /dɪnaɪ/ **denies, denying, denied**
1 VO, V+ING, or V-REPORT If you **deny** something such as an accusation, you say that it is not true. *The President has strenuously denied the accusation... Both men, who denied the claims, have since disappeared... The general denied that the army had violated the ceasefire... Green denied doing anything illegal.*
2 VOor VOO If you **deny** someone something that they want or have a right to, you do not let them have it. *Freedom is denied to the young... A number of people have been denied the right to travel outside Kenya.*

deodorant /diːəʊdərənt/ **deodorants**
N MASS **Deodorant** is a substance that you put on your body to reduce the smell of perspiration.

deodorize /diːəʊdəraɪz/ **deodorizes, deodorizing, deodorized**; also spelt **deodorise.**
VO If you **deodorize** something, you hide or remove unpleasant smells from it; a formal word. *The generator uses minute quantities of ozone to sterilise and deodorise refrigerated food vehicles.* ◆ **deodorized** ADJ *Deodorized towels can cause allergic reactions.*

depart /dɪpɑːt/ **departs, departing, departed**
1 V To **depart** from a place means to leave it. *The rescue ships departed from the area as quickly as possible... She prepared to depart for Italy.*
2 V+from If you **depart** from the normal way of doing something, you do something slightly different. *He said he would depart from tradition by releasing the text of the letter.*

departed /dɪpɑːtɪd/
ADJ **Departed** friends or relatives are people who have died; a formal word. *Let us pray for our departed friends.*

department /dɪpɑːtmənt/ **departments**
NC+SUPP A **department** is one of the sections of a large shop or organization such as a university. *...the cosmetics department of Harrods. ...a Professor in the English department. ...the Department of Health.*

departmental /diːpɑːtmentl/
ADJ ATTRIB **Departmental** is used to describe the activities, responsibilities, and possessions of a department, for example a government department, or a department in a large organization. *The departmental office was full of people... There's a departmental meeting this afternoon.*

department store, department stores
NC A **department store** is a large shop which is divided into lots of sections, each of which sells a particular type of thing. *...the famous London department store, Harrods.*

departure /dɪpɑːtʃə/ **departures**
1 NCorNU **Departure** is the act of leaving a place. *...the week before their departure... Before departure, Iliescu made a statement.*
2 NC If an action is a **departure** from what was previously planned or what is usually done, it is different from it. *Does the budget represent a departure from stated Government policy?*

depend /dɪpend/ **depends, depending, depended**
1 V+onor upon If you **depend** on someone or something,

you need them to survive. *Zambia depends on foreign aid to fund nearly all of its development programmes... These factories depend upon natural resources.*
2 V+on or upon If you can **depend** on someone or something, you know that they will help you when you need them. *Cuba could also depend on the Soviet Union to buy its produce... In-flight computers can lead pilots to depend on them for all their assessments and decisions... The Rapid Reaction Corps is likely to depend upon US air support.*
3 V+on or V-REPORT If you say that one thing **depends** on another, you mean that the first thing will be affected or determined by the second. *The success of the meeting depends largely on whether the chairman is efficient... Depending on what's happened to the signal, you can tell what kind of rocks are under the ground.*
● **Depend** is used in these phrases. ● You use an expression such as '**It depends**' to indicate that you cannot give a clear answer to a question because the answer will be affected or determined by other factors. *'What will you do?' 'I don't know, it depends.'... It all depends on what you mean by democracy.* ● You use **depending on** to say that what happens varies according to the circumstances. *This training takes a variable time, depending on the chosen speciality.*

dependable /dɪpɛndəbl/
ADJ If someone or something is **dependable**, you know that they will always act consistently or do what you need or expect them to do. *...a dependable sort of car... He's very organized and dependable.*

dependant /dɪpɛndənt/ **dependants**; also spelt **dependent**.
NC Your **dependants** are the people who you support financially, such as your children. *The latest tax reforms treat married women on a par with their husbands, instead of being their dependants.*

dependence /dɪpɛndəns/
NU+on or upon **Dependence** on something is a constant need for it in order to be able to live or work properly. *...the increasing dependence of police forces on computers. ...this government's dependence on western economic aid. ...the difference between a dependence upon the United States and a partnership with the United States.*

dependency /dɪpɛndənsi/ **dependencies**
NC A **dependency** is a country which is controlled by another country. *Britain was a Roman dependency for a long period.*

dependent /dɪpɛndənt/
ADJ If you are **dependent** on someone or something, you need them to survive. *West Europe was still heavily dependent on Middle Eastern oil.*

depict /dɪpɪkt/ **depicts, depicting, depicted**
1 VO If you **depict** someone or something, you draw them in a painting or cartoon. *...an art calendar depicting some ancient legend.*
2 VO To **depict** someone or something also means to describe them in words. *Women are constantly depicted as inferior to men.*

depiction /dɪpɪkʃn/ **depictions**
NC or NU A **depiction** of something is a picture of it or a written description of it. *...depictions of the burial of Christ. ...the media depiction of the Havana summit.*

depilatory /dɪpɪlətəⁱri/
ADJ ATTRIB **Depilatory** is used to describe something which removes hair from your body. *...a jar of depilatory cream.*

deplete /dɪpliːt/ **depletes, depleting, depleted**
VO If you **deplete** something, you reduce the amount of it that is available to be used. *We must be careful as we deplete our stocks of resources.* ◆ **depletion** /dɪpliːʃn/ NU *...the depletion of raw material reserves.*

deplorable /dɪplɔːrəbl/
ADJ If you say that something is **deplorable**, you mean that it is extremely bad or unpleasant; a formal word. *The conditions in the prison were deplorable.*

deplore /dɪplɔː/ **deplores, deploring, deplored**
VO If you **deplore** something, you think that it is wrong or immoral; a formal word. *The Social Services Secretary, Mr John Moore, said he deplored*

the action of the strikers.

deploy /dɪplɔɪ/ **deploys, deploying, deployed**
VO To **deploy** troops or resources means to organize or position them so that they are ready for immediate action. *Oman could deploy regular forces of some 15,000.*

deployment /dɪplɔɪmənt/
NU The **deployment** of troops, resources, or equipment is the organization and preparation of them so that they are in a position or condition where they are ready for immediate action. *...protests against the deployment of American cruise missiles in Berkshire.*

depopulate /diːpɒpjʊleɪt/ **depopulates, depopulating, depopulated**
VO If something **depopulates** an area, it greatly reduces the number of people living there. *The arrival of the conquerors depopulated large parts of Central and South America.* ◆ **depopulated** ADJ *The landscape has a depopulated and dreamlike air.* ◆ **depopulation** /diːpɒpjʊleɪʃn/ NU *...the depopulation of the city centre.*

deport /dɪpɔːt/ **deports, deporting, deported**
VO When a government **deports** foreigners, it sends them out of the country because they have committed a crime or because they are there without official permission. *He was deported to France.* ◆ **deportation** /diːpɔːteɪʃn/ **deportations** NU or NC *They were prepared to risk deportation... The deportations were against international law.*

deportee /diːpɔːtiː/ **deportees**
NC A **deportee** is someone who is being deported. *Both Egypt and Jordan have said that they will not accept the deportees.*

deportment /dɪpɔːtmənt/
NU Your **deportment** is the way you behave, especially the way you walk and move; a formal word. *...an age when elegance of appearance and deportment were important.*

depose /dɪpəʊz/ **deposes, deposing, deposed**
VO If a ruler or leader is **deposed**, they are removed from their position by force. *The military ruler was deposed, and forced into exile in neighbouring Egypt.*

deposit /dɪpɒzɪt/ **deposits, depositing, deposited**
1 VO A If you **deposit** something somewhere, you put it there, often so that it will be safe until it is needed again. *He deposited the case in the left luggage office.*
2 NC A **deposit** is a sum of money which you put in a bank account or other savings account. *Most banks are paying 11.25 % on deposits of more than £5,000.*
3 NC A **deposit** is also money given in part payment for goods or services. *We've saved enough for the deposit on a house.*
4 NC A **deposit** is also a sum of money which you give a person you rent or hire something from. The money is returned to you if you do not damage the goods.
5 VO If a substance is **deposited** somewhere, it is left there as a result of a chemical or geological process. *Layers of sand were deposited on top of the peat.*
6 NC A **deposit** is an amount of a substance that has been left somewhere as a result of a chemical or geological process. *...rich mineral deposits.*

deposit account, deposit accounts
NC A **deposit account** is a type of bank account in which the amount of money in it increases because it earns interest. *The attraction of a building society deposit account paying twelve per cent interest per year has increased.*

deposition /depəzɪʃn/ **depositions**
1 NU **Deposition** is a geological process which causes layers of minerals to be formed in the ground or on the surface of the earth over a period of time; a technical term. *For the most part rocks are not built up by deposition but broken down by erosion.*
2 NU The **deposition** of a political leader is the removal of him or her from office. *...after the actual deposition of Haile Selassie in September 1974.*
3 NC A **deposition** is a formal written statement, made for example by a witness to a crime, which can be used in a court of law if the witness cannot be present. *The accused didn't say anything as he heard the deposition submitted by the police.*

depot /dɛpəʊ/ **depots**
1 NC A **depot** is a place where goods and vehicles are kept when they are not being used. *A military inquiry is to be held into a fire at an army equipment depot.*
2 NC A **depot** is also a bus station or a railway station; used in American English. *The bus traffic at the depot in downtown Providence is still busy.*

depraved /dɪpreɪvd/
ADJ Someone who is **depraved** is morally bad. *Few mothers are depraved enough to kill their children.*

depravity /dɪprævəti/
NU **Depravity** is moral corruption; a formal word. *The terrorists have sunk to new levels of wickedness and depravity.*

deprecate /dɛprəkeɪt/ **deprecates, deprecating, deprecated**
VO If you **deprecate** something, you speak critically about it because you disapprove of it; a formal word. *They definitely deprecated education for the masses.*

deprecating /dɛprəkeɪtɪŋ/
ADJ A **deprecating** attitude, gesture, or remark shows that you think something is not very good; a formal word. *Tom waved a deprecating hand... His deprecating air of educated superiority seemed suddenly suspect to her.*

deprecatory /dɛprəkeɪtəri/
ADJ A **deprecatory** attitude or gesture shows that you disapprove of something. *With a deprecatory grunt, Mrs Haze stooped to pick up the offending sock.*

depreciate /dɪpriːʃieɪt/ **depreciates, depreciating, depreciated**
V When something **depreciates**, it loses some of its value. *...an investment that was certain to depreciate.*
◆ **depreciation** /dɪpriːʃieɪʃn/ NU+SUPP *...the depreciation of currency.*

depredation /dɛprədeɪʃn/ **depredations**
NC or NU **Depredations** are attacks which are made in order to steal or destroy something; an old-fashioned word. *...the depredations of the enemy... They expressed grave concern about the vulnerability of the Kampuchean people to the depredations of the Khmer Rouge.*

depress /dɪprɛs/ **depresses, depressing, depressed**
1 VO If something **depresses** you, it makes you feel sad and disappointed. *But the worst blow is the gas rationing, that really depresses people... He said that the war depressed him more each day... He was disoriented and depressed, and found it hard to concentrate... Americans were depressed and divided by the Watergate scandal.*
2 VO If something **depresses** prices, wages, or figures, it causes them to fall in value. *Higher than expected retail sales figures in the United States depressed share prices.*

depressed /dɪprɛst/
1 ADJ If you are **depressed**, you feel sad and disappointed. *We all knew that he was depressed.*
2 ADJ A place that is **depressed** does not have as much business or employment as it used to. *You only have to look at depressed areas and unemployment 'blackspots' to see the stress people are under.*

depressing /dɪprɛsɪŋ/
ADJ Something that is **depressing** makes you feel sad and disappointed. *This was depressing news.*
◆ **depressingly** SUBMOD *It was all depressingly clear.*

depression /dɪprɛʃn/ **depressions**
1 NU or NC **Depression** is a mental state in which someone feels unhappy and has no energy or enthusiasm. *For a time he was in hospital suffering from depression... These depressions can occur in both summer and winter.*
2 NC A **depression** is a time when there is very little economic activity, which results in a lot of unemployment. *...the depression of the 1930's.*
3 NC On a surface, a **depression** is an area which is lower than the rest of the surface. *There was a depression on the seat of the armchair where she had been sitting.*

depressive /dɪprɛsɪv/ **depressives**
1 ADJ Something that is **depressive** causes you to feel sad and lacking in energy. *...the depressive streak in her nature.*

2 NC A **depressive** person is someone who often suffers from depression. *Contrary to expectations, depressive patients often improve after a sleepless night.*

deprivation /dɛprəveɪʃn/ **deprivations**
NU or NC If you suffer **deprivation**, you do not have or are prevented from having something that you want or need. *They suffer from deprivation of political and civil rights. ...several reports of torture, including severe beatings and sleep deprivation... He has urged Poles to accept the necessity of these deprivations and sacrifices.*

deprive /dɪpraɪv/ **deprives, depriving, deprived**
VO+of If you **deprive** someone of something, you take it away from them or prevent them from having it. *He said that the war was depriving thousands of people of food.*

deprived /dɪpraɪvd/
ADJ If you describe someone or something as **deprived**, you mean they do not have the things that you consider to be essential in life. *Some of the remaining money will be used to help deprived youngsters... He was engaged in voluntary social work in a deprived area of London.*

dept, depts
Dept is a written abbreviation for 'department'.

depth /dɛpθ/ **depths**
1 NU or NC The **depth** of something such as a river is the distance between its top and bottom surfaces. *None of the lakes was more than a few yards in depth. ...analysing the temperature at different depths.*
2 NU or NC The **depth** of a solid structure is the distance between its front and back. *The depth of the cupboard was 40 centimetres.*
3 NU+SUPP The **depth** of an emotion is its great intensity. *The depth of his concern was evident enough.*
4 N PL The **depths** of the ocean are the parts which are a long way below the surface. *Submarines enable people to explore the depths of the sea.*
5 N PL+SUPP The **depths** of an area are the parts of it that are very remote. *...his home in the depths of the English countryside. ...the depths of the jungle.*
6 N PL+SUPP In the **depths** of winter means in the middle of winter, when it is coldest. *...queueing for a bus in the depths of a Russian winter.*
● **Depth** is used in these phrases. ● If you deal with a subject in **depth**, you deal with it very thoroughly and consider all the aspects of it. *They'd analysed the current crisis in depth.* ● If you are out of your **depth**, you are in water that is deeper than you are tall and so you have to swim. *Don't go out of your depth in the sea.* ● You can also say that you are out of your **depth** when you are trying to deal with something that is too difficult for you. *They were out of their depth in the World Cup finals in Italy.* ● If you are in the **depths of** despair, you are extremely unhappy. *Karmal spoke of his heavy heart and the depths of his despair while away from his homeland.*

depth charge, depth charges
NC A **depth charge** is a type of bomb which explodes under water and which is used especially to destroy enemy submarines. *They dropped a depth charge after detecting signs of an intruding vessel.*

deputation /dɛpjuteɪʃn/ **deputations**
NC A **deputation** is a small group of people sent to speak or act on behalf of others. *The farmers are to send a deputation to the Agriculture Minister.*

deputize /dɛpjutaɪz/ **deputizes, deputizing, deputized**; also spelt **deputise**.
V+for If you **deputize** for someone, you do something on their behalf, such as attend a meeting or give a speech. *The budget was delivered by Mr Lynch, deputizing for Mr Haughey.*

deputy /dɛpjuti/ **deputies**
NC or N+N A **deputy** is the second most important person in an organization or department. Someone's deputy often acts on their behalf when they are not there. *He and his deputy co-operated well. ...the Deputy Chairman of the Commission.*

derail /dɪreɪl/ **derails, derailing, derailed**
VO If a train is **derailed**, it comes off the track on

which it is running. *A morning passenger train was derailed about thirty miles west of Copenhagen.*

derailment /dɪˈreɪlmənt/ **derailments**
NCorNU A **derailment** is an accident in which a train comes off the track on which it is running. *British Rail are carrying out an inquiry today into the cause of the derailment... In one incident, railway tracks being torn up caused a derailment.*

deranged /dɪˈreɪndʒd/
ADJ Someone who is **deranged** behaves in a wild or strange way, often as a result of mental illness. *He was almost killed by a deranged gunman.*

derby, derbies; pronounced /ˈdɑːbi/ for the meanings in paragraphs 1 and 2 and /ˈdɜːbi/ for the meaning in paragraph 3.
1 N PROP The **Derby** is a famous English horse race which takes place every year. *...an outstanding horse who won the Derby earlier in the month.*
2 NC A **derby** is a sporting event between teams from the same area or city. *52,000 fans turned out for the derby between Liverpool and Everton.*
3 NC In American English, a **derby** is a bowler hat. *...a round-faced old man in a derby and a shabby overcoat.*

derelict /ˈderəlɪkt/
ADJ A **derelict** building or area of land has not been used for some time and is in a bad condition. *Middlesbrough is now a depressing place, full of derelict industrial sites.*

dereliction /ˌderəˈlɪkʃn/
NU If a building or a piece of land is in a state of **dereliction**, it is deserted or abandoned. *The building is still much as it was after being salvaged from dereliction.*

dereliction of duty
NU **Dereliction of duty** is deliberate or accidental failure to do what you should do as part of your job; a formal expression. *I call that a grave dereliction of duty.*

deride /dɪˈraɪd/ **derides, deriding, derided**
VO If you **deride** someone or something, you talk about them in a way that shows that you think they are stupid or have no value. *They have repeatedly derided Hungary's political reforms.*

de rigueur /də rɪˈɡɜː/
ADJ PRED A possession or habit that is **de rigueur** is fashionable and therefore necessary for anyone who wants to avoid being considered old-fashioned or unusual. *Calculators as thin as biscuits are de rigueur for businessmen.*

derision /dɪˈrɪʒn/
NU If you speak of someone or something with **derision**, you show contempt for them. *They speak with derision of amateurs.*

derisive /dɪˈraɪsɪv/
ADJ A **derisive** noise, expression, or remark shows the contempt that you have for someone or something. *Maureen rocked with derisive laughter.* ◆ **derisively** ADV *Desiree snorted derisively.*

derisory /dɪˈraɪsəri/
ADJ Something that is **derisory** is so small or inadequate that it seems silly or not worth considering. *Fines for cruelty to animals are derisory.*

derivation /ˌderɪˈveɪʃn/ **derivations**
NC The **derivation** of something such as a word is the original form or meaning of it. *The derivation of ecology is from the Greek words oikus, meaning 'house', and logos, meaning 'understanding'.*

derivative /dɪˈrɪvətɪv/ **derivatives**
1 NC A **derivative** is something which has developed from something else. *...the modern derivative of the fairy story. ...crack, the highly addictive derivative of cocaine.*
2 ADJ A work or idea that is **derivative** is not new or original, but copies ideas that have been used before; used showing disapproval. *He provides a useful, if rather derivative, survey of the way in which Western artists have treated the nude... You can't be derivative if you're unfamiliar with the works of others.*

derive /dɪˈraɪv/ **derives, deriving, derived**
1 VO If you **derive** a particular feeling from someone or something, you get it from them; a formal use.

The East Germans derived considerable amusement from the predicament of their capitalist neighbours.
2 V-ERG+*from* If something **derives** or is **derived** from another thing, it comes from that thing. *Archbishop Tutu said his theological position derives from the church... The word 'detergent' is derived from the Latin word for 'cleaner'.*

dermatitis /ˌdɜːməˈtaɪtɪs/
NU **Dermatitis** is a disease which makes your skin red and painful.

derogatory /dɪˈrɒɡətəˀri/
ADJ A **derogatory** remark expresses your low opinion of someone or something. *...an interview in which he was quoted as making derogatory remarks about the Prime Minister.*

derrick /ˈderɪk/ **derricks**
1 NC A **derrick** is a simple crane that is used to move cargo on a ship.
2 NC A **derrick** is also a tower built over an oil well which is used to raise and lower the drill.

derv /dɜːv/
NU **Derv** is the fuel that is used in diesel cars and lorries. *The industry consider that derv has been too expensive.*

descale /ˌdiːˈskeɪl/ **descales, descaling, descaled**
VO When you **descale** a kettle, you remove the hard layer which has formed inside it as a result of the action of the chemicals that are in water.

descant /ˈdeskænt/ **descants**
NC A **descant** is a tune which is played or sung above the main tune in a piece of music. *I thought we'd try the descant in the second verse only.*

descend /dɪˈsend/ **descends, descending, descended**
1 V or VO If you **descend** or if you **descend** something, you move downwards; a formal use. *The valley becomes more exquisite as we descend... They descended the stairs.*
2 V If silence or unhappiness **descends** on people or places, it occurs or starts to affect them; a literary use. *Gloom began to descend on all of them.*
3 V If people **descend** on a place, they arrive suddenly. *The whole family descended on us without any warning.*
4 V+*to* If you **descend** to something, you behave in a way that is considered unworthy of you. *All too soon they will descend to spreading scandal and gossip.*

descendant /dɪˈsendənt/ **descendants**
NC Someone's **descendants** are the people in later generations who are related to them. *Many of these settlers are the descendants of convicts.*

descended /dɪˈsendɪd/
ADJ PRED+*from* A person who is **descended** from someone who lived a long time ago is related to them. *...a town full of families like his own, descended from Norwegian settlers.*

descending /dɪˈsendɪŋ/
ADJ ATTRIB When a group of things is arranged in **descending** order, each thing is smaller or less important than the thing before it. *The book lists, in descending order, Britain's millionaires.*

descent /dɪˈsent/ **descents**
1 NC A **descent** is a movement from a higher to a lower level. *He saw an aircraft making a very steep descent.*
2 NU+SUPP Your **descent** is your family's origins. *...Americans of Irish descent.*

describe /dɪˈskraɪb/ **describes, describing, described**
1 VO or V-REPORT When you **describe** something, you say what it is like or what happened. *We asked the author how she would describe her book... I can't describe my feelings when I was led out handcuffed in front of my friends and colleagues... He described how he was kidnapped... They were so seriously injured that they could not describe what happened.*
2 VO or V-REPORT If you **describe** a person or place, you say in words what they look like. *Can you describe your son?... It isn't easy to describe, but I can tell you the path ascends through a winding valley.*
3 VO+*as* If you **describe** someone or something as having a particular quality or being of a particular type, you say that they have that quality or are of that type. *He described Mr Austin's idea as ludicrous... He*

described himself as a political moderate... 79 per cent of those questioned said they would describe Britain as either fairly or very racist.

description /dɪskrɪpʃn/ **descriptions**
1 NC+SUPP A **description** is an account of what someone or something is like. *The police have issued a description of a man arrested at the scene... Quetel's description of life in the prisons is vivid and compassionate. ...a detailed description of the house.*
2 NU **Description** is the act of saying what someone or something is like. *The relationships in his family are so complex that description is almost impossible.*
3 N SING Something of a particular **description** is something of that kind. *Her dress was too tight to have concealed a weapon of any description.*

descriptive /dɪskrɪptɪv/
ADJ **Descriptive** writing describes what something is like. *...a descriptive article about Venice.*

desecrate /desɪkreɪt/ **desecrates, desecrating, desecrated**
VO If someone **desecrates** something considered sacred or special, they deliberately damage it. *The men in Rodez had desecrated the church.*
♦ **desecration** /desɪkreɪʃn/ NU *...the desecration of religious sites.*

desegregate /diːsegrɪgeɪt/ **desegregates, desegregating, desegregated**
VO To **desegregate** something such as a place, institution, or service means to officially cease keeping the people who use it in separate groups according to their race, religion, or sex. *...new legislation to desegregate public facilities.*

desensitize /diːsensɪtaɪz/ **desensitizes, desensitizing, desensitized**; also spelt **desensitise**
VO If you **desensitize** someone, you cause them to react less strongly than they used to react to things such as pain, anxiety, or other people's suffering. *A parent doesn't want the school to desensitize his or her children.*

desert, deserts, deserting, deserted; pronounced /dezət/ when it is a noun and /dɪzɜːt/ when it is a verb.
1 NCorNU A **desert** is a large area of land where there is very little water or rain and very few plants. *...the Sahara Desert. ...large areas of desert.*
2 VO If people **desert** a place, they leave it and it becomes empty. *The medical staff have deserted the city's main hospital.* ♦ **deserted** ADJ *...a deserted village.*
3 VO If someone **deserts** you, they leave you and no longer help or support you. *She deserted her family.*
♦ **desertion** /dɪzɜːʃn/ NU *She could get a divorce on the grounds of desertion.*
4 V If someone **deserts** from the armed forces, they leave without permission. *Many conscripts deserted... They have deserted from his army to join the rebels.*
♦ **desertion, desertions** NUorNC *...the desertion of young conscripts... Desertions have been very common.*

deserter /dɪzɜːtə/ **deserters**
NC A **deserter** is someone who leaves their job in the armed forces without permission. *...a deserter from the British army.*

desertification /dɪzɜːtɪfɪkeɪʃn/
NU **Desertification** happens when a large area of fertile land becomes a desert. *Drought and desertification can be partly attributed to deforestation.*

desert island, desert islands
NC A **desert island** is a small tropical island, where nobody lives. *...marooned on a desert island.*

deserve /dɪzɜːv/ **deserves, deserving, deserved**
VOorV+to-INF If you say that someone **deserves** a reward or punishment, you mean that they should be given it because of their qualities or actions. *These people deserve recognition for their talents... He deserves to get the sack.*

deserved /dɪzɜːvd/
ADJ You say that something is **deserved** when the person getting it is worthy of it. *It was a richly deserved honour.* ♦ **deservedly** /dɪzɜːvɪdli/ ADV *The first prize was won, most deservedly, by Mrs Jones.*

deserving /dɪzɜːvɪŋ/
ADJ If someone or something is **deserving**, they should be helped; a formal word. *There are hordes of deserving people in this world.*

desiccated /desɪkeɪtɪd/
1 ADJ **Desiccated** food has been dried in order to preserve it. *...desiccated coconut.*
2 ADJ Something that is **desiccated** has lost all the moisture that was in it; a literary use. *...hunks of desiccated skin and fat.*

design /dɪzaɪn/ **designs, designing, designed**
1 VO When you **design** something new, you plan what it should be like. *The house was designed by local builders... The company will design and develop new engines for small aircraft.*
2 NU **Design** is the process of planning the form of a new object. *...graphic and industrial design.*
3 NU The **design** of a manufactured object is its form or the way it has been made. *The awkward design of the handles made it difficult to use.*
4 NC A **design** is a drawing of the proposed form of a new object. *He is submitting a design for the new building.*
5 NC A **design** is also a decorative pattern of lines, flowers, or shapes. *The designs on the stamps all come from the original drawings in the library.*
6 V-PASS If something **is designed** for a purpose, it is intended for that purpose. *The laws were designed to protect women... Tests have been designed to assess mathematical ability.*
7 N PL If you have **designs** on something, you want to have it and are planning to get it; used showing disapproval. *The Soviet Union and France have no imperialist designs on the Middle East. ...accusations that Hungary was harbouring territorial designs on its neighbour.*

designate, designates, designating, designated; pronounced /dezɪgneɪt/ when it is a verb and /dezɪgnət/ when it is an adjective.
1 VO When you **designate** someone or something, you formally give them a description or name. *The area was designated a national monument.*
2 VO When you **designate** someone to do a particular job, you formally choose them for that job. *I had been designated to read the lesson.*
3 ADJafterN **Designate** is used to describe someone who has been formally chosen to do a job, but has not yet started doing it. *Mr Bell had been Attorney General designate.*

designation /dezɪgneɪʃn/ **designations**
NC A **designation** is a description or name given to a person or thing; a formal word. *The plane's official designation is SR-71.*

designer /dɪzaɪnə/ **designers**
1 NC A **designer** is a person whose job involves planning the form of a new object. *His real gift was as a designer. ...the designer of Liverpool Cathedral, Sir Gilbert Scott. ...a dress designer.*
2 ADJ ATTRIB **Designer** clothes are expensive, fashionable clothes made by a famous designer or fashion house. *She dressed in expensive designer clothes, travelled on yachts, and collected jewellery... On some days, he wears Italian designer suits.*

desirable /dɪzaɪərəbl/
1 ADJ Something that is **desirable** is worth having or doing. *After an injury an X-ray is often desirable... A fur coat used to be regarded as one of the most glamorous and desirable of all possessions.*
♦ **desirability** /dɪzaɪərəbɪləti/ NU *Both sides were agreed on the desirability of resuming regular meetings.*
2 ADJ Someone who is **desirable** is sexually attractive. *They must keep healthy and fit and handsome and desirable.*

desire /dɪzaɪə/ **desires, desiring, desired**
1 VOorV+to-INF If you **desire** something, you want it. *They desire peace... He passionately desired to continue his career in politics.* ♦ **desired** ADJ *This did not produce the desired effect.*
2 NC A **desire** is a wish to do or have something. *He had not the slightest desire to go on holiday. ...his desire for justice.*

3 VO If you **desire** someone, you want to have sex with them. *He still desired her.*
4 NUorNC **Desire** for someone is a feeling of wanting to have sex with them. *She no longer has any desire for her husband.*

desirous /dɪzaɪərəs/
ADJ PRED+*of* If you are **desirous** of something, you want it very much; a formal word. *Is Miss Paget desirous of travelling to London?*

desist /dɪzɪst/ **desists, desisting, desisted**
V If you **desist** from doing something, you stop doing it; a formal word. *Only then may you desist from your enquiries.*

desk /desk/ **desks**
1 NC A **desk** is a table, often with drawers, which you sit at in order to write or work. *My notebook was lying on the desk.*
2 N SING+SUPP You can refer to the staff of a newspaper or news programme who deal with a particular subject as a particular **desk**. *...Rod Sharpe from our foreign news desk reports. ...and now over to the sports desk.*
3 N SING+SUPP You can refer to the place in a shop, station, or airport where you obtain a particular service as a particular **desk**. *British Rail is advising people to check with the information desk before turning up at the station.*

desk clerk, desk clerks
NC A **desk clerk** is a receptionist in a hotel; used in American English.

desktop /desktɒp/; also spelt **desk-top**.
ADJ ATTRIB **Desktop** machines such as computers are a convenient size for using on a desk or table. *We have our own small desk-top computer.*

desolate /desələt/
1 ADJ A **desolate** place is empty of people and looks depressing. *The port now lies desolate and abandoned after the battle. ...a desolate street of seedy bars.*
2 ADJ If someone is **desolate**, they feel very lonely and depressed. *After their visit the families looked desolate. Several of them were in tears.*

desolation /desəleɪʃn/
1 NU The **desolation** of a place is its depressing emptiness. *Eye witnesses at the border described scenes of utter desolation as the last buses pulled out of the camp.*
2 NU **Desolation** is also a feeling of great unhappiness. *...the sadness and desolation which has descended on the people of Armenia almost two weeks after the earthquake there.*

despair /dɪspeə/ **despairs, despairing, despaired**
1 NU **Despair** is a feeling of hopelessness. *I was in despair... The present troubles reflect a deep despair that cannot be ignored.*
2 V If you **despair**, you lose hope. *She despaired at the thought of it... He suggested that the worst may be over and called on his fellow countrymen not to despair.*
3 V+*of* If you **despair** of something, you feel that there is no hope that it will happen or improve. *She had despaired of completing her thesis... Some fat people despair of ever losing weight.*

despatch /dɪspætʃ/. See **dispatch**.

desperate /despərət/
1 ADJ If you are **desperate**, you are in such a bad situation that you will try anything to change it. *Most of the settlers are desperate because life is very, very hard for them... She killed him in a desperate attempt to free herself.* ◆ **desperately** ADV *He will fight even more desperately if trapped... The Iranian government is desperately trying to reassert its authority.*
2 ADJ If you are **desperate** for something, you want or need it very much indeed. *I was desperate for the money... They are desperate to escape from famine and civil war in their own country... There is a desperate need for dialogue.* ◆ **desperately** ADV *They desperately needed food.*
3 ADJ A **desperate** situation is very difficult or dangerous. *The situation in many African countries is desperate and living standards, already low, are falling fast... The Soviet economy is in a desperate condition.*

desperation /despəreɪʃn/
NU **Desperation** is the feeling that you have when you are in such a bad situation that you will try anything to change it. *Sam's desperation grew worse as his exams approached... 'Let's get out,' he said in desperation.*

despicable /dɪspɪkəbl/
ADJ A **despicable** person or action is extremely nasty or evil. *The attack has been condemned by the Northern Ireland Office as a despicable act.*

despise /dɪspaɪz/ **despises, despising, despised**
VO If you **despise** someone or something, you have a very low opinion of them. *They despise them for their ignorance.*

despite /dɪspaɪt/
1 PREP You use **despite** to introduce a fact which makes the other part of the sentence surprising. *Despite the difference in their ages they were close friends... The programme was broadcast despite government pressure to stop it being screened.*
2 PREP If you do something **despite** yourself, you do it although you did not really intend to. *Rose, despite herself, had to admit that she was impressed.*

despoil /dɪspɔɪl/ **despoils, despoiling, despoiled**
VO To **despoil** a place means to make it less attractive, valuable, or important by taking things away from it or by destroying it; a formal word. *...the way in which man has despoiled his environment.*

despondency /dɪspɒndənsi/
NU **Despondency** is a feeling of unhappiness caused by difficulties that seem hard to overcome. *He was unable to hide his despondency.*

despondent /dɪspɒndənt/
ADJ If you are **despondent**, you are unhappy because you have difficulties that seem hard to overcome. *She felt too despondent to go downstairs.* ◆ **despondently** ADV *Fanny sighed despondently.*

despot /despɒt/ **despots**
NC A **despot** is a ruler or other person who has a lot of power and uses it unfairly or cruelly; a formal word. *...Mrs Thatcher's descriptions of Saddam Hussein as a 'despot and war criminal'.*

despotic /dɪspɒtɪk/
ADJ **Despotic** rulers or governments use their power in an unfair or cruel way; a formal word. *He denounced the despotic rule of his predecessor.*

despotism /despətɪzəm/
NU **Despotism** is cruel, unfair government by a ruler or rulers who have a lot of power; a formal word. *...ruthless centralized despotism.*

dessert /dɪzɜːt/ **desserts**
NUorNC **Dessert** is something sweet, such as fruit or a pudding, that you eat at the end of a meal. *For dessert, I had cheesecake with strawberries.*

dessert spoon, dessert spoons
1 NC A **dessert spoon** is a spoon which is about twice as big as a teaspoon. You use it to eat desserts.
2 NC A **dessert spoon** of food or liquid is the amount that a dessert spoon will hold. *Add two dessert spoons of salt.*

destination /destɪneɪʃn/ **destinations**
NC Your **destination** is the place you are going to. *Members of the group left the country yesterday for an unknown destination.*

destined /destɪnd/
ADJ If someone or something is **destined** for a particular experience, that experience cannot be prevented. *The station was destined for demolition... She felt she was destined to be unhappy for the rest of her life.*

destiny /destəni/ **destinies**
1 NC+SUPP Someone's **destiny** is everything that will happen to them, especially when it is considered to be controlled by someone or something else. *There's an old Chinese belief that one's destiny is linked to the moment of birth... We are the masters of our own destiny.*
2 NU **Destiny** is the force which some people believe controls the things that happen to you. *Destiny gave me a task to perform.*

destitute /dɛstɪtjuːt/
ADJ Someone who is **destitute** has no money or
possessions; a formal word. *They are seriously
worried that they may end up destitute and without a
home.* ▶ Also N PL *She began helping the destitute
and dying in Calcutta nearly forty years ago.*

destitution /dɛstɪtjuːʃn/
NU **Destitution** is the state of having no money or
possessions; a formal word. *The peasantry hovered
on the brink of destitution.*

destroy /dɪstrɔɪ/ **destroys, destroying, destroyed**
VO To **destroy** something means to damage it so much
that it is completely ruined or ceases to exist. *Several
buildings were destroyed by the bomb... They want to
destroy the State.*

destroyer /dɪstrɔɪə/ **destroyers**
NC A **destroyer** is a small warship with a lot of guns.
*Armed sailors from an American destroyer boarded
the merchant ship.*

destruction /dɪstrʌkʃn/
NU **Destruction** is the act of destroying something, or
the state of being destroyed. *It will cause pollution
and the destruction of our seas and rivers... Torrential
rains in Rio have caused heavy casualties and
widespread destruction.*

destructive /dɪstrʌktɪv/
ADJ Something that is **destructive** causes great
damage or distress. *Jealousy is destructive and
undesirable.* ◆ **destructiveness** NU *...the
destructiveness of the problem child.*

desultory /dɛsəltəºri/
ADJ A **desultory** action is done without enthusiasm and
in a disorganized way; a formal word. *There were
some desultory attempts to defend him.*

detach /dɪtætʃ/ **detaches, detaching, detached**
1 VO If you **detach** something from the thing that it is
fixed to, you remove it. *The handle of the saucepan
can be detached.*
2 VO+*from* If you **detach** yourself from something, you
become less involved in it or attached to it than you
used to. *His strategy has been to detach himself from
the socialists.*

detachable /dɪtætʃəbl/
ADJ Something that is **detachable** is made so that it
can be removed from a larger object. *...detachable
collars. ...pens with detachable tops.*

detached /dɪtætʃt/
1 ADJ If you are **detached** from something, you are not
personally involved in it. *...the detached view that
writers must take... He accused the government of
being too detached from ordinary people.*
2 ADJ A **detached** house is not joined to any other
house.

detachment /dɪtætʃmənt/ **detachments**
1 NC A **detachment** of soldiers or military vehicles is
a group of them that is sent away from the main
group to carry out a particular task. *The
Czechoslovak parliament has given its approval for the
deployment of a military detachment to the region. ...a
detachment of armoured vehicles designed to
withstand chemical attack.*
2 NU **Detachment** is the feeling of not being personally
involved in something. *The President should have
detachment, he should delegate... On the platform he
displayed a cool detachment, seeming to confirm his
own admission that he didn't suffer from nerves.*

detail /diːteɪl/ **details, detailing, detailed**
1 NC A **detail** is an individual feature or element of
something. *I can still remember every single detail of
that night... He described it down to the smallest
detail.*
2 NU **Detail** consists of small features which are often
not noticed. *Attention to detail is vital in this job.*
3 N PL **Details** about someone or something are items
of information about them. *You can get details of
nursery schools from the local authority... There are
no further details at the moment.*
4 VO If you **detail** things, you list them or give full
information about them; a formal use. *They have
been asked to detail the costs of staging the event...
General Zhang did not detail the casualties.*

detailed /diːteɪld/
ADJ Something that is **detailed** contains a lot of
details. *They gave a detailed account of what they
had seen.*

detain /dɪteɪn/ **detains, detaining, detained**
1 VO When people such as the police **detain** someone,
they keep them in a place under their control. *We
shall be obliged to detain you here while we continue
the investigation... They were detained under the
Prevention of Terrorism Act.*
2 VO To **detain** someone also means to delay them, for
example by talking to them. *Well, I needn't detain
you any longer.*

detainee /diːteɪniː/ **detainees**
NC A **detainee** is someone who is held prisoner by a
government because of his or her political views or
activities. *The detainees are held under the country's
Internal Security Act... The hotel had previously been
used to house British detainees.*

detect /dɪtɛkt/ **detects, detecting, detected**
VO If you **detect** something, you notice it or find it.
*These animals seem able to detect a shower of rain
falling five miles away... The submarines had to be
detected and destroyed.* ◆ **detection** /dɪtɛkʃn/ NU *...a
campaign to promote early detection of the disease...
The submarines were able to withdraw without
detection.*

detectable /dɪtɛktəbl/
ADJ Something that is **detectable** can be noticed or
discovered. *The differences may be subtle but they
will be detectable.*

detective /dɪtɛktɪv/ **detectives**
NC A **detective** is someone, usually a police officer,
whose job is to discover the facts about a crime or
other situation. *Detectives are investigating the
possibility that sensitive information might have been
stolen.*

detector /dɪtɛktə/ **detectors**
NC+SUPP A **detector** is an instrument which is used to
find or measure something. *The new metal detector
has been designed for use in high security areas, such
as airports, seaports and government buildings... In
some countries the use of domestic smoke detectors is
common.*

detente /deɪtɒnt/; also spelt **détente**.
NU **Detente** is a state of friendly relations between two
countries when previously there had been problems
between them; a formal word. *The atmosphere of
detente between the superpowers was improving.*

detention /dɪtɛnʃn/ **detentions**
NUorNC **Detention** is the arrest or imprisonment of
someone. *Their detention has caused an international
outcry... Over one thousand people are being held in
detention without trial... Public criticism of the policy
has led to detentions.*

detention centre, detention centres
1 NC A **detention centre** or detention camp is a place
where prisoners or refugees are kept on a temporary
basis. *The hijackers are still in a detention centre
near Tel Aviv, and their immediate fate is not clear.*
2 NC In Britain, a **detention centre** is a kind of prison
for young people. *He was sentenced to eight weeks in
a detention centre for a first offence committed on his
fourteenth birthday.*

deter /dɪtɜː/ **deters, deterring, deterred**
VO To **deter** someone from doing something means to
make them unwilling to do it. *Such discrimination
may deter more women from seeking work.*

detergent /dɪtɜːdʒənt/ **detergents**
N MASS **Detergent** is a chemical used for washing
things such as clothes or dishes. *They were washed in
water and detergent. ...stains on clothing that can't be
removed by detergents or even organic solvents.*

deteriorate /dɪtɪərɪəreɪt/ **deteriorates, deteriorating,
deteriorated**
V If something **deteriorates**, it becomes worse. *His
sight had begun to deteriorate... The weather had
deteriorated.* ◆ **deteriorating** ADJ ATTRIB *There have
been reports of deteriorating conditions in the Afghan
refugee camps.* ◆ **deterioration** /dɪtɪərɪəreɪʃn/ NU *She
had suffered progressive deterioration of health.*

determinant /dɪtɜ:mɪnənt/ **determinants**
NC A **determinant** is something that controls or influences what will happen; a formal word. ...*the historical determinants of this development... Inflation is the main determinant of people's sense of economic well-being.*

determination /dɪtɜ:mɪneɪʃn/
NU **Determination** is great firmness about doing what you have decided to do. *Seeing my determination to leave, she demanded her money.*

determine /dɪtɜ:mɪn/ **determines, determining, determined**; a formal word
1 V O or V-REPORT To **determine** the truth about something means to discover it. *Experts are continuing their efforts to determine the cause of Wednesday's crash... It was in the public interest to determine exactly what happened... No attempt has been made to determine whether he may have committed such offences.*
2 V O or V-REPORT If something **determines** what will happen, it controls it. *Economic factors determine the progress which a society can make... The meeting may well determine how far the reforms go.*
3 V O or V-REPORT If you **determine** something, you decide it or settle it. *The date of the match is yet to be determined... He has no greater right than her to determine how their money should be spent.*

determined /dɪtɜ:mɪnd/
ADJ If you are **determined** to do something, you have made a firm decision to do it and will not let anything stop you. *He is determined to win in the end.*
◆ **determinedly** ADV *She determinedly kept the conversation going.*

determiner /dɪtɜ:mɪnə/ **determiners**
NC In grammar, a **determiner** is a word that is used at the beginning of many noun groups in order to say which particular thing or person you are referring to. In the sentences 'The walls were white' and 'I remember his name now', 'the' and 'his' are determiners. Other determiners are 'some', 'both' and 'neither'.

determinism /dɪtɜ:mɪnɪzəm/
NU **Determinism** is the belief that all acts, decisions, and events are the results of things that have already happened, and therefore cannot be altered.

deterministic /dɪtɜ:mɪnɪstɪk/
ADJ A **deterministic** theory or view is based on the ideas of determinism. *We can never know the initial conditions on which to base a deterministic prediction of the future.*

deterrence /dɪterəns/
NU **Deterrence** is the prevention of war by having weapons that are so powerful that people will not dare to attack you. *They believe that NATO's policy of deterrence is justified.*

deterrent /dɪterənt/ **deterrents**
1 NC A **deterrent** is something that makes people afraid to do something. *Severe punishment is the only true deterrent.* ► Also ADJ ATTRIB *These sanctions will have a deterrent effect upon the actions of the government.*
2 NC+SUPP A **deterrent** is also a weapon that is intended to make enemies afraid to attack. *He insisted that a nuclear deterrent would be retained.*

detest /dɪtest/ **detests, detesting, detested**
V O If you **detest** someone or something, you dislike them very much. *In his own lifetime he was detested by almost everybody.*

detestable /dɪtestəbl/
ADJ If you say that someone or something is **detestable**, you mean that you dislike them very strongly. *Mrs Thatcher condemned apartheid as a repulsive and detestable system.*

dethrone /di:θrəʊn/ **dethrones, dethroning, dethroned**
V O If a monarch or other powerful person is **dethroned**, they are removed from their position of power. *The visit will be his first since he was dethroned and went into exile forty-two years ago.*

detonate /detəneɪt/ **detonates, detonating, detonated**
V-ERG If someone **detonates** a bomb or if a bomb **detonates**, it explodes. *The car bomb appeared to have been detonated by remote control... Another*

soldier was killed while handling an explosive device which detonated.

detonation /detəneɪʃn/ **detonations**
1 NC A **detonation** is a large or powerful explosion. *Few people survived the effects of the detonation.*
2 NU **Detonation** is the action of causing a device such as a bomb to explode. *...the possible detonation of a nuclear weapon.*

detonator /detəneɪtə/ **detonators**
NC A **detonator** is a small amount of explosive or a piece of electrical or electronic equipment which is used to explode a bomb or other explosive device. *Police said they had also seized explosives, detonators, grenades and ammunition.*

detour /di:tʊə, di:tɔ:/ **detours**
NC If you make a **detour** on a journey, you go by a route which is not the shortest way, because you want to avoid difficulties or because there is something you want to do on the way. *Exasperated workers have responded by blocking the motorway, forcing heavy motor traffic to make a fifty mile detour along country roads.*

detract /dɪtrækt/ **detracts, detracting, detracted**
V+*from* If one thing **detracts** from another, it makes the other thing seem less good or impressive. *This fact did not detract from her sense of achievement.*

detriment /detrɪmənt/
If something happens to your **detriment**, it harms you; a formal expression. *This discovery has been exploited to the detriment of the poor peasants.*

detrimental /detrɪmentl/
ADJ Something that is **detrimental** has harmful or damaging effects; a formal word. *...actions which may be detrimental to the company.*

detritus /dɪtraɪtəs/
NU+SUPP **Detritus** is the small pieces of rubbish that remain when an event has finished or when something has been used; a literary word. *He walks through the party detritus.*

de trop /də trəʊ/
ADJ PRED Something or someone that is **de trop** is not wanted, because they are unsuitable or unnecessary in a certain situation; a formal expression. *They'll use all their favourite ploys to make you feel uncomfortable and de trop.*

deuce /dju:s/
NU **Deuce** is the score in a game of tennis when both players have forty points. *She took just 42 minutes to beat the French girl Catherine Suire 6-love, 6-love, with only three games going to deuce.*

devalue /di:vælju:/ **devalues, devaluing, devalued**
1 V O If you **devalue** something, you cause it to be thought less important and worthy of respect. *Scientific expertise has been devalued... Our present system can devalue the lives of some of the people most in need of help.*
2 V O To **devalue** the currency of a country means to reduce its value in relation to other currencies. *The President has devalued the dollar... President Gorbachev is said to be planning to devalue the rouble.* ◆ **devaluation** /di:væljueɪʃn/ NU *...the devaluation of sterling in November 1967.*

devastate /devəsteɪt/ **devastates, devastating, devastated**
V O If something **devastates** a place, it damages it very badly or destroys it totally. *A hurricane had devastated the plantation.* ◆ **devastated** ADJ *The BBC Moscow correspondent has been visiting the devastated area.*

devastated /devəsteɪtɪd/
ADJ PRED If you are **devastated** by something, you are very shocked and upset by it. *Bishop Daly said he was devastated by the news of the Cardinal's death.*

devastating /devəsteɪtɪŋ/
1 ADJ Something that is **devastating** severely damages something or destroys it totally. *Had such a quantity of Semtex exploded, the blast would have been devastating.*
2 ADJ If you find something **devastating**, it makes you feel very shocked and upset. *It was a devastating announcement.*

devastation /dɛvəsteɪʃn/
N U or N SING **Devastation** is severe and widespread damage or destruction. *...the threat of nuclear devastation... Relief officials say their efforts are being hampered by the scale of the devastation.*

develop /dɪvɛləp/ **develops, developing, developed**
1 V-ERG When something **develops**, it grows or changes over a period of time into a better, more advanced, or more complete form. *The bud develops into a flower... Her friendship with Harold developed slowly... We had hopes of developing tourism on a big scale.*
♦ **developing** ADJ ATTRIB *...companies who were keen to break into developing markets... He plans to use his developing military power to further his ambitions.*
2 V O To **develop** an area of land means to build houses or factories on it. *The scheme includes plans to develop an island in the Danube with factories, shops and housing.*
3 V O If someone **develops** a new machine, they produce it by improving the original design. *The nine-foot diameter engine has been developed to power commercial aircraft.*
4 V O To **develop** a characteristic, illness, or fault means to begin to have it. *She developed an enormous appetite.*
5 V O When a photographic film is **developed**, negatives or prints are made from it. *I would like to have these pictures developed.*

developed /dɪvɛləpt/
ADJ ATTRIB The **developed** countries are the rich industrialized countries. *In the developed countries, there are now about 2 million deaths a year from smoking... Most large cities in the developed world have difficulty in managing road traffic.*

developer /dɪvɛləpə/ **developers**
1 N C A **developer** is a person or a company that buys land in order to build new houses or factories on it. *The land would have a high commercial value if it were sold to developers... Property developers are pushing to be allowed to build thousands of new homes in the green fields around London.*
2 N C+SUPP If a child is an early **developer**, he or she develops physically or mentally earlier than others of the same age. If a child is a late **developer**, he or she develops later than others. *He was a late developer, intellectually.*

developing /dɪvɛləpɪŋ/
ADJ ATTRIB The **developing** countries are the poorer, less industrialized countries. *Many developing countries are paralysed by the debt burden. ...the North-South dialogue between industrialised and developing nations.*

development /dɪvɛləpmənt/ **developments**
1 N U+SUPP **Development** is the growth or formation of something over a period of time. *...a child's psychological development. ...rapid economic development.*
2 N U or N C **Development** is also the process or result of improving a basic design. *...research and development. ...developments in aircraft engines.*
3 N U+SUPP **Development** is also the process of making an area of land or water more useful or profitable. *...Japanese ventures for the development of Siberia.*
4 N+N or N U **Development** projects and aid are intended to help the poorer, less industrialized countries to develop. *The scheme finances small-scale development projects in remote villages in Northern Pakistan. ...the British Minister for Overseas Development.*
5 N C A **development** is an event which is likely to have an effect on an existing situation. *Recent developments in Latin America suggest that the situation may be improving.*
6 N C A **development** is also an estate of houses or other buildings which have been built by property developers. *Many people live in new housing developments.*

deviance /diːvɪəns/
N U **Deviance** is behaviour which is different from what people consider acceptable. *Everybody knows that deviance from the official norm carries great risks.*

deviant /diːvɪənt/ **deviants**
N C A **deviant** is someone whose behaviour or beliefs are not considered acceptable. *...studies of deviants. ...social deviants.* ▸ Also ADJ *To light a cigarette in company is becoming a deviant act.*

deviate /diːvɪeɪt/ **deviates, deviating, deviated**
V To **deviate** from a way of thinking or behaving means to think or behave differently from what is considered to be normal or acceptable. *He has not deviated from his view that war can never be justified.*

deviation /diːvɪeɪʃn/ **deviations**
N U or N C **Deviation** is a difference in behaviour or belief from what people consider to be normal or acceptable. *Radical deviation from established norms is not possible... There had been a number of deviations from army regulations.*

device /dɪvaɪs/ **devices**
1 N C A **device** is an object that has been made or built for a particular purpose, for example for recording or measuring something. *The device can be used to preserve seeds and grain and prevent damage from insects and moisture... There are already electronic devices for detecting explosives.*
2 N C A **device** is also a method of achieving something. *They used television advertising as a device for stimulating demand.*
3 If you **leave** someone **to their own devices**, you leave them alone to do as they wish. *...a group of people who, left to their own devices, might have been very successful in the business world.*

devil /dɛvl/ **devils**
1 N PROP In Christianity, the **Devil** is the most powerful evil spirit. *They vowed to renounce the Devil and all his works.*
2 N C A **devil** is any evil spirit. *In one of his many self-portraits, he portrays himself as a horned devil.*
3 N C+SUPP You can also use **devil** when showing your opinion of someone. For example, you can call someone a silly **devil** or a lucky **devil**; an informal use. *Oh you lucky devil!*

devilish /dɛvəlɪʃ/
ADJ A **devilish** idea or action is cruel or wicked. *Perhaps they were part of the devilish conspiracy.*

devil's advocate, devil's advocates
N C If you play **devil's advocate** in a debate, you put forward an opposing or unpopular point of view in order to make the argument more interesting, rather than because you really believe it. *The author plays devil's advocate very well.*

devious /diːvɪəs/
1 ADJ A **devious** person is dishonest and does things in a secretive, often complicated way. *...consultants who are prepared to use devious means to justify their actions.*
2 ADJ A **devious** route or path to a place involves many changes in direction. *She led him by devious ways to the meeting place.*

devise /dɪvaɪz/ **devises, devising, devised**
V O If you **devise** a plan, system, or machine, you work it out or design it. *It has been necessary to devise a system of universal schooling.*

devoid /dɪvɔɪd/
ADJ PRED If someone or something is **devoid** of a quality, they have none of it at all; a formal word. *...people who are completely devoid of humour.*

devolution /diːvəluːʃn/
N U **Devolution** is the transfer of authority or power from a central government or organization to local governments or smaller organizations. *They want to negotiate for greater devolution within the framework of a united Sri Lanka.*

devolve /dɪvɒlv/ **devolves, devolving, devolved**
V O A If a central government or organization **devolves** authority or power to local governments or smaller organizations, it transfers it to them; a formal word. *The key question of how much power will be devolved to the republics remains vague... Considerable economic power has been devolved to provincial governments.*

devote /dɪvəʊt/ **devotes, devoting, devoted**
1 V-REFL+to If you **devote** yourself to something, you spend a lot of your time or energy on it. *He devoted*

himself to his studies... He abandoned his political life and devoted himself to business.
2 VO+*to* To **devote** a certain amount of time, energy, or attention to something means to spend that amount of time, energy, or attention on it. *They have devoted all their time to helping the sick... The Sunday papers again devote much space to coverage and analysis of the situation in the Gulf.*
3 VO+*to* A meeting, speech, or document that is **devoted** to a particular subject deals only with that subject. *Mrs Thatcher made a speech devoted largely to listing economic successes... The final session yesterday was devoted mainly to assessments of the options.*

devoted /dɪvəʊtɪd/
ADJ If you are **devoted** to someone or something, you love them very much. *He's devoted to his mother.*

devotee /dɛvətiː/ **devotees**
NC A **devotee** of a subject or activity is someone who is very enthusiastic about it. *The building has an enormous appeal for devotees of history.*

devotion /dɪvəʊʃn/ **devotions**
1 NU **Devotion** is great love for a person or thing. *...their devotion to their children. ...total devotion to the cause.*
2 NU **Devotion** is also strong religious feeling. *We watched them kneel in devotion.*
3 N PL Someone's **devotions** are the prayers that they say. *Attend your local church and continue your devotions.*

devour /dɪvaʊə/ **devours, devouring, devoured**
VO To **devour** something means to eat it quickly and eagerly. *We came upon a black snake devouring a large frog.*

devout /dɪvaʊt/
ADJ A **devout** person has deep religious beliefs. *He was a devout Muslim who prayed regularly.*

dew /djuː/
NU **Dew** is small drops of water that form on the ground during the night. *The ground was still damp from the morning dew.*

dewlap /djuːlæp/ **dewlaps**
NC A **dewlap** is a loose fold of skin that hangs under the throat of animals such as cows and dogs.

dewy /djuːi/ **dewier, dewiest**
ADJ Something that is **dewy** is wet with dew.

dewy-eyed
ADJ Someone who is **dewy-eyed** is innocent and inexperienced. *She and Dan were still dewy-eyed enough to think that they would get full compensation.*

dexterity /dɛkstɛrəti/
NU **Dexterity** is the skill of using your hands, or sometimes your mind, to do something well. *I was unable to do anything which required manual dexterity... He was a master with this knife, and used it with dexterity and a sense of power.*

dexterous /dɛkstrəs/; also spelt **dextrous**.
ADJ Someone who is **dexterous** is very skillful with their hands. *He was a born cook, he was dexterous and quick.*

dextrose /dɛkstrəʊz/
NU **Dextrose** is a natural form of sugar that is found in fruit and honey, and in the blood of animals.

Dhākā /dækə/
Dhākā is the capital of Bangladesh and its largest city. Population: 3,950,000 (1984).

diabetes /daɪəbiːtiːz/
NU **Diabetes** is a medical condition in which someone's body is unable to control the level of sugar in their blood. *Hopes must be high for an eventual cure for diabetes.*

diabetic /daɪəbɛtɪk/ **diabetics**
NC A **diabetic** is a person who suffers from diabetes. *Stabilizing diabetes in this way is an important aspect of their treatment.* ▶ Also ADJ ATTRIB *...an elderly man with a diabetic condition.*

diabolic /daɪəbɒlɪk/
ADJ **Diabolic** is used to describe something that people think is caused by or belongs to the Devil; a formal word. *...the hysterics that led to suspicion of diabolic possession.*

diabolical /daɪəbɒlɪkl/
ADJ **Diabolical** means extremely bad or unpleasant; a literary word. *It gave men the pretext for all sorts of diabolical behaviour.*

diadem /daɪədem/ **diadems**
NC A **diadem** is a small crown with precious stones in it. *When the Queen reaches the House of Lords she takes off her diamond diadem and puts on her imperial state crown.*

diagnose /daɪəgnəʊz/ **diagnoses** /daɪəgnəʊzɪz/; **diagnosing, diagnosed**
VO When a doctor **diagnoses** an illness that someone has, he or she identifies what is wrong. *The doctor has diagnosed it as rheumatism.*

diagnosis /daɪəgnəʊsɪs/ **diagnoses** /daɪəgnəʊsiːz/
NU or NC **Diagnosis** is identifying what is wrong with someone who is ill. *It will make diagnosis something like 99.9 per cent conclusive... This makes it all the more important to be sure of the diagnosis before treatment begins.*

diagnostic /daɪəgnɒstɪk/
ADJ **Diagnostic** devices or methods are used for identifying what is wrong with people who are ill. *...basic diagnostic tests.*

diagonal /daɪægənəl/
ADJ A **diagonal** line goes in a slanting direction, for example from the bottom corner of one side of a rectangle to the top corner of the other side. *There was a diagonal red line on the label.* ◆ **diagonally**
ADV *We drove diagonally across the airfield.*

diagram /daɪəgræm/ **diagrams**
NC A **diagram** is a drawing which is used to explain something. *...a technical manual with diagrams in it to make it easy for people to use. ...a diagram of the brain.*

diagrammatic /daɪəgrəmætɪk/
ADJ **Diagrammatic** means arranged or drawn as a diagram. *The other factors can be shown in diagrammatic form.*

dial /daɪəl/ **dials, dialling, dialled**; spelt **dialing, dialed** in American English.
1 NC The **dial** of a clock, meter, or other device is the part where the time or a measurement is indicated. *The figures on the dial can be seen.*
2 NC On a radio, the **dial** is the controlling part which you move in order to change the frequency. *Set the dial to your local NPR station and wake up to morning news.*
3 NC The **dial** on some telephones is a circle with holes in it which you turn several times in order to telephone someone.
4 VO or V If you **dial** a number, you turn the dial or press the buttons on a telephone in order to phone someone. *Dial 411 and ask the operator for information... He dialled five times with no response.*

dialect /daɪəlekt/ **dialects**
NC or NU A **dialect** is a form of a language spoken in a particular area. *There are many different dialects in Chinese. ...old ballads written in northern dialect.*

dialling code, dialling codes
NC A **dialling code** is a telephone number which you dial before someone's personal number in order to be connected to the right area. *The dialling code for Birmingham is 021.*

dialling tone, dialling tones
NC The **dialling tone** is the noise which you hear when you pick up a telephone receiver and which means that you can dial the number you want.

dialogue /daɪəlɒg/ **dialogues**; spelt **dialog** in American English.
1 NU or NC **Dialogue** is communication or discussion between groups. *The union continued to seek dialogue with the authorities... The EEC wants more political dialogue as well as economic co-operation... The two sides agreed to keep open a dialogue.*
2 NC or NU A **dialogue** is a conversation. *Their dialogue was interrupted by Philip's voice. ...500 words of movie dialogue.*

dial tone, dial tones
NC A **dial tone** is the same as a **dialling tone**; used in American English. *You hear the dial tone and then you dial the number.*

diameter /daɪæmɪtə/ **diameters**
NC The **diameter** of a circle or sphere is the length of a straight line through the middle of it. ...*a giant planet over 30,000 miles in diameter.*

diametrically /daɪəmɛtrɪkli/
If two things are **diametrically opposed** or **diametrically opposite**, they are completely different from each other. *The two systems are diametrically opposed... Iraq and Saudi Arabia have taken diametrically opposite positions on the issue.*

diamond /daɪəmənd/ **diamonds**
1 NCorNU A **diamond** is a hard, bright precious stone. *It is rich in gold and diamonds... The fact that diamond is the hardest known material is well known. ...diamond brooches.*
2 NC A **diamond** is also a shape with four straight sides of equal length which are not at right angles to each other.
3 NU **Diamonds** is one of the four suits in a pack of playing cards.

diamond jubilee, diamond jubilees
NC A **diamond jubilee** is the sixtieth anniversary of an important event. *Mr Gandhi was addressing a gathering of parliamentarians to mark the diamond jubilee of the parliamentary secretariat.*

diamond wedding, diamond weddings
NC Someone's **diamond wedding** is their sixtieth wedding anniversary.

diaper /daɪəpə/ **diapers**
NC A **diaper** is a nappy; used in American English. *I change his diaper every couple of hours.*

diaphanous /daɪæfənəs/
ADJ **Diaphanous** cloth is very thin and almost transparent. *Each window had its own diaphanous blind.*

diaphragm /daɪəfræm/ **diaphragms**
1 NC Your **diaphragm** is a muscle between your lungs and your stomach. *When you breathe in the diaphragm contracts and gives your lungs room to expand.*
2 NC A **diaphragm** is a contraceptive device placed inside a woman's vagina.

diarist /daɪərɪst/ **diarists**
NC A **diarist** is a person who records things in a diary which is later published. ...*the Victorian diarist Francis Kilvert.*

diarrhoea /daɪərɪə/; also spelt **diarrhea**.
NU When someone is ill and they have **diarrhoea**, a lot of liquid faeces comes out of their body. *Dirty water means a spread of diarrhoea, measles and other infections.*

diary /daɪəri/ **diaries**
NC A **diary** is a book which has a separate space for each day of the year. You use a diary to write down things you plan to do, or to record what happens in your life. *This book is made up of the diaries she kept on her travels... An entry was found in his diary which showed that he had held a meeting with them.*

diatribe /daɪətraɪb/ **diatribes**
NC A **diatribe** is an angry speech or article which is extremely critical of someone's ideas or activities. ...*a cynical diatribe against all human sentiments.*

dice /daɪs/ **dices, dicing, diced.** The form **dice** is both the singular and the plural of the noun.
1 NC A **dice** is a small cube with one to six spots on each face. You throw dice in games to decide, for example, how many moves you can make. *They roll dice to see who will go first.*
2 VO When you **dice** food, you cut it into small cubes. *Peel and finely dice the onion.* ◆ **diced** ADJ ...*diced potatoes.*

dicey /daɪsi/
ADJ **Dicey** means slightly dangerous or uncertain; an informal word. *Hitch-hiking's a bit dicey in this area.*

dichotomy /daɪkɒtəmi/ **dichotomies**
NC If there is a very great difference between two things, you can say that there is a **dichotomy** between them; a formal word. *The clearest dichotomy is between the winners and the losers.*

dickens /dɪkɪnz/
The **dickens** is used in questions after words like 'what', 'where', and 'why' to emphasize the fact that you are surprised or annoyed; an old-fashioned, informal expression. *Why the dickens should the boy have any of my money?*

dictate, dictates, dictating, dictated; pronounced /dɪkteɪt/ when it is a verb and /dɪkteɪt/ when it is a noun.
1 VOorV If you **dictate** something, you say it aloud for someone else to write down. *It took him a long time to dictate this letter... Walk about as you dictate.*
2 V+to, VO, orV-REPORT If you **dictate** to someone, you tell them what they must do. *The unions are hardly in a position to dictate to the Labour Party... Landlords can dictate their own conditions... The law dictated that his right hand be cut off.*
3 NC A **dictate** is an order which you have to obey; a formal use. *They obeyed the union's dictates and went on strike.*

dictation /dɪkteɪʃn/ **dictations**
1 NU **Dictation** is the speaking aloud of words for someone else to write down. *Jill took down a story from Frank's dictation.*
2 NCorNU A **dictation** is a test of your knowledge of a language, in which you write down a text that is read aloud to you. *Our teacher was always giving us French dictations... She usually did well on dictation.*

dictator /dɪkteɪtə/ **dictators**
NC A **dictator** is a ruler who has complete power in a country; used showing disapproval. *He called them 'corrupt dictators who had no popular support'.*

dictatorial /dɪktətɔːriəl/
ADJ **Dictatorial** people use their power too forcefully. ...*dictatorial regimes. ...their dictatorial attitude.*

dictatorship /dɪkteɪtəʃɪp/ **dictatorships**
1 NUorNC **Dictatorship** is government by a dictator. *Democracy soon gave way to dictatorship. ...a military dictatorship which lasted for twelve years.*
2 NC A **dictatorship** is a country ruled by a dictator. *Spain remained a dictatorship under General Franco.*

diction /dɪkʃn/
NU Someone's **diction** is how clearly they speak or sing. *Her exquisite intonation, clear diction and easy sense of harmony are renowned.*

dictionary /dɪkʃənəri/ **dictionaries**
1 NC A **dictionary** is a book which lists the words of a language in alphabetical order and explains their meanings. ...*a new edition of the dictionary.*
2 NC A **dictionary** is also a book in which words in one language are listed alphabetically, together with words which have the same meaning in another language. ...*an English-French dictionary.*

dictum /dɪktəm/ **dictums** or **dicta** /dɪktə/
1 NC A **dictum** is a formal statement made by someone who has authority. ...*the General's dictum that 'only patriotic, honest citizens would be allowed these privileges.'*
2 NC A **dictum** is also a saying that describes an aspect of life in an interesting or wise way. *His dictum always was, 'If a job's worth doing, it's worth doing well'.*

did /dɪd, dɪd/
Did is the past tense of **do**.

didactic /dɪdæktɪk/
ADJ Something that is **didactic** is intended to teach people something; a formal word. *Most of the facts are presented in a dry, didactic and sometimes rather ponderous way.*

diddle /dɪdl/ **diddles, diddling, diddled**
VO If you **diddle** someone, you take money from them dishonestly or unfairly; an informal word. *You've been diddled!*

didn't /dɪdnt/
Didn't is the usual spoken form of 'did not'.

die /daɪ/ **dies, dying, died**
1 V When people, animals, and plants **die**, they stop living. *Two demonstrators died during the attack... He died of a heart attack.*
2 V When emotions **die**, they become less intense and disappear; a literary use. *True love never dies.*
3 See also **dying**.
● **Die** is used in these phrases. ● If someone **dies a violent** or **unnatural death**, they die in a violent or unnatural way. *I don't believe Davis died a natural*

death. ● If you are **dying for** something or **dying to** do something, you want very much to have it or to do it; an informal expression. *I'm dying for a drink... They were all dying to go to Paris.* ● If an idea or custom **dies hard**, it changes or disappears very slowly. *Colonial traditions die hard.*

die away PHRASAL VERB If a sound **dies away**, it gradually becomes fainter and disappears. *Now that the cheers had died away, it seemed oddly quiet.*

die down PHRASAL VERB If something **dies down**, it becomes quieter or less intense. *The wind has died down... The ethnic unrest appeared to die down a little.*

die out PHRASAL VERB If something **dies out**, it becomes less and less common and eventually disappears. *Many species died out.*

diehard /daɪhɑːd/ **diehards**
NC A **diehard** is someone who is very strongly opposed to change and new ideas. *With the exception of a few diehards, the committee welcomed the proposals for reform.*

diesel /diːzl/ **diesels**
1 NU **Diesel** is a fuel which is often used in trains, buses, and lorries, and which is also used in some cars. *In recent years diesel has been used more than petrol. ...diesel engines... Diesel fuel will cost about five per cent more from today.*
2 NC A **diesel** is a vehicle with a diesel engine. *This year one car in ten sold in Italy will be a diesel.*

diet /daɪət/ **diets, dieting, dieted**
1 NCorNU Your **diet** is the kind of food you eat. *Her diet consisted of bread and lentils... He said that changing people's diets should be part of state policy... Some cancers are associated with diet.*
2 NC If you are on a **diet**, you are eating special kinds of food because you want to lose weight. *...people who aren't able to stick to a diet. ...diet drinks.*
3 V If you **are dieting**, you are on a diet. *In Hungary only 12% of women ever try to diet.*

dietary /daɪətəᵊri/
ADJ ATTRIB **Dietary** means relating to the kind of food people eat. *We are working on changing dietary habits.*

dietician /daɪətɪʃn/ **dieticians**
NC A **dietician** is someone whose job is to advise people about what they should eat in order to be healthy. *Dieticians tell us that brown bread is a lot healthier than white bread... Cheryl Brown is a nutritionist and dietician working for London's Greenwich Council.*

differ /dɪfə/ **differs, differing, differed**
1 V-RECIP If one thing **differs** from another or if they **differ**, they are unlike each other in some way. *Modern cars differ from the early ones in many ways... He acknowledged that views over sanctions differed.*
2 V If people **differ** about something, they disagree with each other about it. *We differ about moral standards.*

difference /dɪfrəns/ **differences**
1 NCorNU The **difference** between things is the way in which they are different from each other. *There is an essential difference between computers and humans... Look at their difference in size... She expected to find little or no difference between the two groups.*
2 N SING The **difference** between two amounts is the amount by which one is less than the other. *The difference between the actual cost and what they sold it for was made up by the government.*
3 NC If people have their **differences**, they disagree about things. *They had not yet resolved their differences over a strategic arms reduction treaty.*
4 If you say that something **makes a difference**, you mean that it changes a situation. *What difference has the discovery made?... It makes no difference whether he is a citizen or not.*

different /dɪfrənt/
1 ADJ If one thing is **different** from another, it is unlike the other thing in some way. In American English, but not in British English, the structure **different than** is often used. *The meeting was different from any that had gone before... Today*

things are completely different from how they were two years ago... His message is very different to theirs... The speech was a little different than what they expected.* ◆ **differently** ADV *...people who feel very differently about things.*
2 ADJ ATTRIB When you refer to two or more **different** things of a particular kind, you mean two or more separate things of that kind. *I visited 21 different schools.*

differential /dɪfərenʃl/ **differentials**
1 NC A **differential** is a difference between two values in a scale; a technical use in mathematics.
2 NC A **differential** is also a difference between rates of pay for different types of work, especially work done by people in the same industry or company. *Their differentials have been narrowed by inflation.*

differentiate /dɪfərenʃieɪt/ **differentiates, differentiating, differentiated**
1 V+between If you **differentiate** between things, you recognize or show the difference between them. *How can you differentiate between moral and religious questions?*
2 VO If a feature **differentiates** one thing from another, it makes the two things different. *What differentiates a sculpture from an object?* ◆ **differentiation** /dɪfərenʃieɪʃn/ NU *...the differentiation of classes.*

difficult /dɪfɪkəlt/
1 ADJ Something that is **difficult** causes problems, usually because it is not easy to do, understand, or solve. *Why is it so difficult for the rich to help the poor?... That's a very difficult question... He admitted they were in a very difficult position.*
2 ADJ A **difficult** person behaves in an unreasonable and unhelpful way. *All thirteen-year-olds are difficult.*

difficulty /dɪfɪkəlti/ **difficulties**
1 NC A **difficulty** is a problem. *There are lots of difficulties that have to be overcome... A number of universities are facing serious financial difficulties.*
2 NU If you have **difficulty** doing something, you are not able to do it easily. *I was having difficulty breathing... She spoke with difficulty.*
3 If you are **in difficulty** or **in difficulties**, you are having a lot of problems. *He went to the aid of a swimmer in difficulty... Iran is known to be in difficulties over selling its crude oil.*

diffidence /dɪfɪdəns/
NU **Diffidence** is the quality of lacking confidence and being rather shy. *...his natural diffidence... She walked up with some diffidence.*

diffident /dɪfɪdənt/
ADJ **Diffident** people lack confidence and are rather shy. *...a rather diffident, uncommunicative man.* ◆ **diffidently** ADV *He approached the desk diffidently.*

diffuse, diffuses, diffusing, diffused; pronounced /dɪfjuːz/ when it is a verb and /dɪfjuːs/ when it is an adjective. A formal word.
1 V-ERG If light or knowledge **diffuses** or **is diffused**, it spreads. *The light was diffused by leaves... The sun diffuses through the trees... Printing presses have diffused knowledge throughout the world.* ◆ **diffusion** /dɪfjuːʒn/ NU *...the diffusion of scientific knowledge.*
2 ADJ Something that is **diffuse** is spread over a large area rather than concentrated in one place. *...a broad, diffuse organization. ...a faint and diffuse glow of light.*

dig /dɪg/ **digs, digging, dug**
1 VorVO If you **dig**, you use a spade to make a hole in the ground or to move the earth. *Scientists from the geological survey have been digging in the desert... Police and volunteers were digging for survivors... He dug a little hole in the ground... I was digging my garden.*
2 VorVO If an animal **digs**, it makes a hole in the ground using its paws. *This animal can dig faster than any cat or dog.*
3 V-ERGA If you **dig** one thing into another, you press the first thing hard into the second. *She dug her needle into her sewing... Cows and goats have pointed hooves that dig into the soil.*
4 NC A **dig** is a remark which is intended to hurt or embarrass someone. *Whenever she can, she takes a dig at me.*

dig out PHRASAL VERB 1 If you **dig** someone or something **out** of a place where they are buried or trapped, you get them out with some effort or difficulty. *Two hundred workers were dug out alive from the ruins of a collapsed factory.* 2 If you **dig** something **out**, you find it after it has been hidden or stored for a long time. *We dug out our tour books and maps for the holiday.*

dig up PHRASAL VERB 1 If you **dig** something **up**, you remove it from the ground where it has been buried. *Their bodies were dug up at the weekend.* 2 If you **dig up** information that is not widely known, you discover it. *Journalists have dug up some hair-raising facts about the company.*

digest /daɪdʒɛst, dɪdʒɛst/ **digests, digesting, digested** 1 VO If you **digest** information, you think about it and understand it. *Non-communist nations in the region are still digesting the implications of America's move.* 2 VO When you **digest** food, your stomach removes the substances that your body needs and gets rid of the rest. *Both conditions prevent the patient from digesting fat in his food.*

digestible /dɪdʒɛstəbl, daɪdʒɛstəbl/ ADJ Food that is **digestible** is able to be digested easily. *He cut up the meat into small, easily digestible pieces.*

digestion /dɪdʒɛstʃən, daɪdʒɛstʃən/ **digestions** 1 NU **Digestion** is the process of digesting food. *A good walk aids digestion.* 2 NC Your **digestion** is the system in your body which digests your food. *His digestion had always been poor.*

digestive /dɪdʒɛstɪv, daɪdʒɛstɪv/ ADJ ATTRIB **Digestive** refers to the digestion of food. *...the digestive system. ...older people who develop digestive problems.*

digit /dɪdʒɪt/ **digits** 1 NC A **digit** is a written symbol for any of the ten numbers from 0 to 9. *...a two digit number.* 2 NC Someone's **digits** are their fingers, thumbs, or toes; a formal use. *Many animals have five digits.*

digital /dɪdʒɪtl/ 1 ADJ **Digital** systems record or transmit information in the form of thousands of very small signals. *Digital audio tapes have given us more faithful reproductions of live performances... Britain's trunk telephone network is now entirely digital.* 2 ADJ ATTRIB **Digital** instruments such as watches or clocks give information by displaying numbers, rather than by having a pointer which moves over a dial. *...a digital watch... At one end of the instrument is a digital display unit.*

dignified /dɪgnɪfaɪd/ ADJ **Dignified** means calm, impressive, and worthy of respect. *She was tall, handsome, and very dignified. ...a dignified letter.*

dignify /dɪgnɪfaɪ/ **dignifies, dignifying, dignified** VO Something that **dignifies** a place makes it impressive. *They stood admiring the broad steps that dignified the front of the mansion.*

dignitary /dɪgnətəʳri/ **dignitaries** NC A **dignitary** is someone who has a high rank in government or in the Church. *He was treated very much like a visiting dignitary.*

dignity /dɪgnəti/ 1 NU If someone behaves with **dignity**, their behaviour is calm, impressive, and worthy of respect. *Throughout this whole affair we've acted with dignity and honour. ...the dignity with which he faced long spells of imprisonment.* 2 NU **Dignity** is also the quality of being worthy of respect. *Don't discount the importance of human dignity... The aim is to restore the dignity of the armed forces.* 3 N SING+POSS Someone's **dignity** is the sense they have of their own importance or worth. *She said that Iranian women are very free, because they have their dignity... They ask whether the concept of charity threatens the dignity of those in receipt of it.*

digress /daɪgrɛs/ **digresses, digressing, digressed** V If you **digress**, you stop talking about your main subject and talk about something different for a while; a formal word. *I will digress slightly at this stage.*

♦ **digression**, /daɪgrɛʃn/ **digressions** NC *This long digression has led me away from my main story.*

dike /daɪk/. See **dyke.**

dilapidated /dɪlæpɪdeɪtɪd/ ADJ A **dilapidated** building is old and in bad condition. *...a small and somewhat dilapidated hotel.*

dilate /daɪleɪt/ **dilates, dilating, dilated** V-ERG When blood vessels or the pupils of your eyes **dilate**, they become wider. *Exercise makes the body's blood vessels dilate so that more blood can get to the muscles... The cells release histamine, which dilates blood vessels and contracts muscles.*

dilemma /dɪlɛmə, daɪlɛmə/ **dilemmas** NC A **dilemma** is a difficult situation in which you have to choose between two or more alternatives. *It put me in a difficult moral dilemma.*

dilettante /dɪlətænti/ **dilettantes** or **dilettanti** /dɪlətænti/ NC A **dilettante** is someone who seems interested in a subject, especially in art, but who does not really know very much about it; a formal word, used showing disapproval. *He is really a dilettante rather than a working photographer.*

diligence /dɪlɪdʒəns/ NU **Diligence** is careful and conscientious hard work. *I'd been hoping to impress my new boss with my diligence.*

diligent /dɪlɪdʒənt/ ADJ Someone who is **diligent** works hard and carefully. *They are hard-working, diligent people... I have no doubt that diligent research will produce results.* ♦ **diligently** ADV *He read the Bible diligently.*

dill /dɪl/ NU **Dill** is a herb with yellow flowers and a strong sweet smell. It is used in cooking. *...white sauce with dill and mustard.*

dilute /daɪljuːt/ **dilutes, diluting, diluted** 1 VO When you **dilute** a liquid, you add water or another liquid to it in order to make it weaker. *He diluted the solution with 90% water... We gave them vodka diluted with lemonade.* 2 VO To **dilute** someone's power, idea, or role means to make it weaker or less effective. *It was an attempt to dilute the powers of the President... They feel their culture has been diluted... This could dilute the role of the national assembly.*

dim /dɪm/ **dimmer, dimmest; dims, dimming, dimmed** 1 ADJ A **dim** place is rather dark because there is not much light in it. *...a dim hallway.* ♦ **dimly** ADV *...the dimly lit department store.* 2 ADJ Something that is **dim** is not very easy to see. *Bernard peered at the dim figure by the bus-stop.* 3 ADJ If your memory of something is **dim**, you can hardly remember it at all. *I only have a dim recollection of the production.* 4 If you **take a dim view** of someone or something, you disapprove of them or have a low opinion of them. *They must take a very dim view of the government backing down on this issue.* 5 ADJ If you say that someone is **dim**, you think they are stupid; an informal use. *Have you ever met anyone quite so dim?* 6 V-ERG If a light **dims** or if you **dim** it, it becomes less bright. *Then the lights dimmed and the movie began... The lights were dimmed for the night.*

dime /daɪm/ **dimes** NC A **dime** is an American coin worth ten cents. *The farm pays a dime for a hundred cubic feet of water.*

dimension /daɪmɛnʃn/ **dimensions** 1 NC A **dimension** of a situation is a fact or event that affects it. *Most of us were Catholic, and this added an extra dimension to the tension.* 2 N PL You can refer to the measurements of something as its **dimensions**. *...the dimensions of a standard brick.*

diminish /dɪmɪnɪʃ/ **diminishes, diminishing, diminished** V-ERG When something **diminishes** or is **diminished**, its size, importance, or intensity is reduced; a formal word. *As she turned the knob, the sound diminished... His standing has been diminished by the financial* *scandal which erupted in 1987.* ◆ **diminished** ADJ *Money could be saved from reduced spending on defence because of the diminished military threat from Moscow.* ◆ **diminishing** ADJ ATTRIB *They blame outside factors for the country's huge international debt and diminishing foreign earnings.*

diminished responsibility
NU If a court of law accepts that someone committed a crime in a state of **diminished responsibility**, it is considered that the person was mentally ill at the time and should not be punished too severely. *The authorities rejected his plea for clemency on the grounds of diminished responsibility.*

diminutive /dɪˈmɪnjʊtɪv/
ADJ **Diminutive** means very small indeed; a formal word. *...Mrs Bradley, a diminutive figure in black.*

Dimitrov, Philip /ˈfɪlɪp dɪˈmiːtrɒf/
Philip Dimitrov became Prime Minister of Bulgaria in 1991. He was one of the founders of the Green Party, and became leader of the Union of Democratic Forces in 1990. Born: 1955.

dimmer /ˈdɪmə/ **dimmers**
1 NC A **dimmer** or a **dimmer switch** is a switch that allows you gradually to change the brightness of an electric light.
2 **Dimmer** is the comparative of **dim**.

dimple /ˈdɪmpl/ **dimples**
NC A **dimple** is a small hollow in someone's cheek or chin, often one that you can see when they smile. *She still had that dimple he could remember from twelve years ago.*

dimpled /ˈdɪmpld/
ADJ Something that is **dimpled** has small hollows in it. *...the child's dimpled cheeks.*

din /dɪn/
N SING A **din** is a very loud, unpleasant noise. *They were unable to sleep because of the din coming from the bar.*

dine /daɪn/ **dines, dining, dined**
V When you **dine**, you have dinner; a formal word. *They dined at a Hungarian restaurant.*

diner /ˈdaɪnə/ **diners**
1 NC A **diner** in a restaurant is someone who is having a meal there. *The area was packed with theatre-goers and diners.*
2 NC A **diner** is also a small, cheap restaurant; used in American English. *...a crowd eating breakfast at a diner down the street.*

ding-dong /ˈdɪŋdɒŋ/ **ding-dongs**
1 NU or NC **Ding-dong** is used to represent the sound made by a bell.
2 N SING A **ding-dong** is a lively quarrel or fight; an informal use. *There was a bit of a ding-dong outside the pub when we arrived.*
3 ADJ ATTRIB A **ding-dong** contest is one in which first one person seems to be winning, and then the other person does; an informal use. *...the ding-dong nature of the two party system.*

dinghy /ˈdɪŋɡi/ **dinghies**
NC A **dinghy** is a small boat that you sail or row. *As the vessel began to sink the crew took to two dinghies. ...rubber dinghies.*

dingo /ˈdɪŋɡəʊ/ **dingoes**
NC A **dingo** is an Australian wild dog.

dingy /ˈdɪndʒi/
ADJ A **dingy** place or thing is dirty or rather dark. *...a dingy suburb of north-east Paris.*

dining car, dining cars
NC A **dining car** is a carriage on a train where passengers can have a meal. *A fire started in the dining car and swiftly engulfed most of the train.*

dining room, dining rooms
NC The **dining room** is the room in a house or hotel where people have their meals. *They came back to the dining room to wait for dinner.*

dining table, dining tables
NC A **dining table** is a table that you sit at to eat your meals.

dinner /ˈdɪnə/ **dinners**
1 NU or NC **Dinner** is the main meal of the day. Some people use **dinner** to refer to the meal they have in

the middle of the day, and some people use **dinner** to refer to their evening meal. *Only three tables have been set for dinner. ...a candle-lit dinner.*
2 NC A **dinner** is a formal social event in the evening at which a meal is served. *Mrs Thatcher attended a dinner at the Mansion House last night.*

dinner dance, dinner dances
NC A **dinner dance** is a social event that takes place in the evening at a hotel or restaurant where a large number of people come to have dinner and to dance.

dinner jacket, dinner jackets
NC A **dinner jacket** is a black jacket that a man wears with a bow tie at formal social events. *They had to dress up in dinner jackets.*

dinner party, dinner parties
NC A **dinner party** is a social event that takes place in the evening where a small group of people are invited to have dinner at someone's house. *He presented the perfume to her at a dinner party.*

dinner service, dinner services
NC A **dinner service** is a set of plates and dishes that are used for serving meals. *...a ninety-six piece silver dinner service.*

dinner table, dinner tables
NC A **dinner table** is a table which is being used or which is going to be used during a meal. *She was setting the dinner table... His parents won't allow books at the dinner table.*

dinnertime /ˈdɪnətaɪm/
NU **Dinnertime** is the time when dinner is eaten, either at about midday or early in the evening.

dinosaur /ˈdaɪnəsɔː/ **dinosaurs**
NC **Dinosaurs** were large reptiles which lived in prehistoric times. *Why did the dinosaurs become extinct about 70 million years ago?*

dint /dɪnt/
PREP If you achieve a result **by dint of** something, you achieve it by means of that thing; an old-fashioned expression. *By dint of clever cutting, the factory manages to make 110 coats from the same amount of cloth.*

diocesan /daɪˈɒsɪsən/
ADJ ATTRIB **Diocesan** means of or relating to a diocese. *...the diocesan newspaper.*

diocese /ˈdaɪəsɪs/ **dioceses**
NC A **diocese** is the area over which a bishop has control. *...a Roman Catholic Bishop, Dr Cahal Daly, whose diocese includes Belfast.*

Diouf, Abdou /ˈæbduː djuːf/
Abdou Diouf became President of Senegal in 1981. He was Minister of Planning and Industry from 1968 to 1970 and Prime Minister from 1970 to 1980. From 1985 to 1986 he was Chairman of the Organization of African Unity. He is a member of the Socialist Party (PS). Born: 1935.

dioxide /daɪˈɒksaɪd/. See **carbon dioxide, sulphur dioxide.**

dip /dɪp/ **dips, dipping, dipped**
1 V OA If you **dip** something into a liquid or powder, you put it in and then quickly take it out again. *He dipped his pen in the ink... Mosquito nets dipped in insecticide may reduce malaria by up to two-thirds in young children.*
2 V If something **dips**, it makes a downward movement. *The plane's nose dipped... You can see the bird's head dip as its mate approaches.*
3 V If a road or railway line **dips**, it goes down quite suddenly to a lower level. *The railway dips between thick forests.*
4 NC A **dip** in a surface is a place in it that is lower than the rest of the surface. *...a small dip in the ground.*
5 NC or NU A **dip** is a thick creamy mixture which you eat by scooping it up with raw vegetables or biscuits. *...tasty cheese dips.*
6 NC If you have a **dip**, you go for a quick swim. *I think I'll take a dip before the tide comes in.*

diphtheria /dɪfˈθɪəriə, dɪpˈθɪəriə/
NU **Diphtheria** is a dangerous infectious disease. *The authorities in Sudan say an outbreak of diphtheria has been confirmed in the capital, Khartoum.*

diphthong /dɪfθɒŋ, dɪpθɒŋ/ **diphthongs**
NC A **diphthong** is a vowel in which the speaker's
tongue changes position while it is being pronounced,
so that the vowel sounds like a combination of two
other vowels. For example, the vowel sounds in 'cow',
'tail', and 'go' are diphthongs. **Diphthong** is a technical
term in linguistics.

diploma /dɪpləʊmə/ **diplomas**
NC A **diploma** is a qualification lower than a degree
which is awarded by a university or college. ...*a
diploma in theology.*

diplomacy /dɪpləʊməsi/
1 NU **Diplomacy** is the management of relations
between countries. *President Bush might still seek to
conclude the crisis through diplomacy... They have no
previous experience of international diplomacy.* ● See
also **shuttle diplomacy**.
2 NU **Diplomacy** is also the skill of saying or doing
things without offending people. *You will need to
employ a great deal of tact and diplomacy to put this
young man politely in his place.*

diplomat /dɪpləmæt/ **diplomats**
NC A **diplomat** is a government official, usually in an
embassy, who negotiates with another country on
behalf of his or her own country. *Foreign diplomats
will be allowed to accompany the refugees to the
airport.*

diplomatic /dɪpləmætɪk/
1 ADJ ATTRIB **Diplomatic** means relating to diplomacy
and diplomats. *The Hungarians and the Israelis intend
to re-establish diplomatic relations... According to
diplomatic sources, some troops remain opposed to the
President.*
2 ADJ Someone who is **diplomatic** is able to be tactful
and say or do things without offending people.
*Questioned about his views in a live television debate,
he managed to sound slightly more diplomatic.*

diplomatic corps
N SING The **diplomatic corps** is the group of all the
diplomats who work in one city or country. ...*the
smart areas where the diplomatic corps and the
industrialists live.*

diplomatic immunity
NU **Diplomatic immunity** is the freedom from legal
action and from paying taxes that a diplomat has in
the country in which he or she is working. *He should
have been prosecuted for drunken driving, but he was
able to claim diplomatic immunity.*

Diplomatic Service
N PROP The **Diplomatic Service** is the part of the Civil
Service which provides diplomats to work abroad.
*Since joining the Diplomatic Service, Sir David has
served in postings in Moscow, Vienna, and as High
Commissioner in Malaysia.*

dipper /dɪpə/ **dippers**
1 NC A **dipper** is a large spoon or small bowl,
especially one with a long handle, which is used for
taking some of the liquid out of a container. *You use
a dipper of smooth polished wood for tasting the
whisky as it is being distilled.*
2 See also **big dipper**.

dipstick /dɪpstɪk/ **dipsticks**
NC A **dipstick** is a metal rod with notches on the end.
It is used to measure the amount of liquid in a
container, especially the amount of oil in a car
engine. *Check the level of the oil with the dipstick.*

dire /daɪə/
ADJ Something that is **dire** is very bad. ...*the dire
consequences of his actions... The economic situation
is dire.*

direct /dərɛkt, daɪrɛkt/ **directs, directing, directed**
1 ADJ or ADV **Direct** means going or aimed straight
towards a place or object. *Are there any direct flights
to Athens?... Why hadn't he gone direct to the lounge?*
2 ADJ ATTRIB or ADV **Direct** actions are done openly or
without involving anyone else. ...*the direct
intervention of the managing director... This move is a
direct challenge to the government... The Americans
have been calling for direct talks between the Israelis
and the Palestinians... Some of the money comes
direct from industry.* ◆ **directness** NU *She has
acquired many supporters who admire her directness*

and good humour.
3 VOA Something that **is directed** at a particular
person or thing is aimed at them or is intended to
affect them. ...*a question that John had evidently
directed at me... This is a fundamental question to
which we should all be directing our attention.*
4 VOA If you **direct** someone somewhere, you tell
them how to get there; a formal use. *Can you direct
me to the cemetery?*
5 VO If someone **directs** a project or a group of
people, they organize it and are in charge of it. *No
one seemed to be directing the operation.*
6 VOor V If someone **directs** a film, play, or television
programme, they decide how it should be made and
performed. *Peter Brook has produced operas,
directed films and written books... I was beginning to
want to try my hand at directing.*

direct action
NU **Direct action** is something that you do, such as
going on strike or demonstrating, in order to put
pressure on an employer or government and to show
what you want. *We had to decide what forms of direct
action should be used.*

direct current. See **DC**.

direct debit, direct debits
NC A **direct debit** is an instruction that you issue to
your bank or other financial institution to pay an
amount of money from your account to a named
person or company at regular intervals. *Graduates
would be able to pay back by direct debit over a 10
year period.*

direct hit, direct hits
NC A **direct hit** is the hitting of a target exactly with a
bomb, bullet, or other missile. *We fire off dummy
missiles and direct hits are recorded by flashes of
light.*

direction /dərɛkʃn, daɪrɛkʃn/ **directions**
1 NC+SUPP You use **direction** to refer to the general
line that someone or something is moving or pointing
in. *He was driven away from the airport in the
direction of the country districts... We ended up going
in the opposite direction from them.*
2 NC+SUPP You also use **direction** to refer to the
general way in which something is developing or
progressing. *That's why India changed the direction
of its economic policy... He should have understood
what direction the United States and the other
countries would go in.*
3 N PL **Directions** are instructions that tell you what to
do or how to get to a place. *Follow the directions that
your doctor gives you... I asked a policeman for
directions to the hospital.*
4 If you do something **under** someone else's **direction**,
they tell you what to do. *The study was undertaken by
members of the law faculty, under the direction of the
Professor of Law.*

directive /dərɛktɪv, daɪrɛktɪv/ **directives**
NC A **directive** is an official instruction; a formal
word. *The government is obliged to take action
because of EEC directives.*

directly /dərɛktli, daɪrɛktli/
1 ADV **Directly** means straight towards something.
She turned her head and looked directly at them.
2 ADV If you do something **directly**, you do it openly or
without involving anyone else. *She never directly
asked for money... No senior UN official had ever
dealt directly with the rebels.*
3 SUBMOD If you are **directly** involved in something,
you are involved in it without going through another
person. *The Prime Minister and his deputy were both
directly involved in the plot... Local authorities were
alleged to be directly responsible for racial
discrimination.*
4 ADV If one thing is **directly** above, below, or in front
of another, it is in exactly that position. *The sun was
almost directly overhead.*
5 ADV or CONJ **Directly** also means very soon or
immediately. *I'll move back into my old room
directly... Directly he heard the door close he picked
up the telephone.*

direct object, direct objects. See **object**.

director /dərɛktə, daɪrɛktə/ **directors**
1 NC A **director** is someone who decides how a film, play, or television programme is made or performed. *He has also established himself as a major director, with fourteen films to his credit.*
2 NC A **director** is also someone who is on the board of a company or is in charge of a group, institution, or project. *...the Director of the Scottish Prison Service.*

directorate /dərɛktərət, daɪrɛktərət/ **directorates**
1 NC A **directorate** is a board of directors in a company or organization. *...the first meeting of a new directorate.*
2 NC+SUPP A **directorate** is also a part of a government department which is responsible for one particular thing. *...the Rural Affairs Directorate.*

director general, director generals or **directors general**
NC The **director general** of a large organization such as the BBC is the person who is in charge of it. *...a statement which was signed by both the Chairman and the Director General of the BBC. ...the Director General of the Confederation of British Industry.*

directorial /daɪrektɔːriəl/
ADJ ATTRIB **Directorial** means relating to company directors or their work; a formal word. *He was about to begin his directorial duties.*

Director of Public Prosecutions
N PROP The **Director of Public Prosecutions** is the official who is head of the Crown Prosecution Service, and is therefore responsible for all the prosecutions that the police make. *Correspondents say the Director of Public Prosecutions could intervene to stop the case.*

directorship /dərɛktəʃɪp, daɪrɛktəʃɪp/ **directorships**
NC A **directorship** is the job or position of a company director. *Ten people held between them as many as 400 directorships.*

directory /dərɛktəᵘri, daɪrɛktəᵘri/ **directories**
NC A **directory** is a book which gives lists of information such as people's names, addresses, and telephone numbers, usually arranged in alphabetical order. *...a telephone directory. ...the European Directory of Agrochemical Products.*

directory enquiries
NU **Directory enquiries** is a service which you can telephone if you want to find out a person's telephone number. *I'll ring directory enquiries.*

direct rule
NU **Direct rule** is a system in which a central government rules a province which has had its own parliament or law-making organization in the past. *The Soviet authorities are imposing direct rule from Moscow on the disputed territory of Nagorno-Karabakh.*

direct tax, direct taxes
NC A **direct tax** is a tax which a person or organization pays directly to the government, for example income tax. *It will introduce a sales tax of three per cent, while direct taxes on income will be cut.*

direct taxation
NU **Direct taxation** is a system in which a government raises money by means of direct taxes. *Mr Delors said one way of raising funds would be direct taxation of citizens by the EC.*

dirge /dɜːdʒ/ **dirges**
NC A **dirge** is a slow, sad song or piece of music that is often performed at funerals. *Thousands of people stopped to watch as the coffin went by followed by students chanting funeral dirges.*

dirt /dɜːt/
1 NU If there is **dirt** on something, there is dust, mud, or a stain on it. *When sand is fired at the stonework, the dirt and grime come away.*
2 NU **Dirt** is also the earth on the ground. *The bodies had been buried under shallow mounds of dirt... The desert is covered by a layer of tightly packed dirt.*
3 N+N A **dirt** road or track is made from earth without any gravel or tarmac laid on it. *Their simple homes are often miles apart along dusty dirt roads... They headed for a dirt airstrip within fifteen miles of the border.*

dirt-cheap
ADJ or ADV Something that is **dirt-cheap** is very cheap indeed; an informal word. *We have lots of dirt-cheap pieces of technical equipment... We bought it dirt-cheap.*

dirty /dɜːti/ **dirtier, dirtiest; dirties, dirtying, dirtied**
1 ADJ Something that is **dirty** has dust, mud, or stains on it. *In the 1970s Asilah was not a very healthy place to live—it was dirty and it was full of rats. ...dirty marks on the walls.*
2 VO To **dirty** something means to make it dirty. *Even his clothes were stained and dirtied beyond knowing... They have never dirtied their hands on a farm.*
3 ADJ ATTRIB A **dirty** action is unfair or dishonest. *Mr Mesic accused Serbia of waging a dirty and aggressive war against Croatia... The People's Party said he had been the victim of a dirty tricks campaign.*
4 ADJ **Dirty** jokes, books, or language refer to sex in a way that many people find offensive. *Unnecessary sex scenes, bad language and dirty jokes all provoke more complaints than screen violence.*

dis- /dɪs-, dɪs-/
PREFIX **Dis-** is added to words to form other words which refer to an opposite process, quality, or state. *The ball disappeared into the river. ...crowds of discontented people... There was disagreement on the ideal course.*

disability /dɪsəbɪləti/ **disabilities**
NC or NU A **disability** is a severe physical or mental illness that restricts the way that you can live your life. *...different levels of disability... The major disabilities are cerebral palsy and spina bifida.*

disable /dɪseɪbl/ **disables, disabling, disabled**
1 VO If something **disables** you, it injures you physically or mentally and severely affects your life. *...if you are disabled by an accident at work.*
2 VO If someone **disables** a piece of equipment or machinery, they cause so much damage to it that it no longer works properly and is unlikely to do so again. *The Americans disabled two Iranian frigates and damaged another.* ♦ **disabled** ADJ *The partially disabled Hubble telescope continues to peer out into space.*

disabled /dɪseɪbld/
N PL The **disabled** are people who have a physical or mental condition that severely affects their lives. *...a holiday home for the disabled in Lourdes.* ▸ Also ADJ *She has to look after a disabled relative.*

disablement /dɪseɪblmənt/
NU **Disablement** is the state of being disabled or the act of becoming disabled; a formal word. *...unable to work because of disablement caused by an accident.*

disabuse /dɪsəbjuːz/ **disabuses, disabusing, disabused**
VO+of or VO If you **disabuse** someone of something, you tell them or persuade them that what they believe is in fact untrue; a formal word. *'Well, I think I can disabuse you of that notion,' he said solemnly... The paper says he will be rapidly disabused when the United Nations Security Council meets later today.*

disadvantage /dɪsədvɑːntɪdʒ/ **disadvantages**
1 NC A **disadvantage** is a factor in a situation which causes problems. *...the disadvantages of living in cities.*
2 If you are **at a disadvantage**, you have a problem that other people do not have. *These restrictions put banks at a disadvantage.*

disadvantaged /dɪsədvɑːntɪdʒd/
ADJ People who are **disadvantaged** live in bad conditions and do not have the means to improve their situation. *...health care for the nation's minorities and disadvantaged citizens.*

disadvantageous /dɪsædvəntɛɪdʒəs/
ADJ Something that is **disadvantageous** to you puts you in a worse position than other people. *This made the 1988 agreement disadvantageous to the British.*

disaffected /dɪsəfɛktɪd/
ADJ People who are **disaffected** are dissatisfied with an organization or idea and no longer support it. *Our party gained four disaffected UP members.*

disaffection /dɪsəfɛkʃn/
NU **Disaffection** is a feeling of dissatisfaction that

people have with an organization or idea, so that they no longer support it; a formal word. *They were worried about the possibility of disaffection in the army.*

disagree /dɪsəgriː/ **disagrees, disagreeing, disagreed**
1 V-RECIP If you **disagree** with someone, you have a different opinion about something. *I disagree completely with John Taylor... She and I disagree about it.*
2 V+with If you **disagree** with an action or decision, you disapprove of it. *Benn disagreed with the abandonment of the project.*
3 V+with If food or drink **disagrees** with you, you feel ill after you have eaten or drunk it; an informal use. *Oranges and chocolate disagree with me, they give me migraine.*

disagreeable /dɪsəgriːəbl/
1 ADJ Something that is **disagreeable** is unpleasant or annoying. *...a very disagreeable smell.*
2 ADJ A **disagreeable** person is unfriendly or unpleasant. *He sees this disagreeable man ruffling his son's hair.*

disagreement /dɪsəgriːmənt/ **disagreements**
1 NU **Disagreement** is the act of indicating that you object to something that you find unacceptable. *There was no disagreement and the notion was passed unanimously... There was little disagreement over what needed to be done.*
2 NCorNU A **disagreement** is also a dispute or argument in which two or more people cannot agree about something. *We had a serious disagreement about business... There has been disagreement over the results of the report. ...disagreements between the Republican President and the Democratic-controlled Congress.*
3 If people are **in disagreement**, they have different opinions about something. *The international community is in disagreement on what to do with the boat people... Many experts find themselves in total disagreement.*
4 NU **Disagreement** is also differences between two or more accounts, results, totals, etc, which indicate that they cannot all be correct. *There was little disagreement between the results of these tests.*

disallow /dɪsəlaʊ/ **disallows, disallowing, disallowed**
VO If an action or claim is **disallowed**, it is not accepted or not approved by people in authority; a formal word. *The appeals were disallowed by the court.*

disappear /dɪsəpɪə/ **disappears, disappearing, disappeared**
1 V If someone or something **disappears**, they go where they cannot be seen or found. *I saw him disappear round the corner... They were spotted in Central London soon afterwards, but since then have disappeared.*
2 V To **disappear** also means to stop existing or happening. *Hong Kong's notorious working conditions have all but disappeared... They will be able to save varieties of seed which might otherwise have disappeared.*

disappearance /dɪsəpɪərəns/ **disappearances**
1 NCorNU The **disappearance** of a person is a situation in which they cannot be found because no-one knows where they have gone. *No one would enquire too closely into the disappearance of such an unimportant person.*
2 N SING The **disappearance** of an object is a situation in which it cannot be found because it has been lost or stolen. *He mentioned the disappearance of his passport to the manager.*
3 NU+SUPP The **disappearance** of a type of thing, person, or animal is a process in which the type becomes less common and finally no longer exists. *This could lead to their total disappearance within fifty or sixty years.*

disappoint /dɪsəpɔɪnt/ **disappoints, disappointing, disappointed**
VO If things or people **disappoint** you, they are not as good as you had hoped, or do not do what you want. *The results disappointed him... We must not disappoint the hopes of the people.*

disappointed /dɪsəpɔɪntɪd/
ADJ If you are **disappointed,** you are upset because something has not happened or because something is not as good as you hoped it would be. *She was disappointed that Ted had not come... My father was bitterly disappointed in me.*

disappointing /dɪsəpɔɪntɪŋ/
ADJ Something that is **disappointing** is not as good or not as much as you expected it to be. *Finland's Seppo Raty won the javelin event with a disappointing throw of 89.6 metres. ...a disappointing book. ...disappointing attendances at last week's inaugural event.*
♦ **disappointingly** ADV *...the disappointingly small crowd.*

disappointment /dɪsəpɔɪntmənt/ **disappointments**
1 NU **Disappointment** is the state of feeling upset, sad, or let down. *To my disappointment, she came with her mother... The optimism generated earlier in the day had led only to disappointment.*
2 NC A **disappointment** is something which makes you feel upset, sad, or let down. *That defeat was a surprise and a disappointment.*

disapproval /dɪsəpruːvl/
NU If you express **disapproval** of something, you indicate that you do not like it or that you think it is wrong. *...his disapproval of the President's policy.*

disapprove /dɪsəpruːv/ **disapproves, disapproving, disapproved**
V If you **disapprove** of something, you do not like it or you think it is wrong. *The other teachers disapproved of his methods... Even if he and his fellow officers disapprove of the rebels' methods, they agree with their aims.*

disapproving /dɪsəpruːvɪŋ/
ADJ A **disapproving** action or expression indicates that you do not like someone or something or that you think their opinions or actions are wrong. *...a disapproving glance... My parents were slightly disapproving of Ellen.* ♦ **disapprovingly** ADV *He shook his head disapprovingly.*

disarm /dɪsɑːm/ **disarms, disarming, disarmed**
1 VO To **disarm** people means to take away their weapons. *The officer captured and disarmed the two men.*
2 V If a country or organization **disarms**, it gets rid of some of its weapons. *The IRA leadership has disarmed and disbanded one of its units.*
3 VO If an explosive device is **disarmed**, it is no longer dangerous because the detonator has been removed. *The soldiers drilled through the fuse and disarmed the bomb.*
4 VO To **disarm** someone also means to cause them to feel less angry or hostile. *They were so kind that it surprised and disarmed her.*

disarmament /dɪsɑːməmənt/
NU **Disarmament** is the process in which countries agree to reduce the number of weapons that they have. *NATO is promoting detente and disarmament. ...disarmament talks on chemical weapons.*

disarmer /dɪsɑːmə/ **disarmers**
NC+SUPP **Disarmers** are people who try to persuade a government to ban the use of nuclear weapons. *Neil Kinnock won a battle over Labour's out-and-out nuclear disarmers. ...his past image as a particularly forceful and enthusiastic unilateral disarmer.*

disarming /dɪsɑːmɪŋ/
ADJ If someone is **disarming**, they have the ability to make you to feel less angry or hostile. *...Harriet's disarming friendliness. ...a disarming smile.*

disarrange /dɪsəreɪndʒ/ **disarranges, disarranging, disarranged**
VO To **disarrange** something means to make it untidy; a formal word. *The wind was disarranging her hair.*

disarray /dɪsəreɪ/
If people or things are **in disarray**, they have become confused and disorganized; a formal expression. *The Democratic Party was in disarray.*

disassociate /dɪsəsəʊʃieɪt/ **disassociates, disassociating, disassociated**
V-REFL+*from* If you **disassociate** yourself from a person or situation, you show that you are not involved with them; a formal word. *Democratic politicians wanted*

to disassociate themselves from the President.

disaster /dɪzɑːstə/ **disasters**

1 NC A **disaster** is an unexpected event which causes a lot of damage or suffering. *...the Exxon Valdez oil spill disaster in Alaska. ...victims of the Bhopal gas disaster.*

2 NC If you say that something is a **disaster**, you mean that you think it is very unsuccessful or unpleasant. *The last day at the hotel was a disaster... The Chamber's President, Warren Williams, said it would be a disaster for trade in this region.*

3 NU **Disaster** is a situation which affects you very badly. *They had led the country into economic disaster.*

disastrous /dɪzɑːstrəs/

1 ADJ A **disastrous** event causes a lot of damage or suffering. *...disastrous floods.* ♦ **disastrously** ADV *These diseases have increased disastrously.*

2 ADJ **Disastrous** also means very unsuccessful or unpleasant. *'The Independent' describes it as morally wrong and tactically disastrous. ...a disastrous holiday.* ♦ **disastrously** ADV *The team performed disastrously.*

disavow /dɪsəvaʊ/ **disavows, disavowing, disavowed**

VO If you **disavow** something, you say that you are not connected with it or responsible for it; a formal word. *He had refused to disavow his attitudes on human rights.*

disband /dɪsbænd/ **disbands, disbanding, disbanded**

V-ERG When someone **disbands** a group of people or when a group **disbands**, it officially ceases to exist. *She disbanded her team of bodyguards in 1988... The armed Spanish Catalan separatist group, Terra Lliure, says it is to disband... The regiment had been disbanded.*

disbandment /dɪsbændmənt/

NU The **disbandment** of something is the act of it ceasing to exist. *Few would call for the disbandment of NATO... The President ordered the disbandment of the union secretariat.*

disbelief /dɪsbɪliːf/

NU **Disbelief** is not believing that something is true or real. *He shook his head in disbelief... I looked at it with disbelief.*

disbelieve /dɪsbɪliːv/ **disbelieves, disbelieving, disbelieved**

VO If you **disbelieve** someone, you think that they are telling lies; a formal word. *There was no reason to disbelieve reports that the general had gone.*

disburse /dɪsbɜːs/ **disburses, disbursing, disbursed**

VO To **disburse** an amount of money means to pay it out, usually from a fund which has been collected for a particular purpose; a formal word. *During 1974, £213m was disbursed in regional development grants.*

disbursement /dɪsbɜːsmənt/ **disbursements**; a formal word.

1 NU **Disbursement** is the paying out of a sum of money, especially from a fund. *...the disbursement of 9000 million US dollars of assistance.*

2 NC A **disbursement** is a sum of money that is paid out. *Under the initiative, official disbursements of some six thousand million dollars can be expected both this year and next.*

disc /dɪsk/ **discs**; spelt **disk** in American English.

1 NC A **disc** is a flat, circular shape or object. *...a metal disc with a number stamped on it.*

2 NC A **disc** is also a piece of cartilage between the bones in your spine. *He has disc problems in his lower back.*

3 NC A **disc** is also a gramophone record. *The most recent gramophone technology is the compact disc.*

4 See also **disk**.

discard /dɪskɑːd/ **discards, discarding, discarded**

VO If you **discard** something, you get rid of it because it is not wanted. *Pull off and discard the outer leaves.* ♦ **discarded** ADJ *...discarded newspapers.*

discern /dɪsɜːn/ **discerns, discerning, discerned**; a formal word.

1 VO If you can **discern** something, you can see it when you look very carefully. *I could dimly discern his figure.*

2 VO or V-REPORT To **discern** something also means to

notice or understand it, especially by thinking about it or by studying it carefully. *Posy had not discerned the real reason... He is unable to discern what is actually happening.*

discernible /dɪsɜːnəbl/

1 ADJ If something is **discernible**, you can see it when you look very carefully. *Each pebble was clearly discernible.*

2 ADJ If a quality, characteristic, or effect is **discernible**, you can notice it or understand it especially by thinking about it or by studying it carefully. *An element of envy is discernible in his attitude... Privatizing the electricity will not result in discernible improvements.*

discerning /dɪsɜːnɪŋ/

ADJ A **discerning** person is good at judging the quality of something. *Discerning readers have been praising this writer for years.*

discharge, discharges, discharging, discharged; pronounced /dɪstʃɑːdʒ/ when it is a verb and /dɪstʃɑːdʒ/ when it is a noun.

1 VO When someone **is discharged** from hospital, prison, or the armed forces, they are allowed to leave. *...a major study of mentally ill patients who have been discharged from hospital.* ► Also NU *...from the time of his discharge until his re-arrest.*

2 VO If someone **discharges** their duties or responsibilities, they carry them out; a formal use. *He is unable to discharge the duties of his office.*

3 VO To **discharge** an object or substance means to send it out from a place; a formal use. *The city's sewage is discharged into huge lakes.* ► Also NC *...the discharge of mercury from industrial premises.*

4 NC A **discharge** is also the quantity of a substance that comes out from a place; a technical use. *...a discharge from the nose.*

disciple /dɪsaɪpl/ **disciples**

NC A **disciple** is someone who believes, supports, and uses the ideas of their leader or superior. *...Christ washing the feet of his disciples during the Last Supper... He was a firm disciple of President Gorbachev's perestroika programme.*

disciplinarian /dɪsəplɪneəriən/ **disciplinarians**

NC If someone in authority is a **disciplinarian**, they insist that people obey the rules strictly or face severe punishment for failing to do so. *She is a stern disciplinarian and a tough police officer.*

disciplinary /dɪsəplɪnəʳri/

ADJ ATTRIB **Disciplinary** matters are concerned with making sure that people obey rules and punishing those who do not. *...forcing them to take disciplinary action against their own members.*

discipline /dɪsəplɪn/ **disciplines, disciplining, disciplined**

1 NU **Discipline** is the practice of making people obey rules and punishing them when they do not. *She was a harsh mother and imposed severe discipline.*

2 VO To **discipline** someone means to punish them for behaving badly or breaking rules. *They could be disciplined by the union if they refused to strike.*

3 NU **Discipline** is also the quality of always behaving or working in a controlled way. *They admired our patience and discipline.*

4 NU or NC A **discipline** is a particular activity or subject; a formal use. *He won World Cup races in all three disciplines—Downhill, Slalom and Giant Slalom.*

disciplined /dɪsəplɪnd/

ADJ Someone who is **disciplined** behaves or works in a controlled way. *Baker looks as if he lives a disciplined life.*

disc jockey, disc jockeys

NC A **disc jockey** is someone whose job is to play and introduce pop records on the radio or at a disco. *She was the first woman disc jockey to have a daily programme on Radio One.*

disclaim /dɪskleɪm/ **disclaims, disclaiming, disclaimed**

VO If you **disclaim** knowledge of something or **disclaim** responsibility for it, you say that you did not know about it or are not responsible for it; a formal word. *Tess disclaimed any knowledge of it.*

disclaimer /dɪsklҽɪmə/ **disclaimers**
NC A **disclaimer** is a statement in which someone says that they did not know about something or that they are not responsible for it; a formal word. *They thought I was making the usual disclaimers.*

disclose /dɪsklҽʊz/ **discloses, disclosing, disclosed**
V O or V-REPORT If you **disclose** new or secret information, you tell it to someone. *I had no intention of disclosing their names... The English newspaper disclosed that the treaty had been signed.*

disclosure /dɪsklҽʊʒə/ **disclosures**
N U or NC **Disclosure** is the act of revealing new or secret information. *He feared it might lead to the disclosure of his visit to Rome... There were more disclosures about Casey in the press.*

disco /dɪskəʊ/ **discos**
NC A **disco** is a place where people dance to pop records. *Rap has developed and become more widely popular, particularly for dancing in discos... Ecstasy has been a key feature of the disco craze, Acid House.*

discolour /dɪskʌlə/ **discolours, discolouring, discoloured**; spelt **discolor** in American English.
V-ERG If something **discolours** or if something **discolours** it, its original colour changes and it looks unattractive. *The pans may discolour inside. ...the oxidation process which discolours fruit.* ♦ **discoloured** ADJ *...discoloured or damaged teeth.*

discomfit /dɪskʌmfɪt/ **discomfits, discomfiting, discomfited**
V O If you **are discomfited** by something, it causes you to feel slightly embarrassed or confused; a literary word. *I was discomfited to find that he was still there... The Chancellor of the Exchequer will be particularly discomfited by Mr Poehl's dismissal of his plan. ...a pompous authority-figure whom Haynes eventually discomfited.*

discomfiture /dɪskʌmfɪtʃə/
NU **Discomfiture** is a feeling of slight embarrassment or confusion; a literary word. *She seemed delighted at my momentary discomfiture.*

discomfort /dɪskʌmfət/ **discomforts**
1 NU **Discomfort** is an unpleasant or painful feeling in a part of your body. *He was conscious only of physical discomfort.*
2 NU **Discomfort** is also a feeling of worry or embarrassment. *I no longer experienced discomfort in their presence.*
3 N PL+SUPP **Discomforts** are conditions which make you feel uncomfortable or suffer pain. *...the physical discomforts of filming.*

disconcert /dɪskənsɜːt/ **disconcerts, disconcerting, disconcerted**
V O If something **disconcerts** you, it makes you feel worried or embarrassed. *Her cold stare disconcerted me... His statement has surprised and disconcerted the Bush administration.*

disconcerting /dɪskənsɜːtɪŋ/
ADJ Something that is **disconcerting** makes you feel worried or embarrassed. *...his disconcerting habit of pausing before he spoke.* ♦ **disconcertingly** SUBMOD *Harold laughed disconcertingly loudly.*

disconnect /dɪskənҽkt/ **disconnects, disconnecting, disconnected**
1 V O If you **disconnect** things that are joined, you pull them apart. *Can you disconnect all these tubes?*
2 V O If you **disconnect** a piece of equipment, you detach it from its source of power. *I bent down to disconnect the plug.*
3 V O If a gas, electricity, water, or telephone company **disconnects** you, it turns off the connection to your house, usually because you have not paid the bill. *His telephone is said to have been disconnected.*

disconnected /dɪskənҽktɪd/
ADJ **Disconnected** things are not linked in any way. *...a series of disconnected events.*

disconsolate /dɪskɒnsələt/
ADJ Someone who is **disconsolate** is very unhappy or disappointed; a formal word. *...a disconsolate Ivan Lendl as he is knocked out of the Wimbledon Championships.* ♦ **disconsolately** ADV *He walked disconsolately down the path.*

discontent /dɪskəntҽnt/
NU **Discontent** is the feeling of not being satisfied with your situation. *...their discontent with pay and conditions.*

discontented /dɪskəntҽntɪd/
ADJ If you are **discontented**, you are not satisfied with your situation. *Most of the people he saw looked discontented.*

discontinue /dɪskəntɪnjuː/ **discontinues, discontinuing, discontinued**
V O If you **discontinue** an activity, you stop doing it; a formal word. *The party voted to discontinue coalition talks... The daylight patrols have been discontinued.*

discontinuity /dɪskɒntɪnjuːəti/ **discontinuities**; a formal word.
1 NU **Discontinuity** in a process is a lack of smooth or continuous development. *We must see this period as one of discontinuity.*
2 NC+SUPP A **discontinuity** is a break that occurs in a developing process. *...the discontinuities in men's lives.*

discontinuous /dɪskəntɪnjuəs/
ADJ A process that is **discontinuous** happens in stages with intervals between them, rather than continuously; a technical term. *There is a discontinuous impact of material upon the device.*

discord /dɪskɔːd/ **discords**
NU **Discord** is disagreement; a literary word. *He's been a source of discord and worry.*

discordant /dɪskɔːdnt/; a formal word.
1 ADJ Things that are **discordant** are different from each other in an unpleasant way. *...the discordant state of industrial relations.*
2 ADJ A **discordant** sound or musical effect is unpleasant or unattractive to listen to. *Janacek's second string quartet is a clear example of a discordant effect.*

discotheque /dɪskətek/ **discotheques**
NC A **discotheque** is a disco. *Pocket money goes on cigarettes, records and going to discotheques.*

discount, discounts, discounting, discounted; pronounced /dɪskaʊnt/ when it is a noun and /dɪskaʊnt/ when it is a verb.
1 NC A **discount** is a reduction in the price of something. *Our clients receive a 50 per cent discount.*
2 V O If you **discount** something, you reject or ignore it. *I decided to discount the risks.*

discourage /dɪskʌrɪdʒ/ **discourages, discouraging, discouraged**
1 V O If someone or something **discourages** you, they cause you to lose your enthusiasm or become unwilling to do something. *Don't let friends discourage you.* ♦ **discouraging** ADJ *...a difficult and discouraging task.* ♦ **discouraged** ADJ *Whenever I feel discouraged, I read that letter.*
2 V O or V O A To **discourage** an action or to **discourage** someone from doing it means to try and persuade them not to do it. *The organization has in the past discouraged the adoption of babies from abroad... She wanted to discourage him from marrying the girl.*

discouragement /dɪskʌrɪdʒmənt/
1 NU **Discouragement** is the act of trying to persuade someone not to do something. *When I first started, I encountered opposition and discouragement.*
2 N SING A **discouragement** is something that makes you unwilling to do something because you are afraid of the consequences. *The submarines were a constant discouragement to naval movements.*

discourse /dɪskɔːs/ **discourses**; a formal word.
1 NC A **discourse** is something that someone says or writes in order to explain something. *They listened to his discourse on human relations.*
2 NU **Discourse** is spoken or written communication between people. *Let us switch the area of discourse to politics.*

discourteous /dɪskɜːtɪəs/
ADJ Someone who is **discourteous** is rude and has no consideration for the feelings of other people; a formal word. *He was quite the most discourteous young man I have ever met... I realised I had allowed a discourteous pause to develop.* ♦ **discourteously** ADV *We were discourteously ignored.*

discourtesy /dɪskɜːtəsi/

NU **Discourtesy** is rude, ill-mannered behaviour; a formal word. *Any other attitude smacked of discourtesy.*

discover /dɪskʌvə/ **discovers, discovering, discovered**

1 V OorV-REPORT When you **discover** something, you find it or find out about it, especially for the first time. *Herschel discovered a new planet... I discovered that Zapp is Melanie's father... He was dead before anyone discovered him.*

2 VO If an artist or athlete **is discovered,** someone realizes how talented they are and helps them to become famous. *The young black guitarist, Jimi Hendrix, had been discovered playing in Greenwich Village.*

discoverer /dɪskʌvərə/ **discoverers**

NC+SUPP The **discoverer** of something is the first person to find out about it. *Who was the discoverer of the electron?*

discovery /dɪskʌvəri/ **discoveries**

1 N CorNU A **discovery** is the finding of an object or fact that nobody knew about. *His discovery of X-rays heralded the age of modern physics... New scientific discoveries are being made every day.*

2 NC A **discovery** is also something that you find or learn about. *The discovery that he actually wanted to hurt her took her breath away. ...new insights and discoveries.*

discredit /dɪskrɛdɪt/ **discredits, discrediting, discredited;** a formal word.

1 VO To **discredit** someone means to cause other people to stop trusting or respecting them. *...efforts to discredit the government.* ♦ **discredited** ADJ *...the discredited ambassador.*

2 VO To **discredit** an idea or belief means to make it appear false or doubtful. *Scientific discoveries have discredited religious belief.* ♦ **discredited** ADJ *...discredited theories.*

3 NU **Discredit** is shame and disapproval. *It may bring discredit to our city.*

discreditable /dɪskrɛdɪtəbl/

ADJ **Discreditable** behaviour is not acceptable because people consider it to be shameful and wrong; a formal word. *It is a mistake to suppose that there is anything discreditable in this.*

discreet /dɪskriːt/

1 ADJ If you are **discreet,** you avoid causing embarrassment when dealing with secret or private matters. *Make discreet enquiries at his place of employment... I'll certainly be most discreet in my conversation.* ♦ **discreetly** ADV *The king came discreetly up the back stairs.*

2 ADJ Something that is **discreet** is intended to avoid attracting attention. *The police are maintaining a discreet presence.* ♦ **discreetly** ADV *...the discreetly shaded light.*

discrepancy /dɪskrɛpənsi/ **discrepancies**

NC A **discrepancy** is a difference between things that ought to be the same. *...discrepancies between school records and examination results.*

discrete /dɪskriːt/

ADJ ATTRIB **Discrete** things are separate from each other; a formal word. *Do you think he staked out any discrete territory for the Democrats? ...the two discrete hemispheres of the brain.*

discretion /dɪskrɛʃn/

1 NU **Discretion** is the quality of not causing embarrassment or difficulties when dealing with secret or private matters. *The plan was carried out with maximum speed and discretion.*

2 NU **Discretion** is also the ability to judge a situation and to take suitable decisions or actions. *Use your discretion!*

3 If a decision is **at the discretion of** someone in authority, it depends on them and not on a fixed rule. *The issue of these cards is at the discretion of your bank manager.*

discretionary /dɪskrɛʃənəri/

ADJ **Discretionary** matters are not fixed by rules but are decided by the people in authority. *The University has funds for discretionary awards in special cases.*

discriminate /dɪskrɪmɪneɪt/ **discriminates, discriminating, discriminated**

1 V If you can **discriminate** between two things, you can recognize the difference between them. *It teaches him to discriminate between right and wrong... They don't discriminate, you know, they just kill anyone.* ♦ **discrimination** NU *...discrimination between the important and the trivial problems.*

2 V To **discriminate** against someone or in favour of them means to unfairly treat them worse or better than other people. *The law discriminated against women... Opposition parties have called for a boycott, saying that a new constitution would discriminate against Mauritania's black Africans.*

discriminating /dɪskrɪmɪneɪtɪŋ/

ADJ If you are **discriminating,** you recognize and like things that are of good quality. *We offer choices to discriminating readers.*

discrimination /dɪskrɪmɪneɪʃn/

1 NU **Discrimination** is the practice of treating one person or group of people less fairly or less well than other people or groups. *African students in China accuse the Chinese of chronic racial discrimination... The police force has to stamp out sexual discrimination.*

2 NU **Discrimination** is the ability to recognize and like things that are of good quality. *He showed a total lack of discrimination in the way he decorated his room.*

discriminatory /dɪskrɪmɪnətəri/

ADJ Something that is **discriminatory** is unfair in the way it treats one person or group when compared with the way other people or groups are treated by it. *He has fought these discriminatory proposals... Pakistani politicians see this law as discriminatory.*

discursive /dɪskɜːsɪv/

ADJ **Discursive** speech or writing expresses someone's ideas or opinions in a very long and detailed way; a formal word. *He has gone in for discursive footnotes in which tricky critical points are discussed in unusually lengthy fashion. ...a long discursive and emotional news conference.*

discus /dɪskəs/ **discuses**

NC A **discus** is a heavy circular object that athletes try to throw as far as they can in sports competitions. *The Cuban discus thrower has been suspended for using anabolic steroids.*

discuss /dɪskʌs/ **discusses, discussing, discussed**

VO If you **discuss** something, you talk about it seriously with other people. *The issues raised by racial segregation were freely discussed... The two sides are due to meet again in May to continue discussing a ceasefire.*

discussion /dɪskʌʃn/ **discussions**

1 NU **Discussion** is the act of talking seriously about something with other people. *Ten hours were spent in discussion of Boon's papers.*

2 NC A **discussion** is a serious conversation. *I had been involved in discussions about this with Ken and Frank.*

3 If something is **under discussion,** it is being talked about and no decision about it has been reached yet. *The document under discussion deals with the broad outlines of the plan.*

disdain /dɪsdeɪn/ **disdains, disdaining, disdained;** a formal word.

1 NU If you feel **disdain** for someone or something, you think that they have little value or importance. *He spoke of the rebels with disdain... He turned away in disdain.*

2 V OorV+to-INF If you **disdain** something or **disdain** to do something, you reject it or refuse to do it because you think that it is not important or is not good enough for you. *She's always made a point of dressing conservatively, disdaining the vulgar flair favoured by her predecessor... Claire disdained to reply.*

disdainful /dɪsdeɪnfl/

ADJ If you are **disdainful** of someone or something, you think they have little value or importance. *They tend to be disdainful of their colleagues.* ♦ **disdainfully** ADV *She looked away disdainfully.*

disease /dɪzˈiːz/ **diseases**
N C or N U A **disease** is an illness in living things caused by an infection or by a part of them that does not work properly. *I have a rare eye disease. ...diseases such as cancer.*

diseased /dɪzˈiːzd/
ADJ Someone or something that is **diseased** is affected by a disease. *Malnourished, exhausted and diseased, the refugees are survivors of a brief but extremely violent battle. ...an old diseased tree.*

disembark /dɪsɪmbɑːk/ **disembarks, disembarking, disembarked**
V When you **disembark** from a ship or aeroplane, you get off it at the end of your journey; a formal word. *The airliner landed at Paris to disembark a number of French citizens.*

disembodied /dɪsɪmbɒdid/
1 ADJ **Disembodied** means separated from or existing without a body. *...a disembodied head.*
2 ADJ You can also describe something as **disembodied** when it does not seem to be attached to anyone or to come from anyone. *Dawlish's disembodied hands reached into the circle. ...disembodied voices.*

disembowel /dɪsɪmbaʊəl/ **disembowels, disembowelling, disembowelled**; spelt **disemboweling, disemboweled** in American English.
V O To **disembowel** people or animals means to remove their internal organs, especially their stomach, intestines, and bowels. *A soldier was disembowelled and lynched by the mob.*

disenchanted /dɪsɪntʃɑːntɪd/
ADJ If you are **disenchanted** with something, you no longer think that it is good or worthwhile. *Some young people are disenchanted with school.*

disenchantment /dɪsɪntʃɑːntmənt/
N U **Disenchantment** is the feeling of being disappointed with something and no longer thinking that it is good or worthwhile. *...public disenchantment with the war.*

disenfranchise /dɪsɪnfræntʃaɪz/ **disenfranchises, disenfranchising, disenfranchised**
V O To **disenfranchise** someone means to take away their right to vote. *In Southern Rhodesia, the minority white government had all but disenfranchised the black majority. ...small, marginal, disenfranchised minority groups.*

disengage /dɪsɪŋgeɪdʒ/ **disengages, disengaging, disengaged**
V O If you **disengage** things that are linked or connected, you separate them; a formal word. *Melanie attempted to disengage her arms from his grip... He disengaged himself and jumped up.*

disentangle /dɪsɪntæŋgl/ **disentangles, disentangling, disentangled**
V O If you **disentangle** something, you separate it from other things that it has become attached to. *She disentangled her jacket from the coat-hanger... Tom disentangled himself from his wife's arms.*

disestablish /dɪsɪstæblɪʃ/ **disestablishes, disestablishing, disestablished**
V O To **disestablish** a church or religion means to take away its official status, so that it is no longer recognized as a national institution; a formal word. *The Bill would disestablish the church from the State.*

disestablishment /dɪsɪstæblɪʃmənt/
N U The **disestablishment** of a church or religion is the act of taking away its official status; a formal word. *Disestablishment would remove the Church's constitutional links with the government.*

disfavour /dɪsfeɪvə/; spelt **disfavor** in American English.
N U **Disfavour** is dislike or disapproval of someone or something. *He became one of a line of political figures who suddenly fell into disfavour and were removed from power... Lauren stepped back and eyed her twin with disfavour.*

disfigure /dɪsfɪgə/ **disfigures, disfiguring, disfigured**
V O To **disfigure** someone or something means to spoil their appearance; a formal word. *His nose was disfigured in an accident.*

disfigurement /dɪsfɪgəmənt/ **disfigurements**
N C+SUPP A **disfigurement** is something, for example a scar, that spoils a person's appearance. *Kay didn't care about her husband's disfigurement.*

disgorge /dɪsgɔːdʒ/ **disgorges, disgorging, disgorged**; a literary word.
1 V O If something **disgorges** its contents, it empties them out. *...factories disgorging effluent into the river.*
2 V O If you say that a vehicle or building **disgorges** people, you mean that a lot of people leave the vehicle or building. *The buses disgorge crowds on to the pavements... The beaches were full of landing craft disgorging troops.*

disgrace /dɪsgreɪs/ **disgraces, disgracing, disgraced**
1 N U **Disgrace** is a state in which people disapprove of someone or no longer respect them. *My uncle brought disgrace on the family... He himself had come back twice from political disgrace.* ● If you are **in disgrace**, you have done something which makes people disapprove of you or stop respecting you. *He was sent back to his village in disgrace... Nixon was the first President ever to resign the office in disgrace.*
2 N SING Something that is a **disgrace** is totally unacceptable. *The state of Britain's roads is a disgrace!... Britain has described their reports as an absolute disgrace.*
3 N SING You say that someone is a **disgrace** to someone else when their behaviour harms the other person's reputation. *You're a disgrace to the Italians.*
4 V O or V-REFL If you **disgrace** someone, you behave in a way that causes them to be disapproved of. *They have disgraced the whole school... Fanny disgraced herself in London... 'We shall disgrace ourselves before the people,' he declared, 'if we act differently'.*

disgraceful /dɪsgreɪsfl/
ADJ If you say that something is **disgraceful**, you think it is totally unacceptable. *...the disgraceful state of the prisons.* ♦ **disgracefully** ADV *She behaved disgracefully.*

disgruntled /dɪsgrʌntld/
ADJ If you are **disgruntled**, you are cross and dissatisfied about something. *Disgruntled voters smashed ballot boxes.*

disguise /dɪsgaɪz/ **disguises, disguising, disguised**
1 N C A **disguise** is a change in your appearance that is intended to prevent people from recognizing you. *...the disguise he wore when he escaped.* ● If you are **in disguise**, you have changed your appearance to prevent people recognizing you. *The Emperor came aboard the ship in disguise.*
2 V-REFL If you **disguise** yourself, you dress like someone else and behave like them in order to deceive people. *I disguised myself as a French priest.*
3 V O If you **disguise** something, you change it so that people do not recognize it or know about it. *He tried to disguise his voice... It proved difficult to disguise her anxiety.*

disgust /dɪsgʌst/ **disgusts, disgusting, disgusted**
V O If something **disgusts** you, it causes you to have a strong feeling of dislike or disapproval. *The attitudes of the tourists disgusted him even more.* ► Also N U *Many expressed disgust at the use of such weapons... He returned downstairs in disgust.*

disgusted /dɪsgʌstɪd/
ADJ If you are **disgusted**, you have a strong feeling of dislike or disapproval. *She was disgusted with herself.*

disgusting /dɪsgʌstɪŋ/
ADJ If you describe something as **disgusting**, you mean that you think it is extremely unpleasant. *The food was disgusting.* ♦ **disgustingly** SUBMOD *She was disgustingly fat.*

dish /dɪʃ/ **dishes, dishing, dished**
1 N C A **dish** is a shallow container used for cooking or serving food. *...picking from a shared dish with chopsticks.*
2 N C Food that is prepared in a particular style is referred to as a **dish**. *...the traditional British dish of eggs and bacon.*
3 N C A **dish** is also a type of radio or television aerial that picks up or sends signals from a transmitter that is orbiting around the Earth. *...a large satellite dish*

and a high powered transmitter... Magellan will turn its huge dish aerial to face Earth and transmit the data.

dish out PHRASAL VERB If someone **dishes out** something, they give some of it to each person in a group of people, whether it is wanted or not; an informal expression. *She dished out advice to the elderly that they should wear woolly hats indoors to keep warm... The illegal campaigners are said to be dishing out large sums of cash to supporters.*

dish up PHRASAL VERB If you **dish up** food, you serve it; an informal expression. *Off to one side of the market, a woman dishes up plates of raw seafood.*

dishcloth /dɪʃklɒθ/ **dishcloths**
NC A **dishcloth** is a cloth used for washing dishes and cutlery.

disheartened /dɪshɑːtnd/
ADJ If you are **disheartened**, you feel disappointed and have less hope or confidence than you used to. *The American took six out of seven games, as the Swede became increasingly disheartened.*

disheartening /dɪshɑːtəⁿnɪŋ/
ADJ If something is **disheartening**, it makes you feel disappointed and have less hope or confidence than you used to. *Such a defeat is inevitably disheartening.*

dishevelled /dɪʃevld/; spelt **disheveled** in American English.
ADJ If someone is **dishevelled**, their appearance is very untidy. *...dirty and dishevelled travellers.*

dishonest /dɪsɒnɪst/
ADJ Someone who is **dishonest** lies, cheats, or does illegal things, and cannot be trusted. *The smugglers could be regarded as pretty dishonest men.*
♦ **dishonestly** ADV *In my opinion, they have acted dishonestly.*

dishonesty /dɪsɒnəsti/
NU **Dishonesty** is dishonest behaviour. *...allegations of fraud or dishonesty.*

dishonour /dɪsɒnə/ **dishonours, dishonouring, dishonoured**; spelt **dishonor** in American English.
1 VO If you **dishonour** someone, you behave in a way that damages their good reputation; a formal use. *He taught her never to dishonour her family.*
2 NU **Dishonour** is a state in which people disapprove of you and have no respect for you. *There are people who prefer death to dishonour.*

dishonourable /dɪsɒnəⁿrəbl/
ADJ Someone who is **dishonourable** is not honest and does things which you consider to be morally unacceptable. *There is something very dishonourable about him... I think it is dishonourable to maintain your seat in Parliament under the circumstances.*
♦ **dishonourably** ADV *Stephen would never behave dishonourably.*

dishwasher /dɪʃwɒʃə/ **dishwashers**
NC A **dishwasher** is a machine that washes dishes, plates, cutlery, etc. *Dowries range from a car, a washing machine or a dishwasher.*

dishwater /dɪʃwɔːtə/
NU or N SING **Dishwater** is water that plates, saucepans, and cutlery have been washed in. *The dishes were washed without soap so that the dishwater could be used on the garden.* ● If you say that a cup of tea is **as weak as dishwater** or **like dishwater**, you mean that it is very weak and does not have enough flavour.

dishy /dɪʃi/
ADJ If a woman describes a man as **dishy**, she means that she thinks he is very good looking; an informal word. *I saw this really dishy bloke down at the Post Office.*

disillusion /dɪsɪluːʒn/ **disillusions, disillusioning, disillusioned**
1 VO If something **disillusions** you, it makes you realize that something is not as good as you thought. *Above all, it's the poor economic record of the Communists which has disillusioned the Yugoslavs... They were bitterly disillusioned by the performance.*
♦ **disillusioning** ADJ *...the disillusioning failure of the unit.*
2 NU **Disillusion** is the same as **disillusionment**. *...her growing disillusion with her husband.*

disillusioned /dɪsɪluːʒnd/
ADJ If you are **disillusioned**, you feel disappointed because someone or something is not as good as you expected them to be. *My father was thoroughly disillusioned with me... He is facing growing opposition to his policies from a disillusioned electorate.*

disillusionment /dɪsɪluːʒnmənt/
NU **Disillusionment** is the feeling of disappointment you have when you discover that someone or something is not as good as you thought. *...public disillusionment with politics.*

disincentive /dɪsɪnsɛntɪv/ **disincentives**
NC A **disincentive** is something which discourages people from behaving or acting in a particular way; a formal word. *Any further increase in benefits would be a disincentive to work.*

disinclination /dɪsɪnklɪneɪʃn/
N SING **Disinclination** is a feeling that you do not want to do something. *There is a natural disinclination to go out on winter evenings.*

disinclined /dɪsɪnklaɪnd/
ADJ PRED If you are **disinclined** to do something, you do not want to do it. *She was disinclined to talk about that.*

disinfect /dɪsɪnfɛkt/ **disinfects, disinfecting, disinfected**
VO If you **disinfect** something, you clean it using a liquid that kills germs. *Suspect ventilation equipment has been closed down and disinfected.*

disinfectant /dɪsɪnfɛktənt/
N MASS **Disinfectant** is a liquid which contains chemicals that kill germs. *Toluene is widely used as a laboratory disinfectant to kill bacteria.*

disinformation /dɪsɪnfəmeɪʃn/
NU **Disinformation** is false or misleading information, especially information which has been issued by a government or other political organization to discredit someone or something. *...the spread of scandal and disinformation to discredit its opponents. ...a Contra disinformation campaign to undermine the ceasefire.*

disingenuous /dɪsɪndʒɛnjuəs/
ADJ If you describe someone as **disingenuous**, you mean that you think they are slightly dishonest and insincere. *He wasn't being disingenuous... 'Do you mean,' she asked with a disingenuous smile, 'that it was John?'*

disinherit /dɪsɪnhɛrɪt/ **disinherits, disinheriting, disinherited**
VO If you **disinherit** your children, you legally arrange that, when you die, they will not receive any of your money or property. *Her father disowned and disinherited her.*

disinherited /dɪsɪnhɛrɪtɪd/
ADJ You say that people are **disinherited** when they have lost their cultural or social traditions. *As a minority group, they remain trapped, disinherited, and despised.*

disintegrate /dɪsɪntəɡreɪt/ **disintegrates, disintegrating, disintegrated**
1 V If an object **disintegrates**, it breaks into many small pieces. *There was an explosion and the boat disintegrated.*
2 V If a relationship or organization **disintegrates**, it becomes very weak and unsuccessful. *They had seen marriages disintegrate under such pressure.*
♦ **disintegration** /dɪsɪntəɡreɪʃn/ NU *...the disintegration of the army.*

disinter /dɪsɪntɜː/ **disinters, disinterring, disinterred**
1 VO If you **disinter** something, you start using it again after it has not been used for a long time; often used humorously. *An entertaining historical play was disinterred.*
2 VO When a dead body is **disinterred**, it is dug up from out of the ground. *His remains had been disinterred from an unmarked grave.*

disinterest /dɪsɪntrəst/
NU **Disinterest** is a lack of interest or enthusiasm in something. *...the Government's disinterest in conservation.*

disinterested /dɪsɪntrəstɪd/
1 ADJ Someone who is **disinterested** is not involved in a situation and can make fair decisions or judgements

about it. *I'm a disinterested observer... His motives in the affair may not be as disinterested as he suggests... Many people remember his disinterested help to unknown writers.*
2 ADJ If you are **disinterested** in something, you are not interested in it. Some users of English believe that it is not correct to use **disinterested** with this meaning. *Young people are notoriously disinterested in anything that might hurt them.*

disjointed /dɪsdʒɔɪntɪd/
ADJ **Disjointed** words or ideas are not connected in a sensible way and are difficult to understand. *...a number of disjointed statements.*

disk /dɪsk/ **disks**
1 NC A **disk** is part of a large computer which stores information. *The loss was due to the wearing out of a data-recording disk.*
2 NC A **disk** is also a small circular, flexible piece of plastic with a magnetic surface which is used in small computers to store information. *A standard floppy disk is used on personal computers now.*

disk drive, disk drives
NC A **disk drive** is the part of a large computer which contains a disk or the part of a small computer into which a disk can be inserted. The disk drive controls the reading of data to and from the disk. *All you need is an IBM personal computer with a single disk drive.*

dislike /dɪslaɪk/ **dislikes, disliking, disliked**
1 VO If you **dislike** someone or something, you think they are unpleasant and do not like them. *Reverend King disliked black power slogans because they were divisive... Everyone here seems to dislike him.*
2 NU **Dislike** is the feeling of not liking someone or something. *They make little effort to disguise their dislike of Ligachov. ...their dislike of authority.*
3 If you **take a dislike to** someone or something, you begin to dislike them. *What if the next president takes a dislike to it?*
4 N PL Your **dislikes** are the things that you do not like. *She has her likes and dislikes, as we all have.*

dislocate /dɪsləkeɪt/ **dislocates, dislocating, dislocated**
VO If you **dislocate** a part of your body, it is forced out of its normal position and causes you pain. *I had a nasty fall and dislocated my arm.*

dislocation /dɪsləkeɪʃn/
NU **Dislocation** is a situation in which the usual state of affairs has been changed in a way that is disturbing or disruptive. *...the dislocation of traffic caused by the construction of the Thames Barrier.*

dislodge /dɪslɒdʒ/ **dislodges, dislodging, dislodged**
VO If you **dislodge** someone or something, you cause them to move from a place. *Burr put his feet on the table, dislodging papers and books.*

disloyal /dɪslɔɪəl/
ADJ If someone is **disloyal** to their friends, family, or country, they do not support them or they do things that could harm them. *You wanted me to be disloyal to Gareth.*

disloyalty /dɪslɔɪəlti/
NU **Disloyalty** is disloyal behaviour. *...Haldane's disloyalty to the nation.*

dismal /dɪzməl/
1 ADJ Something that is **dismal** is unattractive and depressing. *As dismal as things may appear, there is light at the end of the tunnel. ...one dark, dismal day.*
◆ **dismally** ADV or SUBMOD *The day's events dismally underlined the tenuous nature of their control... His message is dismally unappealing compared to that of his main rival.*
2 ADJ You can also use **dismal** to describe something that is unsuccessful. *Their record over the last decade has been dismal.* ◆ **dismally** ADV *He failed dismally to suggest a way out of the country's difficulties.*

dismantle /dɪsmæntl/ **dismantles, dismantling, dismantled**
1 VO If you **dismantle** a machine or structure, you separate it into its parts. *The Austrian government has decided to dismantle its only nuclear power station... The African National Congress is to dismantle its bases in Angola.*
2 VO To **dismantle** an organization or political system

means to cause it to stop functioning by gradually reducing its power or purpose. *They are urging governments to maintain pressure on South Africa to dismantle apartheid. ...the democratic institutions dismantled by Ferdinand Marcos.*

dismay /dɪsmeɪ/ **dismays, dismaying, dismayed**
1 VO If something **dismays** you, it makes you feel afraid, worried, or disappointed. *He dismayed his friends by his vicious attacks on the English way of life.* ◆ **dismayed** ADJ *Barbara seemed dismayed at my views.*
2 NU **Dismay** is a strong feeling of fear, worry, or disappointment. *I realised with dismay that he had gone.*

dismember /dɪsmɛmbə/ **dismembers, dismembering, dismembered**
VO To **dismember** a person or animal means to tear their body to pieces; a formal word. *...a wild animal dismembering its prey.*

dismemberment /dɪsmɛmbəmənt/; a formal word.
1 NU **Dismemberment** is the pulling off or cutting off of the arms and legs of a person or animal. *The murder was followed by dismemberment and decapitation.*
2 NU **Dismemberment** is also the dividing of a country or area of land into smaller parts. *...the dismemberment of the empire.*

dismiss /dɪsmɪs/ **dismisses, dismissing, dismissed**
1 VO If you **dismiss** something, you decide or say that it is not important enough or not good enough for you to think about. *This plan was dismissed as foolish... Unionist politicians in Northern Ireland dismissed this announcement as meaningless.*
2 VO If you **are dismissed** from your job, your employers get rid of you. *They were dismissed for refusing to join a union... The Bolivian government has announced it will dismiss up to 60 policemen linked to drug trafficking.*
3 VO If someone in authority **dismisses** you, they give you permission to leave; a formal use. *Dismissing the other children, she told me to wait.*

dismissal /dɪsmɪsl/ **dismissals**
1 NU or NC **Dismissal** is the act of getting rid of an employee. *They discussed the dismissal of a teacher. ...a tribunal dealing with unfair dismissals.*
2 NU **Dismissal** is also the act of deciding or stating that something is not important or not good enough. *...this dismissal of the computer's potential.*

dismissive /dɪsmɪsɪv/
ADJ If you are **dismissive** of something, your attitude indicates that you think they are not important or not good enough; a formal word. *She is dismissive of the school.*

dismount /dɪsmaʊnt/ **dismounts, dismounting, dismounted**
V If you **dismount** from a horse or a vehicle, you get down from it; a formal word. *The police officer dismounted from his bicycle.*

disobedience /dɪsəbiːdiəns/
NU **Disobedience** is deliberately not doing what you are told to do by a person in authority. *She would tolerate no argument or disobedience.*

disobedient /dɪsəbiːdiənt/
ADJ If you are **disobedient**, you deliberately do not do what you are told to do. *Mr Weatherill has had to admonish disobedient MPs... He called them disobedient and their actions a scandal.*

disobey /dɪsəbeɪ/ **disobeys, disobeying, disobeyed**
VO or V If you **disobey** a person in authority or an order, you deliberately do not do what you are told to do. *It never occurred to them that they could disobey their parents... If a soldier was ordered to undertake such actions he was duty-bound to disobey.*

disobliging /dɪsəblaɪdʒɪŋ/
ADJ People who are **disobliging** are unwilling to do the things that people want them to do. *He had a somewhat spiteful and disobliging nature.*

disorder /dɪsɔːdə/ **disorders**
1 NU Something that is in **disorder** is very untidy, badly prepared, or badly organized. *The room was in dreadful disorder. ...the vicious circle of over-indebtedness, financial disorder and low growth...*

When enemy armies are defeated, they retreat often in disorder.
2 NU **Disorder** is a situation in which people behave violently. *...a serious risk of public disorder. ...general disorder and bloodshed.*
3 NC A **disorder** is a problem or illness which affects a person's mind or body. *Friends say he is suffering from a worsening liver disorder. ...painful stomach disorders.*

disordered /dɪsˈɔːdəd/
1 ADJ Something that is **disordered** is untidy and not neatly arranged. *...the small disordered room.*
2 ADJ Someone who is mentally **disordered** has an illness which affects their mind. *...the care of mentally disordered patients.*

disorderly /dɪsˈɔːdəli/
1 ADJ Something that is **disorderly** is very untidy. *...their disorderly bedroom.*
2 ADJ People who are **disorderly** behave in an uncontrolled or violent way. *Twelve football supporters were fined for disorderly behaviour. ...two counts of assault and one of disorderly conduct.*

disorganize /dɪsˈɔːɡənaɪz/ **disorganizes, disorganizing, disorganized**; also spelt **disorganise**.
VO If someone **disorganizes** something that is carefully arranged, they interfere with its smooth operation. *I'm too busy. You'll disorganize my whole morning schedule.*

disorganized /dɪsˈɔːɡənaɪzd/; also spelt **disorganised**.
1 ADJ If something is **disorganized**, it is in a confused and badly prepared state. *Everything was disorganised because he had got back late.*
2 ADJ If you are **disorganized**, you do not plan or arrange things well. *The UN aid effort remains disorganized and is still without a co-ordinated base.*

disorient /dɪsˈɔːrient/ **disorients, disorienting, disoriented**
VO If something **disorients** you, you become confused or unsure about where you are. *The shock of the experience disoriented her, and she stumbled back down the hill.* ♦ **disoriented** ADJ *I woke up that afternoon, totally disoriented... The pilot became disoriented in the dense fog.*

disorientate /dɪsˈɔːrienteɪt/ **disorientates, disorientating, disorientated**
VO If something **disorientates** you, you become confused or unsure about where you are. *The plan was to stun, disorientate, and confuse the garrison at the barracks... Putting their cage on a revolving phonograph table disorientates them.* ♦ **disorientated** ADJ *Voters are bewildered and disorientated... People are disorientated, not knowing where to go.*

disorientation /dɪsˌɔːrienˈteɪʃn/
NU **Disorientation** is a feeling of extreme confusion. *...a sense of uncertainty and disorientation. ...a quest for substances to treat disorientation among jet-setters.*

disown /dɪsˈəʊn/ **disowns, disowning, disowned**
VO If you **disown** someone or something, you formally end your connection with them. *If it happened again her family would disown her.*

disparage /dɪsˈpærɪdʒ/ **disparages, disparaging, disparaged**
VO If you **disparage** someone or something, you talk about them with disapproval or lack of respect; a formal word. *The Social Democratic Party was sometimes disparaged by rank-and-file Liberals.*

disparagement /dɪsˈpærɪdʒmənt/
NU **Disparagement** is the act of speaking about someone or something in a way which shows that you do not have a good opinion of them; a formal word. *He made a noise of disparagement.*

disparaging /dɪsˈpærɪdʒɪŋ/
ADJ A **disparaging** remark or comment is critical and scornful. *The newspaper had made disparaging remarks about his wife.* ♦ **disparagingly** ADV *He speaks disparagingly of her 'odious, suburban gentility'.*

disparate /ˈdɪspərət/
ADJ **Disparate** is used to describe things that are very different from each other; a formal word. *Many of the disparate islands which make up the Republic are*

uninhabited. *...the coming together of seemingly disparate social groups.*

disparity /dɪsˈpærəti/ **disparities**
NCorNU A **disparity** between things is a difference between them; a formal word. *...the disparities between rich and poor... There is a disparity in South Africa's favour.*

dispassionate /dɪsˈpæʃənət/
ADJ Someone who is **dispassionate** is calm, reasonable, and not influenced by their emotions. *The dispassionate observer can only be puzzled by this phenomenon.* ♦ **dispassionately** ADV *I shall judge your problems dispassionately.*

dispatch /dɪsˈpætʃ/ **dispatches, dispatching, dispatched**; also spelt **despatch**.
1 VO If you **dispatch** someone or something to a place, you send them there. *Troops were dispatched to the north coast.*
2 NC A **dispatch** is an official report sent to a person or organization by their representative in another place. *...a dispatch from their office in Rome.*

dispel /dɪsˈpel/ **dispels, dispelling, dispelled**
VO To **dispel** an idea or feeling that someone has means to stop them believing in it or feeling it. *All such doubts were now dispelled.*

dispensable /dɪsˈpensəbl/
ADJ If someone or something is **dispensable**, they are not really needed. *These were dispensable luxuries.*

dispensary /dɪsˈpensəri/ **dispensaries**
NC A **dispensary** is a place, for example in a hospital, where medicines are prepared and given out. *The Red Cross has put its dispensaries on alert in Kabul.*

dispensation /ˌdɪspenˈseɪʃn/ **dispensations**
NUorNC A **dispensation** is special permission to do something that is normally not allowed; a formal word. *For centuries royal dispensation was required to hunt here... The club's president asked for a special dispensation but UEFA says he must stick to the rules.*

dispense /dɪsˈpens/ **dispenses, dispensing, dispensed**
1 VO To **dispense** something means to give it to people; a formal use. *The UN intends to dispense aid in the areas they control.*
2 VO If someone **dispenses** medicine, they prepare it and give it to people. *A mobile clinic tours certain areas dispensing methadone.*

dispense with PHRASAL VERB If you **dispense with** something, you stop using it or get rid of it because it is not needed. *We decided to dispense with the services of Mrs Baggot.*

dispenser /dɪsˈpensə/ **dispensers**
NC+SUPP A **dispenser** is a machine or container from which you can get things. *...cash dispensers.*

dispersal /dɪsˈpɜːsl/
NU **Dispersal** is the spreading of people or things over a wide area. *The explosion led to the widespread dispersal of a poisonous chemical into the atmosphere.*

disperse /dɪsˈpɜːs/ **disperses, dispersing, dispersed**
1 V-ERG When a group of people **disperse** or when someone or something **disperses** them, they go away in different directions. *The crowd was dispersing... Police used tear gas to disperse the mob.*
2 V-ERG When something **disperses** or when something **disperses** it, it spreads over a wide area. *Most of the pieces had dispersed. ...a fan system for dispersing smoke.*

dispersion /dɪsˈpɜːʃn/
NU **Dispersion** is the spreading of people or things over a wide area; a formal word. *The dispersion of troops was efficiently accomplished.*

dispirited /dɪˈspɪrɪtɪd/
ADJ If you are **dispirited**, you have lost your confidence or enthusiasm. *Tired and dispirited comrades have drifted back to their campuses.*

dispiriting /dɪˈspɪrɪtɪŋ/
ADJ Something that is **dispiriting** causes you to lose your enthusiasm and excitement. *...the first dismal, dispiriting day of November.*

displace /dɪsˈpleɪs/ **displaces, displacing, displaced**
1 VO If one thing **displaces** another, it forces the other thing out and occupies its position. *London displaced Antwerp as the commercial capital of Europe.*

2 VO If someone **is displaced**, they are forced to move away from the area where they live. *...Greek Cypriots displaced from the North.*

displacement /dɪspleɪsmənt/
1 NU **Displacement** is the removal of something from its usual position by something which then occupies that position. *New techniques led to the displacement of the Fine Art tradition.*
2 NU **Displacement** is also the forcing of people away from the area or country where they live. *...the painful displacement of large masses of people.*
3 NU The **displacement** of a liquid is the weight or volume that is displaced by an object submerged or floating in it, for example the weight of water displaced by a ship floating in it; a technical use.

display /dɪspleɪ/ displays, displaying, displayed
1 VO If you **display** something, you put it in a place where people can see it. *...a small museum where they could display the collection.* ▸ Also NU *He has all his tools on display.*
2 VO If you **display** a quality or emotion, you behave in a way which shows that you have it. *The winner displayed all the courage needed to take one of the world's hardest races.* ▸ Also NC *...a spontaneous display of affection.*
3 NC A **display** is something which is intended to attract people's attention, such as an event, or an attractive arrangement of different things. *...displays of sausages and cheese. ...a firework display.*

displease /dɪspliːz/ displeases, displeasing, displeased
VO If someone or something **displeases** you, they make you dissatisfied, annoyed, or upset; a formal word. *What he saw did not displease him... His decision is bound to displease the business community.*

displeased /dɪspliːzd/; a formal word.
1 ADJ PRED If you are **displeased**, you are annoyed or rather angry about something that has happened. *Don seemed displeased... She didn't sound displeased.*
2 ADJ PRED If you are **displeased** with someone, you are rather angry with them because of something that they have done. *Smith has become displeased with some members of the staff.*

displeasure /dɪspleʒə/
NU **Displeasure** is a feeling of dissatisfaction or annoyance. *Professor Aitken looked at me with displeasure.*

disport /dɪspɔːt/ disports, disporting, disported
V-REFL If you **disport** yourself, you amuse yourself in a happy and energetic way; an old-fashioned word, often used humorously. *They could be seen disporting themselves in the fashionable discotheques.*

disposable /dɪspəʊzəbl/
ADJ **Disposable** things are designed to be thrown away after they have been used once. *Most medical authorities nowadays use disposable syringes for injecting drugs and vaccines. ...disposable nappies.*

disposal /dɪspəʊzl/
1 If you have something **at your disposal**, you can use it at any time. *...a cottage put at her disposal by a friend.*
2 NU **Disposal** is the act of getting rid of something. *...the safe disposal of radioactive waste.*

dispose /dɪspəʊz/ disposes, disposing, disposed
dispose of PHRASAL VERB
If you **dispose of** something that you no longer want or need, you get rid of it. *He could dispose of the house and car.*

disposed /dɪspəʊzd/; a formal word.
1 ADJ PRED+to-INF If you are **disposed** to do something, you are willing to do it. *The President of the United States does not seem disposed to bail out the President of the Soviet Union.*
2 If you are **well disposed** to someone, you feel friendly towards them. *Norway and Sweden are well disposed towards the Sandinistas.*

disposition /dɪspəzɪʃn/ dispositions
1 NC Your **disposition** is your character or mood. *Wuddell was of a cheerful disposition.*
2 NU+to-INF A **disposition** to do something is a willingness to do it; a formal use. *Adam showed no disposition to move.*

dispossess /dɪspəzes/ dispossesses, dispossessing, dispossessed
VO If you **are dispossessed** of land or property, it is taken from you. *Landowners could not be legally dispossessed.*

disproportion /dɪsprəpɔːʃn/
N SING or NU **Disproportion** is a state in which two things are unequal; a formal word. *...the disproportion between philosophical and political developments.*

disproportionate /dɪsprəpɔːʃənət/
ADJ Something that is **disproportionate** is surprising or unreasonable in amount or size. *A disproportionate number of people die shortly after retiring.*
♦ **disproportionately** ADV *Black males form a disproportionately large element of the prison population.*

disprove /dɪspruːv/ disproves, disproving, disproved
V-REPORT or VO If you **disprove** an idea or belief, you show that it is not true. *They can neither prove nor disprove that it is genuine... So far, all examinations of the Turin shroud have failed to prove or disprove its authenticity.*

disputation /dɪspjuːteɪʃn/ disputations
NU or NC **Disputation** is discussion on a subject which people cannot agree about; a formal word. *After much public disputation the plans were approved. ...endless meetings, disputations and clashes.*

dispute, disputes, disputing, disputed; pronounced /dɪspjuːt/ or /dɪspjuːt/ when it is a noun and /dɪspjuːt/ when it is a verb.
1 NC or NU A **dispute** is a disagreement or quarrel between people or groups. *...disputes between unions and employers... There is some dispute about this.*
2 If people are **in dispute**, they disagree with each other. *Two-hundred technicians have been in dispute with the company for nearly three months.*
3 If something is **in dispute**, people disagree about it. *The outcome of the voting is in dispute.*
4 V-REPORT or VO If you **dispute** an opinion, you say that you think it is incorrect. *I don't dispute that children need love... He disputed American claims that their farmers faced unfair competition.* ♦ **disputed** ADJ *...a disputed decision.*
5 VO When people **dispute** something, they fight for control of it. *They continued to dispute the ownership of the territory.* ♦ **disputed** ADJ *...the disputed provinces.*

disqualification /dɪskwɒlɪfɪkeɪʃn/ disqualifications
NU or NC **Disqualification** is the act of stopping someone from taking part in an event, activity, or competition. *He is liable to disqualification from all official events... The jury voted for disqualifications after West Germany lodged a protest.*

disqualify /dɪskwɒlɪfaɪ/ disqualifies, disqualifying, disqualified
VO If someone is **disqualified**, they are officially stopped from doing something because they have broken a law or rule. *They were disqualified from driving... She could be disqualified from standing in a general election... Conner was disqualified in the race when his yacht ran aground.*

disquiet /dɪskwaɪət/
NU **Disquiet** is a feeling of worry or anxiety; a formal word. *Some of them have expressed disquiet at the military regime's excesses.*

disregard /dɪsrɪgɑːd/ disregards, disregarding, disregarded
VO To **disregard** something means to ignore it or not take it seriously. *Men who disregarded the warning were beaten severely.* ▸ Also NU *The centre was built with an obvious disregard for cost.*

disrepair /dɪsrɪpeə/
If something is **in disrepair**, it is broken or has not been looked after properly; a formal expression. *His cycle is in disrepair.*

disreputable /dɪsrepjutəbl/
ADJ If someone is **disreputable**, they are not respectable or trustworthy. *...Ash and his disreputable friends.*

disrepute /dɪsrɪpjuːt/
If something is **brought into disrepute** or falls into

disrepute, it loses its good reputation; a formal expression. *He brought his profession into disrepute.*

disrespect /dɪsrɪspɛkt/
NU If someone shows **disrespect** for a person, law, or custom, they do not behave towards them in a respectful way. *I don't think he intended any disrespect.*

disrespectful /dɪsrɪspɛktfl/
ADJ Someone who is **disrespectful** shows disrespect. *They are arrogant and disrespectful to me.*

disrobe /dɪsrəʊb/ **disrobes, disrobing, disrobed**
V When someone **disrobes**, they remove their clothes; a formal word. *He came upon Mrs Slesers disrobing for her bath.*

disrupt /dɪsrʌpt/ **disrupts, disrupting, disrupted**
VO To **disrupt** an activity, system, or process means to prevent it from continuing normally. *...attempts to disrupt meetings... Trains have been severely disrupted.*

disruption /dɪsrʌpʃn/ **disruptions**
NUorNC When there is **disruption** of an event, system, or process, it is prevented from proceeding or operating easily or peacefully. *...the disruption of rail communications. ...disruptions in routine.*

disruptive /dɪsrʌptɪv/
ADJ If someone is **disruptive**, they prevent an activity or system from continuing normally. *...children who are disruptive in school.*

dissatisfaction /dɪsatɪsfækʃn/
NU If you feel **dissatisfaction** with something, you are not satisfied with it. *There is widespread dissatisfaction with the existing political parties.*

dissatisfied /dɪsatɪsfaɪd/
ADJ If you are **dissatisfied**, you are not contented, or are not satisfied with something. *All of them had been dissatisfied with their lives.*

dissect /dɪsɛkt/ **dissects, dissecting, dissected**
VO If someone **dissects** a dead body or part of a body, they cut it up in order to examine it. *I had to go to the Anatomy Department and spend quite a lot of time dissecting limbs and measuring the muscles... Back at the laboratory, the ovary is dissected and as many as 20 eggs are taken out.* ◆ **dissection** /dɪsɛkʃn/ NU *...the dissection of the earthworm.*

dissemble /dɪsɛmbl/ **dissembles, dissembling, dissembled**
V If someone **dissembles**, they hide their real motives or emotions, for example by pretending to have other motives or emotions; a literary word. *It was not in her nature to dissemble... He has succeeded so far, sometimes by dissembling, sometimes almost by stealth.*

disseminate /dɪsɛmɪneɪt/ **disseminates, disseminating, disseminated**
VO To **disseminate** something such as information means to distribute it to many people; a formal word. *They were faced with the problem of disseminating information among the villages... It will help them to disseminate this type of technology to the other farmers much more quickly and efficiently.* ◆ **dissemination** /dɪsɛmɪneɪʃn/ NU *...the printing and dissemination of news.*

dissension /dɪsɛnʃn/
NU **Dissension** is disagreement and argument; a formal word. *The continued uncertainty and reports of dissension are making back-bench MPs edgy. ...months of discussion, dissension and debate.*

dissent /dɪsɛnt/ **dissents, dissenting, dissented**
1 V If someone **dissents**, they express strong disagreement with established ideas; a formal use. *...anyone dissenting from the prevailing view.* ◆ **dissenting** ADJ ATTRIB *There have been dissenting voices.*
2 NU **Dissent** is strong disagreement or dissatisfaction with a proposal or with established ideas or values. *Healthy societies can tolerate dissent.*

dissenter /dɪsɛntə/ **dissenters**
NC A **dissenter** is someone who expresses disagreement with established ideas; a formal word. *...political and religious dissenters.*

dissertation /dɪsəteɪʃn/ **dissertations**
NC A **dissertation** is a long formal piece of writing, especially for a university degree. *She wrote a dissertation on industrial development.*

disservice /dɪsɜːvɪs/
N SING If you do someone a **disservice**, you do something that harms them; a formal word. *They are guilty of a disservice to their community.*

dissident /dɪsɪdənt/ **dissidents**
NC A **dissident** is someone who criticizes their government or organization; a formal word. *...a prominent Burmese journalist and dissident. ...political dissidents. ...a crackdown on human rights and dissident groups in the country.*

dissimilar /dɪsɪmɪlə/
ADJ If two things are **dissimilar**, they are different from each other; a formal word. *...a proposal not dissimilar to that now adopted by the Government.*

dissimilarity /dɪsɪmɪlærəti/ **dissimilarities**
1 NU If there is **dissimilarity** between two or more things, they are different from each other in particular ways. *You will have noticed the dissimilarity between our organization and the others.*
2 NC A **dissimilarity** is one of the ways in which two things are different from each other. *...the dissimilarities in their characters... Important dissimilarities are often ignored.*

dissimulate /dɪsɪmjʊleɪt/ **dissimulates, dissimulating, dissimulated**
V If someone **dissimulates**, they hide their real motives or emotions, for example by pretending to have other motives or emotions; a formal word. *They learned to conceal, to dissimulate, and to cheat officials.* ◆ **dissimulation** /dɪsɪmjʊleɪʃn/ NU *He was incapable of either dissimulation or duplicity.*

dissipate /dɪsɪpeɪt/ **dissipates, dissipating, dissipated**; a formal word.
1 V-ERG If something **dissipates** or if something **dissipates** it, it gradually becomes less or disappears. *Soon the civilian resistance dissipated, and the troops were all inside the compound... The heat was dissipated by cooling systems.*
2 VO If someone **dissipates** money, time, or effort, they waste it in a foolish way. *The opposition parties seem to dissipate most of their energies in bickering.*

dissipated /dɪsɪpeɪtɪd/
ADJ A **dissipated** person is someone who has harmed their health by spending too much time drinking alcohol and enjoying other physical pleasures. *He was looking rather shabby and dissipated... At university he led a very dissipated life.*

dissipation /dɪsɪpeɪʃn/; a formal word.
1 NU The **dissipation** of something such as a feeling is the process by which it disappears or is made to disappear. *By talking to her mother she managed to bring about the dissipation of all her fears.*
2 NU The **dissipation** of money, time, or effort is the wasting of it. *We must learn to prevent the dissipation of valuable resources such as oil and gas.*
3 NU **Dissipation** is also the leading of a dissipated life, or the state of being dissipated. *His years of dissipation soon ruined his health... He had an easy, confident manner and an air of mild dissipation.*

dissociate /dɪsəʊʃieɪt/ **dissociates, dissociating, dissociated**
1 V-REFL+*from* If you **dissociate** yourself from someone or something, you say that you are not connected with them. *He did all he could to dissociate himself from the Government.*
2 VO+*from* If you **dissociate** one thing from another, you consider them separately. *It is often difficult to dissociate cause from effect.*

dissolute /dɪsəluːt/
ADJ A **dissolute** person does not care about morals and lives in a way that is considered to be wicked. *He misused public funds to support a dissolute and immoral lifestyle.*

dissolution /dɪsəluːʃn/
NU The **dissolution** of an organization or legal relationship is the act of officially ending it; a formal word. *The country's voters approved the dissolution of parliament in a referendum held yesterday.*

dissolve /dɪzɒlv/ **dissolves, dissolving, dissolved**
1 V-ERG If a solid substance **dissolves** or is **dissolved**,

it mixes with a liquid solution until it disappears. *They dissolve in the body over certain periods of time... The drug helps natural body enzymes to dissolve fibrin... Dissolve the sugar in the water.*
2 VO To **dissolve** an organization or legal relationship means to officially end it; a formal use. *They wish to dissolve their union with the United States... They called for parliament to be dissolved and a fresh general election to be held.*
dissolve into PHRASAL VERB If you **dissolve into** tears or laughter, you begin to cry or laugh, because you cannot control yourself. *Eileen dissolved into giggles.*

dissonance /dɪsənəns/
NU **Dissonance** is a lack of agreement or harmony between things; a formal word. *...this dissonance of colours... He said it would be a pity if a voice of dissonance were to emerge from Paris.*

dissuade /dɪsweɪd/ **dissuades, dissuading, dissuaded**
VO If you **dissuade** someone from doing something, you persuade them not to do it; a formal word. *I tried to dissuade David from going.*

distance /dɪstəns/ **distances**
1 NCorNU The **distance** between two places is the amount of space between them. *Farmers were travelling long distances to get supplies... The town is some distance from the sea.*
2 If you are **at a distance** from something, or if you see it or remember it **from a distance**, you are a long way away from it in space or time. *Remembering this disaster at a distance, I think that it was not her fault... From a distance, he heard Jack's whisper.*

distant /dɪstənt/
1 ADJ Something that is **distant** is far away. *...a distant country.*
2 ADJ An event or time that is **distant** is far away in the past or future. *He may return in the not too distant future.*
3 ADJ A **distant** relative is one that you are not closely related to. *Mr Oreta is a distant relative of President Aquino.*
4 ADJ Someone who is **distant** is unfriendly. *Boylan was polite but distant.*
5 ADJ You also use **distant** to say that someone is not paying attention because they are thinking about something else. *His eyes took on a distant look.*

distantly /dɪstəntli/
1 ADV If you see or hear something **distantly**, you hear or see it faintly because it is far away. *From the other end of the street, he could distantly see a figure waiting... The sound of a recorder was distantly audible.*
2 ADV If something happens **distantly**, it happens in a place that is far away; a literary use. *Children laughed distantly in other rooms.*
3 ADV If you are **distantly** related to someone, you are related to them but not closely. *She was distantly connected on her mother's side with the Rothschilds.*
4 ADV If you do something **distantly**, you do it in a cold and emotionally detached way. *He behaved very distantly.*
5 ADV **Distantly** also means that you do something in a way that shows that you are not concentrating on what you are doing but are thinking about something else. *She carried on with her work, smiling distantly.*

distaste /dɪsteɪst/
N SING+SUPP **Distaste** is a feeling of dislike or disapproval. *She looked at him with distaste. ...his distaste for money.*

distasteful /dɪsteɪstfl/
ADJ If something is **distasteful** to you, you dislike or disapprove of it. *...work that is distasteful to him.*

distemper /dɪstempə/
1 NU **Distemper** is a dangerous infectious disease that can be caught by animals, especially dogs. *I was treated like a dog with distemper.*
2 NU **Distemper** is also paint which dissolves in water and which can be used for decorating. *My bedroom was painted with pink distemper.*

distend /dɪstend/ **distends, distending, distended**
VorVO If a part of a person's or animal's body **distends**, it becomes swollen and unnaturally large; a formal word. *The camel had a large lump which*

distended her milk vein.

distended /dɪstendɪd/
ADJ If a part of someone's body is **distended**, it is swollen and unnaturally large; a formal word. *He had a grossly distended stomach.*

distension /dɪstenʃn/ **distensions**; also spelt **distention** in American English.
NCorNU A **distension** is a swelling in a person's or animal's body; a medical term. *The baby cannot consume enough milk to relieve the distension.*

distil /dɪstɪl/ **distils, distilling, distilled**; spelt **distill** in American English.
VO When a liquid is **distilled**, it is heated until it becomes steam and then cooled until it becomes liquid again. This purifies or concentrates the liquid. *We can use solar energy to distil that water.* ◆ **distilled** ADJ *Top up the car battery with distilled water.*
◆ **distillation** /dɪstɪleɪʃn/ NU *Separate the alcohol from the water by distillation.*

distiller /dɪstɪlə/ **distillers**
NC A **distiller** is a person or a company that makes whisky or similar strong alcoholic drinks by a process of distilling. *Japanese distillers raised a few objections. ...the Distillers Scotch Whisky Company.*

distillery /dɪstɪləri/ **distilleries**
NC A **distillery** is a place where whisky or a similar strong alcoholic drink is made by a process of distilling. *There is a large distillery here for distilling spirits which they called Glasgow brandy.*

distinct /dɪstɪŋkt/
1 ADJ If one thing is **distinct** from another, there is an important difference between them. *Our interests were quite distinct from those of the workers.*
2 You use **as distinct from** to indicate exactly which thing you mean by contrasting it with something else. *...parliamentary (as distinct from presidential) systems.*
3 ADJ If something is **distinct**, you can hear or see it clearly. *Looking over the bottom of the foothills, there's a very distinct line where it becomes forest... Each stage of the parasite is distinct.* ◆ **distinctly** ADV *Jones was distinctly seen at the back door.*
4 ADJ ATTRIB You can use **distinct** to emphasize that something is great enough in amount or degree to be noticeable or important. *This speech marks a distinct hardening of their position. ...a distinct possibility of war.* ◆ **distinctly** SUBMOD *...a Frenchwoman with a distinctly un-Latin temperament.*

distinction /dɪstɪŋkʃn/ **distinctions**
1 NC A **distinction** is a difference between similar things. *Remember the distinction between those words.*
2 If you **draw** or **make a distinction** between two things, you say that they are different. *Many animal welfare groups draw a distinction between animals bred in captivity and those caught in the wild... I must make a distinction here between travellers and tourists.*
3 NU **Distinction** is the quality of being excellent. *He is a man of distinction.*

distinctive /dɪstɪŋktɪv/
ADJ Something that is **distinctive** has special qualities that make it easily recognizable. *Irene had a very distinctive voice.* ◆ **distinctively** ADV *...a distinctively African culture.*

distinguish /dɪstɪŋgwɪʃ/ **distinguishes, distinguishing, distinguished**
1 VOorV+between If you can **distinguish** one thing from another, you can see or understand the difference between them. *...animals that cannot distinguish colours... He had never been capable of distinguishing between his friends and his enemies.*
2 VO+from If a feature or quality **distinguishes** one thing from another, it causes the things to be recognized as different. *What distinguishes totalitarian governments from authoritarian ones?* ◆ **distinguishing** ADJ ATTRIB *He had no scars or distinguishing marks.*
3 VO If you can **distinguish** something, you are just able to see it, hear it, or taste it. *The photograph was poor and few details could be distinguished.*
4 V-REFL If you **distinguish** yourself, you do something

that makes you famous, important, or admired. *...prisoners who had distinguished themselves in battle.*

distinguishable /dɪstɪŋgwɪʃəbl/
ADJ If one thing is **distinguishable** from another, you can notice or understand the difference between them. *Berlin is now one city and the East and West portions become less distinguishable from each other every day... Each voice is absolutely distinguishable.*

distinguished /dɪstɪŋgwɪʃt/
ADJ A **distinguished** person is very successful, famous or important. *...rushing to meet the distinguished visitors.*

distort /dɪstɔːt/ **distorts, distorting, distorted**
1 VO To **distort** a fact or idea means to represent it wrongly. *You're distorting his argument.* ♦ **distorted** ADJ *They get a distorted picture of what's going on.*
2 VO If something is **distorted**, it becomes twisted into a different shape. *The objects were scorched and distorted.* ♦ **distorted** ADJ *...her distorted limbs.*

distortion /dɪstɔːʃn/ **distortions**
1 NUorNC **Distortion** is the changing of the meaning or purpose of something into something else that is different in an unacceptable way; used showing disapproval. *...this kind of distortion of history. ...deliberate distortion of an old idea. ...the grotesque distortions put about by the media.*
2 NUorNC **Distortion** is also the changing of the appearance or sound of something in a way that makes it seem strange or unclear. *We want to keep the amount of distortion to an absolute minimum... This kind of filtering produces certain kinds of distortions.*

distract /dɪstrækt/ **distracts, distracting, distracted**
VO If something **distracts** you or **distracts** your attention, it stops you concentrating. *It distracted them from their work.*

distracted /dɪstræktɪd/
ADJ If you are **distracted**, you are not concentrating properly because you are thinking about something else, often because you are worried. *During classes he was distracted and strangely troubled.* ♦ **distractedly** ADV *She began looking distractedly about her.*

distracting /dɪstræktɪŋ/
1 ADJ If something is **distracting**, it causes you to stop concentrating properly; used showing disapproval. *Sub-titles can be very distracting.*
2 ADJ You also use **distracting** to describe something that helps you to stop thinking about your everyday problems; used showing approval. *I find films both relaxing and distracting.*

distraction /dɪstrækʃn/ **distractions**
1 NCorNU A **distraction** is something that takes your attention away from what you are doing. *In spite of numerous modern distractions, children are still reading... She needed to work without interruption or distraction.*
2 NCorNU A **distraction** is also an object or activity that is intended to entertain people. *...the various distractions provided for them. ...wealthy tourists in search of distraction and entertainment.*

distraught /dɪstrɔːt/
ADJ If someone is **distraught**, they are extremely upset or worried. *'What can we do?' she asked, turning a distraught face to me.*

distress /dɪstrɛs/ **distresses, distressing, distressed**
1 NU **Distress** is extreme anxiety, sorrow, or pain. *Delays may cause distress to your family... He was breathing fast and in obvious distress.*
2 NU **Distress** is also the state of being in extreme danger and needing urgent help. *...an aircraft in distress.*
3 VO If someone or something **distresses** you, they cause you to be upset or worried. *I hate to distress you like this, but it is important... The blast, which occurred in a largely commercial area, has puzzled and distressed many Afghans.*

distressed /dɪstrɛst/
1 ADJ Someone who is **distressed** is upset because something unpleasant or alarming has happened or is about to happen. *She was distressed about my having to leave home.*

2 ADJ You also use **distressed** to describe someone who is in a great deal of pain. *Ovett dropped out of the race, clearly distressed and having difficulty breathing.*

distressing /dɪstrɛsɪŋ/
ADJ Something that is **distressing** causes you to feel extremely worried, alarmed, or unhappy. *He had found her tears very distressing... It was a distressing experience for me.* ♦ **distressingly** ADV *The number of emergency telephones was distressingly inadequate.*

distribute /dɪstrɪbjuːt/ **distributes, distributing, distributed**
1 VO If you **distribute** things such as leaflets, you hand them out to people or send them by post. *The government is to distribute a leaflet about the community charge.*
2 VO When goods **are distributed**, they are supplied to the shops or businesses that use or sell them. *They needed trucks to distribute their produce over New York City.*
3 VO To **distribute** something also means to share it among the members of a group. *The queen distributed Maundy money to a group of elderly men and women.*

distribution /dɪstrɪbjuːʃn/ **distributions**
1 NUorNC **Distribution** is the delivering of something to several people or organizations. *The President said he'll also provide technical assistance to help with distribution... This figure represents a sharp increase over August distributions when the relief operation was getting re-started... His job is to organize the distribution of money to students.*
2 NUorNC The **distribution** of something is the sharing out of it among a particular group. *The conference discussed the fair distribution of income and wealth... The survey looks at the age distributions of each ethnic group.*

distributor /dɪstrɪbjʊtə/ **distributors**
NC A **distributor** is a person, company, or organization that supplies goods or provisions to shops, businesses, or countries. *A West German gas distributor, Ruhrgas, obtained over a third of the East German gas network... a group of aid agencies which is the only distributor of relief food in the south. ...the big manufacturers and distributors.*

district /dɪstrɪkt/ **districts**
1 NC+SUPP A **district** is an area of a town or country. *...doctors in country districts. ...a working class district of Paris.*
2 NC A **district** is also an administrative area of a town or country. *...district councils.*

district attorney, district attorneys
NC A **district attorney** is a lawyer who prosecutes criminal cases for the State or Federal government in the United States. *The first witness, the New York District Attorney, Robert Morgenthau, said no action had been taken against him.*

district nurse, district nurses
NC A **district nurse** is a nurse who goes to people's houses to give them medical treatment. *Ask your family doctor, district nurse, or health visitor.*

distrust /dɪstrʌst/ **distrusts, distrusting, distrusted**
VO If you **distrust** someone or something, you think that they are not honest, reliable, or safe. *He keeps his savings under his mattress because he distrusts the banks.* ► Also NU *...their distrust of politicians.*

distrustful /dɪstrʌstfl/
ADJ If you are **distrustful** of someone or something, you think that they are not honest, reliable, or safe. *Both parties were distrustful of his policies.*

disturb /dɪstɜːb/ **disturbs, disturbing, disturbed**
1 VO If you **disturb** someone, you interrupt what they are doing and cause them inconvenience. *If she's asleep, don't disturb her.*
2 VO If something **disturbs** you, it makes you feel upset or worried. *I was disturbed by some of the speeches.*
3 VO To **disturb** something means to change its position or appearance. *The sand had not been disturbed.*

disturbance /dɪstɜːbəns/ **disturbances**
1 NC A **disturbance** is an event in which people behave

violently in public. *...violent disturbances in Liverpool.*
2 NUorNC **Disturbance** is the act of making a situation less peaceful, organized, or stable. *These proposals involved the least disturbance of the status quo... This would cause disturbance to the public.*
3 NC You can use **disturbance** to refer to extreme unhappiness or mental illness. *...serious emotional disturbance.*

disturbed /dɪstɜːbd/
ADJ Someone who is **disturbed** is extremely worried, unhappy, or mentally ill. *...emotionally disturbed youngsters. ...his disturbed childhood.*

disturbing /dɪstɜːbɪŋ/
ADJ Something that is **disturbing** makes you feel worried or upset. *She has written two disturbing books.* ◆ **disturbingly** SUBMOD *The radiation levels are disturbingly high.*

disunite /dɪsjuːnaɪt/ **disunites, disuniting, disunited**
VO If something **disunites** a group of people who have previously had the same ideas and intentions, it causes disagreement and division among them; a formal word. *The success of the campaign was in disuniting the ruling party.* ◆ **disunited** ADJ *Disunited governments are not good for the country.*

disunity /dɪsjuːnəti/
NU **Disunity** is a lack of agreement among people which prevents them from working together effectively; a formal word. *This could provoke serious disunity in the party... There is considerable disunity within the Churches on this issue.*

disuse /dɪsjuːs/
NU **Disuse** is the state of being no longer used. *These methods have fallen into disuse.*

disused /dɪsjuːzd/
ADJ A **disused** place or building is no longer used. *...a disused airfield near Lincoln.*

ditch /dɪtʃ/ **ditches, ditching, ditched**
1 NC A **ditch** is a long, narrow channel cut into the ground at the side of a road or field. *...a muddy ditch.*
2 VO If you **ditch** something, you get rid of it; an informal use. *He had decided to ditch the car.*
3 If you make a **last ditch attempt** or a **last ditch effort** to achieve something, you try for the final time to make a success of it, after all previous attempts have failed. *Mr Gorbachev's proposals sound like a last ditch attempt to secure peace. ...a last ditch effort to assist in the election of Mr Chirac.*

ditchwater /dɪtʃwɔːtə/
If you say that something or someone is **as dull as ditchwater**, you mean that they are extremely boring; an old-fashioned, informal expression.

dither /dɪðə/ **dithers, dithering, dithered**
V If you **are dithering**, you are hesitating because you are unable to make a quick decision. *After dithering about helplessly for a bit, he picked up the phone.*

ditto /dɪtəʊ/
You use **ditto** to represent a word or phrase that you have just used in order to avoid repeating it. In written lists, ditto can be represented by a symbol (") underneath the word or phrase that you want to repeat. *...a cupboard door with mirror, a bathroom door ditto.*

ditty /dɪti/ **ditties**
NC A **ditty** is a short and simple song or poem; an old-fashioned word, often used humorously. *Ditties like 'Jack and Jill' could well be the foundation for appreciating poetry later on in a child's life.*

diurnal /daɪɜːnl/
ADJ **Diurnal** activities happen during the daytime; a formal word. *His domestic life had led him to strictly diurnal habits, and by sundown he was always asleep.*

divan /dɪvæn/ **divans**
NC A **divan** or a **divan bed** is a bed with a thick base under the mattress. *She was sitting on a divan with her shoes off.*

dive /daɪv/ **dives, diving, dived**. The form **dove** is sometimes used as the past tense of the verb in American English.
1 V If you **dive**, you jump head-first into water with your arms straight above your head. *Two survivors escaped by diving into the river.* ▶ Also NC *Ralph did*

a dive into the pool.
2 V To **dive** also means to go under the surface of the sea or a lake, either using special breathing equipment or in a specially designed vessel. *The deepest an unprotected human can dive is about 40 metres... We scrambled below and the submarine prepared to dive.*
3 V When birds and animals **dive**, they go quickly downwards, head-first, through the air or water. *The seals were unable to dive for fish and died of starvation.*
4 VA If you **dive** in a particular direction, you jump or rush in that direction. *He dived after the ball.* ▶ Also N SING *He made a dive for the bag.*
5 VA If you **dive** into a bag or cupboard, you put your hands into it quickly in order to get something out; an informal use. *He suddenly dived into the chest and produced a shirt.*

diver /daɪvə/ **divers**
NC A **diver** is a person who works under water, usually in the sea, using special breathing equipment. *Helicopters, divers and local fishermen all took part in the search.*

diverge /daɪvɜːdʒ/ **diverges, diverging, diverged**
1 V When things **diverge**, they are different, or they become different. *Their interests diverge from those of pensioners... His view is that bears and raccoons diverged from a common ancestor.*
2 V When roads or paths **diverge**, they begin leading in different directions. *The Mujahedeen control a strategic junction where the road also diverges to Lagham.*

divergence /daɪvɜːdʒəns/ **divergences**
NCorNU **Divergence** is a difference between two or more things, attitudes or opinions that are usually expected to be similar to each other; a formal word. *Perhaps more important were divergences in equipment... There is an inseparable divergence of interest... There was much greater divergence on how to handle the crisis.*

divergent /daɪvɜːdʒənt/
ADJ Things that are **divergent** are very different, or opposing, in attitudes or characteristics. *...widely divergent religious groups... They could not work out a compromise between their divergent standpoints.*

diverse /daɪvɜːs/
1 ADJ If a group or range of things is **diverse**, it is made up of a wide variety of things. *...the world's finest and most diverse arts festival. ...a diverse group of children... The films are a diverse mix of animation, short stills and full-length features.*
2 ADJ People, ideas, or objects that are **diverse** are different and distinct from each other. *The United Nations was in the best position to try to bring the diverse groups together. ...a man of diverse talents.*

diversify /daɪvɜːsɪfaɪ/ **diversifies, diversifying, diversified**
VorVO When an organization **diversifies**, it increases the variety of the things that it makes or does. *Many car manufacturers are diversifying as rapidly as they can... It also fits in with government policy to diversify production and grow trees to protect the environment.* ◆ **diversification** /daɪvɜːsɪfɪkeɪʃn/ NU *...a diversification of interests.*

diversion /daɪvɜːʃn/ **diversions**
1 NC A **diversion** is something that distracts your attention and makes you think about something else. *This incident was a diversion from the true message he was trying to get across.*
2 NU **Diversion** is the same as **enjoyment**; a formal use. *They seldom meet even for merriment and diversion.*
3 NC A **diversion** is also a special route arranged for traffic when the normal route cannot be used. *...warnings about roadworks and diversions up ahead.*
4 NUorNC The **diversion** of something involves changing its course or destination, or changing the thing that it is used for. *...the sale of arms to Iran and the subsequent diversion of funds to the Contras... Possible diversions of the troop convoys were considered.*

diversionary /daɪvɜːʃənəri/
ADJ ATTRIB A **diversionary** activity is intended to

attract people's attention away from something which you do not want them to think about or know about. *His speech was widely viewed as a diversionary tactic to disguise the real situation... This was clearly a diversionary proposal.*

diversity /daɪvɜːsəti/ **diversities**
NC+SUPPorNU+SUPP Someone or something's **diversity** is the state of it being varied or the range of its different conditions, qualities, or types. *...a federation of states with strong regional and linguistic diversities... There is an extraordinary diversity of talent, background, class and race... There'll be other populations elsewhere which still have considerable genetic diversity.*

divert /daɪvɜːt/ **diverts, diverting, diverted**
1 VO To **divert** people or vehicles means to change their course or destination. *The police were diverting the traffic.*
2 VOA To **divert** something such as money means to cause it to be used for a different purpose. *We feel it desirable to divert funds from armaments to health and education.*
3 VO If you **divert** someone's attention, you stop them thinking about something by making them think about something else. *The government was trying to divert attention from more pressing problems.*

divest /daɪvest/ **divests, divesting, divested**; a formal word.
1 V-REFL+of If you **divest** yourself of something, you get rid of it or stop being responsible for it. *She divested herself of her bag... Most Western countries have long since divested themselves of their colonies.*
2 VO+of If you **divest** something of a quality or function, you cause it to lose that quality or function. *They are divesting public housing of its welfare role.*

divide /daɪvaɪd/ **divides, dividing, divided**
1 V-ERG If someone **divides** something or if it **divides**, it separates into two or more parts. *...an attempt to divide the country into two social classes... The children are divided into three age groups... The cells begin to divide rapidly.*
2 VO If you **divide** something among a number of people, you give each of them part of it. *The land was divided between the two brothers... Twenty percent of the money will be divided among charities for young people in Britain.*
3 VO If something **divides** two areas or **divides** an area into two, it forms a barrier or boundary between the two areas. *A line of rocks seemed to divide the cave into two... The frontier which divides North and South Korea is reputedly the most heavily fortified in the world.*
4 V-ERG If people **divide** over something or if something **divides** them, they disagree about it. *This question is dividing the people of Wales. ...the British imperial policy of 'divide and rule'.*
5 VO If you **divide** a larger number by a smaller number, you calculate how many times the smaller number can go exactly into the larger number. *This total is then divided by 52 to arrive at your weekly payment.*
6 NC A **divide** is a significant difference between two groups. *The divide between rich and poor was great... This shows a gloomy picture of the North/South divide with Scotland and the North facing the worst of the job cuts.*

divide up PHRASAL VERB If you **divide** something **up**, you share it out among a number of people. *The proceeds had to be divided up among about four hundred people.*

divided /daɪvaɪdɪd/
1 ADJ If something is **divided**, it contains or involves two or more opposing ideas or opinions. *My mind is divided... Public opinion was divided... Many children suffer from divided loyalties when their parents are divorced.*
2 ADJ If a group of people are **divided**, they strongly disagree about something. *The conference was divided on many issues... Christianity is deeply divided on the whole issue of test-tube babies.*

dividend /dɪvɪdend/ **dividends**
NC A **dividend** is the part of a company's profits which

is paid to people who have shares in the company. *The dividend can go up or down depending on the company's profits.* ● If something **pays dividends**, it brings advantages at a later date. *The time she had spent learning German now paid dividends.* ● See also **peace dividend.**

divider /dɪvaɪdə/ **dividers**
1 NC+SUPP A **divider** is something which forms a barrier between two areas of space or two groups of people. *Open shelving makes a most attractive room divider... The two-tier education system is a great social divider.*
2 N PL **Dividers** are an instrument used for measuring lines and for marking points along them. Dividers consist of two pointed arms joined at one end and look rather like a pair of compasses. *...a pair of dividers. ...navigational dividers.*

dividing line, dividing lines
NC A **dividing line** is a distinction or set of distinctions which marks the difference between two types or groups and keeps them separate. *The dividing line between wants and needs is a hard one to define.*

divine /dɪvaɪn/ **divines, divining, divined**
1 ADJ Something that is **divine** belongs or relates to a god or goddess. *These men had been operating under divine inspiration.* ◆ **divinely** ADV *...a divinely appointed prophet.*
2 ADJ Some people use **divine** to describe things that they like or enjoy very much; used in old-fashioned, informal speech. *Darling, how lovely to see you, you look simply divine.*
3 VOorV-REPORT If you **divine** something that you did not know before, you learn it by guessing or by being very sensitive; a literary use. *She had divined something about me... No watcher could have divined that he was really an assassin.*

diving /daɪvɪŋ/
1 NU **Diving** is the activity of working or exploring underwater or at the bottom of the sea, using special breathing equipment. *One ship is used for deep sea diving and submarine rescue.*
2 NU **Diving** is also the sport or activity in which you jump into water head-first with your arms held straight above your head. *I was never any good at diving.*

diving board, diving boards
NC A **diving board** is a board high above a swimming pool from which people can dive into the water. *...a swimming pool diving board wobbling after a dive.*

divinity /dɪvɪnəti/ **divinities**
1 NU **Divinity** is the study of the Christian religion. *Jeffrey John, Dean of Divinity at Magdalen College, Oxford, looks at the gospel of Luke.*
2 NU **Divinity** is also the quality of being divine. *The divinity of the Pharaoh was not doubted.*
3 NC A **divinity** is a god or goddess. *His soul is, to Buddhists, that of a Bodhisattva—a divinity in human form.*

divisible /dɪvɪzəbl/
ADJ PRED A number that is **divisible** by another number can be divided by that number. *Each of these numbers is divisible by two.*

division /dɪvɪʒn/ **divisions**
1 NU The **division** of something is the act of separating it into two or more different parts. *...the division of physical science into chemistry and physics.*
2 NU The **division** of something is also the sharing of it among a number of people. *...the division of responsibility.*
3 NU **Division** is the mathematical process of dividing one number by another.
4 NC A **division** is a difference or conflict between two groups of people. *...a division between hardliners and moderates. ...serious ethnic divisions in the Republics of Estonia, Latvia and Lithuania.*
5 NC A **division** is also one of the groups of teams which make up a football league or other sports league. *Celtic finished fifth in Scotland's Premier Division last season.*
6 NC A **division** is also a group of military units which fight as a single unit. *A rifle division was ordered to*

move in and shoot if necessary.
7 NC A **division** also refers to a department in a large organization. *...the BBC's engineering division.*

division of labour, divisions of labour
NCorNU A **division of labour** is a way of organizing a society or a household so that each member has a particular task to do which contributes to the running of that society or household. *This is a division of labour designed to suit everyone. ...a fundamental change in the world division of labour.*

division sign, division signs
NC A **division sign** is the sign (÷) which is put between two numbers to show that the first number is being divided by the second.

divisive /dɪvaɪsɪv/
ADJ Something that is **divisive** causes hostility between people; a formal word. *...the Government's divisive policy of confrontation. ... the divisive issue of sanctions against South Africa.*

divorce /dɪvɔːs/ **divorces, divorcing, divorced**
1 V-RECIP When someone **divorces** their husband or wife, or when they get divorced, their marriage is legally ended. *His wife Kim divorced him in 1978... In 1984, it became possible to divorce after just one year, instead of the previous minimum of three. ...when my parents got divorced.* ♦ **divorced** ADJ *...a divorced lady.*
2 NCorNU A **divorce** is the legal ending of a marriage. *The report also notes an increase in early divorces... I want a divorce. ...a rising divorce rate... One in three British marriages ends in divorce.*
3 VO If you **divorce** one thing from another, you treat the two things as separate from each other; a formal use. *I don't think it is possible to divorce sport from politics.*

divorcee /dɪvɔːsiː/ **divorcees**
NC A **divorcee** is a person, especially a woman, who is divorced. *For women, the number of divorcees getting married again has fallen.*

divulge /daɪvʌldʒ/ **divulges, divulging, divulged**
VOorV-REPORT If you **divulge** a piece of information, you tell it to someone; a formal word. *I shall divulge the details to no one... He divulged that he had heard reports about Sharp's misbehaviour.*

D.I.Y. /diːaɪwaɪ/
NU **D.I.Y.** is the activity of making or repairing things yourself, especially in your home. **D.I.Y.** is an abbreviation for 'do-it-yourself'. *...D.I.Y. experts.*

dizzy /dɪzi/
1 ADJ If you feel **dizzy**, you feel that you are losing your balance and are about to fall. *I can't climb trees—I get dizzy.* ♦ **dizziness** NU *She was overcome by nausea and dizziness.*
2 If someone reaches the **dizzy heights** of success, they have been very successful in their chosen career. This expression is used especially of people in the entertainment industry. *She first knew such dizzy heights as a top exponent of black American music.*

Djibouti /dʒɪbuːti/
The **Republic of Djibouti** is a country in north-eastern Africa. Djibouti was a French colony, originally called French Somaliland and later the French Territory of the Afars and Issas, from the 19th century until it became independent in 1977. Ethnic violence, between the Issas (50%) and Afars (40%), has been a cause of civil disorder. The Popular Assembly for Progress (RPP) became the sole party in 1981. Hassan Gouled Aptidon, an Issa, became President in 1977. Barkad Gourad Hamadou, an Afar, became Prime Minister in 1978. Djibouti is a member of the Arab League and the Organization of African Unity. There are many refugees in Djibouti from Ethiopia and Somalia. There is also a French garrison. Djibouti produces agricultural products. Large foreign debts are a major economic problem. The capital, which had a population of 200,000 in 1982, is also called **Djibouti**. ♦ **Djibouti** N, ADJ
▪ *per capita GNP:* approximately US$600 ▪ *religion:* Islam (mainly Sunni) ▪ *language:* Arabic and French (official) ▪ *currency:* franc ▪ *capital:* Djibouti ▪ *population:* 483,000 (1987) ▪ *size:* 23,200 square kilometres.

Djohar, Saïd Mohammed
/saɪd məuhæməd dʒəuhə/
Saïd Mohammed Djohar became acting President of the Comoros and leader of the Comoran Union for Progress (UCP or Udzima) in 1989, and was elected President in 1990. He was formerly President of the Supreme Court. Born: 1918.

Dlamini, Obed /dləmiːni/
Obed Dlamini was appointed Prime Minister of Swaziland in 1989. He is the founder and former Secretary-General of the Swaziland Federation of Trade Unions. Born: 1937.

DNA /diːeneɪ/
N PROP **DNA** is a type of acid that is the main constituent of the chromosomes in most living organisms. It is responsible for passing on hereditary characteristics. **DNA** is an abbreviation for deoxyribonucleic acid. *It has all the DNA and genetic information needed to cause infection... We are able to extract DNA from bone.*

do, does, doing, did, done; pronounced /də/ or /duː/ when it is an auxiliary verb and /duː/ when it is a main verb.
1 AUX **Do** is used to form the negative of main verbs, by putting 'not' or '-n't' after the auxiliary and before the main verb in its infinitive form. *You don't have to go... There are lots of words in that newspaper article which they don't understand... He didn't know what was happening.*
2 AUX **Do** is used to form questions, by putting the subject after the auxiliary and before the main verb in its infinitive form. *What did he say?... Do you think that's possible?... Does it cause problems in practical terms for the patient?*
3 AUX **Do** is used to stand for, and refer back to, a previous verbal group. *She meets lots more people than I do... I like cooking and so does John.*
4 AUX **Do** is used in question tags. *She made a lot of mistakes, didn't she?... That doesn't mean that they're causing the disease, does it?... Patrick, this really does look like a complete victory for the rebels, doesn't it?*
5 AUX **Do** is used to give emphasis to the main verb when there is no other auxiliary. *I did buy a map but I must have lost it... Do sit down... So it does look as though few firms will want to sell them.*
6 AUX **Do** is used with '-n't' or 'not' to tell someone not to behave in a certain way. *Don't speak to me like that.*
7 VO When you **do** something, you perform an action, activity, or task. *What are you doing?... I do the cooking and Brian does the cleaning... Each country nominates one official who does much of the groundwork.*
8 VO You use **do** with a noun referring to a thing when you are talking about something regularly done to that thing. *She had done her hair for the party... We have a man to do the garden.*
9 VO To **do** something about a problem means to try to solve it. *They promised that they were going to do something about immigration... There's nothing I can do about it... She was desperately ill and very little could be done for her.*
10 VO You use **do** to say that something has a particular result or effect. *Their policies have done more harm for the working class than ours... They are afraid of what it might do to the children.*
11 VO If you ask someone what they **do**, you are asking what their job is. *What do you want to do when you leave school?*
12 VA If someone **does** well or badly, they are successful or unsuccessful. *I didn't do very well in my exams... It all depends how the Labour Party do at this next election.*
13 VO If you **do** a subject, you study it at school or college. *I'm doing biology.*
14 VO You use **do** when referring to the speed that something achieves or can achieve. *The car's already doing 70 miles per hour.*
15 VorVO If you say that something will **do**, you mean that it is satisfactory. *No other school will do... Two thousand will do me very well.*

16 See also **doings**, **done**.

● **Do** is used in these phrases. ● If you ask someone **what** they **did with** something, you are asking where they put it. *What did you do with the keys?* ● If you ask **what** someone **is doing** in a particular place, you are expressing surprise that they are there. *What are you doing here? I thought you were still in London.* ● If you say that someone **would do well** to do something, you mean that they ought to do it. *She would do well to steer clear of men.* ● What something **has to do with** or **is to do with** is what it is connected or concerned with. *The basic argument has nothing to do with agriculture... It's got something to do with an economic crisis.* ● If you say that you **could do with** something, you mean that you need it. *I think we could all do with a good night's sleep.* ● **'How do you do?'** is a formal way of greeting someone. *'How do you do?'* is a formal way of greeting someone. *'How do you do, sir?'—'How do you do? I'm very happy to be here.'* ● **'How are you doing?'** is an informal way of greeting someone; used in American English. *How are you doing this morning, Bob?*

do away with PHRASAL VERB To **do away with** something means to get rid of it. *Modern medicines have not done away with disease.*

do out of PHRASAL VERB If you **do** someone **out of** something, you unfairly cause them not to have it; an informal expression. *He did me out of £500.*

do over PHRASAL VERB If you **do** something **over**, you do it again; used in American English. *They're going to have to reline it and do it over again.*

do up PHRASAL VERB 1 If you **do** something **up**, you fasten it. *He did his shoelaces up.* 2 To **do up** an old building means to repair and decorate it; an informal expression. *The theatre was horrible, done up as cheaply as possible.*

do without PHRASAL VERB If you **do without** something, you manage or survive in spite of not having it. *Many Victorian households did without a bathroom altogether... If you don't have cigarettes, you must simply do without.*

doc /dɒk/ **docs**
N C or VOCATIVE You can refer to a doctor as **doc**; an informal word. *Have you been to see the doc?... I said, 'Doc, I've got a ringing in my ear. What should I do?'*

docile /dəʊsaɪl/
ADJ A **docile** person or animal is quiet and easily controlled. *Their economic success is achieved on the basis of a cheap and docile workforce.*

dock /dɒk/ **docks, docking, docked**
1 NC A **dock** is an enclosed area of water where ships are loaded, unloaded, or repaired. *The docks were once home to the great Cunard liners that raced across the Atlantic.*
2 V When a ship **docks**, it comes into a dock. *They docked at Southampton.*
3 N SING In a law court, the **dock** is the place where the person accused of a crime stands or sits. *During the five minute court hearing, he sat silently in the dock.*
4 VO To **dock** someone's income means to keep back some of the money. *He docked her pocket money until the debt was paid off.*

docker /dɒkə/ **dockers**
N C A **docker** is a person who works at the docks. *Dockers unloaded the ship, which is expected to leave in a few hours.*

docket /dɒkɪt/ **dockets, docketing, docketed**
1 NC A **docket** is an itemized list which shows the contents of something, such as a parcel or a ship's cargo, that has to be delivered. It also proves who the goods belong to. *He stuffed the docket for the second case into his back pocket.*
2 VO If someone **dockets** a parcel, cargo, or other goods, they attach a docket to it. *They had been examined, categorized, docketed.*

dockland /dɒklənd/ **docklands**
N U or N PL The **dockland** of a town or city is the area around the docks. *The Corporation has reclaimed more than seven hundred acres of derelict dockland to create new businesses... Canary Wharf is a gigantic office block which epitomises the new docklands.*

dock worker, dock workers
N C A **dock worker** is a person who works in the docks, loading and unloading ships. *Dock workers went on strike hitting important exports from Panama.*

dockyard /dɒkjɑːd/ **dockyards**
N C A **dockyard** is a place where ships are built, maintained, and repaired. *The ship is currently undergoing exhaustive tests at a naval dockyard.*

doctor /dɒktə/ **doctors, doctoring, doctored**
1 N C or TITLE A **doctor** is someone qualified in medicine who treats sick or injured people. *AIDS and hepatitis have become a real problem for any medical person: doctor, dentist, nurse... She felt so ill we had to call the doctor... I went to see Doctor Barker this morning.*
2 NC **Doctor** is also the title given to someone who has been awarded the highest academic degree by a university. *He is a doctor of philosophy and a professor at Sofia University.*
3 VO To **doctor** something means to deliberately change it, usually in order to deceive people. *The dispatch from Davis had been doctored.*

doctoral /dɒktərəl/
ADJ ATTRIB A **doctoral** thesis or piece of research is written or done in order to obtain a doctor's degree. *...a doctoral dissertation.*

doctorate /dɒktərət/ **doctorates**
N C A **doctorate** is the highest degree awarded by a university. *He's carrying out research for a higher degree, a doctorate on low cost housing.*

doctrinaire /dɒktrɪneə/
ADJ Someone who is **doctrinaire** accepts particular theories or principles without considering arguments against them; a formal word. *Their attitudes were condemned as doctrinaire.*

doctrinal /dɒktraɪnl/
ADJ **Doctrinal** is used to describe something that is related to doctrines; a formal word. *The discussions had collapsed under the weight of doctrinal arguments between rival factions.*

doctrine /dɒktrɪn/ **doctrines**
1 NC+SUPP or NU+SUPP A **doctrine** is a principle or belief, or a set of principles or beliefs. *...Catholic doctrines. ...the doctrine of permanent revolution... Until now, he has merely been advising Catholic politicians to follow Church doctrine and to oppose abortion.*
2 NC A **doctrine** is also a statement of official government beliefs and aims; used in American English. *That doctrine, first delineated in 1982, spells out how the US military would fight a war... He supports the Supreme Court's one-man one-vote doctrine.*

document, documents, documenting, documented; pronounced /dɒkjəmənt/ when it is a noun and /dɒkjument/ when it is a verb.
1 NC A **document** is an official piece of paper with writing on it. *Dr Savimbi said the document would be signed within the next forty-eight hours. ...travel documents.*
2 VO If you **document** something, you make a detailed record of it on film, tape, or paper. *The Alliance of Human Rights Advocates has documented evidence of torture and executions.*

documentary /dɒkjumentᵊri/ **documentaries**
1 NC A **documentary** is a radio or television programme or a film, which gives information about a particular subject. *...a television documentary on the lives of the Royal Family.*
2 ADJ ATTRIB **Documentary** evidence consists of written information. *Polish researchers were studying the documentary evidence relating to the massacres at first hand.*

documentation /dɒkjumənteɪʃn/
N U **Documentation** consists of documents that provide proof or evidence of something. *There was no suggestion that police documentation showed that the confessions had been cooked up.*

dodder /dɒdə/ **dodders, doddering, doddered**
V If someone **dodders**, they walk in an unsteady or shaky way, usually because they are old.

doddering /dɒdərɪŋ/
ADJ Someone who is **doddering** walks in an unsteady

and shaky way, usually because they are old. *She was doddering and frail.*

doddery /dɒdəri/
ADJ Someone who is **doddery** walks in an unsteady and shaky way, usually because they are old. *He was a new kind of leader, very different from his grey-suited doddery old predecessors.*

doddle /dɒdl/
N SING Something that is a **doddle** is very easy to do; an informal word. *Don't worry about it. It'll be a doddle.*

dodge /dɒdʒ/ **dodges, dodging, dodged**
1 V If you **dodge** somewhere, you move there suddenly to avoid being hit, caught, or seen. *He dodged into the post office.*
2 VO If you **dodge** a moving object, you avoid it by quickly moving aside. *The Minister had to dodge flying tomatoes.*
3 VO If you **dodge** a problem, you avoid thinking about it or dealing with it. *This issue should not be dodged.*

dodgem /dɒdʒəm/ **dodgems**
NC A **dodgem** or **dodgem car** is a small electric car with a wide rubber bumper all round. People drive dodgems around a special enclosure at a fairground. *Let's go on the dodgems.*

dodger /dɒdʒə/ **dodgers**
NC+SUPP A **dodger** is someone who avoids an obligation or duty, such as paying taxes, by using trickery or deceit. *He was accused of being a tax dodger.*

dodgy /dɒdʒi/
ADJ Something that is **dodgy** seems rather risky, dangerous, or unreliable; an informal word. *It's a rather dodgy plan, but it might just work... Relying on the conscience of your rulers is a dodgy thing.*

dodo /dəʊdəʊ/ **dodos** or **dodoes**
1 NC A **dodo** was a very large bird that was unable to fly. Dodos are now extinct. *Every year thousands of species go the way of the dodo, mainly because of man-induced environmental change.*
2 If you say that something is **as dead as a dodo**, you are emphasizing that it no longer exists; an informal expression. *How can something be the law of the land one day and as dead as a dodo the next?*

Dodoma /dədəʊmə/
Dodoma was selected in 1974 to replace Dar es Salaam as the administrative capital of Tanzania. Population: 85,000 (1985).

doe /dəʊ/ **does** /dəʊz/
NC A **doe** is an adult female deer, rabbit, or hare.

doer /duːə/ **doers**
NC A **doer** is a person who does jobs promptly and efficiently and does not spend much time thinking about them. *She is one of the doers of this world.*

does, pronounced /dəz/ or /dʌz/ when it is an auxiliary verb and /dʌz/ when it is a main verb.
Does is the third person singular of the present tense of **do**.

doesn't /dʌznt/
Doesn't is the usual spoken form of 'does not'. *It's something which doesn't effect the environment.*

doff /dɒf/ **doffs, doffing, doffed**
VO If you **doff** your hat you take it off as a way of greeting or saluting someone; an old-fashioned word. *The sailors doffed their hats and cheered as the Royal couple sailed past.*

dog /dɒg/ **dogs, dogging, dogged**
1 NC A **dog** is an animal that is often kept as a pet. Dogs are also used to guard or hunt things. *A person bitten by a dog requested an anti-rabies injection.*
2 NC When you are mentioning the sex of a dog or fox, you refer to the male animal as a **dog**.
3 VO If problems or injuries **dog** you, they keep affecting you. *The project has been dogged by a number of technical problems... Bad luck has dogged me all year.*

dogcart /dɒgkɑːt/ **dogcarts**
NC A **dogcart** is a light cart with two wheels pulled by a horse, which people can ride in.

dog-collar, dog-collars
NC A **dog-collar** is a white collar worn by Christian priests and ministers; an informal word.

dog-eared
ADJ A **dog-eared** book or piece of paper has been used so much that the corners of the pages are turned down or crumpled. *The Commander thumbs through a dog-eared note-pad.*

dogfight /dɒgfaɪt/ **dogfights**
1 NC A **dogfight** is a fight between fighter planes, in which they fly close to one another and manoeuvre very fast. *Iran says its jets shot down an Iraqi war plane in a dogfight over the Gulf.*
2 NC A **dogfight** is also a fight between dogs, especially one that has been illegally organized by people for entertainment.

dogfish /dɒgfɪʃ/; **dogfish** is both the singular and the plural form.
NC A **dogfish** is a small shark. There are several kinds of dogfish.

dogged /dɒgɪd/
ADJ ATTRIB **Dogged** means showing determination to continue with something, even if it is very difficult. *...his dogged refusal to admit defeat.* ◆ **doggedly** ADV *Karen doggedly continued to search.*

doggerel /dɒgərəl/
NU **Doggerel** is poetry which is silly or funny, often written quickly and not intended to be serious. *She wrote some doggerel about it.*

doggie paddle /dɒgi pædl/
NU The **doggie paddle** or **dog paddle** is a swimming stroke which is often used by children or people who are learning to swim.

doggo /dɒgəʊ/
If you **lie doggo**, you lie still and keep very quiet so that people will not find you; an informal expression. *I lay doggo in my tent.*

dog-house
If you are **in the dog-house**, you are in disgrace and people are annoyed with you; an informal expression. *Poor Nigel is in the dog-house.*

dogma /dɒgmə/ **dogmas**
NCorNU A **dogma** is a rigid belief or system of beliefs held by a religious or political group; used showing disapproval. *He had no time for political or other dogmas... It's been a product of crude dogma and bureaucratic mismanagement. ...Christianity in the early days when there was less dogma.*

dogmatic /dɒgmætɪk/
ADJ Someone who is **dogmatic** about something is convinced that they are right and does not consider other points of view. *She was not impressed by his dogmatic assertions.* ◆ **dogmatically** ADV *'This stone,' he said dogmatically, 'is far older than the rest.'*

dogmatism /dɒgmətɪzəm/
NU **Dogmatism** is a strong and confident assertion of opinion, which is made without looking at the evidence and without considering that different opinions might be justified. *His education has taught him a distrust of dogmatism.* ◆ **dogmatist** /dɒgmətɪst/ **dogmatists** NC *England inherited the worst dogmas and dogmatists of the women's movement from America.*

do-gooder /duːgʊdə/ **do-gooders**
NC A **do-gooder** is someone who does things which they think will help other people, although others think that they are interfering. *A Conservative MP called Amnesty International interfering do-gooders.*

dogsbody /dɒgzbɒdi/ **dogsbodies**
NC A **dogsbody** is someone who does the boring jobs that nobody else wants to do; an informal word. *I was employed as a general dogsbody on the project.*

dog-tired
ADJ PRED If you are **dog-tired**, you are extremely tired; an informal word. *I was dog-tired that evening.*

Doha /dəʊhə/
Doha is the capital of Qatar and its largest city. Population: 217,000 (1986).

doily /dɔɪli/ **doilies**
NC A **doily** is a decorative mat made from paper or cloth that has a pattern of tiny holes in it. You put a doily on a plate under something such as a cake or a sandwich. *...a lace doily.*

doings /duːɪŋz/
N PL Someone's **doings** are their activities. *...a magazine about the doings of royalty.*

do-it-yourself
NU **Do-it-yourself** is the activity of making or repairing things in your home yourself, rather than employing other people. *Do-it-yourself home improvement is very popular.*

doldrums /dɒldrəmz/
If an area of activity is **in the doldrums**, nothing new or exciting is happening. *The American market is in the doldrums.*

dole /dəʊl/ doles, doling, doled
N SING The **dole** is money given regularly by the government to people who are unemployed. *This is forcing them to choose between the dole and a job... Nine thousand staff are aware that they may be joining the dole queues in the not-too-distant future.*
● Someone who is **on the dole** is unemployed and receives money regularly from the government. *Adult unemployment usually falls in April, while the number of school leavers on the dole normally rises.*
dole out PHRASAL VERB If you **dole** something **out**, you give a certain amount of it to each person in a group; an informal expression. *...the bureaucrats who dole out government favours.*

doleful /dəʊlfl/
ADJ A **doleful** expression or manner is depressed and miserable. *...a doleful sigh... The tunes are doleful and melancholic.*

doll /dɒl/ dolls
1 NC A **doll** is a child's toy which looks like a small person or baby. *...plastic dolls which they can spend hours dressing up.*
2 NC If you say that someone is a **doll**, you mean that you like them; used in American English. *Oh she's a doll, just a really wonderful worker.*

dollar /dɒlə/ dollars
NC A **dollar** is a unit of money in the USA, Canada, and some other countries. *They spent half a million dollars on the campaign.*

dolled up
ADJ PRED When a woman gets **dolled up**, she puts on smart clothes in order to look attractive; an informal expression. *She was all dolled up in the latest fashion.*

dollop /dɒləp/ dollops
NC A **dollop** of soft or sticky food is an amount of it served in a lump; an informal word. *...a dollop of ice-cream.*

doll's house, doll's houses
NC A **doll's house** is a toy in the form of a small house. *...a toy sailing boat, a robot and a doll's house.*

dolly /dɒli/ dollies
1 NC **Dolly** is a child's word for a doll.
2 NC A **dolly** or a **dolly bird** is a young woman who is considered to be very pretty but not very intelligent; an informal, old-fashioned expression that some people find offensive. *He was too busy chasing the teenage dollies of Paris.*

dolphin /dɒlfɪn/ dolphins
NC A **dolphin** is a mammal with a long snout which lives in the sea, usually in groups. Dolphins often swim with a curved motion on the surface of the ocean. *His life was saved by a school of dolphins which chased the shark away.*

dolt /dəʊlt/ dolts
NC If you say that someone is a **dolt**, you mean that you think that they have done something stupid. *You would have to be a complete dolt to miss the turn-off.*

domain /dəʊmeɪn/ domains; a formal word.
1 NC+POSS Someone's **domain** is the area where they have control or influence. *His domain extended to New York... The huge palace complex was the exclusive domain of the Emperor and his family.*
2 NC+SUPP A **domain** is also a particular area of activity or interest. *This question comes into the domain of philosophy... The book moves into a sort of spiritual domain.*

dome /dəʊm/ domes
NC A **dome** is a round roof. *...the dome of St Peter's.*

domed /dəʊmd/
ADJ Something that is **domed** is in the shape of a dome. *...a typical example of traditional architecture with its superb domed roofs.*

domestic /dəmestɪk/
1 ADJ ATTRIB **Domestic** means concerning matters within a country, rather than its relations with other countries. *...foreign and domestic policy.*
2 ADJ ATTRIB **Domestic** also means concerning your home and family. *...domestic responsibilities.*
3 ADJ ATTRIB **Domestic** items and services are used in people's homes rather than in factories or offices. *Hygiene in domestic kitchens was rated very good compared to the professional centres.*
4 ADJ **Domestic** animals are not wild, and are kept as pets or on farms. *The wild goats had once been domestic animals, but escaped into the wild.*

domesticate /dəmestɪkeɪt/ domesticates, domesticating, domesticated
VO When people **domesticate** wild animals or plants, they bring them under control and use them for work or for food. *Animals like cattle and sheep have come to be domesticated. ...differences between domesticated species and their wild relatives.*

domesticated /dəmestɪkeɪtɪd/
1 ADJ **Domesticated** animals are kept on farms and used for work or food. *There were no domesticated animals for ploughing.*
2 ADJ If someone is **domesticated**, they willingly do household tasks such as cleaning. *He thinks that it is unmanly to be domesticated.*

domesticity /dɒmestɪsəti, dəʊmestɪsəti/
NU **Domesticity** is the habit of spending a lot of time at home with your family; a formal word. *People are willing to give up the freedom of single life for the shackles of domesticity.*

domestic science
NU **Domestic science** is the study of cooking, needlework, and other household skills, usually learned at school. *The report says sport should be integrated with subjects such as biology and domestic science.*

domicile /dɒmɪsaɪl/ domiciles
NC+SUPP Your **domicile** is the place where you live; a formal word. *She took me to what was apparently her own domicile.*

domiciled /dɒmɪsaɪld/
ADJ PRED If you are **domiciled** in a particular place, you live there; a formal word. *She is regarded as domiciled in the UK.*

dominance /dɒmɪnəns/
1 NU If someone has **dominance** over a person, place, or group, they have power or control over them. *The treaty gave them dominance of the sea routes... The cricket world will be watching keenly to see if Pakistan can maintain their dominance in the forthcoming Test series.*
2 NU If something has **dominance**, it is regarded as more important than other similar things. *...the dominance of economics in social sciences.*

dominant /dɒmɪnənt/
ADJ Someone or something that is **dominant** is more powerful, important, or noticeable than similar people or things. *It had a dominant position in the market... She's been dominant in British politics for so long... Faldo was now the dominant force in the game.*

dominate /dɒmɪneɪt/ dominates, dominating, dominated
1 VO To **dominate** a situation means to be the most powerful or important person or thing in it. *Three men dominated the intellectual life of France in the 18th century... The sports news is dominated by Washington.* ◆ **domination** /dɒmɪneɪʃn/ NU *...the company's increasing domination of the UK market.*
2 VO If one country **dominates** another, it has power over it. *He said that Vietnam's aim was still to dominate Cambodia.* ◆ **domination** NU *...the domination of Europe over the rest of the world.*

dominating /dɒmɪneɪtɪŋ/
ADJ Someone who is **dominating** has a strong personality and influences other people a great deal. *He was the dominating figure in a huge conspiracy.*

domineering /dɒmɪnɪərɪŋ/
ADJ Someone who is **domineering** tries to control other people; used showing disapproval. *At the centre of Kafka's insecurity lay his relationship with his domineering father.*

Dominica /dɒmɪniːkə/

The **Commonwealth of Dominica** is a country in the Caribbean. It was a British colony from the 19th century until 1978. Sir Clarence Augustus Seignoret became President in 1983. Mary Eugenia Charles, of the Dominica Freedom Party (DFP), became Prime Minister in 1980. Dominica is a member of the Commonwealth and the Organization of American States. It exports bananas, coconuts, and citrus fruit. Tourism is an important industry. ◆ **Dominican** /dɒmɪniːkən/ N, ADJ ▪ *per capita GNP:* US$1,650 ▪ *religion:* Christianity (mainly Roman Catholic) ▪ *language:* English (official) ▪ *currency:* East Caribbean dollar ▪ *capital:* Roseau ▪ *population:* 82,000 (1989) ▪ *size:* 749 square kilometres.

Dominican Republic /dəmɪnɪkən rɪpʌblɪk/

The **Dominican Republic** is a country in the Caribbean. It was a Spanish colony from the 16th century until 1821, and was part of Haiti until 1844, when it became independent. From 1930 to 1961 it was ruled by General Rafael Trujillo. Dr Joaquín Balaguer Ricardo, of the Social Christian Reformist Party (PRSC), became President in 1986 and again in 1990. The Dominican Republic is a member of the Organization of American States. It exports sugar and ferro-nickel. Tourism is an important industry. Large foreign debts and high inflation are major economic problems. ◆ **Dominican** /dəmɪnɪkən/ N, ADJ ▪ *per capita GNP:* US$680 ▪ *religion:* Christianity (mainly Roman Catholic) ▪ *language:* Spanish ▪ *currency:* peso ▪ *capital:* Santo Domingo ▪ *population:* 7 million (1989) ▪ *size:* 48,072 square kilometres.

dominion /dəmɪnjən/

NU **Dominion** is control or authority; a formal word. *They now had dominion over a large part of southern India.*

domino /dɒmɪnəʊ/ **dominoes**

NUorNC **Dominoes** is a game played using small rectangular blocks marked with two groups of spots on one side. These blocks are called dominoes. *The crowd melted away and went back to playing dominoes... All they gave us was a box of dominoes.*

Do Muoi /dəʊ muɔɪ/

Do Muoi became Secretary General of the Communist Party of Vietnam in 1991. He was Minister of Commerce in 1969, Deputy Prime Minister and Minister of Building from 1976 to 1987, and Prime Minister from 1988 to 1991. Born: 1917.

don /dɒn/ **dons, donning, donned**

1 NC A **don** is a lecturer at Oxford or Cambridge University. *He was a don at Cambridge and they were undergraduates.*
2 VO If you **don** a piece of clothing, you put it on; a literary use. *The two men donned white cotton gloves.*

donate /dəʊneɪt/ **donates, donating, donated**

VO If you **donate** something to a charity or other organization, you give it to them. *The van was donated to us by a local firm.*

donation /dəʊneɪʃn/ **donations**

NC A **donation** is an amount of money, or something else that is valuable, given to a charity or other organization. *They received a large donation from one of the unions.*

done /dʌn/

1 **Done** is the past participle of **do**.
2 ADJ PRED A task that is **done** has been completed. *When her errand was done she ran home.* ● If you say that a situation or task is **over and done with**, you mean that it is finished and you can forget about it. *It will be of central importance to our party to get that review over and done with.*

donkey /dɒŋki/ **donkeys**

NC A **donkey** is an animal like a small horse with long ears. *A mule is the result of mating a horse with a donkey.*

donkey jacket, donkey jackets

NC A **donkey jacket** is a thick, warm jacket, which workmen often wear. *So far there have been no sightings of the three escaped men, who are all dressed in prison denims and donkey jackets.*

donkey work

NU **Donkey work** is hard work which is not very interesting; an informal expression. *Nobody tells me anything that's interesting. I just do the donkey work.*

donnish /dɒnɪʃ/

ADJ Someone who is **donnish** is considered to be rather serious and clever. *I hope you're not too donnish, Tom... It seemed that he might look forward to a donnish life devoted to private study.*

donor /dəʊnə/ **donors**

1 NC+SUPP A **donor** is someone who lets blood or an organ be taken from their body so that it can be given to a patient who needs it. *An appeal has been broadcast for blood donors to help treat the wounded.*
2 NC A **donor** is also someone who gives something such as money to a charity or other organization. *About half this amount comes from individual donors.*

don't /dəʊnt/

Don't is the usual spoken form of 'do not'. *He said, 'I don't believe this'.*

doodad /duːdæd/ **doodads**

NC A **doodad** is the same as a **doodah**; used in American English. *...other optical doodads I couldn't understand and didn't need.*

doodah /duːdɑː/ **doodahs**

NC You can use **doodah** to refer to something whose name you have forgotten or do not know; an informal word.

doodle /duːdl/ **doodles, doodling, doodled**

NC A **doodle** is a pattern or picture that you draw when you are bored or thinking about something else. *He made a few doodles with a ballpoint on the back of the bill.* ► Also V *I used to doodle on my papers.*

doom /duːm/

NU **Doom** is a terrible state or event in the future which you cannot prevent. *I felt as if I were going to my doom... He said there had always been those predicting doom and gloom.*

doomed /duːmd/

1 ADJ PRED If someone is **doomed** to an unpleasant or undesirable experience, they are certain to suffer it. *They are doomed to failure... He was doomed to be killed in a car crash.*
2 ADJ If something is **doomed**, it is certain to fail or be destroyed. *They informed the Prime Minister that his government was doomed.*

doomsday /duːmzdeɪ/

1 NU **Doomsday** is the end of the world. *Several distressed people described it as doomsday... The possibility of the disease affecting humans, he said, was a doomsday scenario.*
2 If you say that something will or could happen until **Doomsday**, you mean that it will or could go on for ever. *I could have knocked until Doomsday and Antonio would not have heard me.*

door /dɔː/ **doors**

1 NC A **door** is a swinging or sliding piece of wood, glass, or metal, which is used to open and close the entrance to a building, room, cupboard, or vehicle. *Do you have a safety chain on your front door?*
2 NC A **door** is also a doorway. *As they passed through the door, they saw Tom at the end of the room.*
3 When you are **out of doors**, you are in the open air, rather than inside a building. *The tremor caused panic among people who had been camping out of doors.*
4 See also **next door**.

doorbell /dɔːbel/ **doorbells**

NC A **doorbell** is a bell which you ring when you want the people inside a house to open the door. *When the doorbell rang, the host opened the door.*

door-handle, door-handles

NC A **door-handle** is the handle on a door which operates the mechanism that holds the door shut. You turn the door-handle to open or close the door.

doorknob /dɔːnɒb/ **doorknobs**

NC A **doorknob** is a round handle on a door.

doorman /dɔːmən/ **doormen**

NC A **doorman** is a person who is on duty at the main entrance of a large building, hotel, or club to help visitors that come to the building and to maintain security. *He was prevented from leaving the hotel by the doorman.*

doormat /dɔːmæt/ **doormats**
NC A **doormat** is a mat by a door which people can wipe their shoes on before going into a house. *You can weave this fibre into very strong rope which can then be woven into doormats.*

doorstep /dɔːstep/ **doorsteps**
NC A **doorstep** is a step on the outside of a building, in front of a door. *She was shot while standing on her doorstep as demonstrations went on nearby.* ● If a place is **on your doorstep**, it is very near to where you live. *The Afghan civil war will remain on Russia's doorstep.*

doorstop /dɔːstɒp/ **doorstops**
NC A **doorstop** is something such as a heavy object that you use to keep a door open and prevent it closing.

door-to-door
ADJ ATTRIB **Door-to-door** activities involve going from one house to another along a street, usually in order to try and sell something or to make official inquiries. *He began his sales career as a door-to-door salesman... Police in Wiltshire are carrying out door-to-door inquiries.*

doorway /dɔːweɪ/ **doorways**
NC A **doorway** is the space in a wall when a door is open. *A child stood in the doorway.*

dope /dəʊp/ **dopes, doping, doped**
1 NU **Dope** is an illegal drug such as cannabis; an informal use. *He was selling dope on a corner... This is the place to buy dope and everyone knows it... He has been allowed to keep his Super-flyweight world title despite failing a dope test.*
2 V O If one person **dopes** another, or **dopes** an animal, they put a drug into their food or drink to make them unconscious. *This will be Bravefoot's first race since he was doped at Doncaster last September.*

dopey /dəʊpi/
1 ADJ Someone who is **dopey** is sleepy, often because they have taken drugs or alcohol. *The pill had already made her dopey.*
2 ADJ If you describe someone as **dopey**, you mean that they are stupid; an informal use. *She's all right but her brother's a bit dopey.*

dorm /dɔːm/ **dorms**
NC A **dorm** is the same as a **dormitory**; an informal word. *At the front of the dorm is a bathroom, a couple of telephones and a small dayroom... They started walking up the hill to their dorms.*

dormant /dɔːmənt/
ADJ Something that is **dormant** has not been active or used for a long time. *The idea had lain dormant in Britain during the fifties.*

dormer /dɔːmə/ **dormers**
NC A **dormer** or a **dormer window** is a window that is built upright in a sloping roof. *...a one-and-a-half storey, stone-built farmhouse with dormer windows.*

dormitory /dɔːmətri/ **dormitories**
NC A **dormitory** is a large bedroom where several people sleep, for example in a boarding school or hostel. *Unmarried men and women live separately, in large dormitories... A whistle is their order to turn out their dormitory lights.*

dormouse /dɔːmaʊs/ **dormice** /dɔːmaɪs/
NC A **dormouse** is a small furry animal like a mouse.

dorsal /dɔːsl/
ADJ ATTRIB **Dorsal** means relating to the back or spine of the body. It is used especially when referring to fish; a technical term. *Its dorsal fin broke water.*

dosage /dəʊsɪdʒ/ **dosages**
NC The **dosage** of a medicine or drug is the amount that should be taken. *...a daily dosage of 150 mg.*

dose /dəʊs/ **doses, dosing, dosed**
1 NC A **dose** of a medicine or drug is a measured amount of it. *This is lethal to rats in small doses.*
2 V-REFL or V O If you **dose** someone, you give them a medicine or drug. *He dosed himself with pills.*

doss /dɒs/ **dosses, dossing, dossed**
doss down PHRASAL VERB If you **doss down** somewhere, usually in an uncomfortable place, you sleep there for a short time; an informal expression.

...a rusty stretcher where he had dossed down once or twice.

Dos Santos, José Eduardo /ʒʊzeɪ dʊs sæntʊs/
José Eduardo dos Santos became President of Angola in 1979. He is a member of the Popular Movement for the Liberation of Angola-Workers' Party (MPLA-PT). He was First Deputy Prime Minister, Minister of Planning, and Head of the National Planning Committee from 1978 to 1979. Born: 1942.

dosser /dɒsə/ **dossers**
NC A **dosser** is a city person who sleeps outside in the streets or in cheap, uncomfortable hotels; an informal word, used showing disapproval. *I wash every morning, get changed, try to look respectable, but people won't give me a job because I'm a dosser.*

doss-house, doss-houses
NC A **doss-house** is a kind of cheap hotel in a city for people who have no home and very little money; an informal word, used showing disapproval.

dossier /dɒsɪeɪ/ **dossiers**
NC A **dossier** is a collection of papers containing information on a particular subject. *The files contain personal dossiers on over 6 million people.*

dot /dɒt/ **dots, dotting, dotted**
1 NC A **dot** is a very small round mark. *She was wearing the red dot which Hindu women wear on their foreheads.*
2 V O If things are **dotted** around a particular area, they are scattered around it in small groups. *There are about forty sizeable resorts dotted around the coast... I can see the hillsides dotted with the shanty homes of thousands of people.*
3 If something happens **on the dot**, it happens at exactly the right time. *At eleven o'clock on the dot the bandsmen drew to attention and the parade began.*

dotage /dəʊtɪdʒ/
If someone is **in their dotage**, they are very old and becoming weak. *Will you look after me in my dotage?*

dote /dəʊt/ **dotes, doting, doted**
V+on or upon If you **dote on** someone, you love them very much and cannot see their faults. *He said a final farewell to his daughter and the two grandsons he doted on. ...the beautiful, demanding, possessive mother who doted upon her children.*

doting /dəʊtɪŋ/
ADJ **Doting** means showing a lot of love for someone or something. *Parents used to buy extra copies to send to doting relatives elsewhere.*

dot matrix printer, dot matrix printers
NC A **dot matrix printer** is a computer printer that uses a set of pins to produce the shape of each letter. *Instead of using a special recorder, we use an ordinary dot matrix printer.*

dotted /dɒtɪd/
ADJ ATTRIB **Dotted** lines are made of a row of dots. *The boundaries are shown on the map by dotted lines.*

dotty /dɒti/
ADJ Someone or something that is **dotty** is strange or slightly mad; an informal word. *He said it was dotty to suggest that the government's bill would be tyrannical.*

Douala /dʊɑːlə/
Douala is the largest city in Cameroon. Population: 1,030,000 (1986).

double /dʌbl/ **doubles, doubling, doubled**
1 ADJ ATTRIB You use **double** to describe things that are unusual because they have two similar parts rather than one. *He is desperate to avoid what could be a double disaster for his country... The relatively high profile of certain charities today serves a double purpose... Bernie Winters teamed up with his brother Mike to become one of the most successful double acts on television.*
2 PREDET If something is **double** the amount or size of another thing, it is twice as large. *British investment abroad was almost double the amount foreign companies invested here... We paid her double what she was getting before.*
3 ADJ ATTRIB You use **double** to describe a quantity of food or drink that is twice the normal size. *...a double gin.*
4 ADJ ATTRIB **Double** before a number or letter

indicates that it occurs twice... *My phone number is nine, double three, two, four... 'Apple' is spelt a, double p, l, e.*

5 ADJ ATTRIB **Double** is also used to describe a pair of similar things. *The double doors were open.*

6 V-ERG If something **doubles** or if you **double** it, it becomes twice as large. *The government is to double the amount spent on roads... If every performance sold out, he would double his investment... The world population is doubling every thirty-five years.*

7 V+as If something **doubles** as something else, it is used for it in addition to its main use. *This bedroom doubles as a study.*

8 NU **Doubles** is a game of tennis or badminton in which two people play against two other people. *Rick Leach and Jim Pugh will team up for the doubles... The women's doubles title was won by Martina Navratilova and Pam Shriver.*

9 If you **bend double**, you bend right over. If you are **bent double**, you are bending right over. *Peasants work throughout the day either hoeing arid soil or bent double planting rice.*

10 **double figures:** see figure.

double up PHRASAL VERB If you **double up** with laughter or pain, you bend your body right over. *The crowd, he says, doubled up with laughter. ...a great pain which causes you to double up.* ♦ **doubled up** ADJ PRED *I was doubled up in pain.*

double agent, double agents
NC A **double agent** is someone who works as a spy for a particular country or organization, but who also works for its enemies. *The Bureau of Counter Intelligence was responsible for infiltrating double agents into East Germany.*

double-barrelled; spelt **double-barreled** in American English.
1 ADJ A gun that is **double-barrelled** has two barrels. *A man armed with a double-barrelled shotgun fired indiscriminately as he walked through the streets of Whitley Bay.*
2 ADJ A surname that is **double-barrelled** has two parts which are joined by a hyphen, for example 'Miss J. Heydon-Smith'.

double bass /dʌbl beɪs/ **double basses**
NC A **double bass** is a large stringed instrument shaped like a violin. You play the double bass standing up. *...no violins, only one viola, three cellos and a double bass.*

double bed, double beds
NC A **double bed** is a bed that is designed for two people to sleep in.

double bill, double bills
NC A **double bill** is a performance in the theatre or the cinema, or a sporting event in which there are two main items on the programme. *The plays have never before been performed as a double bill... The Breland-Lee clash will be part of a welterweight double bill that also features another title fight.*

double blind
ADJ ATTRIB A **double blind** trial or test is a type of scientific test that compares two or more groups of items, usually drugs. Neither the scientists nor the people taking the test know who is using which item until after the test finishes. *In a series of double blind trials, more than 330 patients were given GLA supplements or dummy capsules... What were the results of those double blind trials?*

double bluff, double bluffs
NCorNU A **double bluff** is an attempt to deceive someone by saying exactly what you intend to do when you know that they will assume you are lying. *Perhaps, he thought, it was a kind of double bluff... Rosalind Yarde reports on the game of bluff and double bluff being played out in the corridors of Westminster.*

double-breasted
ADJ A **double-breasted** jacket or coat has two wide sections at the front which overlap when you button them up. *Stockbrokers and solicitors are going back to the classical look—two-button, double-breasted suits with turn-ups.*

double-check, double-checks, double-checking, double-checked
VOorV-REPORT If you **double-check** something, you check it a second time to make sure that it is completely correct or safe. *The police suspect he has been abducted but today's efforts are to double-check that he is not the victim of a tragic accident.*

double chin, double chins
NC Someone who has a **double chin** has a fold of fat under their chin. *He's stocky, with a double chin.*

double cream
NU **Double cream** is very thick cream.

double-cross, double-crosses, double-crossing, double-crossed
VO If someone **double-crosses** you, they betray you, instead of doing what you had planned together; an informal word. *Cook threatened to kill them if they double-crossed him.*

double-dealing
NU **Double-dealing** is deceitful behaviour. *They already have a reputation for political corruption and double-dealing of the worst sort.*

double-decker, double-deckers
NC A **double-decker** or a **double-decker bus** is a bus with two floors.

double Dutch
NU If you say that speech or writing is **double Dutch** you mean that you cannot understand it at all; an informal expression. *It all sounded a bit like double Dutch to me.*

double-edged
1 ADJ A comment that is **double-edged** has two meanings which can both apply to what has been said, but mean the opposite of each other. *She made a very double-edged remark about my work.*
2 ADJ A **double-edged** blade has two sharp edges.
3 If you say that something is a **double-edged sword**, you mean that although it seems to give a lot of benefits, there are also some disadvantages to it. *Success can be a double-edged sword... Their new defence policy is seen as a double-edged sword.*

double entendre /duːbl ɒnˈtɒndrə/ **double entendres;** also spelt **double-entendre**.
NC A **double entendre** is a word or phrase that has two meanings, one of which is rude and often sexual. *They mouthed outrageous double-entendres in crystal clear Edwardian accents.*

double-glaze, double-glazes, double-glazing, double-glazed
VO If you **double-glaze** a house or windows, you fit the windows with a second layer of glass in order to keep the inside of the house warmer or quieter. *Is it really worth double-glazing your house?*

double-glazing
NU **Double-glazing** is an extra layer of glass fitted to a window to keep a room warmer or quieter. *The additional cost of building a house with double-glazing is very small indeed.*

double-jointed
ADJ Someone who is **double-jointed** can bend parts of their body to a much greater degree than is normal.

double negative, double negatives
NC A **double negative** is a grammatical construction in which two negatives are used. In English, only one negative is needed, and double negatives, for example 'I didn't never say that', are considered to be incorrect.

double-park, double-parks, double-parking, double-parked
VorVO If someone **double-parks**, they park a car in the road by the side of another parked car rather than at the kerbside.

double-quick
ADVorADJ If something happens **double-quick** or in **double-quick** time, it happens very quickly indeed. *The police arrived double-quick, and arrested him... They had the rest of us locked up in double-quick time.*

double room, double rooms
NC A **double room** is a bedroom for two people, especially in a hotel. *Check the availability of inexpensive double rooms near the beach.*

double standard, double standards
NC A **double standard** is a set of unfair principles that allows more freedom of behaviour to one group of people than to another. *There were inequalities between men and women and a double standard of morality.*

doublet /dʌblət/ **doublets**
NC A **doublet** is a short, tight-fitting jacket which was worn by men in former times. *He is shown wearing a brown doublet with puffed sleeves.*

double-take, double-takes
If you **do a double-take**, your reaction to something is delayed because you have had to think twice about it, or because it is not what you expected to hear. *When I told him the news, he did a double-take.*

double talk
NU **Double talk** is talk that can deceive people or is difficult to understand because the things which are said have two possible meanings. *Shimon Peres accused the Palestinians of double talk and of making ambiguous statements.*

double vision
NU **Double vision** is a medical condition that makes you see a single object as two separate objects. It is caused by an illness, a blow to the head, or by drinking too much alcohol. *He suffered from double vision.*

doubly /dʌbli/
1 SUBMOD You use **doubly** to say that something has two aspects or features. *He is doubly disadvantaged, both by his age and by his nationality.*
2 SUBMOD You also use **doubly** to say that something happens or is true to a greater degree than usual. *It was doubly difficult for Dora at her age.*

doubt /daut/ **doubts, doubting, doubted**
1 NCorNU If you have **doubts** about something, you have feelings of uncertainty about it. *Frank had no doubts about the outcome of the trial... I had moments of doubt.*
2 V-REPORTorVO If you **doubt** whether something is true or possible, you think it is probably not true or possible. *I doubt if they will ever want vanilla pudding again... Maybe he changed his mind, but I doubt it.*
3 VO If you **doubt** something, you think it might not be true or might not exist. *...men who never doubt their own superiority.*
4 VO If you **doubt** someone or **doubt** their word, you think they might not be telling the truth. *He doubted Mr Savimbi's claim to have forsaken military solutions to the civil war.*
● **Doubt** is used in these phrases. ● If you say there is **no doubt** about something, you are emphasizing that it is true. *Rose was mad, there was no doubt about it.* ● You also use **no doubt** to say that you are assuming that something is true. *As Jennifer has no doubt told you, we are leaving tomorrow.* ● You use **without doubt** or **without a doubt** to emphasize that something is true. *Hugh Scanlon became without doubt one of the most powerful men in Britain.* ● If something is shown to be true **beyond a doubt**, it is shown to be definitely true. *We have established the ownership beyond all doubt.* ● If something is **in doubt** or is **open to doubt**, it is uncertain. *Devaluation had put Concorde's future in doubt.* ● If you are **in doubt** about something, you feel unsure about it. *If in doubt, call the doctor.* ● to **give** someone **the benefit of the doubt**: see **benefit**.

doubter /dautə/ **doubters**
NC A **doubter** is someone who has doubts, especially about their religion or a political system. *They want to show to doubters that the Gorbachov regime can be tough as well as reformist.*

doubtful /dautfl/
1 ADJ Something that is **doubtful** seems unlikely or uncertain. *It is doubtful whether the Chairman would approve... The organization has a doubtful future.*
2 ADJ If you are **doubtful** about something, you are unsure about it. *I was a little doubtful about accepting the job.* ◆ **doubtfully** ADV *Ralph looked at him doubtfully.*

doubtless /dautləs/
ADV SEN If something is **doubtless** the case, it is probably or almost certainly the case. *Over 2,500 species are known and doubtless more are still to be discovered.*

dough /dəu/
NU **Dough** is a mixture, mainly of flour and water, which can be cooked to make bread, pastry, or biscuits. *These ingredients are made into dough, baked and ground into fine powder... It will take an hour if I boil the chicken and mix the dough while it's cooking.*

doughnut /dəunʌt/ **doughnuts**
NC A **doughnut** is a lump or ring of sweet dough cooked in hot fat. *...cream filled doughnuts.*

doughty /dauti/ **doughtier, doughtiest**
ADJ Someone who is **doughty** is brave, determined, and not easily defeated; an old-fashioned word. *...such a doughty fighter.*

doughy /dəui/ **doughier, doughiest**
ADJ Something that is **doughy** has a thick, sticky texture, like dough. *The old man took up the doughy mass and placed it upon the hot stone.*

Douglas /dʌgləs/
Douglas is the capital of the Isle of Man. Population: 20,000 (1986).

Douglas-Home, Sir Alec /ælɪk dʌgləs hjuːm/
Sir Alec Douglas-Home was Prime Minister of the United Kingdom from 1963 to 1964. He is a member of the Conservative Party. He was MP for South Lanark from 1931 to 1945, and for Lanark from 1950 to 1951. In 1951 he succeeded as the 14th Earl of Home. He was Deputy Leader of the House of Lords from 1956 to 1957, and Leader from 1959 to 1960. In 1963 he disclaimed his peerages, and was MP for Kinross and West Perthshire from 1963 to 1974. He was the leader of the Conservative Party from 1963 to 1965. He was Foreign Secretary from 1960 to 1963, and from 1970 to1974. In 1974 he was created Baron Home of the Hirsel of Coldstream. Born: 1903.

dour /duə, dauə/
ADJ Someone who is **dour** has a severe and unfriendly manner. *She faced me with her usual dour expression.* ◆ **dourly** ADV *'Yes,' said Christopher, smiling dourly.*

douse /daus/ **douses, dousing, doused**; also spelt **dowse**.
1 VO If you **douse** a fire or light, you stop it burning or shining. *The lightening starts more fires than the rain douses.*
2 VO If you **douse** something with liquid, you throw the liquid over it. *She had doused herself with perfume.*
3 VO To **douse** a difficult situation means to say or do something to calm it down. *...Mr Gorbachov's suggestions for dousing this major regional conflict.*

dove, doves; pronounced /dʌv/ for the meanings in paragraphs 1 and 2, and /dəuv/ for the meaning in paragraph 3.
1 NC A **dove** is a type of pigeon which is usually white. Doves are often used as a symbol of peace. *The stamp showed a flying dove carrying a letter in its beak.*
2 NC In politics, a **dove** is someone who supports the use of liberal policies or peaceful methods to solve difficult situations. *How can this contradiction between anti-communist hardliner and the dove on social issues be explained? ...the divide between hawks and doves within Israel.*
3 **dove** is a past tense of **dive**; used in American English. *They sprayed bullets as park officials dove for cover.*

dovecote /dʌvkɒt/ **dovecotes**; also spelt **dovecot**.
NC A **dovecote** is a box, shelter, or part of a house built for doves or pigeons to live in.

dovetail /dʌvteɪl/ **dovetails, dovetailing, dovetailed**
1 V-RECIP If two things **dovetail** or if one thing **dovetails** with another, the two things fit together or are compatible with each other in a very neat way. *The two schedules dovetailed together without friction... Every scientist feels elated when the numbers dovetail.*

2 NC A **dovetail** or a **dovetail joint** is a wedge-shaped joint used in carpentry for fitting two pieces of wood tightly together.

dowager /daʊədʒə/ **dowagers**
1 TITLE or NC You use **dowager** to refer to the widow of a duke, emperor, or other high-ranking man. *...the Dowager Duchess of Devonshire... She also sent a private message to Hirohito's widow, the Dowager Empress.*
2 NC A **dowager** is also a rich or grand-looking old lady; a literary use. *...like one of those old dowagers taking the waters.*

dowdy /daʊdi/
ADJ Someone who is **dowdy** is wearing dull and unfashionable clothes.

Dowiyogo, Bernard /bɜːnəd daʊɪjəʊɡəʊ/
Bernard Dowiyogo became President of Nauru in 1989. He was elected an MP in 1973, and has previously served as President from 1976 to 1978. He was Minister of Justice from 1983 to 1989. He is the leader of the Nauru Party. Born: 1946.

down /daʊn, daʊn/
1 PREP or ADV **Down** means towards the ground or a lower level, or in a lower place. *Shall I lift your suitcase down?... They walked down the steps... The rain came down in sheets. ...the house down below.*
2 ADV You use **down** with verbs such as 'fall' or 'pull' to say that something is destroyed or falls to the ground. *The house fell down a week later... He burnt down his school... They are said to have pulled down barbed-wire fences.*
3 ADV If you put something **down**, you put it somewhere, so that you are no longer holding it. *Put that book down.*
4 PREP or ADV If you go **down** a road, you go along it. *The library is halfway down the street... Farther down she stopped at the chemist's... He walked down the road reading a newspaper.*
5 PREP If you go **down** a river, you go along it in the direction that it flows. *...floating down the river.*
6 ADV **Down** is often used to mean in the south or towards the south. *There's a man down in Baltimore who does that.*
7 ADV If the amount or level of something goes **down**, it decreases. *Sheila was trying to get her weight down... The government says its priority is to get inflation down.*
8 ADJ PRED If something is **down** on paper, it has been written on the paper. *That date wasn't down on our news sheet.*
9 ADJ PRED If you are feeling **down**, you are feeling unhappy or depressed; an informal use. *I'm feeling a bit down today.*
10 NU **Down** is the small, soft feathers on young birds. Down is used to make pillows or quilts. *The chicks are covered with down when they emerge from the egg.*
● **Down** is used in these phrases. ● **Down to** a particular detail means including everything, even that detail. *Successful suicides seem to have been planned down to the last detail.* ● If you **go down with** an illness or **are down with** it, you have that illness; an informal expression. *She's down with the flu.* ● **up and down, ups and downs:** see up.

down-and-out, down-and-outs
NC A **down-and-out** is a person who has no job and no home and who has no hope of getting work or finding somewhere to live. *His research took him among the down-and-outs in the city of Liverpool.*

down at heel
ADJ Someone or something that is **down at heel** looks in bad condition, because of lack of money. *He looked somewhat down at heel. ...a crumbling, Victorian resort, slightly down at heel, full of ghosts.*

downbeat /daʊnbiːt/
ADJ Something or someone that is **downbeat** is deliberately casual and restrained; an informal word. *Johnny was hurt that Nino should be so downbeat.*

downcast /daʊnkɑːst/
1 ADJ If you are **downcast**, you are feeling sad and pessimistic. *Glasgow fans were downcast after Rangers lost their European Cup quarter-final two-nil.*

2 ADJ If your eyes are **downcast**, you are looking towards the ground. *The girl could only nod, her eyes downcast.*

downer /daʊnə/ **downers**; an informal word.
1 NC A **downer** is a drug that causes you to feel sleepy or very calm such as a barbiturate drug.
2 If you are **on a downer**, you are feeling depressed and pessimistic.

downfall /daʊnfɔːl/
1 NU The **downfall** of a person or institution is their failure or loss of power. *...the downfall of a dictator.*
2 NU If something was someone's **downfall**, it caused their failure or loss of power. *Bad publicity was our downfall.*

downgrade /daʊnɡreɪd/ **downgrades, downgrading, downgraded**
VO If you **downgrade** something, you give it less importance than it had before. *They were reluctant to downgrade the nuclear element of their defence.*

downhearted /daʊnhɑːtɪd/
ADJ If you are **downhearted**, you are feeling sad and discouraged; an old-fashioned word. *The Kremlin's best known hardliner was not in the least bit downhearted.*

downhill /daʊnhɪl/
1 ADV or ADJ ATTRIB If something is moving **downhill**, it is moving down a slope. *The children were racing downhill on their sledges. ...the Olympic downhill champion.*
2 ADV You say that something is going **downhill** when it is deteriorating. *The National Health Service is going downhill and needs more money... From then on relations went downhill rapidly.*

Downing Street /daʊnɪŋ striːt/
N PROP **Downing Street** is the street in London in which the Prime Minister and the Chancellor of the Exchequer live. **Downing Street** is also used to refer to the Prime Minister and his or her officials. *The demonstrators handed in a letter at the Prime Minister's residence in Downing Street... The paper said that Downing Street had not confirmed that the visit would go ahead... Downing Street is so far refusing to comment on Mr Ridley's latest position.*

down-market
ADJ or ADV Something such as a product or service that is **down-market** looks cheap and is not very good in quality. *We sell a lot of down-market books... Chichester has gone distinctly down-market.*

down payment, down payments
NC A **down payment** is a sum of money that you pay when you first buy something using a credit arrangement or when you are paying for something by instalments. The down payment is a percentage of its total cost. *Banks in general have become very, very conservative and are looking for much higher down payments... It is reported that under the terms of the agreement Lazio will make a down payment of £4m to the London club.*

downpour /daʊnpɔː/ **downpours**
NC A **downpour** is a heavy fall of rain. *The main streets were flooded by a torrential downpour.*

downright /daʊnraɪt/
SUBMOD or ADJ ATTRIB You use **downright** to emphasize that something is bad or unpleasant. *Some of the jobs were downright disgusting... That's a downright lie.*

Down's syndrome /daʊnz sɪndrəʊm/
N PROP **Down's syndrome** is a human genetic disorder that results in physical abnormalities and limited mental ability in those who suffer with it. *People born with the genetic defect causing Down's Syndrome age more quickly.*

downstairs /daʊnsteəz/
1 ADV If you go **downstairs** in a building, you go down a staircase towards the ground floor. *You go downstairs, you have breakfast and you go out.*
2 ADV If something is **downstairs**, it is on the ground floor or on a lower floor than you. *...the photograph on the piano downstairs.*
3 ADJ ATTRIB A **downstairs** room or object is on the ground floor of a building or on a lower floor than where you are. *...the downstairs phone.*

downstream /daʊnstriːm/
ADV Something that is moving **downstream** is moving along a river towards its final destination. *The soil is washed downstream.*

down-to-earth
ADJ **Down-to-earth** people are concerned with practical things, rather than with theories. *...his warm, down-to-earth manner.*

downtown /daʊntaʊn/
ADV or ADJ ATTRIB **Downtown** means in or towards the centre of a city. *We went downtown... It's early afternoon in a downtown Manhattan office. ...downtown Belfast.*

downtrodden /daʊntrɒdn/
ADJ **Downtrodden** people are treated very badly by those who are in a position of power or authority. *Dutch politicians have said they would like to see Surinam's downtrodden minority integrated into the national life.*

downturn /daʊntɜːn/ **downturns**
NC If there is a **downturn** in something such as a country's economy, it becomes worse or less successful. *...a downturn in manufacturing and industry.*

down under
Down under is used to refer to Australia or New Zealand; an informal expression. *...my cousin from down under.*

downward /daʊnwəd/ **downwards**. In normal British English, **downwards** is an adverb and **downward** is an adjective. In formal British English and in American English, **downward** is both an adjective and an adverb.
1 ADV If you move or look **downwards**, you move or look towards the ground or a lower level. *It glides gently downwards... My dad was lying face downward.* ▶ Also ADJ ATTRIB *...a downward glance.*
2 ADV If an amount or rate moves **downwards**, it decreases. *Benefit levels in the national assistance scheme were revised downwards.* ▶ Also ADJ ATTRIB *Prices started a downward plunge.*

downwind /daʊnwɪnd/
ADJ If you are **downwind** of something, the wind is blowing through it or past it towards you. *They are downwind of Johnston Atoll.*

downy /daʊni/
ADJ Something that is **downy** is filled or covered with small, soft feathers, or covered with very fine hairs. *...thick downy feather beds. ...the downy head of the sleeping baby.*

dowry /daʊəri/ **dowries**
NC A woman's **dowry** is the money or goods which her family give to the man that she marries. *Excessive dowry demands can have tragic results for young brides.*

dowse /daʊs/. See **douse**.

doyen /dɔɪən/ **doyens**
NC The **doyen** of a group or profession is the oldest and most experienced and respected member of it; a formal word. *Peter Nichols was the doyen of Times correspondents when he retired last year.*

doyenne /dɔɪen/ **doyennes**
NC The **doyenne** of a group or profession is the woman who is the oldest and most experienced and respected member of it; a formal word. *...Agatha Christie, still regarded as the doyenne of English detective fiction.*

doze /dəʊz/ **dozes, dozing, dozed**
V When you **doze**, you sleep lightly or for a short period. *Thomas dozed in the armchair.* ▶ Also NC *I had a short doze at ten o'clock.*
doze off PHRASAL VERB If you **doze off**, you fall into a light sleep. *He dozed off in front of the fire.*

dozen /dʌzn/ **dozens**
1 NC A **dozen** means twelve. *...a dozen eggs.*
2 QUANT You can use **dozens** to refer vaguely to a large number. *There had been dozens of attempts at reform.*

dozy /dəʊzi/ **dozier, doziest**
ADJ If you are **dozy**, you are feeling sleepy and not very alert. *...a bleeper which would wake the most dozy security man.*

DPP /diːpiːpiː/
N PROP **DPP** is an abbreviation for **Director of Public**

Prosecutions. *The DPP said there was insufficient evidence to bring prosecutions.*

Dr, Drs.
Dr is a written abbreviation for 'Doctor'. *...Dr Franz.*

drab /dræb/ **drabber, drabbest**
ADJ Something that is **drab** is dull and not attractive or exciting. *...the drab old building. ...a drab brown dress.*

drachma /drækmə/ **drachmae** /drækmi/ or **drachmas**
NC The **drachma** is the unit of money used in Greece. *There was a reward of two hundred million drachmas, which is approximately eight hundred thousand pounds.*

draconian /drəkəʊniən/
ADJ ATTRIB **Draconian** laws or measures are extremely harsh; a formal word. *They announced an easing of the draconian measures on immigration... The Government's proposals will mean a more draconian version of the Official Secrets Act.*

draft /drɑːft/ **drafts, drafting, drafted**
1 NC A **draft** of a letter, book, or speech is an early version of it. *A first draft of a new document will be written today by the party president.*
2 VO When you **draft** a letter, book, or speech, you write the first version of it. *They drafted a letter to the local newspaper.*
3 VO If you **are drafted**, you are told to serve in one of your country's armed forces; used in American English. *I was drafted into the navy.*
4 VO When people **are drafted** somewhere, they are moved there to do a particular job. *Extra staff were drafted from Paris to Rome.*
5 See also **draught**.

draft dodger, draft dodgers
NC A **draft dodger** is someone who avoids joining the armed forces when normally they would be obliged to join. *The South African authorities are making heroes of the white draft dodgers.*

draftee /drɑːftiː/ **draftees**
NC A **draftee** is someone who has been drafted into his or her country's armed forces; used in American English. *These men are not draftees. They signed up for the job... In some cities almost no draftees were registered in the fall.*

draftsman /drɑːftsmən/. See **draughtsman**.
draftsmanship /drɑːftsmənʃɪp/. See **draughtsmanship**.
drafty /drɑːfti/. See **draughty**.

drag /dræg/ **drags, dragging, dragged**
1 VO If you **drag** something or someone somewhere, you pull them there with difficulty. *He listened as the body was dragged up the stairs... She grabbed her husband by the wrist and dragged him away.*
2 VOA To **drag** someone somewhere also means to make them go there; an informal use. *I'm sorry to drag you to the telephone, but something awful has happened.*
3 V-REFLA If you **drag** yourself somewhere, you move there slowly because you feel ill or weak or because you do not want to go there. *I was able to drag myself shakily to my feet.*
4 V If an event **drags**, it is very boring and seems to last a long time. *The part of the play which drags is the last half-hour.*
5 If a man is **in drag**, he is wearing women's clothes. *There was a man in evening dress, various others in drag and another in a heavy rubber suit.*
drag into PHRASAL VERB If someone is **dragged into** an unpleasant situation, they are forced to become involved in it against their will. *The party's leadership doesn't want to get dragged into a damaging row.*
drag on PHRASAL VERB If a situation or process **drags on**, it lasts or takes longer than seems necessary. *The civil war drags on. ...negotiations that have been dragging on for years.*
drag out PHRASAL VERB If you **drag** something **out**, you make it last for longer than necessary. *How could we prevent them from dragging out the talks?*

dragon /drægən/ **dragons**
NC In stories and legends, a **dragon** is an animal like a big lizard. It has wings and claws, and breathes out fire. *Unicorns, mermaids, griffins and dragons are*

just some of the imaginary creatures that make up the rich wealth of legends.

dragonfly /drǽgənflaɪ/ **dragonflies**
NC A **dragonfly** is a colourful insect which is often found near water. *...the creation of ponds for dragonflies.*

dragoon /drəgúːn/ **dragoons, dragooning, dragooned**
NC A **dragoon** is a soldier, especially in old European armies. *...the Royal Scots Dragoon Guards.*
dragoon into PHRASAL VERB If you **dragoon** someone **into** something that they do not want to do, you force them to do it. *She seems to have this ghastly need to dragoon us all into her schemes.*

drain /dreɪn/ **drains, draining, drained**
1 VO When people **drain** wet land, they dry it by causing water to flow out of it. *If you drain a mangrove swamp, the earth may be very acidic... Farmers drained the land and brought hundreds of thousands of acres back into cultivation. ...the fountains were drained.*
2 VA When liquid **drains** somewhere, it flows there gradually. *The sewage drains off into the river... It will take several weeks before the floods drain away.*
3 NC A **drain** is a pipe that carries water or sewage away from a place. *This has been designed to get rid of grease blocking up drains... Each time you flush a toilet, two gallons of water go down the drain.*
4 NC A **drain** is also a metal grid in a road, through which rainwater can flow away. *Although the residents paid their local taxes, the roads were unpaved and the drains were never repaired.*
5 VO If you **drain** a glass, you drink the whole of its contents. *Mary picked up the glass and drained it.*
6 VO If something **drains** your strength or resources, it uses them up. *Record bank failures have nearly drained the deposit insurance fund... The project is draining the charity's funds.* ◆ **drained** ADJ *He looks drained, like he's tired of having to answer questions.*
7 N SING If something is a **drain** on your resources, it uses them up. *The banks are facing a large drain on their funds.*

drainage /dreɪnɪdʒ/
NU **Drainage** is the system or process by which water or other liquids are drained from a place. *Because of inadequate drainage, pools of dirty water mixed with garbage remained in the streets. ...drainage ditches.*

draining board, draining boards
NC A **draining board** is a sloping area next to a sink where you put cups, plates, and cutlery to drain.

drainpipe /dreɪnpaɪp/ **drainpipes**
NC A **drainpipe** is a pipe attached to the side of a building, through which water flows from the roof into a drain. *A handful of them crawled up the drainpipe to the roof.*

drake /dreɪk/ **drakes**
NC A **drake** is a male duck.

dram /dræm/ **drams**
NC A **dram** is a small measure of whisky or other alcoholic drink; used in Scottish English. *Would you care for a dram?*

drama /drɑːmə/ **dramas**
1 NC A **drama** is a serious play for the theatre, television, or radio. *It's not a documentary, but a drama based on one man's memories.*
2 NU You refer to plays in general as **drama**. *...an expert on modern drama.*
3 NU or NC You can refer to exciting aspects of a real situation as its **drama**. *After several weeks of high drama, life is returning to normal... The hostage drama at Algiers airport looks set to continue. ...the dramas of this village life.*

dramatic /drəmǽtɪk/ **dramatics**
1 ADJ **Dramatic** change is sudden and noticeable. *I expect to see dramatic improvements.* ◆ **dramatically** ADV *The way in which information is transmitted has changed dramatically.*
2 ADJ You describe something as **dramatic** when it is very exciting. *Landing on the moon was one of the most dramatic scientific adventures of this century.*
3 ADJ If you say or do something **dramatic**, you are trying to surprise and impress people. *In a dramatic statement, General Negovanovic said the country is*

faced with civil war... The Foreign Minister made his dramatic move as a way of highlighting the danger from hardline communists. ...a dramatic gesture.
◆ **dramatically** ADV *He paused dramatically.*
4 ADJ ATTRIB **Dramatic** art or writing is connected with plays and the theatre. *...Browning's dramatic works.*
5 NU **Dramatics** is the performing of plays. *...amateur dramatics.*

dramatis personae /drǽmətɪs pəsə́ʊnaɪ/
N PL The **dramatis personae** of a play are all the characters in it; a formal expression.

dramatist /drǽmətɪst/ **dramatists**
NC A **dramatist** is someone who writes plays. *Shakespeare was a great poet as well as a great dramatist.*

dramatize /drǽmətaɪz/ **dramatizes, dramatizing, dramatized**; also spelt **dramatise**.
1 VO If a book or story is **dramatized**, it is rewritten as a play. *Her autobiography has been dramatized for the theatre.* ◆ **dramatization** /drǽmətaɪzeɪʃn/ **dramatizations** NC *...a dramatization of the story of Ali Baba.*
2 VO If you **dramatize** an event or situation, you try to make it seem more serious or exciting than it really is. *The President took a low-key view of the differences, refusing to dramatize the situation.*

drank /dræŋk/
Drank is the past tense of **drink**.

drape /dreɪp/ **drapes, draping, draped**
1 VOA If you **drape** a piece of cloth somewhere, you place it there so that it hangs down. *He began to drape the shawl over Gertrude's shoulders.*
2 VO+with or in If something is **draped** with a piece of cloth, it is covered by it. *...coffins draped with American flags... His coffin was draped in the Palestinian flag.*
3 N PL **Drapes** are curtains which are made from a heavy material or that hang in folds; used in American English. *The drapes were drawn and the lights were turned on.*

draper /dreɪpə/ **drapers**; an old-fashioned word.
1 NC A **draper** is someone who has a shop which sells cloth.
2 NC The **draper** or the **draper's** is also used to refer to the shop itself.

drapery /dreɪpəri/ **draperies**; an old-fashioned word.
1 NU or N PL You can refer to cloth or clothing hanging in folds as **drapery** or **draperies**. *...fold upon fold of thick drapery... They wore layers of enfolding draperies.*
2 NU **Drapery** is also the cloth that you buy in a shop. *She works in the drapery department.*

drastic /drǽstɪk/
1 ADJ A **drastic** course of action is extreme and is usually taken urgently. *This may force the Government to take drastic measures.*
2 ADJ A **drastic** change is very significant and noticeable. *...the drastic decline in flat-building.*
◆ **drastically** ADV *Because of the snow, visibility was drastically reduced.*

drat /dræt/
You say **'drat'**, **'drat it'**, or **'drat the man'** when you are annoyed about something; used in old-fashioned, informal English. *'Drat the girl,' said Stanley. 'Has she no tact, no sense?'*

draught /drɑːft/ **draughts**; spelt **draft** in American English.
1 NC A **draught** is a current of air coming into a room or vehicle. *The draught from the window stirred the papers on her desk.*
2 NC A **draught** of liquid is a large amount that you swallow. *He gulped the brandy down in one draught.*
3 ADJ ATTRIB **Draught** beer is served from barrels. *...the aroma and flavour of one of Britain's most famous beverages, draught Bass beer.*
4 NU **Draughts** is a game for two people, played with round pieces on a board. *...the chequered board used for the game of chess or draughts.*

draughtboard /drɑːftbɔːd/ **draughtboards**
NC A **draughtboard** is a board divided into 64 squares, on which the game of draughts is played.

draughtsman /drɑːftsmən/ **draughtsmen** /drɑːftsmən/;
spelt **draftsman** in American English.
NC A **draughtsman** is someone whose job is to prepare
technical drawings. *After an early career as a
draughtsman, he earned a degree in architecture.*

draughtsmanship /drɑːftsmənʃɪp/; spelt
draftsmanship in American English.
NU **Draughtsmanship** is the ability to draw well. It
also refers the act of drawing. *The draughtsmanship
of the forgery was excellent.*

draughty /drɑːfti/ **draughtier, draughtiest**; spelt
drafty in American English.
ADJ A **draughty** room or building has currents of cold
air blowing into it. *One had to join the queue in the
draughty, noisy foyer and wait.*

draw /drɔː/ **draws, drawing, drew, drawn**
1 VOorV If you **draw** a picture, pattern, or diagram,
you make it using a pencil, pen, or crayon. *She used
to draw funny pictures... It was on the walls of the
camp that he learnt to draw.*
2 VA When vehicles or people **draw** away, they move
away. When they **draw** near, they move near. *The cab
drew away from the kerb... Jack and Roger drew
near.*
3 VOA If you **draw** someone or something in a
particular direction, you pull them there. *He draws
the document from its folder.*
4 VO If a cart or other vehicle, or an agricultural
implement, **is drawn** by an animal, the animal moves
along pulling the vehicle or implement behind it. *She
saw two-wheeled and four-wheeled vehicles drawn by
huge animals.*
5 VO If you **draw** a curtain or blind, you pull it across
a window to cover it or uncover it. *She drew the
blinds, and turned the lights on.*
6 VOorV If someone **draws** a gun, sword, or knife, they
pull it out of its holder so that it is ready to use. *They
were demonstrating to each other how fast they could
draw their guns when one went off... She drew on me,
but I was too quick for her.*
7 VO If you **draw** a deep breath, you take a lot of air
into your lungs in order to calm you down. If you **draw**
a sharp breath, you take a sudden breath of air into
your lungs because you have been shocked in some
way. *'It's malignant,' he said. My wife drew in a
sharp breath and my brain stopped working.*
8 VOA If you **draw** money out of a bank or building
society, you take it out so that you can use it. *The
chairman had been charged with a number of financial
offences, including drawing money out of a frozen
bank account.*
9 VO If something **is drawn** from a thing or place, it is
obtained from that thing or place. *The committee
members are drawn from all sections of the local
community.*
10 VO If you **draw** a conclusion, distinction, or
comparison, you decide that it exists or is true.
Unfortunately, they drew the wrong conclusions.
11 VO If something that you do **draws** a particular
reaction, that is the way that people react to it. *The
mayor drew criticism for these excesses.*
12 V-RECIP In a game or competition, if one person or
team **draws** with another one, they get the same
number of points and nobody wins. *Australia are
second in the table, after drawing one-all with the
Soviet Union... Iran and Japan drew 2-2 in a non-
championship match in Teheran.* ▶ Also NC *The fifth
game ended in a draw.*
13 See also **drawing, drawn.**
● **Draw** is used in these phrases. ● If you **draw**
people's **attention** to something, you make them aware
of it. *He drew attention to the rising unemployment
rates.* ● When an event or period of time **draws to a
close** or **draws to an end**, it finishes. *About fifteen
rebels surrendered as the crisis drew to a close... As
the second day of talks drew to an end, there were no
signs of progress.* ● to **draw a blank**: see **blank.** ● to
draw the line: see **line.**

draw into PHRASAL VERB If you **draw** someone **into**
something, you cause them to become involved in it.
She refused to be drawn into the conversation.

draw on PHRASAL VERB 1 If you **draw on** or **draw**

upon something, you use it. *...the kind of information
an expert draws on... He valued the performance
aspect of the presidency above anything else and he
drew upon his acting experience.* 2 To **draw on** a
cigarette means to suck it and inhale the smoke.

draw up PHRASAL VERB 1 When you **draw up** a
document, list, or plan, you prepare it and write it
out. *I was busy drawing up plans for the new course.*
2 When a vehicle **draws up**, it comes to a place and
stops. *Just before eleven a bus drew up.*

draw upon PHRASAL VERB See **draw on.**

drawback /drɔːbæk/ **drawbacks**
NC A **drawback** is an aspect of something that makes
it less acceptable than it would otherwise be. *The
major drawback of the system is that the funds are
administered centrally.*

drawbridge /drɔːbrɪdʒ/ **drawbridges**
NC A **drawbridge** is a bridge that can be pulled up, for
example to prevent people from getting into a fortified
building such as a castle or to allow ships to pass
underneath it. *Germany's most modern prison is
surrounded by a moat, with a drawbridge and a
surveillance system.*

drawer /drɔː/ **drawers**
NC A **drawer** is a part of a desk or other piece of
furniture that is shaped like a rectangular box. You
pull it towards you to open it. *He has a file drawer
full of clippings and maps... Her collection of buttons
filled the tables, closets and drawers of her two-storey
home.*

drawing /drɔːɪŋ/ **drawings**
1 NC A **drawing** is a picture made with a pencil, pen,
or crayon. *...an exhibition of children's drawings...
The cabinet can be made locally from drawings that
we've now got available.*
2 NU **Drawing** is the skill or work of drawing
pictures. *She had a passion for drawing and painting.*

drawing board, drawing boards
1 NC A **drawing board** is a large flat board, often fixed
to a metal frame so that it looks like a desk, on which
you place your paper when you are drawing or
designing something. *Two cartoonists hunch over
their drawing boards, ink pot and pen by their side.*
2 If you say that you need to go **back to the drawing
board**, you mean that something you have made or
done has not been successful and that you need to
start again or try another idea. *The theorists have to
go back to the drawing board and start again.*

drawing pin, drawing pins
NC A **drawing pin** is a short nail with a broad, flat top.
It is used for attaching papers to a vertical surface.

drawing room, drawing rooms
NC A **drawing room** is a room in a large house where
people sit and relax, or entertain guests; an old-
fashioned word. *They settled into the chairs in the
elegant drawing room.*

drawl /drɔːl/ **drawls, drawling, drawled**
V-QUOTE or V If someone **drawls**, they speak slowly, with
long vowel sounds. *She shifted lazily on the sofa and
drawled, 'If you want a drink, dear, you'll have to get
it yourself.'* ▶ Also N SING *McCord spoke in a soft
drawl.*

drawn /drɔːn/
1 **Drawn** is the past participle of **draw.**
2 ADJ A **drawn** curtain or blind has been pulled over a
window to cover it. *Many residents suffered a self-
imposed curfew behind drawn curtains and locked
doors.*
3 ADJ If someone looks **drawn**, they look very tired or
ill. *There was a drawn and haggard look about his
eyes.*

drawn-out
ADJ You describe something as **drawn-out** when it
lasts longer than you think it should. *He was tired of
the long drawn-out arguments.*

drawstring /drɔːstrɪŋ/ **drawstrings**
NC A **drawstring** is a cord that goes through a seam
round an opening, for example at the top of a bag or a
pair of trousers. When the cord is pulled tighter, the
opening gets smaller. *...a drawstring bag. ...trousers
with a drawstring waist.*

dread /drɛd/ dreads, dreading, dreaded
VOorV+ING If you **dread** something unpleasant which
may happen, you feel anxious about it. *She had begun
to dread these excursions... Fanny dreaded seeing
Thomas again.* ▸ Also NU *Her dread of returning to
school gets stronger.*
dreaded /drɛdɪd/
ADJ ATTRIB **Dreaded** means terrible and greatly
feared. *Consumption was the most dreaded disease of
the time.*
dreadful /drɛdfl/
1 ADJ If you say that something is **dreadful**, you mean
that it is very unpleasant or very poor in quality. *The
weather was dreadful.*
2 ADJ ATTRIB You can use **dreadful** to emphasize the
degree or extent of something bad. *I was a dreadful
coward... It'll be a dreadful waste.*
dreadfully /drɛdfəli/
1 SUBMOD **Dreadfully** means very or to a very great
extent. *The three girls were dreadfully dull
companions... She was dreadfully upset... I'm so
dreadfully sorry... She was most dreadfully sick all
day.*
2 ADV **Dreadfully** also means in a very bad or
unpleasant way. *He had behaved dreadfully.*
dream /driːm/ dreams, dreaming, dreamed or
dreamt
1 NC A **dream** is an imaginary series of events that
you experience in your mind while you are asleep. *In
his dream he was sitting in a theatre watching a play.*
2 VorV-REPORT If you **dream** when you are asleep, you
experience imaginary events in your mind. *He
became aware that he was dreaming... I dreamt that I
was beaten up by Ernest Hemingway.*
3 NC+SUPP A **dream** is also something which you often
think about because you would like it to happen. *His
dream of being champion had come true... The dream
of a unified, free, and democratic Germany was just a
short step away. ...a dream world.*
4 VorV-REPORT If you **dream**, you think about a
situation or event that you would very much like to
happen. *She dreamed of having a car... Those who
dream that the revolution can be defeated are fooling
themselves.*
5 If you say that you **would not dream of** doing
something, or that you **would never dream of** doing it,
you are emphasizing that you would not do it. *I
wouldn't dream of trying to convince anybody... I
would never dream of causing a riot.*
dream up PHRASAL VERB If someone **dreams up** a
plan, they invent it. *He would never dream up a
desperate scheme like that on his own.*
dreamer /driːmə/ dreamers
NC Someone who is a **dreamer** looks forward to
pleasant things that may never happen, rather than
being realistic and practical. *Many believe Dr Meyers
to be an impractical dreamer.*
dreamily /driːmɪli/
ADV If you do something **dreamily**, you do it without
concentrating, because you are thinking about
something else, especially something that is pleasant.
'It's worth a lot of money,' she said dreamily.
dreamless /driːmləs/
ADJ **Dreamless** sleep is very deep and peaceful, and
without dreams. *He lay down again and soon fell into
a mercifully dreamless sleep.*
dreamlike /driːmlaɪk/
ADJ **Dreamlike** things or situations seem strange and
unreal. *There was a dreamlike quality to the scene...
Already the landscape has a depopulated and
dreamlike air.*
dreamt /drɛmt/
Dreamt is a past tense and past participle of **dream**.
dreamy /driːmi/ dreamier, dreamiest
ADJ Someone with a **dreamy** expression looks as if
they are thinking about something very pleasant. *A
dreamy look came into her eyes.*
dreary /drɪəri/ drearier, dreariest
ADJ Something that is **dreary** is so dull that it makes
you feel bored or depressed. *They don't realise how
dull and dreary their world is... They do only the
dreariest jobs.*

dredge /drɛdʒ/ dredges, dredging, dredged
VO To **dredge** a harbour, river, or other area of water
means to clear it or search for something in it by
removing mud and other unwanted material from the
bottom using a special machine. *Workmen made the
find as they dredged the lake.*
dredger /drɛdʒə/ dredgers
NC A **dredger** is a boat fitted with a special machine
that is used to clear or search harbours, rivers, and
other areas of water, by removing mud and other
unwanted material from the bottom. *The giant
mechanical dredger was working its way through
shallow water in the north-eastern part of the lake.*
dregs /drɛgz/
1 N PL The **dregs** of a liquid are the last drops left at
the bottom of a container, together with any solid bits
that have sunk to the bottom. *She had drunk her
coffee down to the dregs.*
2 N PL+SUPP The **dregs** of a society or community are
the people who you consider to be the worst or the
most useless people in it. *It sees the dissidents as
anti-social elements and the dregs of society.*
drenched /drɛntʃt/
ADJ If you are **drenched**, you have become very wet.
Joseph was drenched with sweat.
dress /drɛs/ dresses, dressing, dressed
1 NC A **dress** is a piece of clothing worn by a woman
or girl which covers her body and extends down over
her legs. *She was wearing a short black dress.*
2 NU You can refer generally to the type of clothes
that people wear as **dress**. *The court ruled that dress
was a matter of individual liberty... Certain forms of
dress have been associated with a rise in religious
fundamentalism. ...sixty men in full battle dress... He
was in evening dress.*
3 V When you **dress**, you put on your clothes; a
literary use. *When he had shaved and dressed, he
went down to the kitchen.*
4 VO If you **dress** someone, you put clothes on them.
*His trembling reduced, he could write, dress himself,
and walk more easily... The argument was still ringing
in her head when she woke and when she dressed her
children... His nurse had dressed him in a stretch suit.*
5 See also **dressed**.
dress up PHRASAL VERB 1 If you **dress up**, you put on
different clothes, in order to make yourself look like
someone else or in order to look smarter. *...carnivals
which give an opportunity for people to dress up in
exotic costumes and have a good time... We're not
against children dressing up or having fun.* 2 If you
dress up something, you try to make it seem more
acceptable to other people by altering details of it or
presenting it differently. *However he may dress up
his position, he is basically in favour of the status quo.
...an unlawful political protest dressed up as a trade
dispute.*
dressage /drɛsɑːʒ/
NU **Dressage** consists of making the horse you are
riding perform controlled movements in response to
your signals, especially in a competition. *...the World
Dressage champion.*
dress circle
N SING The **dress circle** is the first floor balcony in a
theatre. *We sat in the dress circle.*
dressed /drɛst/
1 ADJ PRED If you are **dressed**, you are wearing
clothes rather than being naked. *Both men were fully
dressed.*
2 ADJ PRED If you are **dressed** in a particular way, you
are wearing clothes of a particular kind or colour. *He
was dressed in a black suit.*
3 When you **get dressed**, you put on your clothes.
*After a long soak in the bath we returned to the
anteroom to get dressed.*
4 See also **dress**.
dresser /drɛsə/ dressers
1 NC A **dresser** is a piece of furniture with cupboards
or drawers in the lower part and shelves in the top
part. *...blue and white plates on the stripped pine
dresser.*
2 NC In American English, a **dresser** is a chest of
drawers, usually with a mirror on the top. *He walked

round the beds to the dresser and opened the drawer.
3 NC+SUPP You also use **dresser** to refer to the kind of
clothes that a person wears. For example, if you say
that someone is a neat dresser, you mean that they
dress neatly. *Her husband has often been described as
a drab dresser.*

dressing /drɛsɪŋ/ **dressings**
1 NC A **dressing** is a protective covering that is put on
a wound. *Boiled potato peelings can serve as a
painless dressing for burns, according to research at
the Wadia hospital. ...a surgical dressing.*
2 N MASS A salad **dressing** is a mixture of oil, vinegar,
and herbs, which you pour over a salad. *What kind of
dressing would you like on your salad?... These oils
are ideal for cooking and salad dressing.*

dressing-down
N SING If someone gives you a **dressing-down**, they
speak angrily to you because you have done something
bad or foolish; an informal word. *He received a fierce
dressing-down over Britain's opposition to sanctions
against South Africa.*

dressing gown, dressing gowns
NC A **dressing gown** is a loose-fitting coat worn over
pyjamas or a nightdress when you are not in bed. *She
slid her legs off the bed and reached for her dressing
gown.*

dressing room, dressing rooms
1 NC A **dressing room** is a room in a theatre where
actors prepare for a performance. *She would lock
herself in her dressing room between takes.*
2 NC A **dressing room** is also a room in a sports arena
where athletes get changed. *All the lockers in the
Seattle Mariners' dressing room have names written
above them. ...the referee's dressing room.*

dressing table, dressing tables
NC In a bedroom, a **dressing table** is a small table
with drawers and a mirror. *The cabin had two bunks,
a dressing table and a wardrobe.*

dressing-up
NU **Dressing-up** is the activity of putting on special or
different clothes, especially as part of a game played
by children in which they pretend to be different
people. *...the phenomenon of dressing up to see 'The
Rocky Horror Picture Show'.*

dressmaker /drɛsmeɪkə/ **dressmakers**
NC A **dressmaker** is a person who is paid to make
women's or children's clothes. *She has been unable to
work as a dressmaker because of injuries sustained to
her eyes and hands.*

dress rehearsal, dress rehearsals
NC The **dress rehearsal** of a play, opera, or show is
the final rehearsal before it is performed, in which the
performers wear their costumes and the lights and
scenery are used in the proper way. *Ten thousand
people turned up to watch the free dress rehearsal of
an outside production of Aida.*

dress shirt, dress shirts
NC A **dress shirt** is a special shirt which men wear on
formal occasions with a dinner jacket and a black bow
tie. *I found a couple of suits and half a dozen dress
shirts on hangers.*

dressy /drɛsi/ **dressier, dressiest**
ADJ **Dressy** clothes are elegant clothes which you wear
on formal occasions; an informal word. *The men had
worn suits and ties, the women simple but dressy
clothes.*

drew /druː/
Drew is the past tense of **draw**.

dribble /drɪbl/ **dribbles, dribbling, dribbled**
1 V A When a liquid **dribbles** down a surface, it moves
down it in a thin stream. *Condensation dribbled down
the glass.*
2 V When a person or animal **dribbles**, saliva trickles
from their mouth. *He wore thick glasses and dribbled.*
3 V Oor V In games such as football or basketball, when
a player **dribbles** a ball, they move while keeping
close control of the ball with their feet or their hands.
*Lukic dribbles the ball out of his box and smashes it
60 yards upfield... The forward dribbled past two
defenders before scoring the game's outstanding goal.*
dribble out PHRASAL VERB When someone or
something **dribbles out** from somewhere, they come

out very slowly, often over a long period of time. *The
others began dribbling out of the cafe, eating peanuts
and candy bars... The facts have slowly dribbled out
over the last two weeks.*

dribs and drabs /drɪbsəndræbz/
If people or things arrive **in dribs and drabs**, they
arrive in small numbers over a period of time rather
than arriving all together; an informal expression.
The food came in dribs and drabs.

dried /draɪd/
1 **Dried** is the past tense and past participle of **dry**.
2 ADJ ATTRIB **Dried** food has been preserved by the
removal of liquid from it. *...dried milk.*

dried-up
1 ADJ Someone who is **dried-up** looks old, small, and
very wrinkled, and often also looks bad-tempered and
unpleasant. *A little dried-up old man came to the
door.*
2 See also **dry up**.

drier /draɪə/. See **dryer**.

drift /drɪft/ **drifts, drifting, drifted**
1 V A When something **drifts** somewhere, it is carried
there by the wind or by water. *The clouds drifted
away... A fishing boat was drifting slowly along.*
2 V A When people **drift** somewhere, they move there
slowly. *The crowd started to drift away.*
3 V A To **drift** towards a bad situation means to slowly
reach that situation. *We are drifting towards disaster.*
▶ Also N SING+SUPP *...the drift to violence.*
4 V Aor V When someone **drifts** or **drifts** around, they
travel from place to place without a settled way of
life. *It's hard to get in touch with him because he
drifts around from place to place... They drifted
between luxury homes in New York, Paris, and
Athens.*
5 NC A **drift** is the same as a **snowdrift**. *There were
two-foot drifts in some places.*
drift off PHRASAL VERB If you **drift off** to sleep, you
gradually fall asleep. *I think I drifted off to sleep with
the television on.*

drifter /drɪftə/ **drifters**
NC A **drifter** is a person who does not stay in one
place or in one job for very long. *She was a drifter.
No family, no close friends.*

drift net, drift nets
NC A **drift net** is a very large fishing net that is
supported by floats or attached to a special boat which
is allowed to drift with the tide or current. *Japan says
its fishing fleets will stop using huge drift nets in the
South Pacific this coming season. ...a demonstration
against drift-net fishing.*

driftwood /drɪftwʊd/
NU **Driftwood** is wood which is floating on the sea or a
river, or which has been carried by the water onto the
shore.

drill /drɪl/ **drills, drilling, drilled**
1 NC A **drill** is a tool for making holes. *...an electric
drill.*
2 V Oor V When you **drill** a hole in something, or **drill**
into it, you make a hole in it using a drill. *They are
drilling holes into hot rocks that exist deep
underground.*
3 V When people **drill** for oil or water, they search for
it by drilling deep holes in the ground or in the
seabed. *The licences allow more than seventy
companies to search and drill for oil... The company
confirmed today that it has plans to continue drilling.*
4 NC A **drill** is also a way of learning something by
repeating a routine exercise. *...spelling drills. ...a fire
drill.* ▶ Also V O *He doesn't believe in drilling a class
for more than ten minutes a day... The band were as
tightly drilled as you might expect.*

drily /draɪli/. See **dry**.

drink /drɪŋk/ **drinks, drinking, drank, drunk**
1 V Oor V When you **drink** a liquid, you take it into your
mouth and swallow it. *We sat drinking coffee... He
drank eagerly.*
2 NC A **drink** is an amount of a liquid which you
drink. *I asked for a drink of water.*
3 V To **drink** also means to drink alcohol. *You
shouldn't drink and drive.*
4 NU **Drink** is alcohol, for example beer, wine, or

whisky. *He eventually died of drink.*
5 NC A **drink** is also an alcoholic drink. *He poured himself a drink.*
6 See also **drunk.**
drink to PHRASAL VERB If you **drink to** someone or something, you raise your glass before drinking, and say that you hope they will be happy or successful. *They agreed on their plan and drank to it.*

drinkable /drɪŋkəbl/
1 ADJ Water that is **drinkable** is clean and safe for drinking. *The task of providing a clean, drinkable supply of water is going to become more difficult.*
2 ADJ Wine or beer that is **drinkable** tastes nice and is pleasant to drink. *They have a good range of drinkable wines at reasonable prices.*

drink-driving; also spelt **drink driving.**
NU **Drink-driving** is the offence of driving a vehicle with too much alcohol in your bloodstream. *A junior government minister has resigned after being arrested for a drink-driving offence.*

drinker /drɪŋkə/ **drinkers**
1 NC A **drinker** is someone who drinks alcohol, especially in large quantities. *She had become a secret drinker... The British are not really a nation of heavy drinkers.*
2 NC+SUPP You can use **drinker** to say what kind of drink someone regularly drinks. For example, a beer drinker is someone who regularly drinks beer. *Normally the Japanese are not great wine drinkers.*

drinking /drɪŋkɪŋ/
NU **Drinking** is the activity of drinking alcohol. *There had been some heavy drinking at the party.*

drinking fountain, drinking fountains
NC A **drinking fountain** is a device which supplies running water for members of the public to drink.

drinking water
NU **Drinking water** is water which is safe to drink. *There is no proper sanitation or drinking water.*

drip /drɪp/ **drips, dripping, dripped**
1 V When liquid **drips,** it falls in small drops. *The rain was dripping down our necks.*
2 V When something **drips,** drops of liquid fall from it. *...the dripping of the tap.*
3 NC **Drips** are drops of liquid falling from a place. *She placed a cup under the leak to catch the drips.*

drip-dry
ADJ **Drip-dry** fabric dries without creases when it is hung up wet, and does not need ironing. *...drip-dry shirts.*

dripping /drɪpɪŋ/
1 ADJ Someone or something that is **dripping** wet is very wet. *Judy came out of the bathroom, still dripping wet.*
2 NU **Dripping** is the fat which comes out of meat when it is fried or roasted. It can also be used for frying food in.

drive /draɪv/ **drives, driving, drove, driven**
1 VOorV If you **drive** a vehicle, you control it so that it goes where you want it to go. *He drives fast cars and flies his own plane... The judge was ambushed by gunmen as he drove to work... I have never learned to drive.*
2 VOA If you **drive** someone somewhere, you take them there in a car. *Can I drive you to the airport?*
3 NC A **drive** is a journey in a vehicle such as a car. *It'll be a thirty mile drive.*
4 NC A **drive** is also a private road leading from a public road to a house. *There were several cars parked in the drive.*
5 VO If something **drives** a machine, it supplies the power that makes it work. *Steam can be used to drive generators.*
6 VOA If you **drive** a post or a nail into something, you force it in by hitting it with a hammer. *She stood in front of a stake driven into the gravel.*
7 VOA To **drive** someone or something somewhere means to force them to go there. *Half a million people had been driven out... High local taxes drove industry away.*
8 VOAorVOC To **drive** someone into a bad state means to cause them to be in that state. *The farming venture drove the company into debt... Going on*

holiday with these horrible kids will drive me mad.
9 VO+to-INF If something **drives** people or things to do something that they would not normally do, it causes them to do it. *The gales drove scores of ships to take shelter... Food should not be in such short supply that people are driven to protest on the streets.*
10 VO If someone is **driven** by a feeling or need, this is what makes them behave as they do. *...a man driven by greed or envy.*
11 NU **Drive** is energy and determination. *Northcliffe had great ability and drive.*
12 N SING+SUPP A **drive** is also a special effort by a group of people to achieve something. *The Poles launched a tremendous investment drive... Following a sustained recruitment drive, British universities now have more overseas students than ever before.*
13 If you understand **what** someone is **driving at,** you understand what they are trying to say; an informal use. *She knew at once what I was driving at.*
14 See also **driving, drove.**

drive-in, drive-ins
NC A **drive-in** is a cinema, restaurant, or other place that offers a service to people which allows them to stay in their cars while using the service provided. *Films such as 'Female Jungle' and 'A Bucket of Blood' are screened mostly at drive-ins. ...a drive-in cinema.*

drivel /drɪvl/ **drivels, drivelling, drivelled;** spelt **driveling, driveled** in American English.
NU You refer to something that is written or said as **drivel** when you think it is very silly; an informal word. *You do talk drivel sometimes!*
drivel on PHRASAL VERB If someone **drivels on,** they talk for a long time about things that are boring or irrelevant; an informal expression. *She spent an hour drivelling on about it.*

driven /drɪvn/
Driven is the past participle of **drive.**

driver /draɪvə/ **drivers**
NC A **driver** is someone who drives a motor vehicle. *Some drivers spent the night sleeping in their cars. ...lorry drivers. ...bus drivers.*

driver's licence, driver's licences; spelt **driver's license** in American English.
NC A **driver's licence** is the same as a **driving licence.** *She was found guilty of driving without a valid driver's licence.*

drive shaft, drive shafts
NC A **drive shaft** is a shaft in a car or other vehicle that transfers power from the gear box to the wheels.

driveway /draɪvweɪ/ **driveways**
NC A **driveway** is a private road that leads from a public road to a house or garage. *He was shot dead in the driveway of his home.*

driving /draɪvɪŋ/
1 NU **Driving** is the activity of driving a car, or the way that you drive it. *She was found guilty of dangerous driving.*
2 ADJ ATTRIB The **driving** force behind something is the person or group mainly responsible for it. *The union is the driving force behind the revolution.*

driving licence, driving licences; also spelt **driving license** in American English.
NC A **driving licence** is a card showing that you are qualified to drive. *Apart from one previous offence for speeding, he has a clean driving licence.*

driving school, driving schools
NC A **driving school** is a business that employs instructors who teach people how to drive a car.

drizzle /drɪzl/ **drizzles, drizzling, drizzled**
NU **Drizzle** is light rain falling in very small drops. *Many were standing bare-headed in the evening drizzle.* ► Also V *It was drizzling as I walked home.*

droll /drəʊl/
ADJ **Droll** means amusing; an old-fashioned word. *Bing was witty, in a droll way.*

dromedary /drɒmədəʳri/ **dromedaries**
NC A **dromedary** is a camel with one hump.

drone /drəʊn/ **drones, droning, droned**
V If something **drones,** it makes a low, continuous humming noise. *The engine droned on and on.* ► Also N SING *...the drone of a bee.*

drool /druːl/ **drools, drooling, drooled**
1 v If someone **drools**, they let saliva fall from their mouth. *Some sufferers may live for years, trapped inside a wasted body, drooling, unable to move or speak.*
2 v If you **drool** over someone or something, you look at them with uncontrolled pleasure; used showing disapproval. *Gaskell's drooling over you all the time.*

droop /druːp/ **droops, drooping, drooped**
v If something **droops**, it hangs or leans downwards with no strength or firmness. *His shoulders drooped.*
♦ **drooping** ADJ ...*drooping purple flowers.*

droopy /druːpi/ **droopier, droopiest**
ADJ Something that is **droopy** hangs or leans downwards with no strength or firmness. ...*the waiter with the droopy moustache.*

drop /drɒp/ **drops, dropping, dropped**
1 V-ERG If you **drop** something or if it **drops**, it falls straight down. *Planes dropped huge quantities of incendiary bombs... He dropped his cigar... Ash dropped from his cigarette.*
2 v If a level or amount **drops**, it quickly becomes less. *The temperature of their bodies dropped ten degrees.* ▶ Also NC ...*a drop in income.*
3 V-ERG If your voice **drops** or if you **drop** your voice, you speak more quietly. *Bill's voice dropped when he saw his father on the other side of the room... They dropped their voices as they entered the church.*
4 VOA If the driver of a vehicle **drops** you somewhere or **drops** you off, he or she stops the vehicle and you get out. *He ordered his taxi to drop him at the corner of the street... He dropped him off on the outskirts of Glasgow.*
5 VO If you **drop** what you are doing or dealing with, you stop doing it or dealing with it. *The charges against him were dropped... I was certain he would drop everything to help.*
6 VO If you **drop** a hint, you give someone a hint in a casual way. *Mr Gorbachev has dropped hints that there might be a review of compulsory military service.*
7 If you **drop** someone **a line**, you write them a short letter; an informal expression. *If you want to know more about any of these stories, don't hesitate to drop us a line.*
8 NC A **drop** of a liquid is a very small amount of it shaped like a little ball. *A drop of blood slid down his leg.*
9 N SING+SUPP You use **drop** to talk about vertical distances. For example, a thirty-foot **drop** is a distance of thirty feet between the top of a cliff or wall and the bottom of it. *The cliff plunged in a vertical drop of 300 feet.*
drop by PHRASAL VERB If you **drop by** or **drop round**, you visit someone informally, often without having arranged it beforehand. *If there's anything you want to see, just drop by.*
drop in PHRASAL VERB If you **drop in** on someone, you visit them informally, often without having arranged it beforehand. *I thought I'd just drop in and see how you were... US Secretary of State James Baker dropped in on Ankara last week.*
drop off PHRASAL VERB If you **drop off** to sleep, you go to sleep.
drop out PHRASAL VERB 1 If someone who is participating in an activity **drops out**, they stop participating without finishing what they are doing. *By this stage of the operation Garner and an accomplice had actually dropped out... He had dropped out of medical studies and chosen instead to train as a clergyman.* 2 See also **drop-out**.
drop round PHRASAL VERB See **drop by**.

droplet /drɒplət/ **droplets**
NC A **droplet** is a very small drop of liquid. *The disease is carried in water droplets in the air.*

drop-out, drop-outs; also spelt **dropout**. An informal word.
1 NC **Drop-outs** are people who reject the accepted ways of a society, for example by not having a regular job. *The police are looking into the possibility that teenage drop-outs were involved.*
2 NC **Drop-outs** are also young people who have left

school or college before finishing their studies. ...*a high-school dropout.*

dropper /drɒpə/ **droppers**
NC A **dropper** is a small glass tube with a hollow rubber part on one end. You use it for drawing up and dropping small amounts of liquid. ...*an eye dropper.*

droppings /drɒpɪŋz/
N PL **Droppings** are the faeces of birds and small animals. ...*mouse droppings.*

dropsy /drɒpsi/
NU **Dropsy** is a medical condition in which parts of the body fill up with fluid. It can be caused by various diseases.

dross /drɒs/
1 NU If you describe something as **dross**, you mean that you think it is of a very poor quality. *We can't publish this dross.*
2 NU **Dross** is also the waste material that floats on the surface of a metal such as gold that has been melted.

drought /draut/ **droughts**
NU or NC A **drought** is a long period of time during which no rain falls. ...*the effects of famine and drought... Local problems include diseases and periodic droughts.*

drove /drəuv/ **droves**
1 **Drove** is the past tense of **drive**.
2 N PL **Droves** of people are very large numbers of them. *The Communist Party lost its members in droves.*

drown /draun/ **drowns, drowning, drowned**
1 V-ERG When someone **drowns** or is **drowned**, they die because they have gone under water and cannot breathe. *A man fell from a bridge and drowned... I couldn't make myself drown the poor creature.*
2 VO If one sound **drowns** another, it is louder than the other sound, and therefore makes it impossible to hear. ...*the heckling which drowned his speech.*
drown out PHRASAL VERB If one sound **drowns out** another, it is louder than the other sound, and therefore makes it impossible to hear. *The noise from the aeroplane drowned out the voice from the loudspeaker.*

drowse /drauz/ **drowses, drowsing, drowsed**
v If you **are drowsing**, you are almost asleep or just asleep. *They were drowsing on their duffel bags between flights.*

drowsy /drauzi/ **drowsier, drowsiest**
ADJ If you are **drowsy**, you feel sleepy and cannot think clearly. *I became pleasantly drowsy.* ♦ **drowsily** ADV *I shook my head drowsily.* ♦ **drowsiness** NU *The sound of the waves lulled me into drowsiness.*

drudge /drʌdʒ/ **drudges**
NC A **drudge** is someone who has to do a lot of uninteresting work. It is also used to refer to a task which is uninteresting but necessary. *He works very hard; he's kind of a drudge in the way he goes about it... It was regarded as a chore and a drudge by most of the population.*

drudgery /drʌdʒəri/
NU **Drudgery** is uninteresting work that must be done. *While we were on holiday, we relaxed, far away from the drudgery of home. ...the drudgery of those math courses in high school.*

drug /drʌg/ **drugs, drugging, drugged**
1 NC A **drug** is a chemical substance given to people to treat or prevent illness or disease. *The findings could also be used to develop new drugs for cancer.*
2 NC **Drugs** are also substances that some people smoke or inject into their blood because of their stimulating effects. In most countries, these uses of drugs are illegal. *He was on drugs... She takes drugs... He is wanted on drugs smuggling charges.*
3 VO If you **drug** a person or animal, you give them a chemical substance in order to make them sleepy or unconscious. *The chimp had been drugged with a tranquiliser.* ♦ **drugged** ADJ *She spoke as if she was half asleep or drugged.*
4 VO If food or drink is **drugged**, a chemical substance is added to it in order to make someone unconscious when they eat or drink it. ♦ **drugged** ADJ *Delgado insisted that he was handed a drugged drink after*

completing a mountain stage.

druggist /drʌgɪst/ **druggists**; used in American English.

1 NC A **druggist** is a person who is qualified to prepare and sell drugs and medicines.

2 NC A **druggist** is also a shop where medicines and drugs that have been prescribed by a doctor are sold. *Is there a druggist round here?*

drugstore /drʌgstɔː/ **drugstores**

NC A **drugstore** is a shop where medicines and drugs that have been prescribed by a doctor are sold; used in American English. *Jerry Woods is the pharmacist at the drugstore.*

druid /druːɪd/ **druids**

1 NC A **druid** is a priest of a religion which was followed in Britain, Ireland, and France before Christianity. *The original druids were poets and philosophers as well as spiritual advisers... This druid solstice took place at the famous site of Stonehenge.*

2 NC A **druid** is also someone who follows this religion in modern times. *Modern Druids believe the stones have been the site of Pagan ritual since pre-Christian times.*

drum /drʌm/ **drums, drumming, drummed**

1 NC A **drum** is a musical instrument consisting of a skin stretched tightly over a round frame. You play it by beating it with sticks or with your hands. *To the incessant beat of drums, the crowd dances and stamps as if hypnotised. ...a drum kit.*

2 NC A **drum** is also a large cylindrical container in which fuel is kept. *...oil drums.*

3 V If something is **drumming** on a surface, it is hitting it regularly, making a continuous beating sound. *We sat listening to the rain drumming on the roof.* ● See also **drumming**.

drum into PHRASAL VERB If you **drum** something **into** someone, you keep saying it in order to make them understand or remember it. *These facts had been drummed into him.*

drum up PHRASAL VERB If you **drum up** support, you do things to attract and win people's support. *The organisers failed to drum up much public support.*

drumbeat /drʌmbiːt/ **drumbeats**

NC A **drumbeat** is the sound of a beat on a drum. *He faintly heard the drumbeats and the shouting of dancers in the distance.*

drum major, drum majors

NC A **drum major** is a sergeant in the army who is in charge of the drummers in a military band, or who leads the band when they are marching.

drummer /drʌmə/ **drummers**

NC A **drummer** is a person who plays a drum or drums in a band or group.

drumming /drʌmɪŋ/

NU **Drumming** is the action of playing the drums.

drum roll, drum rolls

NC A **drum roll** is a series of drumbeats that follow each other so quickly that they make a continuous sound. It is sometimes used to introduce someone as they come onto the stage in a theatre. *The new weapon was towed out of a hangar to the accompaniment of a drum roll from a military band.*

drumstick /drʌmstɪk/ **drumsticks**

1 NC A **drumstick** is a stick used for beating a drum. *He tapped his drumsticks on the wooden sides of the drum.*

2 NC A **drumstick** is also the lower part of the leg of a bird such as a chicken which is cooked and eaten. *She took ham and turkey, but not a drumstick.*

drunk /drʌŋk/ **drunks**

1 **Drunk** is the past participle of **drink**.

2 ADJ If someone is **drunk**, they have drunk so much alcohol that they cannot speak clearly or behave sensibly. *He was so drunk he couldn't write a word.*

3 NC A **drunk** is someone who is drunk or who often gets drunk. *A drunk slashed his face with a broken beer glass.*

drunkard /drʌŋkəd/ **drunkards**

NC A **drunkard** is someone who often gets drunk. *He depicts him as a drunkard and even an alcoholic whose drunkenness contributed to the disaster.*

drunken /drʌŋkən/

ADJ ATTRIB **Drunken** behaviour is clumsy, noisy, or foolish behaviour by someone who is drunk. *A long drunken party had just broken up. ...the dangers of drunken driving.* ● **drunkenly** ADV *Their parents fought drunkenly with each other.*

drunkenness /drʌŋkənnəs/

NU **Drunkenness** is the habit of being frequently drunk. *They acquired a reputation for drunkenness and crime.*

dry /draɪ/ **drier** or **dryer, driest; dries, drying, dried**

1 ADJ Something that is **dry** has no water or other liquid on it or in it. *I'll just shake my hands dry... We'll cover the wounds up with a clean dry bandage.* ● **dryness** NU *...the dryness of the air.*

2 V-ERG When you **dry** something or when it **dries**, it becomes dry. *He dried his feet with the towel... The washing hung drying in the sun.*

3 ADJ When the weather is **dry**, there is no rain. *The night was dry and clear... The dry season comes in March.*

4 ADJ **Dry** humour is subtle and sarcastic. *I enjoyed her dry accounts of her work experiences.* ● **drily** or **dryly** ADV *'Thank you,' I said drily. 'It must be nice to be so culturally enlightened.'*

5 ADJ **Dry** sherry or wine does not taste sweet. *They were drinking dry white wine.*

6 See also **dried, dryer**.

dry out PHRASAL VERB 1 If something **dries out** or if you **dry** it **out**, it becomes completely dry. *This causes the rivers to dry out... Eucalyptus is very greedy for water and it actually dries the soil out.* 2 If someone **dries out** or is **dried out**, they are given medical treatment to help them stop being an alcoholic; an informal use. *They sent him to a special hospital to dry out.*

dry up PHRASAL VERB 1 If something **dries up**, it loses all its water or moisture. *The pool dried up in the summer... My mouth always dries up when I'm nervous.* ● **dried-up** ADJ *...a dried-up piece of cake.* 2 When you **dry up** after a meal or **dry** the dishes **up**, you wipe the water off the cutlery and dishes when they have been washed. *Would you like me to dry up?* 3 If a supply or series of things **dries up**, it stops. *If this source of labour were to dry up, the industries would be forced to relocate.*

dry-clean, dry-cleans, dry-cleaning, dry-cleaned

VO When clothes are **dry-cleaned**, they are cleaned with a liquid chemical rather than with water. *I wondered whether he washed or dry-cleaned the silk scarf in his jacket pocket.*

dry cleaner or **dry cleaner's, dry cleaners**

NC A **dry cleaner** or **dry cleaner's** is a shop where clothes and other things made of cloth can be dry-cleaned. *Take it to the dry cleaner's.*

dry-cleaning

1 NU **Dry-cleaning** is the action or work of dry-cleaning things such as suits or overcoats. *...a dry-cleaning shop.*

2 NU **Dry-cleaning** is also clothes and other things made of cloth that have been dry-cleaned, or that are going to be dry-cleaned.

dry dock, dry docks

NC A **dry dock** is a place in a harbour from which water can be removed after a ship has entered it, so that the ship can be repaired or finished. *The Romanian ship is to be towed to a dry dock in Norway today for repairs to her damaged bow.*

dryer /draɪə/ **dryers**; also spelt **drier**.

1 NC A **dryer** is an electric machine that dries washing by using hot air.

2 NC A **dryer** is also any machine or device which dries things. *We designed a very simple dryer.*

3 **Dryer** is also the comparative form of **dry**.

dry-eyed

ADJ Someone who is **dry-eyed** is not crying although you might expect them to be. *Then, dry-eyed, he turned and walked away.*

dry ginger

NU **Dry ginger** is a fizzy ginger-flavoured drink that is used for mixing with whisky or other alcoholic drinks.

dry goods
N PL **Dry goods** are cloth, thread, and other things that are sold at a draper's shop; used in American English.

dry land
NU You say '**dry land**' when contrasting an area of land with the sea or the air. *We'll soon be on dry land again... The aircraft broke up as it landed in the sea just metres from dry land.*

dry rot
NU **Dry rot** is a serious disease in wood, caused by a fungus. It causes the wood to decay. *If you suspect that you have dry rot in your house call a surveyor.*

dry-stone wall, dry-stone walls
NC A **dry-stone wall** is a wall that has been built by fitting stones together without using any mortar. *...the Yorkshire Dales National Park's traditional barns, hay meadows and dry-stone walls.*

DTs /diːtiːz/
N PL If an alcoholic has the **DTs**, he or she shakes uncontrollably and may see things which do not exist.

dual /djuːəl/
ADJ ATTRIB **Dual** means having two parts, functions, or aspects. *The committee has a dual function. ...dual nationality.*

dual carriageway, dual carriageways
N Cor NU A **dual carriageway** is a road with a strip of grass or concrete down the middle to separate traffic going in opposite directions. *Lorries would be restricted to 50 mph on motorways and dual carriageways.*

dualism /djuːəlɪzəm/
NU **Dualism** is the state of having two main parts or aspects, or the belief that something has two main parts or aspects; a formal word. *...the old dualism of God and the devil... He seeks a dualism such as mind and matter.*

dub /dʌb/ **dubs, dubbing, dubbed**
1 VOC If something is **dubbed** a particular name, it is given that name. *London was dubbed 'the insurance capital of the world'.*
2 VO If a film is **dubbed**, the voices on the soundtrack are not those of the actors, but the voices of other actors speaking in a different language. *The series sells in forty-seven countries and has been dubbed into six languages.*

dubbin /dʌbɪn/
NU **Dubbin** is a kind of thick grease that is rubbed on leather to make it soft and waterproof.

dubious /djuːbiəs/
1 ADJ You describe something as **dubious** when you think it is not completely honest, safe, or reliable. *...goods of dubious origin.*
2 ADJ PRED If you are **dubious** about something, you are unsure about it. *She was dubious about Baker's choice of pilot.* ◆ **dubiously** ADV *They looked at him dubiously, not knowing how much to believe.*

Dublin /dʌblɪn/
Dublin is the capital of the Republic of Ireland and its largest city. Population: 921,000 (1986).

ducal /djuːkl/
ADJ ATTRIB **Ducal** places or things belong to or are connected with a duke. *...trees that would not have disgraced a ducal park.*

duchess /dʌtʃɪs/ **duchesses**
N Cor TITLE A **duchess** is a woman who has the same rank as a duke, or who is the wife of a duke. *...the Duchess of Marlborough.*

duchy /dʌtʃi/ **duchies**
NC A **duchy** is the area of land that is owned or ruled by a duke. *...the Grand Duchy of Luxembourg.*

duck /dʌk/ **ducks, ducking, ducked**
1 NC A **duck** is a common water bird with short legs, webbed feet, and a large flat beak. *Threatened species include geese, ducks, and many waders.*
2 NU **Duck** refers to the meat of a duck when it is cooked and eaten. *The chef prepared duck with artichokes and oxtail fondue.*
3 V or VO If you **duck**, you move your head quickly downwards to avoid something that is in your way or that is going to hit you, or to avoid being seen. *A gull flew so close that she ducked... He ducked his head to go out of the tent.*

4 VA If you **duck** into a place, you move there quickly, usually in order to escape danger. *I ducked into the shrubbery.*
5 VO If you **duck** a responsibility or duty, you avoid it. *Israel could not duck its responsibilities any longer... Mr Baker had promised that he would not duck the issue of their pay.*
6 See also **lame duck**.
duck out PHRASAL VERB If you **duck out** of something that you are supposed to do, or if you duck out, you avoid doing it. *It's very difficult to duck out of this role... The Labour opposition accused her of ducking out.*

ducking /dʌkɪŋ/ **duckings**
NC If you give someone a **ducking**, you push them under water. *The child got a nasty ducking.*

duckling /dʌklɪŋ/ **ducklings**
NC A **duckling** is a young duck.

ducks and drakes
NU **Ducks and drakes** is a game in which you throw a flat stone across an area of water in such a way that the stone bounces across the surface.

duct /dʌkt/ **ducts**
1 NC A **duct** is a pipe, tube, or channel through which a liquid or gas is sent. *...air-conditioning ducts.*
2 NC A **duct** is also a tube in your body that a liquid such as tears or bile can pass through. *The liver has one bile duct, one artery, and one main vein going to it. ...the sperm duct.*

dud /dʌd/ **duds**
ADJ or NC You say that something is **dud** or a **dud** when it does not work properly; an informal word. *...dud light bulbs... The new system is a dud.*

dud cheque, dud cheques
NC A **dud cheque** is a cheque which is not worth any money because the person who wrote it does not have any money in their bank account. *He'd been sent to prison for handing out dud cheques all over the country.*

dude /djuːd/ **dudes**
NC A **dude** is a man; used in informal American English. *...every damn dude in the platoon.*

dudgeon /dʌdʒən/
If you are **in high dudgeon**, you are very angry or resentful, usually because your feelings have been hurt by what someone has said or done. *He slammed the door and went off in high dudgeon.*

due /djuː/
1 PREP If an event or situation is **due to** something else, it happens or exists as a result of it. *Over 40 per cent of deaths were due to this disease.*
2 ADJ PRED If something is **due** at a particular time, it is expected to happen or to arrive at that time. *What time is the bus due?... The committee was due to meet on 22 August.*
3 If you say that something will happen **in due course**, you mean that it will happen eventually, when the time is right; a formal expression. *All will be attended to in due course.*
4 N PL **Dues** are sums of money that you pay regularly to an organization that you belong to. *A new form of payment was introduced for collecting members' dues.*
5 ADJ PRED If some money is **due** to you, you have a right to it. *You may get slightly less than the full amount due to you.*
6 ADJ ATTRIB If you give something **due** consideration, you give it the consideration it deserves. *After due consideration of the evidence, the meeting decided that no one had been to blame.*
7 ADV You use **due** to talk about exact compass directions. For example, **due** north means exactly to the north of where you are. *The vessel is now anchored twenty-five miles due east of Ramsgate.*

duel /djuːəl/ **duels**
1 NC A **duel** is a fight between two people in which they use guns or swords in order to settle a quarrel. *The protagonists engage in their deadly duel, fighting up and down a flight of steps.*
2 NC You can refer to any conflict between two people or groups as a **duel**. *There have been sporadic artillery duels in the area over the last month.*

due process; a legal term.
1 N SING In the United States, **due process** or **due process of law** are the procedures which are established in the Constitution to protect the individual's legal rights and liberties. *The Judge said Seebol was denied his Constitutional rights to privacy, equal protection and due process... He says the system in Alabama amounts to a denial of the due process of law guaranteed by the Constitution.*
2 N SING **Due process of law** also refers to the administration of justice according to established rules and principles. *He said that the reason none of them had been tried yet was because the due process of law had to be followed.*

duet /djuːˈet/ **duets**
N C A **duet** is a piece of music sung or played by two people. *She sang a duet from Rossini's Semiramide, with Marilyn Horne.*

duff /dʌf/ **duffs, duffing, duffed**; an informal word.
ADJ PRED Something that is **duff** is useless or broken. *It might look all right, but I'll bet you it's a duff one.*
duff up PHRASAL VERB If you **duff** someone **up**, you fight them and injure them, usually using your fists. *They dragged him into the alley and duffed him up.*

duffel bag /dʌfl bæg/ **duffel bags**; also spelt **duffle bag**.
N C A **duffel bag** is a strong cloth bag shaped like a cylinder, with a drawstring that goes around the top of the bag and is also attached to the bottom. You carry it over your shoulder. *He threw his stuff in a duffel bag and left.*

duffel coat /dʌfl kəʊt/ **duffel coats**; also spelt **duffle coat**.
N C A **duffel coat** is a heavy coat with a hood and barrel-shaped buttons.

duffer /dʌfə/ **duffers**
N C A **duffer** is someone who is unable to learn what someone else is trying to teach them, or who is unable to do something well or properly; an informal word. *I'm a complete golfing duffer.*

dug /dʌg/
Dug is the past tense and past participle of **dig**.

dugout /dʌgaʊt/ **dugouts**; also spelt **dug-out**.
1 N C A **dugout** is a canoe that is made by hollowing out a log. *When we went by water, Colonel Arnold would travel aboard his own dugout, manned by two Indians... Fishermen in dug-out canoes make the rounds of their nets.*
2 N C A **dugout** is also a shelter made by digging a hole in the ground and then covering it or tunnelling so that the shelter has a roof over it. Dugouts are usually made by soldiers. *You can just see the outlines of the Ethiopian trenches, with their dugouts as well.*

duke /djuːk/ **dukes**
N or TITLE A **duke** is a man with a rank just below that of a prince. *...the Duke of York.*

dukedom /djuːkdəm/ **dukedoms**
1 N C A **dukedom** is the rank or title of a duke. *He became the tenth to succeed to the dukedom in 1940.*
2 N C A **dukedom** is also the land owned by a duke.

dulcet /dʌlsɪt/
ADJ ATTRIB **Dulcet** sounds are gentle and pleasant to listen to; a literary word, often used humorously. *I wake up to the dulcet tones of the Radio Four news.*

dull /dʌl/ **duller, dullest; dulls, dulling, dulled**
1 ADJ Something or someone that is **dull** is not interesting. *I thought the book dull and unoriginal. ...dull and mediocre films... He was seen as rather dull and uninspired.* ◆ **dullness** N U *...the dullness of his life.*
2 ADJ You say that someone is **dull** when they show no interest in anything. *She became dull and silent.* ◆ **dully** ADV *They stared dully at the ground.*
3 ADJ ATTRIB A **dull** colour or light is not bright. *The sea had been a dull grey.* ◆ **dully** ADV *The lights of the houses gleamed dully.*
4 ADJ You say that the weather is **dull** when it is cloudy. *It was a dull morning.*
5 ADJ ATTRIB A **dull** sound is not clear or loud. *...a dull thud.*
6 ADJ ATTRIB **Dull** feelings are weak and not intense. *The dull ache in her side began again.* ◆ **dully** ADV

His ankle throbbed dully.
7 V O If something **dulls** a pain or feeling, it causes it to seem less intense. *The leaves are chewed by poor peasants to dull the appetite.*

dullard /dʌləd/ **dullards**
N C A **dullard** is a person who is stupid and unimaginative; an old-fashioned word. *...an incompetent, bumbling dullard.*

duly /djuːli/
ADV If something is **duly** done, it is done in the correct way; a formal word. *She was declared duly elected to Parliament.*

dumb /dʌm/ **dumber, dumbest**
1 ADJ Someone who is **dumb** is completely unable to speak. *...deaf and dumb people.*
2 ADJ PRED If someone is **dumb** on a particular occasion, they cannot speak because they are angry, shocked, or surprised. *We were struck dumb with horror.* ◆ **dumbly** /dʌmli/ ADV *He stared dumbly at the wall.*
3 ADJ **Dumb** also means stupid; an informal use. *In films, she often appeared as the smart blonde, rather than the dumb one.*

dumbbell /dʌmbel/ **dumbbells**
1 N C A **dumbbell** is a short bar with weights on either side which people use for physical exercise to strengthen their arm and shoulder muscles.
2 N C If you call someone a **dumbbell**, you mean that you think they are a stupid person; used in informal American English. *They had watched many a dumbbell turn into a national hero on the baseball pitch.*

dumbfounded /dʌmfaʊndɪd/
ADJ If you are **dumbfounded**, you are so surprised that you cannot speak. *He was watching, dumbfounded.*

dumbstruck /dʌmstrʌk/
ADJ If you are **dumbstruck**, you are so shocked or surprised that you cannot speak. *'I am absolutely dumbstruck. I'm horrified and dismayed.'*

dumb waiter, dumb waiters
N C A **dumb waiter** is a lift used to carry things, such as food or dishes, from one floor of a building to another.

dummy /dʌmi/ **dummies**
1 N C A baby's **dummy** is a rubber or plastic object that you give the baby to suck so that it feels comforted.
2 N C A tailor's **dummy** is a model of a person that is used to display clothes.
3 N+N or N C You use **dummy** to describe things that are not real. For example, a dummy car is not a real car, but has been made to look or behave like a real car. *The test missile with a dummy warhead had just been launched... British officials then switched the crates, replacing the real ones with dummies.*

dummy run, dummy runs
N C A **dummy run** is a trial or test procedure, which is carried out in order to see if something works properly.

dump /dʌmp/ **dumps, dumping, dumped**
1 V O When unwanted waste matter **is dumped**, it is put somewhere and is intended to remain there for a very long period of time. *Nearly 4,000 tons of highly toxic waste had been dumped in a small port in Nigeria.* ◆ **dumping** N U *...the dumping of acid wastes in the North Sea.*
2 V O If you **dump** something somewhere, you put it there quickly and carelessly. *She dumped her bag on Judy's table.*
3 N C A rubbish **dump** is a place where rubbish is left, for example on open ground outside a town. *We're told that this dump is going to contain just household trash... Glass and plastic bottles have ended up on the garbage dump. ...a landfill rubbish dump.*
4 N C+SUPP An ammunition **dump** is a place where weapons are stored, usually by the armed forces. *The guerrillas say they have blown up another ammunition dump... Among the weapons seized from the arms dump was a Soviet-made rocket launcher.*
5 N C If you refer to a place as a **dump**, you mean it is unattractive and unpleasant to live in; an informal use.

dumper truck, dumper trucks
NC A **dumper truck** is a truck whose carrying part can tip backwards so that the load falls out.

dumping ground, dumping grounds
1 NC A **dumping ground** is a place where unwanted waste matter is left. *There has been concern that the Pacific might become a dumping ground for chemical and nuclear waste.*
2 NC+*for* If you refer to a place as a **dumping ground** for a particular thing, you mean that that thing is left there, usually in large quantities. *The house has become a dumping ground for stolen goods.*

dumpling /dʌmplɪŋ/ **dumplings**
NC A **dumpling** is a lump of dough cooked with meat and vegetables in gravy. *...starchy white dumplings called fufu.*

dumpy /dʌmpi/
ADJ A **dumpy** person is short and fat.

dun /dʌn/
ADJ Something that is **dun** is a dull grey-brown colour.

dunce /dʌns/ **dunces**
NC You call someone a **dunce** when they cannot learn what someone is trying to teach them. *I was such a dunce at school.*

dune /djuːn/ **dunes**
NC A **dune** or a sand **dune** is a hill of sand near the sea or in a desert. *They went missing in an area of 900-feet dunes and loose, swirling sand.*

dung /dʌŋ/
NU **Dung** is faeces from large animals. *They've always collected cow dung to fertilize their crops.*

dungarees /dʌŋgəriːz/
N PL **Dungarees** are trousers attached to a piece of cloth which covers your chest and has straps going over your shoulders.

dungeon /dʌndʒən/ **dungeons**
NC A **dungeon** is a dark underground prison in a castle. *One man said he had been held in a dungeon for five years.*

dunk /dʌŋk/ **dunks, dunking, dunked**
VO If you **dunk** something in a liquid, you put it there for a short time before swallowing it; an informal word. *I dunked my bread in the cocoa.*

duo /djuːəʊ/ **duos**
1 NC A **duo** is two musicians or singers who play music or sing together as a pair. *...a world-famous singing duo.*
2 NC+SUPP You can also refer to two people together as a **duo**, especially people who have something in common; an informal use. *When they're together they make a frightening duo.*

duodenal /djuːəʊdiːnl/
ADJ ATTRIB **Duodenal** means relating to or contained in the duodenum; a medical term. *...a duodenal ulcer.*

duodenum /djuːəʊdiːnəm/ **duodenums**
NC Your **duodenum** is the part of your small intestine just below your stomach; a medical term. *The cause of death was cancer of the duodenum.*

dupe /djuːp/ **dupes, duping, duped**
1 VO If someone **dupes** you, they trick you. *I was duped into expressing my thoughts.*
2 NC A **dupe** is someone who has been tricked. *He told them they were fools and dupes to put their hands to such a document... Boren believed Gates was Casey's dupe as much as Congress was.*

duplex /djuːpleks/ **duplexes**
1 ADJ A **duplex** device or process has two parts; a technical use. *This stimulates a duplex transaction.*
2 NC In American English, a **duplex** is a semi-detached house. *The house was an older duplex encircled by nicely shaped hedges.*
3 NC In American English, a **duplex** is also a flat which has rooms on two floors.

duplicate, duplicates, duplicating, duplicated;
pronounced /djuːplɪkeɪt/ when it is a verb and /djuːplɪkət/ when it is a noun or adjective
1 VO If you **duplicate** a piece of writing or a drawing, you make exact copies of it using a machine. *A court in Czechoslovakia has upheld a four-year prison sentence on a religious activist for writing and duplicating illegal printed matter.*
2 NC A **duplicate** is something that is identical to

something else. *Keep duplicates of all data files. ...a duplicate key.*
3 If you have something **in duplicate**, you have two identical copies of it. *Usually now we ask for a draft in duplicate.*
4 VO When an activity is **duplicated**, two people or two groups do the same thing. *They said the ships were at risk because they had no organised defence and operations would be duplicated.* ◆ **duplication** /djuːplɪkeɪʃn/ NU *We try to avoid duplication of work.*

duplicator /djuːplɪkeɪtə/ **duplicators**
NC A **duplicator** is a machine which makes copies of writing or drawings from a specially prepared original. *You can use the typewriter or duplicator.*

duplicity /djuːplɪsəti/
NU **Duplicity** is speech or action that aims to make people believe something which is not true. *I was trying to plan some way of tackling her duplicity.*

durable /djʊərəbl/
ADJ Something that is **durable** is strong and lasts a long time. *...durable products.* ◆ **durability** /djʊərəbɪləti/ NU *...the durability of their love.*

duration /djʊəreɪʃn/
N SING The **duration** of something is the length of time that it lasts for. *He was prepared to do this for the duration of the campaign.*

duress /djʊəres/
If you do something **under duress**, you are forced to do it. *The confessions were made under duress and after ill-treatment.*

Durex /djʊəreks/; **Durex** is both the singular and the plural form.
NC A **Durex** is a condom; **Durex** is a trademark.

during /djʊərɪŋ/
1 PREP Something that happens **during** a period of time happens continuously or repeatedly in that period. *She heated the place during the winter with a huge wood furnace... Fred had worked with her at Oxford during the war.*
2 PREP You also use **during** to say that something happens at some point in a period of time. *He had died during the night.*

Dushanbe /duːʃænbeɪ/
Dushanbe is the capital of Tadjikistan and its largest city. Population: 604,000 (1989).

dusk /dʌsk/
NU **Dusk** is the time just before night when it is not completely dark. *As dusk fell, the sound of automatic weapons could be heard.*

dusky /dʌski/
ADJ Something that is **dusky** is rather dark; a literary word. *...her dusky cheeks.*

dust /dʌst/ **dusts, dusting, dusted**
1 NU **Dust** is dry, fine powder such as particles of earth, dirt, or pollen. *Each car threw up a cloud of white dust. ...the dust on the coffee table.*
2 VOorV When you **dust** furniture or other objects, you remove dust from them using a duster. *She lifted the jugs as she dusted the shelf... He washed, tidied, and dusted.*
3 VO If you **dust** a surface with a powder, you cover it lightly with the powder. *She put on lipstick and dusted her face with powder.*

dustbin /dʌstbɪn/ **dustbins**
NC A **dustbin** is a large container that you put rubbish in. It is usually kept outside. *This waste usually goes into bin bags or into a dustbin.*

dustcart /dʌstkɑːt/ **dustcarts**
NC A **dustcart** is a lorry into which the dustmen put the rubbish from people's dustbins.

dust-cover. See dust-jacket.

duster /dʌstə/ **dusters**
NC A **duster** is a cloth used for removing dust from furniture and other objects. ● See also **knuckle-duster**.

dust-jacket, dust-jackets
NC A **dust-jacket** or a **dust-cover** is a loose paper cover which is put on a book to protect it. It often contains information about the book and its author. *They put his photograph on the dust-jacket of his first novel.*

dustman /dʌstmən/ **dustmen** /dʌstmən/
NC A **dustman** is a person whose job is to empty

dustbins. *Dustmen are now refusing to collect any more rubbish because of the ban.*

dustpan /dʌstpæn/ **dustpans**
NC A **dustpan** is a small flat container for sweeping dust and dirt into.

dustsheet /dʌstʃiːt/ **dustsheets**
NC A **dustsheet** is a large cloth which is used to cover objects such as furniture in order to protect them from dust.

dust-up, dust-ups
NC A **dust-up** is a quarrel or fight; an informal word. *Another dust-up took place on the public beach.*

dusty /dʌsti/ **dustier, dustiest**
ADJ Something that is **dusty** is covered with dust. *...a dusty mountain track. ...a room full of dusty, broken furniture.*

Dutch /dʌtʃ/
1 ADJ **Dutch** means belonging or relating to the Netherlands. *...the world-famous Dutch painter, Vincent Van Gogh.*
2 NU **Dutch** is the language spoken by people who live in the Netherlands. *The country's official language is Dutch.*
3 N PL The **Dutch** are the people who come from the Netherlands. *The province was the very last area of present day Indonesia to be colonised by the Dutch.*

dutiful /djuːtɪfl/
ADJ If you are **dutiful**, you do everything that you are expected to do. *He was a dutiful son.* ♦ **dutifully** ADV *The audience dutifully applauded.*

duty /djuːti/ **duties**
1 NU **Duty** is the work that you have to do as your job. *He reported for duty at the manager's office.*
2 When policemen, doctors, or nurses are **on duty**, they are working. When they are **off duty**, they are not working. *A police constable on duty became suspicious... You can go off duty now.*
3 N PL Your **duties** are the tasks you do as part of your job. *Nursing auxiliaries help qualified nurses with their basic duties... Mrs Thatcher bears the responsibilities and duties of the leader of her party until a successor is in place.*
4 N SING+POSS If you say that something is your **duty**, you mean that you ought to do it because it is your responsibility. *As a doctor, it was my duty to preserve life.*
5 NCorNU **Duties** are taxes which you pay to the government on goods that you buy. *Britain hopes to persuade Japan to lower existing import duties on whisky... The government increased the duty on petrol. ...the list of states allowed to sell goods free of duty in the United States.*

duty-bound
ADJ PRED+to-INF If you are **duty-bound** to do something, you must do it because it is your duty; a formal word. *You are duty-bound to stay by her sick bed.*

duty-free
ADJ **Duty-free** goods are bought at airports or on planes or ships at a cheaper price than usual because they are not taxed. *...duty-free cigarettes.*

duty-free shop, duty-free shops
NC A **duty-free shop** is a shop, for example at an airport, where you can buy duty-free goods.

duvet /duːveɪ/ **duvets**
NC A **duvet** is a large bag filled with feathers or similar material, which you use to cover yourself in bed.

duvet cover, duvet covers
NC A **duvet cover** is a washable cover for a duvet.

dwarf /dwɔːf/ **dwarfs, dwarfing, dwarfed**
1 VO If one thing **dwarfs** another thing, it makes the other thing look small. *David was dwarfed by a huge desk.*
2 ADJ ATTRIB **Dwarf** plants or animals are much smaller than other plants or animals of the same kind. *...dwarf firs.*
3 NC A **dwarf** is a person who is much smaller than most people. *Some children remain as dwarfs because they lack a particular hormone.*

dwarfish /dwɔːfɪʃ/
ADJ Someone or something that is **dwarfish** is surprisingly small. *He was a short, burly man, almost*

dwarfish.

dwell /dwel/ **dwells, dwelling, dwelled** or **dwelt**
VA If you **dwell** somewhere, you live there; an old-fashioned word. *'Pray how long have you dwelt here?' said I... Pinkwater dwells in the arboreal splendor of the Upper Hudson River Valley.*

dwell on PHRASAL VERB If you **dwell on** something or **dwell upon** it, you think, speak, or write about it a great deal. *She began to dwell on memories of her mother... So far we have dwelt upon the negative elements in the situation.*

dweller /dwelə/ **dwellers**
NC+SUPP You use **dweller** to say where someone lives. For example, a city **dweller** is someone who lives in a city. *The train was carrying hostel dwellers home from work.*

dwelling /dwelɪŋ/ **dwellings**
NC A **dwelling** is a house or other place where someone lives; a formal word. *They were five miles from the nearest dwelling.*

dwelt /dwelt/
Dwelt is a past tense and past participle of **dwell**.

dwindle /dwɪndl/ **dwindles, dwindling, dwindled**
V If something **dwindles**, it becomes smaller or less strong. *Their small hoard of money dwindled... Support for CND dwindled.* ♦ **dwindling** ADJ *...an area of rapidly dwindling forest.*

dye /daɪ/ **dyes, dyeing, dyed**
1 VO If you **dye** hair or cloth, you change its colour by soaking it in a coloured liquid. *It will be dyed scarlet and cut to lengths of exactly eighteen inches.* ♦ **dyed** ADJ *...a woman with dyed red hair.*
2 N MASS A **dye** is a substance which is mixed into a liquid and used to change the colour of cloth or hair. *...chemical dyes.*

dyed-in-the-wool
ADJ ATTRIB **Dyed-in-the-wool** means having very strong opinions about something which you refuse to change. *He spoke as a dyed-in-the-wool aristocrat himself.*

dying /daɪɪŋ/
1 **Dying** is the present participle of **die**.
2 N PL The **dying** are people who are so ill or so badly injured that they are likely to die soon. *She cared for the poor, the diseased and the dying.*
3 ADJ ATTRIB A **dying** tradition or industry is becoming less important and is likely to end altogether. *Has reading itself become a dying pastime for children in Britain?*

dyke /daɪk/ **dykes**; also spelt **dike**.
NC A **dyke** is a thick wall that prevents water flooding onto land from a river or from the sea. *France is backing a dyke and water management project to control annual flooding.*

dynamic /daɪnæmɪk/ **dynamics**
1 ADJ A **dynamic** person is full of energy and purpose. *The new President is a dynamic and able man.* ♦ **dynamically** ADV *We would like to see them participate more dynamically.*
2 N PL The **dynamics** of a society or a situation are the forces that cause it to change. *...the dynamics of industrial development... You don't feel that he has an understanding of the dynamics of filmmaking.*

dynamism /daɪnəmɪzəm/
NU Someone's **dynamism** is their energy or ability to produce new ideas. *He has injected a sense of dynamism into Hungarian public life.*

dynamite /daɪnəmaɪt/ **dynamites, dynamiting, dynamited**
1 NU **Dynamite** is an explosive that is made by soaking a substance such as sawdust with nitroglycerin. *...rebels wielding sticks of dynamite.*
2 VO If someone **dynamites** something, they blow it up by using dynamite. *In other attacks, two mineral trains were dynamited and derailed... The rebels dynamited power lines plunging much of the city into darkness.*

dynamo /daɪnəməʊ/ **dynamos**
NC A **dynamo** is a device that uses the movement of a machine to produce electricity. *Faraday's work, including the invention of the first dynamo, paved the way for the large scale generation of electrical power.*

dynastic /dɪnǽstɪk/
ADJ **Dynastic** means typical of or relating to a dynasty. *Most Japanese support the continuation of a dynastic imperial line.*

dynasty /dɪnəsti/ **dynasties**
NC A **dynasty** is a series of rulers of a country who all belong to the same family. *The Manchu dynasty fell in 1911.*

d'you /djə, djuː/
D'you is a short form of 'do you' used in questions in spoken English. *'D'you know what I found?'*

dysentery /dɪsntri/
NU **Dysentery** is an infection that causes severe diarrhoea. *Some are fighting pneumonia, dysentery and other diseases.*

dyslexia /dɪslɛksiə/
NU **Dyslexia** is difficulty with reading, caused by a slight disorder of the brain. *We've heard a lot in recent times about dyslexia, which is sometimes described as word-blindness.*

dyslexic /dɪslɛksɪk/
ADJ Someone who is **dyslexic** has difficulty with reading because of a slight disorder of the brain. *Her younger daughter was dyslexic. ...dyslexic pupils.*

dyspepsia /dɪspɛpsiə/
NU **Dyspepsia** is the same as **indigestion**; a formal word.

dyspeptic /dɪspɛptɪk/
ADJ Someone who is **dyspeptic** is suffering from indigestion or often suffers from it; a formal word.

dystrophy /dɪstrəfi/. See **muscular dystrophy**.

Dzaoudzi /dzaudzi/
Dzaoudzi is the capital of Mayotte. Population: 6,000 (1985).

E e

E, e /iː/ **E's, e's**
1 NC **E** is the fifth letter of the English alphabet.
2 **E** is a written abbreviation for 'east'.

each /iːtʃ/
1 DET or PRON If you refer to **each** thing or person in a group, you are referring to every member and considering them as individuals. *Each county is subdivided into several districts... There were peaches and pears. I opened two tins of each.*
2 PRON You use **each** to emphasize that you are referring to every individual thing or person in a group. *They cost eight pounds each.*
3 PRON You use **each other** when you are saying that each member of a group does something to the others. *She and John looked at each other.*

eager /iːgə/
ADJ If you are **eager** to do or have something, you very much want to do it or have it. *The majority were eager for change.* ◆ **eagerly** ADV *...eagerly waiting for news of a victory.* ◆ **eagerness** NU *...my eagerness to learn.*

eagle /iːgl/ **eagles**
NC An **eagle** is a large bird that lives by eating small animals. *...England's only pair of nesting eagles.*

ear /ɪə/ **ears**
1 NC Your **ears** are the two parts of your body, one on each side of your head, which you hear with. *...a Prime Ministerial aide whispered anxiously in her ear.*
2 N SING+SUPP You can use **ear** to refer to a person's willingness to listen to someone. *He tried to give a sympathetic ear at all times.*
3 NC The **ears** of a cereal plant such as wheat are the top parts containing the seeds. *...an ear of wheat.*
● **Ear** is used in these phrases. ● If you **keep** or **have** your **ear to the ground,** you make sure that you are well informed about what is happening. ● If you can **play** a piece of music **by ear,** you can play it after listening to it, rather than by reading printed music. ● If you **play** a particular situation **by ear,** you make decisions as things happen rather than planning it beforehand. *A spokeswoman said the UN team would 'play it by ear'.* ● If you **turn a deaf ear** to something that is being said, you ignore it. *The Treasury turned a deaf ear to NHS cash pleas.* ● If a request or complaint about something **falls on deaf ears,** it is ignored. *I hope that our appeals will not fall on deaf ears... Those arguments have so far fallen on deaf ears.* ● If you **have the ear** of someone in authority, they listen to your advice and are influenced by it when they make decisions. *Oliver North emerges as the man who had the ear of President Reagan.* ● When someone forgets what you tell them, you can say that it **goes in one ear and out the other.**

earache /ɪəreɪk/
N U or N SING **Earache** is a pain in the inside part of your ear. *...a build up of pressure in the inner ear leading to severe earache... The baby had been screaming all morning with an earache.*

eardrum /ɪədrʌm/ **eardrums**
NC Your **eardrums** are thin pieces of skin inside your ears, which vibrate so that you can hear sounds. *His eardrum had been perforated by a blow.*

earful /ɪəful/
N SING If you say that you gave someone an **earful,** you mean that you spoke angrily to them for quite a long time; an informal word. *I gave him an earful on how he had oppressed me all our married life... If anyone touched him, they'd get an earful.*

earl /ɜːl/ **earls**
N C or TITLE An **earl** is a British nobleman. *Only a few months later the earl was dead. ...the family home of the Earl of Caernarvon.*

earldom /ɜːldəm/ **earldoms**
NC An **earldom** is the rank or state of being an earl. *Mrs Thatcher herself bestowed on a former prime minister, Harold Macmillan, the Earldom of Stockton.*

earlier /ɜːlɪə/
ADV or ADJ **Earlier** is the comparative of **early.** It is also used to refer to a time before the present or before the one you are talking about. *Her parents had died of cholera four years earlier. ...in earlier times, when this fashion was popular.*

earlobe /ɪələub/ **earlobes**
NC Your **earlobes** are the soft parts at the bottom of your ears.

early /ɜːli/ **earlier, earliest**
1 ADV or ADJ ATTRIB **Early** means near the beginning of a period of time, a process, or a piece of work. *I got up early. ...early last week. ...in the early 1980s.*
2 ADV or ADJ If someone or something arrives or happens **early,** they arrive or happen before the expected or normal time. *The day's practice ended early because of bad light. ...her husband's early death.*
● **Early** is used in these phrases. ● **As early as** means at a particular time that is surprisingly early. *As early as 1978 the United States had taken steps to counteract this.* ● **At the earliest** means not before the date or time mentioned. *No developments were expected before August at the earliest.* ● You say it's **early days** when a situation or process has just begun and you do not know what is likely to happen in the future. *It's early days yet, we've just had the first round of meetings.* ● **bright and early**: see **bright**. ● the **early hours**: see **hour**. ● **early night**: see **night**.

early-warning
ADJ ATTRIB An **early-warning** system is a system which gives a warning at the earliest possible moment that something bad is likely to happen, for example if a machine is about to stop working, or an enemy has launched missiles against your country. *For years they have worked on early-warning and other systems to minimise loss of life.*

earmark /ɪəmɑːk/ **earmarks, earmarking, earmarked**
V O If resources such as money **are earmarked** for a particular purpose, they have been reserved for that purpose. *A sum of a hundred and twenty million rupees has already been earmarked for various expansion programmes.*

earn /ɜːn/ **earns, earning, earned**
1 V O If you **earn** money, you receive it in return for work that you do. *...the average worker, earning $15,058... They have to earn a living somehow.*

2 VO If something **earns** money, it produces money as profit. *'Peanuts' by Charles Shultz is featured in more than 2,000 papers, and is estimated to earn 60 million dollars a year.*
3 VO If you **earn** something such as praise, you get it because you deserve it. *He has earned his place in history.*

earner /ˈɜːnə/ **earners**
NC An **earner** is someone or something that earns money or produces profit. *...a reliable wage earner. ...when the woman is either the major or the sole earner.*

earnest /ˈɜːnɪst/
1 ADJ **Earnest** people are very serious and sincere in what they say and do. *...an earnest young man from the University... It is my earnest wish that you use this money to further your research.*
2 If you are **in earnest**, you are sincere. *Is the President in earnest about the desire to negotiate?*
3 If something happens **in earnest**, it happens with much more effort and determination than before. *Work on the tunnel began in earnest soon after.*

earnestly /ˈɜːnɪstli/
1 ADV If you say something **earnestly**, you say it very seriously, often because you believe that it is important. *'Are you sure you can manage it?' she asked earnestly... He was in a corner of the room talking earnestly to Julie.*
2 ADV If you do something **earnestly**, you do it in a thorough and serious way, intending to succeed. *You must promise that you will go into it seriously and earnestly.*

earnings /ˈɜːnɪŋz/
N PL Your **earnings** are the money that you earn by working. *Earnings have been rising by an average 8%.*

earnings-related
ADJ An **earnings-related** payment or benefit provides higher or lower payments according to the amount a person was earning while working. *In that year the government introduced its earnings-related pension scheme.*

earphone /ˈɪəfəʊn/ **earphones**
NC **Earphones** are a piece of equipment which you wear over or inside your ears, so that you can listen to something, often a radio or cassette recorder, without anybody else hearing. *The noise is so loud that it's sometimes hard for the driver to hear instructions over his earphones.*

earpiece /ˈɪəpiːs/ **earpieces**
1 NC The **earpiece** of a telephone receiver, hearing aid, or other device is the part that is held up to or put into your ear. *...a spare earpiece for listening in to the recording.*
2 NC The **earpieces** of a pair of glasses are the parts which fit over your ears to keep the glasses on.

earplug /ˈɪəplʌg/ **earplugs**
NC **Earplugs** are small pieces of soft material or specially made plastic shapes which you put into your ears to keep out noise, water, or cold air. *Drummond brought his earplugs with him when he attended the concert.*

earring /ˈɪərɪŋ/ **earrings**
NC **Earrings** are pieces of jewellery which hang from your ears.

earshot /ˈɪəʃɒt/
If you are **within earshot** of something, you are close enough to be able to hear it. If you are **out of earshot**, you are too far away to hear it. *There was no one within earshot... Keep him out of earshot if possible.*

ear-splitting
ADJ An **ear-splitting** noise is very loud. *...an ear-splitting shriek.*

earth /ɜːθ/ **earths**
1 N PROP The **Earth** is the planet on which we live. *...the Earth and other planets in the solar system.*
2 N SING The **earth** is also the land surface on which we live and move about. *For twenty minutes the earth shook.*
3 NU **Earth** is the substance in which plants grow. *Eight bodies had been removed from a thirty-foot pile of earth.*

4 NC An **earth** is an electrical wire which allows current to pass from an appliance into the ground. It makes the appliance safe even when there is something wrong with it. *Cut back the covers of the neutral and live wires about 1 inch, leaving the earth a bit longer.*
● **Earth** is used in these phrases. ● You use **on earth** with words such as 'how', 'why', 'what', or 'where', to emphasize that there is no obvious answer to a question or problem. *How on earth do we raise half a million dollars?... He was wondering what on earth he should do.* ● If something costs **the earth**, it costs a very large amount of money; an informal expression. *If you go to a commercial photographer he'll charge the earth for it.* ● See also **down-to-earth**.

earth-bound
1 ADJ If something is **earth-bound**, it is unable to leave the surface of the Earth by flying. *...earth-bound insects.*
2 ADJ If you say that someone is **earth-bound**, you mean that they do not have enough imagination to think how things might be different. *...to make comprehensible to our earth-bound senses a vision of divine order.*

earthen /ˈɜːθn/
1 ADJ ATTRIB **Earthen** pots are made of baked clay. *The traditional breakfast of porridge was cooked in earthen pots.*
2 ADJ ATTRIB An **earthen** floor is made of hard earth. *The earthen floor was covered with rugs and cushions.*

earthenware /ˈɜːθnweə/
ADJ ATTRIB **Earthenware** pots are made of baked clay. *...a big earthenware jar.* ▶ Also NU *...bowls of glazed earthenware.*

earthly /ˈɜːθli/
1 ADJ ATTRIB **Earthly** means happening in the material world and not in any spiritual life or life after death. *She believed that our earthly life is all that matters.*
2 ADJ ATTRIB If you say that there is no **earthly** reason for something, you are emphasizing that there is no reason for it. *He said there was no earthly hope of the refugees ever returning.*

earthquake /ˈɜːθkweɪk/ **earthquakes**
NC An **earthquake** is a shaking of the ground caused by movement of the Earth's crust. *The country has been hit by an earthquake... An earthquake struck the northern territories of Australia just before dawn.*

earth-shattering
ADJ Something that is **earth-shattering** is very surprising or shocking. *...an earth-shattering discovery.*

earthwork /ˈɜːθwɜːk/ **earthworks**
NC **Earthworks** are large mounds of earth that have been built for defence, especially mounds which were built a very long time ago. *The earthworks commanded a view of the valley floor.*

earthworm /ˈɜːθwɜːm/ **earthworms**
NC An **earthworm** is a worm that lives under the ground.

earthy /ˈɜːθi/
1 ADJ Someone who is **earthy** does not mind talking openly about things such as sex that other people find embarrassing. *...Deng's earthy and matter-of-fact style. ...an earthy sexuality rooted in everyday life.*
2 ADJ Something that is **earthy** looks, smells, or feels like earth. *...the subtle, earthy fragrance of wild thyme.*

earwig /ˈɪəwɪg/ **earwigs**
NC An **earwig** is a small, thin brown insect that has a pair of pincers at the back end of its body. *The common earwig is a harmless enough insect but gardeners hate it.*

ease /iːz/ **eases, easing, eased**
1 NU **Ease** is lack of difficulty. *She performed this trick with ease.*
2 If you are **at ease**, you feel confident and comfortable. If you are **ill at ease**, you are anxious or worried. *He was at ease with strangers... Brody felt ill at ease and patronized.*
3 V-ERG If something **eases** a difficult or unpleasant situation, or if it **eases**, it becomes less difficult or unpleasant. *The bungalows were built to ease the*

housing shortage. ...a powder which eased the pain...
There's no immediate prospect that the political
pressure on Mr Baker will ease.
4 VOA If you **ease** something somewhere, you move it
there slowly and carefully. *I eased the back door
open.*
ease off PHRASAL VERB If something **eases off**, it
becomes less in degree, quantity, or intensity. *The
rain had eased off... The pace of our activity gradually
eased off.*
easel /iːzl/ **easels**
NC An **easel** is a wooden frame that supports a picture
which an artist is painting.
easily /iːzɪli/
1 ADV If something can be done **easily**, it can be done
without difficulty. *A baby buggy can be easily carried
on a bus or in a car.*
2 ADV You use **easily** to emphasize that something is
very likely to happen, or is certainly true. *She might
easily decide to cancel the whole thing... This car is
easily the most popular model.*
3 ADV You also use **easily** to say that something
happens more quickly than normal. *He tired very
easily.*
east /iːst/
1 N SING The **east** is the direction in which you look to
see the sun rise. *Ben noticed the first faint streaks of
dawn in the east.*
2 N SING The **east** of a place is the part which is
towards the east. *...old people in the east of Glasgow.*
▶ Also ADJ ATTRIB *...East Africa.*
3 ADV **East** means towards the east, or to the east of a
place or thing. *They were heading almost due east.*
4 ADJ ATTRIB An **east** wind blows from the east.
5 N SING The **East** is used to refer either to the
countries in the southern and eastern part of Asia,
including India, China, and Japan. *He was deeply
interested in meditation, the East, and yoga. ...a
breakthrough in East-West relations.*
6 See also **Far East, Middle East.**
eastbound /iːstbaʊnd/
ADJ **Eastbound** roads, cars, and trains lead or are
travelling towards the east. *Morris slouched in the
seat of his eastbound aircraft... The eastbound
carriageway of the M4 was blocked for 2 hours.*
Easter /iːstə/
NU **Easter** is a religious festival when Christians
celebrate the resurrection of Christ after his death.
*School holidays are at Christmas, Easter and during
the summer.*
Easter egg, Easter eggs
NC An **Easter egg** is a chocolate egg given as a
present at Easter. *Many Britons buy huge chocolate
Easter eggs for their children.*
easterly /iːstəli/
1 ADJ **Easterly** means towards the east. *...Barbados,
the most easterly of the Caribbean islands.*
2 ADJ An **easterly** wind blows from the east. *Easterly
winds brought dust from the Sahara desert, thousands
of miles away across the Atlantic.*
eastern /iːstən/
1 ADJ ATTRIB **Eastern** means in or from the east of a
region or country. *...a small town in Eastern
Portugal.*
2 ADJ ATTRIB **Eastern** also means coming either from
the people or countries of the East, such as India,
China, and Japan. *...Eastern philosophy. ...the
Eastern bloc.*
easterner /iːstənə/ **easterners**
NC An **easterner** is a person who was born in or who
lives in the eastern part of a place or country,
especially an American from the East Coast of the
USA. *Like many another easterner, he was impressed
by the California style.*
easternmost /iːstənməʊst/
ADJ ATTRIB The **easternmost** part of an area or the
easternmost thing in a line is the one that is farther
towards the east than any other. *...the easternmost
promontories of the region.*
eastward /iːstwəd/ or **eastwards**
1 ADV **Eastward** or **eastwards** means towards the
east. *An icy winter storm that brought several inches

of snow to the Central and Midwestern states is
moving eastward today... They travelled eastwards.*
2 ADJ ATTRIB **Eastward** is used to describe things
which are moving towards the east or which face
towards the east. *...a grassy eastward slope.*
easy /iːzi/ **easier, easiest**
1 ADJ Something that is **easy** can be done without
difficulty. *The house is easy to keep clean... This new
dancing looked easy.*
2 ADJ **Easy** also means relaxed. *They have a natural,
easy confidence.*
3 ADJ An **easy** life or time is comfortable and without
any problems. *I wanted to make life easier for you.*
● **Easy** is used in these phrases. ● If you **take it easy**
or **take things easy**, you relax and do very little; used
in informal English. *Mr Papandreou has been advised
by his doctors to take it easy.* ● If you **go easy on**
something, you avoid using too much of it; an
informal expression. *Now a word for dentists: go easy
on the drill.* ● You can say **easier said than done** to
indicate that it is difficult to do what someone has just
suggested. *He has made certain steps in that direction
but it is easier said that done... Of course, giving up
smoking is easier said than done.*
easy chair, easy chairs
NC An **easy chair** is a large, comfortable chair. *...the
traditional materials for building easy chairs, unspun
cotton, horsehair, hessian, steel springs and so on.*
easy-going
ADJ An **easy-going** person is not easily annoyed or
upset. *The Colonel is not renowned for possessing an
easy-going temperament.*
easy money
NU **Easy money** is money that you get without having
to work very hard for it. *...the temptation of making
easy money through drugs trafficking.*
easy touch
N SING An **easy touch** is the same as a **soft touch**; an
informal expression.
eat /iːt/ **eats, eating, ate, eaten**
1 VOorV When you **eat** something, you put it into your
mouth, chew it, and swallow it. *He began to eat his
sandwich... He was too tired even to eat.*
2 V To **eat** also means to have a meal. *He said he
would eat at his hotel.*
eat into PHRASAL VERB If a substance such as acid or
rust **eats into** something, it destroys the surface of the
thing.
eat out PHRASAL VERB When you **eat out**, you have a
meal at a restaurant. *The outbreaks of the disease
have caused many people to avoid eating out in
restaurants.*
eat up PHRASAL VERB If you **eat up** your food, you eat
it all.
eatable /iːtəbl/
ADJ Something that is **eatable** is good enough or tasty
enough for people to eat and enjoy. *The food here is
barely eatable.*
eaten /iːtn/
Eaten is the past participle of **eat.**
eater /iːtə/ **eaters**
NC+SUPP You use **eater** to refer to someone who eats
in a particular way or eats a particular thing. *...a
slow eater. ...a meat eater.*
eating /iːtɪŋ/
ADJ ATTRIB An **eating** apple or pear is one that is
usually eaten raw rather than cooked.
eau de cologne /əʊ də kələʊn/
NU **Eau de cologne** is a fairly weak, sweet-smelling
perfume.
eaves /iːvz/
N PL The **eaves** of a house are the lower edges of its
roof. *Hundreds of pigeons fluttered noisily into the air
from the eaves of the buildings.*
eavesdrop /iːvzdrɒp/ **eavesdrops, eavesdropping,
eavesdropped**
V If you **eavesdrop** on someone, you listen secretly to
what they are saying. *U.S. agents tunnelled from
West to East Berlin to eavesdrop on military
conversations.*
eavesdropper /iːvzdrɒpə/ **eavesdroppers**
NC An **eavesdropper** is a person who listens secretly to

what other people are saying; used showing
disapproval. ...*using Latin phrases as a precaution
against telephone eavesdroppers.*

ebb /ɛb/ **ebbs, ebbing, ebbed**
1 v If a feeling or a person's strength **ebbs**, it
weakens; a literary use. *Only then did the strength
ebb from his fingers.*
2 If something is **at a low ebb**, it is not being very
successful or profitable. *George's fortunes at this time
were at a low ebb.*
3 v When the tide or the sea **ebbs**, its level falls.
▶ Also N SING ...*the stormy ebb and flow of the sea.*
4 You talk about the **ebb and flow of** something when
you want to describe a situation in which periods of
progress and success are followed by periods of
trouble or difficulty. *In the ebb and flow of political
struggle it was inevitable that one of them would go
under.*

ebony /ɛbəni/
1 NU **Ebony** is a very hard, dark-coloured wood. ...*a
veneered walnut throne inlaid with ebony, ivory and
mother-of-pearl.*
2 ADJ Something that is **ebony** in colour is very deep
black. *He keeps his hair an almost unbelievable ebony
black.*

ebullience /ɪbʌliəns/
NU **Ebullience** is the quality of being lively and full of
enthusiasm or excitement; a formal word. *Their Irish
ebullience made them outgoing and spontaneous.*

ebullient /ɪbʌliənt/
ADJ An **ebullient** person is lively and full of
enthusiasm; a formal word. *The demonstrators, in
ebullient mood, came to voice their support.*

EC /iː siː/. See **European Community.**

eccentric /ɪksɛntrɪk/ **eccentrics**
1 ADJ An **eccentric** person has habits or opinions that
other people think strange. ...*a slightly eccentric
Frenchman.*
2 NC An **eccentric** is a person with strange habits or
opinions. ...*a bunch of harmless eccentrics.*

eccentricity /ɛksɛntrɪsəti/ **eccentricities**
1 NU **Eccentricity** is unusual behaviour that other
people consider strange and peculiar. *Many questions
have been asked about his eccentricity and reliability.*
2 NC An **eccentricity** is a habit or attitude which other
people think is strange and peculiar. *Despite or
perhaps because of his eccentricities, Pell is one of the
state's best-loved politicians.*

ecclesiastic /ɪkliːziæstɪk/ **ecclesiastics**
NC An **ecclesiastic** is a priest or clergyman in the
Christian Church; a formal word.

ecclesiastical /ɪkliːziæstɪkl/
ADJ **Ecclesiastical** means belonging to or connected
with the Christian Church. *None of Lithuania's 7
ecclesiastical districts has a resident bishop or
archbishop.*

echelon /ɛʃəlɒn/ **echelons**
NC+SUPP An **echelon** is a level of power or
responsibility in an organization; a formal word. ...*the
higher echelons of the party.*

echo /ɛkəʊ/ **echoes, echoing, echoed**
1 NC An **echo** is a sound caused by a noise being
reflected off a surface such as a wall. *Judy listened to
the echo of her shoes clicking on the marble floors.*
2 v If a sound **echoes**, a reflected sound can be heard
after it. *Our footsteps echoed through the large hollow
lobby.*
3 v In a place that **echoes**, a sound continues or is
repeated after the original sound has stopped. *The
bamboo grove echoed with the screams of monkeys.*
♦ **echoing** ADJ ...*echoing halls.*
4 NC An **echo** is also an expression of an attitude,
opinion, or statement which has already been
expressed. *The echo of public sentiment in Congress
was inevitable.*
5 V or V-QUOTE If you **echo** someone's words, you
repeat them or express the same thing. *Todd's
disappointment was echoed by Ian Stark... 'We're very
lucky,' I observed. 'Very, very lucky,' he echoed
soberly.*
6 NC+SUPP A detail or feature which reminds you of
something else can also be referred to as an **echo.**

...*echoes of the past.*

éclair /ɪkleə/ **éclairs**
NC An **éclair** is a long, thin, and very light cake filled
with cream and covered with chocolate.

eclectic /ɪklɛktɪk/
ADJ **Eclectic** means using what seems to be best from
different ideas or beliefs; a formal word. ...*an eclectic
mixture of Western and Asian thought.*

eclipse /ɪklɪps/ **eclipses, eclipsing, eclipsed**
1 NC When there is an **eclipse** of the sun, the moon
comes between the earth and the sun, so that for a
short time you cannot see part or all of the sun. When
there is an **eclipse** of the moon, the earth comes
between the sun and the moon, so that for a short time
the earth's shadow covers the moon. *A few hours ago
a total eclipse of the sun took place across the Pacific
and Central America.*
2 N SING If someone or something suffers an **eclipse,**
they lose some or all of their importance or influence.
...*the eclipse of the radical press.*
3 VO If one thing **eclipses** another, the first thing
becomes more important so that the second thing is no
longer noticed. *Less talented artists were totally
eclipsed.*

eco- /iːkəʊ-/
PREFIX **Eco-** combines with nouns and adjectives to
form new nouns and adjectives. Words formed in this
way indicate that the person or thing mentioned by the
original noun or adjective is connected with the
environment, or with concern for the environment.
*Man is moving into a totally new stage of eco-
technological development... In deference to the
increasing masses of eco-purists, there is a no-smoking
terrace.*

ecological /iːkəlɒdʒɪkl/
1 ADJ ATTRIB **Ecological** means involved with or
concerning the pattern and balance of relationships
between plants, animals, people, and their
environment. *Use of nitrogen fertilizers has damaged
the ecological balance in some of the world's lakes.
...the local ecological impact of removing all the
vegetation.* ♦ **ecologically** SUBMOD or ADV *It was an
ecologically sound system of farm management... The
world in 2000 will be more crowded, more polluted,
less stable ecologically.*
2 ADJ ATTRIB **Ecological** groups, movements, and
people are concerned with the preservation of the
environment and natural resources and improving the
quality of life. *Ecological groups in Brazil say that
nothing is being done to tackle the heart of the
problem.*

ecologist /ɪkɒlədʒɪst/ **ecologists**
NC 1 An **ecologist** is a person who studies the pattern
and balance of relationships between plants, animals,
people, and their environment. *Ecologists estimate
that half of the ancient woodlands in Britain are in
danger of extinction.*
2 An **ecologist** is also a person who believes that the
environment and natural resources should be used
properly and be preserved. ...*amateur ecologists.*

ecology /ɪkɒlədʒi/
1 NU When you talk about the **ecology** of a place, you
are referring to the relationships between living things
and their environment. ...*the delicate ecology of the
rainforest.*
2 NU **Ecology** is the study of the relationship between
living things and their environment. ...*the most recent
research in ecology.*

economic /iːkənɒmɪk, ɛkənɒmɪk/ **economics**
1 ADJ ATTRIB **Economic** means concerned with the
organization of the money, industry, and trade of a
country, region, or social group. ...*a period of
economic and industrial crisis.* ♦ **economically** ADV
...*an economically stable society.*
2 ADJ A business that is **economic** produces a profit.
*We have to keep fares high enough to make it
economic for the service to continue.*
3 NU **Economics** is the study of the way in which
money, industry, and trade are organized in a society.
...*Dr Gramoz Pashko, an economics lecturer at the
University of Tirana.*
4 NU+SUPP The **economics** of a society or industry is

the system of organizing money and trade in it. ...*the economics of the timber trade.*

economical /iːkə**nɒ**mɪkl, ɛkə**nɒ**mɪkl/
1 ADJ Something that is **economical** does not require a lot of money to operate. *This system was extremely economical because it ran on half-price electricity.* ◆ **economically** ADV *This service could be most economically operated.*
2 ADJ If someone is **economical**, they spend money carefully and sensibly. *People are having to be as economical as possible.* ◆ **economically** ADV *We live very economically.*
3 ADJ **Economical** also means using the minimum amount of something that is necessary. *She spoke in short, economical sentences.*

economist /ɪ**kɒ**nəmɪst/ **economists**
NC An **economist** is a person who studies, teaches, or writes about economics. *Lloyds Bank economists are predicting that inflation will rise to five percent this year.*

economize /ɪ**kɒ**nəmaɪz/ **economizes, economizing, economized**; also spelt **economise**.
V If you **economize**, you save money by spending it very carefully. *The loss of business was so great that they had to economize on staff.*

economy /ɪ**kɒ**nəmi/ **economies**
1 NC The **economy** of a country or region is the system by which money, industry, and trade are organized. *New England's economy is still largely based on manufacturing.* ● See also **market economy**.
2 NC The wealth obtained by a country or region from business and industry is also referred to as its **economy**. *Unofficial strikes were damaging the British economy.*
3 NU **Economy** is careful spending or the careful use of things to save money. *His house was small, for reasons of economy.*

ecosystem /iːkəʊsɪstəm/ **ecosystems**
NC An **ecosystem** is all the plants and animals that live in a particular area together with the complex relationship that exists between them and their environment; a technical term in biology. *...the intricate prairie ecosystem. ...highly sensitive and delicately balanced ecosystems.*

ecstasy /ɛkstəsi/ **ecstasies**
1 NU or NC **Ecstasy** is a feeling of very great happiness. *His big face was transfixed in ecstasy.*
2 NU **Ecstasy** is also an illegal drug which acts as a stimulant and can cause hallucinations. *The youngsters taking ecstasy don't realize the harm it may cause now it's so readily available.*

ecstatic /ɪkst**æ**tɪk/
ADJ If you are **ecstatic**, you feel very enthusiastic and happy. *Eddie was ecstatic over his new rifle. ...a wild ecstatic happiness.* ◆ **ecstatically** ADV *...children jumping ecstatically up and down.*

ECU /ɛkjuː/ **ECUs**; also written **ecu**. The plural form can be either **ECUs** or **ECU**.
NC An **ECU** is a unit of money that is based on the value of several different currencies in the European Community. ECU is an abbreviation for 'European Currency Unit'. *...a campaign to turn the ecu into the single currency of the European Community... Mr Ghozali had suggested a figure of eight hundred million ECU... He said the EC would finance the first six months of the programme to the tune of ten million ECUs, or about seven million pounds.*

Ecuador /ɛkwədɔː/
The **Republic of Ecuador** is a country in north-western South America. It includes the Galapagos Islands. It was a Spanish colony from the 16th century until 1822. Rodrigo Borja Cevallos of the Democratic Left (ID), became President in 1988. Ecuador is a member of OPEC and the Organization of American States. High inflation and large foreign debts are major economic problems. Ecuador exports oil, fish, and bananas. Cocaine is illegally produced. ◆ **Ecuadorean** /ɛkwədɔːriən/ N, ADJ
■ *per capita GNP:* US$1,080 ■ *religion:* Christianity (mainly Roman Catholic) ■ *language:* Spanish (official), Quechua ■ *currency:* sucre ■ *capital:* Quito ■ *largest city:* Guayaquil ■ *population:* 11 million (1991)

■ *size:* 270,670 square kilometres.

ecumenical /iːkjuː**me**nɪkl/
ADJ **Ecumenical** is used to describe ideas and movements which try to unite different Christian Churches; a formal word. *...an ecumenical church service is being held in the Marienkirche in East Berlin.*

ecumenicism /iːkjuː**me**nɪsɪzəm/
NU **Ecumenicism** is the belief that all the different branches of the Christian Church should co-operate and be united. *The church here has managed to practise ecumenicism for years.*

ecumenism /ɪkjuː**me**nɪzəm/
NU **Ecumenism** is the same as **ecumenicism**.

eczema /ɛksɪmə/
NU **Eczema** is an uncomfortable skin disease which makes your skin itch and become rough and sore. *The commonest form of allergy in babies is eczema.*

ed., eds.
NC **ed.** is the written abbreviation for editor. *Frank Field (ed.) 'Education and the Urban Crisis'.*

-ed; pronounced as the separate syllable /-ɪd/ after /t/ and /d/; pronounced /-t/ after /p, k, tʃ, f, θ, s, ʃ/. Otherwise it is pronounced /-d/.
1 SUFFIX **-ed** is used to form the past tense of most verbs. *He blinked in the bright light... Tim dodged round the car.*
2 SUFFIX **-ed** is also used to form the past participle of most verbs. The past participles of transitive verbs are often used as adjectives indicating that something has been affected in some way. The past participles of a few intransitive verbs are used as adjectives indicating that a person or thing has done something. Adjectives of this kind are often not defined but are treated with the related verbs. *They had arrived two hours earlier. ...fried eggs. ...an escaped prisoner.*
3 SUFFIX **-ed** is also added to nouns to form adjectives which describe someone or something as having a particular feature. For example, a bearded man is a man with a beard. Adjectives of this kind are sometimes not defined but are treated with the related nouns. *...gabled houses.*

eddy /ɛdi/ **eddies, eddying, eddied**
V If water or wind **eddies**, it moves round and round in no particular direction. *The wind whipped and eddied around the buildings.* ► Also NC *...every eddy of the tide.*

Eden, Sir Anthony /æntəni iːdən/
Sir Anthony Eden was Prime Minister of the United Kingdom and leader of the Conservative Party from 1955 to 1957. He was born in 1897. He was MP for Warwick and Leamington from 1923 to 1957. He served as Foreign Secretary from 1935 to 1938, from 1940 to 1945, and from 1951 to 1955. He was created the 1st Earl of Avon in 1961 and died in 1977.

edge /ɛdʒ/ **edges, edging, edged**
1 NC The **edge** of something is the place or line where it stops and another thing begins. *Little children played at the water's edge... I was stopped at a roadblock on the edge of town... The bird had a white stripe along the front edge of each wing.*
2 NC The **edge** of a flat, thin object is its long side. *...the edge of a ruler.*
3 VO If something is **edged** with a particular thing, it has that thing along its edge. *...a beautiful garden edged with flowering trees.*
4 V A or V O A If you **edge** somewhere, or **edge** your way there, you move there very slowly. *He edged away from the thug... I edged my way to the window.*
5 V A If something such as a currency or a deficit **edges** upwards, it increases slightly in value or amount. If it **edges** downwards, it decreases slightly. *The trade deficit is likely to edge upwards next year... Sales of new homes edged up one per cent in March... In Frankfurt, the dollar edged down less than a quarter of a cent to 1.75.*
6 V A If you **edge** towards a particular state or event, it slowly becomes more and more likely. *...edging towards modest improvements in regional co-operation... The Times says Hungary has edged closer to involvement after Yugoslav air force planes again violated its airspace.*

7 N SING If people are on the **edge** of an event, it is likely to happen soon. *The world had been brought to the edge of war... More than a million people there are on the edge of starvation.*
8 If you are **on edge**, you are nervous and unable to relax. *The prospect was setting his nerves on edge.*
9 N SING If you have an **edge** over someone, you have an advantage over them. *Europe's edge over the rest of the world became marked.*
10 see also **cutting edge**.

edgeways /ɛdʒweɪz/
If you say that you cannot **get a word in edgeways**, you mean that you are unable to say anything because someone else is talking too much; an informal expression. *The conversation was fairly one-sided, with Mr Pelletreau trying but failing to get a word in edgeways.*

edging /ɛdʒɪŋ/ **edgings**
NC An **edging** is something that is put along the sides of something else to make it look attractive. *...a blouse trimmed with bows and lace edgings.*

edgy /ɛdʒi/
ADJ When you are **edgy**, you are nervous and anxious. *The hijackers are edgy, frightened men who can easily be triggered into violent reaction.*

edible /ɛdəbl/
ADJ Something that is **edible** is safe to eat and not poisonous. *...edible mushrooms.*

edict /iːdɪkt/ **edicts**
NC An **edict** is a command given by someone in authority; a formal word. *I told the factory inspector we would defy his edict.*

edifice /ɛdɪfɪs/ **edifices**; a formal word.
1 NC An **edifice** is a large and impressive building. *...the twin-towered edifice of St James' Church.*
2 NC An **edifice** is also a system of beliefs or a traditional institution. *The whole edifice of modern civilization is beginning to sway.*

edify /ɛdɪfaɪ/ **edifies, edifying, edified**
VO If something **edifies** you, it teaches you something useful or interesting; a formal word. *...a series of popular talks intended to edify and entertain.*
♦ **edifying** ADJ *He may come out with all sorts of edifying sentiments.* ♦ **edification** /ɛdɪfɪkeɪʃn/ N U *...books bought for instruction or edification.*

edit /ɛdɪt/ **edits, editing, edited**
1 VO If you **edit** a text, you correct it so that it is suitable for publication. *Lloyd Timberlake was one of those most involved in writing and editing the book.*
♦ **edited** ADJ ATTRIB *This is the edited text.*
2 VO If you **edit** a book, you collect pieces of writing by different authors and prepare them for publication. *...'The Save and Prosper Book of Money,' edited by Margaret Allen.*
3 VO If you **edit** a film or a television or radio programme, you decide which material to include and arrange it in a particular order. *There is not usually time to edit the programme in the studio.* ♦ **edited** ADJ ATTRIB *The edited version was accurate, but not entirely representative.*
4 VO Someone who **edits** a newspaper or magazine is in charge of it and makes decisions concerning the contents. *Wild accusations against him appeared in Pravda, the paper he used to edit.*

edit out PHRASAL VERB If you **edit** something **out** of a book or film, you remove part of it, often because it might be offensive to some people. *We had to edit out the expletives.*

edition /ɪdɪʃn/ **editions**
1 NC+SUPP An **edition** is a particular version of a book, magazine, or newspaper that is printed at one time. *...the city edition of the New York Times.*
2 NC+SUPP An **edition** is also a television or radio programme that is one of a series. *...tonight's edition of Kaleidoscope.*

editor /ɛdɪtə/ **editors**
1 NC The **editor** of a newspaper or magazine is the person who is in charge of all the journalists and who is responsible for making decisions about the contents. *Russell Twisk is the editor of the British edition of Reader's Digest... Before joining ITN Sir Alastair had had a distinguished career as editor of*

The Economist magazine.
2 NC+SUPP The journalist who is responsible for a particular section of a newspaper or magazine is called an **editor**. *David Makovsky, diplomatic editor of the Jerusalem Post, says that Israel is encouraged by this statement... The Independent's Middle East Editor, Patrick Cockburn, believes neither side will trust the other just yet.*
3 NC+SUPP An **editor** is also a senior radio or television journalist who reports on a particular type of news. *From Paris, our Economics Editor, Dominic Harrod, reports. ...BBC Television's Foreign Affairs editor, John Simpson.*
4 NC A person who selects recorded material for a film or for radio or television programmes is also called an **editor**.
5 NC An **editor** is also a person who checks and corrects texts before they are published.
6 NC An **editor** is also a person who collects pieces of writing by different authors and prepares them for publication in a book or series of books. *In his foreword the editor, John Taylor, looks at the trends and changes in today's aircraft business.*
7 NC An **editor** is also a computer program that enables you to make alterations and corrections to stored data. *...a screen editor.*

editorial /ɛdɪtɔːrɪəl/ **editorials**
1 ADJ ATTRIB **Editorial** means involved in preparing a newspaper, magazine, or book for publication. *Hearst expanded his editorial staff.*
2 ADJ ATTRIB **Editorial** also means involving the attitudes, opinions, and contents of a newspaper, magazine, or television programme. *...the paper's editorial policy.*
3 NC An **editorial** is an article in a newspaper which gives the opinion of the editor or publisher on a particular topic. *In an editorial, The Guardian turns its attention to the defence of Western Europe.*

editorialize /ɛdɪtɔːrɪəlaɪz/ **editorializes, editorializing, editorialized**; also spelt **editorialise**.
V If someone such as a journalist **editorializes**, he or she expresses an opinion rather than stating facts, especially in an article which is supposed to be reporting facts rather than giving opinions. *Other papers have editorialized, criticizing the Czech government for rushing to judgement on this individual.* ♦ **editorializing** NU *In spite of all the editorializing, it was well worth reading... This later editorializing style is very well integrated with the humorous beginning.*

editorship /ɛdɪtəʃɪp/
N SING The **editorship** of a newspaper or magazine is the position and authority of its editor. *The paper was considerably improved under McPherson's editorship.*

educate /ɛdʒʊkeɪt/ **educates, educating, educated**
1 VO When someone **is educated**, he or she is taught at a school or college. *Naturally we're interested in how our children are educated... He was educated at a local mission school.*
2 VO To **educate** people also means to teach them better ways of doing something or a better way of living. *Not enough is being done to educate smokers about the benefits of stopping the habit.*

educated /ɛdʒʊkeɪtɪd/
ADJ **Educated** people have reached a high standard of learning. *He's an educated and articulate man, speaking Arabic as well as fluent French.*

educated guess, educated guesses
NC An **educated guess** is a guess which is based on a certain amount of knowledge and therefore likely to be correct. *Would you care to make an educated guess as to how long it might be until we see these new drugs in clinical use?*

education /ɛdʒʊkeɪʃn/
1 N U **Education** consists of teaching people various subjects at a school or college. *...government policies on social services and education... Education standards were relatively high.*
2 NU **Education** is also the process through which a person is taught better ways of doing something or a better way of living. *It's a question of education. Farmers must learn that if they destroy the*

environment it produces less food.
3 See also **further education, higher education.**
educational /ɛdʒʊkeɪʃəˀnəl/
ADJ **Educational** means concerned with and related to education. *...an educational institution.*
♦ **educationally** ADV *...a school for the educationally subnormal.*
educationalist /ɛdʒʊkeɪʃəˀnəlɪst/ **educationalists**
NC An **educationalist** is a specialist in the theories and methods of education. *Testing of pupils is also going to be introduced despite the opposition of many teachers and educationalists.*
educationist /ɛdʒʊkeɪʃənɪst/ **educationists**
NC An **educationist** is the same as an educationalist.
educative /ɛdʒʊkətɪv/
ADJ An **educative** quality or activity is one that teaches you something; a formal word. *The trial was seen by many as an educative experience.*
educator /ɛdʒʊkeɪtə/ **educators**
NC An **educator** is a person who educates people; a formal word. *He was a distinguished educator.*
Edwardian /edwɔːdiən/
ADJ **Edwardian** is used to refer to the style of architecture and dress that was popular in Britain at the beginning of the 20th century. *...Edwardian England.*
EEC /iːiːsiː/
N PROP The **EEC** is a term that was used to refer to the EC; an abbreviation for 'European Economic Community'.
eel /iːl/ **eels**
NC An **eel** is a long, thin, snake-like fish. *Turtle soups, crabs or eels can be surprisingly tasty.*
e'er /eə/
ADV **E'er** means ever; a literary word.
eerie /ɪəri/
ADJ Something that is **eerie** is strange and frightening. *...the eerie feeling that someone was watching me.* ♦ **eerily** ADV *The lights gleamed eerily.*
efface /ɪfeɪs/ **effaces, effacing, effaced**
VO To **efface** something means to remove it completely; a formal word. *In the sand, all the footprints had effaced one another... He hoped to efface the memory of an embarrassing speech.*
effect /ɪfɛkt/ **effects, effecting, effected**
1 NC An **effect** is a change, reaction, or impression that is caused by something or is the result of something. *This has the effect of separating students from teachers. ...the effect of noise on people in the factories... Don't move, or you'll destroy the whole effect.*
2 VO If you **effect** something, you succeed in causing it to happen; a formal use. *Production was halted until repairs could be effected.*
3 See also **greenhouse effect, sound effect.**
● **Effect** is used in these phrases. ● If you do something **for effect**, you do it in order to impress people. *...a pause for effect.* ● You add **in effect** to a statement to indicate that it is not precisely accurate but it is a reasonable summary of a situation. *In effect he has no choice.* ● You use **to this effect, to that effect,** or **to the effect that** when you are summarizing what someone has said, rather than repeating their actual words. *...a rumour to the effect that he had been drunk... He said, 'No, you fool, the other way!' or words to that effect.* ● When something **takes effect** or is **put into effect,** it starts to happen. *The tax cuts take effect on July 1st... Signing the agreement was one thing, putting it into effect was another.*
effective /ɪfɛktɪv/
1 ADJ Something that is **effective** produces the intended results. *...the most effective ways of reducing pollution.* ♦ **effectiveness** NU *Methods vary in effectiveness.*
2 ADJ ATTRIB **Effective** also means having a particular role or result in practice, though not officially. *He assumed effective command of the armed forces.*
3 ADJ PRED When a law or an agreement becomes **effective,** it begins officially to apply. *...the offer of a ceasefire effective from midday today.*

effectively /ɪfɛktɪvli/
ADV You use **effectively** to indicate that what you are saying is a reasonable summary of a situation, although it is not precisely accurate. *The television was on, effectively ruling out conversation.*
effectual /ɪfɛktʃuəl/
ADJ An **effectual** action or plan is one that succeeds in producing the results that were intended; a formal word. *The law would have to be very tough indeed to be effectual.* ♦ **effectually** ADV *He hacked less effectually at several boards.*
effeminacy /ɪfɛmɪnəsi/
NU If you refer to a man's or a boy's **effeminacy,** you mean that he behaves, looks, or sounds like a woman or girl; used showing disapproval. *His timidity, his slight effeminacy, were worrying.*
effeminate /ɪfɛmɪnət/
ADJ When people describe a man as **effeminate,** they mean that he behaves, looks, or sounds like a woman; used showing disapproval. *He was pointedly ridiculed, described as silly and effeminate... I think effeminate voices are a real turn-off.*
effervescence /ɛfəvɛsns/
1 NU **Effervescence** is the releasing of bubbles of gas by a liquid.
2 NU **Effervescence** is also the quality of being lively and enthusiastic in your behaviour. *Kitty's letter gave a calm appraisal of Tom's effervescence.*
effervescent /ɛfəvɛsnt/
1 ADJ An **effervescent** liquid is a liquid that releases bubbles of gas. *...a slightly effervescent wine which is very agreeable. ...an effervescent drink.*
2 ADJ Someone who is **effervescent** is lively and enthusiastic in their behaviour. *...a very effervescent personality.*
effete /ɪfiːt/
ADJ Someone who is **effete** is weak and powerless; a literary word. *The boys would think it vaguely effete to comment on the flowers and plants.*
efficacious /ɛfɪkeɪʃəs/
ADJ Something that is **efficacious** is successful in solving a problem or achieving an aim; a formal word. *Cameron's remedy had been remarkably efficacious... These lotions, usually efficacious in cases of prickly heat, seemed slow in having any beneficial results.*
efficacy /ɛfɪkəsi/
NU **Efficacy** is the ability to do something or do it well and produce the results that were intended; a formal word. *...doubts over the efficacy of his leadership. ...the efficacy of our policy. ...the efficacy of prayer.*
efficiency /ɪfɪʃnsi/
1 NU **Efficiency** is the quality of being able to do a task successfully and without wasting time or energy. *...an increase in business efficiency. ...improve the efficiency of their reading. ...her efficiency in developing ideas.*
2 NU **Efficiency** refers to the difference between the amount of energy a machine needs to make it work, and the amount it produces; a technical term in physics. *Electricity is produced at something like 30% efficiency from the power station.*
efficient /ɪfɪʃnt/
ADJ Something or someone that is **efficient** does a job well and successfully, without wasting time or energy. *Engines and cars can be made more efficient... You need a very efficient production manager.* ♦ **efficiently** ADV *You must work more efficiently.*
effigy /ɛfɪdʒi/ **effigies;** a formal word.
1 NC An **effigy** is a roughly made figure that represents someone you strongly dislike. *The students burned effigies of the president.*
2 NC An **effigy** is also a statue or carving of a famous person. *...unusually good fifteenth-century alabaster effigies.*
effluent /ɛfluənt/ **effluents**
N U or PL **Effluent** is liquid waste material that comes out of factories or sewage works; a formal word. *Every day one thousand million litres of effluent is pumped out into the ocean. ...the effluents from nuclear power stations.*

effort /ˈɛfət/ efforts
1 NCorNU If you make an **effort** to do something, you try hard to do it. *...the efforts of governments to restrain inflation... It's a waste of effort.*
2 NU If you do something with **effort**, it is difficult for you to do. *Robert spoke with effort.*
3 N SING If you say that an action is an **effort**, you mean that an unusual amount of physical or mental energy is needed to do it. *Getting up was an effort.*
4 NC+SUPP If you describe an object or an action as a poor or feeble **effort**, you mean it has not been well made or well done. *It was a rather amateurish effort.*

effortless /ˈɛfətləs/
ADJ You describe an action as **effortless** when it is achieved very easily. *His rise in politics appears to have been effortless.* ◆ **effortlessly** ADV *He slipped back effortlessly into his old ways.*

effrontery /ɪfrˈʌntəri/
NU **Effrontery** is bold, rude, or cheeky behaviour; a formal word. *He has the effrontery to use my office without asking.*

effusion /ɪfjuːˈʒn/ effusions; a literary word.
1 NCorNU An **effusion** is a sudden pouring out of something such as light or a liquid. *...a tremendous effusion of colour, the last glow.*
2 NCorNU **Effusion** is also the expression of your emotions or ideas with more enthusiasm and for longer than is usual or expected. *Her gesture checked my effusion, which would have led to nothing anyway.*

effusive /ɪfjuːˈsɪv/
ADJ An **effusive** person expresses pleasure, gratitude, or approval enthusiastically. *Mrs Schiff was effusive in her congratulations. ...an effusive welcome.* ◆ **effusively** ADV *The doctor thanked him effusively.*

EFL /iːɛfˈɛl/
EFL is used to describe things that are connected with the teaching of English to people whose first language is not English. **EFL** is an abbreviation for 'English as a Foreign Language'. *...EFL dictionaries.*

e.g. /iːdʒiː/
e.g. is an abbreviation that means 'for example'. It is used before a noun or clause, or to introduce another sentence. *...woollens and other delicate fabrics (e.g. lace)... He specialised in trivial knowledge, e.g. that three MPs had glass eyes.*

egalitarian /ɪgælɪtˈɛəriən/
ADJ In an **egalitarian** system or society, all people are equal and have the same rights. *...a more egalitarian educational system.*

egalitarianism /ɪgælɪtˈɛəriənɪzəm/
NU **Egalitarianism** is the belief that all people are equal and should have the same rights and opportunities, or the practice of this belief. *...the absurdly implacable dream of total egalitarianism.*

egg /ɛg/ eggs, egging, egged
1 NC An **egg** is the rounded object produced by a female bird from which a baby bird later emerges. Some other creatures, such as reptiles and fish, also produce eggs. *England's only pair of breeding Golden Eagles have laid another egg at their nest in the Lake District.*
2 NCorNU An **egg** is also a hen's egg considered as food. *I was offered tea and a hard-boiled egg... They always had bacon and egg for breakfast.*
3 NC An **egg** is also a cell in a female person or animal which can develop into a baby. *...stop the fertilized egg implanting itself in the womb.*
egg on PHRASAL VERB If you **egg** someone **on**, you encourage them to do something daring or foolish. *...egged on by his own supporters and Labour MPs Mr Ashdown persisted.*

eggcup /ˈɛgkʌp/ eggcups
NC An **eggcup** is a small container in which you put a boiled egg while you eat it. *It looked like an eggcup suitable for a goose egg.*

egghead /ˈɛghɛd/ eggheads
NC If you call someone an **egghead**, you mean that you think they are too interested in ideas and theories, and not enough in practical actions; an informal word. *...the pompous egghead!*

eggplant /ˈɛgplɑːnt/ eggplants
NCorNU An **eggplant** is the same as an **aubergine**;

used in American English. *I've made you that eggplant dip you like.*

eggshell /ˈɛgʃɛl/ eggshells
NCorNU **Eggshell** or an **eggshell** is the hard covering round a bird's egg. *...fragments of eggshell.*

egg-timer, egg-timers
NC An **egg-timer** is a device that helps you measure the time needed to boil an egg.

egg whisk, egg whisks
NC An **egg whisk** is a device used in cooking for beating eggs or cream into a light, fluffy state.

ego /iːgəʊ, ˈɛgəʊ/ egos
NC Your **ego** is your opinion of your own worth. *It was a blow to my ego.*

egocentric /iːgəʊsˈɛntrɪk, ˈɛgəʊsɛntrɪk/
ADJ If you are **egocentric**, you think only of yourself and what you want, and do not consider the wishes of other people. *...egocentric and authoritarian adults.* ◆ **egocentricity** /iːgəʊsɛntrˈɪsəti, ˈɛgəʊsɛntrɪsəti/ NU *He was accused of pathological egocentricity.*

egoism /iːgəʊɪzəm, ˈɛgəʊɪzəm/
NU **Egoism** is the same as egotism.

egoist /iːgəʊɪst, ˈɛgəʊɪst/ egoists
NC An **egoist** is the same as an egotist.

egoistic /iːgəʊˈɪstɪk, ˈɛgəʊɪstɪk/
ADJ **Egoistic** means the same as egotistic.

egomania /iːgəʊmˈeɪniə, ˈɛgəʊmeɪniə/
NU **Egomania** is a state of mind or a way of behaving in which a person does not care about harming other people in order to get what he or she wants. *He was eaten up with conceit, violent egomania.*

egomaniac /iːgəʊmˈeɪniæk, ˈɛgəʊmeɪniæk/ egomaniacs
NC An **egomaniac** is a person who thinks only of himself or herself and who does not care about harming other people in order to get what he or she wants.

egotism /ˈɛgəʊtɪzəm, iːgəʊtɪzəm/
NU **Egotism** is selfish behaviour which shows that you believe you are more important than other people. *It was a piece of blatant egotism.*

egotist /ˈɛgəʊtɪst, iːgəʊtɪst/ egotists
NC An **egotist** is a person who acts selfishly and believes that he or she is more important than other people. *She was already so much the egotist that her eyes were blind to anyone or anything but herself.*

egotistic /ˌɛgəʊtˈɪstɪk, iːgəʊtɪstɪk/
ADJ If you are **egotistic** or **egotistical**, you believe that you are more important than other people. *Success makes a man egotistic.*

ego trip, ego trips
NC An **ego trip** is an action or a series of actions that someone does for their own satisfaction and enjoyment, often one that shows that they think they are more important than other people. *He's on another one of his ego trips.*

Egypt /iːdʒɪpt/
The **Arab Republic of Egypt** is a country in northern Africa. It became fully independent from Britain in 1936. In 1956 President Nasser nationalized the Suez Canal, resulting in the Suez Crisis. The Yom Kippur War of 1973 was the last in a series of wars between Israel and Egypt, which were ended by the Camp David agreement of 1978. Lieutenant-General Muhammad Hosni Mubarak, of the National Democratic Party (NDP), became President in 1981, when President Anwar Sadat was assassinated. Egypt produces oil, and is a major exporter of cotton and textiles. It is a member of the Arab League and the Organization of African Unity. ◆ **Egyptian** /ɪdʒɪpʃn/ N, ADJ
▪ *per capita GNP:* US$650 ▪ *religion:* Islam (mainly Sunni), Christianity ▪ *language:* Arabic ▪ *currency:* pound ▪ *capital:* Cairo ▪ *population:* 51 million (1988) ▪ *size:* 997,739 square kilometres.

eh /eɪ/; an informal word.
1 You say '**eh**' when you are asking someone to reply to you or to agree with you. *Looks good, eh?... Who knows we're here? Eh?*
2 You also say '**eh**' when you are asking someone to repeat what they have just said because you did not hear it the first time. *'Well, I still have a car.'—'Eh?'—'I said I still have a car.'*

eiderdown /ˈaɪdədaʊn/ **eiderdowns**
NC An **eiderdown** is a bed covering filled with feathers or warm material.

eight /eɪt/ **eights**
Eight is the number 8. *The treaty took eight months of negotiations to draw up.*

eighteen /eɪˈtiːn/ **eighteens**
Eighteen is the number 18. *At least eighteen people were injured.*

eighteenth /eɪˈtiːnθ/
ADJ The **eighteenth** item in a series is the one that you count as number eighteen. *The siege is now in its eighteenth day.*

eighth /eɪtθ/ **eighths**
1 ADJ The **eighth** item in a series is the one that you count as number eight. *...his room on the eighth floor.*
2 NC An **eighth** is one of eight equal parts of something. *It was about an eighth of an inch thick.*

eightieth /eɪˈtiəθ/
ADJ The **eightieth** item in a series is the one that you count as number eighty. *He's just had his eightieth birthday.*

eighty /eɪti/ **eighties**
Eighty is the number 80. *The eighty ships are arriving today.*

Eire /eɪrə/. See **Ireland.**

Eisenhower, Dwight D. /dwaɪt aɪznhaʊə/
General Dwight D. Eisenhower was President of the United States from 1953 to 1961. He was born in 1890 and was a member of the Republican Party. In 1942 he became commander of US troops in Europe, and in 1943 he became supreme commander of the Allied Expeditionary Forces. He was supreme commander of NATO from 1950 to 1952. He died in 1969.

eisteddfod /aɪstɛdfəd/ **eisteddfods**
NC An **eisteddfod** is a Welsh festival at which competitions are held in music, poetry, drama, and art. *The organisers set virtually no restrictions on entrance to the eisteddfod.*

either /aɪðə, iːðə/
1 CONJ You use **either** in front of the first of two or more alternatives, when you are stating the only possibilities or choices that there are. The other alternatives are introduced by 'or'. *I was expecting you either today or tomorrow... You either love him or you hate him.*
2 CONJ You can use **either** in a negative statement in front of the first of two alternatives in order to say that the negative statement refers to both the alternatives. *Dr Kirk, you're not being either frank or fair... I wouldn't dream of asking either Mary or my mother to take on the responsibility.*
3 PRON or DET **Either** refers to one of two possible things, when you want to say that it does not matter which one is chosen. *Either is acceptable... Either way, I can't lose.*
4 PRON or DET You can also use **either** in a negative statement to refer to each of two things when you are saying that the negative statement includes both of them. *'Which one do you want?'—'I don't want either.'... She could not see either man.*
5 ADV **Either** is used by itself at the end of a negative statement to indicate that there is a similarity or connection between a person or thing that you have just mentioned and one that was mentioned earlier. *'I haven't got that address.'—'No, I haven't got it either.'... Not only was he ugly, he was not very interesting either.*
6 DET You can use **either** before a noun that refers to each of two things when you are talking about both of them. *The two ladies sat in large armchairs on either side of the stage... In either case the answer is the same.*

ejaculate /ɪdʒækjʊleɪt/ **ejaculates, ejaculating, ejaculated**
V When a man **ejaculates**, semen comes out through his penis. ◆ **ejaculation** /ɪdʒækjʊleɪʃn/ **ejaculations** NU or NC *The prostate gland is essential for ejaculation... Once two ejaculations are shown to be sperm-free, the man is cleared as infertile.*

eject /ɪdʒɛkt/ **ejects, ejecting, ejected**
1 VO To **eject** something means to push or send it out

forcefully. *The machine ejected a handful of cigarettes.*
2 VO If you **eject** someone from a place, you force them to leave. *British Embassy officials were ejected from the hotel amid angry scenes.*

ejector seat /ɪdʒɛktə siːt/ **ejector seats**
NC An **ejector seat** is a special seat which can throw the pilot out of a fast military aeroplane in an emergency. *The pilot is said to have been killed because his ejector seat had been incorrectly rigged.*

eke /iːk/ **ekes, eking, eked**
eke out PHRASAL VERB 1 If you **eke** something **out**, you make your supply of it last as long as possible. *Migrants send home cash that helps eke out low village incomes.* 2 If you **eke out** a living, you manage to survive with very little money. *...fed up with having to eke out a living on monthly incomes of around 80 dollars.*

elaborate, elaborates, elaborating, elaborated; pronounced /ɪlæbərət/ when it is an adjective and /ɪlæbəreɪt/ when it is a verb.
1 ADJ Something that is **elaborate** is very complex because it has a lot of different parts. *...the elaborate network of canals... Breast-milk is naturally clean and wholesome, whereas powdered milk requires fairly elaborate preparation, using clean water and sterilised bottles.* ◆ **elaborately** ADV *The operation had been elaborately planned by the French security services.*
2 ADJ You also use **elaborate** to describe something that is made with a lot of detailed artistic designs. *...the elaborate embroidered and jewelled headdress.* ◆ **elaborately** ADV *Every inch of its surface was elaborately decorated.*
3 V+on or VO If you **elaborate** on an idea, or if you **elaborate** it, you give more details about it. *It isn't a statement I want to elaborate on... Some of these points will have to be further elaborated as we go along.* ◆ **elaboration** /ɪlæbəreɪʃn/ **elaborations** NC or NU *An elaboration of this idea will follow in Chapter 12... One of the two main tasks should be the elaboration of a social charter.*
4 VO To **elaborate** something also means to make it more complex. *This type of plan could be elaborated.*

elapse /ɪlæps/ **elapses, elapsing, elapsed**
V When a period of time **elapses**, it passes; a formal word. *Too much time had elapsed since I had attempted any serious study.*

elastic /ɪlæstɪk/
1 NU **Elastic** is a rubber material that stretches when you pull it and returns to its original size when you let it go. *It snapped back like a piece of elastic.*
2 ADJ Something that is **elastic** stretches easily. *...a softer, more elastic and lighter material.*
3 ADJ **Elastic** ideas and policies can change in order to suit new circumstances. *Liberal policy was sufficiently elastic to accommodate both views.*

elastic band, elastic bands
NC An **elastic band** is the same as a **rubber band.**

elasticity /iːlæstɪsəti/
1 NU **Elasticity** is the ability to change and adapt in order to suit new circumstances or conditions as they arise. *These simple methods possess a certain elasticity as to their practical application.*
2 NU+SUPP **Elasticity** is also the ability of a material or substance to return to its original shape and size after it has been stretched. *We set up an experiment to measure the elasticity of the thread... The skin eventually loses its elasticity.*

elated /ɪleɪtɪd/
ADJ If you are **elated**, you are extremely happy and excited. *The members left the meeting elated.*

elation /ɪleɪʃn/
NU **Elation** is a feeling of great happiness and excitement. *This little incident filled me with elation.*

elbow /ɛlbəʊ/ **elbows, elbowing, elbowed**
1 NC Your **elbow** is the part in the middle of your arm where it bends. *She sat with her elbows on the table.*
2 VOA If you **elbow** someone away, you push them aside with your elbow. *She elbowed him to one side and walked out... It's often impossible to elbow one's way through the crowds to cross St Mark's Square.*

elbow grease

NU **Elbow grease** is the effort and energy that you use when doing physical work like rubbing or polishing; an informal expression. *Removing all the old paint can be extremely hard work and involves lots of elbow grease.*

elbowroom /ɛlbəurum/

NU **Elbowroom** is the freedom in a particular place or situation to do what you want to do or need to do; an informal word. *Mazowiecki's speech received a standing ovation—but it was also designed to give himself more political elbowroom.*

elder /ɛldə/ elders

1 ADJ The **elder** of two people is the one who was born first. *...his elder brother.*
2 NC The **elders** of a society or religious organization are the older members who have influence and authority, or who hold positions of responsibility; a formal use. *In the narrow allies off the main street, Muslim elders were ordering young men to go home.*
3 NC An **elder** is a small tree or shrub. It has white flowers and red, purple, or black edible berries. *I struggled across the stream and broke through the nettles and elder bushes into the field.*

elderberry /ɛldəbeʳri/ elderberries

1 NC An **elderberry** tree is the same as an elder tree.
2 NC An **elderberry** is one of the edible red or black berries that grow on an elder bush or tree. *...elderberry wine.*

elderly /ɛldəli/

1 ADJ **Elderly** people are old. *The coach was full of elderly ladies.*
2 N PL You can refer to old people in general as the **elderly**. *...unless the elderly are adequately cared for.*

elder statesman, elder statesmen

1 NC An **elder statesman** is an old and respected politician or former politician who still has influence because of his or her experience. *Beaverbrook and Lloyd George were among the elder statesmen who attended these functions.*
2 NC An **elder statesman** is also an experienced member or former member of a company or other organization who still has influence because of his or her experience.

eldest /ɛldɪst/

ADJ The **eldest** person in a group is the one who was born before all the others. *Her eldest son was killed in the First War.*

elect /ɪlɛkt/ elects, electing, elected

1 VOorVOC When people **elect** someone, they choose that person to represent them, by voting for them. *They met to elect a president... Why should we elect him Mayor?* ◆ **elected** ADJ ATTRIB *...a democratically elected government.*
2 V+to-INF If you **elect** to do something, you choose to do it; a formal use. *It has been shown that women who are in ill health don't elect to have children.*

election /ɪlɛkʃn/ elections

1 NCorNU An **election** is a process in which people vote to choose a person or group of people to hold an official position. *I may vote for her at the next election... Mr Lenihan is also one of the candidates standing for election as president.* ● See also by-election, general election.
2 N SING The **election** of a person or a political party is their success in winning an election. *...the election of Mr Heath's government in 1970.*

electioneering /ɪlɛkʃənɪərɪŋ/

NU **Electioneering** is the activities that politicians and their supporters carry out in order to persuade people to vote for them or for their political party in an election, for example making speeches and visiting voters in their homes. *He continued his electioneering tour.*

elective /ɪlɛktɪv/ electives

1 ADJ An **elective** post or committee is one to which people are appointed as a result of winning an election; a formal use. *Blacks began to win elective offices, many of them becoming mayors.*
2 NC An **elective** is a subject which a student can choose to study as part of his or her course; used in American English. *She teaches an elective on black American history.*
3 ADJ **Elective** surgery is surgery that is planned in advance, rather than being carried out in an emergency. *There were some concerns raised: notably, the long waits for elective surgery.*

elector /ɪlɛktə/ electors

NC The **electors** are the people who have the right to vote in an election. *...the support of electors from all parts of the political spectrum.*

electoral /ɪlɛktəʳrəl/

ADJ ATTRIB **Electoral** is used to describe things that are connected with an election. *...a contribution to their electoral funds. ...electoral success.*

electoral register, electoral registers

NC An **electoral register** or **electoral roll** is an official list of all the people who have the right to vote in an election. *She has flatly refused to go on the electoral register in Ripon.*

electorate /ɪlɛktəʳrət/ electorates

N COLL The **electorate** of a country is all the people there who have the right to vote in an election. *In moments of crisis, the Indian electorate has in the past chosen stability... Twenty percent of the electorate were still uncertain about who to vote for.*

electric /ɪlɛktrɪk/

1 ADJ An **electric** device or machine works by means of electricity. *...an electric fan.*
2 ADJ ATTRIB **Electric** is used to describe other things that relate to electricity. *...electric current.*
3 ADJ If a situation is **electric**, people are very excited. *When Drew arrived, the atmosphere was already electric.*

electrical /ɪlɛktrɪkl/

1 ADJ **Electrical** devices or machines work by means of electricity. *...electrical equipment.* ◆ **electrically** ADV *...electrically operated windows.*
2 ADJ ATTRIB **Electrical** engineers and industries are involved in the production or maintenance of electricity or electrical goods. *...the electronic and electrical engineering industries.*

electric blanket, electric blankets

NC An **electric blanket** is a blanket with wires inside it, which carry an electric current that keeps the blanket warm.

electric-blue

ADJ Something that is **electric-blue** in colour is very bright blue. *...electric-blue dragonflies... The sofa set was in electric-blue.*

electric chair

N SING The **electric chair** is a method of execution, used in some parts of the United States, in which a person is strapped to a special chair and killed by a powerful electric current. *The man died in the electric chair despite an international campaign to save his life.*

electrician /ɪlɛktrɪʃn/ electricians

NC An **electrician** is a person whose job is to install and repair electrical equipment. *The strike by electricians has left parts of Rio without light.*

electricity /ɪlɛktrɪsəti/

NU **Electricity** is a form of energy used for heating and lighting, and to provide power for machines. *They generate the electricity in power stations.*

electric shock, electric shocks

NC If you get an **electric shock**, you feel a sudden sharp pain when you touch something connected to a supply of electricity. *He is reported to have suffered an electric shock.*

electrify /ɪlɛktrɪfaɪ/ electrifies, electrifying, electrified

1 VO If something **electrifies** you, it excites you a lot. *...the news that had electrified the world.* ◆ **electrifying** ADJ *...an electrifying speech.*
2 VO If you **electrify** something, you connect it to a supply of electricity. *I toyed with the idea of electrifying the railings... The line has recently been electrified.* ◆ **electrified** ADJ ATTRIB *...electrified wire netting.* ◆ **electrification** /ɪlɛktrɪfɪkeɪʃn/ NU *...the building of roads and the electrification of villages.*

electrocute /ɪlɛktrəkjuːt/ electrocutes, electrocuting, electrocuted

VOorV-REFL If someone is **electrocuted**, they are killed

or badly injured by touching something connected to a source of electricity. *A fifteen-year-old boy was electrocuted and killed when he tried to place a flag on a pylon... Don't touch that wire, you'll electrocute yourself!*

electrode /ɪlɛktrəʊd/ **electrodes**
NC An **electrode** is a small piece of metal that takes an electric current to or from a source of power or a piece of equipment. *We used electrodes to measure the electrical activity of the muscles.*

electrolysis /ɪlɛktrɒləsɪs/
NU **Electrolysis** is the process of passing an electric current through a substance in order to produce chemical changes in the substance; a technical term in physics. *...hydrogen generated from water by electrolysis.*

electrolyte /ɪlɛktrəlaɪt/ **electrolytes**
NC An **electrolyte** is a substance, usually a liquid, which electricity can pass through. *...batteries that functioned perfectly when a new electrolyte, copper sulphate, was added.*

electromagnetic /ɪlɛktrəʊmægnɛtɪk/
ADJ **Electromagnetic** is used to describe magnetic forces and effects produced by an electric current. *...electromagnetic waves.*

electron /ɪlɛktrɒn/ **electrons**
NC An **electron** is a tiny particle of matter smaller than an atom. *...the atoms are split into electrons and protons.*

electronic /ɪlɛktrɒnɪk/ **electronics**
1 ADJ An **electronic** device has transistors, silicon chips, or valves which control and change the electric current passing through it. *...electronic equipment.*
2 ADJ ATTRIB An **electronic** process involves the use of electronic devices. *...electronic surveillance.*
♦ **electronically** ADV *Each vehicle might be electronically tracked.*
3 NU **Electronics** is the technology of using transistors, silicon chips, or valves to make radios, televisions, and computers. *...the British electronics industry.*
4 N PL **Electronics** also refers to the equipment that consists of electronic devices. *The boat carries a mass of sophisticated electronics.*

electronic tagging
NU **Electronic tagging** involves making a person wear an electronic device which gives out signals and tells someone in authority where that person is. *In the USA, electronic tagging is applied to only one prisoner in 1000... The judge has agreed to free him on bail on condition that he wears an electronic tagging device.*

electroplate /ɪlɛktrəpleɪt/ **electroplates, electroplating, electroplated**
VO To **electroplate** something means to put a layer of silver or other metal on it by dipping it in a special liquid through which an electric current is passed; a technical term.

elegance /ɛlɪgəns/
NU If a person or thing has **elegance**, it has a pleasing and graceful appearance, manner, or style. *...the elegance of classical ballet... The street had retained some of its old elegance.*

elegant /ɛlɪgənt/
1 ADJ **Elegant** means pleasing and graceful in appearance. *...a tall, elegant woman. ...the little church with its elegant square tower.* ♦ **elegantly** ADV *...an elegantly dressed woman.*
2 ADJ An **elegant** idea or plan is simple, clear, and clever. *His proposal has an elegant simplicity.*

elegiac /ɛlɪdʒaɪək/
ADJ Something that is **elegiac** expresses or shows sadness; a literary word. *...an elegiac mood.*

elegy /ɛlədʒi/ **elegies**
NC An **elegy** is a sad poem, often about someone who has died. *They mourned their king, chanted an elegy, spoke about that great man.*

element /ɛlɪmənt/ **elements**
1 NC+SUPP An **element** of something is one of the single parts which combines with others to make up a whole. *...the different elements in the play.*
2 N PL+SUPP The **elements** of a subject are the basic and most important points. *...the elements of reading.*

3 NC+SUPP When you talk about **elements** within a society, you are referring to groups of people with similar aims or habits. *...sympathetic elements outside the party.*
4 NC If something has an **element** of a particular quality, it has a certain amount of it. *It contains an element of truth.*
5 NC An **element** is a substance that consists of only one type of atom. For example, gold, oxygen, and carbon are elements.
6 NC The **element** in an electrical appliance is the metal part which changes the electric current into heat. *The element in the mat is powered by a 24 volt transformer.*
7 N PL You can refer to stormy weather as the **elements**. *Her raincoat was buttoned tight against the elements.*
8 If someone is in their **element**, they are doing something that they enjoy and do well. *Mr Mitterrand is in his element as he sets about the task of broadening his majority.*

elemental /ɛlɪmɛntl/
ADJ **Elemental** feelings and behaviour are simple and forceful; a literary word. *...outbursts of elemental rage.*

elementary /ɛlɪmɛntəˀri/
ADJ Something that is **elementary** is very simple, straightforward, and basic. *Most towns had taken some elementary precautions. ...elementary maths.*

elementary school, elementary schools
NC In the United States, an **elementary school** is a school where children are taught for the first six or eight years of their education. *Although Siad went to elementary school, he was largely self-educated.*

elephant /ɛlɪfənt/ **elephants**
NC An **elephant** is a very large animal with a long, flexible nose called a trunk. *Both rhino and elephant herds are being decimated by poachers.*

elephantine /ɛlɪfæntaɪn/
ADJ Something that is **elephantine** is like an elephant, for example because it is large and clumsy; a literary word. *...Amelia's elephantine foot. ...an elephantine attempt at gallantry.*

elevate /ɛlɪveɪt/ **elevates, elevating, elevated**
1 VO When people or things **are elevated**, they are given greater status or importance. *The series elevated Johnson from obscurity to stardom.*
2 VO To **elevate** something means to raise it to a higher level. *Earth movements elevated great areas of the seabed.*

elevated /ɛlɪveɪtɪd/
1 ADJ ATTRIB A person or a job or role that is **elevated** is very important or of very high rank. *...some elevated person like the Home Secretary... It is in keeping with your elevated position in the profession.*
2 ADJ If thoughts or ideas are **elevated**, they are on a high level morally or intellectually. *Let's discuss it on a slightly more elevated plane.*
3 ADJ You say that land or a building is **elevated** when it is higher than the surrounding area. *...a floor elevated two or three feet above the ground.*

elevation /ɛlɪveɪʃn/ **elevations**; a formal word.
1 NU+POSS The **elevation** of someone or something is the act of raising them to a position of greater importance. *...the elevation of the standards of the average man. ...his elevation to the peerage.*
2 NC The **elevation** of a place is its height above sea level. *...a fairly flat plateau at an elevation of about a hundred feet.*

elevator /ɛlɪveɪtə/ **elevators**
NC An **elevator** is a device like a large box, that moves up and down inside a tall building to carry people from one floor to another; used in American English. *I went down in the elevator.*

eleven /ɪlɛvn/ **elevens**
Eleven is the number 11. *What is the legacy of Mrs Thatcher's eleven years in power?*

elevenses /ɪlɛvnzɪz/
NU **Elevenses** is a light snack that you have in the middle of the morning, for example a cup of tea or coffee and biscuits; an informal word. *I went indoors to put on the kettle for our elevenses.*

eleventh /ɪlɛvnθ/
ADJ The **eleventh** item in a series is the one that you count as number eleven. *This is the eleventh round of talks on the issue.*

eleventh hour
N SING The **eleventh hour** is the last possible moment before something happens. *I was asked, at the eleventh hour, to direct the play.*

elf /ɛlf/ **elves** /ɛlvz/
NC An **elf** is a small magical person in fairy stories who plays tricks on people.

elfin /ɛlfɪn/
1 ADJ ATTRIB If you say that someone has **elfin** looks, you mean that they have small, delicate features.
2 ADJ ATTRIB **Elfin** is also used to describe things that are connected with elves.

elicit /ɪlɪsɪt/ **elicits, eliciting, elicited**; a formal word.
1 VO If you **elicit** a response or a reaction, you do something which makes other people respond or react. *Threats to reinstate the tax elicited jeers from the opposition.*
2 VO If you **elicit** a piece of information, you get it by asking careful questions. *In five minutes she had elicited all the Herriard family history.*

elide /ɪlaɪd/ **elides, eliding, elided**
VO If you **elide** a part of a word, you do not pronounce it when you are speaking; a technical term in linguistics.

eligible /ɛlɪdʒəbl/
1 ADJ Someone who is **eligible** for something is qualified or suitable for it. *You may be eligible for a grant... She is only just eligible to vote.* ◆ **eligibility** /ɛlɪdʒəbɪləti/ NU *...the eligibility of applicants.*
2 ADJ An **eligible** man or woman is not yet married but is considered to be a suitable partner. *...an eligible bachelor.*

eliminate /ɪlɪmɪneɪt/ **eliminates, eliminating, eliminated**
1 VO To **eliminate** something means to remove it completely. *Poverty must be eliminated.* ◆ **elimination** /ɪlɪmɪneɪʃn/ NU *...the elimination of spelling errors.*
2 VO When a person or team is **eliminated** from a competition, they are defeated and so take no further part in it. *Four minor candidates were eliminated in the first round.*

elision /ɪlɪʒn/
NU **Elision** is the leaving out of the sound of some part of a word when it is spoken; a technical term in linguistics.

elite /ɪliːt/ **elites**
1 N COLL An **elite** is a group of the most powerful, rich, or talented people in a society. *An elite of about 3,000 families control most of the wealth and power in Bangladesh.*
2 ADJ ATTRIB **Elite** people or organizations are considered to be the best of their kind. *...elite training establishments.*

elitism /ɪliːtɪzəm/
NU **Elitism** is the belief that a society should be ruled by a small group of people who are considered by some to be superior to everyone else. *This kind of elitism is even more marked in public schools.*

elitist /ɪliːtɪst/ **elitists**
1 ADJ **Elitist** people, systems, or ideas practise or support elitism. *It had been a very elitist society. ...elitist arguments.*
2 NC An **elitist** is a person who believes that a society or country should be ruled by a small group of people who are superior to everyone else. *In some ways he's quite like you—an elitist.*

elixir /ɪlɪksə/ **elixirs**
NC An **elixir** is a liquid that is considered to have magical powers. *...their search to find the elixir of life.*

Elizabethan /ɪlɪzəbiːθn/
ADJ Something or someone that is **Elizabethan** happened, was made, or lived in England when Elizabeth the First was Queen in the second half of the sixteenth century. *...the unique nature of Elizabethan painting.*

Elizabeth II /ɪliːzəbəθ! də sɛkənd/
Elizabeth II became Queen of the United Kingdom of Great Britain and Northern Ireland in 1952, after the death of her father, King George VI. She is Head of the Commonwealth. Born: 1926.

elk /ɛlk/ **elks**. The plural form can be either **elks** or **elk**.
NC An **elk** is the largest type of deer, sometimes two metres high at the shoulder and with big, flattened antlers. *Large numbers of elk and deer now roam the forests.*

ellipse /ɪlɪps/ **ellipses** /ɪlɪpsɪz/
NC An **ellipse** is an oval shape like a flattened circle.

ellipsis /ɪlɪpsɪs/ **ellipses** /ɪlɪpsiːz/
NU or NC **Ellipsis** is the missing out of one or more words from a sentence when the sentence can be understood without them; a technical term in linguistics.

elliptic /ɪlɪptɪk/ ADJ
Elliptic means the same as **elliptical**.

elliptical /ɪlɪptɪkl/
1 ADJ Something that is **elliptical** has an oval shape like a flattened circle. *First of all, it will go into a highly elliptical orbit around the poles of Venus.*
2 ADJ Speech or writing that is **elliptical** is difficult to understand, or easily misunderstood, because some words have been missed out. *...elliptical references to problems best not aired in public.*

elm /ɛlm/ **elms**
NC or NU An **elm** is a tree with broad leaves. The wood that is obtained from it is also called **elm**. *An estimated 15 billion elm trees were lost in the USA in the course of the Dutch Elm Disease epidemic.*

elocution /ɛləkjuːʃn/
NU **Elocution** is the art of speaking clearly in public with a standard accent. *He taught elocution at a junior college.*

elongate /iːlɒŋgeɪt/ **elongates, elongating, elongated**
VO If you **elongate** something, you stretch it so that it becomes longer; a formal word. *Rise up on your toes and elongate the complete length of your spine.* ◆ **elongation** /iːlɒŋgeɪʃn/ NU *...the elongation of the circles into ellipses.*

elongated /iːlɒŋgeɪtɪd/
ADJ Something that is **elongated** is very long and thin. *One is nice and round, and another is more elongated and has the shape of a rugby ball.*

elope /ɪləʊp/ **elopes, eloping, eloped**
V-RECIP When two people **elope**, they go away secretly together to get married. *The film tells the tale of two lovers who decide to elope just before the girl is due to marry an older man... Is it true you eloped with her to Florida?*

elopement /ɪləʊpmənt/ **elopements**
NC or NU An **elopement** is an act of eloping. *He had read of her elopement while at Oxford.*

eloquence /ɛləkwəns/
1 NU **Eloquence** is the ability to speak and write well and in a convincing way. *He may have inherited his eloquence from his father, a Christian preacher.*
2 NU **Eloquence** is also the art of speaking or writing well and in a convincing way. *But the eloquence and fluent imagery of that period never returned.*

eloquent /ɛləkwənt/
ADJ **Eloquent** people express themselves well in speech or writing. *He was tall, eloquent, and had fine manners. ...eloquent descriptions.* ◆ **eloquently** ADV *They spoke eloquently of their concern.*

El Salvador /ɛl sælvədɔː/
The **Republic of El Salvador** is a country in Central America. It was a Spanish colony from the 16th century until 1821. Many left-wing guerrilla groups were organized in the 1970s and civil war began in 1979. Since the 1980s the government's main opponent has been the Farabundo Martí National Liberation Movement (FMLN), a coalition of a number of separate guerrilla groups. Successive right-wing governments have been supported by the USA. Alfredo Félix Cristiani Burkard, of the Nationalist Republican Alliance (ARENA), became President in 1989. A peace agreement was signed by the government and the FMLN in 1991 under the auspices of the United Nations. El Salvador is a member of the Organization of American States. High inflation and large foreign debts are major economic problems. Civil war has

seriously damaged the economy. El Salvador exports coffee, sugar, and cotton. ◆ **Salvadoran, Salvadorean** /sælvədɔːrən, sælvədɔːriən/ N, ADJ ▪ *per capita GNP:* US$950 ▪ *religion:* Christianity (mainly Roman Catholic) ▪ *language:* Spanish ▪ *currency:* colón ▪ *capital:* San Salvador ▪ *population:* 5 million (1990) ▪ *size:* 21,393 square kilometres.

else /els/
1 ADV You use **else** after words such as 'anywhere', 'someone', and 'what' to refer vaguely to another place, person, or thing. *Let's go somewhere else... I had nothing else to do. ...someone else's house... Who else was there?*
2 CONJ You use **or else** when you are indicating the unpleasant results that will occur if someone does not do something. *You've got to be very careful or else you'll miss the turn-off into our drive.*
3 CONJ You also use **or else** to introduce the second of two possibilities, when you do not know which one is true. *I think I was at school, or else I was staying with a friend.*

elsewhere /elsweə/
ADV **Elsewhere** means in other places or to another place. *...in Europe and elsewhere... He can go elsewhere.*

ELT /iːeltiː/
ELT is used to describe things that are connected with the teaching of English. **ELT** is an abbreviation for 'English Language Teaching'.

elucidate /ɪluːsɪdeɪt/ **elucidates, elucidating, elucidated**
VO If you **elucidate** something, you make it clear and understandable; a formal word. *...a lesson elucidating the points that have been made in the previous lecture.*

elude /ɪluːd/, **eludes, eluding, eluded**; a formal word.
1 VO If something that you want **eludes** you, you fail to obtain or achieve it. *...the peace she felt had always eluded her. ...the political credibility which has so far always eluded them.*
2 VO If an idea or fact **eludes** you, you cannot understand or remember it. *This is something that still eludes scientists after many years of work... She tried to remember the shape of his face, but it eluded her.*
3 VO If you **elude** someone or something, you manage to escape from them. *...the problems of eluding the police.*

elusive /ɪluːsɪv/
ADJ Something or someone that is **elusive** is difficult to find, achieve, describe, or remember; a formal word. *Happiness is an elusive quality.*

elves /elvz/
Elves is the plural of **elf**.

emaciated /ɪmeɪsieɪtɪd/
ADJ An **emaciated** person is extremely thin because of illness or lack of food. *...the stream of emaciated refugees who've been arriving in the northern part of Sudan.*

emaciation /ɪmeɪsieɪʃn/
NU **Emaciation** is the state of being extremely thin and weak because of illness or lack of food. *They starved themselves into a state of emaciation.*

emanate /eməneɪt/ **emanates, emanating, emanated**
V+from If a quality, idea, or feeling **emanates** from you, it comes from you; a formal word. *These ideas are said to emanate from Henry Kissinger.*

emancipate /ɪmænsɪpeɪt/ **emancipates, emancipating, emancipated**
VO To **emancipate** someone means to free them from unpleasant social, political, or legal restrictions; a formal word. *...a government determined to emancipate the poor.* ◆ **emancipation** /ɪmænsɪpeɪʃn/ NU *Marx spoke of the emancipation of mankind.*

emasculate /ɪmæskjuleɪt/ **emasculates, emasculating, emasculated**
VO If someone or something is **emasculated**, their strength or power is removed so that they become weak or ineffective. *...measures designed to emasculate worker militancy.*

embalm /ɪmbɑːm/ **embalms, embalming, embalmed**
VO When a dead person is **embalmed**, their body is preserved using special substances. *...the mummified internal organs of Psusennes, removed and embalmed separately.* ◆ **embalmed** ADJ *...the embalmed body of Georgi Dimitrov is to be removed from its mausoleum.*

embankment /ɪmbæŋkmənt/ **embankments**
NC An **embankment** is a thick wall or mound of earth that is built to carry a railway or road over an area of low ground, or to prevent water from a river from flooding the area. *...a piece of track lined by steep grassy embankments... the wooded motorway embankment... The river rose several metres and burst its banks along stretches of the embankment.*

embargo /ɪmbɑːgəʊ/ **embargoes**
NC An **embargo** is an order made by a government to stop trade with another country. *The states imposed an embargo on oil shipments. ...a trade embargo.*

embark /ɪmbɑːk/ **embarks, embarking, embarked**
V When you **embark** on a ship, you go on board before the start of a voyage. *She had embarked on the S.S. Gordon Castle at Tilbury.* ◆ **embarkation** /embɑːkeɪʃn/ NU *Passengers without confirmed bookings are being advised to get in touch with the ports of embarkation before leaving home.*
embark on PHRASAL VERB If you **embark on** something new, you start it. *Peru embarked on a massive programme of reform.*

embarrass /ɪmbærəs/ **embarrasses, embarrassing, embarrassed**
1 VO If something **embarrasses** you, it makes you feel shy or ashamed. *It embarrasses me even to think about it.*
2 VO If something **embarrasses** a politician, it causes political problems for them. *The march could embarrass the government.*

embarrassed /ɪmbærəst/
ADJ If you are **embarrassed**, you feel shy or ashamed. *I felt really embarrassed about it... She had been too embarrassed to ask her friends... They were met with embarrassed silence.*

embarrassing /ɪmbærəsɪŋ/
ADJ Something that is **embarrassing** makes you feel shy or ashamed. *He said something that would be embarrassing for me to repeat.* ◆ **embarrassingly** ADV *Their possessions were embarrassingly few.*

embarrassment /ɪmbærəsmənt/ **embarrassments**
1 NU **Embarrassment** is a shy feeling or a feeling of shame. *His cheeks were hot with embarrassment.*
2 NC Someone or something that embarrasses people can be referred to as an **embarrassment**. *It was a political embarrassment.*

embassy /embəsi/ **embassies**
1 NC An **embassy** is a group of officials, headed by an ambassador, who represent their government in a foreign country. *She was attached to the Canadian embassy... He travelled to London today to meet embassy officials from several different countries.*
2 NC The building in which an ambassador and his or her officials work is also called an **embassy**. *They might be prevented from getting into the embassy.*

embattled /ɪmbætld/
ADJ An **embattled** person or group is having a lot of problems. *...supporting an embattled Labour Government... Already weakened by the Iran Contra affair, President Reagan is looking increasingly embattled.*

embed /ɪmbed/ **embeds, embedding, embedded**
1 VO If an object is **embedded** in a mass of surrounding substance, it is fixed there firmly and deeply. *He examined the locks; both were embedded in the woodwork... The plane swerved off the landing strip and ended up with its wheels embedded in mud... The baby is believed to have shrapnel embedded in its spine.*
2 VO If something such as an attitude or feeling is **embedded** in a society or in someone's personality, it has become a permanent and noticeable feature of it. *...racist ideas which had become so deeply embedded. ...a deeply embedded feeling of guilt.*

embellish /ɪmbelɪʃ/ **embellishes, embellishing, embellished**; a formal word.
1 VO If something is **embellished** with other things,

they are added to make it more attractive. ...*a dress embellished with tiny circular mirrors. ...a striking ballet, embellished by Bach's music.*
2 VO If you **embellish** a story, you make it more interesting by adding details which may be untrue. *A translator heavily embellished the Israeli foreign minister's statements.* ◆ **embellished** ADJ ...*embellished accounts of the day's events.*

embellishment /ɪmbɛlɪʃmənt/ **embellishments**
1 NCorNU An **embellishment** is a decoration added to something to make it seem more attractive. ...*a flat surface that seemed to cry out for decorative embellishments... For a long time, embellishment of any kind was frowned upon.*
2 NC An **embellishment** to a story or account of something is a detail added to make it seem more interesting, even if it is not actually true. ...*the exact truth without any exaggerations or embellishments... They were accused of copying articles from other papers and repeating them with embellishments.*

ember /ɛmbə/ **embers**
NC **Embers** are glowing pieces of wood or coal from a dying fire. *Clear the bees away from the comb of honey using embers of fire and smoke.*

embezzle /ɪmbɛzl/ **embezzles, embezzling, embezzled**
VO If someone **embezzles** money, they steal it from an organization that they work for. *More than two-hundred-million dollars of state funds had been embezzled by the head of the bank. ...charges of embezzling union funds.*

embezzlement /ɪmbɛzlmənt/
NU **Embezzlement** is the act or practice of taking or using money illegally for your own purposes, when it belongs to a company or organization that you work for. *It accused him of the embezzlement of public funds. ...charges of forgery and embezzlement.*

embitter /ɪmbɪtə/ **embitters, embittering, embittered**
VO If someone is **embittered** by what happens to them, they feel angry and resentful because of it. *The economic system had embittered and discouraged people... They are in danger of further embittering their enemies.* ◆ **embittered** ADJ *Shaffer portrayed Salieri as an embittered, mediocre composer. ...a demoralized and embittered people.*

emblazoned /ɪmbleɪzənd/
ADJ PRED+*on* or *with* If designs or letters are **emblazoned** on something, they are clearly drawn, printed, or sewn on it. ...*a flag on which the imperial eagle was emblazoned. ...sweatshirts emblazoned with the name of their college.*

emblem /ɛmbləm/ **emblems**
1 NC An **emblem** is a design representing a country or organization. ...*the proposal to restore the crown to Poland's national emblem... The Red Cross takes even minor abuse of its emblem seriously.*
2 NC+SUPP An **emblem** is also something representing a quality or idea. *To the Chinese, the dragon is a symbol of the life force, an emblem of royalty, power, and wealth.*

emblematic /ɛmbləmætɪk/
ADJ Something, such as an object in a painting, that is **emblematic** of something else, such as an abstract idea, stands for it or symbolically represents it. *The lion also has an emblematic function in the painting... We tend to see Mexico as an emblematic country, reflecting the troubles of the continent.*

embodiment /ɪmbɒdɪmənt/
N SING If you describe someone or something as the **embodiment** of a quality or idea, you mean that it is their most noticeable characteristic or the basis of all they do; a formal word. *She was the embodiment of loyalty... To many, including himself, he was the embodiment of the capitalist ethic.*

embody /ɪmbɒdi/ **embodies, embodying, embodied**
1 VO To **embody** a quality or idea means to have it as your most noticeable characteristic or as the basis of everything you do. ...*the institutions which embody traditional values... His aim is to reconcile Tunisia with a brand of Islam that embodies tolerance, progress, and openness.*
2 VO If something **embodies** a particular thing, it contains or consists of that thing. *These proposals were embodied in the Industrial Relations Act... The main draft embodies a proposal that the UN should monitor food supplies to ensure they reach the refugees.*

emboldened /ɪmbəʊldənd/
ADJ PRED If you are **emboldened** by something that happens, it makes you feel confident enough to behave in a particular way. *Demonstrators in Prague have been emboldened by the new spirit of reform in Moscow.*

embolism /ɛmbəlɪzəm/ **embolisms**
NC An **embolism** is a blockage in a vein or artery in the body of a person or animal, caused by a blood clot or air bubble; a medical term. *Although he had been partly paralysed by an air embolism, he had survived.*

embossed /ɪmbɒst/
V-PASS If something such as paper or wood is **embossed** with a design, the design stands up slightly from the surface. *The cigarettes are embossed with the gold emblem of the Palace of Westminster... They're made of water-resistant card, and are embossed with pastel coloured flowers.* ◆ **embossed** ADJ *She jotted down the names on the back of her embossed invitation card.*

embrace /ɪmbreɪs/ **embraces, embracing, embraced**
1 V-RECIP When you **embrace** someone, you put your arms around them in order to show your affection for them. *Before she could embrace him he stepped away... Mr Assad and President Mubarak embraced as they met at the airport.* ▶ Also NC *They greeted us with warm embraces.*
2 VO If something **embraces** a group of people, things, or ideas, it includes them; a formal use. *The course embraces elements of chemistry, physics, and engineering.*
3 VO If you **embrace** a religion, political system, or idea, you start believing in it completely; a formal use. *President Gorbachev is expected to urge the party to embrace democracy... His suggestion will not be eagerly embraced by all.*

embrasure /ɪmbreɪʒə/ **embrasures**; a technical term.
1 NC An **embrasure** is an opening in a wall where a window or door is fixed, when it is wider on the inside than on the outside. *He opened up the interior by fitting window embrasures in the small niches.*
2 NC In fortified buildings such as castles, an **embrasure** is an opening in the wall, through which defenders could shoot at their enemies. *Mr Banks said he had seen roughly constructed brick huts with embrasures for machine guns.*

embrocation /ɛmbrəkeɪʃn/ **embrocations**
N MASS **Embrocation** is a liquid which is rubbed onto the body to reduce pain from aches or bruises. *Used as an embrocation, chamomile oil is a good treatment for neuralgia.*

embroider /ɪmbrɔɪdə/ **embroiders, embroidering, embroidered**
VorVO If you **embroider** fabric, you sew a decorative design onto it. *His mother sits placidly embroidering behind the latticed windows of the salon... She had embroidered the picture onto her dance skirt.* ◆ **embroidered** ADJ *His usual dress is a simple grey embroidered robe.*

embroidery /ɪmbrɔɪdəᵒri/
1 NU **Embroidery** consists of designs sewn onto fabric. *They are immensely elaborate works of applique, embroidery or collage.*
2 NU **Embroidery** is also the activity of sewing designs onto fabric. ...*Jane's first attempts at embroidery.*

embroil /ɪmbrɔɪl/ **embroils, embroiling, embroiled**
VO When someone is **embroiled** in an argument or fight, they become deeply involved in it; a formal word. *An arms deal has embroiled the Indian government in a huge corruption scandal... The Gulf crisis threatens to embroil Israel in a war, which could have serious implications for its relationship with the United Sates.*

embryo /ɛmbriəʊ/ **embryos**
NC An **embryo** is an animal or human in the very early stages of development in the womb. *British scientists believe they have discovered the gene that determines the sex of a human embryo.*

embryonic /ɛmbriɒnɪk/
ADJ Something that is **embryonic** is at a very early stage of its development; a formal word. *Embryonic peasant movements began to emerge... This new consensus between the two nations is as yet embryonic.*

emcee /ɛmsiː/ **emcees**
NC An **emcee** is the same as a **master of ceremonies**; used in American English. *Dennis De Concini was the host and emcee of the party, and took the most active role.*

emend /ɪmɛnd/ **emends, emending, emended**
VO If you **emend** a piece of writing, you correct the mistakes in it. *What you say will be noted down, then typed out for you to read and emend if necessary before you sign.*

emerald /ɛmərəld/ **emeralds**
1 NC An **emerald** is a bright green precious stone. *...a drive to stop foreigners mining for emeralds which are found in the area.*
2 ADJ Something that is **emerald** in colour is bright green. *...in Hawaii, where waves crash against an emerald coastline.*

emerge /ɪmɜːdʒ/ **emerges, emerging, emerged**; a formal word.
1 V When you **emerge** from a place that you have been in for some time, you come out. *As the two men emerged, they were approached by journalists... Mr Primakov emerged from the eighty-minute meeting saying he was carrying a message of peace... The latest reports say that as they emerged from the temple, two of the militants disobeyed orders and were shot dead.*
2 V+from If you **emerge** from a difficult or bad experience, you come to the end of it. *Few emerge from the experience unscathed... The Germans had just emerged from a brutal dictatorship, which put to death millions who belonged to minority ethnic groups.*
3 V+from or V-REPORT If a fact **emerges** from a discussion or investigation, it becomes known as a result of it. *So far, no motive for the hijacking has emerged... One amazing fact emerged from their study—that cats were able to survive a fall of up to 7 storeys... This morning, it emerged that the surveillance operation had been wider than was at first disclosed.*
4 V When something such as an industry or a political movement **emerges**, it comes into existence. *Large-scale industry emerged only gradually... The traditions which have emerged from thousands of years of Chinese civilization are now a major obstacle to progress.*

emergence /ɪmɜːdʒəns/
N SING The **emergence** of something is the process or event of its coming into existence. *...the emergence of new ideas... One of the high points of contemporary music was Judith Weir's emergence as an important composer... The Prime Minister has come here to celebrate the emergence of new democracies in Europe.*

emergency /ɪmɜːdʒənsi/ **emergencies**
NCorNU An **emergency** is an unexpected and dangerous situation, which must be dealt with quickly. *The bells were only used in emergencies. ...what to do in case of emergency... The plane made an emergency landing.*

emergency services
N PL The **emergency services** are the public organizations who take quick action to deal with emergencies when they occur, especially the fire brigade, the police, and the ambulance service. *Mr Channon paid tribute to the emergency services who fought to save lives on the night of the fire.*

emergent /ɪmɜːdʒənt/
ADJ ATTRIB An **emergent** country, political group, or way of life is becoming powerful or is coming into existence; a formal word. *The main focus of emergent nationalism is in the Baltic States... He strongly supports Bangladesh as an emergent nation.*

emeritus /ɪmɛrɪtəs/
ADJ ATTRIB or ADJ after N **Emeritus** is used with a professional title to indicate that the person has

retired but keeps the title as an honour. *...Emeritus Professor of Anthropology... Their emeritus chairman is Father Basil Wrighton. ...the Professor Emeritus of Theology.*

emery /ɛməri/
NU **Emery** is a hard grey metal, which is often ground to a powder and stuck onto paper, cardboard, or cloth to make a tool for smoothing or polishing surfaces. *A fine surface was produced by working down the various grades of emery paper.*

emery board, emery boards
NC An **emery board** is a long, narrow piece of wood or cardboard with a rough surface, which is used for smoothing and shaping people's fingernails.

emetic /ɪmɛtɪk/ **emetics**; a medical term.
1 NC An **emetic** is something that is given to someone to swallow, in order to make them vomit. *Cardamon is an emetic that should only be used under trained supervision.*
2 ADJ Something that is **emetic** makes you vomit. *This remedy must not be used in pregnancy, as it has emetic tendencies.*

emigrant /ɛmɪgrənt/ **emigrants**
NC An **emigrant** is a person who has left their own country to live in another country. *The number of Jewish emigrants from the Soviet Union has steadily increased this year.*

emigrate /ɛmɪgreɪt/ **emigrates, emigrating, emigrated**
V If you **emigrate**, you leave your native country to live in another country. *He received permission to emigrate to Canada... He tried to escape his troubles by feigning suicide and emigrating to Australia.*

emigration /ɛmɪgreɪʃn/
NU **Emigration** is the act or process of leaving your native country to live in another country. *...the encouragement given to peasant emigration. ...restrictions on emigration will be relaxed.*

émigré /ɛmɪgreɪ/ **émigrés**
NC An **émigré** is someone who has left their country for political reasons. *Increasing numbers of émigrés are being refused admittance as refugees. ...the Russian émigré community in New York.*

eminence /ɛmɪnəns/
1 NU **Eminence** is the quality of being very well-known and highly respected. *Jimmie was a man of some local eminence. ...a mathematician of eminence.*
2 TITLE The expression **Your Eminence** is used to address a Roman Catholic cardinal.

eminent /ɛmɪnənt/
ADJ **Eminent** people are important and respected. *...one of the most eminent scientists in Britain.*

eminently /ɛmɪnəntli/
SUBMOD You use **eminently** with a word referring to a positive quality to say that the quality is very noticeable in someone or something. *He already has international stature, and seems eminently well-qualified for the post of President... Hennessey's book is eminently readable.*

emir /emɪə/ **emirs**
NC An **emir** is a Muslim ruler, especially in South-West Asia and West Africa. *The Emir of Gwandu is the most senior figure in the caliphate after the Sultan.*

emirate /ɛmərət/ **emirates**
NC An **emirate** is a country that is ruled by an emir. *...the United Arab Emirates... Kuwait is a tiny but vastly wealthy emirate.*

emissary /ɛmɪsəri/ **emissaries**
NC An **emissary** is a messenger or representative sent by a government or leader; a formal word. *The Secretary General has invited high level emissaries from Iran and Iraq to come to New York. ...the Soviet emissary, Mr Yevgeny Primakov.*

emission /ɪmɪʃn/ **emissions**
NCorNU When there is an **emission** of gas or radiation, it is released into the atmosphere; a formal word. *...measures to control carbon dioxide emissions... The lake has become polluted by effluent discharge and smoke emission from a pulp factory nearby.*

emit /ɪmɪt/ **emits, emitting, emitted**
1 VO If something **emits** heat, light, or a smell, it sends it out by means of a physical or chemical

process. ...*the rays of heat that are emitted by the warm earth... The foam, which caught fire, emitted a toxic gas which is believed to have killed most of the victims.*
2 VO To **emit** a sound or noise means to produce it so that other people can hear it. *He stands surrounded by 100 or so women and children, emitting a chorus of cries and coughs... Giant pandas are unlike other bears, and they emit a gentle bleat instead of a mighty roar.*

emollient /ɪmˈplɪənt/ **emollients**
N MASS An **emollient** is a liquid or cream which you put on your skin to soften it; a formal word. *Jojoba is such a wonderful emollient, and is used instead of whale oil.*

emolument /ɪmˈpljuːmənt/ **emoluments**
NC An **emolument** is money or some other form of payment which a person receives for doing work; a formal word. *Emoluments earned by UK residents abroad may be taxed.*

emotion /ɪˈməʊʃn/ **emotions**
NC or NU An **emotion** is a feeling such as fear, love, anger, or jealousy. *It wasn't proper for a man to show his emotions... She looked around her without emotion.*

emotional /ɪˈməʊʃənəl/
1 ADJ **Emotional** means relating to your feelings. *...the emotional needs of children... He claimed damages for the emotional stress he had suffered.*
♦ **emotionally** ADV *He felt physically and emotionally exhausted.*
2 ADJ When someone is **emotional**, they experience a strong emotion and show it openly, especially by crying. *The newspapers report Miss Bhutto as being emotional after her election defeat... After an emotional reunion with their grandparents, they were taken to a local hospital for a check-up.*

emotive /ɪˈməʊtɪv/
ADJ Something that is **emotive** is likely to make people feel strong emotions. *Jerusalem, as a city sacred to Muslims, Christians, and Jews, is always an emotive issue... He was careful to avoid emotive or condemnatory language.*

empathize /ˈempəθaɪz/ **empathizes, empathizing, empathized**; also spelt **empathise**.
V If you **empathize** with someone, you understand their situation, problems, and feelings, because you have been in a similar situation. *Josh had understood. At last he empathized with the woman's dilemma... The idea is to encourage students to empathize with people from different backgrounds.*

empathy /ˈempəθi/
NU **Empathy** is the ability to share another person's feelings as if they were your own; a formal word. *The reader is encouraged to understand the depth of Abu Rish's empathy with the suffering of his people... Townsend's gift is that he commands a great deal of audience empathy.*

emperor /ˈempərə/ **emperors**
NC An **emperor** is a man who rules an empire. *...the former Ethiopian emperor, Haile Selassie.*

emphasis /ˈemfəsɪs/
1 NU or N SING **Emphasis** is special importance that is given to an activity or to a part or aspect of something. *Too much emphasis is being placed on basic research... There's a new emphasis on assessing the food needs of the Soviet Union during the coming winter.*
2 NU or N SING **Emphasis** is also extra force that you put on a word in order to make it seem more important. *'They had four cars,' he repeated with emphasis... I think this may be—and the emphasis is on the word may—an important development.*

emphasize /ˈemfəsaɪz/ **emphasizes, emphasizing, emphasized**; also spelt **emphasise**.
V-REPORT or VO To **emphasize** something means to indicate that it is particularly important or true, or to draw special attention to it. *The SPLA has emphasized that there will be no ceasefire until the agreement has been endorsed... He emphasized the need for national unity.*

emphatic /ɪmˈfætɪk/
1 ADJ An **emphatic** statement or opinion is made forcefully. *...an emphatic refutation.*
2 ADJ PRED If you are **emphatic**, you use forceful language, to show that what you are saying is important. *Mr Heath brushed off, with an emphatic 'no', the charge that his visit was handing the Iraqi leader a propaganda coup... They are emphatic that a diplomatic solution is still possible.*
3 ADJ If someone gives an **emphatic** performance or achieves an **emphatic** victory, they have been successful in a complete, forceful, or positive way. *There were emphatic performances in the European Cup competition from Real Madrid and Glasgow Rangers... The newspaper sees it as an emphatic victory for the ruling United National Party.*

emphatically /ɪmˈfætɪkli/
1 ADV If you say something **emphatically**, you say it in a way that shows that you feel strongly about it. *'I hope it does,' she said emphatically.*
2 ADV SEN You also use **emphatically** to indicate that something is definitely true. *She is emphatically not a recluse.*

empire /ˈempaɪə/ **empires**
1 NC An **empire** is a group of countries controlled by one country. *...the Roman Empire.*
2 NC You can also refer to a large group of companies controlled by one person as an **empire**. *His publishing empire was flourishing.*

empirical /ɪmˈpɪrɪkl/
ADJ **Empirical** knowledge or study is based on practical experience and observation rather than theories; a formal word. *They based their radical conclusions on empirical sociological data.*
♦ **empirically** ADV *The theory could be tested empirically.*

empiricism /ɪmˈpɪrɪsɪzəm/
NU **Empiricism** is the belief that people should rely on practical experience rather than theories as a basis for knowledge and action; a formal word. *They deny the possibility of acquiring knowledge through any means other than empiricism.*

employ /ɪmˈplɔɪ/ **employs, employing, employed**
1 VO If you **employ** someone, you pay them to work for you. *He was employed as a research assistant... They have to cut production costs, and they often do that by employing children.*
2 VO To **employ** something means to use it; a formal use. *You will need to employ a great deal of tact... The weapon makers are now employing all of the techniques of modern biochemistry.*

employable /ɪmˈplɔɪəbl/
ADJ Something or someone that is **employable** is capable of being employed or used in a job. *She has no employable skills... Only one-third of the population of employable age are actually working.*

employee /ɪmˈplɔɪiː/ **employees**
NC An **employee** is a person who is paid to work for an organization or for another person. *Several thousand employees of the state broadcasting system have gone on strike... He and a second man, also a British Rail employee, were taken to hospital for treatment.*

employer /ɪmˈplɔɪə/ **employers**
NC Your **employer** is the organization or person that you work for. *Employers want to make sure that new recruits fit in with the rest of the people in the office... British Rail is an Equal Opportunities employer... The textile industry is a large employer, and therefore politically sensitive.*

employment /ɪmˈplɔɪmənt/
NU **Employment** is the position of having a paid job. *He had retired from regular employment... the government's commitment to full employment.*

employment agency, employment agencies
NC An **employment agency** is an organization that earns money by helping people to find work. *...Manpower, the huge international employment agency.*

emporium /emˈpɔːriəm/ **emporiums** or **emporia** /emˈpɔːriə/
NC An **emporium** is a large shop that sells a lot of

different things; an old-fashioned word. *Leon took them to Garretts, a downtown emporium where they bought cheese, and caramel popcorn.*

empower /ɪmpaʊə/ **empowers, empowering, empowered**
VO+*to*-INF When someone is **empowered** to do something, they have the authority or power to do it; a formal word. *The police are empowered to stop anyone to search for illegal drugs... He had been empowered by the Mozambique government to set up peace talks. The United Nations charter would empower it to use military measures.*

empress /ɛmprəs/ **empresses**
NC An **empress** is a woman who rules an empire, or the wife of an emperor. *...Empress Eugenie of France.*

emptiness /ɛmptɪnəs/
1 NU A feeling of **emptiness** is an unhappy or frightening feeling that nothing is worthwhile. *...the inner sense of emptiness she felt... One feels an emptiness where there might be friendship and affection.*
2 NU The **emptiness** of a place is the fact that it has nothing in it. *...the largely unexplored emptiness of the Indian Ocean... Many of the soldiers desert, and wander off into the vast emptiness of Siberia.*

empty /ɛmpti/ **emptier, emptiest; empties, emptying, emptied**
1 ADJ An **empty** place, vehicle, or container has no people or things in it. *Tourists have been put off by the fighting, and most hotels are empty... The school was empty at the time of the fire, and there were no injuries... Recycling paper and taking your empty bottles to the bottle bank won't save the world.*
2 ADJ A gesture, threat, or relationship that is **empty** has no real value or meaning. *The pardons are a conciliatory, if empty gesture... They ignored his threats as empty rhetoric... The Guardian have said there is too much hype and empty ceremonial.*
3 ADJ If you describe a person's life or a period of time as **empty**, you mean that nothing interesting or valuable happens in it. *How shall I exist during the empty days ahead?... She felt tired, nervous, empty, and sexually frustrated.*
4 VO If you **empty** a container, you remove its contents. *She picked up an ashtray and emptied it into a wastepaper basket.*
5 VOA If you **empty** a substance or object out of a container, you pour or tip it out of the container. *Empty the water out of those boots... The crew were unable to empty a tank holding waste water.*
6 V If a room or building **empties**, everyone in it goes out. *The play was over and the auditorium began to empty... The halls empty quickly when the day is done at West Springfield.*
7 V If a container **empties**, everything in it flows out or disappears from it. *The regulator will control the pressure within the can as it empties.*

empty-handed
ADJ PRED If you come back from somewhere **empty-handed**, you have failed to get what you intended to get. *Two armed men ambushed a van outside a factory but escaped empty-handed... The delegation in Detroit are coming back empty-handed after failing to persuade Ford to build a plant near Dundee.*

empty-headed
ADJ If you say that someone is **empty-headed**, you mean that they do not think sensibly and often do silly or stupid things. *He was putting on an act to impress an empty-headed girl.*

emu /iːmjuː/ **emus**
NC An **emu** is a large flightless Australian bird with long legs. *The modern kiwi is more closely related to the Australian emus and cassowaries.*

EMU /iːmjuː, iːemjuː/
EMU is an abbreviation for 'European Monetary Union', a system that would mean that members of the European Community would all use the same currency. *Discussions on EMU displaced the issue of farm subsidies at the summit this weekend. ...fierce opposition to EMU.*

emulate /ɛmjʊleɪt/ **emulates, emulating, emulated**
VO If you **emulate** someone or something, you imitate them because you admire them; a formal word. *The Soviet Union wants Czechoslovakia to emulate its own reform programme... Ian Botham is attempting to emulate the feat of Hannibal two thousand years ago in crossing the Alps.*

emulsifier /ɪmʌlsɪfaɪə/ **emulsifiers**
NC An **emulsifier** is a substance used in food manufacturing which helps to combine liquids of different thicknesses. *...food additives such as thickeners, flavour enhancers, emulsifiers, colourings, to name a few.*

emulsify /ɪmʌlsɪfaɪ/ **emulsifies, emulsifying, emulsified**
V-ERG When two liquids of different thicknesses **emulsify** or when something **emulsifies** them, they combine; a technical term. *Spraying operations from aircraft have dispersed or emulsified much of the thousand tonnes of oil that were spilt.*

emulsion /ɪmʌlʃn/ **emulsions, emulsioning, emulsioned**
1 NU **Emulsion** or **emulsion paint** is a water-based paint which is used for painting walls and ceilings. *...dark brown carved wood set against white emulsion.*
2 VO If you **emulsion** something, you paint it with emulsion paint. *...an ordinary, flat emulsioned wall.*
3 NUorNC **Emulsion** is a substance that is used to make photographic film sensitive to light; a technical use. *There was a fault in the photographic emulsion... Photo stencil emulsions can be used for screen printing.*

-en /-n, -ən/
SUFFIX **-en** is used instead of '-ed' to form the past participle of some verbs, such as 'take' and 'give'. See **-ed.**

enable /ɪneɪbl/ **enables, enabling, enabled**
VO+*to*-INF If someone or something **enables** you to do something, they make it possible for you to do it. *...the feathers that enable a bird to fly... They made a donation to the Prince's Trust charity to enable 250 young people to start a business of their own.*

enact /ɪnækt/ **enacts, enacting, enacted**; a formal word.
1 VO When a government **enacts** a proposal, they make it into a law. *They do have to obey laws enacted by Congress... In the meantime, Serbia will enact a new constitution, establishing a legal basis for multi-party politics.*
2 VO If people **enact** a story or play, they act it. *This beautiful woman could enact the most passionate love-affairs on the screen... The children enact games of being soldiers, which help them through their fears.*

enactment /ɪnæktmənt/ **enactments**; a formal word.
1 NUorNC The **enactment** of a law is the process in a parliament or legislative assembly by which it is agreed upon and made official. *They succeeded in forcing the Bill's acceptance and immediate enactment... The enactment of political reforms is less certain.*
2 NU The **enactment** of a play, story, or character is the performance of it by an actor or group of actors. *...his dramatic enactment of Marcus's plight... Three men had their hands nailed to crosses in an enactment of the Crucifixion.*

enamel /ɪnæml/
1 NU **Enamel** is a substance like glass which can be heated and used to decorate or protect metal, glass, or pottery. *It is made from top quality materials with a stove enamel all-weather finish.*
2 NU **Enamel** is also the hard white substance that forms the outer part of a tooth. *It adheres directly to the tooth enamel without the drilling required to fix a conventional filling.*

enamelled /ɪnæmld/; spelt **enameled** in American English.
ADJ ATTRIB Something that is **enamelled** is decorated or covered with enamel. *...a line of enamelled blue pennants.*

enamoured /ɪnæməd/; spelt **enamored** in American English.
ADJ PRED+*of* If you are **enamoured** of someone or

something, you like them very much; a literary word.
*I was, of course, always enamoured of the theatre...
The ladies at the court of Elizabeth were enamoured
of the startlingly pale faces produced by heavy white
make-up.*

en bloc /ɒnᵒ blɒk/
ADV **En bloc** means as a group; a formal expression.
*...a system which teaches the young, en bloc, a
number of beliefs.*

encamp /ɪŋkæmp/ **encamps, encamping, encamped**
V When people **encamp**, they set up their camp; a
formal word. *His tribe had encamped for the summer
up at the quarry... The army was encamped outside
the walls.*

encampment /ɪŋkæmpmənt/ **encampments**
NC An **encampment** is a group of tents or other
shelters put together in one place, for example by
soldiers or gypsies. *We made our way down to the
encampment below.*

encapsulate /ɪŋkæpsjʊleɪt/ **encapsulates,
encapsulating, encapsulated**
VO If something **encapsulates** facts or ideas, it
contains or represents them in a very small space or
in a single object or event; a formal word. *A play
was written, encapsulating the main arguments... The
same year, he married the woman who encapsulated
the Hollywood dream— Marylin Monroe.*

encase /ɪŋkeɪs/ **encases, encasing, encased**
VO If something **is encased** in a container or material,
it is completely enclosed within it or covered by it.
*Her feet were encased in a pair of old baseball boots...
Left behind were hundreds of tons of explosives, many
now encased in ice.*

-ence /-əns, -ns/
SUFFIX **-ence** and **-ency** are added to adjectives,
usually in place of '-ent', to form nouns. These nouns
usually refer to states, qualities, or behaviour. Nouns
of this kind are often not defined but are treated with
the related adjectives. *...signs of affluence. ...the
prevention of delinquency.*

enchant /ɪntʃɑːnt/ **enchants, enchanting, enchanted**
1 VO If someone or something **enchants** you, they fill
you with a feeling of great delight. *Her charisma
managed to enchant the audience... He could pick up
the sax and enchant listeners with its sound.*
2 VO To **enchant** someone or something also means to
put a magic spell on them, especially in fairy stories.
*In the legend, the nightingale sings all night and
enchants the snake.*

enchanted /ɪntʃɑːntɪd/
1 ADJ If you are **enchanted** by something or someone,
you find them very pleasing. *When I found it was
about someone's experience on a mountain, I was
enchanted.*
2 ADJ If you describe a place or event as **enchanted**,
you mean that it seems as lovely or strange as
something in a fairy story. *...an enchanted island.*

enchanter /ɪntʃɑːntə/ **enchanters**
NC An **enchanter** is a person who uses magic to put
spells on people, for example in fairy stories. *Their
enchanter is the evil von Rothbart.*

enchanting /ɪntʃɑːntɪŋ/
ADJ **Enchanting** means lovely or very pleasing. *...the
most enchanting smile... We walked through narrow
cobbled streets, past enchanting 14th and 15th century
buildings.*

enchantment /ɪntʃɑːntmənt/ **enchantments**
1 NU **Enchantment** is the feeling of great delight that
something very beautiful or mysterious gives you.
*Those woods where he played as a boy still retained
for him a secret, subtle enchantment... His simple line
drawings lend a childlike enchantment to a scene.*
2 NC An **enchantment** is a magic spell, for example in
fairy stories. *Her novel 'Possession' has lots of spells
and enchantments in it.*

enchantress /ɪntʃɑːntrəs/ **enchantresses**
NC An **enchantress** is a woman who uses magic to put
spells on people, for example in fairy stories. *The role
of the evil enchantress Odile presents a challenge to
the performer.*

encircle /ɪnsɜːkl/ **encircles, encircling, encircled**
VO To **encircle** someone or something means to

surround them completely. *'Not now,' she said,
encircling me with her arms... He has defended his
belief that the grasslands encircling London should be
developed for housing.*

enclave /eŋkleɪv/ **enclaves**
NC An **enclave** is a place that is different in some way
from the areas surrounding it, for example because
the people there are from a different culture; a formal
word. *...the Armenian enclave of Karabakh in
Azerbaijan.*

enclose /ɪŋkləʊz/ **encloses, enclosing, enclosed**
1 VO If an object is **enclosed** by something solid, it is
completely surrounded by it. *The statue is enclosed in
a heavy glass cabinet... The mature oaks will be
enclosed by railings and a security man will guard
them... Buried inside the concrete shell enclosing the
nuclear reactor is 20km of pipework.* ◆ **enclosed** ADJ
The reaction takes place within an enclosed space.
2 VO If you **enclose** something with a letter, you put it
in the same envelope. *I enclose a small cheque... An
appropriate answer is sent, often with a small gift
enclosed.* ◆ **enclosed** ADJ *...the enclosed list.*

enclosed /ɪŋkləʊzd/
ADJ An **enclosed** community or existence is kept
separate from the normal and typical activities of the
outside world. *They lived in an enclosed community.*

enclosure /ɪŋkləʊʒə/ **enclosures**
NC An **enclosure** is an area of land surrounded by a
wall or fence and used for a special purpose. *...the
public enclosure of a racecourse.*

encode /ɪŋkəʊd/ **encodes, encoding, encoded**
VO To **encode** a message or some information means
to put it into code. *...encoding missile test data...
We're built according to the design encoded in our
genes.*

encompass /ɪŋkʌmpəs/ **encompasses, encompassing,
encompassed**
VO If something **encompasses** certain things, it
includes all of them; a formal word. *...a policy which
encompasses all aspects of conservation... The area
known as Transcaucasia encompasses the Soviet
republics of Armenia, Azerbaijan, and Georgia... Do
you have any projects which encompass whole
villages?*

encore, encores; pronounced /ɒŋkɔː/ for the meaning
in paragraph 1 and /ɒŋkɔː/ for the meaning in
paragraph 2.
1 An audience shouts **'Encore!'** at the end of a concert
when they want the performer to perform an extra
item. *Thomas laughed as he heard the applause—
'Encore!' they shouted. 'Give us another!'*
2 NC An **encore** is an additional item that is
performed at the end of a concert. *I often use this
song as an encore... She returned for four encores.*

encounter /ɪŋkaʊntə/ **encounters, encountering,
encountered;** a formal word.
1 VO If you **encounter** someone, you meet them. *On
their journey they encountered an English couple...
The residents are possibly the least attractive group of
people I've encountered.*
2 VO If you **encounter** something, you experience it,
often for the first time. *They've never encountered
any discrimination... Her staff say it was one of the
largest crowds she had ever encountered. ...the
indigenous cultures and religions which they
encountered in their attempts to convert the world to
Christianity.*
3 VO If you **encounter** problems or difficulties, you
experience them. *The main problem that we
encountered was that there is no reliable way that can
be used to produce crystals... His proposals are likely
to encounter fierce opposition... The main danger is to
fishermen who may encounter snakes tangled in their
gear.*
4 NC An **encounter** with someone is a meeting with
them, particularly one that is unexpected or
significant. *This was the first official encounter
between the Roman Catholic Church and the
Communist government there... He had many
meetings with Bette Davis, after their first encounter
in 1972 until her death in 1989.*
5 NC+SUPP You can also refer to an experience of a

particular type as an **encounter**. *Some people acquired the virus as a result of a single sexual encounter... For many blacks, their first encounter with their own history comes at college or university.*

encourage /ɪŋkʌrɪdʒ/ **encourages, encouraging, encouraged**

1 VO If you **encourage** someone to do something, you tell them that you think that they should do it, or that they should continue doing it. *Her husband encouraged her to get a car... Peasant families should be encouraged, by incentives, to grow alternative crops.*

2 VO If you **encourage** a particular activity, you support it actively. *Group meetings in the factory were always encouraged... There was a period in the mid-seventies when political activity was encouraged. ...allegations that the CIA encouraged a wave of terrorist attacks.*

3 VO If something **encourages** an attitude or a kind of behaviour, it makes it more likely to happen. *This encouraged the growth of Marxism... Ministers are embarrassed by criticism that their policies are encouraging corruption.*

encouragement /ɪŋkʌrɪdʒmənt/

NU If someone gives you **encouragement**, they tell you that what you are doing is good and that you should continue to do it. *All I need is some encouragement!... With the encouragement from his high school English teacher, Carl entered the Tennessee State College in Nashville.*

encouraging /ɪŋkʌrɪdʒɪŋ/

ADJ Something that is **encouraging** gives you hope or confidence. *...a piece of encouraging news.*

♦ **encouragingly** ADV *Rachel smiled encouragingly.*

encroach /ɪŋkrəʊtʃ/ **encroaches, encroaching, encroached**

1 V+*on* or *upon* Something that **encroaches** on your time or rights gradually takes up or takes away more and more of these things. *The new law doesn't encroach on the rights of the citizen... In recent years, the central government has steadily encroached on the State's autonomy... There are elements in society who will defend the public sector against any attempts to encroach upon it.*

2 V, V+*on*, or V+*upon* If something **encroaches** on or upon an area of land or water, it gradually covers more and more of it. *Land shortages are a problem, especially where the desert has been encroaching. ...pastures encroached on by deserts.*

3 V+*on* or *into* To **encroach** on or into a restricted area that is controlled by someone else means to enter it illegally. *The Syrians killed five soldiers when they encroached on positions near the airport... A fishing vessel loaded with squid had encroached into Argentine waters.*

encroachment /ɪŋkrəʊtʃmənt/ **encroachments**

NCorNU An **encroachment** is an act of taking all or part of something away from someone or something. *...encroachments of civil liberties. ...an encroachment on their property.*

encrustation /ɪŋkrʌsteɪʃn/ **encrustations**

1 NCorNU An **encrustation** is a layer that has built up on a surface during the course of a period of time. *The scab-like blemishes sound as if they are an encrustation caused by skin oils... Going down the tunnel, I found this rather large encrustation which had built up within the tunnel.*

2 NCorNU An **encrustation** is also a layer of jewels, gold, silver, and so on, that is decorating something. *...the waist-length plumes, the encrustations of gold lace.*

encrusted /ɪŋkrʌstɪd/

ADJ If a surface is **encrusted** with something, it is covered with it. *There are sumptuous pieces of gold and silver work, encrusted with precious stones... We scrambled up the snow encrusted mountain paths.*

encumber /ɪŋkʌmbə/ **encumbers, encumbering, encumbered**

VO If you **are encumbered** with something, you find it difficult to move or to do something; a formal word. *...passengers who were encumbered with suitcases.*

encumbrance /ɪŋkʌmbrəns/ **encumbrances**

NC An **encumbrance** is something or someone that limits your personal freedom or hinders your movements; a formal word. *Encumbrances had been deftly removed.*

-ency /-ənsi, -nsi/. See **-ence**.

encyclical /ɪnsɪklɪkl/ **encyclicals**

NC An **encyclical** is an official letter written by the Pope and sent to all Roman Catholic bishops, usually in order to make a statement about the official teachings of the Church. *The encyclical concerns itself with moral rights and responsibilities. ...the Pope's recent encyclical letter on social justice.*

encyclopedia /ɪnsaɪkləpiːdiə/ **encyclopedias**; also spelt **encyclopaedia**.

NC An **encyclopedia** is a book or set of books in which many facts are arranged for reference, usually in alphabetical order. *The material is laid out, as in an encyclopedia, for easy reference.*

encyclopedic /ɪnsaɪkləpiːdɪk/; also spelt **encyclopaedic**.

ADJ Something that is **encyclopedic** is very full, complete, and thorough in the amount of knowledge or information that it has. *She knew her subject with encyclopedic thoroughness... David Caute's book is wide-ranging without being encyclopaedic.*

end /end/ **ends, ending, ended**

1 N SING The **end** of a period of time, event, or piece of writing is the last part of it. *...at the end of August... Germany was divided into two states at the end of World War Two... She read the first draft from beginning to end... At the end of the novel, Henchard is ruined materially and emotionally.*

2 N SING If something puts an **end** to an activity or situation, the activity or situation stops. *He urged an immediate end to all armed attacks... That was the end of the matter.*

3 NC+SUPP The **end** of something long and narrow is one of the extreme points furthest from the centre. *Sharpen a stick at both ends.*

4 NC+SUPP The **end** is also the point on something long and narrow that is farthest away from you, or farthest from the point where it is attached to something else. *The house is located at the end of a dirt road in a field of waist-high weeds... The end of its tail quivered... The rhino is the only animal in the world with a horn growing from the end of its nose.*

5 NC+SUPP **End** is also used to refer to either of the two extreme points of a scale. *Those on the higher end of the pay scale can usually find other jobs... Worse off are the Republicans who are at the other end of the political spectrum.*

6 NC+SUPP You can refer to a place that you are telephoning or travelling to as the other **end**. *The phone at the other end rang... The main task is to find out who should conduct the investigation at the European end.*

7 NC An **end** is the purpose for which something is done. *...their use of industrial power for political ends... To that end, Mr Baker will now fly on from Paris to Yemen.*

8 NC Someone's **end** is their death; a literary use. *He did not deserve such a cruel end.*

9 V-ERG If a situation or activity **ends** or if you **end** it, it stops. *The play ends with all the children playing and reciting... The trail ends one mile from Bakewell... I joined the club because I'd ended a relationship, and I wanted to get out and about without getting involved... He refused to end his nine-week-old hunger strike... I'd like to end with a poem by Denise Levertoff.*

10 V An object that **ends** with or in something has that thing on its tip or as its last part. *Each finger ends with a sharp claw.*

11 See also **ending**.

● **End** is used in these phrases. ● If something is **at an end**, it is finished. *The evacuation of the Armenian earthquake zone is nearly at an end... Are his days as a force in the Lebanon at an end?* ● If something **comes to an end**, it stops. *The general's seven year rule of South Korea comes to an end at midnight tonight... Their period in national service had come to* *an end.* ● **In the end** means finally, after a considerable time. *She went back to England in the end... If this in the end would produce more love and understanding, I would be very surprised.* ● If something is **an end in itself**, it is desirable, even though you may achieve nothing by it. *They do not see political pluralism as an end in itself... From its early beginnings, Mexican art has never been an end in itself, but a bridge to the past.* ● You say **at the end of the day** when you are talking about what appears to be the case after you have considered all the relevant facts. *The question at the end of the day is whether the house is actually worth that amount... The Foreign Secretary said that at the end of the day it is the German people who will decide.* ● If you manage to **make ends meet**, you have just enough money to live on. *Firms that fail to make ends meet are warned they could go out of business.* ● **No end** means a lot; an informal expression. *She had no end of trouble at school... I pleased her no end when I recognised the tune.* ● Something that happens for days or weeks **on end** happens continuously during that time. *The sound of transport planes can be heard for hours on end... The negotiators were locked up together for days and nights on end.* ● If you do something **to the bitter end**, you continue to do it for as long as possible, although it is very difficult or unpleasant. *The guerillas would fight to the bitter end, he said, in order to achieve their main goal... They will hold on to power to the bitter end, rejecting all intervention from the outside world.* ● **to get the wrong end of the stick**: see **stick**. ● **at a loose end**: see **loose**. ● See also **dead end**, **odds and ends**.

end up PHRASAL VERB If you **end up** in a particular place or situation, you are in that place or situation after a series of events, even though you did not intend to be. *Many of their friends have ended up in prison... We ended up taking a taxi there.*

endanger /ɪndeɪndʒə/ **endangers, endangering, endangered**
1 vo If something **endangers** people, animals, or places, it causes them to be in a situation in which they might be harmed. *The herbicides did not endanger human life... We must develop industrial processes which will not endanger the environment.* ◆ **endangered** ADJ *...endangered species of animals.*
2 vo If you **endanger** something, you do something that may damage it, destroy it, or put it at risk. *The result of the decision may be to endanger Austria's international reputation... This crisis could endanger the stability of the European continent... Ms Harman claims she did nothing to endanger national security.*

Endara Galimany, Guillermo
/giːljeəməu endɑːrə gælɪmɑːni/
Guillermo **Endara Galimany** became the President of Panama in 1989, after the overthrow of Manuel Noriega. He is the leader of the Democratic Civic Opposition Alliance (ADOC). Born: 1937.

endear /ɪndɪə/ **endears, endearing, endeared**
V-REFL or VO If someone's behaviour **endears** them to you, it makes you fond of them; a formal word. *He endeared himself to the ordinary people of the city... It was this approach that endeared Chiang Ching-Kuo to the people of Taiwan.*

endearing /ɪndɪərɪŋ/
ADJ If someone's behaviour is **endearing**, it makes you fond of them; a formal word. *...an endearing smile... He is in a very endearing way an emotional man.* ◆ **endearingly** ADV *...endearingly childish behaviour.*

endearment /ɪndɪəmənt/ **endearments**
NCorNU **Endearments** are words or phrases that you use to show affection; a formal word. *...murmuring endearments. ...terms of endearment.*

endeavour /ɪndevə/ **endeavours, endeavouring, endeavoured;** spelt **endeavor** in American English.
1 V+to-INF If you **endeavour** to do something, you try to do it. *He endeavoured to adopt a positive but realistic attitude... Both men have endeavoured to work together in a relatively peaceful fashion.*
2 NCorNU An **endeavour** is an attempt to do something, especially if it is new and original. *We must wish him good fortune in his endeavours. ...this*

exciting new field of endeavour.

endemic /endemɪk/
ADJ A condition or illness that is **endemic** in a particular place is found naturally or commonly among the people there; a formal word. *Until the 1940's, malaria was endemic in Ceylon.*

ending /endɪŋ/ **endings**
NC The **ending** of something such as a story or a play is the last part of it. *The best kind of story is the one with a happy ending.*

endive /endɪv/ **endives**
1 NCorNU An **endive** is a plant with crisp, curly leaves that are eaten in salads. *At nine came dishes of carrots, sprouts, endive and stuffing.*
2 NU **Endive** is the same as **chicory**; used in American English.

endless /endləs/
1 ADJ If you describe something as **endless**, you mean that it lasts so long that it seems as if it will never end. *...an endless search for food... The local radio plays an endless selection of nationalist songs. ...the ambulance crews, ancillary staff, medical secretaries; the list seems endless.* ◆ **endlessly** ADV *She used to nag me endlessly.*
2 ADJ **Endless** also means very large or long, with no variation. *...an endless sandy waste... Walking around the endless corridors of the palace of Westminster, one can often see MPs at work.*

endocrine /endəkraɪn/
ADJ ATTRIB **Endocrine** refers to the system of glands that secrete hormones directly into the bloodstream, such as the pituitary or thyroid glands; a medical term. *It would diminish the risk for endocrine related tumours like breast cancer.*

endorse /ɪndɔːs/ **endorses, endorsing, endorsed**
vo If you **endorse** someone or something, you say publicly that you support or approve of them. *The Germans and Italians endorsed the plan... A ten-point charter was unanimously endorsed, calling on the government to end racial discrimination.*

endorsement /ɪndɔːsmənt/ **endorsements**
1 NCorNU An **endorsement** is a formal or public statement that you support or approve of something or someone. *George Bush made one of the most positive endorsements of a single European market ever voiced by an American president... The Pope has issued his fullest endorsement ever of the Solidarity trade union movement.*
2 NCorNU An **endorsement** on someone's driving licence is a note saying that they have been found guilty of a driving offence. *He's already got three endorsements.*
3 NCorNU If you make an **endorsement** of a document or cheque, you write a note on the document or write your name on the back of the cheque.

endow /ɪndaʊ/ **endows, endowing, endowed**
1 vo If someone or something is **endowed** with a quality, they have it or are given it; a formal use. *O'Neill had been endowed with film star looks... He's the seventh son of a seventh son, which according to gypsy tradition endows him with psychic powers.*
2 vo If someone **endows** an institution, they give it a large amount of money. *The Association is trying to raise a million pounds to endow a research team.*

endowment /ɪndaʊmənt/ **endowments**
1 NC An **endowment** is a gift of money that is made to an institution such as a school or hospital. *Every penny of our endowment is spent on equipment... Most American universities depend on endowments and donations from benefactors.*
2 NC Someone's **endowments** are their natural qualities and abilities; a formal use. *His natural endowments made him specially suited to the work.*

endowment policy, endowment policies
NC An **endowment policy** is an insurance policy which will give you a sum of money after a certain number of years. *This policy offers life-time cover with flexibility to convert to an endowment policy.*

end product
N SING The **end product** of an activity or process is the thing that it produces. *The end product is an anti-cancer antibody.*

end result
N SING You can describe the result of a lengthy process or activity as its **end result**. *Diplomats say the talks are the end result of lengthy painstaking preparations... Although the conflicts differ, the end result is always the same.*

endurance /ɪndjʊərəns/
NU **Endurance** is the ability to bear an unpleasant or painful situation calmly and patiently. *They admired the troops for their courage and endurance... Kruger had competed in motorcycle endurance races.*

endure /ɪndjʊə/ **endures, enduring, endured**
1 VO If you **endure** a painful or difficult situation, you bear it calmly and patiently. *It was more than I could endure... There is no end to the humiliations you may have to endure.*
2 V If something **endures**, it continues to exist. *...a city which will endure for ever... A world lay ahead where peace endured.* ◆ **enduring** ADJ *...hopes for an enduring peace.*

endways /ɛndweɪz/
ADV Something that is **endways** to something else is placed at right angles to it. *The cottage is built endways to the road.*

enema /ɛnəmə/ **enemas**
NC An **enema** is a solution which is put into a person's rectum in order to empty their bowels, for example before an operation is performed. *...unconventional cancer treatment, such as caffeine enemas.*

enemy /ɛnəmi/ **enemies**
1 NC You can describe someone who intends to harm you as your **enemy**. *...an enemy of society... His angry and uncompromising style won him many enemies.*
2 N COLL In a war, the **enemy** is the army or country that you are fighting. *The enemy had been forced back. ...enemy aircraft.*

energetic /ɛnədʒɛtɪk/
1 ADJ Someone who is **energetic** shows a lot of enthusiasm and determination. *He is an energetic campaigner in the cause of road safety... He described British workers as loyal, adaptable, and energetic.* ◆ **energetically** /ɛnədʒɛtɪkli/ ADV *This right is energetically denied.*
2 ADJ An **energetic** person or activity does or involves a lot of physical movement. *...energetic young children... Do something energetic, play golf, swim, or ski.* ◆ **energetically** ADV *...acrobats energetically tumbling across the stage.*

energize /ɛnədʒaɪz/ **energizes, energizing, energized;** also spelt **energise**.
VO If something **energizes** you, it gives you the enthusiasm and determination to do something. *...a sparkling friendliness which had a curious energizing effect on Tom... On the other hand, this may energize black voters to go out and vote.*

energy /ɛnədʒi/ **energies**
1 NU **Energy** is the ability and willingness to be active, because you do not feel tired. *He has neither the time nor the energy to play with the children. ...a woman of energy and ambition.*
2 NC+POSS Your **energies** are your effort and attention, which you direct towards a particular aim. *Men like Muhammed Abdu poured their energies into religious reform.*
3 NU **Energy** is also power obtained from sources such as electricity, coal, or water, that makes machines work or provides heat. *...nuclear energy... Energy conservation groups have dubbed it a tragedy.*

enervated /ɛnəveɪtɪd/
ADJ If you feel **enervated**, you feel that you have lost your strength and liveliness; a formal word. *I leaned back, already enervated.*

enervating /ɛnəveɪtɪŋ/
ADJ If you feel that something is **enervating**, you feel that it takes away your strength and liveliness. *...a particularly enervating day.*

enfant terrible /ɒnfɒnⁿ terɪbl/ **enfants terribles**
NC An **enfant terrible** is a clever but unconventional person whose unusual behaviour or ideas cause anger or embarrassment among their friends or colleagues; a literary expression. *Jacques Derrida was an enfant*

terrible of the French intelligentsia.

enfeebled /ɪnfiːbld/
ADJ Someone or something that is **enfeebled** has become very weak. *...enfeebled through age... The dispute leaves his administration increasingly enfeebled. ...an enfeebled economy.*

enfold /ɪnfəʊld/ **enfolds, enfolding, enfolded**; a literary word.
1 VO If you **enfold** something in your hand or in your arms, you put your hand or arms around it. *Their arms reached out to enfold him.*
2 VO If something **enfolds** you, it surrounds you. *...this darkness that enfolds me.*

enforce /ɪnfɔːs/ **enforces, enforcing, enforced**
1 VO If people in a position of authority **enforce** a law or rule, they make sure that it is obeyed. *...officials who refused to enforce the immigration laws... The Indian army are enforcing a curfew and searching houses.*
2 VO If you **enforce** a particular condition, you force it to be done or to happen. *He enforced high standards. ...their ability to win—or enforce—the loyalty of peasants.* ◆ **enforced** ADJ ATTRIB *...a life of enforced inactivity... The rumour is that he has been sent on an enforced holiday.*

enforceable /ɪnfɔːsəbl/
ADJ A rule or agreement that is **enforceable** can be enforced. *...a civil contract enforceable by law... How enforceable or indeed effective do you think the blockade will be?*

enforcement /ɪnfɔːsmənt/
NU If someone carries out an **enforcement** of an act or rule, they enforce it. *...the enforcement of discipline. ...drug enforcement agencies.*

enfranchise /ɪnfræntʃaɪz/ **enfranchises, enfranchising, enfranchised**
VO To **enfranchise** someone means to give them the right to vote in elections; a formal word. *...the reform Acts of 1884 and 1918 enfranchised working men and women.*

enfranchisement /ɪnfræntʃɪzmənt/
NU **Enfranchisement** is the condition of someone having the right to vote in elections; a formal word. *...the enfranchisement of the masses.*

engage /ɪŋgeɪdʒ/ **engages, engaging, engaged;** a formal word.
1 V A or V-PASS If you **engage** in an activity, you do it. If you **are engaged** in it, you are doing it. *It was considered inappropriate for a former President to engage in commerce... The work we're engaged in is a study of heat transfer.*
2 VO If something **engages** you or **engages** your attention or interest, it keeps you interested in it and thinking about it. *Boredom has a chance to develop if the child's interest is not engaged.*
3 If you **engage** someone **in conversation**, you have a conversation with them. *The two men were engaged in an animated conversation.*
4 VO If you **engage** someone to do a particular job, you appoint them to do it. *The barristers are engaged by solicitors who brief them on the case... In Britain, two companies have engaged Soviet dancers in their companies.*
5 VO If a military force **engages** the enemy, it attacks them and starts a battle. *Guerillas of the ULA have engaged the security forces in gun battles.*

engaged /ɪŋgeɪdʒd/
1 ADJ If two people are **engaged**, they have agreed to marry each other. *We all get enormous pleasure from seeing a couple get engaged... It was love at first sight, and they were engaged in three months.*
2 ADJ If someone's telephone is **engaged**, it is already in use, so that you cannot get through on it. *Receptionists' telephones are always engaged.*
3 ADJ PRED If a public toilet is **engaged**, it is already being used.

engagement /ɪŋgeɪdʒmənt/ **engagements**
1 NC An **engagement** is an appointment that you have with someone; a formal use. *Mr Takishita's final engagement was with the Defence Secretary, Mr Frank Carlucci.*
2 NC An **engagement** is also an agreement that two

people have made to get married, or the period during which they are engaged. *Their engagement was officially announced on 5th August... Could this mean the end of Clark Kent's long engagement to Lois?*
3 NC A military **engagement** is an armed conflict between two enemies. *After 13 years of military engagement in Angola, Cuba is claiming part of the credit for the peace agreement. ...the rules of engagement.*

engagement ring, engagement rings
NC An **engagement ring** is a ring worn by a woman when she is engaged to be married. *The groom has spent nearly £300 on the engagement ring.*

engaging /ɪngeɪdʒɪŋ/
ADJ Someone who is **engaging** is pleasant and charming. *Lineker has the ability to say uncontroversial things in an engaging way.*

engender /ɪndʒendə/ **engenders, engendering, engendered**
VO If someone or something **engenders** a particular feeling, atmosphere, or situation, they cause it to occur; a formal word. *This engenders a sense of responsibility... The sense of desperation and hopelessness that this engenders is the number one political issue in Poland.*

engine /endʒɪn/ **engines**
1 NC The **engine** of a vehicle is the part that produces the power to make it move. *The Viscount used jet engine technology to drive the propellers.*
2 NC An **engine** is also the large vehicle that pulls a railway train. *It was 50 years ago that the Mallard railway engine set a world speed record of 126 miles per hour.*

engineer /endʒɪnɪə/ **engineers, engineering, engineered**
1 NC An **engineer** is a skilled person who uses scientific knowledge to design and construct machinery, electrical devices, or roads and bridges. *The railway locomotive, the Rocket, was built by the famous engineer George Stephenson.*
2 NC An **engineer** is also a person who repairs mechanical or electrical devices. *...a telephone engineer.*
3 NC In American English, an **engineer** is someone who drives a train. *It takes at least four—an engineer, two brakemen, and a conductor—to ensure a safe transit from A to B.*
4 VO If you **engineer** an event or situation, you cause it to happen in a clever or indirect way. *It was Dr Martin who had engineered Miss Jackson's dismissal.*

engineering /endʒɪnɪərɪŋ/
NU **Engineering** is the work involved in designing and constructing machinery, electrical devices, or roads and bridges. *Italian companies used to be noted for large-scale construction and engineering projects.*

England /ɪŋglənd/
England is a country of the United Kingdom of Great Britain and Northern Ireland. The population in 1989 was 48 million, which is more than four-fifths the population of the United Kingdom. England is divided into 46 counties and contains 130,439 square kilometres. London is the capital of England and of the United Kingdom.

English /ɪŋglɪʃ/
1 ADJ **English** means belonging or relating to England. *...the English countryside.*
2 NU **English** is the language spoken by people who live in Great Britain and Ireland, the United States, Canada, Australia, and many other countries. *Half the letter was in Swedish and the rest in English.*
3 N PL The **English** are the people who come from England. *She has been accused of being the most ambitious person in Westminster—not a trait the English admire.*

English breakfast, English breakfasts
NC or NU An **English breakfast** is a breakfast which consists of cooked food, such as bacon and eggs, in addition to toast and marmalade and tea or coffee. *The ticket includes a full English breakfast and a bottle of champagne.*

Englishman /ɪŋglɪʃmən/ **Englishmen** /ɪŋglɪʃmən/
NC An **Englishman** is a man who comes from

England. *For the first time, an Englishman has been elected to head the Order.*

Englishwoman /ɪŋglɪʃwʊmən/ **Englishwomen**
NC An **Englishwoman** is a woman who comes from England. *An Englishwoman was refused a job because she could not speak Welsh.*

engrave /ɪngreɪv/ **engraves, engraving, engraved**
1 VO If you **engrave** something with a design or inscription or if you **engrave** a design on it, you cut the design into its surface. *Dem Deutscher Volker, 'To the German People' is engraved in huge lettering on the Reichstag.* ♦ **engraved** ADJ *...engraved copper trays.*
2 VO+on or upon If you say that something is **engraved** on your mind, memory, or heart, you mean that you will never forget it; a literary use. *The events on the night of the crash were forever engraved on the minds and hearts of the townspeople.*

engraver /ɪngreɪvə/ **engravers**
NC An **engraver** is someone who cuts designs or inscriptions on metal, glass, wood, etc. *He learnt to be a wood engraver.*

engraving /ɪngreɪvɪŋ/ **engravings**
NC An **engraving** is a picture or design that has been either cut into a surface or printed from an engraved plate. *Among the museum's delights are many engravings derived from the work of the original explorers.*

engrossed /ɪngrəʊst/
ADJ PRED If you are **engrossed** in something, it holds your attention completely. *The hotel porter was engrossed in Pasternak's Dr Zhivago.*

engrossing /ɪngrəʊsɪŋ/
ADJ Something that is **engrossing** is so interesting that you do not want to do or think about anything else. *...two of the most engrossing books I have ever read.*

engulf /ɪngʌlf/ **engulfs, engulfing, engulfed**; a literary word.
1 VO If something is **engulfed**, it is completely covered and hidden by another thing, often suddenly. *The town was quickly engulfed in volcanic ash... After the crash, it exploded and was engulfed in flames... One day, the island will be engulfed by the rising sea.*
2 VO If something such as a feeling **engulfs** you, you are strongly affected by it. *...a world engulfed in hatred and intolerance... He warned that the Afghan conflict could engulf Pakistan.*

enhance /ɪnhɑːns/ **enhances, enhancing, enhanced**
VO To **enhance** something means to improve its value, quality, or attractiveness. *It would enhance his standing in the community... Public confidence is enhanced by public access to important information... The capacity of underground stations would be enhanced by the building of new short tracks.*

enhancement /ɪnhɑːnsmənt/
NU The **enhancement** of something is the improvement of it in relation to its value, quality, or attractiveness. *The Countryside Commission promotes the conservation and enhancement of rural areas in England and Wales. ...the enhancement of women's economic status.*

enigma /ɪnɪgmə/ **enigmas**
NC Someone or something that is an **enigma** is mysterious and difficult to understand. *Mrs Yule remains an enigma, revealing nothing of herself... He describes their views on Soviet naval policy as something of an enigma.*

enigmatic /enɪgmætɪk/
ADJ **Enigmatic** means mysterious and difficult to understand. *Donne is the most enigmatic of all our poets. ...an enigmatic smile.* ♦ **enigmatically** ADV *'You can try,' he said enigmatically.*

enjoin /ɪndʒɔɪn/ **enjoins, enjoining, enjoined**; a formal word.
1 VO+to-INF If you **enjoin** someone to do something, you order them to do it, especially when you are in a position of authority. *He enjoined them to be fierce and uncompromising... They were enjoined to be submissive.*
2 VO If you **enjoin** a particular kind of behaviour on someone, you order or recommend that they behave in that way, especially when you are in a position of

authority. *Zoe put a finger to her lips to enjoin silence... This religion enjoins poverty upon all its followers.*

enjoy /ɪndʒɔɪ/ **enjoys, enjoying, enjoyed**
1 V Oor V+ING If you **enjoy** something, it gives you pleasure and satisfaction. *I asked him if he still enjoyed politics, now he was retired... I hope you've enjoyed this brief visit as much as I have... Painting is something that I really enjoy doing... You will thoroughly enjoy reading it.*
2 VO To **enjoy** something also means to be lucky enough to have it. *They enjoyed exceptional living standards... Unlike Sikhs, for example, Muslims have not until now enjoyed protection against discrimination... Party members have enjoyed privileges that were denied the rest of the population.*
3 V-REFL If you **enjoy** yourself, you do something you like doing. *I'll now have more time to enjoy myself.*

enjoyable /ɪndʒɔɪəbl/
ADJ Something that is **enjoyable** gives you pleasure. *It certainly strikes me as a city which is an enjoyable city to be in... So this novel is not only enjoyable, it is also important in literary history.*

enjoyment /ɪndʒɔɪmənt/
NU **Enjoyment** is the feeling of pleasure you get from something you enjoy. *...the enjoyment that reading brings.*

enlarge /ɪnlɑːdʒ/ **enlarges, enlarging, enlarged**
V-ERG If you **enlarge** something or if it **enlarges**, it becomes bigger. *The original windows were enlarged by Christopher Wren. ...a natural chemical which makes the blood vessels enlarge.* ◆ **enlarged** ADJ *...abnormally enlarged tonsils.*

enlarge on PHRASAL VERB If you **enlarge on** or **enlarge upon** a subject, you give more details about it; a formal expression. *He enlarged on the glorious future he had in mind.*
enlarge upon PHRASAL VERB See **enlarge on**.

enlargement /ɪnlɑːdʒmənt/ **enlargements**
1 NU **Enlargement** is the process or result of making something larger. *The X-ray showed moderate enlargement of the heart... He opposed the enlargement of the Community to Portugal and Spain.*
2 NC An **enlargement** is a photograph that has been made bigger.

enlighten /ɪnlaɪtn/ **enlightens, enlightening, enlightened**
VO To **enlighten** someone means to give them more knowledge about something; a formal word. *The object is to amuse and enlighten the reader.*
◆ **enlightening** ADJ *...a most enlightening book.*

enlightened /ɪnlaɪtnd/
ADJ If you describe someone as **enlightened**, you mean that they have sensible, modern attitudes and ways of dealing with things. *Our enlightened social policies are much admired... He is campaigning for less military spending and a more enlightened foreign policy.*

enlightenment /ɪnlaɪtnmənt/
NU **Enlightenment** is the act of enlightening or the state of being enlightened. *These talks were intended to bring culture and enlightenment to the hearers.*

enlist /ɪnlɪst/ **enlists, enlisting, enlisted**
1 V-ERG If someone **enlists** or is **enlisted**, they join the armed forces. *He had enlisted in the Marines... They were enlisted into the 21st Regiment.*
2 VO If you **enlist** someone or **enlist** their help or support, you persuade them to help you. *...the opportunity to enlist so powerful an ally as Germany... General Merid enlisted the support of the commander of the air force.*

enlisted /ɪnlɪstɪd/
ADJ An **enlisted** man or woman is a member of the United States army or navy who is below the rank of an officer. *...two officers and four enlisted men.*

enlistment /ɪnlɪstmənt/ **enlistments**
1 NU **Enlistment** is the act of joining the army, navy, or air force. *...enlistment in the Air Force.*
2 NC An **enlistment** is the period of time for which someone is a member of one of the armed forces. *...a normal five-year enlistment.*

enliven /ɪnlaɪvn/ **enlivens, enlivening, enlivened**
VO If something **enlivens** an event or situation, it makes it more lively or cheerful. *The journey was enlivened by noisy goings-on in the next carriage.*

en masse /ɒn mæs/
ADV If a group of people do something **en masse**, they all do it together. *They threatened to resign en masse.*

enmeshed /ɪnmeʃt/
ADJ PRED If you are **enmeshed** in a situation, you are involved in it and find it difficult to escape; a formal word. *He was being enmeshed in the family business against his will.*

enmity /enməti/
NU **Enmity** is a long-lasting feeling of hatred towards someone; a formal word. *It had earned him the enduring enmity of the farmers.*

ennoble /ɪnəʊbl/ **ennobles, ennobling, ennobled**
VO To **ennoble** someone or something means to make them more noble and dignified; a formal word. *Suffering does not ennoble people.*

ennui /ɒnwiː/
NU **Ennui** is a feeling of tiredness, boredom, and dissatisfaction; a literary word.

enormity /ɪnɔːmɪti/ **enormities**
1 N SING The **enormity** of a problem or difficulty is its great size and seriousness. *Smith did not grasp the enormity of the danger involved... Only then can you grasp the full enormity of his task.*
2 NC An **enormity** is an action that is considered to be totally unacceptable. *Last night's programme set out the enormity of recent IRA outrages... The enormities of his régime were finally uncovered.*

enormous /ɪnɔːməs/
ADJ **Enormous** means extremely large in size, amount, or degree. *...an enormous cat... To his enormous delight he was elected.*

enormously /ɪnɔːməsli/
ADV You use **enormously** to emphasize the scale or extent of something. *It has increased enormously the demand for food in the third world... I became enormously fond of her. ...an enormously long room.*

enough /ɪnʌf, ənʌf/
1 DET or PRON **Enough** means as much as you need. *I haven't enough room... I hope it's enough... I had not seen enough of his work.* ▶ Also ADJ after N *The fact that he did so much is proof enough.*
2 PRON or DET If you say that something is **enough**, you mean that you do not want it to continue or get any worse. *I've had enough of the both of you... Don't tell me. I've got enough problems.* ▶ Also ADV *This thing is complicated enough already.*
3 ADV You use **enough** to say that someone or something has the necessary amount of a quality, or that something is happening to the necessary extent. *He was old enough to understand... The student isn't trying hard enough.*
● **Enough** is used in these phrases. ● You use expressions such as **strangely enough** and **interestingly enough** to indicate that you think a fact is strange or interesting. *The loss of my son had, strangely enough, made God more real to me... Interestingly enough, pregnancy rates were shown to be completely unaffected by consumption of alcohol.* ● **sure enough**: see **sure**.

en passant /ɒn pæsɒn/
ADV If you deal with or speak about something **en passant**, you do it quickly while you are doing something else, especially because you do not think it is important; a literary expression. *She felt that it was unimportant and could be dealt with en passant.*

enquire /ɪnkwaɪə/. See **inquire**.
enquirer /ɪnkwaɪərə/. See **inquirer**.
enquiry /ɪnkwaɪəri/. See **inquiry**.

enrage /ɪnreɪdʒ/ **enrages, enraging, enraged**
VO If something **enrages** you, it makes you very angry. *She was enraged by these remarks... This is likely to enrage British war veterans who feel that no British Royal should attend the funeral... Farmers are enraged because of a lack of guaranteed minimum prices.* ◆ **enraged** ADJ *Letters flooded in to MPs from enraged constituents.*

enraptured /ɪnræptʃəd/
ADJ Someone who is **enraptured** is filled with fascination, joy, and delight about something; a literary word. *We would gaze enraptured at the sunsets.*

enrich /ɪnrɪtʃ/ **enriches, enriching, enriched**
1 VO To **enrich** something means to improve its quality by adding something to it. *Pig manure has long been used to enrich soils... An awareness and understanding of death can enrich children's lives... In the beginning there's an idea. Then it's developed and enriched.* ◆ **enriched** ADJ *...enriched breakfast cereals.*
2 VO To **enrich** someone means to make them richer; a formal use. *The purpose of the colonies was to enrich the colonists. ...a ruler accused of enriching himself at his people's expense.*
3 VO To **enrich** a substance means to increase the proportion of one component in relation to the others; a technical term in physics. *Australia has denied allegations that the uranium has been illegally enriched, making it usable for nuclear weapons... The evidence shows that strontium 87 was enriched in the rock 65 million years ago.*

enrichment /ɪnrɪtʃmənt/
1 NU **Enrichment** is the act of improving the quality of something. *They seem to have gained a great deal of spiritual enrichment from the experience.*
2 NU **Enrichment** is also the act of making someone richer. *He told journalists that claims about his alleged enrichment were baseless... Mr Hurd declared that enrichment of the individual and the family should only be part of the Conservative agenda.*
3 NU The process of increasing the proportion of one component in a substance in proportion to the others is called **enrichment**; a technical term in physics. *New evidence indicates the existence of three programmes for uranium enrichment... They were using a form of enrichment technology which is now considered outdated.*

enrol /ɪnrəʊl/ **enrols, enrolling, enrolled**; also spelt **enroll** in American English.
V-ERG If you **enrol** on a course or if someone **enrols** you, you officially join it and pay a fee. *I enrolled at the University of Vienna. ...claims that those enrolled at the school were not genuine students.*

enrolment /ɪnrəʊlmənt/ **enrolments**; spelt **enrollment** in American English.
1 NU **Enrolment** is the act of enrolling or the state of being enrolled at an institution or on a course. *...the enrolment of Prince Charles at the University. ...organizing the enrolment of pupils.*
2 NC An **enrolment** is the number of people who are enrolled at an institution or on a course. *University enrolments had risen by 50 per cent.*

en route /ɒn ruːt/
ADV If you are **en route** to a place, you are travelling there. *You'll see plenty to interest you en route.*

ensconce /ɪnskɒns/ **ensconces, ensconcing, ensconced**
V-REFL or V A If you **ensconce** yourself or are **ensconced** in a particular place, you put yourself there firmly and comfortably, with no immediate intention of moving away. *I knew she'd ensconce herself in the corner by the fire... Karl was happily ensconced at West Point.*

ensemble /ɒnˢɒmbl/ **ensembles**
1 NC An **ensemble** is a small group of musicians who regularly play or sing together. *The Amadeus Quartet is one of the most famous ensembles in the world.*
2 NC You can refer to a matching set of clothes as an **ensemble**; a formal use. *A black silk tie completed the ensemble.*
3 NC An **ensemble** is also a group of things or people considered as a whole rather than as separate individuals. *The ultimate goal is always an ensemble of inner attitudes, whose consequence is to make us act efficiently... The virtue of the Mall is its ensemble, the irregular facade joined to balconies, gardens, and paths.*

enshrined /ɪnʃraɪnd/
ADJ If something such as an idea or a right is **enshrined** in a society or a law, it is permanent and protected; a formal word. *The universities' autonomy*

is enshrined in their charters.

enshroud /ɪnʃraʊd/ **enshrouds, enshrouding, enshrouded**
VO To **enshroud** something means to cover it completely so that it can no longer be seen; a literary word. *Gases and debris enshrouded the centre of the explosion.*

ensign, ensigns; pronounced /ɛnsn/ for the meanings in paragraphs 1 and 2, and /ɛnsaɪn/ for the meaning in paragraph 3.
1 NC An **ensign** is a flag flown on a ship to show what country that ship belongs to. *A huge red ensign bearing the names of all one hundred and six ships that took part was presented to the Chairman.*
2 NC An **ensign** is also a junior officer in the United States navy.
3 NC Until the late nineteenth century, an **ensign** was also a junior officer in the British army.

enslave /ɪnsleɪv/ **enslaves, enslaving, enslaved**
1 VO To **enslave** someone means to make them into a slave. *He was enslaved and ill-treated.* ◆ **enslaved** ADJ *...enslaved peoples.*
2 VO To **enslave** people also means to keep them in a difficult situation from which they cannot escape. *Men were enslaved by developing industrialism... Mr Chairman, you do not enslave one nation in order to free another.*

enslavement /ɪnsleɪvmənt/
1 NU **Enslavement** is the act of making someone into a slave or the state of being a slave. *...the systematic enslavement and exploitation of the masses.*
2 NU **Enslavement** is also the state of being caught or trapped in a situation from which it is difficult to escape. *...enslavement to the status quo.*

ensnare /ɪnsneə/ **ensnares, ensnaring, ensnared**
1 VO If you **ensnare** an animal, you catch it in a trap or snare. *The dolphins become ensnared in salmon nets.*
2 VO If you **ensnare** someone, you gain power or control over them, especially by using dishonest or devious methods. *A look would ensnare and enchant her completely... I decided to try to ensnare Mr Peake into doing it.*

ensue /ɪnsjuː/ **ensues, ensuing, ensued**
V If something **ensues**, it happens immediately after something else; a formal word. *The police pushed the crowd towards the town centre, where some ugly scuffles ensued... A long legal battle ensued as the British authorities tried to secure his extradition.*

ensuing /ɪnsjuːɪŋ/
ADJ ATTRIB **Ensuing** means happening immediately afterwards. *He had half killed the policeman in the ensuing fight. ...the ensuing months.*

ensure /ɪnʃɔː/ **ensures, ensuring, ensured**; spelt **insure** in American English.
V-REPORT or VO To **ensure** that something happens means to make certain that it happens. *I shall try to insure that your stay is a pleasant one... The government provided protection to the relief agencies to ensure the rice went to needy residents... The door did not lock, but at least it ensured a reasonable amount of privacy.*

entail /ɪnteɪl/ **entails, entailing, entailed**
VO If one thing **entails** another, it necessarily involves it or causes it. *The move entailed radical changes in lifestyle... An attack on Kabul was unacceptable because of the number of civilian casualties it would entail.*

entangle /ɪntæŋgl/ **entangles, entangling, entangled**
1 V-PASS A If something is **entangled** in something such as a rope, wire, or net, it is caught in it very firmly. *Suddenly she was entangled in the seaweed... A little white dog ran into the street and became entangled in the soldier's legs.* ◆ **entangled** ADJ ATTRIB *...the mass of entangled boughs.*
2 V-PASS A If you are **entangled** in something, you are involved in difficulties from which it is hard to escape. *The military did not want to get entangled in another war... The country became entangled in a grave economic crisis.* ◆ **entangled** ADJ *The oar got entangled in the weeds.*
3 V-PASS If you are **entangled** with someone, you are

involved in a relationship with them that causes problems or difficulties. *She got entangled with a pretty awful crook herself... A professional should do his work and not become entangled emotionally.*

entanglement /ɪntæŋglmənt/ **entanglements**
NCorNU An **entanglement** is a relationship with someone, especially a sexual relationship, that results in damage to your reputation; used showing disapproval. *Her role as his wife led to boredom and then an entanglement with Bartholomew... The decision represents a degree of entanglement the government probably does not want.*

entente /ɒnˈtɒnt/ **ententes**
NCorNU An **entente** or an **entente cordiale** is a friendly agreement between two or more countries. *The two leaders signed a treaty of entente and cooperation... Agreement by Britain and France to produce the new missiles together would give the entente cordiale new meaning, says the Independent.*

enter /ˈentə/ **enters, entering, entered**
1 VorVO When you **enter** a place, you come or go into it. *They stopped talking as soon as they saw Brody enter... Tom timidly entered the bedroom... During the raids, Dutch and Belgian premises were also entered.*
2 VO When you **enter** an organization, institution, or profession, you become a member of it or become involved in it. *He decided to enter college... She entered politics... After she finished her degree, she entered a firm of chartered accountants and married her boss... She announced that at this stage she would not enter a coalition government.*
3 VO If a new quality or feature **enters** something, it appears in it. *A note of resolution entered the bishop's voice... Concepts such as profit, loss, and productivity are beginning to enter Soviet economic life.*
4 VO When something **enters** a new period in its development or history, this period begins. *The industry entered a period of lower growth... The peace process has now entered a critical stage... I've said many times that we have entered a new era in world affairs.*
5 VOorV+for If you **enter** a competition or race or if you **enter** for it, you take part in it. *They are planning to increase the number of tournaments they enter... In the Americas Cup, the United States entered a catamaran against a conventional mono-hull... The two cars will be entered for this year's 24 hour race at Le Mans.*
6 VO If you **enter** a conversation with someone, you start to have a conversation with them. *She did not decide lightly to enter a moral debate about her policies... They are more concerned with job security than entering a debate about improving standards in schools.*
7 VO When you **enter** something in a book or computer, you write or type it in. *Enter it in the cash book... If we want to start a letter, you type this code, and that's the word 'Dear' entered into the computer.*
enter into PHRASAL VERB 1 When you **enter into** something important or complicated, you start doing it or become involved in it. *The Labour Government refused to enter into negotiations... They will now be entering into the unfamiliar world of international competition.* 2 If you **enter into** a discussion with someone, you start it or become involved in it. *...the decision of the United States to enter into a dialogue with the PLO... Instead of walking away, he entered into an argument with an Israeli colonel.* 3 Something that **enters** into something else is a factor in it. *Obviously personal relationships enter into it... The fourth member state, Italy, barely enters into this struggle.*

enterprise /ˈentəpraɪz/ **enterprises**
1 NC An **enterprise** is a company or business. *...large industrial enterprises. ...twenty of the country's largest and most profitable enterprises.*
2 NC An **enterprise** is also something new, difficult, or important that you do or try to do. *He had doubts about the whole enterprise... A conventional war would be a complex enterprise involving more than sheer size of forces... A spokesman said today the trip would be a fruitless enterprise.*

3 NU **Enterprise** is a system of business, especially one in a particular country. *Selling the state telephone network to private enterprise is an important test case.*
4 NU **Enterprise** is also willingness to try out new ways of doing and achieving things. *...men of enterprise, energy, and ambition.*

enterprising /ˈentəpraɪzɪŋ/
ADJ Someone who is **enterprising** is willing to try out new ways of doing and achieving things. *You are no longer the enterprising cook that once you were... An enterprising young Russian woman and her partner have come up with a new venture with a difference.*

entertain /entəˈteɪn/ **entertains, entertaining, entertained**
1 VorVO If you **entertain** people, you do something that amuses or interests them. *...keeping their children entertained... We entertained the guests with a detailed description of the party.*
2 VorVO To **entertain** people also means to give them food and hospitality, for example at your house. *The government is to reduce money spent on entertaining foreign guests... The delegates were entertained in fine style.*
3 VO If you **entertain** an idea or suggestion, you consider it; a formal use. *I wondered what could have led me to entertain so ludicrous a suspicion. ...their refusal to entertain Japan's claim to a group of islands off Hokkaido.*

entertainer /entəˈteɪnə/ **entertainers**
NC An **entertainer** is a person whose job is to entertain audiences, for example by telling jokes, singing, or dancing. *Josephine Baker became one of the world's leading entertainers in the 1920s.*

entertaining /entəˈteɪnɪŋ/
1 ADJ People or things that are **entertaining** are amusing or interesting and give you pleasure. *The plays are entertaining and accessible. ...Timothy Ward's entertaining account of his time spent in a Buddhist monastery.*
2 NU **Entertaining** involves giving guests food and talking to them. *...business entertaining... This reflects the quantity of entertaining the Queen has to carry out.*

entertainment /entəˈteɪnmənt/ **entertainments**
1 NU **Entertainment** consists of performances, films, plays, and so on that people watch for pleasure. *...a guide to London entertainment. ...the entertainment business.*
2 NC An **entertainment** is a performance which people watch. *...extravagant musical entertainments.*

enthral /ɪnˈθrɔːl/ **enthrals, enthralling, enthralled;**
spelt **enthrall, enthralled** in American English.
VO To **enthral** someone means to hold their attention and interest completely. *This extraordinary performer retains the power to enthral audiences... He also plays the saxophone, and was enthralled with Parker's music.* ◆ **enthralled** ADJ *400 people listened enthralled to an account of her journey.* ◆ **enthralling** ADJ *From the confines of Communist Europe there have sprung new, enthralling fashions.*

enthrone /ɪnˈθrəʊn/ **enthrones, enthroning, enthroned;**
a formal word.
1 V-PASS When kings, queens, or bishops are **enthroned**, they officially take on their role during a ceremony in which they are placed on a throne. *He was enthroned as Archbishop of Cape Town... The bewildered child was taken from his home to be enthroned as the fourteenth Dalai Lama.*
2 VOorVOA To **enthrone** an idea means to give it a prominent place in your life or thoughts because you consider it to be very important. *They wanted to help their Russian brethren to enthrone socialism.*

enthronement /ɪnˈθrəʊnmənt/ **enthronements**
1 NC An **enthronement** is a ceremony to mark the start of the reign of a king, queen, or bishop. *...the enthronement of George Neville as Archbishop of York... During the enthronement, the ensemble will sing Taize chants.*
2 N SING+SUPP **Enthronement** is also the act of giving something a prominent place in your life or thoughts because you consider it to be very important. *...the*

enthronement of reason.

enthuse /ɪnˈθjuːz/ **enthuses, enthusing, enthused**
V or V-QUOTE If you **enthuse** over something, you say excitedly how wonderful or pleasing it is. *...enthusing over a weekend spent in the Lake District... 'Brilliant,' he enthused.*

enthusiasm /ɪnˈθjuːziæzəm/ **enthusiasms**
NU or NC **Enthusiasm** is great eagerness to do something or to be involved in something. *He had embarked with great enthusiasm on an ambitious project. ...her enthusiasm for the theatre... You can get in touch, person to person, with someone who has the same enthusiasms as yourself.*

enthusiast /ɪnˈθjuːziæst/ **enthusiasts**
NC An **enthusiast** is a person who is very interested in a particular activity or subject. *The club opened a year ago to cater to gun enthusiasts living in the area... The death of Sherlock Holmes is being remembered around the world today by Holmes enthusiasts.*

enthusiastic /ɪnθjuːziˈæstɪk/
ADJ If you are **enthusiastic** about something, you want to do it very much or like it very much, and show this in an excited way. *Sarah is very enthusiastic about learning to read... There was an enthusiastic welcome for the several hundred who returned home this weekend.* ◆ **enthusiastically** ADV *I responded very enthusiastically... Abortion opponents hailed the decision enthusiastically.*

entice /ɪnˈtaɪs/ **entices, enticing, enticed**
VO To **entice** someone means to try to persuade them to go somewhere or to do something. *He wants to create a Church that can entice reasonable people back into it... Some retailers are trying to entice Christmas shoppers to buy their presents now.*

enticing /ɪnˈtaɪsɪŋ/
ADJ Something that is **enticing** is extremely attractive; a literary word. *Tanya's invitation seemed too enticing to refuse.*

entire /ɪnˈtaɪə/
ADJ ATTRIB **Entire** is used to refer to the whole of something. *He had spent his entire career on Wall Street... Almost the entire family have gathered in Delhi... They promised to pay compensation for the entire post-war period.*

entirely /ɪnˈtaɪəli/
ADV **Entirely** means completely. *It was entirely my own fault... I agree entirely... He had told them something entirely different.*

entirety /ɪnˈtaɪərəti/
If you refer to something in its **entirety**, you mean all of it; a formal expression. *If published, it must be published in its entirety.*

entitle /ɪnˈtaɪtl/ **entitles, entitling, entitled**
VO+to or VO+to-INF If something **entitles** you to have or do something, it gives you the right to have it or do it. *Their qualifications entitle them to a higher salary... They are entitled to argue their case in print.*

entitled /ɪnˈtaɪtld/
ADJ PRED You use **entitled** when you are mentioning the title of something such as a book, film, or painting. *...a report entitled 'Attitudes Towards Geriatrics'.*

entitlement /ɪnˈtaɪtlmənt/ **entitlements**
NC or NU An **entitlement** to something is the right to have or do it; a formal word. *...entitlements to welfare and tax benefits... Manual workers were limited to a shorter period of entitlement.*

entity /ˈentəti/ **entities**
NC An **entity** is something that exists separately from other things and has a clear identity; a formal word. *Increasingly, inner cities and suburbs are separate entities.*

entomb /ɪnˈtuːm/ **entombs, entombing, entombed**; a formal word.
1 VO If something is **entombed**, it is buried or trapped underground. *The site is now entombed in the foundations of a block of luxury flats.*
2 VO When a person's dead body is **entombed**, it is put into a grave or tomb. *...the linen cloth in which the body of Christ was entombed.*

entomology /entəˈmɒlədʒi/
NU **Entomology** is the study of insects. *The entomology department are working on various fungal pathogens of insects.*

entourage /ˈɒntʊrɑːʒ/ **entourages**
NC The **entourage** of someone famous or important is the group of assistants or other people who travel with them. *Among his entourage was a retired general.*

entrails /ˈentreɪlz/
N PL The **entrails** of people or animals are their intestines; a literary word. *Haggis, the Scottish national dish, is made of sheep's entrails.*

entrance, **entrances**, **entrancing**, **entranced**; pronounced /ˈentrəns/ when it is a noun and /ɪnˈtrɑːns/ when it is a verb.
1 NC An **entrance** is a way into a place, for example a door or gate. *...the entrance to the National Gallery... A guard pointed out the entrance, a thick steel and wire door.*
2 NC Someone's **entrance** is their arrival in a room. *Her father would make a sudden entrance... He makes a grand entrance, embracing everyone.*
3 NU If you gain **entrance** to a place, profession or institution, you are able to go into it or are accepted as a member of it. *Entrance to the professions is open to many more people... Brian Eno made a flamboyant entrance into rock music in the early 1970s.*
4 VO If something **entrances** you, it makes you feel delight and wonder. *He was entirely entranced by her... His flute playing is so hypnotic that even he becomes entranced by it.* ◆ **entranced** ADJ *Everyone sat entranced.*

entrance fee /ˈentrəns fiː/ **entrance fees**
NC An **entrance fee** is a sum of money which you pay before you enter a cinema, museum, etc, or which you have to pay in order to join an organization. *He used to look at the pictures outside cinemas, unable to afford the entrance fee.*

entrant /ˈentrənt/ **entrants**
NC An **entrant** is a person who officially enters a competition or institution. *Each entrant plays the music of their choice.*

entrap /ɪnˈtræp/ **entraps, entrapping, entrapped**
VO If you **entrap** someone or something, you trap them by tricking or deceiving them; a formal word. *A game warden conspired to entrap the poachers into a situation where they could be killed.*

entrapment /ɪnˈtræpmənt/
NU **Entrapment** is the practice of arresting someone by using unfair or illegal methods; a legal term. *Colonel Pakhtusov was caught in a so-called sting or entrapment operation mounted by FBI agents.*

entreat /ɪnˈtriːt/ **entreats, entreating, entreated**
VO+to-INF If you **entreat** someone to do something, you ask them very humbly and seriously to do it; a formal word. *He entreated her not to be angry.*

entreaty /ɪnˈtriːti/ **entreaties**
NC or NU An **entreaty** is a humble and serious request; a formal word. *Nobody listened to my entreaties... He would turn his eyes to me in dumb entreaty.*

entrée /ˈɒntreɪ/ **entrées**
1 N SING+SUPP The **entrée** to a particular place or group of people is the right to enter that place or to be accepted by that group. *I have the entrée into his house... She hopes one day to regain her entrée to polite society.*
2 NC An **entrée** is the main course of a meal or, in very formal banquets, a dish eaten immediately before the main course. *He ordered the most expensive hors d'oeuvre and entrée that the restaurant offered.*

entrenched /ɪnˈtrentʃt/
ADJ If something such as power, a custom, or an idea is **entrenched**, it is firmly established and difficult to change; a formal word. *...strongly entrenched ideas.*

entrepreneur /ˌɒntrəprəˈnɜː/ **entrepreneurs**
NC An **entrepreneur** is a person who sets up businesses. *The British entrepreneur, Richard Branson, has accepted an offer to become the director of a Soviet travel agency.*

entrepreneurial /ˌɒntrəprəˈnɜːriəl/
ADJ **Entrepreneurial** means having the qualities that are needed for people to succeed as entrepreneurs.

His energy and entrepreneurial spirit are legendary...
Southerners are seen as being ambitious,
entrepreneurial, snobbish, and wealthy.

entropy /ˈentrəpi/
NU **Entropy** is a state of disorder, confusion, and
disorganization; a formal word. *A decrease in entropy*
is always associated with an increase in organisation.

entrust /ɪnˈtrʌst/ **entrusts, entrusting, entrusted**
VO If you **entrust** something important to someone or
if you **entrust** them with it, you make them responsible
for it. *It was a task the Foreign Secretary had*
entrusted to him... Children are too young to be
entrusted with family money.

entry /ˈentri/ **entries**
1 NC An **entry** is something that you produce in order
to take part in a competition, for example a piece of
work or the answers to a set of questions. *...the five*
winning entries... The award is given, according to the
entry form, to an unpublished work of fiction set in the
future.
2 NC Something written under a particular heading in
a diary, account book, dictionary, or encyclopedia is
also called an **entry**. *Let me look up the entries for*
mid-June... In one diary entry, Bass admits to his
fantasy of witnessing the destruction of the trees.
3 NC An **entry** is also a way into a place, for example
a door or gate. *...the pretty screen at the entry to*
Hyde Park.
4 NC+POSS A person's **entry** is their arrival in a room.
At Derek's entry a few heads turned.
5 NU If you are allowed **entry** into a country or place,
you are allowed to go in it. *Many of his associates*
were refused entry into Britain... Several hearings are
required for entry into Canada... Soldiers have barred
entry to those who don't work in the building.
6 NU Someone's **entry** into a society, group, or activity
is the act of joining it. *...her entry into national*
politics... I myself opposed our entry into this war.
7 The words **no entry** are used on signs to indicate
that you are not allowed to go into a particular area or
through a particular door or gate. *The sign on the*
gate read 'no entry'.
8 NU **Entry** in a competition is the act of taking part
in it. *Entry is free to all readers.*

entwine /ɪnˈtwaɪn/ **entwines, entwining, entwined**
V-ERG If something **entwines** with something else or if
you **entwine** it, you twist one thing in and around
another thing. *The roots grow down and entwine in*
the mesh... One second later her fingers were entwined
in my own.

E number /ˈiː nʌmbə/ **E numbers**
NC **E numbers** are numbers which appear on food
labels to identify additives that have been approved by
the European Community as suitable preservatives to
be used in the product. People also refer to the
additives themselves as **E numbers**. *Everyone*
assumes that E numbers are terrible things, but
vitamin C has an E number.

enumerate /ɪnˈjuːməreɪt/ **enumerates, enumerating,**
enumerated
VO When you **enumerate** a list of things, you name
each one in turn; a formal word. *...a number of*
explanations, which he declined to enumerate.

enunciate /ɪnˈʌnsieɪt/ **enunciates, enunciating,**
enunciated; a formal word.
1 VOorV When you **enunciate** a word or part of a word,
you pronounce it clearly.
2 VO When you **enunciate** a thought, idea, or plan, you
express it clearly and formally. *The importance of*
Adam Smith today is that, to me, he enunciated some
eternal truths... He announced that there was no
change in the government policy enunciated by the
President.

envelop /ɪnˈveləp/ **envelops, enveloping, enveloped**
VO If something soft **envelops** an object, it covers or
surrounds it completely. *Mist was rising, enveloping*
the grey tree trunks.

envelope /ˈenvələʊp, ˈɒnvələʊp/ **envelopes**
1 NC An **envelope** is the rectangular paper cover in
which you send a letter through the post. *The result*
has been placed in a sealed envelope and is not due to
be opened until tomorrow.

2 NC An **envelope** is also a substance that covers
another object, completely enclosing it. *...an envelope*
of membrane around the cell. ...the earth's magnetic
envelope.

enviable /ˈenviəbl/
ADJ You describe something such as a quality as
enviable when someone else has it and you wish that
you had it yourself. *She learned to speak foreign*
languages with enviable fluency.

envious /ˈenviəs/
ADJ Someone who is **envious** of someone else wishes
they could have the things that the other person has.
Envious, angry, and determined to get back his
money, he bullied her into working off the debt... I
remember this girl in college, I was always very
envious of her. ◆ **enviously** ADV *They were watched*
enviously by the rest of the crowd.

environment /ɪnˈvaɪərənmənt/ **environments**
1 NCorNU Your **environment** is everything around you
that affects your daily life, for example where you live
and the people and things that affect you. *Could the*
college provide a stimulating environment?... Are we
more influenced by environment or heredity?
2 N SING The **environment** is the natural world of land,
sea, air, plants, and animals. *We are fighting pollution*
to protect the environment. ...the Secretary of State
for the Environment.

environmental /ɪnˌvaɪərənˈmentl/
1 ADJ ATTRIB **Environmental** means concerned with or
relating to the natural world. *...environmental*
pollution... The environmental group Greenpeace is
sending a ship to assess the damage.
2 ADJ ATTRIB **Environmental** also means relating to the
surroundings in which a person or animal lives.
Corals are very demanding in their environmental
requirements.

environmentalist /ɪnˌvaɪərənˈmentəlɪst/
environmentalists
NC An **environmentalist** is a person who wants to
protect and preserve the natural environment.
Environmentalists have expressed concern about
safety at the nuclear plant.

environmentally /ɪnˌvaɪərənˈmentəli/
ADV You use **environmentally** to describe the effect
that something has on the natural world, such as
plants, animals, and the atmosphere. *Retailers hope*
to cash in on environmentally conscious shoppers in
search of low-energy light bulbs or non-toxic
cleaners... Not only are bicycles environmentally
friendly, they're also quicker in traffic jams... This is
not only expensive, it's environmentally damaging.

environs /ɪnˈvaɪərənz/
N PL+POSS If you talk about a place and its **environs**,
you are referring to the place and the area
immediately surrounding it; a formal word. *...Fleet*
Street and its environs.

envisage /ɪnˈvɪzɪdʒ/ **envisages, envisaging, envisaged**
VOorV-REPORT If you **envisage** a situation or event, you
imagine it, or think that it is likely to happen. *The*
last forecast envisaged inflation falling to about 10 per
cent... The party envisages that socialism can come
without civil war.

envision /ɪnˈvɪʒn/ **envisions, envisioning, envisioned**
VO If you **envision** something, you envisage it; used in
American English. *This envisioned a 10-15 per cent*
cut in weapons by 1994.

envoy /ˈenvɔɪ/ **envoys**
1 NC An **envoy** is a country's diplomatic
representative who is sent to a foreign country in
order to deliver a message or to take part in talks of
some kind. *A senior envoy from the Indian Prime*
Minister has arrived in Sri Lanka in an attempt to
diffuse the row between the two countries.
2 NC An **envoy** is also a diplomat in an embassy who
is immediately below the ambassador in rank. *Mr*
Basti was Iran's envoy in London until earlier this
week.

envy /ˈenvi/ **envies, envying, envied**
1 VOorVOO If you **envy** someone, you wish that you
had the same things or qualities that they have. *It*
would be unfair to envy him his good fortune...
Suchard also envies Rowntree its many different

brands and its skill in marketing them.
2 NU **Envy** is the feeling you have when you wish you had the same thing or quality that someone else has. *Her undisputed good looks caused envy and admiration.*
3 If you have something that other people wish they had, you can say that it is the **envy** of these people. *It has a robust economy that is the envy of its neighbours.*

enzyme /ɛnzaɪm/ **enzymes**
NC An **enzyme** is a chemical substance that is found in living creatures. An enzyme produces changes in other substances without being changed itself; a technical term in biology. *In the liver there are two families of enzymes called the cytochromes P450 and cytochromes P448. ...a rare enzyme deficiency.*

eon /iːɒn, iːɒn/. See **aeon**.

EP /iːpiː/ **EPs**
NC An **EP** is a record which is designed to be played at either 33 rpm or 45 rpm and which lasts for about 8 minutes on each side. EP is an abbreviation for 'extended play'. *This is from an EP called 'Crackers International', featuring four songs.*

epaulet /ɛpəlɛt/ **epaulets**; also spelt **epaulette**.
NC An **epaulet** is a decoration worn on the shoulder of certain uniforms, especially military ones. *There were narrow gold epaulets at the shoulders of his tunic.*

épée /eɪpeɪ/ **épées**
NC An **épée** is a thin, light sword that is used in the sport of fencing. *Thomas Gerull has won the individual épée event.*

ephemeral /ɪfɛmərəl/
ADJ Something that is **ephemeral** lasts only for a short time; a literary word. *The sad regression in that country showed how ephemeral progress could be... Stage performances, ephemeral by nature, are particularly hard to analyze.*

epic /ɛpɪk/ **epics**
1 NC An **epic** is a long book, poem, or film which usually tells a story of heroic deeds. *...Homer's epic poems 'The Iliad' and 'The Odyssey'.*
2 ADJ Something that is described as **epic** is considered very impressive or ambitious. *...his triumphant return after his epic voyage.*

epicentre /ɛpɪsɛntə/ **epicentres**
NC The **epicentre** of an earthquake is the place where the earthquake starts. *We could see that the damage was worse as the epicentre was approached.*

epicure /ɛpɪkjʊə/ **epicures**
NC An **epicure** is a person who enjoys eating food which is of very good quality; a literary word.

epidemic /ɛpɪdɛmɪk/ **epidemics**
1 NC An **epidemic** is an occurrence of a disease which spreads quickly and affects a large number of people. *The feared epidemic of cholera has not materialised. ...stemming the AIDS epidemic.*
2 NC An **epidemic** of something is the rapid way it develops and spreads. *He said pickpocketing had reached epidemic proportions... Marriages are down, and divorce has become an epidemic.*

epidermis /ɛpɪdɜːmɪs/
N SING Your **epidermis** is the thin, protective, outer layer of your skin. *These cells are just under the epidermis.*

epiglottis /ɛpɪglɒtɪs/ **epiglottises**
NC Your **epiglottis** is the thin flap at the back of your tongue which closes when you swallow food in order to prevent the food from going down your windpipe.

epigram /ɛpɪɡræm/ **epigrams**
NC An **epigram** is a short saying or poem which expresses an idea in a very clever and amusing way. *...brilliant epigrams of his own invention.*

epigrammatic /ɛpɪɡrəmætɪk/
ADJ Something that is **epigrammatic** is like an epigram. *...almost epigrammatic jokes.*

epilepsy /ɛpɪlɛpsi/
NU **Epilepsy** is a brain condition which causes a person to lose consciousness and have fits. *About 1 in every 100 people suffers from epilepsy to some extent.*

epileptic /ɛpɪlɛptɪk/ **epileptics**
1 ADJ Someone who is **epileptic** suffers from epilepsy. *This is a very useful aid in dealing with epileptic*

children. ► Also NC *The welterweight world champion Terry Marsh quit after being diagnosed as an epileptic.*
2 ADJ ATTRIB **Epileptic** also means caused by epilepsy. *The symptoms include panic attacks and epileptic fits.*

epilogue /ɛpɪlɒɡ/ **epilogues**
NC An **epilogue** is a passage added to the end of a book or play as a conclusion. *The book contains an epilogue with an update of the most recent events.*

Epiphany /ɪpɪfəni/
NU **Epiphany** is a Christian festival held on January 6th, which commemorates the arrival of the three wise men who came to see Jesus Christ soon after he was born. *The site is opened once a year for the Greek Orthodox clergy to celebrate Epiphany.*

episcopal /ɪpɪskəpl/
ADJ ATTRIB **Episcopal** means belonging or relating to a bishop; a formal word. *The Pope made four episcopal appointments this year.*

Episcopal Church
N PROP The **Episcopal Church** is a self-governing branch of the Anglican faith which is based in Scotland and the United States of America. *The Episcopal Church in the United States counts President Bush among its members.*

episcopalian /ɪpɪskəpeɪliən/ **episcopalians**
1 ADJ ATTRIB **Episcopalian** means belonging to the Episcopal Church. *Six Bishops of the Episcopalian Church are opposed to the ordination of women... They were married by an Episcopalian minister in Boston.*
2 NC An **Episcopalian** is a member of the Episcopal Church. *The parishoners are largely well-to-do Episcopalians of an evangelical persuasion.*

episode /ɛpɪsəʊd/ **episodes**
1 NC An **episode** is an important or memorable event or series of events. *A wartime episode had demonstrated his judgement of men... The episode has left doubts about the President's long-term health.*
2 NC An **episode** is also one of the programmes in a serial on television or radio. *In a recent episode of 'The Archers', the wall of Walter's cottage collapsed.*

episodic /ɛpɪsɒdɪk/
ADJ Something that is **episodic** happens at irregular and infrequent intervals; a formal word. *The book then returns to the beginning of the story and in rather an episodic, erratic sequence, describes the development of the project.*

epistle /ɪpɪsl/ **epistles**
1 NC An **epistle** is a letter; a formal, often humorous, use. *...a smudged, greasy, and tear-stained epistle which I received the other day.*
2 NC+SUPP An **Epistle** is also one of the books in the New Testament which were originally written as letters to early Christians by the apostles. *...the First Epistle to the Corinthians.*

epistolary /ɪpɪstələri/
ADJ ATTRIB An **epistolary** novel or story is one that is presented in the form of a series of letters; a literary word. *There's a whole chapter on how to write an epistolary novel.*

epitaph /ɛpɪtɑːf/ **epitaphs**
NC An **epitaph** is something written on a person's gravestone, or a sentence or short poem that summarizes a person's character. *Walter Mondale wrote his own epitaph, and said, 'I never really warmed up to television and television never really warmed up to me.'*

epithet /ɛpɪθɛt/ **epithets**
NC An **epithet** is an adjective or a short descriptive phrase; a formal word. *One of the kinder epithets applied to it in the press today is 'unfortunate'.*

epitome /ɪpɪtəmi/
N SING If you say that someone or something is the **epitome** of a particular thing, you mean that they are a perfect example of it; a formal word. *He was considered the epitome of a gentleman.*

epitomize /ɪpɪtəmaɪz/ **epitomizes, epitomizing, epitomized**; also spelt **epitomise**.
VO If you say that someone or something **epitomizes** a particular thing, you mean that they are a perfect example of it. *His failure epitomizes that of the whole movement... With his low-slung holster and well-worn*

hat, John Wayne epitomizes the American Cowboy.

epoch /iːppk/ **epochs**
NC An **epoch** is a long period of time in history; a formal word. *We are at the end of a historical epoch.*

epoch-making
ADJ Something that is **epoch-making** is considered to be extremely important or significant. *...Needham's epoch-making account of Chinese science and civilization.*

eponymous /ɪppnɪməs/
ADJ ATTRIB An **eponymous** hero or heroine is the character in a play or book whose name is the title of that play or book; a literary word. *...Cedric, the eponymous hero of Little Lord Fauntleroy.*

Epsom salts /epsəm sɔːlts/
N PL **Epsom salts** are a white powder which you can mix with water and drink as a medicine to help you empty your bowels. *Add Epsom salts and borax to the footbath water.*

equable /ekwəbl/
ADJ An **equable** person is calm and reasonable, and does not get angry quickly. *His qualities of sound judgement, combined with an equable temperament and a great capacity for friendship, marked him out as a physician of exceptional ability.* ◆ **equably** /ekwəbli/ ADV *'It suits me,' I said equably.*

equal /iːkwəl/ **equals, equalling, equalled**; spelt **equaling, equaled** in American English.
1 ADJ If two things are **equal** or if one thing is **equal** to another, they are the same in size, amount, or degree. *The cake was divided into twelve equal parts... The nurses marched through the city, demanding equal pay with their counterparts in the West... The commander of the Turkish contingent will be equal in rank to the commander in the full force.*
2 ADJ ATTRIB If people have **equal** rights, they have the same rights as each other. *...equal opportunities for men and women... All three factions are to have equal status.*
3 ADJ PRED If you say that people are **equal**, you mean that everyone has or should have the same rights and opportunities. *According to the Constitution everyone is equal before the law.*
4 NC+POSS Someone who is your **equal** has the same ability, status, or rights that you have. *We treat our enemies as equals. ...a woman conversing as an equal with the clerics.*
5 If two people do something **on equal terms**, neither person has any advantage over the other. *This law enables British shipbuilders to compete on equal terms with foreign yards... They have agreed to meet on reasonably equal terms.*
6 VC If something **equals** a particular amount, it is equal to it. *79 minus 14 equals 65.*
7 VO To **equal** something or someone means to be as good as or as great as them. *There are few film artists who can equal this man for sheer daring... His singing style was often copied but never equalled.*
8 ADJ PRED+to If someone is **equal** to a job or situation, they have the necessary abilities, strength, or courage to deal successfully with it; a formal use. *He was confident that the two people would be equal to the task ahead of them... He is determined to show that his government is equal to the problems facing South Korea.*

equality /ɪkwpləti/
NU **Equality** is a situation or state where all the members of a society or group have the same status, rights, and opportunities. *...equality between men and women... People favour socialism because of its fundamental fairness, equality, freedom, and democracy.*

equalize /iːkwəlaɪz/ **equalizes, equalizing, equalized**; also spelt **equalise**.
1 VO To **equalize** a situation, society, or system means to give everyone the same rights or opportunities in a particular area, for example society, education, wealth, etc. *It was thought that comprehensive schools would help to equalize society... Capital taxation will play a major part in equalizing the distribution of wealth.* ◆ **equalization** /iːkwəlaɪzeɪʃn/ NU *...the equalization of wealth through taxation.*

2 V In a game such as football, if a team or player **equalizes**, they score a goal that makes the score of the two teams equal. *England equalized at the beginning of the second half.*

equalizer /iːkwəlaɪzə/ **equalizers**
NC In a game such as football, an **equalizer** is a goal that makes the score of the two teams equal. *The equalizer came only minutes before the final whistle.*

equally /iːkwəli/
1 ADV **Equally** means in sections, amounts, or spaces that are the same size as each other. *On his death the land was divided equally between them... They are to combine to form a new company equally controlled by News International and the shareholders of BSB.*
2 SUBMOD or ADV **Equally** also means to the same degree or extent. *He was a superb pianist. Irene was equally brilliant... Are parents meant to love all their children equally?... The United States is equally anxious to preserve its status in Europe.*
3 ADV SEN **Equally** is used to introduce a comment which balances or contrasts with another comment that has just been made. *Each country must find its own solution to unemployment. Equally, each must find its own way of coping with inflation... The polls show that the party would have a better chance of winning if Mr Hestletine was the leader. Equally, there are many who may not like Mrs Thatcher much, but are not happy with Mr Hestletine either.*

Equal Opportunities Commission
N PROP The **Equal Opportunities Commission** is an organization which was set up by the government to make sure that the law on equal pay and the laws against sexual and racial discrimination are not broken. *The Equal Opportunities Commission report has shown that women in the NHS are discriminated against.*

equals sign, equals signs
NC An **equals sign** is the sign '='.

equal time
NU **Equal time** is the practice of giving all the candidates in an election or all the participants in a debate the same amount of broadcasting time on radio or television; used in American English. *Don Park, of Minnesota, believes we owe the interested parties some equal time.*

equanimity /ekwənɪməti/
NU **Equanimity** is a calm state of mind; a formal word. *They were content to accept their defeat with equanimity.*

equate /ɪkweɪt/ **equates, equating, equated**
VO If you **equate** one thing with another, you say or believe that it is the same thing; a formal word. *War should on no account be equated with glory. ...an old way of thinking which still equates energy growth with economic success.*

equation /ɪkweɪ3n/ **equations**
1 NC An **equation** is a mathematical statement saying that two amounts or values are the same, for example $6 \times 4 = 12 \times 2$.
2 NC An **equation** is also a situation where two or more parts must be considered together in order that the whole situation can be understood. *The hostage situation is part of a complex equation... Today's incident illustrated both sides of the equation.*

Equator /ɪkweɪtə/
N PROP The **Equator** is an imaginary line round the middle of the earth, halfway between the North and South poles. *Kourou on the coast of French Guiana is just 5 degrees north of the Equator.*

equatorial /ekwətɔːriəl/
ADJ ATTRIB **Equatorial** is used to describe places and conditions near or at the Equator. *...the southern equatorial regions.*

Equatorial Guinea /ekwətɔːriəl gɪni/
The **Republic of Equatorial Guinea** is a country in western Africa. It includes the islands of Bioko (formerly Fernando Póo), Corisco, Great and Small Elobey, and Annobón (formerly Pagalu). It was a Spanish colony, known as Spanish Guinea, from 1778 until independence in 1968. Lieutenant-Colonel Teodoro Obiang Nguema Mbasogo became President in a coup in 1979. He is a member of the Democratic Party of

Equatorial Guinea (PDGE), the only legal party, although a multi-party system is to be introduced. Lieutenant-Colonel Cristino Seriche Bioke Malabo became Prime Minister in 1982. Equatorial Guinea is a member of the Organization of African Unity. It exports cocoa, coffee, and timber. ◆ **Equatorial Guinean** /ɛkwətɔːriəl gɪniən/ N, ADJ ▪ *per capita GNP:* US$350 ▪ *religion:* Christianity (mainly Roman Catholic) ▪ *language:* Spanish (official), Fang, Bubi ▪ *currency:* CFA franc ▪ *capital:* Malabo ▪ *largest city:* Bata ▪ *population:* 344,000 (1989) ▪ *size:* 28,051 square kilometres.

equerry /ɪkwɛri/ **equerries**
NC An **equerry** is an officer of a royal household or court who acts as a personal assistant to a member of the royal family. *He is to be replaced by Commander Richard Aylard, a former equerry to the Princess of Wales.*

equestrian /ɪkwɛstriən/
ADJ ATTRIB **Equestrian** means connected with the activity of riding horses; a formal word. *Following the death of 19 horses last week, the future of the equestrian event is causing concern.*

equidistant /iːkwɪdɪstənt/
ADJ PRED A place that is **equidistant** from two other places is the same distance from each of them. *Six-inch stakes equidistant from the house marked the perimeter of her garden.*

equilateral /iːkwɪlætərᵊl/
ADJ An **equilateral** triangle has sides that are all the same length; a technical term in mathematics. *On the plan, the building is two 98 cm equilateral triangles placed back to back.*

equilibrium /iːkwɪlɪbriəm/
NU **Equilibrium** is a balance between several different forces, groups, or aspects of a situation; a formal word. *I believe this state of equilibrium will be maintained... Suffering helps to maintain a moral equilibrium in a society that is often motivated by greed.*

equine /ɛkwaɪn/
ADJ **Equine** means connected with or relating to horses. *...research into equine health.*

equinox /iːkwɪnɒks, ɛkwɪnɒks/ **equinoxes**
NC An **equinox** is one of the two days in the year when the hours of daylight and darkness are of equal length. *...the autumn equinox.*

equip /ɪkwɪp/ **equips, equipping, equipped**
1 V-REFL+*with* or VO+*with* If you **equip** yourself with something, or if someone **equips** you with it, you obtain it for a particular purpose. *They equip themselves with a great variety of gadgets... The enemy troops were equipped with tanks, aircraft and missiles.* ◆ **equipped** ADJ+SUPP *By contrast, their competitors were superbly equipped. ...locally recruited defence forces pitted against a much better equipped Federal Army.*
2 VO+*with* If something is **equipped** with a particular feature, it has it. *The card will be equipped with a built-in computer chip... It would be easier to equip the missiles with chemical than nuclear warheads.*
3 VO+*for* If something **equips** you for a task or experience, it prepares you mentally for it. *Little in their history has equipped them for coping with this problem.* ◆ **equipped** ADJ+SUPP *They were poorly equipped to deal with the situation... The paper believes that he is intellectually equipped for the task.*

equipment /ɪkwɪpmənt/
NU **Equipment** consists of the things which are needed for a particular activity. *...kitchen equipment.*

equipoise /ɛkwɪpɔɪz/
NU **Equipoise** is a balance existing between several different influences or aspects of a situation so that none of them is more important or powerful than the others; a formal word.

equitable /ɛkwɪtəbl/
ADJ In an **equitable** system, everyone is treated equally; a formal word. *...a more equitable distribution between Muslims and Christians on a 50/50 parity basis.*

equity /ɛkwəti/ **equities**
1 NU **Equity** is the quality of being fair and reasonable

in a way that gives equal treatment to everyone. *...an assurance of equity and social justice.*
2 NU **Equity** is the principle used in law which allows a fair judgement to be made in a case where the existing laws do not provide a reasonable answer to the problem; a legal use.
3 NCorNU If you have **equities** in a company, you have shares in that company whose rate of interest is not fixed; a technical term in economics. *The strategists advised investment in equities. ...a new factory in a developing country where shareholders equity was involved.*

equivalence /ɪkwɪvələns/
NU If there is **equivalence** between two things, they have the same use, function, size, or value. *Can we establish the equivalence of these two values?... There is some sort of moral equivalence between his regime and the Western democracies.*

equivalent /ɪkwɪvələnt/ **equivalents**
ADJ If things are **equivalent**, they have the same use, function, size, or value. *Women were paid less than men doing equivalent work... His job was roughly equivalent to that of the State Department's chief.*
► Also NC *A good quilt is the equivalent of at least three blankets.*

equivocal /ɪkwɪvəkl/
ADJ If something that you say or do is **equivocal**, it is deliberately ambiguous or hard to understand; a formal word. *He limited himself to an equivocal grunt.*

equivocate /ɪkwɪvəkeɪt/ **equivocates, equivocating, equivocated**
V When someone **equivocates**, they deliberately use vague and ambiguous language in order to deceive people or to avoid speaking the truth. *The temptation to equivocate was especially strong.*

er /ɜː, ə/
1 **Er** is used in writing to represent the sound that people make when they hesitate while they are deciding what to say next. *...and it was not until 1845 that, er, Texas became part of the USA.*
2 **Er** is the sound that people make when they want to attract someone's attention before speaking. *Er, ladies and gentlemen, dinner is served.*

-er /-ə/ **-ers**
1 SUFFIX You add **-er** to adjectives with one or two syllables to form comparative adjectives. You also add it to some adverbs that do not end in '-ly' to form comparative adverbs. *They are faced with a much harder problem... He apologized for not returning sooner.*
2 SUFFIX **-er** is added to verbs to form nouns referring to people or things that perform a particular action. For example, a reader is someone who reads. *...successive waves of invaders.*
3 SUFFIX **-er** is also used to form nouns that refer to a person with a particular job or to a person of a particular kind. *My grandfather was a miner. ...elderly pensioners.*

era /ɪərə/ **eras**
NC An **era** is a period of time that is considered as a single unit because it has a particular feature. *...a throwback to the Stalinist era... Her candidacy marked the beginning of a new era for the party.*

eradicate /ɪrædɪkeɪt/ **eradicates, eradicating, eradicated**
VO To **eradicate** something means to destroy or remove it completely; a formal word. *...the failure of the welfare state to eradicate poverty.* ◆ **eradication** /ɪrædɪkeɪʃn/ NU *...the eradication of apartheid.*

erase /ɪreɪz/ **erases, erasing, erased**
1 VO If you **erase** a thought or feeling, you get rid of it. *He cannot erase the memories of childhood.*
2 VO If you **erase** writing, you remove it by rubbing it with a rubber or cloth. *Gateshead erased Jenkins' name from the page.*
3 VO To **erase** sound or an image which has been recorded on a tape or information which has been stored in a computer means to remove it completely. *Teenage thieves erased vital details from the computer software.*
4 VO To **erase** something also means to remove it so

that it no longer exists; a formal use. ...*a campaign to erase hunger from the world.*

eraser /ɪreɪzə/ **erasers**
NC An **eraser** is a piece of rubber used for rubbing out writing; used in American English. *I like my pencils sharp and they have to have an eraser.*

ere /eə/
PREP or CONJ **Ere** means the same as **before** when it is used to refer to time; a literary word. *Sam well knew this habit of hers and had ere now taken advantage of it.*

erect /ɪrekt/ **erects, erecting, erected**
1 VO If you **erect** something, you build it or set it up so that it can be used; a formal use. *It would be splendid to erect a memorial to the regiment... This kind of tent is easily erected.*
2 ADJ People or things that are **erect** are straight and upright. *In the door, small but erect, stood an old man... She held herself erect.*

erection /ɪrekʃn/ **erections**
1 NU The **erection** of something is the act of building it or placing it in an upright position. *The building was badly damaged shortly after its erection. ...the erection of a gravestone.*
2 NC If a man has an **erection**, his penis is erect, because he is sexually aroused.

ergonomics /ɜːgənɒmɪks/
NU **Ergonomics** is the study of how working conditions, machines, and equipment can be arranged, in order that people can work with them more efficiently. *Ergonomics could be called the science of good design.*

ermine /ɜːmɪn/
NU **Ermine** is expensive white fur that is obtained from stoats. *...red robes trimmed with white ermine fur.*

erode /ɪrəʊd/ **erodes, eroding, eroded**
1 V-ERG If something such as someone's authority or their rights **are eroded** or someone **erodes** them, these authorities or rights are gradually destroyed or removed. *Our freedom is being eroded... Some provisions of the Bill erode civil liberties... Confidence in the dollar has eroded.*
2 V-ERG If rock or soil **erodes** or if water **erodes** it, it is gradually destroyed or removed. *...as one island erodes and another expands... The river has eroded the rocks.*

erogenous zone /ɪrɒdʒənəs zəʊn/ **erogenous zones**
NC An **erogenous zone** is a part of your body where sexual pleasure can be felt or caused; a formal word.

erosion /ɪrəʊʒn/
NU **Erosion** is the gradual removal or destruction of something. *Soil erosion is an increasing problem in the humid tropics. ...the loss of farmland by erosion. ...the erosion of individual freedom.*

erotic /ɪrɒtɪk/
1 ADJ **Erotic** feelings and activities involve sexual pleasure or desire. *...an erotic experience... The effect is titillating rather than erotic.*
2 ADJ **Erotic** paintings, books, and films are intended to produce feelings of sexual pleasure. *...an anthology of erotic verse.*

erotica /ɪrɒtɪkə/
NU **Erotica** refers to works of art that show and describe people engaged in sexual activity. It is intended to sexually arouse a viewer or reader, usually in a skilful and artistic way.

eroticism /ɪrɒtɪsɪzəm/
1 NU **Eroticism** is sexual interest and excitement. *...the helpless rapture of adolescent eroticism.*
2 NU **Eroticism** is the erotic quality of a book, picture, film, or sculpture. *The powerful eroticism of the book was a revelation.*

err /ɜː/ **errs, erring, erred**
1 V If you **err**, you make a mistake; a formal use. *Undoubtedly we have erred in giving such low status to our nurses.*
2 If you **err on the side of** a particular way of behaving, you tend to behave in that way. *Often one finds that advisers err on the side of caution.*

errand /erənd/ **errands**
NC If you go on an **errand** for someone, you go a short

distance in order to do something for them, for example to buy something from a shop. *They were forced to act as servants for senior boys, for whom they ran errands.*

errant /erənt/; a formal word.
1 ADJ ATTRIB **Errant** is used to describe someone whose behaviour or actions are considered unacceptable or wrong by other people. *They came straight up to me, like errant children, begging forgiveness. ...errant capitalist intellectuals.*
2 ADJ ATTRIB **Errant** is also used to describe a husband or wife who is unfaithful to his or her partner. *...laws that compel an errant husband to support his ex-wife.*

errata /erɑːtə/
N PL **Errata** are the mistakes that are made during the printing of a book; a technical term.

erratic /ɪrætɪk/
ADJ Something that is **erratic** does not follow a regular pattern, but happens at unexpected times or moves in an irregular way. *...the country's erratic attempts to move into the future... I made my erratic way through the dining room.* ◆ **erratically** ADV *Bullets whiz past erratically.*

erroneous /ɪrəʊniəs/
ADJ **Erroneous** beliefs or opinions are incorrect; a formal word. *These erroneous views have often led to discrimination against people with the HIV infection... This idea seemed to me totally erroneous.*
◆ **erroneously** ADV *They erroneously imagined that they had become wiser.*

error /erə/ **errors**
1 NC or NU An **error** is a mistake. *The doctor committed an appalling error of judgement... A degree of error is inevitable.*
2 If something happens **in error**, it happens by mistake. *Another village had been wiped out in error.*
3 **trial and error**: see **trial**.

ersatz /eəzæts/
ADJ Something that is described as **ersatz** is a poor imitation of the original thing; used showing disapproval. *It tasted more like ersatz coffee to me. ...an ersatz TV newscast featuring a mock TV anchorman introducing mock reporters.*

erstwhile /ɜːstwaɪl/
ADJ ATTRIB You use **erstwhile** to describe someone or something that used to have the job, position, or role indicated, but no longer has it; a formal word. *My erstwhile brother-in-law wants to see me.*

erudite /eruːdaɪt/
ADJ **Erudite** is the quality of showing great academic knowledge, and is used to refer to people and the things that they produce; a formal word. *...a highly erudite understanding of literature... She has a reputation for lengthy, erudite literary fictions.*

erudition /eruːdɪʃn/
NU **Erudition** is great academic knowledge; a formal word. *...a thinker of great originality and immense erudition.*

erupt /ɪrʌpt/ **erupts, erupting, erupted**
1 V When a volcano **erupts**, it throws out lava, ash, and steam. *The Nevado Del Ruiz volcano erupted in 1985.* ◆ **eruption** /ɪrʌpʃn/ **eruptions** NU or NC *...rock flowing out of the area in volcanic eruptions. ...a volcano on the point of eruption.*
2 V If violence or fighting **erupts**, it suddenly begins or intensifies. *Violence erupted after the demonstrators attempted to march to the presidential mansion... Widespread fighting erupted in the wake of Slovenia's and Croatia's independence declarations.* ◆ **eruption** NU or NC *This may have stopped the eruption of a major war between the superpowers... Albanian riots may spark off a new eruption of violence.*
3 V If an issue or a situation **erupts**, it happens suddenly or intensifies unexpectedly. *Controversy has erupted in Poland over the death of a Warsaw priest... A war of words has erupted between Saudi Arabia and Iran over this year's Hajj... The Cuban Missile Crisis had erupted.*
4 V When people in a place suddenly become angry or violent, you can say that they **erupt** or that the place **erupts**. *Anti-American riots erupted after the arrest of an alleged drug trafficker... The inhabitants had*

erupted in massive protests.

escalate /ˈɛskəleɪt/ **escalates, escalating, escalated**
V-ERG If someone **escalates** a situation or if an unpleasant situation **escalates**, it becomes greater in size, seriousness, or intensity. *Democrats were escalating their attack on the power of the President... Tension is escalating once again in the Afghan conflict... There is a danger that the conflict might escalate to a nuclear confrontation.* ♦ **escalation** /ˌɛskəˈleɪʃn/ **escalations** N U or N C *...a steady escalation of violence... There's always a danger of escalation.*

escalator /ˈɛskəleɪtə/ **escalators**
N C An **escalator** is a moving staircase which takes people from one level of a building to another. *The passenger stopped the escalator with its emergency button.*

escalope /ˈɛskəlɒp/ **escalopes**
N C An **escalope** is a thin boneless slice of meat, especially veal. Escalopes are often coated in egg and breadcrumbs, and then fried.

escapade /ˈɛskəpeɪd/ **escapades**
N C An **escapade** is an exciting and sometimes dangerous adventure. *She enjoyed the escapade... The whole school knew every detail of this mad escapade.*

escape /ɪskeɪp/ **escapes, escaping, escaped**
1 V A or V If you **escape** from a place, you succeed in getting away from it. *On 7 October Eva escaped from prison... He escaped to Britain... He was shot by a gunman who escaped on foot.* ♦ **escaped** ADJ ATTRIB *He had shot and killed two escaped convicts.*
2 N U or N C An **escape** is the act of escaping from a particular place or situation. *Unsuccessful escapes have ended in death... Those seeking escape from poverty in Latin America.*
3 V C or V A You can say that you **escape** when you survive something such as an accident. *Fortunately we all escaped unhurt... The minister escaped without a scratch.*
4 V O If you **escape** something or someone, you succeed in avoiding them. *Only the Interior Minister escaped arrest... Ralph was thankful to have escaped responsibility... She would marry the first man who asked her, in order to escape her father.*
5 N C An **escape** is a way of avoiding difficulties or responsibilities. *Reading is an escape from reality.*
6 V O If something **escapes** you or **escapes** your attention, you do not know about it or do not remember it. *I doubt that such tactics escaped their notice... Their names escaped him.*
7 V When a gas or liquid **escapes**, it leaks from a pipe or container. *...air escaping from a tyre.*
8 See also **fire escape**.

escapism /ɪskeɪpɪzəm/
N U **Escapism** consists of thoughts or activities involving pleasant ideas instead of the boring aspects of your life. *Thinking about the future is a form of escapism.*

escapist /ɪskeɪpɪst/ **escapists**
1 ADJ **Escapist** stories and films concentrate on pleasant or fantastic subjects and are intended to entertain an audience rather than involve them in complex or serious themes. *It is accepted by all as light, escapist, television stuff... The film is an escapist fantasy.*
2 N C An **escapist** is someone who thinks a lot about imaginary things in order to avoid thinking about their ordinary life.

escapologist /ˌɛskəˈpɒlədʒɪst/ **escapologists**
N C An **escapologist** is someone who entertains audiences by being tied up and placed in a dangerous situation, such as a tank full of water, and escaping from it.

escarpment /ɪskɑːpmənt/ **escarpments**
N C An **escarpment** is a wide, steep slope on a ridge or mountain. *The foot of the spectacular escarpment marks the northern edge of the Gebel Gharbi range.*

eschew /ɪstʃuː/ **eschews, eschewing, eschewed**
V O If you **eschew** something, you deliberately avoid doing it or becoming involved in it; a formal word. *Evans eschewed costly ideas such as financing new prisons... A civilized leader must eschew violence.*

escort, escorts, escorting, escorted; pronounced /ˈɛskɔːt/ when it is a noun and /ɪskɔːt/ when it is a verb.
1 N C An **escort** is a person who goes somewhere with you to protect you. *The guests will get a police escort.* ● If someone is taken somewhere **under escort**, they are accompanied by guards, either because they have been arrested or because they are very important. *...to prevent remand prisoners being brought long distances under escort to attend court.*
2 V O A If you **escort** someone somewhere, you go there with them to make sure that they leave a place or get to their destination. *He escorted me to the door.*

ESL /iːɛsɛl/
N U **ESL** is used to refer to things that are connected with the teaching of English to people whose first language is not English. ESL is an abbreviation for 'English as a second language'.

esophagus /iːsɒfəgəs/. See **oesophagus**.

esoteric /ˌɛsəʊterɪk, ˌiːsəʊterɪk/
ADJ Something that is **esoteric** is understood by only a small number of people who have a special knowledge or interest in the subject; a formal word, used showing disapproval. *...an esoteric script that few people can read.*

ESP /iːɛspiː/
1 N U **ESP** is used to refer to things that are connected with the teaching of English to people who need it for a particular purpose. ESP is an abbreviation for 'English for specific purposes' or 'English for special purposes'.
2 N U **ESP** also refers to the ability that some people are believed to have of using their mind rather than their other senses to obtain details about their environment. ESP is an abbreviation for 'extra sensory perception'.

esp.
Esp. is a written abbreviation for 'especially'. *Everyone in the area, esp. children under 5, is at risk.*

especial /ɪspɛʃl/
ADJ ATTRIB **Especial** means exceptional or special in some way; a formal word. *He took especial care to vary his routine.*

especially /ɪspɛʃəli/
1 ADV SEN You use **especially** to indicate that what you are saying applies more to one thing than to any other. *He was kind to his staff, especially those who were sick or in trouble... Double ovens are a good idea, especially if you are cooking several meals at once.*
2 SUBMOD You use **especially** with an adjective to emphasize a quality. *He found his host especially irritating... These viruses are especially difficult to treat.*

Esperanto /ˌɛspəˈræntəʊ/
N U **Esperanto** is an invented language which consists of parts of several European languages, and which was designed to help people from different countries communicate easily with each other. *Iris Murdoch's books have been translated into 26 languages including Icelandic and Esperanto.*

espionage /ˈɛspiənɑːʒ/
N U **Espionage** is the activity of finding out the political, military, or industrial secrets of your enemies or rivals. *The Swiss threatened to throw them in jail for espionage.*

esplanade /ˌɛspləneɪd/ **esplanades**
N C An **esplanade** is a wide, open road where people walk for pleasure, especially by the sea in seaside towns. *She would meet me for lunch in the King's Hotel on the Esplanade.*

espousal /ɪspaʊzl/
N SING+SUPP The **espousal** of a particular policy, cause, or plan is the act of strongly supporting it; a formal word. *This espousal of disarmament lost him many friends.*

espouse /ɪspaʊz/ **espouses, espousing, espoused**
V O If you **espouse** a policy or plan, you support it; a formal word. *Both candidates espouse centre-left policies. ...the free-market philosophy espoused by Mrs Thatcher.*

espresso /ɛspresəʊ/ **espressos**
N MASS **Espresso** is a coffee drink that is made by

forcing steam or boiling water through ground coffee beans. ...*espresso coffee machines.*

esprit de corps /esprit̩ də kɔː/
NU **Esprit de corps** is a feeling of loyalty and pride that is shared by the members of a group who consider themselves to be different from other people in some special way; a formal expression. *The regimental system must be maintained for the esprit de corps that it brings to our front-line battalions.*

espy /ɪspaɪ/ **espies, espying, espied**
VO If you **espy** something, you see or notice it; an old-fashioned word, often used humorously. *Peter went right in and at this point espied the briefcase in the corner of the room.*

Esq.
Esq. is sometimes written after a man's name if he has no other title. **Esq.** is an abbreviation for 'esquire'. ...*James Dickson, Esq.*

esquire /ɪskwaɪə/
Esquire is a formal title that can be used after a man's name if he has no other title, especially on an envelope that is addressed to him.

essay /eseɪ/ **essays**
1 NC An **essay** is a short piece of writing on one particular subject written by a student. *I had to produce an essay on Herrick for my tutor.*
2 NC An **essay** is also a short piece of writing on one particular subject that is written by a writer for publication. *I read some of his political essays.*

essayist /eseɪɪst/ **essayists**
NC An **essayist** is someone who writes essays for publication. ...*the best political essayist in the country.*

essence /esns/
1 N SING The **essence** of something is its basic and most important characteristic which gives it an individual identity. *Competition is the essence of all games.*
2 ADV SEN You use **in essence** to indicate that you are talking about the most important aspect of something. *But this is not in essence a book about religion.*
3 NU **Essence** is a concentrated liquid used to flavour food. ...*vanilla essence.*

essential /ɪsenʃl/ **essentials**
1 ADJ Something that is **essential** is extremely important or absolutely necessary to a particular subject, situation, or activity. *Land is essential for food and for work. ...an essential qualification for a journalist... It is essential to set your targets realistically.*
2 NC An **essential** is something that is absolutely necessary for the situation you are in or the task you are doing. *I always considered a washing machine an essential. ...other essentials such as fuel and clothing... I had only the bare essentials.*
3 ADJ ATTRIB The **essential** aspects of something are its most basic or important aspects. ...*the essential feature of the situation.*
4 N PL **Essentials** are also the most important parts or facts of a particular subject. *Amendments are possible only if they do not alter the essentials of the plan.*

essentially /ɪsenʃəli/
1 ADV You use **essentially** to emphasize a quality that something or someone has, and to say that this quality is their most important one. *Phyllis was essentially a soft, caring person... We were living in a country not essentially different from our own.*
2 ADV You use **essentially** to indicate that what you are saying is generally true, and that other factors are not necessary for you to make your point. *Such theories are essentially correct... She essentially stopped eating.*
3 ADV SEN You can also use **essentially** to say what you think is the most important and relevant feature of someone or something, and to say that you are not describing it in detail. *Essentially, gravity is something which we feel we all understand.*

-est /-ɪst, -əst/
SUFFIX You add **-est** to adjectives that have one or two syllables to form superlatives. You also add it to some adverbs that do not end in -ly. ...*the prettiest girl she*

had ever seen... *It's the winning blow that strikes hardest.*

establish /ɪstæblɪʃ/ **establishes, establishing, established**
1 VO If you **establish** an organization or a system, you create it in a way that is intended to be permanent. *He had set out to establish his own business.*
♦ **established** ADJ ATTRIB ...*the established institutions of society. ...well established principles.*
2 VO If you **establish** contact with a group of people, you start to have discussions with them. *Liu Binyan said the Front would try to establish contacts with the underground groups within China... The Angolan government is keen to establish diplomatic ties with the United States.*
3 VO or V-REPORT If you **establish** that something is true, you prove that it is definitely true. *So far they have been unable to establish the cause of death... A court of enquiry established that there were faults on both sides.*
4 V-REFL+as or VOA If you **establish** yourself as something, or **establish** your reputation as something, you get a reputation for being that thing. *The Liberals established themselves as the major alternative... He quickly established his reputation as a radical... He established a reputation for extraordinary holiness.*

establishment /ɪstæblɪʃmənt/ **establishments**
1 NC+SUPP An **establishment** is a shop, business, or some other sort of institution. ...*the transformation of the old hotel into a five-star establishment... It is an essential defence establishment.*
2 N SING You refer to a group of people as the **establishment** when they have special power and influence in the running of a country or organization. ...*the British Establishment. ...the university establishment.*
3 N SING The **establishment** of an organization or system is the act of creating it. ...*the establishment of free trade unions.*

estate /ɪsteɪt/ **estates**
1 NC An **estate** is a large area of land in the country which is owned by one person or organization. *He bought an estate near Oxford.*
2 NC Someone's **estate** is the money and property they leave when they die. *She left her estate to her grandchildren.*
3 See also **housing estate, industrial estate, real estate, trading estate.**

estate agent, estate agents
NC An **estate agent** is someone who works for a company selling houses and land. *The code requires estate agents to explain fully all fees and charges.*

estate car, estate cars
NC An **estate car** is a car with a long body, a door at the rear, and space behind the back seats. *Just before the estate car drove up, a telephone call was made to the garage.*

esteem /ɪstiːm/
NU **Esteem** is admiration and respect; a formal word. *I know the high esteem you feel for our colleague here... Zapp had no great esteem for his fellow lecturers.*

esteemed /ɪstiːmd/
ADJ You use **esteemed** to describe someone who you greatly admire and respect; an old-fashioned word. ...*our esteemed employer, Otto Gerran.*

esthete /iːsθiːt/. See aesthete.
esthetic /iːsθetɪk/. See aesthetic.

estimable /estɪməbl/
ADJ Someone or something that is **estimable** deserves respect and admiration; a formal word. ...*valuable and estimable characteristics.*

estimate, estimates, estimating, estimated; pronounced /estɪmeɪt/ when it is a verb and /estɪmət/ when it is a noun.
1 VO If you **estimate** an amount or a quantity, you calculate it approximately or say what it is likely to be. *They were not able to estimate the cost.*
♦ **estimated** ADJ *In 1975 there were an estimated 6,000 children in community homes.*
2 NC An **estimate** is an approximate calculation. *According to some estimates the number of farms has*

increased by 50 per cent.

3 NC An **estimate** from a builder or plumber is a written statement of how much a job is likely to cost. *It is a good idea to get at least two written estimates to compare costs.*

4 V O or V-REPORT If you **estimate** something, you make a judgement about it based on the available evidence. *How would you estimate our chances?... It is estimated that about 150 people are now taking refuge in the four embassies.*

5 NC An **estimate** is also a judgement made about a person or a situation. *Thomas wasn't living up to my estimate of him.*

estimation /ɛstɪmeɪʃn/ **estimations**
1 NC An **estimation** is an approximate calculation, or the result obtained by it. *...an estimation of the speed of the air leaving the lungs.*
2 N SING Your **estimation** of a person or situation is your opinion of them. *His comments were, in my estimation, correct and most useful.*

Estonia /ɛstəʊnɪə/
The **Republic of Estonia** became independent of the USSR in 1991. It is one of the Baltic States located in the north-west of the former USSR on the Baltic Sea. It was an independent country from 1918 until 1940, when it was occupied by Soviet troops and became part of the USSR. Arnold Rüütel became President in 1990. Estonia produces oil and gas, chemicals, and textiles. ◆ **Estonian** /ɛstəʊnɪən/ N, ADJ
▪ *per capita GNP:* US$6,240 ▪ *religion:* Christianity (mainly Lutheran) ▪ *language:* Estonian ▪ *currency:* rouble, to be replaced by kroon ▪ *capital:* Tallinn ▪ *population:* 1.5 million (1989) ▪ *size:* 45,100 square kilometres.

estranged /ɪstreɪndʒd/
1 ADJ If you are **estranged** from your husband or wife, you no longer live with them. *The president has been sued by his estranged wife.*
2 ADJ PRED If you are **estranged** from your family or friends, you have quarrelled with them and no longer speak to them. *He knows I am estranged from my father.*

estrangement /ɪstreɪndʒmənt/ **estrangements**
NU or NC **Estrangement** is the state of being estranged from someone or the length of time for which you are estranged; a formal word. *...his estrangement from his son... This sense of isolation and estrangement was easy enough to understand.*

estrogen /iːstrədʒən/. See **oestrogen**.

estuary /ɛstʃʊri/ **estuaries**
NC An **estuary** is the wide part of a river where it joins the sea. *A project to build a dam across a river estuary on the Black Sea coast. ...the Thames estuary.*

et al. /ɛt æl/
The expression **et al.** is used after a name or a list of names to indicate that other people are also involved. *...an admirable paper by Harris et al.*

etc
etc is used at the end of a list to indicate that there are other items which you could mention if you had enough time or space. **Etc** is an abbreviation for 'et cetera'. *...window frames, floorboards, beams, etc... She had to cook, do the cleaning, make beds etc, etc.*

et cetera /ɛt sɛtrə/. See **etc**.

etch /ɛtʃ/ **etches, etching, etched**
1 V O or V If you **etch** a design or pattern on a surface, you cut it into the surface using a sharp tool. *The artists must have spent many hours etching the images on the walls. ...tiny conductors etched on the chip itself.*
2 VO If something **is etched** on your memory, it has made a very deep impression on you. *His face will remain permanently etched on my memory.*

etching /ɛtʃɪŋ/ **etchings**
NC An **etching** is a picture printed from a metal plate that has had a design cut into it. *His etchings and drawings never went out of fashion.*

eternal /ɪtɜːnl/
1 ADJ If something is **eternal**, it lasts for ever. *...the promise of eternal bliss.* ◆ **eternally** ADV *Something remained eternally unspoiled in him.*
2 ADJ **Eternal** truths and values never change and are

thought to be true in all situations. *...a society which lives by eternal principles.*

eternal triangle
N SING You use the expression **eternal triangle** to refer to an emotional relationship involving love and jealousy between two men and a woman or two women and a man.

eternity /ɪtɜːnəti/ **eternities**
1 NU **Eternity** is time without an end, or a state of existence that is outside time, especially the state which some people believe they will pass into after they have died. *The preacher promised us eternity.*
2 NC You can refer to a period of time as an **eternity** when it seems very long; an informal use. *I lay there for an eternity, coughing and gasping.*

ether /iːθə/
1 NU **Ether** is a colourless liquid that burns easily. It is used in industry as a solvent and in medicine as an anaesthetic.
2 N SING The **ether** is the air; a literary use. *...a stutter of Morse code whispering through the ether.*

ethereal /ɪθɪəriəl/
ADJ Something that is **ethereal** is so light and delicate that it seems almost supernatural. *...her ethereal beauty.*

ethic /ɛθɪk/ **ethics**
1 N SING+SUPP A particular **ethic** is a moral belief that influences people's behaviour, attitudes, and ideas. *...the American ethic of expansion and opportunity.*
2 N PL **Ethics** are moral beliefs and rules about right and wrong. *The episode underlines the power of the press but raises several questions about its ethics. ...medical ethics.*

ethical /ɛθɪkl/
ADJ ATTRIB **Ethical** means influenced by a system of moral beliefs about right and wrong. *She had no ethical objection to drinking. ...high ethical standards.*

Ethiopia /iːθiəʊpiə/
The **People's Democratic Republic of Ethiopia** is a country in north-eastern Africa. The main ethnic groups include Amhara, Tigréans, Oromos, Somalis, and Afars. In 1974 the emperor Haile Selassie was deposed and Ethiopia became a one-party state, ruled by a military committee, the Provisional Military Administrative Council (the Dergue). Lieutenant-Colonel Mengistu Haile Mariam came to power in 1977. By the 1980s there were several armed secessionist movements, including the Eritrean People's Liberation Front (EPLF) and the Tigré People's Liberation Front (TPLF). Somalia claimed the Ogaden region, which it invaded in 1977. Civil war between the armies of the various factions and the government severely damaged the economy and recurrent droughts caused widespread famine in the 1980s. In 1989 the Ethiopian People's Democratic Movement (EPDM) and the TPLF formed a coalition called the Ethiopian People's Revolutionary Democratic Front (EPRDF) which was allied with the EPLF. In 1991 the EPRDF entered Addis Ababa without resistance. Meles Zenawi, the leader of the EPRDF, became President of the interim government. The EPLF immediately announced plans to secede from Ethiopia. Ethiopia exports coffee. Huge foreign debts are a major economic problem. Ethiopia is a member of the Organization of African Unity.
◆ **Ethiopian** /iːθiəʊpiən/ N, ADJ
▪ *per capita GNP:* US$120 ▪ *religion:* Christianity (mainly Ethiopian Orthodox), Islam, animism
▪ *language:* Amharic (official) ▪ *currency:* birr
▪ *capital:* Addis Ababa ▪ *population:* 49 million (1989)
▪ *size:* 1,251,282 square kilometres.

ethnic /ɛθnɪk/
ADJ ATTRIB **Ethnic** means connected with different racial or cultural groups of people. *...the ethnic composition of the voters of New York. ...ethnic minorities.* ◆ **ethnicity** /ɛθnɪsəti/ NU *The Estonians are cousins to the Finns in terms of ethnicity, culture and language.*

ethnographic /ɛθnəgræfɪk/
ADJ Something that is **ethnographic** is connected with or relates to ethnography. *...minorities of an ethnographic kind.*

ethnography /eθnɒgrəfi/
NU **Ethnography** is the branch of anthropology in which different cultures are studied and described. *...the Institute of Ethnography of the U.S.S.R.*

ethnologist /eθnɒlədʒɪst/ **ethnologists**
NC An **ethnologist** is a person who studies and describes different cultures. *Mr Leiris was a noted ethnologist, specialising in African civilizations.*

ethnology /eθnɒlədʒi/
NU **Ethnology** is the branch of anthropology in which the organization and culture of different races of people are studied and compared.

ethos /iːθɒs/
N SING The **ethos** of a group of people is the set of ideas and attitudes associated with it. *There is a much more competitive ethos in British society. ...moral and religious ethos.*

etiquette /etɪket/
NU **Etiquette** is a set of customs and rules for polite behaviour in particular classes of people or professions. *...a book on etiquette.*

etymological /etɪmɒlɒdʒɪkl/
ADJ **Etymological** means concerned with or relating to etymology. *...an etymological dictionary.*

etymology /etɪmɒlədʒi/ **etymologies**
1 NU **Etymology** is the study of the origins and historical development of words.
2 NC The **etymology** of a particular word is its history.

eucalyptus /juːkəlɪptəs/ **eucalyptuses**. The plural form can be either **eucalyptuses** or **eucalyptus**.
NCorNU A **eucalyptus** is an evergreen tree. It is grown to provide timber, gum, and for its oil that is used in medicines. *...a forest of pines and eucalyptus.*

Eucharist /juːkərɪst/ **Eucharists**
N SINGorNC The **Eucharist** is the Christian religious ceremony in which Christ's last meal with his disciples is celebrated by the symbolic consecration of bread and wine at Mass during Holy Communion. *He celebrated the Eucharist every morning.*

Eucharistic /juːkərɪstɪk/
ADJ **Eucharistic** means concerned with or relating to the Eucharist. *The Pope said Mass at the end of the week-long eucharistic congress.*

eugenics /juːdʒenɪks/
NU **Eugenics** is the study of how to improve the human race by carefully selecting parents who will produce stronger children; a technical term. *...the problems and ethical issues arising out of eugenics.*

eulogize /juːlədʒaɪz/ **eulogizes, eulogizing, eulogized**; also spelt **eulogise**.
VAorVO If you **eulogize** over something or **eulogize** it, you praise it very much; a formal word. *On 28 May 1356, Bishop Henry was eulogizing over what Geoffrey had done. ...a new brand of literature that eulogized peasant life.*

eulogy /juːlədʒi/ **eulogies**
NC A **eulogy** is a speech or piece of writing praising someone or something; a formal word. *Countless eulogies have been written about her.*

eunuch /juːnək/ **eunuchs**
NC A **eunuch** is a man who has had his testicles removed. *A certain eunuch is attracting crowds in his home town.*

euphemism /juːfəmɪzəm/ **euphemisms**
NCorNU A **euphemism** is a polite word or expression that people use to talk about something they find unpleasant or embarrassing. *...those who are classified as unemployed, or 'waiting for jobs', to use the official euphemism.*

euphemistic /juːfəmɪstɪk/
ADJ **Euphemistic** language consists of polite words or expressions for things that people find unpleasant or embarrassing. ♦ **euphemistically** ADV *Then came what the French euphemistically call 'the events of May'—the student revolution.*

euphoria /juːfɔːriə/
NU **Euphoria** is a feeling of great happiness. *She shared Dan's euphoria over the play.*

euphoric /juːfɒrɪk/
ADJ If you are **euphoric**, you feel extremely happy. *The Palestinian mood was euphoric.*

Eurasian /juəreɪʒn/ **Eurasians**
1 ADJ **Eurasian** means concerned with or relating to both Europe and Asia. *...the Eurasian land-mass.*
2 NC A **Eurasian** is a person who has one European and one Asian parent; an old-fashioned use.

eureka /juriːkə/
Someone might say '**eureka**!' when they suddenly discover something, or when they solve a mystery or a problem; often used humorously. *All we get is sand— no nuggets, no gold and no one yells 'Eureka!'*

Euro- /juərəu-/
PREFIX **Euro-** is added to words to form other words that describe something which is connected with Europe or with the EC. *...at the Euro-summit. ...the Euro-tunnel. ...a Euro-MP.*

Europe /juərəp/
Europe is the world's second smallest continent, consisting of approximately 10 million square kilometres. Its population in 1986 was about 700 million, which is about one sixth of the world's population. Mont Blanc (4,807 metres) is the highest point in Europe. Main rivers include the Volga, Danube, Rhine, Vistula, Elbe, Rhône, and Oder.

European /juərəpiːən/ **Europeans**
1 ADJ **European** means coming from or relating to Europe. *President Mubarak of Egypt is seeking greater European support for the Middle East peace process.*
2 NC A **European** is a person who comes from Europe. *There aren't many Europeans living here.*

European Community (EC) /juərəpiːən kəmjuːnəti/
The Treaty of Rome in 1958 established the **European Economic Community** (EEC), with the intention of creating a Common Market in Europe. The Single European Act of 1987 aimed to create a single market within the EC by 1992. The headquarters of the European Commission and the Council of Ministers are in Brussels. The European Court of Justice is in Luxembourg. The European Parliament meets in Strasbourg and Luxembourg. Members of the EC are: Belgium, Denmark, France, Germany, Greece, Ireland, Italy, Luxembourg, Netherlands, Portugal, Spain, and the United Kingdom.

European Currency Unit. See ECU.

euthanasia /juːθənɔɪziə/
NU **Euthanasia** is the practice of painlessly killing a sick or injured person to relieve their suffering when they cannot be cured. *The Ministry would not intervene if hospitals decided to practise euthanasia on terminally ill patients.*

evacuate /ɪvækjueɪt/ **evacuates, evacuating, evacuated**
VO If people **are evacuated** from a place, they are moved out of it because it has become dangerous. *The entire complex was being evacuated... I was evacuated to Swindon in 1941... The authorities evacuated nearby villages.* ♦ **evacuation** /ɪvækjueɪʃn/
NU *Orders went out to prepare for the evacuation of the city... The evacuation of Indian nationals from Kuwait has continued.*

evacuee /ɪvækjuiː/ **evacuees**
NC An **evacuee** is someone who has been sent away from a place because it has become too dangerous to stay there, especially in war. *We crowded into the village hall, to await the arrival of the evacuees from Liverpool. ...bringing the women and children to evacuee camps in Jordan.*

evade /ɪveɪd/ **evades, evading, evaded**
1 VO If you **evade** something that you do not want to be involved with, you avoid it. *I evaded the issue... He had found a way of evading responsibility.*
2 VO If you **evade** someone or something that is moving towards you, you succeed in not being touched by them. *Tim tried to catch her arm but she evaded him.*
3 VO If something such as success or love **evades** you, you never manage to achieve it. *Military glory had evaded him throughout his long career.*

evaluate /ɪvæljueɪt/ **evaluates, evaluating, evaluated**
VO If you **evaluate** something, you decide how valuable it is after considering all its features. *He*

was asked to evaluate the situation.

evaluation /ɪvæljueɪʃn/ **evaluations**
NCorNU An **evaluation** is a decision about how significant or valuable something is, based on a careful study of its good and bad features. *...a realistic evaluation of the working of Britain's economy... They can help develop our powers of critical evaluation.*

evangelical /iːvændʒelɪkl/
ADJ People and beliefs that are **evangelical** are Christian and emphasize the importance of the four gospels of the New Testament. *...an article about evangelical Christianity. ...a minister who is evangelical and charismatic in his beliefs.*

evangelism /ɪvændʒəlɪzəm/
NU **Evangelism** is the teaching of Christianity, especially to people who are not Christians. *Many of these students are involved in evangelism.*

evangelist /ɪvændʒəlɪst/ **evangelists**
NC An **evangelist** is someone who travels from place to place in order to try to convert people to Christianity. *...Christian evangelists... The former television evangelist, Pat Robertson.*

evangelize /ɪvændʒəlaɪz/ **evangelizes, evangelizing, evangelized;** also spelt **evangelise.**
VorVO To **evangelize** means to try to convert people to Christianity. *US religious groups are being encouraged to come in and evangelize.*

evaporate /ɪvæpəreɪt/ **evaporates, evaporating, evaporated**
1 V When a liquid **evaporates**, it changes into a gas, usually because it has been heated. *All the water has evaporated.* ♦ **evaporation** /ɪvæpəreɪʃn/ NU *Be careful not to lose too much liquid by evaporation.*
2 V If a feeling or attitude **evaporates**, it gradually becomes less and eventually disappears. *My nervousness evaporated.*

evaporated milk
NU **Evaporated milk** is thick unsweetened milk from which some water has been removed.

evasion /ɪveɪʒn/ **evasions**
NUorNC **Evasion** is the act of deliberately not doing something that you ought to do. *He is guilty of gross tax evasion. ...an evasion of our responsibilities... He continued with his evasions and lies.*

evasive /ɪveɪsɪv/
1 ADJ If you are being **evasive**, you are deliberately not talking about something. *They had been evasive and refused to cooperate with the investigators. ...an evasive answer.* ♦ **evasively** ADV *The Count had answered evasively.*
2 If you **take evasive action**, you deliberately move away from things so that you avoid crashing into them. *The pilot had been obliged to take evasive action to avoid the fighter.*

eve /iːv/
N SING The **eve** of an event is the day before it. *...a devastating attack on the eve of the election.* ● See also **Christmas Eve, New Year's Eve.**

even /iːvn/ **evens, evening, evened**
1 ADV SEN You use **even** to emphasize that what precedes it or follows it in the sentence is surprising. *Even Anthony enjoyed it... She liked him even when she was quarrelling with him... I often lend her money even now.*
2 ADV You use **even** with comparative adjectives for emphasis. *Barber had something even worse to tell me. ...an even brighter light... I must be even more tired than I thought.*
3 ADJ If a measurement or rate is **even**, it stays at about the same level. *...an even body temperature.* ♦ **evenly** ADV *Mary was breathing quietly and evenly.*
4 ADJ **Even** surfaces are smooth and flat. *...a nice even surface... The road wasn't very even.*
5 ADJ If there is an **even** distribution or division of something, each person, group, or area involved has an equal amount. *The distribution of land was much more even than in Latin America.* ♦ **evenly** ADV *Opinion seems to be fairly evenly divided.*
6 ADJ If a contest or competition is **even**, the people taking part are all equally skilful. *It was a pretty even game.* ♦ **evenly** ADV *Government and rebel*

soldiers are evenly matched.
7 ADJ An **even** number can be divided exactly by the number two. *Cars can only enter the city on alternate days, depending on whether their licence plates end in odd or even numbers.*
● **Even** is used in these phrases. ● If there is an **even chance** of something happening, the probability of it happening or not happening is equal. *She would have had only an even chance of being saved.* ● You use **even if** or **even though** to indicate that a particular fact does not make the rest of your statement untrue. *Even if you disagree with her, she's worth listening to... I was always rather afraid of men, even though I had lots of boyfriends.* ● You use **even so** to introduce a surprising fact that relates to what you have just said. *Their feathers are regularly shed and renewed. Even so they need constant care.* ● If you say you will **get even** with someone, you mean that you intend to harm them because they have harmed you; an informal expression. *I always knew that one day I would get even with her.*

even out PHRASAL VERB When an amount of something **evens out** or when you **even it out**, it becomes more evenly distributed or steadier. *Irrigation systems help to even out the supply of water over the growing season.*

even-handed
ADJ Someone who is **even-handed** is completely fair, especially when they are judging or testing other people. *He had been a fair and even-handed assessor.* ♦ **even-handedly** ADV *She dispensed justice even-handedly.*

evening /iːvnɪŋ/ **evenings**
NCorNU The **evening** is the part of each day between the end of the afternoon and the time you go to bed. *...with the dark winter evenings closing in... He arrived about six in the evening... He was silently finishing his evening meal.*

evening class, evening classes
NC An **evening class** is a course of study for adults that is taught in the evening. *Over half a million adults study at polytechnics, specialist colleges and evening classes.*

evening dress, evening dresses
1 NC An **evening dress** is a special dress, usually a long one, that a woman wears on a formal occasion in the evening. *Britain's best known woman conductor, Jane Glover, wears an evening dress for grand occasions.*
2 NU **Evening dress** refers to the clothes worn by people at formal occasions that take place in the evening. *...the appearance of a couple in black evening dress.*

evensong /iːvnsɒŋ/
NU **Evensong** is an evening service held in the Church of England.

event /ɪvent/ **events**
1 NC An **event** is something that happens, especially something unusual or important. *Next day the newspapers reported the event. ...the most important event in family life.*
2 N PL You can refer to all the things that are happening in a particular situation as **events**. *Events now moved swiftly... The authorities were quite unable to control events.*
3 NC In sport, an **event** is one of the activities or special disciplines that are part of an organized competitive meeting. *Lord Exeter presented the medals for this event.*
4 You say **in the event of** something, **in the event that** something happens, or **in that event**, when you are talking about a possible future situation, especially when you are planning what to do if it occurs; a formal expression. *The focus has shifted to how the Gulf's oil supplies can best be secured in the event of regional attacks... In the unlikely event that they give you any real trouble, give me a ring... In that event, a constitutional conference will be held.*

even-tempered
ADJ Someone who is **even-tempered** is usually calm and does not easily get angry. *She was a happy, even-tempered woman.*

eventful /ɪvɛntfl/
ADJ An **eventful** period of time is full of exciting or important events. *His middle and later years could never have been as eventful as his early life. ...the most exhausting and eventful day of his life.*

eventual /ɪvɛntʃuəl/
ADJ ATTRIB The **eventual** result of a process or series of events is what happens at the end of it. *...the company's eventual collapse in 1971.*

eventuality /ɪvɛntʃuælətɪ/ **eventualities**
NC An **eventuality** is a possible future event; a formal word. *We are insured against all eventualities... United Nations officials want to be prepared for any eventuality.*

eventually /ɪvɛntʃuəlɪ/
1 ADV or ADV SEN If something happens **eventually**, it happens after a lot of delays or problems. *Rodin eventually agreed that Casson was right... Eventually they got through to the hospital.*
2 ADV **Eventually** also means happening as the final result of a process or series of events. *The three firms eventually became Imperial Airways.*

ever /ɛvə/
1 ADV **Ever** means at any time in the past or future. *I don't think I'll ever be homesick here... I am happier than I have ever been.*
2 ADV You also use **ever** in questions beginning with words such as 'why', 'when', and 'which' when you want to emphasize your surprise or shock. *'I'm sorry. I'd rather not say.'—'Why ever not?.'... Who ever would have thought that?*
● **Ever** is used in these phrases. ● You use **ever since** to emphasize that something has been true all the time since the time mentioned, and is still true now. *'How long have you lived here?'—'Ever since I was married.'* ● You use **ever so** and **ever such** to emphasize the degree of something; an informal expression. *They are ever so kind... I had ever such a nice letter from her.*

ever- /ɛvə-/
PREFIX **Ever-** is used in expressions like 'ever increasing' and 'ever-present' to indicate that something exists or continues all the time. *...an ever-increasing prison population. ...an ever-present sense of danger.*

evergreen /ɛvəgriːn/ **evergreens**
NC An **evergreen** is a tree or bush which never loses its leaves. *...the rolling evergreen hills.*

everlasting /ɛvəlɑːstɪŋ/
ADJ Something that is **everlasting** never ends or never seems to change; a literary word. *...the everlasting snows of the mighty Himalayas.* ◆ **everlastingly** ADV *He was everlastingly optimistic.*

evermore /ɛvəmɔː/
ADV **Evermore** means for all the time in the future; a literary word. *Watch over us, now and for evermore.*

every /ɛvrɪ/
1 DET You use **every** to indicate that you are referring to all the members of a group or all the parts of something. *She spoke to every person at the party... I loved every minute of it.*
2 DET You also use **every** to indicate that something happens at regular intervals. *They met every day... I visit her once every six months... Every so often, she spends a weekend in London.*
3 You use **every** to say how often something happens. For example, if something happens **every second** day or **every other** day, it happens on one day in each period of two days. *We only take a vacation every other year.*
4 DET You use **every** before a number to say what proportion of people or things something applies to. *One woman in every two hundred is a sufferer... Since 1976, nine women have lost jobs for every five men.*
5 DET If something shows **every** sign of happening, or if there is **every** chance that it will happen, it is very likely to happen. *They show every sign of continuing to succeed.*
6 DET If someone has **every** reason to do something, they would be justified in doing it. *She had every reason to be pleased.*

everybody /ɛvrɪbɒdɪ/. See **everyone**.

everyday /ɛvrɪdeɪ/
1 ADJ ATTRIB You use **everyday** to describe something which is part of normal life, and is not especially interesting. *People could resume a normal everyday life. ...their role in everyday affairs.*
2 ADJ ATTRIB You also use **everyday** describe something that happens or is used each day. *Exercise is part of my everyday routine.*

everyone /ɛvrɪwʌn/
1 PRON INDEF **Everyone** or **everybody** means all the people in a group. *She was genuinely interested in everyone she met... Everybody in the office laughed.*
2 PRON INDEF You can use **everyone** or **everybody** to refer to all the people in the world. *Everyone has their own ideas about it.*

everything /ɛvrɪθɪŋ/
1 PRON INDEF You use **everything** to refer to all the objects, activities, or facts in a situation. *I don't agree with everything he says... I will arrange everything.*
2 PRON INDEF You can also use **everything** to refer to all possible or likely actions, activities, or situations. *That's your answer to everything... You think of everything.*
3 PRON INDEF **Everything** also means life in general. *Is everything all right?... Everything went on just as before.*

everywhere /ɛvrɪweə/
1 ADV You use **everywhere** to refer to a whole area or to all the places in a particular area. *Everywhere in Asia it is the same... People everywhere are becoming aware of the problem.*
2 ADV You also use **everywhere** to refer to all the places that someone goes to. *Everywhere I went, people were angry or suspicious... She always carried a gun with her everywhere.*

evict /ɪvɪkt/ **evicts, evicting, evicted**
VO When people **are evicted**, they are officially forced to leave the house where they are living. *If evicted, they would have nowhere else to go... There's no question of using riot police to evict the squatters by force.*

eviction /ɪvɪkʃn/ **evictions**
N U or NC **Eviction** is the act or process of officially forcing someone to leave a house or piece of land. *The family faces eviction for non-payment of rent... There had been mass evictions and deportations of people on ethnic grounds.*

evidence /ɛvɪdəns/
NU **Evidence** is the things you see, experience, or are told which make you believe that something is true. *We saw evidence everywhere that a real effort was being made to promote tourism... There was no evidence of quarrels between them... The scientific evidence is somewhat scant.*
● **Evidence** is used in these phrases. ● If you **give evidence** in a court of law, you say what you know about something. *Alma gave evidence in the witness box, pinning the guilt on to her young lover.* ● If someone or something is **in evidence**, they are present and can be clearly seen. *Violence was particularly in evidence in the towns.*

evident /ɛvɪdənt/
ADJ If it is **evident** that something exists or is true, people can easily see that it exists or is true. *It was evident that his faith in the Government was severely shaken... Mr Hurd said he was encouraged by the evident will to negotiate.*

evidently /ɛvɪdəntlɪ/
ADV SEN You use **evidently** to say that something is obviously true. *They said it would come, but evidently they failed to send it... I found her in bed, evidently in great pain.*

evil /iːvl/ **evils**
1 NU **Evil** is all the wicked and bad things that happen in the world. *...promising social revolution as man's final deliverance from evil.*
2 ADJ An **evil** person is wicked and cruel. *Evil and nasty people are trying to murder and intimidate both communities.*
3 NC The **evils** of a situation are all the bad or

harmful things in it. ...*the evils of drink. ...a programme to eradicate these evils... We can educate our children to say no to the evil of drugs.*
4 ADJ Something that is **evil** is harmful. *Slavery was the most evil system of labour ever devised.*
5 If you have two choices, but you think that they are both bad, you can call the one that is less bad the **lesser of two evils** or the **lesser evil**. *Many people see it as the lesser of two evils... Admission of defeat will seem a lesser evil than the continuation of the war.*

evildoer /iːvldʊːə/ **evildoers**
NC An **evildoer** is a person whose behaviour is wicked and who causes harm and suffering to others. ...*the first major case against an alleged Nazi evildoer to be held in Israel since 1962.*

evil eye
N SING The **evil eye** refers to the supposed magical power of casting an evil spell on someone or something by looking at them; also used to refer to the actual look that someone with this power gives to someone or something. *She gave me the evil eye.*

evince /ɪvɪns/ **evinces, evincing, evinced**
VO If someone **evinces** a feeling or quality, they show it very clearly; a formal word. *I have never heard one of our boys evince any interest in the movement.*

evocation /iːvəkeɪʃn/ **evocations**
NCorNU An **evocation** of a place or a past event is an experience in which you are reminded of it. ...*evocations of rural America... It was disturbing, this evocation of her youth.*

evocative /ɪvɒkətɪv/
ADJ Something that is **evocative** makes you think about or remember a place or a past event. ...*an evocative description.*

evoke /ɪvəʊk/ **evokes, evoking, evoked**
VO If something **evokes** an emotion, memory, or response, it causes it to be recalled or expressed; a formal word. *The quarrel seemed to evoke the bitterest passions... He said his return evoked both pleasant and unpleasant memories.*

evolution /iːvəluːʃn/
1 NU **Evolution** is a process of gradual change during which animals and plants change some of their characteristics to cope with a different environment, and sometimes develop into new species. *The processes of evolution are still going on. ...the thousands of years of man's evolution.*
2 NU+SUPP You can use **evolution** to refer to any gradual process of change and development. ...*the evolution of parliamentary democracy.*

evolutionary /iːvəluːʃənəʳri/
ADJ ATTRIB **Evolutionary** means related to evolution. *Palaeoanthropologists believe that modern man developed in a single evolutionary event in Africa... Stability requires evolutionary rather than revolutionary political advance.*

evolve /ɪvɒlv/ **evolves, evolving, evolved**
1 V When animals and plants **evolve**, they gradually change and develop into different forms or species. *The earliest fish have evolved into some 30,000 different species.*
2 V-ERG When something **evolves** or someone **evolves** it, it gradually develops from something simple into something more complex or advanced. *It was fascinating to see how the film evolved... How did Giotto evolve his very personal and original style?*

ewe /juː/ **ewes**
NC A **ewe** is an adult female sheep. *Normally a ewe will reject a lamb that's not its own.*

ewer /juːə/ **ewers**
NC A **ewer** is a large jug with a wide opening; an old-fashioned word.

ex /eks/
N SING+SUPP Someone's **ex** is their ex-wife, ex-husband, ex-girlfriend, etc; an informal word. ...*jilted lovers getting their own back on their ex.*

ex- /eks-, ɪks-, ɪgz-/
PREFIX **Ex-** is added to nouns to indicate that someone or something is no longer the thing referred to by the noun. For example, an ex-farmer is someone who is no longer a farmer. ...*the ex-Beatle, Paul McCartney. ...ex-president Marcos.*

exacerbate /ɪgzæsəbeɪt/ **exacerbates, exacerbating, exacerbated**
VO To **exacerbate** a bad situation means to make it worse; a formal word. *Other statements have tended to exacerbate the tension in both countries.*

exact /ɪgzækt/ **exacts, exacting, exacted**
1 ADJ Something that is **exact** is correct, accurate, and complete in every way. *He noted the exact time. ...an exact replica of Hamburg airport.*
2 You say **to be exact** when you want give more detailed information. *Birds are supposed to have evolved from reptiles—dinosaurs, to be exact.*
3 VO If someone **exacts** something from you, they demand and obtain it, because they are more powerful than you are; a formal use. *They exacted absolute obedience from their followers.*

exacting /ɪgzæktɪŋ/
ADJ An **exacting** person or task requires you to work very hard or take a great deal of care. *The railway inspectorate should be more intrusive and exacting. ...an exacting job... The state of repair failed to measure up to their exacting standards.*

exactitude /ɪgzæktɪtjuːd/
NU **Exactitude** is the quality of being very accurate and careful. *He copied the words which followed with exactitude. ...military exactitude.*

exactly /ɪgzæktli/
1 ADV **Exactly** means with complete accuracy and precision. *You've exactly one hour to do this... That's exactly what they told me.*
2 ADV If you do something **exactly**, you do it very accurately. *Sam answered the owl's cry, imitating it exactly.*
3 ADV You can use **exactly** to emphasize how similar two things are. *He's exactly like a little baby.*
4 You can say '**Exactly**' to agree with what has just been said. *'Do you mean that we are stuck here?'—'Exactly, my dear.'*
5 ADV You can use **not exactly** to indicate that something is not quite true. *He didn't exactly block me, but he didn't move either... 'She's taken the day off.'—'Is she sick?'—'Not exactly.'*

exactness /ɪgzæktnəs/
NU **Exactness** is the quality of being accurate and very precise. *He chose to express himself delicately and with great exactness.*

exaggerate /ɪgzædʒəreɪt/ **exaggerates, exaggerating, exaggerated**
1 VorVO If you **exaggerate**, you make the thing that you are talking about seem larger, worse, or more important than it actually is. *I am exaggerating a little... It is impossible to exaggerate the horrors of the system.* ◆ **exaggeration** /ɪgzædʒəreɪʃn/ **exaggerations** NCorNU *Isn't that a bit of an exaggeration?... All parties to this complex conflict seem prone to exaggeration.*
2 VO To **exaggerate** something such as a gesture means to make it very obvious. *Ballet exaggerates ordinary body movements.*

exaggerated /ɪgzædʒəreɪtɪd/
ADJ Something that is **exaggerated** is or seems larger, better, worse, or more important than it needs to be. *Brody heaved an exaggerated sigh... He described the report's allegations as exaggerated.*

exalt /ɪgzɔːlt/ **exalts, exalting, exalted**; a formal word.
1 VO To **exalt** someone means to praise them very highly. *Some historians exalt Churchill as a war leader.*
2 VO If you **exalt** someone, you raise them to a higher position in society. *The Prime Minister exalted many of his friends.*

exaltation /egzɔːlteɪʃn/; a formal word.
1 NU **Exaltation** is an intense feeling of great joy and happiness. ...*peasants in a state of religious exaltation.*
2 NU **Exaltation** is the act of praising something or someone very highly. ...*the exaltation of nature and the soil.*

exalted /ɪgzɔːltɪd/
ADJ An **exalted** person is very important; a literary word. ...*someone in his exalted position.*

exam /ɪgzæm/ **exams**
NC An **exam** is the same as an **examination**. *Many teachers are reserving judgement on the GCSE until the exam results are published.*

examination /ɪgzæmɪneɪʃn/ **examinations**
1 NC An **examination** is a formal test that you take to show your knowledge of a subject. *...a three-hour written examination.*
2 NCorNU If you make an **examination** of something, you look at it or consider it very carefully. *So far all examinations of the shroud have failed to prove or the disprove its authenticity... The hospital's ethical credibility is under severe examination.*
3 NCorNU A medical **examination** is a check by a doctor to find out how healthy you are. *Medical examinations showed there were no signs of radiation effects on people... Although Mr Bush would require further examination, there was no sign that he had had a heart attack.*

examine /ɪgzæmɪn/ **examines, examining, examined**
1 VO If you **examine** something, you look at it carefully. *I examined the lighter, then handed it back... She sat back in her chair and examined her fingernails.*
2 VO When people **examine** an idea, proposal, plan, etc, they consider or discuss it very carefully. *An EC meeting on Tuesday examined a French proposal to send a peacekeeping force... A spokesman said the plan would be carefully examined.*
3 VO If an official investigation **examines** something, it looks at or inspects every part of it as carefully as possible in order to discover something about it. *Police are examining a car that was used in the raid... Safety Officers are examining a Boeing 727 after a section of its fuselage was torn off.*
4 VO If a doctor **examines** you, he or she looks at your body to check your health. *Each child is medically examined.*
5 VO If a teacher **examines** you, he or she finds out how much you know by asking you questions or by making you take an examination. *These people were examined in a total of 39 subjects.*

examiner /ɪgzæmɪnə/ **examiners**
NC An **examiner** is a person who sets or marks a test or an examination. *If I knew that my driving examiner was going to be with me, I would drive sanely and sensibly.*

example /ɪgzɑːmpl/ **examples**
1 NC An **example** is something which represents or is typical of a particular group of things. *It's a very fine example of traditional architecture... Could you give me an example?*
2 NC If someone is an **example** to other people or sets an **example**, they behave in a way that other people should copy. *They are a shining example to progressive people everywhere... She set such a good example to us all.*
● **Example** is used in these phrases. ● You use **for example** to show that you are giving an example of a particular kind of thing. *Japan, for example, has two languages.* ● If you **follow** someone's **example**, you copy their behaviour. ● If you **make an example** of someone, you punish them severely so that other people will not behave in the same way. *Mr Gorbachev may have chosen to make an example of the republic and send in troops to assert his authority.*

exasperate /ɪgzɑːspəreɪt/ **exasperates, exasperating, exasperated**
VO If someone or something **exasperates** you, they annoy you and make you feel frustrated. *She frequently exasperates her friends.* ◆ **exasperated** ADJ *He had an exasperated look on his face.* ◆ **exasperating** ADJ *I have seldom had a more exasperating day.*

exasperation /ɪgzɑːspəreɪʃn/
NU **Exasperation** is the feeling of annoyance you have when someone or something does not behave in the way that you would like. *He looked at the little boy in exasperation.*

excavate /ekskəveɪt/ **excavates, excavating, excavated**
VorVO To **excavate** a piece of land means to remove

earth carefully from it and look for the remains of pots or buildings, in order to find out about the past. *The early excavators at the turn of the century were using dynamite to excavate... The tomb was not properly excavated until the 1960's.* ◆ **excavation** /ekskəveɪʃn/ **excavations** NCorNU *Excavations at the cave have been under way since the 1930s. ...the excavation of a Neolithic village.*

excavator /ekskəveɪtə/ **excavators**
NC An **excavator** is a very large machine that is used for digging, for example on a building site. *He urged factory managers to send excavators, trucks, bulldozers and other equipment.*

exceed /ɪksiːd/ **exceeds, exceeding, exceeded**
1 VO If something **exceeds** a particular amount, it is greater than that amount. *Average annual temperatures exceed 20° centigrade.*
2 VO If you **exceed** a limit, you go beyond it. *A motorist was caught exceeding the speed limit... The company is not allowed to exceed its budget.*

exceedingly /ɪksiːdɪŋli/
SUBMOD **Exceedingly** means very much indeed; an old-fashioned word. *The Colonel was exceedingly wealthy.*

excel /ɪksel/ **excels, excelling, excelled**
VA If someone **excels** at or in something, they are very good at it. *He excels at sports... Though his acting was limited, he excelled in the plays of Shaw.*

excellence /eksələns/
NU **Excellence** is the quality of being extremely good at something. *Sport is an area in which excellence is still treasured.*

Excellency /eksələnsi/ **Excellencies**
TITLE People use **Your Excellency, His Excellency,** or **Excellency** to refer to or address important officials. *His Excellency desires to see you... I shall do my best, Your Excellency.*

excellent /eksələnt/
ADJ Something that is **excellent** is very good indeed. *I think the teaching here is excellent... That's an excellent idea.* ◆ **excellently** ADV *The system works excellently.*

except /ɪksept/
PREP or CONJ You use **except** or **except for** to introduce the only thing or person that a statement does not apply to. *All the boys except Piggy started to giggle... There was little I could do except wait... They ran out of food, except for some sugar.*

excepted /ɪkseptɪd/
PREP You use **excepted** after you have mentioned a person or thing to show that you do not include them in a group mentioned in your statement. *...a gentleman for whom other people—Rhoda excepted—put on their biggest smiles... It is more worth seeing than any city I ever saw, London excepted.*

excepting /ɪkseptɪŋ/
PREP You use **excepting** to introduce the only thing that prevents a statement from being completely true. *He was the only human male for miles around (excepting an old handyman).*

exception /ɪksepʃn/ **exceptions**
NC An **exception** is a thing, person, or situation that is not included in a general statement. *Women, with a few exceptions, are not involved in politics.*
● **Exception** is used in these phrases. ● You use **without exception** to indicate that your statement is true in all cases. *Almost without exception, the fastest-growing cities are in Africa.* ● If you **take exception** to something, you feel offended or annoyed by it. *There are three things you've just said that I take exception to.*

exceptionable /ɪksepʃ⁰nəbl/
ADJ Something that is **exceptionable** causes you to feel offended or annoyed, usually with the result that you complain about it. *What I do find really quite exceptionable in his argument is the idea that a woman is unfit to run a company.*

exceptional /ɪksepʃ⁰nəl/
1 ADJ An **exceptional** person is unusually talented or clever. *My brother isn't exceptional; there are plenty of youngsters like him.*
2 ADJ **Exceptional** situations or events are unusual or

rare. *Permission will be granted only in very exceptional circumstances.*

exceptionally /ɪksepʃəⁿnəli/

1 SUBMOD You use **exceptionally** to emphasize how very good, important, or bad something is. *...an exceptionally fine meal... February had been exceptionally wet.*

2 ADV SEN You also use **exceptionally** to indicate that what you are talking about is unusual and is only likely to happen very rarely. *Exceptionally, with the approval of the University, a degree will be awarded to a candidate who did not take all the exams.*

excerpt /eksɜːpt/ **excerpts**

NC An **excerpt** is a short piece of writing or music that is taken from a longer piece of work. *Here are a few excerpts from her diary... You'll hear the oboe in this final excerpt.*

excess, excesses; usually pronounced /ɪkses/ when it is a noun and /ekses/ when it is an adjective.

1 N SING An **excess** of something is a larger amount than is necessary or normal. *Inflation results from an excess of demand over supply... This report should discourage us all from eating an excess of fat.* ► Also ADJ ATTRIB *The body gets rid of excess water through the urine.*

2 If you do something **to excess**, you do it too much. *He spent all his time cleaning and tidying to excess.*

3 N PL **Excesses** are acts which are extreme, cruel, or immoral. *...the worst excesses of the French Revolution.*

excessive /ɪksesɪv/

ADJ If something is **excessive**, it is too great in amount or degree. *Their profits were excessive.*
◆ **excessively** ADV *He walked excessively fast.*

exchange /ɪkstʃeɪndʒ/ **exchanges, exchanging, exchanged**

1 VO If people **exchange** things, they give them to each other at the same time. *The three of us exchanged addresses... Gertie and Dolly exchanged glances.* ► Also NC *...an exchange of information... They signed a two-year cultural exchange agreement.*

2 VO If you **exchange** one thing for another, you replace the first thing with the second. *The sales girl refused to exchange the sweater... She exchanged the jewels for money.*

3 If someone carries out something **in exchange** or **in exchange for** something else, they do one thing in return for another thing. *Giving development aid did not prevent donor countries demanding humanitarian guarantees in exchange... The ANC is to end its armed struggle in exchange for the release of political prisoners.*

4 NC An **exchange** is a brief conversation; a formal use. *Throughout these exchanges I had a curious feeling of detachment.*

5 NC An **exchange** is an event during a war when armies or nations use weapons against each other; a military use. *There has been a heavy exchange of fire between para-military forces... One of the gunmen was also killed in the exchange.*

6 See also **stock exchange, telephone exchange**.

exchange rate, exchange rates

NC The **exchange rate** is the number of units of one country's currency that can be exchanged for an equivalent amount in another country's currency. *An over-valued exchange rate discourages exports.*

Exchequer /ɪkstʃekə/

N PROP The **Exchequer** is the department in the British government which is responsible for receiving, issuing and accounting for money belonging to the state. *The new housing benefit scales will save the Exchequer about six hundred and fifty million pounds a year.*
● See also **Chancellor of the Exchequer**.

excise /eksaɪz/

NU **Excise** is a tax that the government of a country puts on goods produced for sale in that country; a technical term. *Companies like Texaco pay an excise tax to the government... Excise duties on alcohol and cigarettes are to rise from thirty to forty per cent.*
● See also **customs and excise**.

excitable /ɪksaɪtəbl/

ADJ An **excitable** person becomes excited very easily.

She was deliberately unreasonable, emotional and excitable.

excite /ɪksaɪt/ **excites, exciting, excited**

1 VO If something **excites** you, it makes you interested and enthusiastic. *The idea of journalism excited me... The Liberal Democrats have not yet excited the public with their key policy.*

2 VO If someone or something **excites** you, they give you strong feeling of happiness, nervousness, or worry that make you unable to react. *'What happened, doctor?'—'Don't excite yourself, please. Everything is normal.'*

3 VO If something **excites** a feeling or reaction, it causes it to happen; a formal use. *These rumours excited suspicion... The monarchy does not excite strong feelings among the majority of Romanians.*

excited /ɪksaɪtɪd/

ADJ If you are **excited**, you are very happy and cannot relax because you are looking forward to something very eagerly. *He was so excited he could hardly sleep... There were hundreds of excited children to meet us.* ◆ **excitedly** ADV *They were excitedly discussing plans.*

excitement /ɪksaɪtmənt/ **excitements**

1 NU **Excitement** is the state of being excited. *Struggling to conceal his excitement, he accepted her invitation... He was trembling with excitement... Unmanned aircraft are causing great excitement in the aeronautical world.*

2 NCor NU An **excitement** is something that causes you to feel excited. *In the 1950s, pop groups sang about the excitements of dancing and kissing and cuddling. ...all the excitements of London. ...youths looking for excitement after another hot day in depressed inner city areas.*

exciting /ɪksaɪtɪŋ/

ADJ Something that is **exciting** makes you feel excited. *Growing up in the heart of London was exciting... What an exciting idea!*

exclaim /ɪkskleɪm/ **exclaims, exclaiming, exclaimed**

V-QUOTE or V-REPORT When you **exclaim**, you say something suddenly because you are excited, shocked, or angry. *'Oh, you poor child!' exclaimed Mrs Socket... He exclaimed that it was more than he could have hoped for.*

exclamation /ekskləmeɪʃn/ **exclamations**

NC An **exclamation** is a sound, word, or sentence that is spoken suddenly and emphatically in order to express excitement, admiration, shock, or anger. *He drew back with a sharp exclamation... They embraced him with exclamations of joy.*

exclamation mark, exclamation marks

NC An **exclamation mark** is the punctuation mark (!).

exclamation point, exclamation points

NC An **exclamation point** is an exclamation mark; used in American English.

exclude /ɪkskluːd/ **excludes, excluding, excluded**

1 VOA or VO If you **exclude** something from an activity or discussion, you deliberately do not include that thing in it. *He managed to have the issue excluded from the agenda... He refused to exclude the possibility of a deal.*

2 VO If you **exclude** a possibility, you reject it. *A fake call from some local phone box was not excluded.*

3 VOA or VO If you **exclude** someone from a place or activity, you prevent them from entering the place or taking part in the activity. *...jobs from which the majority of workers are excluded... Those responsible for the genocide have to be excluded.*

excluding /ɪkskluːdɪŋ/

PREP You use **excluding** before mentioning a person or thing to show that you are not including them in your statement. *We are open seven days a week, excluding Christmas Day... The retail prices index, excluding housing costs, rose by 646.6 per cent.*

exclusion /ɪkskluːʒn/

1 NU The **exclusion** of something from a speech, piece of writing, or legal document is the act of deliberately not including it. *...the exclusion of any mention of her good qualities... The bill already has an exclusion clause.*

2 NU **Exclusion** is the act of preventing someone from

entering a place or from taking part in an activity.
...*the laws relating to the admission and exclusion of
aliens.* ...*their exclusion from the rights and liberties
that others enjoy.*

exclusion zone, exclusion zones
NC An **exclusion zone** is an area from which people
have been evacuated, or in which a particular activity
is not allowed. ...*people evacuated from the thirty-
kilometre exclusion zone... More and more countries
seek modern warships to patrol economic exclusion
zones around their coasts.*

exclusive /ɪksklu:sɪv/
1 ADJ Something that is **exclusive** is available only to
people who are rich or who belong to a high social
class. ...*an exclusive residential district.*
2 ADJ ATTRIB **Exclusive** means used or owned by only
one person or group. *They have exclusive use of the
machine.*
3 ADJ If two things are mutually **exclusive**, they
cannot exist together. *There is no reason why these
two functions should be mutually exclusive.*
4 ADJ ATTRIB An **exclusive** story in a magazine or
newspaper is one that is published in that paper and in
no other. *The Mail On Sunday leads with what it says
is an exclusive story on a secret security operation.*
...*an exclusive interview.*

exclusively /ɪksklu:sɪvli/
ADV You use **exclusively** to refer to situations that
involve only the things mentioned, and nothing else.
...*young people who devote their lives exclusively to
sport.*

excommunicate /ˌɛkskəmju:nɪkeɪt/ **excommunicates,
excommunicating, excommunicated**
VO If a Roman Catholic is **excommunicated** by the
church as a punishment for a major wrong that they
have done, it is publicly and officially stated that the
person is no longer allowed to be a member of the
Roman Catholic church. *She was excommunicated by
Cardinal Manning.*

excommunication /ˌɛkskəmju:nɪkeɪʃn/
excommunications
NU or NC **Excommunication** is the state of being
excommunicated or the act of excommunicating
someone. ...*the penalty of automatic
excommunication.*

excrement /ˈɛkskrəmənt/
NU **Excrement** is the solid waste matter that is passed
out of your body through your bowels; a formal word.
*There are no sanitation facilities—garbage and
excrement are piling up all around.*

excrescence /ɪkskrɛsns/ **excrescences**
NC An **excrescence** is a lump or growth on the surface
of an animal or plant; a formal word.

excreta /ɪkskri:tə/
NU **Excreta** is waste matter such as urine, sweat, or
faeces, which is passed out of a person's or animal's
body; a formal word. *The silk worm excreta is put
into the pond as fertilizer.*

excrete /ɪkskri:t/ **excretes, excreting, excreted**
VO or V When you **excrete** waste matter from your
body, you get rid of it, usually through your bowels; a
formal word. *They're given drugs which enable them
to excrete this excess iron in their urine... Dimethyl
sulphide is known to be excreted by many planktonic
organisms in the sea.* ...*canals where people can wash
and excrete.* ♦ **excretion** /ɪkskri:ʃn/ **excretions**
NC or NU ...*the burglar spoiling valuable clothing with
secretions and excretions... HDL takes cholesterol to
the liver where it is broken down for excretion.*

excruciating /ɪkskru:ʃieɪtɪŋ/
1 ADJ **Excruciating** pain is very painful indeed.
Cystitis causes excruciating pain on passing urine.
2 ADJ An **excruciating** situation or experience is
extremely difficult to bear. ...*excruciating
unhappiness.*

excursion /ɪkskɜ:ʃn/ **excursions**
1 NC An **excursion** is a short journey, especially one
that has been organized for a particular reason or for
a particular group of people. ...*a shopping excursion.*
...*a party of high-school students on a school holiday
excursion.*
2 NC An **excursion** into a new activity is an attempt to

do it or understand it for the first time. ...*a rare
excursion into contemporary music.*

excusable /ɪkskju:zəbl/
ADJ If a mistake or wrong action is **excusable**, you can
forgive it, because of the circumstances in which it
was made. *He made an excusable mistake.*

excuse, excuses, excusing, excused; pronounced
/ɪkskju:s/ when it is a noun and /ɪkskju:z/ when it is a
verb.
1 NC An **excuse** is a reason which you give to explain
why something has been done, has not been done, or
will not be done. *She should not use the crisis as an
excuse for Tory failures... There is no excuse for this
happening in a new building... I have no excuses for
losing the match today.*
2 V-REFL or VO If you **excuse** yourself or **excuse**
something wrong that you have done, you say why you
did it, in an attempt to defend yourself. *He felt the
need to excuse himself publicly for having written the
article... The Vice-President admitted taking bribes,
excusing it as a momentary weakness.*
3 VO or VOO If you **excuse** someone for something
wrong that they have done, you forgive them for it. *I
could never excuse him for being so rude... I excused
him much of his prejudice.*
4 VO If you **excuse** someone from a duty or
responsibility, you free them from it. *He was excused
military service because he had very poor vision in
one eye.* ...*a certificate excusing him from games at
school.*
5 VO If you ask someone to **excuse** you, you are
asking them to allow you to leave. *You'll have to
excuse me; I ought to be saying goodnight.*
● **Excuse** is used in these phrases. ● You say 'excuse
me' to attract someone's attention when you want to
ask them a question. *Excuse me, but is there a fairly
cheap restaurant near here?* ● You also say 'excuse
me' before correcting someone. *Excuse me, but I
think you have misunderstood.* ● You also say 'excuse
me' to apologize for disturbing or interrupting
someone, or for doing something slightly impolite such
as burping. *Excuse me for disturbing you at home.*
● In American English, you say 'excuse me' when you
want someone to repeat what they have just said.
*'You can tell that it's going to die out.'—'Excuse
me?'—'You can tell that it's going to die out.'*

ex-directory /ˌɛksdərɛktəˀri/
ADJ In Britain, if a person or his or her telephone
number is **ex-directory**, the number is not listed in the
telephone directory, and the telephone company will
refuse to give it to people who ask for it.

execrable /ˈɛksɪkrəbl/
ADJ If you say that something is **execrable**, you mean
that it is very bad or very unpleasant; a formal word.
The food is execrable.

execute /ˈɛksɪkju:t/ **executes, executing, executed**
1 VO To **execute** someone means to kill them as a
punishment for a crime. *A man has been executed for
the murder of thirty-three women.* ♦ **execution**
/ˌɛksɪkju:ʃn/ **executions** NC or NU *He sent a message to
the President protesting about the executions... In the
US more than two thousand people are still awaiting
execution.*
2 VO If you **execute** a plan, you carry it out; a formal
use. ...*a carefully executed crime.* ♦ **execution** NU
...*obstructing an officer in the execution of his duty.*
3 VO If you **execute** a difficult action or movement,
you perform it. *The pilot began to execute a series of
aerobatics.*

executioner /ˌɛksɪkju:ʃənə/ **executioners**
NC An **executioner** is a person who has the job of
executing criminals. ...*Sanson, the executioner in
revolutionary Paris.*

executive /ɪgzɛkjutɪv/ **executives**
1 NC An **executive** is someone employed by a
company at a senior level. *He joined a bank, and
quickly rose to become one of its senior executives.*
2 ADJ ATTRIB The **executive** sections and members of
an organization are concerned with making important
decisions. *Tomorrow, the union's executive committee
is to decide on further action.* ...*the executive director
of UNICEF.*

3 N COLL The **executive** of an organization is a committee which has the authority to make important decisions. *...the executive of the National Union of Teachers.*

executor /ɪgzɛkjʊtə/ **executors**
1 NC Your **executor** is the person who you appoint to deal with your affairs after your death; a legal use. *In his will, he explicitly forbids his executors from giving details of his death.*
2 NC The **executor** of an order, wish, or policy is the person who carries it out. *He described him as a good executor of a bad foreign policy.*

exegesis /ɛksɪdʒiːsɪs/ **exegeses** /ɛksɪdʒiːsiːz/
NC An **exegesis** is an explanation and interpretation of a piece of writing, especially a religious piece of writing, after very careful study; a technical term. *...a lengthy exegesis on classical Marxist theory.*

exemplar /ɪgzɛmplɑː/ **exemplars**; a formal word.
1 NC An **exemplar** is a typical example of a group or class of things.
2 NC An **exemplar** is also someone or something that is considered to be so good that they should be copied or imitated. *They are the pillars of society, our exemplars of success and social attainment.*

exemplary /ɪgzɛmplərɪ/
1 ADJ If you describe something as **exemplary**, you mean that you think it is so good that it should be copied or imitated. *He carried out all the tasks entrusted to him with exemplary efficiency. ...an exemplary father.*
2 ADJ An **exemplary** punishment is an unusually harsh one which is intended to discourage other people from committing similar crimes. *He handed out exemplary punishments to criminals convicted of particularly hideous crimes.*

exemplify /ɪgzɛmplɪfaɪ/ **exemplifies, exemplifying, exemplified**
1 VO If you say that someone or something **exemplifies** a situation or quality, you mean that they are a typical example of it. *He exemplified the new liberalism.*
2 VO If you **exemplify** something, you give an example of it. *I'm going to exemplify one or two of these points.*

exempt /ɪgzɛmpt/ **exempts, exempting, exempted**
1 ADJ PRED If you are **exempt** from a rule or duty, you do not have to obey it or perform it. *Harold was exempt from military service.*
2 VO To **exempt** a person from a rule or duty means to state officially that they do not have to obey it or perform it. *Farmers were exempted from rates.*
◆ **exemption** /ɪgzɛmpʃn/ **exemptions** N U or NC *Farmers have also been asking for exemption from the payment of these bills... This provides tax relief and exemptions for industries concentrating on exports.*

exercise /ɛksəsaɪz/ **exercises, exercising, exercised**
1 NC or NU **Exercises** are energetic movements which you do to make yourself fit and healthy. *...gymnastic exercises... The benefits of exercise are now well known.*
2 NC An **exercise** is a short piece of work which is designed to help you learn something. *One learns one's native language at one's mother's knee, without grammar exercises and without writing the language.*
3 NC **Exercises** are also repeated actions in which you practise something, for example playing a musical instrument. *I always start my singing practice with scales and exercises.*
4 NC **Exercises** are also practice operations or manoeuvres performed by the armed forces. *Reservists have been mobilised for military exercises to test how quickly they could be sent into action.*
5 NC+SUPP An **exercise** in something is an activity intended to achieve a particular purpose. *The rally was organized by the state as an exercise in patriotism... The President's persistence may partly be a public relations exercise to prove his government is interested in peace.*
6 V or VO When you **exercise**, you move your body energetically in order to become fit and remain healthy. *Exercising reduces the risk of heart attacks and can increase life expectancy... Even on days when*

you miss your training, it is a good idea to stretch and exercise your muscles.
7 VO If something **exercises** your mind, you think about it a great deal; a formal use. *This mystery has exercised the minds of many throughout the ages.*
8 VO To **exercise** authority, rights, or responsibilities means to use them; a formal use. *They exercise considerable influence in all western countries... He chose to exercise his right under Italian law not to appear in court.* ▶ Also N SING+of *...the exercise of personal responsibility.*

exercise book, exercise books
NC An **exercise book** is a small book with blank pages used for doing school work.

exert /ɪgzɜːt/ **exerts, exerting, exerted**
1 VO If you **exert** influence or pressure, you use it to achieve something. *These departments exert pressure on the schools to get them to agree.*
2 V-REFL If you **exert** yourself, you make a physical or mental effort to do something. *He had to exert himself to make conversation with the visitor.*

exertion /ɪgzɜːʃn/ **exertions**
N U or NC **Exertion** is physical effort or exercise. *He was panting with exertion... Tired out by the day's exertions and disasters, he had been sleeping more soundly than usual.*

ex gratia /ɛks greɪʃə/
ADJ An **ex gratia** payment or grant is one that is given as a favour or gift and not because it is legally necessary; a formal expression. *It will be up to the company to decide whether it wants to make an ex gratia payment.*

exhale /ɛksheɪl/ **exhales, exhaling, exhaled**
V or VO When you **exhale**, you breathe out; a formal word. *He exhaled slowly and smiled... He exhaled another great billow of cigar smoke.*

exhaust /ɪgzɔːst/ **exhausts, exhausting, exhausted**
1 VO If something **exhausts** you, it makes you very tired. *His efforts exhausted him.* ◆ **exhausted** ADJ *All three men were hot, dirty, and exhausted.*
◆ **exhausting** ADJ *...a difficult and exhausting job.*
2 VO If you **exhaust** a supply of something such as money or food, you use it all up. *The Community's aid budget has been exhausted by the after-effects of the Gulf War... They soon exhausted the food resources... Many factories were on the point of exhausting stockpiles of raw materials.*
3 VO If you **exhaust** a subject, you talk about it so much that there is nothing else to say. *Clearing up the issue of the massacres, from a Polish point of view, does not exhaust the subject of Soviet wartime misdeeds.*
4 NC An **exhaust** or an **exhaust pipe** is a pipe which carries the gas out of the engine of a motor vehicle. *A woman brought a van in to be fitted with a new exhaust. ...the black soot billowing from the exhaust pipe of a lorry straining to climb a hill.*
5 NU **Exhaust** is the gas produced by the engine of a motor vehicle. *Oil particles from the motor's exhaust are released into the atmosphere.*

exhaustible /ɪgzɔːstəbl/
ADJ Something that is **exhaustible** exists only in a limited quantity. *...possible long term shortages of exhaustible resources.*

exhaustion /ɪgzɔːstʃən/
N U **Exhaustion** is the state of being so tired that you have no energy left. *She was almost fainting with exhaustion.*

exhaustive /ɪgzɔːstɪv/
ADJ An **exhaustive** study or search is very thorough. *You might have to make many more exhaustive surveys.* ◆ **exhaustively** ADV *The political implications of that have been exhaustively analysed.*

exhibit /ɪgzɪbɪt/ **exhibits, exhibiting, exhibited**
1 VO If you **exhibit** an ability or feeling, it can be seen clearly by other people; a formal use. *He still exhibited signs of stress.*
2 VO When something is **exhibited**, it is put in a public place for people to look at. *The paintings are exhibited in chronological sequence.*
3 NC An **exhibit** is something shown in a museum or art gallery. *Our local museum has over a thousand*

exhibits. ...a broad range of exhibits on show.
4 NC An **exhibit** is also something shown in a court as evidence. *Exhibit number two is a diary belonging to the accused.*
5 NC In American English, an **exhibit** is also the same as an **exhibition**. *The Mapplethorpe exhibit drew 81,000 people during its seven-week run last spring.*

exhibition /ˌeksɪbɪʃn/ **exhibitions**
1 NC An **exhibition** is a collection of pictures or other objects shown in a public place. *A new exhibition of Robert Rauschenberg works opens at the National Gallery of Art today.*
2 NU **Exhibition** is the showing of pictures or other objects in a public place. *The film was refused a licence for public exhibition.*

exhibitionism /ˌeksɪbɪʃənɪzəm/
NU **Exhibitionism** is a type of behaviour in which someone tries to get people's attention all the time; a formal word. *...the exhibitionism of the world of show business.* ◆ **exhibitionist, exhibitionists** NC *As a child I was inclined to be an exhibitionist.*

exhibitor /ɪgzɪbɪtə/ **exhibitors**
NC An **exhibitor** is a person whose work is being exhibited. *Ruskin Spear was a regular exhibitor at the Royal Academy Summer Exhibition.*

exhilarate /ɪgzɪləreɪt/ **exhilarates, exhilarating, exhilarated**
VO If you **are exhilarated** by something, you feel great happiness and excitement. *The refugees were exhilarated by the news.* ◆ **exhilarated** ADJ *After a short run, you will feel exhilarated and less tired than you imagine.* ◆ **exhilarating** ADJ *...an exhilarating experience.*

exhilaration /ɪgzɪləreɪʃn/
NU **Exhilaration** is a strong feeling of excitement and happiness. *There was a sense of exhilaration about being alone on the beach.*

exhort /ɪgzɔːt/ **exhorts, exhorting, exhorted**
VO If you **exhort** someone to do something, you try hard to persuade them to do it; a formal word. *I exhorted the men not to drink too much.* ◆ **exhortation** /ˌegzɔːteɪʃn/ **exhortations** NCorNU *...fervent exhortations to revolutionary action. ...the exhortation to commit acts of violence.*

exhume /eksˈhjuːm/ **exhumes, exhuming, exhumed**
VO When a body is **exhumed**, permission is given for it to be taken out of the ground where it is buried. *His body has already been exhumed from an unmarked grave.*

exigency /ˈeksɪdʒənsi/ **exigencies**
NCorNU The **exigencies** of a situation or a job are the difficulties that you have to deal with as part of it; a formal word. *King Fahd has just cancelled a visit to the US because of the exigencies of the Lebanese situation... The government was compelled by military exigency to introduce many reforms.*

exile /ˈeksaɪl/ **exiles, exiling, exiled**
1 NU If someone lives in **exile**, they live in a foreign country because they cannot live in their own country, usually for political reasons. *Mr Mokhele has been living in exile for fourteen years... Many more are thought to be returning from exile in southern India.*
2 VO If someone is **exiled**, they are sent away from their own country and are not allowed to return. *I was exiled from Ceylon for a year.* ◆ **exiled** ADJ *...the exiled King.*
3 NC An **exile** is someone who lives in exile. *Thirty-thousand political exiles are expected to return to South Africa in the near future.*

exist /ɪgzɪst/ **exists, existing, existed**
1 V If something **exists**, it is present in the world as a real or living thing. *Communities who live by hunting still exist... That word doesn't exist in English... Nobody can actually know God exists.*
2 See also **existing**.

existence /ɪgzɪstəns/ **existences**
1 NU **Existence** is the state of existing. *Do you believe in the existence of God?*
2 NC+SUPP You can use **existence** to refer to someone's way of life. *The family lived a more or less vagabond existence.*

existential /ˌegzɪstenʃl/
ADJ **Existential** means relating to human existence and experience; a formal word. *Another composer, B. Leza, was a master of existential anguish.*

existentialism /ˌegzɪstenʃəlɪzəm/
NU **Existentialism** is a philosophical belief which stresses the importance of human experience and says that everyone is responsible for the results of their own actions. *Her works include books on existentialism.*

existentialist /ˌegzɪstenʃəlɪst/ **existentialists**
NC An **existentialist** is a person who agrees with the philosophy of existentialism. *...the writings of the Existentialists.* ▶ Also ADJ *...an existentialist approach.*

existing /ɪgzɪstɪŋ/
ADJ ATTRIB You use **existing** to describe something which is now in use or in operation. *We have to find ways of making the existing system work better.*

exit /ˈeksɪt/ **exits**
1 NC An **exit** is a door through which you can leave a public building. *He hurried towards the exit.*
2 NC An **exit** is also a place where traffic can leave a motorway. *I missed my exit from the motorway and had to drive on some distance.*
3 If you **make an exit** from a room, you leave it; a formal expression. *He made a hasty exit from the Men's Room.*

exit poll, exit polls
NC In an election, an **exit poll** is a survey which is carried out as people leave the polling stations, in which they are asked who they voted for. *The Communists, now renamed the Bulgarian Socialist Party, are heading for a clear victory, according to several exit polls.*

exit visa, exit visas
NC An **exit visa** is an official stamp in someone's passport, or an official document, which allows them to leave a particular country. *In 1990, more than 450,000 Soviet citizens were granted exit visas—but more than twice as many actually applied for them.*

exodus /ˈeksədəs/
N SING When there is an **exodus**, a lot of people leave a place together. *There's still the possibility of a mass exodus from Kuwait and Iraq.*

ex officio /ˌeks əfɪʃiəʊ/
ADJ ATTRIBorADV Ex **officio** is used to indicate that someone is entitled to something because of their rank, office or position; a formal expression. *...an ex officio member of the University Council... The WPA committee was composed of 24 members from different nations and, ex officio, the six members of the Executive Committee.*

exonerate /ɪgzɒnəreɪt/ **exonerates, exonerating, exonerated**
VO To **exonerate** someone means to show that they are not responsible for something wrong that has happened; a formal word. *His evidence might exonerate me from the crimes they had charged me with.*

exorbitant /ɪgzɔːbɪtənt/
ADJ If you describe something as **exorbitant**, you mean that it is much more expensive than it should be. *...the exorbitant rates of interest charged by Western banks.*

exorcism /ˈeksɔːsɪzəm/ **exorcisms**
NUorNC **Exorcism** is the removing of evil spirits from a place or person by using prayer. *Why is there such a revival of interest in the supernatural, in exorcism, demon possession and the black arts?*

exorcize /ˈeksɔːsaɪz/ **exorcizes, exorcizing, exorcized;** also spelt **exorcise.**
1 VO To **exorcize** an evil spirit or to **exorcize** a place or person means to force the spirit to leave the place or person by means of prayers and religious ceremonies. *They've gone to San Francisco to exorcize the evil spirits which they say have taken over the city.*
2 VO If you **exorcize** a painful or unhappy memory, you succeed in removing it from your mind. *He exorcized his harrowing memories through writing a book.*

exotic /ɪgzɒtɪk/
ADJ Something that is **exotic** is unusual and interesting because it comes from or is related to a distant country. *...rich exotic foods. ...distant and exotic holiday destinations.*

expand /ɪkspænd/ **expands, expanding, expanded**
V-ERG When something **expands**, it becomes larger. *Natural materials expand with heat... The city's population expanded by 12 per cent. ...major measures to expand the Royal Air Force.*
expand on PHRASAL VERB If you **expand on** or **expand upon** something, you give more information or details about it. *Perhaps you could expand on this a little bit... I went on to expand upon this theme.*

expanse /ɪkspæns/ **expanses**
NC+*of* An **expanse** of sea, sky, or land is a very large area of it; a literary word. *...the wide expanse of snowy fields.*

expansion /ɪkspænʃn/
NU **Expansion** is the process of becoming greater in size or amount. *...the rapid expansion of British agriculture.*

expansionism /ɪkspænʃənɪzəm/
NU **Expansionism** is the policy of expanding the economy of a country or increasing the amount of land that it rules. *The treaty contains an important clause to quell fears of territorial expansionism.*
♦ **expansionist** /ɪkspænʃənɪst/ ADJ *He accused Israel of pursuing aggressive and expansionist policies.*

expansive /ɪkspænsɪv/
ADJ If you are **expansive**, you talk a lot, because you are happy and relaxed. *Mr Gorbachev was in expansive mood as he greeted the Foreign Secretary.*

expatiate /ɪkspeɪʃieɪt/ **expatiates, expatiating, expatiated**
V A If you **expatiate** on or about something, you write or speak in detail or at great length about it; a formal word.

expatriate /ekspætriət/ **expatriates**
NC An **expatriate** is someone who lives in a country which is not their own. *Sir James Spicer hosted a reception for British expatriates.* ► Also ADJ *...the large Tunisian expatriate community in France.*

expect /ɪkspɛkt/ **expects, expecting, expected**
1 V O+*to*-INF, V+*to*-INF, or V-REPORT If you **expect** something to happen, you believe that it will happen. *Nobody expected the strike to succeed... He didn't expect to be so busy... When do you expect that this material will be available?*
2 V O If you **are expecting** something, you believe that it is going to happen or arrive. *We are expecting rain... Dr Willoughby was expecting him.* ♦ **expected** ADJ *We would resist this expected attack.*
3 V O or V+*to*-INF If you **expect** something, you believe that it is your right to get it or have it. *We expect sincerity from our politicians... I expect to be treated with respect.*
4 V O+*to*-INF If you **expect** someone to do something, you require them to do it as a duty or obligation. *He is expected to put his work before his family.*
5 You say 'I expect' when you mean that what you are saying is likely to be correct. *I expect you can hear the sound of the planting going on... I expect you agree.*
6 V O or V If a woman is **expecting** a baby, she is pregnant. *She's expecting her third baby.*

expectancy /ɪkspɛktənsi/
NU **Expectancy** is a feeling that something exciting is about to happen. *There's a certain air of expectancy about the city.* ● See also **life expectancy**.

expectant /ɪkspɛktənt/
1 ADJ If you are **expectant**, you think something is going to happen. *Expectant crowds have been lining the streets for several hours.* ♦ **expectantly** ADV *She looked at him expectantly.*
2 ADJ ATTRIB An **expectant** mother or father is someone whose baby is going to be born soon. *The supplies are intended in particular for children and expectant mothers.*

expectation /ekspekteɪʃn/ **expectations**
NC or NU **Expectations** are hopes or beliefs that something will happen. *The plan has succeeded beyond our expectations... There was a great deal of expectation about the visit.*

expectorant /ɪkspɛktərənt/ **expectorants**
NC An **expectorant** is a cough medicine that helps to loosen phlegm in your chest.

expediency /ɪkspiːdiənsi/
NU **Expediency** is behaviour in which you do what is convenient, rather than what is morally right; a formal word. *They have abandoned principle for expediency.*

expedient /ɪkspiːdiənt/ **expedients**; a formal word.
1 NC An **expedient** is an action that achieves a particular purpose, but may not be morally acceptable. *Incomes controls were used only as a short-term expedient.*
2 ADJ If it is **expedient** to do something, it is useful or convenient to do it. *The President did not find it expedient to attend the meeting.*

expedite /ekspədaɪt/ **expedites, expediting, expedited**
V O If you **expedite** something, you cause it to be done more quickly; a formal word. *We must do more to expedite development... This helped to expedite the army's withdrawal.*

expedition /ekspədɪʃn/ **expeditions**
1 NC An **expedition** is an organized journey that is made for a particular purpose such as exploration. *They were detained for illegally entering a restricted area while on a scientific expedition... The expedition is being sponsored by a Japanese firm.*
2 NC You can also refer to the people who go on an expedition as an **expedition**. *Stephen Hillen and David Tyson were part of a four-person expedition which scaled Makrong Chhish, a mountain in northern Pakistan.*
3 NC An **expedition** is also a short journey or outing, often one that you make for pleasure. *...a shopping expedition.*

expeditionary force /ekspədɪʃənəri fɔːs/ **expeditionary forces**
NC An **expeditionary force** is a group of soldiers who are sent to fight in a foreign country. *He refused to allow Mr.Chirac to send an expeditionary force to Chad.*

expeditious /ekspədɪʃəs/
ADJ **Expeditious** means quick and efficient; a formal word. *...the most expeditious method of obtaining reduced hours.* ♦ **expeditiously** ADV *The reports will be examined as expeditiously as possible.*

expel /ɪkspɛl/ **expels, expelling, expelled**
1 V O If someone **is expelled** from a school or organization, they are officially told to leave because they have behaved badly. *He had been expelled from his previous school for stealing.*
2 V O When people **are expelled** from a place, they are made to leave it, usually by force. *Peasants were expelled from their villages.*
3 V O If a gas or liquid **is expelled** from a place, it is forced out of it; a formal use. *Water is sucked in at one end and expelled at the other.*

expend /ɪkspɛnd/ **expends, expending, expended**
V O To **expend** energy, time, or money means to spend or use it; a formal word. *We will have to expend all our energies on development rather than on party political squabbles.*

expendable /ɪkspɛndəbl/
ADJ Someone or something that is **expendable** is no longer needed and can be got rid of; a formal word. *To the planners, foreign workers have the advantage of being readily available, and, as seen this week, highly expendable.*

expenditure /ɪkspɛndɪtʃə/ **expenditures**
1 NU or NC Your **expenditure** on something is the total amount of money you spend on it. *We restricted our expenditure on food... The cabinet agreed that public expenditure would have to be kept under strict control... Their expenditures reach almost 200,000 million dollars a year.*
2 NU+SUPP **Expenditure** of energy or time is energy or time used for a particular purpose. *This was done with a minimum expenditure of energy.*

expense /ɪkspɛns/ **expenses**
1 NU or NC **Expense** is the money that something costs

or that you need to pay for something. ...*the roads they're building at vast expense... People won't be left with enough to pay for basic everyday expenses.*
2 N PL Your **expenses** are the money you spend while doing something connected with your work, which is paid back to you afterwards. *MPs must account for their campaign expenses... Pay the bill and claim it on expenses.*
● **Expense** is used in these phrases. ● If you do something at someone's **expense**, they provide the money for it. *He circulated the document at his own expense.* ● If you make a joke at someone's **expense**, you do it to make them seem foolish. *The tabloid newspapers have not been able to resist an outbreak of jokes at Edwina's expense.* ● If you achieve something at someone's **expense**, you do it in a way that harms them. *They increase their own income at the expense of the rural masses.*

expense account, expense accounts
NC An **expense account** is an arrangement that is made by the company you work for, which allows you to spend their money on things that are part of your job, for example travelling or looking after their clients. *As an executive, you will be entitled to an expense account. ...an expense-account lunch.*

expensive /ɪkspɛnsɪv/
ADJ **Expensive** things cost a lot of money. ...*young men dressed in expensive Italian clothes.*
◆ **expensively** ADV *We can do that fairly easily and not too expensively.*

experience /ɪkspɪəriəns/ **experiences, experiencing, experienced**
1 NU If you have had **experience** of something, you have seen it, done it, or felt it. *The new countries have no experience of democracy... I had no military experience.*
2 NU You can refer to all the things that have happened to you as **experience**. *Everyone learns best from his own experience. ...speaking from personal experience.*
3 NC+SUPP An **experience** is something that happens to you or something you do. *Moving house can be a traumatic experience.*
4 VO If you **experience** a situation or feeling, it happens to you or you are affected by it. *Similar problems have been experienced by other students.*

experienced /ɪkspɪəriənst/
ADJ **Experienced** is used to describe someone who has done a particular job for a long time. *He is a very experienced journalist.*

experiment /ɪkspɛrɪmənt/ **experiments, experimenting, experimented**
1 NCorNU An **experiment** is a scientific test done to prove or discover something. *The most important part of the experiment was analysing the radiation given off by the missiles. ...new information gathered by observation or experiment.*
2 NC If you do something new to see what effects it has, you can refer to your action as an **experiment**. *The new simplified system is being introduced as an experiment.*
3 VA If you **experiment** with something or experiment on it, you do a scientific test on it. *He experimented with young white rats.* ◆ **experimentation** /ɪkspɛrɪmenteɪʃn/ NU *They might be able to confirm the results by some careful experimentation on human volunteers.*
4 VAorV To **experiment** also means to try out something such as an idea or method in order to see what it is like or how it works. *They are willing to experiment with new economic ideas... Only 3 per cent of parents questioned say that their teenage son or daughter is likely to experiment with soft drugs such as cannabis... I'd like them to see us as a band who needs to change, who needs to experiment.*

experimental /ɪkspɛrɪmentl/
1 ADJ Something that is **experimental** uses new ideas or methods to see how they work. *A small number of towns have begun experimental bans on drinking alcohol in public... There has been a call for television cameras to be allowed into the courts on an experimental basis.* ◆ **experimentally** /ɪkspɛrɪmentəli/

ADV ...*the first parking meters, introduced experimentally in 1958.*
2 ADJ **Experimental** also means relating to scientific experiments. *There is now experimental evidence to show that pigs can become infected with human flu viruses.* ◆ **experimentally** ADV *They are measured experimentally and the results compared.*

experimenter /ɪkspɛrɪmentə/ **experimenters**
1 NC An **experimenter** is someone who does scientific tests in order to prove a theory or discover what happens to things in particular conditions. *For many years experimenters thought that very high temperatures and pressures were essential to the process.*
2 NC An **experimenter** is also someone who likes trying new ideas or methods. *He was an incessant experimenter.*

expert /ɛkspɜːt/ **experts**
1 NC An **expert** is a person who is very skilled at doing something or who knows a lot about a particular subject. *Experts were called in to dismantle the bomb... Mr Oleg Sokolov is an acknowledged expert on American policy.*
2 ADJ Someone who is **expert** at doing something is very skilled at it. *They sought help from expert money advisers.* ◆ **expertly** ADV *Burke drove expertly.*

expertise /ɛkspɜːtiːz/
NU **Expertise** is special skill or knowledge. *The Soviet Union desperately wants Japanese industrial expertise.*

expiate /ɛkspieɪt/ **expiates, expiating, expiated**
VO If you **expiate** guilty feelings or bad behaviour, you do something to indicate that you are sorry for what you have done; a formal word. *He hoped to expiate his guilt over leaving her.* ◆ **expiation** /ɛkspieɪʃn/ NU *He sought expiation by demanding punishment.*

expiration /ɛkspəreɪʃn/ **expirations**
1 NU The **expiration** of a period of time is its ending; a formal use. ...*the expiration of the sixty-day truce and negotiating period.*
2 NCorNU **Expiration** is also the action of breathing air out of your lungs; a medical use.

expire /ɪkspaɪə/ **expires, expiring, expired**
1 V When something **expires**, it reaches the end of the period of time for which it is valid; a formal use. *My passport is due to expire in three months.*
2 V When someone **expires**, they die; a literary use. *The old lady expired within the hour.*

expiry /ɪkspaɪəri/
NU The **expiry** of something such as a licence or passport is the fact that it ceases to be valid; a formal word. *The French licences have no expiry date.*

explain /ɪkspleɪn/ **explains, explaining, explained**
1 VOorV-REPORT If you **explain** something, you give details about it so that it can be understood. *John went on to explain the legal situation... My father suggested that I ask one of his brothers, who, he told me, was very good at explaining such things... I explained that I was trying to write a book... There have been endless TV and radio programmes explaining how it all works.*
2 VOorV If you **explain** something that has happened, you give reasons for it. *He never wrote to me to explain his decision... Just a minute. Let me explain.*
explain away PHRASAL VERB If you **explain away** a mistake, you try to indicate that it is not very important or that it is not really your fault. *Their leaders are clearly having problems explaining away recent failures.*

explanation /ɛkspləneɪʃn/ **explanations**
NCorNU If you give an **explanation**, you say why something happened, or describe something in detail. *There's been no official explanation of how the tragedy happened. ...a note of explanation.*

explanatory /ɪksplænətəri/
ADJ Something that is **explanatory** explains something by giving details about it. *They produce free explanatory leaflets on heating.*

expletive /ɪksplitɪv/ **expletives**
NC An **expletive** is a rude word or expression such as 'Damn!' which you say loudly and suddenly when you are annoyed, excited, or in pain; a formal word. *I*

heard all sorts of expletives being yelled in my direction.

explicable /ɪksplɪkəbl/

ADJ Something that is **explicable** can be explained and understood; a formal word. *For no explicable reason your mind goes blank.*

explicate /ɛksplɪkeɪt/ **explicates, explicating, explicated**

VO To **explicate** something means to explain it and make it clear; a formal word. *...informal activities that help the student define, explicate and test his values.*

explicit /ɪksplɪsɪt/

1 ADJ Something that is **explicit** is shown or expressed clearly and openly, without hiding anything. *Egypt is the only Arab country which has given explicit support to the plan... The album's lyrics include sexually explicit language.* ◆ **explicitly** ADV *...explicitly violent scenes.*

2 ADJ If you are **explicit** about something, you express yourself clearly and openly. *She was not explicit about what she really felt.* ◆ **explicitly** ADV *I don't think that he stated that explicitly.*

explode /ɪkspləʊd/ **explodes, exploding, exploded**

1 V-ERG When a bomb **explodes**, it bursts with great force. *A bomb had exploded in the next street... They exploded a nuclear device.*

2 VA You can say that a person **explodes** when they express strong feelings suddenly and violently. *She exploded with rage.*

3 V When something increases suddenly and rapidly in number or intensity, you can say that it **explodes**. *The US prison population has exploded since 1980, growing by almost 134 per cent... It could be that they have had a hand in escalating the tensions which have now exploded into violence.*

4 VO If you **explode** a theory, you prove that it is wrong or impossible. *...new evidence exploding the myth that light or moderate drinking can protect against heart attack.*

exploit, exploits, exploiting, exploited; pronounced /ɪksplɔɪt/ when it is a verb and /ɛksplɔɪt/ when it is a noun.

1 VO If someone **exploits** you, they unfairly use your work or ideas and give you little in return. *For centuries tribal people have been exploited by settlers.* ◆ **exploitation** /ɛksplɔɪteɪʃn/ NU *The shopworkers' unions are afraid of exploitation of their members.*

2 VO If you **exploit** a situation, you make use of it in order to achieve something or gain some advantage. *They were accused of exploiting the Gulf crisis for political and economic gain.* ◆ **exploitation** NU *...his skilful exploitation of the differences between the Mujahedin forces.*

3 VO To **exploit** something such as a raw material or an idea means to develop it in order to make money out of it. *Many groups believe that multinational companies are exploiting Brazil's rich natural resources.* ◆ **exploitation** NU *...the exploitation of the Earth's resources.*

4 NC Someone's **exploits** are the brave or interesting things they have done. *The Brigade have earned the nickname The Desert Rats after their exploits in the Second World War.*

exploitable /ɪksplɔɪtəbl/

1 ADJ Something that is **exploitable** can be used as a basis for making money. *This is not really an exploitable resource... None of these species is commercially exploitable.*

2 ADJ People who are **exploitable** can be made to work for very low pay. *...a large and easily exploitable work force.*

exploitative /ɪksplɔɪtətɪv/

ADJ An **exploitative** person or organization treats people unfairly by using their work or ideas and giving them very little in return. *Their rule over the Congo was ruthlessly exploitative.*

exploiter /ɪksplɔɪtə/ **exploiters**

NC You refer to people as **exploiters** when they use other people or things in order to make money in an uncaring way. *...the misuse of power by property-hungry exploiters.*

exploratory /ɪksplɒrətəʳri/

ADJ **Exploratory** actions are done to discover something or to learn something; a formal word. *...an exploratory operation on his knee... He is due to go to Israel tomorrow for exploratory talks.*

explore /ɪksplɔː/ **explores, exploring, explored**

1 VO If you **explore** a place, you travel in it to find out what it is like. *He explored three continents by canoe.* ◆ **exploration** /ɛkspləreɪʃn/ **explorations** NU or NC *The greatest journey of exploration was undertaken by Captain Cook in the eighteen century... He helped them with their underwater explorations.*

2 VO If you **explore** something with your hands, you touch it so that you can feel what it is like. *With widespread hands he explored the wet grass.*

3 VO If you **explore** an idea, you think about it carefully to decide whether it is a good one. *The conference explored the possibility of closer trade links.*

explorer /ɪksplɔːrə/ **explorers**

NC An **explorer** is someone who travels to places about which very little is known, in order to discover what is there. *The British explorer, Sir Ranulph Fiennes, has abandoned an attempt to reach the North Pole.*

explosion /ɪkspləʊʒn/ **explosions**

1 NC An **explosion** is a sudden, violent burst of energy, for example one caused by a bomb. *Twenty men were killed in the explosion.*

2 NC+SUPP An **explosion** of something is a large and rapid increase of it. *A succession of good rains led to a population explosion amongst desert locusts.*

3 NC An **explosion** of a feeling is a sudden, intense, and often unexpected expression of it. *He said that these proposals would be greeted by an explosion of anger... There has been an explosion of interest in fashion.*

explosive /ɪkspləʊsɪv/ **explosives**

1 NC or NU An **explosive** is a substance or device that can cause an explosion. *They had been found in possession of arms and explosives. ...the manufacturer of the plastic explosive, Semtex.*

2 ADJ Something that is **explosive** is capable of causing an explosion. *...a powerful explosive device.*

3 ADJ A sudden loud noise can be described as **explosive**. *The final applause was explosive.*

4 ADJ An **explosive** situation is likely to have serious or dangerous effects. *Unemployment has become the most explosive political issue.*

exponent /ɪkspəʊnənt/ **exponents**; a formal word.

1 NC+SUPP An **exponent** of an idea, theory, or plan is someone who speaks or writes in support of it. *They see Mr Lilley as one of the most ardent exponents of the Thatcher revolution.*

2 NC+SUPP An **exponent** of a particular skill or activity is a person who is good at it. *He was a great exponent of chamber music.*

exponential /ɛkspənɛnʃl/

ADJ **Exponential** means growing or increasing very rapidly; a formal word. *...a period of exponential growth.*

export, exports, exporting, exported; pronounced /ɪkspɔːt/ when it is a verb and /ɛkspɔːt/ when it is a noun.

1 VO To **export** goods means to sell them to another country and send them there. *Raw materials are exported at low prices.*

2 NU The **export** of goods is the sale and sending of them to another country. *The export of military equipment is already forbidden... They grow coffee and bananas for export.*

3 NC **Exports** are goods which are sold to another country and sent there. *Burma has been badly hit by falling prices for some of its major exports, such as rice and teak... A ban has been put on all food exports.*

4 VO To **export** ideas or values means to introduce them into other countries. *This is a system which has been exported to scores of other countries around the world.*

5 **export credit**: see credit.

exportable /ɪkspɔːtəbl/

ADJ **Exportable** means suitable to be exported. *The*

drink will now become exportable anywhere in the EC... Only two countries, Ivory Coast and Gambia, have exportable surpluses.

exporter /ɪkspɔːtə/ **exporters**
NC An **exporter** is a country, firm, or person that sells and sends goods to another country. *Ivory Coast is the world's largest cocoa producer and exporter.*

expose /ɪkspəʊz/ **exposes, exposing, exposed**
1 VO To **expose** something means to uncover it and make it visible. *The rocks are exposed at low tide.*
2 VO To **expose** someone means to reveal the truth about them, especially when it involves dishonest or shocking behaviour. *Anthony Blunt was exposed as a spy in 1979... Their highly profitable dealings in imported Japanese cars were exposed.*
3 VO+to If you **are exposed** to something dangerous, you are put in a situation in which it might harm you. *They had been exposed to radiation.*

exposé /eksp<u>əu</u>zeɪ/ **exposés**
NC An **exposé** is a piece of writing which reveals the truth about something, especially something involving dishonest or shocking behaviour.

exposed /ɪkspəʊzd/
ADJ If a place is **exposed**, it has no natural protection against bad weather or enemies, for example because it has no trees or is on very high ground. *The house is in a very exposed position. ...the most exposed of seaside promenades... When the animal has left the exposed feeding grounds it is safe from attack.*

exposition /ekspəzɪʃn/ **expositions**
NC An **exposition** of an idea or theory is a detailed explanation of it; a formal word. *Mr Reagan's speech contained a strong exposition of Western-style freedom and democracy.*

expostulate /ɪkspɒstjʊleɪt/ **expostulates, expostulating, expostulated**
V or V-QUOTE If you **expostulate**, you express strong disagreement with someone; a formal word. *He was expostulating with the porter... 'What's got into you, Hilary?' Morris expostulated.*

exposure /ɪkspəʊʒə/ **exposures**
1 NU **Exposure** to something dangerous means being in a situation where you are affected by it. *He was suffering from exposure to nuclear radiation.*
2 NU **Exposure** is also the harmful effect on your body caused by very cold weather. *The group's leader died of exposure.*
3 NU **Exposure** is also publicity. *The petition has received no exposure in the local press.*
4 NU The **exposure** of a well-known person is the revealing of the truth about them, especially when it involves dishonest or shocking behaviour. *She said that public exposure of MPs would bring the Commons into disrepute... The chairman resigned following the exposure of corruption.*
5 NC In photography, an **exposure** is a single photograph. *...a camera capable of taking a hundred exposures before the film needs changing.*

expound /ɪkspaʊnd/ **expounds, expounding, expounded**
VO If you **expound** an idea or opinion, you give a clear and detailed explanation of it; a formal word. *Schmidt continued to expound his views on economics and politics.*

express /ɪkspres/ **expresses, expressing, expressed**
1 VO or V-REFL When you **express** an idea or feeling, you show what you think or feel by saying or doing something. *The Defence Minister has expressed concern at the possibility of war... A statement said Egypt had so far expressed no opinion... You may not like either what she has to say or the way in which she expresses herself... She expresses herself through art.*
2 V-REFL If an idea or feeling **expresses** itself in some way, it can be clearly seen in someone's actions; a formal use. *That increased confidence expressed itself in other ways.*
3 VO If you **express** a quantity in a particular form, you write it down in that form. *Here it is expressed as a percentage.*
4 ADJ ATTRIB An **express** command or order is stated clearly; a formal use. *The chapel was built in 1943 at*

the express wish of the then Prime Minister.
♦ **expressly** ADV *Jefferson had expressly asked her to invite Freeman.*
5 ADJ ATTRIB An **express** intention or purpose is deliberate or specific. *She came with the express purpose of causing trouble.* ♦ **expressly** ADV *They bought the house expressly for her.*
6 ADJ ATTRIB An **express** service is one in which things are done faster than usual. *...an express letter.*
7 NC An **express** is a fast train or coach which stops at very few places. *The express was travelling from Mandalay.*

expression /ɪkspreʃn/ **expressions**
1 NU or NC The **expression** of ideas or feelings is the showing of them through words, actions, or art. *The authorities seemed prepared to tolerate the expression of liberal ideas... We parted with many expressions of goodwill.*
2 NC or NU Your **expression** is the way that your face shows what you are thinking or feeling. *...a shabby-looking soldier who shuffled around with a bored expression... Anthony's face showed not a flicker of expression.*
3 NC An **expression** is a word or phrase, especially one that you are explaining or commenting on. *I prefer to use the expression 'joint venture'.*

expressionism /ɪkspreʃənɪzəm/
NU **Expressionism** is a style of art, literature, and music, which uses symbolism and exaggeration in order to represent emotions as opposed to physical reality.

expressionless /ɪkspreʃnləs/
ADJ If someone's face or voice is **expressionless**, it does not show their feelings. *He described the terror he felt at the cold, expressionless eyes of one of the hijackers.*

expressive /ɪkspresɪv/
1 ADJ Something that is **expressive** indicates clearly a person's feelings or intentions. *She had given Lynn an expressive glance.* ♦ **expressively** ADV *He drew a finger expressively across his throat.*
2 ADJ Someone's **expressive** ability is their ability to speak or write clearly and interestingly. *...evaluating the child's expressive powers.*

expressway /ɪkspresweɪ/ **expressways**
NC An **expressway** is a wide road designed so that a lot of traffic can move along it very quickly. *The thirty mile long six-lane road—to be known as the Midlands Expressway—will skirt the city of Birmingham, one of the worst traffic bottlenecks in the country.*

expropriate /eksprəʊprieɪt/ **expropriates, expropriating, expropriated**
VO If someone **expropriates** something, they take it away from its owner; a formal word. *The surplus will be expropriated by the government.*

expulsion /ɪkspʌlʃn/ **expulsions**; a formal word.
1 NU or NC **Expulsion** is the expelling of someone from a school or organization. *The officials were warned that they faced expulsion from the party. ...resolutions protesting against the expulsions of four key reformers from the party.*
2 NU or NC **Expulsion** is also the act of forcing people to leave a place. *...the expulsion of military advisers... No official reason has been given for the expulsions.*

expunge /ɪkspʌndʒ/ **expunges, expunging, expunged**
VO To **expunge** something means to remove it completely, for example from a piece of writing or from your memory, because it causes problems or bad feelings; a formal word. *...his battle to expunge the clause from the contract... He had tried to expunge memories of the failure.*

expurgate /ekspəgeɪt/ **expurgates, expurgating, expurgated**
VO To **expurgate** a piece of writing means to remove parts of it before it is published in order to avoid offending or shocking people; a formal word. *He still hopes to see a Chinese version of his book—it would be expurgated of course—published in China.*
♦ **expurgated** ADJ *...the expurgated version of Shakespeare by Thomas Bowdler.*

exquisite /ɪkskwɪzɪt, ɛkskwɪzɪt/
1 ADJ **Exquisite** means extremely beautiful. *She has the most exquisite face. ...exquisite jewellery.*
◆ **exquisitely** ADV *Their children were exquisitely dressed.*
2 ADJ **Exquisite** pleasure or pain is very great. *...sipping the water slowly with exquisite relief.*

ex-serviceman, ex-servicemen
NC An **ex-serviceman** is a man who used to be in a country's army, navy, or air force. *Mr Mitterrand awarded medals of honour to a group of ex-servicemen.*

extant /ekstænt/
ADJ Something that is **extant** still exists although it is very old; a formal word. *...one Spanish law that is still extant in California.*

extemporize /ɪkstempəraɪz/ **extemporizes, extemporizing, extemporized**; also spelt **extemporise**.
V or VO If you **extemporize**, you speak, act, or perform something immediately, without any rehearsing or preparation; a formal word. *Certain performers are funnier when they extemporize.*

extend /ɪkstend/ **extends, extending, extended**
1 VA If something **extends** for a particular distance, it continues for that distance. *The road now extends two kilometres beyond the river.*
2 VA If an object **extends** from a surface, it sticks out from it. *...metal slabs extending from the wall.*
3 VA If an event or activity **extends** for a period of time, it continues for that time. *His working day often extends well into the evening.*
4 VA If a situation **extends** to particular people or things, it includes or affects them. *The consequences of unemployment extend well beyond the labour market.*
5 VO If you **extend** something, you make it bigger, or make it last longer or include more. *Have you ever thought of extending your house?... The authorities extended her visa... Congress wants the law extended to cover all states.*
6 VO If you **extend** a part of your body, you straighten it or stretch it out. *He extended his hand, and Brody shook it.*
7 VO To **extend** an offer or invitation to someone means to make it; a formal use. *He extended an invitation for President Suharto to visit India.*

extendable /ɪkstendəbl/
1 ADJ Something that is **extendable** can be made longer in length. *Some species have small extendable tentacles. ...an extendable ladder.*
2 ADJ You can also use **extendable** to say that something can be made to exist or be valid for a longer period of time. *The tenancy of the Lodge was only extendable on a weekly basis.*

extended /ɪkstendɪd/
ADJ Something that is **extended** is bigger or longer than usual or includes more people or things than usual. *They should face a compulsory extended driving test. ...a tribal society grouped in huge extended families.*

extension /ɪkstenʃn/ **extensions**
1 NC An **extension** is a new room or building which is added to an existing building. *...a new extension to the library.*
2 NC or NU An **extension** is also an extra period of time for which something continues to exist or be valid. *Applications for visa extensions by four students have been rejected... He asked for extension of his residence permit.*
3 NC or NU The **extension** of something is its development to include or affect more things. *The legislation was updated in line with the latest extensions of the United Nations sanctions... Nationalist leaders demanded the extension of democratic rights.*
4 NC A telephone **extension** is one of several telephones connected to the switchboard of an organization, each with its own number. *If you require a ticket please phone Jamethy Close on extension 2838.*

extensive /ɪkstensɪv/
1 ADJ If something is **extensive** in area, it covers a large area. *...an extensive Roman settlement in north-west England.*
2 ADJ **Extensive** means very great in effect. *Many buildings suffered extensive damage in the blast.*
◆ **extensively** ADV *The aircraft were extensively modified.*
3 ADJ **Extensive** also means covering many details, ideas, or items. *We had fairly extensive discussions.*
◆ **extensively** ADV *I have quoted extensively from it in the following pages.*

extent /ɪkstent/
1 N SING+POSS The **extent** of a situation or difficulty is its size or scale. *The full extent of the problem is not yet known.*
2 N SING+POSS The **extent** of something is its length, area, or size. *The extent of the area infested is probably bigger than in the 1950s.*
● **Extent** is used in these phrases. ● You use phrases such as **to a large extent**, **to some extent**, or **to a certain extent** to indicate that something is partly but not entirely true. *Well I think to a certain extent it's true... The agreement was supported to a large extent by Cuba and the United States.* ● You use phrases such as **to what extent**, **to that extent**, or **to the extent** that when discussing how true a statement is. *To what extent are diseases linked with genes?... A computer is intelligent only to the extent that it can store information.* ● You use phrases such as **to the extent of** or **to such an extent that** to indicate that a situation has reached a particular stage. *Membership of the party also meant blind obedience to the party, even to the extent of killing people... Sanitary conditions had deteriorated to such an extent that there was widespread danger of disease.*

exterior /ɪkstɪərɪə/ **exteriors**
1 NC The **exterior** of something is its outside surface. *Keep your car exterior in good condition.*
2 NC+SUPP Your **exterior** is your usual outward appearance and behaviour. *Beneath his professional doctor's exterior, he was wildly fun-loving and reckless.*
3 ADJ ATTRIB **Exterior** means situated or happening outside a person or thing. *Exterior drains must be kept clear.*

exterminate /ɪkstɜːmɪneɪt/ **exterminates, exterminating, exterminated**
VO When a group of animals or people are **exterminated**, they are all killed. *Fishing must stop before the species is completely exterminated.*
◆ **extermination** /ɪkstɜːmɪneɪʃn/ NU *We must find a way to prevent the extermination of these animals.*

exterminator /ɪkstɜːmɪneɪtə/ **exterminators**
NC An **exterminator** is a person whose job is to kill animals such as rats or mice, because they are a nuisance or a danger. *...a rodent exterminator.*

external /ɪkstɜːnl/ **externals**
1 ADJ **External** means happening, coming from, or existing outside a place, person, or area of activity. *...the external walls of the chimneys... They did it in response to external pressures.* ◆ **externally** /ɪkstɜːnəli/ ADV *It should be applied externally.*
2 ADJ ATTRIB **External** is used to describe people who come into an organization from outside to do a job there. *Their accounts are audited by a firm of external auditors.*
3 N PL The **externals** of a situation are features in it which are obvious but not important; a formal use. *The popular historian is concerned only with externals.*

externalize /ɪkstɜːnəlaɪz/ **externalizes, externalizing, externalized**; also spelt **externalise**.
VO If you **externalize** your ideas or feelings, you express them in words or actions; a formal word. *He tried to externalize his thoughts in pencilled images... Their discontent was externalised in political action.*

extinct /ɪkstɪŋkt/
1 ADJ If a species of animals is **extinct**, it no longer has any living members. *The dodo became extinct about 300 years ago... One of the very rare Asian species of rhino could be extinct by the end of the century if the trade in poached horns is not stopped.*

2 ADJ An **extinct** volcano does not erupt or is unlikely to erupt. *...an extinct volcano on the island of St Lucia.*

extinction /ɪkstɪŋkʃn/
NU The **extinction** of a species of animal is the death of all its remaining members. *Apes are in danger of extinction.*

extinguish /ɪkstɪŋgwɪʃ/ **extinguishes, extinguishing, extinguished**; a formal word.
1 VO If you **extinguish** a fire or a light, you stop it burning or shining. *A fire on board a cargo ferry in the English Channel has been extinguished.*
2 VO To **extinguish** a quality, idea or feeling means to destroy it. *However great evil may seem, it will never finally extinguish good when men fight with courage.*

extinguisher /ɪkstɪŋgwɪʃə/. See **fire extinguisher**.

extol /ɪkstəʊl/ **extols, extolling, extolled**
VO If you **extol** something, you praise it and talk about it enthusiastically; a formal word. *He was extolling the virtues of female independence.*

extort /ɪkstɔːt/ **extorts, extorting, extorted**
VO If someone **extorts** money from you, they get it by using force or threats. *Soldiers, some of them drunk, commandeered cars and extorted money.*

extortion /ɪkstɔːʃn/
1 NU **Extortion** is the crime of obtaining something from someone, especially money, by using force or threats. *...a criminal specializing in extortion... He faces trial on extortion charges.*
2 NU You also describe someone's behaviour as **extortion** if you think they are trying to obtain more money for something than it is worth; used showing disapproval. *'It's extortion,' she said. 'He's not worth this much.'*

extortionate /ɪkstɔːʃəⁿnət/
ADJ **Extortionate** demands or prices are much greater than you consider to be fair. *They lend to these women at extortionate rates, usually around three hundred per cent per year.*

extra /ekstrə/ **extras**
1 ADJ or ADV An **extra** thing, person, or amount is another one that is added to others of the same kind. *Take an extra pair of shoes... India is to introduce extra security measures along its border with Pakistan in the Punjab area... You have to pay extra for breakfast.*
2 NC **Extras** are things that are not necessary but make something more comfortable, useful, or enjoyable. *With the extras, the car cost £4,000.*
3 N PL **Extras** are also additional amounts of money added to the basic price of something. *There are no hidden extras.*
4 NC An **extra** is a person who plays an unimportant part in a film. *The cast included hundreds of Japanese American extras who were bused 100 miles to the site each day.*
5 SUBMOD If you are **extra** polite or **extra** careful, you are more polite or careful than usual. *He was extra polite to his superiors.*

extra- /ekstrə-, ɪkstræ-/
PREFIX **Extra-** is used to form adjectives that describe something as being outside something else. For example, extra-parliamentary activities are political activities that take place outside parliament; used in formal English. *The president was forced to take extra-constitutional steps.*

extract, extracts, extracting, extracted; pronounced /ɪkstrækt/ when it is a verb and /ekstrækt/ when it is a noun.
1 VO If you **extract** something from a place, you take or pull it out; a formal use. *Mrs Oliver extracted a small notebook from her bag.*
2 VO To **extract** a raw material means to get it from the ground or to separate it from another substance. *The Japanese extract ten million tons of coal each year.*
3 VO If you **extract** information from someone, you get it from them with difficulty. *Sir James had extracted from Francis a fairly detailed account.*
4 VO+*from* If someone **extracts** advantage from a situation, they use the situation in order to gain advantage; a formal use. *They will extract the*

maximum propaganda value from this affair.
5 NC An **extract** from a piece of writing or music is a small part of it that is printed or played separately. *She began by reading an extract from one of the stories.*

extraction /ɪkstrækʃn/
1 NU Your **extraction** is the country or people that your family originally comes from; a formal use. *Alistair was of Scottish extraction.*
2 NU The **extraction** of something is the act or process of removing it. *They discussed the technology required for the cleaner and more efficient extraction of minerals.*

extractor /ɪkstræktə/ **extractors**
NC An **extractor** or extractor **fan** is a device in a window or wall which draws steam or hot air out of a room or building.

extra-curricular /ekstrəkərɪkjʊlə/
ADJ **Extra-curricular** activities are activities for students that are not part of their course; a formal word. *Forty per cent of schools have reported a cut-back in extra-curricular activities in the last two years.*

extradite /ekstrədaɪt/ **extradites, extraditing, extradited**
VO If someone is **extradited**, they are officially sent back to their own country to be tried for a crime that they have been accused of; a formal word. *Finland has extradited a Soviet man who hijacked a plane last month.* ◆ **extradition** /ekstrədɪʃn/ NU *France requested their extradition from the United States.*

extradition warrant, extradition warrants
NC An **extradition warrant** is a legal document that is issued by one country and sent to another asking them to hand over someone who is accused of a crime in the country of issue. *Britain may issue an extradition warrant asking the Irish authorities to return him.*

extra-marital /ekstrəmærɪtl/; also spelt **extramarital**.
ADJ You use **extra-marital** to describe a sexual relationship between a married person and someone who is not their husband or wife; a formal word. *He said he was resigning because he had been having an extra-marital affair.*

extra-mural
ADJ ATTRIB You use **extra-mural** to refer to courses in a college or university which are involved mainly with part-time students. *...the Department of Extra-mural Studies.*

extraneous /ɪkstreɪniəs/
ADJ Something that is **extraneous** happens or concerns things outside the situation or subject that you are talking about; a formal word. *We must avoid all extraneous issues.*

extraordinary /ɪkstrɔːdənəⁿri/
1 ADJ If you describe someone or something as **extraordinary**, you mean that they have some special or extreme qualities. *In her book Mary Wilson assesses the career of this extraordinary man... We lived an extraordinary life of luxury.* ◆ **extraordinarily** SUBMOD *...an extraordinarily beautiful girl.*
2 ADJ You can also say that something is **extraordinary** when it is unusual or surprising. *What an extraordinary thing to say... The latest figures are extraordinary.* ◆ **extraordinarily** SUBMOD *...extraordinarily high levels of radiation.*
3 ADJ ATTRIB An **extraordinary** meeting is arranged specially to deal with a particular problem. *The EC will hold an extraordinary meeting of its foreign affairs council next week.*

extrapolate /ɪkstræpəleɪt/ **extrapolates, extrapolating, extrapolated**
V or VO If you **extrapolate** from known facts, you examine them and use logic or reason in order to calculate a quantity or make statements about what is likely to happen in the future; a formal word. *...the inadequacy of extrapolating from the experience of English-speaking students... To assess future needs, the Department simply extrapolated past demand trends.*

extrapolation /ɪkstræpəleɪʃn/ **extrapolations**; a formal word
1 NU **Extrapolation** is the act or process of

extrapolating. *Extrapolation of their results suggests that regular doses could eliminate the disease.*
2 NC An **extrapolation** is a quantity, idea, or calculation which is the result of extrapolating from existing ones. *...one simple extrapolation from existing technology. ...simple extrapolations from current events.*

extrasensory perception /ɛkstrəsensəri pəsɛpʃn/
NU **Extrasensory perception** is an ability that some people think exists, by which people can feel or know things that they could not have felt or known through the ordinary senses such as touch, sight, or hearing.

extraterrestrial /ɛkstrətərɛstriəl/ **extraterrestrials**
1 ADJ **Extraterrestrial** means happening, existing, or coming from somewhere beyond the planet Earth; a formal use. *...a concentrated search for extraterrestrial life.*
2 NC An **extraterrestrial** is a living creature that some people think exists or may exist in another part of the universe. *...the first to contact intelligent extraterrestrials.*

extra time
NU In sport, **extra time** is an additional period of time that is added to the end of a match in which the two teams are level, as a way of allowing the teams more time to produce a conclusive result.

extravagance /ɪkstrævəgəns/ **extravagances**
1 NU **Extravagance** is the spending of more money than is reasonable or than you can afford. *It is easy to criticize governments for extravagance and waste.*
2 NC An **extravagance** is something that you spend money on but cannot really afford. *It was a little extravagance of my father's to buy new plants every year.*

extravagant /ɪkstrævəgənt/
1 ADJ An **extravagant** person spends more money than they can afford or uses more of something than is reasonable. *He was extravagant and liked to live well... She considered him extravagant with electricity.* ◆ **extravagantly** ADV *I lived extravagantly, taking cabs everywhere.*
2 ADJ Something that is **extravagant** costs more money than you can afford or uses more of something than is reasonable. *...extravagant gifts. ...machines that are extravagant in their requirements of energy.* ◆ **extravagantly** SUBMOD *...merchandise known to be extravagantly priced.*
3 ADJ **Extravagant** behaviour is exaggerated and is done to create a particular effect; a formal use. *He raised his eyebrows in extravagant surprise.* ◆ **extravagantly** SUBMOD *Harold was extravagantly affectionate with his daughters.*
4 ADJ **Extravagant** ideas or claims are unrealistic and impractical; a formal use. *They do not generally make such extravagant claims for success.*
5 ADJ **Extravagant** entertainments or designs are elaborate and impressive. *...an extravagant display of colourful lights.*

extravaganza /ɪkstrævəgænzə/ **extravaganzas**
NC An **extravaganza** is a very elaborate and expensive public activity or performance. *China launched the eleventh Asian games with a three hour extravaganza of colour, sound and ceremony.*

extreme /ɪkstriːm/ **extremes**
1 ADJ ATTRIB **Extreme** means very great in degree or intensity. *He died in extreme poverty... You must proceed with extreme caution.* ◆ **extremely** SUBMOD *...an extremely difficult task... Ralph and I always got on extremely well.*
2 ADJ **Extreme** situations and behaviour are much more severe or unusual than you would expect. *People are capable of surviving in extreme conditions... Their methods may seem extreme.*
3 ADJ **Extreme** opinions, beliefs, or political movements are unacceptably severe or unreasonable. *Some deputies loyal to Mr Yeltsin did share those extreme views. ...the extreme Right Wing of the Party.*
4 ADJ ATTRIB The **extreme** point or edge of something is its farthest point or edge. *...the extreme south of the country.*
● **Extreme** is used in these phrases. ● If someone is

going to extremes, or is taking something to extremes, their behaviour is so severe or foolish that it is unacceptable. *This clause will give prejudiced councils a chance of going to extremes... There may be some women who take the diet to extremes.* ● You use **in the extreme** to emphasize how bad or undesirable something is. *I thought the suggestion dangerous in the extreme.*

extremis /ɪkstriːmɪs/. See **in extremis**.

extremism /ɪkstriːmɪzəm/
NU **Extremism** is the behaviour or beliefs of extremists. *He warned of the dangers of extremism.*

extremist /ɪkstriːmɪst/ **extremists**
NC An **extremist** is a person who wishes to bring about political or social change by using severe or unreasonable methods. *Sikh extremists have shot and killed a former minister in the Punjab government.* ▶ Also ADJ *...extremist groups opposed to the Afghan government.*

extremity /ɪkstrɛməti/ **extremities**
1 NC The **extremities** of something are its farthest points or edges; a formal use. *The Durand line was originally the north western extremity of British India.*
2 N PL Your **extremities** are the farthest parts of your body, especially your hands and feet. *The warmth spread outwards till it reached his extremities.*
3 NC An **extremity** is a very serious situation; a formal use. *She tried to remember how things had ever reached such an extremity.*
4 NU If someone talks or behaves in an extreme way, you can talk about the **extremity** of their views or behaviour; a formal use.

extricate /ɛkstrɪkeɪt/ **extricates, extricating, extricated**; a formal word.
1 V Oor V-REFL If you **extricate** someone from a difficult situation, you free them from it. *How are their new leaders going to extricate the country from economic chaos?... She found it impossible to extricate herself from the relationship.*
2 V Oor V-REFL If you **extricate** someone from a place where they are trapped, you get them out. *It was exceedingly difficult to extricate her from the hole.*

extrovert /ɛkstrəvɜːt/ **extroverts**
NC An **extrovert** is a person who is active, lively, and sociable. *The English see the Pope as a charming extrovert.* ▶ Also ADJ *People with an extrovert personality are more likely to enjoy sports.*

extrude /ɪkstruːd/ **extrudes, extruding, extruded**
V-ERG When something **extrudes** or is **extruded**, it is forced or squeezed out through a small opening; a formal word. *The meat gradually extrudes out through the holes... The plastic can be extruded into many shapes or forms.*

exuberance /ɪgzjuːbəᵊrəns/
NU **Exuberance** is behaviour which is energetic, excited, and cheerful. *She always greeted him with the same exuberance.*

exuberant /ɪgzjuːbəᵊrənt/
ADJ Someone who is **exuberant** is full of energy, excitement, and cheerfulness. *...the exuberant director of the Theatre Royal.*

exude /ɪgzjuːd/ **exudes, exuding, exuded**; a formal word.
1 VO If someone **exudes** a quality or feeling, they show that they have it to a great extent. *She exuded vitality, enthusiasm, and generosity.*
2 V-ERG If something **exudes** a substance or smell, the substance or smell comes out of it. *The Glycladium would exude this chemical into the soil... Some frogs exude a poisonous chemical from their skins.*

exult /ɪgzʌlt/ **exults, exulting, exulted**
Vor V-QUOTE If you **exult**, you feel and show great pleasure because of a success that you have had. *I exulted at my fortune... 'I've never played golf like I did last week,' he exulted.*

exultant /ɪgzʌltənt/
ADJ If you are **exultant**, you feel very happy and triumphant; a formal word. *Her voice was loud and exultant.*

Eyadéma, Gnassingbe /njæsiːŋbeɪ eɪɑːdeɪmə/
General Gnassingbe Eyadéma , of the Togolese People's Assembly (RPT), became President of Togo

in 1967, when he led an army coup. In 1991 he was forced to accept the appointment of Kokou Koffigoh as Prime Minister. *Born: 1937.*

eye /aɪ/ **eyes, eyeing** or **eying, eyed**

1 NC Your **eyes** are the two things in your face that you see with. *She went into hospital for an operation on her left eye... After a while my eyes became accustomed to the dark... She opened her eyes.*

2 N SING+*for* If you have an **eye** for something, you can recognize it and make good judgements about it. *The artist has a marvellous eye for detail.*

3 VO If you **eye** something, you look at it carefully or suspiciously. *Posy was eyeing the man thoughtfully.*

● **Eye** is used in these phrases. ● If you **cast** or **run** your **eye over** something, you look quickly at every part of it. *He ran his eye over the article.* ● If something **catches** your **eye**, you suddenly notice it. *The flowers in your window caught my eye.* ● If you try to **catch** someone's **eye**, you try to attract their attention. *Can you catch the waiter's eye?* ● If someone **is keeping** an **eye on** or **has** their **eye** on a situation or person, they are watching to see how the situation develops or how the person behaves. *We're going to be keeping a close eye on the latest developments in Yugoslavia... I've had an eye on you for a long time.* ● To **keep an eye on** someone or something also means to watch them and make sure that they are safe. *Can you keep an eye on the baby while I go shopping?* ● If something is true **in** your **eyes**, this is your opinion. *Her children could do no wrong in her eyes.* ● If there is **more to** a situation **than meets the eye**, it is more complicated than it seemed at first. ● If an event **opens** your **eyes**, it makes you aware of something for the first time. *The uprising had opened the eyes of the world to their plight.* ● If you don't **see eye to eye** with someone, you disagree with them. *The Soviet Union and the US do not see eye to eye about Afghanistan.* ● If you are **up to** your **eyes in** something, you are very busy with it. *Sal is still up to her eyes in kids and housework.*

eyeball /aɪbɔːl/ **eyeballs**

NC Your **eyeballs** are the parts of your eyes that are like white balls.

eyebrow /aɪbraʊ/ **eyebrows**

NC Your **eyebrows** are the lines of hair which grow above your eyes. *...her exquisite face, with its arched eyebrows and wide-set eyes.* ● If something causes you to **raise an eyebrow** or to **raise** your **eyebrows**, it causes you to feel surprised or disapproving. *Eyebrows were raised at their behaviour.*

eye-catching

ADJ Something that is **eye-catching** is very noticeable. *One of the most eye-catching displays belonged to a British firm.*

eyeful /aɪfʊl/

1 N SING An **eyeful** of dust or liquid is an amount of it which has got into someone's eye. *...an eyeful of sand.*

2 N SING If you get an **eyeful** of someone or something, you have a good look at them; an informal use.

3 N SING If men refer to a woman as an **eyeful**, they mean that they find her very attractive; an informal use.

eyelash /aɪlæʃ/ **eyelashes**

NC Your **eyelashes** are the hairs which grow on the edges of your eyelids. *These enormous eyelashes prevent the sand entering the eyes.*

eyelet /aɪlət/ **eyelets**

NC An **eyelet** is a small hole with a metal or leather ring round it, which is made in cloth. You can put cord, rope, or string through it, for example in the sails of a boat or in the flaps of tents.

eyelid /aɪlɪd/ **eyelids**

1 NC Your **eyelids** are the two flaps of skin which cover your eyes when they are closed.

2 If you **don't bat an eyelid** when something happens, or if you do something **without batting an eyelid**, you remain completely calm and are not at all shocked or surprised; used in informal English. *In the distance, a drunk slumps unconscious into the hedgerow; no one bats an eyelid... Mr Yeltsin said the conspirators would have killed thousands of people without batting an eyelid.*

eye-opener

N SING If you say that something is an **eye-opener**, you mean that you find it very surprising and that you have learned something from it which you did not know before; an informal word. *The book is quite an eye-opener.*

eye patch, eye patches

NC An **eye patch** is a piece of material which you wear over your eye when you have damaged or injured it.

eyepiece /aɪpiːs/ **eyepieces**

NC The **eyepiece** of a microscope or telescope is the piece of glass at one end, where you put your eye in order to look through the instrument.

eye-shadow

NU **Eye-shadow** is a substance which some women put on their eyelids to colour them.

eyesight /aɪsaɪt/

NU Your **eyesight** is your ability to see. *His eyesight was excellent.*

eye socket, eye sockets

NC Your **eye sockets** are the two bony parts on either side of your face, which hold your eyeballs.

eyesore /aɪsɔː/ **eyesores**

NC If you say that something is an **eyesore**, you mean that it is extremely ugly. *He said the abandoned base was an appalling eyesore.*

eye strain

NU **Eye strain** is pain that you feel around your eyes or at the back of your eyes when you are very tired or should be wearing glasses. *Care should be taken that the position of the screen and lighting are adjusted to prevent eye strain and headaches.*

eye tooth, eye teeth

1 NC Your **eye teeth** are the two pointed teeth towards the front of your upper jaw.

2 If you say that you would **give** your **eye teeth** for something, you mean that you want it very much and you would do anything to get it; an informal expression. *I'd give my eye teeth for such a lot of money.*

eyewash /aɪwɒʃ/

1 NU **Eyewash** is a liquid which you use for bathing your eyes when they are sore.

2 NU If you say that something is **eyewash**, you mean that it is not true or that you do not believe it; an informal, old-fashioned use. *That report is a load of old eyewash.*

eyewitness /aɪwɪtnəs/ **eyewitnesses**; also spelt **eye-witness**.

NC An **eyewitness** is a person who has seen an event and can therefore describe it, for example in a law court. *Eyewitnesses near the scene of the disaster said the plane had exploded in a ball of fire... The papers carry eyewitness accounts of how the ground shook like an earthquake.*

eyrie /ɪəri, eəri/ **eyries**

1 NC An **eyrie** is the nest of an eagle, falcon, or other similar bird, that is usually built high up in rough, mountainous country. *The golden eagles have produced a second egg at their eyrie in the Lake District.*

2 NC An **eyrie** is also a place, such as a house or a castle, that is built high up and is difficult to reach. *He was invited to Hitler's mountain eyrie in Berchtesgaden.*

F f

F, f /ɛf/ **F's, f's**
  1 NC **F** is the sixth letter of the English alphabet.
  2 **F** is an abbreviation for 'Fahrenheit'. *...when the temperature outside is 30°F.*

fab /fæb/
  ADJ If you say that something is **fab**, you are expressing your approval of it; an old-fashioned, informal word. *I think Ted's rather fab, don't you?*

fable /ˈfeɪbl/ **fables**
  NC A **fable** is a traditional story which teaches a moral lesson. *There are many fables which represent how important maize was to many of the tribes.*

fabled /ˈfeɪbld/
  ADJ ATTRIB **Fabled** places, things, or people are well-known because a lot of stories are told about them. *The greatest of all its cities was the fabled Timbuktu.*

fabric /ˈfæbrɪk/ **fabrics**
  1 N MASS **Fabric** is cloth that is used for making clothes, curtains, and so on. *...silks and other soft fabrics. ...a bit of fabric.*
  2 N SING The **fabric** of a society is its structure and customs; a formal use. *Their economic and social policies threatened to tear apart the social fabric of the French nation... He said the fabric of society was threatened by groups of criminals involved with drugs, fraud, violence and robbery.*
  3 N SING The **fabric** of a building is its walls, roof, and other parts; a formal use. *This amount was enough to maintain the fabric of the house.*

fabricate /ˈfæbrɪkeɪt/ **fabricates, fabricating, fabricated**
  VO If you **fabricate** information, you invent it in order to deceive people; a formal word. *They fabricated evidence and threatened witnesses.* ♦ **fabrication** /fæbrɪˈkeɪʃn/ **fabrications** N C or N U *The story was a fabrication... a tissue of lies and fabrication.*

fabulous /ˈfæbjʊləs/
  1 ADJ You use **fabulous** to say how wonderful or impressive something is; an informal use. *What a fabulous place this is!* ♦ **fabulously** SUBMOD *...a fabulously rich family.*
  2 ADJ ATTRIB **Fabulous** creatures, places, or things occur in stories or legends, but are not real or true; a literary use. *...the legend of the Cretan minotaur, the fabulous and deadly monster who was half-man, half-bull.*

facade /fəˈsɑːd/ **facades**; also spelt **façade**.
  1 NC The **facade** of a large building is the outside of its front wall. *...the ornate facade of the Palace.*
  2 N SING You say that something is a **facade** when it gives a wrong impression of the true nature of a situation. *...the grim facts behind the facade of gaiety.*

face /feɪs/ **faces, facing, faced**
  1 NC Your **face** is the front of your head from your chin to your forehead. *Tears were pouring down her face. ...the expression on her face... There was severe bruising on his face... The girl's face was unhappy.*
  2 NC A **face** of something such as a cliff or a mountain is a surface or side of it. *...the north face of the Eiger... The machine cut through the last few inches of rock face and the tunnel was completed.*

  3 N+N The coal **face** is the part of a mine from which miners dig coal or minerals. *They were being taken to the coal face a thousand feet underground.*
  4 NC The **face** of a clock or watch is the surface which shows the time. *Surrounding the clock face is a series of figures.*
  5 N SING+SUPP The **face** of a place or activity is its appearance or nature. *...the transformation of the face of London... The riots completely changed the political face of the country.*
  6 N SING+SUPP You also use **face** to refer to the impression created by a political party or by its policies. *The Party can now show its caring face... Dubček had tried to bring in 'Socialism with a human face' in 1968.*
  7 V O or V A If someone or something **faces** in a particular direction, their front is towards that direction. *The boys faced each other... The seats face forward.*
  8 VO If you **face** a difficulty, challenge, or choice, or if you **are faced** with it, you have to deal with it. *It is the biggest problem he has ever faced... The Albanians are now faced with a stark choice... Faced with 70 per cent price inflation, the workforce is demanding more pay... The political and economic challenge facing his government is daunting.*
  9 VO If you **face** the truth, you accept it, even though it is unpleasant. *...the campaign to get rid of the blank spots in Soviet history and face the truth... We simply must face facts.*
  10 V O or V+ING If you cannot **face** something, you do not feel able to deal with it because it seems so difficult or unpleasant. *I just couldn't face the idea of going back there... She could not face speaking to them.*
  ● **Face** is used in these phrases. ● If something is **face down**, its front points downwards. If it is **face up**, its front points upwards. *Lay three cards face up on the table... He was dragged out of bed and made to lie face down on the floor.* ● If two people are **face to face**, they are looking directly at each other. *I suddenly came face to face with Karen... This will be the first face-to-face meeting between the American and Soviet Defence Ministers since 1979.* ● If you are brought **face to face** with a difficulty or unpleasant fact, you cannot avoid it and have to deal with it. *It brings patients face to face with their problems.* ● If you **make** or **pull a face**, you put on an ugly expression to show your dislike of something. *The children made faces at the teacher... He pulled a face and seemed about to argue.* ● You say 'let's face it' when you are saying something which is unpleasant or which you do not really want to admit. *Let's face it, a lot of their behaviour was incredibly obnoxious.* ● If you **lose face**, people lose respect for you because you cannot achieve what you said you would. If you do something to **save face**, you do it in order to avoid losing people's respect. *Do you dismiss the idea, or back his enthusiasm and risk losing money and face?... His task is to find a peace formula which allows Iran's hardliners to save face, and is also acceptable to Iraq.* ● If you do something **in the face of** a particular problem or difficulty, you do it even though this

problem or difficulty exists. *They carry on smiling in the face of adversity.* ● You say **on the face of it** to indicate that you are describing what something seems to be like but that its real nature may be different. *On the face of it, it sounds like a good idea.* ● If you **set your face against** something, you oppose it strongly. *Britain has set its face against production controls.* ● **at face value**: see **value**. ● **to put a brave face on** something: see **brave**.

face up to PHRASAL VERB If you **face up to** a difficult situation, you accept it and deal with it. *They had to face up to many setbacks.*

face cloth, face cloths
NC A **face cloth** is the same as a **face flannel**.

face cream, face creams
N MASS **Face cream** is a thick substance that you rub into your face in order to clean or soften it.

-faced /-feɪst/
SUFFIX **-faced** is added to some adjectives to make another adjective that describes someone's face or expression. *...a chubby-faced shy teenager... The city is patrolled by grim-faced soldiers and riot policemen.*

face flannel, face flannels
NC A **face flannel** is a small piece of towelling which you use for washing yourself.

faceless /ˈfeɪsləs/
ADJ ATTRIB **Faceless** people are dull and boring, and have no individuality. *...the faceless bureaucrats against whom he can do nothing and whom he never even sees.*

face lift, face lifts
1 NC A **face lift** is an operation in which a surgeon tightens the skin on someone's face in order to make them look younger.
2 NC If you give a place or thing a **face lift**, you do something that will make it look better or more attractive. *The Hotel is to close for more than a year for a £72 million face lift.*

face pack, face packs
NC A **face pack** is a thick substance which you spread on your face, leave to dry for a short time, then remove, in order to clean your skin thoroughly.

face powder, face powders
N MASS **Face powder** is a very fine, soft, flesh-coloured powder that you put on your face to make it look smoother.

face-saver, face-savers
NC If something acts as a **face-saver**, it provides an excuse which prevents damage to your reputation or the loss of people's respect for you. *Senior American officials suggest the agreement offers an important political face-saver to the Ambassador.*

face-saving
ADJ ATTRIB A **face-saving** action is done in order to avoid losing people's respect. *He is apparently still proposing a face-saving formula, under which there would be a complete withdrawal of troops from the region.*

facet /ˈfæsɪt/ **facets**
1 NC A **facet** of something is a part or aspect of it. *...an interesting facet of his character.*
2 NC The **facets** of a stone are the flat surfaces on its outside.

facetious /fəˈsiːʃəs/
ADJ If someone is being **facetious**, they are making humorous remarks in a serious situation. *Mrs Pringle ignored this facetious interruption.*

facial /ˈfeɪʃl/
ADJ ATTRIB **Facial** is used to describe things that relate to your face. *...facial muscles.*

facie. See **prima facie.**

facile /ˈfæsaɪl/
ADJ A **facile** remark or argument is simple and obvious, and has not been thought about carefully enough. *It would be facile to call it a conspiracy.*

facilitate /fəˈsɪləteɪt/ **facilitates, facilitating, facilitated**
VO To **facilitate** a process means to make it easier; a formal word. *...legislation to facilitate the sale of homes.*

facility /fəˈsɪləti/ **facilities**
1 NC **Facilities** are buildings or equipment provided for a particular purpose. *...play facilities for young children... The educational facilities available to them are inadequate... The two nations will sign an agreement not to attack each other's nuclear facilities.*
2 NC+SUPP You can refer to something that is built or set up for a particular purpose as a particular **facility**. *...the largest jail facility in the world. ...a repair facility for Soviet fishing vessels.*
3 NC+SUPP A **facility** is a useful feature in something. *...a computer with a message-swapping facility.*
4 NCorNU If you have a **facility** for a particular activity, you find it easy and do it well; a formal use. *He developed a facility for writing melodies in the key of F sharp... Not everyone easily acquires facility in foreign languages.*

facing /ˈfeɪsɪŋ/ **facings**
1 NU **Facing** is a second layer of material which is stitched inside the cuffs, collar and some other parts of clothes in order to strengthen them and make them look neat.
2 N PL The **facings** of a uniform, jacket, or coat are its collar and cuffs when they are made of a different fabric from the main part.
3 NCorNU A **facing** on a wall is a layer of stone, concrete, or other material that is spread over its surface in order to make it look attractive.
4 See also **face**.

facsimile /fækˈsɪməli/ **facsimiles**
1 NC A **facsimile** of something is an exact model or copy of it. *The Financial Times carries a facsimile of the four-page issue it published a hundred years ago.*
2 NCorN+N A **facsimile** is also the same as a **fax**; a formal use. *There was a facsimile machine in the conference centre.*

fact /fækt/ **facts**
1 NC A **fact** is a statement or piece of information that is true. *The report is full of facts and figures... He told me a few facts about her.*
2 NC You also use **fact** when you are referring to a situation that exists or to something that happened. *...the fact of belonging to a certain race... He'll be asking ministers to reveal what they know of the facts of the affair... The situation is complicated by the fact that a conflict has occurred.*
3 NU If you say that a story or statement is **fact**, you mean that it is true. *How much of the novel is fiction and how much is fact?*
4 You say **in fact, in point of fact, in actual fact,** or **as a matter of fact** to emphasize that something really happened or is true, or to introduce some information, especially more precise information. *This is, in fact, what happened... A temporary halt to the fighting is in fact the only positive outcome of the pact... In actual fact, we don't have all that much more leisure time than we used to... As a matter of fact, I just got it this afternoon.*
5 See also **fact of life.**

fact-finding
ADJ ATTRIB A **fact-finding** trip or mission is one whose purpose is to get information about a particular situation, especially for an official group. *A United Nations fact-finding mission is to be sent to the area.*

faction /ˈfækʃn/ **factions**
N COLL A **faction** is an organized group of people within a larger group, with their own ideas and beliefs. *...arguments between rival factions. ...the breakaway faction of Prince Johnson... The Solidarity movement has appeared to be splitting into two factions.*

factional /ˈfækʃəⁿl/
ADJ **Factional** means caused by or relating to factions. *About thirty more people have been killed in factional fighting in the townships around Johannesburg.*

factionalism /ˈfækʃəⁿəlɪzəm/
NU **Factionalism** is the state of having one or more factions within a group. *The party has a long history of factionalism.*

factitious /fækˈtɪʃəs/
ADJ **Factitious** means artificial, as opposed to natural or genuine; a formal word.

facto. See de facto.

fact of life, facts of life

1 NC You say that something which is not pleasant is a **fact of life** when there is nothing that you can do to change it so you must accept it. *Hunger is already a fact of life in some areas... Traffic congestion is now a daily fact of life in many of the world's major cities... The harsh economic facts of life may prevent him from making much headway with some of his policies.*
2 N PL If you tell a child the **facts of life**, you tell him or her about sexual intercourse and explain how babies are born. *You should get your family doctor to tell her the facts of life... A childish interest in the facts of life and in some aspects of sex is quite normal.*

factor /fǽktə/ **factors**

1 NC+SUPP A **factor** is one of the things that affects an event, decision, or situation. *Confidence is the key factor in any successful career... There are other important factors to be considered. ...social and economic factors.*
2 NC+*of* If an amount increases or decreases by a **factor** of a particular number, it becomes that number of times bigger or smaller. *Its weight went up by a factor of eight... I diluted it by a factor of 100.*
3 NC A **factor** of a whole number is a smaller whole number which can be multiplied with another whole number to produce the first whole number. *2 and 5 are factors of 10.*
4 N SING+SUPP You can use **factor** to refer to a particular level on a scale of measurement. *The factor 2 sun tan oil is for skin that tans easily.*

factory /fǽktri/ **factories**

1 NC A **factory** is a large building or group of buildings where machines are used to make large quantities of goods. *They have denied that the factory is producing nuclear weapons. ...industrial pollution from old-fashioned factories.*
2 See also **bomb factory.**

factory farming

NU **Factory farming** is a system of farming which involves keeping animals indoors with very little space, and giving them special food so that they grow more quickly or produce more eggs or milk. *They are campaigning against factory farming.*

factory floor

N SING The **factory floor** refers to all the workers in a factory, especially in contrast to the management. It can also refer to the area where they work. *Concern has also come from the factory floor itself... This profitability came from productivity increases on the factory floor... In a small laboratory, off the factory floor, Geoffrey explained how his system works.*

factory ship, factory ships

NC A **factory ship** is a large fishing boat which has equipment for processing the fish that are caught, for example by cleaning or freezing them, whilst still at sea. *Namibia's other great resource, fish, has been nearly exhausted by foreign factory ships.*

factotum /fæktə́utəm/ **factotums**

NC A **factotum** is a servant who is employed to do a wide variety of jobs for someone; a formal word.

fact sheet, fact sheets

NC A **fact sheet** is a piece of paper with information about a particular subject, especially a summary of information that has been given on a radio or television programme. *Write to this address for our fact sheet on National Savings certificates.*

factual /fǽktʃuəl/

ADJ Something that is **factual** contains or refers to facts rather than theories or opinions. *Mr King is expected to restrict his statement to a factual account of Saturday's events... They called on the world's media to provide factual and balanced information on the disease.* ◆ **factually** ADV *They said her comments were factually incorrect and highly irresponsible.*

faculty /fǽklti/ **faculties**

1 NC Your **faculties** are your physical and mental abilities. *He is said to be in full control of his faculties. ...the faculty of imagination.*
2 NC A **faculty** in a university or college is a group of related departments. *...the Arts Faculty.*

3 N COLL You can refer to all the staff of a particular group of related departments in a University or College as the **faculty.** *The faculty is extremely outraged over this decision.*

fad /fǽd/ **fads**

NC A **fad** is something which is very popular for a short time. *...taking up the latest fad about 'whole foods' or 'biological farming'.*

faddy /fǽdi/ **faddier, faddiest**

ADJ Someone who is **faddy** has very strong likes and dislikes which you think are unreasonable; an informal word. *He's rather faddy about his food.*

fade /féɪd/ **fades, fading, faded**

1 V If something **fades**, it slowly becomes less bright, less loud, or less intense. *The afternoon light was fading... The applause faded... Interest in the story will fade.*
2 V-ERG When a coloured object **fades**, it gradually becomes paler in colour. *The wallpaper may have faded... How can I stop the sun from fading the carpet?* ◆ **faded** ADJ *...an old man in a faded blue shirt.*

fade away PHRASAL VERB When something **fades away**, it slowly becomes less intense or strong until it ends completely. *Your enthusiasm for running will soon fade away... They will watch the last days of summer fade away.*

fade out PHRASAL VERB 1 When something **fades out**, it slowly becomes less intense, strong, or important, until it disappears. *Astronomers are predicting that the pulsations will fade out completely in the next few years.* 2 To **fade out** a sound or picture on the radio or television means to make it disappear gradually.

faeces /fíːsiːz/; spelt **feces** in American English.

NU or N PL **Faeces** is the solid waste that people or animals get rid of from their body, for example when a person goes to the toilet; a formal word. *The ground is covered in faeces... Human feces transmit cholera bacteria.*

faff /fǽf/ **faffs, faffing, faffed**

faff about PHRASAL VERB If someone **is faffing about** or is **faffing around**, they are wasting time by doing things in a very disorganized way or by doing things that are unnecessary; used in informal English. *He's been faffing about all morning.*

fag /fǽg/ **fags**

1 NC A **fag** is a cigarette; an informal use. *...a packet of fags.*
2 NC In informal American English, a **fag** is a homosexual man; an offensive use.

fag end, fag ends; an informal expression

1 NC A **fag end** is the last bit of a cigarette, which people throw away when they have smoked the rest.
2 NC+*of* The **fag end** of something is the last or worst part of it. *...the fag end of the day.*

fagged /fǽgd/

ADJ PRED If someone is **fagged** or **fagged out**, they are very tired; used in informal English. *'You look fagged to death,' said Kate.*

faggot /fǽgət/ **faggots**

NC In American English, a **faggot** is a homosexual man; an offensive word.

Fahd ibn Abdul Aziz, King /fǽhəd bɪn æbdəl əzíːz/ **King Fahd ibn Abdul Aziz** succeeded to the throne of Saudi Arabia in 1982, on the death of his brother. He became Crown Prince in 1975. Born: 1923.

Fahrenheit /fǽrənhaɪt/

NU **Fahrenheit** is a scale for measuring temperature, in which water freezes at 32° and boils at 212°. *The temperature doesn't normally drop below 80 degrees Fahrenheit.*

fail /féɪl/ **fails, failing, failed**

1 V If someone **fails** to do something that they were trying to do, they do not succeed in doing it. *Their party failed to win a single seat... He admits that restructuring the Soviet Union is harder than he ever imagined; he knows he might fail.* ◆ **failed** ADJ ATTRIB *He was a failed novelist and poet.*
2 V If an activity, attempt, or plan **fails**, it is not successful. *Should military force be used if sanctions against Iraq fail?... Earlier attempts at negotiations failed because neither side could agree on an*

acceptable venue for talks... Three thousand businesses in the London area failed in the first few months of this year. ♦ **failed** ADJ ATTRIB *Several soldiers involved in a failed coup attempt have been sentenced to death.*
3 V+*to*-INF If someone **fails** to do something that they should have done, they do not do it. *He was fined for failing to complete the census form... The incident has brought into focus the dilemma facing troops when civilians fail to respond to orders to stop... This move is justified on the grounds that the unions fail to represent their members' interests.*
4 VOorV If someone **fails** a test, examination, or course, they do not reach the standard that is required. *I passed the written part but failed the oral section... Every submarine captain qualifies for command by taking the incredibly difficult 'Perisher course', so called because a large proportion fail.*
5 V If something **fails**, it stops working properly, or does not do what it is supposed to do. *Her lighter failed. ...people whose sight is failing... Stocks of grain were already low before the rains failed.*
6 VO If someone **fails** you, they do not do what you expected or trusted them to do. *Our leaders have failed us.*

failing /ˈfeɪlɪŋ/ **failings**
1 NC A **failing** is a fault or unsatisfactory feature. *The present system has many failings.*
2 You say **failing that** to introduce an alternative, in case what you previously said is not possible. *Wear your national dress or, failing that, a suit.*

fail-safe
ADJ Something that is **fail-safe** is designed or made in such a way that nothing dangerous can happen if a part of it goes wrong. *British Rail said there was a fail-safe system so that if anything went wrong with this signal it would switch immediately to red.*

failure /ˈfeɪljə/ **failures**
1 NU **Failure** is a lack of success in doing or achieving something. *...a desperate initiative which ended in failure... I think that the risk of failure is too great.*
2 NC If something is a **failure**, it is unsuccessful. *The meeting was a failure... The whole policy has proved a failure and should be abandoned.*
3 NC Someone who is a **failure** has not succeeded in doing something that they were trying to do. *He was sacked by his employers and condemned by his son as a failure.*
4 NU+*to*-INF Your **failure** to do something is the fact that you do not do it although you were expected to. *They remarked on his failure to appear at the party... It draws attention to the underlying cause of the violence—the government's failure to enforce the law.*
5 NU+SUPP or NC+SUPP When there is a **failure** of something, it stops working or does not do what it is supposed to do. *Four thousand people in Britain develop kidney failure each year... We don't yet know the precise cause of the engine failure... Investment levels have fallen, while the number of business failures has risen... There's now likely to be a total crop failure.*

fain /feɪn/
ADV+INF If someone says that they would **fain** do something, they mean that they would like to do it; an old-fashioned word. *The Prime Minister himself would fain wait upon him at breakfast.*

faint /feɪnt/ **fainter, faintest; faints, fainting, fainted**
1 ADJ Something that is **faint** is not strong or intense. *There was a faint smell of gas... Her cries grew fainter. ...a faint hope. ...a faint smile.*
2 V If you **faint**, you lose consciousness for a short time. *He nearly fainted from the pain.*
3 ADJ Someone who feels **faint** feels dizzy and unsteady. *Glasses of water were given to those who felt faint.*

faint-hearted
ADJ If a person or their behaviour is **faint-hearted**, they lack confidence and do not try very hard because they are afraid of failing. *The picket was well-intentioned, but faint-hearted... It was a pretty faint-hearted attempt, if you ask me.*

faintly /ˈfeɪntli/
1 SUBMOD You can use **faintly** to indicate that something is true only to a very slight degree. *It was faintly possible.*
2 ADV If something happens **faintly**, it happens with very little strength or intensity. *She turned and smiled faintly.*

fair /feə/ **fairer, fairest; fairs**
1 ADJ Something or someone that is **fair** is reasonable, right, and just. *It wouldn't be fair to disturb the children... She won't get a fair trial... They claim they have never had a fair share of the country's oil wealth.* ● See also **fair play**.
2 ADJ ATTRIB A **fair** number, size, or amount is quite a large number, size, or amount. *We've got a fair number of postgraduate students. ...a fair-sized bedroom.*
3 ADJ ATTRIB If you have a **fair** guess or a **fair** idea about something, you are likely to be correct. *Most ministers have a fair idea of what the future holds for them.*
4 ADJ ATTRIB If you have a **fair** chance of doing something, it is likely that you will be able to do it. *I've think I've got a fair chance of evading them altogether.*
5 ADJ Someone who is **fair** or who has **fair** hair has light, gold-coloured hair. *She was fair and blue-eyed.*
6 ADJ **Fair** skin is pale in colour. *Unprotected fair skin gets sunburned quickly.*
7 ADJ When the weather is **fair**, it is quite sunny and not raining; a formal use. *It will be fair and warm.*
8 NC A **fair** is an event held in a park or field at which people pay to ride on various machines for amusement or try to win prizes in games. *...the doll I won at the fair.*
9 NC A **fair** is also an event at which people display or sell goods. *...the Leipzig Trade Fair... Some publishers have already withdrawn from the Teheran book fair.*

fair copy, fair copies
NC A **fair copy** of a piece of writing is a neat copy with no mistakes or alterations.

fair game
NU If you say that someone is **fair game**, you mean that it is acceptable to criticize or attack them, usually because of the way they behave. *When we're in public we're fair game. When we're in private, we're in private.*

fairground /ˈfeəɡraʊnd/ **fairgrounds**
NC A **fairground** is an area of land where a fair is held.

fairly /ˈfeəli/
1 SUBMOD **Fairly** means to quite a large degree. *The information was fairly accurate... I wrote the first part fairly quickly.*
2 ADV If something is said or done **fairly**, it seems reasonable and just. *The car could fairly be described as sluggish and noisy... You haven't played the game fairly.*

fairness /ˈfeənəs/
1 NU **Fairness** is the quality of being reasonable and just. *Even a child sees the fairness of reasonable penalties.*
2 You use expressions such as **in all fairness** and **in fairness to** someone in order to correct or balance a previous unfavourable statement. *In all fairness, I must say that I was not the only one... Yet in fairness to him, one must add that he was often correct.*

fair play
NU If you want **fair play**, you want everyone to be treated in a reasonable and just way. *They appealed to his sense of fair play.*

fair sex
N SING The **fair sex** refers to women in general; an old-fashioned expression, often used humorously.

fairway /ˈfeəweɪ/ **fairways**
NC The **fairway** on a golf course is the long strip of short grass between every tee and green. *...a group of golfers playing on an adjoining fairway.*

fair-weather
ADJ ATTRIB You use **fair-weather** to describe someone who takes part in an activity or offers help only when

it is easy; used showing disapproval. ...*a fair-weather sailor... She was not just a fair-weather friend.*

fairy /fˈeəri/ **fairies**
NC **Fairies** are imaginary creatures that look like small people with wings.

fairyland /fˈeərilænd/ **fairylands**
1 NU **Fairyland** is the imaginary place where fairies live.
2 NC If you describe a place as a **fairyland**, you mean that it has a delicate beauty. *By night, the scene is a brilliant fairyland of blazing neon lights.*

fairy lights
N PL **Fairy lights** are small, coloured electric lights that are hung up as decorations, for example on a Christmas tree.

fairy tale, fairy tales
1 NC A **fairy tale** or a **fairy story** is a story for children involving magical events and imaginary creatures. *As psychologists from Jung onwards have tried to show, there are unsuspected depths to fairy tales... In fairy stories good girls end up marrying the prince.*
2 N+N A **fairy tale** success is one which is very surprising because it represents a success for someone who is not expected to succeed. *Once again the FA Cup has produced a fairy tale story in Football; the non-league side, Sutton United, beat First Division Coventry City by two goals to one.*
3 NC You can describe an account or explanation of something as a **fairy tale** when you consider that it is untrue and intended to deceive people. *His reports are little more than fairy tales designed to reinforce the prejudices of his bored listeners.*

fait accompli /fˌeɪt əkˈompli/
N SING If something is a **fait accompli**, it has already been done and cannot be changed; a formal expression. *Local church leaders accepted these changes as a fait accompli.*

faith /fˈeɪθ/ **faiths**
1 NU If you have **faith** in someone or something, you feel confident about their ability or goodness. *I had faith in Alan—I knew he could take care of me.*
2 NC A **faith** is a particular religion, such as Christianity or Buddhism. *...its tolerant attitude to other faiths.*
3 NU **Faith** is strong religious belief. *...her deep religious faith.*
● **Faith** is used in these phrases. ● If you **break faith** with someone, you fail to behave in the way that you promised or were expected to. If you **keep faith** with them, you continue to behave as you promised or were expected to. *I will not break faith with the students here... The government is not keeping faith with its promises to honour a peaceful transfer of power.* ● If you do something **in good faith**, you sincerely believe that what you are doing is right, honest, or legal, even though this may not be the case. *The statement added that Mr De Wet had acted in good faith.*

faithful /fˈeɪθfl/
1 ADJ If you are **faithful** to a person, organization, or idea, you remain firm in your support for them. *Bond remained faithful to his old teacher.* ◆ **faithfully** ADV *The party rallied round him faithfully.*
2 ADJ Someone who is **faithful** to their husband, wife, or lover does not have a sexual relationship with anyone else. *She has been a faithful wife to him.*
3 ADJ A **faithful** account, translation, or adaptation of a book represents the facts or the original book accurately. *Do you think the film was faithful to the book?* ◆ **faithfully** ADV *Their activities were faithfully described in the newspapers.*

faithfully /fˈeɪθfəli/
When you start a letter with 'Dear Sir' or 'Dear Madam', you write '**Yours faithfully**' before your signature.

faith healer, faith healers
NC A **faith healer** is someone who practises faith healing. *He was working as a faith healer.*

faith healing
NU **Faith healing** is the treatment of a sick person by someone who believes that they can heal people through prayer and the power of religious faith.

A debate has developed over the right of people who believe in faith healing to refuse conventional medical treatment for their children.

faithless /fˈeɪθləs/
ADJ A **faithless** person is disloyal or dishonest. *The friend had turned out to be faithless.*

fake /fˈeɪk/ **fakes, faking, faked**
1 NC A **fake** is something that is made to look like something valuable or real in order to deceive people. *They swore that the pictures were fakes... The youth claimed to have a hand grenade, though this later proved to be a fake.* ▶ Also ADJ *...a fake passport... He smuggled a fake bomb onto an aircraft and flew to the United States.*
2 VO If someone **fakes** something, they make it look like something valuable or real in order to deceive people. *In the nineteenth century, they faked antiques of all kinds... The signatures on the purchasers' cheques were faked... Fourteen years ago he faked suicide and fled the country in an attempt to evade financial ruin.* ◆ **faked** ADJ *...spies entering the country with faked passports.*
3 VO If you **fake** a feeling or reaction, you pretend that you are experiencing it. *Thomas faked a yawn.*

falcon /fˈɔːlkən, fˈælkən/ **falcons**
NC A **falcon** is a bird of prey that can be trained to hunt other birds and animals. *He removes the hood from one of his falcons, and the powerful bird of prey soars up above the runway.*

falconer /fˈɔːlkəⁿnə, fˈælkəⁿnə/ **falconers**
NC A **falconer** is someone who trains and uses falcons for hunting. *Many birds of prey fetch a high price from falconers.*

falconry /fˈɔːlkənri, fˈælkənri/
NU **Falconry** is the skill of training falcons to hunt, and the sport of using them to hunt. *A League spokesman said falconry was a blood sport.*

Falkland Islands /fˈɔːlklənd aɪləndz/
The **Falkland Islands** are a territory of the United Kingdom, lying in the South Atlantic Ocean, east of Argentina. They were claimed by Britain, in spite of opposition by Argentina, in 1833. Argentine forces invaded and occupied the islands in 1982, but surrendered to a British task force two months later. The Falkland Islands export wool. ◆ **Falkland Islander** /fˈɔːlklənd aɪləndə/ N
■ *religion:* Christianity ■ *language:* English ■ *currency:* pound ■ *capital:* Stanley ■ *population:* 2,000 (1989) ■ *size:* 12,173 square kilometres.

fall /fˈɔːl/ **falls, falling, fell, fallen**
1 V If someone or something **falls** from an upright position, they become unbalanced and drop to the ground. *She lost her balance and fell... He fell off his ladder... The cup fell from her hand and shattered on the floor... Yesterday an engine fell off a Boeing 737 shortly after the plane took off.* ▶ Also NC *He was rushed to hospital after a 40-foot fall.* ◆ **fallen** ADJ ATTRIB *The equipment needed to move the heavy fallen masonry is not available.*
2 V If something **falls**, it moves downwards onto or towards the ground. *The snow was still falling... Tears fell from Mother's eyes.*
3 V If people in a position of power **fall**, they suddenly lose that position. *The regime had fallen.* ▶ Also N SING+POSS *This led to the Government's fall.*
4 V If a place **falls** in a war or election, an enemy army or a different political party takes control of it. *A number of smaller towns are said to have fallen to rebel guerillas... Greater London will fall to Labour.* ▶ Also N SING+POSS *...the fall of France.*
5 V If someone **falls** in battle, they are killed; a literary use. *...the elegant Martyrs' Monument, which commemorates those who fell in the war.*
6 V If something **falls** in amount, value, or strength, it decreases. *Share prices fell sharply during the day in New York... Their voices could be heard rising and falling... Anyone found sleeping outdoors when the temperature falls below freezing should be taken to a shelter or hospital.* ▶ Also N SING *There's been a sharp fall in the price of oil. ...a fall in moral standards.* ◆ **falling** ADJ *Some nations were uneasy about their falling birth rates.*

7 V When night or darkness **falls**, night begins and it becomes dark. *As darkness falls the noise of the helicopters is beginning to fade.*

8 V A When light or shadow **falls** on something, it covers it. *A shadow fell over her book and she looked up.*

9 V If silence or a feeling of sadness or tiredness **falls** on a group of people, they become silent, sad, or tired; a literary use. *An expectant hush fell on the gathering.*

10 V Cor V A You can use **fall** to show that someone or something passes into another state. For example, if someone **falls** ill, they become ill. *After a while I fell asleep... Their ideas had simply fallen into disuse and been forgotten.*

11 V A To **fall** into a particular group or category means to belong in that group or category. *Human beings fall into two types... My work really falls into three parts... The present case falls outside our jurisdiction.*

12 V A If an event **falls** on a particular date, that is the date when it happens. *Their New Year Festival falls on February 17th... The first of May fell on a Sunday this year.*

13 N PL You can refer to a waterfall as the **falls**. *...Niagara Falls... He said the power station would not be visible from the falls themselves.*

14 N U or N C In American English, the **fall** is autumn. *His second novel was published here last fall.*

15 to **fall flat**: see **flat**. to **fall in love**: see **love**. to **fall short**: see **short**.

fall about PHRASAL VERB If you say that people are **falling about**, you mean that they are very amused by something; an informal expression. *When he complained, they fell about laughing.*

fall apart PHRASAL VERB **1** If something **falls apart**, it breaks into pieces because it is old or badly made. *...cheap beds that fell apart.* **2** If an organization or system **falls apart**, it becomes disorganized and unable to work effectively. *The nation is falling apart.*

fall away PHRASAL VERB If something **falls away** from the surface it is attached to, it breaks off. *Patches of plaster had fallen away between the windows.*

fall back PHRASAL VERB If you **fall back**, you move quickly away from someone or something. *I saw my husband fall back in horror.*

fall back on PHRASAL VERB If you **fall back on** something, you do it or use it after other things have failed. *Often you give up and fall back on easier solutions.*

fall behind PHRASAL VERB If you **fall behind**, you do not make progress or move forward as fast as other people. *...children who fall behind with their reading.*

fall down PHRASAL VERB **1** If someone or something **falls down** from an upright position, they become unbalanced and drop to the ground. *He tripped and fell down.* **2** If something such as a building or bridge **falls down**, it collapses and breaks into pieces because it is old, weak, or damaged. *Part of the ceiling fell down.*

fall for PHRASAL VERB **1** If you **fall for** someone, you are strongly attracted to them and start loving them. *Richard fell for her the moment he set eyes on her.* **2** If you **fall for** a lie or trick, you believe it even though it is not true; an informal expression. *The working class were not going to fall for this one.*

fall in PHRASAL VERB If a roof or ceiling **falls in**, it collapses and falls to the ground. *People stampeded out of the cinema after the roof fell in.*

fall in with PHRASAL VERB If you **fall in with** an idea, plan, or system, you accept it and do not try to change it. *Instead of challenging the lie, she falls in with it.*

fall off PHRASAL VERB If the degree, amount, or rate of something **falls off**, it decreases. *We knew that the numbers of overseas students would fall off drastically.*

fall on PHRASAL VERB If your eyes suddenly **fall on** something or **fall upon** it, you suddenly see it or notice it. *His gaze fell on a small white bundle.*

fall out PHRASAL VERB **1** If a person's hair or a tooth **falls out**, it becomes loose and separates from their body. *After about two weeks, the victim's hair starts*

to fall out. **2** If you **fall out** with someone, you have an argument with them and stop being friendly. *I've fallen out with certain members of the band.* **3** See also **fallout**.

fall over PHRASAL VERB If someone or something **falls over** from an upright position, they become unbalanced and drop to the ground. *The pig became nervous and aggressive, lost its appetite and started falling over.*

fall through PHRASAL VERB If an arrangement **falls through**, it fails to happen. *We wanted to book a villa but it fell through.*

fall to PHRASAL VERB If a responsibility or duty **falls** to someone, it becomes their responsibility or duty; a formal expression. *It fell to Philip to act the part of host.*

fall upon PHRASAL VERB See **fall on**.

fallacious /fəleɪʃəs/
ADJ A **fallacious** idea or argument is based on incorrect information or a fault in logic; a formal word. *This point of view is exposed as fallacious by Emerson.*

fallacy /fæləsi/ **fallacies**
N C A **fallacy** is an idea or argument which is incorrect or illogical; a formal word. *It is a fallacy that women are more pure-minded than men.*

fallback /fɔːlbæk/
ADJ ATTRIB In negotiations, a **fallback** position is a more moderate policy or set of demands that is put forward if the original policy or set of demands is not accepted; used in American English. *Meanwhile, as a fallback position, Denver mayor Federico Pena is proposing a deal with another airline.*

fallen /fɔːlən/
Fallen is the past participle of **fall**.

fallen arches
N PL If you have **fallen arches**, the hollow part at the bottom of each of your feet has become flat and does not support the rest of your foot properly when you walk.

fall guy, fall guys
N C A **fall guy** is someone who has been tricked by another person so that the other person could get something deceitfully without taking any blame; an informal expression. *He was probably a fall guy for men too powerful to be touched.*

fallible /fæləbl/; a formal word
1 ADJ If you say that someone is **fallible**, you mean that they may make mistakes. *It is now obviously permitted to say that previous Soviet leaders were fallible.* **2** ADJ If something is **fallible**, it may be wrong or unreliable. *Mary was conscious how fallible this method was.*

falling-off
N SING If there is a **falling-off** in something, it decreases. *A falling-off in business was expected.*

falling-out
N SING A **falling-out** is a quarrel; used in American English. *He had a falling-out with a former collaborator... Wasn't some sort of falling-out inevitable?*

falling star, falling stars
N C A **falling star** is the same as a **meteor**.

fallopian tube /fələʊpiən tjuːb/ **fallopian tubes**
N C A woman's **fallopian tubes** are the two tubes in her body along which eggs pass from her ovaries to her uterus. *They found out I had blocked fallopian tubes.*

fallout /fɔːlaʊt/
1 N U **Fallout** is the radiation that affects an area after a nuclear explosion. *North Wales received a considerable dose of nuclear fallout during the disaster... An extensive network of nuclear fallout shelters had been built.* **2** N U+SUPP You can refer to the unpleasant consequences of an event or action as the **fallout** from it. *In view of the fallout from last year's events, the repercussions could be very serious indeed... The political fallout from the election has been extraordinary... The economic fallout of international sanctions could well go beyond a cut-back in luxuries.*

fallow /fæləu/
ADJ If land is lying **fallow**, no crops have been planted in it, so that the soil has a chance to rest and improve. *...plots of fallow land.*

fallow deer; **fallow deer** is both the singular and the plural form.
NC A **fallow deer** is a small deer with a reddish coat that develops white spots in summer. *I believe that the fallow deer are the loveliest of all forest creatures.*

false /fɔːls/
1 ADJ If something is **false**, it is untrue or based on a mistake or wrong information. *What you're saying is false... I had a false impression of him... We did not come here to create false hopes. ...to save her from false imprisonment.* ◆ **falsely** ADV *...falsely accusing him of a crime.* ● **under false pretences**: see pretence.
2 ADJ **False** things are made so that they appear real although they are not. *He was given a disguise of a false beard and toupee... He is said to be using a false passport.*
3 ADJ Behaviour that is **false** is not sincere. *...a false smile. ...false modesty.* ◆ **falsely** ADV *She laughed, falsely, to cheer him up.*

false alarm, **false alarms**
NC When you are warned of something dangerous and it does not happen, you say that the warning was a **false alarm**. *A series of false alarms were also raised during the evening in four other towns.*

falsehood /fɔːlshʊd/ **falsehoods**; a formal word.
1 NU The **falsehood** of something is the fact that it is untrue. *We must establish the truth or falsehood of the various rumours.*
2 NC A **falsehood** is a lie. *The list is likely to be riddled with inaccuracies, mistakes and falsehoods.*

false move, **false moves**
NC A **false move** is an action or movement which turns out to be a mistake and which can put you in a position of great risk or danger. *Barbara soon realized that this was a false move... One false move, and I might have slipped two hundred feet.*

false start, **false starts**
1 NC A **false start** is an attempt to start something which fails because you are not properly prepared. *The ship is on her way to the Gulf again, after a false start earlier this week. ...natural speech with all its hesitations and false starts.*
2 A **false start** is also the beginning of a race when one competitor moves before the starter has given the signal. *He made a false start in a 25 yard event.*

falsetto /fɔːlsetəu/ **falsettos**
NC If a man speaks or sings in a **falsetto**, he uses a high-pitched voice. *I heard him singing in a clear, high falsetto. ...a falsetto whine.*

falsify /fɔːlsɪfaɪ/ **falsifies**, **falsifying**, **falsified**
VO If someone **falsifies** information, they change it so that it is no longer true, in order to deceive people. *The facts concerning my birth have been falsified.* ◆ **falsification** /fɔːlsɪfɪkeɪʃn/ **falsifications** NU or NC *...falsification of accounts... The book was rejected in Romania as a falsification.*

falsity /fɔːlsəti/
NU The **falsity** of something is the fact that it is untrue; a formal word. *...the falsity of this evidence.*

falter /fɔːltə/ **falters**, **faltering**, **faltered**
1 V If something **falters**, it becomes weaker or slower, and may stop completely. *The engines faltered and the plane lost height.*
2 V If you **falter**, you hesitate and become unsure or unsteady. *From that moment onwards he never faltered in his resolve... He faltered when answering questions on his defence and foreign policy.*

faltering /fɔːltərɪŋ/
ADJ A **faltering** attempt or effort is hesitant and uncertain because you are nervous or do not really know what to do. *She made faltering attempts to write letters in German. ...Britain's faltering steps towards a fourth television channel... 'I still believe freedom and democracy will win in the end,' he added in a faltering voice.*

fame /feɪm/
NU If you achieve **fame**, you become well-known and admired by many people. *She was jealous of Ellen's fame... He rose rapidly to fame.*

famed /feɪmd/
ADJ If you are **famed** for something, you are well-known and admired because of it; a literary word. *The women there were famed for the pots they made.*

familial /fəmɪliəl/
ADJ ATTRIB **Familial** means concerning families in general or one family in particular; a formal word. *...social and familial influences.*

familiar /fəmɪliə/
1 ADJ If someone or something is **familiar** to you, you recognize them or know them well. *His name was familiar to me. ...my pleasure at seeing all the familiar faces again.* ◆ **familiarity** /fəmɪliærəti/ NU *...the familiarity of the surroundings.*
2 ADJ PRED+with If you are **familiar** with something, you know it well. *I am of course familiar with your work.* ◆ **familiarity** NU *...his familiarity with the system gave him a considerable advantage.*
3 ADJ If you behave in a **familiar** way towards someone, you treat them very informally, so that you may offend them if you are not close friends. *...disliking intensely the burly man's familiar tone.* ◆ **familiarly** ADV *He spoke of them casually and familiarly by their first names.* ◆ **familiarity** NU *They greeted him with familiarity.*

familiarize /fəmɪliəraɪz/ **familiarizes**, **familiarizing**, **familiarized**; also spelt **familiarise**.
V-REFL+with or VO+with If you **familiarize** yourself with something, or if someone **familiarizes** you with it, you learn all about it and get to know it. *He had to familiarize himself with the ship. ...to familiarize their colleagues with the principles.*

family /fæməli/ **families**
1 N COLL or NU A **family** is a group of people who are related to each other, especially parents and their children. *...an English family on holiday. ...the central role of the family in ensuring a better life for children. ...help offered by family and friends... He left Iraq 40 years ago but still has family in Baghdad.*
2 N COLL or NU When parents talk about their **family**, they mean their children. *...mothers with large families... I just want to find out if he was married or had any family.*
3 N+N You use **family** to describe things which can be used or enjoyed by both parents and children. *...a family car. ...family entertainment.*
4 N COLL You can also use **family** to refer to all your ancestors. *Her mother's family had lived there for generations... Ben worked in the family business.*

family doctor, **family doctors**
NC A **family doctor** is the same as a **GP**. *Family doctors have no time these days to make regular calls.*

family man, **family men**
1 NC A **family man** is a man who is very fond of his wife and children and likes to spend a lot of time with them. *He was essentially a family man who enjoyed best of all the company of his wife and their son and daughter.*
2 NC You can also use **family man** to refer to a man who has a wife and children. *Wages are so low in relation to the cost of living that a family man cannot survive on them.*

family name, **family names**
NC Your **family name** is your surname. *...a tomb with our family name inscribed on it.*

family planning
NU **Family planning** is the practice of using contraception to control the number of children in a family. *...the ever-growing world population and the need for family planning. ...a network of family planning centres across the country.*

family tree, **family trees**
NC A **family tree** is a chart that shows all the people in your family over many generations and the relationships between them.

famine /fæmɪn/ **famines**
NU or NC A **famine** is a serious shortage of food in a country, which may cause many deaths. *...the effects of famine and drought... There are fears of a famine... The aid workers were taking part in a famine relief operation... Emergency supplies will*

soon be resumed to famine victims in the north of the country.

famished /fǽmɪʃt/
ADJ If you say that you are **famished**, you mean that you are very hungry; an informal word. *He must be absolutely famished.*

famous /féɪməs/
ADJ Someone or something that is **famous** is very well-known. *...a famous writer... California is famous for raisins.*

famously /féɪməsli/
1 ADV SEN You use **famously** to refer to the fact that someone or something is well-known. *That's why the Supreme Court has always opposed it, most famously in the 1971 case of the Pentagon papers.*
2 If you **get on famously** with someone, you are very friendly with each other and enjoy meeting and being together. *But for all that the two men got on famously and had several rounds of private talks.*

fan /fæn/ **fans, fanning, fanned**
1 NC If you are a **fan** of someone or something, you like them very much and are very interested in them. *Whitney Stine became a Bette Davis fan at the age of 8... Of all the world's football fans, the English have the worst reputation.*
2 NC A **fan** is a flat object that you hold in your hand and wave in order to move the air and make yourself cooler.
3 V-REFL If you **fan** yourself, you wave a fan or other flat object in order to move the air and make yourself cooler. *She took up some sheets of paper and fanned herself with them.*
4 NC A **fan** is also a piece of electrical equipment with revolving blades which keeps a room or machine cool or which gets rid of unpleasant smells. *...an industrial fan driven by an electric motor.*
5 VO To **fan** a fire means to create a current of air so that the fire burns more strongly. *...fires that were fanned by the outward moving winds.*
6 VO To **fan** an emotion such as fear or hatred means to cause people to feel it more strongly. *They had been fanning national hatred and poisoning the country's political mood... Chinese-African tensions have been fanned by Chinese resentment at the more comfortable living conditions of most African students.*
7 to fan the **flames**: see **flame**.
fan out PHRASAL VERB When people or things **fan out**, they move forwards together from the same point, while moving farther apart from each other. *The five of us fanned out at intervals of not more than fifteen feet.*

fanatic /fənǽtɪk/ **fanatics**
1 NC A **fanatic** is a person with strong religious or political beliefs who behaves in an extreme or violent way. *Mr Chirac was at pains to point out that he did not regard all Muslims as fanatics.*
2 NC A **fanatic** is also a person who is very enthusiastic about a subject or activity. *...a sports fanatic.*

fanatical /fənǽtɪkl/
ADJ Someone who is **fanatical** feels very strongly about something and behaves in an extreme way because of this. *...an army officer considered by many to be a fanatical nationalist... The meeting was broken up by fanatical mobs who surrounded the party headquarters and attacked the participants.*
● **fanatically** ADV *The hijackers are fanatically dedicated to their cause.*

fanaticism /fənǽtɪsɪzəm/
NU **Fanaticism** is fanatical behaviour. *He took to abstract painting with an obsessive fanaticism.*

fan belt, fan belts
NC A **fan belt** is a belt in a car engine that drives the fan which keeps the engine cool. *Cars are having trouble with over-heating and broken fan belts.*

fancier /fǽnsɪə/ **fanciers**
1 NC+SUPP An animal or plant **fancier** is a person who breeds animals or plants of a particular type or who is very interested in them. *...a pigeon fancier.*
2 **Fancier** is the comparative form of **fancy**.

fanciful /fǽnsɪfl/
1 ADJ **Fanciful** ideas or stories are based on someone's imagination and not on reality. *He had heard fanciful tales about their work.*
2 ADJ Something that is **fanciful** is unusual and elaborate rather than plain; used showing disapproval. *He considered this name far too fanciful.*

fan club, fan clubs
NC A **fan club** is an organized group of people who all admire the same person or thing such as a pop singer, film star, or football club, and who arrange trips to concerts or publish newsletters for club members. *There are 29 Cliff Richard fan clubs in Britain.*

fancy /fǽnsi/ **fancies, fancying, fancied; fancier, fanciest**
1 VOorV+ING If you **fancy** something, you want to have it or do it; an informal use. *She fancied a flat of her own... I don't fancy going back alone.*
2 VO If you **fancy** someone, you feel attracted to them in a sexual way; an informal use. *I fancied you when I was young, but I never had the nerve to say so.*
3 V-REFL If you **fancy** yourself, you think that you are especially clever, attractive, or good at something; used in informal English, showing disapproval. *I've heard that this man Bond fancies himself with a pistol... We all fancied ourselves as leaders.*
4 You say **'fancy'** when you want to express surprise; an informal use. *Fancy seeing you here!*
5 V-REPORT If you **fancy** that something is the case, you think or suppose that it is true; a formal use. *I fancied I could hear a baby screaming.*
6 ADJ Something that is **fancy** is special, unusual, or elaborate; an informal use. *...good plain food: nothing fancy... The concert will be a fancy occasion.*
7 NCorNU A **fancy** is an idea that is unlikely or untrue; a formal use. *His mind was filled with weird fancies... It is difficult to separate fact from fancy.*
● **Fancy** is used in these phrases. ● If you **take a fancy to** someone or something, you start liking them, usually for no understandable reason; an informal expression. *Fortunately, she took a fancy to me.* ● If something **takes your fancy** when you see or hear it, you like it; an informal expression. *Visitors are free to come and browse round and buy anything that takes their fancy.*

fancy dress
NU **Fancy dress** is clothing that you wear for a party where people dress to look like particular characters, for example from history or stories. *...ladies in fancy dress. ...a fancy dress ball.*

fancy-free
ADJ Someone who is **fancy-free** is free to do what they like, usually because they have no responsibilities or are not married. *There I was, footloose and fancy-free.*

fancy man, fancy men
NC A woman's **fancy man** is her lover or boyfriend; an old-fashioned, informal expression, used showing disapproval.

fancy woman, fancy women
NC A man's **fancy woman** is his lover or girlfriend; an old-fashioned, informal expression, used showing disapproval.

fandango /fændǽŋgəʊ/ **fandangos**
NC A **fandango** is a Spanish dance in which two people dance very close together.

fanfare /fǽnfeə/ **fanfares**
1 NC A **fanfare** is a short, loud tune played on trumpets to announce a special event. *A trumpeter gave a fanfare from a balcony.*
2 NC+SUPPorNU+SUPP You also use **fanfare** to say that something happens or is announced in a way that is intended to make people notice it. *The three hostages were released amid a fanfare of publicity... It was launched with much fanfare more than eighteen months ago.*

fang /fæŋ/ **fangs**
NC If an animal has **fangs**, it has long, sharp teeth. *They capture their prey by injecting a fatal venom with their fangs.*

fanlight /fǽnlaɪt/ **fanlights**
NC A **fanlight** is a small window above a door. *...the stained glass fanlight above the front door.*

fanny /fǽni/ **fannies**
1 NC In British English, a woman's **fanny** is her genitals; an offensive use.
2 NC In American English, someone's **fanny** is their bottom; an informal, rude use.

fantasize /fǽntəsaɪz/ **fantasizes, fantasizing, fantasized**; also spelt **fantasise**.
V or V-REPORT If you **fantasize**, you think imaginatively about something that you would like to happen but that is unlikely. *I have often fantasized about these occasions... She had fantasized that she and Wendy would live in this house.*

fantastic /fæntǽstɪk/
1 ADJ People say that something is **fantastic** when they like or admire it very much; an informal use. *He chewed it and said, 'Fantastic!'... He scored the most fantastic goal I have ever seen.*
2 ADJ ATTRIB You use **fantastic** to emphasize the size, amount, or degree of something. *Dr O'Shea seemed to spend a fantastic amount of time on the road. ...her fantastic power.* ◆ **fantastically** SUBMOD *They were fantastically strict.*
3 ADJ You describe something as **fantastic** when it seems strange and wonderful or unlikely. *...fantastic images of gods... He was in love with her—fantastic though that may seem.* ◆ **fantastically** SUBMOD *...fantastically shaped islands.*

fantasy /fǽntəsi/ **fantasies**
1 NC A **fantasy** is a situation or event that you think about or imagine, although it is unlikely to happen or be true. *It's hard to explain—when people ask you what it's like on stage; it's like fulfilling a fantasy.*
2 NU or NC **Fantasy** refers to the activity of imagining things, or the things that you imagine. *To a child, fantasy and reality are very close to each other... His novels were fantasies.*

far /faː/ **farther** or **further, farthest** or **furthest**. **Farther** and **farthest** are used mainly when talking about distance. See also separate entries for **further** and **furthest.**
1 ADV If one place, thing, or person is **far** away from another, there is a great distance between them. *He sat far away from the others. ...a villa not far from Hotel Miranda. ...a little farther south.*
2 ADV **Far** is used in questions and statements about distance. *How far is Amity from here?... Vita went as far as Bologna.*
3 ADJ ATTRIB You use **far** to refer to the part of an area that is the greatest distance from the centre in a particular direction. *...in the far north of the country. ...on the far right of the page.*
4 ADJ ATTRIB When there are two similar things somewhere, you use **far** to refer to the one that is a greater distance from you. *...the far end of the room.*
5 ADV A A time or event that is **far** in the future or the past is a long time from the present. *The Fourth of July isn't far off. ...as far back as the twelfth century.*
6 ADV You use **far** to indicate the extent or degree to which something happens. *Prices will not come down very far... None of us would trust them very far. ...using her methods as far as possible.*
7 ADV **Far** is used in questions and statements about extent or degree. *How far have you got in developing this?... Mr Petrakov went as far as describing the parliaments of the Russian Republic and the Soviet Union itself as the greatest threat to economic reform.*
8 ADV You can use **far** in comparisons to emphasize that one thing is much greater or better than another. *...a far greater problem... It was far more than I expected... The firm had far outstripped its rivals.*
9 ADJ ATTRIB You can describe people with extreme left-wing or right-wing political views as the **far** left or the **far** right. *The far left has been keeping a low profile... Mr Rocard started his political career on the far left... He'll have to find a way of winning over these far-right voters without alienating the centrists.*
◆ **Far** is used in these phrases. ◆ If something happens **far and wide**, it happens in a lot of places or over a large area. *People would come from far and wide to hear him.* ◆ You can use **by far** or **far and away** in comparisons to emphasize that something is better or greater than anything else. *She was by far*

the camp's best swimmer... *This is far and away the most important point.* ◆ If an answer or idea is **not far wrong, not far out,** or **not far off,** it is almost correct. *I had guessed at one point five million, so I was not very far out... He may not have been far wrong when he predicted that one day they would all come back.* ◆ You can use **far from** to emphasize that something is the opposite of what it could have been or of what you expected. *His hands were far from clean... Far from speeding up, the tank slithered to a halt.* ◆ So **far** means up until the present point in time or the present stage in a situation. *What do you think of the town so far?... No details of their discussions have so far been released.* ◆ If you say that someone is going too **far,** you mean that they are behaving in an unacceptable or extreme way; an informal expression. *Mr Tebbit has warned Prince Charles not to go too far in his comments about social issues.* ◆ **as far as** something is concerned: see **concerned.** ◆ **few and far between:** see **few.** ◆ See also **insofar as.**

faraway /fáːrəweɪ/
1 ADJ ATTRIB **Faraway** means a long distance away from you. *...news from faraway villages. ...the faraway sound of a waterfall.*
2 ADJ ATTRIB If someone has a **faraway** look, they seem to be thinking deeply and are not paying attention to what is happening. *There was a dreamy, faraway look on his face.*

farce /faːs/ **farces**
1 NC or NU A **farce** is a humorous play in which the characters become involved in unlikely and complicated situations. *...a classical farce from Poland's leading playwright... This new play is a combination of satire, history, tragedy, and farce.*
2 NC or NU If you say that something is a **farce,** you mean that it is very disorganized or unsatisfactory. *His education had been a farce... The press is asking whether the trial is sliding into farce.*

farcical /fáːsɪkl/
ADJ If you describe a situation or event as **farcical,** you mean that it is completely ridiculous. *They say that the election was farcical and that this parliament carries no credibility.*

fare /feə/ **fares, faring, fared**
1 NC The **fare** is the money that you pay for a journey by bus, taxi, train, boat, or aeroplane. *Coach fares are cheaper than rail fares.*
2 NU+SUPP You can refer to a particular type of food as a particular **fare.** *Army kitchens serve better fare than some hotels... Rice, beans, and corn the basic fare of the Nicaraguans.*
3 V A If you **fare** badly in a particular situation, you are unsuccessful or are treated badly. If you **fare** well, you are successful or are treated well; a formal use. *They fared badly in the 1978 elections.*

Far East
N PROP The **Far East** consists of all the countries of Eastern Asia, including China and Japan. *He has also served abroad, mainly in the Far East and in Cyprus.*

farewell /feəwél/ **farewells**
1 **Farewell** means goodbye; an old-fashioned use. *Farewell, my dear child... He bade farewell to his family.* ▸ Also NC *...tearful farewells.*
2 ADJ ATTRIB A **farewell** act or gesture is performed by or for someone who is leaving a particular post or career. *President Reagan has delivered a farewell speech to the American people... He was speaking at a farewell dinner in his constituency.*

far-fetched
ADJ A **far-fetched** story, idea, or plan is exaggerated or unlikely. *The theory is too far-fetched to be considered.*

far-flung
1 ADJ ATTRIB **Far-flung** places are a long distance away. *...some far-flung corner of the world.*
2 ADJ ATTRIB **Far-flung** means covering a very wide area or extending to distant places. *...the produce of a far-flung empire.*

farm /faːm/ **farms, farming, farmed**
1 NC A **farm** is an area of land consisting of fields and buildings, where crops are grown or animals are raised. *My father worked on a farm. ...the European*

Community's policy of farm subsidies.
2 VOorV If you **farm** an area of land, you grow crops or raise animals on it. *The hill land is farmed by Mike Keeble... Many of these are young men who have never farmed.*

farmer /fɑ:mə/ **farmers**
NC A **farmer** is a person who owns or manages a farm. *The implication is that some dairy farmers will go out of business... The bulk of them are peasant farmers, working on scattered areas of not more than half an acre.*

farm hand, farm hands
NC A **farm hand** is a person who is employed to work on a farm.

farmhouse /fɑ:mhaʊs/ **farmhouses**
NC A **farmhouse** is a house on a farm, especially the house in which a farmer lives. *He saw the old farmhouse where his grandmother lived.*

farming /fɑ:mɪŋ/
NU **Farming** is the activity of growing crops or raising animals on a farm. *...an economy based on farming and tourism. ...sheep farming.*

farmland /fɑ:mlænd/
NU **Farmland** is land which is farmed or which is suitable for farming. *Tens of thousands of acres of farmland have been flooded.*

farmyard /fɑ:mjɔ:d/ **farmyards**
NC A **farmyard** is an area on a farm surrounded by buildings or walls. *We've now come to another very smart, tidy farmyard.*

Faroe Islands /feərəʊ aɪləndz/
The **Faroe Islands** are a territory of Denmark in the North Atlantic, between Iceland and Norway. Streymoy is the largest and most populous of the 18 islands. Fishing is the main industry. ◆ **Faroese** /feərəʊi:z/ N,N PL, ADJ
▪ *per capita GNP:* US$14,600 ▪ *religion:* Christianity (mainly Evangelical Lutheran) ▪ *language:* Faroese, Danish ▪ *currency:* Faroese and Danish krone ▪ *capital:* Tórshavn ▪ *population:* 48,000 (1989) ▪ *size:* 1,399 square kilometres.

far-off
1 ADJ A **far-off** place is a long distance away. *...a far-off country.*
2 ADJ A **far-off** time is a long time away in the future or past. *...looking back at that far-off day.*

far out
ADJ **Far out** means unusual or strange, and very different from other things of the same kind; an informal expression. *That may sound far out, but it had happened a couple of times before... The possibility of creating new, far-out forms of man for space exploration.*

far-reaching
ADJ **Far-reaching** means affecting something greatly, in many ways. *It could have far-reaching implications for the economy.*

farrier /færiə/ **farriers**
NC A **farrier** is a person who fits horseshoes onto horses.

farrow /færəʊ/ **farrows, farrowing, farrowed**
V When a female pig **farrows**, she gives birth to piglets; a technical term. *...small tin-roofed huts in which the pigs can shelter from the weather and farrow.*

far-sighted
1 ADJ If someone is **far-sighted**, they are good at guessing what will happen in the future and making suitable plans. *Over twenty years ago some far-sighted farmers in Britain set up the Rare Breeds Survival Trust.*
2 ADJ In American English, **far-sighted** means the same as **long-sighted**.

fart /fɑ:t/ **farts, farting, farted**; an informal or rude word which some people find offensive.
1 V If someone **farts**, they allow air to be forced out of their body through their anus.
2 NC If you call someone an old **fart**, you are indicating that you think that they are boring and that you do not respect them.

fart about PHRASAL VERB If you say that someone is **farting about** or **is farting around**, you mean that they

are wasting time doing silly things instead of doing what needs to be done; an informal expression which some people find offensive.

farther /fɑ:ðə/
Farther is a comparative of **far**.

farthest /fɑ:ðɪst/
Farthest is a superlative of **far**.

farthing /fɑ:ðɪŋ/ **farthings**
NC In old British currency, a **farthing** was a coin that was worth a quarter of a penny.

fascia /feɪʃə/ **fascias**; a formal word
1 NC The **fascia** in a car is the part surrounding the instruments and dials.
2 NC The **fascia** on a shop front is the flat surface above the shop window, on which the name of the shop is written.

fascinate /fæsɪneɪt/ **fascinates, fascinating, fascinated**
VO If something or someone **fascinates** you, you find them very interesting. *I love history, it fascinates me.*
◆ **fascinated** ADJ *He became fascinated with their whole way of life.* ◆ **fascinating** ADJ *It's a fascinating book.*

fascination /fæsɪneɪʃn/
NU **Fascination** is the state of being greatly interested in something. *...a fascination with Hokkaido's wild country.*

fascism /fæʃɪzəm/
NU **Fascism** is a right-wing political philosophy that believes in the importance of having strong rules, state control, and the prevention of political opposition. *The task now was to build a strong and normal society in which the seeds of fascism could never again flourish.*

fascist /fæʃɪst/ **fascists**
1 NC A **fascist** is someone who believes in fascism. *...the monstrous crimes of the fascists during the war.*
2 NC If you call someone a **fascist**, you mean that their opinions are very right-wing; used showing disapproval. *The Association is saying all except confessed criminals and what they call 'fascists' should be freed.*
3 ADJ **Fascist** is used to describe people and things that are connected with fascism, or with very right-wing ideas. *...a party that many observers regard as having fascist tendencies.*

fashion /fæʃn/ **fashions, fashioning, fashioned**
1 N SING+SUPP If you do something in a particular **fashion**, you do it in that way. *He greeted us in his usual friendly fashion... The authorities appear to have abandoned any attempt to distribute food and water in an orderly fashion.*
2 NU **Fashion** is the area of activity that involves styles of clothing and appearance. *...the fashion industry. ...a fashion show at the Opera House featuring some of the world's top designers.*
3 NC A **fashion** is a style of clothing or a way of behaving that is popular at a particular time. *...the latest Parisian fashions.* ● If something is **in fashion**, it is popular and approved of at a particular time. If it is **out of fashion**, it is not popular or approved of. *Books about spying are in fashion now... This is a policy that is increasingly out of fashion.*
4 VO If you **fashion** something, you create it; a formal use. *The crew fashioned a raft from the wreckage... The Japanese authorities want to fashion a new political role for the country.*
5 See also **old-fashioned**.

fashionable /fæʃənəbl/
ADJ Something that is **fashionable** is popular or approved of at a particular time. *...the striped shirts that were fashionable in 1963. ...a sophisticated and fashionable lifestyle... Marxism was very fashionable amongst the students.* ◆ **fashionably** ADV *...fashionably dressed ladies.*

fast /fɑ:st/ **faster, fastest; fasts, fasting, fasted**
1 ADJorADV **Fast** means moving, acting, or happening with great speed. *...a fast car. ...producing goods at a faster rate... I ran as fast as I could... News travels pretty fast.*
2 ADJorADV **Fast** is used in questions and statements about speed. *...looking out of the windows to see how*

fast we were going... How fast does it lay the surface?... It will not be a very fast vehicle, it will be going 20 miles per hour.
3 ADV **Fast** also means happening without any delay. *She needed medical help fast... Treat stains as fast as possible.*
4 ADJ If a watch or clock is **fast**, it is showing a time that is later than the real time.
5 ADV If something is held or fixed **fast**, it is held or fixed very firmly. *He saw a small man, his leg held fast in the lion trap, making desperate efforts to free himself.*
6 V If you **fast**, you eat no food for a period of time, usually for religious reasons. *He fasts for a whole day every week.* ▶ Also NC *During my fast I lost fifteen pounds.*
● **Fast** is used in these phrases. ● Someone who is **fast asleep** is completely asleep. *MPs have been kept in the chamber right through the night, many of them slumped over their desks and fast asleep.* ● If you **hold fast** to an idea or course of action, you firmly continue believing it or doing it. *He was determined to hold fast to his beliefs.* ● **to make a fast buck**: see **buck**. ● **thick and fast**: see **thick**. ● See also **hard and fast**.

fast breeder reactor, fast breeder reactors
NC A **fast breeder reactor** or a **fast breeder** is a kind of nuclear reactor that produces more plutonium than it uses. *Vast amounts of money have already been invested in fast breeder reactors... They argue that fast breeders will never be viable.*

fasten /ˈfɑːsn/ **fastens, fastening, fastened**
1 V-ERG If you **fasten** something, you fix it in a closed position with a button, strap, or other device. *He fastened his seat-belt... The case fastened at the top.*
2 VOA If you **fasten** one thing to another, you attach the first thing to the second. *The bench had been fastened to the pavement.*
3 V-ERG A If you **fasten** your hands or teeth around or onto something, you grasp it firmly with your hands or teeth. *He fastened his hands round the spear... Her hands fastened on the climbing rope.*
fasten on PHRASAL VERB If you **fasten on** to someone or something, you concentrate your attention or efforts on them. *Once she had fastened on to a scheme she did not let go.*

fastener /ˈfɑːsnə/ **fasteners**
NC A **fastener** is a device such as a button, zip, or safety pin that fastens something, especially clothing.

fastening /ˈfɑːsnɪŋ/ **fastenings**
NC A **fastening** is a device that keeps something fixed or closed. *...the fastenings of her gown.*

fast food
NU **Fast food** is hot food such as hamburgers that is served quickly after you order it, but which is not considered to be good for you if you eat it too often. *The survey portrays the British as a nation addicted to television, fast food, beer and gambling.*

fastidious /fæˈstɪdɪəs/
ADJ Someone who is **fastidious** is fussy and likes things to be clean, tidy, and properly done; a formal word. *...with noses wrinkled in fastidious distaste.*
◆ **fastidiously** ADV *The process was fastidiously checked.*

fastness /ˈfɑːstnəs/ **fastnesses**
NC+SUPP A **fastness** is a safe place, usually one that is difficult to get to; a literary word. *...this island fastness.*

fat /fæt/ **fatter, fattest; fats**
1 ADJ A **fat** person has a lot of flesh on their body and weighs too much. *...a small fat man.* ◆ **fatness** NU *He was embarrassed to hear her discussing his fatness.*
2 NU **Fat** in the bodies of animals and people is the layer of flesh which is used to store energy and to keep them warm. *We don't really know why we have so much body fat.*
3 N MASS **Fat** is a substance contained in many foods and used by your body to produce energy. *If the diet were much lower in saturated fat and cholesterol, they would not have the abnormality. ...a diet containing protein, fats, carbohydrates, and vitamins.*

4 N MASS **Fat** is also a substance used in cooking which is obtained from vegetables or the flesh of animals. *...a smell of fried fat. ...add high energy foods such as oils or fats into the gruel.*
5 ADJ A **fat** book, case, or other object is very thick or wide. *...a fat briefcase.*
6 ADJ ATTRIB A **fat** profit is a large one. *They expect fat profits from the operation.*

fatal /ˈfeɪtl/
1 ADJ A **fatal** action has undesirable results. *I made the fatal mistake of letting her talk.* ◆ **fatally** ADV *Their leaders are fatally mistaken... The basic design is fatally flawed.*
2 ADJ A **fatal** accident or illness causes someone's death. *...Pollock's fatal car crash.* ◆ **fatally** ADV *Four men were fatally stabbed.*

fatalism /ˈfeɪtəlɪzəm/
NU **Fatalism** is the belief that people cannot prevent or control events. *...the fatalism of the masses.*

fatalistic /feɪtəˈlɪstɪk/
ADJ Someone who is **fatalistic** believes that human beings cannot influence or control events. *She had a far more fatalistic approach... You get to be terribly fatalistic in combat.*

fatality /fəˈtælətɪ/ **fatalities**
1 NC A **fatality** is a person's death, caused by an accident or violence. *All nine people aboard the helicopter were injured but there were no fatalities.*
2 NU **Fatality** is the feeling or belief that people cannot prevent or control events; a formal use. *The modern world is dominated by a sense of fatality.*

fate /feɪt/ **fates**
1 NU **Fate** is a power believed by some people to control everything that happens. *Fate was against me.*
2 NC+SUPP Someone's **fate** is what happens to them. *Several other companies suffered a similar fate... Their other worry must be the fate of the President himself.*

fated /ˈfeɪtɪd/
ADJ If you say that someone is **fated** to do something, or that something is **fated**, you mean that nothing can be done to prevent what will happen to them. *We were fated to dislike one another... What actually did happen to the fated Boeing 737 we shall soon know.*

fateful /ˈfeɪtfl/
ADJ ATTRIB If you describe an action or event as **fateful**, you mean that it had important, and often bad, effects on later events. *The President made his fateful announcement.*

fat-free
ADJ **Fat-free** food does not contain any fat. *...a new type of ground beef that is 91 percent fat-free. ...a little pot of fat-free yoghurt.*

fathead /ˈfæthed/ **fatheads**
NC If you say that someone is a **fathead**, you mean that you think they are very stupid; an old-fashioned, offensive word. *Should my income suffer because some fathead swears in front of a prospective parent?*

father /ˈfɑːðə/ **fathers, fathering, fathered**
1 NC or VOCATIVE Your **father** is your male parent. *The Duchess's father is travelling with them... Father! Save me!*
2 VO When a man **fathers** a child, he makes a woman pregnant and their child is born; a literary use. *...children fathered by American troops during the war.*
3 N SING If you say that a man is the **father** of something, you mean that he invented or started it. *Chaucer is often said to be the father of English poetry.*
4 TITLE or VOCATIVE In some Christian churches, priests are addressed or referred to as **Father**. *On Friday morning, Father Boff and the priests and nuns held a demonstration.*
5 N PROP or VOCATIVE Christians often refer to God as our **Father** or address him as **Father**. *Heavenly Father, hear our prayers.*

Father Christmas
N PROP **Father Christmas** is an imaginary old man with a long white beard and a red coat. Young children believe that he brings their Christmas

presents. *It's generally accepted that Father Christmas comes from the land of snow somewhere in the north. ...half-a-million letters posted by youngsters to Father Christmas in Reindeerland.*

father figure, father figures
NC A **father figure** is a man who is not your father but provides support and authority in a similar way to a father. *He was a quiet father figure during his years of power... They regarded him as a father figure.*

fatherhood /ˈfɑːðəhʊd/
NU **Fatherhood** is the state of being a father. *Attitudes to fatherhood are changing.*

father-in-law, fathers-in-law
NC Your **father-in-law** is the father of your husband or wife. *He was joined on the flight by his father-in-law and daughter.*

fatherland /ˈfɑːðəlænd/ **fatherlands**
NC Someone's **fatherland** is the country in which they or their ancestors were born; a literary word. *They were fighting for their fatherland.*

fatherless /ˈfɑːðələs/
ADJ You describe children as **fatherless** when their father has died or does not live with them. *Because they grew up fatherless, very few of them ever finished school.*

fatherly /ˈfɑːðəli/
ADJ ATTRIB You say that someone behaves in a **fatherly** way when they behave like a kind father. *Let me give you some fatherly advice.*

Father's Day
N SING or NU In Britain, **Father's Day** is the third Sunday in June, celebrated in honour of fathers. *'I just wanted to wish you a happy Father's Day'... On Father's Day this year I decided to call him... This was my first Father's Day at home.*

fathom /ˈfæðəm/ **fathoms, fathoming, fathomed**
1 NC A **fathom** is a unit of length used for describing the depth of the sea. One fathom is equal to 6 feet or approximately 1.8 metres. *He was at work 60 fathoms deep.*
2 VO If you cannot **fathom** something, you cannot understand it properly even though you think about it carefully. *I couldn't fathom the meaning of her remarks... The political reasoning behind this is difficult to fathom.*

fathom out PHRASAL VERB If you cannot **fathom** something **out**, you cannot understand it properly even though you think about it carefully. *What I can't fathom out is why he did it... Doctors are trying to fathom out what it is about the building that makes them sick.*

fathomless /ˈfæðəmləs/
ADJ Something that is **fathomless** cannot be measured or understood because it is very deep, obscure, or complicated. *She looked at him with calm, fathomless eyes. ...a fathomless truth.*

fatigue /fəˈtiːɡ/ **fatigues, fatiguing, fatigued**
1 NU **Fatigue** is a feeling of extreme physical or mental tiredness. *He was dizzy with hunger and fatigue. ...his voice hoarse with fatigue.*
2 NU+SUPP You can also say that people are suffering from a particular kind of **fatigue** when they have been doing something for a long time and feel they can no longer continue to do it. *Food quantities given to the refugees now are smaller because of donor fatigue... The low turn out was probably due to voter fatigue and the hot weather.* ● See also **metal fatigue**.
3 VO If something **fatigues** you, it makes you extremely tired; a formal use. *Some people say eating fatigues them.* ◆ **fatigued** ADJ *She was utterly fatigued.*

fatted /ˈfætɪd/
If you **kill the fatted calf**, you have a celebration to welcome a person you have not seen for a long time; a literary expression.

fatten /ˈfætn/ **fattens, fattening, fattened**
V-ERG If you **fatten** an animal or if it **fattens**, it gains weight as a result of eating a lot of food. *Soya is excellent for fattening pigs.*

fatten up PHRASAL VERB If you **fatten up** an animal, you give it a lot of food to eat so that it reaches the desired weight. *Their cattle take twice as long to*

fatten up as European cattle.

fattening /ˈfætənɪŋ/
ADJ **Fattening** food tends to make people fat. *We only had time for fattening fast food.*

fatty /ˈfæti/
ADJ **Fatty** food contains a lot of fat. *Avoid eating fatty foods such as chocolate. ...the fatty diets of the middle-aged.*

fatuous /ˈfætjuəs/
ADJ A **fatuous** remark, action, or plan is extremely foolish. *In her letter she addresses me in the most fatuous kind of way.*

faucet /ˈfɔːsɪt/ **faucets**
NC A **faucet** is a tap, for example on a sink or bath; used in American English. *I can hear the faucet running someplace over there.*

fault /fɔːlt/ **faults, faulting, faulted**
1 N SING+POSS If a bad situation is your **fault**, you caused it or are responsible for it. *It was entirely my own fault... The disruption is the fault of a government committed to confrontation... Many unauthorized workers feel they are branded as criminals through no fault of their own.*
2 NC A **fault** in something is a weakness or imperfection in it. *Computer faults are commonplace... The pilots were trying to repair a fault in the plane when it crashed.*
3 VO If you say that you cannot **fault** someone, you mean that they are doing something so well that you cannot criticize them. *I couldn't fault him on that one.*
4 NC A **fault** is also a large crack in the Earth's surface; a technical use in geology. *A New Mexico scientist predicted a damaging earthquake along the fault in December.*
● **Fault** is used in these phrases. ● If you are **at fault**, you are incorrect or have done something wrong. *It was 1976, I believe, if my memory is not at fault.* ● If you **find fault** with something, you complain about it. *If he'd done a poor job, I'm sure she'd have more to find fault with.*

faultless /ˈfɔːltləs/
ADJ Something that is **faultless** contains no mistakes. *...faultless German.*

faulty /ˈfɔːlti/
ADJ A **faulty** machine or piece of equipment is not working properly. *...a faulty transformer.*

faun /fɔːn/ **fauns**
NC A **faun** is an imaginary creature which is like a man with goat's legs and horns. *...Debussy's 'Prelude to the Afternoon of a Faun'.*

fauna /ˈfɔːnə/
N PL The **fauna** in a place are all the animals, birds, fish, and insects there; a formal word. *...the flora and fauna of Africa.*

faux pas /ˌfəʊ ˈpɑː/; **faux pas** is both the singular and the plural form. The plural is pronounced /ˌfəʊ ˈpɑːz/.
NC A **faux pas** is a socially embarrassing action or mistake; a formal expression. *They behaved as if they were fearful of committing a faux pas.*

favour /ˈfeɪvə/ **favours, favouring, favoured**; spelt **favor** in American English.
1 NU If you regard something or someone with **favour**, you like or support them. *I think the company will look with favour on your plan... Is this just an attempt to win his favour?*
2 NC If you do someone a **favour**, you do something for them even though you do not have to. *I've come to ask a favour.*
3 VO If you **favour** something, you prefer it to the other choices available. *...those who favour disarmament.*
4 VO Something that **favours** a person or event makes it easier for that person to be successful or for that event to happen. *The weather favoured the attacking army.*
5 VO If you **favour** someone, you treat them better than you treat other people. *Parents may favour the youngest child in the family.*
6 VO+with If you **favour** someone with your attention or presence, you give it to them; a formal use. *The minister favoured us with an interview.*
● **Favour** is used in these phrases. ● If you are **in**

favour of something, you think that it is a good thing. *They are in favour of reforming the tax laws... The Croatian authorities are confidently predicting a vote in favour of separation.* ● If someone makes a judgement in your **favour**, they say that you are right about something or they give some advantage to you rather than to someone else. *Sufferers fighting for compensation have welcomed an appeal court ruling in their favour... The umpire ruled in her favour.* ● Something that is in your **favour** gives you an advantage. *The system is biased in favour of young people.* ● If one thing is rejected in **favour of** another, the second thing is done or chosen instead of the first one. *The plans for a new airport have been scrapped in favour of an extension to the old one.* ● If something is in **favour**, people like or support it. If something is **out of favour**, people no longer like or support it. *Their views are very much out of favour now.* ● to **curry favour**: see **curry**.

favourable /feɪvəʳrəbl/; spelt **favorable** in American English.
1 ADJ If you are **favourable** to something, you agree with it or approve of it. *Her request met with a favourable response. ...the republics that were favourable to the idea of the Union Treaty.* ◆ **favourably** ADV *Many reacted favourably to the plan.*
2 ADJ If something makes a **favourable** impression on you, you like it or approve of it. *My impression of Bulgaria was very favourable.* ◆ **favourably** ADV *Her application had impressed him very favourably.*
3 ADJ If you present something in a **favourable** light, you try to make people like it or approve of it. *Officials gave a favourable account of the meetings. ...presenting the government's policies in a favourable light.*
4 ADJ **Favourable** conditions make something more likely to succeed. *This creates an atmosphere favourable to expansion... Conditions for growing food were generally favourable.*
5 ADJ If you make a **favourable** comparison between two things, you say that the first is at least as good as the second. *Visitors come to take advantage of favourable prices, good quality and variety.* ◆ **favourably** ADV *...a service which compares favourably with that of other countries.*

favourite /feɪvəʳrət/ **favourites**; spelt **favorite** in American English.
1 ADJ Your **favourite** thing of a particular type is the one that you like most. *What is your favourite television programme?... Well, a favourite definition of a weed is a plant in the wrong place.*
2 NC The **favourite** in a competition is the person or animal that is expected to win it. *A year and a half ago he was the hot favourite to become the next Chancellor... The race was won by the joint favourite, Ballyhane... Dixon is the odds-on favorite to succeed Marion Barry.*

favourite son, favourite sons
NC The **favourite son** of a particular place, group of people, or organization is a person who is very popular with the people in that place, group, or organization. *Nelson Mandela is more than the favourite son of this wind-swept landscape—he's a tribal prince. ...the last appearance of one of the sport's favourite sons... People in Touba were sad about the fall from power of their favourite son.*

favouritism /feɪvəʳrətɪzm/; spelt **favoritism** in American English.
NU **Favouritism** is the practice of unfairly helping or supporting one person or group more than another. *There must be no favouritism in the allocation of contracts.*

fawn /fɔːn/ **fawns, fawning, fawned**
1 ADJ Something that is **fawn** is pale yellowish-brown. *...a fawn overcoat.*
2 NC A **fawn** is a very young deer. *Last summer, all the does had twin fawns instead of singles.*
3 V If people **fawn** on powerful or rich people, they flatter them to get something for themselves; used showing disapproval. *...courtiers who had once flattered and fawned on him.*

fax /fæks/ **faxes, faxing, faxed**
1 V Oor VOO If you **fax** a document, you cause a copy of it to be made in a different place by sending information electronically along a telephone line. *The messages were faxed to a recruitment agency in the City... The Post Office faxed me a list of rules set up by Soviet Customs.*
2 NC or NU A **fax** or a **fax** machine is the piece of equipment used to copy documents by sending information electronically along a telephone line. *I find that if I've got telephones or faxes, or televisions, it's simply a distraction... These days, of course, cartoonists send their work in by fax. ...teaching people how to work computers and fax machines.*
3 NC A **fax** is also the copy that is made when you fax a document. *He sent me a fax of the original memo... Telexes and faxes sent to the bank from Bangladesh had so far not been answered, he said.*

faze /feɪz/ **fazes, fazing, fazed**
V O If something **fazes** you, it interrupts what you are doing because it is confusing, upsetting, or amazing. *Nothing seemed to faze them... Even this master of the unstoppable flow of scepticism was fazed.*

FBI /ˌefbiːˈaɪ/
N PROP In the United States, the **FBI** is a state agency that investigates crimes in which a national law is broken or in which the country's security is threatened. **FBI** is an abbreviation for 'Federal Bureau of Investigation'. *...his refusal to hand over tapes to the FBI.*

fealty /fiːəlti/ **fealties**
NU or NC In former times, when someone swore **fealty** to their lord or ruler, they promised to be loyal to him or her. *...swearing eternal fealty to each other.*

fear /fɪə/ **fears, fearing, feared**
1 NU **Fear** is the unpleasant feeling of worry that you get when you think that you are in danger or that something horrible is going to happen. *They huddled together, quaking with fear... She was brought up with no fear of animals... Many homosexual priests now live in fear.*
2 NC A **fear** is a thought that something unpleasant might happen or might have happened. *My worst fears were quickly realized... I think it's a very unrealistic fear.*
3 If you do not do something **for fear** of something happening, you do not do it because you do not wish that thing to happen. *They did not mention it for fear of offending him... Few of us are prepared to admit to being happy for fear that we will be thought stupid.*
4 VO If you **fear** someone or something, they make you feel nervous or worried; a formal use. *He fears nothing... The old man feared banks and was said to keep his money under his bed.*
5 VO or V-REPORT If you **fear** something unpleasant, you are worried that it might happen, or might have happened; a formal use. *An epidemic of plague was feared... They fear that their new-found independence might be lost... More demonstrations are feared.*
6 V If you say that you **fear** that something is the case, you mean that you are sorry or sad about it; a formal use. *It is usually, I fear, the parents who are responsible.*

fear for PHRASAL VERB If you **fear for** something, you worry that it might be in danger; a formal expression. *Morris began to fear for the life of Mrs Reilly.*

fearful /fɪəfl/; a formal word.
1 ADJ Someone who is **fearful** is very afraid of something. *They are fearful of letting their feelings take over.* ◆ **fearfully** ADV *The boys looked at each other fearfully.*
2 ADJ Something that is **fearful** is very unpleasant or bad. *...the fearful risks of the operation.*

fearless /fɪələs/
ADJ A **fearless** person or animal is not afraid. *He was fearless in his condemnation of terrorism—fearless in his fight for the truth. ...his fearless bravery and dedication to attack.* ◆ **fearlessly** ADV *The broadcasting staff had faced danger fearlessly and stood fast at their posts... We get on and tackle the real issues fearlessly and positively.*

fearsome /fɪ̯əsəm/
ADJ A **fearsome** thing is terrible or frightening; a
literary word. *The dog had a fearsome set of teeth...*
The sight of so many armed men, clearly in a war-like
mood, is truly fearsome.

feasible /fiːzəbl/
ADJ Something that is **feasible** can be done, made, or
achieved. *The electric car is technically feasible.*
♦ **feasibility** /fiːzəbɪ̯ləti/ NU ...*the technical feasibility*
of a supersonic aircraft... They agreed to a feasibility
study on the dumping of toxic waste.

feast /fiːst/ **feasts, feasting, feasted**
1 NC A **feast** is a very large meal, usually prepared
for a special occasion. *They held a Thanksgiving*
service and invited Americans to a feast. ...*a wedding*
feast.
2 V If you **feast**, you take part in a feast; a literary
use. *He sprawled there, feasting off cold roast duck...*
We've feasted not only on doves, turkey, and quail, but
robins, squirrels and, only once, a possum. ♦ **feasting**
NU *At the end of Ramadan, usually it's a time of*
feasting and celebration.
3 N SING You can also refer to something as a
particular kind of **feast** when it includes a large
number of things that you think are very good,
interesting, or enjoyable. *The finished film is a feast*
for the senses. ...*a feast of top class tennis.* ...*that*
annual feast of the arts, the Edinburgh Festival.
4 If you **feast** your **eyes** on something, you look at it
for a long time because you like it very much. *I*
feasted my eyes upon her lovely face.

feat /fiːt/ **feats**
NC+SUPP A **feat** of some kind is an impressive and
difficult act or achievement. ...*a brilliant feat of*
engineering... The paper says it is a remarkable feat
to have secured his party's nomination so early.

feather /fɛðə/ **feathers**
NC A bird's **feathers** are the light, soft things covering
its body. ...*a bird with delicate trailing feathers.*
...*ostrich feathers.*

feather-bedding
NU **Feather-bedding** is the practice of allowing work to
be done slowly or inefficiently so that all the jobs in a
particular firm are protected; used in informal
English, showing disapproval. ...*the feather-bedding of*
agriculture.

feather boa /fɛðə bəʊə/ **feather boas**
NC A **feather boa** is a long, thin scarf made of soft
feathers.

feather-brained
ADJ Someone who is **feather-brained** is rather silly and
forgetful.

feather duster, feather dusters
NC A **feather duster** is a stick with a bunch of feathers
attached which is used for dusting. ...*ornaments that*
seem to have had no more handling than the flick of a
feather duster.

feathered /fɛðəd/
ADJ ATTRIB **feathered** means covered with feathers or
made of feathers. ...*girls in feathered head-dresses.*

featherweight /fɛðəweɪt/ **featherweights**
1 NC A **featherweight** is a boxer who weighs between
53.5 and 57 kilograms, which is one of the lowest
weight ranges. *Fenech was named as the number one*
featherweight.
2 NC A **featherweight** is also someone or something
that does not weigh very much. *He was only 5 feet 8*
inches tall, but he would lift me up as if I was a
featherweight. ...*a featherweight shuttlecock.*
3 NC You can also refer to someone or something that
is of very little importance as a **featherweight**. *Mr*
McPeak took pains to paint them as a potentially
worthy opponent. 'They are no featherweights,' he
said... It was a featherweight distraction, a fleeting
annoyance.

feathery /fɛðə⁰ri/
ADJ Something that is **feathery** reminds you of
feathers, usually because of its softness or shape.
...*feathery palm trees.*

feature /fiːtʃə/ **features, featuring, featured**
1 NC+SUPP A **feature** of something is an interesting or
important part or characteristic of it. *Every car will*

have built-in safety features. ...*the natural features of*
the landscape.
2 N PL Your **features** are your eyes, nose, mouth, and
other parts of your face. ...*a small, slightly built man*
with lively features,... He has the family features—a
long thin face and a prominent nose.
3 VO When a film or exhibition **features** someone or
something, they are an important part of it. *This film*
features two of my favourite actors.
4 V+in To **feature** in something means to be an
important and noticeable part of it. *This is not the*
first time he has featured in allegations of violence...
According to the Prime Minister, the question of
Afghanistan features large.
5 NC A **feature** is also a special article in a newspaper
or magazine, or a special programme on radio or
television. *The local newspaper ran a feature on drug*
abuse... Ever popular features include a vocabulary
quiz called 'It Pays to Increase Your Word Power'.
6 NC A full-length film in a cinema is also called a
feature or a **feature film**. ...*the soundtrack of the*
smash hit feature film.

featureless /fiːtʃələs/
ADJ Something that is **featureless** has no interesting
features or characteristics. ...*a featureless expanse of*
sand. ...*featureless rooms.*

Feb.
Feb. is a written abbreviation for 'February'. *The*
ceremony takes place tomorrow (Feb. 13).

febrile /fiːbraɪl/
ADJ **Febrile** behaviour is intensely and nervously
active; a literary word. ...*her febrile state of*
creativity.

February /fɛbruəri/
NU **February** is the second month of the year in the
western calendar. ...*cold sunny days in February.*

feces /fiːsiːz/. See **faeces**.

feckless /fɛkləs/
ADJ A **feckless** person lacks strength of character, and
cannot run their life properly; a literary word.
...*children with drunken or feckless parents.*

fecund /fiːkənd, fɛkənd/
ADJ A living thing or place that is **fecund** is fertile or
very productive; a literary word. ...*fecund soil... The*
latest dramatists are less fecund than the generation
before.

fed /fɛd/
Fed is the past tense and past participle of **feed**. ♦ See
also **fed up**.

federal /fɛdə⁰rəl/
ADJ ATTRIB In a **federal** country or system, a group of
states is controlled by a central government. *Mr*
Delors is outspoken in his belief in the need for a
federal Europe. ...*other economic legislation approved*
by the federal Parliament. ...*the Federal Republic of*
Germany.

federalism /fɛdə⁰rəlɪzəm/
NU **Federalism** is belief in or support for a federal
system of government, or this system itself. ...*a party*
dedicated to federalism... Nothing is more likely than
federalism to upset economic equilibrium. ♦ **federalist**,
federalists NC *They will be trying to convince the*
less enthusiastic federalists.

federate /fɛdəreɪt/ **federates, federating, federated**
V-RECIP When one state or society **federates** with
another, or when they **federate**, or **are federated**, they
join together for a common purpose. *They said they*
would willingly federate with Jordan... They want to
federate after independence, not before... Afterwards,
the whole world will be federated under a single
government. ♦ **federated** ADJ ATTRIB ...*a federated*
Moroccan state.

federation /fɛdəreɪʃn/ **federations**
NC A **federation** is a group of organizations or states
that have joined together for a common purpose.
...*the National Federation of Women's Institutes.*

fed up
ADJ PRED If you are **fed up**, you are bored or annoyed;
an informal expression. *You sound a bit fed up... The*
young men are fed up with washing their own clothing.

fee /fiː/ **fees**
1 NC A **fee** is a sum of money that you pay to be

allowed to do something. *They spend the afternoons looking at the pictures outside cinemas, unable to afford the entrance fee.*
2 NC A **fee** is also the money that you pay for a particular job or service. *Agencies charge a fee to find an au pair.*

feeble /fiːbl/ **feebler, feeblest**
1 ADJ Someone or something that is **feeble** has very little power, strength, or energy. *The creature is physically feeble, with poor vision and dull senses... Vietnam is in desperate need of aid, trade and investment to revive its feeble economy.* ♦ **feebly** ADV *He waved his hands feebly.*
2 ADJ If you describe something that someone says as **feeble**, you mean that you think it is not very good, convincing or effective. *This feeble answer is of course a lie. ...a feeble joke.* ♦ **feebly** ADV *'They seemed all right to me,' I explained feebly.*

feeble-minded
ADJ Someone who is **feeble-minded** is unable to think or understand things very quickly. *...using feeble-minded people for their own advantage... She was classified as 'feeble-minded' and sent to an institution for the mentally ill.*

feed /fiːd/ **feeds, feeding, fed**
1 VOorVOO If you **feed** a baby or an animal, you give it food. *We plant sunflowers in order to feed the bees... When the mixture is ready, you begin to feed it to the sick person, a sip at a time... She fed the baby some milk.* ▶ Also NC *What time is his next feed?*
2 V When an animal or baby **feeds**, it eats something. *Not all bats feed on insects... The geese feed in large flocks.*
3 N MASS **Feed** is food that is given to an animal. *It shouldn't be fed as a sole source of feed, but as part of a balanced diet. ...cattle feed.*
4 VOorV-REFL If you **feed** your family or a community, you supply or prepare food for them. *The farmers grew too little to feed even their own families... Are you feeding yourself properly?*
5 V+onorVO If something **feeds** on something else or is fed by it, it grows stronger as a result of it. *Anger feeds on disappointment... The fires were being fed by escaping gas.*
6 VO+into If you **feed** something into a container, store, or other object, you gradually put it in. *You can feed the seeds into the funnel by hand... We need accurate weather data to feed into the computer.*

feedback /fiːdbæk/
NU When you get **feedback**, you get comments about something that you have done or made. *There's no feedback from the national media on these issues. ...negative feedback.*

feeder /fiːdə/ **feeders**
1 ADJ ATTRIB A **feeder** road, railway line, or air route is a minor one that connects with a major one. *The sacks were loaded onto the feeder flight to Frankfurt... The new policy targets interstate highways and feeder routes for federal aid.*
2 NC A **feeder** is a device that is used for feeding animals or sick people. *Last year, there was enthusiasm about an automatic pig feeder for dry sows... She developed a simple feeder from which sick patients can drink when they like.*
3 NC+SUPP If a baby or animal is a slow **feeder**, a fussy **feeder**, and so on, it feeds in that particular way. *...a baby who is a listless, sleepy feeder.*

feeding-bottle, feeding-bottles
NC A **feeding-bottle** is a small bottle with a special rubber top through which a baby can drink. *They suck gently, as they would from a teat on a feeding-bottle.*

feeding ground, feeding grounds
NC The **feeding ground** of a group of birds or animals is the place where they find food and eat. *Migration takes them to feeding grounds on the other side of the Atlantic.*

feel /fiːl/ **feels, feeling, felt**
1 VO,VC,orVA If you **feel** an emotion or a sensation, you experience it. *Mrs Oliver felt a sudden desire to burst out crying... I was feeling hungry... She felt a fool... I felt like a murderer.*

2 V-REPORT,VC,orVOC If you **feel** that something is the case, it is your opinion that it is the case. *He felt I was making a terrible mistake... I felt obliged to invite him in... He felt it necessary to explain why he had come.*
3 VA If you **feel** a particular way about something, you have that attitude or reaction to it. *She knew how I felt about totalitarianism.*
4 VCorVA If you talk about how an experience **feels**, you are talking about the emotions and sensations connected with it. *It felt good to be back... What does it feel like to watch yourself on TV?*
5 VCorVA The way something **feels** is the way it seems to you when you touch or hold it. *It does feel a bit warm... It feels like a normal fabric.* ▶ Also N SING+SUPP *...the cool feel of armchair leather.*
6 VOorV-REFL If you **feel** something, you are aware that it is touching or happening to your body. *They felt the wind on their damp faces... He could feel himself blushing.*
7 VO To **feel** something also means to be aware of it, even though you cannot see or hear it. *He had felt Binta's presence in the hut.*
8 VO If you **feel** a physical object, you touch it deliberately, in order to find out what it is like. *Eric felt his face. 'I'm all rough. Am I bleeding?'*
9 VO If you **feel** the effect or result of something, you experience it. *Stock exchanges in Sao Paulo and Rio were already feeling the effects of the new recession.*
10 N SING+for If you have a **feel** for something, you understand it well and are able to deal with it skilfully. *I was actually pleasantly surprised that he has a good feel for the music.*
11 N SING+SUPP The **feel** of something, for example a place, is the general impression that it gives. *The Brazilian Amazon has the feel of a tropical wild west.*
12 See also **feeling, felt.**
● **Feel** is used in these phrases. ● If you **feel like** doing or having something, you want to do or have it. *I felt like saying, 'Why don't you shut up?'... I feel like a stroll.* ● If you **do not feel yourself**, you feel slightly ill. *I don't really feel myself today.*

feel for PHRASAL VERB 1 If you **feel for** an object, you try to find it using your hands rather than your eyes. *She felt in her bag for her key.* 2 If you **feel for** someone, you have a lot of sympathy for them. *So it's very tough and we feel for them, and that's why we're trying to do what we can to offer them some retraining.*

feeler /fiːlə/ **feelers**
1 NC An insect's **feelers** are the two thin stalks on its head which it touches and senses things with. *It has two feelers at the front of the head.*
2 NC A **feeler** is also a suggestion that you make in a tentative way in order to find out what people's reactions will be before making a decision or putting a plan into action. *Already feelers were out about another script... Why did they put this statement out? Was it really a feeler for peace?*

feeling /fiːlɪŋ/ **feelings**
1 NCorNU A **feeling** is an emotion or attitude. *She tried to hide her feelings... Their strongest feeling for the Royal family was one of respect. ...a voice rich in real feeling.*
2 NC+SUPP A **feeling** is also a physical sensation. *...an itchy feeling. ...feelings of nausea.*
3 NU If you have no **feeling** in a part of your body, you do not know when that part is being touched.
4 NC If you have a **feeling** that something is the case or that something is going to happen, you think that it is probably the case or that it will probably happen. *My feeling is that it would work very well... I have a nasty feeling you're right... This has encouraged a feeling that General Ne Win will probably continue to exert great influence behind the scenes.*
5 NU **Feeling** for someone or something is affection or sympathy for them. *He may be moved by feeling for his fellow-citizens. ...a cold, calculating woman with little feeling for anything or anyone beyond her husband and a small circle of friends.*
● **Feeling** is used in these phrases. ● **Bad feeling** or **ill feeling** is resentment or hostility between people.

There was none of the bad feeling of the semi-final...
He said he hoped the ill feeling on the other side could
be dissipated through diplomatic contact in the future.
● If you **hurt** someone's **feelings**, you upset them. *He*
said the remarks had hurt the feelings of the Chinese
people. ● If you have no **hard feelings** towards
someone who has upset you, you do not feel angry
with them. *'There are no hard feelings,' Mr Bush*
declared 'now the election is over.'

fee-paying
ADJ ATTRIB A **fee-paying** school is a private school that
charges fees, rather than one which is run by the
state. *The number of foreign students at independent*
fee-paying schools is falling.

feet /fiːt/
Feet is the plural of **foot.**

feign /feɪn/ **feigns, feigning, feigned**
VO If you **feign** a feeling, you pretend to experience it;
a literary word. *Her efforts to feign cheerfulness*
weren't convincing. ◆ **feigned** ADJ *...with feigned*
surprise.

feint /feɪnt/ **feints, feinting, feinted**
NC In a fight or battle, a **feint** is a misleading action
or movement which is intended to deceive your
opponent. *There will be feints, skirmishes, and raids*
such as we saw yesterday. ► Also V *Green feinted*
with his right.

Felber, René /rəneɪ felbeə/
René Felber became the President of Switzerland
for 1992. He was Vice President from 1990 to 1991.
He is a member of the Social Democratic Party.
Born: 1933.

felicity /fəlɪsəti/ **felicities;** a formal or literary word.
1 NU **Felicity** is great happiness and pleasure. *It has*
little or nothing to do with the felicity of marriage.
2 NU **Felicity** is also the quality of being good,
pleasant, or desirable. *...small moments of*
architectural madness and felicity amidst acres of
monotony.
3 NC **Felicities** are particularly suitable or well-chosen
remarks. *I don't think young people pay much*
attention to wit anymore, to felicities of expression.

feline /fiːlaɪn/
1 ADJ **Feline** means belonging or relating to the cat
family. *...the feline leukaemia virus.*
2 ADJ A **feline** person looks or moves like a cat. *...her*
feline charm.

fell /fel/ **fells, felling, felled**
1 **Fell** is the past tense of **fall.**
2 VO If you **fell** a tree, you cut it down. *The thieves*
felled hundreds of oaks and beech trees in Pear
wood... Trees have been felled in order to block
roads.

fellow /feləu/ **fellows**
1 NC A **fellow** is a man; an informal use. *Doug is an*
exceedingly amiable fellow.
2 ADJ ATTRIB You use **fellow** to describe people who
have something in common with you. *...a fellow*
passenger. ...fellow Americans. ► Also N PL+POSS *He*
sought the approval of his fellows.
3 NC A **fellow** of a society or academic institution is a
senior member of it. *I spent the time as a senior*
research fellow at Columbia University.

fellow feeling
NU **Fellow feeling** is sympathy and friendship that
exists between people who have shared similar
experiences or difficulties. *He demonstrated his fellow*
feeling with the President when he criticized the
treaty.

fellowship /feləuʃɪp/ **fellowships**
1 NU **Fellowship** is a feeling of friendship that people
have when they are doing something together. *...the*
atmosphere of cheerful good fellowship.
2 NC+SUPP A **fellowship** is a group of people that join
together for a common purpose. *...the Socialist*
Fellowship.

felon /felən/ **felons**
NC A **felon** is a person who is guilty of a felony; a
legal term. *I was stopped by the police twice because*
I allegedly resembled a felon.

felony /feləni/ **felonies**
NC In countries where the legal system distinguishes

between very serious crimes and less serious ones, a
felony is a very serious crime, for example armed
robbery; a legal term. *He was convicted of lying*
under oath, a felony... She faces a felony charge of
criminal mischief.

felt /felt/
1 **Felt** is the past tense and past participle of **feel.**
2 NU **Felt** is a type of thick cloth made by pressing
short threads together. *Jim handed me a rectangle of*
felt, an armband with the words 'Hall Guard,
Lieutenant' sewn onto it.

felt-tip, felt-tips
NCorN+N A **felt-tip** or a **felt-tip** pen has a nib made out
of fibres that have been pressed together. *Alcock's*
artistic career started with birthday cards for friends
drawn with felt-tips. ...a sack with 'explosives' written
in felt-tip pen.

fem.
Fem. is a written abbreviation for 'female' or
'feminine'.

female /fiːmeɪl/ **females**
1 NC You can refer to any creature that can produce
babies from its body or lay eggs as a **female.** *The*
genes are inherited through the male or the female.
► Also ADJ *...a female toad.*
2 NC Women and girls are sometimes referred to as
females; some people find this use offensive. *...a lone*
female staying at a hotel.
3 ADJ ATTRIB **Female** means concerning or relating to
women, or being a woman. *...traditionally female*
areas of work... There are only nineteen female
members of parliament.

feminine /femənɪn/
ADJ **Feminine** means relating to women or considered
typical of or suitable for them. *...feminine clothes.*

femininity /femənɪnəti/
1 NU A woman's **femininity** is the fact that she is a
woman. *Not surprisingly, some of her male colleagues*
make much issue of her femininity.
2 NU **Femininity** is also the qualities that are
considered to be typical of women. *The fashion*
industry responded to the new mood of femininity.

feminism /femənɪzəm/
NU **Feminism** is the belief that women should have the
same rights, power, and opportunities as men. *The*
first two-thirds of the book is a discussion on
feminism. ...opposition to abortion and feminism.

feminist /femənɪst/ **feminists**
NC A **feminist** is a person who believes in and supports
feminism. *Claudia thought of herself as a feminist.*
...the feminist response to the new law.

femme fatale /fæm fətɑːl/ **femmes fatales**
NC A **femme fatale** is a mysterious, attractive and
seductive woman who is likely to lead men into
dangerous or difficult situations by her charm. *In her*
early silent films, she was immediately successful as a
'femme fatale', conveying intense sensuality.

femur /fiːmə/ **femurs** or **femora.**
NC Your **femur** is the large bone in the upper part of
your leg. *In the rubble, archaeologists have*
discovered the femur of a brown bear.

fen /fen/ **fens**
N PLorNU An area of low, flat, very wet land is
referred to as the **fens** or as **fen.** *...the landscape of*
the fens. ...areas of marsh and fen.

fence /fens/ **fences, fencing, fenced**
1 NC A **fence** is a barrier made of wood or wire
supported by posts. *The barrier was a ten foot high*
wall with an electric fence... barbed wire fences.
2 VO If you **fence** an area of land, you surround it
with a fence. ◆ **fenced** ADJ *...a fenced enclosure.*
3 If you **sit on the fence,** you avoid supporting any
side in a discussion or argument. *He described the*
government as sitting on the fence instead of hitting
back at its critics.
fence in PHRASAL VERB If you **fence** something **in,** you
surround it with a fence. *The unfortunate animals*
were fenced in and unable to roam very far.
fence off PHRASAL VERB If you **fence off** an area of
land, you build a fence round it. *Conservation is not*
just a matter of fencing off an area and preventing
human access.

fencing /fɛnsɪŋ/
1 NU **Fencing** is a sport in which two competitors fight using very thin swords. *In fencing, China beat South Korea to win the women's épée team gold. ...members of Cuba's fencing team.*
2 NU **Fencing** is also materials used to make fences. *...cedar wood fencing.*

fend /fɛnd/ **fends, fending, fended**
If you **fend for yourself**, you look after yourself without relying on help from anyone else. *Grown-up children should leave home and fend for themselves.*
fend off PHRASAL VERB 1 If you **fend off** someone who is attacking you, you use your arms or a stick to defend yourself. *...a picture of a man fending off a policeman's rifle.* 2 If you **fend off** questions or requests, you avoid answering them. *Mr Mandela fended off further questions, saying he would deal with them at a news conference.*

fender /fɛndə/ **fenders**
1 NC A **fender** is a low metal wall that surrounds a fireplace.
2 NC A **fender** is also a fireguard.
3 NC A **fender** is also a solid but soft object, such as an old tyre or a coil of rope, which hangs over the side of a boat to protect it when it comes alongside other boats or a harbour wall.
4 NC In American English, a **fender** is a wing of a car. *You can see the places where it's hitting the fender.*

Fenech Adami, Dr Edward /ɛdwəd fɛnɛk ədɑːmi/
Dr Edward Fenech Adami became Prime Minister of Malta in 1987. He became a member of Parliament in 1969 and the leader of the Nationalist Party (PN) in 1977. He was leader of the Opposition from 1977 to 1982, and from 1983 to 1987. In 1979 he became Vice President of the European Union of Christian Democrat Parties. Born: 1934.

fennel /fɛnl/
NU **Fennel** is an edible plant with a crisp rounded base and feathery leaves. *They are using a steam distiller to obtain the essential oils from aromatic plants like thyme and fennel.*

feral /fɪərəl, fɛrəl/
ADJ ATTRIB **Feral** means wild or uncultivated. **Feral** is used especially to describe animals that used to be kept by people but have now become wild; a formal word. *Very young feral kittens may settle well into domestic life. ...the feral instinct.*

ferment, ferments, fermenting, fermented;
pronounced /fɜːment/ when it is a noun and /fəmɛnt/ when it is a verb.
1 NU **Ferment** is excitement and unrest caused by change or uncertainty. *Portugal was in ferment. ...the ferment of religious rivalry.*
2 V-ERG When something such as wine, beer, or fruit **ferments** or is **fermented**, a chemical change takes place in it, often producing alcohol. *They drank anything that would ferment... Traditionally, the porridge is fermented for a few days before being eaten... He will ferment his wine to the point where he gets just the taste he wants.* ◆ **fermented** ADJ *...the whiff of fermented apples.*

fermentation /fɜːmenteɪʃn/
NU **Fermentation** is the process by which wine, beer, or food ferments. *In the course of his work on fermentation, Pasteur was drawn into controversy. ...the fermentation is too slow.*

fern /fɜːn/ **ferns**
NC A **fern** is a plant with long stems, feathery leaves, and no flowers. *...a primitive fern that grows in the desert.*

ferocious /fərəʊʃəs/
ADJ A **ferocious** animal, person, or action is fierce and violent. *...two years of ferocious fighting.*
◆ **ferociously** ADV *The buck shook his antlers ferociously.*

ferocity /fərɒsəti/
NU When something is done with **ferocity**, it is done in a fierce and violent way. *The attack was resumed with a new ferocity.*

ferret /fɛrɪt/ **ferrets, ferreting, ferreted**
NC A **ferret** is a small, fierce animal that is used for

hunting rabbits and rats. *The evacuation includes household pets, such as cats, dogs, birds, and ferrets.*
ferret out PHRASAL VERB If you **ferret out** information, you discover it by searching thoroughly; an informal expression. *...spies all over Britain, said to be ferreting out national secrets.*

ferrous /fɛrəs/
ADJ ATTRIB **Ferrous** means containing or relating to iron. *...ferrous metals. ...ferrous sulphate.*

ferrule /fɛruːl, fɛrəl/ **ferrules**
NC A **ferrule** is a protective metal or rubber cap that is fixed onto the end of a stick or post. *The black rubber ferrule on the end was unscrewed and revealed three shining caps.*

ferry /fɛri/ **ferries, ferrying, ferried**
1 NC A **ferry** is a boat that carries passengers or vehicles across a river or a narrow bit of sea. *We got back to London by train and ferry. ...anxiety over the design of car ferries.*
2 VO To **ferry** people or goods somewhere means to transport them there. *They were ferried from one building to another.*

ferryboat /fɛribəʊt/ **ferryboats**
NC A **ferryboat** is a boat used as a ferry. *I had hoped we might find an unofficial ferryboat crossing or footbridge.*

fertile /fɜːtaɪl/
1 ADJ Land is **fertile** if plants grow easily in it. *...light, fertile soil.* ◆ **fertility** /fɜːtɪləti/ NU *...soil fertility.*
2 ADJ ATTRIB If someone has a **fertile** mind or imagination, they produce a lot of good or original ideas. *His mental condition fuelled an already fertile imagination to produce bizarre and fantastic writings.*
3 ADJ You describe a place or situation as **fertile** ground when you think that something is likely to succeed or develop there. *Britain is not fertile ground for news magazines... The climate of unrest is proving fertile ground for fundamentalists.*
4 ADJ People who are **fertile** are able to produce babies. *...sperm from an anonymous, fertile donor... They monitored all fertile women and subjected them to monthly check-ups.* ◆ **fertility** NU *Fertility rates have declined.*

fertilize /fɜːtəlaɪz/ **fertilizes, fertilizing, fertilized;** also spelt **fertilise.**
1 VO When an egg or plant is **fertilized**, the process of reproduction begins by sperm joining with the egg, or by pollen coming into contact with the reproductive part of a plant. *She became pregnant after eggs were fertilized in a test tube and then implanted in the womb.* ◆ **fertilized** ADJ *The fertilised egg remains where it is for one more week.* ◆ **fertilization** /fɜːtəlaɪzeɪʃn/ NU *...the small amount of pollen necessary for fertilization. ...in vitro fertilization.*
2 VO To **fertilize** land means to spread manure or chemicals on it to make plants grow well. *If the farmer is going to feed his livestock from such a small area of land, it will have to be fertilized a lot... The snail faeces contains nitrogen, and it is that which fertilises the desert soil.*

fertilizer /fɜːtəlaɪzə/ **fertilizers;** also spelt **fertiliser.**
N MASS **Fertilizer** is a substance that you spread on the ground to make plants grow more successfully. *The harvest has been bad because of a shortage of fertilizer and pesticides. ...careless use of chemical fertilisers.*

fervent /fɜːvnt/
ADJ Someone who is **fervent** about something has strong and enthusiastic feelings about it. *...a fervent belief in God.* ◆ **fervently** ADV *'Oh, I am glad!' Scylla said fervently.*

fervid /fɜːvɪd/
ADJ ATTRIB **Fervid** means the same as **fervent**; a formal word. *...full of fervid and misplaced loyalties.*

fervour /fɜːvə/; spelt **fervor** in American English.
NU **Fervour** is a very strong feeling in favour of something; a formal word. *'She's marvellous,' said Mrs Moffatt with fervour.*

festal /fɛstl/
ADJ ATTRIB **Festal** means relating to a festival or celebration; a formal word. *...as though some*

primitive festal act was taking place.

fester /fɛstə/ festers, festering, festered
1 V If an unpleasant situation, feeling, or thought **festers**, it grows worse. *...the bitter row still festering between them.*
2 V When a wound **festers**, it becomes infected and produces pus. ◆ **festering** ADJ *When the mixture has cooled, it can be applied to the festering wounds of cattle and other animals.*

festival /fɛstɪvl/ festivals
1 NC A **festival** is an organized series of events and performances. *...the London Film Festival... Some threatened to boycott the festival.*
2 NC A **festival** is also a day or period when people have a holiday and celebrate some special event, often a religious one. *...hundreds celebrating Tibet's annual prayer festival.*

festive /fɛstɪv/
ADJ Something that is **festive** is full of colour and happiness, especially because of a holiday or celebration. *A correspondent who was at the stadium described a happy and festive scene. ...a festive occasion.*

festive season
N SING You can refer to the period when people celebrate Christmas as the **festive season.** *The festive season should be a time for resting, not rushing around the shops and organizing family gatherings.*

festivity /fɛstɪvəti/ festivities
1 NU **Festivity** is the celebrating of something in a happy way. *...four days of festivity.*
2 N PL **Festivities** are things that people do to celebrate something. *The week is crammed with festivities.*

festoon /fɛstuːnd/ festoons, festooning, festooned
VO If something is **festooned** with objects, the objects are hanging across it in large numbers. *The counters were festooned with rainbow-coloured scarves... Flags festooned the roadside.*

fetch /fɛtʃ/ fetches, fetching, fetched
1 VO or VOO If you **fetch** something or someone, you go and get them from where they are. *He fetched a bucket of water from the pond... Scylla ran to fetch her guardian a long cool drink.*
2 VO If something **fetches** a particular amount of money, it is sold for that amount. *His pictures fetch very high prices.*
3 See also **far-fetched.**
fetch up PHRASAL VERB If you **fetch up** somewhere, you arrive there, usually without intending to; used in American English. *After stumbling around in swamps, starving, Hiro fetches up at an artist's colony.*

fetching /fɛtʃɪŋ/
ADJ If a woman looks **fetching**, she looks attractive. *Melanie looked remarkably fetching in a white dress.*

fête /feɪt/ fêtes, fêting, fêted; also spelt fete.
1 NC A **fête** is an event held out of doors that includes competitions, entertainments, and the selling of home-made goods. *...the church fête.*
2 VO If someone important is **fêted**, a public welcome is provided for them. *In New York, Karen Blixen was being fêted by everyone who knew her work.*

fetid /fɛtɪd, fiːtɪd/
ADJ **Fetid** water or air has a strong, unpleasant smell; a formal word. *...a priest who lives and works with the poor in one of the many fetid shanty towns on the outskirts of Lima.*

fetish /fɛtɪʃ/ fetishes
1 NC A **fetish** is a strong liking or need for a particular object or activity which gives a person sexual pleasure and excitement. *Stealing knickers is a well recognized minor fetish.*
2 NC A **fetish** is also an activity that you have an extremely strong and excessive desire to do. *Cleanliness is almost a fetish with her.*

fetishism /fɛtɪʃɪzəm/
NU **Fetishism** is the condition of having a fetish.

fetlock /fɛtlɒk/ fetlocks
NC A horse's **fetlock** is the back part of its leg, just above the hoof.

fetter /fɛtə/ fetters, fettering, fettered; a literary word.
1 VO If something **fetters** you, it prevents you from behaving in a free and natural way. *...the forces that fetter our souls.*
2 NC **Fetters** are things that prevent you from behaving in a free and natural way. *...freed from the fetters of control.*

fettle /fɛtl/
To be **in fine fettle** means to be in very good condition or health; an informal expression. *They began the week in fine fettle.*

fetus /fiːtəs/. See foetus.

feud /fjuːd/ feuds, feuding, feuded
1 NC A **feud** is a long-lasting and bitter dispute. *His feud with the Premier proceeded remorselessly. ...a violent feud between the two families.*
2 V-RECIP If two people or groups **feud**, there is a feud between them. *They have feuded with each other instead of carrying on the fight... Now some worried Conservatives see the Tory party feuding for another week.* ◆ **feuding** ADJ *Can feuding neighbours ever become good friends?*

feudal /fjuːdl/
ADJ ATTRIB **Feudal** means relating to feudalism. *...a feudal society.*

feudalism /fjuːdəlɪzəm/
NU **Feudalism** was a system in which people were given land or protection by people of higher rank, and worked and fought for them in return. *They considered it to be a form of medieval feudalism.*

fever /fiːvə/ fevers
1 NCorNU If you have a **fever**, your temperature is higher than usual because you are ill. *The President, who was to have presided at the meeting, is ill with a fever... The symptoms are vomiting, headache, fever and a rash.* ● See also **hay fever, scarlet fever, yellow fever.**
2 NC A **fever** is also extreme excitement or agitation. *He stayed calm through the fever of the campaign. ...election fever.*

fevered /fiːvəd/
ADJ ATTRIB **Fevered** means the same as feverish. *...a day of fevered anticipation. ...the fevered political atmosphere... Will his fevered body relax back into comfort?*

feverish /fiːvəʳrɪʃ/
1 ADJ **Feverish** emotion or activity shows great excitement or agitation. *...the feverish excitement in his voice. ...a feverish race against time. ...feverish speculation in literary circles.* ◆ **feverishly** ADV *They worked feverishly.*
2 ADJ If you are **feverish**, you are suffering from a fever. *Medical witnesses testified that the boy must have been feverish, vomiting and in pain.*

fever pitch
NU If something is at **fever pitch**, it is characterized by a state of extreme excitement. *Our excitement reached fever pitch on the day of the wedding.*

few /fjuː/ fewer, fewest
1 QUANT or PRON **Few** is used to indicate a small number of things or people. *The window opened a few inches... A few were smoking.*
2 QUANT or PRON **Few** is also used to indicate that a number of things or people is smaller than is desirable or than was expected. *Very few people survived... There are fewer trains at night... Few of them ever reach their potential.*
● **Few** is used in these phrases. ● Things that are **few and far between** are very rare or uncommon. *News bulletins are few and far between.* ● You use **no fewer than** to suggest that a number is surprisingly large. *No fewer than five cameramen lost their lives.* ● You use **quite a few** and **a good few** when you are referring to quite a lot of things or people. *We had quite a few friendly arguments... I spent a good few years of my life there.*

fey /feɪ/
ADJ Someone or something that is **fey** is rather strange, unnatural, or seems to belong to a different world; a literary word. *The overall enchantment of the play makes the fey moments easily forgivable.*

fez /fɛz/ **fezzes**
NC A **fez** is a round, red hat which has a flat top with a tassel hanging from it and no brim. *She shaved her head and wore the traditional tasselled fez.*

ff
When **ff** is written after a particular page, line, etc has been mentioned, it means 'and the following pages, lines, etc'. *See p. 28 ff.*

fiancé /fiɒnseɪ/ **fiancés**; spelt **fiancée** when referring to a woman.
NC Your **fiancé** or **fiancée** is the person you are engaged to. *The woman was murdered by her jilted fiancé.*

fiasco /fiæskəʊ/ **fiascos**
NC When something fails completely, you can describe it as a **fiasco**, especially if it seems ridiculous or disorganized. *The meeting was a fiasco.*

fiat /fiːæt, faɪæt/ **fiats**
NC A **fiat** is an official order given by someone in authority; a formal word. *The rest of the wars were declared only by presidential fiat to which Congress in due time gave assent.*

fib /fɪb/ **fibs, fibbing, fibbed**; an informal word.
1 NC A **fib** is a small lie which is not very important. *Clearly either Waddell or Carmichael was telling fibs.*
2 V If you **are fibbing**, you are telling lies, but not very important ones. *It isn't true! You're fibbing!... Well, I didn't lie exactly, I fibbed.*

fibber /fɪbə/ **fibbers**
NC A **fibber** is someone who tells fibs; an informal word.

fibre /faɪbə/ **fibres**; spelt **fiber** in American English.
1 NCorNU A **fibre** is a thin thread of a natural or artificial substance, especially one used to make cloth or rope. *Fibres from curtains, carpets and clothes can cause allergic reactions. ...curtains made of cheap sisal fibre.*
2 NU **Fibre** consists of the parts of plants that your body cannot digest and absorb. *Scientists are recommending people to eat more fibre.*
3 NC A **fibre** is also a thin piece of flesh like a thread which connects nerve cells in your body or which muscles are made of. *...nerve fibres.*

fibreglass /faɪbəɡlɑːs/; spelt **fiberglass** in American English.
NU **Fibreglass** is plastic strengthened with short threads of glass. *...a fibreglass boat.*

fibre optic, fibre optics
1 NU **Fibre optics** is the use of long thin threads of glass to carry information in the form of light. *In fibre optics, the digital information is transmitted by a tiny laser beam.*
2 ADJ ATTRIB **Fibre optic** means relating to or involved in fibre optics. *...a fibre optic cable.*

fibrous /faɪbrəs/
ADJ Something that is **fibrous** contains a lot of fibres. *They eat a great deal of fibrous twigs and woody material.*

fibula /fɪbjʊlə/ **fibulae** /fɪbjʊliː/ or **fibulas**
NC Your **fibula** is the outer bone of the two bones in the lower part of your leg; a medical term.

fickle /fɪkl/
ADJ A **fickle** person keeps changing their mind about what they like or want; used showing disapproval. *The Prince has objected to being described as fickle. ...trying to win back his fickle supporters.*

fiction /fɪkʃn/ **fictions**
1 NUorNC **Fiction** is stories about imaginary people and events. *I enjoy reading fiction... She writes lengthy, erudite fictions, including 'The Virgin in the Garden'.*
2 NU A statement or account that is **fiction** is not true. *The crisis meant an even greater need to distinguish fact from fiction, truth from propaganda.*
3 NC A **fiction** is something you pretend is true, although you know it is not. *We had to keep up the fiction of being a normal couple. ...the fiction of civility.*

fictional /fɪkʃəⁿəl/
1 ADJ **Fictional** people and events are not real, but occur in stories, plays, and films. *...a fictional composer called Moony Shapiro.*
2 ADJ ATTRIB **Fictional** means relating to novels and stories. *...the fictional treatment of adultery.*

fictionalize /fɪkʃəⁿəlaɪz/ **fictionalizes, fictionalizing, fictionalized**; also spelt **fictionalise**.
VO If you **fictionalize** an account of something that actually happened, you tell it as a story, with some details changed or added. *What precisely is the point of fictionalising such well-known historical events?*
♦ **fictionalized** ADJ *...a fictionalized autobiography.*

fictitious /fɪktɪʃəs/
ADJ Something that is **fictitious** is false or does not exist. *They bought the materials under fictitious names.*

fiddle /fɪdl/ **fiddles, fiddling, fiddled**
1 V If you **fiddle** with something, you keep moving it or touching it with your fingers. *He sat nervously fiddling with his spectacles.*
2 VO When people **fiddle** documents that concern money, they alter them dishonestly in order to get money for themselves; an informal use. *He had fiddled the figures in the transaction... Many members, while not technically fiddling their expenses, frequently underspend deliberately.*
3 NC A **fiddle** is a dishonest action or scheme to get money; an informal use. *Laing had worked some fiddle.*
4 NC A **fiddle** is also a violin; an informal use. *As a young man he played the fiddle at local dances. ...Irish fiddle music.*
5 If you **play second fiddle** to someone, your position is less important than theirs in something that you are doing together. *He has had to play second fiddle to his deputy, but now all that is likely to change.*
fiddle around PHRASAL VERB If you **fiddle around** or **fiddle about** with something, you keep moving it or touching it with your fingers. *You can fiddle around with them, bend them into amusing shapes and link them together in long chains... He was fiddling about in the parlour with his stamp collection.*

fiddler /fɪdlə/ **fiddlers**
1 NC A **fiddler** is a person who plays the violin, especially one who plays traditional or folk music. *In Brooklyn park, a fiddler plays on the corner.*
2 NC A **fiddler** is also someone who lies or dishonestly alters documents that concern money in order to get money for themselves; an informal use. *The main perpetrators are small-time fiddlers claiming grants.*

fiddling /fɪdⁿlɪŋ/
1 NU **Fiddling** is the practice of getting money dishonestly by altering something such as an account; an informal use. *A lot of fiddling goes on in these companies.*
2 ADJ Something that is **fiddling** is small, unimportant, or difficult to do. *One reason for the lack of progress is the daunting amount of fiddling technical detail.*

fiddly /fɪdⁿli/
ADJ Something that is **fiddly** is difficult to do or use, because it involves small or complicated objects; an informal word. *...a very fiddly job... It gives them a better hold on those fiddly little foil caps.*

fidelity /fɪdɛləti/; a formal word.
1 NU **Fidelity** is the quality of remaining firm in your beliefs and loyalties. *There's nothing like a dog's fidelity.*
2 NU **Fidelity** is also the state of having a sexual relationship with only one person, especially your husband or wife. *The Pope has insisted that Catholic family values and fidelity to a single partner are the best ways to stop the infection. ...vows of eternal love and fidelity.*
3 NU The **fidelity** of a report, translation, or adaptation is its degree of accuracy. *...fidelity to the author's intentions.*

fidget /fɪdʒɪt/ **fidgets, fidgeting, fidgeted**
V If you **fidget**, you keep moving your hands or feet or changing position slightly, because you are nervous or bored. *The children are starting to fidget.*

fidgety /fɪdʒəti/
ADJ Someone who is **fidgety** keeps fidgeting.

fief /fiːf/ **fiefs**
1 NC In former times, a **fief** was a piece of land given to someone by their lord. In return, the person who

was given the land had to provide particular services to the lord.
2 See also fiefdom.

fiefdom /fiːfdəm/ **fiefdoms**
NC A **fiefdom** or a **fief** is something such as an area or organization that one person has total control over. *He runs his businesses, according to Margaret Pagono, like a personal fiefdom... The NRC had a clean sweep at Sokoto—the fief of the Sultan who is spiritual leader of Nigeria's Muslims... In their regional fiefdoms with the backing of local people, militias are likely to be stronger and more difficult to disarm.*

field /fiːld/ **fields, fielding, fielded**
1 NC A **field** is an enclosed area of land where crops are grown or animals are kept. *...fields of wheat. ...ploughing the field.*
2 NC A sports **field** is a grassy area where sports are played. *...a football field... He was sent off the field for hitting another player in the face.*
3 NC An oil **field**, gas **field**, etc is an area of land or sea bed under which oil or gas has been found. *He ran Britain's energy policy when the North Sea oil fields were being developed.*
4 NC+SUPP A magnetic or gravitational **field** is an area in which a force such as magnetism or gravity has an effect. *There is no evidence to suggest that the moon has a magnetic field.*
5 NC+SUPP Your **field** of vision is the area that you can see without turning your head. *A brown figure dressed in red crept into her field of vision.*
6 NC+SUPP A particular **field** is a subject or area of interest. *...the political field. ...an expert in the field of race relations.*
7 ADJ ATTRIB A **field** trip or a **field** study involves research that is done in a real, natural environment rather than in a theoretical way. *Ecology is essentially a subject for field study... Tell us how you organise those field trips you've been going on.*
8 ADJ ATTRIB You can use **field** to refer to equipment or buildings that are used in a battlefield. *...deliveries of field guns... He contacted the BBC by field telephone.*
9 VO If a political party **fields** a candidate, they put that candidate up for election. *The party intends to establish itself by fielding more green candidates in the next election... The opposition parties are fielding candidates in less than half the parliamentary constituencies.*
10 VO If a sports team **fields** a particular number or type of players, those players are chosen to play for the team on a particular occasion. *Real Madrid fielded only three regular first time players.*
11 VO If you **field** questions or criticisms, you deal with them in a skilful way. *The officer fielded questions with great confidence from Western and Soviet journalists... Mr Walesa was in ebullient form, cracking jokes and fielding an eclectic range of questions.*
12 V The team that is **fielding** in a game of cricket or baseball is the team trying to catch the ball. *They were fielding for a second-rate team.*
13 You can say that someone has a **field day** when they do something that is very exciting or enjoyable, especially when they are able to do it to a much greater extent than normal. *The Japanese press is having a field day exposing fraud... The opposition has had a field day attacking the government.*

fielder /fiːldə/ **fielders**
NC A **fielder** is a player in cricket, baseball, or rounders who is fielding or one who has a particular skill at fielding. *The ball soared over the fielders' heads... He's an excellent fielder.*

field event, field events
NC A **field event** is an athletics contest such as the high jump or throwing the discus or javelin, rather than a race. *Japan have been celebrating gold medals in track and field events.*

field glasses; also spelt field-glasses.
N PL **Field glasses** are binoculars.

field hockey
NU **Field hockey** is the same as **hockey;** used in American English. *...the field hockey World Cup.*

field hospital, field hospitals
NC A **field hospital** is a temporary hospital that is set up near a battlefield to deal with casualties. *He said his country might set up a military field hospital.*

field marshal, field marshals
TITLE or NC A **field marshal** is an army officer of the highest rank. *...Field Marshal Montgomery.*

fieldmouse /fiːldmaʊs/ **fieldmice**
NC A **fieldmouse** is a mouse with a long tail that lives in fields and woods.

field sports
N PL Hunting, shooting birds, and angling are referred to as **field sports** when they are done mainly for pleasure. *Field sports do lure a well-heeled clientele.*

field-test, field-tests, field-testing, field-tested
VO If you **field-test** a new piece of equipment, you test it in a real, natural environment. *It hasn't been field-tested yet.* ▶ Also NC *It has undergone several field-tests.*

fieldwork /fiːldwɜːk/
NU **Fieldwork** is the task of gathering of information about a certain subject by carrying out an investigation directly, rather than by reading about it or discussing it. *The course included a lot of fieldwork.*

fiend /fiːnd/ **fiends**
1 NC If you call someone a **fiend**, you mean that they are very wicked or cruel; a literary use. *I have no idea who this murderous fiend may be... It's very difficult to work out the twisted minds of these fiends.*
2 NC+SUPP You can use **fiend** to describe someone who is very interested in a particular thing or who likes it very much; an informal use. *...that health fiend.*

fiendish /fiːndɪʃ/
1 ADJ A **fiendish** person is very cruel. *That was considered a diabolical act—just fiendish and inhumane. ...a fiendish despot.*
2 ADJ A **fiendish** problem or task is very difficult; an informal use. *...a task of fiendish complexity.*
♦ **fiendishly** SUBMOD *...fiendishly difficult jigsaw-puzzles.*

fierce /fɪəs/ **fiercer, fiercest**
1 ADJ **Fierce** means very aggressive or angry. *During the debate there was a fierce exchange of views. ...fierce dogs.* ♦ **fiercely** ADV *'Don't assume anything!' said Martha fiercely.*
2 ADJ **Fierce** also means extremely strong or intense. *...the fierce loyalty of these people. ...a fierce storm.*
♦ **fiercely** ADV *...a fiercely dedicated group of people.*

fiery /faɪəri/
1 ADJ Something that is **fiery** is burning strongly or contains fire. *...clouds of fiery gas.*
2 ADJ **Fiery** also means bright red. *The tonsils become fiery red and swollen.*
3 ADJ A **fiery** person behaves or speaks in an angry way. *...this fiery young man. ...a fiery speech.*

fiesta /fiestə/ **fiestas**
NC A **fiesta** is a time of public entertainment and parties on a special religious day, especially in Spain or Latin America. *They were attacked as they walked back from a fiesta at night.*

fife /faɪf/ **fifes**
NC A **fife** is a small pipe-shaped musical instrument. *...marching to fife and drum.*

fifteen /fɪftiːn/
Fifteen is the number 15. *He has been campaigning for fifteen years.*

fifteenth /fɪftiːnθ/
ADJ The **fifteenth** item in a series is the one that you count as number fifteen. *...June the fifteenth.*

fifth /fɪfθ/ **fifths**
1 ADJ The **fifth** item in a series is the one that you count as number five. *Mr Lawson's fifth budget could also be his last.*
2 NC A **fifth** is one of five equal parts of something. *Only one fifth of the surface area of Africa is farmland.*

fifth column
N SING A **fifth column** is a group of people who secretly support and help the enemies of the country or organization they are working for. *He warned that there is a fifth column that is trying to soften the*

revolutionary spirit of the Cubans through capitalist ideology.

fifth columnist, fifth columnists
NC A **fifth columnist** is someone who secretly supports and helps the enemies of the country or organization they are in. *They found themselves accused of being fifth columnists and separatists.*

fifth generation
ADJ **Fifth generation** is used to describe advanced computer technology that is concerned with artificial intelligence. *...fifth generation nuclear missiles.*

fiftieth /fɪftiəθ/
ADJ The **fiftieth** item in a series is the one that you count as number fifty. *...the fiftieth anniversary of the Battle of Britain.*

fifty /fɪfti/ **fifties**
Fifty is the number 50. *At least ten people died and fifty were injured.*

fifty-fifty
1 ADV or ADJ When something is divided **fifty-fifty** between two people, each person gets half. *Profits were to be split fifty-fifty between us.*
2 ADJ If the chances of something happening are **fifty-fifty**, it is equally likely to happen as not to happen. *...a fifty-fifty chance of survival.*

fig /fɪg/ **figs**
NC A **fig** is a soft, sweet, tropical fruit that is full of tiny seeds. *Things like Barbadian cherries, figs and flowers. ...fig trees.*

fig., figs.
Fig. is used in writing to refer to a particular diagram. **Fig.** is an abbreviation for 'figure'. *The piston moves into a horizontal position (see fig. 3).*

fight /faɪt/ **fights, fighting, fought**
1 V or VO If you **fight** something, you try in a determined way to stop it. *You can't fight against progress... I remember the day the doctor told me to take more exercise—I argued, I fought, but he was adamant... Brian has fought fires for the Red Adair Company all over the world for 13 years.* ▶ Also NC *...the fight against illegal drugs.*
2 V+for If you **fight** for something, you try in a determined way to get it or achieve it. *They will fight for their rights... Once before, Shaw fought for his job and won.* ▶ Also NC *...the fight for equality.*
3 V or VO You can say that someone **fights**, if they take part in a battle or war. *He had fought in the First World War. ...both sides fought each other with automatic weapons... The two countries fought a naval battle over the islands in 1988.* ◆ **fighting** NU *We were only metres away from the fighting.*
4 V or VO When people **fight**, they try to hurt each other physically. *The children continued to fight... I learned how to fight other boys.* ◆ **fighting** NU *He was a powerfully built man with a reputation for fighting.*
5 NC A **fight** is a situation in which people hit or try to hurt each other physically. *There would be fights sometimes between the workers... I congratulate Bob and Jack on a tough fight.*
6 V-RECIP When people **fight** about something, they quarrel. *They fought about money... It's nice not having to fight you about housework.*
7 VO When politicians **fight** an election, they try to win it. *They are determined they will never again fight government-rigged elections... A major fund-raising drive will be needed to enable them to fight the campaign.*
8 VO When you **fight** an emotion or desire, you try very hard not to feel it, show it, or act on it. *He fought the urge to cry.*
● **Fight** is used in these phrases. ● If you **fight** your way somewhere, you get there with difficulty, usually because there are a lot of people in your way. *They fought, and kicked and grabbed their way towards the truck.* ● If you **put up a fight**, you fight strongly against someone who is stronger than you are. *Mohammed decided to leave Canada without putting up a fight.* ● If you **fight shy** of doing something, you try to avoid doing it. *He recalled the conditions of the early settlers, and didn't fight shy of referring to the native Aborigines.*

fight back PHRASAL VERB 1 If you **fight back** against

someone who has attacked you or made difficulties for you, you try to protect yourself and stop them or beat them. *The importing countries could fight back with laws of their own... It's hoped the antibodies will help the ill patients fight back.* 2 When you **fight back** an emotion, you try very hard not to feel it, show it, or act on it. *She fought back the tears.*

fight off PHRASAL VERB 1 If you **fight off** something unpleasant or unwanted, you succeed in getting rid of it or overcoming it. *We can fight off most minor ailments... He may find himself fighting off a challenge for the Presidency... The confectionary group, Rowntrees, has said it intends to fight off a takeover bid by the Swiss food conglomerate, Nestlés.* 2 If you **fight off** someone who has attacked you, you succeed in driving them away by fighting them. *They sent in troops to try and fight off the invasion.*

fight out PHRASAL VERB When two people or groups **fight** something **out**, they fight or argue until one of them wins. *The European nations were fighting it out on the battlefield. ...while the two sides fight out a seemingly endless legal battle.*

fighter /faɪtə/ **fighters**
1 NC A **fighter** or a **fighter plane** is a fast military aircraft used for destroying other aircraft. *A Soviet fighter has crashed at an air show in northern Italy... They have asked to buy forty fighter bombers from the U.S.*
2 NC You can refer to a person as a **fighter** when they keep trying to achieve or prevent something and are not put off by difficulties or opposition. *He was a brave and courageous fighter for Irish views in Westminster. ...a freedom fighter... I'm a fighter by character, and I began to fight the system.*
3 NC A **fighter** is also someone who physically fights another person. *He's the first British fighter to win the title three times.*

fig leaf, fig leaves
1 NC A **fig leaf** is a large leaf which comes from the fig tree. A fig leaf is sometimes used in painting and sculpture to cover the genitals of a nude body. *They sat down on the grass—her face darkened with shade from the fig leaves.*
2 N SING A **fig leaf** is also something that someone says or does in order to try and hide something unpleasant or embarrassing and to keep people's respect. *Their trade with East Germany was carried out practically on a barter basis, only feebly covered by the fig leaf of the transferable rouble... He has indicated throughout that he is not going to withdraw without some kind of a fig leaf.*

figment /fɪgmənt/ **figments**
NC If you say that something is a **figment** of someone's imagination, you mean that it does not really exist and that they are imagining it. *The mineral wealth of Antarctica is a figment of a lot of people's imaginations.*

figurative /fɪgərətɪv/
1 ADJ If you use a word or expression in a **figurative** sense, you use it with a more abstract or imaginative meaning than its ordinary one. *He imprisoned her, in a figurative sense.*
2 ADJ **Figurative** art is a style of art in which people and things are shown as they actually look. *It wasn't until much later that figurative work like his was taken seriously.*

figuratively /fɪgərətɪvli/
ADV When someone is speaking **figuratively**, they are using a word or expression with a more abstract or imaginative meaning than its usual one. *'She said I killed him.'—'She was speaking figuratively.'*

figure /fɪgə/ **figures, figuring, figured**
1 NC A **figure** is a particular amount expressed as a number, especially a statistic. *...unemployment figures. ...the total casualty figure.*
2 NC A **figure** is also any of the ten written symbols from 0 to 9 that are used to represent a number. *...a three-figure number.*
3 NC A **figure** is the shape of a person you cannot see clearly. *I could see a small female figure advancing towards us... The small but bulky figure of Yasser Arafat.*

4 NC+SUPP Someone who is referred to as a particular type of **figure** is well-known and important in some way. *He was a key figure in the independence struggle. ...the country's two most important political figures... No-one could be in any doubt that a major operatic figure of the first rank had arrived.*
5 NC+SUPP If you say that someone is, for example, a mother **figure** or a hero **figure**, you mean that they have the qualities typical of a mother or hero. *In terms of sculpture, Moore was a father figure. ...authority figures. ...a figure of hero worship.*
6 NC Your **figure** is the shape of your body. *She's got a fabulous figure... He was always worrying about his figure.*
7 NC A **figure** is also a drawing or diagram in a book. *The original design was modified (see Figure 4.).*
8 V-REPORT or V-QUOTE If you **figure** that something is the case, you think or guess that it is the case; an informal use. *They figured it was better to stay where they were... I wanted to throw a drink in his face, but I figured 'Why waste the gin?'*
9 V A thing or person that **figures** in something appears in it or is included in it. *Loneliness figures quite a lot in his conversation.*
● **Figure** is used in these phrases. ● A number in **double figures** is between ten and ninety-nine. A number in **single figures** is between nought and nine. *The survey shows that inflation has reached double figures... They persuaded the unions to keep wage demands down to single figures.* ● When you **put a figure on** an amount, you say exactly how much it is. *They said defence spending should be raised but put no figure on the increase they wanted.*
figure out PHRASAL VERB If you **figure out** a solution to a problem or the reason for something, you work it out; an informal expression. *She had not yet figured out what she was going to do... The actuaries have figured it out, and they're not losing money.*
figure eight, figure eights
NC A **figure eight** is the same as a figure of **eight**; used in American English.
figurehead /fɪgəhed/ **figureheads**
NC If you refer to the leader of a movement or organization as a **figurehead**, you mean that he or she has little real power. *Whoever is the victor, they will prove to be only a figurehead.*
figure of eight, figures of eight
NC A **figure of eight** is something, for example a knot or a movement done by a skater, that has the shape of the number 8.
figure of speech, figures of speech
NC A **figure of speech** is an expression or word that is used with a more abstract or imaginative meaning than its original one. *'What do you mean, dinky?'— 'Sorry, a figure of speech.'*
figure skating
NU **Figure skating** is skating in an attractive pattern, usually with spins and jumps included.
figurine /fɪgəriːn/ **figurines**
NC A **figurine** is a small ornamental model of a person. *Artefacts so far recovered have included hand-painted porcelain, wine in stone jars and Grecian-style figurines.*
Fiji /fiːdʒiː/
The **Republic of Fiji** is a country in the South Pacific, east of Australia. There are over 300 islands in the archipelago. The population is almost equally divided between native Fijians and those of Indian descent. Most of the population live on Viti Levu and Vanua Levu. The area was settled by Britain from the late 18th century and became a colony in 1874. In 1970 Fiji became independent. In 1987, following a coup, it became a republic and allowed its membership of the Commonwealth to lapse. Ratu Sir Penaia Ganilau became President in 1987. Ratu Sir Kamisese Mara, of the Alliance Party (AP), became Prime Minister in 1970. Fiji exports sugar, gold, coconuts, and ginger. Tourism is an important industry. ◆ **Fijian** /fiːdʒiːən/ N, ADJ
■ *per capita GNP:* US$1,540 ■ *religion:* Christianity, Hinduism ■ *language:* Fijian, Hindi, English
■ *currency:* dollar ■ *capital:* Suva ■ *population:* 727,000

(1989) ■ *size:* 18,333 square kilometres.
filament /fɪləmənt/ **filaments**
NC A **filament** is a very thin piece or thread of something. *They are reinforced with strong plastic filaments. ...the carbon filaments of the ordinary light bulb.*
filch /fɪltʃ/ **filches, filching, filched**
VO If someone **filches** something, they steal it; an informal word. *The letters had been filched from his private files.*
file /faɪl/ **files, filing, filed**
1 NC A **file** is a box or folder in which documents are kept. *He closed the file and looked up at Rodin... He went to his office to leaf through his file—a black binder jammed with articles.*
2 NC A **file** is also a collection of information about a particular person or thing. *Get me the personal file on Victor Kowalski... The evidence is a thick file compiled by the secret police.*
3 VO If you **file** a document, you put it in the correct file. *Bills are not filed under B; but under U for unpleasant.*
4 NC In computing, a **file** is a set of related data with its own name. *Then all the cards, we call them files, are stored on disc.*
5 VO or V+for When you **file** a complaint or request, you make it officially. *I'm filing for divorce. ...a lawsuit they have filed.*
6 VA When a group of people **files** somewhere, they walk one behind the other in a line. *They filed out in silence... They have been paying their last respects, filing past his casket at the family home.*
7 NC A **file** is also a tool with rough surfaces, used for smoothing and shaping hard materials. *He wanted to make an engine that could be made by someone with a drill, a file, and a hacksaw.*
8 VO If you **file** an object, you smooth or shape it with a file. *...filing her fingernails.*
● **File** is used in these phrases. ● Something that is on **file** or on the **files** is recorded in a collection of information. *All the addresses were kept on file... The police had both men on their files.* ● A group of people who are moving along in **single file** are in a line, one behind the other. *They were allowed to walk to the building in single file to deliver the petition.*
filial /fɪlɪəl/
ADJ **Filial** means relating to the status or duties of a son or daughter; a formal word. *...a sense of filial obligation.*
filibuster /fɪlɪbʌstə/ **filibusters, filibustering, filibustered**
NC A **filibuster** is a long slow speech or a series of long slow speeches which are used as a method of preventing laws from being passed by the legislature, because the debating time runs out before the debate is over, so that a vote cannot be taken. *I could not prolong a filibuster indefinitely.* ► Also V *We had agreed that we would not filibuster... Filibustering is not technically allowed at Westminster.*
filigree /fɪlɪgriː/
NU **Filigree** is delicate ornamental designs made with gold or silver wire. *You might look at some of the embroidery and filigree silver.*
filing cabinet, filing cabinets
NC A **filing cabinet** is a piece of office furniture with deep drawers in which files are kept. *Filing cabinets had been forced open.*
filing clerk, filing clerks
NC A **filing clerk** is a person whose job is to file documents in an office.
Filipino /fɪlɪpiːnəʊ/ **Filipinos**
1 NC A **Filipino** is a person who comes from the Philippines. *Many people believe that as a Filipino, he has the right to be buried in his homeland.*
2 ADJ **Filipino** means belonging to or coming from the Philippines. *Twenty Filipino crew members are still missing.*
fill /fɪl/ **fills, filling, filled**
1 VO If you **fill** a container or area, you put a large amount of something into it, so that it is full. *Fill the teapot with boiling water... Work began this week on filling the huge reservoir east of the capital.*

2 vo If something **fills** a space, it is so big or there are such large numbers or amounts of it that there is very little room left. *Enthusiastic crowds filled the streets... Heavy rains filled the mine with floodwaters.* ◆ **filled** ADJ PRED ...*a large hall filled with rows of desks.*

3 v To **fill** means to become full of things, people, or a substance. *Madeleine's eyes filled with tears... The dam is filling with water and villages are being flooded.*

4 vo If something **fills** you with an emotion or if an emotion **fills** you, you experience this emotion strongly. *His son's lies filled him with anger... Their enforced exile will probably fill them with dread.*

5 vo If something **fills** a need or gap, its activity or existence satisfies or removes it. *The Alliance filled the political vacuum... Her mother has been filling the gap by making public appearances on her behalf... All charities should try to finally fill the need for which they exist.*

6 vo Something that **fills** a role or position performs a particular function or has a particular place within a system. *It has filled this role in a most satisfactory way for many years... That leaves only one post to be filled in Mr Bush's administration.*

7 If you **have had your fill of** something, you do not want to experience it or do it any more; an informal expression. *I've had my fill of this job.*

8 See also **filling**.

fill in PHRASAL VERB 1 When you **fill in** a form, you write information in the spaces on it. *Fill in your name and address... Many people are repelled at the idea of filling in a donor card.* 2 If you **fill** someone **in**, you give them detailed information about something. *I'll fill you in on the details now... He's less compelling when he's filling in the necessary background.* 3 If you **fill in** for someone else, you do their job for them in their absence. *What is needed is people who are prepared to fill in for them.*

fill out PHRASAL VERB 1 When you **fill out** a form, you write information in the spaces on it. *I've filled out the death certificate. ...the lengthy process of filling out passport application forms.* 2 If a thin person **fills out**, he or she becomes fatter. *He'd filled out a lot since I'd last seen him.*

fill up PHRASAL VERB 1 If you **fill up** a container, you put a large amount of something into it, so that it is full. *Fill up his seed bowl twice a day... Take a deep breath, filling your lungs up completely.* 2 If a place **fills up**, it becomes full of things or people. *His office began to fill up with people.*

filler /fɪlə/ **fillers**
1 NU **Filler** is a substance used for filling cracks or holes, especially in walls, car bodies, or wood. ...*tooth filler.*
2 N MASS A **filler** is also a substance used to increase the weight or size of something. *They say pecan shells used as filler can make the stuff much stronger. ...a cheap filler to increase the bulk of other materials. ...organic fillers like nutshell flours.*

filler cap, filler caps
NC A **filler cap** is the lid that covers the hole through which you put petrol or oil into a vehicle. *The oil filler cap was so hot it burned my fingers right through my gloves.*

fillet /fɪlɪt/ **fillets, filleting, filleted**
1 NCorNU A **fillet** of fish or meat is a piece without bones. ...*a two hour banquet of veal fillet and asparagus tips. ...roast fillet of pork.*
2 vo If you **fillet** a piece of fish or meat, you remove the bones from it. *She could fillet a catfish in 11 seconds.*

filling /fɪlɪŋ/ **fillings**
1 NC A **filling** is a small amount of metal or plastic that a dentist puts in a hole in a tooth. *What happens when you lose a filling while on holiday?*
2 N MASS The **filling** in a pie, chocolate, sandwich, or cake is the mixture inside it. ...*delicious chocolates with cream fillings.*
3 N MASS The **filling** in a piece of soft furniture such as a sofa is the material inside the cushions. ...*inflammable sofa filling.*

4 ADJ Food that is **filling** makes you feel full when you have eaten it. *The stuff tastes great and is less filling.*

filling station, filling stations
NC A **filling station** is a place where you can buy petrol and oil for your car. *There are already reports of long queues of motorists at filling stations... In some areas petrol tanker drivers are refusing to make deliveries to the filling stations.*

fillip /fɪlɪp/ **fillips**
NC A **fillip** is a sudden improvement or increase in excitement or energy. *The choice of films is wide and gives an added fillip to the classroom lessons.*

filly /fɪli/ **fillies**
NC A **filly** is a young female horse. *The trainer is threatening to withdraw if conditions don't suit the filly.*

film /fɪlm/ **films, filming, filmed**
1 NCorNU A **film** consists of moving pictures that have been recorded so that they can be shown in a cinema or on television. *Shall we go and see a film?... The broadcast began with close-up film of babies crying. ...his contribution to the art of film.*
2 VorVO If you **film** someone or something, you use a camera to take moving pictures which can be shown in a cinema or on television. *The TV crews couldn't film at night... He was inside, filming an episode for a BBC television science programme... The monkeys were filmed during each meeting and the number of times they groomed each other was noted.*
3 NUorNC A **film** is also the roll of thin plastic that you use in a camera to take photographs. ...*a roll of film. ...long exposure films.*
4 NC A **film** of powder, liquid, or grease is a very thin layer of it. *It left a thin film of oil on the final product.*

filming /fɪlmɪŋ/
NU **Filming** is the activity of making a film, including acting, directing, and operating of the cameras. *I found filming exhausting.*

film star, film stars
NC A **film star** is a famous actor or actress who appears in films. ...*the young British film star, Daniel Day Lewis.*

film-strip, film-strips
NC A **film-strip** is a series of still pictures on a piece of film that are shown one after the other on a screen. ...*an educational film-strip.*

filmy /fɪlmi/ **filmier, filmiest**
ADJ A fabric or substance that is **filmy** is very thin and almost transparent. ...*a filmy black nightie.*

Filofax /faɪləfæks/ **Filofaxes**
NC A **Filofax** is a type of personal filing system in the form of a small, ring-bound book that you can carry around with you. **Filofax** is a trademark. ...*a rule book in Filofax form.*

filter /fɪltə/ **filters, filtering, filtered**
1 vo To **filter** a substance means to pass it through a device which is designed to remove particles from it. *Water would have to be filtered many times to remove any radioactive matter... The ozone layer helps to filter harmful rays from the sun.*
2 NC A **filter** is a device through which something is filtered. *It looks a bit like a coffee filter.*
3 va When light or sound **filters** into a place, it comes in faintly. ...*with the morning light already filtering through the curtains.*
4 va When news or information **filters** through to people, it gradually reaches them. *Relatives back in Britain had to wait for news to filter through... Disturbing rumours filtered back from the East.*

filter out PHRASAL VERB To **filter out** something from a substance means to remove it by passing the substance through a filter. *First we would have to filter out some of the tar particles... And then again, you have to filter the particles out of the gas.*

filter tip, filter tips
NC A **filter tip** is a small device at the end of a cigarette that reduces the amount of nicotine that is inhaled by the smoker. *The inclusion of enzymes in the filter tip of a cigarette would be of great benefit to smokers.*

filter-tipped
ADJ A **filter-tipped** cigarette has a filter tip.

filth /fɪlθ/
1 NU **Filth** is a large amount of dirt that disgusts you. *...the filth and decay of the villages.*
2 NU People can use **filth** to refer to people or behaviour that they consider to be bad and corrupt. *He is quoted as saying that his tenants are 'absolute filth'.*
3 NU People refer to words or pictures as **filth** when they think that they describe or represent something such as sex or nudity in a very rude way. *That filth should never be shown on television.*

filthy /fɪlθi/ **filthier, filthiest**
1 ADJ Something that is **filthy** is very dirty indeed. *...a really filthy oven.*
2 ADJ People describe words or pictures as **filthy** when they think that they describe or represent sex or nudity in a disgusting way. *...a filthy book.*

fin /fɪn/ **fins**
NC A fish's **fins** are the flat objects which stick out of its body and help it to swim. *...dorsal fins.*

final /faɪnl/ **finals**
1 ADJ ATTRIB In a series of events, things, or people, the **final** one is the last one, or the one that happens at the end. *...on the final morning of the festival... We made our final attempt to beat the record... The final applause was explosive.*
2 ADJ If a decision is **final**, it cannot be changed or questioned. *The judge's decision is final.*
3 ADJ ATTRIB **Final** also means the greatest or most severe that is possible. *He paid the final penalty for his crime... The final irony is that he died two days before it was completed.*
4 NC The **final** is the last game or contest in a series which decides the overall winner. *...the Scottish League Cup final at Hampden Park.*
5 N PL You can also refer to the last few games or contests in a series as the **finals**. *It will be the first time the two countries have met in the finals of the competition.*
6 N PL **Finals** are also the last and most important examinations in a university or college course. *He will be taking his finals at Cambridge University in Land Economy.*

finale /fɪnɑːli/ **finales**
NC The **finale** is the last section of a show or a piece of music. *...the finale of Beethoven's Violin Concerto.*

finalise /faɪnəlaɪz/. See **finalize**.

finalist /faɪnəlɪst/ **finalists**
NC A **finalist** is someone who takes part in the final of a competition. *...an Olympic finalist.*

finality /faɪnælɪti/
NU If you say something with **finality**, it is clear that you will not say anything else relating to that matter; a literary word. *Margaret said quietly but with finality: 'Well, we'll just have to disagree over this.'*

finalize /faɪnəlaɪz/ **finalizes, finalizing, finalized**; also spelt **finalise**.
VO If you **finalize** something that you are arranging, you complete the arrangements for it. *I'm hoping to finalize things with the builders next week.*

finally /faɪnəli/
1 ADV If you say that something **finally** happened, you mean that it happened after a long time. *They finally realized that the whole thing was a joke.*
2 ADV You use **finally** to indicate that something is the last in a series. *Trotsky lived in Turkey, France, Norway and finally Mexico.*
3 ADV SEN You also use **finally** to introduce a final point, question, or topic. *Finally, Carol, are you encouraged by the direction education is taking?... Let's come finally to the question of pensions.*

finance /faɪnæns, fɪnæns/ **finances, financing, financed**; usually pronounced /fɪnæns/ when it is a verb and /faɪnæns/ when it is a noun.
1 VO If you **finance** something such as a project, you provide money for it. *A private company will finance and build the pipeline.*
2 NU **Finance** for a project or purchase is the money needed to pay for it. *The Group raises finance for oil drilling.*

3 NU **Finance** is also the management of money, especially on a national level. *...public-sector finance. ...a successful job in high finance.*
4 N PL Your **finances** are the amount of money that you have. *Whether it can be done depends, of course, on your finances.*

financial /faɪnænʃl, fɪnænʃl/
ADJ **Financial** means relating to or involving money. *The company was in deep financial difficulties.*
♦ **financially** SUBMOD *The venture was not financially successful.*

Financial Times Share Index
N SING The **Financial Times Share Index** is an index of share prices produced by the Financial Times which is based on the average price of shares in thirty British companies, and which is used by shareholders and investors to check general changes in share prices. *The Financial Times Share Index has risen about 15 per cent since January.*

Financial Times Stock Exchange 100 Index
N SING The **Financial Times Stock Exchange 100 Index** or the **Financial Times Stock Exchange Index** is an index of share prices produced by the Financial Times which is based on the average price of one hundred securities, and which is used by shareholders and investors to check the daily changes in share prices. The **Financial Times Stock Exchange 100 Index** is also referred to as the **One-hundred Share Index** and the **FTSE 100 Index**. *By lunchtime, the most reliable index, the Financial Times Stock Exchange 100 Index had fallen by more than forty points... In the City, share prices had a good day, with the Financial Times Stock Exchange Index up about ten points.*

financial year, financial years
NC The **financial year** is a period of twelve months, used by government, business, and other organizations according to which they plan and assess their budgets, profits, and losses. In Britain, the financial year used by government for tax collection starts on 5th April. *...the government's economic forecast for the coming financial year.*

financier /faɪnænsiə, fɪnænsiə/ **financiers**
NC A **financier** is a person who provides money for projects or enterprises. *...the multi-millionaire American financier, Sir John Templeton... The unions are still the main financiers of the Labour Party.*

finch /fɪntʃ/ **finches**
NC A **finch** is a small bird with a short strong beak.

find /faɪnd/ **finds, finding, found**
1 VO If you **find** someone or something either by chance or when you are looking for them, you discover them, see them, or learn where they are. *She found a crack in one of the tea-cups... She looked up to find Tony standing there... He thinks I'm lost, I can't find the bridge.*
2 VO If you **find** something that you need or want, you succeed in getting it. *He cannot find work... I had not yet found the answer.*
3 NC If you describe something that has been discovered as a **find**, you mean that it is interesting, good, or useful. *Among the finds so far are pottery and jewellery... Liz Pym, who plays the heroine, is a real find.*
4 V-REPORT or VOC If you **find** that something is the case, you become aware of it or realize it. *When I got back, I found that the reading lamp would not work... He found it hard to make friends.*
5 V-PASS If you say that something is **found** in a particular place, you mean that it is in that place. *Four different species of lungfish are found in Africa.*
6 VOC or V-REPORT If you say that you **find** that something has a particular quality, you are expressing your opinion about it. *I don't find that funny at all... Do you find that there are a lot more fires in the summer?*
7 V-REFL+ING If you **find** yourself doing something, you do it without intending to. *He found himself giggling uncontrollably.*
8 VO If you **find** the time to do something, you manage to do it even though you are busy. *How do you find time to write these books?*
9 VOC When a court or jury **finds** a person guilty or

not guilty, they decide if that person is guilty or innocent. *He was found guilty of murder.*
10 If you **find** your **way** somewhere, you get there by choosing the right way to go. *They were tested to see if they could remember how to find their way through a maze.*
11 to **find fault**: see **fault**.
12 See also **found**.
find out PHRASAL VERB 1 If you **find** something **out**, you learn it, often by making a deliberate effort. *I found out the train times.* 2 If you **find** someone **out**, you discover they have been doing something dishonest. *The manager had found him out and was going to sack him.*

finding /ˈfaɪndɪŋ/ **findings**
NC Someone's **findings** are the information they get as the result of an investigation or some research. *...the findings of the committee.*

fine /faɪn/ **finer, finest; fines, fining, fined**
1 ADJ You use **fine** to describe something that is very good. *From the top there is a fine view.*
2 ADJ PRED If something is **fine**, it is satisfactory or acceptable. *'Do you want it stronger than that?'—'No, that's fine.'* ▶ Also ADV *We get on fine.*
3 ADJ PRED If you say that you are **fine**, you mean that you are feeling well and quite happy. *'How are you?'—'Fine, thanks.'*
4 ADJ When the weather is **fine**, it is sunny and not raining. *...much of the country enjoying fine weather over the last two weeks.*
5 ADJ Something that is **fine** consists of very small or narrow parts. *...fine hair. ...handfuls of fine sand.*
◆ **finely** ADV *...finely chopped meat.*
6 ADJ A **fine** adjustment or distinction is very delicate or exact. *Their eyes are trained to see the fine detail.*
◆ **finely** ADV *...finely balanced systems.*
7 VO If you **are fined**, you are punished by being ordered to pay a sum of money. *The demonstrators were fined £5 each for breach of the peace.*
8 NC A **fine** is a sum of money which someone has to pay as a punishment. *He paid a £10,000 fine for income tax evasion.*

fine art, fine arts
NU or N PL **Fine art** is painting, sculpture, and objects which are made to be admired rather than to be useful. *...a fine art course... He was no expert in the fine arts.*

fine print
NU The **fine print** of a contract or agreement is the part of it written in very small print, especially when this is considered as referring to unfavourable conditions which the person signing the contract might overlook. *We still have to see the fine print before the document can be signed.*

finery /ˈfaɪnəri/
NU **Finery** is beautiful and impressive clothing and jewellery; a literary word. *The ladies were dressed up in all their finery.*

finesse /fɪˈnɛs/
NU If you do something with **finesse**, you do it with great skill and elegance. *Towns in the North of England were built quickly without finesse throughout the 1800s.*

fine-tooth comb /ˌfaɪntuːθ ˈkəʊm/
If you **go over** or **through** something **with a fine-tooth comb** or **fine-toothed comb**, you look at it very carefully and consider every detail of it. *They went over the company's records with a fine-tooth comb but could find nothing wrong.*

finger /ˈfɪŋɡə/ **fingers, fingering, fingered**
1 NC Your **fingers** are the four long parts at the end of each of your hands. *She ran her fingers through the cool grass... He held it between his finger and thumb.*
2 VO If you **finger** something, you touch or feel it with your finger. *Eric fingered his split lip.*
3 VO If you **finger** someone, such as a criminal, you identify them; used in informal, American English. *In New York City, people who have fingered drug dealers have been assassinated.*
4 See also **green fingers**.
● **Finger** is used in these phrases. ● If you say that someone did not **lay a finger on** someone else, you

mean that they did not touch or harm them. *Stop yelling! He didn't lay a finger on you.* ● If you say that someone did not **lift a finger** or **raise a finger** to help someone else, you mean that they did nothing at all to help them. *He's never raised a finger to help you with the baby.* ● If you **put your finger on** a reason or problem, you identify it. *He immediately put his finger on what was wrong.* ● To **point the finger** at someone means to blame them or accuse them of something. *The Soviet official pointed a finger at the United States, accusing them of arming the Mujahedin.*

finger bowl, finger bowls
NC A **finger bowl** is a small bowl with water in it which you can wash your fingers in during a formal meal.

fingering /ˈfɪŋɡərɪŋ/
NU **Fingering** is the method of using the most suitable finger to play each note when you are playing a musical instrument, especially the piano. *I haven't learnt the fingering for this piece yet.*

fingermark /ˈfɪŋɡəmɑːk/ **fingermarks**
NC A **fingermark** is a mark which is made when someone puts a dirty or greasy finger onto a clean surface. *You've put fingermarks all over my mirror.*

fingernail /ˈfɪŋɡəneɪl/ **fingernails**
NC Your **fingernails** are the hard areas on the ends of your fingers. *Sometimes it's impossible to open a parcel without losing your fingernails.*

finger painting
NU **Finger painting** is painting, done mainly by small children, in which the paint is put onto the paper with the fingers rather than with a brush.

fingerprint /ˈfɪŋɡəprɪnt/ **fingerprints, fingerprinting, fingerprinted**
1 NC A **fingerprint** is a mark made by the tip of your finger showing the lines on the skin. *He was careful, leaving no fingerprints.*
2 V When the police **fingerprint** someone or take their **fingerprints**, they make them press their fingers onto an inky pad and then onto paper, so that they can identify them with their fingerprints. *...regulations that require them to be fingerprinted and carry identity cards.*
3 VO If the police **fingerprint** an object, they put a layer of special dust on it so that any fingerprints that are on it can be seen. *We're fingerprinting their house even though we don't know if any fingerprints exist there.*
4 See also **genetic fingerprinting**.

fingertip /ˈfɪŋɡətɪp/ **fingertips**
NC Your **fingertips** are the ends of your fingers. *...words in braille that can be read with the fingertips.*

finicky /ˈfɪnɪki/
ADJ Someone who is **finicky** is fussy; an informal word. *He was a very finicky eater.*

finis /ˈfɪnɪs/
Finis means 'the end'; sometimes written at the end of a book or film.

finish /ˈfɪnɪʃ/ **finishes, finishing, finished**
1 VO When you **finish** something, you reach the end of it and complete it. *I've finished reading your book... Brody finished his sandwich.* ● The **finishing touches** are the last, detailed thing you have to do in order to complete something. *She had been putting the finishing touches to her make-up.*
2 V When something **finishes**, it ends. *The course starts in October and finishes in June.*
3 N SING The **finish** of something such as a race is the last part of it. *In a thrilling finish, she won by two shots.*
4 VO If you **finish** work at a particular time, you stop working or studying at that time. *I finish work at 3.*
5 V A or V C In a race or competition, the position that someone **finishes** in is the position they are in at the end. *Two other Kenyans finished in second and fourth place... He finished fifth.*
6 NU or NC An object's **finish** is the appearance or texture of its surface. *Metallic finish is standard on this car. ...a fabric which has a special finish.*
7 See also **finished**.
finish off PHRASAL VERB 1 When you **finish** something

off, you do the last part of it. *He finished off his thesis.* 2 When you **finish off** something that you have been eating or drinking, you eat or drink the last part of it. *He finished off the wine with a couple of swallows.* 3 If someone **finishes off** a person who is already badly injured, they kill them. *The captain finished him off with his revolver.*

finish up PHRASAL VERB If you **finish up** in a particular place or situation, you are in that place or situation after doing something. *She'll be starting in Southampton and finishing up in London... They finished up serving in a shop.*

finish with PHRASAL VERB When you **finish with** someone or something, you stop being involved with them or dealing with them. *I haven't finished with you yet.*

finished /fɪnɪʃt/
1 ADJ PRED If you are **finished** with something, you are no longer dealing with it, or are no longer interested in it. *He won't be finished for at least half an hour... He was finished with marriage.*
2 ADJ PRED If someone or something is **finished**, they no longer exist or are no longer important. *All that is finished now... If that happens, Richard is finished.*

finishing school, finishing schools
NCorNU A **finishing school** is a private school where upper-class young women are taught manners and other social skills. *I would have gone to finishing school in Virginia.*

finite /faɪnaɪt/
ADJ Something that is **finite** has a limited size which cannot be increased; a formal word. *We have a finite number of places.*

fink /fɪŋk/ **finks**
NC A **fink** is someone who tells the authorities that a person they know has done something illegal or wrong; used in informal American English, showing disapproval.

Finland /fɪnlənd/
The **Republic of Finland** is a country in northern Europe. It became independent from Russia during the Russian Revolution and became a republic in 1919. The Soviet Union invaded Finland in 1939 and annexed Finnish Karelia and the eastern shore of the Gulf of Finland. Dr Mauno Koivisto, of the Social Democratic Party (SDP), became President in 1982. Esko Aho, of the Centre Party (KESK or KP), became Prime Minister in 1991. Finland exports timber, pulp, and paper. ◆ **Finn** /fɪn/ N **Finnish** /fɪnɪʃ/ ADJ
▪ *per capita GNP:* US$18,610 ▪ *religion:* Christianity (mainly Evangelical Lutheran) ▪ *language:* Finnish, Swedish ▪ *currency:* markka ▪ *capital:* Helsinki (Helsingfors) ▪ *population:* 5 million (1989) ▪ *size:* 304,623 square kilometres.

Finnbogadóttir, Vigdís /vɪɡdɪs fɪnbɒɡədɒtɪə/
Vigdís Finnbogadóttir became President of Iceland in 1980. She is not affiliated to a political party. Born: 1930.

fiord /fjɔːd, fiːɔːd/. See **fjord**.

fir /fɜː/ **firs**
NC A **fir** is a tall, pointed, evergreen tree. It has needle-like leaves and brown cones. *...silver birch and fir trees.*

fire /faɪə/ **fires, firing, fired**
1 NU **Fire** is the hot, bright flames produced by things that are burning. *The hijacked plane exploded in a ball of fire.*
2 NCorNU A **fire** is an occurrence of uncontrolled burning. *A fire had severely damaged the school... His neighbour's house is not insured against fire.*
3 NC A **fire** is also a burning pile of fuel that you have set light to, often in order to keep yourself warm. *He lit a fire and cooked a meal.*
4 NC A device that uses electricity or gas to give out heat is also called a **fire**. *An electrical current goes through the bar and heats the fire.*
5 VorV-ERG If someone **fires**, or if a gun or any other type of firearm **fires**, a bullet is sent from it. *I fired three or four times in quick succession. ...rifles firing high velocity bullets... Six Republicans appeared briefly to fire the ceremonial volley.* ◆ **firing** N SING *The firing stopped.*

6 NU Shots fired from a gun or guns are referred to as **fire**. *We climbed up the hill under fire.*
7 VO If you **fire** questions at someone, you say a lot of them quickly. *He was faced with a battery of press cameramen and reporters firing questions.*
8 VO If your employer **fires** you, he or she dismisses you from your job; an informal use. *Graffman fired him for incompetence.*
● **Fire** is used in these phrases. ● Something that is **on fire** is burning and is being destroyed. *Two vehicles were on fire.* ● If something **catches fire**, it starts burning. *...houses where foam-filled furniture had caught fire.* ● If you **set fire to** something, you start it burning. *He set fire to the church.*

fire alarm, fire alarms
NC A **fire alarm** is a device that makes a noise, for example with a bell, to warn people when there is a fire. *What did you hear before the fire alarm went off?... Many got out as soon as the fire alarm was raised but others were saved by firemen.*

firearm /faɪərɑːm/ **firearms**
NC **Firearms** are guns; a formal word. *She appeared in court on charges of possessing firearms and explosives.*

fireball /faɪəbɔːl/ **fireballs**
NC A **fireball** is a ball of fire, for example one at the centre of a nuclear explosion. *There was a massive explosion, followed by a huge fireball and a pall of black smoke.*

firebomb /faɪəbɒm/ **firebombs**
NC A **firebomb** is a bomb that is made in a particular way so that it burns after it has exploded. *Sixteen youths were charged with throwing firebombs.*

firebrand /faɪəbrænd/ **firebrands**
NC You describe someone as a **firebrand** when they are very active in politics and try to make other people take strong action. *He is represented by the media as a dangerous firebrand.*

firebreak /faɪəbreɪk/ **firebreaks**
NC A **firebreak** is an area of open land that has been cleared in a wood or forest to stop a fire from spreading. *Heavy machinery has been used to clear firebreaks and helicopters have dropped fire repellents.*

firebrick /faɪəbrɪk/ **firebricks**
NCorNU A **firebrick** is a type of brick which cannot be damaged by heat and which is used to line furnaces.

fire brigade, fire brigades
N SINGorNC The **fire brigade** is an organization which puts out fires. *Army and police personnel are helping the fire brigade in the rescue operation.*

firecracker /faɪəkrækə/ **firecrackers**
NC A **firecracker** is a firework that makes several loud bangs when you light it. *People set off strings of firecrackers.*

fire department, fire departments
N SINGorNC The **fire department** is the same as the **fire brigade**; used in American English. *Teams from four fire departments spent all night trying to reach the boy.*

fire door, fire doors
NC A **fire door** is one of a number of special doors in a building that must be kept closed whenever possible in order to stop a fire from spreading if one breaks out. *You exit through the fire door.*

fire drill, fire drills
NCorNU When a **fire drill** takes place in a particular building, the people who work or live there practise what to do if there is a fire. *They staged a fire drill without informing the local fire brigade in advance. ...a Swedish vessel with the crew subject to regular fire drill.*

fire-eater, fire-eaters
1 NC A **fire-eater** is a performer who puts flaming rods into his or her mouth to entertain people. *Street theatre companies jostle for space with jugglers, clowns, fire-eaters and unicyclists.*
2 NC If you call someone a **fire-eater**, you mean that they are very quarrelsome.

fire engine, fire engines
NC A **fire engine** is a large vehicle that is used to carry firemen and their equipment. *A fire engine arrived with siren blaring and lights flashing.*

fire escape, fire escapes
NC A **fire escape** is a metal staircase on the outside of a building which people can use to escape from a fire in the building. *Many of them complained that the hotel had only one fire escape.*

fire extinguisher, fire extinguishers
NC A **fire extinguisher** is a metal cylinder containing water or chemicals which can put out fires. *He couldn't get a fire extinguisher aimed at the flames.*

firefighter /faɪəfaɪtə/ **firefighters**
NC A **firefighter** is a person whose job is putting out fires. *Firefighters reported that the blaze was under control.*

fire-fighting
NU **Fire-fighting** is the work of putting out fires. *...fire-fighting equipment.*

firefly /faɪəflaɪ/ **fireflies**
NC A **firefly** is an insect that glows in the dark. *...nocturnal animals like moths and fireflies.*

fireguard /faɪəgɑːd/ **fireguards**
NC A **fireguard** is a screen made of strong wire mesh that you put in front of a fire so that people cannot accidentally burn themselves.

fire hydrant, fire hydrants
NC A **fire hydrant** is a pipe in the street from which firemen can obtain water that they can use to put out a fire.

fire-irons
N PL **Fire-irons** are tools that you use for putting coal or wood on a fire, or for cleaning the fireplace.

firelight /faɪəlaɪt/
NU **Firelight** is the light that comes from a fire. *...bodies moving in and out of the firelight.*

fire lighter, fire lighters
NC A **fire lighter** is a small block of a material that can be lit easily, and which is used to start a fire burning.

fireman /faɪəmən/ **firemen** /faɪəmən/
NC A **fireman** is a person whose job is to put out fires. *Firemen turned their hoses on the flames.*

fireplace /faɪəpleɪs/ **fireplaces**
NC A **fireplace** is a space in the wall of a room, usually opening into a chimney, that is used as a place to light a fire in. *There was a portrait of his wife over the fireplace.*

fireplug /faɪəplʌg/ **fireplugs**
NC A **fireplug** is the same as a **fire hydrant**; used in American English.

firepower /faɪəpaʊə/
NU The **firepower** of an army, ship, tank, or aircraft is the amount of ammunition it can fire. *Every two days, the world's arsenals gain a firepower equal to the whole of that used in the Second World War.*

fireproof /faɪəpruːf/
ADJ **Fireproof** things cannot be damaged by fire. *...fireproof clothing.*

fire-raising
NU **Fire-raising** is the act of deliberately starting a fire in order to damage or destroy something, usually a building.

fire service, fire services
N SING or NC The **fire service** is the same as the **fire brigade**. *There was a quick response from the police, the ambulances, and the fire service... The police, ambulance and fire services were hampered by heavy snow.*

fireside /faɪəsaɪd/ **firesides**
NC If you sit by the **fireside** in a room, you sit near the fire. *...sitting comfortably by his fireside. ...a fireside chat.*

fire station, fire stations
NC A **fire station** is a building where fire engines are kept.

fire-storm, fire-storms
NC A **fire-storm** is a fire that is burning uncontrollably in a place that has been bombed.

fire trap, fire traps
NC If you describe a building or parts of a building as a **fire trap**, you mean that it could easily catch fire or would be difficult to escape from if there was a fire. *Mr Dobson pointed to the narrowing of platforms and the new ticket barriers, which he said must be fire traps in an emergency.*

firewater /faɪəwɔːtə/
NU **Firewater** is very strong alcoholic drink such as whisky; an informal word, often used humorously.

firewood /faɪəwʊd/
NU **Firewood** is wood that has been prepared for burning on a fire. *There's a shortage of tents, firewood and hot food.*

firework /faɪəwɜːk/ **fireworks**
1 NC **Fireworks** are small objects with chemicals inside them that burn with coloured sparks or smoke when you light them. Fireworks are lit on special occasions to entertain people. *A few fireworks went off. ...a firework display.*
2 N PL **Fireworks** are also angry arguments or words. *Despite the verbal fireworks both governments have agreed to negotiate in search of an agreement.*

firing squad, firing squads
NC A **firing squad** is a group of soldiers who have been ordered to kill by shooting a person who has been sentenced to death. *Seven soldiers were executed by firing squad at dawn this morning.*

firm /fɜːm/ **firms; firmer, firmest**
1 NC A **firm** is a business that sells goods or services. *He was a partner in a firm of solicitors.*
2 ADJ Something that is **firm** does not move easily when pressed, pushed, or shaken. *...a firm mattress. ...a firm ladder.* ◆ **firmly** ADV *Each block rested firmly on the block below it.*
3 ADJ A **firm** grasp or push is one which is strong and controlled. *I took a firm hold on the rope. ...firm pressure.* ◆ **firmly** ADV *She grasped the cork firmly.*
4 ADJ A **firm** decision, opinion, or piece of information is definite and unlikely to change. *...a person with firm views... No firm evidence had come to light.* ◆ **firmly** ADV *His sister was firmly of the belief that he was crazy.*
5 ADJ A **firm** person behaves with authority and shows that they will not change their mind. *...firm leadership... 'No,' said Mother in a firm voice.* ◆ **firmly** ADV *I shall tell her quite firmly that it is not any business of hers.* ◆ **firmness** NU *She treated the children with kindliness and firmness.*
6 If you **stand firm**, you refuse to change your mind. *The government should stand firm against such threats.*

firmament /fɜːməmənt/
N SING The **firmament** is the sky or the heavens; a literary word.

firmware /fɜːmweə/
NU **Firmware** consists of a series of fixed instructions that are built into the hardware of a computer, and which remain unchanged unless the system's hardware is altered in some way.

first /fɜːst/
1 ADJ The **first** thing, person, event, or period of time is the one that is earlier than all the others of the same kind. *...the first man in space. ...the first two years of age.*
2 ADV If you do something **first**, you do it before anyone else does it, or before you do anything else. *Ralph spoke first... First I went to see the editor of the Dispatch.*
3 ADJ or ADV When something happens or is done for the **first** time, it has never happened or been done before. *For the first time in our lives something really exciting has happened... Vita and Harold first met in the summer of 1910.*
4 N SING An event that is described as a **first** has never happened before. *It's a first for me too.*
5 ADJ The **first** thing, person, or place in a line is the one that is nearest to the front or nearest to you. *They took their seats in the first three rows.*
6 PRON The **first** you hear of or know about something is the time when you first become aware of it. *The first Mr Walker knew about it was when he saw it in the local paper.*
7 ADV SEN You say **first** when you are about to mention the first in a series of items. *There were several reasons for this. First, four submarines had been sighted.*
8 ADJ **First** refers to the best or most important thing

or person of a particular kind. *She won first prize...
The first duty of the state is to ensure that law and
order prevail.*
9 ADV If you put someone or something **first**, you treat
them as more important than anything else. *Put your
career first... Your family must always come first.*
● **First** is used in these phrases. ● You use **at first**
when you are talking about what happens in the early
part of an event or experience, in contrast to what
happens later. *At first I was reluctant.* ● If you do
something **first thing**, you do it at the beginning of the
day, before you do anything else. *I'll tell her first
thing tomorrow.* ● **at first glance: see glance.**

first aid
NU **First aid** is medical treatment given as soon as
possible to a sick or injured person. *The wounded
were given first aid. ...my first-aid kit.*

first-born
N SING or ADJ You can refer to someone's first child as
their **first-born** or their **first-born** child; a literary
word. *We'll stand by you. You are our first-born. ...his
first-born son.*

first-class, also written **first class.**
1 ADJ Something or someone that is **first-class**, is of
the highest quality. *...a first-class administrator. ...a
first class honours degree in applied chemistry.*
2 ADJ **First-class** accommodation on public transport
is the best and most expensive type of
accommodation. *...a first-class rail ticket.* ► Also ADV
...flying first class.
3 ADJ or ADV In Britain, **first-class** mail is the quicker
and more expensive type of postage. *Two first-class
stamps, please... I sent it first class on Friday.*

first cousin, first cousins
NC Your **first cousin** is the son or daughter of your
aunt or uncle. *King Olav is staying as a guest of the
Queen, who is his first cousin.*

first-day cover, first-day covers
NC A **first-day cover** is an envelope on which a set of
special stamps has been stuck and which is post-
marked on the first day that the stamps were issued.

first-degree
1 ADJ ATTRIB A **first-degree** burn is one of the least
severe kind, where only the surface layer of the skin
has been burnt.
2 ADJ ATTRIB In the United States, **first-degree** murder
is the most serious type, where the act is planned
before it is carried out. *A suspect has been arrested
and charged with first-degree murder.*

first-ever
ADJ ATTRIB Something that is the **first-ever** one of its
kind has never happened before. *...the first-ever
Piccadilly Festival.*

first floor
1 N SING In Britain, the **first floor** of a building is the
floor immediately above the ground floor. *Cracks
developed in a wall on the first floor of the building.*
2 N SING In the United States, the **first floor** of a
building is the ground floor.

first fruits
N PL The **first fruits** of a project or activity are the
earliest results or profits. *The first fruits are likely to
be trivial.*

first-hand
ADJ ATTRIB **First-hand** information or experience is
gained directly, rather than from other people or from
books. *They have first-hand experience of charitable
organizations.* ► Also ADV *This sort of experience can
only be gained first-hand.*

First Lady, First Ladies
1 NC The **First Lady** in a country or state is the wife
of the president or state governor. *The Ivory Coast's
First Lady was beautifully dressed... There's been
speculation that the two First Ladies don't get on.*
2 N SING A woman who is referred to as the **first lady**
of something is considered to be better than any other
at the thing mentioned. *Ella Fitzgerald—'The First
Lady of Song', as she is affectionately known—is
celebrating her 70th birthday.*

first language, first languages
NC Someone's **first language** is the language that they
learnt first and speak best; used especially when they

speak more than one language. *Her first language is
English but her father has always spoken Czech to
her.*

firstly /fɜːstli/
ADV SEN You use **firstly** when you are about to mention
the first in a series of items. *There are two reasons.
Firstly I have no evidence that the original document
has been destroyed.*

first name, first names
NC Your **first name** is the first of the names that you
were given when you were born, as opposed to your
surname. *Nobody called Daintry by his first name
because nobody knew it.* ● If you are on **first name
terms** with someone, you use your first names rather
than your titles or surnames when you speak to each
other because you know each other well and do not
have to respect formalities. *It was a day on which an
American President put himself on first name terms
with a Soviet communist leader.*

first night, first nights
NC The **first night** of a show or play is the first public
performance of it. *...Broadway first nights.*

first offender, first offenders
NC A **first offender** is a person who has been found
guilty of a crime for the first time. *...concern about a
young first offender spending many years in prison.*

first person
N SING The **first person** refers to yourself when you are
speaking or writing, and is expressed as 'I' or 'we'
with the form of a verb which is used with 'I' or 'we'.
*Charles is the first person story-teller of the book. ...a
narrative in the first person.*

first-rate
ADJ Someone or something that is **first-rate** is
excellent and of the highest quality. *...a first-rate
golfer. ...first-rate performances.*

first school, first schools
NC In Britain, a **first school** is a school for children
aged between five and nine.

first-time buyer, first-time buyers
NC A **first-time buyer** is someone who is buying a
house for the first time. *Britain's biggest building
society is to cut its mortgage rate for first-time buyers
by one per cent... Basic houses have been taken way
beyond the range of first-time buyers.*

First World War
N PROP The **First World War** or the **First War** is the
major war that was fought between 1914 and 1918 in
Europe. *He had fought in the First World War.*

fiscal /fɪskl/
ADJ ATTRIB **Fiscal** is used to describe something
relating to finances controlled by the government,
especially taxation; a formal word. *...fiscal controls.*

fiscal year, fiscal years
NC The **fiscal year** is the same as the **financial year**;
used in American English. *The US Senate Intelligence
Committee has voted to cut aid to the Afghan
resistance by a third for the next fiscal year.*

fish /fɪʃ/ **fishes, fishing, fished.** The plural of the noun
is usually **fish**, but **fishes** is also used.
1 NC A **fish** is a creature with a tail and fins that lives
in water. *The hunting down of alligators will mean
the proliferation of piranha fish.*
2 NU **Fish** is the flesh of a fish eaten as food. *...fish
and chips.*
3 V If you **fish**, you try to catch fish. *They went
fishing and caught half a dozen trout.*
4 VO If you **fish** a particular area of water, you try to
catch fish there. *It was the first trawler ever to fish
those waters.*
5 VA If you **fish** for information or praise, you try to
get it indirectly. *I think he was just fishing for
compliments.*
6 VOA If you **fish** something out of a liquid or a
container, you remove it; an informal use. *He fished a
gold watch from his pocket.*

fish and chip shop, fish and chip shops
NC A **fish and chip shop** is a place where you can buy
fried fish, fishcakes, sausages, chips, and other fried
foods to take away and eat.

fishcake /fɪʃkeɪk/ **fishcakes**
NC A **fishcake** is a mixture of fish and mashed potato

that is made into a flat round shape, covered in breadcrumbs and fried.

fisherman /fɪʃəmən/ **fishermen** /fɪʃəmən/
NC A **fisherman** is a man who catches fish as a job or for sport. *Scottish fishermen depend on haddock as the mainstay of their catch.*

fishery /fɪʃəri/ **fisheries**
NC **Fisheries** are areas of the sea where many fish are caught. *...a fisheries treaty between Canada and France.*

fish finger, fish fingers
NC **Fish fingers** are small oblong pieces of fish, covered in breadcrumbs and usually sold in frozen form.

fishing /fɪʃɪŋ/
NU **Fishing** is the sport, hobby, or business of catching fish. *Fishing has been a profitable industry lately. ...a small fishing boat.*

fishing net, fishing nets
NC A **fishing net** is a large net that fishermen use to catch fish from a boat. *The Taiwanese vessel damaged a Chinese fishing net.*

fishing rod, fishing rods
NC A **fishing rod** is a pole with a line and hook attached to it which is used for fishing.

fishing tackle
NU **Fishing tackle** consists of all the equipment that is used in the sport of fishing, such as fishing rods, lines, hooks, and bait.

fish knife, fish knives
NC A **fish knife** is a knife that has a broad blade without a sharp edge and is used when you eat fish.

fishmonger /fɪʃmʌŋgə/ **fishmongers**
NC A **fishmonger** is a shopkeeper who sells fish.

fish slice, fish slices
NC A **fish slice** is a kitchen tool which consists of a flat part with slits in it attached to a handle. It is used for turning or serving fish or other food that is cooked in a frying pan.

fishwife /fɪʃwaɪf/ **fishwives**
NC If you refer to a woman as a **fishwife**, you mean that she is coarse or bad-tempered and has a loud voice; an informal word.

fishy /fɪʃi/
1 ADJ Something that smells or tastes **fishy** smells or tastes like fish. *It had a fishy flavour.*
2 ADJ If something or someone seems **fishy** to you, they seem dishonest or suspicious; an informal use. *There seems to be something fishy going on... The film world is full of barmy and fishy people.*

fission /fɪʃn/
NU Nuclear **fission** is the splitting of the nucleus of an atom to produce a large amount of energy. *Neutrinos are very small particles which are thought to take part in nuclear reactions such as fusion and fission.*

fissure /fɪʃə/ **fissures**
NC A **fissure** is a deep crack in rock or in the ground; a formal word. *...fracture or fissure formations.*

fist /fɪst/ **fists**
NC You refer to someone's hand as their **fist** when they have bent their fingers to touch their palm. *I shook my fist... The Marine held it tightly in his fist.*

fistful /fɪstfʊl/ **fistfuls**
NC A **fistful** of things is the number of them that you can hold in your fist. *He handed me a fistful of letters.*

fisticuffs /fɪstikʌfs/
NU **Fisticuffs** is fighting in which people try to hit each other with their fists; an old-fashioned word, often used humorously. *I do not choose to engage in fisticuffs with you.*

fit /fɪt/ **fits, fitting, fitted; fitter, fittest**. The form fit can also be used for the past tense and past participle of the verb in American English.
1 V, VO, or VA If something **fits**, it is the right size and shape to go onto a person's body or onto a particular object. *Does the lid fit?... The boots fitted Rudolph perfectly... The metal cover fits over the tap.*
2 N SING If something is a good fit, it fits well. *She tried the dress on. It was a perfect fit.*
3 VA If something **fits** into something else, it is small enough to be able to go in it. *All my clothes fit into one suitcase.*

4 VOA If you **fit** something into a particular space or place, you put it there. *Philip fitted his key into the lock.*
5 VO You can also say that something **fits** a person or thing when it is suitable for them. *The description fits women more than it fits men.*
6 VO If you **fit** something somewhere, you attach it there, or put it there carefully and securely. *Castors can be fitted to a bed to make it easier to pull... The kitchen has been fitted with a stainless steel sink.*
7 ADJ PRED If someone or something is **fit** for a particular purpose, they are suitable or appropriate for it. *The houses are now fit for human habitation... She regarded herself as fit to be a governess.*
8 ADJ Someone who is **fit** is healthy and physically strong. *She works hard at keeping fit.* ◆ **fitness** NU *They were trained to a peak of physical fitness.*
9 NC If someone has a **fit**, they suddenly lose consciousness and their body makes uncontrollable movements. *...an epileptic fit.*
10 NC+SUPP If you have a **fit** of coughing or laughter, you suddenly start coughing or laughing in an uncontrollable way. *She had a coughing fit.*
11 NC+*of* If you do something in a **fit** of anger or panic, you are very angry or afraid when you do it. *In a fit of rage, he had flung Paul's violin out of the window.*
12 See also **fitted, fitter, fitting**.
● Fit is used in these phrases. ● If someone sees **fit** to do something, they decide that it is the right thing to do; a formal expression. *The present government has seen fit to cut back on spending.* ● Something that happens in **fits and starts** keeps happening and then stopping again. *The fighting in southern areas of Lebanon has been going on in fits and starts since last April.* ● not in a **fit** state: see state.

fit in PHRASAL VERB 1 If you manage to **fit** a person or task **in**, you manage to find time to deal with them. *You seem to fit in an enormous amount every day.*
2 If you **fit in** as part of a group, you seem to belong there because you are similar to the other people in it. *I am very happy with the way the three new guys have fitted in.* 3 If you say that someone or something **fits in**, you understand how they form part of a particular situation or system. *It's difficult to know where these books fit in.*

fit into PHRASAL VERB If you **fit into** a particular group, you seem to belong there because you are similar to the other people in it. *These children are unable to fit into ordinary society when they leave school.*

fitful /fɪtfl/
ADJ Something that is **fitful** happens for irregular periods of time. *He dozed off into a fitful sleep.*

fitment /fɪtmənt/ **fitments**
NC A **fitment** is a piece of furniture, for example a cupboard, which is fixed to the wall of a room but which can be removed. *...kitchen fitments.*

fitted /fɪtɪd/
1 ADJ PRED If you are **fitted** to something or **fitted** to do something, you have the right qualities for it; a formal use. *Those best fitted to their surroundings will survive.*
2 ADJ ATTRIB **Fitted** clothes or furnishings are designed to be exactly the right size for their purpose. *Dolly wore a grey dress with a fitted bodice. ...a fitted carpet.*
3 ADJ ATTRIB **Fitted** furniture is designed to fill a particular space and is fixed in place. *...fitted wardrobes.*

fitter /fɪtə/ **fitters**
NC A **fitter** is a person whose job is to put together or install machinery or equipment. *He got a job as an electrical fitter.*

fitting /fɪtɪŋ/ **fittings**
1 ADJ If something is **fitting**, it is right or suitable; a formal use. *As I was the eldest, it was fitting that I should go first.*
2 NC A **fitting** is a small part on the outside of a piece of equipment or furniture, such as a handle or a tap. *...bathroom fittings. ...brass fittings.*
3 N PL **Fittings** are things such as cookers or electric fires that are fixed inside a building but can be

removed to another building. *Make sure you know what fixtures and fittings will be left at your new home.*

five /faɪv/ **fives**
Five is the number 5.

five-o'clock shadow, five-o'clock shadows
NC If a man has a five-o'clock shadow, his chin and the sides of his face look dark because his beard has grown a little during the day after he has shaved in the morning.

fiver /faɪvə/ **fivers**
NC A **fiver** is five pounds, or a note worth five pounds; an informal word. *You owe me a fiver.*

fix /fɪks/ **fixes, fixing, fixed**
1 VOA If you **fix** something somewhere, you attach it or put it there firmly and securely. *He had the sign fixed to the gate... She fixed a jewelled brooch on her dress.*
2 VO+on If you **fix** your eyes or attention on something, you look at it or think about it with complete attention. *She fixed her brown eyes on him.*
3 VO If you **fix** the date or amount of something, you decide and arrange exactly what it will be. *All that remained was to fix the date of the wedding.*
4 VO To **fix** something means to repair it. *I learned how to fix radios in the Army.*
5 VO If someone **fixes** a race or a competition, they make unfair or illegal arrangements which affect its result. *If the government tried to fix the results of the elections, there would be social unrest.*
6 VO To **fix** someone a drink or some food means to prepare it for them; an informal use. *Would you like me to fix you a drink?*
7 NC A **fix** is an injection of an addictive drug such as heroin; an informal use. *He looked like he needed a fix.*
8 See also **fixed, quick fix.**

fix up; an informal expression PHRASAL VERB 1 If you **fix** someone **up** with something they need, you provide it. *They told me that they could fix me up with tickets.* 2 If you **fix** something **up**, you arrange it. *The holiday is all fixed up.*

fixated /fɪkseɪtɪd/
ADJ PRED Someone who is **fixated** on a particular thing thinks about it to an extreme and excessive degree. *He remains fixated on objects which remind him of his mother.*

fixation /fɪkseɪʃn/ **fixations**
NC A **fixation** is an extreme or obsessive interest in something. *...the sport fixation of the British.*

fixative /fɪksətɪv/ **fixatives**
1 NU or NC **Fixative** or a **fixative** is a liquid used to preserve the surface of a drawing, photograph, etc. *You should spray it with fixative.*
2 NU or NC **Fixative** is also a liquid used to hold things in place, for example dentures.

fixed /fɪkst/
1 ADJ A **fixed** amount, pattern, method, or opinion always stays the same. *The signal goes on sounding at fixed intervals. ...a fixed pattern of behaviour... Children can be raised without fixed ideas and prejudices.*
2 ADJ PRED If something is **fixed** in your mind, you remember it well. *The scene was firmly fixed in all our minds.*

fixedly /fɪksɪdli/
ADV If you stare **fixedly** at someone or something, you look at them steadily and continuously. *She was staring out of the window fixedly.*

fixed-wing
ADJ ATTRIB **Fixed wing** aircraft are military planes with rigid wings that restrict them to land-based runways when they are taking off and landing and which cannot be carried on board an aircraft carrier. *Helicopters, fixed-wing aircraft and surface vessels are continuing to search for the missing men.*

fixity /fɪksəti/
NU The **fixity** of a person's gaze, concentration, or attitude is the quality it has of not changing or weakening; a formal word. *...the fixity of his stare... He showed a remarkable fixity of purpose.*

fixture /fɪkstʃə/ **fixtures**
1 NC A **fixture** is a piece of furniture or equipment which is fixed inside a building and which remains there when you move. *...the light fixture on the ceiling.*
2 NC If something or someone is a **fixture** in a particular place, they are always there. *Pool seems likely to become a fixture in working-class pubs.*
3 NC In sport, a **fixture** is a match or event arranged for a particular date. *We had to cancel a lot of fixtures... Most athletic clubs produce their own fixture lists.*

fizz /fɪz/ **fizzes, fizzing, fizzed**
V If a liquid, especially a drink, **fizzes**, it produces lots of little bubbles of gas.

fizzle /fɪzl/ **fizzles, fizzling, fizzled**
fizzle out PHRASAL VERB If something **fizzles out**, it ends in a weak or disappointing way; an informal expression. *The strike fizzled out after three days.*

fizzy /fɪzi/
ADJ A **fizzy** drink is full of little bubbles of gas. *...fizzy lemonade.*

fjord /fjɔːd, fiːɔːd/ **fjords;** also spelt **fiord.**
NC A **fjord** is a strip of sea that comes into the land between high cliffs, especially in Norway. *...the Murmansk fiord.*

flab /flæb/
NU **Flab** is loose flesh on the body of someone who is fat. *She was ashamed of her flab. ...formerly athletic bodies that have gone to flab.*

flabbergasted /flæbəgɑːstɪd/
ADJ If you are **flabbergasted**, you are extremely surprised; an informal word. *I stared at him, flabbergasted.*

flabby /flæbi/
ADJ **Flabby** people are fat and have loose flesh on their bodies. *...her flabby arms.*

flaccid /flæsɪd, flæksɪd/
ADJ Something that is **flaccid** is soft and loose or limp, rather than firm; a formal word. *Her lips went flaccid, her eyes glazed over.*

flag /flæg/ **flags, flagging, flagged**
1 NC A **flag** is a piece of coloured cloth used as a sign or a signal, or a symbol of something such as a country. *...a ship flying a foreign flag... The guard blew his whistle and waved his flag.*
2 V If you **flag** or your efforts **flag**, you begin to lose enthusiasm or energy. *I started to flag a bit after a while... Mr Heseltine's undeclared campaign to succeed Mrs Thatcher has flagged a little of late.*
♦ **flagging** ADJ *She tried to revive their flagging energies.*

flag down PHRASAL VERB If you **flag down** a vehicle, you signal to the driver to stop. *A grenade was thrown at a police car that was flagged down by a bystander.*

flag day, flag days
NC A **flag day** is a day on which people collect money for a charity from people in the street and give them a small badge or paper flag to show that they have given money.

flagellate /flædʒəleɪt/ **flagellates, flagellating, flagellated;** a formal word.
1 V O or V-REFL If someone **flagellates** themselves or someone else, they beat themselves or the other person, for example as an act of religious penance. *...a painting of a saint flagellating himself.*
2 V O or V-REFL If you **flagellate** yourself or someone else, you criticize yourself or them very severely. *I did not like the way he flagellated me in his speech.*

flagged /flægd/
ADJ A **flagged** path or area of ground is paved with flagstones.

flag of convenience, flags of convenience
NC If a ship flies under a **flag of convenience**, it has been registered in a country with lower safety standards and lower taxation than its country of origin. *...ferries flying a flag of convenience, crewed by men who work for low wages.*

flagon /flægən/ **flagons**
NC A **flagon** is a large wide bottle or jug for cider or wine; an old-fashioned word.

flagpole /flægpəʊl/ **flagpoles**
NC A **flagpole** is a tall pole used to display a flag.
*Three marines walked slowly to the Embassy flagpole
and solemnly lowered the Stars and Stripes.*

flagrant /fleɪgrənt/
ADJ ATTRIB **Flagrant** actions or situations are openly
shocking and bad. *...a flagrant violation of human
rights. ...flagrant injustices.* ◆ **flagrantly** ADV *The
report concludes that the government has flagrantly
disregarded the principles of law... He has described
the management as 'flagrantly incompetent'.*

flagship /flægʃɪp/ **flagships**
1 NC A **flagship** is the most important ship in a fleet.
The QE2 is Cunard's flagship.
2 NC The **flagship** of a group of things or ideas that
are owned or produced by a particular organization is
the most important one. *...the BBC TV's flagship
current affairs programme Panorama... The flagship
of Mr Douglas's economic programme has been the
introduction of a single income tax rate.*

flagstaff /flægstɑːf/ **flagstaffs**
NC A **flagstaff** is the same as a flagpole.

flagstone /flægstəʊn/ **flagstones**
NC **Flagstones** are big, flat, square pieces of stone
used for paving. *Many cathedrals are adorned from
flagstone floor to soaring roof with magnificent
coloured windows.*

flag-waving
NU **Flag-waving** is the expression of patriotic feelings
in an excessively loud or exaggerated way. *All this
flag-waving disgusts me. ...flag-waving patriots.*

flail /fleɪl/ **flails, flailing, flailed**
V-ERG If you **flail** your arms or legs about or if they
flail, they wave about wildly. *The baby flailed her
little arms... Two men fell on each other, arms
flailing.*

flair /fleə/
1 N SING or NU A **flair** for doing something is a natural
ability to do it. *He had a flair for this branch of law...
Wilson was impressed by his political flair.*
2 NU **Flair** is also the ability to do things in an
original, interesting, and stylish way. *She showed her
usual flair and cunning.*

flak /flæk/
1 NU **Flak** is a large number of explosive shells being
fired at planes from the ground. *I saw one of the
Dakotas hit by flak.*
2 NU You can also refer to severe criticism as **flak**;
an informal use. *...the readiness of the government to
take political flak over the affair.*

flake /fleɪk/ **flakes, flaking, flaked**
1 NC A **flake** is a small thin piece of something that
has broken off a larger piece. *...flakes of burnt paper
from a bonfire.*
2 NC A **flake** is also a snowflake. *Crystals of snow
may join together to form anything from big flat flakes
to tiny round balls.*
3 V If paint **flakes**, small pieces of it come off. *The
paint was flaking off the walls.*
flake out PHRASAL VERB If you **flake out**, you collapse
or go to sleep because you are very tired; an informal
expression. *When I got to the top I just flaked out.*

flak jacket, flak jackets
NC A **flak jacket** is a thick sleeveless jacket that
soldiers and policemen sometimes wear to protect
themselves against bullets. *...in full combat gear,
wearing flak jackets and armed with sub-machine
guns.*

flaky /fleɪki/
ADJ Something that is **flaky** breaks easily into flakes or
tends to come off in flakes. *The car was flaky with
rust... This gives the pastry a flaky texture.*

flaky pastry
NU **Flaky pastry** is a rich pastry consisting of very
thin layers.

flambé /flɒmbeɪ/ **flambés, flambéing, flambéed**
VO If you **flambé** food, you serve or cook it in flaming
brandy. *...flambéed steaks.*

flamboyance /flæmbɔɪəns/
1 NU **Flamboyance** is behaviour that is very
noticeable, confident, and exaggerated. *James was a
gentle man, despite his flamboyance.*

2 NU **Flamboyance** is also the quality of being brightly
coloured or of a very noticeable shape or design.

flamboyant /flæmbɔɪənt/
1 ADJ **Flamboyant** people behave in a very noticeable,
confident, and exaggerated way. *He has been accused
of being too flamboyant on stage.*
2 ADJ Something that is **flamboyant** is very brightly
coloured and noticeable. *...a flamboyant quilted
bathrobe.*

flame /fleɪm/ **flames**
1 NCorNU A **flame** is a long, pointed stream of burning
gas that comes from something that is burning. *The
flames and smoke rose hundreds of feet into the air...
The aircraft disappeared in a ball of flame.*
2 N SING+SUPP You can also use **flame** to refer to a
person's or a group's spirit of resistance or to their
determination to achieve something. *The spark that
ignited the flame of Solidarity came a year earlier...
Whatever happens, the flame of resistance must not go
out.*
● **Flame** is used in these phrases. ● If something is in
flames, it is on fire. *My parents' home was in flames.*
● If something **bursts into flames**, it suddenly starts
burning. *The satellite burst into flames and
disintegrated.* ● If you **fan the flames** or **add fuel to
the flames** of a difficult situation, the things that you
say or do make the situation worse. *If spending is not
stopped it will fan the flames of inflation... The
warning adds fuel to the flames of discord between
Serbs and Croats.*

flamenco /fləmeŋkəʊ/
NU **Flamenco** is a Spanish dance that is danced to a
special type of guitar music. *...flamenco dancers.*

flameproof /fleɪmpruːf/
ADJ Something that is **flameproof** is made of a
substance that is not easily damaged by fire or heat.

flame-thrower, flame-throwers
NC A **flame-thrower** is a gun that can send out a
stream of burning liquid and is used as a weapon or
for clearing plants from an area of ground. *...a full-
scale assault on the security post using flame-
throwers, rocket-launchers, automatic weapons and
two large bombs.*

flaming /fleɪmɪŋ/
1 ADJ ATTRIB **Flaming** things are burning and
producing flames. *...planes diving down with flaming
wings.*
2 ADJ Something that is **flaming** red or **flaming** orange
is very bright in colour. *She had flaming red hair.*

flamingo /fləmɪŋgəʊ/ **flamingos** or **flamingoes**
NC A **flamingo** is a bird with pink feathers, long thin
legs, and a curved beak. *Why do flamingoes stand on
one leg?*

flammable /flæməbl/
ADJ Something that is **flammable** catches fire easily.
*The fire broke out after flammable substances leaked
in a refining unit.*

flan /flæn/ **flans**
NCorNU A **flan** is a kind of tart made of pastry and
filled with fruit or something savoury. *...onion flan.*

flange /flændʒ/ **flanges**
NC A **flange** is a projecting edge on an object used for
strengthening it or for attaching it to another object; a
technical term.

flank /flæŋk/ **flanks, flanking, flanked**
1 V-PASS If something is **flanked** by things, it has them
on both sides of it. *They were flanked by airport
security men... Billy was seated at the table, flanked
by the two women.*
2 NC An animal's **flanks** are its sides. *Their legs
gripped the flanks of the ponies.*
3 NC The **flank** of an army or fleet is the part at one
side of it when it is ready for battle or involved in a
battle. *Their fire on the enemy's flank could not stop
his southward advance.*

flannel /flænl/ **flannels**
1 NU **Flannel** is a lightweight cloth used for making
clothes. *...a grey flannel suit.*
2 NC A **flannel** is a small cloth used for washing
yourself.

flannelette /flænəlet/
NU **Flannelette** is a soft cloth made from cotton and

used especially for making sheets and nightclothes.

flap /flæp/ **flaps, flapping, flapped**

1 V-ERG If a piece of cloth or paper **flaps** or if you **flap** it, it moves quickly up and down or from side to side. *His long robes flapped in the breeze... She leant out of the window and furiously flapped the blanket.*

2 V-ERG When a bird **flaps** its wings, it moves them quickly up and down. *...huge brown birds flapping their wings... Its wings flapped weakly.*

3 NC A **flap** is a flat piece of something that moves freely because it is attached by only one edge. *...looking out through a tent flap.*

4 Someone who is **in a flap** is very excited or frightened; an informal expression. *My parents were understandably in a flap about it all.*

flapjack /flæpdʒæk/ **flapjacks**

1 NU **Flapjack** is a thick chewy biscuit made from oats, butter, and syrup or treacle.

2 NC In American English, a **flapjack** is a pancake.

flare /fleə/ **flares, flaring, flared**

1 NC A **flare** is a small device that produces a bright flame. Flares are used as signals. *He stood ready to fire a warning flare.*

2 V If a fire **flares**, the flames suddenly become larger. *The candle flared to a bright light.*

3 V If something such as violence, conflict, or anger **flares**, it starts or becomes worse. *From time to time violence flared.*

flare out PHRASAL VERB Something that **flares out** spreads outwards at one end to form a wide shape. *She pirouetted, making the skirt flare out.*

flare up PHRASAL VERB 1 If fire or a flame **flares up**, it suddenly burns very fiercely and brightly. *The fire flared up high and showed their little group clearly.*

2 If something such as violence, a conflict, or an emotion **flares up**, it suddenly becomes very intense or serious. *The fighting flared up when a blockade was imposed.*

flared /fleəd/

ADJ ATTRIB **Flared** skirts or trousers become wider towards the hem or towards the bottom of the legs.

flash /flæʃ/ **flashes, flashing, flashed**

1 NC A **flash** of light is a sudden, short burst of light. *Suddenly there was a flash of lightning.*

2 V-ERG If a light **flashes** or if you **flash** it, it shines brightly for a very short time. *...with sirens blaring and lights flashing... I'll flash my headlights to make sure he sees us.*

3 NU **Flash** is the use of flashbulbs to give more light when taking a photograph. *I think this needs flash.*

4 VA If something **flashes** past you, it moves very fast. *Something white flashed past the van.*

5 V+through If something **flashes** through your mind, you think of it suddenly and briefly. *It flashed through his mind that he might never get back.*

6 NC+SUPP If you have a **flash** of intuition or insight, you suddenly realize something. *Sarah guessed it with a flash of intuition.*

7 VO+at If you **flash** a look or a smile at someone, you look or smile at them quickly and briefly. *He flashed a conspiratorial grin at them.*

flashback /flæʃbæk/ **flashbacks**

NC A **flashback** is a scene in a film, play, or book where the story suddenly goes back to events in the past. *It's a humorous story, told in the form of an interview with flashbacks.*

flashbulb /flæʃbʌlb/ **flashbulbs**

NC A **flashbulb** is a small light bulb that can be fixed to a camera. It makes a bright flash of light so that you can take photographs indoors.

flash burn, flash burns

NC A **flash burn** is a burn that you get if you are near an extremely bright, hot flash, for example a flash caused by an exploding bomb.

flashcube /flæʃkjuːb/ **flashcubes**

NC A **flashcube** is a small cube containing four flashbulbs, which turns on the top of a camera so that you can take four photographs without changing the bulb.

flasher /flæʃə/ **flashers**

1 NC A **flasher** on a vehicle is a signal light which flashes to show that the vehicle is going to turn left or

right. *People use their nearside flashers when they're going to stop.*

2 NC A **flasher** is a man who deliberately exposes his penis to people in public, usually because he has a form of mental illness.

flash flood, flash floods

NC A **flash flood** is a sudden rush of water over dry land, usually caused by a great deal of rain. *Storms have killed hundreds of people in flash floods.*

flashgun /flæʃgʌn/ **flashguns**

NC A **flashgun** is a device that you can attach to, or that is part of, a camera and that causes a flashbulb to work automatically when the shutter opens.

flashing /flæʃɪŋ/

NU **Flashing** is waterproof material used to cover joins in a roof that might otherwise leak. *Someone got up on our roof and stripped away all the lead flashing.*

flashlight /flæʃlaɪt/ **flashlights**

NC A **flashlight** is a lamp that you can carry around, which is powered by batteries; used in American English. *We had to depend on our flashlight to see our way around.*

flashpoint /flæʃpɔɪnt/ **flashpoints**

1 NC A **flashpoint** is the moment at which emotional or political conflict reaches a climax and becomes violent. *The crisis in that troubled country neared a flashpoint last week.*

2 NC A **flashpoint** is also a place which people think is dangerous because political trouble may start there and then spread to other towns or countries. *This country is another very possible flashpoint, precisely because it is so weak.*

3 NC The **flashpoint** of a substance is the lowest temperature at which it will produce sufficient vapour to ignite when a small flame is put close to it.

flashy /flæʃi/ **flashier, flashiest**

ADJ **Flashy** things look smart, bright, and expensive in a rather vulgar way; an informal word. *...a flashy sports car.*

flask /flɑːsk/ **flasks**

1 NC A **flask** is a bottle used for carrying alcoholic or hot drinks around with you. *He took out a flask of brandy and poured a measure.* ● See also **hip flask**.

2 NC You can use **flask** to refer to a container for liquids and its contents, or to the contents only. *...a flask of coffee.*

flat /flæt/ **flats; flatter, flattest**

1 NC A **flat** is a set of rooms for living in, usually on one floor of a large building. *...a block of flats.*

2 ADJ Something that is **flat** is not sloping, curved, or pointed. *Every flat surface in our house is covered with junk... He took the handkerchief and smoothed it flat.*

3 ADV A If something is **flat** against a surface, the front or broadest part of it is touching the surface. *She let the blade of her oar rest flat upon the water.*

4 ADJ A **flat** tyre does not have enough air inside it. *A flat tyre forced him to stop.*

5 ADJ ATTRIB A **flat** refusal, denial, or rejection is definite and firm. *Their earnest request met with a flat refusal.* ◆ **flatly** ADV *She has flatly refused to go.*

6 ADJ If something, such as a performance or piece of writing, is **flat**, it is not exciting or interesting. *The writing is mostly flat... The contrived boldness of many of the exhibits seems quite flat today.*

7 ADJ A **flat** voice is cold and unemotional. *Arnold went on, his voice flat, neither menacing nor inviting.* ◆ **flatly** ADV *'She is dead,' said Ash flatly.*

8 ADV If something is done in a particular amount of time **flat**, it is done quickly in exactly that amount of time. *They will be able to hit the targets in four minutes flat.*

9 NC or ADJ after N In music, **flat** is used to refer to the note which is a semitone lower than the note which is stated with it. For example A flat is a semitone lower than A. *This piece has a lot of flats in it. ...the Scherzo in B flat minor.*

10 ADV or ADJ If a musical note is played or sung **flat**, it is slightly lower in pitch than it should be. *Just don't play flat... The tenor was a bit flat.*

11 ADJ ATTRIB A **flat** charge or fee is the same for everyone whatever the circumstances are. *We charge*

a flat rate of £2.00.
12 ADJ A **flat** battery has lost some or all of its electrical power. *The batteries have gone flat.*
13 ADJ A drink that is **flat** has lost the bubbles of gas it previously contained. *This beer's flat.*
● **Flat** is used in these phrases. ● If an event or attempt to do something **falls flat**, it fails. *His little joke fell flat.* ● If you do something **flat out**, you do it as fast or as hard as you can. *Our staff are working flat out.*

flat cap, flat caps
NC A **flat cap** is a cloth cap with a stiff peak at the front, worn by men.

flatfish /flætfɪʃ/ **flatfishes.** The plural form can be either flatfishes or flatfish.
NC A **flatfish** is a sea fish that has a wide, flat body, for example a plaice or sole.

flat-footed /flætfʊtɪd/
1 ADJ Someone who is **flat-footed** has feet with arches that are too low.
2 ADJ **Flat-footed** is also used to describe someone who is unable to move quickly, easily, or gracefully. *I'm a rather flat-footed dancer, I'm afraid.*
3 ADJ You can also use **flat-footed** to describe someone who is rather clumsy, stupid, or insensitive in what they say or do. *That's typical of his flat-footed approach to things!*

flatiron /flætaɪən/ **flatirons**
NC A **flatiron** is an old type of iron that was heated on a fire or stove rather than by electricity.

flatlet /flætlət/ **flatlets**
NC A **flatlet** is a small flat. *There's a flatlet for rent in Bridge Road.*

flatmate /flætmeɪt/ **flatmates**
NC Someone's **flatmate** is the person who shares a flat with them.

flat racing
NU **Flat racing** is horse racing which does not involve jumping over fences. *A French horse is favourite to win the opening Classic of the English flat racing season, the 1000 guineas.*

flat-screen
ADJ ATTRIB **Flat-screen** television sets and computer consoles make use of a liquid display crystal instead of a cathode ray tube to create an image on the screen. They are smaller and flatter than sets produced in the past and have a sharper image. *Scientists believe these materials may be developed to make flat-screen TV sets that could hang on the wall like pictures.*

flatten /flætn/ **flattens, flattening, flattened**
1 VO If you **flatten** something, you make it flatter. *...a bulldozer flattening out the ruts in the road... The steel rod had been slightly flattened.*
2 V-REFL+*against* If you **flatten** yourself against something, you press yourself flat against it. *She flattened herself against the door to avoid detection.*
3 VO To **flatten** buildings or crops means to destroy them by knocking them down. *Huge areas of Queen Victoria Street were flattened by bombs.*
flatten out PHRASAL VERB If you **flatten** something **out**, or if it **flattens out**, it becomes flat or flatter. *The lump had flattened out, almost.*

flattened /flætnd/
1 ADJ A **flattened** object has been squashed flat. *...flattened paper cups.*
2 ADJ ATTRIB You can also use **flattened** to describe something that has a flatter shape than usual. *...a grotesque creature with a flattened body.*

flatter /flætə/ **flatters, flattering, flattered**
1 VO If you **flatter** someone, you praise them in an exaggerated way, either to please them or to persuade them to do something. *Ginny knew that he was saying all this just to flatter her.*
2 V-REFL If you **flatter** yourself that something is the case, you believe, perhaps wrongly, something good about yourself. *I flatter myself on being a good judge of character.*

flattered /flætəd/
ADJ If you are **flattered** by something, you are pleased because it makes you feel important. *I was flattered that he remembered my name.*

flattering /flætərɪŋ/
1 ADJ If someone's behaviour towards you is **flattering**, it is pleasing because it shows that they have a high opinion of you. *They listened to him with a flattering interest.*
2 ADJ If a picture or piece of clothing is **flattering**, it makes you appear more attractive than you usually do. *It is not a flattering picture.*

flattery /flætəri/
NU **Flattery** is flattering words or behaviour. *He was immune to the flattery of political leaders.*

flatulence /flætjʊləns/
NU **Flatulence** is too much gas in a person's stomach or bowels, which causes an uncomfortable feeling. *They had less fever and bowel problems, though they did suffer from flatulence.*

flaunt /flɔ:nt/ **flaunts, flaunting, flaunted**
VO If you **flaunt** something that you possess, you display it in a very obvious way. *They flaunt their engagement rings... The leader of the group wanted to flaunt his authority.*

flautist /flɔ:tɪst/ **flautists**
NC A **flautist** is someone who plays the flute, especially as their job. *The distinguished flautist was at one time a player in the Berlin Philharmonic.*

flavour /fleɪvə/ **flavours, flavouring, flavoured**; spelt **flavor** in American English.
1 NCorNU The **flavour** of a food or drink is its taste. *Raw fish has a very delicate flavour... You can try adding salt to give it some flavour.*
2 VO If you **flavour** food or drink, you add something to give it a particular taste. *Milk can be flavoured with vanilla.*
3 NU You can refer to a special quality that something has as its **flavour**. *Pimlico has its own peculiar flavour and atmosphere.*

flavouring /fleɪvə⁰rɪŋ/ **flavourings**; spelt **flavoring** in American English.
N MASS **Flavouring** is a substance used in food or drink to give it a particular taste. *...flavouring and colouring additives. ...beans, peas, some flavouring seeds, herbs and spices.*

flaw /flɔ:/ **flaws**
1 NC A **flaw** in something is a fault or mistake in it that spoils it or makes it unsatisfactory. *There is a flaw in this policy... The law contained a flaw which made it unworkable.*
2 NC A **flaw** in someone's character is an undesirable quality which they have. *It demonstrates a personality flaw, but not an irremediable one.*

flawed /flɔ:d/
ADJ Something that is **flawed** has a flaw of some kind. *We are all flawed in some way. ...flawed arguments.*

flawless /flɔ:ləs/
ADJ Something that is **flawless** is perfect. *...a flawless performance. ...her flawless complexion.*

flax /flæks/
NU **Flax** is a plant used for making rope and cloth.

flaxen /flæksn/
ADJ **Flaxen** hair is pale yellow in colour; a literary word.

flay /fleɪ/ **flays, flaying, flayed**
VO If someone **flays** a dead animal, they cut off its skin.

flea /fli:/ **fleas**
NC A **flea** is a small jumping insect that sucks human or animal blood. *...pets and their fleas.*

flea market, flea markets
NC A **flea market** is an outdoor market selling cheap second-hand goods and sometimes also antiques. *Jones looks for bells everywhere he goes: at antique shows and shops, flea markets, auctions and junk shops.*

fleapit /fli:pɪt/ **fleapits**
NC A **fleapit** is an old, shabby cinema or theatre; an informal word.

fleck /flek/ **flecks**
NC **Flecks** are small marks on a surface, or objects that look like small marks. *...the grey flecks in his eyes... Little flecks of white powder floated on top.*

flecked /flekt/
ADJ PRED+*with* If a surface is **flecked** with small marks,

it is covered with them. *Her eyes were dull grey, and flecked with dots of milky white.*

fled /flɛd/
Fled is the past tense and past participle of flee.

fledgling /flɛdʒlɪŋ/ **fledglings**
1 NC A **fledgling** is a young bird.
2 ADJ ATTRIB You use **fledgling** to describe an inexperienced person, organization, or political system; used in formal written English. *...fledgling industries. ...the fledgling democracies of Eastern Europe.*

flee /fliː/ **flees, fleeing, fled**
V or VO If you **flee**, you run away from a place, a person, or a thing. *He fled the country... The city's population prepared to flee the heat for the relative cool of the rivers... He had to flee to Tanzania.*

fleece /fliːs/ **fleeces, fleecing, fleeced**
1 NC A sheep's **fleece** is its wool. *...sheep with full fleeces waiting to be clipped.*
2 NC A **fleece** is a sheep's wool when it is cut off in one piece.
3 VO If you **are fleeced** by someone, they get a lot of money from you dishonestly; an informal use. *There were allegations that he was being fleeced of his vast fortune by his three guardians.*

fleecy /fliːsi/
1 ADJ Something that is **fleecy** is made of a soft, slightly fluffy material. *...a nylon tracksuit with a fleecy lining.*
2 ADJ You can also use **fleecy** to describe something that is light, soft and fluffy in appearance. *...fleecy clouds.*

fleet /fliːt/ **fleets**
1 NC A **fleet** is an organized group of ships. *Britain had to increase her battle fleet. ...a trawling fleet.*
2 NC You can also refer to a group of vehicles as a **fleet**. *...fleets of buses.*
3 If someone is **fleet of foot**, or if they are **fleet footed**, they are quick and agile when they run; a literary expression. *For many of us, the less fleet of foot, the thought of a marathon is just short of insanity. ...a fleet footed challenger.*

fleeting /fliːtɪŋ/
ADJ ATTRIB **Fleeting** is used to describe things which last for only a very short time. *I got only fleeting glimpses of them.* ♦ **fleetingly** ADV *...a way to assert power, however fleetingly.*

Fleet Street
N PROP **Fleet Street** is a street in London where some British newspapers have their offices; often used to refer to these newspapers and to the journalists who work for them. *Things in Fleet Street are very bad just now. ...a possible Fleet Street job.*

flesh /flɛʃ/ **fleshes, fleshing, fleshed**
1 NU Your **flesh** is the soft part of your body between your bones and your skin. *The fangs are driven into the victim's flesh.*
2 NU You can also refer to a person's skin as their **flesh**. *...the whiteness of her flesh.*
3 NU The **flesh** of a fruit or vegetable is the soft inner part. *...the seedling's tender young flesh.*
• **Flesh** is used in these phrases. • If you see someone **in the flesh**, you actually see them rather than, for example, seeing them in a film or on television. *...the crowd wildly enthusiastic to see their hero in the flesh for the first time.* • Someone who is your own **flesh and blood** is a member of your own family. *We believe that these people are our flesh and our blood.* • See also **flesh-and-blood**.
flesh out PHRASAL VERB If you **flesh** something **out**, you add more details to it. *We're now seeing the proposal fleshed out for the first time.*

flesh-and-blood
ADJ ATTRIB **Flesh-and-blood** means real and alive, rather than imaginary or artificial. *...a game between a computer and a flesh-and-blood chess master.*

fleshly /flɛʃli/
ADJ **Fleshly** means relating to sensual and sexual feelings and desires. *...a particularly luscious and fleshly poem.*

fleshpot /flɛʃpɒt/ **fleshpots**
NC A **fleshpot** is a place such as a striptease club or brothel, where people go for sexual pleasure; often used humorously. *...the fleshpots of Soho.*

fleshy /flɛʃi/ **fleshier, fleshiest**
1 ADJ If you describe someone as **fleshy**, you mean that they have a lot of extra weight on their bodies.
2 ADJ **Fleshy** parts of the body, a plant, or a fruit are thick and soft. *...fleshy tap roots.*

flew /fluː/
Flew is the past tense of fly.

flex /flɛks/ **flexes, flexing, flexed**
1 NC or NU A **flex** is a long plastic tube with two or three wires inside which is used for carrying electricity. *...a length of flex.*
2 VO If you **flex** part of your body, you bend, move, or stretch it to exercise it. *Film directors asked no more of him than to flex his muscles and grunt at the camera.*
3 When a group of people or a country **flexes** their muscle, they use their power to gain an advantage or to win a victory over an opponent. *They'll be flexing their military muscle from the safety of an air base at Palmerola... The action has encouraged workers in the oil industry to flex their industrial muscle.*

flexible /flɛksəbl/
1 ADJ A **flexible** object or material can be bent easily without breaking. *The tube is flexible but tough.*
2 ADJ A **flexible** arrangement can be adapted to different conditions. *...flexible working hours.*
♦ **flexibility** /flɛksəbɪləti/ NU *This called for some flexibility of approach.*

flexitime /flɛksitaɪm/
NU **Flexitime** is a system that allows employees to vary the time that they start or finish work, provided that an agreed total number of hours are spent at work each week, month, or some other period.

flick /flɪk/ **flicks, flicking, flicked**
1 V-ERG A If something **flicks** in a particular direction or if someone or something **flicks** it in a particular direction, it moves there with a short, sudden movement. *Its tongue flicks in and out of its tiny mouth. ...flicking its tail backwards and forwards.* ▶ Also NC *...a quick upward flick of the arm.*
2 V O A If you **flick** something away, you remove it with a quick movement of your finger or hand. *He flicked the dust from his suit... She sat there, flicking ash into the ashtray.*
3 VO If you **flick** something such as a whip or a towel, you hold one end and move your hand quickly up and then forward, so that the other end moves. *He flicked a leather thong across the animal's back.* ▶ Also NC *He gave a flick of the whip.*
4 VO You also **flick** something when you hit it sharply with your fingernail by pressing the fingernail against your thumb and suddenly releasing it. *I flicked the hollow door with my finger.*
5 VO If you **flick** a switch or catch, you press it sharply so that it moves. *She flicked on the lamp.*
flick through PHRASAL VERB If you **flick through** a book or magazine, you turn the pages quickly. *He flicked through the passport, not understanding a word.*

flicker /flɪkə/ **flickers, flickering, flickered**
1 V If a light or flame **flickers**, it shines unsteadily. *The candle flickered by the bed.* ▶ Also NC *...a faint flicker of lightning.*
2 NC A **flicker** of feeling is a brief experience of it. *There was a flicker of fear in the man's eyes.*
3 V A If an expression **flickers** across your face, it appears briefly. *A rather sad smile flickered across her face.*
4 V You can also say that something **flickers** when it moves lightly and quickly, especially up and down or backwards and forwards. *Her eyelids flickered and closed again.*

flick-knife, flick-knives
NC A **flick-knife** is a knife with a blade that is hidden in the handle and that springs out when a button is pressed. *Several weapons were found, including flick-knives, coshes and a handgun.*

flier /flaɪə/. See flyer.

flight /flaɪt/ **flights**
1 NC A **flight** is a journey made by flying, especially in

an aeroplane. *It had been his first flight.*
2 NC A **flight** is also an aeroplane carrying passengers on a particular journey. *Can you tell me what time Flight No. 172 arrives?*
3 NU **Flight** is the action of flying. *...a bird in flight... Supersonic flight is very expensive.*
4 NC A **flight** of birds is a group of them flying together. *...a flight of duck.*
5 NU **Flight** is also the act of running away from a dangerous or unpleasant situation; a formal use. *He was born at sea during his parents' flight from the revolution.*
6 NC A **flight** of steps is a row of them leading from one level to another. *She led the way down a short flight of steps.*

flight deck, flight decks
1 NC The **flight deck** of an aircraft carrier is the flat open surface on the deck where aircraft take off and land. *The huge flight deck, one thousand feet long, is bigger than many airports on land.*
2 NC The **flight deck** of a large aeroplane is the area at the front where the pilot works and where all the controls are. *The Boeing's pilot came from the flight deck to look out of the window.*

flightless /flaɪtləs/
ADJ ATTRIB A **flightless** bird or insect is unable to fly because it does not have the necessary type of wings. *On the islands of the Indian Ocean, huge flightless pigeons evolved.*

flight lieutenant, flight lieutenants
NC A **flight lieutenant** is an officer in the British air force of the rank below squadron leader.

flight recorder, flight recorders
NC The **flight recorder** on an aeroplane is the instrument which records all the information about the flight. It is also known as the black box. *The flight recorder of the 707 has been retrieved from the debris.*

flighty /flaɪti/
ADJ People, especially women, are described as **flighty** when they are not serious, steady, or reliable; an old-fashioned word. *...the disrespectful way in which these flighty females carry out their duties.*

flimsy /flɪmzi/ **flimsier, flimsiest**
1 ADJ Something that is **flimsy** is easily damaged because it is badly made or made of a weak material. *Mudslides buried families inside their flimsy homes.*
2 ADJ A **flimsy** excuse or **flimsy** evidence is not very good or convincing. *His lawyers say the findings were based on flimsy evidence... He said a youth was being arrested for the flimsiest of reasons.*
3 ADJ **Flimsy** cloth or clothing is thin and does not give much protection. *She was wearing a glamorous but flimsy chiffon dress.*

flinch /flɪntʃ/ **flinches, flinching, flinched**
1 V If you **flinch** when you are startled or hurt, you make a small, sudden movement without meaning to. *Even stroking the skin of whales causes their whole bodies to flinch... The battle-hardened people now hardly flinch at the sound of a gunshot.*
2 V If you **flinch** from something unpleasant, you are unwilling to do it or think about it. *They flinched from the prospect of starting again.*

fling /flɪŋ/ **flings, flinging, flung**
1 VOA If you **fling** something somewhere, you throw it there quickly and carelessly or with a lot of force. *She was flinging a few things into her handbag... He had intended to fling two cockerels on to the pitch at yesterday's international... One woman picked up handfuls of dirt and began flinging it at the American Embassy.*
2 V-REFLA If you **fling** yourself somewhere, you move or jump there with a lot of force. *He flung himself down at Jack's feet.*
3 NC If someone has a **fling**, they have a brief sexual relationship; an informal use. *She had a brief fling while her husband was away.*
4 NC To have a **fling** also means to enjoy yourself briefly in an energetic way. *...a last fling at the disco... Maybe they're having one last fling, one final spending binge before they expect things to tighten up.*

flint /flɪnt/ **flints**
NUorNC **Flint** is a very hard, greyish-black stone

which produces sparks when struck. *...the grey flint parish church... The burnt flint remains have allowed the Neanderthal remains to be dated at about 35,000 years old.*

flintlock /flɪntlɒk/ **flintlocks**
NC A **flintlock** is a type of gun that was used in the past. Sparks struck from a flint inside the gun would light gunpowder to fire it.

flinty /flɪnti/
1 ADJ A **flinty** expression or **flinty** eyes look uncaring, hard, and cold. *The colonel was a short, balding man with flinty eyes.*
2 ADJ ATTRIB A **flinty** building or piece of land is made of flints or contains flints.

flip /flɪp/ **flips, flipping, flipped**
1 VOA If you **flip** something that weighs very little into a different position, you quickly push it into that position. *He flipped open his notebook.*
2 VO If you **flip** a switch or **flip** a light or a machine on or off, you turn it on or off. *As soon as he flipped the switch on, the thing started to play... Drivers in New York will be required to flip on their headlights when they are using their windshield wipers... Cantanco flipped on the transmitter.*
3 V If you **flip**, you suddenly become angry because of something that has happened; an informal use. *When her employers said they might prosecute, she flipped... My parents would probably flip if I married a white person.*
flip over PHRASAL VERB If something **flips over**, or if someone **flips** something **over**, it turns over suddenly and sometimes crashes. *His boat is reported to have hit a wave and to have flipped over... The helicopter's down draught flipped the plane over.*
flip through PHRASAL VERB If you **flip through** a book or file, you turn the pages and look at them quickly to get a rough idea of their contents. *It looks like the kind of thing you might want to flip through rather than a real newspaper which demands to be read.*

flip-flop, flip-flops, flip-flopping, flip-flopped
1 NC **Flip-flops** are sandals which are held on your foot by a V-shaped strap that goes between your big toe and the next toe.
2 V If someone, especially a politician, **flip-flops** on something, they suddenly change their point of view about it; used in American English. *He appears to flip-flop, first saying that he supports more taxes for the rich, then saying he doesn't... Boschwitz flip-flopped on the civil rights bill.* ► Also NC *...the President's apparent flip-flop over the last three days.*

flippancy /flɪpənsi/
NU **Flippancy** means behaving or speaking in a flippant way. *'This is no time for flippancy,' he said angrily.*

flippant /flɪpənt/
ADJ If someone is **flippant**, or has a **flippant** attitude, they do not seem to take things seriously. *It encourages people to have a flippant attitude towards marriage... Throughout the trial he has acted in a relaxed and even flippant manner.* ♦ **flippantly** ADV *'How do you get admitted to Welfare Hostel anyway?' said Lynn flippantly.*

flipper /flɪpə/ **flippers**
1 NC The **flippers** of an animal such as a seal are the two or four flat limbs that it uses for swimming. *Like today's whales, it had front flippers to steer it through the water.*
2 NC **Flippers** are also flat pieces of rubber that you can wear on your feet to help you swim more quickly.

flipping /flɪpɪŋ/
ADJ ATTRIBorSUBMOD You can use **flipping** to emphasize the following word, especially when you are annoyed; used in informal speech. *'It's flipping impossible!'*

flip side; an informal expression.
1 N SING The **flip side** of a gramophone record is the side that does not have the main song on it.
2 N SING The **flip side** of an argument, idea, situation, and so on is a less well known or less popular aspect of it. *As we gain ability to control disease, the flip side of that knowledge is that we can now induce disease.*

flirt /flɜːt/ **flirts, flirting, flirted**

1 V-RECIP If you **flirt** with someone, you behave as if you are sexually attracted to them, in a not very serious way. *She never even flirted with other men. ...like a film star, kissing babies, hugging mothers and flirting with sisters.* ◆ **flirtation** /flɜːteɪʃn/ **flirtations** NC *He had a mild flirtation with two Danish blondes.*
2 NC A **flirt** is someone who flirts a lot. *They should give him the nickname Casanova because he's a flirt.*
3 V+with If you **flirt** with the idea of doing or having something, you consider doing or having it, without making any definite plans. *Burlington has flirted for years with the idea of a wood-burning electrical generator.*
4 V+with If a politician, political group, or country **flirts** with another person, group, country, or idea, they have contact with them, and may use or join them, but they do not commit themselves. *The Christian Democrats may be planning to undermine the government coalition as they flirt with extreme nationalists.* ◆ **flirtation** /flɜːteɪʃn/ **flirtations** NC *Despite brief flirtations with both the Soviet Union and China, the country's real future lay as an ally of the West.*

flirtatious /flɜːteɪʃəs/
ADJ If someone is flirting, you can say they are being **flirtatious**. *She kept giving him flirtatious looks.*

flit /flɪt/ **flits, flitting, flitted**
1 V A To **flit** about means to fly or move quickly from one place to another. *Bats flitted about... The President flitted from continent to continent.*
2 V A If an expression **flits** across your face or if an idea **flits** through your mind, it is there for only a short time. *An expression of pain flitted across Lo's face... A picture of three boys walking along a bright beach flitted through his mind.*

float /fləʊt/ **floats, floating, floated**
1 V If something is **floating** in a liquid, it is lying or moving slowly on the surface. *There was seaweed floating on the surface of the water.*
2 V Something that **floats** through the air moves slowly through it, because it is very light. *Six dollar bills floated down on to the table.*
3 VO If you **float** a plan, idea, or suggestion, you introduce it to other people, who may decide whether to use it or not. *Suggestions were being floated at the end of last year that Mrs Thatcher would visit South Africa... It recently floated the idea of a regional trade pact.*
4 VO If a director or a government **floats** a company, they sell shares in it to the public. *Some of the newly privatised firms will be floated on the Hungarian Stock Market.*
5 V-ERG If a government **floats** its country's currency, or things like prices or interest rates **float**, their values are allowed to change freely without interference. *The government may sell part of the industry to a private company rather than floating it on the stock exchange... The government was thinking of using a fixed exchange rate rather than letting it float... Mrs Thatcher wanted to let the pound float freely against other currencies.* ◆ **floating** ADJ ATTRIB *The Bulgarian National Bank introduced a floating exchange rate for non-commercial purchases of hard currency.*
6 NC A **float** is a light object that is used to help someone or something float in water. *A drift net is a huge nylon curtain, supported by floats. ...plastic floats.*
7 NC A **float** is also a lorry that is decorated in some way and often carries people in costume as part of a festival procession. *There will be a procession of decorated floats with music, clowns and all types of entertainment.*
8 N SING A **float** is also a small amount of money that shopkeepers keep in their cash till before they start selling things in order to be able to give customers change if necessary. *Have you got the float ready for the jumble sale tomorrow.*

floatation /fləʊteɪʃn/. See **flotation**.

floating population
N SING If a country or a city has a **floating population**, people are constantly arriving, leaving and changing address. *Now there's a largely floating population without formal employment.*

floating voter, floating voters
NC A **floating voter** is a person who is not a firm supporter of any political party. *A lot of those floating voters voted FIS partly as a way of saying no, we don't want more FLN.*

flock /flɒk/ **flocks, flocking, flocked**
1 N COLL A **flock** of birds, sheep, or goats is a group of them. *...a flock of seagulls.*
2 N COLL+POSS Someone's **flock**, especially a clergyman's, is the group of people that they are responsible for; an old-fashioned use. *The Pope insisted that a prior condition must be permission to visit his Roman Catholic flock there.*
3 V A or V+to-INF If people **flock** to a place or event, a lot of them go there, because it is pleasant or interesting. *Thousands of young Sri Lankans flocked into Colombo yesterday to apply to join the army... British tourists flocked to Tunisian holiday resorts in vast numbers... Consumers have always flocked in to buy such luxuries as underwear, coffee and toothpaste.*

floe /fləʊ/. See **ice floe**.

flog /flɒg/ **flogs, flogging, flogged**
1 VO To **flog** someone means to hit them hard with a whip or stick as a punishment. *Three of the officials were ordered to be flogged.* ◆ **flogging, floggings** NUorNC *People are in detention in Khartoum awaiting execution of their sentences of flogging or amputation... He was sentenced to receive a public flogging.*
2 VO If you **flog** something, you sell it; an informal use. *It was a black market flogging American aid stolen or diverted by corrupt officials.*

flood /flʌd/ **floods, flooding, flooded**
1 NC If there is a **flood**, a large amount of water covers an area which is usually dry, for example when a river overflows. *Devastating floods have again hit Brazil... The latest death brings the total killed in the recent floods to twenty-five... The authorities may have to place the city on flood alert.*
2 V-ERG If something **floods** an area or if an area **floods**, it becomes covered with water. *When we took the plug out the kitchen flooded... The rice fields were flooded.* ◆ **flooding** NU *There has been heavy rain in many areas, resulting in widespread flooding.*
3 V If a river **floods**, it overflows, usually after very heavy rain. *Swollen rivers have overflowed and flooded large parts of the area.*
4 NC A **flood** of things is a large number of them. *She received a flood of grateful letters.*
5 V A If people or things **flood** into a place, large numbers of them come there. *...a substantial increase in the number of refugees flooding into the country.*

floodgates /flʌdgeɪts/
If someone or something **opens the floodgates**, they make it possible for a large number of people to do something for the first time. *They were afraid of opening the floodgates to mass democracy... If the government opened the floodgates, some ten thousand foreign workers would find jobs here.*

floodlight /flʌdlaɪt/ **floodlights**
NC **Floodlights** are powerful lamps which are used to light sports grounds and the outsides of public buildings when it is dark. *England prepare to play under floodlights at Perth. ...the famous Brandenburg Gate lit up with floodlights.*

floodlit /flʌdlɪt/
ADJ If a building or place is **floodlit**, it is lit by floodlights. *The cathedral is floodlit at night.*

floodwater /flʌdwɔːtə/ **floodwaters**
NUorN PL **Floodwater** or **floodwaters** is the water produced by flooding. *Although much of the floodwater receded, heavy rainstorms are hampering relief efforts... At least 1,000 people have been evacuated as floodwaters rose over riverbanks this morning.*

floor /flɔː/ **floors, flooring, floored**
1 NC The **floor** of a room is the flat part that you walk on. *The walls and the floor are damp... Many will spend the night sleeping on the floor of the ferry terminal.*
2 NC A **floor** of a building is all the rooms on a

particular level. *She escaped through a ground floor window... They took the lift to the fourth floor.*
3 N SING The **sea floor** or the **ocean floor** is the surface of the bottom of the sea. *The original echo changes in sound quality depending on the composition of the sea floor... Only about four percent of the ocean floor has been mapped in detail.*
4 NC+SUPP The **floor** of the stock exchange is the large open area where the trading is done. *No buyers could be found for roughly half the stocks traded on the floor of the exchange... There is a trading floor where investors can buy and sell bonds issued by the government.*
5 N SING The **floor** is also used to refer to the place where official debates are held, especially between Members of Parliament. *Government and opposition members face each other across the floor of the House of Commons... There were two further nominations from the floor of the conference... These people have preferred to pass notes to the presidium, rather than take the floor themselves.*
6 VO If a boxer **floors** his opponent, he knocks him down but the opponent is able to get up and continue the fight. *Although Rivera floored Mitchell in the second round, the champion controlled the fight from then on.*
7 VO If a remark or question **floors** you, you are so surprised or confused by it that you cannot answer it. *Bing appeared to be floored by this casual remark.*
8 See also **factory floor, shop floor**.

floorboard /flɔːbɔːd/ **floorboards**
NC **Floorboards** are the long pieces of wood that a floor is made of. *The floorboards are up in the press area. ...under the kitchen floorboards.*

floor show, floor shows
NC A **floor show** is a series of performances by dancers, singers, or comedians at a night club. *In the casino's night club, there is a break in the floor show.*

flop /flɒp/ **flops, flopping, flopped**
1 VA If you **flop** onto something, you sit or lie down suddenly and heavily because you are tired. *She flopped into an armchair.*
2 NC Something that is a **flop** is a total failure; an informal use. *Not one of his numerous musicals was a flop.*
3 V If something **flops**, it is a total failure; an informal use. *One of their space projects flopped... The British government's sale of its stake in BP flopped.*

flophouse /flɒphaʊs/ **flophouses**
NC A **flophouse** is the same as a **doss-house**; used in informal American English. *He was living in a flophouse, sleeping on a bare mattress in what was, essentially, a closet.*

floppy /flɒpi/ **floppies**
1 ADJ Something that is **floppy** is loose and flexible rather than stiff, and tends to hang downwards. *...ladies in floppy hats... Alsatians must have stiff, not floppy ears.*
2 NC A **floppy** is a floppy disk. *Think of a single floppy as being nearly one megabyte.*

floppy disk, floppy disks; also spelt **floppy disc**.
NC A **floppy disk** is a small flexible magnetic disk used for storing data and programs. Floppy disks are used with micro-computers. *Businesses are increasingly storing information in computers and on microfilm, tape and floppy disks.*

flora /flɔːrə/
N PL The **flora** in a place are all the plants there; a formal word. *...the flora and fauna of our countryside.*

floral /flɔːrəl/
1 ADJ ATTRIB **Floral** cloth, paper, or china has a pattern of flowers on it. *...floral dresses. ...floral wallpaper.*
2 ADJ ATTRIB You also use **floral** to describe something that is made of flowers. *...floral decorations.*

florid /flɒrɪd/; a literary word.
1 ADJ Something that is **florid** is complicated and extravagant rather than plain and simple; used showing disapproval. *Get rid of that greed for adjectives and florid writing. ...florid verse.*
2 ADJ Someone who is **florid** has a red face. *...a large man with a florid complexion.*

florin /flɒrɪn/ **florins**
NC A **florin** was a British coin that was worth two shillings.

florist /flɒrɪst/ **florists**
1 NC A **florist** is a shopkeeper who sells flowers and indoor plants. *...a brilliant florist who works for Buckingham Palace.*
2 NC A **florist** or a **florist's** is a shop where flowers and indoor plants are sold. *...a vast bronze jar filled with leaves and a few poppies—whatever was cheap at the florist.*

floss /flɒs/
NU **Floss** is soft threads of some kind, for example hair. *Spiders exude a silky floss... Use dental floss to clean between your teeth.* ● See also **candy floss**.

flotation /fləʊteɪʃn/; also spelt **floatation**.
1 N SING The **flotation** of a company happens when its owners sell shares in it to the public. *It will be the biggest flotation so far in its privatisation campaign... It is considering a private sale, rather than a public flotation.*
2 N+N A **flotation** tank or compartment helps something to float because it is filled with air or gas.

flotilla /flətɪlə/ **flotillas**
NC A **flotilla** is a group of small ships, usually military ships. *His immediate concern was the flotilla of minesweepers several miles ahead.*

flotsam /flɒtsəm/
1 NU **Flotsam** or **flotsam and jetsam** is rubbish, for example bits of wood, that is floating on the sea or has been left by the sea on the shore. *They searched for several weeks for identifiable flotsam from the lost planes... The roofs of submerged houses bobbed like flotsam above a vast sea of brown mud.*
2 NU People who do not have homes or jobs and perhaps have had to leave their own country or area may be referred to as **flotsam** or **flotsam and jetsam**. *They counted themselves as wanderers, misfits, flotsam and jetsam.*

flounce /flaʊns/ **flounces, flouncing, flounced**
VA When people **flounce** somewhere, they walk there quickly in an angry way, trying to draw attention to themselves. *She flounced into the bedroom, slamming the door behind her.*

flounder /flaʊndə/ **flounders, floundering, floundered**
1 V If you **flounder** in water or mud, you move in an uncontrolled way, trying not to sink. *Firm sand can disintegrate in seconds, leaving vehicles floundering.*
2 V If a movement, talks, or an economy **flounders**, it has many problems and may soon collapse completely. *But if the right is floundering, the left also has its problems... America is resigned to war as peace initiatives flounder... The UN sponsored peace talks have floundered.* ◆ **floundering** ADJ ATTRIB *...to restore the floundering economy.*
3 V You can also say that someone **is floundering** when they cannot think what to say or do. *Suddenly she asked me: 'What do you think?' I floundered for a moment.*

flour /flaʊə/
NU **Flour** is a white or brown powder that is made by grinding grain. It is used to make bread, cakes, and pastry. *It contained wheat flour and sugar and some baking powder.*

flourish /flʌrɪʃ/ **flourishes, flourishing, flourished**
1 V If something **flourishes**, it is active or successful, or it is developing quickly and strongly. *Democracy cannot possibly flourish in such circumstances... The arts flourished.* ◆ **flourishing** ADJ *The result is rampant inflation and a flourishing black market.*
2 V If a plant or animal **flourishes**, it grows well or is healthy because the conditions are right for it. *In these waters, bacteria flourish.*
3 VO If you **flourish** an object, you wave it about so that people notice it. *She rushed in flourishing a document... She flourished an enormously long cigarette holder.*
4 NC If you do something with a **flourish**, you do it with a bold sweeping movement. *Jack drew his knife with a flourish.*

floury /flaʊəri/
1 ADJ Something that is **floury** is covered with flour or

tastes of flour. *She wiped her floury hands on her apron.*
2 ADJ **Floury** potatoes go fluffy and break up when they are cooked.

flout /flaʊt/ **flouts, flouting, flouted**
VO If you **flout** a law, order, or rule of behaviour, you deliberately disobey it. *Too many motorists continue to flout the law on drinking and driving... No government should be able to pass laws flouting basic human rights.*

flow /fləʊ/ **flows, flowing, flowed**
1 VA If a river **flows** somewhere, it moves in that direction. *The river flows south-west to the Atlantic Ocean.* ▶ Also NU+SUPP *Turkish engineers partially closed down the flow of the River Euphrates to divert the water into a reservoir.*
2 VA If a liquid, gas, or electrical current **flows** somewhere, it moves steadily and continuously. *Lithuania says that supplies of Soviet oil are once again flowing to the Baltic republic... The magnetic field controls the way an electric current flows through a superconducting material.* ▶ Also NU+SUPP *The blood flow is cut off.*
3 VA You can also say that people or things **flow** somewhere when they move freely or steadily from one place to another. *European scientists, engineers and technicians are flowing into the United States... They expect donations to continue flowing into banks and building societies.* ▶ Also NU+SUPP *...the free flow of information and ideas... The escape roads were open; the endless flow of refugees resumed.*
4 VA If someone's hair or clothing **flows** about them, it hangs freely and loosely. *She let her hair down so that it flowed over her shoulders.* ◆ **flowing** ADJ *...women in long flowing robes.*
5 V+*from* If a quality or situation **flows** from something, it results naturally from it; a literary use. *The love for one another flows from that unity.*

flow chart, flow charts
NC A **flow chart** or a **flow diagram** is a diagram which shows a series of actions and the way they follow on from each other in a process.

flower /flaʊə/ **flowers, flowering, flowered**
1 NC The **flowers** on a plant are the coloured parts that grow on its stems, as opposed to its leaves. *Romance is not about an occasional card or bunch of flowers... A number of people lit candles and laid flowers on the grave. ...wild flowers.*
2 NC **Flowers** are also small plants that are grown for their flowers, as opposed to trees, shrubs, and vegetables. *He planted flowers on the banks... There's everything for the gardener at Chelsea Flower Show.*
3 V When a plant or tree **flowers**, its flowers appear and open. *It flowers well throughout the heat of a desert summer... Pick all the buds so that the plant won't flower again.*
4 V When an idea, artistic style, or political movement **flowers**, it develops fully and is successful; a literary use. *Since the return to democracy, Spain's relations with Latin America have flowered... Goodwill had briefly flowered in 1988.*

flowerbed /flaʊəbed/ **flowerbeds**
NC A **flowerbed** is an area of earth in which you grow plants. *...gardeners tending the flowerbeds.*

flowered /flaʊəd/
ADJ **Flowered** cloth, paper, or china has a pattern of flowers on it. *...flowered wall-papers. ...flowered hats.*

flowering /flaʊərɪŋ/
1 ADJ ATTRIB **Flowering** shrubs, trees, or plants produce flowers. *...garden centres selling all kinds of flowering plants and shrubs.*
2 NU The **flowering** of an idea, artistic style, or political movement is its successful development; a literary use. *...that flowering of eighteenth century intellectual creativity known as the Scottish Enlightenment. ...the maturing and flowering of the Philippine nation.*

flower people
N PL The **flower people** were people who belonged to a cult of the late 1960s which believed in peace and love, and used the flower as a symbol.

flowerpot /flaʊəpɒt/ **flowerpots**
NC A **flowerpot** is a small container which a plant is grown in.

flowery /flaʊəri/
1 ADJ Something that is **flowery** has a pattern of flowers on it or smells of flowers. *...flowery clothes.*
2 ADJ **Flowery** speech or writing contains long, complicated words and literary expressions; used showing disapproval. *Behind the flowery words and the mutual praise lies an element of mistrust.*

flown /fləʊn/
Flown is the past participle of **fly**.

fl. oz.
fl. oz. is a written abbreviation for 'fluid ounce'. *Add 3 fl. oz. methylated spirits.*

flu /fluː/
NU **Flu** is an illness which is like a bad cold. When you have flu, you feel weak and your muscles ache. *Most people who got flu went home to bed and got better... Last year there was a flu epidemic.*

fluctuate /flʌktʃueɪt/ **fluctuates, fluctuating, fluctuated**
V If something **fluctuates**, its amount, level, or nature keeps changing. *Prices fluctuated between 1970 and 1972... The level of the drug in the body fluctuates over time... Friendships blossomed, fluctuated, and died.*
◆ **fluctuation** /flʌktʃueɪʃn/ **fluctuations** NC *There have been wild fluctuations in the value of the dollar. ...currency fluctuations.*

flue /fluː/ **flues**
NC A **flue** is a chimney or a pipe that acts as a chimney. *Dutch scientists have come up with new ways to rid carbon dioxide from the flues of power stations... Not only did flue gases create acid rain but they could travel thousands of kilometres.*

fluency /fluːənsi/
NU **Fluency** is the quality or the state of being fluent. *She could speak German with great fluency. ...the clarity and fluency of his diction. ...subjects that require fluency in the written word.*

fluent /fluːənt/
1 ADJ Someone who is **fluent** in a foreign language can speak or write it easily and correctly. *He spoke good fluent German with an East German accent. ...a fluent Spanish speaker.* ◆ **fluently** ADV *He spoke both languages fluently.*
2 ADJ Someone whose speech, reading, or writing is **fluent** speaks, reads, or writes easily and clearly. ◆ **fluently** ADV *By the time she was six she could read fluently.*

fluff /flʌf/ **fluffs, fluffing, fluffed**
1 NU **Fluff** is the small masses of soft, light thread that you find on clothes or in dusty corners of a room. *He brushed some fluff from his jacket.*
2 VO If you **fluff** something or **fluff** it out, you shake it or brush it in order to make it seem larger and lighter. *She fluffed her hair out in big waves.*

fluffy /flʌfi/
ADJ Something that is **fluffy** is very soft and furry. *...a fluffy kitten.*

fluid /fluːɪd/ **fluids**
1 NCorNU A **fluid** is a substance that can flow, especially a liquid. *...petrol and cleaning fluids. ...body fluids such as blood... You really need to change the brake fluid every three months.* ▶ Also ADJ *After a month it was still completely fluid at the centre.*
2 ADJ A situation, idea, or arrangement that is **fluid** is likely to change, or can be changed. *Opinion in the trade unions is very fluid as regards this question.*
◆ **fluidity** /fluːɪdəti/ NU *...the fluidity of the situation.*

fluid ounce, fluid ounces
NC A **fluid ounce** is a unit of volume for liquids. There are twenty fluid ounces in an imperial pint, and sixteen in an American pint.

fluke /fluːk/ **flukes**
NC If something good that happens is a **fluke**, it happens accidentally rather than because of someone's skill or plan; an informal word. *Chanet's success dispelled any suggestion that his points win over Williams had been a fluke... An army spokesman described the attack as a fluke, with tragic results.*

flummox /flˈʌməks/ **flummoxes, flummoxing, flummoxed**
VO If someone is **flummoxed**, they are confused and do not know what to do or say; an informal word. *Both Mr Kohl and Mr Genscher were somewhat flummoxed by the Soviet suggestion... He completely flummoxed me.*

flung /flʌŋ/
Flung is the past tense and past participle of **fling**.

flunk /flʌŋk/ **flunks, flunking, flunked**; used in informal American English.
1 VO or V If you **flunk** an exam or a course, you fail it because you do not reach the required standard. *He flunked all his science courses... They're more likely to be labelled special education and they're much more likely to flunk.*
2 VO If an examiner **flunks** someone, he or she gives them a low mark or assessment for an exam or course, so that they fail it. *Who is he? Some PhD student I flunked?*
flunk out PHRASAL VERB If you **flunk out**, you are dismissed from a school or college because your work is not good enough. *'You're gonna flunk out if you just sit there watching me study!'*

flunkey /flˈʌŋki/ **flunkeys**; also spelt **flunky**. An informal word.
1 NC A **flunkey** is a man who acts as a servant in a large house and who wears ceremonial dress. *We went up some steps, where a flunkey took our cards.*
2 NC A **flunkey** is a person who follows someone who is important and who does small jobs for them in the hope of being rewarded; used showing disapproval. *She went out of the door before any of the flunkeys in the restaurant had time to push it open it for her.*

fluorescence /flɔːˈrɛsns/
NU **Fluorescence** is the very bright appearance that fluorescent things have, as if light is shining from them. *It also has sensors for fluorescence and light level. ...the fluorescence of healthy natural teeth.*

fluorescent /flɔːˈrɛsnt/
ADJ ATTRIB A **fluorescent** light shines with a very hard, bright light. *...fluorescent lighting... Later models were often painted fluorescent red or orange.*

fluoridation /flɔːrɪˈdeɪʃn/
NU **Fluoridation** is the action or process of adding fluoride to a water supply. *...literature that claims that fluoridation is harmful.*

fluoride /flˈɔːraɪd/
NU **Fluoride** is a mixture of chemicals that is sometimes added to a water supply or to toothpaste because it is good for people's teeth. *It's more than thirty years since the chemical fluoride was introduced into water supplies to prevent tooth decay... People should clean their teeth regularly with toothpaste containing fluoride.*

flurried /flˈʌrɪd/
ADJ Someone or something that is **flurried** is confused and disorganized because they are being rushed. *The child wandered about, deserted, flurried and bewildered... This flurried christening proved unnecessary.*

flurry /flˈʌri/ **flurries**
1 NC A **flurry** of activity or speech is a short, energetic amount of it. *There has been a flurry of diplomatic activity... The decision raised a flurry of objections.*
2 NC A **flurry** of snow or wind is a small amount of it that moves suddenly and quickly along. *...snow flurries.*

flush /flʌʃ/ **flushes, flushing, flushed**
1 V If you **flush**, your face goes red because you are embarrassed or because you feel hot or unwell. *She knew she was flushing hotly.*
2 N SING If there is a **flush** in your face, it is slightly red. *There was a flush in his cheeks.* ♦ **flushed** ADJ *Her face was flushed.*
3 V-ERG When you **flush** a toilet or when it **flushes**, the handle is pressed or pulled and water flows into the toilet bowl. *...laws that impose fines for urinating in public places or failing to flush a public toilet after use... She heard the toilet flush.*
4 ADJ ATTRIB A **flush** toilet has a handle that you press

or pull after use, to clean the bowl with water. *We have washing facilities, and we have a very nice flush toilet.*
5 ADJ PRED If something is **flush** with a surface, it is level with it and does not stick up. *The problem is with an insulation seal where the cargo doors close flush with the vehicle.*
flush out PHRASAL VERB If you **flush** people or animals out, you force them to come out. *They will advise the President of what steps should be taken to flush Iraqi troops out of Kuwait... Government troops were drafted in to flush out the small bands of rebels.*

flushed /flˈʌʃt/
ADJ PRED Someone who is **flushed** with success or pride is very pleased and excited as a result of achieving something. *...flushed by their apparent triumph.*

fluster /flˈʌstə/ **flusters, flustering, flustered**
VO If something **flusters** you, it makes you feel nervous and confused. *Go away, you're flustering me.* ♦ **flustered** ADJ *He was so flustered he forgot to close the door.*

flute /fluːt/ **flutes**
NC A **flute** is a musical instrument in the shape of a long tube with holes in it. You play it by holding it horizontally and blowing over a hole near one end. *...a piano, a flute or a full orchestra. ...flute music by Bach.*

fluted /flˈuːtɪd/
ADJ Something that is **fluted** has long grooves cut or shaped into it. *...fluted columns.*

flutist /flˈuːtɪst/ **flutists**
NC A **flutist** is the same as a **flautist**; used in American English.

flutter /flˈʌtə/ **flutters, fluttering, fluttered**
1 V-ERG If something **flutters** or if you **flutter** it, it waves up and down or from side to side. *His long robe fluttered in the wind... Courting male birds flutter their wings like chicks.*
2 VA If something light **flutters** somewhere, it moves through the air with small quick movements. *The pieces of paper flutter down like butterflies.*
3 N SING A **flutter** of panic, excitement, or pleasure is a slight feeling of panic, excitement, or pleasure. *The unabashed admiration of the stranger caused a flutter of pleasure.*
4 NC If you have a **flutter**, you have a small bet on something such as a horse race; an informal use. *Just about everyone has a little flutter on the Grand National.*

flux /flʌks/
NU If something is in a state of **flux**, it is changing constantly. *...years of political flux... International politics are in a state of flux, following the INF agreement.*

fly /flaɪ/ **flies, flying, flew, flown**
1 NC A **fly** is a small insect with two wings. There are many types of flies, and the most common are black in colour. *Keep away flies and other insects... Scientists were able to breed fruit flies which lived 80 percent longer.*
2 V When a bird, insect, or aircraft **flies**, it moves through the air. *My canary flew away... There are bound to be mishaps when so many planes are flying so often.* ● See also **flying**.
3 VA If you **fly** somewhere, you travel there in an aircraft. *You can fly from Cardiff to Ostend.*
4 VO When someone **flies** an aircraft, they control its movement in the air. *Once I was flying my plane and ran into a storm over San Francisco.* ♦ **flying** NU *New restrictions on civil flying over Britain have been confirmed... That's only fifty minutes flying time from the Iraqi border.*
5 VOA If you **fly** someone or something somewhere, you send them there by plane. *Exotic fruits were specially flown in for the occasion.*
6 VA If something **flies** about, it moves about freely and loosely in the air. *He jumped onto the platform with his cloak flying.*
7 V-ERG When a flag is **flying** or when people **fly** a flag, it is displayed at the top of a pole. *The Red Cross flag flew at each corner of the compound. ...oil tankers flying the American flag.*

8 VA If something **flies** in a particular direction, it moves there with a lot of speed or force. *His glasses flew off and smashed on the rocks.*
9 V+at If you **fly** at someone or let **fly** at them, you attack them, either by hitting them or by insulting them. *One day the man flew at me in a temper... He really let fly on the subject of racism.*
10 NC The front opening on a pair of trousers is referred to as the **fly** or the **flies**. *She started to button up the flies of her shorts.*
● **Fly** is used in these phrases. ● If you say that **time flies**, you mean that it seems to pass very quickly. ● If you **send** someone or something **flying** or if they **go flying**, they fall over with a lot of force. *Earthquakes have sent local residents scurrying for shelter as glass and chinaware is sent flying... I tripped over his foot and went flying.* ● If people are **dropping like flies** or **dropping off like flies**, large numbers of people are dying within a short space of time. *People were dropping like flies from diabetes, malnutrition, and heart disease.* ● If you say that someone **wouldn't hurt a fly** or **wouldn't harm a fly**, you mean they are very kind and gentle. *...a religious leader who wouldn't hurt a fly.* ● with **flying colours**: see **colour**. ● to **fly off the handle**: see **handle**.
fly into PHRASAL VERB If you **fly into** a rage or a panic, you suddenly become very angry or anxious. *She flies into a temper if I make a mistake.*

flyaway /ˈflaɪəweɪ/
ADJ ATTRIB **Flyaway** hair is very soft, fine, and difficult to control. *This shampoo is recommended for flyaway hair.*

flyblown /ˈflaɪbləʊn/
ADJ Something that is **flyblown** is covered with dirty spots or marks. *She took two cakes out of the flyblown display case.*

flyby /ˈflaɪbaɪ/ **flybys**
NC A **flyby** is the same as a **flypast**; used in American English. *The display ends with a flyby of more than a hundred military aircraft.*

fly-by-night
ADJ ATTRIB A **fly-by-night** business or person in business is unreliable because they are interested only in making money very quickly, often in illegal ways. *...stories of fly-by-night operators who do shoddy work, overcharge, or fail to complete jobs.*

flyer /ˈflaɪə/ **flyers**; also spelt **flier**.
1 NC If a bird or insect is a skilled **flyer**, it can fly well or quickly. *Hawkmoths are among the swiftest insect flyers.*
2 NC People who fly aircraft are sometimes referred to as **flyers**. *...dashing young flyers.*
3 NC A **flyer** is the same as a **handbill**; used in American English. *Kansas City Post Office mailed out flyers to area residents. ...pamphlets and fliers.*

fly-fishing
NU **Fly-fishing** is a kind of fishing in which a silk or nylon model of a small winged insect is used as bait. *He had a fervour for fly-fishing that captivated all who met him.*

flying /ˈflaɪɪŋ/
1 ADJ ATTRIB If you take a **flying** leap or jump, you run forward and jump. *She took a flying leap at the fence.*
2 ADJ ATTRIB A **flying** animal is able to fly. *...flies and other flying insects.* ● See also **fly**.
3 If you **get off to a flying start**, you start something very well, for example a race or a new job. *China and Japan have got off to a flying start in the swimming events.*
4 with **flying colours**: see **colour**.

flying buttress, flying buttresses
NC A **flying buttress** is an arch and vertical column that supports the outside of a wall, usually the wall of a large church; a technical term in architecture.

flying doctor, flying doctors
NC A **flying doctor** is a doctor, especially in Australia, who travels by aircraft to visit patients who live in isolated areas. *A flying doctor service is vital in such a large, sparsely-populated country.*

flying fish, flying fishes. The plural form can be either **flying fishes** or **flying fish**.
NC A **flying fish** is a type of fish that is able to jump out of the water and move forward in the air by using its large fins.

Flying Fish Cove /ˌflaɪɪŋ fɪʃ ˈkəʊv/
Flying Fish Cove is the capital of Christmas Island and its principal settlement.

flying picket, flying pickets
NC A **flying picket** is a group of trade union members that travels to different places of work during a strike in order to persuade people there to join the strike. *Flying pickets have persuaded men at eighteen other collieries not to work.*

flying saucer, flying saucers
NC People refer to oval shaped flat objects that they see in the sky which they believe to be spacecraft from other planets as **flying saucers**. *16% of women and 25% of men believe in flying saucers. ...a flying saucer flying over the landscape.*

flying squad, flying squads
N COLL The **flying squad** is a group of police officers who are always ready to travel quickly to the scene of a serious crime. *Officers from Scotland Yard's flying squad were involved.*

flying visit, flying visits
NC A **flying visit** is a visit that only lasts a very short time. *I'm afraid this will only be a flying visit, as I have to be back in London tonight.*

flyleaf /ˈflaɪliːf/ **flyleaves**
NC The **flyleaf** of a book is a page at the front that has nothing printed on it, or just the title and the author's name. *'To Aunt Agnes' was written in a bold hand on the flyleaf.*

flyover /ˈflaɪəʊvə/ **flyovers**
NC A **flyover** is a structure which carries one road above another one. *...to build flyovers and expressways. ...a massive new motorway flyover. ...a road crash involving four vehicles on the A27 Shoreham flyover in West Sussex.*

flypaper /ˈflaɪpeɪpə/
NU **Flypaper** is a long piece of sticky paper that you hang up in a room in order to catch flies.

flypast /ˈflaɪpɑːst/ **flypasts**
NC When a **flypast** takes place on a ceremonial occasion or as a display, a group of aircraft fly through the sky in a special formation. *The Royal Family have been watching the flypast.*

flyposting /ˈflaɪpəʊstɪŋ/
NU **Flyposting** means putting advertisements or posters in unauthorized places. *There have already been some arrests for illegal flyposting.*

flysheet /ˈflaɪʃiːt/ **flysheets**
NC The **flysheet** of a tent is the waterproof outer part that covers the inner part and protects it from rain.

flyweight /ˈflaɪweɪt/ **flyweights**
NC A **flyweight** is a boxer who weighs less than 51 kilos if he is a professional, or between 48 and 51 kilos if he is an amateur. *Fidel Bassa has retained his WBA world flyweight title in Belfast.*

flywheel /ˈflaɪwiːl/ **flywheels**
NC A **flywheel** is a heavy wheel that is part of a machine and makes it work at a steady speed. *A flywheel keeps the generator speed steady as the airflow increases.*

foal /fəʊl/ **foals**
NC A **foal** is a very young horse. *One of the most popular race mares of all, Pebbles, has had her first foal. ...a new-born foal.*

foam /fəʊm/ **foams, foaming, foamed**
1 NU **Foam** consists of a mass of small bubbles. It is formed when air and a liquid are mixed together violently. *...the line of white foam where the waves broke. ...the pale yellow foam on their coffee.*
2 NU **Foam** also refers to a substance that consists of a mass of very small bubbles. It is formed into a chemical so that it is suitable to be used for a particular purpose. *...products such as hairsprays, deodorants and shaving foam. ...a foam carpet cleaner.*
3 NU **Foam** or **foam rubber** is soft rubber full of small holes which is used, for example, to make mattresses and cushions. *...the use of foam in the upholstery of household furniture. ...foam packaging for fast food containers.*

4 V If a liquid **is foaming**, it has lots of small bubbles in it or on its surface. *...mysteriously foaming dark pools.*

foamy /fəʊmi/ **foamier, foamiest**
1 ADJ A liquid that is **foamy** has a mass of small bubbles on its surface. *The sea was all glossy and pale and foamy like ginger beer.*
2 ADJ Something such as blossom or lace that is described as **foamy** is pale in colour and made up of many delicate parts or strands; a literary use. *...foamy clusters of cream-coloured flowers.*

fob /fɒb/ **fobs, fobbing, fobbed**
fob off PHRASAL VERB If you **fob off** someone who needs something, you give them something that is not very good or is not really what they wanted, although you pretend it is; an informal expression. *He may try to fob you off with a prescription for pills.*

focal /fəʊkl/
1 ADJ ATTRIB **Focal** is used to describe something relating to the point at which several rays or lines meet. *...the focal crossroads, grandly named the 'Place des Nations'.*
2 ADJ ATTRIB **Focal** is used to describe something that is very important. *In most developing countries, the state is a focal institution.*

focal point
N SING The **focal point** of people's interest or activity is the thing they concentrate on or the place they are most active. *The United Nations is likely to remain the focal point for negotiations... The focal point of these celebrations was the local church.*

focus /fəʊkəs/ **focuses, focusing, focused**; also spelt **focusses, focussing, focussed**
1 V-ERG When you **focus** a camera on something or when a camera **focuses** on it, you adjust it so that it takes clear pictures. *They reportedly plan to release a satellite that will focus cameras on the Middle East... The cameras focused on the men, but they never said anything out loud... We film sideways since people feel irritated if you focus at them.* ● If a photograph or telescope is **in focus**, the photograph or the thing you are looking at is clear and sharp. If it is **out of focus**, the photograph or the thing you are looking at is blurred. *The only part of the picture which was in clear focus was a small child.*
2 V-ERG If people **focus** their attention on something or if their attention is **focused**, they are concentrating on one thing or thinking and talking about that thing. *This kind of dilemma prevents the league from focusing their attention on more pressing problems... International attention has been focussed on airport security... Previous crime campaigns have focused on crimes like burglary and theft.*
3 V-ERG When you **focus** your eyes or when your eyes **focus**, you adjust them so that you can see clearly. *He tried to focus his eyes on a painting above Ellen's head... His eyes would not focus... I shook my head and tried to focus.*
4 VO If you **focus** a ray of light, you direct it towards a particular point. *I focused the beam of the spotlight on them.*
5 NU If special attention is being paid to something, you can say that it is the **focus** of interest or attention. *Changes in the urban environment are the focus of public interest and discussion... British issues are the main focus of attention.*

fodder /fɒdə/
NU **Fodder** is food that is given to animals such as cows or horses. *The extra soya beans are being used as animal fodder to improve meat production. ...fodder crops for the cows.*

foe /fəʊ/ **foes**
NC Your **foe** is your enemy; an old-fashioned word. *He's neither friend nor foe. ...bitter foes.*

foetal /fiːtl/; also spelt **fetal**.
ADJ ATTRIB **Foetal** is used to describe something relating to or like a foetus. *The drug may cause foetal abnormalities... Foetal tissue is already used to treat diabetes... I was curled up in a foetal position.*

foetus /fiːtəs/ **foetuses**; also spelt **fetus**.
NC A **foetus** is an unborn animal or human being, used especially to refer to the period of its development

from eight weeks until birth. *The genetic material can be obtained by taking a sample from the cord joining the foetus to the womb.*

fog /fɒg/ **fogs**
NU or NC When there is **fog**, there are tiny drops of water in the air which form a thick cloud and make it difficult to see things. *Snow and fog are blocking the airport.*

fog bank, fog banks
NC A **fog bank** is an area of thick fog, especially at sea.

fogbound /fɒgbaʊnd/
ADJ A place or building that is **fogbound** cannot operate as usual, because of fog. *For much of the night the airport was fogbound.*

fogey /fəʊgi/ **fogeys**; also spelt **fogy**.
NC A **fogey** is a boring, old-fashioned person; an informal word. *Don't be such an old fogey!*

foggy /fɒgi/ **foggier, foggiest**
ADJ When it is **foggy**, there is fog. *...on a foggy morning... The weather is foggy and cold.*

foghorn /fɒghɔːn/ **foghorns**
NC A **foghorn** is a loud horn that is used when it is foggy to warn ships about the positions of land and other ships. *That wail belongs to the foghorn that warns vessels away from Alcatraz Island.*

fog lamp, fog lamps
NC A **fog lamp** or a **fog light** is a special, powerful light on a car or other vehicle which you use when you are driving in fog.

fogy /fəʊgi/. See **fogey**.

foible /fɔɪbl/ **foibles**
NC A **foible** is a rather strange or foolish habit, but one which is considered unimportant and allowable; a literary word. *She knows his moods and foibles.*

foil /fɔɪl/ **foils, foiling, foiled**
1 NU **Foil** is metal in the form of a thin sheet. *...the foil wrapper of a bar of chocolate.*
2 VO If you **foil** someone's plan or attempt at something, you prevent it from being successful. *It is thought that police foiled a plot to assassinate Mr De Mita in February... Another attempt to hijack a Soviet airliner has been foiled.*
3 N SING Something that is a good **foil** for something else contrasts with it and makes its good qualities more noticeable. *She had bronzed skin, for which her yellow swimsuit was a perfect foil.*

foist /fɔɪst/ **foists, foisting, foisted**
foist on PHRASAL VERB If you **foist** something **on** someone, you force them to have it or experience it without their approval. *They were out to foist their views on the people.*

fold /fəʊld/ **folds, folding, folded**
1 VO If you **fold** a piece of paper or cloth, you bend it so that one part covers another part. *Fold the sheets and blankets back at the top.*
2 VO If you **fold** something, you make it into a smaller shape by bending it over on itself several times. *They folded the tent neatly.*
3 NC A **fold** in a piece of cloth or paper is a bend that you make in it when you put one part of it over another part of it. It is also used to refer to the curved shapes that are formed in a piece of cloth when it is not lying flat. *You need to make three folds in the paper along lines A, B, and C... Snow had collected in the folds of my clothes.*
4 N SING The **fold** is an organization or group towards which people feel a strong sense of loyalty and belonging. *He has succeeded in bringing several senators into the Liberal Party fold... Others might be encouraged to join the fold.*
5 VO If you **fold** a piece of furniture or equipment, you change its shape by bending or closing parts of it.
6 V If a piece of furniture or equipment **folds**, you can change its shape and make it smaller by bending or closing parts of it. *The rear seat folds down... It folds actually to twelve and a half centimetres.* ● See also **folding**.
7 V If a business or organization **folds**, it is unsuccessful and has to close. *The project in Swaziland folded several years ago.*
8 VO If you **fold** your arms or hands, you bring them

together and cross them or link them. *He sat with his arms folded across his chest... Policemen watched with their arms folded.*

fold up PHRASAL VERB If you **fold** something **up**, you make it into a smaller shape by bending it over on itself several times. *She folded up some shirts... Someone had folded up the piece of paper beforehand.*

-fold /-fəʊld/

1 SUFFIX **-fold** combines with numbers to say that something has a particular number of kinds or parts. *The problems were two-fold: it was difficult to get finance, and there weren't enough trained people available.*

2 SUFFIX **-fold** is also used to indicate that something is multiplied a particular number of times. *The number of visitors rose twenty-five-fold in the eighteen years from 1971... Both countries would see their populations increase four-fold.*

fold-away

ADJ ATTRIB A **fold-away** piece of furniture or equipment is one that can be folded into a smaller shape for convenience or storage. *...a fold-away table.*

folder /fəʊldə/ **folders**

NC A **folder** is a thin piece of cardboard folded into the shape of a container or cover, in which you can keep documents. *He took a sealed envelope from the folder on his desk.*

folding /fəʊldɪŋ/

ADJ ATTRIB A **folding** table, bicycle, or other object can be folded into a smaller shape to make it easier to carry or store. *...folding seats and umbrellas.*

fold-up

ADJ ATTRIB A **fold-up** piece of furniture or equipment is one that can be folded into a smaller shape for convenience or storage. *...fold-up desks. ...fold-up bicycles.*

foliage /fəʊliɪdʒ/

NU The leaves of plants and trees can be referred to as **foliage**. *Nearly a quarter of our trees are sick, dead or dying—that is, they've suffered severe loss of foliage.*

folio /fəʊliəʊ/ **folios**

NC A **folio** is a book made with paper of a large size, especially from the early centuries of European printing. *...a copy of Shakespeare's first folio of 1623. ...a folio volume of Italian paintings.*

folk /fəʊk/ **folks**

1 ADJ ATTRIB **Folk** music, art, and customs are traditional or typical of a particular community or nation. *...Russian folk songs. ...Scottish folk dances.*

2 N PL You can refer to people as **folk**. *The folk in this area have a great tradition of hospitality. ...old folk.*

3 N PL Your **folks** are your close relatives, especially your parents; used in informal American English. *I don't even have time to write letters to my folks.*

folklore /fəʊklɔː/

NU The traditional stories and customs of a community or nation are referred to as its **folklore**. *...children's stories based on African folklore. ...ancient herbal folklore remedies.*

folksy /fəʊksi/

ADJ Something that is **folksy** is simple and has a style that is characteristic of folk craft and tradition. *...her full and folksy long skirt... He flooded the airways with his folksy anti-crime messages.*

follicle /fɒlɪkl/ **follicles**

NC A **follicle** is one of the small hollows in the skin which hairs grow from. *The technique involves removing from the scalp the tiny sacs or follicles from which the hair grows.*

follow /fɒləʊ/ **follows, following, followed**

1 VOorV If you **follow** someone who is moving, you move along behind them. *He followed Sally into the yard... Lynn got up and made for the stairs and Marsha followed.*

2 VO If one person or country **follows** another, they do the same thing after the other. *The Guardian believes Norway will soon follow Sweden in seeking membership... The Portuguese government may want to follow the Spanish precedent.*

3 VOorV If you **follow** someone who has gone to a

place, you go there yourself. *He followed them to Venice.*

4 VOorV Something that **follows** a particular event happens after it. *The announcement followed a meeting yesterday to discuss the country's transition to full democracy... Decisions on a single European currency should follow three years later.*

5 VOA If someone **follows** one action by another, they complete one action and then start another which may be connected in some way. *The aim is to establish a scientific base on the Moon and to follow that by a manned flight to Mars... The farmers will plant one crop, then follow it by a slightly later crop.*

6 VO If a particular thing that happens is **followed** by another thing, this thing happens first and then the other thing happens. *Use carbon tetrachloride followed by soap and water.*

7 V-REPORT or V If you say that something **follows**, you mean that it is true because something else is true. *The German economy is the strongest in Europe, but it does not follow that Germany will dominate the Community... You must interpret the idea of multiplication and the product rule follows.*

8 You use **as follows** to introduce a list of things or a description of the way something is done. *The contents are as follows: one black desk, one grey wastepaper bin, two red chairs.*

9 VO If you **follow** a path or river, you go along it. *Radio waves follow the curvature of the Earth... We were able to follow the river.*

10 VO If you **follow** someone's instructions, advice, or example, you do what they say or do what they have done. *The issue was one on which China tended to follow Pakistan's advice... Failure to follow the instructions could result in closure.*

11 VO If you **follow** a particular course of action, you do something in a planned way. *Each country would be free to follow its own policy on direct aid... Patients had to follow a strict daily routine.*

12 VOorV If you can **follow** an explanation or the plot of a story, you can understand it. *They were having some difficulty in following the plot... He could not really quite follow what Dr Hochstadt was attempting to say.*

13 VO If you **follow** a series of events or a television serial, you take an interest in it and keep informed about what happens. *If you follow scientific developments you'll know that researchers have already succeeded in putting genes from one creature into another.* ● to **follow suit**: see suit.

follow up PHRASAL VERB 1 If you **follow** something **up**, you try to find out more about it. *It's an idea which has been followed up by a group of researchers at Birmingham.* 2 If you **follow** one thing **up** with another, you do the second thing after you have done the first, often in support of it. *He followed up this criticism with a personal attack on the Prime Minister.* ● See also **follow-up**.

follower /fɒləʊə/ **followers**

NC The **followers** of a person or belief are the people who support the person or accept the belief. *...the followers of Chinese communism.*

following /fɒləʊɪŋ/

1 ADJ ATTRIB The **following** day, week, or year is the day, week, or year after the one you have just mentioned. *They compete in a semifinal on a Saturday and then play the final the following day. ...early the following morning.*

2 PREP **Following** a particular event means after that event, and often as a result of it. *Several people have been taken to hospital following a bomb explosion in West Belfast... Britain's economy also comes under close scrutiny following the biggest rise in unemployment for four years.*

3 ADJ ATTRIB You can refer to the things that you are about to mention as the **following** things. *This could be achieved in the following way... He issued the following statement.*

4 N SING A person or organization that has a **following** has a group of people who support their beliefs or actions. *They gained a huge following of young fans.*

5 ADJ ATTRIB If something such as a boat or an aeroplane, or someone such as an athlete has a **following** wind, the wind is moving in the same direction as that vehicle or that person. *His jump did not qualify for the record because of a following wind.*

follow-my-leader

NU **Follow-my-leader** is a children's game in which one child is followed by all the others in a line, and his or her actions are copied.

follow-on, follow-ons

NU or NC A **follow-on** is something that comes after something else or someone else, or as a result of it. *He proposed an early start for the first group with a follow-on of two more groups the next day... the basis of further follow-on agreements.*

follow-through, follow-throughs

1 NC A **follow-through** is the completion of an action or planned series of actions. *This wouldn't halt the attack but it would at least blunt the follow-through.*
2 NC A **follow-through** is the completion of a movement such as hitting a ball. *He held his follow-through pose for 10 seconds.*

follow-up, follow-ups

ADJ ATTRIB **Follow-up** work or action is done as a continuation of something. *...follow-up treatment... The parties had agreed that a follow-up meeting should take place in Africa itself.* ▶ Also NC *This conference is a follow-up to an earlier one... This song is the follow-up to their No.2 smash 'Get a Life'.*

folly /fɒli/ **follies**

NU or NC If you say that an action or way of behaving is **folly** or a **folly**, you mean that it is foolish; a literary word. *Any other course would be political folly. ...the lies and follies of governments.*

foment /fəʊmɛnt/ **foments, fomenting, fomented**

VO If someone or something **foments** trouble, especially political trouble, they cause it to develop or increase; a formal word. *They were accused of fomenting trouble... The demonstrations were fomented by foreign forces.* ▶ Also NU *His move towards a market economy have been halted by the nationalist foment.*

fond /fɒnd/ **fonder, fondest**

1 ADJ PRED+*of* If you are **fond** of someone, you feel affection for them. *I'm very fond of you.*
2 ADJ PRED+*of* If you are **fond** of something, you like it. *I am not fond of salad... Etta was fond of shopping.* ◆ **fondness** NU *...my fondness for red wine.*
3 ADJ ATTRIB You use **fond** to describe people or their behaviour when they show affection. *His fond parents looked on. ...looking at me with fond eyes.* ◆ **fondly** ADV *He used to gaze at the old car fondly. ...fondly remembered.*
4 ADJ ATTRIB **Fond** hopes, wishes, or expectations are a little bit foolish and unlikely to be fulfilled. *One fond dream has been to harness the sun's rays.* ◆ **fondly** ADV *He had fondly imagined that it would be a simple matter.*

fondant /fɒndənt/ **fondants**

NC A **fondant** is a sugary sweet that melts in your mouth.

fondle /fɒndl/ **fondles, fondling, fondled**

VO If you **fondle** someone, you touch them or stroke them gently, usually to show your affection. *Every baby needs to be smiled at, talked to, played with, fondled—gently and lovingly.*

fondue /fɒndjuː/ **fondues**

NC or NU A **fondue** is a hot sauce, often made with cheese, which you dip small pieces of bread, meat, or vegetable into and eat. *The fondue is made with the fontina cheese and a little bit of egg yolk. ...oxtail fondue.*

font /fɒnt/ **fonts**

NC The **font** in a church is a bowl which holds the water used for baptisms.

food /fuːd/ **foods**

1 N MASS **Food** is what people and animals eat. *Bring enough food and water for the trip... There are genuine shortages of food... Even such basic foods as salt and flour are to be rationed. ...pet foods.*
2 If something gives you **food for thought**, it causes you to think how it will effect future events. *The*

timing of the arrests, just two days before parliamentary elections, gives food for thought.

food aid

NU **Food aid** is supplies of food sent to a country which does not have enough food for its people, usually because of a disaster or emergency. *The government has appealed to the United Nations for urgent food aid... Up to fifteen hundred tons of food aid must be delivered every month.*

food chain, food chains

NC A **food chain** is a series of living things which are considered as being linked because each thing feeds on the thing below it in the series. *Some of the fertilizers get into the food chain and damage humans.*

food mixer, food mixers

NC A **food mixer** is an electrical machine which people use in the kitchen to mix things like cake mixture.

food poisoning

NU **Food poisoning** is an illness that gives people sickness and diarrhoea. It is caused by eating food that has gone bad. *19 patients died and over 400 were ill with food poisoning as a result of bad hygiene practices.*

food stamp, food stamps

NC In the United States, **food stamps** are stamps that are given to people on a low income by the government in order to help them buy food. *A record number of people applied for public assistance and food stamps from public agencies. ...foodstamps and welfare benefits.*

foodstuff /fuːdstʌf/ **foodstuffs**

NC **Foodstuffs** are substances which people eat. *They produce sugar and other basic foodstuffs.*

fool /fuːl/ **fools, fooling, fooled**

1 NC If you call someone a **fool**, you mean that they are silly or have done something silly. *You stupid fool!*
2 VO If you **fool** someone, you deceive or trick them. *He fooled them with false promises.*
● **Fool** is used in these phrases. ● If you **make a fool** of someone, you make them appear silly by telling people about something silly that they have done, or by tricking them. *Mind you, I wasn't the only man she made a fool of.* ● If you **make a fool of** yourself, you behave in a way that makes you appear silly. *He had never learned to dance and was not prepared to make a fool of himself.* ● If you **play the fool**, you behave in a playful and silly way. *I must seriously ask you not to play the fool.*

fool about or **fool around** PHRASAL VERB If you **fool about** or **fool around**, you behave in a playful and silly way. *He was always fooling about.*

foolery /fuːləri/

NU **Foolery** is foolish behaviour. *Stop this foolery of sleeping on the sitting-room sofa.*

foolhardy /fuːlhɑːdi/

ADJ **Foolhardy** behaviour is foolish because it involves taking risks; a formal word. *When Zaguary tested an early vaccine on himself, some described the act as foolhardy. ...this very costly and foolhardy policy.* ◆ **foolhardiness** NU *The police criticised the windsurfers for their foolhardiness.*

foolish /fuːlɪʃ/

1 ADJ If you say that someone's behaviour is **foolish**, you mean that it is not sensible. *What I did was foolish in the extreme... Stop this foolish nonsense.* ◆ **foolishly** ADV or ADV SEN *He thought he'd behaved foolishly... Foolishly, we said we would do the decorating.* ◆ **foolishness** NU *Have I killed him by my foolishness?*
2 ADJ You can also say that people are **foolish** when they are so silly that they make you want to laugh. *They looked foolish... The leadership has been made to look foolish.* ◆ **foolishly** ADV *Would the whole thing appear foolishly melodramatic?*

foolproof /fuːlpruːf/

ADJ A plan, system, or machine that is **foolproof** is so good or easy to use that it cannot go wrong or be used wrongly. *...foolproof safety devices... Such an ambitious system could never be foolproof.*

foolscap /fuːlzkæp/

NU **Foolscap** is paper which is about 34 centimetres by

43 centimetres in size. *...three sheets of foolscap. ...foolscap paper.*

fool's errand, fool's errands
NC If someone is sent on a **fool's errand**, they are sent to do a task which is impossible or pointless; a literary expression. *It was a fool's errand; he'll never change his mind.*

fool's gold
NU **Fool's gold** is a substance that is found in rock and that looks rather like gold but is not valuable.

fool's paradise
N SING If you say that someone is living in a **fool's paradise**, you mean that they are in a state of great happiness which is threatened by change, but they are not aware of this threat.

foot /fʊt/ **feet; foots, footing, footed.** The form **feet** is the plural of the noun. The form **foots** is the third person singular, present tense, of the verb in the final phrase.
1 NC Your **feet** are the parts of your body that are at the ends of your legs and that you stand on. *She accidentally stood on someone's foot... He lost his foot in a motorcycle accident six years ago.*
2 N SING The **foot** of something is the bottom or lower end of it. *...at the foot of the stairs... He sat at the foot of her bed.*
3 NC A **foot** is a unit of length, equal to 12 inches or approximately 30.48 centimetres. The plural can be either 'foot' or 'feet'. *We were a few feet away from the edge. ...a 40-foot fall. ...drifting snow up to a foot deep in places.* ● to **have** or **get cold feet**: see **cold**.
● **Foot** is used in these phrases. ● If you go somewhere **on foot**, you walk, rather than use any form of transport. *They wandered from one holy place to another, on foot and without money.* ● When you are **on your feet**, you are standing up. *He's portrayed as sometimes too drunk to stay on his feet.* ● When someone is **on their feet** again after an illness or a difficult period of time, they have recovered. *He's had an operation but Spur's say he'll be back on his feet in six months. ...an economic programme to put the country back on its feet.* ● If you **get to your feet**, you stand up. *He rose hurriedly to his feet.* ● To **set foot** in a place means to go there. *It was a long time before I set foot in a theatre again... President F.W. de Klerk set foot on Dutch soil this morning.* ● If someone in authority **puts their foot down**, they say that something must not happen or continue. *President Mitterrand put his foot down.* ● If you **put your feet up**, you relax by sitting with your legs supported by something. *She likes to put her feet up after a day's work.* ● If you **put your foot in it**, you cause embarrassment by doing or saying something tactless; an informal expression. ● If someone has to **stand on their own two feet**, they have to manage without help from other people. *The government is keen to be seen able to stand on its own two feet... They should become more able to take initiatives and stand on their own two feet.* ● If you **foot the bill** for something, you pay for it. *One hundred thousand people have simply refused to pay it, leaving the airlines to foot the bill... The taxpayer should be made to foot the bill.*

footage /fʊtɪdʒ/
NU **Footage** of a particular event is a film or part of a film which shows this event. *...some spine-chilling footage on the effects of nuclear war.*

foot-and-mouth disease
NU **Foot-and-mouth disease** is a serious disease that affects cattle, sheep, pigs, and goats. As a result of the disease blisters form in the animal's mouth and around its hooves, and it has to be slaughtered. *British meat has been banned in the Caribbean because of fears of foot-and-mouth disease. ...an outbreak of foot-and-mouth disease.*

football /fʊtbɔːl/ **footballs**
1 NU **Football** is a game played between two teams of eleven players who kick a ball around a field in an attempt to score goals. *The children are playing football... Swindon Town Football Club will play in Division Two next season. ...English football fans.*
2 NU In the United States, **football** is a game played between two teams of eleven players who carry the ball in their hands or throw it to each other in an attempt to score goals that are called touchdowns. *Former Washington Redskins defensive end Dexter Manley can play professional football again... Red Grange was playing college football in Illinois. ...the National Football League.*
3 NC A **football** is the large ball which is used in the game of football. *He was hit in the face by a football. ...a very lightweight plastic football.*

footballer /fʊtbɔːlə/ **footballers**
NC A **footballer** is a person who plays football, usually as a job. *After leaving school he became a professional footballer. ...European footballer of the year.*

footballing /fʊtbɔːlɪŋ/
ADJ ATTRIB **Footballing** means related to football. *A serious knee injury brought his footballing career to an abrupt end. ...footballing countries. ...his footballing achievements.*

football pools
N PL **Football pools** are the same as the pools: see **pool**.

footbridge /fʊtbrɪdʒ/ **footbridges**
NC A **footbridge** is a narrow bridge that you can walk but not drive across. *He was seen walking across a footbridge away from the playing fields.*

footfall /fʊtfɔːl/ **footfalls**
NC A **footfall** is the sound that is made by someone walking each time they take a step; a literary word. *Suddenly he heard heavy footfalls behind him.*

foothills /fʊthɪlz/
N PL **Foothills** are low hills at the base of a mountain or at the edge of a mountain range. *...the foothills of the Himalayas. ...in the foothills of central Tuscany.*

foothold /fʊthəʊld/ **footholds**
1 NC **Footholds** are ledges or hollows where you can put your feet when you are climbing. *He cut footholds in the side of the ravine.*
2 N SING If you get a **foothold** when you are trying to achieve something, you establish yourself in a strong position from which you can make progress. *I tried to gain a foothold in the organization.*

footing /fʊtɪŋ/
1 NU If you lose your **footing**, your feet slip, and you fall. *He lost his footing, and stumbled to the floor.*
2 N SING+SUPP You use **footing** to describe the basis on which something is done. *We've had to get this on a more official footing.*
3 N SING Your **footing** with someone is your relationship with them. *The laws will allow the private sector to operate on an equal footing with the state sector... Talks have put relations between Britain and Japan on a new and more secure footing.*

footlights /fʊtlaɪts/
N PL The **footlights** in a theatre are the lights that are in a row along the front of the stage. *There was a string orchestra already playing in the pit and the bottom of the pit was lit by the footlights.*

footling /fuːtlɪŋ/
ADJ Something that is **footling** is very unimportant and not worth taking seriously; an old-fashioned word, used showing disapproval. *Don't let's have a lot of footling excuses for not going.*

footloose /fʊtluːs/
ADJ Someone who is **footloose** has no responsibilities or commitments and so is free to do what they want. *...numerous footloose young men from other villages... She's still footloose and fancy-free.*

footman /fʊtmən/ **footmen** /fʊtmən/
NC A **footman** is a male servant who does jobs such as opening doors or serving food. *The Queen has to employ around 300 staff. These are mainly footmen, housemaids and grooms.*

footmark /fʊtmɑːk/ **footmarks**
NC A **footmark** is a mark that someone's foot or shoe has made on a surface. *...the marks of wheels, hoof-prints and footmarks.*

footnote /fʊtnəʊt/ **footnotes**
1 NC A **footnote** is a note at the bottom of a page which gives more information about something on the page. *Here is a history book that doesn't overload*

every page with footnotes and references.

2 NC+SUPP A **footnote** in history is an event which will probably be remembered but is not very important. *A footnote in the history of international broadcasting was written today... I'm afraid that Marx will now become a footnote in history.*

footpath /fʊtpɑːθ/ **footpaths**

NC A **footpath** is a path for people to walk on, especially in the country. *A bicycle has no legal right to be on a footpath.*

footplate /fʊtpleɪt/ **footplates**

NC A **footplate** is the platform on a steam locomotive where the driver and fireman stand.

footprint /fʊtprɪnt/ **footprints**

NC **Footprints** are the marks that your feet leave in soft ground or when they are wet. *...footprints in the snow.*

footsie /fʊtsi/

1 If someone **plays footsie** with you, they touch your feet with their own feet, for example under a table, often as a playful way of expressing their romantic or sexual feelings towards you; an informal expression. *I wouldn't mind playing footsie with that Mr Hooper.*

2 N SING The Financial Times Stock Exchange 100 Index is sometimes referred to as the **Footsie**; an informal word. *On Friday, the stock market drifted lower, with the Footsie falling 17.5 points... Profit-taking is expected to reverse part of the recent Footsie rise.*

footsore /fʊtsɔː/

ADJ If you are **footsore**, you have sore or tired feet after walking a long way. *She was tired and footsore and desperately weary of travelling.*

footstep /fʊtstep/ **footsteps**

NC Your **footsteps** are the sounds that your feet make when you walk. *They heard footsteps and turned.* ● If you **follow in** someone's **footsteps**, you do the same things as they did earlier. *I followed in my father's footsteps and became a gamekeeper.*

footstool /fʊtstuːl/ **footstools**

NC A **footstool** is a low stool that you can rest your feet on when you are sitting in a chair.

footwear /fʊtweə/

NU **Footwear** refers to shoes, boots, and sandals; a formal word. *...the price of clothes, footwear and household goods... You can tell a great deal about people from their footwear.*

footwork /fʊtwɜːk/

1 NU **Footwork** is the way in which you move your feet, especially in sports such as boxing, football, or tennis, or in dancing. *...attention to footwork, angle of the racket, smoothness of strokes.*

2 NU Fancy **footwork** is a clever way of dealing with a difficult situation. *...an economic system that will require some fancy footwork indeed.*

foppish /fɒpɪʃ/

ADJ A man who is **foppish** is vain and dresses in fancy, elegant clothes; an old-fashioned word, used showing disapproval. *He dresses with an almost foppish elegance.*

for /fə, fɔː/

1 PREP If something is **for** someone, they are intended to have it or benefit from it. *He left a note for her on the table... I am doing everything I can for you.*

2 PREP You use **for** when you are describing the purpose of something, the reason for something, or the cause of something. *...a knife for cutting linoleum... This area is famous for its spring flowers.*

3 PREP If you work **for** someone, you are employed by them. *He works for British Rail.*

4 PREP If you speak or act **for** someone, you do it on their behalf. *We are speaking for the majority of the British people.*

5 PREP You use **for** when you are saying how something affects someone. *I knew it was difficult for him to talk like this... It was a frightening experience for a boy.*

6 PREP You also use **for** when you are mentioning a person or thing that you have feelings about. *I felt sorry for my wife. ...Kurt's contempt for people.*

7 PREP You use **for** when you are mentioning two things that are equivalent or can be substituted in

some way. *'Carte' is the French word for card. ...a substitute for natural rubber.*

8 PREP You also use **for** after such words as 'time', 'space', or 'money' when you are saying how much of it there is and what use could be made of it. *There was room for a table... He didn't have the concentration required for doing the job.*

9 PREP You use **for** to say how long something lasts or continues. *I have known you for a long time.*

10 PREP You also use **for** to say how far something extends. *Black cliffs rose sheer out of the water for a hundred feet or more.*

11 PREP If something is planned **for** a particular time, it is planned to happen then. *The meeting has been scheduled for August 30.*

12 PREP If you leave **for** a place or if you take a train, plane, or boat **for** a place, you are going there. *...one morning, before he left for the fields.*

13 PREP You use **for** when you are talking about the cost of something. *You can buy the paperback for about two pounds.*

14 PREP You also use **for** when you state the second part of a ratio. *About nine women have lost their jobs for every five men.*

15 PREP You can use **for** when you say that someone or something is surprising in relation to other aspects of them. *She wore rather too much make-up for her age.*

16 PREP If you are **for** something, you are in favour of it. *There was a majority of 294 for war, with only 6 voting against.*

17 CONJ **For** is sometimes used to mean 'because'; an old-fashioned use. *This was where he spent his free time, for he had nowhere else to go.*

● **For** is used these phrases. ● You use an expression such as **for the first time** when you are saying how many times or on which occasion something has happened. *The guide returned for the third time.* ● If you are **all for** something, you are very much in favour of it. ● **as for**: see **as**. ● **but for**: see **but**. ● **for all**: see **all**.

forage /fɒrɪdʒ/ **forages, foraging, foraged**

1 V When animals or people **forage**, they search for food. *They had to hunt and forage to stay alive... The two were attempting to forage for food near the village of Firanc.*

2 V A If you **forage** for something, you search busily for it.

foray /fɒreɪ/ **forays**

1 NC If a group of soldiers make a **foray** into an area, they make a quick attack there, usually in order to steal supplies. *The rebels use the jungle as a base from which to launch forays into Batticaloa itself.*

2 NC If you make a **foray** into a new area of activity or interest, you start to become involved in it. *This wasn't her first foray into singing... Mr Gorbachov has made tentative forays into capitalist methods.*

forbade /fəbæd, fəbeɪd/

Forbade is the past tense of **forbid**.

forbear /fɔːbeə/, **forbears, forbearing, forbore, forborne**

V If you **forbear** from doing something, you do not do it although you have the opportunity or the right to do it; a formal word. *The military forbore from taking over government entirely... He forbore to use them in that way, for they were his friends.*

forbearance /fɔːbeərəns/

NU **Forbearance** is patience and kindness; a formal word. *...urging them to display greater patience and forbearance.*

forbearing /fɔːbeərɪŋ/

ADJ Someone who is **forbearing** is patient and kind; a formal word. *She remembers her mother as mild and forbearing.*

forbid /fəbɪd/, **forbids, forbidding, forbade, forbidden**

1 V O If you **forbid** someone to do something, you order them not to do it. *I forbid you to tell her.*

2 V O If something **forbids** an event or course of action, it makes it impossible for it to happen; a literary use. *Mexico City's altitude forbids such exertions.*

forbidden /fəbɪdn/

1 ADJ PRED If something is **forbidden**, you are not

allowed to do it or have it. *It is forbidden to bathe in the sea here... Indoor football is forbidden.*
2 ADJ A **forbidden** place is one that you are not allowed to visit or enter. *...forbidden ground.*
3 ADJ A **forbidden** subject is one that you must not mention. *The multi-party system mustn't be a forbidden theme. We must talk about it.*

forbidden fruit, forbidden fruits
N UorNC **Forbidden fruit** is a source of pleasure that involves breaking a rule or doing something that you are not supposed to do. *Some people might still prefer the taste of forbidden fruit... He could fall in love only with forbidden fruit, with women who were married or engaged... The authorities had created an attractive 'forbidden fruit'.*

forbidding /fəbɪdɪŋ/
ADJ Someone or something that is **forbidding** has a severe and unfriendly appearance. *...a bleak, forbidding stretch of grey water.*

force /fɔːs/ **forces, forcing, forced**
1 VO If you **force** someone to do something, you make them do it, although they are unwilling. *They forced him to resign... She forced herself to kiss her mother's cheek... Around fifty-thousand children have been forced into such schemes and made to work against their will.* ◆ **forced** ADJ ATTRIB *One of their planes did make a forced landing. ...forced labour.*
2 VO If a situation or event **forces** you to do something, it makes it necessary for you to do it. *Weekend gales forced him to change his plans... Technical problems on board the American space shuttle have forced astronauts to abandon the first of their planned experiments... An eye injury forced him to retire for three years.*
3 VOA If you **force** something into a particular position, you use a lot of strength to make it move there. *I forced his head back... Topson forced open the tin of bacon... They forced David into a small room.*
4 VO If you **force** a lock, door, or safe, you break the lock in order to open it. *They had to force the lock on the trunk.*
5 NU **Force** is the use of physical violence or strength. *We have renounced the use of force to settle our disputes... I hit him with all the force I could muster.*
6 NCorNU A **force** in physics is the pulling or pushing effect that one thing has on another. *...magnetic forces... If force is applied to the lock it will be absorbed.*
7 NC Someone or something that is a **force** in a situation has a great effect or influence on it. *Britain is re-establishing itself as a powerful force in world affairs... The 14-nation Cairns group has emerged as the driving force behind the reforms.*
8 NC A **force** is also an organized group of soldiers or other armed people. *...the United States armed forces... Security forces were patrolling the streets. ...a guerrilla force.*
● **Force** is used in these phrases. ● If you **force** your **way** into a place, you succeed in getting there although there are people, things or problems that are trying to prevent you from doing so, or are in your way. *The thieves forced their way in through a first floor window. ...attempting to force his way into territory sealed off from the outside world.* ● If you do something from **force of habit**, you do it because you have always done it in the past. *Many of them stayed from force of habit until the shooting began.* ● A law or system that is **in force** exists or is being used. *A state of emergency is now in force... The new liberal passport law technically doesn't come into force until September the first.* ● If people do something **in force**, they do it in large numbers. *Animal rights campaigners turned up in force... Tanks and soldiers were out in force last night.* ● If you **join forces** with someone, you work together to achieve a common aim or purpose. *In South Wales, the government has joined forces with the local authorities... Six Western countries have joined forces to try to halt the spread of advanced missile technology.*

forced /fɔːst/
1 ADJ ATTRIB A **forced** action is one that you only do because you have no choice. *They promised to abolish forced labour.*
2 ADJ Something that is **forced** does not happen naturally and easily. *...a forced smile.*

force-feed, force-feeds, force-feeding, force-fed
VO If you **force-feed** a person or animal, you make them eat or drink by pushing food or drink down their throat. *Prisoners who went on hunger strike were force-fed.*

forceful /fɔːsfl/
1 ADJ Someone who is **forceful** expresses their opinions in a strong and confident way. *...a forceful and assertive man.* ◆ **forcefully** ADV *Her views were forcefully expressed.*
2 ADJ Something that is **forceful** causes you to think or feel something very strongly. *...a forceful reminder of the risks involved.*

forceps /fɔːseps/
N PL A pair of **forceps** is an instrument consisting of two long narrow arms which is used by a doctor for holding things. *...artery forceps.*

forcible /fɔːsəbl/
1 ADJ ATTRIB **Forcible** actions involve physical force or violence. *...the forcible imposition of military control.* ◆ **forcibly** ADV *Children were taken forcibly from their mothers.*
2 ADJ ATTRIB A **forcible** reminder, example, or statement is very powerful or emphatic. *The survey made certain very forcible recommendations.* ◆ **forcibly** ADV *This point has been forcibly expressed by Tories.*

ford /fɔːd/ **fords, fording, forded**
VO If you **ford** a stream or river, you cross it by walking or driving through a shallow part of it. *They used bulldozers to level the bank to make it easier to ford the river by car.* ► Also NC *We'll have to walk downstream and see if we can find a ford, or a boatman who will take us across.*

Ford, Gerald /dʒerəld fɔːd/
Gerald Ford was President of the United States from 1974 to 1977. He is a member of the Republican Party and was a member of the House of Representatives from 1949 to 1973. He was appointed by Richard Nixon as Vice President in 1973 and became President in 1974 when Richard Nixon resigned. He was the first unelected holder of these posts. Born: 1913.

fore /fɔː/
When something or someone comes **to the fore**, they suddenly become important or popular. *The issue of civil rights had come to the fore.*

forearm /fɔːrɑːm/ **forearms**
NC Your **forearms** are the parts of your arms between your elbows and your wrists. *...disorders affecting the shoulder, elbow, forearm, wrist, hand and finger.*

forebear /fɔːbeə/ **forebears**
NC Your **forebears** are your ancestors; a literary word. *...the lands from which their forebears had been driven.*

foreboding /fɔːbəudɪŋ/ **forebodings**
N UorNC **Foreboding** is a strong feeling that something terrible is going to happen. *Tim's absence filled her with foreboding. ...dismal forebodings.*

forecast /fɔːkɑːst/, **forecasts, forecasting, forecasted.**
The past tense and past participle of the verb can be either **forecasted** or **forecast**.
1 NC A **forecast** is a prediction of what is expected to happen in the future. *...forecasts of military involvement in British politics. ...the weather forecast.*
2 VO If you **forecast** future events, you say what you think is going to happen. *Some warm weather had been forecast.*

foreclose /fɔːkləuz/ **forecloses, foreclosing, foreclosed**
V If the person or organization that lent someone money **forecloses**, they take possession of the property that was bought with the borrowed money, for example because regular repayments have not been made; a technical term. *My bank foreclosed on me.*

forecourt /fɔːkɔːt/ **forecourts**
NC The **forecourt** of a large building is an open area

at the front. *...the forecourt of the railway station.*
...an elderly forecourt salesman in a petrol station.

forefather /fɔːfɑːðə/ **forefathers**
NC Your **forefathers** are your ancestors, especially
your male ancestors; a literary word. *...the land*
which my forefathers paid for in instalments of blood.

forefinger /fɔːfɪŋgə/ **forefingers**
NC Your **forefinger** is the finger next to your thumb.
...twirling a lock of his hair around his forefinger.

forefoot /fɔːfʊt/ **forefeet**
NC A four-legged animal's **forefeet** are its two front
feet. *It swims by paddling with its webbed forefeet*
and steering with its hind feet.

forefront /fɔːfrʌnt/
N SING Someone or something that is in the **forefront** or
at the **forefront** of an activity is important in its
development. *The Save the Children Fund has been in*
the forefront of the worldwide campaign to try and
improve conditions... British meteorologists continue to
be at the forefront of this kind of research.

forego /fɔːgəʊ/ **foregoes, foregoing, forewent,**
foregone; also spelt **forgo.**
VO If you **forego** something, you give it up or do not
insist on having it; a formal word. *Lilian agreed to*
forego her holiday.

foregoing /fɔːgəʊɪŋ/
ADJ ATTRIB You can use **foregoing** refer to something
that has just been said; a formal word. *...the*
foregoing analysis. ► Also N SING *In the foregoing we*
have seen how people differ in their approach to
problems.

foregone /fɔːgɒn/
If the result of something is **a foregone conclusion**, it
is certain what the result will be. *The outcome was*
assumed to be a foregone conclusion.

foreground /fɔːgraʊnd/
N SING The **foreground** of a picture is the part that
seems nearest to you. *...Constable's 'The Cornfield' in*
the foreground of which lies a boy drinking water from
a stream.

forehand /fɔːhænd/ **forehands**
NC A **forehand** is a shot in tennis or squash in which
the palm of your hand faces the direction in which you
are hitting the ball. *...accurate first serves and*
forehand passing shots.

forehead /fɒrɪd, fɔːhed/ **foreheads**
NC Your **forehead** is the flat area at the front of your
head above your eyebrows and below where your hair
grows. *He wiped his forehead with his hand.*

foreign /fɒrɪn/
1 ADJ Something that is **foreign** belongs or relates to a
country that is not your own. *...a policy of restricting*
foreign imports. ...children from foreign countries.
2 ADJ ATTRIB A **foreign** minister is a government
minister who deals with matters involving other
countries besides his or her own. *...talks with the*
Soviet Foreign Minister, Mr Shevardnadze. ...Labour's
foreign affairs spokesman, Mr Gerald Kaufman.
3 ADJ ATTRIB A **foreign** object has got into something,
usually by accident, and should not be there; a formal
use. *...food containing foreign matter.*
4 ADJ You can say that something is **foreign** to a
person or thing when it is unknown to them or not
typical of them; a formal use. *...that strange gloomy*
mood that was so foreign to him.

foreign body, foreign bodies
NC A **foreign body** is an object that has got into
something else, usually by accident, and should not be
in it; a formal expression. *...a complaint about a*
foreign body in some food.

foreigner /fɒrɪnə/ **foreigners**
NC You refer to someone as a **foreigner** when they
belong to a country that is not your own. *More than a*
million foreigners visit the USA every year.

foreign exchange
1 N+N or N PL The **foreign exchange** markets are the
systems by which one country's currency is changed
into another country's currency. *In the City the*
foreign exchange markets were calm again after
Friday's hectic trading. ...the latest news from the
stock markets and foreign exchanges... The dollar has
fallen on the foreign exchanges.

2 NU **Foreign exchange** is also one country's currency
which is held by another country. *The country now*
has only two months' worth of foreign exchange left in
its banks... Taiwan had over $50,000 million in foreign
exchange in the bank.

foreign national, foreign nationals
NC You use **foreign national** to refer to someone who
is staying in a country other than the country of which
they are a citizen. *Other attempts are underway to*
secure the release of foreign nationals... Foreign
nationals said there had been a fierce battle for the
town over the weekend.

Foreign Office
N PROP The **Foreign Office** is the government
department, especially in Britain, which has
responsibility for the government's dealings and
relations with foreign governments. *A Foreign Office*
spokesman said Britain would look forward to doing
business with such a government.

foreknowledge /fɔːnɒlɪdʒ/
NU **Foreknowledge** is knowledge of an event or
situation before it actually happens; a formal word.
He had foreknowledge of the plot and he took
advantage of it.

foreleg /fɔːleg/ **forelegs**
NC The **forelegs** of an animal are its two front legs. *It*
has short silky fur, powerful forelegs, and a stumpy
tail.

forelock /fɔːlɒk/ **forelocks**
1 NC A **forelock** is a piece of hair that falls over your
forehead. *People often used to pull their forelocks to*
show respect for other people of a higher class than
they were. People began to move aside, touching their
forelocks.
2 If you say that one person **tugs their forelock** to
another person, you mean that the first person shows
the second person too much respect or is unnecessarily
worried about their opinions. *The decision to sack*
their technicians means they have stopped tugging
their forelocks to the unions.

foreman /fɔːmən/ **foremen** /fɔːmən/
1 NC A **foreman** is a person who is in charge of a
group of workers. *Alf Sensen has been the foreman in*
charge of the Corkscrew ride for the past 7 years.
2 NC The **foreman** of the jury is their leader. *The*
foreman of the jury, one of the three woman jurors,
pronounced the verdicts as the charges were read out
one at a time.

foremost /fɔːməʊst/
1 ADJ The **foremost** of a group of things is the most
important or best. *...India's foremost centre for hand-*
made shoes.
2 **First and foremost** means more than anything else.
Rugby is first and foremost a team game.

forename /fɔːneɪm/ **forenames**
NC Your **forenames** are your first names, as opposed
to your surname; a formal word. *...her fondness for*
outlandish forenames.

forensic /fərɛnsɪk/
ADJ ATTRIB When a **forensic** analysis is done, objects
are examined scientifically in order to discover
information about a crime. *...forensic tests for*
detecting the presence of blood.

forepart /fɔːpɑːt/ **foreparts**
NC The **forepart** of something, especially an animal, is
the front part of it; a formal word. *The forepart and*
head remain raised.

foreplay /fɔːpleɪ/
NU **Foreplay** is an activity such as kissing and
stroking which takes place before sexual intercourse.

forerunner /fɔːrʌnə/ **forerunners**
NC The **forerunner** of something is a similar thing that
existed before it. *...the forerunners of the*
International Socialists.

foresee /fɔːsiː/ **foresees, foreseeing, foresaw,**
foreseen
VO or V-REPORT If you **foresee** something, you believe
that it is going to happen. *Do you foresee any*
problems with the new system?... It has forced the
alliance to adapt to circumstances that were not
foreseen in December 1989... It was possible to foresee
that the coming winter would be a hard one.

foreseeable /fɔːˈsiːəbl/
When you talk about **the foreseeable future**, you are referring to the period of time in the future during which it is possible to say what will happen. *Nobody is likely to find a cure in the foreseeable future.*

foreshadow /fɔːˈʃædəʊ/ **foreshadows, foreshadowing, foreshadowed**
VO If one thing **foreshadows** another, it suggests that the other thing will happen. *These later movements had been foreshadowed in much of the work of the late 1950s.*

foreshore /fɔːˈʃɔː/ **foreshores**
NC The **foreshore** is the part of the shore that is between the points reached by the high tide and the low tide. *...collecting shells on a strip of foreshore.*

foreshorten /fɔːˈʃɔːtn/ **foreshortens, foreshortening, foreshortened**
VO Something that **is foreshortened** is drawn or seen from such an angle that its two ends appear closer together than they really are. ♦ **foreshortened** ADJ *...the foreshortened bulks of two old women, seen from above.*

foresight /ˈfɔːsaɪt/
NU **Foresight** is the ability to see what is likely to happen, which is shown in the action that someone takes. *He showed remarkable foresight. ...a lack of foresight.*

foreskin /ˈfɔːskɪn/ **foreskins**
NC A man's **foreskin** is the skin that covers the end of his penis.

forest /ˈfɒrɪst/ **forests**
1 NCorNU A **forest** is a large area where trees grow close together. *...plans for the preservation of tropical rain forests. ...a clearing in the forest. ...a primitive paradise of swamp and forest.*
2 NC A **forest** of tall, narrow objects is a group of them standing or sticking upright. *Generals lined up, behind walls of multi-coloured medals and a forest of salutes.*

forestall /fɔːˈstɔːl/ **forestalls, forestalling, forestalled**
VO If you **forestall** someone, you realize what they are likely to do and prevent them from doing it. *There were heavy police patrols to forestall any repetition of the riots in February.*

forester /ˈfɒrɪstə/ **foresters**
NC A **forester** is a person whose job is to look after the trees in a forest and to plant new ones. *A local forester started to encourage people to plant long, straight lines of trees.*

forestry /ˈfɒrɪstri/
NU **Forestry** is the science or skill of growing trees in forests. *...a social forestry programme of replanting and controls on cutting.*

foretaste /ˈfɔːteɪst/
N SING+*of* You say that an event is a **foretaste** of a future situation when it suggests to you what that future situation will be like. *The episode was a foretaste of the bitter struggle that was to come.*

foretell /fɔːˈtel/ **foretells, foretelling, foretold**
VOorV-REPORT If you **foretell** something, you say correctly that it will happen in the future; a literary word. *The Almanack claims to have foretold the atomic bomb explosion at Hiroshima... There have been many prophets who have foretold the end of the world... Who ever foretell that Paul would turn traitor?*

forethought /ˈfɔːθɔːt/
NU **Forethought** is the practice of thinking carefully about what will be needed, or about what the consequences of something will be. *With a bit of forethought, life can be made a lot easier.*

foretold /fɔːˈtəʊld/
Foretold is the past participle of **foretell**.

forever /fərˈevə/. The form **for ever** is also used, except for the meaning in paragraph 3.
1 ADV Something that will happen or continue **forever** will always happen or continue. *They thought that their empire would last forever.*
2 ADV Something that has gone **forever** has gone and will never reappear. *This innocence is lost forever.*
3 ADV If you say that someone is **forever** doing something, you mean that they do it very often; used

in informal English showing disapproval. *Babbage was forever spotting errors in their calculations.*

forewarn /fɔːˈwɔːn/ **forewarns, forewarning, forewarned**
VOorVO-REPORT If you **forewarn** someone, you warn them that something is going to happen. *Mr Baker said that the Chinese had been forewarned... Prison chiefs were forewarned of the escape plot... We were forewarned that the food would be unusual.*

forewent /fɔːˈwent/
Forewent is the past tense of **forego**.

foreword /ˈfɔːwɜːd/ **forewords**
NC The **foreword** to a book is an introduction by the author or by someone else. *In his foreword, the editor looks at the trends and changes in today's aircraft business.*

forfeit /ˈfɔːfɪt/ **forfeits, forfeiting, forfeited**
1 VO If you **forfeit** a right, privilege, or possession, you have to give it up because you have done something wrong. *He has forfeited the right to be the leader of this nation... If she doesn't compete then she may forfeit an Olympic place.*
2 NC A **forfeit** is something that you have to give up, or an unpleasant task that you have to perform because you have done something wrong. *...his reluctance to exact from them a forfeit they could not pay.*

forfeiture /ˈfɔːfɪtʃə/
NU **Forfeiture** is the action of forfeiting something. *If convicted, the couple face twenty years' imprisonment together with the forfeiture of at least $250,000,000 of personal property.*

forgave /fəˈgeɪv/
Forgave is the past tense of **forgive**.

forge /fɔːdʒ/ **forges, forging, forged**
1 VO If someone **forges** banknotes, documents, or paintings, they copy them or make false ones in order to deceive people. *I learnt how to forge someone else's signature.*
2 VO If you **forge** an alliance or relationship, you succeed in creating it. *They forged links with the French Communist Party.*
3 NC A **forge** is a place where metal things such as horseshoes are made. *They have commissioned a forge to construct the iron components.*

forge ahead PHRASAL VERB If you **forge ahead**, you make a lot of progress, or you make more progress than someone else. *He seems determined to forge ahead, at least on higher productivity.*

forger /ˈfɔːdʒə/ **forgers**
NC A **forger** is someone who forges things such as banknotes, documents, or paintings. *The master forger had inadvertently left the 'u' out of 'Banque de France'.*

forgery /ˈfɔːdʒəri/ **forgeries**
1 NU **Forgery** is the crime of forging things such as banknotes, documents, or paintings. *...awaiting trial on charges of forgery and embezzlement.*
2 NC You can refer to a forged banknote, document, or painting as a **forgery**. *Handwriting experts contend that it is a manifest forgery.*

forget /fəˈget/ **forgets, forgetting, forgot, forgotten**
1 VOorV-REPORT If you **forget** something or **forget** how to do something, you cannot think of it, although you knew it in the past. *I never forget a face... I forgot what I was going to say... She had forgotten how to ride a bicycle... It's sometimes forgotten that what we're talking about is only the Northern half of the country.* ♦ **forgotten** ADJ *...a forgotten event in her past.*
2 VOorV If you **forget** to do something, you do not remember to do it. *They forgot to apply for American visas... I forgot to mention that John is a musician.*
3 VO If you **forget** something that you had intended to bring with you, you do not remember to bring it. *Sorry to disturb you—I forgot my key.*
4 VO You also say that someone **forgets** something when they deliberately do not think about it any more. *If you want my advice I think you ought to forget her.* ● You say **forget it** to someone as a way of telling them not to worry or bother about something that you have done to help them or something they

have done wrong. *'What do I owe you for lunch?'*— *'Forget it.'*

5 V-REFL If you **forget** yourself, you behave in an uncontrolled or unacceptable way, usually because you are feeling very emotional. *'Oh darling!' cried Judy, forgetting herself.*

forgetful /fəɡɛtfl/
ADJ Someone who is **forgetful** often forgets things. *I had been hopelessly vague, forgetful and sloppy.* ♦ **forgetfulness** NU *...his growing forgetfulness.*

forget-me-not, forget-me-nots
NC A **forget-me-not** is a small plant with tiny blue flowers. *Wild forget-me-nots are blooming along woodland paths.*

forgettable /fəɡɛtəbl/
ADJ Something that is **forgettable** is not unusual or special in any way. *It was a little bit of football history in what was otherwise a thoroughly mundane and forgettable second division match. ...thousands of entirely forgettable men working at obscure jobs in the city.*

forgivable /fəɡɪvəbl/
ADJ If you say that something is **forgivable**, you mean that you can understand it and can forgive it. *Her lack of sympathy was perhaps forgivable.*

forgive /fəɡɪv/ **forgives, forgiving, forgave, forgiven**
1 V O or V O O If you **forgive** someone who has done something wrong, you stop being angry with them. *I'll never forgive you for what you did... I forgave him everything.*
2 V-PASS If you say that someone could **be forgiven** for doing a particular thing, you mean that you can understand the reasons for such behaviour. *We could be forgiven for thinking that we were still in London.*

forgiveness /fəɡɪvnəs/
NU If you ask someone for their **forgiveness**, you are asking them to forgive you for something wrong that you have done.

forgiving /fəɡɪvɪŋ/
ADJ Someone who is **forgiving** is willing to forgive people. *...a forgiving father.*

forgo /fɔːɡəʊ/. See **forego**.

forgot /fəɡɒt/
Forgot is the past tense of **forget**.

forgotten /fəɡɒtn/
Forgotten is the past participle of **forget**.

fork /fɔːk/ **forks, forking, forked**
1 NC A **fork** is a tool that you eat food with. It consists of three or four prongs on the end of a handle. *The milk shakes could be mixed with a fork as well. ...using a knife and fork.*
2 NC A **fork** is also a tool that you dig your garden with. It consists of three or four long prongs attached to a long handle. *...a scheme to share tools such as spades and forks.*
3 NC A **fork** in a road, path, or river is the point at which it divides into two parts in the shape of a 'Y'. *When you come to the fork turn left.*
4 V If something such as a path or river **forks**, it divides into two parts in the shape of a 'Y'. *...where the road forks.*

fork out PHRASAL VERB If you **fork out** for something, you pay for it; an informal expression. *...the fortune I had already had to fork out on her education.*

fork over PHRASAL VERB To **fork over** means the same as to **fork out**; used in American English. *If you're a smoker you now have to fork over between five and seven dollars for a pack of cigarettes.*

forked /fɔːkt/
ADJ Something that is **forked** divides into two parts in the shape of a 'Y'. *...an adder's forked tongue.*

forked lightning
NU **Forked lightning** is lightning that is seen as jagged lines of light dividing into two or more parts near the ground. *Suddenly there was a flash and a zig-zag of forked lightning.*

fork-lift truck, fork-lift trucks
NC or N+N A **fork-lift** or a **fork-lift truck** is a small vehicle with two movable arms on the front that are used to lift heavy loads. *They're loading up and down a ladder and haven't the space to use a fork-lift.*

forlorn /fəlɔːn/
1 ADJ If you are **forlorn**, you are lonely and unhappy. *The child looked very forlorn. ...a forlorn cry.* ♦ **forlornly** ADV *He was standing forlornly by the ticket office.*
2 ADJ ATTRIB A **forlorn** attempt or hope has no chance of success. *...the forlorn hope of achieving full employment.*

form /fɔːm/ **forms, forming, formed**
1 NC+SUPP A **form** of something is a type or kind of it. *He begged for any form of transport that would take him to the ferry... Leukaemia is a rare form of cancer... They speak a form of Turkish.*
2 NC The **form** in which a particular thing occurs is one of several ways that it can be expressed. *The broadcast took the form of an interview... There was still twenty-eight days to decide what form the action should take... Half the money will be for humanitarian assistance in the form of cash for housing, emergency public works and loans for businesses.*
3 V-ERG When a particular shape **forms** or is **formed** people or things move or are arranged so that this shape is made. *Long queues had formed... They formed a ring... The men formed themselves into a line.*
4 NC The **form** of something is its shape. *The middle finger was touching the end of the thumb in the form of a letter O.*
5 NC You can refer to someone or something that you see as a **form**; a literary use. *She gazed with deep affection at his slumbering form... We saw a slender ghostly form.*
6 VC If something **forms** a thing with a particular structure or function, it has this structure or function. *The chair folds back to form a couch. ...red rocks forming a kind of cave.*
7 VC The things or people that **form** a particular thing are what it consists of. *The contents of the house will form the basis of a major exhibition... Breast milk continues to form part of the diet for at least 13 weeks... Germans form the country's second largest minority.*
8 VO If you **form** an organization, group, or company, you start it. *The League was formed in 1959.*
9 V-ERG When something **forms** or is **formed**, it begins to exist. *Features like mountains, valleys and beaches are forming slowly all the time... The islands are volcanic and were formed comparatively recently.*
10 NC A **form** is a piece of paper with questions printed on it. You write the answers on the same piece of paper. *...application forms... Fill in this form.*
11 NC In a school, a **form** is a class, or all the classes containing children of a similar age. *...the fifth form.*
● **Form** is used in these phrases. ● Someone who is **on form** is performing their usual activity very well. Someone who is **off form** is not performing as well as they usually do. *Lester Piggott is also on form... Noah's serve was off form in the first two sets but it picked up later.* ● If someone's behaviour is **true to form**, it is typical of them. *Watson, true to form, made an instant decision.*

formal /fɔːml/
1 ADJ **Formal** speech or behaviour is correct, rather than relaxed and friendly, and is used especially in official situations. *The letter was stiff and formal.* ♦ **formally** ADV *Everyone was formally lined up to meet the king.* ♦ **formality** /fɔːmæləti/ NU *The elders conversed with strict formality.*
2 ADJ ATTRIB A **formal** statement or action is one that is done officially. *No formal declaration of war had been made.* ♦ **formally** ADV *He had already formally announced his candidacy.*
3 ADJ **Formal** occasions are ones at which people wear smart clothes and behave correctly rather than casually. **Formal** clothes are clothes suitable for formal occasions. *...a formal dinner.* ♦ **formally** ADV *He dressed rather formally.*
4 ADJ A **formal** garden or room is arranged in a neat and regular way. *...formal flowerbeds.*
5 ADJ ATTRIB **Formal** education or training is given officially, usually in a school or college. *...formal qualifications.*

6 See also **formality**.

formaldehyde /fɔːmældɪhaɪd/
NU **Formaldehyde** is a strong-smelling gas, used especially to preserve specimens in biology. ...*such chemicals as formaldehyde and benzene.*

formalise /fɔːməlaɪz/. See **formalize**.

formalism /fɔːməlɪzəm/
NU **Formalism** is a style, especially in art, in which great attention is paid to the outward form or appearance of things rather than to their inner reality or meaning. *I think that as a doctrine formalism has done damage.* ◆ **formalist, formalists** NC *My quarrel with the formalists is about the nature of sculpture itself.*

formality /fɔːmælətɪ/ **formalities**
1 NC **Formalities** are formal actions that are carried out on particular occasions. *The pre-funeral formalities had to be attended to.*
2 NC If you say that a particular action is a **formality**, you mean that it must be done but it will not change what is being arranged in any way. *Official acceptance was merely a formality... The decision is seen there as a formality, and is not expected to have much effect in local financial markets.*
3 See also **formal**.

formalize /fɔːməlaɪz/ **formalizes, formalizing, formalized**; also spelt **formalise**.
VO If you **formalize** a plan or arrangement, you make it official. *Their marriage vows will be formalized.*

format /fɔːmæt/ **formats**
NC+SUPP The **format** of something is the way it is arranged and presented. *I think there's little chance that either will be continued in the same format... They failed to reach an accord on a format for national elections... Nine out of ten people chose the VHS format for home video recorders in preference to Betamax.*

formation /fɔːmeɪʃn/ **formations**
1 NU+SUPP The **formation** of something is its start or creation. ...*the formation of the United Nations.* ...*the physical process of rock formation.* ...*the formation of new ideas.*
2 NU If things are in a particular **formation**, they are arranged in a particular pattern. ...*aircraft flying in formation.*
3 NC A rock **formation** or a cloud **formation** is rock or clouds of a particular shape. ...*a mysterious cloud formation.*

formative /fɔːmətɪv/
ADJ ATTRIB A **formative** period in your life has an important influence on your character and attitudes. *Bettelheim's formative years as an adolescent were spent in Vienna... The work with Miles Davis was the most formative for Hancock as a musician.*

former /fɔːmə/
1 ADJ ATTRIB **Former** is used to indicate what someone or something used to be, but no longer is. ...*former President Richard Nixon.* ...*their former home.*
2 ADJ ATTRIB If something happened or existed in **former** days or **former** years, it happened or existed in the past. ...*a selection of items published in former years.*
3 N SING or N PL When two people or things have just been mentioned, you can refer to the first of them as the **former**. *The former is approved by nearly all scientists and doctors involved... The former believe in a strong centralized government.* ► Also ADJ *Lack of space forbids the former alternative.*

formerly /fɔːməli/
ADV If something happened **formerly**, it happened in the past. *Some of my salesmen formerly worked for this company.*

Formica /fɔːmaɪkə/
NU **Formica** is a hard plastic that is used for covering surfaces such as kitchen worktops; **Formica** is a trademark. ...*the coffee-stained formica of the local student union bar.*

formidable /fɔːmɪdəbl, fəmɪdəbl/
1 ADJ Something that is **formidable** is difficult to deal with or overcome. *He had earned the reputation of being a formidable opponent.* ◆ **formidably** ADV ...*formidably equipped armies.*

2 ADJ **Formidable** also means impressive because it is so good or great. ...*the formidable army of brains that are at the Prime Minister's disposal.*

formless /fɔːmləs/
ADJ Something that is **formless** does not have a clear shape or structure; a formal word. *The movie is formless and shapeless.* ...*formless chaos.*

form letter, form letters
NC A **form letter** is a standardized letter that is copied and sent to many people; used in American English. *It includes a form letter that can be signed, clipped and mailed... The State Department would send a two paragraph letter back which was a form letter.*

formula /fɔːmjʊlə/ **formulae** /fɔːmjʊliː/ or **formulas**
1 NC A **formula** is a group of letters, numbers, or other symbols which represents a scientific or mathematical rule. *He knew the formula for converting kilometres into miles.*
2 NC The **formula** for a substance is an abbreviation showing what other substances, in what proportions, it contains. ...*changing the formula of the polypropylene tubes.*
3 NC A **formula** is a plan that is made as a way of dealing with a problem. ...*a peace formula.*
4 NU+SUPP Infant **formula** or baby **formula** is powder that can be mixed with water to make food for babies; used in American English. *Young mothers often have no choice in whether or not to buy infant formula.*

formulaic /fɔːmjʊleɪɪk/
ADJ A **formulaic** way of saying something has been used many times before in similar situations; a literary word. *And doesn't that lead to maybe some formulaic type of stories?*

formulate /fɔːmjʊleɪt/ **formulates, formulating, formulated**
1 VO If you **formulate** a plan or proposal, you develop it, thinking about the details carefully. *We had formulated our own strategy.* ◆ **formulation** /fɔːmjʊleɪʃn/ **formulations** NU or NC ...*the formulation of a common foreign policy... Not everyone agrees with this formulation.*
2 VO If you **formulate** a thought or opinion, you express it in words. *The statement, formulated by the working group, condemns in harsh language certain individuals and groups.*

fornicate /fɔːnɪkeɪt/ **fornicates, fornicating, fornicated**
V-RECIP To **fornicate** means to have sex with someone who you are not married to; a literary word used showing disapproval.

forsake /fəseɪk/ **forsakes, forsaking, forsook, forsaken**; a literary word.
1 VO If you **forsake** someone, you stop helping them or stop looking after them. *Their leaders have forsaken them.*
2 VO If you **forsake** something, you stop doing or having it. ...*if you forsake religion.*

forsaken /fəseɪkn/
ADJ A **forsaken** place is no longer lived in or no longer looked after; a literary word. ...*a dusty, forsaken prairie village.*

forswear /fɔːsweə/ **forswears, forswearing, forswore, forsworn**
VO If you **forswear** something, you stop doing it, having it, or using it, or you promise that you will; a formal word. *Harold had forsworn fighting.*

forsythia /fɔːsaɪθɪə/
NU **Forsythia** is a bush that has yellow flowers on it in the spring before the leaves have grown. ...*a feathery branch of forsythia... The forsythia bloomed in the blackthorn winter.*

fort /fɔːt/ **forts**
NC A **fort** is a strong building that is used as a military base for soldiers to defend a particular area. *The prison at Walata is housed in an old colonial fort in the desert.*

Fort-de-France /fɔː də frɑːns/
Fort-de-France is the capital of Martinique and its largest city. Population: 102,000 (1990).

forte /fɔːteɪ/ **fortes**
NC+SUPP You can say that an activity is your **forte** if you are very good at it. *Cooking is hardly my forte.*

forth /fɔːθ/; a literary word.

1 ADV To go **forth** from a place means to leave it. *The goats came bounding forth from their pens.*
2 ADV When something is brought **forth**, it is brought out into a place where you can see it. *He reached into his briefcase and brought forth a file.*
3 and so forth: see **so. back and forth:** see **back.**

forthcoming /fɔːθkʌmɪŋ/; a formal word.

1 ADJ ATTRIB A **forthcoming** event is going to happen soon. *...the forthcoming election.*
2 ADJ PRED When something such as help or information is **forthcoming**, it is provided or made available. *No evidence was forthcoming.*
3 ADJ PRED If someone is **forthcoming**, they willingly give you information when you ask. *He was not forthcoming on the way in which he had risen to power.*

forthright /fɔːθraɪt/

ADJ Someone who is **forthright** says clearly and strongly what they think. *...his forthright opposition to the war.*

forthwith /fɔːθwɪθ/

ADV **Forthwith** means immediately; a literary word. *He would take up his new duties forthwith.*

fortieth /fɔːtiəθ/

ADJ The **fortieth** item in a series is the one that you count as number forty. *...NATO's fortieth anniversary.*

fortification /fɔːtɪfɪkeɪʃn/ **fortifications**; a formal word.

1 NC **Fortifications** are buildings, walls, or ditches that are built to protect a place against attack. *...coastal defence fortifications.*
2 NU The **fortification** of a place is the act of fortifying it. *...the fortification of Florence.*

fortified wine, fortified wines

NC or NU **Fortified wines** are various types of alcoholic drink that are made by mixing wine with a small amount of brandy or strong alcohol. *...brandies and fortified wines such as ports and sherries.*

fortify /fɔːtɪfaɪ/ **fortifies, fortifying, fortified**

1 VO If people **fortify** a place, they make it stronger and less easy to attack, often by building a wall or ditch round it. *...the tiny fortified town.*
2 VO Things that **fortify** you make you feel stronger and more full of energy. *....huddled in warm coats and fortified by a tot of brandy... To fortify himself, he began thinking about how pleased his wife would be.*

fortissimo /fɔːtɪsɪməʊ/

ADV A piece of music that is played **fortissimo** is played very loudly; a technical term in music. *The band continued playing fortissimo.* ▶ Also ADJ *...a fortissimo passage of the score.*

fortitude /fɔːtɪtjuːd/

NU If someone who is in pain or danger shows **fortitude**, they do not complain and remain brave and calm; a formal word. *He hoped that the people of Pakistan would face the crisis with fortitude and calm.*

fortnight /fɔːtnaɪt/ **fortnights**

NC A **fortnight** is a period of two weeks. *I went to Rothesay for a fortnight.*

fortnightly /fɔːtnaɪtli/

ADJ ATTRIB or ADV A **fortnightly** event or magazine happens or appears once a fortnight. *...a fortnightly newspaper... The group meets fortnightly.*

fortress /fɔːtrəs/ **fortresses**

NC A **fortress** is a castle or other large strong building which is difficult for enemies to enter. *...a ten-million dollar concrete fortress laced with sophisticated security apparatus.*

fortuitous /fɔːtjuːɪtəs/

ADJ You describe an event as **fortuitous** when it happens by chance and helps someone; a formal word. *...a fortuitous discovery.*

fortunate /fɔːtʃənət/

1 ADJ Someone who is **fortunate** is lucky. *...those who are fortunate enough to get jobs.*
2 ADJ You say that an event is **fortunate** when it is lucky for someone. *It was fortunate for Mr Fox that he decided to wait.* ◆ **fortunately** ADV SEN *Fortunately she didn't mind.*

fortune /fɔːtʃuːn, fɔːtʃən/ **fortunes**

1 NU **Fortune** or good **fortune** is good luck. Ill **fortune** is bad luck. *He has since had the good fortune to be promoted.*
2 N PL+POSS If you talk about someone's **fortunes**, you are referring to the extent to which they are doing well or being successful. *In the following years, Victor's fortunes improved considerably.*
3 NC A **fortune** is a very large amount of money. *His father left him an immense fortune... His personal fortune is estimated at more than £50,000,000.*
4 When someone **tells** your **fortune**, they tell you what will happen to you in the future.

fortune-teller, fortune-tellers

NC A **fortune-teller** is someone who tells people's fortunes, often in exchange for money. *...the fortune-teller's curse that he would kill his father and marry his mother.*

forty /fɔːti/ **forties**

Forty is the number 40.

forum /fɔːrəm/ **forums**

NC A **forum** is a place or event in which people exchange ideas and discuss things. *...Parliament's role as a forum for debate.*

forward /fɔːwəd/ **forwards, forwarding, forwarded.**

Forward can be used as an adverb, an adjective, or a verb. **Forwards** is only used as an adverb.
1 ADV or ADJ ATTRIB **Forward** or **forwards** is the direction in front of you. *Suddenly she leaned forward. ...his forward movement.*
2 ADV or ADJ after N **Forward** or **forwards** is also used to indicate that something progresses or becomes more modern. *...moving society forward into a better world... Obviously it's a great step forward for you.*
3 ADV or ADJ ATTRIB If you look **forward** in time, you look into the future. *When I was your age I could only look forward. ...forward planning.* ● See also **look forward to.**
4 VO If you **forward** a letter that has been sent to someone who has moved, you send it to them at the place where they are now living.

forwarding address, forwarding addresses

NC A **forwarding address** is an address that you give to someone when you go and live somewhere else so that they can send your mail on to you. *She had gone to Spain, leaving no forwarding address.*

forward-looking

ADJ Someone who is **forward-looking** thinks about the future or has modern ideas. *As a publisher, Ernest Benn was forward-looking and imaginative.*

forwent /fɔːwent/

Forwent is the past tense of **forgo.**

fossil /fɒsl/ **fossils**

NC A **fossil** is the hardened remains of a prehistoric animal or plant, or a print that it leaves in rock.

fossil fuel, fossil fuels

N MASS **Fossil fuels** are fuels such as coal, oil, and peat that are formed from the decayed remains of plants and animals. *...carbon dioxide emissions produced by burning fossil fuels... Gas is a fossil fuel the same as oil and coal... The best way to reduce the warming of the atmosphere is to burn less fossil fuel.*

fossilize /fɒsəlaɪz/ **fossilizes, fossilizing, fossilized;** also spelt **fossilise.**

V-ERG When the remains of an animal or plant **fossilize** or **are fossilized**, they become hard, or leave a print, and form a fossil. *In time minerals will come in and fossilise the protein... The carcass floated out to sea where it was buried and fossilised... Brains do not fossilize.*

fossilized /fɒsəlaɪzd/; also spelt **fossilised.**

1 ADJ A **fossilized** animal or plant is one whose remains have become hard and formed a fossil in prehistoric times. *American geologists have found fossilised skeletons of 40 million year old whales. ...the fossilized remains of the dinosaur.*
2 ADJ If ideas, attitudes, or ways of behaving are **fossilized**, they are fixed and unlikely to change; used showing disapproval. *Efforts were made two or three years ago to breathe some new life into these fossilized organisations.*

foster /fɒstə/ **fosters, fostering, fostered**
1 ADJ ATTRIB **Foster** parents are people who officially take a child into their family for a period of time, without becoming the child's legal parents. The child is referred to as their **foster** child. *The couple must first become the twins' foster parents, and then adopt them... He would live with a foster family in Zimbabwe.*
2 V O or V If you **foster** children, you take them into your family for a period of time, without becoming their legal parents. *Bertram and Beryl Pringle have fostered three boys from Dr Barnados... The case involved a 17 month old black child who was fostered from the age of 6 days... People who can't have children of their own sometimes foster.*
3 V O If you **foster** a feeling, activity, or idea, you help it to develop. *The local council has a policy of fostering music, drama, and crafts. ...sound policies which foster confidence in both domestic and foreign investors.*

fought /fɔːt/
Fought is the past tense and past participle of **fight**.

foul /faʊl/ **fouler, foulest; fouls, fouling, fouled**
1 ADJ Something that is **foul** is dirty or smells unpleasant. *The water in the pools became tepid and foul.*
2 ADJ **Foul** language contains swear words or rude words. *...using subversive and foul language.*
3 ADJ If someone has a **foul** temper, they become angry or violent suddenly and easily.
4 If you **fall foul of** someone or something, you do something which gets you into trouble with them. *Three American technicians fell foul of the government and ended up in detention.*
5 V O If you **foul** something, you make it dirty; a formal use. *The deck would soon be fouled with blood... MPs protested and complained of the problems caused by dogs fouling the streets.*
6 NC In a game or sport, a **foul** is an action that is against the rules. *The team's record of fouls was among the worst... Two men were sent off for fouls in the second half.* ▶ Also V O or V *He has meanwhile told World Cup referees to send off any player who deliberately fouls a man in a goal scoring position... Last year's English Amateur champion Mark Rowing, fouled, giving Duggan a free ball.*
foul up PHRASAL VERB If you **foul up** something such as a plan, you spoil it by doing something wrong or stupid; an informal use. *There are 147 ways to foul up a relationship.*

foul-mouthed
ADJ If someone is **foul-mouthed**, their language is offensive and contains unacceptable words such as swear words and rude words related to sex or other bodily functions. *...eight noisy foul-mouthed women, all shouting at once.*

foul play
NU **Foul play** is criminal violence or activity that results in someone's death or other serious consequences. *The circumstances of his death suggest foul play... There was no evidence of foul play.*

foul-up, foul-ups
NC A **foul-up** is a state of disorder or trouble which is the result of mistakes or carelessness; an informal word. *The Centre hates that kind of foul-up.*

found /faʊnd/ **founds, founding, founded**
1 **Found** is the past tense and past participle of **find**.
2 V O If someone **founds** a town or an organization, they cause it to be built or to exist. *The Constituency Labour Party was founded in 1918 by Walter Ayles and others... The theatre was founded in 1720.* ● See also **founding father.**
3 V O+on or upon If something is **founded** on a particular thing, it is based on it. *...a political system founded on force... It was founded upon charity, without any settled endowment.* ● See also **well-founded.**

foundation /faʊndeɪʃn/ **foundations**
1 NC+SUPP The **foundation** of something such as a belief or way of life is the idea, attitude, or experience on which it is based. *Respect for the law is the foundation of civilised living.*
2 N PL The **foundations** of a building or other structure

are the layers of bricks or concrete below the ground that it is built on. *...concrete foundations would not be laid for the time being.*
3 N SING When a new institution or organization is created, you can refer to this event as its **foundation**. *...since the foundation of the university.*
4 NC A **foundation** is an organization which provides money for a special purpose. *...the National Foundation for Educational Research.*
5 NU If a story, idea, or argument has no **foundation**, there are no facts to prove that it is true. *The suggestion is absurd and without foundation.*

foundation course, foundation courses
NC In Britain, a **foundation course** is a course that you do at some colleges and universities in order to prepare you for a longer or more advanced course. *They have been told to begin work on foundation courses allowing people without A levels to join degree courses.*

foundation stone, foundation stones
NC A **foundation stone** is a large block of stone built into a large public building. It is usually unveiled at a ceremony when the building is complete and has words cut into it which record the event. *The foundation stone was laid by the Duke of Edinburgh.*

founder /faʊndə/ **founders, foundering, foundered**
1 NC The **founder** of a town or organization is the person who caused it to be built or exist. *...Thomas Kemp, the founder of Kemp Town.*
2 V If something **founders**, it fails; a formal use. *Without their assistance the arrangement would have foundered.*
3 V If a ship **founders**, it fills with water and sinks. *A fully laden tanker has foundered on a reef off the coast of Alaska.*

founder member, founder members
NC A **founder member** of a club, group, or organization is one of the original members. *Saudi Arabia was a founder member of the Arab Organization for Industrialization.*

founding /faʊndɪŋ/
N SING The **founding** of an organization, tradition, or club is the action of creating it. *...the fortieth anniversary of the founding of the National Health Service. ...NATO's founding charter... He is better known for being a founding member of the super group Genesis.* ● See also **found.**

founding father, founding fathers
1 NC The **founding father** of an institution, organization or idea is the person who sets it up or who first develops it; a literary expression. *...the founding fathers of the university... If economics has a founding father, it is Smith.*
2 N PL The **Founding Fathers** of the United States were the members of the American Constitutional Convention of 1787. *The clear and unambiguous intention of the founding fathers was that the American electorate should be kept as well-informed as possible.*

foundling /faʊndlɪŋ/ **foundlings**
NC A **foundling** is a baby which has been abandoned by its parents, often in a public place, and then been found by someone; an old-fashioned word.

foundry /faʊndri/ **foundries**
NC A **foundry** is a place where metal or glass is melted and formed into particular shapes. *...a railway brake block foundry near Cairo.*

fount /faʊnt/
N SING+of If you describe a person or thing as the **fount** of something, you mean that they are the best source or supply of it; a literary word. *...the Encyclopaedia Britannica, the fount of all knowledge.*

fountain /faʊntɪn/ **fountains**
NC A **fountain** is an ornamental feature in a pool which consists of a jet of water that is forced up into the air by a pump. *The square will be adorned by spectacular fountains.*

fountain pen, fountain pens
NC A **fountain pen** is a pen with a container inside which you fill with ink. *Among the relics housed in the museum is an old fountain pen and a pair of spectacles.*

four /fɔː/ **fours**
1 **Four** is the number 4.
2 If you are **on all fours**, you are crawling or leaning on your hands and knees. *Claud slipped through the hedge on all fours.*

four-letter word, four-letter words
NC **Four-letter words** are short words that people consider to be rude or offensive, usually because they refer to sex or other bodily functions. *...using four-letter words and indulging in indecencies.*

four-ply
ADJ **Four-ply** wool, rope, wood, and so on has four layers or strands.

four-poster, four-posters
N C or N+N A **four-poster** or a **four-poster bed** is a large old-fashioned bed that has a tall post at each corner and curtains that can be drawn around it. *The rooms are decked out in antique furniture and four-poster beds.*

foursome /fɔːsəm/ **foursomes**
NC A **foursome** is a group of four people. *We functioned well as a foursome.*

four-square
1 ADJ If something is **four-square**, it looks solid and square in shape. *...a four-square house, with corner turrets and battlements.*
2 ADV or ADJ Something that is **four-square** is straight and placed or balanced firmly on something. *...with his regulation chef's hat four-square on his greying clipped hair.*
3 ADJ If something is **four-square** it is strong and steady, and unlikely to be affected by changing situations. *...the four-square rock-like quality of the old religion... The armed forces are now four-square behind the democratic process.*

fourteen /fɔːtiːn/
Fourteen is the number 14.

fourteenth /fɔːtiːnθ/
ADJ The **fourteenth** item in a series is the one that you count as number fourteen.

fourth /fɔːθ/ **fourths**
1 ADJ The **fourth** item in a series is the one that you count as number four.
2 NC A **fourth** is one of four equal parts of something; used in American English. *They conceded him three-fourths or more of the spending cuts he sought.*

fourth dimension
N SING The **fourth dimension**, in physics, is time. The other three dimensions are length, breadth, and height.

Fourth of July
N SING The **Fourth of July** is a holiday in the United States when people celebrate the Declaration of Independence in 1776. *The Fourth of July has always been an occasion for displaying patriotic sentiments.*

four-wheel drive
ADJ ATTRIB A **four-wheel drive** vehicle is one in which all four wheels are connected to the engine. *Apart from the more intrepid breed of traveller equipped with a four-wheel drive vehicle, few visitors venture this far. ...the world-famous four-wheel drive Land-Rovers.*

fowl /faul/ **fowls**. The plural form can be either **fowls** or **fowl**.
NC A **fowl** is a bird, especially one that can be eaten as food. *More than two million water fowl depend upon Britain's estuaries for food and winter refuge.*

fox /fɒks/ **foxes, foxing, foxed**
1 NC A **fox** is a wild animal which looks like a dog and has reddish-brown fur. *Foxes killing lambs can cost farmers as much as five-hundred pounds a year.*
2 VO If something **foxes** you, you cannot understand it or solve it; an informal use. *We were foxed by the calculations.*

foxglove /fɒksglʌv/ **foxgloves**
NC A **foxglove** is a tall plant that has pink or white flowers shaped like bells growing up the stem. *...two of the many species of foxglove.*

foxhole /fɒkshəul/ **foxholes**
NC A **foxhole** is a small pit that soldiers dig where they can shelter from and shoot at the enemy. *...in foxholes under fire.*

foxhound /fɒkshaund/ **foxhounds**
NC A **foxhound** is a type of dog that is bred and trained for hunting foxes. *Many gamekeepers around the country manage quite well without a pack of foxhounds.*

fox-hunting
NU **Fox-hunting** is a sport in which people riding horses chase foxes across the countryside. *...fox-hunting, stag-hunting and hare coursing.*

foxy /fɒksi/ **foxier, foxiest**
1 ADJ If someone is **foxy**, they are deceitful in a clever, secretive way. *...a certain foxy gentleman... He is a foxy character, and has a few tricks yet up his sleeve.*
2 ADJ If a man describes a woman as **foxy**, he means that she is sexually attractive; used in informal American English.

foyer /fɔɪeɪ, fwaɪeɪ/ **foyers**
NC The **foyer** of a large building such as a theatre, cinema, or hotel is the large area just inside the main doors where people meet or wait. *Mr Deng emerged to greet Mr Gorbachov in the foyer of the Great Hall of the People. ...the foyer of a major hotel in Moscow.*

Fr.
1 **Fr.** is a written abbreviation for 'French' and 'franc'. *Men's Singles—Second Round: Aaron Krickstein (USA) beat Stephane Grenier (Fr).*
2 **Fr.** is also a written abbreviation for 'Father' which is used in titles before the name of a Catholic priest. *...a free thinking Catholic priest, Fr. Pat Buckley.*

fracas /frækɑː/
N SING A **fracas** is a rough, noisy quarrel or fight; a formal word. *They got involved in another fracas.*

fraction /frækʃn/ **fractions**
1 NC You can refer to a small amount or proportion of something as a **fraction** of it. *For a fraction of a second, I hesitated... The door opened a fraction.*
2 NC In arithmetic, a **fraction** is an exact division of a number. For example, $\frac{1}{4}$ and $\frac{1}{3}$ are fractions of 1.

fractional /frækʃəⁿəl/
ADJ If something is **fractional**, it is very small in size or degree. *...a fractional hesitation.*

fractionally /frækʃəⁿəli/
ADV **Fractionally** means very slightly. *They're only fractionally different.*

fractious /frækʃəs/
ADJ If someone, especially a child, is **fractious**, they become upset or angry very quickly about small unimportant things, often because they are tired; a formal word. *She was fractious with other children. ...in a fractious mood.*

fracture /fræktʃə/ **fractures, fracturing, fractured**
1 NC A **fracture** is a crack or break in something, especially a bone. *...a fracture of the left shoulder blade.*
2 V-ERG If something such as a bone **fractures** or is **fractured**, cracks appear in it or it breaks. *Osteoporosis causes the bones to fracture more easily... Valery Lioukin has fractured his arm falling off the horizontal bar.* ◆ **fractured** ADJ *...a broken leg and collar-bone and a suspected fractured skull.*

fragile /frædʒaɪl/
ADJ **Fragile** things are easily broken or harmed. *...constructions built of fragile materials. ...extremely fragile economies.* ◆ **fragility** /frədʒɪləti/ NU *...the softness and fragility of baby animals.*

fragment, fragments, fragmenting, fragmented; pronounced /frægmənt/ when it is a noun and /frægment/ when it is a verb.
1 NC A **fragment** of something is a small piece or part of it. *...a small fragment of bone... This was only a fragment out of a long conversation with John.*
2 V-ERG If something **fragments** or is **fragmented**, it breaks or separates into small pieces. *The opposition has fragmented even further with several new parties being formed... Farms are constantly being fragmented into smaller holdings.* ◆ **fragmentation** /frægmenteɪʃn/ NU *What they most want to see is the fragmentation of Ethiopia into small nations.*

fragmentary /frægməntəⁿri/
ADJ Something that is **fragmentary** is made up of small or unconnected pieces. *...the fragmentary*

evidence for this story.

fragmented /frǽgmentɪd/
ADJ Something that is **fragmented** consists of a lot of different parts which seem unconnected with each other. *It's a book that is very fragmented in its structure.*

fragrance /fréɪgrəns/ **fragrances**
NC You can refer to a sweet or pleasant smell as a **fragrance**. *The scent resembles the fragrance of a freshly opened packet of tea. ...a selection of sweet-smelling fragrances.*

fragrant /fréɪgrənt/
ADJ Something that is **fragrant** has a sweet or pleasant smell. *...fragrant flowers.*

frail /freɪl/ **frailer, frailest**
1 ADJ A **frail** person is not strong or healthy. *Visitors who have met him in recent weeks say he has been looking frail. ...a frail old man.*
2 ADJ Something that is **frail** is easily broken or damaged. *...a frail structure.*

frailty /fréɪlti/ **frailties**
1 N PLorNU If you talk about someone's **frailties** or **frailty**, you are referring to their weaknesses; a literary use. *...our vanities and frailties. ...such consequences of human frailty.*
2 NU **Frailty** is also the condition of being weak in health. *...the advanced age and frailty of some of the inhabitants.*

frame /freɪm/ **frames, framing, framed**
1 NC A **frame** is a structure inside which you can fit something such as a window, door, or picture. *...gold-painted picture frames.*
2 NC A **frame** is also an arrangement of bars that give an object its shape and strength. *...a bunk made of canvas laced to a steel frame.*
3 N PL The **frames** of a pair of glasses are the wire or plastic part which holds the lenses in place. *...new glasses in a variety of fashionable colours—yellow frames, blue, white and red.*
4 NC If someone has a big or small **frame**, they have a big or small body. *His big frame was gaunt and weak.*
5 VO If you **frame** a picture or photograph, you put it in a frame. *Are you having your picture professionally framed?* ♦ **framed** ADJ ATTRIB *...a framed photograph of her mother.*
6 VOA If you **frame** something in a particular kind of language, you express it in that way. *Laws are invariably framed in tortuous jargon.*
7 VO If someone **frames** you, they make it seem that you have committed a crime, although you have not. *I was framed by the authorities.*

frame of mind
N SING Your **frame of mind** is the mood that you are in at a particular time. *I'm not in the right frame of mind for riddles.*

frame of reference, frames of reference
NC A **frame of reference** is a particular set of beliefs, ideas, or observations on which you base your judgement of things. *Their frame of reference was totally American.*

frame-up, frame-ups
NC A **frame-up** is a situation where someone pretends that an innocent person has committed a crime by deliberately lying or inventing evidence; an informal word. *The girl snorted that it was a frame-up and went off in search of the true culprit.*

framework /fréɪmwɜːk/ **frameworks**
1 NC A **framework** is a structure that forms a support or frame for something. *There are nine large panels set in a richly carved framework.*
2 NC+SUPP A **framework** is also a set of rules, ideas, or beliefs which you use in order to make sense of facts or events or to decide how to behave. *They were able to absorb these changes within the framework of traditional institutions and ideas.*

franc /fræŋk/ **francs**
NC The **franc** is one of the different units of money of France, Switzerland, Belgium, and of some other countries where French is spoken. *The franc plunged to its lowest rate against the dollar for a year... It cost twenty thousand Belgian francs.*

France /frɑːns/
The **French Republic** is a country in western Europe. It was occupied by Germany from 1940 to 1944. General Charles de Gaulle dominated French politics from the end of the Second World War until 1969. The Socialist Party (PS) came to power in 1981, when François Mitterrand became President. Pierre Bérégevoy became Prime Minister in 1992. France is a member of the European Community. It exports grain, wine, steel, and aluminium. ♦ **Frenchman, Frenchwoman** /frɛntʃmən, frɛntʃwʊmən/ N **French** /frɛntʃ/ ADJ,N PL
■ *per capita GNP:* US$16,080 ■ *religion:* Christianity (mainly Roman Catholic) ■ *language:* French ■ *currency:* franc ■ *capital:* Paris ■ *population:* 56 million (1988) ■ *size:* 543,965 square kilometres.

franchise /frǽntʃaɪz/ **franchises**
1 N SING The **franchise** is the right to vote in an election, especially one to elect a parliament; a formal use. *...a policy of universal franchise.*
2 NC A **franchise** is an authority that is given by a company to someone, allowing them to sell its goods or services. *...two new companies which were awarded franchises for round-the-clock broadcasting. ...the sale of independent television franchises.*

frank /fræŋk/ **franker, frankest; franks, franking, franked**
1 ADJ If someone is **frank**, they state things in an open and honest way. *...a frank discussion.* ♦ **frankness** NU *He seemed to be speaking with complete frankness.*
2 VO To **frank** a letter or parcel means to put a mark or message on it, usually to show that no stamp is needed. *For the next six weeks, all letters, parcels and magazines posted here will also be franked with a slogan: 'Jesus Is Alive'.*

frankfurter /frǽŋkfɜːtə/ **frankfurters**
NC A **frankfurter** is a type of smoked sausage.

frankincense /frǽŋkɪnsens/
NU **Frankincense** is a substance that is burned as incense and is obtained from trees that produce gum. *Some of the first people to visit the baby Jesus were wise men bringing gifts of gold, frankincense and myrrh.*

frankly /frǽŋkli/
1 ADV SEN You use **frankly** when boldly stating a feeling or opinion. *Frankly, this has all come as a bit of a shock.*
2 ADV If you say or do something **frankly**, you say or do it in an open and honest way. *He asked me to tell him frankly what I wished to do.*

frantic /frǽntɪk/
1 ADJ If you are **frantic**, you behave in a wild and desperate way because you are frightened or worried. *We were frantic with worry.* ♦ **frantically** ADV *...frantically searching for David.*
2 ADJ When there is **frantic** activity, things are done hurriedly and in a disorganized way. *...a frantic week of high-level discussions.* ♦ **frantically** ADV *They worked frantically throughout the day.*

fraternal /frətɜːnl/
ADJ **Fraternal** means having strong links of friendship with another group of people; a formal word. *Fraternal greetings were received from the Communist Party of the Soviet Union.*

fraternity /frətɜːnəti/ **fraternities**; a formal word.
1 NU **Fraternity** refers to feelings of friendship between groups of people. *A call to strengthen the fraternity of the peoples of the USSR.*
2 NC+SUPP You can refer to a group of people with the same profession or interests as a **fraternity**. *...the banking fraternity.*
3 N COLL In the United States, a **fraternity** is a society of male students that is formed for social purposes. *...men's college fraternities.*

fraternize /frǽtənaɪz/ **fraternizes, fraternizing, fraternized**; also spelt **fraternise**.
V-RECIP If you **fraternize** with someone, you associate with them in a friendly way, even though they may be from a different country or social group; a formal word. *Ash fraternized with their sons and grandsons.*

fratricide /frǽtrɪsaɪd/
NU **Fratricide** is the crime of killing your brother.

fraud /frɔːd/ **frauds**
1 NU **Fraud** is the crime of gaining money by deceit or trickery. *His closest adviser is under indictment for fraud.*
2 NC A **fraud** is something that deceives people in an illegal or immoral way. *The case involves allegations of a fraud worth at least $200 million. ...the victim of a fraud.*
3 NC Someone who is a **fraud** is not the person they pretend to be or does not have the abilities or status they pretend to have. *She rounded on a young man wearing a medal and accused him of being a fraud.*

fraudulence /frɔːdjʊləns/
NU **Fraudulence** is the quality of being deliberately deceitful or dishonest. *He was aware of the fraudulence of what he was proposing.*

fraudulent /frɔːdjʊlənt/
ADJ Something that is **fraudulent** is deliberately deceitful, dishonest, or untrue. *The promise Mrs Haze had made was a fraudulent one.*

fraught /frɔːt/
1 ADJ PRED+with If something is **fraught** with problems or difficulties, it is full of them. *Any further moves would be fraught with danger.*
2 ADJ Someone who is **fraught** is very worried or anxious. *Everyone's rather tense and fraught tonight.*
3 ADJ If a situation is **fraught**, it is tense and awkward. *It was a fraught evening altogether.*

fray /freɪ/ **frays, fraying, frayed**
1 V-ERG If something such as cloth or rope **frays** or is **frayed**, its threads or strands become worn and it is likely to tear or break. *His shirts were frayed. ...the fraying edge of the carpet.*
2 N SING You can refer to an exciting activity, fight, or argument that you are involved in as the **fray**. *Mr Mitterrand has up to now kept out of the political fray... The army has now entered the fray.*
3 V-ERG If your nerves **fray** or your temper **frays**, you feel irritable and tense. *As the day wore on tempers frayed and disgruntled voters smashed ballot boxes... It's very, very hot and tempers are frayed.* ♦ **frayed** ADJ *It can help soothe the frayed nerves of parents.*

frazzle /frǽzl/; an informal word.
1 If you are **worn to a frazzle**, you are exhausted and irritable because of worry, problems, or overwork. *She was worn to a frazzle by her selfless devotion.*
2 If something is **burned to a frazzle**, it is burned because it has been cooked for too long or because it has been in the sun for too long. *Tourists just want to come and lie on the beach and get burnt to a frazzle.*

frazzled /frǽzld/; an informal word.
1 ADJ If you are **frazzled**, you are exhausted and often confused or irritable because of worry, problems, or overwork. *...a frazzled mother of five.*
2 ADJ If something is **frazzled**, it is burned or dried up because it has been cooked for too long or because it has been in the sun for too long. *I was frazzled and burned black by the sun.*

freak /friːk/ **freaks, freaking, freaked**
1 NC People call someone a **freak** when their behaviour or attitudes are unusual or when they are physically abnormal in some way. *A woman is considered a freak if she puts her career first. ...hair-raising freaks, including a two-headed Indian.*
2 N+N A **freak** event or action is unusual and unlikely to happen. *My mother died in a freak accident, struck by lightning at a picnic.*
freak out PHRASAL VERB If you **freak out**, you become extremely confused, upset, or angry; an informal expression. *My kids kind of freaked out when they came home from school.*

freakish /friːkɪʃ/
ADJ You describe something as **freakish** when it is very unusual. *...an isolated, freakish event. ...freakish-looking people.*

freaky /friːki/ **freakier, freakiest**
ADJ If someone or something is **freaky**, they are very unusual or frightening in some way; an informal word. *The whole thing was freaky.*

freckled /frekld/
ADJ Someone who is **freckled** has freckles. *...her freckled face.*

freckles /freklz/
N PL **Freckles** are small, light brown spots on someone's skin, especially their face. *She had red hair and freckles.*

free /friː/ **freer, freest; frees, freeing, freed**
1 ADJ Someone or something that is **free** is not controlled or limited. *Within the EEC there is free movement of labour... Algeria already possesses one of the freest presses in the Arab world... The leaders are free to discuss what they like.*
2 ADJ or ADV Someone who is **free** is no longer a prisoner or a slave. *I wish to return to London, this time as a free man... One prisoner in seven had been set free.*
3 VO If you **free** a prisoner or a slave, you release them. *She was arrested but freed after three weeks... They overpowered the policemen on duty in the station and freed the prisoner.*
4 VO If you **free** someone of something unpleasant or restricting, you get rid of it for them. *Romania had freed itself from pro-Moscow elements in its Communist hierarchy. ...the attempt to free France of the Dictator.*
5 ADJ PRED A person or thing that is **free** of something unpleasant does not have it or is not affected by it. *The area will be free of pollution by the year 2000. ...free from all financial worry.*
6 VO If you **free** something such as money or resources, you make it available for a task or purpose. *We could cut defence expenditure, freeing vital resources for more useful purposes... The Soviet Union tried to rely more on coal and nuclear power in order to free oil reserves for export.*
7 ADJ If you have a **free** period of time or are **free** at a particular time, you are not busy then. *They don't have much free time... Are you free for lunch?*
8 ADJ A place, seat, or machine that is **free** is not occupied or not being used. *Is that seat free?*
9 ADJ If something is **free**, you can have it or use it without paying. *...free school meals... National museums and galleries have traditionally been free to visitors.*
10 ADV If something is cut or pulled **free**, it is moved so that it is no longer attached to something or trapped. *I shook my jacket free and hurried off.*
11 VO If you **free** something that is fixed or trapped, you remove or loosen it from the place where it was. *He freed his arms.*
12 ADJ PRED If someone is **free** with something, they give or use it a lot; used showing disapproval.
13 to give someone a **free hand**: see **hand**.

-free /-friː, -fri/
SUFFIX **-free** is added to nouns to form adjectives that indicate that something does not have the thing mentioned. *Each submarine reported a trouble-free launch. ...error-free computer programs.*

free agent, free agents
NC You say that someone is a **free agent** when they can do whatever they want because they are not responsible to anyone. *They're completely independent observers, free agents who draw their own conclusions.*

free-and-easy
ADJ **Free-and-easy** people and things are relaxed, casual, and informal. *...a free-and-easy relationship.*

freebie /friːbi/ **freebies**
NC A **freebie** is something that you are given without having to pay for it, usually by a company; an informal word. *The industry vows to quit giving away freebies in places where kids hang out.*

freedom /friːdəm/ **freedoms**
1 NU or NC **Freedom** is the state of being allowed to do or say what you want. *Political freedom is still rare. ...freedom of speech. ...the erosion of basic freedoms.*
2 NU When slaves or prisoners escape or are released, you can say that they gain their **freedom**. *Many slaves buy their freedom with what they save from farming.*
3 NU When someone or something has **freedom** of

movement, they can move about without restriction.
...*increased freedom of movement between the two
countries.*
4 NU+*from* When there is **freedom** from something
unpleasant, people are not affected by it. ...*freedom
from hunger and starvation.*

freedom fighter, freedom fighters
NC **Freedom fighters** are people who try to overthrow
the government of their country, using violent
methods; used showing approval. *He said they were
in no way idealists or freedom fighters.* ...*an eminent
freedom fighter who had a deep commitment to the
welfare of the poor.*

free enterprise
NU **Free enterprise** is an economic system in which
businesses compete for profit without much
government control. ...*the ideals of democracy and
free enterprise.*

free fall
1 NU In parachuting, **free fall** is the part of the jump
before the parachute opens. ...*free fall parachute
jumps from six miles high.*
2 NU If things such as prices go into **free fall**, they
start to fall uncontrollably. *Coffee prices went into
free fall yesterday... the main share index appears to
have gone into free fall.*

Freefone /fri:fəʊn/
NU **Freefone** is a system in Britain which allows you
to phone particular organizations without paying for
the call. You ask the operator for Freefone and give a
special number; **Freefone** is a trademark. *Police are
asking witnesses to contact them on a special hotline.
The number is freefone 0800 789 321.*

free-for-all, free-for-alls
NC A **free-for-all** is a disorganized fight, argument, or
attempt to get something, in which everybody joins
in. *The fight turned into a free-for-all... This would
result in a free-for-all on wage bargaining.*

freehand /fri:hænd/
ADJ A **freehand** drawing is drawn without using
instruments such as a ruler or a pair of compasses.
▶ Also ADV *She drew it freehand.*

freehold /fri:həʊld/
1 N SING If you have the **freehold** of a building or piece
of land, you own it for life and there are no conditions
regarding your ownership; compare **leasehold**. *The
person with the freehold has absolute title to the
land... The freehold belongs officially to the Polish
state.*
2 ADJ If a building or piece of land is **freehold**, you
can own it for life. ...*freehold property.* ...*leasehold
or freehold ownership.*

free house, free houses
NC A pub that is a **free house** is not owned by a
particular brewery and can sell whatever beers it
chooses to. *Brewers with more than two thousand
pubs will have to convert thousands of their premises
into free houses.*

free kick, free kicks
NC When there is a **free kick** in a game of football, the
ball is given to a member of one side to kick without
opposition because a member of the other side has
broken a rule. *The third goal was scored direct from
a free kick.*

freelance /fri:lɑ:ns/
ADJ or ADV A **freelance** journalist or photographer is not
employed by one organization, but is paid for each
piece of work that they do by the organization that
they do it for. ...*freelance writing... I work freelance.*

freeloader /fri:ləʊdə/ **freeloaders**
NC A **freeloader** is someone who takes advantage of
the generosity of other people to provide them with
food, accommodation.

free love
NU **Free love** is the practice of having sexual
relationships without marrying, often several
relationships at the same time; an old-fashioned
expression. *He founded a sect dedicated to free love.*
...*the free love attitudes left over from the 60s.*

freely /fri:li/
1 ADV You say that something is done **freely** when it is
done often or in large quantities. *He spends fairly*

freely. ...*perspiring freely.*
2 ADV Someone or something that can move or act
freely is not controlled or limited by anything. *British
goods were allowed to move freely from one state to
another... If people are allowed to travel more freely,
they will be more likely to return.*
3 ADV If you can talk **freely**, you do not need to be
careful about what you say. *We are all comrades here
and I may talk freely.*
4 SUBMOD Something that is **freely** available can be
obtained easily. *These drugs are freely available in
most cities.*
5 ADV Something that is given or done **freely** is given
or done willingly. ...*freely given affection.*

freeman /fri:mən/ **freemen** /fri:mən/
NC Someone who is a **freeman** of a particular city has
been given the freedom of that city as a special
honour. *Nelson Mandela was made a freeman of this
city when he was still a prisoner in Cape Town.*

free market, free markets
N+N or NC In a country with a **free market** economy the
production of goods is controlled by individual people
and organizations rather than by the government.
*East German businesses were beginning to adapt to a
free market system... Currencies in a free market are
naturally volatile... A plan for scrapping the
centralised, state-run system and creating a free
market economy.* ● See also **market economy.**

Freemason /fri:meɪsn/ **Freemasons**
NC A **Freemason** is a member of a large secret
society whose members promise to help each other
and use a system of secret signs to recognize other
members. *The document criticised the Freemasons'
selective use of the Bible.*

freemasonry /fri:meɪsnri/
1 NU **Freemasonry** is the natural friendly feeling that
exists between people who are of the same kind. *A
happy freemasonry exists between expense account
fiddlers.*
2 NU **Freemasonry** is the organization of the
Freemasons and their beliefs and practices. *The
Methodist Church found many aspects of Freemasonry
incompatible with church membership.*

free pardon, free pardons
NC If someone who has been found guilty of a crime is
given a **free pardon,** they are allowed to go free.
*President Mugabe granted a second free pardon to a
government minister last week.*

free pass, free passes
NC A **free pass** is an official document that allows a
person to travel or to enter a particular building
without having to pay.

free port, free ports
NC A **free port** is a port or airport where goods can be
brought in from foreign countries without payment of
duty if they are going to be exported again. ...*the free
port of Monrovia was now safe for shipping.*

Freepost /fri:pəʊst/
NU **Freepost** is a system in Britain by which an
organization pays the postage when someone writes to
them. 'Freepost' is written on the envelope as part of
the address; **Freepost** is a trademark. *Return it to:
Lloyds Bank PLC, FREEPOST, Birmingham.*

freer /fri:ə/
Freer is the comparative of **free.**

free-range
1 ADJ A **free-range** chicken is a hen that is allowed to
move and feed freely on an area of open ground.
...*the perception that a free-range chicken leads a
happier life.*
2 ADJ **Free-range** eggs or meat products come from
free-range animals. *Free-range eggs take twelve
percent of the egg market in England's richer
southern counties.* ...*a low-cholesterol, free-range
product.*

freesia /fri:zɪə/ **freesias**
NC or NU A **freesia** is a plant with fragrant yellow, pink,
white, or purple tubular flowers. ...*a bed of freesias
that were beginning to run wild.* ...*green-tipped
snowdrops, as well as the papery narcissi and pale
gold freesia.*

free spirit, free spirits
NC Someone who is a **free spirit** is independent and lives as he or she wants to live rather than in a conventional way. *Pope needed money to remain a free spirit in an age of political patronage.*

freest /friːst/
Freest is the superlative of **free**.

free-standing
ADJ A **free-standing** piece of furniture or other object is not fixed to anything or stands on its own away from other things. *...a free-standing bath.*

freestyle /friːstaɪl/
N SING **Freestyle** refers to sports competitions, especially swimming and wrestling, in which competitors can use any style or method they like. *She won the 100 metres freestyle.*

freethinker /friːθɪŋkə/ **freethinkers**
NC A **freethinker** is someone who works out their own ideas rather than accepting generally accepted views. *...a political radical and freethinker.*

Freetown /friːtaʊn/
Freetown is the capital of Sierra Leone and its largest city. Population: 470,000 (1985).

free trade
NU **Free trade** is trade that is done between different countries without restrictions or taxes on what is bought or sold. *Eighty percent of Canadian trade with the Americans is free trade... He said he would appeal directly to the people for approval of the free trade agreement.*

freeway /friːweɪ/ **freeways**
NC A **freeway** is a road with several lanes and controlled places where vehicles join it, so that people can travel quickly; used in American English. *He turned off the freeway.*

freewheel /friːwiːl/ **freewheels, freewheeling, freewheeled**
V If you **freewheel**, you travel, usually downhill, on a bicycle without using the pedals, or in a vehicle without using the engine.

freewheeling /friːwiːlɪŋ/
ADJ ATTRIB A **freewheeling** person behaves in a casual, bold way without feeling restricted by rules or accepted ways of doing things. *...all the trappings one associates with freewheeling urban youth. ...the versatility of his poetic, freewheeling style.*

free will
1 NU If you believe in **free will**, you believe that people are able to choose what they do and not that their actions are decided by God, Fate, or scientific processes. *...notions of predestination and free will.*
2 If you do something of your **own free will**, you do it by choice and not because you are forced. *The Foreign Ministry spokesman said that the refugees left of their own free will... He has come back of his own free will.*

freeze /friːz/ **freezes, freezing, froze, frozen**
1 V When a liquid **freezes**, it becomes solid because it is so cold. *The water froze in the wells... It opened a supply route to Russia that could be used when the northern sea lanes froze in the winter.*
2 VO If you **freeze** food, you preserve it by storing it at a temperature below freezing point. *...catching fish, freezing it and distributing it to cold stores. ...simply freeze the whole shrimp.*
3 V When it **freezes** outside, the temperature falls below freezing point. *I think it'll freeze tonight.* ▸ Also N SING *The current freeze has burst pipes in some LA and San Francisco suburbs.*
4 V If you **freeze**, you become very cold; an informal use. *You'll freeze to death out there.*
5 V You can also say that someone **freezes** when they suddenly stop moving and become completely still and quiet. *Then she sensed something moving about. She froze... The crowd at first froze and then began to stampede.*
6 VO To **freeze** something such as wages or prices means to state officially that they will not be allowed to increase during a particular period of time. *Various attempts to control or freeze wages have failed... Last month the Senate froze $95,000,000 in economic and military aid to Peru.* ▸ Also NC A

parliamentary committee has proposed a freeze in government spending. ...a freeze in the nuclear arms race.*
7 VO If you **freeze** something such as a bank account, you obtain a legal order which prevents anyone, including the holder, from using it. *He has had one of his bank accounts frozen because of his refusal to pay the controversial local tax... It was the Bank of England which led a worldwide operation to freeze most of the bank's assets last Friday.*
8 See also **deep freeze, freezing, frozen.**
freeze over PHRASAL VERB If something **freezes over** it becomes completely covered with a layer of ice. *The lakes were frozen over last winter.*
freeze up PHRASAL VERB If something **freezes up**, it becomes completely covered or blocked with ice. *The lock has frozen up.*

freeze-dried
ADJ **Freeze-dried** food has been preserved by a process of rapid freezing and drying. *...freeze-dried instant coffee.*

freeze-frame, freeze-frames
1 NC A **freeze-frame** from a film is an individual picture from it, produced by stopping the film at that point. *...a freeze-frame of Finney reaching out to Keaton.*
2 NC The **freeze-frame** on a video is a device that allows you to stop the film, for example to look at an individual picture.

freezer /friːzə/ **freezers**
NC A **freezer** is a large container in which you can store food for long periods of time, because the temperature inside is kept below freezing point. *Shopkeepers have had to throw food away as freezers turn themselves off.*

freeze-up, freeze-ups
NC When a **freeze-up** occurs, ice completely covers or blocks something such as a pipe, machine, or river. *We kept the water moving enough to prevent a complete freeze-up.*

freezing /friːzɪŋ/
1 ADJ If something or someone is **freezing**, or feels freezing, they are very cold indeed. *It's freezing outside... The water was freezing.*
2 NU **Freezing** is also the same as **freezing point**. *The air temperature was now well below freezing.*

freezing point, freezing points
1 NU **Freezing point** is 0° Celsius, the temperature at which water freezes. *The temperature was well above freezing point.*
2 NC The **freezing point** of a particular substance is the temperature at which it freezes.

freight /freɪt/
1 NU **Freight** refers to the movement of goods by lorries, trains, ships, or aeroplanes. *It is going by air freight.*
2 NU **Freight** is the goods that are transported by lorries, trains, ships, or aeroplanes. *Thirty-seven percent of the nation's freight moves by rail.*

freight car, freight cars
NC A **freight car** is a wagon on a train in which goods are transported; used in American English. *A passenger train slammed into some parked freight cars.*

freighter /freɪtə/ **freighters**
NC A **freighter** is a ship or aeroplane that is designed to carry goods. *The shipment arrived in Jamaica from Lisbon on board a Panamanian freighter.*

freight train, freight trains
NC A **freight train** is a train that carries goods rather than people. *...a freight train transporting fuel oil.*

French /frentʃ/
1 ADJ **French** means belonging or relating to France. *...the French ambassador.*
2 NU **French** is the language spoken by people who live in France and in parts of Belgium, Canada, and Switzerland. *...experts in languages ranging from French and Arabic to Turkish.*
3 N PL The **French** are the people who come from France. *The French have generally supported German resistance to British demands.*

French bean, French beans
NC **French beans** are long, rounded green beans which you cook and eat as a vegetable. ...*use 8 oz. fresh or frozen French beans.*
French bread
NU **French bread** is bread which is baked in long, thin, crusty loaves.
French door, French doors
NC **French doors** are the same as **French windows**. *He saw her cross the kitchen and go out by the French door.*
French dressing
NU **French dressing** is a thin sauce made of oil, vinegar, and spices which you put on salad.
French fries
N PL **French fries** are thin sticks of potato fried in oil. *Foods like hamburgers, hot dogs and French fries are still dominating school lunch menus.*
French Guiana /frɛntʃ giɑːnə/
French Guiana is a territory of France, in northern South America. It was settled by France from 1637 and was used as a penal colony until 1937. Fish, gold, and rice are exported. ♦ **French Guianese, French Guianan** /frɛntʃ giəniːz, giɑːnən/ N, ADJ ▪ *religion:* Christianity (mainly Roman Catholic) ▪ *language:* French (official), Creole ▪ *currency:* French franc ▪ *capital:* Cayenne ▪ *population:* 115,000 (1990) ▪ *size:* 90,000 square kilometres.
French horn, French horns. See **horn**.
French loaf, French loaves
NC A **French loaf** is a long, thin loaf of bread.
Frenchman /frɛntʃmən/ **Frenchmen** /frɛntʃmən/
NC A **Frenchman** is a man who comes from France. *...a suave, worldly, charming Frenchman.*
French polish
NU **French polish** is a type of varnish which is painted onto wood so that the wood has a hard, shiny surface. *Layers of shellac have been rubbed down and built up to get the gleaming finish of French polish.*
French Polynesia /frɛntʃ pɒlɪniːziə/
French Polynesia is a territory of France in the South Pacific. It consists of five archipelagos: Society Archipelago (including Tahiti and Moorea), Tuamotu Archipelago, Gambier Islands, Austral Islands, and the Marquesas. Tahiti and other islands in the group were settled by France from 1842. Tourism is an important industry. Tahiti exports cultured black pearls and coconut oil. ♦ **French Polynesian** /frɛntʃ pɒlɪniːziən/ N, ADJ ▪ *religion:* Christianity (mainly Protestant) ▪ *language:* French (official), Tahitian ▪ *currency:* Pacific franc ▪ *capital:* Papeete ▪ *population:* 195,000 (1990) ▪ *size:* 4,000 square kilometres.
French stick, French sticks
NC A **French stick** is the same as a **French loaf**. *Don't forget the cheeseboard and the French sticks to go with it.*
French window, French windows
NC **French windows** are glass doors which lead onto a garden or balcony.
frenetic /frənɛtɪk/
ADJ **Frenetic** activity or behaviour is fast, energetic, and uncontrolled. *...New York's reputation as a frenetic twenty-four-hours-a-day city... The diplomatic timetable continues at a frenetic pace.*
frenzied /frɛnzid/
ADJ **Frenzied** actions are wild, excited, and uncontrolled. *...frenzied cheers. ...a frenzied mob of students.*
frenzy /frɛnzi/
N U or N SING Someone who is in a **frenzy** has lost control of their feelings and is acting in a very excited and violent or uncontrolled way. *There was an element of frenzy and desperation in the singing... It would drive Thomas into a frenzy.*
frequency /friːkwənsi/ **frequencies**
1 NU The **frequency** of an event is the number of times it happens. *Disasters appear to be increasing in frequency. ...the frequency of their appearance.*
2 NC or NU The **frequency** of a sound or radio wave is the number of times it vibrates within a specified period of time; a technical use in physics. *The higher*

the frequency, the further the signal penetrates the ground... The brain recognizes three constituents of sound: frequency, amplitude and phase.
frequent, frequents, frequenting, frequented;
pronounced /friːkwənt/ when it is an adjective and /frɪkwɛnt/ when it is a verb.
1 ADJ You say that something is **frequent** when it happens often. *George's absences were frequent... They move at frequent intervals.* ♦ **frequently** ADV *This question is frequently asked... He frequently saw her sitting out on the lawn, reading.*
2 VO If you **frequent** a place, you go there often. *Jo liked to frequent the bars... The bomb exploded in a shopping centre that is frequented by tourists.*
fresco /frɛskəʊ/ **frescoes**
NC A **fresco** is a picture painted onto a wet plastered wall. *...'The Last Supper', Leonardo's fresco on the wall of Santa Maria delle Grazie in Milan.*
fresh /frɛʃ/ **fresher, freshest**
1 ADJ ATTRIB A **fresh** thing or amount replaces or is added to a previous one. *Rose had given him fresh instructions... He poured himself a fresh drink... Fresh criticism has been directed at the Federal government.*
2 ADJ Something that is **fresh** has been done or experienced recently. *...fresh footprints in the snow... Memories of the war are fresh in both countries... We want to talk to people while it's still fresh in their minds.*
3 ADJ **Fresh** food has been produced or picked recently, and has not been preserved. *...fresh and frozen fish... The valley is the country's biggest producer of fresh oranges in the winter.*
4 ADJ If you describe something as **fresh**, you mean you like it because it is new and exciting. *He has a fresh approach... Does the Congress have any fresh ideas for turning the economy around?* ♦ **freshness** NU *This gives the novel freshness and charm... There was a freshness and enthusiasm about the new party which many found attractive.*
5 ADJ If something smells, tastes, or feels **fresh**, it is pleasant and refreshing. If something looks **fresh**, it is pleasantly clean in appearance. *The air is cool and fresh. ...the fresh dawn light.*
6 ADJ **Fresh** water is water that is suitable for drinking, for example because it is not salty or is not polluted. *The main problem now is the lack of fresh water and adequate medical care... The dam would prevent salt water from mixing with the fresh water supplies.* ● See also **freshwater**.
7 ADJ If the weather is **fresh**, it is fairly cold and windy. *The wind is fresh and strong in the pine trees outside the house.*
8 ADJ PRED If you are **fresh** from a place, you have been there very recently. *...coming fresh from the junior school... Both of you are fresh from the election campaign in Poland.*
fresh- /frɛʃ-/
PREFIX **fresh-** is added to past participles in order to form adjectives which describe something as having been recently made or done. *...a vase of fresh-cut flowers... The smell of peanuts, hot dogs, and fresh-cut grass is in the air.*
fresh air
N U or N SING If you say that you want some **fresh air**, you mean that you want to go outside or open a window, often because the room or building you are in is uncomfortably warm. *Get out in the fresh air... What you need is plenty of sun and fresh air.*
freshen /frɛʃn/ **freshens, freshening, freshened**
1 VO If you **freshen** something, you make it cleaner and fresher. *The air freshened his lungs... Keith freshened himself with a wash.*
2 V If the wind **freshens**, it becomes stronger. *The winds have gone round to the south-west and are freshening.*
freshen up PHRASAL VERB If you **freshen up**, you have a quick wash and tidy yourself up. *Sarah and Barry returned to their hotel to freshen up.*
fresher /frɛʃə/ **freshers**
NC A **fresher** is a student who has just started university or college. *Some units have been reserved*

for first year students under the 'freshers on Campus' scheme.

freshly /ˈfrɛʃli/
ADV If something has been **freshly** made or done, it has been made or done recently. *...freshly cooked food. ...a crowded graveyard of more than 100 freshly dug graves.*

freshman /ˈfrɛʃmən/ **freshmen** /ˈfrɛʃmən/
NC A **freshman** is a student who is in his or her first year at university or college; used in American English. *I searched the crowds of freshmen for others who were black... He had finished his freshman year of science.*

freshwater /ˈfrɛʃwɔːtə/
1 ADJ ATTRIB A **freshwater** lake or pool contains water that is not salty. *This is fairly shallow water, free of freshwater outlets from rivers.*
2 ADJ ATTRIB A **freshwater** fish or other animal lives in a river, lake, or pool that is not salty. *...the life-cycle of the freshwater snail.*

fret /frɛt/ **frets, fretting, fretted**
V If you **fret**, you feel anxious and worried about something. *Daniel was fretting about money... Many parents fret over the sort of music their children are listening to.*

fretful /ˈfrɛtfl/
ADJ If someone is **fretful**, they behave in a way that shows that they are worried or uncomfortable. *...fretful babies... His visit is intended to give the appearance of activity to a fretful American public.*

fretted /ˈfrɛtɪd/
ADJ ATTRIB A **fretted** wooden or stone object has been decorated by cutting bits out of it. *...the fretted roof of the station arch.*

fretwork /ˈfrɛtwɜːk/
NU or N+N **Fretwork** is wood or metal that has been decorated by cutting bits of it out to make a pattern. *...the creation of an artist skilled in fretwork. ...fretwork bookcases.*

Freudian /ˈfrɔɪdiən/
ADJ **Freudian** means relating to the ideas and methods of the psychiatrist Sigmund Freud, especially to his ideas about people's subconscious sexual feelings. *...the Freudian concept of infant sexuality.*

Freudian slip, Freudian slips
NC If someone accidentally says something that reveals their subconscious feelings, especially their sexual feelings, this is referred to as a **Freudian slip**.

Fri.
Fri. is an abbreviation for 'Friday'.

friable /ˈfraɪəbl/
ADJ A substance that is **friable** is easily broken up rather than being firm or hard; a technical word. *Do not collect fossils from friable cliffs in the fragile fen area... The mixture is moulded into a friable tablet that dissolves under the tongue... The fallopian tubes are affected by pregnancy, and are enlarged, friable, and heavy with veins.*

friar /ˈfraɪə/ **friars**
NC or TITLE A **friar** is a member of a Catholic religious order. *...Franciscan friars... One of Robin's trusted friends was a fat and jolly priest called Friar Tuck.*

fricassee /ˈfrɪkəsiː, ˌfrɪkəˈseɪ/ **fricassees**
NC or NU A **fricassee** consists of pieces of meat, especially chicken or veal, cooked and served in a white sauce. *...chicken fricassee... There's also fricassee of lobster in Chinon wine.*

friction /ˈfrɪkʃn/ **frictions**
1 NU **Friction** is the force that prevents things from moving freely when they are touching each other. *If you have a lot of air in the chamber, it will exert some friction on the ball.*
2 NU **Friction** is also the rubbing of one thing against another. *...ball bearings and rollers minimise the effects of wear and friction.*
3 NU or N PL **Friction** between people is disagreement and quarrels. *...friction between Healy and his colleagues. ...family frictions.*

Friday /ˈfraɪdeɪ, ˈfraɪdi/ **Fridays**
NU or NC **Friday** is the day after Thursday and before Saturday. *The talks will take place in Luxembourg on Friday.*

fridge /frɪdʒ/ **fridges**
NC A **fridge** is a large metal container for storing food at low temperatures to keep it fresh. *Customers should ensure that they purchase an energy efficient fridge, freezer or television.*

friend /frɛnd/ **friends**
1 NC A **friend** is someone you know well. *He was my best friend at Oxford. ...an old friend of the family... We all escaped down the street to a friend's house.*
2 N PL If you are **friends** with someone, you like each other and enjoy spending time together. *You used to be friends with him, didn't you?... They are discouraged from becoming friends with foreigners.*
3 If you **make friends** with someone, you begin a friendship with them. *The message for unmarried middle-aged men is to learn how to make friends and look after yourself better. ...his talent for making friends with people of all races and backgrounds.*
4 N PL The people who help and support a cause or a country are often referred to as its **friends**. *All friends of Ireland should support us... We will not be isolated, and I hope our many friends will understand our position.*

friendless /ˈfrɛndləs/
ADJ A **friendless** person has no friends. *She remained friendless and miserable... She arrived in Britain penniless, friendless, and with nowhere to go.*

friendly /ˈfrɛndli/ **friendlier, friendliest; friendlies**
1 ADJ A **friendly** person is kind and pleasant. *The women had been friendly to Lyn. ...a friendly smile... He was a nice dog too, very friendly.* ◆ **friendliness** NU *The friendliness was gone from his voice.*
2 ADJ If you are **friendly** with someone, you like each other and behave to each other like friends. *I became friendly with a young engineer... The rebel leader was friendly with a dissident officer who was dismissed last year.*
3 ADJ A **friendly** place or object makes you feel comfortable and reassured. *...a small room lit by friendly lamps. ...the friendly clang of the cable cars.*
4 ADJ In warfare, a **friendly** country or armed force is one that is your ally. *Some friendly ships have been stopped at least 15 times... He described Iran as a friendly state which had shown its good intentions.*
5 ADJ A **friendly** fight or argument is not serious. *We have a little friendly competition with New York... AZAPO was formed as friendly rival to the underground organization, the ANC.*
6 NC A **friendly** is a sports match that is played for practice and not as part of a competition. *In an international friendly in Warsaw, Poland were beaten 3-2 by the United States... Denmark held Hungary to a 2-all draw in a friendly match in Budapest.*

friendly fire
NU In warfare, **friendly fire** is gunfire or bombing that comes from your own side, especially when it kills or injures members of its own army. *Seven marines died from friendly fire, the victims of a missile launched from an American aircraft.*

friendly society, friendly societies
NC In Britain, a **friendly society** is an organization to which people regularly pay small amounts of money and which then gives them money when they retire or when they are ill. *The main friendly society the Workers' Circle, wound up more recently.*

friendship /ˈfrɛndʃɪp/ **friendships**
1 NC or NU A **friendship** is a relationship or state of friendliness between two people who like each other. *My friendship with her had taught me a great deal... Friendship is based on shared interests.*
2 NU **Friendship** between countries is a relationship in which they help and support each other. *...his efforts to promote Anglo-German friendship. ...establishing a firm friendship with Poland.*

frieze /friːz/ **friezes**
NC A **frieze** is a long, narrow decorative feature along the top of a wall. *Lord Elgin, for example, removed a marble frieze from the Parthenon temple in Athens.*

frig /frɪg/ **frigs, frigging, frigged**; a rude, informal word.
frig about PHRASAL VERB If you say that someone is **frigging about** or **frigging around**, you mean that they

are wasting time when they should be doing a task or job.

frig around PHRASAL VERB See **frig about**.

frigate /frɪɡət/ **frigates**
NC A **frigate** is a small, fast ship used by the navy to protect other ships. *The British frigate Battleaxe is leading the Royal Navy's permanent patrol in the Gulf.*

frigging /frɪɡɪŋ/
ADJ ATTRIB People use **frigging** before a noun when they are expressing their anger or annoyance about something; a rude, informal word.

fright /fraɪt/ **frights**
1 NU **Fright** is a sudden feeling of fear. *I heard Amy cry out in fright... He was paralysed with fright.*
2 If someone **takes fright**, they experience a sudden feeling of fear. *The animals took fright and ran away... As a result of seeing the eclipse, the local people took fright and consulted a priest.*
3 NC A **fright** is an experience which gives you a sudden feeling of fear. *She gave me a nasty fright with those rabbits... The top seed was given a fright in the first set, but came back to win 7-6... It was the worst fright of my life.*

frighten /fraɪtn/ **frightens, frightening, frightened**
VO If something **frightens** you, it makes you feel afraid, nervous, or worried. *Rats and mice don't frighten me... This was something that really frightened me about the future.*
frighten away PHRASAL VERB If you **frighten** someone **away**, you scare them so that they go away and do not come any closer. *He waved his torch to frighten away some animal.*
frighten into PHRASAL VERB If you **frighten** someone **into** doing something, you force them to do it by making them afraid. *They tried to frighten me into talking... It was a plan to frighten the reformers into giving more power to President Gorbachev.*
frighten off PHRASAL VERB To **frighten** a person **off** means to make them unwilling to become involved in something. *Cliff was less encouraging, seeking to frighten him off.*

frightened /fraɪtnd/
1 ADJ If you are **frightened**, you are afraid of something that has happened or that may happen. *The men led their frightened families to safety... When you were a child, were you frightened of the dark?*
2 ADJ PRED If you are **frightened**, you are worried or nervous about something. *I was frightened of making a fool of myself... I am frightened to look... They were frightened that you might talk to the police.*

frightening /fraɪtᵊnɪŋ/
ADJ Something that is **frightening** makes you feel afraid or worried. *...the most frightening sight he had ever seen... It is frightening to think what a complete search would reveal.* ◆ **frighteningly** ADV *It was happening frighteningly fast.*

frightful /fraɪtfl/
ADJ Something that is **frightful** is very bad or unpleasant; an old-fashioned word. *...help for the refugees trapped in frightful conditions... A journey through the subconscious can be distressing and frightful.* ◆ **frightfully** ADV *She had behaved frightfully.*

frigid /frɪdʒɪd/
1 ADJ If someone says that a woman is **frigid**, they mean that she does not easily become sexually aroused.
2 ADJ A **frigid** place or type of weather is very cold. *The pay bonus for working in frigid Siberia can't buy a better place to live. ...the frigid cold desert night air.*

frill /frɪl/ **frills**
1 NC A **frill** is a long, narrow, folded strip of cloth which is attached to something as a decoration. *...a white pillow with a blue frill round it.*
2 N PL If something has no **frills**, it is simple and has no unnecessary or additional features. *...a house with no frills. ...the necessities of life but none of the frills.*

frilled /frɪld/
ADJ If a piece of clothing is **frilled**, it is decorated with a frill or frills. *...a white frilled blouse.*

frilly /frɪli/
ADJ **Frilly** clothes or objects are decorated with many frills. *...a frilly nightdress.*

fringe /frɪndʒ/ **fringes**
1 NC A **fringe** is hair which is cut so that it hangs over your forehead.
2 NC A **fringe** is also a decoration attached to clothes and other objects, consisting of a row of hanging threads. *...silk shawls with fringes.*
3 NC The **fringes** of a place are the parts farthest from the centre. *...on the western fringe of London.*
4 NC You can use **fringe** or the **fringes** to refer to the parts of an activity or organization that are the most unusual or extreme, or which are only loosely connected with it. *...the radical fringe of the Labour Party... Henry Jaglum works on the fringes of American cinema. ...fringe theatre.*

fringe benefit, fringe benefits
NC **Fringe benefits** are extra things that you get from a particular job, for example a car, a house, or free insurance which you are given in addition to your salary. *They have stopped work, demanding more pay and improved fringe benefits.*

fringed /frɪndʒd/
1 ADJ **Fringed** clothes are decorated with a fringe. *...a fringed leather jacket.*
2 ADJ PRED A If a place or object is **fringed** with things, they are situated along its edges. *Her eyes were large, fringed with long eyelashes. ...a bay of blue water fringed by palm trees.*

frippery /frɪpəri/ **fripperies**
NUorN PL Objects are referred to as **frippery** or **fripperies** when they are cheap, vulgar, and do not serve any useful purpose. *...a case full of frippery. ...the mass manufacture of fripperies and novelties of all kinds.*

Frisbee /frɪzbiː/ **Frisbees**
NC A **Frisbee** is a light plastic disc that one person throws to another as part of a game; **Frisbee** is a trademark. *There's everything from Elvis body lotion to commemorative Frisbees.*

frisk /frɪsk/ **frisks, frisking, frisked**
1 VO If someone **frisks** you, they search you quickly with their hands to see if you are hiding a weapon; an informal use. *Two policemen grabbed his arms while another one frisked him.*
2 V When animals **frisk**, they run around in a happy, energetic way. *...his nine dogs frisking round him.*

frisky /frɪski/ **friskier, friskiest**
ADJ A **frisky** animal or person is energetic and wants to have fun. *...frisky young ponies. ...the frisky schoolboy lurking underneath.*

frisson /friːsɒn/ **frissons**
NC A **frisson** is a short, sudden feeling of excitement or fear; a literary word. *There's a particular frisson in looking at these rooms as they would have been used hundreds of years ago... Mr Gorbachev must have felt a frisson of nostalgia when he sat down to breakfast with Mr Reagan.*

fritter /frɪtə/ **fritters, frittering, frittered**
NC **Fritters** consist of fruit or vegetables dipped in batter and fried. *...banana fritters.*
fritter away PHRASAL VERB If you **fritter away** time, money, or opportunities, you waste them or do not take advantage of them. *She would not fritter away her vacation on reading... England earlier frittered away their chances and were all out for one hundred and fifty.*

frivolity /frɪvɒləti/
NU **Frivolity** is silly, light-hearted behaviour. *Harry tolerated the younger man's frivolity.*

frivolous /frɪvələs/
1 ADJ A **frivolous** person is being silly when they should be serious or sensible. *Forgive me. I didn't mean to sound frivolous.*
2 ADJ **Frivolous** objects and activities are amusing or silly, rather than useful. *I spend a lot of my salary on frivolous things... He accused Congress of wasting time on frivolous measures while dragging its feet on major legislation.*

frizz /frɪz/ **frizzes, frizzing, frizzed**
1 VO If you **frizz** your hair, you brush or perm it so

that it has a lot of stiff, wiry curls. ◆ **frizzed** ADJ *Her hair is frizzed and pretty.*
2 NC A **frizz** of hair has a lot of stiff, wiry curls. *...a cerise bow crowning the black frizz of hair.*

frizzle /frɪzl/ **frizzles, frizzling, frizzled**
V-ERG If something **frizzles** or if you **frizzle** it, it becomes burned and crisp or hard, because of very strong heat. *The gas dried up her hair and frizzled the ends.* ◆ **frizzled** ADJ *...frizzled bacon.*

frizzy /frɪzi/
ADJ **Frizzy** hair has stiff, wiry curls. *...a youth with a mop of frizzy hair... Her school friends mocked her frizzy red hair, and she withdrew into books.*

fro /frəʊ/
to and fro: see **to**.

frock /frɒk/ **frocks**
NC A **frock** is the same as a **dress**; an old-fashioned word. *...a white lace frock.*

frock coat, frock coats
NC A **frock coat** is a long coat that was worn by men in the 19th century. *...actors in wigs and frock coats.*

frog /frɒg/ **frogs**
1 NC A **frog** is a small creature with smooth, often green skin, big eyes, and long back legs which it uses for jumping. Many frogs live near water. *...Japanese tree frogs.*
2 If you **have a frog in** your **throat**, you cannot speak properly because your throat is partly blocked by mucus; an informal expression.

frogman /frɒgmən/ **frogmen** /frɒgmən/
NC A **frogman** is a person whose job involves diving and working underwater. *Police frogmen have discovered a car with two bodies inside it at a docks near Lancaster.*

frog-march, frog-marches, frog-marching, frog-marched
VO If you **are frog-marched** somewhere, you are forced to walk there by two people, each holding one of your arms. *I was frog-marched down to the police station.*

frogspawn /frɒgspɔːn/
NU **Frogspawn** is a soft, jelly-like substance which contains the eggs of a frog. *Every year I take note of the time that the frogspawn appears.*

fro-ing /frəʊɪŋ/
See **to-ing and fro-ing**.

frolic /frɒlɪk/ **frolics, frolicking, frolicked**
1 V When animals or children **frolic**, they run around and play in a lively way. *The children frolicked on the sand... For the first three years I never saw a single crow, but now they frolic and play in sight.*
2 NC A **frolic** is lively, happy, and carefree behaviour. *What started as a frolic might turn into something different. ...late night frolics on the lawn.*

from /frəm, frɒm/
1 PREP You use **from** to say where the source, origin, or starting point of something is. *...wisps of smoke from a small fire... She came from Ilford... Get the leaflet from a post office. ...a song from his latest film... The shafts were cut from heavy planks of wood.*
2 PREP If someone or something moves or is taken **from** a place, they leave it or are removed, so that they are no longer there. *They drove down from Leeds... We scrambled from our trucks and ran after them... We went around clearing rubbish from the fields.*
3 PREP If you take something **from** an amount, you reduce the amount by that much. *This will be deducted from your pension... Four from seventeen leaves thirteen.*
4 PREP If you are away **from** a place, you are not there. *They were away from home... He was absent from school for two weeks.*
5 PREP If you return **from** doing something, you return after doing it. *The men had not yet come back from fishing... I went to meet my children from school.*
6 PREP If you see or hear something **from** a particular position, you are in that position when you see it or hear it. *From the top of the bus you could look down on people below... From here you cannot see the water itself.*

7 PREP Something that sticks out or hangs **from** an object is attached to it or touches it. *...buckets hanging from a bamboo pole... From his left hand dangled Piggy's broken glasses.*
8 PREP You can use **from** when giving distances. For example, if one place is fifty miles **from** another, the distance between them is fifty miles. *From our back door to their back door was just a few yards... From Parkington I still had a hundred miles to go.*
9 PREP If a road goes **from** one place to another, you can travel along it between the two places. *...on the main road from Paris to Marseilles.*
10 PREP If something happens **from** a particular time, it begins to happen then. *She was deaf from birth... We had no rain from March to October.*
11 PREP If something changes **from** one thing to another, it stops being the first thing and becomes the second thing. *They enlarged the committee from 17 members to 30. ...translating from one language to another.*
12 PREP You say **from** one thing to another when you are stating the range of things that are possible. *The process takes from two to five weeks... The flowers may be anything from pink to crimson.*
13 PREP You use **from** to give the reason for an opinion. *I could see from her face that she felt disappointed... I am speaking from personal experience.*
14 PREP If one thing happens **from** another, it happens as a result of it. *From nervousness she said a few more stupid things... My eyes hurt from the wind.*

frond /frɒnd/ **fronds**
NC **Fronds** are long spiky leaves. *...palm fronds.*

front /frʌnt/ **fronts, fronting, fronted**
1 NC The **front** of something is the part of it that faces you or faces forward. *...jackets with six buttons down the front... The policeman searched the front of the car.* ▸ Also ADJ ATTRIB *...the front gate... One of his front teeth was gone.*
2 ADJ The **front** page or **front** cover of a newspaper or magazine is the outside part on which the first words or pictures are printed. *The front page of The Independent is dominated by a close-up picture of Mr Hurd... Every woman's magazine has a picture on the front cover.*
3 N SING In warfare, the **front** is the place where two armies are fighting each other. *...fourteen miles from the front... His greatest poems were written out of his experiences of life at the front.*
4 NC+SUPP If something happens on a particular **front**, it happens with regard to a particular situation or activity. *On the intellectual front, little advance has been made... He has also taken decisive action on the cocaine front.*
5 N SING If someone puts on a **front**, they pretend to have feelings which they do not have. *They will be fooling only themselves if they try to maintain a front of unity... The Europeans and Americans are anxious to present a solid front.*
6 NC An organization or activity that is a **front** for an illegal or secret activity is used to hide it. *They argue that the incident proves the government is simply a front for the old military regime... Sometimes these clinics are a front for unscrupulous surgeons cashing in on a lucrative industry.*
7 NC The word **Front** is used in the titles of political organizations with a particular aim. *...the Ethiopian People's Revolutionary Democratic Front.*
8 NC A **front** is also the line where a mass of cold air meets a mass of warm air; a technical use. *The torrential rains have been caused by a cold front.*
9 VO A pop group that is **fronted** by a particular person has that person as its lead singer. *The band are fronted by 20 year old Ruth Joy.*
● **Front** is used these phrases. ● If someone or something is **in front**, they are ahead of other people or things who are in the same group or who are doing the same activity. *Jay walked in front and Simon and Val behind him. ...a lady in the row in front.* ● If you are **in front** in a competition or contest, you are winning. *After two missed penalty strokes, England were in front.* ● If you do something **in front of**

someone, you do it in their presence. *Instead of being opened in front of the representatives, the ballot boxes were taken to the police station... There will be a preliminary hearing in front of three judges... I couldn't tell you in front of Sam.* ● If someone or something is **in front of** a particular thing, they are facing it or close to the front part of it. *A car was drawing up in front of the house... There was a man standing in front of me.*

frontage /frʌntɪdʒ/ **frontages**
NC The **frontage** of a building is the side facing the street; a formal word. *...the Victorian frontage of the Treasury.*

frontal /frʌntl/
1 ADJ ATTRIB A **frontal** attack is direct and obvious. *...a frontal attack on the unions.*
2 ADJ ATTRIB **Frontal** also means concerning the front of something. *...a frontal view... Memory is housed in the frontal lobes.*

front bench, front benches
NC The **front bench** or the **front benches** are British members of Parliament who are ministers in the Government or who hold official positions in an opposition party. *...the debating strength of the front bench... He was appointed front-bench spokesman on transport.* ● See also **bench**, **backbench**.

frontbencher /frʌntbentʃə/ **frontbenchers**
NC A **frontbencher** is a member of the British Parliament who is a minister in the Government or who holds an official position in an opposition party. *...a Tory frontbencher.*

front crawl
NU **Front crawl** is a type of swimming stroke that you do lying on your front. *Now we really just have the four strokes: backstroke, breaststroke, butterfly and front crawl.*

front door, front doors
NC The **front door** of a house or other building is the main door, which is usually in the wall that faces a street. *It hadn't got any steps up to the front door.*

frontier /frʌntɪə, frʌntɪə/ **frontiers**
1 NC A **frontier** is a border between two countries. *...the remote frontier between Iran and Pakistan... The discussions took place in a shabby frontier post.*
2 NC+SUPP The **frontiers** of a subject are the limits to which it can be known or done. *They are doing work on the frontiers of discovery... Archaos have expanded the frontiers of circus.*

frontispiece /frʌntɪspiːs/ **frontispieces**
NC The **frontispiece** of a book is a picture at the beginning, opposite the page with the title on.

front line
1 N SING The **front line** is the place where two armies are fighting each other. *We came to within a mile of the front line. ...front-line troops.*
2 Someone who is **in the front line** has to play a very important part in defending or achieving something. *By assuming extra powers, Mr Gorbachov has put himself directly in the front line. ...countries in the front line of the drug war.*

front man, front men
1 NC A **front man** is someone who represents a particular group and acts on their behalf. *Mohammed was the comparatively respectable front man of the team... His inexperience and proximity to Mrs Thatcher will turn him into her front man.*
2 NC A **front man** is someone who presents a television or radio programme, or who is the lead singer of a pop group. *Bob's known as a good front man who's carried the band without any pretensions of being a good singer.*

front-page
ADJ ATTRIB **Front-page** articles or pictures are printed on the front page of a newspaper because they are very important or interesting. *Several papers carried front-page stories about the murdered girl... A front-page report in The Times says that such a challenge could damage his credibility.*

front-runner, front-runners
NC In a competition or contest, the **front-runner** is the person who seems most likely to win it. *...George Smith, the current front-runner for the job.*

frost /frɒst/ **frosts**
NCorNU When there is a **frost**, the outside temperature drops below freezing and the ground is covered with ice crystals. *Even into April the frosts continued... There was a touch of frost this morning... The lawn was sparkling with frost.*

frostbite /frɒstbaɪt/
NU **Frostbite** is a condition caused by extreme cold which can damage your fingers, toes, and ears. *He was crippled with frostbite... People trapped in buildings are very vulnerable to frostbite.*

frostbitten /frɒstbɪtn/
ADJ If someone or a part of their body is **frostbitten**, they are suffering from frostbite. *My tongue hurt because it was frost-bitten.*

frosted /frɒstɪd/
ADJ ATTRIB **Frosted** glass has a rough surface that you cannot see through. *...the frosted glass pane in the door.*

frosting /frɒstɪŋ/
NU **Frosting** is the same as **icing**; used in American English. *...the frosting on the cake.*

frosty /frɒsti/
1 ADJ If the weather is **frosty**, the temperature is below freezing. *...a still and frosty night.*
2 ADJ If you refer to someone's behaviour as **frosty**, you think that person is unfriendly. *...a frosty glance... He reportedly got a frosty reception from the Japanese Foreign Minister... Relations between Pretoria and the General have been distinctly frosty.*

froth /frɒθ/ **froths, frothing, frothed**
1 V If a liquid **froths**, small bubbles appear on the surface. *...the water frothing at his feet... The river roared through the gates, frothing like flowing snow.*
2 NU **Froth** is a mass of small bubbles on the surface of a liquid. *...a ring of white froth appeared on the surface... It's a good beer, which keeps its taste even when the froth is blown away.*

frothy /frɒθi/
1 ADJ A **frothy** liquid has lots of bubbles on its surface. *...frothy beer... You see this frothy, brown stuff washing up on the shore.*
2 ADJ You can use **frothy** to describe things that are light-hearted and not serious at all. *The operetta generally has a frothy plot, at least in Europe. ...the kind of frothy song you hear in Shakespeare.*

frown /fraʊn/ **frowns, frowning, frowned**
V If you **frown**, you move your eyebrows close together because you are annoyed, worried, or thinking hard. *He frowned as though deep in thought... His face froze each time he frowned.* ▸ Also NC *...a frown of disappointment... His frown lines are getting deeper and deeper.*
frown on or **frown upon** PHRASAL VERB If something is **frowned on** or is **frowned upon**, people disapprove of it. *This practice has been frowned on by health workers... Non-membership of a union is frowned upon... His family were Quakers who frowned on movie-going... Islam, however, frowns on astronomy and other unorthodox forms of fortune-telling.*

froze /frəʊz/
Froze is the past tense of **freeze**.

frozen /frəʊzn/
1 **Frozen** is the past participle of **freeze**.
2 ADJ If water is **frozen** or **frozen** over, its surface has turned into ice because it is very cold. *...the frozen canal... The Missouri was frozen over.*
3 ADJ **Frozen** food has been preserved by freezing. *...a packet of frozen peas.*
4 ADJ If you are **frozen**, you are very cold. *'Poor Oliver,' she said. 'You're frozen.'*

frugal /fruːgl/
1 ADJ Someone who is **frugal** spends very little money. *She lived a careful, frugal life.* ◆ **frugality** /fruːgælɪti/ NU *...the tendency towards frugality and simplicity.*
2 ADJ A **frugal** meal is small and cheap. *...his frugal breakfast... Some shoppers have indicated they're planning a frugal Christmas.*

fruit /fruːt/ **fruits.** The plural form for the meaning in paragraph 1 is usually **fruit**, but **fruits** is also used.
1 NCorNU A **fruit** is something which grows on a tree

or a bush and which contains seeds or a stone covered by a substance that you can eat. Apples, oranges, and bananas are all fruit. Fruit is often eaten raw, or cooked as a dessert. *...citrus fruits... Concentrate on eating lots of fruit and plenty of fresh food... They've planted fruit trees over on the right here.*
2 NC+*of* The **fruit** or **fruits** of an action are its results, especially good ones. *...the fruit of his visits to China... The fruits of our labours were tremendous.*
● If an action **bears fruit**, it produces good results; a formal expression. *The good work of this year will continue to bear fruit... The plans to relieve economic conditions in the occupied territories are yet to bear fruit.*

fruitcake /ˈfruːtkeɪk/ **fruitcakes**
NCorNU A **fruitcake** is a cake containing dried fruit. *We settled for some apple chutney and a rich dark fruitcake... The Americans sent 17,000 pounds of fruitcake.*

fruit cocktail, fruit cocktails
NCorNU A **fruit cocktail** is a mixture of pieces of different kinds of fruit which is usually eaten as the first course of a meal.

fruit fly fruit flies
NC A **fruit fly** is a small flying insect which lays its eggs on leaves. *Fruit flies breed very quickly, so you can use them to study genetics.*

fruitful /ˈfruːtfl/
ADJ Something that is **fruitful** produces good and useful results. *...hours of fruitful discussion. ...the fruitful use of funds.*

fruition /fruˈɪʃn/
When something **comes to fruition**, it starts to produce the intended results; a formal expression. *At last his efforts were coming to fruition... Hefner had a brilliant idea which he brought to fruition, and then he kind of loused it up.*

fruitless /ˈfruːtləs/
ADJ Something that is **fruitless** does not produce any results or achieve anything worthwhile. *...making fruitless inquiries. ...their fruitless search for the plane.*

fruit machine, fruit machines
NC A **fruit machine** is a machine used for gambling which pays out money when you get a particular pattern of symbols on a screen. *London's casinos, gaming clubs and fruit machine arcades attract international gamblers.*

fruit salad, fruit salads
NUorNC **Fruit salad** is a mixture of pieces of different kinds of fruit in juice which is eaten as a dessert. *It's a sort of cross between a potato salad and a fruit salad.*

fruity /ˈfruːti/ **fruitier, fruitiest**
1 ADJ Something that is **fruity** smells or tastes of fruit. *...cheap, fruity wines.*
2 ADJ A **fruity** laugh or voice is rich and deep.

frump /frʌmp/ **frumps**
NC When people refer to a woman as a **frump**, they mean that she is old-fashioned, dull, and uninteresting.

Frunze /ˈfrʊnzə/. See **Bishkek**

frustrate /frʌˈstreɪt/ **frustrates, frustrating, frustrated**
1 VO If a situation **frustrates** you, it stops you doing what you want to do, and it angers or upsets you. *The lack of money depressed and frustrated him... Fatima says she's getting increasingly frustrated and angry with government officials.* ◆ **frustrated** ADJ *...the sobbing wife and the angry, frustrated husband.*
◆ **frustrating** ADJ *It was frustrating to live at the sea's edge and be unable to swim.*
2 VO If someone or something **frustrates** a plan or hope, they prevent the event that was planned or hoped for from taking place. *The government have frustrated further advance towards European union... Their united stand frustrated an effort by the ruling family to divide the opposition.* ◆ **frustrated** ADJ *The play is about a woman with frustrated ambitions.*

frustrated /frʌˈstreɪtɪd/
ADJ ATTRIB If you refer to someone as a **frustrated** poet or a **frustrated** teacher, for example, you mean that the person would like to be a poet or a teacher, but has been unable to become one. *I read that Art*

Blakey was a sort of frustrated pianist... So you wouldn't say you were a frustrated puzzle player?

frustration /frʌˈstreɪʃn/ **frustrations**
1 NUorNC **Frustration** is a feeling of anger or distress because you cannot do what you want to do. *...screaming with frustration. ...the frustrations of poverty.*
2 NU+SUPP **Frustration** is also the prevention of a plan or hope that should have taken place. *...the frustration of hopes.*

fry /fraɪ/ **fries, frying, fried**
1 V-ERG When food **fries** or when you **fry** it, you cook it in a pan containing hot fat. *...the smell of frying onions... Ellen was frying an egg.* ◆ **fried** ADJ *...fried potatoes.*
2 See also **small fry**.

frying pan, frying pans
NC A **frying pan** is a flat, metal pan with a long handle, used for frying food. *...non-stick frying pans.*

fry-up, fry-ups
NC A **fry-up** is a meal consisting of food that has been fried; an informal word. *Passengers will be able to order the traditional fry-up of sausages, tomatoes, bacon, and mushrooms.*

ft
ft is a written abbreviation for 'foot' or 'feet' in measurements. *...cages less than 4 ft high.*

FTSE 100 Index
N SING The **FTSE 100 Index** or the **FTSE Index** is an abbreviation for the **Financial Times Stock Exchange 100 Index**. *In London, the FTSE Index closed down 34.5 at 2304.5.*

fuchsia /ˈfjuːʃə/ **fuchsias**
NC A **fuchsia** is a plant or a small bush with pink, purple, or white flowers which hang downwards, with their outer petals curved backwards. *Several hundred plant growers were there, showing off their blooms: roses, orchids, fuchsias, and azaleas.*

fuck /fʌk/ **fucks, fucking, fucked**; a rude and offensive word which you should avoid using.
1 **Fuck** and **fucking** are used as swear words in order to emphasize a word or phrase.
2 **Fuck** and **fucking** are used in order to emphasize something that makes you feel angry or annoyed.
3 **Fuck all** is used to mean 'nothing at all'.
4 VorV-RECIP To **fuck** someone means to have sex with them.
fuck about PHRASAL VERB To **fuck about** or **fuck around** means to behave in a way that is silly, stupid, or unnecessary and that annoys other people; a rude and offensive expression.
fuck off PHRASAL VERB **Fuck off** is an insulting and offensive way of telling someone to go away.
fuck up PHRASAL VERB If you **fuck** something **up**, you make a mess of it; a rude and offensive expression.

fuddled /ˈfʌdld/
ADJ If you are **fuddled**, you are confused and unable to think clearly. *I was fuddled with drink... You have some fuddled idea that each of us carries his own destiny.*

fuddy-duddy /ˈfʌdidʌdi/ **fuddy-duddies**
NC You describe people as **fuddy-duddies** when you think they are old-fashioned and dull in their appearance or attitudes. *...two old fuddy-duddies.*
► Also ADJ *They consider boxer shorts old-fashioned and fuddy-duddy... They have appointed a public relations firm to improve their fuddy-duddy image.*

fudge /fʌdʒ/ **fudges, fudging, fudged**
1 NU **Fudge** is a soft, brown sweet made from butter, milk, and sugar. *...fudge, peanut brittle and other goodies.*
2 VO If you **fudge** something, you avoid making clear or definite decisions about it. *...an attempt to fudge this issue by concealing the facts... The problem of the centre's relationship with the provinces has been fudged.* ► Also NC *The resolution has been described as a classic fudge... They're going now for another fudge instead of a straight, clear proscription.*

fuel /ˈfjuːəl/ **fuels, fuelling, fuelled**; spelt **fueling, fueled** in American English.
1 N MASS **Fuel** is a substance such as wood or petrol that is burned to supply heat or power. *The cost of*

fuel is a worry for old people. ...the increase in world fuel consumption. ● See also **fossil fuel.**
2 VO A machine or vehicle that **is fuelled** by a particular substance works by burning that substance. ...boilers fuelled by coal. ...heavy industries mainly fuelled by highly-polluting lignite coal.
3 VO If something **fuels** a bad situation or feeling, it makes it worse. Hugh's anger was fuelled by resentment... The whole affair has fuelled speculation about the consequences of army involvement... The discontent has been fuelled by resentment about corruption in high places.

fug /fʌg/
N SING A **fug** is an airless, usually smoky and rather smelly atmosphere; an informal word. ...a thick fug of cigarette smoke.

fugitive /fjuːdʒətɪv/ fugitives
N COR N+N A **fugitive** is someone who is avoiding their enemies or an unpleasant situation. ...political fugitives from Algeria. ...a fugitive American.

fugue /fjuːg/ fugues
N COR NU A **fugue** is a piece of music that begins with a short, simple tune, which is then repeated by other voices or instrumental parts with small variations; a technical term in music. Bach wrote some of his fugues in Eisenach. ...'Prelude, Fugue and Riffs', by Leonard Bernstein.

Fujimori, Alberto Keinyo
/ælbeɑtəʊ keiːnjəʊ fuːdʒimɔːri/
Alberto Keinyo Fujimori became President of Peru in 1990. He is the founder of Change 90. Born: 1938.

-ful /-fʊl/ -fuls
SUFFIX **-ful** is used to form nouns referring to the amount of a substance that an object contains. ...two cupfuls of sugar. ...every mouthful of food.

fulcrum /fʊlkrəm/
N SING A **fulcrum** is the point at which something is balancing or pivoting; a technical term. ...a direct connection to the pump rod through a fulcrum.

fulfil /fʊlfɪl/ fulfils, fulfilling, fulfilled; spelt fulfill, fulfills in American English.
1 VO If you **fulfil** a promise or hope, you carry it out or achieve it. They failed to fulfil their promises to revive the economy... I had fulfilled many of my ambitions.
2 VO If you **fulfill** conditions or requirements that are asked of you, you are able to complete them successfully. They are threatening to boycott the elections if these conditions are not fulfilled... They may not have fulfilled Community requirements for a public hearing.
3 VO OR V-REFL If what you are doing **fulfils** you or if you **fulfil** yourself, you feel happy and satisfied. This way of life no longer fulfils the individuals concerned... They felt free to fulfil themselves. ◆ **fulfilling** ADJ ...creative and fulfilling jobs. ◆ **fulfilled** ADJ The children gain if both parents are living fulfilled lives.
4 VO To **fulfil** a role or function means to do what is required by it. He could no longer fulfil his function as breadwinner for the family... Helicopters fulfilled a variety of roles.

fulfilment /fʊlfɪlmənt/; spelt **fulfillment** in American English.
1 NU **Fulfilment** is a feeling of satisfaction that you get from doing or achieving something. People find fulfilment in working for a common goal... The members of the committee could look back on the process with a feeling of fulfilment.
2 NU The **fulfilment** of a promise or hope is the fact of it happening. ...the fulfilment of their dreams... They feel that the union has failed on the fulfilment of promises.

full /fʊl/ fuller, fullest
1 ADJ Something that is **full** contains as much of a substance or as many objects as it can. The bucket's almost full... All the car parks are absolutely full.
2 ADJ PRED+of If a place is **full** of things or people, it contains a large number of them. ...a garden full of pear and apple trees... His office was full of policemen.
3 ADJ PRED+of If someone or something is **full** of a feeling or quality, they have a lot of it. I was full of

confidence... His dark eyes were full of fury.
4 ADJ ATTRIB You can use **full** to indicate the greatest possible amount of something. ...a return to full employment... Make full use of your brains.
5 ADJ ATTRIB You can use **full** when you are referring to the whole of something. I haven't got his full name. ...my last full day in Warsaw.
6 ADJ ATTRIB You can use **full** to emphasize how great an amount or degree is. Here you can see the full squalor of the buildings... I paused to allow the full impact of this to strike home.
7 ADV When machinery or equipment is **full** on, it is working at its greatest power. The gas fire was full on... The volume was turned up full.
8 ADJ If someone has a **full** life, they do a lot of pleasant and interesting things, and are always busy. Everyone is entitled to a full life.
9 ADJ When there is a **full** moon, the moon appears as a bright circle. The lights went out, but fortunately there was a full moon.
● **Full** is used these phrases. ● Something that has been done **in full** has been done or finished completely. The bill has been paid in full... The report will be published in full tomorrow. ● **full of beans**: see bean.

full-back, full-backs
N C A **full-back** is a defending player in football, hockey, or rugby who stands close to the goal or line that he or she is defending. Chelsea's full-back Tony Dorigo may get a chance to play for England in the European Championships.

full-blooded
ADJ ATTRIB **Full-blooded** is used to describe things that are intense or complete. ...without the full-blooded support of the Opposition parties.

full-blown
ADJ ATTRIB **Full-blown** things are complete and fully developed. ...a full-blown military operation... So far, official statistics logged only 23 full-blown AIDS cases.

full board
NU If a hotel provides **full board**, you can get all your meals there.

full dress
NU Someone who is in **full dress** is wearing all the clothes needed for a ceremony or formal occasion. A Zulu in full dress looked magnificent... Round the corner marched a full-dress regiment of soldiers.

full-face
ADJ OR ADV A **full-face** photograph or portrait is one of someone who is facing you directly rather than having their head turned away or downwards. Send a full-face photograph of yourself... The face is seen both in profile and full-face.

full-fledged
Full-fledged means the same as **fully-fledged**; used in American English.

full-grown
ADJ An animal or plant that is **full-grown** has reached its natural size and has stopped growing. A full-grown male giraffe can stand over nineteen feet tall... When full-grown, the larva will spin a cocoon.

full house, full houses
N C If a theatre has a **full house** for a particular performance, it has as large an audience as it can hold. I can remember when we'd have a full house every night.

full-length
1 ADJ ATTRIB Something that is **full-length** is the normal length, rather than being shorter than normal. 'The Birthday Party' was Harold Pinter's first full-length play. ...a full-length television documentary.
2 ADV Someone who is lying **full-length** is lying down flat and stretched out.

full marks
N PL If you get **full marks** in a test or exam, you answer every question correctly.

fullness /fʊlnəs/
1 NU If you talk about the **fullness** of something, you mean that it is very intense, or full of many things; a literary use. ...the fullness of her love. ...life in all its fullness.
2 If something will happen **in the fullness of time**, it

will eventually happen after a long time. *Only in the fullness of time will it become clear whether they do indeed bear fruit.*

full-page

ADJ ATTRIB A **full-page** advertisement, picture, or article covers a whole page of a newspaper or magazine. *The Sunday Times art review has a full-page interview with the Russian dancer, Mikhail Baryshnikov.*

full-scale

ADJ ATTRIB **Full-scale** things have all the features that are possible and are done to the greatest possible extent. *...a full-scale war. ...plans to complete a full-scale highway across the Sahara.*

full-size

1 ADJ **Full-size** or **full-sized** things have finished growing and will not become any larger. *...full-size trees.*

2 ADJ ATTRIB You can also use **full-size** to describe things that are the same size as the thing they represent. *...a full-size model of a vehicle... If the prototype is successful, the way will be clear to design and build a full-sized version.*

full stop, full stops

NC A **full stop** is the punctuation mark (.). *...even something only the size of a full stop.*

full-throated

ADJ ATTRIB A **full-throated** shout or laugh is very loud. *She gave a full-throated laugh.*

full-time

1 ADJ or ADV **Full-time** work or study takes up the whole of each normal working week. *...a full-time job... Bob and I worked full time.*

2 NU In games such as football **full time** is the end of a match. *England equalised a few minutes from full time with a penalty by Lineker.*

full up

1 ADJ PRED If something is **full up**, it contains as much of something as it can and there is no room for anything else. *The car parks were all full up.*

2 ADJ PRED If you are **full up**, you have eaten so much that you cannot eat any more; an informal expression.

fully /fʊli/

1 ADV **Fully** means to the greatest degree or extent possible. *The secrets of its success are still not fully understood.*

2 ADV You use **fully** to indicate that a process is completely finished, and that no details have been omitted or forgotten. *It was weeks before he fully recovered... She answered his questions fully.*

fully-fledged

ADJ ATTRIB **Fully-fledged** means having completely developed into the type of thing or person mentioned. *...fully-fledged members of the association. ...a fully-fledged war.*

fully-grown

Fully-grown means the same as **full-grown**.

fulminate /fʊlmɪneɪt, fʌlmɪneɪt/ **fulminates, fulminating, fulminated**

V+against If you **fulminate** against someone or something, you criticize them angrily; a formal word. *He paced up and down, fulminating against Thomas.* ◆ **fulmination** /fʊlmɪneɪʃn, fʌlmɪneɪʃn/ **fulminations** NC or NU *...the fulminations of preachers in the eighteenth century.*

fulsome /fʊlsəm/

ADJ **Fulsome** apologies or expressions of gratitude or admiration are very exaggerated or excessive; a formal word. *...with fulsome compliments and extravagant gifts.*

fumble /fʌmbl/ **fumbles, fumbling, fumbled**

1 V If you **fumble** with an object, you handle it clumsily. *His awkwardness made him fumble with the key... He fumbled with his chopsticks, and dropped a piece of food in his lap.*

2 V If you **fumble** for something, you search for it clumsily because you are not able to see what you are doing properly. *He fumbled in his pocket for his whistle... I fumbled for the script on my knee and began reading it in the wrong place.*

3 V If you **fumble** when you are trying to say or do something, you talk or act in a confused way. *The*

New York Times devotes three columns trying to figure out why Mr Bush fumbled so badly... Moments later, Newbridge fumbled, missed a penalty, and the final whistle went.

fume /fjuːm/ **fumes, fuming, fumed**

1 N PL **Fumes** are unpleasantly strong or harmful gases or smells. *...the exhaust fumes of a car. ...tobacco fumes.*

2 V or V-QUOTE If you **fume**, you show impatience and anger. *His rivals fumed over his calmness... I was fuming with rage... 'It's monstrous!' Jackie fumed.*

fumigate /fjuːmɪɡeɪt/ **fumigates, fumigating, fumigated**

VO If you **fumigate** something, you disinfect it, for example in order to get rid of germs or insects, by using special chemicals. *Your things will probably need fumigating.*

fun /fʌn/

1 NU **Fun** is something such as an activity or situation that is pleasant and enjoyable and that causes you to feel happy. *It's fun working for him... However, university life itself is often not much fun... Hallowe'en is just a bit of harmless fun... Thousands of people have come down here to join in the fun.*

2 NU If someone is **fun**, they are good company because they are interesting or amusing. *He was fun to be with... It's a pleasant place to be in, the people are fun, and there's great music.*

● **Fun** is used these phrases. ● If you do something for **fun** or for the fun of it, you do it because you enjoy doing it, and not for any other reason. *...things that you do for fun in your spare time... You don't come to work just for the fun of it.* ● If you **make fun of** someone or something, you tease them or make jokes about them. *Don't make fun of my father... If you came to school wearing trainers, everyone would make fun of you.* ● If you **poke fun at** someone or something, you make jokes about them in a way that is sometimes hurtful. *They like to poke fun at figures of authority... His satirical drawings poked fun at many Middle East governments.*

Funafuti Atoll /fuːnəfuːti ætɒl/

Funafuti Atoll is the capital of Tuvalu and its largest settlement. Population: 3,000 (1985).

function /fʌŋkʃn/ **functions, functioning, functioned**

1 NC The **function** of something or someone is its purpose or role. *The essential function of trade unions is to bargain with employers... The brain performs three functions: recording, recalling, and analysing.*

2 V If a machine or system **functions**, it works. *The phone didn't function at all. ...an idea of how the civil service functions... The government's job is to ensure that political institutions continue to function.*

3 V+as If someone or something **functions** as a particular thing, they do the work or fulfil the purpose of that thing. *The room had previously functioned as a playroom... I found myself functioning as an ambassador.*

4 NC If one thing is a **function** of another, its amount or nature depends on the other thing; a formal use. *The supply of money was a function of the amount of gold discovered.*

5 NC A **function** is also a large formal dinner or party. *He had been invited to a function at the college... Her normal activities, such as opening hospitals and attending charity functions, are far from glamorous.*

6 NC In computing, a **function** is a sequence of operations performed by the computer when a single key is pressed; a technical use. *...the memory function. ...the function keys on the keyboard.*

functional /fʌŋkʃ(ə)nəl/

1 ADJ **Functional** things are useful and practical rather than attractive. *...functional modern furniture... I always try to use a functional language in my books.*

2 ADJ If something is **functional**, it is working properly. *How long has the machine been functional?... Officials say the Libyan plant is not yet fully functional.*

3 ADJ ATTRIB **Functional** also means relating to the way something works. *...a functional description of*

the motorcycle... We train them in functional
management, areas like marketing, cost, and design.
functionary /fʌŋkʃənəʰri/ **functionaries**
NC A **functionary** is a person who has an official
administrative job in an organization, especially in a
government or a political party; a formal word. *Mr*
Calfa worked as a high functionary in the Cabinet of
the Communist government.
fund /fʌnd/ **funds, funding, funded**
1 N PL **Funds** are amounts of money that are available
for spending. *...how to raise funds for a commercial*
project... They are on trial for embezzling company
funds.
2 NC A **fund** is an amount of money that is collected
for a particular purpose. *He made a generous*
donation to our campaign fund.
3 NC If you have a **fund** of something, you have a lot
of it. *...a large fund of scientific knowledge.*
4 VO To **fund** something means to provide money for
it. *The work is being funded both by governments and*
private industry. ◆ **funding** NU *They provide funding*
in the form of loans.
fundamental /fʌndəmẹntl/ **fundamentals**
1 ADJ If something is **fundamental**, it is very
important or basic. *...the fundamental principles on*
which it is based... The differences are in some
respects fundamental.
2 N PL The **fundamentals** of a subject or activity are
its most important and basic parts. *...the*
fundamentals of police work... Their test really gets
down to fundamentals.
fundamentalism /fʌndəmẹntəlɪzəm/
NU **Fundamentalism** is belief in the original form of a
religion, without accepting any later ideas. *...the*
resurgence of fundamentalism in the United States.
◆ **fundamentalist** /fʌndəmẹntəlɪst/ **fundamentalists**
N Cor N+N *...Hindu fundamentalists. ...a fundamentalist*
preacher.
fundamentally /fʌndəmẹntəli/
ADV or ADV SEN You use **fundamentally** to indicate that
you are talking about the real or basic nature of
something. *Our criminal code is based fundamentally*
on fear... I disagreed fundamentally with the Party...
Fundamentally, we are not a part of the community.
fund-raising
NU **Fund-raising** is the activity of collecting money for
a particular purpose. *Mrs Thatcher praised the*
hospital's own efforts at fund-raising... Ethiopia is due
to receive money from the recent Comic Relief fund-
raising campaign.
funeral /fjuːnəʰrəl/ **funerals**
NC A **funeral** is a ceremony for the burial or
cremation of someone who has died. *Relatives were*
gathering for a funeral. ...a funeral service.
funerary /fjuːnərəri/
ADJ ATTRIB **Funerary** means relating to funerals,
burials, or cremations; a formal word. *The funerary*
ceremonies occupied two days.
funereal /fjuːnɪərɪəl/
ADJ If you describe something as **funereal**, you mean
that it is very sad, serious, and depressing; a literary
word. *The atmosphere in the cabin was almost*
funereal... The Telegraph adopts the same funereal
theme in its headline.
funfair /fʌnfeə/ **funfairs**
NC In Britain, a **funfair** is a form of entertainment
that consists of a collection of large machines on
which you can have exciting rides, and stalls where
you can win things. *I promised to take them to the*
funfair on Saturday.
fungal /fʌŋgl/
ADJ ATTRIB **Fungal** means caused by, consisting of, or
relating to fungus. *Corn has little natural resistance*
to fungal infections... This area of research
investigates the way trees protect themselves against
fungal attack.
fungi /fʌŋgiː, fʌndʒaɪ/
Fungi is the plural of **fungus**.
fungicide /fʌŋgɪsaɪd, fʌndʒɪsaɪd/ **fungicides**
N Cor NU A **fungicide** is a chemical that can be used to
kill fungus or to prevent it from growing. *They will*
soon be testing the fungicide in Australia and

Thailand. ...a capsule containing chemical fungicide.
fungoid /fʌŋgɔɪd/
ADJ **Fungoid** means consisting of or covered with
fungus, or reminding you of fungus; a formal word.
fungus /fʌŋgəs/ **fungi**
1 NC **Fungi** are plants such as mushrooms and
toadstools which have no leaves or stem, and grow on
other living things. *...trees that are affected by*
fungi... Truffles are fungi which grow underground...
The new stamps show a swan, a waterlilly, and an
edible fungus.
2 NU **Fungus** is a soft, furry growth that appears on
dead or diseased animals or plants. *The disease*
comes from chemicals produced by mould or fungus
growing on the stored crops... A patch of white fungus
covers her shin.
funicular /fjuːnɪkjʊlə/ **funiculars**
NC A **funicular** is a special railway which runs up a
very steep hill or mountain. A machine at the top of
the slope pulls the carriage up the rails by a steel
rope. *A funicular on the other side carries you up to*
the neo-Baroque Royal Palace.
funk /fʌŋk/
NU **Funk** is a style of music based on jazz and blues,
with a strong, repeated bass part. *They have roots in*
Little Richard and Jimi Hendrix but blend that with
Funk, Reggae and Hip Hop.
funky /fʌŋki/
1 ADJ **Funky** jazz, blues, or pop music has a very
strong, repeated bass part. *...the music's funky roots.*
2 ADJ You can use **funky** to describe something that
you like or admire; an informal use. *The theatre*
looks hip, and the couches are funky pieces from the
1950s.
funnel /fʌnl/ **funnels, funnelling, funnelled**; spelt
funneling, funneled in American English.
1 NC A **funnel** is an object with a wide top and a tube
at the bottom, which is used to pour substances into a
container. *Fill a bottle through a funnel... The sample*
is poured into this funnel, and suction applied to draw
it through.
2 NC A **funnel** is also a chimney on a ship or railway
engine. *...a ship with a yellow funnel.*
3 V-ERG If something **funnels** or is **funnelled**
somewhere, it is directed through a narrow space or
through a limited number of places. *...gales funnelling*
between the islands... Some of the gas would funnel
down the hole and make it luminous... The sunlight
which bounces off the mirror is funnelled through the
concentrator to produce a spot of intense light... We
funnel water in from outside the state through a whole
system of aqueducts.
4 VOA If you **funnel** money or resources somewhere,
you send them there from several sources.
...funnelling aid to the resistance groups... In addition,
the United States has been funnelling about twenty
million dollars to the non-Communists.
funnily /fʌnɪli/
You say **funnily enough** to indicate that something is
surprising, but true. *I started here at about the same*
time as you, funnily enough.
funny /fʌni/ **funnier, funniest**
1 ADJ You say that something is **funny** when it is
strange, surprising, or puzzling. *...a funny little white*
hat... It's a funny thing to write... The funny thing is,
we went to Arthur's house just yesterday.
2 ADJ **Funny** things or people are amusing and make
you smile or laugh. *...funny stories... It did look*
funny upside down... She laughed. 'What's funny?' he
asked... Brian Patten is a funny, honest, and
unpretentious English poet.
3 ADJ PRED If you feel **funny**, you feel slightly ill; an
informal use.
funny bone, funny bones
NC Your **funny bone** is the part of your elbow that
gives you a tingling feeling when it is hit; an informal
expression.
fur /fɜː/ **furs**
1 NU **Fur** is the thick hair that grows on the bodies of
many animals. *Moles have short silky fur... The Yeti*
was about 2 metres tall and covered in fur about 6-7
cms. in length.

2 N MASS You use **fur** to refer to the fur-covered skin of an animal used to make clothes or rugs. *They were jailed for their part in hunting pandas for their fur. ...a campaign to protest at the sale of fur coats. ...companies involved in the fur trade.*
3 NU **Fur** is also a soft, artificial material that resembles fur.
4 NC A **fur** is a coat made from real or artificial fur. *Clutching an elegant fur befitting a Countess, Rita stands by the train. ...a tax on expensive cars, jewellery, furs, and yachts.*

furbish /ˈfɜːbɪʃ/ **furbishes, furbishing, furbished**
VO If you **furbish** something, you make it look better, for example by painting or repairing it; a formal word. *...my freshly furbished dining room.*

furious /ˈfjʊərɪəs/
1 ADJ If someone is **furious**, they are extremely angry. *I was furious and told them to get out of my house... She was furious with him.* ◆ **furiously** ADV *'Who is this man?' the Prince exclaimed furiously.*
2 ADJ ATTRIB You can use **furious** to indicate that something involves great energy, speed, or violence. *...a furious battle. ...the furious efforts they were making.* ◆ **furiously** ADV *She ran furiously up the hill.*

furl /fɜːl/ **furls, furling, furled**
VO When you **furl** something such as an umbrella, sail, or flag, you roll or fold it up because it is not going to be used. ◆ **furled** ADJ *...a ship with its sails furled... His black umbrella was furled tight.*

furlong /ˈfɜːlɒŋ/ **furlongs**
NC A **furlong** is an imperial unit of length that is equal to 220 yards or 201.2 metres. *We could predict which horse would win over five furlongs.*

furnace /ˈfɜːnɪs/ **furnaces**
NC A **furnace** is a container for a very hot fire that is being used to melt metal or burn rubbish. *Gradually, coal furnaces were replaced by gas and electric ones.*

furnish /ˈfɜːnɪʃ/ **furnishes, furnishing, furnished**
1 VO When you **furnish** a room, you put furniture in it. *Do you enjoy decorating and furnishing a house?*
2 VO To **furnish** something means to provide it or supply it; a formal use. *They were not prepared to furnish the necessary troops... Luckily, they have furnished us with a translation.*

furnished /ˈfɜːnɪʃt/
1 ADJ A **furnished** room or house is rented with furniture already in it. *They were living in a furnished flat near Finchley Station. ...a lack of furnished accommodation.*
2 ADJ When you say how a room or house is **furnished**, you are describing the kind or amount of furniture that it has in it. *The bedroom was scantily furnished. ...a large room furnished with low tables and cushions.*

furnishings /ˈfɜːnɪʃɪŋz/
N PL The **furnishings** of a room are the furniture and fittings, such as curtains or carpets, that are in it. *The tables and stools were the sole furnishings of the room.*

furniture /ˈfɜːnɪtʃə/
NU **Furniture** consists of the large movable objects in a room such as tables or chairs. *She arranged the furniture... The only piece of furniture was an old wardrobe.*

furore /fjʊˈrɔːri, fjʊəˈrɔː/; spelt **furor** in American English.
N SING A **furore** is a very angry or excited reaction by people to something. *The lecture caused an enormous furore. ...the present furore over drugs.*

furrier /ˈfʌrɪə/ **furriers**
NC A **furrier** is a person who makes or sells clothes made from fur.

furrow /ˈfʌrəʊ/ **furrows, furrowing, furrowed**
1 NC A **furrow** is a long line in the earth made for planting seeds. *...a field with parallel furrows running down it.*
2 NC The **furrows** in someone's skin are deep folds or lines. *...the deep furrows in his cheeks.*
3 V-ERG When your brow **furrows** or when you **furrow** it, you frown. *His brow furrowed in anguish... The pain caused him to furrow his brow.*

furry /ˈfɜːri/ **furrier, furriest**
1 ADJ A **furry** animal is covered with thick, soft hair. *It had a long furry tail... A spider, brown and furry, crouched on a tree trunk.*
2 ADJ Something that is **furry** resembles fur. *...a furry coat.*

further /ˈfɜːðə/ **furthers, furthering, furthered.**
Further is a comparative of **far**, and it is also a verb.
1 ADV **Further** means to a greater degree or extent. *The situation was further complicated by uncertainty about the future... He sank further into debt... Japan went even further, cutting energy expenditure by half.*
2 ADV If someone or something goes **further** or takes something **further**, they progress to a more advanced or detailed stage. *They never got any further... Let's go a step further... He hoped the new offer would develop matters a stage further.*
3 ADJ or ADJ after N A **further** thing or amount is an additional one. *We need a further five hundred pounds... Do you have nothing further to say?*
4 **Further to** is used in business letters to indicate that you are referring to a previous letter or conversation; a formal expression. *Further to your enquiry of the 16th, I am happy to enclose the new contract.*
5 ADV **Further** means a greater distance than before or than something else. *I walked further than I intended... They moved further away from the street.*
6 VO If you **further** something, you help it to progress or to be successful. *...a plot by Morris to further his career... A spokesman said Israel was working on ideas furthering the peace plan... The image of Austria as a brave little nation was furthered by films such as 'The Sound of Music'.*

furtherance /ˈfɜːðərəns/
NU+SUPP If you do something in **furtherance** of something else, you do it in order to help this other thing to be achieved; a formal word. *He did it solely in the furtherance of his own interests. ...acting in furtherance of a lawful trade dispute.*

further education
NU **Further education** is education received at a college after leaving school, but not at a university or polytechnic. *The state is pouring money into further education. ...further education courses.*

furthermore /ˌfɜːðəˈmɔː/
ADV SEN **Furthermore** is used to introduce a statement adding to or supporting the previous one. *He carried out orders without questioning them. Furthermore, he was not bothered by hard work... It is nearly dark, and furthermore it's going to rain.*

furthermost /ˈfɜːðəməʊst/
ADJ ATTRIB The **furthermost** one of a number of similar things is the one that is the greatest distance away from a particular place. *We made our way to the furthermost hut.*

furthest /ˈfɜːðɪst/. **Furthest** is a superlative of **far**.
1 ADV or ADJ **Furthest** means to a greater extent or degree than ever before. *...countries where commercialized farming has advanced furthest. ...the furthest limits of democracy.*
2 ADJ or ADV The **furthest** one of a number of things is the one that is the greatest distance away. *...the furthest reaches of the solar system. ...the fields which lay furthest from his farm.*

furtive /ˈfɜːtɪv/
ADJ **Furtive** behaviour is secretive and sly. *His funeral was not the furtive, private affair which would have been suitable to a spy... Mr Dobson accused the government of being underhand and furtive over the matter. ...a furtive glance.* ◆ **furtively** ADV *He looked round, furtively... There was a couple sitting together, holding hands furtively.*

fury /ˈfjʊəri/
NU **Fury** is violent or very great anger. *He clenched his fists in fury... There was fury in Miss Lenaut's dark eyes.*

fuse /fjuːz/ **fuses, fusing, fused**
1 NC In an electrical appliance, a **fuse** is a wire safety device which melts and stops the electric current if there is a fault. *Have you checked the fuse?*
2 V-ERG When an electric device **fuses** or when someone or something **fuses** it, it stops working

because of a fault. *Several of the street lamps had fused... If the cables had met, they would have fused the lights.*
3 NC A **fuse** is also part of a bomb or firework which delays the explosion and gives people time to move away. *Dynamite, fuses, revolvers and ammunition were said to have been found in the car... The bomb fuse has been removed, and it is due to be detonated in a controlled explosion this morning.*
4 V-ERG When objects **fuse** or when you **fuse** them, they join together because of heat or a biological process. *During fertilization the sperm and egg fuse... Surgeons used a piece of bone from his pelvis to fuse together two of his vertebrae. ...the materials which one is trying to fuse at very high temperatures.*
5 V-ERG If you **fuse** ideas, methods, or systems that are different from each other, you combine them in an interesting, unexpected, and exciting way. *...an attempt to fuse radical and more conservative plans... King Juan Carlos praised Mr Fuentes for the way in which he had fused Spanish and Latin American culture... Many of the papers fuse comments from Mr Major on interest rate cuts with a warning from the CBI that the economy is in recession. ..the man who fused Big Band Swing and Country and Western music.*

fuse box, fuse boxes
NC A **fuse box** is a box that is usually fixed to a wall in a house or other building and that contains the fuses for all the electric circuits in the building.

fuselage /fjuːzəlɑːʒ/ **fuselages**
NC The **fuselage** of an aeroplane or rocket is its main part. *The search party have located the four engines, both wings and most of the fuselage... It came to rest with smoke billowing from its fuselage.*

fuse wire
NU **Fuse wire** is the metal wire that is used in fuses.

fusillade /fjuːzəleɪd/
N SING+*of* A **fusillade** of shots is a large number of them fired at the same time. *Both men were killed in a fusillade of bullets fired at close range.*

fusion /fjuːʒn/ **fusions**
1 NU or NU When two or more ideas, methods, or systems are combined, you can say that there is a **fusion** of them. *...the fusion of radical and socialist ideals... The painting is a rich fusion of several elements.*
2 NU The process in which atomic particles combine to produce nuclear energy is called nuclear **fusion**; a technical use. *It could be useful for exploring the physics of nuclear fusion.*

fuss /fʌs/ **fusses, fussing, fussed**
1 N SING or NC **Fuss** is unnecessarily anxious or excited behaviour. *They're making a fuss about the wedding... He accepted the statement without fuss... What the hell is all the fuss about?*
2 V When people **fuss**, they behave in an unnecessarily anxious or excited way. *Stop fussing, mother... Ted fussed with his camera... The children fussed and fidgeted, ill after a month in the mountains and a two-day journey.*
● **Fuss** is used in these phrases. ● If you **make a fuss** of someone, you pay a lot of attention to them. *They like to be flattered and made a fuss of.* ● If you **make a fuss** or **kick up a fuss**, you become angry or upset about something, often unnecessarily. *An indignant passenger, making a fuss, could distract officials' attention from a potential terrorist... It's going to be very difficult for them to make a fuss over this... He's likely to kick up a fuss if he's left off the list.*

fuss over PHRASAL VERB If you **fuss over** someone or something, you pay them too much attention or worry about them too much. *She was inclined to fuss over her health... I hated being fussed over as a child.*

fusspot /fʌspɒt/ **fusspots**
NC A **fusspot** is a person who is always complaining and is difficult to please; an informal word. *Sit down and stop being such a fusspot, Karen.*

fussy /fʌsi/ **fussier, fussiest**
1 ADJ Someone who is **fussy** is too concerned with unimportant details and is difficult to please. *I am very fussy about my food... The majority of insects are fussy about where they lay their eggs... Some countries were accused of being too fussy about their conditions.*
2 ADJ You can use **fussy** to describe things such as clothes or furniture that are too elaborate or detailed. *...fussy lace curtains... Before Crosby, there were the fussy, formal style of operatic singers.*

fusty /fʌsti/ **fustier, fustiest**
1 ADJ Something that is **fusty** is old-fashioned in attitudes or ideas; used showing disapproval. *I was sent to a fusty old school in the country.*
2 ADJ Something that smells **fusty** has a stale, unpleasant smell because it is old or neglected. *The sleeping bag smelt fusty... The family home, now a museum, is poky and fusty but full of memorabilia.*

futile /fjuːtaɪl/
ADJ A **futile** action is one which is not successful, and is unlikely ever to be successful. *...a series of costly and futile wars... Lucy knew how futile it was to argue with her father.* ◆ **futility** /fjuːtɪləti/ NU *...the futility of their attempts. ...the injustice and futility of terrorism... There was a deepening sense of frustration, despair, and futility.*

future /fjuːtʃə/ **futures**
1 N SING The **future** is the period of time after the present. *It might be possible in the future... What plans do you have for the future? ...not within the foreseeable future.* ► Also ADJ ATTRIB *Let's meet again at some future date. ...future generations... He may be a future Prime Minister.*
2 You use **in future** when you are telling someone what you want or expect to happen from now on. *Be more careful in future... We will be able to avoid it in future... In future, political parties will be able to operate.*
3 NC Your **future** is your life or career after the present time. *I decided that my future lay in medicine... Their task is to plan Quebec's future.*
4 N SING Something that has a **future** is likely to be successful. *Does the engine have a future?... Members of the public may wonder if this scheme has any future at all.*
5 N PL **Futures** are commodities that are bought or sold on the stock exchange at an agreed price that is paid at a later date. *Oil futures are higher this morning on the New York Mercantile Exchange. ...the volatile futures market.*

future tense
N SING In grammar, the **future tense** is used to refer to things that will come after the present.

futuristic /fjuːtʃərɪstɪk/
ADJ You describe something as **futuristic** when it looks or seems unusual, as if belonging to some period of time in the future. *...the futuristic shape of the buildings... Ballard is a much admired writer of futuristic novels... Sounds very futuristic, but it's not exactly a new idea is it?*

fuzz /fʌz/
NU **Fuzz** is a mass of short curly hairs or threads. *...the light, blond fuzz on his cheeks.*

fuzzy /fʌzi/ **fuzzier, fuzziest**
1 ADJ **Fuzzy** hair sticks up in a soft, curly mass. *His fuzzy head was cradled in his arms. ...a little white, fuzzy poodle.*
2 ADJ A **fuzzy** picture, image, or sound is unclear and hard to see or hear. *The Navy videos were fuzzy and hard to interpret... The inner ear is damaged, and what they hear is distorted, fuzzy, or blurred... Expect fuzzy radio communications, power problems, and a light snow.*
3 ADJ If you or your thoughts are **fuzzy**, you are confused and cannot think clearly. *My mind was tired and a bit fuzzy... It's just that he gets fuzzy and confused over his objectives.*

G g

G, g /dʒiː/ **G's, g's**
1 NC **G** is the seventh letter of the English alphabet.
2 **g.** is used after a number as a written abbreviation
for 'gram'. ...*257g.*

gab /gæb/
If you say that someone has **the gift of the gab**, you
mean that they have the ability to speak easily,
confidently, and in a persuasive way; an informal
expression. ...*people with the incredible gift of the gab
for the language of love.*

gabardine /gæbədiːn/ **gabardines**; also spelt
gaberdine.
NU **Gabardine** is a fairly thick cloth which is used
especially for making coats. ...*a grey gabardine suit.*

gabble /gæbl/ **gabbles, gabbling, gabbled**
V-QUOTE, V, or VO If you **gabble**, you talk so quickly that
it is difficult for people to understand you; an informal
word. '*Look here,' he gabbled, 'It's about the Harvest
Festival.'... He gabbled excitedly into Marcus's ear...
He gabbled his last words.* ► Also N SING *There was a
gabble of conversation in the pub.*

gable /geɪbl/ **gables**
NC A **gable** is the triangular part at the top of the end
wall of a building, between the two sloping sides of the
roof. *The gable ends of two warehouse buildings have
been turned into projection screens.*

gabled /geɪbld/
ADJ **Gabled** is used to describe houses that have a
gable or gables. ...*a red-bricked gabled mansion.*

Gabon /gæbɒn/
The **Republic of Gabon** is a country in western Africa.
It was part of French Equatorial Africa from 1886 and
became independent in 1960. Albert-Bernard Bongo
(now Omar Bongo) became President of Gabon in
1967. The Democratic Party of Gabon (PDG) became
the only legal party in 1969. Political parties were
legalized in 1990. Gabon exports oil. It is a member of
OPEC and the Organization of African Unity. It also
exports manganese, timber, and uranium. ◆ **Gabonese**
/gæbəniːz/ N, ADJ
▪ *per capita GNP:* US$2,970 ▪ *religion:* Christianity,
animism ▪ *language:* French (official), Fang
▪ *currency:* CFA franc ▪ *capital:* Libreville
▪ *population:* 1 million (1989) ▪ *size:* 267,667 square
kilometres.

Gaborone /xæburuːni/
Gaborone is the capital of Botswana and its largest
city. Population: 111,000 (1988).

gad /gæd/ **gads, gadding, gadded**
gad about PHRASAL VERB If you **gad about** or **gad
around**, you go to a lot of different places looking for
amusement and entertainment; an old-fashioned
word. *This is hardly the time to be gadding around.*

Gaddafi, Muammar al- /muʌmər əl gədɑːfi/ See
Qaddafi

gadget /gædʒɪt/ **gadgets**
NC A **gadget** is a small machine or device which does
a useful job. ...*household gadgets.*

gadgetry /gædʒɪtri/
NU **Gadgetry** consists of small machines or devices
that do something useful. *New developments will
make the present gadgetry look very old-fashioned.*

Gaelic /geɪlɪk/
1 NU **Gaelic** is a language spoken by people in Ireland
and parts of Scotland. *In her acceptance speech,
given in English and Gaelic, she pledged to help solve
the problems in Northern Ireland.*
2 ADJ Something that is **Gaelic** is written or spoken in
Gaelic, or is associated with the culture of Gaelic
people. ...*an old Gaelic proverb.* ...*the fiery
imagination of Gaelic Ireland.*

gaff /gæf/
If you **blow the gaff** you let someone know a secret
that other people do not want them to know, especially
by mistake or without meaning to; an informal
expression. *Was Mrs Welch there when he blew the
gaff about the phone call?*

gaffe /gæf/ **gaffes**
NC A **gaffe** is something that you say or do which is
considered socially incorrect. *I had no idea of the
gaffe which I was committing.*

gaffer /gæfə/ **gaffers**; an informal word.
1 NC The **gaffer** in a business, a factory, or on a
building site is the man in charge, for example the
owner or a foreman. *You'll have to ask the gaffer.*
2 NC Some people use **gaffer** to refer to any man,
especially an old man. ...*an old gaffer not famous for
his tact.*

gag /gæg/ **gags, gagging, gagged**
1 NC A **gag** is a piece of cloth that is tied round or put
inside someone's mouth to stop them from speaking.
Some of the audience put gags over their mouths.
2 VO If someone **gags** you, they tie a piece of cloth
round your mouth to stop you from speaking. *Three
men broke into his house and bound and gagged a
guard.*
3 VO If a person in authority or the government **gags**
someone, they prevent them from expressing their
opinion or from publishing certain information. *He
said the government was not seeking to gag the press.*
4 NC A **gag** is also a joke told by a comedian; an
informal use. ...*gag writers.*

gaga /gɑːgɑː/
ADJ Someone who is **gaga** is slightly mad or senile; an
informal word. *She's seventy-seven and rather gaga.*

gaggle /gægl/ **gaggles**
NC You can use **gaggle** to refer to a group of people;
often used humorously. ...*the agreeable past-time of
budget speculation with a gaggle of analysts.*

gaiety /geɪəti/
NU **Gaiety** is a feeling or attitude of liveliness and
fun. ...*fresh youthful gaiety.*

gaily /geɪli/
1 ADV If you do something **gaily**, you do it in a lively,
happy way. *Off we set, with Pam chattering gaily all
the way.*
2 ADV Something that is **gaily** decorated is decorated
in a bright, pretty way. *Guests offered gaily wrapped
presents.*

gain /geɪn/ **gains, gaining, gained**
1 VO or V+in If you **gain** a quality, you get it gradually.
*The speaker began to gain confidence... The opposition
party is gaining in popularity.*
2 V+from or VO If you **gain** from something, you get

some advantage from it. *It is not only banks who will gain from the coming of electronic money... They would gain substantial additional tax revenues from cigarette imports.*
3 NC A **gain** is an improvement or increase. *The company has made notable gains in productivity.*
4 NU If you do something for **gain**, you do it in order to get some profit for yourself; a formal use. *He did it for financial gain.*
5 VorVO If a clock or watch **gains**, the hands move round slightly faster than they should. *My watch gains about ten minutes every day.*
gain on PHRASAL VERB If you **gain on** someone or something, you gradually catch them up. *Bayern Munich were unable to gain on the West German League leaders Werder Bremen.*

gainful /ˈgeɪnfl/
ADJ ATTRIB **Gainful** means useful or profitable; a formal word. *...gainful employment. ...all manner of professions and gainful pursuits.* ◆ **gainfully** ADV *Clearly there was nothing that could gainfully be said. ...gainfully employed.*

gainsay /geɪnˈseɪ/ **gainsays, gainsaying, gainsaid**
VO If something cannot be **gainsaid** or there is no **gainsaying** it, it is true or correct and cannot be denied or contradicted; a formal word. *Teachers have expertise that cannot be gainsaid... This was such an evident truth that there was no gainsaying it.*

gait /geɪt/ **gaits**
NC Someone's **gait** is their way of walking; a formal word. *...their faltering gait... Seven friends walking down the street with a gait, an attitude that smacked of toughness.*

gaiter /ˈgeɪtə/ **gaiters**
NC **Gaiters** are coverings made of cloth, leather, or other material for your legs below your knees. Gaiters were commonly worn in former times, but are now mainly worn by climbers and skiers or as part of an old-fashioned uniform. *...a fat man in breeches and gaiters.*

gal /gæl/ **gals**
NC **Gal** is used in written English to represent the word 'girl' pronounced this way in a particular accent. *Since she's known you she's a different gal. ...a very nice, ladylike gal.*

gala /ˈgɑːlə/ **galas**
NC A **gala** is a special public celebration, entertainment, or performance. *He was speaking at a gala in his honour. ...the special guest on a gala occasion.*

galactic /gəˈlæktɪk/
ADJ ATTRIB **Galactic** means relating to galaxies. *The Universe, far from being evenly filled with galaxies and galactic clusters, has huge areas of void.*

galaxy /ˈgæləksi/ **galaxies**
NC A **galaxy** is a huge group of stars and planets extending over millions of miles. *Every planet in the Solar System, every star in our galaxy, and every galaxy in the Universe is made of atoms.*

gale /geɪl/ **gales**
NC A **gale** is a very strong wind. *...a howling gale. ...gale force winds.*

gall /gɔːl/ **galls, galling, galled**
1 N SING If someone has the **gall** to do something dangerous or dishonest, they have the daring to do it; used showing disapproval. *They haven't the gall to steal.*
2 VO If something **galls** you, it makes you angry or annoyed; an old-fashioned use. *It galled him to have to ask permission.*

gallant /ˈgælənt/; also pronounced /gəˈlænt/ for the meaning in paragraph 2.
1 ADJ A **gallant** person is very brave and honourable when in danger or difficulty. *They have put up a gallant fight over the years.* ◆ **gallantly** ADV *Gallantly they battled on.*
2 ADJ A **gallant** man is polite and considerate towards women. *'Allow me,' said the gallant policeman.* ◆ **gallantly** ADV *He gallantly offered to carry her cases to the car.*

gallantry /ˈgæləntri/
1 NU **Gallantry** is bravery shown by someone who is

in danger, especially in a war. *He was awarded the Military Cross for gallantry in combat.*
2 NU **Gallantry** is also polite and considerate behaviour by men towards women. *...expectations of old-fashioned gallantry.*

gall bladder, gall bladders
NC Your **gall bladder** is the organ in your body which stores bile. It is next to your liver. *Research indicates that aspirin and related drugs completely prevent the formation of gallstones in the gall bladder. ...gall-bladder surgery.*

galleon /ˈgæliən/ **galleons**
NC A **galleon** is a sailing ship with three masts that was used as a warship or for carrying large cargoes from the fifteenth to the eighteenth century. *...Spanish galleons.*

gallery /ˈgæləri/ **galleries**
1 NC A **gallery** is a building or room where works of art are exhibited, and sometimes sold. *...the National Gallery.*
2 NC In a theatre or large hall, the **gallery** is a raised area at the back or sides where the audience can sit. *...the public gallery at Parliament.* ◆ If you **play to the gallery**, you do something in public in a way which you hope will impress people. *I think Walesa has a tendency generally to play to the gallery.*

galley /ˈgæli/ **galleys**
NC A **galley** is a kitchen in a ship or an aircraft. *Each submarine leaves crammed full of eatables in the galley.*

Gallic /ˈgælɪk/
ADJ Something that is **Gallic** belongs to or is associated with French culture or the French people; a formal word. *...the Gallic nation. ...the famous rationalist strain in Gallic philosophy.*

gallivant /ˈgælɪvænt/ **gallivants, gallivanting, gallivanted**
gallivant about PHRASAL VERB If you **gallivant about** or **gallivant around**, you go to a lot of different places looking for amusement and entertainment; an old-fashioned word. *You're here to do a job, not go gallivanting around all those country clubs.*

gallon /ˈgælən/ **gallons**
1 NC In Britain, a **gallon** is a unit of volume for liquids equal to eight imperial pints or approximately 4.55 litres. *...three gallons of water.*
2 NC In the United States, a **gallon** is a unit of volume for liquids equal to eight American pints or approximately 3.79 litres. *Gasoline fell over two cents a gallon, down to $1.23.*

gallop /ˈgæləp/ **gallops, galloping, galloped**
1 V When a horse **gallops**, it runs very fast so that all four legs are off the ground at the same time between strides. *The horse galloped down the road.* ▶ Also N SING *All the animals broke into a gallop.*
2 VorVO If you **gallop**, you ride a horse that is galloping. *He swung onto his horse, saluted, and galloped off... We galloped the horses up to the moor.*
3 NC A **gallop** is also a ride on a galloping horse. *...a brisk morning's gallop.*

galloping /ˈgæləpɪŋ/
ADJ ATTRIB **Galloping** is used to describe something that is increasing or developing so fast that it is difficult to control. *The oil crisis brought galloping inflation on an international scale.*

gallows /ˈgæləʊz/; **gallows** is both the singular and the plural form.
NC A **gallows** is a wooden frame on which criminals used to be hanged. *The condemned man was led to the gallows.*

gallstone /ˈgɔːlstəʊn/ **gallstones**
NC A **gallstone** is a small and painful lump which can develop in your gall bladder. *It is thought that their diet makes certain people liable to suffer from gallstones.*

Gallup poll /ˈgæləp pəʊl/ **Gallup polls**
NC A **Gallup poll** is a survey by the American Institute of Public Opinion or its British counterpart in which a group of people, specially chosen to represent all the people in a country, are asked for their opinion on something, such as how they will vote in an election. *A Gallup poll carried out for the BBC suggests that*

four out of five voters are unclear what the new party stands for.

galore /gəlɔ:/
ADJ after N **Galore** means existing in very large numbers. *...restaurants and night clubs galore.*

galoshes /gəlɒʃɪz/
N PL **Galoshes** are waterproof shoes that can be worn over ordinary shoes to prevent them from getting wet.

galvanize /gælvənaɪz/ **galvanizes, galvanizing, galvanized**; also spelt **galvanise**.
VO To **galvanize** someone means to cause them to do something suddenly by making them feel excited, afraid, or angry. *The lecture galvanized several others into action.*

galvanized /gælvənaɪzd/; also spelt **galvanised**.
ADJ **Galvanized** metal has been covered with zinc to protect it from rust. *...galvanized iron.*

Gambia /gæmbɪə/
The **Republic of the Gambia** is a country in western Africa. It was a British colony from the 19th century until independence in 1965. Sir Dawda Kairaba Jawara, of the People's Progressive Party (PPP), became Premier in 1962, Prime Minister at independence in 1965, and President when Gambia became a republic in 1970. Gambia is a member of the Commonwealth and the Organization of African Unity. It exports groundnuts. Tourism is becoming an important industry. ◆ **Gambian** /gæmbɪən/ N, ADJ
▪ *per capita GNP:* US$220 ▪ *religion:* Islam ▪ *language:* English (official), Madinka, Wolof, Fula ▪ *currency:* dalasi ▪ *capital:* Banjul ▪ *largest city:* Serekunda ▪ *population:* 848,000 (1989) ▪ *size:* 11,295 square kilometres.

gambit /gæmbɪt/ **gambits**
1 NC A **gambit** is something that you do or say in a situation or game in order to try to gain an advantage. *The initiative was widely seen as a cynical gambit to widen the existing ethnic rifts. ...an opening gambit in a constitutional chess-match which may last quite some time. ...a good gambit for attracting attention.*
2 NC A **gambit** is also something you say to someone in order to start a conversation with them. *...suitable opening gambits for dinner parties.*

gamble /gæmbl/ **gambles, gambling, gambled**
1 N SING A **gamble** is a risky action or decision taken in the hope of gaining money or success. *We took a gamble, and lost. ...a gamble that paid off for us.*
► Also V,VO,or V+on *The hardliners in the Kremlin gambled and lost... The company gambled all on the new factory... I was gambling on the assumption that the file had been lost.*
2 V,VO,or V+on If you **gamble**, you bet money in a game or on the result of a race or competition. *There was little to do except gamble and drink beer... Fred gambled his profits away... He gambled heavily on the horses.* ◆ **gambling** NU *If you're going to make money on gambling, you have to know more than the bookie... He used the firm's money to pay off gambling debts.*

gambler /gæmblə/ **gamblers**
NC A **gambler** is someone who bets money in games or on the results of races or competitions. *...a compulsive gambler.*

gambol /gæmbl/ **gambols, gambolling, gambolled**; also spelt **gamboling, gamboled** in American English.
V If animals or people **gambol**, they run or jump about in a playful way. *...with his dogs gambolling round him.*

game /geɪm/ **games**
1 NC A **game** is an enjoyable activity with a set of rules which is played by individuals or teams against each other. *You need two people to play this game. ...word games.*
2 NC A **game** is also a particular occasion on which a game is played. *Did you go to the baseball game?*
3 NC In sports such as tennis, a **game** is part of a match, consisting of a fixed number of points. *Becker leads by four games to one.*
4 N PL **Games** are sports played at school or in a competition. *I was hopeless at games at school. ...the Olympic Games.*

5 NC A **game** is also the equipment needed to play a particular indoor game. *...a box of toys and games.*
6 NC You can describe a way of behaving as a **game** when it is used to try to gain advantage. *...these games that politicians play.*
7 NU **Game** is wild animals or birds that are hunted for sport or food. *...game and poultry.*
8 ADJ Someone who is **game** is willing to do something new, unusual, or risky. *I'm game for anything!*
● **Game** is used in these phrases. ● If you beat someone at their **own game**, you use their own methods to gain an advantage over them. *Mr Beregovoy encouraged a consortium sympathetic to the socialists to try to beat Mr Chirac at his own game and launch raids on the firms concerned.* ● If you say **the game is up**, you mean that someone's secret plans or activities have been discovered. *When the last attempt failed, he realised that the game was up.* ● If someone or something **gives the game away**, they reveal a secret. *I can't tell you the exact amount because that would give the game away.*

gamekeeper /geɪmki:pə/ **gamekeepers**
NC A **gamekeeper** is a person employed to look after game animals and birds on someone's land. *...a gamekeeper on the estate.*

gamesmanship /geɪmzmənʃɪp/
NU **Gamesmanship** is the art or practice of winning a game by methods that are not against the rules but are very close to cheating. *It is gamesmanship to make a loud noise while your opponent is playing.*

gaming /geɪmɪŋ/
NU **Gaming** is the same as **gambling**; a formal word. *...gaming clubs. ...the Betting and Gaming Act of 1960.*

gamma /gæmə/ **gammas**
NCorNU **Gamma** is the third letter of the Greek alphabet, sometimes used as a mark or grade given for a student's work, indicating an average or poor piece of work.

gamma rays
N PL **Gamma rays** are a type of electromagnetic radiation that has a shorter wavelength and higher energy than X-rays. *Neutron stars give out nearly all of their radiation as gamma rays.*

gammon /gæmən/
NU **Gammon** is smoked or salted meat from a pig, similar to bacon.

gamut /gæmət/
N SING+of You use **gamut** to refer to the whole range of things in a varied situation or activity; a literary word. *...the entire gamut of London politics.*

gander /gændə/ **ganders**
NC A **gander** is a male goose.

gang /gæŋ/ **gangs, ganging, ganged**
N COLL A **gang** is a group of people who join together for some purpose, often criminal. *Five members of the eight man gang who plotted to overthrow him are under arrest. ...a gang of terrorists.*
gang up PHRASAL VERB If people **gang up** on you, or if they **gang up** against you, they unite against you; an informal expression. *The UN can work effectively as a forum when sufficient nations are of like mind in ganging up against an aggressor... National groups are ganging up to claim their rights.*

gangland /gæŋlænd, gæŋlənd/
ADJ ATTRIB **Gangland** is used to describe activities or people that are involved in organized crime. *They were all gangland killers. ...a New York gangland boss.*

gangling /gæŋglɪŋ/
ADJ A **gangling** young person is tall, thin, and clumsy; used in written English. *...a tall, slender, gangling young man with big feet.*

gangly /gæŋgli/
ADJ **Gangly** means the same as **gangling**. *...gangly teenagers stalking the streets of urban America.*

gangplank /gæŋplæŋk/ **gangplanks**
NC A **gangplank** is a short bridge or platform that can be placed between the side of a ship or boat and the shore, so that people can get on or off. *The gangplank was again lowered and they were put ashore.*

gangrene /ˈgæŋgriːn/
NU **Gangrene** is decay in part of a person's body, caused by insufficient blood flowing to it. *He has developed frostbite in his foot and is taking anti-biotics to stop gangrene from setting in.*

gangrenous /ˈgæŋgrɪnəs/
ADJ **Gangrenous** is used to describe a part of a person's body that has been affected by gangrene. *They had to amputate the gangrenous leg.*

gangster /ˈgæŋstə/ **gangsters**
NC A **gangster** is a member of a group of violent criminals. *The Kray twins were two of London's most feared gangsters.*

gangway /ˈgæŋweɪ/ **gangways**
1 NC A **gangway** is a passage left between rows of seats for people to walk along. *The Jumbo was to have a wide body with two gangways and an upper deck.*
2 NC A **gangway** is also a short bridge or platform leading onto a ship.

Ganilau, Ratu Sir Penaia
/ˈrɑːtuː sə pənaɪə ˈgænɪlaʊ/
Ratu Sir Penaia Ganilau became the first President of Fiji following the military coup of 1987. He held numerous cabinet posts from 1961, served as Deputy Prime Minister from 1973 to 1983, and was Governor General from 1983 to 1987. Born: 1918.

gantry /ˈgæntri/ **gantries**
NC A **gantry** is a high metal structure that supports a crane, a set of road signs, railway signals, or other equipment. *There was only one metal ladder up to the gantry... The gantry was crammed with photographic lights.*

gaol /dʒeɪl/. See jail.
gaoler /ˈdʒeɪlə/. See jailer.

gap /gæp/ **gaps**
1 NC A **gap** is a space between two things or a hole in something solid. *She had gaps in her teeth. ...a gap in the hedge.*
2 NC A **gap** is also a period of time when you are not involved in a particular activity. *After a gap of two years, she went back to college.*
3 NC If there is something missing from a situation which prevents it from being satisfactory or complete, you can also say that there is a **gap**. *This book fills a major gap.*
4 NC A **gap** is also a great difference between two things, people, or ideas. *The gap between rich and poor regions widened.* ◆ See also **generation gap**.

gape /geɪp/ **gapes, gaping, gaped**
1 V If you **gape**, you look at someone or something in surprise, with your mouth open. *Jackson gaped in astonishment at the result.* ◆ **gaping** ADJ *...gaping tourists.*
2 V If something **gapes**, it opens wide or comes apart. *The shirt gaped to reveal his chest.* ◆ **gaping** ADJ ATTRIB *The dressing gown had a gaping hole in it.*

gappy /ˈgæpi/
ADJ If someone has **gappy** teeth or a **gappy** smile, they have a lot of gaps between their teeth. *She plunged her gappy teeth into it.*

gap-toothed
ADJ A **gap-toothed** person has wide spaces between their teeth. *...a genial gap-toothed man. ...a gap-toothed grin.*

garage /ˈgærɑːʒ, ˈgærɪdʒ/ **garages**
1 NC A **garage** is a building in which you keep a car. *He parked his car in the open, rather than in a lock-up garage.*
2 NC A **garage** is also a place where you can get your car repaired, buy a car, or buy petrol. *Cars serviced in many garages are being handed back to their owners in an unroadworthy condition.*

garb /gɑːb/
N SING+SUPP Someone's **garb** is the clothes that they are wearing; a literary word. *...military garb.*

garbage /ˈgɑːbɪdʒ/
1 NU **Garbage** is rubbish, especially kitchen waste; used in American English. *...the garbage in the streets.*
2 NU You can refer to ideas that are stupid or worthless as **garbage**; an informal use. *He talked a lot of garbage on the subject.*

garbage can, garbage cans
NC A **garbage can** is a container that you put rubbish into; used in American English. *He threw his beer bottle into the garbage can.*

garbage collector, garbage collectors
NC A **garbage collector** is a person whose job is to empty the rubbish from people's dustbins and take it away to be disposed of; used in American English. *...garbage collectors striking for higher pay.*

garbage truck, garbage trucks
NC A **garbage truck** is a lorry into which the dustmen put the rubbish from people's dustbins; used in American English. *I was there to grab it from the jaws of a garbage truck.*

garbled /ˈgɑːbld/
ADJ If a message or explanation is **garbled**, the details are confused or wrong. *I got a garbled telephone message.*

garden /ˈgɑːdn/ **gardens, gardening, gardened**
1 NC A **garden** is an area of land next to a house, with plants, trees and grass. *...sitting in the back garden. ...the vegetable garden.*
2 V If you **garden**, you do work in your garden such as weeding or planting. *Vita is busy gardening.* ◆ **gardening** NU *It is too hot to do any gardening.*
3 NC **Gardens** are a park with plants, trees, and grass. *...the botanical gardens.*

garden centre, garden centres
NC A **garden centre** is a place where you can buy things for your garden such as plants, gardening tools, and fertilizers. *...your local garden centre or tree nursery.*

garden city, garden cities
NC A **garden city** is a town that has been planned and built to include a lot of open spaces, trees, and grass. *...the garden city was never completed according to plan.*

gardener /ˈgɑːdnə/ **gardeners**
NC A **gardener** is someone who looks after a garden, either as a job or a hobby. *...a keen gardener.*

gardenia /gɑːˈdiːnɪə/ **gardenias**
NC A **gardenia** is a large white or yellow flower that has a very pleasant smell; used also of the bush on which it grows. *...a gardenia in her hair.*

garden party, garden parties
NC A **garden party** is a formal party held in a large private garden, usually in the afternoon. *...open air events such as summer flower shows or garden parties.*

gargantuan /gɑːˈgæntjuən/
ADJ Something that is **gargantuan** is very large; a literary word. *The Times says that the budget deficit has been caused by the American government's gargantuan appetite for borrowing.*

gargle /ˈgɑːgl/ **gargles, gargling, gargled**
V When you **gargle**, you wash your throat by filling your mouth with liquid, tilting your head back, and breathing out through your mouth, making a bubbling noise.

gargoyle /ˈgɑːgɔɪl/ **gargoyles**
NC A **gargoyle** is a decorative stone carving on old buildings. It is usually shaped like the head of a strange and ugly creature, and water drains through it from the roof of the building. *A gargoyle is a functioning work on architectural buildings.*

garish /ˈgeərɪʃ/
ADJ Something that is **garish** is unpleasantly bright and noticeable. *...a garish yellow tie.*

garland /ˈgɑːlənd/ **garlands**
NC A **garland** is a circle of flowers and leaves, worn round the neck or head. *He hung a garland of flowers round my neck.*

garlic /ˈgɑːlɪk/
NU **Garlic** is the small round white bulb of an onion-like plant with a very strong smell and taste. *Add a crushed clove of garlic.*

garment /ˈgɑːmənt/ **garments**
NC A **garment** is a piece of clothing; a formal word. *...happy people with golden skins scantily dressed in light, multi-coloured garments. ...fashion garments.*

garner /gɑːnə/ garners, garnering, garnered
VO If you **garner** something, you collect it, often with some difficulty; a formal word. *The aim was to garner ideas on how to maintain American leadership into the next century... The last Australian batsman had studiously garnered 27 runs in 65 minutes before being caught.*

garnet /gɑːnɪt/ garnets
NC A **garnet** is a hard shiny stone that is used in making jewellery. *It had an exquisite golden garnet pommel.*

garnish /gɑːnɪʃ/ garnishes, garnishing, garnished
1 NCorNU A **garnish** is a small amount of food that you use to decorate cooked or prepared food. *...a garnish of parsley.*
2 VO To **garnish** food means to decorate it with small amounts of a different food. *Garnish the fish with cucumber slices.*

garret /gærət/ garrets
NC A **garret** is a very small room at the top of a house. *...a Parisian garret.*

garrison /gærɪsən/ garrisons
NC A **garrison** is a group of soldiers whose job is to guard a town or building. *Captain Cherstakov of the Moscow garrison presented the Guard of Honour.*

garrotte /gərɒt/ garrottes, garrotting, garrotted; also spelt **garrote** or **garotte**.
1 VO To **garrotte** someone means to kill them by strangling them or breaking their neck, using a device such as a piece of wire or a metal collar.
2 NC A **garrotte** is a piece of wire or a metal collar used to garrotte someone.

garrulous /gærələs/
ADJ A **garrulous** person talks a lot. *...a foolish, garrulous woman.*

garter /gɑːtə/ garters
NC A **garter** is a piece of elastic worn round the top of a stocking or sock to prevent it slipping down. *Hollywood's moral watchdog banned low-cut necklines, garters and women's navels.*

gas /gæs/ gases; gasses, gassing, gassed. The form **gases** is the plural of the noun. The form **gasses** is the 3rd person singular, present tense of the verb.
1 NU **Gas** is a substance like air that is neither liquid nor solid and burns easily. It is used as a fuel for heating and cooking. *He remembered to turn the gas off before leaving home.*
2 NCorNU A **gas** is any air-like substance that is neither liquid nor solid, such as oxygen or hydrogen. *The gases in question are chlorofluorocarbons... Helium is a gas at room temperature.* ● See also **tear gas.**
3 ADJ **Gas** fires and **gas** cookers use gas as a fuel. *The gas fire was full on.*
4 NU **Gas** is also the same as **petrol**; used in American English. *...a gallon of gas.*
5 VOorV-REFL To **gas** a person or animal means to kill them with poisonous gas. *In the old days people shot or gassed pests without a thought... She tried to gas herself.*
6 N SING If you refer to an event or situation as a **gas**, you mean that it is very lively, amusing, and enjoyable; used in informal American English. *You should have seen his first lesson, it was a real gas.*

gasbag /gæsbæg/ gasbags
NC If you call someone a **gasbag**, you mean that they talk a lot, especially about things that are not important; an offensive word. *I spent three hours with the old gasbag and I couldn't get a word in edgeways.*

gas chamber, gas chambers
NC A **gas chamber** is a room that can be filled with poisonous gas in order to kill people or animals. *...California's gas chamber at San Quentin prison.*

gaseous /gæsiəs, geɪʃəs/
ADJ ATTRIB **Gaseous** describes substances which are neither solid nor liquid; a formal word. *...liquid or gaseous fuels.*

gas-fired
ADJ **Gas-fired** power or heating uses gas as its fuel. *National Power wants to build more profitable gas-fired power stations.*

gash /gæʃ/ gashes, gashing, gashed
1 NC A **gash** is a long, deep cut. *Zeleika had a large gash in her head.*
2 VO If you **gash** something, you make a long, deep cut in it. *He gashed his arm on a window last night.*

gasholder /gæshəʊldə/ gasholders
NC A **gasholder** is the same as a **gasometer**. *The view would be alright if it weren't for the gasholder.*

gasket /gæskɪt/ gaskets
NC A **gasket** is a flat piece of soft material that you put between two joined surfaces in a pipe or engine in order to make sure that gas or liquid cannot escape. *...automotive gaskets.*

gas light, gas lights
NC A **gas light** is a lamp that produces light by burning gas. *She turned up the gas light.*

gasman /gæsmæn/ gasmen
NC A **gasman** is a man whose job is to install and repair gas appliances, or to read gas meters; an informal word. *Don't turn the gas on again until the gasman tells you it's safe to do so.*

gas mask, gas masks
NC A **gas mask** is a device that you wear over your face to protect you from breathing poisonous gases. *People waited with only the protection of a gas mask to see if this warhead was a chemical weapon.*

gasoline /gæsəliːn/
NU **Gasoline** is the same as **petrol**; used in American English. *...unleaded gasoline. ...cans of gasoline.*

gasometer /gæsɒmɪtə/ gasometers
NC A **gasometer** is a very large metal container that is the size of a building, which stores gas and then supplies it through pipes to buildings which have gas appliances. *The view would be all right if it weren't for the gasometer.*

gasp /gɑːsp/ gasps, gasping, gasped
1 NC A **gasp** is a short, quick intake of breath through your mouth, especially when you are surprised or in pain. *I listened to him breathing in short gasps. ...a gasp of horrified surprise.*
2 VorV-QUOTE If you **gasp**, you take a short, quick breath through your mouth, especially when you are surprised or in pain. *He was gasping for air... 'Call the doctor!' she gasped.*
3 V+for If you **are gasping** for a drink, you are extremely thirsty; an informal expression. *Would you like a cup of tea? You must be gasping.*

gas ring, gas rings
NC A **gas ring** is a circular gas pipe on a cooker, which has several holes in it and directs the flames under pans.

gas station, gas stations
NC A **gas station** is a place where petrol is sold; used in American English. *Drivers hear that the price of crude oil has dropped, then pass a gas station where prices are still high.*

gassy /gæsi/ gassier, gassiest
ADJ Drinks that are **gassy** have a lot of bubbles. *This beer's a bit too gassy for my taste.*

gastric /gæstrɪk/
ADJ ATTRIB **Gastric** describes processes, pains, or illnesses occurring in the stomach. *...non-communicable diseases such as cancer, strokes, diabetes or gastric ulcers.*

gastroenteritis /gæstrəʊentəraɪtɪs/; also spelt **gastro-enteritis.**
NU **Gastroenteritis** is an illness in which your stomach and intestines become swollen and painful, causing diarrhoea and sickness; a medical term. *...an attack of gastro-enteritis.*

gastronomic /gæstrənɒmɪk/
ADJ ATTRIB **Gastronomic** means concerned with good food; a formal word. *...the gastronomic reputation of France.*

gastronomy /gæstrɒnəmi/
NU **Gastronomy** is the activity and knowledge involved in preparing and appreciating good food; a formal word. *But above all, France is noted for its gastronomy.*

gasworks /gæswɜːks/; **gasworks** is both the singular and the plural form.
NC A **gasworks** is a kind of factory where gas is made

or processed, and from where it is piped to people's homes for heating and cooking. *Then the city's gasworks blew up, and the fire began.*

gate /geɪt/ **gates**
1 NC A **gate** is a door-like structure used at the entrance to a field, a garden, or the grounds of a building. *The prison gates closed behind him.*
2 NC In an airport, a **gate** is an exit through which passengers reach their aeroplane. *The helicopter had just landed and was manoeuvring into position at Gate Number Ten when the accident happened.*
3 NC The **gate** at a sporting event is the total number of people who attended. *He hoped that compulsory membership cards would increase the gate at Southend's home matches. ...record gate receipts.*

gateau /ˈgætəʊ/ **gateaux** /ˈgætəʊz/; also spelt **gâteau.**
NCorNU A **gateau** is a rich cake, usually with cream in it. *...a large slice of gateau. ...a cream gateau.*

gatecrash /ˈgeɪtkræʃ/ **gatecrashes, gatecrashing, gatecrashed**
VorVO If you **gatecrash** a party, you go to it when you have not been invited; an informal word. *I haven't gatecrashed a party since I was eighteen.*

gatecrasher /ˈgeɪtkræʃə/ **gatecrashers**
NC A **gatecrasher** is a person who goes to a party or other social event without having been invited; an informal word. *The party was so boring, even the gatecrashers left early.*

gatehouse /ˈgeɪthaʊs/ **gatehouses**
NC A **gatehouse** is a small house next to a gate into a park or estate, usually one in which the park-keeper lives. *They used to deliver parcels of food to the man who lived in the gatehouse.*

gatekeeper /ˈgeɪtkiːpə/ **gatekeepers**
NC A **gatekeeper** is a person who is in charge of a gate and who allows people through it; an old-fashioned word.

gate money
NU **Gate money** is the total amount of money that is paid by the spectators who attend a sporting event such as a football match. *Gate money accounts for only two-thirds of the club's income.*

gatepost /ˈgeɪtpəʊst/ **gateposts**
NC A **gatepost** is a post in the ground which a gate is fastened to. *They stuck the object onto a school gatepost.*

gateway /ˈgeɪtweɪ/ **gateways**
1 NC A **gateway** is an entrance where there is a gate. *They passed through an arched gateway.*
2 NC+*to* Something that is considered the entrance to a larger or more important thing can be described as the **gateway** to the larger thing. *Maralal is the gateway to northern Kenya. ...examinations are the gateways to some professions.*

gather /ˈgæðə/ **gathers, gathering, gathered**
1 V-ERG When people **gather** somewhere or when you **gather** them somewhere, they come together in a group. *The villagers gathered around him... He whistled to gather the whole squad in a group.*
2 VO If you **gather** things, you collect them or bring them together in one place. *I gathered my maps together and tucked them into the folder... The team worked for about a year and a half to gather data.*
3 VO If something **gathers** speed, momentum, or force, it gradually becomes faster or stronger. *The train gathered speed as it left the town... The disintegration of the USSR appears to be gathering momentum.* ● See also **gathering.**
4 Something that is **gathering dust** is not being used regularly. *...livestock research being done in Africa, much of it unpublished and probably gathering dust.*
5 V-REPORT If you **gather** that something is true, you learn from what someone says that it is true. *I gathered that they were not expected to eat with us... His wife had been ill, I gather, for some time.*
6 VO If you **gather** a piece of cloth, you sew a thread through it and then pull the thread tight so that the cloth forms very small folds or pleats. *I've nearly finished gathering the sleeves on my frock.*

gather up PHRASAL VERB If you **gather up** a number of things, you bring them together into a group. *She watched Willie gather up the papers.*

gathering /ˈgæðəʳrɪŋ/ **gatherings**
1 NC A **gathering** is a group of people meeting for a particular purpose. *...political and social gatherings.*
2 ADJ ATTRIB **Gathering** darkness or a **gathering** storm is beginning to become visible. *We walked in the gathering dusk... He told parliament of a gathering storm which the Republic's militia would not be able to control.*

gauche /gəʊʃ/
ADJ Someone who is **gauche** is awkward and uncomfortable in the company of other people. *She seemed rather gauche and fat and to have grown much shyer.*

gaudy /ˈgɔːdi/
ADJ Something that is **gaudy** is very brightly coloured; used showing disapproval. *...young men in gaudy shirts.*

gauge /geɪdʒ/ **gauges, gauging, gauged**
1 VOorV-REPORT If you **gauge** an amount or quantity, you measure or calculate it, often by means of a device. *With a modern machine, you can gauge the number of stitches... They waited, trying to gauge whether it was dark enough.*
2 NC A **gauge** is a device that shows the amount of something. *The fuel gauge dropped swiftly towards zero.*
3 VOorV-REPORT If you **gauge** people's feelings, actions, or intentions in a particular situation, you carefully consider and judge them. *The Times sent reporters out to gauge support for the new party. ...a method for the teacher to gauge what the child is doing.*
4 NC+SUPP A **gauge** is also a fact that can be used to judge a situation. *The increase in attendance was used as a gauge of the course's success.*

gaunt /gɔːnt/
1 ADJ A **gaunt** person looks very thin and unhealthy. *She looked very weak, her face gaunt and drawn.*
2 ADJ Something that is **gaunt** looks bare and unattractive. *...the gaunt outlines of the houses.*

gauntlet /ˈgɔːntlət/ **gauntlets**
NC **Gauntlets** are long, thick, protective gloves. *The policemen pulled on their white gauntlets.*
● **Gauntlet** is used in these phrases. ● If you **throw down the gauntlet,** you challenge someone to argue or compete with you. If you **take up the gauntlet,** or if you **pick up the gauntlet,** you accept someone's challenge. *The leaders of the Russian Federation have thrown down the gauntlet to the central Soviet government... Whoever decides to take up the gauntlet and challenge Mrs Thatcher will have a tough battle.*
● If you **run the gauntlet,** you go through an unpleasant experience in which people attack or criticize you. *Communist forces ran the gauntlet of artillery fire to reach the open sea.*

gauze /gɔːz/
NU **Gauze** is a light, soft cloth with tiny holes in it. *...gauze or cotton wool that they find in their first aid kits at home.*

gauzy /ˈgɔːzi/
ADJ ATTRIB **Gauzy** means light, soft, and thin, so that you can see through it. *...a gauzy nightdress. ...a blur of gauzy wings.*

gave /geɪv/
Gave is the past tense of **give.**

gavel /ˈgævl/ **gavels**
NC A **gavel** is a small wooden hammer that you bang on a table to get attention when you are officially in charge of a formal event such as a meeting. *The chairman rapped sharply with his gavel. ...the banging of the judge's gavel.*

Gaviria Trujillo, César /ˌseɪsə gævˈɪərɪə truˈhiːjəʊ/
César Gaviria Trujillo became President of Colombia in 1990. He was elected to the Chamber of Deputies in 1972. He served as Minister of Finance in 1986, and of the Interior in 1990. He is a member of the Liberal Party (PL).

Gawd /gɔːd/
Gawd is used in written English to represent the word 'God' pronounced this way in a particular accent or tone of voice, especially in phrases expressing boredom, irritation, or shock such as 'Oh Gawd, here

we go again' or 'Oh my Gawd'.
gawk /gɔːk/ **gawks, gawking, gawked**
v If someone is **gawking**, they are staring at someone or something in a rude, stupid, or unthinking way; an informal word. *Come along, girl! Don't just stand there gawking!... They would remain quaint villagers to be gawked at.*
gawky /gɔːki/
ADJ A **gawky** person stands and moves awkwardly and clumsily. *...a gawky young woman.*
gawp /gɔːp/ **gawps, gawping, gawped**
v If you **gawp** at someone or something, you stare at them in a rude or stupid way. *Don't stand there gawping, come away!*
gay /geɪ/ **gays; gayer, gayest**
1 ADJ A person who is **gay** is homosexual. *We understand more about Hockney's art when we know that he's gay. ...a radical group of lesbians and gay men.* ▶ Also NC *...a holiday spot for gays.*
2 ADJ ATTRIB **Gay** organizations and magazines are for homosexual people. *...an active Gay Group. ...the editor of Gay News, a newspaper for homosexuals.*
3 ADJ **Gay** also means lively and bright; an old-fashioned use. *What gay and exciting place are you taking me to?*
Gayoom, Maumoun Abdul
/maʊmuːn æbdʊl gɑːjuːm/
Maumoun Abdul Gayoom became President of the Maldives in 1978. He was Minister of Transport from 1977 to 1978. Born: 1937.
gaze /geɪz/ **gazes, gazing, gazed**
1 v A If you **gaze** at someone or something, you look steadily at them for a long time. *She turned to gaze admiringly at her husband... He gazed down into the water.*
2 NC Someone's **gaze** is the long and steady way they are looking at someone or something. *He sat without shifting his gaze from the television.*
gazelle /gəzel/ **gazelles**
NC A **gazelle** is a kind of small antelope. *She ran like a gazelle.*
gazump /gəzʌmp/ **gazumps, gazumping, gazumped**
v O If you are **gazumped** by someone, they agree to sell their house to you, but then sell it to someone else who offers to pay a higher price; used showing disapproval. *...advice to house-buyers on how to avoid being gazumped.*
GB /dʒiːbiː/
GB is a written abbreviation for 'Great Britain'.
GCC /dʒiːsiːsiː/. See **Gulf Co-operation Council**
GCE /dʒiːsiːiː/ **GCE's**
NC **GCE** Advanced level examinations are taken by British school students at the age of seventeen or eighteen. **GCE** is an abbreviation for 'General Certificate of Education'. *In some cases you may be advised to follow a GCE Advanced Level course.* ● See also **A level, O level.**
GCSE /dʒiːsiːesiː/ **GCSE's**
NC **GCSE** examinations are taken by British school students at the age of fifteen or sixteen. The GCSE examination was introduced in Britain in 1988 to replace the GCE Ordinary level examination. GCSE is an abbreviation for 'General Certificate of Secondary Education'. *The main GCSE papers are now over. ...students who return to school or college to retake GCSE's.*
gear /gɪə/ **gears, gearing, geared**
1 NC A **gear** is a piece of machinery, for example in a car or on a bicycle, which controls the rate at which energy is converted into motion. *John checked the gear on the bicycle.*
2 NCorNU A **gear** is also one of the different ranges of speed or power which a machine or vehicle has. *We slow down to first gear and ten miles an hour... The basic model has three gears. ...a nine-speed gear mechanism.*
3 NU The **gear** for a particular activity is the equipment and special clothes that you use. *...camping gear.*
4 v O A If someone or something is **geared** to a particular purpose, they are organized or designed to be suitable for it. *They were not geared to armed combat. ...a policy geared towards rehabilitation.*
gear up PHRASAL VERB If someone is **geared up** to do something, they are prepared and able to do it. *Hotels like this are not geared up to cater for parties.*
gearbox /gɪəbɒks/ **gearboxes**
NC A **gearbox** is the system of gears in an engine or vehicle. *...an automatic gearbox.*
gear lever, gear levers
NC A **gear lever** is the lever that you use to change gear in a car or other vehicle. *A carphone had been placed so near the gear lever that the driver could not get it into reverse.*
gearshift /gɪəʃɪft/ **gearshifts**
NC A **gearshift** is the same as a **gear lever**; used in American English.
gee /dʒiː/
Some people say '**gee**' when they are surprised or excited; used in informal American English. *Gee, what fun!*
geese /giːs/
Geese is the plural of **goose**. *...snow geese.*
geezer /giːzə/ **geezers**
NC Some people use **geezer** to refer to a man; an informal word. *This other geezer comes along and takes his shoes.*
Geiger counter /gaɪgə kaʊntə/ **Geiger counters**
NC A **Geiger counter** is a device which detects and measures radioactivity. *When he stood for several minutes on top of it, his Geiger counter had ticked away madly.*
Geingob, Hage /hɑːgeɪ gaɪngɒb/
Hage Geingob became Prime Minister of Namibia in 1990 when Namibia became independent. He was Chairman of the Constituent Assembly from 1989 to 1990.
geisha /geɪʃə/ **geishas**
NC A **geisha** is a Japanese woman who is specially trained in music, dancing, and the art of conversation, and whose job is to entertain men. *...the art of the geisha.*
gel /dʒel/ **gels, gelling, gelled**; also spelt **jell.**
1 v If a liquid **gels**, it changes into a thicker, firmer, jelly-like substance. *It's been formulated to gel very quickly and solidifies to form a film over the surface.*
2 N MASS **Gel** is a smooth, soft, jelly-like substance, especially one used to keep your hair in the style of your choice. *...gel for his dreadlocks.*
3 v If an unclear shape, thought, or idea **gels**, it becomes clearer or easier to understand. *After talking to you things really began to gel.*
gelatin /dʒelətɪn/
N MASS **Gelatin** is a clear, tasteless powder used to make liquids firm. *It's transparent and resembles a piece of hardened gelatin.*
gelatine /dʒelətiːn/
Gelatine is the same as **gelatin.**
gelatinous /dʒəlætɪnəs/
ADJ Something that is **gelatinous** is thick and often sticky, like a jelly. *He put his fork into something gelatinous on his plate. ...eggs laid within gelatinous masses.*
gelding /geldɪŋ/ **geldings**
NC A **gelding** is a male horse which has been castrated in order to make it less aggressive or to make it jump better in races or competitions. *Devil's Elbow, a four year old gelding, has tested positive for three banned substances after winning at Worcester.*
gelignite /dʒelɪgnaɪt/
NU **Gelignite** is an explosive similar to dynamite. *...explosives such as gelignite and TNT.*
gem /dʒem/ **gems**
1 NC A **gem** is a jewel. *...a bracelet of solid gold, studded with gems.*
2 NC You can refer to someone or something as a **gem** if they are especially good or pleasing. *...this gem of wisdom... This house is a gem.*
gemstone /dʒemstəʊn/ **gemstones**
NC A **gemstone** is a jewel or stone used in jewellery. *Intense heat and pressure conditions make the diamond crystallise as a gemstone.*
gen /dʒen/ **gens, genning, genned**
NU If you say someone has the **gen** on something, you

mean that they have all the information about it; an informal word. *Let me have the gen on the deal by lunchtime.*

gen up PHRASAL VERB If you **gen up** on something, you find out as much information as possible about it. *He's genning up on the legal position before he signs it.* ● See also **genned up**.

Gen.
Gen. is a written abbreviation for 'General'; used to indicate a person's rank in the armed forces. *...Gen. de Gaulle.*

gendarme /ʒɒnˈdɑːm/ **gendarmes**
NC A **gendarme** is a member of the French police force. *The second car was driven by a gendarme.*

gender /ˈdʒɛndə/ **genders**
1 NU or NC A person's **gender** is their characteristic of being male or female. *...differences of race or gender... People of a variety of races and both genders compete for equal pay among a dwindling number of jobs.*
2 NC or NU In the grammar of some languages, **gender** is used to refer to the classification of nouns as masculine, feminine, and neuter.

gene /dʒiːn/ **genes**
NC **Genes** are parts of cells which control the physical characteristics, growth, and development of living things. They are passed on from one generation to another. *...an exciting new discovery about how genes may be transferred by a naturally occurring process... The gene for maleness must be somewhere on the Y-chromosome.*

genealogical /ˌdʒiːniəˈlɒdʒɪkl/
ADJ **Genealogical** means concerning the history of families; a formal word. *...evidence of genealogical relationships. ...answers to genealogical queries.*

genealogy /ˌdʒiːniˈælədʒi/ **genealogies**; a formal word
1 NU **Genealogy** is the study of the history of families. ♦ **genealogist, genealogists** NC *...an amateur genealogist attempting to trace the family of his wife.*
2 NC A **genealogy** is the history of a particular family, describing who each person married and who their children were. *Sarah's genealogy is illustrious: she is a direct descendent of the 17th Century king, Charles II.*

genera /ˈdʒɛnərə/
Genera is the plural of **genus**. *We have fishes which are placed in 6, 8 or 10 different genera.*

general /ˈdʒɛnərəl/ **generals**
1 ADJ You use **general** when describing something that relates to the whole of something, or to most of it, rather than to any particular detail or part. *The general standard of education there is very high. ...general business expenses... Principles have to be stated in very general terms.* ♦ **generally** ADV or ADV SEN *His account was generally accurate... It's wonderful for information on things generally.*
2 ADJ You also use **general** to describe something that involves or affects most people in a group. *There was a general movement to leave the table. ...a topic of general interest.* ♦ **generally** ADV *When will this material become generally available?*
3 ADJ ATTRIB **General** also describes a statement or opinion that is true or suitable in most situations. *As a general rule, consult the doctor if the baby has a temperature.* ♦ **generally** ADV *Generally speaking, there are union instructions about such situations.*
4 ADJ ATTRIB You also use **general** to describe an organization or business that offers a variety of services or goods. *...a general grocery store. ...a general hospital.*
5 ADJ ATTRIB **General** is also used to describe someone's job, to indicate that they have complete responsibility for the administration of an organization. *...the general manager of the hotel.*
6 ADJ ATTRIB **General** is also used to describe a person who does a variety of unskilled jobs. *...unskilled general labourers.*
7 NC or TITLE A **general** is an army officer of very high rank. *...purging the army of its corrupt generals. ...General Colin Powell.*
● **General** is used in these phrases. ● You say **in general** when you are talking about the whole of a

situation without going into details, or when you are referring to most people or things in a group. *They want shorter shifts, and shorter working hours in general. ...his contemptuous attitude to society in general.* ● **In general** is also used to indicate that a statement is true in most cases. *The industrial processes, in general, are based on man-made processes.*

general delivery
NU If you send a letter by **general delivery**, you send it to a particular post office, where the person who it is addressed to can collect it; used in American English.

general election, general elections
NC A **general election** is an election for a new government, in which all the citizens of a country may vote. *A record number of people turned out to vote in yesterday's general election.*

generalise /ˈdʒɛnərəlaɪz/. See **generalize**.

generalissimo /ˌdʒɛnərəˈlɪsɪməʊ/ **generalissimos**
NC A **generalissimo** is a supreme commander of combined military, naval, and air forces, especially one who wields political as well as military power. *...Generalissimo Chiang Kai-shek.*

generality /ˌdʒɛnəˈrælətɪ/ **generalities**
NC A **generality** is a statement that is not very detailed; a formal word. *She spoke in short simple generalities.*

generalization /ˌdʒɛnərəlaɪˈzeɪʃn/ **generalizations**; also spelt **generalisation**.
NC A **generalization** is a statement that is true in most cases. *It is easy to make sweeping generalizations about someone else's problems.*

generalize /ˈdʒɛnərəlaɪz/ **generalizes, generalizing, generalized**; also spelt **generalise**.
V If you **generalize**, you say something that is true in most cases. *I don't think you can generalize about that.* ♦ **generalization** /ˌdʒɛnərəlaɪˈzeɪʃn/ NU *Generalization is usually unwise.*

generalized /ˈdʒɛnərəlaɪzd/; also spelt **generalised**.
ADJ ATTRIB **Generalized** means relating to a large number or variety of people, things, or situations. *The problem is one of generalized human needs. ...generalised remarks about the futility of love.*

general knowledge
NU **General knowledge** is knowledge about many different things, rather than about one particular subject. *Her general knowledge is amazing.*

general practice, general practices
1 NU **General practice** is the work of a doctor who treats people at a surgery or in their homes, and who does not specialize. *If he's going into general practice, he must have further training.*
2 NC A **general practice** is a place where such a doctor works. *Some hospital doctors are also attached to general practices.*

general practitioner. See **GP**.

general public
N COLL The **general public** consists of people in general, usually contrasted with people who are specialists in a particular field. *An independent official appointed to protect the interests of the general public... The lecture will interest both musicians and members of the general public.*

general strike, general strikes
NC A **general strike** is the refusal to work by all or most people in a country or state. *...demands for a general strike to force the government to concede.*

generate /ˈdʒɛnəreɪt/ **generates, generating, generated**
1 VO To **generate** something means to cause it to begin and develop; a formal use. *This book will continue to generate excitement for a long time.*
2 VO To **generate** electricity or other forms of energy means to produce it. *More than half of Scotland's electricity is due to be generated by nuclear energy.*

generation /ˌdʒɛnəˈreɪʃn/ **generations**
1 NC A **generation** is all the people in a group or country who are of a similar age. *...an older generation of intellectuals... Few actresses of her generation could play the part well.*
2 NC A **generation** is also the period of time, usually

considered to be about thirty years, that it takes for children to grow up and become adults and have children of their own. *We have had a generation of peace in Europe.*
3 NC+SUPP A stage of development in the design and manufacture of machines or equipment is also called a **generation**. *...the new generation of missiles.*
4 NU The **generation** of energy is its production. *Electric power generation had ceased.*

generation gap
N SING A **generation gap** is a difference in attitude and behaviour between older people and younger people. *The dispute really centres around a generation gap with the younger Party members.*

generative /dʒɛnəʳrətɪv/
ADJ **Generative** means capable of producing something; a formal word. *...generative powers. ...generative forces. ...generative rules.*

generator /dʒɛnəreɪtə/ **generators**
NC A **generator** is a machine which produces electricity. *...gas-powered generators.*

generic /dʒənɛrɪk/
ADJ ATTRIB **Generic** means applying to a whole group of similar things; a formal word. *Software is a generic term for the sets of programs which control a computer.*

generosity /dʒɛnərɒsəti/
NU Someone's **generosity** is their characteristic of doing or giving more than is usual or expected. *You shouldn't take advantage of his generosity.*

generous /dʒɛnəʳrəs/
1 ADJ A **generous** person gives more of something, especially money, than is usual or expected. *That's very generous of you... They aren't very generous with pensions... Saudi Arabia has so far been by far the most generous single donor to Bangladesh.*
♦ **generously** ADV *She was paid generously.*
2 ADJ **Generous** also means friendly, helpful, and willing to see the good qualities in people or things. *She was a kind and generous soul... The most generous interpretation is that he didn't know.*
♦ **generously** ADV *Mrs Hutchins has generously agreed to be with us today.*
3 ADJ Something that is **generous** is much larger than is usual or necessary. *...a generous measure of cognac.* ♦ **generously** ADV *...a generously illustrated book.*

genesis /dʒɛnəsɪs/
N SING The **genesis** of something is its beginning, birth, or creation; a formal word. *I explained the genesis of my idea as well as I could.*

genetic /dʒənɛtɪk/ **genetics**
1 NU **Genetics** is the study of how characteristics are passed from one generation to another by means of genes. *The field of genetics helps to throw some light on the line of evolution that led to modern people.*
2 ADJ **Genetic** means concerned with genetic or genes. *...genetic defects.* ♦ **genetically** ADV *...genetically programmed behaviour.*

genetic engineering
NU **Genetic engineering** is the science of changing the genetic structure of a living organism in order to make it stronger or more suitable for a particular purpose. *Aren't there dangers associated with genetic engineering?*

genetic fingerprinting
NU **Genetic fingerprinting** is a method of identifying an individual by examining the unique pattern of DNA molecules that are present in their blood, saliva, or skin tissue. *British doctors are now using genetic fingerprinting to diagnose a type of cancer at a very early stage. ...a national database of genetic fingerprinting.*

geneticist /dʒənɛtɪsɪst/ **geneticists**
NC A **geneticist** is a person who studies or specializes in genetics. *...a plant geneticist.*

genial /dʒiːniəl/
ADJ A **genial** person is good-humoured and friendly. *...his reputation as a genial and moderate man. ...a genial smile.* ♦ **genially** ADV *He waved genially to people as they passed.* ♦ **geniality** /dʒiːniælətɪ/ NU *...his general air of geniality.*

genie /dʒiːni/ **genies**
NC In stories that originate from Arabia and Persia, a **genie** is a magical being that obeys the orders of the person who controls it. *He had disappeared overnight, in a puff of dust, like a genie.*

genital /dʒɛnɪtl/ **genitals**
1 N PL A person's or an animal's **genitals** are their external sexual organs. *They were subjected to electric shocks to the head, body and genitals.*
2 ADJ ATTRIB **Genital** means relating to a person's external sexual organs. *The mortality from genital cancers amongst pill users is being slightly reduced.*

genitalia /dʒɛnɪteɪliə/
N PL A person's or an animal's **genitalia** are their external sexual organs; a formal word.

genitive /dʒɛnətɪv/
ADJ In the grammar of some languages, the **genitive** case is a case used for nouns, pronouns, and other words that indicates a relationship of ownership, possession, or association between one thing and another. ▸ Also N SING *Both the adjective and the noun are in the genitive.*

genius /dʒiːniəs/ **geniuses**
1 NC A **genius** is a highly intelligent, creative, or talented person. *Beethoven was a genius. ...the famous maths genius.*
2 NU **Genius** is very great ability or skill in something. *...his genius for improvisation.*
3 NU **Genius** is also an excellent quality which makes something distinct from everything else; a literary use. *That is the genius of the system.*

genned up /dʒɛnd ʌp/
ADJ PRED If you are **genned up**, you have all the details or information about something that you need; an informal expression. ● to gen up: see gen.

genocide /dʒɛnəsaɪd/
NU **Genocide** is the murder of a whole community or race; a formal word. *They should withdraw all forms of support for the Khmer Rouge leaders responsible for acts of genocide.*

genre /ʒɒnʳrə/ **genres**
NC A **genre** is a particular form or style of literature, art, or music; a formal word. *...a whole new genre of sentimental fiction.*

gent /dʒɛnt/ **gents**
1 NC A **gent** is a gentleman; an informal word. *They are very tough gents.*
2 N SING A **gents** or the **gents** is a public toilet for men. *The gents was situated in a small yard outside.*

genteel /dʒɛntiːl/
ADJ A **genteel** person or place is quiet, respectable, and refined. *Now I know they will lobby Parliament from time to time—but in a very genteel and polite way... The town of Eastbourne is a genteel resort on the south coast.*

gentian /dʒɛnʃn/ **gentians**
NC A **gentian** is a small plant with a blue or purple flower shaped like a trumpet which grows in mountain regions.

Gentile /dʒɛntaɪl/ **Gentiles**
NC A **Gentile** is a person who is not Jewish. *She seemed to regard me, an Englishman and a Gentile, with some suspicion.* ▸ Also ADJ *...the gentile world.*

gentility /dʒɛntɪlətɪ/; a formal word.
1 NU **Gentility** is the respectability and high social status of the upper classes. *The family had made a swift descent from gentility to near-poverty.*
2 NU **Gentility** is also polite and well-mannered behaviour. *...the courtesy and gentility of these beautiful girls.*

gentle /dʒɛntl/ **gentler, gentlest**
1 ADJ A **gentle** person is kind, mild, and pleasantly calm. *He was a kind, gentle, old-fashioned romantic... I should have done it better by being more gentle and more caring.* ♦ **gently** ADV *'You have nothing to worry about,' he said gently.* ♦ **gentleness** NU *...the virtues of gentleness and compassion.*
2 ADJ If someone's voice or expression is **gentle**, it is calm, quiet, and kind. *He greeted me with a very gentle voice... She had very gentle blue eyes.*
3 ADJ **Gentle** movements are even and calm. *...the gentle rocking of his mother's chair... There was a*

gentle breeze. ◆ **gently** ADV *I shook her gently and she opened her eyes.*
4 ADJ **Gentle** scenery has soft shapes and colours that people find pleasant and relaxing. *The beach stretched away in a gentle curve.* ◆ **gently** ADV *...gently sloping hills.*
5 ADJ ATTRIB **Gentle** jokes or hints are kind and not intended to hurt people. *...a very gentle parody of American life.*

gentlefolk /dʒɛntlfəʊk/
N PL **Gentlefolk** are people who come from the middle or upper classes; an old-fashioned word. *...a rest home for retired gentlefolk.*

gentleman /dʒɛntlmən/ **gentlemen** /dʒɛntlmən/
1 NC A **gentleman** is a man from a family of high social standing. *...a country gentleman.*
2 NC A **gentleman** is also a man who is polite and well-educated. *He was a terribly nice man—a real gentleman.*
3 NC You can refer politely to a man as a **gentleman**. *Good afternoon, ladies and gentlemen.*

gentlemanly /dʒɛntlmənli/
ADJ A man who is **gentlemanly** behaves very politely and kindly. *...a courteous, gentlemanly gesture.*

gentlewoman /dʒɛntlwʊmən/ **gentlewomen**; an old-fashioned word.
1 NC A **gentlewoman** is a woman of high social standing. *Skill with the needle was considered a necessary quality of a gentlewoman in the early nineteenth century.*
2 NC A **gentlewoman** is a woman who is cultured, educated, and refined in her manners.

gentry /dʒɛntri/
N PL The **gentry** are people of high social status; a formal word. *...landed gentry.*

genuflect /dʒɛnjʊflɛkt/ **genuflects, genuflecting, genuflected**
V If you **genuflect**, you bend one or both knees, especially in church, as a sign of respect for someone or something. *They both genuflected and crossed themselves.*

genuine /dʒɛnjuɪn/
1 ADJ Something that is **genuine** is real and exactly what it appears to be. *...genuine Ugandan food... The experts decided that the painting was a genuine Constable... She looked at me in genuine astonishment.* ◆ **genuinely** ADV *...genuinely democratic countries.*
2 ADJ Someone who is **genuine** is honest and sincere. *They seemed nice, genuine fellows.*

genus /dʒɛnəs, dʒiːnəs/ **genera** /dʒɛnərə/
NC A **genus** is a class or group of similar animals or plants; a technical term. *Tool-making set apart members of the genus Homo from the rest of the animal kingdom.*

geographer /dʒiɒɡrəfə/ **geographers**
NC A **geographer** is a person who studies geography or is an expert in it. *...professional geographers.*

geographic /dʒiːəɡræfɪk/ or **geographical** /dʒiːəɡræfɪkl/
ADJ Something that is **geographic** or **geographical** involves geography. *...geographic and political boundaries. ...the characteristics of any geographical region.* ◆ **geographically** ADV *...geographically separated species.*

geography /dʒiɒɡrəfi/
1 NU **Geography** is the study of the countries of the world and of such things as land formations, seas, climate, towns, and populations. *He will be sampling the diversity of Bolivia's geography and people.*
2 NU The **geography** of a place is the way that its physical features are arranged within it. *...the geography of the United States.*

geological /dʒiːəlɒdʒɪkl/
ADJ **Geological** means relating to geology. *...an interesting geological site.*

geology /dʒiɒlədʒi/
1 NU **Geology** is the study of the Earth's structure, surface, and origins. *The most familiar group that appears in most geology text books are the frondose fossils.* ◆ **geologist, geologists** NC *For many years these questions puzzled geologists.*

2 NU The **geology** of an area is the structure of its land. *...techniques to study the earth's surface, its geology, its meteorology and many other areas.*

geometric /dʒiːəmɛtrɪk/ or **geometrical** /dʒiːəmɛtrɪkl/
1 ADJ ATTRIB **Geometric** or **geometrical** is used to refer to something which relates to geometry. *...a geometrical problem.*
2 ADJ **Geometric** or **geometrical** designs and shapes consist of regular shapes and lines, and sharp angles. *...abstract geometrical designs.*

geometry /dʒiɒmətri/
N U **Geometry** is a mathematical science concerned with the measurement of lines, angles, curves, and shapes. *Theories of gravity describe the geometry of space and time.*

geophysical /dʒiːəʊfɪzɪkl/
ADJ **Geophysical** means relating to or concerned with geophysics. *Any geophysical survey is done by profiling.*

geophysicist /dʒiːəʊfɪzəsɪst/ **geophysicists**
NC A **geophysicist** is someone who studies or specializes in geophysics. *Senior geophysicist, Andy Green, demonstrates how underground microphones reveal clues to the mini earthquakes that happen as rocks split.*

geophysics /dʒiːəʊfɪzɪks/
N U **Geophysics** is the branch of geology that uses physics to examine the Earth's structure, climate, and oceans. *The Tehrān University geophysics centre reported that there were twenty-two tremors overnight.*

geopolitical /dʒiːəʊpəlɪtɪkl/
ADJ **Geopolitical** means relating to or concerned with geopolitics. *...those problems are political in nature, not geopolitical.*

geopolitics /dʒiːəʊpɒlətɪks/
N U **Geopolitics** is the study of politics on a worldwide scale, especially as it affects the relations between countries. *Gorbachev was reticent about the geopolitics of the Mediterranean area as applied to the Middle East.*

George Town /dʒɔːdʒ taʊn/
George Town is the capital and largest town of the Cayman Islands. It is on Grand Cayman Island. Population: 13,000 (1989).

Georgetown /dʒɔːdʒtaʊn/
Georgetown is the capital of Guyana and its largest city. Population: 188,000 (1983).

Georgia /dʒɔːdʒə/
The **Republic of Georgia** became independent of the USSR in 1991. It lies in the south of the former USSR, between the Black and Caspian Seas. Zviad Gamsakhurdia, of Round Table (a pro-independence party), became President in 1990 and was deposed in 1991. Eduard Shevardnadze was appointed President of the State Council in 1992. ◆ **Georgian** /dʒɔːdʒən/ N, ADJ ▪ *per capita GNP:* US$4,410 ▪ *religion:* Christianity, Islam ▪ *language:* Georgian ▪ *currency:* rouble ▪ *capital:* Tbilisi ▪ *population:* 5 million (1989) ▪ *size:* 69,700 square kilometres.

Georgian /dʒɔːdʒən/
ADJ **Georgian** is used in Britain to describe the eighteenth century and the style of architecture and the arts that was popular at the time. *...a large late Georgian house.*

geranium /dʒəreɪniəm/ **geraniums**
NC A **geranium** is a plant with small red, pink, or white flowers, often grown in houses.

gerbil /dʒɜːbl/ **gerbils**
NC A **gerbil** is a small, furry animal with long back legs that is often kept as a pet.

geriatric /dʒɛriætrɪk/
ADJ **Geriatric** is used to describe very old people, their illnesses, and their treatment; a medical term. *...a geriatric ward.*

germ /dʒɜːm/ **germs**
1 NC A **germ** is a very small organism that causes disease. *...a flu germ. ...keep things clean and free of germs.*
2 NC+SUPP The **germ** of something such as an idea or plan is the beginning of it which may develop or become more important. *There may have been the*

germ of a rational idea there, but it quickly became irrational.

German /dʒɜːmən/ **Germans**
1 ADJ **German** means belonging or relating to Germany. *...the German Institute for Economic Research. ...German reunification.*
2 NC A **German** is a person who comes from Germany. *The orchestra was founded by a German, Karl Hallé.*
3 NU **German** is the language spoken by people who live in Germany, Austria, and parts of Switzerland. *Our conversation in German was more successful.*

germane /dʒɜːmeɪn/
ADJ PRED+*to* Something that is **germane** to a situation or idea is connected with it in an important way; a formal word. *It is clearly not germane to present-day conditions. ...issues most germane to socialist policy.*

Germanic /dʒɜːmænɪk/
1 ADJ If you describe someone or something as **Germanic**, you think that their appearance or behaviour is typical of German people or things. *...his Germanic nature. ...very Germanic in everything they did.*
2 ADJ **Germanic** is also used to describe the ancient culture and people of northern Europe, and the language they spoke, from which the modern Scandinavian languages and English, German, and Dutch derive. *...a Germanic tribe. ...Germanic mythology.*

German measles
NU **German measles** is the same as **rubella**. *In Europe, rubella, or German measles, commonly precedes rheumatoid arthritis.*

Germany /dʒɜːmənɪ/
The **Federal Republic of Germany** is a country in central Europe. At the end of the Second World War, Germany was divided into zones occupied by USA, UK, France, and USSR. Berlin was similarly divided. In 1949 the western zones were joined to form the Federal Republic of Germany (FRG), also called West Germany, a democratic country with its capital at Bonn. The Soviet zone became the German Democratic Republic (GDR), also called East Germany, a Communist country with its capital at East Berlin. Berlin had a special status. In 1961 the Berlin Wall was built to prevent East Germans escaping into West Germany. Erich Honecker was General Secretary of the Socialist Unity Party of Germany (SED), the Communist party of East Germany, from 1971 until his resignation in the face of pro-democracy demonstrations in 1989. The Berlin Wall was dismantled in 1989 and Germany was reunified in 1990. Dr Richard von Weizsäcker, of the Christian Democratic Union (CDU), became President in 1984. Dr Helmut Kohl (CDU) became Chancellor in 1982. Germany is a member of the European Community and NATO. At the time of reunification, West Germany was one of the world's leading industrial countries with an extremely strong economy, while East Germany was in serious industrial and economic decline. Germany produces machinery and other manufactured goods, chemicals, and agricultural products. ◆ **German** /dʒɜːmən/ N, ADJ ▪ *per capita GNP:* approximately US$20,750 ▪ *religion:* Christianity ▪ *language:* German ▪ *currency:* Deutsche Mark ▪ *capital:* Berlin (the seat of government remains temporarily in Bonn) ▪ *population:* 79 million (1990) ▪ *size:* 356,945 square kilometres.

germinal /dʒɜːmɪnl/
ADJ Something that is **germinal** is in an early stage of its development, or is causing something else to develop; a formal word. *...a germinal force in re-establishing industry.*

germinate /dʒɜːmɪneɪt/ **germinates, germinating, germinated**
1 V-ERG If a seed **germinates**, or if you **germinate** a seed, it starts to grow. *You need cool, moist weather for the seed to germinate... How do we germinate the seed?* ◆ **germination** /dʒɜːmɪneɪʃn/ NU *Temperature is most important for seed germination.*
2 V-ERG If an idea, plan, or feeling **germinates**, or if something **germinates** it, it comes into existence and

begins to develop; a formal use. *New concepts germinate before your eyes... Farmers rely on the gentle pre-monsoon rains to help germinate their crops.*

germ warfare
NU **Germ warfare** is the use of bombs which contain harmful germs by an army in order to cause disease in enemy troops or to destroy crops that they might use as food. *This treaty bans germ warfare.*

gerontology /dʒerɒntɒlədʒi/
NU **Gerontology** is the study of the process by which we get old, how our bodies change, and the problems that old people have. *I've been doing experimental gerontology all my life, and that deals with time.*

gerrymandering /dʒerɪmændərɪŋ/
NU **Gerrymandering** is the act of altering political boundaries in order to give an unfair advantage to one political party or group of people. *They and other opposition parties regard it as a piece of gerrymandering.*

gerund /dʒerənd/ **gerunds**
NC In grammar, a **gerund** is a noun formed from a verb and expressing an action or state. In English, gerunds end in '-ing'.

gestation /dʒesteɪʃn/
1 NU **Gestation** is the process in which babies grow inside their mother's body before they are born; a medical use. *...the gestation period.*
2 NU **Gestation** is also the process in which an idea or plan develops; a formal use. *The road had been sixty years in gestation.*

gesticulate /dʒestɪkjʊleɪt/ **gesticulates, gesticulating, gesticulated**
V If you **gesticulate**, you make movements with your hands and arms, often while you are talking, for example because you are describing something that is difficult to express in words; a formal word. *Stuart gesticulated angrily.*

gesticulation /dʒestɪkjʊleɪʃn/ **gesticulations**
1 NC **Gesticulations** are movements that you make with your hands and arms, often while you are talking, for example because you are describing something that is difficult to express in words; a formal word. *...the gesticulations that accompany conversation.*
2 NU **Gesticulation** is the act of gesticulating.

gestural /dʒestʃərəl/
ADJ ATTRIB **Gestural** means consisting of or relating to gestures; a formal word. *We share the same kind of gestural language.*

gesture /dʒestʃə/ **gestures, gesturing, gestured**
1 NC A **gesture** is a movement that you make with your hands or your head to express emotion or to give information. *She made an angry gesture with her fist.*
2 V-REPORT or V A If you **gesture**, you use your hands or your head to express emotion or to give information. *She gestured that I ought to wait... He gestured to me to lie down... She gestured towards the bookshelves.*
3 NC A **gesture** is also something that you say or do in order to express your attitude or intentions, often something you know will not have much effect. *The demonstration is a gesture of defiance.*

get /get/ **gets, getting, got**. The form **gotten** is often used for the past participle in American English.
1 VC **Get** often has the same meaning as 'become'. For example, if something **gets** cold, it becomes cold. *She began to get suspicious... If things get worse, you'll have to come home... It's getting late.*
2 AUX+PAST PARTICIPLE **Get** can be used instead of 'be' to form passives. *Suppose someone gets killed... He failed to get re-elected.*
3 V A If you **get** into a particular state or situation, you start being in that state or situation. *He got into trouble with the police... I began to get in a panic.*
4 V A To **get** somewhere means to move or arrive somewhere. *Nobody can get past... I got there about 8 o'clock... When we got to Firle Beacon we had a rest... What time do they get back?*
5 V O A or V O C If you **get** someone or something into a particular position, state, or situation, you cause them to be in that position, state, or situation. *I got Allen into his bunk... The girl finally got the door open... He got her pregnant.*

6 VO+to-INF If you **get** someone to do something, you ask or tell them to do it, and they do it. *She gets Stuart to help her.*

7 VO+PAST PARTICIPLE If you **get** something done, you cause it to be done. *I got safety belts fitted.*

8 VO If you **get** something, you obtain it. *He's trying to get a flat... Get advice from your local health department.*

9 VO To **get** something also means to receive it. *I got the anorak for Christmas... He was with us when we got the news.*

10 VOO or VO+for If you **get** someone something, or if you **get** it for them, you bring it to them or obtain it for them. *Get me a glass of water... He got her a job with the telephone company... How do you get loans for small businessmen?*

11 VO If you **get** the time or opportunity to do something, you have the time or opportunity to do it. *We get little time for sewing.*

12 VO If you **get** a particular idea or feeling, you have it or experience it. *I got the impression he'd had a sleepless night... She got a lot of fun out of it.*

13 VO If you **get** an illness or disease, you become ill with it. *She got chicken pox.*

14 V+to-INF If you **get** to do something, you eventually do it. *The Prime Minister got to hear of the rumours... I got to like the whole idea... We never got to see the play.*

15 V+ING If you **get** moving or **get** going, you begin to move or to do something. *We can't seem to get moving.*

16 V A If you **get** to a particular stage in an activity, you reach that stage. *You have got to an important stage in your career... I got as far as dismantling the plug.*

17 VO When you **get** a train or bus, you make a journey by train or bus. *We got the train to Colchester.*

18 VO If you **get** a person or an animal, you catch, trap, or shoot them. *The police got him in the end.*

19 V+to If something **is getting** to you, it is making you suffer physically or mentally. *The fatigue and backache are getting to me now.*

20 VO If something **gets** you, it annoys you; used in speech. *'What gets me is the way Janet implies that I'm lazy.'*

21 VO If you **get** a joke or **get** the point of something, you understand it. *I don't really get the point of the story.*

22 People often say **'you get'** instead of 'there is' or 'there are' when they are saying that something exists, happens, or can be experienced. *You get some rather curious effects.*

23 See also **got**.

24 to **get** your way: see **way**. to **get** used to something: see **used**.

get about PHRASAL VERB See **get around**.

get across PHRASAL VERB If you **get** an idea or argument **across**, you succeed in making people understand it. *This is a very clever way, of course, of getting the message across.*

get ahead PHRASAL VERB If you **get ahead**, you are successful in your career; an informal expression. *He learned the hard way about who gets ahead and who's left behind in America.*

get along PHRASAL VERB If you **get along** with someone, you have a friendly relationship with them. *The two men get along well.*

get around PHRASAL VERB **1** If you **get around**, you go to a lot of different places as part of your way of life. *Cycling is actually a quicker way to get around London.* **2** If news **gets around**, **gets about**, or **gets round**, it is told to lots of people and becomes well known. *The news got around... Startling rumours began to get about.* **3** If you **get around** or **get round** a difficulty or restriction, you manage to avoid it or you deal with it. *To help get around this problem, some tanks are now equipped with radar.*

get around to PHRASAL VERB See **get round to**.

get at PHRASAL VERB **1** If you **get at** something, you manage to reach it or obtain it. *The goats bent down to get at the short grass.* **2** If you ask someone what

they **are getting at**, you ask them to explain what they mean; an informal use. *I don't know what you are getting at.* **3** If someone **is getting at** you, they are criticizing or teasing you in an unkind way; an informal use. *You're always getting at me.*

get away PHRASAL VERB **1** If you **get away** from somewhere, you succeed in leaving it. *You've got to get away from home.* **2** If someone **gets away** or if you get someone **away**, they escape. *They got away through Mrs Barnett's garden.* ● See also **getaway**. **3** If you **get away**, you go away for your holidays. *Is there any chance of you getting away this summer?*

get away with PHRASAL VERB If you **get away with** something that you should not have done, you are not punished for doing it. *He bribed her—and got away with it.*

get back PHRASAL VERB **1** If you **get back** something that you used to have, you have it once again. *He hoped he would get back his old job.* **2** If you tell someone to **get back**, you are telling them to move away from something or someone.

get back to PHRASAL VERB **1** If you **get back to** what you were doing before, you start doing it again. *Eddie wanted to get back to sleep... He got back to work again.* **2** To **get back to** a previous state or level means to return to it. *Things would soon get back to normal.*

get by PHRASAL VERB If you **get by** in a situation, you succeed in surviving or in dealing with it. *He had managed to get by without much reading or writing.*

get down PHRASAL VERB **1** If something **gets** you **down**, it makes you unhappy; an informal use. *The loneliness really started to get my mother down after a few months.* **2** If you **get down** what someone is saying, you write it down. *I keep repeating myself so that you can get it down.* **3** If you **get** food **down**, you manage to swallow it, but for some reason it is difficult to do so; an informal use. *I eventually managed to get it down.*

get down to PHRASAL VERB When you **get down to** something, you start doing it. *I got down to work.*

get in PHRASAL VERB **1** When a train, bus, or plane **gets in**, it arrives. *What time does the coach get in?* **2** When a political party or a politician **gets in**, they are elected. *If the two parties both put up candidates all over the country, it will severely damage the chances of either getting in.* **3** In a conversation, if you **get** a remark **in**, you eventually manage to say something. *'What I wanted to say,' I finally got in, 'is that I've a set of instructions at home.'*

get in on PHRASAL VERB If you **get in on** an activity, you start taking part in it, perhaps without being invited; an informal expression. *'He even gets in on the photography shows,' she said indignantly.*

get into PHRASAL VERB **1** If you **get into** an activity, you start doing it or being involved in it. *I always get into arguments with people... He was determined to get into politics.* **2** If you **get into** a particular habit, you start doing that thing regularly. *She'd got into the habit of sulking.* **3** If you **get into** a school, college, or university, you are accepted there as a pupil or student. *Darwin failed to get into medical school at Cambridge.* **4** You ask what has **got into** someone when they are behaving in an unexpected way; an informal use. *What's got into her?*

get off PHRASAL VERB **1** If you **get** something **off**, you remove it. *Get your shirt off... I got most of the mud off your clothes.* **2** If someone is given a very small punishment for breaking a law or rule, you can say that they **got off** with this punishment. *He expressed relief that he had got off so lightly.* **3** You say **'Get off'** or **'Get your hands off'** to someone when you are telling them not to touch something.

get off with PHRASAL VERB If you **get off with** someone, you begin a romantic or sexual relationship with them; an informal expression. *Mike thinks I'm trying to get off with his girlfriend.*

get on PHRASAL VERB **1** If you **get** a piece of clothing **on**, you put it on. *Get your coat on.* **2** If you **get on** with someone, you have a friendly relationship with them. *Mother and I get on very well.* **3** If you **get on** with an activity, you continue doing it or start doing it. *Perhaps we can get on with the meeting now.* 4 If someone is **getting on** well or badly, they are making good or bad progress. *I always get on far better if I can draw a diagram... How's he getting on?* 5 To get **on** also means to be successful in your career. *She's got to study to get on.* 6 If you say that someone is **getting on**, you mean that they are old; an informal use. *This puts a great strain on Members of the House of Lords, especially on those who are getting on in years.* 7 If something is **getting on for** a particular amount, it is nearly that amount; an informal use. *They have getting on for a hundred stores.*

get on to PHRASAL VERB 1 If you **get on to** a particular topic, you start talking about it. *Somehow we got on to grandparents.* 2 If you **get on to** someone, you contact them. *I'll get on to her right away.*

get out PHRASAL VERB 1 If you **get out** of a place or organization, you leave it. *I'm going to get out of New York... The sooner we get out the better.* 2 If you **get** something **out**, you take it from the place where it is kept. *He got out a book and read.* 3 If you **get out** of doing something, you avoid doing it. *She always got out of washing up.* 4 If news or information **gets out**, it becomes known. *The word got out that he would go ahead with the merger.* 5 To **get** a stain **out** means to remove it. *I couldn't get the stain out of your green dress.*

get over PHRASAL VERB 1 If you **get over** an unpleasant experience or an illness, you recover from it. *Have you got over the shock?* 2 If you **get over** a problem, you manage to deal with it. *One mother got over this problem by leaving her baby with someone else.* 3 If you **get** your meaning **over**, people understand what you are saying or what you have written. *He got his meaning over to Jo at the fourth time of trying.*

get over with PHRASAL VERB If you decide to **get** something unpleasant **over with**, you decide to do it or endure it. *Can we just get this questioning over with?*

get round PHRASAL VERB See **get around.**

get round to PHRASAL VERB If you **get round** or **get around to** doing something, you do it after a delay, because you were previously too busy or were reluctant to do it. *The Church, they suggest, hasn't even got round to buying the land needed... Psychologists haven't really got round to looking at humans properly in any real detail.*

get through PHRASAL VERB 1 If you **get through** a task, you succeed in completing it. *It is extremely difficult to get through this amount of work in such a short time.* 2 If you **get through** an unpleasant experience or time, you manage to live through it. *They helped me to get through that time.* 3 If you **get through** a large amount of something, you completely use it up. *I got through about six pounds worth of drink.* 4 If you **get through** to someone, you succeed in making them understand what you are trying to say; an informal use. *Howard, how do I get through to you?* 5 When you are telephoning someone, if you **get through**, you succeed in contacting them. *I finally got through at twenty past ten.*

get together PHRASAL VERB 1 When people **get together**, they meet in order to discuss something or to spend time together. *He warned that revolution and bloodshed could result if the government and opposition failed to get together to carry out real economic reforms.* ● See also **get-together.** 2 If you **get** something **together**, you make it or organize it. *He's spent a whole afternoon trying to get the barbecue together.*

get up PHRASAL VERB 1 If you are sitting or lying and then **get up**, you rise to a standing position. *The woman got up from her chair with the baby in her arms.* 2 When you **get up** in the morning, you get out of bed. *You've got to get up at eight o'clock.* 3 See also **get-up.**

get up to PHRASAL VERB What someone **gets up to** is what they do, especially when it is something that you do not approve of. *When I found out what they used to get up to I was horrified.*

getaway /ɡɛtəweɪ/ **getaways**
NC When someone makes a **getaway**, they leave a

place in a hurry, often after committing a crime; an informal word. *Duffield was already making his getaway down the stairs... The gang picked up the money and made their getaway... He waited at the wheel of the getaway car.*

get-together, get-togethers
NC A **get-together** is an informal meeting or party. *We must have a get-together some evening.*

get-up, get-ups
NC A **get-up** is a strange or unusual set of clothes; an informal word. *She was wearing her arty get-up.*

gewgaw /ɡjuːɡɔː/ **gewgaws**
NC A **gewgaw** is an attractive and brightly-coloured ornament or piece of jewellery that has little value; used showing disapproval. *...a bag of fancy gewgaws.*

geyser /ɡiːzə/ **geysers**
NC A **geyser** is a hole in the Earth's surface from which hot water and steam are forced out. *And then that particular geyser will settle down and another one will be erupting somewhere else.*

Ghali, Dr Boutros Boutros /buːtrɒs buːtrɒs ɡɑːli/
Dr Boutros Boutros Ghali became Secretary General of the United Nations in 1992. He was the Egyptian Minister for Foreign Affairs from 1978 to 1989. Born: 1922.

Ghana /ɡɑːnə/
The **Republic of Ghana** is a country in western Africa, formerly known as the Gold Coast. It was a British colony from 1874 until 1957, when the Gold Coast merged with British Togoland to form Ghana. Dr Kwame Nkrumah of the Convention People's Party (CPP) was the first President. He was overthrown in 1966. In 1981 Flight-Lieutenant Jerry Rawlings established the Provisional National Defence Council (PNDC) and outlawed all political parties. Ghana is a member of the Commonwealth and the Organization of African Unity. It exports cocoa, timber, and gold. Large foreign debts and high inflation are serious economic problems. ◆ **Ghanaian** /ɡɑːneɪən/ N, ADJ ▪ *per capita GNP:* US$400 ▪ *religion:* Christianity, animism, Islam ▪ *language:* English (official), Akan ▪ *currency:* cedi ▪ *capital:* Accra ▪ *population:* 14 million (1989) ▪ *size:* 238,533 square kilometres.

ghastly /ɡɑːstli/
1 ADJ You describe things, situations, or people as **ghastly** when they are very unpleasant or when you dislike them a lot. *...the ghastly news of the murder. ...ghastly office blocks.*
2 ADJ PRED You can say that someone looks **ghastly** when they look very ill; an informal use. *She was crying, blowing her nose and looking simply ghastly.*

gherkin /ɡɜːkɪn/ **gherkins**
NC A **gherkin** is a small cucumber which has been pickled in vinegar. *...gherkins and cocktail onions.*

ghetto /ɡɛtəʊ/ **ghettos** or **ghettoes**
NC A **ghetto** is a part of a city which is inhabited by many people of a particular nationality, colour, religion, or class; used especially to refer to a poor area of a city. *...a black kid growing up in the ghetto.*

ghetto-blaster, ghetto-blasters
NC A **ghetto-blaster** is a large portable tape player with built-in speakers. *In the film, Radio Raheem walks about with loud music playing on his ghetto-blaster.*

ghost /ɡəʊst/ **ghosts**
1 NC When people think that they see a **ghost**, they think that they can see the spirit of a dead person. *...the ghost of Mrs Dowell.*
2 NC+SUPP The **ghost** of something, especially something bad that has happened, is the memory of it. *The ghosts of Tiananmen are still haunting the Chinese leadership... They hoped the historian's report would help to lay the ghosts of the past. ...the ghost of Anti-Americanism.*
● **Ghost** is used in these phrases. ● If you say that someone **has given up the ghost**, you mean they have died; an informal expression. *The victim had given up the ghost and the floor was slippery with his blood.*
● If you say that a machine **has given up the ghost**, you mean that it has stopped working completely and cannot be repaired; an informal expression. *The car took us all the way across Europe, only giving up the*

ghost in the last stages of the journey. • If you say that someone has not got **the ghost of a chance** of doing something, you mean that they have very little chance of succeeding in doing it; an informal expression. *We have not the ghost of a chance of changing father's will.*

ghostly /gəʊstli/
ADJ Something that is **ghostly** is frightening because it does not seem real or natural, or because it seems supernatural in some way. *...ghostly rumbling noises... At Halloween, the ghostly forms of the dead were said to haunt the earth.*

ghost town, ghost towns
NC A **ghost town** is a town which used to be busy and prosperous but which people no longer live in. *Mogadishu is said to be a virtual ghost town, deserted by two-thirds of its residents.*

ghost-write, ghost-writes, ghost-writing, ghost-wrote, ghost-written
VO If an article, speech, or book is **ghost-written**, it is written by someone on behalf of a famous person, who then publishes it or uses it as their own work. *The speech was in fact mostly ghost-written by Stockman.*
♦ **ghost-writing** NU *...a piece of ghost-writing on Mailer's part.*

ghost-writer, ghost-writers
NC A **ghost-writer** is someone who writes articles, speeches, or books for other people.

ghoul /guːl/ **ghouls**
1 NC A **ghoul** is an imaginary evil spirit, especially one that eats dead bodies. *...ghouls and supernatural beasts.*
2 NC If you call someone a **ghoul**, you mean that they show an interest in things that are shocking or unpleasant such as torture, death, and dead bodies. *Police described sightseers who want to see this terrible catastrophe as ghouls.*

ghoulish /guːlɪʃ/
ADJ If you refer to someone or something as **ghoulish**, you think that they show an unhealthy interest in shocking or unpleasant things such as torture or death. *Tim took a ghoulish interest in the murders. ...a ghoulish and horrifying form of entertainment.*

Ghozali, Sid Ahmed /siːd aːxmed gəʊzɒːli/
Sid Ahmed Ghozali was appointed Prime Minister of Algeria in 1991. He is a member of the National Liberation Front (FLN). He was Minister of Energy and Petrochemicals from 1977 to 1979, Minister of Finance from 1988 to 1989, and Foreign Secretary from 1989 to 1991. Born: 1937.

GHQ /dʒiːeɪtʃkjuː/
NU **GHQ** is the place where the people work who organize military forces or a military operation. **GHQ** is an abbreviation for 'General Headquarters'. *She agreed to meet him at GHQ at four-thirty.*

GI /dʒiː aɪ/ **GIs**
NC A **GI** is a soldier in the United States army; an informal word. *More than two hundred people were injured, most of them American GIs stationed in the city.*

giant /dʒaɪənt/ **giants**
1 NC In myths and children's stories, a **giant** is a huge, very strong person. *...stories of cruel giants.*
2 NC+SUPP You can use **giant** to refer to a very large or successful organization or country. *...the US car giant, General Motors. ...the Communist giants China and the Soviet Union... Have they got what it takes to become international music giants?*
3 N SING You can use **giant** to refer to something that is much larger than its usual size. *...a giant of a man.*
▶ Also ADJ ATTRIB *...giant Christmas trees... His giant leap of two metres forty four is still a world record.*

giant killer, giant killers
NC In sport, you can refer to a weak, unknown team as **giant killers** when they beat a strong, well-known team. *Denmark could be emerging as the unlikely giant killers of the first round.*

giant killing, giant killings
NC In sport, when a weak, unknown team beats a strong, well-known team, you can refer to their success as a **giant killing**. *The giant killings didn't end with the non-league clubs, though... The small*

Romanian club, Timisoara, have pulled off a *giant-killing* act in the UEFA cup, knocking out the powerful Atletico Madrid side in Spain.

giant panda, giant pandas. See **panda**.

gibber /dʒɪbə/ **gibbers, gibbering, gibbered**
V or V-QUOTE To **gibber** means to talk very fast in a confused manner. *...men gibbering in their terror... 'I shouldn't have told you,' she gibbered.*

gibberish /dʒɪbəʳrɪʃ/
NU **Gibberish** is talk which does not make any sense. *He said the wording was gibberish and ordered the authorities to pay all costs of the legal action... Let other parents work on their kid's verbal skills and I'll stick with my daughter's gibberish.*

gibbet /dʒɪbɪt/ **gibbets**
NC A **gibbet** is a gallows; an old-fashioned word. *Will you erect a gibbet in every field and hang up men like scarecrows?*

gibbon /gɪbən/ **gibbons**
NC A **gibbon** is an ape with very long arms.

gibe /dʒaɪb/. See **jibe**.

giblets /dʒɪbləts/
N PL The **giblets** of a chicken or other bird are the parts such as its heart and liver which you remove before you cook the bird, but which may also be cooked and eaten.

Gibraltar /dʒɪbrɔːltə/
Gibraltar is a British Crown Colony in southern Europe, on the north of the Strait of Gibraltar, which connects the Mediterranean and the Atlantic. It was ceded to Britain in 1713, but Spain disputes Britain's claim to sovereignty. Gibraltar's strategic importance led to its development as a military base. Tourism, shipping, and banking are important industries.
♦ **Gibraltarian** /dʒɪbrɔːltɛəriən/ N, ADJ **Gibraltar** /dʒɪbrɔːltə/ ADJ
■ *religion:* Christianity (mainly Roman Catholic)
■ *language:* English (official), Spanish ■ *currency:* pound ■ *population:* 31,000 (1989) ■ *size:* 5.5 square kilometres.

giddy /gɪdi/
1 ADJ If you feel **giddy**, you feel that you are about to fall over, usually because you are not well. *He had a headache and felt giddy.* ♦ **giddiness** NU *...a sensation of extreme giddiness.*
2 ADJ **Giddy** behaviour is very happy, excited, and slightly reckless behaviour. *They goof around with the giddy excitement of fourteen-year-olds.*
3 ADJ If something makes you **giddy**, you find it confusing. *It made me giddy to hear so much analysis.*

gift /gɪft/ **gifts**
1 NC A **gift** is something that you give someone as a present. *...a gift from the Russian ambassador to Charles II. ...the gift of a handful of primroses.*
2 NC If someone has a **gift** for a particular activity, they have a natural ability for doing it. *John has a real gift for conversation. ...his gifts as a story-teller.*

gifted /gɪftɪd/
1 ADJ A **gifted** person has a natural ability for a particular activity. *...a gifted actress.*
2 ADJ A **gifted** child is very intelligent or talented. *Individual schools vary in their approach to gifted children.*

gift-wrapped
ADJ **Gift-wrapped** presents are wrapped in pretty paper. *Your tickets will arrive gift-wrapped.*

gig /gɪg/ **gigs**
NC A **gig** is a live performance by a pop musician, comedian, or disc jockey; an informal word. *They started out doing free gigs in bars.*

gigantic /dʒaɪgæntɪk/
ADJ Something that is **gigantic** is extremely large. *...a gigantic rubbish heap. ...a gigantic effort.*

giggle /gɪgl/ **giggles, giggling, giggled**
V or V-QUOTE If you **giggle**, you make quiet laughing noises, because you are amused or because you are nervous or embarrassed. *The absurd sound made her giggle... 'Oh dear,' she giggled, 'I forgot.'* ▶ Also NC *...a nervous giggle.*

giggly /gɪgəʳli/
ADJ If people are **giggly**, they giggle a lot, either

because they are happy and amused or because they are slightly nervous. *They returned, rather giggly.*

gigolo /ˈʒɪɡəˌləʊ/ **gigolos**
NC A **gigolo** is a man who is paid to be the lover and companion of a rich, older woman; used showing disapproval. *She had a drunken row with her gigolo.*

gild /ɡɪld/ **gilds, gilding, gilded**
1 VO To **gild** a surface means to cover it in a thin layer of gold or gold paint.
2 VO If something **is gilded**, it appears golden; a literary use. *The hedges were gilded by the sun. ...his face gilded in the glow from the stove.*
3 If someone **is gilding the lily**, they are trying to improve something that is already beautiful or perfect, and which therefore does not need improving.

gilded /ˈɡɪldɪd/
ADJ ATTRIB You use **gilded** to describe something that has been covered with a thin layer of gold or gold paint. *...the ornate gilded mirror.*

gilding /ˈɡɪldɪŋ/
NU The **gilding** on something is a thin layer of gold or gold paint that covers it. *The gilding is thinner than he expected.*

gill, gills; pronounced /ɡɪl/ for the meaning in paragraph 1 and /dʒɪl/ for the meaning in paragraph 2.
1 NC **Gills** are the organs on the sides of a fish through which it breathes. *Most species have gills.*
2 NU A **gill** is a unit of measurement for liquids that is equal to a quarter of a pint or 0.142 litres. *...a gill of rum a day.*

gilt /ɡɪlt/ **gilts**
1 NU **Gilt** is a thin layer of gold or gold paint that you use to decorate something. *The gilt had been chipped.*
▶ Also ADJ ATTRIB *...paintings in dark gilt frames.*
2 N PL **Gilts** are gilt-edged stocks or securities. *...its gilts and Euro-market operations.*

gilt-edged
ADJ **Gilt-edged** stocks or securities are issued by the government for people to invest in for a fixed period of time at a fixed rate of interest. With gilt-edged stocks there is very little risk of investors losing their money. *Almost three hundred and eighty-seven thousand pounds had been made by selling gilt-edged stocks.*

gimcrack /ˈdʒɪmkræk/
ADJ ATTRIB **Gimcrack** things look attractive but are badly made and so are of little use or value. *...some flashy gimcrack boat.*

gimlet /ˈɡɪmlət/ **gimlets**
1 NC A **gimlet** is a small sharp tool used for making small holes in wood.
2 ADJ ATTRIB If someone has **gimlet** eyes, they look at things very carefully and notice every detail. *His gimlet eyes blinked at her.*

gimmick /ˈɡɪmɪk/ **gimmicks**
NC A **gimmick** is an unusual action, object, or device which is intended to attract interest or publicity. *The manufacturer needed a new sales gimmick.*

gimmickry /ˈɡɪmɪkri/
NU **Gimmickry** is actions or objects that are not necessary or important but whose main purpose is to attract interest or publicity. *...computers loaded with gimmickry... No legal gimmickry will save the animals.*

gimmicky /ˈɡɪmɪki/
ADJ Something that is **gimmicky** contains a lot of unnecessary or unimportant things that have been included to attract interest or publicity; an informal word. *The production was rather gimmicky... Good ideas become standard, gimmicky ones die quickly.*

gin /dʒɪn/ **gins**
N MASS **Gin** is a colourless alcoholic drink. *Spirits (whisky, gin and vodka, for instance) are not advertised on British television... The delegates were sipping a couple of gin and tonics.*

ginger /ˈdʒɪndʒə/
1 NU **Ginger** is the root of a plant which has a spicy, hot flavour and is used in cooking. *I added a chopped onion and a little ginger.*
2 ADJ Something that is **ginger** in colour is bright orange-brown. *...a man with ginger hair. ...a ginger cat.*

ginger ale, ginger ales
N MASS **Ginger ale** is a fizzy non-alcoholic drink flavoured with ginger, which is often mixed with an alcoholic drink. *'Give me a whisky and a ginger ale on the side.'*

ginger beer, ginger beers
N MASS **Ginger beer** is a fizzy drink flavoured with ginger, which is sometimes slightly alcoholic. *Sunday lunch was ginger beer and a potato.*

gingerbread /ˈdʒɪndʒəbred/
NU **Gingerbread** is a sweet cake or biscuit that is flavoured with ginger. It is often made in the shape of a person.

ginger group, ginger groups
NC A **ginger group** is a group of people with similar ideas who work together, especially within a larger organization, to try to persuade others to accept or approve of their ideas. *...an independent ginger group in the union.*

gingerly /ˈdʒɪndʒəli/
ADV If you do something **gingerly**, you do it carefully and perhaps nervously. *They walked gingerly over the rotten floorboards.*

gingery /ˈdʒɪndʒərⁱ/
1 ADJ **Gingery** means slightly ginger in colour. *...his curly gingery locks. ...a gingery tweed jacket.*
2 ADJ **Gingery** also means slightly ginger in taste or smell. *It smelled of earth, of herbs and exotic gingery scents.*

gingham /ˈɡɪŋəm/
NU **Gingham** is cotton cloth that has small squares or stripes. *...a pink gingham shirt.*

ginseng /ˈdʒɪnseŋ/
NU **Ginseng** is the root of a plant found in China, Korea, and North America which some people believe is good for your health.

gipsy /ˈdʒɪpsi/ **gipsies.** See gypsy.

giraffe /dʒɪˈrɑːf/ **giraffes**
NC A **giraffe** is an African animal with a very long neck, long legs, and dark patches on its body.

gird /ɡɜːd/ **girds, girding, girded**
If someone **is girding** their **loins** or **girding up** their loins, they are preparing to do something difficult or dangerous; a literary expression. *Bonn and Vienna are girding their loins to cope with another influx of refugees from East Germany.*

girder /ˈɡɜːdə/ **girders**
NC A **girder** is a long, thick piece of steel or iron that is used in the frameworks of buildings and bridges. *The girder had been hoisted into position.*

girdle /ˈɡɜːdl/ **girdles, girdling, girdled**
1 NC A **girdle** is a piece of women's underwear that fits tightly around the stomach and hips. *...bras and girdles.*
2 VO If you **girdle** something, you surround it with a circle; a literary word. *Within a decade optical cables will girdle the Earth.*

girl /ɡɜːl/ **girls**
1 NC A **girl** is a female child. *...when you were a little girl. ...an eight-year-old girl... She has two girls and a boy. ...a girls' school.*
2 NC You can also refer to a young woman as a **girl**; some people find this use offensive. *There were a lot of pretty girls there.*
3 N PL You can refer to a group of women as **girls**. *...the other girls at work.*

girlfriend /ˈɡɜːlfrend/ **girlfriends**
1 NC A man's or boy's **girlfriend** is the woman or girl with whom he is having a romantic or sexual relationship. *He had had an argument with his girlfriend.*
2 NC A woman's **girlfriend** is a female friend; used in American English. *She went to the movies with some girlfriends.*

girl guide, girl guides
NC A **girl guide** is a member of the Girl Guides Association. Girl guides are encouraged to be disciplined and to learn practical skills. *About fifteen thousand Scouts and Girl Guides have begun a ten-day jamboree in Australia.*

girlhood /ˈɡɜːlhʊd/
NU **Girlhood** is the time during which a female person

is a girl. *She had a healthy and happy girlhood.*
girlie /gɜːli/
ADJ ATTRIB **Girlie** magazines or calendars show
photographs of naked or almost naked women; an
informal word. *He was reading a girlie magazine...
The survey shows that a quarter of the men resorted
to girlie magazines, the rest to what's described as
'solitary vices'.*
girlish /gɜːlɪʃ/
ADJ If a woman is **girlish**, she is like a young girl in
appearance or behaviour. *...a girlish laugh.*
girl scout, girl scouts
NC In the United States, a **girl scout** is a member of
the Girl Scouts Association. Girl scouts are encouraged
to be disciplined and to learn practical skills.
giro /dʒaɪrəʊ/ **giros**
1 NU In Britain, **Giro** is a system by which a bank or
post office can transfer money from one account to
another. *...a Bank Giro paying in slip... With a Giro
account you can put in and draw out cash during
normal Post Office hours.*
2 NC In Britain, a **giro** or **giro cheque** is a cheque that
is given to a person who is unemployed or ill by the
government. *She clapped him about the head with a
saucepan when she heard he'd spent the Giro on drink.*
girth /gɜːθ/ **girths**
NC The **girth** of something is the measurement around
it; a formal word. *He was a vigorous man for his
girth. ...a 52-inch girth.*
gist /dʒɪst/
N SING The **gist** of a speech, conversation, or piece of
writing is its general meaning. *We began to get the
gist of her remarks.*
give /gɪv/ **gives, giving, gave, given**
1 VO or VOO **Give** is often used with nouns that describe
actions, especially physical actions. The whole
expression refers to the performing of the action. For
example, 'She gave a smile' means almost the same
as 'She smiled'. *Jill gave an immense sigh... She gave
Etta a quick, shrewd glance... She gave the door a
push... Any aircraft carrying the Prime Minister is
given a thorough check.*
2 VOO or VO+*to* You use **give** to say that a person does a
particular thing for someone else. For example, if you
give someone help, you help them. *He gave her a lift
back to London. ...a tutor who came to give lessons to
my son.*
3 VO, VOO, or VO+*to* You also use **give** with nouns that
refer to information, opinions, or greetings. For
example, if you **give** someone some news, you tell it to
them. *That's the best advice I can give... 13% gave
bad housing as their main source of worry... Castle
gave the porter the message... Give my regards to
your daughter.*
4 VO If you **give** a speech or a performance, you
speak or perform in public. *He was due to give a
lecture that evening.*
5 VO+*to* or VOO If you **give** attention or thought to
something, you concentrate on it, deal with it, or think
about it. *More attention must be given to industrial
investment, research and development... She hadn't
bothered to give it particular thought.*
6 VOO, VO+*to*, or VO If you **give** someone something, or if
you **give** it to them, you offer it to them, for example
as a present. *They gave me a handsome little wooden
box... He gave it to me, it's mine... It was the only
thing she had to give.*
7 VOO or VO+*to* To **give** someone something also means
to hand it over to them or to provide them with it.
Give me your key... He gave a card to Beynon.
8 VOO If something **gives** you a particular feeling,
quality, idea, or right, it causes you to have it or
experience it. *Working on the car has given me an
appetite... What gave you that idea?... His leadership
gives him the right to command.*
9 VO If you **give** a party, you organize it. *Every year
he gives a lunch for his family and friends.*
10 VOO You also use **give** to say that you estimate
something to be a particular amount, level, or value.
*The polls had given the President a 10 to 15 point
lead... I give him a week before he has a nervous
breakdown.*

11 V If something **gives**, it collapses or breaks under
pressure. *His legs gave beneath him.*
12 See also **given.**
● **Give** is used in these phrases. ● If you **would give
anything** or **would give your right arm** to do or have
something, you are very keen to do or have it. *She
said she would give anything to stay in China.* ● If
someone **gives as good as** they get in a fight or
argument, they fight or argue as hard as their
opponent. ● **Give or take** is used to indicate that an
amount is approximate. For example, if something is
fifty years old **give or take** a few years, it is
approximately fifty years old. *It's three hundred miles
to Edinburgh, give or take ten... The results turned out
to be exactly the same, give or take one percent.* ● If
one thing **gives way** to another, it is replaced by it.
Her look of joy gave way to one of misery. ● If a
structure **gives way**, it collapses. *The floor gave way.*
● If you **give way** to someone, you agree to allow them
to do something, although you do not really want to.
*In the long run it proved easier to give way to his
demands.* ● If you **give way** when you are driving a
car, you slow down or stop in order to allow other
traffic to go in front of you. *Give way to traffic from
the right.* ● to **give evidence**: see **evidence.** ● to **give
ground**: see **ground.** ● to **give rise to** something: see
rise.
give away PHRASAL VERB 1 If you **give** something
away, you give it to someone, often because you no
longer want it. *She has given away jewellery worth
millions of pounds.* 2 If you **give away** information
that should be kept secret, you reveal it to other
people. *Mr King seems certain to be pressed for
further details, but he is unlikely to give much away.*
3 See also **give-away.**
give back PHRASAL VERB If you **give** something **back**,
you return it to the person who gave it to you. *If I
didn't need the money, I would give it back again.*
give in PHRASAL VERB When you **give in**, you agree to
do something you do not want to, or accept that you
will not be able to do something that you do want to
do. *We mustn't give in to threats... I resolved not to
give in.*
give off PHRASAL VERB If something **gives off** heat,
smoke, or a smell, it produces it and sends it out into
the air. *...the tremendous heat given off by the fire.*
give out PHRASAL VERB 1 If you **give out** a number of
things, you distribute them among a group of people.
Howard gave out drinks to his guests. 2 If something
gives out it stops working, usually because it is old or
broken. *The fuse within a plug will give out
occasionally.*
give over PHRASAL VERB If something is **given over** to
a particular use, it is used only for that purpose.
...land given over to agriculture.
give up PHRASAL VERB 1 If you **give up** something,
you stop doing it or having it. *He gave up smoking to
save money... She never completely gave up hope.* 2 If
you **give up**, you admit that you cannot do a particular
thing and stop trying to do it. *I don't know. I give up.*
3 If you **give up** your job, you resign from it. *It's
widely believed that he might give up active politics
for an academic career.*
give up on PHRASAL VERB If you **give up on** something
or someone, you stop trying to understand or change
what they are doing, because the task seems a waste
of effort. *Many women give up on men after pursuing
them.*
give-and-take
NU **Give-and-take** is willingness to listen to other
people's opinions and to make compromises. *How far
they will go will be a matter of give-and-take.*
give-away, give-aways
1 N SING or N+N A **give-away** is something that reveals a
truth that is not clearly visible or that someone is
trying to hide. *He ate a banana with a knife and
fork—to modern minds a clear give-away if ever there
was one. ...a give-away remark... Such producers
make sure any give-away signs are erased from their
products.*
2 NC A **give-away** is also something that you are given
free, for example when you buy something. *Many*

stores are trying various promotions, including give-aways and unannounced sales, to lure in shoppers before Christmas. ...such give-aways as free lunch for all schoolchildren.
3 ADJ ATTRIB **Give-away** also means extremely cheap. *The houses were sold off to their tenants at give-away prices.*

given /gɪvn/
1 **Given** is the past participle of **give**.
2 ADJ ATTRIB A **given** date or time is one that has been fixed or decided on previously. *At a given moment we all cheered.*
3 If you talk about **any given** time, **any given** situation, and so on, you mean any time, situation, or so on that you choose to mention. *Often people don't know what's happening at any given moment... One cannot look at the problems of any given society in isolation from the rest of the world.*
4 PREP or CONJ If something is the case **given** a particular thing, it is the case if you take that thing into account. *Given the months of bitter fighting that preceded this meeting, it was a major breakthrough that the warring parties were able to come together at all... It seemed churlish to send him away, given that he only wanted to take photographs.*
5 ADJ PRED+to If you say that someone is **given** to doing something, you mean that they often do it; a formal use. *He was given to claiming that he was related to the Queen.*

given name, **given names**
NC Your **given name** is your first name, which you were given at birth in addition to your surname; used in American English. *Until a few months ago, Imbana Cantanco went by his given name, Duane Retos.*

glacé /glæseɪ/
ADJ ATTRIB **Glacé** fruits have been preserved in a thick sugary syrup. *...glacé cherries.*

glacial /gleɪʃl, gleɪsɪəl/
ADJ ATTRIB **Glacial** means relating to glaciers or ice. *...a glacial landscape.*

glacier /glæsɪə/ **glaciers**
NC A **glacier** is a huge mass of ice which moves very slowly, often down a mountain valley. *This may hasten the rate at which glaciers and snowfields melt in the mountains, threatening people downstream with the possibility of flooding.*

glad /glæd/
1 ADJ PRED If you are **glad** about something, you are happy and pleased about it. *I'm so glad that your niece was able to use the tickets... Ralph was glad of a chance to change the subject...* ◆ **gladly** ADV *He gladly accepted their invitation.*
2 ADJ PRED+to-INF If you say that you are **glad** to do something, you mean that you are willing to do it. *I will be glad to be of assistance.* ◆ **gladly** ADV *We will gladly do it if it is within our power.*

gladden /glædn/ **gladdens**, **gladdening**, **gladdened**
VO If something **gladdens** you, it makes you happy and pleased; a formal word. *It gladdened him to be home.*

glade /gleɪd/ **glades**
NC A **glade** is a grassy space without trees in a wood or forest; a literary word. *You'd need those cereal crops in clearings or glades where there is more sun.*

gladiator /glædɪeɪtə/ **gladiators**
NC A **gladiator** was a man who, in the time of the Roman Empire, used to fight other men or wild animals in order to entertain an audience. *These would have been the doorways from which the gladiators would have emerged into the vast open arena.*

glad-rags
N PL Your **glad-rags** are smart clothes which you wear for special occasions such as parties; an informal word, often used humorously. *Go and put your glad-rags on!*

glamor /glæmə/. See **glamour**.

glamorize /glæmərɑɪz/ **glamorizes**, **glamorizing**, **glamorized**; also spelt **glamorise**.
VO If you **glamorize** something, you make it look or seem more attractive than it really is. *The truth is sometimes glamorised.*

glamorous /glæməʳrəs/
ADJ People, places, or jobs that are **glamorous** are attractive and exciting. *...the most glamorous star in motion pictures.*

glamour /glæmə/; also spelt **glamor** in American English.
NU People, places, or jobs that have **glamour** are attractive and exciting. *It lacks the glamour of the Bolshoi Ballet. ...the superficial glamour of television. ...an image of glamour and power.*

glance /glɑːns/ **glances**, **glancing**, **glanced**
1 V A If you **glance** at something, you look at it very quickly and then look away. *Jacqueline glanced at her watch... Rudolph glanced around to make sure nobody was watching.* ▸ Also NC *He cast a quick glance at his friend.*
2 V O+through or at If you **glance** through or at a newspaper or book, you spend a short time looking at it without reading it carefully. *During breakfast he glances through the morning paper... He glanced at the sleeve notes of an Eddie Cochran album.*
● **Glance** is used in these phrases. ● If you can see or recognize something **at a glance**, you can see or recognize it immediately. *She can tell at a glance whether they are married.* ● If you say that something is true or seems to be true **at first glance**, you mean that it seems to be true when you first see it or think about it, but that your first impression may be wrong. *At first glance, it all seems bizarre... At first glance, they were united in denouncing yesterday's incident, but on closer reading, important differences emerged.*
glance off PHRASAL VERB If something **glances off** another object, it hits it at an angle and bounces away in another direction. *Stones hit him on the shoulder and one glanced off his skull.*

glancing /glɑːnsɪŋ/
ADJ ATTRIB A **glancing** blow hits something at an angle rather than from directly in front or behind. *It hit him a glancing blow on the forehead.*

gland /glænd/ **glands**
NC **Glands** are organs in your body that make substances that are vital to your body or that allow substances to pass out of your body. *The President's heart condition was caused by an overactive thyroid gland... As the disease progresses, there is often profound fatigue and swollen lymph glands.*

glandular /glændjʊlə/
ADJ ATTRIB **Glandular** means relating to your glands. *...glandular changes. ...the virus causing glandular fever.*

glare /gleə/ **glares**, **glaring**, **glared**
1 V If you **glare** at someone, you look at them angrily. *The two brothers glared at each other.* ▸ Also N SING *He shot a suspicious glare at me.*
2 V If a light **glares**, it shines very brightly and makes things difficult to see. *A harsh light glared through the windows.* ▸ Also N SING *The windows were tinted to reduce the glare.*
3 N SING If you are in the **glare** of publicity or public attention, you are constantly being watched and talked about by people. *At home he can relax once he's away from the glare of publicity.*

glaring /gleərɪŋ/
ADJ If you refer to something bad as **glaring**, you mean that it is very obvious. *...glaring inequalities of wealth... There is one glaring omission.* ◆ **glaringly** ADV *It was glaringly obvious that he had no idea what he was doing.*

glasnost /glæznɒst/
NU **Glasnost** is a policy of frankness and accountability of a government to its people and to other nations. **Glasnost** was first developed in the former Soviet Union under President Gorbachev. *...the East German government's reluctance to introduce Soviet-style glasnost. ...the tidal wave of glasnost which has been sweeping over the Soviet political system.*

glass /glɑːs/ **glasses**
1 NU **Glass** is the hard transparent substance that windows and bottles are made from. *He sweeps away the broken glass... They crept up to the glass doors and peeped inside.*

2 NC A **glass** is a container made of glass which you can drink from. *I put down my glass and stood up.*
3 NC You can use **glass** to refer to a glass and its contents, or to the contents only. *He poured Ellen a glass of wine.*
4 NU Glass objects that you have in your house can be referred to as **glass**. *...a house crammed with beautiful furniture, glass and china.*
5 N PL **Glasses** are two lenses in a frame that some people wear in front of their eyes in order to see better. *...a girl with glasses. ...a pair of glasses.*
6 See also **dark glasses**, **magnifying glass**, **stained glass**.

glass fibre; spelt **glass fiber** in American English.
NU **Glass fibre** is a strong material made from short thin threads of glass. It is used to keep heat inside buildings or to strengthen plastic. *Oil companies are showing an interest in plastic reinforced with glass fibre... The minehunters have glass fibre hulls to make them less vulnerable to magnetic mines.*

glasshouse /glɑːshaʊs/ **glasshouses**
NC A **glasshouse** is a large greenhouse. *Some people have compared this to the effect of being in a glasshouse on a summer's day.*

glassware /glɑːsweə/
NU **Glassware** is objects made of glass, for example bowls, drinking containers, and ornaments. *There are also some fine examples of Bugatti furniture and art nouveau glassware.*

glassy /glɑːsi/
1 ADJ Something that is **glassy** is smooth and shiny, like glass; a literary use. *...the glassy sea... The instructions promised it would restore the roughed out curve to glassy smoothness.*
2 ADJ If someone's eyes are **glassy**, they show no feeling or understanding in their expression. *He gazed at the street with dull, glassy eyes.*

glaucoma /glɔːkəʊmə/
NU **Glaucoma** is an eye disease which can cause a person to go gradually blind. *Glaucoma is a major cause of blindness worldwide.*

glaze /gleɪz/ **glazes**, **glazing**, **glazed**
1 NC A **glaze** is a thin layer of a hard shiny substance on a piece of pottery. *Her trademark is the vibrant glazes she uses on her bowls and vases.*
2 VO When you **glaze** food such as pastry, you spread a layer of beaten egg, milk, or other liquid onto it before you cook it in order to give it an attractive shiny surface. *We're going to glaze the sweet potatoes.*
glaze over PHRASAL VERB If someone's eyes **glaze over**, they become dull and lose all expression, usually because of boredom. *Constitutional reform is often an arid subject causing eyes to glaze over.*

glazed /gleɪzd/
1 ADJ If someone's eyes are **glazed**, their expression is dull or dreamy, because they are tired, bored, or affected by drink or drugs. *His eyes took on a slightly glazed, distant look.*
2 ADJ If pottery is **glazed**, it is covered with a thin layer of a hard shiny substance. *...glazed clay pots.*
3 ADJ A **glazed** window or door has glass in it. *...see-through escalators and glazed shopping malls.*

gleam /gliːm/ **gleams**, **gleaming**, **gleamed**
1 V If an object or a surface **gleams**, it shines because it is reflecting light. *He polished the gold until it gleamed.* ► Also N SING *...a gleam of water.*
♦ **gleaming** ADJ *...the gleaming white dome of the Presidential Palace.*
2 V When a small light shines brightly, you can say that it **gleams**. *The lighthouses of the islands gleam and wink above the surf.*
3 V If your face or eyes **gleam** with a particular feeling, they show it. *His eyes gleamed with pleasure.* ► Also N SING *A gleam of triumph crossed the woman's face.* ♦ **gleaming** ADJ *...a gleaming smile.*

glean /gliːn/ **gleans**, **gleaning**, **gleaned**
VO If you **glean** information about something, you obtain it slowly and with difficulty. *Much of the information he gleaned was of no practical use.*

glee /gliː/
NU **Glee** is a feeling of happiness and excitement,

often caused by someone else's misfortune. *...the glee with which the media report scientific calamities.*

gleeful /gliːfl/
ADJ Someone who is **gleeful** is happy or excited, often because of someone else's misfortune. *...clicking her teeth in gleeful disapproval.* ♦ **gleefully** ADV *He gleefully rubbed his hands.*

glen /glen/ **glens**
NC A **glen** is a deep, narrow valley, especially in Scotland or Ireland. *Here in the glen the clear water rushes between low oaks, birches and alders... Hundreds of skiers were cleared from the slopes of Glen Shee after heavy snow falls.*

glib /glɪb/
ADJ You describe someone's behaviour as **glib** when they talk too quickly and confidently, making difficult things sound easy, so that you feel that you cannot trust them. *MacIver was always ready with glib promises.* ♦ **glibly** ADV *They still talk glibly of a return to full employment.*

glide /glaɪd/ **glides**, **gliding**, **glided**
1 V If you **glide** somewhere, you move there smoothly and silently. *Tim glided to the door and down the stairs... The canoes glided by.*
2 V When birds or aeroplanes **glide**, they float on air currents. *...an owl gliding silently over the fields.*

glider /glaɪdə/ **gliders**
NC A **glider** is an aircraft without an engine, which flies by floating on air currents. *In the late nineteenth century people had gone up in gliders.*

gliding /glaɪdɪŋ/
NU **Gliding** is the sport or activity of flying in a glider.

glimmer /glɪmə/ **glimmers**, **glimmering**, **glimmered**
1 V If something **glimmers**, it produces a faint, often unsteady light. *The pearl glimmered faintly as she moved.* ► Also N SING *The sky was pink with the first, far-off glimmer of the dawn.*
2 NC+SUPP A **glimmer** of something is a faint sign of it. *He showed no glimmer of interest in them.*

glimmering /glɪmərɪŋ/ **glimmerings**
NC+SUPP A **glimmering** of something is a faint sign of it. *...the first glimmerings of hope... A glimmering of new understanding brightens the bleak horizons of Muscular Dystrophy.*

glimpse /glɪmps/ **glimpses**, **glimpsing**, **glimpsed**
1 VO If you **glimpse** something, you see it very briefly and not very well. *...a village they had glimpsed through the trees.* ► Also NC *...the first glimpse I caught of Fanny.*
2 VO You can also say that you **glimpse** something when you experience or think about it briefly, and begin to understand it better. *She glimpses something of what life ought to be about.* ► Also NC *...glimpses of his kindness.*

glint /glɪnt/ **glints**, **glinting**, **glinted**
1 V If something **glints**, it produces or reflects a quick flash of light. *His spectacles glinted in the sunlight... The sun glinted on the walls.* ► Also N SING *...a glint of metal.*
2 V If someone's eyes **glint**, they shine and express a particular emotion. *Her green eyes glinted with mockery.* ► Also N SING *There was an ironic glint in his eyes.*

glisten /glɪsn/ **glistens**, **glistening**, **glistened**
V If something **glistens**, it shines, because it is smooth, wet, or oily. *His face glistened with sweat.*
♦ **glistening** ADJ *...glistening lips.*

glitch /glɪtʃ/ **glitches**; used in informal American English.
1 NC A **glitch** is a small problem that stops something from working properly or being successful. *NASA blames a technical glitch for the delay... Are there likely to be any last-minute glitches holding up agreement?*
2 NC A **glitch** is also a false electronic signal caused by a sudden increase in electrical power. *The army says that they think a computer software glitch let a SCUD missile slip past their defences.*

glitter /glɪtə/ **glitters**, **glittering**, **glittered**
1 V If something **glitters**, it shines and sparkles. *Her jewellery glittered under the spotlight... Stars glittered in a clear sky.* ► Also N SING *...the glitter of the sea.*

2 v If someone's eyes **glitter**, they are very bright and shiny because they are feeling a particular emotion. *Tony gazed with glittering eyes around him.*
3 NU You can also use **glitter** to refer to something's superficial attractiveness or to the excitement and glamour associated with a situation. *...the glitter of consumer gadgetry. ...showbusiness glitter. ...the glitter and glitz of Hollywood.*

glittering /glɪtəᵊrɪŋ/
ADJ ATTRIB You can describe something as **glittering** when it is very impressive. *...a glittering career.*

glittery /glɪtəᵊri/
ADJ Something that is **glittery** shines with a sparkling light. *...glittery jewellery.*

glitz /glɪts/
NU Something that has **glitz** is superficially attractive, in a very noticeable and exaggerated way; an informal word. *Hollywood has once again been celebrating its annual festival of glitz and glamour.*

glitzy /glɪtsi/ **glitzier, glitziest**
ADJ Something that is **glitzy** is superficially attractive, in a very noticeable and exaggerated way; an informal word. *To judge the book by its cover, it seems fairly glitzy and glamorous.*

gloat /gləʊt/ **gloats, gloating, gloated**
v When someone **gloats**, they show great pleasure at their own success or at other people's failure. *They were gloating over my bankruptcy.*

glob /glɒb/ **globs**
NC A **glob** of liquid or of a soft substance is a small amount of it with a round shape; an informal word. *...a glob of milk. ...globs of foam.*

global /gləʊbl/
ADJ **Global** means concerning or including the whole world. *...protests on a global scale.* ◆ **globally** ADV *Deforestation has a considerable impact on weather patterns, both globally and locally.*

global warming
NU **Global warming** is the problem of the gradual rise in temperature in the Earth's atmosphere. It happens because heat that is absorbed from the sun cannot leave the atmosphere because of a build-up of carbon dioxide and other gases. *We've heard a lot in the past couple of years about cutting greenhouse gas emissions and slowing global warming.*

globe /gləʊb/ **globes**
1 N SING You can refer to the Earth as the **globe**. *...countries on the far side of the globe.*
2 NC A **globe** is a spherical object with a map of the world on it. *How come not one of my students could find Baltimore or Kuwait on a globe?*
3 NC Any object shaped like a ball can be referred to as a **globe**. *...the orange globe of the sun.*

globetrotter /gləʊbtrɒtə/ **globetrotters**
NC A **globetrotter** is someone who spends a lot of time visiting places all over the world. *Mr Mulroney is not the only globetrotter, the Japanese Prime Minister is in the US on the first leg of a trip.*

globular /glɒbjʊlə/
ADJ Something that is **globular** is round like a ball; a formal word. *...a globular helmet. ...the globular front part of the tadpole.*

globule /glɒbjuːl/ **globules**
NC A **globule** of liquid is a tiny round drop of it; a formal word. *...a globule of blood.*

gloom /gluːm/
1 N SING **Gloom** is partial darkness in which there is still a little light. *He peered through the gloom at the dim figure. ...the gloom of their cell.*
2 NU **Gloom** is also a feeling of unhappiness or despair. *He viewed the future with gloom.*

gloomy /gluːmi/ **gloomier, gloomiest**
1 ADJ Something that is **gloomy** is dark and rather depressing. *...the gloomy prison. ...a gloomy day.*
2 ADJ If someone is **gloomy**, they are unhappy and have a feeling of hopelessness. *He looked gloomy... There was a gloomy silence.* ◆ **gloomily** ADV *'Trouble,' Rudolph said gloomily.*
3 ADJ If a situation is **gloomy**, it does not give you much hope of success or happiness. *The outlook is particularly gloomy among manufacturers... The Saudi ambassador delivered a gloomy assessment today of the crisis in the Persian Gulf.*

glorified /glɔːrɪfaɪd/
ADJ ATTRIB You use **glorified** to say that something is not really any more important or impressive than its name suggests. For example, if you describe a lake as a glorified pond, you mean that it is really no bigger than a pond. *I can't stay here, though. I'm just a sort of glorified lodger.*

glorify /glɔːrɪfaɪ/ **glorifies, glorifying, glorified**
vo If you **glorify** someone or something, you praise them or make them seem more important than they really are. *His newspapers glorified his charitable donations.* ◆ **glorification** N SING+SUPP *...the glorification of violence.*

glorious /glɔːriəs/
1 ADJ Something that is **glorious** is very beautiful and impressive. *...the most glorious flowers I have ever seen.* ◆ **gloriously** SUBMOD *...gloriously embroidered pictures.*
2 ADJ Things that are **glorious** are very pleasant and make you happy. *...a glorious carefree feeling of joy... We had glorious sunshine.* ◆ **gloriously** SUBMOD *We got gloriously drunk... The first few days were gloriously hot.*
3 ADJ **Glorious** events or periods involve great fame or success. *...the glorious future opening before them.*

glory /glɔːri/ **glories, glorying, gloried**
1 NU **Glory** is fame and admiration that you get for an achievement. *The warriors valued glory and honour above life itself... I did it for the theatre, not for my own personal glory.*
2 NU+SUPP The **glory** of something is the fact of its being very beautiful or impressive. *...the glory of the classical theatre.*
3 N PL+SUPP The **glories** of a person or group are the occasions on which they have done something famous or admirable. *...a shrine to the glories of the French Army.*
4 N PL+SUPP The **glories** of a culture or place are the things that people find most attractive or impressive about it. *...the glories of Venice.*

glory in PHRASAL VERB If you **glory in** a situation or activity, you enjoy it very much. *The women were glorying in this new-found freedom.*

gloss /glɒs/ **glosses, glossing, glossed**
N SING A **gloss** is a bright shine on a surface. *The wood has a high gloss.*

gloss over PHRASAL VERB If you **gloss over** a problem or mistake, you try to make it seem unimportant by ignoring it or by dealing with it very quickly. *This may seem a convenient means of glossing over summit differences, and reaching some form of compromise agreement.*

glossary /glɒsəᵊri/ **glossaries**
NC The **glossary** of a book or a subject is an alphabetical list of the special or technical words used in it, with explanations of their meanings. *Each man has been given a glossary of key terms in three different languages.*

gloss paint
NU **Gloss paint** is paint that looks shiny when it is dry. *There are many different resins used in paint: vinyl for emulsion and alkyds for gloss paints.*

glossy /glɒsi/
1 ADJ Something that is **glossy** is smooth and shiny. *She had glossy brown hair.*
2 ADJ You can describe something as **glossy** when you mean that it has an attractive appearance but is really quite poor in quality or of little practical value. *The glossy images promise only illusion. ...glossy movie script dialogue.*
3 ADJ ATTRIB **Glossy** photographs, booklets, and so on are produced on expensive, shiny paper. *Glossy brochures cannot conceal the simple fact that there's virtually no new money.*

glossy magazine, glossy magazines
NC A **glossy magazine** is a magazine printed on expensive, shiny paper with colour photographs, usually of fashionable clothes, famous people, expensive houses, and so on. *...the fashion models you see in glossy magazines... The glossy magazines carried detailed pictures of the Royal Wedding.*

glove /glʌv/ **gloves**

NC A **glove** is a piece of clothing which covers your hand and wrist and has individual sections for each finger. *He pulled his gloves on.*

glove compartment, glove compartments

NC The **glove compartment** in a car is a small cupboard or shelf below the front windscreen. *He took the gun out of the glove compartment of his car.*

gloved /glʌvd/

ADJ **Gloved** is used to describe a person's hand when they are wearing a glove. *He gripped it with his gloved hands... She bent her gloved fingers over it.*

glow /gləʊ/ **glows, glowing, glowed**

1 NC A **glow** is a dull, steady light. *...the blue glow of a police station light.*

2 N SING A **glow** on someone's face is the pink colour that it has when they are excited or when they have done some exercise. *The conversation brought a glow to her cheeks.*

3 N SING A **glow** is also a strong feeling of pleasure or satisfaction. *I felt a glow of pleasure.*

4 V If something **glows**, it produces a dull, steady light or looks bright by reflecting light. *A cluster of stars glowed above us... They blew into the charcoal until it glowed red.*

5 V If someone **glows** or if their face **glows**, their face is pink as a result of excitement or physical exercise. *Aunt Agnes glowed with joy... Her face glowed with a healthy red sheen.*

glower /glaʊə/ **glowers, glowering, glowered**

V If you **glower** at someone, you look at them angrily. *He glowered resentfully at Ash.*

glowing /gləʊɪŋ/

ADJ A **glowing** description of someone or something praises them very highly. *...the book, of which I had read such glowing reports.*

glow-worm, glow-worms

NC A **glow-worm** is a beetle that produces a greenish light from its body.

glucose /ɡluːkəʊz/

NU **Glucose** is a type of sugar that gives you energy. *An electronic sensor is able to measure directly the level of glucose in a patient's bloodstream.*

glue /gluː/ **glues, glueing** or **gluing, glued**

1 N MASS **Glue** is a sticky substance used for joining things together. *The hat seems to be stuck on with glue.*

2 V OA If you **glue** one object to another, you stick them together using glue. *A new piece was glued into place.*

glued /gluːd/

1 ADJ PRED You can use **glued** to say that one thing is firmly fixed to another. *...a chop glued to the plate by a thick sauce.*

2 ADJ PRED If someone is **glued** to the television or radio, they are giving it all their attention; an informal use. *Those unlucky enough not to have a ticket will be glued to their television sets.*

3 ADJ PRED If someone's eyes are **glued** to a particular thing, they are watching it with all their attention; an informal use. *Their eyes were glued to the scene below.*

glue sniffing

NU **Glue sniffing** is the dangerous practice of inhaling the vapour from glue in order to experience pleasant sensations.

gluey /gluːi/

ADJ **Gluey** means very sticky. *...gluey sweets.*

glum /glʌm/

ADJ Someone who is **glum** is sad and quiet, because someone or something has disappointed them. *I was also a little glum because I had just broken up with my girlfriend. ...his glum face.* ♦ **glumly** ADV *'It's no use,' Eddie said glumly.*

glut /glʌt/ **gluts**

NC If there is a **glut** of something such as goods or raw materials, there is so much of it that it cannot all be sold or used. *The oil glut has forced price cuts.*

glutinous /gluːtɪnəs/

ADJ **Glutinous** food or substances are very sticky. *...glutinous rice.*

glutton /glʌtn/ **gluttons**

1 NC A **glutton** is a greedy person who eats too much. *You're just a glutton eating steak and eggs every day.*

2 NC+for If someone keeps having or doing something which you consider undesirable, you can say that they are a **glutton** for it. *He was a glutton for work.*

gluttonous /glʌtənəs/

ADJ A **gluttonous** person eats too much, in a greedy way; a literary word. *...over-fed women and their gluttonous husbands.*

gluttony /glʌtəni/

NU **Gluttony** is the habit or act of eating too much; a literary word. *...the gluttony of the Christmas season.*

glycerine /glɪsəᵊrɪn/; spelt **glycerin** in American English.

NU **Glycerine** is a thick, colourless liquid that is used in making medicine and explosives. *The antibiotic is mixed with a glycerin derivative to ease the spread of the ointment.*

gm, gms

gm is a written abbreviation for 'gram'. *...250 gms of sugar.*

GMT /dʒiːemtiː/

GMT is the standard time in Britain which is used to calculate the time in the rest of the world. **GMT** is an abbreviation for 'Greenwich Mean Time'. *It departs Bermuda 12.42 GMT 17th Jan.*

gnarled /nɑːld/

ADJ If something is **gnarled**, it is old, rough, and twisted. *...gnarled and twisted trees. ...gnarled peasant's hands.*

gnash /næʃ/ **gnashes, gnashing, gnashed**

VO If you **gnash** your teeth, you grind them together hard because you are angry or in pain. *I lay gnashing my teeth in despair.*

gnat /næt/ **gnats**

NC A **gnat** is a small flying insect that bites. *It is effective against gnats, ticks and fleas as well as mosquitoes.*

gnaw /nɔː/ **gnaws, gnawing, gnawed**

1 VOorVA If animals or people **gnaw** something or **gnaw** at it, they bite it repeatedly. *...watching her puppy gnaw a bone... A couple of mice are gnawing at the root... The ant tried to gnaw through the thread.*

2 VA If a feeling **gnaws** at you or **gnaws** away at you, it causes you to keep worrying; a literary use. *These desires gnaw away at us constantly.* ♦ **gnawing** ADJ ATTRIB *...gnawing doubts about the future of civilisation.*

gnome /nəʊm/ **gnomes**

1 NC In children's stories, a **gnome** is a tiny old man with a beard and pointed hat.

2 NC A **gnome** is also a statue of a gnome that some people put in their garden for decoration. *...red-nosed garden gnomes.*

gnomic /nəʊmɪk/

ADJ Something that is **gnomic** seems to be very wise but is also slightly puzzling; a literary word. *...his calm and gnomic face. ...gnomic questions.*

GNP /dʒiːenpiː/

NU In economics, **GNP** is the total value of all the goods produced and services provided by a country in one year. **GNP** is an abbreviation for 'Gross National Product'. *Japanese GNP is now probably fifteen per cent of world GNP... A country that size has a GNP that is in the trillions of dollars.*

gnu /nuː/ **gnus**

NC A **gnu** is a large African antelope.

go /gəʊ/ **goes, going, went, gone** In most cases the past participle of go is 'gone', but in paragraphs 1, 2, 3, and 4 'been' is sometimes used: see **been**.

1 V When you **go** somewhere, you move or travel there. *I went to Stockholm... She went into the sitting-room... He went to get some fresh milk... Mr Mann went to the airport to meet Mr Singh.*

2 V When you **go**, you leave the place where you are. *Our train went at 2.25... 'I must go,' she said.*

3 V+ING or V+for If you **go** and do a particular thing, you move from one place to another in order to do it. *Let's go fishing... They went for a walk.*

4 V+and+INF If you **go** and do a particular thing, you move from one place to another in order to do it. *I'll go and see him in the morning... It's an amazing thing*

for us to be able to go and explore these caves.
5 V+*to* If you **go** to school, church, or work, you attend regularly. *She went to London University for three years... Neil Kinnock went to Cardiff University. ...if a blind child goes to school in England.*
6 V A If a road **goes** somewhere, it leads to that place. *There's a little road that goes off to the right.*
7 V Cor V A You can also use **go** to say that something changes or becomes something else. For example, if your hair is **going** grey, it is becoming grey. *The village thought we had gone crazy... They let firms go bankrupt.*
8 V C You can use **go** to say that someone or something is in a particular state. For example, if something **goes** unnoticed, nobody notices it. *Her decision went unchallenged... When our clothes wore out, we went naked.*
9 V A **Go** is also used to say how a particular event, activity, or period of time passes. *How did school go?... Everything went pretty smoothly... He expressed his satisfaction at the way the visit went.*
10 V You say that a machine or device is **going** when it is in operation. *The tape recorder was still going.*
11 V When a bell or alarm **goes**, it makes a noise. *When the alarm goes, he has to leave his work.*
12 V You can say that something is **going** or has **gone** when it no longer works. *Her eyesight is going... I think the batteries must have gone.*
13 V A If money or resources **go** into or on something such as a plan or project, they support or finance it. *Most of the aid has gone into urban projects... 40% of his income goes on rent.*
14 V+*to* If something **goes** to someone, it is given to them. *8,960 votes went to General Mulinge... The job is to go to a private contractor... One of the biggest cheers of the day went to an army officer in full uniform.*
15 V-RECIP If two things **go** together, they match or are appropriate to each other. *I got the shoes to go with my coat... The colours go so very well together.*
16 V A If something **goes** in a particular place, it fits in that place or belongs there. *The silencer went on easily... Where do the pans go?*
17 V-QUOTE or V A You can use **go** before a word representing a noise or before quoting something. *As the song goes: 'I fell in love with eyes of blue'. ...American sirens which instead of going 'Ow-wow' go 'Whoop-whoop'... It goes something like this.*
18 N C A **go** is an attempt to do something. *He passed the test first go... I'll have a go at mending it.*
19 N C+POSS If it is your **go** in a game, it is your turn to do something such as put a card down or move a piece. *It's Pam's go.*
20 See also **going, gone.**
● **Go** is used in these phrases. ● If there is a particular thing **to go**, it remains to be done or dealt with. If there is a particular period of time **to go**, it has not yet passed. *With only four matches to go, they're eight points behind... There are only eight days to go before Britain's local elections.* ● You say **there goes** a particular thing to express disappointment that you cannot have it; an informal expression. *There goes my chance of a job.* ● If you say that something **goes to show** or **goes to prove** something interesting, you mean that it shows or proves it. *All of which goes to show that people haven't changed.* ● If you **have a go** at someone, you criticize or attack them; an informal expression. *You are always open to attack from people who want to have a go at you.* ● If something happens **from the word go**, it happens throughout a situation. *She complained from the word go.* ● If someone **makes a go** of a business or relationship, they try very hard to make it successful; an informal expression. ● If someone is always **on the go**, they are busy and active; an informal use. ● If you have a particular project or activity **on the go**, you are dealing with it or are involved in it. *She's always got several schemes on the go.* ● If you say that someone **has gone and done** something, you are expressing annoyance at what they have done. *That idiot Antonio has gone and locked our door.* ● People say '**Here goes**' before they do something difficult,

dangerous, or exciting; an informal expression. ● If you say '**It's all go**' you mean that the situation you are in is very busy or exciting. ● **to go easy on** something: see **easy.** ● **to go without saying**: see **say.**
● **there you go**: see **there.**

go about PHRASAL VERB If you **go about** a task or your usual activities, you do them. *She told me how to go about it... How do you actually go about making things better?*
go after PHRASAL VERB If you **go after** something, you try to get it. *My husband had gone after a job.*
go against PHRASAL VERB **1** If something **goes against** an idea, it conflicts with it. *When things go against my wishes, I threaten to resign.* **2** If you **go against** someone's advice, you do something different from what they want you to do. *She went against the advice of her Cabinet and called a general election.* **3** If a decision **goes against** someone, for example in a court of law, they lose. *The judgement went against the Greek government.*
go ahead PHRASAL VERB **1** If someone **goes ahead** with a plan or idea, they begin to do it. *They are going ahead with the missile... 'Would you like to hear it?'—'Go ahead.'* **2** If an organized event **goes ahead**, it takes place. *The May Day marches could go ahead.* **3** See also **go-ahead.**
go along with PHRASAL VERB If you **go along with** a decision or idea, you accept it and obey it. *How could you go along with such a plan?... East Germany is expected to go along with Bonn's wishes.*
go around PHRASAL VERB **1** If you **go around**, or **go round** doing something that other people disapprove of, you have the habit of doing it. *I don't go around deliberately hurting people's feelings... It's British companies who are going round buying up the world.* **2** If you **go around** or **go round** with a person or group of people, you regularly meet them as friends. *He had no intention of letting her go around with those scruffy students. ...the local people who go round with them.* **3** If a piece of news or a joke is **going around** or is **going round**, it is being told by many people. *...the gossip that went around years ago.*
go away PHRASAL VERB **1** If you **go away**, you leave a place or a person's company. *They went away empty-handed.* **2** If you **go away**, you leave a place and spend a period of time somewhere else, usually as a holiday. *She had gone away for a few days.*
go back on PHRASAL VERB If you **go back on** a promise, you do not do what you promised to do. *President Bush has had to go back on his promise not to cut taxes.*
go back to PHRASAL VERB **1** If you **go back to** an activity or a particular topic, you start doing it again or talking about it again. *She had gone back to staring out of the window... Going back to your point about standards, I agree that they have fallen.* **2** If something **goes back to** a particular time in the past, it was made or built then. *The shop goes back to 1707.*
go before PHRASAL VERB Something that **has gone before** has happened or been discussed at an earlier time. *The meeting was unlike any that had gone before.*
go by PHRASAL VERB **1** If a period of time **has gone by**, it has passed. *Eight years went by and the children grew up... The days went by slowly.* **2** If you **go by** something, you use it as a basis for a judgement or action. *I try to go by reason as far as possible.*
go down PHRASAL VERB **1** If an amount or level **goes down**, it becomes lower. *The average age of farmers has gone down.* **2** If something like a speech or performance **goes down** well, people like it. *It was a message that went down well with the Czechoslovak leaders.* **3** When the sun **goes down**, it sets. *As the sun went down behind the distant mountains, a cool quiet came over the fields.*
go down with PHRASAL VERB If you **go down with** an illness, you catch it. *Nick Grundy went down with suspected tonsillitis.*
go for PHRASAL VERB **1** If you **go for** a particular type of product or method, you like it or prefer it. *Children go for the brightly coloured ones.* **2** If you **go for** someone, you attack them. *He went for me with the*

bread-knife. 3 If a statement about one person or thing **goes for** another, it is also true of the second person or thing. *Western Europe can expect much slower economic growth this year—and this also goes for countries which have remained buoyant in recent years.*

go in for PHRASAL VERB If you **go in for** something, you decide to do it or have it on a regular basis. *I thought of going in for teaching... They go in for vintage port.*

go into PHRASAL VERB 1 If you **go into** something, you describe it or examine it in detail. *I won't go into what I've suffered.* 2 If you **go into** a particular occupation, you decide to do it as your career. *Have you ever thought of going into journalism?* 3 The amount of time, effort, or money that **goes into** something is the amount that produces it. *Three years of research went into the making of those films.* 4 If a vehicle **goes into** a particular movement, it starts moving in that way. *The plane went into a nose dive.*

go off PHRASAL VERB 1 If you **go off** something or someone, you stop liking them. *He's suddenly gone off the idea.* 2 If something **goes off**, it explodes or makes a sudden loud noise. *I could hear the bombs going off... The alarm went off.* 3 If a device or machine **goes off**, it stops operating. *The light only goes off at night.* 4 If an organized event **goes off** well, it is successful. *The meeting went off well.*

go off with PHRASAL VERB If someone **goes off with** something belonging to another person, they take it away with them. *She had let him go off with her papers.*

go on PHRASAL VERB 1 If you **go on** doing something, you continue to do it. *I went on writing... They can't go on with their examinations.* 2 If you **go on** to do something, you do it after you have done something else. *He went on to get his degree.* 3 If you **go on** somewhere, you go there from a place that you have already reached. *We had gone on to Clare's house.* 4 If you **go on**, you continue talking. *'You know,' he went on, 'it's extraordinary.'... 'Sounds serious,' I said. 'Go on.'* 5 If you **go on** about something or **go on** at someone, you keep talking in a boring way; an informal use. *Don't go on about it... I went on at my father to have safety belts fitted.* 6 If a particular activity is **going on**, it is taking place. *There's a big argument going on... A lot of cheating goes on.* ● See also **goings-on**. 7 You say '**Go on**' to someone to encourage them to do something. *Go on, have a biscuit.* 8 If you **go on** a piece of information, you base your actions or opinion on it. *They had nothing more to go on than an anonymous phone call.* 9 If a device or machine **goes on**, it starts operating. *The light goes on automatically.*

go out PHRASAL VERB 1 If you **go out** with someone, you spend time with them socially and often have a romantic or sexual relationship with them. *I went out with him a long time ago.* 2 If something that produces light or heat **goes out**, it stops producing light or heat. *The lights went out in the big tent... The fire went out... My cigar's gone out.* 3 If something **goes out**, it stops being popular. *Steam went out and diesel was introduced.*

go over PHRASAL VERB If you **go over** something, you examine or consider it very carefully. *He went over this in his mind.*

go over to PHRASAL VERB 1 If someone **goes over to** a different method, they change to it. *We went over to the American system.* 2 If you **go over to** an organization, you join them after previously belonging to one with very different ideas. *Anyone joining the police is going over to the other side.*

go round PHRASAL VERB 1 If there is enough of something to **go round**, there is enough of it for everyone. *By 1984 there was enough grain to go round and a surplus for export too.* 2 See also **go around**.

go through PHRASAL VERB 1 If you **go through** an unpleasant event, you experience it. *I'm too old to go through that again.* 2 If you **go through** a number of things, you look at them or refer to each of them in turn. *Go through the files again... You'd better go through the names.* 3 If a law or official decision goes

through, it is officially approved. *The adoption went through.*

go through with PHRASAL VERB If you **go through with** something difficult or unpleasant, you do it. *Would he go through with the assassination?*

go towards PHRASAL VERB If an amount of money **goes towards** something, it is used as part of the cost of that thing. *The money will go towards famine relief.*

go under PHRASAL VERB If a business **goes under**, it fails. *Scores of firms will go under because there isn't the money to help them.*

go up PHRASAL VERB 1 If an amount or level **goes up**, it increases. *The price of food will go up.* 2 When a building or other structure **goes up**, it is built. *The barricades went up at dawn.* 3 If something **goes up**, it explodes or starts to burn fiercely. *In seconds it had gone up in flames.*

go with PHRASAL VERB If one thing **goes with** another, you always get the first thing if you get the second one. *The house went with the job.*

go without PHRASAL VERB If you **go without** something, you do not get it or have it. *If they couldn't get coal, they had to go without... The family went without food all day.*

goad /gəʊd/ **goads, goading, goaded**
VO If you **goad** someone, you make them feel angry, often deliberately, so that they react by doing something. *She was being goaded into denouncing her own friend.*

goad on PHRASAL VERB If you **goad** someone **on**, you encourage them. *...the spontaneous uprising of masses goaded on by student activists.*

go-ahead
1 N SING If you give someone the **go-ahead**, you give them permission to do something. *The Greek government today gave the go-ahead for five major road schemes.*
2 ADJ A **go-ahead** person or organization tries hard to succeed, often by using new methods. *The economy is modern and go-ahead.*

goal /gəʊl/ **goals**
1 NC The **goal** in games such as football or hockey is the space into which the players try to get the ball in order to score a point for their team. *Robson completely missed his kick in front of the goal.*
2 NC You also use **goal** to refer to an instance in which a player succeeds in getting the ball into the goal, and the point they score by doing this. *It was his guile that gave Chelsea the decisive goal.*
3 NC+SUPP Your **goal** is something that you hope to achieve. *The main goal is ending the war.*
4 See also **own goal**.

goal difference
N U In football leagues, when two teams have the same number of points for wins, losses, and draws, their relative positions are decided on their **goal difference**. This is the proportion of goals they have scored to the goals other teams have scored against them. *United are still level on points with Forest but stay third on goal difference... The Italian League could be decided on goal difference.*

goalie /gəʊli/ **goalies**
NC A **goalie** is a goalkeeper; an informal word. *Tretiak was the top goalie with the Soviet national team.*

goalkeeper /gəʊlkiːpə/ **goalkeepers**
NC A **goalkeeper** is the player in a sports team whose job is to guard the goal. *Their goalkeeper saved a penalty in the second half.*

goalpost /gəʊlpəʊst/ **goalposts**
1 NC A **goalpost** is one of the two upright posts connected by a crossbar which form the goal in games like football and hockey. *They tore down one set of goalposts and started fighting with police.*
2 If someone **moves the goalposts** in a certain situation, they unfairly change the rules or requirements, often making it harder for people to succeed. *It is apparent that the administration is shifting the goalposts and changing its demands... The commerce department has moved the goalposts to make the performance look better.*

goat /gəʊt/ goats
NC A **goat** is an animal which is a bit bigger than a sheep and has horns. ...*a new breed of goat which can provide twice as much milk as local goats.*

goatee /gəʊtiː/ goatees
NC A **goatee** is a very short pointed beard that a man wears on his chin but not on his cheeks. *Yusaf, a small man with a well-trimmed goatee, announced that he was Egyptian.*

goatherd /gəʊthɜːd/ goatherds
NC A **goatherd** is a person who is responsible for looking after a group of goats.

goatskin /gəʊtskɪn/ goatskins
NU or NC **Goatskin** is leather made from the skin of a goat. ...*heavy goatskin drums.*

gob /gɒb/ gobs
1 NC Someone's **gob** is their mouth; an informal use, which some people find offensive. *You shut your gob!*
2 NC A **gob** of something is a mass of thick liquid, especially saliva; an informal use. *He spat out a big gob of spit.*

gobbet /gɒbɪt/ gobbets
NC A **gobbet** of something soft, especially food, is a small lump or piece of it; an informal word. *Most animals simply bolt their food in gobbets.*

gobble /gɒbl/ gobbles, gobbling, gobbled
VO If someone **gobbles** food, they eat it quickly and greedily. *Still hungry, I gobbled a second sandwich.*
gobble down PHRASAL VERB If you **gobble down** food or **gobble** it **up**, you eat all of it very quickly. *He gobbled down the two remaining eggs. ...truck drivers gobbling up hot-dogs.*

gobbledygook /gɒbldɪguːk/; also spelt **gobbledegook**.
NU **Gobbledygook** is language, often in official statements, which you cannot understand at all; an informal word. *He talked complicated gobbledygook.*

gobbler /gɒblə/ gobblers
NC A **gobbler** is a turkey; an informal word.

go-between, go-betweens
NC A **go-between** is a person who takes messages between people who are not able or willing to meet each other. *He denied he is acting as a go-between in talks with Sinn Fein and with the British government.*

goblet /gɒblət/ goblets
NC A **goblet** is a type of cup without handles and usually with a long stem. *He took care not to spill his goblet of wine.*

goblin /gɒblɪn/ goblins
NC A **goblin** is a small ugly creature in fairy stories. ...*goblins and devils and demons, and things we fear, without knowing why.*

go-cart, go-carts
NC A **go-cart** is a small vehicle that children ride in or pull along.

god /gɒd/ gods
1 N PROP The name **God** is given to the spirit or being who is worshipped as the creator and ruler of the world, especially by Christians, Jews, and Muslims. *Two thirds of British people say they believe in God.*
2 People sometimes use **God** in exclamations for emphasis, or to express surprise, fear, or excitement; some people find this use offensive. *My God, John, what are you doing here at this hour?*
3 NC A **god** is one of the spirits or beings believed in many religions to have power over an aspect of the world. ...*the Saxon god of war.*
● **God** is used in these phrases. ● If you say **God knows**, you are emphasizing that you don't know something or that you find a fact very surprising. *He was interested in shooting and God knows what else... God knows how they knew I was coming.* ● **for God's sake**: see sake. ● **thank God**: see thank.

god-awful
ADJ **God-awful** is a swear word used to describe something that the speaker thinks is very bad indeed. *The real horrors of war are so God-awful that they cannot be depicted to most people.*

godchild /gɒdtʃaɪld/ godchildren
NC If someone is your **godchild**, you are their godparent, which means that you have agreed to take responsibility for their religious upbringing.

goddammit /gɒddæmɪt/
Goddammit is a swear word that is used to express annoyance, anger, or irritation; used in American English.

goddamn /gɒdæm/; also spelt **goddam**.
ADJ **Goddamn** is a swear word that is used for emphasis, usually to express a strong emotion such as excitement, anger, or irritation; used in American English. *'We have no goddamn choice,' he said.*

goddamned /gɒdæmd/
Goddamned means the same as **goddamn**; an informal word used in American English.

goddaughter /gɒddɔːtə/ goddaughters
NC A **goddaughter** is a female godchild.

goddess /gɒdes/ goddesses
NC A **goddess** is a female god. *She was killed in a ritual sacrifice to the goddess.*

godfather /gɒdfɑːðə/ godfathers
1 NC A **godfather** is a male godparent. *Prince Charles became godfather to the daughter of a close friend.*
2 N SING **Godfather** is sometimes used to refer to a very powerful man who is at the head of a criminal organization. *The Mafia family fight with rival gangs and the Godfather struggles to keep control over his volatile relatives... This man was obviously the Godfather.*

god-fearing
ADJ Someone who is **god-fearing** is religious and behaves according to the moral rules of their religion. *The rebel leader says that as a God-fearing Christian he's not going to become another dictator.*

god-forsaken
ADJ ATTRIB A **god-forsaken** place is somewhere without any interesting scenery or culture, and which most people find very depressing. *The ranch was a lonely run-down god-forsaken place.*

godhead /gɒdhed/
NU The **godhead** is the divine nature of God; a literary word. *Unlike the pagan gods, the Christian godhead was believed to be wholly and stainlessly good.*

godless /gɒdləs/
ADJ A **godless** person does not believe in God and has no moral principles; used showing disapproval. *These men were dirty, drunken, and both godless and lawless.*

godly /gɒdli/
ADJ Someone who is **godly** is deeply religious and shows obedience to the rules of their religion. ...*a godly courageous statesman... You can have a godly world, it doesn't have to be a godless one.*

godmother /gɒdmʌðə/ godmothers
NC A **godmother** is a female godparent. *She might be chosen as godmother to the young Princess.*

godparent /gɒdpeərənt/ godparents
NC Someone's **godparent** is a man or woman who agrees to take responsibility for their religious upbringing.

godsend /gɒdsend/
N SING Something that is a **godsend** arrives or happens unexpectedly and helps you very much in some way. *The extra twenty dollars a week was a godsend.*

godson /gɒdsʌn/ godsons
NC A **godson** is a male godchild. *She began studying him and discovered a biography written in 1974 by his godson.*

Godthab /gɒdhɔːb/. See **Nuuk**

-goer /-gəʊə/ -goers
SUFFIX **-goer** is added to words such as 'church' and 'film' to form nouns that refer to people who regularly go to a particular place or event. *They were both enthusiastic playgoers.*

gofer /gəʊfə/ gofers; also spelt **gopher**.
NC A **gofer** is someone who is employed to help someone by fetching things, and generally carrying out unimportant tasks; an informal word. *These chefs are under strict instructions not to do any cooking, but to act as gofers, finding the right pans, helping with oven temperatures, and ensuring dishes are presented on time... Either he didn't trust the waiters or he was accustomed to treating his bodyguards as gofers.*

go-getter, go-getters
NC A **go-getter** is a person who is very ambitious and

energetic. *We are forced into competition, forced to be go-getters and achieve great things.*

goggle /gɒgl/ **goggles, goggling, goggled**
1 V If you **goggle** at something, you stare at it with your eyes wide open; an informal use. *She goggled at the dreadful suit.*
2 N PL **Goggles** are large glasses that fit closely to your face around your eyes to protect them. *She was wearing big green-tinted snow goggles.*

goggle box
N SING The **goggle box** is the television; an informal expression. *He sits watching the goggle box all day.*

goggle-eyed
ADJ If you are **goggle-eyed**, your eyes are wide open in surprise; an informal word. *...Father Christmas dispensing gifts to goggle-eyed children.*

go-go /gəʊgəʊ/
ADJ ATTRIB **Go-go** is used to describe a type of dancing performed to pop music in places like pubs and clubs by young women wearing very few clothes. *...go-go dancing... In these go-go bars they're now presenting safer sex cabarets.*

Goh Chok Tong /gəʊ tʃɒk tɒŋ/
Goh Chok Tong became Prime Minister of Singapore in 1990. He is a member of the People's Action Party (PAP). He became a member of Parliament in 1976. He served as Minister of Finance from 1977 to 1979, of Trade and Industry from 1979 to 1981, of Health from 1981 to 1982, and of Defence from 1982 to 1984. He was Deputy Prime Minister and Minister of Defence from 1985 to 1990. Born: 1941.

going /gəʊɪŋ/
1 V+to-INF You use **be going to** to express future time. For example, if you say that something **is going to** happen, you mean that it will happen or that you intend it to happen. *She told him she was going to leave her job... I'm not going to be made a scapegoat.*
2 NU The **going** is the conditions that affect your ability to do something. *When the going gets tough, we run back to our parents... It was hard going at first.*
3 ADJ ATTRIB The **going** rate for something is the usual and expected rate for it. *The going rate is about £1,000 a head.*
4 You say **'That's good going'** or **'That's not bad going'** if you are impressed at someone's speed or progress. *About three quarters are on no drugs by the time they've left, which is pretty good going.*
5 See also **go**.
● **Going** is used in these phrases. ● If you **get going**, you start doing something, especially after a delay. *It remains to be seen whether he will take the same line when the talks get going.* ● If you **keep going**, you continue doing something difficult or tiring. *If somebody was feeling down, I would try to help them to keep going.* ● If you **have** something **going for** you, you have an advantage or useful quality. *She had so much going for her in the way of wealth and success.*

going-over, goings-over; an informal word.
1 NC A **going-over** is an examination that you make of something in order to make sure that it is all right. *I gave the engine a thorough going-over.*
2 NC A **going over** is also a violent physical attack on someone, especially as a punishment or a warning. *The boys gave him a going-over.*

goings-on
N PL **Goings-on** are strange, amusing, or improper activities. *...exciting goings-on between Scarlett O'Hara and the dashing Rhett Butler.*

goitre /gɔɪtə/
NU **Goitre** is a disease of the thyroid gland that makes a person's neck very swollen; a medical term. *People who do not eat enough iodine may develop goitre.*

go-kart /gəʊkɑːt/ **go-karts**
NC A **go-kart** is a very small motor vehicle with four wheels, used for racing.

go-karting /gəʊkɑːtɪŋ/
NU **Go-karting** is the sport of racing or riding on go-karts. *Warwick injured his back in a go-karting incident.*

gold /gəʊld/ **golds**
1 NU **Gold** is a valuable yellow-coloured metal used

for making jewellery. It is also used as an international currency. *...gold bracelets. ...a fixed exchange rate for the dollar against gold.*
2 NU **Gold** is also jewellery and other things that are made of gold. *They stole an estimated 12 million pounds worth of gold and jewels.*
3 ADJ Something that is **gold** in colour is bright yellow. *...a cap with gold braid all over it.*
4 NCorNU A **gold** is the same as a **gold medal**. *Japan won a gold in one of the shooting categories... Nigeria's Chioma Ajunwa took gold in the women's long jump.*
● **Gold** is used in these phrases. ● If someone has a **heart of gold**, they are very good, kind, and considerate. *Steve Condos was known as the man with the heart of gold.* ● If a child or an animal is **as good as gold**, it behaves very well.

gold dust
If you say that something is **like gold dust**, you mean that it is very difficult to obtain, especially because everyone wants it; an informal expression. *Biros are like gold dust in this office.*

golden /gəʊldən/
1 ADJ Something that is **golden** in colour is bright yellow. *...a girl with bright golden hair.*
2 ADJ **Golden** things are made of gold. *She wore a golden cross.*
3 ADJ You use **golden** to describe something that is excellent or ideal. *The summit has given them the golden opportunity to talk face to face.*

golden age, golden ages
NC A **golden age** is a period of time during which a very high level of achievement is reached in a particular subject, especially in art or literature. *...the golden age of jazz.*

golden handshake, golden handshakes
NC A **golden handshake** is a large sum of money that a company gives to an employee when he or she retires, as a reward for long service or good work. *His golden handshake will amount to nearly £1 million.*

golden jubilee, golden jubilees
NC A **golden jubilee** is the 50th anniversary of an important or special event. *The company is celebrating its golden jubilee.*

golden rule, golden rules
NC A **golden rule** is an important thing to remember to do in order to be successful at something. *The golden rule for candidates is to let the voters see your face.*

golden syrup
NU **Golden syrup** is a sweet, sticky, yellow type of food that is made from sugar.

golden wedding, golden weddings
NC A **golden wedding** or a **golden wedding anniversary** is the fiftieth anniversary of a wedding.

goldfish /gəʊldfɪʃ/; **goldfish** is both the singular and the plural form.
NC A **goldfish** is a small orange-coloured fish which people keep in ponds or bowls. *We had never seen goldfish before in this river. ...a goldfish bowl.*

gold medal, gold medals
NC A **gold medal** is a medal made of gold which is awarded as first prize in a contest or competition. *David Wilkie won the gold medal for the 200 metres breaststroke.*

goldmine /gəʊldmaɪn/ **goldmines**
NC You can refer to something that produces large profits as a **goldmine**. *Farm subsidies and controls are a goldmine to those who know how to work the system... The opposition parties see the community charge as a political goldmine.*

gold-plated
ADJ Something that is **gold-plated** is covered with a very thin layer of gold. *...a long list of items from fancy china and linens to gold-plated bathroom fixtures.*

gold-rimmed
ADJ **Gold-rimmed** is used to describe something that has a golden edge or border. *...a pair of gold-rimmed reading glasses. ...an enormous gold-rimmed cup.*

goldsmith /gəʊldsmɪθ/ **goldsmiths**
NC A **goldsmith** is a person whose job is making

jewellery and other objects using gold.

golf /gɒlf/
NU **Golf** is a game in which you use long sticks called clubs to hit a ball into holes that are spread out over a large area of grass. *Hal Sutton leads the New Orleans Open Golf tournament after the first round.*

golf ball, golf balls; spelt **golfball** for the meaning in paragraph 2.
1 NC A **golf ball** is a small, hard white ball which people use when they are playing golf. *The children invented a new game of hitting the golf ball from one tee to all the greens on the golf course.*
2 NC A **golfball** or **golfball typewriter** is an electric typewriter in which the letters and symbols are on a round piece of metal that moves across the paper when you type.

golf club, golf clubs
1 NC A **golf club** is a stick which you use to hit the ball in golf. *He always seemed to be on camera with a tennis racket, a golf club or a fishing reel in his hand... David Szewczul lost his luggage and golf clubs on the trip.*
2 NC A **golf club** is also an organization whose members play golf, or the place where they play golf. *There are plans for an informal get together at the golf club.*

golf course, golf courses
NC A **golf course** is a large area of grass where people play golf. *The local council wants to turn the land into a golf course.*

golfer /gɒlfə/ **golfers**
NC A **golfer** is a person who plays golf for pleasure or as a profession. *The British golfer, Nick Faldo, has won the Open Championship at St. Andrews.*

golfing /gɒlfɪŋ/
NU **Golfing** is the activity of playing golf. *Most people took advantage of the special holiday to go golfing or stay at home with a video. ...a golfing holiday.*

golliwog /gɒliwɒg/ **golliwogs;** also spelt **gollywog.**
NC A **golliwog** is a child's toy, usually made out of soft material, with a black face, large white eyes, and spiky black hair. Some people consider golliwogs to be racially offensive.

golly /gɒli/ **gollies**
1 People say **'golly'** to indicate that they are very surprised by something; an informal, old-fashioned use. *'Golly!' cried Dot. 'Have you seen the time!'... 'Golly, I didn't know he was an expert.'*
2 People say **'by golly'** to emphasize that something did happen or should happen; an informal, old-fashioned use. *He said he'd do it, and by golly he's succeeded.*
3 NC A **golly** is the same as a **golliwog.**

Göncz, Arpád /ɔːpɑːd gɜːnts/
Árpád Göncz became President of Hungary in 1990. He was previously Speaker of the National Assembly. He is a member of the Alliance of Free Democrats (SzDSz).

gondola /gɒndələ/ **gondolas**
NC A **gondola** is a long narrow boat that is used especially in Venice. It has a flat bottom and curves upwards at both ends. A person stands at one end of the gondola and uses a long pole to move and steer it.

gondolier /gɒndəlɪə/ **gondoliers**
NC A **gondolier** is a person whose job is to take people from one place to another in a gondola.

gone /gɒn/
1 **Gone** is the past participle of **go.**
2 ADJ PRED Someone or something that is **gone** is no longer present or no longer exists. *He turned the corner and was gone... What will happen now that Indian troops have gone from Sri Lanka?... The days are gone when women worked for half pay.*
3 PREP If it is **gone** a particular time, it is later than that time; an informal use. *It's gone tea-time.*

goner /gɒnə/ **goners**
NC If you say that someone is a **goner,** you mean that they are about to die, or in such danger that nobody can save them; an informal, old-fashioned word. *'Thanks for rescuing me.'—'I thought you were a goner.'*

gong /gɒŋ/ **gongs**
NC A **gong** is a flat, circular piece of metal that you hit with a hammer to make a loud sound. *The President was welcomed with the banging of drums and gongs.*

gonna, /gɒnə, gənə/
Gonna is used in written English to represent the words 'going to' when they are pronounced informally. *What are we gonna do?*

González Márquez, Felipe
/felɪːpeɪ gɒnθɑːleθ mɑːkeθ/
Felipe González Márquez became Prime Minister of Spain in 1982. He became leader of the Socialist Workers' Party (PSOE) in 1974. Born: 1942.

goo /guː/
NU You can use **goo** to refer to any thick, sticky substance, for example mud or paste; an informal word. *...animals sinking in the goo offshore.*

good /gʊd/ **better, best; goods.** See also separate entries at **better** and **best.**
1 ADJ Something that is **good** is pleasant, acceptable, or satisfactory. *They had a good time... Hello! It's good to see you. ...a very good school... She speaks good English... The chances for success look good.*
2 ADJ ATTRIB Someone who is in a **good** mood is cheerful and pleasant to be with. *He was clearly in a good mood and wanted to share this with his audience... He was in good spirits.*
3 ADJ If you are good at something, you are skilful and successful at it. *Alex is a good swimmer... He was very good at his job... He was good at games... He was very good at talking me out of things.*
4 ADJ A **good** person is kind and thoughtful. *He's always been good to me... It's good of you to come.*
5 ADJ You also use **good** to describe someone who is morally correct in their attitudes and behaviour. *There was no trace of evil in her—she was good.*
6 ADJ A child or animal that is **good** is well-behaved. *Were the kids good?... 'Good dog.'*
7 NU **Good** is moral and religious correctness. *...the conflict between good and evil.*
8 N SING+POSS If something is done for the **good** of a person or organization, it is done in order to benefit them. *Casey should quit for the good of the agency... It was for her own good.*
9 NU You use **good** with a negative to say that something will not succeed or be of any use. *It's no good worrying any more tonight... Even if I came, what good would it do?*
10 ADJ ATTRIB You use **good** to emphasize the extent or degree of something. *He took a good long look at it. ...a good while ago.*
11 N PL **Goods** are things that are made to be sold. *...a wide range of electrical goods.* ● See also **consumer goods.**
● **Good** is used in these phrases. ● If you say **it's a good thing** or **it's a good job** that something is the case, you mean that it is fortunate. *It's a good thing I wasn't there.* ● If you say that someone **has done a good job** of doing something, you mean that they have been successful in doing that thing. *Japan has done a good job cleaning up the domestic environment.* ● If you say that something will **do** someone **good,** you mean that it will benefit them or improve them. *It'll do you good to get a bit of fresh air.* ● People say **'Good for you'** to express approval. *'I've told him I won't do it.'—'Good for you.'* ● If something happens **for good,** the situation it produces will never change. *They had gone for good. ...the real possibility of the company closing for good.* ● You use **as good as** before an adjective or a verb to indicate that something is almost true. *Without her glasses she was as good as blind... He had as good as abdicated.* ● If you **make good** some damage or a loss, you repair the damage or replace what has been lost. *This would be a good year for the treasury to begin making good the underfunding.* ● If you **deliver the goods** or **come up with the goods,** you do what is expected of you; an informal expression. *Such an unwieldy system is unable to deliver the goods... You could always rely on her to come up with the goods.* ● in **good time:** see **time.** ● as **good as** one's **word:** see **word.**

good afternoon
You say 'Good afternoon' in the afternoon when you are greeting someone; a formal expression. *'Good afternoon. Could I speak to Mr Duff, please.'*

goodbye /gʊdbaɪ/; also spelt **good-bye**.
You say 'Goodbye' to someone when leaving, or at the end of a telephone conversation. *We said good-bye to Charlie and walked back.*

good day
People sometimes say 'Good day' to each other instead of 'Hello' or 'Goodbye', or when they want to indicate that they want to go away; an old-fashioned expression. *As he walked in he nodded gravely, and said as he went into his office, 'Good day to you.'... 'I see,' he said. 'Then we understand each other. Good day, Monsieur Goossens.'*

good evening
You say 'Good evening' in the evening when you are greeting someone; a formal expression. *'Good evening, Mr Castle. I'm sorry I'm late.'*

good-for-nothing, good-for-nothings
NC A **good-for-nothing** is a lazy or irresponsible person. *'That good-for-nothing!' muttered Liz. ...his good-for-nothing son.*

Good Friday
NU **Good Friday** is the day on which Christians remember the crucifixion of Jesus Christ. It is the Friday before Easter Sunday. *Hot Cross buns were traditionally eaten for breakfast on Good Friday morning.*

good-humoured
ADJ Someone who is **good-humoured** is pleasant and cheerful. *The crowd was loud and boisterous but good-humoured.*

goodie /gʊdi/. See **goody**.

good-looking
ADJ A **good-looking** person has an attractive face. *...a smartly dressed, good-looking man.*

good looks
N PL If you talk about someone's **good looks**, you are referring to the attractive appearance of their face. *...his striking good looks and charm... She seems to have everything, intelligence, good looks, a comfortable home.*

goodly /gʊdli/
ADJ ATTRIB A **goodly** amount or part of something is a fairly large amount or part of it, often more than was expected; a formal word. *A goodly part of her income went on travel... He sold it for a goodly sum.*

good morning
You say 'Good morning' in the morning when you are greeting someone. *Good morning, darling. Another beautiful day.*

good-natured
ADJ A person or animal that is **good-natured** is friendly, pleasant, and has an even temper. *Student leaders and writers have been addressing the good-natured crowd.*

goodness /gʊdnəs/
1 People say 'My goodness' or 'Goodness' to express surprise. *My goodness, this is a difficult one.* • **thank goodness**: see **thank**.
2 NU **Goodness** is the quality of being kind and considerate. *...a belief in the goodness of human nature.*
3 NU **Goodness** is the healthy, nourishing quality that some foods have.

goodnight /gʊdnaɪt/; also spelt **good night**.
You say 'Goodnight' to someone late in the evening, before going home or going to sleep. *We all said good night and went to our rooms.*

goods train, goods trains
NC A **goods train** is a train that transports goods and not people. *A goods train was derailed spilling a cargo of highly toxic liquid.*

goods wagon, goods wagons
NC A **goods wagon** is a carriage on a train that carries goods and not people. *Hundreds of trains and thousands of goods wagons were standing idle.*

good-tempered
ADJ A **good-tempered** person is cheerful and does not get angry easily. *The delays could make an otherwise good-tempered crowd turn hostile.*

goodwill /gʊdwɪl/
NU **Goodwill** is a friendly or helpful attitude towards other people, countries, or organizations. *He counts on West German goodwill to a great extent in his foreign policy... The hostages were released as a goodwill gesture... Goodwill messages came in from around the world.*

goody /gʊdi/ **goodies**; also spelt **goodie**. **Goody** is an informal word.
1 Children, say '**goody**' to express pleasure. *Oh goody, there's some cake!*
2 N PL **Goodies** are pleasant, exciting, or attractive things. *She opened the bag of goodies... They made off with $150 worth of fudge, peanut brittle and other goodies.*
3 NC A **goody** is a person in a film or book who supports the people or ideas that you approve of.

goody-goody, goody-goodies
NC A **goody-goody** is a person who behaves extremely well in order to please people in authority; an informal word used showing disapproval.

gooey /guːi/
ADJ A **gooey** substance is very soft and sticky; an informal word. *...gooey fudge.*

goof /guːf/ **goofs, goofing, goofed**; an informal word.
1 V If you **goof**, you make a foolish mistake. *They had their chance, and they goofed... The reason the enemy has military capability today is that the State Department goofed on two counts.*
2 NC A **goof** is a foolish person, especially someone who is easily deceived; used in American English. *That poor goof wouldn't know.*

goof off PHRASAL VERB When someone **goofs off**, they waste time. *...the type of person who might steal or goof off on the job.*

goofy /guːfi/ **goofier, goofiest**
ADJ Something that is **goofy** is silly or ridiculous, often in a strange or unusual way; an informal word used in American English. *It's the sort of goofy idea that Zoe would have.*

goon /guːn/ **goons**
NC A **goon** is a person who is paid to hurt or threaten people. *You know he has guards, he has goons... Troops belatedly arrive and immediately begin behaving like barbaric goons.*

goose /guːs/ **geese** /giːs/
NC A **goose** is a large bird with a long neck and webbed feet. *Geese are quite vicious animals.*

gooseberry /gʊzbəᵊri/ **gooseberries**
1 NC A **gooseberry** is a small, round, green fruit that grows on a bush. *Gooseberry bushes, if left alone, drop their branches.*
2 If someone is **playing gooseberry**, they are with two other people who are in love and who want to be alone together. *I'd hate to play gooseberry to you and your boyfriend.*

gooseflesh /guːsfleʃ/
NU **Gooseflesh** refers to a condition of your skin when you are cold or scared. The hairs on the skin stand up so that it is covered with tiny bumps. *The sudden chill raised gooseflesh on the girl's arms.*

goose pimples
N PL **Goose pimples** are the same as **gooseflesh**. *Wild irritation was bringing her out in goose pimples.*

goose-step, goose-steps, goose-stepping, goose-stepped
V If soldiers **goose-step**, they march in such a way that they lift their legs high and do not bend their knees. *Two sentries with white gloves were goose-stepping up and down.*

gopher /gəʊfə/ **gophers**
1 NC A **gopher** is a small animal rather like a rat which has short legs and cheek pouches, and which lives underground. *Brown bears are omnivorous, and eat plants, nuts, fish, chipmunks, gophers, and carrion.*
2 See also **gofer**.

Gorbachev, Mikhail /mɪːxaɪːl gɔːbətʃɒf/
Mikhail Gorbachev became the leader of the USSR in 1985, when he succeeded Konstantin Chernenko as General Secretary of the Communist Party of the Soviet Union (KPSS). From 1988 to 1990 he was

Chairman of the Supreme Soviet. In 1990 he became the first President of the USSR. He introduced the policies of perestroika (restructuring) to revive the Soviet economy and glasnost (openness), which permitted more political and cultural freedom. He was temporarily deposed in a coup in 1991 and resigned from the Presidency at the dissolution of the USSR in 1991. Born: 1931.

Gorbunovs, Anatolijs /ænətəʊlɪs gɔːbʊnɒfs/ Anatolijs Gorbunovs became President of Latvia in 1990. He was Secretary of the Central Committee of the Latvian Communist Party from 1985 to 1988, and Chairman of the Presidium of the Latvian Supreme Soviet from 1988 to 1990. Born: 1942.

Gordian knot /gɔːdiən nɒt/ **Gordian knots**
NC A **Gordian knot** is a very difficult and complicated problem or situation; a formal expression. *Planners were busy by-passing the Gordian knot.* ● If you **cut** or **untie** the **Gordian knot** in a particular situation, you solve a difficult problem by taking bold or forceful actions. *The way to socialism and democracy was a Gordian knot which could not be cut... A generous system of child benefits unties this Gordian knot.*

gore /gɔː/ **gores, goring, gored**
1 VO If an animal **gores** someone, it wounds them badly with its horns or tusks. *...if a bull gores someone to death.*
2 NU **Gore** is unpleasant-looking blood from a wound. *...a horror film full of gore.*

gorge /gɔːdʒ/ **gorges, gorging, gorged**
1 NC A **gorge** is a narrow steep-sided valley. *The road winds through rocky gorges and hills.*
2 V-REFL or V If you **gorge** or **gorge** yourself, you eat a lot of food very greedily. *Even though there are abundant supplies of food they do not gorge themselves... Money is so tight you can't afford the new pants you need after gorging over the holidays.*

gorgeous /gɔːdʒəs/
ADJ Someone or something that is **gorgeous** is extremely pleasant or attractive. *'Look what David gave me.'—'Oh it's absolutely gorgeous.'... Isn't it a gorgeous day?*

gorilla /gərɪlə/ **gorillas**
NC A **gorilla** is an animal which resembles a very large ape. *The mountain gorilla colony is the only one of its kind in the world.*

gormless /gɔːmləs/
ADJ If you say that someone is **gormless**, you think that they are stupid because they often have a blank facial expression and do not seem understand things very quickly; an informal word. *He is soft and vulnerable, though not gormless.*

gorse /gɔːs/
NU **Gorse** is a dark green bush which has sharp prickles and yellow flowers. *...a gentle place, covered in flowering gorse, temperate woodland and little patchworks of fields.*

gory /gɔːri/
ADJ **Gory** situations involve people being injured or dying in a horrible way. *The film contains no gory violence.*

gosh /gɒʃ/
You say **'Gosh'** to indicate surprise or shock; an informal, old-fashioned word. *'Gosh, this is a good system.'... 'Gosh, don't you find it really difficult?'*

gosling /gɒzlɪŋ/ **goslings**
NC A **gosling** is a baby goose. *...a newly hatched gosling.*

go-slow, go-slows
NC A **go-slow** is a protest by workers in which they deliberately work slowly. *They are likely to continue their campaign of passive disobedience through strikes, go-slows and boycotts... The lay-offs have already led to strikes and go-slows.*

gospel /gɒspl/ **gospels**
1 NC The **Gospels** are the four books of the Bible describing the life and teachings of Jesus Christ. *...the Gospel according to St Mark.*
2 NC+SUPP A **gospel** is also a set of ideas that someone believes in very strongly. *They continue to preach their gospel of self-reliance.*
3 ADJ If you regard something as **gospel** or as **gospel**

truth, you believe strongly that it is true. *You can take it as gospel truth that he is busy.*
4 ADJ ATTRIB **Gospel** music is a style of religious music involving strong rhythms and people singing in harmony. *His mother was a gospel singer.*

gossamer /gɒsəmə/
1 NU **Gossamer** is the very light, fine thread that spiders use to make cobwebs. *...shining ends of flying gossamer.*
2 NU **Gossamer** is very thin and delicate cloth; a literary use. *Pink gossamer curtains draped the walls.*

gossip /gɒsɪp/ **gossips, gossiping, gossiped**
1 NU or NC **Gossip** is informal conversation, often about other people's private affairs. *...a nice, chatty letter, full of news and gossip. ...the usual gossip about the Royal family. ...friendly gossips over our garden gates.*
2 V If you **gossip** with someone, you talk informally with them about local people and events. *I mustn't stay gossiping with you any longer... She knows almost everyone you've ever heard of—but she doesn't gossip about them much.*
3 NC A **gossip** is a person who enjoys talking about other people's private affairs. *Gossips have insisted that he is more than just another friend... Isn't he a bit of a gossip himself?*

gossip column, gossip columns
NC A **gossip column** is the part of a newspaper or magazine where the activities of famous people are discussed. *His flamboyant lifestyle often got him into the gossip columns.*

gossipy /gɒsɪpi/
1 ADJ A **gossipy** person enjoys gossiping; used showing disapproval. *...a lot of gossipy old women.*
2 ADJ Speech or writing that is **gossipy** is informal and full of news about your own affairs or about other people. *...a controversial and gossipy book.*

got /gɒt/
1 **Got** is the past tense and past participle of **get**.
2 VO You can use **have got** instead of the more formal 'have' when talking about possessing things: see **have**. *We haven't got a car... Have you got any brochures on Holland?... I've got nothing to hide... That door's got a lock on it.*
3 V+to-INF You can use **have got to** instead of the more formal 'have to' or 'must' when talking about something that must be done. *It's got to be approved... We've got to get up early tomorrow... There's got to be some motive.*

Gothic /gɒθɪk/
1 ADJ A building such as a cathedral that is **Gothic** has a style of architecture that is distinguished by tall pillars, high vaulted ceilings, and pointed arches. *The church was Gothic, grey, and stark on the outside.* ▶ Also NU *...the transition from Gothic to Renaissance.*
2 ADJ **Gothic** is used to describe stories in which strange, mysterious adventures happen in dark and lonely places such as the ruins of a castle. *...a Gothic horror story.*
3 ADJ **Gothic** is a style of printing or writing in which the letters are very ornate, and which is used especially in things such as signs or book titles. *'Hotel Metropole' was inscribed in Gothic letters above the door.*

gotta /gɒtə/
Gotta is used in written English to represent the words 'got to' when they are pronounced informally, as a way of saying 'have to' or 'must'. *I've gotta get back.*

gotten /gɒtn/
Gotten is often used for the past participle of **get** in American English. *The situation has gotten badly out of hand.*

gouge /gaʊdʒ/ **gouges, gouging, gouged**
VO If you **gouge** something, you make a hole in it with a pointed object. *You've gouged a hole in the wall with the end of the pole.*
gouge out PHRASAL VERB If you **gouge** something **out**, you force it out of a hole using your fingers or a sharp tool. *I can see the huge drill bit gouging out the rock ahead of us.*

Gouled Aptidon, Hassan /hæsæn guːlɛd æptɪdɒn/
Hassan Gouled Aptidon became President of Djibouti
in 1977. He served as Minister of Education from 1963
to 1967 and became Chairman of the Popular
Assembly for Progress (RPP) in 1979. Born: 1916.

Gourad Hamadou, Barkad
/bɑːkæt guəræt hæmɑːduː/
Barkad Gourad Hamadou became Prime Minister of
Djibouti in 1978. He was Minister of Education from
1960 to 1964, and of Health from 1964 to 1966. He is a
member of the Popular Assembly for Progress (RPP),
the sole party, and is an Afar.

gourd /ɡʊəd, ɡɔːd/ **gourds**
1 NC A **gourd** is a large fruit that is similar to a
marrow. *These are wild squash, melons, gourds and
cucumbers that we have found that will develop roots
very rapidly.*
2 NC A **gourd** is also a container made from a gourd.
...a gourd full of milk.

gourmand /ɡʊəmənd, ɡɔːmənd/ **gourmands**
NC A **gourmand** is a person who enjoys eating and
drinking, especially in large amounts; a formal word.
*He was an enormous gourmand and gambler as well
as a splendid actor.*

gourmet /ɡʊəmeɪ, ɡɔːmeɪ/ **gourmets**
1 NC A **gourmet** is a person who enjoys good food and
who knows a lot about cooking and wine. *...a variety
of snails truly prized by gourmets.*
2 ADJ ATTRIB You use **gourmet** to describe food which
is intended to be enjoyed by gourmets. *Chrétien
offered them French gourmet cuisine... Gourmet
menus may soon be available in hospitals.*

gout /ɡaʊt/
NU **Gout** is an illness which causes swollen joints.
*Only about three in every thousand people ever suffer
from gout.*

gouty /ɡaʊti/
ADJ Someone who is **gouty** suffers from gout.

govern /ɡʌvn/ **governs, governing, governed**
1 V or VO Someone who **governs** a country rules it, for
example by making and revising the laws, managing
the economy, and controlling public services. *Many
civil servants are sure that they can govern better
than the politicians. ...the party which has governed
Algeria since independence.* ◆ **governing** NU *They
believed that they still had a role to play in the
governing of Indonesia.* ● See also **governing**.
2 VO Something that **governs** an event or situation has
control and influence over it. *Poverty governed our
lives. ...rules governing the conduct of students.*

governess /ɡʌvəˈnəs/ **governesses**
NC A **governess** is a woman employed by a family to
live with them and educate their children. *In the old
days girls lived in the country—they had a governess
and they never came to London until they were 17 or
18.*

governing /ɡʌvəˈnɪŋ/
ADJ The **governing** party is the political party in power
in a country. *The governing Labour Party in
Australia has voted to abandon its traditional
opposition to privatisation.*

governing body, governing bodies
NC A **governing body** is a committee that is
responsible for making and enforcing the rules which
control a public organization or group of professional
people. *He's directly responsible to the governing
bodies of the university.*

government /ɡʌvnmənt/ **governments**
1 N COLL A **government** is the group of people who are
responsible for governing a country or state. *The
Wilson Government came to power in 1964... The
government has had to cut back on public
expenditure... He explained his policy to government
officials.*
2 NU **Government** is the organization and methods
involved in governing a country or state. *Most of his
ministers had no previous experience of government...
Government has become much more difficult today.*

governmental /ɡʌvnˈmɛntl/
ADJ ATTRIB **Governmental** means concerned with and
related to government. *The necessary resources can
only come at governmental level.*

governor /ɡʌvəˈnə/ **governors**
1 NC A **governor** is a person who is responsible for the
political administration of a region, or for the
administration of an institution. *The new governor of
Tamil Nadu state is to be Mr P. C. Alexander.
...Governor John Connally of Texas.*
2 NC A **governor** is a person who is on a committee
which controls an organization such as a school or a
hospital. *He said the government wanted to see
authorities handing over more to school governors.
...the chairman of the BBC's Board of Governors,
Marmaduke Hussey.*

Governor General, Governors General or
Governor Generals.
NC A **Governor General** is a person who, in a former
colony, is the chief representative of the country which
used to control that colony. *Instructions had been
communicated to the Governor General.*

govt.
Govt. is an abbreviation for **government**.

gown /ɡaʊn/ **gowns**
1 NC A **gown** is a long dress which women wear on
formal occasions. *...a sumptuous gown of purple
velvet... Brides mostly want to have bridal gowns of
their own, rather than hiring them.*
2 NC A **gown** is also a loose black cloak which is worn
on formal occasions by people such as judges and
lawyers. *The students and academics were wearing
their university gowns... Traditionally they wore silk
gowns that distinguished them from other barristers.*

GP /dʒiːpiː/ **GPs**
NC A **GP** is a doctor who treats all types of illness,
instead of specializing in one area of medicine. GP is
an abbreviation for 'general practitioner'. *Parents
should contact their GP if children develop severe
headaches, stiff necks or vomiting.*

grab /ɡræb/ **grabs, grabbing, grabbed**
1 VO If you **grab** something, you take it or pick it up
roughly. *She grabbed my arm... When the policeman
tried to grab him, the young man opened fire.*
2 V+at If you **grab** at something, you try to take it or
pick it up. *She fell on her knees to grab at the money.*
▶ Also NC *He made a grab for the knife.*
3 VO If you **grab** some food or sleep, you manage to
get some quickly. *I'll grab a sandwich before I go.*
4 VO or V+at If you **grab** an opportunity, you take
advantage of it eagerly. *Why didn't you grab the
chance to go to New York?... The mediators grabbed
at the new proposal.*
5 If something is **up for grabs**, it is generally available
to anyone who is interested in it; an informal
expression. *His job is up for grabs.*

grace /ɡreɪs/ **graces, gracing, graced**
1 NU Someone's **grace** is the smooth, elegant and
attractive way they move. *She moved with an
extraordinary grace.*
2 TITLE You use expressions such as **Your Grace** and
Her Grace to address or refer to a Duke, Duchess, or
Archbishop. *His Grace will receive you now.*
3 VO If you say that something or someone **graces** a
place or an event, you mean that they are present and
that they make the place or event more attractive or
enjoyable; a formal use. *...the plants that grace our
conservatories... He had been invited to grace a
function at the college.*
● **Grace** is used in these phrases. ● If you do
something unpleasant **with good grace**, or **with a good
grace**, you do it without complaining. *She should have
retired with good grace instead of pursuing a fight that
is bound to ruin her.* ● If you **have the grace** or **have
the good grace** to do something, you do something
which shows that you are sorry for having done
something to upset someone. *At least he had the
grace to drop his smile and look away from me.*

graceful /ɡreɪsfl/
1 ADJ Someone or something that is **graceful** moves in
a smooth and elegant way or has an attractive,
pleasing shape. *They're very graceful animals. ...the
graceful little white wooden building... The writing is
graceful, elegant, and clear.* ◆ **gracefully** ADV *Learn
how to move gracefully on a stage.*
2 ADJ **Graceful** behaviour is polite, kind, and

pleasant. *She turned with graceful solicitude to Anthea.* ♦ **gracefully** ADV *He accepted gracefully and gratefully.*

graceless /ˈgreɪsləs/
1 ADJ Something that is **graceless** is unattractive and dull, rather than elegant. *...a large, graceless industrial city.*
2 ADJ If someone is **graceless**, they behave in an impolite way; a formal use showing disapproval. *He was so graceless, so eager to shock.*

gracious /ˈgreɪʃəs/
1 ADJ If someone is **gracious**, they are polite and pleasant, especially towards people who have a lower social position than them. *She could also be witty, very ladylike, and gracious... The people of this state have always been gracious and hospitable.* ♦ **graciously** ADV *The lady assured him graciously that it had all been a mistake.*
2 ADJ ATTRIB You use **gracious** to describe the comfortable way of life of wealthy people, especially in former times. *...places of recreation and gracious living. ...a gracious marble-halled conference palace.*
3 You can use '**Good gracious!**' and '**Goodness gracious!**' to express surprise or annoyance; an informal, old-fashioned use. *'Good gracious me! Look at that!'*

gradation /grəˈdeɪʃn/ **gradations**
NC+SUPP A **gradation** is a small change, or one of the stages in the process of change. *...the subtle colour gradations.*

grade /greɪd/ **grades, grading, graded**
1 VO If you **grade** something, you judge or measure the quality of it and give it a number or name which indicates how good or bad it is. *The reports are graded 1 to 6.*
2 NC The **grade** of a product is its quality. *...ordinary grade petrol.*
3 NC Your **grade** in an examination is the mark you get, usually in the form of a letter or number. *She passed the exams with good grades.*
4 NC+SUPP Your **grade** in a company or organization is your level of importance or your rank. *...separate dining rooms for different grades of staff.*
5 NC At schools in the United States a **grade** is a group of classes in which all the children are of a similar age. *She had entered the sixth grade at eleven.*
6 If you **make the grade**, you succeed in something by reaching the required standard; an informal expression. *The produce will not make the grade on the export market.*

grade crossing, grade crossings
NC A **grade crossing** is a level crossing; used in American English.

graded /ˈgreɪdɪd/
ADJ ATTRIB **Graded** is used to describe something that is gradually sloping or changing. *...a nicely graded curve.*

gradient /ˈgreɪdiənt/ **gradients**
NC A **gradient** is a slope or the angle of a slope. *The floor has a minimum gradient of one in five. ...roads with sharp bends and varying gradients.*

gradual /ˈgrædʒuəl/
ADJ Something that is **gradual** happens over a long period of time rather than suddenly. *It's a process of gradual development.* ♦ **gradually** ADV *Things change gradually in engineering.*

gradualism /ˈgrædʒuəlɪzəm/
NU **Gradualism** is the policy of trying to change a situation or achieve a goal slowly rather than quickly or violently. *In Eastern Europe there's been argument within governments about the merits of this policy compared with gradualism.*

graduate, graduates, graduating, graduated; pronounced /ˈgrædʒuət/ when it is a noun and /ˈgrædʒueɪt/ when it is a verb.
1 NC A **graduate** is a student who has successfully completed a first degree at a university or college. *...a psychology graduate of Stanford University.*
2 NC+SUPP In the United States, a **graduate** is a student who has successfully completed high school or another educational course. *All of the soldiers must*

be high school graduates.
3 N+N **Graduate** students are students who have a first degree and are studying for a higher one. *...graduate students in the philosophy department.*
4 V When a student **graduates**, he or she has successfully completed a degree course at a university or college and receives a certificate that shows this. *She recently graduated from law school.*
5 V In the United States, when someone **graduates**, they have successfully completed high school and receive a certificate or diploma that shows this. *Seventeen-year-old Laura has now graduated from public high school and is off to college in Minnesota.*
6 V If you **graduate** from one thing to another, you go from a less important job or position to a more important one. *Start on a local paper, and then graduate to a provincial paper.*

graduated /ˈgrædʒueɪtɪd/
ADJ **Graduated** is used to describe something that increases by regular amounts or grades. *...a graduated form of payment of the Community Charge. ...several graduated ridges down the side of the can.*

graduate school, graduate schools
NCorNU A **graduate school** is a department in a North American university or college where postgraduate students are taught. *...the Graduate School of Business at McGill University... I intended to study philosophy in graduate school.*

graduation /ˌgrædʒuˈeɪʃn/
1 NU **Graduation** is the successful completion of a course of study at a university or college, and, in the United States, high school. *He should get a good job after graduation.*
2 N SING The ceremony at which students from university or college, and, in the United States, high school, receive their degrees or diplomas is also called a **graduation**. *He had just attended his daughter's graduation.*

graffiti /grəˈfiːti/
NU **Graffiti** is words or pictures that are written or drawn on walls, signs, and posters in public places. Graffiti is usually rude, funny, or contains a political message. *Litter bins overflow with rubbish and there is graffiti in subways, trains, and buses.*

graft /grɑːft/ **grafts, grafting, grafted**
1 VO If you **graft** a part of one plant onto another, you join them so that they will grow together and become one plant. *We grafted tomatoes onto plants that were resistant to certain diseases.*
2 VO If you **graft** one idea or system onto another, you try to join one to the other. *...modern federal structures grafted on to ancient cultural divisions.*
3 VO If doctors **graft** a piece of healthy tissue to a damaged part of your body, they attach it by a medical operation in order to replace the damaged part. *...new veins grafted to his heart.* ► Also NC *Laverne had skin grafts on her thighs.*
4 NU **Graft** means hard work; an informal use. *Julie returns to work today knowing that the really hard graft was done last week.*
5 NU **Graft** is also the act of obtaining money dishonestly by using your position of authority. *...charges of corruption and graft... He vowed to resign if he could not suppress graft in official circles.*

grain /greɪn/ **grains**
1 NC A **grain** of wheat, rice, or other cereal crop is a seed from it. *...a hen pecking round for grains of corn. ...no bigger than grains of rice.*
2 N MASS **Grain** is a cereal crop, especially wheat or corn, that has been harvested for food. *...subsidies to encourage farmers to grow grain... Grain is now being brought south by boat... They thought the country would produce 208 million tonnes of wheat and other grains.*
3 NC A **grain** of something such as sand or salt is a tiny hard piece of it. *...small particles, no heavier than grains of sand.*
4 N SING A **grain** of a quality is a very small amount of it; a literary use. *He did not have a grain of humour... Both remarks contain a grain of truth.*
5 NC The **grain** in wood is the natural pattern and direction of lines on its surface. *He took the pipe and*

examined the grain in the bowl... The wood has to have been dead for ten to fifteen years before the patina and grain appear.
6 If an idea or action **goes against the grain**, it is very difficult to accept it or do it, because it conflicts with your beliefs. *The scheme goes against the grain of the country's history and character.*

grained /greɪnd/
ADJ **Grained** is used after adjectives and adverbs to describe substances that consist of particles of a particular size. *...a coarse grained clay.*

grainy /greɪni/
1 ADJ ATTRIB Something that is **grainy** has a rough surface or texture. *...the grainy wood of the table.*
2 ADJ A **grainy** photograph or film is of poor quality and appears to be made up of black, grey, or coloured spots. *...a grainy black and white photograph of three men. ...shot in irritating high contrast grainy film.*

gram /græm/ **grams**; also spelt **gramme**.
NC A **gram** is a unit of weight equal to one thousandth of a kilogram. *...500 grams of flour.*

grammar /græmə/ **grammars**
1 NU **Grammar** is the rules of a language which describe how sentences are formed. *Every dialect of English has rules of grammar.*
2 NU You can also refer to someone's **grammar** when you are describing the way in which they either obey or do not obey the rules of grammar when they write or speak. *I'm constantly having to correct their grammar.*
3 NC A **grammar** is a book that describes the rules of a language. *...an old French grammar.*

grammarian /grəmeəriən/ **grammarians**
NC A **grammarian** is a person who specializes in studying and writing books about grammar.

grammar school, grammar schools
NC A **grammar school** is a school in Britain for children aged between eleven and eighteen with a high academic ability. *...the head of modern languages at a London grammar school.*

grammatical /grəmætɪkl/
1 ADJ ATTRIB **Grammatical** is used to describe something that relates to grammar. *This sentence is very complex in its grammatical structure.*
♦ **grammatically** ADV *His English was usually grammatically correct.*
2 ADJ If someone's language is **grammatical**, it is correct because it obeys the rules of grammar. *He speaks perfectly grammatical English.*

gramme /græm/. See gram.

gramophone /græməfəʊn/ **gramophones**
NC A **gramophone** is an old-fashioned type of record player. *...a small hand-driven gramophone.*

gran /græn/ **grans**
NCor VOCATIVE Your **gran** is your grandmother; an informal word. *I went to stay with my Gran over Christmas.*

granary /grænəri/ **granaries**
1 NC A **granary** is a building in which grain is stored. *..a bakery and granary that have just been expanded.*
2 ADJ ATTRIB **Granary** bread is bread which contains whole grains of wheat; **granary** is a trademark. *Wholemeal bread often gets confused with brown bread or Granary bread.*

grand /grænd/ **grander, grandest**. The form **grand** is both the singular and the plural of the noun.
1 ADJ **Grand** buildings are splendid or impressive. *...the grand Kremlin palace. ...the grand country house she lived in.* ♦ **grandly** ADV *Its interior is grandly elegant.*
2 ADJ ATTRIB Plans and actions that are **grand** are intended to achieve important results. *...his grand schemes for totally redefining science. ...last year's grand strategy for redefining the party.*
3 ADJ People, jobs, or appearances that are **grand** seem important or socially superior. *...all sorts of grand people... The job isn't as grand as it sounds.* ♦ **grandly** ADV *He announced grandly that he 'had no time for women.'*
4 ADJ ATTRIB **Grand** moments or activities are exciting and important. *Finally, the grand moment comes when you make your first solo flight.*

5 ADJ ATTRIB A **grand** total is the final amount of something. *In 1886 Levers, the soap firm, spent a grand total of £50 on advertising.*
6 NC A **grand** means a thousand pounds or a thousand dollars; an informal use. *That still leaves you with fifty grand.*

grandad /grændæd/ **grandads**; also spelt **granddad**.
NCor VOCATIVE Your **grandad** is your grandfather; an informal word.

grandaddy /grændædi/ **grandaddies**; also spelt **granddaddy**.
NCor VOCATIVE Your **grandaddy** is your grandfather; an informal word used in American English.

grandchild /græntʃaɪld/ **grandchildren**
NC Your **grandchild** is the child of your son or daughter. *The baby will be the Queen's fifth grandchild.*

granddaughter /grændɔːtə/ **granddaughters**
NC Your **granddaughter** is the daughter of your son or daughter. *He had come out to lunch with his granddaughter.*

grandeur /grændʒə/
1 NU **Grandeur** is the quality in something which makes it seem impressive and elegant. *...the grandeur of Lansdowne House... Television and radio advertisements will focus on Africa's scenic grandeur and its ancient and proud civilisation.*
2 NU A person's **grandeur** is the great importance and social status that they have. *His wealth gave him grandeur. ...a bureaucrat with delusions of grandeur.*

grandfather /grændfɑːðə/ **grandfathers**
NC Your **grandfather** is the father of your father or mother. *These vineyards were planted by my grandfather, 76 years ago... A grandfather was amongst those killed.*

grandfather clock, grandfather clocks
NC A **grandfather clock** is a clock in a tall wooden case which stands on the floor.

grandiloquent /grændɪləkwənt/
ADJ Language or behaviour that is **grandiloquent** uses words that are unnecessarily complicated and difficult to understand, or exaggeratedly impressive gestures; a formal word. *...a grandiloquent announcement. ...a grandiloquent gesture against the system of education.*
♦ **grandiloquently** ADV *...gesturing grandiloquently.*

grandiose /grændiəʊs/
ADJ **Grandiose** is used to describe something which is bigger or more elaborate than necessary and thereby seems ridiculous. *Huge tracts of forest have been given over to grandiose development projects. ...grandiose schemes for industrial ventures.*

grand jury, grand juries
NC A **grand jury** is a jury, usually in the United States, which considers a criminal case in order to decide if someone should be tried in a court of law. *A grand jury in Miami indicted the General on drugs charges.*

grandma /grænmɑː/ **grandmas**
NCor VOCATIVE Your **grandma** is your grandmother; an informal word. *...hot pepper sauces the way her grandma used to make them.*

grandmaster /grændmɑːstə/ **grandmasters**
NC In chess, a **grandmaster** is a player who has reached the very highest standard, measured in ranking points. *...the Cuban chess grandmaster, Guillermo Garcia.*

grandmother /grænmʌðə/ **grandmothers**
NC Your **grandmother** is the mother of your father or mother. *She was staying with her grandmother... I met a sixty-four year old grandmother going home.*

grandpa /grænpɑː/ **grandpas**
NCor VOCATIVE Your **grandpa** is your grandfather; an informal word. *She had 14 grandchildren, but I was the only one named after Grandpa so I thought I was special.*

grandparent /grænpeərənt/ **grandparents**
NC Your **grandparents** are the parents of your father or mother. *She was sent to her grandparents in Somalia.*

grand piano, grand pianos
NC A **grand piano** is a large piano. *All eyes are on Joseph Payne, who sits at the grand piano.*

Grand Prix /grɒnⁿ priː/. The plural form can be
written **Grands Prix** or **Grand Prix**, and is pronounced
/grɒnⁿ priː/ or /grɒnⁿ priːz/.
NC A **Grand Prix** is one of a series of races for very
powerful racing cars; also used sometimes in the
names of competitions in other sports. *The Monaco
Grand Prix was won by the French driver, Alain
Prost. ...the $130,000 Grand Prix tennis tournament
being held at Guaruja in Brazil.*

grand slam, grand slams
NC A **grand slam** is the achievement of winning all the
matches or major tournaments in a season in a
particular sport, for example in tennis or rugby. *In
1988 she became the first woman to win the Grand
Slam since 1970.*

grandson /grænsʌn/ **grandsons**
NC Your **grandson** is the son of your son or daughter.
He lived with his grandson in Mexico City.

grandstand /grændstænd/ **grandstands**
NC A **grandstand** is a covered stand for spectators at
sporting events. *They were sitting in the top row of
the grandstand... At least one £14 grandstand ticket
changed hands in Edinburgh for £800.*

grand tour, grand tours
1 NC A **grand tour** is a journey round the main cities
of Europe that young men from rich families used to
make in former times as part of their education. *Part
of his education was the traditional Grand Tour.*
2 NC If you are given a **grand tour** of a place, you are
taken all round it and shown everything. *Come round
and we'll give you a grand tour of the house!*

grange /greɪndʒ/ **granges**
NC A **grange** is a farmhouse, especially one that has
several other buildings attached to it.

granite /grænɪt/
NU **Granite** is a very hard rock used in building. *...an
old granite quarry in Cornwall.*

granny /græni/ **grannies**; also spelt **grannie**.
N or VOCATIVE Your **granny** is your grandmother; an
informal word. *The story of Edward is told by an old
granny to a little girl... When I was about 12, I said,
'Granny, you've got to write this down for me.'*

grant /grɑːnt/ **grants, granting, granted**
1 NC A **grant** is an amount of money that the
government gives to a person or an organization for a
particular purpose such as education or home
improvements. *They get a grant from the council.
...government plans to replace part of the student
grant with a loan.*
2 VOO or VO+to If someone in authority **grants** you
something, they give it to you. *Proposals have been
made to grant each displaced family £25,000... He was
finally granted a visa... He has granted an amnesty to
those imprisoned for their attempts to overthrow his
government.*
3 V-REPORT or VO If you **grant** that something is true,
you admit that it is true; a formal use. *I grant that
sincerity has its awkward moments... That joy ride, I
grant you, was a silly stunt.*
● **Grant** is used in these phrases. ● If you **take it for
granted** that something is true, you believe that it is
true without thinking about it. *It is taken for granted
that every child should learn mathematics.* ● If you
take someone **for granted**, you benefit from them
without showing that you are grateful. *He just takes
me absolutely for granted.*

granular /grænjʊlə/
ADJ Something that is **granular** is composed of a lot of
granules, or has the texture or appearance of being
composed of a lot of granules; a formal word. *...a
special, granular form of a plastic material.*

granulated /grænjʊleɪtɪd/
ADJ ATTRIB **Granulated** sugar is in the form of coarse
grains. *...a bag of granulated sugar.*

granule /grænjuːl/ **granules**
NC A **granule** is a small round piece of something.
...sea salt sold in the form of granules.

grape /greɪp/ **grapes**
NC **Grapes** are small green or purple fruit that can be
eaten raw or used for making wine. *...a bunch of
grapes.*

grapefruit /greɪpfruːt/ **grapefruits**. The plural form
can be either **grapefruits** or **grapefruit**.
NU or NC A **grapefruit** is a large, round, yellow fruit,
similar to an orange, that has a sharp, sour taste.
*...sixteen thousand tons of grapefruit and oranges.
...fresh jaffa grapefruit juice... The Ministry advised
people who had bought grapefruit recently not to eat
them.*

grapevine /greɪpvaɪn/ **grapevines**
1 NC A **grapevine** is a climbing plant on which grapes
grow.
2 N SING A **grapevine** is a network of people who pass
on news in an informal way. *Every community has a
grapevine... They had just heard through the
grapevine that I had been transferred to the tenth
floor.*

graph /grɑːf/ **graphs**
NC A **graph** is a mathematical diagram, usually a line
or curve, which shows the relationship between two or
more sets of numbers or measurements. *The results
were plotted on a graph.*

graphic /græfɪk/ **graphics**
1 ADJ **Graphic** descriptions or accounts are very clear
and detailed. *...his graphic stories of persecution.*
♦ **graphically** ADV *The cruelty of this is graphically
described by the old farmer.*
2 ADJ ATTRIB Something that is **graphic** is concerned
with drawing, especially the use of strong lines and
colours. *...graphic and industrial design.*
3 N PL **Graphics** are drawings and pictures that are
made using simple lines and sometimes strong
colours. *...computer generated graphics.*

graphite /græfaɪt/
NU **Graphite** is a hard black substance that is a form
of carbon. It is used to make the centre part of
pencils. *He described the new material as being very
like graphite.*

graphology /græfɒlədʒi/
NU **Graphology** is the science of examining people's
handwriting in order to discover what sort of
personality they have; a technical term. *The
personality traits that can be identified from
graphology depend on various elements of the
handwriting.*

graph paper
NU **Graph paper** is paper that has small squares
printed on it so that you can use it for drawing
graphs. *The plastic model was sliced into strips,
traced out on graph paper and then projected by
computer to full size.*

grapnel /græpnəl/ **grapnels**
NC A **grapnel** is a device which consists of several
hooks that are joined together and attached to one end
of a rope. Grapnels are used especially in sailing; a
technical term. *The grapnel was caught between
rocks and we had to cut the rope.*

grapple /græpl/ **grapples, grappling, grappled**
1 V If you **grapple** with someone, you take hold of
them and struggle or fight with them. *We grappled
with him and took the guns from him.*
2 V+with If you **grapple** with a problem, you try hard
to solve it. *I grappled with this moral dilemma.*

grappling iron, grappling irons
NC A **grappling iron** is the same as a **grapnel**.

grasp /grɑːsp/ **grasps, grasping, grasped**
1 VO If you **grasp** something, you take it with your
hand and hold it firmly. *Edward grasped Castle's
arm.*
2 N SING+SUPP A **grasp** is a firm hold or grip. *The
animal had a powerful grasp.*
3 VO or V-REPORT If you **grasp** something complicated,
you understand it. *The concepts were difficult to
grasp... I grasped quite soon what was going on.*
4 N SING+SUPP If you have a **grasp** of something, you
have an understanding of it. *He had a sound grasp of
tactics.*
● **Grasp** is used in these phrases. ● If something is
within your **grasp**, it is likely that you will achieve it.
A peaceful solution was within his grasp. ● If
something is **in** your **grasp**, you hold it or control it. If
something escapes or slips **from** your **grasp**, you no
longer hold it or control it. *He must now feel he has*

his party's nomination in his grasp... Victory was
snatched from his grasp.

grasping /grɑːspɪŋ/
ADJ A **grasping** person wants to get as much money as
possible; used showing disapproval. ...a grasping
woman who would stoop to any device to lay her
hands on Sir John's money.

grass /grɑːs/ **grasses**
N MASS **Grass** is a very common green plant with
narrow leaves that forms a layer covering an area of
ground. They lay on the grass. ...prairie grasses.

grasshopper /grɑːshɒpə/ **grasshoppers**
NC A **grasshopper** is an insect with long back legs that
jumps high into the air and makes a high, vibrating
sound. For most farmers it is the locust and
grasshopper swarms that will be the worst headache.

grassland /grɑːslænd/ **grasslands**
NU or NC **Grassland** is land covered with wild grass.
The animals run short of native grassland for shelter
and food and die off. ...a vast but sparsely populated
country of grasslands and savannah woodlands.

grass roots
N PL The **grass roots** of an organization are the
ordinary people in it, rather than its leaders. ...to
strengthen democracy at the grass roots.
...implementing government programmes at a grass
roots level.

grassy /grɑːsi/
ADJ A **grassy** area of land is covered in grass. ...a
steep grassy slope.

grate /greɪt/ **grates, grating, grated**
1 NC A **grate** is a framework of metal bars in a
fireplace. A fire was burning in the grate.
2 VO When you **grate** food, you shred it into very
small pieces using a grater. ...not every cassava gets
grated, you get lumps coming out. ♦ **grated** ADJ
...grated lemon peel.
3 V-ERG If something **grates** or if you **grate** it, it rubs
against something else, making a harsh, unpleasant
sound. He could hear her shoes grating on the steps...
He grated his teeth.
4 V If a noise **grates** on you, it irritates you. That
shrill laugh grated on her mother.
5 See also **grating**.

grateful /greɪtfl/
ADJ If you are **grateful** for something that someone
has given you or done for you, you are pleased and
wish to thank them. I am ever so grateful to you for
talking to me... I'd be so grateful if you could do it.
♦ **gratefully** ADV He accepted the money gratefully.

grater /greɪtə/ **graters**
NC A **grater** is a small metal tool with a rough surface
which is used for shredding food into very small
pieces. For example, they found out that this grater
becomes blunt within about three weeks.

gratify /grætɪfaɪ/ **gratifies, gratifying, gratified**; a
formal word.
1 VO If you **are gratified** by something, it gives you
pleasure or satisfaction. He was gratified that his
guess had been proved right. ♦ **gratifying** ADJ It was
gratifying to see so many people present... It makes a
gratifying change. ♦ **gratification** /grætɪfɪkeɪʃn/ NU To
my immense gratification, he fell into the trap.
2 VO If you **gratify** a desire, you satisfy it. His
smallest wish must be gratified. ♦ **gratification** NU
...action directed towards the gratification of desire.

grating /greɪtɪŋ/ **gratings**
1 NC A **grating** is a metal frame with rows of bars
across it fastened over a hole in a wall or in the
ground. The storm sewers in the street have a grating
over them.
2 ADJ A **grating** sound is harsh and unpleasant. ...a
grating voice.

gratis /grætɪs, grɑːtɪs/
ADV or ADJ PRED If something is done or provided **gratis**,
it does not have to be paid for; a formal word. He
works gratis for his creditor... It is yours, gratis.

gratitude /grætɪtjuːd/
NU **Gratitude** is the state of feeling grateful. I must
express my gratitude to the BBC.

gratuitous /grətjuːɪtəs/
ADJ An action that is **gratuitous** is unnecessary, and

usually harmful or upsetting; a formal word.
...gratuitous acts of vandalism. ♦ **gratuitously** ADV
She had no wish to wound his feelings gratuitously.

gratuity /grətjuːəti/ **gratuities**
1 NC A **gratuity** is a gift of money to someone who has
done something for you; a formal use. Is one allowed
to offer gratuities to the guides?
2 NC A **gratuity** is also a large gift of money given to
someone when they leave their employment, especially
when they leave the armed forces. He resigned from
the service and applied for a gratuity instead of a
pension.

grave /greɪv/ **graves; graver, gravest**
1 NC A **grave** is a place where a dead person is
buried. Flowers had been put on the grave. ...the
cemetery where the mass grave was discovered.
2 If you say that someone who is dead would **turn in**
their **grave**, you mean that they would be very
shocked or upset by something that is happening now,
if they were alive.
3 ADJ A situation that is **grave** is very serious. The
state is facing a grave financial crisis... The Forum
has expressed grave concern at the proposals.
♦ **gravely** ADV His father was gravely ill.
4 ADJ A person who is **grave** is quiet and serious; a
literary use. ...a grave, courteous man... She
returned, looking even graver. ♦ **gravely** ADV Roger
understood and nodded gravely.

gravedigger /greɪvdɪgə/ **gravediggers**
NC A **gravedigger** is a person whose job is to dig
graves for dead people to be buried in. The dead were
left unburied as gravediggers went on strike... The
gravediggers continue the grim job of exhuming the
layers of skeletons.

gravel /grævl/
NU **Gravel** consists of very small stones. It is often
used to make paths. ...the sound of his feet on the
gravel.

gravelled /grævld/; spelt **graveled** in American
English.
ADJ A **gravelled** path has a surface made of gravel.
We walked together along the gravelled paths. ...a
gravelled strip of ground outside the lecture rooms.

gravelly /grævəli/
1 ADJ An area of land that is **gravelly** is covered in
small stones. ...gravelly soil.
2 ADJ A **gravelly** voice is low and rough. His rugged
face and gravelly voice came to epitomize the tough
but decent Englishman.

graven /greɪvn/
ADJ ATTRIB A **graven** image is one that has been
carved, especially for use in religious worship; a
literary word.

graveside /greɪvsaɪd/ **gravesides**
NC The **graveside** is the area around a grave; used
especially when talking about burying someone. At
the graveside he made a little speech.

gravestone /greɪvstəʊn/ **gravestones**
NC A **gravestone** is a large stone with words carved
into it, which is placed on a grave. The book says
gravestones tell the history of a parish and are an
integral part of the churchyard's character. ...a
marble gravestone.

graveyard /greɪvjɑːd/ **graveyards**
NC A **graveyard** is an area of land where dead people
are buried. The child is buried in a crowded
graveyard between 100 other freshly dug graves.

gravitas /grævɪtæs/
NU Someone who has **gravitas** is able to talk about
important things in a serious, intelligent way, so that
their views are respected. He looks younger than he
is. He looks less serious than he is. He doesn't have
that quality called 'gravitas'.

gravitate /grævɪteɪt/ **gravitates, gravitating,
gravitated**
V + towards or to If you **gravitate** towards a place or
activity, you are attracted by it and go to it or get
involved in it. Albania has already shown signs of
gravitating towards the West economically and
diplomatically... Spokesmen maintain that wherever
they are sent in Pakistan, they would gravitate to
Karachi for jobs.

gravitation /ˌɡrævɪˈteɪʃn/
NU **Gravitation** is the force which causes objects to be attracted towards each other; a technical term in physics. *...a unified theory of all forces, including gravitation.*

gravitational /ˌɡrævɪˈteɪʃəʰnəl/
ADJ ATTRIB **Gravitational** means relating to or resulting from the force of gravity. *...the earth's gravitational force. ...a low gravitational field.*

gravity /ˈɡrævəti/
1 NU **Gravity** is the force which makes things fall when you drop them. *...the effects of gravity... The idea that gravity acts equally on all matter was mooted as long ago as the 17th century.*
2 NU+SUPP The **gravity** of a situation is its importance and seriousness. *...the gravity of the threat to shipping.*

gravy /ˈɡreɪvi/
NU **Gravy** is a thin savoury sauce that is served with meat. *Pour the gravy over the mixture and stir... On the menu today: turkey, gravy, sweet potatoes, and cranberry sauce.*

gravy boat, gravy boats
NC A **gravy boat** is a long, shallow jug that is used for serving gravy.

gravy train, gravy trains
NC If you describe something such as a job or business as a **gravy train**, you mean that you get a lot of money from it without much effort; an informal expression. *...a private gravy train subsidized from public funds... I've been riding the gravy train all my life.*

gray /ɡreɪ/. See grey.

graze /ɡreɪz/ **grazes, grazing, grazed**
1 V-ERG or VO When an animal **grazes**, it eats grass. *The horses graze peacefully... The people of the town fought for the right to graze cattle on the Common. ...land grazed by sheep and cattle.*
2 VO If you **graze** a part of your body, you injure the skin by scraping against something. *I grazed my legs as he pulled me up.* ▶ Also NC *...cuts and grazes.*

grazing /ˈɡreɪzɪŋ/
NU **Grazing** or **grazing land** is land on which animals graze or are grazed. *...the lack of good grazing.*

grease /ɡriːs/ **greases, greasing, greased**
1 N MASS **Grease** is a thick substance that is used to oil the moving parts of machines. *...thick layers of grease and fluff... Presumably there's been some contamination with oils and greases used to lubricate.*
2 NU **Grease** is also an oily substance that is produced by your skin. *...grease marks on sofa backs and arms.*
3 NU **Grease** is also animal fat that is produced by cooking meat. *Try a light touch of cooking oil or grease.*
4 VO If you **grease** something, you put grease or fat on it. *Clean and grease the valve thoroughly.*

grease gun, grease guns
NC A **grease gun** is a device for forcing grease into special holes in machines so that their moving parts work smoothly.

greasepaint /ˈɡriːspeɪnt/
NU **Greasepaint** is an oily substance used by actors as make-up. *Groucho's moustache consisted entirely of greasepaint, as anyone could see.*

greaseproof paper /ˌɡriːspruːf ˈpeɪpə/
NU **Greaseproof paper** does not allow grease to pass through it. It is used especially when cooking. *Line a tin with greased greaseproof paper.*

greasy /ˈɡriːsi/
ADJ Something that is **greasy** is covered with grease or contains a lot of grease. *...greasy tools. ...greasy hamburgers.*

great /ɡreɪt/ **greater, greatest**
1 ADJ You use **great** to describe something that is very large in size, amount, or degree. *...a great black cloud of smoke... There is a great amount of conflict... He had great difficulty in selling his house.*
2 ADJ Something or someone that is important, famous, or exciting can be described as **great**. *...the great cities of the Rhineland. ...the great issues of the day. ...a great actor.* ♦ **greatness** NU *...the*

greatness *of Germany. ...Boltzmann's greatness as a physicist.*
3 ADJ If something is **great**, it is very good; an informal use. *It's a great idea.*
4 You say **'great'** when you want to express approval or excitement about something; an informal use. *Great! Thanks very much.*
5 SUBMOD or ADJ ATTRIB You also use **great** for emphasis. *...a great big gaping hole... He was a great friend of Huxley.*

great- /ɡreɪt-/
PREFIX **Great-** combines with nouns that refer to members of a family. Nouns formed in this way refer to a relative who is two or more generations away from you. For example, your great-grandfather is the grandfather of one of your parents. *Mrs Regan has three daughters, nine grandchildren, and seven great-grandchildren. ...a precious family heirloom passed down from great-grandma.*

Great Britain /ˌɡreɪt ˈbrɪtn/
N PROP **Great Britain** is the island consisting of England, Scotland, and Wales, which together with Northern Ireland makes up the United Kingdom. See also **United Kingdom**. *In Great Britain, nationalists in Wales complain about the influx of English people unwilling to learn Welsh... The Great Britain women's hockey team have beaten New Zealand by 3 goals to 1 in Christchurch.*

greatcoat /ˈɡreɪtkəʊt/ **greatcoats**
NC A **greatcoat** is a long thick overcoat that is worn especially as part of a uniform. *...an army greatcoat.*

greater /ˈɡreɪtə/
1 ADJ ATTRIB **Greater** is used with or as part of the names of large cities, when you are referring to the whole city including the suburbs and not just to the central area. *...Greater London. ...the eight million people in greater Calcutta.*
2 ADJ ATTRIB **Greater** is also used with the name of a nation to describe the area which extends beyond its current border, but which used to belong to it, or which some people consider should belong to it. *He accused Serbia of waging a dirty war against his people, with the aim of creating a Greater Serbia.*

greatly /ˈɡreɪtli/
ADV You use **greatly** to emphasize the degree of something. *I was greatly influenced by Sullivan... He was not greatly surprised.*

Greece /ɡriːs/
The **Hellenic Republic** is a country in south-east Europe. It includes 1,400 islands, in addition to the mainland. Occupation by Germany from 1941 to 1944 was followed by civil war until 1949. A military junta ruled from 1967 to 1974. Greece is a member of the European Community and NATO. A New Democracy (ND) government was elected in 1990, when Konstantinos Karamanlis became President and Konstantinos Mitsotakis became Prime Minister. Greece exports grain, cotton, and other agricultural products. Tourism is an important industry. ♦ **Greek** /ɡriːk/ N, ADJ
▪ *per capita GNP:* US$4,790 ▪ *religion:* Christianity (mainly Greek Orthodox) ▪ *language:* Greek
▪ *currency:* drachma ▪ *capital:* Athens ▪ *population:* 10 million (1988) ▪ *size:* 131,957 square kilometres.

greed /ɡriːd/
NU **Greed** is a desire for more of something than is necessary or fair. *...opposition claims that her policies have encouraged greed and selfishness.*

greedy /ˈɡriːdi/ **greedier, greediest**
ADJ Someone who is **greedy** wants more of something than is necessary or fair. *People got richer and also greedier.* ♦ **greedily** ADV *They were eating greedily.*

Greek /ɡriːk/ **Greeks**
1 ADJ **Greek** means belonging or relating to Greece. *...a Greek airforce transport plane. ...Greek and Roman mythology. ...traditional Greek music.*
2 NC A **Greek** is a person who comes from Greece. *Most Greeks tend not to see the group as a threat to them... For the Greeks in general it is the social problems which are causing concern. ...the ancient Greeks.*
3 NU **Greek** is the language spoken by people living in

Greece. *Departments have been opened for the study of Bulgarian, Hungarian, Polish and modern Greek.*
4 NU **Greek** or **Ancient Greek** was the language used in Greece in ancient times. *They abandoned Latin and Greek, and taught more practical subjects instead.*

green /griːn/ **greener, greenest; greens**
1 ADJ Something that is **green** is the colour of grass or leaves. *She had blonde hair and green eyes.*
2 ADJ A place that is **green** is covered with grass and trees. *...the tranquillity of the lush green countryside.*
3 ADJ **Green** is used to describe political movements that are particularly concerned about protecting the environment. *This move is being hailed by green campaigners as a major step forward... Dr Runcie said he hoped the charter would help to spread awareness of green issues.*
4 NC **Greens** are members of green political movements. *...the success of the Greens in Germany.*
5 NC A **green** is an area of grass in a town or village. *...the village green.*
6 NC A **green** is also a smooth, flat area of grass around a hole on a golf course. *Lyle was off the edge of the green.*
7 N PL You can refer to the cooked green leaves of vegetables such as cabbage or spinach as **greens**. *People are living mostly on boiled greens and milkless tea.*
8 ADJ PRED+*with* If someone is **green** with envy, they are very envious indeed. *...a building which is due to be opened in a month's time and which will make British MPs green with envy.*
9 ADJ If someone is **green**, they are inexperienced. *...green recruits, new to the traditions.*

greenback /griːnbæk/ **greenbacks**
1 NC A **greenback** is any American banknote; used in informal American English.
2 N SING **Greenback** is also used to refer to the American dollar as a unit of currency. *The greenback rose against all major currencies... In Paris, the greenback was lower by four-fifths of a cent.*

green belt, green belts
NC A **green belt** is an area of land with fields or parks around a town or city, where people are not allowed to build houses or factories by law. *They've planted 20,000 green belts around villages and around Nairobi. ...a green belt area near Budapest.*

Green Beret, Green Berets
NC A **Green Beret** is a British or American commando; an informal expression. *...the elite American Green Beret regiment.*

green card, green cards
NC A **green card** is an official document which gives permission for someone who is not a citizen of the United States to live and work there. *Most of those who inquire are turned away because they have neither US citizenship nor proper immigration identification, namely a green card.*

greenery /griːnəri/
NU Plants that make a place look attractive are referred to as **greenery**. *...the lush greenery of the region.*

green fingers
N PL If you say that someone has **green fingers**, you mean that they are very good at growing vegetables, plants, or flowers. *I don't seem to have green fingers at all!*

greenfly /griːnflaɪ/ **greenflies**. The plural form can be either **greenfly** or **greenflies**.
NC **Greenfly** are small, green, winged insects that damage plants. *Marigolds are also grown in temperate climates to protect roses from greenfly.*

greengage /griːngeɪdʒ/ **greengages**
NC A **greengage** is a greenish-yellow coloured plum with a sweet taste.

greengrocer /griːngrəʊsə/ **greengrocers**
1 NC A **greengrocer** is a person who runs a shop where you can buy fruit and vegetables. *In Preston one greengrocer actually rushed around his shop gathering bananas and oranges which he insisted that I take with me.*
2 NC A **greengrocer** or **greengrocer's** is a shop where you can buy fruit and vegetables.

greenhorn /griːnhɔːn/ **greenhorns**; an informal word.
1 NC A **greenhorn** is someone who has recently come to live in America; used in American English. *They made him feel a foreigner, a greenhorn.*
2 NC A **greenhorn** is also a person who has had very little experience of life or of a particular job.

greenhouse /griːnhaʊs/ **greenhouses**
1 NC A **greenhouse** is a glass building in which you grow plants that need to be protected from bad weather. *He's been growing them in greenhouses at first.*
2 ADJ ATTRIB **Greenhouse** also describes things that cause or relate to the greenhouse effect. *...increasing emissions of greenhouse gases. ...greenhouse warming from carbon dioxide and methane.*

greenhouse effect
N SING The **greenhouse effect** is the problem caused by a build-up of gases such as carbon dioxide in the air around the Earth. These gases trap the heat from the sun, and cause a gradual rise in the temperature of the Earth's atmosphere. *...a report calling for further action to protect the ozone layer so as to limit the so-called greenhouse effect. ...global warming due to the accelerating greenhouse effect.*

greenish /griːnɪʃ/
ADJ Something that is **greenish** is slightly green. *...a greenish blue.*

Greenland /griːnlənd/
Greenland is a self-governing territory of Denmark in the Arctic Ocean, north-east of Canada. It is the world's largest island. Only one-sixth of Greenland is ice-free and habitable. Fishing is the main industry.
♦ **Greenlander** /griːnləndə/ N **Greenlandic** /griːnlændɪk/ ADJ
■ *per capita GNP:* US$8,780 ■ *religion:* Christianity (mainly Evangelical Lutheran) ■ *language:* Greenlandic and Danish (official) ■ *currency:* Danish krone ■ *capital:* Nuuk ■ *population:* 56,000 (1990) ■ *size:* 2,175,600 square kilometres.

green light
N SING If someone gives you the **green light** to do something, they give you permission to do it. *Congress has just given the green light to go ahead with the plan... The British Foreign Secretary, Mr Douglas Hurd, told the BBC the resolution was not a green light for war.*

Green Paper, Green Papers
NC In Britain, a **Green Paper** is a document containing ideas about a particular subject; it is published by the Government so that people can discuss the ideas before any decisions are made. *A government Green Paper published later today will outline far-reaching changes to the probation service... The proposals are in the form of a Green Paper discussion document.*

Green Party
N PROP The **Green Party** is a political party that is particularly concerned about protecting the environment. *They've had strong pressures put upon them by the environmental lobby and indeed by the Green Party in their parliament.*

green pepper, green peppers
NC A **green pepper** is an unripe pepper that is used in cooking or eaten raw in salads. *Cook the onions, green pepper and tomatoes, and mix that in there too.*

green revolution
N SING The **green revolution** is the increase in agricultural production in developing countries that has been made possible by the use of new types of crops and new farming methods. *...India's green revolution, which enabled a great leap in agricultural productivity.*

greenroom /griːnruːm, griːnrʊm/ **greenrooms**
NC The **greenroom** is a room in a theatre or television studio where performers can rest. *We were standing in the greenroom after the concert.*

green salad, green salads
NCorNU A **green salad** is a salad made mainly with lettuce and other green vegetables.

greenstuff /griːnstʌf/
NU **Greenstuff** is green vegetables that are used for food.

Greenwich Mean Time /grɛnɪtʃ miːn taɪm/. See GMT.

greet /griːt/ **greets, greeting, greeted**
1 vo When you **greet** someone, you express friendliness or pleasure when you meet them, or when they arrive somewhere, for example by saying 'hello' or by shaking their hand. *His eldest daughter was there to greet him... Tens of thousands of Hungarians turned out to greet Mr Bush as he arrived in Budapest.*
2 voa If you **greet** something in a particular way, you react to it in that way. *The news will be greeted with shock and surprise.*
3 vo If something **greets** you, it is the first thing you notice in a place; used in written English. *The smell of coffee greeted us as we entered.*

greeting /griːtɪŋ/ **greetings**
NCorNU A **greeting** is something friendly that you say or do on meeting someone. *...a friendly greeting... Families come to the fence and shout greetings to each other... She smiled in greeting.*

greetings card, greetings cards
NC A **greetings card**, or, in American English, a **greeting card**, is a folded card with a picture on the front and greetings inside that you give or send to someone, for example on their birthday. *Thank you for the anniversary greetings card.*

gregarious /grəgɛəriəs/
ADJ Someone who is **gregarious** enjoys being with other people. *...somebody who is gregarious, outgoing, an extrovert.*

gremlin /grɛmlɪn/ **gremlins**
NC A **gremlin** is a tiny imaginary evil spirit that people say is the cause of a problem, especially in a machine, which they cannot explain properly or locate. *Engineers have conquered the gremlins that have plagued front-wheel drive cars.*

Grenada /grəneɪdə/
The State of **Grenada** is a country in the Caribbean. It was a British colony from 1762 to 1974. In 1983 the assassination of the Prime Minister, Maurice Bishop, led to the invasion of Grenada by troops from the US and Caribbean countries. Nicholas Brathwaite, of the National Democratic Congress (NDC), became Prime Minister in 1990. Grenada is a member of the Commonwealth and the Organization of American States. It is the second largest producer of nutmeg in the world. Tourism is an expanding industry.
♦ **Grenadian** /grəneɪdiən/ N, ADJ
▪ *per capita GNP:* US$1,370 ▪ *religion:* Christianity (mainly Roman Catholic) ▪ *language:* English ▪ *currency:* East Caribbean dollar ▪ *capital:* St George's ▪ *population:* 102,000 (1988) ▪ *size:* 344 square kilometres.

grenade /grəneɪd/ **grenades**
NC A **grenade** is a small bomb that can be thrown by hand. *A grenade has exploded inside the police headquarters in Londonderry... Unknown attackers threw a hand grenade and fired shots.*

grew /gruː/
Grew is the past tense of **grow**.

grey /greɪ/ **greyer, greyest**; spelt **gray** in American English.
1 ADJ Something that is **grey** is the colour of ashes or of clouds on a rainy day. *...a grey suit. ...the grey-haired driver.*
2 ADJ If someone is going **grey**, their hair is becoming grey. *She went grey in about a year.*
3 ADJ If someone looks **grey**, they look pale and ill. *He had gone grey and his hands trembled slightly.*
♦ **greyness** NU *There was an awful greyness about his face.*
4 ADJ You can describe someone or something as **grey** if you consider that they are rather boring and unattractive, and very similar to other people or things. *He's always appeared in the past as a rather grey, cautious figure. ...this grim, grey city.*
5 ADJ If the weather is **grey**, the sky is very cloudy and the light is dull. *It's very gray and very gloomy.*
6 See also **greying**.

grey area, grey areas
NC A **grey area** is an aspect of something that people

are not sure how to deal with because it is not clearly defined or because there is not enough information about it. *The book is an attempt to cast some light on a very grey area. ...a mechanism for dealing with what he called the 'grey area of political prisoners'.*

greyhound /greɪhaʊnd/ **greyhounds**
NC A **greyhound** is a kind of dog that has a thin body and long thin legs and that can run very fast. *...his pet greyhound... Greyhound racing is no longer necessarily the domain of the working class.*

greying /greɪɪŋ/; spelt **graying** in American English.
ADJ Someone who has **greying** hair or who is **greying** has hair that is going grey. *His graying hair is cut short... He's tall, greying, very tanned and very handsome.*

greyish /greɪɪʃ/; spelt **grayish** in American English.
ADJ Something that is **greyish** is slightly grey. *It was bluish, greyish, in colour.*

grid /grɪd/ **grids**
1 NC A **grid** is a pattern of straight lines that cross over each other to form squares. *...a grid of small streets.*
2 N+N **Grid** maps have a grid drawn over them. The lines are numbered, so that you can refer to any place on the map by using the numbers of the lines. *Air-traffic controllers, for example, need to know not only the grid reference of aeroplanes, but also the altitude.*
3 NC A **grid** is also a large number of connecting power lines that transmit electricity over the whole of a particular country or area. *The plant will sell the electricity to area boards supplying the national grid. ...an agreement linking East Germany into the West German electricity grid. ...the possibility of setting up a regional grid.*

griddle /grɪdl/ **griddles**
NC A **griddle** is a round, flat, heavy piece of metal which is placed on a stove or fire and used for cooking.

gridlock /grɪdlɒk/; used in American English.
1 NU **Gridlock** is the situation that exists when all the roads in a particular place are full of vehicles which cannot move because there are too many of them. *Thousands of troops and civilians have been leaving the city, causing gridlock and other problems... We were stuck there in gridlock for 45 minutes... We left at eleven and ran into an immediate gridlock of people fleeing north.*
2 NU **Gridlock** is also a state of affairs in an argument or dispute in which neither side is willing to give in, and so no agreement can be reached. *...a sort of political gridlock, a mutual veto power over any change in the status quo... We're asking them to get the UN system to work, which is presently at gridlock.*

grief /griːf/
1 NU **Grief** is extreme sadness. *That helped to ease his grief.*
2 If someone or something **comes to grief**, they fail or are harmed. *I ran away once but came to grief.*

grief-stricken
ADJ If someone is **grief-stricken**, they are extremely sad about something that has happened. *She had looked so utterly grief-stricken. ...the grief-stricken widow.*

grievance /griːvns/ **grievances**
1 NC A **grievance** is a complaint that you make about something which you feel is unfair. *They may well have a genuine grievance... We wish you to continue to work and use the laid-down grievance procedures so that we can resolve this dispute.*
2 NCorNU A **grievance** is also a feeling that something that has been done is unfair. *Now it seems as though the same old grievances which have bedevilled attempts to resolve the problem have not gone away... He seems still to be harbouring a deep sense of grievance against the President for allegedly misrepresenting him.*

grieve /griːv/ **grieves, grieving, grieved**
1 v If you **grieve**, you feel very sad about something that has happened. *She was grieving for the dead baby.*
2 vo If something **grieves** you, it makes you feel very sad. *I was grieved to hear that he had been captured.*

grievous /ɡriːvəs/
ADJ Something that is **grievous** is extremely serious or worrying in its effects; a formal word. ...*a grievous mistake.* ◆ **grievously** ADV *He had been grievously wounded.*

grievous bodily harm
NU If someone is accused of **grievous bodily harm**, they are accused of causing very serious physical injury to someone; a legal expression. ...*assault with intent to commit grievous bodily harm.*

grill /ɡrɪl/ **grills, grilling, grilled**
1 V-ERG When you **grill** food, you cook it using strong heat directly above or below it. *I usually grill or fry beef... She put the breakfast sausages on to grill.* ◆ **grilled** ADJ ...*a grilled chop.*
2 NC A **grill** is a part of a cooker where food is cooked by strong heat from above. *Heat just the surface of the food, under a grill or in a pan... Arrange the slices on the grill pan.*
3 NC A **grill** is also a flat frame of metal bars on which you cook food over a fire. *On the patio outside, the barbecue grill is sizzling.*
4 NC A **grill** is also a dish which consists of food that has been grilled. *I asked for a mixed grill.*
5 VO If you **grill** someone, you ask them a lot of questions in an intense way; an informal use. *At the police station, she was grilled for twenty-four hours.*

grille /ɡrɪl/ **grilles**
NC A **grille** is a framework of metal bars or wire that is placed in front of a window or a piece of machinery, for protection. ...*steel shutters on the windows, steel grilles on the doors. ...the air-conditioning grille.*

grim /ɡrɪm/ **grimmer, grimmest**
1 ADJ A situation or news that is **grim** is unpleasant and makes people feel unhappy or pessimistic. ...*the grim aftermath of World War I. ...the grim facts.*
2 ADJ A **grim** place is unattractive and depressing. *The new housing blocks are austere and grim. ...grim dormitory towns with block after block of drab municipal housing.*
3 ADJ If someone is **grim**, they are very serious or stern. ...*his grim determination not to cry. ...grim-faced guards.* ◆ **grimly** ADV *'Smoke,' Eddie announced grimly.*

grimace /ɡrɪmeɪs, ɡrɪməs/ **grimaces, grimacing, grimaced**
NC A **grimace** is a twisted, ugly expression on your face that shows you are displeased, disgusted, or in pain. *Thomas made a little grimace. Perhaps he thought the wine was sour.* ► Also V *She made a bad gear-change and grimaced.*

grime /ɡraɪm/
NU **Grime** is dirt on the surface of something. *The windows were thick with grime.*

grimy /ɡraɪmi/
ADJ Something that is **grimy** is very dirty. ...*a grimy office.*

grin /ɡrɪn/ **grins, grinning, grinned**
1 V If you **grin**, you smile broadly. *He grinned at her.* ► Also NC *The pilot was unhurt and climbed out with a cheerful grin.*
2 If you **grin and bear it**, you accept a difficult or unpleasant situation without complaining; an informal expression. *I'd just have to grin and bear it for the next two hours.*

grind /ɡraɪnd/ **grinds, grinding, ground**
1 VO When something such as corn or coffee is **ground**, it is crushed until it becomes a fine powder. *She has been especially interested in introducing mills for grinding maize. ...freshly ground black pepper.*
2 VOA If you **grind** something into a surface, you press it hard into the surface. *He ground his cigarette in the ashtray.*
3 VO If you **grind** the edge of something, you make it smooth or sharp by pressing it against a hard surface or on a machine. *There was a knife being ground on a wheel.*
4 V If a machine **grinds**, it makes a harsh scraping noise. *The lift grinds in the shaft.*
5 N SING You can refer to tiring, boring, and routine work as the **grind**. ...*the long and tiresome grind of preparing themselves for college entrance.*

6 to **grind to a halt**: see **halt**. See also **grinding, ground.**

grind down PHRASAL VERB If you **grind** someone **down**, you treat them very harshly, so that they do not have the will to resist you. *They sought an end to the socialist system that had ground them down and made their country one of the poorest in the world... Morale has been ground down further by continuous warnings.*

grind up PHRASAL VERB If you **grind** something **up**, you crush it until it becomes a fine powder, especially in a machine. *They dry the grain, then they grind it up and make flour out of it.*

grinder /ɡraɪndə/ **grinders**
NC A **grinder** is a machine or device which crushes something into small pieces. ...*a coffee grinder.*

grinding /ɡraɪndɪŋ/
ADJ ATTRIB **Grinding** describes a situation that never seems to change, and makes you feel unhappy, tired, or bored. ...*grinding poverty.*

grindstone /ɡraɪndstəʊn/ **grindstones**
1 NC A **grindstone** is a large round stone that turns like a wheel and is used for sharpening knives and tools or for grinding grain. *At first people had no grindstones and complained that they had to eat their food raw because they couldn't make it into flour.*
2 If you keep your **nose to the grindstone**, you work very hard all the time. *They are going to have to get their noses to the grindstone... Everybody's nose was to the grindstone here.*

gringo /ɡrɪŋɡəʊ/ **gringos**
NC **Gringo** is sometimes used by people from Spain and Latin America to refer to foreigners, especially people from the United States or Britain; an offensive word. ...*crowds shouting, 'Gringos out of Honduras.'*

grip /ɡrɪp/ **grips, gripping, gripped**
1 VO If you **grip** something, you take hold of it with your hand and continue to hold it firmly. *Lomax gripped the boy's arm.* ► Also NC *I tightened my grip on the handrail.*
2 N SING+SUPP A **grip** on someone or something is control over them. *He now took a firm grip on the management side of the newspaper... She felt herself in the grip of a sadness she could not understand.*
3 VO If something **grips** you, it suddenly affects you strongly. *He seemed to be gripped by a powerful desire to laugh.*
4 VO If you **are gripped** by something, your attention is concentrated on it. *I was really gripped by the first few pages.* ◆ **gripping** ADJ ...*a gripping film.*
● **Grip** is used in these phrases. ● If you **get** or **come to grips with** a problem, you start taking action to deal with it. *It's taken us eighteen years to get to grips with our inadequacies.* ● If you **are losing** your **grip**, you are becoming less able to deal with things. *He seems to be losing his grip.*

gripe /ɡraɪp/ **gripes, griping, griped**
V If you **gripe** about something, you keep complaining about it; an informal word. *Farmers often gripe about outsiders, especially foreigners, buying farmland in their area.*

griping /ɡraɪpɪŋ/
ADJ ATTRIB A **griping** pain is a sudden, stabbing pain in your stomach or bowels.

grisly /ɡrɪzli/
ADJ Something that is **grisly** is extremely nasty and horrible. ...*a grisly experiment. ...the grisly proof of our inhumanity.*

grist /ɡrɪst/
If you say that something is **grist to the mill**, you mean that it is something that it is useful for a particular purpose. *All this conflict was grist to the mill for the various Left groups.*

gristle /ɡrɪsl/
NU **Gristle** is a tough, rubbery substance found in meat. *Cheaper beefburgers contain a high proportion of fat, gristle and other substances.*

gristly /ɡrɪsəli/
ADJ Meat that is **gristly** has a lot of gristle in it.

grit /ɡrɪt/ **grits, gritting, gritted**
1 NU **Grit** consists of tiny pieces of stone. *High winds had blown grit onto the track.*
2 VO If people **grit** a road, they put grit on it to make

it less slippery in icy or snowy weather.

3 NU If you say that someone has **grit**, you mean that they have determination and courage. *He said Mr Bush was a man of strength, vision and true grit.* ● Grit is used in these phrases. ● If you **grit** your **teeth**, you press your upper and lower teeth together. *She nodded at me sternly. I gritted my teeth, but she didn't notice my anger.* ● If you **grit** your **teeth** in a difficult situation, you decide to carry on. *'You just had to sort of, you know, grit your teeth and bear it.'*

gritty /grɪti/
ADJ Something that is **gritty** is covered with grit or has a texture like grit. *...the gritty carpet.*

grizzle /grɪzl/ **grizzles, grizzling, grizzled**; an informal word.
1 V If a baby or child **grizzles**, it keeps crying and whining. *The baby grizzles all night.*
2 V If someone **grizzles**, they continuously complain about something in a whining manner. *Rhoda was grizzling because she had lost.*

grizzled /grɪzld/
ADJ A **grizzled** person or a person with **grizzled** hair has hair that is grey or streaked with grey. *...a grizzled beard.*

grizzly /grɪzli/ **grizzlies**
NC A **grizzly** or a **grizzly bear** is a large, fierce, greyish-brown bear which lives in western North America. *The area is crucial for wildlife populations, including the federally protected grizzly bear... Two grizzly bear cubs are in need of a permanent home.*

groan /grəʊn/ **groans, groaning, groaned**
1 V,V-QUOTE,or VA If you **groan**, you make a long, low sound of pain, unhappiness or disapproval. *I could hear her crying out in pain, gasping and groaning... 'This was one of the longest days of my life,' he groaned... I remember groaning at the realization that I had entirely wasted my prime.* ► Also NC *A chorus of groans greeted his joke.*
2 V If wood **groans**, it makes a loud creaking sound. *The wind roared, the trees groaned.*

grocer /grəʊsə/ **grocers**
1 NC A **grocer** is a person who sells foods such as flour, sugar, and tinned foods, and some other products that people use in their homes. *The second measure is backed by farm groups and grocers.*
2 NC A **grocer's** is a shop where you can buy foods such as flour, sugar, and tinned foods, and some other products that people use in their homes. *...growing from a small grocer's shop to a factory employing thousands.*

grocery /grəʊsəri/ **groceries**
1 NC In America, a grocer's shop is called a **grocery**. *This morning, the Red Apple Grocery Store was busy with customers. ...the Main Street grocery.*
2 N PL **Groceries** are foods such as flour, sugar, and tinned foods. *...a shopping-basket containing groceries. ...supplies of fruit and vegetables and other groceries.*

grog /grɒg/
NU **Grog** is a drink made by diluting a strong spirit, such as rum or whisky, with water; an old-fashioned word. *He returned with two glasses of hot grog.*

groggy /grɒgi/
ADJ If you feel **groggy**, you feel weak and ill; an informal word. *I expect you're feeling a bit groggy with the injections.*

groin /grɔɪn/ **groins**
NC Your **groin** is the part of your body where your legs meet your abdomen. *He limped off the field after straining a groin muscle... Barnes has been having treatment for a groin injury.*

groom /gruːm/ **grooms, grooming, groomed**
1 NC A **groom** is a person who looks after horses in a stable.
2 NC A **groom** is also the same as a **bridegroom**. *The wedding feast went on until midnight but the bride and groom left before that.*
3 VO If you **groom** an animal, you brush its fur. *We helped to groom Brown's horse.*
4 VO If you **groom** a person for a special job, you prepare them by teaching them the skills they will need. *He was, in fact, never groomed for the political*

leadership... *I had been chosen to be groomed as editor... He has not groomed an obvious successor.*

groomed /gruːmd/
ADJ You use **groomed** after an adverb to describe someone's appearance. *Well groomed and imperturbable, he has the rare advantage of being untainted by scandal... The manager was a beautifully groomed young man.*

groove /gruːv/ **grooves**
NC A **groove** is a line cut into a surface. *...a steel plate with grooves cut in it.*

grooved /gruːvd/
ADJ Something that is **grooved** has grooves on its surface. *The upper jaw is deeply grooved.*

groovy /gruːvi/
ADJ Something that is **groovy** is attractive, fashionable, or exciting; an informal, old-fashioned word. *It's quite a groovy game, actually.*

grope /grəʊp/ **gropes, groping, groped**
1 V A If you **grope** for something that you cannot see, you search for it with your hands. *I groped for the timetable I had in my pocket.*
2 VOA If you **grope** your way to a place, you move there using your hands to feel the way because you cannot see anything. *I groped my way out of bed and downstairs.*
3 V A If you **grope** for something such as the solution to a problem, you try to think of it, when you have no real idea what it could be. *We are groping for ways to get the communities together.*

gross /grəʊs/ **grosser, grossest; grosses, grossing, grossed.** The form **gross** is both the singular and the plural of the noun. The form **grosses** is the third person singular, present tense, of the verb.
1 ADJ ATTRIB You use **gross** to describe something which is unacceptable or unpleasant and which is very great in amount or degree. *...children whose parents are guilty of gross neglect.* ◆ **grossly** ADV *They were both grossly overweight.*
2 ADJ Speech or behaviour that is **gross** shows lack of taste, or is very rude. *He felt he had said something gross, indecent.*
3 ADJ Something that is **gross** is very large and ugly. *...the gross architecture of the Piccadilly frontages.*
4 ADJ ATTRIBor ADV **Gross** is used to describe a total amount of something, after all relevant amounts have been added but before any deductions have been made. *His gross income will very likely exceed $900,000 this year... She earns £20,000 gross.*
5 ADJ ATTRIBor ADV **Gross** describes the total weight of something, including its container. *...8,000 merchant ships with a gross tonnage of 20 million... It weighs 12kg gross.*
6 VO If a person or something such as a business **grosses** a particular amount of money, that is the total amount of money they earn before any deductions have been made. *His mail order business selling T-shirts grosses around a million dollars a year... The sale grossed at least two-thirds more than the auctioneers had reckoned.*
7 NC A **gross** is a group of 144 things. *He bought them by the gross.*

gross national product
NUorN SING In economics, the **gross national product** is the total value of all the goods produced and services provided by a country in one year. *Official aid increased both in value and as a share of gross national product... He announced a 6.1% increase in the Gross National Product.*

grotesque /grəʊtesk/
1 ADJ Something that is **grotesque** is exaggerated, and is ridiculous or frightening. *...grotesque comedy.* ◆ **grotesquely** ADV *I knew I had been perfectly ridiculous, over-acting grotesquely.*
2 ADJ **Grotesque** also means very ugly. *...grotesque figures carved into the stonework.*

grotto /grɒtəʊ/ **grottoes or grottos**
NC A **grotto** is a small attractive cave. *...a landscaped park with grottoes and streams and mini-waterfalls throughout. ...ancient wall paintings in Buddhist grottos.*

grotty /grɒti/
ADJ Something that is **grotty** is unpleasant or of poor quality; an informal word. *...a grotty little building.*

grouch /grautʃ/ **grouches, grouching, grouched**; an informal word.
1 V If you **grouch**, you complain about something in a bad-tempered way. *He is always grouching about his children.*
2 NC A **grouch** is someone who is always complaining in a bad-tempered way. *I am a grouch before my first cup of coffee.*

grouchy /grautʃi/
ADJ Someone who is **grouchy** is bad-tempered and complains a lot; an informal word. *He was a miserable grouchy man. ...a grouchy old woman.*

ground /graund/ **grounds, grounding, grounded**
1 N SING The **ground** is the surface of the Earth. *He set down his bundle carefully on the ground.*
2 NU **Ground** is land. *...a rocky piece of ground. ...a patch of waste ground near the airport.*
3 NC+SUPP A **ground** is an area of land which is used for a particular purpose. *He was taken to an army training ground where he saw a mock battle. ...a burial ground. ...football grounds.*
4 N PL The **grounds** of a building are the land which surrounds it and belongs with it. *...the school grounds.*
5 NC A **ground** is an electrical wire which allows current to pass from an appliance into the ground. It makes the appliance safe even when there is something wrong with it; used in American English. *...ground wires.*
6 NU+SUPP You can also use **ground** to refer to a subject or range of things when you are considering it as an area to be covered or dealt with. *This course covers the same ground as the undergraduate degree in Social Administration.*
7 N PL+SUPP Something that is **grounds** for something else is a reason or justification for it. *It's less likely that he will ever be allowed back to his homeland, even on compassionate grounds... You have no real grounds for complaint.*
8 NU If you gain **ground**, you make progress or get an advantage. If you lose **ground**, you find yourself at a disadvantage. *Godley's views are gaining political ground... His party is losing ground to its more nationalist opponents... He tried to regain lost ground.*
9 NU+SUPP or NC+SUPP You also use **ground** to refer to a place or situation in which particular ideas, attitudes, or organizations can develop and be successful. *This very English corner of South Wales is not fertile ground for the Welsh nationalists... This diversity is fertile ground for different perspectives to flourish... The waterlogged city is a potential breeding ground for disease.*
10 N+N **Ground** is also used to describe people or things that operate or are found on the surface of the Earth, rather than in the air. *Both airports have been hit by a strike by ground staff. ...pulses of radio waves beamed into the sky from a ground station. ...the Commander-in-Chief of the Soviet ground forces.*
11 VO If aircraft or pilots **are grounded**, they are not allowed to fly. *Eastern Airlines grounded all of its flights as of midnight last night... The space shuttle fleet has been grounded since May.*
12 VOA If an argument or opinion **is grounded** in or on something, it is based on that thing. *...a delusion grounded in fear.*
13 **Ground** is also the past tense and past participle of **grind**.
• **Ground** is used in these phrases. • **On grounds of, on the grounds of,** and **on the grounds that** introduce the reason for a particular action. *He was always declining their invitations on grounds of ill health.*
• When you talk about what is happening **on the ground,** you are talking about what is really happening in a situation, rather than what the people who are in control are saying or thinking about it. *Whatever may be happening on the ground, the authorities deny an official policy of expulsions... The question is whether a new agreement between top politicians can still be made to work on the ground.* • If you **go to ground,** you hide somewhere for a period of time. *All the*

people involved have gone to ground in cheap hotels.
• If you **run** something **to ground,** you find it after a long, difficult search. *It was run to ground in the nearby woods.* • If you **break fresh ground** or **break new ground,** you make a discovery or start a new activity. *The programme broke fresh ground for the Soviet media... A frame on this scale has never been tried before so we've really broken new ground.* • If you **get** something **off the ground,** you get it started. *There was a hurry to get the new film off the ground.*
• If you **stand** your **ground** or **hold** your **ground** when people are opposing you, you do not retreat or do not accept something that you do not want to accept. *Most sides in the conflict seem to be holding their ground... He stood his ground to the last.* • If you **give ground** when people are opposing you, you retreat or accept something that you do not want to accept. *The German government is unlikely to give ground on this question. ...a stubborn refusal to give any ground.*
• to **have** your **ear to the ground:** see **ear.** • **thin on the ground:** see **thin.** • See also **common ground, home ground.**

groundcloth /graundklɒθ/ **groundcloths**
NC A **groundcloth** is the same as a **groundsheet**; used in American English.

ground floor
1 N SING In Britain, the **ground floor** of a building is the floor that is level with the ground outside. *The fire broke out among the archives on the ground floor... These are the ground floor rooms that are actually underneath the gallery.*
2 If you **get in on the ground floor,** you get involved in an activity when it is just beginning, so that you have a very good chance of succeeding. *You can participate in this exciting new industry and have the opportunity to make hundreds of thousands of dollars by getting in on the ground floor now.*

grounding /graundɪŋ/
N SING A **grounding** in a subject is instruction in the basic facts or principles of it. *Schools must provide a firm grounding in the basics—reading, writing, arithmetic.*

groundless /graundləs/
ADJ A fear or suspicion that is **groundless** is not based on reason or evidence. *Your fears are groundless... His allegations, when investigated, proved groundless.*

ground level
NU **Ground level** is used to refer to the ground or to the floor of a building which is at the same level as the ground. *The trees are sliced right down to ground level before planting takes place... The moisture seems to have been caused by faulty plumbing at ground level.*

groundnut /graundnʌt/ **groundnuts**
NC A **groundnut** is the same as a **peanut.** *The farmers' price for groundnuts, Senegal's chief export crop, was being reduced by more than twenty percent.*

ground plan, ground plans
1 NC A **ground plan** is a plan of the ground floor of a building.
2 NC You can refer to a basic plan for future action as a **ground plan.**

ground rent, ground rents
NU or NC **Ground rent** is rent which is paid by the owner of a flat or house to the owner of the land on which it is built. *Ground rents in London can be nearly twenty times higher than in Wales.*

ground rules
N PL The **ground rules** for something are the basic principles on which future action will be based. *They sat down to work out the ground rules for the project.*

groundsheet /graundʃiːt/ **groundsheets**
NC A **groundsheet** is a piece of waterproof material that you put on the ground to sleep on when you are camping. *There were groundsheets, waterproofed sleeping bags, a paraffin lamp, a small stove and a barbecue set.*

groundsman /graundzmən/ **groundsmen** /graundzmən/
NC A **groundsman** is a person whose job is to look after a park or sports ground. *The groundsman spotted smoke and flames but was unable to prevent the flames spreading to the rear of the stand.*

ground staff
N COLL **Ground staff** are people who are paid to maintain a sports ground. *As usual, the ground staff have done a magnificent job.*

groundswell /ˈgraʊndswel/
N SING+SUPP A **groundswell** is the rapid growth of a feeling or opinion about something in a society or group of people. *There was a groundswell of outrage against him. ...the groundswell of opinion against reform.*

ground-to-air
ADJ ATTRIB **Ground-to-air** missiles are fired from the ground at aeroplanes and other missiles, rather than at targets on the ground. *The plane was hit by a ground-to-air missile... What do the Angolans have in the way of ground-to-air defences?*

groundwork /ˈgraʊndwɜːk/
N SING If you do the **groundwork** on something, you do the early work which forms the basis for further work. *They had already provided the groundwork for economic progress.*

group /gruːp/ groups, grouping, grouped
1 N COLL A **group** is a number of people or things which are together in one place at one time. *...a group of buildings. ...standing in a group in the centre of the room.*
2 N COLL+SUPP A **group** is a set of people or things which have something in common. *...children of his age group. ...a parents' action group.* ● See also blood group, peer group, pressure group.
3 N COLL A **group** is also a number of musicians who perform pop music together. *...a personal appearance by the group's original bass player.*
4 N COLL A **group** is also a number of separate firms that all have the same owner. *The Dolphin Group— which is London based—has subsidiaries in Kenya and India.*
5 V OA When you **group** a number of things or people in a particular way, you arrange them in one or more sets or places. *Researchers noticed that they could group the cells into two sorts... The changes involve a reduction in the number of portfolios, with several former ministries grouped together... The 700 participants from around the world grouped themselves into various committees... The remaining forces would surrender their arms and be grouped in camps.*
group together PHRASAL VERB If people **group together**, they come together in one place or within one organization or system, often in order to achieve a particular aim. *The survivors grouped together, hampered by wreckage... They encouraged workers and consumers to group together.*

groupie /ˈgruːpi/ groupies
N C A **groupie** is someone who is very keen on a particular pop group, singer, or other famous person, and follows them around and tries to meet them; an informal word. *...the legions of groupies that stuck to the sensual, poetic and alcoholic lead singer.*

grouping /ˈgruːpɪŋ/ groupings
N C+SUPP A **grouping** of people or things is a set of them with something in common. *Communists in Yugoslavia's biggest republic have formed a new political grouping. ...a new opposition grouping whose formation was announced yesterday.*

group practice, group practices
N C A **group practice** is a small organization of doctors who work together in the same place.

group therapy
N U **Group therapy** is a form of psychiatric treatment in which people discuss their problems with each other in a group. *Social worker Ken Eugafusa leads group therapy sessions for juvenile sex offenders.*

grouse /graʊs/ grouses, grousing, groused. The form **grouse** is both the singular and the plural of the noun. The form **grouses** is the third person singular, present tense, of the verb.
1 N C A **grouse** is a kind of small fat bird. Grouse are often shot for sport and can be eaten. *In recent years the hunting of game birds such as grouse and pheasant has had to be restricted. ...a day's grouse shooting.*

2 V, V-REPORT, or V-QUOTE If you **grouse**, you complain. *It was a sad end to her career but she never grumbled or groused... US chip makers have long groused that Japanese companies resist buying American chips, even when they're technologically superior... 'They don't have to do it every week,' groused Carl.*

grove /grəʊv/ groves
N C A **grove** is a group of trees that are close together. *...an olive grove.*

grovel /ˈgrɒvl/ grovels, grovelling, grovelled; spelt groveling, groveled in American English.
1 V If you **grovel**, you behave very humbly towards someone because you think they are important; used showing disapproval. *They are going to make you grovel.* ◆ **grovelling** ADJ *He sent a letter of grovelling apology to the publisher.*
2 V A To **grovel** also means to crawl on the floor, for example in order to find something. *He was grovelling under his desk for a dropped pencil.*

grow /grəʊ/ grows, growing, grew, grown
1 V If something **grows**, it increases in size, amount or degree. *Babies who are small at birth grow faster... Jobs in industry will grow by 11 per cent... As tension grew in Moscow, the Secretary General of the United Nations issued an urgent appeal for restraint.*
2 V If a plant or tree **grows** in a particular place, it is alive there. *An oak tree grew at the edge of the lane.*
3 V O When you **grow** plants, you put them in the ground and look after them as they develop. *The district grew peas on a large scale.*
4 V If you **grow** your hair, you do not cut it and it gradually becomes longer.
5 V O If a man **grows** a beard or a moustache, he lets it develop by not shaving. *People began to say 'It's quite nice to see you clean-shaven,' and so I never grew a beard again.*
6 V A, V C, or V+to-INF If something **grows** into a particular state, it changes gradually until it is in that state. *Small ailments left unchecked grow into larger problems... The sun grew so hot that they were forced to stop working... I grew to dislike working for the cinema.*
7 V If one idea **grows** out of another, it develops from it. *My own idea grew out of seeing this film.*
8 See also **grown**.
grow apart PHRASAL VERB If people **grow apart**, they gradually begin to have different interests and opinions from each other. *My siblings and I started growing apart.*
grow into PHRASAL VERB When children **grow into** a piece of clothing that is too big for them, they get bigger so that it fits them properly. *It's a bit big, but she'll soon grow into it.*
grow on PHRASAL VERB If something **grows on** you, you start to like it more and more; an informal expression. *She was someone whose charm grew very slowly on you.*
grow out of PHRASAL VERB 1 If you **grow out of** a type of behaviour or an interest, especially one that people consider is childish or immature, you stop behaving in that way or having that interest. *He'll grow out of it.* 2 When children **grow out of** a piece of clothing, they become so big that it no longer fits them. *It cost a small fortune and she grew out of it in three months.*
grow up PHRASAL VERB 1 When someone **grows up**, they gradually change from being a child into being an adult. *They grew up in the early days of television.* 2 If you tell someone to **grow up**, you are telling them to stop behaving in a childish or silly way; an informal use. 3 When something such as an idea or organization **grows up**, it starts to exist and becomes more important or larger. *The idea has grown up that science cannot be wrong... The Afghan resistance grew up around local commanders.* 4 See also **grown-up**.

grower /ˈgrəʊə/ growers
N C A **grower** is a person who grows large quantities of a particular plant or crop in order to sell them. *...a British lily grower... Growers in the southern counties were making large profits.*

growing pains
N PL **Growing pains** are the temporary difficulties and

problems that an organization has when it starts to exist, or starts to develop. *...a company's growing pains.*

growing season, growing seasons
NC The **growing season** in a particular country or area is the period in each year when the weather and temperature is usually right for plants and crops to be able to grow. *If rains are late, the growing season is cut short.*

growl /graʊl/ **growls, growling, growled**
1 v When an animal **growls**, it makes a low rumbling noise, usually because it is angry. *The dog growled at me.* ▶ Also NC *He did not hear the growl of the leopard.*
2 v or V-QUOTE If someone **growls**, they use a low, rough, rather angry voice. *He growled in frustration... 'There's a visitor here,' he growled.* ▶ Also NC *'Yeah,' said John in a low growl.*

grown /grəʊn/
1 **Grown** is the past participle of **grow**.
2 ADJ ATTRIB A **grown** man or woman is an adult. *I have two grown daughters and a teenage son... As a grown man, he wrote about his experiences.*

grown-up, grown-ups
1 NC Children often refer to adults as **grown-ups**. *Until the grown-ups come to fetch us we'll have fun.*
2 ADJ Someone who is **grown-up** is no longer a child. *...older couples with grown-up children.*
3 ADJ You also describe someone as **grown-up** when they behave in an adult way, especially if he or she is, in fact, still a child. *Your brother's awfully grown-up for his age.*

growth /grəʊθ/ **growths**
1 NU+SUPP The **growth** of something is its increase or development in size, wealth, or importance. *...India's population growth... Its economic growth rate is second only to Japan's. ...the growth of political opposition.*
2 NU **Growth** in a person, animal, or plant is the process of increasing in size and development. *He noticed that this drug seemed to inhibit bacterial growth.*
3 NC A **growth** is an abnormal lump that grows inside or on a person, animal, or plant. *Malignant cancerous growths are stiffer than ordinary healthy organs. ...conventional ways of treating these growths.*

grub /grʌb/ **grubs, grubbing, grubbed**
1 NC A **grub** is a worm-like young insect which has just come out of an egg. *It taps away at tree bark, and then picks out the grubs that it finds.*
2 NU **Grub** is food; an informal use. *I don't like going without my grub.*
3 v A If you **grub** about for something, you search for it by moving things or digging. *The fish grubs around on the river bed.*

grubby /grʌbi/ **grubbier, grubbiest**
ADJ Something that is **grubby** is rather dirty; an informal word. *...their grubby hands.*

grudge /grʌdʒ/ **grudges, grudging, grudged**
1 NC If you have a **grudge** against someone, you have unfriendly feelings towards them because they have harmed you in the past. *They had to do it, and I bear them no grudge... It isn't in her nature to hold grudges.*
2 v OO or VO+*to* If you **grudge** someone something, you give it to them unwillingly or are not pleased that they have it. *We need not grudge them their mindless pleasures... Not that I grudge the use of my kitchen to you.*

grudging /grʌdʒɪŋ/
ADJ A **grudging** feeling or response is one that you feel or make very unwillingly. *Others stood watching with grudging respect... It does appear to mark a grudging realisation by the authorities that some concessions may be necessary.* ◆ **grudgingly** ADV *'Okay,' he said grudgingly, 'I suppose I was to blame.'*

gruel /gruːəl/
NU **Gruel** is a cheap food made by boiling something such as oats with water or milk. *He drank several teaspoons of vegetable gruel. ...rice gruel with milk and sugar.*

gruelling /gruːəlɪŋ/; spelt **grueling** in American English.
ADJ Something that is **gruelling** is extremely difficult and tiring. *I was exhausted after a gruelling week.*

gruesome /gruːsəm/
ADJ Something that is **gruesome** involves death or injury and is very shocking. *...gruesome tales of child murder.*

gruff /grʌf/
ADJ A **gruff** voice is low, rough, and unfriendly. *He hid his feelings behind a kind of gruff abruptness.* ◆ **gruffly** ADV *She said gruffly, 'Put on your clothes.'*

grumble /grʌmbl/ **grumbles, grumbling, grumbled**
V, V+*about*, V-REPORT, or V-QUOTE If you **grumble**, you complain about something, usually in a low voice and not forcefully. *The shoppers grumbled, of course, because they could no longer afford to hoard food... They will grumble about having to do the work... They grumble that the writers are not free to express themselves... 'It's awful,' Posy grumbled.* ▶ Also NC *There were angry grumbles from the British ranks.* ◆ **grumbling, grumblings** NU or N PL *Until that happens there will be lots of grumbling, and at best a grudging acceptance of the new methods... This demand is a reaction to grumblings in the ranks that activists are being left out of critical decisions.*

grumpy /grʌmpi/
ADJ A **grumpy** person is bad-tempered and miserable; an informal word. *Don't be so grumpy and cynical about it.*

grunt /grʌnt/ **grunts, grunting, grunted**
1 v If you **grunt**, you make a low, rough noise, usually because you are uninterested or disapproving. *His father looked up and grunted, then went back to his work.* ▶ Also NC *He gave a sceptical grunt.*
2 v When a pig **grunts**, it makes a low, rough noise. *Wild pigs grunted and snorted.* ▶ Also NC *It sounded like a pig's grunt.*

G-string /dʒiːstrɪŋ/ **G-strings**
NC A **G-string** is a narrow band of cloth that is worn between a person's legs to cover his or her sexual organs, and that is held up by a piece of string round the waist. *The law banning all public nudity requires that dancers wear at least a G-string.*

Guadeloupe /ɡwɑːdəluːp/
Guadeloupe is a territory of France in the Caribbean. The islands were settled by France in 1635. Bananas and sugar are exported. Tourism is an important industry. ◆ **Guadeloupian** /ɡwɑːdəluːpiən/ N **Guadeloupe** /ɡwɑːdəluːp/ ADJ
▪ *religion:* Christianity (mainly Roman Catholic)
▪ *language:* French (official), Creole ▪ *currency:* French franc ▪ *capital:* Basse-Terre ▪ *largest city:* Les Abymes ▪ *population:* 387,000 (1990) ▪ *size:* 1,780 square kilometres.

Guam /ɡwɑːm/
Guam is a self-governing territory of the United States in the Pacific. It is the largest of the Mariana Islands. Guam was a Spanish colony from 1565 until it was ceded to the United States in 1898. It was occupied by Japan from 1941 to 1944. Guam is an important military base and its economy is based on military spending and tourism. ◆ **Guamanian** /ɡwɑːmeɪniən/ N, ADJ
▪ *per capita GNP:* US$5,470 ▪ *religion:* Christianity (mainly Roman Catholic) ▪ *language:* English (official), Japanese, Chamorro ▪ *currency:* US dollar ▪ *capital:* Agaña ▪ *population:* 133,000 (1990) ▪ *size:* 549 square kilometres.

guano /ɡwɑːnəʊ/
NU **Guano** is the excrement of sea birds. It is used as a fertilizer. *...rich guano deposits.*

guarantee /ɡærəntiː/ **guarantees, guaranteeing, guaranteed**
1 v OO or VOO If one thing **guarantees** another, the first is certain to cause the second thing to happen. *This method guarantees success... Supporters argue that the pact will guarantee Canada's prosperity... His actions have guaranteed him a serious challenge in 1992.*
2 v O, v OO, V+*to*-INF, or V-REPORT If you **guarantee** something, you promise that it will definitely happen,

or that you will do it or provide it. *His personal safety should be guaranteed... They have guaranteed him some sort of award... They guarantee to hold interest rates down until next year... I'm not guaranteeing that this will work.*
3 V-PASS+*to*-INF If you say that something is **guaranteed** to happen, you mean that you are certain that it will happen. *This state of affairs is guaranteed to continue indefinitely.*
4 NC Something that is a **guarantee** of a particular thing makes it certain that it will happen or that it is true. *There is no guarantee that they are telling the truth... The jury system is one of the guarantees of democracy.*
5 NC A **guarantee** is also a promise that something will happen. *We want some guarantee that an enquiry will be held. ...guarantees of full employment.*
6 VO If a company **guarantees** a product or work that they do, they give a written promise that if it has any faults within a particular time it will be repaired, replaced, or redone free of charge.
7 NC A **guarantee** is also a written promise by a company that if a product or work that they do has any faults within a particular time, it will be repaired, replaced, or redone free of charge. *How long does the guarantee last?*
guarantor /gærəntɔː/ **guarantors**
NC A **guarantor** is a person who gives a guarantee or who is bound by one; a legal term. *Mr Gorbachov said Moscow was ready to serve as a guarantor. ...the army's role as guarantor of national security.*
guard /gɑːd/ **guards, guarding, guarded**
1 VO If you **guard** a place, person, or object, you watch them in order to protect them. *Scotland Yard sent an officer to guard his house.*
2 VO To **guard** someone also means to watch them in order to stop them from escaping. *She had been locked in her room and was guarded night and day.*
3 NCorN COLL A **guard** is a person or group of people that protect or watch someone or something. *When other guards noticed the escape, they opened fire... They will give him an armed guard.*
4 NC A **guard** is also a railway official on a train. *The guard blew his whistle.*
5 N PL The **Guards** is the name of some regiments in the British army. *...the Queen's Dragoon Guards.*
6 VO If you **guard** something important or secret, you protect or hide it. *The professions, as you might expect, guard their secrets closely.* ◆ **guarded** ADJ *The contents of the lists were a closely guarded secret.*
7 NC A **guard** is also a device which covers a dangerous part of something. *When the guard is taken off the motor the machine can't start.*
8 See also **guarded.**
● **Guard** is used in these phrases. ● If you **stand guard** over someone or something, you guard them. *You will be expected to stand guard over the village.*
● Someone who is **on guard** is responsible for guarding a particular place or person. *The trial opened under tight security with armed soldiers and riot police on guard.* ● If you are **on** your **guard**, you are being careful because a situation might become difficult or dangerous. *Busy parents have to be on their guard against being bad-tempered with their children.* ● If you **catch** someone **off guard**, you surprise them by doing something when they are not expecting it. *Privately senior ANC members have admitted they were caught off guard by the speed of recent events.*
guard against PHRASAL VERB If you **guard against** something, you are careful to avoid it happening or avoid being affected by it. *...ideas which the trained mind of a judge knows to guard against.*
guard dog, guard dogs
NC A **guard dog** is a fierce dog that has been specially trained to protect a particular place. *Meanwhile, police with guard dogs maintain an uneasy patrol in the prison precincts.*
guarded /gɑːdɪd/
1 ADJ Someone who is **guarded** is careful about what they say, either because they are not sure about something, or because they do not want to give away information. *There is guarded optimism about the*

future... Mr Hurd gave a guarded welcome to the President's statement... His statements were guarded.
◆ **guardedly** ADV *They only echo the views that have been expressed more guardedly by Mr Lawson... Officials there are guardedly optimistic.*
2 See also **guard.**
guardian /gɑːdiən/ **guardians**
1 NC A **guardian** is someone who has been legally appointed to look after a child. *He became the legal guardian of his brother's daughter.*
2 NC A **guardian** is also someone who is considered a protector or defender of things; a literary use. *...guardians of morality.*
guardian angel, guardian angels
NC A **guardian angel** is a spirit who is believed to protect and to guide a particular person. *Through a still and starry night we fly as if guided by guardian angels back to our husbands, our wives, our children, our friends.*
guardianship /gɑːdiənʃɪp/
NU **Guardianship** is the position of being a guardian. *She was placed under her mother's guardianship.*
guard-rail, guard-rails
NC A **guard-rail** is a railing that is sometimes placed along roads, paths, and staircases to protect people. *He walked past me and looked over the guard-rail.*
guardsman /gɑːdzmən/ **guardsmen** /gɑːdzmən/
NC A **guardsman** is a soldier who is a member of the Guards. *...the scarlet coats and bearskins of the guardsmen.*
guard's van, guard's vans
NC The **guard's van** of a train is a small carriage in which the guard travels. *We oughtn't to be in the guard's van at the back, we ought to be in the driver's cab at the front.*
Guatemala /gwætɪmɑːlə/
The **Republic of Guatemala** is a country in Central America. It was a Spanish colony from the 16th century, and became an independent Republic in 1839. Politics were dominated by the military until the restoration of civilian rule in 1986. Conflicts between the army and guerilla groups, most notably URNG (Guatemalan National Revolutionary Unity), remain a source of civil disorder and violence. Jorge Serrano Elías became President in 1991. He is a member of the Solidarity and Action Movement (MAS). Guatemala is a member of the Organization of American States. It exports coffee, bananas, and sugar. Large foreign debts and high inflation are serious economic problems. ◆ **Guatemalan** /gwætɪmɑːlən/ N, ADJ
▪ *per capita GNP:* US$920 ▪ *religion:* Christianity (mainly Roman Catholic) ▪ *language:* Spanish (official) ▪ *currency:* quetzal ▪ *capital:* Guatemala City ▪ *population:* 9 million (1990) ▪ *size:* 108,889 square kilometres.
Guatemala City /gwætɪmɑːlə sɪti/
Guatemala City is the capital of Guatemala and its largest city. Population: 754,000 (1981).
guava /gwɑːvə/ **guavas**
NC A **guava** is a round yellow tropical fruit with pink or white flesh and hard seeds. *The fruit trees used are mango and guava.*
Guayaquil /gwaɪækiːl/
Guayaquil is the largest city in Ecuador. Population: 1,764,000 (1990).
gubernatorial /guːbəʳnətɔːriəl/
ADJ **Gubernatorial** means relating to or connected with the post of governor. *He's seeking the Republican gubernatorial nomination.*
guerrilla /gərɪlə/ **guerrillas**; also spelt **guerilla.**
NC A **guerrilla** is a person who fights as part of an unofficial army, usually against an official army or police force. *The President repeated the government's desire to negotiate with the guerrillas... The guerrillas fired rockets and fire bombs at a police station and other buildings.* ▶ Also ADJ ATTRIB *This week, rival factions in Angola signed an agreement that could end 30 years of guerilla warfare.*
guess /ges/ **guesses, guessing, guessed**
1 V, V-REPORT, V A, or VO If you **guess** something, you give an answer or an opinion about something when you do not know whether it is correct. *It's not as severe as*

*you might guess... She guessed that she was fifty
yards from shore... We can only guess at the number
of deaths it has caused... It's impossible at this stage
to guess the number of casualties.*
2 V or VO You also say that you **guess** something when
you give the correct answer to a problem or question,
although you did not know the answer for certain.
*How did you guess?... I had guessed the identity of her
lover.*
3 NC A **guess** is an attempt to give the right answer to
something when you do not know what the answer is.
I don't know the name but I'll take a guess at it.
● **Guess** is used in these phrases. ● If you say that
something is **anyone's guess** or **anybody's guess**, you
mean that nobody can be certain about what will
really happen or what is really the case. *How this will
affect procedure is anyone's guess... What we shall
find at other sites is anybody's guess.* ● You say
'Guess what' to draw attention to something exciting,
surprising, or interesting that you are about to tell
someone. *Guess what, you're going to be a granny!*
● You say **I guess** to indicate that you think that
something is true or likely; used in informal American
English. *'What's that?'—'Some sort of blackbird, I
guess.'... 'Sure?'—'I guess so.'* ● If you **keep** someone
guessing, you do not tell them what they want to
know. *Throughout the year, he kept the world
guessing as to the date of the general election.*
guesstimate /gɛstɪmət/ **guesstimates, guesstimating,
guesstimated**; also spelt **guestimate**.
NC A **guesstimate** is an approximate calculation that
is based mainly or entirely on guesswork; an informal
word. *...Anglo's guesstimate of £17 million.* ▶ Also
VO *Analysts guesstimate their potential at about 2.5p
of earnings per share.*
guesswork /gɛswɜːk/
NU **Guesswork** is the process or result of trying to
guess something. *This is pure guesswork at this stage.*
guest /gɛst/ **guests**
1 NC A **guest** is someone who is staying in your home
or is attending an event because they have been
invited. *We're here as guests of the National Theatre.
...wedding guests... With guest speakers including
William Waldegrave and Sir Peter Imbert, there was
tight security at the conference.*
2 NC A **guest** is also someone who is staying in a
hotel. *...hotel guests.*
guest book, guest books
NC A **guest book** is a book in which guests write their
names and addresses when they have been staying in
someone's house or in a hotel or guest house. *A
fragile woman answers the phone and asks visitors to
sign the guest book.*
guest house, guest houses
NC A **guest house** is a small hotel. *A splendid complex
of government guest houses and apartments.
...hoteliers and guest house managers.*
guestimate /gɛstɪmət/. See **guesstimate**.
guest of honour, guests of honour; spelt **guest of
honor** in American English.
NC The **guest of honour** is the most important guest at
a dinner or other social occasion. *The Queen, as head
of the Commonwealth, was guest of honour at the
ceremony.*
guest-room, guest-rooms
NC A **guest-room** is a bedroom in someone's house for
visitors to sleep in. *He was lodged in the guest-rooms
reserved for dignitaries.*
guff /gʌf/
NU If you say that something that is said or written is
guff, you mean that it is nonsense; an informal word.
guffaw /gʌfɔː/ **guffaws, guffawing, guffawed**
NC A **guffaw** is a very loud laugh. *Martin let out a
delighted guffaw.* ▶ Also V *He guffawed and thumped
his friend on the shoulder.*
guidance /gaɪdns/
NU **Guidance** is help and advice. *Several delegates
expressed regret that he was leaving office and called
on him to continue giving guidance. ...guidance from
an expert.*
guide /gaɪd/ **guides, guiding, guided**
1 NC A **guide** is someone who shows tourists round

places such as museums or cities. *He provided the
groups with jeeps and guides for sight-seeing.*
2 VO If you **guide** someone round a city or building,
you show it to them and explain points of interest. *A
young woman guided us on a tour of the museum.*
● **guided** ADJ ATTRIB *We went on a guided tour of
Paris.*
3 NC A **guide** is also someone who leads the way
through difficult country. *With me is Goitom, who's
going to be my guide over the next few days.*
4 VO To **guide** someone or something means to cause
them to move in the right direction. *Men crossing the
ocean would use the stars to guide them.*
5 N SING A **guide** is also something that helps you to
plan your actions or to form an opinion about
something. *As a rough guide, 1 cubic foot stores 25lb
frozen food... Looking at Eastern Europe's share of
world trade is not a good guide to its true economic
potential.*
6 NC A **guide** is also a book which gives you
information or instructions to help you do or
understand something. *This book is meant to be a
practical guide to healthy living.*
7 NC A **guide** is also the same as a **guidebook**. *...a
guide to New York City.*
8 NC A **guide** or a **girl guide** is a member of the Girl
Guides Association. Guides are encouraged to be
disciplined and to learn practical skills. *The Guides
object strongly to the notion that they are 'goody
goodies' who never do anything exciting... In Britain,
the scouts have always been a male bastion separate
from the girl guides.*
9 VO If someone or something **guides** you, they
influence your actions or decisions. *Politicians will in
the end always be guided by changes in public opinion.*
● See also **guiding**.
guidebook /gaɪdbʊk/ **guidebooks**
NC A **guidebook** is a book which gives information for
tourists about a town, area, or country. *We'll write a
guidebook at the end of our trek. ...an impressively
detailed guidebook.*
guided missile, guided missiles
NC A **guided missile** is a missile whose course can be
controlled while it is in the air. *Some guided missiles
used by these helicopters were not effective... They
fired surface-to-surface guided missiles.*
guide dog, guide dogs
NC A **guide dog** is a dog that has been trained to lead
a blind person. *Will it be as useful as a guide dog is
for the blind at the moment?*
guideline /gaɪdlaɪn/ **guidelines**
NC A **guideline** is a piece of advice about how to do
something. *...government pay guidelines.*
guiding /gaɪdɪŋ/
ADJ ATTRIB Someone's **guiding** principles or **guiding**
force are the principles, ideas, or people that strongly
influence their actions, especially moral decisions.
*The paper thinks that realism will be Mr Bush's
guiding principle... He said the party would remain the
guiding force... For Adam Smith, the guiding light was
not self-interest.*
guild /gɪld/ **guilds**
NC A **guild** is an organization of people who do the
same job or who share an interest. *Many Guild
members are angry with their union leadership. ...the
Screen Actors' Guild.*
guilder /gɪldə/ **guilders**
NC A **guilder** is a unit of money that is used in the
Netherlands. *This year the Dutch government made
available sixty million guilders in so-called interim
aid.*
guildhall /gɪldhɔːl/ **guildhalls**
NC A **guildhall** is a building near the centre of a town
or city where members of a guild used to meet.
guile /gaɪl/
NU **Guile** is cunning and deceit. *He was a man
without guile.*
guillotine /gɪlətiːn/ **guillotines, guillotining,
guillotined**
1 NC A **guillotine** is a device which was used to
execute people by cutting off their heads, especially in
France in the past. *...a French aristocrat lies prone*

beneath the plunging blade of the guillotine.
2 VO To **guillotine** someone means to kill them using a guillotine. *Up to three thousand were guillotined in Paris alone.*
3 NC A **guillotine** is also a device used for cutting and trimming paper. *...a paper guillotine.*
4 VO In parliament, if the government **guillotines** a debate, it officially limits the amount of time for discussion before a vote must be taken. *Labour MPs were furious with government Whips for deciding to guillotine further debate on the bill.*
5 N SING If the government puts a **guillotine** on a debate in parliament, it guillotines it. *The government have decided to put a guillotine on the health bill which MPs have been debating.*

guilt /gɪlt/
1 NU **Guilt** is an unhappy feeling that you have because you have done something wrong. *I had agonizing feelings of shame and guilt.*
2 NU **Guilt** is the fact that you have done something wrong or illegal. *He at last made a public admission of his guilt.*

guilt complex, guilt complexes
NC A **guilt complex** is a feeling of guilt that someone has which they cannot get rid of, and which may eventually lead to mental illness. *...an obsessive guilt complex.*

guiltless /gɪltləs/
ADJ If someone is **guiltless**, they have not done anything wrong. *Nor were governments guiltless in this matter.*

guilty /gɪlti/
1 ADJ If you feel **guilty**, you feel unhappy because you have done something wrong. *They feel guilty about seeing her so little.* ◆ **guiltily** ADV *I blushed and looked away guiltily.* ● **guilty conscience:** see conscience.
2 ADJ ATTRIB You use **guilty** to describe an action or fact that you feel guilty about. *...a guilty secret.*
3 ADJ If someone is **guilty**, they have committed a crime or done something wrong. *He was found guilty of passing on secret papers to a foreign power.*

guinea /gɪni/ **guineas**
NC A **guinea** is an old British unit of money worth £1.05. Guineas are sometimes still used, for example in some auctions. *Mr Poulson paid one million four hundred thousand guineas for a horse called Ravellina.*

Guinea /gɪni/
The **Republic of Guinea** is a country in western Africa. It was a French colony, known as French Guinea, from 1849 until independence in 1958. Ahmed Sekou Touré became the first President and established a one-party state. General Lansana Conté became President in a coup following the death of Sekou Touré in 1984. There are no political parties. Guinea is a member of the Organization of African Unity. It is the world's second largest producer of bauxite. It also exports alumina and diamonds. Large foreign debts and high inflation are serious economic problems. ◆ **Guinean** /gɪniən/ N, ADJ
▪ *per capita GNP:* US$430 ▪ *religion:* Islam ▪ *language:* French (official), Soussou, Manika ▪ *currency:* franc ▪ *capital:* Conakry ▪ *population:* 5 million (1988) ▪ *size:* 245,857 square kilometres.

Guinea-Bissau /gɪni bɪsaʊ/
The **Republic of Guinea-Bissau** is a country in western Africa. It was a Portuguese colony, known as Portuguese Guinea, from the 15th century until it became independent in 1974. Brigadier-General João Bernardo Vieira became President in a coup in 1980. He is a member of the African Party for the Independence of Guinea and Cape Verde (PAIGC). In 1991 the post of Prime Minister was re-established and given to Carlos Correia of the PAIGC. Guinea-Bissau is a member of the Organization of African Unity. It exports cashews, fish, and peanuts. Large foreign debts and high inflation are serious economic problems. ◆ **Guinea-Bissauan** /gɪni bɪsaʊən/ N, ADJ
▪ *per capita GNP:* US$180 ▪ *religion:* animism, Islam ▪ *language:* Portuguese (official), Creole, Balante ▪ *currency:* peso ▪ *capital:* Bissau ▪ *population:* 943,000 (1989) ▪ *size:* 36,125 square kilometres.

guinea fowl; guinea fowl is both the singular and the plural form.
NC A **guinea fowl** is a large grey African bird. *The term 'poultry' covers not only chickens, but guinea fowl, ducks, geese and other birds.*

guinea pig, guinea pigs
1 NC A **guinea pig** is a small furry animal without a tail which is often kept as a pet. *She keeps a veritable menagerie of animals, including a parrot, three dogs and a guinea pig called Oscar.*
2 NC A **guinea pig** is also a person that is used in an experiment; an informal use. *...experimentation on human guinea pigs.*

guise /gaɪz/ **guises**
NC+SUPP You use **guise** to refer to the outward appearance or form of something. *A lot of nonsense was talked, under the guise of philosophy.*

guitar /gɪtɑː/ **guitars**
NC A **guitar** is a wooden musical instrument with six strings which are plucked or strummed. *You would play it exactly the way you would play a guitar. ...an artful combination of bass guitar, jazz saxophonist and keyboards.*

guitarist /gɪtɑːrɪst/ **guitarists**
NC A **guitarist** is someone who plays the guitar. *...the group's lead singer and guitarist. ...the gypsy guitarist Django Reinhardt.*

gulch /gʌltʃ/ **gulches**
NC A **gulch** is a long, narrow valley with steep sides which has been made by a stream flowing through it; used in American English. *...the Grand Gulch.*

gulf /gʌlf/ **gulfs**
1 NC A **gulf** is an important difference between two people, things, or groups. *The gulf between the cultures was too great to be easily bridged.*
2 NC A **gulf** is also a very large area of sea which extends a long way into the surrounding land. *...the Gulf of Mexico.*

Gulf Co-operation Council (GCC)
The Co-operation Council for the Arab States of the Gulf, commonly known as the **Gulf Co-operation Council**, was established in 1981 to foster economic, defence, social, and cultural co-operation. The members are: Bahrain, Kuwait, Oman, Qatar, Saudi Arabia, and the United Arab Emirates. The headquarters are in Riyadh.

Gulf Stream
N PROP The **Gulf Stream** is a warm ocean current which flows from the Gulf of Mexico, along the south-east coast of the United States, and north-eastwards in the Atlantic Ocean. *The Solar heat absorbed in the tropics is carried north and south by great currents such as the Gulf Stream.*

gull /gʌl/ **gulls**
NC A **gull** is a common sea bird. *Up the coast, gulls land on a wind-blown beach.*

gullet /gʌlɪt/ **gullets**
NC Your **gullet** is the tube from your mouth to your stomach. *...acid from the stomach flowing the wrong way, upwards into the gullet.*

gulley /gʌli/. See gully.

gullible /gʌləbl/
ADJ A **gullible** person is easily tricked. *Most of the girls were gullible and poorly-educated, and were tricked into thinking they were leaving home to work or study.*

gully /gʌli/ **gullies**
NC A **gully** is a long, narrow valley with steep sides. *The men stop at the edge of a ridge; from here they can look down on a steep gully filled with snow.*

gulp /gʌlp/ **gulps, gulping, gulped**
1 VO If you **gulp** something, you drink or eat it very quickly by swallowing large quantities of it at a time. *She gulped her coffee.* ► Also NC *She took a gulp of whisky.*
2 V If you **gulp**, you swallow air, usually because you are nervous. *He gulped and stammered for me to call back.* ► Also NC *I gave a little gulp.*

gulp down PHRASAL VERB If you **gulp** something **down**, you quickly drink or eat all of it by swallowing large quantities of it at a time. *After gulping down his breakfast, he hurried to the station.*

gum /gʌm/ **gums, gumming, gummed**
1 NU **Gum** is a kind of sweet which you chew but do not swallow. *Ignoring hygiene, I popped the gum back into my mouth and chewed it while I pondered my next move.* ● See also **bubble gum, chewing gum.**
2 NU **Gum** is also a type of glue that you use to stick paper together. *The tiny piece of paper, fixed by gum to the envelope, served as a receipt of pre-payment of postage.*
3 VOA If you **gum** one thing to another, you stick them together.
4 NC Your **gums** are the areas of firm, pink flesh inside your mouth, which your teeth grow out of. *...defects such as teeth that stick inwards and cut the gums. ...gum disease runs in our family.*

gumbo /gʌmbəʊ/
NU **Gumbo** is a type of soup that is thickened with a vegetable called okra; used in American English. *Some volunteers had made a big pot of chicken gumbo for the runners.*

gumboot /gʌmbuːt/ **gumboots**
NC **Gumboots** are long, waterproof, rubber boots.

gummy /gʌmi/ **gummier, gummiest**
1 ADJ Something that is **gummy** is sticky. *...a special gummy substance.*
2 ADJ A **gummy** smile or grin shows the gums of your mouth. *She liked to think he had a special gummy grin for her.*

gumption /gʌmpʃn/
NU **Gumption** is the quality of being able to think what it would be sensible to do in a particular situation, and to do it; an informal word. *I'd never have had the gumption to do what he had done.*

gum tree, gum trees
1 NC You can refer to any tree that produces gum, for example a eucalyptus tree, as a **gum tree**. *...arguments going on in political and forestry circles about the gum tree.*
2 If you say that someone is **up a gum tree**, you mean that they are in a difficult situation which they cannot get out of easily; an informal expression.

gun /gʌn/ **guns, gunning, gunned**
1 NC A **gun** is a weapon from which bullets are fired. *He was discovered dead in the bedroom with a gun in his hand... The last escapee was captured after a gun battle in the Ghamrah district of Cairo.*
2 VO If you **gun** an engine or a vehicle, you start the engine or increase the engine speed by pressing on the accelerator pedal; used in American English. *He gunned his engine and drove off... She would drive the truck down to the edge of the pond and gun the engine.* ● **Gun** is used in these phrases. ● If you **jump the gun**, you do something before the proper time; an informal expression. *Newspapers began to jump the gun and talk about resignations.* ● If you **stick to** your **guns**, you continue to have your own opinion about something even though other people disagree; an informal expression. *The Estonians seem to be sticking to their guns and show little sign of backing down... Both leaders stuck to their guns.*

gun down PHRASAL VERB If you **gun** someone **down**, you shoot at them and kill or injure them. *About a dozen people were gunned down. ...the men who gunned down innocent civilians and soldiers during the violent days of the revolution.*

gun for PHRASAL VERB If someone is **gunning for** you, they are trying to harm you or cause you trouble in some way. *Only the most diehard conservatives will be gunning for Mr Gorbachev at the congress.*

gunboat /gʌnbəʊt/ **gunboats**
NC A **gunboat** is a small ship which has several large guns fixed on it. *...protecting as many as five tankers at a time from attack by plane or gunboat.*

gundog /gʌndɒg/ **gundogs**
NC A **gundog** is a dog that has been trained to work with a hunter or gamekeeper, especially to find and carry back birds or animals that have been shot.

gunfire /gʌnfaɪə/
NU **Gunfire** is the repeated shooting of guns. *There were regular bursts of gunfire and the occasional sound of artillery.*

gunge /gʌndʒ/
NU You use **gunge** to refer to a soft and sticky substance, especially if it is unpleasant; an informal word. *It's solidifying into a sort of brown gunge.*

gung-ho /gʌŋhəʊ/
ADJ You use **gung-ho** to describe a person or their attitude when they are very enthusiastic about something, especially about going to war; used showing disapproval. *If they want to take a gung-ho attitude and go out there and fight, that's entirely up to them... Up until Aristide announced his candidacy, the United States was gung-ho in support of these elections.*

gunk /gʌŋk/
NU You use **gunk** to refer to a substance that is soft, sticky, and unpleasant; an informal word. *When you stop smoking your lungs start to work again, and so you start to cough up some of the gunk that's been accumulating there.*

gunman /gʌnmən/ **gunmen** /gʌnmən/
NC A **gunman** is someone who uses a gun to commit a crime. *A lone gunman who hijacked a domestic airliner has died in a shoot-out with police.*

gunmetal /gʌnmetl/
NU **Gunmetal** is a dark grey metal which is made of copper mixed with tin and zinc. *...one grey gunmetal desk lamp.*

gunner /gʌnə/ **gunners**
NC A **gunner** is a member of the armed forces who is trained to use guns. *The gunner sitting next to us began to fire his weapon. ...an anti-aircraft gunner.*

gunnery /gʌnəri/
NU **Gunnery** is the technique of firing large guns. *...a gunnery officer.*

gunpoint /gʌnpɔɪnt/
If someone holds you or forces you to do something **at gunpoint**, they have a gun and threaten to shoot you if you do not obey them. *He held the three men at gunpoint... They were forced to hand over the keys at gunpoint.*

gunpowder /gʌnpaʊdə/
NU **Gunpowder** is an explosive substance. *The gunpowder is thought to have been ignited by a cigarette... They went on the rampage, setting shops and houses on fire with petrol and gunpowder.*

gun-runner, gun-runners
NC A **gun-runner** is someone who takes or sends guns into a country secretly and illegally, especially so that the guns can be used by people who are opposed to the government.

gun-running
NU **Gun-running** is the activity of taking or sending guns into a country secretly and illegally, especially so that the guns can be used by people who are opposed to the government. *He has been indicted on charges of murder, gun-running and resisting arrest.*

gunship /gʌnʃɪp/. See **helicopter gunship.**

gunshot /gʌnʃɒt/ **gunshots**
NC A **gunshot** is a single firing of a gun. *...the sound of gunshots.*

gunsmith /gʌnsmɪθ/ **gunsmiths**
NC A **gunsmith** is someone who makes and repairs guns. *...a Georgia gunsmith who has the backing of the National Rifle Association.*

guppy /gʌpi/ **guppies**
NC A **guppy** is a small, brightly-coloured tropical fish. People sometimes keep guppies in aquariums. *The institute also intends to increase the number of guppies because these fish feed on the mosquito larvae.*

gurgle /gɜːgl/ **gurgles, gurgling, gurgled**
1 V When water **gurgles**, it makes a bubbling sound. *We stared into the gloomy crack where water gurgled between the rocks.*
2 V When a baby **gurgles**, it makes bubbling sounds in its throat. *Kicking and gurgling, his little brother looked up at him.* ► Also NC *...gurgles of pleasure.*

guru /gʊruː/ **gurus**
1 TITLE or NC A **guru** is a spiritual leader and teacher, especially in Hinduism. *The Sikh religion was founded in the fifteenth century by Guru Nanak. ...guru Maharishi Mahesh Yogi.*

2 NC A **guru** is also a respected adviser. *He's something of a pension fund guru.*

gush /gʌʃ/ **gushes, gushing, gushed**
1 VA When liquid **gushes** out of something, it flows out very quickly and in large quantities. *Tears were gushing from her closed eyes.* ► Also N SING *...a gush of blood.*
2 V or V-QUOTE If someone **gushes**, they express their admiration or pleasure in an exaggerated way. *He, poor soul, was listening to me gushing on about how much I enjoyed his books... 'Amy!' he gushed. 'How good to see you again.'* ♦ **gushing** ADJ *She's always described with gushing reverence in the official media.*

gusset /gʌsɪt/ **gussets**
NC A **gusset** is a small strip of cloth that is sewn into a garment in order to make it wider, stronger, or more comfortable. *...nylon briefs with a cotton gusset.*

gust /gʌst/ **gusts**
1 NC A **gust** is a short, strong rush of wind. *...a sudden gust of wind.*
2 N SING+*of* If you feel a **gust** of emotion, you feel the emotion suddenly and intensely; a literary use. *A gust of pure happiness swept through her.*

gusto /gʌstəʊ/
If you do something **with gusto**, you do it with energy and enthusiasm. *It will be a job which we and others will do with gusto.*

gusty /gʌsti/
ADJ **Gusty** is used to describe weather in which there are very strong, irregular winds. *...gusty winds.*

gut /gʌt/ **guts, gutting, gutted**
1 N PL Your **guts** are your internal organs, especially your intestines. *Other strains produce a sort of toxin which, when it gets into our guts, causes diarrhoea and vomiting.*
2 N SING The **gut** is the tube inside your body through which food passes while it is being digested. *American scientists have found that eating spicy foods doesn't damage the stomach lining or gut... Antibodies are transferred from the milk through the wall of the gut into the baby animal's bloodstream.*
3 N SING Someone's **gut** is their stomach, especially when it is very large and sticks out; an informal use. *He would hit him first in the knee and then in the gut.*
4 VO If you **gut** a fish, you remove the organs from inside it.
5 NU If you have **guts**, you are brave or courageous; an informal use. *Sam hasn't got the guts to leave... Was it incompetence or just lack of guts?*
6 If you **hate** someone's **guts**, you feel an extremely strong sense of dislike towards them. *They hated my guts when I first got elected.*
7 N+N A **gut** feeling is based on instinct or emotion rather than on reason. *My immediate gut reaction was to refuse.*
8 VO If a building or vehicle **is gutted**, the inside is destroyed. *The whole house was gutted by fire.* ♦ **gutted** ADJ ATTRIB *The streets have been cleared of rubble and gutted vehicles.*
9 See also **gutted**.

gutless /gʌtləs/
ADJ Someone who is **gutless** has a weak character and lacks courage or determination. *...that yellow, gutless worm, Claude.*

gutsy /gʌtsi/; an informal word.
1 ADJ Someone who is **gutsy** shows courage or determination. *That's so gutsy, you've really got to admire her for doing it.*
2 ADJ Something that is **gutsy** expresses a meaning or idea very powerfully and vividly. *The play used red-hot, gutsy, four-letter words.*

gutted /gʌtɪd/
1 ADJ PRED If you are **gutted**, you feel extremely disappointed or depressed by something that has happened; an informal word. *Ninety-nine per cent of Birmingham City's supporters will be absolutely gutted if he leaves the club.*
2 See also **gutted**.

gutter /gʌtə/ **gutters**
1 NC The **gutter** is the edge of a road next to the pavement, where rain collects and flows away. *The motorbike lay on its side in the gutter.*

2 NC A **gutter** is also a plastic or metal channel fixed to the edge of a roof, which rain water drains into. *At the lower end of the corrugated iron roof there's a gutter going right the way across.*
3 N SING If someone describes a person as living in the **gutter**, they mean that he or she is living in extremely poor and degrading circumstances. *He was talking to one of the residents about the courage it must have taken to pull himself out of the gutter and kick the habit.*

guttering /gʌtərɪŋ/
NU **Guttering** consists of the plastic or metal channels fixed to the edge of the roof of a building, which rain water drains into. *There was damp because the guttering had not been fixed for years.*

gutter press
N SING The **gutter press** refers to newspapers and magazines that contain more stories about people's private affairs, and about scandals involving sex or violence, than about international, political, or economic affairs; an informal expression, used showing disapproval. *That sort of sensational reporting is typical of the gutter press.*

guttural /gʌtərəl/
ADJ **Guttural** sounds are harsh sounds that are produced at the back of a person's throat. *...a strange, loud, guttural cry.*

guy /gaɪ/ **guys**; an informal word.
1 NC A **guy** is a man. *...the guy who drove the bus.*
2 N PL Americans sometimes address a group of people as **guys** or **you guys**. *Listen, guys, I'm not going to be with you next week... You guys can go back to work.*

Guyana /gaɪænə/
The **Co-operative Republic of Guyana** is a country in northern South America. Guyana was a British colony called British Guiana from 1831 until independence in 1966. The People's National Congress (PNC) has been the ruling party since independence. Hugh Desmond Hoyte became President in 1985. Although opposition parties are allowed, electoral malpractice has been widely alleged and Guyana has been a virtual one-party state since independence. Electoral reforms were agreed in 1990. Guyana is a member of the Commonwealth and of the Organization of American States. Large foreign debts and high inflation are major economic problems. Guyana exports bauxite and sugar. ♦ **Guyanese, Guyanan** /gaɪəniːz, gaɪænən/ N, ADJ
▪ *per capita GNP:* US$410 ▪ *religion:* Christianity, Hinduism ▪ *language:* English (official), Hindi, Urdu ▪ *currency:* dollar ▪ *capital:* Georgetown ▪ *population:* 800,000 (1990) ▪ *size:* 214,969 square kilometres.

guzzle /gʌzl/ **guzzles, guzzling, guzzled**
VO If you **guzzle** something, you drink or eat it quickly and greedily; an informal word. *The Cherry Wine was being guzzled like lemonade.*

gym /dʒɪm/ **gyms**
1 NC A **gym** is the same as a **gymnasium**. *He was always at the gym.*
2 NU **Gym** is the same as **gymnastics**. *We did an hour of gym.*

gymkhana /dʒɪmkɑːnə/ **gymkhanas**
NC A **gymkhana** is an event in which people ride horses in competitions. *...the large paddock where the gymkhana was being held.*

gymnasium /dʒɪmneɪziəm/ **gymnasiums**
NC A **gymnasium** is a room with equipment for physical exercise; a formal word. *There are two squash courts, saunas, an indoor swimming pool and gymnasium.*

gymnast /dʒɪmnæst/ **gymnasts**
NC A **gymnast** is someone who is trained in gymnastics. *...three top Soviet coaches who've been training British gymnasts.*

gymnastic /dʒɪmnæstɪk/ **gymnastics**
1 N PL **Gymnastics** are physical exercises, which develop your agility and strength. *...impressive displays of gymnastics... The Chinese won almost all the golds in gymnastics, swimming and shooting.*
2 ADJ ATTRIB **Gymnastic** is used to describe things relating to gymnastics. *...gymnastic ability.*

gymslip /dʒɪmslɪp/ **gymslips**
NC A **gymslip** is a sleeveless dress that schoolgirls used to wear over a blouse or jumper as part of their school uniform.

gynaecology /gaɪnɪkɒlədʒi/; also spelt **gynecology**.
NU **Gynaecology** is the branch of medical science which deals with women's diseases and medical conditions, especially in the reproductive system. *In gynaecology, for example, the instrument could be used for cervical investigations.* ◆ **gynaecologist**, **gynaecologists** NC ...*a study organised by consultant gynaecologist, Mr John Studd.*

gypsum /dʒɪpsəm/
NU **Gypsum** a soft white substance which looks like chalk and which is used to make plaster of Paris. ...*a kind of mortar made of ground limestone, with a little clay and some powdered gypsum.*

gypsy /dʒɪpsi/ **gypsies**; also spelt **gipsy**.
NC A **gypsy** is a member of a race of people who travel from place to place in caravans rather than living in one place. *The majority of gypsies in the country, especially the younger ones, do not speak the Romany language... Even here, there is said to be harassment of gypsies.*

gyrate /dʒaɪreɪt/ **gyrates, gyrating, gyrated**
v If something **gyrates**, it turns round and round in a circle, usually very fast; a formal word. ...*a small gyrating plastic advertisement for a brand of lager.*

gyration /dʒaɪreɪʃn/ **gyrations**
NU or N PL **Gyration** is the act of gyrating. *Jack broke out of his gyration and stood facing Ralph. ...their bodily gyrations and contortions.*

gyroscope /dʒaɪrəskəʊp/ **gyroscopes**
NC A **gyroscope** is a device that contains a disc rotating on an axis which can turn freely in any direction, so that the disc maintains the same position whatever the position or movement of the surrounding structure. *The gyroscope system consists of four of these rotating spheres.*

H h

H, h /eɪtʃ/ H's, h's
NC **H** is the eighth letter of the English alphabet.
ha /hɑː/; also spelt **hah**.
You say **ha** to show that you are very surprised,
pleased, or annoyed about something; an informal
word. *'Ha!' she said, 'Isn't that wonderful?'*... *Hah!
Scared you, didn't I?* ● See also **ha ha**.
habeas corpus /heɪbɪəs kɔːpəs/
NU **Habeas corpus** is a law that exists in many
countries. It states that a person cannot be kept in
prison unless he or she has been brought before a
judge or a magistrate, who must decide whether it is
lawful for that person to be kept in prison. *It is of
little consolation to a poor peasant that habeas corpus
exists, if he cannot get a lawyer... Two days later he
was released at the habeas corpus hearing.*
haberdasher /hæbədæʃə/ **haberdashers**
1 NC A **haberdasher** is a shop or shopkeeper selling
small articles for sewing and dressmaking, for
example buttons and zips. *Arthur Lewis was a very
fashionable haberdasher with a shop called Lewis &
Allenby's.*
2 NC In the United States, a **haberdasher** is a shop or
shopkeeper selling men's clothing.
haberdashery /hæbədæʃəᵊri/
1 NU **Haberdashery** is buttons, zips, thread, and other
small things that you need for sewing.
2 NU In the United States, **haberdashery** is men's
clothing sold in a shop.
habit /hæbɪt/ **habits**
1 NCorNU A **habit** is something that you do often or
regularly. *It became a habit for the fans to use the
office... More out of habit than anything else, I stopped
and went in.* ● If you are **in the habit of** doing
something, or if you **make a habit** of doing it, you do it
regularly and often. *Once a month Castle was in the
habit of taking Sarah for an excursion... They made a
habit of lunching together twice a week.*
2 NC A **habit** is also an action which is considered bad
that someone does repeatedly and finds difficult to stop
doing. *He had a nervous habit of biting his nails...
After twenty years as a chain smoker, Mr Kamal Nath
has given up the habit.*
3 NC+SUPP A drug **habit** is an addiction to a drug.
*Groups exist to help those who want to kick the
marijuana habit... Her drug habit had made her a
liability.*
4 NC A **habit** is also a piece of clothing shaped like a
long loose dress, which a nun or monk wears. *With
his vibrant voice, white hair and black monk's habit,
the Cardinal is an impressive figure.*
habitable /hæbɪtəbl/
ADJ If a place is **habitable**, it is suitable for people to
live in. *Only four percent of the land is habitable.*
habitat /hæbɪtæt/ **habitats**
NC+SUPP The **habitat** of an animal or plant is its
natural environment. *Their habitat is being destroyed.
...the open woodland that is their natural habitat.*
habitation /hæbɪteɪʃn/ **habitations**; a formal word.
1 NU **Habitation** is the activity of living somewhere.
*The Government declared the area unfit for human
habitation.*

2 NC A **habitation** is a place where people live.
...squalid human habitations.
habitual /həbɪtʃuəl/
ADJ A **habitual** action is one that someone usually does
or often does. *'Sorry I'm late,' David said with his
habitual guilty grin.* ◆ **habitually** ADV *Anybody who
habitually keeps his office door shut is suspect.*
habituate /həbɪtʃueɪt/ **habituates, habituating,
habituated**
V-PASS+*to* If you **are habituated** to something, you have
got used to it; a formal word. *The people of these
countries have been habituated to authoritarian
traditions.*
habitué /həbɪtʃueɪ/ **habitués**
NC A **habitué** is someone who often visits a particular
place or attends a particular kind of event; a formal
word. *...nightclub habitués.*
Habyarimana, Juvénal /ʒuveɪnəl hæbjæriːmɑːnə/
Major-General Juvénal Habyarimana became
President of Rwanda in a coup in 1973. He was
Commander of the Armed Forces from 1963 to 1965,
and Minister for the National Guard and Chief of Staff
of Police from 1965 to 1973. He founded the National
Revolutionary Movement for Development (MRND),
in 1975. Born: 1937.
hack /hæk/ **hacks, hacking, hacked**
1 VAorVO If you **hack** something, you cut it with a
sharp tool, using strong, rough strokes. *...hacking
away at the branches... They were ambushed and
hacked to death.*
2 NC A **hack** is a professional writer who produces
work fast, without worrying about its quality; an
informal use. *...tabloid hacks, always eager to find
victims in order to sell newspapers. ...a hack writer.*
3 V When someone **hacks** into a computer system,
they try to break into it in order to get secret
information. *The saboteurs had demanded money in
return for revealing how they hacked into the systems.*
◆ **hacking** NU *The act of hacking is not an offence.*
4 If you say that someone **can't hack** it, you mean that
they are incapable of doing something, or of dealing
with a problem; an informal expression. *He wakes up
one day and says 'Juliet, I can't hack it. I have to
go.'... Times are hard, you've got no bread on your
table, and your parents can't hack it.*
hacker /hækə/ **hackers**
NC A computer **hacker** is someone who tries to break
into computer systems, especially in order to get
secret or confidential information that is stored there.
*The company says that hackers have broken into the
banks' central computer systems.*
hacking /hækɪŋ/
1 ADJ ATTRIB A **hacking** cough is a dry, painful cough
with a harsh, unpleasant sound. *His hacking cough
could be heard next door.*
2 See also **hack**.
hacking jacket, hacking jackets
NC A **hacking jacket** is a jacket made of tweed with a
slit at the bottom on either side and with slanting
pockets. Hacking jackets are often worn by people who
go riding on horseback.

hackles /ˈhæklz/
1 If your **hackles rise**, you begin to feel angry and hostile because of something that has happened. *To this day, my hackles rise when I hear actors talking about 'getting laughs'. ...a move which is bound in advance to get the hackles of the other side up.*
2 N PL The **hackles** of a dog or cat are the hairs on the back of its neck, which rise when the animal is angry or frightened. *At certain parts of the house our dogs' hackles always rose when there was no one there.*
3 N PL The **hackles** of a cock, turkey, pheasant, or other male bird are long feathers on the back of its neck that stand up when it is angry or ready to fight.

hackneyed /ˈhæknid/
ADJ A **hackneyed** expression is meaningless because it has been used too often. *'Of course I love you. With all my heart.' The hackneyed phrase came unintended to his lips.*

hacksaw /ˈhæksɔː/ **hacksaws**
NC A **hacksaw** is a small saw used for cutting metal. *He is said to have used a hacksaw to remove the bars of his cell door.*

hackwork /ˈhækwɜːk/
NU **Hackwork** is uninteresting and unoriginal work, especially pieces of writing done simply to earn money rather than out of genuine interest. *The volume was judged to be such uncreative hackwork that it isn't worthy of federal copyright protection.*

had /həd, hæd, hæd/
Had is the past tense and past participle of **have**.

haddock /ˈhædək/; **haddock** is both the singular and the plural form.
NCorNU A **haddock** is a fish that lives in the sea that you can eat. *He said there would soon be no cod or haddock left to fish in the North Sea.*

hadn't /ˈhædnt/
Hadn't is the usual spoken form of 'had not'.

haemoglobin /ˌhiːməˈɡləʊbɪn/; also spelt **hemoglobin**.
NU **Haemoglobin** is a substance that carries oxygen in red blood cells; a technical term in biology. *...the red blood pigment, haemoglobin.*

haemophilia /ˌhiːməˈfɪliə/; also spelt **hemophilia**.
NU **Haemophilia** is a disease in which a person's blood does not clot properly, so that they bleed for a long time if they are injured. *Around 5,000 men and boys in Britain suffer from haemophilia.*

haemophiliac /ˌhiːməˈfɪliæk/ **haemophiliacs**; also spelt **hemophiliac**.
NC A **haemophiliac** is a person who suffers from haemophilia. *At the moment there are some 5,000 haemophiliacs in Britain alone.*

haemorrhage /ˈhemərɪdʒ/ **haemorrhages, haemorrhaging, haemorrhaged**; also spelt **hemorrhage**.
1 NCorNU A **haemorrhage** is serious bleeding inside a person's body. *He had died of a brain haemorrhage... Haemorrhage during or just after an operation is a problem, as is infection.*
2 N SING+SUPP A **haemorrhage** of people or resources is a rapid loss of them from a group or a place, severely weakening its position. *It's unlikely to slow down the steady haemorrhage of liberals from the party's ranks. ...this haemorrhage of funds from the poor should stop... He said the move would stem the haemorrhage of talent and enterprise from the colony.*
3 V If a group or a place is **haemorrhaging**, it is losing people or resources rapidly and is becoming weak. *One broker said bluntly that Hong Kong was haemorrhaging badly, losing both people and capital.*
♦ **haemorrhaging** NU *General Motors confirmed that the hemorrhaging began last year. ...the latest incident of self-inflicted haemorrhaging in South Africa's black community.*

haemorrhoids /ˈhemərɔɪdz/; also spelt **hemorrhoids**.
N PL **Haemorrhoids** are painful swellings that appear in the veins inside a person's anus; a medical term. *He was forced out of the match because of haemorrhoids.*

hag /hæɡ/ **hags**
NC A **hag** is an ugly and unpleasant woman; an offensive word. *He called her a sinister, selfish and inhuman old hag.*

haggard /ˈhæɡəd/
ADJ A **haggard** person looks very tired and worried. *There was a haggard look about his eyes. ...As she got older she got haggard.*

haggis /ˈhæɡɪs/
NU **Haggis** is a Scottish dish made with oatmeal and the internal organs of a sheep or calf. *Burns' Night continues to be celebrated with the eating of haggis.*

haggle /ˈhæɡl/ **haggles, haggling, haggled**
V-RECIP If you **haggle**, you argue about something before reaching an agreement, especially about the cost of something that you are buying. *The twelve heads of government had haggled into the early hours... They haggled with shopkeepers in the bazaar.*

hah /hɑː/. See **ha**.

ha ha /ˌhɑːˈhɑː/; also spelt **ha-ha**.
1 Ha ha is used in writing to represent the sound that people make when they laugh.
2 You sometimes say ha ha sarcastically, when you are not amused and are only pretending to laugh. *I watched as the man made mistakes. 'Ha ha,' I sneered to myself.*

hail /heɪl/ **hails, hailing, hailed**
1 N SING **Hail** consists of tiny balls of ice that fall from the sky. *The hail battered on the windows... Violent rain and hail had devastated crops in the Meknes region.*
2 V When it **hails**, hail falls from the sky. *It hailed all afternoon.*
3 N SING A **hail** of small objects is a large number of them that fall down on you at the same time with great force. *He was dead, killed in a hail of bullets... Riot police were met with a hail of stones and petrol bombs.*
4 VO If you **hail** someone, you call to them; a literary use. *A voice hailed him from the steps.*
5 VO If you **hail** a taxi, you signal to the driver to stop. *They hailed a taxi which took them to a tube station north-west of central London.*
6 VO+as If you **hail** a person, event, or achievement as important or successful, you praise them publicly. *They were hailed as heroes... The discovery was hailed as the scientific sensation of the century.*

hailstone /ˈheɪlstəʊn/ **hailstones**
NC **Hailstones** are tiny balls of ice that fall from the sky when it hails. *Freak hailstones over a wide area of the country have killed more than seventeen people.*

hailstorm /ˈheɪlstɔːm/ **hailstorms**
NC A **hailstorm** is a storm during which it hails. *They were caught in a hailstorm as they returned home from school.*

hair /heə/ **hairs**
1 NU Your **hair** is the large number of hairs that grow in a mass on your head. *...a young woman with long blonde hair.*
2 NC **Hairs** are the long, fine strands that grow in large numbers on your head and other parts of your body. *...black hairs on the back of his hands.*
3 NCorNU **Hairs** are also very fine thread-like strands that grow on some animals, insects, and plants. *The adult beetle has silken hairs on its body... The plumes have always been made from hair cut from the soft underbelly of the yak.*
● **Hair** is used in these phrases. ● Something that makes your **hair stand on end** shocks or horrifies you. *She did it with an ease that made his hair stand on end.* ● If you **let your hair down**, you relax completely and enjoy yourself. *The ball was a chance for them to let their hair down.* ● If you say that someone is **splitting hairs**, you mean that they are making unnecessary distinctions or paying too much attention to unimportant details. *Am I splitting hairs here? I think not, because this is an important distinction.*

hairbrush /ˈheəbrʌʃ/ **hairbrushes**
NC A **hairbrush** is a brush that you use to brush your hair.

haircut /ˈheəkʌt/ **haircuts**
1 NC If you have a **haircut**, someone cuts your hair for you. *He needed a haircut.*
2 NC A **haircut** is also the style in which your hair has been cut. *The girls had short, neat haircuts.*

hairdo /heɪduː/ **hairdos**

NC A **hairdo** is the style in which your hair has been cut and arranged; an informal word. *I went to a salon and had a new hairdo.*

hairdresser /heɪdresə/ **hairdressers**

1 NC A **hairdresser** is a person who cuts, washes, and styles people's hair. *...late night shopping or an evening visit to the hairdresser.*

2 NC A **hairdresser's** is a place where you can have your hair cut, washed, and styled. *There are two hairdressers in the High Street.*

hairdressing /heɪdresɪŋ/

NU **Hairdressing** is the occupation or activity of cutting, washing, and styling people's hair. *...a small hairdressing business in Barnet.*

hairdryer /heɪdraɪə/ **hairdryers**; also spelt **hairdrier**.

NC A **hairdryer** is a machine that you use to dry your hair.

hair-grip, hair-grips

NC A **hair-grip** is a small metal or plastic clip that women use to hold their hair in position.

hairless /heələs/

ADJ A part of your body that is **hairless** has no hair on it. *...his hairless chest.*

hairline /heəlaɪn/ **hairlines**

1 NC Your **hairline** is the edge of the area where your hair grows on the front part of your head. *His hairline was receding.*

2 ADJ ATTRIB A **hairline** crack or gap is very narrow or fine. *...a tiny hairline fracture.*

hairnet /heənet/ **hairnets**

NC A **hairnet** is a small net that some women wear over their hair in order to keep it tidy.

hairpiece /heəpiːs/ **hairpieces**

NC A **hairpiece** is a piece of false hair that some people wear on their head if they are bald or if they want to make their own hair seem longer or thicker. *He took off his hairpiece.*

hairpin /heəpɪn/ **hairpins**

NC A **hairpin** is a thin piece of bent metal used to hold hair in position.

hairpin bend, hairpin bends

NC A **hairpin bend** is a very sharp bend in a road, where the road turns back in the opposite direction. *I was nearly killed on a hairpin bend near Sparrowpit.*

hair-raising

ADJ Something that is **hair-raising** is very frightening or disturbing. *The ride was bumpy and at times hair-raising.*

hair's breadth

N SING If something happens by a **hair's breadth**, it nearly did not happen at all. *A national strike has been averted by no more than a hair's breadth... Giscard staged a brilliant campaign that earned him a hair's breadth victory over Mitterrand in the second round.*

hair slide, hair slides

NC A **hair slide** is a decorative clip that girls and women put in their hair to hold it in position.

hairsplitting /heəsplɪtɪŋ/

NU **Hairsplitting** is the act of making distinctions between things or ideas when the differences between them are very small and not at all important or useful. *They did not take his theoretical hairsplitting seriously.*

hairstyle /heəstaɪl/ **hairstyles**

NC Your **hairstyle** is the style in which your hair has been cut or arranged. *...a new hairstyle.*

hairy /heəri/ **hairier, hairiest**

1 ADJ Someone or something that is **hairy** is covered with hair. *...a big, hairy man.*

2 ADJ If you describe a situation as **hairy**, you mean that it is frightening or worrying but rather exciting; an informal use. *It got a little hairy when we drove him to the station with only two minutes to spare.*

Haiti /heɪti/

The **Republic of Haiti** is a country in the Caribbean on the island of Hispaniola. It was a French colony from 1659 until independence in 1804 following a slave uprising led by Toussaint l'Ouverture. It was governed by the United States from 1915 to 1934. Dr François Duvalier, called Papa Doc, was President from 1957 until his death in 1971. His son, Jean-Claude Duvalier, called Baby Doc, ruled until 1986, when he went into exile. Father Jean-Bertrand Aristide became the first democratically elected President in 1990. He was overthrown in a coup led by Brigadier-General Raoul Cedras, the Commander-in-Chief of the Army, in 1991. Joseph Nerette was appointed President and Jean Jacques Honorat was appointed Prime Minister in 1991. Haiti is a member of the Organization of American States. It produces manufactured goods and coffee. Tourism, formerly an important industry, has been severely affected by the political instability.
◆ **Haitian** /heɪʃn/ N, ADJ
▪ *per capita GNP:* US$400 ▪ *religion:* Christianity (mainly Roman Catholic), Voodoo ▪ *language:* French and Creole (official) ▪ *currency:* gourde ▪ *capital:* Port-au-Prince ▪ *population:* 7 million (1990) ▪ *size:* 27,750 square kilometres.

hake /heɪk/

NU **Hake** is a big fish, similar to cod, that is eaten in Europe and North America. *They sell grilled sole, fried plaice and hake in a tomato sauce.*

halcyon /hælsiən/

ADJ ATTRIB A **halcyon** time is a peaceful or happy one; a formal word. *...the halcyon days of the alliance in the 1980's.*

hale /heɪl/

ADJ If you describe someone as **hale**, you mean that they are healthy; a literary word. *They had hale old parents who lived on farms in the country.*

half /huːf/ **halves** /hɑːvz/

1 QUANT, PREDET, or PRON **Half** of an amount or object is one of the two equal parts that together make up the whole amount or object. *I went to Poland four and a half years ago... Half of the patients are not receiving the drug... Half his front teeth are missing... Roughly half are French.* ▶ Also NC *The changes will have repercussions for both halves of Germany.*

2 ADJ ATTRIB You also use **half** to refer to a half of something. *...a half chicken... The film wouldn't end for another half hour.*

3 ADV You also use **half** to say that something is only partly the case or happens to only a limited extent. *He half expected to see Davis there... His eyes were half-closed. ...his half empty glass.*

4 SUBMOD You can use **half** to say that someone has parents of different nationalities. For example, if you are **half** German, one of your parents is German. *He is half English and half Belgian.*

5 ADV You use **half** with 'past' to refer to a time that is thirty minutes after a particular hour. For example, if it is **half** past two, thirty minutes have passed since two o'clock. *The raid took place at half past four this morning.*

6 NC In games such as football and rugby, matches are divided into two equal periods of time which are called **halves**. *Abazi scored the only goal ten minutes into the second half.*

7 NC A **half** is also half a pint of a drink such as beer or cider. *...a half of lager.*

● **Half** is used in these phrases. ● If you increase something **by half**, half of the original amount is added to it. If you decrease it **by half**, half of the original amount is taken away from it. *She reckoned she cut her costs by half.* ● If something is divided **in half**, it is divided into two equal parts. *He tore it in half.* ● If two people **go halves**, they divide the cost of something equally between them. *Janet is going halves with Cheryl.* ● If you say that someone does not do things **by halves**, you mean that they always do things very thoroughly. *He can't do anything by halves.*

half-baked

ADJ **Half-baked** ideas or plans have not been properly thought out, and so are usually stupid or impractical. *...your half-baked political opinions.*

half board

NU If you have **half board** at a hotel, you have your breakfast and evening meal there, but not your lunch.

half-brother, half-brothers

NC Your **half-brother** is a boy or man with either the same mother or the same father as you. *Mr Regalado is the half-brother of the Honduran armed forces chief.*

half-caste
ADJ Someone who is **half-caste** has parents of different races; some people find this word offensive. *There is a new willingness by half-caste Australians to identify publicly with their aboriginal background.*

half cock
If something goes off **half cock** or **at half cock**, it happens, but not fully or successfully, or not in the way that it was planned; an informal expression.

half-day, half-days
NC A **half-day** is a day when you work only in the morning or in the afternoon, but not all day. *Saturday is his half-day.*

half-hearted
ADJ Someone or something that is **half-hearted** shows no real effort or enthusiasm. *She made a half-hearted attempt to break away.* ◆ **half-heartedly** ADV *I stayed home, studying half-heartedly.*

half-life, half-lives
NC The **half-life** of a radioactive substance is the time that it takes to lose half its radioactivity. *The half-life of iodine 125 is 60 days.*

half-mast
If a flag is flying **at half-mast**, it is flying from the middle of the pole as a sign of mourning. *Flags are flying at half-mast on all official buildings.*

half-note, half-notes
NC A **half-note** is a minim; used in American English.

halfpenny /heɪpni/ **halfpennies** or **halfpence** /heɪpns/
NC A **halfpenny** is a small British coin which used to be worth one half of a penny.

half-price
ADJ If something is **half-price**, you can buy it for half of its usual price. *...half-price electricity.*

half-sister, half-sisters
NC Your **half-sister** is a girl or woman with either the same mother or the same father as you. *He will meet the half-sister he has not seen since 1931.*

half-term
NU **Half-term** is a short holiday in the middle of a school term. *...people from Britain travelling to France for the school half-term holiday.*

half-timbered /hɑːftɪmbəd/
ADJ Buildings that are **half-timbered** have a framework of wooden beams which you can see from the outside. *...whitewashed half-timbered houses.*

half-time
NU **Half-time** is the short break between the two parts of a sports match, when the players have a rest. *The Italians led 9-3 at half-time.*

halftone /hɑːftəʊn/ **halftones**
1 NC A **halftone** is an illustration in a newspaper or book that consists of a very large number of very small dots, each of which is either black or white.
2 NC A **halftone** is the same as a **semitone**; used in American English.

halfway /hɑːfweɪ/
1 ADV **Halfway** means at the middle of a place or in between two points. *She was halfway up the stairs.*
2 ADV **Halfway** also means at the middle of a period of time or an event. *Dr O'Shea usually fell asleep halfway through the programme.*
3 If you **meet** someone **halfway**, you accept some of the points they are making so that you can come to an agreement. *He spoke of the need for an official willingness to meet the demands of the people halfway.*

halfway house, halfway houses
1 NC A **halfway house** is a hostel where people who have recently left prison or another institution can live for a short time while they learn to live on their own again. *Rose will now spend three months in a Cincinnati halfway house while he performs 1,000 hours of community service.*
2 N SING A **halfway house** is also a compromise between two different points of views or plans, or a situation which contains elements that are normally opposed to each other. *While the controversy over SDI is a great as ever, there's growing support for a kind of halfway house.*

half-wit, half-wits
NC If you call someone a **half-wit**, you are showing that you think they have behaved in a stupid, silly, or irresponsible way; an informal use.

half-witted /hɑːfwɪtɪd/
ADJ Some people use **half-witted** to describe behaviour that they think is very stupid, silly, or irresponsible; an informal word. *Well, that was a pretty half-witted thing to do.*

half-yearly
ADJ ATTRIB A **half-yearly** event happens every six months. *...the half-yearly meeting of the International Cocoa Organisation... The International Monetary Fund has published its half-yearly forecasts.*

halibut /hælɪbət/ **halibuts**
NCorNU A **halibut** is a large flat fish that you can eat.

halitosis /hælɪtəʊsɪs/
NU If someone has **halitosis**, they have breath that smells unpleasant, usually because they have a throat infection or decayed teeth.

hall /hɔːl/ **halls**
1 NC A **hall** is the area just inside the front door of a house. *We began bringing down our suitcases and putting them in the hall... He crept down the hall to their rooms.*
2 NC A **hall** is also a large room or building used for public events such as concerts, exhibitions, and meetings. *We organized a concert in the village hall... One thousand students returned to their lecture halls today.*
3 Students who live **in hall** live in university or college accommodation.

hallelujah /hælɪluːjə/; also spelt **halleluiah** and **alleluia**.
Some Christians say **hallelujah** in church as an exclamation of praise and thanks to God.

hallmark /hɔːlmɑːk/ **hallmarks**
1 NC+SUPP A **hallmark** is the most typical quality or feature of something or someone. *Nobody has admitted responsibility but the killings bear the hallmarks of the IRA... An air of melancholy is a hallmark of their songs.*
2 NC A **hallmark** is also an official mark put on objects made of precious metals which indicates their value, origin, and quality.

hallo /hələʊ/. See **hello**.

hall of residence, halls of residence
NC **Halls of residence** are blocks of rooms or flats belonging to universities or colleges and which are used by students. *The government has ordered students to leave the halls of residence.*

hallowed /hæləʊd/
ADJ If something is **hallowed**, it is respected, usually because it is old or important; a literary word. *...those hallowed offices on State Street.*

Halloween /hæləʊiːn/; also spelt **Hallowe'en**.
NU **Hallowe'en** is October 31st. It is traditionally said to be the night on which ghosts and witches can be seen, and so children often dress up as ghosts and witches. *Many rituals grew up around Hallowe'en.*

hallstand /hɔːlstænd/ **hallstands**
NC A **hallstand** is a piece of furniture on which you hang coats and hats.

hallucinate /həluːsɪneɪt/ **hallucinates, hallucinating, hallucinated**
v If you **hallucinate**, you see things that are not really there, either because you are ill or because you have taken a drug. *He started hallucinating, seeing members of the public as animals ready to attack him.*

hallucination /həluːsɪneɪʃn/ **hallucinations**
1 NCorNU A **hallucination** is the experience of seeing something that is not really there because you are ill or have taken a drug. *Larry's drug-enhanced hallucinations became more intense... Symptoms include damage to the central nervous system, hallucination and poor co-ordination.*
2 NC A **hallucination** is also something that is not real that someone sees when they are ill or have taken a drug. *She was no hallucination, her breath misted his windscreen.*

hallucinatory /həluːsɪnətᵊri/
ADJ Something that is **hallucinatory** is like a hallucination or is the cause of a hallucination. *I had a sudden hallucinatory vision of him... There was no*

question of my having been given a hallucinatory
drug.
hallucinogenic /həluːsɪnədʒenɪk/
ADJ A **hallucinogenic** drug is one that causes you to
hallucinate. *The drug, known as 'Ecstasy', has
hallucinogenic effects and loosens inhibitions.*
hallway /hɔːlweɪ/ **hallways**
NC A **hallway** is the entrance hall of a house or other
building. *In pride of place in their hallway stands the
piano.*
halo /heɪləʊ/ **haloes** or **halos**
NC A **halo** is a circle of light that is drawn in pictures
round the head of a holy figure such as a saint or
angel. *Although appearing to be Christ, the figure
bears no halo.*
halt /hɔːlt/ **halts, halting, halted**
1 V-ERG When a person or vehicle **halts** or when
something **halts** them, they stop moving. *He took a
step and halted... He tried to push past, but the girl
halted him... A second lorry was halted yesterday in
the Turkish port of Mersin.*
2 V-ERG When growth, development, or activity **halts**
or when you **halt** it, it stops completely. *A strike by
Brazil's oil workers has halted production at about
half of the country's refineries... The firm halted its
imports of nylon. ...if population growth were to halt
overnight.*
3 If something such as growth, development, or an
activity **comes** or **grinds to a halt**, or if it **is brought to
a halt**, it stops completely. *There were signs that last
year's steady progress in human rights policy had
come to a halt... The talks in Berlin ground to a halt...
Up to one thousand protesters gathered in University
Square, bringing traffic to a halt.*
4 If someone **calls a halt to** an activity, they decide
not to continue with it. *Peter Brooke called a halt to
the current talks a week ago.*
halter /hɔːltə/ **halters**
NC A **halter** is a strap made from leather or rope that
is fastened round the head of a horse so that it can be
led easily. *I tied Bub with his halter to the tree.*
halterneck /hɔːltənek/
ADJ A woman's **halterneck** dress or top is one that is
held in place by a narrow band of cloth round the back
of the neck, so that no shoulder straps are necessary.
halting /hɔːltɪŋ/
ADJ If you speak in a **halting** way, you speak
uncertainly with a lot of pauses. *...his halting
admission of guilt.*
halve /hɑːv/ **halves, halving, halved**
1 V-ERG When you **halve** something or when it **halves**,
it is reduced to half its previous size or amount. *This
could halve rail fares... If that happened, sales would
halve overnight.*
2 VO If you **halve** something, you divide it into two
equal parts. *Halve the avocado pears and remove the
stones.*
3 **Halves** is the plural of **half.**
ham /hæm/
NU **Ham** is salted meat from a pig's leg. *...a ham
sandwich... You can load the boot of your car with
caviar, champagne, hams and brandy.*
hamburger /hæmbɜːgə/ **hamburgers**
NC A **hamburger** is a flat round mass of minced beef,
fried and eaten in a bread roll. *Townspeople come
here at noon for coffee and hamburgers... A diet of too
many cream-cakes, hamburgers and chips accounts
for the deaths of many people in the West.*
ham-fisted /hæmfɪstɪd/
ADJ Someone who is **ham-fisted** is clumsy, usually in
the way that they use their hands. *Even the most
ham-fisted cook can take pleasure in his effort.*
Hamilton /hæmltən/
Hamilton is the capital of Bermuda and its largest
town. Population: 6,000 (1988).
hamlet /hæmlət/ **hamlets**
NC A **hamlet** is a small village. *...a remote mountain
hamlet.*
hammer /hæmə/ **hammers, hammering, hammered**
1 NC A **hammer** is a tool used for hitting things,
consisting of a heavy piece of metal at the end of a
handle. *If you could get a sample of the rock and hit

it with a hammer it would shatter.*
2 VO If you **hammer** something, you hit it with a
hammer. *I hammered a peg into the crack.*
3 VOorVA If you **hammer** a surface or **hammer** on it,
you hit it several times. *He hammered the table and
told us he wanted results... Men used to hammer on
our door late at night.*
4 NC A **hammer** is also a heavy weight attached to a
piece of wire, that is thrown as a sport. *...the
American hammer thrower, Ken Flax.*
5 VOA If you **hammer** an idea into people, you keep
repeating it in order to influence them. *...ideas
hammered into their heads by a stream of movies.*
6 VO If something **is hammered**, it is severely
damaged; an informal use. *Financial confidence in
Japan was hammered at the end of last year when
inflation seemed to be rising.*
hammer out PHRASAL VERB If you **hammer out**
something such as an agreement or plan, you reach an
agreement about it after a long or difficult discussion.
*Many practical details need to be hammered out.
...procedures hammered out over recent years.*
hammock /hæmək/ **hammocks**
NC A **hammock** is a piece of strong cloth which is
hung between two supports and used as a bed. *He
went to sleep on the garden hammock.*
hamper /hæmpə/ **hampers, hampering, hampered**
1 VO If you **hamper** a person or their actions, you
make it difficult for them to move or make progress.
*They were hampered by a constant stream of
visitors... Efforts to clear the area had been hampered
by lack of equipment.*
2 NC A **hamper** is a large basket with a lid, used for
carrying food or storing clothes. *...clothes on the floor
and in hampers.*
hamster /hæmstə/ **hamsters**
NC A **hamster** is a small rodent similar to a mouse,
which is often kept as a pet. *Hamsters eat almost
anything.*
hamstring /hæmstrɪŋ/ **hamstrings, hamstringing,
hamstrung**
1 NC A **hamstring** is a tendon behind your knee joining
the muscles of your thigh to the bones of your lower
leg. *Nicholas suffered a hamstring injury at the start
of the season.*
2 VO If you **hamstring** someone, you make it very
difficult for them to take any action; a literary use.
*The economic growth of the West is hamstrung by the
lack of purchasing power.*
hand /hænd/ **hands, handing, handed**
1 NC Your **hands** are the parts of your body at the end
of your arms. Each hand has four fingers and a
thumb. *He took her hand and squeezed it... The
injured man suffered burns to his hands.*
2 NC The **hands** of a clock or watch are the thin pieces
of metal or plastic that indicate what time it is. *...a
watch with a second hand.*
3 N SING If you ask someone for a **hand** with
something, you are asking them to help you. *Give me
a hand with this desk, will you?... Do you need a hand
with that?*
4 VOO If you **hand** something to someone, you give it
to them. *Could you hand me that piece of wood?... He
scribbled four lines and handed the note to the Field
Marshal.*
5 N SING The **hand** of someone or something is an
effective influence that that person or thing has on
events. *...moves that would resist the heavy hand of
state control over the economy... This has
strengthened the hand of the opposition moderates.*
6 PREFIX **Hand** can be added to some nouns that refer
to objects such as tools, machines, or vehicles to form
new nouns that carry the meaning of operated by hand
rather than automatically. *She was sitting on a stool
looking at herself in a hand-mirror... If the water
demand were quite small a hand pump would be
perfectly adequate.*
7 NC A **hand** is also someone who is employed to do
hard physical work; an old-fashioned use. *...farm
hands.*
● **Hand** is used in these phrases. ● You use **on the one
hand** when mentioning one aspect of a situation, and in

the next sentence or paragraph you use **on the other hand** when mentioning another, contrasting aspect. *On the one hand, it declared that the State would not interfere in the affairs of religious organisations. On the other, it forbade all religious teaching in schools.* ● If you have a responsibility or problem **on** your **hands**, you have to deal with it. When it is **off** your **hands**, it is no longer your responsibility. *They've still got an economic crisis on their hands.* ● The job or problem **in hand** is the one that you are currently dealing with. *Let's get on with the job in hand.* ● If you have something **in hand**, you have something that you have not used yet, which you can use later to gain an advantage over your rivals. *Warwickshire's lead in the championship is 14 points, although Essex have a game in hand.* ● If you have some time **in hand**, you have some time free. *He arrived with half an hour in hand and went for a walk.* ● A situation that you have **in hand** is one that you have under control. *The Prime Minister has the situation well in hand.* ● If you know something **off hand**, you can think of it straight away without asking someone else or checking it in a book. *I can't think off hand what the answer is.* ● If someone is **on hand**, they are near and ready to help. *A medical orderly is now on hand to deal with any further casualties.* ● If you have something **to hand**, you have it ready to use when needed. *...using the material most readily to hand.* ● Something that is **at hand** or **close at hand** is very near in time or place. *I picked up a book that happened to lie at hand.* ● If you do something **by hand**, you do it using your hands rather than a machine. *Planting by hand is tedious and time-consuming.* ● Two people who are **hand in hand** are holding each other's hand. *She spent the next five minutes or so walking hand in hand with Trudy.* ● Two things that **go hand in hand** are closely connected. *Military superiority went hand in hand with organizational superiority.* ● If you **know** a place **like the back of your hand**, you know it extremely well. *A London cabbie knows the city like the back of his hand.* ● If you **try** your **hand** at a new activity, you attempt to do it. *I had tried my hand at milking years ago.* ● If you **have a hand** in a situation, you are actively involved in it. *I had a hand in drafting the appeal.* ● If you **take** someone **in hand**, you take control of them and show them how to behave or what to do. *I'm going to take that boy in hand and teach him a lesson or two.* ● If someone gives you **a free hand**, they allow you to do a particular task exactly as you want. *Mr Yeltsin has made clear that he believes the treaty gives him a free hand to begin replacing existing communist structures of power.* ● If an audience gives a singer, actor, or sports player a **big hand**, they clap their hands loudly and cheer in order to show their appreciation of them; an informal expression. *Williams gained a big hand from his team for a hard-earned championship point.* ● If you **force** someone's **hand**, you make them do something sooner than they had planned to do it. *They had been resisting making the names public, but a leading newspaper forced their hand by printing most of the details.* ● If you **have** your **hands full**, you are very busy. *The new Prime Minister already has his hands full.* ● If you reject an idea **out of hand**, you reject it immediately and completely. *The initiative was rejected out of hand by the United States.* ● If a person or a situation **gets out of hand**, you are no longer able to control them or it. *There are fears that any quarrel could rapidly get out of hand.* ● If a possession **changes hands**, it is sold or given away. *The fifty acres of land changed hands four times.* ● If you **wash** your **hands** of someone or something, you refuse to take any more responsibility for them. *The government may wish to wash its hands of all responsibility for the impending disaster.*

hand down PHRASAL VERB 1 If possessions, skills, or knowledge **are handed down**, they are given or left to people who are younger or who belong to a younger generation. *This brooch has been handed down in our family for two hundred years... Such knowledge was handed down from father to son.* 2 If people in authority **hand down** a decision, they make it public;

used in American English. *That was one of the two important decisions handed down by the High Court yesterday... The panel's recommendations must be handed down within 65 days.*

hand in PHRASAL VERB If you **hand in** a written paper, you give it to someone in authority. *I haven't yet marked the work you handed in... I was tempted to hand in my resignation at once.*

hand on PHRASAL VERB If you **hand** something **on to** someone, you give it or leave it to them. *They handed on their knowledge to their children... The question may have to be handed on to his successor.*

hand out PHRASAL VERB 1 If you **hand out** a set of things, you give one to each person in a group. *Hand out the books.* 2 When people in authority **hand out** advice or punishment, they give it to people. *Family doctors handed out information on treatment.* 3 See also **handout**.

hand over PHRASAL VERB 1 If you **hand** something **over** to someone, you give it to them. *Samuel was clearly about to hand over large sums of money to this man.* 2 If you **hand over** to someone, you make them responsible for something which you were previously responsible for. *Sir John handed over to his deputy and left.*

handbag /ˈhændbæg/ **handbags**
NC **Handbags** are small bags which many women carry with them and use to keep things like their money and diaries in. *He is accused of stealing money from a handbag.*

hand baggage. See **hand luggage.**

handball /ˈhændbɔːl/
NU **Handball** is a game, usually played by two teams, in which you hit the ball with the palm of your hand. *Their men took the Handball title, beating Yugoslavia by 29 points to 27.*

handbill /ˈhændbɪl/ **handbills**
NC A **handbill** is a small printed notice which is used to advertise a particular company, service, or event. *Thousands of handbills were distributed to shops and offices announcing a revolutionary new accounting system.*

handbook /ˈhændbʊk/ **handbooks**
NC A **handbook** is a book giving advice or instructions. *He has written a handbook of bee-keeping for beginners.*

handbrake /ˈhændbreɪk/ **handbrakes**
NC A **handbrake** is a brake in a car which is operated by hand. *Mr Boggis released the handbrake.*

handcart /ˈhændkɑːt/ **handcarts**
NC A **handcart** is a small two-wheeled cart which is pushed or pulled along and is used for transporting goods.

handclap /ˈhændklæp/
N SING A **slow handclap** is slow rhythmic clapping by an audience to show that they do not like what they are seeing or hearing.

handcuff /ˈhændkʌf/ **handcuffs, handcuffing, handcuffed**
1 N PL **Handcuffs** are two metal rings linked by a short chain which are locked round a prisoner's wrists. *The defendant was led into the top security courtroom in handcuffs.*
2 VO If you **handcuff** someone, you put handcuffs around their wrists. *They were searched and handcuffed.*

handful /ˈhændfʊl/ **handfuls**
1 NC A **handful** of something is a small quantity of it that you can hold in one hand. *Roger gathered a handful of stones.*
2 N SING If there is only a **handful** of people or things, there are not very many of them. *The firm employs only a handful of workers.*
3 NC If you describe a child as a **handful**, you mean that he or she is difficult to control; an informal use. *Malcolm's a bit of a handful at the moment.*

handgun /ˈhændgʌn/ **handguns**
NC A **handgun** is a gun that you can hold, carry, and fire with one hand. *The man opened fire with a handgun.*

hand-held
ADJ ATTRIB A **hand-held** machine is one that is small

enough to use or carry in your hand. ...*a hand-held instrument containing the measuring components... It's no bigger than a hand-held shaver.*

handicap /ˈhændɪkæp/ **handicaps, handicapping, handicapped**

1 NC A **handicap** is a physical or mental disability. *These changes have made the campus an easier place for people with handicaps... Any woman who's given birth to a baby with a handicap will want to protect her next child from a similar fate.*

2 NC A **handicap** is also a situation that makes it harder for you to do something. *His chief handicap is that he comes from a broken home... The lack of good roads, railways, transport and communications is one glaring handicap to development.*

3 VO If an event or a situation **handicaps** someone, it makes it difficult for them to act or to do something. *We were handicapped by the darkness.*

4 NC A **handicap** is also a disadvantage given to someone who is good at a particular sport, in order to make the competition between them and the other competitors more equal. *A fellow golfer asked him what his handicap was.*

handicapped /ˈhændɪkæpt/

1 ADJ Someone who is **handicapped** has a physical or mental disability. *A friend of his had a handicapped daughter.*

2 N PL You can refer to people who are handicapped as **the handicapped**. ...*establishments for the mentally or physically handicapped.*

handicraft /ˈhændɪkrɑːft/ **handicrafts**

1 NC **Handicrafts** are activities such as embroidery and pottery which involve making things with your hands in a skilful way. *She teaches handicrafts.*

2 NC **Handicrafts** are also the objects that are produced by people doing handicrafts. *Handicrafts were produced by families to be sold in local shops.*

handiwork /ˈhændɪwɜːk/

NU+POSS If you refer to something as your **handiwork**, you mean that you made it yourself. *He stood back and surveyed his handiwork.*

handkerchief /ˈhæŋkətʃɪf/ **handkerchiefs**

NC A **handkerchief** is a small square of fabric or paper used when you blow your nose. *He dabbed his face with his handkerchief. ...linen handkerchiefs intricately embroidered with coloured silk and gold threads.*

handle /ˈhændl/ **handles, handling, handled**

1 NC A **handle** is the part of an object that you hold in order to carry it or operate it. *He tugged at the metal handle. ...a broom handle.*

2 VO When you **handle** something, you hold it and move it about in your hands. *The child handled the ornaments carefully and seldom broke anything.*

3 VO To **handle** something also means to use or control it effectively. *She had handled a machine gun herself.*

4 VA If something **handles** well, it is easy to use or control. *This car handles very nicely.*

5 VO If you **handle** a problem or a particular area of work, you deal with it or are responsible for it. *You don't have to come. Hendricks and I can handle it... He handles all the major accounts.* ◆ **handling** NU *His handling of these important issues was condemned by the opposition.*

6 VO If you can **handle** people, you are good at getting them to respect you and do what you want them to. *The principal was a genius in the way he handled us.*

7 N SING If you have a **handle** on a subject, you have a way of approaching it that helps you to understand it. ...*changes which we don't have a very good handle on... That will give us for the first time a really good handle on the individual masses of both Pluto and Charon.*

8 If you **fly off the handle**, you completely lose your temper; an informal expression.

handlebar /ˈhændlbɑː/ **handlebars**

NC The **handlebars** of a bicycle consist of the curved metal bar with handles at each end which are used for steering. *It doesn't have a steering wheel at all, it's got handlebars very similar to a motorcycle.*

handler /ˈhændlə/ **handlers**

NC+SUPP A **handler** is someone whose job is to be in charge of a particular type of thing. *Baggage handlers at London's Heathrow Airport say they checked all baggage with extreme thoroughness... A search is being carried out today involving a police helicopter and dog handlers.*

hand luggage

NU Your **hand luggage** or **hand baggage** is the bags or cases, that you keep with you during the journey when you travel on an aeroplane or coach. *Passengers are advised that only one small item of hand luggage may be taken into the aircraft cabin... The bomb could have been contained in his hand baggage.*

handmade /ˈhændmeɪd/

ADJ If something is **handmade**, it is made without using machines. ...*beautiful handmade clothes.*

handmaiden /ˈhændmeɪdn/ **handmaidens**

1 NC A **handmaiden** or a **handmaid** is a female servant; an old-fashioned use.

2 NC+of or to A **handmaiden** or **handmaid** is also something which plays a lesser but important supporting role to something else. *The Party regarded the trade unions as the handmaid of the political movement.*

hand-me-down, hand-me-downs

NC **Hand-me-downs** are things, especially clothing, which have been used by other people before you and which have been given to you for your use. ...*my elder sister's hand-me-downs. ...hand-me-down clothes.*

handout /ˈhændaʊt/ **handouts**

1 NC A **handout** is money, clothing, or food which is given free to poor people. *We said that we wouldn't be relying on handouts from anyone for our future.*

2 NC A **handout** is also a document, copies of which are given to a number of people in a meeting or a class. ...*a pile of unread public relations handouts and shiny magazines.*

hand-picked

ADJ If someone is **hand-picked**, they have been carefully chosen for a particular purpose or job. *Each of the officers had been hand-picked by the general.*

handrail /ˈhændreɪl/ **handrails**

NC A **handrail** is a long piece of metal or wood fixed near stairs or high places. ...*holding onto the bright brass handrails.*

handset /ˈhændset/ **handsets**

NC The **handset** of a portable telephone is the part that you hold near your ear and speak into. *There is a way of recording your conversation by fitting something to the telephone handset.*

handshake /ˈhændʃeɪk/ **handshakes**

NC If you give someone a **handshake**, you grasp their right hand with your right hand and move it up and down as a sign of greeting or to show that you have agreed about something. *Their handshake appeared to be a gesture of reconciliation.*

hands-off /ˌhændz ˈɒf/

ADJ ATTRIB If someone has a **hands-off** approach to a situation or problem, they let it develop or resolve itself, while intervening as little as possible. *It's unlikely that the Bush administration's hands-off policy will change... Labour is preparing to criticize what it sees as a hands-off approach to the issue of repayment.*

handsome /ˈhænsəm/

1 ADJ A **handsome** man has an attractive face with regular features. *He was a tall, dark, and undeniably handsome man.*

2 ADJ A woman who is **handsome** has an attractive, smart appearance with large, regular features rather than small, delicate ones. ...*a strikingly handsome woman.*

3 ADJ ATTRIB A **handsome** sum of money is a large or generous amount; a formal use. *The rate of return on these farmers' outlay was a handsome 57 per cent.* ◆ **handsomely** ADV *There's no doubt that we have contributed to those profits and contributed handsomely... He was paid handsomely.*

hands-on /ˌhændz ˈɒn/

1 ADJ ATTRIB If you have **hands-on** experience of something, especially a computer, you have actually

used it rather than just learned or read about it. *We could take that actual hands-on shipbuilding experience and sawmill experience... I brought games to the classroom. I taught everything with hands-on materials.*
2 ADJ ATTRIB If someone has a **hands-on** approach to a situation or problem, they intervene a great deal in it to try to solve it. *George Bush is an extraordinarily engaged, hands-on president in foreign affairs.*

handstand /hændstænd/ **handstands**
NC If you do a **handstand**, you balance upside down on your hands with your body and legs straight up in the air.

hand-to-hand
ADJ ATTRIB A **hand-to-hand** fight is one in which people are fighting very close together, with their hands or knives. *Some reports spoke of hand-to-hand fighting in the streets.*

hand-to-mouth
ADJ ATTRIB or ADV A **hand-to-mouth** existence is a way of life in which you have hardly enough food or money to live on. *He is living a hand-to-mouth existence with his father... Many peasant farmers live hand-to-mouth.*

handwriting /hændraɪtɪŋ/
NU Your **handwriting** is your style of writing with a pen or pencil. *He looked at his son's laborious handwriting.*

handwritten /hændrɪtn/
ADJ A piece of writing that is **handwritten** is one that has been written using a pen or pencil rather than a typewriter or other machine. *The handwritten, unsigned statement, was delivered to the offices of an international news agency in Beirut.*

handy /hændi/ **handier, handiest**
1 ADJ Something that is **handy** is useful and easy to use. *An electric kettle is very handy.*
2 ADJ after N A thing or place that is **handy** is nearby and convenient; an informal use. *I looked to see whether there was a glass handy.*
3 ADJ Someone who is **handy** with a particular thing is skilful at using it; an informal use. *...village boys who had a handy way with horses.*

handyman /hændimæn/ **handymen**
NC A **handyman** is a man who is good at making or repairing things. *An eighteen year old boy joined the household as chauffeur and handyman.*

hang /hæŋ/ **hangs, hanging, hung** /hʌŋ/. The form **hanged** is used as the past tense and past participle for the meaning in paragraph 3.
1 V OA If you **hang** something on a hook or rail, you place it so that its highest part is supported and the rest of it is not. *He was hanging his coat in the hall.*
2 V A If something is **hanging** somewhere, the top of it is attached to something and the rest of it is free and not supported. *...some washing hanging on a line. ...yellow ribbons hanging from lamp posts.*
3 V O or V-REFL To **hang** someone means to kill them by tying a rope around their neck and taking away the support from under their feet so that they hang in the air. *Rebecca Smith was hanged in 1849... He tried to hang himself.*
4 V+over If a future event or a possibility **hangs** over you, it worries you. *...the threat of universal extinction hanging over all the world today.*
5 If you **get the hang** of something, you begin to understand how to do it; an informal expression. *Once you have got the hang of it, you'll be alright.*
6 See also **hanging**.

hang about PHRASAL VERB See **hang around**.
hang around PHRASAL VERB If you **hang around**, **hang about**, or **hang round** somewhere, you stay in a particular place doing nothing often because you are waiting for someone; used in informal English. *We would have to hang around for a while... She was left to hang about the platform on her own.*
hang on PHRASAL VERB 1 If you ask someone to **hang on**, you mean you want them to wait for a moment; an informal expression. *Hang on a minute.* 2 If you **hang on**, you manage to survive until a situation improves. *I can't keep hanging on here much longer.* 3 If one thing **hangs on** another, it depends on it. *Everything hangs on money at the moment.*

hang onto PHRASAL VERB 1 If you **hang onto** something, you hold it very tightly. *Claude hung on to Tom's shoulder.* 2 If you **hang onto** a position that you have, you try to keep it. *Fear is a powerful motive for hanging onto power.*
hang out PHRASAL VERB When you **hang out** washing, you hang it on a clothes line to dry. *Mrs Poulter was hanging out her washing.*
hang round PHRASAL VERB See **hang around**.
hang up PHRASAL VERB 1 If you **hang** something **up**, you place it so that its highest part is supported and the rest of it is not. *Howard hangs up his scarf on the hook behind the door.* 2 If something is **hanging up** somewhere, the top of it is attached to something and the rest of it is free and not supported. *There are some old tools hanging up in the shed.* 3 If you **hang up** when you are on the phone, you end the phone call by putting the receiver back on the rest. *'Thank-you. Goodbye.' He hung up.*
hang up on PHRASAL VERB If you **hang up on** someone, you end a phone call to them suddenly and unexpectedly by putting the receiver back on the rest. *He didn't answer. He just hung up on me.*

hangar /hæŋə/ **hangars**
NC A **hangar** is a large building where aircraft are kept. *The client intends to house two jumbo jets within the hangar.*

hangdog /hæŋdɒg/
ADJ ATTRIB Someone who has a **hangdog** expression looks miserable or guilty.

hanger /hæŋə/ **hangers**
NC A **hanger** is a curved piece of metal or wood used for hanging clothes on. *I brought a load of clothes hangers.*

hanger-on, hangers-on
NC A **hanger-on** is a person who tries to be friendly with a richer or more important person or group, especially for his or her own advantage. *...a small group of writers, artists and assorted hangers-on.*

hang-glider, hang-gliders
NC A **hang-glider** is a type of large kite, which someone can hang from and use to help them fly through the air. *...the multi-coloured triangle of his hang-glider. ...hang-glider pilots.*

hang-gliding
NU **Hang-gliding** is the activity of flying in a hang-glider. *Larger numbers of people have tackled the joys and hazards of hang-gliding.*

hanging /hæŋɪŋ/ **hangings**
1 NU **Hanging** is the practice of executing people by hanging them. *Every one of them was in favour of hanging... This is the third occasion when extremists have killed their victims by hanging.*
2 NC A **hanging** is the act of killing a person by hanging them. *The report mentions six public hangings.*
3 NC A **hanging** is also a piece of cloth used as a decoration on a wall. *...silk and damask hangings.*

hangman /hæŋmən/ **hangmen** /hæŋmən/
NC A **hangman** is a man whose job is to execute people by hanging them.

hangover /hæŋəʊvə/ **hangovers**
1 NC A **hangover** is a headache and feeling of sickness that people have after drinking too much alcohol. *He woke up this morning with a hangover.*
2 NC+SUPP A **hangover** from the past is something which results from ideas or attitudes which people had but which are no longer generally held. *...a hangover from earlier, more primitive times.*

hang-up, hang-ups
NC If you have a **hang-up** about something, you have a feeling of anxiety or embarrassment about it; an informal word. *He's got a hang-up about flying.*

hank /hæŋk/ **hanks**
NC A **hank** is a length of loosely-wound wool, rope, or string; a technical term. *...spinning wool from a hank onto a wooden spindle.*

hanker /hæŋkə/ **hankers, hankering, hankered**
V+after or V+for If you **hanker** after something or **hanker** for it, you want it very much. *We always hankered after a bungalow of our own.*

hankering /ˈhæŋkəᵊrɪŋ/ **hankerings**
NC+for A **hankering** for something is a great desire for it. *If you give way to this hankering for food you will become fat.*

hanky /ˈhæŋki/ **hankies**; also spelt **hankie**.
NC A **hanky** is the same as a **handkerchief**; an informal word. *She discreetly wiped her fingers on a lace hanky.*

hanky-panky /ˈhæŋki ˈpæŋki/
NU **Hanky-panky** is improper but not very serious sexual activity between two people; an informal word, used humorously. *I caught them having a little hanky-panky in the car.*

Hanoi /hænˈɔɪ/
Hanoi is the capital of Vietnam and its second largest city. It was formerly the capital of French Indochina and was the capital of North Vietnam from 1954 to 1976. Population: 1,089,000 (1989).

Hans Adam II, Prince of Liechtenstein /hæns ˈædəm/
Prince Hans Adam II became Prince of Liechtenstein in 1989, at the death of his father, Franz Josef II. He had previously assumed executive authority in 1984. Born: 1945.

hansom /ˈhænsəm/ **hansoms**
NC A **hansom** or a **hansom cab** is a horse-drawn carriage with two wheels and a fixed hood. Hansom cabs were used in former times.

haphazard /hæpˈhæzəd/
ADJ Something that is **haphazard** is not organized according to a plan. *It was done on a haphazard basis.* ♦ **haphazardly** ADV *...all the papers haphazardly strewn on desks.*

hapless /ˈhæpləs/
ADJ ATTRIB A **hapless** person is unlucky; a literary word. *...the hapless victim of a misplaced murder attempt.*

happen /ˈhæpn/ **happens, happening, happened**
1 V When something **happens**, it occurs or is done without being planned. *The explosion had happened at one in the morning. ...a court of inquiry into what happened... He had no knowledge of what was happening.*
2 V+to When something **happens** to you, it takes place and affects you. *...all the ghastly things that had happened to him.*
3 V+to-INF If you **happen** to do something, you do it by chance. *He happened to be at their base when the alert began.*
4 You say '**as it happens**' before a statement in order to introduce a new fact. *As it happens, I brought the note with me.*

happening /ˈhæpəᵊnɪŋ/ **happenings**
NC A **happening** is something that happens, often in an unexpected way. *...some very bizarre happenings in Europe.*

happy /ˈhæpi/ **happier, happiest**
1 ADJ Someone who is **happy** feels pleasure, often because something nice has happened. *I was happy to hear that you passed your exam... The old man's not very happy. ...a happy smile.* ♦ **happily** ADV *We laughed and chatted happily together.* ♦ **happiness** NU *Money did not bring happiness.*
2 ADJ A time or place that is **happy** is full of pleasant and enjoyable feelings, or has an atmosphere in which people feel happy. *...a happy childhood. ...the happiest time of their lives.*
3 ADJ PRED If you are **happy** about a situation or arrangement, you are satisfied with it. *We are not too happy about this turn of events... Are you happy with that, Diana?*
4 ADJ PRED+to-INF If you are **happy** to do something, you are willing to do it. *I was happy to work with George.*
5 ADJ ATTRIB You use **happy** in greetings to say that you hope someone will enjoy a special occasion. *Happy birthday!... Happy New Year!* ● **many happy returns**: see **return**.
6 ADJ ATTRIB You use **happy** to describe something that is appropriate or lucky; a formal use. *I appreciate that this is not a happy comparison... By a happy coincidence, we were all on the same train.*

♦ **happily** ADV SEN *That trend reversed itself, happily.*

happy-go-lucky
ADJ Someone who is **happy-go-lucky** enjoys life and does not worry about the future. *They are happy-go-lucky people who are happiest leaning on a shovel doing manual work. ...the traditional happy-go-lucky attitude.*

Harald V, King /ˈhærəld/
Harald V succeeded his father, Olav V, as King of Norway in 1991. He served as regent from 1990 to 1991. Born: 1937.

harangue /həˈræŋ/ **harangues, haranguing, harangued**; used showing disapproval.
1 NC A **harangue** is a long, forceful, persuasive speech. *...blazing harangues about the wickedness of the Government.*
2 VO If someone **harangues** you, they try to persuade you to accept their opinions or ideas in a forceful way. *Smith harangued his fellow students and persuaded them to walk out.*

Harare /həˈrɑːri/
Harare is the capital of Zimbabwe and its largest city. It was formerly called Salisbury. Population: 656,000 (1982).

harass /ˈhærəs/ **harasses, harassing, harassed**
VO If you **harass** someone, you continually trouble them or annoy them. *Some governments have chosen to harass and persecute the rural poor.*

harassed /ˈhærəst/
ADJ Someone who is **harassed** feels worried because they have too much to do or too many problems. *As the pressure gets worse, people get more harassed.*

harassing /ˈhærəsɪŋ/
ADJ Something that is **harassing** makes you feel worried because you have too much to do. *I have had a particularly busy and harassing day.*

harassment /ˈhærəsmənt/
NU **Harassment** is behaviour which is intended to trouble or annoy someone. *...alleged police brutality and harassment.*

harbinger /ˈhɑːbɪndʒə/ **harbingers**
NC A person or thing that is a **harbinger** of something is a sign that that thing is going to happen in the future; a formal word. *The sudden oil price rise was a harbinger of future problems.*

harbour /ˈhɑːbə/ **harbours, harbouring, harboured**; spelt **harbor** in American English.
1 NC A **harbour** is an area of deep water which is protected from the sea by land or walls, so that boats can be left there safely. *The ship had just entered Havana harbour.*
2 VO If you **harbour** an unpleasant emotion, you have it for a long period of time; a literary use. *I was unable to dismiss the fears I harboured for my safety.*
3 VO If you **harbour** someone who is wanted by the police, you hide them secretly in your house. *You could get into trouble for harbouring her.*

hard /hɑːd/ **harder, hardest**
1 ADJ or ADV If something feels **hard** when you touch it, it is very firm and is not easily bent, cut, or broken. *The green fruits were as hard as rocks... The ground was baked hard.* ♦ **hardness** NU *We gave them cushions to ease the hardness of the benches.*
2 ADJ If something is **hard** to do or to understand, it is difficult to do or understand. *He found it hard to make friends... That is a very hard question to answer.*
3 ADV If you try **hard** or work **hard**, you make a great effort to achieve something. *I cannot stand upright, no matter how hard I try... He had worked hard all his life... Think hard about what I'm offering.*
4 ADJ **Hard** work involves a lot of effort. *This has been a long hard day... It was very hard work in the shop.*
5 ADV **Hard** also means with a lot of force. *She slammed the door hard... The government's first reaction to the riots was to clamp down hard.*
6 ADJ Someone who is **hard** shows no kindness or pity. *His hard grey eyes began to soften a little.*
7 ADJ PRED+on To be **hard** on someone or something means to treat them unkindly or severely. *Don't be hard on her... It seemed rather hard on the women... This work's hard on the feet.*

8 ADJ If your life or a period of time is **hard**, it is difficult and unpleasant. *He finds life at sea hard.*
9 ADJ A **hard** winter or **hard** frost is very cold or severe. *Militants in the Kashmir valley are preparing themselves for a long hard winter.*
10 ADJ ATTRIB **Hard** facts are definitely true. *We have no hard evidence to indicate that he is the culprit.*
11 ADJ ATTRIB **Hard** drugs are strong illegal drugs such as heroin or cocaine. *Officials from the Home Office are to hold urgent talks with the Dutch authorities about the smuggling of hard drugs into Britain.*
12 If you feel **hard done by**, you feel you have been treated unfairly. *Not everybody is satisfied and there are many people who feel they've been hard done by.*
13 to **follow hard on the heels of** someone: see **heel**. See also **hard left**, **hard right**.

hard and fast
ADJ ATTRIB **Hard and fast** rules cannot be changed. *There isn't any hard and fast rule about this.*

hardback /ˈhɑːdbæk/ **hardbacks**
N C or N U A **hardback** is a book which has a stiff cover. *...recent hardbacks. ...a hardback edition... It was published in hardback.*

hardball /ˈhɑːdbɔːl/
1 N U **Hardball** is the same as **baseball**; used when comparing it with softball.
2 If you say that people **play hardball**, you mean they are prepared to be very tough and forceful in order to get what they want; used in American English. *Analysts are calling on the United States to play hardball to get the peace process going.*
3 ADJ ATTRIB **Hardball** can be used to describe methods which are very tough and forceful; used in American English. *The old style of cautious diplomacy has been replaced by a hardball pursuit of one goal.*

hard-bitten
ADJ **Hard-bitten** people are determined to get what they want without having any sympathy for the people they might hurt or affect. *He is out of step with many of his hard-bitten colleagues.*

hardboard /ˈhɑːdbɔːd/
N U **Hardboard** is a thin, flexible sheet of wood made by pressing wood fibres very closely together.

hard-boiled
ADJ A **hard-boiled** egg has been boiled in its shell until the yolk and the white are hard. *I am offered tea and a hard-boiled egg.*

hard cash
N U **Hard cash** is real money, rather than promises of money or credit. *There have been no promises of hard cash or investment.*

hardcore /ˈhɑːdkɔː/
1 N SING You can refer to the members of a group who are most involved with it as the **hardcore**. *There is a hardcore of committed communists amongst the Afghan army officers.*
2 ADJ ATTRIB **Hardcore** pornography shows sexual acts in very explicit detail. *They have been the main producers of hardcore child pornography since the late 1960's... Until now, obscenity prosecutions usually have focused on hardcore pornography and the commercial sex industry.*

hard currency, hard currencies
N U or N C A **hard currency** is one which can be traded internationally and so is considered to be a good one to have or to invest in. *...the lack of hard currency to purchase vital imports... Is sterling any longer a hard currency?*

hard disk, hard disks
N C A **hard disk** is a piece of stiff plastic which is coated with a magnetic substance on which computer information can be stored. A hard disk can store much more information than a floppy disk. *At present information is stored on the micro-computer's hard disk.*

hard drink
N U **Hard drink** is strong alcoholic drink such as whisky, gin, or brandy.

hard-drinking
ADJ ATTRIB A **hard-drinking** person is one who frequently drinks large quantities of alcohol. *...an*

impetuous, loud-mouthed, hard-drinking actor.

harden /ˈhɑːdn/ **hardens, hardening, hardened**
1 V-ERG When something **hardens**, it becomes stiff or firm. *The glue dries very fast and hardens in an hour... This is then dipped in cold water to harden the wax.*
2 V-ERG When your ideas or attitudes **harden**, they become fixed and you become determined not to change them. *The organization has hardened its attitude to the crisis... The economic warfare has hardened General Noriega's resolve not to step down... Now, however, the tone has hardened.* ◆ **hardening** N U *It would almost certainly result in a hardening of Allied opposition and determination.*
3 V O When events **harden** people, they make them become less sympathetic and gentle than they were before. *Life in the camp had hardened her considerably.*

hardened /ˈhɑːdnd/
ADJ **Hardened** means having so much experience of something that you are no longer affected by it in the way that other people would be. *The report claims that young people put in prison are corrupted by hardened criminals. ...a world hardened to political injustice.*

hard-headed
ADJ A **hard-headed** person is practical and determined. *It's not difficult to see why hard-headed businessmen have invested in this way.*

hard-hearted
ADJ A **hard-hearted** person is unsympathetic and does not care about other people. *...a hard-hearted approach to the needy in society.*

hard-hit
ADJ If someone or something is **hard-hit** by a particular problem, they are very badly affected by it. *Britain's farmers have been hard-hit by cuts in EEC subsidies... The organisation aims to assist countries hard-hit by the Gulf crisis.*

hard-hitting
ADJ ATTRIB A **hard-hitting** speech or article, is one in which the speaker or author is not afraid to discuss all aspects of a particular subject, usually in a very critical way. *...a hard-hitting account of the Nigerian Civil War... The leader of the opposition has made a hard-hitting speech denouncing the government's economic and social policies.*

hard labour; spelt **hard labor** in American English.
N U **Hard labour** is hard physical work which people have to do as punishment for a crime. *He was condemned to six months hard labour.*

hard left; also written **hard-left**.
N SING or N PL The **hard left** refers to those members of a left wing political group or party who have the most extreme beliefs about the sort of society they want to create and about the sort of policies their group should adopt to achieve this. *It's thought that the hard left have gained a majority. ...an attempt by the hard-left to destabilize the government.*

hard line
N SING If someone takes a **hard line** on something, they have a firm policy which they refuse to change. *He applauded the president's hard line on the issue.*

hardliner /ˈhɑːdlaɪnə/ **hardliners**
N C A **hardliner** is a person who supports a strict, fixed set of ideas that are often extreme, and who refuses to accept any change in them. *Political power in this country alternates between hardliners and moderates within the ruling party.*

hard luck
You can say 'Hard luck' to someone to say that you are sorry they have not got what they wanted; an informal expression.

hard-luck story, hard-luck stories
N C If you tell someone a **hard-luck story**, you tell them about some awful things that have happened to you in order to get help, sympathy, or money from them.

hardly /ˈhɑːdli/
1 ADV You use **hardly** to say that something is only just true. *I was beginning to like Sam, though I hardly knew him... The boy was hardly more than seventeen... She had hardly any money... Her bedroom*

was so small that she could hardly move in it.
2 ADV If you say **hardly** had one thing happened when
something else happened, you mean that the first
event was followed immediately by the second.
*Hardly had he uttered the words when he began
laughing.*
3 ADV You can use **hardly** in an ironic way to
emphasize that something is certainly not true. *I will
hardly need to remind you to be polite... In the
circumstances, it is hardly surprising that he resigned.*

hard-nosed
ADJ **Hard-nosed** people are tough and realistic, and
take decisions on practical grounds rather than
emotional ones; an informal word. *...hard-nosed
economists... Audiences are favouring a more hard-
nosed, realistic acting style.*

hard of hearing
ADJ If someone is **hard of hearing**, they are not able to
hear properly. *This makes it much easier for me
because I'm a little hard of hearing.*

hard palate, hard palates
NC Your **hard palate** is the hard top part of the inside
of your mouth, from your teeth back towards your
throat: compare **soft palate**.

hard porn
NU **Hard porn** is pornography that shows sex in a very
explicit, violent, or unpleasant way.

hard-pressed
ADJ If someone is **hard-pressed**, they are under a
great deal of strain and worry. *The Department of
Education is particularly hard-pressed at the moment.*

hard right; also written **hard-right**.
N SING or N PL The **hard right** refers to those members
of a political group or party who have the most
extreme right-wing beliefs about the sort of society
they want to create and about the sort of policies their
group should adopt to achieve this. *They faced a
challenge from the hard right. ...a power struggle
going on between the more moderate side of the party
and the hard-right.*

hard sell
N SING The **hard sell** is a method of selling in which
the salesperson puts a lot of pressure on someone to
make them buy something. *They weren't given the
hard sell.* ▶ Also ADJ ATTRIB *I don't like his hard sell
approach.*

hardship /hɑːdʃɪp/ hardships
NU or NC **Hardship** is a situation in which someone
suffers from difficulties and problems, often because
they do not have enough money. *...a period of
considerable hardship and unhappiness... You know
the hardships we have suffered.*

hard shoulder
N SING The **hard shoulder** is the area at the side of a
motorway where you are allowed to stop if your car
has broken down. *All three carriageways and the
hard shoulder were blocked solid.*

hard-up
ADJ If you are **hard-up**, you have very little money; an
informal word. *...a hard-up divorcee struggling to
bring up a sick child on social security payments.*

hardware /hɑːdweə/
1 NU **Hardware** is tools and equipment for use in the
home and garden. *The components are readily
available in hardware shops and are used in domestic
appliances.*
2 NU Military **hardware** is machinery that is used in
war, for example, tanks, aircrafts, or missiles. *China
is now the fifth largest exporter of military hardware
in the world.*
3 NU Computer **hardware** is the machinery of a
computer as opposed to the programs that are written
for it. *In addition to the basic hardware and software,
several other components will be needed.*

hard-wearing
ADJ Something that is **hard-wearing** is strong and lasts
for a long time. *These blankets are hard-wearing, but
not so warm as wool.*

hard-won
ADJ A **hard-won** victory or success, is one that you
have achieved, even though it was difficult. *...the
country's hard-won independence... They have always*

tried to avoid damaging their hard-won reputation.

hardwood /hɑːdwʊd/ hardwoods
NC or NU A **hardwood** is a tree such as an oak tree that
produces very strong, hard wood. **Hardwood** also
refers to the wood produced by such a tree, which is
often used for making good quality furniture. *Papua
New Guinea is one of the world's major producers of
tropical hardwoods... Intensive logging for hardwood
also changes the flora of certain areas. ...hardwood
floors.*

hardy /hɑːdi/ hardier, hardiest
ADJ People, animals, and plants that are **hardy** are
strong and able to endure difficult conditions. *Their
children are remarkably hardy... Strawberries are
hardy and easy to grow in all soils.*

hare /heə/ hares
NC A **hare** is an animal like a large rabbit with long
ears, long legs, and a small tail. *They rejected a call
to stop the hunting of foxes, hares and mink.*

harebrained /heəbreɪnd/
ADJ **Harebrained** plans or ideas are foolish and
unlikely to succeed. *A senior American official has
dismissed these plans as harebrained.*

harelip /heəlɪp/ harelips
NC or NU If someone has a **harelip**, their upper lip is
split slightly because it did not grow properly before
they were born.

harem /hɑːriːm, hɑːriːm/ harems
NC A **harem** is a group of wives or mistresses
belonging to one man, especially in Muslim societies.
She'd been born and brought up in a harem.

haricot /hærɪkəʊ/ haricots
NC **Haricots** or **haricot beans** are small, pale beans.
They are usually sold dried. *...the next crop of haricot
beans.*

hark /hɑːk/ harks, harking, harked
hark back PHRASAL VERB If someone or something
harks back to an event or situation in the past, they
remember it or remind you of it. *Increasingly she
harked back to our 'dear little cottage'.*

harlequin /hɑːləkwɪn/
ADJ ATTRIB **Harlequin** means having a lot of different
colours which are usually arranged in a diamond
pattern. *...a harlequin jacket.*

harlot /hɑːlət/ harlots
NC A **harlot** is a prostitute, or a woman who looks or
behaves like a prostitute; an old-fashioned word, used
showing disapproval. *'That yonder wicked harlot doth
bewitch me.'*

harm /hɑːm/ harms, harming, harmed
1 VO To **harm** someone means to physically injure
them in some way. *I stood very still, hoping they
wouldn't harm my sister and me... The military
campaign risks harming civilians.*
2 VO If you **harm** something, you damage it or make
it less successful in some way. *Washing cannot harm
the fabric... This can harm the child's psychological
development... The British stance on South Africa had
harmed relations with other members of the
Commonwealth.*
3 NU **Harm** is physical injury or damage which is
caused to someone or something. *He went in danger
of physical harm... Do prisons do more harm than
good?*
● **Harm** occurs in these phrases. ● If you say that
someone or something will **come to no harm** or that **no
harm will come** to them, you mean that they will not
be hurt or damaged. *I know that I can walk safely
through the streets of West Belfast and that I will
come to no harm at all... No harm would come to the
Prime Minister or to the other hostages.* ● If someone
or something is **out of harm's way**, they are in a safe
place. *He was concerned about the physical safety of
his family and wanted to get them out of harm's way.*
● If you say that **there is no harm in** doing something,
you mean that you want to do it and you do not think
that it is wrong. *There's no harm in asking.*

harmful /hɑːmfl/
ADJ Something that is **harmful** has a bad effect on
someone or something else. *Too much salt can be
harmful to a young baby.*

harmless /hɑːmləs/
1 ADJ Something that is **harmless** is safe to use, touch, or be near. ...*harmless butterflies.* ◆ **harmlessly** ADV *The rocket thudded harmlessly to the ground.*
2 ADJ A **harmless** action is unlikely to annoy or worry people. *Singing in the bath gives him a little harmless pleasure.* ◆ **harmlessly** ADV *His column deals harmlessly with the antics of film stars.*

harmonic /hɑːmɒnɪk/ **harmonics**
1 ADJ ATTRIB **Harmonic** means composed, played, or sung using two or more notes which sound right and pleasing together. ...*the newer harmonic structures he was always reaching for.*
2 NC A **harmonic** is a musical note which is produced as an overtone of another note. *His work exposes in its harmonics a whole region of sound neglected until now.*

harmonica /hɑːmɒnɪkə/ **harmonicas**
NC A **harmonica** is a small musical instrument which you play by moving it across your lips and blowing and sucking air through it. ...*'Eleanor Rigby' played by Tommy Reilly on his specially made silver harmonica.*

harmonious /hɑːməʊnɪəs/
1 ADJ A relationship, agreement, or discussion that is **harmonious** is friendly and peaceful. ...*a generally harmonious debate.* ◆ **harmoniously** ADV *Harold and I worked harmoniously together.*
2 ADJ Something that is **harmonious** has parts which go well together. *The different parts of the garden fit together in a harmonious way.*

harmonize /hɑːmənaɪz/ **harmonizes, harmonizing, harmonized;** also spelt **harmonise.**
1 V-ERG If two or more things **harmonize** with each other or if you **harmonize** them, they fit in well with each other. *Such events harmonized with one's view of society.* ...*the dancers' costumes harmonizing with their choice of colours... The Prince has made comments about architects being incapable of harmonizing their buildings with the environment.*
2 VO or VA When people **harmonize** ideas or issues, they agree about them in a friendly way. *The Presidents of all five countries did agree to harmonize their economic policies... It's difficult to get world leaders to harmonize on the important issues.*

harmony /hɑːməni/ **harmonies**
1 NU If people are living in **harmony** with each other, they are in a state of peaceful agreement and co-operation. *Industry and the universities have worked together in harmony.*
2 NU or NC **Harmony** is the pleasant combination of different notes of music played at the same time. *They sing in harmony.* ...*the harmonies of Ravel and Debussy.*
3 N SING+SUPP The **harmony** of something is the way in which its parts are combined into a pleasant arrangement. ...*the harmony of nature.*

harness /hɑːnɪs/ **harnesses, harnessing, harnessed**
1 VO If you **harness** something such as a source of energy, you bring it under your control and use it. *Techniques harnessing the energy of the sun are being developed... Martin Luther King harnessed popular support in opposing racial segregation.*
2 NC A **harness** is a set of straps which fit under a person's arms and round their body to hold equipment or to prevent them from moving too much. ...*your safety harness.*
3 NC A **harness** is also a set of leather straps and metal links fastened round a horse's head or body so that it can pull a carriage, cart, or plough. ...*a simple breast-band harness for the donkey.*
4 VO If you **harness** an animal such as a horse, you put a harness on it. ...*tips to improve the way you harness up your oxen or buffalo... Farmers have got problems with harnessing their carts.*

harp /hɑːp/ **harps, harping, harped**
NC A **harp** is a large musical instrument consisting of a triangular frame with vertical strings which you pluck with your fingers. ...*a full size concert harp.* ...*harps and lutes.*
harp on PHRASAL VERB If you **harp on** about something, you keep talking about it; an informal

expression, used showing disapproval. *She continued to harp on the theme of her wasted life.*

harpist /hɑːpɪst/ **harpists**
NC A **harpist** is a person who plays the harp.

harpoon /hɑːpuːn/ **harpoons**
NC A **harpoon** is a spear with a long rope attached to it. It is fired from a gun by people hunting whales. *Mr Wilkinson said that protesters would try to prevent the firing of the ship's harpoons.*

harpsichord /hɑːpsɪkɔːd/ **harpsichords**
NC A **harpsichord** is a musical instrument which looks like a small piano. When you press the keys, strings are plucked mechanically rather than hit by hammers as in a piano. *His international reputation has been made—brilliantly—at the harpsichord.* ...*playing the sparkling finale of a harpsichord concerto by Joseph Haydn.*

harpy /hɑːpi/ **harpies**
NC If you refer to a woman as a **harpy**, you mean that she is very unpleasant or violent; a literary word. ...*preserving the male of the species from what are termed 'vipers, harpies and housewives'.*

harrow /hærəʊ/ **harrows**
NC A **harrow** is a piece of farm equipment that is used on ploughed land to break up large lumps of soil. *The harrow is dragged as fast as possible across the ground.* ...*animal drawn harrows.*

harrowing /hærəʊɪŋ/
ADJ A **harrowing** situation or experience is very upsetting or disturbing. *The film is deeply harrowing.*

harry /hæri/ **harries, harrying, harried**
VO If you **harry** someone, you constantly ask them for something or tell them what to do, so that they feel anxious or annoyed; a formal word. *He set to work harrying people for donations.* ◆ **harried** ADJ ...*a waiter with a full tray and a harried expression.*

harsh /hɑːʃ/ **harsher, harshest**
1 ADJ A **harsh** condition or way of life is severe and difficult. *His family wouldn't survive the harsh winter.* ◆ **harshness** NU ...*the harshness of their nomadic life.*
2 ADJ **Harsh** behaviour and actions are cruel and unkind. ...*her harsh, cold, contemptuous attitude.* ◆ **harshly** ADV *You've marked his essay rather harshly.* ◆ **harshness** NU *Disobedience is treated with special harshness.*
3 ADJ A **harsh** light or sound is unpleasantly bright or loud. *Harsh daylight fell into the room... She spoke in a harsh whisper.* ◆ **harshly** ADV *'What is it?' he said harshly.*

harvest /hɑːvɪst/ **harvests, harvesting, harvested**
1 N SING The **harvest** is the gathering of a crop. *Their stock of rice wouldn't last until the harvest.* ► Also VO *We harvested what we could before the rains came.*
2 NC A crop is called a **harvest** when it is gathered. *Their sons always came home to help bring in the harvest.*

harvester /hɑːvɪstə/ **harvesters**
1 NC A **harvester** is a machine which gathers crops such as wheat, corn, or vegetables. ...*a new harvester which is adaptable for a number of crops.*
2 NC You can refer to a person who cuts and collects the harvest as a **harvester**. *Using a sickle instead of the traditional knife cuts the average number of harvesters needed by more than half.*

harvest festival, harvest festivals
NC A **harvest festival** is a special Christian church service held every year to thank God for the harvest.

has; pronounced /həz, hæz/ when it is an auxiliary verb and /hæz/ when it is a main verb.
Has is the third person singular of the present tense of **have.**

has-been /hæzbiːn/ **has-beens**
NC A **has-been** is a person who used to be important or successful, but is not now; an informal word. ...*a political has-been.*

hash /hæʃ/
1 If you **make a hash of** a job, you do it very badly; an informal expression. *The paper says that Washington is making the most pathetic hash of it.*
2 NU **Hash** is a mixture of cooked meat and vegetables that is usually baked or fried; used in

American English. ...*cans of corned beef hash.* ...*a waitress in a hash house.*

hashish /hæʃiːʃ/
NU **Hashish** is a drug made from the hemp plant which some people smoke in cigarettes. Hashish is illegal in many countries. *Dutch customs arrested three people suspected of smuggling the drug hashish.*

hasn't /hæznt/
Hasn't is the usual spoken form of 'has not'.

hasp /hɑːsp/ **hasps**
NC A **hasp** is a flat piece of metal with a slot in it that is fastened to the edge of a door or lid to form part of the lock. To close the door or lid, you push the slot over a metal loop fastened to the other section and put a padlock through the loop.

Hassan II, King of Morocco /hæsən/
Hassan II succeeded his father, Mohammed V, as King of Morocco in 1961. He was named Crown Prince in 1957. He served as Commander-in-Chief of the Armed Forces from 1956 to 1963, Minister of Defence and Vice Premier from 1960 to 1961, as Prime Minister from 1961 to 1963 and from 1965 to 1967, and as Minister of Defence from 1972 to 1973. He became Commander-in-Chief of the Army in 1972. Born: 1929.

Hassanali, Noor Mohammed /nuə məuhæmməd hæsənɑːli/
Noor Mohammed Hassanali became President of Trinidad and Tobago in 1987. He was a Supreme Court judge from 1978 to 1985. He is a member of the National Alliance for Reconstruction (NAR). Born: 1918.

hassle /hæsl/ **hassles, hassling, hassled;** an informal word.
1 NCorNU If you say that something is a **hassle**, you mean that it is difficult to do or causes a lot of trouble. *The saving wouldn't be worth the added hassle.* ...*the hustle and hassle of city life... I didn't want any hassle from the other women.*
2 VO If someone **hassles** you, they keep annoying you, for example by telling you to do things that you do not want to. *A number of people have been attacked and hassled a lot.*

hassock /hæsək/ **hassocks**
NC A **hassock** is a cushion for kneeling on in a church.

haste /heɪst/
1 NU **Haste** is the act of doing things quickly. *I immediately regretted my haste... It was written quickly and published in haste.*
2 To **make haste** means to hurry; an old-fashioned expression. *They want to try and make all haste to capture Kabul.*

hasten /heɪsn/ **hastens, hastening, hastened;** a formal word.
1 VO If you **hasten** something, you make it happen faster or sooner. *Two factors hastened the formation of the new party.*
2 V+*to*-INF If you **hasten** to do something, you are quick to do it. *He hastened to remark that he was not against television.*
3 VA If you **hasten** somewhere, you hurry there. *He hastened back into the forest.*

hasty /heɪsti/
1 ADJ If you are **hasty**, you do things suddenly and quickly, often without thinking properly about them. *He made a hasty, unsuitable marriage.* ◆ **hastily** ADV *Philip hastily changed the subject... Decisions on economic and political reform may have been made too hastily.*
2 ADJ A **hasty** action is done quickly because you do not have much time.* ...*a hasty meal.* ◆ **hastily** ADV *He dressed himself hastily.*

hat /hæt/ **hats**
1 NC A **hat** is a covering that you wear on your head. *The Duchess of York wore a huge broad-rimmed hat to protect her from the midday sun.* ...*hats decorated with flowers and ribbons.*
2 N SING+SUPP If you say that someone is wearing a particular **hat**, you mean they are doing the particular job indicated at the time, although they also perform other tasks as well. *I've got my teacher's hat on today... Wearing his other hat, as Party General Secretary, Mr Gorbachov fought off a strong challenge.*

● **Hat** is used in these phrases. ● If something is described as **old hat**, it is so well known that it has become boring. *His views may have been radical a few years ago, but now they're old hat.* ● If you **pass the hat** or **pass the hat round**, you collect money from a group of people in order to pay for something or buy something for someone. *The locals passed the hat for the Red Cross... Whenever someone retires from this office we pass the hat round.* ● If you say that you **take off** your **hat** or **take** your **hat off** to someone, you mean that you admire them for something they have done. *I take my hat off to her for the way she did it... I think you not only have to take your hat off to him, but really admire the way he's handled this crisis.* ● If you **throw** your **hat into the ring**, you indicate your willingness to take up a particular challenge. *John Prescott is expected to throw his hat into the ring as the third candidate for Labour's deputy leadership.*

hatband /hætbænd/ **hatbands**
NC A **hatband** is a strip of cloth that is put round a hat above the brim as a decoration. *He wore a brown fedora with a grey silk hatband.*

hatbox /hætbɒks/ **hatboxes**
NC A **hatbox** is a cylindrical box in which a hat can be carried and stored.

hatch /hætʃ/, **hatches, hatching, hatched**
1 V-ERG When an egg **hatches**, or when a bird, insect, or other animal **hatches** an egg, the egg breaks open and a baby animal comes out. *After ten days, the eggs hatch... The larva hatches out and lives in the soil... The locust needs damp soil to hatch its eggs.*
2 VO To **hatch** a plot or scheme means to plan it. *I've heard about the grand plot that you two gentlemen are hatching.*
3 NC A **hatch** is an opening in the deck of a ship, which is used by people for coming on deck or going below, or during loading and unloading cargo. *The captain died whilst trying to close an outside hatch in a desperate effort to save the crew.* ...*the forward cargo hatch.*
4 NC A **hatch** is also a small opening in a wall, especially between a kitchen and a dining room, which you can pass something such as food through. ...*bland food appeared through a hatch... We were supposed to queue up at the hatch to receive our morning pills.*

hatchback /hætʃbæk/ **hatchbacks**
NC A **hatchback** is a car with an extra door at the back which opens upwards. ...*a red Vauxhall Cavalier hatchback.* ...*the versatility of a hatchback.*

hatchery /hætʃəri/ **hatcheries**
NC A **hatchery** is a place where people control the hatching of eggs, especially fish eggs. *There are about 600 fish farms or hatcheries altogether.* ...*a small freshwater hatchery.*

hatchet /hætʃit/ **hatchets**
1 NC A **hatchet** is a small axe. *If you cut them, you can do it with a knife or a small hatchet.*
2 If two people **bury the hatchet**, they become friendly again after a quarrel or disagreement. *The Soviet Union and Germany have at last buried the hatchet... The hatchet is now well and truly buried.*

hatchet job, hatchet jobs
NC A **hatchet job** is a violent written or spoken attack on someone or something that seeks out to destroy their reputation; an informal expression. *Stryker had done a hatchet job on him.*

hatchet man, hatchet men
NC A **hatchet man** is a man who is employed by someone to destroy things or do unpleasant tasks for them; an informal expression. *Posner described Kravchenko as a hatchet man carrying out the Kremlin's policies.*

hatchway /hætʃweɪ/ **hatchways**
NC A **hatchway** is the same as a **hatch**.

hate /heɪt/ **hates, hating, hated**
1 VO, V-REFL, V+ING, or V+*to*-INF If you **hate** someone or something, you have an extremely strong feeling of dislike for them. *I hate milk... She was aware of what she was doing and she hated herself for it... I used to hate going to lectures... I would hate to move to another house.* ◆ **hated** ADJ ...*the most hated man in America.*

2 NU **Hate** is an extremely strong feeling of dislike for someone or something. *He was a violent bully, destructive and full of hate.* ● **Hate** is used in these phrases. ● You say 'I **hate to say it**' to introduce something that you regret having to say, because it is unpleasant. *There is unfortunately—I hate to say it—a substantial amount of racism in our cities.* ● to **hate** someone's **guts**: see **gut**.

hateful /ˈheɪtfl/
ADJ **Hateful** means extremely unpleasant; an old-fashioned word. *It was going to be a hateful week.*

hatpin /ˈhætpɪn/ **hatpins**
NC A **hatpin** is a metal pin which can be pushed through a woman's hat and through her hair to keep the hat in position.

hatred /ˈheɪtrəd/
NU **Hatred** is an extremely strong feeling of dislike. *...their hatred of technology... She felt hatred towards his sister.*

hatstand /ˈhætstænd/ **hatstands**
NC A **hatstand** is an upright pole with hooks at the top on which hats can be hung.

hatter /ˈhætə/
If you say that someone is **as mad as a hatter**, you mean that they do very foolish or strange things. *You may think at first I'm as mad as a hatter.*

hat trick, hat tricks
NC A **hat trick** is a series of three achievements, especially in a sports match, for example three goals scored by the same person in a football match or three wickets taken by one bowler with consecutive balls in cricket. *Robson scored two fine goals and narrowly missed a hat trick.*

haughty /ˈhɔːti/
ADJ **Haughty** people think that they are better than others; used showing disapproval. *He had an air of haughty aloofness.* ◆ **haughtily** ADV *'Very well,' he replied haughtily.*

haul /hɔːl/ **hauls, hauling, hauled**
1 VO A or V-REFL A If you **haul** something heavy somewhere, you pull it there with a great effort. *They hauled the pilot clear of the wreckage... Ralph hauled himself onto the platform.*
2 If something is a **long haul**, it takes a long time and a lot of effort. *We began the long haul up the cobbled street. ...as women begin the long haul to equality.*
haul up PHRASAL VERB If someone **is hauled up** before a court of law, they are made to appear before the court; an informal expression. *He got hauled up in court for assaulting a student.*

haulage /ˈhɔːlɪdʒ/
NU **Haulage** is the business of transporting goods by road. *It stresses distribution in particular, including road haulage and warehouses. ...long-distance haulage drivers.*

haulier /ˈhɔːlɪə/ **hauliers**
NC A **haulier** is a person who runs a business that transports goods by road. *...a system of licenses obliges hauliers to apply for permits to move goods between countries.*

haunch /hɔːntʃ/ **haunches**
NC Your **haunches** are your buttocks and the tops of your legs. *He squatted down on his haunches.*

haunt /hɔːnt/ **haunts, haunting, haunted**
1 VO If a place **is haunted**, people believe that a ghost appears there regularly. *The building is apparently haunted by a poltergeist... They wouldn't want to tell their children that the house was haunted because they wouldn't want to frighten them.*
2 VO If something unpleasant **haunts** you, you keep thinking or worrying about it over a long period of time. *...a mystery that had haunted me for most of my life.*
3 VO Something that **haunts** a person or an organization regularly causes them problems over a long period of time. *Communal violence has been haunting India ever since independence... East Germany's Stalinist past still haunts its fledgling democracy.*
4 NC+SUPP Someone's **haunts** are places which they often visit. *Their old haunts have been ruined by*

becoming too popular.

haunted /ˈhɔːntɪd/
1 ADJ A **haunted** building or other place is one where people believe that a ghost regularly appears. *...a haunted house.*
2 ADJ Someone who has a **haunted** expression looks very worried or troubled. *Her face took on a haunted quality.*

haunting /ˈhɔːntɪŋ/
ADJ Something that is **haunting** remains in your thoughts because it is very beautiful or sad. *He repeated the haunting melody.*

Hau Pei-tsun /xaʊ beɪ tsʊn/
General **Hau Pei-tsun** became Premier of Taiwan in 1990. He was Commander-in-Chief of the Army and Chief of General Staff from 1978 to 1989, and Minister of Defence from 1989 to 1990. He became a member of the Central Committee of the Kuomintang (KMT) in 1984. Born: 1918.

hauteur /əʊˈtɜː/
NU **Hauteur** is haughtiness; a formal word. *...icy aristocratic hauteur.*

Havana /həˈvænə/
Havana is the capital of Cuba and its largest city. Population: 2,096,000 (1989).

have, has, having, had; pronounced /həv, hæv/ when it is an auxiliary verb and /hæv/ when it is a main verb. **Have** is often contracted to **'ve**, **has** to **'s**, and **had** to **'d**.
1 AUX You use **have** in front of a past participle in order to form the perfect tenses of the verb. *We have already done that... It hasn't rained for a month... Officials said that the two men had at last signed an agreement... I had just finished when you arrived.*
2 AUX You use **having** in front of a past participle in order to introduce a clause that mentions an action which had already happened before another related action began. *Quite a few of the shop fronts were still boarded up, having closed down in 1930 or 1931... We were back in Edinburgh at ten past twelve, having driven straight across the bridge again.*
3 V+to-INF You can use **have** followed by an infinitive with 'to' to say that something must be done or must happen. 'Have got' is also used in this way: see **got**. *Then he had to sit down because he felt dizzy... I have to speak to your father... There are plenty of jobs; she doesn't have to go to Canada.*
4 VO You can use **have** with nouns which describe actions in order to say that the action is happening, or to give more information about it. *You go and have a look... I had a little stroll round the garden this morning... We're having a meeting. Come and join in.*
5 VO **Have** is used with nouns which refer to the effect one thing has on another. *What effect will this have on transportation?... If this has no result, try a weak solution of bleach.*
6 VO **Have** can also be used to form nouns from verbs. *It's worth having a try... We've had a think about what to do.*
7 VO In normal speech or writing, you often use **have** where in more formal language you would use a specific verb. For example, you normally say 'I have a sandwich every lunchtime' rather than 'I eat a sandwich every lunchtime'. *I had a boring afternoon... They all had an injection when they left Britain... Boylan had his back to the window.*
8 VO **Have** is often used with nouns which refer to the attributes, qualities, or characteristics of someone or something. *He had beautiful manners... It's nice to have an excuse. ...machines which have dangerous moving parts.*
9 VO You can use **have** to say that you own something, or to talk about things and people that are associated with you. 'Have got' is also used in this way: see **got**. *What's the point in having a mink coat?... He had a small hotel... They don't have any money... I have lots of friends.*
10 VO+PAST PARTICIPLE **Have** is used in front of a past participle to say that you arrange for something to happen, or to say that something happens to you without your doing anything about it. *You should have your car cleaned... Isn't it time you had your hair*

cut?... She had her purse stolen... Children love to have stories read to them.
11 VO+to-INF You use **have** with an object and an infinitive with 'to' to say that you are responsible for something. *She had a huge department to administer... I've never had so much work to finish.*
12 VO If you **have** an illness or disability, you suffer from it. *She began to have attacks of chest pain... I thought he was having a heart attack.*
13 VO When a woman **has** a baby, she gives birth to it. *My mother had six children in nine years.*
14 VO+to If you **have** something to yourself, you are the only person there. *They had the bar to themselves.*
● **Have** occurs in these informal phrases. ● If you **have it in for** someone, you are determined to make life difficult for them because you dislike them or are angry with them. *He had it in for me.* ● If you **have been had**, you have been deliberately tricked by someone, who has, for example, sold you something at too high a price. ● If you say that someone **has had it**, you mean that they will be in trouble because of something they have done. *Oh Lord, she's had it now!* ● If you say that you **have had it**, you mean that you are too exhausted to continue with what you were doing. *They both look as if they've about had it.* ● If you **are had up** for something, you appear in court for a crime that you have committed. *He was had up for indecent exposure.* ● If you **are having** someone **on**, you are teasing them; an informal expression.
Havel, Václav /vɑ̀ːtslæf hǽvəl/
Václav Havel became President of Czechoslovakia in 1989. He is a playwright and was formerly a spokesman for Charter 77, a human rights movement. He was a founder of Civic Forum in 1989. Born: 1936.
haven /héɪvn/ **havens**
NC A **haven** is a place where people feel safe and secure. *They have made the park a haven for weary Londoners... Military commanders are preparing to extend the safe haven to protect Kurdish refugees.*
have-nots /hǽvnɒts/
N PL The **have-nots** are people who have little money or few possessions in contrast to people who are rich and own a lot of possessions. *One result of all these developments, however, is a visibly growing gap between the haves and the have-nots.*
haven't /hǽvnt/
Haven't is the usual spoken form of 'have not'. *I haven't done anything wrong.*
haversack /hǽvəsæk/ **haversacks**
NC A **haversack** is a canvas bag worn on your back and used for carrying things when you are out walking. *...British marines carrying haversacks.*
haves /hǽvz/
N PL The **haves** are people who have a lot of money and possessions. *President Mitterrand warned against a new division of Europe into haves and have-nots.*
havoc /hǽvək/
1 NU **Havoc** is a state of great disorder. *After the havoc of the war, England had to be rebuilt.*
2 To **play havoc with** something means to cause great disorder and confusion. *Rain has been playing havoc with the schedule at the Australian Open.*
haw /hɔː/ **haws, hawing, hawed**
1 NC **Haws** are the red berries produced by hawthorn trees in autumn.
2 Writers sometimes use **'haw haw'** to show that one of their characters is laughing, especially in a rather unpleasant or superior way. *'He cut himself eating peas last night.'—'Haw haw.'*
3 Haw is used as a verb only in the expression 'to hum and haw'; see **hum**.
hawk /hɔːk/ **hawks, hawking, hawked**
1 NC A **hawk** is a large bird with a hooked bill, sharp claws, and very good eyesight. *A hawk hovered, motionless, in the blue sky.*
2 NC A **hawk** is also a politician who believes in using the threat of force when dealing with other countries, rather than more peaceful diplomatic methods. *Another self-confessed hawk and reactionary expressed satisfaction that Mr Shevardnadze had gone... Both hawks and doves have expanded their*

conditions for ending the war.
3 VO If you **hawk** something around, you try to sell it by taking it from place to place; often used showing disapproval. *His writings were being hawked round German publishers.*
hawker /hɔ́ːkə/ **hawkers**
NC A **hawker** is a person who travels from place to place selling things. *The hawkers set up temporary stalls on the roadside. ...illegal street hawkers.*
hawk-eyed /hɔ́ːkaɪd/
ADJ Someone who is **hawk-eyed** has very good eyesight and seems to see absolutely everything that is happening.
hawkish /hɔ́ːkɪʃ/
ADJ Someone who is **hawkish** believes in using force and violence to achieve something rather than using more peaceful or diplomatic methods. *His aides evidently feared that he had been too hawkish.*
hawser /hɔ́ːzə/ **hawsers**
NC A **hawser** is a large heavy rope, especially one used on a ship. *The Lowland Radar had been towing a barge when a hawser snapped and hit the men.*
hawthorn /hɔ́ːθɔːn/ **hawthorns**
NCorNU A **hawthorn** is a small tree. It has sharp thorns, white flowers and red fruit called haws. *...the flowering cycle of the apple plants, which is different from the hawthorn plants.*
hay /heɪ/
NU **Hay** is grass which has been cut and dried so that it can be used to feed animals. *...40 bales of hay.*
hay fever
NU **Hay fever** is an allergy to pollen and grass which makes some people sneeze a lot. *...it could also help anyone who suffers from hay fever.*
haystack /héɪstæk/ **haystacks**
1 NC A **haystack** is a large neat pile of hay, usually in a field. *Last night police were investigating a suspected arson after a haystack caught fire.*
2 If you say that trying to find something is like looking for **a needle in a haystack**, you mean that it is extremely difficult or impossible to find. *Helicopters are searching for the missing men, but it's like looking for a needle in a haystack.*
haywire /héɪwaɪə/
ADJ PRED If something goes **haywire**, it becomes completely disordered or out of control; an informal word. *The body's functions have gone haywire, their whole body is not working properly.*
hazard /hǽzəd/ **hazards, hazarding, hazarded**
1 NC A **hazard** is something which could be dangerous to you. *...a natural hazard, like an earth tremor... Drinking alcohol is a real health hazard if carried to excess.*
2 V-REPORT or V-QUOTE If you **hazard** a guess, you make a suggestion which is only a guess. *As to the author of the letter, I will hazard a guess that it is Howard... 'How much do you think he makes a year?'—'Fifteen thousand,' Rudolph hazarded.*
hazardous /hǽzədəs/
ADJ Something that is **hazardous** is dangerous to people's health or safety. *...hazardous chemicals... Breathing smoky air may be hazardous to health.*
haze /heɪz/
N SING+SUPP A **haze** is a kind of mist caused by heat or something such as dust in the air. *The room became cloudy with a blue haze of smoke.*
hazel /héɪzl/ **hazels**
1 NCorNU A **hazel** is a small tree which has edible nuts.
2 ADJ **Hazel** eyes are greenish-brown.
hazelnut /héɪzlnʌt/ **hazelnuts**
NC **Hazelnuts** are nuts from a hazel tree.
hazy /héɪzi/ **hazier, haziest**
1 ADJ When the sky or a view is **hazy**, you cannot see it clearly because there is a haze. *...a hazy blue view beyond railings on a mountain pass.*
2 ADJ PRED If you are **hazy** about things or if your thoughts are **hazy**, you are unclear or confused. *She was hazy about her mother's origins... The details are getting a bit hazy in my mind now.*
H-bomb /éɪtʃ bɒm/ **H-bombs**
NC An **H-bomb** is a nuclear bomb in which energy is

released from hydrogen atoms. **H-bomb** is an abbreviation for 'hydrogen bomb'. *Nuclear fusion powers the sun and the H-bomb.*

he /hi, hiː/. **He** is used as the subject of a verb.
1 PRON You use **he** to refer to a man, boy, or male animal that has already been mentioned, or whose identity is known. *Bill had flown back from New York and he and his wife took me out to dinner.*
2 PRON **He** can also be used to refer to a person whose sex is not known or stated; some users of English prefer 'he or she' or 'they' to be used instead. *A teacher should do whatever he thinks best.*

head /hed/ **heads, heading, headed**
1 NC Your **head** is the top part of your body which has your eyes, mouth, and brain in it; used also to refer to the same part of an animal's body. *She shook her head... Her fingers moved over the fur on the cat's head.*
2 N SING+SUPP The **head** of something is the top, start, or most important end. *Howard stood at the head of the stairs. ...standing at the head of the queue.*
3 NC The **head** of an organization, school, or department is the person in charge of it. *...the head of the English department.* ▸ Also N+N *...the head gardener.*
4 ADV When you toss a coin and it comes down **heads**, you can see the side of the coin with a person's head on it.
5 VO If something **heads** a list, it is at the top of it. *...with Tower Hamlets heading the list.*
6 VO If you **head** an organization, you are in charge of it. *The firm is headed by John Murray.*
7 VO You can mention the title of a piece of writing by saying how it **is headed.** *...an article headed 'An Open Letter to the Prime Minister.'*
8 VA If you **head** in a particular direction, you go in that direction. *Julie headed for the cupboard.*
9 V+*for* If you **are heading** for an unpleasant situation, you are behaving in a way that makes the situation more likely. *You may be heading for disaster.*
10 VO In football, when a player **heads** a ball, he hits it with his head. *Rush headed home a cross from Barnes... In the 85th minute Burrows headed the equalizer.* ◆ **headed** ADJ ATTRIB *United were undone by two excellent headed goals by Bright.*
11 See also **heading.**
● **Head** occurs in these phrases. ● The cost or amount **a head** or **per head** is the cost or amount for each person. *The trip will cost £5,000 per head.* ● If you are speaking **off the top of** your **head**, the information you are giving may not be accurate, because you have not had time to check it or think about it. *It was something he invented more or less off the top of his head, on the spur of the moment.* ● If you are laughing, crying, or shouting your **head off**, you are doing it very noisily; an informal expression. *...people were screaming their heads off.* ● If you **bite** or **snap** someone's **head off**, you speak to them very angrily; an informal expression. ● If something **comes** or is **brought to a head**, it reaches a state where you have to do something urgently about it. *The power struggle seems likely to come to a head at the Party Congress in December. ...a strike ballot which would bring the nineteen week long dispute to a head.* ● If alcohol goes to your **head**, it makes you drunk. *The champagne went straight to my head.* ● If praise or success goes to your **head**, it makes you conceited. *All this, the critics say, went to Mitterrand's head when he was re-elected for a second term.* ● In a difficult situation, if you **keep** your **head**, you stay calm. If you **lose** your **head**, you panic. *I hope this hysterical step doesn't indicate that people in authority are losing their heads.* ● If you **keep** your **head down**, you try to avoid trouble. *They learned that it is safer to keep their heads down and their mouths shut... When the takeover happened, Jacob kept his head down and hoped for the best.* ● If you cannot **make head nor tail of** something, you cannot understand it at all; an informal expression. ● **head and shoulders above:** see **shoulder.**

headache /hedeɪk/ **headaches**
1 NC If you have a **headache**, you have a pain in your

head. *Aspirin is something most of us take when we have a headache.*
2 NC If you say that something is a **headache**, you mean that it causes you difficulty or worry. *Rivalry between the two industries presents a big headache for government.*

headband /hedbænd/ **headbands**
NC A **headband** is a narrow strip of material which you can wear round your head across your forehead, usually to keep hair or sweat out of your eyes. *...cheerleaders in red headbands.*

headboard /hedbɔːd/ **headboards**
NC A **headboard** is an upright board at the end of a bed where your head is.

head boy, head boys
NC The **head boy** of a school is the boy who is the leader of the prefects and who often represents the school on public occasions.

head count, head counts
NC If you do a **head count**, you count the number of people in a particular place. *Now that the nation's head count is over, the Census Bureau is to send the individual states the information.*

headdress /heddres/ **headdresses**; also spelt **head-dress.**
NC A **headdress** is something worn on a person's head for decoration. *The dancers wore face masks and tall head-dresses. ...traditional Kurdish headdress.*

headed notepaper
NU **Headed notepaper** is notepaper which has the name and address of the person or organization it belongs to printed at the top of each sheet. *The doctor sent me a letter on headed notepaper.*

header /hedə/ **headers**
1 NC A **header** is the act of hitting a ball with your head in football. *...a spectacular diving header in the 72nd minute.*
2 N SING A **header** is also a jump or dive in a particular direction with your head going first. *She took a header into the bushes.*

head-first
ADV If you fall somewhere **head-first**, your head is the part of your body that is furthest forward as you fall. *He had fallen head-first into the ditch.*

headgear /hedgɪə/
NU You can refer to hats or other things worn on people's heads as **headgear**. *Whether it was a small cap or bonnet or a large-brimmed hat, the headgear was trimmed with ribbons.*

head girl, head girls
NC The **head girl** of a school is the girl who is the leader of the prefects and who often represents the school on public occasions.

head-hunter, head-hunters
NC A **head-hunter** is a person who tries to persuade someone to leave their job and take another job which has better pay and more status. *She was approached by a head-hunter and offered a job with another company.*

heading /hedɪŋ/ **headings**
NC A **heading** is the title of a piece of writing, written or printed at the top of it. *The figures were put forward under the heading 'World Fuel Requirements in the 1990s'.*

headlamp /hedlæmp/ **headlamps**
NC A **headlamp** is the same as a **headlight**. *The area was in pitch darkness, the only light coming from car headlamps.*

headland /hedlənd/ **headlands**
NC A **headland** is a narrow piece of land which sticks out into the sea. *...the boat rounded the headland in sight of Copacabana beach. ...perched on a headland overlooking the Atlantic.*

headless /hedləs/
ADJ A **headless** body has no head. *A headless body could be seen in the sea.*

headlight /hedlaɪt/ **headlights**
NC A car's **headlights** are the large bright lights at the front. *Two cars appeared in front of me both with their headlights full on.*

headline /hedlaɪn/ **headlines**
1 NC A **headline** is the title of a newspaper story,

printed in large letters. *The headlines that day were full of news of the kidnapping.*
2 N PL The **headlines** are also the main points of the news which are read on radio or television. *And now for the main headlines again.*

headlong /hɛdlɒŋ/
1 ADV If you move **headlong** in a particular direction, you move there very quickly. *The frightened elephants ran headlong through the forest.*
2 ADV or ADJ If you rush **headlong** into something, you do it quickly without thinking carefully about it. *They dropped headlong into trouble. ...a headlong rush to sell.*

headman /hɛdmən/ **headmen** /hɛdmən/
NC A **headman** is a chief or tribal leader in a village. *...village and family leaders such as the headman.*

headmaster /hɛdmɑːstə/ **headmasters**
NC A **headmaster** is a man who is the head teacher of a school. *He is now a secondary school headmaster in Birmingham. ...the headmaster of the local school.*

headmistress /hɛdmɪstrəs/ **headmistresses**
NC A **headmistress** is a woman who is the head teacher of a school. *...the headmistress of what is said to be the largest girls' comprehensive school in Europe.*

head of state, heads of state
NC A **head of state** is the leader of a country, for example a president, king, or queen. *A number of African heads of state are gathering in Benin for a three-day meeting.*

head-on
1 ADV or ADJ ATTRIB If two vehicles hit each other **head-on**, they hit each other with their front parts pointing towards each other. *The motor cycle ran head-on into the lorry. ...a head-on collision.*
2 ADJ ATTRIB or ADV A **head-on** disagreement is firm and direct and has no compromises. *...a head-on confrontation with the unions... It had to meet the threat head-on.*

headphones /hɛdfəʊnz/
N PL **Headphones** are small speakers which you wear over your ears in order to listen to music or other sounds without other people hearing. *She listened to the record on her headphones.*

headquartered /hɛdkwɔːtəd/
ADJ PRED If an organization or group of people is **headquartered** in a particular place, their headquarters are in that place; used in American English. *...a meeting of the Organization of the Islamic Conference, an international group which is headquartered in Saudi Arabia... This is where the militant groups are headquartered.*

headquarters /hɛdkwɔːtəz/
N PL The **headquarters** of an organization are its main offices. *Captain Meadows was ordered to report to headquarters the following day.*

headrest /hɛdrest/ **headrests**
NC A **headrest** is an object which is attached to the back of a seat and which you can lean your head on, especially one on the front seat of a car.

headroom /hɛdruːm, hɛdrʊm/
NU **Headroom** is the amount of space below a roof or bridge.

headscarf /hɛdskɑːf/ **headscarves**
NC A **headscarf** is a scarf which is worn on the head by women. *...both girls wore a headscarf.*

headset /hɛdset/ **headsets**
NC A **headset** is the same as **headphones**; used in American English. *Put on your headset and listen in. ...stereo headsets.*

headship /hɛdʃɪp/ **headships**
NC A **headship** is the position or job of being a leader, especially a head teacher in a school. *Two new headships have been created by the education authority.*

head-shrinker, head-shrinkers
NC A **head-shrinker** is a psychiatrist; an informal word.

headstand /hɛdstænd/ **headstands**
NC If you do a **headstand**, you balance upside down with your head and your hands on the ground and your legs up in the air.

head start, head starts
NC If you have a **head start** on other people, you have an advantage over them in a competition or race. *A university degree would give you a head start in getting a job.*

headstone /hɛdstəʊn/ **headstones**
NC A **headstone** is a large stone at one end of a grave, showing the name of the dead person. *Forty-three graves were attacked, their headstones overturned and in one case smashed to fragments.*

headstrong /hɛdstrɒŋ/
ADJ A **headstrong** person is determined to do what they want and will not let anyone stop them. *Luce was stubborn and headstrong.*

head teacher, head teachers
NC A **head teacher** is a teacher who is in charge of a school. *In many areas education authorities are having difficulties recruiting new head teachers.*

headway /hɛdweɪ/
If you **make headway**, you make progress towards achieving something. *The emergency services began to make some headway in restoring order to the devastated area.*

headwind /hɛdwɪnd/ **headwinds**
NC A **headwind** is a wind blowing in the opposite direction to the way you are moving. *Strong headwinds caused his microlight plane to use up more fuel than expected.*

headword /hɛdwɜːd/ **headwords**
NC A **headword** is a word which is followed by a phrase or paragraph which explains the word's meaning, especially in a dictionary. *A headword may have more than one meaning.*

heady /hɛdi/
ADJ A **heady** drink, atmosphere, or experience strongly affects your senses, for example by making you feel drunk or excited. *...heady perfumes. ...the heady days of the sixties.*

heal /hiːl/ **heals, healing, healed**
1 V-ERG When something **heals** or is **healed**, it becomes healthy and normal again. *...damage to the ecology that would take a hundred years to heal... This ointment should heal the cut in no time.*
2 VO If someone **heals** you when you are ill, they make you well again. *He had been miraculously healed of his illness.*
heal up PHRASAL VERB When an injury **heals up**, it becomes completely healthy again. *His hoof had healed up.*

healer /hiːlə/ **healers**
NC A **healer** is a person who heals people, especially by unconventional methods. *...claims by traditional healers that the barks and leaves of certain trees can cure dysentery and stomach ache.*

health /hɛlθ/
1 NU Your **health** is the condition of your body. *Cigarette smoking is dangerous to your health... My mother was in poor health.*
2 NU **Health** is a state in which you are fit and well. *They were glowing with health. ...a soldier who was nursed back to health.*
3 When you **drink** to someone's health or **drink** their health, you drink as a sign of wishing them health and happiness. *Holidaymakers and locals alike, all were ready to drink her health.*
4 NU+SUPP The **health** of an organization or system is the success that it has and the fact that it is working well. *The company's health is shown by this year's high profits. ...the health of the British film industry.*

health care; also spelt **healthcare** or **health-care**.
N+N or NU A country's **health care** system or organization involves everything, for example, hospitals, nurses, and doctors, that are supposed to help keep people healthy, or look after them and try to make them well again if they become ill. *...protest action by nurses and other healthcare workers. ...a fair supply of food, decent housing and health care. ...escalating health-care costs.*

health centre, health centres
NC A **health centre** is a building in which several doctors in a particular district have offices where their patients can visit them. *Mr Mazilu is ill and*

undergoing treatment at a health centre... The money will go towards more than a thousand health centres and hospitals.

health food, health foods
N MASS **Health foods** are natural foods without artificial ingredients which people buy because they consider them to be good for them. *...high-fibre health foods... It can be bought over the counter in numerous health food shops.*

Health Service
N SING In Britain, the **Health Service** is the same as the **National Health Service.** *...a meeting between the nursing unions and the Health Service management.*

healthy /ˈhelθi/ **healthier, healthiest**
1 ADJ A **healthy** person is well and not suffering from any illness. *As a result of the diet, he feels fitter and healthier... At the age of 48, Mrs Anthony gave birth to three healthy babies.* ♦ **healthily** ADV *It is perfectly possible to live healthily on a meat-free diet.*
2 ADJ If a feature or quality that you have is **healthy,** it shows that you are well. *The children have healthy appetites. ...healthy skin.* ♦ **healthily** SUBMOD *...the dreamless slumber of the healthily tired man.*
3 ADJ Something that is **healthy** is good for you and likely to make you fit and strong. *...healthy seaside air.*
4 ADJ A **healthy** organization or system is successful. *...a healthy economy... Today it is a thriving, healthy community that attracts visitors from all over the country.*
5 ADJ A **healthy** amount of something is a large amount that shows success. *...healthy profits. ...healthy trade and current account figures... China's economy has shown healthy growth in the first half of this year.*
6 ADJ If you have a **healthy** attitude about something, you show good sense. *We should maintain a healthy scepticism about reports coming out of Yugoslavia.*

heap /hiːp/ **heaps, heaping, heaped**
1 NC A **heap** of things is an untidy pile of them. *The earthquake had turned the town into a heap of ruins.*
2 VOA If you **heap** things in a pile, you arrange them in a large pile. *...food heaped on platters.*
3 VO+on or upon If you **heap** praise or criticism on someone or something, you give them a lot of praise or criticism. *Bush says that it is wrong to heap all the blame on the Reagan administration.*
4 QUANT **Heaps** or a **heap** of something is a large quantity of it; an informal use. *We've got heaps of time.*
5 If someone collapses **in a heap,** they fall heavily and do not move. *A Sunday Mirror journalist was tripped up and left in a heap.*
heap up PHRASAL VERB If you **heap** things **up,** you make them into a pile. *The sand and gravel was heaped up into a sort of monstrous yellow cone.*

heaped /hiːpt/
1 ADJ A **heaped** spoonful has the contents of the spoon piled up above the edge. *Add one heaped tablespoon of salt.*
2 ADJ If a surface is **heaped** with things, it has a lot of them on it in a pile. *The desk was heaped with magazines.*

hear /hɪə/ **hears, hearing, heard**
1 V O or V When you **hear** sounds, you are aware of them because they reach your ears. *He heard a distant voice shouting... Etta hated to hear Mrs Hochstadt talk like that... She could hear clearly.*
2 VO When a judge or a court **hears** a case or **hears** evidence, they listen to it officially in order to make a decision about it. *The court has agreed to hear the case early in June.*
3 V+from If you **hear** from someone, you receive a letter or a telephone call from them. *They'll be delighted to hear from you again.*
4 VO, V-REPORT, or V+of If you **hear** some news or information, you learn it because someone tells it to you or it is mentioned on the radio or television. *My first meeting with the woman confirmed everything I had heard about her... I was glad to hear that things are quietening down... He came to hear of their difficulties.*

5 **'Hear hear'** is something people such as politicians say during a debate to show they agree with what the speaker is saying.
● **Hear** occurs in these phrases. ● If you **won't hear of** someone doing something, you refuse to let them do it. *I asked her to step down and give the people a chance to elect a new leadership, but she wouldn't hear of it.* ● If you **have never heard of** someone or something, you do not know anything about them, or you may not even know that they exist. *Nobody had ever heard of him.*
hear out PHRASAL VERB If you **hear** someone **out,** you listen to everything they have to say without interrupting them. *It was considered inattentive to hear out a speaker in silence for any length of time.*

hearer /ˈhɪərə/ **hearers**
NC Your **hearers** are the people who are listening to you speak; a formal word. *I have limited myself not only to a small audience but to a small number of hearers.*

hearing /ˈhɪərɪŋ/ **hearings**
1 NU **Hearing** is the sense which makes it possible for you to be aware of sounds. *Her limbs were weak, her hearing almost gone.*
2 NC A **hearing** is an official meeting held to collect facts about an incident or problem. *A Congressional hearing in Washington has expressed concern at the number of refugees leaving Vietnam.*
● **Hearing** occurs in these phrases. ● If you are **in** or **within** someone's **hearing,** you are so close to them that they can hear what you are saying. *She began to grumble about it within his hearing.* ● If someone gives you **a hearing** or **a fair hearing,** they listen to you when you give your opinion about something. *The High Court passed its verdict without giving a hearing to the Chief Minister... Everybody is entitled to a fair hearing.* ● See also **hard of hearing.**

hearing aid, hearing aids
NC A **hearing aid** is a device which people with hearing difficulties wear in their ear to enable them to hear better. *We decided that we would fit good quality hearing aids.*

hearsay /ˈhɪəseɪ/
NU **Hearsay** is information which you have been told indirectly, but which you do not personally know to be true. *He said he'd found a lot of the evidence exaggerated and much of it had been hearsay.*

hearse /hɜːs/ **hearses**
NC A **hearse** is a large car that carries the coffin at a funeral. *Mourners marched behind the hearse.*

heart /hɑːt/ **hearts**
1 NC Your **heart** is the organ in your chest that pumps the blood around your body. *She could hear her heart beating... Her heart condition was much improved by the operation. ...the first successful human heart transplant.*
2 NC You can also talk about someone's **heart** to refer to their emotions or character. *...the troubled heart of the younger man... He's got a very soft heart.*
3 NU **Heart** is used in various expressions referring to courage and determination. *It was a bad time and people were losing heart... No one had the heart to tell her... Mr Reagan told his audience that they should be encouraged and take heart from this meeting.*
4 N SING+of The **heart** of something is the most important part of it. *At the heart of the deadlock is a wide disparity over reducing subsidies to farmers. ...the heart of the problem.*
5 N SING+of The **heart** of somewhere is the most central part of it. *Thousands of protesters marched into the heart of San Francisco... University Square is in the heart of Bucharest.*
6 NC A **heart** is also a shape like a real heart; used especially as a symbol of love.
7 NU **Hearts** is one of the four suits in a pack of playing cards.
8 See also **purple heart.**
● **Heart** occurs in these phrases. ● If someone is a particular kind of person **at heart,** this is what they are really like. *He was at heart a kindly man.* ● If you know something such as a poem **by heart,** you can remember it perfectly. *There was a tradition in*

English schools of learning poetry by heart. ● If you have a **change of heart**, your feelings about something change. *The Soviet authorities, in a sudden change of heart, have given her permission to leave.* ● If you say something **from the heart** or **from the bottom of your heart**, you are being sincere. *You can perhaps sympathize with this cry from the heart... How can one be happy? I may laugh, but not from the heart.* ● If your **heart isn't in** what you are doing, you have very little enthusiasm for it. *His heart is not in the course he's taking but he realises that there is no real alternative.* ● If someone can do something to their **heart's content**, they can do it as much as they want. *John could talk and plan to his heart's content, it would make no difference now.* ● If someone or something **breaks** your **heart**, they make you very unhappy. *Every time I hear that someone has breached the public trust, it breaks my heart.* ● If something is **close to** or **dear to** your **heart**, you care deeply about it. *The author is one of those who lets passion take over when the subject is very close to his heart. ...attacking fundamental principles dear to the heart of most Latin American leaders.* ● If your **heart leaps**, you suddenly feel very excited and happy. If your **heart sinks**, you suddenly feel very disappointed or unhappy. *He said his heart leapt for joy when the Hungarian people cast off Communist rule... I found there were six of us auditioning and my heart sank.* ● If you have **set** your **heart on** something, you want it very much. *She had set her heart on going.* ● If you **take** an experience **to heart**, you are deeply affected and upset by it. *President Mobutu took the criticism too much to heart.* ● If you say that someone's **heart is in the right place**, you mean they are kind and considerate.

heartache /hɑːteɪk/ **heartaches**
NUorNC **Heartache** is very great sadness and emotional suffering. *I was young enough to suffer adolescent heartache. ...all the trials and heartaches that followed.*

heart attack, heart attacks
NC If someone has a **heart attack**, their heart begins to beat very irregularly or stops completely. *Unskilled workers die early of causes such as heart attacks, strokes and lung cancer.*

heartbeat /hɑːtbiːt/ **heartbeats**
1 N SING Your **heartbeat** is the regular movement of your heart as it pumps blood around your body. *He could hear the pounding rhythm of her heartbeat.*
2 NC A **heartbeat** is one of the movements of your heart. *Doctors say his heartbeat is still irregular.*

heartbreak /hɑːtbreɪk/
NU **Heartbreak** is very great sadness or unhappiness. *...tragedy and heartbreak.*

heartbreaking /hɑːtbreɪkɪŋ/
ADJ Something that is **heartbreaking** makes you feel extremely sad and upset. *...a heartbreaking letter from an American friend whose wife had died.*

heartbroken /hɑːtbrəʊkən/
ADJ Someone who is **heartbroken** is extremely sad and upset. *Sylvia would be heartbroken if one of her cats died.*

heartburn /hɑːtbɜːn/
NU **Heartburn** is a painful burning sensation in your chest, caused by acid from your stomach. *It may be possible to relieve the pain of angina by treating the heartburn.*

hearten /hɑːtn/ **heartens, heartening, heartened**
VO If you **are heartened** by something, it encourages you and makes you cheerful. *I am very heartened by her success.* ◆ **heartening** ADJ *...some heartening news.*

heart failure
NU **Heart failure** is a serious medical condition in which someone's heart stops working as well as it should, sometimes stopping completely so that they die. *My mother had heart failure the year before last.*

heartfelt /hɑːtfelt/
ADJ ATTRIB You use **heartfelt** to indicate that someone feels or believes something deeply and sincerely. *...a heartfelt wish that it will never happen.*

hearth /hɑːθ/ **hearths**
NC A **hearth** is the floor of a fireplace. *A bright fire was burning in the hearth.*

hearthrug /hɑːθrʌg/ **hearthrugs**
NC A **hearthrug** is a rug which is put in front of a fireplace.

heartland /hɑːtlænd/ **heartlands**
NC+SUPP You can refer to the area where something is based as a **heartland**, for example, the industrial **heartland** of a country or region is the area where most of its industry is based and where industry is very important. *...Kosovo, Serbia's historical heartland. ...the Tory heartlands in the south east of England. ...the industrial heartlands of western Europe.*

heartless /hɑːtləs/
ADJ If someone is **heartless**, they are cruel and unkind. *...a heartless cynic.* ◆ **heartlessly** ADV *...defenceless creatures being heartlessly destroyed.*

heartrending /hɑːtrendɪŋ/
ADJ If something is **heartrending**, it makes you feel great sadness and pity. *Isabel's sigh was heartrending.*

heartstrings /hɑːtstrɪŋz/
When sights, sounds, events, and so on **tug at** your **heartstrings**, they cause you to feel very emotional. *It's wonderful music—it really tugs at your heartstrings.*

heartthrob /hɑːtθrɒb/ **heartthrobs**
NC A **heartthrob** is a man such as an actor who is very physically attractive to women. *Johnnie Ray was one of popular music's first heartthrobs.*

heart-to-heart, heart-to-hearts
NCorN+N A **heart-to-heart** is an intimate conversation between two people, especially close friends, in which feelings and personal problems are talked about openly. *I had quite a heart-to-heart with her last night... Maybe we ought to have a heart-to-heart talk.*

heart-warming
ADJ Something that is **heart-warming** causes you to feel pleased and very happy. *It was a heart-warming spectacle... Is there a sight more heart-warming than a family reunion?*

hearty /hɑːti/ **heartier, heartiest**
1 ADJ **Hearty** people or actions are loud, cheerful, and energetic. *...hearty soccer fans... He had a big hearty laugh.* ◆ **heartily** ADV *Etta laughed heartily.*
2 ADJ ATTRIB **Hearty** feelings or opinions are strongly felt or strongly held. *I have a hearty hatred of all examinations.* ◆ **heartily** ADV *Why should one pretend to like people one actually heartily dislikes?*
3 ADJ ATTRIB A **hearty** meal is large and very satisfying. *Mr Tracy had eaten a hearty breakfast including ham and eggs.*

heat /hiːt/ **heats, heating, heated**
1 VO When you **heat** something, you raise its temperature. *Don't heat more water than you need. ...accommodation that is difficult to heat.*
2 NU **Heat** is warmth or the quality of being hot. *Water retains heat much longer than air. ...loss of body heat... You shouldn't go out in this heat.*
3 NU+SUPP **Heat** also refers to the temperature of something that is warm. *It should be equivalent to body heat.*
4 N SING **Heat** is also a source of heat, for example a cooking ring. *Don't put pans straight on to a high heat.*
5 NU+SUPP You also use **heat** to refer to a state of strong emotional feeling, especially anger or excitement. *'You're a fool,' Boylan said, without heat.*
6 N SING+SUPP The **heat** of a particular activity is the point where there is the greatest activity or excitement. *Last week in the heat of an election campaign, the Prime Minister left for America!*
7 NC A **heat** is a race or competition whose winners take part in another one, against winners of similar races or competitions. *...the first heat of a women's World Cup slalom race at Cormayeur in Italy.* ● See also **dead heat**.
8 See also **heated, heating**.

heat up PHRASAL VERB 1 When something **heats up**, it gradually becomes hotter. *The water is being heated* *up by these hot rocks.* 2 When you **heat up** food that has already been cooked, you make it hot again. *He considered heating up the pot roast.*

heated /hi:tɪd/
ADJ If someone is **heated** about something, they are angry and excited about it. *...a heated argument.*
♦ **heatedly** ADV *Naturalists argued heatedly about the issue for nearly a century.*

heater /hi:tə/ **heaters**
NC A **heater** is a piece of equipment which is used to warm a room or to heat water. *Mel had left the car heater on.* ● See also **immersion heater**.

heath /hi:θ/ **heaths**
NC A **heath** is an area of open land covered with rough grass or heather. *Heath fires caused by the hot weather have also been causing problems.*

Heath, Edward /edwəd hi:θ/
Edward Heath was Prime Minister of the United Kingdom from 1970 to 1974, and was responsible for taking the United Kingdom into the European Community. He is a member of the Conservative Party. He was MP for Bexley from 1950 to 1974, for Bexley Sidcup from 1974 to 1983, and became MP for Old Bexley and Sidcup in 1983. He was Secretary of State for Industry and Trade from 1963 to 1964, and leader of the Opposition from 1965 to 1970. Born: 1916.

heathen /hi:ðn/ **heathens**
NC Christians used to refer to people from other countries who were not Christians as **heathens**; an old-fashioned word. *He carried out a mission to baptize and spread the message amongst the heathens.*
▶ Also ADJ *...the ancient heathen inhabitants of this place.*

heather /heðə/
NU **Heather** is a plant with small purple, pink, or white flowers that grows wild on hills and moorland. *...the regeneration of native woodlands and heather moors.*

heating /hi:tɪŋ/
NU **Heating** is the process or equipment involved in keeping a building warm. *The rent was £7 a week including heating.* ● See also **central heating**.

heat-stroke
NU People sometimes suffer from **heat-stroke** when they have been exposed to high temperatures for too long. *Twenty-three people have died of heat-stroke in Delhi.*

heatwave /hi:tweɪv/ **heatwaves**
NC A **heatwave** is a period when the weather is much hotter than usual. *...this year's blistering heatwave.*

heave /hi:v/ **heaves, heaving, heaved**
1 VOorV To **heave** something means to push, pull, or lift it using a lot of effort. *Lee heaved himself with a groan from his chair.* ▶ Also NC *With one single determined heave I pulled everything down.*
2 V If something **heaves**, it moves up and down or in and out with large regular movements. *His shoulders heaved silently.* ♦ **heaving** ADJ *...a sailing ship battered by heaving waves.*
3 V To **heave** also means to vomit or feel sick. *The sight of all the soapy scum made her stomach heave.*
4 If you say that someone has **heaved a sigh of relief**, you mean that they are very glad and thankful that something has happened. *He somehow managed to shoot straight at the keeper and Liverpool heaved a sigh of relief.*

heaven /hevn/ **heavens**
1 N PROP **Heaven** is where God is believed to live, and where good people are believed to go when they die. *...rising like prayers to heaven. ...the promise of a place in heaven after a glorious death.*
2 NU If you say that a place is **heaven**, you mean that it gives you a lot of pleasure; an informal use. *Mrs Duncan's cottage is just heaven... He said Kuwait used to be like heaven on earth.*
3 N PL The **heavens** are the sky; a literary use. *The moon was high in the heavens.*
● **Heaven** occurs in these phrases. ● You say '**heaven knows**' to emphasize that you do not know something or that you find something very surprising. *Heaven knows what I would do without it... He ended up, heaven knows why, in the Geological Museum.* ● You

say '**good heavens**' or '**heavens**' to express surprise or to emphasize that you agree or disagree. *Heavens, is that the time?... 'Oh, good heavens, no,' said Etta.*
● **thank heavens**: see **thank**. ● **for heaven's sake**: see **sake**.

heavenly /hevnli/
1 ADJ ATTRIB **Heavenly** describes things relating to heaven. *The heavenly spirits were displeased with the people.*
2 ADJ If you describe something as **heavenly**, you mean that it is very pleasant and enjoyable; an old-fashioned, informal use. *...a big steaming pot of the most heavenly stew.*

heavenly body, heavenly bodies
NC **Heavenly body** is used to refer to a planet, star, moon, or other natural object in space. *Much of astrology relies on the alignments, the relative positions of these heavenly bodies.*

heaven-sent
ADJ Something that is **heaven-sent** is unexpected but very welcome because it happens at just the right time. *...a heaven-sent opportunity.*

heavenward /hevnwəd/ or **heavenwards** /hevnwədz/
ADV **Heavenward** means up towards the sky or to heaven; a literary word. *Mr Menzies turned his eyes heavenward... The old lady's husband had departed heavenwards during the night.*

heavily /hevɪli/
1 ADV If someone says something **heavily**, they say it in a slow way, showing sadness, tiredness, or annoyance. *'I don't understand you,' he said heavily.*
2 See also **heavy**.

heavy /hevi/ **heavier, heaviest; heavies**
1 ADJ Something that is **heavy** weighs a lot. *He dumped the heavy suitcases by the door.*
2 ADJ **Heavy** also means great in amount, degree, or intensity. *There would be heavy casualties. ...a heavy responsibility.* ♦ **heavily** ADV *It began to rain more heavily.*
3 ADJ You also use **heavy** to describe something that has a solid, thick appearance or texture. *...spectacles with heavy black frames. ...heavy clay soil.* ♦ **heavily** ADV *I've never seen anyone so heavily built move quite so fast.*
4 ADJ PRED+*with* Something that is **heavy with** things is full of them or loaded with them; a literary use. *The trees were heavy with fruit and blossoms.*
5 ADJ **Heavy** breathing is very loud and deep. *She lay sleeping, her breathing heavy.* ♦ **heavily** ADV *She sighed heavily.*
6 ADJ ATTRIB A **heavy** movement or action is done with a lot of force or pressure. *A heavy blow with a club knocked him senseless. ...a heavy lumbering trot.*
♦ **heavily** ADV *He sat down heavily.*
7 ADJ If you have a **heavy** schedule, you have a lot of work. *I've had a heavy week.*
8 ADJ **Heavy** work requires a lot of physical strength. *I cannot do heavy work in the fields.*
9 ADJ **Heavy** air or weather is unpleasantly still, hot, and damp. *Such heavy weather is common in this part of the Gulf.*
10 ADJ If your heart is **heavy**, you are sad about something. *Rescue teams were leaving the stricken area with heavy hearts.*
11 ADJ A situation that is **heavy** is serious and difficult to cope with; an informal use. *It was all a bit heavy yesterday.*
12 NC A **heavy** is a strong man who is employed to protect a person or place, often by using violence; an informal use. *He had a couple of heavies with him so we didn't push our luck.*
13 to **make heavy weather** of something: see **weather**. See also **heavily**.

heavy-duty
ADJ ATTRIB A **heavy-duty** piece of equipment is strong and can be used a lot. *...a heavy-duty combination padlock.*

heavy-handed
ADJ Someone who is **heavy-handed** acts or speaks forcefully and thoughtlessly. *We are incensed at the government's heavy-handed economic policies.*

heavy industry, heavy industries
NU or NC **Heavy industry** is industry in which large machines are used to produce raw materials or to make large objects. *...areas of heavy industry such as shipbuilding... Most of the migrant workers are employed in heavy industries.*

heavy metal
NU **Heavy metal** is a type of loud rock music with a strong beat. *...the new breed of heavy metal bands. ...imitators of the punk and heavy metal movements.*

heavy-set
ADJ Someone who is **heavy-set** has a large, solid body; used in American English. *She is a graying, heavy-set woman who seems to have aged beyond her years.*

heavyweight /hɛviweɪt/ **heavyweights**
1 NC A **heavyweight** is a boxer or wrestler in the heaviest class. *...the undisputed world heavyweight boxing champion.*
2 N+N A **heavyweight** is also an important person in a particular field, subject, or activity who has a lot of experience and influence. *He has received the backing of several political heavyweights, including the Environment Secretary and the Defence Secretary.*

Hebrew /hiːbruː/
NU **Hebrew** is a language spoken by Jews in former times. A modern form of Hebrew is spoken now in Israel. *The agreements were drawn up in English, Hebrew and Arabic.*

heck /hɛk/; an informal word.
1 Some people use **the heck** after words such as 'how', 'why', or 'what', to emphasize a question. *Why the heck is she so polite?*
2 People use **a heck of** to emphasize how big something is or how much of it there is. *Jean has done a heck of a lot for us.*

heckle /hɛkl/ **heckles, heckling, heckled**
V or V If people **heckle** public speakers, they interrupt them by making rude remarks. *Crowds on Red Square began to heckle Mr Gorbachov... Unscheduled speakers took over the rostrum or heckled from the floor.* ◆ **heckling** NU *His words were almost drowned out by the heckling from the opposition benches.*

heckler /hɛkəˀlə/ **hecklers**
NC A **heckler** is someone who interrupts a speaker at a public meeting by shouting or making rude remarks. *He had a reputation as something of a parliamentary heckler.*

hectare /hɛkteə/ **hectares**
NC A **hectare** is a unit of area equal to 10,000 square metres. *The tiny 0.2 hectare farm has over 50 different useful crop plants growing on it.*

hectic /hɛktɪk/
ADJ A **hectic** situation involves a lot of rushed activity. *The strain of his hectic schedule has left him extremely tired.*

hector /hɛktə/ **hectors, hectoring, hectored**
VO If you **hector** someone, you talk to them aggressively or criticize them, especially when you want them do something. *...wooing the voters instead of hectoring them.* ◆ **hectoring** ADJ *He adopted a threatening and hectoring tone.*

he'd /hɪd, hiːd/
1 **He'd** is the usual spoken form of 'he had', especially when 'had' is an auxiliary verb. *He said he'd been held in solitary confinement.*
2 **He'd** is also a spoken form of 'he would'. *He said that he'd give me a lift.*

hedge /hɛdʒ/ **hedges, hedging, hedged**
1 NC A **hedge** is a row of bushes along the edge of a garden, field, or road. *...a very thorny, densely growing bush, which provides very good hedges.*
2 V If you **hedge**, you avoid answering a question or committing yourself to something. *Since then, the military leadership have hedged.*
3 N SING A **hedge** against an unpleasant situation or event is something that you hope will protect you from its effects. *...a hedge against the current threats to economic and financial stability.*
4 If you **hedge your bets**, you avoid the risk of losing a lot by supporting more than one person or thing; an informal expression. *They're hedging their bets awaiting the outcome of today's results.*

hedgehog /hɛdʒhɒg/ **hedgehogs**
NC A **hedgehog** is a small brown animal with sharp spikes covering its back. *At one hedgehog sanctuary, fourteen animals and twelve babies were brought in in a state of dehydration.*

hedgerow /hɛdʒrəʊ/ **hedgerows**
NC A **hedgerow** is a row of bushes, trees, and plants, usually growing along a country lane or between fields. *Britain has lost 125,000 miles of hedgerows and almost half its ancient woodlands.*

hedonism /hiːdənɪzəm/
NU **Hedonism** is the belief that having pleasure is the most important thing in life; a formal word. *The sanctions of religion and custom have gone, to be replaced with a greedy hedonism.*

hedonist /hiːdənɪst/ **hedonists**
NC A **hedonist** is someone who believes that having pleasure is the most important thing in life. *My son, being somewhat of a hedonist, prefers the attractions of the city.* ◆ **hedonistic** /hiːdənɪstɪk/ ADJ *...lives of unending hedonistic delight.*

heed /hiːd/ **heeds, heeding, heeded**; a formal word.
1 VO If you **heed** someone's advice, you pay attention to it. *David wished that he had heeded his father's warnings.*
2 If you **take heed** of what someone says or if you **pay heed** to them, you consider carefully what they say. *The Daily Mail urges the British Chancellor to take heed of the Confederation's warning... Few people are paying much heed to the calls for a peaceful poll.*

heedless /hiːdləs/
ADJ If you are **heedless** of someone or something, you do not take any notice of them; a formal word. *She stood glued to the radio, heedless of the bustle about her. ...heedless passers-by hurrying through the market place.*

hee-haw /hiːhɔː/ **hee-haws**
NC **Hee-haw** is used in writing to represent the sound that a donkey makes.

heel /hiːl/ **heels**
1 NC Your **heel** is the back part of your foot, just below your ankle. *Runners have the major impact on the front of their feet rather than on the heels.*
2 NC The **heel** of a sock or shoe is the part covering or below the heel. *All I could hear was the click of my own heels.*
3 See also **Achilles heel.**
● **Heels** is used in these phrases. ● If you **dig your heels in**, you refuse to be persuaded to do something. *So what if he does dig his heels in and says: 'No, we cannot have a united Germany in NATO?'* ● If one event or situation follows **hard on the heels** or **hot on the heels** of another, it happens very quickly after it. *The latest discovery comes hard on the heels of an attempt to smuggle nuclear trigger devices into Iraq through Britain.* ● If you **take to your heels**, you run away; a literary expression. *As soon as he saw me he took to his heels.*

hefty /hɛfti/ **heftier, heftiest**
ADJ **Hefty** means very large in size, weight, or amount; an informal word. *...a broad, hefty Irish nurse... Many workers have lodged hefty pay demands.*

hegemony /hɪgɛməni/
NU **Hegemony** is the domination or control of one country, organization, or social group over a group of others; a formal word. *He denounced what he saw as Punjabi hegemony crushing the smaller provinces of Pakistan.*

heifer /hɛfə/ **heifers**
NC A **heifer** is a young female cow. *...a nice black heifer.*

height /haɪt/ **heights**
1 NU+SUPP or NC+SUPP The **height** of a person or thing is their measurement from bottom to top. *The redwood grows to 100 metres in height... He was of medium height... This enables them to grow to considerable heights.*
2 NU **Height** is the quality of being tall. *You'll recognize her because of her height.*
3 NU+SUPP or NC+SUPP A particular **height** is the distance that something is above the ground. *The*

aircraft reaches its maximum height of 80,000 feet in about ten minutes... The bag had been dropped from about shoulder height.
4 N SING A **height** is a position or place that is a long way above the ground. *He'd had to climb down to the village from a height.*
5 N PL You use **heights** to refer to the top of a hill or cliff. *...fierce fighting on the heights above the bay.*
6 N SING+SUPP When an activity, situation, or organization is at its **height**, it is at its most successful, powerful, or intense. *At the height of their racing career, the Jaguar team were unbeatable... It is the height of the tourist season.*
7 N SING+of You can use **height** to emphasize how extreme a quality is. For example, if you say that something is the **height** of absurdity, you mean that it is extremely absurd. *It seemed to me the height of luxury.*
8 N PL+SUPP If something reaches great **heights**, it becomes very extreme or intense. *The rate of inflation has reached unprecedented heights.*
heighten /haɪtn/ **heightens, heightening, heightened;**
a formal word.
V-ERG When something **heightens** a feeling or state or when it **heightens**, it increases in degree or intensity. *Tensions were heightened by the campaign for independence... As their hardship heightened, so did their desperation and anger.* ◆ **heightened** ADJ ATTRIB *She is in a state of heightened emotion.*
heinous /heɪnəs/
ADJ **Heinous** means extremely evil; a formal word. *...heinous crimes.*
heir /eə/ **heirs**
1 NC Someone's **heir** is the person who will inherit their money, property, or title when they die. *...Thompson's son and heir... The Prince of Wales is heir to the throne.*
2 NC+SUPP If someone or something is the **heir** of a person or system that was important in the past, they continue to think or work in the way of that person or system. *The organisers of last week's coup undoubtedly see themselves as the legitimate heirs of Bolshevism... John Major is being portrayed as the true heir to Mrs Thatcher.*
heiress /eəres/ **heiresses**
NC An **heiress** is a woman who will inherit property, money, or a title. *...tobacco heiress Doris Duke.*
heirloom /eəlu:m/ **heirlooms**
NC An **heirloom** is an object that has belonged to a family for a very long time. *...jewels and other family heirlooms.*
heist /haɪst/ **heists**
NC A **heist** is a robbery, especially of a large amount of money or extremely valuable objects; used in American English. *It was the biggest art heist in the history of the country. ...the heist of a shipment of gold ore by a Mississippi gang.*
held /held/
Held is the past tense and past participle of **hold**.
helicopter /helɪkɒptə/ **helicopters**
NC A **helicopter** is an aircraft with no wings, but with large blades which rotate above it. *A helicopter that was flying from Missouri to Texas went down in heavy fog last night.*
helicopter gunship, helicopter gunships
NC A **helicopter gunship** is a helicopter which has several large guns fixed on it. *The city has been bombarded by long-range artillery and helicopter gunships... Helicopters and planes gave air support and one helicopter gunship was reported to have been shot down.*
heliport /helɪpɔːt/ **heliports**
NC A **heliport** is a place where helicopters land and take off.
helium /hiːliəm/
NU **Helium** is a gas that is lighter than air and that is used to fill balloons and airships. *Ken was filling up helium balloons and giving them away.*
hell /hel/
1 N PROP In Christianity and some other religions, **hell** is the place where wicked people are believed to go and be punished when they die. *...a torrid landscape,*

reminiscent of the fires of hell.
2 NU If you say that a situation is **hell**, you mean that it is extremely unpleasant; an informal use. *Meal times were hell—he would throw food at me, stamp, or lash out.*
3 People use **hell** when they are angry or excited about something; an informal or rude use which some people find offensive. *Bloody hell, I thought, I've come all this way for nothing.*
● **Hell** is used in these informal phrases. ● If you say that **all hell broke loose**, you mean that there was suddenly a lot of arguing or fighting. *When Darwin asserted that men were descended from apes, all hell broke loose.* ● If someone **gives** you **hell**, they are very severe and cruel to you. *I bet these ladies gave their secretaries hell.* ● To **play hell with** something means to have a bad effect on it. *The new extension will play hell with the plumbing.* ● If someone does something **for the hell of it**, they do it for fun or for no particular reason. *I don't want to offend people for the hell of it.* ● People use **a hell of** or **one hell of** to emphasize the amount or size of something. *There was a hell of a lot of traffic.* ● Some people use **like hell** to emphasize how strong an action or quality is. *It hurt like hell.* ● People say **to hell with** something when they want to show that they do not care about it. *To hell with what happens later... They don't debate, they have their viewpoint, and to hell with everyone else.* ● People sometimes use **the hell** after words such as 'what', 'who', 'where' and 'why' to emphasize a question; a rude or offensive expression. *Why the hell should I help you? ...wondering where the hell to start.*
he'll /hɪl, hiːl/
He'll is the usual spoken form of 'he will'. *He'll be having talks with Government leaders.*
hell-bent; also written **hell bent.**
ADJ PRED+on If you are **hell-bent** on doing something, you are very determined to do it, however bad the consequences might be. *The two sides seem hell-bent on another meaningless trial of strength... They are hell bent on paying the interest on their bank overdrafts.*
Hellenic /helːnɪk, helenɪk/
ADJ **Hellenic** is used to describe the people, language, and culture of Ancient Greece. *...Orpheus wandering the Hellenic world from one port to the next.*
hellish /helɪʃ/
ADJ If something is **hellish**, it is extremely unpleasant; an informal word. *It's hellish being a student without a grant.*
hello /hələʊ, heləʊ/ **hellos;** also spelt **hallo** and **hullo.**
You say 'Hello' when you are greeting someone or starting a telephone conversation. *Hello boys, how are you?... Hello, Tony Durham here.* ► Also NC *Do come over and say hello to the group.*
helm /helm/ **helms**
1 NC The **helm** of a boat or ship is its wheel or tiller and the position from which the boat is controlled; a technical term. *The company's chairman took the helm of the huge ship for two minutes.*
2 When someone is **at the helm** or when they **take over the helm**, they are in a position of leadership or control. *With any lesser figure at the helm the party's prestige will be diminished... He took over the helm of state in 1948.*
helmet /helmɪt/ **helmets**
NC A **helmet** is a hard hat which you wear to protect your head. *Diving helmet design has improved considerably.*
helmsman /helmzmən/ **helmsmen** /helmzmən/
NC The **helmsman** of a boat is the person who is steering it; a technical term. *Investigators will be interviewing the captain, third mate and helmsman.*
help /help/ **helps, helping, helped**
1 V or V O If you **help** someone, you make something easier for them, for example by doing part of their work or by giving them advice or money. *Something went wrong with his machine so I helped him fix it... The Solidarity leader offered to help.*
2 V or VO If something **helps**, it makes a difficult situation or task easier to deal with. *I've got 40 pence, will that help?... Good weather helped the clean-up*

operations on the East Coast.
3 V+*to*-INF or V+INF If something **helps** to achieve a particular result, it is one of the things that combine to achieve it. *One of the things that can help to keep prices down is high productivity... Having a job helps keep them off the streets.*
4 V-REFL If you **help** yourself, you serve yourself with food or drink. *Mr Stokes helped himself to some more rum.*
5 V O or V+ING If you can't **help** the way you feel or the way you behave, you cannot change it or stop it happening. *You can't help who you fall in love with... I can't help feeling that it was a mistake to let him go.*
6 NU If you give **help** to someone, you assist them in some way, for example by giving them money or advice, or by doing part of their work for them. *The organization gives help to single women.*
7 N SING or N U If someone or something is a **help**, they make things better or easier by assisting you in some way. *He was a great help with some of the problems... That isn't much help.*
8 If something **is of help**, it makes things better or easier. *Having a sober mind around might prove to be of some help.*
9 NU **Help** is also the assistance that someone gives when they go to rescue a person who is in danger. *They were crying and running outside into the street, waiting for help.*
10 If you are in danger, you shout '**help**!' in order to attract someone's attention. *Oh no, my God, help! Don't let him!*
help out PHRASAL VERB If you **help out** or **help** someone **out**, you do them a favour, such as lending them money or doing part of their work. *I think her colleagues did help her out on that occasion.*
helper /hɛlpə/ **helpers**
NC A **helper** is a person who gives advice, assistance, or money in order to help another person or group, usually with an organized activity. *All the helpers for this organization are voluntary.*
helpful /hɛlpfl/
1 ADJ If someone is **helpful**, they help you by doing work for you or by giving you advice or information. *They were all very pleasant and extremely kind and helpful.* ◆ **helpfully** ADV *Doctor Percival said helpfully, 'I'd advise you not to go'.* ◆ **helpfulness** NU *I was greatly impressed by the efficiency and helpfulness of the stage crew.*
2 ADJ Something that is **helpful** makes a situation more pleasant or easier to deal with. *It is often helpful during an illness to talk to other sufferers.*
helping /hɛlpɪŋ/ **helpings**
NC A **helping** of food is the amount that you get in a single serving. *I gave him a second helping of pudding.*
helping hand
N SING If you give someone a **helping hand**, you do something which helps them. *Douglas Hurd is in the Middle East, trying to give a helping hand to America's peace initiative... Why do they need this extra helping hand to find someone?*
helpless /hɛlpləs/
ADJ If you are **helpless**, you are unable to do anything useful or to protect yourself, for example because you are very weak. *...a helpless baby... Sam raised his arms in a helpless gesture.* ◆ **helplessly** ADV *She stood there helplessly crying.* ◆ **helplessness** NU *She took advantage of my utter helplessness.*
helpline /hɛlplaɪn/ **helplines**
NC A **helpline** is a telephone line that is reserved for callers who need to contact a particular organization about a specific problem. *Mr Waldegrave said the new centre would work closely with the Gulf Helpline.*
Helsinki /hɛlsɪŋki/
Helsinki is the capital of Finland and its largest city. Population: 491,000 (1989).
helter-skelter /hɛltəskɛltə/ **helter-skelters**
1 ADJ ATTRIB You use **helter-skelter** to describe something that is hurried or disorganized. *...the last minute helter-skelter rush for the bus... They must try and re-impose some kind of order on this increasingly helter-skelter corruption.* ▶ Also ADV *Yugoslavia may*

be heading helter-skelter towards bloodshed.
2 NC A **helter-skelter** is a tall, spiral-shaped tower which you can slide down for fun, usually at fairgrounds.
hem /hɛm/ **hems, hemming, hemmed**
1 NC The **hem** of a garment or piece of cloth is an edge which is folded over and sewn. *...hems on evening gowns.*
2 VO If you **hem** a piece of cloth, you fold the edge over and sew it to make it neat. *She had hemmed a set of handkerchiefs.*
hem in PHRASAL VERB If you **are hemmed in** by something, you are surrounded by something and cannot move, or are limited in some way in what you can do. *Two heavily reinforced battalions were hemmed in in the barracks... His administration is still hemmed in by the legacy of military rule.*
he-man, he-men
NC A **he-man** is a strong man, especially one who likes to show how strong he is; an informal word.
hemisphere /hɛmɪsfɪə/ **hemispheres**
1 NC A **hemisphere** is one half of the earth. *...the first day of autumn in the northern hemisphere, the first day of spring in the southern hemisphere. ...the greatest empires in the western hemisphere.*
2 NC The left and right **hemispheres** are the two halves of the brain. *The left hemisphere is the hemisphere of speech.*
hemispheric /hɛmɪsfɛrɪk/
ADJ ATTRIB **Hemispheric** means relating to one half of the Earth. *President Bush is apparently now keen to create a sense of hemispheric identity. ...a hemispheric free trade zone stretching from Point Barrow in Alaska to the Straits of Magellan. ...a meeting in late October of Western hemispheric nations in Porto Rico.*
hemline /hɛmlaɪn/ **hemlines**
NC The **hemline** of a dress or skirt is the bottom edge of it.
hemlock /hɛmlɒk/
NU **Hemlock** is a poison made from a plant with small white flowers, a spotted stem, and finely divided leaves. *...condemned to death by drinking hemlock.*
hemoglobin /hiːməglə͡ʊbɪn/. See **haemoglobin**.
hemophilia /hiːməfɪliə/. See **haemophilia**.
hemorrhage /hɛmə͡ʊrɪdʒ/. See **haemorrhage**.
hemorrhoids /hɛmərɔɪdz/. See **haemorrhoids**.
hemp /hɛmp/
NU **Hemp** is a plant grown in Asia. It is used for making rope and in the production of the drug cannabis.
hemstitch /hɛmstɪtʃ/
NU **Hemstitch** is a special sewing stitch used for sewing hems.
hen /hɛn/ **hens**
1 NC **Hens** are female chickens, often kept for their eggs. *The modern battery hen is a living production line for eggs.*
2 NC or N+N A **hen** is also any female bird. *...a hen pheasant.*
hence /hɛns/; a formal word.
1 ADV SEN **Hence** means for the reason just mentioned. *The computer has become smaller and cheaper and hence more available to a greater number of people.*
2 ADV If something will happen a particular length of time **hence**, it will happen that length of time from now. *The tunnel will open in 1993, seven years hence.*
henceforth /hɛnsfɔːθ/
ADV SEN **Henceforth** means from this time on; a formal word. *The companies will henceforth have to operate on commercial lines.*
henchman /hɛntʃmən/ **henchmen** /hɛntʃmən/
NC+POSS **Henchmen** are people employed by a powerful person to do violent or dishonest work. *He signed the papers and left it to his henchmen to do the work.*
Heng Samrin /hɛŋ sæmrɪn/
Heng Samrin became President of Cambodia in 1979. From 1981 to 1991 he was General Secretary of the Kampuchean People's Revolutionary Party (KPRP), now renamed the Cambodian People's Party (CPP).

He defected to Vietnam in 1978. Heng Samrin remained President at the return of Prince Sihanouk as head of the Supreme National Council in 1991. Born: 1934.

henna /ˈhenə/ **hennas, hennaing, hennaed**
1 NU **Henna** is a reddish-brown dye that is used for colouring hair or skin. It is made from the leaves of a shrub that grows in Asia and North Africa. *...her hair freshly coloured with henna.*
2 VO When you **henna** your hair or your skin, you dye it using henna. *My hair was still crimson from having been persistently hennaed for seven years.* ◆ **hennaed** /ˈhenəd/ ADJ *...slightly curly, hennaed hair.*

hen party, hen parties
NC A **hen party** is a party or gathering at which only women are present; they are usually held shortly before a woman gets married.

henpecked /ˈhenpekt/
ADJ If you describe a man as **henpecked**, you mean that he is completely dominated by a woman who orders him about and tells him what to do. *Macbeth can be seen as the henpecked husband of a domineering wife.*

hepatitis /hepəˈtaɪtɪs/
NU **Hepatitis** is a serious disease which affects the liver. *As a major health risk hepatitis is second only to smoking.*

heptagon /ˈheptəgən/ **heptagons**
NC A **heptagon** is a geometric shape with seven straight sides.

heptagonal /hepˈtægənl/
ADJ A **heptagonal** object or shape has seven straight sides.

her /hə, hɜː/
1 PRON **Her** is used as the object of a verb or preposition. You use **her** to refer to a woman, girl, or female animal that has already been mentioned, or whose identity is known. *I knew your mother—I was at school with her... They gave her the job.*
2 DET You also use **her** to indicate that something belongs or relates to a woman, girl, or female animal that has already been mentioned, or whose identity is known. *She opened her bag... Her name is Cynthia.*
3 DET You also use **her** in some titles. *...Her Majesty the Queen.*

herald /ˈherəld/ **heralds, heralding, heralded**; a formal word.
VO Something that **heralds** a future event or situation is a sign that it is going to happen or appear. *His rise to power heralded the end of the liberal era.* ▶ Also NC+*of* *The festival was the herald of a new age.*

heraldic /həˈrældɪk/
ADJ ATTRIB **Heraldic** means relating to heraldry. *...the heraldic motto.*

heraldry /ˈherəldri/
NU **Heraldry** is the study of coats of arms and of the history of the families who are entitled to have them. *The new design, it is said, would follow 'the correct rules' of European heraldry.*

herb /hɜːb/ **herbs**
NC A **herb** is a plant which is used to flavour food, or as a medicine. *...dried herbs and spices.*

herbaceous /hɜːˈbeɪʃəs/
ADJ **Herbaceous** plants are soft and fleshy rather than hard and woody.

herbaceous border, herbaceous borders
NC A **herbaceous border** is a strip of ground containing a mixture of plants that flower every year.

herbal /ˈhɜːbl/
ADJ ATTRIB **Herbal** means made from herbs or relating to herbs. *...herbal medicine. ...herbal tea.*

herbalist /ˈhɜːbəlɪst/ **herbalists**
NC A **herbalist** is a person who grows or sells herbs that are used in medicine. *Herbalists and witch-doctors are experimenting with potions and plant extracts.*

herbicide /ˈhɜːbɪsaɪd/ **herbicides**
NCorNU A **herbicide** is a chemical that is used to destroy plants especially on a large scale, for example in farming. *Using herbicides can be ecologically disastrous... The company applied herbicide not fertilizer.*

herbivore /ˈhɜːbɪvɔː/ **herbivores**
NC A **herbivore** is an animal that only eats plants. *Normally sheep and deer are herbivores and don't eat meat.*

herbivorous /hɜːˈbɪvəʳrəs/
ADJ A **herbivorous** animal is one that only eats plants. *...herbivorous fish.*

herculean /hɜːkjuˈliːən/
ADJ ATTRIB A **herculean** task or effort is very difficult and requires great strength; a literary word. *You must make a herculean effort not to talk to them about it.*

herd /hɜːd/ **herds, herding, herded**
1 NC A **herd** of animals is a large group of them living together. *...a herd of goats.*
2 VO If you **herd** people or animals, you make them move together to form a group. *...men herding cattle... The chained people were herded back into the dark cellar.*

herdsman /ˈhɜːdzmən/ **herdsmen** /ˈhɜːdzmən/
NC A **herdsman** is a man who looks after a herd of animals such as cattle or goats. *The people of Lesotho are mostly farmers or herdsmen.*

here /hɪə/
1 ADV **Here** refers to the place where you are or to a place which has been mentioned. *She left here at eight o'clock... Elizabeth, come over here... You've been here for a number of years.*
2 ADV You use **here** when you are referring to a place, person, or thing that is near you. *You have to sign here and acknowledge the receipt... I have here a very important message that has just arrived.*
3 ADV You can also use **here** to refer to a particular time, situation, or subject. *The autumn's really here at last... I think that what we're talking about here is role-playing.*
4 ADV You can use **here** at the beginning of a sentence in order to draw attention to something or to introduce something. *Here is the News... Here she is... Here's how it's done.*
5 You can say '**here**' when you are offering or giving something to someone. *He pushed a piece of paper across the table. 'Here you are. My address.'... 'Here, hold this while I go and get a newspaper.'*
● **Here** is used in these phrases. ● You say '**Here's to us**' or '**Here's to your new job**', for example, as a way of wishing someone success or happiness. ● Something that is happening **here and there** is happening in several different places at the same time. *Panic here and there was only to be expected.*

hereabouts /hɪərəˈbaʊts/
ADV Something that is **hereabouts** is near to you or in the same general area as you are. *Is there a fellow American hereabouts?*

hereafter /hɪərˈɑːftə/
1 N SING The **hereafter** is the life which some people believe exists after they die. *The hereafter, for all we know, may be an eternal state of boredom.*
2 ADV **Hereafter** or **hereinafter** is used to introduce information about what you are going to call something in a document after you have referred to it for the first time; a legal use. *...the South Australia Housing Trust (hereafter called the Trust).*

hereby /hɪəˈbaɪ/
ADV **Hereby** is used in formal statements and documents to emphasize that they are official. *I hereby resign. ...He is hereby licensed to drive motor vehicles of Groups A and E.*

hereditary /həˈredətri/
1 ADJ A **hereditary** characteristic or illness is passed on to a child from its parents before it is born. *...a progressive, hereditary disease of certain glands.*
2 ADJ A **hereditary** title or position in society is passed on from parent to child. *...the hereditary right to belong to the House of Lords.*

heredity /həˈredəti/
NU **Heredity** is the biological process by which characteristics are passed on from parents to their children before the children are born. *Do you think we are influenced more by environment or heredity?*

herein /hɪərˈɪn/
ADV **Herein** means in this place, situation, or

document; a formal word. *Herein lies the real danger. ...the undeniable facts contained herein.*

hereinafter /hɪərɪnɑːftə/. See **hereafter**.

heresy /hɛrəsi/ **heresies**
1 NUorNC **Heresy** is a belief or way of behaving that seriously disagrees with the principles of a particular religion. *The Islamic council said illustrating the Koran with profane pictures constituted sacrilege and heresy. ...a minority sect traditionally despised for their religious heresy.*
2 NUorNC **Heresy** is a belief or way of behaving that disagrees with generally accepted beliefs. *...bitter complaints about the heresies of the group... To the left such sentiments are heresy.*

heretic /hɛrətɪk/ **heretics**
1 NC A **heretic** is a person whose beliefs seriously disagree with the principles of the particular religion they belong to. *Images of the Inquisition burning and torturing heretics.* ◆ **heretical** ADJ *The bishops jailed him for heretical and blasphemous words.*
2 NC A **heretic** is a person whose beliefs are generally thought to be wrong. *In the past she and her sociologist colleagues were regarded as heretics... The late President Tito was long denounced by Moscow as a communist heretic.* ◆ **heretical** ADJ *In a way though, this is not such a heretical view, for it contains echoes of speeches by many leaders.*

heretofore /hɪətuːfɔː/
ADV **Heretofore** means before this time; a formal word. *I devoted all my heretofore unchannelled enthusiasm to it.*

herewith /hɪəwɪð/; a formal word.
1 ADV You use **herewith** to say that you are enclosing something in a letter that you are sending. *I herewith return your cheque.*
2 ADV **Herewith** also means the same as **hereby**. *I herewith declare myself Dictator.*

heritage /hɛrətɪdʒ/
N SING+POSS A country's **heritage** consists of all its old buildings and monuments, and the qualities and traditions that have continued over many years, especially when they are considered to be of historical importance. *...Britain's national heritage. ...the rich heritage of Russian folk music.*

hermaphrodite /hɜːmæfrədaɪt/ **hermaphrodites**
NC A **hermaphrodite** is a person, animal, or flower that has both male and female reproductive organs; a technical term in biology. *Slugs and snails are hermaphrodites.*

hermetic /hɜːmɛtɪk/
1 ADJ ATTRIB If a container has a **hermetic** seal, it is very tightly closed so that no air can get in or out. *It solidified and formed a perfect hermetic seal.*
◆ **hermetically** ADV *...plastic packs of food, hermetically sealed.*
2 ADJ ATTRIB If you describe the situation you are in as **hermetic**, you mean that you feel socially or physically separated from other people. *...the hermetic seclusion of the hotel... They found themselves shut within small hermetic circles.*
◆ **hermetically** ADV *They acted as though the poor were hermetically sealed off from social influences.*

hermit /hɜːmɪt/ **hermits**
NC A **hermit** is a person who deliberately lives alone, away from people and society. *...the learned hermit and abbot Joachim of Fiore.*

hermit crab, hermit crabs
NC A **hermit crab** is a small crab that lives in the empty shells of other shellfish. *Hermit crabs and lobsters are very close relatives.*

hernia /hɜːniə/ **hernias**
NCorNU A **hernia** is a medical condition which is often caused by strain or injury; it results in one of your inner organs sticking through a weak point in the surrounding tissue. *A minor hernia was diagnosed. ...hernia, appendicitis and gall bladder operations.*

hero /hɪərəʊ/ **heroes**
1 NC The **hero** of a book, play, or film is its main male character. *His peculiar Christian name comes from the hero of one of her novels.*
2 NC A **hero** is also someone who has done something brave or good and is admired by a lot of people. *...one*

of the heroes of the Battle of Britain.
3 NC+POSS If you describe a man as your **hero**, you mean that you admire him greatly. *Bill Hook was my first rugby hero.*

heroic /hɪrəʊɪk/
ADJ **Heroic** actions or people are brave, courageous, and determined. *They are heroic figures in the fight against cancer... He was strong, self-reliant, a one-man cavalry—he was heroic.* ◆ **heroically** ADV *They fought heroically.*

heroin /hɛrəʊɪn/
NU **Heroin** is a powerful drug which some people take for pleasure, but which they can become addicted to. *They found a quarter of a ton of hashish, along with heroin, cocaine and other drugs.*

heroine /hɛrəʊɪn/ **heroines**
1 NC The **heroine** of a book, play, or film is its main female character. *The ballet expresses in dance the feelings of its heroine.*
2 NC A **heroine** is also a woman who has done something brave or good and is admired by a lot of people. *...the heroine of their great 1967 election triumph.*
3 NC If you describe a woman as your **heroine**, you mean that you admire her greatly. *One old woman had come all the way from her village just to see her heroine.*

heroism /hɛrəʊɪzəm/
NU **Heroism** is great courage and bravery. *...an act of heroism.*

heron /hɛrən/ **herons**
NC A **heron** is a large bird which eats fish. *...the mournful cry of the curlew and the deep call of the heron.*

herpes /hɜːpiːz/
NU **Herpes** is a disease which causes painful red spots to appear on the skin. *Like other viruses, herpes first has to get into a cell.*

herring /hɛrɪŋ/ **herrings**. The plural form can be either **herrings** or **herring**.
1 NCorNU A **herring** is a long silver-coloured fish that lives in the sea. *Soviet fishermen will be allowed a sizeable quota of herring. ...fifteen tons of herrings and sardines.*
2 See also **red herring**.

herringbone /hɛrɪŋbəʊn/
NU **Herringbone** is a pattern used in fabrics or brickwork which consists of short lines of V shapes.

herring gull, herring gulls
NC A **herring gull** is a large bird that is found on the coasts of Britain. It has white feathers, black tips on its wings, and pink legs.

hers /hɜːz/
PRON You use **hers** to indicate that something belongs or relates to a woman, girl, or female animal that has already been mentioned, or whose identity is known. *He laid his hand on hers... You were an old friend of hers.*

herself /həsɛlf/
1 PRON REFL You use **herself** as the object of a verb or preposition to refer to the same woman, girl, or female animal that is mentioned as the subject of the clause, or as a previous object in the clause. *She groaned and stretched herself out flat on the sofa... Barbara stared at herself in the mirror... On the way home Rose bought herself a piece of cheese for lunch.*
2 PRON REFL You also use **herself** to emphasize the female subject or object of a clause, and to make it clear who you are referring to. *Sally herself came back... How strange that he should collide with Melanie Byrd herself,'... Their audience was of middle-aged women like herself.*
3 PRON REFL If a girl or woman does something **herself**, she does it without any help or interference from anyone else. *She had printed the little card herself.*

Herzog, Chaim /xaɪm hɛətsɒg/
General Chaim Herzog became President of Israel in 1983. He was Director of Military Intelligence from 1959 to 1962, and the Permanent Representative to the United Nations from 1975 to 1978. He was a member of the Knesset from 1981 to 1983. He is a member of the

Labour Party. Born: 1918.

he's /hɪz, hiːz/
1 **He's** is the usual spoken form of 'he is'. *He's a reporter... He's going away soon.*
2 **He's** is also the usual spoken form of 'he has', especially when 'has' is an auxiliary verb. *I hope he's got some money left... He's gone.*

hesitancy /hɛzɪtənsi/
NU **Hesitancy** is unwillingness to do something, usually because you are uncertain, embarrassed, or worried. *There was no hesitancy in his words.*

hesitant /hɛzɪtənt/
ADJ If you are **hesitant** about doing something, you do not do it quickly or immediately, usually because you are uncertain, embarrassed, or worried. *He was hesitant about accepting the invitation... He seemed hesitant to confirm the bad news. ...a hesitant, almost boyish smile.* ◆ **hesitantly** ADV *'Maybe you could teach me,' said Marsha hesitantly.*

hesitate /hɛzɪteɪt/ **hesitates, hesitating, hesitated**
1 V If you **hesitate**, you pause slightly while you are doing something or just before you do it, usually because you are uncertain, embarrassed, or worried. *She put her hand on the phone, hesitated for a moment, then picked up the receiver.* ◆ **hesitation** /hɛzɪteɪʃn/ **hesitations** NUorNC *'Well, no,' Karen said, with some hesitation. ...a slight hesitation.*
2 V+*to*-INF If you **hesitate** to do something, you are unwilling to do it because you are not certain whether it is correct or right. *Don't hesitate to go to a doctor if you have any unusual symptoms.* ◆ **hesitation** NUorNC *After some hesitation he agreed to allow me to write the article... Bamuthi's hesitations were overcome.*

hessian /hɛsiən/
NU **Hessian** is a thick rough fabric that is used for making sacks. *...unspun cotton, horsehair, hessian.*

heterodox /hɛtərɒdɒks/
ADJ **Heterodox** beliefs, opinions, or ideas are different from the accepted or official ones; a formal word. *...conventional policies or the more heterodox variety.*

heterogeneous /hɛtərədʒiːniəs/
ADJ Something that is **heterogeneous** consists of many different types of things; a formal word. *Arts and sciences are contained in one heterogeneous collection.*

heterosexual /hɛtərəsɛkʃuəl/ **heterosexuals**
1 ADJ A **heterosexual** relationship is a sexual one between a man and a woman. *The minimum age of consent for heterosexual relationships in Britain is 16.*
2 ADJ Someone who is **heterosexual** is sexually attracted to people of the opposite sex. *He said it was vital that heterosexual people protect themselves by using condoms.* ▶ Also NC *It is not only drug users and homosexuals who are at risk from AIDS, but heterosexuals as well.*

heterosexuality /hɛtərəsɛkʃuæləti/
NU **Heterosexuality** is sexual attraction or sexual activity between a man and a woman. *...the problems of heterosexuality.*

het up /hɛt ʌp/
ADJ PRED If you get **het up**, you get very excited or anxious about something; an informal expression. *...when he gets all het up about some business problem.*

heuristic /hjuərɪstɪk/
ADJ **Heuristic** methods of learning involve using reasoning and past experience rather than formulas or solutions that are given to you; a formal word.

hew /hjuː/ **hews, hewing, hewed, hewn**
VO If someone **hews** a shape out of stone or wood, they cut large pieces out of it roughly; a literary word. *They made him hew out his cross and drag it to Calvary.*

hexagon /hɛksəgən/ **hexagons**
NC A **hexagon** is a geometric shape that has six straight sides. *The soccer ball is composed of a pattern of hexagons and pentagons.*

hexagonal /hɛksægənl/
ADJ A **hexagonal** object or shape has six straight sides. *...each about two metres across, hexagonal in shape.*

hey /heɪ/
You say or shout **'hey'** to attract someone's attention or to show surprise, interest, or annoyance. *'Hey, Ben!' he called. There was no reply.*

heyday /heɪdeɪ/
N SING+POSS The **heyday** of a person, nation, or organization is the time when they are most powerful, successful, or popular. *...the heyday of Christianity.*

hi /haɪ/
You say **'hi'** when you are greeting someone informally. *'Hi, Uncle Harold,' Thomas said.*

hiatus /haɪeɪtəs/
N SING A **hiatus** is a pause in which nothing happens; a formal word. *They began talking with the PLO after a hiatus of 13 years.*

hibernate /haɪbəneɪt/ **hibernates, hibernating, hibernated**
V Animals that **hibernate** spend the winter in a state like a deep sleep. *Squirrels don't hibernate.* ◆ **hibernation** /haɪbəneɪʃn/ NU *...a brown bear emerging from hibernation.*

hibiscus /hɪbɪskəs/ **hibiscuses**
NC A **hibiscus** is a bush with large yellow or red bell-shaped flowers. *...waiting under the palms and hibiscus in the shady courtyard.*

hiccup /hɪkʌp/ **hiccups, hiccupping, hiccupped**; also spelt **hiccough**; **hiccup** and **hiccough** are pronounced in the same way.
1 NC A **hiccup** is a small problem or difficulty, usually one which can be put right fairly easily. *This project has had some kind of a hitch, or hiccup. ...this is just an economic hiccup... British Rail deny any design fault in either the old or new equipment, but blame a hiccup in the changeover.*
2 NC If you have **hiccups**, you make repeated sharp sounds in your throat, often because you have been eating or drinking too quickly. *In contrast to sneezing or coughing, hiccups have no obvious function... Most people get hiccups occasionally.*
3 V When you **hiccup**, you make repeated sharp sounds in your throat. *She turned over on her side, hiccupped once or twice and went to sleep... A London doctor has a new explanation for why we hiccup.*

hick /hɪk/ **hicks**
NC You can refer to someone who comes from the country and is not used to living in a city as a **hick**; used in informal American English showing disapproval. *'You're so sophisticated. How can you be from Texas?' 'Well, you know, we're not all hicks down here.'*

hid /hɪd/
Hid is the past tense of **hide**.

hidden /hɪdn/
1 **Hidden** is the past participle of **hide**.
2 ADJ A place that is **hidden** is difficult to find. *...hidden valleys.*
3 ADJ Something that is **hidden** is not easily noticed. *...the hidden disadvantages of a cheque book.*

hidden agenda, hidden agendas
NC If you say that politicians have a **hidden agenda**, you mean that they are keeping some of their intentions secret; used showing disapproval. *There are suspicions about a so-called hidden agenda in the recent talks... The group claim the SDP has a hidden agenda.*

hide /haɪd/ **hides, hiding, hid, hidden**
1 VO To **hide** something means to cover it or put it somewhere so that it cannot be seen. *The women managed to steal and hide a few knives... Much of his face was hidden by a beard.*
2 VorV-REFL If you **hide**, you go somewhere where you cannot easily be seen or found. *There was nowhere to hide... He went off and hid himself from them.*
3 VO If you **hide** what you feel or know, you keep it a secret, so that nobody else knows about it. *I couldn't hide this fact from you.*
4 NCorNU The **hide** of a large animal is its skin which is used for making leather. *...unwanted carcass components, like the hide, the liver and the gut.*

hide-and-seek
NU **Hide-and-seek** is a game in which one player covers his or her eyes until the other players have

hidden themselves, and then he or she tries to find them. *Bushes all over the world are the children's paradise because hide-and-seek is a universal game... Their warships play a deadly game of hide-and-seek in the world's oceans.*

hideaway /haɪdəweɪ/ **hideaways**
NC A **hideaway** is a place where you go to get away from other people. *After stocking up our hideaway with luxuries, we drove up the mountain to watch the sunset.*

hidebound /haɪdbaʊnd/
ADJ People who are **hidebound** are unwilling to change their ideas, or to accept new ones, even when they obviously should do so. *The members of committees are often hidebound, unimaginative and even incompetent... He hated the hidebound conservatism of his superiors.*

hideous /hɪdiəs/
ADJ Something that is **hideous** is extremely unpleasant or ugly. *...the hideous conditions of trench warfare... They're ugly, hideous brutes.* ◆ **hideously** SUBMOD *...hideously mutilated bodies. ...a hideously difficult task.*

hideout /haɪdaʊt/ **hideouts**
NC A **hideout** is a place where someone goes secretly because they do not want anyone to find them, for example because they are running away from the police. *Police raided a flat which was used as a hideout by IRA terrorists.*

hiding /haɪdɪŋ/ **hidings**
1 If someone is **in hiding**, or goes **into hiding**, they have secretly gone somewhere where they cannot be found. *...an unending flood of illegals, now in hiding in parts of Cape Town... He has not been heard from since going into hiding in June.*
2 NC If you give someone a **hiding**, you beat them as a punishment; an old-fashioned use. *He told us to stop, or else we'd get a good hiding.*

hiding place, hiding places
NC A **hiding place** is a special place where things or people can be hidden. *You need to find a new hiding place for that key.*

hierarchical /haɪərɑːkɪkl/
ADJ A **hierarchical** system or organization is one in which people have different ranks or positions, depending on how important they are. *...ancient hierarchical societies.*

hierarchy /haɪərɑːki/ **hierarchies**; a formal word.
1 NC A **hierarchy** is a system in which people have different ranks or positions depending on how important they are. *...a society in which people are prepared to observe their correct place in the hierarchy. ...a tier in the hierarchy of state management.*
2 NC The **hierarchy** of an organization is the group of people who manage and control it. *The university hierarchy decided that it was best to ignore the situation.*

hieroglyph /haɪərəglɪf/ **hieroglyphs**
NC **Hieroglyphs** are symbols in the form of pictures which are used in some writing systems, for example that of ancient Egypt. *A combination of hieroglyphs represent place names of a conquered location.*

hieroglyphics /haɪərəglɪfɪks/
1 N PL **Hieroglyphics** are symbols in the form of pictures which are used in some writing systems, for example that of ancient Egypt. *Reading from the ancient hieroglyphics she shows how wholesome the ancient Egyptian diet was.*
2 N PL You can also refer to written symbols or words that you cannot understand as **hieroglyphics**. *On the blackboards were hieroglyphics which I was told were called logarithms.*

hi-fi /haɪfaɪ/ **hi-fis**
NC A **hi-fi** is a set of stereo equipment which you use to play records, tapes, and compact discs. *...listening to music on the hi-fi.*

higgledy-piggledy /hɪɡldɪpɪɡldi/
ADJ If things are **higgledy-piggledy**, they are in a great muddle or disorder. *The books were higgledy-piggledy on the table.* ► Also ADV *He thrust clothes higgledy-piggledy into plastic bags.*

high /haɪ/ **higher, highest; highs**
1 ADJ A **high** structure or mountain measures a long distance from the bottom to the top. *...the high walls of the prison.*
2 ADJ or ADJ after N **High** is used in questions and statements about height. *How high are the walls? ...a 200 foot high crag.*
3 ADJ or ADV If something is **high**, it is a long way above the ground, above sea level, or above a person. *The bookshelf was too high for him to reach... I threw the shell high up into the air.*
4 ADJ **High** also means great in amount, degree, or intensity. *Her works fetch high prices. ...areas of high unemployment... Their diet is high in saturated fat.*
5 ADJ If the quality or standard of something is **high**, it is very good indeed. *...high quality colour photographs... Lord Mackay said high standards of conduct were essential to the administration of justice.*
6 ADJ ATTRIB **High** is also used with approximate numbers. For example, if a number or level is in the **high** eighties, it is more than eighty-five, but not as much as ninety.
7 ADJ ATTRIB You can also use **high** to mean advanced or complex. *...a successful job in high finance... The questions he'd asked were at a higher level than other people's.*
8 ADJ A **high** position in a profession or society is an important one. *She is high enough up in the company to be able to help you. ...high social status.*
9 ADJ If someone has a **high** opinion of a person or thing, they respect them very much. *...a man who shared his high opinion of The Times... They are clearly held in high regard and their presence is welcomed.*
10 ADJ If someone has **high** principles or standards, they are morally good. *...patriotism and high principle.*
11 ADJ A **high** sound is close to the top of a range of notes. *...a high squeaky voice.*
12 ADJ If your spirits are **high**, you are happy and confident about the future. *They were not at all depressed, but in high spirits.*
13 ADJ If you are **high** on drugs, you are under the influence of them. *...roaming the night clubs, getting high on speed or amphetamines.*
14 NC+SUPP A **high** is the greatest level or amount that something reaches. *Prices on the stock exchange reached another record high last week.*
15 If you say that it is **high time** something was done, you mean that it should be done now, and that it should have really been done before now. *It's high time for serious political dialogue.*

high altar, high altars
NC The **high altar** in a church is the most important altar there. *The great window behind the high altar at York Minster.*

high and mighty
ADJ If you say that someone's behaviour is **high and mighty**, you mean that they think they are very important and are confident that their opinions are right; used showing disapproval. *There's no need to be so high and mighty about it!*

highborn /haɪbɔːn/
ADJ A **highborn** person has parents who belong to the nobility; a literary word.

highbrow /haɪbraʊ/
ADJ Something that is **highbrow** appeals to educated or cultured people and is often difficult to understand. *...highbrow radio programmes.*

high chair, high chairs
NC A **high chair** is a chair for a small child to sit in while they are eating. **High chairs** have long legs and a tray at the front to hold the food. *...a cotton harness which keeps children sitting safely in shopping trolleys, dining chairs and high chairs.*

High Church
ADJ Someone or something that is **High Church** belongs or relates to a section of the Church of England which emphasizes the importance of ceremony and ritual. *...a High Church Mass. ...practising his religion as a devout high church Anglican.*

high-class
ADJ Something that is **high-class** is of very good quality and high social status. *...big hotels and high-class restaurants.*

high command
N SING The **high command** is the group that consists of the most senior officers in a nation's armed forces. *...senior army officers, including members of the high command.*

High Commission, High Commissions
N COLL A **High Commission** is an office which houses the High Commissioner and his or her staff. *...the acting head of the British High Commission.*

High Commissioner, High Commissioners
NC A **High Commissioner** is an ambassador who represents one Commonwealth country in another. *...the Zambian High Commissioner.*

High Court, High Courts
NC In England and Wales, the **High Court** is a court of law which deals with important cases. *The case was heard in the High Court. ...a distinguished High Court judge.*

higher /haɪə/ **highers**
1 **Higher** is the comparative form of **high**.
2 ADJ ATTRIB A **higher** exam or qualification is of an advanced standard or level. *They have their first degrees and are studying for higher degrees.*
3 NC In Scotland, **highers** are exams that are taken by school students at the age of 16 or 17. *...other British qualifications such as Scottish Highers.*

higher education
NU **Higher education** is education at universities, polytechnics, and some colleges. *The Central Committee has approved a number of reforms in secondary and higher education.*

highfalutin /haɪfəluːtɪn/
ADJ **Highfalutin** behaviour is pompous, false, and foolish; an old-fashioned word. *I'm sick of her and her highfalutin ways!*

high fidelity
ADJ A **high fidelity** tape recorder is one of good quality which produces very accurate recordings. *...a high fidelity digital recording.*

high-flier, high-fliers. See **high-flyer.**

high-flown
ADJ **High-flown** language or ideas are too grand, and sound pompous or silly. *...high-flown compliments.*

high-flyer, high-flyers; also spelt **high-flier.**
NC A **high-flyer** is someone who is very ambitious and who is likely to be very successful in their career. *We offer a tough four-year course for high-flyers.*

high-flying
ADJ A **high-flying** person is very ambitious and is likely to be successful in their career. *They were all very high-flying people, but I think we still managed to impress them. ...a high-flying life style and an extensive bank account.*

high-handed
ADJ A **high-handed** person uses their authority in an unnecessarily forceful way without considering other people's feelings. *There was really no need for such high-handed behaviour.* ♦ **high-handedness** NU *The incident was quoted as another example of the high-handedness of the police chief.*

high-heeled
ADJ **High-heeled** shoes have a high narrow heel at the back. *...her well-crafted coiffure and high-heeled shoes.*

high heels
N PL **High heels** are the same as **high-heeled** shoes. *Her suit and high heels were very stylish and smart.*

high jinks
NU **High jinks** is lively, excited behaviour in which people do things for fun; an old-fashioned, informal expression. *They have learned to expect high jinks as part of the show.*

high jump
N SING The **high jump** is an athletics event which involves jumping over a raised bar. *Kostadinova broke her own indoor world high jump record.*

highlands /haɪləndz/
N PL **Highlands** are mountainous areas. *...the*

highlands of New Guinea.

high-level
ADJ ATTRIB **High-level** talks or discussions involve very senior politicians, officials, or businesspeople. *A month ago, President Bush proposed high-level talks with Iraq... A high-level German delegation is in Moscow to examine how best to provide food aid.*

high life
N SING The **high life** is an exciting and luxurious way of living involving a great deal of entertainment, going to parties, and eating good food. *She has a taste for the high life.*

highlight /haɪlaɪt/ **highlights, highlighting, highlighted**
1 VO If you **highlight** a point or problem, you draw attention to it. *The survey highlighted the needs of working women.*
2 NC+SUPP The **highlights** of an event, activity, or period of time are the most interesting or exciting parts of it. *...the highlights of the first day's play... This visit provided the real highlight of the morning.*
3 N PL **Highlights** are light-coloured streaks in someone's hair. *She's just had blonde highlights put in her hair.*

highly /haɪli/
1 SUBMOD You use **highly** to emphasize that a particular quality exists to a great degree. *The report is highly critical of these policies... It is highly improbable that they will accept. ...highly-educated people.*
2 SUBMOD **Highly** is also used to indicate that something is very important. *...a highly placed negotiator. ...a highly classified document.*
3 ADV If you praise someone **highly** or speak **highly** of them, you praise them a lot. *They spoke highly of Harold... Ross Thompson obviously thought very highly of him.*

highly-strung
ADJ Someone who is **highly-strung** is very nervous and easily upset.

High Mass
NU **High Mass** is a church service held in a Catholic church in which there is more ceremony than in an ordinary mass. *The pilgrimage culminated with a High Mass at St Vitus cathedral.*

high-minded
ADJ Someone who is **high-minded** has strong moral principles. *...high-minded idealists from overseas.*

Highness /haɪnəs/ **Highnesses**
TITLE You use expressions such as **Your Highness** and **His Highness** to address or refer to a prince or princess. *...Her Royal Highness, Princess Alexandra.*

high noon
1 NU **High noon** is a time at which conflict or crisis occurs which is intended to settle a dispute. *The Times describes it as high noon for South Africa.*
2 NU **High noon** also means the same as **noon**; a literary use. *Only at high noon did the sun finally cut through the grimy blackness.*

high-pitched
ADJ A **high-pitched** sound is high and shrill. *...a high-pitched whine.*

high point, high points
NC+SUPP The **high point** of an event, activity, or period of time is the most exciting or enjoyable part of it. *His speech was the high point of the evening.*

high-powered
1 ADJ A **high-powered** machine or piece of equipment is powerful and efficient. *...high-powered microscopes.*
2 ADJ A **high-powered** activity is very advanced and successful. *...high-powered advertising... The course is high-powered.*

high-rise
ADJ **High-rise** buildings are very tall modern buildings. *...high-rise flats.*

highroad /haɪrəʊd/ **highroads**
1 NC A **highroad** is a main road. *The A10 highroad in South Tottenham.*
2 NC+to The **highroad** to something is the easiest or most successful way to achieve it. *Political power is the highroad to self-advancement.*

high school, high schools
1 In Britain, **High School** is sometimes used in the names of schools for people aged between eleven and eighteen. ...*Acton High School in west London*.
2 NCorNU In the United States, a **high school** is a school for people aged between fifteen and eighteen. *In the United States high school students don't come out of school with the kind of skills that they need*.

high season
N SING The **high season** is the time of year when holiday resorts, hotels, tourist attractions, and so on, receive most visitors. *It is hoped that other types of tourism can be developed as an alternative to mass high season travel*.

high-sounding
ADJ **High-sounding** language or ideas seem very grand and important, although often they are not at all important. ...*altruism and other high-sounding principles*.

high-spirited
ADJ Someone who is **high-spirited** is very lively. ...*a characteristically high-spirited style of story telling*.

high spot, high spots
NC The **high spot** of an event, activity, or period of time is the most exciting or enjoyable part of it. *The temple was the high spot of the tour*.

high street, high streets
1 NC The **high street** of a town is the main street where most of the shops and banks are. *They had a little flat off Kensington High Street*.
2 ADJ ATTRIB **High street** retailers are large companies which have branches in the main shopping areas of most towns. *The law allows only certain shops to open while restricting big high street retailers... There was a further fall in the level of high street sales last month*.

high summer
NU **High summer** is the middle of summer. *They serve lunches here only in high summer*.

high tea
NU In Britain, **high tea** is a meal that some people eat in the late afternoon, often with tea to drink. *The children have high tea at about 5.30, but we don't eat until 8*.

high technology; also written **high-technology**.
NU **High technology** is the development and use of advanced electronics and computers. ...*a new leap forward into an age of high technology*. ...*high-technology equipment*. ● See also **hi tech**.

high-tension; also written **high tension**.
ADJ ATTRIB A **high-tension** electricity cable is one which carries a very powerful current. *A passenger plane has crashed near Paris after hitting high tension electricity lines*.

high tide, high tides
NUorNC At the coast, **high tide** is the time when the sea is at its highest level. ...*a pool which the sea only reached at high tide... The heavy seas are the product of strong winds and high tides*.

high treason
NU **High treason** is a very serious crime which puts your country or the King or Queen in danger. *Police in Finland say they have arrested two people suspected of high treason*.

high-up, high-ups
NC A **high-up** is an important person with a lot of authority and influence; an informal word. *They put out a statement saying the talk of half-heartedness amongst high-ups was false*.

high water
NU **High water** is the time when the water in a river or sea is at its highest level. *We'll have to wait for high water before we can reload the boat*.

high-water mark, high-water marks
1 NC A **high-water mark** is the level reached by the sea at high tide or by a river in a flood. *Just below the high-water mark there are thick clumps of green seaweed*.
2 NC The highest or most successful stage of achievement in a process is called the **high-water mark**. *Life in the court of Urbino was one of the high-water marks of western civilization*.

highway /haɪweɪ/ **highways**
1 NC In American English, a **highway** is a large road that connects towns or cities. ...*inter-state highways*.
2 NC A **highway** is also a main road; a legal use. *She was charged with obstructing the highway*.

Highway Code
N SING In Britain, the **Highway Code** is an official booklet published by the Department of Transport containing the rules which tell people how to use public roads safely. *I would drive sanely and sensibly in accordance with the Highway Code*.

highwayman /haɪweɪmən/ **highwaymen** /haɪweɪmən/
NC In former times, **highwaymen** were robbers on horseback who used to threaten to shoot travellers if they did not hand over their money and valuable possessions. ...*the most famous highwayman, Dick Turpin*.

high wire, high wires
NC A **high wire** is a length of rope or wire stretched tight high above the ground and used for balancing acts.

hijack /haɪdʒæk/ **hijacks, hijacking, hijacked**
VO If someone **hijacks** a plane or other vehicle, they illegally take control of it by force while it is travelling from one place to another. *If you are taken hostage or hijacked, try to strike up a relationship with your kidnappers*. ► Also NC *The hijack began on Tuesday during a flight from Bangkok*.

hijacker /haɪdʒækə/ **hijackers**
NC A **hijacker** is a person who hijacks a plane or other vehicle. ...*security men and passengers overpowered the hijacker*.

hijacking /haɪdʒækɪŋ/ **hijackings**
NCorNU A **hijacking** is an incident in which a group of people illegally take control of a plane or other vehicle. *There have been more than fifty attempted hijackings there in the last fifteen years*. ...*the problem of hijacking and terrorism*.

hike /haɪk/ **hikes, hiking, hiked**
1 NC A **hike** in prices, wages, or interest rates is a large increase in them. *This has led to a hike in prices of between five and fifteen percent... The economy has suffered from unrealistic wage hikes and corruption*.
2 NC A **hike** is a long walk in the country. *We're going on a four mile hike tomorrow*.
3 V If you **hike**, you go on long country walks for pleasure. *We used to walk or hike around St Blasien in the summer*. ◆ **hiking** NU *We have maps of the area where we hope to do some hiking*.

hiker /haɪkə/ **hikers**
NC A **hiker** is someone who is going for a long walk in the countryside or in the hills, for pleasure. *I watched the hikers scrambling up the gully*.

hilarious /hɪleəriəs/
ADJ Something that is **hilarious** is extremely funny and makes you laugh a lot. ...*the hilarious tale of how Harold got stuck in a lift*.

hilarity /hɪlærəti/
NU **Hilarity** is great amusement and laughter; a formal word. *The noise of hilarity in the restaurant below kept him awake*.

hill /hɪl/ **hills**
NC A **hill** is an area of land that is higher than the land that surrounds it, but not as high as a mountain. *I started to walk up the hill*. ...*the Malvern Hills of Worcestershire*.

hillbilly /hɪlbɪli/ **hillbillies**
NC In the United States, a **hillbilly** is a person who comes from a mountainous country area, especially one who is considered by people who live in towns to be unintelligent or uneducated. *They remind me of hillbillies with leaky roofs*.

hillock /hɪlək/ **hillocks**
NC A **hillock** is a small hill; a literary word. *The view was broken up into many little valleys and small hillocks*.

hillside /hɪlsaɪd/ **hillsides**
NC A **hillside** is the side of a hill. ...*the steep hillsides of North Wales*. ...*a hillside town*.

hilltop /hɪltɒp/ **hilltops**
NC A **hilltop** is the top of a hill. ...*a barren rocky*

hilltop. ...the hilltop village of Combe.

hilly /hɪli/

ADJ **Hilly** land has many hills. They drove around the hilly area behind the town.

hilt /hɪlt/ **hilts**

1 NC The **hilt** of a sword or knife is its handle. A knife, embedded up to its hilt, had been driven into the back of his neck.

2 If you support or defend someone **to the hilt**, you give them all the support that you can. She had backed me to the hilt in all my projects.

him /hɪm/. **Him** is used as the object of a verb or preposition.

1 PRON You use **him** to refer to a man, boy, or male animal that has already been mentioned or whose identity is known. He asked if you'd ring him back when you got in... There's no need for him to worry.

2 PRON **Him** can also be used to refer to someone whose sex is not known or stated; some users of English prefer 'him or her' or 'them' to be used instead.

himself /hɪmsɛlf/

1 PRON REFL You use **himself** as the object of a verb or preposition to refer to the same man, boy, or male animal that is mentioned as the subject of the clause, or as a previous object in the clause. Mr Boggis introduced himself. ...his lack of confidence in himself.

2 PRON REFL You also use **himself** to emphasize the male subject or object of a clause, and to make it clear who you are referring to. Forman himself became Minister of International Affairs... It was easy for a clever young man like himself to make a good living.

3 PRON REFL If a man or boy does something **himself**, he does it without any help or interference from anyone else. Mr Watson will put up most of the money himself.

hind /haɪnd/

ADJ ATTRIB The **hind** legs of an animal are at the back of its body. When they run, they get most of their forward motion from their hind legs.

hinder /hɪndə/ **hinders, hindering, hindered**

VO If something **hinders** you, it makes it more difficult for you to do something. Her career was not hindered by the fact that she had three children.

hindquarters /haɪndkwɔːtəz/

N PL The **hindquarters** of an animal with four legs are the back part of it, including its two back legs.

hindrance /hɪndrəns/ **hindrances**

1 NC A **hindrance** is a person or thing that makes it more difficult for you to do something. New ideas may be more of a hindrance than an asset.

2 NU **Hindrance** is the act of hindering someone or something. Now they can construct tunnel systems without hindrance.

hindsight /haɪndsaɪt/

NU **Hindsight** is the ability to understand something after it has happened. With hindsight, what could we learn from their mistakes?

Hindu /hɪnduː/ **Hindus**

NC A **Hindu** is a person who believes in Hinduism. This meeting point of the two rivers is a particularly sacred place for Hindus... A group of Hindu holy men chant religious hymns to the glory of Rama.

Hinduism /hɪnduːɪzəm/

NU **Hinduism** is an Indian religion, which has many gods and teaches that people have another life on earth after they die. ...believers in Islam, Hinduism and Buddhism.

hinge /hɪndʒ/ **hinges, hinging, hinged**

NC A **hinge** is a moveable joint made of metal, wood, or plastic that joins two things so that one of them can swing freely. The door was ripped from its hinges.

hinge on PHRASAL VERB If something **hinges on** or **hinges upon** a fact or event, it depends on it. Everything hinged on what happened to the United States economy.

hinge upon PHRASAL VERB See **hinge on**

hinged /hɪndʒd/

ADJ An object that is **hinged** is joined to another object with a hinge. ...the hinged flap of the counter.

hint /hɪnt/ **hints, hinting, hinted**

1 NC A **hint** is a suggestion about something that is made in an indirect way. As yet no hint had appeared as to who was going to be the next Foreign Secretary. ● If you **drop a hint**, you suggest something in an indirect way. He had dropped several hints that he knew where Mary was. ● If you **take a hint**, you understand something that is suggested indirectly, often something that people are too polite to say to you openly. She may take the hint and become more organized.

2 V or V-REPORT If you **hint** at something, you suggest something in an indirect way. Harold hinted at what she had already guessed... I tried to hint that I deserved an increase in salary.

3 NC A **hint** is also a helpful piece of advice. The magazine had the usual hints on fashion and cookery.

4 N SING A **hint** of something is a very small amount of it. There was a hint of disapproval in her face.

hinterland /hɪntəlænd/ **hinterlands**

NC The **hinterland** of a piece of coastline or a large river is the area of land behind it or around it. ...a small town somewhere in the hinterland of Watermouth.

hip /hɪp/ **hips**

1 NC Your **hips** are the two areas at the sides of your body between the tops of your legs and your waist. ...a pistol at his hip... He limped off with a hip injury.

2 ADJ If you say that something or someone is **hip**, you mean that they are very modern and follow all the latest fashions; an informal use. They mixed easily with the hip New York artists.

hip-bath, hip-baths

NC A **hip-bath** is a small bath which is big enough for you to sit in but not to lie down in.

hip flask, hip flasks

NC A **hip flask** is a small metal container in which brandy, whisky, or other spirits can be carried, usually in the pocket of a jacket. ...a curved hip flask made of pewter.

hip hop

NU **Hip hop** refers to a style of music, dance, and art that originated in the United States and is associated with rap music, graffiti art, and break dancing. He talks about what can be done in this style of music and voices his opinion on the merits of and future for hip hop.

hippie /hɪpi/ **hippies**; also spelt **hippy**.

NC A **hippie** is someone who has rejected conventional ideas and wants to live a life based on peace and love. ...the days when Afghanistan was a haven for hippies.

hippo /hɪpəʊ/ **hippos**

NC A **hippo** is a hippopotamus. ...wild animals like hippos and crocodiles.

Hippocratic oath /hɪpəkrætɪk əʊθ/

N SING The **Hippocratic oath** is a solemn promise made by newly qualified doctors, saying that they will follow the standards set by their profession and try to save life. The decision hindered him from carrying out his Hippocratic oath.

hippopotamus /hɪpəpɒtəməs/ **hippopotamuses** or **hippopotami**

NC A **hippopotamus** is a large African animal with short legs and thick, wrinkled skin which lives near water. They spent some time on land and some time in water, like hippopotami.

hippy /hɪpi/. See **hippie**.

hire /haɪə/ **hires, hiring, hired**

1 VO If you **hire** something, you pay money to use it for a period of time. We hired a car and drove across the island. ► Also NU+SUPP Hire of a van costs about £30 a day.

2 If something is **for hire**, you can hire it. ...boats for hire.

3 VO If you **hire** someone, you pay them to do a job for you. You've got to hire a private detective to make enquiries.

hire out PHRASAL VERB If you **hire out** something, you allow it to be used in return for payment. Holborn library hires out pictures.

hireling /ˈhaɪəlɪŋ/ **hirelings**
NC A **hireling** is a person who does not care who they work for and who is willing to do something bad or illegal as long as they are paid for it. *...hireling soldiers.*

hire purchase
NU **Hire purchase** is a way of buying goods gradually. You make regular payments to the seller until you have paid the full price and the goods belong to you. *Have you bought anything on hire purchase?*

hirsute /ˈhɜːsjuːt/
ADJ Someone who is **hirsute** is hairy; a literary word, often used humorously. *He says he'll remain hirsute in the hope that it will bring his side luck.*

his /hɪz/
1 DET You use **his** to indicate that something belongs or relates to a man, boy, or male animal that has already been mentioned, or to refer to someone whose sex is not known or stated. *He had his hands in his pockets... To each according to his need.* ▶ Also PRON *Willie had a job on a magazine that a friend of his had just started.*
2 DET You also use **his** in titles when you are referring to a man. *...his Lordship.*

hiss /hɪs/ **hisses, hissing, hissed**
1 V To **hiss** means to make a sound like a long 's'. *If you shove a hot frying pan into water it will hiss and buckle.* ▶ N SING *...the soft hiss of roasting meat.*
2 V-QUOTE or V-REPORT If you **hiss** something, you say it in a strong, angry whisper. *He pointed a shaking finger at my friend and hissed through clenched teeth: 'You, you get out!'*
3 V or VO When an audience **hisses**, they express their dislike of a performance by making long loud 's' sounds. *The crowd hissed and booed... The Algerian crowd booed and hissed the Egyptian team.*

historian /hɪˈstɔːrɪən/ **historians**
NC A **historian** is a person who studies history. *He writes as a historian with an interest in social anthropology... An historian of science said it was a radical and ambitious plan.*

historic /hɪˈstɒrɪk/
ADJ Something that is **historic** is important in history. *...a historic change.*

historical /hɪˈstɒrɪkl/
1 ADJ ATTRIB **Historical** people or situations existed in the past and are considered to be a part of history. *...actual historical events. ...autographs and manuscripts of historical interest.* ◆ **historically** ADV *Historically, Labour was strongly opposed to the powers of the House of Lords.*
2 ADJ ATTRIB **Historical** books and pictures describe or represent people or things of a type that existed in the past. *...historical novels.*

history /ˈhɪstri/ **histories**
1 NU You can refer to the events of the past as **history**. *...one of the most dramatic moments in Polish history... Each city has its own history and character.* ● Someone who **makes history** does something which will be remembered for a long time, usually because it is the first time it has been done. *Lawyers said they believed the case made legal history... An all-female yacht crew have made history by becoming the first to sail round the world.* ● If someone or something **goes down in history** they will be remembered for a special reason. *Gorbachev will go down in history as a revolutionary leader... I want this election to go down in history as one in which there was a choice.*
2 NU **History** is also the study of the past. *I adored history and hated geography. ...a history book, not a novel.*
3 NC+SUPP A **history** is a description of the important events that have happened in a particular subject. *...a television history of the United States.*
4 NC+SUPP Someone's **history** is a set of facts or a particular fact that is known about their past. *There is a family history of coronary heart disease. ...information about the children's social and economic background and their medical histories.*
5 See also **natural history**.

histrionic /ˌhɪstrɪˈɒnɪk/ **histrionics**
1 ADJ ATTRIB **Histrionic** behaviour is very dramatic and exaggerated, but is not sincere; a formal use. *A performance could cheapen into a merely histrionic display.*
2 N PL You can describe dramatic and exaggerated behaviour as **histrionics**. *What was needed was a lot of clear and cool thinking not histrionics.*

hit /hɪt/ **hits, hitting**. The form **hit** is used in the present tense and is also the past tense and past participle of the verb.
1 VO To **hit** someone or something means to strike them forcefully. *He hit the burglar on the head with a candlestick... He never hit the ball very far.*
2 VO When one thing **hits** another, it touches it with a lot of force. *The helicopter hit an electricity cable in the southern port of Rameswaram... It burst into flames as it hit the ground.*
3 VO If a bomb or other missile **hits** its target, it reaches it. *Three ships were hit... More than 20 mortar bombs are understood to have hit the palace.*
4 NC A **hit** is the action or fact of a bomb or other missile hitting its target. *The tanks were designed to withstand anything except a direct hit.*
5 VO If something **hits** a person, place, or thing, it affects them badly. *Spectator sport has been badly hit by the increase in ticket prices... Luanda was hit by a similar cholera epidemic last year... Transport has been badly hit.*
6 VO When a feeling or an idea **hits** you, it suddenly comes into your mind. *The shock of her death kept hitting me afresh... Suddenly it hit me: my diary had probably been read by everyone in the office.*
7 NC A **hit** is a record, play, or film that is very popular and successful. *'Right Back Where We Started From' was originally a hit for Maxine Nightingale when it reached No.8 in the British charts... The play became a tremendous hit.*
8 If two people **hit it off**, they like each other and become friendly as soon as they meet. *The two men did not hit it off during the Soviet president's visit to Cuba.*

hit back PHRASAL VERB If you **hit back** at someone who has criticized or harmed you, you criticize or harm them in return. *Edward Heath hit back using very strong language, accusing Mrs Thatcher of small-mindedness.*

hit on PHRASAL VERB If you **hit on** an idea or **hit upon** it, you think of it. *He hit on the idea of cutting a hole in the door to let the cat in.*

hit out PHRASAL VERB If you **hit out** at someone, you criticize them strongly. *The Prime Minister hit out at her colleagues in Europe.*

hit upon PHRASAL VERB See **hit on**

hit and miss
ADJ Something that is **hit and miss** happens in an unplanned way, so that you cannot predict what the result will be. *Navigation was very hit and miss and we were totally off course.*

hit-and-run
1 ADJ ATTRIB A **hit-and-run** car accident is one in which the driver does not stop. *She was killed by a hit-and-run motorist.*
2 ADJ ATTRIB In warfare, a **hit-and-run** attack is a raid on an enemy position that relies on surprise and speed for its success. *The guerrillas have switched from hit-and-run attacks on isolated targets to large scale operations.*

hitch /hɪtʃ/ **hitches, hitching, hitched**
1 NC A **hitch** is a slight problem or difficulty. *There had also been one or two technical hitches.*
2 V or VO If you **hitch** a lift, you hitch-hike. *He hitched south towards Italy... I can hitch a ride the rest of the way.*
3 VOA If you **hitch** something onto an object, you fasten it there. *...ponies hitched to rails.*

hitch up PHRASAL VERB If you **hitch up** a piece of clothing, you pull it up into a higher position. *He hitched up his trousers.*

hitch-hike, hitch-hikes, hitch-hiking, hitch-hiked
V If you **hitch-hike**, you travel by getting lifts from passing vehicles without paying. *She went off with a*

friend intending to hitch-hike to Turkey.

hitch-hiker, hitch-hikers
NC A **hitch-hiker** is someone who is hitch-hiking, or someone who hitch-hikes regularly. *...foreign hitch-hikers in Sardinia.*

hi tech /haɪ tek/; also spelt **high tech.**
ADJ Something that is **hi tech** uses very modern methods and equipment. *Can hi tech revive Zambian agriculture?*

hither /hɪðə/; a literary word
ADV **Hither** is used to describe movement towards the place where you are at present. *...my journey hither.*
● Something that moves **hither and thither** moves in all directions. *She ran hither and thither in the orchard.*

hitherto /hɪðətuː/
ADV If something has been happening **hitherto**, it has been happening until now; a formal word. *She had hitherto been nice to me.*

hit list, hit lists
NC A **hit list** is a list that terrorists or gangsters have of the people they intend to kill. *Police say his name featured on an IRA hit list discovered in a raid on a house in London.*

hit man, hit men
NC A **hit man** is a person who is hired by terrorists or gangsters to kill people. *One hostage was killed last week, allegedly by hit men.*

hit or miss
ADJ **Hit or miss** means the same as **hit and miss**. *It is really a hit or miss activity trying to discover these new antibiotics.*

hit parade
N SING The **hit parade** is the list of pop records which have sold most copies over the previous week or month; an old-fashioned expression.

HIV /eɪtʃaɪviː/
1 NU **HIV** is a virus that reduces people's resistance to illness and can cause AIDS. **HIV** is an abbreviation for 'human immunodeficiency virus'. *In New York City one in sixty pregnant women are already infected with HIV... Needle sharing is the one of the major causes for the spread of HIV... She specializes in patients with AIDS and HIV infections.*
2 If a person is **HIV positive**, they are infected with the HIV virus, and may develop AIDS. *Many of them are now HIV positive and suffering from AIDS. ...babies whose mothers became HIV positive through infected needles used to inject drugs... There are currently fifty-nine prisoners who have been diagnosed as HIV positive, but none has developed full-blown AIDS.*

hive /haɪv/ **hives**
1 NC A **hive** is a beehive. *The stand has to be strong enough to hold a hive full of bees and its honey.*
2 NC+of You describe a place as a **hive** of a particular kind of activity when there is a lot of that activity there. *Calcutta is a hive of industry and trade.*
hive off PHRASAL VERB If you **hive off** part of a business, you transfer it to new ownership, usually by selling it. *Some observers have suggested that Reuters may hive off its news operation.*

HM /eɪtʃem/
HM is the abbreviation for 'Her Majesty's' or 'His Majesty's'; used as part of the name of some British government organizations, or as part of a person's title. *HM Customs and Excise must be notified. ...HM Forces.*

h'm /həm, m/; also spelt **hm.**
You say '**h'm**' when you are hesitating, for example because you are thinking about something. *H'm, well, I know that's a problem... H'm, I wonder how long he's been there—you know.*

HMI /eɪtʃemaɪ/ **HMI's**
NC An **HMI** is a government official in Great Britain who is responsible for supervising teaching and administration in schools. **HMI** is an abbreviation for 'Her Majesty's Inspector' or 'His Majesty's Inspector'. *There's been a recent HMI's report on foreign language teaching in primary schools.*

HMS /eɪtʃemes/
HMS is used before the names of ships in the British Royal Navy. **HMS** is an abbreviation for 'Her Majesty's Ship' or 'His Majesty's Ship'. *...HMS Churchill.*

HNC /eɪtʃensiː/ **HNCs**
NCor NU An **HNC** is a group of examinations in technical subjects such as electronics and engineering, which you can take at a British college or polytechnic. **HNC** is an abbreviation for 'Higher National Certificate'. *She's doing an HNC course in electronics.*

hoard /hɔːd/ **hoards, hoarding, hoarded**
1 VO If you **hoard** things, you save or store them, often in secret, because they are valuable or important to you. *People here have hoarded vast quantities of food in anticipation of the recent price rises... Is it better to spend your money today or hoard every penny in the bank for tomorrow?*
2 N SING A **hoard** is a store of things you have saved. *...a small hoard of coins.*

hoarding /hɔːdɪŋ/ **hoardings**
NC A **hoarding** is a large board used for advertising which stands at the side of a road. *I scanned the hoardings for election posters.*

hoarse /hɔːs/ **hoarser, hoarsest**
ADJ If your voice is **hoarse**, it sounds rough and unclear, and you can hardly speak. *When he spoke his voice was hoarse with rage.* ◆ **hoarsely** ADV *'Go in there,' he whispered hoarsely.* ◆ **hoarseness** NU *I noticed a peculiar hoarseness in Johnny's voice.*

hoary /hɔːri/
ADJ A **hoary** problem or subject is old and familiar. *...the hoary old question of Namibia and the Cuban troops.*

hoax /həʊks/ **hoaxes**
NC A **hoax** is a trick in which someone tells people something that is not true. *It wasn't a hoax, there really was a fire.*

hob /hɒb/ **hobs**
NC A **hob** is a surface on top of a cooker which can be heated and which usually contains gas rings or electric rings for putting saucepans on. *He turned on all the gas taps and left a chip pan on a lighted hob.*

hobble /hɒbl/ **hobbles, hobbling, hobbled**
1 V If you **hobble**, you walk in an awkward way because you are in pain. *He hobbled along as best he could.*
2 VO If you **hobble** an animal, you tie its legs together so that it cannot run away. *...the camel's legs, hobbled in a perfect fold under its enormous body.*

hobby /hɒbi/ **hobbies**
NC A **hobby** is something that you enjoy doing in your spare time. *Music is his chief hobby.*

hobby-horse, hobby-horses
1 NC You describe a subject or idea as your **hobby-horse** if you have strong feelings on it and like talking about it whenever you have the opportunity. *Film censorship is a personal hobby-horse of mine... Oh dear, he's on his hobby-horse again.*
2 NC A **hobby-horse** is a toy that looks like a horse's head on a stick and which a child can pretend to ride like a horse.

hobnail boot /hɒbneɪl buːt/ **hobnail boots**
NC **Hobnail boots** or **hobnailed boots** are heavy boots with short nails put in underneath to make them wear out less quickly.

hobnob /hɒbnɒb/ **hobnobs, hobnobbing, hobnobbed**
V+with If you **hobnob** with someone, you are friendly and spend time with them; an informal word, used showing disapproval. *He's a working class lad who hobnobs with Popes and Presidents.*

hobo /həʊbəʊ/ **hobos** or **hoboes**
NC A **hobo** is someone who has no home or work and often travels from town to town; used in American English.

Hobson's choice /hɒbsnz tʃɔɪs/
You describe a situation as **Hobson's choice** when, although there appear to be alternatives, in fact there is only one thing you can do. *I'm afraid it's a case of Hobson's choice.*

Ho Chi Minh City /həʊ tʃiː mɪn sɪti/
Ho Chi Minh City, formerly known as Saigon, is the largest city in Vietnam. It was the capital of South Vietnam from 1954 to 1975. Population: 3,169,000 (1989).

hock /hɒk/
N MASS **Hock** is a type of dry white wine from Germany. ...*a glass of hock.*

hockey /hɒki/
NU **Hockey** is an outdoor game played between two teams using long curved sticks to hit a small ball. *English men's hockey is to have its first national league.* ● See also **ice hockey**.

hocus-pocus /həukəspəukəs/
NU **Hocus-pocus** is something that is done or said in order to trick or confuse someone; used showing disapproval. *There's been a bit of hocus-pocus going on here... The rest of your question I find rhetorical hocus-pocus.*

hod /hɒd/ **hods**
NC A **hod** is a container that workmen on a building site use for carrying bricks. It consists of a box-shaped holder attached to a long handle.

hodge-podge /hɒdʒpɒdʒ/
N SING A **hodge-podge** is a confused or disorderly mixture of different types of things; an informal word. ...*a hodge-podge of modern building.* ● See also **hotchpotch**.

hoe /həu/ **hoes, hoeing, hoed**
1 NC A **hoe** is a long-handled gardening tool which is used to remove small weeds. *The gardening hoe has long been a part of the gardener's toolkit.*
2 V or VO If you **hoe** an area of land, you use a hoe to remove the weeds there. *The land has to be ploughed, then hoed and harvested. ...when you are old and can no longer hoe the fields.*

hog /hɒg/ **hogs, hogging, hogged**
1 NC A **hog** is a large male pig, usually one that has been castrated. *It isn't as difficult for larger cattle and hog farmers.*
2 VO If you **hog** something, you take all of it in a selfish or impolite way; an informal use. ...*a huge lorry hogging the centre of the road.*
3 If you **go the whole hog**, you do something bold or extravagant in the most complete way possible. *If we can't negotiate some sort of compromise then we might as well go the whole hog and attack.*

Hogmanay /hɒgmənei/
NU **Hogmanay** is New Year's Eve in Scotland and the celebrations that take place at that time. *Hogmanay is a traditional time of celebration for Scotsmen everywhere.*

hogwash /hɒgwɒʃ/
NU If you describe something that someone says as **hogwash**, you mean that it is nonsense; an informal word. *This is all hogwash as far as I'm concerned.*

ho ho /həu həu/
Ho ho is used to represent laughter in written English.

hoi polloi /hɔɪ pəlɔɪ/
N PL The **hoi polloi** are ordinary people considered as a group, rather than people who are rich, well-educated, or upper-class; used showing disapproval. *Avocado pears used to be fashionable but now the hoi polloi eat them in wine bars.*

hoist /hɔɪst/ **hoists, hoisting, hoisted**
1 VOA If you **hoist** something somewhere, you lift it or pull it up there. *She hoisted the child onto her shoulder.*
2 VO If you **hoist** a flag or a sail, you pull it up to its correct position using ropes. *The American flag was hoisted.*
3 NC A **hoist** is a machine for lifting heavy things. ...*an electric hoist.*

hoity-toity /hɔɪti tɔɪti/
ADJ Someone who is **hoity-toity** behaves in a proud and haughty way; an informal word, used showing disapproval.

hold /həuld/ **holds, holding, held**
1 VO When you **hold** something, you carry or support it, usually using your fingers or your arms. *He was holding a bottle of milk... I held the picture up to the light... He held her in his arms.*
2 NU If you take **hold** of something, you put your hand tightly round it. *She took hold of my wrist... He still had hold of my jacket... She resumed her hold on the rope.*
3 VO or V-REFL If you **hold** your body or part of your

body in a particular position, you keep it in that position. *Etta held her head back... Mrs Patel held herself erect.*
4 VO or V If one thing **holds** another thing, it keeps it in position. *There was just a rail holding it... The glue held.*
5 VO If something **holds** a particular amount of something, it can contain that amount. *The theatre itself can hold only a limited number of people.*
6 VO or VOO If you **hold** someone, you keep them as a prisoner. *I was held overnight in a cell... Three people are being held... The young private had been held a prisoner by the guerrillas.*
7 VO If you **hold** power or office, you have it. *The ruling Liberal Democratic Party has held power continuously for thirty-five years. ...one of the greatest Prime Ministers who ever held office.*
8 N SING If you have a **hold** over someone, you have power or control over them. *The party tightened its hold on the union... Mr Gorbachov has dropped his ideological hold over eastern Europe.*
9 N SING If you have a **hold** over someone, you know something about them that you can use to make them do something for you. *The farmer had a hold over me. He had discovered my illegal whiskey still.*
10 VO If you **hold** a qualification, licence or other official document, you have it. *You need to hold a work permit... She held a BA degree in psychology.*
11 VO If you **hold** an event, you organize it and it takes place. *They're also expected to hold separate informal meetings with a number of other nations... An anniversary lunch is to be held in his honour... Nicaragua will hold elections in three weeks' time.*
12 VO If you **hold** a conversation with someone, you talk with them. *They held a long and friendly conversation.*
13 VO You can use **hold** to say that something has a particular quality or characteristic. *These legends hold a romantic fascination for many Japanese... We will have to see what the future holds.*
14 VO or V-REPORT If you **hold** a particular opinion, that is your opinion. *People who hold this view are sometimes dismissed as cranks... Marxists hold that people are all naturally creative.*
15 V or VO If someone asks you to **hold** or to **hold** the line when you have made a telephone call, they are asking you to wait until they can connect you. *The line's engaged; will you hold?*
16 VO If you **hold** someone's interest or attention, you keep them interested. *He was finding it a strain to hold the students' attention.*
17 V If an offer or invitation still **holds**, it is still available. *Will you tell her the offer still holds?*
18 V If your luck **holds** or if the weather **holds**, it remains good. *If my luck continues to hold, I think I've got a fair chance.*
19 NC The **hold** of a ship or aeroplane is the place where cargo is stored. *A fire occurred in the plane's cabin or cargo hold.*
● **Hold** is used in these phrases. ● If you **hold tight**, you hold something very firmly. ● When something **takes hold**, it starts to have a great effect. *Then the fire took hold.* ● If you **get hold** of something or someone, you manage to get them or find them. *Can you get hold of a car this weekend?* ● If you say '**Hold it**' or '**Hold everything**', you are telling someone to stop what they are doing. *Hold it, what are you doing?* ● If you put a process **on hold**, you stop it temporarily, or delay its start. *The peace process is now on hold... Mike Tyson's bid to regain his world title could be put on hold.* ● If you **hold** your **own**, you are not defeated by someone or do not have worse results than them. *She was still able to hold her own with the Prime Minister.* ● To **hold sway** see **sway**.

hold against PHRASAL VERB If someone has done something wrong and you **hold** it **against** them, you treat them more severely because they did it. *His refusal to cooperate will be held against him.*

hold back PHRASAL VERB 1 If you **hold back**, you hesitate before doing something. *Police have held back from going into such a holy place.* 2 If you **hold** someone or something **back**, you prevent them from advancing or increasing. *If she is ambitious, don't try to hold her back... The rise in living standards has been held back for so long.* 3 If you **hold** something **back**, you do not tell someone the full details about it. *I want the truth now, with nothing held back.*

hold down PHRASAL VERB If you **hold down** a job, you manage to keep it. *He was surprised to find her holding down a successful job in high finance.*

hold off PHRASAL VERB If you **hold** something **off**, you prevent it from reaching or affecting you. *The French and British wanted to hold off Portuguese textile competition.*

hold on PHRASAL VERB 1 If you **hold on**, you keep your hand firmly round something. *He tried to pull free but she held on tight.* 2 If you ask someone to **hold on**, you are asking them to wait for a short time. *Hold on a moment, please.*

hold onto PHRASAL VERB 1 If you **hold onto** something, you keep your hand firmly round it. *He has to hold onto something to steady himself.* 2 To **hold onto** something also means to keep it and not lose it. *Politicians want to hold on to power at all costs.*

hold out PHRASAL VERB 1 If you **hold out** your hand or something that is in your hand, you move it away from your body, usually towards someone. *'John?' Esther held out the phone.* 2 If you **hold out**, you stand firm and manage to resist opposition. *Women all over the country are holding out for more freedom... I can't hold out forever.* 3 If you **hold out** on someone, you refuse to give them information that they want; an informal expression. *I'm sure he's holding out on them.*

hold up PHRASAL VERB If someone or something **holds** you **up**, they delay you. *The whole thing was held up about half an hour.* ● See also **hold-up**.

hold with PHRASAL VERB If you do not **hold with** something, you do not approve of it; used in formal speech. *...a man who did not hold with these notions.*

holdall /ˈhəʊldɔːl/ **holdalls**
NC A **holdall** is a large bag in which you put clothes and other things when you are going away from home. *The bomb weighed less than twenty pounds and could have been carried into the barracks in a holdall.*

holder /ˈhəʊldə/ **holders**
1 NC A **holder** is a container for putting objects in or keeping them in position. *The cup was held in a brown plastic holder.*
2 NC A **holder** is also someone who owns, controls, or has something. *...ticket-holders. ...holders of anti-government opinions. ...Luton Town, the Littlewoods cup holders.*

holding /ˈhəʊldɪŋ/ **holdings**
1 NC+SUPP If you have a **holding** in a company, you own shares in it. *We should sell the government holding in British Gas.*
2 NC A **holding** is also an area of farm land rented or owned by the person who cultivates it. *78 per cent of holdings are below 5 hectares.*
3 ADJ ATTRIB You use **holding** to describe a temporary action which is intended to prevent a situation from becoming worse. *The rest of the campaign was a holding operation.*

holdout /ˈhəʊldaʊt/ **holdouts**
NC A **holdout** is someone who does not want to agree to something that others want to do; used in American English. *Miners in western Siberia, the last major holdouts in the strike, have agreed to return to work... Thatcher was the single holdout against the first steps toward creating a European central bank.*

holdover /ˈhəʊldəʊvə/ **holdovers**
NC A **holdover** is something or someone that remains from a previous time or event; used in American English. *Another holdover from the steam engine era is the measurement of a day's work... Of the 19 candidates named today for ministries, five of them are holdovers from the previous Cabinet.*

hold-up, hold-ups
1 NC A **hold-up** is a situation in which someone is threatened with a weapon in order to make them hand over money. *...the victim of a masked hold-up.*
2 NC A **hold-up** is also something which causes a delay. *...traffic hold-ups.*

hole /həʊl/ **holes, holing, holed**
1 NC A **hole** is an opening or hollow space in something solid. *What do you recommend for filling holes and cracks? ...a deep hole in the ground... He was wearing grey socks with holes in them.*
2 If you **pick holes in** an argument or theory, you find weak points in it; an informal expression.
3 NC You can describe an unpleasant place as a **hole**; an informal use. *Why don't you leave this awful hole and come to live with me?*
4 VO If a building or a ship is **holed**, holes are made in it. *The buildings were holed by shrapnel.*

hole up PHRASAL VERB If you **hole up** somewhere, you hide there to avoid trouble; an informal expression. *Mao formed his ideas while he was a guerrilla, holed up in the barren north-west.*

holiday /ˈhɒlədeɪ/ **holidays**
1 NCorNU A **holiday** is a period of time spent away from home for relaxation. *I went to Marrakesh for a holiday... Remember to turn off the gas when you go on holiday.*
2 NCorNU A **holiday** is also a period of time during which you are not working. *New Year's Day is a national holiday... The company offers three weeks paid holiday.* ● See also **bank holiday**.

holiday camp, holiday camps
NC A **holiday camp** is a place which provides holiday accommodation and entertainment for large numbers of people. *Most of the group spent a week at Pontin's holiday camp in Somerset.*

holidaymaker /ˈhɒlədeɪmeɪkə/ **holidaymakers**
NC A **holidaymaker** is a person who is away from home on holiday. *A record number of holidaymakers are travelling to Bangkok, Australia and Florida.*

holiness /ˈhəʊlɪnəs/
1 NU **Holiness** is the state or quality of being holy. *She could feel the holiness of the place.*
2 TITLE You use expressions such as **Your Holiness** and **His Holiness** to address or refer to the Pope or to leaders of some other religions. *His Holiness was in London for religious reasons.*

holism /ˈhəʊlɪzəm/
NU **Holism** is a set of beliefs in which everything in nature is seen as being connected in some way.

holistic /həʊˈlɪstɪk/
ADJ **Holistic** means based on the principles of holism. *This is an attempt to address the enormous problems facing the Soviet Union in an holistic way. ...we must take a more holistic approach.*

Holland /ˈhɒlənd/. See **Netherlands**.

holler /ˈhɒlə/ **hollers, hollering, hollered**
V If you **holler**, you shout or weep loudly; used in informal American English. *You should have heard him holler!... He was tired of me hollering at him... They keep hollering for school reform.*

hollow /ˈhɒləʊ/ **hollows, hollowing, hollowed**
1 ADJ Something that is **hollow** has a hole or space inside it. *...a hollow tube. ...a large hollow container.*
2 ADJ A surface that is **hollow** curves inwards or downwards. *...a lean, hollow-cheeked man.*
3 NC A **hollow** is an area that is lower than the surrounding surface. *Davis hid in a hollow surrounded by bracken.*
4 ADJ A **hollow** situation or opinion has no real worth or effectiveness; a formal use. *Their independence is hollow... His outward optimism rang hollow.*
5 ADJ ATTRIB If someone gives a **hollow** laugh, they laugh in a way that shows that they do not really find something funny. ◆ **hollowly** ADV *He laughed hollowly. 'And what a mess we made of that!'*
6 ADJ A **hollow** sound is dull and echoing. *The door closed with a hollow clang behind him.* ◆ **hollowly** ADV *His footsteps sounded hollowly on the uncarpeted stairs.*

hollow out PHRASAL VERB If you **hollow** something **out**, you remove the inside part of it. *They hollowed out large tree trunks into boats.*

holly /ˈhɒli/
NU **Holly** is a small evergreen tree. It has prickly leaves and red berries. Holly is used by many people as a Christmas decoration. *All parts of the holly plant are harmful if eaten.*

Hollywood /hɒliwʊd/
N PROP **Hollywood** is the place in Los Angeles where a large number of American films are made; used also to refer to the part of the American film industry that makes these films. *This film has made Clint Eastwood the highest paid star in Hollywood. ...heroines in old Hollywood movies.*

holocaust /hɒləkɔːst/ **holocausts**
NCorNU A **holocaust** is very great destruction and loss of life, especially in war or by fire. *...a nuclear holocaust. ...a danger of war and holocaust.*

hologram /hɒləgræm/ **holograms**
NC A **hologram** is a three-dimensional photographic image created by laser beams. *...holograms on credit cards.*

holograph /hɒləgrɑːf/ **holographs**
1 NC A **holograph** is the same as a **hologram**.
2 NC A **holograph** is also a book or document written in the author's own handwriting; a formal use.

hols /hɒlz/
N PL Your **hols** are the same as your **holiday**; an informal, old-fashioned word. *She was down from Oxford for the hols. ...the last day of the Christmas hols.*

holster /həʊlstə/ **holsters**
NC A **holster** is a holder for a gun worn on a belt. *...a revolver holster on his hip.*

holy /həʊli/ **holier, holiest**
1 ADJ Something that is **holy** relates to God or to a particular religion. *...holy pictures and statues.*
2 ADJ Someone who is **holy** is religious and leads a pure and good life. *The simple villagers are willing to donate generously to the holy man... Several holy men have begun a hunger-strike.*

Holy Communion
N PROP **Holy Communion** is the most important religious service in the Christian church, in which people share bread and wine as a symbol of the Last Supper and the crucifixion of Christ. *...young church-goers going to Holy Communion.*

Holy Father
N PROP The **Holy Father** is the Pope. *The Pontiff wished peace on all Nicaraguans and the President replied, yes Holy Father, we must bring about peace.*

Holy Ghost
N PROP The **Holy Ghost** is the same as the **Holy Spirit**.

holy of holies
1 N SING A **holy of holies** is a place that is considered to be especially holy for a particular religion.
2 N SING A **holy of holies** is a place that is considered to be very private and special so that only certain people are allowed to enter. *I had been summoned into that holy of holies, the headmaster's study.*

Holy Spirit
N PROP In the Christian religion, the **Holy Spirit** is one of the three aspects of God, together with God the Father and God the Son. *I came to know Christ as my Lord and Saviour through the power and presence of the Holy Spirit.*

Holy Week, Holy Weeks
N PROP In the Christian religion, **Holy Week** is the week before Easter, when Christians remember the events leading up to the crucifixion of Christ. *Palm Sunday marks the beginning of Holy Week.*

Holy Writ
N PROP **Holy Writ** is another name for a book, such as the Bible, regarded as sacred by followers of a religion; an old-fashioned expression.

homage /hɒmɪdʒ/
NU **Homage** is respect shown towards someone you admire or who is in authority. *Many of Roth's fans paid homage to him at a San Francisco gallery... This is another homage to those who, like Warhol, have been part of his life.*

home /həʊm/ **homes, homing, homed**
1 NUorNC Your **home** is the place where you live. *She gave up her job and stayed at home to care for her children. ...a normal home life... Many of them found it hard to find homes and jobs.*
2 NU Your **home** is also the area or country that you come from or live in. *Once they're home, they hanker after the new and delicious foods they tried abroad.*

3 ADV **Home** means to or at the place where you live. *I want to go home... Here we are, home at last.*
4 If you are **at home** in a particular situation, you feel comfortable and relaxed in it. *I felt at home at once, because I recognized familiar faces.* ● If you say to a guest **'Make yourself at home'**, you are inviting them to feel relaxed in your home. *Make yourself at home. I'll be back in half an hour.*
5 N+NorNU **Home** also means relating to your own country rather than to foreign countries. *The government had promised to maintain an expanding home market... Newspapers both at home and abroad ignored the incident.*
6 NC A **home** is also a building where people who cannot care for themselves are looked after. *...a children's home. ...a home for the elderly.*
7 N SING+SUPP The **home** of something is the place where it began or where it is found. *...that home of free enterprise, the United States.*
8 If you **bring** or **drive** something **home** to someone, you make them understand how important it is. *He raised his voice to drive home the point.*
9 ADJ ATTRIB A **home** game is played on your team's own ground. *They watched every single game, home or away.*
10 See also **homing**.

home in PHRASAL VERB If a missile **homes in** on something, it finds it. *It can thus home in on the target with pinpoint accuracy.*

home-brew
NU **Home-brew** is beer made in someone's home rather than in a brewery.

homecoming /həʊmkʌmɪŋ/ **homecomings**
NC+POSS Your **homecoming** is your return to your home or country after you have been away for a long time. *There were 120,000 people at his homecoming.*

home computer, home computers
NC A **home computer** is a computer that is kept at home for personal use. It is often used for playing computer games or for running simple programs. *It's a case of programming your home computer.*

home economics
NU **Home economics** is a school subject dealing with how to run a house well and efficiently. *The lab has been doing some home economics studies and found it could replace butter in recipes... Subjects the pass rate has risen the most in are art and design, business studies, home economics, and music.*

home ground
If you are **on home ground** in a particular situation, you know exactly what to do because the place or the situation is familiar to you. *This setback on home ground is a humiliating defeat for Ms Bhutto.*

home-grown
ADJ **Home-grown** fruit and vegetables have been grown in your own garden, area, or country. *He uses 100 per cent home-grown fruit from California's Bajaro Valley.*

home help, home helps
NC A **home help** is a person employed, often by a local government authority, to help sick or old people with their housework. *In Warwickshire they have introduced charges for home helps.*

homeland /həʊmlænd/ **homelands**
NC Your **homeland** is your native country. *A Chinese student has made a dramatic return to his homeland.*

homeless /həʊmləs/
1 ADJ If people are **homeless**, they have nowhere to live. *Floods in north-eastern India made 233,000 people homeless.* ◆ **homelessness** NU *For a growing number of young people, homelessness is becoming a way of life.*
2 N PL You can refer to people who are homeless as **the homeless**. *The mayor has also requisitioned a giant sports stadium to house the homeless.*

homely /həʊmli/
ADJ If something is **homely**, it is simple and ordinary. *We stayed in the Hotel Claravallis, a homely and comfortable establishment.*

home-made
ADJ Something that is **home-made** has been made in someone's home, rather than in a shop or factory.

...home-made bread. ...home-made clothes.

Home Office
N PROP The **Home Office** is the department of the British Government which is responsible for the police, immigration, and broadcasting. *...the three great offices of state—the Foreign Office, the Home Office and the Treasury.*

homeopath /ˈhəʊmɪəpæθ/ **homeopaths;** also spelt **homoeopath.**
N C A **homeopath** is someone who treats illness by homeopathy.

homeopathic /ˌhəʊmɪəˈpæθɪk/; also spelt **homoeopathic.**
ADJ **Homeopathic** means related to or used in homeopathy. *...homeopathic remedies.*

homeopathy /ˌhəʊmɪˈɒpəθi/; also spelt **homoeopathy.**
N U **Homeopathy** is a way of treating illness in which the patient is given very small amounts of drugs which are prepared from natural substances. *The growing popularity of homeopathy has offended parts of the medical profession.*

homeowner /ˈhəʊməʊnə/ **homeowners**
N C A **homeowner** is someone who owns their own home. *A large number of homeowners have been hit hard by the recent interest rate rise.*

Home Secretary, Home Secretaries
N PROP or N C The **Home Secretary** is the member of the British government who is in charge of the Home Office. *The Home Secretary, Mr Hurd, acknowledged that the prison population was continuing to grow... The paper wishes she had found a Home Secretary who offers deeds as well as words to combat crime.*

homesick /ˈhəʊmsɪk/
ADJ If you are **homesick,** you are unhappy because you are away from home. *The smell of the grass made her homesick for her parents' farm.*
♦ **homesickness** N U *...a sudden spasm of homesickness.*

homespun /ˈhəʊmspʌn/
ADJ Beliefs, opinions, or comments that are **homespun** are simple and uncomplicated. *They believed in simple living and homespun virtues.*

homestead /ˈhəʊmsted/ **homesteads**
N C A **homestead** is a farmhouse and the land around it; used in American English. *He was born on a failing homestead in Nebraska.*

home stretch
1 N SING The **home stretch** or the **home straight** is the last part of a race.
2 N SING You can also refer to the last part of any activity that lasts for a fairly long time as **the home stretch,** especially if the activity is difficult or boring.

home time
N U **Home time** is the time of day when children finish school and go home; an informal expression.

home town, home towns
N C Your **home town** is the town where you were born or spent your childhood. *My own home town is thousands of miles away. ...Robin Hood's home town of Nottingham.*

home truth, home truths
N C **Home truths** are unpleasant facts that you learn about yourself, usually from someone else. *They're concentrating on some hard facts, some home truths.*

homeward /ˈhəʊmwəd/ **homewards.** In normal British English, **homewards** is an adverb and **homeward** is an adjective. In formal British English and in American English, **homeward** is both an adjective and an adverb.
ADV **Homewards** or **homeward** means towards home. *The time had come to drive the goats homewards.*
▶ Also ADJ ATTRIB *The tank blew up on its homeward journey.*

homeward-bound
ADJ People or things that are **homeward-bound** are on their way home. *...homeward-bound commuters. ...homeward-bound ships.*

homework /ˈhəʊmwɜːk/
1 N U **Homework** is work that teachers give pupils to do at home. *He never did any homework and he got terrible results in school.*
2 N U **Homework** is also research that is done in preparation for a written article or speech. *Aiken did*

his homework and worked out a convincing commercial case.

homey /ˈhəʊmi/
ADJ If you describe a place as **homey,** you mean that you feel comfortable and relaxed there; an informal word. *My second flat was more homey than the first.*

homicidal /ˌhɒmɪˈsaɪdl/
ADJ Someone who is **homicidal** is likely to commit murder. *...homicidal maniacs.*

homicide /ˈhɒmɪsaɪd/ **homicides**
N C or N U **Homicide** is the crime of murder; used in American English. *1990 has seen a record number of homicides... A motorist has been charged with homicide for failing to put his child in a restraining seat.*

homily /ˈhɒməli/ **homilies**
N C A **homily** is a speech or a piece of writing in which someone complains about something or tells people how they ought to behave; a formal word. *We listened to her homily about the rising cost of living.*

homing /ˈhəʊmɪŋ/
1 ADJ ATTRIB A weapon or a piece of equipment that has a **homing** system is able to guide itself to a target, or to give out a signal that guides people to it. *Even small missiles have built-in homing devices... The flight recorders are of an older type and don't send out a homing signal when activated.*
2 ADJ ATTRIB An animal that has a **homing** instinct is able to remember a place and return there. *They have a highly accurate homing instinct that leads them to sea cliffs.*

homing pigeon, homing pigeons
N C A **homing pigeon** is trained to return to a particular place, especially in races with other pigeons. *The four-hundred mile race should have taken the homing pigeons around twenty-four hours to complete.*

homoeopath /ˈhəʊmɪəpæθ/. See **homeopath.**
homoeopathic /ˌhəʊmɪəˈpæθɪk/. See **homeopathic.**
homoeopathy /ˌhəʊmɪˈɒpəθi/. See **homeopathy.**

homogeneity /ˌhɒmədʒəˈniːɪti/
N U **Homogeneity** is the quality of being homogeneous. *...emphasis on the unity of the nation and the homogeneity of society.*

homogeneous /ˌhɒməˈdʒiːnɪəs/
ADJ A thing or group that is **homogeneous** has parts or members which are all the same. *The working class is not very homogeneous.*

homogenized /həˈmɒdʒənaɪzd/
ADJ **Homogenized** milk has had the cream on top of it broken up so that the cream and milk are evenly mixed.

homogenous /həˈmɒdʒənəs/
ADJ **Homogenous** means the same as **homogeneous.** *Culturally, China was much more homogenous than the Soviet Union.*

homo sapiens /ˌhəʊməʊ ˈsæpienz/
N U **Homo sapiens** is used to refer to human beings considered as a type of animal in relation to other animals. *Homo erectus, our immediate ancestor, was giving rise to homo sapiens.*

homosexual /ˌhəʊməˈsekʃuəl/ **homosexuals**
ADJ Someone who is **homosexual** is sexually attracted to people of the same sex. *In an opinion poll, 61 per cent of British people thought that homosexual relationships between adults should be legal... Jarman's most recent film is a meditation on being homosexual in a time of plague.* ▶ Also N C *...clubs and bars for homosexuals.* ♦ **homosexuality** /ˌhəʊməsekʃuˈælɪti/ N U *...the reform of the laws on homosexuality.*

Hon.
TITLE **Hon.** is a written abbreviation for 'honourable' and 'honorary' when they are used as part of a person's title. *The Duke and Duchess of Kent, and Princess Alexandra, the Hon. Lady Ogilvy and the Hon. Sir Angus Ogilvy were also present.*

Honduras /hɒnˈdjʊərəs/
The **Republic of Honduras** is a country in Central America. It was a Spanish colony from the 16th century until it became independent in 1838. Rafael Leonardo Callejas, of the National Party (PN),

became President in 1990. Honduras is a member of the Organization of American States. It exports bananas, coffee, shrimp, and lobsters. Large foreign debts and high inflation are serious economic problems. ◆ **Honduran** /hɒndjuərən/ N, ADJ ▪ *per capita GNP:* US$900 ▪ *religion:* Christianity (mainly Roman Catholic) ▪ *language:* Spanish ▪ *currency:* lempira ▪ *capital:* Tegucigalpa ▪ *population:* 5 million (1990) ▪ *size:* 112,088 square kilometres.

hone /həʊn/ **hones, honing, honed**
1 VO If you **hone** something such as a blade or a stone, you sharpen it. *Grind it down to shape and hone it to a fine edge.*
2 VO If you **hone** someone or something, you carefully prepare and develop them for a special purpose over a long period of time. *...intellectuals honed in the ancient universities to direct the nation.*

honest /ɒnɪst/
1 ADJ Someone who is **honest** about something is completely truthful about it. *At least you're honest about why you want the money... To be perfectly honest, up until three weeks ago I had never set foot in a nightclub... Not all scientists are as honest as Pasteur was.*
2 ADJ Someone who is **honest** does not cheat or break the law and can be trusted with valuable things. *He's very honest in money matters.*
3 ADV SEN You say '**honest**' to emphasize that you are telling the truth; an informal use. *It's true as I'm sitting here, Mabel, honest it is.*

honest broker, honest brokers
NC An **honest broker** is someone who negotiates with the two sides in an international dispute in order to try to end it. *Algeria prefers to act as an honest broker on these occasions, without taking sides.*

honestly /ɒnɪstli/
1 ADV or ADV SEN You use **honestly** to emphasize that you really and truthfully believe what you are saying. *I'll tell you honestly: I don't like it... He didn't honestly think he would miss them.*
2 ADV SEN You also use **honestly** to emphasize that you are telling the truth and that you want your listeners to believe you. *I'll go if you like. I don't mind, honestly.*
3 You also use **honestly** to indicate annoyance or impatience. *Honestly, Flora, this is getting ridiculous.*
4 ADV If you do something **honestly**, you do without cheating or telling lies. *He insisted that the bank had operated honestly... He said it would only be possible to find a common future by looking honestly at the past.*

honesty /ɒnɪsti/
NU **Honesty** is the quality of being honest. *...the need for complete honesty.*

honey /hʌni/
NU **Honey** is a sweet sticky substance made by bees. You eat honey and use it as a sweetener. *...tea sweetened with honey.*

honeybee /hʌnibiː/ **honeybees**
NC A **honeybee** is a bee that makes honey. *Honeybees are social insects living and working together in large numbers.*

honeycomb /hʌnikəʊm/ **honeycombs**
NC or NU A **honeycomb** is a wax structure consisting of rows of six-sided holes where bees store honey. *...a hollow honeycomb structure. ...colonies of bees on large honeycombs suspended from supports... They sell it as honeycomb.*

honeydew melon /hʌnidjuː mɛlən/ **honeydew melons**
NC A **honeydew melon** is a type of melon with a yellow skin.

honeyed /hʌnid/
ADJ If someone speaks **honeyed** words or speaks with a **honeyed** voice, what they say is soft and pleasant to listen to, although it is often untrue. *She was soothed by his honeyed words.*

honeymoon /hʌnimuːn/ **honeymoons**
1 NC A **honeymoon** is a holiday taken by a newly-married couple. *They spent their honeymoon at Petersburg, Florida.*
2 NC A **honeymoon** is also a period of time after the start of a new job or government when everyone is pleased with the people concerned. *The honeymoon period is over.*

honeysuckle /hʌnisʌkl/
NU **Honeysuckle** is a climbing plant with sweet-smelling flowers.

Hong Kong /hɒŋ kɒŋ/
The **Territory of Hong Kong** is a colony of the United Kingdom. The colony consists of Hong Kong Island, the Kowloon Peninsula, and the New Territories on the mainland. The island was ceded to the British crown in 1841. In 1898 the rest of the territory was leased to Britain for 99 years. Hong Kong was occupied by Japan from 1941 to 1945. In 1984 China and Britain agreed that sovereignty over the whole of the territory would revert to China in 1997. Hong Kong exports clothing and electrical products. Banking, shipping, and tourism are important industries.
▪ *per capita GNP:* US$10,320 ▪ *religion:* Buddhism, Christianity ▪ *language:* English and Cantonese (official) ▪ *currency:* dollar ▪ *capital:* Victoria ▪ *population:* 6 million (1990) ▪ *size:* 1,075 square kilometres.

Honiara /hɒniɑːrə/
Honiara is the capital of the Solomon Islands and its largest city. It is on the island of Guadalcanal. Population: 35,000 (1990).

honk /hɒŋk/ **honks, honking, honked**
V-ERG If you **honk** the horn of a vehicle or if the vehicle's horn **honks**, it produces a short loud sound. *...driving their cars, honking their horns in noisy parades. ...the usual cacophony of car horns honking aggressively away.*

honor /ɒnə/. See **honour**.
honorable /ɒnərəbl/. See **honourable**.
honorary /ɒnərəri/
1 ADJ ATTRIB An **honorary** title is given to someone as a mark of respect and does not require the usual qualifications. *...an honorary degree.*
2 ADJ ATTRIB An **honorary** job is an official job that is done without payment. *...the honorary Treasurer.*

Honorat, Jean Jacques /ʒɒnˠ ʒæk ɒnɒrɑː/
Jean Jacques Honorat was appointed Prime Minister and Foreign Minister of Haiti in 1991. He was formerly Director of the Haitian Centre for Human Rights.

honorific /ɒnərɪfɪk/ **honorifics**
ADJ ATTRIB An **honorific** title is one that is given to someone as a sign of respect or honour. *Hirohito was reinstated to several honorific titles which he had been stripped of during the war.* ▶ Also NC *Retired military personnel are to be denied the right to use their rank as an honorific.*

honour /ɒnə/ **honours, honouring, honoured**; spelt **honor** in American English.
1 NU **Honour** is a feeling of pride that you have when you believe that you are behaving in the best way so that other people admire or respect you. *A debt is a thing of family honour... He was able to withdraw from the battle with honour.*
2 NC An **honour** is a special award or job that is given to someone for something they have done. *It was a richly deserved honour.*
3 N SING If you describe something that has happened to you as an **honour**, you mean that you are pleased and proud about it; a formal use. *He is one of the most interesting people I have had the honour of meeting... She did me the honour of attending my exhibition.*
4 NU **Honours** is a type of university degree which is of a higher standard than an ordinary degree. *...a first class honours degree in French.*
5 VO If you **honour** someone, you give them public praise or a medal for something they have done. *The people came to honour their leader... In 1949, he was honoured with the Grand Cross.*
6 VO To **honour** someone also means to treat them with special attention and respect. *When President Gorbachev lunches with the Queen today, he will become the first Soviet leader to be so honoured.*
◆ **honoured** ADJ ATTRIB *Rose was the honoured guest.*
7 VO If you **honour** an arrangement or promise, you keep to it; a formal use. *The government has solemn*

commitments and must honour them.
● **Honour** is used in these phrases. ● If something is arranged **in honour of** a person or an event, it is arranged specially for that person or to celebrate that event. *The ceremony was held in honour of the Queen's birthday.* ● You address a judge in court as **your honor**; used in American English. *One of the jurors declared, 'Your Honor, I've already made up my mind. She's guilty.'*

honourable /ɒnərəbl/; spelt **honorable** in American English.
1 ADJ Someone who is **honourable** is honest and worthy of respect. *...an honourable man... Major Vane had always tried to do the honourable thing.*
◆ **honourably** ADV *He served his master honourably until his death.*
2 ADJ ATTRIB In debates in the British parliament, one member of parliament refers to another as the **honourable** member, the **honourable** gentleman, the **honourable** lady, or their **honourable** friend. *...the honourable member for Malmesbury is mistaken... I am sure the honourable gentleman will agree... Is My Honourable Friend aware that his refusal to back the experiment will be greeted with great disappointment?*

honourable mention, honourable mentions
NC If something that you do in a competition is given an **honourable mention**, it receives a mark of special praise although it does not actually win a prize. *British designs got a $5,000 second prize and a $2,000 honourable mention.*

honours list, honours lists
NC The **honours list** is a list of people who are going to receive an official honour, such as a knighthood. Honours lists are published several times a year. *The New Year's honours list, recognising leading figures in British life, is published today... He has been knighted in the Queen's birthday honours list.*

Hons.
Hons. is a written abbreviation for 'Honours'; used after the name of a university degree. *...BA Hons. History, Cambridge.*

hooch /huːtʃ/
NU **Hooch** is alcoholic drink; an informal word. *Otto brought out his private hooch supplies.*

hood /hʊd/ **hoods**
1 NC A **hood** is a part of a coat which covers your head. *He held both sides of the hood closed against the snow.*
2 NC A **hood** is also a covering on a vehicle or a piece of equipment, which is usually curved and can be moved. *...a pram which had its hood folded down.*
3 NC The **hood** of a car is the same as its **bonnet**; used in American English. *...the hood of the station wagon.*

hooded /hʊdɪd/
1 ADJ ATTRIB A **hooded** piece of clothing has a hood. *...a hooded duffel coat.*
2 ADJ ATTRIB A **hooded** person is difficult to recognize because they have a hood or a piece of cloth pulled down over their face. *Five hooded men burst into his hotel room and overpowered him. ...a procession of bishops and hooded monks.*
3 ADJ ATTRIB Someone with **hooded** eyes has large eyelids that are partly closed. *...hooded eyes glaring intensely.*

hoodlum /huːdləm/ **hoodlums**
NC A **hoodlum** is a violent criminal, especially one who is part of a gang; an informal word. *...people who have been knifed and robbed by hoodlums.*

hoodwink /hʊdwɪŋk/ **hoodwinks, hoodwinking, hoodwinked**
VO If you **hoodwink** someone, you trick or deceive them. *He is too often hoodwinked by flashy external appearances.*

hooey /huːi/
NU If you describe something that someone says as **hooey**, you mean that it is nonsense; used in informal speech. *That's a load of hooey.*

hoof /huːf/ **hoofs** or **hooves** /huːvz/
NC An animal's **hoofs** are the hard parts of its feet. *...animals with cloven hoofs... He can look at a set of hoof prints and tell if the horses are loaded down.*

hook /hʊk/ **hooks, hooking, hooked**
1 NC A **hook** is a bent piece of metal or plastic used for holding things or hanging things on. *Howard hangs up his coat on the hook behind the door. ...curtain hooks.*
2 VOA If you **hook** one thing onto another, you attach it there using a hook. *One after the other they were hooked to the moving cable.*
● **Hook** is used in these phrases. ● If you take the phone **off the hook**, you take the receiver off the part that it normally rests on, so that the phone will not ring. *...a telephone with its receiver off the hook.* ● If your telephone **is ringing off the hook**, so many people are trying to telephone you that it is ringing constantly; used in American English. *The phones at donation centers have been ringing off the hook with first-time volunteers.* ● If someone **gets off the hook**, they manage to get out of a difficult or dangerous situation; an informal expression. *He felt he had got off the hook perhaps too easily.*

hook up PHRASAL VERB If you **hook up** a computer or other electronic machine, you connect it to other similar machines or to a central power supply.

hookah /hʊkə/ **hookahs**
NC A **hookah** is a Middle Eastern pipe for smoking tobacco or marijuana. It consists of a long flexible stem and a jar of water, through which the smoke is sucked in order to cool it. *The crowd melted away and went back to playing dominoes and smoking their hookahs.*

hook and eye, hooks and eyes
NC A **hook and eye** is a small metal hook and bar that together form a fastening for clothes such as dresses or skirts.

hooked /hʊkt/
1 ADJ Something that is **hooked** is shaped like a hook. *...huge hooked claws. ...a long, rather hooked nose.*
2 ADJ PRED If you are **hooked** on something, you enjoy it so much that it takes up a lot of your interest and attention; an informal use. *I'm really hooked on those kids.*
3 ADJ PRED If you are **hooked** on a drug, you are addicted to it. *Some people seem more susceptible than others to becoming hooked on alcohol.*

hooker /hʊkə/ **hookers**
NC A **hooker** is a prostitute; used in informal American English. *...hookers who pick up tricks in a bar.*

hook-nosed
ADJ Someone who is **hook-nosed** has a large nose that curves out in the middle.

hook-up, hook-ups
NC A **hook-up** is an electronic or radio connection between computers, satellites, or radios. *...a telephone hook-up.*

hooky /hʊki/; also spelt **hookey**.
A child who **plays hooky** deliberately stays away from school without permission; used in American English. *Paul is a shy, stammering boy who plays hooky and keeps to his bedroom practising his guitar.*

hooligan /huːlɪgən/ **hooligans**
NC A **hooligan** is a young person who behaves in a noisy and violent way in public places. *...groups of skinheads, who are juvenile hooligans.*

hooliganism /huːlɪgənɪzəm/
NU **Hooliganism** is the behaviour and action of hooligans. *...an increase in football hooliganism.*

hoop /huːp/ **hoops**
1 NC A **hoop** is a large ring made of wood, metal, or plastic. *...boys holding hoops, kites, and marbles.*
2 If one person makes another **jump through hoops**, they make them do something difficult, boring, or unpleasant which is usually not necessary. *They do not wish to be seen jumping through hoops for groups they regard as terrorists.*

hoop-la /huːplɑː/ **hoop-las**
NCorNU The **hoop-la** is a game at a fair in which you try to throw small hoops over objects in order to win them.

hooray /hʊreɪ/; also spelt **hurray**.
People sometimes shout '**Hooray!**' when they are very happy and excited. *'Hooray, it's over, let's go home.'*

hoot /huːt/ **hoots, hooting, hooted**
1 V or V-ERG If you **hoot** the horn on a vehicle or if the horn **hoots**, it makes a loud noise. *Tug boats hooted at it... Drivers hooted their horns... The horn hooted once.* ► Also NC *I heard a hoot and saw Martin driving by.*
2 V If you **hoot**, you make a loud high-pitched noise when you are laughing. *They pointed and hooted with enjoyment.* ► Also NC *At this Etta gave a hoot of laughter.*
3 V When an owl **hoots**, it makes a sound like a long 'oo'. *Outside, an owl hooted among the pines.* ► Also N SING *He heard the hoot of an owl.*

hooter /huːtə/ **hooters**
1 NC A **hooter** is a device which makes a loud noise as a warning or to signal the beginning and end of factory shifts or some sports matches. *It controls an automatic warning system which sounds a hooter in a drivers cabin when a signal is red... You used to open your windows and listen to the noise in the factories, the hooters blowing, the trains.*
2 NC You can refer to someone's nose as their **hooter**, especially if it is very large; an informal use.

hoover /huːvə/ **hoovers, hoovering, hoovered**
1 NC A **Hoover** is a vacuum cleaner; **Hoover** is a trademark. *There was no Hoover for the carpets.*
2 V or VO If you **hoover** a carpet, you clean it using a vacuum cleaner. *She began the daily round of washing and hoovering.*

hooves /huːvz/
Hooves is a plural of **hoof**. *Cows and goats have pointed hooves that dig into the soil.*

hop /hɒp/ **hops, hopping, hopped**
1 V If you **hop**, you move along by jumping on one foot. *...hopping clumsily up and down in their chains.* ► Also NC *They began jumping up and down together in short hops.*
2 V When birds and some small animals **hop**, they move in small jumps using both feet together. *A hare hopped straight into the doorway.* ► Also NC *...a bird so heavy that it could make only short, low hops through the brush.*
3 V A If you **hop** somewhere, you move there quickly or suddenly; an informal use. *He hopped out of bed... Let's hop in my car and drive out there.*
4 NC **Hops** are flowers that are dried and used for making beer. *...the hop gardens of Sussex.*

hope /həʊp/ **hopes, hoping, hoped**
1 V-REPORT, V+to-INF, or V+for If you **hope** that something is true or will happen, you want it to be true or to happen. *The authorities also hoped that the system would help save petrol... She hoped she wasn't going to cry... 'You haven't lost the ticket, have you?'—'I hope not.'... I sat down, hoping to remain unnoticed... He paused, hoping for evidence of interest.*
2 NU or NC **Hope** is a feeling of confidence that what you want to happen might happen. *She never completely gave up hope. ...his hopes of a reconciliation.*
3 N SING+SUPP If there is a **hope** of something desirable happening, there is a chance that it may happen. *There is no hope of regular employment as an agricultural labourer.*
● **Hope** is used in these phrases. ● If you do something **in the hope** of achieving a particular thing, you do it because you want to achieve that thing. *Tourists were waiting outside the palace in the hope of getting a look at the king.* ● If something **raises** your **hopes**, it makes you feel that what you want to happen will happen. *The new agreement raised hopes for conditions of prosperity.*

hopeful /həʊpfl/ **hopefuls**
1 ADJ If you are **hopeful**, you are fairly confident that something that you want to happen will happen. *He sounded hopeful that she would come.*
2 ADJ An outcome, method, or event that is **hopeful** makes you feel that what you want to happen will happen. *...the most astonishing and hopeful results... This seems to be a hopeful way of tackling the problem.*
3 NC If you refer to someone as a **hopeful**, you mean that they have an ambition and it is possible that they

will achieve it. *Almost a hundred hopefuls stood in a queue outside the theatre.*

hopefully /həʊpfəˀli/
1 ADV If you do something **hopefully**, you do it in a way which shows that you are fairly confident that what you want to happen will happen. *He smiled hopefully.*
2 ADV SEN **Hopefully** is often used when mentioning something that you hope and are fairly confident will happen. Some careful speakers of English think that this use of **hopefully** is incorrect. *The new legislation, hopefully, will lead to some improvements.*

hopeless /həʊpləs/
1 ADJ If you feel **hopeless**, you feel desperate because there seems to be no possibility of comfort or success. *I walked away in an agony of hopeless grief and pity.*
◆ **hopelessly** ADV *She shook her head hopelessly.*
◆ **hopelessness** NU *...the hopelessness of the poor.*
2 ADJ Someone or something that is **hopeless** is certain to be unsuccessful. *I knew my love was as hopeless as ever... The situation was hopeless.*
3 ADJ ATTRIB You use **hopeless** to emphasize how bad an event or situation is. *Her room is in a hopeless muddle... He was hopeless at games.* ◆ **hopelessly** SUBMOD *She was hopelessly impulsive.*

hopper /hɒpə/ **hoppers**
NC A **hopper** is a device shaped like a large funnel, in which substances such as grain, coal, animal food, or sand can be stored. *Large trailers came along and tipped it into a big hopper.*

horde /hɔːd/ **hordes**
NC A **horde** is a large, rather frightening crowd of people or animals. *...hordes of screaming children. ...rioting hordes.*

horizon /həraɪzn/ **horizons**
1 NC The **horizon** is the distant line where the sky seems to touch the land or the sea. *...the smoke on the horizon.*
2 If something is **on the horizon**, it is going to happen or appear soon. *A new type of drug is on the horizon.*
3 NC Your **horizons** are the limits of what you want to do or of what you are involved in. *...the spontaneous expansion of human horizons.*

horizontal /hɒrɪzɒntl/
ADJ Something that is **horizontal** is flat and level with the ground, rather than at an angle to it. *...horizontal stripes.* ◆ **horizontally** ADV *The lower branches spread out almost horizontally.*

hormonal /hɔːməʊnl/
ADJ **Hormonal** means relating to or involving hormones. *...hormonal changes. ...hormonal activity.*

hormone /hɔːməʊn/ **hormones**
NC A **hormone** is a chemical produced by your body. *...the male hormone testosterone.*

horn /hɔːn/ **horns**
1 NC The **horn** on a vehicle is the thing that makes a loud noise as a signal or warning. *A car passed him at top speed, sounding its horn... It was me driving the car, me honking the horn.*
2 NC **Horns** are the hard pointed things that grow out of the heads of cows, goats, and some other animals. *...the horns of a bull.*
3 NU **Horn** is the hard substance that the horns of animals are made of. *...ceremonial daggers with rhino horn handles.*
4 NC A **horn** or a **French horn** is a musical instrument consisting of a long brass tube wound round in a circle with a funnel at the end. *Ed used to play the French horn with the New York City Ballet Orchestra... It recalls some of the great jazz horn players.*

horned /hɔːnd/
ADJ ATTRIB **Horned** is used to describe animals that have horns or parts of their body that look like horns. *...the great horned owl. ...the horned toad.*

hornet /hɔːnɪt/ **hornets**
1 NC A **hornet** is a flying insect like a large wasp which has a very painful sting. *Towards the end of the summer, the bees are threatened by hornets.*
2 If you describe a situation as a **hornet's nest**, you mean that it is extremely unpleasant or difficult to deal with; an informal expression. *The affair has stirred up a hornet's nest of bitter recrimination.*

horn-rimmed
ADJ **Horn-rimmed** spectacles have plastic frames that look as though they are made of horn. *She wore enormous horn-rimmed glasses.*
horny /hɔːni/ **hornier, horniest**
1 ADJ Something that is **horny** is hard, strong, and made of horn or a substance like horn. *It has an armour of horny scales... Their skeleton is flexible and horny.*
2 ADJ You can describe someone's skin as **horny** when it is very hard, tough, or wrinkled. *He crunched Philip's fingers in his huge, horny hand.*
3 ADJ If you describe someone as **horny**, you mean that they are sexually aroused or easily aroused; an informal use. *The picture shows two horny teenagers being expelled from the garden. ...a mindless tussle with a hot horny youth.*
horoscope /hɒrəskəʊp/ **horoscopes**
NC Your **horoscope** is a forecast of future events, based on the position of the stars on the day you were born. *Many people still consult their horoscopes in the popular papers.*
horrendous /hɒrɛndəs/
ADJ Something that is **horrendous** is extremely unpleasant and shocking. *...the horrendous murder of a prostitute... The economic woes in some of the Balkan States are just horrendous... Some cities, such as Tokyo, have horrendous smog problems.*
horrible /hɒrəbl/
1 ADJ You describe something as **horrible** when you do not like it at all. *The hotel was horrible... I've never had such a horrible meal... We've been made to think of history as a dull, boring, horrible subject.*
2 ADJ Something that is **horrible** causes you to feel fear, shock, or disgust. *They knew that all wars are horrible... That was a terrifying and horrible experience.* ◆ **horribly** ADV *The man had begun to scream horribly.*
3 ADJ ATTRIB You use **horrible** to emphasize how bad something is. *Everything's in a horrible muddle... I've got a horrible suspicion this thing won't work.* ◆ **horribly** SUBMOD *Everything has gone horribly wrong.*
horrid /hɒrɪd/
ADJ Something or someone that is **horrid** is very unpleasant. *...a horrid little flat... I don't mean to be horrid to you.*
horrific /hɒrɪfɪk/
ADJ Something that is **horrific** is so unpleasant that people are horrified and shocked by it. *They are both serving life sentences for a series of horrific child murders. ...these horrific events.*
horrify /hɒrɪfaɪ/ **horrifies, horrifying, horrified**
VO If you **are horrified** by something, it makes you feel alarmed and upset. *He was horrified by their poverty... Both Mr Faulds and his daughter were horrified at the proposal... All this horrifies opponents of military toys... The prospect of oil exploration there horrifies environmentalists.* ◆ **horrifying** ADJ *...horrifying stories.*
horror /hɒrə/ **horrors**
1 NU **Horror** is a strong feeling of alarm caused by something extremely unpleasant. *The boys shrank away in horror.*
2 N SING If you have a **horror** of something, you are afraid of it or dislike it strongly. *Despite a horror of violence, John allowed himself to be drafted into the army.*
3 N PL You can refer to extremely unpleasant experiences as **horrors**. *His mind would dwell on the horrors he had been through.*
4 N+N A **horror** film or story is intended to be very frightening. *...the star of countless horror films, Peter Cushing.*
5 N+N A **horror** story can also be a story that is true and very unpleasant. *So far there have been no television pictures of suffering children, or horror stories.*
horror-stricken or **horror-struck**
ADJ Someone who is **horror-stricken** or **horror-struck** feels very great horror or dismay at something that has happened. *Roland was horror-stricken at what*

he'd done... The mass of people were horror-struck at the war which was being thrust upon them.
hors de combat /ɔː də kɒmbɑː/
ADJ PRED If someone is **hors de combat**, they have been injured, and so are unable to do something such as fight or play a sport; a literary term. *All civilians and all those hors de combat must be protected from acts of violence.*
hors d'oeuvre /ɔːdɜːv/ **hors d'oeuvres**
N PL **Hors d'oeuvres** are dishes of cold food eaten before the main course of a meal. *They went back to the lounge, where hors d'oeuvres were just being served.*
horse /hɔːs/ **horses**
NC A **horse** is a large animal which you can ride. Some horses are used for pulling ploughs and carts. *In the first race, his horse was only narrowly beaten... He would ride the horse into Calhoun... When it's time to plough his fields, Savaski uses a horse.*
horseback /hɔːsbæk/
1 If you are **on horseback**, you are riding a horse. *The police on foot and on horseback eventually cleared the pitch.*
2 ADJ ATTRIB **Horseback** is used to describe things that relate to riding horses; used in American English. *...visitors taking a horseback ride amongst the ruins... The line of floats, bands, and horseback riders stretches on for three miles.*
horse box, horse boxes
NC A **horse box** is a vehicle like a removal van which is used to transport horses. *He will miss the first race, after an accident in his horse box.*
horse chestnut, horse chestnuts
1 NC A **horse chestnut** is a large tree. It has big leaves and shiny reddish-brown nuts covered with a spiky case. *Squirrels also like larch, maple, and horse chestnut.*
2 NC A **horse chestnut** is also the nut of this tree. A more common name for the nut is conker. *Don't confuse them with horse chestnuts, whose inedible conkers look very similar to sweet chestnuts inside their spiny husks.*
horse-drawn
ADJ A **horse-drawn** vehicle is pulled by one or more horses. *She saw a picture of Piccadilly almost jammed with horse-drawn traffic in about 1875... Most of their artillery would have been horse-drawn.*
horseflesh /hɔːsfleʃ/
NU **Horseflesh** or **horsemeat** is meat from a horse, especially when it is fed to other animals or eaten by people. *They imported Australian horsemeat for pet food.*
horsefly /hɔːsflaɪ/ **horseflies**
NC A **horsefly** is a large fly that stings horses, cattle, and people and sucks their blood. *The wild stallion bucked, as if stung by horseflies.*
horsehair /hɔːsheə/
NU **Horsehair** is hair from horses' manes or tails, that was used in the past to stuff mattresses and furniture. *The Colonel reclined on a horsehair sofa.*
horseman /hɔːsmən/ **horsemen** /hɔːsmən/
NC A **horseman** is a man who is riding a horse, or a man who rides horses well. *It ended with the ceremonial firing of guns and a spectacular charge by horsemen.*
horsemanship /hɔːsmənʃɪp/
NU **Horsemanship** is the ability to ride horses well. *The Queen will watch a display of traditional horsemanship before flying home.*
horseplay /hɔːspleɪ/
NU **Horseplay** is rough play in which people push and hit each other, or behave boisterously in a silly way. *She was engaged in some horseplay involving the hiding of her swimming-costume... Employees did not wear protective clothing, and horseplay at the plant was common.*
horsepower /hɔːspaʊə/
NU **Horsepower** is a unit of power. It is used for measuring how powerful an engine is. *He started up the outboard motor—5 horsepower only, but enough for a fourteen-foot dinghy... The self-loading Muck Truck has a 6 horsepower engine which operates two*

individually controlled hydraulic motors.

horseradish /hɔːsrædɪʃ/
NU **Horseradish** is the white root of a plant similar to a mustard plant. It has a very strong, sharp taste and is used in sauces. *Get just the right amount of horseradish, two tablespoons, no more.*

horse sense
NU **Horse sense** is the same as **common sense**; an informal expression. *He showed his political horse sense in a carefully worded speech.*

horseshoe /hɔːsʃuː/ **horseshoes**
NC A **horseshoe** is a piece of metal shaped like a U which is fixed to a horse's hoof. *She was given six silver spoons, all engraved with a lucky horseshoe.*

horse trading
NU **Horse trading** is bargaining which takes place unofficially and which often involves exchanges rather than payment. *At the beginning of term there is horse trading over timetables... But the real political horse trading began yesterday, as leaders set out their positions.*

horsewhip /hɔːswɪp/ **horsewhips, horsewhipping, horsewhipped**
1 NC A **horsewhip** is a long thin piece of leather on the end of a short, stiff handle.
2 VO If someone **horsewhips** a person or animal, they hit them several times with a horsewhip in order to hurt or punish them. *The man was tied to a tree and horsewhipped.*

horsewoman /hɔːswʊmən/ **horsewomen**
NC A **horsewoman** is a woman who is riding a horse or a woman who rides horses well. *...the Princess Royal—a keen horsewoman herself.*

horsey /hɔːsi/; also spelt **horsy**.
1 ADJ Someone who is **horsey** is very keen on horses or is fond of riding horses; an informal use. *We watched her show-jumping at a gymkhana, in her horsy phase.*
2 ADJ If you describe a woman as **horsey**, you mean that her face reminds you of a horse; an offensive use.

horsy /hɔːsi/. See **horsey**.

horticultural /hɔːtɪkʌltʃərəl/
ADJ **Horticultural** means concerned with or relating to horticulture. *Food Focus is a guide to fresh agricultural and horticultural produce from Britain.*
● See also **horticulture**.

horticulturalist /hɔːtɪkʌltʃərəlɪst/ **horticulturalists**
NC A **horticulturalist** is a person who grows flowers, fruit, and vegetables, especially as their job. *Zimbabwean horticulturalists have made their mark on the exotic flowers and fruit market in Germany.*

horticulture /hɔːtɪkʌltʃə/
NU **Horticulture** is the study and practice of growing plants. *The Festival will celebrate the highest standards in horticulture.* ● See also **horticultural**.

hose /həʊz/ **hoses, hosing, hosed**
1 NC A **hose** is a long, flexible pipe through which water is carried. *Protestors were sprayed with high pressure water hoses... They tried to fight the fire with a hose.*
2 VO If you **hose** something, you wash it or spread water on it using a hose. *Hose the soil well immediately after planting rose bushes.*

hosepipe /həʊzpaɪp/ **hosepipes**
NC A **hosepipe** is the same as a **hose**. *Several water companies have imposed hosepipe bans.*

hosiery /həʊziəri/
NU **Hosiery** is garments such as tights and stockings that are for sale in a shop; a formal word. *Recently, textile, hosiery, and meat processing plants have been built in the province.*

hospice /hɒspɪs/ **hospices**
NC A **hospice** is a hospital which looks after the dying, counselling them and giving practical help as well as medical care. *He raised money for a Cambridgeshire hospice. ...other local charities including a hospice for those who have terminal illnesses.*

hospitable /hɒspɪtəbl/
ADJ If you are **hospitable**, you are friendly and welcoming towards guests or strangers. *Mr Steinberg was a good-natured and hospitable man... She behaved in a generous and hospitable fashion.*

hospital /hɒspɪtl/ **hospitals**
NCorNU A **hospital** is a place where sick and injured people are looked after by doctors and nurses. *They were taken to hospital but neither is said to be seriously injured... Two others are still in hospital, one of them in a serious condition... There is a lack of transport for staff to get to the hospitals.*

hospitality /hɒspɪtælɪti/
1 NU **Hospitality** is friendly, welcoming behaviour towards guests or strangers. *I thanked him for his hospitality... We were delighted with the friendliness and hospitality of these simple people. ...a call to all Kenyans to accord hospitality to the fleeing Somali nationals.*
2 NU **Hospitality** is also the food, drink, and other privileges which large organizations provide for their visitors or clients. *He described the embarrassingly lavish hospitality the Koreans had laid on... Hospitality at the President's guest house was graciously declined... Some of the teams travel in a hospitality coach.* ● See also **corporate hospitality**.

hospitalize /hɒspɪtəlaɪz/ **hospitalizes, hospitalizing, hospitalized**; also spelt **hospitalise**.
VO If someone is **hospitalized**, they are sent to hospital. *She contracted pneumonia and had to be hospitalized.* ◆ **hospitalization** /hɒspɪtəlaɪzeɪʃn/ NU *Psychiatrists play safe and opt for hospitalization.*

host /həʊst/ **hosts, hosting, hosted**
1 NC The **host** in a house or at a party is the person who has invited the guests. *She will today be holding talks with her host, President Moi.*
2 N+N A **host** country provides the facilities for an event, or gives people from another country a place to live. *The host country won more than half the gold medals in the Games... There are now more than thirteen million refugees in the world, which has placed enormous burdens on host countries.*
3 VO If a place or a country **hosts** an event, it is held there and all the facilities are supplied by that place or country. *The World Cup takes place every four years and there's always stiff competition to host it... The United States will host the two Grand Prix meets... In four weeks time, Nigeria is hosting the OAU summit.*
4 N SING A **host** of things is a lot of them; a formal use. *...Lesotho, Swaziland, Botswana and a host of other African countries... This conjures up a host of ideas for the future.*
5 NC A **host** is also an animal or plant that has smaller animals, often insects, living and feeding on it. *Like most parasitic diseases, it doesn't kill its host.*
6 NC The **host** of a radio or television show is the person who introduces it and talks to the people taking part. *...a former radio chat show host... A smooth, suave television show host, he shows an unusual grasp of facts and figures.* ► Also VO *The entertainment part of the programme was hosted by Roger Moore.*
7 If a person or country **plays host** to other people or countries, they receive them as guests, usually for a special event. *Agatha Christie's hometown, Torquay, plays host to the annual Crime Writers' Conference.*

hostage /hɒstɪdʒ/ **hostages**
NC A **hostage** is someone who has been captured by a person or organization and who may be killed or injured if people do not do what the person or organization wants. *There are twenty-five hostages in the TV station held by about fifty gunmen.*
● **Hostage** is used in these phrases. ● If someone is **taken hostage** or is **held hostage**, they are captured and kept as a hostage. *Some passengers and the driver escaped—the rest were taken hostage... They are being held hostage until our demands are met.*
● If you are a **hostage to** something, or are **hostage to** it, you are prevented from changing your plans because of previous arrangements or promises you have made. *He did not want to become a hostage to his own promises... They wanted to demonstrate that they were no longer hostage to the ANC's confused agenda... It is uncertain whether he will be running the KGB, or will become hostage to it.*

host computer, host computers
NC A **host computer** is a computer whose programs

and data are available to be used by other computers that are connected to it.

hostel /hɒstl/ **hostels**
1 NC A **hostel** is a house owned by local government authorities or charities where people can stay cheaply for a short time. *...a hostel for the homeless in London... They may find hostel accommodation but only a few move on to more permanent housing.*
2 NC A **hostel** is also the same as a **youth hostel**. *They're heading for a hot shower and a mattress at a hostel known as 'The Place'.*

hostess /hǝustɪs/ **hostesses**
1 NC The **hostess** at a party is the woman who has invited the guests. *My favorite part of breakfast is when the hostess offers us champagne.*
2 See also **air hostess**.

hostile /hɒstaɪl/
1 ADJ If you are **hostile** to someone or something, you disagree with them or disapprove of them. *Employers are adopting an increasingly hostile approach towards unions... The Prime Minister was confronted by hostile elements in the crowd.*
2 ADJ A **hostile** person is unfriendly and aggressive. *Frank was a reserved, almost hostile person... I was in a depressed and hostile mood.*
3 ADJ **Hostile** situations and conditions make it difficult for you to achieve something. *...hostile weather. ...the problem of running machinery in hostile environments.*

hostility /hɒstɪlǝti/ **hostilities**
1 N PL You can refer to fighting between two countries or groups as **hostilities**; a formal use. *They agreed to cease hostilities while negotiations were in progress... He said his country might also set up a military field hospital if hostilities broke out.*
2 NU **Hostility** is unfriendly and aggressive behaviour. *Their friendship is regarded with suspicion and hostility... Correspondents believe the attack was prompted by hostility to foreigners.*
3 NU **Hostility** is also opposition to something you do not approve of. *American spokesmen made clear their hostility to the new proposals.*

hot /hɒt/ **hotter, hottest; hots, hotting, hotted**
1 ADJ If something is **hot**, it has a high temperature. *The metal is so hot I can't touch it... The hot, sunny weather has continued over many parts of Britain today... Many people in the capital waited for hours in the hot sun... Yesterday was the hottest May day in Britain since records began.*
2 ADJ ATTRIB A **hot** issue or topic is one that is currently very important and that is receiving a lot of publicity. *Education has become a hot election issue in Britain... The control of growth is currently a hot topic in biology.*
3 ADJ PRED If you are **hot**, your body is at an unpleasantly high temperature. *Hot and perspiring, John toiled up the hill... The British doctors therefore suggest that parents should feel their babies to see if they are hot.*
4 ADJ ATTRIB **Hot** food has been cooked and should be eaten before it becomes cold. *Free milk and hot meals are being handed out... Sometimes it's only bread and cheese; more often there are hot dishes.*
5 ADJ **Hot** food can also mean food that has a strong burning taste caused by spices. *...hot curries. ...hot chilli pepper sauces.*
6 ADJ ATTRIB The **hot** favourite is the person or team that people consider most likely to win a race or competition. *The West German team is a hot favourite.*
7 ADJ PRED If someone is **hot** on something, they know a lot about it; an informal use. *I'm not so hot on linguistic theory.*
8 ADJ Someone with a **hot** temper gets angry very easily. *...the maestro's notoriously hot temper.*
9 See also **hot air, hot dog, hot flush, hot line, hot potato, hot seat, hot spot, hot stuff.**

hot up PHRASAL VERB If a situation **hots up**, it becomes more tense and more activity takes place. *The drugs war is likely to hot up still further in the next few months... Poland's presidential campaign is hotting up.*

hot air
NU **Hot air** means speeches that are made mainly to impress people rather than be accurate; an informal expression, used showing disapproval. *His speech was just hot air. ...innumerable explosions of hot air from the opposition parties.*

hot-air balloon, hot-air balloons
NC A **hot-air balloon** is a large balloon with a basket hanging from it in which people can travel. *...spectacular stunts like flying a hot-air balloon across the Atlantic.*

hotbed /hɒtbed/ **hotbeds**
NC+*of* If you say that a place is a **hotbed** of a particular kind of an activity, usually one that you do not approve of, you mean that a lot of this activity happens there. *The universities are hotbeds of intrigue... They would become a hotbed of terrorism.*

hot-blooded /hɒtblʌdɪd/
ADJ Someone who is **hot-blooded** quickly and easily expresses their feelings, especially those of anger or love. *For some reason, Charleston, the first state to secede, had more hot-blooded people than any of the others... The kings were either hot-blooded lechers or men who knew nothing but restraint.*

hotchpotch /hɒtʃpɒtʃ/
N SING A **hotchpotch** is a disorderly mixture of different types of things; an informal word. *...a hotchpotch of uncoordinated schemes.*

hot dog, hot dogs
NC A **hot dog** is a long bread roll with a sausage in it. *The smell of peanuts, hot dogs and fresh cut grass is in the air. ...a hot dog stall.*

hotel /hǝutel/ **hotels**
NC A **hotel** is a building where people stay, for example when they are on holiday, and pay for their rooms and meals. *They are insisting on accommodation in a luxury hotel in the centre of the city.*

hotelier /hǝutelɪǝ, hǝutelɪeɪ/ **hoteliers**
NC A **hotelier** is a person who owns or manages a hotel. *He is constantly receiving complaints from hoteliers.*

hot flush, hot flushes
NC A **hot flush** is a sudden hot feeling in the skin which women often experience at the time of their menopause. *The problem is that it makes you menopausal sometimes, with all the problems of hot flushes and weak bones.*

hotfoot /hɒtfʊt/
ADV If someone goes somewhere **hotfoot**, they go there quickly and eagerly; an informal word. *...the kindly doctor goes hotfoot to the rescue of suffering mankind.*

hothead /hɒthed/ **hotheads**
NC A **hothead** is someone who does things hastily and without thinking what the consequences will be; used showing disapproval. *He was regarded as a hothead, a man whose career could be blunted by his rashness. ...I hope you're not a hothead like your brother.*

hot-headed /hɒthedɪd/
ADJ Someone who is **hot-headed** acts hastily and without thinking what the consequences will be. *He criticised his deputy as a hot-headed youth.*

hothouse /hɒthaʊs/ **hothouses**
1 NC A **hothouse** is a heated glass building in which plants and flowers grow. *Florists say supplies have been held up because the recent windy weather damaged hothouses in Holland.*
2 NC A **hothouse** is a place where there is a lot of intense intellectual or emotional activity. *Belgrade, previously a hothouse of cultural pluralism and dissent, now stands firmly behind the party line... In a closed situation, it's easy for the hothouse atmosphere to boil over.*

hot line, hot lines
1 NC A **hot line** is a direct telephone line between heads of government for use in an emergency. *He used the Washington-Moscow hot line to put the suggestion to Mr Gorbachev.*
2 NC A **hot line** is also a telephone line that the public can use to contact the police or other services with information about a particular situation. *The police are asking witnesses to contact them on a special hot*

line... Anti-corruption hot lines at reporting centres
have been set up.

hotly /hɒtli/
ADV If people discuss, argue, or say something **hotly**,
they speak in a lively or angry way, because they feel
strongly. *The issue has been hotly debated at two
consecutive meetings... The television companies hotly
deny that they are on the side of terrorism.*

hot-plate, hot-plates
NC A **hot-plate** is a flat surface, often on a cooker,
which is heated by electricity and which you can cook
food on. *All he owns in this world is a few pans, a
hot-plate, and his personal papers.*

hotpot /hɒtpɒt/ **hotpots**
NCorNU A **hotpot** is a dish made from a mixture of
meat, vegetables, and gravy with sliced potatoes on
top, which is cooked slowly in the oven. *They serve
one of London's greatest dishes, hotpot of eel, belly
pork and garlic.*

hot potato, hot potatoes; an informal expression.
NC A problem or issue that is a **hot potato** is a very
difficult or awkward one that nobody wants to deal
with. *The issue has become a domestic hot potato...
Base closures have been a political hot potato, leading
as they do to the loss of hundreds of civilian jobs.* • If
you **drop** a person or a project **like a hot potato**, you
suddenly stop being involved with them. *She dropped
him like a hot potato when she found out.*

hot seat
Someone who is **in the hot seat** is in a position in
which they have to make very important decisions; an
informal expression. *It's certainly going to be a hot
seat for anyone who gets it... Looking back on his time
in the hot seat, he was philosophical.*

hot spot, hot spots; used in informal English.
1 NC A **hot spot** is an exciting place where there is a
lot of activity or entertainment. *...Birmingham's
fashionable hot spots.*
2 NC A **hot spot** is also an area where there is some
form of trouble such as fighting or political unrest.
*The situation along the Thai-Cambodian border, for
years one of the hot spots of the conflict, is now
relatively quiet. ...towns and cities which have been
identified as election hot spots by the authorities.*

hot stuff; an informal expression.
1 NU If you think someone is **hot stuff**, you find them
exciting and attractive, especially sexually. *We stood
there pretending to be hot stuff.*
2 NU An activity that is **hot stuff** is very popular.
Skateboarding is hot stuff in East Anglia.

hot-water bottle, hot-water bottles
NC A **hot-water bottle** is a rubber container which you
fill with hot water and use to warm a bed. *Apply
gentle external heat with things like hot-water bottles.*

hot-wire, hot-wires, hot-wiring, hot-wired
VO If someone **hot-wires** a car, they start the engine
without using the key, usually in order to steal the
car. *Some of the GIs were taught how to hot-wire a
car... A good thief can force open a car door and hot-
wire the ignition in less than a minute.*

hound /haʊnd/ **hounds, hounding, hounded**
1 NC A **hound** is a type of dog used for hunting or
racing. *...large packs of hounds.*
2 VO If someone **hounds** you, they constantly disturb
you or criticize you. *He was hounded by the press.*

Houphouët-Boigny, Dr Félix
/feɪliːks uɪfwet bwænji/
Dr Félix **Houphouët-Boigny** became Premier of Côte
d'Ivoire in 1959 and President in 1960. He was a
member of the French Assembly from 1946 to 1959 and
served in the French cabinet from 1957 to 1960. He
became President of the Democratic African
Assembly, now called the Democratic Party of Côte
d'Ivoire (PDCI), in 1959. Born: 1905.

hour /aʊə/ **hours**
1 NC An **hour** is a period of sixty minutes. *They slept
for two hours... Miners have begun a series of twenty-
four hour strikes. ...speaking in a BBC interview
within the last hour... The road has a speed limit of
sixty miles per hour.*
2 N PL You can refer to the period of time that
something happens each day as the **hours** that it

happens. *...our demands for shorter working hours.*
3 NC+SUPP You can refer to a particular time in the
day as a particular **hour**. *There was little traffic at
this hour... He began teaching at nine o' clock in the
morning, an unearthly hour for most students.*
• **Hour** is used in these phrases. • Something that
happens **on the hour** happens at one o'clock, at two
o'clock, and so on at regular intervals of one hour.
Buses for London leave on the hour. • If something
happens in the **early hours** or in the **small hours**, it
happens in the early morning after midnight. *He was
taken from his home in the early hours of the
morning... The noise kept him awake until the small
hours.* • See also **eleventh hour, rush-hour.**

hourglass /aʊəglɑːs/ **hourglasses**
NC An **hourglass** is a device that is used to measure
an hour of time. It has two linked glass sections, and
sand flows slowly from the top one into the lower one,
taking an hour to do so. *Going through the black hole
will be a little bit like sand going through an
hourglass.*

hour hand, hour hands
NC The **hour hand** on a clock or watch is the hand that
points to the number of hours that have passed since
twelve o'clock.

hourly /aʊəli/
1 ADJ ATTRIB An **hourly** event happens once every
hour. *It was run as one of the later items in a regular
hourly bulletin... There were hourly hook-ups with
Mission Control.* ▶ Also ADV *The ground rules change
daily and sometimes hourly.*
2 ADJ ATTRIB Your **hourly** earnings are the amount of
money that you earn each hour. *The strikers are
demanding increases in hourly wages... Up until now,
barristers have been forbidden from advertising their
hourly rates.*

house, houses, housing, housed. The noun is
pronounced /haʊs/ in the singular and /haʊzɪz/ in the
plural. The verb is pronounced /haʊz/.
1 NC A **house** is a building in which people live. *He
has a house in Pimlico... Details such as whether the
house is damp or mouldy or has fitted carpets will also
be recorded.*
2 NC A building which is used for a special purpose
such as an office, business, theatre, and so on is
referred to as a **House**, often as part of its name. *The
opera house quickly fell into disrepair... Here at Bush
House, senior management has reacted with delight
and surprise at the news... House of Fraser stores
nationwide are selling a wide range of Christmas
tableware.*
3 NC+SUPP A **house** is also a company, especially one
which publishes books, lends money, or designs
clothes. *...a University Publishing House.*
4 NC A country's parliament or one section of it is
often referred to as a **House**; a formal use. *The
Canadian government is headed towards crisis in the
non-elected Upper House or Senate. ...twenty-two
members drawn from both Houses. ...the House of
Representatives.*
5 NC In a theatre or cinema, the **house** is the part
where the audience sits. *We stood at the back of the
packed house.*
6 If you are given something in a restaurant **on the
house**, you do not have to pay for it.
7 VO When someone is **housed**, they are provided with
a house or flat. *They are better housed than ever
before. ...rows and rows of small back to back homes
built in the 1800s to house workers.*
8 VO If a building **houses** something, that thing is kept
in the building; a formal use. *This is the building
which houses the library.*
9 NC A **house** is also a group of children of different
ages in a school who compete against other groups in
sports and other activities. Each house usually has a
name. *Our house won the prize for the best exam
results.*
10 See also **boarding house, public house.**

house arrest
NU If someone is put under **house arrest**, they are not
allowed to leave their house. This is a form of
punishment in some countries. *He was placed under*

house arrest in October last year. ...years of jail, house arrest and exile.

houseboat /ˈhaʊsbəʊt/ **houseboats**
NC A **houseboat** is a small boat on a river or canal which people live in. *This is at a point on the River Wye where people are living on houseboats.*

housebound /ˈhaʊsbaʊnd/
ADJ Someone who is **housebound** is unable to leave their house because they are ill or old. *He told the court that he had been housebound without his specially adapted car.*

houseboy /ˈhaʊsbɔɪ/ **houseboys**
NC A **houseboy** is a man or boy who cleans and does other jobs in someone else's house; an old-fashioned word. *Most of them are employed as low paid plantation workers or houseboys with little social security.*

housebreaker /ˈhaʊsbreɪkə/ **housebreakers**
NC A **housebreaker** is someone who enters another person's house, for example by breaking the locks or windows, in order to steal their possessions. *He described the former police chief as a self-confessed killer, housebreaker, and liar.*

housebreaking /ˈhaʊsbreɪkɪŋ/
NU **Housebreaking** is the crime of entering another person's house, for example by breaking the locks or windows, in order to steal their possessions. *He was arrested by the police on charges of housebreaking... The country was experiencing a high rate of armed robbery, housebreaking, and car theft.*

housecoat /ˈhaʊskəʊt/ **housecoats**
NC A **housecoat** is a long loose coat that some women wear during the day when they are in their house. *The company makes nightdresses and housecoats for customers throughout Europe and the Middle East.*

housefather /ˈhaʊsfɑːðə/ **housefathers**
NC A **housefather** is a man who looks after a particular group of children in an institution such as a children's home.

houseful /ˈhaʊsfʊl/ **housefuls**
N SING A **houseful** of people or things is a number of them all together in one house, which makes the house very full. *A houseful of children is easier than dealing with one lazy husband... You've got quite a houseful.*

house guest, house guests
NC A **house guest** is a person who is staying at someone's house for a period of time. *He was her house guest in Paris.*

household /ˈhaʊshəʊld/ **households**
1 NC A **household** consists of all the people in a family or group who live together in a house. *He loved being part of a huge household... Only 8 per cent of households owned a fridge.*
2 N SING The **household** is your home and everything connected with looking after it. *My daughter managed the entire household... A total of 142 products are now being rationed, varying from bread to clothes to household appliances.*

householder /ˈhaʊshəʊldə/ **householders**
NC A **householder** is the legal owner or tenant of a house. *Two thirds of householders own their homes... The government has appealed to industry and householders to make greater efforts to conserve water.*

household name, household names
NC Someone or something that is a **household name** is very well known and often talked about. *Why are so few black comedians household names in Britain?*

housekeeper /ˈhaʊskiːpə/ **housekeepers**
NC A **housekeeper** is a person employed to cook and clean a house for its owner. *The cat is now being cared for by Mrs Walker's housekeeper.*

housekeeping /ˈhaʊskiːpɪŋ/
1 NU **Housekeeping** is the work and organization involved in running a home. *Women were also responsible for the housekeeping.*
2 NU The **housekeeping** is the money that you use each week to buy food, cleaning materials, and other things for your home; an informal use. *She spent all the housekeeping on a new coat.*

housemaid /ˈhaʊsmeɪd/ **housemaids**
NC A **housemaid** is a female servant who cleans and

does other work in someone else's house; an old-fashioned word. *His domestic staff consisted of three cooks, three waitresses, a housemaid and a gardener.*

houseman /ˈhaʊsmən/ **housemen** /ˈhaʊsmən/
NC A **houseman** is a doctor who has a junior post in a hospital. *She is assisted by housemen, nurses, and consultants.*

house martin, house martins
NC A **house martin** is a small black and white bird with a forked tail. *House martins are building their mud nests under the eaves of houses.*

housemaster /ˈhaʊsmɑːstə/ **housemasters**
NC A **housemaster** is a male teacher who is in charge of one of the houses in a school. *The housemaster was in charge of approximately fifty boys in one house.*

housemistress /ˈhaʊsmɪstrəs/ **housemistresses**
NC A **housemistress** is a female teacher who is in charge of one of the houses in a school.

housemother /ˈhaʊsmʌðə/ **housemothers**
NC A **housemother** is a woman who looks after a particular group of children in an institution such as a children's home.

House of Commons
1 N PROP The **House of Commons** is the more powerful of the two parts of parliament in Britain or Canada. Members of Parliament are elected to the House of Commons by the adult population of the country. *He made his statement to the House of Commons on April 30... One week later the House of Commons debated the entire business.*
2 N PROP You can also refer to the building where Members of Parliament meet as the **House of Commons**. *Look over the road on your left to the House of Commons.*

house of God, houses of God
NC A Christian church or chapel is sometimes referred to as a **house of God**. *They supported measures taken to preserve the security of pilgrims in the house of God.*

House of Lords
1 N PROP The **House of Lords** is the less powerful of the two parts of parliament in Britain. Its members have the right of office because they come from noble families or are appointed by the government. *...the campaign for the abolition of the House of Lords. ...Archbishops and Bishops, of whom twenty-four sit in the House of Lords.*
2 N PROP You can also refer to the building where the Lords meet as the **House of Lords**. *Beyond this, as ante-room to the actual House of Lords, is the Prince's chamber.*

House of Representatives
N PROP The **House of Representatives** is the less powerful of the two parts of Congress in the United States, or the equivalent part of the system of government in some other countries. *Last week the House of Representatives approved a $136 billion order.*

house-party, house-parties
NC A **house-party** is a party held at a big house in the country, usually at a weekend, where the guests stay for a few days. *Shelley, Byron and Dr John Polidori all attended the house-party at the Villa Diodati on the shores of Lake Geneva.*

houseplant /ˈhaʊsplɑːnt/ **houseplants**
NC A **houseplant** is a plant which grows in a pot indoors. *It has numerous uses in growing and caring for houseplants, shrubs and cuttings.*

houseproud /ˈhaʊspraʊd/
ADJ A **houseproud** person spends a lot of time cleaning and decorating their house, because they want other people to admire it. *People who are houseproud will be appalled to find out they are providing a comfortable home for millions of mites and bacteria.*

houseroom /ˈhaʊsruːm, ˈhaʊsrʊm/
If you say that you **wouldn't give** something **houseroom**, you mean that you dislike it and would not want to consider it; an informal expression. *He knew the smarter shops just wouldn't give him houseroom.*

house servant, house servants
NC A **house servant** is a person who works in someone else's house and does their cooking and cleaning; an

old-fashioned expression.

Houses of Parliament
1 N PROP In Britain, the **Houses of Parliament** are the British parliament which consists of two parts, the House of Commons and the House of Lords. *The measure will have to go to the Houses of Parliament.*
2 N PROP You can also refer to the buildings in London where each part of the British parliament does its work as the **Houses of Parliament**. *The road leads to the Houses of Parliament.*

house-to-house
ADJ ATTRIB If the police carry out a **house-to-house** search, they search all the houses in an area. *Troops have surrounded local villages and conducted house-to-house searches... Police said it was useless to continue after fruitless house-to-house enquiries.*

housetrain /ˈhaʊstreɪn/ **housetrains, housetraining, housetrained**
VO If you **housetrain** a pet animal, you teach it to urinate and defecate out of doors or in a special container indoors, rather than on the floor indoors. *Housetrain your puppy by saying 'no' in a firm voice.* ◆ **housetrained** ADJ *Are the kittens housetrained?*

house-warming, house-warmings
NC A **house-warming** is a party that you give for friends when you have just moved into a new house. *When's the house-warming going to be?*

housewife /ˈhaʊswaɪf/ **housewives**
NC A **housewife** is a married woman who does not have a job outside her home. *They describe themselves as workers, students and housewives... She grumbles about prices like any ordinary housewife.*

housework /ˈhaʊswɜːk/
NU **Housework** is the work such as cleaning and cooking that you do in your home. *The men shared all the housework.*

housing /ˈhaʊzɪŋ/
1 NU **Housing** is the buildings that people live in. *Employment, housing, food and transport are all posing problems for the local population... Housing is just not affordable.*
2 NCorN+N **Housing** is also the job of providing houses for people to live in. *...the housing department.*

housing association, housing associations
NC A **housing association** is an organization which owns houses and helps its members to rent or buy them more cheaply than usual. *Ms West has formed a housing association to build homes for single mothers.*

housing development, housing developments
NC A **housing development** is an area of new houses or accommodation. *They live in a housing development for poor families.*

housing estate, housing estates
NC A **housing estate** is a large number of houses or flats built close together at the same time. *...a row of shops on a housing estate... The incident happened on a housing estate in the town.*

housing project, housing projects
NC A **housing project** is the same as a **housing estate**; used in American English. *...East Lake Meadows, a housing project in southeast Atlanta. ...tenants from housing projects.*

hovel /ˈhɒvl, ˈhʌvl/ **hovels**
NC A **hovel** is a small, dirty hut or house that people live in and that is in bad condition. *They lived in overcrowded hovels.*

hover /ˈhɒvə/ **hovers, hovering, hovered**
1 V When a bird, insect, or aircraft **hovers**, it stays in the same position in the air. *The Harrier can hover and even fly backwards, more or less like a helicopter... A police helicopter hovered overhead.*
2 V If someone is **hovering**, they are hesitating about doing something because they cannot make a decision. *A figure hovered uncertainly in the doorway... We hovered between the two possibilities.*

hovercraft /ˈhɒvəkrɑːft/ **hovercrafts.** The plural form can be either **hovercrafts** or **hovercraft**.
NC A **hovercraft** is a vehicle that travels across water by floating on a cushion of air. *A number of cross-Channel and Irish Sea ferry and hovercraft services aren't operating this morning.*

how /haʊ, haʊ/
1 ADVorCONJ You use **how** to ask about or refer to the way in which something is done. *How have you been treated out there?... They must be allowed to choose how to protect their own health... Lesley Kerwin looks at how the world's financial markets reacted.*
2 ADV You can use **how** to refer to the extent to which something is true. *He was asked how serious the situation has become... They certainly knew how dangerous the area could be... How fair and free will the election be?*
3 ADV You can use **how** at the beginning of a clause to introduce a statement or fact. *It's amazing how he survived to 94... We are all aware of how an odour or sound can bring back happy memories.*
4 ADV You use **how** to ask about or refer to a measurement, amount, or quantity. *How many languages do you speak?... How many people do you think they have in London, operating at the moment?... The Administration hasn't said how much it will be asking Congress to provide... The depth of the recession will depend on how long the crisis lasts.*
5 ADV You use **how** in questions when you are asking someone whether something was successful or enjoyable. *How did school go?... How was Paris?*
6 ADV You also use **how** to ask about or refer to someone's health. *'How are you?'—'Fine, thanks.'... I'm going to see how Davis is.*
7 ADV You can use **how** in exclamations to emphasize an adjective, adverb, or statement. *How pretty you look!... How I dislike that man!... How I love those joke drawings.*
● **How** is used in these phrases. ● You can say **How about you?** when you are asking someone their opinion. *How about you, Dorothy, what do you want?* ● You can say **how about** something or **how would you like** something when you are making an offer or suggestion. *If there isn't a playgroup locally, how about starting one?... How would you fancy a few months on the continent?*

howdah /ˈhaʊdə/ **howdahs**
NC A **howdah** is a seat that is put on an elephant's back for people to ride on it. *...plodding elephants draped in brocade and carrying silver howdahs full of bejewelled guests.*

howdy /ˈhaʊdi/
Howdy is an informal way of saying 'Hello'; used in American English. *'Howdy, Jefferson,' he said.*

however /haʊˈevə/
1 ADV SEN You use **however** when you are adding a comment which contrasts with what has just been said. *They disagreed about much; they agreed, however, about more... The doctors warn however, that the treatment would have to continue for life... However a police spokesman said the man was not being held.*
2 ADV You can use **however** before an adjective or adverb to emphasize that the degree or extent of something cannot change a situation. *For the victim of an inaccurate newspaper story, however damaging it may be, there is really no adequate redress... There is no doubt that progress, however faltering, is being made.*
3 You use **however many** or **however much** after 'or' at the beginning of a clause to indicate that you do not know the exact quantity or size of something, and that it is not important; an informal use. *...the twelve or eleven people on the jury or however many there are.*

howl /haʊl/ **howls, howling, howled**
1 V If a wolf or a dog **howls**, it utters a long, loud crying sound. *Jackals howled among the ruins... Traditional signs of an earthquake include dogs howling, and horses refusing to enter their stables.*
2 V If a person **howls**, they make a long, loud cry, expressing pain, anger, or unhappiness. *I put back my head and howled... He howled at the top of his lungs about the inherent racism of not having been given the award.* ▶ Also NC *...a howl of pain... She let out a bit of a howl when he put her finger in the basin of water... Changes to the constitution would raise howls of protest from the opposition.*
3 V When the wind **howls**, it blows hard and makes a

loud noise. *The wind's howling and it's 20 below zero.*
◆ **howling** ADJ ATTRIB *Six inches of snow fell last night
in a howling blizzard... We were sitting in a howling
draught.*
4 v If you **howl** with laughter, you laugh very loudly.
*Every man in the audience was howling as Steve
did his act... You may laugh, but the Republicans
howled when they heard it.*
howl down PHRASAL VERB If people **howl** you **down**,
they shout loudly to stop you speaking. *He was howled
down by monarchists... Two years ago, these proposals
would have been howled down.*
howler /haʊlə/ **howlers**
NC A **howler** is a stupid, but often funny, mistake; an
informal word. *He made such awful howlers that even
the teacher laughed... His advisors urged him to say
as little as possible, fearful that he would only make
more howlers.*
howling /haʊlɪŋ/
ADJ ATTRIB A **howling** success is an extremely great
success. *Her new play was a howling success.*
Hoyte, Hugh Desmond /hjuː dezmənd hɔɪt/
Hugh Desmond Hoyte became President of Guyana in
1985. He was elected MP in 1968. He served as
Minister of Home Affairs from 1969 to 1971, of Finance
from 1971 to 1972, of Works and Communications from
1972 to 1975, and of Economic Development from 1975
to 1981. He was Vice President from 1981 to 1984, and
Prime Minister from 1984 to 1985. He became leader of
the People's National Congress (PNC) in 1985. Born:
1929.
HP /eɪtʃpiː/
HP is an abbreviation for 'hire purchase'. *Buy an
electric typewriter on HP as soon as you can afford it.*
HQ /eɪtʃkjuː/ **HQs**
NC HQ is an abbreviation for 'headquarters'. *Panther
1 to HQ, we're heading eastbound on Christopher
Street.*
hr, hrs
hr is a written abbreviation for 'hour'. *He won the
Cardiff run in 2hrs 26mins 4secs.*
Hrawi, Elias /ɪljæs hrɑːwi/
Elias Hrawi became President of Lebanon in 1989,
following the assassination of René Mouawad. He is a
Maronite, and served as Minister of Public Works and
Transport from 1980 to 1982. Born: 1930.
HRH
HRH is a written abbreviation for 'His Royal
Highness' or 'Her Royal Highness'. HRH is used as
part of the title of a prince or princess. *...HRH Prince
Charles.*
hub /hʌb/ **hubs**
1 NC+*of* If you describe a place as the **hub** of a
district, you mean that it is the most important or
exciting part. *It's the business hub of the area...
Illinois is at the hub of American business and politics.*
2 NC The **hub** of a wheel is the part at the centre.
Attach your lamp to the hub and spin the wheel.
hubbub /hʌbʌb/
1 N SING A **hubbub** is a noise made by a lot of people
all talking or shouting at the same time. *There was
an increasing hubbub from the great reception hall
below... It was easy to talk on and on amid that
hubbub of voices.*
2 N SING A **hubbub** is also great confusion or
excitement that is created in a particular situation.
*He would have been pardoned long ago if it had not
been for the hubbub created by the newspapers.*
hubby /hʌbi/ **hubbies**
NC+POSS A woman can refer to her husband as her
hubby; an informal word. *I can't wait to get home
and tell my hubby about it!*
hubcap /hʌbkæp/ **hubcaps**
NC A **hubcap** is a metal disc that covers and protects
the hub of a wheel on motor vehicles. *Remove the
hubcap and loosen the nuts with a spanner.*
hubris /hjuːbrɪs/
NU **Hubris** is arrogant pride; a formal word. *Filled
with entrepreneurial hubris, they bought a brewery six
times larger than their original plans... We have to be
careful of hubris. We cannot be overconfident.*

huckster /hʌkstə/ **hucksters**
NC A **huckster** is someone who sells small, cheap
things in the street or at the doors of houses; used in
American English. *...Senegalese hucksters with their
fake silver jewellery... The idea of curing baldness
with 'hair restorer' has long been associated with
quacks and hucksters.*
huddle /hʌdl/ **huddles, huddling, huddled**
1 V A If you **huddle** somewhere, you sit, stand, or lie
there holding your arms and legs close to your body,
because you are cold or frightened. *She huddled
among the untidy bedclothes... Outside the building,
thousands huddled under plastic sheeting to listen to
live broadcasts of the speech... Huddled in bars and
tearooms, the fans watched the screens anxiously.*
◆ **huddled** ADJ *In the evening he would sit huddled
near the stove... We drove past the huddled survivors
to the Zacamil district.*
2 NC A **huddle** of people or things is a small group
standing or sitting close together. *They flopped down
in a huddle. ...a huddle of huts.*
hue /hjuː/ **hues**
NC A **hue** is a colour; a literary word. *Mrs
Partridge's face took on a deeper hue.*
huff /hʌf/
1 If someone is **in a huff**, they are behaving in a bad-
tempered way because they are annoyed or offended;
an informal expression. *The people all left in a huff.*
2 If you **huff and puff** about something, you express
your anger, annoyance, or dissatisfaction with it. *In
the past, no-one has ever believed them when they
have huffed and puffed, and threatened this and that.*
huffy /hʌfi/ **huffier, huffiest**
ADJ Someone who is **huffy** is obviously annoyed or
offended about something; an informal word. *He
became huffy and said he'd scrap the whole idea.*
◆ **huffily** ADV *Arthur rose huffily and left.*
hug /hʌg/ **hugs, hugging, hugged**
1 V-RECIP When you **hug** someone, you put your arms
around them and hold them tightly because you like
them or are pleased to see them. *During our infancy,
our parents cuddle and hug us... In an instant we were
hugging and kissing... They hugged each other when
they met this morning... When she found her daddy,
she just hugged and hugged him.* ► Also NC *He
greeted his mother with a hug... I only want to give
you a big hug and a kiss.*
2 VO If you **hug** something, you hold it close to your
body with your arms tightly round it. *...a basket
which she hugged tight on her lap... He hugged the
trunk of a palm tree all night during the hurricane.*
3 VO Something that **hugs** the ground or a stretch of
land or water stays very close to it. *...the wide
boulevard that hugs the Algiers coastline... A dark
storm cloud hugs mountaintops in the distance... The
usual policy, of flying fast and hugging the ground, will
be dropped... The coastguard plane spotted the fishing
vessel suspiciously hugging the coastline.*
huge /hjuːdʒ/
ADJ Something that is **huge** is extremely large in size,
amount, or degree. *Mr Singh has been drawing huge
crowds in the Hindi-speaking states... Some lost huge
sums of money as share prices plunged.* ◆ **hugely**
ADV *He enjoyed a hugely successful career in
management... Gardener was enjoying himself hugely.*
huh /hʌ, hʌ/
Some people say '**huh?**' at the end of a question; used
in informal spoken American English. *'You been
away, huh?'—'Yes,' I said.*
hula hoop /huːlə huːp/ **hula hoops**
NC A **hula hoop** is a large hoop that children play with
by putting it around their waist and moving their
waist and hips so that the hoop spins quickly around
their waist. *...hula hoops used by the disabled
children.*
hulk /hʌlk/ **hulks**
NC You can refer to something or someone that is
large and heavy as a **hulk**. *The Abbey is a great
cross-shaped, blackish hulk... He disappeared while
investigating the hulk of the ship in Scapa Flow.*
hulking /hʌlkɪŋ/
ADJ ATTRIB A **hulking** person or object is extremely

large and heavy. *The path is channelled deep between hulking masonry on each side.*

hull /hʌl/ **hulls**

NC The **hull** of a boat or ship is the main part of its body. *Ships' hulls are traditionally made of steel plates cut and welded together.*

hullabaloo /hʌləbəluː/ **hullabaloos**

NC If you make a **hullabaloo**, you make a lot of noise or fuss about something; an old-fashioned word. *You can't imagine what a hullabaloo they've been making about it at College.*

hullo /hələʊ/. See **hello**.

hum /hʌm/ **hums, humming, hummed**

1 V If something **hums**, it makes a low continuous noise. *The air-conditioning hummed.* ▸ Also N SING *The only sound she heard was the hum of a machine in the basement.*

2 V or VO When you **hum**, you sing a tune with your lips closed. *I began to hum... She started humming the school song.* ● If you **hum and haw**, you take a long time to say something because you cannot think of the right words. *Spear hummed and hawed, trying to express himself.*

human /hjuːmən/ **humans**

1 ADJ **Human** means relating to or concerning people. *It is a thriller revealing the darker side of human nature. ...the human body. ...one of the most exciting periods in human history.*

2 ADJ If you call feelings, errors, or people **human**, you mean that they are, or have, weaknesses which are typical of people rather than machines. *I don't think there's any human error involved... The Prime Minister is human and her record is not perfect.*

3 NC You can refer to people as **humans** when you are comparing them with animals or machines. *Could a computer ever beat a human at chess?*

human being, human beings

NC A **human being** is a man, woman, or child. *This is the longest time any human being has spent in space... He was surprised that a human being could treat another in such a way.*

humane /hjuːmeɪn/

ADJ **Humane** behaviour or a **humane** person or society is considerate and respectful of people's and animals' rights. *He accused the government of ignoring international agreements on the humane treatment of prisoners... It has a duty to maintain order but in as humane a way as possible... He said that his government was determined to help in the creation of a more just and humane society. ...the fundamental issue of humane ways of killing whales.* ◆ **humanely** ADV *Animals must be killed humanely.*

humanise /hjuːmənaɪz/. See **humanize**.

humanism /hjuːmənɪzəm/

NU **Humanism** is the belief that people can achieve happiness and fulfilment without having a religion. *They have done away with the Socialist terminology, but have retained the philosophy of humanism.* ◆ **humanist, humanists** NC *...the humanist's belief in man.*

humanistic /hjuːmənɪstɪk/

ADJ A **humanistic** idea, condition, or system relates to humanism. *The vacuum left by religion has been filled by a kind of humanistic materialism. ...trying to build up a society based on humanistic values.*

humanitarian /hjuːmænəteərɪən/

ADJ If a person or society has **humanitarian** behaviour or attitudes, they try to avoid making people suffer. *It was decided to grant him political asylum on humanitarian grounds... It was described as a good and humanitarian solution to the problem... Amnesty International explained that its motives were purely humanitarian.*

humanitarianism /hjuːmænəteərɪənɪzəm/

NU **Humanitarianism** is the concern for the welfare of all people and desire to improve their lives. *They believed in some ideal of justice and humanitarianism in this often inhumane world.*

humanity /hjuːmænəti/ **humanities**

1 NU **Humanity** means all the people in the world. *...a crime against humanity... The greatest threat to the future of humanity comes from environmental*

degradation. *...one group of humans, isolated from the rest of humanity.*

2 NU **Humanity** is also the quality of being kind, thoughtful, and sympathetic. *...a man of remarkable humanity... All efforts to bring about more humanity and justice in society had come to nothing.*

3 NU A person's **humanity** is their state of being a human being, rather than an animal or an object; a formal use. *They denied him his humanity.*

4 N PL The **humanities** are subjects such as literature, philosophy, and history which are concerned with human ideas and behaviour. *She has a background in humanities and modern languages.*

humanize /hjuːmənaɪz/ **humanizes, humanizing, humanized**; also spelt **humanise**.

1 VO If you **humanize** a situation or condition, you improve it by changing it in a way which makes it more suitable and pleasant for people. *...the need to humanise the factory environment.* ◆ **humanization** /hjuːmənaɪzeɪʃn/ NU *...promoting work humanization in a number of key industries.*

2 VO If you **humanize** an animal or a machine, you give it human characteristics or qualities. *What he's done by putting them on stage is to humanize them.*

humankind /hjuːmənkaɪnd/

NU **Humankind** is the same as **mankind**. *This man was from the dregs of humankind.*

humanly /hjuːmənli/

If something is **humanly** possible, it is possible or reasonable for people to do it. *You were asked to reply within twenty-four hours whenever this was humanly possible.*

human nature

NU **Human nature** is the natural qualities and behaviour that most people have. *You can't change human nature... A love of rousing songs is part of human nature.*

humanoid /hjuːmənɔɪd/ **humanoids**

1 ADJ Something that is **humanoid** is not human but has the characteristics of a human being. *The doll has a twist-and-turn waist that makes her more humanoid than before.*

2 NC A **humanoid** is a robot, or a creature in science fiction, that looks and acts like a human being. *...life-like computer-controlled humanoids capable of moving their arms and legs.*

human race

N SING You can refer to the whole of mankind as the **human race**. *The future of the human race might now be at stake.*

human rights

N PL **Human rights** are the basic rights which all people should have. *...a violation of human rights.*

humble /hʌmbl/ **humbler, humblest**

1 ADJ A **humble** person is not proud and does not believe that they are better than other people. *In his victory speech, Mr Bush was both conciliatory and humble in his acknowledgement of the democratic process... Jim bore this with humble patience.* ◆ **humbly** ADV *'You know much more about it, Sir, than I do,' said John humbly.*

2 ADJ A **humble** thing or place is unpretentious and not special in any way. *The humble office plant can do more than just brighten the office, it cleans the air... The museum has on display objects which probably would not find a place anywhere else—the humble vacuum cleaner, for example, or the telephone.*

3 ADJ People with low social status are sometimes described as **humble**. *...men and women from very humble backgrounds... His humble origins have greatly influenced his political outlook.*

humbled /hʌmbld/

V-PASS If someone is **humbled**, they are defeated and made to feel inferior. *He was humbled in Stockholm 6-1, 6-4 by an obstinate Dan Goldie... The rebels were humbled and forced to accept a peaceful solution.*

humbug /hʌmbʌg/ **humbugs**

1 NC A **humbug** is a hard striped sweet that tastes of peppermint. *My sister was chewing her humbug very quietly.*

2 NU **Humbug** is speech or writing that is dishonest

and may be intended to deceive people.
*...parliamentary humbug... The British public can still
recognise humbug when they hear it.*

humdinger /hʌmdɪŋə/ **humdingers**
NC If you describe someone or something as a
humdinger, you mean that they are very good and you
are impressed by them; an informal word. *...a
humdinger of a show.*

humdrum /hʌmdrʌm/
ADJ Something that is **humdrum** is ordinary and dull.
*...their humdrum lives... Ministerial committees deal
with the more everyday, humdrum decisions... The
scandal promises to give spice to an otherwise
humdrum regional election.*

humerus /hju:mərəs/ **humeruses** or **humeri** /hju:mərai/
NC Your **humerus** is the bone between your shoulder
and your elbow; a medical term. *Among the
collection of bones, Bob found that the lower jaw bone
and the humerus were the most common.*

humid /hju:mɪd/
ADJ In **humid** places, the weather is hot and damp.
*...humid jungles... The disease is common in children
in the humid areas of West Africa.*

humidify /hju:mɪdɪfai/ **humidifies, humidifying,
humidified**
VO To **humidify** somewhere such as a room means to
release more water into the air and thus make it more
moist. *A small room is preferable as a sickroom
because you can humidify it more easily.*

humidity /hju:mɪdəti/
NU **Humidity** is dampness in the air. *...diseases and
weeds, encouraged by heat and humidity.*

humiliate /hju:mɪlieɪt/ **humiliates, humiliating,
humiliated**
VO If you **humiliate** someone, you say or do something
that makes them feel ashamed or foolish. *She had
humiliated him in front of his friends.* ◆ **humiliated**
ADJ *I could die. I feel so humiliated.*

humiliating /hju:mɪlieɪtɪŋ/
ADJ Something that is **humiliating** embarrasses you
and makes you feel ashamed and stupid. *He said it
was humiliating for him that his wife should go out to
work.* ◆ **humiliatingly** ADV *It is not certain that he is
yet ready to return to the city from which he was
humiliatingly expelled five years ago.*

humiliation /hju:mɪlieɪʃn/ **humiliations**
NU **Humiliation** is the experience of feeling helpless or
stupid, especially in front of other people. *The
prisoners suffered constant public humiliation... Use of
force as a means of punishment or humiliation was
against the law.*

humility /hju:mɪləti/
NU Someone who has **humility** is not proud and does
not believe that they are better than other people. *He
has sufficient humility to acknowledge his own
imperfections.*

hummingbird /hʌmɪŋbɜ:d/ **hummingbirds**
NC A **hummingbird** is a very small brightly coloured
bird with small powerful wings that make a humming
sound as they vibrate. *Why should the bumblebee and
the hummingbird differ from other insects, birds, and
indeed aeroplanes?*

humor /hju:mə/. See **humour**.

humorist /hju:mərist/ **humorists**
NC A **humorist** is writer who makes jokes or writes in
a humorous way. *He's been the most consistently
inventive humorist in the English language for the last
fifteen years. ...the humorist Miles Kington.*

humorous /hju:mərəs/
ADJ If someone or something is **humorous**, they are
amusing and witty. *...humorous books... The pupils
were imaginative, quick, and humorous.* ◆ **humorously**
ADV *They often humorously referred to themselves as
caretakers.*

humour /hju:mə/ **humours, humouring, humoured;**
spelt **humor** in American English.
1 NU **Humour** is the ability to see when something is
funny and to say amusing things. *He appealed to
them with his direct style and wry humour. ...a great
sense of humour... His sense of humour is intact, as is
his faith.*
2 NU If something has **humour**, it is funny and makes

you want to laugh. *She could appreciate the humour
of the remark... Even his serious films are punctuated
by humour.*
3 NU+SUPP If you are in a good **humour**, you feel
happy and cheerful. *The work was proceeding with
efficiency and good humour. ...an atmosphere of quiet
good humour.*
4 VO If you **humour** someone who is behaving
strangely, you try to please them or pretend to agree
with them, so that they will not become upset. *He had
bought it to humour Julie.*

humourless /hju:mələs/; spelt **humorless** in American
English.
ADJ Someone who is **humourless** is very serious and
does not find things amusing. *These people were
humourless and rude, and I'm furious.*

hump /hʌmp/ **humps, humping, humped**
1 NC A **hump** is a small hill or raised piece of ground.
...the humps and hollows of the old golf course.
2 NC A camel's **hump** is the large lump on its back.
The hump is full of fat and water.
3 VO If you **hump** something heavy somewhere, you
carry it there with difficulty; an informal use. *You
will probably have to hump your own luggage to the
airport.*

humpback /hʌmpbæk/ **humpbacks**
1 NC A **humpback** is the same as a **hunchback**; an
offensive word.
2 ADJ ATTRIB A **humpback** bridge is the same as a
humpbacked bridge.

humpbacked /hʌmpbækt/
1 ADJ ATTRIB A **humpbacked** animal has a hump on its
back. *...the humpbacked whale.*
2 ADJ ATTRIB A **humpbacked** bridge is a small bridge
which curves very steeply upwards. *To see the effect,
you have to stand on the humpbacked bridge over the
River Teifi.*

hunch /hʌntʃ/ **hunches, hunching, hunched**
1 NC A **hunch** is an idea that you have which is
accompanied by a strong feeling that it is correct or
true, although you have not really thought about it or
got any proof; an informal use. *Morris had a hunch
that she was a good cook... Watson frequently acted on
a hunch.*
2 V If you **hunch** somewhere, you draw your shoulders
towards each other and lower your chin towards your
chest. *I was cold as I hunched over my meagre fire...
The children hunched in the bushes, watching the
grown-ups.* ◆ **hunched** ADJ *I saw a small hunched
figure wheeling a pram... Mr Read arrived in
Damascus, haggard, hunched and unable to walk
without great difficulty.*

hunchback /hʌntʃbæk/ **hunchbacks**
1 NC A **hunchback** is a person who has a large lump
on their back because their spine is deformed; an
offensive word. *...a song about the hunchback of
Notre Dame.*
2 NC A **hunchback** is also a large lump on someone's
back that is caused by a deformity of the spine. *He
has a withered arm, a leg brace, and a hunchback.*

hundred /hʌndrəd/ **hundreds**
1 A **hundred** or one **hundred** is the number 100. *The
government was defeated by a hundred and fifty
votes... Five hundred people have been wounded in the
last nine days.*
2 QUANT You can use **hundreds** to refer to a very large
number. *He handed me hundreds of forms.*
3 If you say that something is **a hundred per cent**
true, you mean that it is completely true; an informal
expression. *Your assessment of Otto is a hundred per
cent wrong... I agree one hundred per cent with Carol.*

hundredth /hʌndrədθ/ **hundredths**
1 ADJ The **hundredth** item in a series is the one that
you count as number one hundred. *...the hundredth
anniversary of tennis championships at Wimbledon.*
2 NC A **hundredth** is one of a hundred equal parts of
something. *...one hundredth of a second.*

hundredweight /hʌndrədweɪt/ **hundredweights**. The
plural form can be either **hundredweights** or
hundredweight.
NC A **hundredweight** is a unit of weight equal to 112
pounds in Britain and 100 pounds in the United States.

The tenor bell in St Paul's Cathedral weighs sixty-two hundredweight.

hung /hʌŋ/
1 **Hung** is the past tense and past participle of most senses of **hang**.
2 ADJ ATTRIB A **hung** jury, parliament, or other decision-making body, is one in which there is no overall majority. *It is very possible that the result of the National Assembly's elections will be a hung parliament... Both trials ended in hung juries... All of them were previously hung councils.*

Hungary /hʌŋgəri/
The **Republic of Hungary** is a country in central Europe. It was a member of the former Warsaw Pact. Occupied by Germany from 1944 to 1945, it became a Communist state in 1949. Soviet military intervention in 1956 ended a period of reform under Imre Nagy. Gradual liberalization preceded the declaration of a new republic in 1989. Árpád Göncz, of the Alliance of Free Democrats (SzDSz), became President in 1990. József Antall, of the Hungarian Democratic Forum (MDF), became Prime Minister in 1990. Hungary produces coal and agricultural products. Large foreign debts and high inflation are major economic problems.
♦ **Hungarian** /hʌŋgɛəriən/ N, ADJ
▪ *per capita GNP:* US$2,460 ▪ *religion:* Christianity (mainly Roman Catholic) ▪ *language:* Hungarian ▪ *currency:* forint ▪ *capital:* Budapest ▪ *population:* 10 million (1989) ▪ *size:* 93,033 square kilometres.

hunger /hʌŋgə/ **hungers, hungering, hungered**
1 NU **Hunger** is the feeling of weakness or discomfort that you get when you need something to eat. *Babies show their hunger by waking up to be fed.*
2 NU **Hunger** is also a serious lack of food which causes suffering or death. *But his wife and two children died of hunger. ...a vicious circle of hunger and poverty.*
3 V+*for or after* If you **hunger** for or **hunger** after something, you want it very much; a formal use. *...Spaniards who hunger for Flamenco music.*

hunger strike, hunger strikes
NU or NC If someone goes on **hunger strike**, they stop eating in order to protest about something, often a political issue. *They have been on hunger strike for more than two months... They have begun a hunger strike in protest at their imprisonment... Many have been freed as a result of their hunger strikes.*

hunger striker, hunger strikers
NC A **hunger striker** is a person who has stopped eating in order to protest about something, often a political issue. *More than forty hunger strikers have joined the campaign... Prison authorities have refused any comment on the hunger strikers.*

hung over
ADJ Someone who is **hung over** has a headache and feels sick because they drank too much alcohol on the previous day. *We're all really hung over this morning.*

hungry /hʌŋgri/ **hungrier, hungriest**
1 ADJ When you are **hungry**, you want food because you have not eaten for a time, and you have an uncomfortable feeling in your stomach. *I'm tired and hungry and I want some supper. ...a hungry baby.*
♦ **hungrily** ADV *I ate hungrily.*
2 If people go **hungry**, they suffer from hunger because there is no food for them to eat. *There's no famine as such, but people might go hungry. ...areas of acute poverty, with people going hungry at this time of the year.*
3 ADJ If you are **hungry** for something, you want it very much. *They were hungry for news... After seven decades of centralized rule, the republics are hungry for freedom.*

hung up
ADJ If you are **hung up** on something or **hung up** about it, you are constantly nervous or worried about it because you do not understand how to deal with it; an informal expression. *You're hung up about your father.*

hunk /hʌŋk/ **hunks**
1 NC A **hunk** of something solid is a large piece of it. *...a hunk of brown bread. ...a hunk of beeswax.*
2 NC If you refer to a man as a **hunk**, you mean that

he is big and strong and that people find him sexually attractive. *In the next issue, they used hunks, in full-body semi-nude poses.*

hunker /hʌŋkə/ **hunkers, hunkering, hunkered**
hunker down PHRASAL VERB If someone **hunkers down**, they sit or lie down in order to defend themselves or to prepare themselves for something; used in American English. *I think people have hunkered down then for a fight... So he's hunkering down, looking for bad times.*

Hun Sen /hun sɛn/
Hun Sen became Prime Minister of Cambodia in 1985. He was Minister for Foreign Affairs from 1979 to 1986, and Vice Chairman of the Council of Ministers from 1981 to 1985. He remained Prime Minister in 1991, when Prince Sihanouk returned to Cambodia as head of the Supreme National Council. Hun Sen became Vice Chairman of the Central Committee of the Cambodian People's Party (CPP) in 1991. Born: 1951.

hunt /hʌnt/ **hunts, hunting, hunted**
1 VO or V When people or animals **hunt**, they chase wild animals and kill them for food or as a sport. *It's perfectly legal to use packs of trained dogs to hunt wild foxes or hares... The whale has been commercially hunted for its meat and oil... Hyenas usually hunt at night.* ▶ Also NC *They sighted a zebra and the hunt began.* ♦ **hunting** NU *The government's ban on commercial seal hunting came as no surprise. ...a hunting accident.*
2 VO If you **hunt** for someone or something, you search for them. *The man now being hunted by the police is white... The kids hunted for treasure.* ▶ Also NC *The hunt continues for those responsible for the car bombing... The police have launched a nationwide hunt for the stolen plane.*
3 See also **witch-hunt**.
hunt down PHRASAL VERB If you **hunt** someone or something **down**, you succeed in finding them after searching for them. *Those who do not give themselves up will be hunted down.*

hunter /hʌntə/ **hunters**
1 NC A **hunter** is a person who hunts wild animals for food or as a sport. *For once hunters and conservationists are on the same side... Eleven panda hunters and fur sellers were given jail sentences today.*
2 NC+SUPP People who search for things of a particular kind are often referred to as **hunters**. *...bargain hunters... December is never a good month for job hunters.*

hunting ground, hunting grounds
NC A **hunting ground** is a place where people who have a particular interest are likely to find something that they are looking for. *This street has always been a happy hunting ground for antique collectors.*

huntsman /hʌntsmən/ **huntsmen**
NC A **huntsman** is a person who hunts wild animals, especially one who hunts foxes using dogs. *...a cunning fox which was trying to escape from a pack of baying hounds and horn-blowing huntsmen.*

hurdle /hɜːdl/ **hurdles**
1 NC A **hurdle** is a difficulty that you must overcome in order to achieve something. *Its first hurdle is to survive a vote of confidence in Parliament tomorrow... The peace process must still overcome several major hurdles.*
2 NC **Hurdles** are fences that runners jump over in some races. *The men's 110 metre hurdles was won by Yu Zhicheng of China.*

hurl /hɜːl/ **hurls, hurling, hurled**
1 VO If you **hurl** something, you throw it with a lot of force. *I took all his books and hurled them out of the window.*
2 VO If you **hurl** abuse or insults at someone, you shout abuse or insults at them. *Abuse was hurled at the police.*

hurling /hɜːlɪŋ/
NU **Hurling** is an outdoor game that is played with special sticks and a ball between two teams of 15 players each. *...the all-Ireland hurling final.*

hurly-burly /hɜːlibɜːli/
N SING The **hurly-burly** of a place is the noise and

activity created by the people and things that are
there. ...*the hurly-burly of excited children*... *He
found all the noise and hurly-burly tiresome.*
hurray /hʊreɪ/. See **hooray**.
hurricane /hʌrɪkən, hʌrɪkeɪn/ **hurricanes**
NC A **hurricane** is a very violent wind or storm. *The
island is in the path of the hurricane.*
hurricane lamp, hurricane lamps
NC A **hurricane lamp** is a paraffin lamp in which the
flame is specially protected by glass. *A few people
ran about swinging hurricane lamps.*
hurried /hʌrid/
ADJ Something that is **hurried** is done very quickly or
suddenly. ...*a hurried lunch.* ...*a hurried glance.*
♦ **hurriedly** ADV *He had dressed hurriedly.*
hurry /hʌri/ **hurries, hurrying, hurried**
1 VA If you **hurry** somewhere, you go there quickly.
*He hurried off down the street... The people hurried
home... The white doors open, and the dancers hurry
through it.*
2 V or V+*to*-INF If you **hurry** to do something, you start
doing it as soon as you can. *If we hurry, we can catch
them before they go back underground... They hurried
to help him... Traders hurried to buy up supplies
before the long weekend.*
3 VO If you **hurry** someone or something, you try to
make them do something more quickly. *Efforts to
hurry them only make them angry... In other words,
he really doesn't want to be hurried.*
4 N SING If you are in a **hurry**, you need to do
something quickly. If you do something in a **hurry**, you
do it quickly. *She was always in a hurry... Otto had to
leave in a great hurry... The meeting was arranged in
something of a hurry... In the middle of all this hurry,
he dropped the bag.*
● **Hurry** is used in these phrases. ● If you say to
someone **'There's no hurry'** or **'I'm in no hurry'**, you
are telling them that there is no need to do something
immediately. *There's no hurry. You've got until nine
o'clock... I'm in no particular hurry to call an election,
there's too much to do.* ● You can also say that you
are **in no hurry** to do something when you are very
unwilling to do it. *He was in no hurry to confront
Abraham Chase... The European Community is in no
hurry to extend its commitments.* ● If you say **'What's
the hurry?'**, you want to know why something must be
done quickly. *'Drink up, Sarah!'—'What's the hurry?'*
hurry up PHRASAL VERB 1 If you tell someone to
hurry up, you are telling them to do something more
quickly. *Hurry up, it's getting late... Just hurry up
and search me and let me get the hell out of here...
Well, I'd better hurry up and finish this interview and
let you get back.* 2 If you **hurry** something **up**, you
make it happen faster or sooner than it would have
done. *You can hurry the process up by leaving the
door open.*
hurt /hɜːt/ **hurts, hurting**. The form **hurt** is used in the
present tense and is also the past tense and past
participle of the verb.
1 V-REFL or VO If you **hurt** yourself or **hurt** a part of
your body, you injure yourself. *Prince Charles has
hurt himself in the past several times... She pulled up
because she had hurt her back and could not control
the horse.*
2 ADJ If you are **hurt**, you have been injured. *No one
was killed or badly hurt... It may be only a matter of
time before someone is hurt... Two policemen were
also hurt.*
3 VO If someone **hurts** you, they injure you or cause
you pain. *Rescuers were extremely cautious for fear
of hurting children still trapped... They did say that
they had hurt one hostage.*
4 V If a part of your body **hurts**, you feel pain there.
My leg was beginning to hurt... Their eyes hurt.
5 VO You can say that something **hurts** someone or
something when it has a bad effect on them. *The
housing boom has hurt as well as helped people... The
country has needed help and has been badly hurt by
that decision.*
6 VO If someone **hurts** you, they upset you by saying
or doing something rude or inconsiderate. *He told the
court he was surprised and hurt by the ban... He*

didn't want to hurt her feelings. ► Also ADJ ...*a tone
of hurt surprise.*
7 NU A feeling of **hurt** is a feeling that you have when
you have been treated badly. ...*feelings of anger and
hurt.* ...*that sense of hurt that our credentials and
values have been questioned.*
hurtful /hɜːtfl/
ADJ **Hurtful** remarks or actions upset people. *Some of
the things they say are hurtful.*
hurtle /hɜːtl/ **hurtles, hurtling, hurtled**
V If something **hurtles** somewhere, it moves very
quickly, often in a dangerous way. *He watched the
plane as it hurtled down the runway.*
husband /hʌzbənd/ **husbands**
NC A woman's **husband** is the man she is married to.
*She met her husband in 1942. ...a change in the law so
that husbands and wives would be independently
taxed.*
husbandry /hʌzbəndri/
NU **Husbandry** is farming, especially when it is done
carefully and well. ...*animal husbandry... Good
husbandry keeps pests and diseases in check.*
hush /hʌʃ/ **hushes, hushing, hushed**
1 If you say **'Hush!'** to someone, you are telling them
to be quiet.
2 N SING You say that there is a **hush** when everything
is quiet and peaceful, or suddenly becomes quiet. *An
expectant hush fell on the gathering... There was an
unusual hush in the infirmary.*
hush up PHRASAL VERB If people in authority **hush**
something **up**, they prevent the public from knowing
about it. *The police had hushed the matter up.*
hushed /hʌʃt/
1 ADJ A **hushed** place is quiet and peaceful; a literary
word. *We walked in silence through the hushed
valley... He told a hushed Congress that the Prime
Minister's life was not thought to be in danger.*
2 ADJ If you say something in a **hushed** voice, you say
it very quietly. *In the hotel lobby, people were talking
in hushed tones... The conversations are hushed, and
no lights are allowed.*
hush-hush
ADJ Something that is **hush-hush** is secret and not to
be discussed with other people; an informal
expression. *'We work in the same office.'—'One of
those hush-hush jobs, isn't it?'*
hush money
NU **Hush money** is money that is given to someone to
persuade them to keep secret something that they
know. *He also paid the girl hush money out of church
funds to keep her quiet.*
husk /hʌsk/ **husks**
NC **Husks** are the outer coverings of grains or seeds.
...*the outer husk of the seed... Rice husks are also
burned for fuel in the USA.*
husky /hʌski/ **huskier, huskiest; huskies**
1 ADJ If someone's voice is **husky**, it sounds rough or
hoarse, often in an attractive way. *Her voice is husky.
...masculine characteristics like a husky voice and
facial hair.*
2 NC A **husky** is a strong, furry dog which is used to
pull sledges across the snow. *Each sled is pulled by
eight to twelve Alaskan and Siberian huskies. ...an
outbreak of distemper among husky dogs.*
Hussain, Saddam /sædɑːm huseɪn/
Saddam Hussain became President of Iraq and leader
of the Arab Baath Socialist Party in 1979. In 1990 he
ordered Iraq's invasion of Kuwait. Born: 1937.
Hussein ibn Talal, King of Jordan
/huseɪn ɪbn təlæl/
Hussein ibn Talal became King of Jordan in 1952,
succeeding his father. He was named heir apparent in
1951. Born: 1935.
hussy /hʌsi/ **hussies**
NC If you refer to a girl or woman as a **hussy**, you
think that her behaviour is immoral, especially in a
sexual way; an old-fashioned word. *The stereotyped
rape victim is a bra-less hussy, attacked in a dark
alley by a stranger she had been eyeing up in the pub.*
hustings /hʌstɪŋz/
N PL The political activities such as speeches and
interviews that take place before an election are

sometimes referred to as the **hustings**. *...her presence at the hustings in December... I heard nothing about it anywhere on the hustings.*

hustle /hʌsl/ **hustles, hustling, hustled**
1 VO If you **hustle** someone, you try to hurry them into doing something, for example by talking persuasively to them, or by pulling or pushing them. *He hustled Fanny through the door... Five demonstrators ran onto the course but they were hustled away by police... How can they avoid being hustled into some premature commitment?... He accused them of trying to hustle Britain into economic and monetary union.*
2 V If you **hustle**, you try very hard, perhaps by using dishonest or devious means, to get something such as money or promises from someone; used in American English. *...encounters with rickshaw-pullers hustling for incredibly high fares... Supporters are hustling to get as many votes as they can.*

hustler /hʌslə/ **hustlers**; an informal word used in American English.
1 NC A **hustler** is a person who tries to earn money or gain an advantage from a situation, often by using dishonest or illegal methods. *...a fast-talking street-wise hustler... Unscrupulous hustlers can cash in on the subtle fascination of astrology.*
2 NC A **hustler** is also a male prostitute. *...a haunt of pimps and bookies and hustlers and dope pedlars.*

hut /hʌt/ **huts**
NC A **hut** is a small, simple building, often made of wood, mud, or grass. *Tents and huts have been put up to shelter the homeless. ...mud huts.*

hutch /hʌtʃ/ **hutches**
NC A **hutch** is a cage that rabbits or other small pet animals are kept in. It is usually made of wood. *...a rabbit hutch.*

hyacinth /haɪəsɪnθ/ **hyacinths**
NC A **hyacinth** is a plant with a lot of small, sweet-smelling flowers growing closely around a single stem. *The perfumes, which contain lemon, hyacinth, and rose, are intended to reduce stress.*

hyaena /haɪiːnə/ **hyaenas**. See hyena.

hybrid /haɪbrɪd/ **hybrids**
1 NCorN+N A **hybrid** is an animal or plant bred from two different types of animal or plant; a technical use in biology. *Scientists confirmed that they had discovered a new hybrid of the speckled owl and the barn owl... They are working with several different hybrids. ...hybrid roses.*
2 NC Anything that is a mixture of two different things can be called a **hybrid**. *...a hybrid of business and art... A typical American solution would be a hybrid.* ▶ Also ADJ *...hybrid systems of heat storage.*

hybridization /haɪbrɪdaɪzeɪʃn/; also spelt **hybridisation**.
NU **Hybridization** is the process in which two different species of animal or plant together produce a new type of animal or plant; a technical term in biology. *The two groups of birds were closely related, so hybridisation could have occurred... They are doing some hybridization with the heavy bodied fish and the coloured fish.*

hydrant /haɪdrənt/ **hydrants**
NC A fire **hydrant** is a pipe in the street which supplies water for putting out fires. *Their initial attempt to bring the fire under control was hampered by a damaged hydrant.*

hydrate /haɪdreɪt/ **hydrates**
NC A **hydrate** is a chemical that contains water; a technical term. *Deep underground you find methane as solid hydrates.*

hydraulic /haɪdrɒlɪk/ **hydraulics**
1 ADJ Something that is **hydraulic** involves or is operated by a fluid that is under pressure, such as water or oil. *The car, controlled by powerful hydraulic brakes, travels at 80kph... Basically, the machine is powered by a hydraulic motor.*
2 NU **Hydraulics** is the study and use of systems that work using hydraulic pressure. *The captain announced a mechanical problem, and it was the hydraulics this time.*

hydrocarbon /haɪdrəkɔːbən/ **hydrocarbons**
NC A **hydrocarbon** is a chemical compound that is a mixture of hydrogen and carbon; a technical term in chemistry. *Numerous companies have replaced CFCs entirely by hydrocarbon gases such as butane.*

hydro-electric /haɪdrəʊɪlektrɪk/
ADJ ATTRIB **Hydro-electric** power is electrical power obtained from the energy of running water. *...state-run nuclear and hydro-electric power stations and oilfields... Damage had been done by hydro-electric dams.*

hydro-electricity /haɪdrəʊɪlektrɪsəti/
NU **Hydro-electricity** is electricity made from the energy of running water. *Lesotho will also benefit from cheap hydro-electricity.*

hydrofoil /haɪdrəfɔɪl/ **hydrofoils**
NC A **hydrofoil** is a boat which can travel above the surface of the water by resting on a pair of special fins. Hydrofoil is also used to refer to the fins themselves. *Travel between the two cities takes place on a large number of ferries and hydrofoils.*

hydrogen /haɪdrədʒən/
NU **Hydrogen** is the lightest gas and the simplest chemical element in nature. *Levels of hydrogen and of methane rise quite dramatically before an earthquake occurs... Hydrogen has the smallest molecule of any element.*

hydrogen bomb, hydrogen bombs
NC A **hydrogen bomb** is a nuclear bomb in which energy is released from hydrogen atoms. *They had just exploded a powerful hydrogen bomb.*

hydrogen peroxide
NU **Hydrogen peroxide** is a chemical that is used as a bleach for hair and as an antiseptic. *...the minute amounts of ozone and hydrogen peroxide that are normally present in the atmosphere.*

hydrophobia /haɪdrəfəʊbiə/
NU **Hydrophobia** is the same as rabies; an old-fashioned word.

hydroplane /haɪdrəpleɪn/ **hydroplanes, hydroplaning, hydroplaned**
1 NC A **hydroplane** is a speedboat which rises out of the water when it is travelling fast.
2 V When a speedboat **hydroplanes**, it travels forward quickly, rising out of the water. *They hydroplaned back into Brazil in April 1935.*

hydroponics /haɪdrəpɒnɪks/
NU **Hydroponics** is a method of growing plants in water rather than in soil; a technical term in biology. *They've done this by a technique known as hydroponics... In that case hydroponics has an advantage.*

hydropower /haɪdrəpaʊə/
NU **Hydropower** is the same as **hydro-electric** power. *When you generate hydropower from the Columbia River, you're making it harder for the salmon to travel upstream. ...renewable resources, such as solar and hydropower.*

hydrotherapy /haɪdrəʊθerəpi/
NU **Hydrotherapy** is a method of treating people with some diseases or injuries by making them swim or do exercises in water. *As well as its use as a swimming aid, the float is of great importance in hydrotherapy and other water-based treatments.*

hyena /haɪiːnə/ **hyenas**; also spelt **hyaena**.
NC A **hyena** is an African animal that looks like a wolf and often hunts in groups. It makes a sound like laughter. *...the howling of the hyenas.*

hygiene /haɪdʒiːn/
NU **Hygiene** is the practice of keeping yourself and your surroundings clean, especially to avoid illness or the spread of diseases. *...personal hygiene... Investigations are underway to improve standards of food hygiene. ...disease related to bad hygiene and poor food.*

hygienic /haɪdʒiːnɪk/
ADJ Something that is **hygienic** is clean and unlikely to cause illness. *It's more hygienic to use disposable paper tissues.*

hymen /haɪmen/ **hymens**
NC A **hymen** is a piece of skin that often covers part of a girl's or woman's vagina and breaks either when

she has sex for the first time, or earlier; a technical term. *One reason mothers gave for not wanting their daughters to use tampons is that it would break the hymen.*

hymn /hɪm/ **hymns**
NC A **hymn** is a song sung by Christians to praise God. *After prayers and hymns, wreaths were cast into the sea.*

hymnal /hɪmnəl/ **hymnals**
NC A **hymnal** is a book of hymns; a formal word. *She pulls a hymnal out of her purse and starts to sing.*

hype /haɪp/ **hypes, hyping, hyped**
1 NU **Hype** is the promotion of someone or something by using intensive or extravagant methods of publicity. *The evidence, once stripped of its media hype, was extremely weak... He accused them of engaging in political hype... They dismiss the arguments as largely hype.*
2 VO To **hype** a product means to advertize it using intensive or extravagant methods of publicity. *Christmas is hyped on the media... How much is the intrigue and rivalry between the players deliberately hyped?*
hype up PHRASAL VERB If you **hype up** someone, you deliberately make them very excited. *I realized the job was not to hype up the team, but to calm them all down.* ◆ **hyped up** ADJ *I was going to bed tired, but I was so hyped up.*

hyper- /haɪpə-/
PREFIX **Hyper-** is used to form adjectives that describe someone as having too much of a particular quality. For example, someone who is hyper-cautious is too cautious. *I'm curious about these hyper-fastidious people who are obsessed with their own health.*

hyperactive /haɪpəræktɪv/
ADJ Someone who is **hyperactive** is unable to relax or concentrate, and is always in a state of great agitation or excitement. *Doctors have assured the parents of hyperactive children that they are not to blame.* ◆ **hyperactivity** /haɪpəræktɪvəti/ NU *Lead poisoning causes lowering of the intelligence, hyperactivity and general illness... The symptoms range from hyperactivity to epilepsy.*

hyperbola /haɪpɜːbələ/ **hyperbolas**
NC A **hyperbola** is a smooth curve that gets steeper or flatter at a constant rate; a technical term in mathematics.

hyperbole /haɪpɜːbəli/
NU **Hyperbole** is a style of speech or writing which uses exaggeration in order to achieve its effect. *The speech certainly contained an element of hyperbole... A jewel of extraordinary beauty set in the Indian Ocean, it is tempting to employ hyperbole when speaking of Mauritius.*

hyper-inflation
NU **Hyper-inflation** is extremely severe inflation. *The economy is plunging towards hyper-inflation and recession. ...hyper-inflation running at 50 per cent a month.*

hypermarket /haɪpəmɑːkɪt/ **hypermarkets**
NC A **hypermarket** is a very large supermarket. *They also now run a chain of do-it-yourself shops and hypermarkets.*

hypersensitive /haɪpəsɛnsətɪv/
1 ADJ Someone who is **hypersensitive** is extremely sensitive to certain drugs, chemicals, changes in temperature, and so on. *There is a small risk to soldiers who are hypersensitive to some component of the vaccine.*
2 ADJ If you refer to someone as **hypersensitive**, you mean that they are very easily annoyed or offended; used showing disapproval. *He was hypersensitive on this issue... Emily is fastidious and hypersensitive.*

hypertension /haɪpətɛnʃn/
NU **Hypertension** is a medical condition in which a person has very high blood pressure. *...overwork and hypertension... Most people do not have to be hospitalized for hypertension.*

hyphen /haɪfn/ **hyphens**
NC A **hyphen** is a punctuation mark used to join words together. For example, the word 'left-handed' has a hyphen in the middle of it. *Every answer in this part of the quiz is a word that has two hyphens.*

hyphenated /haɪfəneɪtɪd/
ADJ A word that is **hyphenated** is written with a hyphen between two or more of its parts. *The surname Gregory-Smith is hyphenated.*

hypnosis /hɪpnəʊsɪs/
NU **Hypnosis** is the practice or skill of hypnotizing people. *Aromatherapy, acupuncture and hypnosis are just a few of the alternative treatments on offer... He described his use of hypnosis to explore his patients' past-life experiences.* ● If you are **under hypnosis**, you have been hypnotized. *Is it true that a person could be made to commit a crime under hypnosis?*

hypnotic /hɪpnɒtɪk/
ADJ Something that is **hypnotic** makes you feel as if you have been hypnotized. *The rhythmic clapping was having a hypnotic effect on Ginny.*

hypnotise /hɪpnətaɪz/. See **hypnotize**.

hypnotism /hɪpnətɪzəm/
NU **Hypnotism** is the same as **hypnosis**.

hypnotize /hɪpnətaɪz/ **hypnotizes, hypnotizing, hypnotized**; also spelt **hypnotise**.
1 VO If someone **hypnotizes** you, they put you into a state in which you seem to be asleep but in which you can still respond to things that are said to you. *I was able to hypnotize him into doing things against his own will.*
2 VO If you **are hypnotized** by something, you are so fascinated by it that you cannot think of anything else. *The child was hypnotized by the machine.*

hypochondria /haɪpəkɒndriə/
NU Someone who has **hypochondria** continually worries about their health, although there is usually nothing wrong with them. *Many elderly people fail to report their symptoms because they fear the all-too common accusation of hypochondria.*

hypochondriac /haɪpəkɒndriæk/ **hypochondriacs**
NC A **hypochondriac** is someone who worries about their health, often when there is nothing wrong with them. *He was a bit of a hypochondriac... She was a confirmed hypochondriac, and devoted all her energies to looking after her children with excessive solicitude.*

hypocrisy /hɪpɒkrəsi/
NU **Hypocrisy** is behaviour in which someone pretends to have beliefs, principles, or feelings that they do not really have. *Opposition MPs angrily accused him of dishonesty and hypocrisy... There are double standards and hypocrisy in these negotiations.*

hypocrite /hɪpəkrɪt/ **hypocrites**
NC A **hypocrite** is someone who pretends to have beliefs, principles, or feelings that they do not really have. *People have found his straightforwardness refreshing. He's certainly no hypocrite.*

hypocritical /hɪpəkrɪtɪkl/
ADJ If someone is being **hypocritical**, they are pretending to have beliefs, principles, or feelings that they do not really have. *They send you their love. It would be hypocritical of me to do the same... Many Columbians feel their country was pushed into the firing line by a hypocritical United States.*

hypodermic /haɪpədɜːmɪk/ **hypodermics**
ADJ A **hypodermic** needle or syringe is a medical instrument with a hollow needle, which is used to give injections. *It's possible to live a nearly normal life with one's hypodermic needle and supply of insulin... One of the ways in which hepatitis and AIDS are transmitted is through unsterilized hypodermic syringes.* ► Also NC *With the new Bates hypodermic you can't do that, because it will only work once... The sterilizer lock would reset automatically when the hypodermics were properly sterilized.*

hypotenuse /haɪpɒtənjuːz/ **hypotenuses**
NC The **hypotenuse** of a right-angled triangle is the side opposite the right angle; a technical term in mathematics.

hypothermia /haɪpəθɜːmiə/
NU If a person has **hypothermia**, their body temperature has become unusually low as a result of being in severe cold for a long time; a medical term. *Hypothermia is one of the main causes of death among the elderly.*

hypothesis /haɪpɒθəsɪs/ **hypotheses** /haɪpɒθəsiːz/
NC A **hypothesis** is an explanation or theory which has not yet been proved to be correct; a formal word. *People have proposed all kinds of hypotheses about what these things are.*

hypothesize /haɪpɒθəsaɪz/ **hypothesizes, hypothesizing, hypothesized**; also spelt **hypothesise**.
V If you **hypothesize** about something, you suggest an explanation or theory about it based on your ideas, not on facts. *We can only hypothesise as to how much unrest they will cause.*

hypothetical /haɪpəθetɪkl/
ADJ Something that is **hypothetical** is based on possible situations rather than actual ones; a formal word. *Let me put a hypothetical question to you.*

hysterectomy /hɪstərektəmi/ **hysterectomies**
NC A **hysterectomy** is a surgical operation to remove a woman's womb; a medical term. *...women who have had their ovaries removed during a hysterectomy operation.*

hysteria /hɪstɪəriə/
1 NU **Hysteria** among a group of people is a state of uncontrolled excitement, anger, or panic. *On occasions there was mass hysteria... Nothing could be achieved in an atmosphere of hysteria.*
2 NU A person who is suffering from **hysteria** is in a state of violent and disturbed emotion as a result of shock; a medical use. *Many new cases of hysteria,*

epilepsy and hypertension are being monitored by the unit.

hysterical /hɪsterɪkl/
1 ADJ Someone who is **hysterical** is in a state of uncontrolled excitement, anger, or panic, as a result of a shock or unpleasant experience. *...a mob of hysterical vigilantes. ...Farlow's hysterical letter. ...stress leading to irrational and hysterical behaviour.*
♦ **hysterically** ADV *A man was screaming hysterically.*
2 ADJ **Hysterical** laughter is loud and uncontrolled. *The wail of the saxophone gives way to a prolonged passage of hysterical laughter.* ♦ **hysterically** ADV *We laughed hysterically at their startled expressions.*
3 ADJ If you describe something as **hysterical**, you mean that it is extremely funny; an informal use.
♦ **hysterically** SUBMOD *...jokes which people find hysterically funny.*

hysterics /hɪsterɪks/
1 N PL If someone is in **hysterics** or is having **hysterics**, they are in a state of uncontrolled excitement, anger, or panic. *If she didn't get home early, there would probably be hysterics from her mother.*
2 N PL You can also say that someone is in **hysterics** or is having **hysterics** when they are laughing uncontrollably; an informal use. *The audience was in hysterics.*

I i

I, i /aɪ/ **I's, i's**
NC **I** is the ninth letter of the English alphabet.

I /aɪ/
PRON **I** is used as the subject of a verb. A speaker or writer uses **I** to refer to himself or herself. *I like your dress... He and I were at school together.*

IBA /aɪbiːeɪ/
N PROP The **IBA** is an organization which controls all the broadcasting companies in the United Kingdom except the BBC. **IBA** is an abbreviation for 'Independent Broadcasting Authority'. *Religious advisers are appointed jointly by the BBC and the IBA.*

-ibility /-əbɪləti/ **-ibilities**
SUFFIX **-ibility** is added in place of '-ible' at the end of adjectives to form nouns. Nouns of this kind are often not defined but are treated with the related adjectives. *...the need to provide flexibility. ...the impossibility of any change.*

-ic /-ɪk/
SUFFIX **-ic** is added to nouns to form adjectives indicating that someone or something has a particular quality or relates to a particular thing. *...parasitic insects. ...an opportunistic foreign policy.*

ice /aɪs/ **ices, icing, iced**
1 NU **Ice** is frozen water. *Snow falls and builds up into a layer of ice.*
2 NU **Ice** is also pieces of ice used to keep food or drink cool. *...two tall glasses of pineapple juice, soda and ice.*
3 VO To **ice** cakes means to cover them with icing. *Have you iced your Christmas cake yet?*
4 NC An **ice** is an ice cream. *He went over and bought ices and lollipops for the children.*
5 If you **break the ice**, you make people feel relaxed, for example at the beginning of a party or a meeting. *This new initiative could indeed break the ice between the two sides.*
6 See also **iced, icing**.
ice over PHRASAL VERB If something **ices over**, it becomes covered with ice. *The lake began to ice over.*
ice up PHRASAL VERB When something **ices up**, it becomes so cold that ice forms around it or inside it so that it cannot function properly. *The lock, in these conditions, may ice up and become unusable.*

Ice Age
N PROP The **Ice Age** was a period of time lasting many thousands of years, during which a lot of the earth's surface was covered with ice. *The Ice Age arrived about 60 million years after the dinosaurs had departed.*

iceberg /aɪsbɜːg/ **icebergs**
NC An **iceberg** is a large, tall mass of ice floating in the sea. *Nine tenths of an iceberg is below water.*
● **tip of the iceberg**: see tip.

ice-blue
ADJ **Ice-blue** is a very pale blue colour. *...ice-blue eyes.*

icebox /aɪsbɒks/ **iceboxes**
NC An **icebox** is a refrigerator; used in American English. *You take the container out of the freezer and put it in the icebox to thaw it out.*

ice-bucket, ice-buckets
NC An **ice-bucket** is a container which holds ice cubes or cold water and ice. You can use it to provide ice cubes to put in drinks, or to put bottles of wine in and keep the wine cool.

ice-cap, ice-caps
NC An **ice-cap** is a layer of thick ice and snow that permanently covers a particular area of land. *The penguin can survive on the Antarctic ice-cap in winter. ...the polar ice-caps.*

ice-cold
ADJ **Ice-cold** means very cold indeed. *...ice-cold beer.*

ice cream, ice creams
1 NU **Ice cream** is a very cold sweet food made from milk. *...a diet of chips, ice cream and sweets.*
2 NC An **ice cream** is a portion of ice cream, usually wrapped in paper or in a container. *...an ice cream cone.*

ice-cream soda, ice-cream sodas
NU or NC **Ice-cream soda** is a dessert made from ice cream, fruit-flavoured syrup, and soda water. It is usually served in a tall glass. *...a glass of ice-cream soda... Karen gobbled an ice-cream soda.*

ice cube, ice cubes
NC An **ice cube** is a small block of ice that you put into a drink to make it cold. *He dropped in a few ice cubes.*

iced /aɪst/
1 ADJ ATTRIB An **iced** drink has been made very cold. *...an iced beer.*
2 ADJ An **iced** cake is covered with icing. *There were trays of tea and sandwiches and little iced cakes.*

ice floe, ice floes
NC An **ice floe** is a large area of ice floating in the sea. *A group of Soviet scientists are trapped on a drifting ice floe in the Arctic sea.*

ice hockey
NU **Ice hockey** is a game like hockey played on ice. *The United States have failed to reach the medals stages of the ice hockey competition at the Winter Olympics.*

Iceland /aɪslənd/
The **Republic of Iceland** is a country in the North Atlantic. It became independent from Denmark in 1944. It is a member of NATO. Vigdís Finnbogadóttir (independent) became President in 1980. Davíd Oddsson, of the Independence Party (IP), became Prime Minister in 1991. Fishing is the main industry.
◆ **Icelander** /aɪsləndə/ N **Icelandic** /aɪslændɪk/ ADJ
■ *per capita GNP:* US$20,160 ■ *religion:* Christianity (mainly Evangelical Lutheran) ■ *language:* Icelandic ■ *currency:* króna ■ *capital:* Reykjavík ■ *population:* 254,000 (1990) ■ *size:* 103,000 square kilometres.

ice lolly, ice lollies
NC An **ice lolly** is a piece of flavoured ice or ice cream on a stick.

ice rink, ice rinks
NC An **ice rink** is a level area of ice, usually inside a building, that has been made artificially and kept frozen so that people can skate on it. *The action moved to the ice rink and the free section of the men's figure skating.*

ice-skate, ice-skates
NC **Ice-skates** are shoes with metal bars attached to them that you wear when you skate on ice.

ice-skating
NU **Ice-skating** is the activity or sport of skating on ice. ...*a fortnight of skiing and ice-skating.*

icicle /ˈaɪsɪkl/ **icicles**
NC An **icicle** is a long pointed piece of ice hanging from a surface. *The domes of the Kremlin were fringed with the icicles that mark the first thaw of spring.*

icing /ˈaɪsɪŋ/
NU **Icing** is a sweet substance made from powdered sugar that is used to cover cakes. ...*marzipan icing.*
● If you describe something as **the icing on the cake**, you mean that it is an attractive addition to something. *West Germany produced some more icing on President Bush's cake by announcing a two billion dollar contribution to help pay for US forces in Saudi Arabia.*

icing sugar
NU **Icing sugar** is white sugar that has been ground to a very fine powder. It is used for making icing and sweets. *Add half the quantity of icing sugar gradually.*

icon /ˈaɪkɒn/ **icons**; also spelt **ikon.**
NC An **icon** is a picture of Christ or a saint painted on a wooden panel. Icons are regarded as holy by some Christians. *For many people, Byzantine means religious art, glorious churches, icons and murals.*

iconoclast /aɪˈkɒnəklæst/ **iconoclasts**
NC An **iconoclast** is a person who criticizes beliefs that are generally accepted in a society; a formal word. *The image presented of him is of a mindless iconoclast... He was an iconoclast who wanted to throw away the whole tradition.*

iconoclastic /aɪkɒnəˈklæstɪk/
ADJ **Iconoclastic** ideas, theories, etc contradict established beliefs; a formal word. ...*his iconoclastic theories about language.*

icy /ˈaɪsi/ **icier, iciest**
1 ADJ **Icy** air or water is extremely cold. *As I opened the door a gust of icy air struck me.*
2 ADJ An **icy** road has ice on it and is dangerous because it is slippery. *Their car skidded on an icy road and collided with another vehicle.*
3 ADJ You say that someone's behaviour is **icy** when they show their dislike or anger in a quiet, controlled way. *Bowman spoke with an icy calm.* ◆ **icily** ADV *'That is quite out of the question,' said Thomas icily.*

I'd /aɪd/
I'd is the usual spoken form of 'I had', especially when 'had' is an auxiliary verb. **I'd** is also a spoken form of 'I would'. *I'd just had a letter from her... I'd like to make my views clear.*

idea /aɪˈdɪə/ **ideas**
1 NC An **idea** is a plan or possible course of action. *It's a good idea to get some instruction... I don't like the idea of going to ask for money.*
2 NC Your **idea** of something is your belief about what it is like or what it should be like. *People had some odd ideas about village children... What's your idea of a good party?... They had many ideas on how films should be made.*
3 N SING+SUPP If you have an **idea** of something, you know about it to some extent. *He has a good idea of how the Civil Service functions... Have you any idea how much it would cost?*
4 N SING+SUPP If you have an **idea** that something is the case, you suspect that it is the case. *My friends had an idea that something was wrong.*
5 If you have **no idea** about something, you do not know anything about it. *They had no idea of the route taken by the aircraft... The engineers have no idea of the size of the leak.*
6 N SING The **idea** of an action or activity is its aim or purpose. *The idea is to try and avoid further expense.*

ideal /aɪˈdɪəl/ **ideals**
1 NC An **ideal** is a principle, idea, or standard that seems very good and worth trying to achieve. *He believed in parliamentary democracy as an ideal.*
2 N SING Your **ideal** of something is the person or thing

that seems to you to be the best possible example of it. *He idolizes her as his feminine ideal.*
3 ADJ The **ideal** person or thing for a particular purpose is the best one for it. *He is the ideal person for the job.*
4 ADJ ATTRIB An **ideal** society or world is the best possible one that you can imagine. *He set down his theory of an ideal society based on absolute reason, absolute sincerity and equality between men and women... In an ideal world, South-East Asia would want to wave goodbye to all foreign soldiers.*

idealise /aɪˈdɪəlaɪz/. See **idealize.**

idealism /aɪˈdɪəlɪzəm/
NU **Idealism** is the behaviour and beliefs of someone who has strong ideals and tries to base their behaviour on these ideals. *The enormous hopes and idealism of the French Revolution were soon dissipated.* ◆ **idealist**, **idealists** NC *He was an idealist, too good for the world of action.*

idealistic /aɪdɪəˈlɪstɪk/
ADJ **Idealistic** people base their behaviour on ideals. *I was a teenager and had all these idealistic visions of brotherhood and fraternity.*

idealize /aɪˈdɪəlaɪz/ **idealizes, idealizing, idealized**; also spelt **idealise.**
VorVO If you **idealize** someone or something, you think of them as perfect or much better than they really are. *Romantic love and motherhood are sentimentally idealized... If that war was designed to frustrate air power, this one seemed to idealize it.* ◆ **idealized** ADJ *The boy yearned to be like his idealized father.*

ideally /aɪˈdɪəli/
1 ADV SEN If you say that **ideally** something should happen, you mean that you would like it to happen, although it may not be possible. *The government should ideally be run by the people.*
2 ADV If someone is **ideally** suited for something, they are as suitable for it as possible. *He considered himself ideally suited for the job.*

identical /aɪˈdɛntɪkl/
ADJ Things that are **identical** are exactly the same. ...*two women in identical pinafores.* ◆ **identically** ADV *All of them were identically dressed for the occasion.*

identical twin, identical twins
NC **Identical twins** are twins of the same sex who look exactly the same. *The likelihood of having identical twins is the same the world over.*

identifiable /aɪˌdɛntɪˈfaɪəbl/
ADJ Something that is **identifiable** can be recognized. ...*a much more easily identifiable hand signal.*

identification /aɪˌdɛntɪfɪˈkeɪʃn/
1 NU The **identification** of people or things is the process of recognizing or choosing them. ...*the identification of requirements and resources.*
2 NU When someone asks for your **identification**, they are asking to see something such as a driving licence which proves who you are. *They presented Lebanese passports as identification.*
3 NU+*with* **Identification** with someone or something is a feeling of sympathy and support for them. ...*identification with the People's Republic of China.*

identify /aɪˈdɛntɪfaɪ/ **identifies, identifying, identified**
1 VO If you can **identify** someone or something, you can recognize them and say who or what they are. *The guard had been identified as Victor Kowalski.*
2 VO If something **identifies** you, it makes it possible for people to recognize you. *Wear on your third finger an iron ring, which will identify you.*
3 V+*with* If you **identify** with someone or something, you feel that you understand them or their feelings. *He couldn't identify with other people's troubles.*
4 VO+*with* If you **identify** one thing with another, you consider them to be the same thing; a formal use. *He said that there was a tendency to identify democracy with multi-party pluralism.*

identikit /aɪˈdɛntɪkɪt/ **identikits**
NC An **identikit** or an **identikit** picture is a drawing, made up from a special set of smaller drawings, of the face of someone the police want to question. It is made from descriptions given to them by witnesses to a crime. *The police have now released an identikit*

portrait of the two men still wanted in connection with the crime.

identity /aɪdɛntəti/ **identities**
1 NC+POSS Your **identity** is who you are. *Glenn whipped off the mask to reveal his identity.*
2 NCorNU The **identity** of a person or place is the characteristics they have that distinguish them from others. *...your sense of identity, of who you are and what you are. ...a region with its own cultural identity... We are losing our identity as a Panamanian country.* ● **mistaken identity**: see **mistaken**.

identity card, identity cards
NC An **identity card** is a card with a person's name, date of birth, and other information on it, which people in some countries have to carry in order to prove who they are. *The idea of personal identity cards has always aroused fierce opposition in Britain.*

ideological /aɪdiəlɒdʒɪkl/
ADJ **Ideological** means relating to principles or beliefs. *...the ideological aspects of the dispute.*
♦ **ideologically** ADV *I was ideologically attracted to Liberalism.*

ideology /aɪdiɒlədʒi/ **ideologies**
NCorNU An **ideology** is a set of beliefs, especially the political beliefs on which people, parties, or countries base their actions. *...the capitalist ideology of the West. ...the Polish Communist Party's head of ideology in Stalin's time... He argues that there is no room for ideology in economics.*

idiocy /ɪdiəsi/
NU The **idiocy** of something is the fact that it is very stupid; a formal word. *...the idiocy of the plan.*

idiom /ɪdiəm/ **idioms**
1 NC An **idiom** is a group of words which have a different meaning when used together from the one they would have if you took the meaning of each word individually. *During the war in the Gulf he's heard plenty of intriguing idioms: 'collateral damage', for instance.*
2 NC+SUPP The **idiom** of something such as speech, writing, or music, is its particular style; a formal use. *He demonstrated the unfathomable depths and potential of this musical idiom.*

idiomatic /ɪdiəmætɪk/
ADJ In **idiomatic** speech or writing, words are used in a way that sounds natural to native speakers of the language. *Her English was fluent and idiomatic.*

idiosyncrasy /ɪdiəsɪŋkrəsi/ **idiosyncrasies**
NC Someone's **idiosyncrasies** are their own rather unusual habits or likes and dislikes. *She adjusted to her husband's many idiosyncrasies.*

idiosyncratic /ɪdiəsɪŋkrætɪk/
ADJ If someone's behaviour or likes and dislikes are **idiosyncratic**, they are personal to them, and are often rather unusual. *...the band's highly idiosyncratic approach to music.*

idiot /ɪdiət/ **idiots**
NC If you call someone an **idiot**, you mean that they are very stupid. *That idiot Antonio has gone and locked our door.*

idiotic /ɪdiɒtɪk/
ADJ Someone or something that is **idiotic** is very stupid. *It was an idiotic question to ask.*

idle /aɪdl/ **idler, idlest; idles, idling, idled**
1 ADJ Someone who is **idle** is not doing anything, especially when they should be doing something. *He always wanted to make a comedy about the idle rich.*
♦ **idly** ADV *...those who sit idly by while you slave over a hot stove.* ♦ **idleness** NU *No one can afford to pay troops to sit about in idleness.*
2 ADJ PRED Machines or factories that are **idle** are not being used. *The machinery could not be converted, and so stood idle.*
3 ADJ If you say that it would be **idle** to do something, you mean that nothing useful would be achieved by it; a formal use. *It would be idle to look for a solution at this stage.*
4 ADJ ATTRIB You use **idle** to describe something that you do for no particular reason, often because you have nothing better to do. *Idle curiosity is certainly a vice... Sudhir and Judy carried on long, idle conversations.* ♦ **idly** ADV *She glanced idly down the*

list of contents.
5 ADJ ATTRIB You can describe something that someone has said or done that you do not take seriously as **idle**. *It was something of an idle gesture... This is no idle threat.*
6 V If a car engine is **idling**, it is running slowly because it has not been put in gear and is not moving. *I can take my foot off the accelerator and it'll idle.*
7 VO When workers or their workplaces are **idled**, the workplaces close down because the employers have no more work for them to do, or because the workers go on strike; used in American English. *At its peak, the strike idled 300,000 of the country's 1.2 million miners... GM, Ford and Chrysler will idle a dozen US and Canadian assembly lines later this week.*
idle away PHRASAL VERB If you **idle away** a period of time, you spend it doing very little. *...three old men, idling away the summer afternoon under the trees.*

idler /aɪdlə/ **idlers**
NC If you call someone an **idler**, you mean that they are lazy and should be working. *...a state full of idlers.*

idol /aɪdl/ **idols**
1 NC An **idol** is someone such as a film star or pop star, who is greatly admired or loved by the public. *...young pop idols.*
2 NC An **idol** is also a statue that is worshipped by people who believe that it is a god. *Hindus claim that an idol of Rama miraculously appeared inside the mosque.*

idolatrous /aɪdɒlətrəs/
ADJ Something that is **idolatrous** treats a particular person or group of people as an idol; used showing disapproval. *No newspaper could have been more idolatrous of the generals who commanded the campaign.*

idolatry /aɪdɒlətri/
NU Someone who practises **idolatry** worships idols; used showing disapproval. *Now they were punished for their heresy, now they would suffer for their idolatry.*

idolize /aɪdəlaɪz/ **idolizes, idolizing, idolized**; also spelt **idolise**.
VO If you **idolize** someone such as a film star or a pop star, you admire them very much. *They idolize Bob Dylan.*

idyll /ɪdl/ **idylls**
NC An **idyll** is an idyllic situation. *...the myth of an unchanging idyll of rural England.*

idyllic /ɪdɪlɪk/
ADJ Something that is **idyllic** is extremely pleasant and peaceful without any difficulties. *...an idyllic place to raise a young child.*

i.e. /aɪ iː/
i.e. is used to introduce a word or sentence expressing what you have just said in a different and clearer way. *To keep a dog costs twice as much, i.e. £110 a year.*

if /ɪf/
1 CONJ You use **if** in conditional sentences to mention an event or situation that might happen, might be happening, or might have happened. *If all goes well, Voyager 2 will head on to Uranus... If any questions occur to you, then don't hesitate to write... If I could afford it I would buy a boat... It would have been better if you had explained more clearly what you meant.*
2 CONJ You also use **if** in indirect questions. *I asked her if I could help her... I wonder if you'd give the children a bath?*
3 CONJ **If** can also be used to introduce an exception to a general statement you have already made. *It was an excellent concert. If I had any disappointment, it was all at the end.*
4 CONJ You can also use **if** to introduce a comment or request. *If you don't mind me saying so, I think you are partly responsible... If you can sign that for me. Thank you.*
● **If** is used in these phrases. ● You use **if not** to suggest, for example, that an amount might be bigger or that a time might be sooner than one you have just mentioned. *They have hundreds of thousands if not*

millions of pounds of investment... I'd like to see you tonight, if not sooner. ● You can say **'if I were you'** when you are giving someone advice. If I were you I'd take the money. ● You use **if anything** when you are saying something which confirms a negative statement that you have just made. It certainly wasn't an improvement. We were, if anything, worse off than before. ● You use **if only** when you are mentioning a reason for doing something. I'll have a glass myself, if only to stop you from drinking it all. ● You also use **if only** to express a wish or desire, especially one that cannot be fulfilled. If only she could have lived a little longer. ● You use **as if** when you are describing the way something is done by comparing it with something else. She folded her arms as if she were cold.

iffy /ɪfi/
ADJ PRED If you are **iffy** about something, you are uncertain about whether you are going to do it or not; an informal word. 'Are you going to the party?'—'I'm a bit iffy about it at the moment.'

igloo /ɪglu:/ **igloos**
NC An **igloo** is a round house made from blocks of snow. Eskimoes spend much of their winter inside their igloos.

igneous /ɪgniəs/
ADJ **Igneous** rocks are formed by volcanic action; a technical term in geology.

ignite /ɪgnaɪt/ **ignites, igniting, ignited**
V-ERG When something **ignites** or when you **ignite** something, it starts burning. Rockets of all shapes and sizes ignited and flew up in every direction... The device was supposed to ignite the fireworks.

ignition /ɪgnɪʃn/
N SING The **ignition** is the part of a car's engine which ignites the fuel and starts the car; also used of the keyhole where you put a key in order to start the engine. Have you switched the ignition on?... He stuck the key in the ignition and started the engine.

ignoble /ɪgnəʊbl/
ADJ An **ignoble** person behaves in a cowardly or morally unacceptable way which makes people lose respect for them; a formal word. His career was a procession of lies and deception; cynicism, ruthlessness and ignoble acts.

ignominious /ɪgnəmɪniəs/
ADJ **Ignominious** means shameful or very embarrassing; a formal word. The marriage was considered especially ignominious since she was of royal descent... Many believe it will end in ignominious defeat for her. ◆ **ignominiously** ADV They were ignominiously defeated in the general election.

ignominy /ɪgnəmɪni/
NU **Ignominy** is shame or public disgrace; a formal word. ...a life of prostitution and ignominy.

ignoramus /ɪgnəreɪməs/ **ignoramuses**
NC If you call someone an **ignoramus**, you mean that you think that they have very little knowledge; an offensive word. He is not dealing with uneducated ignoramuses, he is dealing with highly intelligent men.

ignorance /ɪgnərəns/
NU **Ignorance** of something is lack of knowledge about it. Individuals suffer through ignorance of their rights.

ignorant /ɪgnərənt/
1 ADJ If you are **ignorant** of something, you do not know about it. The masses were largely ignorant of the options open to them.
2 ADJ You say that people are **ignorant** when they behave in an impolite or inconsiderate way. Some users of English believe that it is not correct to use **ignorant** with this meaning. She is an ignorant woman.

ignore /ɪgnɔ:/ **ignores, ignoring, ignored**
1 VO If you **ignore** someone or something, you deliberately take no notice of them. I ignored him and looked at Judith... Ralph ignored Jack's question.
2 VO Something that **ignores** an important aspect of a situation fails to take it into account. These proposals ignore the court's existing power... It's a political agreement which ignores the scientific facts.

ikon /aɪkɒn/. See **icon**.

Iliescu, Ion /jɒn ɪljesku:/
Ion Iliescu became President of Romania in 1990. He served on the Central Committee of the Romanian Communist Party from 1968 to 1984. He was Chairman of the National Salvation Front (NSF) from 1989 to 1990. Born: 1930.

ilk /ɪlk/
N SING Something of a particular **ilk** is something of a particular type mentioned. ...Joan Baez and vocalists of that ilk. ...blueberries and many small berries of that ilk.

ill /ɪl/ **ills. Worse** is sometimes used as the comparative for the meaning in paragraph 1.
1 ADJ Someone who is **ill** is suffering from a disease or health problem. I feel ill... She is ill with cancer... Don't refreeze food, it could make you ill. ...a hospital for the mentally ill.
2 N PL Difficulties or problems can be referred to as **ills**; a literary use. ...the ills of old age. ...the country's economic ills.
3 ADV **Ill** means badly; a literary use. The programme was ill researched.
4 ADJ ATTRIB **Ill** also means harmful; a formal use. Did you get any ill effects when you had your blood transfusion? ...protection against ill fortune.
● **Ill** is used in these phrases. ● If you **fall ill** or are **taken ill**, you become ill suddenly. ● If you **speak ill of** someone, you criticize them. Don't expect me to speak ill of my employer. ● **ill at ease**: see **ease**.

I'll /aɪl/
I'll is the usual spoken form of 'I will' or 'I shall'. I'll ring you tomorrow morning.

ill- /ɪl-/
PREFIX **Ill-** is added to words, especially adjectives and past participles, to add the meaning 'badly' or 'inadequately'. For example, 'ill-written' means badly written. He makes ill-conceived and ridiculous comments.

ill-advised
ADJ An **ill-advised** action is not sensible or wise. The paper calls it an ill-advised mission and says the visit could cause severe damage.

ill-assorted
ADJ Things that are in an **ill-assorted** group do not suit or match each other. ...an ill-assorted collection of books.

ill-bred
ADJ If you say that someone is **ill-bred,** you think that they have bad manners. He's just an ill-bred lout.

ill-disposed
ADJ A person who is **ill-disposed** towards something or someone is unwilling to support them or to be sympathetic towards them. The defence might be undone by ill-disposed judges... He has accused them of being ill-disposed towards talks to find a peaceful solution.

illegal /ɪli:gl/
1 ADJ If an activity, possession, or organization is **illegal**, the law says that it is not allowed. It is illegal in many countries for women to work on night shifts... Marijuana is illegal in the United States. ◆ **illegally** ADV ...illegally parked cars.
2 ADJ ATTRIB An **illegal** immigrant is a person who has entered a country without official permission. The British government regarded him as an illegal immigrant after his permit expired.

illegible /ɪledʒɪbl/
ADJ **Illegible** writing is so unclear that you cannot read it. ...a short illegible hand-scrawled paragraph.

illegitimacy /ɪlɪdʒɪtɪməsi/
NU **Illegitimacy** is the fact of being born illegitimate. Victoria was not told of her illegitimacy until she was ten.

illegitimate /ɪlɪdʒɪtɪmət/
1 ADJ A person who is **illegitimate** was born of parents who were not legally married to each other. ...an illegitimate child.
2 ADJ An **illegitimate** activity is not allowed or approved by law or social customs. All parties regarded the treaty as illegitimate... They are resorting to force as a way of achieving illegitimate aims.

ill-equipped
ADJ Someone who is **ill-equipped** to do something does not have the ability, qualities, or equipment necessary to do it. *The police were plainly ill-equipped to deal with the riot.*

ill-fated
ADJ If you describe something as **ill-fated,** you mean that it ended in an unfortunate or tragic way; a literary word. *Alice recounted the story of her ill-fated boating expedition.*

ill-founded
ADJ Something that is **ill-founded** is not based on any proper proof or evidence. *He warned that their confidence was ill-founded.*

ill-gotten gains
N PL **Ill-gotten gains** are things that you have gained, received, or achieved in a dishonest or deceitful way. *...legislation to stop drug barons benefiting from their ill-gotten gains.*

ill health; also written **ill-health.**
NU Someone who suffers from **ill health** has an illness or keeps feeling unwell for long periods of time. *He retired in 1987, suffering from ill-health... Alcohol misuse is responsible for a vast amount of ill health.*

illiberal /ɪlɪbəᵊrəl/
ADJ A law or system that is **illiberal** allows people very little freedom or choice of action. *...the very illiberal laws on divorce... The government was overthrown by an even more illiberal regime.*

illicit /ɪlɪsɪt/
ADJ ATTRIB An **illicit** activity or substance is not allowed by law, or is not acceptable according to the social customs of a country. *They were prosecuted for illicit liquor selling... Naturally, they had their vices, their illicit pleasures.*

illiteracy /ɪlɪtᵊrəsi/
NU **Illiteracy** is the inability of people to read or write. *Mr Munala said that because of the high illiteracy rate among these people, a recorded version of the Bible had been produced.*

illiterate /ɪlɪtᵊrət/
ADJ Someone who is **illiterate** cannot read or write. *40 per cent of the country is reckoned to be illiterate.*

illness /ɪlnəs/ **illnesses**
1 NU **Illness** is the fact or experience of being ill. *I haven't been able to work because of illness.*
2 NC An **illness** is a particular disease such as a cold, measles, or pneumonia. *She died of a mysterious illness.*

illogical /ɪlɒdʒɪkl/
ADJ An **illogical** feeling or action is not reasonable or sensible. *It is clearly illogical to maintain such a proposition.* ◆ **illogically** ADV *I felt illogically that my own years there counted for nothing.*

ill-omened
ADJ If you describe something as **ill-omened,** you mean that you know that it is going to be unlucky or end in an unfortunate or tragic way; a literary word. *...the start of an ill-omened marriage.*

ill-starred
ADJ If you describe someone or something as **ill-starred,** you mean that you know that they are going to be unlucky, or that unfortunate or tragic things are going to happen to them; a literary word. *...Prince Henry, the ill-starred brother of Charles I.*

ill-tempered
1 ADJ Someone who is **ill-tempered** has a bad temper. *Victoria Station was full of anxious ill-tempered travellers.*
2 ADJ An **ill-tempered** occasion is one in which the people involved are aggressive or unfriendly towards each other. *...an ill-tempered fringe meeting at the conference. ...West Germany's defeat of the reigning champions, Argentina, in an ill-tempered match.*

ill-timed
ADJ Something that is **ill-timed** happens or is done at the wrong time, so that it is inappropriate or rude. *Her comments were ill-timed.*

ill-treat, ill-treats, ill-treating, ill-treated
VO If someone **ill-treats** you, they treat you cruelly. *Amnesty's evidence shows that hundreds of Yemenis have been tortured or ill-treated.*

ill-treatment
NU **Ill-treatment** is harsh or cruel treatment. *...creatures who are the victims of man's ill-treatment.*

illuminate /ɪluːmɪneɪt/ **illuminates, illuminating, illuminated**
1 VO To **illuminate** something means to shine light on it. *Lamps were arranged to illuminate his work.*
2 VO If you **illuminate** something that is difficult to understand, you make it clearer by explaining it or giving examples. *Their doctrine illuminates much that might seem obscure in the Muslim teaching.*
◆ **illuminating** ADJ *...his illuminating book on the subject.*

illuminated /ɪluːmɪneɪtɪd/
1 ADJ Something that is **illuminated** is lit up, usually by electric lighting. *...Vienna's most spectacularly illuminated church.*
2 ADJ **Illuminated** old books, manuscripts, and official documents have brightly coloured drawings and designs, often using gold paint. *One exhibition shows the story of the Bible through the religious illuminated manuscripts.*

illumination /ɪluːmɪneɪʃn/ **illuminations**
1 NU **Illumination** is the lighting that a place has. *The dusty bulb gave barely adequate illumination.*
2 N PL **Illuminations** are coloured lights which are put up in towns, especially at Christmas, as a decoration. *Prince Edward threw the switch to light the illuminations. ...Blackpool illuminations.*

illumine /ɪluːmɪn/ **illumines, illumining, illumined**
VO To **illumine** something means the same as to **illuminate** it; a literary word.

illusion /ɪluːʒn/ **illusions**
1 NC or NU An **illusion** is a false idea or belief. *She had no illusions about the army's ability to prevent her from taking power... We have an illusion of freedom... He said it would be an illusion to expect spectacular results soon.*
2 NC An optical **illusion** is something that looks like one thing but is really something else or is not there at all. *Cirrus clouds formed in arches across the sky, giving the illusion of travelling inside the body of an enormous animal.*

illusory /ɪluːzəᵊri/; a formal word.
1 ADJ Something that is **illusory** seems to exist, but does not really exist. *The difference is largely illusory.*
2 ADJ An **illusory** hope or belief makes you believe in something that does not exist or is not possible. *...illusory hopes that he would soon find a new job.*

illustrate /ɪləstreɪt/ **illustrates, illustrating, illustrated**
1 VO If you **illustrate** a point, you make it clear by using examples or stories. *The Muslims tell a story to illustrate the fact that power changes people... Nothing illustrates his selfishness more clearly than his behaviour to his wife.*
2 VO To **illustrate** a book means to put pictures or diagrams into it. *He is an architect and illustrates the book with photographs of his own buildings.*
◆ **illustrated** ADJ *...illustrated books of fairy tales.*

illustration /ɪləstreɪʃn/ **illustrations**
1 NC An **illustration** is an example or story used to make a point clear. *I've included a few specific examples as illustrations of the difficulty of our work.*
2 NC An **illustration** in a book is a picture or diagram. *...a cookery book with marvellous colour illustrations.*

illustrative /ɪləstrətɪv/
ADJ An **illustrative** picture or action is an example or explanation of something; a formal word. *These incidents are illustrative of the range of political actions being undertaken.*

illustrator /ɪləstreɪtə/ **illustrators**
NC An **illustrator** is an artist who draws pictures and diagrams for books and magazines. *...an illustrator of children's books.*

illustrious /ɪlʌstriəs/
ADJ An **illustrious** person is famous and distinguished; a formal word. *He is a member of an illustrious family... He described them as people who were illustrious.*

ill will

NU **Ill will** is a feeling of hostility towards someone. *He assured me he felt no ill will toward me... The tax had created a lot of ill will.*

ill wind

N SING An **ill wind** is an event which you expect to be unpleasant, but which in fact has a good result. The expression occurs in the proverb 'It's an ill wind that blows nobody any good', meaning that however bad something is, it usually has one or two good aspects at least. *Even an ill wind can bring good in some ways as long as you put it to good purpose.*

I'm /aɪm/

I'm is the usual spoken form of 'I am'. *I'm not blaming you... I'm afraid I can't come.*

image /ˈɪmɪdʒ/ **images**

1 NC If you have an **image** of someone or something, you have a picture or idea of them in your mind. *To most people, the term 'industrial revolution' conjures up images of smoky steel mills or clanking machines.*

2 NC The **image** of a person or organization is the way that they appear to other people. *His attempts to improve the Post Office's image were criticised as 'gimmicks'.*

3 NC An **image** is also a picture or reflection of someone or something. *He began to dress, never taking his eyes off his image in the mirror.*

4 NC An **image** is also a picture or theme in a work of art such as a painting or a book. *He was one of the few painters who produced convincing images of life in contemporary America.*

imagery /ˈɪmɪdʒri/

NU **Imagery** is the mental pictures or ideas created by poetic language, art, or music. *...religious imagery... Poetry allows him to use surreal imagery.*

imaginable /ɪˈmædʒɪnəbl/

ADJ ATTRIB or ADJ after N You use **imaginable** when referring to the most extreme example of a particular thing that you can think of. *...the narrowest imaginable range of interests. ...the most horrible punishments imaginable.*

imaginary /ɪˈmædʒɪnəʳri/

ADJ Something that is **imaginary** exists only in your mind. *Many children develop fears of imaginary dangers.*

imagination /ɪˌmædʒɪˈneɪʃn/ **imaginations**

NCorNU Your **imagination** is your ability to form new ideas or to think about things which you cannot see or which do not exist in real life. *You need a very good imagination to get to grips with these kinds of ideas... He asked them, using their imagination, to describe what they would see if they were in the central square in Milan.*

imaginative /ɪˈmædʒɪnətɪv/

ADJ Someone who is **imaginative** is able to form ideas of new or exciting things. *...an imaginative writer. ...imaginative and original theories.* ◆ **imaginatively** ADV *...an imaginatively designed bathroom.*

imagine /ɪˈmædʒɪn/ **imagines, imagining, imagined**

1 V-REPORT or VO If you **imagine** a situation, you think about it and try to form a picture or idea of it in your mind. *Try to imagine you're sitting on a cloud... It's hard to imagine a greater biological threat.*

2 V-REPORT or VO If you say that someone **imagined** something, you mean that they thought they saw or heard it, although it did not really happen or exist. *A reader imagined that Guthrie must have been with the pioneers to know so much about their lives... 'I saw a thing on the mountain.'—'You only imagined it.'*

3 V-REPORT If you say that you **imagine** something is true, you mean that you think it is true. *I imagine that the Libyan military have gone on full alert... I should imagine he wants you to hold his hand.*

imaginings /ɪˈmædʒɪnɪŋz/

N PL **Imaginings** are things that you think you have seen or heard, although actually you have not; a literary word. *The myth derives from their feverish imaginings.*

imbalance /ɪmˈbæləns/ **imbalances**

NCorNU If there is an **imbalance** in a situation, things are not evenly or fairly arranged. *...the imbalance between the rich and poor countries... He accused the council of gross imbalance and disregard for the real situation.*

imbecile /ˈɪmbəsiːl/ **imbeciles**

NC If you call someone an **imbecile**, you are saying that you think they are stupid. *For two years that imbecile spent his money like water.*

imbibe /ɪmˈbaɪb/ **imbibes, imbibing, imbibed**; a formal word.

1 VOorV If you **imbibe** alcohol, you drink it. *He had imbibed some much stronger beers in his young days in Manchester... 'Whisky?' 'Thank you,' I said, 'but I never imbibe.'*

2 VO If you **imbibe** ideas or arguments, you listen to them and believe that they are right or true. *You have been imbibing too many of their doctrines.*

imbroglio /ɪmˈbrəʊliəʊ/ **imbroglios**

NC An **imbroglio** is a very confusing or complicated situation; a literary word. *His solution had from the start of the whole imbroglio been to put down the rebellion by force.*

imbue /ɪmˈbjuː/ **imbues, imbuing, imbued**

VO If you **imbue** something with a quality, you fill it with that quality; a literary word. *...Mondrian's desire to imbue his art with mystical properties.* ◆ **imbued** ADJ PRED *...a unified society deeply imbued with Marxist convictions.*

IMF /ˌaɪemˈef/

N PROP The **IMF** is an international agency which is part of the United Nations and which tries to promote trade and improve economic conditions in the countries which belong to it. The IMF also lends money to its members to help them to develop industries, etc. **IMF** is an abbreviation for 'International Monetary Fund'. *...institutions like the World Bank and IMF... The IMF is also expected to approve a second loan of more than two thousand million dollars in October.*

imitate /ˈɪmɪteɪt/ **imitates, imitating, imitated**

VO If you **imitate** someone or something, you copy what they say or do. *He tried to imitate the girl's voice... The University of London imitated the German tradition of scholarship.*

imitation /ˌɪmɪˈteɪʃn/ **imitations**

1 NC An **imitation** is a copy of something else. *Computers so far are just bad imitations of our brains.*

2 NCorNU If you give an **imitation** of someone, you copy the way they speak or behave. *'Come here, my dear,' she said, giving a reasonable imitation of Isabel Travers... Boys can be seen to pat one another on the head in imitation of what their fathers do.*

3 ADJ ATTRIB **Imitation** things are not genuine but are made to look genuine. *...a pocket diary bound in black imitation leather.*

imitative /ˈɪmɪtətɪv/

ADJ Behaviour that is **imitative** copies someone else's behaviour; a formal word. *The film was withdrawn because of the imitative violence it was producing in some of the teenagers who watched it.*

imitator /ˈɪmɪteɪtəʳ/ **imitators**

NC An **imitator** of someone is a person who copies them or who behaves in the same way as them. *...successful designers and their imitators.*

immaculate /ɪˈmækjʊlət/

1 ADJ Something that is **immaculate** is perfectly clean or tidy. *Her apartment was immaculate.* ◆ **immaculately** ADV *Sir Oswald was immaculately dressed.*

2 ADJ **Immaculate** also means without any mistakes. *Your timing and technique will have to be immaculate.*

immaterial /ˌɪməˈtɪəriəl/

ADJ Something that is **immaterial** is not important or not relevant; a formal word. *The price was immaterial.*

immature /ˌɪməˈtjʊə, ˌɪməˈtʃɔː/

1 ADJ Something that is **immature** is not yet fully developed. *...the baby's immature digestive system.*

2 ADJ If you describe someone as **immature**, you mean that they do not behave in a sensible and adult way. *...an immature desire to shock.* ◆ **immaturity** /ˌɪməˈtjʊərəti/ NU *...complaints about my immaturity and lack of judgement.*

immeasurable /ɪmɛʒəºrəbl/
ADJ An amount or distance that is **immeasurable** is too large to be measured or counted. *The gap between them now seems immeasurable.*

immeasurably /ɪmɛʒəºrəbli/
SUBMOD You use **immeasurably** to emphasize that something has a particular quality to a very great extent. *Paul Getty had always been immeasurably wealthy.*

immediacy /ɪmiːdiəsi/
NU When you talk about the **immediacy** of something, you mean that it seems to be happening now or that it makes you feel directly involved with it; a formal word. *It is the immediacy of events which makes television so popular.*

immediate /ɪmiːdiət/
1 ADJ Something that is **immediate** happens without any delay. *They called for an immediate meeting of the Security Council.*
2 ADJ ATTRIB **Immediate** needs and concerns must be dealt with quickly. *He was occupied with more immediate matters.*
3 ADJ ATTRIB **Immediate** also means next in time or position. *Charlie was more honest than his immediate predecessor... To the immediate south we can see the mountains.*
4 ADJ ATTRIB Your **immediate** family are your close relatives such as your parents, brothers, and sisters. *The President has provided political favours to members of his immediate family.*

immediately /ɪmiːdiətli/
1 ADV If something happens **immediately**, it happens without any delay. *I have to go to Brighton immediately. It's very urgent.*
2 ADV You can use **immediately** when you are talking about something that can be understood or used without delay. *The connections are not immediately apparent.*
3 ADV **Immediately** also means next in time or position. *The church is immediately on your right... The sequence of events immediately preceding the tragedy is uncertain.*
4 ADV **Immediately** is also used to show that something is closely and directly involved in a situation. *The countries most immediately threatened are those in the south.*
5 CONJ You also use **immediately** when you are saying that something happens as soon as something else has happened. *Immediately I finish the show I get changed and go home.*

immemorial /ɪməmɔːriəl/
ADJ ATTRIB You use **immemorial** to describe things which are so old that nobody can remember a time when they did not exist. *...the immemorial custom of all Western societies.* ● If something has been happening **from time immemorial**, it has been happening for longer than anyone can remember. *They go on acting just as they did from time immemorial.*

immense /ɪmɛns/
ADJ **Immense** means extremely large. *Squids grow to an immense size... This development has been of immense importance.* ◆ **immensity** /ɪmɛnsəti/ NU+SUPP *...the immensity of the building.*

immensely /ɪmɛnsli/
ADV **Immensely** means to a very great extent or degree. *The issue is immensely complex... I enjoyed the course immensely.*

immerse /ɪmɜːs/ **immerses, immersing, immersed**
1 V-REFL+*in* If you **immerse** yourself in something, you become completely involved in it. *That year I immersed myself totally in my work.* ◆ **immersed** ADJ PRED *He became immersed in the activities of the union.*
2 VO If you **immerse** something in a liquid, you put it into the liquid so that it is completely covered. ◆ **immersion** /ɪmɜːʃn/ NU *You must be baptized by total immersion in our pool.*

immersion heater, immersion heaters
NC An **immersion heater** is an electric heater which provides hot water.

immigrant /ɪmɪgrənt/ **immigrants**
NC An **immigrant** is a person who has come to live in a country from another country. *...a Russian immigrant... East London has a large immigrant community.*

immigrate /ɪmɪgreɪt/ **immigrates, immigrating, immigrated**
VA If a person **immigrates**, they come to live in a country from another country. *...the great Indian forward, Darshan Koolar, who immigrated to the Midlands some years ago.*

immigration /ɪmɪgreɪʃn/
1 NU **Immigration** is the coming of people into a country in order to live and work there. *...government controls on immigration.*
2 NU **Immigration** is also the place at a port, airport, or border where officials check the passports of people coming into a country. *They are whisked through immigration and customs formalities in a matter of minutes.*

imminence /ɪmɪnəns/
NU The **imminence** of an event is the near certainty that it will happen very soon. *They seemed unaware of the imminence of the invasion. ...the imminence of world revolution.*

imminent /ɪmɪnənt/
ADJ Something that is **imminent** will happen very soon. *I believed that war was imminent. ...his imminent departure.*

immobile /ɪmaʊbaɪl/
ADJ **Immobile** means not moving, or unable to move. *Boylan sat immobile, staring straight ahead... Sea-snakes have fangs that are short and immobile.* ◆ **immobility** /ɪmaʊbɪləti/ NU *She had drugged herself into immobility.*

immobilize /ɪmaʊbəlaɪz/ **immobilizes, immobilizing, immobilized**; also spelt **immobilise.**
VO If someone or something **is immobilized**, they are made unable to move. *When you ring the alarm it immobilizes the lift.*

immoderate /ɪmɒdəºrət/
ADJ **Immoderate** is used to describe people, behaviour, or beliefs that are considered to be too extreme; used showing disapproval. *We were taught by Brother Byrne, who was so immoderate in using the strap that the class started a campaign against him.* ◆ **immoderately** ADV *She laughed immoderately.*

immodest /ɪmɒdɪst/
1 ADJ Behaviour that is **immodest** shocks or embarrasses some people because they think that it is rude. *Breast feeding in public may seem immodest to some people.*
2 ADJ Someone who is **immodest** is boastful. *He said it might be immodest for him to quote the next two lines of the review.*

immoral /ɪmɒrəl/
ADJ If you describe someone or their behaviour as **immoral**, you mean that they are morally wrong. *...the cruel and immoral use of animals in medical research.* ◆ **immorality** /ɪməræləti/ NU *...a denunciation of other people's immorality.*

immortal /ɪmɔːtl/
1 ADJ Someone or something that is **immortal**, is famous and will be remembered for a long time. *The play contained one immortal line.* ◆ **immortality** /ɪmɔːtæləti/ NU *You're not going to achieve immortality by writing a book like that.*
2 ADJ In stories, someone who is **immortal** lives for ever. *...old legends of immortal creatures.*

immortalize /ɪmɔːtəlaɪz/ **immortalizes, immortalizing, immortalized**; also spelt **immortalise.**
VO To **immortalize** someone or something means to cause them to be remembered for a very long time. *We talked about her gangster parts immortalised on film.*

immovable /ɪmuːvəbl/
1 ADJ An **immovable** object is fixed and cannot be moved. *...an immovable pillar.*
2 ADJ **Immovable** attitudes or opinions are firm and will not change. *...immovable conservatism.*

immune /ɪmjuːn/
1 ADJ PRED If you are **immune** to a disease, you cannot be made ill by it. *She thought that women might be immune to lung cancer.* ◆ **immunity** /ɪmjuːnəti/ NU *Babies receive immunity to a variety of infections.*
2 ADJ PRED If you are **immune** to something harmful, it cannot affect you or happen to you. *He was immune to the flattery of political leaders. ...targets that the West had considered immune from air attack.* ◆ **immunity** NU *He had been granted immunity from prosecution.*

immunize /ɪmjʊnaɪz/ **immunizes, immunizing, immunized;** also spelt **immunise.**
VO If you **are immunized** against a disease, you are made immune to it, usually by being given an injection. *They should have their children immunised against diphtheria.* ◆ **immunization** /ɪmjʊnaɪzeɪʃn/ NU *Measles can be prevented by immunization.*

immutable /ɪmjuːtəbl/
ADJ Something that is **immutable** will never change; a formal word. *...behaving according to a set of immutable rules.*

imp /ɪmp/ **imps**
1 NC An **imp** is a small creature in a fairy story that has magical powers and often causes trouble in a playful way. *...a mischievous imp.*
2 NC If you call a child an **imp**, you mean that they are naughty, but in a playful way that does not cause any serious harm.

impact /ɪmpækt/ **impacts**
1 NC+SUPP If something makes an **impact** on a situation or person, it has a strong effect on them. *...the impact of computing on routine office work... British authors make relatively little impact abroad.*
2 NU The **impact** of one object on another is the force with which it hits it. *Many modern bullets produce an explosive effect upon impact.*

impacted /ɪmpæktɪd/
ADJ An **impacted** tooth is unable to grow through your gum properly. *...an impacted wisdom tooth that had to be taken out.*

impair /ɪmpeə/ **impairs, impairing, impaired**
VO If you **impair** something, you damage it so that it stops working properly; a formal word. *His digestion had been impaired by his recent illness.* ◆ **impaired** ADJ *...children with impaired hearing.*

impale /ɪmpeɪl/ **impales, impaling, impaled**
VO or V-REFL If you **impale** something, you stick a sharp pointed object through it; a formal word. *He cut off a piece of the meat and impaled it on his fork... He was holding a branch, and impaled upon it was the bloody head of a leopard.*

impart /ɪmpɑːt/ **imparts, imparting, imparted;** a formal word.
1 VO If you **impart** information to someone, you tell it to them. *He had a terrible piece of news to impart.*
2 VO If something **imparts** a particular quality, it gives that quality to something else. *Carrots impart a delicious flavour to stews.*

impartial /ɪmpɑːʃl/
ADJ Someone who is **impartial** is able to act fairly because they are not personally involved in a situation. *He gave an impartial view of the state of affairs in Northern Ireland.* ◆ **impartially** ADV *These men will judge the people impartially.* ◆ **impartiality** /ɪmpɑːʃiæləti/ NU *The BBC was dedicated to impartiality.*

impassable /ɪmpɑːsəbl/
ADJ If a road or path is **impassable**, you cannot use it because it is blocked or in bad condition. *The onset of the rainy season makes roads impassable.*

impasse /æmpæs, ɪmpæs/
N SING An **impasse** is a difficult situation in which it is impossible to make any progress; a formal word. *The talks had reached an impasse over the issue.*

impassioned /ɪmpæʃnd/
ADJ When you speak in an **impassioned** way, you express powerful emotion because you feel very strongly about something; a literary word. *After three hours of impassioned debate the motion was defeated.*

impassive /ɪmpæsɪv/
ADJ If your face is **impassive**, it does not show any emotion. *...the impassive face of a carnival mask... His impassive features have given us no clues.* ◆ **impassively** ADV *He looked at me impassively.*

impatience /ɪmpeɪʃns/
1 NU Someone's **impatience** is their feeling of annoyance at having to wait for something. *The British Foreign Secretary revealed impatience with the pace of the EEC's negotiations.*
2 NU If you show **impatience** to do something, you are eager to do it. If you show **impatience** for something to happen, you want it to happen immediately. *He was awaiting the outcome with impatience... Yesterday's demonstration reflected public impatience for change.*

impatient /ɪmpeɪʃnt/
1 ADJ If you are **impatient**, you are annoyed because you have had to wait too long for something. *Albanians have become impatient with the slow pace of liberalisation in the country.* ◆ **impatiently** ADV *Oliver stood waiting impatiently.*
2 ADJ If you are **impatient** to do something, you are eager to do it. If you are **impatient** for something to happen, you want it to happen immediately. *Philip was impatient to inspect his place of work.* ◆ **impatiently** ADV *He looked forward impatiently to Kumar's next visit.*

impeach /ɪmpiːtʃ/ **impeaches, impeaching, impeached**
VO In the United States, if a government official or politician is **impeached**, they are charged with committing a serious crime in connection with their job. *President Nixon was impeached by the House Judiciary Committee and decided to resign.*

impeachable /ɪmpiːtʃəbl/
ADJ In the United States, an **impeachable** crime or offence is one for which a public official can be impeached. *He committed impeachable crimes.*

impeachment /ɪmpiːtʃmənt/
NU In the United States, the **impeachment** of a public official is their trial for a serious crime committed in office. *They were deciding on the crimes that would justify impeachment.*

impeccable /ɪmpekəbl/
ADJ Something that is **impeccable** is perfect. *He had impeccable manners.* ◆ **impeccably** ADV *As usual, he was impeccably dressed.*

impecunious /ɪmpəkjuːniəs/
ADJ Someone who is **impecunious** has very little money; a formal word. *The powers of the central government have steadily dwindled as it has become more impecunious.*

impede /ɪmpiːd/ **impedes, impeding, impeded**
VO To **impede** someone or something means to make their movement or development difficult; a formal word. *...procedures that would impede an effective investigation.*

impediment /ɪmpedɪmənt/ **impediments**
1 NC If something is an **impediment** to a person or thing, it makes their movement or development difficult; a formal use. *The new taxes were a major impediment to economic growth.*
2 NC A speech **impediment** is a disability such as a stammer which makes speaking difficult. *We are trying to understand better the complexities of this common speech impediment.*

impedimenta /ɪmpedɪmentə/
N PL A person's **impedimenta** are the bags and other things that slow them down on a journey, used especially to refer to the equipment carried by an army; a literary word. *He included among his impedimenta a wife and three children.*

impel /ɪmpel/ **impels, impelling, impelled**
VO When an emotion **impels** you to do something, you feel forced to do it; a formal word. *I feel impelled to express grave doubts about the project.*

impending /ɪmpendɪŋ/
ADJ ATTRIB You use **impending** to describe something that will happen very soon; a formal word. *...impending disaster.*

impenetrable /ɪmpenətrəbl/
1 ADJ An **impenetrable** wall or barrier is impossible to

get through. ...*the impenetrable mountain terrain.*
2 ADJ **Impenetrable** also means impossible to understand. *The law seems mysterious and impenetrable.*

imperative /ɪmpɛrətɪv/ **imperatives**
1 ADJ Something that is **imperative** is very important and needs to be considered or dealt with urgently; a formal use. *It's imperative that we take care of Liebermann immediately.*
2 NC An **imperative** is an action, command, or task that is very urgent and must be dealt with quickly or urgently; a formal use. *The military imperative has had to give way to the political and diplomatic imperative of holding together the coalition.*
3 NC In grammar, an **imperative** is a verb in the form that is typically used for giving instructions or making informal invitations. For example, in 'Turn left at the next crossroads' and 'Have another biscuit', 'turn' and 'have' are imperatives.

imperceptible /ɪmpəsɛptəbl/
ADJ Something that is **imperceptible** is so small or slight that it exists or happens without being felt or noticed. ...*an almost imperceptible sensation.*
◆ **imperceptibly** ADV *The room had grown imperceptibly warmer.*

imperfect /ɪmpɜːfɪkt/
1 ADJ Something that is **imperfect** has faults. *We live in an imperfect society.*
2 N SING In grammar, the **imperfect** or the **imperfect tense** is used in describing continuous actions in the past. It is also called the 'past continuous'.

imperfection /ɪmpəfɛkʃn/ **imperfections**
NU or NC An **imperfection** is a fault or weakness. ...*a state of imperfection... This world is riddled with imperfection... Americans do not tolerate such imperfections in themselves.*

imperfectly /ɪmpɜːfɪktli/
ADV If you do something **imperfectly**, you do not do it completely or satisfactorily. ...*a world which we only imperfectly understand.*

imperial /ɪmpɪərɪəl/
1 ADJ ATTRIB **Imperial** means belonging or relating to an empire, emperor, or empress. ...*the decline of Britain as an imperial power.* ...*the Imperial Palace.*
2 ADJ ATTRIB The **imperial** system of measurement uses miles, feet and inches, pounds and ounces, and gallons and pints.

imperialism /ɪmpɪərɪəlɪzəm/
NU **Imperialism** is a system in which a rich and powerful country controls other countries. ...*the struggle against imperialism.* ◆ **imperialist**, **imperialists** NC or N+N ...*rival imperialists.* ...*imperialist powers.*

imperil /ɪmpɛrəl/ **imperils, imperilling, imperilled;** spelt **imperiling, imperiled** in American English.
VO Something that **imperils** you puts you in danger; a formal word. *A whole range of policies could imperil the next Superpower Summit... Roy Hattersley accused the government of imperilling industrial relations.*

imperious /ɪmpɪərɪəs/
ADJ An **imperious** person is proud and expects to be obeyed; a formal word. *All of them share the same qualities: imperious manner, striking appearance and fearless spirit.*

imperishable /ɪmpɛrɪʃəbl/
ADJ Something that is **imperishable** cannot disappear or be destroyed; a formal word. *There was a certain quality which was imperishable.*

impermanence /ɪmpɜːmənəns/
NU **Impermanence** is a quality of not being permanent; a formal word. ...*a sense of fragile impermanence.*

impermanent /ɪmpɜːmənənt/
ADJ Something that is **impermanent** is likely to change; a formal word. *Changes come slowly and are generally impermanent.*

impermeable /ɪmpɜːmiəbl/
ADJ Something that is **impermeable** will not allow fluid to pass through it; a formal word. ...*impermeable membranes.*

impersonal /ɪmpɜːsəⁿnəl/
1 ADJ An **impersonal** place or activity makes you feel that you are not important and that your personality, feelings, and opinions do not matter. ...*a vast, impersonal organization.* ...*dull, repetitive, impersonal work.*
2 ADJ **Impersonal** also means not concerned with any particular person. ...*impersonal selection procedures.*
◆ **impersonally** ADV ...*written examinations marked impersonally and with no knowledge of the candidate.*
3 ADJ ATTRIB In grammar, an **impersonal** pronoun is one that does not refer to a person or a particular object, for example, 'it' in the sentence 'It was very late when we arrived'.
4 ADJ ATTRIB In grammar, an **impersonal** verb does not have a subject and is used only after 'it' or 'there', as in 'It is raining'.

impersonate /ɪmpɜːsəneɪt/ **impersonates, impersonating, impersonated**
VO If you **impersonate** someone, you pretend to be that person, either to deceive people or to entertain them. *I ought to be arrested for impersonating an officer.* ◆ **impersonation** /ɪmpɜːsəneɪʃn/ **impersonations** NC or NU ...*his impersonation of a Russian prince.* ...*our powers of impersonation.*

impersonator /ɪmpɜːsəneɪtə/ **impersonators**
NC An **impersonator** is a stage performer who impersonates famous people. *Almost all the Elvis impersonators do the aging, jumpsuited, Vegas Elvis.*

impertinence /ɪmpɜːtɪnəns/
NU **Impertinence** is behaviour that is not polite or respectful. *They might be offended by such impertinence.*

impertinent /ɪmpɜːtɪnənt/
ADJ Someone who is being **impertinent** is not being polite or respectful. *It would be rather impertinent of me to express an opinion.* ...*impertinent questions.*

imperturbable /ɪmpətɜːbəbl/
ADJ Someone who is **imperturbable** remains calm and untroubled, even in a situation that is disturbing. *She had been admirably calm, imperturbable, and reasoning over the death of the cat.*

impervious /ɪmpɜːvɪəs/
1 ADJ If you are **impervious** to someone's actions, you are not affected by them. *They were impervious to any outside pressures.*
2 ADJ If something is **impervious** to water, water cannot pass through it. *At the same time the material is impervious to water and very strong.*

impetuous /ɪmpɛtʃuəs/
ADJ Someone who is **impetuous** acts quickly and suddenly without thinking. *She has transformed herself from an impetuous, inexperienced 33 year old into a responsible and moderate politician.*

impetus /ɪmpɪtəs/
NU+SUPP The **impetus** of something is the strong effect it has in causing something to happen. *The present conflict might provide fresh impetus for peace talks.*

impiety /ɪmpaɪəti/
NU **Impiety** is a lack of respect or religious reverence that a person shows; a formal word, used showing disapproval.

impinge /ɪmpɪndʒ/ **impinges, impinging, impinged**
V+on or upon Something that **impinges** on you has an effect on you, often by restricting the way that you can behave; a formal word. *Your political opinions will necessarily impinge on your public life... They are worried about work that could impinge upon civil liberties.*

impious /ɪmpɪəs, ɪmpaɪəs/
ADJ Someone who is **impious** shows a lack of respect or religious reverence; a formal word, used showing disapproval. *The Muslim authorities have described the book as impious and have called for it to be banned.*

impish /ɪmpɪʃ/
ADJ Someone who has an **impish** quality appears cheeky or naughty in a playful way. *He had an impish, rather wicked humour.*

implacable /ɪmplækəbl/
ADJ Someone who is **implacable** has strong feelings of anger or dislike that you cannot change. ...*our most*

implacable opponent. ...the implacable hatred that workers feel for their employers. ◆ **implacably** ADV *They are implacably hostile.*

implant, implants, implanting, implanted; pronounced /ɪmˈplɑːnt/ when it is a verb and /ˈɪmplɑːnt/ when it is a noun.
1 VO To **implant** something into a person's body means to put it there by means of an operation. *...Poland's first successful operation to implant an artificial heart. ...experiments in which mice will be implanted with human cells.*
2 NC An **implant** is something implanted into a person's body. *...hormone implants.*

implausible /ɪmˈplɔːzəbl/
ADJ Something that is **implausible** is not easy to believe, and unlikely to be true. *...a very implausible romantic thriller.*

implement, implements, implementing, implemented; pronounced /ˈɪmpləment/ when it is a verb and /ˈɪmpləmənt/ when it is a noun.
1 VO If you **implement** a plan, system, or law, you carry it out. *...policies that they would like to see implemented.* ◆ **implementation** /ɪmpləmenˈteɪʃn/ NU *...the implementation of the desired reforms.*
2 NC An **implement** is a tool or other piece of equipment. *...basic agricultural implements.*

implicate /ˈɪmplɪkeɪt/ **implicates, implicating, implicated**
VO If you **implicate** someone in an unpleasant event or situation, you show that they were involved in it. *He was implicated in the murder of a teacher.*

implication /ɪmplɪˈkeɪʃn/ **implications**
1 NC An **implication** is something suggested or implied by a situation, event, or statement. *The clear implication is that violence is suspected... Spencer began to query the political implications of Macaulay's statement.*
2 If something is true **by implication**, a statement, event, or fact suggests or implies that it is true. *He made it fairly clear, by implication, where he thought the violence stemmed from... It has happened before, so, by implication, it could happen again.*

implicit /ɪmˈplɪsɪt/
1 ADJ **Implicit** criticisms or attitudes are expressed in an indirect way. *...advertisements containing implicit racial prejudice... Artists, writers and actors gathered to protest at the censorship implicit in the measure.* ◆ **implicitly** ADV *Mr Biffen implicitly criticised the idea.*
2 ADJ If you have an **implicit** belief or faith in something, you believe it completely and have no doubts about it. *I declare that I have implicit faith in Marxism.* ◆ **implicitly** ADV *I believe implicitly in the concept of Europe.*

implore /ɪmˈplɔː/ **implores, imploring, implored**
VO+to-INF or V-QUOTE If you **implore** someone to do something, you beg them to do it; a literary word. *She implored me to come... 'Before you go,' she implored, 'can you tell me how to get there.'*

imply /ɪmˈplaɪ/ **implies, implying, implied**
1 VO or V-REPORT If you **imply** that something is true, you suggest that it is true without actually saying so. *At one point she implied she would marry me... He implied that the government lacked a commitment to negotiation.* ◆ **implied** ADJ *...implied criticism.*
2 V-REPORT or VO If a situation **implies** that something is the case, it makes it seem that it is the case. *These discoveries imply that the sea-bed is rich in fossil fuels... The Justice Minister said it implied recognition of a multi party system.*

impolite /ɪmpəˈlaɪt/
ADJ **Impolite** behaviour is rude and offends people. *It was very impolite of him to ask.*

impolitic /ɪmˈpɒlɪtɪk/
ADJ An **impolitic** action is unwise and likely to cause difficulty or embarrassment; a formal word. *It seemed impolitic to draw too much attention to this.*

imponderable /ɪmˈpɒndərəbl/ **imponderables**
ADJ ATTRIB **Imponderable** is used to describe something that is impossible or very difficult to assess or estimate; a literary word. *...the great imponderable forces of nature.* ► Also NC *...such*

imponderables as power and knowledge.

import, imports, importing, imported; pronounced /ɪmˈpɔːt/ when it is a verb and /ˈɪmpɔːt/ when it is a noun.
1 VO When goods or services **are imported**, they are bought from another country and sent to your own country. *He tried to import orchids to England. ...imported sugar.* ◆ **importation** /ɪmpɔːˈteɪʃn/ NU *...the illegal importation of drugs into Britain.*
2 NC **Imports** are products or raw materials bought from another country for use in your own country. *Imports may include industrial raw materials and machinery as well as a limited range of consumer goods.*
3 NU The **import** of something is the importance that it has because of the way that it is likely to affect people or events; a formal use. *The future of the school may be of little import... Mr Giraud said that this was of no import to France.*

importance /ɪmˈpɔːtns/
1 NU+SUPP The **importance** of something is its quality of being significant, valuable, or necessary. *...the importance of mathematics to science. ...Stonehenge's historic importance.*
2 NU The **importance** of a person is the social influence or power that he or she has. *Was he related to anyone of importance?*

important /ɪmˈpɔːtnt/
1 ADJ Something that is **important** is very significant, valuable, or necessary. *This is the most important part of the job... It is important to get on with your employer and his wife.* ◆ **importantly** ADV *The problems the Chinese face differ importantly from those facing Africa.*
2 ADJ An **important** person has influence or power. *...the list of important people who are coming on state visits.*

importer /ɪmˈpɔːtə/ **importers**
NC An **importer** is a person, country, or business that buys goods or services from another country for use in their own country. *Britain is the world's third largest importer of canned tuna.*

importunate /ɪmˈpɔːtjʊnət/
ADJ Someone who is **importunate** is persistent in trying to get something that they want; a formal word. *She holds out her hand for money, importunate, insistent, desperate.*

importune /ɪmˈpɔːtjuːn/ **importunes, importuning, importuned**
VO If you **importune** someone, you persistently ask them for something or urge them to do something; a formal word. *He began to importune her with offers of marriage.*

importunity /ɪmpɔːtjuːnəti/ **importunities**
NU or NC **Importunity** or an **importunity** is an example of importunate behaviour; a formal word. *I was there to protect her from the importunities of unscrupulous and lascivious men.*

impose /ɪmˈpəʊz/ **imposes, imposing, imposed**
1 VO If you **impose** something on people, you force them to accept it. *She was a harsh mother and imposed severe discipline on her children. ...the proposal to impose a 20p admission charge for museums.* ◆ **imposition** /ɪmpəˈzɪʃn/ NU *...the imposition of a wages freeze.*
2 V If someone **imposes** on you, they expect you to do something for them which you do not want to do. *She would hate to feel that she was imposing on anyone.* ◆ **imposition, impositions** NC *I'd be so grateful, though really it's an imposition.*

imposing /ɪmˈpəʊzɪŋ/
ADJ Someone or something that is **imposing** has an impressive appearance or manner. *Mrs Sabawala's house was large and imposing.*

impossible /ɪmˈpɒsəbl/
1 ADJ Something that is **impossible** cannot be done, cannot happen, or cannot be believed. *It was an impossible task... Staying awake all night was virtually impossible.* ◆ **impossibly** SUBMOD *He had impossibly thin legs.* ◆ **impossibility** /ɪmpɒsəˈbɪləti/ NU *...the impossibility of change.*
2 ADJ You can say that a situation or person is

impossible when they are very difficult to deal with. *They are in an impossible position on this matter... You're an impossible man to please.* ♦ **impossibly** SUBMOD *Flats make life impossibly restrictive for energetic young children.*

impostor /ɪmpɒstə/ **impostors**; also spelt **imposter**. NC An **impostor** is someone who pretends to be someone else in order to get what they want. *Dr Thomas believes the Germans sent an imposter posing as Hess to Scotland.*

impotence /ɪmpətəns/
1 NU **Impotence** is a lack of power over people or events; a formal use. *...the inadequacies of planning law and the impotence of planners.*
2 NU **Impotence** is also a man's inability to perform the sex act because he cannot have an erection. *His fear of impotence had affected him physically.*

impotent /ɪmpətənt/
1 ADJ You say that someone is **impotent** when they have no power over people or events; a formal use. *Those who do not conform must be rendered impotent.*
2 ADJ If a man is **impotent**, he is unable to have sex. *Sterilization is not going to make a person impotent.*

impound /ɪmpaʊnd/ **impounds, impounding, impounded**
VO If policemen or other officials **impound** something that you own, they legally take possession of it; a formal word. *Security Police had come to our house and impounded all our belongings.*

impoverish /ɪmpɒvərɪʃ/ **impoverishes, impoverishing, impoverished**
VO To **impoverish** someone or something means to make them poor. *They were impoverished by a prolonged spell of unemployment... Its use spreads disease and impoverishes the land.* ♦ **impoverished** ADJ *...an impoverished Third World country.*

impoverishment /ɪmpɒvərɪʃmənt/
NU **Impoverishment** is the state of being poor, or the process of becoming poor. *...a period of very severe impoverishment.*

impracticable /ɪmpræktɪkəbl/
ADJ If a course of action is **impracticable**, it cannot be carried out. *It would be impracticable to ban all food additives.*

impractical /ɪmpræktɪkl/
ADJ An **impractical** idea or course of action is not sensible, realistic, or practical. *...a totally impractical view.*

imprecation /ɪmprɪkeɪʃn/ **imprecations**
NC An **imprecation** is something insulting that someone says to a person they are very angry with; a formal word. *He was exposed to the sleeve-tugging and imprecations of the crowd.*

imprecise /ɪmprɪsaɪs/
ADJ Something that is **imprecise** is not clear or accurate. *...imprecise data.*

impregnable /ɪmpregnəbl/
ADJ Something that is **impregnable** is so strong or solid that it cannot be broken into. *The old Dutch fort with its thick high walls and backing onto the sea looks virtually impregnable.*

impregnate /ɪmpregneɪt/ **impregnates, impregnating, impregnated**
VO If you **impregnate** something with a substance, you make the substance pass into it and spread through it. *...paper that has been impregnated with chemicals.*

impresario /ɪmprəsɑːriəʊ/ **impresarios**
NC An **impresario** is a person who arranges for plays, concerts, and musicals to be performed. *...a theatrical impresario.*

impress /ɪmpres/ **impresses, impressing, impressed**
1 VO If you **impress** someone, you make them admire and respect you because of your qualities, abilities, or achievements. *I was hoping to impress my new boss with my diligence... I was greatly impressed by the pianist.*
2 VO+on or upon If you **impress** something on someone, you make them understand the importance of it; a formal use. *She impressed on the Government the danger of making too many cuts... He's been striving to impress upon them the need to wear gloves when handling circuit boards.*

impression /ɪmpreʃn/ **impressions**
1 NC Your **impression** of someone or something is the way they seem to you. *They give the impression of not working... I had the impression that he didn't trust me.*
2 NC An **impression** is also an amusing imitation of a well-known person. *Have you seen her impressions of the TV newscasters?*
● **Impression** is used in these phrases. ● If you are **under the impression** that something is true, you believe it is true, usually when it is not. *They were under the impression I had come to stay.* ● If you **make an impression**, you have a strong effect on people, causing them to remember you. *She did not fail to make an impression.*

impressionable /ɪmpreʃənəbl/
ADJ Someone who is **impressionable** is easy to influence. *...an impressionable young girl.*

Impressionism /ɪmpreʃənɪzəm/
NU **Impressionism** is a style of painting developed in France between 1870 and 1900 that concentrated on showing the effects of light on a subject rather than on clear and exact detail. *...from Impressionism to contemporary art.*

impressionist /ɪmpreʃənɪst/ **impressionists**
1 NC An **Impressionist** was an artist who painted in the style of Impressionism. *When I was young, I liked the Impressionists.* ▶ Also ADJ *The farm is like an impressionist painting, splashed with colour in the early morning light.*
2 NC An **impressionist** is a person who entertains by means of funny imitations of people's behaviour and ways of talking, usually of well-known people. *The Soviet Union's most popular impressionist, Gennady Khazanov, has been sending Moscow audiences into hysterics with a sketch about President Gorbachev.*

impressionistic /ɪmpreʃənɪstɪk/
ADJ A view of something that is **impressionistic** relies on general aspects of the thing rather than dealing with the real facts or details. *Are these notes properly finished or are they simply meant to be impressionistic?*

impressive /ɪmpresɪv/
ADJ Something that is **impressive** impresses you, usually because it is large or important. *The list of speakers was impressive.* ♦ **impressively** ADV *...an impressively large mansion.*

imprint, imprints, imprinting, imprinted; pronounced /ɪmprɪnt/ when it is a noun and /ɪmprɪnt/ when it is a verb.
1 NC If something leaves an **imprint** on your mind or on a place, it has a strong, lasting effect on it. *These things have left a deep imprint on our thinking... The town still bears the imprint of its industrial origins.*
2 VO If something is **imprinted** on your memory, you cannot forget it. *This sunset will be forever imprinted in my mind.*
3 NC An **imprint** is a mark made by the pressure of an object on a surface. *In its centre was the imprint of his hand.*
4 VO If an object is **imprinted** onto a surface, it is pressed hard onto the surface so that it leaves a mark. *...the hand imprinted in the sand.*

imprison /ɪmprɪzn/ **imprisons, imprisoning, imprisoned**
VO To **imprison** someone means to lock them up in a prison. *An appeals court has set free six Irishmen that it says have been falsely imprisoned for sixteen years.*

imprisonment /ɪmprɪznmənt/
NU **Imprisonment** is the state of being locked up in a prison. *They were sentenced to life imprisonment.*

improbable /ɪmprɒbəbl/
ADJ Something that is **improbable** is unlikely to be true or to happen. *His explanation seems highly improbable.*

impromptu /ɪmprɒmptjuː/
ADJ An **impromptu** activity is not planned or organized. *I got drawn into a kind of impromptu party downstairs.*

improper /ɪmprɒpə/
1 ADJ If you describe someone's behaviour as

improper, you mean that it is rude or shocking. *Charlotte thought my mirth improper.* 2 ADJ **Improper** activities are illegal or dishonest. *...allegations of improper business dealings.* ◆ **improperly** ADV *There were charges that Hugel had improperly provided them with cash.* 3 ADJ **Improper** conditions or methods of treatment are not suitable or adequate. *...the cruel and improper treatment of cattle.* ◆ **improperly** ADV *Bottled milk, improperly handled, is a lethal carrier of disease.*

impropriety /ˌɪmprəˈpraɪəti/ NU **Impropriety** is improper behaviour; a formal word. *...the impropriety of publicly reading private letters.*

improve /ɪmˈpruːv/ **improves, improving, improved** 1 V-ERG If something **improves** or if you **improve** something, it gets better. *The weather improved later in the day... These houses have been improved by the addition of bathrooms.* ◆ **improved** ADJ *In underdeveloped countries, improved health and education are urgently needed.* 2 V-ERG If a skill you have **improves** or if you **improve** a skill, you get better at it. *His French was improving... She went to the club to improve her tennis.* 3 V+*on or upon* If you **improve** on an achievement, you achieve a better standard or result than the previous one. *He thinks he's improving on my work. ...terms which cannot be improved upon.*

improvement /ɪmˈpruːvmənt/ **improvements** N C or N U If there is an **improvement** in something, it gets better. *...improvements in living conditions. ...the gradual improvement of relations between East and West.*

improvidence /ɪmˈprɒvɪdəns/ NU **Improvidence** is improvident behaviour; a formal word.

improvident /ɪmˈprɒvɪdənt/ ADJ Someone who is **improvident** is wasteful and does not think about the future; a formal word. *...a childhood that had caused him to turn out feckless and improvident... They have lived improvident lives.*

improvise /ˈɪmprəvaɪz/ **improvises, improvising, improvised** 1 V or VO When you **improvise**, you make something using whatever materials you have rather than the proper ones, or you carry out an activity without planning it in advance. *We had to improvise as we went along... When the old, highly centralized political structures give way, the only recourse is to improvise local structures.* ◆ **improvised** ADJ *Tanks were crossing the river on improvised bridges.* 2 V or VO When actors or musicians **improvise**, they make up the words or music while they are performing. *He began to improvise on the piano before receiving any formal tuition... They're suspicious of anyone who spends most of their time improvising the music they play.* ◆ **improvisation** /ˌɪmprəvaɪˈzeɪʃn/ **improvisations** N U or N C *There was a good deal of improvisation. ...his improvisations on the organ.*

imprudent /ɪmˈpruːdnt/ ADJ **Imprudent** behaviour is not sensible or careful; a formal word. *It would be imprudent of you to make enemies.*

impudence /ˈɪmpjʊdəns/ NU· **Impudence** is impudent behaviour or speech. *He claimed with astounding impudence that the trials were fabricated.*

impudent /ˈɪmpjʊdənt/ ADJ Someone who is **impudent** behaves or speaks rudely or in a way that shows disrespect. *The impudent child extended her legs across my lap.* ◆ **impudently** ADV *...somebody who impudently defies my order.*

impugn /ɪmˈpjuːn/ **impugns, impugning, impugned** VO Someone who **impugns** something such as a quality criticizes it, especially by expressing doubt about it; a formal word. *They were daring to impugn the profession of medicine... He may attempt to impugn the reputation of his victim... There is no ground to*

impugn the sincerity of his belief.

impulse /ˈɪmpʌls/ **impulses** 1 NC An **impulse** is a sudden desire to do something. *I had a sudden impulse to turn around and walk out.* ● If you do something **on impulse**, you do it suddenly without planning it. *A waiting period does force some people to reconsider buying a gun on impulse.* 2 NC An **impulse** is also a short electrical signal sent along a wire or nerve or through the air. *...the impulse frequency.*

impulse buy, impulse buys NC An **impulse buy** is something that you buy because you see it and like it rather than because you planned to buy it.

impulsion /ɪmˈpʌlʃn/ **impulsions** NC An **impulsion** to do something is a strong desire to do it, usually a desire that you cannot control; a literary word. *We all felt the impulsion to act out our roles.*

impulsive /ɪmˈpʌlsɪv/ ADJ Someone who is **impulsive** does things suddenly without thinking about them first. *We must do nothing foolish or impulsive.* ◆ **impulsively** ADV *She kissed him impulsively.*

impunity /ɪmˈpjuːnəti/ If you do something wrong **with impunity**, you are not punished for it; a formal expression. *Landlords were simply ignoring the law with impunity.*

impure /ɪmˈpjʊə, ɪmˈpjɔː/ 1 ADJ A substance that is **impure** is not of good quality because it has other substances mixed with it. *...drinking water made impure by over-frequent recycling.* 2 ADJ **Impure** thoughts and actions are concerned with sex and are regarded as sinful.

impurity /ɪmˈpjʊərəti, ɪmˈpjɔːrəti/ **impurities** NC **Impurities** are substances that are present in another substance, making it of a low quality. *There are traces of impurities in the gold.*

impute /ɪmˈpjuːt/ **imputes, imputing, imputed** VO+*to* If you **impute** something such as blame, a crime, or a change to a person or thing, you say that this person or thing is responsible for it or is the cause of it; a formal word. *No blame can be imputed to him... It is hard to impute a rise in output to any one factor.*

in /ɪn, ɪn/ 1 PREP or ADV Something that is **in** something else is enclosed by it or surrounded by it. *We put them away in a big box... We've just found a body in the water... She opened her bag and put her diary in.* 2 PREP If something is **in** a place, or happens **in** a place, it is there, or it happens there. *I could not sleep because of the pain in my feet... I wanted to play in the garden... She locked herself in the bathroom... In Hamburg the girls split up.* 3 ADV If you are **in**, you are present at your home or place of work. *He's never in when I phone.* 4 ADV If a train, boat, or plane is **in** or has come **in**, it has arrived. *The train's not in yet.* 5 ADV When someone comes **in**, they enter a room or building. *There was a knock at Howard's door. 'Come in,' he shouted... He had his meals brought in.* 6 ADV When the sea or tide comes **in**, the sea moves towards the shore rather than away from it. *We were thigh-deep in water when the tide came in.* 7 PREP Something that is **in** a window, especially a shop window, is just behind the window so that you can see it from outside. *How much is the hat in the window?* 8 PREP When you see something **in** a mirror, you see its reflection. *Try not to look at your face in the mirror.* 9 PREP Someone who is **in** a piece of clothing is wearing it. *Martin was in his pyjamas.* 10 PREP If something is **in** a book, film, play, or picture, you can read it or see it there. *She dies in the last act... In Chapter 7 this point is discussed.* 11 PREP If you are **in** a play, race, or other activity, you are one of the people taking part. *She took part in a marathon.* 12 PREP If you are **in** business, computing, television, or another field of work, that is the type of work that you do. *His father had made a lot of money in business... She's in television.*

13 PREP If someone or something is **in** a group or collection, they are part of it. *She waited in the queue... This is one of the finest beetles in the collection.*

14 PREP If something happens **in** a particular year, month, or season, it happens during that time. *In 1872, Chicago was burned to the ground... It'll be warmer in the spring.*

15 PREP If something happens **in** a particular situation, it happens during it or when it is going on. *He escaped in the confusion... In these circumstances prices and profits would remain stable.*

16 PREP If you do something **in** a particular period of time, that is how long it takes you to do it. *I told him the money would be paid back in six months.*

17 PREP Something that will happen **in** a particular length of time, will happen after that length of time. *In another five minutes it'll be pitch dark.*

18 PREP If you are **in** a particular state or situation, that is your present state or situation. *We are in a position to advise our Indian friends.*

19 PREP If you are **in** love, distress, or another feeling or emotion, you have the feeling or emotion mentioned. *She was very much in love with him... I found her in low spirits.*

20 PREP You use **in** to mention the feeling or emotion that causes someone to behave in a particular way. *He shook his head in admiration... In his excitement, Billy had forgotten the letter.*

21 PREP You use **in** to specify a general subject or field of activity. *...recent advances in mathematics... She's an expert in children's literature.*

22 PREP You use **in** to indicate how many people or things do something. *Students flocked to the SDP in considerable numbers.*

23 PREP You use **in** to indicate approximate ages or temperatures. For example, if someone is in their fifties, they are between 50 and 59 years old. If the temperature is in the seventies, it is between 70 and 79 degrees. *In her twenties and thirties she had had no difficulty finding jobs.*

24 PREP You use **in** to express a ratio, proportion, or probability. *Only one acre in five was previously uncultivated... He has only a one in ten chance of being reunited with his family.*

25 PREP You use **in** to indicate how something is expressed. *I need your complaints in writing... She spoke in a calm, friendly voice... They were speaking in French.*

26 PREP You use **in** to describe the arrangement or shape of something. *The students sit in a circle on the floor.*

27 PREP You use **in** to specify what quality or aspect of something you are referring to. *It grew to eight metres in length... We need a change in direction.*

28 ADJ Something that is **in** is fashionable; an informal use. *Bright colours are in this year.*

29 PREP+ING You use **in** with a present participle to indicate that when you do something, something else happens as a consequence. *In accepting this view, he was admitting the possibility that he was mistaken earlier.*

● **In** is used in these phrases. ● If something has a particular quality **in itself**, it has this quality because of its nature. *This was an achievement in itself... It is foolish to believe that punishment in itself can induce a sense of responsibility.* ● You use **in that** to explain or justify a statement that you have just made. *He's a good listener in that he never interrupts you with thoughts of his own.* ● If you say that someone **is in for** a shock or a surprise, you mean they are going to experience it. *Those who pass nightmares off as a result of having eaten too much are in for a shock.* ● If someone **has it in for** you, or if they **have got it in for** you, they dislike you and try to cause problems for you; an informal expression. *She's really got it in for me.* ● If you are **in on** something, you are involved in it or know about it; an informal expression. *I'd like to be in on the scheme.* ● See also **ins and outs**.

in., ins. The plural form can be either **ins.** or **in.** **In.** is a written abbreviation for 'inch'. *...6 x 4 ins.*

in- /ɪn-, ɪn-/
PREFIX **In-** is added to some words to form other words that have the opposite meaning. For example, something that is incorrect is not correct. *He was obviously insincere... 'No, Father,' she said, almost inaudibly.*

inability /ɪnəbɪləti/
NU+to-INF Someone's **inability** to do something is the fact that they are unable to do it. *She despises her husband for his inability to work.*

inaccessible /ɪnəksɛsəbl/
1 ADJ An **inaccessible** place is impossible or very difficult to reach. *...the most inaccessible reaches of the jungle.* ◆ **inaccessibility** /ɪnəksɛsəbɪləti/ NU *The hilltop church attracted good congregations, in spite of its inaccessibility.*
2 ADJ If something such as music or art is **inaccessible**, it is hard for people to understand or appreciate; a formal use. *The music of Bartok is considered inaccessible by many people.*

inaccuracy /ɪnækjʊrəsi/ **inaccuracies**
1 NU The **inaccuracy** of something is the fact that it is not correct in some way. *...the inaccuracy of my estimates.*
2 NC An **inaccuracy** is a statement that is not correct. *The report contained a number of inaccuracies.*

inaccurate /ɪnækjʊrət/
ADJ Something that is **inaccurate** is not correct in some way. *...a wildly inaccurate editorial.*

inaction /ɪnækʃn/
NU+POSS If you refer to someone's **inaction**, you mean that they are doing nothing. *We do not accept this as an excuse for government inaction.*

inactive /ɪnæktɪv/
ADJ A person, animal, or thing that is **inactive** is not doing anything. *Crocodiles are inactive for long periods.* ◆ **inactivity** /ɪnæktɪvəti/ NU *...a time of inactivity.*

inadequacy /ɪnædɪkwəsi/ **inadequacies**
1 NU+SUPP The **inadequacy** of something is the fact that there is not enough of it or that it is not good enough. *...the inadequacy of education facilities in Britain... They want to draw attention to what they see as the government's inadequacy in handling the Health Service.*
2 NU If someone has feelings of **inadequacy**, they feel they do not have the qualities necessary to do something or to cope with life. *He looks respectable, but inside he's probably seething with feelings of inadequacy and incompleteness.*
3 NC An **inadequacy** is a weakness or fault in a person or thing. *...the inadequacies of a superficial education. ...his inadequacies as a vote catcher.*

inadequate /ɪnædɪkwət/
1 ADJ If something is **inadequate**, there is not enough of it or it is not good enough. *His income is inadequate to meet his basic needs. ...an inadequate lunch.* ◆ **inadequately** ADV *...inadequately heated accommodation.*
2 ADJ If you say that someone is **inadequate**, you mean that they do not have the qualities necessary to do something or to cope with life. *We were apparently too inadequate to join his exclusive club... He makes me feel totally inadequate.*

inadmissible /ɪnədmɪsəbl/
ADJ **Inadmissible** evidence cannot be used as evidence in a court of law. *They told him his evidence would be inadmissible on the basis of hearsay testimony.*

inadvertent /ɪnədvɜːtnt/
ADJ An **inadvertent** action is one that you do unintentionally without thinking or without realizing. *The suffering is inadvertent and unwanted.* ◆ **inadvertently** ADV *...a dog that has been kicked inadvertently by a friend.*

inadvisable /ɪnədvaɪzəbl/
ADJ PRED A course of action that is **inadvisable** is not sensible and should not be done. *It is inadvisable to plant lettuces too early.*

inalienable /ɪneɪliənəbl/
ADJ An **inalienable** right is one that cannot be taken

away; a formal word. ...*the inalienable right to do anything you want.*

inane /ɪneɪn/
ADJ **Inane** remarks or actions are silly or meaningless. *He condemned Mr Ridley's remarks as inane ramblings.* ♦ **inanely** ADV *He smiled rather inanely.*

inanimate /ɪnænɪmət/
ADJ An **inanimate** object has no life. ...*a 16th century Italian monk whose belief that all inanimate objects were alive got him burned at the stake.*

inapplicable /ɪnəplɪkəbl, ɪnæplɪkəbl/
ADJ Something that is **inapplicable** to something that you are considering is not relevant or appropriate to it. *The phrase seemed inapplicable to the tall young man.*

inappropriate /ɪnəprəʊprɪət/
ADJ Something that is **inappropriate** is not suitable for a particular occasion. ...*inappropriate clothes.*

inapt /ɪnæpt/
ADJ Something that is **inapt** is not useful or suitable for a particular occasion or purpose; a formal word. ...*an inapt term.*

inarticulate /ɪnɑːtɪkjʊlət/
ADJ If you are **inarticulate**, you cannot express yourself easily in speech. ...*the caricature of the English footballer as a dull-witted, inarticulate individual.*

inasmuch /ɪnəzmʌtʃ/; also spelt **in as much.**
CONJ **Inasmuch as** is used to introduce a clause in which you say something that explains the preceding statement, or that limits it in some way; a formal expression. *This was important inasmuch as it showed just what human beings were capable of... The United Nations bore responsibility for the war inasmuch as it's being waged to enforce UN resolutions.*

inattention /ɪnətenʃn/
NU **Inattention** is lack of attention to what is being said or done. ...*scolding the maid for inattention.*

inattentive /ɪnətentɪv/
ADJ Someone who is **inattentive** is not paying attention. ...*children who are inattentive and doing poorly in school.*

inaudible /ɪnɔːdəbl/
ADJ **Inaudible** means not loud enough to be heard. *Her voice became inaudible.*

inaugural /ɪnɔːgjʊrəl/
ADJ ATTRIB An **inaugural** meeting or speech is the first one of a new organization or leader. ...*his inaugural address as President.*

inaugurate /ɪnɔːgjʊreɪt/ **inaugurates, inaugurating, inaugurated**
1 VO When a new leader is **inaugurated**, they are established in their new position at an official ceremony. *Mr Shankar will be inaugurated in two weeks' time for a five year term.* ♦ **inauguration** /ɪnɔːgjʊreɪʃn/ **inaugurations** NU or NC ...*the inauguration of a new President. ...his inauguration speech.*
2 VO If you **inaugurate** a system or organization, you start it; a formal use. *She also inaugurated a new telephone exchange set up with British aid... The Bluebell Railway project was inaugurated by Paul Channon, the Secretary of State.* ♦ **inauguration** NU *The Council is to meet for the first time since its inauguration five years ago.*

inauspicious /ɪnɔːspɪʃəs/
ADJ An **inauspicious** occasion seems unlucky and gives signs that success is unlikely; a formal word. *When Angola achieved independence, the circumstances under which it did so appeared inauspicious... Sir Len's career got off to an inauspicious start when he scored nought in his first Test Match.*

inborn /ɪnbɔːn/
ADJ **Inborn** qualities are ones which you are born with. ...*a virus to which there is no inborn maternal immunity... Are these qualities inborn, or can they be learned?*

inbred /ɪnbred/
1 ADJ An **inbred** quality is one that is inborn. ...*the inbred suspicion of strangers.*

2 ADJ People who are **inbred** have ancestors who are all closely related to each other. ...*the inbred royal family.*

inbreeding /ɪnbriːdɪŋ/
NU **Inbreeding** is the repeated breeding of closely related animals or people. *Animals naturally avoid their own kin because that leads to inbreeding which is dangerous for the species.*

inbuilt /ɪnbɪlt/
ADJ An **inbuilt** quality is one that someone is born with, or one that something has had from the time it was produced. *Babies have an inbuilt ability to understand musical scales... Women's right to equal treatment was denied because of inbuilt social and economic discrimination.*

Inc. /ɪŋk/
ADJ after N In the United States, **Inc.** is used as the written abbreviation for **Incorporated** in the names of companies. ...*the UK subsidiary of Safeway Stores Inc. of the USA.*

inc. or **incl.**
1 In advertisements, **inc.** or **incl.** is a written abbreviation for 'including'. ...*large garden inc. rockery. ...fully fitted kitchen incl. washing machine and freezer.*
2 In advertisements, **inc.** or **incl.** is also a written abbreviation for 'inclusive'. ...*cost £250 inc. of VAT. ...£150 pcm incl. of gas and elec.*

incalculable /ɪŋkælkjʊləbl/
ADJ Something that is **incalculable** is so great that it cannot be estimated. *The loss to the race as a whole is incalculable.*

incandescence /ɪŋkændesns/
NU **Incandescence** is the quality that something has of giving out a lot of light when heated; a formal word. *The metal gleamed with a snowy incandescence.*

incandescent /ɪŋkændesnt/
ADJ Something that is **incandescent** gives out a lot of light when heated; a formal word. ...*sparks of incandescent pink.*

incantation /ɪŋkænteɪʃn/ **incantations**
NC An **incantation** is a magic spell that is chanted or sung. *The film concentrates on the ceremonies, the uniforms, the parades, and incantations.*

incapable /ɪŋkeɪpəbl/
1 ADJ PRED+of Someone who is **incapable** of doing something is unable to do it. *She is incapable of grasping what self-discipline means... I had believed him to be incapable of lying.*
2 ADJ An **incapable** person is weak and helpless or stupid. *He's both incapable and dishonest... But Sir John says policing is too important to be left in incapable hands.*

incapacitate /ɪŋkəpæsɪteɪt/ **incapacitates, incapacitating, incapacitated**
VO If something **incapacitates** someone, it weakens them so much that they become unable to do certain things; a formal word. ...*those not yet incapacitated by seasickness.*

incapacity /ɪŋkəpæsəti/
NU The **incapacity** of a person, society, or system is their inability to do something; a formal word. ...*her incapacity to forgive herself... 6.8 million days of certified incapacity for work resulted from this disease.*

incarcerate /ɪŋkɑːsəreɪt/ **incarcerates, incarcerating, incarcerated**
VO If someone is **incarcerated**, they are put in prison; a formal word. *Thousands of innocent people had been murdered, injured or incarcerated... Twice during the seventies she was forcibly incarcerated in psychiatric hospitals.* ♦ **incarceration** /ɪŋkɑːsəreɪʃn/ NU ...*the incarceration of political dissenters.*

incarnate /ɪŋkɑːnɪt/
ADJ after N Someone who is a thing or quality **incarnate** represents that thing or quality in human form to a great degree. ...*evil incarnate... They made me out to be that hideous reality incarnate.*

incarnation /ɪŋkɑːneɪʃn/ **incarnations**
1 NC An **incarnation** is one of the lives that a person has, according to some religions.

2 NC The **incarnation** of a god is that god's appearance in human form. *The Dalai Lama is revered both as the incarnation of the deity and as the rightful ruler of Tibet.*
3 NC Someone or something that is the **incarnation** of a particular quality or thing represents or is typical of that quality or thing in an extreme form. *Mr Le Pen is just the most recent incarnation of the extreme Right tradition in French politics... He was a fat little boy who later became the incarnation of the handsome, attractive lover.*

incautious /ɪnkɔːʃəs/
ADJ Someone who is **incautious** does not take enough care over what they say or do; a formal word. *...an incautious remark.*

incendiary /ɪnsɛndiəri/
ADJ ATTRIB **Incendiary** attacks or weapons involve setting fire to something. *...an incendiary bomb... A group calling itself the Liberation Front says it was responsible for the incendiary device.*

incense, incenses, incensing, incensed; pronounced /ɪnsens/ when it is a noun and /ɪnsɛns/ when it is a verb.
1 NU **Incense** is a substance that is burned for its sweet smell, often during a religious ceremony. *The smell of incense filled the sparkling new building. ...incense holders.*
2 VO Something that **incenses** you makes you extremely angry; a formal use. *The proposed pay freeze has incensed the men... The charges apparently incensed Botham, who said the walk would raise millions for charity.* ◆ **incensed** ADJ PRED *Korean businessmen are particularly incensed at the government's new policy.*

incentive /ɪnsɛntɪv/ **incentives**
NCorNU An **incentive** is something that encourages you to do something. *Money is being used as an incentive... He has no incentive to make permanent improvements.*

inception /ɪnsɛpʃn/
NU+SUPP The **inception** of an institution or activity is its start; a formal word. *It's being regarded as NATO's most important meeting since its inception forty years ago... He managed one of the biggest winning margins since the inception of world bowls.*

incessant /ɪnsɛsnt/
ADJ An **incessant** activity never stops. *...long centuries of almost incessant warfare. ...incessant rain.* ◆ **incessantly** ADV *She drank tea incessantly.*

incest /ɪnsest/
NU **Incest** is sexual intercourse between two people who are closely related, for example a brother and sister. *...pregnancies arising from rape or incest.*

incestuous /ɪnsɛstjuəs/
1 ADJ An **incestuous** relationship is one involving incest. *He experienced a succession of violent, erotic, incestuous dreams concerning his daughter.*
2 ADJ An **incestuous** group of people is a small group of people who all know each other well and do not associate with anyone outside the group; used showing disapproval. *The relationship of the banks with enterprise managers and politicians is often incestuous.*

inch /ɪntʃ/ **inches, inching, inched**
1 NC An **inch** is a unit of length, equal to approximately 2.54 centimetres. *Five inches of snow had fallen.*
2 V-ERGA If you **inch** somewhere, you move there very slowly and carefully. If you **inch** something somewhere, you move it there very slowly and carefully. *You can only enter the caves by inching through a narrow tunnel on your stomach... Howard inched the van forward.*

inchoate /ɪnkəʊeɪt, ɪnkəʊeɪt/
ADJ ATTRIB **Inchoate** ideas or attitudes are newly formed and therefore not yet properly developed or organized; a formal word. *...the student's inchoate political awareness.*

incidence /ɪnsɪdəns/
N SING+of The **incidence** of something is how often it occurs. *There is a high incidence of heart disease among middle-aged men.*

incident /ɪnsɪdənt/ **incidents**
NC An **incident** is an event, especially one involving something unpleasant. *...a shooting incident... No casualties occurred in these incidents.*

incidental /ɪnsɪdɛntl/
ADJ ATTRIB Something that is **incidental** occurs in connection with something more important. *...incidental expenses. ...incidental music for a film.*

incidentally /ɪnsɪdɛntəli/
ADV SEN You use **incidentally** when you add information or change the subject. *Incidentally, I suggest that you have the telephone moved to the sitting-room.*

incident room, incident rooms
NC An **incident room** is a special room set up in a police station, or near the place where a serious crime was committed, from where the police carry out the investigation into that crime. *Detectives have now launched a murder enquiry and are setting up an incident room at Southwark police station.*

incinerate /ɪnsɪnəreɪt/ **incinerates, incinerating, incinerated**
VO If you **incinerate** a large quantity of something, you burn it completely; a formal word. *Tons of paper are incinerated every year.* ◆ **incineration** /ɪnsɪnəreɪʃn/ NU *...the incineration of rockets containing nerve gas... The US claims that the incineration will be harmless.*

incinerator /ɪnsɪnəreɪtə/ **incinerators**
NC An **incinerator** is a furnace for burning rubbish. *...the destruction of chemicals in a special incinerator.*

incipient /ɪnsɪpiənt/
ADJ ATTRIB **Incipient** means starting to happen or appear; a formal word. *...incipient baldness.*

incise /ɪnsaɪz/ **incises, incising, incised**
VO If you **incise** something, you cut into it carefully with a sharp instrument; a formal word. *We learn how to lance, incise and stitch the wound... His name was incised on the stone.*

incision /ɪnsɪʒn/ **incisions**
NC An **incision** is a careful cut made in something, for example by a surgeon; a formal word. *...a device for holding back the edges of wounds and incisions.*

incisive /ɪnsaɪsɪv/
ADJ **Incisive** speech or writing is clear and forceful; a formal word. *...an incisive critique of our society.*

incisor /ɪnsaɪzə/ **incisors**
NC An **incisor** is one of the teeth at the front of your mouth which you use for biting into food. *Every upper central incisor that has been found in any Chinese fossil has this feature.*

incite /ɪnsaɪt/ **incites, inciting, incited**
VO If you **incite** people to do something violent or unpleasant, you encourage them to do it. *He accused the lawyer of advocating anarchy and inciting citizens to riot... There's a fine line between raising awareness about AIDS and inciting panic... They had been accused of inciting violence.*

incitement /ɪnsaɪtmənt/
NU+oforto **Incitement** is the activity of inciting particular behaviour or feelings. *He made his reputation as a newspaper editor specializing in the incitement of hatred... His rhetoric amounted to deliberate incitement to terrorist activities.*

incl. See **inc.**

inclement /ɪnklɛmənt/
ADJ **Inclement** weather is unpleasantly cold or stormy; a formal word. *In spite of some inclement holiday weather here, play has been possible this morning in two of the matches.*

inclination /ɪnklɪneɪʃn/ **inclinations**
NCorNU An **inclination** is a feeling that makes you want to act in a particular way. *He did not show any religious inclinations... Some parents have no time or inclination to play with their children.*

incline, inclines, inclining, inclined; a formal word, pronounced /ɪnklaɪn/ when it is a noun and /ɪnklaɪn/ when it is a verb.
1 NC An **incline** is a slope. *They have to be put on these stretchers, then carried up this steep incline, which is muddy and slippery.*

2 VO If you **incline** your head, you bend your neck so that your head is leaning forward. *...graciously inclining their heads.*
3 V+*to*-INF or V A If you **incline** to act in a certain way, or if you **incline** towards a particular opinion, you are likely to act that way or to accept that opinion. *Some of the Senators currently incline to reject the treaty on nationalist grounds... Some incline more towards Social-Democratic ideas.*

inclined /ɪŋklaɪnd/
1 ADJ PRED+*to*-INF If you are **inclined** to behave in a particular way, you often behave in that way, or you want to do so. *My father was inclined to be very moody... Why are some people inclined to be criminals? ...Maybe both regimes will be more inclined to compromise.*
2 ADJ PRED+*to*-INF If you say that you are **inclined** to have a particular opinion, you are saying that you have that opinion. *Defence experts are inclined to agree... The Secretary General is inclined to see the crisis as an internal affair.*
3 ADJ PRED Someone who is mathematically **inclined** or artistically **inclined**, for example, has a natural ability to do mathematics or art. *...democratically inclined reformers.*

include /ɪŋkluːd/ **includes, including, included**
1 VO If one thing **includes** another, it has the other thing as one of its parts. *The four-man crew included one Briton... The proposals included the nationalization of major industries.*
2 VOA If you **include** one thing in another, you make it part of the second thing. *Carpets and curtains are to be included in the purchase price.*

included /ɪŋkluːdɪd/
ADJ after N You use **included** to emphasize that someone or something is part of a group. *All of us, myself included, had been totally committed to the project.*

including /ɪŋkluːdɪŋ/
PREP You use **including** when mentioning one or more members of a group of people or things. *Nine persons were injured, including two wounded by gunfire.*

inclusion /ɪŋkluːʒn/
NU The **inclusion** of one thing in another involves making it a part of the second thing. *...the inclusion of the Old Testament in the Christian Bible.*

inclusive /ɪŋkluːsɪv/
1 ADJ An **inclusive** price includes payment for all the separate parts of something or for one particular part that is being specified. *All prices are inclusive of the return flights from London.*
2 ADJ after N You use **inclusive** to indicate that the things mentioned are included in a series, as well as the things between them. *...ages 17 to 27 inclusive.*

incognito /ɪŋkɒgniːtəʊ/
ADV Someone famous who is travelling **incognito** is travelling in disguise or using another name so that they will not be recognized. *Earlier this month he resigned as mayor and flew incognito to Argentina.*

incoherence /ɪŋkəʊhɪərəns/
NU The **incoherence** of something is the fact that it is unclear and difficult to understand. *...the incoherence of his talk.*

incoherent /ɪŋkəʊhɪərənt/
1 ADJ If something is **incoherent**, it is unclear and difficult to understand. *The aims were incoherent. ...incoherent policies and inept official measures.*
2 ADJ If someone is **incoherent**, they are talking in an unclear way. *He was incoherent with joy... He'll be fine and maybe dazed and amazed but certainly not incoherent.* ◆ **incoherently** ADV *Marcus stood up, muttering incoherently.*

income /ɪŋkʌm/ **incomes**
N C or NU A person's or country's **income** is the money that they earn or receive. *At present, the earnings of a married woman are treated as part of her husband's income... ...people on low incomes. The country's external debt stands at about seven and a half times Zaire's annual income.*

income support
NU In Britain, **income support** is an amount of money that people who have a very low income, or no income, and who do not qualify for any other state

benefits can claim from the government. *Magistrates will be given the power to instruct local social security offices to deduct income support or unemployment benefit at source to help pay those fines.*

income tax, income taxes
N U or N C **Income tax** is the tax that you have to pay regularly to the government and which is a certain percentage of your income. *The Government has increased the standard rate of income tax... The legislation would leave income taxes unchanged.*

incoming /ɪŋkʌmɪŋ/
1 ADJ ATTRIB **Incoming** means coming into a place. *...incoming passengers. ...incoming data.*
2 ADJ ATTRIB An **incoming** official or government has just been appointed or elected. *The incoming President sees economic reform as leading the way to a revival of the party's fortunes.*

incommunicado /ɪŋkəmjuːnɪkɑːdəʊ/
ADV If you are being kept **incommunicado**, you are not allowed to talk to anyone outside the place where you are. *They returned to their cabins, where they would remain incommunicado for the next ten hours.*

incomparable /ɪŋkɒmpərəbl/
ADJ Something that is **incomparable** is very good or great in degree; a formal word. *...a movement of incomparable grace. ...a writer of incomparable prose.* ◆ **incomparably** SUBMOD *...an incomparably superior education.*

incompatible /ɪŋkəmpætəbl/
ADJ Two people or things that are **incompatible** cannot exist or work together. *Somehow the two men were incompatible... Their styles of life were incompatible... His actions are totally incompatible with the group's safety.* ◆ **incompatibility** /ɪŋkəmpætəbɪləti/ **incompatibilities** N U or N C *There is a fundamental incompatibility between the management and the unions.*

incompetence /ɪŋkɒmpɪtəns/
NU If you refer to someone's **incompetence**, you are referring to their inability to do a particular job or activity successfully. *...the incompetence and corruption of our senior ministers... Graffman fired him for incompetence.*

incompetent /ɪŋkɒmpɪtənt/
ADJ Someone who is **incompetent** does their job badly. *Our secret services are completely incompetent.*

incomplete /ɪŋkəmpliːt/
1 ADJ Something that is **incomplete** does not have all the parts that it should have or has not been finished. *...this short and incomplete account of my life.*
2 ADJ You can also use **incomplete** to describe something that is not as great in extent or degree as it could be. *...the consequences of incomplete military success.* ◆ **incompletely** ADV *...incompletely cooked meat.*

incomprehensible /ɪŋkɒmprɪhɛnsəbl/
ADJ Something that is **incomprehensible** is impossible to understand. *Most critics thought the play was boring and incomprehensible... Mr Caputo said his government was concerned over the incomprehensible attitude of the United Kingdom.*

incomprehension /ɪŋkɒmprɪhɛnʃn/
NU **Incomprehension** is the state of being unable to understand something. *He went on staring in incomprehension.*

inconceivable /ɪŋkənsiːvəbl/
ADJ If you describe something as **inconceivable**, you think it cannot possibly happen or be true. *He found it inconceivable that Belov was insane.*

inconclusive /ɪŋkənkluːsɪv/
ADJ If something such as a discussion or experiment is **inconclusive**, it does not lead to any clear decision or result. *Tests indicated that she had taken steroids, but later tests proved inconclusive... They are likely to get bogged down in an inconclusive debate... I think the evidence is at the moment inconclusive.*

incongruity /ɪŋkɒŋgruːəti/ **incongruities**
N U or N C The **incongruity** of something is the strangeness of it, usually because it does not fit in with the rest of the event or the situation; a formal word. *I was struck by the glaring incongruity of the scene. There I was, my face dirty, my clothes torn, and there*

he was, immaculate as usual... It is clear that tensions arise from incongruities between cultural elements in a society.

incongruous /ɪnkɒŋgruəs/
ADJ Something that is **incongruous** seems strange because it does not fit in with the rest of the situation. *He was an incongruous figure among the tourists.*
♦ **incongruously** ADV *...a fat lady, dressed incongruously in black satin.*

inconsequential /ɪnkɒnsɪkwɛnʃl/
ADJ Something that is **inconsequential** is not very important. *...some inconsequential conversation.*

inconsiderable /ɪnkənsɪdə⁰rəbl/
If you describe something as **not inconsiderable**, you mean that it is large. *The country's not inconsiderable army was mobilized.*

inconsiderate /ɪnkənsɪdə⁰rət/
ADJ **Inconsiderate** people do not care how their behaviour affects other people. *...offences such as failing to report an accident or inconsiderate driving.*

inconsistency /ɪnkənsɪstənsi/ **inconsistencies**
1 NU **Inconsistency** is behaviour which is unpredictable because it changes from one occasion to another; used showing disapproval. *He had noticed the President's inconsistency on abortion and marijuana... The girls adopted a fairly cynical attitude to their mother's inconsistencies.*
2 NC If there is an **inconsistency** between two facts, one of them cannot possibly be true if the other is true. *We have a logical inconsistency here.*

inconsistent /ɪnkənsɪstənt/
1 ADJ If someone is **inconsistent**, they behave differently or say different things in similar situations; used showing disapproval. *The blame was laid on an inconsistent government... In what he says, he is often notoriously inconsistent.*
2 ADJ Something that is **inconsistent** does not stay the same, being sometimes good and sometimes bad. *They play very inconsistent football.*
3 ADJ If two facts are **inconsistent**, one cannot possibly be true if the other is true. *Some of your answers are rather inconsistent... The charges, he said, were patently inconsistent and contradictory.*
4 ADJ PRED+*with* Something that is **inconsistent** with a particular set of ideas or values is not in accordance with them. *...a monarch whose behaviour they judged to be inconsistent with Hindu religious values... The allegation was unfounded and inconsistent with the improved relations between Washington and Moscow.*

inconsolable /ɪnkənsəʊləbl/
ADJ Someone who is **inconsolable** is very sad and cannot be comforted. *When his daughter was murdered Adam was inconsolable.* ♦ **inconsolably** ADV *Iris was inconsolably distressed.*

inconspicuous /ɪnkənspɪkjuəs/
ADJ Something that is **inconspicuous** is not at all noticeable. *I have asked the children to make themselves as inconspicuous as possible.*
♦ **inconspicuously** ADV *He slipped into the nearest bar as inconspicuously as he could.*

incontinence /ɪnkɒntɪnəns/
1 NU **Incontinence** is the inability to control your bladder and bowels. *My father was on the verge of senility and incontinence.*
2 NU **Incontinence** is also the inability to control your physical desires, especially your desire for sex; a formal use. *He was renowned for his incontinence and profligacy.*

incontinent /ɪnkɒntɪnənt/
ADJ Someone who is **incontinent** is unable to control their bladder or bowels. *Fewer patients are incontinent and most are walking on their own.*

incontrovertible /ɪnkɒntrəvɜːtəbl/
ADJ **Incontrovertible** evidence or proof shows that something is definitely true; a formal word. *His picture collection was incontrovertible evidence of his wealth... Two facts about Congress politics in India are incontrovertible.*

inconvenience /ɪnkənviːnɪəns/ **inconveniences, inconveniencing, inconvenienced**
1 NU or NC If something causes **inconvenience**, it causes problems or difficulties. *I'm very sorry to have*

caused so much inconvenience... You have to put up with these inconveniences as best you can.
2 VO If you **inconvenience** someone, you cause problems or difficulties for them. *I am very sorry for people who are inconvenienced by this or hurt by it, but there is no alternative.*

inconvenient /ɪnkənviːnɪənt/
ADJ Something that is **inconvenient** causes problems or difficulties for you. *I seem to have come at an inconvenient time.*

incorporate /ɪnkɔːpəreɪt/ **incorporates, incorporating, incorporated**
1 VO+*into or in* If one thing is **incorporated** into another, it becomes a part of the second thing. *The decision will be incorporated into Brazil's new constitution... He indicated that ideas put forward by Japan could be incorporated in the UN plan.* ♦ **incorporation** /ɪnkɔːpəreɪʃn/ NU *...the incorporation of Austria into the German Empire.*
2 VO If one thing **incorporates** another, it includes the second thing as one of its parts. *The 1990 models incorporated a specially developed anti-theft alarm... These houses usually incorporated a long gallery.*

Incorporated
ADJ after N In the United States, **Incorporated** is used after the name of a company to indicate that the company has been legally formed into a corporation. **Incorporated** has the written abbreviation **Inc.** *Businessland Incorporated once was one of the country's largest computer retailers.*

incorrect /ɪnkərɛkt/
ADJ Something that is **incorrect** is wrong or untrue. *Sonny dismissed the information as incorrect. ...incorrect English.* ♦ **incorrectly** ADV *The problem has been incorrectly defined.*

incorrigible /ɪnkɒrɪdʒəbl/
ADJ Someone who is **incorrigible** has faults that will never change; a formal word. *...incorrigible criminals.*

incorruptible /ɪnkərʌptəbl/
ADJ Someone who is **incorruptible** cannot be bribed or persuaded to do things that they should not do. *Those on duty in the main part of the airport are incorruptible in the fight against terrorism and drugs.*

increase, increases, increasing, increased; pronounced /ɪnkriːs/ when it is a verb and /ɪnkriːs/ when it is a noun.
1 V-ERG If something **increases**, or if you **increase** it, it becomes larger in amount. *Crime has increased by three per cent in the past year. ...men seeking to increase their knowledge.* ♦ **increased** ADJ *...increased productivity.* ♦ **increasing** ADJ *Japanese industry is making increasing use of robots.*
2 NC An **increase** is a rise in the number, level, or amount of something. *They demanded a sharp increase in wages.*
3 If something is **on the increase**, it is becoming more frequent. *Crime is on the increase.*

increasingly /ɪnkriːsɪŋli/
SUBMOD or ADV You use **increasingly** to indicate that a situation or quality is becoming greater in intensity or more common. *It was becoming increasingly difficult to find jobs... Men increasingly find that they need more training.*

incredible /ɪnkrɛdəbl/
1 ADJ Something that is **incredible** is very surprising. *They were wearing incredible uniforms... The news is shocking and incredible.* ♦ **incredibly** ADV SEN *Upstairs, incredibly, the beds were already made.*
2 ADJ If you say that something is **incredible**, you mean that you do not believe that it can be true. *You've no basis for this incredible suggestion... The account cannot be dismissed as incredible.*
3 ADJ If you describe something that you have experienced or seen as **incredible**, you mean that it was exceptionally good. *He failed to match his incredible long jump performance in Tokyo... It was an incredible experience.*
4 ADJ **Incredible** also means very great in amount or degree. *They get an incredible amount of money... The curfew led to an incredible amount of hardship.*
♦ **incredibly** SUBMOD *The water was incredibly hot.*

incredulity /ɪnkrədjuːlətɪ/
NU **Incredulity** is total disbelief of something that is
said or done. *...an expression of sheer incredulity...
His decision produced shock and incredulity.*

incredulous /ɪnkrɛdjʊləs/
ADJ If someone is **incredulous**, they cannot believe
what they have just heard. *'You left her all alone?'
He sounded incredulous.* ♦ **incredulously** ADV *I stared
at him incredulously.*

increment /ɪnkrəmənt/ **increments**
NC An **increment** is an addition to something,
especially a regular addition to someone's salary; a
formal word. *There were political reasons for the
strike as well as the demand for pay increments...
Each increment of confidence-building was in his view
an improvement.*

incremental /ɪnkrəmɛntl/
ADJ Something that is **incremental** increases in value
or in amount, often by a regular amount; a formal
word. *Lecturers enjoy job security, steady
incremental increases in salary, and more or less
regular working hours.*

incriminate /ɪnkrɪmɪneɪt/ **incriminates,
incriminating, incriminated**
VO If something **incriminates** you, it indicates that you
are the person responsible for a crime. *They raided
his laboratory to seize any papers that might
incriminate them.* ♦ **incriminating** ADJ
...incriminating evidence.

incubate /ɪnkjʊbeɪt/ **incubates, incubating, incubated**
1 V-ERG If a bird's eggs **incubate** or if they **are
incubated**, they develop in a warm environment until
they hatch; a technical use in biology. *The vegetation
keeps the nest warm and helps the eggs to incubate...
The eggs are incubated at high temperatures, about 32
degrees Celsius.* ♦ **incubation** /ɪnkjʊbeɪʃn/ NU *...a way
of determining the sex of a hen's egg before
incubation.*
2 V-ERG When something such as bacteria **incubates**,
or when it is **incubated**, it remains inactive for a while
and then slowly develops into a disease; a medical
use. *It took four days for the plague to incubate...
Overcrowded, badly lit and ventilated houses help to
incubate disease.* ♦ **incubation** NU *Though some show
AIDS soon after infection, the average incubation is
eight years... There's a long incubation period where
nothing appears to be wrong.*

incubator /ɪnkjʊbeɪtə/ **incubators**
NC An **incubator** is a piece of hospital equipment in
which a sick or weak newborn baby is kept. *...a tiny
little mite in her incubator, pink and vulnerable
looking.*

inculcate /ɪnkʌlkeɪt/ **inculcates, inculcating,
inculcated**
VO+*in or into* If you **inculcate** an idea in someone, you
teach it to them so that it becomes fixed in their mind;
a formal word. *We want to inculcate the values of
marriage and family life into our children.*

incumbent /ɪnkʌmbənt/ **incumbents**; a formal word.
1 ADJ PRED+*on or upon* If it is **incumbent** on or upon you
to do something, it is your duty to do it. *It is
incumbent upon any sailor to respond to save life
where life is in danger.*
2 NC An **incumbent** is the person who holds a
particular post at a particular time. *The previous
incumbent resigned last Thursday... The term of office
of the incumbent Prime Minister comes up for renewal
in October.*

incur /ɪnkɜː/ **incurs, incurring, incurred**
VO If you **incur** something, especially something
unpleasant, it happens to you because of what you do;
a formal word. *...the risk of incurring her displeasure.
...business expenses incurred outside the office.*

incurable /ɪnkjʊərəbl, ɪnkjɔːrəbl/
1 ADJ An **incurable** disease cannot be cured.
...incurable cancer.
2 ADJ ATTRIB You can use **incurable** to describe people
with a fixed attitude or habit. *...incurable optimists.*
♦ **incurably** SUBMOD *...the incurably servile
housekeeper.*

incurious /ɪnkjʊərɪəs/
ADJ Someone who is **incurious** does not pay very much
attention to what is happening, either near them or in
the world in general; a formal word. *Ordinary
country people are incurious—and proud of it.*
♦ **incuriously** ADV *The girl raised her eyes and
looked, briefly and incuriously, at them.*

incursion /ɪnkɜːʃn/ **incursions**
NC An **incursion** is a small military invasion, often
temporary or accidental; a formal word. *...their
incursion into Yugoslavia... He said the Israeli
operation was an invasion rather than an incursion.
...cross-border incursions.*

indebted /ɪndɛtɪd/
1 ADJ PRED+*to* If you are **indebted** to someone, you owe
them gratitude for something. *I am indebted to Bob
Waller for many of the ideas expressed here.*
♦ **indebtedness** NU *I readily acknowledge my
indebtedness to my friends.*
2 ADJ PRED If you are **indebted**, you owe someone
money; used in American English. *I'm indebted for
six months after I graduate.* ♦ **indebtedness** NU *Home
ownership involves higher indebtedness than renting.*

indecency /ɪndiːsnsɪ/
NU If you refer to the **indecency** of something or
someone, you are referring to the fact that they are
morally or sexually offensive. *...laws concerning
indecency, obscenity, and violence.*

indecent /ɪndiːsnt/
1 ADJ Something that is **indecent** is shocking, usually
because it relates to sex or nakedness. *...indecent
jokes.*
2 ADJ You can also describe something that breaks the
rules of good behaviour or morality as **indecent**. *She
was granted a British passport with indecent haste
before the 1984 Los Angeles Olympics.*

indecipherable /ɪndɪsaɪfərəbl/
ADJ If writing is **indecipherable**, you cannot read it; a
formal word. *The writing, he says, was almost
indecipherable, but had been written along the port
bow of the ship.*

indecision /ɪndɪsɪʒn/
NU **Indecision** is uncertainty about what you should
do. *Many are interpreting his silence as a sign of
weakness and indecision. ...weeks of chronic indecision
and uncertainty.*

indecisive /ɪndɪsaɪsɪv/
1 ADJ If you are **indecisive**, you find it difficult to
make decisions. *The President has become indecisive,
and sometimes downright incompetent.*
2 ADJ An **indecisive** result, for example in a vote or
election, is one which does not have a clear result one
way or the other. *In Denmark, the process is
underway to elect a new government after an
indecisive general election there... He is partly to
blame for this indecisive outcome.*

indeed /ɪndiːd/
1 ADV SEN You use **indeed** to confirm or agree with
something that has just been said. *'I think you knew
him.'—'I did indeed.'*
2 ADV SEN You use **indeed** at the end of a clause to
give extra force to the word 'very', or to emphasize a
particular word. *We have very little information
indeed... The possibility of rescue now seemed remote
indeed.*
3 ADV SEN You also use **indeed** when adding
information which strengthens the point you have
already made. *This act has failed to bring women's
earnings up to the same level. Indeed the gulf is
widening... How do you get over that problem, indeed
if you can get over it?*
4 ADV SEN You can also use **indeed** to express anger or
scorn; used in spoken English. *'She wants to go
too.'—'Does she indeed!'*

indefatigable /ɪndɪfætɪgəbl/
ADJ People who are **indefatigable** never get tired of
doing something; a formal word. *She was an
indefatigable traveller.*

indefensible /ɪndɪfɛnsəbl/
ADJ Statements, actions, or ideas that are **indefensible**
are wrong and cannot be justified; a formal word. *He
denounced the judge's savage attack as totally
indefensible.*

indefinable /ɪndɪfaɪnəbl/
ADJ A quality or feeling that is **indefinable** cannot easily be described. *It's a unique shellfish which has a delicious and indefinable taste.* ♦ **indefinably** ADV *Terry had somehow indefinably altered.*

indefinite /ɪndɛfəⁿnət/
1 ADJ If something is **indefinite**, people have not decided when it will end. *...an indefinite strike... An indefinite curfew was imposed this morning in parts of the city.* ♦ **indefinitely** /ɪndɛfəⁿnətli/ ADV *All waiting lists have been frozen indefinitely.*
2 ADJ If something such as a plan is **indefinite**, it is not exact or clear. *Milner advised him not to answer so indefinite a proposal.*

indefinite article, indefinite articles
NC In grammar, the words 'a' and 'an' are sometimes called **indefinite articles**. In this dictionary, 'a' and 'an' are called determiners.

indelible /ɪndɛləbl/
1 ADJ If a mark or stain is **indelible**, it cannot be removed or washed out. *His fingertips had turned an indelible black. ...indelible ink.*
2 ADJ **Indelible** memories will never be forgotten. *The defeat left an indelible mark on Irish history... Another indelible influence on Tutu was his visit to Britain.* ♦ **indelibly** ADV *The number was printed indelibly on her brain.*

indelicate /ɪndɛlɪkət/
ADJ **Indelicate** behaviour is rude or offensive; a formal word. *Simon was hungry, but felt it would be indelicate to make too much fuss about it.*

indemnity /ɪndɛmnəti/ **indemnities**
1 NU If something provides **indemnity**, it provides insurance or protection against damage or loss, especially in the form of financial compensation. *...the Engineering Employers' Indemnity Fund. ...indemnity against prosecution.*
2 NC An **indemnity** is an amount of money or goods that is received by someone as compensation for some damage or loss they have suffered. *The families of the two young men paid an indemnity to the victim after the accident.*

indent /ɪndɛnt/ **indents, indenting, indented**
1 VO When you **indent** a word, a line, or a paragraph, you start it further in from the margin than you start the other lines. *Give the name of the speaker in capitals and indent the speech.*
2 V+for If you **indent** for goods, you order them by filling in a special form; a technical term. *He indented for 5,000 miles of rubber tubing.*

indentation /ɪndɛnteɪʃn/ **indentations**
1 NC An **indentation** is a dent in the surface or edge of something; a formal word. *The high heels of her boots made little indentations in the carpet.*
2 NC You can also use **indentation** to refer to a space at the beginning of a line of writing, between the margin and the beginning of the writing.

indented /ɪndɛntɪd/
1 ADJ Something that is **indented** has notches or marks on its edge or its surface. *...the wooden block, indented by chopper and saw.*
2 ADJ A word, a line, or a paragraph that is **indented**, starts further in from the margin than the other lines.

independence /ɪndɪpɛndəns/
1 NU If a country has **independence**, it is not ruled by any other country. *The country has had 24 years of independence... Members of the police are to be sent to oversee the country's transition to independence.*
2 NU If you refer to someone's **independence**, you are referring to the fact that they do not rely on other people. *She shows great independence of mind... Maxwell always had this intellectual independence.*

Independence Day
NU A country's **Independence Day** is the day on which the population celebrate their independence from another country that ruled them in the past. *Tomorrow, on Israel's Independence Day, the US Secretary of State will arrive in Jerusalem for talks. ...an independence day parade.*

independent /ɪndɪpɛndənt/
1 ADJ Something that is **independent** exists, happens, or acts separately from other people or things. *Two*

independent studies came to the same conclusions. ...20 clinics which are independent of the National Health Service. ♦ **independently** ADV *Agriculture developed independently in many parts of the globe.*
2 ADJ Someone who is **independent** does not rely on other people. *I became financially independent.*
3 ADJ An **independent** school, broadcasting company, or other organization does not receive money from the government. *...an independent radio station in Moscow. ...a documentary broadcast on British independent television.*
4 ADJ **Independent** countries and states are not ruled by other countries and have their own governments. *Independent Angola was at war again. ...the Polisario movement which says that the disputed Western Sahara should be independent.*
5 ADJ ATTRIB An **independent** inquiry or opinion is held by people who are not involved in a situation and so are able to make a fair judgement. *The Labour Party are calling for an independent inquiry into the export of the uranium... There are no independent accounts of the fighting.*

in-depth
ADJ ATTRIB An **in-depth** investigation or analysis is very thorough and detailed. *There is now much more in-depth analysis of social and economic problems... He has demanded an in-depth inquiry into the death of the former minister.*

indescribable /ɪndɪskraɪbəbl/
ADJ Something that is **indescribable** is too intense or extreme to be described. *The smell was indescribable.* ♦ **indescribably** ADV *The air was getting indescribably foul. ...an indescribably sad cry.*

indestructible /ɪndɪstrʌktəbl/
ADJ Something that is **indestructible** cannot be destroyed. *...a new type of thermometer which appears to be indestructible and is very easy to read. ...an indestructible bond.*

indeterminable /ɪndɪtɜːmɪnəbl/
ADJ An **indeterminable** number, amount, or quantity is unable to be counted or measured exactly. *There is an indeterminable number of factors.*

indeterminacy /ɪndɪtɜːmɪnəsi/
NU **Indeterminacy** is the quality of being uncertain or vague. *...the indeterminacy of thought and values that characterizes contemporary life.*

indeterminate /ɪndɪtɜːmɪnət/
ADJ If something is **indeterminate**, you cannot say exactly what it is. *...a figure of indeterminate sex.*

index /ɪndɛks/ **indexes, indexing, indexed; indices.**
The plural form of the noun is **indexes** for the meanings in paragraphs 1 and 2, and **indices** for the meanings in paragraphs 3 and 6.
1 NC An **index** is an alphabetical list at the back of a book saying where particular things are referred to in the book. *They pick up the book, look at the index, and are delighted to find that they understand it.*
2 NC A card **index** is a set of cards with information on them, arranged in alphabetical order. *...a pocket-sized card index and diary system.*
3 NC An **index** is also a system by which changes in the value of something can be compared or measured. *...a 0.3 per cent rise in the wholesale prices index... You can take each of the indices in the social sector and compare them with those of twenty years ago.*
4 NSING If one thing is an **index** of another thing, it is a sign of the changes that are taking place in the other thing. *Coal was the perfect index to Britain's situation.*
5 VO+to If you **index** one thing to something else, you arrange it so that when one thing increases or decreases, the other thing also increases or decreases. *...state university professors, who have been striking for the past three months to demand their salaries be indexed to the inflation rate.*
6 NC In mathematics, **indices** are the little numbers that show how many times you must multiply a number by itself. In the equation $3^2 = 9$, the number 2 is an index.

indexation /ɪndɛkseɪʃn/
NU **Indexation** is the system of making wages, interest rates, pensions and so on linked to an index which

measures inflation or the cost of living. *The indexation of private sector salaries is to be phased out... The President is serious in his efforts to reject wage indexation.*

index card, index cards
NC A **index card** is a small card on which you can write information about someone or something in order to file it and consult it when necessary. *The Federal Public Prosecutor's office in Berne has nine-hundred-thousand names on index cards and files.*

index finger, index fingers
NC Your **index finger** is the finger that is next to your thumb. *The knife slipped and she severed a nerve in her index finger.*

index-linked
ADJ **Index-linked** pensions, payments, and so on are linked to the index which measures inflation or the cost of living, and so change every time inflation or the cost of living changes. *The workers are demanding index-linked salary adjustments.*

India /ɪndɪə/
The **Republic of India** is a country in southern Asia. It has the second largest population in the world. India became independent from Britain in 1947. Jawaharlal Nehru was the first Prime Minister of India and led the Congress Party until his death in 1964. His daughter Indira Gandhi dominated Indian politics from 1966 until her assassination in 1984. Her son, Rajiv Gandhi, was Prime Minister from 1984 to 1989, and was assassinated during the election of 1991, won by the Congress (I) Party. Ramaswami Venkataraman became President in 1987. P V Narasimha Rao became Prime Minister in 1991. India is a member of the Commonwealth. Cotton, tea, rice, and spices are the main agricultural exports. ♦ **Indian** /ɪndɪən/ N, ADJ ▪ *per capita GNP:* US$330 ▪ *religion:* Hinduism (80%), Islam (11%) ▪ *language:* Hindi, English (16 regional languages are also recognized) ▪ *currency:* rupee ▪ *capital:* Delhi ▪ *largest city:* Calcutta ▪ *population:* 833 million (1989) ▪ *size:* 3,287,263 square kilometres.

Indian /ɪndɪən/ **Indians**
1 ADJ **Indian** means belonging or relating to India. *Indian attitudes may have to change.*
2 NC An **Indian** is a person who comes from India. *This tends to favour certain groups such as Pakistanis and Indians.*
3 NC An **Indian** is also someone descended from the people who lived in North, South, or Central America before Europeans arrived. *...square dancing teams, along with Blackfoot Indians, cowboys and mounted police.*

Indian ink
NU **Indian ink** is a black ink which is used especially for drawing.

Indian summer, Indian summers
NC An **Indian summer** is a period of warm weather during the autumn. *The turnout was expected to be low, but Germany is currently enjoying an Indian summer, encouraging people to get out and vote.*

india rubber, india rubbers
NUorNC **India rubber** is rubber used for erasing pencil marks and making balls, toys, and so on.

indicate /ɪndɪkeɪt/ **indicates, indicating, indicated**
1 VOorV-REPORT If something **indicates** a fact or situation, it shows that it exists. *This absurd action indicated the level of their intelligence... The poll indicates a drop in support for the Conservatives... These studies indicate that it's best to change your car every two years.*
2 VOorV-REPORT If you **indicate** a fact, you mention it in a rather indirect way. *President Castro's speech indicates a few of the things he will be telling his visitor... I indicated that I had not seen enough of his work to be able to judge it.*
3 VO If you **indicate** something to someone, you point to it. *She sat down in the armchair that Mrs Jones indicated.*
4 VorV-REPORT When a driver **indicates**, flashing lights on the car show which way he or she is going to turn. *He indicated that he was turning left.*

indication /ɪndɪkeɪʃn/ **indications**
NCorNU An **indication** is a sign which gives you an idea of what someone feels, what is happening, or what is likely to happen. *The President gave a clear indication yesterday of his willingness to meet the visitors... All the indications are that the National Party will be soundly defeated... There was no indication that he ever noticed my absence.*

indicative /ɪndɪkətɪv/
1 ADJ PRED+of If something is **indicative** of the existence or nature of something, it is a sign of it; a formal use. *He regarded their action as indicative of their lack of courage... It is indicative of how the ceasefire agreement has thrown the Contra movement into disarray.*
2 N SING If a verb is in the **indicative**, it is in the form used for making statements. Compare **imperative** and **interrogative**.

indicator /ɪndɪkeɪtə/ **indicators**
1 NC+SUPP An **indicator** of something tells you whether it exists or what it is like; a formal use. *Price is not always an indicator of quality... The Commission's representative said there were hopeful indicators of economic recovery.*
2 NC A car's **indicators** are the lights used to show when it is turning left or right.

indices /ɪndɪsiːz/
Indices is a plural of **index**.

indict /ɪndaɪt/ **indicts, indicting, indicted**
VO When someone is **indicted** for a crime, they are officially charged with it; a legal term. *An interesting aspect of the case was whether or not Stephen could be legally indicted. ...a decision to indict the General on charges of smuggling.*

indictable /ɪndaɪtəbl/
ADJ An **indictable** offence is one for which you can be officially charged; a legal term. *The inquiry did not accuse Mr Scargill of any indictable offences.*

indictment /ɪndaɪtmənt/ **indictments**
1 NC+SUPP If you say that a fact or situation is an **indictment** of something, you mean that it shows how bad that thing is; a formal use. *It is a striking indictment of our educational system that so many children cannot read or write.*
2 NCorNU An **indictment** is a criminal charge against someone; a legal term. *The indictment was read to the jury... Robbins is under indictment for fraud.*

indifference /ɪndɪfərəns/
NU **Indifference** is a complete lack of interest in something or someone. *Halliday's presence or absence was a matter of total indifference to him... After years of official indifference, the state nursery school campaign seems to be making progress.*

indifferent /ɪndɪfərənt/
1 ADJ If you are **indifferent** to something, you have no interest in it. *Children fail to progress if their parents seem indifferent to their success.* ♦ **indifferently** ADV *She looked at me indifferently as I pulled up a stool.*
2 ADJ **Indifferent** also means of a rather low standard. *He was an indifferent actor.*

indigenous /ɪndɪdʒɪnəs/
ADJ Something that is **indigenous** comes from the country in which it is found; a formal word. *...the indigenous population... The elephant is indigenous to India.*

indigestible /ɪndɪdʒestəbl/
ADJ Food that is **indigestible** cannot be digested easily. *Cereal such as maize contains an indigestible material called phytate which is rich in iron.*

indigestion /ɪndɪdʒestʃən/
NU **Indigestion** is pain that you get when you cannot digest food. *Food that is too fatty may cause indigestion.*

indignant /ɪndɪgnənt/
ADJ If you are **indignant**, you are shocked and angry, often because you consider you have been treated unfairly. *Many taxpayers are indignant at what they regard as an illegal use of public funds.* ♦ **indignantly** ADV *'Why not?' cried Judy indignantly.*

indignation /ɪndɪgneɪʃn/
NU **Indignation** is shock and anger. *She seethed with indignation.*

indignity /ɪndɪgnəti/ **indignities**
N or NU An **indignity** is something that makes you feel embarrassed or humiliated; a formal word. *He hated the rules and the petty indignities of prison life. ...the indignity of slavery.*

indigo /ɪndɪgəʊ/
ADJ Something that is **indigo** is dark purple. *...an indigo sky.*

indirect /ɪndərekt, ɪndaɪrekt/
1 ADJ Something that is **indirect** is not done or caused directly, but by means of something or someone else. *A sudden increase in oil prices would have serious indirect effects... Many of the deaths are the indirect result of Brazil's massive debts.* ◆ **indirectly** ADV *I suppose I was indirectly responsible for the whole thing.*
2 ADJ An **indirect** route or journey does not use the shortest way between two places. *The pilots have a system of identifying themselves through their speed and their indirect approach.*
3 ADJ An **indirect** answer or reference does not openly mention the thing that is actually being talked about. *Pakistan has rejected an indirect allegation that they have been supplying weapons to the Sikhs... He listened impassively to indirect but pointed criticisms of his term in office.*

indirect object, indirect objects. See **object**.

indirect tax, indirect taxes
NC An **indirect tax** is a tax on goods and services which is added to the price of these goods and services. VAT and import duty are indirect taxes: compare **direct tax**. *Economists are expecting a sharp rise in indirect taxes.*

indirect taxation
NU **Indirect taxation** is the raising of money by a government by means of indirect taxes. *He's indicated his support for a Bill which recommends indirect taxation.*

indiscernible /ɪndɪsɜːnəbl/
ADJ Something that is **indiscernible** cannot be seen or understood clearly; a formal word. *For some indiscernible reason she wants to marry him.*

indiscipline /ɪndɪsəplɪn/
N U **Indiscipline** is a lack of discipline. *Murphy was found guilty of indiscipline on the field. ...violence and indiscipline in schools.*

indiscreet /ɪndɪskriːt/
ADJ If you are **indiscreet**, you talk about or do things openly when you should keep them secret. *...an indiscreet comment.*

indiscretion /ɪndɪskreʃn/ **indiscretions**
N or NU **Indiscretion** is behaviour that is unacceptable by being incautious, tactless, or by revealing secrets. *How could she commit such an indiscretion?... He has shown acute political indiscretion and is unbelievably naive.*

indiscriminate /ɪndɪskrɪmɪnət/
ADJ An **indiscriminate** action does not involve any careful choice. *Television watchers tend to be indiscriminate in their viewing habits.* ◆ **indiscriminately** ADV *He reads widely and indiscriminately.*

indispensable /ɪndɪspensəbl/
ADJ If something is **indispensable**, it is absolutely essential. *In my job, a telephone is indispensable.*

indisposed /ɪndɪspəʊzd/
ADJ PRED If someone, especially a performer or important person, is **indisposed**, they are suffering from a slight illness; a formal word. *His Excellency is indisposed.*

indisposition /ɪndɪspəzɪʃn/ **indispositions**
N U or NC **Indisposition** is slight illness which prevents you from doing something you had planned to do; a formal word. *He was prevented from finishing his lecture through sudden indisposition.*

indisputable /ɪndɪspjuːtəbl/
ADJ If a fact is **indisputable**, it is obviously and definitely true. *We're going to have a very hard time. That's indisputable.* ◆ **indisputably** ADV *The book is indisputably a masterpiece.*

indissoluble /ɪndɪsɒljʊbl/
ADJ An **indissoluble** relationship or link can never be

ended; a formal word. *...the indissoluble ties of mother to child.*

indistinct /ɪndɪstɪŋkt/
ADJ Something that is **indistinct** is unclear and difficult to see or hear. *His words were faint and often indistinct.* ◆ **indistinctly** ADV *I mumbled indistinctly through a mouthful of food.*

indistinguishable /ɪndɪstɪŋgwɪʃəbl/
ADJ If two or more things are **indistinguishable** from each other, they are so similar that it is impossible to tell them apart. *In his dress, manner, and command of English, he was quite indistinguishable from the club's members. ...an indistinguishable jumble of words.*

individual /ɪndɪvɪdʒʊəl/ **individuals**
1 ADJ ATTRIB **Individual** means relating to one person or thing, rather than to a large group. *...individual tuition... We can identify each individual whale by its song.* ◆ **individually** ADV *Each fruit should be wrapped individually in paper.*
2 NC An **individual** is a person. *...the freedom of the individual.*

individualism /ɪndɪvɪdʒʊəlɪzəm/
1 NU **Individualism** is behaviour that is quite different from anyone else's behaviour. *Why should we put such emphasis on individualism?*
2 NU **Individualism** is also the belief that economics and politics should not be controlled by the state. *He is opposed to individualism and free-market capitalism. ...rabid individualism.*

individualist /ɪndɪvɪdʒʊəlɪst/ **individualists**
NC An **individualist** is someone who likes to do things in their own way. *Academics are such individualists.*

individualistic /ɪndɪvɪdʒʊəlɪstɪk/
ADJ If you are **individualistic**, you like to do things by yourself and in your own way. *Group communication reduced the need for individualistic artistic expression.*

individuality /ɪndɪvɪdʒʊæləti/
NU If something has **individuality**, it is different from all other things and is therefore interesting. *The advertisement lacks any individuality.*

individualize /ɪndɪvɪdʒʊəlaɪz/ **individualizes, individualizing, individualized**; also spelt **individualise**.
VO If you **individualize** something, you make it different from other things so that it can be recognized or identified; a formal word. *...all the subtle smells and textures that individualize any situation.*

indivisible /ɪndɪvɪzəbl/
ADJ If something is **indivisible**, it cannot be divided into different parts. *...the ancient Greek belief that the atom is indivisible.*

Indo- /ɪndəʊ-/
PREFIX **Indo-** is used to form adjectives which describe something as connected both with India and with another country or continent. *She has an Indo-Portuguese background.*

indoctrinate /ɪndɒktrɪneɪt/ **indoctrinates, indoctrinating, indoctrinated**
VO If you **indoctrinate** someone, you teach them a particular belief with the aim that they will not consider other beliefs; used showing disapproval. *The officials told the committee that the separatists were out to indoctrinate their compatriots... The masses who we have indoctrinated will certainly support us and we shall seize the final victory.* ◆ **indoctrination** /ɪndɒktrɪneɪʃn/ N U *It is difficult to overcome the early indoctrination of children.*

indolence /ɪndələns/
N U **Indolence** is laziness; a formal word. *...the indolence of his movements.*

indolent /ɪndələnt/
ADJ Someone who is **indolent** is lazy; a formal word. *...an indolent smile.*

indomitable /ɪndɒmɪtəbl/
ADJ Someone who is **indomitable** never admits that they have been defeated; a formal word. *The boy had been kept alive by his indomitable spirit.*

Indonesia /ɪndəʊniːziə/
The **Republic of Indonesia** is a country in the Pacific, off the coast of south-east Asia. It consists of over 13,000 islands and is the largest archipelago in the

world. The main islands are Sumatra, Java, part of Borneo (known as Kalimantan), Sulawesi (Celebes) and Irian Jaya (West New Guinea). It was a Dutch colony from the 17th century until 1949 and was occupied by Japan from 1942 to 1945. Dr Sukarno, the first President, ruled until 1967. Indonesia annexed East Timor in 1975, but has failed to gain international recognition for the new territory. General Suharto became President in 1968. Indonesia produces oil and is a member of OPEC. It is also a member of the Association of South East Asian Nations. It is the world's second largest producer of natural rubber. Large foreign debts are a major economic problem. ♦ **Indonesian** /ɪndəuniːziən/ N, ADJ ▪ *per capita GNP:* US$430 ▪ *religion:* Islam, Christianity ▪ *language:* Bahasa Indonesia (official) ▪ *currency:* rupiah ▪ *capital:* Jakarta ▪ *population:* 175 million (1988) ▪ *size:* 1,904,569 square kilometres.

indoor /ˈɪndɔː/
ADJ ATTRIB You use **indoor** to describe things inside a building rather than outside. *...indoor games such as table tennis.*

indoors /ɪnˈdɔːz/
ADV If something happens **indoors**, it happens inside a building. *We'd better go indoors.*

indrawn /ɪnˈdrɔːn/
ADJ ATTRIB An **indrawn** breath is one in which you breathe in suddenly. *There were one or two indrawn breaths from around the table.*

indubitable /ɪnˈdjuːbɪtəbl/
ADJ Something that is **indubitable** is definite and cannot be doubted; a formal word. *There have been indubitable signs already.* ♦ **indubitably** ADV *There was Thomas, dirty and muddy but indubitably alive.*

induce /ɪnˈdjuːs/ **induces, inducing, induced**
1 VO To **induce** a particular state or condition means to cause it. *Blame was put on the shortage of fuel induced by allied attacks on oil fields and refineries. ...pills guaranteed to induce sleep.*
2 VO+to-INF To **induce** someone to do something means to persuade or influence them to do it. *What on earth had induced her to marry a man like that?*
3 VO If doctors **induce** labour or birth, they cause a pregnant woman to start giving birth by the use of drugs or other medical means. *They induced labour for her second pregnancy.*

inducement /ɪnˈdjuːsmənt/ **inducements**
NC An **inducement** is something which might persuade someone to do a particular thing. *These tax advantages provide the main inducement to become a home-owner.*

induct /ɪnˈdʌkt/ **inducts, inducting, inducted**
1 VO If you **induct** someone, you officially place them in a particular job, rank, or position; a formal use. *They will be inducted into service sometime around the end of the year.*
2 VO If someone is **inducted** into the army, they are required by law to start military service; used in American English. *Her son had refused to be inducted into the U.S. Army.*

induction /ɪnˈdʌkʃn/ **inductions**
1 NUorNC A person's **induction** in a new job or way of life is their formal introduction to it. *They are said to oppose her induction in politics... Next month there will be the ceremony of induction of the new chancellor.*
2 NU **Induction** into the army is the legal requirement for someone to begin military service; used in American English. *Forty per cent of the conscripts failed to turn up for induction.*
3 NU **Induction** is used to refer to a way of reasoning in which you use individual ideas or facts to give you a general rule or conclusion. *My argument follows the rules of logical induction... Induction, not deduction, was his method.*
4 NU **Induction** is also the act of beginning or stimulating a natural process, such as pregnancy. *These chemicals seem to be involved in the induction of the cancer process.*
5 NU The process by which electricity or magnetism is passed between two objects or circuits without them touching each other is also referred to as **induction**.

Faraday discovered electromagnetic induction and invented the first dynamo.

induction coil, induction coils
NC An **induction coil** is a transformer that is used to produce a high voltage from a low voltage. *Researchers are almost ready to do away with external wiring by using induction coils buried under the skin.*

induction course, induction courses
NC An **induction course** is a course arranged for people who are new to a job or place, in order to show them what they are expected to do and where things are. *The next stage was what the Foreign Office called their induction course.*

inductive /ɪnˈdʌktɪv/
ADJ **Inductive** reasoning is based on the process of induction.

indulge /ɪnˈdʌldʒ/ **indulges, indulging, indulged**
1 V+in, VO, or V-REFL If you **indulge** in something or **indulge** a hobby or interest, you allow yourself to have or do something that you enjoy. *Let us indulge in a little daydreaming... Jack had spent the previous three weeks indulging his passion for climbing... He indulged himself by smoking another cigarette.*
2 VO If you **indulge** someone, you let them have or do whatever they want, even if this is not good for them. *He was usually prepared to indulge his sister.*

indulgence /ɪnˈdʌldʒəns/ **indulgences**
1 NC An **indulgence** is something pleasant that you allow yourself to do or have. *Smoking was his one indulgence... For Britain's meat-eating majority, Christmas time is the ultimate indulgence.*
2 NU **Indulgence** is being kind to people and not criticizing their weaknesses. *Simon listened to her with indulgence... I'd ask your indulgence.*

indulgent /ɪnˈdʌldʒənt/
ADJ If you are **indulgent**, you treat a person with special kindness, often in a way that is not good for them. *...an indulgent father.* ♦ **indulgently** ADV *He smiled indulgently at her.*

industrial /ɪnˈdʌstriəl/
1 ADJ ATTRIB **Industrial** means relating to industry. *The report says the disaster was caused by sabotage, not industrial accident. ...industrial and technical change.*
2 ADJ An **industrial** city, country, or area is one in which industry is important or highly developed. *Britain, like many other industrial countries, has drastically reduced its dependence on oil... Wolverhampton is the industrial heartland of Britain.*

industrial action
NU When a group of workers take **industrial action**, they stop working or take other action to protest about their pay or working conditions. *Prison officers will be stepping up their industrial action over staffing levels.*

industrial estate, industrial estates
NC An **industrial estate** is an area which has been specially planned for a lot of factories. *The glass factory is a modern plant on a new industrial estate.*

industrialise /ɪnˈdʌstriəlaɪz/. See **industrialize**.

industrialism /ɪnˈdʌstriəlɪzəm/
NU **Industrialism** is the state of having an economy based on industry.

industrialist /ɪnˈdʌstriəlɪst/ **industrialists**
NC An **industrialist** is a person who owns or controls large amounts of money or property in industry. *One such influential person was the American industrialist Henry Ford... The bank would be able to lend to entrepreneurs and industrialists.*

industrialize /ɪnˈdʌstriəlaɪz/ **industrializes, industrializing, industrialized**; also spelt **industrialise**.
V-ERG When a country **industrializes** or when people **industrialize** it, it develops a lot of industries. *The only way we're going to compete with the West is to industrialize. ...the funds needed to industrialize all the underdeveloped countries.* ♦ **industrialization** /ɪnˌdʌstriəlaɪˈzeɪʃn/ NU *...the rising cost of industrialization.*

industrialized /ɪnˈdʌstriəlaɪzd/
ADJ An **industrialized** society or place is one in which society depends heavily on industry. *...the*

industrialized world. ...those societies which became industrialized during the last century.

industrial relations
N PL **Industrial relations** are the relationship between employers and workers. *He identified the need for an inquiry into industrial relations in the car industry.*

industrious /ɪndʌstriəs/
ADJ Someone who is **industrious** works very hard; a formal word. *...an industrious student.*

industry /ɪndəstri/ **industries**
1 NU **Industry** is the work and processes involved in making things in factories. *Japanese industry is making increasing use of robots. ...higher state subsidies to industry. ...the department of Trade and Industry.*
2 NC+SUPP A particular **industry** consists of all the people and the processes that are involved in manufacturing, producing, or commercializing a particular thing. *The textile industry is a large employer here... The report has provoked a furious response from the tobacco industry. ...concern about the effects of the expanding tourist industry.*
3 NU **Industry** is also the quality of working very hard; a formal word. *...the old virtues of self-reliance, industry, and frugality.*

inebriate /ɪniːbriət/ **inebriates**
ADJ An **inebriate** person drinks a lot of alcohol and is regularly drunk; a formal word. *...his inebriate father.* ► Also NC *He had died in a home for inebriates.*

inebriated /ɪniːbrieɪtɪd/
ADJ Someone who is **inebriated** is drunk; a formal word. *I was part of a hopelessly inebriated audience.*

inedible /ɪnɛdəbl/
ADJ Something that is **inedible** is poisonous or too unpleasant to eat. *Bamboo is inedible when it is in flower.*

ineffable /ɪnɛfəbl/
ADJ Something that is **ineffable** is so wonderful or great that it cannot be described in words; a formal word. *Sometimes music can produce an ineffable joy. ...the ineffable story-teller, P.G. Wodehouse.*
♦ **ineffably** ADV *They were ineffably sad.*

ineffective /ɪnɪfɛktɪv/
ADJ Something that is **ineffective** has no effect. *He found it hard to understand why they thought sanctions would be ineffective... The Environment Minister said that dog registration would be expensive and ineffective.* ♦ **ineffectiveness** NU *He was disgusted by the ineffectiveness of the government.*

ineffectual /ɪnɪfɛktʃuəl/
ADJ Something that is **ineffectual** does not do what it is supposed to do. *...ineffectual policies.*
♦ **ineffectually** ADV *...trying ineffectually to brush the mud off his jacket.*

inefficiency /ɪnɪfɪʃnsi/
NU If you refer to the **inefficiency** of a person, organization, or system, you are referring to the fact that they are badly organized and do not use resources, equipment, or time in the best possible way. *He criticised the inefficiency of public authorities.*

inefficient /ɪnɪfɪʃnt/
ADJ A person, organization, system, or machine that is **inefficient** is badly organized and does not use resources, equipment, or time in the best possible way. *...shutting down aging and inefficient refineries. ...inefficient farming.* ♦ **inefficiently** ADV *She works slowly and inefficiently.*

inelegant /ɪnɛlɪgənt/
ADJ Something that is **inelegant** is not attractive or graceful. *Glass chandeliers have been replaced by inelegant plastic ones. ...his inelegant dressing gown.*

ineligible /ɪnɛlɪdʒəbl/
ADJ If you are **ineligible** for something, you are not qualified for it or entitled to it; a formal word. *I am ineligible for unemployment benefit.*

ineluctable /ɪnɪlʌktəbl/
ADJ ATTRIB **Ineluctable** describes something that nobody can escape from; a formal word. *...a world of ineluctable corruption.*

inept /ɪnɛpt/
ADJ Someone who is **inept** does something with a complete lack of skill. *...the government's inept handling of the crisis.*

ineptitude /ɪnɛptɪtjuːd/
NU **Ineptitude** is a complete lack of skill; a formal word. *...his record of political ineptitude.*

inequality /ɪnɪkwɒləti/ **inequalities**
NUorNC **Inequality** is a difference in wealth or opportunity between groups in a society. *...reform aimed at reducing inequality... We found great inequalities of opportunity.*

inequitable /ɪnɛkwɪtəbl/
ADJ Something that is **inequitable** is unfair or unjust; a formal word. *...the inequitable division of wealth. ...inequitable taxation.*

inequity /ɪnɛkwəti/ **inequities**
NUorNC The **inequity** of something is the fact that it is unfair and unjust; a formal word. *...the government's unique combination of inequity and incompetence. ...glaring inequities between the black and white communities.*

ineradicable /ɪnɪrædɪkəbl/
ADJ Something that is **ineradicable** cannot be removed; a formal word. *...an ineradicable tendency to be frivolous.*

inert /ɪnɜːt/
1 ADJ Someone or something that is **inert** does not move at all and appears to be lifeless. *I carried her, still inert, up the stairs to her room.*
2 ADJ An **inert** substance or gas is one which does not react with other chemical substances; a technical use in chemistry. *Like other fairly inert chemicals DNA can survive for millennia.*

inertia /ɪnɜːʃə/
1 NU If you have a feeling of **inertia**, you feel very lazy and unwilling to do anything. *Though I wanted to go, I stayed from sheer inertia.*
2 NU You can also use **inertia** to refer to a government's or an organization's lack of energy or initiative in dealing with a problem. *But the UN's role remains limited by national rivalries and internal inertia.*
3 NU **Inertia** is also the tendency of a physical object to remain still, or to continue moving if it is already moving, unless a force is applied to it; a technical use in physics.

inescapable /ɪnɪskeɪpəbl/
ADJ If something is **inescapable**, it cannot be avoided. *...an inescapable conclusion.*

inessential /ɪnɪsɛnʃl/ **inessentials**
1 ADJ Something that is **inessential** is unnecessary. *She thought she would sell any inessential furniture.*
2 N PL The **inessentials** are the things that you do not really need. *I felt that my life was suddenly stripped of inessentials such as worries about money.*

inestimable /ɪnɛstɪməbl/
ADJ Something that is **inestimable** is extremely great or good; a formal word. *Maria's advice proved of inestimable value.*

inevitable /ɪnɛvɪtəbl/
1 ADJ If something is **inevitable**, it cannot be prevented or avoided. *If this policy continues, then violence is inevitable.* ♦ **inevitability** /ɪnɛvɪtəbɪləti/ NU *You must recognize the inevitability of change.*
2 N SING The **inevitable** is something that cannot be prevented or avoided. *I resigned myself to the inevitable.*

inevitably /ɪnɛvɪtəbli/
ADV SEN If something **inevitably** happens or will happen, it is the only possible result. *A household of this size inevitably has problems.*

inexact /ɪnɪgzækt/
ADJ Something that is **inexact** is not precise or accurate. *Lip reading is an incomplete, inexact form of comprehending for the deaf.*

inexcusable /ɪnɪkskjuːzəbl/
ADJ Something that is **inexcusable** is too bad to be justified or tolerated. *...an inexcusable act of destruction.*

inexhaustible /ɪnɪgzɔːstəbl/
ADJ An **inexhaustible** supply of something is so great

that it will never be used up. *The sun is an inexhaustible source of energy... His patience must be inexhaustible.*

inexorable /ɪnɛksəºrəbl/
ADJ Something that is **inexorable** cannot be prevented from continuing; a formal word. *...the inexorable rise in the cost of living.* ◆ **inexorably** ADV *These facts led inexorably to one conclusion.*

inexpensive /ɪnɪkspɛnsɪv/
ADJ Something that is **inexpensive** does not cost much. *...an inexpensive wine.*

inexperience /ɪnɪkspɪərɪəns/
NU If you refer to someone's **inexperience**, you are referring to the fact that they have little or no experience of a particular activity. *You're bound to make a few mistakes through inexperience.*

inexperienced /ɪnɪkspɪərɪənst/
ADJ If you are **inexperienced**, you have little or no experience of a particular activity. *...an inexperienced swimmer.*

inexpert /ɪnɛkspɜːt/
ADJ Something that is **inexpert** shows a lack of skill. *...Harris's inexpert but conscientious gardening.*

inexplicable /ɪnɪksplɪkəbl/
ADJ If something is **inexplicable**, you cannot explain it. *I still find this incident inexplicable.* ◆ **inexplicably** ADV *Anita had inexplicably disappeared.*

inexpressible /ɪnɪksprɛsəbl/
ADJ An **inexpressible** feeling is too strong to be expressed in words. *It was an inexpressible relief.*

inexpressive /ɪnɪksprɛsɪv/
ADJ If someone's face or eyes are **inexpressive**, you cannot tell what the person is thinking. *...his inexpressive eyes.*

in extremis /ɪn ɪkstriːmɪs/; a formal expression.
1 If someone is **in extremis**, they are about to die. *He is in extremis and unlikely to see the night out.*
2 You can also use **in extremis** to indicate that someone is in a very difficult situation and has to use extreme methods in order to solve their problems. *The US methods are alternatives, and only to be used in extremis.*

inextricable /ɪnɪkstrɪkəbl, ɪnɛkstrɪkəbl/
ADJ You use **inextricable** to describe complicated things that cannot be separated or considered separately; a formal word. *He painted a picture of a world bound together by inextricable economic ties.* ◆ **inextricably** ADV *Social and economic factors are inextricably linked.*

infallible /ɪnfæləbl/
ADJ Someone or something that is **infallible** is never wrong. *Doctors aren't infallible... He criticised party leaders who thought of themselves as infallible.*

infamous /ɪnfəməs/
ADJ **Infamous** people or things are well-known because of something bad. *...the infamous Khmer Rouge leader, Pol Pot... How well I remember that infamous night.*

infamy /ɪnfəmi/
NU **Infamy** is the state of being infamous. *This is a day that will live in infamy... He was returned to fame—or rather infamy— a few years later in the film Amadeus.*

infancy /ɪnfənsi/
1 NU **Infancy** is the period in your life when you are a very young child. *The child died in infancy.*
2 If something is **in its infancy**, it has only just started. *The private economy is only in its infancy in Bulgaria, Romania and the five interested Soviet republics.*

infant /ɪnfənt/ **infants**; a formal word.
1 NC An **infant** is a very young child or baby. *He was sent to be looked after by his aunt while he was still an infant. ...infant mortality.*
2 ADJ An **infant** organisation, country, or movement is new and has not developed much. *At the outset, the Sultan supported the infant Republic and the social change it represented... Today's warning to the infant opposition party is the toughest yet issued by the authorities.*

infanticide /ɪnfæntɪsaɪd/
NU **Infanticide** is the crime of killing a young child. *In*

pre-revolutionary days, female infanticide was not uncommon.

infantile /ɪnfəntaɪl/
1 ADJ You use **infantile** to describe the diseases or behaviour of very young children; a formal use. *...infantile paralysis.*
2 ADJ Someone who is **infantile** behaves in a foolish and childish way. *Darwin thought emotions were bestial and infantile. ...infantile arguments.*

infantry /ɪnfəntri/
N COLL The **infantry** are the soldiers in an army who fight on foot rather than in tanks or on horses. *...difficulties in recruiting, especially for the infantry. ...The Second Light Infantry Division.*

infantryman /ɪnfəntrɪmən/ **infantrymen** /ɪnfəntrɪmən/
NC An **infantryman** is a soldier in an infantry regiment. *The Ghurkas have won fame as infantrymen and jungle fighters.*

infant school, infant schools
NC An **infant school** is a school for children aged five to seven. *Children should be tested on their abilities when they start infant school.*

infatuated /ɪnfætjueɪtɪd/
ADJ If you are **infatuated** with someone, you have a strong feeling of love for them that other people think is ridiculous. *Sartre had become infatuated with a younger woman, Olga.* ◆ **infatuation** /ɪnfætjueɪʃn/ **infatuations** NCorNU *This is not love but a foolish infatuation.*

infect /ɪnfɛkt/ **infects, infecting, infected**
VO To **infect** people, animals, plants, or food means to cause them to suffer from germs or to carry germs. *Imported birds can infect their owners with an unpleasant illness... If the virus infects human cells, it can easily be spread from one person to another.*

infected /ɪnfɛktɪd/
1 ADJ An **infected** wound or part of your body is unable to heal properly because of germs. *She had a large infected gash in her head.*
2 ADJ An **infected** place is one where an infection or disease is present and spreading among people and animals. *Keep outside the infected area.*

infection /ɪnfɛkʃn/ **infections**
1 NCorNU An **infection** is a disease caused by germs. *I had an ear infection... Radiation lessened bodily resistance to infection.*
2 NU **Infection** is the state of becoming infected. *There is little risk of infection.*

infectious /ɪnfɛkʃəs/
1 ADJ If you have an **infectious** disease, people near you can catch it from you. *One in ten children believe that cancer is infectious. ...toxins produced by infectious bacteria.*
2 ADJ If a feeling is **infectious**, it spreads to other people. *Don't you find her enthusiasm infectious?*

infer /ɪnfɜː/ **infers, inferring, inferred**
VO+from, V-REPORT, or VO If you **infer** something that is not stated directly, you decide that it is true, on the basis of information you have; a formal word. *What can be inferred from the Archbishop's words?... He infers from the actual place-names that they preserve the names of local gods... As a result of this simple statement, I could infer a lot about his former wives.*

inference /ɪnfəºrəns/ **inferences**
NC An **inference** is a conclusion that you draw about something. *The inferences drawn from data have led to some major changes in our policy.*

inferior /ɪnfɪərɪə/ **inferiors**
1 ADJ Someone or something that is **inferior** is not as good or important as other people or things. *Charlie, aged sixteen, felt inferior to lads of his own age... It was a cheap and inferior product.* ◆ **inferiority** /ɪnfɪərɪɒrəti/ NU *...feelings of inferiority.*
2 NC Your **inferiors** are people who have a lower position or status than you. *Those cultures ignore their own regional inferiors, whom they considered to be primitive.*

inferiority complex, inferiority complexes
NC If someone has an **inferiority complex**, they often feel that they are less important or worthwhile than other people. *...a boy who had an inferiority complex about his size.*

infernal /ɪnfɜːnl/
ADJ ATTRIB You use **infernal** to describe something that is very unpleasant; an old-fashioned word. *Will you stop that infernal noise?... You know how people would have voted, and that infernal bill would have become law.*

inferno /ɪnfɜːnəʊ/ **infernos**
NC An **inferno** is a very large dangerous fire; a literary word. *The platform in the North Sea was engulfed by an inferno last July.*

infertile /ɪnfɜːtaɪl/
1 ADJ Someone who is **infertile** cannot have children. *She learned she was infertile... Supporters of the research say it will help infertile couples.* ◆ **infertility** /ɪnfətɪləti/ NU *...an infertility clinic.*
2 ADJ **Infertile** soil is of poor quality, and so plants cannot grow well in it. *...a bleak, inhospitable, infertile land.*

infest /ɪnfest/ **infests, infesting, infested**
VO When insects, rats, or other animals **infest** a plant or a place, they spread in large numbers and cause damage. *...the vermin that infest the crops... The back yard was infested by rats.* ◆ **infested** ADJ *He claimed his cell was infested with red poultry mites... Often the only cure is to destroy infested furniture.* ◆ **infestation** /ɪnfesteɪʃn/ **infestations** NUorNC *So far, there have not been any cases of screw worm infestation... Spraying has been carried out against infestations.*

infidel /ɪnfɪdəl/ **infidels**
NC An **infidel** is a person whose religion is different from that of the speaker; a literary word, used showing disapproval. *...the spiritual duty of liberating the infidels.* ▶ Also ADJ ATTRIB *...the wicked opinions of her infidel son.*

infidelity /ɪnfɪdeləti/ **infidelities**
NUorNC **Infidelity** is the act of being unfaithful to your husband, wife, or lover. *...lurid stories of sex orgies, rape, and sexual infidelity. ...the infidelities of her callous, debonair, secretly bisexual husband.*

in-fighting
NU **In-fighting** is rivalry or quarrelling between members of the same organization. *Their resistance crumbled because of factional in-fighting.*

infiltrate /ɪnfɪltreɪt/ **infiltrates, infiltrating, infiltrated**
VOorV+into If people **infiltrate** an organization or **infiltrate** into it, they join it secretly in order to spy on it or influence it. *Police officers infiltrated a notorious gang of soccer thugs... He had allowed the British civil service to be infiltrated by secret agents... One reporter tried to infiltrate into the prison by mingling with a group of prisoners.* ◆ **infiltration** /ɪnfɪltreɪʃn/ **infiltrations** NUorNC *...gradual infiltration of the security forces... They have been placed on high alert because of the recent infiltrations.*

infiltrator /ɪnfɪltreɪtə/ **infiltrators**
NC An **infiltrator** of an organization is a person who infiltrates it. *Numbers of police agents had been discovered to be infiltrators inside the party.*

infinite /ɪnfɪnət/
ADJ Something that is **infinite** is extremely large in amount or degree, or has no limit. *Qualified doctors are found in an infinite variety of careers... The variations are in fact infinite.* ◆ **infinitely** SUBMOD *The process of unloading had been infinitely easier than putting the stuff on.*

infinitesimal /ɪnfɪnɪtesɪml/
ADJ **Infinitesimal** means extremely small; a formal word. *The chances that the company will have any problems are infinitesimal.*

infinitive /ɪnfɪnətɪv/ **infinitives**
NC In grammar, the **infinitive** of a verb is its base form or simplest form, such as 'do', 'take', and 'eat'. The infinitive can either be used on its own or with 'to' in front of it.

infinity /ɪnfɪnəti/
1 NU **Infinity** is a number that is larger than any other number and so can never be given an exact value. *The bottom of the equation is zero, so the actual quantity shoots up to infinity. ...an infinity of possible combinations.*
2 NU **Infinity** is also a point that is further away than

any other point and so can never be reached. *There was nothing but darkness stretching away to infinity.*

infirm /ɪnfɜːm/; a formal word.
ADJ A person who is **infirm** is weak or ill. *His grandfather was over eighty, infirm and totally blind.* ▶ Also N PL *...the needs of the old and infirm.* ◆ **infirmity**, /ɪnfɜːməti/ **infirmities** NCorNU *...physical infirmity or weakness. ...the infirmities of old age.*

infirmary /ɪnfɜːməri/ **infirmaries**
NC Some hospitals are called **infirmaries**. *He is now at the town's Royal Infirmary with grave injuries.*

inflame /ɪnfleɪm/ **inflames, inflaming, inflamed**
VO If something **inflames** you, it makes you very angry or excited. *Her question seemed to inflame him all the more... The affair has inflamed Muslim feelings all over the world... The deployment of soldiers only inflamed the situation more.*

inflamed /ɪnfleɪmd/
ADJ If part of your body is **inflamed**, it is red or swollen because of an infection or injury; a formal word. *He underwent minor surgery to drain fluid from an inflamed left lung.*

inflammable /ɪnflæməbl/
ADJ An **inflammable** material or chemical burns easily. *It gives out light, but not heat and so is safe to use near inflammable liquids.*

inflammation /ɪnfləmeɪʃn/
NUorN SING When **inflammation** occurs on a part of your body, that part becomes swollen and red. *...inflammation of the ears.*

inflammatory /ɪnflæmətəʳri/
ADJ An **inflammatory** speech or action is likely to make people very angry or hostile. *...an inflammatory speech about terrorists.*

inflatable /ɪnfleɪtəbl/
ADJ An **inflatable** object can be filled with air. *...inflatable lifejackets.*

inflate /ɪnfleɪt/ **inflates, inflating, inflated**
1 V-ERG When you **inflate** something or when it **inflates**, it becomes bigger as it is filled with air or another gas. *The breathing machine can inflate the lungs with oxygen... He may be the only head coach in the Easter Collegiate Conference who has to inflate his own footballs... Two of the life rafts failed to inflate properly.* ◆ **inflated** ADJ *...the large inflated tyre they used as a raft.*
2 VO If someone **inflates** an amount, figure, or the effect of something, they exaggerate it and say it is higher, bigger, or more important than it really is. *...zealous officials inflating the Socialist share of the vote... The usual figure of between 30,000 and 40,000 soldiers given by Western sources is probably much inflated... Proportional representation has the effect of inflating the role of smaller parties.*

inflated /ɪnfleɪtɪd/
1 ADJ If you have an **inflated** opinion of yourself, you think you are much more important than you really are. *...his inflated self-image. ...making inflated boasts about the system they had founded.*
2 ADJ An **inflated** price or salary is higher than is considered reasonable. *...food and clothing which had to be bought at inflated prices. ...plans to bring artificially inflated prices closer to world market levels.*

inflation /ɪnfleɪʃn/
NU **Inflation** is a general increase in the prices of goods and services in a country. *Chile has reduced its inflation in the past year from a hundred per cent to fifty.*

inflationary /ɪnfleɪʃənəʳri/
ADJ An **inflationary** action or event causes inflation; a formal word. *...inflationary wage demands.*

inflect /ɪnflekt/ **inflects, inflecting, inflected**
V If a word **inflects**, its ending or form changes in order to show its grammatical function or number. For example, 'makes', 'making', and 'made' are inflected forms of 'make'. ◆ **inflected** ADJ *German is an inflected language.*

inflection /ɪnflekʃn/ **inflections**; also spelt **inflexion**.
1 NCorNU An **inflection** is a change in the sound of your voice when you speak. *This enables you to listen to the fine inflections in someone's voice. She spoke in*

a low voice, always without inflection.
2 NCorNU An **inflection** is also a change in the form of a word that shows its grammatical function or number. *...French and Spanish names with inflections.*

inflexible /ɪnflˈɛksəbl/
ADJ Someone or something that is **inflexible** cannot be altered. *Neither Mr Hurd nor Mr Major are expected to be as inflexible in their positions as Mrs Thatcher... Nursery schools have inflexible hours.* ◆ **inflexibility** NU *...dogmatic inflexibility in the face of change.*

inflexion /ɪnflˈɛkʃn/. See **inflection.**

inflict /ɪnflˈɪkt/ **inflicts, inflicting, inflicted**
VO If you **inflict** something unpleasant on someone, you make them suffer it. *...the dreadful way she had inflicted her problems on him.*

in-flight
ADJ ATTRIB You use **in-flight** to describe things that are used or take place on board an aeroplane. *Many people would fly more frequently if in-flight smoking was stopped... Libya has developed an in-flight refuelling system.*

influence /ˈɪnfluəns/ **influences, influencing, influenced**
1 NUorNC **Influence** is power to affect people's actions. *Moscow retains some influence over their affairs... His teachings still exert a strong influence... Economic changes were having a very positive influence on relations between London and Moscow.*
● If you are **under the influence** of someone or something, you are being affected or controlled by them. *He was under the influence of friends who were highly conservative.*
2 NC+SUPP If you are an **influence** on people or things, you have an effect on them. *He was a bad influence on the children.*
3 VO To **influence** a person, thing, or situation means to have an effect on the way that person acts or on what happens. *I didn't want him to influence me in my choice.*

influential /ˌɪnfluˈɛnʃl/
ADJ Someone who is **influential** has a lot of influence over people. *...a powerful and influential politician.*

influenza /ˌɪnfluˈɛnzə/
NU **Influenza** is flu; a formal word. *...an epidemic of influenza.*

influx /ˈɪnflʌks/ **influxes**
NC+SUPP An **influx** of people or things into a place is their arrival there in large numbers. *...a massive influx of refugees... Customs officers fear an influx of cheap Soviet vodka... The Sudan cannot handle new influxes of destitute and hungry people.*

info /ˈɪnfəʊ/
NU **Info** is the same as **information**; an informal word. *...the info on where the meeting was.*

inform /ɪnfˈɔːm/ **informs, informing, informed**
1 VO+of, V-REPORT, or V-QUOTE If you **inform** someone of something, you tell them about it. *He intended to see Barbara to inform her of his objections... I informed her that I was unwell... 'They are late,' he informed her.* ● See also **informed.**
2 V+onoragainst If someone **informs** on or against a person, they give information about that person, for example to the police, with the result that he or she is accused of committing a crime or is shown to be guilty of something. *It can be difficult for a child to inform on someone he knows.*

informal /ɪnfˈɔːml/
1 ADJ You use **informal** to describe behaviour and speech that is relaxed or casual rather than correct, official or serious. *...a relaxed and quite informal discussion.* ◆ **informally** ADV *...people talking informally together.* ◆ **informality** /ɪnfɔːmˈælɪti/ NU *...an atmosphere of informality.*
2 ADJ You can also use **informal** to describe something that is done officially. *We have informal contacts with over 500 firms.*

informant /ɪnfˈɔːmənt/ **informants**
1 NC An **informant** is someone who gives another person a piece of information. *They were finally tipped off about the location by a civilian informant.*
2 NC An **informant** is also the same as an **informer.** *They are charged with the murder of 40 people suspected of being government informants.*

information /ˌɪnfəmˈeɪʃn/
NU If you have **information** about a particular thing, you know something about it. *I'm afraid I have no information on that... She provided me with a very interesting piece of information about his past.*

information technology
NU **Information technology** is the theory and practice of using computers to store and analyze information. *In the West, the technological revolution, particularly in the area of information technology, is proceeding apace.*

informative /ɪnfˈɔːmətɪv/
ADJ Something that is **informative** gives you useful information. *...an informative guidebook.*

informed /ɪnfˈɔːmd/
1 ADJ Someone who is well **informed**, or badly **informed**, knows a lot about, or not much about, what is happening in the world. *She's an extremely well informed woman... Television has made people better informed.*
2 ADJ ATTRIB An **informed** guess or source is likely to be quite accurate because it is based on some knowledge. *Hence the director's informed guess of 600,000 cases around the world... Informed sources say the coup leader is still in Pakistan.*

informer /ɪnfˈɔːmə/ **informers**
NC An **informer** is someone who tells the police that another person has done something wrong. *...trials based on the evidence of informers.*

infra dig /ˌɪnfrə dˈɪg/
ADJ PRED If you feel that it is **infra dig** to do something, you feel that you are too good or too important to do it; an old-fashioned word. *There's an idea today that going out and reporting is infra dig, you know, it's what journalists do.*

infra-red /ˌɪnfrəˈrɛd/
ADJ **Infra-red** light is below the colour red in the spectrum and cannot be seen. *All fibre optic transmissions use infra-red light. ...infra-red cameras.*

infrastructure /ˈɪnfrəstrʌktʃə/ **infrastructures**
NC The **infrastructure** of a country, society, or organization is the structure which helps it to function effectively, such as the facilities, services and equipment that are provided. *Western technology needs a reliable infrastructure which is sometimes lacking in developing countries.*

infrequent /ɪnfrˈiːkwənt/
ADJ If something is **infrequent**, it does not happen often. *...her sister's infrequent letters.* ◆ **infrequently** ADV *My parents were only able to visit us infrequently.*

infringe /ɪnfrˈɪndʒ/ **infringes, infringing, infringed**
1 VO If you **infringe** a law or an agreement, you break it; a formal use. *They occasionally infringe the law by parking near a junction.*
2 VOorV+on If you **infringe** people's rights, you do not allow people the rights or freedom that they are entitled to. *They were citizens with legal rights, which were being infringed... We must fight them when they infringe on our children's right to freedom.*

infringement /ɪnfrˈɪndʒmənt/ **infringements**
1 NCorNU An **infringement** of a law, rule, or agreement is the breaking of it. *...small infringements of prison discipline... Infringement of the rules on foam furniture fillings should carry stiffer penalties.*
2 NC+oforon If an action is an **infringement** on your rights, it restricts you unfairly. *His arrest and detention was an infringement of his civil liberties... The new law is inflexible, an infringement on free speech.*

infuriate /ɪnfjˈʊərieɪt/ **infuriates, infuriating, infuriated**
VO If something or someone **infuriates** you, they make you extremely angry. *Old jeans and T-shirts infuriated him.* ◆ **infuriating** ADJ *...her infuriating habit of criticizing people all the time.* ◆ **infuriated** ADJ *...a group of infuriated little boys.*

infuse /ɪnfjˈuːz/ **infuses, infusing, infused**
1 VO+intoorVO+with If you **infuse** a certain quality into someone or you **infuse** them with it, you fill them with it; a formal use. *The appearance of young soldiers infused new hope and morale into the army. ...ways of*

*infusing academic research with youthful talent...
Japan's political scene has become infused with a new
sense of ethics and equity.*
2 V-ERG If you **infuse** a drink or medicine, you pour
hot water onto herbs or leaves and leave it for the
liquid to absorb the flavour. *Add the tea leaves and
leave to infuse for five minutes.*

infusion /ɪnfjuːʒn/ **infusions**
1 NC+*of*orNU+*of* An **infusion** of one thing into another is
a case in which the first thing is added to the second
and so gives it new life and vigour; a formal use.
*...an infusion of new capital of £2 billion... He said
yesterday that his country will need a massive
infusion of Western aid... I was writing a story on how
the large infusion of troops has affected the local
economy.*
2 NUorNC If a patient is given an **infusion** of blood or
a drug, it is given to them very slowly by injection.
*Continuous infusion of the drug apomorphine is helping
one group of sufferers. ...equipment for giving
infusions.*
3 NCorNU An **infusion** is also a liquid made by leaving
herbs in hot water until the flavour is strong.
*...infusions of camomile tea... The syrup contained an
infusion of cocaine.*

-ing /-ɪŋ/
SUFFIX **-ing** is added to verbs to form present
participles or uncount nouns referring to activities.
Present participles are often used as adjectives that
describe a person or thing as doing something. Nouns
and adjectives of this kind are often not defined but
are treated with the related verbs. *I was walking
along the road... Farming was something I really
enjoyed. ...the dazzling sun.*

ingenious /ɪndʒiːnɪəs/
ADJ An **ingenious** idea, plan, or device is very clever.
...an ingenious method of forecasting economic trends.
♦ **ingeniously** ADV *The hangers were ingeniously fixed
to the wardrobe by pieces of wire.*

ingénue /ˈænˈʒeɪnjuː/ **ingénues**
NC You use **ingénue** to describe a young, innocent
woman, especially when this is actually a role being
played by an actress; a formal word. *I played the
poor, innocent little ingénue. ...ingénue roles.*

ingenuity /ɪndʒənjuːəti/
NU **Ingenuity** is skill at inventing things or at working
out plans. *With a bit of ingenuity you can do almost
anything.*

ingenuous /ɪndʒenjuəs/
ADJ Someone who is **ingenuous** is innocent, trusting,
and honest. *Aristotle and Pythagoras, all those years
ago, were just as ingenuous as you or I... He concludes
that his suggestion is either ingenuous beyond belief,
or a frivolous piece of mischief making.*

inglorious /ɪnglɔːrɪəs/
ADJ Something that is **inglorious** is shameful and
brings dishonour to the person involved. *Rudolph's
choice was inglorious.* ♦ **ingloriously** ADV *In the
nineteen fifties he had briefly and ingloriously been
Prime Minister.*

ingot /ɪŋgət/ **ingots**
NC An **ingot** is a lump of metal, usually shaped like a
brick. *...an ingot of genuine gold. ...cast iron ingots.*

ingrained /ɪŋgreɪnd/
ADJ **Ingrained** habits and beliefs are difficult to
change. *The belief that one should work hard is
ingrained in our culture.*

ingratiate /ɪŋgreɪʃɪeɪt/ **ingratiates, ingratiating,
ingratiated**
V-REFL+*with* If you try to **ingratiate** yourself with other
people, you try to make them like you; used showing
disapproval. *They resented his knack for ingratiating
himself with officers.* ♦ **ingratiating** ADJ *...an
ingratiating smile.*

ingratitude /ɪŋgrætɪtjuːd/
NU **Ingratitude** is lack of gratitude for something that
has been done for you. *I was shocked and enraged at
such ingratitude.*

ingredient /ɪŋgriːdɪənt/ **ingredients**
1 NC The **ingredients** of something that you cook or
prepare are the different foods that you use. *Mix the
ingredients to a soft dough.*

2 NC+SUPP An **ingredient** of a situation is one of the
essential parts of it. *The most essential ingredient in
economic progress is investment.*

ingrowing /ɪŋgrəʊɪŋ/
ADJ An **ingrowing** toenail is one which is growing into
your toe, often causing pain.

inhabit /ɪnhæbɪt/ **inhabits, inhabiting, inhabited**
VO If a place or region is **inhabited**, people live there.
*The town was a seaside resort, inhabited by fishermen
and hoteliers.*

inhabitant /ɪnhæbɪtənt/ **inhabitants**
NC The **inhabitants** of a place are the people who live
there. *Many Yugoslavian inhabitants are dissatisfied
with the system... The company outraged Free
Presbyterian inhabitants of the Outer Hebrides by
starting a ferry service on Sunday.*

inhale /ɪnheɪl/ **inhales, inhaling, inhaled**
VorVO When you **inhale**, you breathe in. *She put the
cigarette between her lips and inhaled deeply.
...inhaling the scent of haymaking.*

inherent /ɪnherənt, ɪnhɪərənt/
ADJ Characteristics that are **inherent** in someone or
something are a natural part of them. *...my inherent
laziness. ...the dangers inherent in this kind of political
system.* ♦ **inherently** ADV *Power stations are
inherently inefficient.*

inherit /ɪnherɪt/ **inherits, inheriting, inherited**
1 VO If you **inherit** something such as a situation or
attitude, you take it over from people who came
before you. *They inherited a weak economy... He had
doubts about Communism, inherited from his mother
whose family was a victim of the purges.*
2 VO If you **inherit** money or property, you receive it
from someone who has died. *His fortune was
estimated at one billion dollars, and Christina
inherited nearly half of it.*
3 VO If you **inherit** a characteristic, you are born with
it, because your parents or ancestors had it. *This kind
of brain damage may be inherited... One person in 4
inherits a tendency to diabetes.*

inheritance /ɪnherɪtəns/ **inheritances**
1 NCorNU An **inheritance** is money or property which
you receive from someone who is dead. *He had no
motive for depriving his son of the inheritance. ...the
customs of inheritance in Asia.*
2 NC+SUPP An **inheritance** is also a situation or thing
which you have taken over from people who came
before you. *...our alphabet, an inheritance from the
Greeks.*
3 NU **Inheritance** is the fact of being born with
characteristics which your parents or ancestors had.
*To what extent does human nature depend on genetic
inheritance?*

inheritor /ɪnherɪtə/ **inheritors**
NC+SUPP People who are the **inheritors** of something
inherited it from people who came before them. *...the
inheritors of a literary tradition.*

inhibit /ɪnhɪbɪt/ **inhibits, inhibiting, inhibited**
VO If something **inhibits** growth or development, it
prevents it or slows it down. *The drugs with which the
animals are fed inhibit their development.*

inhibited /ɪnhɪbɪtɪd/
ADJ If you are **inhibited**, you find it difficult to behave
naturally and show your feelings. *Her severe
upbringing had left her inhibited.*

inhibition /ɪnɪbɪʃn/ **inhibitions**
NCorNU **Inhibitions** are feelings of fear or
embarrassment that make it difficult for you to behave
naturally. *...a child who is free from inhibitions...
She's prepared to argue without inhibition.*

inhospitable /ɪnhɒspɪtəbl/
1 ADJ An **inhospitable** place is unpleasant to live in.
*...inhospitable deserts... Venus is known to be
profoundly inhospitable, with clouds of sulphuric acid
covering the surface.*
2 ADJ If you are **inhospitable**, you do not make people
feel welcome when they visit you. *I don't like to be
inhospitable, but you can see I've got an awful lot here
that needs doing.*

in-house
ADJ ATTRIBorADV **In-house** work or equipment is done
or used within a company or an organisation, rather

than being subcontracted to other companies or organisations. ...*corporations with large in-house systems and multiple lines... They've had a lot of in-house training... We do it all in-house.*

inhuman /ɪnˈhjuːmən/
1 ADJ Behaviour that is **inhuman** is extremely cruel. ...*barbarous and inhuman atrocities.*
2 ADJ Something that is **inhuman** is not human or does not seem human, and is strange or frightening. *Their faces looked inhuman, covered with scarlet and black paint.*

inhumane /ɪnhjuːˈmeɪn/
ADJ **Inhumane** treatment is extremely cruel. *The police had acted in an inhumane way and overstepped the limits of a democratic state... He condemned the use of these terrible and inhumane weapons.*

inhumanity /ɪnhjuːˈmænəti/
NU **Inhumanity** is cruelty or lack of feeling. ...*man's inhumanity to man.*

inimical /ɪˈnɪmɪkl/
ADJ PRED+*to* Conditions that are **inimical** to something make it hard for it to develop or survive; a formal word. *Her dislike of state intervention was seen by environmentalists as inimical to proper control on pollution... The very nature of society is inimical to freedom.*

inimitable /ɪˈnɪmɪtəbl/
ADJ **Inimitable** is used to praise a special person or a special quality that someone has; a formal word. *The Welsh rugby team have their own inimitable style.*

iniquitous /ɪˈnɪkwɪtəs/
ADJ **Iniquitous** means very bad and unfair; a formal word. ...*this iniquitous policy.*

iniquity /ɪˈnɪkwəti/ **iniquities**
NCorNU An **iniquity** is something that is wicked or unjust; a formal word. *We fought a revolution to put an end to such iniquities. ...Rose's iniquity and selfishness.*

initial /ɪˈnɪʃl/ **initials, initialling, initialled**; spelt **initialed, initialing** in American English.
1 ADJ ATTRIB You use **initial** to describe something that happens at the beginning of a process. ...*the initial stages of learning English... My initial reaction was one of great relief.*
2 N PL **Initials** are the capital letters which begin each word of a name. ...*a flag bearing the initials of the National Liberation Front... You can engrave your initials on it or incorporate the logo of your company.*
3 VO When someone **initials** a written agreement or treaty, they put their initials on it to show that they approve of it before agreeing to sign it formally and make it binding. *After the agreement was initialled in June, the Community made it clear it was not ready to fix a date for its signature... He and the Soviet Foreign Minister initialled a bilateral treaty of close cooperation.*

initially /ɪˈnɪʃəli/
ADV **Initially** means in the early stages of a process. *I don't remember who initially conceived the idea.*

initiate /ɪˈnɪʃieɪt/ **initiates, initiating, initiated**; pronounced /ɪˈnɪʃieɪt/ when it is a verb and /ɪˈnɪʃiət/ when it is a noun.
1 VO If you **initiate** something, you cause it to start. *Congress immediately initiated hearings to investigate what had happened... We should initiate direct talks with the trades unions.* ◆ **initiation** /ɪnɪʃiˈeɪʃn/ NU ...*the initiation of a new revolutionary practice.*
2 VO+*into* If you **initiate** someone into a group, you conduct a ceremony or teach them special things so that they become a member. *He initiated people into groups under high priestesses... To understand, one must be initiated into great mysteries.* ◆ **initiation** NU *They investigated over a hundred complaints of bullying, violence and degrading initiation. ...an initiation ceremony.*
3 NC An **initiate** is a person who has recently been allowed to join a particular group and who has been taught special things. ...*an initiate into the world of politics.*

initiative /ɪˈnɪʃətɪv/ **initiatives**
1 NC An **initiative** is an important act that is intended to solve a problem. ...*launching various initiatives to*

tackle real or imagined problems... He has not revealed the details of his new peace initiative. ...foreign policy initiatives.*
2 N SING If you have the **initiative**, you are in a stronger position than your opponents. *They had lost the initiative. ...the efforts of the Hungarian government to recapture the initiative.*
3 NU If you have **initiative**, you are able to take action without needing other people to tell you what to do. *In special circumstances we have to use our initiative.*
● **Initiative** is used in these phrases. ● If you do something **on** your **own initiative**, you do it without being told to do it by someone else. *On their own initiative they have started a local campaign against the use of tobacco.* ● If you **take the initiative**, you are the first person to do something. *In Sweden, employers have taken the initiative in promoting health insurance schemes.*

inject /ɪnˈdʒekt/ **injects, injecting, injected**
1 VOA If you **inject** someone with a liquid, or **inject** a liquid into them, you use a syringe to get it into their body. *An increasing number of young people have started injecting themselves with alcohol... The research team injected glucose into the bloodstream of the volunteers.* ◆ **injection** /ɪnˈdʒekʃn/ **injections** NC *You had a smallpox injection when you were five.*
2 VO+*into* If you **inject** a quality such as excitement or interest into a situation, you do something that adds this quality to the situation. *She was trying to inject some fun into the grim proceedings... The Committee debated bills on scrapping central planning and injecting competition into the banking system.*
3 VO+*into* If you **inject** money into a business or organization, you provide it with more money. *Enormous sums of money are injected each year into teaching... The year after the riot, the Government injected around £1 million into the area.* ◆ **injection** NC+*of* ...*massive injections of commercial funds.*

injudicious /ɪndʒuːˈdɪʃəs/
ADJ Something or someone that is **injudicious** shows poor judgement; a formal word. *He thought it would be injudicious to question her.*

injunction /ɪnˈdʒʌŋkʃn/ **injunctions**
NC An **injunction** is a court order which is issued to stop someone from doing something. *We will apply to the courts for an injunction against the march.*

injure /ˈɪndʒə/ **injures, injuring, injured**
VOorV-REFL If you **injure** someone, you damage a part of their body. *No-one was injured in the fire... Peter injured his right hand in an accident... I feared they might injure themselves.*

injured /ˈɪndʒəd/
1 ADJ An **injured** person or animal is damaged in some part of the body, usually as a result of an accident or fighting. *She was not badly injured but she couldn't speak... The soldiers were dragging their injured comrades with them.*
2 N PL A group of injured people can be referred to as the **injured**. *We must provide medical attention to the injured.*
3 ADJ If you feel **injured**, you feel upset because something unjust or unfair has happened to you. *One feels faintly injured if the buses don't come on time... Haggerty's injured professional pride quite overcame any desire for reconciliation.*

injured party, injured parties
NC If you describe someone as the **injured party**, you mean that they have been treated unfairly, especially when they are involved in a court case to try and get justice; a legal expression.

injurious /ɪnˈdʒʊəriəs/
ADJ **Injurious** means harmful or damaging; a formal word. *A strike could be gravely injurious to the national economy. ...an injurious effect.*

injury /ˈɪndʒəri/ **injuries**
NCorNU An **injury** is damage done to a person's body. *The earthquake caused many deaths and severe injuries... Louis received an injury to his head... He was weakened by illness and injury... They have withdrawn from the tournament because of injury.*
● If you say that a person is going to **do** someone **an injury**, you mean that he or she is going to damage a

part of their body in some way; often used humorously. *He's going to do someone an injury and I'm not going to be around... He would do himself an injury doing that one day.*

injury time

NU **Injury time** is the period of time added to the end of a football match because play was interrupted during the match when players were injured. *It was only during injury time in last night's match that the title was decided.*

injustice /ɪndʒʌstɪs/ **injustices**

1 NUorNC **Injustice** is a lack of fairness in a situation. *There's social injustice everywhere... He contemplated the injustices of life.*

2 If you have **done** someone **an injustice**, you have judged them too harshly or unfairly. *...a grievous injustice had been done to the immigrant workers by not recognising their skills.*

ink /ɪŋk/ **inks**

N MASS **Ink** is the coloured liquid used for writing or printing. *Please write in ink. ...acrylic-based inks.*

inkling /ɪŋklɪŋ/

If you **have an inkling** of something, you suspect what it is or suspect that it is the case. *He had an inkling of what was going on... I had no inkling that she was interested in me.*

inkstand /ɪŋkstænd/ **inkstands**

NC An **inkstand** is a container for ink bottles and pens.

inkwell /ɪŋkwel/ **inkwells**

NC An **inkwell** is a container for ink in a desk.

inky /ɪŋki/

1 ADJ **Inky** means very black or dark; a literary use. *...an inky sky.*

2 ADJ **Inky** also means covered in ink. *...an inky handkerchief.*

inland; pronounced /ɪnlənd/ when it is an adjective and /ɪnlænd/ when it is an adverb.

ADJorADV **Inland** means away from the coast of a country. *The Sahara was once an inland sea... Donkeys bear goods inland to the towns and villages.*

Inland Revenue

N PROP In Britain, the **Inland Revenue** is the government authority which collects income tax and some other taxes. *...an alleged conspiracy to defraud the Inland Revenue.*

in-laws /ɪnlɔːz/

N PL Your **in-laws** are the parents and close relatives of your husband or wife. *...once married she follows her husband back to her in-laws.*

inlay, **inlays**, **inlaying**, **inlaid**; pronounced /ɪnleɪ/ when it is a noun and /ɪnleɪ/ when it is a verb.

1 NCorNU An **inlay** is a design or pattern on an object which is made by putting materials such as wood, gold, or silver into the surface of the object. *...a writing desk of rosewood with ebony inlay.*

2 NCorNU An **inlay** is also a substance such as gold or porcelain which is used by dentists to fill a damaged tooth. *Biting on an apple, I pulled an inlay out of my tooth.*

3 VO+*with* To **inlay** an object with a substance means to put a design or pattern made from that substance into its surface. *The box must have been inlaid with lead.* ◆ **inlaid** ADJ *...a lavishly inlaid table.*

inlet /ɪnlət/ **inlets**

1 NC An **inlet** is a narrow strip of water which goes from a sea or lake into the land. *...the Golden Horn, an inlet from the Bosphorus Sea.*

2 NC An **inlet** is also a part on a machine through which a flow of liquid or gas enters. *The device draws air through an inlet tube into a chemical solution.*

in loco parentis /ɪn ləʊkəʊ pərentɪs/

If you are **in loco parentis**, you are, for a short time, in the position of a parent towards someone else's children. Teachers are often regarded as being in loco parentis; a legal expression.

inmate /ɪnmeɪt/ **inmates**

NC The **inmates** of a prison or a psychiatric hospital are the prisoners or patients who are living there. *Senior staff from other prisons have been brought in to look after the inmates.*

inmost /ɪnməʊst/

ADJ ATTRIB **Inmost** means the same as **innermost**. *You*

read my inmost thoughts.

inn /ɪn/ **inns**

NC An **inn** is a small hotel or a pub; an old-fashioned word. *...the Pilgrim's Inn.*

innards /ɪnədz/

1 N PL The **innards** of a person or animal are the organs inside the body.

2 N PL A machine's **innards** are the parts inside it. *...a wooden tiger with complicated mechanical innards.*

innate /ɪneɪt/

ADJ An **innate** quality or ability is one which a person is born with. *They believed intelligence was innate, and unlikely to change. ...an innate talent for music.* ◆ **innately** ADV *I don't think that anybody is innately good.*

inner /ɪnə/

1 ADJ ATTRIB You use **inner** to describe something which is contained or enclosed inside something else. *There were several flats overlooking the inner courtyard... The structures the scientists have been studying are the tiny hairs in the inner ear.*

2 ADJ ATTRIB **Inner** feelings are feelings which you do not show to other people. *...his inner feelings of failure. ...inner doubts.*

inner city, inner cities

NC The **inner city** is the area around the centre of a city, where people live. *This is one of the most serious problems in the inner cities. ...inner-city children.*

innermost /ɪnəməʊst/

ADJ ATTRIB Your **innermost** thoughts and feelings are your most personal and secret ones. *...her innermost wishes.*

inner tube, inner tubes

NC An **inner tube** is a rubber tube inside a car tyre or bicycle tyre, containing air.

innings /ɪnɪŋz/. **Innings** is both the singular and the plural form.

NC An **innings** is a period in a game of cricket during which a particular player or team is batting. *Australia are at 101 for no wickets in their second innings... Graeme Hick scored a record-breaking innings of 405 runs.*

innkeeper /ɪnkiːpə/ **innkeepers**

NC An **innkeeper** is someone who looks after an inn; an old-fashioned word. *...a guide for coachmen and innkeepers.*

innocence /ɪnəsəns/

1 NU **Innocence** is the quality of having no experience of the more complex or unpleasant aspects of life. *He had a peculiar air of childlike innocence.*

2 NU **Innocence** is also the quality of not being guilty of a crime. *He desperately protested his innocence.*

innocent /ɪnəsənt/

1 ADJ If someone is **innocent**, they are not guilty of a crime. *He was accused of a crime of violence of which he was innocent. ...the suffering that would be inflicted upon innocent people.*

2 ADJ If you are **innocent**, you have no experience of the more complex or unpleasant aspects of life. *I was very young, and very innocent.*

3 ADJ An **innocent** remark or action is not meant to offend people, even if it does so. *It was an innocent question.* ◆ **innocently** ADV *'What did I do wrong?' asked Howard, innocently.*

innocuous /ɪnɒkjuəs/

ADJ **Innocuous** means not at all harmful; a formal word. *Most of these substances are relatively innocuous... Even seemingly innocuous words, in certain contexts, are taken to be offensive.*

innovate /ɪnəveɪt/ **innovates**, **innovating**, **innovated**

V To **innovate** means to introduce changes and new ideas. *...the industry's capacity to respond swiftly to market changes and to innovate.*

innovation /ɪnəveɪʃn/ **innovations**

1 NC An **innovation** is a new thing or new method of doing something. *...major innovations such as antibiotics. ...a series of remarkable innovations in textile manufacturing.*

2 NU **Innovation** is the introduction of new things or new methods. *...a period of technological innovation.*

innovative /ɪnəveɪtɪv/
1 ADJ Something that is **innovative** is new and original. *...their innovative campaign style.* *...innovative ideas.*
2 ADJ An **innovative** person introduces changes and new ideas. *...a pioneering and innovative banker.*
innovator /ɪnəveɪtə/ **innovators**
NC An **innovator** is someone who introduces changes and new ideas. *The Pope thought of himself as an innovator.*
innovatory /ɪnəveɪtəri/
ADJ Something that is **innovatory** is new and original. *His music was innovatory in its time.*
innuendo /ɪnjuˈendəʊ/ **innuendoes** or **innuendos**
NU or NC **Innuendo** is indirect reference to something rude or unpleasant. *...a campaign of innuendo and gossip. ...sexual innuendoes.*
innumerable /ɪnjuːmərəbl/
ADJ **Innumerable** means too many to be counted. *The industrial age has brought innumerable benefits.*
inoculate /ɪnɒkjʊleɪt/ **inoculates, inoculating, inoculated**
VO If you **are inoculated** against a disease, you are injected with a weak form of the disease as a way of being protected against it. *A pedigree pup should have been inoculated against serious diseases.*
inoculation /ɪnɒkjʊleɪʃn/ **inoculations**
NC or NU If you are given an **inoculation**, you are injected with a weak form of a disease as a way of being protected against it. *It's a good idea to keep a record of all your children's inoculations. ...prevention of disease by inoculation.*
inoffensive /ɪnəfensɪv/
ADJ **Inoffensive** means harmless or not unpleasant. *...a nice, quiet, inoffensive little fellow.*
inoperable /ɪnɒpərəbl/
ADJ An **inoperable** medical condition such as a tumour or cancer is one that cannot be removed or cured by a surgical operation.
inoperative /ɪnɒpərətɪv/
ADJ An **inoperative** rule, principle, or tax is one that does not work any more or that cannot be made to work. *All inmates convicted under the now inoperative Article 70 of the Criminal Code have been released.*
inopportune /ɪnɒpətjuːn/
1 ADJ Something that is **inopportune** is done or happens at an unsuitable time, and causes trouble or embarrassment because of this. *...an inopportune remark.*
2 ADJ An **inopportune** moment or time is one that is unsuitable for a particular thing to happen. *You've called at a rather inopportune moment.*
inordinate /ɪnɔːdɪnət/
ADJ **Inordinate** means much greater than you would expect or than is necessary; a formal word. *Alan always spent an inordinate length of time in the bathroom.* ◆ **inordinately** SUBMOD *...an achievement of which I was inordinately proud.*
inorganic /ɪnɔːgænɪk/
ADJ **Inorganic** substances are substances such as stone and metal that do not come from living things. *...inorganic fertilizers.*
in-patient, in-patients
NC An **in-patient** is someone who stays in hospital while they receive treatment. *...psychiatric in-patients. ...Czechoslovakia's first in-patient treatment centre for drug addiction.*
input /ɪnpʊt/ **inputs, inputting, inputted**
1 NU or NC **Input** consists of resources such as money, power, or workers that are given to something such as a machine or a project to make it work. *Incineration requires a large energy input... The project requires the input of more labour.*
2 NU or NC Your **input** into a discussion or activity is your contribution to it. *We've had input from everybody who can read and write... Our input to the general conversation might be just an odd sentence here and there.*
3 NU **Input** is also information that is put into a computer. *The computer can tell the position of an object from the input data.*

4 VO If you **input** information into a computer, you feed it in, for example by typing it on a keyboard. *The text of a speech can be inputted and updated at any time.*
inquest /ɪnkwest/ **inquests**
NC An **inquest** is an official inquiry into the cause of someone's death. *There have been demands from his family for an inquest.*
inquire /ɪnkwaɪə/ **inquires, inquiring, inquired**; also spelt **enquire**.
VA, V-REPORT, V-QUOTE, or V If you **inquire** about something, you ask for information about it; a formal word. *He went to enquire about the times of trains to Edinburgh... He inquired whether it was possible to leave his case at the station... 'What will it cost?' inquired Miss Musson... Vernon could have found that out, too—if he had taken the trouble to inquire.*
inquire after PHRASAL VERB If you **inquire after** someone, you ask how they are. *She enquired after Mrs Carstair's daughter, who had just had a baby.*
inquire into PHRASAL VERB If you **inquire into** something, you investigate it. *The police inquired into the deaths of two young girls.*
inquirer /ɪnkwaɪərə/ **inquirers**
NC An **inquirer** is a person who asks for information about something or someone; a formal word. *We told all inquirers to phone again later.*
inquiring /ɪnkwaɪərɪŋ/; also spelt **enquiring**.
1 ADJ ATTRIB If you have an **inquiring** mind, you have a great interest in learning new things. *...the inquiring mind that produces a technical breakthrough.*
2 ADJ If you have an **inquiring** expression on your face, you show that you want to know something. *...the people's inquiring faces.* ◆ **inquiringly** ADV *I looked at her inquiringly.*
inquiry /ɪnkwaɪəri/ **inquiries**; also spelt **enquiry**, especially for the meaning in paragraph 1.
1 NC An **inquiry** is a question which you ask in order to get information. *I shall make some enquiries.*
2 NC An **inquiry** is also an official investigation. *Opposition MPs have called for a public inquiry.*
3 NU **Inquiry** is the process of asking about something to get information. *On further enquiry, I discovered that there had been nobody at home.*
inquisition /ɪnkwɪzɪʃn/ **inquisitions**
NC An **inquisition** is an official investigation, especially one which is very thorough and uses harsh methods of questioning. *Galileo was put on trial by the Holy Inquisition and forced to retract his theories that the sun, not the earth, is the centre of the Universe... In his letter of resignation, Mr Shevardnadze described the investigation into his activities as an inquisition.*
inquisitive /ɪnkwɪzətɪv/
ADJ An **inquisitive** person likes finding out about things, especially secret things. *He tried not to sound inquisitive.* ◆ **inquisitively** ADV *I glanced inquisitively through the open doorway.*
inquisitor /ɪnkwɪzɪtə/ **inquisitors**
NC An **inquisitor** is someone who asks questions in an inquisition. *The old man glared at him like an inquisitor.*
inquisitorial /ɪnkwɪzətɔːriəl/
ADJ Someone or something that is **inquisitorial** asks questions in a very thorough and harsh way, as if in an inquisition. *...an inquisitorial voice.*
inroads /ɪnrəʊdz/
N PL If one thing makes **inroads** into another, it starts affecting it or destroying it. *The Liberal Democrats made deep inroads into traditional Conservative strongholds in southern England... They are highly sensitive to any inroads upon their independence.*
insalubrious /ɪnsəluːbriəs/
ADJ A place or climate that is **insalubrious** is likely to make you unhealthy; a formal word. *The site was surrounded by insalubrious swamps.*
ins and outs
N PL The **ins and outs** of a situation are all the detailed points and facts about it. *We had to discuss all the ins and outs of the proposal. ...a man who knows the ins and outs of America's political capital like the back of his hand.*

insane /ɪnseɪn/
1 ADJ Someone who is **insane** is mad. *She went insane and died after giving birth to a still-born child. ...special hospitals for the criminally insane.* ♦ **insanity** /ɪnsænəti/ NU *He saw the beginnings of insanity in her.*
2 ADJ You can also describe someone as **insane** when they behave very foolishly. *You'd be insane to do that.* ♦ **insanely** SUBMOD *I must admit that I was insanely jealous.* ♦ **insanity** NU *I laughed at the insanity of it all.*

insanitary /ɪnsænɪtəⁿri/
ADJ Something that is **insanitary** is so dirty that it is likely to have a bad effect on people's health; a formal word. *They are living in insanitary conditions.*

insatiable /ɪnseɪʃəbl/
ADJ An **insatiable** desire or greed is very great. *...an insatiable curiosity. ...criminals whose sole motivation is an insatiable thirst for power.* ♦ **insatiably** ADV *She was insatiably curious.*

inscribe /ɪnskraɪb/ inscribes, inscribing, inscribed
VOA If words **are inscribed** on an object or if an object **is inscribed** with them, the words are written or carved on the object; a formal word. *The names of the dead were inscribed on the wall... Each stamp is inscribed with the date and place where a sea battle or event takes place in the history of the Armada. ...a ring inscribed 'To My Darling'.*

inscription /ɪnskrɪpʃn/ inscriptions
NC An **inscription** is words that are written or carved on something. *The inscription above the door was in English.*

inscrutable /ɪnskruːtəbl/
ADJ Someone who is **inscrutable** does not show what they are really thinking. *The candidates are pretty inscrutable.*

insect /ɪnsekt/ insects
NC An **insect** is a small creature with six legs and usually wings. Ants, flies, and butterflies are all insects. *...the war against crop-destroying insects. ...insect-borne diseases.*

insecticide /ɪnsektɪsaɪd/ insecticides
N MASS **Insecticide** is a chemical used to kill insects. *...mosquito nets that have been soaked in insecticide... Farmers have come to rely on chemical insecticides.*

insecure /ɪnsɪkjʊəⁿ/
1 ADJ If you feel **insecure**, you feel that you are not good enough or are not loved. *What had I done to make you so insecure and frightened?* ♦ **insecurity** /ɪnsɪkjʊərəti/ NU *...feelings of insecurity.*
2 ADJ Something that is **insecure** is not safe or protected. *The evidence is clear that he was responsible for the insecure site and the escape of the chemicals... It's a very insecure job these days... Their place in society is insecure.* ♦ **insecurity** NU *...financial insecurity.*

inseminate /ɪnsemɪneɪt/ inseminates, inseminating, inseminated
VO To **inseminate** a female animal means to put a male's sperm into her in order to make her pregnant. *He intends to inseminate cows with sperm from some of the world's top breeds of bulls.* ♦ **insemination** /ɪnsemɪneɪʃn/ NU *...the artificial insemination of cows and sheep.*

insensible /ɪnsensəbl/; a formal word.
1 ADJ PRED A person or animal that is **insensible** to a physical sensation is unable to feel it. *We believe that all animals should be rendered insensible to pain before slaughter.*
2 ADJ PRED Someone who is **insensible** of something that has happened is unaware of it. *She seemed wholly insensible of the honour done to her. ...children that lived and died insensible of their misery.*

insensitive /ɪnsensətɪv/
ADJ Someone who is **insensitive** is not aware of or sympathetic to other people's feelings. *...bad-mannered, loud, insensitive oafs. ...the insensitive attitude of the government.* ♦ **insensitivity** /ɪnsensətɪvəti/ NU *There were times when he showed a curious insensitivity.*

inseparable /ɪnsepəⁿrəbl/
1 ADJ If two things are **inseparable**, they cannot be

considered separately; a formal use. *Culture is inseparable from class... The social and ecological costs are inseparable.*
2 ADJ Friends who are **inseparable** are always together. *Soon they were inseparable.*

insert, inserts, inserting, inserted; pronounced /ɪnsɜːt/ when it is a verb and /ɪnsɜːt/ when it is a noun.
1 VO If you **insert** an object into something, you put the object inside it. *He inserted the wooden peg into the hole.* ♦ **insertion** /ɪnsɜːʃn/ NU *After insertion, this extra material has to be removed.*
2 VO If you **insert** a comment in a piece of writing or a speech, you include it. *The President inserted one unscripted item in his speech.* ♦ **insertion, insertions** NU or NC *...the insertion of the sentence at an advanced stage of the preparatory work.*
3 NC An **insert** is something that is inserted somewhere, especially an advertisement on a piece of paper that is placed inside a magazine or newspaper. *...advertising inserts. ...supportive shoes with special inserts... We will be working on the many inserts that have to go in.*

inset, insets; pronounced /ɪnset/ when it is an adjective and /ɪnset/ when it is a noun.
1 ADJ Something that is **inset** with a decoration or piece of material has the decoration or material set inside it. *...gold or silver inset with gems... The eyes are alabaster ovals with inset pupils of ivory.*
2 NC An **inset** is a small picture, diagram, or map that is inside a larger one. *Several newspapers have the picture of the man arriving under guard, and a photo inset of the victim.*

inshore /ɪnʃɔː/
ADJ ATTRIB or ADV **Inshore** means in the sea but quite close to the land. *...inshore fishermen... These fish are not found inshore.*

inside /ɪnsaɪd/ insides. The form **inside of** can also be used as a preposition, especially in American English.
1 PREP or ADV Something or someone that is **inside** a place, container, or object is in it or surrounded by it. *Two minutes later we were inside the taxi... Fifty per cent of the money goes to charities inside of Baltimore... You left your lighter inside... It is a fruit with a seed inside.* ▸ Also ADJ ATTRIB *The door had no inside bolt.*
2 NC The **inside** of something is the part or area that its sides surround or contain. *The inside of my mouth was dry. ...the inside of the castle.*
3 ADJ ATTRIB You have **inside** information about a particular situation when you are involved in it and know more about it than other people, or have been told about it by someone who is involved in it. *They would be prevented from passing on inside information about new share offers... This inside knowledge of how America's political system works undoubtedly gives him a great advantage... There is evidence that the attackers had inside information about the targets.*
4 N PL Your **insides** are your internal organs, especially your stomach; an informal use. *What we all need is a bit of food in our insides.*
5 ADV or PREP If you say that someone has a feeling **inside**, you mean that they have not expressed this feeling. *Deep inside I didn't know exactly how to feel because I was split between them a lot after the separation occurred. ...expressing what they feel inside themselves... Dealing with all the garbage we have buried inside of us is hard.*
6 ADJ ATTRIB On a wide road, the **inside** lane is the left-hand lane in countries where you drive on the left, and the right-hand lane in countries where you drive on the right. *All the lorries were in the inside lane.*
7 PREP If you do something **inside** a particular time, you do it before the end of that time; an informal use. *Inside three hours, we were back again... Many countries anticipated that sanctions would work inside of three and a half months.*
8 ADV You can say that someone is **inside** when they are in prison; an informal use. *He ran the racket while he was inside for another offence.*
9 If something such as a piece of clothing is **inside out**, the inside part has been turned so that it faces outwards. *Eskimos coped with extreme cold by*

turning their furs inside out to trap in the heat.

insider /ɪnsaɪdə/ **insiders**
1 NC An **insider** is someone who is involved in a situation and who knows more about it than other people. *According to one insider, the government is getting worried.*
2 N+N **Insider** dealing is the practice of illegally buying or selling shares on the stock market for profit when you know more about a particular company than other people, often because you are involved with it in some way. *He became involved in doubtful financial dealings, including insider trading. ...the sort of information that is of use to insider dealers.*

insidious /ɪnsɪdiəs/
ADJ Something that is **insidious** is unpleasant and develops gradually without being noticed; a formal word. *The leaflets were a more insidious form of propaganda.*

insight /ɪnsaɪt/ **insights**
N U or N C **Insight** into a complex situation or problem is an understanding of it. *...a reading of insight, verve, and courage. ...interesting psychological insights.*

Insignia /ɪnsɪgniə/. Insignia is both the singular and the plural form.
NC An **insignia** is a badge or sign which shows that a person or object belongs to a particular organization. *...military insignia. ...a plane bearing the insignia of the Condor Legion.*

insignificance /ɪnsɪgnɪfɪkəns/
NU **Insignificance** is the quality of being insignificant. *This emergency plunges all her other problems into insignificance.*

insignificant /ɪnsɪgnɪfɪkənt/
ADJ Something that is **insignificant** is not at all important. *Whatever I write seems so insignificant. ...an insignificant minority.*

insincere /ɪnsɪnsɪə/
ADJ Someone who is **insincere** pretends to have feelings that they do not have. *...people whose admiration is extravagant and often insincere.*
♦ **insincerity** /ɪnsɪnserəti/ N U *The young are quick to recognize insincerity.*

insinuate /ɪnsɪnjueɪt/ **insinuates, insinuating, insinuated**
1 V-REPORT If you **insinuate** that something is true, you hint in an unpleasant way that it is true. *He insinuated that my wife had betrayed my trust in her.*
2 V-REFL+*into* If you **insinuate** yourself into a particular position, you manage slowly and cleverly to get yourself into that position; used showing disapproval. *He eventually insinuated himself into a key position in the Party.*

insipid /ɪnsɪpɪd/
1 ADJ Someone or something that is **insipid** is dull and boring. *I used to find him insipid.*
2 ADJ **Insipid** food or drink has very little taste. *...gigantic insipid tomatoes, huge flavourless lettuces.*

insist /ɪnsɪst/ **insists, insisting, insisted**
1 V-REPORT or V-QUOTE If you **insist** that something must happen or that something is true, you say it very firmly and refuse to change your mind. *She insisted that Jim must leave... 'But you know that she's innocent,' the girl insisted.*
2 V+*on* or V If you **insist** on something, you say very firmly that you must do it or have it, and refuse to change your mind. *He insisted on paying for the meal... We were right to insist on reform... He was firm about not letting us through, but we insisted and he finally gave up.*

insistence /ɪnsɪstəns/
NU Someone's **insistence** on something is the fact that they keep saying firmly that it must be done. *...my insistence on secrecy... In 1987, at Polish insistence, a joint commission to investigate the issue was set up.*

insistent /ɪnsɪstənt/
1 ADJ Someone who is **insistent** keeps saying firmly that something must be done. *...insistent demands that more should be done.* ♦ **insistently** ADV *No-one has spoken more insistently on the subject of education than her.*
2 ADJ If a noise or action is **insistent**, it continues for a long time and gets your attention. *...the insistent*

ringing of the telephone. ♦ **insistently** ADV *I tugged insistently at his jacket.*

in situ /ɪn sɪtjuː/
ADV If something remains **in situ**, especially while something is done to it, it remains where it is; a formal expression. *They will carry out further analysis in situ.*

insofar as /ɪnsəfɑːr əz/
CONJ You use **insofar as** when giving the reason for something or when showing the extent of something. *They were contemptuous of the traditional culture, except insofar as it provided precious metals.*

insole /ɪnsəʊl/ **insoles**
NC The **insole** of a shoe is the soft layer of material inside it, which the sole of your foot rests on. *Blistering can be prevented by using foot powder, soft insoles and two pairs of socks.*

insolence /ɪnsələns/
NU **Insolence** is behaviour which is very rude or impolite. *I was taken to the headmistress for my insolence.*

insolent /ɪnsələnt/
ADJ An **insolent** person is very rude or impolite. *...an insolent remark.*

insoluble /ɪnsɒljʊbl/
1 ADJ An **insoluble** problem cannot be solved. *The second question is insoluble. ...locked into an apparently insoluble conflict between blacks and whites.*
2 ADJ An **insoluble** substance does not dissolve or break down. *Roughage is an insoluble fibre.*

insolvency /ɪnsɒlvənsi/
NU **Insolvency** is the state of a person or organization that does not have enough money to pay their debts. *The bank had forced him into insolvency.*

insolvent /ɪnsɒlvənt/
ADJ A person or organization that is **insolvent** does not have enough money to pay their debts; a formal word. *He revealed that he was insolvent by 1.2m pounds.*

insomnia /ɪnsɒmniə/
NU Someone who suffers from **insomnia** finds it difficult to sleep. *...suffering from chronic insomnia.*

insomniac /ɪnsɒmniæk/ **insomniacs**
NC An **insomniac** is a person who finds it difficult to sleep. *...disorientation among jet-setters, night workers and some types of insomniacs.*

insouciance /ɪnsuːsiəns/
NU **Insouciance** is lack of concern shown by a person; a literary word. *She smiled and shook her head with pert insouciance.*

insouciant /ɪnsuːsiənt/
ADJ An **insouciant** action or quality shows a lack of concern; a literary word. *...sitting side-saddle in the most dashing and insouciant style.*

inspect /ɪnspekt/ **inspects, inspecting, inspected**
V O If you **inspect** something, you examine it carefully. *She inspected his scalp for lice... The kitchens were now amongst the cleanest he had inspected.* ♦ **inspection** /ɪnspekʃn/ **inspections** N U or N C *Closer inspection revealed crabs among the rocks. ...an inspection of the kitchen.*

inspector /ɪnspektə/ **inspectors**
1 NC An **inspector** is someone's whose job is to inspect things. *...the factory inspector... The inspector's report was released to the public.*
2 NC or TITLE An **inspector** is also an officer in the police force who is above a sergeant in rank. *He is a police inspector. ...Inspector Connell.*

inspectorate /ɪnspektəʳrət/ **inspectorates**
NC An **inspectorate** is a group of inspectors who are employed to work on the same issue or area. *...the Nuclear Inspectorate's report on a leak of radioactive waste.*

inspector of taxes, inspectors of taxes
NC An **inspector of taxes** is a person who is employed by the government to calculate the amount of tax that people should pay.

inspiration /ɪnspəreɪʃn/ **inspirations**
1 NU **Inspiration** is a feeling of excitement and enthusiasm gained from new ideas. *I have derived inspiration from Freud.*

2 N SING+SUPP The **inspiration** for something such as a piece of work or a theory is the thing that provides the basic idea or example for it. *He became the inspiration for the comic strip character, Superman.*
3 NU If you get **inspiration**, you suddenly think of a good idea. *He paused, searching for inspiration.*

inspirational /ɪnspəreɪʃ°nəl/
ADJ Something that is **inspirational** provides you with inspiration. *The book was of the greatest inspirational value.*

inspire /ɪnspaɪə/ **inspires, inspiring, inspired**
1 VO If someone or something **inspires** you, they make you want to do something by giving you new ideas and enthusiasm. *Not even Churchill could inspire the Party to reform... They were too gloomy to be inspired by his enthusiasm.*
2 VO Someone or something that **inspires** a particular emotion in people makes them feel this emotion. *...a man who inspired confidence in women.*

inspired /ɪnspaɪəd/
1 ADJ Someone who is **inspired** is brilliant and very creative in their work. *Ian McKellen is an inspired actor as well as being a political activist. ...works of inspired beauty.*
2 ADJ An **inspired** guess is very clever and accurate. *It was just an inspired guess.*

inspiring /ɪnspaɪərɪŋ/
ADJ Something or someone that is **inspiring** is exciting and makes you enthusiastic and interested. *It was an inspiring occasion... I'm afraid it may not be inspiring to watch.*

inst.
1 You write **inst.** as an abbreviation for 'instant' in formal letters to refer to the current month. *Thank you for your letter of 28th inst.*
2 Inst. is a written abbreviation for 'Institute'; used as part of the name of a particular institute. *...Inst. of Archaeology.*

instability /ɪnstəbɪləti/ **instabilities**
NU or NC **Instability** is a lack of stability in a place, situation, or person. *It was just one more sign of his instability... Reductions in East-West tensions will bring regional instabilities into sharper focus.*

install /ɪnstɔːl/ **installs, installing, installed**
1 VO If you **install** a piece of equipment, you put or fit it somewhere so that it is ready for use. *We have just installed central heating.*
2 VO If you **install** someone in an important job or position, you give them that job or position. *He installed a man named Briceland as head of the advertisement department.*
3 V-REFLA If you **install** yourself in a place, you settle there. *He installed himself in Victoria Street shortly after the election.*

installation /ɪnstəleɪʃn/ **installations**
1 NC An **installation** is a place that contains equipment and machinery which are used for a particular purpose. *...North Sea oil and gas installations. ...missile installations.*
2 NU The **installation** of a piece of equipment involves putting it into place and making it ready for use. *...the installation of the colour TV.*

instalment /ɪnstɔːlmənt/ **instalments**; spelt **installment** in American English.
1 NC If you pay for something in **instalments**, you pay small sums of money at regular intervals over a period of time. *I paid one hundred dollars in four monthly instalments.*
2 NC If a story is published in **instalments**, part of it is published each day, week, or month. *...the first instalment of the story.*

instance /ɪnstəns/ **instances**
1 You use **for instance** when giving an example of the thing you are talking about. *I mean, for instance, a man like Tom... For instance, an electric fire is a relatively expensive method of heating a room.*
2 NC An **instance** is a particular example of an event, situation, or person. *I do not think that in this instance the doctor was right. ...instances of government injustice.*
3 You say **in the first instance** when mentioning something that is the first step in a series of actions.

They agreed to meet privately for, in the first instance, fifteen minutes... They will need many things, but in the first instance, expertise will be crucial.

instant /ɪnstənt/ **instants**
1 NC An **instant** is an extremely short period of time. *Bal hesitated for an instant... It was all gone in a single instant.*
2 N SING+SUPP A particular **instant** is the actual moment when something happens. *At that instant, an angry buzzing began.*
3 CONJ If you do something **the instant** something else happens, you do it as soon as it happens. *She must have dashed out the instant I grabbed the phone.*
4 ADJ You use **instant** to describe something that happens immediately. *Herschel did not have instant success.* ♦ **instantly** ADV *He was killed instantly.*
5 ADJ **Instant** food is food that you can prepare very quickly, for example by just adding hot water. *...instant coffee.*

instantaneous /ɪnstənteɪniəs/
ADJ Something that is **instantaneous** happens immediately and very quickly. *Death was instantaneous.* ♦ **instantaneously** ADV *The pain passed instantaneously.*

instead /ɪnsted/
PREP or ADV SEN If you do one thing **instead of** another or if you do it **instead**, you do the first thing rather than the second thing. *If you want to have your meal at seven o'clock instead of five o'clock, you can... He would have sat back, but instead his mind began to consider a more ambitious scheme.*

instep /ɪnstep/ **insteps**
NC Your **instep** is the middle part of your foot, where it curves upwards. *Michael Harrison pulled out because of an instep injury.*

instigate /ɪnstɪgeɪt/ **instigates, instigating, instigated**
VO To **instigate** an event or situation means to cause it to happen; a formal word. *Further prosecutions were instigated privately.* ♦ **instigation** /ɪnstɪgeɪʃn/ NU *One husband, at the instigation of his wife, called the police.*

instigator /ɪnstɪgeɪtə/ **instigators**
NC The **instigator** of an event or situation is the person who causes it to happen; a formal word. *The instigator of the plot was Colonel Fletcher.*

instil /ɪnstɪl/ **instils, instilling, instilled**; spelt **instill, instills** in American English.
VO If you **instil** an idea or feeling into someone, you make them think it or feel it. *The presence of the guard was supposed to instil awe and fear in us.*

instinct /ɪnstɪŋkt/ **instincts**
1 NC or NU An **instinct** is the natural tendency that a person or animal has to behave or react in a particular way. *...a fundamental instinct for survival. ...the maternal instinct... She knew, by instinct, that he wouldn't come back.*
2 NC If it is your **instinct** to do something, you feel that it is right to do it. *My first instinct was to resign.*

instinctive /ɪnstɪŋktɪv/
ADJ An **instinctive** feeling, idea, or action is one that you have or do without thinking. *Brody took an instinctive dislike to the man... My instinctive reaction was to take a couple of rapid steps backwards.* ♦ **instinctively** ADV *Charles instinctively understood I wanted to be alone.*

instinctual /ɪnstɪŋktjuəl/
ADJ An **instinctual** feeling, action, or idea is the same as an **instinctive** one. *...instinctual impulses.*

institute /ɪnstɪtjuːt/ **institutes, instituting, instituted**
1 NC An **institute** is an organization set up to do a particular type of work, especially research or teaching. *I visited a number of research institutes in Asia. ...the Massachusetts Institute of Technology.*
2 VO If you **institute** a system, rule, or course of action, you start it; a formal use. *Mr Wilson was in Opposition when the scheme was instituted.*

institution /ɪnstɪtjuːʃn/ **institutions**
1 NC An **institution** is a custom or system that is an important or typical feature of a society or group. *...the institution of marriage.*
2 NC An **institution** is also a large organization, such

as a university, bank, or hospital. *These universities accept lower grades than the more prestigious institutions. ...financial institutions... He may end up in a mental institution.*

institutional /ɪnstɪtjuːʃəʰnəl/
1 ADJ ATTRIB **Institutional** means relating to a large organization, such as a university, bank, or hospital. *The child has been in institutional care for many years.*
2 ADJ ATTRIB **Institutional** also means relating to the customs or systems that are an important or typical feature of a society or group. *...the political and institutional changes needed for the transition to a market economy.*

institutionalize /ɪnstɪtjuːʃəʰnəlaɪz/ **institutionalizes, institutionalizing, institutionalized;** also spelt **institutionalise.**
1 VO If you **institutionalize** someone, you put them in an institution, for example a hospital for people who are mentally ill, or a home for children with no parents. *His wife persuaded him to institutionalize his ageing mother.*
2 VO To **institutionalize** something means to establish it as an important or typical feature of a society or group. *What is required is a means of institutionalizing the new power of labour.*

institutionalized /ɪnstɪtjuːʃəʰnəlaɪzd/; also spelt **institutionalised.**
1 ADJ If someone is **institutionalized**, they have been living in an institution such as a hospital or a prison for so long that they find it hard to look after themselves. *...institutionalized children.*
2 ADJ If a custom or system becomes **institutionalized**, it becomes an important and typical feature of a society or group. *...institutionalized religion.*

instruct /ɪnstrʌkt/ **instructs, instructing, instructed**
1 VO+to-INF, VO-QUOTE, VO-REPORT, or V-REPORT If you **instruct** someone to do something, you tell them to do it; a formal use. *I've been instructed to take you to London... 'Breathe in,' he instructed her... The Committee has now instructed that all official business should be conducted in Punjabi.*
2 VO Someone who **instructs** people in a subject or skill teaches it to them. *...the Japanese woman who instructed her in the Japanese language and customs.*

instruction /ɪnstrʌkʃn/ **instructions**
1 NC An **instruction** is something that someone tells you to do. *She was only following the instructions of her supervisor.*
2 N PL **Instructions** are clear and detailed information on how to do something. *Read the instructions before you switch on the engine. ...an instruction manual.*
3 NU **Instruction** in a subject or skill is teaching that someone gives you about it. *...school-based language instruction.*

instructive /ɪnstrʌktɪv/
ADJ Something that is **instructive** gives you useful information. *The very order in which he places these concerns is instructive. ...an instructive case study of the modern-day politics of Islam.*

instructor /ɪnstrʌktə/ **instructors**
NC An **instructor** is a teacher, especially of driving, skiing, or swimming. *...a Swiss ski instructor.*

instrument /ɪnstrəmənt/ **instruments**
1 NC An **instrument** is a tool or device that is used to do a particular task. *...surgical instruments. ...instruments of torture.*
2 NC A musical **instrument** is an object such as a piano, guitar, or flute which you play in order to produce music. *...stringed instruments.*
3 NC+SUPP Something that is an **instrument** for achieving a particular aim is used by people to achieve that aim; a formal use. *Incomes policy is a weak instrument for reducing inflation.*

instrumental /ɪnstrəmentl/
1 ADJ Someone or something that is **instrumental** in a process or event helps to make it happen. *The organization was instrumental in getting a ban on certain furs.*
2 ADJ **Instrumental** music is performed using musical instruments and not voices. *He talks about playing the saxophone and even demonstrates his instrumental*

style in the studio.

instrumentalist /ɪnstrəmentəlɪst/ **instrumentalists**
NC An **instrumentalist** is a person who plays a musical instrument. *...a band of instrumentalists who play flutes, fiddles, bagpipes and drums.*

instrumentation /ɪnstrəmenteɪʃn/
1 NU **Instrumentation** is a group or collection of instruments, usually ones that are part of the same machine. *Other electronic problems involving cockpit instrumentation had been solved.*
2 NU **Instrumentation** also refers to the writing or adapting of music that is intended to be played by a number of different musical instruments. *He is seldom praised for his instrumentation... I've used the same type of instrumentation that they used in those days.*

instrument panel, instrument panels
NC An **instrument panel** is the panel in a vehicle or on a machine where the dials and switches are located. *A button is pressed and the amount of acid is shown up on the instrument panel. ...the design of the instrument panel.*

insubordinate /ɪnsəbɔːdɪnət/
ADJ Someone who is **insubordinate** is disobedient; a formal word. *...to punish insubordinate behaviour.*

insubordination /ɪnsəbɔːdɪneɪʃn/
NU **Insubordination** is disobedient behaviour; a formal word. *...charges of insubordination.*

insubstantial /ɪnsəbstænʃl/
1 ADJ **Insubstantial** things are not large, solid, or strong. *Lynn's shoulder was bony and insubstantial. ...a feathery, insubstantial plant.*
2 ADJ You also use **insubstantial** to describe something such as a policy or action which is weak or ineffective. *..weak and insubstantial policies... This was no insubstantial threat.*

insufferable /ɪnsʌfəʰrəbl/
ADJ If someone or something is **insufferable**, they are very unpleasant or annoying. *He was becoming an insufferable pest with his stealing.*

insufficiency /ɪnsəfɪʃnsi/
NU **Insufficiency** is the state of something not being large enough in amount for a particular purpose; a formal word. *...fighting against economic insufficiency. ...an insufficiency of Vitamin C in the diet.*

insufficient /ɪnsəfɪʃnt/
ADJ Something that is **insufficient** is not enough for a particular purpose; a formal word. *Insufficient research has been done... These steps will be insufficient to change our economic decline.*
♦ **insufficiently** ADV *My hand had proved insufficiently strong to open the door.*

insular /ɪnsjʊlə/
ADJ **Insular** people are unwilling to meet new people or to consider new ideas. *He lived a rather insular life.*

insulate /ɪnsjʊleɪt/ **insulates, insulating, insulated**
1 VO If a material or substance **insulates** something, it keeps its temperature constant by covering it in a thick layer. *The function of a mammal's hair is to insulate the body.*
2 VO If you **insulate** a person from harmful things, you protect them from those things; a formal use. *They could insulate the local population from these dangerous influences. ...in a sheltered, womb-like world, insulated against the events of life outside.*
3 VO If you **insulate** an electrical device, you cover it with rubber or plastic to prevent electricity passing through it and giving the person using it an electric shock. *...electric cables which are insulated with rubber or plastic.*

insulation /ɪnsjʊleɪʃn/
NU **Insulation** is a thick layer of material that is used to stop heat from escaping from something. *...a long roll of roof insulation. ...cavity wall insulation.*

insulator /ɪnsjʊleɪtə/ **insulators**
NC An **insulator** is material that insulates something. *Few substances can equal fur as an insulator.*

insulin /ɪnsjʊlɪn/
NU **Insulin** is a substance that most people produce naturally in their body and which controls the level of

sugar in their blood. *Many diabetics require regular injections of insulin.*

insult, insults, insulting, insulted; pronounced /ɪnsˈʌlt/ when it is a verb and /ˈɪnsʌlt/ when it is a noun.
1 vo If you **insult** someone, you offend them by saying or doing something that is rude. *You don't have to apologize to me. You didn't insult me.* ◆ **insulting** ADJ *He did use insulting language.*
2 NC An **insult** is a rude remark or action which offends someone. *The older boys yelled out insults... I would take it as an insult if you left.*
3 You say 'to add insult to injury' when you are mentioning an action or fact that makes an unfair or unpleasant situation even worse. *To add insult to injury, second and third generation Koreans in Japan are obliged to be finger-printed as aliens... A union official said this was adding insult to injury.*

insuperable /ɪnsˈjuːpərəbl/
ADJ A problem that is **insuperable** cannot be solved; a formal word. *It would be an insuperable barrier to unity.*

insupportable /ɪnsəpˈɔːtəbl/
ADJ If you find something **insupportable**, you find it so unpleasant that you cannot accept it; a formal word. *Accusations of that kind are quite insupportable.*

insurance /ɪnʃˈʊərəns, ɪnʃˈɔːrəns/
1 NU **Insurance** is an agreement in which you pay a fixed sum of money to a company, usually each year. Then, if you become ill or if your property is damaged or stolen, the company pays you a sum of money. *...private health insurance. ...insurance companies.*
2 N SING If you do something as an **insurance** against something unpleasant, you do it in order to protect yourself in case the unpleasant thing happens. *They build up supplies as an insurance against drought.*
3 See also **national insurance**.

insurance policy, insurance policies
NC An **insurance policy** is a written agreement which you sign in order to insure someone or something. *We must find out if there is any insurance policy covering the mortgage.*

insure /ɪnʃˈʊə, ɪnʃˈɔː/ **insures, insuring, insured**
1 V-REFL or VO If you **insure** yourself or your property, you pay money to an insurance company so that, if you become ill or if your property is damaged or stolen, the company will pay you a sum of money. *He insured himself against all eventualities... Insure your baggage before you leave home.* ◆ **insured** ADJ PRED *The house is not insured against fire.*
2 V+*against* If you **insure** against something unpleasant happening, you do something to protect yourself in case it happens. *In years of good rainfall they expand their stocks to insure against drought.*
3 See also **ensure**.

insurer /ɪnʃˈʊərə, ɪnʃˈɔːrə/ **insurers**
NC An **insurer** is a company that sells insurance. *Lloyds has estimated that insurers will end up paying out around one billion dollars as a result of the accident.*

insurgent /ɪnsˈɜːdʒənt/ **insurgents**
NC **Insurgents** are people who are fighting against the government or army of their own country; a formal word. *Insurgents partially damaged the embassy.*

insurmountable /ɪnsəmˈaʊntəbl/
ADJ An **insurmountable** problem cannot be solved; a formal word. *...other, seemingly insurmountable obstacles to a peaceful transition. ...what many observers see as insurmountable difficulties in achieving this goal.*

insurrection /ɪnsərˈekʃn/ **insurrections**
N Cor NU An **insurrection** is violent action taken by a group of people against the rulers of their country. *...an armed insurrection... Such policies were intended to prevent insurrection.*

intact /ɪntˈækt/
ADJ Something that is **intact** is complete and has not been damaged or spoilt. *...the window remained intact... They are fighting to keep village life intact.*

intake /ˈɪnteɪk/ **intakes**
1 NU+SUPP Your **intake** of food, drink, or air is the amount that you eat, drink, or breathe in, or the process of taking it into your body. *Nurses kept*

measuring her fluid intake.
2 NC+SUPP The people who are accepted into an institution or organization at a particular time are referred to as a particular **intake**. *...the army's huge emergency intake of soldiers.*

intangible /ɪntˈændʒəbl/
ADJ A quality or idea that is **intangible** is hard to define or explain. *...the intangible and unquantifiable nature of the other benefits.*

integer /ˈɪntɪdʒə/ **integers**
NC An **integer** is an exact whole number such as 1, 7, or 24, as opposed to a number with fractions or decimals; a technical term in mathematics.

integral /ˈɪntɪgrəl/
ADJ If one thing is an **integral** part of another thing, it is an essential part of it. *The Young Socialists were an integral feature of the Labour movement... The concept of loyalty is integral to the story.*

integrate /ˈɪntɪgreɪt/ **integrates, integrating, integrated**
1 V-ERG or V-RECIP If people **integrate** into a social group, they mix with people in that group. *...helping the individual integrate quickly into the community. ...ways of integrating handicapped children into ordinary schools... A senior cabinet minister said recently that the ethnic Chinese should make efforts to integrate with the rest of the Indonesian community... He said yesterday that countries must be serious about integrating.* ◆ **integration** /ˌɪntɪgrˈeɪʃn/ NU *He campaigned for the integration of immigrants into British society.*
2 V-RECIP If you **integrate** things, you combine them so that they are closely linked or so that they form one thing. *The two regional railway systems were integrated. ...one of three European countries helping to integrate UNITA and government troops into a single national army... We integrate contemporary dance with acrobatics.* ◆ **integration** NU *...greater European economic integration.*

integrated /ˈɪntɪgreɪtɪd/
ADJ An **integrated** institution is intended for use by people of all races or groups. *...an integrated school for Protestants and Catholics... In theory, all schools should already be integrated.*

integrity /ɪntˈegrəti/
1 NU **Integrity** is the quality of being honest and firm in your moral principles. *He was particularly respected for his integrity. ...a man of the highest integrity.*
2 NU+POSS The **integrity** of something such as a group of people is its quality of being one united thing. *They were totally committed to the survival and integrity of the nation... Somalia had received full moral and material backing in its bid to preserve its territorial integrity and national sovereignty.*

intellect /ˈɪntəlekt/ **intellects**
1 NU or NC **Intellect** is the ability to think and to understand ideas and information. *...the intellect of modern man. ...the idea of computers with intellects.*
2 NU **Intellect** is also the quality of being very intelligent or clever. *...a family noted for its intellect.*

intellectual /ˌɪntəlˈektʃuəl/ **intellectuals**
1 ADJ ATTRIB **Intellectual** means involving a person's ability to think and to understand ideas and information. *...children in need of extra emotional or intellectual stimulation. ...his tremendous intellectual powers.* ◆ **intellectually** ADV *...an intellectually challenging occupation.*
2 NC An **intellectual** is someone who spends a lot of time studying and thinking about complicated ideas. *...scholars and intellectuals.* ► Also ADJ *...an intellectual conversation.*

intelligence /ɪntˈelɪdʒəns/
1 NU Someone's **intelligence** is their ability to understand and learn things. *...a person of average intelligence.*
2 NU **Intelligence** is the ability to think and understand instead of doing things by instinct or automatically. *Do hedgehogs have intelligence? ...computer intelligence.*
3 NU **Intelligence** is also information gathered by the government about their country's enemies.

...American intelligence services.

intelligent /ɪntɛlɪdʒənt/
1 ADJ An **intelligent** person has the ability to understand and learn things well. *Jo is an intelligent student. ...a very intelligent question.* ◆ **intelligently** ADV *They dealt with that problem intelligently.*
2 ADJ An animal or computer that is **intelligent** has the ability to think and understand instead of doing things by instinct or automatically. *Computers can be intelligent.*

intelligentsia /ɪntɛlɪdʒɛntsɪə/
N COLL The **intelligentsia** in a community are the most educated people in it. *Class structure in society is changing in favour of the technical and creative intelligentsia.*

intelligible /ɪntɛlɪdʒəbl/
ADJ Something that is **intelligible** can be understood. *Describe it in a way that would be intelligible to an outsider.*

intemperate /ɪntɛmpərət/
ADJ **Intemperate** behaviour or opinions are unreasonably strong and uncontrolled; a formal word. *...an organization about which Charles had made several intemperate and highly publicized remarks.*

intend /ɪntɛnd/ **intends, intending, intended**
1 V+to-INF or V+ING If you **intend** to do something, you have decided to do it or have planned to do it. *This is my job and I intend to do it... He woke later than he had intended... He had intended staying longer.*
2 VO+to-INF, V O A, or VO-REPORT If you **intend** something to happen or to have a particular effect or function, you have planned that it should happen or should have that effect or function. *We never intended the scheme to be permanent... It is intended as a handbook, for frequent reference... They are not yet intended for use... It had been intended that a second group should be assembled.*
3 VO+for Something that is **intended** for a particular person has been planned or provided for that person. *The man had drunk what had been intended for me.*

intended /ɪntɛndɪd/
ADJ ATTRIB You use **intended** to describe the thing that you are trying or planning to achieve, do, or affect. *What is the intended result? ...his intended victim.*

intense /ɪntɛns/
1 ADJ Something that is **intense** is very great in strength or degree. *The effects of the drug are intense and brief. ...the intense heat... The row caused her intense unhappiness.* ◆ **intensely** ADV *She had suffered intensely.* ◆ **intensity** /ɪntɛnsəti/ NU *The debates are renewed with great intensity.*
2 ADJ An **intense** person is serious all the time. *...Tereza, an intense young girl from the country.*

intensify /ɪntɛnsɪfaɪ/ **intensifies, intensifying, intensified**
V-ERG If you **intensify** something or if it **intensifies**, it becomes greater in strength or degree. *The search was intensified using dogs... In the late 1960s the pressures suddenly intensified.* ◆ **intensified** ADJ ATTRIB *...intensified international competition.*

intensive /ɪntɛnsɪv/
ADJ An **intensive** activity involves a very great concentration of energy, resources, or people on one particular task. *...the last intensive preparation for my exams... He has expressed his concern about modern intensive farming methods.* ◆ **intensively** ADV *The land was developed very intensively in the mid 1930s.*

intensive care
NU **Intensive care** is extremely thorough care provided by hospitals for people who are very seriously ill. *Eight victims are still in a critical condition in the intensive care unit.*

intent /ɪntɛnt/ **intents**
1 NU A person's **intent** is their intention to do something; a formal use. *The conference declared its intent to organize a national movement... They signed a declaration of intent.*
2 ADJ When you look **intent**, you show that you are paying great attention. *She was brushing her hair, intent on her face in the mirror.* ◆ **intently** ADV *I stood behind a parked van, watching intently.*

3 ADJ PRED+on or upon If you are **intent** on doing something, you are determined to do it. *They were intent on keeping what they had... The government was intent upon deceiving the Commission.*
4 You say **to all intents and purposes** to suggest that a situation is not exactly as you describe it but the effect is the same as if it were. *She was to all intents and purposes the infant's mother.*

intention /ɪntɛnʃn/ **intentions**
N or NU An **intention** is an idea or plan of what you are going to do. *He confirmed his intention to leave next April... She had no intention of spending the rest of her life working as a waitress.*

intentional /ɪntɛnʃəⁿnəl/
ADJ Something that is **intentional** is deliberate. *...intentional misrepresentation.* ◆ **intentionally** ADV *I banged the door. Not intentionally.*

inter /ɪntɜː/ **inters, interring, interred**
VO To **inter** someone means to bury them; a formal word. *Thomas was interred next to his grandmother.*

inter- /ɪntə-/
PREFIX **Inter-** combines with adjectives and nouns to form adjectives that describe something as moving, existing, or happening between similar things or groups of people. For example, inter-governmental relations are relations between governments. *...an inter-city express train. ...inter-racial marriages.*

interact /ɪntərækt/ **interacts, interacting, interacted**
V-RECIP The way that two people or things **interact** is the way that they communicate or work in relation to each other. *Mothers and babies interact in a very complex way... The tidal currents interacted with the discharge from a river estuary.* ◆ **interaction** /ɪntərækʃn/ **interactions** NU or NC *There is a need for more interaction between staff and children. ...the creature's interactions with the world around it.*

interactive /ɪntəræktɪv/
ADJ **Interactive** use of a computer is use in which the user and the computer communicate directly with each other by means of a keyboard and a screen; a technical term in computing. *We used the interactive facilities of the graphics to move one towards the other. ...large interactive computer games.*

inter alia /ɪntər eɪlɪə/
ADV SEN You use **inter alia** when you want to say that there are other aspects of something apart from the one you are mentioning; a formal expression. *Buckingham Palace houses, inter alia, a fine collection of paintings.*

intercede /ɪntəsiːd/ **intercedes, interceding, interceded**
V If you **intercede** with a person, you talk to them in order to try to end a disagreement that they have with another person; a formal word. *I had interceded for him with his employer.*

intercept /ɪntəsɛpt/ **intercepts, intercepting, intercepted**
VO If you **intercept** someone or something that is travelling from one place to another, you stop them. *Two army patrol boats intercepted a cargo ship off the harbour of Jiyeh... Telex messages had been intercepted and misinterpreted.*

interceptor /ɪntəsɛptə/ **interceptors**
NC An **interceptor** is a fighter aircraft designed to intercept and attack enemy planes. *The defending forces will deploy interceptor aircraft.*

intercession /ɪntəsɛʃn/ **intercessions**
NU or NC **Intercession** is an act of trying to end a disagreement between two people; a formal word. *Mr Arafat said that his American visa was obtained after intercession by President Mubarak... Through the intercession of a friend, my request was granted.*

interchange, interchanges, interchanging, interchanged; pronounced /ɪntətʃeɪndʒ/ when it is a noun and /ɪntətʃeɪndʒ/ when it is a verb.
1 NU+SUPP or NC+SUPP The **interchange** of things, people, or ideas is the exchange of them between a number of people or groups. *...interchange between the classes. ...a regular forum for the interchange of information and ideas.*
2 V-ERG or V-RECIP If things or ideas **interchange** or are **interchanged**, they change places or are exchanged

with each other. *What we intend is to link up the information in Asia and the Pacific and in Africa so that it can be interchanged and readily available from one place to another... In nature we know that genes interchange with each other.*
3 NC An **interchange** on a motorway is a junction where it meets another main road. *...the interchange in Birmingham known as Spaghetti Junction.*

interchangeable /ɪntətʃeɪndʒəbl/
ADJ Things that are **interchangeable** can be exchanged with each other without making any difference. *We tend to use these terms as if they were freely interchangeable.* ◆ **interchangeably** ADV *...the word 'fascist' was used interchangeably with the word 'racist'.*

intercom /ɪntəkɒm/ **intercoms**
NC An **intercom** is a device like a small box with a microphone and loudspeaker which you use to talk to people in another room. *A voice on the intercom said, 'It's Mr Vaughan.'*

interconnect /ɪntəkənɛkt/ **interconnects, interconnecting, interconnected**
V-ERG or V-RECIP Things that **interconnect** or that are **interconnected** are connected with each other. *There's a need for all these areas to interconnect... Monarch, court and government were all interconnected... This service must be able to interconnect with millions of others.*

intercontinental /ɪntəkɒntɪnɛntl/
ADJ **Intercontinental** is used to describe something that exists or happens between continents. *...an intercontinental flight.*

intercourse /ɪntəkɔːs/
NU If people have **intercourse**, they have sex; a formal word. *They have to decide whether to have sexual intercourse.*

interdependence /ɪntədɪpɛndəns/
NU **Interdependence** is the condition of a group of people or things all depending on each other. *...the interdependence of economies.*

interdependent /ɪntədɪpɛndənt/
ADJ People or things that are **interdependent** all depend on each other. *Plants and animals are strongly interdependent.*

interdisciplinary /ɪntədɪsəplɪnəⁿri/
ADJ **Interdisciplinary** means involving more than one academic subject. *...an interdisciplinary course in African studies.*

interest /ɪntrəst, ɪntərest/ **interests, interesting, interested**
1 N SING or NU If you have an **interest** in something, you want to learn or hear more about it. *None of them had the slightest interest in music... Brody was beginning to lose interest.*
2 NC Your **interests** are the things that you enjoy doing. *He had two consuming interests: rowing and polo.*
3 VO If something **interests** you, you want to learn more about it or to continue doing it. *Young men should always look for work which interests them.*
4 VO If you **interest** someone in something, you persuade them to do it or to buy it. *Can I interest you in yet another horror movie?*
5 NC If you have an **interest** in something being done, you want it to be done because you will benefit from it. *They had no interest in the overthrow of the established order... They would protect the interests of their members.* ● Something that is **in the interests** of a person or group will benefit them in some way. *It is not in the interests of any of us to have a weak government.* ● See also **vested interest**.
6 NC A person or organization that has **interests** in a particular type of business owns shares or companies of this type. *...an industrialist with business interests in Germany... British companies still retain a considerable interest in the industry.*
7 NU **Interest** is extra money that you receive if you have invested a sum of money, or money that you pay if you have borrowed money. *...the interest you pay on your mortgage. ...high interest rates.*

interested /ɪntrəstɪd/
1 ADJ PRED If you are **interested** in something, you

think it is important or worthwhile and you want to know more about it or want to develop it further. *I'm very interested in birds... He looked interested... My sister is interested in becoming a nurse.*
2 ADJ ATTRIB An **interested** party or group of people is affected by or involved in a particular event or situation. *We talked to scientists and other interested parties.*

interest-free; also written **interest free.**
ADJ An **interest-free** loan has no interest charged on it: see **interest.** ▶ Also ADV *...if you lent someone money interest free.*

interest group, interest groups
NC An **interest group** is an organization or group of people who want certain things to happen or to be done because they will benefit from them. *The Congress building is packed with lobbyists and interest groups staging protests against the bill.*

interesting /ɪntrəstɪŋ/
ADJ If you find something **interesting**, it attracts you or holds your attention. *That's a very interesting question... He was not very interesting to talk to.*

interestingly /ɪntrəstɪŋli/
ADV SEN You use **interestingly** to introduce a piece of information that you think is interesting and unexpected. *Interestingly enough, America is now dependent on Africa for oil imports.*

interface /ɪntəfeɪs/ **interfaces**
NC The **interface** between two subjects or systems is the area in which they affect each other or have links with each other. *...new ways of involving young people with the interface between technology and design.*

interfere /ɪntəfɪə/ **interferes, interfering, interfered**
1 V A or V If you **interfere** in a situation, you become involved in it although it does not really concern you; used showing disapproval. *My mother interferes in things... Don't interfere.* ◆ **interfering** ADJ *...an interfering old woman.*
2 V A Something that **interferes** with a situation, process, or activity has a damaging effect on it. *Child-bearing will not interfere with a career.*

interference /ɪntəfɪərəns/
1 NU **Interference** is the act of interfering in something. *I wanted to do the thing on my own without outside interference or help... They didn't want any interference from their national government.*
2 NU When there is **interference**, a radio signal is affected by other radio waves so that it cannot be received properly. *The satellite changes the radio frequency to avoid interference.*

interim /ɪntərɪm/
ADJ ATTRIB **Interim** describes things that are intended to be used until something permanent is arranged. *Some groups are still calling for the establishment of an interim government to oversee elections. ...an interim report.*

interior /ɪntɪəriə/ **interiors**
1 NC The **interior** of something is the inside part of it. *Very little is known about the deep interior of the earth... The castle has its interior well preserved.* ▶ Also ADJ ATTRIB *...an interior room without windows.*
2 ADJ ATTRIB An **interior** minister or political department deals with affairs in their own country. *The Interior Minister emphasized that dealing with these illegal immigrants was an internal matter.*

interior designer, interior designer
NC An **interior designer** is a person whose job is to plan the way that the inside of a house looks by choosing the colours and designs of its wallpaper, carpets, and furniture.

interject /ɪntədʒɛkt/ **interjects, interjecting, interjected**
V, V-QUOTE, or VO If you **interject**, you say something when someone else is speaking; a formal word. *Time and again, he interjected to point out that he agreed with the President... 'No, no,' interjected Schmidt. ...if I may interject a word here.*

interjection /ɪntədʒɛkʃn/ **interjections**
1 NC An **interjection** is something you say when someone else is speaking; a formal use. *They would*

have to avoid the lengthy interjections that held up the summer's proceedings.
2 NC In grammar, an **interjection** is a word or expression expressing a feeling of surprise, pain, or horror.

interlaced /ɪntəleɪst/
ADJ Things that are **interlaced** are joined closely together as if they are woven. *...interlaced branches... She sat cupping a knee with interlaced fingers.*

interlink /ɪntəlɪŋk/ **interlinks, interlinking, interlinked**
V-RECIP or V-ERG If things **are interlinked**, they are connected with each other in some way. *Geoffrey Bindman explains how the political and legal processes are interlinked... The question of repatriation is closely interlinked with the need for economic recovery. ...profound long-term effects that interlink with social and economic transformation.* ◆ **interlinked** ADJ *...the two interlinked key issues of the Kampuchean problem.*

interlock /ɪntəlɒk/ **interlocks, interlocking, interlocked**
1 V-RECIP or V-ERG Things that **interlock** with each other fit into each other and are firmly joined. *All the units interlock with one another rigidly... Slide the fingers along the backs of the hands until they interlock... He interlocked his fingers.*
2 V-ERG If systems, situations, or plans **are interlocked**, they are very closely connected. *The two companies were financially interlocked to the degree that he and two other English directors graced the board of the American company... The tragedies begin to interlock and choke us all.* ◆ **interlocking** ADJ ATTRIB *Two historic and interlocking agreements are to be signed at the United Nations today.*

interlocutor /ɪntəlɒkjʊtə/ **interlocutors**
NC Your **interlocutor** is the person with whom you are having a conversation; a formal word. *He looked at his interlocutor across the table.*

interloper /ɪntələʊpə/ **interlopers**
NC An **interloper** is a person who interferes in something or who is in a place where they are not supposed to be. *Any interloper who heckled would be removed from the meeting.*

interlude /ɪntəluːd/ **interludes**
NC An **interlude** is a short period of time during which an activity or event stops. *After this interlude, the band started up again.*

intermarriage /ɪntəmærɪdʒ/
NU **Intermarriage** is marriage between people from different social, racial, or religious groups. *There will be intermarriage between our people and yours.*

intermarry /ɪntəmæri/ **intermarries, intermarrying, intermarried**
V When people from different social, racial, or religious groups **intermarry**, they marry each other. *The two communities intermarried and coexisted quite peacefully.*

intermediary /ɪntəmiːdiəri/ **intermediaries**
NC An **intermediary** is a person who passes messages between two people or groups. *He dealt through an intermediary with Beaverbrook himself.*

intermediate /ɪntəmiːdiət/
1 ADJ ATTRIB An **intermediate** stage is one that occurs between two other stages. *One group of animals developed into another by way of intermediate forms.*
2 ADJ **Intermediate** students are no longer beginners, but are not yet advanced. *...an English course, intermediate level, for adult students.*

interment /ɪntɜːmənt/
NU The **interment** of a dead person is their burial; a formal word. *They brought back their lamented comrade's remains for interment on the farm.*

interminable /ɪntɜːmɪnəbl/
ADJ Something that is **interminable** continues for such a long time that it seems as if it will never end; used showing disapproval. *I was glad of company for this interminable flight.* ◆ **interminably** ADV *MPs argued each point interminably.*

intermingle /ɪntəmɪŋgl/ **intermingles, intermingling, intermingled**
V-RECIP When people or things **intermingle**, they mix

with each other; a formal word. *It would not be the first time that extremes of right and left cross over or intermingle... The police intermingled with the crowds.*

intermission /ɪntəmɪʃn/ **intermissions**
NC An **intermission** is an interval between two parts of something such as a film, play, or opera. *The ballet, in three acts with two intermissions, was called Corsair.*

intermittent /ɪntəmɪtnt/
ADJ Something that is **intermittent** happens occasionally rather than continuously. *I became aware of a faint, intermittent noise.* ◆ **intermittently** ADV *The magazine had been published intermittently since the war.*

intern, interns, interning, interned; pronounced /ɪntɜːn/ when it is a verb and /ɪntɜːn/ when it is a noun.
1 VO To **intern** someone means to put them in prison or a prison camp, for political reasons. *...the camp where thousands of western civilians were interned... They said they had been interned without trial.*
2 NC An **intern** is a senior student or a graduate who is gaining supervised work experience, especially a medical graduate who is working in a hospital as a junior doctor; used in American English. *This extra money essentially subsidizes medical education; it pays for residents and interns to treat patients... They are working as interns at IBM.*

internal /ɪntɜːnl/
1 ADJ ATTRIB You use **internal** to describe things that exist or happen inside a place, person, or object. *You should lag internal pipes to prevent them from freezing... Our internal human system uses about 100 watts of energy.* ◆ **internally** ADV *The house has been rebuilt internally.*
2 ADJ ATTRIB **Internal** is also used to describe something that exists or happens within a particular organization. *...an internal bank memorandum.* ◆ **internally** ADV *The ruling Liberals are split internally in many regions.*
3 ADJ ATTRIB **Internal** also means relating to the political and commercial activities inside a country. *...the internal politics of France.* ◆ **internally** ADV *Haiti's problems must be solved internally.*
4 ADJ **Internal** ideas or images exist in your mind. *We have both external and internal values.*

internal combustion engine, internal combustion engines
NC An **internal combustion engine** is an engine that creates its energy by burning fuel inside itself. *Most cars have an internal combustion engine. It was quite common in the past to use gas generators to power internal combustion engines.*

internalize /ɪntɜːnəlaɪz/ **internalizes, internalizing, internalized**; also spelt **internalise**.
VO If you **internalize** something such as a belief or a set of values, you make it become a part of your attitude or way of thinking; a formal word. *He has not yet internalized that knowledge.* ◆ **internalization** /ɪntɜːnəlaɪzeɪʃn/ NU *They were weighed down by this internalization of the belief in their own superiority.*

international /ɪntənæʃəⁿl/ **internationals**
1 ADJ **International** means involving different countries. *...international affairs. ...an international agreement on nuclear waste.* ◆ **internationally** ADV *She's an internationally famous historian.*
2 NC In sport, an **international** is a match that is played between teams from two countries. *England have won the third and final one-day international against the West Indies.*
3 NC An **international** is also a sportsman or sportswoman who plays in an international. *...a former England international.*

internationalism /ɪntənæʃəⁿəlɪzəm/
NU **Internationalism** is the belief that countries should co-operate with one another and try to understand one another. *This is an age of internationalism.*

international relations
N PL **International relations** consist of the political relationships between different countries. *What effect will this incident have on international relations?*

internecine /ɪntəniːsaɪn/
ADJ ATTRIB An **internecine** conflict, war, or quarrel is

one which causes destruction to both sides; a formal word. ...*internecine struggles*. ...*internecine warfare*.

internee /ɪntɜːˈniː/ **internees**
NC An **internee** is a person who has been imprisoned for political reasons. *We try to help the families of internees*.

internment /ɪntɜːnmənt/
NU **Internment** is imprisonment for political reasons. *A former Justice Minister called for the internment of suspected terrorists*.

interpersonal /ɪntəpɜːˈsəʊnəl/
ADJ ATTRIB **Interpersonal** means relating to relationships between people. *There are also interpersonal problems that will occur*. ...*a whole new concept of interpersonal relationships based on sharing rather than owning*.

interplay /ˈɪntəpleɪ/
NU The **interplay** between two or more things is the way that they react or work with each other; a formal word. ...*the interplay between practical and theoretical constraints*. ...*the interplay of market forces*.

Interpol /ˈɪntəpɒl/
N PROP **Interpol** is an international police organization which, with the help of the police forces in individual countries, tries to fight international crime. *His description had been circulated to the local police force by Interpol... Public prosecutors and the police searched the company's offices and Interpol has also been alerted*.

interpolate /ɪntɜːpəleɪt/ **interpolates, interpolating, interpolated**
V O or V-QUOTE If you **interpolate** a comment or piece of writing, you insert it into a conversation or text as an addition; a formal word. *'It was last Friday', interpolated Sheila... A later edition interpolated the following passage*.

interpolation /ɪntɜːpəleɪʃn/ **interpolations**
NC An **interpolation** is an addition to a piece of writing. *Interpolations in brackets are the author's*.

interpose /ɪntəpəʊz/ **interposes, interposing, interposed**
V-QUOTE If you **interpose**, you interrupt with a comment or question; a formal word. *'Enough of this!' interposed Miss Musson*.

interpret /ɪntɜːprɪt/ **interprets, interpreting, interpreted**
1 VO If you **interpret** something in a particular way, you decide that this is its meaning or significance. *I'm not quite sure how to interpret that question... The election result is being interpreted as a serious setback for the government... It's difficult to interpret those findings*.
2 V or VO If you **interpret** what someone is saying, you translate it immediately into another language. *Paul had to interpret for us... He interpreted the opening words of section 16*.

interpretation /ɪntɜːprɪteɪʃn/ **interpretations**
1 NC or NU An **interpretation** of something is an explanation of what it means, often one of several different explanations. *This passage is open to a variety of interpretations... It's hard to know if this is simply a difference of interpretation*.
2 NC or NU A performer's **interpretation** of a piece of music or a dance is the particular way in which they choose to perform it. *Do you find his interpretation of Chopin satisfactory?... He's become known for his sensitive interpretation of music and a vibrant sense of humour*.

interpretative /ɪntɜːprɪtətɪv/
ADJ ATTRIB You use **interpretative** to describe something or someone that gives an interpretation. ...*an interpretative article*.

interpreter /ɪntɜːprɪtə/ **interpreters**
NC An **interpreter** is a person whose job is to translate what someone is saying into another language. *Ngugi Wa Thiong'o, the Kenyan novelist, spoke to the audience through an interpreter*.

interregnum /ɪntəregnəm/ **interregnums** or **interregna** /ɪntəregnə/
NC or NU An **interregnum** is the period between the end of one ruler's reign and the beginning of the next

ruler's reign. *After a brief interregnum, Britain entered upon the reign of the second Harold... From today's viewpoint, this time can be seen as one of interregnum in Moscow*.

interrelate /ɪntərɪleɪt/ **interrelates, interrelating, interrelated**
V-ERG If two or more things **interrelate** or are **interrelated**, there is a connection between them and they have an effect on one another; a formal word. *These courses interrelate in a variety of ways... All three factors are interrelated*.

interrelationship /ɪntərɪleɪʃnʃɪp/ **interrelationships**
NC An **interrelationship** is a close relationship between two or more things. *The report focuses on the interrelationship between population, resources, the environment and development*.

interrogate /ɪnterəgeɪt/ **interrogates, interrogating, interrogated**
VO If someone, especially a police officer or an army officer, **interrogates** you, they question you thoroughly for a long time, in order to get information from you. *They had been interrogated for 20 hours about political demonstrations*.

interrogation /ɪnterəgeɪʃn/ **interrogations**
NU or NC **Interrogation** is the act or process of interrogating someone. *We've had him under interrogation for 36 hours... Waddell had undergone a lengthy interrogation*.

interrogative /ɪntərɒgətɪv/ **interrogatives**; a technical term in grammar.
1 ADJ An **interrogative** sentence is one that has the form of a question. For example, 'What is your name?' is interrogative.
2 NC An **interrogative** is a word such as 'who', 'how', or 'why', which can be used to ask a question.

interrogator /ɪntərəgeɪtə/ **interrogators**
NC An **interrogator** is a person, especially a police officer or an army officer, who questions someone thoroughly for a long time. *She managed to stand up to her interrogator because she was angry instead of being intimidated*.

interrupt /ɪntərʌpt/ **interrupts, interrupting, interrupted**
1 V, VO, or V-QUOTE If you **interrupt** someone who is speaking, you say or do something that causes them to stop. *Don't interrupt... Sorry to interrupt you... 'Enough,' interrupted Koda Dad roughly*.
2 VO If you **interrupt** an activity, you temporarily prevent it from continuing. *Bain had interrupted his holiday to go to Hamburg*.

interruption /ɪntərʌpʃn/ **interruptions**
1 NC An **interruption** is something which temporarily prevents an activity from continuing. *She hates interruptions when she's working*.
2 NU **Interruption** is the act of interrupting someone or something. *We should be safe from interruption*.

intersect /ɪntəsekt/ **intersects, intersecting, intersected**
1 V-RECIP When roads or lines **intersect**, they cross each other. *The highway intersected Main Street in a busy crossing... What if the two lines do not intersect?*
2 VO If an area or surface is **intersected** by something such as roads or lines, they cross the area or surface and divide it into smaller areas. *The centre of Caracas is intersected by broad avenues... The marshes were intersected by a maze of ditches*.

intersection /ɪntəsekʃn/ **intersections**
NC An **intersection** is a place where roads cross each other. ...*a city at the intersection of three motorways*.

intersperse /ɪntəspɜːs/ **intersperses, interspersing, interspersed**
VO If one thing is **interspersed** with a number of other things, these things occur here and there. ...*a street of old shops and houses interspersed with modern offices and banks... They've been interspersing programmes with decrees and announcements*.

interstate, interstates; pronounced /ɪntəsteɪt/ when it is a noun and /ɪntəsteɪt/ when it is an adjective.
1 NC In the United States, an **interstate** is a main road that goes between states. *Bowater is a mile away from the interstate... Clean-up crews are expected to work throughout the day trying to reopen the*

southbound lanes of Interstate 75.
2 ADJ ATTRIB **Interstate** means between states; used especially of the United States. *...the interstate highway... Less certain are the prospects for interstate banking.*

interstellar /ɪntəstelə/
ADJ ATTRIB **Interstellar** means between the stars; a formal word. *...interstellar travel. ...the nature of interstellar space.*

interstice /ɪntɜːstɪs/ **interstices**
NC **Interstices** are small gaps or cracks between things that are very close together; a formal word. *...pieces of limestone and granite, the interstices padded with wet earth.*

intertwine /ɪntətwaɪn/ **intertwines, intertwining, intertwined**
V-ERG or V-RECIP If two things **intertwine** or are **intertwined**, they are joined together in a very close or complicated way. *Their tails intertwine... Reality and art are intertwined... Gold was intertwined with silver round the handle of the goblet.*

interval /ɪntəvl/ **intervals**
1 NC The **interval** between two events or dates is the period of time between them. *...the interval between supper and bedtime. ...after an interval of ten years.*
2 NC At a play or concert, an **interval** is a break between two of the parts. *The audience were going out for the interval.*
● **Interval** is used in these phrases. ● If something happens **at intervals**, it happens several times, with gaps or pauses in between. *At intervals, the carriage was halted... They were not checked at regular intervals.* ● If things are placed at particular **intervals**, there are spaces of a particular size between them. *They were scattered through the forest, at varying intervals.*

intervene /ɪntəviːn/ **intervenes, intervening, intervened**
1 V If you **intervene** in a situation, you become involved in it and try to change it. *Two officers intervened to stop their recording... The State may intervene in disputes between employers and workers... So far the federal government has not intervened.*
2 V If you **intervene** when someone is speaking, you interrupt in order to say something. *Mr Gorbachev intervened to say he favoured these proposals.*
3 V You can say that something such as an event or bad weather **intervenes** when it delays something or prevents it from happening. *The weather intervened, and strong winds prevented the spray planes from flying and the small boats from sailing.*

intervening /ɪntəviːnɪŋ/
ADJ ATTRIB An **intervening** period of time is one which separates two events or points in time. *What happened in the intervening years?*

intervention /ɪntəvenʃn/ **interventions**
1 NU or NC **Intervention** is an attempt to change a situation by becoming involved in it. *He was against American intervention in the war... The other pressure was military intervention. ...the interventions of government.*
2 NC An **intervention** during a discussion is an interruption. *...the angry interventions of Lord Grant.*

interview /ɪntəvjuː/ **interviews, interviewing, interviewed**
1 NC or NU An **interview** is a formal meeting at which someone is asked questions in order to find out if they are suitable for a job or a course of study. *I had an interview for a job on a newspaper... He was invited for interview at three universities.*
2 NC An **interview** is also a conversation in which a journalist asks a famous person questions. *Earlier, Mr Gorbachev, in an interview with American journalists, indicated he would welcome a further summit... In a BBC television interview, he said the idea was to create people committed to a system which delivered prosperity.*
3 VO When an employer **interviews** you, he or she asks you questions in order to find out whether you are suitable for a job. *I was once interviewed for a part in a film.*

4 VO When the police **interview** someone, they ask them questions about a crime that has been committed. *A police spokesman said this morning that the man had been arrested and interviewed about the murder.*
5 VO When a famous person is **interviewed**, a journalist asks them a series of questions. *Hopkins was interviewed by Wyndham for Queen magazine.*

interviewee /ɪntəvjuːiː/ **interviewees**
NC An **interviewee** is a person who is being interviewed. *The interviewee was an unknown factory worker.*

interviewer /ɪntəvjuːə/ **interviewers**
NC An **interviewer** is the person who asks questions in an interview. *Television interviewers were being too aggressive.*

interweave /ɪntəwiːv/ **interweaves, interweaving, interwove, interwoven**
V-ERG or V-RECIP If two or more things **interweave** or are **interwoven**, they are joined together in a very close or complicated way. *You could see the columns of smoke interweaving... The four voices were interwoven in a beautifully sung quartet... The new show is a mystical fairy-tale, interweaving all the themes of comedy and dark unsettling menace.*

interwoven /ɪntəwəʊvn/
ADJ If things are **interwoven**, they are very closely connected. *Social and international unity have become interwoven. ...one of many interwoven trends.*

intestate /ɪntesteɪt/
ADV If someone dies **intestate**, they die without having made a will.

intestinal /ɪntestɪnl/
ADJ ATTRIB **Intestinal** means relating to the intestines. *...an intestinal infection.*

intestine /ɪntestɪn/ **intestines**
NC Your **intestines** are the tubes in your body through which food from your stomach passes. *...pains in the intestine.*

intimacy /ɪntɪməsi/
NU When there is **intimacy** between people, they have a very close relationship. *Never before had he known such intimacy with another person.*

intimate, intimates, intimating, intimated;
pronounced /ɪntɪmət/ when it is an adjective and /ɪntɪmeɪt/ when it is a verb.
1 ADJ If two people have an **intimate** relationship, they are very good friends. *...her best and most intimate friend.* ◆ **intimately** ADV *I don't know any girls intimately.*
2 ADJ **Intimate** also means personal and private. *...the most intimate details of their personal lives.* ◆ **intimately** ADV *...women talking intimately to other women.*
3 ADJ To be **intimate** with someone means to have a sexual relationship with them; an old-fashioned use. *He had been intimate with a number of women.*
4 ADJ An **intimate** connection is a very close one. *...its intimate bonds with government.* ◆ **intimately** ADV *These two questions are intimately linked.*
5 ADJ ATTRIB If you have an **intimate** knowledge of something, you know it in great detail. *...someone with an intimate knowledge of the station.* ◆ **intimately** ADV *He knew the contents of the files intimately.*
6 V-REPORT or VO If you **intimate** that something is the case, you say it in an indirect way; a formal use. *Forbes intimated that he would prefer to do this later... Let me ask you about something that you intimated.*

intimation /ɪntɪmeɪʃn/ **intimations**
NC+SUPP If you have an **intimation** of something, you feel that it exists or is true; a literary word. *For the first time I felt some intimation of danger. ...the first intimations of a new idea.*

intimidate /ɪntɪmɪdeɪt/ **intimidates, intimidating, intimidated**
VO To **intimidate** someone means to frighten them, usually as a deliberate way of making them do something. *In 1972 his neighbours intimidated his family into leaving.* ◆ **intimidation** /ɪntɪmɪdeɪʃn/ NU *Young suffered imprisonment and intimidation... The authorities reacted with intimidation, physical violence*

and imprisonment.

intimidated /ɪntɪmɪdeɪtɪd/
ADJ If you are **intimidated** by someone, you are afraid of them and have no confidence in yourself. *Theo was intimidated by so many strangers.*

intimidating /ɪntɪmɪdeɪtɪŋ/
ADJ If someone or something is **intimidating**, it causes you to feel afraid and to lose confidence in yourself. *The rooms were huge and intimidating. ...Police deny there will be any intimidating police presence.*

into /ɪntə, ɪntu, ɪntuː/
1 PREP If you put one thing **into** another thing, you put the first thing inside the second thing. *Pour some water into a glass... He slipped the note into his pocket.*
2 PREP If one thing goes **into** another, the first thing moves from the outside to the inside of the second thing, by breaking or damaging the surface of it. *She stuck her knitting needles into the ball of wool... She bit into the apple.*
3 PREP If you go **into** a place or get **into** a vehicle, you go inside it. *He walked into a police station... They got into the car.*
4 PREP If one thing gets **into** another thing, the first thing enters the second thing and becomes part of it. *Drugs may get into the milk. ...Britain's entry into the Common Market.*
5 PREP If you bump or crash **into** something, you hit it accidentally. *I bumped into a chair.*
6 PREP If you get **into** a piece of clothing, you put it on. *She changed into her best dress.*
7 PREP To get **into** a particular state means to start being in that state. *The Labour Government came into power in 1974... The assembly was shocked into silence.*
8 PREP If something is changed **into** a new form or shape, it then has this new form or shape. *The bud develops into a flower... The play was made into a movie... I tore her letter into eight pieces.*
9 PREP An investigation **into** a subject or event is concerned with that subject or event. *...research into emotional problems... Some MPs demanded a full enquiry into the incident.*
10 PREP If you move or go **into** a particular career, you start working in it. *I'd like to move into marketing.*
11 PREP If you are very interested in something and like it very much, you can say that you are **into** it; an informal use. *Teenagers are into those romantic novels.*

intolerable /ɪntɒlərəbl/
ADJ If something is **intolerable**, it is so bad that people cannot tolerate it or accept it. *They were protesting at an economic crisis which has made their lives intolerable.* ◆ **intolerably** ADV *The days were still intolerably hot.*

intolerance /ɪntɒlərəns/
NU **Intolerance** is unwillingness to let other people act in a different way or hold different opinions from you; used showing disapproval. *She accused the men of ignorance and intolerance... He complained about the intolerance of the party. ...a world engulfed in hatred and intolerance.*

intolerant /ɪntɒlərənt/
ADJ **Intolerant** people disapprove of behaviour and opinions that differ from their own; used showing disapproval. *He was intolerant of other people's weakness... We are giving support to intolerant regimes.*

intonation /ɪntəneɪʃn/ **intonations**
NU or NC Your **intonation** is the way your voice rises and falls when you speak. *...the subtleties of middle-class intonation. ...their accents and intonations.*

intone /ɪntəʊn/ **intones, intoning, intoned**
V or V-QUOTE If you **intone** something, you say it in a slow and serious way, not allowing your voice to rise and fall very much; a literary word. *They intoned the afternoon prayers... A dark voice intoned 'except a man die and be born again'.*

intoxicant /ɪntɒksɪkənt/ **intoxicants**
NC You refer to alcohol as an **intoxicant** when you are emphasizing the fact that it can cause you to become

drunk; a formal word.

intoxicated /ɪntɒksɪkeɪtɪd/
1 ADJ If someone is **intoxicated**, they are drunk; a formal use. *He was charged with driving while intoxicated.*
2 ADJ PRED If you are **intoxicated** by an event, idea, or feeling, it makes you behave in an excited and uncontrolled way; a literary use. *Intoxicated by victory, he was dancing... They became intoxicated with pride.*

intoxicating /ɪntɒksɪkeɪtɪŋ/
1 ADJ An **intoxicating** drink contains alcohol and can make you drunk. *...a fruity, intoxicating wine.*
2 ADJ Something that is **intoxicating** causes you to be very excited and to behave in an uncontrolled or foolish way. *The euphoria in the Baltic states has been intoxicating as they attempt to reassert their identities. ...her intoxicating beauty.*

intoxication /ɪntɒksɪkeɪʃn/
1 NU **Intoxication** is the state of being drunk. *They were in an advanced state of intoxication.*
2 NU **Intoxication** is also the state of being so excited that you behave in an uncontrolled or foolish way. *...the intoxication of success.*

intractable /ɪntræktəbl/; a formal word.
1 ADJ **Intractable** people are stubborn and difficult to influence or control. *On one issue Luce was intractable.*
2 ADJ **Intractable** problems seem impossible to deal with. *Labour problems can be more intractable.*

intransigence /ɪntrænsɪdʒəns/
NU+POSS **Intransigence** is refusal to behave differently or to change your attitude to something; a formal word, used showing disapproval. *...the intransigence of the landowners. ...the Government's intransigence over price controls.*

intransigent /ɪntrænsɪdʒənt/
ADJ If someone is **intransigent**, they refuse to change their behaviour or opinions; a formal word, used showing disapproval. *...their intransigent attitude over our debts.*

intransitive /ɪntrænsətɪv/
ADJ An **intransitive** verb does not have an object.

intravenous /ɪntrəviːnəs/
ADJ ATTRIB **Intravenous** foods or drugs are given to sick people through their veins, rather than their mouths. *We fed them an intravenous sugar solution... The intravenous fluids kept him alive.* ◆ **intravenously** ADV *Steve had been fed intravenously.*

in tray, in trays
NC An **in tray** is a tray or shallow basket used in offices to put letters and documents in when they arrive or when they are waiting to be dealt with. *There are all sorts of bits of paper coming into the in tray, and they have all got to be filed sometime.*

intrepid /ɪntrepɪd/
ADJ An **intrepid** person acts bravely, ignoring difficulties and danger; a literary word. *...the route of those intrepid explorers.*

intricacy /ɪntrɪkəsi/ **intricacies**
1 N PL The **intricacies** of a situation are its complicated or subtle details. *...the intricacies of American politics.*
2 NU The **intricacy** of something is the fact that it has many parts or details. *...the technical intricacy of modern industry.*

intricate /ɪntrɪkət/
ADJ Something that is **intricate** has many small parts or details. *They were painted in intricate patterns. ...long, intricate discussions.* ◆ **intricately** ADV *...an intricately carved door.*

intrigue, intrigues, intriguing, intrigued; pronounced /ɪntriːg/ when it is a noun and /ɪntriːg/ when it is a verb.
1 NU or NC **Intrigue** is the making of secret plans that are intended to harm other people. *...a great deal of political intrigue. ...financial intrigues.*
2 VO If something **intrigues** you, you are fascinated by it and curious about it. *The idea seemed to intrigue him.* ◆ **intriguing** ADJ *That sounds most intriguing.*

intrigued /ɪntriːgd/
ADJ If you are **intrigued** by something, you are

fascinated by it and curious about it. *She seemed intrigued by all the smaller birds... Intrigued, I followed the instructions.*

intrinsic /ɪntrɪnsɪk/
ADJ ATTRIB The **intrinsic** qualities of something are its important and basic qualities; a formal word. *...the intrinsic idiocy of the plan. ...objects which have no intrinsic value.* ♦ **intrinsically** ADV *His material was intrinsically interesting.*

introduce /ɪntrədjuːs/ **introduces, introducing, introduced**
1 VO or V-REFLIf you **introduce** one person to another, you tell them each other's name, so that they can get to know each other. *Hogan introduced him to Karl... At a party in Hollywood, I was introduced to Charlie Chaplin... I had better introduce myself—I'm Mark Rodin.*
2 VO To **introduce** something means to cause it to exist in a place or system for the first time. *The British government is to introduce new legislation aimed at cutting funds to terrorist organisations... Vehicle manufacturers should introduce more safety factors... Rabbits had been introduced into Australia by Europeans.*
3 VO When someone **introduces** a television or radio programme which consists of a number of different reports, they tell you at the beginning of each report what it will be about and who will present it. *Tonight's edition was introduced by Paul Allen.*
4 VO If you **introduce** a subject in a talk or lecture, you begin to talk about it for the first time, usually in a general way. *This afternoon, I want to introduce the subject of metaphor.*
5 VO+to If you **introduce** someone to something, you cause them to have their first experience of it. *We introduced them to the new methods... He was first introduced to politics as a child.*

introduction /ɪntrədʌkʃn/ **introductions**
1 NU+SUPP The **introduction** of something is the occasion when it is caused to exist in a place or system for the first time. *The Government saw the introduction of new technology as vital.*
2 N SING Your **introduction** to something is the occasion when you experience it for the first time. *This was my first real introduction to agriculture.*
3 NC The **introduction** to a book or talk comes at the beginning and tells you what the rest of the book or talk is about. *This is a point which he makes in the introduction to his new book.*
4 NC When you make an **introduction**, you tell two people each other's names so that they can get to know each other. *Such first visits are usually an occasion for introductions and pleasantries.*

introductory /ɪntrədʌktəri/
ADJ ATTRIB **Introductory** remarks, books, or courses are intended to give you a general idea of a particular subject, often before more detailed information is given. *...a good introductory chapter on forests.*

introspection /ɪntrəspekʃn/
NU **Introspection** is the examining of your own thoughts, ideas, and feelings. *Such a move would signal the end of the Bush administration's period of introspection, which critics say has already gone on too long.*

introspective /ɪntrəspektɪv/
ADJ **Introspective** people spend a lot of time examining their own thoughts, ideas, and feelings. *The boy was downcast and introspective.*

introvert /ɪntrəvɜːt/ **introverts**
NC An **introvert** is a person who finds it difficult to talk to people and to make friends because he or she is quiet and shy. *...a bashful introvert.*

introverted /ɪntrəvɜːtɪd/
ADJ **Introverted** people find it difficult to talk to people and to make friends because they are quiet and shy. *Rosa was quiet and introverted.*

intrude /ɪntruːd/ **intrudes, intruding, intruded**
1 VA If someone **intrudes**, they go into a place where they are not supposed to be. *India accused Pakistan of trying to intrude into its territory... Mr Ryzhkov rejected allegations that Soviet submarines have been intruding into Swedish waters. ...a report from Tibet*

that unspecified Indian aircraft had intruded in the last few days.
2 V If you **intrude** on someone, you disturb them when they are in a private place or having a private conversation. *He felt that he couldn't intrude... I don't want to intrude on your family.*
3 V+on If something **intrudes** on your mood or your life, it disturbs it or has an unpleasant effect on it. *I shall not intrude on your grief.*

intruder /ɪntruːdə/ **intruders**
NC An **intruder** is a person who enters a place without permission. *An intruder had come into his home.*

intrusion /ɪntruːʒn/ **intrusions**
1 NC If someone disturbs you when you are in a private place or having a private conversation, you can describe their behaviour as an **intrusion**. *I must ask your pardon for this intrusion.*
2 NCorNU An **intrusion** is also something that affects your work or way of life in an unwelcome way. *...the bank's intrusions into Mr Wheeler's operations... Government could enforce the law with minimal intrusion.*

intrusive /ɪntruːsɪv/
ADJ If someone or something is **intrusive**, they disturb your mood or life in an unwelcome way. *...Gordon's intrusive interest in our religious activities.*

intuit /ɪntjuːɪt/ **intuits, intuiting, intuited**
V-REPORT If you **intuit** something, you guess it by using your feelings, rather than your knowledge; a formal word. *She intuited that Peter would be glad to see her.*

intuition /ɪntjuɪʃn/ **intuitions**
NUorNC If your **intuition** tells you that something is the case, or if you have an **intuition** about it, you feel that it is the case although you have no evidence or proof. *My intuition told me to stay away. ...arguments based on intuition... I've got an intuition that something is wrong.*

intuitive /ɪntjuːətɪv/
ADJ **Intuitive** ideas or feelings tell you that something is the case although you have no evidence or proof. *I got a strong intuitive feeling that he was lying. ...his intuitive understanding of nature.* ♦ **intuitively** ADV *I felt intuitively that they would not return.*

inundate /ɪnʌndeɪt/ **inundates, inundating, inundated**
1 VO If you **are inundated** with things, you receive so many of them that you cannot deal with them all. *She was inundated with telephone calls.*
2 VO If an area of land **is inundated**, it becomes covered in water; a formal use. *Rio's shanty towns have been inundated by overflowing rivers.*

inure /ɪnjuə/ **inures, inuring, inured**
V-REFL+toor V-PASS+to If you **inure** yourself to something unpleasant, you experience it so often that you learn to accept it; a formal word. *...people who inure themselves to tragedy. ...a man who was inured to disappointment.*

invade /ɪnveɪd/ **invades, invading, invaded**
1 VO To **invade** a country means to enter it by force with an army. *...Kennedy's secret plan to invade Cuba... In October 1940 Italian troops invaded Greece.*
2 VO When people or animals **invade** a place, they enter it in large numbers. *The town was invaded by reporters.*
3 VO If someone or something **invades** your privacy, they disturb you when you want to be left alone. *There are frequent complaints that journalists and press photographers invade people's privacy.*

invader /ɪnveɪdə/ **invaders**
1 N PL **Invaders** are soldiers who are invading a country. *Heavy fire greeted the invaders... They were cruel and sadistic invaders.*
2 N SING You can refer to a country or army that has invaded or is about to invade another country as the **invader**. *It will be no easy task to repel the invader... We may have to make peace with the invader.*

invalid, invalids; pronounced /ɪnvəlɪd/ for the meaning in paragraph 1, and /ɪnvælɪd/ for the meanings in paragraphs 2 and 3.
1 NCorN+N An **invalid** is someone who is very ill or disabled and needs to be cared for by someone else. *The family treated her like an invalid. ...her invalid*

mother who needed constant attention.
2 ADJ If an argument, conclusion, or result is **invalid**, it is not correct. *The comparison is invalid.*
♦ **invalidity** /ɪnvəlɪdəti/ NU *My experiments show the invalidity of his argument.*
3 ADJ If an official process, contract, or document is **invalid**, it is not legally acceptable. *The court ruled his election invalid... The result was declared invalid because less than fourteen per cent of the population turned out to vote.*

invalidate /ɪnvælɪdeɪt/ **invalidates, invalidating, invalidated**; a formal word.
1 VO If something **invalidates** an argument, conclusion, or result, it proves that it is wrong. *Such exceptions do not invalidate the rule.*
2 VO If something **invalidates** an official process, contract, or document, it makes it legally unacceptable. *The marriage would invalidate any earlier will.*

invaluable /ɪnvæljuəbl/
ADJ If someone or something is **invaluable**, they are extremely useful. *This experience proved invaluable later on.*

invariable /ɪnveəriəbl/
ADJ Something that is **invariable** always happens or never changes. *They followed an invariable routine... This process, however, was not invariable.*
♦ **invariably** /ɪnveəriəbli/ ADV *The conversation invariably returns to politics.*

invasion /ɪnveɪʒn/ **invasions**
1 NCorNU When there is an **invasion** of a country, an army enters it by force. *...the invasion of Europe by the Allies in 1944... It enabled us to remain free from invasion.*
2 NU+SUPP You can refer to the arrival of large numbers of things or people as an **invasion** of them. *...the invasion of Italian movies in the fifties.*

invective /ɪnvektɪv/
NU **Invective** is very rude and unpleasant things that people say when they are very angry or annoyed with someone; a formal word. *...women hurling invective at us... A torrent of invective awaited them.*

inveigh /ɪnveɪ/ **inveighs, inveighing, inveighed**
V+*against* If you **inveigh** against something, you criticize it strongly; a formal word. *It is fashionable in some quarters to inveigh against a 'competitive ladder' society.*

inveigle /ɪnveɪgl/ **inveigles, inveigling, inveigled**
VO+*into* or VO If you **inveigle** someone into doing something, you cleverly persuade them to do it when they do not really want to; a formal word. *The Duke tried to inveigle him into his service... He was inveigled into meeting a few more people... He could not inveigle Benny as he had the others.*

invent /ɪnvent/ **invents, inventing, invented**
1 VO If you **invent** something, you are the first person to think of it or make it. *...the men who invented the sewing machine... He invented this phrase himself.*
2 VO If you **invent** a story or excuse, you try to persuade people that it is true when it is not. *...lies invented for a political purpose.*

invention /ɪnvenʃn/ **inventions**
1 NC An **invention** is a machine or system that has been invented by someone. *Writing was the most revolutionary of all human inventions.*
2 NC If you refer to someone's account of something as an **invention**, you mean that it is not true and that they have made it up. *The account was a deliberate and malicious invention.*
3 NU+SUPP When someone creates something that has never existed before, you can refer to this event as the **invention** of the thing. *...the invention of printing.*
4 NU **Invention** is also the ability to have clever and original ideas. *...his powers of invention.*

inventive /ɪnventɪv/
ADJ An **inventive** person is good at inventing things or has clever and original ideas. *He is inventive in dealing with physical problems.* ♦ **inventiveness** NU *The musicians can play, even if they do lack inventiveness.*

inventor /ɪnventə/ **inventors**
NC An **inventor** is a person who has invented

something, or whose job it is to invent things. *She was the inventor of modern ballet. ...a novel wind turbine devised by a British inventor.*

inventory /ɪnvəntəri/ **inventories**
1 NC An **inventory** is a written list of the assets, resources, goods, etc that an organization owns or that are in a place. *Provincial governments have been instructed to make inventories of all their assets... An inventory was made of all the objects in Highclere Castle.*
2 NCorNU An **inventory** is also a supply or stock of something; used in American English. *Mr Bush also dropped his insistence that the US be allowed to retain a small inventory of chemical weapons for self-defense... After Christmas what retailers are trying to do is unload the excess inventory that they've got.*

inverse /ɪnvɜːs/; a formal word.
1 ADJ If there is an **inverse** relationship between two things or amounts, one of them decreases as the other increases. *The time spent varies in inverse proportion to the amount of work done.*
2 N SING The **inverse** of something is its exact opposite. *It represents the inverse of everything I find worth preserving... The inverse case is also worth considering.*

inversion /ɪnvɜːʃn/ **inversions**
NC When there is an **inversion** of something, it is changed into its opposite; a formal word. *...this curious inversion of facts. ...an inversion of the expected order.*

invert /ɪnvɜːt/ **inverts, inverting, inverted**
VO If you **invert** something, you turn it upside down; a formal word. *The chairs are inverted on the tables.*
♦ **inverted** ADJ *It was shaped like an inverted cone.*

invertebrate /ɪnvɜːtɪbrət/ **invertebrates**
NC An **invertebrate** is a creature without a spine, for example an insect, worm, or octopus. *The fish and invertebrate creatures there differ in many respects from those in warmer waters.*

inverted commas
N PL **Inverted commas** are the punctuation marks (' ') or (" ") that are used in writing to indicate where speech or a quotation begins and ends.

invest /ɪnvest/ **invests, investing, invested**
1 VO, VO+*in*, or V+*in* If you **invest** an amount of money, or **invest** it in something, you pay it into a bank or buy something such as shares or property with it, because you think that you will be able to earn more money from it. *£20 million of public money had been invested... Much of the money was invested in property... A unit trust is an attractive way of investing in stocks and shares... They invest in horses which they hope will make them a fortune in stud fees some time in the future.*
2 V+*in* If you **invest** in something useful, you buy it because it will help you to do something more efficiently or cheaply or because it will last a long time. *A number of people have invested in night storage heaters... Good shoes are worth investing in even though they are expensive.*
3 VOorV If you **invest** money, time, or energy in something, you use it to try to make the thing successful; a formal use. *They are willing to invest energy in a European disarmament campaign... They have failed to invest in job creation in the cities.*
4 VO+*with* To **invest** someone with rights or responsibilities means to give them those rights or responsibilities legally or officially; a formal use. *The law invests the shareholders alone with legal rights.*

investigate /ɪnvestɪgeɪt/ **investigates, investigating, investigated**
VOorV If you **investigate** an event, situation, or allegation, you examine all the facts connected with it in order to discover the truth. *He had come to investigate a murder... The Senate decided to set up a committee to investigate allegations of corruption in the government... I sent my men to investigate.*

investigation /ɪnvestɪgeɪʃn/ **investigations**
NCorNU An **investigation** is a process in which you examine all the facts connected with an event, situation, or allegation in order to discover the truth. *...the results of their investigations... She was*

admitted to hospital for further investigation... He is now under investigation in connection with the murder of a Protestant priest.

investigative /ɪnvɛstɪgətɪv/
ADJ ATTRIB **Investigative** activities involve examining all the facts connected with an event, situation, or allegation in order to discover the truth. He was doing investigative work on Kennedy. ...investigative reporters.

investigator /ɪnvɛstɪgeɪtə/ **investigators**
NC An **investigator** is someone whose job is to investigate events, situations, or allegations. Aircraft accident investigators got to the scene quickly.

investigatory /ɪnvɛstɪgətri/
ADJ ATTRIB **Investigatory** activities or organizations are concerned with investigating all the facts connected with an event, situation, or person. The CIR should be retained, but with its investigatory role only.

investiture /ɪnvɛstɪtʃə/ **investitures**
NC An **investiture** is a ceremony in which someone is given an official title. ...plans for the Investiture of Prince Charles as Prince of Wales.

investment /ɪnvɛstmənt/ **investments**
1 NU **Investment** is the activity of buying shares or of putting money into a bank account in order to obtain a profit. We aim to encourage investment... This would enable them to attract foreign investment.
2 NC An **investment** is an amount of money that you pay into a bank or buy something such as shares or property with, because you think that you will be able to earn more money from it. ...a better return on the investment... How safe are these investments?
3 NC You can refer to something that you buy as an **investment** when you think that you will be able to earn more money from it. Property is still a good investment.
4 N SING You can refer to something useful that you buy as an **investment**. The tractors proved a superb investment.

investor /ɪnvɛstə/ **investors**
NC An **investor** is a person who buys shares or who pays money into a bank in order to receive a profit. The investor is entitled to a reasonable return on his money... Investors sought to recover losses sustained earlier in the week.

inveterate /ɪnvɛtərət/.
ADJ ATTRIB You use **inveterate** to say that someone has been doing something for a long time and that they are not likely to stop doing it. For example, an **inveterate** liar is someone who has always told lies and who will probably continue to tell lies; a formal word. Hubert had been an inveterate hunter. ...their inveterate distrust of others.

invidious /ɪnvɪdiəs/
1 ADJ An **invidious** task or job is unpleasant to do, because it is likely to make you unpopular. The role of a critic can be an invidious one.
2 ADJ An **invidious** comparison or choice between two things is unfair because the two things cannot really be compared, or because there is only one thing you can choose. He defended American police against invidious comparisons with Scotland Yard... This involves an invidious choice.

invigilate /ɪnvɪdʒɪleɪt/ **invigilates, invigilating, invigilated**
V orV If a teacher **invigilates** an examination, she or he supervises the people who are taking it in order to ensure that it starts and finishes at the correct time, and also to prevent cheating. He wrote this whilst invigilating a biology examination.

invigilator /ɪnvɪdʒɪleɪtə/ **invigilators**
NC An **invigilator** is someone who supervises the people taking an examination. ...attempts made by invigilators to stop the students cheating.

invigorated /ɪnvɪgəreɪtɪd/
ADJ If you feel **invigorated**, you feel more energetic than you did because you have just been involved in something that has refreshed you. He felt invigorated... The audience left fresh and invigorated.

invigorating /ɪnvɪgəreɪtɪŋ/
ADJ Something that is **invigorating** makes you feel more energetic. The air here is invigorating. ...an invigorating bath.

invincible /ɪnvɪnsəbl/
ADJ An **invincible** army or sports team is very powerful and difficult to defeat; a formal word. They are invincible in battle. ...the invincible Real Madrid side of the early sixties.

inviolable /ɪnvaɪələbl/
ADJ If a principle or law is **inviolable**, you cannot or must not break it; a formal word. Tradition was considered inviolable.

inviolate /ɪnvaɪələt/
ADJ Something that is **inviolate** has not been or cannot be harmed or affected; a formal word. The rule of law is inviolate... The church's seclusion is inviolate.

invisible /ɪnvɪzəbl/
1 ADJ If something is **invisible**, you cannot see it, because it is hidden or because it is very small or faint. Her legs were invisible beneath the table. ...hairs invisible to the naked eye. ♦ **invisibly** SUBMOD ...draw the lines almost invisibly pale. ♦ **invisibility** /ɪnvɪzəbɪləti/ NU The main advantage is the submarine's invisibility.
2 ADJ ATTRIB **Invisible** earnings are the money that a country makes as a result of services such as banking and tourism, rather than by producing goods. Invisible exports such as tourism and foreign labour are down... The large deficit in trade in goods was partly offset by a sixty-million pound surplus on trade in invisible items.
3 ADJ In stories, **invisible** people or things cannot be seen by anyone. He waves his magic wand and turns himself invisible.

invitation /ɪnvɪteɪʃn/ **invitations**
1 NC An **invitation** is a written or spoken request to come to an event such as a party, meal, or meeting. Cindy accepted invitations to cocktail parties... I had an invitation to go and talk to the cadets.
2 NC The card or paper on which an invitation is written is also called an **invitation**. Jenny was waving the invitation.
3 N SING+SUPP Behaviour that encourages you to do something can be referred to as an **invitation**. Houses left unlocked are an open invitation to burglary.

invitational /ɪnvɪteɪʃəºnəl/
ADJ ATTRIB An **invitational** sports event is one in which players can only compete if they have been invited to compete. The Scottish basketball team, Livingstone, won the annual World Invitational Tournament at Crystal Palace in London last night. ...the Las Vegas Invitational Tournament.

invite /ɪnvaɪt/ **invites, inviting, invited**
1 VO If you **invite** someone to a party or a meal, you ask them to come to it. Leggett invited me for lunch at the hotel.
2 VO If you **are invited** to do something, you are formally asked to do it. I was invited to attend future meetings... He was invited for interview.
3 VO To **invite** something such as confidence or disbelief means to cause people to have this attitude towards you; a formal use. This kind of statement invites disbelief.
4 VO To **invite** danger or trouble means to make it more likely; a formal use. To speak of it to others would invite danger.

inviting /ɪnvaɪtɪŋ/
ADJ If you say that something is **inviting**, you mean it is attractive and desirable. The place was green and inviting. ...large dark eyes, shy but inviting. ♦ **invitingly** ADV The packet of cigarettes lay invitingly open.

invocation /ɪnvəkeɪʃn/ **invocations**
NCorNU An **invocation** is a spoken request to a god for help or forgiveness. They murmured invocations to the gods.

invoice /ɪnvɔɪs/ **invoices, invoicing, invoiced**
1 NC An **invoice** is an official document that lists the goods or services that you have received from a person or company and says how much money you owe them. The families were stunned when they read invoices billing them for several thousand dollars.
2 VO To **invoice** someone means to send them an invoice. Have they invoiced us for the stationery yet?

invoke /ɪnvˈəʊk/ **invokes, invoking, invoked;** a formal
word.
1 vo If you **invoke** a law, you use it to justify what
you are doing. *The Government invoked the
Emergency Powers Act.*
2 vo To **invoke** feelings of a particular kind means to
cause someone to feel them. *They tried to invoke
popular enthusiasm for the war.*

involuntary /ɪnvˈɒləntəʳri/
1 ADJ An **involuntary** action is one that is done
suddenly and unintentionally because you are unable
to control yourself. *There were one or two involuntary
exclamations... 'Ugh!' he exclaimed with an
involuntary shudder.* ◆ **involuntarily** ADV *I shivered
involuntarily.*
2 ADJ You use **involuntary** to describe an action or
situation when the people who are affected by it are
forced to accept it, usually by someone in authority.
*...a scheme of involuntary repatriation for all those
who are found not to be genuine refugees... The Police
Commission has put him on paid involuntary leave for
sixty days while it continues its investigation.*
◆ **involuntarily** ADV *Some are mental patients who
have been confined to institutions involuntarily.*

involve /ɪnvˈɒlv/ **involves, involving, involved**
1 vo or v+ING If an activity **involves** something, that
thing is included or used in it. *Some of the
experiments involve the equipment you've seen... The
report follows a number of incidents involving police
use of firearms... Caring for a one-year-old involves
changing nappies.*
2 vo Something that **involves** you concerns or affects
you. *Workers are never told about things which
involve them.*
3 V-REFL If you **involve** yourself in something, you
take part in it. *They involve themselves deeply in
community affairs.*
4 vo If you **involve** someone else in something, you
get them to take part in it. *Did you have to involve
me in this?*

involved /ɪnvˈɒlvd/
1 ADJ PRED or ADJ after N If you are **involved** in a
situation or activity, you are taking part in it. *Should
religious leaders get involved in politics?... He
appealed to all the parties involved to show restraint.*
2 ADJ PRED If you are deeply **involved** in something
you are doing, you feel very strongly or
enthusiastically about it. *I was deeply involved in my
work... She became terribly involved with writing.*
3 ADJ after N or ADJ PRED The things **involved** in
something such as a job or system are the things that
are required in order to do it or understand it. *There
is quite a lot of work involved... Explain the principles
involved... What is involved in making a television
programme?*
4 ADJ If you describe a situation or activity as
involved, you mean that it is very complicated. *We
had long involved discussions.*
5 ADJ PRED If you are **involved** with another person,
you are having a close relationship with them. *He had
become involved with her in Brussels.*

involvement /ɪnvˈɒlvmənt/
1 NU Your **involvement** in something is the fact that
you are taking part in it. *...parental involvement in
schools. ...the active involvement of workers... He
would not rule out military involvement by the United
States.*
2 NU **Involvement** is also the concern and enthusiasm
that you feel about something. *...his deep involvement
with socialism.*

invulnerable /ɪnvˈʌlnərəbl/
ADJ If someone or something is **invulnerable**, they
cannot be harmed or damaged. *The nuclear
submarine is almost invulnerable to attack.*
◆ **invulnerability** /ɪnvˌʌlnərəbˈɪləti/ NU *There's this
dangerous sense of invulnerability, of immortality.*

inward /ɪnwəd/ **inwards.** In normal British English,
inwards is an adverb and **inward** is an adjective. In
formal British English and in American English,
inward is both an adjective and an adverb.
1 ADJ ATTRIB Your **inward** thoughts or feelings are the
ones that you do not express or show to other people.

...my inward happiness. ◆ **inwardly** ADV *I remained
inwardly unconvinced.*
2 ADV If something moves or faces **inward** or **inwards**,
it moves or faces towards the inside or centre of
something. *The door swung inward... His cell faced
inwards. ...an inward flow of air.*

inward-looking
ADJ **Inward-looking** people and societies are more
interested in themselves than in other people or
societies. *Mrs Thatcher is against a tightly-formed,
inward-looking European Community.*

inwards /ɪnwədz/. See **inward**.

iodine /ˈaɪədiːn/
NU **Iodine** is a dark-coloured substance used in
medicine and photography. *The next thing to do is to
apply a disinfectant such as alcohol or iodine.*

ion /ˈaɪən, ˈaɪɒn/ **ions**
NC **Ions** are electrically charged atoms; a technical
term. *...calcium ions. ...ions of nitrogen.*

-ion /-jən, -ən/ **-ions.** See **-ation.**

ioniser /ˈaɪənaɪzə/ **ionisers**
NC An **ioniser** is a device which emits negative ions
into the atmosphere of a room. This is believed to
have a good effect on people. *Ionisers negatively
charge the air to refresh it. They don't actually
remove pollutants.*

iota /aɪˈəʊtə/
N SING You can refer to an extremely small amount of
something as an **iota**. *I don't feel one iota of guilt... I
don't think you've changed an iota.*

IOU /ˌaɪəʊjuː/ **IOUs**
NC An **IOU** is a written promise to pay back money
that you have borrowed. **IOU** represents 'I owe you'.
He wrote out an IOU for five thousand dollars.

IPA /ˌaɪpiːˈeɪ/
N U or N SING **IPA** is the most widely used system of
representing the sounds of human speech. The
pronunciations in this dictionary use IPA symbols. **IPA**
is an abbreviation for 'International Phonetic
Alphabet'.

IQ /ˌaɪkjuː/ **IQs**
NU+SUPP Your **IQ** is your level of intelligence,
measured by a special test. **IQ** is an abbreviation for
'intelligence quotient'. *I think an IQ of 120 is enough
for anything... Modern researchers also believe that a
high IQ is not the key to genuine creativity.*

IRA /ˌaɪɑːrˈeɪ/
N PROP The **IRA** is an organization that wants
Northern Ireland to become independent of the United
Kingdom and to be united politically with the Irish
Republic. It sometimes uses violence to try to achieve
this. **IRA** is an abbreviation for 'Irish Republican
Army'. *The prison hunger strike increased support for
the IRA... Four men were shot dead in an IRA
ambush yesterday.*

Iran /ɪrˈɑːn/
The **Islamic Republic of Iran** is a country in western
Asia, east of Iraq. It was ruled by Shah Pahlavi from
1941 to 1979, when the Ayatollah Khomeini returned
from exile and the Shah fled the country. The
Ayatollah opposed the increasing westernization of
Iran and called for a return to traditional Muslim
values. Iran was at war with Iraq from 1980 until 1988.
Ayatollah Khomeini was the Wali Faqih (spiritual
leader) until his death in 1989 and was succeeded by
Ayatollah Ali Khamenei. Hojatoleslam Hashemi Ali
Akbar Rafsanjani, of the Islamic Republican Party,
became President in 1989. Iran produces oil and is a
member of OPEC. ◆ **Iranian** /ɪrˈeɪniən/ N, ADJ
▪ *per capita GNP:* approximately US$3,716 ▪ *religion:*
Islam (mainly Shia) ▪ *language:* Farsi (Persian)
(official) ▪ *currency:* rial ▪ *capital:* Tehrän
▪ *population:* 50 million (1989) ▪ *size:* 1,648,000 square
kilometres.

Iraq /ɪrˈɑːk/
The **Republic of Iraq** is a country in western Asia,
west of Iran. The Arab Baath Socialist Party has been
in power since 1968. Saddam Hussain became
President in 1979. In 1980 Iraq invaded Iran, beginning
the Iran-Iraq War, which continued until a ceasefire in
1988. In 1990 Iraq invaded Kuwait. In the Gulf War of
1991, the US and its allies expelled Iraqi troops from

Kuwait. Iraq produces oil, but all its pipelines were closed after the invasion of Kuwait. It is a member of OPEC and the Arab League. ◆ **Iraqi** /ɪrɑːki/ N, ADJ ▪ *per capita GNP:* approximately US$3,654 ▪ *religion:* Islam ▪ *language:* Arabic (official), Kurdish ▪ *currency:* dinar ▪ *capital:* Baghdad ▪ *population:* 18 million (1989) ▪ *size:* 438,317 square kilometres.

irascible /ɪræsəbl/
ADJ An **irascible** person becomes angry very easily; a formal word. *He is irascible and violent. ...Jeff's irascible outbursts.*

irate /aɪreɪt/
ADJ If you are **irate**, you are very angry; a formal word. *The Bishop looked irate. ...irate customers. ...an irate letter.*

ire /aɪə/
NU **Ire** is anger; a literary word. *He incurred the ire of the authorities.*

Ireland (Eire) /aɪələnd/
The **Republic of Ireland** is a country in north-west Europe. When it achieved independence from Britain in 1920, the six northern counties known as Northern Ireland or Ulster remained part of the United Kingdom. IRA opposition to the partition of Ireland has caused civil unrest to the present. The Republic of Ireland is a member of the European Community. Mary Robinson, an independent, became President in 1990. Albert Reynolds, of Fianna Fáil, became Prime Minister in 1992 following the resignation of Charles Haughey. Ireland exports meat and dairy products. Tourism is an important industry. ◆ **Irishman, Irishwoman** /aɪrɪʃmən, aɪrɪʃwumən/ N **Irish** /aɪrɪʃ/ ADJ, N PL ▪ *per capita GNP:* US$7,480 ▪ *religion:* Christianity (mainly Roman Catholic) ▪ *language:* English, Irish ▪ *currency:* punt ▪ *capital:* Dublin ▪ *population:* 4 million (1989) ▪ *size:* 70,283 square kilometres.

iridescent /ɪrɪdesnt/
ADJ Something that is **iridescent** has bright colours that seem to keep changing; a literary word. *...the iridescent blue and orange glow. ...iridescent feathers.*

iris /aɪrɪs/ **irises**
1 NC The **iris** in your eye is the round coloured part. *The irises were of flecked grey. ...inflammation of their irises.*
2 NC An **iris** is also a tall plant with long leaves and large purple, yellow, or white flowers. *The cottage gardens blaze with irises, lilies, and peonies.*

Irish /aɪrɪʃ/
1 ADJ **Irish** means belonging or relating to the Republic of Ireland, or to any part of Ireland. *...the Irish Prime Minister... She spoke with an Irish accent.*
2 N PL The **Irish** are the people who come from Ireland. *The majority of the Irish accept these proposals.*

Irishman /aɪrɪʃmən/ **Irishmen** /aɪrɪʃmən/
NC An **Irishman** is a man who comes from Ireland. *The UN will supply a monitoring team of military officers including Finns, Austrians, Swedes, Irishmen and Canadians.*

Irishwoman /aɪrɪʃwumən/ **Irishwomen**
NC An **Irishwoman** is a woman who comes from Ireland. *Two Irishmen and an Irishwoman have pleaded not guilty at the Crown Court in Winchester.*

irk /ɜːk/ **irks, irking, irked**
VO If something **irks** you, it irritates or annoys you; a formal word. *What seems to irk the Moldavians most of all is the apparent unexpectedness of the demands.*

irksome /ɜːksəm/
ADJ If something is **irksome**, it irritates or annoys you; a formal word. *He would find these constraints most irksome... The impact on the taxpayer was irksome and unwarranted.*

iron /aɪən/ **irons, ironing, ironed**
1 NU or N+N **Iron** is a hard, dark metal used to make steel, and also to make objects such as gates and fences. Very small amounts of iron occur in your blood and in food. *...a lump of iron. ...an iron bar. ...the iron and steel industries... Seaweed has a high iron content.*
2 NC An **iron** is an electrical device with a heated flat metal base. You rub it over clothes to remove creases. *If it's cotton or linen, use a hot iron.*
3 VO If you **iron** clothes, you remove the creases from them using an iron. *I can't iron shirts.* ◆ **ironing** NU *She's doing the ironing.*
4 ADJ ATTRIB You can use **iron** to describe the character or behaviour of someone who is very firm in their decisions and actions, or who can control their feelings well. *He was able to enforce his iron will. ...her iron composure.*

iron out PHRASAL VERB If you **iron out** difficulties, you make them disappear; an informal expression. *There are still a few points to be ironed out before the meeting can be concluded.*

Iron Age
N PROP The **Iron Age** was a period of time which began when people started making things from iron, about three thousand years ago. *This year, for probably the first time since the Iron Age, this land has not felt the heavy hand of man. ...an Iron Age sword, thought to be up to two thousand five hundred years old.*

Iron Curtain
1 N PROP People used to refer to the border that separated the former Soviet Union and its East European allies from the Western European countries as the **Iron Curtain**. *...the Soviet side of the Iron Curtain.* ● When people talked about things happening **behind the Iron Curtain**, they meant that they happened in the former Soviet Union or in one of the East European countries that were allied to it. *Sales of his novels were most brisk behind the Iron Curtain. ...as democracy spreads in Eastern Europe, and more information becomes available from behind the now demolished Iron Curtain.*
2 N+N People used to refer to the Soviet Union and its former East European allies as the **Iron Curtain** countries. *I have been to a number of Iron Curtain countries.*

iron fist
N SING You use **iron fist** to refer to the fact that a leader or government treats people in a very harsh and unfair way. *He did not hesitate to use an iron fist to crush any sign of opposition to his absolute rule... The President rules his country with an iron fist... The Commission condemned what it called their iron fist policy.*

iron-grey; also spelt **iron-gray** in American English.
ADJ **Iron-grey** hair is a dark grey colour. *He had iron-grey hair cut at medium length... He looked down at the iron-grey head.*

ironic /aɪrɒnɪk/
1 ADJ An **ironic** remark or gesture is inappropriate in the situation in which it is made, and is intended as a joke or insult. *It was possible that his thanks were ironic.*
2 ADJ An **ironic** situation is strange or amusing because it is the opposite of what you expect. *It is ironic that the people who complain most loudly are the ones who do least to help.*

ironical /aɪrɒnɪkl/
ADJ **Ironical** means the same as **ironic**. *It is ironical that the absentees include those who are forever accusing the government of not doing enough.*

ironically /aɪrɒnɪkli/
1 ADV SEN You say **ironically** to draw attention to a situation which is strange or amusing, because it is the opposite of what you expect. *Ironically, the intelligence chief was the last person to hear the news.*
2 ADV If you say something **ironically**, you say it as a joke or insult, because it is an inappropriate thing to say in the particular situation. *'Do you want to search the apartment?' she enquired ironically.*

ironing board, ironing boards
NC An **ironing board** is a long, narrow board covered with cloth, on which you iron clothes. *His mom set up the ironing board to press his uniform.*

ironmonger /aɪənmʌŋgə/ **ironmongers**
NC An **ironmonger** or an **ironmonger's** is a shop which sells tools, nails, pans, and many other things that you need for doing jobs in your house or garden. *Insecticides should be available from big stores or ironmongers.*

ironmongery /aɪənmʌŋgəˀri/
NU **Ironmongery** is the metal things that an ironmonger sells. *I was surprised to find ironmongery all over the place.*
ironstone /aɪənstəʊn/
NU **Ironstone** is rock that contains a lot of iron. *...an outcrop of ironstone. ...great ironstone boulders.*
ironwork /aɪənwɜːk/
NU You refer to iron objects or the iron parts of buildings as **ironwork**. *The staircase has fine ironwork. ...ironwork gates.*
irony /aɪrəni/ **ironies**
1 NU **Irony** is a way of speaking in which you say something which is inappropriate, as a joke or insult. *She said with slight irony, 'Bravo.'*
2 NUorNC The **irony** of a situation is an aspect of it which is strange or amusing, because it is the opposite of what you expect. *The irony is that many politicians agree with him... History has many ironies.*
irradiate /ɪreɪdɪeɪt/ **irradiates, irradiating, irradiated**
1 VO If you **are irradiated**, you are exposed to a large amount of radioactivity. *People in the area could be blinded or irradiated.* ♦ **irradiation** /ɪreɪdɪeɪʃn/ NU *...nuclear irradiation studies.*
2 VO To **irradiate** food means to expose it to radiation in order to kill bacteria and make it safe to eat for a longer period of time. *Do we really need to irradiate food, and is it safe?* ♦ **irradiation** NU *Is food irradiation dangerous?*
irrational /ɪræʃənl/
ADJ **Irrational** feelings or behaviour are not based on logical reasons or thinking. *His anxiety was irrational. ...an irrational child.* ♦ **irrationally** ADV *They were accused of acting irrationally.*
♦ **irrationality** /ɪræʃənæləti/ NU *...the irrationality of contemporary economics.*
irreconcilable /ɪrekənsaɪləbl/
1 ADJ If two ideas are **irreconcilable**, they are so different from each other that it is impossible to believe or accept both of them; a formal use. *Their views had been irreconcilable from the beginning.*
2 ADJ If two parties in an argument are **irreconcilable**, their beliefs or aims are so different that it is unlikely that they will ever reach an agreement. *They have been trying to appease irreconcilable groups.*
3 ADJ An **irreconcilable** disagreement is so serious that it cannot be settled. *...an irreconcilable clash of loyalties.*
irredeemable /ɪrɪdiːməbl/
ADJ If someone has an **irredeemable** fault in their character or personality, it cannot ever be corrected; a formal word. *...a complete and irredeemable selfishness.* ♦ **irredeemably** SUBMOD *I saw him as old, corrupt and irredeemably evil.*
irreducible /ɪrɪdjuːsəbl/
ADJ Something that is **irreducible** cannot be reduced in amount or cannot be made simpler; a formal word. *...the irreducible essence of art... The fifth theory is irreducible to simpler terms.*
irrefutable /ɪrɪfjuːtəbl/
ADJ An **irrefutable** statement cannot be shown to be incorrect; a formal word. *That is an opinion, not an irrefutable fact.*
irregular /ɪregjʊlə/ **irregulars**
1 ADJ Something that is **irregular** is not smooth or straight, or does not form a regular pattern. *...its rough, irregular surface. ...dark, irregular markings on the photos.* ♦ **irregularly** ADV *...irregularly shaped fields.*
2 ADJ **Irregular** is also used to say that a series of events happens with different periods of time between them. *...feeding them at irregular intervals... The newspaper's appearance became increasingly irregular.* ♦ **irregularly** ADV *He went home, irregularly, at weekends.* ♦ **irregularity** /ɪregjʊlærəti/ **irregularities** NCorNU *This is more likely to produce irregularities of heart rate... These illnesses can be caused by irregularity in feeding.*
3 ADJ **Irregular** behaviour is unusual and not acceptable. *It isn't signed. This is irregular. ...a highly irregular request.* ♦ **irregularity** NC *He rejected allegations of financial irregularities.*

4 NC **Irregulars** are soldiers who do not belong to an official national army. *...an operation to confront and disarm Armenian irregulars.*
5 ADJ An **irregular** verb, noun, or adjective does not inflect in the same way as most other verbs, nouns, or adjectives in the language. 'Go' and 'be' are irregular verbs in English.
irrelevance /ɪreləvəns/
NU The **irrelevance** of something is the fact that it is not connected with what you are talking about or dealing with, and is therefore not important. *'By the way,' he added with apparent irrelevance, 'will you be locking it?'*
irrelevancy /ɪreləvənsi/ **irrelevancies**
NC You can refer to a fact, activity, or institution that you think has no useful purpose as an **irrelevancy**; a formal word. *School is an irrelevancy... He should not waste his time with irrelevancies.*
irrelevant /ɪreləvənt/
ADJ If something is **irrelevant**, it is not connected with what you are talking about or dealing with, and is therefore not important. *The book was full of irrelevant information... He felt that right and wrong were irrelevant to the situation.*
irreligious /ɪrɪlɪdʒəs/
ADJ An **irreligious** person does not accept the beliefs of any particular religion, or opposes all religions. *My family were completely irreligious. ...an irreligious society. ...irreligious attitudes.*
irremediable /ɪrɪmiːdiəbl/
ADJ If a situation or state is **irremediable**, it is very bad and cannot be improved; a formal word. *Irremediable damage has been done.*
irreparable /ɪrepərəbl/
ADJ **Irreparable** damage is so severe that it cannot be repaired or put right; a formal word. *Many of the country's most valuable natural habitats will suffer irreparable damage unless something is done soon... If the crisis continues, it will cause irreparable damage to Hungary's reputation abroad.*
irreplaceable /ɪrɪpleɪsəbl/
ADJ Things or people that are **irreplaceable** are so special that they cannot be replaced if they are lost or destroyed, or if they leave. *A spokesman at the British Museum points out that transferring irreplaceable objects between countries is impractical because of prohibitive insurance costs... No man in politics is irreplaceable.*
irrepressible /ɪrɪpresəbl/
ADJ **Irrepressible** people are lively, energetic, and cheerful. *Basil is irrepressible, funny, and affectionate.*
irreproachable /ɪrɪprəʊtʃəbl/
ADJ If someone's behaviour or character is **irreproachable**, it is so good or correct that it cannot be criticized. *He had done an irreproachable job of presiding over the tribunal. ...McKinley's irreproachable character.*
irresistible /ɪrɪzɪstəbl/
1 ADJ If your wish to do something is **irresistible**, you cannot prevent yourself doing it. *The urge to laugh was irresistible.*
2 ADJ If you describe someone or something as **irresistible**, you mean that they are very attractive. *He found her irresistible... His charm was irresistible to them.* ♦ **irresistibly** SUBMOD *The songs are irresistibly catchy.*
3 ADJ An **irresistible** force cannot be stopped or controlled. *They put irresistible pressure upon the government.* ♦ **irresistibly** ADV *The waves take you irresistibly onwards.*
irresolute /ɪrezəluːt/
ADJ If you are **irresolute**, you cannot decide what to do; a formal word. *The worst reason to launch an attack would be a fear of seeming irresolute or appearing to back down.*
irrespective /ɪrɪspektɪv/
PREP If something is true or happens **irrespective of** other things, those things do not affect it; a formal word. *They demanded equal pay irrespective of age or sex. ...available to all students, irrespective of where they live.*

irresponsible /ɪrɪspɒnsəbl/
ADJ **Irresponsible** people do things without properly considering their possible consequences; used showing disapproval. *You've behaved like an irresponsible idiot... It would be irresponsible of me to encourage you.* ♦ **irresponsibly** ADV *...acting unfairly and irresponsibly.* ♦ **irresponsibility** /ɪrɪspɒnsəbɪləti/ NU *...youthful irresponsibility.*

irretrievable /ɪrɪtriːvəbl/
1 ADJ **Irretrievable** harm is so severe that it cannot be put right again; a formal use. *...the irretrievable damage done to the Earth.* ♦ **irretrievably** ADV *The war was irretrievably lost.*
2 ADJ If a situation is **irretrievable**, it is so bad that there is no chance of it ever being put right. *There have been indications during the morning that the situation will not be irretrievable.*

irreverence /ɪrɛvᵊrəns/
NU **Irreverence** is behaviour in which you talk to someone, or talk about them, without showing the respect for them that people would expect. *His irreverence has frequently landed him in trouble... Should irreverence towards God really be a criminal offence?*

irreverent /ɪrɛvᵊrənt/
ADJ If you are **irreverent**, you do not show the respect for someone or something that people would expect. *...rude and irreverent comments.*

irreversible /ɪrɪvɜːsəbl/
ADJ If a change is **irreversible**, the thing affected cannot be changed back to its original state. *The damage may be irreversible.*

irrevocable /ɪrɛvəkəbl/
ADJ Actions or decisions that are **irrevocable** cannot be stopped or changed; a formal word. *The US has given its irrevocable commitment to the Russians.* ♦ **irrevocably** ADV *The world had changed irrevocably.*

irrigate /ɪrɪgeɪt/ **irrigates, irrigating, irrigated**
VO To **irrigate** land means to supply it with water in order to help crops to grow. *A small pump will irrigate about an acre of land.* ♦ **irrigated** ADJ *...the irrigated areas of the Ganges plain.* ♦ **irrigation** /ɪrɪgeɪʃn/ NU *...the area under irrigation. ...a complex irrigation system.*

irritable /ɪrɪtəbl/
ADJ If you are **irritable**, you are easily annoyed. *Judy was feeling hot, tired, and irritable.* ♦ **irritably** ADV *'What do you want me to do?' she said irritably.* ♦ **irritability** /ɪrɪtəbɪləti/ NU *...periods of irritability.*

irritant /ɪrɪtənt/ **irritants**
NC If something keeps annoying you, you can refer to it as an **irritant**; a formal word. *Lack of national independence was a strong irritant.*

irritate /ɪrɪteɪt/ **irritates, irritating, irritated**
1 VO If something **irritates** you, it keeps annoying you. *His style irritated some officials... Dixon, irritated by this question, said nothing.* ♦ **irritated** ADJ *...an irritated gesture.*
2 VO If something **irritates** a part of your body, it causes it to itch or be sore. *The detergent can irritate sensitive feet.*

irritating /ɪrɪteɪtɪŋ/
ADJ Something that is **irritating** keeps annoying you. *...an irritating noise.* ♦ **irritatingly** SUBMOD *She was irritatingly slow.*

irritation /ɪrɪteɪʃn/ **irritations**
1 NU **Irritation** is a feeling of annoyance about something that someone continues to do. *I began to feel the same irritation with all of them.*
2 NC An **irritation** is something that keeps annoying you. *...the irritations of everyday existence.*
3 NU **Irritation** in a part of your body is a feeling of slight pain and discomfort there. *...eye irritation.*

is /ɪz/
Is is the third person singular of the present tense of be.

-ise /-aɪz/ **-ises, -ising, -ised.** See **-ize**.

-ish /-ɪʃ/
1 SUFFIX **-ish** is added to adjectives to form other adjectives which indicate that something has a quality to a limited extent. For example, 'reddish' means slightly red. *He had a yellowish complexion... He was a biggish fellow.*
2 SUFFIX **-ish** is also added to nouns to form adjectives which indicate that someone or something has the qualities of a particular kind of thing or person. For example, someone who is childish behaves like a child. *She was a beautiful kittenish creature.*

Islam /ɪzlɑːm/
NU **Islam** is the religion of the Muslims, which teaches that there is only one God and that Mohammed is His prophet. *Islam is to be made the state religion.*

Islāmābād /ɪslɑːməbæd/
Islāmābād is the capital of Pakistan and its twelfth largest city. Population: 204,000 (1981).

Islamic /ɪzlæmɪk/
ADJ ATTRIB **Islamic** means belonging or relating to Islam. *...the Islamic civilisation. ...Islamic laws... Islamic fundamentalists have been gaining strength in North Africa.*

island /aɪlənd/ **islands**
NC An **island** is a piece of land that is completely surrounded by water. *There are pigs on the island. ...the Channel Islands. ...four Soviet-held islands off the northern coast of Japan.*

islander /aɪləndə/ **islanders**
NC **Islanders** are people who live on an island. *The islanders had never seen a car. ...the Falkland Islanders.*

isle /aɪl/ **isles**
NC **Isle** is used in the names of some islands. *...the Isle of Wight. ...the British Isles.*

Isle of Man /aɪl əv mæn/
The **Isle of Man** is a British crown dependency in the Irish Sea between England and Ireland. It is self-governing. Britain is responsible for its defence and foreign affairs. Tourism is a major industry.
♦ **Manxman, Manxwoman** /mæŋksmən, mæŋkswʊmən/ N **Manx** /mæŋks/ ADJ
▪ *religion:* Christianity ▪ *language:* English ▪ *currency:* pound sterling ▪ *capital:* Douglas ▪ *population:* 64,000 (1986) ▪ *size:* 572 square kilometres.

islet /aɪlət/ **islets**
NC An **islet** is a small island; a literary word. *They live on a small islet... There is one taverna on this tiny islet.*

-ism /-ɪzəm/ **-isms**
1 SUFFIX **-ism** is used to form nouns that refer to political or religious movements and beliefs. *...the emergence of nationalism. ...the importance of Hinduism as a unifying force.*
2 SUFFIX **-ism** is also used to form nouns that refer to attitudes or behaviour. *Clem's eyes gleamed with fanaticism. ...an opportunity for heroism.*

isn't /ɪznt/
Isn't is the usual spoken form of 'is not'.

isobar /aɪsəbɑː/ **isobars**
NC An **isobar** is a line on a weather map joining points of equal atmospheric pressure.

isolate /aɪsəleɪt/ **isolates, isolating, isolated**
1 VO or V-REFL If something **isolates** you or if you **isolate** yourself, you become physically or socially separated from other people. *His wealth isolated him... They isolated themselves in order to build a new society.* ♦ **isolated** ADJ *Often they feel lonely and isolated.*
2 VO or V-REFL To **isolate** a country or government means to cause it to become politically or economically separated from other countries or governments. *Algiers now accepts that its attempts to isolate Morocco diplomatically have had no impact on the war... The US cannot afford to isolate itself economically.* ♦ **isolated** ADJ *All this left North Korea more isolated than ever.*
3 VO To **isolate** a substance means to separate it from other substances so that it can be examined in detail; a technical use. *You can isolate genes and study how they work.*
4 VO If you **isolate** a sick person or animal, you keep them apart from other people or animals, so that their illness does not spread. *David had to be isolated for whooping cough.*

isolated /ˈaɪsəleɪtɪd/
1 ADJ An **isolated** place is a long way away from any town or village. *Many of the refugee villages are in isolated areas and access to them is difficult. ...an isolated farmhouse.*
2 ADJ An **isolated** example or incident is one that is rare and not part of a general pattern. *...a few isolated acts of violence... The protest passed off peacefully except for a few isolated incidents.*

isolation /ˌaɪsəˈleɪʃn/
1 NU **Isolation** is a state in which you feel separate from other people, because you live far away from them or because you do not have any friends. *...mothers living in isolation and poverty.*
2 NU **Isolation** is also the state in which a country or government has become politically or economically separated from other countries or governments. *Romania has suffered international isolation ever since the events of last June... China is keen to end its economic isolation.*
3 If something exists or happens **in isolation**, it exists or happens separately from other things of the same kind. *These questions can't be answered in isolation from each other.*

isolationism /ˌaɪsəˈleɪʃəˈnɪzəm/
NU **Isolationism** is the policy of a country when it avoids becoming involved in relationships with or disputes between other countries; used showing disapproval. *The report blames British isolationism.*
♦ **isolationist, isolationists** NC *He was still an isolationist. ...isolationist attitudes.*

isometric /ˌaɪsəmˈetrɪk/ **isometrics**
N PL **Isometrics** or **isometric exercises** are exercises in which you make your muscles work against each other or against something else, for example by pressing your hands together. *Isometrics may increase muscle bulk.*

isosceles triangle /aɪˈsɒsəliːz ˈtraɪæŋgl/ **isosceles triangles**
NC An **isosceles triangle** is a triangle which has two sides that are the same length; a technical term in mathematics. *...a cabinet that's shaped like an isosceles triangle.*

isotope /ˈaɪsətəʊp/ **isotopes**
NC **Isotopes** are atoms which have the same atomic number but which have different physical properties because they do not have the same number of neutrons; a technical term. *Tritium is one of the mildest radioactive isotopes.*

Israel /ˈɪzreɪəl/
The **State of Israel** is a country in south-west Asia, on the Mediterranean. Since 1967 it has occupied the Gaza Strip, Golan Heights and the West Bank, which are known collectively as the Occupied Territories. Israel was founded in 1948 by immigrants from Europe and the rest of the world, who wished to establish a Jewish homeland. Civil war left about 800,000 Palestinian Arabs homeless. A Palestinian uprising, called the intifada, began in 1987. In 1991 Israel was attacked by Iraqi Scud missiles in the Gulf War. General Chaim Herzog, of the Labour Party, became President in 1983. Itzhak Shamir, of Likud, became Prime Minister in 1986. Israel exports polished diamonds, citrus and other fruits, and textiles. ♦ **Israeli** /ɪzˈreɪli/ N, ADJ
▪ *per capita GNP:* US$8,650 ▪ *religion:* Judaism (82%), Islam (14%) ▪ *language:* Hebrew, Arabic (official), ▪ *currency:* shekel ▪ *capital:* Jerusalem (but many countries refuse to move their embassies from Tel Aviv) ▪ *population:* 5 million (1990) ▪ *size:* 21,501 square kilometres (including the Occupied Territories).

issue /ˈɪʃuː, ˈɪsjuː/ **issues, issuing, issued**
1 NC An **issue** is an important problem or subject that people are discussing or arguing about. *I raised the issue with him... Many other contentious issues were settled earlier this year... The problem of drug abuse among the young is a key issue in his campaign... Another topic was the issue of European security... Environmental issues are high on this year's agenda.*
2 N SING If something is the **issue**, it is the thing you consider to be the most important part of a situation or discussion. *That's just not the issue... You cannot*

go on evading the issue.
3 NC An **issue** of a magazine or newspaper is a particular edition of it. *The article had appeared in the previous day's issue.*
4 VO If someone **issues** a statement, they make it formally or publicly. *The statement issued after the meeting does not indicate whether there has been any change in their attitude... They issued a serious warning.*
5 VO If you **are issued** with something or if it **is issued** to you, it is officially given to you. *She was issued with travel documents... Radios were issued to the troops.*
6 V+from When something **issues** from a place, it comes out of it; a literary use. *...the smells issuing from the kitchen.*
● **Issue** is used in these phrases. ● The thing **at issue** is the thing that is being argued about. *The point at issue is this.* ● If you **make an issue of** something, you make a fuss about it. *They didn't make an issue of their wish to join NATO.*

-ist /-ɪst/ **-ists**
1 SUFFIX **-ist** is added to nouns which end in '-ism' to form adjectives and new nouns. Adjectives formed in this way describe something related to or based on a particular set of beliefs. Nouns formed in this way refer to a person whose behaviour is based on a particular set of beliefs. For example, socialist ideas are based on socialism and a pacifist believes in pacifism. In this dictionary, these nouns and adjectives are sometimes not defined but are treated with the related nouns. *The demonstrators want to establish a fascist government... She was a very early feminist in the post war period.*
2 SUFFIX **-ist** is also added to nouns to form new nouns which refer to a person who does a particular thing. For example, a violinist is someone who plays the violin. *A pianist, Leon McCawley, played Rachmaninov's notoriously difficult third piano concerto. ...a physicist from Princeton University.*

Istanbul /ˌɪstænˈbʊl/
Istanbul is the largest city in Turkey. It was formerly known as Byzantium and Constantinople. Population: 5,476,000 (1985).

isthmus /ˈɪsməs/ **isthmuses**
NC An **isthmus** is a narrow area of land connecting two larger areas; a technical term. *...the Isthmus of Panama.*

it /ɪt/. It is used as the subject of a verb or as the object of a verb or preposition.
1 PRON You use **it** to refer to an object, animal, or other thing that has already been mentioned or whose identity is known. *...a tray with glasses on it... The man went up to the cat and started stroking it... The strike went on for a year before it was settled.*
2 PRON You also use **it** to refer to a situation or fact, or to give your opinion or express your attitude towards a particular situation or fact. *She was frightened, but tried not to show it... He found it hard to make friends... It was very pleasant at the Hochstadts... It is madness for Great Britain to remain opposed to the deal... It seems to be a big problem.*
3 PRON You also use **it** when you are talking about the weather, the time, the date, or the day of the week. *It's hot... It's raining here... It is nearly one o'clock.*
4 PRON You also use **it** when you are stating or asking who is speaking on the telephone or who is present. *Who is it?... It's me—Mary.*
5 PRON It also occurs in structures which are used to emphasize or draw attention to something. *It's my mother I'm worried about.*

Italian /ɪˈtæljən/ **Italians**
1 ADJ **Italian** means belonging or relating to Italy. *Diana has an Italian mother and a Jamaican father.*
2 NC An **Italian** is a person who comes from Italy. *The other four were Italians.*
3 NU **Italian** is the language spoken by people who live in Italy. *Special language courses for business people are starting up all over Britain to teach French, German, Italian, Dutch, and even Japanese.*

italics /ɪtælɪks/
N PL **Italics** are letters printed so that they slope to the right. Italics are often used to emphasize a word or sentence. The examples in this dictionary are printed in italics.
Italy /ɪtəli/
The **Italian Republic** is a country in southern Europe. It includes the islands of Sicily, Sardinia, and Elba. Mussolini, the leader of the Fascist Party, came to power in 1922. Italy was allied with Germany in the Second World War, until it was invaded by the Allies in 1943. The modern state was founded in 1946. Italy is a member of the European Community and NATO. Francesco Cossiga, of the Christian Democrats (DC), became President in 1985. Giulio Andreotti (DC) became Prime Minister in 1989. Textiles and clothing, metals, cars, fruit, and wine are important exports. Tourism is an important industry. ♦ **Italian** /ɪtæliən/ N, ADJ
■ *per capita GNP:* US$13,320 ■ *religion:* Christianity (mainly Roman Catholic) ■ *language:* Italian ■ *currency:* lira ■ *capital:* Rome (Roma) ■ *population:* 58 million (1988) ■ *size:* 301,277 square kilometres.
itch /ɪtʃ/ **itches, itching, itched**
1 V If you **itch** or if a part of your body **itches**, you have an unpleasant feeling on your skin that makes you want to scratch. *My toes are itching like mad.*
2 NC An **itch** is an unpleasant feeling on your skin that makes you want to scratch.
3 V+*to*-INF If you **itch** to do something, you are very impatient to do it; an informal use. *I was itching to get away.*
itchy /ɪtʃi/
ADJ If you are **itchy** or if a part of your body is **itchy**, you have an unpleasant feeling on your skin that makes you want to scratch. *Don't you feel all itchy?... My skin became dry and itchy.*
it'd /ɪtəd/
It'd is a spoken form of 'it had', especially when 'had' is an auxiliary. **It'd** is also a spoken form of 'it would'. *It'd just been killed... If I went on the train, it'd be cheaper.*
item /aɪtəm/ **items**
1 NC An **item** is one of a collection or list of objects. *They maintained a constant store of foodstuffs, medicines and household items... What if they urgently need an item that is in short supply?... The cost of many items will double.*
2 NC An **item** is also one of a number of matters you are dealing with. *I had two items of business to attend to before lunch... The main item on the agenda at this morning's first session is aid to the Soviet Union.*
3 NC An **item** in a newspaper or magazine is a report or article. *The contest for the leadership of the British Conservative Party is again the main item in the papers.*
itemize /aɪtəmaɪz/ **itemizes, itemizing, itemized**; also spelt **itemise**.
VO If you **itemize** a number of things, you make a list of them. *The contents of his pockets were itemized and confiscated.*
itinerant /ɪtɪnərənt/
ADJ ATTRIB **Itinerant** people travel around a region, living or working for short periods in different places; a formal word. *...the huge migrant population of itinerant workers.*
itinerary /ɪtɪnəʳrəri/ **itineraries**
NC An **itinerary** is a plan of a journey, including the route and the places that will be visited. *A detailed itinerary is supplied.*
it'll /ɪtl/
It'll is a spoken form of 'it will'. *It'll be quite interesting.*
its /ɪts/
DET You use **its** to indicate that something belongs or

relates to a thing, place, or animal that has just been mentioned or whose identity is known. *The creature lifted its head... The group held its first meeting last week.*
it's /ɪts/
It's is a spoken form of 'it is' or 'it has', especially when 'has' is an auxiliary verb. *It's very important... It's snowing... It's been nice talking to you.*
itself /ɪtself/
1 PRON REFL You use **itself** as the object of a verb or preposition to refer to the same thing or animal that is mentioned as the subject of the clause, or as a previous object in the clause. *Britain must bring itself up to date... It wraps its furry tail around itself.*
2 PRON REFL You also use **itself** to emphasize the subject or object of a clause, and to make it clear what you are referring to. *The town itself was very small.*
3 If you say that something has a particular quality in itself, you mean that it has this quality because of its own nature, regardless of any other factors. *The process is, in itself, an act of worship.*
ITV /aɪtiːviː/
N PROP **ITV** refers to a group of several British commercial television channels. **ITV** is an abbreviation for Independent Television. *Subsequent episodes will be broadcast on Tuesdays on ITV.*
-ity /-əti/ **-ities**
SUFFIX **-ity** is added to adjectives to form nouns. These nouns usually refer to states, qualities, or behaviour. In this dictionary nouns of this kind are often not defined but are treated with the related adjectives. *Their function is to give rigidity... About this there is unanimity among sociologists.*
IUD /aɪjuːdiː/ **IUDs**
NC An **IUD** is a piece of plastic or metal which is put inside a woman's womb in order to prevent her from becoming pregnant. **IUD** is an abbreviation for 'intra-uterine device'. *He claimed that breastfeeding your baby can be as effective a form of contraception as the IUD.*
I've /aɪv/
I've is the usual spoken form of 'I have', especially when 'have' is an auxiliary. *I've never met her... I've only been there once.*
ivory /aɪvəʳri/
NU **Ivory** is the substance which forms the tusks of elephants. It is valuable, and is often used to make ornaments. *China is to join an international ban on ivory trading. ...ivory chess sets.*
Ivory Coast /aɪvəʳri kəʊst/ See **Côte d'Ivoire.**
ivory tower, ivory towers
NC If you describe someone as living in an **ivory tower**, you mean that they deliberately keep themselves away from the practical problems of everyday life; used showing disapproval. *We hope that people here don't just live in an ivory tower... This isn't an ivory tower, this is part of the real world.*
ivy /aɪvi/
NU **Ivy** is a plant that grows up walls and trees. *...a dirty little track all overgrown with ivy.*
Ivy League
N PROP The **Ivy League** is a group of eight important universities in the eastern part of the United States. *...professors who helped those schools to match the Ivy League in reputation. ...eight Ivy League colleges.*
-ize /-aɪz/ **-izes, -izing, -ized**; also spelt **-ise, -ises, -ising, -ised**.
SUFFIX Verbs that can end in either '-ize' or '-ise' are dealt with in this dictionary as ending in '-ize'. Some verbs ending in **-ize** are derived from adjectives. These verbs describe processes by which things or people are changed to a particular state or condition. For example, when something is popularized, it is made popular. *Parliament finally legalized trade unions.*

J j

J, j /dʒeɪ/ **J's, j's**
NC J is the tenth letter of the English alphabet.
jab /dʒæb/ **jabs, jabbing, jabbed**
1 V OR If you **jab** something somewhere, you push it there with a quick, sudden movement. *She jabbed her knitting needles into a ball of wool... He jabbed his finger at me.* ► Also NC *...the rhythmic jab and parry of professional boxing.*
2 NC A **jab** is an injection of a substance into your blood to prevent illness; an informal use. *Diabetics may soon be offered a pill to replace their daily jabs.*
jabber /dʒæbə/ **jabbers, jabbering, jabbered**
V Someone who is **jabbering** is talking very quickly and excitedly; an informal word. *The children began to jabber among themselves... She was jabbering in Italian to her husband.*
jack /dʒæk/ **jacks, jacking, jacked**
1 NC A **jack** is a device for lifting a heavy object off the ground. *It was moved around on hydraulic jacks.*
2 NC A **jack** is also a playing card with a picture of a young man on it. *...the Jack of Diamonds.*
jack in PHRASAL VERB If you **jack in** something such as an activity or job, you stop doing it; an informal expression. *One of these days I'm going to jack this job in and sail around the world.*
jack up PHRASAL VERB If you **jack up** the price or the value of something, you increase its cost or importance above the level of what is reasonable; an informal expression. *They either cancel the policy or jack the prices up so high small companies can't afford it anymore... These rises were blamed on store operators who had jacked up prices.*
jackal /dʒækɔːl, dʒækl/ **jackals**
NC A **jackal** is a wild animal that looks like a dog, has long legs and pointed ears, and lives in Africa and Southern Asia. *Now and again the jackals howled.*
jackass /dʒækæs/ **jackasses**
NC If you call someone a **jackass**, you mean that you think they are a stupid and foolish person; an old-fashioned word. *He's the biggest jackass we have ever had as president.*
jackboot /dʒækbuːt/ **jackboots**
1 N PL **Jackboots** are heavy, long boots that come up to the knee. They used to be worn by soldiers, especially in the cavalry. *...right wing military conservatives with crew cuts and jackboots.*
2 If you say that a country or a group is **under the jackboot** of someone such as a dictator, you mean that it is suffering from harsh and unjust government by them. *National culture was crushed under the invader's jackboot.*
jackdaw /dʒækdɔː/ **jackdaws**
NC A **jackdaw** is a large black and grey bird that is similar to a crow, and lives in Europe and Asia. *...jackdaws hopping around.*
jacket /dʒækɪt/ **jackets**
1 NC A **jacket** is a short coat. *...a tweed sports jacket.* ● See also **dinner jacket, lifejacket.**
2 NC The **jacket** of a baked potato is its skin. *...potatoes in their jackets.*
3 NC The **jacket** of a book is the paper cover that protects it. *...the author's biography on the book jacket... He believed that books should be placed on library shelves with their jackets off.*
jack-in-the-box, jack-in-the-boxes
NC A **jack-in-the-box** is a child's toy which consists of a box with a doll inside it that springs out when the lid is opened.
jack-knife, jack-knifes, jack-knifing, jack-knifed; jack-knives. The form **jack-knifes** is the third person singular, present tense, of the verb. The form **jack-knives** is the plural of the noun.
1 V If an articulated lorry **jack-knifes**, the trailer swings round at a sharp angle to the cab, sending it into an uncontrollable skid. *Traffic was stopped after an articulated truck jack-knifed in heavy rain.*
2 NC A **jack-knife** is a large knife with a blade that can be folded into the handle. *He fumbled in his pocket and pulled out an ordinary jack-knife.*
jack of all trades, jacks of all trades
NC Someone who is a **jack of all trades** is able to do a variety of different jobs; often used to suggest that they are not expert at any particular one.
jackpot /dʒækpɒt/ **jackpots**
NC The **jackpot** is the most valuable prize in a game or lottery. *They shared a $51.4 million jackpot in a record Californian lottery.*
Jacobean /dʒækəbiːən/
ADJ A building, piece of furniture, or literature that is **Jacobean** was built or produced in the style of the period between 1603 and 1625. *...a Jacobean house on a great estate.*
Jacuzzi /dʒəkuːzi/ **Jacuzzis**
NC A **Jacuzzi** is a large circular bath which is fitted with a device that makes the water swirl around; **Jacuzzi** is a trademark. *They have fitted kitchens, jacuzzis and two cars.*
jade /dʒeɪd/
NU **Jade** is a hard green stone used for making jewellery and ornaments. *...a small carved jade statue of the Buddha.*
jaded /dʒeɪdɪd/
ADJ If you are **jaded**, you have no enthusiasm because you are tired of something or because you have had too much of the same thing. *...jaded housewives who'd like to try something different.*
Jaffa /dʒæfə/
NU **Jaffa** is a brand of fruit that comes from Israel; **Jaffa** is a trademark. *...a batch of Jaffa brand grapefruit.*
jagged /dʒægɪd/
ADJ Something that is **jagged** has a rough, uneven shape with lots of sharp points. *...small pieces of jagged metal.*
jaguar /dʒægjuə/ **jaguars**
NC A **jaguar** is a large member of the cat family with dark spots on its back. *...endangered species such as jaguars.*
jail /dʒeɪl/ **jails, jailing, jailed;** also spelt **gaol.**
1 NC or NU A **jail** is a place where people are kept locked up, usually because they have been found guilty of a crime. *He applied for an immediate move to a British jail... He went to jail for attempted robbery. ...a heavy jail sentence.*

2 vo If someone **is jailed**, they are put into jail. *He was jailed for five years.*

jailbird /dʒeɪlbɜːd/ **jailbirds**; also spelt **gaolbird**.

NC A **jailbird** is a person who is in prison or who has been to prison; an old-fashioned, informal word.

jailbreak /dʒeɪlbreɪk/ **jailbreaks**

NC A **jailbreak** is an escape from jail. *The jailbreak follows hunger strikes and unrest in other prisons.*

jailer /dʒeɪlə/ **jailers**; also spelt **gaoler**.

NC A **jailer** is a person in charge of a jail; an old-fashioned word. *The prison warden denied a report that inmates died because the jailers refused to unlock the doors to the dormitory.*

Jakarta /dʒəkɑːtə/

Jakarta is the capital of Indonesia and its largest city. It is the headquarters of the Association of South East Asian Nations. Population: 7,348,000 (1983).

jalopy /dʒəlɒpi/ **jalopies**

NC A **jalopy** is an old, unreliable car; an old-fashioned word, often used humorously. *Many Cubans will be happy to exchange their pre-1959 American jalopies for a Chinese bicycle.*

jam /dʒæm/ **jams, jamming, jammed**

1 N MASS **Jam** is a food made by cooking fruit with sugar. You usually spread it on bread. *...pots of raspberry and blackcurrant jam... You just get fruit and you preserve it or you make it into jams or purees.*

2 vo A If you **jam** something somewhere, you push it there roughly. *Reporters jammed microphones in our faces... Then he jammed his hat back on.*

3 v-ERG If something **jams** or if you **jam** it, it becomes fixed in one position and cannot move freely or work properly. *The machines jammed and broke down... I jammed the window shut.*

4 vo If a lot of things **are jammed** into a place, they are packed tightly together and can hardly move. *The town was jammed with traffic.*

5 NC A traffic **jam** is a situation where there are so many vehicles on a road that none of them can move. *There were traffic jams, and police clearing people away... The strike has disrupted train and bus services and brought severe jams on the roads.*

6 NC If you are in a **jam**, you are in a difficult situation; an informal use. *He finds himself in exactly the same jam as his brother was in ten years before.*

7 vo To **jam** a radio or electronic signal means to interfere with it and prevent it being received clearly. *Iran repeated allegations that the American Navy had jammed the communications network of Iranian warships.*

8 v When musicians **jam**, they play jazz or rock music informally, not following parts that have been written down or planned in advance. *...while Paul, George and Ringo jammed on the piano.*

Jamaica /dʒəmeɪkə/

Jamaica is a country in the Caribbean. It was a British colony from 1655 to 1962. It is a member of the Commonwealth and the Organization of American States. P.J. Patterson, of the People's National Party (PNP), became Prime Minister in 1992. Important exports are bauxite, alumina, sugar, and bananas. Cannabis is illegally produced. Tourism is an important industry. High inflation and large foreign debts are major economic problems. ♦ **Jamaican** /dʒəmeɪkən/ N, ADJ

▪ *per capita GNP:* US$1,080 ▪ *religion:* Christianity (mainly Protestant) ▪ *language:* English ▪ *currency:* dollar ▪ *capital:* Kingston ▪ *population:* 2 million (1988) ▪ *size:* 10,991 square kilometres.

jamb /dʒæm/ **jambs**

NC A **jamb** is a post that forms the side part or upright of a door frame or window frame. *...a bell on the jamb of the door.*

jamboree /dʒæmbəriː/ **jamborees**

NC A **jamboree** is a party or celebration which a large number of people go to. *...an open-air jamboree that attracted 250,000 people.*

Jamestown /dʒeɪmztaʊn/

Jamestown is the capital of St Helena and its largest town. Population: 1,500 (1987).

jam-jar, jam-jars

NC A **jam-jar** is a glass jar which is used for keeping jam in.

jammy /dʒæmi/ **jammier, jammiest**; an informal word.

1 ADJ Something that is **jammy** is dirty and sticky because it is covered with jam. *Be careful where you put those jammy fingers.*

2 ADJ If you say that a person or something that a person does is **jammy**, you mean that they are very lucky because something good has happened by chance. *You jammy so-and-so!... He'll get a jammy job somewhere.*

jam-packed

ADJ A place that is **jam-packed** is so full of people or things that there is no room for any more; an informal word. *The streets were jam-packed that day.*

Jan.

Jan. is a written abbreviation for 'January'. *...Jan. 6th, 1931.*

jangle /dʒæŋgl/ **jangles, jangling, jangled**

1 v-ERG If metal objects **jangle** or if you **jangle** them, they make a ringing noise by hitting against each other. *I ran upstairs, the keys jangling in my pockets... An ice-cream truck drives up and jangles its bell.* ▶ Also N SING *...the jangle of armour.*

2 v-ERG If something **jangles** your nerves, or make your nerves **jangle**, it makes you feel very nervous or agitated. *The klaxon of action stations always jangled a man's nerves... The slightest rumour now sets nerves jangling and shares go down yet again.*

janitor /dʒænɪtə/ **janitors**

NC A **janitor** is a person whose job is to look after a building. *He was hired as a janitor.*

January /dʒænjuəri/

NU **January** is the first month of the year in the Western calendar. *...an unusually cold January.*

Japan /dʒəpæn/

Japan is a country in the Pacific, off the eastern coast of Asia. The four principal islands are Hokkaido, Honshu, Shikoku, and Kyushu. Japan entered the Second World War by attacking the US Navy at Pearl Harbour in 1941. The first use of atom bombs at Hiroshima and Nagasaki led to the end of the war in 1945. After the Second World War Japan developed high technology industries and it is now the world's largest producer of cars, washing machines, and watches. It also exports computers, stereos, televisions, and video recorders. Emperor Akihito succeeded his father, Emperor Hirohito, in 1989. Kiichi Miyazawa, of the Liberal Democratic Party (LDP), became Prime Minister in 1991. ♦ **Japanese** /dʒæpəniːz/ ADJ, N PL, N

▪ *per capita GNP:* US$21,040 ▪ *religion:* Shintoism, Buddhism ▪ *language:* Japanese ▪ *currency:* yen ▪ *capital:* Tokyo ▪ *population:* 123 million (1989) ▪ *size:* 377,815 square kilometres.

Japanese /dʒæpəniːz/. **Japanese** is the singular and plural of the noun.

1 ADJ **Japanese** means belonging or relating to Japan, its people or its culture. *...the Japanese electronics firm, Matsushita.*

2 NC The **Japanese** are the people who come from Japan. *The Japanese eat rice often and are particular about its taste.*

3 NU **Japanese** is the language spoken by people who live in Japan. *...language courses to teach French, German, Italian and Japanese.*

jar /dʒɑː/ **jars, jarring, jarred**

1 NC A **jar** is a glass container with a lid that is used for storing food. *The liquid should be allowed to settle in a sealed jar for 4 to 5 weeks.*

2 NC You can use **jar** to refer to a jar and its contents, or to the contents only. *...a jar of peanut butter.*

3 v If something **jars** on you, you find it unpleasant or annoying. *The harsh, metallic sound jarred on her... He had a way of speaking that jarred.*

4 vo If something **jars** you, it gives you an unpleasant shock. *He was evidently jarred by my appearance.* ♦ **jarring** ADJ *...a jarring experience.*

5 v-ERG If things **jar** or if you **jar** them, they strike

against each other with quite a lot of force. *The house shook and his bones were jarred... A steel beam jarred loose by the quake fell on her.* ▶ Also NC *Knocks and jars can cause weakness in the spine.*

jargon /dʒɑːgən/
NU **Jargon** consists of words and expressions that are used in special or technical ways by particular groups of people. *...complex legal jargon.*

jarring /dʒɑːrɪŋ/
1 ADJ Something that is **jarring** irritates or upsets you, often because it seems strange or unsuitable in its surroundings. *There's a jarring addition to the landscape: a purple, red and yellow building... At times the contrast can be jarring.*
2 See also **jar**.

jasmine /dʒæzmɪn/
NU **Jasmine** is a climbing plant which has small white or yellow flowers with a pleasant smell. *She was sent a sweet-smelling jasmine flower by a 16-year-old boy.*

jaundice /dʒɔːndɪs/
NU **Jaundice** is a serious illness that makes your skin and eyes yellow. *They can pass into the bile duct and cause jaundice.*

jaundiced /dʒɔːndɪst/
ADJ A **jaundiced** attitude or view is pessimistic and not at all enthusiastic; a literary word. *He takes a rather jaundiced view of societies and clubs.*

jaunt /dʒɔːnt/ **jaunts**
NC A **jaunt** is a short journey which you go on for pleasure. *We got lost on a motor jaunt to Marrakesh.*

jaunty /dʒɔːnti/
ADJ **Jaunty** means light-hearted, full of confidence, and energetic. *He spoke suddenly in a jaunty tone... She adjusted her hat to a jaunty angle.*

javelin /dʒævəlɪn/ **javelins**
NC A **javelin** is a long spear that is thrown in sports competitions. *Backley became the first man to throw the javelin over 90 metres.*

jaw /dʒɔː/ **jaws**
1 NC Your **jaw** is the part of your face below your mouth which moves up and down when you eat. *His jaw dropped in surprise.*
2 NC Your **jaw** is also one of the two bones in the lower part of your face which your teeth are attached to. *...the upper jaw... The panther held a snake in its jaws.*

Jawara, Sir Dawda Kairaba
/daʊdə kaɪrɑːbə dʒəwɑːrə/
Sir Dawda Kairaba Jawara became Premier of Gambia in 1962, Prime Minister of independent Gambia in 1965, and President when Gambia became a republic in 1970. He was Minister of Education from 1960 to 1961. He founded the People's Progressive Party (PPP) in 1960. Born: 1924.

jawbone /dʒɔːbəʊn/ **jawbones**
NC A **jawbone** is the bone in the lower jaw of a person or animal. *...slaying the Philistines with the jawbone of an ass.*

jay /dʒeɪ/ **jays**
NC A **jay** is a brownish-pink bird with blue and black wings that lives in Europe and Asia. *The problem with hazelnuts is that the squirrels and the jays will get there first.*

jaywalker /dʒeɪwɔːkə/ **jaywalkers**
NC A **jaywalker** is a person who crosses roads in a careless and dangerous way. *The trouble with driving in the city is that there are so many jaywalkers.*

jaywalking /dʒeɪwɔːkɪŋ/
NU **Jaywalking** is the act of crossing a road or walking in a road in a careless and dangerous way. *In some countries you can be arrested for jaywalking.*

jazz /dʒæz/ **jazzes, jazzing, jazzed**
NU **Jazz** is a style of music that is usually played with drums, saxophones, and trumpets and that often involves improvisation. *Outside the US where it was born, jazz took rather longer to become respectable... Miles Davis, the legendary jazz trumpeter.*
jazz up PHRASAL VERB If you **jazz** something **up**, you make it look more colourful, interesting, or exciting; an informal expression. *They've certainly jazzed this place up since the last time I was here.*

jazzed-up
ADJ Music that is **jazzed-up** has been changed in order to make it sound more like popular music or jazz; an informal word. *...a jazzed-up version of one of the Brandenburg Concertos.*

jazzy /dʒæzi/ **jazzier, jazziest**
1 ADJ If you describe something as **jazzy**, you mean that it is colourful and modern; an informal use. *He was dressed in a jazzy suit and a large yellow cravat.*
2 ADJ Music that is **jazzy** is in the style of jazz. *...a large orchestra playing jazzy rhythms.*

JCB /dʒeɪsiːbiː/ **JCBs**
NC A **JCB** is a type of construction machine used for digging earth; **JCB** is a trademark. *The superstition among the urban manual labourers was so strong that they wouldn't go near it with their JCBs or their machines.*

jct.
On maps and roadsigns, **jct.** is used as a written abbreviation for 'junction' and refers to the places where junctions are found on roads, railways, and motorways.

jealous /dʒeləs/
1 ADJ If you are **jealous**, you feel anger or bitterness towards someone who has something that you would like to have. *I often felt jealous because David could go out when he wished... They may feel jealous of your success.*
2 ADJ If you are **jealous**, you feel that you must try to keep someone that you have a close relationship with, or something that you have, because you think someone else might take them away from you. *She was a very jealous woman... He was jealous of his wife and suspected her of adultery.* ◆ **jealously** ADV *They were jealously guarding their independence.*

jealousy /dʒeləsi/ **jealousies**
NU or NC **Jealousy** is the quality of being jealous. *Jimmie felt a surge of jealousy... He was good at talking me out of my suspicions and jealousies.*

Jean, Grand Duke of Luxembourg /ʒɒnˈ/
Jean became Grand Duke of Luxembourg in 1964, after the abdication of his mother, Grand Duchess Charlotte. Born: 1921.

jeans /dʒiːnz/
N PL **Jeans** are casual trousers made of strong denim. *Levi American blue jeans remain as popular as ever. ...a pair of jeans.*

Jeddah /dʒedə/
Jeddah is the administrative capital of Saudi Arabia and its largest city. Population: 1,500,000 (1983).

jeep /dʒiːp/ **jeeps**
NC A **Jeep** is a small four-wheeled vehicle that can travel over rough ground; **Jeep** is a trademark. *A jeep pulled up and a marine jumped out.*

jeer /dʒɪə/ **jeers, jeering, jeered**
V, VO, or V A If you **jeer** at someone, you say rude and insulting things to them. *Tens of thousands of opposition demonstrators booed and jeered when the expected announcement was not made... Unofficial demonstrators on Red Square jeered President Gorbachev and his colleagues off the platform... Students also leaned out of their dormitory windows and jeered at police on the streets outside.* ◆ **jeering** ADJ *...the jeering crowd.*

Jehovah /dʒɪhəʊvə/
N PROP **Jehovah** is the name given to God in the Old Testament. *...the wrath of Jehovah.*

Jehovah's Witness, Jehovah's Witnesses
NC A **Jehovah's Witness** is a member of a religious organization which accepts some Christian ideas and believes that the world is going to end very soon. *Sixty members of the Jehovah's Witness religious sect are in prison in Poland.*

jejune /dʒɪdʒuːn/
ADJ Something that is **jejune** is considered to be very simple and unsophisticated; a literary word. *...a jejune notion that she'd seen it all.*

jell /dʒel/. See **gel**.

jellied /dʒelid/
ADJ **Jellied** food is prepared and eaten in a jelly. *If you don't like oysters, you probably won't like jellied eels.*

Jell-O /dʒɛləʊ/
NU In the United States, Jell-O is a flavouring that is used in making jelly desserts; Jell-O is a trademark. *...orange Jell-O.*

jelly /dʒɛli/ **jellies**
1 N MASS Jelly is a clear food made from gelatine, fruit juice, and sugar, which is eaten as a dessert. *Her mother passed around plates of jelly and custard. ...a jelly on a plate.*
2 N MASS Jelly is also a kind of jam made by boiling fruit juice and sugar. *...slices of bread, smeared with butter and jelly... The jelly is a deliciously dark orange... From these fruits they're making preserved products, such as jams and jellies.*
3 NU Jelly can also mean any substance which is clear and partly liquid, partly solid. *The ointment resembles petroleum jelly when it's made up. ...a laboratory plate containing a special jelly.*

jellyfish /dʒɛlifɪʃ/. Jellyfish is both the singular and the plural form.
NC A jellyfish is a sea creature with a clear soft body and tentacles which can sting you. *Shoals of giant jellyfish have been spotted at resorts in Devon and Cornwall.*

jemmy /dʒɛmi/ **jemmies**
NC A jemmy is a heavy metal bar which is curved at one end and which is used as a tool especially by criminals for forcing things open. *Any filing cabinet will yield to a jemmy and a bit of brute force.*

jeopardize /dʒɛpədaɪz/ **jeopardizes, jeopardizing, jeopardized;** also spelt **jeopardise.**
VO If you jeopardize a situation, you do something that may destroy or damage it. *This judgment may jeopardize his job... I didn't want to jeopardize my relationship with my new friend.*

jeopardy /dʒɛpədi/
If something or someone is in jeopardy, they are in a dangerous situation, where they might fail, be lost, or be destroyed. *She had placed herself in jeopardy in order to save my life... Their future is in jeopardy.*

jerk /dʒɜːk/ **jerks, jerking, jerked**
1 V-ERG If something jerks or if you jerk someone or something, it is moved suddenly and forcefully. *The door of the van was jerked open... The driver jerked the wheel and yanked the gear lever, gesturing out of the window... That means that your muscles suddenly jerk as you're falling asleep.* ▶ Also NC *The man pulled the girl back with a jerk.*
2 VA If you jerk in a particular direction or in a particular way, you move with a very sudden and quick movement. *She jerked away from him... Jerking suddenly awake, he lay very still and listened.*
3 NC If you call someone a jerk, you mean that they are very stupid; an offensive use. *He called his successor at Houston a jerk.*

jerkin /dʒɜːkɪn/ **jerkins**
NC A jerkin is a sleeveless jacket worn by men and women, especially in former times. *...a big youth in a black leather jerkin.*

jerky /dʒɜːki/
ADJ Movements that are jerky are sudden and abrupt and do not flow smoothly. *She lit a cigarette with quick, jerky movements.*

jerry-built /dʒɛribɪlt/
ADJ If houses or blocks of flats are jerry-built, they have been built very quickly and cheaply, without much care for safety or quality. *Everybody was out of work and the jerry-built houses had been neglected.*

jersey /dʒɜːzi/ **jerseys**
1 NC A jersey is a knitted garment that covers the upper part of your body and your arms. You pull it on over your head. *...her striped jersey... He took the race leader's yellow jersey yesterday, winning the morning time trial.*
2 NU Jersey is a knitted fabric used to make clothing. *I have always loved using jersey, preferably cotton jersey. ...her plain lilac jersey dress.*

Jerusalem /dʒəruːsələm/
Jerusalem is Israel's largest city. It became the capital of Israel in 1967, but many countries refuse to move their embassies from Tel Aviv. Population: 447,000 (1985).

jest /dʒɛst/ **jests**
NC A jest is an amusing comment or a joke; an old-fashioned use. *He'd obviously enjoyed the jest.* ● If you say something in jest, you do not mean it seriously, but want to be amusing. *It was said half in jest.*

jester /dʒɛstə/ **jesters**
NC A jester is a man in former times whose job it was to amuse the king or queen, for example by telling jokes or performing tricks. *...the medieval Court Jester.*

Jesuit /dʒɛzjuɪt/ **Jesuits**
NC A Jesuit is a Catholic priest who belongs to the Society of Jesus, which does a lot of missionary work and is especially loyal to the Pope. *The Silesians are the Roman Catholic Church's third largest order after the Jesuits and the Franciscans.*

Jesus /dʒiːzəs/
1 N PROP Jesus or Jesus Christ is the name of the man who Christians believe was the son of God, and whose teachings are the basis of Christianity. *Easter is here, and Christians are remembering the death and resurrection of Jesus Christ.*
2 Some people use Jesus as a swear word used to express surprise, shock, or annoyance, or to emphasize what they are saying; an informal use, which many people find offensive. *Jesus, this place looks like Cape Canaveral.*

jet /dʒɛt/ **jets, jetting, jetted**
1 NC A jet is an aeroplane that is powered by a jet engine. *She woke just as the big jet from Hong Kong touched down.*
2 VA If you jet somewhere, you travel there in a fast aeroplane. *...jetting around the world in a Jumbo.*
3 NC A jet of water or gas is a strong, fast, thin stream of it. *He blew a jet of water into the air.*
4 NU Jet is a hard black stone that is used in jewellery.

jet-black
ADJ Something that is jet-black is very dark black in colour. *His hair was jet-black. ...their jet-black wings.*

jet engine, jet engines
NC A jet engine is an engine, especially in an aeroplane, in which hot air and gases are pushed out at the back. *Rolls-Royce says it has successfully tested the world's largest jet engine.*

jetlag /dʒɛtlæg/
NU Jetlag is a feeling of confusion and tiredness that people experience after a long journey in an aeroplane, especially when they cross time zones. *With jetlag still a problem, I almost fell asleep during the meeting.*

jet-lagged /dʒɛtlægd/
ADJ If you are jet-lagged, you are suffering from jetlag. *Poor hotel service is just one of the problems facing any jet-lagged business traveller.*

jet-propelled
ADJ An aeroplane that is jet-propelled uses jet engines to provide its power. *Heinkel built the world's first jet-propelled aircraft.*

jetsam /dʒɛtsəm/
NU Jetsam is rubbish that is floating on the sea or that has been left by the sea on the shore; a formal word.

jet set
N SING The jet set are rich and successful people, especially young people, who live in a luxurious way. *...the whole French and Italian jet set.*

jet-setter, jet-setters
NC A jet-setter is a member of the jet set. *An international jet-setter, she was often photographed in glittering company, a friend of the rich and famous.*

jet-setting /dʒɛtsetɪŋ/
ADJ ATTRIB Jet-setting is used to refer to the activities and life-style of the jet set. *Currently the preserve of jet-setting businessmen, supersonic flight could become a routine form of travel in the 21st century.*

jettison /dʒɛtɪsən/ **jettisons, jettisoning, jettisoned**
VO If you jettison something, you deliberately reject it or throw it away; a formal word. *The system allows the tank to be jettisoned when it's empty. ...ideas too valuable, too sacred, to jettison.*

jetty /dʒeti/ jetties
NC A **jetty** is a wide stone wall or wooden platform at the edge of the sea or a river, where people can get on and off boats. *The boat was tied up alongside a crumbling limestone jetty.*

Jew /dʒuː/ Jews
NC A **Jew** is a person who believes in and practises the religion of Judaism. *They were practising astrology, which the Jews regarded with disapproval.*

jewel /dʒuːəl/ jewels
1 NC A **jewel** is a precious stone used to decorate valuable things that you wear, such as rings or necklaces. *She was wearing even more jewels than the Queen Mother!*
2 If you describe an achievement or thing as the **jewel** in someone's **crown**, you mean that that achievement or thing is the one they are most proud of. *Of all the measures which the Labour administration introduced, the creation of the National Health Service was the jewel in its crown.*

jewelled /dʒuːəld/; spelt **jeweled** in American English.
ADJ ATTRIB **Jewelled** items and ornaments are decorated with precious stones. *...a jewelled brooch.*

jeweller /dʒuːələ/ jewellers; spelt **jeweler** in American English.
1 NC A **jeweller** is a person who makes, sells, and repairs jewellery and watches. *The jewel encrusted, gold eggs were made by the jeweller Carl Fabergé.*
2 NC A **jeweller** or a **jeweller's** is a shop where jewellery and watches are sold and repaired. *...the famous jeweller, Van Cleef & Arpels.*

jewellery /dʒuːəlri/; spelt **jewelry** in American English.
NU **Jewellery** consists of ornaments that people wear such as rings, bracelets, and necklaces. *She thought some of her jewellery was missing. ...a jewellery box.*

Jewess /dʒuːes/ Jewesses
NC A **Jewess** is a woman or girl who is Jewish; an old-fashioned word which many people find offensive.

Jewish /dʒuːɪʃ/
ADJ **Jewish** means belonging or relating to the religion of Judaism or to its followers. *...the Orthodox Hasidic Jewish community.*

Jewry /dʒuəri/
NU **Jewry** is all the people who believe in and practise the religion of Judaism; a formal word. *...her championing of the rights of Soviet Jewry.*

Jiang Zemin /dʒɑːŋ dʒəmɪn/
Jiang Zemin succeeded Deng Xiaoping as Chairman of the Chinese Communist Party (CCP) Central Military Commission in 1989. He also became General Secretary of the CCP in 1989. He was Mayor of Shanghai from 1985 to 1988. He became a member of the Central Committee of the CCP in 1982 and of the Politburo in 1987. Born: 1934.

jib /dʒɪb/ jibs, jibbing, jibbed
v If a horse or donkey **jibs**, it stops suddenly and refuses to continue. *Once again the donkey jibbed and would not pass it.*
jib at PHRASAL VERB If you **jib at** something, you are unwilling to do it or to accept a new situation; an old-fashioned expression. *He had begun to jib at carrying out the orders of his masters.*

jibe /dʒaɪb/ jibes, jibing, jibed; also spelt **gibe** for the meaning in paragraph 1.
1 NC A **jibe** is a rude or insulting remark about someone. *He swallowed and tried to smile at the jibe.*
2 V+with If one account or claim **jibes** with another, it agrees with it; used in informal American English. *He did not elaborate, but the comments jibe with recent reports.*

jiffy /dʒɪfi/
If you say that you will do something **in a jiffy**, you mean that you will do it quickly and very soon; an informal expression. *I'll be back in a jiffy.*

jig /dʒɪg/ jigs
1 NC A **jig** is a lively folk dance. *...a traditional Irish jig.*
2 NC A **jig** is also a device for holding something steady when it is being machined by a tool such as a drill. *Most of the tools are actually jigs which are clamped onto the end of the bone to align the cutters.*

jiggery-pokery /dʒɪgəripəukəri/
NU **Jiggery-pokery** is behaviour or activity that involves mischief, trickery, or dishonesty, and is often done in secret; an informal expression. *He thought there was jiggery-pokery going on in the stables.*

jiggle /dʒɪgl/ jiggles, jiggling, jiggled
VO If you **jiggle** something, you move it quickly up and down or from side to side; an informal word. *She jiggled the front door handle.*

jigsaw /dʒɪgsɔː/ jigsaws
1 NC A **jigsaw** or **jigsaw puzzle** is a toy consisting of a picture on cardboard or wood that has been cut up, and which has to be put back together again. *Their products range from card games and jigsaws to computers.*
2 N SING You can refer to a complicated situation that involves more than one issue or more than one person as a **jigsaw** or **jigsaw puzzle**. *By the mid-1780s many pieces of the revolutionary jigsaw were in place... Karachi is a complicated jigsaw of different communities.*

jihad /dʒɪhæd/
N SING A **jihad** is a holy war which Islam allows Muslims to fight against those who reject its teachings. *The basic motivation behind their struggle is seen as a jihad in defence of Islam.*

jilt /dʒɪlt/ jilts, jilting, jilted
VO If you **jilt** someone who you have promised to marry, you end your relationship with them suddenly. *He had jilted her to marry a maidservant.*

Jim Crow /dʒɪm krəʊ/
ADJ ATTRIB **Jim Crow** is used to describe racist laws and attitudes; used in American English. *It was passed into law 37 years ago and it was the main Jim Crow law segregating public facilities by race.*

jimmy /dʒɪmi/ jimmies
NC A **jimmy** is the same as a **jemmy**; used in American English.

jingle /dʒɪŋgl/ jingles, jingling, jingled
1 V-ERG When something **jingles** or when you **jingle** it, it makes a gentle ringing noise, like small bells. *...waving her arms in the air so that her charm bracelet jingled... People jingle coins in their pockets for good luck.* ► Also N SING *I can hear the jingle of bracelets coming up behind me in the dark.*
2 NC A **jingle** is a short and simple tune, often with words, used to advertise a product on radio or television. *That's the musical jingle for London's Spectrum Radio.*

jingoism /dʒɪŋgəʊɪzəm/
NU **Jingoism** is enthusiastic and unreasonable belief in the superiority of your country, especially when it involves support for a war against another country; used showing disapproval. *In the United States there was a rift between jingoism and calm counsel.*

jingoistic /dʒɪŋgəʊɪstɪk/
ADJ Something that is **jingoistic** shows enthusiastic and unreasonable belief in the superiority of a particular country, especially in support of a war against another country. *...jingoistic songs, flag-waving, and patriotic orations.*

jinx /dʒɪŋks/ jinxes
NC A **jinx** is bad luck, or something that is thought to bring bad luck. *...Muck Hall: the farm with the jinx on it.*

jinxed /dʒɪŋkst/
ADJ Something that is **jinxed** is considered to be unlucky or to bring bad luck. *The Boston Red Sox have been jinxed ever since.*

jitters /dʒɪtəz/
N PL The **jitters** are feelings of extreme nervousness that you get just before you have to do something important or when you are expecting important news; an informal word. *To keep her from getting the jitters, I pretended to know what I was doing.*

jittery /dʒɪtəri/
ADJ Someone who is **jittery** feels extremely nervous; an informal word. *Her government has survived six coup attempts and the mood in Manila is still jittery.*

jive /dʒaɪv/ jives, jiving, jived
1 N SING The **jive** is a dance which became popular in the 1940s and 1950s, at first performed to jazz music

and later to rock and roll music. *The frenetic pace of jive music suited the juke box very well.*
2 v To **jive** means to dance the jive. *You don't have to know how to twist and jive.*

Jnr.
Jnr. is a written abbreviation for 'Junior' that is used after someone's name to distinguish them from an older member of the family who has the same name. *...Fred A. Hartley Jnr.*

Job /dʒəʊb/
1 If you say that someone has **the patience of Job**, you mean that they are extremely patient; an old-fashioned expression.
2 If you call someone a **Job's comforter**, you mean that they make someone who is unhappy or in trouble even more unhappy by talking about his or her troubles; an old-fashioned expression.

job /dʒɒb/ **jobs**
1 NC A **job** is the work that someone does to earn money. *Gladys finally got a good job as a secretary... Several senior executives running the project will lose their jobs.*
2 NC A **job** is also a particular task. *There are always plenty of jobs to be done round here. ...a repair job.*
3 NC+POSS The **job** of a particular person or thing is their duty or function. *It's not their job to decide what ought to be the law... His job was to guide this giant project to completion in 1993.*
4 N SING If you say that you had a **job** doing something, you are emphasizing how difficult it was; an informal use. *I had a difficult job sneaking into the house.*
● **Job** is used in these phrases. ● If you say that something is **just the job**, you mean that it is exactly what you wanted or needed; an informal expression.
● If you refer to work as **jobs for the boys**, you mean that it has been created to provide employment for someone's friends or relatives; an informal expression, used showing disapproval. *The programme was in danger of looking like jobs for the boys.* ● **It's a good job**: see **good**.

jobbing /dʒɒbɪŋ/
ADJ ATTRIB A **jobbing** worker does not work for someone on a regular basis, but does particular jobs when they are asked to. *...a jobbing builder.*

jobless /dʒɒbləs/
ADJ Someone who is **jobless** does not have a job, but would like one. *During the depression millions were jobless and homeless.* ▶ Also N PL *We have to do more for the poor and the jobless.*

job lot, job lots
NC A **job lot** is a number of things of a similar kind which are sold together, for example in an auction. *He bought a job lot of 50 books for £3.*

job sharing
NU **Job sharing** is the arrangement by which two people work part-time at the same job, for example one person working in the morning and the other in the afternoon. *We must begin to look seriously at the whole question of job sharing.*

jock /dʒɒk/ **jocks**
NC A **jock** is someone who is good at sport, particularly at school or college; used in informal American English. *...some high school jock she's been watching every afternoon in the gym where she goes.*

jockey /dʒɒki/ **jockeys, jockeying, jockeyed**
1 NC A **jockey** is someone who rides a horse in a race. *Jockey Willie Carson will still ride the favourite in Sunday's Prix de L'Arc de Triomphe.*
2 In a struggle for fame or power, if someone is **jockeying for position**, they are using various methods to gain an advantage over their rivals. *As President Endara's star wanes, his two vice-presidents seem to be jockeying for position to replace him.*

Jockey Shorts
N PL **Jockey Shorts** are men's underpants that are shaped like the shorts worn for playing sports, and cover the top part of the thighs; **Jockey Shorts** is a trademark. *I found out that in jockey shorts, I don't look so perfect.*

jockstrap /dʒɒkstræp/ **jockstraps**
NC A **jockstrap** is a piece of clothing worn by

sportsmen under their shorts or trousers to support their genitals. *If he had his way, Michelangelo's David would be sheathed in a jockstrap.*

jocose /dʒəʊkəʊs/
ADJ **Jocose** means amusing or humorous; a literary word. *He said this in a tone of jocose raillery.*
◆ **jocosely** ADV *...after twenty months of cold labour, as one of them jocosely put it.*

jocular /dʒɒkjʊlə/; a literary word.
1 ADJ Someone who is **jocular** is cheerful and often makes jokes. *...a jocular English visitor.*
2 ADJ Something that is **jocular** is intended to make people laugh. *...a jocular remark.*

jodhpurs /dʒɒdpəz/
N PL **Jodhpurs** are close-fitting trousers worn when riding a horse. *Herr Stangl ordered specially tailored riding boots and white jodhpurs and a jacket.*

jog /dʒɒg/ **jogs, jogging, jogged**
1 v If you **jog**, you run slowly, often as a form of exercise. *...people who jog or play squash.* ◆ **jogging** NU *...the current enthusiasm for jogging.*
2 N SING A **jog** is a slow run. *I speeded up to a jog and moved up the road briskly.*
3 VO If you **jog** something, you push or bump it slightly so that it shakes or moves. *Be careful not to jog the table.*
4 If someone or something **jogs** your **memory**, they remind you of something. *He had demonstrated the sound to jog my memory.*

jogger /dʒɒgə/ **joggers**
NC A **jogger** is a person who runs at a jogging pace as a form of exercise. *...a couple of track-suited joggers.*

joggle /dʒɒgl/ **joggles, joggling, joggled**
VO If you **joggle** something, you move or shake it gently and repeatedly, especially up and down. *She joggled the baby on her arm.*

john /dʒɒn/ **johns**
NC A **john** is the same as a **toilet**; used in informal American English. *...the bathrooms and the johns and the showers... They don't have to wait in line to get into the john.*

John Paul II, Pope /dʒɒn pɔːl/
John Paul II became Pope in 1978. Born Karol Wojtyla, he was ordained in 1946. In 1954 he was appointed Professor of Social Ethics at Lublin Catholic University. He was Archbishop of Cracow from 1963 to 1978 and became a Cardinal in 1967. Born: 1920.

Johnson, Lyndon Baines /lɪndən beɪnz dʒɒnsn/
Lyndon Baines Johnson was President of the United States from 1963 to 1969. He was born in 1908 and was a member of the Democratic Party. He was a member of the Senate from 1948 to 1960. He served as Vice President from 1961 to 1963, and became President following the assassination of John F Kennedy. He died in 1973.

joie de vivre /ʒwɑː də viːvrə/
NU **Joie de vivre** is a feeling of happiness and enjoyment of life; a literary expression. *They were filled with joie de vivre.*

join /dʒɔɪn/ **joins, joining, joined**
1 VO If one person or vehicle **joins** another, the two people or vehicles come together in the same place, so that both of them can do something together. *He went for a walk before joining his brother for tea... The helicopter was quickly joined by a second.*
2 VO If you **join** a queue, you go and stand at the end of it. *They went off to join the queue for coffee... The van joined the row of cars.*
3 V-RECIP If two roads or rivers **join**, or if one **joins** the other, they meet or come together at a particular point. *The torrents join and increase in strength, washing away people, houses, roads... This road joins the motorway at junction 16.*
4 VOorV If you **join** an organization, you become a member of it. *Paul joined the amateur group that John was leading... Both Portugal and Spain joined the European Community in 1986... It had decided to join.*
5 VO If you **join** an activity, you become involved in it. *They were invited to join the feasting... Thousands of people joined the strike.* ● **to join forces**: see **force**.
6 VO To **join** two things means to fix or fasten them

together. *Cut them down the middle and join the two outside edges together.*

7 vo If a line, a path, or a bridge **joins** two places, it connects them. *Draw a straight line joining these two points... The cities are joined by telecommunication links... The two ends of the Channel Tunnel were linked and Britain was once again joined to continental Europe.*

8 NC A **join** is a place where two things are fastened or fixed together. *The repair was done so well, you could hardly see the join.*

join in PHRASAL VERB If you **join in** an activity, you become involved in it. *Parents should join in these discussions... He tries to join in.*

join up PHRASAL VERB **1** If someone **joins up**, they become a member of the armed forces. *At eighteen, just before joining up and going abroad, I met Elizabeth.* **2** If you **join up** two or more things, you fasten or connect them together. *I used to join up all his paper clips in a long chain.*

joiner /dʒɔɪnə/ **joiners**
NC A **joiner** is a person who makes wooden window frames, door frames, and doors. *With the dry weather came the chance for builders, joiners and slaters to get to work on the houses.*

joinery /dʒɔɪnəri/
NU **Joinery** is the skill and work of a joiner. *In the seventeenth century improved joinery techniques produced the open wooden staircase.*

joint /dʒɔɪnt/ **joints**
1 ADJ ATTRIB **Joint** means shared by or belonging to two or more people. *We have opened a joint account at the bank... The presentation was a joint effort.* ♦ **jointly** ADV *It was built jointly by France and Germany.*
2 NC A **joint** is a part of your body such as your elbow or knee where two bones meet and are able to move together. *He can feel the rheumatism in his joints. ...the joints of the fingers.*
3 NC A **joint** is also a place where two things, such as pieces of wood, are fastened or fixed together. *Cracks appeared at the joints between the new plaster and the old.*
4 NC A **joint** of meat is a fairly large piece of meat suitable for roasting. *...a joint of roast beef.*
5 NC You can also refer to a place where people go for some form of entertainment such as a nightclub as a **joint**; an informal use. *...strip joints.*
6 NC Some people refer to a cigarette which contains cannabis as a **joint**; an informal use. *They have a picture of four ounces of marijuana and a picture of 290 fat joints you can roll from four ounces.*

jointed /dʒɔɪntɪd/
ADJ Something that is **jointed** has joints that move. *The doll had jointed legs and arms.*

joint-stock company, joint-stock companies
NC A **joint-stock company** is a business company that is owned by the people who have bought shares in that company; a technical term in business. *The government enacted legislation allowing the formation of joint-stock companies.*

joist /dʒɔɪst/ **joists**
NC A **joist** is a long thick piece of wood, metal, or concrete that is used in buildings or other structures, especially to support a floor or ceiling. *...a roof joist.*

joke /dʒəʊk/ **jokes, joking, joked**
1 NC A **joke** is something that is said or done to make you laugh, for example a funny story. *Dave was telling me this joke about a penguin.*
2 v If you **joke**, you tell funny stories or say things that are amusing and not serious. *Don't worry, I was only joking.*
3 N SING If you say that someone or something is a **joke**, you mean that they are ridiculous and not worthy of respect; an informal use. *His colleagues regard him as a joke.*
4 If you say that something is **no joke**, you mean that it is difficult or unpleasant. *The North slope of Alaska is desolate. Working outside is no joke.*

joker /dʒəʊkə/ **jokers**
1 NC Someone who is a **joker** likes making jokes or doing amusing things. *He was an adventurer and*

practical joker.
2 NC The **joker** in a pack of cards is a card which does not belong to any of the four suits. ● If you refer to someone or something as the **joker in the pack**, you mean that their behaviour or attitude is different from other people's, and is unpredictable and possibly mischievous. *Even if you did reach some common accord, you still have the jokers in the pack—the terrorist splinter groups.*

jokey /dʒəʊki/
ADJ Something that is **jokey** is amusing and does not have any serious meaning; an informal word. *They all had jokey nicknames.*

jokingly /dʒəʊkɪŋli/
ADV If you say or do something **jokingly**, you do it to amuse someone or without seriously meaning it. *My friend said jokingly that George had lost around two hundred pounds.*

jollity /dʒɒləti/
NU **Jollity** is cheerful behaviour; an old-fashioned word. *He admired her high spirits and her jollity.*

jolly /dʒɒli/; an old-fashioned word.
1 ADJ A **jolly** person is happy and cheerful. *Buddy's mother was a jolly, easy-going woman.*
2 ADJ A **jolly** event is lively and enjoyable. *I had a very jolly time.*
3 SUBMOD You can use **jolly** to emphasize something. *That will be a jolly good investment for the future... You work jolly hard here, you know.*
4 ADV You can use **jolly well** to emphasize what you are saying, especially when you are annoyed or upset. *I'm jolly well not going to ring her up!*

jolt /dʒəʊlt/ **jolts, jolting, jolted**
1 V-ERG If something **jolts** or if you **jolt** it, it moves suddenly and fairly violently. *...enormous loads that jolted and swayed... She jolted his arm.* ► Also NC *I came down slowly at first, but then with a jolt.*
2 vo If you **are jolted** by something, it gives you an unpleasant surprise or shock. *I was jolted awake by a bright light.* ► Also N SING *The aim of Detention Centres is to give kids a jolt.*

Jordan /dʒɔːdən/
The **Hashemite Kingdom of Jordan** is a country in south-west Asia. Jordan was a part of the Ottoman Empire until the First World War. It was then ruled by Britain under a League of Nations mandate and was known as Transjordan. It became independent in 1946. In 1967 Israel occupied the West Bank and East Jerusalem. There are about 1 million Palestinian refugees in Jordan, about 200,000 of them living in refugee camps. Approximately 500,000 Arabs and Asians fled into Jordan following Iraq's invasion of Kuwait in 1990. King Hussein ibn Talal succeeded his father in 1952. Field Marshal Sharif Zaid ibn Shaker became Prime Minister in 1991. Legislation to legalize political parties was introduced in 1991. Jordan exports fruit and vegetables, and phosphates. Large foreign debts and high inflation are major economic problems. Jordan is a member of the Arab League. ♦ **Jordanian** /dʒɔːdeɪniən/ N, ADJ
▪ *per capita GNP:* US$1,500 ▪ *religion:* Islam (mainly Sunni) ▪ *language:* Arabic ▪ *currency:* dinar ▪ *capital:* Amman ▪ *population:* 4 million (1989) ▪ *size:* 97,740 square kilometres.

joss stick /dʒɒs stɪk/ **joss sticks**
NC A **joss stick** is a thin stick covered with a substance that burns very slowly and fills the air with a perfumed smell.

jostle /dʒɒsl/ **jostles, jostling, jostled**
V OR V If people **jostle** or if they **jostle** each other, they bump against or push each other in a crowd. *Several of his team-mates pushed and jostled the referee... The crowd jostled to keep their position.*

jot /dʒɒt/ **jots, jotting, jotted**
vo If you **jot** something down, you write it down in the form of a short informal note. *I asked you to jot down a few ideas... I jot odd notes in the back of the diary.*

jotter /dʒɒtə/ **jotters**
NC A **jotter** is a pad or notebook that you write things in, usually in the form of short informal notes. *I looked up a scribbled formula I had in a jotter.*

jottings /dʒɒtɪŋ/

N PL **Jottings** are brief notes that you make about something. *For the purpose of writing my statement, I looked up some old jottings.*

joule /dʒuːl/ **joules**

NC A **joule** is a unit of energy or work; a technical term in physics. *The Nova Laser is able to is able to concentrate 10 thousand Joules of energy into a single flash of light.*

journal /dʒɜːnl/ **journals**

1 NC A **journal** is a magazine which is devoted to a particular subject or area of interest. *...the New England Journal of Medicine. ...a trade journal.*

2 NC A **journal** is also a daily or weekly newspaper, especially one that uses the term 'journal' in its title. *...the Wall Street Journal.*

3 NC A **journal** is also an account which you write of your daily activities. *For nearly three months he had been keeping a journal.*

journalese /dʒɜːnəliːz/

NU **Journalese** is a style of writing which is found in some newspapers or magazines. A typical feature of journalese is the frequent use of cliches or exaggerations.

journalism /dʒɜːnəlɪzəm/

NU **Journalism** is the job of collecting, writing, and publishing news in newspapers and magazines and on television and radio. *Have you ever thought of going into journalism?*

journalist /dʒɜːnəlɪst/ **journalists**

NC A **journalist** is a person who writes, usually about current affairs, for newspapers, magazines, television, or radio. *Two western journalists are missing... She worked as a journalist on The Times.*

journalistic /dʒɜːnəlɪstɪk/

ADJ ATTRIB **Journalistic** means relating to the work of a journalist. *I had no journalistic experience in Britain.*

journey /dʒɜːni/ **journeys, journeying, journeyed**

1 NC When you make a **journey**, you travel from one place to another. *Severe traffic congestion has made the journey to and from work very slow... He went on a journey to London.*

2 VA If you **journey** somewhere, you travel there; a literary use. *The nights became colder as they journeyed north.*

journeyman /dʒɜːnimən/ **journeymen** /dʒɜːnimən/

NC A **journeyman** is a worker who has finished learning a trade but who is employed by someone else rather than working on his or her own; an old-fashioned word. *The printing press employed a small number of journeymen and apprentices.*

joust /dʒaʊst/ **jousts, jousting, jousted**

1 V In medieval times, when two knights on horseback **jousted**, they fought against each other, using lances. ♦ **jousting** NU *...in a land of jousting tournaments, complete with black knights and distressed damsels.*

2 V When two or more people **joust**, they compete with each other for superiority; a literary use. *The deciding match in the men's hockey has old rivals India and Pakistan jousting for gold.* ♦ **jousting** NU *The protest began after a day of political jousting between Mikhail Gorbachev and the Russian Parliament. ...technical jousting between defence and prosecution counsel.*

Jove /dʒəʊv/

By **Jove** is used to emphasize that you are surprised; an old-fashioned, informal expression. *By Jove, he's got a talent.*

jovial /dʒəʊviəl/

ADJ A **jovial** person behaves in a cheerful and happy way. *He was a big, heavy, jovial man. ...a jovial smile.*

jowl /dʒaʊl/ **jowls**

NC Your **jowls** are the lower parts of your cheeks, especially when they hang down and cover your jawbones. *...an old woman with heavy jowls and a double chin.*

joy /dʒɔɪ/ **joys**

1 NU **Joy** is a feeling of great happiness. *She shouted with joy when I told her she was free... His face showed his joy the moment he saw me.*

2 NC+SUPP Something that is a **joy** makes you feel happy or gives you great pleasure. *She discovered the joy of writing... 'Your joys are our joys,' he said, 'your tears are our tears.'*

joyful /dʒɔɪfl/

1 ADJ Something that is **joyful** causes happiness and pleasure. *I still felt sad even after you'd announced the joyful tidings.*

2 ADJ A **joyful** person is extremely happy. *The joyful parents named him Lexington.* ♦ **joyfully** ADV *We welcomed him joyfully to the club.*

joyless /dʒɔɪləs/

ADJ **Joyless** means producing or experiencing no pleasure. *...years and years of joyless married life.*

joyous /dʒɔɪəs/

ADJ **Joyous** means extremely happy and enthusiastic; a literary word. *I spread my arms wide and felt joyous and exalted and free.* ♦ **joyously** ADV *He flung back the curtains joyously and let the sunlight pour in.*

joyride /dʒɔɪraɪd/ **joyrides**

NC If someone goes for a **joyride**, they steal a car and drive it around at high speed for fun. *We've had subway trains taken for joyrides, buses stolen, and found in other parts of the city... The joyride ended when police stopped the bus two miles down the road.*

joyrider /dʒɔɪraɪdə/ **joyriders**

NC A **joyrider** is someone who steals a car and drives it around at high speed for fun. *Fighting broke out when police tried to stop joyriders driving around the streets of a housing estate. ...tougher penalties for joyriders.*

joyriding /dʒɔɪraɪdɪŋ/

NU **Joyriding** is the activity of stealing a car and driving it around at high speed for fun. *...the acute problem of joyriding in Catholic areas of west Belfast... Joyriding by youths has been a factor in recent inner city riots. ...the deaths of two teenagers involved in a joyriding incident.*

joystick /dʒɔɪstɪk/ **joysticks**

1 NC The **joystick** is a lever in an aeroplane which the pilot uses in order to control the direction or height of the aeroplane. *Easing the joystick back she brought the plane in to land.*

2 NC A **joystick** is a lever attached to a computer, which you use to play certain types of computer games.

JP /dʒeɪpiː/ **JPs**

NC A **JP** is a local magistrate. JP is an abbreviation for 'Justice of the Peace'. *The three JPs, acting as judges, gave a 'not guilty' verdict.*

Jr.

Jr. is a written abbreviation for 'Junior' that is used after someone's name to distinguish them from an older member of the family who has the same name; used in American English. *...Alfred P. Sloan Jr.*

Juan Carlos, King of Spain /xwæn kɑːləʊs/

Juan Carlos became King of Spain in 1975 at the death of General Franco, who appointed him his successor in 1969. He is the grandson of King Alfonso XIII of Spain. He initiated the restoration of democracy in Spain. Born: 1938.

jubilant /dʒuːbɪlənt/

ADJ If you are **jubilant**, you feel extremely happy and successful. *...a jubilant Labour Party Conference.*

jubilation /dʒuːbɪleɪʃn/

NU **Jubilation** is a feeling of great happiness and success; a formal word. *There was a general air of jubilation.*

jubilee /dʒuːbɪliː/ **jubilees**

NC A **jubilee** is a special anniversary of an important event, especially the 25th or 50th anniversary. *...Queen Victoria's jubilee.*

Judaic /dʒuːdeɪɪk/

ADJ ATTRIB **Judaic** means belonging or relating to Judaism; a formal word. *Christianity was able to maintain a close link with the Judaic tradition.*

Judaism /dʒuːdeɪɪzəm/

NU **Judaism** is the religion of the Jewish people, which is based on the Old Testament of the Bible and the Talmud or book of laws and traditions. *...the moral teachings of Judaism.*

Judas /dʒuːdəs/ **Judases**
  NC A **Judas** is someone who betrays a friend. *You're a traitor, a liar, a phony, and a Judas.*
judder /dʒʌdə/ **judders, juddering, juddered**
  V If something **judders**, it shakes and vibrates violently. *Lorries judder along beneath my window.*
judge /dʒʌdʒ/ **judges, judging, judged**
  1 NCorTITLE A **judge** is the person in a court of law who decides how the law should be applied, for example how criminals should be punished. *Last week she appeared before a judge... Judge Arnason set Miss Davis free on bail.*
  2 NC+SUPP If someone is a good **judge** of something, they can understand it and make sensible decisions about it. If they are a bad **judge** of something, they often make the wrong decisions about it. *He was a good judge of character.*
  3 VOorV If you **judge** someone or something, you form an opinion about them based on the evidence or information that you have. *It's impossible to judge her age... He judged it wiser to put a stop to this quarrel... I'm not in a position to judge.*
  4 VO If you **judge** a competition, you decide who the winner is. *The competition was judged by the local mayor.*
  5 NC A **judge** is also a person who chooses the winner of a competition. *The panel of judges consisted of a variety of famous people.*
  6 VO If you **judge** someone, you decide whether they are good or bad after you have observed their character or behaviour; used showing disapproval. *She seemed to be watching him, judging him... Social workers declare that they are not out to judge people, but simply want to help.*
judgement /dʒʌdʒmənt/ **judgements**; also spelt **judgment**.
  1 NC A **judgement** is an opinion that you have or express after thinking carefully about something. *I shall make my own judgement on this matter when I see the results... In our judgment, her plan has definitely succeeded.*
  2 NC A **judgement** is also a decision made by a judge or by a court of law. *The final judgment will probably be made in court.*
  3 NU **Judgement** is the ability to make sensible guesses about a situation or sensible decisions about what to do. *My father did not permit me to question his judgement. ...an error of judgement.*
  4 NUorNC **Judgement** is also the process of deciding how good something or someone is. *I have a great fear of judgment... During her career a scientist must survive many judgments.*
  5 NC A **judgement** is also something unpleasant that happens to you and that is considered to be a punishment from God. *War is a judgement on us all for our sins.*
  ● **Judgement** is used in these phrases. ● If you **pass judgement** on something, you give your opinion about it, especially if you are making a criticism. *Pope John Paul has told churchmen that at times it was right for the church to pass judgement on political matters.* ● If you **reserve judgement** about something, you do not give an opinion about it until you know more about it. *Many teachers are reserving judgement on the GCSE until the exam results are published.* ● If something is **against** your **better judgement**, you believe that it would be more sensible not to do it. *Mr King denied there was a danger of Britain being sucked into hostilities against its better judgement.*
judicial /dʒuːdɪʃl/; a formal word.
  1 ADJ ATTRIB **Judicial** means relating to judgement in a court of law. *I would like to go through proper judicial procedures. ...a judicial inquiry.*
  2 ADJ ATTRIB **Judicial** also means showing or using careful judgement in thinking about something. *...examined with judicial care.*
judiciary /dʒuːdɪʃəri/
  N SING The **judiciary** is the branch of authority in a country which is concerned with justice and the legal system. *The judiciary in Malaysia has a reputation of fairness. ...Northern Ireland's judiciary.*

judicious /dʒuːdɪʃəs/; a formal word.
  ADJ An action or decision that is **judicious** shows good judgement and sense. *They made judicious use of government incentives.* ◆ **judiciously** ADV *You put your case most judiciously.*
judo /dʒuːdəʊ/
  NU **Judo** is a Japanese sport or martial art in which two people fight and try to throw each other to the ground. *In the men's judo competition, Japan won the middleweight gold.*
jug /dʒʌg/ **jugs**
  1 NC A **jug** is a container which is used for holding and pouring liquids. *...a big white jug full of beer. ...the milk jug.*
  2 NC You can use **jug** to refer to a jug and its contents, or to the contents only. *...a jug of water.*
jugged hare /dʒʌgd heə/
  NU **Jugged hare** is a stew of hare cooked in a casserole. *...a meal of country paté and jugged hare.*
juggernaut /dʒʌgənɔːt/ **juggernauts**
  1 NC A **juggernaut** is a very large lorry. *...moves to restrict the number of juggernaut lorries en route to northern Europe.*
  2 NC A **juggernaut** is also any large organization or group who are extremely powerful; used showing disapproval. *...the military juggernaut in Iraq... A lot of the Western banks were afraid that the Bank of America juggernaut would just roll over them.*
juggle /dʒʌgl/ **juggles, juggling, juggled**
  1 V+withorVO If you **juggle**, you entertain people by throwing things into the air, catching each one and throwing it up again so that there are several of them in the air at the same time. *...juggling with half a dozen balls... The jugglers juggle chain saws.*
  2 VOorV+with If you **juggle** numbers or ideas, or **juggle** with them, you rearrange them repeatedly in order to make them fit the pattern that you want them to. *Both of them juggle their working hours to be with the children... He was still juggling with figures.*
juggler /dʒʌglə/ **jugglers**
  NC A **juggler** is someone who juggles in order to entertain people. *I had watched a juggler practising his act.*
Jugnauth, Aneerood /ænɪruːd dʒʌgnʌt/
  Aneerood Jugnauth became Prime Minister of Mauritius in 1982. He was elected to the Legislative Assembly in 1963. He served as Minister of State and Development from 1965 to 1967, and of Labour in 1967. He was leader of the Opposition from 1976 to 1982. He founded the Socialist Movement of Mauritius (MSM) in 1983. Born: 1930.
jugular /dʒʌgjʊlə/ **jugulars**
  NC Your **jugular** or **jugular vein** is a large vein in your neck that carries blood from your head back to your heart. *...the channels that drain the blood from the brain into the jugular... His unknown attacker, who used a broken bottle, missed his jugular vein by an inch.* ● If you say that someone **goes for the jugular**, you mean that they ruthlessly attack an opponent's weakest point. *He went for the jugular in his opponent, fighting what has been criticized as a dirty campaign.*
juice /dʒuːs/ **juices**
  1 N MASS **Juice** is the liquid that can be obtained from a fruit or a plant. *...two glasses of pineapple juice... I remember sitting in my grandmother's kitchen drinking grape juice and ginger ale... Most of all I want a beer, a cigarette and an orange juice.*
  2 NCorNU The **juices** of a joint of meat are the liquid that comes out of it when you cook it. *...spooning the juices over the top of a leg of lamb.*
  3 N PL The **juices** in your stomach are the fluids that help you to digest food. *...digestive juices.*
juicy /dʒuːsi/ **juicier, juiciest**
  1 ADJ A fruit or other food that is **juicy** has a lot of juice in it. *...juicy, ripe tomatoes.*
  2 ADJ **Juicy** also means interesting or exciting, or containing scandal; an informal use. *...juicy gossip.*
jukebox /dʒuːkbɒks/ **jukeboxes**
  NC A **jukebox** is a record player in places such as pubs and bars. You put a coin in and choose the record that you want to hear. *My favorite song is on*

the jukebox.

Jul.
Jul. is a written abbreviation for 'July'. *...Tuesday Jul. 31st, 1990.*

July /dʒʊlaɪ/
NU **July** is the seventh month of the year in the Western calendar. *...the summer holidays in July.*

jumble /dʒʌmbl/ **jumbles, jumbling, jumbled**
1 N SING A **jumble** is a lot of different things that are all mixed together in a confused or untidy way. *...a chaotic jumble of motor vehicles of every description... It was an indistinguishable jumble of words.*
2 VO If you **jumble** things, or **jumble** them up, you mix them together so that they are not in the correct order. *The bits and pieces were jumbled up with a lot of stuff that would never be needed again.*

jumble sale, jumble sales
NC A **jumble sale** is a sale of cheap second-hand goods, usually held to raise money for charity. *...the church jumble sale.*

jumbo /dʒʌmbəʊ/ **jumbos**
1 ADJ ATTRIB **Jumbo** means very large; used especially in advertising. *...jumbo steaks.*
2 NC A **jumbo** or a **jumbo jet** is a type of large wide-bodied jet aeroplane; an informal use. *...a Pan Am Boeing 747 Jumbo Jet... Three ambulances drove the half mile from the terminal to the jumbo.*

jump /dʒʌmp/ **jumps, jumping, jumped**
1 V When you **jump**, you push your feet against the ground and move upwards quickly into the air. *The horse jumps over a small stream... He jumped down from the terrace.* ▶ Also NC *It was a spectacular jump.*
2 VO If you **jump** something such as a fence, you jump over it or across it. *Some protesters had jumped the fence to get inside the compound.*
3 VA To **jump** also means to move quickly and suddenly. *Ralph jumped to his feet... He jumped up and went across to the large bookcase.*
4 V If you **jump**, you make a sudden movement because you have just been frightened or surprised by something. *A sudden noise made me jump.*
5 V If an amount or level **jumps**, it increases by a large amount in a short time. *The population jumped to nearly 10,000.* ▶ Also NC *...a massive jump in expenditure.*
6 VO If someone **jumps** a queue, they move to the front of it or are served or dealt with before it is their turn. *Public opinion about refugees jumping the queue caused pressure on the government to restrict refugee entry.*
● **Jump** is used in these phrases. ● If you **keep one jump ahead** of an opponent or rival, you manage always to be in a better position than they are. *Her absence this week will give her rivals a chance to get one jump ahead.* ● to **jump the gun**: see gun.
jump at PHRASAL VERB If you **jump at** an offer or opportunity, you accept it eagerly as soon as it is offered to you. *He jumped at the idea.*

jumped-up
ADJ ATTRIB **Jumped-up** people consider themselves to be more important than they really are; an informal expression. *...a jumped-up office boy.*

jumper /dʒʌmpə/ **jumpers**
NC A **jumper** is a knitted garment that covers the upper part of your body and your arms. *He was dressed in an anorak, a black jumper and blue jeans.*

jump jet, jump jets
NC A **jump jet** is a jet aircraft that can take off and land vertically. *...the Harrier, Britain's revolutionary jump jet.*

jump leads
N PL **Jump leads** are two thick wires with connecting clips that can be used to start a car with a flat battery by connecting it to the battery of another car.

jump-start, jump-starts, jump-starting, jump-started
1 VO If you **jump-start** a car's engine, you start it by using the power from another battery. *He was huddled with the manager trying to jump-start his car.*
2 VO If someone **jump-starts** a project or a situation

that has come to a halt, they put in a lot of effort in a short time in an attempt to start it moving again. *He hopes that a free trade agreement will bring in massive foreign investment to jump-start the Mexican economy... US officials came to the meeting armed with several new ideas for jump-starting the failed talks.*

jump suit, jump suits
NC A **jump suit** is a piece of clothing in the form of a top and trousers in one continuous piece. *She had blonde hair and wore a green jump suit.*

jumpy /dʒʌmpi/
ADJ If you are **jumpy**, you are nervous or worried about something; an informal word. *The very thought of it makes me feel slightly jumpy.*

Jun.
Jun. is a written abbreviation for 'June'. *...Thursday Jun. 14, 1990.*

junction /dʒʌŋkʃn/ **junctions**
NC A **junction** is a place where roads or railway lines join. *...the junction of Cortez Avenue and Main Street.*

junction box, junction boxes
NC A **junction box** is a closed earthed box inside which electrical wires are connected. *Even telephone junction boxes were searched.*

juncture /dʒʌŋktʃə/
At a particular **juncture** means at a particular time, especially when it is an important point in a series of events; a formal expression. *She knew that any move on her part at this juncture would be interpreted as a sign of weakness.*

June /dʒuːn/
NU **June** is the sixth month of the year in the Western calendar. *...Friday, June 14th... The unemployment rate reached its highest since June of 1987.*

jungle /dʒʌŋgl/ **jungles**
1 NCorNU A **jungle** is a forest in a hot country where tall trees and other plants grow very closely together. *...the hills and jungles of Central America. ...the Amazon jungle. ...immense tracts of impenetrable jungle.*
2 N SING+SUPP You can refer to a situation in which it is very hard to get what you want because everything is very complicated and there are other people trying to get what they want, as a **jungle**. *...the jungle of real politics.*

junior /dʒuːniə/ **juniors**
1 ADJ Someone who is **junior** holds a position that is less important than others in an organization or profession. *We could give the job to somebody more junior.* ▶ Also NC *Police officers later blamed their juniors.*
2 N SING+POSS If you are someone's **junior**, you are younger than they are. *...a man seventeen years her junior.*
3 TITLE When there are two people in one family who have the same name, **Junior** is sometimes used after the younger person's name in order to prevent confusion. *His son, Al Junior, rang him up.* ● See also **Jnr.**
4 NC In the United States, a student in the third year of a high school or university course is called a **junior**. *Moshe Adams is a junior in black history... In his junior year, Red Grange once scored four touchdowns in twelve minutes.*

junior school, junior schools
NCorNU A **junior school** in England or Wales is a school for children between the ages of about seven and eleven. *...junior schools and high schools. ...six hundred infant and junior school children... In an age when swimmers are often still at junior school, Biondi started competitive swimming late in life.*

juniper /dʒuːnɪpə/ **junipers**
NCorNU A **juniper** is an evergreen bush with purple berries which can be used in cooking and medicine. *Everywhere you look, pine trees and junipers scattered the hillside. ...the incense of burning juniper.*

junk /dʒʌŋk/; an informal word.
1 NU **Junk** is an amount of old or useless things. *Look, get that junk off the table, will you!*
2 N+N **Junk** shops sell second-hand goods very cheaply. *We got most of our furniture from junk*

shops and jumble sales.

junk bond, junk bonds

NC A **junk bond** is a security that may earn a very high rate of interest, although there is also quite a high risk of losing money. *...investment in the high risk, high return securities known as junk bonds... The company was financed by junk bonds.*

junket /dʒʌŋkɪt/ **junkets**

1 NC A **junket** is a trip or visit made by an official or a group of officials and paid for with public money; an informal word, used showing disapproval. *It's over £500 per person for fares and lodging, but a comparable junket to Hawaii costs only £389.*

2 NU or NC **Junket** is a sweet dessert food made with milk and rennet. *There are all the milk puddings from junket to rice pudding... In a few hours it will have set to the consistency of a light junket.*

junketing /dʒʌŋkɪtɪŋ/

NU **Junketing** is entertainment arranged for visiting officials and usually paid for with public money; an informal word, used showing disapproval.

junk food, junk foods

N MASS **Junk food** is food that is not very good for your health but is easy and quick to prepare. *Stay away from junk food and get some exercise... Junk foods are easy for people to buy, but perhaps not the most desirable things for them to be eating.*

junkie /dʒʌŋki/ **junkies**

1 NC A **junkie** is a drug addict; an informal word. *Don't get ripped off by the junkies or drug dealers who hang out on nearby street corners. ...a 17 year old junkie from north London.*

2 NC +SUPP A **junkie** is also a person who is obsessively interested in something. *...news junkies.*

junk mail

NU **Junk mail** is advertising and publicity materials that you receive through the post, even though you have not asked for them; used showing disapproval. *...the deluge of newspapers, magazines, reports, letters, junk mail and bulletins that hits us daily.*

junta /dʒʌntə, hʊntə/ **juntas**

NC A **junta** is a military government that has taken power by force, and not through elections. *They were members of the ruling military junta.*

jurisdiction /dʒʊərɪsdɪkʃn/

NU **Jurisdiction** is the power that a court of law or someone in authority has to carry out legal judgements or enforce laws. *The Governor had no jurisdiction over prices.*

jurisprudence /dʒʊərɪspruːdns/

NU **Jurisprudence** is the study of law and the principles on which laws are based; a legal term. *The Islamic Assembly of Jurisprudence has ruled that Baha'ism is not a religion.*

jurist /dʒʊərɪst/ **jurists**

NC A **jurist** is a person who is an expert on law; a formal word. *Their decision was based on the authority of leading jurists.*

juror /dʒʊərə/ **jurors**

NC A **juror** is a member of a jury. *The jurors gave their verdict.*

jury /dʒʊəri/ **juries**

1 N COLL A **jury** is a group of people in a court of law who listen to the facts about a crime and decide whether the person accused is guilty or not. *A jury would never convict on that evidence. ...trial by jury... Judges and juries are not allowed to draw any conclusions from a suspect's silence.*

2 N COLL A **jury** is also a group of people who choose the winner of a competition. *She is a novelist and one of the judges on the Booker jury.*

jury box, jury boxes

NC The **jury box** is the place in a court where the jury sits.

just /dʒʌst/

1 ADV If you say that something has **just** happened, you mean that it happened a very short time ago. *I've just sold my car... A new survey of British lifestyles has just been published... She had only just moved in.*

2 ADV If you say that you are **just** doing something, you mean that you will finish doing it very soon. If you say that you are **just** going to do something, you mean

that you will do it very soon. *I'm just making us some coffee... They were just about to leave.*

3 ADV You can also use **just** to emphasize that something happens or happened at exactly the moment you are talking about. *The telephone rang just as I was about to serve up the dinner... Judy didn't like to tell him just then.*

4 **Just now** means now or a very short time ago. *Nasty weather we're having just now... She was here just now.*

5 You say '**just a minute**', '**just a moment**', or '**just a second**' when you are asking someone to wait for a short time. *'Have you got John's address?'—'Just a minute. I'll have a look.'*

6 ADV You also use **just** to indicate that something is not very important, interesting, difficult, or great. *It's just a story... Just add boiling water... It is not just a children's film.*

7 ADV **Just** is also used to indicate that you are talking about a small part or sample, not the whole of an amount. *These are just a few of the enquiries... These are just some of the environmental problems which will face the Romanian government.*

8 ADV **Just** also indicates that what you are saying is the case, but only to a very small degree. *The heat was just bearable... He could only just hear them... It might just help.*

9 ADV You can use **just** to give emphasis to what you are saying. *I just know there's something wrong... Just listen to that noise... She was as fat as he was and just as unattractive.*

10 ADV **Just** also means exactly or precisely. *That's just what I wanted to hear... Just the opposite kind of thing can happen.*

11 ADV You can use **just** with words such as 'person' or 'thing' to indicate that they are exactly what is needed. *Sam would be just the person!... He knew just the place.*

12 ADV **Just** is also used in polite requests and interruptions, and to make opinions sound less forceful and more polite. *Can I just use your lighter please?... I just think that we should bring this matter to everyone's attention.*

13 You use **just about** to say that something is so close to a particular level or state that it can be regarded as having reached it. *She was just about his age... Everything is just about ready.*

14 ADJ Someone or something that is **just** is reasonable and fair. *...a just punishment. ...a just and civilised society.* ◆ **justly** ADV *I believe that I have acted justly.*

justice /dʒʌstɪs/

1 NU **Justice** is fairness in the way that people are treated. *The concept of justice is very basic in human thought. ...economic justice.*

2 NU **Justice** is also the legal system that a country uses in order to deal with people who break the law. *The courts are a very important part of our British system of justice.*

3 NU+SUPP The **justice** of a claim, argument, or cause is its quality of being reasonable and right. *They believe in the justice of their cause.*

4 TITLE **Justice** is used before the names of judges. *Lord Justice Wolf and Mr Justice Pill declared that the current guidance was unlawful.* ● **Justice** is used in these phrases. ● If a criminal is **brought to justice**, he or she is caught and punished. *No one should weep when this tyrant is brought to justice.* ● If you **do justice** to something, you deal with it properly and completely. *I am the only man in Europe capable of doing it justice, of making a perfect job of it.*

Justice of the Peace, Justices of the Peace

NC A **Justice of the Peace** is an officer of the court who judges cases that come before the lower courts. *It requires a bit of life experience to be a Justice of the Peace.*

justifiable /dʒʌstɪfaɪəbl/

ADJ An opinion, action, or fact that is **justifiable** is acceptable or correct because there is a good reason for it. *I hope this is a justifiable interpretation.* ◆ **justifiably** ADV *The Government is justifiably* *unpopular. She was justifiably proud of her achievements.*

justifiable homicide, justifiable homicides
NU or NC **Justifiable homicide** is an act of killing someone which is considered to be excusable or lawful, for example if you kill someone in self-defence; a legal term. *He escaped on a verdict of justifiable homicide... They claimed that the killing of Gregory Clark was a 'justifiable homicide.'*

justification /dʒʌstɪfɪkeɪʃn/ **justifications**
NC or NU A **justification** for something is a good reason or explanation for it. *We all have justifications for what we do... There was no justification for higher interest rates.*

justified /dʒʌstɪfaɪd/
1 ADJ PRED If you think that someone is **justified** in doing something, you think that they have good reasons for doing it. *I think he was quite justified in refusing to help her.*
2 ADJ An action that is **justified** is reasonable and acceptable. *In these circumstances, massive industrial action is justified and necessary.*

justify /dʒʌstɪfaɪ/ **justifies, justifying, justified**
V O, V-REFL, or V+ING If someone **justifies** an action or idea, they give a good reason why it is sensible or necessary. *The decision has been fully justified... I'm not going to try and justify myself... How did they justify putting that on a gallery wall?*

jut /dʒʌt/ **juts, jutting, jutted**
V A If something **juts** out, it sticks out above or beyond a surface. *A line of rocks jutted into the sea.*

jute /dʒuːt/
NU **Jute** is a substance that is used to make cloth and rope. It comes from a plant which grows mainly in South-East Asia. *...jute fibre. ...jute sacks.*

juvenile /dʒuːvənaɪl/ **juveniles**
1 NC A **juvenile** is a child or young person who is not yet old enough to be regarded as an adult; a formal use. *17% of all crime in 1983 was committed by juveniles.*
2 ADJ ATTRIB **Juvenile** activity or behaviour involves young people who are not adults. *...the increase in juvenile crime.*
3 ADJ You can describe someone's behaviour as **juvenile** if you think that it is silly or immature. *Mike has a somewhat juvenile sense of humour.*

juvenile court, juvenile courts
NC A **juvenile court** is a court which deals with crimes committed by young people who are not yet old enough to be considered as adults. *A sixteen year old boy has appeared at juvenile court accused of firearm offences.*

juvenile delinquency
NU **Juvenile delinquency** is vandalism and other criminal behaviour that is committed by young people who are not yet old enough to be legally considered as adults. *High unemployment has produced a growing problem of juvenile delinquency.*

juvenile delinquent, juvenile delinquents
NC A **juvenile delinquent** is a young person who is guilty of committing crimes, especially vandalism and violence. *None of these parents wanted to see their kids as juvenile delinquents.*

juxtapose /dʒʌkstəpəʊz/ **juxtaposes, juxtaposing, juxtaposed**
V O or V O+with If you **juxtapose** two things or ideas, you put them next to each other, or compare them, often in order to emphasize the difference between them; a formal word. *In certain areas of London, enormous wealth is juxtaposed against tremendous social deprivation... She juxtaposes her photographs with illustrations of flowers.* ◆ **juxtaposition** /dʒʌkstəpəzɪʃn/ **juxtapositions** NC or NU *This has produced a stark juxtaposition of affluence and squalor in the capital... It's the juxtaposition and combination of these words that makes the image that you remember.*

K k

K, k /keɪ/ **K's, k's**
NC **K** is the eleventh letter of the English alphabet.
Kabul /kɑːbʊl/
Kabul is the capital of Afghanistan and its largest city. Population: 1,036,000 (1982).
kaftan /kæftæn/ **kaftans.** See **caftan**.
kale /keɪl/
NU **Kale** is a vegetable that is similar to a cabbage. It has curly leaves which you can cook and eat. *...good vegetable production, for crops such as spinach, cabbage, kale and broccoli.*
kaleidoscope /kəlaɪdəskəʊp/ **kaleidoscopes**
1 NC A **kaleidoscope** is a tube that you hold in your hand. When you look through one end and turn the tube, you see a changing pattern of colours.
2 N SING+SUPP You can refer to any pattern of colours or images that keeps changing as a **kaleidoscope**; a literary use. *Several hundred people twirl around the dancefloor in a kaleidoscope of colour in motion.*
3 N SING+SUPP If you refer to a political situation that is in a state of constant change as a **kaleidoscope**. *India now has to find a new place in Asia's political kaleidoscope... The revolutions which shook the kaleidoscope of East and Central Europe have left some strange political configurations.*
kaleidoscopic /kəlaɪdəskɒpɪk/
1 ADJ ATTRIB **Kaleidoscopic** patterns and images are made up of rapidly changing colours and shapes. *An old-fashioned chandelier cast its kaleidoscopic colours onto her paper.*
2 ADJ ATTRIB **Kaleidoscopic** changes to social or political situations happen quickly, without any fixed or certain pattern. *The students also supported the kaleidoscopic succession of Solidarity Campaigns... The steel industry in recent years has undergone the most kaleidoscopic change.*
kamikaze /kæmɪkɑːzi/
ADJ ATTRIB If you perform a **kamikaze** act, you attack the enemy knowing that you will be hurt or killed doing it. *It was a kamikaze mission. ...the army's emphasis on personal daring and its echoes of the cult of the kamikaze suicide pilots, with a similar disregard for human life.*
Kampala /kæmpɑːlə/
Kampala is the capital of Uganda and its largest city. Population: 458,000 (1980).
kangaroo /kæŋgəruː/ **kangaroos**
NC A **kangaroo** is a large Australian animal which moves by jumping on its back legs. Female kangaroos carry their babies in a pouch on their stomachs. *Many kangaroos have died in the flooded outback areas of New South Wales.*
kangaroo court, kangaroo courts
NC A **kangaroo court** is an unofficial trial of a member of an organization who is accused of having seriously broken the rules of that organization. *Suspected collaborators are to be tried in kangaroo courts... He said the businessman was a victim of a kangaroo court, with no-one there to defend him.*
kapok /keɪpɒk/
NU **Kapok** is a soft white fluffy material that is used for stuffing cushions, or is put inside sleeping bags and

jackets to provide warmth.
kaput /kəpʊt/
ADJ PRED If you say that something is **kaput**, you mean that it is broken; an informal word. *The record player seems to be kaput.*
Karáchi /kərɑːtʃi/
Karáchi is the largest city in Pakistan and the capital of Sind province. Population: 5,181,000 (1981).
Karamanlis, Konstantinos
/kɒnstændiːnɒs kærəmænliːs/
Konstantinos Karamanlis was President of Greece from 1980 to 1985, and again became President in 1990. He was an MP from 1935 to 1967, and from 1974 to 1980. He served as Prime Minister from 1955 to 1958, 1958 to 1961, and from 1961 to 1963. From 1963 until 1974 he was in exile, and on his return to Greece he founded the New Democracy Party. He was leader of the New Democracy Party and Prime Minister of Greece from 1974 to 1980. Born: 1907.
Karami, Umar /uːmɑː kərɑːmi/
Umar Karami became Prime Minister of Lebanon in 1990. He is a Sunni Muslim, and the brother of the former Prime Minister, Rashid Karami, who was assassinated in 1987. He was Minister of Education from 1989 to 1990. Born: 1936.
karaoke /kæriəʊki/
NUorN+N **Karaoke** is a form of entertainment found in some bars and clubs in which people take it in turns to sing well-known songs to a pre-recorded tape, following the words as they are shown on a television screen. *There's free drink, karaoke, inflated bouncy castles, and arm-wrestling... Friday night is karaoke night here... We actually have a recording session for the best karaoke singer on the night.*
karate /kərɑːti/
NU **Karate** is a sport in which people fight using their hands, elbows, feet, and legs. *...the flying fists and feet of karate... The blow could have been a karate chop delivered by someone versed in martial arts.*
Karimov, Islam /ɪslɑːm kəriːməf/
Islam Karimov became President of Uzbekistan in 1990. He was Minister of Finance and Deputy Chairman of the Council of Ministers of the Uzbek Soviet Socialist Republic from 1983 to 1986, and First Secretary of the Central Committee of the Uzbek Communist Party from 1989 to 1990. He became Chairman of the People's Democratic Party of Uzbekistan in 1991. Born: 1938.
Karl-I-Bond, Nguza /ŋguːzə kɑːl iː bɒnd/
Nguza Karl-I-Bond became Prime Minister of Zaïre in 1991. He was State Commissioner for Foreign Affairs and International Co-operation from 1972 to 1974, from 1976 to 1977, from 1979 to 1980, and from 1988 to 1990. He formerly served as Prime Minister from 1980 to 1981. Born: 1938.
karma /kɑːmə/
NU In the Buddhist religion, **karma** is the belief that your actions in one life affect all your other lives after that one. *In Buddhist societies, monks are so revered that mistreatment of them is believed to be devastating to one's karma.*

Karoui, Hamed /hɑːmɪd kærəwi/
Hamed Karoui became Prime Minister of Tunisia in 1989. He was elected to the National Assembly in 1964. He served as Minister for Youth and Sports from 1986 to 1987, and for Justice from 1988 to 1989. He is a member of the Democratic Constitutional Assembly (RCD). Born: 1927.

Kāthmāndu /kætmændɯː/
Kāthmāndu is the capital of Nepal and its largest city. Population: 235,000 (1981).

kayak /kaɪæk/ **kayaks**
NC A **kayak** is a particular type of canoe, especially used by Eskimos or in the sport of canoeing. *In canoeing, Birgit Schmidt took the kayak singles gold medal in 1980.*

Kazakhstan /kəzɑːkstɑːn/
Kazakhstan became independent of the USSR in 1991. It is located in the east of the former USSR, bordering on China. Territorially it was the second largest of the Soviet republics. Nursultan Nazarbayev, of the Kazakh Communist Party, became President in 1990. Kazakhstan produces metals, manufactured goods, and wheat. In 1991 it joined the Commonwealth of Independent States. ◆ **Kazakh** /kəzɑːk/ N, ADJ
▪ *per capita GNP:* US$3,720 ▪ *religion:* Islam (mainly Sunni), Christianity ▪ *language:* Kazakh, Russian ▪ *currency:* rouble ▪ *capital:* Alma Ata ▪ *population:* 17 million (1990) ▪ *size:* 2,717,300 square kilometres.

Keating, Paul /pɔːl kiːtɪŋ/
Paul Keating became Prime Minister of Australia in 1991 after the resignation of Bob Hawke. He was first elected to the House of Representatives in 1969. He was Minister for Northern Australia in 1975, and Treasurer from 1983 to 1991. He also served as Deputy Prime Minister from 1990 to 1991. He is a member of the Australian Labor Party (ALP). Born: 1944.

kebab /kəbæb/ **kebabs**
NC A **kebab** consists of small pieces of meat and vegetables that have been put on a thin rod and grilled. *...27 identical meat kebabs on skewers.*

kedgeree /kedʒəriː/
NU **Kedgeree** is a cooked dish consisting of rice, fish, and eggs.

keel /kiːl/ **keels, keeling, keeled**
1 NC The **keel** of a boat is the long specially shaped piece of wood or metal that runs along the bottom. It forms part of the boat's structure and helps to strengthen it and keep it steady. *One yacht overturned after losing its keel off the South coast.*
2 If something is **on an even keel**, it is working or proceeding smoothly and satisfactorily. *Most governments are able to keep their economies on an even keel.*
keel over PHRASAL VERB If something or someone **keels over**, they fall over sideways. *One of the athletes suddenly keeled over.*

keen /kiːn/ **keener, keenest**
1 ADJ PRED If you are **keen** to do something, you want to do it very much. *Her solicitor was keener to talk than she was... He didn't seem all that keen on having it... He's not keen for Charlotte to know.*
2 ADJ You use **keen** to show that someone enjoys a particular sport or activity and does it a lot. *He was not a keen gardener... Boys are as keen on cooking as girls are.*
3 ADJ **Keen** people are enthusiastic and are interested in everything they do. *They were highly-motivated students, very keen.*
4 ADJ If you have a **keen** interest or desire, your interest or desire is very strong. *He took a keen interest in domestic affairs.* ◆ **keenly** ADV *I was keenly interested in outdoor activities.*
5 ADJ If you have **keen** sight or hearing, you can see or hear very well. *It takes a keen eye to spot them. ...keen powers of observation.*
6 ADJ A **keen** contest or competition is one in which the competitors are all trying very hard to win. *The competition for the first prize was keen.* ◆ **keenly** ADV *...a keenly contested football match.*

keenly /kiːnli/
1 ADV If you watch or listen **keenly**, you watch or listen with great concentration. *People browse along,*

looking keenly at price tags.
2 See also **keen**.

keep /kiːp/ **keeps, keeping, kept**
1 VOA To **keep** someone or something in a particular state or place means to cause them to remain in that state or place. *They had been kept awake by nightingales... She kept her arm around her husband as she spoke... He bought a guard dog to keep out intruders... Sorry to keep you waiting.*
2 VC or VA If you **keep** in a particular state or place, you remain in that state or place. *They've got to hunt for food to keep alive... Keep in touch... They kept away from the forest.* ● If a sign says **'Keep Out'**, it is warning you not to go somewhere. *There's a 'Keep Out' sign on the gate.*
3 V+ING If you **keep** doing something, or **keep** on doing it, you do it repeatedly or continually without stopping. *I keep making the same mistake... The men just kept walking... They kept on walking for a while in silence... I kept on getting up and staring out of the window.*
4 VO If you **keep** something, you continue to have it. *Why didn't Daddy let me keep the ten dollars?... She would not be able to keep her job.*
5 VOA If you **keep** something in a particular place, you always have it there so that you can find it easily. *...the shelf where the butter and cheese were kept... Keep a spare key in your bag.*
6 VO **Keep** is used with some nouns to indicate that someone continues to do something. For example, if you keep a grip on something, you continue to hold it or control it. *They would keep a look-out for him.*
7 VO+from To **keep** someone or something from doing something means to prevent them from doing it. *She had to hold the boy tight, to keep him from falling.*
8 VO If something **keeps** you, it makes you arrive somewhere later than expected. *Am I keeping you from your party?... What kept you?*
9 VO When you **keep** something such as a promise or an appointment, you do what you said you would do. *Hearst kept his word.*
10 VO+from If you **keep** something from someone, you do not tell them about it. *Why did you keep it from me?*
11 VO If you **keep** a record of a series of events, you make a written record of it. *We keep a record of the noise levels.*
12 VO People who **keep** animals own them and take care of them. *My dad kept chickens.*
13 N SING+POSS Your **keep** is the cost of food and other things that you need every day. *The grant includes £19 for your keep during the vacation.*
14 to **keep** someone **guessing**: see **guess**. to **keep** your **head**: see **head**. See also **keeping**.
keep back PHRASAL VERB 1 If you **keep** part of something **back**, you make sure that you do not use or give away all of it, so that you still have some to use at a later time. *Remember to keep back enough cream to make the topping.* 2 If you **keep** some information **back**, you do not tell everything you know about something. *You can't write an autobiography without keeping something back.*
keep down PHRASAL VERB If you **keep** a number or amount **down**, you do not allow it to increase. *The French are very concerned to keep costs down.*
keep off PHRASAL VERB If you **keep** something **off**, you prevent it from reaching you and harming you. *They built a bamboo shelter to keep the rain off.*
keep on PHRASAL VERB If someone **keeps on** about something, they talk about it a lot in a boring or irritating way. *She kept on about the car.*
keep on at PHRASAL VERB If someone **keeps on at** you, they repeatedly ask or tell you to do something, in an irritating way. *I made no reply but he kept on at me.*
keep to PHRASAL VERB 1 If you **keep to** a rule, plan, or agreement, you do as it says. *We must keep to the deadlines.* 2 If you **keep** something **to** a particular amount, you limit it to that amount. *Keep it to a minimum.*
keep up PHRASAL VERB 1 If one person or thing **keeps up** with another, the first one moves, progresses, or increases as fast as the second. *I started to run, so*

that she had to hurry to keep up with me... Pensions were increased to keep up with the rise in prices. **2** If you **keep up** with what is happening, you make sure that you know about it. *Even friends have trouble keeping up with each other's whereabouts.* **3** If people **keep up**, they deal successfully with a situation, especially one that is changing quickly or to a great extent. *...the struggle to keep up with inflation... It has increased so much that our imagination can't keep up.*

keeper /kiːpə/ **keepers**
NC A **keeper** is a person who takes care of animals, for example, in a zoo. *At London Zoo's insect house Paul Pearce-Kelly, the head keeper of invertebrates introduced me to the species. ...a zoo keeper.*

keep-fit
NU **Keep-fit** is the activity of keeping your body in good condition by doing regular exercise. *...her image as a keep-fit fanatic. ...playing tennis with his keep-fit trainer.*

keeping /kiːpɪŋ/
1 If you say that something is **in keeping** with a particular situation or activity, you mean that it seems to be suitable and appropriate. *White socks and brown shoes were not quite in keeping with her beautiful satin evening dress... In keeping with the government policy of non-interference, they refused to take any action.*
2 If something is **out of keeping** with a particular situation or activity, it is not considered to be suitable or appropriate. *Her costume was quite out of keeping with the character she was supposed to be playing.*
3 N SING+POSS If something is in your **keeping**, you are looking after it and are responsible for it. *He entrusted the book to my keeping.*

keepsake /kiːpseɪk/ **keepsakes**
NC A **keepsake** is a small present that someone gives you so that you will not forget them. *I want you to have this keepsake that my mother brought from Sweden.*

keg /keg/ **kegs**
1 NC A **keg** is a small barrel used for storing something such as beer or other alcoholic drinks. *Fill the jugs with wine from big wooden kegs.*
2 NU **Keg** is a kind of beer which is kept under pressure in a metal barrel. *...fizzy, keg beers.*
3 See also **powder keg**.

ken /ken/
If something is **beyond** your **ken**, you do not have enough knowledge to be able to understand it; an old-fashioned expression.

Kennedy, John Fitzgerald
/dʒɒn fɪtsdʒerəld kenədi/
John F Kennedy was President of the United States from 1961 to 1963. He was born in 1917 and was a member of the Democratic Party. He was a member of the House of Representatives from 1947 to 1953, and of the Senate from 1953 to 1961. He was assassinated in 1963.

kennel /kenl/ **kennels**
1 NC A **kennel** is a small hut made for a dog to sleep in. *A spokesman said a new four-storey building with two-hundred kennels was necessary to cope with the growing number of unwanted dogs.*
2 N PLor N SING **Kennels** or a **kennel** is a place where people can leave their pet dogs when they go on holiday, or where dogs are bred. *A spokeswoman for the kennels said there was no chance that the dog had spread the disease. ...a dog kennel housing police dogs.*

Kenya /kenjə/
The **Republic of Kenya** is a country in eastern Africa. It became a British colony in the 19th century. The Mau Mau rising, a Kikuyu independence movement which aimed to expel European settlers from Kenya, occurred from 1952 to 1956. Kenya became independent in 1963. Jomo Kenyatta, of the Kenya African National Union (KANU), was the first president and ruled until his death in 1978. KANU was the sole legal party from 1969 until 1991, when political parties were legalized. Daniel T arap Moi succeeded Kenyatta as President in 1978. Kenya is a member of the Commonwealth and the Organization of African Unity. It exports coffee

and tea. Cannabis is illegally produced. Tourism is an important industry. Large foreign debts and high inflation are major economic problems. ◆ **Kenyan** /kenjən/ N, ADJ
■ *per capita GNP:* US$360 ■ *religion:* animism, Christianity ■ *language:* Kiswahili (official), English, Kikuyu, Luo ■ *currency:* shilling ■ *capital:* Nairobi ■ *population:* 25 million (1989) ■ *size:* 582,646 square kilometres.

kept /kept/
Kept is the past tense and past participle of **keep**.

kerb /kɜːb/ **kerbs**; spelt **curb** in American English.
NC The **kerb** is the part of a pavement that is immediately next to the road. *The taxi pulled into the kerb. ...standing on the kerb.*

kerb-crawling
NU **Kerb-crawling** is the illegal activity of driving slowly along a kerb in order to hire a prostitute.

kerchief /kɜːtʃɪf/ **kerchiefs**
NC A **kerchief** is a piece of cloth that you can wear on your head or round your neck; an old-fashioned word. *He was dressed in a black silk shirt with a red kerchief knotted round his throat.*

kerfuffle /kəfʌfl/ **kerfuffles**
NC A **kerfuffle** is a noisy and disorderly incident often resulting from an argument; an informal word. *Fletcher enjoyed the resulting kerfuffle.*

kernel /kɜːnl/ **kernels**
NC The **kernel** of a nut is the part inside the shell. *Many people are living on wild food such as palm nut kernels and edible leaves.*

kerosene /kerəsiːn/
NU **Kerosene** is the same as **paraffin**; used in American English. *The area used to supply neighbouring regions with petrol, kerosene and other fuels. ...wooden-frame homes heated by kerosene stoves.*

kestrel /kestrəl/ **kestrels**
NC A **kestrel** is a type of small falcon.

ketch /ketʃ/ **ketches**
NC A **ketch** is a type of sailing ship that has two masts. *The skipper of the ketch and a crew member were missing, presumed drowned.*

ketchup /ketʃəp/
NU **Ketchup** is a thick, cold sauce made from tomatoes. *...tomato ketchup and its spicier variety, Worcestershire sauce.*

kettle /ketl/ **kettles**
NC A **kettle** is a covered container that you use for boiling water. It has a handle and a spout. *...just about enough power to boil a kettle.*

kettledrum /ketldrʌm/ **kettledrums**
NC A **kettledrum** is a large drum with a curved bottom, which usually stands on a tripod.

key /kiː/ **keys**
1 NC A **key** is a specially shaped piece of metal which fits in a lock and is turned in order to open or lock a door, drawer, or suitcase. *He refused to hand over his car keys... There's a security alert at Wandsworth jail because of the disappearance of a bunch of keys.*
2 NC The **keys** of a typewriter, computer keyboard, or cash register are the buttons that you press in order to operate it. *By punching a few keys on his computer, he drew the outline of the freighter on his screen... The operator only uses five keys to operate the word-processing facility.*
3 ADJ ATTRIB The **key** things or people in a group are the most important ones. *The country's key industries are coal, engineering, and transport... Unemployment was a key issue during the election campaign... He became a key figure in the anti-apartheid movement.*
4 NC The **key** to a desirable situation or result is the way in which it can be achieved. *Education became the key to progress... This reflects the line that he has recently been emphasizing as a key to economic reform.*
5 NC The **key** to a map, diagram, or technical book is a list of the symbols and abbreviations used in it, and their meanings. *You will find a key at the front of the book.*
6 NC The **keys** of a piano or organ are the black and white bars that you press in order to play it. *If you*

push down a piano key, the note will last until you lift your finger.
7 NC In music, a **key** is a scale of musical notes that starts at one particular note. *...an orchestral passage that returns throughout the movement in different keys. ...the key of D.*

keyboard /kiːbɔːd/ **keyboards**
1 NC The **keyboard** of a typewriter or a computer terminal is the set of keys that you press in order to operate it. *I only have to use a small proportion of the keys on the keyboard... They might well use the system as it stands, just typing on the computer keyboard.*
2 NC The **keyboard** of a piano or organ is the set of black and white keys that you press in order to play it. *She reached out her hands to the keyboard and began to play.*

keyboarder /kiːbɔːdə/ **keyboarders**
NC A **keyboarder** is someone whose job is typing information into a computer or word processor using a keyboard.

keyboarding /kiːbɔːdɪŋ/
NU **Keyboarding** is the activity of typing information into a computer or word processor using a keyboard.

keyed up /kiːd ʌp/
ADJ PRED If you are **keyed up**, you are very excited or nervous before an important or dangerous event. *Everybody's keyed up, especially in the quarter finals.*

keyhole /kiːhəʊl/ **keyholes**
NC A **keyhole** is the hole in a lock that you put a key in. *The front door had several keyholes.*

keynote /kiːnəʊt/ **keynotes**
N+NorNC The **keynote** of a policy, speech, or idea is the part which is emphasized or given the most importance. *In a keynote speech, Mr Takeshita said Japan wanted a greater role in bringing peace and stability to the world. ...the keynote address of his current tour... The keynote for Labour policy, he saw, was planning. ...themes that have since become the keynotes for civil rights campaigners around the world.*

key-ring /kiːstɔːn/ **key-rings**
NC A **key-ring** is a ring which you use to keep your keys together.

keystone /kiːstəʊn/ **keystones**
1 NC+SUPP You can use **keystone** to refer to an important part of a process, which is the basis for later developments. *The first National Insurance Bill was the keystone of the future Welfare State... This treaty is the keystone under international law that makes unity acceptable to Germany's neighbours.*
2 NC A **keystone** is a stone at the top of an arch, which keeps the other stones in place by its weight and position.

kg
Kg is a written abbreviation for 'kilogram' or 'kilograms'. *Increase the load by 100 kg.*

khaki /kɑːki/
ADJ Something that is **khaki** is yellowish-brown in colour. *The boys looked smart in khaki and polished brass. ...khaki shorts.*

Khaleqiar, Fazl Haq /fæzl hæk xɑːlɪkjɑː/
Fazl Haq Khaleqiar became Prime Minister of Afghanistan in 1990. He was Minister for Financial and Economic Affairs from 1985 to 1988, and Governor of Herat Province from 1988 to 1989. Born: 1934.

Khalifa, Sheikh Isa bin Sulman al-
/iːsə bɪn sʊlmæn æl xæliːfə/
Sheikh Isa bin Sulman al-Khalifa became the Amir of Bahrain on the death of his father in 1961. He was named Crown Prince in 1958. Born: 1933.

Khamenei, Ayatollah Ali /aɪjətɒlə æliː xɑːməneiː/
Ayatollah Ali Khamenei became the Wali Faqih (spiritual leader) of Iran on the death of Ayatollah Khomeini in 1989. He was a student of Ayatollah Khomeini. He served as President of Iran from 1981 to 1989, and was Secretary General of the Islamic Republican Party from 1980 to 1987. Born: 1939.

Khan, Ghulam Ishaq /gʊlɑːm ɪshɑːk kɑːn/
Ghulam Ishaq Khan became President of Pakistan in 1988. He was Chairman of the Water and Power Development Authority (WAPDA) from 1961 to 1966,

Finance Secretary from 1966 to 1970, Cabinet Secretary from 1970 to 1971, Governor of the State Bank of Pakistan from 1971 to 1975, Minister of Finance from 1978 to 1985, and Chairman of the Senate from 1985 to 1988. Born: 1915.

Khartoum /kɑːtuːm/
Khartoum is the capital of Sudan. With Khartoum North and Omdurman, it forms the largest urban conurbation in Sudan. Population: 476,000 (1983).

Khraprayūn, Suchinda /sʊtʃɪndə kræpraɪjuːn/
General Suchinda Khraprayun became Supreme Commander of the armed forces of Thailand in 1991 and acting Prime Minister of Thailand in 1992.

kibbutz /kɪbʊts/ **kibbutzes** or **kibbutzim** /kɪbʊtsiːm/
NC A **kibbutz** is a place of work in Israel, for example a farm or factory, where the workers live together and share all the duties and income. *He wrote to the Jewish agency asking to visit a kibbutz.*

kibosh /kaɪbɒʃ/
If something **puts the kibosh on** an event, situation, or someone's plans, it completely ruins them; an informal expression. *It would certainly put the kibosh on any lingering hopes they might have had.*

kick /kɪk/ **kicks, kicking, kicked**
1 VO If you **kick** someone or something, you hit them with your foot. *He protested violently, and threatened to kick me... We caught sight of Christopher, kicking a tin can down the High Street.* ▶ Also NC *He gave him a good kick.*
2 V If you **kick**, you move your feet violently or suddenly, for example when you are dancing or swimming. *Simon was floating in the water and kicking with his feet.*
3 If someone **gets a kick** from something, they get pleasure or excitement from it; an informal expression. *They loved debate, and got a kick out of court proceedings.*
4 VO If you **kick** a habit, you stop having that habit; an informal use. *She had kicked her cocaine habit... One of the reasons smokers find it so hard to kick the habit is their addiction to nicotine.*
5 See also **free kick**.

kick about PHRASAL VERB See **kick around**.
kick around PHRASAL VERB If something is **kicking around** or **kicking about**, it is lying there and has been forgotten; an informal expression. *There's a lot of difference between a fresh herring and one which may have been kicking around in a deep freeze for months... His old bike has been kicking about under the bushes for days.*
kick off PHRASAL VERB When you **kick off** an event or a discussion, you start it; an informal expression. *They kicked off a two-month tour of the U.S. with a party in Washington.*
kick out PHRASAL VERB If you **kick** someone **out**, you make them leave a place; an informal expression. *She kicked me out of the room... Zoe was kicked out of school at 15 for being a bad influence.*
kick up PHRASAL VERB If you **kick up** a fuss or a row, you get very annoyed or upset; an informal expression. *When I told him, he kicked up a fuss.*

kickback /kɪkbæk/ **kickbacks**
NC A **kickback** is a sum of money that is paid to someone illegally, for example money paid to an agent by a company because the agent can arrange for the company to be chosen to do an important job. *He has always denied that he received any kickbacks from contractors.*

kick-off, kick-offs
NUorNC **Kick-off** or the **kick-off** is the time at which a football game starts. *Kick-off is at 2.30... Heavy rain set in just before the kick-off.*

kick-start, kick-starts, kick-starting, kick-started
1 NC A **kick-start** or a **kick-starter** is the lever that you press with your foot to start a motorbike. *They leaned across their machines, stabbed at the kick-starters and moved forward.*
2 VO If you **kick-start** a motorcycle, you press the lever that starts it with your foot. *He spoke about keeping together on the road and then signalled them to kick-start their bikes.*
3 VO If you **kick-start** something which has stopped

working or reached a deadlock, you take a course of action that will start the process going again. *Labour has said there should be a one percent interest rate cut to kick-start the economy out of the recession... It is an attempt to kick-start the negotiating process into life again.*

kid /kɪd/ **kids, kidding, kidded**
1 NC You can refer to a child as a **kid**; an informal use. *...five-year-old kids... I can remember the feelings I had when I was a kid. ...his wife and kids.*
2 NC Young people who are no longer children are sometimes referred to as **kids**; used in informal American English. *GM's college kids pay only $1,200 tuition.*
3 ADJ ATTRIB You can refer to someone's younger brother or sister as their **kid** brother or sister; used in informal American English. *For their finale of the show, they brought out their kid sister who was 11 years old.*
4 V If someone says that they **are kidding**, they mean that what they have said is not really true and is meant as a joke; an informal use. *They're not sure whether I'm kidding or not... I'm not kidding, Jill. He could have taken it if he'd wanted.* ● You say '**No kidding**' to emphasize that you are serious or that something is true; an informal expression. *No kidding, Ginny, you look good.*
5 VO If you **kid** someone, you tease them. *Tim's friends kidded him about his odd clothes.*
6 V-REFL If people **kid** themselves, they allow themselves to believe something that is not true. *They like to kid themselves they're keeping fit... We don't want to kid ourselves but we think there are some good opportunities.*
7 NC A **kid** is also a young goat that is less than one year old. *It didn't really have a great deal of effect on the growth of the kid or the lamb.*

kiddie /kɪdi/ **kiddies**
NC A **kiddie** is a very young child; an informal word. *His young kiddie was in hospital.*

kid gloves
If you **treat** or **handle** someone **with kid gloves**, you are very careful in the way you deal with them because you do not want to make them angry or upset. *Treat him with kid gloves and you won't get your head bitten off.*

kidnap /kɪdnæp/ **kidnaps, kidnapping, kidnapped**
1 VO If someone **kidnaps** you, they take you away by force, usually in order to demand money from your family, employer, or government. *He was kidnapped by terrorists just over a month ago.* ◆ **kidnapping**, **kidnappings** NU or NC *They charged me with murder and kidnapping. ...the kidnapping of a royal child.*
2 NU **Kidnap** is the crime of kidnapping someone. *...the threat of kidnap or assassination. ...a kidnap victim.*

kidnapper /kɪdnæpə/ **kidnappers**
A **kidnapper** is a person who has kidnapped someone and may be demanding money from their family, employers, or government in return for their release. *I had given up all hope of tracing her kidnapper.*

kidney /kɪdni/ **kidneys**
NC Your **kidneys** are the two organs that filter waste matter from your bloodstream and send it out of your body in its urine. *He had kidney trouble.*

kidney bean, kidney beans
NC **Kidney beans** are beans that have the same shape as a kidney, and which you can eat. *She mixed ground meat with tomatoes, kidney beans, and chilli powder.*

kidney machine, kidney machines
NC A **kidney machine** is a machine that is used to do the work of a kidney for people whose own kidneys are diseased or do not work properly. *Treatment with an artificial kidney machine—dialysis—keeps patients alive.*

Kiev /kiːef/
Kiev is the capital of Ukraine and its largest city. Population: 2,602,000 (1989).

Kigali /kɪgɑːli/
Kigali is the capital of Rwanda and its largest city. Population: 157,000 (1981).

kill /kɪl/ **kills, killing, killed**
1 VO, V, or V-REFL When someone or something **kills** a person, animal or plant, they cause the person, animal, or plant to die. *They eat meat only once or twice a month when they kill a chicken... The state police killed three people when they fired on the crowd. ...a desire to kill... The sun had killed most of the plants... He had tried to kill himself five times.*
2 NC The act of killing an animal after hunting it is referred to as the **kill**. *The hunters move in for the kill.*
3 VO If something **kills** an activity, process, or feeling, it prevents it from continuing. *His behaviour outraged me and killed our friendship... These latest measures killed all hope of any relaxation of the system.*
● **Kill** is used in these phrases. ● When you **kill time**, you do something unimportant or uninteresting while you are waiting for something to happen. *He spent long hours keeping out of the way, killing time.* ● to **kill two birds with one stone**: see **bird**.
kill off PHRASAL VERB If you **kill** something **off**, you completely destroy it. *This discovery killed off one of the last surviving romances about the place... The bacteria had been killed off.*

killer /kɪlə/ **killers**
1 NC A **killer** is a person who has killed someone. *He became a ruthless killer.*
2 NC You can refer to anything that causes death as a **killer**. *The lion is one of the most efficient killers in the animal world... Heart disease is the major killer.*

killer instinct
N SING A **killer instinct** is a great determination to get what you want, even though it might involve causing harm to other people. *He has a competitive killer instinct that makes everything he does a challenge.*

killer whale, killer whales
NC A **killer whale** is a black and white whale that usually hunts in packs and eats large fish and seals.

killing /kɪlɪŋ/ **killings**
NC A **killing** is an act in which one person deliberately kills another. *...a brutal killing.*

killjoy /kɪldʒɔɪ/ **killjoys**
NC A **killjoy** is someone who stops other people from enjoying themselves, often by reminding them of something unpleasant. *Don't be such a killjoy!*

kiln /kɪln/ **kilns**
NC A **kiln** is an oven used to bake pottery and bricks. *They don't have a kiln that will fire the terracotta at a high enough temperature. ...a brick kiln.*

kilo /kiːləʊ/ **kilos**
NC A **kilo** is the same as a **kilogram**. *Tomatoes sell at more than twenty dinars a kilo... A kilo of meat costs the equivalent of £15.*

kilogram /kɪləgræm/ **kilograms**; also spelt **kilogramme**.
NC A **kilogram** is a unit of weight equal to one thousand grams. *His wife gave birth to their daughter who weighed less than one kilogram. ...the official price of four hundred francs a kilogram.*

kilohertz /kɪləhɜːts/. **Kilohertz** is both the singular and the plural form.
NC A **kilohertz** is a unit of measurement of radio waves that is equal to one thousand hertz. *...a ten kilohertz sound, which is very high pitched.*

kilometre /kɪləmiːtə, kɪlɒmɪtə/ **kilometres**; spelt **kilometer** in American English.
NC A **kilometre** is a unit of distance equal to one thousand metres. *We could see rain falling about a kilometre away.*

kilowatt /kɪləwɒt/ **kilowatts**
NC A **kilowatt** is a unit of power that is equal to one thousand watts. *...the amount of electricity needed to produce one kilowatt of power for one hour... A one kilowatt fire uses one unit in one hour.*

kilowatt hour, kilowatt hours
NC A **kilowatt hour** is a unit of energy that is equal to the energy provided by a thousand watts in one hour. *Friends of the Earth claim that every kilowatt hour of electricity used in Britain is responsible for the emission of approximately one kilogram of carbon dioxide.*

kilt /kɪlt/ **kilts**

NC A **kilt** is a short pleated skirt that men sometimes wear as part of their country's traditional costume, especially in Scotland. Kilts can also be worn by women and girls. *Patriotic though he was, Burns never wore the kilt or any other tartan garment.*

Kim Il Sung /kɪm ɪl sʊŋ/

Marshal Kim Il Sung became the ruler of North Korea in 1946. He led the Korean People's Revolutionary Army in the war against Japan from 1932 to 1945 and was supreme commander of the North Korean army in the Korean War. He proclaimed the Democratic People's Republic of Korea in 1948, served as Premier from 1948 to 1972, and became President in 1972. He founded the Korean Workers' Party (KWP) in 1945 and became General Secretary of the Central Committee of the KWP in 1966. Born: 1912.

kimono /kɪməʊnəʊ/ **kimonos**

NC A **kimono** is an item of Japanese clothing. It is long, shaped like a coat and has wide sleeves. *...a loose-fitting, comfortable kimono.*

kin /kɪn/

NU Your **kin** are your relatives; an old-fashioned word. *It's natural for those of them that have kin outside the Soviet Union to want to renew contact.* ● See also next of kin, kith and kin.

kind /kaɪnd/ **kinds; kinder, kindest**

1 NC+SUPP or NU+SUPP If you talk about a particular **kind** of thing, you are talking about one of the classes or sorts of that thing. *Composers, artists, writers, pray for inspiration of that kind... The threat to the environment from emissions of a variety of kinds has been known for a long time... These thoughts weren't the kind he could share with anyone... Was he carrying a weapon and, if so, what kind of weapon?* 2 ADJ A **kind** person is gentle, caring, and helpful. *We were much kinder to one another after that night... It was kind of you to come.* ◆ **kindly** ADV *'You're not to blame yourself, Smithy,' Rick said kindly.* ● **Kind** is used in these phrases. ● You use a **kind of** to say that something can be roughly described in a particular way; an informal expression. *He spoke in a kind of sad whisper.* ● **Kind of** is used to say that something is partly true; used in informal American English. *I felt kind of sorry for him.* ● You use **of a kind** to say that something belongs to a particular class of things, but that it is not really satisfactory. *A solution of a kind has been found to this problem.* ● Payment **in kind** is payment in the form of goods or services, rather than money. *We have asked them to contribute in kind to this operation... Germany promised 3.3 billion marks of which 2 billion have been paid in kind, in equipment and in various other services.*

kindergarten /kɪndəgɑːtn/ **kindergartens**

NC or NU A **kindergarten** is a school for young children who are not old enough to go to a primary school. *There's a kindergarten and summer camp for workers' children... Her six year-old daughter attends kindergarten there.*

kind-hearted

ADJ Someone who is **kind-hearted** is caring, loving, and gentle.

kindle /kɪndl/ **kindles, kindling, kindled**

1 VO If something **kindles** an idea or feeling in you, it starts you thinking about that idea or feeling; a literary use. *...the aspirations kindled in us in early childhood.* 2 VO If you **kindle** a fire, you light paper or wood in order to start it. *The flame was kindled using a mirror to catch the fierce rays of the morning sun.*

kindling /kɪndəlɪŋ/

NU **Kindling** is small pieces of dry wood that you use to start a fire. *They would pull up the blackened stalks for kindling.*

kindly /kaɪndli/

1 ADJ ATTRIB A **kindly** person is kind, caring, and sympathetic. *Being a kindly and reasonable man, he at once apologized.* ◆ **kindliness** NU *...the great virtues of humility and kindliness.* 2 ADV If you ask someone to **kindly** do something, you are asking them in a way that shows your annoyance.

Kindly take your hand off my knee. 3 See also **kind.** ● **Kindly** is used in these phrases. ● If someone **looks kindly** on something, they approve of it. *The White House will look more kindly on a robust economy.* ● If someone **does not take kindly** to something, they do not like it. *They are unlikely to take kindly to this suggestion.*

kindness /kaɪndnəs/ **kindnesses**

1 NC A **kindness** is a helpful or considerate act. *She thanked them both many times for all their kindnesses.* 2 NU **Kindness** is the quality of being gentle, caring, and helpful. *He treated his labourers with kindness and understanding.*

kindred spirit /kɪndrəd spɪrɪt/ **kindred spirits**

NC Someone who is a **kindred spirit** has the same view of life that you have. *When I saw his work I recognized him as a kindred spirit... Mr Zhu will probably not have to look too hard to find kindred spirits in Moscow.*

kinetic /kɪnɛtɪk/ **kinetics**

1 ADJ ATTRIB **Kinetic** is used to describe something that is concerned with movement. *The kinetic ring is related to the flywheel... These are thrilling kinetic spectacles that send you out of the theatre dazzled.* 2 NU **Kinetics** is the scientific study of the way energy behaves when something moves; a technical term in physics. *That is where we marry the enzyme kinetics to electro-chemistry.*

kinetic art

NU **Kinetic art** is visual art, especially sculpture, which has parts that move. *We have a tremendous kinetic sculpture that you play with and look at as it changes. ...a work of kinetic art.*

kinetic energy

NU **Kinetic energy** is the energy that is produced when something moves; a technical term in physics. *...the amount of kinetic energy of a meteorite hitting the earth.*

king /kɪŋ/ **kings**

1 NC or TITLE A **king** is a man who is a member of the royal family of his country, and who is considered to be the Head of State of that country. *...medieval Saxon kings. ...King Hassan of Morocco. ...the King of Spain.* 2 NC If you describe a man as the **king** of something, you mean that he is particularly good at what he does or is the best in his particular field. *Elvis Presley is the king of Rock and Roll.* 3 NC In chess, the **king** is the piece which each player has, and that his opponent must try to capture. 4 NC A **king** is also a playing card with a picture of a king on it.

kingdom /kɪŋdəm/ **kingdoms**

1 NC A **kingdom** is a country or region that is ruled by a king or queen. *Relations between the kingdom of Spain and its former colony are far from good.* 2 N SING+SUPP All the animals, birds, and insects in the world can be referred to together as the animal **kingdom**. All the plants can be referred to as the plant **kingdom**. *Ageing is a fascinating subject, relevant to the entire animal kingdom including, of course, man. ...a protein which is found everywhere throughout the animal and plant kingdom.*

kingfisher /kɪŋfɪʃə/ **kingfishers**

NC A **kingfisher** is a small, brightly-coloured bird which lives near rivers and lakes and catches fish.

kingpin /kɪŋpɪn/ **kingpins**

NC+SUPP The **kingpin** of a particular organization is the most important person in it. *It was revealed he was the kingpin of an illegal organization... The United States wants to see drug kingpins behind bars for long terms.*

kingship /kɪŋʃɪp/

NU **Kingship** is the fact or position of being a king. *...an emblem of kingship.*

king-size

ADJ ATTRIB **King-size** things or **king-sized** things are of the largest size that you can get. *...his king-size bed. ...king-size cigarettes.*

Kingston /kɪŋztən/
Kingston is the capital of Jamaica and its largest city. Population: 104,041 (1982).

Kingston /kɪŋztən/
Kingston is the capital of Norfolk Island and its largest settlement.

Kingstown /kɪŋztaʊn/
Kingstown is the capital of St Vincent and the Grenadines and its largest city. Population: 19,000 (1989).

kink /kɪŋk/ **kinks, kinking, kinked**
1 NC A **kink** is a curve or twist in something such as a piece of wire which is otherwise straight. *I'm trying to get the kinks out of my hair.*
2 V If something **kinks**, it has, or it develops, a curve or twist in it. *Don't press the cable too much or it will kink.*
3 NC A **kink** is also a particular quality or feature of a person's mind or character, especially one which is thought to be unusual or abnormal; an informal use. *He got to know their individual habits, kinks, and procedures.*

kinky /kɪŋki/
ADJ If you describe someone's behaviour as **kinky**, you mean that it is strange, and probably connected with unusual sexual practices; an informal word. *There must be something very kinky going on.*

Kinnock, Neil /niːl kɪnək/
Neil Kinnock was elected leader of the Labour Party in Great Britain in 1983 and so became Leader of the Opposition until 1992, when he resigned. He was MP for Bedwellty from 1970 to 1983, and was elected MP for Islwyn in 1983. Born: 1942.

Kinshasa /kɪnʃɑːsə/
Kinshasa is the capital of Zaïre and its largest city. It was formerly called Léopoldville. Population: 3,500,000 (1985).

kinship /kɪnʃɪp/
1 NU **Kinship** is the relationship between members of the same family; a formal use. *Their ties of kinship mean a lot to them.*
2 NU+SUPP If you feel **kinship** with someone, you feel close to them because you share their ideas or feelings; a literary use. *He felt a deep kinship with the other students.*

kinsman /kɪnzmən/ **kinsmen**
NC A **kinsman** is a male relative; an old-fashioned word. *...the descendants of a distant kinsman named McCaslin.*

kinswoman /kɪnzwʊmən/ **kinswomen**
NC A **kinswoman** is a female relative; an old-fashioned word.

kiosk /kiːɒsk/ **kiosks**
1 NC A **kiosk** is a small building similar to a hut where things such as sandwiches and newspapers are sold. *There have been daily protests at Moscow's cigarette kiosks, where supplies have been short for several weeks. ...a newspaper kiosk.*
2 NC A telephone **kiosk** is the same as a **telephone box**. *The final report shows that just over ninety-two percent of phone kiosks are working properly.*

kip /kɪp/ **kips, kipping, kipped**; an informal word.
1 V If you **kip**, you sleep. *Why don't you go up and kip on my bed?*
2 N SING A **kip** is a period of sleep. *I might leave Ian at your place and get some kip... I feel like a kip.*
kip down PHRASAL VERB If you **kip down** somewhere, you go to sleep at a place that is not your home; an informal expression. *Why don't you kip down here?*

kipper /kɪpə/ **kippers**
NC A **kipper** is a herring which has been preserved by being hung in smoke. *Consumption of fatty fish such as kippers can reduce the risk of death after a heart attack.*

Kirghizia /kɜːgɪziə/ See **Kyrgyzstan**

Kiribati /kɪrɪbæs/
The **Republic of Kiribati** is a country in the Pacific. There are about 33 islands, including the Gilbert Islands, Phoenix Islands, and Line Islands. They came under British control in the late 19th and early 20th centuries. Kiribati became independent in 1979. Ieremia Tabai, an independent, became President in

1979. Kiribati is a member of the Commonwealth. It exports copra and fish. Tourism is an important industry. ◆ **Kiribati** /kɪrɪbæs/ N, ADJ
■ *per capita GNP:* US$650 ■ *religion:* Christianity
■ *language:* English (official), I-Kiribati ■ *currency:* Australian dollar ■ *capital:* Bairiki ■ *population:* 68,000 (1988) ■ *size:* 861 square kilometres.

kirsch /kɪəʃ/
NU **Kirsch** is a strong, colourless, alcoholic drink made from cherries which is usually drunk after a meal. *...a glass of kirsch. ...pineapples in kirsch.*

Kishinev /kiːʃɪnjɒf/
Kishinev is the capital of Moldavia and its largest city. Population: 720,000 (1989).

kiss /kɪs/ **kisses, kissing, kissed**
VO, V-RECIP, or V If you **kiss** someone, you touch them with your lips to show affection or to greet them. *He opened his eyes when I kissed his cheek... I kissed her goodbye and drove away... They stopped and kissed.*
▶ Also NC *Give me a kiss.*

kiss of death
N SING If you say that something is the **kiss of death**, you mean that it is certain to make something go drastically wrong or fail completely. *It's the kiss of death whenever Paul says he'll help with the cooking.*

kiss of life
1 N SING If you give someone the **kiss of life**, you put your mouth onto their mouth and breathe into their lungs to make them start breathing again, for example because they have nearly drowned. *She pulled him out of the lake and gave him the kiss of life.*
2 N SING The **kiss of life** is something which gives new life or energy to something else which is failing. *Government investment would be the kiss of life to the coal industry.*

kit /kɪt/ **kits, kitting, kitted**
1 NC+SUPP A **kit** is a group of items that are kept together because they are used for similar purposes. *...my first-aid kit. ...a tool kit.*
2 NU Your **kit** is the special clothing you use for a particular sport. *Have you brought your squash kit?*
3 NC A **kit** is also a set of parts that can be put together in order to make something. *...a do-it-yourself radio kit.*
kit out PHRASAL VERB If you **kit** someone or something **out**, you provide them with everything they need at that particular time, for example clothing, equipment, furniture, and so on; an informal expression. *...dustmen kitted out in smart new overalls... Prison officers kitted out in full riot gear entered the ruins of the prison.*

kitbag /kɪtbæg/ **kitbags**
NC A **kitbag** is a bag in which people keep clothing and personal belongings or things that they need for a particular purpose such as their work. *Soviet troops are packing their kitbags and loading up the transport planes. ...a really valuable tool in a doctor's kitbag.*

kitchen /kɪtʃɪn/ **kitchens**
NC A **kitchen** is a room used for cooking and for jobs such as washing up. *...the women preparing food in their kitchens. ...kitchen utensils.* ● See also **soup kitchen**.

kitchenette /kɪtʃɪnɛt/ **kitchenettes**
NC A **kitchenette** is a small kitchen, or a part of a larger room that is used for cooking. *...two small rooms, with a kitchenette and a tiny bathroom.*

kitchen garden, kitchen gardens
NC A **kitchen garden** is a part of a garden in which vegetables, herbs, and fruit are grown.

kitchen sink
If you go somewhere and take **everything but the kitchen sink**, you take a lot of things with you, many of which are unnecessary; often used humorously.

kite /kaɪt/ **kites**
1 NC A **kite** is an object consisting of a light frame covered with paper or cloth. It has a long string which you hold while the kite flies in the air. *He was interested in aviation and was flying kites of all sorts of designs.*
2 If you say that someone is **kite-flying**, or that they are **flying a kite**, you mean that you think they are only suggesting something in order to see how people

react, rather than because they definitely believe it or intend to do it. *His views, even though they might be a form of kite-flying, had to be carefully studied and considered... Mr Gerasimov described the proposal as no more than 'flying a kite' and suggested that it was not serious.*

kith and kin /kɪθ n kɪn/
NU Your **kith and kin** are your friends and relatives; an old-fashioned expression. *Their own kith and kin were on the verge of being exterminated.*

kitsch /kɪtʃ/
NU **Kitsch** is used to describe objects or works of art which are very elaborate and often very colourful. *He dismissed the exhibition as commercial kitsch.* ▶ Also ADJ *...a kitsch design.*

kitten /kɪtn/ **kittens**
NC A **kitten** is a very young cat. *...a wide-eyed, intelligent kitten, looking ready for some playful mischief.*

kittenish /kɪtənɪʃ/
ADJ A woman who is **kittenish** flirts with men by behaving in a playful and affectionate way. *She was feminine, sprightly, spoiled and kittenish.*

kitty /kɪti/ **kitties**
NC A **kitty** is an amount of money consisting of contributions from several people, which is spent on things that they will share or use together. *After we paid the phone bill there was nothing left in the kitty.*

kiwi /kiːwi/ **kiwis**
1 NC A **kiwi** is a type of bird which cannot fly that lives in New Zealand. *The kiwi had been chewed up a bit, there were dog tooth marks on it and there were feathers scattered.*
2 NC You can also refer to a person who comes from New Zealand as a **Kiwi**. *The 20 year-old Kiwi recovered in the third set and took a crucial 3-love lead... The cup has now been awarded to the Kiwis.*

kiwi fruit, kiwi fruits. The plural form can be either **kiwi fruits** or **kiwi fruit**.
NC A **kiwi fruit** is a fruit with a brown hairy skin and green flesh. *Kiwi fruits are almost essential for the complete fruit salad.*

klaxon /klæksən/ **klaxons**
NC A **klaxon** is a loud horn that used to be used in emergencies, for example on police cars, fire engines, and ambulances to warn other people and traffic; an old-fashioned word. *...waving flags and sounding klaxons.*

Kleenex /kliːnɛks/ **Kleenexes.** The plural form can be either **Kleenexes** or **Kleenex**.
NU or NC **Kleenex** is a soft tissue paper that is used as a handkerchief; **Kleenex** is a trademark. *...a packet of Kleenex... Have you got a Kleenex?*

kleptomania /klɛptəmeɪniə/
NU **Kleptomania** is a strong and uncontrollable desire to steal things, often occurring as a mental illness; a technical term in psychiatry.

kleptomaniac /klɛptəmeɪniæk/ **kleptomaniacs**
NC A **kleptomaniac** is a person who cannot control the desire to steal things, often because of a mental illness. *His life would be in ruins if it became known he was a kleptomaniac.*

km
Km is a written abbreviation for 'kilometres' or 'kilometre'. *My older sister lives about 10km from our village.*

knack /næk/
N SING+SUPP If you have the **knack** of doing something, you are able to do it, although other people may find it difficult. *He is the consummate politician with the knack of appealing to the ordinary masses... He's got a clear voice, and a knack for writing melodies.*

knackered /nækəd/
ADJ PRED If you are **knackered**, you are very tired; an informal word. *Is it much further? I'm knackered.*

knapsack /næpsæk/ **knapsacks**
NC A **knapsack** is a canvas or leather bag that you carry strapped over your back or slung over your shoulder. *They were carrying knapsacks with medical supplies. ...an army issue knapsack.*

knave /neɪv/ **knaves**
NC A **knave** is a dishonest man; an old-fashioned

word. *You take me for a fool as well as a knave.*

knavery /neɪvəri/
NU **Knavery** is dishonesty; an old-fashioned word. *It really upsets me to contemplate such knavery.*

knead /niːd/ **kneads, kneading, kneaded**
VO When you **knead** dough, you press and squeeze it with your hands to make it smooth. *Knead dough on a well-floured surface.*

knee /niː/ **knees**
1 NC Your **knee** is the place where your leg bends. *Your knee's bleeding.*
2 NC If something or someone is on your **knee**, they are resting or sitting on the upper part of your legs when you are sitting down. *She sat with Marcus by her side and Maria on her knee.*
3 N PL If you are on your **knees**, you are kneeling. *Kurt threw himself on his knees... The woman got up off her knees.*
4 If something **brings** a country to its **knees**, it almost destroys it. *The cost of the war would have brought the kingdom to its knees.*

kneecap /niːkæp/ **kneecaps**
NC Your **kneecaps** are the bones at the front of your knees.

kneecapping /niːkæpɪŋ/ **kneecappings**
NC A **kneecapping** is the act of shooting someone in the knee, which is carried out by some terrorist organizations as a form of punishment. *A thief who had his knees damaged by gunshots—so-called kneecapping—was arrested at the wheel of a stolen car only weeks later. ...punished by regular beatings or even kneecappings by local paramilitary groups.*

knee-deep
ADJ PRED+in If you are **knee-deep** in something, it is as high as your knees. *He stood there knee-deep in the grass.*

knee-high
ADJ If something is **knee-high**, it is as high as your knees. *I crept through a mass of knee-high nettles.*

knee-jerk
N+N If you have a **knee-jerk** reaction to something, you react in a very predictable way, often without thinking. *Opposition to this round of reforms is, in part, a knee-jerk reaction against sales taxes. ...automatic knee-jerk conservatives on all issues.*

kneel /niːl/ **kneels, kneeling, knelt** or **kneeled**
1 V If you **are kneeling**, your legs are bent under you with your knees touching the ground and supporting the rest of your body. *Ralph was kneeling by the fire.* ◆ **kneeling** ADJ ATTRIB *The kneeling figure was Mary Darling.*
2 V If you **kneel** or **kneel** down, you bend your legs and lower your body until your knees are on the ground. *Together they kneeled in prayer... I knelt down beside her.*

knees-up, knees-ups
NC A **knees-up** is a party or celebration; an informal word. *We'll be having a bit of a knees-up on Thursday evening after work.*

knell /nɛl/
N SING+SUPP If you say that the **knell** of something sounds or tolls, you mean that it is going to end soon; a literary word. *The knell of her carefree childhood was sounding.*

knelt /nɛlt/
Knelt is a past tense and past participle of **kneel**.

knew /njuː/
Knew is the past tense of **know**.

knickerbockers /nɪkəbɒkəz/
N PL **Knickerbockers** are loose trousers which reach as far as the knees. They were usually worn by women or children. *She wore knickerbockers, a white frilled blouse and a velvet jacket.*

knickers /nɪkəz/
N PL **Knickers** are a piece of underwear worn by women and girls which have holes for the legs and elastic around the top. *...a pair of knickers.*

knick-knacks /nɪknæks/
N PL **Knick-knacks** are small ornaments. *Their house was full of plants and attractive knick-knacks.*

knife /naɪf/ **knives; knifes, knifing, knifed.** The form **knives** is the plural of the noun. The form **knifes** is the third person singular, present tense, of the verb.

1 NC A **knife** is an object consisting of a sharp, flat piece of metal attached to a handle. You use a knife to cut things. *...knives and forks. ...men armed with knives. ...a knife blade.*

2 VO To **knife** someone means to attack and injure them with a knife. *A man shot and knifed a group of French tourists in the centre of Amman... Rausenberger had been knifed and robbed near his home.* ◆ **knifing, knifings** NC *There were often knifings or brawls.*

3 See also **carving knife, penknife.**

knife-edge, knife-edges
NC A **knife-edge** is a situation that is extremely difficult, because you are not sure what is going to happen or what you should decide. *He seemed perpetually balanced on the knife-edge of agonizing decisions... The rest of the country is on a knife-edge... The Soviet leader is walking a difficult, dangerous knife-edge between encouragement and control.*

knight /naɪt/ **knights, knighting, knighted**
1 NC In medieval times, a **knight** was a man of noble birth, who served his lord in battle. *...knights in armour.*

2 NC In modern times, a **knight** is a man who has been given a knighthood. *Mr Weinberger was appointed an honorary Knight Grand Cross in the civil division of the Most Excellent Order of the British Empire.*

3 NC In chess, a **knight** is a piece shaped like a horse's head.

4 VO If a man is **knighted**, he is given a knighthood. *He was knighted by Queen Anne in 1705.*

knighthood /naɪthʊd/ **knighthoods**
NC In Britain, a **knighthood** is a title given to a man by the Queen or King for outstanding achievements or for service to his country. A man with a knighthood puts 'Sir' in front of his name. *Within hours of completing his journey, he received a telegram from the Queen honouring him with a knighthood.*

knightly /naɪtli/
ADJ ATTRIB **Knightly** means characteristic of a knight, especially by showing chivalry, bravery and fairness; an old-fashioned word. *...the pursuit of the knightly ideal.*

knit /nɪt/ **knits, knitting, knitted**
1 VOorV When someone **knits** something, they make it from wool or a similar thread using knitting needles or a machine. *During World War II she knitted socks and sweaters for the troops... The old lady sat in her doorway and knitted.* ◆ **knitted** ADJ *...a knitted shawl.*

2 If you **knit** your **brows**, you frown because you are angry or worried; a literary expression. *He sat there knitting his brows and twisting his napkin.*

3 ADJ A group of people who are close **knit** or tightly **knit** feel closely linked to each other. *It's a very close-knit community... They live in tightly knit families.*

knitter /nɪtə/ **knitters**
NC A **knitter** is a person who knits. *She was a great knitter.*

knitting /nɪtɪŋ/
1 NU **Knitting** is something that is being knitted. *She picked up her knitting.*

2 NU You also use **knitting** to refer to the action or process of knitting. *...a distraction like knitting which the child can do while watching television... There's a huge business in New Zealand in creative knitting.*

knitting machine, knitting machines
NC A **knitting machine** is a machine that you can use at home for knitting things.

knitting needle, knitting needles
NC **Knitting needles** are thin plastic or metal rods which you use when you are knitting.

knitwear /nɪtweə/
NU **Knitwear** is clothing that has been knitted. *...the family knitwear business.*

knives /naɪvz/
Knives is the plural of **knife.**

knob /nɒb/ **knobs**
1 NC A **knob** is a round handle on a door or drawer. *He turned the knob. ...polished brass knobs.*

2 NC A **knob** is also a rounded lump on top of a stick or post. *Her umbrella is elegantly capped with a glass knob.*

3 NC A round switch on a machine or device is also called a **knob.** *...the knobs on his tape recorder.*

knobbly /nɒbli/
ADJ Something that is **knobbly** is uneven with large lumps on it. *...knobbly old hands.*

knobby /nɒbi/
ADJ **Knobby** means the same as **knobbly**; used in American English. *He caught her by her thin knobby wrist.*

knock /nɒk/ **knocks, knocking, knocked**
1 V, V+on, or V+at If you **knock** at a door or window, you hit it, usually several times, in order to attract someone's attention. *He didn't even knock as he burst inside... He knocked softly on the door.* ▶ Also NC *There was a knock at the door.*

2 VOAorVO If you **knock** something, you hit it roughly, so that it moves or falls over. *In the excitement he knocked over his chair... The glass had been knocked out from the windows.* ▶ Also NC *Knocks can cause weaknesses in the spine.*

3 VOAorVOC If you **knock** someone down or **knock** them unconscious, you hit them so hard that they fall down or become unconscious. *Dad knocked him to the floor... Rudolph had seen him knock Thomas unconscious with his fist.*

4 VO If you **knock** someone or something, you criticize them; an informal expression. *He was always knocking the performance of fellow-actors.*

knock about PHRASAL VERB 1 If someone is **knocked about** or **knocked around**, they are hit several times; an informal expression. *He did not like the thought of a woman being knocked about.* 2 Someone who **has knocked about** or **knocked around** has had experience in a lot of different places or situations; an informal expression. *I'm a bachelor, I've knocked around the world a bit.*

knock around PHRASAL VERB See **knock about.**

knock back PHRASAL VERB If you **knock back** a drink, you drink it quickly; an informal expression. *...knocking back drinks in the Basitka bar.*

knock down PHRASAL VERB 1 If a vehicle **knocks** someone **down**, it hits them so that they are killed or injured. *He was knocked down by a bus.* 2 If you **knock down** a building, you deliberately destroy it or remove it. *I'd knock the wall down between the two rooms.*

knock off PHRASAL VERB 1 If someone **knocks** an amount **off** the price of something, they reduce the price by that amount. *He knocked £50 off the price, because it was scratched.* 2 If someone **knocks** something **off**, they steal it; an informal expression. *He was planning to knock off a few videos.*

knock out PHRASAL VERB 1 If someone **knocks** you **out**, they hit you so hard that they cause you to be unconscious. *He hit me so hard he knocked me out.* 2 If a drug **knocks** you **out**, you become unconscious after taking it. *The tablet had knocked her out for four hours.* 3 If a person or team is **knocked out** of a competition, they are defeated in a game, so that they do not play any more games. *The second favourites, Saudi Arabia, were surprisingly knocked out.* 4 If something **knocks** you **out**, it shocks or impresses you, because it is not what you expected; an informal expression. *The news absolutely knocked me out... Her performance really knocked me out.*

knockdown /nɒkdaʊn/; an informal word.
1 ADJ ATTRIB A **knockdown** price is one that is a lot lower than it would be normally. *I got it for a knockdown price.*

2 ADJ ATTRIB A **knockdown** argument or piece of reasoning is very strong and powerful and difficult to argue against. *Opponents of expansion believe they have a knockdown argument.*

knocker /nɒkə/ **knockers**
NC A **knocker** is a piece of metal attached to the door of a building, which you use to hit the door in order to attract the attention of the people inside. *...a yellow ribbon attached to the door knocker.*

knock knees

N PL Someone who has **knock knees** has legs which turn inwards at the knees. *They all had the same golden hair, knock knees, and upturned noses.*

knock-on

ADJ ATTRIB If something has a **knock-on** effect, it causes a series of events to happen, one after another. *We need to find a solution that doesn't have so many knock-on effects. ...a dramatic indication of the knock-on repercussions of the invasion.*

knockout /nɒkaʊt/ **knockouts**

1 NC In boxing, a **knockout** is a blow that makes one of the boxers fall to the floor and unable to stand up before the referee has counted to ten. *Davies won by a knockout.*
2 ADJ ATTRIB A **knockout** competition is one in which the winner of each match goes on to the next round, until one competitor or team is the winner. *Last year we won the knockout cup.*

knock-up, knock-ups

NC A **knock-up** is a period of time in which the players practise hitting a ball or shuttlecock to each other before beginning a game of tennis, squash, or badminton. *Let's have a knock-up before we start.*

knoll /nəʊl/ **knolls**

NC A **knoll** is a small hill; a literary word. *...a grassy knoll on the outskirts of Waltham.*

knot /nɒt/ **knots, knotting, knotted**

1 NC A **knot** is a place in a piece of string, rope, or cloth where one end has been passed through a loop and pulled tight. You tie a knot in order to join two things together or to keep something firmly in place. *He had tied a crude knot... The knot of her headscarf hung beneath her chin.*
2 VO If you **knot** a piece of string, rope, or cloth, you pass one end of it through a loop and pull it tight. *She knotted the handkerchief corners and tied it tight.*
♦ **knotted** ADJ *...a knotted handkerchief.*
3 VOA If you **knot** one thing around another, you fasten them together using a knot. *He knotted a towel about his neck... I set off with the rope knotted round my waist.*
4 N SING+SUPP A **knot** of people is a group of them standing very close together. *...watched by a knot of sightseers.*
5 NC A **knot** is also a unit used for measuring the speed of ships and aircraft, equal to approximately 1.85 kilometres per hour. *...an underwater object moving at over 150 knots.*

knotty /nɒti/

ADJ ATTRIB A **knotty** problem is complicated and difficult to solve; an informal word. *He and Don had solved many a knotty problem in this room. ...a knotty question.*

know /nəʊ/ **knows, knowing, knew, known**

1 V-REPORT, VO, or V If you **know** something, you have it in your mind and are certain that it is correct. *I knew that she had recently graduated from law school... I don't know her address... 'Will they come back?'—'I don't know.'... We knew what to expect... No one knew how to repair it.*
2 V+of or V+about If you **know** of something or **know** about it, you have heard about it. *Many people did not even know of their existence... Claude knew about the killing.*
3 VO If you **know** a language, you can understand it and speak it. *Shanti knew a few words of English.*
4 VA If you **know** about a subject, you have studied it and have some knowledge of it. *They knew a lot about films... I don't know much about physics, I'm afraid.*
5 VO If you **know** a place or thing, you are familiar with it. *He knew London well... Do you know the poem 'Kubla Khan'?*
6 VO If you **know** someone, you are familiar with them because you have met them and talked to them. *Do you know David?... She knew old Willie very well.*
7 V-PASS+as You can use **know** in the passive to say what people call someone or something. For example, if a forest is **known** as the Big Thicket, people call it the Big Thicket.
8 See also **knowing, known**.
● **Know** is used in these phrases. ● If you **let** someone

know about something, you tell them about it. *I'll find out about the car and let you know what happened.*
● If you **get to know** a person or a place, you find out what they are like. *I'd like the chance to get to know him.* ● If you **know better** than someone else, your ideas are more sensible or more correct than theirs. *The experts, who knew better, laughed at the idea.*
● If you say that someone ought to **know better**, you mean that they ought to behave in a more sensible and acceptable way. *Brian is old enough to know better.*
● If you say that someone **knows best**, you mean that they are always right about what should be done. *Parents always know best.* ● You say '**I know**' to indicate that you agree with what has just been said, or to indicate that you realize something is true. *'It's quite extraordinary.'—'I know.'... I get frightened in the night sometimes—it's silly, I know.* ● Someone who is **in the know** has information about something that only a few people have. *Those in the know are confidently predicting that the titles will stay in Asia.*
● You say '**you know**' to emphasize something or to make your statement clearer. *You were very naughty, you know... You know, most of the time he seems like a fool. ...the old desk. You know, the one that's broken.* ● People say '**you know**' to fill in a gap in a conversation, for example when they are unsure about what they are saying or what they are going to say next. *She thought a lot about her appearance, you know, and spent a lot of her money on clothes.*

knowable /nəʊəbl/

ADJ Things that are **knowable** can be known about. *The answers are knowable in advance.*

know-all, know-alls

NC A **know-all** is someone who thinks that they know a lot more than other people; an informal word, used showing disapproval.

know-how

NU **Know-how** is knowledge about how to do scientific or technical things; an informal word. *They now had the facilities and know-how to produce advanced weapons.*

knowing /nəʊɪŋ/

ADJ ATTRIB A **knowing** gesture or remark shows that you understand something, even though it has not actually been mentioned directly. *This is usually greeted with deep sighs and knowing looks. ...a knowing smile.*

knowingly /nəʊɪŋli/

1 ADV If you do something wrong **knowingly**, you are aware that it is wrong when you do it. *They knowingly broke laws that ban trade in rare reptiles.*
2 ADV If you look, smile, or wink **knowingly**, you do it in a way that shows that you understand something, even though it has not actually been mentioned directly. *The girls looked knowingly at each other.*

know-it-all, know-it-alls

NC A **know-it-all** is the same as a **know-all**; used in informal American English. *He's a bit of a know-it-all, but that's not surprising.*

knowledge /nɒlɪdʒ/

1 NU **Knowledge** is information and understanding about a subject, which someone has in their mind. *...advances in scientific knowledge... All knowledge comes to us through our senses. ...a knowledge of income-tax legislation.*
2 If you say that something is true **to the best of** your **knowledge**, you mean that you think that it is true, although you are not completely sure. *...a play which to the best of my knowledge has never been performed in Britain.*

knowledgeable /nɒlɪdʒəbl/

ADJ A **knowledgeable** person knows a lot about many different things or a lot about a particular subject. *He was surprisingly knowledgeable about what was going on in the theatre.*

known /nəʊn/

1 **Known** is the past participle of **know**.
2 ADJ If something is **known** to people, they are aware of it and have information about it. *There's no known cure for a cold. ...the most dangerous substance known to man... He was a known criminal.*
3 If you let it be **known** that something is the case,

you make sure that people know it, without telling them directly; a formal expression. *She let it be known that she wanted to leave China.*
4 See also **well-known**.

knuckle /nʌkl/ **knuckles, knuckling, knuckled**
NC Your **knuckles** are the rounded pieces of bone where your fingers join your hands, and where your fingers bend. *As he fell, he scraped the skin off his knuckles.*
knuckle down PHRASAL VERB If someone **knuckles down**, they begin to work or study very hard, especially after a period when they have done very little work; an informal expression. *It's high time you knuckled down to some hard study.*
knuckle under PHRASAL VERB If you **knuckle under**, you do what someone else tells you to do or what a situation forces you to do; an informal expression. *He blames foreigners for putting pressure on Japan and the Japanese for knuckling under to that pressure... The United States, he said, did not knuckle under to demands.*

knuckle-duster, knuckle-dusters
NC A **knuckle-duster** is a weapon made from a piece of metal shaped like rings that have been joined together. It is designed to be worn on someone's hand, and makes a punch much harder. *Among the weapons on the list are high-powered catapults, knuckle-dusters, and a wide variety of knives.*

KO /keɪ əʊ/ **KO's, KO'd**; also written **k.o.**
1 NC **KO** is an abbreviation for 'knockout'. *Davis won by a KO in the 4th round.*
2 VO To **KO** someone means to hit them so hard that they become unconscious; an informal expression.

koala /kəʊɑːlə/ **koalas**
NC A **koala** or a **koala bear** is an Australian animal which looks like a small bear with grey fur and small tufted ears. Koalas live in trees and eat leaves. *Police in Australia are adopting new tactics to try to protect koala bears... Koalas are an endangered species.*

Koffigoh, Joseph Kokou /dʒəʊzɪf kəʊku: kɒfigəʊ/
Joseph Kokou Koffigoh was appointed interim Prime Minister of Togo by a pro-democracy conference in 1991. He was previously President of the Bar Association and Chairman of the Human Rights League of Togo. Born: 1943.

kohl /kəʊl/
NU **Kohl** is a cosmetic used to darken the edge of a person's eyelids.

Kohl, Dr Helmut /hɛlmuːt kəʊl/
Dr Helmut Kohl became Chancellor of West Germany in 1982 and of re-united Germany in 1990. He was Minister-President of the Rhineland-Palatinate from 1969 to 1976. He was Deputy Chairman of the Christian Democratic Union (CDU) from 1969 to 1973, and became Chairman in 1973. Born: 1930.

Koirala, Girija Prasad /gɪriːdʒə prəsɑːd kɔɪrɑːlə/
Girija Prasad Koirala was elected Prime Minister of Nepal in 1991. His brother, Bisheswar Prasad Koirala, was Prime Minister of Nepal from 1959 to 1960. He became General Secretary of the Nepali Congress Party (NCP) in 1980. Born: 1926.

Koivisto, Dr Mauno /maʊnəʊ kɔɪvɪstəʊ/
Dr Mauno Koivisto became President of Finland in 1982. He served as Minister of Finance from 1966 to 1967, and was Prime Minister from 1968 to 1970, and from 1979 to 1982. He is a member of the Social Democratic Party (SDP). Born: 1923.

Kolingba, André /ɒnᵒdreɪ kɒliːŋbə/
General André Kolingba became President of the Central African Republic in a coup in 1981. He founded the Central African Democratic Assembly (RDC) in 1986.

Koran /kɔːrɑːn/
N PROP The **Koran** is the sacred book on which the religion of Islam is based. *They went through a brief religious ceremony of blessing, kissing the Holy Koran and touching it with their foreheads. ...one of several original copies of the Koran, dictated personally by the Caliph Osman.*

Koranic /kɔːrænɪk/
ADJ ATTRIB **Koranic** is used to describe things which belong or relate to the Koran. *...Koranic verses.*

Korea /kəriːə/ See **North Korea, South Korea**

Koror /kɒrɔː/
Koror is the capital of Belau and its largest town. Population: 10,000 (1990).

kosher /kəʊʃə/
ADJ **Kosher** food is approved of by the laws of Judaism. *Rabbi Schneier said there was now greater access to kosher food, bibles, and prayer books. ...kosher butchers and shops that close for the Sabbath.*

kow-tow /kaʊ taʊ/ **kow-tows, kow-towing, kow-towed**
V+*to* If you **kow-tow** to someone, you behave very humbly and respectfully towards them, especially because you hope to get something from them; an informal expression. *He rather resents having to kow-tow to anyone.*

kph
kph is a written abbreviation for 'kilometres per hour'; used after a number to indicate the speed at which something is moving. *Airships can travel in excess of 240 kph.*

kraal /krɑːl/ **kraals**
NC A **kraal** is a type of village in southern Africa in which the buildings are surrounded by a wooden fence. *He had to learn always to be truthful to the people of his own tribe and kraal.*

Kravchuk, Leonid /leɪənɪːd krɒftʃuːk/
Leonid Kravchuk became President of Ukraine in 1991. He was a Secretary of the Central Committee of the Ukrainian Communist Party from 1989 to 1990, and Chairman of the Ukrainian Supreme Soviet from 1990 to 1991. Born: 1934.

Kremlin /krɛmlɪn/
N COLL The **Kremlin** is a group of buildings in the centre of Moscow which houses the government offices of the Russian Republic. The word **Kremlin** was also used to refer to the central government of the former Soviet Union. *This change was welcomed by the Kremlin... Soviet spokesmen have repeatedly said the Kremlin has no intention of doing this... There was a chance that Kremlin leaders would give their approval.*

krugerrand /kruːgərænd/ **krugerrands**
NC A **krugerrand** is a South African gold coin which some people buy as an investment. *Mr Botha presented him with a gold krugerrand coin.*

Kuala Lumpur /kwɑːlə lʊmpə/
Kuala Lumpur is the capital of Malaysia and its largest city. Population: 959,000 (1982).

Kučan, Milan /miːlæn kuːtʃæn/
Milan Kučan became President of Slovenia in 1990. He was a member of the Central Committee of the League of Communists of Yugoslavia from 1982 to 1986, and President of the Presidium of the Central Committee of the League of Communists of Slovenia from 1986 to 1989. He is now a member of the Party of Democratic Reform. Born: 1941.

kudos /kjuːdɒs/
NU **Kudos** is fame or admiration that someone gets as a result of a particular action or achievement. *He enjoys all the kudos that goes with being a successful doctor.*

Kung Fu /kʌŋ fuː/
NU **Kung Fu** is a Chinese style of fighting which involves using only your hands and feet. *...Kung Fu classes.*

Kuwait /kuːweɪt/
The State of Kuwait is a country in the Gulf. The Sabah family has ruled it since the 19th century. Sheikh Jaber al-Ahmad al-Sabah became Amir in 1977. The Crown Prince, Sheikh Saad al-Abdullah al-Salem al-Sabah, became Prime Minister in 1978. There are no political parties. Iraq invaded Kuwait in 1990, but its troops were driven out by the US and its allies in 1991. Kuwait possesses nearly 10 per cent of the world's oil reserves. It is a member of OPEC, the Arab League, and the Gulf Co-operation Council. ◆ **Kuwaiti** /kuːweɪti/ N, ADJ
▪ *per capita GNP:* US$13,680 ▪ *religion:* Islam (mainly Sunni) ▪ *language:* Arabic ▪ *currency:* dinar ▪ *capital:* Kuwait City ▪ *population:* 2 million (1989) (73% foreign nationals) ▪ *size:* 17,818 square kilometres.

Kuwait City /kuːweɪt sɪti/
   Kuwait City is the capital of Kuwait and its largest
   city. Population: 44,335 (1985).
kW
   kW is a written abbreviation for 'kilowatt'; used
   especially after a number to indicate a measurement
   of electrical power. *...a 1kW electric fire.*
Kyrgyzstan /kɪəgɪstɑːn/
   The **Republic of Kyrgyzstan** became independent of
   the USSR in 1991. It is in the extreme south-east of the
former USSR, on the border with China. Askar
Akayev, of the Kyrgyz Communist Party, became
President in 1990. Kyrgyzstan produces metals, coal,
and agricultural products. In 1991 it joined the
Commonwealth of Independent States. ◆ **Kyrgyzstani**
/kɪəgɪstɑːn/ N **Kyrgyz** /kɪəgɪz/ ADJ
   ▪ *per capita GNP:* US$3,030 ▪ *religion:* Islam
   ▪ *language:* Kyrgyz ▪ *currency:* rouble ▪ *capital:*
   Bishkek (formerly Frunze) ▪ *population:* 4 million
   (1990) ▪ *size:* 198,500 square kilometres.

L l

L, l /el/ **L's, l's**
1 NC **L** is the twelfth letter of the English alphabet.
2 **L** is the symbol for 'learner driver'. In Britain, a large red 'L' on a white background is attached to cars in which people are learning to drive.
3 **L** or **l** is also an abbreviation for 'litre'.

lab /læb/ **labs**
NC A **lab** is a laboratory; an informal word. *Your X-rays have just come back from the lab.*

label /leɪbl/ **labels, labelling, labelled**; spelt **labeling, labeled** in American English.
1 NC A **label** is a piece of paper, cloth, or plastic that is attached to an object to give information about it. *The bottles got wet and all the labels came off... Manufacturers should be required by law to mark all pre-packed foods with a standard label giving information about ingredients.*
2 VO If you **label** something, you attach a label to it. *...the brown pot labelled 'Salt'.*
3 NC+SUPP A **label** is also a word or phrase that people use to describe you; used showing disapproval. *He was not willing to accept the label of anarchist.*
4 VO If people **label** you as something, they describe you or think of you in that way; used showing disapproval. *Once you are labelled as a secretary you will never become anything else... There were theoretical reasons for a reluctance to label a child as depressed.*
5 NC You can refer to a company that produces and promotes records as a particular **label**. *Written and produced by Midge, this is his first release on his new record label... He made some of his best recordings for the illustrious Blue Note record label.*

labial /leɪbɪəl/
ADJ A **labial** sound is produced with your lips; a technical term in linguistics.

labor /leɪbə/. See **labour**.

laboratory /ləbɒrətri/ **laboratories**
1 NC A **laboratory** is a building or room where scientific experiments and research are carried out. *The geologists took the samples back to the laboratory... A number of nuclear research laboratories were badly damaged.*
2 NC A **laboratory** in a school or university is a room containing scientific equipment where students are taught science subjects such as chemistry. *The laboratory belongs to the Faculty of Science. ...combined courses where one subject involves significant laboratory or workshop-based activities.*
● See also **language laboratory**.

laborious /ləbɔːrɪəs/
ADJ A **laborious** task takes a lot of time and effort. *Clearing the forest is a laborious business.*
♦ **laboriously** ADV *...laboriously hand-written books.*

labor union, labor unions
NC In the United States, a **labor union** is an organization that has been formed by workers in order to represent their rights and interests to their employers, for example in order to improve working conditions or wages. *The strike was called by left-wing labor unions.*

labour /leɪbə/ **labours, labouring, laboured**; spelt **labor** in American English.
1 N PROP You can use **Labour** to refer to the Labour Party. *The party's deputy leader, Mr Roy Hattersley, said Labour was already committed to a united Ireland... Mr Hurd's decision has been attacked by Labour. ...the Labour MP for Pontypridd.*
2 NU or NC **Labour** is very hard work. *As in many developing countries the women do a lot of the agricultural labour. ...a terrified population ravaged by forced labour in the fields. ...a pleasant distraction from his political labours.*
3 V A If you **labour** at something, you do it with difficulty. *A team of technicians has laboured hard at cleaning each frame of the original print... Tim had laboured over a letter to Gertrude.* ♦ **laboured** ADJ *McKellen's breathing was laboured.*
4 NU **Labour** is used to refer to the people who work in a country or industry. *...a shortage of skilled labour... Employers rely far more now on casual and seasonal labour... They fear job losses as industry moves south to where there is cheap labour.*
5 NU **Labour** is also the work done by a group of workers. *They are threatening a withdrawal of labour in support of their claims.*
6 V+under If you **labour** under a misapprehension or delusion, you continue to believe something which is not true. *He laboured under the misapprehension that nobody liked him.*
7 VO If you **labour** a point or an argument, you talk about it in great and unnecessary detail. *There is no need to labour the point.*
8 NU **Labour** is also the last stage of pregnancy, in which a woman gives birth to a baby. *She was in labour for seven hours. ...the risk of high blood loss in labour.*

labourer /leɪbəʳrə/ **labourers**; spelt **laborer** in American English.
NC A **labourer** is a person who does a job which involves a lot of hard physical work. *...a farm labourer.*

labour force
N SING 1 The **labour force** consists of all the people in a particular country who are able to work. *The labour force is growing at a rate of about one million a year... Unemployment will continue to grow to reach eight and a half per cent of the labour force or around two and a quarter million next year.*
2 N SING The **labour force** can also refer to all the people who work for a particular company. *The company has made cuts in the labour force of two thirds since 1980.*

labour-intensive
ADJ Industries or techniques that are **labour-intensive** need or use a lot of workers. *...the traditional labour-intensive manufacturing industries.*

labour market
N SING The **labour market** consists of all the people who want work at a particular time, or the demand for work, especially in relation to the amount of work available; a technical term in economics. *...women wanting to break into the labour market.*

Labour Party; also spelt **Labor Party** in Australian English.
N PROP The **Labour Party** is the main left-of-centre party in the United Kingdom. It has a long association with the Trade Unions. It believes in social justice within a market economy, properly funded public services and a measure of constitutional reform. *Half our unions are affiliated to the Labour Party... He declined to speak at the Labour Party rally in Hyde Park last month.*

labour-saving
ADJ A machine or method that is **labour-saving** saves you a lot of hard work or effort. *....the labour-saving devices of the early twentieth century, such as the electric iron or the washing machine.*

laburnum /ləbɜːnəm/ **laburnums**
NC A **laburnum** is a small tree. It has long stems of yellow flowers and poisonous seeds. Laburnums are often planted in gardens.

labyrinth /læbərɪnθ/ **labyrinths**
NC A **labyrinth** is a complicated series of paths or passages, through which it is difficult to find your way; a literary word. *He wandered through the labyrinths of the Old Town.*

labyrinthine /læbərɪnθaɪn/; a literary word.
1 ADJ Something that is **labyrinthine** is like a labyrinth. *The castle is labyrinthine, dark, and mysterious.*
2 ADJ **Labyrinthine** also means very complicated and difficult to understand. *...a nightmare of labyrinthine bureaucratic procedures.*

Lacalle Herrara, Luis Alberto
/luːɪs ælbeətəʊ lækæljeɪ erɑːrə/
Luis Alberto Lacalle Herrara became President of Uruguay in 1990. He was elected to the Legislative Assembly in 1971 and became a Senator in 1984. He is a member of the National Party (PN), also known as the Blanco Party. Born: 1941.

lace /leɪs/ **laces, lacing, laced**
1 NC **Laces** are pieces of cord or string that you put through holes along the two edges of something and tie in order to fasten them together. *...tying the laces of his shoes.*
2 NU **Lace** is very delicate cloth which has a pattern of holes in it. *...a white lace handkerchief.*

lace up PHRASAL VERB If you **lace** something **up**, you fasten it by pulling two ends of a lace tight and tying them together. *He bent and laced up his shoes.*

lacerate /læsəreɪt/ **lacerates, lacerating, lacerated**
VO If something **lacerates** your skin, it cuts it deeply. ♦ **lacerated** ADJ *The thirty-year old woman was suffering from a badly lacerated hand.*

laceration /læsəreɪʃn/ **lacerations**
NC A **laceration** is a bad cut on your skin. *She had terrible lacerations on her legs and arms.*

lace-up, lace-ups
NC **Lace-ups** or **lace-up** shoes are shoes which are fastened with laces. *Maria's lace-ups had got holes in the toes.*

lachrymose /lækrɪməʊs/
ADJ Someone who is **lachrymose** cries very easily and very often; a literary word. *She was irritable and lachrymose.*

lack /læk/ **lacks, lacking, lacked**
1 N SING or NU If there is a **lack** of something, there is not enough of it, or there is none at all. *The junior grades are suffering from a severe lack of sleep... Lack of proper funding is making our job more difficult.*
2 V-ERG If you **lack** something, or if something is **lacking**, you do not have enough of it, or you do not have any at all. *They lack the confidence to make friends... The advertisement lacks any individuality... What is lacking is any of the excitement and extraordinary power of his music.*
3 If you say that there is **no lack of** something, you mean that there is a great deal of it, and perhaps more than you need. *There was no lack of schools to choose from.*
4 See also **lacking**.

lackadaisical /lækədeɪzɪkl/
ADJ Someone who is **lackadaisical** does not show any

interest or enthusiasm and acts as if they are daydreaming. *She was annoyingly lackadaisical and impractical.*

lackey /læki/ **lackeys**
NC If you call someone a **lackey**, you mean that they follow someone's orders completely, without ever questioning them; used showing disapproval. *They said that the police were lackeys of the Establishment.*

lacking /lækɪŋ/
1 ADJ PRED+*in* If someone or something is **lacking** in a particular quality, they do not have enough of it or have none of it at all. *But he was also lacking in charity... Its ideology is sterile and lacking in originality... Philip was not lacking in intelligence.*
2 ADJ PRED If a quality is **lacking**, it is not there, although you would expect it to be there. *But once in power, political confidence appeared lacking... Innovation has been sadly lacking.*
3 See also **lack**.

lacklustre /læklʌstə/; also spelt **lackluster** in American English.
ADJ Something or someone that is **lacklustre** has no brightness or liveliness. *The pianist gave a lacklustre performance.*

laconic /ləkɒnɪk/
ADJ A **laconic** comment uses very few words to say something, so that the person who makes it seems very casual. *In a laconic statement to Finance Ministry officials he said he had no regrets. ...the laconic entries in his diary.* ♦ **laconically** ADV *Sam was laconically directed to an office in a nearby street.*

lacquer /lækə/ **lacquers**
1 N MASS **Lacquer** is a special type of paint which is put on wood or metal to protect it and make it shiny. *The usual method is to apply synthetic lacquer over the surface of the object.*
2 N MASS **Lacquer** is also a liquid which some people spray on their hair to hold it neatly in place.

lacquered /lækəd/
ADJ **Lacquered** wood or metal has been covered in lacquer. *...a lacquered box. ...a lacquered wooden spoon.*

lacrosse /ləkrɒs/
NU **Lacrosse** is an outdoor game played between two teams of players. They use long sticks with nets at the end to catch and throw a small ball, in order to try and score goals. *They play traditional schoolgirl games like hockey and lacrosse.*

lactation /lækteɪʃn/
NU **Lactation** is the production of milk by women and female mammals during the period before and after they give birth; a formal word. *If there's a food shortage during lactation, the milk supply drops.*

lactic acid /læktɪk æsɪd/
NU **Lactic acid** is a type of acid which is found in sour milk and is also produced by your muscles when you have been exercising a lot. *A build up of lactic acid causes painful muscular cramps.*

lactose /læktəʊs/
NU **Lactose** is a type of sugar which is found in milk and which is sometimes added to food. *They will only metabolise complicated sugars like sucrose or lactose when the much simpler glucose has been used up.*

lacy /leɪsi/
ADJ Something that is **lacy** is made from lace or has pieces of lace attached to it. *...a lacy dress.*

lad /læd/ **lads**
NC A **lad** is a boy or young man; an informal word. *He used to collect stamps when he was a lad.*

ladder /lædə/ **ladders**
NC A **ladder** is a piece of equipment used for climbing up something such as a wall or a tree. It consists of two long pieces of wood, metal, or rope with steps fixed between them. *The man got his young son through the smoke and flames and escaped down a ladder.*

laddie /lædi/ **laddies**
N C or VOCATIVE A **laddie** is a young man or boy; an informal word. *...this little laddie, aged about four... You've been in a fight, laddie.*

laden /leɪdn/
ADJ PRED If someone or something is **laden** with a lot

of heavy things, they are holding or carrying them; a literary word. *The trees were laden with fruit... Ken arrived laden with presents... A cargo ship laden with rice has left South Korea.*

la-di-da /lɑːdidɑː/; also spelt **lah-di-dah.**
ADJ or ADV Someone who is **la-di-da** has an upper-class way of behaving or speaking, which seems very affected; an old-fashioned, informal word, used showing disapproval. *...his la-di-da family, as she called them. ...a posh twit, talking so la-di-da I had to leave the room.*

ladies' man, ladies' men
NC A **ladies' man** is a man who enjoys flirting with women in a way that they also enjoy; an old-fashioned expression. *Mr Spencer was a great ladies' man.*

ladies' room
N SING The **ladies' room** is a public toilet for women, especially in a large public building. *Can you tell me where the ladies' room is?*

ladle /leɪdl/ **ladles, ladling, ladled**
1 NC A **ladle** is a large, round, deep spoon with a long handle, used for serving soup or stew.
2 VO If you **ladle** food such as soup or stew, you serve it using a ladle. *...ladling the soup into bowls.*

lady /leɪdi/ **ladies**
1 NC You can use **lady** as a polite way of referring to a woman. *...a rich American lady. ...elderly ladies living on their own.*
2 VOCATIVE You can say **'ladies'** when you are addressing a group of women. *Ladies, could I have your attention, please?... Good evening, ladies and gentlemen.*
3 NC If you say that a woman is a **lady**, you mean that she behaves in a polite, dignified, and graceful way, especially if she comes from a high social class; an old-fashioned use. *A lady never crosses her legs... I'm not a lady and never will be.*
4 TITLE **Lady** is a title used in front of the names of some women from the upper classes. *...Lady Diana Cooper... Lady Gibbs is seventy-eight.*
5 N SING Some people refer to a public toilet for women as the **ladies**. *Where's the ladies?*

ladybird /leɪdibɜːd/ **ladybirds**
NC A **ladybird** is a small, round, red beetle with black spots. *In our garden, my wife tries to encourage ladybirds to get rid of pests.*

ladybug /leɪdibʌg/ **ladybugs**
NC A **ladybug** is the same as a **ladybird**; used in American English. *There's a long tradition of using ladybugs for the control of pests.*

lady friend, lady friends
NC A man's **lady friend** is his girlfriend; an old-fashioned expression. *I overheard the servants discuss his various lady friends.*

lady-in-waiting, ladies-in-waiting
NC A **lady-in-waiting** is a woman from the aristocracy or upper classes, who acts as a companion to a female member of the royal family. *The Queen was accompanied by three ladies-in-waiting.*

ladykiller /leɪdikɪlə/ **ladykillers**
NC A **ladykiller** is an attractive man who enjoys flirting with or seducing women, but who soon leaves each woman to search for someone new; an old-fashioned word.

ladylike /leɪdilaɪk/
ADJ If you say that a woman or girl is **ladylike**, you mean that she behaves in a polite, dignified, and graceful way. *Alice's mother had always considered Jill to be ladylike and discreet... She took little ladylike sips of the cold drink.*

Lady Muck
N PROP If you refer to a woman or girl as **Lady Muck**, you are showing that you think she is too bossy and has too high an opinion of herself; an informal expression. *Who the hell does she think she is? Lady Muck?*

Ladyship /leɪdɪʃɪp/ **Ladyships**
TITLE **Ladyship** is used in the expressions 'Your Ladyship', 'Her Ladyship', and 'Their Ladyships' as a respectful way of addressing or talking about a female member of the nobility or the wife of a knight or peer. *Her Ladyship will see you in the library, sir.*

lady's maid, lady's maids
NC A **lady's maid** was a female servant, especially in 18th or 19th century Britain, who worked for a rich woman, doing things such as looking after her clothes, helping her to dress, or doing her hair.

lag /læg/ **lags, lagging, lagged**
1 V If you **lag** behind someone or something, you move or progress more slowly than they do. *He now lags 10 points behind the champion overall... Mr Lamont said economic transformation had lagged behind political reform throughout eastern Europe.*
2 V When something such as trade or investment **lags**, it slows down or there is less of it than there was before. *Production lagged and unemployment rose.*
3 NC+SUPP A time **lag** is a period of time between two related events. *There is usually a long time lag between infection by HIV and actually developing full-blown AIDS... There will be a one-year lag between the time I write this book and its publication.*
4 VO If you **lag** a pipe, a water tank, or the inside of a roof, you cover it with a special material in order to prevent heat escaping from it. *Hot water pipes and tanks need to be lagged with insulating material to prevent heat loss and save money... These supports are lagged with asbestos as a fire precaution.*

lager /lɑːgə/ **lagers**
N MASS **Lager** is a kind of light beer. *...a glass of lager... The traditional British pint of beer has been overtaken by lager... They may opt for a glass of fruit juice or a non-alcoholic lager.*

lager lout, lager louts
NC **Lager louts** are young men who behave in a noisy or aggressive way because they are drunk; an informal expression. *Many of the lager louts are young people with high disposable incomes.*

laggard /lægəd/ **laggards**
NC A **laggard** is someone who is slower than everyone else, especially in their work; an old-fashioned word.

lagging /lægɪŋ/
NU **Lagging** is special material which is used to cover pipes, water tanks, or the inside of a roof in order to prevent heat escaping. *The problem with some forms of lagging is that they don't always completely cover the pipes.*

lagoon /ləguːn/ **lagoons**
NC A **lagoon** is an area of calm sea water that is separated from the ocean by reefs or sand. *The coastal lagoons of the Nile Delta are important wildlife centres.*

Lagos /leɪgɒs/
Lagos is the largest city in Nigeria. It was formerly the capital, and while a new capital was constructed at Abuja, many government offices remained in Lagos. Population: 1,097,000 (1983).

lah-di-dah /lɑː di dɑː/. See **la-di-da.**

laid /leɪd/
Laid is the past tense and past participle of **lay**.

laid-back
ADJ Someone who is **laid-back** behaves in a calm, relaxed way as if nothing will ever worry them; an informal word. *James believed in a laid-back approach.*

laid up
ADJ If you are **laid up**, you have to stay in bed because you are ill. *He had been laid up for five days with a bad cold.*

lain /leɪn/
Lain is the past participle of some meanings of **lie**.

lair /leə/ **lairs**
NC A **lair** is a place where a wild animal lives, usually a place which is underground or well-hidden. *...animals that refuse to come out of their lairs.*

laird /leəd/ **lairds**
NC A **laird** is a landowner in Scotland who owns a large area of land.

laissez-faire /leɪseɪfeə/
NU **Laissez-faire** is the policy which is based on the idea that governments and the law should not interfere with business, finance, or the conditions of people's working lives. *...the self-defeating ideology of laissez-faire.* ▶ Also ADJ *It is therefore unlikely that a laissez-faire policy will succeed... The traditionalists*

want a laissez-faire approach to the economy.

laity /leɪəti/; a formal word.
1 N PL The **laity** are all the people involved in the work of a church who are not clergymen, monks, or nuns. *...the Catholic laity. ...a human rights watchdog organisation formed by churchmen and laity.*
2 N PL You also refer to all the people who do not belong to a particular profession as the **laity**. *He called all professions conspiracies against the laity.*

lake /leɪk/ **lakes**
NC A **lake** is a large area of fresh water, surrounded by land. *Two fishermen were sitting in a boat in the middle of a beautiful lake. ...Lake Michigan.*

lakeside /leɪksaɪd/
N SING The **lakeside** is the area of land around the edge of a lake. *We got up to walk along the lakeside at an early hour... He had lunch at a lakeside restaurant.*

lam /læm/ **lams, lamming, lammed**
V Oor V+*into* To **lam** someone or something or to **lam** into someone or something means to hit them very hard; an informal word. *If he says it again, lam him.*

lama /lɑːmə/ **lamas**
NC A **lama** is a Buddhist priest or monk in Tibet and Mongolia. *...the Panshen Lama, who is a spiritual leader of Tibetan Buddhists.*

lamb /læm/ **lambs**
1 NC A **lamb** is a young sheep. *It's the heart of Welsh sheep-rearing country—more lambs are produced here than anywhere else in Britain... He claimed that it is largely untrue that foxes kill young lambs.*
2 NU **Lamb** is the flesh of a sheep or lamb eaten as food. *I went in the farmhouse, and there I had roast lamb... Sales of pork, lamb and poultry had risen.*

lambing /læmɪŋ/
NU **Lambing** is the time in the spring when female sheep give birth to lambs. *...the lambing season.*

lambskin /læmskɪn/ **lambskins**
NUorNC **Lambskin** is the skin of a lamb, usually with the wool still on it, used for making slippers, coats, and rugs. *...a lambskin hat. ...lambskin slippers.*

lame /leɪm/
1 ADJ If someone is **lame**, they cannot walk properly because an injury or illness has damaged one or both of their legs. *The illness left her permanently lame... They frequently suffer from hip displacements, which make them go lame. ...a lame horse.*
2 ADJ A **lame** excuse, argument, or remark is poor or weak. *My lame excuse was that I had too much else to do... Mr Gorbachev said the rumours were lame fabrications.* ♦ **lamely** ADV *'I didn't recognize you,' Claude said lamely.*

lamé /lɑːmeɪ/
NU **Lamé** is cloth that has threads of gold or silver woven into it, which make it sparkle. *Revellers flaunt their golden lamé, lace and leather costumes as they walk up the street.*

lame duck, lame ducks
1 NC A **lame duck** is someone who is not successful and who needs to be helped by other people. *He was yet another of my sister's lame ducks.*
2 ADJ **Lame duck** is also used to describe people in official positions whose term of office is about to end, and who have not been re-elected; used in American English. *Mr Reagan is a lame duck president, and Mr Bush is still putting together his National Security team.*

lament /ləment/ **laments, lamenting, lamented**
VO, V-REPORT, V-QUOTE, or V If you **lament** something, you express your sadness or regret about it; a literary word. *He laments the changing pattern of life in the countryside... He lamented that they didn't have the opportunity that he was having that day... 'All the flour is wet!' lamented Miss Mutton... There is little ministers can do but lament.* ▶ Also NC *'It's a dying industry,' is his lament.*

lamentable /læməntəbl/
ADJ If you describe something as **lamentable**, you mean that it is very unfortunate or disappointing; a literary word. *...the lamentable state of the industry in the Sixties.* ♦ **lamentably** SUBMOD or ADV SEN *...the lamentably inadequate plans for retraining officers...*

The policies needed to nurture the country back to health will be exceptional and, lamentably, very harsh.

lamentation /læmenteɪʃn/ **lamentations**
NCorNU A **lamentation** is an expression of grief or great sorrow; a formal word. *...tears and lamentations... a cry of lamentation went up.*

laminated /læmɪneɪtɪd/
1 ADJ Material such as wood, glass, or plastic that is **laminated** consists of several thin sheets or layers that are stuck together. *...windscreens made of laminated glass.*
2 ADJ A product that is **laminated** is covered with a thin sheet of clear plastic in order to protect it. *...an advertisement, glossy and laminated... They'll then apply for the new laminated cards being issued from June the first.*

lamp /læmp/ **lamps**
NC A **lamp** is a light that works by using electricity or by burning oil or gas. *She turned on the bedside lamp. ...the street lamp outside.*

lamplight /læmplaɪt/
NU **Lamplight** is the light produced by a lamp. *...her hair gleaming in the lamplight.*

lamplit /læmplɪt/
ADJ If something is **lamplit**, it can be seen because there is light from a lamp. *We saw the lamplit windows ahead.*

lampoon /læmpuːn/ **lampoons, lampooning, lampooned**
1 VO If you **lampoon** someone or something, you criticize them very strongly, but using humorous means. *The governor was lampooned by the Journal's cartoonists... The Premier was lampooned as Bumbling Baldwin in the Express.*
2 NC A **lampoon** is a piece of writing or speech which criticizes someone or something very strongly, but using humorous means. *Lampoons were written and passed from hand to hand.*

lamp-post, lamp-posts
NC A **lamp-post** is a tall metal or concrete pole beside a road with a light at the top. *There are posters in the shop windows and stuck on the lamp-posts to greet the Pope's arrival.*

lampshade /læmpʃeɪd/ **lampshades**
NC A **lampshade** is a decorative covering over an electric light bulb which makes the light softer. *The silk lampshades matched the curtains.*

lance /lɑːns/ **lances, lancing, lanced**
1 VO If you **lance** a boil on someone's body, you pierce it with a sharp instrument in order to let the pus drain out. *The doctor lanced the abscess.*
2 NC A **lance** is a long spear used in former times, especially by soldiers on horseback.

lancet /lɑːnsɪt/ **lancets**
NC A **lancet** is a small knife with a sharp point and two sharp edges. It is used by doctors for cutting people's skin.

land /lænd/ **lands, landing, landed**
1 NU **Land** is an area of ground. *It's good agricultural land. ...a piece of land... The next stage will be the sale of land and houses.*
2 N+POSS If you refer to someone's **land** or **lands**, you mean an area of land which they own. *...the terrible Thirty Years' War that devastated the German lands and most of Central Europe... Their lands are occupied and they have no political rights.*
3 NUorN SING **Land** or the **land** refers to the part of the world that is solid ground rather than sea or air. *We turned away from land and headed out to sea... Unless huge quantities of relief supplies can be got to them by sea, land and air, many more people will perish. ...a river that has cut deep into the land.*
4 NC A particular **land** is a particular country; a literary use. *...a land where there is never any rain... Australia is the land of opportunities.*
5 V If someone or something **lands** somewhere, they come down to the ground or in water after moving through the air. *The pilot told the control tower that he'd run into technical trouble and tried to land... His plane lands at six-thirty... The last man slipped and landed in the water.*

6 VO To **land** people or goods somewhere means to unload them there at the end of a journey, especially a journey by ship. ...*small ships sailing from Florida to land arms and combatants.*

7 V-ERG If you **land** in an unpleasant situation or if something **lands** you in it, you come to be in it; an informal use. *Twenty years ago, an advocate of capitalism would have landed in prison... The trip landed them both in trouble.*

8 VO+*with* If you **land** someone with something that causes difficulties, you cause them to have to deal with it; an informal use. *You landed us with that awful man.*

land up PHRASAL VERB If you **land up** in a particular place or situation, you arrive in it after a long journey or at the end of a long series of events. *She landed up in Rome.*

landau /ˈlændɔː/ **landaus**
NC A **landau** is a covered four-wheeled carriage pulled by four horses and used especially in the 19th century.

landed /ˈlændɪd/
ADJ ATTRIB **Landed** people own large areas of land. *The protestors say the land reforms will still protect the interests of the landed classes.*

landfall /ˈlændfɔːl/ **landfalls**
NUorNC **Landfall** is the first bit of land which you see or arrive at after a voyage at sea. ...*four more days without landfall, water running short, no fresh meat... The south-eastern coast of Texas is the first landfall of most birds migrating north from the Yucatan and Central America.*

landfill /ˈlændfɪl/
1 NC A **landfill** or a **landfill site** is a place where large amounts of waste materials are disposed of by burying them in a very large, deep hole. *For years, the military dumped solvents and motor oil into a leaky landfill on the base... Burying poisonous waste in landfill sites is not acceptable.*
2 NU You can also use **landfill** to refer to the process of disposing of large amounts of waste materials by burying them in a large hole. *We are running out of holes in the ground for landfill.*

landing /ˈlændɪŋ/ **landings**
1 NC In a building, a **landing** is an area at the top of a staircase, with rooms leading off it. *I switched on the light on the landing. ...the first-floor landing.*
2 NCorNU When the pilot of an aircraft makes a **landing**, he or she brings the aircraft down to the ground. *We had to make an emergency landing... They have blocked the runway with buses and other vehicles to prevent landings by military aircraft... They have been unable to unload their supplies three days after landing.*

landing craft; landing craft is both the singular and the plural form.
NC A **landing craft** is a small boat designed for the landing of soldiers and military equipment on the shore. ...*slow-moving landing craft, heavily loaded with troops and supplies.*

landing stage, landing stages
NC A **landing stage** is a wooden platform used for landing goods and passengers from a boat. ...*holiday houses, each with its own landing stage.*

landing strip, landing strips
NC A **landing strip** is a long flat piece of land from which aircraft can take off and land, especially one used only by private or military aircraft. *They are believed to have destroyed the aircraft on the landing strip.*

landlady /ˈlændleɪdɪ/ **landladies**
1 NC A **landlady** is a woman who owns a house, flat, or room which she allows other people to live in, in return for rent. *Ellen gave the landlady a cheque.*
2 NC A woman who owns or runs a pub is also called a **landlady**. *The landlady refused to serve him.*

landless /ˈlændləs/
ADJ Someone who is **landless** is prevented from owning the land that they farm, usually by large landowners or by the economic system. ...*landless agricultural labourers.* ▶ Also N PL The **landless** is used to refer to people who are landless. *It raised expectations among the landless.* ◆ **landlessness** NU ...*an increase in*

landlessness and poverty.

landlocked /ˈlændlɒkt/
ADJ A country that is **landlocked** is surrounded by other countries and has no sea coast. *If Ethiopia was to lose these ports, it would become a landlocked country.*

landlord /ˈlændlɔːd/ **landlords**
1 NC A **landlord** is a man who owns a house, flat, or room which he allows other people to live in, in return for rent. *Thousands of families in London are homeless, unable to afford the very high rents charged by private landlords.*
2 NC A man who owns or runs a pub is also called a **landlord**. *Behind the bar was a genial landlord.*

landlubber /ˈlændlʌbə/ **landlubbers**
NC A **landlubber** is a person who is not used to or does not like travelling by boat or ship, and is not knowledgeable about the sea; an old-fashioned word.

landmark /ˈlændmɑːk/ **landmarks**
1 NC A **landmark** is a noticeable building or feature of the land, which you can use to judge your position. *The city's most famous landmark is not a gate as such, but a massive classical arch... The Chamberlain tower is a landmark visible for miles.*
2 NC You can also refer to an important stage in the development of something as a **landmark**. *The discovery of penicillin was a landmark in medicine... This was a landmark meeting with President Gorbachev.*

land mass, land masses
NC A **land mass** is a very large area of land such as a continent. *The air over the great land mass heats up and rises. ...the Eurasian land mass... An asteroid more than one to two kilometres wide hitting a land mass would cause immense damage.*

landmine /ˈlændmaɪn/ **landmines**
NC A **landmine** is an explosive device which is placed on or under the ground and explodes when a person or vehicle touches it. *One man died and another was seriously wounded when their car hit a landmine.*

landowner /ˈlændəʊnə/ **landowners**
NC A **landowner** is a person who owns land, especially a large amount of land. ...*a rich landowner who had a house near the temple... Banks lend to the big landowners at much lower rates. ...conflicts between peasants and landowners.*

landowning /ˈlændəʊnɪŋ/
ADJ ATTRIB **Landowning** is used to describe people who own a lot of land, especially when they are considered as a group within society. *The landowning class opposed the spread of education. ...a wealthy landowning family.*

land reform, land reforms
NUorNC **Land reform** is a change in the system of land ownership, especially when it involves giving land to the people who actually farm it and taking it away from people who own large areas for profit. *They formed themselves into trade-union style associations to press for land reform... There were also protests against the failure to carry out land reforms.*

land registry, land registries
NC A **land registry** is a government office where records are kept about each area of land in a country or region, its exact size and location, and its owner.

Land-Rover /ˈlænd ˌrəʊvə/ **Land-Rovers**
NC A **Land-Rover** is a strong four-wheeled motor vehicle which can travel over rough or steep ground, and is used especially by farmers and other people who work in rural areas. **Land-Rover** is a trademark. *The firm used a Land-Rover to break down the glass doors to the building.*

Landsbergis, Vytautas /ˈvɪtautæs ˈlænsbeəgɪs/
Vytautas Landsbergis became President of Lithuania in 1990. He founded Sajudis (the Popular Front for Perestroika) in 1988. Born: 1932.

landscape /ˈlændskeɪp/ **landscapes, landscaping, landscaped**
1 NC The **landscape** is everything that you can see when you look across an area of land, including hills, rivers, buildings, and trees. ...*the beauty of the Welsh landscape... The photo shows a landscape strewn with oil-drums and cable wheels.*

2 N SING+SUPP The **landscape** of a particular situation is its background and all the features that affect it. *The collapse of local Communist Parties has already transformed the political landscape. ...the realities of the international landscape.*
3 NC A **landscape** is a painting of the countryside. *She painted landscapes and portraits.*
4 VO If an area of land **is landscaped**, someone alters it to create a pleasing effect, for example by creating different levels and planting trees and bushes. *The Professor's office overlooked the landscaped grounds.*

landscape architect, landscape architects
NC A **landscape architect** is the same as a **landscape gardener**.

landscape gardener, landscape gardeners
NC A **landscape gardener** is a person who designs gardens or parks so that they look more attractive. *He's a self-employed landscape gardener.*

landslide /lændslaɪd/ **landslides**
1 N SING If an election is won by a **landslide**, it is won by a large number of votes. *Taylor should win by a landslide... The National League for Democracy won a landslide victory in last year's multi-party elections.*
2 NC A **landslide** is also a large amount of earth and rocks falling down the side of a mountain. *The slightest noise might set off a landslide.*

landslip /lændslɪp/ **landslips**
NC A **landslip** is a small movement of soil and rocks down a slope. *A landslip had made the house unsafe.*

landward /lændwəd/
ADJ ATTRIB **Landward** means nearest to the land or facing the land, rather than the sea. *...the cottage with its recent additions on the landward side.*

lane /leɪn/ **lanes**
1 NC A **lane** is a narrow road in the country. *He was driving home down a quiet country lane.*
2 NC Roads, race courses, and swimming pools are sometimes divided into **lanes**. These are parallel strips separated from each other by lines or ropes. *He changed lanes to make a left turn.*

language /læŋgwɪdʒ/ **languages**
1 NC A **language** is a system of sounds and written symbols used by the people of a particular country, area, or tribe to communicate with each other. *...the English language... I can speak six languages... I have never liked my situation of living here and not knowing the language... Many have English as a first or second language.*
2 NU **Language** is the ability to use words in order to communicate. *This research helps teachers to understand how children acquire language.*
3 NU+SUPP You can refer to the words used in connection with a particular subject as the **language** of that subject. *...the language of sociology.*
4 NU The **language** of a piece of writing or a speech is the style in which it is written or spoken. *I admire the directness of the language. ...her characteristically blunt language.*
5 NUorNC **Language** is also used to refer to other means of communication such as sign language, computer languages, and animal language. *The way that they usually communicate with others is by using sign language. ...higher level languages such as Fortran and Basic.*

language lab, language labs
NC A **language lab** is the same as a language laboratory; an informal word.

language laboratory, language laboratories
NC A **language laboratory** is a classroom equipped with tape recorders and headphones where people can improve their knowledge of foreign languages. *Our institution had no language laboratory of its own.*

languid /læŋgwɪd/
ADJ Someone who is **languid** lacks interest and energy; a literary word. *...languid ladies in elegant evening gowns.* ◆ **languidly** ADV *He looked up languidly.*

languish /læŋgwɪʃ/ **languishes, languishing, languished**
V You say that people **languish** when they are forced to remain and suffer in an unpleasant situation; a literary word. *A few people enjoyed rich lifestyles*

while the majority languished in poverty.

languor /læŋgə/
NU **Languor** is a pleasant feeling of being relaxed and not having any energy or interest in anything; a literary word. *...the languor of the summer afternoon.*

languorous /læŋgərəs/
ADJ If you describe something as **languorous**, you mean that it is lazy, relaxed, and not energetic, usually in a pleasant way. *...Helen's languorous waves of the hand. ...the perfect, languorous, endless hot summer.*

lank /læŋk/
ADJ If someone's hair is **lank**, it is long and perhaps rather greasy and it lies or hangs in a dull and unattractive way. *Her lank, sandy locks dangled limply about her neck.*

lanky /læŋki/
ADJ Someone who is **lanky** is tall and thin and moves rather awkwardly. *Quentin was a lanky boy with long skinny legs.*

lantern /læntən/ **lanterns**
NC A **lantern** is a lamp in a metal frame with glass sides. *They are seen singing in the street in the late evening by the light of a lantern.*

lanyard /lænjəd/ **lanyards**
NC A **lanyard** is a piece of thick string, usually with a whistle or knife attached to it and worn around someone's neck as part of a uniform. *...sailor dress complete with a lanyard.*

Laos /lɑːɒs/
The **Lao People's Democratic Republic** is a country in south-east Asia. Laos was part of French Indochina from the late 19th century. It was occupied by Japan from 1940 to 1945, and returned to French control after the Second World War. It became independent, as the Kingdom of Laos, in 1953. After many years of civil war, the Pathet Lao (PL) gained control and proclaimed the People's Democratic Republic of Laos in 1975. Several armed groups continued to oppose the government throughout the 1970s and 1980s. The ruling party is the Lao People's Revolutionary Party (LPRP). Kaysone Phomvihane became Prime Minister in 1975 and President in 1991. General Khamtay Siphandone became Prime Minister in 1991. Laos exports timber, coffee, and tin. Opium and cannabis are illegally exported. Large foreign debts and high inflation are serious economic problems.
◆ **Lao, Laotian** /laʊ, laʊʃən/ N, ADJ
▪ *per capita GNP:* US$170 ▪ *religion:* Buddhism
▪ *language:* Lao or Laotian ▪ *currency:* kip ▪ *capital:* Vientiane ▪ *population:* 4 million (1989) ▪ *size:* 236,800 square kilometres.

lap /læp/ **laps, lapping, lapped**
1 NC In a race, you say that a competitor has completed a **lap** when he or she has gone round the course once. *Three laps later he overtook Niall MacKenzie of Scotland.*
2 VO If you **lap** another competitor in a race, you pass them while they are still on the previous lap. *Senna and Gerhard Berger lapped the whole of the field by half-way.*
3 NC+POSS Your **lap** is the flat area formed by your thighs when you are sitting down. *Her youngest child was asleep in her lap... Nowadays you can use a computer on your lap.*
4 VA When water **laps** against something, it touches it gently and makes a soft sound. *Waves lapped against the side of the boat.*
5 VAorVO When an animal **laps** a drink, it uses its tongue to flick the liquid into its mouth. *The cat was lapping at a saucer of milk.*

lap up PHRASAL VERB 1 When an animal **laps up** a drink, it drinks it up very eagerly. *It was lapping up the milk as if it had not been fed for days.* 2 If someone **laps up** information or attention, they accept it eagerly, often when it is not really true or sincere. *It was a lie, but millions of newspaper readers lapped it up... America lapped up all of these scandals.*

La Paz /læ pæs/
La Paz is the administrative capital of Bolivia and its largest city. Population: 1,050,000 (1988).

lapel /ləpɛl/ **lapels**
NC The **lapels** of a jacket or coat are the two parts at the front that are folded back on each side and join the collar. *They wore black ribbons in their lapels as a sign of mourning.*

lapis lazuli /læpɪs læzjʊlaɪ/
NU **Lapis lazuli** is a bright blue semi-precious stone, used especially in making jewellery. *They found thousands of artifacts of gold, silver and lapis lazuli.*

lap of honour, laps of honour
NC A **lap of honour** is a slow run or drive around a race track or sports field by the winner of a race or a game in order to receive the applause of the crowd. *Arsenal carried the trophy around the field in a lap of honour... The two teams took a lap of honour together at the end of the match.*

lapse /læps/ **lapses, lapsing, lapsed**
1 N SING+SUPP A **lapse** of time is a period of time that is long enough for a situation to change. *After a certain lapse of time it would be safe for Daisy to return... He was not conscious of the time lapse.*
2 V If a period of time **lapses**, it passes. *Hours lapsed between each phone call.*
3 V If a situation, relationship, or legal contract **lapses**, it is allowed to end or to become invalid. *Fiji's membership of the Commonwealth had lapsed... The legislation which gave the power to do this lapsed in March last year.*
4 NC+SUPP If you have a **lapse** of memory or a **lapse** of concentration, you forget about something or fail to concentrate on something. *Mr Reagan's testimony was marked by many lapses of memory, and observers found it inconclusive.*
5 NC A **lapse** is also a piece of bad behaviour by someone who usually behaves well. *I intended to make up for this lapse in manners at the next party.*
6 V+*into* If you **lapse** into a particular kind of behaviour, you start behaving that way. *He lapsed into an unhappy silence.*

lap-top
ADJ ATTRIB A **lap-top** computer is small enough for you to carry with you and for you to use without a desk. *The system is controlled by a lap-top computer.*

lapwing /læpwɪŋ/ **lapwings**
NC A **lapwing** is a small bird with dark green feathers, a white breast, and a tuft of feathers on its head. *Lapwings live mainly in fields and on moorland.*

Laraki, Dr Azzedine /æzediːn ləraːki/
Dr Azzedine Laraki became Prime Minister of Morocco in 1986. He served as Minister of National Education from 1977 to 1986. He is an independent. Born: 1929.

larceny /laːsəni/
NU **Larceny** is the crime of theft; a legal term. *The youth was charged with larceny. ...petty larceny.*

larch /laːtʃ/ **larches**
NC A **larch** is a tree with needle-shaped leaves. *Many of the oldest larches have been cut down.*

lard /laːd/
NU **Lard** is soft white fat obtained from pigs. It is used in cooking. *...a diet of too many cream-cakes, hamburgers and chips fried in lard.*

larder /laːdə/ **larders**
NC A **larder** is a room or cupboard in which food is kept. *...a well-stocked larder.*

large /laːdʒ/ **larger, largest**
ADJ Something that is **large** is greater in size or amount than is usual or average. *...a large house... We have to spend quite large sums of money... They seized a large quantity of weapons... They have been sold in large numbers to Saudi Arabia... Both projects are very large.*
• **Large** is used in these phrases. • You use **at large** to indicate that you are talking about most of the people mentioned. *Opposition is building up against him both in the country at large and within his own party.* • If you say that a dangerous person, thing, or animal is **at large**, you mean that they have escaped and have not yet been captured or made safe. *Two of the attackers have given themselves up but six others are still at large... The CFCs being released today will still be at large in the atmosphere.* • You use **by and**

large to indicate that a statement is mostly but not completely true. *By and large, they were free to do as they wished... This year's two day festival was, by and large, a peaceful event.*

largely /laːdʒli/
1 ADV You use **largely** to say that a statement is mostly but not completely true. *The evidence shows them to be largely correct... Her work is largely confined to the cinema.*
2 ADV You also use **largely** to introduce the main reason for an event or situation. *We were there largely because of the girls... He was acquitted, largely on the evidence of a tape recording.*

large-scale
1 ADJ ATTRIB A **large-scale** action or event happens over a wide area or involves a lot of people or things. *In December a large-scale earthquake in Armenia killed 25,000 people... Last year brought the first large-scale anti-government protests in decades.*
2 ADJ ATTRIB A **large-scale** map or diagram represents a small area of land or a building or machine on a scale that is large enough for small details to be shown. *The difficulty has been getting pictures accurate enough in detail for large-scale maps.*

largesse /laːʒɛs/; also spelt **largess**.
NU **Largesse** is kindness or generosity, especially when this involves giving more money than was expected or asked for; a formal word. *Harold's largesse did not equal Lord Nuffield's £50,000... I was going to give him five dollars, but thought the largesse might be misconstrued.*

largish /laːdʒɪʃ/
ADJ **Largish** means fairly large. *...a largish man. ...a largish town.*

lark /laːk/ **larks, larking, larked**
NC A **lark** is a small brown bird that has a pleasant song.
lark about PHRASAL VERB If you **lark about**, you enjoy yourself doing silly things; an informal expression.

larva /laːvə/ **larvae** /laːviː/
NC A **larva** is an insect at the stage before it becomes an adult. Larvae look like short, fat worms. *The larvae of the weevil tunnel into the potato tubers.*

larval /laːvl/
ADJ **Larval** means concerning insect larvae or in the state of being an insect larva. *They go through a larval stage for the first fortnight or so.*

laryngitis /lærɪndʒaɪtɪs/
NU **Laryngitis** is an infection of the throat in which your larynx becomes swollen and painful, making it difficult for you to speak.

larynx /lærɪŋks/ **larynxes** or **larynges** /lærɪndʒiz/
NC Your **larynx** is the top part of the passage that leads from your throat to your lungs and contains your vocal cords; a medical term. *Talking above the noise of an aircraft for long periods strains the larynx.*

lascivious /ləsɪviəs/
ADJ **Lascivious** people have a strong desire for sex; used showing disapproval.

laser /leɪzə/ **lasers**
1 NC A **laser** is a narrow beam of concentrated light that is used especially for cutting very hard materials and in surgery. *A laser beam would cut into it.*
2 NC A **laser** is also a machine which produces lasers. *...a beam of light from a laser.*

laser printer, laser printers
NC A **laser printer** is a printer that is connected to a computer and produces words or pictures that are extremely clear, by using laser light. *The information has been printed out via the laser printer.*

lash /læʃ/ **lashes, lashing, lashed**
1 NC Your **lashes** are the hairs that grow on the edge of your eyelids. *He had nice sad eyes with beautiful lashes... Tear drops fell from her long lashes.*
2 NC A **lash** is the thin strip of leather at the end of a whip. *He gasped as the lash hit him.*
3 NC A **lash** is also a blow with a whip on someone's back as a punishment. *...a public flogging of thirty-nine lashes.*
4 VO If one person **lashes** another, they hit them with a whip. *They snatched up whips and lashed the backs of those who had fallen.*

5 V Oor V A If the wind or rain **lashes** something, it hits it violently; a literary use. *High winds lashed the branches of the elm... Snow was lashing against the windows.*
6 V O If you **lash** one thing to another, you tie them firmly together. *We lashed our boats together.*

lash out PHRASAL VERB 1 If you **lash out**, you suddenly try to hit someone with your hands or feet or with a weapon. *When cornered, they lash out with savage kicks.* 2 You can also say that someone **lashes out** when they criticize or scold people angrily. *Harris lashed out against the Committee.*

lashing /læʃɪŋ/ **lashings**
1 NC **Lashings** are ropes or cables used to tie something firmly to something else. *They began to remove the lashings from the deck cargo.*
2 NC A **lashing** is a punishment in which a person is hit with a whip. *Some of them never recovered from the shock of these lashings.*
3 NC A **lashing** is also a cruel and angry speech, criticizing or scolding someone or something. *She was determined to give him a lashing with her tongue.*
4 N PL **Lashings** of something means a large quantity or amount of it; an old-fashioned use. *We had scones, and lashings of cream.*

lass /læs/ **lasses**
NC In some parts of Britain, a young woman or girl is referred to as a **lass**. *She'd worked on the farm as a lass.*

lassie /læsɪ/ **lassies**
N C or VOCATIVE A **lassie** is a young woman or girl; used in informal Scottish English. *The lassies here will miss him... That's all right, lassie.*

lassitude /læsɪtjuːd/
NU **Lassitude** is a state of tiredness, laziness, or lack of interest; a formal word. *...symptoms of irritability and profound lassitude.*

lasso /læsuː/ **lassoes, lassoing, lassoed;** also spelt **lassoo.**
1 NC A **lasso** is a long rope with a noose at one end, used especially by cowboys for catching cattle and horses.
2 V O If you **lasso** an animal such as a cow or horse, you catch it by throwing the noose of a lasso round its neck and pulling it tight.

last /lɑːst/ **lasts, lasting, lasted**
1 ADJ You use **last** to describe the most recent period of time, event, or thing. *I went to a party last night. ...the last four years. ...the last British general election... Their last album 'Pop Art' made the Top 5 in the charts.*
2 ADJ or PRON The **last** thing or part is the one that comes at the end or after all the others. *He missed the last bus. ...the last classroom along that passage... The Pope is now in Malawi, the last stop on his tour of southern Africa... Hooper was the last to leave.*
3 ADJ or PRON **Last** is also used to refer to the only thing or part that remains. *She removed the last traces of make-up... Otto drank the last of the brandy.*
4 ADJ or PRON You can use **last** to emphasize that you do not want to do something or that something is unlikely to happen. *The last thing I want to do is offend you... I would be the last to suggest that.*
5 ADV If something **last** happened on a particular occasion, it has not happened since then. *They last saw their homeland nine years ago... It's a long time since we met last.*
6 ADV If something happens **last**, it happens after everything else. *He added the milk last.*
7 V If something **lasts**, it continues to exist or happen. *His speech lasted for exactly fourteen minutes... Profits are as high as ever. It won't last.*
8 V To **last** also means to remain in good condition. *A fresh pepper lasts about three weeks.*
9 V O A or V A If a quantity of something **lasts** for a period of time, there is enough of it for someone to use during that period. *He had only £8 left to last him till he reached Bury... A cheap box of toothpowder lasts two years.*
10 See also **lasting.**
● **Last** is used in these phrases. ● If something has happened **at last** or **at long last**, it has happened after

a long period of time. *At last Ralph stopped work and stood up... At long last I've found a girl that really loves me.* ● You use **the last** to indicate that something did not happen or exist again after a particular time, or that it will never happen or exist again. *That was the last I ever saw of Northcliffe.* ● You use expressions such as **to the last detail** or **to the last man** to emphasize that you are including every single thing or person. *The robbery was planned down to the last detail.*

last-ditch
ADJ ATTRIB You can refer to your final attempt to do something that you have previously failed to do as a **last-ditch** attempt. *The Treasury made a last-ditch attempt to intervene.*

lasting /lɑːstɪŋ/
ADJ ATTRIB Something that is **lasting** continues to exist or to be effective for a very long time. *This may provide a lasting solution to our problems. ...lasting friendships.* ● See also **last.**

Last Judgement; also spelt **Last Judgment.**
N PROP In the Christian religion, the **Last Judgement** is the last day of the world, on which God will judge everyone. *They sang the praises of God in preparation for the Last Judgement.*

lastly /lɑːstlɪ/
1 ADV SEN You use **lastly** when you want to make a final point that is connected with the ones you have already mentioned. *Lastly, I would like to ask you about your future plans.*
2 ADV You also use **lastly** when you are saying what happens after everything else in a series of actions or events. *Lastly he jabbed the knife into the trunk of the tree.*

last-minute
ADJ ATTRIB A **last-minute** action is done just before something else which is planned to happen at a fixed time. *...a last-minute attempt to stop the school being closed.* ● If you do something **at the last minute**, or if you leave it **to the last minute**, you do it at the last possible time that it can be done. *Her instructions from the State Department had been changed at the last minute... Why do you always leave things to the last minute?*

last rites
N PL The **last rites** are a religious ceremony performed by a Christian priest for a dying person. It consists of prayers and readings, and sometimes a short service of Holy Communion. *A priest gave her the last rites.*

latch /lætʃ/ **latches, latching, latched**
1 NC A **latch** is a fastening on a door or gate. It consists of a metal bar which is held in place to lock the door and which you lift in order to open the door. *He closes the front door, checking the latch twice.*
2 V O If you **latch** a door or gate, you fasten it by means of a latch. *Latch that gate.*
3 If a door with a lock that locks automatically is **on the latch**, the lock has been set so that it does not lock automatically when you shut the door. *He closed the door and left it on the latch in case Tom had forgotten his key.*

latch onto PHRASAL VERB If you **latch onto** someone or something, you become very involved with them, because you are interested in them or find them useful; an informal expression. *She latched onto someone with a family business.*

latchkey /lætʃkiː/ **latchkeys**
NC A **latchkey** is a key for a latch; an old-fashioned word. *When he arrived at the house he found that he had forgotten his latchkey.*

latchkey child, latchkey children
NC A **latchkey child** is a child whose parent or parents are not at home when they get home from school and who has a key to the house so that he or she can get in; an old-fashioned expression, used showing disapproval. *...the problem of latchkey children.*

late /leɪt/ **later, latest**
1 ADV or ADJ ATTRIB **Late** means near the end of a period of time, a process, or a piece of work. *...late in 1952... Very late at night, I got a phone call... Decker arrived in late September. ...in the late afternoon...*

He was a well built man in his late forties with a strong cockney accent. ...Picasso's late work.
2 ADJ or ADV If you are **late** for something or if you arrive **late**, you arrive after the time that was arranged. *I was ten minutes late for my appointment... I apologize for my late arrival... Etta arrived late.*
3 ADJ or ADV You use **late** to describe things that happen after the normal time. *We had a late lunch at the hotel. ...if you get up late.*
4 ADJ ATTRIB You use **late** when you are talking about someone who is dead. *...the late Harry Truman.*
5 See also **later, latest.**
● **Late** is used in these phrases. ● **As late as** means at a particular time or period that is surprisingly late. *Even as late as 1950 coal provided over 90% of our energy.* ● If it is **too late** for something, that thing is no longer possible or useful. If something happens **too late**, the right time for it has passed. *I realized my mistake too late... It's too late to change that now.*

latecomer /leɪtkʌmə/ **latecomers**
NC A **latecomer** is someone who arrives after the time that they should have arrived.

lately /leɪtli/
ADV If something has happened or been happening **lately**, it has happened or been happening in the recent past. *John has seemed worried lately.*

latent /leɪtnt/
ADJ **Latent** is used to describe something which is hidden and not obvious at the moment, but which may develop further in the future. *Everyone has a latent mathematical ability.*

later /leɪtə/
1 **Later** is the comparative form of **late.**
2 ADV You use **later** or **later on** to refer to a time or situation that is after the one that you have been talking about or after the present one. *I returned four weeks later... See you later... Later on this evening, we shall have some music.*
3 ADJ ATTRIB You also use **later** to refer to the last part of someone's life. *This may cause illness in later life.*

lateral /lætəᵊrəl/
ADJ ATTRIB **Lateral** means relating to the sides of something, or moving in a sideways direction. *All of these primitive sea creatures had well developed lateral fins.*

lateral thinking
NU **Lateral thinking** is a method of solving problems by using your imagination to help you think of solutions that are not at first obvious, rather than by using logic or other conventional ways of thinking. *When a new idea is required, then lateral thinking should be used.*

latest /leɪtɪst/
1 **Latest** is the superlative form of **late.**
2 ADJ You use **latest** to describe something that is the most recent thing of its kind. *...the latest news. ...her latest book.*
3 You use **at the latest** to emphasize that something must happen at or before a particular time. *Changes will become necessary by the autumn at the latest.*

latex /leɪteks/
NU **Latex** is a substance obtained from some kinds of trees, which is used to make products like rubber and glue. *Latex adhesive can be removed with special remover.*

lath /lɑːθ/
NU **Lath** consists of strips of thin wood which are put onto the inside walls of houses or other buildings and are then covered with plaster; a technical term. *The narrow corridor had walls of plastered lath.*

lathe /leɪð/ **lathes**
NC A **lathe** is a machine for shaping wood or metal. It works by turning the wood or metal against a tool which cuts it. *This is a manually operated lathe.*

lather /lɑːðə/
N SING or NU **Lather** is a white mass of bubbles which is produced by mixing soap or washing powder with water. *The lather should be left on the skin for some time. ...a good lather.*

Latin /lætɪn/
1 NU **Latin** is the language which the ancient Romans used to speak. *The Vice-Chancellor addressed us in Latin... Many universities would only accept students who had some proficiency in Latin.*
2 ADJ **Latin** is used to refer to people who come from the countries where French, Italian, Spanish, and Portuguese are spoken. *He had Latin blood... Cuba was one of the least Catholic of the Latin countries.*

Latin American, Latin Americans
1 ADJ **Latin American** means relating or belonging to the countries of South and Central America. *Eight Latin American countries have urged Britain to call off the military exercises. ..the BBC Latin American correspondent.*
2 NC A **Latin American** is someone who lives in or comes from South or Central America. *At present over two hundred million Latin Americans live below the poverty line.*

latitude /lætɪtjuːd/ **latitudes**
1 N C or N U The **latitude** of a place is its distance to the north or south of the Equator: compare **longitude.** *Many people in higher latitudes get a bit depressed as winter arrives... New York City is 41 degrees north latitude.*
2 NU **Latitude** is freedom to choose how to do something; a formal use. *She was given considerable latitude in how she spent the money.*

latrine /lətriːn/ **latrines**
NC In the army, the **latrines** are the toilets. *He was forced to clean the latrines.*

latter /lætə/
1 N SING or N PL When two people or things have just been mentioned, you refer to the second one as the **latter.** *The leading publications are the two weeklies, Moscow News and Ogonyok. The latter is a very colourful magazine... American people no longer appear to prefer tax cuts to additional spending, provided the latter is on things they care about.* ► Also ADJ *The novel was made into a film in 1943 and again in 1967: I prefer the latter version to the former.*
2 ADJ You use **latter** to describe the second part of a period of time. *By the latter half of July the total was well over two million... The United States enjoyed a healthy trade surplus with China in the latter half of the 1980s.*

latter-day
ADJ ATTRIB **Latter-day** is used to describe a person or thing that is a modern equivalent of someone or something in the past. *...the latter-day martyr, Edith Cavell.*

latterly /lætəli/
ADV or ADV SEN **Latterly** means recently; a formal word. *It's only more latterly that we've come to see this as an issue... Latterly, he has been sharply critical of Mr Kadar's old-guard style of leadership.*

lattice /lætɪs/ **lattices**
NC A **lattice** is a pattern or structure made of strips which cross over each other diagonally leaving holes in between. *...a lattice of bamboo.*

latticed /lætɪst/
ADJ ATTRIB Something that is **latticed** is decorated with or in the form of a lattice. *Mrs Halliday was wearing a hat with a latticed brim.*

lattice window, lattice windows
NC A **lattice window** or a **latticed window** is a window which is decorated with a pattern of strips of lead which cross over each other diagonally. *The houses had little arches and pillars and latticed windows.*

latticework /lætɪswɜːk/
NU **Latticework** is any structure that is made in the form of a lattice. *...a latticework of silver.*

Latvia /lætviə/
The **Republic of Latvia** became independent of the USSR in 1991. It is one of the Baltic States, located in the north-west of the former USSR on the Baltic Sea. Latvia was an independent country from 1918 until 1940, when it became part of the USSR. Anatolijs Gorbunovs became President in 1990. Latvia produces electronic and telecommunications equipment, and other manufactured goods. ♦ **Latvian, Lett** /lætviən, let N **Latvian, Lettish** /letɪʃ/ ADJ

■ *per capita GNP:* US$6,740 ■ *religion:* Christianity (mainly Lutheran) ■ *language:* Latvian, Russian ■ *currency:* lat ■ *capital:* Riga ■ *population:* 3 million (1989) ■ *size:* 64,589 square kilometres.

laud /lɔːd/ **lauds, lauding, lauded**
vo If you **laud** someone, you praise and admire them; an old-fashioned word. *They exalted his heroic life and lauded his daring deeds.*

laudable /lɔːdəbl/
ADJ If you describe something as **laudable**, you mean that it deserves to be praised or admired; a formal word. *The programme was inspired by laudable motives of improving housing conditions.*

laudanum /lɔːdən̩əm/
NU **Laudanum** is a drug containing opium, which was popular in Victorian times and was used to help people sleep. *Later she died from an overdose of laudanum.*

laudatory /lɔːdətə⁰ri/
ADJ If a piece of writing or speech is **laudatory**, it expresses praise or admiration for someone; a formal word. *For several days now official organizations have been sending laudatory messages of congratulation.*

laugh /lɑːf/ **laughs, laughing, laughed**
vorVA When you **laugh**, you make the sound which shows that you are happy or amused. *He grinned, then started to laugh... The young men laughed at his jokes.* ▸ Also NC *'Hurry up,' said Tony with a laugh.*
● **Laugh** is used in these phrases. ● If someone has the **last laugh**, they succeed after appearing to have been defeated. *Henry had outlived all the others to have the last laugh.* ● If you **laugh** your **head off**, you laugh very loudly for a long time. *The fishermen were laughing their heads off.* ● If you do or say something **for a laugh**, you do or say it for fun rather than for any other reason. *I gave him the wrong address just for a laugh.*
laugh at PHRASAL VERB If you **laugh at** someone or something, you mock them or make jokes about them. *I don't think it's nice to laugh at people's disabilities.*
laugh off PHRASAL VERB If you **laugh off** a serious situation, you try to suggest that it is amusing and unimportant. *Northcliffe attempted to laugh the matter off.*

laughable /lɑːfəbl/
ADJ You say that something is **laughable** when it seems amusing because it is so obviously unsuccessful, foolish, or poor in quality. *It's almost laughable to talk about a 'policy'.* ◆ **laughably** SUBMOD *They appear almost laughably pompous.*

laughing gas
NU **Laughing gas** is a type of anaesthetic gas. It sometimes has the effect of making people laugh uncontrollably if it is sniffed in small quantities. *The pain of having teeth pulled and filled was first banished by laughing gas.*

laughing stock
If you say that someone or something is a **laughing stock**, you mean that they are supposed to be important or serious but have been made to seem ridiculous. *Arthur's garden was the laughing stock of the neighbourhood.*

laughter /lɑːftə/
NU **Laughter** is the act of laughing, or the sound of people laughing. *We roared with laughter... Their talk grew louder and so did their laughter.*

launch /lɔːntʃ/ **launches, launching, launched**
1 vo When a ship is **launched**, it is put into water for the first time. *A newly-refurbished research ship was officially launched at Tilbury.*
2 vo To **launch** a rocket, missile, or satellite means to send it into the air or into space. *Soviet rockets launched more satellites into orbit.* ▸ Also NC *They gave only a few minutes' warning of the missile launch.*
3 vo To **launch** a large and important activity, for example a political movement or a military attack, means to start it. *The government has launched a massive literacy campaign.*
4 vo If a company **launches** a new product, it starts to make it available to the public. *A magazine called 'The Week' was launched in January 1964.* ▸ Also NC

We are already selling millions of copies just one year after the launch.
5 NC A **launch** is a large motorboat. *A motor launch has sunk in the central Philippines.*
launch into PHRASAL VERB If you **launch into** a speech, fight, or other activity, you start it enthusiastically. *He launched into an outspoken condemnation of their policy.*

launching pad, launching pads
1 NC A **launching pad** is a platform from which rockets, missiles, or satellites are launched. *The space port would be the launching pad for commercial satellites.*
2 NC A **launching pad** is also a situation which you can use in order to go forward to something better or more important. *The Conservative Conference this week may be the launching pad for a possible General Election... Sometimes a first job can act as a launching pad into something else.*

launder /lɔːndə/ **launders, laundering, laundered**
1 vo When you **launder** clothes, sheets, and towels, you wash and iron them; an old-fashioned use. *Six hundred costumes had to be laundered, labelled, packed and sent on to the next theatre.*
2 vo To **launder** money that has been obtained illegally means to send it to a legitimate business or foreign bank, so that when it is brought back nobody knows that it was illegally obtained. *...a system to launder money earned from the cocaine trade.*
◆ **laundering** NU *He was indicted for drug trafficking and money laundering.*

launderette /lɔːndrɛt/ **launderettes**
NC A **launderette** is a shop where there are washing machines and dryers which you can pay to use. *In some launderettes there is also an automatic dry-cleaning machine.*

Laundromat /lɔːndrəmæt/ **Laundromats**
NC In the United States, a **Laundromat** is a launderette; **Laundromat** is a trademark. *Sylvia is with Chris at a Laundromat doing the laundry.*

laundry /lɔːndri/ **laundries**
1 NUorN SING **Laundry** is clothes, sheets, and towels that are dirty and need to be washed, or which have just been washed. *The washing machine takes about two hours to do my laundry... She still made me do all the housework and the laundry.*
2 NC A **laundry** is a firm that washes and irons clothes, sheets, and towels for people. *Many of Soho's patisseries, laundries and food stores are run by people who come from non-English ethnic backgrounds.*
3 NC A **laundry** is also a room in a house or hotel where clothes, sheets, and towels are washed. *They are making the other kitchen into a laundry.*

laurel /lɒrəl/ **laurels**
1 NC A **laurel** is a small evergreen tree. It has shiny leaves that have a pleasant smell and are used in cooking as a flavouring. *...a species of laurel which occurs on the coast.*
2 If you say that someone is **resting on** their **laurels**, you mean that they feel satisfied with what they have already achieved and are not making any more effort. *We have no cause to rest on our laurels.*

lava /lɑːvə/
NU **Lava** is the hot liquid rock that comes out of a volcano and becomes solid as it cools. *Latest reports say lava is continuing to flow from the volcano.*

lavatory /lævətri/ **lavatories**
1 NC A **lavatory** is the same as a **toilet**. *Forty-three percent of British men never clean the lavatory.*
2 NC A **lavatory** is the same as a **washbasin**; used in American English.

lavatory paper
NU **Lavatory paper** is the same as **toilet paper**.

lavender /lævɪndə/
NU **Lavender** is a garden plant with sweet-smelling, bluish-purple flowers. *...essential oil made from lavender.*

lavender water
NU **Lavender water** is a light perfume that is made from and smells of lavender.

lavish /lǽvɪʃ/ **lavishes, lavishing, lavished**
1 ADJ If you are **lavish** with your money or time, you are very generous in the way that you spend it for other people's benefit. *...the lavish hospitality of Indian princes.* ◆ **lavishly** ADV *Rich merchants lavishly entertained travelling tradesmen.*
2 ADJ Something that is **lavish** is very large, or has an appearance of great wealth and extravagance. *The portions would be lavish... The high cost of weddings has not put couples off lavish ceremonies.* ◆ **lavishly** ADV *The building has been lavishly restored to a fresh brilliance.*
3 VO+*on* or *upon* If you **lavish** money, affection, or time on someone or something, you spend a lot of money on them or give them a lot of affection or attention; a literary use. *He lavished presents on her... Mr Bush has lavished praise on Turkey and on President Ozal.*

law /lɔː/ **laws**
1 N SING or NU The **law** is a system of rules that a society or government develops in order to deal with business agreements, social relationships, and crime. *It's against the law to demonstrate here... She was caught breaking the law... Every company must by law submit accounts annually.*
2 NU+SUPP **Law** is used to refer to a particular branch of the law, for example company **law**. *They are registered in countries where company law is notoriously lax... The soldiers faced charges under military law.*
3 NC A **law** is one of the rules in a system of law which deals with a particular type of agreement, relationship, or crime. *Many of the laws passed by Parliament are never enforced. ...proposals for a revision of the divorce laws.*
4 NC A **law** is also a rule or set of rules for good behaviour which seems right and important for moral, religious, or emotional reasons. *Children soon accept social laws.*
5 NU or N SING **Law** or the **law** is all the professions which deal with advising people about the law, representing people in court, or giving decisions and punishments. *I was planning a career in law... There are curious parallels between medicine and the law. ...a New York law firm.*
6 When someone **lays down the law**, they give other people orders because they think that they are right and the other people are wrong; used showing disapproval. *They tend to lay down the law and run the place in rather a strict way.*
7 NC+SUPP You also use **law** to refer to a natural process in which a particular event or thing always leads to a particular result. *...the laws of nature... The laws that govern the behaviour of light are universal.*
8 NC+SUPP A scientific rule that explains natural processes is also called a **law**. *...the second law of heat distribution.*

law-abiding
ADJ A **law-abiding** person always obeys the law. *...respectable, law-abiding citizens.*

law and order
NU When there is **law and order** in a country, the laws are generally accepted and obeyed there. *There were periods of unrest and a breakdown of law and order.*

law-breaking
ADJ ATTRIB **Law-breaking** is used to describe a person or an action involved in doing something that is illegal. *...policies to keep law-breaking youngsters off the streets.*

law court, law courts
NC A **law court** is a place where legal matters are decided by a judge and jury or by a magistrate. *As the hearing went on, about fifty supporters of Mr Mendis demonstrated outside the law courts.*

law-enforcement
NU **Law-enforcement** agencies or officials are those such as the police and government legal departments that are responsible for making sure that people do not break the laws of a country or state; used in American English. *The authorities should provide for adequate law-enforcement... The bank's transaction was criticized by law-enforcement officials.*

lawful /lɔːfl/
ADJ **Lawful** activities, organizations, and products are allowed by law; a formal word. *Use all lawful means to persuade employers.* ◆ **lawfully** ADV *The tenant cannot be lawfully evicted.*

lawless /lɔːləs/
ADJ **Lawless** actions break the law; a formal word. *...the lawless activities of these gangs.* ◆ **lawlessness** NU *...our disapproval of lawlessness and violence.*

Law Lord, Law Lords
NC In Britain, the **Law Lords** are legally qualified members of the House of Lords who operate as the highest court of appeal in the country. *The Law Lords overturned an earlier ruling by the High Court that the weapons were not illegal. ...a senior Law Lord.*

lawn /lɔːn/ **lawns**
NC or NU A **lawn** is an area of grass that is kept cut short. A lawn is usually part of a garden or park. *I'm going to mow the lawn... They sat in rows on the lawn... For five months they lived on a patch of lawn.*

lawnmower /lɔːnməʊə/ **lawnmowers**
NC A **lawnmower** is a machine for cutting grass on lawns. *The government is being asked to improve safety standards for lawnmowers.*

lawn tennis
1 NU **Lawn tennis** is the same as **tennis**; a formal use. *...Wimbledon, for many years the home of lawn tennis.*
2 NU **Lawn tennis** is also used to refer to tennis played on grass, rather than on a hard court.

lawsuit /lɔːsuːt/ **lawsuits**
NC A **lawsuit** is a case in a court of law which concerns a dispute between two people or organizations, rather than the prosecution of a criminal by the police; a formal word. *He had sought to bring a lawsuit against the airline.*

lawyer /lɔːjə/ **lawyers**
NC A **lawyer** is a person who is qualified to advise people about the law and represent them in court. *The inquiry is to be headed by a British lawyer, Mr John Scott.*

lax /læks/
ADJ If someone's behaviour or a system is **lax**, the rules are not being obeyed or standards are not being maintained. *Procedures are lax, discipline is weak. The minister was criticised for being too lax...*

laxative /lǽksətɪv/ **laxatives**
NC A **laxative** is a medicine that stops you being constipated. *There are some stomach aches for which a laxative is dangerous.*

lay /leɪ/ **lays, laying, laid**
1 **Lay** is the past tense of some meanings of **lie**.
2 VOA If you **lay** something somewhere, you place it there so that it rests there. *She laid the baby gently down on its bed... She laid a hand on his shoulder... They laid flowers and lit candles in Wenceslas Square.*
3 VO When you **lay** the table, you arrange the knives, forks, plates, and other things on a table before a meal. *I'm not laying a place at table for him.*
4 VO If you **lay** something such as a carpet or a cable, you put it on the floor or in the ground in its proper position. *They're laying water pipes and electricity cables.*
5 VO or V When a female bird or animal **lays** an egg, the egg comes out of its body. *All birds lay eggs... She lays at night.*
6 VO If you **lay** the basis for something, you make preparations for it in order to make sure that it will happen in the way you want it to. *Her new policy helped to lay the foundations of electoral success.*
7 ADJ ATTRIB You use **lay** to describe people who are involved with a Christian church but are not members of the clergy, monks, or nuns. *...a lay preacher.*
8 ADJ ATTRIB You also use **lay** to describe someone who is not trained or qualified in a particular subject or activity. *The computer has become much more accessible to the lay person.*
● **Lay** is used in these phrases. ● If you **lay** someone **open to** criticism or attack, you do something which is likely to make people criticize or attack them. *That kind of behaviour can lay you open to the charge of wasting the company's time.* ● If you **lay emphasis on**

something, you emphasize it. *He is expected to lay strong emphasis on human rights.* ● **to lay claim to:** see **claim**.

lay before PHRASAL VERB If you **lay** an idea or problem **before** someone, you present it to them, for example in order to obtain their approval or advice; a formal expression. *What exactly was the scheme he intended to lay before them?*

lay down PHRASAL VERB 1 If rules or people in authority **lay down** what people must do, they tell people what they must do. *...the conditions laid down by the Department of Health.* ● **to lay down the law:** see **law**. 2 If someone **lays down** their life in a war or struggle, they are killed while fighting for something; a literary use. *He added that three men had laid down their lives in service of their country.*

lay into PHRASAL VERB If you **lay into** someone, you start attacking them physically or criticizing them severely. *She really laid into the management.*

lay off PHRASAL VERB 1 If workers **are laid off** by their employers, they are told to leave their jobs, usually because there is no more work for them to do. *Yesterday more than five hundred workers were laid off.* 2 If you tell someone to **lay off**, you are telling them to leave you alone; an informal use. *She appealed to the press to lay off... Lay off that book— it's mine.*

lay on PHRASAL VERB If you **lay on** food, entertainment, or a service, you provide it. *We laid on a great show for them.*

lay out PHRASAL VERB 1 If you **lay out** a group of things, you spread them out and arrange them. *Clothes, jewels, and ornaments were laid out on the ground.* 2 You can describe the design of a garden, building, or town by saying how it **is laid out**. *Their settlement is laid out traditionally as a small village.* 3 See also **layout**.

layabout /leɪəbaʊt/ **layabouts**
NC If you say that someone is a **layabout**, you mean that they are idle and lazy; an informal word. *He's just a drunken layabout.*

lay-by, lay-bys
NC A **lay-by** is a short strip of road by the side of a main road, where cars can stop for a while. *Pull into the next lay-by.*

layer /leɪə/ **layers**
NC A **layer** is a flat piece of something or a quantity of something that covers a surface or that is between two other things. *Insulate yourself by wrapping up in as many layers as possible... A fine layer of dust covered everything. ...the ozone layer.*

layette /leɪet/ **layettes**
NC A **layette** is a set of the things that you need for a baby, such as clothes and nappies; a formal word.

layman /leɪmən/ **laymen** /leɪmən/
NC A **layman** is a person who is not qualified or experienced in a particular subject or activity. *...a task for industrial experts rather than for laymen.*

layoff /leɪɒf/ **layoffs**
NC When there are **layoffs** in a company, people are made unemployed because there is no more work for them in the company. *Textile companies announced 2,000 fresh layoffs last week... It has been agreed there will be no more immediate layoffs in the public sector.*

layout /leɪaʊt/ **layouts**
NC+SUPP The **layout** of a garden, building, or piece of writing is the way in which the parts of it are arranged. *He knew the airport layout intimately.*

laze /leɪz/ **lazes, lazing, lazed**
V If you **laze** somewhere, you relax and enjoy yourself, not doing anything that requires any effort. *...a swimming pool where she could laze and drowse.*

laze about PHRASAL VERB See **laze around**.

laze around PHRASAL VERB If you **laze around**, or **laze about**, you relax, not doing anything that requires any effort. *They just lazed around and had a good time.*

lazy /leɪzi/ **lazier, laziest**
1 ADJ **Lazy** people try to avoid doing any work. *His maths teacher thought he was bright but lazy.*
◆ **laziness** NU *Only laziness prevented him from doing it.*
2 ADJ ATTRIB **Lazy** actions are done slowly without

making very much effort. *She gave a lazy smile.*
◆ **lazily** ADV *Philip was lazily combing his hair.*

lazybones /leɪzibəʊnz/
N SING If you say that someone is a **lazybones**, you mean that they are very lazy indeed.

lb, lbs. The plural form can be either **lbs** or **lb**. You use **lb** as a written abbreviation for 'pound' when you are giving the weight of something. *...a 2 lb bag of sugar. ...a fish weighing about 10 lbs.*

LCD /elsiːdiː/
LCD is an abbreviation for **liquid crystal display**.

lead, leads, leading, led; pronounced /liːd/ for the meanings in paragraphs 1 to 18 and for the phrases and phrasal verbs, and /led/ for the meanings in paragraphs 19 and 20.
1 V O A If you **lead** someone somewhere, you take them there. *My mother takes me by the hand and leads me downstairs... Mr Vaz led a deputation of BCCI depositors and staff to the Prime Minister's office.*
2 V O If you **lead** a group of moving people, you walk or ride in front of them. *He led a demonstration through the City... Jenny was leading and I was at the back.*
3 V A If something such as a road, pipe, or wire **leads** somewhere, it goes there. *...the main street leading to the centre of the city... The steps lead down to his basement.*
4 V A If a door or gate **leads** to a place, you can get to the place by going through it. *There was a gate on our left leading into a field... The outer door leads to a heavy soundproofed inner door.*
5 V or V O If you **lead** in a race or competition, you are winning. *He now leads by an hour and 50 minutes... Nick Faldo leads the group on 213.*
6 N SING If you are in the **lead** in a race, competition, or election, you are winning. *This win gave him the overall lead... Recent opinion polls show Walesa slightly in the lead.*
7 V O or V If you **lead** a group or organization, you are officially in charge of it. *The government will be led by a new Prime Minister... He lacked any desire to lead.*
8 V O If you **lead** an activity, you start it or guide it. *The rioting was led by students. ..in 1953, Fidel Castro led his first armed attack against the army of Cuban dictator Fulgencio Batista.*
9 V+to If one thing **leads** to another, it causes the second thing to happen. *The new producer prices will also lead to higher prices in the shops next year... This would lead almost certainly to long prison sentences.*
10 V O+to-INF or V O+to If something **leads** you to do, feel, or believe something, it influences or affects you so that you do, feel, or believe that thing. *Recent evidence is leading historians to reassess that event... This led him to a somewhat pessimistic view of Africa's future.*
11 NC If you give a **lead**, you do something which is considered a good example to follow. *The European Community should give a lead... Other firms are now following the company's lead.*
12 V O You can describe the way you live by saying that you **lead** a particular kind of life. *He led a life of some luxury and pleasure... Many lead a double life.*
13 NC A dog's **lead** is a long, thin chain or piece of leather which you attach to the dog's collar so that you can keep it under control. *The pit bull terrier had slipped its lead and attacked her for ten minutes.*
14 NC A **lead** in a piece of electrical equipment is a piece of wire which supplies electricity to the equipment. *Check that the leads to the battery are in good condition.*
15 N SING The **lead** in a play or film is the most important role in it. *Richard was signed up to play the lead.*
16 ADJ ATTRIB The **lead** story in a newspaper or news report is the piece of news that is given the most importance. *According to the lead story in the Sun, the final decision will be taken by the Prime Minister.*
17 ADJ ATTRIB The **lead** singer in a pop group is the main singer. *Lead singer Marti Pellow has a voice of pop, rock and soul all rolled into one.*
18 NC A **lead** is also a piece of information which may

help the police to solve a crime or scientists to discover something. *Scientists really have to look at every lead they can.*
19 NU **Lead** is a soft, grey, heavy metal. *Lead is a poison that can produce high blood pressure in adults... Paint chips and lead pollution in dust and dirt are the main problems.*
20 NC The **lead** in a pencil is the centre part of it which makes a mark on paper. *It is about the size of a number 2 lead pencil.*
21 See also **leading**.
● **Lead** is used in these phrases. ● If you **lead the way**, you go in front of someone in order to show them where to go. *I led the way to Andrew's cabin.* ● If you **take the lead**, you start doing something before other people do. *France took the lead in the development of the airbus.*
lead off PHRASAL VERB **1** If a road, corridor, or room **leads off** from a place, it goes away from it. *There is a lane leading off right beside the Restaurant du Canal.* **2** If someone **leads off** in a meeting, conversation, or performance, they start the meeting, conversation, or performance. *The chairman led off with a financial statement.*
lead up to PHRASAL VERB **1** Events that **lead up to** a situation happen one after the other until they cause that situation to exist. *...the chain of events that led up to her death.* **2** If you **lead up to** a particular subject in a conversation, you gradually guide the conversation to a point where you can introduce that subject. *Ever since you came in you've been leading up to this one question.*
leaded /lɛdɪd/
1 ADJ **Leaded** fuels contain a small amount of lead which was added to make the engine use the fuel more efficiently. *She said that motorists were still not changing from leaded to unleaded petrol.*
2 ADJ **Leaded** glass or windows are made of small pieces of glass held together in a pattern by strips of lead placed between each piece. *...solid brass chandeliers, stencilled ceilings and Victorian leaded glass.*
leaden /lɛdn/; a literary word.
1 ADJ A **leaden** sky or sea is dark grey and has no movement of clouds or waves. *...under a leaden grey sky.*
2 ADJ If your movements are **leaden**, you move slowly and heavily, because you are tired. *He took two leaden steps forward.*
3 ADJ **Leaden** conversation or writing is very dull. *...the leaden clichés of the Communist Party phrasebook.*
leader /liːdə/ **leaders**
1 NC The **leader** of a country, an organization, or a group of people is the person who is in charge of it and who represents it. *...the Chinese leader. ...the leader of the opposition party... His skills are much more those of a manager than a leader.*
2 NC A **leader** is also a person or company who is one of the biggest or most successful in its field. *Lloyds has developed into a world leader in the essential business of insuring risks.*
3 NC The **leader** in a race or competition is the person who is winning at a particular time. *He remains the rally's overall leader... The race leader finished fourth after the 674 kilometre stage.*
4 NC The **leader** in a newspaper is the main article in it, usually expressing the editor's opinion on the most important news item of the day. *The Times leader begins with a sombre statement.*
leadership /liːdəʃɪp/
1 N SING You can refer to the people who are in charge of a country, a group, or an organization as the **leadership**. *...the gap between the leadership and the men they represent.*
2 N SING The **leadership** is also the position or state of being in control of a group or organization. *...the election of Wilson to the leadership of the Labour Party. ...an independent group under the leadership of Jones.*
3 NU **Leadership** refers to the qualities that make someone a good leader. *...a task calling for energy*

and firm leadership.
lead-in /liːdɪn/ **lead-ins**
NC A **lead-in** is what is said or done as an introduction before the main subject or event, especially the introduction to a radio or television programme. *...a typical lead-in to a news report. ...a good lead-in to the final phase.*
leading /liːdɪŋ/
1 ADJ ATTRIB The **leading** people or things in a group are the most important ones. *Some of Britain's leading businessmen express their concern about the level of pay claims... Alberto Moravia has been one of Italy's leading literary figures for more than half a century.*
2 ADJ ATTRIB The **leading** role in a play or film is the main one. *...their leading lady, Yvonne Printemps.*
3 ADJ ATTRIB If a person or country plays a **leading** role in something, their actions are very important to the creation or development of it. *For over three centuries, Britain played a leading role in the scientific revolution that changed our lives.*
leading article, leading articles
NC The **leading article** in a newspaper is the main article in it, usually expressing the editor's opinion on the most important news item of the day. *He was able to continue his attack in a leading article of 30th October.*
leading light, leading lights
NC If someone is a **leading light** in an organization or campaign, they are one of the most important, active, and influential people in it. *Strauss has been a leading light in the Democratic party.*
leading question, leading questions
NC A **leading question** is a question that is asked in such a way that it seems that a particular answer is expected; used showing disapproval. *...the child is asked leading questions.*
lead-up
N SING The **lead-up** to an event is the time before the event when preparations are being made for it. *...in the lead-up to 1992 and the creation of a single European market.*
leaf /liːf/ **leaves; leafs, leafing, leafed.** The form **leaves** is the plural of the noun. The form **leafs** is the third person singular, present tense, of the phrasal verb.
1 NC The **leaves** of a tree or plant are the parts that are flat, thin, and usually green. *There are a large number of root and leaf vegetables in the garden.*
● When trees are **in leaf**, they have leaves on their branches. *The trees and shrubs were in full leaf.*
2 If you decide to **turn over a new leaf** or to **turn a new leaf**, you decide to try and behave in a better or more acceptable way. *Seventy-four percent of them had turned over a new leaf after a year... The message spoke of turning a new leaf in the two countries' relations.*
leaf through PHRASAL VERB If you **leaf through** a book or newspaper, you turn the pages quickly without looking at them carefully. *Leaf through the pages until you come to one you recognise.*
leaflet /liːflət/ **leaflets, leafleting, leafleted**
1 NC A **leaflet** is a little book or a piece of paper containing information about a particular subject. *He and his team devised a new sales leaflet to promote the Electrodyne... They reported that a worker had been arrested for distributing leaflets harmful to the state.*
2 VO If you **leaflet** a place, you distribute leaflets there. *All the local houses and shops had been leafleted.*
leafy /liːfi/
1 ADJ **Leafy** trees and plants have a lot of leaves. *...leafy green vegetables.*
2 ADJ You say that a place is **leafy** when there are a lot of trees and plants there. *...a leafy suburb.*
league /liːg/ **leagues**
1 N COLL A **league** is a group of people, clubs, or countries that have joined together for a particular purpose or because they share a common interest. *...the National Book League... He became the youngest manager in the Football League.*

2 If you are **in league with** someone, you are working with them for a particular purpose, often secretly. *They are in league with the police.*
League of Arab States See **Arab League**
league table, league tables
NC When things, such as teams or organizations, are presented in a **league table**, they are listed according to the scores or results they have obtained, with the most successful at the top and the least successful at the bottom. *This survey produced a league table of the numbers of tourists who got food poisoning on holiday... France is the head of the league table.*
leak /liːk/ **leaks, leaking, leaked**
1 V If a container or other object **leaks**, there is a hole or crack in it which lets liquid or gas escape. *The roof leaks. ...leaking drain pipes.* ▶ Also NC *Engineers are repairing a leak in a one centimetre diameter pipe.*
2 V A When liquid or gas **leaks** through an object or **leaks** out of it, it escapes through a hole or crack in it. *The water was still slowly leaking out.* ▶ Also NC *If the problem had gone undetected it might eventually have led to a radiation leak... Jacques Cousteau has described the oil leak as a catastrophe.*
3 VO If someone **leaks** a piece of secret information, they let other people know about it. *He made sure the story was leaked to the media... An IRA informer leaked details of the route the army bus was taking.* ▶ Also NC *...the possibility of a security leak... Like many reports in journalism it comes from a leak.*
leak out PHRASAL VERB If information that you want to keep secret **leaks out**, it becomes known to other people. *There was plainly a political purpose in allowing a story to leak out which had been kept secret for six months.*
leakage /liːkɪdʒ/ **leakages**
NC If there is a **leakage** of liquid or gas, it escapes from a pipe or container through a hole or crack. *A leakage in the hydraulic system was diagnosed.*
leaky /liːki/
ADJ Something that is **leaky** has holes or cracks in it which liquids or gases can escape through. *...a leaky roof.*
lean /liːn/ **leans, leaning, leaned** or **leant**
1 V A When you **lean** in a particular direction, you bend your body in that direction. *He was sitting on the edge of his chair and leaning eagerly forwards... I leaned out of the window.*
2 V A or VO A If you **lean** on something, you rest against it so that it partly supports your weight. If you **lean** an object on something, you place the object so that its weight is partly supported by the thing it is resting against. *He leaned against a tree... He leaned the bike against a railing.*
3 ADJ A **lean** person is thin but looks strong and fit. *...a lean, handsome man.*
4 ADJ **Lean** meat does not have very much fat. *People buying meat want lean meat with not too much fat.*
5 ADJ A **lean** period of time is one in which people do not have very much food, money, or success. *These are lean years for the Ministry of Defence... The Financial Times predicts lean times ahead for the economy.*
lean on or **lean upon** PHRASAL VERB **1** If you **lean on** or **lean upon** someone, you try to influence them by threatening them. *They can lean on the administration by threatening to withhold their subscriptions.* **2** To **lean on** or **lean upon** someone also means to depend on them for support and encouragement. *They lean heavily upon each other for support.*
lean towards PHRASAL VERB If you **lean towards** a particular idea or action, you approve of it and behave in accordance with it. *...parents who naturally lean towards strictness... Yet the country is leaning towards the Democratic candidate.*
leaning /liːnɪŋ/ **leanings**
NC+SUPP If you have a **leaning** towards a particular belief or type of behaviour, you tend to have that belief or to behave in that way. *...their different political leanings.*

leant /lent/
Leant is a past tense and past participle of **lean**.
lean-to, lean-tos
NC A **lean-to** is a shed which is attached to one wall of a house, garage, or other building. *The refugees have set up hundreds of shacks and lean-tos. ...little lean-tos made out of plastic sheeting.*
leap /liːp/ **leaps, leaping, leaped** or **leapt**
1 V A If you **leap** somewhere, you jump high in the air or jump a long distance. *She leaps off a 30 metre high building... Others were killed leaping from windows on the upper floor... He leapt to safety.* ▶ Also NC *She took a flying leap at the fence... He made leaps of 8.4 and 8.7 metres.*
2 V A To **leap** somewhere also means to move there suddenly and quickly. *She leapt into a taxi... The crowds leapt to their feet.*
3 V A You can say that things **leap** when they suddenly advance or increase by a large amount. *The number of computers in the world is leaping upwards daily... Unemployment has leapt from less than 10,000 to over half a million.* ▶ Also NC *...a leap in oil prices.*
4 If something changes **by leaps and bounds**, it changes very quickly. *Japanese aid in the form of low interest loans has grown by leaps and bounds... The cost of the health service expanded by leaps and bounds.*
leap at PHRASAL VERB If you **leap at** a chance or opportunity, you accept it quickly and eagerly. *David would have leaped at the chance to go.*
leapfrog /liːpfrɒg/ **leapfrogs, leapfrogging, leapfrogged**
1 NU **Leapfrog** is a game which children play, in which one group of children bend over, while others jump over their backs.
2 V A or VO If one group of people **leapfrogs** into a particular position or **leapfrogs** someone else, they use the achievements of another person or group in order to make advances of their own. *It gives the third world a chance to leapfrog into the space age.*
leapt /lept/
Leapt is a past tense and past participle of **leap**.
leap year, leap years
NC A **leap year** is a year in which there are 366 days instead of 365. The extra day is the 29th February. There is a leap year every four years.
learn /lɜːn/ **learns, learning, learned** or **learnt**
1 VO, V, or V+to-INF If you **learn** something, you obtain knowledge or a skill through studying or training. *Children learn foreign languages very easily... The best way to learn is by practical experience... He had never learnt to read and write.*
2 VO If you **learn** a poem, song, or the script of a play, you study or repeat the words so that you can remember them. *We have to learn the whole poem.*
3 V+to-INF If people **learn** to behave in a particular way, their attitudes gradually change and they start behaving that way. *If only these people could learn to live together.*
4 V A, VO, or V-REPORT If you **learn** of something, you find out about it. *They offered help as soon as they learnt of the accident. ...the night when he learned the truth about Sam... She was extremely upset to learn that he had died.*
learned /lɜːnɪd/
1 ADJ **Learned** people have gained a lot of knowledge by studying. *He was one of that rare breed of wise and learned men.*
2 ADJ ATTRIB **Learned** books or papers have been written by someone with a lot of academic knowledge. *...new ideas announced in learned journals.*
learner /lɜːnə/ **learners**
NC A **learner** is someone who is learning about a particular subject or how to do something. *She is a very slow learner. ...learners of English. ...a learner driver.*
learning /lɜːnɪŋ/
NU **Learning** is knowledge that has been gained through studying. *...a man of learning.*
learnt /lɜːnt/
Learnt is a past tense and past participle of **learn**.

lease /liːs/ **leases, leasing, leased**

1 NC A **lease** is a legal agreement under which someone pays money to use a building or piece of land for a period of time. *The house was let on a 99-year lease.*

2 VOorVOO If you **lease** property from someone or if they **lease** it to you, they allow you to use it in return for money. *They leased a house at Cospoli... He had persuaded the local council to lease him a house.*

3 If someone who seemed to be weak or failing has **a new lease of life**, they are now more lively or successful. *After her marriage it was as though she'd got a new lease of life.*

leasehold /liːshəʊld/

ADJ If a building or land is described as **leasehold**, you can live there or make use of it in return for payment of money as arranged according to a lease. *...a leasehold property.*

leaseholder /liːshəʊldə/ **leaseholders**

NC A **leaseholder** is a person who is allowed to use a property according to the terms of a lease. *Collective farms could be turned over to leaseholders.*

leash /liːʃ/ **leashes**

NC A dog's **leash** is a long thin piece of leather or a chain, which you attach to the dog's collar. *I kept Sandy on the leash.*

least /liːst/

1 ADJ ATTRIB You use **least** when comparing two or more things, to say that the amount of one of the things is the smallest of the two or of the group. *...the thinner animals, who had the least muscle over their bones.*

2 ADV You also use **least** to say that something is true to as small a degree or extent as is possible. *He came out when I least expected it... They're the ones who need it the least.*

3 SUBMOD You also use **least** to say that something has less of a particular quality than most other things of its kind. *...one of the smallest and least powerful of the African states.*

4 QUANT You can also use **least** to emphasize that a particular situation or thing is much less important or serious than other ones. *That was the least of her worries.*

● **Least** is used in these phrases. ● You use **at least** to say that the number or amount mentioned is the smallest that is likely, and that the actual number or amount may be greater. *He drank at least half a bottle of whisky a day... I must have slept twelve hours at least.* ● You also use **at least** to say that something is the minimum which should be done in the circumstances, although in fact you think that more than this ought to be done. *Go to see the administrator or at least write a letter.* ● **At least** can also be used to indicate an advantage that exists in spite of the disadvantage or bad situation that has just been mentioned. *The process looks rather laborious but at least it is not dangerous.* ● When you want to correct something that you have just said, you can also use **at least**. *A couple of days ago I spotted my ex-wife; at least I thought I did, I wasn't sure.* ● You can use **in the least** and **the least bit** to emphasize a negative. *I don't mind in the least, I really don't... She wasn't the least bit jealous.* ● You can use **to say the least** to suggest that a situation is actually much more extreme or serious than you say it is. *...a development which will have, to say the least, intriguing effects.* ● You can use **not least** when giving an important example or reason. *...for a whole variety of reasons, not least because people have begun to find that it is too expensive.* ● You can use **least of all** after a negative statement to emphasize that it applies especially to a particular person or thing. *Nobody seemed amused, least of all Jenny.*

leather /leðə/

NU **Leather** is treated animal skin which is used for making shoes, clothes, bags, and furniture. *...leather jackets.*

leathery /leðəri/

ADJ If something has a **leathery** texture, it is tough, like leather. *The wrinkled, leathery face broke into a smile.*

leave /liːv/ **leaves, leaving, left**

1 VOorV When you **leave** a place, you go away from it. *He left Karachi on Sunday afternoon... He wanted to have his poems published before he left his native land forever... Experts working in the country will leave as soon as they complete the project... My train leaves at 11.30.*

2 VOA If you **leave** a person or thing somewhere, they stay there when you go away. *It's difficult for us to leave friends and colleagues here... I had left my raincoat in the restaurant.*

3 VOorV If you **leave** a place or institution, you go away permanently from it. *What do you want to do when you leave school?... Many nurses are leaving the profession for a variety of reasons... All they want to do is leave at 16 and get a job.*

4 VO If you **leave** an amount of something, you do not use it, and so it remains available to be used later. *Leave some of the stew for the boys... He drained what was left of his drink.* ● See also **left**.

5 VOAorVA To **leave** someone or something in a particular state or position means to cause them to remain or be in that state or position. *The result has left everybody dissatisfied... Leave a space between the fridge and the wall... Left alone, the child would have been unable to breathe.*

6 VO+to-INF If you **leave** someone or something to do something, you go away and let them continue to do what they were doing without interfering. *Leave it to soak for about fifteen minutes... They would be left to make their own decisions.*

7 VO If someone **leaves** the person they are having a relationship with, they finish the relationship and stop living with them. *My husband had left me for another woman.*

8 VO If something **leaves** a mark, effect, or impression, it causes that mark, effect, or impression to remain as a result. *I didn't want him to leave a trail of wet footprints... Does it leave a stain?*

9 VO If you **leave** something to someone, you give them the responsibility for dealing with it. *He said the whole business should be left to the courts... Government policy has largely been to leave the whole matter to the operation of market forces.*

10 VOA If you **leave** something until a particular time, you delay dealing with it. *Why do you always leave things to the last minute? We decided to leave the opening of presents until morning.*

11 VO If you **leave** a particular subject, you stop talking about it and start discussing something else. *Let's leave the budget and go on to another question.*

12 VOAorVO If you **leave** property or money to someone, you arrange for it to be given to them after you have died. *He left all his property to his wife... She did not leave a very large legacy.*

13 NU **Leave** is a period of time when you are on holiday from your job or absent for another reason. *All police leave has been cancelled... He had been on sick leave for the past three years.*

14 **Leaves** is also the plural form of **leaf**.

leave behind PHRASAL VERB 1 If you **leave** someone or something **behind**, you go away permanently from them. *I hated having to leave behind all my friends.* 2 If you **leave** an object or a situation **behind**, it remains after you have left a place. *Millie had left her watch behind... They had been forced to leave all their possessions behind. ...leaving behind an unsolved mystery.*

leave off PHRASAL VERB 1 If you **leave** someone or something **off** a list, you do not include them in that list. *Hopper was too important to be left off the guest list.* 2 If you continue doing something **from where** you **left off**, you start doing it again at the point where you had previously stopped doing it. *He sat down at the piano again and started playing from where he left off.*

leave out PHRASAL VERB If you **leave** a person or thing **out**, you do not include it in something. *The selectors said both players were left out because of their poor performances... One or two scenes in the play had to be left out of the performance.*

leaven /levn/ **leavens, leavening, leavened**

1 VO If someone or something **leavens** a situation or

activity, they change it gradually, usually making it more interesting or acceptable. *Bitter humour does leaven the movie's violence.*
2 NU **Leaven** is the same as **yeast**; an old-fashioned use.

leavened /lɛvnd/
ADJ **Leavened** bread or dough has had yeast added to it. *Leavened bread stays fresh longer than unleavened bread.*

leave of absence, leaves of absence
N U or N C If you have **leave of absence**, you have permission to be away from work for a certain period. *Weiner took leave of absence from his police job. ...At issue in the case is whether employers must, under federal law, grant extended leaves of absence for military training.*

leaves /liːvz/
1 **Leaves** is the plural of **leaf**.
2 **Leaves** is the third person singular form of **leave**.

leavings /liːvɪŋz/
N PL **Leavings** are the things that remain after something has been finished, for example, food on a plate or rubbish. *We had littered the tables with our messy leavings of cake-crumbs and broken meat.*

Lebanon /lɛbənən/
The **Republic of Lebanon** is a country in west Asia, on the Mediterranean. When it became independent from France in 1941, the National Covenant established that the government would reflect the religious composition of the country: the president would be a Maronite Christian, the prime minister a Sunni Muslim, the speaker of the National Assembly a Shia Muslim, and the chief of staff of the armed forces a Druze Muslim. Since independence, the proportion of Muslims has drastically increased, largely because of the influx of Palestinian refugees. Increasing tensions between Muslim and Christians resulted in civil war, which lasted from 1975 to 1990. The war has caused a complete breakdown of civil order. The main factions involved in the fighting include: the Phalangists, a right-wing, Maronite Christian group; the Progressive Socialist Party (PSP), composed of left-wing, mainly Druze Muslims; the Amal group, which is Shia Muslim and pro-Syrian; Hezbollah, which is also Shia Muslim, but backed by Iran; and Murabitoun, a Sunni Muslim militia. Elias Hrawi, a Maronite, became President in 1989. Umar Karami, a Sunni, became Prime Minister in 1990. Lebanon was once an important commercial and industrial nation, but the civil war has destroyed its economy. It produces agricultural products, chemicals, and textiles. Opium and cannabis are illegally exported. Large foreign debts and high inflation are major economic problems. Lebanon is a member of the Arab League. ◆ **Lebanese** /lɛbəniːz/ N, ADJ
▪ *religion:* Islam (57%), Christianity (43%) (these figures are estimates as there has been no reliable census information for many years) ▪ *language:* Arabic (official), French ▪ *currency:* pound ▪ *capital:* Beirut ▪ *population:* 3 million (1988) ▪ *size:* 10,452 square kilometres.

lecher /lɛtʃə/ **lechers**
NC A **lecher** is a man who behaves towards women in a way which shows that he is only interested in them sexually; used showing disapproval.

lecherous /lɛtʃərəs/
ADJ A **lecherous** man behaves towards women in a way which shows he is only interested in them sexually; used showing disapproval. *The historian concludes that the President was 'selfish, petty and lecherous'.*

lechery /lɛtʃəri/
NU **Lechery** is the behaviour of men who are only interested in women sexually; used showing disapproval. *...a shameless glance of lechery. ...cold-blooded lechery.*

lectern /lɛktən/ **lecterns**
NC A **lectern** is a high sloping desk on which someone puts their notes or a book when they are standing up and talking or reading to an audience. *The bomb was discovered under the speaker's lectern shortly before the start of the conference.*

lecture /lɛktʃə/ **lectures, lecturing, lectured**
1 NC A **lecture** is a talk that someone gives in order to teach people about a particular subject. *...a series of lectures on literature.*
2 V If you **lecture**, you give a lecture or series of lectures. *He lectured on Economic History at the University.*
3 VOA If someone **lectures** you about something, they criticize you or tell you how you should behave. *I had always been lectured about not talking with my mouth full.*
4 NC A **lecture** is also strong criticism that someone makes about something that they do not like. *He'll give her a lecture on her responsibilities.*

lecturer /lɛktʃərə/ **lecturers**
NC A **lecturer** is a teacher at a university or college. *...a lecturer in sociology.*

lectureship /lɛktʃəʃɪp/ **lectureships**
NC A **lectureship** is a position of lecturer at a university or college. *...a lectureship at Birmingham University.*

led /lɛd/
Led is the past tense and past participle of **lead**.

ledge /lɛdʒ/ **ledges**
1 NC A **ledge** is a narrow, flat place in the side of a cliff or mountain. *Only a bird could get to that ledge.*
2 NC A **ledge** is also a narrow shelf along the bottom edge of a window. *...students sitting on the window ledges.*

ledger /lɛdʒə/ **ledgers**
NC A **ledger** is a book in which a company or organization writes down the amounts of money it spends and receives. *Investigators looking into the commission's books found four separate ledgers containing conflicting information.*

lee /liː/ **lees**; a formal word.
1 N SING The **lee** of a place is the shelter that it gives from the wind or bad weather. *...in the lee of a rock.*
2 ADJ ATTRIB The **lee** side of a ship is the one that is away from the wind; a technical use. *I stepped out onto the starboard ladder on the lee side.*
3 N PL The **lees** are the sediment that collects at the bottom of a bottle of wine or of a barrel of beer.

leech /liːtʃ/ **leeches**
1 NC A **leech** is a small animal which looks like a worm and lives in water. Leeches feed by attaching themselves to other animals and sucking their blood. *The pond was full of leeches.*
2 NC If you call someone a **leech**, you mean that they deliberately depend on other people, usually for money. *He's nothing but a leech.*

leek /liːk/ **leeks**
NC A **leek** is a long thin vegetable which is white at one end and has long green leaves. *Now they grow garlic and shallots and leeks.*

leer /lɪə/ **leers, leering, leered**
V If someone **leers** at you, they smile in an unpleasant way, usually because they are sexually interested in you. *He leaned over and leered at them.* ► Also NC *He was staring down with a leer on his face.*

leery /lɪəri/
ADJ PRED If you are **leery** about something, you feel suspicious of it or frightened that it may happen; used in American English. *That country has been leery of foreign competition... Many businesses are leery of a recession and are not hiring.*

Lee Teng-hui /liː dʌŋ xweɪ/
Lee Teng-hui became President of Taiwan in 1988. He was Mayor of Taipei from 1978 to 1981 and Governor of Taiwan Province from 1981 to 1984. He was Vice President of Taiwan from 1984 to 1988. He is a member of the Kuomintang (KMT). Born: 1923.

leeway /liːweɪ/
1 NU **Leeway** is the flexibility that someone has to change their plans, for example by taking more time or money than they had originally intended. *It doesn't give you much leeway, does it?... This will give the Russians ten days leeway to cope with poor weather.*
2 NU If you have **leeway** to make up, you have to work very hard because you do not have much time to reach a particular goal.

left /left/
1 **Left** is the past tense and past participle of **leave**.
2 ADJ PRED or ADJ after N If there is an amount of something **left**, it remains after the rest has gone or been used. *I only had two pounds left. ...what was left of the Berlin Wall.*
3 ADJ PRED or ADJ after N If there is an amount of something **left over**, it remains after the rest has gone, because you did not need to use it. *We had a bit of time left over. ...the money which is left over each week after a person has paid living expenses.*
4 N SING The **left** is one of two opposite directions, sides, or positions. In the word 'to', the 't' is to the left of the 'o'. *The trees that stood to the boy's left had been cut down... There was a gate on our left leading into a field. ...the third door to the left.* ▶ Also ADV or ADJ ATTRIB *He turned left and began strolling down the street... Each stamp had a unique set of letterings in the bottom left corners... In his left hand he clutched a book.*
5 N SING The **Left** is used to refer to the people or groups who support socialism rather than capitalism. *...the extreme left. ...many critics on both left and right... The left even has its own publishing houses.* ▶ Also ADJ ATTRIB *That's the view of some extreme left people.*

left-hand
ADJ ATTRIB **Left-hand** refers to something which is on the left side. *She noted it down on the left-hand page.*

left-hand drive
ADJ ATTRIB A **left-hand drive** car, van, or lorry has the steering wheel on the left side and is designed to be driven on the right-hand side of the road. *She has a left-hand drive mini that she got in France.*

left-handed
ADJ or ADV **Left-handed** people use their left hand rather than their right hand for activities such as writing and throwing a ball. *They both play golf left-handed. ...left-handed batsmen.*

left-hander /lefthændə/ **left-handers**
NC A **left-hander** is someone who uses their left hand rather than their right hand for activities such as writing and throwing a ball. *Da Vinci, Michelangelo, Raphael, and Picasso were all left-handers.*

leftie /lefti/ **lefties**; also spelt **lefty**.
1 NC If you refer to someone as a **leftie**, you mean that they have socialist beliefs; used showing disapproval. *...troublemakers and lefties.*
2 NC In informal American English, a **leftie** is someone, especially a sports player, who is left-handed. *It's tough enough being left-handed in a right-handed world but two weeks ago, the outlook for lefties seemed bleak.*

leftist /leftist/ **leftists**
NC Socialists and communists are sometimes referred to as **leftists**. ▶ Also ADJ ATTRIB *...extreme leftist activities.*

left-luggage office, left-luggage offices
NC In a railway station or airport, you can pay to leave your luggage in a **left-luggage office**.

left-of-centre
ADJ **Left-of-centre** people or political parties support political ideas which are closer to socialism than to conservatism and a market economy. *...left-of-centre MPs. ...a mildly left-of-centre government.*

leftover /leftəʊvə/ **leftovers**
1 N PL The **leftovers** from a meal are the food that has not been eaten. *The dogs eat the leftovers... They sleep on floors and survive on scraps and leftovers from their employers' meals.*
2 ADJ ATTRIB You use **leftover** to describe an amount of something that remains after the rest has been used. *...a bottle of leftover perfume.*

leftward /leftwəd/. The form **leftwards** is also used.
ADJ ATTRIB **Leftward** or **leftwards** means on or towards a political position that is closer to socialism than to capitalism. *...the leftward shifts in his party since 1945... The Labour Party moved in a leftwards direction.* ▶ Also ADV *...a more leftward looking Democratic Party... The party has moved leftwards while in opposition.*

left-wing; spelt **left wing** for the meaning in paragraph 2.
1 ADJ **Left-wing** people have political ideas that are close to socialism or communism. *...left-wing journalists. ...the influential left-wing newspaper.*
2 N SING The **left wing** of a political party consists of the members of it whose beliefs are closer to socialism or communism than those of its other members. *...the left wing of the Labour Party.*

left-winger, left-wingers
NC A **left-winger** is a person whose political beliefs are close to socialism or communism, or closer to them than most of the other people in the same group or party. *...a small number of left-wingers seeking to exploit the unrest.*

leg /leg/ **legs**
1 NC Your **legs** are the two long parts of your body between your hips and feet which you use for walking and running. *One of the hostages was shot in the leg... Hill life develops strong shoulder, back and leg muscles.*
2 NC The **legs** of an animal, bird, or insect are the thin parts of its body that it uses to stand on or to move across the ground. *...creatures with short legs and long tails.*
3 NC+SUPP A **leg** of lamb or pork is a piece of meat from the thigh of a sheep, lamb, or pig. *...putting a leg of lamb in the deep-freeze... There is a leg of ham and a bowl of sausages.*
4 NC+SUPP The **legs** of a table or chair are the thin vertical parts that touch the floor. *He leaned back, tipping the legs of his chair.*
5 NC A **leg** of a tour, journey, or visit is one part of it. *President Mubarak is about to arrive in Brussels on the first leg of a European tour. ...a British Airways plane which had flown them on the final leg from Frankfurt.*
6 NC A **leg** of a long race or competition is one stage or part of it. *The fifth and final leg was won by Britain's Malcolm Elliot... The teams fought out a one-all draw in their first leg game in Bucharest.*
● **Leg** is used in these phrases. ● If someone **pulls your leg**, they tell you something untrue as a joke. *'You're pulling my leg.'—'No, it's true.'* ● If you say that someone **does not have a leg to stand on**, you mean that what they have done or said cannot be justified or proved. ● Something that is **on its last legs** is in a very bad condition and will soon stop working or break; an informal use. *It was obvious to everyone that the Ottoman empire was on its last legs.*

legacy /legəsi/ **legacies**
1 NC A **legacy** is money or property which someone leaves to you when they die. *...a legacy of five thousand pounds.*
2 NC+SUPP The **legacy** of an event or period of history is something which is a direct result of it and which continues to exist after it is over. *He said the legacy of the Cold War years must be cleared away... The border war left a legacy of bitterness and humiliation.*

legal /liːgl/
1 ADJ ATTRIB **Legal** is used to refer to things that relate to the law. *Mr Pearce could still face further lengthy legal battles to prove his case... The government has pursued similar legal action in Australia. ...legal experts.* ◆ **legally** ADV *Throughout history, women have been legally and economically subordinate to men.*
2 ADJ An action or situation that is **legal** is allowed or required by law. *Capital punishment is legal in many countries. ...circumstances under which abortion in Britain is legal.* ◆ **legally** ADV *...to make the contracts legally binding... They are urging that parents should be made legally responsible for the actions of their children.*

legal aid
NU **Legal aid** is financial assistance given by the government or another organization to people who cannot afford to pay for a lawyer. *She has applied for legal aid.*

legalise /liːgəlaɪz/. See **legalize**.

legalistic /liːgəlɪstɪk/
ADJ **Legalistic** means using, expressing, or

understanding the law in a very precise and careful way, often showing excessive attention to its details. *Daintry's got a very legalistic mind.*

legalistically /liːgəlɪstɪkli/
ADV If something is done **legalistically**, it is done with special attention to legal points. *It is a lengthy document, legalistically expressed.*

legality /liːgælɪti/
NU+SUPP The **legality** of an action or situation concerns whether or not it is allowed by law. *He disputed the legality of the invasion.*

legalize /liːgəlaɪz/ **legalizes, legalizing, legalized**; also spelt **legalise**.
VO If something **is legalized**, a law is passed that makes it legal. *He rejected suggestions that drugs should be legalised to take them out of the criminal sector. ...steps to legalise alternative political parties.*

legal tender
NU **Legal tender** is money, especially a particular coin or banknote, which is officially part of a country's currency at a particular time. *At midnight local time the East German mark ceased to be legal tender and was replaced by the Deutschmark.*

legate /legət/ **legates**
NC A **legate** is a person who is the official representative of another person, especially the Pope's official representative in a particular country; a formal word. *...the Pope's legate in France. ...the papal legate.*

legation /lɪgeɪʃn/ **legations**; a technical word.
1 NC A **legation** is a group of government officials and diplomats who work in a foreign country and represent their government in that country. *...the large staff of the legation.*
2 NC A **legation** is also the building in which a legation works. *...the huge front windows of the legation.*

legend /ledʒənd/ **legends**
1 NCorNU A **legend** is a very old story that may be based on real events. *...folk tales, legends, and myths... The original inhabitants, according to legend, were blacksmiths.*
2 NC If you refer to someone as a **legend**, you mean that they are very famous and admired. *Brook has become something of a legend.*

legendary /ledʒəndri/
1 ADJ A **legendary** person or thing is very famous and a lot of stories are told about them. *...one of his many legendary acts of courage.*
2 ADJ **Legendary** also means described in an old legend. *...the legendary king.*

-legged /-legɪd/
SUFFIX **-legged** is added to numbers to form adjectives describing how many legs something has. *...the first four-legged creatures. ...a three-legged table.*

leggings /legɪŋz/
N PL **Leggings** are an outer covering of leather or other strong material, often in the form of trousers, that you wear over your normal trousers in order to protect them. *...farmers in leather breeches and leggings.*

leggy /legi/ **leggier, leggiest**
ADJ If you describe someone, usually a woman, as **leggy**, you mean that they have very long legs. *...the sultry, leggy Marlene Dietrich. ...a beautiful girl: leggy, Italian-looking.*

legibility /ledʒəbɪləti/
NU If you talk about the **legibility** of a piece of writing, you are referring to how easy or difficult it is to read.

legible /ledʒəbl/
ADJ **Legible** writing is clear enough to be read. *...a crumpled but still legible document.*

legion /liːdʒən/ **legions**
1 TITLE **Legion** is sometimes used in the names of large sections of an army. *...the Condor Legion.*
2 NC A **legion** of people is a large number of them. *...legions of foreign visitors.*
3 ADJ PRED You can say that things are **legion** when there are many of them; a formal use. *Stories about him are legion.*

legionnaires' disease /liːdʒəneəz dɪziːz/
NU **Legionnaires' disease** is a serious lung infection

that can kill people. *Fewer than 200 people have died of Legionnaires' Disease since it was discovered in 1976.*

legislate /ledʒɪsleɪt/ **legislates, legislating, legislated**
VAorVO When a government **legislates**, it passes a new law; a formal word. *The organization wants all countries to legislate on banning smoking in public places... Parliament must eventually legislate against fox-hunting... They would legislate new revenue sources for the poor.*

legislation /ledʒɪsleɪʃn/
NU+SUPP **Legislation** consists of a law or laws passed by a government; a formal word. *...tax legislation. ...the introduction of legislation to govern industrial relations... Further legislation and action will be required.*

legislative /ledʒɪslətɪv/
ADJ ATTRIB **Legislative** means involving or relating to the process of making and passing laws; a formal word. *The Government should consider further legislative reforms.*

legislator /ledʒɪsleɪtə/ **legislators**
NC A **legislator** is someone involved in making or passing laws; a formal word. *Many of the legislators who drafted the bill are landowners.*

legislature /ledʒɪslətʃə/ **legislatures**
NC The **legislature** of a state or country is the group of people with the power to make and pass laws; a formal word. *The legislature appointed an 11 member commission to draw up a list of conditions... Its legislature is considering more than 20 bills.*

legitimacy /lɪdʒɪtɪməsi/
NU The **legitimacy** of something is the fact that it is reasonable, acceptable, or legal. *...the legitimacy of our complaint.*

legitimate, legitimates, legitimating, legitimated; pronounced /lɪdʒɪtɪmət/ in paragraphs 1 to 3 and /lɪdʒɪtɪmeɪt/ in paragraph 4.
1 ADJ Something that is **legitimate** is acceptable according to the law. *...a legitimate business transaction... Both claim to be the legitimate government of all China... They would not regard any negotiations without their presence as legitimate.* ◆ **legitimately** ADV *This material is legitimately owned by our Swiss associates.*
2 ADJ Something, such as a claim or an argument, that is **legitimate** is reasonable and justified. *Some said they appeared to have a legitimate claim. ...the legitimate interests of others... They feel it's legitimate for them to develop chemical and nuclear weapons.* ◆ **legitimately** ADV *He apologized, quite legitimately blaming his assistant for the mistake.*
3 ADJ Someone who is **legitimate** was born of parents who were legally married at the time, and can claim a share of their wealth or possessions when they die. *...evidence that he was his father's legitimate son.*
4 VO To **legitimate** something means the same as to legitimize it. *Like Napolean, he created a Consitution to legitimate his own, successful, palace coup.*

legitimize /lɪdʒɪtɪmaɪz/ **legitimizes, legitimizing, legitimized**; also spelt **legitimise**.
VO To **legitimize** something means to officially allow it, accept it, or approve of it; a formal word. *...the process was legitimized in the Enclosure Acts... If a group is not legitimized, their meetings can be forbidden.* ◆ **legitimization** /lɪdʒɪtɪmaɪzeɪʃn/ NU *...the need for legitimization by elections.*

legless /legləs/
1 ADJ ATTRIB If someone is **legless**, they have no legs, for example as the result of an accident. *...the legless beggars who pull themselves along the pavement.*
2 ADJ If you say that someone is **legless**, you mean that they are extremely drunk; an informal use. *He was more or less legless already and we were only on our third pint.*

leg room
NU **Leg room** is the amount of space, especially in a car or other vehicle, that is left in front of your seat for your legs. *...the lack of leg room in a modern jet.*

leisure /leʒə/
1 NU **Leisure** is time when you do not have to work and can do things that you enjoy. *Not everybody*

wants more leisure. ...a leisure industry.
2 If you do something **at leisure** or **at your leisure**, you do it when you want to, without hurrying. *You could then view it at your leisure.*

leisure centre, leisure centres
NC A **leisure centre** is a large building containing different facilities for leisure activities, such as a sports hall, swimming pool, and rooms for meetings. *The aim is to construct a leisure centre that will be one of Britain's biggest tourist attractions. ...schools, parks, housing estates and leisure centres.*

leisured /lɛ̃ʒəd/
1 ADJ ATTRIB **Leisured** people are people who do not work, usually because they are rich. *Culture was for the leisured classes.*
2 ADJ ATTRIB **Leisured** activities are done in a relaxed way or do not involve work. *...a leisured life in the suburbs... He ate a leisured luncheon.*

leisurely /lɛ̃ʒəli/
ADJ A **leisurely** action is done in a relaxed and unhurried way. *My wife went off for a leisurely walk round the gardens.* ▶ Also ADV *He strolled leisurely away from the bar.*

lemming /lɛmɪŋ/ **lemmings**
1 NC A **lemming** is an animal that looks like a large rat with thick fur. When migrating in large numbers, lemmings sometimes rush over the edge of cliffs and die.
2 NC If you say that people are acting like **lemmings**, you mean that they are behaving in a self-destructive or suicidal way. *Everybody's following her like lemmings over the precipice.*

lemon /lɛmən/ **lemons**
NCorNU A **lemon** is a yellow citrus fruit with sour juice. *...fruits as ordinary as oranges, lemons and bananas. ...slices of lemon.*

lemonade /lɛmənɛɪd/
1 NU **Lemonade** is a clear, sweet, fizzy drink. *They were given a glass of lemonade.*
2 NU In the United States, **lemonade** is a drink which is made from fresh lemons with water and sugar added. *I packed lunch and a bottle of lemonade.*

lemon curd
NU **Lemon curd** or **lemon cheese** is a thick, sweet yellow substance made of lemons which you can spread on bread or put in tarts. *...a pot of lemon curd.*

lemon sole, lemon soles
NCorNU A **lemon sole** is a flat fish that can be cooked and eaten.

lemur /liːmə/ **lemurs**
NC A **lemur** is an animal that looks like a small monkey and has thick fur, a long snout and a long tail. Lemurs are active at night. *...unique plants and wildlife such as the rare monkeylike lemur.*

lend /lɛnd/ **lends, lending, lent**
1 VOOorVO+to If you **lend** someone money or something that you own, you allow them to have or use it for a period of time. *I had to lend him a pound... She was reading a book I had lent her.*
2 VOOorVO+to When people or organizations such as banks **lend** you money, they give it to you and you agree to pay it back at a future date, often with an extra amount of interest. *The World Bank said it would lend India one-hundred-and-fifty million dollars to help pay for oil imports. ...the Council of Mortgage Lenders, representing the institutions which lend money to homebuyers.* ◆ **lending** NU *The Bank will double its educational lending over the next three years... It is imposing stricter conditions on any future lending.*
3 VOorVO+to If you **lend** your support to a person or group, you support them. *He was there lending advice and support... They are lending their support to a series of workshops.*
4 VOorVO+to If something **lends** a particular quality to something else, it gives it that quality. *...lending the place a festive look... It would lend credibility to her arguments.*
5 V-REFL+to If something **lends** itself to being dealt with or considered in a particular way, it is easy to deal with or consider it in that way. *...problems*

which do not lend themselves to simple solutions.

lender /lɛndə/ **lenders**
NC A **lender** is a person or an institution that lends money to people. *They were considered a good risk by lenders. ...loans made by banks and other lenders.*

lending library, lending libraries
NC A **lending library** is a library which allows people to take books away with them for a period of time, rather than read them inside the library. *...a lending library containing one thousand five hundred books and documents in the Vietnamese language.*

lending rate, lending rates
NC The **lending rate** is the rate of interest that you have to pay when you are repaying a loan. *...the 12 per cent minimum lending rate... Bank lending rates have to rise.*

length /lɛŋθ/ **lengths**
1 NCorNU The **length** of something is the amount that it measures from one end to the other. *It grows to a length of three or four metres... The snake was a metre and a half in length... People are presented with lines of different lengths.*
2 NUorNC The **length** of a book, film, or speech is the amount of writing or material that is contained in it. *It is of sufficient length for it to be divided into chapters... It is a film which should appeal to a general audience, despite its length. ...a length of text.*
3 NCorNU The **length** of an event, activity, or situation is the time it lasts. *There is no time limit for the length of the inquiry... He has raised the possibility of a reduction in the length of military service.*
4 NU The **length** of something is also its quality of being long. *...given the length and bitterness of the war... The defendants were stunned by the length of the sentences.*
5 NC In horse or boat racing, a **length** is the distance from the front to the back of the horse or boat, and is used as a unit of measurement. *Another French colt, Squill, was half a length behind in third place... Oxford beat Cambridge by two and a half lengths in the 135th University Boat Race.*
6 NC+SUPP A **length** of wood, string, cloth, or other material is a piece of it. *...a length of rope. ...a short length of steel chain.*
7 N SING If something happens or exists along the **length** of something, it happens or exists for the whole way along it. *They travelled the length of the island... It is now being fought out across the length and breadth of this vast country.*
8 NC If you swim a **length** in a swimming pool, you swim from one end to the other.
● **Length** is used in these phrases. ● If someone does something **at length**, they do it after a long time; a literary expression. *There was another silence. At length Claire said, 'You mean you're not going?'*
● You can also use **at length** to refer to the fact that someone does something in great detail or for a long time; a formal expression. *She spoke at unusual length about the enormous pressures and demands on all modern parents.* ● If someone **goes to great lengths** to achieve something, they try very hard and perhaps do extreme things in order to achieve it. *They are going to go to great lengths to find out what the terms of the contract are... She was visibly shocked by the lengths to which reporters went.*

lengthen /lɛŋθən/ **lengthens, lengthening, lengthened**
V-ERG When something **lengthens** or is **lengthened**, it becomes longer. *The waiting lists are lengthening... The money has been spent on lengthening the runway.*

lengthways /lɛŋθweɪz/
ADV **Lengthways** or **lengthwise** means in a direction or position along the length of something. *The marrow is sliced in half lengthways... The blanket had to be folded lengthways.*

lengthy /lɛŋθi/
ADJ Something that is **lengthy** lasts for a long time. *...lengthy explanations... Hundreds of holiday-makers are facing lengthy delays at the port of Dover.*

leniency /liːniənsi/
NU **Leniency** is a lenient attitude or lenient behaviour. *...pleading for leniency... She was grateful for his leniency.*

lenient /líːniənt/
ADJ When someone in authority is **lenient**, they are not as strict or as severe as expected. *Fines were low and magistrates often too lenient. Those who co-operated can expect lenient treatment.* ◆ **leniently** ADV *Offenders had been treated leniently by the judge.*

lens /lɛnz/ **lenses**
NC A **lens** is a thin, curved piece of glass or plastic which is part of something such as a camera, telescope, or pair of glasses. You look through a lens in order to see things larger, smaller, or more clearly. *...a camera with a zoom lens. ...light-frame spectacles with non-glare lenses.*

lent /lɛnt/
1 **Lent** is the past tense and past participle of **lend**.
2 NU In the Christian calendar, **Lent** is the period of forty days before Easter, during which some Christians give up doing something that they enjoy. *Today is Ash Wednesday, the beginning of Lent.*

lentil /lɛntl/ **lentils**
NC **Lentils** are dried seeds taken from a particular plant which are cooked and eaten. *She has a two week supply of flour, six pounds of chickpeas and two of lentils.*

leonine /líːənaɪn/
ADJ ATTRIB **Leonine** means like a lion, and is used especially to describe men with a lot of hair on their head, or with big beards; a literary word. *...her husband's leonine head. ...his leonine beard.*

leopard /lɛpəd/ **leopards**
NC A **leopard** is a type of large, wild cat. Leopards have yellow fur and black spots, and live in Africa and Asia. *What about this leopard skin jacket?*

leotard /líːətɑːd/ **leotards**
NC A **leotard** is a tight-fitting piece of clothing, covering the body but not the legs, that some people wear when they practise dancing or do exercises. *...with her bright green leotard on.*

leper /lɛpə/ **lepers**
1 NC A **leper** is a person who has leprosy. *...a leper hospital.*
2 NC If you refer to someone as a **leper**, you mean that people in their community avoid them because they have done something that has shocked or offended people. *South Africa has been a sporting leper in the world because of its apartheid policies.*

leprosy /lɛprəsi/
NU **Leprosy** is a serious infectious disease that damages people's flesh. *Six leprosy sufferers were given doses of the drug DFS over a period of six months.*

Les Abymes /leɪz æbiːm/
Les Abymes is the largest city in Guadeloupe. Population: 63,000 (1990).

lesbian /lɛzbiən/ **lesbians**
NC A **lesbian** is a woman who is sexually attracted to women. *...two periodicals for lesbians.* ▶ Also ADJ *It's about time you started working with our community on the human rights of lesbian and gay people.*

lesbianism /lɛzbiənɪzəm/
NU **Lesbianism** refers to sexual relationships between women or the preference that a woman shows for sexual relationships with women. *There is no law relating to lesbianism.*

lesion /líːʒn/ **lesions**
NC A **lesion** is an injury or wound to someone's body; a medical term. *Most of the lesions were superficial.*

Lesotho /ləsúːtuː/
The **Kingdom of Lesotho** is a country in southern Africa. It was a British colony, known as Basutoland, from the 19th century until independence in 1966. Major General Justin Lekhanya came to power in 1986 and banned all political activity. King Letsie III succeeded his father, who went into exile, in 1990. Colonel Elias Phisoana Ramaema became Chairman of the Military Council in 1991 and promised multi-party elections by 1992. Lesotho is a member of the Commonwealth and the Organization of African Unity. It exports clothing, footwear, and wool. Tourism is an important industry. Many Basotho work in South Africa. ◆ **Mosotho** /məsúːtuː/ N SING **Basotho** /bəsúːtuː/

N PL **Lesothan** /ləsúːtən/ N, ADJ
▪ *per capita GNP:* US$410 ▪ *religion:* Christianity, animism ▪ *language:* Sesotho and English (official) ▪ *currency:* loti ▪ *capital:* Maseru ▪ *population:* 2 million (1989) ▪ *size:* 30,355 square kilometres.

less /lɛs/
1 QUANT or DET **Less** means not as much in amount or degree as before or as something else. *With practice it becomes less of an effort... We had less than three miles to go... Sixty per cent of them are aged 20 or less... A shower uses less water than a bath.*
2 SUBMOD **Less** also means not having as much of a quality as before or as something else. *From this time on, I felt less guilty... Fires occurred less frequently outside this area. ...the less developed countries.*
3 ADV If you do something **less** than before or **less** than someone else, you do it to a smaller extent or not as often. *You probably use them less than I do... The more I hear about him, the less I like him.*
4 PREP You can also use **less** to show that the second of two numbers or amounts is subtracted from the first number or amount. *He earns £200 a week, less tax.*
5 See also **lesser**.
● **Less** is used in these phrases. ● You use **less and less** to say that something is becoming smaller all the time in degree or amount. *He found them less and less interesting... They had less and less to talk about.* ● You use **less than** to say that something does not have a particular quality. For example, something that is less than perfect is not perfect. *It would have been less than fair.* ● You can use **no less** as an emphatic way of expressing surprise or admiration at the importance of someone or something. *...the President of the United States, no less.* ● You can use **no less than** before an amount to indicate that you think the amount is surprisingly large. *By 1880, there were no less than fifty-six coal mines. ...no less than 40 per cent of the material.* ● **more or less:** see **more**.

-less /-ləs/
SUFFIX **-less** is added to nouns to form adjectives that indicate that someone or something does not have the thing that the noun refers to. *...landless peasants. ...meaningless sounds.*

lessen /lɛsn/ **lessens, lessening, lessened**
V-ERG If something **lessens** or is **lessened**, it becomes smaller in amount or degree. *Their financial hardship has lessened... Separating the sick from the healthy lessens the risk of infection.* ◆ **lessening** NU+SUPP *...a lessening of his power.*

lesser /lɛsə/
1 ADJ **Lesser** is used to indicate that something is smaller in degree, importance, or amount than another thing that is mentioned. *These customs are common in Czechoslovakia and to a lesser extent in Hungary and Romania. ...charges of attempted murder and lesser crimes.*
2 The **lesser of two evils** or the **lesser evil:** see **evil**.

lesson /lɛsn/ **lessons**
1 NC A **lesson** is a short period of time during which people are taught something. *He had begun flying lessons. ...a history lesson in Russian politics.*
2 NC If an experience teaches you a **lesson**, it makes you realize the truth or realize what should be done. *The lesson for other British companies is that no firm is safe from take-over... What lessons can be learnt from this achievement? ...the lessons of history.*
3 If you **teach** someone a **lesson**, you punish them for something they have done, so that they do not do it again. *They decided to teach him a lesson.*

lest /lɛst/
CONJ If you do something **lest** something unpleasant should happen, you do it to try to prevent the unpleasant thing from happening; a literary word. *I had to grab the iron rail at my side lest I slipped off.*

let /lɛt/ **lets, letting.** The form **let** is used in the present tense and is also the past tense and past participle of the verb.
1 VO If you **let** something happen, you allow it to happen, without doing anything to stop it. *People here sit back and let everyone else do the work... Don't let it go to waste.*

2 VO If you **let** someone do something, you give them your permission to do it. *My parents wouldn't let me go out with boys... If you just open your mouth and let me look inside.*
3 VOA If you **let** someone in, out, or through, you make it possible for them to go there. *'I rang the bell,' Rudolph said, 'and your friend let me in.'... I asked him to stop the car and let me out.*
4 You use **let** when you are making a suggestion, recommendation, or request. *Here, let me try!*
5 You use **let's** or **let us** when you are making a suggestion. *Let's go... Let us hope that's the case.*
6 VO If you **let** your house or land to someone, you allow them to use it in exchange for regular payments. *Part of the nurses' accommodation next door would be let to tourists.*
● **Let** is used in these phrases. ● If you **let go** of someone or something, you stop holding them. *Let go of me.* ● If you say that something is not the case, **let alone** something else, you mean that since the first thing is not the case, the second thing cannot be, because it is more difficult, complicated, or unusual. *...without the knowledge—let alone the consent—of the government... Letters which arrived last October were only opened—let alone dealt with—in December.*
let down PHRASAL VERB **1** If you **let** someone **down**, you disappoint them, usually by not doing something that you said you would do. *The six member states feel badly let down by the United States.* **2** If you **let down** something filled with air, such as a tyre, you allow air to escape from it. *When I came down this morning all my tyres had been let down.*
let in PHRASAL VERB If something **lets in** water or air, it has a hole or crack which allows the water or air to get into it. *My old boots had been letting in water.*
let in for PHRASAL VERB If you wonder what you have **let** yourself **in for**, you think that you may be getting involved in something difficult or unpleasant; an informal expression. *What have we let ourselves in for?*
let in on or **let into** PHRASAL VERB If you **let** someone **in on** a secret or **let** someone **into** a secret, you tell it to them. *Congress hasn't been let in on it.*
let off PHRASAL VERB **1** If you **let** someone **off** a duty or task, you say that they do not have to do it. *We have been let off our homework.* **2** If you **let** someone **off**, you give them no punishment, or a less severe punishment than they expect. *There must be at least a chance that he will be let off... The magistrates let him off with a fine of eighty pounds.* **3** If you **let off** a gun or a bomb, you fire it or cause it to explode. *The boy let off a fire extinguisher in the house... The guerrillas have let off four car bombs.*
let on PHRASAL VERB If you do not **let on** about something secret, you do not tell anyone about it. *Don't let on we went to that dance.*
let out PHRASAL VERB **1** If you **let out** something such as water, air, or breath, you allow it to flow out freely. *He let the water out and refilled the bath.* **2** If you **let out** a particular sound, you make that sound. *Monclair let out a low whistle.*
let up PHRASAL VERB If something **lets up**, it stops or becomes less. *Day followed day and still the heat did not let up.*
letdown /lɛtdaʊn/ **letdowns**
NC If you say that something is a **letdown**, you mean that it is disappointing; an informal word. *For the visitor expecting something special, this is rather a letdown. His decision has been a major let down for many blacks in this city.*
lethal /liːθl/
ADJ Something that is **lethal** can kill people or animals. *The chemical is lethal to rats but safe for cattle. ...a lethal weapon.*
lethargic /ləθɑːdʒɪk/
ADJ If you are **lethargic**, you have no energy or enthusiasm. *The more sleep you lose, the less you want to do, the more lethargic you become... Everyone has lost weight and children are skinny and lethargic.*
lethargy /lɛθədʒi/
NU **Lethargy** is a condition in which you have no energy or enthusiasm; a formal word. *He was*

determined to shake them out of their lethargy.
let's /lɛts/
Let's is the usual spoken form of 'let us'.
Letsie III, King of Lesotho /letsiːə/
Letsie III became King of Lesotho in 1990, when his father, King Moshoeshoe II, was forced to abdicate and went into exile. Born: 1963.
letter /lɛtə/ **letters**
1 NC When you write a **letter**, you write a message on paper and send it to someone, usually through the post. *Peter received a letter from his wife... They informed Victor by letter... They published an open letter asking the help of Mrs Thatcher.*
2 NC. **Letters** are also written symbols which represent the sounds of a language. *Think of a name of an animal starting with the letter F.*
letter-bomb, letter-bombs
NC A **letter-bomb** is a small bomb which is disguised as a letter and sent to someone through the post. *Offices are asked to be on the look-out for letter-bombs in the weeks before Christmas.*
letterbox /lɛtəbɒks/ **letterboxes**
1 NC A **letterbox** is a rectangular hole in a door through which letters are delivered. *It was pushed through the letterbox of an estate agents.*
2 NC A **letterbox** is also the same as a **post-box**.
lettered /lɛtəd/
ADJ Something that is **lettered** is covered or decorated with letters or words. *...a crudely lettered banner.*
letterhead /lɛtəhɛd/ **letterheads**
NC A **letterhead** is the name and address of a person, company, or organization which is printed at the top of their writing paper. *When he gave her the envelope, she immediately recognized the letterhead.*
lettering /lɛtərɪŋ/
NU+SUPP **Lettering** is writing, especially when you are describing the type of letters used. *Underneath it, in smaller lettering, was a name.*
lettuce /lɛtɪs/ **lettuces**
NCorNU A **lettuce** is a plant with large green leaves that you eat in salads. *The cold has caused major damage to the citrus, lettuce and avocado crops.*
let-up, let-ups
NUorNC If there is a **let-up** of something unpleasant, there is a reduction in the intensity of it. *There was a noticeable let-up of violence... There is no sign yet of any let-up.*
leukaemia /luːkiːmiə/; also spelt **leukemia**.
NU **Leukaemia** is a serious illness which affects the blood. *Results of the first trials on people suffering from leukaemia have been remarkable.*
level /lɛvl/ **levels, levelling, levelled**; spelt **leveling, leveled** in American English.
1 NC+SUPP A **level** is a point on a scale, for example a scale of amount, importance, or difficulty. *Mammals maintain their body temperature at a constant level... Interest rates will remain at their present level for some time to come... Inflation has risen to ten point nine percent—its highest level for eight years.*
2 NC+SUPP A **level** is also a particular point or stage in a political or business hierarchy or system. *A similar process is also taking place on the diplomatic level. ...to try and resolve the issue at a local level... The meeting will be at ministerial level.*
3 N SING The **level** of a lake or river, or the **level** of a liquid in a container, is the height of its surface. *In 1987 the lake level began to go down quite dramatically... Check the oil level and tyre pressure of your car regularly.* ● See also **sea level**.
4 N SING+SUPP If one thing is at the **level** of another thing, it is at the same height. *He had a pile of books which reached to the level of his chin.*
5 ADJ PRED If one thing is **level** with another thing, it is at the same height. *He had his hands in front of him, level with his chest.*
6 ADJ PRED If something such as trade stays **level** with something else, it gets larger or smaller at the same rate. *Food production is going to keep level with population growth.*
7 ADV If you are going somewhere and you draw **level** with someone, you get closer to them until you are at their side. *Coming towards me was a man and when*

we drew level, I smiled.
8 ADJ Something that is **level** is completely flat, with no part higher than any other. *The floor is quite level... Improved safety is now possible with a convertible platform that can be used on stairs or level ground.*
9 VO If you **level** an area of land, you make it flat. *...gardeners digging and levelling the ground.*
10 VO If people **level** something such as a building or a wood, they knock it down completely so that there is nothing left. *Specially built tractors levelled more than 1,000 acres of forest... It looks as if it's been levelled by a powerful bomb.*
11 VO If you **level** a criticism or accusation at or against someone, you criticize or accuse them. *...criticisms he has levelled against gangsters. ...a series of drug charges that have been levelled against him.*
12 See also **A level, O level.**
level off PHRASAL VERB 1 If something that has been increasing or decreasing **levels off**, it stops increasing or decreasing. *Economic growth was starting to level off.* 2 When an aircraft **levels off** it travels horizontally after it has been travelling upwards or downwards. *The plane levelled off at 35,000 feet.*
level out PHRASAL VERB **Level out** means the same as **level off.**
level crossing, level crossings
NC A **level crossing** is a place where a railway line crosses a road at the same level. *A bus hit an express train this afternoon on a level crossing.*
level-headed
ADJ If you are **level-headed**, you act calmly in difficult situations. *Level-headed and determined, he guided the team to the championship.*
lever /líːvə/ **levers**
1 NC A **lever** is a handle or bar that you pull or push to operate a piece of machinery. *...the gear lever.*
2 NC A **lever** is also a bar, one end of which is placed under a heavy object so that when you press down on the other end you can move the object. *...conveyor belts and levers.*
3 NC+SUPP A **lever** is also something that you can use as a means of getting someone to do something. *Industrial action may be threatened as a political lever... The army is the only effective lever still left in the hands of the Federal leadership.*
leverage /líːvərɪdʒ/
1 NU **Leverage** is the ability to influence people. *Relatively small groups can exert immense political leverage... The United States did have considerable economic leverage.*
2 NU **Leverage** is also the force that is applied to an object when a lever is used. *They use their weight as leverage in the same way that humans do in wrestling.*
leviathan /ləváɪəθən/ **leviathans**
NC A **leviathan** is something which is extremely large and difficult to control, and which you find rather frightening; a literary word. *...the leviathan of the nation-state.*
levitate /lévɪteɪt/ **levitates, levitating, levitated**
VO If someone **levitates** something, they make it rise into the air without any visible support. Some people believe that they can do this through meditation or magic. *Their trains are levitated by helium-cooled superconducting magnets in the track.* ◆ **levitation** /lévɪteɪʃn/ NU *The huge form in the chair rose as if by levitation.*
levity /lévɪti/
NU **Levity** is behaviour in which someone treats serious matters in a light-hearted way; a formal word. *I've been appalled by the levity with which some politicians discuss this issue.*
levy /lévi/ **levies, levying, levied**
1 NC A **levy** is a sum of money that you pay in tax. *Among the new taxes will be a business petroleum levy, taxing all oil products.*
2 VO When a government or organization **levies** a tax, it demands it from people. *He has it within his power to set prices and levy taxes... It has levied fines totaling more than $72,000.*

lewd /ljʊːd/
ADJ Someone whose behaviour is **lewd** is interested in sex in a crude and unpleasant way. *She had a look almost of lewd abandon. ...a lewd joke.* ◆ **lewdness** NU *She winked with a lewdness that would have shocked Mrs Townsend.*
lexical /léksɪkl/
ADJ **Lexical** means concerning the words or vocabulary of a language; a technical term in linguistics.
lexicographer /léksɪkɒgrəfə/ **lexicographers**
NC A **lexicographer** is someone whose job is to write and edit dictionaries. *Lexicographers are daily discovering new facts about words.*
lexicography /léksɪkɒgrəfi/
NU **Lexicography** is the activity or profession of writing and editing dictionaries. *...the long history of lexicography.*
lexicon /léksɪkən/ **lexicons**
1 N SING If you talk about a particular **lexicon**, you are referring to all the acceptable ideas or principles associated with a particular group or organization. *'Revisionist' is a strong word in the communist lexicon... For them it seems the word 'compromise' is not in the lexicon.*
2 NC A **lexicon** is an alphabetical list of words of a language or of a particular subject.
3 NC A **lexicon** is also a dictionary, especially of a very old language such as Greek or Hebrew; an old-fashioned use.
liability /láɪəbɪləti/ **liabilities**
1 NC If someone or something is a **liability**, they cause a lot of problems or embarrassment. *My car's a real liability... The president finally decided he was more of a liability than an asset.*
2 NC A company's **liabilities** are the money that it owes; a technical use. *The company has had to undertake heavy liabilities.*
3 NU If you have **liability** for a debt or accident, you are legally responsible for it; a legal use. *...accept liability for damage caused by the war.*
liable /láɪəbl/
1 ADJ PRED+*to*-INF Something that is **liable** to happen is very likely to happen. *The play is liable to give offence to many people.*
2 ADJ PRED+*to* If people or things are **liable** to something, they are likely to experience it; a formal use. *I was liable to sea-sickness.*
3 ADJ PRED If you are **liable** for a debt or accident, you are legally responsible for it. *It is liable for about a billion dollars of tickets.*
4 ADJ PRED If you are **liable** for punishment by the authorities, you may be punished for something you have done. *She becomes liable for deportation back to Vietnam. ...a law to make them liable for prosecution.*
liaise /liéɪz/ **liaises, liaising, liaised**
V-RECIP When organizations or people **liaise**, they work together and keep each other informed. *Members can help by liaising with the press... Police forces are liaising.*
liaison /liéɪzn, liéɪzɒ̃/ **liaisons**
1 NU **Liaison** is co-operation and communication between different organizations or between different sections of an organization. *...better liaison between the health and social services.*
2 NC A **liaison** is a sexual relationship; used in formal English showing disapproval. *...his seven-year liaison with the Viennese prostitute.*
liar /láɪə/ **liars**
NC A **liar** is someone who tells lies. *I think the man is a coward and a liar. ...compulsive liars.*
lib /lɪb/
1 NU **Lib** is an abbreviation for 'liberation'. It is used in the names of some political movements that are concerned with freeing people from governments or traditional ideas which the members believe to be oppressive. *I don't believe in women's lib and all that.*
2 See **ad-lib.**
libation /laɪbéɪʃn/ **libations**
NC A **libation** was a liquid such as wine which was poured as an offering to the gods in ancient Greece and Rome; a literary word. *...a libation to the gods.*

libel /ˈlaɪbl/ **libels, libelling, libelled;** spelt **libeling, libeled** in American English.
1 NU or NC **Libel** is something in writing which wrongly accuses someone of something, and which is therefore against the law. *Hinds brought an action for libel against him... This was a gigantic libel.*
2 VO To **libel** someone means to write or print something in a book or newspaper which wrongly damages that person's reputation and is therefore against the law. *A district court ruled that the newspaper had libelled the President... The newspaper has paid substantial damages for libelling him last September.*

libellous /ˈlaɪbələs/; spelt **libelous** in American English.
ADJ If something that is written is **libellous**, it wrongly accuses someone of something, and is therefore against the law. *The police say that the film could be criminally libellous... Mr Nair has denied he made libellous remarks about Mr Lee in media interviews.*

liberal /ˈlɪbərəl/ **liberals**
1 ADJ Someone who is **liberal** is tolerant of different behaviour or opinions. *My school was traditional, but more liberal than other public schools. ...a liberal democracy.* ▸ Also NC *...a pair of enlightened liberals.*
2 ADJ **Liberal** also means giving, using, or taking a lot of something. *Could any man make a more liberal offer?* ◆ **liberally** ADV *Tim helped himself liberally to some more wine.*
3 NC You can also use **Liberal** to refer to someone who belongs to any political party called the Liberals. *The Liberals and Conservatives might agree that they're frustrated, but they don't agree on the cause of that frustration. The party still holds less than a third of the seats held by the Liberals.*

Liberal Democrat, Liberal Democrats
N PROP or NC The **Liberal Democrats** are the third largest party in the United Kingdom and the main centre party. The party was formed from a merger of the Liberal Party and the majority of the Social Democratic Party in 1988. It believes in reforming the constitution and establishing proportional representation for British elections. *Mr Ashdown said the Liberal Democrats had rediscovered the art of winning. The Prime Minister's remarks came as the Liberal Democrat party began its annual conference in Bournemouth.*

liberalism /ˈlɪbərəlɪzəm/
NU **Liberalism** is the belief that people should have a lot of political and individual freedom. *...the chance to put liberalism into practice... Massachusetts has a reputation for liberalism.*

liberalize /ˈlɪbərəlaɪz/ **liberalizes, liberalizing, liberalized;** also spelt **liberalise.**
VO When a country **liberalizes** its laws or its attitudes, it makes them less strict and allows people more freedom. *There was a move to liberalize the state abortion laws... In January, the Soviet government is expected to liberalize foreign travel for its citizens.* ◆ **liberalization** /ˌlɪbərəlaɪˈzeɪʃn/ NU *He called for the liberalization of the laws relating to immigration.*

Liberal Party
N PROP In Britain, the **Liberal Party** was a political party which believed in limited controls on industry, the provision of welfare services, and more local government and individual freedom. 'Liberal Party' is also used to refer to similar parties in some other countries. *His party is trailing 17 points behind the opposition Liberal Party in the opinion polls... the leader of the Liberal Party was outed.*

liberate /ˈlɪbəreɪt/ **liberates, liberating, liberated;** a formal word.
1 VO To **liberate** a place means to free it from the control of another country, area, or group of people. *President Habré has vowed to liberate the Aozou Strip from Libyan control... Iraq says its forces have completely liberated the town of Shalamcheh on the southern war front.* ◆ **liberation** /ˌlɪbəˈreɪʃn/ NU *... the liberation of Jerusalem by the Crusaders in the 11th century.*
2 VO To **liberate** people means to free them from

captivity or from an unpleasant situation. *The crowd stormed the jail and liberated the three men... He claimed that socialism alone could liberate black people... Many of the passengers liberated from the Kuwaiti Airways Boeing 747 are expected to fly home today.* ◆ **liberation** NU *....the kidnappers' conditions for the liberation of their captives.*
3 See also **liberation.**

liberated /ˈlɪbəreɪtɪd/
1 ADJ People who are **liberated** behave in a less restricted way than is traditional in their society. *Today's liberated women still seem interested in the qualities that would have appealed to their grandmothers.*
2 ADJ A **liberated** area or country is one which has been freed from the control of another country or group of people. *They have failed to produce any real achievements, such as gaining liberated territory. ...an attempt to eliminate Tito's small liberated state centred in South East Bosnia... In the words of the jubilant villagers, this is now a liberated zone.*

liberation /ˌlɪbəˈreɪʃn/
1 NU **Liberation** is used in the names of some political movements that are concerned with freeing people from governments or traditional ideas which the members of the movements believe to be oppressive. *...an organisation called the Students' Liberation Front.*
2 See also **liberate.**

liberation theology
NU **Liberation theology** is a belief based on a radical interpretation of the Scriptures which says that social conditions should be changed by engaging in active politics in oppressive and exploitative countries and regimes. *...the emergence of political priests advancing liberation theology... Europe has to learn from Latin America, where new ideas are coming from the liberation theology movement.*

liberator /ˈlɪbəreɪtə/ **liberators**
NC A **liberator** is someone who frees people from a system, situation, or set of ideas that restricts them in some way; a formal word. *...Joan of Arc, the liberator of her people... Flags were being prepared to welcome the liberators.*

Liberia /laɪˈbɪəriə/
The **Republic of Liberia** is a country in western Africa. The country was partly settled by freed American slaves and a republic was declared in 1847. Samuel Doe came to power in a coup in 1980. Civil war broke out in 1989. When the government of Samuel Doe collapsed and Doe was killed in 1990, Dr Amos Sawyer, of the Liberian People's Party (LPP), became interim President. Liberia is a member of the Organization of African Unity. It exports iron ore, rubber, and coffee. Shipping is an important industry. The civil war has severely disrupted the economy.
◆ **Liberian** /laɪˈɪəriən/ N, ADJ
▪ *per capita GNP:* US$450 ▪ *religion:* Christianity, animism, Islam ▪ *language:* English (official)
▪ *currency:* dollar ▪ *capital:* Monrovia ▪ *population:* 3 million (1989) ▪ *size:* 97,754 square kilometres.

libertarian /ˌlɪbəˈteəriən/ **libertarians**
NC A **libertarian** is someone who believes that people should be free to think and behave as they want to; a formal word. *Education is a topic in which libertarians have taken a close interest.* ▸ Also ADJ *Smith's name has come to be identified with what amounts to a new libertarian ideology.*

libertine /ˈlɪbətiːn/ **libertines**
NC A **libertine** is a person who is immoral and unscrupulous in their sexual activities; an old-fashioned word. *I had convinced her that he was a notorious libertine. ...libertine playboys.*

liberty /ˈlɪbəti/ **liberties;** a formal word.
1 NU or N PL **Liberty** is the freedom to choose how you want to live, without interference from others. *The President has made a strong plea for greater individual liberty in eastern Europe... The debate about the protection of liberties will continue... He compared the victims to his fellow countrymen who'd been forced to choose between death and liberty.* ● See also **civil liberty.**

2 NU **Liberty** is the freedom to go wherever you want. ...*that fundamental aspect of imprisonment, the loss of liberty.* ● **Liberty** is used in these phrases. ● A criminal who is **at liberty** has not yet been caught, or has escaped from prison. *The hijackers are at liberty, and in a position to launch another attack.* ● If you are **not at liberty** to do something, you are not allowed to do it. *He said he was not at liberty to reveal the content of his private conversations with the President.*

libidinous /lɪbɪdɪnəs/
ADJ **Libidinous** people have strong sexual feelings and show them in their behaviour; a literary word. *She behaved in a libidinous way with the men. ...the libidinous spark in Willie's eye.*

libido /lɪbiːdəʊ/ **libidos**
NCorNU Your **libido** is the part of your personality that is considered to cause your sexual desires; a technical term. *...a reaction against repression of the libido.*

librarian /laɪbreəriən/ **librarians**
NC A **librarian** is a person who is in charge of a library or who has been trained to do responsible work in a library. *...the assistant librarian of the college.*

library /laɪbrəri, laɪbri/ **libraries**
1 NC A **library** is a building where books and newspapers are kept for people to read. You can borrow books and sometimes records from libraries for a limited period of time. *A list of the one-hundred writers whose books were the most popular in public libraries last year. ...a new extension to the library.*
2 NC A **library** is also a private collection of books or records. *The Linnean Society owns a priceless library.*

librettist /lɪbretɪst/ **librettists**
NC A **librettist** is a person who writes the words that are used in an opera or musical play. *...a fine poet and librettist.*

libretto /lɪbretəʊ/ **librettos** or **libretti**
NC The **libretto** of an opera is the words that are sung in it. *He knew the libretto well, and he admired it.*

Libreville /liːbrəviːl/
Libreville is the capital of Gabon and its largest city. Population: 352,000 (1988).

Libya /lɪbiə/
The Socialist People's Libyan Arab Jamahiriya is a country in northern Africa. It was an Italian colony from 1911 until the Second World War and became independent in 1951. In 1969 Colonel Muammar al-Qaddafi became the leader of Libya and established the Arab Socialist Union (ASU) as the only party. The governments of the United States and Europe have criticized Qaddafi for supporting terrorism worldwide. In 1986 the United States bombed Tripoli and Benghazi in retaliation for terrorist attacks. Libya exports oil. It is a member of OPEC, the Arab League, and the Organization of African Unity. ◆ **Libyan** /lɪbiən/ N, ADJ ▪ *per capita GNP:* US$5,410 ▪ *religion:* Islam (mainly Sunni) ▪ *language:* Arabic ▪ *currency:* dinar ▪ *capital:* Tripoli ▪ *population:* 4 million (1989) ▪ *size:* 1,775,500 square kilometres.

lice /laɪs/
Lice is the plural of **louse**. *DDT killed the lice that carried typhus.*

licence /laɪsns/ **licences**; spelt **license** in American English.
1 NC A **licence** is an official document which gives you permission to do, use, or own something. *The Department of Trade and Industry issued an export licence for the equipment. ...the government's decision to abolish dog licences.*
2 If someone does something **under licence**, they do it by special permission from the authorities. *...a list of items which could only be imported under licence.*
3 See also **off-licence**.

license /laɪsns/ **licenses, licensing, licensed**
VO To **license** a person, organization, or activity means to give official permission for the person or organization to do something or for the activity to happen. *The Royal College examines and licenses surgeons... At present about thirty individuals are licensed to work specific plots of land.* ◆ **licensing** ADJ ATTRIB *...a licensing authority.*

licensed /laɪsnst/
1 ADJ If you are **licensed** to do something, you have official permission from a government or other authority to do it. *These men are licensed to carry firearms. ...a licensed pilot... He had worked for Israeli intelligence and was licensed to carry a gun... The canoe was licensed to carry twenty people.*
2 ADJ If something that you own or use is **licensed**, you have official permission to own it or use it. *The car is licensed and insured. ...a licensed hand gun.*
3 ADJ If a restaurant, hotel, or club is **licensed**, it is allowed to sell alcoholic drinks. *...an increase in the number of off-licences and licensed clubs.*

licensee /laɪsnsiː/ **licensees**
NC A **licensee** is a person who has been given a licence, especially a licence to sell alcoholic drinks. *They were incensed because the licensee was selling alcohol to Aborigines.*

license plate, license plates
NC A vehicle's **license plates** are the signs on the front and back that show its registration number. *...a car with an Israeli license plate.*

licensing hours
N PL **Licensing hours** are the times of the day when a pub is allowed to sell alcoholic drinks. *The delegates backed a motion in support of Sunday trading and the extension of licensing hours.*

licensing laws
N PL **Licensing laws** are the laws which control the sale of alcoholic drinks. *In Scotland the licensing laws were relaxed in 1977.*

licentious /laɪsenʃəs/
ADJ A **licentious** person is very immoral, especially in their sexual behaviour; a formal word. *They had become wicked, licentious and corrupt.*

lichee /laɪtʃiː/. See **lychee**.

lichen /laɪkən/ **lichens**
N MASS **Lichen** is a cluster of tiny plants that looks like moss and grows on rocks, trees, and walls. *...a stone stairway covered with lichen. ...mosses and lichens.*

lick /lɪk/ **licks, licking, licked**
1 VO When you **lick** something, you move your tongue across its surface. *He licked the last of the egg off his knife... The cat was licking its paw... The dog was happy, jumping up and down, wagging his tail and licking my hand.* ▶ Also NC *...a few licks and nibbles.*
2 VO When flames **lick** something, they touch it very lightly and briefly; a literary use. *There were a few last flames licking the city.*
3 NC A **lick** is a short musical phrase, played on one instrument; an informal use. *Listen to that album, and you'll hear every lick the band ever played in those songs... Licks are part of any good blues guitarist's repertoire.*
● **Lick** is used in these phrases. ● If you **lick your lips**, you move your tongue across your lips, as you think eagerly about something. *She looked at the plate and licked her lips.* ● If you say that someone is **licking their wounds**, you mean that they are recovering after being defeated or humiliated. *He said it was time schools stopped licking their wounds and started trumpeting their success... Two weary countries sat back to lick the wounds of death, debt and destruction.*

licking /lɪkɪŋ/ **lickings**; an informal word.
1 NC If you take a **licking**, you are heavily defeated in a fight, battle, or competition. *The team got another licking on Saturday... The general took a sound licking and lost Nazareth.*
2 NC A **licking** is a punishment which involves beating someone several times; an old-fashioned use. *You'll get a good licking if your father catches you.*

licorice /lɪkərɪʃ/. See **liquorice**.

lid /lɪd/ **lids**
1 NC The **lid** of a container is the top which you open to reach inside it. *She was opening and closing the lid of her tin.*
2 NC Your **lids** are the same as your **eyelids**. *She looked round from under half-closed lids.*

lido /liːdəʊ/ **lidos**
NC A **lido** is an outdoor swimming pool, or a part of a beach, which is used for swimming, sunbathing, or water sports. *Porter wrote songs about people who*

were at the lido, or on ocean-going liners.

lie /laɪ/. The forms **lie**, **lies**, **lying**, **lay**, **lain** are used for the verb in paragraphs 1 to 6 and for the phrasal verbs. The forms **lie**, **lies**, **lying**, **lied** are used for the verb in paragraph 7. **Lies** is also the plural form of the noun.

1 V A or V C If you **are lying** somewhere, you are in a horizontal position and are not standing or sitting. *There were two wounded soldiers lying among the dead... She lay in the sun... I lay there trying to remember what he looked like.*

2 V A or V C If an object **lies** in a particular place, it is in a flat position in that place. *Several dictionaries lay on a shelf. ...the folder lying open before him... The coffin lay undisturbed for centuries... The bomb lay buried until its discovery early this year.*

3 V A or V C If a place **lies** in a particular position, it is situated there. *The bridge lies beyond the docks... Frankfurt lay only 100 kilometres from the demarcation line... The worst hit areas are coastal areas, as Bangladesh is low-lying.*

4 V A If you say that the cause of something or the solution to a problem **lies** somewhere, you are indicating what the cause or the solution is. *Its attraction lay in its simplicity... The causes of this lie deep in the history of society... This break should help us to see where our true interests lie.*

5 V A If something **lies** ahead, it is going to happen in the future. *Endless hours of pleasure lie before you. ...an unwelcome foretaste of what lay in store.*

6 V C or V A You can use **lie** to say what position someone is in during a competition. For example, if they **are lying** third, they are third at the moment. *Tomba is currently lying 10th overall after a poor start... She was lying in eighth position after the first run.*

7 V or V-QUOTE If someone is **lying**, they are saying something which they know is untrue. *There are financial considerations here, and anyone who tells you otherwise is lying... I would be lying if I did not say I have considerable money in my account, I do... You lied to me... 'Certainly not,' I lied.*

8 N C A **lie** is something that someone says which they know is untrue. *You're telling lies now... This myth is a lie, and it's always been a lie... His confession is a lie.*

9 See also **lying**.

lie about PHRASAL VERB **1** If you **lie about** or **lie around**, you spend your time relaxing and being lazy. *They spent the day lying about in their rooms... We lay around smoking.* **2** If things are left **lying about** or **lying around**, they are left somewhere in an untidy way. *The bottles were left lying around overnight... an old boot which someone had left lying about.*

lie ahead PHRASAL VERB If an event or situation **lies ahead**, it is likely to happen in the future. *He warned that setbacks and sacrifices lie ahead... I am confident that our nation will emerge stronger and more united to face the challenges and opportunities that lie ahead.*

lie around PHRASAL VERB See **lie about**.

lie behind PHRASAL VERB The thing that **lies behind** a situation or event is the reason or explanation for it. *Alan Lipke of the BBC examines what lies behind the offer... We've been hoping the problem lying behind it could be solved peacefully.*

lie down PHRASAL VERB **1** When you **lie down**, you move into a horizontal position, usually in order to rest. *He lay down on the couch... She twisted around so that she could lie down alongside me.* **2** If you **take** unfair treatment **lying down**, you accept it without complaining or resisting; an informal expression. *She was never one to take bullying lying down... Each time the American people and government lie down and beg to free the hostages, we are sending a signal of weakness to other governments.*

lie with PHRASAL VERB If the responsibility for something **lies with** you, it is your responsibility; a formal expression. *Are you saying that the fault generally lies with the management?... The responsibility will always lie with the person carrying the gun... The greater the number of hostages, the greater the advantage lying with the hi-jackers.*

Liechtenstein /lɪxtənʃtaɪn/

The **Principality of Liechtenstein** is a country in central Europe. It declared its neutrality in 1868 and since 1919 Switzerland has been responsible for its foreign affairs. Hans Adam II succeeded as Prince at the death of his father, Franz Josef II, in 1989. Hans Brunhart, of the Patriotic Union (VU), became Head of Government in 1978. Liechtenstein exports dental products, machinery, and stamps. Banking and tourism are important industries. ♦ **Liechtensteiner** /lɪxtənʃtaɪnə/ N **Liechtenstein** /lɪxtənʃtaɪn/ ADJ ▪ *per capita GNP:* approximately US$30,270 ▪ *religion:* Christianity (mainly Roman Catholic) ▪ *language:* German (official) ▪ *currency:* Swiss franc ▪ *capital:* Vaduz ▪ *population:* 29,000 (1990) ▪ *size:* 160 square kilometres.

lie-down

N SING If you have a **lie-down**, you have a short rest, usually lying on a bed.

lie-in

N SING If you have a **lie-in**, you stay in bed later than usual in the morning. *I really need a lie-in as well, I'm up every day at eight.*

lieu /ljuː/

In lieu means instead of something or as a replacement for it; a formal expression. *...proposals to pay teachers overtime or give them time off in lieu for taking part in weekend training... You may offer a dissertation in lieu of part of the final examination.*

Lieut.

Lieut. is a written abbreviation for 'lieutenant' when it is a person's title. *...Lieut. Collings.*

lieutenant /leftenənt, luːtenənt/ **lieutenants**

N C or TITLE A **lieutenant** is a junior officer in the army or navy. *A major and two lieutenants are under military detention... The medal was presented to Lieutenant William Leefe Robinson.*

life /laɪf/ **lives** /laɪvz/

1 N U **Life** is the quality which people, animals, and plants have when they are not dead and which objects and substances do not have. *...her last hours of life... He said he was saddened by the needless loss of life.*

2 N U **Life** is things or groups of things which have the quality of being alive. *Is there life on Jupiter? ...plant life.*

3 N PL You can use **lives** to refer to people who have died or been rescued in an accident or disaster. *The police accept that pure luck saved many lives... The unrest is now in its third week, having claimed several hundred lives... The military operation has cost hundreds of civilian lives.*

4 N C Someone's **life** is their state of being alive, or the period of time during which they are alive. *He nearly lost his life... People spend their lives worrying about money... He spent the rest of his life rejecting the guru status which others had thrust upon him... Many of the victims are said to have been crippled for life.*

5 N U **Life** is also the events and experiences that happen to people. *Life is probably harder for women... I don't know what you want out of life... Garbo is said to have had few love affairs in her private life.*

6 N U If someone is sentenced to **life**, they are sentenced to stay in prison for the rest of their lives. *He sentenced Quinn to life, but did not recommend a minimum sentence... The man serving life for the Brighton bombing has just had his appeal rejected.*

7 N U A person, place, or something such as a book or a film that is full of **life** is full of activity and excitement. *His book is well written and full of life.*

8 N SING The **life** of a machine, object, or substance is the period of time that it lasts for. *Using bleach shortens the life of any fabric.*

● **Life** is used in these phrases. ● If someone or something that has been inactive **comes to life**, they become active again. *Their political movement came to life again.* ● If you **hold on** to something **for dear life**, you hold on very tightly; an informal expression. *I held on to the ledge for dear life.* ● If you **live your own life**, you live in the way that you want to, without interference from other people. *She was 18 after all, entitled to live her own life.* ● If someone **takes a** person's **life**, they kill that person; a formal expression. *On the eve of his conviction, he took his own life.* ● to **risk life and limb:** see limb. ● See also **way of life.**

life-and-death
ADJ ATTRIB A **life-and-death** situation or problem is an extremely serious or dangerous one. *...creatures engaged in a life-and-death struggle... Such courts are far less qualified to make life-and-death decisions.*

life assurance
NU **Life assurance** is the same as **life insurance.**

lifebelt /ˈlaɪfbelt/ lifebelts
NC A **lifebelt** is a large ring used to keep a person afloat in water. *Neither the number of passengers nor the number of lifebelts was counted.*

lifeblood /ˈlaɪfblʌd/
1 N SING+SUPP The **lifeblood** of something is the most important thing that it needs in order to exist, develop, or be successful. *Fast communications are the lifeblood of any successful business... Self-confidence is the lifeblood of real democracy.*
2 N SING A person's **lifeblood** is their blood when it is being considered as the power that keeps them alive; a literary use. *She felt her lifeblood ebb away.*

lifeboat /ˈlaɪfbəʊt/ lifeboats
1 NC A **lifeboat** is a boat which is sent out from a port or harbour to rescue people who are in danger at sea. *Helicopters and lifeboats were involved in a thirteen hour search for two people that had been reported missing.*
2 NC A **lifeboat** is also a small boat which is carried on a ship and which is used if the ship is in danger of sinking. *The ferry's lifeboats were lowered into the water for emergency exercises.*

lifebuoy /ˈlaɪfbɔɪ/ lifebuoys
NC A **lifebuoy** is the same as a **lifebelt.**

life-cycle, life-cycles
NC The **life-cycle** of an animal or plant is the series of changes it passes through from the beginning of its life until its death. *...the life-cycle of the salmon.*

life expectancy, life expectancies
N COR NU The **life expectancy** of an animal or plant is the length of time that they are normally likely to live. *Women have a longer life expectancy than men... Bogota has one of the highest life expectancies of the continent.*

life form, life forms
NC+SUPP A **life form** is any living thing. *Many of the deep-sea life forms feed directly on bacteria.*

lifeguard /ˈlaɪfgɑːd/ lifeguards
NC A **lifeguard** is a person at a beach or swimming pool whose job is to rescue people who are in danger of drowning. *The Princess posed for photographers with six lifeguards on a beach.*

life imprisonment
NU When criminals are sentenced to life **imprisonment**, they are sentenced to stay in prison for the rest of their lives. *If convicted, he faces a maximum sentence of life imprisonment.*

life insurance
NU **Life insurance** is a form of insurance in which you make regular payments to an insurance company. In return, a sum of money is paid to you when you reach a certain age or to your wife, husband, or children when you die. *I always keep my life insurance payments up to date.*

lifejacket /ˈlaɪfdʒækɪt/ lifejackets
NC A **lifejacket** is a sleeveless jacket which keeps you afloat in water. *They were stored under the seats with the lifejackets.*

lifeless /ˈlaɪfləs/
1 ADJ A person or animal that is **lifeless** is dead; a literary use. *...the lifeless body of Lieutenant Dowling.*
2 ADJ You use **lifeless** when you want to emphasize that an object is not a living thing. *...a lifeless chunk of rock.*
3 ADJ A **lifeless** place has nothing living or growing there. *...a time when the earth was completely lifeless.*
4 ADJ You can say that people or things are **lifeless** when you find them dull and unexciting. *...a lifeless voice... The interpretation is predictable in this perfect*

but *lifeless recording... Sean gave one of the most listless and lifeless performances in recent history.*

lifelike /ˈlaɪflaɪk/
ADJ Something that is **lifelike** looks real or alive. *...extremely lifelike computer-controlled robots... It's the upper torso of a dummy which is very lifelike.*

lifeline /ˈlaɪflaɪn/ lifelines
1 NC A **lifeline** is something that is very important in helping people to survive, or in helping an activity to continue. *The household became my lifeline, my only link with the outside world. ...the oil lifeline of Western Europe... As long as these lifelines of aid stay in place, they have little incentive to end the war.*
2 NC A **lifeline** is also a rope which you throw to someone who is in danger of drowning. *Police rescued the girl by throwing lifelines to her over the sea wall.*

lifelong /ˈlaɪflɒŋ/
ADJ ATTRIB **Lifelong** means existing or happening for the whole of a person's life. *...her friend and lifelong companion... He is a lifelong dissident who now stands accused of collaborating with the Communist regime.*

life peer, life peers
NC In Britain, a **life peer** is a person who is given a title such as 'Lord' or 'Lady' which they can use for the rest of their life but which they cannot pass on when they die. *...his first television interview since being created a Life Peer in the New Year's Honours list.*

life preserver, life preservers
NC A **life preserver** is the same as a **lifejacket;** used in American English. *Life preservers were not used on the ferry that sank off Bangladesh.*

lifer /ˈlaɪfə/ lifers
NC A **lifer** is a criminal who has been sent to prison for the rest of his or her life; an informal word. *The prisoners broke out of the lifers' wing after overpowering nine guards.*

life science, life sciences
NC The **life sciences** are sciences such as zoology, botany, and anthropology, which are concerned with human beings, animals, and plants. *This time, the shuttle's mission is dedicated entirely to life sciences.*

life sentence, life sentences
NC When criminals receive a **life sentence,** they are sentenced to stay in prison for the rest of their lives. *He's serving a life sentence after being convicted of spying.*

life-size
ADJ **Life-size** paintings or models are the same size as the person or thing that they represent. *...a life-size statue... They are probably using life-size decoys of weapon systems.*

life-sized
ADJ **Life-sized** means the same as **life-size.**

lifespan /ˈlaɪfspæn/ lifespans
1 NC+SUPP The **lifespan** of a person, animal, or plant is the period of time during which they are alive. *...the human lifespan... Why do all the species on earth seem to have their own allotted lifespan?*
2 NC+SUPP The **lifespan** of a product, organization, or idea is the period of time during which it exists or is used. *This job had a planned lifespan of five years.*

lifestyle /ˈlaɪfstaɪl/ lifestyles
NC+SUPP Your **lifestyle** is the way you live, for example the things you normally do. *Patients these days expect their doctors to advise them on a healthy lifestyle... They have consistently promoted smoking as being associated with a cool, sophisticated and fashionable lifestyle... His flamboyant lifestyle in his later years was legendary.*

life-support machine, life-support machines
NC A **life-support machine** is a special machine which keeps someone alive when they are severely ill or disabled. *He was on one of those life-support machines, and they were monitoring him all the time... The search is on for a heart donor to save the life of a baby boy who is on a life-support machine at Great Ormond Street hospital.*

life-support system, life-support systems
1 NC A **life-support system** is special equipment that is used to keep a person alive, for example when they are very ill or in a dangerous environment. *His task*

was to monitor the life-support systems, checking oxygen levels.
2 A **life-support system** is also the combination of all the things that living things need to survive. *...the destruction of our environment and life-support systems. ...the Earth's basic life-support systems.*

lifetime /laɪftaɪm/ **lifetimes**
1 NC A **lifetime** is the length of time that someone is alive. *I've seen a lot of changes in my lifetime... Throughout his lifetime, the great Irish playwright Bernard Shaw received correspondence from all over the world.*
2 N SING+POSS The **lifetime** of something is the period of time that it lasts. *...during the lifetime of this parliament... The cost over the lifetime of the machine would be comparable with present systems.*

lift /lɪft/ **lifts, lifting, lifted**
1 VO If you **lift** something, you move it to another position, usually upwards. *He lifted the glass to his mouth... She lifted her feet on to the settee... She lifted her eyes from the ground and fixed them on me... Many of the pictures show him in the gym, straining against the weight he is lifting.*
2 NC A **lift** is a device like a large box which carries people from one floor to another in a building. *I took the lift to the eighth floor... Only 2 of the 32 lifts were operating.*
3 NC If you give someone a **lift**, you drive them in your car from one place to another. *She offered me a lift home... Are you able to go Dave? Because I'll give you a lift.*
4 V When fog or mist **lifts**, it disappears. *Around midday, the fog lifted... A violet haze was lifting from the sea.*
5 VO If people in authority **lift** a law, rule, or other restriction that prevents people from doing something, they end it. *He lifted the ban on the People's Party... Officials have said that before the sanctions are lifted, Iraq must meet certain conditions... In Gaza, only women are allowed to go out when the curfew is lifted... The authorities said they were prepared to lift the arms embargo.*

lift-off
NU **Lift-off** is the launching of a rocket into space. *The spacecraft exploded shortly after lift-off... They have gone to watch the lift-off of the Soyuz-seven rocket.*

ligament /lɪgəmənt/ **ligaments**
NC A **ligament** is a band of strong tissue in your body, which connects bones and muscles. *He had torn a ligament in his knee.*

light /laɪt/ **lights, lighting, lit** or **lighted; lighter, lightest.** The form **lit** is more usual as the past tense and past participle, but **lighted** is also sometimes used.
1 NU **Light** is the brightness that lets you see things, and that comes from the sun, the moon, lamps, or fire. *We are dependent on the sun for heat and light... By the light of a torch, she began to read. ...a beam of concentrated light.*
2 NC A **light** is anything that produces light, especially an electric bulb. *She went into her daughter's room and turned on the light. ...a portable electric light... There's a little red light here, flashing on and off.*
3 VO A place or object that is **lit** by something has light shining in it or on it. *...a room lit by candles... The stage was starkly lit by crude white lights.*
♦ **lighted** ADJ ATTRIB *He looked up thoughtfully at the lighted windows.*
4 ADJ If a building or room is **light**, it has a lot of natural light in it, for example because it has large windows. *The room is light and airy.*
5 ADJ PRED If it is **light** outside, it is daytime. *It was before light that the Prime Minister arrived to talk to the hunger strikers.*
6 VO If you **light** something, you make it start burning. *The fire took a long time to light... How easy is the stove to light?... They're only allowed to light cigarettes in recreational areas.*
7 N SING If someone asks you for a **light**, they want a match or a cigarette lighter so they can start smoking their cigarette. *Here's the matches—oh, you've got a light have you?*

8 N SING+SUPP If you see something in a particular **light**, you think about it in that way. *We were now seeing things in a different light... Today's attack puts the elections in a new light... There are some who see him in a less flattering light.*
9 ADJ Something that is **light** does not weigh very much. *The bag was very light, as though there were nothing in it... But we need to make the structure much lighter if we are to use it effectively.* ♦ **lightness** NU *...the extreme lightness of this particular shoe.*
10 ADJ You can also say that something is **light** when it is not very great in amount or intensity. *A light rain was falling... Light winds have slowed down the leaders on the first day of the race... The traffic on the highway was light that day... Casualties were described as light... The two officers convicted of political offences received lighter sentences.*
11 ADJ **Light** equipment and machines are small and easily moved. *...a light railway engine... This is essential in these days of lighter and lighter yachts... The force will be armed with light defensive weapons.*
12 ADJ **Light** work does not involve much physical effort. *He has grown much weaker and is now capable of only light work... Fatigue after prolonged light exercise could be a consequence of fatigued nerves.*
13 ADJ Movements and actions that are **light** are graceful or gentle. *She runs up the stairs two at a time with her light graceful step.* ♦ **lightly** ADV *He kissed his wife lightly on the cheek.* ♦ **lightness** NU *For a heavy man he moves with surprising lightness and speed.*
14 ADJ **Light** colours are very pale, and not deep or intense. *They were wearing light blue scarves to match the school uniform... One was six feet tall and wearing jeans and a light coloured shirt.*
15 ADJ A **light** meal is small in quantity. *So a light meal, a piece of toast or a snack, is okay, but not a full meal.*
16 ADJ **Light** books, plays, or pieces of music entertain you without making you think very deeply. *...light entertainment and comedy... There'll always be light musical theatre as long as there are theatres to put it into.*
17 See also **green light, lighting, lightly.**
● **Light** is used in these phrases. ● If you **set light to** something, you make it start burning. *The rebels set light to the vehicles while people were still inside.* ● If a new piece of information **throws, casts**, or **sheds light on** something, it makes it easier to understand. *His diaries throw a new light upon certain incidents... Fresh light has been cast on his reasons for surrendering... The inquest will try to shed light on the death of Mr Markov.* ● If something **comes to light** or **is brought to light**, it becomes known. *It has come to light that he was lying... The incident has taken several weeks to come to light... The paper was undoubtedly correct to bring to light such a horrendous event.* ● **In the light of** something means considering it or taking it into account. *This development is significant in the light of what happened later... The authors say that in the light of their success, the therapy should be made available to all cancer patients.* ● If someone **sees the light**, they finally understand something after having thought about it. *We all just woke up one morning, and saw the light... Merchandisers have at last seen the light, and are selling low-calorie ice-cream, beer, and cheesecake.* ● If you talk about **the light at the end of the tunnel**, you are indicating that although a present situation is bad, you feel optimistic that it will improve soon. *For the first time in many years, they are finding it difficult to see the light at the end of the tunnel. ...part of a process which clearly indicates the light at the end of the tunnel.*

light up PHRASAL VERB **1** If something **lights up** a place or object, it shines light on all of it. *The fire was still blazing, lighting up the sky.* **2** If your face or eyes **light up**, you suddenly look very happy. *His face lit up at the sight of Cynthia.* **3** If you **light up** a cigarette or pipe, you start smoking. *George lit up and puffed away for a while... Smokers are finding* *fewer and fewer places to light up.*

light aircraft; light aircraft is both the singular and the plural form.
NCorNU A **light aircraft** is a type of small aeroplane. *We ought to be able to produce light aircraft in this country.*

light bulb, light bulbs
NC A **light bulb** is the central glass part of an electric lamp which light shines from. *...a fluorescent light bulb.*

lighten /laɪtn/ **lightens, lightening, lightened**
1 V-ERG When something **lightens** or is **lightened**, it becomes less dark. *After the rain stops, the sky lightens a little... The face of the watch darkens and lightens in response to a tiny electrical current... Constant exposure to the sun had lightened my hair... Andrea had the front door open, letting the sun lighten the nearly windowless living room.*
2 V-ERG If a situation **lightens**, or if you **lighten** it, it becomes less serious or boring. *My mood began to lighten in the spring. ...an attempt to lighten the tedium of lessons... Both the Times and the Guardian try to lighten their comments on the furore.*
3 V If someone's face or expression **lightens**, it becomes more cheerful, happy, and relaxed. *Her whole expression lightened... His sternly earnest face lightens like a sunrise when he laughs.*
4 You can say that something **lightens** your **burden** when it makes a bad situation better. *The equality of opportunity women are supposed to enjoy has done little to lighten their burden. ...the need to lighten the burden of interest repayments... The fact is that the Thatcher years have failed to lighten the economic burden of government.*

lighter /laɪtə/ **lighters**
1 NC A **lighter** or a **cigarette lighter** is a small device for lighting cigarettes. *It was a blue plastic disposable lighter.*
2 **Lighter** is the comparative of **light**.

light-fingered /laɪtfɪŋgəd/
ADJ If you say that someone is **light-fingered**, you mean that they steal things; an informal expression. *We lost a camera, ornaments, and other bits and pieces to light-fingered clients.*

light-headed
ADJ If you are **light-headed**, you feel dizzy and faint. *If you become aware of your heartbeat or feel light-headed as you relax, don't be alarmed.*

light-hearted
ADJ Someone or something that is **light-hearted** is cheerful and entertaining. *He was in a light-hearted mood... Let me finish with a slightly more light-hearted question.* ◆ **light-heartedly** ADV *...I would have to do it light-heartedly, not solemnly.*

lighthouse /laɪthaus/ **lighthouses**
NC A **lighthouse** is a tower near the sea which contains a powerful flashing lamp to guide ships or to warn them of danger. *...a lighthouse on the disputed Diaoyutai Islands.*

light industry, light industries
NUorNC **Light industry** is industry in which only small items are made, for example household goods and clothes. *The party's political programme would put more emphasis on light industry and small businesses... Three ministries were created covering energy, electronics, and light industries.*

lighting /laɪtɪŋ/
NU The **lighting** in a place is the way that it is lit, or the quality of the light in it. *...artificial lighting. ...poorly designed street lighting.*

lightly /laɪtli/
ADV If you say that something is not done **lightly**, you mean that it is not done without serious thought. *This is not a charge to make lightly against the government... He knew it was not being said lightly... These are not threats that can be taken lightly.* ◆ See also **light**.

lightning /laɪtnɪŋ/
1 NU **Lightning** is the bright flashes of light in the sky that you see during a thunderstorm. *...a flash of lightning... He was struck by lightning, and nearly died.*

2 ADJ ATTRIB **Lightning** describes things that happen very quickly or last for only a short time. *He drew his gun with lightning speed... Two days ago, they launched a lightning raid into Saudi Arabia... Rapid jumps and lightning turns are performed by the dancers with bravura and enjoyment.*

lightning conductor, lightning conductors
NC A **lightning conductor** is a long, thin piece of metal on top of a building that attracts lightning and allows it to reach the ground safely. *A few years ago, they came up with a simple and cheap lightning conductor for rural areas.*

lightning rod, lightning rods
NC A **lightning rod** is the same as a **lightning conductor**; used in American English.

lightning strike, lightning strikes
NC A **lightning strike** is a strike in which workers stop work suddenly and without any warning, in order to protest about something. *Groups of employees have staged lightning strikes... Building workers went on a lightning strike and a demonstration.*

light pen, light pens
NC A **light pen** is an electronic device shaped like a pen, that is used to read black and white codes on products such as books and packets of food.

lightship /laɪtʃɪp/ **lightships**
NC A **lightship** is a small ship that stays in one place and that has a powerful flashing lamp like a lighthouse. It is used to guide ships or to warn them of danger.

lightweight /laɪtweɪt/ **lightweights**
1 ADJ Something that is **lightweight** weighs less than most other things of the same type. *...a grey lightweight suit. ...lightweight cameras.*
2 N+N A **lightweight** boxer weighs between 130 and 135 pounds. *The World Boxing Council lightweight title has been retained by Jose-Luis Ramirez.*
3 NC You also describe someone as a **lightweight** when you think that they are not very important in a particular area of activity, or that they are not very good at it. *There had been a widespread tendency to dismiss him as a political lightweight.*

light-year, light-years
1 NC A **light-year** is the distance that light travels in a year; a technical use in physics. *The nearest star is about four and a half light-years away.*
2 NC **Light-years** means a very long time; an informal use. *Last Tuesday seemed light-years away already.*

likable /laɪkəbl/. See **likeable**.

like /laɪk/ **likes, liking, liked**
1 PREP If one person or thing is **like** another, they have similar characteristics or behave in similar ways. *He looked like Clark Gable... She's very like her younger sister... The lake was like a bright blue mirror... She began to shake like a jelly.*
2 PREP If you ask someone what something is **like**, you are asking them to describe it. *What was Essex like?... What did they taste like?*
3 PREP **Like** can introduce an example of the thing that you have just mentioned. *We are sending special reporters to countries like Afghanistan.*
4 PREP You can use **like** to say that someone is in the same situation as another person. *He, like everybody else, had worried about it.*
5 CONJ If you say that something is **like** you remembered it or **like** you imagined it, you mean that it is the way you remembered or imagined it; an informal use. *Is it like you remembered it?... It didn't work out quite like I intended it to.*
6 VO,V+ING,orV+to-INF If you **like** something, you find it pleasant or attractive, or you approve of it. *She's a nice girl, I like her... They didn't like what they saw... I like reading... Her folks like her to get in early.*
7 V,VO,V+to-INF,orVO+to-INF If you say that you would **like** something or would **like** to do something, you are expressing a wish or desire. *He can stay here if he likes... Would you like some coffee?... I'd like to marry him... I'd like you to come.*
8 See also **liking**.

◆ **Like** is used in these phrases. ◆ You say **'if you like'** when you are offering to do something for someone. *I'll drive, if you like.* ◆ You say **'and the like'** to indicate there are other similar things or people that can be included in what you are saying. ...*the activities of ruthless mine owners and the like.* ● You say **'like this', 'like that'**, or **'like so'** when you are showing someone how something is done. *Twist it round and put it on here, like that.* ● You can sometimes use **nothing like** instead of 'not' when you want to emphasize a negative statement. *The cast is nothing like as numerous as one might suppose.* ● You use **something like** to indicate that a number or quantity is an estimate, not an exact figure. *Something like ninety per cent of the crop was destroyed.*

-like /-laɪk/
SUFFIX **-like** is added to nouns to form adjectives that describe something as being similar to the thing referred to by the noun. ...*a rock-like hump.*

likeable /ˈlaɪkəbl/; also spelt **likable.**
ADJ If someone is **likeable**, they are pleasant and friendly. ...*a very attractive and likeable young man.*

likelihood /ˈlaɪklihʊd/
N SING The **likelihood** of something happening is the fact that it is likely to happen. *There is every likelihood that she will succeed... This increases the likelihood of an attack.*

likely /ˈlaɪkli/ **likelier, likeliest**
1 ADJ If something is **likely**, it is probably true or will probably happen. *It seemed hardly likely that they would agree... What kind of change is likely?*
2 ADJ PRED+*to*-INF If you are **likely** to do something, you will probably do it. *They were not likely to forget it.*
3 ADV SEN **Very likely** or **most likely** means probably. *Most likely it will be a woman.*
4 ADJ ATTRIB You use **likely** to describe people who will probably be suitable for a particular purpose. *The local committee is always looking out for likely recruits.*

like-minded
ADJ People who are **like-minded** have similar opinions, or interests. ...*Hubbard and his like-minded colleagues.*

liken /ˈlaɪkən/ **likens, likening, likened**
VO+*to* If you **liken** one thing to another thing, you say that they are similar. *It has a mildly nutty taste which has been likened to new potatoes.*

likeness /ˈlaɪknəs/ **likenesses**
1 N SING If one thing has a **likeness** to another, it is similar to it in appearance. ...*a china dog that bore a likeness to his aunt.*
2 NC+SUPP If a picture of someone is a good **likeness** of them, it looks very much like them. *That's certainly, I would say, a good likeness.*

likewise /ˈlaɪkwaɪz/
1 ADV SEN You use **likewise** when you are comparing two things and saying that they are similar. *In Yugoslavia there was a special local way of doing it, likewise in Italy.*
2 ADV If you do one thing, and someone else does **likewise**, they do the same thing. *He is relaxing and invites them to do likewise.*

liking /ˈlaɪkɪŋ/
N SING+SUPP If you have a **liking** for someone or something, you like them. *I took an enormous liking to Davies the moment I met him... She was developing a liking for Scotch.*
● **Liking** is used in these phrases. ● If something is **to** your **liking**, you like it. *Such a compromise will not be to everyone's liking.* ● If something is too big or too fast **for** your **liking**, you would prefer it to be smaller or slower. *You are progressing too fast for his liking.*

lilac /ˈlaɪlək/ **lilacs**
1 NCorNU A **lilac** is a small tree. It has pleasant-smelling white or purple flowers that are also called lilacs. ...*lilac bushes in the garden... Once in a while, she'd give me some lilacs to take home.*
2 ADJ Something that is **lilac** in colour is pale pinkish-purple. ...*her plain lilac dress.*

Lilliputian /ˌlɪlɪˈpjuːʃn/
ADJ **Lilliputian** means very small indeed; a literary word. ...*a Lilliputian chest of drawers.*

Lilo /ˈlaɪləʊ/ **Lilos**
NC A **Lilo** is a long plastic mattress that is filled with air and used for lying on; Lilo is a trademark.

Lilongwe /lɪˈlɒŋgwi/
Lilongwe became the capital of Malawi in 1975 and is Malawi's second largest city. Population: 234,000 (1987).

lilt /lɪlt/ **lilts**
NC A **lilt** in someone's voice is its pleasant rising and falling sound. *There was something familiar in the lilt of her voice. ...his Irish lilt.*

lilting /ˈlɪltɪŋ/
ADJ A **lilting** voice or song rises and falls in pitch in a pleasant way. *The lark sings its lilting song... She spoke to him in her lilting Arabic.*

lily /ˈlɪli/ **lilies**
NC A **lily** is a plant with large flowers that are often white. *The new stamps show a lily, a swan, and a fungus.*

lily-livered /ˌlɪliˈlɪvəd/
ADJ If you describe someone as **lily-livered**, you mean that they are cowardly; an old-fashioned word. *Nobody was going to tell me I was too lily-livered to get my hands dirty with some real work.*

lily of the valley, lilies of the valley. The plural form can be either **lilies of the valley** or **lily of the valley.**
NUorNC **Lily of the valley** is a small plant with large leaves and small, white, bell-shaped flowers. *She carried a bouquet of British-grown flowers—gardenias, roses, and lily-of-the-valley.*

Lima /ˈliːmə/
Lima is the capital of Peru and its largest city. Population: 5,008,400 (1985).

limb /lɪm/ **limbs**
1 NC Your **limbs** are your arms and legs. *He was very tall with long limbs... We cough, yawn, and stretch our limbs.*
2 NC The **limbs** of a tree are its branches; a literary use. *Thick smoke rose into the tree's upper limbs.*
● **Limb** is used in these phrases. ● If someone is **out on a limb**, they are isolated, usually because they have done or said something that other people do not agree with. *President Gorbachov is rather out on a limb with his endorsement of Washington's policy on the Gulf.* ● If someone **risks life and limb**, they do something very dangerous. *This was the experience that people through the ages had been sacrificing life and limb to achieve. ...the cost to life and limb.*

limber /ˈlɪmbə/ **limbers, limbering, limbered**
limber up PHRASAL VERB If you **limber up**, you prepare for a sport by doing exercises. *We had no time to limber up on the practice range.*

limbo /ˈlɪmbəʊ/
1 NU If you are in **limbo**, you are in a situation where you do not know what will happen next and you have no control over things. *Refugees may remain in limbo for years... The republic's status is still in limbo... Few novels have depicted the particular limbo of Asians living in America.*
2 N SING The **limbo** is a West Indian dance in which you have to pass under a low bar while leaning backwards. *We've got a band over from Kingston, calypso singers, limbo, all the jazz.*

lime /laɪm/ **limes**
1 NC A **lime** is a large tree. It has pale green leaves and edible fruit. ...*the long avenue of limes.*
2 NC A **lime** is a small, round, citrus fruit with dark green skin that grows on lime trees. ...*the lime harvest.*
3 NU **Lime** or **lime juice** is a non-alcoholic drink that is made from the juice of limes. ...*vodka and lime. ...the world's largest exporters of lime juice.*
4 NUorN+N **Lime** is also a chemical substance which is used in cement, in whitewash, and as a fertilizer. *There's been a fantastic improvement in the quality of the lime we produce. ...a lime quarry.*

limelight /ˈlaɪmlaɪt/
N SING If someone is in the **limelight**, they are getting a lot of attention. *The Royal Family are used to the limelight.*

limerick /lɪmərɪk/ **limericks**
NC A **limerick** is a humorous poem which has five lines. *Edward Lear was the 19th century English author of nonsense rhymes and limericks.*

limestone /laɪmstəʊn/
NU **Limestone** is a white rock which is used for building and making cement. *...the limestone with which much of York is built.*

limey /laɪmi/ **limeys**
NC Some Americans refer to British people as **limeys** in a disapproving or humorous way. *I told those limey bastards to take you to a hospital. ...the guy's limey accent.*

limit /lɪmɪt/ **limits, limiting, limited**
1 NC A **limit** is the greatest amount, extent, or degree of something that is possible or allowed. *The powers of the human brain are stretched to the limit. ...a motorist exceeding the speed limit... There is no limit to the risks they are prepared to take.*
2 N PL The **limits** of a situation are the facts involved in it which make only some actions or results possible. *...the problems of applying that system within the limits of a weekly, two-hour meeting.*
3 VO If you **limit** something, you prevent it from becoming greater than a particular amount or degree. *Japanese exports would be limited to 1.68m vehicles.*
4 VOorV-REFL If someone or something **limits** you, or if you **limit** yourself, the number of things that you have or do is reduced. *Why should the people of this country limit me that way?... Will he limit himself to seeing that the enterprise is approved?* ♦ **limiting** ADJ *Many of these customs were narrow and limiting.*
5 VO If something **is limited** to a particular place or group of people, it exists only in that place, or is had or done only by that group. *This problem is not limited to Sweden.*
6 See also **age limit**.
● **Limit** is used in these phrases. ● If a place is **off limits**, you are not allowed to go there. *The Eastern Zone was now off limits to me... A judge declared part of a school playground off limits because it's too close to a power line.* ● You say that someone **is the limit** when you are very annoyed with them; an informal expression. ● You can add **within limits** to a statement to indicate that it applies only to reasonable or normal situations. *The Covenant allows signatories, within limits, to restrict their citizens' activities on grounds of national security.*

limitation /lɪmɪteɪʃn/ **limitations**
1 NU **Limitation** is the control or reduction of something. *...the limitation of trade union power.*
2 N PL If you talk about the **limitations** of someone or something, you mean that they can only do some things and not others, or that they can only achieve a fairly low degree of success or excellence. *It's important to know your own limitations... The technique has its limitations.*
3 NC When there are **limitations** on something, it is not allowed to grow or extend beyond certain limits. *All limitations on earnings must cease.*

limited /lɪmɪtɪd/
1 ADJ Something that is **limited** is rather small in amount or degree. *The choice was very limited. ...a painter of limited abilities.*
2 A **limited** company is one in which the shareholders are legally responsible for only a part of any money that it may owe if it goes bankrupt. The word **limited** is often part of a company's name, and has the written abbreviation **Ltd**. *The Foundation had become a limited company. ...Hourmont Travel Limited.*

limited edition, limited editions
NC A **limited edition** is a work of art, such as a book or a painting, which is only produced in very small numbers, so that each one will be valuable in the future. *Both albums were released as limited editions.*

limitless /lɪmɪtləs/
ADJ You say that something is **limitless** when it is extremely large in amount or extent. *...the computer's limitless memory. ...our limitless fascination with toys and games.*

limousine /lɪməziːn/ **limousines**
NC A **limousine** is a very comfortable car. Limousines are usually driven by a chauffeur and are used by rich or important people. *The President's limousine swung through the gates.*

limp /lɪmp/ **limps, limping, limped**
1 V If you **limp**, you walk in an uneven way because one of your legs or feet is hurt. *He picked up his bag and limped back to the road... Two of the dogs were limping badly.* ► Also NC *He walks with a limp... She had a slight limp.*
2 ADJ If someone is **limp**, they have no strength or energy and their body can be moved easily. *Her hand felt limp and damp.* ♦ **limply** ADV *The tiny baby lay limply on her arm.*
3 ADJ Something that is **limp** is soft and not stiff or firm. *...a dressing-gown of limp, shiny fabric.* ♦ **limply** ADV *The rope fell limply to the ground.*

limpet /lɪmpɪt/ **limpets**
NC A **limpet** is a small sea animal with a cone-shaped shell and which attaches itself tightly to rocks. *Other forms of bait are limpets, mussels, slices of herring or mackerel.*

limpet mine, limpet mines
NC A **limpet mine** is a device containing explosives which is attached to its target by a magnet or adhesive and which is very difficult to remove. *Two limpet mines were planted at the Court building but failed to explode.*

limpid /lɪmpɪd/; a literary word.
1 ADJ Something that is **limpid** is so clear that you can see through it easily. *...a pool of limpid water. ...a limpid and cloudless sky.*
2 ADJ ATTRIB **Limpid** speech or writing is clear and easy to understand. *...Heissman's limpid prose... He spoke exquisite, limpid Castilian.*

linchpin /lɪntʃpɪn/ **linchpins**; also spelt **lynchpin**.
NC+SUPP The **linchpin** of something is the most important person or thing involved in it; a formal word. *Gold was, until quite recently, the linchpin of major currencies... As the linchpin of Mr Callaghan's government, Mr Foot was the obvious candidate.*

linctus /lɪŋktəs/ **linctuses**
N MASS A **linctus** is a thick liquid medicine that you take for a sore throat or a cough.

line /laɪn/ **lines, lining, lined**
1 NC A **line** is a long, thin mark on a surface. *...a diagonal red line on the label. ...a straight line joining those two points. ...the hard thin line of Lynn's mouth... The experts had to work out the frequency by measuring the wiggly lines.*
2 NC The **lines** on someone's face are the wrinkles or creases in it. *When I look at Paul, I can see that he's got heavier lines from his cheek to his mouth.*
3 NC A **line** of people or things is a number of them that are arranged in a row. *...long lines of poplar trees... The men formed themselves into a line... The crews are refusing to cross the picket lines... One way of creating a living fence is to grow trees in lines and connect them with barbed wire.*
4 NC You can refer to a long piece of string or wire as a **line** when it is being used for a particular purpose. *...washing hanging on a line... The fish was heavy at the end of my line.*
5 NC **Line** is also used to refer to a route along which people or things move or are sent. *The strong winds brought down many trees and power lines... Several carriages were strewn across the railway lines... A computer sorts the information and passes it to each customer over telephone lines.*
6 NC+SUPP You can use **line** to refer to the edge, outline, or shape of something. *...the firm, delicate lines of Paxton's buildings.*
7 NC+SUPP The **lines** are the set of physical defences or patrols that have been set up along the boundary of an area occupied by an army. *They were dropped by parachute behind enemy lines... She has been marooned for several days behind rebel lines... As the relief operation gets underway, they will be crossing battle lines along roads that are believed to be mined.*
8 NC+SUPP The **line** between similar things, peoples, or actions is the point at which you judge them to belong

to different classes or types. *The traditional social dividing lines are becoming blurred... She will be living below the poverty line... There's a thin line between obscenity and art.*

9 NC A **line** is also one of the rows of words in a piece of writing or a remark said by an actor in a play or film. *I have read every line... She found it impossible to remember her lines... These lines, called iambic pentameters, are the basic unit of Shakespeare's long poems.*

10 NC+SUPP The particular **line** that someone has towards a problem or topic is the attitude or policy they have towards it. *...the official line of the Labour Party... The President takes a much harder line... He maintained a somewhat cautious line.*

11 NC+SUPP The **line** in an activity is the way in which the activity develops or the method you use in doing it. *It became clear that the majority of the republics opposed this line of action... The new research throws some light on the line of evolution that led to modern people... Mr Gorbachov tends to follow this line of reasoning.*

12 N SING+POSS Your **line** of business, work, or research is the kind of work or research that you do. *A man in my line of business has to take precautions. ...his particular line of research.*

13 NC A **line** is also a type of product that a company makes or sells. *Unprofitable lines will be discontinued. ...GM's first new car line for 60 years... We have 300 lines of merchandise.*

14 N SING+SUPP A particular **line** of people or things is a series of them, all connected in some way, that has existed over a period of time. *...the long line of American Presidents... Lenin was not the pre-eminent socialist thinker, but just one in a long line of theorists.*

15 VO If people or things **line** a road or room, they are present in large numbers along its edges or sides. *Earlier, thousands of people lined the 10-mile funeral procession... The streets were lined with cars... The wrecks of Iraqi warplanes line the approach road... Hundreds of Albanians could be seen lining the decks, whistling and chanting.*

16 VO If you **line** a container or a piece of clothing, you cover its inside surface with paper or cloth. *Line the cupboards and drawers with paper. ...a coffin lined with velvet. ...a new way of lining pipes.*

17 VO If something **lines** a container or an area inside a person, animal, or plant, it forms a layer on the inside surface. *...tiny hairs lining the nose... The cilia that line the passage to your lungs are paralysed.*

18 See also **lined**, **lining**, and **front line**, **hard line**, **hot line**.

● **Line** is used in these phrases. ● If people or cars are **in line**, they are in a row, one behind another. *Many of the children standing in line were taking the goods to sell at a profit.* ● If you are **in line** for something, you are likely to get it. *You are next in line for promotion... Poland and Yugoslavia are also in line to join the Council.* ● If one person or group is **in line** with others, it is doing the same thing as the others. *Africa may bring itself in line with the rest of the world on this matter... They wanted a Communist country as a neighbour, in line with Poland and Hungary.* ● If something is done **in line** with a policy or guideline, it is done following that policy or guideline. *...the restoration of diplomatic relations with Iran in line with the policy of Mr Chirac... In line with instructions, the Captain did not resist the order to divert to Muscat.* ● If you keep someone **in line**, you make them behave in the way that they are supposed to. *Travel restrictions and physical assault were still frequently used to keep people in line... The Speaker occasionally intervenes to keep the politicians in line.* ● If you are **on line** when you are using a large computer system, what you type on the keyboard goes directly into the computer system. *We're now able to do this analysis on line.* ● You can say someone is **on the line** when they are talking on the telephone to you. *We have a caller on the line, Sylvia Delany from Michigan... On the line from the courtroom now is Dean Olsher.* ● If your job or reputation is **on the line**,

you may lose it or harm it as a result of doing something brave or foolish. *I didn't dare fight and put my job on the line, so I went along with them... The person who heads the Commission's career is on the line when he makes the report.* ● If something happens **on** or **along** particular **lines**, it happens in that way. *The population is split along religious lines... In Philadelphia, voters usually choose a candidate along racial lines... Yes, I have to think on those lines too.* ● You use **on the lines of** and **along the lines of** when you are giving a general description of what someone has said or of what you want. *Driberg opened with a question on the lines of: 'What do you think about the present political situation?'... Headlines appeared with monotonous regularity on the lines of 'pandamonium' and 'uproar in Parliament'.* ● If someone is **on the right lines**, they are acting in a way that is sensible or likely to produce useful results. *Do his policies strike you as being on the right lines?* ● If someone is **out of line** or **steps out of line**, they do not behave in the way that they are supposed to. *The Transport Worker's leader, Ron Todd, has ensured none of the larger unions step out of line... We cannot show ourselves to be too out of line at such a time of great change.* ● If you **draw the line** at a particular activity, you refuse to do it, because it is more than you are prepared to do. *There is a point at which they will have to draw the line... The idea of terminating that person's life I find abhorrent, and I just drew the line, that's all.* ● If something happens somewhere **along the line**, it happens during a process or activity. *We slipped up somewhere along the line... Maybe later on, down along the line, they'll realise.* ● to **drop** someone a **line**: see **drop**. ● to **read between the lines**: see **read**.

line up PHRASAL VERB **1** If people **line up** or if you **line** them **up**, they stand in a row or form a queue. *They lined us up and marched us off.* **2** If something is **lined up** for someone, it is arranged for them. *A formal farewell party was lined up.* **3** See also **line-up**.

lineage /ˈlɪniɪdʒ/ **lineages**
N U or NC Someone's **lineage** is the series of families from which they are directly descended; a formal word. *...the names and lineage of the women. ...those who can prove their Kuwaiti lineage. ...respect for the lineages of their neighbours.*

lineal /ˈlɪniəl/
ADJ ATTRIB If someone is a **lineal** descendant of a particular person or family, they are directly descended from that person or family; a formal word. *...in direct lineal descent of a soldier of the period.*

lineament /ˈlɪniəmənt/ **lineaments**
N PL+SUPP Someone's **lineaments** are the outlines and features of their face; a literary word. *...the exquisite lineaments of his face.*

linear /ˈlɪniə/; a formal word.
1 ADJ A **linear** process is one in which things always happen one at a time and in a particular order. *...linear thinking. ...events occurring simultaneously rather than in a linear sequence.* **2** ADJ A **linear** shape consists of lines. *...the defined linear boundary that a modern state requires.*

lined /laɪnd/
1 ADJ If someone's skin is **lined**, it has wrinkles on it. *Their faces are lined, immeasurably sad.* **2** ADJ **Lined** paper has lines printed across it. *He was writing on a lined pad.*

line drawing, **line drawings**
NC A **line drawing** is a drawing which consists only of lines, in which darker or lighter areas are shown by the spacing and thickness of the lines. *It's very well illustrated, with 180 charts, diagrams and line drawings.*

lineman /ˈlaɪnmən/ **linemen** /ˈlaɪnmən/; used in American English.
1 NC A **lineman** is someone whose job is to take care of railway lines or telephone or electricity wires. *Thirty-nine-year-old Jerry Thom is a power company lineman.* **2** NC A **lineman** is also a football player who plays in the forward attacking line. *They imposed a lifetime ban on former Washington Redskins defensive lineman Dexter Manley.*

linen /lɪnɪn/
1 NU **Linen** is a kind of cloth that is used for making tea-towels, tablecloths, sheets, and clothes. *...a white linen suit.*
2 NU You can refer to tablecloths, sheets, and similar things as **linen**. *...bed linen.*

line of sight
N SING Your **line of sight** is an imaginary line that stretches between your eye and the object that you are looking at. *The laser crossed his line of sight.*

line of vision
N SING Your **line of vision** is the same as your **line of sight**.

line printer, line printers
NC A **line printer** is a printer that is attached to a computer and prints a line at a time rather than a single character, and so can operate very quickly.

liner /laɪnə/ **liners**
1 NC A **liner** is a large passenger ship. *...a cargo ship which collided with a liner in 1986. ...the world's largest cruise liner.*
2 NC+SUPP A bin **liner** is a plastic bag that you put inside a waste bin or dustbin. *...black polythene bin liners.*

linesman /laɪnzmən/ **linesmen** /laɪnzmən/
NC A **linesman** is an official in games such as football and tennis who watches the boundary lines and indicates when the ball goes outside them. *...the referee and linesmen for the Cup match.*

line-up, line-ups
1 NC A **line-up** is a group of people that are brought together to be members of a team or to take part in a particular event. *...the line-up for the next game. ...the Prime Minister's new cabinet line-up... The star-studded line-up included Stevie Wonder.*
2 NC A **line-up** in a political situation is the way that the people involved have grouped themselves into different sides or parties. *...the new Middle East line-up after the Amman summit... A new line-up emerged in Philippine politics.*

linger /lɪŋgə/ **lingers, lingering, lingered**
1 V If something **lingers**, it continues to exist for a long time. *The resentment and the longings lingered... This tradition apparently manages to linger on.*
♦ **lingering** ADJ ATTRIB *...a lingering sense of guilt... The time had come to remove any lingering doubts and suspicions.*
2 VA If you **linger** somewhere, you stay there for a longer time than is necessary, for example because you are enjoying yourself. *Davis lingered for a moment in the bar. ...lingering over their meals.*

lingerie /lænʒəri/
NU **Lingerie** is women's underwear and night-clothes.

lingo /lɪŋgəʊ/ **lingoes**; an informal word.
1 NC A **lingo** is a foreign language, especially one which you cannot speak or understand. *...some of the problems of learning the lingo.*
2 NC A **lingo** is also a range of vocabulary or a style of language which is used in a special context or by a small group of people. *...the lingo of Pentagon officials... I had mastered the commercial lingo at least.*

lingua franca /lɪŋgwə fræŋkə/ **lingua francas**
NC A **lingua franca** is a language or way of communicating which is used by people who do not speak the same native language; a formal expression. *Pope John Paul addressed worshippers in Swahili, East Africa's lingua franca.*

linguist /lɪŋgwɪst/ **linguists**
1 NC A **linguist** is someone who is involved in the study of linguistics. *...Professor Noam Chomsky, the distinguished American linguist. ...a linguist at the London School of Economics.*
2 NC A **linguist** is also someone who can speak several languages; an informal use. *It will be some time before Britain's youngest budding linguists will be able to try out their skills.*

linguistic /lɪŋgwɪstɪk/ **linguistics**
1 NU **Linguistics** is the study of the way in which language works. *...experts in such disparate fields as linguistics, archaeology and biology. ...the Department of Applied Linguistics at the University of London.*
2 ADJ **Linguistic** abilities or ideas relate to language. *...linguistic development between the ages of nought and four. ...his linguistic ability. ...regardless of political, linguistic and religious considerations.*
♦ **linguistically** ADV *They have been discriminated against linguistically and economically. ...conversations which are linguistically perfect.*

liniment /lɪnəmənt/ **liniments**
N MASS **Liniment** is a liquid that you rub into your skin in order to reduce pain or stiffness. *...a liniment that a sportsman would use for painful muscles. ...a cream liniment containing Japanese peppermint oil.*

lining /laɪnɪŋ/ **linings**
NC A **lining** is a material attached to the inside of something such as a piece of clothing, to make it warmer or more comfortable, or to protect it. *...a white cloak with a scarlet lining.*

link /lɪŋk/ **links, linking, linked**
1 VO Two things **are linked** when there is a relationship between them. *Evidence has been offered linking the group to a series of bomb attacks... He said the tragedy of Palestine was closely linked to British policies in the past.*
2 NC A **link** is a relationship between two things or situations, in which one thing is believed to cause the other to exist. *There seems to be a link between the rising rate of unemployment and the rise in crime... There's a strong link between humour and creativity.*
3 NC You can refer to an organization or relationship that connects two or more things and enables them to work together as a **link**. *The arts centre is probably the most obvious link between the university and the wider community... They said that they would re-open diplomatic links with Nicaragua.*
4 VO Two places or objects **are linked** when there is a physical connection between them so that you can travel or communicate between them. *The television camera had been linked to a computer. ...a canal linking the Pacific and Atlantic oceans.*
5 NC A **link** between two places is a physical connection between them. *They opened a rail link between the two towns. ...a telephone link between Washington and Moscow.*
6 VO If you **link** two things, you join them loosely. *She linked her hand through the crook of his elbow... It ended with the crowd linking arms and singing the pop song 'We are the World'.* ♦ **linked** ADJ *They walked along, arms linked.*
7 NC A **link** of a chain is one of the rings in it.
8 You can talk about a group of connected items or events as **links in a chain**. *...the central link in a chain of six air bases. ...another vital link in the long chain of moves that will eventually release the hostages.*

link up PHRASAL VERB 1 If you **link up** two items or places, or if they **link up**, you connect them to each other. *This computer can be linked up to other computers... Future shuttle flights are expected to link up with an orbiting space station.* 2 If one person or group **links up** with another, they decide to work or act together to do something. *Students tried to link up with other young people and march across the bridge... It's ten years since Rover first linked up with Honda to build Japanese-designed cars in Britain... The Social Democrats in East and West Germany have linked up.*

linkage /lɪŋkɪdʒ/ **linkages**
1 NU or NC The **linkage** between two things is the connection between them. *...the linkage between causes and effects. ...the linkage of truth and beauty... They are trying to develop linkages with the institute in Spain.*
2 NU In politics, **linkage** is the deliberate connecting of two situations, and agreeing to change one of them only if the other one changes as well. *The timing reflects political sensitivities to linkage of Namibian independence with the presence of Cuban troops in Angola... She appeared to relent on her linkage of economic aid to reform.*

linkman /lɪŋkmæn/ **linkmen**
NC A **linkman** is a television or radio broadcaster who speaks between items or programmes and tells you

what is coming next or makes other announcements.

link-up, link-ups

1 NC A **link-up** is a physical connection between two machines or communication systems. *...the link-up of the US Apollo and Soviet Soyuz spacecraft. ...a television satellite link-up with studios in China and India.*
2 NC A **link-up** is also a relationship or partnership between two organizations. *...British Airways' proposed link-up with the Dutch airline KLM and Sabena of Belgium. ...link-ups between enterprises on its territory and large West German concerns.*

link verb, link verbs

NC In grammar, a **link verb** is a verb such as 'be', 'seem' or 'appear'. These verbs are followed by a complement.

lino /ˈlaɪnəʊ/

NU **Lino** is the same as **linoleum**. *...a landing with cracked lino on the floor.*

linoleum /lɪˈnəʊliəm/

NU **Linoleum** is a floor covering with a shiny surface; an old-fashioned word. *The linoleum felt cool and smooth against his bare feet.*

Linotype /ˈlaɪnəʊtaɪp/

N+N A **Linotype** is a printing machine that is operated by a keyboard like a typewriter, and that stores each line on a piece of metal before printing it; **Linotype** is a trademark. *I went over and stared at a Linotype machine.*

linseed oil /ˈlɪnsiːd ɔɪl/

NU **Linseed oil** is an oil made from seeds of the flax plant. It is normally used to make paints and inks, or to rub into wooden surfaces to protect them.

lint /lɪnt/

NU **Lint** is cotton or linen fabric which is used especially for covering cuts and wounds on people's bodies. *...several rolls of lint bandages.*

lintel /ˈlɪntl/ **lintels**

NC A **lintel** is a piece of stone or wood over a door or window, which supports the bricks above the door or window; a technical term. *...using a bolt that fits into the lintel above the door. ...a lintel from one of the most well-known Thai temples.*

lion /ˈlaɪən/ **lions**

1 NC A **lion** is a large, wild member of the cat family found in Africa. Lions have yellowish fur, and male lions have long hair on their head and neck. *Kenya's elephants, lions and other game are a great tourist attraction... The laws against circuses are to protect wild animals such as lions and tigers.*
2 See also **lion's share**.

lioness /ˈlaɪənes/ **lionesses**

NC A **lioness** is a female lion. *After nearly two hours, we found a lioness and her kill—a wildebeest... It's the lioness who defends her cubs.*

lion's share

N SING If you get the **lion's share** of something, you get the largest part of it, leaving very little for other people. *The lion's share of investment has gone to a few favoured companies... The lion's share of the credit belongs to Mr Gorbachev.*

lip /lɪp/ **lips**

1 NC Your **lips** are the top and bottom edges of your mouth. *He had a freshly lit cigarette between his lips.*
2 If you keep a **stiff upper lip**, you do not show any emotion, even though it is difficult not to. *They have kept a stiff upper lip in recent days, as it became increasingly clear that they might well be defeated... So many cultures admire those who keep their feelings hidden and maintain a stiff upper lip.*

Li Peng /ˌliː ˈpʌŋ/

Li Peng became Prime Minister of China in 1988. He served as Minister of the Electric Power Industry from 1981 to 1982 and Minister in Charge of the State Education Commission from 1985 to 1988. He was Acting Prime Minister from 1987 to 1988. He became a member of the Central Committee of the Chinese Communist Party (CCP) in 1982. Born: 1928.

lip-read, lip-reads, lip-reading. The form lip-read is used in the present tense, pronounced /ˈlɪpriːd/, and is also the past tense and past participle, pronounced /ˈlɪpred/.

V If someone can **lip-read**, they can understand what you are saying by watching your lips. Deaf people sometimes do this. *Papa lip-reads; you must face him when you speak.*

lip-service

If someone **pays lip-service** to an idea, they pretend to be in favour of it, but they do not do anything to support it; used showing disapproval. *Our major political parties pay lip-service to the ideal of community participation... According to Dubček, the present leaders in Czechoslovakia are only paying lip service to Mr Gorbachev's ideas.*

lipstick /ˈlɪpstɪk/ **lipsticks**

N MASS **Lipstick** is a coloured substance which women put on their lips. It comes in the form of a small stick. *She was wearing lipstick and mascara. ...a lipstick that re-moisturises the lips.*

liquefy /ˈlɪkwɪfaɪ/ **liquefies, liquefying, liquefied**

V-ERG When a gas or solid substance **liquefies** or is **liquefied**, it changes its form and becomes liquid. *Under these conditions hydrogen liquefies... A lot of energy is wasted liquefying the methane.* ♦ **liquefied** ADJ ATTRIB *...imported two million tons of liquefied natural gas. ...a pipe feeding liquefied hydrogen to the shuttle's main engines.*

liqueur /lɪˈkjʊə/ **liqueurs**

N MASS A **liqueur** is a strong, usually sweet, alcoholic drink, often drunk after a meal. *...imported liqueur brought in from Singapore.*

liquid /ˈlɪkwɪd/ **liquids**

1 N MASS A **liquid** is a substance such as water which is not solid and which can be poured. *...a yellowish, evil-smelling liquid... Some of the gases are cooled down so that they condense into liquid... It's difficult to mix the liquids accurately.*
2 ADJ Something that is **liquid** is in the form of a liquid rather than being solid or a gas. *...liquid polish. ...frozen and stored in liquid nitrogen.*

liquidate /ˈlɪkwɪdeɪt/ **liquidates, liquidating, liquidated**

1 VO When a company is **liquidated**, it is closed down, usually because it is in debt, and its assets are sold to repay the debts. *...eight state banks were to be liquidated. ...if it permitted the industry to be liquidated because of the present glut of oil.* ♦ **liquidation** /ˌlɪkwɪˈdeɪʃn/ NU *By April 1969, the group faced liquidation.*
2 VO When someone **liquidates** people who are causing problems, they have them killed. *All his supporters were expelled, exiled, or liquidated... The government has ruthlessly liquidated its enemies.*

liquidator /ˈlɪkwɪdeɪtə/ **liquidators**

NC A **liquidator** is a person who is responsible for settling the affairs of a company that is being liquidated. *The liquidators said that much of the evidence could be prejudicial to the investigation. ...investors who turned up to hear the latest report from the liquidators.*

liquid crystal, liquid crystals

NC A **liquid crystal** is a liquid that has some of the qualities of crystals, for example reflecting light from different directions in different ways. *Liquid crystals are strange materials half-way between solids and liquids.*

liquid crystal display, liquid crystal displays

NC A **liquid crystal display** is a display of information on a screen, which uses liquid crystals that become visible when electricity is passed through them. *...liquid crystal displays on digital watches.*

liquidity /lɪˈkwɪdəti/

NU **Liquidity** is having enough cash, or things that can easily be converted into cash, to pay any debts or sudden needs; a technical term in economics. *Another growing economic problem in former East Germany is the lack of liquidity for state and local governments. ...its long-term commitment to help Yugoslavia tackle its liquidity crisis.*

liquidize /ˈlɪkwɪdaɪz/ **liquidizes, liquidizing, liquidized**; also spelt **liquidise**.

VO If you **liquidize** food, you mash it in a liquidizer in order to make it liquid. *...either liquidize the vegetables or pass them through a sieve.*

liquidizer /lɪkwɪdaɪzə/ **liquidizers**
NC A **liquidizer** is an electrical machine that you use to mash food and make it liquid.
liquid lunch, liquid lunches
NC A **liquid lunch** is a lunch that consists mostly of alcoholic drinks; often used humorously.
liquor /lɪkə/ **liquors**
N MASS **Liquor** is strong alcoholic drink; used in American English. *They had been drinking home-made liquor and most of them were drunk... The bill makes petrol, liquor, tobacco, and luxury goods more expensive.*
liquorice /lɪkərɪʃ/; also spelt **licorice**.
NU **Liquorice** is a firm black substance with a strong taste used for making sweets.
lira /lɪərə/ **lire** /lɪərə/ or **liras**
1 NC A **lira** is the unit of money that is used in Italy. *The hire charge for two days was ten thousand lire.*
2 NC A **lira** is also the unit of money that is used in Turkey and in Syria. *...a decline in the market value of the Turkish lira.*
Lisbon /lɪzbən/
Lisbon is the capital of Portugal and its largest city. Population: 807,937 (1981).
lisp /lɪsp/ **lisps, lisping, lisped**
1 NC Someone with a **lisp** pronounces the sounds 's' and 'z' as if they were 'th'. For example, they say 'thing' instead of 'sing'. *He spoke with a perceptible lisp.*
2 V or V-QUOTE If someone **lisps**, they speak with a lisp. *When people asked him what he wanted to be when he grew up he would lisp childishly 'a policeman'.*
lissom /lɪsəm/; also spelt **lissome**.
ADJ Someone who is **lissom** is slim and graceful; a literary word. *...heroes in leather flying jackets, and lissom sweethearts left behind on the tarmac.*
list /lɪst/ **lists, listing, listed**
1 NC A **list** is a set of things which are written down one below the other. *Look at your list of things to be mended... Find out all their names and make a list... The list includes sofas, air-conditioners, cameras, motorbikes, and even buses.* ● See also **shopping list, short-list, waiting list.**
2 VO To **list** a set of things means to mention them all one after the other. *There was a label on each case listing its contents.*
3 VO If something **is listed**, it is included as an item on a list, especially an official list. *He is still listed in the files by his code name, the Jackal... Hundreds of men are still listed as missing, feared dead. ...companies listed on the British stock market.*
4 V If a ship **is listing**, it is leaning over to one side, often because it is damaged or sinking. *At about ten hours GMT the Mare began listing and sank... The vessel is still afloat, though listing heavily.*
listed /lɪstɪd/
ADJ **Listed** buildings are protected by law from being demolished or altered, because they are old or important. *It was designated as a listed building because of its historical and architectural interest.*
listen /lɪsn/ **listens, listening, listened**
1 V If you **listen** to someone who is talking or to a sound, you give your attention to the person or the sound. *Paul, are you listening?... Listen carefully to what he says... They listen to some music or read until I put them to bed.*
2 V+for If you **listen** for a sound, you keep alert, ready to hear it if it occurs. *She sat quite still, listening for her baby's cry.*
3 V To **listen** to someone also means to believe them or accept their advice. *No one here will listen to you, not without proof... He refused to listen to reason.*
listen in PHRASAL VERB 1 If you **listen in** to a private conversation, you secretly listen to it. *...a young man in a restaurant listening in to a conversation at a distant table... Telephone calls are taped, and the police can listen in. ...a satellite capable of listening in to military and diplomatic communications.* 2 If you **listen in** to a radio programme, you listen to it. *...anyone who has listened in to the broadcasts from the House of Commons... He was listening in to the World Cup game on his radio.*

listener /lɪsə⁰nə/ **listeners**
1 NC People who listen to the radio are often referred to as **listeners**. *...a weekly English language programme for overseas listeners... The song was chosen from seven others by BBC viewers and listeners.*
2 NC A **listener** in a particular situation is a person who is listening rather than one who is speaking or playing music. *The President reassured his listeners that they had nothing to fear... Heavy, repetitious music seems to have an exciting effect on the listener.*
listeria /lɪstɪəriə/
NU **Listeria** is a kind of bacteria that can cause severe food poisoning. *...the latest scare about listeria in some pre-cooked foods on supermarket shelves... There is an average of more than one death per week from listeria infection in Britain.*
listing /lɪstɪŋ/ **listings**
NC A **listing** is a list, or an item in a list. *She checked the telephone directory and found a listing for E. Howard Hunt, Jr., in Potomac, Maryland... Grechko was shown in the listings as a naval captain, third rank.*
listless /lɪstləs/
ADJ If you are **listless**, you have no energy or enthusiasm. *She became listless and bored.*
◆ **listlessly** ADV *Rose watched him listlessly.*
lit /lɪt/
Lit is a past tense and past participle of **light**.
litany /lɪtəni/ **litanies**
1 NC A **litany** is part of a church service in which the priest says a fixed group of words and the people reply, also using a fixed group of words.
2 NC A **litany** is also something, especially a list of things, that is repeated often or repeated in a boring or insincere way. *The officer on the door chanted the litany 'Who are you and where are you going?' ...a litany of complaints.*
liter /liːtə/. See **litre**.
literacy /lɪtə⁰rəsi/
NU **Literacy** is the ability to read and write. *Mass literacy was only possible after the invention of printing. ...a national agency in Britain which works for adult literacy.*
literal /lɪtə⁰rəl/
1 ADJ The **literal** meaning of a word is its most basic meaning. *She was older than I was, and not only in the literal sense.*
2 ADJ ATTRIB A **literal** translation is one in which you translate each word separately, rather than expressing the meaning in a more natural way. *...a literal translation from the German.*
3 ADJ If you say that something is the **literal** truth or a **literal** fact, you are emphasizing that it is true. *This is a literal fact that applies to every married person.*
literally /lɪtə⁰rəli/
1 ADV You use **literally** to emphasize what you are saying, even though it is exaggerated or surprising. Some careful speakers of English think that this use of **literally** is incorrect. *I have literally begged my son for help... The motorway is literally seconds away from our house.*
2 ADV You also use **literally** to indicate that a word or expression is being used in its most basic sense. *They are people who have literally and spiritually left home.*
3 ADV If you translate a word or expression **literally**, you give its most basic meaning. *...a wati-pulka (literally 'big man').*
literary /lɪtə⁰rəri/
1 ADJ ATTRIB **Literary** means connected with literature. *The text has some literary merit. ...literary critics.*
2 ADJ **Literary** words are rather unusual ones which are used to create a special effect in a poem, speech, or novel.
literate /lɪtə⁰rət/
1 ADJ Someone who is **literate** is able to read and write. *Only half the children in this class are literate.*
2 ADJ Someone who is highly **literate** is well educated and intelligent. *...the children of highly literate parents.*

literati /lɪtərɑːti/
N PL **Literati** are well-educated people who are interested in literature; a formal word. *...legendary gatherings of literati.*

literature /lɪtrətʃə/
1 NU Novels, plays, and poetry are referred to as **literature**, especially when they are considered to have artistic qualities. *I envy you having a friend with whom you can discuss art and literature. ...a degree in English Literature.*
2 NU **Literature** is also printed information about something. *All major political parties print literature for hopeful candidates.*

lithe /laɪð/
ADJ A **lithe** person or animal moves and bends their body easily and gracefully; a literary word. *He looked out at the jewelled sea and the lithe brown girls walking along the beach.*

lithium /lɪθiəm/
NU **Lithium** is the lightest known metal. It is used in batteries, medicines, and chemical processes, especially to make other metals. *..the country's rich deposits of the metal lithium.*

lithograph /lɪθəgrɑːf/ **lithographs**
NC A **lithograph** is a printed picture made by the method of lithography. *...the lithograph of Queen Victoria over the mantlepiece.*

lithographic /lɪθəgræfɪk/
ADJ ATTRIB **Lithographic** processes and equipment are used in lithography. *...a type of stone ideal for use in lithographic printing.*

lithography /lɪθɒgrəfi/
NU **Lithography** is a method of printing in which a piece of stone or metal is specially treated so that ink sticks to some parts of it and not to others. *The poster is so big that two lithography stones had to be used.*

Lithuania /lɪθjueɪniə/
Lithuania became independent of the USSR in 1991. It is one of the Baltic States, located in the north-west of the former USSR on the Baltic Sea. It was an independent country from 1919 until 1940. Vytautas Landsbergis became President in 1990. Lithuania exports agricultural products, electrical goods, and machinery. ♦ **Lithuanian** /lɪθjueɪniən/ N, ADJ
▪ *per capita GNP:* US$5,880 ▪ *religion:* Christianity (mainly Catholic) ▪ *language:* Lithuanian ▪ *currency:* lit ▪ *capital:* Vilnius ▪ *population:* 4 million (1989) ▪ *size:* 65,200 square kilometres.

litigant /lɪtɪgənt/ **litigants**
NC A **litigant** is a person who makes a formal complaint about someone to a civil court of law, or the person that the complaint is made about; a legal term. *In my experience litigants nearly always deceive their solicitors.*

litigate /lɪtɪgeɪt/ **litigates, litigating, litigated**
VO or V If you **litigate** a case, you take it to a civil court of law for a decision; a legal term. *He asked that the case be thrown out of court on the grounds that to litigate it would jeopardize state secrets... They probably have no intention of litigating the matter in court... It's going to be expensive to litigate.*

litigation /lɪtɪgeɪʃn/
NU **Litigation** is the process of fighting or defending a case in a civil court of law; a formal word. *It was not unusual for the bank to be involved in litigation over failed companies.*

litigious /lɪtɪdʒəs/
ADJ Someone who is **litigious** often makes formal complaints about people to a civil court of law; a formal word. *He was incredibly litigious.*

litmus paper /lɪtməs peɪpə/
NU **Litmus paper** is paper which has a chemical in it that makes it turn red when it touches an acid and blue when it touches an alkali. *Soldiers carry pocket detector kits which use a kind of litmus paper or chemical solutions to identify harmful liquids or vapors.*

litmus test /lɪtməs test/ **litmus tests**
NC A **litmus test** of something is a simple and effective way of proving it or measuring it. *...one of the litmus tests by which Mr Gorbachev's so-called*

new thinking would be judged. *...arms control, the traditional litmus test of superpower relations.*

litre /liːtə/ **litres**; spelt **liter** in American English.
1 NC A **litre** is a unit of volume for liquids and gases equal to a thousand cubic centimetres or approximately 1.76 pints. *...a litre of wine. ...a price of 28 pence per litre... The Indian government has raised the price of petrol by one rupee a litre.*
2 NC+SUPP You also use **litre** when talking about the capacity of a car engine. *...a 1.3 litre Vauxhall Astra.*

litter /lɪtə/ **litters, littering, littered**
1 NU **Litter** is rubbish which is left lying around outside. *There were piles of litter in the streets.*
2 VO If a number of things **litter** a place, they are scattered around in it. *Papers littered every surface... The floor was littered with ashtrays.*
3 NC A **litter** is a group of animals born to the same mother at the same time. *It was the finest puppy in a litter of six.*

litter bin, litter bins
NC A **litter bin** is a container into which people can put rubbish, usually in a street, park, or public building. *...places where litter bins overflow with rubbish. ...a litter bin outside Barclays Bank.*

litterbug /lɪtəbʌg/ **litterbugs**
NC A **litterbug** is the same as a **litter lout**; used in American English. *It was drilled into their heads since the time they were in first grade, 'Don't be a litterbug'.*

litter lout, litter louts
NC A **litter lout** is a person who drops or leaves rubbish in public places. *...treating them as if they were shoplifters or litter louts... The problem is not just the odd careless farmer or a bunch of litter louts.*

little /lɪtl/. For the meanings in paragraphs 5 and 6, the comparative is **less** and the superlative is **least**: see the separate entries for these words.
1 ADJ ATTRIB **Little** things are small in size or number, or short in length or duration. *...a little table with a glass top. ...little groups of people. ...after he had walked for a little way... She lay awake a little while longer. ...a little chat.*
2 ADJ A **little** child is very young. *...two little girls... I often heard him do that when I was little.*
3 ADJ ATTRIB Your **little** sister or brother is younger than you are. *There's also Marie's little brother to think about.*
4 ADJ ATTRIB **Little** also means not important. *Don't bother me with little things like that. ...annoying little mishaps.*
5 QUANT or DET You also use **little** to emphasize that there is only a small amount of something. *Little of the equipment was standardized... There is little to worry about... John and I had very little money left... They paid little attention to cost and deliveries... Mr Maude made little, if any, progress... There seems little doubt that fighting is still going on.*
6 ADV **Little** means not very often or to only a small extent. *Richardson interrupted very little... She seemed little changed... We are talking too much and doing too little.*
7 QUANT or DET A **little** of something is a small amount of it. *The waiter poured a little of the wine into a glass... He spoke a little French.*
● **Little** is used in these phrases. ● A **little** or a **little bit** means to a small extent or degree. *He frowned a little... I felt a little uncomfortable... I thought he was a little bit afraid.* ● If something happens **little by little**, it happens gradually. *Then I learnt, little by little, the early history of her family.* ● **precious little**: see **precious**.

little finger, little fingers
NC Your **little finger** is the smallest finger on your hand. *...the tips of his two little fingers.* ● to **twist** someone **round** your **little finger**: see **twist**.

little-known
ADJ ATTRIB A **little-known** person or thing is one that is not famous or familiar. *The importance of one article by a little-known journalist in Pravda should not be overestimated. ...a little-known masterpiece by the German playwright Dietrich Grabbe.*

liturgical /lɪtɜːdʒɪkl/
ADJ Liturgical things are used in or relate to church services. *It illustrates how Jews and early Christians often shared the same liturgical music and mythology. ...a liturgical text.*

liturgy /lɪtədʒi/ **liturgies**
1 NU The religious services that are carried out in a fixed way in the Christian Church are referred to as **liturgy.** *The Eastern Church already differed from the Roman Church in language, liturgy, and other respects.*
2 NC A **liturgy** is a particular form of religious service, usually one that is approved by the Christian Church. *Part of the liturgy was sung to Indian music... They urged the use of non-sexist language in the liturgy... She would have preferred a simpler liturgy.*

live, lives, living, lived. Live is pronounced /lɪv/ when it is a verb and /laɪv/ when it is an adjective or adverb.
1 VA If someone **lives** in a particular place, their home is there. *Where do you live?... I used to live in Grange Road. ...those who leave our country to live abroad... My Grandmother lived with us for fifteen years.*
2 V A or VO The way someone **lives** is the kind of life they have, or the circumstances they are in. *We lived very simply... We live in a technological society. ...condemned a third of its people to live under foreign rule. ...the number of people living below the poverty line... They are forced to live entirely artificial lives.*
3 V To **live** means to be alive. *Women seem to live longer than men... She lost her will to live.*
4 ADJ ATTRIB **Live** animals or plants are alive, rather than being dead or artificial. *They grasp live snakes while dancing to bring rain. ...the export of live sheep to France.*
5 ADJ or ADV A **live** television or radio programme is one in which an event is broadcast at the time that it happens. *...live pictures of a man walking on the moon. ...live coverage of the Papal visit... The concert will be broadcast live on Radio Three.*
6 ADJ or ADV A **live** performance is one that is done in front of an audience. *...live theatre... I would like to perform live as much as possible.*
7 ADJ A **live** wire or piece of electrical equipment is directly connected to a source of electricity. *...live power cables.*
8 ADJ ATTRIB **Live** ammunition or bullets are made of metal, rather than rubber or plastic, and are intended to kill people rather than injure them. *The army opened fire with live ammunition. ...the feeling that live bullets were used too soon and too recklessly.*
9 If you **live it up,** you have a very enjoyable and exciting time, for example by going to parties; an informal expression. *There's no reason why you couldn't, you know, live it up once in a while.*
10 See also **living, short-lived.**

live down PHRASAL VERB If you cannot **live down** a mistake or failure, you cannot make people forget it. *If you were beaten by Jack, you'd never live it down.*
live for PHRASAL VERB If you **live for** a particular thing, it is the most important thing in your life. *...a man who lived for pleasure.*
live in PHRASAL VERB If someone **lives in,** they live in the place where they work or study. *The rest of the students tend to live in.*
live off PHRASAL VERB If you **live off** a particular source of money, you get from it the money that you need. *They were living off welfare.*
live on PHRASAL VERB 1 If you **live on** a particular amount of money, you have that amount of money to buy things. *I don't have enough to live on.* 2 If you **live on** a particular kind of food, it is the only kind you eat. *She lived on berries and wild herbs.* 3 If something **lives on,** it is remembered for a long time. *The Marilyn Monroe legend lives on in Hollywood.*
live out PHRASAL VERB 1 If you **live out** your life in a particular place or in particular circumstances, you stay in that place or remain in those circumstances until the end of your life. *He lived out the remaining years of his life in London. ...a young woman who is living out her life by helping other people.* 2 If

someone **lives out,** they do not live in the place where they work or study.
live through PHRASAL VERB If you **live through** an unpleasant event, you experience it and survive. *...those who lived through the Second World War.*
live together PHRASAL VERB If two people **live together,** they live in the same house and have a sexual relationship but are not married to one another. *The survey shows that couples who live together without getting married enjoy a more harmonious relationship.*
live up to PHRASAL VERB If someone or something **lives up to** people's expectations, they are as good as they were expected to be. *She succeeded in living up to her extraordinary reputation.*
live with PHRASAL VERB 1 If you **live with** someone, you live in the same house as them and have a sexual relationship with them, but are not married to them. *The Social Security people found out she was living with a man. ...men who live with a partner without marriage.* 2 If you have to **live with** an unpleasant situation, you have to accept it and carry on with your life or work. *They have to live with the consequences of their decision.*

live-in
1 ADJ ATTRIB A **live-in** employee is one who lives in the place where they work, for example in their employer's house or a hotel. *Many wealthy middle-class couples are choosing to employ live-in nannies... Only the very rich have live-in servants.*
2 ADJ ATTRIB **Live-in** boyfriends or girlfriends live in the same house as the person they are having a relationship with. *They should be able to take time off work if their live-in partner is sick or has died.*

livelihood /laɪvlɪhʊd/ **livelihoods**
N C or NU Your **livelihood** is the job or the source of your income. *The players say that their livelihoods would be at risk. ...the fear of losing their livelihood. ...the only source of livelihood for many in the occupied territories.*

livelong /lɪvlɒŋ/
If something happens **all the livelong day,** it happens over what seems a long and tedious time; a literary expression. *All the livelong day, Father and Mother strove to please their darling child.*

lively /laɪvli/ **livelier, liveliest**
1 ADJ **Lively** people are active, enthusiastic, and cheerful. *Four lively youngsters suddenly burst into the room.*
2 ADJ **Lively** also means interesting and exciting. *...a lively debate. ...a lively evening.*
3 ADJ ATTRIB You also use **lively** to describe a feeling which is strong and enthusiastic. *She took a lively interest in everything.*

liven /laɪvn/ **livens, livening, livened**
liven up PHRASAL VERB 1 If a place or event **livens up** or if you **liven** it **up,** it becomes more interesting and exciting. *There are lots of new shops and things. The place is really livening up.* 2 If people **liven up** or if something **livens** them **up,** they become more cheerful and energetic. *At least the incident livened her up.*

liver /lɪvə/ **livers**
1 NC Your **liver** is a large organ in your body which cleans your blood. *Drink rots your liver.*
2 NU **Liver** is the liver of some animals, which is cooked and eaten. *The government has warned pregnant women not to eat liver. ...products such as liver pate and liver sausage.*

liveried /lɪvərid/
ADJ ATTRIB A **liveried** servant is a servant who wears a special uniform. *...a liveried doorman outside London's Dorchester hotel.*

liverish /lɪvərɪʃ/
ADJ Someone who is **liverish** feels slightly sick; an old-fashioned word.

livery /lɪvəri/ **liveries**
1 NU or NC A servant's **livery** is the special uniform that he or she wears, especially a uniform that is worn only by the servants of a particular person. *Sixteen servants in rich livery waited on them... They wore his badge and livery.*

2 NC The **livery** of a particular company is the special design or set of colours that are associated with it and are put on its products and possessions. *...the aircraft's sleek design and blue and grey livery. ...the dark blue, grey and red livery of British Airways.*

lives
Lives is both the third person singular, present tense, of the verb **live**, when it is pronounced /lɪvz/, and the plural of the noun **life**, when it is pronounced /laɪvz/.

livestock /laɪvstɒk/
N COLL Animals kept on a farm are referred to as **livestock**. *They encourage farmers to keep more livestock... Half of the country's livestock has been lost since 1979... Large numbers of livestock have drowned.*

live wire /laɪv waɪə/ **live wires**
NC If you describe someone as a **live wire**, you mean that they are lively and energetic; an informal expression.

livid /lɪvɪd/
1 ADJ Someone who is **livid** is extremely angry; an informal use. *He said, 'No, you won't.' I was absolutely livid.*
2 ADJ Something that is **livid** is an unpleasant dark purple or greyish blue colour; a literary use. *...livid bruises.*

living /lɪvɪŋ/
1 ADJ ATTRIB A **living** person or animal is alive. *I have no living relatives... All living things take up carbon from the environment. ...living organisms in the soil or water.*
2 N SING The work that you do for a **living** is the work that you do to earn the money that you need. *I never expected to earn my living as an artist... He made a modest living by painting.*
3 NU+SUPP You use **living** when talking about the quality of people's daily lives. *The quality of urban living has been damaged by excessive noise levels. ...more awareness of the benefits of healthy living.*
4 ADJ ATTRIB You also use **living** when talking about places where people relax when they are not working. *...the living quarters of the hotel staff... We are trying to improve living conditions at sea.*
5 the **living daylights**: see **daylights**. **within living memory**: see **memory**. See also **live, cost of living, standard of living**.

living room, living rooms
NC The **living room** in a house is the room where people sit and relax. *She went back into the living room... The cottage had a living room and two bedrooms.*

living standards
N PL When you refer to **living standards**, you are referring to the level of comfort in which people live, which usually depends on how much money they have. *...a fall in real living standards. ...the demand for better living standards.*

living wage
N SING A **living wage** is a wage which is large enough to enable you to buy food, clothing, and other necessary things. *It's impossible to employ so many people and go on paying them a living wage.*

lizard /lɪzəd/ **lizards**
NC A **lizard** is a reptile with short legs and a long tail. *...a small lizard native to the islands... There are a lot of lizards in the garden.*

Ljubljana /ljuːbljɑːnə/
Ljubljana is the capital of Slovenia and its largest city. Population: 305,000 (1981).

-'ll /-l/
SUFFIX **-'ll** is a short form of 'will' or 'shall' used in spoken English and informal written English. *He'll come back... That'll be all right.*

llama /lɑːmə/ **llamas**
NC A **llama** is a South American animal with thick hair, which looks like a small camel without a hump. *The llamas, alpacas and guanacos would be bred for their fine coats.*

lo /ləʊ/
ADV SEN **Lo**, or **lo and behold**, is used to draw attention to a surprising or interesting event that is about to be mentioned; a literary use. *For lo, the winter is past,* *the rain is over and gone... In the end they gave up and adopted a child, and lo and behold all her tensions disappeared and she became pregnant.*

load /ləʊd/ **loads, loading, loaded**
1 VO If you **load** a vehicle or container or **load** things into it, you put things into it. *...when they came to load the van with their things... We started loading the pheasants into the sacks... The uranium was loaded onto a ship bound for Sweden.*
2 NC A **load** is something which is being carried. *We took up our heavy load and trudged back... Its load of minerals was dumped at sea.*
3 NC+SUPP A bus **load**, car **load**, etc is the number or the quantity of something that can be carried by a particular vehicle. *The team is flying to Yerevan with a plane load of emergency supplies... They expect five boat loads of refugees to arrive tomorrow.*
4 VO When someone **loads** a weapon, they put ammunition such as bullets into it, so that it is ready to be fired. *The crews put on full protective gear, loaded the guns, and took up action stations.*
5 VO When someone **loads** a camera or other piece of equipment, or **loads** a film, tape, etc into it, they put the film, tape, etc into it. *...loading the video into the recorder, starting it, and moving the picture forwards. ...a disk which can be loaded into a computer... The result depends on the type of program that has been loaded into the computer.*
6 QUANT **Loads** of something or a **load** of something means a lot of it; an informal use. *We talked about loads of things... It's a load of old rubbish... Dr Owen described the document as a load of nonsense.*

loaded /ləʊdɪd/
1 ADJ If something is **loaded** with things, it has a large number of them in it or on it. *...a truck loaded with bricks. ...waitresses with loaded trays.*
2 ADJ If a weapon is **loaded**, it has ammunition such as bullets in it. *...started work without noticing that the weapon was loaded... He is reported to have threatened people with a loaded gun.*
3 ADJ PRED If you say that someone is **loaded**, you mean that they have a lot of money; an informal use. *All right, you're loaded. How's about lending us a buck?*
4 ADJ A **loaded** remark or question has more significance, meaning, or purpose than it appears to have. *Proliferation is a very loaded word in this context. ...asking loaded questions in parliament.*

loaf /ləʊf/ **loaves**
NC A **loaf** of bread is bread in a shape that can be cut into slices. *...the cost of a loaf of bread. ...three loaves per person per day.*

loafer /ləʊfə/ **loafers**
NC A **loafer** is someone who spends their time not working, or not doing the things that they ought to be doing; an informal word. *...a pack of idle loafers.*

loam /ləʊm/
NU **Loam** is soil that is good for growing crops and plants in because it contains a lot of decayed vegetable matter, and not too much sand or clay.

loan /ləʊn/ **loans, loaning, loaned**
1 NC A **loan** is a sum of money that you borrow, usually from a bank or government, and have to pay back in smaller amounts with interest every week, month, or year. *They found it impossible to get a bank loan... He insists they will have no problem with any loan repayments. ...an Ethiopian request for a loan worth some $200 million... It will be giving fewer interest-free loans to Third World countries.* ● See also **bridging loan**.
2 N SING If someone gives you a **loan** of something, you borrow it from them. *He asked for the loan of twelve dozen glasses.*
3 If a book or picture is **on loan**, it has been borrowed. *Most of his books are on loan from the library.*
4 VO+too or VOO If you **loan** something to someone, you lend it to them. *He never loaned his car to anybody... I'll loan you fifty dollars. ...the estimated 10,000 million dollars loaned to them by Kuwait.*

loan shark, loan sharks
NC A **loan shark** is someone who lends money to

people at very high rates of interest, and sometimes uses illegal methods or violence to make sure they pay it back; an informal expression, used showing disapproval. *...a debt he owes to a loan shark. ...poorer people often fall into the clutches of loan sharks.*

loath /ləʊθ/; also spelt **loth**.
ADJ PRED+*to*-INF If you are **loath** to do something, you are unwilling to do it. *Governments have been loath to impose any sanctions.*

loathe /ləʊð/ **loathes, loathing, loathed**
V O If you **loathe** something or someone, you dislike them very much. *I particularly loathed team games at school.*

loathing /ləʊðɪŋ/
NU **Loathing** is a feeling of great dislike. *He remembered his school days with loathing.*

loathsome /ləʊðsəm/
ADJ **Loathsome** means very unpleasant. *I hate the loathsome way you use other people.*

loaves /ləʊvz/
Loaves is the plural of **loaf**.

lob /lɒb/ **lobs, lobbing, lobbed**
1 V O If you **lob** something, you throw it high in the air. *She wrapped a piece of paper round a stone and lobbed it into the next garden... Teargas grenades were lobbed into the barricade.*
2 V O If you **lob** the ball in tennis, you hit it high into the air so that it lands behind your opponent. *Miss Evert reached to lob a return of Miss Wade's.* ▶ Also NC *...high lobs to the backhand corner. ...the final game, which Hlasek won with a perfect lob.*

Lobamba /lɒbɡæmbə/
Lobamba is the legislative capital of Swaziland and, as the residence of the Queen Mother, was the traditional Swazi capital. Population: 6,000 (1976).

lobby /lɒbi/ **lobbies, lobbying, lobbied**
1 NC The **lobby** of a building is the main entrance area with corridors and staircases leading off it. *I rushed into the hotel lobby.*
2 N COLL+SUPP A **lobby** is also a group of people who try to persuade the government that something should be done. *...the anti-nuclear lobby. ...the victim of a farming lobby that is far too powerful.*
3 V O or V A If you **lobby** a member of a government, you try to persuade them that a particular thing should be done. *He lobbied the Home Secretary and other members of parliament. ...lobbying for stricter controls on guns... British football clubs are lobbying to be allowed back into Europe.*

lobbyist /lɒbiist/ **lobbyists**
NC A **lobbyist** is someone who actively tries to persuade a government or council that a law should be changed or that a particular thing should be done. *...the activities of parliamentary lobbyists... Lobbyists for the rebels persuaded the US Congress to bring forward the date.*

lobe /ləʊb/ **lobes**
1 NC The **lobe** of your ear is the soft part at the bottom.
2 NC+SUPP A **lobe** is also one of the parts of your brain, your lungs, or your liver; a technical use. *For the typical right-handed person, language is usually under the control of the left temporal lobe of the brain. ...the observation that infection starts in a single lobe of the lungs.*

lobotomy /ləbɒtəmi/ **lobotomies**
NCor NU A **lobotomy** is a surgical operation in which some of the nerves in the brain are cut in order to treat severe mental illness; a medical term.

lobster /lɒbstə/ **lobsters**
NC A **lobster** is a sea creature with a hard shell, two large claws, and eight legs. *At this stage the lobsters are 56 millimetres long, measured from the eye to the tail... There was lobster and veal on the menu.*

lobster pot, lobster pots
NC A **lobster pot** is a trap in the shape of a basket that is used for catching lobsters. *Their boat has not been seen since last night, when they set out to check lobster pots.*

local /ləʊkl/ **locals**
1 ADJ **Local** means existing in or belonging to the area

where you live or work. *...a picture in the local paper... Telephone your local police station. ...acting against the wishes of local residents. ...a local radio station.* ◆ **locally** ADV *Everything we used was bought locally. ...the main equipment, which is being locally produced. ...using locally available materials, simple equipment and local labour.*
2 ADJ ATTRIB A **local** council is responsible for the government of a part of a country. *...over half the local authorities in England and Wales. ...local elections. ...the new system of raising funds for local government.* ◆ **locally** ADV *Should housing policy be decided nationally or locally?*
3 NC You can refer to the people who live in a particular district as the **locals**; an informal use. *The locals view these road improvements with alarm... Locals said at least two others had been hit.*
4 ADJ A **local** anaesthetic affects only a small area of your body. *The operation was carried out under a local anaesthetic and lasted two-and-a-half hours.*

local colour
NU **Local colour** is experience or knowledge of a particular place or period of history and the way this is used in a book or a film in order to make it seem more realistic. *It all gives local colour to the book.*

locale /ləʊkɑːl/ **locales**
NC A **locale** is a small area, for example the place where something happens or where the action of a book or film is set; a literary word. *They were born, grew up, and died in the same locale... We hope your holiday is spent in a more serene locale than Grimm, Pennsylvania.*

locality /ləʊkæləti/ **localities**
NC A particular **locality** is an area of a country or city. *...the anxiety of people living in the same locality.*

localize /ləʊkəlaɪz/ **localizes, localizing, localized**; also spelt **localise**.
1 V O If you **localize** a difficult situation, you restrict it to a small area or group, and prevent it spreading to other areas or groups. *...an attempt to localize the effect of these disturbances... One course of action would be to try to localise the strikes... In other times, this whole dispute might have been localized and diffused.*
2 V O If you **localize** something, you find out exactly where it is. *As I reported earlier, I can't localise the trouble. ...so that we can localize exactly the position of the tumour within their body... Barn owls turned out to be extremely accurate at localising sounds.*

localized /ləʊkəlaɪzd/; also spelt **localised**.
ADJ Something that is **localized** exists or occurs only in one place or in a small area. *...a localized pain in the back of her head. ...localized shortages of motor fuel... Elsewhere in eastern Africa the problems are more localised, but no less urgent.*

local time
NU **Local time** is the official time in a particular region or country. *The plane arrives in London at 17.50 local time... The ceasefire will take effect at midnight local time (2100 GMT).*

locate /ləʊkeɪt/ **locates, locating, located**
1 V O If you **locate** something or someone, you find them; a formal use. *If you do locate him, call me.*
2 V-PASS A If something **is located** in a particular place, it is in that place. *The house was located in the heart of the city.*
3 V A If an organization **locates** in a particular place, they move to that place and start working there. *Ford decided to locate in Dundee... There's concern that dropping trade barriers will encourage US businesses to locate in Mexico.*

location /ləʊkeɪʃn/ **locations**
1 NC+SUPP A **location** is a place, especially the place where something happens or is situated. *Election officials ran out of ballot papers at six locations... The new job involves a new employer and a new location. ...the size and location of your office... The interview was recorded at a secret location nearly a month ago.*
2 If a film is made **on location**, it is made in natural surroundings rather than with artificial scenery on a set or in a studio. *...the film was shot on location in*

the city of Bombay.

loch /lɒx, lɒk/ **lochs**
NC A **loch** is a large area of water in Scotland. *...Loch Lomond.*

loci /ˈləʊsaɪ/
Loci is the plural of **locus**.

lock /lɒk/ **locks, locking, locked**
1 VO When you **lock** something, you fasten it using a key. *Lock the door after you leave.* ◆ **locked** ADJ *...the locked cupboard.*
2 VO If you **lock** something in a cupboard, room, or drawer, you put it inside and lock the door or drawer. *He had locked all his papers in the safe... He locked them away in a drawer.*
3 V-ERG You say that something **locks** or is **locked** in a position when it moves into that position and is held firmly there. *Smoothly the rod locked into place... There's no danger of it collapsing on you once properly locked into position.*
4 V-PASS A If people are **locked** in a fight or argument, they cannot stop fighting or arguing. *Rebel groups and government forces are locked in a fierce battle for control of the country.*
5 NC The **lock** on something such as a door is the part which fastens it when you turn a key in it. *The key rattling in the lock startled me.* ● If something is **under lock and key**, it is in a locked room or container. *She would keep any sensitive documents under lock and key.*
6 NC A **lock** on a canal is a section between barriers, where the water level can be raised or lowered so that boats can move to a higher or lower section of the canal. *The canal operators use stored fresh water to fill up the locks. ...a lock that the Swedish freighter had to pass through before reaching the open sea.*
7 NC A **lock** of hair is a small bunch of hairs; a literary use. *A lock of hair had fallen down over her eyes... He shook his black locks.*

lock in PHRASAL VERB 1 If you **lock** someone **in**, you put them in a place and lock the door so that they cannot get out. *He didn't allow any member of his staff to conduct business because they were all locked in.* 2 If you **lock** yourself **in**, you go into a place and lock the door so that no one else can come in. *The university confirmed that a few foreign students had locked themselves in... By eight in the evening every family locked itself in.*

lock out PHRASAL VERB If you **lock** someone **out**, you prevent them from getting into a place by locking the doors. *She had been locked out of the house.*

lock up PHRASAL VERB 1 If someone is **locked up**, they are put in prison or in a special psychiatric hospital. *The idea of being locked up in jail filled her with horror.* 2 When you **lock up**, you make sure that all the doors and windows of a building are properly closed or locked. *...a Portuguese woman who had been locking up her shop.*

locker /ˈlɒkə/ **lockers**
NC A **locker** is a small metal cupboard with a lock, where you can put your personal belongings temporarily, for example in a school, a place of work, or a sports club. *The sailors have just a tiny bunk space and locker. ...a line of metal lockers.*

locker room, locker rooms
NC A **locker room** is a room in which there are a lot of lockers, for example in a school, a place of work, or a sports club. *The locker room should be opened for just 20 minutes after a game.*

locket /ˈlɒkɪt/ **lockets**
NC A **locket** is a piece of jewellery containing something such as a picture which a woman wears on a chain round her neck.

lockout /ˈlɒkaʊt/ **lockouts**
NC A **lockout** is a situation in which employers close a place of work and prevent workers from entering it until they accept the employers' new proposals on pay or conditions of work. *A lockout has been declared at the shipyard... The management has announced a lockout of workers.*

locksmith /ˈlɒksmɪθ/ **locksmiths**
NC A **locksmith** is someone whose job is to make and mend locks.

lockup /ˈlɒkʌp/ **lockups**
NC A **lockup** is a jail or cell; used in American English. *They hustled him off and put him in the lockup.*

lock-up garage, lock-up garages
NC A **lock-up garage** is a garage situated away from your home which you rent in order to store your car or other belongings securely. *He parked his car in the open, rather than in a lock-up garage.*

locomotion /ˌləʊkəˈməʊʃn/
NU **Locomotion** is the ability to move and the act of moving from one place to another; a technical term. *The child begins to experience the power of locomotion. ...the enormous variety of locomotion techniques of which the human frame is capable.*

locomotive /ˌləʊkəˈməʊtɪv/ **locomotives**
NC A **locomotive** is a railway engine; a formal word. *...a model of a famous early railway locomotive... China is still justly famous for her steam locomotives.*

locum /ˈləʊkəm/ **locums**
NC A **locum** is a doctor or priest who temporarily does the work of another doctor or priest who is ill or on holiday. *It would be more expensive for health authorities to employ locum doctors.*

locus /ˈləʊkəs/ **loci**
NC+of The **locus** of something is the place where it happens, or the most important area or point with which it is associated; a formal word. *The locus of the conflict has been shifting... The Middle East was the locus of virtually all the spare capacity.*

locust /ˈləʊkəst/ **locusts**
NC **Locusts** are large insects that are similar to grasshoppers and live in hot countries. They fly in large groups and eat crops. *Reports from Mozambique say swarms of locusts have destroyed eighty per cent of crops. ...helping to fight a plague of locusts in Tunisia.*

locution /ləˈkjuːʃn/ **locutions**
NC+SUPP A particular **locution** is a particular way of expressing something in words; a formal word. *...employing a locution characteristic of California.*

lodge /lɒdʒ/ **lodges, lodging, lodged**
1 NC A **lodge** is a small house at the entrance to the grounds of a large house. *...seven hundred acres of land, nine cottages and three lodges.*
2 NC A **lodge** is also a hut or small house where people stay on holiday. *They went to a shooting lodge in Scotland for the weekend. ...a hunting lodge deep in the woods.*
3 NC+SUPP In some organizations, a **lodge** is a local branch or meeting place of the organization. *One masonic lodge is said to be composed entirely of police... Every town and village in Northern Ireland has an Orange lodge.*
4 V-ERG A If you **lodge** in someone else's house for a period of time, you live there, usually paying rent. *He had arranged for me to lodge with his daughter... Rebel and government delegates were lodged in different hotels.*
5 V-ERG A If something **lodges** somewhere or is **lodged** there, it becomes stuck there. *The bullet had lodged a quarter of an inch from his spine... I had somehow got the bone lodged in my throat... One missile did not explode and was lodged in the framework of the ship.*
6 VO If you **lodge** a complaint, you formally make it; a formal use. *...the charges that had been lodged against them. ...a complaint lodged with the local police... The appeals were lodged yesterday in the supreme court.*

lodger /ˈlɒdʒə/ **lodgers**
NC A **lodger** is a person who pays money to live in part of someone else's house. *She allowed her student lodgers a lot of freedom.*

lodging /ˈlɒdʒɪŋ/ **lodgings**
1 NU If you are provided with **lodging**, you are provided with a place to stay for a period of time. *They were offered free lodging in first-class hotels.* ● See also **board and lodging**.
2 N PL If you live in **lodgings**, you live in part of someone's house and pay them for this. *They have to find lodgings in the village.*

loft /lɒft/ **lofts**
NC A **loft** is the space inside the roof of a house, often used for storing things. *...domestic energy can be saved by improving loft insulation and draught proofing.*

lofty /lɒfti/; a literary word.
1 ADJ Something that is **lofty** is very high. *We explored lofty corridors.*
2 ADJ A **lofty** idea or aim is noble, important, and admirable. *...trying to maintain a lofty principle... Such lofty goals justify any means.*
3 ADJ Someone who behaves in a **lofty** way behaves in a proud and rather unpleasant way. *She hated his lofty manner.* ◆ **loftily** ADV *'I can't permit that,' Otto said loftily.*

log /lɒg/ **logs, logging, logged**
1 NC A **log** is a piece of a thick branch or of the trunk of a tree. *He threw another log on the fire.*
2 NC A **log** is also an official written record of what happens each day, for example on board a ship. *The Controller entered this in his log.*
3 VO If you **log** an event or fact, you record it officially, for example in writing or on a computer. *The death must be logged... There are systems here for logging the data.*

log in PHRASAL VERB See **log into**.
log into PHRASAL VERB When someone **logs into** a computer system, **logs in**, or **logs on**, they gain access to the system, usually by typing their name or identity code and a password.
log on PHRASAL VERB See **log into**.
log out PHRASAL VERB When someone who is using a computer system **logs out**, they finish using the system by typing a particular command.

loganberry /lɔʊgənbəᵊri/ **loganberries**
NC A **loganberry** is a purplish red fruit that is similar to a raspberry.

logarithm /lɒgərɪðəm/ **logarithms**
NC In mathematics, the **logarithm** of a number is another number that is used to represent it, in order to make a difficult multiplication or division sum simpler. Mathematics books often contain a list of logarithms. *Multiplication of any two numbers is achieved by adding their logarithms.*

log book, log books
NC A **log book** is a book in which someone records details and events relating to something, especially to their car. *Keep the test certificate, the log book, and the insurance certificate at home... The log book showed the aircraft had been on fourteen combat missions.*

logger /lɒgə/ **loggers**
NC **Loggers** are people whose job is to cut down trees in a forest. *The loggers say their jobs are faced with extinction because of declining timber sales.*

loggerheads /lɒgəhedz/
If people are **at loggerheads**, they disagree strongly, and often use every opportunity to argue or fight with each other. *The Christian Democrats were at loggerheads with the Social Democrats... The Americans and Europeans are still at loggerheads over the question of farm subsidies.*

logging /lɒgɪŋ/
NU **Logging** is the activity of cutting down trees in order to sell the wood. *...forests where illegal logging had been reported.* ● See also **log**.

logic /lɒdʒɪk/
1 NU **Logic** is a way of reasoning that involves a series of statements, each of which must be true if the statement before it is true. *The proposals should be debated on the basis of fact and logic. ...an exercise in logic.*
2 NU+SUPP Different kinds of **logic** are different ways of thinking and reasoning. *Economic logic dictated the policy of centralization... The logic behind this is simple: the fewer restrictions there are, the faster trade will grow. ...mistakes for which the logic of Marxism-Leninism could provide no explanation.*

logical /lɒdʒɪkl/
1 ADJ In a **logical** argument or analysis, each statement is true if the statement before it is true. *I made little attempt at logical argument.* ◆ **logically** ADV *Everything has to be logically analysed.*
2 ADJ A **logical** conclusion or result is the only one that can reasonably result. *There is only one logical conclusion... To him violence was a logical inevitability.* ◆ **logically** ADV *It follows logically that one of them is lying.*
3 ADJ A **logical** course of action seems reasonable or sensible in the circumstances. *Wouldn't it have been more logical for them to make the arrest downstairs?* ◆ **logically** ADV SEN *Therefore, logically, he had to go.*

logician /lədʒɪʃn/ **logicians**
NC A **logician** is a person who is a specialist in logic.

logistical /lədʒɪstɪkl/ or **logistic** /lədʒɪstɪk/
1 ADJ ATTRIB In a military situation, **logistical** or **logistic** means concerning the organization of transport, supplies, and maintenance, for troops and equipment; a technical use. *West Germany says it's willing to provide logistical support, but that it cannot subsidize the American troop buildup. ...where the rebels have their main logistic bases.*
2 ADJ ATTRIB **Logistical** or **logistic** means relating to the organization of something complicated. *Moving the government to Berlin is going to be a logistical nightmare and will cost a fortune. ...the logistical problems of the aid programme.*

logistics /lədʒɪstɪks/
1 N PLorNU In a military situation, **logistics** is the organization of transport, supplies, and maintenance, for troops and equipment; a technical use. *The revolutionary guards, acting with army support, are now quite effective, but logistics still present problems... And if we get into a war, we certainly want to have the logistics backup and support to be able to sustain it.*
2 N PLorNU You can refer to the skilful organization of anything complicated as the **logistics** of it; a formal use. *...the tiresome logistics of modern broadcasting... They would meet as soon as possible to discuss the logistics of forming an alliance.*

logjam /lɒgdʒæm/
N SING If a situation has been impossible to change for a long time, especially because people are unable to agree about something, and you talk about someone or something breaking the **logjam**, you mean that they may be able to change it. *...talks aimed at breaking the political logjam in the province... If Washington accepts the idea of an international conference, then the present logjam will have been broken.*

logo /lɔʊgəʊ/ **logos**
NC The **logo** of a company or organization is the special design that it puts on all its products, publicity material, and possessions. *You will be welcome at all hotels displaying our logo. ...the new party logo of the Liberal Democrats.*

loin /lɔɪn/ **loins**
1 N PL Someone's **loins** are the front part of their body between their waist and thighs, especially their sexual organs; a literary use. *My loins still tingle when I think of her. ...Sam, the son of his loins.*
2 NUorNC **Loin**, or a **loin**, is a piece of meat which comes from the back or sides of an animal, quite near the tail end. *...loin chops. ...loin of veal in cream and brandy.*
3 If you **gird up** your **loins** or **gird** your **loins**, you prepare to do something difficult or dangerous; a literary expression. *It's time for them to leave their cushioned chairs, gird up their loins and stride out into the world... Bonn and Vienna are girding their loins to cope with another influx of refugees.*

loincloth /lɔɪnklɒθ/ **loincloths**
NC A **loincloth** is a piece of cloth sometimes worn by men to cover their sexual organs, especially in hot countries where it is too hot to wear anything else. *...the traditional image of iron-age Britons in loincloths.*

loiter /lɔɪtə/ **loiters, loitering, loitered**
V If you **loiter** somewhere, you remain there for a while without any real purpose. *Remember not to loiter on the way.*

loll /lɒl/ **lolls, lolling, lolled**
1 VA If you **loll** somewhere, you sit or lie in a very relaxed position. *The students lolled in the grass.*

2 v If your head or tongue **lolls**, it hangs loosely.
*...feeling so sleepy, head lolling, eyes closing... Her
tongue lolled out, her eyes were rolled back.*
loll about PHRASAL VERB If you **loll about** or **loll
around** somewhere, you lie or stay there in a lazy
way, doing nothing in particular. *He kept saying he
should be at home and not lolling about in the summer
sun. ...walking up hills, taking photographs, and
generally lolling around.*
loll around PHRASAL VERB See **loll about.**

lollipop /lɒlipɒp/ **lollipops**
NC A **lollipop** is a sweet on the end of a stick. *She was
sitting on the front step sucking a lollipop.*

lollipop lady, lollipop ladies
NC A **lollipop lady** is a woman whose job is to help
children cross a particular road safely. She carries a
pole with a circular sign at the top that tells traffic to
stop.

lollipop man, lollipop men
NC A **lollipop man** is a man who does the same job as
a lollipop lady.

lolly /lɒli/ **lollies**; an informal word.
1 NC A **lolly** is a piece of flavoured ice or ice cream
on a stick.
2 NC A **lolly** is also a lollipop.

Lomé /ləʊmeɪ/
Lomé is the capital of Togo and its largest city.
Population: 283,000 (1980).

London /lʌndən/
London is the capital of the United Kingdom and its
largest city. Population: 6,735,000 (1988).

lone /ləʊn/
ADJ ATTRIB A **lone** person or thing is alone or is the
only one in a particular place; a literary word. *They
saw ahead a lone figure walking towards them... It is
thought a lone gunman fired through a window, using
an automatic weapon... The lone dissenter, as usual,
was Britain's Prime Minister Thatcher. ...the lone
survivor.*

lonely /ləʊnli/ **lonelier, loneliest**
1 ADJ Someone who is **lonely** is unhappy because they
are alone or do not have any friends. *...lonely widows.*
♦ **loneliness** NU *They suffer from isolation, poverty
and loneliness.*
2 ADJ A **lonely** situation or period of time is one in
which you feel unhappy because you are alone or do
not have any friends. *...that lonely night in Dakota.*
3 ADJ A **lonely** place is one where very few people
come. *...lonely country roads.*

lonely hearts
N+N A **lonely hearts** section in a newspaper, or a
lonely hearts club, is used by people who are trying to
find someone to be their lover or friend. *...the lonely
hearts column of a fashionable magazine... Many of
those who use lonely hearts columns are divorced
people.*

loner /ləʊnə/ **loners**
NC A **loner** is a person who likes being alone. *Some
may be loners who would scorn any assistance. ...an
unemployed loner who was convicted in 1983 on drugs
charges... He was described by colleagues as being
something of a loner.*

lonesome /ləʊnsəm/
ADJ **Lonesome** means the same as **lonely;** used in
informal American English. *I get lonesome
sometimes. ...a lonesome valley.*

long /lɒŋ/ **longer** /lɒŋgə/ **longest** /lɒŋgɪst/; **longs,
longing, longed**
1 ADV **Long** means a great amount of time or for a
great amount of time. *I haven't known her long...
Sorry it took so long... Our oil won't last much
longer... I had guessed long ago... Six weeks may be
too long to wait.*
2 ADV or ADJ after N **Long** is used in questions and
statements about duration. *'How long have you been
married?'—'Five years.'... His speeches are never less
than two hours long.*
3 ADJ A **long** event or period of time lasts or takes a
great amount of time. *There was a long pause... They
are demanding longer holidays... This work is being
done over a long period of time.*
4 ADJ If you talk about **long** hours, days, or years, you

mean that people worked for longer than usual, or that
a situation seemed to last longer because of hardship
or worry. *Doctors had always been expected to work
long hours... Troops and police have spent another
long day in their search for victims and wreckage...
He will find that relatively little has changed after the
long years he has spent in jail.*
5 ADJ Something that is **long** measures a great
distance from one end to the other. *She had long dark
hair. ...a long line of cars. ...long tables. ...the very
long, smooth runways that such aircraft need... There
were long queues at many polling stations... We drove
a long way the next day. ...a four mile long, shallow
ditch. ...the world's longest tunnel.*
6 ADV or ADJ after N **Long** is used in questions and
statements about length or distance. *How long is that
side? ...an area 3,000 feet long and 900 feet wide. ...an
oil slick sixteen miles long. ...a report five-hundred
pages long.*
7 ADJ A **long** book or other piece of writing contains a
lot of words. *...an enormously long novel.*
8 V+for or V+to-INF If you **long** for something, you want it
very much. *They longed for green trees and open
spaces... They're longing to see you.*
9 See also **longing.**
● **Long** is used in these phrases. ● **For long** means for
a great amount of time. *Men have been indoctrinated
for too long... It didn't stay there for long.* ● You use
long with 'all' and 'whole' to emphasize that something
happens for the whole of a particular time. *We row
all day long... They play the whole day long.*
● Something that **no longer** happens, or does **not**
happen **any longer,** used to happen in the past but does
not happen now. *We can no longer afford to live
there... I couldn't stand it any longer.* ● **Before long**
means soon. *They're bound to catch him before long.*
● If one thing is true **as long as** or **so long as** another
thing is true, it is true only if the other thing is true.
*We were all right as long as we kept our heads down...
Phone quality doesn't matter so long as it is adequate
for conversation.* ● People shout **'Long live'** a
particular person, country, or thing as a way of
showing their support for that person, country, or
thing. *The whole crowd chanted 'Long live Havel,
long live Havel!'... Long live the Republic! Long live
France!* ● You can say **'So long'** to say goodbye; an
informal expression. *'Well, so long.' He turned and
walked back to the car.* ● **at long last:** see **last.**

long- /lɒŋ-/
1 PREFIX **Long-** combines with past participles of
verbs to form adjectives that emphasize that
something happened, or started happening, a long time
ago. *The United Nations has a long-established flood
disaster programme. ...its long-held position as the
world's leading rice exporter.*
2 PREFIX **Long-** combines with adjectives formed from
nouns by adding '-ed', to form other adjectives that
indicate that something is long. *...long-haired louts.
...wearing a long-sleeved shirt and long trousers.*
3 PREFIX **Long-** combines with present participles of
verbs to form adjectives that emphasize that an action
takes place, or has been taking place, for a long time.
*...staffed by loyal long-serving employees. ...their
eleventh long-playing record.*
4 PREFIX **Long-** combines with nouns to form modifiers
that indicate that something happens over a long
distance or for a long time. *Several long-haul flights
have been delayed. ...long-stay visas.*
5 PREFIX **Long-** combines with adjectives to form
other adjectives that indicate that something happens
for a long time or over a long distance. *...Mats
Wilander's bid for a long-overdue tournament victory.
...a long-extinct creature.*

long-awaited
ADJ ATTRIB A **long-awaited** event is one that someone
has been waiting for for a long time. *His long-awaited
opportunity had now at last come. ...a long-awaited
shipment of food.*

longbow /lɒŋbəʊ/ **longbows**
NC A **longbow** is a weapon for firing arrows, which
was used especially by medieval archers. *The
medieval longbow was deadly accurate.*

long-distance
ADJ ATTRIB **Long-distance** vehicles, travel, or communications involve long journeys or places that are far apart. *...long-distance buses and lorries. ...long-distance phone calls. ...a long-distance runner. ...85% of the long-distance routes around the world.*

long division, long divisions
N U or N C **Long division** is a method of dividing one large number by another, which involves writing out each stage in the calculation.

long-drawn-out
ADJ ATTRIB A **long-drawn-out** process or conflict lasts an unnecessarily long time. *...the long-drawn-out peace talks. ...a long-drawn-out struggle.*

long drink, long drinks
N C A **long drink** is a large drink which contains very little alcohol or no alcohol.

longed-for
ADJ ATTRIB A **longed-for** thing or event is one that someone wants very much. *At last the longed-for refreshment arrived.*

longevity /lɒndʒevəti/
N U **Longevity** is long life; a formal word. *...improved health care resulting in increased longevity.*

longhand /lɒŋhænd/
N U If you write something down in **longhand**, you write it by hand using complete words and normal letters, rather than typing it or using shortened forms or special symbols. *The clerk had to write all the evidence down in longhand.*

longing /lɒŋɪŋ/ **longings**
N C or N U A **longing** is a rather sad feeling of wanting something very much. *People have a longing for normality... He gazed with longing and apprehension into the future.*

longingly /lɒŋɪŋli/
ADV If you think **longingly** about something, you think about it with a feeling of desire. *I began to think longingly of bed.*

longitude /lɒndʒɪtjuːd/ **longitudes**
N U or N C The **longitude** of a place is its distance to the west or east of a line passing through Greenwich in England: compare **latitude**. *...lines of latitude and longitude.*

longitudinal /lɒndʒɪtjuːdɪnl/
ADJ ATTRIB A **longitudinal** measurement, axis, cross-section, etc goes from one end of an object to the other rather than across it from side to side; a technical term. *It then falls, spinning rapidly about its longitudinal axis.* ◆ **longitudinally** ADV *The fibres run longitudinally.*

long johns /lɒŋ dʒɒnz/
N PL **Long johns** are warm underpants with long legs.

long jump
N SING The **long jump** is an athletics contest which involves jumping as far as you can from a marker which you run up to. *...the result of the men's long jump... Carl Lewis made up for the disappointment of losing the 100 metres, by winning the long jump.*

long-lasting, longer-lasting
ADJ Something that is **long-lasting** lasts for a long time. *The failure of the dam is unlikely to have long-lasting environmental consequences... So is there any prospect of a longer-lasting vaccine?*

long-life
ADJ ATTRIB **Long-life** milk, fruit juice, and batteries are treated or made so that they last longer than ordinary kinds. *...two new and improved long-life batteries.*

long-lived
ADJ Something that is **long-lived** lives or lasts for a long time. *Bats are surprisingly long-lived creatures. ...a long-lived rebellion.*

long-lost
ADJ ATTRIB You use **long-lost** to describe someone or something that you have not seen for a long time. *She greeted me like a long-lost daughter... Archaeologists have uncovered the long-lost palace of King Edward the Second.*

long-range, longer-range
1 ADJ ATTRIB A **long-range** piece of military equipment operates over long distances. *...a modern long-range strategic missile. ...long-range bombers. ...the need to secure cuts in longer-range nuclear weapons.*
2 ADJ ATTRIB A **long-range** plan or prediction relates to a period extending a long time into the future. *...the necessity for long-range planning. ...a longer-range plan for economic development.*

long-running, longest-running
ADJ ATTRIB Something that is **long-running** has been in existence, or has been performed, for a long time. *...a long-running soap opera. ...one of the longest-running controversies in the history of science. ...The Mousetrap, London's longest-running play.*

longshoreman /lɒŋʃɔːmən/ **longshoremen** /lɒŋʃɔːmən/
N C A **longshoreman** is a person who works in the docks, loading and unloading ships; used in American English. *...a shop steward for the Longshoremen's Union, the dockers of Brooklyn.*

long-sighted
ADJ If you are **long-sighted**, you cannot see things near you clearly, but you can see things a long way away. *Long-sighted people are less likely to suffer from cataracts.*

long-standing, longer-standing, longest-standing
ADJ A **long-standing** situation has existed for a long time. *...a long-standing feud. ...its longest-standing political detainee.*

long-suffering
ADJ Someone who is **long-suffering** patiently bears continual trouble or bad treatment. *...his noble, long-suffering wife.*

long-term, longer-term
1 ADJ **Long-term** things are intended to exist for a long time in the future. *...hopes for a long-term solution to the problem... I hesitated before making a long-term commitment... The government has also announced a series of longer-term measures.*
2 N SING When you talk about what happens in the **long term**, you are talking about what happens over a long period of time. *The results, in the long-term, were successful... And in the longer-term, unification is expected to assure Germany of privileged access to Central European markets.*

long-time
ADJ ATTRIB **Long-time** is used of something that has existed or been a particular thing for a long time. *He set off, accompanied by his long-time friend and travelling companion Ralph Taylor. ...a wildlife photographer with a long-time interest in owls. ...a longtime rival to the Prime Minister.*

long vacation, long vacations
N C The **long vacation** is the period of time during the summer when universities, colleges, and schools are closed. *One solution is to use the long vacations to go abroad on a working holiday.*

long wave
N U **Long wave** is a range of radio waves which are used for broadcasting. *This programme will be broadcast on long wave only... You can get Radio 4 on 200 kHZ long wave.*

long-winded
ADJ If something that has been written or said is **long-winded**, it is boring because it is longer than necessary. *...long-winded prayers. ...the five yearly review may have been long-winded.*

loo /luː/ **loos**
N C People sometimes refer to a toilet as the **loo**; an informal word. *...the downstairs loo... Somebody is in the loo.*

loofah /luːfə/ **loofahs**
N C A **loofah** is an object like a long, rough sponge, which you use to wash yourself in the bath.

look /lʊk/ **looks, looking, looked**
1 v If you **look** in a particular direction, you turn your eyes in that direction in order to see what is there. *She turned to look out of the window... They looked at each other... He blushed and looked away.* ► Also N SING *Take a good look... Did you have a look at the shop?*
2 v+at To **look** at something also means to read, examine, or consider it. *'I'd like to look at his medical history,' Percival said... Let's look at the implications of these changes.* ► Also N SING *Tony, I've had a look at that book you wrote... They will also*

be taking a hard look at their future relationship.
3 V+*at* If you **look** at a situation from a particular point of view, you judge it from that point of view. *If you're a Democrat, you look at things one way, and if you're a Republican you look at them very differently.*
4 VCorVA You use **look** to describe the impression someone or something has on you, or to describe their appearance. *You look very pale... The plan looks impressive enough on paper... Looks as if we're going to be late... He looked as if he hadn't slept very much... 'What does he look like?'—'Pale, thin, dark-haired.'*
5 NC If you give someone a particular kind of **look**, you look at them in a way that shows what you are thinking. *Don't give me such severe looks. What have I done?*
6 N SING+SUPP If someone or something has a particular **look**, they have that appearance or expression. *He didn't have the look of a man who was thinking... There is a nervous look in their eyes.*
7 N PL You refer to someone's **looks** when you are referring to how beautiful or handsome they are. *She had lost her looks... I didn't marry him for his looks.*
8 V A If a window, room, or building **looks** out onto something, it has a view of it. *The kitchen window looks out onto a yard.*
9 You say **'look'** or **'look here'** when you want someone to pay attention to what you are saying. *Look, Mrs Kintner, you've got it wrong.*
10 V You also use **look** with a word such as 'who' or 'what' or with 'at' to draw attention to something, for example when you are angry or surprised. *Now look what you've done... Goodness, look at the time. I promised I'd be home at six.*
look after PHRASAL VERB 1 If you **look after** someone or something, you take care of them. *Your husband ought to be looking after the baby.* 2 If you **look after** something, you are responsible for it. *The duty of the local authority is to look after the interests of local people.*
look back PHRASAL VERB If you **look back**, you think about things that happened in the past. *People can often look back and reflect on happy childhood memories.*
look down on PHRASAL VERB If you **look down on** someone, you think that they are inferior. *Farm labourers used to be looked down on.*
look for PHRASAL VERB If you **look for** someone or something, you try to find them. *I've been looking for you... She looked around for some paper. ...people looking for work.*
look forward to PHRASAL VERB If you **are looking forward** to something, you want it to happen. *I'm quite looking forward to it... I look forward to seeing you.*
look into PHRASAL VERB If you **look into** something, you find out about it. *A working party was set up to look into the problem.*
look on PHRASAL VERB 1 If you **look on** while something happens, you watch it. *His parents looked on with a triumphant smile.* 2 If you **look on** something as a particular thing, you think of it as that thing. *She looked on us as idiots.*
look out PHRASAL VERB You say **'look out'** to warn someone of danger. *'Look out,' I said. 'There's something coming.'* ● See also lookout.
look out for PHRASAL VERB If you **look out for** something, you try to make sure that you notice it. *It's a film we shall look out for in the next couple of months.*
look round PHRASAL VERB If you **look round** a place, you walk round it and look at the different parts of it. *Shall we look round the Cathedral this afternoon?*
look through PHRASAL VERB If you **look through** something, you examine it to find what you are looking for. *He looked through the clothing on the bed.*
look to PHRASAL VERB 1 If you **look to** someone for something such as help or advice, you hope that they will provide it. *Many people in the community will be looking to us for leadership.* 2 If you **look to** the future, you think about it. *Some New Englanders look to the future with a certain anxiety.*

look up PHRASAL VERB 1 If you **look up** information, you find it out by looking in a book. *He looked up the meaning of 'legislation' in the dictionary.* 2 If you **look** someone **up**, you visit them after you have not seen them for a long time; an informal use. *It was such a fine day he thought he'd look me up.* 3 If a situation is **looking up**, it is improving; an informal use. *That summer, things began looking up.*
look upon PHRASAL VERB If you **look upon** something as a particular thing, you think of it as that thing. *Houses are looked upon as investments.*
look up to PHRASAL VERB If you **look up to** someone, you respect and admire them. *His younger brothers look up to him.*
look-alike, look-alikes.
NC A person's **look-alike** is someone who looks very like them. *It was only the Minister's look-alike.*
looker-on /lʊkər ɒn/ **lookers-on**
NC A **looker-on** is someone who watches an activity or event without taking any part in it themselves.
look-in
N SING If you do not get a **look-in**, you do not get the chance to do something because too many other people are doing it; an informal word. *James talks so much that all the others barely get a look-in.*
-looking /-lʊkɪŋ/
1 SUFFIX **-looking** is added to some adjectives to make other adjectives describing what something looks like. *A glossy woman's magazine has also voted the young-looking Waldegrave Britain's sexiest MP. ...a very tired-looking Mr Mandela.*
2 SUFFIX **-looking** is added to some adverbs to describe the way a person is thinking. *It is certainly more precise and forward-looking than the last report. ...a more outward-looking foreign policy.*
looking-glass, looking-glasses
NC A **looking-glass** is the same as a **mirror**; an old-fashioned word. *She took a glance into Mrs Taswell's looking glass on the office wall.*
lookout /lʊkaʊt/ **lookouts**
1 NC A **lookout** is a place from which you can see clearly in all directions. *When she returned to her lookout, she discovered a large tabby cat crouched under the tree.*
2 NC A **lookout** is also someone who is watching for danger. *Two of the burglars were tipped off by a lookout and escaped.*
3 If you are **on the lookout** for something, you are watching out for it; an informal expression. *I'm on the lookout for a second-hand car... They were told to be on the lookout for more of the explosive devices.*
loom /luːm/ **looms, looming, loomed**
1 V A If something **looms** in a particular place or in a particular way, it appears as a tall, unclear, and often frightening shape. *A black thundercloud loomed above Ramsdale's white church tower... She walked past the school, a huge Victorian edifice that loomed up against the dirty sky... He collided with a tall figure looming abruptly out of the mist.*
2 VorVA If a difficult event or situation **looms**, it will soon happen. *The next general election loomed. ...the possibility of a trade war with the United States looming up... There are more diplomatic problems looming on the horizon.*
3 If a problem or event **looms large**, it is likely to be very important or significant, and you feel anxious about it because you cannot avoid it. *It is expected that the Afghan problem will loom large on the agenda... Concern for the environment looms large in this month's issue of Social Trends.*
4 NC A **loom** is a machine that is used for weaving thread into cloth. *A series of rods carry the threads onto the loom.*
loony /luːni/ **loonies**; an informal word.
1 ADJ **Loony** people, ideas, or behaviour seem mad, strange, or eccentric. *They sent me to this loony doctor... She works for a TV station full of loony characters.*
2 NC If you call someone a **loony**, you mean that they behave in a way that seems mad or eccentric. *...some poor old loony repeating the same bit of nonsense.*

loony bin, loony bins
NC A **loony bin** is a psychiatric hospital; an informal expression which some people find offensive. *Depression drove him to the loony bin.*

loop /luːp/ **loops, looping, looped**
1 NC A **loop** is a curved or circular shape in something long, such as a piece of string. *...loops of blue and pink ribbon.*
2 VO If you **loop** a rope or string around an object, you tie a length of it in a loop around the object. *The king had pearls looped round his neck.*
3 V If something **loops**, it goes in a circular direction, making the shape of a loop. *Birds loop and weave through the tall trees.*

loophole /luːphəʊl/ **loopholes**
NC A **loophole** in the law is a small mistake or omission which allows you to avoid doing something that the law intends you to do. *A number of obvious loopholes exist for tax avoidance... He was freed after a sympathetic judge exploited a legal loophole.*

loose /luːs/ **looser, loosest**
1 ADJ Something that is **loose** is not firmly held or fixed in place. *The doorknob is loose and rattles. ...loose strands of wire.* ◆ **loosely** ADV *Willie held the phone loosely.*
2 ADJ You also use **loose** to describe things that are not attached to anything else. *...a few loose sheets of paper.*
3 ADJ **Loose** clothes are rather large and do not fit closely. *He wears baggy shorts and a loose shirt— typical gang attire.* ◆ **loosely** ADV *His black garments hung loosely from his powerful shoulders.*
4 ADJ A **loose** grouping or arrangement is not rigidly controlled or organized. *...the creation of a loose confederation of genuinely autonomous republics... The country has a loose federal structure... He wanted the agenda to be as loose as possible.* ◆ **loosely** ADV *The film is loosely based on the experiences of John Huston. ...loosely associated groups of like-minded people.*
5 ADJ You also use **loose** to describe something such as the wording of a document to say that it is vague. *They are worried by the loose wording of the draft law now under debate.* ◆ **loosely** ADV *The proposals are on the whole loosely worded.*
6 ADV When something that has been held securely breaks or tears **loose**, or when someone or something lets it **loose**, it becomes unattached. *The cable car broke loose and crashed about 600 metres into the ground... They engaged in an act of environmental terrorism by letting loose over a million barrels of oil into the sea... The tremor cut loose a wall of water that went racing down into the valley.*
7 ADV If animals or people break **loose** or are let **loose**, they are freed after they have been restrained, and can do whatever they want. *A group of protesters set about two hundred pigs loose on the road... Her first thought was to turn the dog loose... They let loose two professional militias there with devastating results.*
8 ADV To let **loose** something such as ammunition means to release a large amount of it suddenly, for example by firing it. *Police and army men let loose a hail of gun and mortar fire... They even let loose a couple of rounds of ammunition... The chemical explosives let loose a fine mist of liquid agents.*
9 ADV If you let **loose** criticism, abuse, remarks, and so on, you suddenly say something without restraining yourself. *He let loose a barrage of criticism, describing Britain's news media as less than free... The defendant let loose a torrent of abuse against his prosecutors.*
10 ADJ If your hair is **loose**, it is hanging freely rather than being tied back. *She shook her hair loose... Her long brown hair hangs loose against her shoulders.*
11 ADJ A **loose** woman or someone with **loose** morals or behaviour is willing to have sex with lots of people; used in old-fashioned English, showing disapproval. *Many women would not go into pubs on their own, for fear of being thought loose... She started to go out unveiled, risking the assumption that she was a loose woman. ...excessive drinking and loose behaviour.*

● **Loose** is used in these phrases. ● If people **cut loose**, they become free from the influence or authority of other people. *He just told me to cut loose and have fun... The younger generation have tended to cut loose from the influence of class background.* ● If a dangerous person is **on the loose**, they are free, especially because they have escaped. *A bandit leader was on the loose in the hills.* ● If you tell someone to **hang loose**, you are telling them to relax; used in American English. *The wind will settle down a bit soon, so just hang loose.* ● If you refer to someone or something as a **loose cannon**, you mean that they are likely to be dangerous in a particular situation because they are out of control; used in American English. *Well, Ambassador Gillespie wasn't the loose cannon that her superiors made her out to be... We knew the army was out there, a sort of loose cannon in the region.*

loose cover, loose covers
NC A **loose cover** is a removable cover for something such as a chair or cushion.

loose end, loose ends
NC A **loose end** is a part of a story, situation, or crime that has not been explained. *There are too many loose ends in this case.*
● **Loose end** is used in these phrases. ● If you are **at a loose end**, you have nothing to do and are bored. *Some of them have left school without completing their education, and are at a loose end.* ● If you **tie up** the loose ends on a deal or arrangement, you complete it by attending to all the small details that you need to attend to. *Their job is to tie up the loose ends of this most unusual case... Now, I'm sure there are lots of loose ends you'd like to tie up.*

loose-fitting
ADJ **Loose-fitting** clothes are rather large and do not fit tightly on your body. *...the loose-fitting, comfortable kimono.*

loose-leaf
ADJ ATTRIB A **loose-leaf** book or folder has pages in it which can be removed and replaced. *...copies of a loose-leaf cookbook.*

loosely-knit
ADJ A **loosely-knit** organization or arrangement is one that does not have rigid rules, but instead is flexible and likely to change. *Some strange alliances have emerged within President Aquino's loosely-knit coalition... The Forum is not an organisation, but a loosely-knit movement.*

loosen /luːsn/ **loosens, loosening, loosened**
1 V-ERG If something **loosens**, or is **loosened**, it becomes undone or less tightly held in place. *The tyre on one of his wheels had loosened... The wind had loosened some leaves.*
2 VO If you **loosen** something that is tied or fastened, you undo it slightly. *He took off his jacket and loosened his tie.*
loosen up PHRASAL VERB If you **loosen up** or if something **loosens** you **up**, you become more relaxed and less anxious; an informal expression. *As the day wore on he loosened up and became more chatty... Her second drink loosened her up.*

loot /luːt/ **loots, looting, looted**
1 VOorV When people **loot** shops or houses, they steal things from them during a battle, riot, or other disturbance. *Shops were looted and wrecked in London... Soldiers continued to loot during the dusk to dawn curfew.* ◆ **looting** NU *There was widespread looting of stores and shops.*
2 NU **Loot** is stolen money or goods; an informal use. *He told his wife where the loot was hidden.*

looter /luːtə/ **looters**
NC **Looters** are people who steal things from shops and houses while there is a riot, war, or other disturbance going on. *...smouldering shops set alight by looters... Police now guard wrecked homes because looters have been at work in abandoned areas.*

lop /lɒp/ **lops, lopping, lopped**
VO If you **lop** a tree, you cut off some of its branches. *You need to lop the tree at about 12 inches above the ground.*

lop off PHRASAL VERB 1 If you **lop** something **off**, you cut it off with a quick, strong stroke. ...*a guillotine that probably lopped off many a head... They lop off all the branches that are affected.* 2 If you **lop** a part of something **off**, you make it smaller in length or amount. *He often lops off the first and last stanzas of a poem... If oil prices settle, it could lop a full percentage point off the current rate of economic growth.*

lope /ləʊp/ **lopes, loping, loped**
V A When people or animals **lope** somewhere, they run in a relaxed way with long strides. *The camel is an ungainly animal, but graceful when loping across the desert.*

lopsided /lɒpsaɪdɪd/
ADJ Something that is **lopsided** is uneven because one side is lower or heavier than the other. ...*a lopsided smile... The crystals are shaped like lopsided cubes.*

loquacious /ləkweɪʃəs/
ADJ People who are **loquacious** talk a lot; a formal word. *He is an easy, loquacious man.*

lord /lɔːd/ **lords**
1 TITLE In Britain, **Lord** is the title used in front of the name of peers, judges, bishops, and officials of very high rank. ...*Lord Harewood. ...the Lord Mayor of London. ...the Lord Chief Justice.*
2 NC A **lord** is a man with a high rank in the British nobility. ...*lords and ladies.*
3 N PROP In the Christian church, people refer to God and to Jesus Christ as **Lord** or **the Lord**. *Blessed are they who sow peace in the name of the Lord.*

lordly /lɔːdli/
ADJ A **lordly** person is proud and arrogant and shows that they think they are better than other people. ...*the lordly elder brother... His lordly manners were quite repulsive.*

Lordship /lɔːdʃɪp/ **Lordships**
TITLE Your **Lordship** or his **Lordship** is a respectful way of addressing or talking about a judge, bishop, or lord. *I'm sorry, sir, his Lordship is in his bath... Their Lordships were late for dinner.*

Lord's Prayer
N PROP The **Lord's Prayer** is a very important Christian prayer that was originally taught by Jesus Christ to his disciples. ...*a feminist version of the Lord's Prayer.*

lore /lɔː/
NU+SUPP The **lore** of a particular country or culture is its traditional stories and history. ...*Jewish mystical lore.* ● See also **folklore**.

lorgnette /lɔːnjet/ **lorgnettes**
N C A **lorgnette** is an old-fashioned pair of glasses with a handle which you use to hold the glasses to your eyes. *Lady Montague looked through her lorgnette at him.*

lorry /lɒri/ **lorries**
N C A **lorry** is a large motor vehicle which is used to transport goods by road. ...*a convoy of seventeen lorries... A lorry driver was injured when his vehicle overturned.*

lose /luːz/ **loses, losing, lost**
1 V O If you **lose** something, you cannot find it, for example because you have forgotten where you put it. *You haven't lost the ticket, have you?... She's always losing her cigarette lighter... They lost their way in the woods.*
2 V O You also say you **lose** something when you no longer have it, although you would like to have it, usually because it has been taken away from you or destroyed. *I might lose my job. ...a complete list of all the goods lost in the fire... At least 15 thousand people are believed to have lost their homes.*
3 V O If you **lose** a quality or characteristic, you do not have it any more. *Brody was beginning to lose interest... The government had lost all credibility in the eyes of the people... I felt degraded and isolated— I'd lost all my self-respect... The unions have lost patience with the Prime Minister.*
4 V O If you **lose** blood or fluid from your body, it leaves your body so that you have less of it. *He has lost a large amount of blood from internal bleeding... Enough water must be drunk to replace the fluid that*

has been lost.
5 V O If you **lose** weight, you become thinner. *I was losing weight and some of my hair fell out.*
6 V O If you **lose** a part of your body, it is cut off in an operation or in a violent accident. ...*victims of the earthquake who were paralysed or who had lost limbs... One of the farmers lost a leg in an accident.*
7 V O If you **lose** a relative or friend, they die. *I lost my father when I was nine... Some people who have lost relatives will be given compensation.*
8 V O If you **lose** an opportunity or **lose** time, you waste it. *He will lose his chances of promotion... Bill lost no time in telling everyone about his idea.*
9 V O If a business **loses** money, it earns less than it spends. *They've lost a lot of their revenue on transportation... The creditors want the airline grounded before it loses any more money.*
10 V O If a clock or watch **loses** time, it shows a time that is earlier than the real time.
11 V O or V If you **lose** a competition or argument, someone does better than you and defeats you. *He was found guilty of assaulting a referee after his team lost the match... The Government have lost the argument over the pace of reform... Mr Mazowiecki said that if he lost, he would be part of a critical but loyal opposition.* ♦ **losing** ADJ ATTRIB *Taylor scored 150 but still ended up on the losing side as Leicestershire reached their target of 252.*
12 See also **lost**.
● **Lose** is used in these phrases. ● If you **have something to lose**, you may suffer if you do something unsuccessfully. *The price was too high and he had too much to lose... They had absolutely nothing to lose.*
● If someone **loses their life**, they die in a sudden, violent way, for example in an accident or a war. *We grieve for all those who lost their lives, and extend profound sympathy to the relatives. ...riots in which thousands of citizens lost their lives.* ● If you **lose sight of** something, you can no longer see it. *They lost sight of the land and drifted across the busy Malacca Straits.* ● If you **lose sight of** an aim, objective, or important fact, you forget about it because you are distracted by other, less important things. *I don't think we should lose sight of the fact that we all agree on the overall goals.* ● **to lose face**: see **face**. ● **to lose your head**: see **head**. ● **to lose your temper**: see **temper**. ● **to lose touch**: see **touch**.
lose out PHRASAL VERB If you **lose out**, you do not succeed in what you are doing and so suffer a loss or disadvantage. *They did not lose out in the struggle to keep up with inflation.*

loser /luːzə/ **losers**
1 NC The **loser** of a game, contest, or struggle is the person who is defeated. *It was a victory for all, and there were no winners or losers.* ● A **good loser** is someone who accepts that they have lost a game or contest without complaining. A **bad loser** is someone who hates losing and complains a lot about it. *They urged her to be a good loser, and accept the result... His team have been on top since 1945, and they're bad losers.*
2 NC A **loser** is a person or a thing that is always going to be unsuccessful; an informal use. *I think we are only losers if we allow ourselves to be... He's a born loser.*
3 NC Someone who is the **loser** as the result of an action or event is in a worse situation because of it. *The typical losers will be working-class males in their forties... The Republican Party will be the biggest losers as a result of this budget fiasco.*

loss /lɒs/ **losses**
1 NU **Loss** is the fact of no longer having something or of having less of it than before. ...*temporary loss of vision. ...the loss of liberty. ...heat loss.*
2 NU or NC **Loss** of life occurs when people die. *The loss of life was appalling... Artillery fire caused heavy losses.*
3 NU+SUPP The **loss** of a relative or friend is their death. ...*the loss of my daughter and husband.*
4 NC If a business makes a **loss**, it earns less than it spends. *The company announced a huge loss for the first half of the year. ...a profit and loss account.*

● **Loss** is used in these phrases. ● If you are **at a loss**, you do not know what to do. *I was at a complete loss as to how I could lay my hands on the money.* ● If a business sells something **at a loss**, they sell it at a price which is less than it cost them to produce it or to buy it. *Timber owners have often produced lumber at a loss, but have survived the downturn in demand.* ● If you **cut** your **losses**, you stop doing what you were doing and accept defeat, in order to stop a bad situation becoming worse. *You ought to cut your losses and start again.* ● If you say that someone or something is a **dead loss**, you mean they are completely useless or unsuccessful; an informal expression. *Laurence made it clear that he thought she was a dead loss.*

lost /lɒst/
1 Lost is the past tense and past participle of **lose**.
2 ADJ If you are **lost**, you do not know where you are or you are unable to find your way. *There was that time when we got lost in Dennington... Drivers should plan long journeys so as not to get lost or caught in traffic jams.*
3 ADJ If something is **lost**, you cannot find it, for example because you have forgotten where you put it. *Shopping lists on old envelopes tend to get lost... The emergence of previously lost or hitherto unknown Stradivari violins is always an event in the musical world.*
4 ADJ Someone or something that is **lost** is no longer possessed by the person that they originally belonged to or were associated with. *...farmers whose livelihood is lost or reduced... They can be expected to regain some of their lost prestige.*
5 ADJ PRED+*without* If you say that you would be **lost** without someone or something, you mean that you would be very unhappy or unable to work properly without them. *His charisma bound the people to his presence and made them feel lost without him.*
6 ADJ PRED+*on* If advice or a comment is **lost** on someone, they do not understand it, or they ignore it. *The lesson was not lost on the committee... The symbolism of the sculpture would be lost on them.*
7 If you tell someone to **get lost**, you tell them rudely to go away; an informal expression.

lost cause, lost causes
NC You use **lost cause** to refer to something that you are trying to achieve which has no chance of succeeding. *...a champion of lost causes.*

lost property
NU **Lost property** consists of things that people have lost in a public place such as a railway station. *Claimants of lost property should apply to this office. ...the lost property office.*

lot /lɒt/ **lots**
1 QUANT A **lot** of something or **lots** of it is a large amount of it. *We owed a lot of money... This is a subject that worries a lot of people... I feel that we have a lot to offer. ...a big house with lots of windows.*
2 N SING+SUPP You can refer to a group of people as a particular **lot**; an informal use. *They were a rather arrogant, boring lot.*
3 NC You can refer to a set or group of things as a particular **lot**. *...two sets of cards, one lot written in blue, the other in red... I get two lots of everything.*
4 NC At an auction, a particular **lot** is one of the objects that is being sold. *Lot No 359 was a folder of 11 original sketches.*
5 NC A **lot** is also a small area of land that belongs to a particular person or company. *He's advertising his lot for sale... One vacant lot contains the concrete rubble from an old paint factory.* ● See also **parking lot**.
6 N SING+POSS Your **lot** is the kind of life you have or the things that you have or experience. *He also warned that it would take time to improve the lot of the Russian people... Young Cubans are increasingly dissatisfied with their lot.*
● **Lot** is used in these phrases. ● A **lot** means very much or very often. *The man in the photograph looked a lot like Mr Williams... The weather's a lot warmer there... He laughs a lot.* ● You can use **lots and lots** to emphasize that there are very many things

of a particular kind. *...people with lots and lots of money... Electrical fires are always accompanied by lots and lots of smoke.* ● You can use **the lot** to refer to the whole of an amount which you have just mentioned; an informal expression. *Wilks bet his last ten pounds and lost the lot.* ● If people **draw lots** or **cast lots** to decide who will do something, they each take a piece of paper from a container. One or more pieces of paper is marked, and the people who take marked pieces are chosen. *Two names were selected by drawing lots.* ● If you **throw in** your **lot with** a particular person or group, you decide to work with them and support them from then on, whatever happens. *He may now throw in his lot with the social democrats.*

loth /ləʊθ/. See **loath**.

lotion /ləʊʃn/ **lotions**
N MASS A **lotion** is a liquid that you use on your skin or hair to clean, protect, or improve it. *Until the 1950s treatment consisted of applying various lotions, which were largely ineffective. ...a bottle of suntan lotion.*

lottery /lɒtəri/ **lotteries**
1 NC A **lottery** is a type of gambling game in which people buy numbered tickets. Several numbers are then chosen, and the people who have those numbers on their tickets win a prize. *He won one-and-a-half million pounds in Britain's weekly football lottery. ...a lottery ticket.*
2 N SING If you describe a contest as a **lottery**, you mean that the result depends entirely on luck or chance; used showing disapproval. *The process of setting a figure for compensation is little more than a lottery... He's still philosophical about the lottery element of book prizes.*

lotus /ləʊtəs/ **lotuses**
NC A **lotus** is a type of water-lily that grows in Africa and Asia. *...a lotus of countless petals.*

lotus-eater, lotus-eaters
NC A **lotus-eater** is someone who lives an idle, comfortable life and does not think or care very much about anything.

lotus position
N SING The **lotus position** is a position used in yoga or meditation in which you sit with your legs crossed and your feet resting on the tops of your thighs. *We sat in the lotus position in front of the low table.*

loud /laʊd/ **louder, loudest**
1 ADJ or ADV When a noise is **loud**, the level of sound is very high. *His voice was loud and savage... There was a loud explosion... He spoke louder.* ◆ **loudly** ADV *The audience laughed loudly.*
2 ADJ If someone is **loud** in their support or condemnation of something, they express their opinion forcefully. *The newspapers were loud in their condemnation of British sentimentality.* ◆ **loudly** ADV *Most people loudly allege that all this is just another excuse.*
3 ADJ A **loud** piece of clothing has very bright colours or a striking pattern; used showing disapproval. *...young men in loud shirts and jackets.*
4 If you say something **out loud**, you say it, rather than just thinking it. *She was praying out loud... I laughed out loud at the thought.*

loudhailer /laʊdheɪlə/ **loudhailers**
NC A **loudhailer** is a hand-held device shaped like a cone that you can use to make your voice heard over a long distance. *The colonel, using a loudhailer, tried to reassure the residents.*

loudmouth /laʊdmaʊθ/ **loudmouths** /laʊdmaʊðz/
NC A **loudmouth** is someone who talks a lot, especially in an unpleasant, offensive, or stupid way. *Geldof himself was sometimes portrayed as an unruly loudmouth.*

loud-mouthed /laʊd maʊðd/
ADJ A **loud-mouthed** person talks a lot in an unpleasant or offensive way. *...a loud-mouthed, hard-drinking actor.*

loudspeaker /laʊdspiːkə/ **loudspeakers**
NC A **loudspeaker** is a device that turns electrical signals into sound. Loudspeakers are used so that the words spoken into a microphone, or the sound from a radio or record player, can be heard. *...an*

announcement over the loudspeaker.

lounge /laʊndʒ/ **lounges, lounging, lounged**

1 NC A **lounge** is a room in a house or hotel where people can sit and relax. *In the lounge, there were a dozen or so people plainly in good spirits.*

2 NC A **lounge** at an airport is a large room where passengers wait. *No sooner had he arrived than an official guided him straight to the VIP lounge. ...the arrivals lounge.*

3 NC The **lounge** or **lounge bar** in a pub or hotel is a comfortably furnished bar.

4 VA If you **lounge** somewhere, you lie on something or lean against it lazily. *She lounged on the rug. ...a picture of Mr Quayle in his youth, lounging against a car.*

lounge about or **lounge around** PHRASAL VERB If you **lounge about** or **lounge around**, you spend your time in a relaxed and lazy way, avoiding work that requires any effort. *...people who were lounging about, apparently with nothing to do... On the upper deck, about 80 passengers lounge around in hammocks.*

lounge suit, lounge suits

NC A **lounge suit** is an ordinary suit that is worn by men on fairly formal occasions. *Most of them are dressed in dark lounge suits, but Bernie stood out in traditional African robes.*

louse /laʊs/ **lice; louses, lousing, loused.** The form **lice** is the plural of the noun. The form **louses** is the third person singular, present tense, of the phrasal verb.

NC **Lice** are small insects that live on the bodies of people or animals. *...prisoners rotting in dungeons, covered with lice and rats.*

louse up PHRASAL VERB If a plan, situation, or system **louses up**, or if you **louse** it **up**, it fails; used in informal American English. *If your toilet system louses up, then you're in trouble... Hugh had a brilliant idea, then he kind of loused it up with his personal behaviour.*

lousy /laʊzi/; an informal word.

1 ADJ If you describe something as **lousy**, you mean that it is of very bad quality. *The hotels are lousy. ...a lousy hockey game.*

2 ADJ PRED If you feel **lousy**, you feel ill. *I feel really lousy tonight.*

lout /laʊt/ **louts**

NC If you call a young man a **lout**, you mean that he behaves in an impolite or aggressive way. *...gangs of drunken louts.*

loutish /laʊtɪʃ/

ADJ **Loutish** behaviour is impolite and aggressive. *He had a scruffy appearance and loutish manners.*

louvre /luːvə/ **louvres**; also spelt **louver** in American English.

N Cor N+N A **louvre** or a **louvre** door or window is a door or window with flat, sloping pieces of wood or glass across its frame.

louvred /luːvəd/; also spelt **louvered** in American English.

ADJ A **louvred** door or window has flat, sloping pieces of wood or glass across its frame. *I observed them through the louvred window.*

lovable /lʌvəbl/

ADJ A **lovable** person is pleasant and easy to like. *...a mischievous but lovable child.*

love /lʌv/ **loves, loving, loved**

1 VO If you **love** someone, you feel romantically or sexually attracted to them, and they are very important to you. *I do not think I love him enough to marry him... 'I love you, Colin.'—'I love you too, Janet.'*

2 VO You also say that you **love** someone when their happiness is very important to you, so that you behave in a kind and caring way towards them. *...a little baby to love... They make us feel safe and secure, loved and wanted.*

3 VO If you **love** something, you like it very much. *Sarah loves playing the flute... The English love gardening.*

4 VO You also say that you **love** something when you consider that it is very important and want to protect or support it. *They don't love their village in the way that their parents did... He told the congregation they*

should love both their church and their country.

5 NU **Love** is a very strong feeling of affection for someone who you are romantically or sexually attracted to. *Her love for him never wavered... You are not marrying for love.*

6 NU **Love** is also the feeling that a person's happiness is very important to you, and the way that you show this feeling in your behaviour towards them. *Mr Bush expressed his great love for his grandchildren.*

7 NU **Love** is also a strong liking for something, or a belief that it is very important. *...a man with a genuine love of literature. ...the party's effort to identify patriotism with love of socialism.*

8 V+to-INF or VO If you would **love** to do or have something, you want very much to do it or have it. *Posy said she'd love to stay... I would love a photograph of Edith Evans.*

9 VOCATIVE Some people use **love** as an affectionate way of addressing someone; an informal use. *Thanks a lot, love... Yes, Nora, my love.*

10 You can write **love** or **love from,** followed by your name, when you end an informal letter. *Hope you are all well at home. Love, Dan.*

11 In tennis, **love** is a score of zero. *...six games to love in the third set.*

12 See also **loving.**

● **Love** is used in these phrases. ● If you are **in love** with someone, you feel romantically or sexually attracted to them, and they are very important to you. *They are in love with each other and wish to marry... I tell you, I'm in love.* ● If you **fall in love** with someone, you start to be in love with them. *I fell madly in love with Ellen the first time I saw her. ...the romantic story of a country girl who falls in love.* ● When two people **make love**, they have sex. *The survey shows that twenty-one per cent of women would like to make love less often... He denied all the charges, including one of making love to the President's wife.* ● If there is **no love lost** between two people or groups, they do not like each other at all. *It's no secret that there's little love lost between Mr Mitterrand and Mr Chirac.*

love affair, love affairs

NC A **love affair** is a sexual or romantic relationship between two people. *Later, Andy was to begin a very involved love affair with an actress.*

lovebirds /lʌvbɜːdz/

N PL You can refer in a humorous way to two people as **lovebirds** when they are obviously very much in love. *I shared a compartment with the lovebirds.*

love child, love children

NC A **love child** is someone whose parents have never been married to each other; an old-fashioned expression. *...thirty-five infants, all the pathetic love children of women betrayed.*

loved ones

N PL **Loved ones** is used to refer to members of your family and other people that you care about when something unpleasant or dangerous has happened to them. *Prayers were said for all those who'd lost loved ones in the disaster. ...anxious relatives waiting at Gatwick for their loved ones to arrive.*

love-hate relationship

N SING If you have a **love-hate relationship** with someone or something, your attitude towards them often changes, so that sometimes you like them a great deal or strongly approve of them, and sometimes you strongly dislike them or disapprove of them. *China has had a love-hate relationship with intellectuals and students since well before the 1949 Communist Revolution.*

loveless /lʌvləs/

ADJ ATTRIB In a **loveless** relationship or situation, there is no love. *...a loveless marriage.*

love letter, love letters

NC A **love letter** is a letter that you write to someone in order to tell them that you love them. *...investigating the past through the original nineteenth century love letters.*

love life, love lives

NC Someone's **love life** consists of their romantic and sexual relationships. *Among the more notorious* incidents of his love life was the time he stole the wife of an ex-spy.

lovely /lʌvli/ **lovelier, loveliest**
1 ADJ If you describe someone or something as **lovely**, you mean that they are very beautiful and therefore pleasing to look at or listen to. *'Doesn't she look lovely, Albert?' she whispered... To me Hong Kong was one of the loveliest places in the world.* ◆ **loveliness** NU *...a girl of film-star loveliness.*
2 ADJ You also say that something is **lovely** when you want to show the pleasure that you have from it, or your appreciation of it. *Lovely day, isn't it?... It was lovely to hear from you again.*
3 ADJ You can describe someone as **lovely** when they are friendly, kind, and generous. *We've got lovely neighbours... She's the sweetest, loveliest person.*

love-making
NU **Love-making** refers to sexual activities that take place between two people. *His worries even made him lose interest in love-making.*

love potion, love potions
NC A **love potion** is a drink that is supposed to cause sexual desire in the person who drinks it. *They have no need of love potions.*

lover /lʌvə/ **lovers**
1 NC Your **lover** is someone who you are having a sexual relationship with but are not married to. *Jenny and I were lovers... He was her lover for two stormy years.*
2 NC You can refer to people as **lovers** when they are in love with each other. *Since Romeo and Juliet, young lovers have seen hard times.*
3 NC+SUPP You can also use **lover** to refer to someone who enjoys a particular activity or subject. *...a music lover. ...animal lovers.*

love-story, love-stories
NC A **love story** is a novel, short story, or film about a love affair. *...a familiar love story, in which the man and woman are faced with terrible dilemmas.*

loving /lʌvɪŋ/
1 ADJ Someone who is **loving** feels or shows love to other people. *...a loving, beautiful wife.* ◆ **lovingly** ADV *For a moment she looked at her grandson lovingly.*
2 ADJ ATTRIB **Loving** actions are done with great enjoyment and care. *...tending the gardens with loving care.* ◆ **lovingly** ADV *The Society of Antiquaries have lovingly restored the building.*

low /ləʊ/ **lower, lowest; lows**
1 ADJ Something that is **low** measures a short distance from the bottom to the top. *He tried to hide on the low roof of the hotel. ...a small low wall. ...a luxury home he had built at great cost on a low hill outside the capital.*
2 ADJ or ADV You also say that something is **low** when it is close to the ground. *She made a low curtsey... The race had to be stopped because of low clouds... Military helicopters have been seen flying low over the square.*
3 ADV You also use **low** to say that something is close to the bottom of something. *Glass is at risk if stored too high, too low, or too far back in a cupboard... She saw the scar low on his spine.*
4 ADJ or ADV A dress or blouse that is described as **low** leaves a woman's neck and the top part of her chest bare. *...a low neckline... Her dress was cut low in front.*
5 ADJ **Low** means small in amount, value, or degree. *...a low tar cigarette... There is widespread concern about low wages and rapid price increases. ...people with a low resistance to infection.*
6 ADJ ATTRIB You can use **low** with numbers to give an approximate amount. For example, if a number is 'in the low twenties', it is more than twenty but less than twenty-five. *The temperature is in the low eighties.*
7 ADJ PRED If a supply of something is **low**, there is less than what is needed or less than there should be. *His blood pressure has stayed dangerously low, in spite of transfusions. ...a diet low in vitamins... The pilot sent a message saying he was low on fuel.*
8 ADJ If the quality or standard of something is **low**, it is below what it should be. *...a low standard of*

living... Morale in the teaching profession is low.
9 ADJ **Low** is used to describe people who are near the bottom of a particular scale. *...a junior executive of a fairly low grade. ...the lowest 85 per cent of the working population.*
10 ADJ If you have a **low** opinion of someone, you disapprove of them or dislike them. *We've all come across people who have a low opinion of themselves.*
11 ADJ or ADV You use **low** to describe people or actions which you disapprove of. *...mixing with low company... Well I'm not doing that. I haven't sunk that low.*
12 ADJ A **low** sound has a deep tone. *...a long low note on the horn.*
13 ADJ or ADV You can also describe a quiet sound as **low**. *Smithy spoke to him in a low and urgent voice... He turned the radio on low.*
14 ADJ A **low** light is dim rather than bright. *...low light levels at dusk and dawn.*
15 ADJ Someone who is feeling **low** is unhappy. *I've never been as low as I was last Saturday.*
● **Low** is used in these phrases. ● If you **are lying low**, you are avoiding being seen in public; an informal expression. *She'll have to lie low for a couple of years.* ● If something is **at an all-time low** or **at a record low**, the situation is much worse than it has ever been before. *The row has brought relations between the two countries to an all-time low... Output was at a record low.*

lowbrow /ləʊbraʊ/
ADJ Entertainment, art, music, and so on that is **lowbrow** is simple and easy to understand rather than being intellectual or complicated; used showing disapproval. *...lowbrow culture. ...lowbrow entertainment.*

low-cut
ADJ **Low-cut** dresses and blouses leave a woman's neck, shoulders, and the top part of her chest bare. *Her low-cut dress scandalized audiences.*

low-down; used in informal English.
1 If you have **the low-down on** something, you know all the important information about it. *They are dying to get the low-down on what's going on in Birmingham.*
2 ADJ ATTRIB **Low-down** also means dishonest or unfair. *He's a low-down, rotten bum... What a nasty, low-down trick.*

lower /ləʊə/ **lowers, lowering, lowered**
1 **Lower** is the comparative of **low**.
2 ADJ ATTRIB **Lower** is used to describe the bottom one of a pair of things. *Thomas was lying in the lower bunk... Jane sucked at her lower lip.*
3 ADJ ATTRIB **Lower** is also used to describe the bottom part of something. *The bullet had penetrated the lower left corner of his back... One wall of the lower section of the parliament building is almost completely obscured by a banner.*
4 ADJ ATTRIB You also use **lower** to describe people or things that are less important than similar people or things. *He could argue his case in the lower court. ...the lower levels of the organization.*
5 VO If you **lower** something, you move it slowly downwards. *He lowered his glass... Lynn lowered herself into the water... She lowered her eyes and remained silent.*
6 VO To **lower** an amount, value, or quality means to make it less. *The voting age was lowered to eighteen... Mexican hotels are lowering their rates sharply.* ◆ **lowering** N SING+SUPP *...the lowering of examination standards.*
7 VO If you **lower** your voice, you speak more quietly. *I lowered my voice, and said 'I'm a guy'.*

lower case
N+N or NU **Lower case** letters are small letters, not capital letters. *...signs in lower case lettering... Both initials go in lower case.*

lower class, lower classes
NC Some people use **lower class** or **lower classes** to refer to people who they consider to be in a lower social class than other people. *Cocaine arrived among the upper classes, from where it spread to the artists, and then to the lower classes.*

lowest common denominator, lowest common denominators
1 NC The **lowest common denominator** in a situation is the most basic or simple thing about it that interests or is understood by most people in a particular group; used showing disapproval. *...debased arguments from populism, pandering to the lowest common denominator... Trade associations and employer groups tend to reflect the lowest common denominator among their members.*
2 NC In mathematics, the **lowest common denominator** is the smallest number that all the numbers on the bottom of a particular group of fractions can be divided into; a technical use.

low-key
ADJ Something that is **low-key** is not obvious or intense. *The organization lent us support in its own low-key way... The debate was low-key, with fewer than thirty MPs in their seats.*

lowlands /ˈləʊləndz/
N PL **Lowlands** are an area of flat, low land. *...the Scottish Lowlands.*

lowly /ˈləʊli/ **lowlier, lowliest**
ADJ Something that is **lowly** is low in rank, status, or importance. *...a lowly employee. ...his lowly social origins.*

low-lying
ADJ **Low-lying** land is at, near, or below sea level. *All the low-lying areas were affected by the recent floods.*

low-minded
ADJ If you describe someone as **low-minded**, you mean that you consider them to be crude and vulgar, especially because they think or talk about sex a lot. *Certain low-minded individuals would laugh every time sex was even mentioned.*

low-necked
ADJ **Low-necked** means the same as **low-cut**.

low-paid
ADJ Workers who earn only a small amount of money are described as **low-paid**. *...low-paid workers. ...women in low-paid jobs.*

low-pitched
1 ADJ A sound that is **low-pitched** is deep. *...a low-pitched whistle.*
2 ADJ A voice that is **low-pitched** is very soft and quiet. *Normally he spoke rather deliberately in a low-pitched voice.*

low-rise
ADJ A **low-rise** building has only a few storeys. *The basilica towers incongruously over the mud huts and low-rise buildings.*

low season
N SING The **low season** is the time of year when a holiday resort, hotel, or tourist attraction receives the fewest number of visitors. *Going to Venice in the low season is bound to be a lot cheaper.*

low-spirited
ADJ If you are **low-spirited**, you are depressed.

low-tech
ADJ **Low-tech** designs, systems, or practices do not use modern, up-to-date methods or equipment. *This low-tech pump is driven by wind, hand, or animal power... The theatre has a distinctly low-tech feel to it.*

low tide
NU At the coast, **low tide** is the time when the sea is at its lowest level. *The rocks are exposed at low tide.*

low water
NU **Low water** is the same as **low tide**.

loyal /ˈlɔɪəl/
ADJ A **loyal** person remains firm in their friendship or support for someone or something. *Most Tories remained loyal to the Government. ...a loyal friend.*
♦ **loyally** ADV *For thirty years she had served him loyally.*

loyalist /ˈlɔɪəlɪst/ **loyalists**
NC A **loyalist** is a person who remains firm in their support for a government or ruler. *Thatcher's loyalists are worried about the future... A few hours later, the rebel stronghold was ringed by loyalist forces and tanks.*

loyalty /ˈlɔɪəlti/ **loyalties**
1 NU **Loyalty** is behaviour in which you stay firm in your friendship or support for someone or something. *I am convinced of your loyalty to the cause.*
2 NC **Loyalties** are feelings of friendship, support, or duty. *...their loyalties to the church.*

lozenge /ˈlɒzɪndʒ/ **lozenges**
NC A **lozenge** is a tablet which you suck when you have a sore throat. *...a glass jar filled with lozenges.*

LP /ˌelˈpiː/ **LPs**
NC An **LP** is a record with about 25 minutes of music or speech on each side. *...his long-awaited new LP 'Green Thoughts'.*

L-plate /ˈel pleɪt/ **L-plates**
NC **L-plates** are small signs with an 'L' on them which you attach to a car when you are learning to drive.

LSD /ˌelesˈdiː/
NU **LSD** is a very powerful drug which causes hallucinations. LSD is often taken illegally. *Drugs, including LSD, cannabis and amphetamines, were seized.*

Lt.
Lt. is a written abbreviation for 'lieutenant'. *...Lt Horst. ...Lt. Col. Ferguson.*

Ltd.
Ltd. is a written abbreviation for 'Limited' when it is used after the name of a company. *...Cobuild Ltd.*

Luanda /luˈændə/
Luanda is the capital of Angola and its largest city. Population: 1,134,000 (1987).

Lubbers, Rudolph /ˈruːdɒlf ˈlʌbəz/
Rudolph Lubbers became Prime Minister of the Netherlands in 1982. He was Minister of Economic Affairs from 1973 to 1977. He is a member of the Christian Democratic Appeal (CDA). Born: 1939.

lubricant /ˈluːbrɪkənt/ **lubricants**
NCorNU A **lubricant** is a substance such as oil which you put on the surfaces or parts of a machine to make the parts move smoothly. *It's a bit more expensive than ordinary lubricants. ...a can of spray lubricant.*

lubricate /ˈluːbrɪkeɪt/ **lubricates, lubricating, lubricated**
VO If you **lubricate** part of a machine, you put oil onto it to make it move smoothly. *The chain might need lubricating.* ♦ **lubrication** /ˌluːbrɪˈkeɪʃn/ NU *...the lubrication system of the engine.*

lubricious /luːˈbrɪʃəs/
ADJ **Lubricious** means having or indicating a strong interest in sex; a literary word, used showing disapproval. *...the landlady's lubricious daughter... He uttered a lubricious chuckle.*

lucerne /luːˈsɜːn/
NU **Lucerne** is a plant that is grown for animals to eat and in order to improve the soil. *...fodder crops like clover and lucerne.*

lucid /ˈluːsɪd/; a formal word.
1 ADJ **Lucid** writing or speech is clear and easy to understand. *...a brief and lucid account.* ♦ **lucidly** ADV *Her ideas are very lucidly set out in his book.* ♦ **lucidity** /luːˈsɪdəti/ NU *He expresses himself with quiet lucidity.*
2 ADJ When someone is **lucid**, they are able to think clearly again after being ill. *There was a ringing in my head, yet I was lucid.* ♦ **lucidity** NU *...in one of his moments of lucidity.*

luck /lʌk/ **lucks, lucking, lucked**
NU **Luck** or good **luck** is success or good things that happen to you, that do not come from your own abilities or efforts. Bad **luck** is lack of success or bad things that happen to you, that have not been caused by yourself or other people. *Perhaps what the three winners had in common was determination, hard work, and luck... The children couldn't believe their luck when they were told they had to go back home because there was no-one to teach them... They said goodbye, and wished each other good luck... Why is Friday the thirteenth so widely regarded as a day that brings bad luck?*
● **Luck** is used in these phrases. ● If you say '**Bad luck**', '**Hard luck**', or '**Tough luck**' to someone, you are expressing sympathy when something has gone badly for them. *Tough luck, Barrett. You played a great game.* ● You say '**Good luck**' or '**Best of luck**' to someone when you hope that they will be successful.

Thank you Sarah, and good luck with the novel...
Thank you for writing in to us, and best of luck. ● If
someone is **in luck**, they are lucky on a particular
occasion. *I think you may be in luck today Charlie,*
because this puzzle's on the easy side. ● If you say
that someone is **pushing** their **luck**, you mean that they
are taking a risk and may get into trouble or face
problems as a result. *Things had been going so well*
that she did not want to push her luck... The longer
they continue to smoke, the more they are pushing
their luck. ● When someone **tries** their **luck** at
something, they try to succeed at it. *He came to*
England to try his luck at a musical career. ● You
can add **with luck** to a statement to say that you hope
a particular thing will happen; an informal
expression. *This one should work with a bit of luck...*
With any luck they might forget all about it.
luck out PHRASAL VERB If you **luck out**, you are
fortunate or lucky in something; used in informal
American English. *Boy, I tell you I really lucked out*
here.
luckily /lʌkəli/
ADV SEN You add **luckily** to your statement to indicate
that you are glad that something happened. *Luckily,*
Saturday was a fine day... Luckily for you, I happen to
have the key.
luckless /lʌkləs/
ADJ Someone or something that is **luckless** is
unsuccessful or unfortunate; an old-fashioned word.
This trip of ours has been singularly luckless.
lucky /lʌki/ **luckier, luckiest**
1 ADJ You say that someone is **lucky** when they have
something that is very desirable or when they are in a
very desirable situation. *I'm lucky in having an*
excellent teacher... Francis is lucky to be alive... He
was the luckiest man in the world.
2 ADJ You also describe someone as **lucky** if they
always seem to have good luck. *Are you lucky at*
cards?... Mr Lawson seems to have recovered his
lucky touch.
3 ADJ If you describe an event or situation as **lucky**,
you mean that it had good effects or consequences,
although it happened by chance and not as a result of
planning or preparation. *It was lucky that I had*
cooked a big joint. ...astonishing tales of lucky
escapes.
4 ADJ People describe something as **lucky** when they
believe that it helps them to be successful. *...his lucky*
sweater. ...a lucky charm.
lucky dip, lucky dips
NUor NC **Lucky dip** is a game in which you take an
object out of a covered container containing many
different objects, and then find out what you have
chosen.
lucrative /luːkrətɪv/
ADJ A **lucrative** business or activity earns you a lot of
money; a formal word. *It had been an exciting and*
lucrative business. ...the lucrative trade in tea and
porcelain.
lucre /luːkə/
NU **Lucre** is money or profit, often when it is obtained
by dishonest means or in an inappropriate situation;
an old-fashioned word. *...marketed for lucre in the*
name of liberty. ...a share of the lucre.
Luddite /lʌdaɪt/ **Luddites**
NC A **Luddite** is someone who strongly opposes
changes in industrial methods, especially the
introduction of new machines and modern methods; a
formal word, used showing disapproval. *...the nation's*
leading Luddite. ...fighting in a Luddite way against
improvements and productivity.
ludicrous /luːdɪkrəs/
ADJ Something that is **ludicrous** is extremely foolish,
unreasonable, or unsuitable. *I had a ludicrous feeling*
of pride in him. ...one teacher for every 100 pupils, it
was ludicrous. ◆ **ludicrously** ADV *...a ludicrously low*
price.
lug /lʌg/ **lugs, lugging, lugged**
VOA If you **lug** a heavy object somewhere, you carry
it there with difficulty; an informal word. *She lugged*
the suitcase out into the hallway.

luggage /lʌgɪdʒ/
NU **Luggage** is the suitcases and bags that you take
when you travel. *They did not have much luggage.*
● See also **left-luggage office**.
lughole /lʌgəʊl/ **lugholes**
NC Your **lugholes** are your ears; an informal word.
lugubrious /ləguːbrɪəs/
ADJ **Lugubrious** means sad and dull, and not lively; a
formal word. *...a lugubrious face. ...lugubrious*
hymns.
lukewarm /luːkwɔːm/
1 ADJ Something that is **lukewarm** is only slightly
warm. *...lukewarm water.*
2 ADJ If someone is **lukewarm** towards something or
someone, they do not show much enthusiasm for them
or interest in them. *Reaction to the White Paper has*
been generally lukewarm... Some members have
criticised Denmark for their apparently lukewarm
attitude to the alliance.
lull /lʌl/ **lulls, lulling, lulled**
1 NC A **lull** is a period of quiet or of little activity. *...a*
lull in the conversation... After a lull of several
weeks, there has been a resumption of bombing.
2 VO+into If you are **lulled** into feeling calm or safe,
someone or something makes you feel calm or safe,
especially as a deliberate plan to attack or cheat you.
The strikers were lulled into a false sense of security...
He lulled me into thinking I had won.
lullaby /lʌləbaɪ/ **lullabies**
NC A **lullaby** is a quiet song which you sing to help a
child go to sleep. *...a mother's lullaby.*
lumbago /lʌmbeɪgəʊ/
NU **Lumbago** is a severe pain in the lower part of your
back. *Many of the devices are aimed at people with*
lumbago.
lumbar /lʌmbə/
ADJ ATTRIB **Lumbar** means existing or occurring in the
lower part of your back; a medical term. *...the five*
lumbar joints. ...the lumbar region of the spine.
lumber /lʌmbə/ **lumbers, lumbering, lumbered**
1 NU **Lumber** consists of wood that has been roughly
cut up; used in American English. *...piles of lumber.*
...a lumber company.
2 VA If someone **lumbers** somewhere, they move there
slowly and clumsily. *He lumbered upstairs looking for*
the bathroom... Donkeys lumbered by.
lumber with PHRASAL VERB If you **are lumbered** with
a task, you have to do it even though you do not want
to; an informal expression. *Women are still lumbered*
with the cooking and cleaning.
lumberjack /lʌmbədʒæk/ **lumberjacks**
NC A **lumberjack** is a man whose job is to cut down
trees.
lumberyard /lʌmbəjɑːd/ **lumberyards**
NC A **lumberyard** is a place where freshly cut wood is
stored or sold; used in American English. *...hunks of*
wood straight from the lumberyard.
luminary /luːmɪnəʳri/ **luminaries**
NC A **luminary** is someone who is famous or who is an
expert in a particular subject or activity; a literary
word. *...visits by such luminaries as Elizabeth Taylor.*
...a major luminary of British architecture. ...legal
luminaries.
luminescence /luːmɪnesns/
NU **Luminescence** is a soft, glowing light; a literary
word. *...a dim room lit by a pinkish luminescence...*
The sky became suffused with a pale, milky
luminescence.
luminosity /luːmɪnɒsəti/
NU **Luminosity** is bright light; a literary word.
...twinkling points of pale luminosity... Mysterious
patterns of luminosity glowed in the night.
luminous /luːmɪnəs/
ADJ Something that is **luminous** shines or glows in the
dark. *...the luminous hands of my watch.*
lump /lʌmp/ **lumps, lumping, lumped**
1 NC A **lump** of something is a solid piece of it.
...lumps of clay. ...a lump of butter.
2 NC A **lump** on someone's body is a small, hard
swelling that has been caused by an injury or an
illness. *...a small lump, a little growth just above the*
right eye.

3 NC A **lump** of sugar is a small cube of it. *Black coffee, two lumps, please.*
4 VO If you **lump** different people or things together, you consider them as a group. *'Don't lump me and Dave together,' he interrupted... The old rural counties were lumped together into new units.*
5 If someone has a **lump** in their **throat**, they have a tight feeling in their throat and feel as if they are going to cry, because of a strong emotion such as sorrow or gratitude. *That the sight of the ship's launch brings a lump to his throat is understandable.*

lump sum, lump sums
NC A **lump sum** is a large amount of money that is given or received all at once. *He has been offered a tax-free lump sum of $4,000.*

lumpy /lʌmpi/ **lumpier, lumpiest**
ADJ Something that is **lumpy** contains lumps or is covered in lumps. *...sitting on his lumpy mattress... Her face tends to be puffy and lumpy.*

lunacy /luːnəsi/
NU **Lunacy** is behaviour which seems very strange or foolish. *This comment would have seemed sheer lunacy to his ancestors... It would be lunacy to marry.*

lunar /luːnə/
1 ADJ ATTRIB **Lunar** means relating to the moon; a formal use. *...the lunar surface.*
2 ADJ ATTRIB The **lunar** calendar measures months by the length of time it takes the moon to go round the earth once. *The Chinese will usher in the lunar New Year with the customary celebrations... When his age is reckoned in lunar years, it comes out at 88.*

lunatic /luːnətɪk/ **lunatics**
1 NC If you describe someone as a **lunatic**, you mean that they behave in a dangerous, stupid, or annoying way; an informal use. *The man's a bloody lunatic... The attack was carried out by a lone lunatic gunman acting independently.*
2 ADJ **Lunatic** behaviour is foolish and likely to be dangerous. *...what he referred to as the lunatic excesses of the Common Agricultural Policy... His organisation's aims verge on the lunatic.*

lunatic asylum, lunatic asylums
NC A **lunatic asylum** was a place where mentally disturbed people used to be locked up. *...a chilling portrait of a sane man trapped for life in a lunatic asylum.*

lunatic fringe
N SING If you refer to a group of people as the **lunatic fringe**, you mean that they are very extreme in their opinions or behaviour. *...the lunatic fringe of the movement... To allow a lunatic fringe to dictate the workings of a democracy would set a poor precedent.*

lunch /lʌntʃ/ **lunches, lunching, lunched**
1 NUorNC **Lunch** is a meal that you have in the middle of the day. *What did you have for lunch?... They sat tucking into a lunch of rice, beans and beer.*
2 NC A **lunch** is a formal social event in the middle of the day, at which a meal is served. *The Princess Royal toured the palace and attended a lunch in her honour.*
3 V When you **lunch**, you eat lunch; a formal use. *Why don't you two lunch with me tomorrow?*

luncheon /lʌntʃən/ **luncheons**
NUorNC **Luncheon** is a formal meal in the middle of the day. *I was planning something hot for luncheon... He chose to celebrate his 90th birthday with a special luncheon for his 1,800-strong workforce.*

luncheonette /lʌntʃənɛt/ **luncheonettes**
NC A **luncheonette** is a place where light lunches are served; used in American English. *Luncheonette owners put 'Support Our Troops' stickers in their windows.*

luncheon meat
NU **Luncheon meat** is a mixture of meat and cereal which is sold in tins and eaten cold. *It was luncheon meat, and more beans.*

luncheon voucher, luncheon vouchers
NC **Luncheon vouchers** are vouchers that are given by a company to its employees. They can be exchanged for food in some restaurants. *The 1968 survey found that only 8.7 per cent of employers provided luncheon vouchers.*

lunch hour, lunch hours
NC Your **lunch hour** is the period in the middle of the day when you stop work in order to have a meal. *The secretaries were just back from their lunch hour... They spend their lunch hours in smoky pubs.*

lunchtime /lʌntʃtaɪm/ **lunchtimes**
NUorNC **Lunchtime** is the time in the middle of the day when people have lunch. *She's going to see him at lunchtime... It's full most lunchtimes and evenings.*

lung /lʌŋ/ **lungs**
NC Your **lungs** are the two organs inside your chest which you use for breathing. *Two years ago, she was given a new heart and lungs by pioneering surgeon Magdi Yacoub... Passive smoking can increase the risk of lung cancer.*

lunge /lʌndʒ/ **lunges, lunging, lunged**
VA If you **lunge** in a particular direction, you move there suddenly and clumsily. *When the man lunged at the officer, she was forced to fire, striking him in the chest.* ▸ Also NC *One competitor performed a series of aggressive leaps, lunges, punches, and kicks.*

lurch /lɜːtʃ/ **lurches, lurching, lurched**
1 VorVA To **lurch** means to make a sudden, jerky movement. *He lurched and fell... The boat lurched ahead.* ▸ Also NC *With a tremendous lurch he fell over me.*
2 VA If you **lurch** from one thing to another, you suddenly change your opinions or behaviour. *After lurching away from Socialism in 1976, they now seem to be lurching back.*
3 If someone **leaves** you **in the lurch**, they stop helping you at a very difficult time; an informal expression. *...the need to reassure supporters that they are not being left in the lurch.*

lure /ljʊə/ **lures, luring, lured**
1 VO To **lure** someone means to attract them and cause them go to a particular place, or to do something that they should not. *The price also lures students... Why else had Halliday come up, if not to lure me away?*
2 NC A **lure** is something such as bait which is used to attract prey to a certain place so that they can be caught. *The jar contains a lure to attract the fruitfly.*
3 NC+SUPP A **lure** is an attractive quality that something has, or something that you find attractive. *That's always the lure of a patriotic war... Many economists have succumbed to the fatal lure of mathematics.*

lurgy /lɜːgi/
N SING The **lurgy** is an illness which is not serious, for example a cold; an informal word, used humorously. *Oh no, I think I've got the dreaded lurgy again.*

lurid /ljʊərɪd/
1 ADJ Something that is **lurid** involves a lot of violence or sex; used showing disapproval. *...lurid stories about the war. ...lurid novels.*
2 ADJ **Lurid** things are very brightly coloured. *...lurid polyester skirts.* ◆ **luridly** ADV *...a luridly coloured advertisement.*

lurk /lɜːk/ **lurks, lurking, lurked**
1 VA To **lurk** somewhere means to wait there secretly. *Wild boars and wolves lurked near the isolated camp.*
2 V If something such as a memory, suspicion, or danger **lurks**, it exists, but you are only slightly aware of it. *...outdated prejudices lurking in the minds of individuals.*

Lusaka /lusɑːkə/
Lusaka is the capital of Zambia and its largest city. Population: 870,000 (1988).

luscious /lʌʃəs/
1 ADJ If you describe someone or something as **luscious**, you mean that you find them extremely attractive. *She was looking luscious in faded overalls and a flannel shirt.*
2 ADJ **Luscious** fruit is juicy and delicious. *...a basket of luscious figs.*

lush /lʌʃ/ **lusher, lushest**
1 ADJ Fields or gardens that are **lush** have a lot of very healthy grass or plants. *...a landscape of lush green meadows.*
2 ADJ Places or ways of life that are **lush** are rich and

full of luxury. ...*lush restaurants in London and Paris.*
3 NC A **lush** is a person who is very often drunk; used in informal American English. *It's a terrible myth that you have to be a lush or some kind of addict to be creative.*

lust /lʌst/ **lusts, lusting, lusted**; used showing disapproval.
1 NU **Lust** is a feeling of strong sexual desire for someone. ...*a comic novel of lust and love.*
2 N SING or NU A **lust** for something is a very strong and eager desire to have it. ...*a damaging and unseemly lust for deals at any price... I think he's moved by lust for power.*
lust after or **lust for** PHRASAL VERB 1 If you **lust after** something or **lust for** it, you have a very strong desire to possess it. *They lusted after the gold of El Dorado... He accused them of trying to destroy the People's Front, who were lusting for power.* 2 If you **lust after** someone or **lust for** them, you feel a very strong sexual desire for them. ...*a man who lusts after pretty girls.*

lustful /lʌstfl/
ADJ **Lustful** means feeling or expressing strong sexual desire; used showing disapproval. *The book was once denounced as tending to 'induce lustful thoughts in the minds of those who read it'.*

lustre /lʌstə/; spelt **luster** in American English. A literary word.
1 NU **Lustre** is gentle shining light that is reflected from a surface. *Vegetable dyes give a particularly beautiful lustre and quality to the silk.*
2 NU Someone or something that loses their **lustre** loses the qualities which made them exciting, interesting, or attractive. *Benazir undoubtedly did lose her luster during her period in power... Only the Chinese Theater across the street retains something of its former luster.*

lustrous /lʌstrəs/
ADJ Something that is **lustrous** is smooth and shines brightly and gently. *She had lustrous grey-green eyes... The feathers are so fine and lustrous that they look like rich black velvet.*

lusty /lʌsti/ **lustier, lustiest**
ADJ **Lusty** means healthy and strong; a literary word. ...*a strong and lusty boy of whom any father could be proud.* ◆ **lustily** ADV *They stood waving their Union Jacks and singing lustily.*

lute /luːt/ **lutes**
NC A **lute** is an old-fashioned musical instrument with strings, which is played like a guitar. *He idly plucked the strings of the lute.*

luv /lʌv/
VOCATIVE **Luv** is an informal written form of the word 'love' when it is being used as a way of addressing someone. *It's different with you, luv.*

Luxembourg /lʌksəmbɜːg/
The **Grand Duchy of Luxembourg** is a country in western Europe. It was occupied by Germany from 1940 to 1944. It is a member of NATO and the European Community. Grand Duke Jean became the head of state in 1964. Jacques Santer, of the Christian Social Party (PCS), became Prime Minister in 1984. Luxembourg produces iron and steel. Banking is an important industry. ◆ **Luxembourger** /lʌksəmbɜːgə/ N, ADJ
■ *per capita GNP:* US$22,600 ■ *religion:* Christianity (mainly Roman Catholic) ■ *language:* Letzeburgish (official), French, German ■ *currency:* franc ■ *capital:* Luxembourg-Ville ■ *population:* 375,000 (1988) ■ *size:* 2,586 square kilometres.

Luxembourg-Ville /luːksɒmbuəviːl/
Luxembourg-Ville is the capital of Luxembourg and its largest city. It is the headquarters of the European Parliament, the Court of Justice of the European Communities, and the European Investment Bank. Population: 77,500 (1988).

luxuriance /lʌgzjuəriəns/
NU You use **luxuriance** to refer to plants, gardens, trees, and so on which are healthy and growing well; a literary word. ...*the dark luxuriance of the forest.*

luxuriant /lʌgzjuəriənt/; a literary word.
1 ADJ **Luxuriant** plants, trees, and gardens are large

and healthy. ...*luxuriant forests.*
2 ADJ **Luxuriant** hair is very thick and healthy. ...*his pale lined face and luxuriant, flowing hair.*

luxuriate /lʌgzjuərieɪt/ **luxuriates, luxuriating, luxuriated**
V+in If you **luxuriate** in something, you relax in it and enjoy it very much. *I luxuriated in my retirement.*

luxurious /lʌgzjuəriəs/
1 ADJ Something that is **luxurious** is very comfortable and expensive. ...*big, luxurious cars.* ◆ **luxuriously** ADV *We lived luxuriously.* ...*huge suites, furnished very luxuriously.*
2 ADJ **Luxurious** actions express great pleasure and comfort. *She took a deep luxurious breath.*
◆ **luxuriously** ADV *She stretched luxuriously.*

luxury /lʌkʃəri/ **luxuries**
1 NU **Luxury** is very great comfort among beautiful and expensive surroundings. *We lived in great luxury.* ...*a life of ease and luxury.*
2 NC A **luxury** is something expensive which is not necessary but which gives you pleasure. *Her mother provided her with clothes and little luxuries.*
3 N SING+SUPP A **luxury** is also a pleasure which you do not often experience. *Privacy was an unknown luxury.*

luxury goods
N PL **Luxury goods** are things which are not necessary, but which give you pleasure or make your life more comfortable. Record players, jewellery, and perfume are examples of luxury goods. ...*a new tax on luxury goods.*

LV, LVs
LV is a written abbreviation for 'luncheon voucher'. ...*salary £9,375 per annum, plus LV's.*

-ly /-li/
SUFFIX **-ly** is added to adjectives to form adverbs that indicate the manner or nature of an action. For example, 'rudely' means in a rude way. Adverbs of this kind are usually not defined but are treated with the related adjectives. *He walked slowly down the street... 'I was hoping you would,' Morris said mischievously.*

lychee /laɪtʃiː/ **lychees**; also spelt **lichee**.
NC A **lychee** is a Chinese fruit with pinkish-white flesh and a large stone in the centre. *In this area, there's mangoes, lychees, and breadfruit.*

lychgate /lɪtʃgeɪt/ **lychgates**
NC A **lychgate** is a gate with a roof, which you sometimes see at the entrance to an old churchyard. *They were standing now under the arch of the lychgate.*

lying /laɪɪŋ/
1 **Lying** is the present participle of **lie**.
2 ADJ ATTRIB A **lying** person is dishonest or deceitful. ...*those lying journalists.*
3 NU **Lying** is the act of telling lies. *She's incapable of lying... She shook her fist at the prosecutors, and accused them of lying.*

lying-in
NU A woman's **lying-in** is the time that she needs to spend resting when she gives birth to a child; an old-fashioned word. *Nowadays the lying-in period is usually less than a week.*

lymph gland /lɪmf glænd/ **lymph glands**
NC A **lymph gland** is a small mass of tissue in your body where white blood cells are formed; a medical expression. *As the disease progresses, there is profound fatigue, swollen lymph glands, and depression.*

lynch /lɪntʃ/ **lynches, lynching, lynched**
VO If a person is **lynched**, they are killed, especially by being hanged, by an angry crowd of people who believe that the person has committed a crime. *At one point he was in danger of being lynched.*
◆ **lynching, lynchings** NC *The article mentions executions without trial and lynchings that have taken place in some regions.*

lynchpin /lɪntʃ pɪn/. See **linchpin**.

lynx /lɪŋks/ **lynxes**
NC A **lynx** is a wild animal rather like a cat, with a short tail and very good eyesight. *The lynx, the prairie wolf and the long-tailed weasel are three*

species in Canada that are being pushed to the brink of extinction.

lyre /laɪə/ **lyres**
NC A **lyre** is a stringed musical instrument rather like a small harp which was used in ancient Greece. *He was plucking at a lyre.*

lyric /lɪrɪk/ **lyrics**
1 ADJ ATTRIB **Lyric** poetry is written in a simple and direct style, and usually expresses personal emotions such as love. *The other side of the cassette is Cyril Cusack reading Joyce's lyric poems.*
2 N PL The **lyrics** of a song are its words. *Don Black is in the process of writing the lyrics. ...sexist lyrics.*

lyrical /lɪrɪkl/
1 ADJ Something that is **lyrical** is poetic, musical, and romantic. *He tries to bring into his plays a special lyrical quality. ...a dreamy, lyrical study of the Covent Garden flower market.*
2 to **wax lyrical**: see **wax**.

lyrically /lɪrɪkli/
ADV If you write or speak **lyrically** about someone or something, you write or speak about them in a way that shows your great admiration for them. *It was Johnson, I remember, who had written so lyrically about Woolley.*

lyricism /lɪrɪsɪzəm/
NU **Lyricism** is gentle and romantic emotion, often expressed in poetic writing or in music. *A new group of writers seem to revel in the sort of lyricism once regarded as sentimental.*

lyricist /lɪrɪsɪst/ **lyricists**
NC A **lyricist** is someone who writes the words for modern songs or for musicals. *...the lyricist Alan Jay Lerner.*

M m

M, m /ɛm/ **M's, m's**
1 NC **M** is the thirteenth letter of the English alphabet.
2 **m** is a written abbreviation for 'metres' or 'metre'.
*...a crater more than 10m wide... Each panel
measures 2.44m by 1.22m.*
3 NC **M** is also a written abbreviation for the number
'million'. *This will allow the state to save 60,000 m
roubles a year... The project will cost $10 m.*

ma /mɑː/ **mas**
VOCATIVE or NC Some people address or refer to their
mother as **ma**; an informal, old-fashioned word.
'Look, Ma, look!'... Don't tell Ma or Pa.

M.A. /ɛm eɪ/ **M.A.s**
NC An **M.A.** is a higher degree in the arts or social
sciences. **M.A.** is an abbreviation for 'Master of Arts'.
...an M.A. in Applied Linguistics.

ma'am /mæm/
VOCATIVE **Ma'am** is a spoken abbreviation for
'madam'; an old-fashioned word. *A gentleman has
called, ma'am.*

mac /mæk/ **macs**
NC A **mac** is a raincoat. *...a transparent plastic mac.*

macabre /məkɑːbrə/
ADJ A **macabre** event or story is very strange and
horrible. *...the macabre shooting.*

Macao /məkaʊ/
Macao is a Special Territory of Portugal in south-east
China. It consists of the Macao peninsula and the
islands of Taipa and Coloane. It became a Portuguese
colony in 1557. By an agreement made between China
and Portugal in 1987, Macao will revert to Chinese
ownership in 1999. Clothing and toys are exported.
Tourism and gambling are important industries.
◆ **Macanese** /mækəniːz/ N **Macao** /məkaʊ/ ADJ
▪ *religion:* Christianity (mainly Roman Catholic),
Buddhism ▪ *language:* Portuguese and Chinese
(official) ▪ *currency:* pataca ▪ *capital:* Macao
▪ *population:* 452,000 (1989) ▪ *size:* 17 square
kilometres.

macaroni /mækərəʊni/
NU **Macaroni** is a kind of pasta made in the shape of
short hollow tubes. *You can't eat cold macaroni.*

macaroon /mækəruːn/ **macaroons**
NC A **macaroon** is a sweet biscuit flavoured with
almonds or coconut.

mace /meɪs/ **maces**
1 NC A **mace** is an ornamental stick carried by an
official or placed somewhere as a symbol of authority.
*The Lord Chancellor presides over the House, with the
mace behind him.*
2 NU **Mace** is a spice, usually sold in the form of a
powder, made from the shell of nutmegs. It is used in
cooking. *Remove the onion and mace and add the
breadcrumbs.*

Macedonia /mæsɪdəʊniə/
Macedonia is a country in South Eastern Europe. It
was a republic of Yugoslavia until 1992, when it
declared its independence. The capital is Skopje.

machete /məʃeti/ **machetes**
NC A **machete** is a large knife with a broad blade. *I
used the machete to chop up some of the larger pieces
of wood... They were heavily armed with guns, knives,*
axes, and machetes.

Machiavellian /mækiəvelɪən/
ADJ **Machiavellian** behaviour is behaviour in which
someone tries to get what they want by deceiving and
cheating people in clever ways; a literary word.
You've got to be positively Machiavellian.

machinations /mækɪneɪʃnz/
N PL **Machinations** are secret and complicated plans to
gain power or harm someone; used showing
disapproval. *He could no longer endure the
machinations of his colleagues.*

machine /məʃiːn/ **machines, machining, machined**
1 NC A **machine** is a piece of equipment which uses
electricity or an engine in order to do a particular
kind of work. *He has even devised a simple machine
for cutting the fibre up... They can operate the
machine very easily.* ● See also **fruit machine, kidney
machine.**
2 VO To **machine** something means to make it or work
on it using a machine. *And then it's machined, the
metal cutting is done, and then it goes into metal
finishing.* ◆ **machining** NU *The work of machining a
part is very slow.*
3 N SING+SUPP You also use **machine** to refer to a
well-controlled system or organization. *...the might of
the enemy war machine... They had perfected their
own propaganda machine...*

machine code
NU **Machine code** is a language that can be read by a
computer, and which expresses a set of instructions
that the computer can perform; a technical expression
in computing. *...instructions for translating the
program into machine code.*

machine gun, machine guns
NC A **machine gun** is a gun which fires a lot of bullets
very quickly one after the other. *They said machine
guns and rocket launchers were used in the attacks.*

machinery /məʃiːnəri/
1 NU **Machinery** is machines in general, or machines
that are used in a factory. *Machinery is being
introduced to save labour.*
2 NU+SUPP The **machinery** of a government or
organization is the system that it uses to deal with
things. *The party controls the state machinery.*

machine tool, machine tools
NC A **machine tool** is a machine driven by power that
cuts, shapes, or finishes metal or other materials; a
technical expression. *Four hundred of them worked
busily making machine tools. ...the machine-tool
industry.*

machinist /məʃiːnɪst/ **machinists**
NC A **machinist** is a person whose job is to operate a
machine, especially in a factory. *She works as a
machinist, making trousers for shops.*

machismo /mətʃɪzməʊ/
NU **Machismo** is aggressively masculine behaviour or
attitudes. *...the powerful machismo of the hero.*

macho /mætʃəʊ/
ADJ A man who is **macho** behaves or dresses in an
aggressively masculine way; an informal word. *He
emerged with a macho swagger.*

macintosh /mækɪntɒʃ/. See **mackintosh**.
mackerel /mækrəl/; mackerel is both the singular and the plural form.
N Cor NU **Mackerel** are green-blue sea fish which are often caught and eaten. ...*shoals of mackerel... Eat plenty of fish, preferably oily fish such as mackerel.*
mackintosh /mækɪntɒʃ/ **mackintoshes**; also spelt **macintosh**.
N C A **mackintosh** is a raincoat; an old-fashioned word. *He took off his black mackintosh.*
Macmillan, Harold /hærəld məkmɪlən/
Harold Macmillan was Prime Minister of the United Kingdom from 1957 to 1963. He was born in 1894 and was a member of the Conservative Party. He was MP for Stockton on Tees from 1924 to 1929, and from 1931 to 1945, and for Bromley from 1945 to 1964. He was Minister of Housing from 1951 to 1954, and of Defence from 1954 to 1955. He served as Foreign Secretary in 1955, and was Chancellor of the Exchequer from 1955 to 1957. He was created 1st Earl of Stockton in 1984 and died in 1986.
macro- /mækrəu-/
PREFIX **Macro-** occurs in technical or scientific words that refer to or describe things that are large in size or scope. *You could magnify it to macroscopic proportions. ...macro-economic policies.*
macrobiotic /mækrəubaɪɒtɪk/
ADJ **Macrobiotic** food consists of unrefined grains and vegetables grown without chemical additives; a technical term. ...*the macrobiotic food store.*
macrocosm /mækrəukɒzəm/ **macrocosms**
N C A **macrocosm** is an organized system such as the universe or a society, which is considered as a complete unit. ...*the microcosm of the human body and the macrocosm of nature.*
mad /mæd/ **madder, maddest**
1 ADJ Someone who is **mad** has a mental illness which makes them have strange ideas and sometimes behave oddly. *She was married to a man who'd gone mad.* ◆ **madness** NU ...*the terrible madness that overtook the king.*
2 ADJ You describe someone as **mad** when they do or say things that you think are very foolish. *They think I am mad to live in such a place.* ◆ **madness** NU *It is madness for them to remain unarmed.*
3 ADJ ATTRIB You also use **mad** to describe wild, uncontrolled behaviour. *I was dashing around in the usual mad panic.*
4 ADJ PRED You can say that someone is **mad** when they are very angry; an informal use. *They're mad at me.*
5 ADJ PRED+*about* If you are **mad** about something or someone, you like them very much indeed; an informal use. *For years he's been mad about opera.*
● **Mad** is used in these phrases. ● If you say that someone is driving you **mad** or that they **will drive** you **mad**, you mean that they are annoying you very much. *These blinking kids will drive me mad.* ● If you do something like **mad**, you do it very energetically or enthusiastically; an informal expression. *They were still arguing like mad.*
Madagascar /mædəgæskə/
The **Democratic Republic of Madagascar** is a country in the Indian Ocean, off the east coast of Africa. It was a French colony from 1896 until 1960, when it became independent as the Malagasy Republic. It changed its name to the Democratic Republic of Madagascar in 1975, when Admiral Didier Ratsiraka became President and established the Vanguard of the Malagasy Revolution (AREMA) as the only party. Political parties were legalized in 1990. Guy Willy Razanamasy was appointed Prime Minister in 1991. Madagascar exports coffee, vanilla, sugar, and cloves. Large foreign debts and high inflation are serious economic problems. It is a member of the Organization of African Unity. ◆ **Malagasy** /mæləgɑːsi/ N, ADJ
■ *per capita GNP:* US$180 ■ *religion:* animism, Christianity ■ *language:* French, Malagasy ■ *currency:* franc ■ *capital:* Antananarivo (formerly Tananarive) ■ *population:* 11 million (1989) ■ *size:* 587,041 square kilometres.

madam /mædəm/
VOCATIVE **Madam** is a formal and polite way of addressing a woman. 'Dear Madam' is often used at the beginning of letters. *Good evening, Madam.*
madcap /mædkæp/
ADJ ATTRIB A **madcap** plan or scheme is very foolish and not likely to succeed. ...*some madcap scheme that he had devised.*
mad cow disease
NU **Mad cow disease** is the same as BSE; an informal expression. *BSE—or mad cow disease—has killed thousands of cattle in Britain.*
madden /mædn/ **maddens, maddening, maddened**
VO If something **maddens** you, it makes you feel very angry or annoyed. *The colonel's calmness maddened Pluskat.* ◆ **maddening** ADJ ...*a maddening clicking noise.*
made /meɪd/
Made is the past tense and past participle of **make**.
-made /-meɪd/
SUFFIX **-made** is added to words such as 'factory', 'British', and 'machine' to form adjectives that indicate that something has been made or produced at a particular place or in a particular way. *It's factory-made. ...locally-made goods.* ● See also **home-made, man-made, ready-made, self-made.**
made-to-measure
ADJ A **made-to-measure** suit or shirt is one that is made by a tailor to fit you exactly, rather than one that you buy ready-made in a shop.
made-up
1 ADJ If you or your face, lips, or eyes are **made-up**, you are wearing make-up such as eyeshadow and lipstick. ...*freshly made-up lips... She had magnificent eyes, heavily made-up.*
2 ADJ ATTRIB Something that is **made-up** has already been prepared. *Add 1 teaspoonful white vinegar to 1 pint made-up carpet shampoo.*
3 ADJ A **made-up** story or account is invented and not actually true. *The students were taught a series of made-up facts.* ● See also **make up.**
madhouse /mædhaus/ **madhouses**
N C You say that a place is a **madhouse** when it is full of noise and confusion. *In a statement, he said his country had turned into what he called a madhouse... This place will be a madhouse when they arrive.*
madly /mædli/
1 ADV If you do something **madly**, you do it in a fast, excited, or eager way. *We began rushing around madly in the dark.*
2 If you are **madly in love** with someone, you love them very much in a romantic way. *I fell madly in love with Ellen the first time I ever saw her.*
madman /mædmən/ **madmen** /mædmən/
1 N C You can refer to a foolish or irresponsible person as a **madman**. *I have had enough trouble with that madman Smith.*
2 N C A **madman** is also a man who is mad; an old-fashioned use. *They locked him up as a madman.*
Madonna /mədɒnə/ **Madonnas**
1 N PROP In Christianity, the **Madonna** is Mary, the mother of Jesus. *Walesa thanked the Madonna for what he called these great young people.*
2 N C A **Madonna** is a painting or sculpture of Mary, the mother of Jesus. ...*Raphael's Madonna. ...little ivory madonnas.*
Madrid /mədrɪd/
Madrid is the capital of Spain and its largest city. Population: 3,101,000 (1987).
madrigal /mædrɪgl/ **madrigals**
N C A **madrigal** is a song which is sung by several singers without any instruments. Madrigals were especially popular in England in the sixteenth century. ...*a six-part madrigal.*
maelstrom /meɪlstrom/
N SING A **maelstrom** is a situation which is extremely confused and violent, and usually destructive; a literary word. *Then the country was plunged into the maelstrom of the First World War.*
maestro /maɪstrəu/ **maestros**
N Cor VOCATIVE A **maestro** is someone who is extremely skilful at something, especially conducting or playing

music. *He was an absolute maestro on the piano.*

mafia /mæfiə/ **mafias**
1 N COLL The **Mafia** is a secret criminal organization that was founded in Sicily and organizes many illegal activities in the United States. *He says for the past forty or fifty years the industry has largely been controlled by the Mafia.*
2 N COLL People describe any criminal organization that operates in a similar way to the Mafia as a **mafia**. *Last month the party daily Pravda returned to the attack, virtually accusing Mr Demirchyan of running a local mafia... The problem for Colombia is that drugs mafias have infiltrated all sectors of society.*

mag /mæg/ **mags**
NC A **mag** is a weekly or monthly publication which contains articles, stories, photographs, and advertisements; an informal word. *The most amusing parts of the mag are the ads.*

magazine /mægəzi:n/ **magazines**
1 NC A **magazine** is a weekly or monthly publication which contains articles, stories, photographs, and advertisements. *I got the recipe from a woman's magazine... The editor said the government had been unhappy about the latest edition of the magazine.*
2 NC On radio or television, a **magazine** is a programme made up of several items about different issues, people, and events. *Newsbeat is the popular news magazine on Radio 1.*

magenta /mədʒentə/
ADJ Something that is **magenta** is of a dark, reddish-purple colour. *He was wearing a silk shirt and magenta slacks.* ▶ Also NU *It's a kind of magenta.*

maggot /mægət/ **maggots**
NC **Maggots** are tiny creatures that look like very small worms. Maggots turn into flies. *They're just like the sort of maggots you'd use in fishing. ...maggots of the common house fly.*

Magi /meɪdʒaɪ/
N PL In Christianity, the **Magi** were the wise men who visited Jesus soon after he was born, bringing gifts for him. *...the Adoration of the Magi.*

magic /mædʒɪk/
1 NU In fairy stories, **magic** is a special power that can make apparently impossible things happen. For example, it can control events in nature or make people disappear. *She was accused of inflicting bad fortune on them through evil magic.* ▶ Also ADJ ATTRIB *How fast the magic potion worked!*
2 NU or N+N **Magic** is also the art of performing tricks to entertain people, for example by seeming to make things appear and disappear. *We were trying to find someone to do some magic at the children's party... He was in his bedroom practising magic tricks.*
3 NU The **magic** of something is a special quality that makes it seem wonderful and exciting. *Here was a team caught up in the magic of baseball, and nobody could have beaten them... They need a bit of magic in their lives.* ▶ Also ADJ *...a truly magic moment.*

magical /mædʒɪkl/
1 ADJ Something that is **magical** uses or can produce magic. *I used to believe my mother had magical powers. ...a stream of magical water.*
2 ADJ You can also say that something is **magical** when it has a special, slightly mysterious quality that makes it seem wonderful and exciting. *The journey had lost all its magical quality.* ◆ **magically** ADV *The horizon was magically filling with ships.*

magic carpet, magic carpets
NC In stories, a **magic carpet** is a special carpet that can carry people through the air.

magician /mədʒɪʃn/ **magicians**
1 NC A **magician** is a person who performs tricks as a form of entertainment, for example by seeming to make things appear and disappear. *This process is very effectively used by stage magicians.*
2 NC In stories, a **magician** is a man who has magic powers. *...an island ruled by the magician Prospero.*

magic lantern, magic lanterns
NC A **magic lantern** is an old-fashioned kind of projector which uses large pieces of glass as slides to project a picture on to a screen.

magisterial /mædʒɪstɪəriəl/; a formal word.
1 ADJ If your behaviour or manner is **magisterial**, you act or speak as if you were in a position of authority. *...the colonel's somewhat magisterial manner... He began to address me in a magisterial voice.* ◆ **magisterially** ADV *'Supper,' announced Winifred magisterially.*
2 ADJ ATTRIB **Magisterial** also means relating to a magistrate. *...the magisterial district of East London.*

magistrate /mædʒɪstreɪt/ **magistrates**
NC A **magistrate** is an official who acts as a judge in a law court which deals with minor crimes or disputes. *You'll have to appear before the magistrate. ...the magistrates' court.*

magnanimity /mægnənɪmɪti/
NU **Magnanimity** is generosity towards someone else, especially after you have beaten them in a fight or contest; a formal word. *He displayed extraordinary magnanimity towards his adversary.*

magnanimous /mægnænɪməs/
ADJ **Magnanimous** people are generous and forgiving, especially towards people they have beaten in a fight or contest. *We must encourage new regimes to be magnanimous towards their former oppressors.*

magnate /mægneɪt/ **magnates**
NC+SUPP A **magnate** is someone who is very rich and powerful in business. *...a rich shipping magnate. ...a press magnate.*

magnesium /mægni:ziəm/
NU **Magnesium** is a metallic element which is used for making fireworks and flares because it burns very brightly. *The water contains high amounts of magnesium. ...magnesium flares.*

magnet /mægnət/ **magnets**
NC A **magnet** is a piece of iron which attracts iron or steel towards itself. *The pin was extracted with a magnet.*

magnetic /mægnetɪk/
1 ADJ Something that is **magnetic** has the power of a magnet to attract iron or steel towards it. *He took a carving knife from a magnetic board on the wall.*
2 ADJ ATTRIB People who are described as **magnetic** have qualities which other people find very attractive. *Without magnetic appeal, the politician is unlikely to succeed.*

magnetic field, magnetic fields
NC A **magnetic field** is an area around a magnet, or something functioning as a magnet, in which its power to pull things towards it is felt. *There is a huge magnetic field around Jupiter.*

magnetic north
NU **Magnetic north** is the direction that a compass needle points to.

magnetic tape, magnetic tapes
NU or NC **Magnetic tape** is narrow plastic tape covered with a magnetic substance. It is used for recording sounds, film, or computer information. *He has developed a material that could be used in laser discs which could be erased and recorded as easily as magnetic tape... A magnetic tape goes across the recording head.*

magnetise /mægnətaɪz/. See **magnetize**.

magnetism /mægnətɪzəm/
1 NU **Magnetism** is a power that attracts some substances towards others. *...the forces of electricity and magnetism.*
2 NU Someone with **magnetism** has unusual and exciting qualities which people find attractive. *He had immense personal magnetism.*

magnetize /mægnətaɪz/ **magnetizes, magnetizing, magnetized**; also spelt **magnetise**.
VO If you **magnetize** a substance or object, you give it the power to draw iron or steel towards it.

magnification /mægnɪfɪkeɪʃn/ **magnifications**
1 NU **Magnification** is the process of making something appear bigger than it actually is, for example, by using a microscope. *Magnification shows a structure of great burning curved streamers and spikes.*
2 NU or NC The **magnification** of a microscope, telescope, or pair of binoculars is the degree to which it can magnify things. *All the images, even under the*

*highest magnification, were simply points of light.
...the fundamental problem of producing high
magnifications in optical microscopes.*

magnificence /mægnɪfɪsəns/
NU **Magnificence** is the quality of being very beautiful
or impressive. *...the magnificence of the forest.*

magnificent /mægnɪfɪsənt/
ADJ Something that is **magnificent** is extremely good,
beautiful, or impressive. *It's a magnificent book... Her
dress is magnificent.* ◆ **magnificently** ADV *They
performed magnificently.*

magnify /mægnɪfaɪ/ **magnifies, magnifying,
magnified**
1 VO When a microscope or magnifying glass
magnifies an object, it makes it appear bigger than it
actually is. *The lenses magnified his eyes to the size
of dinner plates.*
2 VO To **magnify** something also means to make it
seem more important than it actually is. *His fears
have greatly magnified the true dangers.*

magnifying glass, magnifying glasses
NC A **magnifying glass** is a piece of glass which
makes objects appear bigger than they actually are.
*It was so tiny I needed to buy a magnifying glass to
see it.*

magnitude /mægnɪtjuːd/
NU The **magnitude** of something is its great size or
importance. *They do not recognize the magnitude of
the problem.*

magnolia /mægnəʊliə/ **magnolias**
NC A **magnolia** is a tree. It has white, pink, yellow, or
purple flowers. *The azaleas are beginning to pop out,
and so are the Japanese magnolias.*

magnum /mægnəm/ **magnums**
NC A **magnum** is a wine bottle holding the equivalent
of two normal bottles, approximately 1.5 litres. *To
mark yesterday's achievement, he was presented with
a magnum of champagne.*

magnum opus
N SING A **magnum opus** is the greatest or most
important single work done by a writer, painter,
composer, or other artist. *Now she has completed
what looks to me like her magnum opus.*

magpie /mægpaɪ/ **magpies**
NC A **magpie** is a black and white bird with a long
tail. Magpies are attracted by shiny objects and take
them to their nests.

maharaja /mɑːhərɑːdʒə/ **maharajas**
NCor TITLE A **maharaja** is the head of one of the royal
families that used to rule parts of India. *Today the
Maharaja lives in the family's ancestral home in north
Calcutta... Kashmir was ruled at the time by a Hindu,
Maharaja Hari Singh.*

Mahathir bin Mohamed, Dr
/məhʌdiə bɪn məʊhʌməd/
Dr Mahathir bin Mohamed became Prime Minister of
Malaysia and President of the New United Malays
National Organization (UMNO (Baru)) in 1981. He was
a member of the House of Representatives from 1964
to 1969, and was re-elected in 1974. He served as
Minister of Education from 1974 to 1977, and for Trade
and Industry from 1977 to 1981. He was Deputy Prime
Minister from 1976 to 1981. Born: 1925.

mahogany /məhɒgəni/
NU **Mahogany** is a dark reddish-brown wood that is
used to make furniture. *...a tall mahogany bookcase.*

maid /meɪd/ **maids**
NC A **maid** is a female servant. *Perla was seventeen
when she left the Philippines to work as a maid for a
rich Kuwaiti family.*

maiden /meɪdn/ **maidens**
1 NC A **maiden** is a young woman; a literary use.
Maidens performed graceful dances.
2 ADJ ATTRIB The **maiden** voyage or flight of a ship or
aeroplane is the first official journey that it makes.
*The vessel was to have made its maiden voyage in
1974.*

maiden aunt, maiden aunts
NC A **maiden aunt** is an aunt who is quite old and has
never married; an old-fashioned expression.

maiden name, maiden names
NC A married woman's **maiden name** was her

surname before she got married and took her
husband's surname. *Her stage name came from her
half-Brazilian mother, whose maiden name was
Fontes.*

maiden speech, maiden speeches
NC Someone's **maiden speech** is the first formal
speech that they make as a Member of Parliament in
the House of Commons or as a Peer in the House of
Lords. *He broke with precedent by making his
maiden speech on a controversial subject.*

maid of honor, maids of honor
NC A **maid of honor** is the chief bridesmaid at a
wedding; used in American English. *What exactly are
the responsibilities of the maid of honor to the bride?*

mail /meɪl/ **mails, mailing, mailed**
1 NU **Mail** is the letters and parcels that the post
office delivers. *If there's anything urgent in the mail,
I'll deal with it... Minnie was alone in the post office,
sorting mail.*
2 N SING The **mail** is the system used by the post office
for collecting and delivering letters and parcels. *He
said that he had lost the check in the mail... Send it to
me by mail.*
3 VO If you **mail** something, you post it. *The books
had to be mailed directly from the publisher.*

mailbag /meɪlbæg/ **mailbags**
NC A **mailbag** is a large bag used by the post office for
carrying letters and parcels. *The British Post Office
traditionally used mailbags sewn by prisoners.*

mailbox /meɪlbɒks/ **mailboxes**; used in American
English. .
1 NC A **mailbox** is a box outside your house where
letters are delivered. *...checking the mailbox at the
end of the day for letters.*
2 NC A **mailbox** is also the same as a **post-box**.

mailing list, mailing lists
NC A **mailing list** is a list of names and addresses that
an organization has so that it can send people
information. *Does anyone wish to be put on the
mailing list?*

mailman /meɪlmæn/ **mailmen**
NC A **mailman** is a man whose job is to deliver letters
and parcels that are sent by post; used in American
English.

mail order
NU If you buy things by **mail order**, you choose them
from a catalogue or an advertisement and they are
delivered to your address. *The record is available by
mail order. ...a mail-order firm.*

maim /meɪm/ **maims, maiming, maimed**
VO To **maim** someone means to injure them so badly
that part of their body is permanently damaged.
These people kill and maim innocent civilians.

main /meɪn/ **mains**
1 ADJ ATTRIB The **main** thing is the most important
one. *His main aim was to reassure people... What are
the main reasons for going to university?... Mrs Foster
hurried through the main entrance.*
2 If something is true **in the main**, it is generally true,
although there may be exceptions; a formal
expression. *The Worthingtons are in the main decent,
friendly folk.*
3 NC The **mains** are the pipes or wires which supply
gas, water, or electricity to buildings, or which take
sewage from them. *The radio we have at home plugs
into the mains... You needn't turn off the mains
water... A bulldozer had cut a gas main.*

main clause, main clauses
NC In grammar, a **main clause** is a clause that can
stand alone as a complete sentence.

mainframe /meɪnfreɪm/ **mainframes**
NC A **mainframe** is a large computer which can be
used by many people at the same time, and which can
do very large or complicated tasks. *...a £60 million
pound project to design the next generation of
advanced mainframe computers.*

mainland /meɪnlənd/
N SING The **mainland** is the main part of a country, in
contrast to the islands around it. *The motorboat was
waiting to ferry him back to the mainland. ...the coast
of mainland Greece.*

main line, main lines
NC A **main line** is an important route on a railway system, usually linking one large city with another. *The advantage of Weybridge is that it's on the main line and you can get to London in twenty-five minutes.*

mainline /ˈmeɪnlaɪn/ **mainlines, mainlining, mainlined**
1 ADJ ATTRIB A **mainline** station is one that lies on a main line. *He took a taxi straight to the mainline station.*
2 V or VO If drug addicts **mainline** or if they **mainline** a drug, they inject a drug into themselves. *People either smoke or mainline the stuff.*

mainly /ˈmeɪnli/
ADV You use **mainly** to say that a statement is true in most cases or to a large extent. *The political groups have more power, mainly because of their larger numbers... I'll be concentrating mainly on French.*

main road, main roads
NC A **main road** is a large important road that leads from one town or city to another. *We turned off the main road shortly after Alcester.*

mainspring /ˈmeɪnsprɪŋ/
N SING+SUPP The **mainspring** of something is the most important reason for it or the thing that is essential to it; a formal word. *Technology was the mainspring of economic growth.*

mainstay /ˈmeɪnsteɪ/ **mainstays**
NC+SUPP The **mainstay** of something is the most important part of it. *Cotton is the mainstay of the economy.*

mainstream /ˈmeɪnstriːm/
N SING People or ideas that are part of the **mainstream** are regarded as normal and conventional because they belong to a group that most people or ideas belong to. *We feel isolated from the mainstream of social life in the community... All of the new ministers come from the political mainstream. ...mainstream education... All three men belonged to the mainstream Fatah group within the PLO.*

maintain /meɪnˈteɪn/ **maintains, maintaining, maintained**
1 VO If you **maintain** something, you continue to have it, and do not let it stop or grow weaker. *I wanted to maintain my friendship with her... For twenty-five years they had failed to maintain law and order.*
2 VO If you **maintain** something at a particular rate or level, you keep it at that rate or level. *One has to maintain the temperature at a very high level.*
3 VO To **maintain** someone means to provide them with money and the things that they need. *I need the money to maintain me until I start a job.*
4 VO If you **maintain** a building, vehicle, road, or machine, you keep it in good condition. *...the rising cost of maintaining the equipment.*
5 V-REPORT or VO If you **maintain** that something is true, you state your opinion very strongly. *Mrs Camish always maintained that he had been a brilliant thinker... The government maintains that spending on the health service has been above the general level of inflation... He maintains his innocence.*

maintenance /ˈmeɪntənəns/
1 NU The **maintenance** of a building, road, vehicle, or machine is the process of keeping it in good condition. *Who's responsible for the care and maintenance of this building?... He learnt tractor maintenance.*
2 N SING The **maintenance** of a state or process consists of making sure that it continues. *...the maintenance of law and order. ...the maintenance of the same rate of expansion.*
3 NU **Maintenance** is also money that someone gives regularly to another person to pay for the things that the person needs. *...the government's plan to make absent fathers pay maintenance for their children.*

maisonette /ˌmeɪzəˈnet/ **maisonettes**
NC A **maisonette** is a small flat on two floors of a larger building. *She shared an upper maisonette with two other girls.*

maize /meɪz/
NU **Maize** is a tall plant which produces corn. The corn grows on long round parts called cobs. *...a field planted with maize.*

Maj.
Maj. is a written abbreviation for 'major'. *...Maj. James Johnson.*

majestic /məˈdʒestɪk/
ADJ **Majestic** means very beautiful, dignified, and impressive. *...the majestic proportions of the great Pyramid... She looked majestic in her large, soft hat.*
♦ **majestically** ADV *Wet clouds, heavy with rain, moved majestically overhead.*

Majesty /ˈmædʒəsti/ **Majesties**
TITLE **Your Majesty, Her Majesty,** or **Their Majesties** are used to address or refer to kings or queens. *...Her Majesty the Queen... Thank you, Your Majesty.*

major /ˈmeɪdʒə/ **majors, majoring, majored**
1 ADJ ATTRIB You use **major** to describe something that is more important, serious, or significant than other things. *Finding a solicitor had been a major problem... One major factor was the revolution in communications... This is likely to become one of the major civil liberties issues of the '90s.*
2 NC or TITLE A **major** is an army officer of medium rank. *...a retired army major. ...Major Burton-Cox.*
3 ADJ In European music, a **major** scale is one in which the third note is two tones higher than the first. *They're both in D major.*
4 V+in If you **major** in a particular subject, you study it as your main subject at university; used in American English. *I decided to major in French... An increasing number of blacks are majoring in science.*

Major, John /dʒɒn ˈmeɪdʒə/
John Major became the Prime Minister of the United Kingdom and the leader of the Conservative Party in 1990. He served as Foreign Secretary in 1989 and as Chancellor of the Exchequer from 1989 to 1990. Born: 1943.

major-domo /ˌmeɪdʒəˈdəʊməʊ/ **major-domos**
NC A **major-domo** is the chief servant in charge of the other servants in a large house; an old-fashioned word.

majorette /ˌmeɪdʒəˈret/ **majorettes**
NC A **majorette** is a girl or young woman who marches at the front of a musical band in a procession. Majorettes wear a uniform and carry sticks which they spin with their fingers and sometimes throw into the air and catch. *Men on horseback, drum majorettes, brass bands, countless schoolchildren—they all took part as thousands more watched.*

major general, major generals
NC or TITLE A **major general** is a senior officer in the army, one rank above a brigadier. *In 1965 he was promoted to commandant of the army and became a major general. ...Major General Alfred Glay.*

majority /məˈdʒɒrəti/ **majorities**
1 N SING The **majority** of people or things in a group is more than half of them. *...mass movements involving the overwhelming majority of the people... Most polls show that Germans support the Allied war effort in the Gulf, but only by a narrow majority.* ● If a group is in **a majority** or **in the majority,** they form more than half of a larger group. *Armenians are being intimidated into leaving the disputed area of Nagorno-Karabakh, where they are in a majority... There's little doubt that the pro-merger faction is in the majority.*
2 NC In an election, a **majority** is the difference between the number of votes gained by the winner and the number gained by the person or party that comes second. *Benn was returned by a majority of 15,479... He now has an overwhelming majority in parliament... If neither candidate wins a clear majority, a second round of voting will take place.* ● See also **absolute majority, overall majority, simple majority.**

majority rule
NU **Majority rule** is government by representatives who are elected under a system in which everyone in a country has the right to vote, rather than under a system in which only a small, privileged group can vote. *He said there would be no end to strife in South Africa until there was majority rule... The party was the first organization to call for black majority rule.*

Majuro Atoll /məˈdʒʊərəʊ ˈætɒl/
Majuro Atoll is the capital of the Marshall Islands and

its largest settlement. Population: 13,000 (1988).

make /meɪk/ **makes, making, made**

1 VO You use **make** to say that someone performs an action. For example, if someone **makes** a suggestion, they suggest something. *I made the wrong decision... He made the shortest speech I've ever heard... We have got to make a really serious effort... He had two phone calls to make.*

2 VO+INF If something **makes** you do something, it causes you to do it. If someone **makes** you do something, they force you to do it. *A sudden noise made Brody jump... Make him listen!... They were made to sit and wait.*

3 VOCorVO+*into* You use **make** to say that someone or something is caused to be a particular thing or to have a particular quality. For example, if something **makes** someone happy, it causes them to be happy. *I'd like to make the world a better place... They're making the old kitchen into a little bedroom.*

4 VO+*of* You use **make** to say how well or badly someone does something. For example, if you **make** a success of something, you do it well. *Let's not make a mess of this.*

5 VOO If you **make** something, you produce it or construct it. *I like making cakes. ...the greatest film ever made... You can make petroleum out of coal... Martin, can you make us a drink?*

6 V-PASS+*of*or*from* If something **is made** of a particular substance, that substance was used to form or construct it. *The houses were made of brick. ...a flute made from bone.*

7 VO If you **make** a sound, you produce it. *Try not to make so much noise.*

8 VC You use **make** to say what two numbers add up to. For example, if two numbers **make** 12, they add up to 12.

9 VOC You use **make** to say what the time is, or to give the result of a calculation. For example, if you **make** it 4 o'clock, your watch says it is 4 o'clock. If you **make** the answer to a calculation 144, you calculate it to be 144.

10 VO If you **make** money, you get it by working for it or by investing money. *He was making ninety dollars a week... She made a £200 profit.*

11 VC You use **make** to say that someone or something is suitable for a particular task or role. For example, if someone would **make** a good secretary, they have the right qualities to be a good secretary. *Do garden tools make good gifts?*

12 VO You can use **make** to say that a part or aspect of something is responsible for that thing's success. *Nicholson's acting really makes the film.*

13 VO If you **make** a place, you manage to get there. *I made Ramsdale by dawn.*

14 VO If you **make** friends or enemies, you cause people to become your friends or enemies. *Karen made friends with several children... Roger made a number of enemies.*

15 to **make good**: see **good**. to **make love**: see **love**. to **make way**: see **way**. See also **making**.

make for PHRASAL VERB If you **make for** a place, you move towards it. *We joined the crowd making for the exit.*

make of PHRASAL VERB If you ask someone what they **make of** something, you want to know what their impression or opinion of it is. *He didn't know what to make of his new boss... Can you make anything of it?*

make off PHRASAL VERB If you **make off**, you leave somewhere as quickly as possible. *The vehicle made off at once.*

make off with PHRASAL VERB If you **make off with** something, you steal it. *Otto made off with the last of the brandy.*

make out PHRASAL VERB 1 If you can **make** something **out**, you can see, hear, or understand it. *He could just make out the number plate of the car... She tried to make out what was being said.* 2 If you **make out** that something is the case, you try to cause people to believe it. *He's not really as hard as people make out.* 3 When you **make out** a cheque or receipt, you write all the necessary information on it. *I made a cheque out for £1200... Did you make out a receipt?*

make up PHRASAL VERB 1 If a number of things **make up** something, they form it. *...the various groups which make up society... All substances are made up of molecules.* 2 If you **make up** a story or an explanation, you invent it, sometimes in order to deceive someone. *He's very good at making up excuses.* 3 If you **make** yourself **up**, you put cosmetics on your face. ● See also **make-up**. 4 If you **make up** an amount, you add to it so that it is as large as it should be. *Government would have to make up the difference out of its welfare budget.* 5 If two people **make up** or **make it up**, they become friends again after a quarrel. *He and Frank made it up.* 6 To **make up** for something that is lost or missing means to replace it or compensate for it. *If babies put on very little weight at first, eventually they will gain rapidly to make up for it.* 7 If you **make it up to** someone for disappointing them, you do something for them to show how sorry you are.

make-believe

NU You refer to someone's behaviour as **make-believe** when they pretend that things are better or more exciting than they really are. *His whole life these days was a game of make-believe.*

maker /meɪkə/ **makers**

NC+SUPP The **maker** of something is the person or company that makes it. *...film maker and critic, Iain Johnstone... The maker's label was carefully removed.*

makeshift /meɪkʃɪft/

ADJ **Makeshift** things are temporary and of poor quality. *The accommodation was makeshift. ...makeshift barricades.*

make-up

1 NU **Make-up** is coloured creams and powders which some people, especially women, put on their faces to make themselves look more attractive. *She had a lot of make-up on. ...eye make-up.*

2 NU+SUPP The **make-up** of something is the different parts that it consists of, and the way these parts are arranged. *...the psychological make-up of primitive man.*

make-weight, make-weights

NC A **make-weight** is something which is added to something else so that there is the right amount, or in order to compensate for something that is missing. *They are good added whole to apple pies, or added as a make-weight to blackberry jelly... I'm only in the team as a sort of make-weight.*

making /meɪkɪŋ/ **makings**

NU+SUPP The **making** of something is the act or process of producing it. *At the end of his life he turned to the making of beautiful books. ..the making of resolutions.*

● **Making** is used in these phrases. ● If a problem is of your **own making**, you caused it. *The trouble here is of the President's own making.* ● If something **is the making of** a person or thing, it is the reason that they are successful. *The description of Belfast is the making of the book.* ● If you say that a person or thing has the **makings** of something, you mean that they seem likely to develop in that way. *She perceived that here might be the makings of the friendship that had so eluded her.*

Maktoum, Shaikh Maktoum bin Rashid al- /ʃeɪk mʌktuːm bɪn rɑːʃɪd əl mʌktuːm/

Shaikh Maktoum bin Rashid al-Maktoum became Ruler of Dubai and Prime Minister of the United Arab Emirates in 1990, at the death of his father. He served as Deputy Prime Minister from 1979 to 1990. Born: 1943.

Malabo /məlɑːbəʊ/

Malabo is the capital of Equatorial Guinea and its second largest town. It is on the island of Bioko (Fernando Póo) and was formerly known as Santa Isabel. Population: 15,000 (1983).

maladjusted /mælədʒʌstɪd/

ADJ **Maladjusted** children have psychological problems and behave in socially unacceptable ways.

maladjustment /mælədʒʌstmənt/ **maladjustments**

NUorNC **Maladjustment** is the state of having psychological problems and behaving in a way which is not acceptable to society. *Over-eating is often a* *symptom of loneliness or maladjustment... Certain maladjustments do occur, of course.*

maladroit /mælədrɔɪt/
ADJ Something that is **maladroit** is done in a clumsy, awkward, or tactless way; a formal word. *...maladroit public relations.* ◆ **maladroitness** NU *It is from their very naivety and maladroitness that their appeal flows.*

malady /mælədi/ **maladies**
NC A **malady** is an illness; an old-fashioned word. *Was she affected by the same malady?*

malaise /maleɪz/
NU **Malaise** is a state in which you feel dissatisfied or unhappy but do not know exactly what is wrong; a formal word. *Malaise had set in with the coming of the twentieth century.*

malaria /maleəriə/
NU **Malaria** is a serious disease caught from mosquitoes and which causes periods of fever. *A few weeks ago we heard about new hope for a vaccine against malaria... The malaria parasite has an extremely complicated life cycle.*

Malawi /məlɑːwi/
The **Republic of Malawi** is a country in southern Africa. It became a British colony in 1891 and from 1907 it was known as Nyasaland. From 1953 to 1964 it was joined with Northern and Southern Rhodesia to form the Federation of Rhodesia and Nyasaland. Malawi became independent in 1964 and Dr Hastings Kamuzu Banda became President. The only party is the Malawi Congress Party (MCP). Malawi is a member of the Commonwealth and the Organization of African Unity. Over 750,000 refugees from the civil war in Mozambique have fled to Malawi. It exports tobacco, tea, and sugar. Large foreign debts and high inflation are serious economic problems. ◆ **Malawian** /məlɑːwiən/ N, ADJ
▪ *per capita GNP:* US$160 ▪ *religion:* Christianity, animism, Islam ▪ *language:* English (official), Chichewa ▪ *currency:* kwacha ▪ *capital:* Lilongwe ▪ *largest city:* Blantyre ▪ *population:* 8 million (1989) ▪ *size:* 118,484 square kilometres.

Malaysia /məleɪziə/
The **Federation of Malaysia** is a country in south-east Asia. It includes part of the Malay Peninsula and Sarawak and Sabah on the island of Borneo (Kalimantan). Malaysia became a British colony in the 19th century. It was occupied by Japan from 1941 until 1946. Communist guerrillas fought for independence from 1948 until the mid-1950s. Malaysia became independent in 1957 and in 1963 the Federation of Malaysia (consisting of Malaya, Sarawak, Sabah, and Singapore) was established. Singapore left the Federation in 1965. Ethnic conflict between the Malay, Chinese, and Indian communities has been a source of civil disorder. Sultan Azlan Muhibbuddin Shah became head of state in 1989. Dr Mahathir bin Mohamed, of the New United Malays National Organization (UMNO (Baru), became Prime Minister in 1981. Malaysia is a member of the Commonwealth and the Association of South East Asian Nations. It exports manufactured goods, oil, and gas. It is the world's largest producer of rubber and palm oil. Tourism is an important industry. ◆ **Malaysian** /məleɪziən/ N, ADJ
▪ *per capita GNP:* US$1,870 ▪ *religion:* Islam, Buddhism ▪ *language:* Bahasa Malaysia (official) ▪ *currency:* ringgit ▪ *capital:* Kuala Lumpur ▪ *population:* 17 million (1988) ▪ *size:* 329,758 square kilometres.

malcontent /mælkəntent/ **malcontents**
NC A **malcontent** is a person who is unhappy with the way society is organized and who wants to try and change it; a formal word, used showing disapproval. *The rioters were not the usual run of urban malcontents but men of responsibility.*

Maldives /mɔːldɪvz/
The **Republic of the Maldives** is a country in the Indian Ocean, south-west of India. It consists of about 1,200 islands. The Maldives were a British protectorate from the 19th century until independence in 1965. Maumoun Abdul Gayoom became President in 1978. The Maldives are a member of the Commonwealth.

Fish is exported. Tourism is an important industry. ◆ **Maldivian** /mɔːldɪviən/ N, ADJ
▪ *per capita GNP:* US$410 ▪ *religion:* Islam (mainly Sunni) ▪ *language:* Dhivehi ▪ *currency:* rufiyaa ▪ *capital:* Malé ▪ *population:* 206,000 (1989) ▪ *size:* 298 square kilometres.

male /meɪl/ **males**
1 NC A **male** is a person or animal that belongs to the sex that cannot give birth to babies or lay eggs. *The males establish a breeding territory.* ▸ Also ADJ *...male hamsters.*
2 ADJ ATTRIB Something that is **male** concerns or affects men rather than women. *...male unemployment.*

Malé /mɑːleɪ/
Malé is the capital of the Maldives and its largest city. Population: 56,000 (1990).

male chauvinism
NU **Male chauvinism** is the belief which some men have that men are naturally better and more important than women; used showing disapproval. *...a symptom of the male chauvinism in our society.*

male chauvinist, male chauvinists
NC A **male chauvinist** is a man who believes that men are naturally better and more important than women; used showing disapproval. *The men in my office are all blatant male chauvinists. ...a male chauvinist remark.*

malefactor /mælɪfæktə/ **malefactors**
NC A **malefactor** is someone, often a criminal, who does something bad; a literary word. *He prosecuted malefactors vigorously.*

malevolence /məlevələns/
NU **Malevolence** is the act of deliberately causing harm, or the feeling of wanting to; a literary word. *...the victims of his malevolence.*

malevolent /məlevələnt/
ADJ **Malevolent** people want to cause harm; a literary word. *These people seemed hard and malevolent.*

malformed /mælfɔːmd/
ADJ If something is **malformed**, it does not have its normal or correct shape; a formal word. *...his hideously malformed legs.*

malfunction /mælfʌŋkʃn/ **malfunctions, malfunctioning, malfunctioned**
V If a machine or a computer **malfunctions**, it fails to work properly. *It does seem almost certain that both engines malfunctioned in some way.* ▸ Also NC *...a malfunction of the generator.*

Mali /mɑːli/
The **Republic of Mali** is a country in western Africa. It was a French colony from the 19th century to 1960. General Moussa Traoré came to power in an army coup in 1968 and established a one-party state. Lieutenant-Colonel Toumani Touré, of the Transition Committee for the Salvation of the People (CTSP), became President in 1991. He promised a new constitution and free elections. Soumana Sacko (CTSP) was appointed Prime Minister in 1991. Mali exports cotton, groundnuts, and fish. It is a member of the Organization of African Unity. ◆ **Malian** /mɑːliən/ N, ADJ
▪ *per capita GNP:* US$230 ▪ *religion:* Islam, animism ▪ *language:* French (official), Bambara ▪ *currency:* CFA franc ▪ *capital:* Bamako ▪ *population:* 8 million (1989) ▪ *size:* 1,240,192 square kilometres.

malice /mælɪs/
NU **Malice** is a desire to harm people. *'So I notice,' he added with a touch of malice.*

malicious /məlɪʃəs/
ADJ **Malicious** talk or behaviour is intended to harm someone or their reputation. *She described the charges as malicious.* ◆ **maliciously** ADV *There isn't anyone who has deliberately and maliciously set out to try and fool the department.*

Malietoa Tanumafili II /mælietəʊə tænuməfiːli/
Malietoa Tanumafili II became joint head of state of Western Samoa in 1962 and became the sole head of state in 1963. Born: 1913.

malign /məlaɪn/ **maligns, maligning, maligned;** a formal word.
1 VO If you **malign** someone, you say unpleasant and

untrue things about them. *He had maligned both women.*

2 ADJ **Malign** behaviour is intended to harm someone. *His speeches are open to all sorts of malign interpretation.*

malignancy /məlɪgnənsi/

1 NU **Malignancy** is the uncontrolled state of a disease, for example a tumour, which is likely to cause death. *The next step depends on the malignancy of the patient's condition.*

2 NU **Malignancy** is also the desire or intention to harm people; a literary use. *The rat, in Rosenberg's poetry, is always a symbol of the malignancy of fate.*

malignant /məlɪgnənt/

1 ADJ A **malignant** disease, for example a tumour, is uncontrollable and likely to cause death. *...a malignant growth.*

2 ADJ **Malignant** behaviour is harmful and cruel; a literary use. *...the consequence of a malignant plot.*

malinger /məlɪŋgə/ **malingers, malingering, malingered**

V If you are **malingering**, you are pretending to be ill in order to avoid working. *I'm not malingering, really I'm not.*

malingerer /məlɪŋgərə/ **malingerers**

NC A **malingerer** is a person who pretends to be ill in order to avoid doing work.

mall /mɔːl, mæl/ **malls**

NC A **mall** is a shopping area where cars are not allowed. *...a bookstore in a local mall.*

mallard /mælɑːd/ **mallards**. The plural form can be either **mallards** or **mallard**.

NC A **mallard** is a very common kind of wild duck. *He's now doing research on mallard mating habits.*

malleable /mæliəbl/; a formal word.

1 ADJ Someone who is **malleable** is easily influenced or controlled by other people. *He was kind and malleable. ...a cheap and malleable labour force.*

2 ADJ A substance that is **malleable** can easily be changed into a new shape. *The clay is of the right consistency, solid but malleable.*

mallet /mælɪt/ **mallets**

NC A **mallet** is a wooden hammer with a square head.

malnourished /mælnʌrɪʃt/

ADJ If someone is **malnourished**, they are physically weak because they have not eaten enough food of the right kind. *The majority of the population is malnourished... Many of the refugees were severely malnourished.*

malnutrition /mælnjuːtrɪʃn/

NU **Malnutrition** is physical weakness caused by not eating enough food of the right kind. *He is showing the first signs of malnutrition.*

malodorous /mæləʊdərəs/

ADJ Something that is **malodorous** has an unpleasant smell; a literary use. *The air outside was almost as dank and malodorous as inside.*

malpractice /mælpræktɪs/ **malpractices**

N U or N C **Malpractice** is behaviour in which someone breaks the law or the rules of their profession in order to gain some personal advantage; a legal term. *Both sides have accused the other of malpractice during Sunday's voting... There had been a number of irregularities and malpractices.*

malt /mɔːlt/

NU **Malt** is a substance made from grain that is used to make some alcoholic drinks. *...malt and barley for beer making. ...a bottle of malt whisky.*

Malta /mɔːltə/

The **Republic of Malta** is a country in the Mediterranean. It includes the islands of Malta, Gozo, and Comino. Malta was a British colony from 1814 until independence in 1964. Dr Vincent Tabone, of the Nationalist Party (PN), became President in 1989. Dr Edward Fenech Adami (PN) became Prime Minister in 1987. Malta is a member of the Commonwealth. It exports clothing and other manufactured items. Tourism is an important industry. ◆ **Maltese** /mɔːltiːz/ N, ADJ, N PL

▪ *per capita GNP:* US$5,050 ▪ *religion:* Christianity (mainly Roman Catholic) ▪ *language:* Maltese and English (official) ▪ *currency:* lira ▪ *capital:* Valletta

▪ *largest city:* Birkirkara ▪ *population:* 349,000 (1988) ▪ *size:* 316 square kilometres.

malted milk, malted milks

N MASS **Malted milk** is a drink made from a special powder that contains malt. *He ordered a malted milk.*

maltreat /mæltriːt/ **maltreats, maltreating, maltreated**

VO If people or animals **are maltreated**, they are treated badly. *We do not intervene unless the children are being physically maltreated.*

maltreatment /mæltriːtmənt/

NU **Maltreatment** involves treating someone or something in a way that will damage or hurt them. *In these circumstances, you are more vulnerable to maltreatment.*

mama /məmɑː/ **mamas**; also spelt **mamma**.

VOCATIVE or N C **Mama** means the same as **mother**; an old-fashioned word. *Oh mama, I am so unhappy... I shall tell your mamma what you did.*

Mamaloni, Solomon /spləmən mæmələʊni/

Solomon **Mamaloni** became Prime Minister of the Solomon Islands in 1989. He was MP for Makira from 1970 to 1976 and for West Makira from 1976 to 1977. He was again elected MP for West Makira in 1980. He was Chief Minister from 1974 to 1976, and Prime Minister from 1981 to 1985. He became the leader of the People's Alliance Party (PAP) in 1980. Born: 1943.

Mammadov, Yagub /jæguːb mæmɑːdof/

Yagub **Mammadov** became President of Azerbaijan in 1992. He was formerly the speaker of parliament.

mammal /mæml/ **mammals**

NC **Mammals** are particular types of animals. Most female mammals give birth to babies rather than laying eggs, and feed their young with milk. Humans, dogs, lions, and whales are all mammals. *This research will have implications for other mammals, including humans.*

mammary /mæməri/

ADJ **Mammary** means relating to the breasts; a technical term. *...the mammary gland.*

mammoth /mæməθ/ **mammoths**

1 ADJ ATTRIB **Mammoth** means very large indeed. *...the immense foyer with its mammoth mirrors. ...a mammoth task.*

2 NC **Mammoths** were animals like elephants with very long tusks and long hair. Mammoths no longer exist. *Miners in the Soviet Union have dug up the remains of a prehistoric mammoth.*

Mamoudzou /mæmuːdzuː/

Mamoudzou is the largest town on the island of Mayotte. Population: 12,000 (1985).

man /mæn/ **men; mans, manning, manned**. The form **men** is the plural of the noun. The form **mans** is the third person singular, present tense, of the verb.

1 NC A **man** is an adult male human being. *Larry was a handsome man in his early fifties... The picture shows a man carrying a Christmas tree... The two men are expected to meet at a conference in the New Year... Men have more time to spare than women.*

2 NU or NC Human beings in general are sometimes referred to as **man**. *Why does man seem to have more diseases than animals? ...a deserted island where no man could live.*

3 N PL The **men** in an army are the ordinary soldiers, rather than the officers. *In all, some 70,000 officers and men died.*

4 VO When soldiers or other people who are on duty **man** a place or a machine, they look after it or operate it. *...a checkpoint manned by British soldiers... They manned the phones all night.*

5 the **man in the street**: see **street**. See also **best man, manned, manning, man-to-man.**

-man /-mæn/

SUFFIX **-man** is added to numbers to make adjectives showing that something involves or is intended for that number of people. *It has a three-man crew... He's competing in the four-man event.*

manacle /mænəkl/ **manacles, manacling, manacled**

1 NC **Manacles** are metal devices attached to a prisoner's wrists or legs in order to prevent the prisoner from moving easily or escaping. *Carleson locked the manacles around the man's wrists.*

2 VO To **manacle** someone means to attach manacles to their wrists or legs in order to prevent them moving easily or escaping. *Were any of them manacled to the floor?*

manage /mænɪdʒ/ **manages, managing, managed**
1 V or VO If you **manage** to do something, you succeed in doing it. *How he managed to find us is beyond me... I'm sure you'll manage perfectly... We'll manage it somehow.*
2 VO If someone **manages** an organization, business, or system, they are responsible for controlling it. *She manages a chain of pet shops.*
3 V If you say that someone **manages**, you mean that they have an acceptable way of life, although they do not have much money. *I don't want charity. I can manage... I've always managed on a teacher's salary.*

manageable /mænɪdʒəbl/
ADJ Something that is **manageable** can be dealt with because it is not too big or complicated. *It is a perfectly manageable task.*

management /mænɪdʒmənt/ **managements**
1 NU The **management** of an organization or situation is the process or act of controlling and organizing it. *The newly created post is intended to relieve Mr Gorbachev of the day-to-day management of party affairs... Opponents of the government accuse it of bad economic management... It's a question of good management.*
2 NU or NC The people who control an organization are also called the **management**. *...communication between management and the workforce... The response from the management has been rapid.*

manager /mænɪdʒə/ **managers**
1 NC A **manager** is the person responsible for running an organization. *What you need is advice from your bank manager. ...the general manager of Philips Ltd in Singapore.*
2 NC The **manager** of a pop star or other entertainer is the person who looks after the star's business interests. *He was so struck by Hendrix's singing and playing that he became his manager and persuaded him to move to Britain.*
3 NC The **manager** of a sports team is the person responsible for organizing and training it. *John Barnwell has been appointed as the new manager of second division Walsall.*

manageress /mænɪdʒərɛs/ **manageresses**
NC A **manageress** is a woman who runs an organization such as a shop or restaurant. *...the manageress of a bookshop.*

managerial /mænɪdʒɪəriəl/
ADJ ATTRIB **Managerial** means relating to the work of a manager or manageress. *...technical and managerial skills.*

managing director, managing directors
NC The **managing director** of a company is a director who is also responsible for the way that the company is managed. *...the appointment of Mr Paul Fox as the new managing director of BBC Television.*

Managua /mənægwə/
Managua is the capital of Nicaragua and its largest city. Population: 682,000 (1985).

Manama /mənɑːmə/
Manama is the capital of Bahrain and its largest city. Population: 122,000 (1981).

mandarin /mændərɪn/ **mandarins**
1 NU **Mandarin** or **Mandarin Chinese** is the official language of China. *BBC programmes in English and Mandarin can be heard now by a potential audience of one billion Chinese... She has had lessons in Mandarin.*
2 NC A **mandarin** is a small orange which is easy to peel.

mandate /mændeɪt/ **mandates, mandating, mandated**
1 NC When someone is given a **mandate** to carry out a policy or task, they are given the authority to do it, or are instructed to do it. *Representatives will debate an amendment calling for any military strike to be backed by a United Nations mandate... My mandate is to find the best team.* ◆ Also VO *He'd now been mandated to go in and to enforce a ceasefire.*
2 NC A government's **mandate** is the authority that it has to carry out particular policies or tasks as a result

of winning an election. *It was widely rumoured that Mr Botha would seek a new mandate for reform by calling a snap general election... The President will be able to claim that he has a mandate for the task that lies ahead.*
3 NC You can refer to the fixed length of time that a country's leader or government remains in office as their **mandate**. *Mr Mitterrand would be willing to reduce the presidential mandate from seven to five years.*
4 V O or V-REPORT To **mandate** something means to make it mandatory; used in American English. *The Clean Air Act mandates a 15% reduction in auto fuel emissions by 1995... The way around that, of course, is to mandate that all health care workers be tested for the AIDS virus.* ◆ **mandated** ADJ ATTRIB *Locally mandated water rationing went into effect in areas of Southern California today.*

mandatory /mændətəʳri/
ADJ If something is **mandatory**, a law states that it must be done. *The testing of cosmetics is not mandatory here.*

mandible /mændɪbl/ **mandibles**
NC A **mandible** is a jawbone, especially the jawbone of an animal, bird, or fish; a technical term.

mandolin /mændəlɪn, mændəlɪn/ **mandolins**; also spelt **mandoline**.
NC A **mandolin** is a musical instrument like a small guitar with four pairs of metal strings. *He had Nino playing the mandolin as accompaniment.*

mane /meɪn/ **manes**
NC A horse's or lion's **mane** is the long thick hair that grows from its neck. *It's about the size of a squirrel, with a mane like a lion and a black and gold coat.*

man-eater, man-eaters
NC A **man-eater** is an animal which eats human beings. *The tigers are a protected species in the region, except when they have turned man-eater.*

man-eating
ADJ ATTRIB A **man-eating** animal is an animal which has eaten human beings and is very dangerous. *...man-eating lions.*

maneuver /mənuːvə/. See **manoeuvre**.

manfully /mænfəli/
ADV If someone does something **manfully**, they do it in a determined way; often used humorously. *I could see Simon manfully wielding a shovel.*

manganese /mæŋgəniːz/
NU **Manganese** is a greyish-white metal that is used in making steel. *Gabon is also a significant producer of manganese and uranium.*

manger /meɪndʒə/ **mangers**
NC A **manger** is a feeding box in a stable or barn. *The horses were crunching their straw and oats at their manger.*

mangle /mæŋgl/ **mangles, mangling, mangled**
VO If something is **mangled**, it is crushed and twisted. *They had their arms mangled in motorcycle crashes.*

mangled /mæŋgld/
ADJ ATTRIB You use **mangled** to describe something that has been crushed and twisted. *A hundred and fifty firemen spent several hours trying to free the injured from the mangled wreckage.*

mango /mæŋgəʊ/ **mangoes** or **mangos**
NC A **mango** is a large, sweet, yellowish fruit which grows in hot countries. *Around the pig pen there is a pawpaw tree, a mango tree and pumpkin vines.*

mangrove /mæŋgrəʊv/ **mangroves**
NC A **mangrove** is a tree that grows in hot countries. Mangroves stand on roots which are above the ground and grow very close together along the banks of rivers. *A number of other fish and shellfish are dependent on mangroves for some stage of their life cycles.*

mangy /meɪndʒi/
ADJ A **mangy** animal has lost a lot of its hair through disease. *...a mangy cat.*

manhandle /mænhændl/ **manhandles, manhandling, manhandled**
VO If you **manhandle** someone, you treat them very roughly. *He had been manhandled on the street by police.*

manhole /ˈmænhəʊl/ **manholes**
NC A **manhole** is a covered hole in the ground leading to a drain or sewer. *...an open manhole. ...manhole covers.*

manhood /ˈmænhʊd/
NU **Manhood** is the state of being a man rather than a boy, or the period of a man's adult life. *...the dubious rewards of manhood... He had millions of dollars to play with in his early manhood.*

man-hour, man-hours
NC You use **man-hour** to refer to the amount of time that a piece of work will take. For example, if a job takes 15 man-hours, it takes one person 15 hours to do it or three people five hours to do it. *One firm spent a total of 370,000 man-hours on the job.*

manhunt /ˈmænhʌnt/ **manhunts**
NC A **manhunt** is a search for someone who has escaped or disappeared. *A big manhunt was launched after he escaped.*

mania /ˈmeɪniə/ **manias**
1 NCorNU A **mania** for something is an excessively strong liking for it. *She had a mania for cleanliness... At times the urge to preserve the past took on the proportions of mania.*
2 NU A **mania** is also a mental illness. *...persecution mania.*

maniac /ˈmeɪniæk/ **maniacs**
NC A **maniac** is a mad person who is violent and dangerous. *She was attacked by a maniac.*

maniacal /məˈnaɪəkl/
ADJ **Maniacal** behaviour is violent, uncontrolled, and dangerous. *His maniacal raving alarmed the butler... She was shrieking maniacal invective at the terrified girl.* ◆ **maniacally** ADV *Flynn laughed maniacally.*

manic /ˈmænɪk/
ADJ You use **manic** to describe behaviour which is very energetic, because the person concerned is excited or anxious. *Weston finished his manic typing.*

manic-depressive, manic-depressives
NC A **manic-depressive** is a person who is sometimes excited and confident and at other times very depressed, and who cannot control these feelings. *He's a bit of a manic-depressive.* ▶ Also ADJ *Mother may have had a manic-depressive personality.*

manicure /ˈmænɪkjʊə/ **manicures, manicuring, manicured**
VO If you **manicure** your hands or nails, you care for them by softening the skin and cutting and polishing the nails. *She was sitting manicuring her nails.* ▶ Also NC *His sister gave him a manicure once a month.*

manicurist /ˈmænɪkjʊərɪst/ **manicurists**
NC A **manicurist** is a person whose job is manicuring people's hands and nails. *I decided to treat myself and go to the manicurist.*

manifest /ˈmænɪfest/ **manifests, manifesting, manifested;** a formal word.
1 ADJ If something is **manifest,** people can easily see that it exists or is true. *It was not just his manifest disapproval that stopped her short. ...a manifest breach of Britain's regulatory system... The symptoms should become manifest early on.*
◆ **manifestly** ADV *Hopper was manifestly too important to be left off the guest list.*
2 VOorV-REFL If you **manifest** something or if it **manifests** itself, people are made aware of it. *We should manifest our resistance... His inventiveness most often manifested itself as a skill in lying.*

manifestation /ˌmænɪfesˈteɪʃn/ **manifestations**
NC+SUPP A **manifestation** of something is a sign that it is happening or exists; a formal word. *...the first manifestations of the Computer Revolution.*

manifesto /ˌmænɪˈfestəʊ/ **manifestos** or **manifestoes**
NC A **manifesto** is a written statement in which a political party says what its aims and policies are. *...Shirley Williams' election manifesto.*

manifold /ˈmænɪfəʊld/
ADJ Things that are **manifold** are of many different kinds; a literary word. *Her good works were manifold.*

manila /məˈnɪlə/; also spelt **manilla.**
ADJ ATTRIB A **manila** envelope or folder is made from a strong brown paper. *...a stack of manila envelopes.*

Manila /məˈnɪlə/
Manila is the capital of the Philippines and its largest city. It is located on Luzon Island. Population: 1,599,000 (1990).

manioc /ˈmæniɒk/
NU **Manioc** is a tropical plant with thick roots that is grown for food. It is also called 'cassava'. *At present one of the crops the small farmers like to grow is manioc.*

manipulate /məˈnɪpjʊleɪt/ **manipulates, manipulating, manipulated**
1 VO If you **manipulate** people, you cause them to behave in the way that you want them to; used showing disapproval. *Small children sometimes manipulate grown-ups... They were mere puppets manipulated by men in search of other ends.*
◆ **manipulation** /məˌnɪpjʊˈleɪʃn/ NU *...his unscrupulous manipulation of people.*
2 VO If you **manipulate** an event, you control it to produce a particular result; used showing disapproval. *There is a widely held suspicion that he still wields great power and is manipulating events behind the scenes... The government has no plans to manipulate the economy to produce an economic boom for an early election.* ◆ **manipulation** NU *...the careful manipulation of circumstances.*
3 VO If you **manipulate** a piece of equipment, you control it in a skilful way; a formal use. *Lawrence manipulated the knobs on his tape recorder.*
◆ **manipulation, manipulations** NC *I had bent to watch the mechanic's manipulations.*

manipulative /məˈnɪpjʊlətɪv/
ADJ **Manipulative** behaviour is behaviour where one person skilfully causes another to act in exactly the way that he or she wants them to; used showing disapproval. *...the manipulative powers of the ruler... His colleagues find him manipulative, cunning, and extremely short-tempered.*

manipulator /məˈnɪpjʊleɪtə/ **manipulators**
NC A **manipulator** is a person who skilfully controls events, systems, or people. *...the expert financial manipulator... The President has shown once again that he is second to none as a political manipulator.*

mankind /mænˈkaɪnd/
NU You can refer to all human beings as **mankind** when you are considering them as a group. *You have performed a valuable service to mankind. ...the greatest scientific triumph in the history of mankind.*

manly /ˈmænli/
ADJ **Manly** behaviour is typical of a man rather than a woman or boy; used showing approval. *He laughed a deep, manly laugh.*

man-made
ADJ Something that is **man-made** is made by people, rather than formed naturally. *...man-made fibres.*

manned /mænd/
1 ADJ A **manned** vehicle such as a spacecraft has people in it who are operating its controls. *The Americans are now discussing the possibility of a manned flight to Mars... MIR is the world's first permanently manned space station... They released special underwater manned vehicles.*
2 See also **man.**

mannequin /ˈmænɪkɪn/ **mannequins;** an old-fashioned word.
1 NC A **mannequin** is a life-sized model of a person which is used to display clothes, hats, or shoes, especially in shop windows.
2 NC A **mannequin** is also a woman who displays clothes, hats, or shoes by wearing them, especially in fashion shows or in fashion photographs.

manner /ˈmænə/ **manners**
1 N SING+SUPP The **manner** in which you do something is the way that you do it. *They filed the report in a routine manner... Their manner of rearing their young is extremely unusual.*
2 N PL If you have good **manners,** you behave and speak very politely... *His courteous manners made him stand out from other senior officials. She had beautiful manners... His manners were charming.*
● **Manner** is used in these phrases. ● **All manner of**

things means things of many different kinds. *There were four canvas bags filled with all manner of tools.*
● You say in **a manner of speaking** to indicate that what you have just said is not absolutely or literally true, but is true in a general way. *If he hadn't been her boss, in a manner of speaking, she would have reported him to the police.*

mannered /mǽnəd/
ADJ If someone's speech or behaviour is **mannered**, it is very artificial, as if they were trying to impress people; used showing disapproval. *His conversation is a trifle mannered.*

mannerism /mǽnərɪzəm/ **mannerisms**
NC Someone's **mannerisms** are gestures or ways of speaking which are typical of them. *As she grew older, her mannerisms became more pronounced.*

manning /mǽnɪŋ/
NU An argument or discussion about **manning** is an argument or discussion about the number of workers employed in a company or on a particular job. *Seamen there have been on strike in a row over manning and pay... The company says it needs to reduce its manning levels.*

Manning, Patrick /pǽtrɪk mǽnɪŋ/
Patrick Manning became Prime Minister of Trinidad and Tobago in 1991. He became the leader of the People's National Movement (PNM) in 1987. He was Minister of Information, and of Industry and Commerce in 1981, and of Energy from 1981 to 1986. Born: 1946.

mannish /mǽnɪʃ/
ADJ People describe a woman as **mannish** when they think that she looks or behaves more like a man than a woman; used showing disapproval. *Her voice was low and almost mannish. ...her mannish shirt and tie.*

manoeuvre /mənúːvə/ **manoeuvres, manoeuvring, manoeuvred**; spelt **maneuver** in American English.
1 V Oor V If you **manoeuvre** something into or out of an awkward position, you skilfully move it there. *She held the door open while I manoeuvred the suitcases into the back... Hooper started the car and manoeuvred out of the parking space.* ▸ Also NC *Most people seem to manage this manoeuvre without causing havoc.*
2 NC A **manoeuvre** is also something clever which you do in order to change a situation to your advantage. *These results have been achieved by a series of political manoeuvres.*
3 If you have **room for manoeuvre**, you have the opportunity to change your plans if it becomes necessary or desirable. *This gives the Secretary General more room for manoeuvre... The government's popularity has drastically declined since it took office, further reducing its room for manoeuvre.*
4 N PL Military **manoeuvres** are training exercises which involve the movement of soldiers and equipment over a large area. *Every spring up to two hundred thousand American and Korean troops stage air, land, and sea manoeuvres.*

manor /mǽnə/ **manors**
NC A **manor** is a large private house and land in the country, especially a house that was built in the Middle Ages. *The local planning authority is insisting that the manor should only be used either as a country club, hotel or luxury apartments... The helicopter took Mr Mitterrand to Waddesdon Manor in Buckinghamshire this morning.*

manor house, manor houses
NC A **manor house** is the main house that is or was on a medieval manor. *...the eldest son of a wealthy family, brought up in a manor house.*

manorial /mənɔ́ːriəl/
ADJ ATTRIB **Manorial** means relating to a medieval manor or manors. *The manorial system was already well established. ...manorial records.*

manpower /mǽnpaʊə/
NU People refer to workers as **manpower** when considering them as a means of producing goods. *The country is in need of skilled manpower.*

manqué /mɒ́ŋkeɪ/
ADJ after N An actor **manqué**, writer **manqué**, etc is a person who never succeeded in becoming a

professional actor, writer, etc although they tried to become one or, in your opinion, might have become one. *My father was a barber manqué. ...a master printer manqué.*

manse /mǽns/ **manses**
NC A **manse** is the house provided for a minister in certain Christian churches, for example in the Church of Scotland. *The manse he lived in was old and damp.*

manservant /mǽnsɜːvnt/ **menservants**
NC A **manservant** is a man who works as a servant in a private house; an old-fashioned word. *The door was opened by a manservant.*

mansion /mǽnʃn/ **mansions**
NC A **mansion** is an extremely large house. *Their wealth was enormous, and the family mansion housed at least six hundred servants.*

manslaughter /mǽnslɔːtə/
NU **Manslaughter** is the killing of a person by someone who may intend to injure them but does not intend to kill them; a legal term. *He was sentenced to two years for manslaughter... The deer hunter who shot and killed a woman in Maine has been acquitted of manslaughter charges.*

mantelpiece /mǽntlpiːs/ **mantelpieces**; also spelt **mantlepiece**.
NC A **mantelpiece** is a shelf over a fireplace.

mantle /mǽntl/ **mantles**
1 N SING If you take on the **mantle** of something such as a profession or an important job, you take on the responsibilities and duties which must be fulfilled by anyone who has this profession or job; a literary use. *...those who would inherit the mantle of office... He had assumed the mantle of newspaper proprietorship.*
2 N SING+SUPP The Earth's **mantle** is the part of the Earth between the crust and the core; a technical use. *...the inner molten rock of the earth's mantle.*
3 NC A **mantle** is a layer of something covering a surface, for example a layer of snow on the ground; a literary use. *The earth bore a thick green mantle of vegetation.*
4 NC A **mantle** is a piece of clothing without sleeves that people used to wear over their other clothes.

mantlepiece /mǽntlpiːs/. See **mantelpiece**.

man-to-man
ADJ ATTRIB A **man-to-man** conversation or discussion involves two men talking honestly and openly, and treating each other as equals. *I think we need to have a man-to-man discussion about this some time.*

manual /mǽnjuəl/ **manuals**
1 ADJ **Manual** work involves using physical strength rather than mental skills. *Some women are still engaged in heavy manual labour.*
2 ADJ ATTRIB **Manual** also means operated by hand, rather than by electricity or by a motor. *...an old manual typewriter.* ◆ **manually** ADV *Such pumps can be operated manually.*
3 NC A **manual** is a book which tells you how to do something. *The instruction manuals are printed in German.*

manufacture /mǽnjʊfǽktʃə/ **manufactures, manufacturing, manufactured**
1 V O To **manufacture** things means to make them in a factory. *Many companies were manufacturing desk calculators... An investor wants to manufacture a new kind of computer chip.* ◆ **manufactured** ADJ ATTRIB *These also have much higher levels of tar and nicotine than the manufactured cigarettes.* ◆ **manufacturing** NU *New England's economy is largely based on manufacturing, farming and tourism.*
2 NU The **manufacture** of something is the making of it in a factory. *...the manufacture and maintenance of vehicles.*
3 V O If you **manufacture** information, you invent it. *She had manufactured the terrorist story to put everyone off.*

manufactured goods
N PL A country's **manufactured goods** are things such as cars which have been produced in that particular country's factories, especially products that can be sold overseas. *Japan and Germany are the leading exporters of manufactured goods... The demand for US manufactured goods fell sharply last month.*

manufacturer /mænjʊfæktʃərə/ **manufacturers**
NC A **manufacturer** is a business that makes goods in large quantities, or the person who owns it. *...the country's major vehicle manufacturer.*

manure /mənjʊə/
NU **Manure** is animal faeces that is spread on the ground in order to improve the growth of plants. *Farmers will only be allowed to spread manure onto their fields from spring onwards.*

manuscript /mænjʊskrɪpt/ **manuscripts**
1 NC A **manuscript** is the typed or handwritten version of a book before it is printed. *She approached a major publisher with the manuscript of her latest novel.*
2 NC A **manuscript** is also an old document that was written by hand before the printing press was invented. *...a medieval manuscript.*

Manx /mæŋks/
ADJ **Manx** is used to describe people or things that belong to or concern the Isle of Man and the people who live there. *The first Manx President is Sir Charles Kerruish.*

many /meni/ The comparative form is **more** and the superlative form is **most**: see the separate entries for these words.
1 QUANT If there are **many** people or things, there are a lot of them. *Many people have been killed. ...the many brilliant speeches that had been made... Many of the old people were blind.*
2 QUANT You also use **many** in questions or statements about quantity. *How many children has she got?... I used to get a lot of sweets. As many as I liked.*
● **Many** is used these phrases. ● You use **a good many** or **a great many** to refer to a very large number of things or people. *The information has proved useful to a great many people.* ● You use **as many** as before a number when you want to say how surprisingly large it is. *He has written as many as five books in eighteen months.* ● **many happy returns**: see return. ● **in so many words**: see word.

many-sided
ADJ Something that is **many-sided** is composed of many different parts or aspects. *The views which Plato formulates there are many-sided... Rabinsky became fascinated by the many-sided Arab character.*

map /mæp/ **maps, mapping, mapped**
NC A **map** is a drawing of an area as it would appear if you saw it from above. A map shows the main features of an area and sometimes has special information on it. *On the map it is quite a brief strip of road.*
map out PHRASAL VERB If you **map out** a plan or task, you work out how you will do it. *The meeting took place in order to map out a future programme for the negotiations.*

maple /meɪpl/ **maples**
NC A **maple** is a tree. Its leaves have five points and appear as a symbol on the Canadian flag. The wood obtained from this tree, which is used to make furniture and flooring, is also called **maple**. *...the delicate green branches of a maple.*

Maputo /məpuːtəʊ/
Maputo, formerly known as Lourenço Marques, is the capital of Mozambique and its largest city.
Population: 1,007,000 (1987).

mar /mɑː/ **mars, marring, marred**
VO To **mar** something means to spoil it; a formal word. *Graffiti marred the sides of buildings.*

Mar.
Mar. is a written abbreviation for 'March'. *...Tues. 19th Mar. 1991.*

Mara, Ratu Sir Kamisese
/rɑːtu: sə kɑːmɪseɪseɪ mɑːrə/
Ratu Sir Kamisese Mara became Prime Minister of Fiji in 1970. He was elected to the Legislative Council in 1953 and founded the Alliance Party (AP) in 1960. He served as Chief Minister from 1967 to 1970. Born: 1920.

marathon /mærəθən/ **marathons**
1 NC A **marathon** is a race in which people run about 26 miles (about 42 km) along roads. *...the London Marathon.*
2 ADJ ATTRIB A **marathon** task takes a long time to do

and is very tiring. *You need stamina to get through such a marathon production.*

marauder /mərɔːdə/ **marauders**
NC **Marauders** are people or animals who are looking for something to steal or kill; an old-fashioned word. *...ancient fortifications where the inhabitants once stored their grain to protect it from marauders. ...foxes, crows, and other marauders.*

marauding /mərɔːdɪŋ/
ADJ ATTRIB A **marauding** person or animal is looking for something to steal or kill; an old-fashioned word. *The countryside was being ravaged by marauding bands.*

marble /mɑːbl/ **marbles**
1 NU **Marble** is a very hard rock used to make statues, fireplaces, and so on. It often has a pattern made up of irregular lines and patches of colour. *...a monument in black marble.*
2 NU **Marbles** is a children's game played with small glass balls. *...a bunch of kids playing marbles.*
3 NC A **marble** is one of the small balls used by children in the game of marbles.

marbled /mɑːbld/
ADJ Something that is **marbled** has a pattern or colouring like that of marble; a literary word. *The building is an urban jewel, all glass with marbled floors, a monument to success... There was a marbled moon coming up. ...marbled linoleum.*

march /mɑːtʃ/ **marches, marching, marched**
1 NU **March** is the third month of the year in the Western calendar. *He hoped that the elections would take place in March.*
2 V When soldiers **march**, they walk with regular steps, as a group. *They marched through Norway.* ► Also NC *We were woken in the middle of the night for a long march.*
3 V When a large group of people **march**, they walk somewhere together in order to protest about something. *The crowds of demonstrators marched down the main street.* ► Also NC *A million people took part in last year's march.*
4 V A If you **march** somewhere, you walk there quickly, for example because you are angry. *He marched out of the store.*
5 VOA If you **march** someone somewhere, you force them to walk there with you by holding their arm. *He marched me out of the door.*
6 N SING+SUPP The **march** of something is its steady development or progress. *...the march of science.*

marchioness /mɑːʃənes/ **marchionesses**
NC A **marchioness** is the wife or widow of a marquis, or a woman with the same rank as a marquis.

mare /meə/ **mares**
NC A **mare** is an adult female horse. *...a six year-old thoroughbred mare.*

margarine /mɑːdʒəriːn/
NU **Margarine** is a substance similar to butter that is made from vegetable oil and animal fats. *...brown bread and margarine.*

marge /mɑːdʒ/
NU **Marge** is the same as **margarine**; an informal word. *Would you prefer butter or marge on your toast?*

margin /mɑːdʒɪn/ **margins**
1 NC+SUPP If you win a contest by a large or small **margin**, you win it by a large or small amount. *They won by the small margin of five seats... She is currently top of the World Cup standings, leading by a wide margin.*
2 NC+SUPP A **margin** of something is an extra amount which allows you more freedom in doing something. *What is the margin of safety?*
3 NC The **margins** on a page are the blank spaces at each side. *They get a red tick in the margin to show that it's right.*

marginal /mɑːdʒɪnl/
1 ADJ Something that is **marginal** is small and not very important. *The effect will be marginal. ...making marginal adjustments.*
2 ADJ A **marginal** seat or constituency is a political constituency where elections are won by a very small majority. *The recently formed Islamic Party may*

field candidates in marginal constituencies.

marginalize /mɑːdʒɪnəlaɪz/ **marginalizes, marginalizing, marginalized**; also spelt **marginalise.**
VO If someone or something is **marginalized**, they are made to seem unimportant because of other people or events. *We need to ensure that African countries are not marginalized in the future.*

marginally /mɑːdʒɪnəªli/
SUBMOD **Marginally** means to only a small extent. *The prices of new houses are marginally higher than old houses.*

Margrethe II, Queen /mɑːgreɪtə/
Queen **Margrethe II** became the Queen of Denmark in 1972, when she succeeded her father, King Frederik IX. Born: 1940.

Mariana Islands See **Northern Mariana Islands**

Mariehamn /mæriːəhɑːmn/
Mariehamn is the capital and largest town of the Åland Islands. Population: 10,000 (1985).

marigold /mærɪgəʊld/ **marigolds**
NC A **marigold** is a type of yellow or orange flower. *...a cottage garden with roses and marigolds climbing over the doorways.*

marijuana /mærɪwɑːnə/
NU **Marijuana** is an illegal drug which is smoked in cigarettes. *The room reeked of marijuana.*

marina /məriːnə/ **marinas**
NC A **marina** is a small harbour for pleasure boats. *The boat was found to have been moored in a marina all the time.*

marinade /mærɪneɪd/ **marinades, marinading, marinaded**
1 NC A **marinade** is a sauce of oil, vinegar, spices, and so on, which you pour over meat or fish some time before you cook it, in order to add flavour, or to make the meat or fish softer. *Brush the fillets with the marinade.*
2 V-ERG To **marinade** food means the same as to **marinate** it.

marinate /mærɪneɪt/ **marinates, marinating, marinated**
V-ERG If you **marinate** meat or fish or if it **marinates**, you soak it in vinegar, oil, and spices before cooking it, in order to flavour it. *Marinate this meat in wine or vinegar overnight... Ceviche is made of raw fish that is marinated with lemon juice.*

marine /məriːn/ **marines**
1 NC A **marine** is a soldier with the American Marine Corps or the British navy. *No casualties were reported among the marines.*
2 ADJ ATTRIB **Marine** is used to describe things relating to the sea. *...marine life. ...marine biology.*

Marine Corps
N PROP The **Marine Corps** is a particular section of soldiers who are part of the American Navy. *Lieutenant-Colonel Oliver North has announced his retirement from the United States Marine Corps.*

mariner /mærɪnə/ **mariners**
NC A **mariner** is a sailor; an old-fashioned word. *Many shipwrecked mariners died along this coast.*

marionette /mæriənet/ **marionettes**
NC A **marionette** is a puppet which you control by strings or wires.

marital /mærɪtl/
ADJ ATTRIB **Marital** means relating to marriage. *...marital happiness.*

marital status
NU Your **marital status** is whether you are single, married, widowed, or divorced; a formal expression. *The letter states their ages, marital status and the number of children.*

maritime /mærɪtaɪm/
ADJ ATTRIB **Maritime** means relating to the sea and to ships; a formal word. *...the National Maritime Museum.*

marjoram /mɑːdʒərəm/
NU **Marjoram** is a kind of herb.

mark /mɑːk/ **marks, marking, marked**
1 NC A **mark** is a small stain or damaged area on a surface. *There seems to be a dirty mark on it. ...grease marks.*
2 NC A **mark** is also a number or letter which

indicates your score in a test or examination. *You need 120 marks out of 200 to pass... When the final marks were posted for the term, Rudolph had an A in history. ...anxious for good marks.*
3 NC+SUPP When something reaches a particular **mark**, it reaches that stage. *Unemployment is well over the three million mark... Once past the halfway mark he found that he was running more easily.*
4 NC+*of* A **mark** of something is a sign or typical feature of it. *I took this smile as a mark of recognition... The scene bore all the marks of a country wedding.*
5 NC A **mark** is also a written or printed symbol, for example a short line or a letter of the alphabet. *The page was covered with dozens of little marks... McNicoll made a few marks with his pen.*
6 V-ERG If a substance **marks** a surface, or if a surface **marks**, the substance damages it or leaves a stain. *Vinegar, lemon juice, egg and salt can mark cutlery... This type of cloth marks very easily.*
7 VO When a teacher **marks** a student's work, he or she decides how good it is and writes comments or a score on it. *They spend their evenings marking exercise books.*
8 VO If you **mark** something, you put a written symbol or words on it. *...reports marked Top Secret... See that everything is marked with your initials.*
9 VO If something **marks** a place or position, it shows where a particular thing is or was. *The area of burned clay marks the position of several Roman furnaces.*
10 VO If an event **marks** a particular change or anniversary, it takes place at the time of that change or anniversary and draws attention to it. *The film marks a turning point in Allen's career... The concert is to mark the 75th Anniversary year of the composer's death.*
11 VO+*as* Something that **marks** you as a particular type of person indicates that you are that type of person. *These signs marked him as a bachelor eager to wed.*
12 VO If a particular quality **marks** a person's life or career, that person shows that quality during their life or career. *The missionary element has marked his glittering career... His cricket has always been marked by courage and determination.*
13 See also **marked, marking.**
● **Mark** is used these phrases. ● If you are **slow off the mark**, you respond to a situation slowly. If you are **quick off the mark**, you respond to a situation quickly. *Neighbours were always quick off the mark to ask him round when his wife was away.* ● If you **make** or **leave** your **mark** on something, you have an important influence on it. *He intended to make his mark on the international stage.* ● If something is **wide of the mark**, it is a long way from being correct. *His assessment of the situation might be rather wide of the mark.* ● If you **are marking time**, you are doing something boring or unimportant while you wait for something else to happen. *I've been marking time reading books.*

mark off PHRASAL VERB If you **mark off** an item on a list, you indicate that it has been dealt with. *Each day was marked off with a neat X.*

mark-down, mark-downs
NC A **mark-down** is a reduction in the price of something. *Departments doing particularly well in the sale were those with big mark-downs on normal prices.*

marked /mɑːkt/
ADJ A **marked** quality or change is very obvious and easily noticed. *He said that the Warsaw Pact now has a marked superiority in conventional forces... This is seen as a marked change of policy... It's been dry and bright, in marked contrast to the recent heavy rain.*
◆ **markedly** /mɑːkɪdli/ SUBMOD or ADV *Business in Nigeria is markedly different from that in Europe... Soviet relations with Egypt and Jordan improved markedly.*

marker /mɑːkə/ **markers**
1 NC A **marker** is an object used to show the position of something. *The post served as a boundary marker.*

2 If a person or an organization **puts down a marker**, they do something that acts as a clear sign of what they want to happen or what they intend to do. *Mrs Thatcher put down her own marker on what the next election manifesto should say on child benefit.*

market /mɑːkɪt/ **markets, marketing, marketed**
1 NC A **market** is a place, usually in the open air, where people sell various goods such as household items, food, animals, and so on. *These women sell fish in the markets. ...a crowded market. ...a market stall.*
2 NC The **market** for a product is the number of people who want to buy it, or the area in the world where it is sold. *...the declining commercial vehicle market... The factories produce plastics for the Soviet market.*
3 N SING The **market** is also used to refer to the amount of a product sold in a particular country over a particular period of time. *The company supplies only about fifteen per cent of the market... He warned that British Coal would have to be a reliable supplier if it was to retain its share of the market.*
4 N SING The stock **market** is sometimes referred to as the **market**. *A recent trend has seen the market drop to its lowest level since February 1987.*
5 N+N **Market** is used to describe an economic situation in which the price of something is decided by how much there is of it, and how many people want to buy it. *The republics would be able to develop trading links based on market forces. ...a socialist government which has become dedicated to market policies... He said that the country must embrace market principles.*
6 N SING The **market** for jobs is the number of people looking for work, and the number of jobs available. *They fear that they will be discriminated against in the job market... The government believes these measures aren't enough to encourage people back into the labour market.*
7 VO To **market** a product means to organize its sale, for example, by deciding on its price, the shops and areas it should be supplied to, and how it should be advertised. *The felt-tip pen was first marketed by a Japanese firm.*
8 See also **marketing, black market**.
● **Market** is used in these phrases. ● If something is **on the market**, it is available for people to buy. *It's one of the slowest cars on the market... It's been on the market for three years.* ● If something is **on the open market**, is it freely available for people to buy. *Most of the items are not available on the open market, and can only be purchased with ration cards.*
● If a person or an organization is **in the market** for something, they are interested in buying it. *Indonesia may be in the market for a cheaper fighter-aircraft... The Libyans are also thought to be in the market for Brazilian missiles of various types.*

marketable /mɑːkɪtəbl/
ADJ If a product is **marketable**, it can be sold, because people want to buy it. *It was their only marketable commodity.*

market economy, market economies
NC In a **market economy** the price of a particular type of thing is decided by how much of it there is and how many people want to buy it. *...the transition to democracy and market economies.* ● See also **free market**.

market garden, market gardens
NC A **market garden** is a small farm where vegetables and fruit are grown for sale. *They bought land, created market gardens, and sold the produce to Durban.*

market gardener, market gardeners
NC A **market gardener** is a person who works on a market garden.

market gardening
NU **Market gardening** is the business of growing vegetables and fruit for sale. *...the prospect of plentiful water for market gardening and grain growing all year round.*

marketing /mɑːkɪtɪŋ/
1 NU **Marketing** is the organization of the sale of a product, for example, deciding on its price, the shops and areas it should be supplied to, and how it should

be advertised. *Gulfstream is totally responsible for the marketing of the aeroplane worldwide... John Abbot is Sales and Marketing Director for General Logistics.*
2 NU **Marketing** is also the same as **shopping**; used in American English. *He and his wife will drive one mile or so once a week to do the marketing.*

market place, market places
1 N SING You can refer to the **market place** when talking about the buying and selling of products. *Its products must compete in the international market place.*
2 NC A **market place** is a small area in a town where a market is held and goods are sold there. *Beggars crowded in every market place.*

market research
NU **Market research** is research into what people want, need, and buy. *According to market research, more than half the population were regular readers of books in 1987.*

marking /mɑːkɪŋ/ **markings**
1 NC **Markings** are shapes, patterns, or designs on the surface of something. *Look at the markings on the petals.*
2 NU When a teacher does some **marking**, he or she reads a student's work and writes comments or a score on it. *There is just no way to keep up with all the marking.*

marksman /mɑːksmən/ **marksmen** /mɑːksmən/
NC A **marksman** is a person who can shoot very accurately. *A police marksman was ordered to open fire.*

marksmanship /mɑːksmənʃɪp/
NU **Marksmanship** is the ability to shoot accurately. *It was an impressive display of marksmanship.*

mark-up, mark-ups
NC A **mark-up** is an increase in the price of something, for example the difference between its cost and the price that you sell it for. *The cost is increased by the sales mark-up... The speculation of the last few days has led to a mark-up of prices by commerce and industry.*

marmalade /mɑːməleɪd/
N MASS **Marmalade** is a food like jam made from citrus fruits such as oranges or lemons. *...stalls selling home-made marmalade, jams and cakes.*

marmoset /mɑːməzet/ **marmosets**
NC A **marmoset** is a very small South American monkey which has claws on its fingers and toes.

maroon /məruːn/
ADJ Something that is **maroon** in colour is a dark reddish-purple. *...a maroon jacket.*

marooned /məruːnd/
ADJ If you are **marooned** in a place, you cannot leave it. *...a story about a group of young boys marooned on a desert island.*

marquee /mɑːkiː/ **marquees**
1 NC A **marquee** is a large tent which is used at an outdoor event. *The show is held in the world's largest marquee.*
2 NC In American English, a **marquee** is also a cover over the entrance of a building, for example, a hotel or a theatre. *...the magnificent marquees of Broadway.*

marquis /mɑːkwɪs/ **marquises**; also spelt **marquess**.
NC A **marquis** is a male member of the nobility who has the rank between duke and earl. *...the Marquis of Stafford.*

marriage /mærɪdʒ/ **marriages**
1 NCorNU A **marriage** is the relationship between a husband and wife, or the state of being married. *It has been a happy marriage. ...in their early years of marriage.*
2 NCorNU A **marriage** is also the act of marrying someone. *Victoria's marriage to her cousin was not welcomed by her family... On marriage, she moves to her husband's family home.*

marriage of convenience, marriages of convenience
1 NC If one person marries another only in order to have the right to live in the other person's country, you can refer to this as a **marriage of convenience**.

...the rule preventing people entering Britain for marriages of convenience.
2 NC When two organizations or political parties which usually oppose each other join together in order to achieve an advantage, such as a parliamentary majority, you can also refer to this as a **marriage of convenience**. *He described the opposition alliance as a marriage of convenience.*

married /mærid/
1 ADJ If you are **married**, you have a husband or wife. *She's married to an Englishman.*
2 If you **get married**, you marry someone. *A person can get married at the age of 16.*
3 ADJ ATTRIB **Married** also means involving or relating to marriage. *...twenty years of happy married life.*

marrow /mærəʊ/ **marrows**
1 NU **Marrow** or **bone marrow** is the substance in the centre of human and animal bones. *Red blood cells are made in the marrow of big bones in the body... He recovered completely when he was given a bone marrow transplant.*
2 NCorNU A **marrow** is a long, thick, green vegetable with white flesh.
3 If you feel an emotion such as shock or a sensation such as cold **to the marrow**, you feel intensely affected by it. *Some films chill you to the marrow of your bones.*

marrow bone, marrow bones
NCorNU A **marrow bone** is a bone that contains a lot of marrow and that is used in cooking.

marry /mæri/ **marries, marrying, married**
1 V-RECIP When a man and a woman **marry**, they become each other's husband and wife during a special ceremony. *They are in love with each other and wish to marry... I want to marry you.*
2 VO When a member of the clergy or a registrar **marries** two people, he or she is in charge of their marriage ceremony. *The story is told by Friar Lawrence, who married the tragic couple.*

marsh /mɑːʃ/ **marshes**
NCorNU A **marsh** is a very wet, muddy area of land. *I went off into the marsh. ...a dense plantation bounded by marsh.*

marshal /mɑːʃl/ **marshals, marshalling, marshalled;**
spelt **marshaling, marshaled** in American English.
1 VO If you **marshal** things or people, you gather them together and organize them. *He hesitated, marshalling his thoughts... Shipping was being marshalled into convoys.*
2 NC A **marshal** is an official who helps to organize a public event. *If you undergo difficulties, please contact the nearest marshal.*
3 NC In the United States, a **marshal** is the chief officer of a police or fire-fighting force. *Anyway, the fire marshal would never have permitted it.*
4 NC In the United States, a **marshal** is also a federal officer who has been appointed to carry out court orders. *US marshal Tony Bennett is overseeing security for the trial.*
5 See also **field marshal**.

Marshall Islands /mɑːʃl aɪləndz/
The **Republic of the Marshall Islands** is a self-governing state in free association with the United States in the Pacific. The islands include Bikini and Eniwetak, former US nuclear test sites. Germany took control of the islands from Spain in the late 19th century. Japan controlled them from the First World War until 1944, when US forces took possession. In 1986 a Compact of Free Association between the Marshall Islands and the United States came into effect. Tourism is an important industry. ◆ **Marshallese** /mɑːʃəliːz/ N, ADJ
■ *religion:* Christianity (mainly Roman Catholic)
■ *language:* English, Marshallese (official) ■ *currency:* US dollar ■ *capital:* Majuro Atoll ■ *population:* 43,000 (1988) ■ *size:* 180 square kilometres.

marshmallow /mɑːʃmæləʊ/ **marshmallows**
1 NU **Marshmallow** is a soft, spongy, sweet food.
2 NC **Marshmallows** are sweets made from marshmallow. *After grabbing a snack of marshmallows and Easter eggs, Charlie joins the family at the table.*

marshy /mɑːʃi/
ADJ **Marshy** land is covered in marshes. *...a stretch of marshy coastline.*

marsupial /mɑːsuːpiəl/ **marsupials**
NC A **marsupial** is an animal such as a kangaroo or an opossum. Female marsupials carry their babies in a pouch at the front of their body until the babies are fully mature and can live by themselves. *The opossum became the first marsupial to be known in Europe.*

martial /mɑːʃl/
ADJ ATTRIB **Martial** describes things that relate to soldiers or war; a formal word. *...the martial tradition of the fiercely independent tribes... The paper was banned under the martial regime of General Erchad.* ● See also **court-martial**.

martial arts
N PL The **martial arts** are the techniques of self-defence that come from the Far East, for example karate and judo. *...a master of the martial arts.*

martial law
NU **Martial law** is control of an area that is established and maintained by soldiers instead of civilians. *He was interned for a year after martial law was imposed... A revolt broke out following the violent suppression of demonstrations under martial law.*

Martian /mɑːʃn/ **Martians**
1 NC A **Martian** is an imaginary creature from the planet Mars. *'The War Of The Worlds' describes a Martian invasion of the United States.*
2 ADJ Something that is **Martian** exists on or relates to the planet Mars. *We know little of the chemistry of Martian rock.*

martinet /mɑːtɪnet/ **martinets**
NC A **martinet** is a person who believes in strict discipline and expects all their orders to be obeyed; a formal word. *Denis was quite a martinet.*

Martinique /mɑːtɪniːk/
Martinique is a territory of France in the Caribbean. The French began to colonize it in 1635. Bananas, rum, and sugar are produced. Tourism is an important industry. ◆ **Martiniquais** /mɑːtɪniːkeɪ/ N, ADJ
■ *religion:* Christianity (mainly Roman Catholic)
■ *language:* French (official), Creole ■ *currency:* French franc ■ *capital:* Fort-de-France ■ *population:* 360,000 (1990) ■ *size:* 1,100 square kilometres.

martyr /mɑːtə/ **martyrs, martyred**
1 NC A **martyr** is someone who is killed because of their religious or political beliefs. *St Sebastian was a Christian martyr... He described Abu Jihad as a martyr who died while carrying out his duty.*
2 V-PASS If someone is **martyred**, they are killed because of their religious or political beliefs. *This is where St Peter was supposed to have been martyred... He described the soldier as having been martyred.*
3 See also **martyred**.

martyrdom /mɑːtədəm/
NU **Martyrdom** is the murder or enforced suffering of someone because of their religious or political beliefs. *...the martyrdom of St Thomas... The hijackers said they would continue their mission until victory or martyrdom.*

martyred /mɑːtəd/
ADJ ATTRIB A **martyred** expression or way of speaking is one that shows that you have suffered a lot, especially when you are exaggerating the suffering in order to get sympathy or praise from someone. *Mr Rogers wore a martyred expression. ...a brave, martyred sigh.*

marvel /mɑːvl/ **marvels, marvelling, marvelled;**
spelt **marveling, marveled** in American English.
1 V A, V-REPORT, V, or V-QUOTE If you **marvel** at something, it fills you with surprise or admiration. *Early travellers marvelled at the riches of Mali... We marvelled that so much could happen in such a short time... They were mostly sightseers who came to marvel but had little interest in the mysteries of Egypt... 'My God,' Foster marvelled, 'I've never seen so much money.'*
2 NC A **marvel** is something that makes you feel great surprise or admiration. *Paestum is one of the marvels*

of Greek architecture... It's a marvel that I'm still alive.

marvellous /mɑːvləs/; spelt **marvelous** in American English.
ADJ If you say that people or things are **marvellous**, you mean that they are wonderful or excellent. *What a marvellous idea!* ◆ **marvellously** SUBMOD *Her plots were marvellously ingenious.*

Marxism /mɑːksɪzəm/
NU **Marxism** is a political philosophy based on the writings of Karl Marx which stresses the importance of the struggle between different social classes. *Today Marxism is no longer fashionable.*

Marxist /mɑːksɪst/ **Marxists**
1 ADJ Something that is **Marxist** is based on or relates to Marxism. *The Emperor was overthrown and replaced with a Marxist government.*
2 NC A **Marxist** is a person who believes in the philosophy of Marxism. *The Marxists were forced to revise their plans.*

marzipan /mɑːzɪpæn/
NU **Marzipan** is a paste made of almonds, sugar, and egg. It is sometimes put on top of cakes, or used to make small sweets. *...a confection of marzipan and barley sugar spun into tear drops.*

masc.
Masc. is a written abbreviation for 'masculine'.

mascara /mæskɑːrə/
NU **Mascara** is a substance used to colour eyelashes. *She suffered an eye infection from the type of mascara and eye makeup she'd used.*

mascot /mæskət, mæskɒt/ **mascots**
NC A **mascot** is an animal or toy which is thought to bring good luck. *Emblems of the giant panda, the mascot of the Games, can be seen on posters all over Beijing... The company uses a rhino as its mascot.*

masculine /mæskjʊlɪn/
ADJ **Masculine** characteristics or things relate to or are typical of men, rather than women. *I think it must have something to do with masculine pride.*

masculinity /mæskjʊlɪnəti/
NU **Masculinity** is the fact of being a man or having qualities considered typical of a man. *His masculinity was now in question.*

Maseru /məseɑːruː/
Maseru is the capital of Lesotho and its largest city. Population: 109,000 (1986).

mash /mæʃ/ **mashes, mashing, mashed**
VO If you **mash** vegetables, you crush them after cooking them. *Mash the lentils well.* ◆ **mashed** ADJ *...mashed potatoes.*

Masire, Dr Quett /kwɛt məzɪəri/
Dr Quett Masire became President of Botswana in 1980. He is a member of the Botswana Democratic Party (BDP). He became a member of the Legislative (now National) Assembly in 1965. He served as Deputy Prime Minister from 1965 to 1966, and was Vice President and Minister of Finance from 1966 to 1980. Born: 1925.

mask /mɑːsk/ **masks, masking, masked**
1 NC A **mask** is something which you wear over your face for protection or as a disguise. *...a surgical mask... The thieves were wearing masks.*
2 VO If you **mask** something, you hide it. *Her eyes were masked by huge, round sunglasses... They couldn't mask their disappointment.*

masked /mɑːskt/
ADJ Someone who is **masked** is wearing a mask. *Three armed and masked men suddenly burst in.*

masked ball, masked balls
NC A **masked ball** is a dance at which all the guests wear masks. They were especially popular in the 17th and 18th century. *The Mardi Gras is a lively season of masked balls and parties.*

masking tape
NU **Masking tape** is plastic or paper tape which is sticky on one side and is used, for example, when you are painting something and want to protect a part of the surface from getting paint on it.

masochism /mæsəkɪzəm/
NU **Masochism** involves getting pleasure from your own suffering. *...masochism in the classical sense of*

sexual excitement in situations of deprivation.

masochist /mæsəkɪst/ **masochists**
NC A **masochist** is someone who gets pleasure from their own suffering. *Unless you are a complete masochist, you are unlikely to derive much pleasure from the show.*

masochistic /mæsəkɪstɪk/
ADJ If a person behaves in a **masochistic** way, they suffer pain of some kind on purpose in order to get pleasure from their own suffering. *There are some actors with strong masochistic streaks who wish to hear only criticisms.*

mason /meɪsn/ **masons**
1 NC A **mason** is a person who makes things out of stone. *A skilled mason can build a tank like this very quickly.*
2 NC A **Mason** is the same as a **Freemason**. *Members of the Masons take an oath of loyalty to each other... He said he was not a Mason.*

masonic /məsɒnɪk/
ADJ ATTRIB **Masonic** is used to describe things relating to the beliefs, traditions, or organization of Freemasons. *...a masonic lodge. ...a masonic dinner.*

masonry /meɪsənri/
NU **Masonry** is the bricks or pieces of stone which form part of a wall or building. *Large chunks of masonry were beginning to fall.*

masquerade /mæskəreɪd, mɑːskəreɪd/ **masquerades, masquerading, masqueraded**
VA If you **masquerade** as something, you pretend to be that thing. *He might try to masquerade as a policeman... He might be masquerading under an assumed name.*

mass /mæs/ **masses, massing, massed**
1 QUANT A **mass** of things is a large amount of them. *Bruce stuffed a mass of papers into his briefcase.*
2 QUANT **Masses** of something means a large amount of it; an informal use. *They've got simply masses of money.*
3 NC A **mass** of a particular substance is a large amount of it. *...a mass of warm air laden with water vapour.*
4 ADJ ATTRIB You use **mass** to describe something which involves a very large number of people. *...the power of mass communication. ...mass unemployment.*
5 N PL You can use the **masses** to refer to the ordinary people in society as a group. *We want to produce opera for the masses.*
6 V When people or things **mass**, they gather together into a large crowd or group. *The students massed in Paris.*
7 NUorNC The **mass** of an object is its weight or the amount of physical matter that it has; a technical use in physics. *The velocity depends on the mass of the object... The atoms were sorted according to their masses.*
8 NUorNC In the Roman Catholic church, **Mass** is the ceremony in which bread and wine is consecrated and eaten by people in the congregation in remembrance of Christ's death and resurrection. *Fewer than ten percent of the people go to mass... The Bishop's letter is to be read at masses across the country.*
9 See also **massed, land mass.**

massacre /mæsəkə/ **massacres, massacring, massacred**
NCorNU A **massacre** is the killing of many people in a violent and cruel way. *...the massacre of twelve thousand soldiers... Enmity between them runs very deep, resulting often in bloodshed and massacre.*
▶ Also VO *The police had massacred crowds of people.*

massage /mæsɑːʒ/ **massages, massaging, massaged**
VO If you **massage** someone, you rub their body to make them relax or to stop their muscles from hurting. *Could you massage the back of my neck?*
▶ Also NUorNC *We can relax our muscles by massage... Let me give you a massage.*

masse /mæs/. See **en masse.**

massed /mæst/
ADJ ATTRIB You can describe people as **massed** when they have been brought together in large numbers for a particular purpose. *...the massed groups of rival*

supporters. ...massed artillery.

masseur /mæsɜː/ **masseurs**
NC A **masseur** is a person whose job is to give people massages.

masseuse /mæsɜːz/ **masseuses**
NC A **masseuse** is a woman whose job is to give people massages.

massif /mæsiːf, mæsiːf/ **massifs**
NC A **massif** is a group of mountains that form part of a mountain range. *...the Beni Bousera massif in northern Morocco. ...the mountains of the Massif Central and the province of Auvergne.*

massive /mæsɪv/
ADJ Something that is **massive** is extremely large in size, quantity, or extent. *He opened the massive oak front doors. ...a massive increase in oil prices.*
◆ **massively** ADV *We invested massively in West German machinery.*

mass media
N COLL The **mass media** are television, radio, and newspapers. *The mass media now play an increasing role in shaping our opinions.*

mass noun, mass nouns
NC In grammar, a **mass noun** is a noun which usually has no plural, but which can have a plural when it refers to quantities or types of something. For example, you can either say that someone ordered two cups of coffee, or that they ordered two coffees.

mass-produce, mass-produces, mass-producing, mass-produced
VO When people **mass-produce** something, they make it in large quantities by repeating the same process many times. *...a vaccine which can be mass-produced cheaply.* ◆ **mass-produced** ADJ *...cheap mass-produced exports.*

mass-production
NU **Mass-production** is the production of something in large quantities. *Soon the car will go into mass-production.*

mast /mɑːst/ **masts**
1 NC The **masts** of a boat are the tall upright poles that support its sails. *The boat we're standing on right now has a mast of around 11 meters.*
2 NC A radio or television **mast** is a very tall pole that is used as an aerial to transmit sound or television pictures. *The telecommunications center was destroyed, though its mast was intact.*

mastectomy /mæstektəmi/ **mastectomies**
NC A **mastectomy** is a surgical operation to remove a woman's breast. *Instead of a mastectomy the surgeon may opt for a lumpectomy if the tumour is smaller.*

master /mɑːstə/ **masters, mastering, mastered**
1 NC A servant's **master** is the man he works for; an old-fashioned use. *Sometimes there was no dispute between a master and his slave.*
2 NC A **master** is also a male teacher. *...the science master.* ● See also **headmaster**.
3 NU+SUPP If you are **master** of a situation, you have control over it. *This was before man was total master of his environment.*
4 ADJ ATTRIB You use **master** to describe someone who is extremely skilled in a particular job or activity. *...master bakers.*
5 VO If you **master** something, you manage to learn it or cope with it. *Slowly, one begins to master the complex skills involved. ...once we have mastered the basic problems.*

master bedroom, master bedrooms
NC The **master bedroom** in a large house is the largest bedroom.

masterful /mɑːstəfl/
ADJ Someone who is **masterful** behaves in a way which shows that they can control people or situations. *His voice had become more masterful.*

master key, master keys
NC A **master key** is a key that can be used to open any of a particular set of locks, each of which is normally opened by its own individual key.

masterly /mɑːstəli/
ADJ A **masterly** action is very skilful. *It was a masterly performance.*

mastermind /mɑːstəmaɪnd/ **masterminds, masterminding, masterminded**
1 VO If you **mastermind** a complicated activity, you plan it in detail and make sure that it happens successfully. *A young accountant masterminded the take-over of the company.*
2 NC+SUPP The **mastermind** of a complicated activity is the person who is responsible for planning and organizing it. *The mastermind of the expedition was a Frenchman... He was a financial mastermind.*

Master of Arts, Masters of Arts
NC A **Master of Arts** is a person with a higher degree in an arts or social science subject.

master of ceremonies, masters of ceremonies
1 NC The **master of ceremonies** is the person who announces the events or names of speakers at very formal occasions such as a banquet.
2 NC A **master of ceremonies** is also the person who introduces the singers, comedians, and actors who appear in a variety show.

Master of Science, Masters of Science
NC A **Master of Science** is a person with a higher degree in a science subject.

masterpiece /mɑːstəpiːs/ **masterpieces**
NC A **masterpiece** is an extremely good painting, novel, film, or other work of art. *It is one of the great masterpieces of European art.*

master plan, master plans
NC A **master plan** is a clever plan that is intended to help someone succeed in a very difficult or very important task. *...a master plan for the development of Thailand's north eastern region.*

master's
N SING If someone has a **master's** or a **master's** degree, they have a degree such as an MA or an MSc. *In the fall he'll begin work on his master's in physics. ...an architect with a master's degree from MIT.*

masterstroke /mɑːstəstrəʊk/ **masterstrokes**
NC A **masterstroke** is something you do which is unexpected but very clever and which helps you to achieve something. *Phoning your mother was a masterstroke.*

master switch, master switches
NC A **master switch** is a switch that can be used to turn on or turn off all the lights, machines, and so on of a particular set at the same time. *The lights in the corridor and cells were turned off by a master switch.*

mastery /mɑːstəri/
1 NU+SUPP **Mastery** of a skill or art is excellence in it. *...his mastery of the language.*
2 NU **Mastery** is also complete power or control over something. *His sons were struggling to obtain mastery of the country.*

masthead /mɑːsthed/ **mastheads**
1 NC A ship's **masthead** is the highest part of its mast. *A green flag flew from the masthead.*
2 NC A newspaper's **masthead** is its name as it appears in big letters at the top of the front page. *On the market came a paper that puts on its masthead that it wants reform, and to tell the truth as it sees it.*

masticate /mæstɪkeɪt/ **masticates, masticating, masticated**
V or VO If you **masticate**, you chew; a formal word. *Rhoda went on masticating her toast.*

mastiff /mæstɪf/ **mastiffs**
NC A **mastiff** is a large, powerful, short-haired dog. *...ferocious-looking dogs like the Neopolitan Mastiff.*

masturbate /mæstəbeɪt/ **masturbates, masturbating, masturbated**
V If someone **masturbates**, they stroke or rub their own genitals in order to get sexual pleasure. *He was trying to hide the fact that he had masturbated and felt guilty about it.* ◆ **masturbation** /mæstəbeɪʃn/ NU *Tell the child that there is nothing sinful about masturbation.*

mat /mæt/ **mats**
1 NC A **mat** is a small piece of cloth, card, or plastic which you put on a table to protect it. *She set his food on the mat before him. ...beer mats.*
2 NC A **mat** is also a small piece of carpet or other thick material that you put on the floor. *...a 'welcome' mat.*

3 See also **matt**.

matador /mætədɔː/ **matadors**
NC A **matador** is a person in a bullfight whose job is to
kill the bull. *...a matador engaging the bull with his
red cape.*

Mata-Utu /mætəuːtuː/
Mata-Utu is the capital and principal settlement of the
Wallis and Futuna Islands. Population: 800 (1983).

match /mætʃ/ **matches, matching, matched**
1 NC A **match** is an organized game of football,
cricket, chess, or other sport. *...a football match. ...a
one-day cricket match.*
2 NC A **match** is also a small wooden stick with a
substance on one end that produces a flame when you
pull or push it along the side of a matchbox. *..a large
box of matches.*
3 V-RECIP If one thing **matches** another, the two things
are similar. *The captain's feelings clearly matched
my own... The windmill blades will be adjustable to
match wind speeds.* ◆ **matching** ADJ ATTRIB *...a blue
jacket with matching shirt.*
4 V-RECIP If you **match** one thing with another, you
decide that one is suitable for the other, or that there
is a connection between them. *The lampshades
matched the curtains... All you have to do is correctly
match the famous personalities with the towns they
come from.*
5 VO To **match** something means to be equal to it in
speed, size, or quality. *They are trying to upgrade
their cars to match the foreign competition... She
walked at a pace that Morris's short legs could hardly
match.*
6 If something **is no match for** another thing, it is
inferior to it. *A machine gun is no match for a tank.*
match up PHRASAL VERB If you **match** one thing **up**
with another, you decide that the two things are
suitable for each other, or are connected in some
way. *Can you match the tops up with the bottoms?*

matchbox /mætʃbɒks/ **matchboxes**
NC A **matchbox** is a small box that matches are sold
in.

matched /mætʃt/
1 ADJ If two people are well **matched**, they are suited
to one another and are likely to have a successful
relationship. *I thought we were perfectly matched.*
2 ADJ If two people or groups are evenly **matched**,
they have the same strength or ability. *Government
and rebel soldiers are evenly matched.*

matchless /mætʃləs/
ADJ You use **matchless** to describe something that is
so good that you think nothing else could be as good; a
formal word. *...men and women of matchless honesty.*

matchmaker /mætʃmeɪkə/ **matchmakers**
NC A **matchmaker** is someone who tries to encourage
other people they know to form relationships or to get
married. *She is the village gossip and matchmaker.*

matchmaking /mætʃmeɪkɪŋ/
NU **Matchmaking** is the activity of encouraging people
you know to form relationships or get married. *He
loved matchmaking.*

match point, match points
NCorNU A **match point** is a situation in a game of
tennis when the player who is in the lead can win the
match if they win the next point. *Connors has two
match points... At match point, she served a double
fault.*

matchstick /mætʃstɪk/ **matchsticks**
NC A **matchstick** is the stick of wood from a match.
*He was removing the ashes from the bowl of his pipe
with a matchstick.*

matchwood /mætʃwʊd/
NU **Matchwood** is used in expressions like 'reduced to
matchwood' or 'smashed to matchwood' when you
want to say that something wooden has been
completely destroyed and is in a lot of little bits. *The
table had been smashed to matchwood.*

mate /meɪt/ **mates, mating, mated**
1 NC Your **mates** are your friends; an informal use.
*He supposed his old mate Kowalski would be with
them.*
2 NC An animal's **mate** is its sexual partner. *The
females are about half the size of their mates.*

3 NC You can also refer to your wife or husband as
your **mate**; used in American English. *She admitted
that most people who attend the fair are looking for a
mate.*
4 V-RECIP When a male animal and a female animal
mate, their sex organs come together so that
fertilization can take place. *Male wild cats sometimes
mate with domestic females... The queen bee is likely
to mate with two or three drones.* ◆ **mating**
ADJ ATTRIB *...the mating season.*
5 N SING The **mate** or **first mate** on a ship is the officer
who is next in importance to the captain. *The
spokesman said that the first mate had recently been
dismissed.*
6 See also **running mate**.

material /mətɪəriəl/ **materials**
1 NCorNU A **material** is a solid substance. *...synthetic
substitutes for natural materials. ...decaying material.*
2 N MASS **Material** is cloth. *The sleeping bags are
made of acrylic material. ...delicate materials, like
silk.*
3 N PL **Materials** are the equipment or things that you
need for a particular activity. *They are providing
building materials such as cement, steel, and glass...
They also discovered guns and other bomb making
materials.*
4 NU Ideas or information that are used as a basis for
a book, play, or film can be referred to as **material**.
*She hoped to find material for some articles... They
researched a lot of background material.*
5 ADJ ATTRIB **Material** things are related to possessions
or money, rather than to more abstract things. *...the
material comforts of life.* ◆ **materially** ADV *Children
can gain materially and psychologically when both
parents work.*

materialise /mətɪəriəlaɪz/. See **materialize**.

materialism /mətɪəriəlɪzəm/
NU **Materialism** is the attitude of people who think
that money and possessions are the most important
things in life. *They were determined to renounce the
materialism of the society they had been brought up
in.*

materialist /mətɪəriəlɪst/ **materialists**
NC A **materialist** is a person who thinks that money
and possessions are the most important things in life.
He was an atheist and a materialist.

materialistic /mətɪəriəlɪstɪk/
ADJ A **materialistic** person or society believes that
money and possessions are the most important things
in life. *This society has made people greedy and
materialistic.*

materialize /mətɪəriəlaɪz/ **materializes,
materializing, materialized**; also spelt **materialise**.
V If a possible event **materializes**, it actually happens.
Fortunately, the attack did not materialize.

maternal /mətɜːnl/
ADJ **Maternal** is used to describe things relating to a
mother. *...the powerful maternal bonds that tie a
mother to her newborn child.*

maternity /mətɜːnəti/
N+N **Maternity** is used to describe things relating to
pregnancy and birth. *She took her cousin to the
maternity hospital... All women will be given a
minimum of 14 weeks paid maternity leave.*

matey /meɪti/
ADJ Someone who is being **matey** is being very
friendly, as if they were your close friend; an informal
word.

math /mæθ/
NU **Math** is the same as **mathematics**; used in
American English. *According to a new government
study, the average public school student cannot
perform simple math.*

mathematical /mæθəmætɪkl/
ADJ ATTRIB **Mathematical** means relating to numbers
and calculations. *Galileo's mathematical calculations
proved that the earth really did move round the sun.'
◆ **mathematically** ADV *...a mathematically provable
law.*

mathematician /mæθəˈmətɪʃn/ **mathematicians**
NC A **mathematician** studies problems involving
numbers and calculations. *...the British scientist and*

mathematician, Sir Isaac Newton.

mathematics /mæθəˈmætɪks/
NU **Mathematics** is a subject which involves the study of numbers, quantities, or shapes. *...a campaign to generate interest in mathematics among primary school pupils.*

maths /mæθs/
NU **Maths** is the same as **mathematics**. *...a first class honours degree in maths. ...the teaching of maths.*

matinee /ˈmætɪneɪ/ **matinees**; also spelt **matinée**.
NC A **matinee** is an afternoon performance of a play or showing of a film. *The play can be seen in repertory, matinee and evening, every Saturday.*

matins /ˈmætɪnz/; also spelt **mattins**.
NU **Matins** is a Christian religious service which is held in the morning. *I'll see you after Sunday matins.*

matriarch /ˈmeɪtriɑːk/ **matriarchs**
1 NC A **matriarch** is a woman who rules in a society in which power passes from mother to daughter.
2 NC A **Matriarch** is an old and powerful female member of a family, for example, a grandmother. *She is the matriarch of one of the most important families in Nicaragua.*

matriarchal /ˌmeɪtriˈɑːkl/
1 ADJ A **matriarchal** society or system is one in which the ruler is female and the power is passed from mother to daughter. *There are traces of the old matriarchal society still present in their culture.*
2 ADJ A **matriarchal** system of inheritance is one in which family property is traditionally inherited from women and not from men.

matriarchy /ˈmeɪtriɑːki/ **matriarchies**
1 NUorNC **Matriarchy** is a system of government in which the ruler is female and the power is passed from mother to daughter.
2 NUorNC **Matriarchy** is a system of inheritance in which family property is traditionally inherited from women and not from men.

matrices /ˈmeɪtrɪsiːz/
Matrices is the plural of **matrix**.

matriculate /məˈtrɪkjʊleɪt/ **matriculates, matriculating, matriculated**
V If you **matriculate**, you register as a student at a university, having got the right qualifications; a formal word. *There are far more black South Africans that matriculated on leaving school this year than there were white.* ◆ **matriculation** /məˌtrɪkjʊˈleɪʃn/ NU *Work for a degree counts only from the date of matriculation.*

matrimonial /ˌmætrɪˈməʊniəl/
ADJ ATTRIB **Matrimonial** means concerning marriage or married people; a formal word. *...matrimonial difficulties.*

matrimony /ˈmætrɪməni/
NU **Matrimony** is the state of being married; a formal word. *So far he has managed to resist the joys of matrimony.*

matrix /ˈmeɪtrɪks/ **matrixes or matrices**
1 NC+SUPP A **matrix** is the environment in which something such as a society develops and grows; a formal use. *Attitudes are formed in a matrix of psychological and social complications.*
2 NC In mathematics, a **matrix** is a rectangular arrangement of numbers, symbols, or letters, written in rows and columns and use in solving certain problems.

matron /ˈmeɪtrən/ **matrons**
1 NC In a hospital, the **matron** is a senior nurse. *Tell matron to take him off the danger list.*
2 NC At a boarding school, the **matron** is a woman who looks after the health of the children. *Jessie Crawford became barrack matron, looking after the girls who were billeted in Dunedan.*

matronly /ˈmeɪtrənli/
ADJ A woman who is **matronly** is middle-aged and slightly overweight. *Mrs Frieda was solid and matronly.*

matt /mæt/; also spelt **mat**.
ADJ A **matt** surface is dull rather than shiny. *...matt black.*

matted /ˈmætɪd/
ADJ Something that is **matted** is twisted together

untidily. *Their hair was matted.*

matter /ˈmætə/ **matters, mattering, mattered**
1 NC+SUPP A **matter** is a situation which you have to deal with. *It was a purely personal matter... She's very honest in money matters... This is a matter for the police.*
2 NPL You use **matters** to refer to the situation that you are talking about. *The absence of electricity made matters worse.*
3 NU You can also use **matter** to refer in a general way to all substances or any particular substance; a formal use. *An atom is the smallest indivisible particle of matter... The termites feed on vegetable matter.*
4 NU+SUPP You can refer to books and magazines as reading **matter**; a formal use. *The glossy monthly magazine 'Marxism Today' is fashionable reading matter in intellectual circles.*
5 V If something **matters**, it is important and is something that you care about or that worries you. *My family were all that mattered to me.*
6 V If something does not **matter**, it is not important because it does not have an effect on the situation. *It does not matter which method you choose.*
● **Matter** is used these phrases. ● You say '**What's the matter?**' or '**Is anything the matter?**' when you think that someone has a problem and you want to know what it is. *What's the matter, Cynthia? You sound odd... What's the matter with your hand?* ● You use **no matter** in expressions such as 'no matter how' and 'no matter what' to indicate that something is true or happens in all circumstances. *I told him to report to me after the job was completed, no matter how late it was... They smiled continuously, no matter what was said.* ● If you do something as a **matter of** principle or policy, you do it for that reason. *Merchant banks recruit women as a matter of policy.* ● You use **matter** in expressions such as 'a matter of days' when you are drawing attention to how short a period of time is. *Within a matter of weeks she was crossing the Atlantic.* ● If you say that something is just a **matter of time**, you mean that it is certain to happen at some time in the future. *It appeared to be only a matter of time before they were caught.* ● If you say that something is just a **matter of** doing something, you mean it is easy and can be achieved just by doing that thing. *Skating's just a matter of practice.* ● You say **for that matter** to emphasize that a statement you have made about one thing is also true about another. *He's shaking with the cold. So am I, for that matter.* ● as a **matter of course**: see **course**. ● as a **matter of fact**: see **fact**.

matter-of-fact
ADJ Someone who is being **matter-of-fact** is not showing any emotion such as anger or surprise, especially in a situation where they would be expected to do so. *'I see,' she said, trying to seem matter-of-fact.*

matting /ˈmætɪŋ/
NU **Matting** is a thick material woven from rope or straw, which is used as a floor covering. *...coconut matting.*

mattins /ˈmætɪnz/. See **matins**.

mattress /ˈmætrəs/ **mattresses**
NC A **mattress** is a large, flat layer of padding which is put on a bed to make it comfortable to sleep on. *The room was small and contained just a mattress, table, and chair.*

mature /məˈtʃʊə/ **matures, maturing, matured**
1 V If someone **matures**, their personality and their emotional behaviour become more fully developed and controlled. *He had matured and quietened down considerably.*
2 ADJ **Mature** people behave in a sensible, well-balanced way. *She's in some ways mature and in some ways rather a child.* ◆ **maturity** /məˈtʃʊərəti/ NU *I have long felt that you lacked maturity.*
3 V To **mature** means to develop or to reach a state of complete development. *...the great casks where the wine matured.*
4 ADJ **Mature** means fully developed. *...mature plants.* ◆ **maturity** NU *Only half of the young birds*

may live to reach maturity.

mature student, mature students
NC In a British college or university, a **mature student** is someone who starts doing their first degree when they are over 21 years old.

maudlin /ˈmɔːdlɪn/
ADJ If you become **maudlin**, you become sad and sentimental about your life; often used of people who have been drinking alcohol. *Don't get so maudlin... She continued in the same rather maudlin tone.*

maul /mɔːl/ **mauls, mauling, mauled**
VO If an animal **mauls** someone, it attacks and injures them. *A hyena mauled four people in a Kenyan village.*

Maundy Thursday /ˈmɔːndi ˈθɜːzdeɪ/
NU **Maundy Thursday** is the Thursday before Easter Sunday.

Mauritania /ˌmɒrɪˈteɪnɪə/
The **Islamic Republic of Mauritania** is a country in north-west Africa. It was part of French West Africa from the 19th century until independence in 1960. It became a one-party state in 1964 and all political activity was banned in 1978. Spain ceded the Spanish Sahara (now called Western Sahara) to Morocco and Mauritania in 1975. Mauritania fought the Polisario Front, who wanted to establish an independent Western Sahara, until 1979, when Mauritania renounced all claims to the Western Sahara. Colonel Maawiya Ould Sid'Ahmed Taya became President in 1984. In 1990 he announced reforms leading to multi-party elections. Ethnic conflict between the Arab-speaking majority and the French-speaking black minority has been a source of civil disorder. Mauritania is a member of the Arab League and the Organization of African Unity. It exports fish and iron ore. ◆ **Mauritanian** /ˌmɒrɪˈteɪnɪən/ N, ADJ
▪ *per capita GNP:* US$480 ▪ *religion:* Islam (mainly Malekite) ▪ *language:* French and Arabic (official) ▪ *currency:* ouguiya ▪ *capital:* Nouakchott ▪ *population:* 2 million (1989) ▪ *size:* 1,030,700 square kilometres.

Mauritius /məˈrɪʃəs/
Mauritius is a country in the Indian Ocean, east of Madagascar. It was a French possession until 1810, and then a British colony until independence in 1968. Aneerood Jugnauth, of the Socialist Movement of Mauritius (PSM), became Prime Minister in 1982. Mauritius is a member of the Commonwealth and the Organization of African Unity. It exports textiles and sugar. Tourism is an important industry. Mauritius claims the islands of Diego Garcia and Tromelin. ◆ **Mauritian** /məˈrɪʃən/ N, ADJ
▪ *per capita GNP:* US$1,810 ▪ *religion:* Hinduism, Christianity, Islam ▪ *language:* English (official), Creole, Hindi, Bhojpuri ▪ *currency:* rupee ▪ *capital:* Port Louis ▪ *population:* 1 million (1989) ▪ *size:* 2,040 square kilometres.

mausoleum /ˌmɔːsəˈliːəm/ **mausoleums**
NC A **mausoleum** is a building containing the grave of someone famous or rich. *...the embalmed body of Lenin, lying in the Mausoleum in Red Square.*

mauve /məʊv/
ADJ Something that is **mauve** in colour is pale purple. *...servants carrying massive mauve parasols.*

maverick /ˈmævərɪk/ **mavericks**
NC A **maverick** is someone who thinks and acts in a very independent way. *He is something of a maverick in foreign policy matters.* ▶ Also ADJ ATTRIB *He is a self-confessed maverick Marxist.*

mawkish /ˈmɔːkɪʃ/
ADJ Something that is **mawkish** shows too much affection, admiration, or some other emotion and seems rather awkward or silly. *...mawkish verses... Claud's flat bovine face glimmered with a mawkish pride.*

max.
max. is a written abbreviation for 'maximum'. *...max. 17°C... The cost will be £90 max.*

maxim /ˈmæksɪm/ **maxims**
NC A **maxim** is a short saying recommending a particular form of behaviour. *Instant action: that's my maxim.*

maximize /ˈmæksɪmaɪz/ **maximizes, maximizing, maximized**; also spelt **maximise**.
VO To **maximize** something means to make it as great in amount or importance as you can. *The company's main objective is to maximize profits.*

maximum /ˈmæksɪməm/
1 ADJ ATTRIB The **maximum** amount of something is the largest amount possible. *They held the prisoner under maximum security conditions... Never exceed the maximum daily dosage of 150 mg.*
2 N SING The **maximum** is the largest amount possible. *Conscription should be limited to a maximum of six months' service.*

may; pronounced /meɪ/ or /meɪ/ when it is a modal and /meɪ/ when it is a noun.
1 MODAL If you say that something **may** happen or be true, you mean that it is possible. *We may be here a long time... You may be right... A gigantic meteorite may have wiped out the dinosaurs 65 million years ago... They struggle to cure diseases so that people may live longer.*
2 MODAL If someone **may** do something, they are allowed to do it. *If the verdict is unacceptable, the defendant may appeal... May I have a word with you, please?*
3 MODAL You can use **may** when saying that, although one thing is true, another contrasting thing is also true. *They may be seven thousand miles away but they know what's going on over here... Ingenious though these techniques may be, they can hardly be regarded as practical.*
4 MODAL You can also use **may** to express a wish that something will happen; a formal use. *Long may it continue.*
5 NU **May** is the fifth month of the year in the Western calendar. *He has held office since May 1979.*

maybe /ˈmeɪbiː/
1 ADV SEN You use **maybe** to indicate that something is possible, but you are not certain about it. *Maybe he'll be prime minister one day... Well, maybe you're right.*
2 ADV SEN You also use **maybe** to show that a number is approximate. *There were maybe half a dozen men there... He's in his fifties, I'd say. Fifty-five, maybe.*

May Day
N PROP **May Day** is the first day of May, which is celebrated as a festival in several countries, especially as a workers' day in Socialist countries. *The strikers believe that the authorities would feel bound to find a compromise before May Day... Today is May Day, observed around the world as a workers' holiday.*

mayday /ˈmeɪdeɪ/ **maydays**
NC A **mayday** or a **mayday signal** is a radio signal which someone in a plane or ship sends out as a call for help when the plane or ship is in serious difficulty. *The crew would have noticed a fall in cabin air pressure and sent a mayday signal for help.*

mayfly /ˈmeɪflaɪ/ **mayflies**
NC A **mayfly** is an insect which lives near water and only lives for a very short time as an adult.

mayhem /ˈmeɪhem/
NU **Mayhem** is an uncontrolled and confused situation. *The kids began to create mayhem in the washrooms.*

mayn't /ˈmeɪənt/
Mayn't is a spoken form of 'may not'.

mayonnaise /ˌmeɪəˈneɪz/
NU **Mayonnaise** is a pale, thick, uncooked sauce made from egg yolks and oil. *...large jars of cheap mayonnaise.*

mayor /meə/ **mayors**
NC The **mayor** of a town is the person who has been elected to lead and to represent it for a year. *The Mayor officially welcomed the royal couple... Five candidates are running for the office of mayor.*

mayoress /ˈmeərɛs/ **mayoresses**
1 NC A woman who holds the office of mayor is sometimes referred to as a **mayoress**. *...a former mayoress of Bilbao.*
2 NC You can also refer to the wife of a mayor as a **mayoress**.

Mayotte /maːˈjɒt/
Mayotte, one of the Comoro Islands, is a territory of

France in the Indian Ocean between Madagascar and the east coast of Africa. It became a French colony in 1841. The Comoros became independent in 1975, but Mayotte chose to retain its links with France. Mayotte is claimed by the Comoros. It exports oil of ylang-ylang and vanilla. Fishing is an important industry.
◆ **Mahorian** /məhɔ:riən/ N, ADJ
▪ *religion:* Islam ▪ *language:* French (official), Mahorian ▪ *currency:* French franc ▪ *capital:* Dzaoudzi (largest town Mamoudzou) ▪ *population:* 73,000 (1988) ▪ *size:* 374 square kilometres.

may've /meɪəv/
May've is a spoken form of 'may have', especially when 'have' is an auxiliary verb.

maze /meɪz/ **mazes**
1 NC A **maze** is a system of complicated passages which it is difficult to find your way through. *Mice were trained to find their way through a maze.*
2 NC+SUPP You can refer to a large number of ideas or subjects which are all connected to each other in a complicated way as a particular kind of **maze.** *Companies are looking for extra guidance to steer them through the financial maze. ...the impenetrable maze of Chinese politics.*

Mbabane /mbəbɑ:ni/
Mbabane is the capital of Swaziland and its largest city. Population: 40,000 (1986).

Mbasogo, Teodoro Obiang Nguema
/teɪədɔ:rəʊ əʊbjæn ŋgwɛɪmə mbæsəʊgəʊ/
Brigadier-General Teodoro Obiang Nguema Mbasogo became President of Equatorial Guinea in a coup in 1979. He is a member of the Democratic Party of Equatorial Guinea (PDGE), which was the only legal party until 1991 when opposition parties were legalized.

MBE /ɛmbi:i:/ **MBEs**
An **MBE** is a British honour granted to a person by the King or Queen for a particular achievement. **MBE** is an abbreviation for 'Member of the Order of the British Empire'. The letters are used after the name of the person who has been awarded the honour. *He was awarded an MBE in the New Year's Honours list. ...Miss May Walley MBE.*

MC /ɛmsi:/ **MCs**
NC **MC** is an abbreviation for 'master of ceremonies'. *'Welcome back', says the MC after the first act.*

McCoy /məkɔɪ/
If you describe someone or something as **the real McCoy**, you mean that they are the genuine person or thing and not an imitation or fake; an informal expression.

MCP /ɛmsi:pi:/ **MCPs**
NC **MCP** is an abbreviation for 'male chauvinist pig'. An **MCP** is a man who behaves as though he thinks men are superior to women and far more important than them; an informal expression, used showing disapproval. *He's a real MCP!*

MD /ɛmdi:/ **MDs**
1 **MD** is an abbreviation for 'Doctor of Medicine'. The letters are usually used after a person's name. *...Richard Selzer, MD.*
2 NC **MD** is also an abbreviation for 'managing director'. *The MD wants to see you.*

me /mi, mi:/
PRON Me is used as the object of a verb or preposition. A speaker or writer uses me to refer to himself or herself. *He told me about it... He looked at me reproachfully.*

mead /mi:d/
NU **Mead** is an alcoholic drink made of honey, spices, and water.

meadow /mɛdəʊ/ **meadows**
NC A **meadow** is a field with grass and flowers growing in it. *...cows grazing on lush green meadows.*

meagre /mi:gə/; spelt **meager** in American English.
ADJ Something that is **meagre** is very small in quantity or quality, and is only just enough. *...a meagre crop of potatoes. ...his meagre wages.*

meal /mi:l/ **meals**
1 NC A **meal** is an occasion when people eat. It is also the food that they eat on that occasion. *...the evening meal. ...a simple meal of bread and cheese.*
2 NU **Meal** is the edible part of part of any grain or

bean pulse that has been ground to a powder. *...soybean meal.*

mealie meal /mi:li mi:l/
NU **Mealie meal** is cereal made of maize that has been ground to a fine powder for use as a food product. *With the end of the general subsidy, the price of mealie meal on the open market has more than doubled.*

meals-on-wheels
N PL **Meals-on-wheels** is a service provided by a local authority by which hot meals are taken to the homes of very old or sick people. *Mother is getting meals-on-wheels.*

meal ticket, meal tickets
1 NC A **meal ticket** is a luncheon voucher; used in American English.
2 N SING A **meal ticket** is also somebody or something that gives you an income or enables you to earn one; an informal use. *I can't leave Bob. He's my meal ticket.*

mealtime /mi:ltaɪm/ **mealtimes**
NC A **mealtime** is an occasion when you eat a meal. *I had a glass of juice three times a day at mealtimes.*

mealy /mi:li/ **mealier, mealiest**
ADJ Vegetables or fruit that are **mealy** are unpleasant to eat because they are dry and powdery. *We ate flavourless mealy bananas.*

mealy-mouthed /mi:limaʊðd/
ADJ Someone who is **mealy-mouthed** is unwilling to speak in a simple or open way because they want to avoid talking directly about something unpleasant; used showing disapproval. *...mealy-mouthed politicians. ...mealy-mouthed excuses.*

mean /mi:n/ **means, meaning, meant; meaner, meanest**
1 VO You ask what a word, expression, or gesture **means** when you want it to be explained to you. *What does 'imperialism' mean?... What is meant by the term 'mental activity'?*
2 V, VO, or V-REPORT What someone **means** is what they are referring to or intending to say. *But what do we mean by 'education'?... I know the guy you mean... I thought you meant you wanted to take your own car.*
3 VO+to If something **means** a lot to you, it is important to you. *These were the friends who had meant most to her since childhood.*
4 V OR V-REPORT If one thing **means** another, it shows that the second thing is true or makes it certain to happen. *A cut in taxes will mean a cut in government spending... Water running down the outside of a wall may mean that the gutters are blocked.*
5 VO If you **mean** something, you are serious about it and not joking, exaggerating, or just being polite. *I'm going. I mean it... Anyone can program a computer. And I do mean anyone.*
6 V+to-INF If you **mean** to do something, you intend to do it. *I meant to ring you but I'm afraid I forgot... I'm sorry, I didn't mean to be rude.*
7 V O+to-INF or V O+for If something is **meant** to be a particular thing or is **meant** for a particular purpose, that is what you intended or planned. *Sorry, I'm not very good at drawing, but that's meant to be a cube... 'That hurts!'—'It's meant to!'... His smile was meant for me.*
8 V-PASS+to-INF If something is **meant** to happen or exist, it is strongly expected to happen or exist. *I found a road that wasn't meant to be there.*
9 V-PASS+to-INF You also use **meant** when you are talking about the reputation that something has. *They're meant to be excellent cars.*
10 NC+SUPP A **means** of doing something is a method or thing which makes it possible. 'Means' is both the singular and plural. *Scientists are working to devise a means of storing this type of power... We have the means to kill people on a massive scale.*
11 N PL You can refer to the money that someone has as their **means**; a formal use. *Sutcliffe has a house in Mayfair so he obviously has means.*
12 ADJ Someone who is **mean** is unwilling to spend much money or to use very much of a particular thing. *I used to be very mean about hot water.*
◆ **meanness** NU *These employers were famous for their meanness.*

13 ADJ If you are **mean** to someone, you are unkind to them. *She had apologized for being so mean to Rudolph.* ◆ **meanness** NU *...his meanness to his sisters.*
14 NC In mathematics, the **mean** is the average of a set of numbers. *What you do first is to calculate the mean.*
● **Mean** is used in these phrases. ● You say '**I mean**' when you are explaining something more clearly or justifying what you have said, or when you are correcting yourself. *If you haven't any climbing boots, you can borrow them. I mean dozens of people have got boots... This is Herbert, I mean Humbert.* ● If something is **a means to an end**, you do it only because it will help you to achieve what you want. *Talks would only be a means to an end, namely peace.* ● If you do something **by means of** a particular method or object, you do it using that method or object. *The rig is anchored in place by means of steel cables.* ● You say '**by all means**' as a way of giving someone permission; a formal expression. *By all means take a day's holiday.* ● **By no means** is used to emphasize that something is not true. *It is by no means certain that this is what he did.* ● You use **no mean** to emphasize that someone or something is especially good or remarkable; a formal expression. *Sir George Gilbert Scott, himself no mean architect, approved the plans... Persuading John to come was no mean feat.*
meander /miˈændə/ **meanders, meandering, meandered**
1 V If a river or road **meanders**, it has a lot of bends in it. *A stream meandered towards the sea.*
2 VA To **meander** also means to move slowly and indirectly. *We meandered along eating nuts and blackberries.*
meanie /ˈmiːni/ **meanies**
NC A **meanie** is a person who is unkind to someone, for example by hurting their feelings or by not allowing them to do something; an informal word.
meaning /ˈmiːnɪŋ/ **meanings**
1 NCorNU The **meaning** of something is what it refers to or the idea that it expresses. *The word 'guide' is used with various meanings... The meaning of the remark was clear.*
2 NU If something has **meaning** for you, it seems to be worthwhile and to have a real purpose. *We yearn for beauty, truth, and meaning in our lives.*
meaningful /ˈmiːnɪŋfl/
1 ADJ A **meaningful** sentence or event has a meaning that you can understand. *Nobody has ever explained electricity to me in a meaningful way.*
2 ADJ A **meaningful** look, expression, or remark is intended to express an attitude or opinion. *They exchanged meaningful glances.* ◆ **meaningfully** ADV *'Goodnight, and call again. Anytime,' Boon added meaningfully.*
3 ADJ Something that is **meaningful** is serious and important. *He felt the need to establish a more meaningful relationship with people. ...meaningful discussions.* ◆ **meaningfully** ADV *At least you'd be filling your time meaningfully.*
meaningless /ˈmiːnɪŋləs/
1 ADJ If something, such as a text, is **meaningless**, it has no meaning that you can understand. *These songs are largely meaningless. ...one thousand giga electron volts, which may be a meaningless number to your person in the street.*
2 ADJ You can also use **meaningless** to say that something, such as a declaration, a gesture, or someone's life, has no purpose and is not worthwhile. *Other leaders called the agreement meaningless... Egypt has little time for such gestures which it dismisses as politically meaningless.*
means test, means tests
NC A **means test** is a test in which your income is assessed in order to see if you are eligible for certain state grants or benefits. If your income is above a certain amount, you are not eligible. *The economic programme was to include the introduction of a means test (to see if recipients are really poor enough to need it).*

means-tested
ADJ A grant or benefit that is **means-tested** varies in amount depending on a means test. *...means-tested benefits.*
meant /ment/
Meant is the past tense and past participle of **mean**.
meantime /ˈmiːntaɪm/
In the **meantime** means in the period of time between two events. *I will call Doctor Ford. In the meantime you must sleep.*
meanwhile /ˈmiːnwaɪl/
1 ADV SEN **Meanwhile** means while something else is happening. *She ate an olive. Nick, meanwhile, was talking about Rose.*
2 ADV SEN **Meanwhile** also means in the period of time between two events. *But meanwhile a number of steps will have to be taken... In the meanwhile, I enjoy the game we're all playing.*
measles /ˈmiːzlz/
NU **Measles** is an infectious illness that gives you red spots on your skin. *...children vaccinated against measles. ...an unconventional strain of measles virus.* ● See also **German measles**.
measly /ˈmiːzəli/
ADJ A **measly** amount of something is very small or inadequate; an informal word. *One measly tomato, that's all we've had from this plant!*
measurable /ˈmeʒərəbl/
ADJ If something is **measurable**, it is large enough to be noticed or to be significant; a formal word. *Some measurable progress had been made.*
measure /ˈmeʒə/ **measures, measuring, measured**
1 VO When you **measure** something, you find out how big or great it is, for example by using an instrument such as a ruler, thermometer, or set of scales. *He measured the diameter... The explosive force is measured in tons.*
2 VC If something **measures** a particular distance, its length, width, or depth is that distance. *...slivers of glass measuring a few millimetres across. ...a square area measuring 900 metres.*
3 NC **Measures** are actions that are carried out by people in authority in order to achieve a particular result; a formal use. *Measures had been taken to limit the economic decline... The federal authorities have put strict security measures in place to protect against any violence... She said police were on the scene as a precautionary measure.*
4 N SING+of You can use **measure** to refer to an amount or degree of something abstract; a formal use. *Everyone is entitled to some measure of protection. ...a large measure of public support.*
5 N SING+of If something is a **measure** of a particular thing, it shows how great or remarkable it is; a formal use. *It is a measure of their achievement that the system has lasted so long.*
6 NC A **measure** of an alcoholic drink such as brandy or whisky is an amount of it in a glass. *...a generous measure of cognac.*
7 If something is done **for good measure**, it is done in addition to a number of other actions. *The waiter had taken away the plates, and, for good measure, had removed his glass.*
8 See also **tape measure**.
measure up PHRASAL VERB If someone or something **measures up** to a standard or to someone's expectations, they are good enough to achieve the standard or fulfil the person's expectations. *He wants to believe that his kids have measured up to his high expectations... The repair failed to measure up to their standards.*
measured /ˈmeʒəd/
ADJ **Measured** behaviour is careful and deliberate; a literary word. *...walking at the same measured pace. ...his cool, measured speech.*
measurement /ˈmeʒəmənt/ **measurements**
1 NC A **measurement** is a result that you obtain by measuring something. *Check the measurements first. ...the exact measurements of the office.*
2 NU **Measurement** is the activity of measuring something. *...the first actual measurement of the speed of sound.*

3 N PL Your **measurements** are the size of your chest, waist, hips, and other parts of your body.

measuring /mɛʒərɪŋ/
ADJ ATTRIB A **measuring** jug or spoon is one that is specially designed for measuring quantities, especially in cooking. *You can use any measuring jug marked in ounces.*

meat /miːt/ **meats**
N MASS **Meat** is the flesh of a dead animal that people cook and eat. *The government imposed rationing of essential foodstuffs such as meat, flour and oil. ...the Community's ban on imports of some American meat products.*

meaty /miːti/ **meatier, meatiest**
1 ADJ **Meaty** is used to describe someone's body or a part of their body when it is fat and heavy. *Along came the porters, immensely meaty, in bloodstained blue or white... He extended his meaty, jeweled hands.*
2 ADJ A meal that is **meaty** contains a lot of meat. *They liked an occasional meaty supplement to their diet.*
3 ADJ ATTRIB A **meaty** thing has a lot of substance, and is interesting or important. *It's a very meaty role for an actress who has specialized in playing tough women... The newspaper suggests that here is a meaty issue waiting to be tackled.*

mecca /mɛkə/ **meccas**
1 N PROP **Mecca** is a city in Saudi Arabia, which is the holiest city in Islam because the Prophet Mohammed was born there. *He is a devout Muslim who regularly makes the pilgrimage to Mecca. ...the sacred shrines at Mecca.*
2 NC+SUPP If you say that a place is a **mecca** for people of a particular kind, you mean that many of them go there because there is something there that interests or attracts them. *The United States is still a mecca for film-makers.*

mechanic /məkænɪk/ **mechanics**
1 NC A **mechanic** is someone who mends and maintains machines and engines as a job. *The car had been left for a mechanic to collect and carry out some repairs... He is training to be a motor mechanic.*
2 N PL+of You can refer to the way in which something works or is done as the **mechanics** of it. *...the mechanics of reading... This factor complicates the mechanics of the whole negotiating process.*

mechanical /məkænɪkl/
1 ADJ A **mechanical** device has moving parts and uses power in order to do a particular task. *They were using a mechanical shovel to clear up the streets.*
◆ **mechanically** ADV *The glass doors slid open mechanically as she approached them.*
2 ADJ ATTRIB Someone who has a **mechanical** mind understands how machines work. *...a given level of mechanical ability.*
3 ADJ A **mechanical** action is done automatically, without thinking about it. *...mindless and mechanical repetitions.* ◆ **mechanically** ADV *'How are you?'—'Oh, fine, thanks,' said Philip mechanically.*

mechanise /mɛkənaɪz/. See **mechanize.**

mechanism /mɛkənɪzəm/ **mechanisms**
1 NC A **mechanism** is a part of a machine that does a particular task. *...a locking mechanism. ...steering mechanisms in cars.*
2 NC+SUPP A **mechanism** is also a way of getting something done within a system. *There's no mechanism for changing the decision.*
3 NC+SUPP **Mechanism** is used to refer to a part of your behaviour that is automatic. *...the defence mechanism of disbelief.*

mechanize /mɛkənaɪz/ **mechanizes, mechanizing, mechanized**; also spelt **mechanise.**
VO If a type of work is **mechanized**, it is done by machines. ◆ **mechanized** ADJ *Housework has become highly mechanised.* ◆ **mechanization** /mɛkənaɪzeɪʃn/ NU *...the mechanization of the postal service.*

medal /mɛdl/ **medals**
NC **Medals** are small metal discs that are given as awards for bravery or as prizes in sporting events. *He won six gold medals.*

medallion /mədælɪən/ **medallions**
NC A **medallion** is a round metal disc which is worn as an ornament on a chain round a person's neck. *A company is marketing peace medallions made from the metal of dismantled nuclear missiles.*

medallist /mɛdəlɪst/ **medallists**; spelt **medalist** in American English.
NC A **medallist** is a person who has won a medal in sport. *...the world champion and Olympic gold medallist.*

meddle /mɛdl/ **meddles, meddling, meddled**
V, V+in, or V+with If you **meddle** in something, you try to influence or change it without being asked; used showing disapproval. *Conservative Member of Parliament, Mr Ivan Lawrence, has told Mr Benn to 'stop meddling'... He's never wanted me to meddle in his affairs... I dared not meddle with my wife's plans.*
◆ **meddling** NU *Serbia has opposed any further European intervention as unwanted meddling... This measure was designed to reduce bureaucratic meddling in the economy.*

meddlesome /mɛdlsəm/
ADJ **Meddlesome** describes behaviour in which someone becomes involved in things that do not really concern them and tries to influence what happens; used showing disapproval. *Her detachment was a mask for a meddlesome nature. ...meddlesome parents.*

media /miːdiə/
1 N COLL You can refer to television, radio, and newspapers as the **media**. *These problems have been exaggerated by the media.* ● See also **mass media.**
2 **Media** is a plural of **medium.**

mediaeval /mɛdiiːvl/. See **medieval.**

median /miːdiən/
ADJ ATTRIB The **median** value of a set of values is the middle value when the values are arranged in order; a technical term in mathematics. *2.7 billion people live in countries with a median income below £300 a head... The median age group in unfurnished renting was sixty to sixty-five.*

mediate /miːdieɪt/ **mediates, mediating, mediated**
V If you **mediate** between two groups, you try to settle a dispute between them. *I mediated for him in a quarrel with his brother.*

mediator /miːdieɪtə/ **mediators**
NC A **mediator** is someone who tries to settle a dispute between two groups. *Tom Hagen was busy trying to find a mediator satisfactory to both parties.*

medic /mɛdɪk/ **medics**
NC A **medic** is a doctor or medical student; an informal word. *Navy medics operated on the foot... We had more law students than medics.*

medical /mɛdɪkl/ **medicals**
1 ADJ ATTRIB **Medical** means relating to the treatment of illness and injuries and to the prevention of illness. *She had to undergo medical treatment. ...the medical care of babies.*
2 NC A **medical** is a thorough examination of your body by a doctor. *They were all set to give him a medical.*

medicament /mədɪkəmənt/ **medicaments**
NC A **medicament** is a medicine; a formal word. *Morell gave him more powerful medicaments.*

Medicare /mɛdɪkeə/
N PROP In the United States, **Medicare** is a system of health care that is administered by the government. *...the range of outpatient services covered under Medicare... The administration's budget seeks a new savings by cutting into the Medicare program.*

medication /mɛdɪkeɪʃn/ **medications**
NU or NC **Medication** is medicine that is used to cure an illness. *The doctor can prescribe medication to relieve the symptoms... Don't forget your medication.*

medicinal /mədɪsəⁿnəl/
ADJ **Medicinal** substances are used to treat and cure illness. *...a medicinal herb.*

medicine /mɛdsn, mɛdɪsən/ **medicines**
1 N MASS A **medicine** is a substance that you drink or swallow in order to cure an illness. *...a medicine for his cold. ...cough medicines.*
2 NU **Medicine** is the treatment of illness and injuries by doctors and nurses. *...the professions of medicine and dentistry.*

medieval /mɛdiˈiːvl/; also spelt **mediaeval**.
ADJ Medieval things belong or relate to the period in European history between the end of the Roman Empire in 476 AD and about 1500 AD. ...*a medieval church.* ...*a form of medieval feudalism.*

mediocre /miːdiˈəʊkə/
ADJ Mediocre things are of poor quality. *He spent much of his time reading mediocre paperbacks.*
♦ **mediocrity** /miːdiˈɒkrəti/ NU *He was dismayed by the mediocrity of the people working with him.*

meditate /ˈmɛdɪteɪt/ **meditates, meditating, meditated**
1 V+on To meditate on something means to think about it carefully and deeply for a long time. *He was left alone to meditate on his sins.* ♦ **meditation** /mɛdɪˈteɪʃn/ **meditations** NU or NC ...*the subject of my meditation... I hope we will not disturb your meditations.*
2 V If you meditate, you remain in a calm, silent state for a period of time, often as part of a religious training or practice. ...*meditating in the wilderness for seven days.* ♦ **meditation** NU *He was deeply interested in meditation and yoga.*

meditative /ˈmɛdɪtətɪv/
ADJ A meditative action shows that you are thinking carefully about something. *Daniel took a meditative sip of tea... We were both quiet and meditative.*
♦ **meditatively** ADV *He was leaning meditatively on his elbow.*

medium /ˈmiːdiəm/ **mediums** or **media**. The plural of the noun is either **mediums** or **media** for the meaning in paragraph 3, and **mediums** for the meaning in paragraph 4.
1 ADJ If something is of medium size, it is neither large nor small. ...*a medium screwdriver... He was of medium height.*
2 ADJ If something is of a medium colour, it is neither light nor dark. ...*medium brown.*
3 NC A medium is the means that you use to communicate or express something; a formal use. ...*sending messages through the medium of paper and printed word... He made collages and mixed media sculptural pieces.*
4 NC A medium is also a person who claims to communicate with people who are dead. *The Oscar for best supporting actress went to Whoopi Goldberg for her portrayal of the reluctant medium in the film 'Ghost'... People have been turning to spirit mediums for protection from the violence of the war.*

medium-dry
ADJ Medium-dry wine or sherry is not very sweet.

medium term
N SING The medium term is the period of time which lasts a few months or years beyond the present time, in contrast with the short term or the long term. *We must now look at the medium term and see how costs can be reduced.* ...*medium-term programming.*

medium wave
NU Medium wave is a range of radio waves which are used for broadcasting. *BBC World Service can be heard on 463m or 648kHz medium wave in Northern Europe.*

medley /ˈmɛdli/ **medleys**
1 NC A medley is also a collection of different tunes or songs that are played one after the other as a single piece of music. *And now, with a medley of forties favourites, here's Vera Lynn.* ...*a rendition of Douglas' Latin medley.*
2 NC A medley of different things is a mixture of them, especially one that produces an odd or interesting effect. *The skyline was a medley of great and small domes.*
3 NC A medley is also a swimming race in which the four main swimming strokes must be used one after the other. *Japan won two swimming gold medals in the Men's 400 metre Individual Medley and the men's 4 x 200 metres Freestyle Relay.*

meek /miːk/
ADJ A meek person is quiet or timid and does what other people say. ...*his meek acceptance of insult.*
♦ **meekly** ADV *'I'm sorry dear,' Gretchen said meekly.*

meet /miːt/ **meets, meeting, met**
1 V-RECIP When two people meet for the first time, they happen to be in the same place and are introduced or get to know each other. *I met a Swedish girl on the train... They met each other at a party in London... The band originally met at college in their native Athens... Come and meet Tony and Rick.*
2 V-RECIP When two people arrange to meet, they arrange to arrive separately at the same place and at the same time, in order to do something together. *They met every day... Meet me under the clock.*
3 VO If you meet someone who is travelling or if you meet their train, plane, or bus, you go to the station, airport, or bus stop in order to be there when they arrive. *As Ms Makarova stepped off the plane, she was met by her mother and other relatives.*
4 V When a group of people meet, they gather together for a purpose. *Teachers in Tokyo met to discuss our methods.*
5 VO If something meets a need, requirement, or condition, it is satisfactory or sufficiently large to fulfil it. *His income is inadequate to meet his basic needs.*
6 VO If you meet a problem or challenge, you deal satisfactorily with it. *On the Punjab problem, Mr Venkataraman said the challenge was being met.*
7 VO If you meet the cost of something, you provide the money for it. *The cost of paying for the scheme is being met by Portugal.*
8 VO To meet a situation or attitude means to experience it. *Where had I met this kind of ignorance before?*
9 V-RECIP When one object meets another, it hits or touches it. *The heavy club met his head with a crack... Their fingers met.*
10 V-RECIP If your eyes meet someone else's, you both look at each other at the same time. *Their eyes meet, and they smile... Her eyes rose to meet mine.*
11 V-RECIP The place where two areas or lines meet is the place where they are next to one another or join. ...*where this road meets the one from Lairg... Parallel lines never meet.*
12 to make ends meet: see end. to meet someone halfway: see halfway.

meet up PHRASAL VERB If you arrange to meet up with someone, you arrange to arrive separately at the same place and at the same time, in order to do something together. *We planned to meet up with them in Florence.*

meet with PHRASAL VERB 1 If you meet with someone, you have a meeting with them; used in American English. *We can meet with the professor Monday night.* 2 If something meets with or is met with a particular reaction, people react to it in that way. *All appeals for aid meet with refusal... His approaches had been met with ill-concealed disdain.* 3 You can say that someone meets with success or failure when they are successful or unsuccessful. *Mr Filali told the United Nations General Assembly that the peace proposals should soon meet with success.*

meeting /ˈmiːtɪŋ/ **meetings**
1 NC A meeting is an event in which people discuss things and make decisions. *The committee will consider the proposal at its next meeting... I held a meeting that afternoon.* ...*a meeting of physicists.*
2 N SING You can refer to the people at a meeting as the meeting. *The meeting agreed with him.*
3 NC A meeting is also an occasion when you meet someone. ...*his first meeting with Alice.*

meeting place, meeting places
NC A meeting place is a place where people meet, usually on a regular basis. *Their house became a meeting place for all the radical students.*

megahertz /ˈmɛgəhɜːts/; megahertz is both the singular and the plural form.
NC A megahertz is a unit of frequency, used especially for radio frequencies. One megahertz equals one million cycles per second. ...*a persistent beeping at 20.005 megahertz.*

megalith /ˈmɛgəlɪθ/ **megaliths**
NC A megalith is a very large stone that stands on the ground and that is thought to have been put there by people a long time ago; a technical term. ...*a ring of*

megaliths on some local hill.

megalomania /mɛgəˈləʊmeɪnɪə/
NU **Megalomania** is the belief that you are more powerful and important than you really are. Megalomania is sometimes a mental illness. *Early success may lead to megalomania.*

megalomaniac /mɛgəˈləʊmeɪnɪæk/ **megalomaniacs**
NC A **megalomaniac** is someone who enjoys being powerful, or who believes that they are more powerful or important than they really are. *...the wilder instincts of one of the 20th Century's most dangerous megalomaniacs.*

megaphone /mɛgəfəʊn/ **megaphones**
NC A **megaphone** is a cone-shaped device for making your voice sound louder in the open air. *The speeches had to be delivered through a hand held megaphone.*

megaton /mɛgətʌn/ **megatons**
NC A **megaton** is one million tons. A one megaton nuclear weapon has the same power as one million tons of TNT; a technical term. *...a 15 megaton thermonuclear device.*

megawatt /mɛgəwɒt/ **megawatts**
NC A **megawatt** is one million watts of electrical power. *Most power stations are designed to generate 250 to 400 megawatts.*

melancholy /mɛlənkɒli/; a literary word
1 ADJ If you feel **melancholy**, you feel sad. *They tend to look rather sullen and melancholy.* ► Also NU *...a touch of melancholy in his voice.*
2 ADJ Something that is **melancholy** makes you feel sad. *...melancholy music.*

mélange /meɪlɑːnʒ/; also spelt **melange**.
N SING A **mélange** is a mixture of people or things. *A strange mélange of women emerged from the cells.*

mêlée /mɛleɪ/ **mêlées**; also spelt **melee**.
NC A **mêlée** is a crowd of people rushing about in different directions and doing different things. *I was caught in the mêlée...*

Meles Zenawi /mɛles zenɑːwi/
Meles Zenawi became President of Ethiopia in 1991. In 1989 he became leader of the Tigre People's Liberation Front (TPLF) and he led the coalition Ethiopian People's Revolutionary Democratic Front (EPRDF), which captured Addis Ababa and deposed President Mengistu in 1991.

mellifluous /mɛlɪfluəs/
ADJ A **mellifluous** voice or piece of music is very pleasant to listen to; a formal word. *They all had mellifluous voices... I particularly savoured the mellifluous second movement.*

mellow /mɛləʊ/ **mellows, mellowing, mellowed**
1 ADJ **Mellow** light is soft and golden. *...the mellow sunlight.*
2 ADJ A **mellow** sound is smooth and pleasant to listen to. *...a nice mellow voice. ...mellow ballads.*
3 V-ERG If someone **mellows** or if something **mellows** them, they become more pleasant or relaxed. *He mellowed considerably as he got older... He says that age should have mellowed me.*
4 ADJ ATTRIB **Mellow** stone or brick has a pleasant soft colour because it is old.

melodic /məlɒdɪk/
ADJ **Melodic** means relating to melody; a technical term in music. *Handel's operas contain wonderful melodic inventions... The instruments produce one melodic line.*

melodious /məlɒdɪəs/
ADJ A **melodious** sound is pleasant to listen to; a formal word. *...a low melodious laugh.*

melodrama /mɛlədrɑːmə/ **melodramas**
NCorNU A **melodrama** is a story or play in which there are a lot of exciting or sad events and in which people's emotions are very exaggerated. *These films were send-ups of steamy Hollywood melodramas... Some of the prose overplays itself into melodrama towards the end.*

melodramatic /mɛlədrəmætɪk/
ADJ If you are being **melodramatic**, you treat a situation as much more serious than it really is. *I think we're getting a bit too melodramatic.*

melody /mɛlədi/ **melodies**
NCorNU A **melody** is a tune; a formal word. *He developed a facility for writing melodies in the key of F sharp... His grasp of melody was faultless.*

melon /mɛlən/ **melons**
NCorNU A **melon** is a large juicy fruit with a thick green or yellow skin. *Some of them are picking cantaloupe melons. ...a piece of melon.*

melt /mɛlt/ **melts, melting, melted**
1 V-ERG When a solid substance **melts** or if someone **melts** it, it changes to a liquid because of being heated. *The snow and ice had melted... Melt the margarine in a saucepan.*
2 V If something **melts**, it gradually disappears. *Lynn's inhibitions melted.*

melt away PHRASAL VERB If something **melts away**, it gradually disappears. *Their differences melted away.*

melt down PHRASAL VERB If you **melt down** a metal or glass object, you heat it until it melts. *Railings were melted down for cannon.*

melting pot, melting pots
NC A **melting pot** is a place or situation in which people, cultures, and ideas of different kinds get mixed together. *The city is a melting pot of races.*

member /mɛmbə/ **members**
1 NC+SUPP A **member** of a group is one of the people, animals, or things belonging to the group. *Babies usually have milder colds than older members of the family. ...a member of the opposite sex.*
2 NC A **member** of an organization is a person, group, or country that has joined it in order to take part in its activities. *...members of trade unions. ...prospects for better co-operation amongst OPEC members.*
3 ADJ ATTRIB The states or countries that have joined an international organization are called the **member** states or countries. *All the member countries are under pressure to conform.*
4 NC A **member** is also a Member of Parliament. *...John Parker, the Labour member for Dagenham.*

Member of Parliament, Members of Parliament
NC A **Member of Parliament** is a person who has been elected to represent people in a country's parliament. *Labour Members of Parliament have been fiercely critical of the government's budget.*

membership /mɛmbəʃɪp/ **memberships**
1 NU **Membership** is the fact or state of being a member of an organization. *Deacon was questioned about his membership of the Nationalist Party. ...South Korea's bid for UN membership.*
2 N COLLorNU The **membership** of an organization is the people who belong to it, or the number of people who belong to it. *The membership for Feminists for Life is still quite small. ...practical, organisational problems of coping with ever-increasing membership.*

membrane /mɛmbreɪn/ **membranes**
NC A **membrane** is a thin piece of skin which connects or covers parts of a person's or animal's body; a technical term. *...the delicate membranes of the throat.*

memento /məmɛntəʊ/ **mementos** or **mementoes**
NC A **memento** is an object which you keep to remind you of a person or a special occasion. *...a memento of the singer's farewell concert.*

memo /mɛməʊ/ **memos**
NC A **memo** is an official note from one person to another within the same organization. *He wrote a memo to the War Department asking for more soldiers.*

memoir /mɛmwɑː/ **memoirs**
1 N PL A person's **memoirs** are a book which they write about people who they have known and events that they remember. *He was writing his memoirs of his career abroad. ...Memoirs of a Conservative.*
2 NC A **memoir** is a book or article that you write about someone you have known well.

memorabilia /mɛməˈræbɪlɪə/
N PL **Memorabilia** are things that you collect because they are connected with a person, organization, and so on in which you are interested. *He had a large collection of war memorabilia.*

memorable /mɛməˈrəbl/
ADJ **Memorable** things are likely to be remembered because they are special or unusual. *...a memorable train journey.*

memorandum /mɛmərændəm/ **memoranda** or **memorandums**

1 NC A **memorandum** is a written report that is prepared for a person or a committee in order to provide them with information about a particular matter. *A Government memorandum to Parliament's Foreign Affairs Committee says it was Iraq which invaded Iran in 1980.*
2 NC A **memorandum** is also an informal diplomatic communication between governments which often summarizes a particular point of view. *The two Foreign Ministers signed a memorandum agreeing to a number of measures designed, they said, to build mutual confidence.*
3 NC An office **memorandum** is a note which is sent to other people or departments within a company that contains information relating to work; a formal use.

memorial /məmɔːriəl/ **memorials**

1 NC A **memorial** is a structure built in order to remind people of a famous person or event. *...a memorial to Queen Alexandra. ...a war memorial.*
2 ADJ ATTRIB A **memorial** event or prize is in honour of someone who has died, so that they will be remembered. *...funerals and memorial services.*

Memorial Day

N PROP In the United States, **Memorial Day** is a public holiday at the end of May when people who have been killed in wars are remembered. *He marked the day before Memorial Day with a visit to a local war monument... It's a Bush family tradition to spend the Memorial Day holiday in Maine.*

memorize /mɛməraɪz/ **memorizes, memorizing, memorized**; also spelt **memorise**.

VO If you **memorize** something, you learn it so that you can remember it exactly. *I was able to read a whole page and memorise it in under three minutes.*

memory /mɛməºri/ **memories**

1 NCorNU Your **memory** is your ability to remember things. *A few things stand out in my memory... A man was found wading in a river in northern France apparently suffering from loss of memory.*
2 NC+SUPP A **memory** is something that you remember about the past. *My memories of a London childhood are happy ones.*
3 NC A computer's **memory** is the capacity of the computer to store information. *IBM unveiled a computer memory chip which is three times faster than the current generation.*
● **Memory** is used in these phrases. ● If you **lose** your **memory**, you forget things that you used to know. *He lost his memory for names.* ● If you do something **from memory**, for example recite a poem or play a piece of music, you do it without looking at anything written or printed. *He would sit down at the piano and play from memory anything you had asked for.* ● If you do something **in memory of** someone who has died, you do it in order to remember that person. *They will hold prayers in memory of the dead.* ● If something has happened **in living memory** or **within living memory**, there are people alive who can remember it happening. *In the Australian outback, farmers are facing the worst economic crisis in living memory. ...the most humiliating episode in the nation's political life within living memory.* ● to **commit** something **to memory**: see **commit**.

men /mɛn/

Men is the plural of **man**.

menace /mɛnɪs/ **menaces, menacing, menaced**

1 NC Something or someone that is a **menace** is likely to cause serious harm. *These riots are a menace to democracy... Next we'll have to face the menace of cholera and other epidemics.*
2 NU **Menace** is the quality of being threatening. *There was anger and menace in his eyes.*
3 VO If someone or something **menaces** you, they threaten to harm you or are likely to do so. *We were menaced by drunks. ...the formidable threat that menaces Europe.*

menacing /mɛnɪsɪŋ/

ADJ If someone's behaviour is **menacing**, they seem to be intending to harm you. *He advanced on me in a menacing fashion.* ◆ **menacingly** ADV *Joy scowled at*

him and waved her knife menacingly.

menage /meɪnɑːʒ/ **menages**; also spelt **ménage**.

N SING+SUPP A **menage** is a group of people living together in one house; a formal word. *...a member of the O'Shea menage.*

ménage à trois /meɪnɑːʒ æ trwæ/ **ménages à trois**

NC You refer to three people as a **ménage à trois** when they live together, and one of them is having a sexual relationship with both of the others; a literary expression. *I'm not asking you to come out and join a ménage à trois.*

menagerie /mənædʒºri/ **menageries**

NC A **menagerie** is a collection of wild animals. *Underneath its water-logged timbers swim a menagerie of muskrat, alligators, catfish and trout.*

mend /mɛnd/ **mends, mending, mended**

VO If you **mend** something that is damaged or broken, you repair it, so that it works or can be used again. *I mended some toys for her... He spent the evening mending socks.*
● **Mend** is used in these phrases. ● If you are **on the mend**, you are recovering from an illness or an injury; an informal expression. *He had some colour in his cheeks and was plainly on the mend.* ● If a relationship or a situation is **on the mend**, it is improving after a difficult or unsuccessful period; an informal expression. *East-West relations in general were once again on the mend... Mr Major painted a picture of an economy on the mend.* ● If someone **mends** their **ways**, they begin to behave better than they did before. *Disaffected MPs are once more saying that Mrs Thatcher should mend her ways.*

mendacious /mɛndeɪʃəs/

ADJ A **mendacious** statement or remark is not truthful; a formal word. *At best, such talk is foolish. At worst, it is mendacious and malevolent.*

mending /mɛndɪŋ/

NU **Mending** is clothes that you have collected together to be mended. *...his mother's basket of mending.*

Menem, Dr Carlos Saúl /kɑːləʊs saʊl mɛnɛm/

Dr Carlos Saúl Menem became President of Argentina in 1989. He is a member of the Justicialist Party. He was Governor of La Rioja Province from 1973 to 1989. Born: 1935.

menfolk /mɛnfəʊk/

N PL+POSS When women refer to their **menfolk**, they mean the men in their family or community. *The wives and mothers would do anything to protect their menfolk.*

menial /miːniəl/

ADJ **Menial** work is boring and tiring, and the people who do it have a low status. *The workload has become heavier and more menial. ...menial tasks.*

meningitis /mɛnɪndʒaɪtɪs/

NU **Meningitis** is a serious infectious illness which affects your brain and spinal cord. *...an outbreak of meningitis in the Malvern area.*

menopause /mɛnəpɔːz/

N SINGorNU The **menopause** is the time during which a woman stops menstruating, usually when she is about fifty. *Scientists are developing drugs which could have benefits for sufferers from calcium loss after the menopause... The boy's mother suffered a premature menopause six years ago.*

men's room, men's rooms

NC The **men's room** is a toilet for men in a public building such as a restaurant; used in American English. *She used the men's room because the line for the ladies' room was too long.*

menstrual /mɛnstruəl/

ADJ ATTRIB **Menstrual** means relating to menstruation. *...the menstrual cycle.*

menstruate /mɛnstrueɪt/ **menstruates, menstruating, menstruated**

V When a woman **menstruates**, blood flows from her womb. Women who are fertile menstruate once a month unless they are pregnant; a formal word. *Young women who train hard for athletic events often stop menstruating altogether.* ◆ **menstruation** /mɛnstrueɪʃn/ NU *...the onset of menstruation.*

menswear /mɛnzweə/

NU **Menswear** is clothing for men, used especially to

refer to the shops that sell men's clothes. *...the American menswear chain, Brooks Brothers.*

-ment /-mənt/ **-ments**
SUFFIX **-ment** is used to form nouns that refer to actions or states. When these nouns are formed directly from verbs, they are often not defined but are treated with the related verbs. *...the commencement of the flight. ...disillusionment with politics.*

mental /mentl/
1 ADJ ATTRIB **Mental** means relating to the process of thinking. *...mental effort. ...one's mental ability.*
♦ **mentally** ADV *She looked at the bouquets, mentally pricing the blooms.*
2 ADJ ATTRIB **Mental** also means relating to the health of a person's mind. *...mental illness.* ♦ **mentally** ADV *He was a sick man, mentally and physically.*
3 ADJ ATTRIB A **mental** act is one that involves only thinking and not physical action. *...mental arithmetic.*
♦ **mentally** ADV *They had all mentally worked out where it would appear.*

mental hospital, mental hospitals
NC A **mental hospital** is a hospital for people who are suffering from mental illness. *He has been confined in a mental hospital since October.*

mentality /mentælətɪ/ **mentalities**
NC+SUPP Your **mentality** is your attitudes or ways of thinking. *She says I have a slave mentality.*

menthol /menθɒl/
NU **Menthol** is a substance that smells a bit like peppermint, and that you can use to clear your nose when you have a cold. *They smelled of garlic and menthol eucalyptus.*

mentholated /menθəleɪtɪd/
ADJ Something that is **mentholated** contains menthol. *...mentholated throat lozenges.*

mention /menʃn/ **mentions, mentioning, mentioned**
1 V-REPORT or V O If you **mention** something, you say something about it, usually briefly. *I mentioned to Tom that I was thinking of going back to work... Penny decided not to mention her cold.*
2 NC or NU A **mention** is a reference to something or someone. *Many of them are famous names, yet they get only very brief mentions... Perhaps we'll hear a mention of cutting capital gains tax... My brother used to go purple in the face at the very mention of my name.*
3 You use **not to mention** when adding something to a list in an emphatic way. *He's always travelling to Buenos Aires and Delhi, not to mention London and Paris.*

mentor /mentɔ:/ **mentors**
NC Someone's **mentor** is a person who teaches them and gives them advice; a formal word. *...Harold, my mentor from my student days.*

menu /menju:/ **menus**
NC A **menu** is a list of the food that you can order to eat in a particular restaurant. *He ordered the most expensive items on the menu.*

MEP /emi:pi:/ **MEPs**
NC An **MEP** is a person who has been elected to the European Parliament. **MEP** is an abbreviation for 'Member of the European Parliament'. *MEP Barbara Simmons was speaking in Strasbourg this morning.*

mercantile /mɜ:kəntaɪl/
ADJ ATTRIB **Mercantile** means relating to merchants or trading; a formal word. *...the overseas expansion of European mercantile and industrial civilization.*

mercenary /mɜ:sənəri/ **mercenaries**
1 NC A **mercenary** is someone who is paid to fight for countries or groups that they do not belong to. *He said they had recruited a group of mercenaries and former soldiers to kill the Pope.*
2 ADJ If something is done in a **mercenary** way or if you say that someone is **mercenary**, you mean they are interested only in the money they can get. *Labour members said Britain should not continue to promote trade in a mercenary manner.*

merchandise /mɜ:tʃəndaɪz/
NU **Merchandise** is goods that are bought, sold, or traded. *I'd like to examine the merchandise.*

merchant /mɜ:tʃənt/ **merchants**
1 NC A **merchant** is a person who buys or sells goods

in large quantities, especially someone who imports and exports goods. *...a textile merchant.*
2 ADJ ATTRIB **Merchant** seamen or ships are involved in carrying goods for trade. *They are considering using Brazilian dockyards to build ships for the Cuban merchant fleet.*

merchant bank, merchant banks
NC A **merchant bank** is a bank that deals mainly with businesses and investment. *He raised the money from a consortium of European banks led by the British merchant bank Hill Samuel.*

merciful /mɜ:sɪfl/
1 ADJ If you describe an event or situation as **merciful**, you mean that it seems fortunate, especially because it stops someone suffering. *Death came as a merciful release.* ♦ **mercifully** ADV *In the end Mrs Paget mercifully died.*
2 ADJ A **merciful** person shows kindness and forgiveness to people who are in their power. *I begged him to be merciful.*

merciless /mɜ:sɪləs/
ADJ A **merciless** person is very strict or cruel and does not show any forgiveness towards people. *He had a reputation as a merciless foe of gambling.*
♦ **mercilessly** ADV *Unarmed peasants were beaten mercilessly.*

mercurial /mɜ:kjʊəriəl/
ADJ Someone who is **mercurial** frequently changes their mind or mood without warning; a literary word. *He was as mercurial as the weather. ...a mercurial temperament.*

mercury /mɜ:kjuri/
NU **Mercury** is a silver-coloured metal that exists as a liquid. It is used, for example, in thermometers. *Water, fish and crops register alarming levels of mercury poisoning... The wind chill factor pushed the mercury to -60 degrees in some Western states.*

mercy /mɜ:si/
1 NU If you show **mercy** to someone, you do not punish them or treat them as severely as you could. *He pleaded for mercy.*
2 If you are **at the mercy of** someone or something, they have complete power over you. *This action would leave them at the mercy of industrialised countries.*

mercy killing, mercy killings
NU **Mercy killing** is the act of killing someone who is very ill, in order to stop them suffering any more pain. *An attempt to legalise mercy killing in Britain has been decisively defeated in the House of Commons.*

mere /mɪə/ **merest. Merest** is used to give emphasis, rather than in comparisons.
1 ADJ ATTRIB **Mere** is used to say how unimportant, minor, or small something is. *They were mere puppets manipulated by men in search of power... He had found out only by the merest accident... In Tanganyika, a mere 2 per cent of the population lived in towns.*
2 ADJ ATTRIB You also use **mere** to refer to something very simple which has a surprisingly strong effect. *They feared the impact the mere presence of a political prisoner would have... The merest suggestion of marital infidelity enrages him.*

merely /mɪəli/
1 ADV You use **merely** to emphasize that something is only what you say and not better, bigger, more important, or more exciting. *This is not genuine. It's merely a reproduction... We accept ideas like this merely because they have never been challenged.*
2 ADV You use **not merely** before the less important of two statements, as a way of emphasizing the more important statement. *Much of this new industry was not merely in India; it was Indian-owned.*

meretricious /merətrɪʃəs/
ADJ Something that is **meretricious** looks attractive but is in fact of little value; a formal word. *Advertisements convey an impression, however meretricious, of the importance of the goods being sold.*

merge /mɜ:dʒ/ **merges, merging, merged**
1 V-RECIP or V-ERG If one thing **merges** with another or if someone **merges** them, they combine together to

make a larger thing. *This suggests that in the next few years Moldavia and Romania will merge... The best solution was for BCCI to merge with an established bank... The government is proposing to merge a number of army regiments... Tibet agreed to merge its armed forces into the People's Liberation army.*
2 V+*into* If something **merges** into the darkness or the background, you can no longer see it clearly as a separate object. *They were painted so that they would merge into the landscape... His bulky form merged into the shadows.*

merger /mɜːdʒə/ **mergers**
NC When a **merger** takes place, two organizations join together. *...a merger between the two organizations.*

meridian /mərɪdɪən/ **meridians**
NC A **meridian** is an imaginary line from the North Pole to the South Pole. Meridians are drawn on maps to help you specify the position of a place.

meringue /mərӕŋ/ **meringues**
NCorNU A **meringue** is a type of crisp, sweet food, made with sugar and egg white. *A meringue goes on top of the vanilla flavoured egg custard.*

merit /merɪt/ **merits, meriting, merited**
1 NU If something has **merit**, it is good or worthwhile; a formal use. *...a work of high literary merit.*
2 NC The **merits** of something are its advantages or good qualities. *...the relative merits of cinema and drama.* ● If you judge something **on its merits**, your opinion of it is based on its own qualities, rather than your personal feelings. *We endeavour to assess any case on its merits.*
3 VO If something **merits** a particular treatment, it is good enough or important enough to be treated in this way; a formal use. *This experiment merits closer examination... It was not important enough to merit a special discussion.*

meritocracy /merɪtɒkrəsi/ **meritocracies**
NCorNU A **meritocracy** is a society or social system in which people have power or prestige because of their abilities and intelligence, rather than because of their wealth or social status; also used to refer to the people themselves. *The position of the old ruling families was destroyed and a new kind of classless meritocracy to some extent has grown up... It is a place of openness and true meritocracy.*

mermaid /mɜːmeɪd/ **mermaids**
NC In children's stories, a **mermaid** is a woman with a fish's tail instead of legs, who lives in the sea. *Unicorns, mermaids, griffins and dragons are just some of the imaginary creatures that make up the wealth of legends in many countries.*

merrily /merɪli/
1 ADV You use **merrily** to say that something happens or is done without people thinking properly about it or about the problems involved. *Before you skip merrily on to the next page, pause.*
2 See also **merry**.

merriment /merɪmənt/
NU **Merriment** means laughter; an old-fashioned word. *She put a hand to her mouth to stifle her merriment.*

merry /meri/
1 ADJ **Merry** means happy and cheerful; an old-fashioned use. *My in-laws, a merry band from Bath, had joined us. ...his merry blue eyes. ...merry music.*
◆ **merrily** ADV *Dr Mason laughed merrily.*
2 People say **Merry Christmas** to each other at Christmas time. *...Merry Christmas and a Happy New Year.*
3 See also **merrily**.

merry-go-round, merry-go-rounds
1 NC A **merry-go-round** is a large circular platform with wooden or plastic animals and vehicles on it which children ride on as it turns round. *'Oh no,' my daughter says when the merry-go-round slows down, looking up from her pink pony.*
2 NC If you describe an activity or a situation as a **merry-go-round**, you mean that it is one in which events occur rapidly one after the other. *British football's managerial merry-go-round continues with the sacking of Celtic's Billy McNeill.*

merry-making
NU **Merry-making** is the activities of people who are enjoying themselves together by singing, dancing, drinking alcohol, etc. *The merry-making continued late into the night.*

mesh /meʃ/ **meshes, meshing, meshed**
1 NU **Mesh** is material like a net made from wire, thread, or plastic. *...a fence made of stout wire mesh. ...fibre woven into a mesh.*
2 V-RECIP If two things **mesh** or if someone **meshes** one thing with another, the two things fit together closely or correspond suitably. *All the numbers do mesh properly... It is not clear how his quieter persona will mesh with Mr Reagan.*
3 VO If a person or organization **meshes** or **meshes** together separate things, they bring them together into one balanced and unified whole. *The 34 nations will attempt to mesh together a Europe beyond ideological and military divisions.*

mesmerize /mezməraɪz/ **mesmerizes, mesmerizing, mesmerized**; also spelt **mesmerise**.
VO If you **are mesmerized** by something, you are so interested in it or so attracted to it that you cannot judge it properly or think about anything else. *Blanche was mesmerized by his voice.*

mess /mes/ **messes, messing, messed**
1 N SING or NU You use **mess** to refer to something that is very untidy and dirty or disorganized. *We cleared up the mess... I know the place is a mess, but make yourself at home... They went back to see how much mess they'd left behind.* ● If a place is **in a mess**, it is untidy or disorganized. *Her hair was in a terrible mess... The US economy is now in a mess.*
2 NC If a situation is a **mess**, it is full of problems and trouble. *My life is such a mess... It seemed a way out from the mess I'd got myself into.*
3 NC A **mess** is also a room or building in which members of the armed forces eat. *...a bomb attack on an officers' mess.*

mess about PHRASAL VERB 1 If you **mess about** or **mess around**, you do things without any particular purpose and without achieving anything; an informal expression. *Some of the lads had been messing around when they should have been working.* 2 If you **mess about** or **mess around** with something, you interfere with it and make it worse; an informal expression. *She didn't want you coming and messing about with things.* 3 If you **mess** someone **about** or **around**, you continually change plans which affect them; an informal expression. *You've been messing me around all summer, and I'm fed up with it.*

mess around PHRASAL VERB See **mess about**.

mess up PHRASAL VERB 1 If you **mess up** something that has been carefully made or done, you spoil it. *That will mess up the whole analysis.* 2 If you **mess up** a room, you make it untidy or dirty. *I was used to him messing up the kitchen.*

mess with PHRASAL VERB If you **mess with** someone or something dangerous, you become involved with them; an informal expression. *We don't mess with heroin or any of that stuff.*

message /mesɪdʒ/ **messages**
1 NC A **message** is a piece of information or a request that you send to someone or leave for them. *Oh, there was a message. Professor Marvin rang. He'd like to meet you on Tuesday... He sent a message to Sir Ian Hamilton saying he was returning.*
2 NC+SUPP A **message** is also the idea that someone tries to communicate to people, for example in a play or a speech. *The play's message is that in the end good and right always triumph.*

messenger /mesndʒə/ **messengers**
NC A **messenger** is someone who takes a message to someone else or who takes messages regularly as their job. *By the time the messenger reached him, the damage had been done.*

messiah /məsaɪə/ **messiahs**
1 N PROP For Jews, the **Messiah** is the King of the Jews, who will be sent to them by God. *...the coming of the Messiah.*
2 N PROP For Christians, the **Messiah** is Jesus Christ. *...the birth of the Messiah.*

3 NC A **messiah** is any person who promises to rescue or succeeds in rescuing people from a very difficult or dangerous situation. *In our history we have been plagued with false messiahs.*

messianic /mɛsiænɪk/; a formal word.
1 ADJ ATTRIB **Messianic** means relating to the belief that a divine being has been born, or will be born, who will change the world. *...messianic cults.*
2 ADJ ATTRIB **Messianic** also means relating to the belief that there will be a complete change in the social order in a country or in the world. *Social democracy is not a messianic creed that promises to change the world.*

Messrs /mɛsəz/
Messrs is used before the names of two or more people as part of the name of the business; a formal word. *Messrs Brant and Prout are dealers in hats.*

mess-up, mess-ups
NC A **mess-up** is a situation in which something has been done very badly or wrongly; an informal word. *There was some mess-up over the availability of dates... What did you think of the mess-up he made of his commentary?*

messy /mɛsi/; an informal word.
1 ADJ **Messy** means dirty or untidy. *...messy bits of food... I disliked the messy farmyard.*
2 ADJ A **messy** person or activity makes things dirty or untidy. *Sometimes I'm neat, sometimes I'm messy... I hate picnics; they're so messy.*
3 ADJ A **messy** situation is confused or complicated, and involves trouble for people. *Brown had been caught in a messy diplomatic dispute.*

met /mɛt/
Met is the past tense and past participle of **meet**.

metabolic /mɛtəbɒlɪk/
ADJ ATTRIB **Metabolic** means relating to a person's or an animal's metabolism; a technical term. *...the gradual slowing down of metabolic processes. ...basic metabolic needs.*

metabolism /mətæbəlɪzəm/ **metabolisms**
NCorNU Your **metabolism** is the chemical process in your body that causes food to be used for growth and energy; a technical term. *Some people's metabolism is more efficient than others... Tumours require the body's own tissue to activate them, by this process of metabolism.*

metal /mɛtl/ **metals**
N MASS **Metal** is a hard substance such as iron, steel, copper, or lead. *It was made of glass and metal. ...a metal spoon.*

metal fatigue
NU If something suffers from **metal fatigue**, the metal has been weakened by repeated movement and it might break. *The crash was thought to have been caused by metal fatigue and poor maintenance.*

metallic /mətælɪk/
1 ADJ A **metallic** sound is like one piece of metal hitting another. *I heard the metallic click of a door handle.*
2 ADJ **Metallic** colours shine like metal. *Her hair was a metallic gold.*
3 ADJ **Metallic** things consist of metal; a technical use. *...metallic ores.*

metallurgist /mɛtælədʒɪst/ **metallurgists**
NC A **metallurgist** is an expert in metallurgy. *...a senior metallurgist with Stocksbridge Engineering Steels.*

metallurgy /mɛtælədʒi/
NU **Metallurgy** is the scientific study of the properties and uses of metals. *...a young assistant professor in metallurgy.*

metalwork /mɛtlwɜːk/
NU **Metalwork** is the activity of making objects out of metal. *Refugees are taught skills like metalwork which they can use when they can return home.*

metamorphose /mɛtəmɔːfəuz/ **metamorphoses, metamorphosing, metamorphosed**
V-ERG When someone or something **metamorphoses** or if they are **metamorphosed** by something, they change into something completely different; a formal word. *The headstrong girl metamorphoses into the loving wife and mother... Young girls are metamorphosed into stunning stars of the screen.*

metamorphosis /mɛtəmɔːfəsɪs/ **metamorphoses** /mɛtəmɔːfəsiːz/
NUorNC When a **metamorphosis** occurs, a person or thing changes into something completely different; a formal word. *...this important metamorphosis from childhood to sexual maturity... Science fiction may be undergoing a metamorphosis.*

metaphor /mɛtəfə/ **metaphors**
NCorNU A **metaphor** is a way of describing something by saying that it is something else which has the qualities that you are trying to describe. For example, if you want to say that someone is shy and timid, you might say that they are a mouse. *We reject metaphors such as 'war on drugs' or 'war on crime' that imply violence... Bertolucci says, 'Literature speaks the language of metaphor, and cinema speaks the language of reality.'*

metaphorical /mɛtəfɒrɪkl/
ADJ You use the word **metaphorical** to indicate that you are not using words with their ordinary meaning, but are describing something by means of an image or symbol. *I had sprouted metaphorical wings.*
♦ **metaphorically** ADV *I was speaking metaphorically.*

metaphysical /mɛtəfɪzɪkl/
ADJ **Metaphysical** means relating to theories about what exists and how we know that it exists. *...the metaphysical and religious ideas in his writings. ...the metaphysical truths which lay at the root of human suffering.*

metaphysics /mɛtəfɪzɪks/
NU **Metaphysics** is the part of philosophy which is concerned with theories about what exists and how we know that it exists. *At the time I was not at all interested in metaphysics. ...the problem of demarcating science from metaphysics.*

mete /miːt/ **metes, meting, meted**
mete out PHRASAL VERB To **mete out** a punishment means to order that someone shall be punished in that way; a formal expression. *Magistrates meted out fines of £1,000.*

meteor /miːtiə/ **meteors**
NC A **meteor** is a piece of rock or metal that burns very brightly when it enters the Earth's atmosphere from space. *...meteor showers.*

meteoric /miːtiɒrɪk/
ADJ A **meteoric** rise to power or success happens very quickly. *He enjoyed a meteoric rise to power in Callaghan's government.*

meteorite /miːtiəraɪt/ **meteorites**
NC A **meteorite** is a large piece of rock or metal from space that has landed on the Earth. *...a meteorite crater.*

meteorological /miːtiərəlɒdʒɪkl/
ADJ ATTRIB **Meteorological** means relating to the weather or to weather forecasting; a technical term. *Meteorological conditions were reasonably good.*

meteorology /miːtiərɒlədʒi/
NU **Meteorology** is the study of the processes in the Earth's atmosphere that cause weather conditions. Meteorology is used especially for giving weather forecasts. *...techniques to study the earth's surface, its geology, its atmosphere, meteorology and many other areas.* ♦ **meteorologist** /miːtiərəlɒdʒɪst/ **meteorologists** NC *...the latest forecasts of the meteorologists.*

meter /miːtə/ **meters**
1 NC A **meter** is a device that measures and records something such as the amount of gas or electricity that you have used. *Someone comes to read the gas and electricity meters.*
2 See also **metre**.

methane /miːθeɪn/
NU **Methane** is a colourless gas that has no smell. Natural gas consists mostly of methane. *Methane and carbon dioxide are produced.*

method /mɛθəd/ **methods**
NCorNU A **method** is a particular way of doing something. *...a change in the method of electing the party's leader... He said that force could be the only method of obtaining the necessary solution. ...an empirical method.*

methodical /məθɒdɪkl/
ADJ A **methodical** person does things carefully and in order. *With methodical thoroughness they demolished the prison.* ◆ **methodically** ADV *He worked quickly and methodically.*
Methodism /mɛθədɪzəm/
NU **Methodism** is the beliefs and practices of Methodists. *The programme is devoted to the history of Methodism.*
Methodist /mɛθədɪst/ **Methodists**
1 NC **Methodists** are Christians who follow the teachings of John Wesley and who have their own branch of the Christian church and their own kind of worship. *His family were strict Methodists.*
2 ADJ **Methodist** means relating to Methodists, their church, and their beliefs. *...the Methodist church. ...his local Methodist chapel. ...Methodist preachers.*
methodology /mɛθədɒlədʒi/ **methodologies**
NCorNU A **methodology** is a system of methods and principles for doing something, for example for teaching or for carrying out research; a formal term. *The Japanese programme is based on an ill-conceived methodology. ...practical teaching methodology. ...a postgraduate course in research methodology.*
meths /mɛθs/
NU **Meths** is methylated spirits; an informal word. *Use a spot of meths by itself on a piece of cotton wool. ...meths drinkers.*
methylated spirit /mɛθəleɪtɪd spɪrɪt/ **methylated spirits**
NU **Methylated spirit** is a liquid made from alcohol and other chemicals. It is used for removing stains and as a fuel in small lamps and heaters. *We set off to clean up the house, with mops and methylated spirits... Try a little methylated spirit rubbed on with a soft cloth.*
meticulous /mətɪkjʊləs/
ADJ A **meticulous** person does things very carefully and with great attention to detail. *He had prepared himself with meticulous care. ...the neatest and most meticulous of girls.* ◆ **meticulously** ADV *...meticulously folded newspapers.*
metier /mɛtieɪ/ **metiers**; also spelt **métier**.
NC Your **metier** is the type of work that you have a natural talent for and do well. *This was assuredly not my metier... He's found his metier at last.*
metre /miːtə/ **metres**; spelt **meter** in American English.
NC A **metre** is a unit of length equal to 100 centimetres. *The blue whale grows to over 30 metres long.*
metric /mɛtrɪk/
ADJ ATTRIB **Metric** units are the ones used in the metric system, for example the metre, the kilogram, and the litre. *NASA has just announced that it won't use metric units on their space stations. ...150 metric tonnes.*
metrication /mɛtrɪkeɪʃn/
NU **Metrication** is the process of changing from measuring things in imperial units to measuring them in metric units. *The Trade Secretary said maximum advantage was being taken of the exemptions from metrication allowed by the European Community.*
metric system
N SING The **metric system** is the system of measurement that uses metres, centimetres, grammes, litres, and so on.
metro /mɛtrəʊ/ **metros**
NC The **metro** is the underground railway system that operates in some cities, for example in Paris. *The strike has disrupted train and bus services and the underground metro system.*
metronome /mɛtrənəʊm/ **metronomes**
NC A **metronome** is a device which is used by people playing music to indicate the speed of a piece of music. It has an arm which swings from side to side making a clicking sound, and which can be adjusted to make the sound at different speeds. *The metronome ticked on slowly. ...the composer's metronome markings.*
metropolis /mətrɒpəlɪs/ **metropolises**
NC A **metropolis** is a very large city; a formal word.

Sydney, a vast metropolis of four million people, has spread its suburbs 120 kilometres along the coast.
metropolitan /mɛtrəpɒlɪtən/
ADJ ATTRIB **Metropolitan** means belonging to or typical of a large busy city. *...seven metropolitan districts in the Midlands.*
Metropolitan Police
N PL The **Metropolitan Police** is the part of the British police force that works in London. *...the Commissioner of the Metropolitan Police.*
mettle /mɛtl/
1 If you are on your **mettle**, you are ready to do something as well as you can, because you know that you are being tested or challenged. *I felt I was on my mettle. It was my first big chance in America... The new speed restrictions will put a keen driver on his mettle.*
2 If you **show** your **mettle** or you **prove** your **mettle**, you show that you are capable of doing something well. *He had no chance to show his mettle... They think she has proved her mettle trying to restore democracy.*
mew /mjuː/ **mews, mewing, mewed**
V When a cat **mews**, it makes a soft high-pitched noise. *The cat was mewing for its supper.*
Mexico /mɛksɪkəʊ/
The **United Mexican States** is a country in Central America. It was a Spanish colony until 1821. Carlos Salinas de Gortari, of the Institutional Revolutionary Party (PPI), became President in 1988. In 1982 Mexico declared it could no longer meet payments on its foreign debts, which were second in size only to Brazil's. High inflation and large foreign debts continue to be major economic problems. Mexico exports oil, engines, and seafood. Cannabis is illegally produced. Tourism is an important industry. Mexico is a member of the Organization of American States.
◆ **Mexican** /mɛksɪkən/ N, ADJ
▪ *per capita GNP:* US$1,820 ▪ *religion:* Christianity (mainly Roman Catholic) ▪ *language:* Spanish ▪ *currency:* peso ▪ *capital:* Mexico City ▪ *population:* 86 million (1989) ▪ *size:* 1,908,691 square kilometres.
Mexico City /mɛksɪkəʊ sɪti/
Mexico City is the world's largest city and one of the fastest growing metropolitan areas in the world. It is the capital of Mexico. Population: 17,322,000 (1986).
mezzanine /mɛzəniːn/ **mezzanines**
NC A **mezzanine** is a small floor which is built between two stories in a building, for example between the ground floor and the first floor. *...his office on the executive mezzanine.*
mezzo-soprano /mɛtsəʊsəpranəʊ/ **mezzo-sopranos**
NC A **mezzo-soprano** is a female singer who sings with a higher range than a contralto but a lower range than a soprano. *She was a large mezzo-soprano who'd once had a good voice... Sophia spoke in an unexpectedly passionate mezzo-soprano.*
mg
mg is a written abbreviation for 'milligram' or 'milligrams'. *It contained 65mg of Vitamin C.*
MI5 /ɛmaɪfaɪv/
N PROP **MI5** is a British government organization which is concerned with the security of the United Kingdom. **MI5** is an abbreviation for 'Military Intelligence Section 5'. *Lady Hargreaves had been vetted by MI5.*
MI6 /ɛmaɪsɪks/
N PROP **MI6** is a British government organization which tries to obtain secret information about the political and military affairs of other countries. **MI6** is an abbreviation for 'Military Intelligence Section 6'. *...the daily report from MI6.*
miaow /miaʊ/ **miaows, miaowing, miaowed**
NC When a cat goes 'miaow', it makes a short high-pitched sound. *That sounds like the miaow of a cat.*
▸ Also V *There was a cat miaowing outside.*
miasma /miæzmə/ **miasmas**
NCorNU A **miasma** is a very unpleasant smell in the air all around you; a literary word. *It covered the entire ranch in a foul miasma. ...a miasma of mothballs.*

mice /maɪs/
Mice is the plural of **mouse**.

mickey /mɪki/
If you **take the mickey** out of someone, you make fun of them; an informal expression. *Musn't take the mickey out of George... You're always taking the mickey.*

micro /maɪkrəʊ/ **micros**
NC A **micro** is the same as a **micro-computer**. *...the generation of computers before the micros.*

micro- /maɪkrəʊ-/
PREFIX **Micro-** is used to form nouns that refer to a very small example of a particular type of thing. For example, a micro-organism is a very small organism such as a virus. *...diseases caused by micro-organisms. ...the invention of the microcassette.*

microbe /maɪkrəʊb/ **microbes**
NC A **microbe** is a very small living thing, which you can only see with a microscope. *...the microbes in the human gut.*

microchip /maɪkrəʊtʃɪp/ **microchips**
NC A **microchip** is a small piece of silicon inside a computer, on which electronic circuits are printed. *...the cost of microchip design.*

micro-computer, micro-computers
NC A **micro-computer** is a small computer, that is usually used by one person in a small business, a school, or in the home. *Information is stored on the micro-computer's hard disk.*

microcosm /maɪkrəkɒzəm/ **microcosms**
NC A place or event that is a **microcosm** of a larger one has all the main features of the larger one and seems like a smaller version of it. *Bristol was a microcosm of urban England in the 1970s.*

microfiche /maɪkrəʊfiːʃ/ **microfiches**
NCorNU A **microfiche** is a small sheet of film on which information is stored in very small print. Microfiches are read on special machines which magnify them. *The Periodicals Catalogue is now on microfiche.*

microfilm /maɪkrəʊfɪlm/ **microfilms, microfilming, microfilmed**
1 NUorNC **Microfilm** is film that is used for photographing information and storing it in a reduced form which can then be read by putting the film into a machine which magnifies it. *The library has a lot of Russian newspapers on microfilm. ...a microfilm reader. ...to replace lost books, microfilms and electronic data.*
2 VO If you **microfilm** maps, documents, or other papers, you photograph them using a microfilm. *They waited while the plans were microfilmed. ...900,000 rolls of microfilmed documents.*

Micronesia /maɪkrəʊniːzɪə/
The **Federated States of Micronesia** is a self-governing territory in free association with the United States. It is located in the Caroline Islands in the Pacific. The islands became a Spanish colony in 1874 and were sold to Germany in 1899. Japan controlled them from the First World War until 1945, when they were occupied by the United States. In 1982 a Compact of Free Association was agreed between Micronesia and the United States. Coconuts, cassava, and sweet potatoes are exported. Tourism and fishing are important industries. ◆ **Micronesian** /maɪkrəʊniːzɪən/ N, ADJ
▪ *per capita GNP:* US$1,500 ▪ *religion:* Christianity (mainly Roman Catholic) ▪ *language:* English (official) ▪ *currency:* US dollar ▪ *capital:* Palikir ▪ *population:* 102,000 (1989) ▪ *size:* 700 square kilometres.

microorganism /maɪkrəʊɔːgənɪzəm/ **microorganisms**
NC A **microorganism** is a microbe; a technical term. *...bacteria, viruses, and other microorganisms.*

microphone /maɪkrəfəʊn/ **microphones**
NC A **microphone** is a device that is used to make sounds louder or to record them on a tape recorder. *Some recording engineers don't put microphones in the best places.*

microprocessor /maɪkrəʊprəʊsesə/ **microprocessors**
NC A **microprocessor** is a microchip which can be programmed to do a large number of tasks or calculations. *High energy particles can cause damage in electronic components, like memories and microprocessors.*

microscope /maɪkrəskəʊp/ **microscopes**
NC A **microscope** is an instrument which magnifies very small objects so that you can study them. *The slides are examined under the microscope.*

microscopic /maɪkrəskɒpɪk/
1 ADJ Something that is **microscopic** is very small and can only usually be seen through a microscope. *...microscopic forms of life.*
2 ADJ A **microscopic** examination of something is very detailed and thorough. *...a microscopic study of medieval customs.*

microwave /maɪkrəweɪv/ **microwaves**
1 NC A **microwave** or a **microwave oven** is a cooker which cooks food very quickly by using short-wave radiation rather than by heat. *Food in microwave ovens is subjected to very high power densities.*
2 NC **Microwaves** are a type of electromagnetic radiation that fall within the wavelength range of 0.3 to 0.001 metres that are used in telecommunications, radar, cooking, and so on. *The satellite will have infra-red cameras and microwave radar devices. ...short range microwave communications.*

mid- /mɪd-/
PREFIX **Mid-** is used to form nouns or modifiers that refer to the middle part of a place or period of time. *...the Dyfi Valley in mid-Wales. ...studies published in the mid-1970s. ...the mid-morning sun.*

mid-air
NU If something happens in **mid-air**, it happens in the air rather than on the ground. *The bird turned in mid-air and darted away. ...a mid-air collision.*

midday /mɪddeɪ/
1 NU **Midday** is twelve o'clock in the middle of the day. *Just before midday the telephone rang.*
2 N+N **Midday** is used to describe things that happen or occur at midday, or in the middle part of the day, from late morning to early afternoon. *...a midday meal... The Duchess of York wore a huge broad-brimmed hat to protect her from the midday sun.*

middle /mɪdl/ **middles**
1 NC The **middle** of something is the part that is farthest from its edges, ends, or outside surface. *In the middle of the lawn was a great cedar tree... He sat down in the middle of the front row. ...the white lines painted along the middle of the highway... Test the meat to see if it is cooked in the middle.*
2 ADJ ATTRIB The **middle** thing or person in a row or series is the one with an equal number of things or people on each side, or before it and after it. *...the middle button of her black leather coat... She was the middle child of the three.*
3 NC Your **middle** is the front part of your body at your waist. *He had a large green towel wrapped round his middle.*
4 N SING The **middle** of an event or period of time is the part that comes after the first part and before the last part. *We landed at Canton in the middle of a torrential storm. ...the middle of December.* ▶ Also ADJ ATTRIB *He was in his middle thirties.*
5 If you are **in the middle of** doing something, you are busy doing it. *I'm in the middle of washing up.*
6 ADJ ATTRIB The **middle** course or way is a moderate course of action that lies between two opposite and extreme courses. *Between Fascism or revolution there is a middle course.*

middle age
NU **Middle age** is the period in your life when you are between about 40 and 60 years old. *...a grave, courteous man in late middle age.*

middle-aged
ADJ **Middle-aged** people are between the ages of about 40 and 60. *...a middle-aged businessman.*

Middle Ages
N PL In European history, the **Middle Ages** were the period between the end of the Roman Empire in 476 AD and about 1500 AD. *Freemasonry arose from the association of travelling stonemasons back in the Middle Ages.*

middle class, middle classes
NC The **middle classes** are the people in a society who are not working class or upper class, for example managers, doctors, and lawyers. *...the new Indian*

middle classes. ▶ Also ADJ *...middle-class families... Watson's upbringing was comfortably middle class.*

middle distance

N SING The **middle distance** is the area or space between the foreground and the distance in a view or in a painting. *He stood at the gate, gazing into the middle distance.*

Middle East

N PROP The **Middle East** is a part of Asia. It includes Iran and all the countries in Asia that are to the west and south-west of Iran. *The Under Secretary General is currently in Egypt at the end of a scheduled tour of the Middle East.*

Middle Eastern

ADJ ATTRIB **Middle Eastern** means coming from or relating to the Middle East. *...Middle Eastern oil.*

middleman /mɪdlmæn/ **middlemen**

1 NC A **middleman** is someone who buys things from the people who produce them and sells them to other people at a profit. *It launched the idea of cutting out the middleman and selling produce at 20 per cent less than the prevailing price.*
2 NC In political discussions, a **middleman** is someone who mediates between the parties concerned. *The Japanese Prime Minister has agreed to act as middleman in improving Sino-South Korean relations.*

middle name, middle names

NC A person's **middle name** is a name that they have which comes between their first name and their surname. *Mary is her middle name.*

middle-of-the-road

ADJ **Middle-of-the-road** politicians or opinions are moderate, not extreme. *...middle-of-the-road Labour MPs.*

middle school, middle schools

NC A **middle school** is a school that children go to between the ages of 8 or 9 and 12 or 13. *Primary schools will reopen on 19th June and middle schools in the third week in August.*

Middle West

N PROP The **Middle West** is the central part of the United States of America. *...my home town in the Middle West.*

middling /mɪdlɪŋ/

ADJ ATTRIB **Middling** means of average quality. *...a woman of middling intellectual attainments.*

midge /mɪdʒ/ **midges**

NC **Midges** are very small flying insects which can bite people. *This year plagues of midges have infested the lagoons.*

midget /mɪdʒɪt/ **midgets**

NC A **midget** is a very small person; an offensive word. *The only midgets I would see were at the circus.*

midi system /mɪdi sɪstəm/ **midi systems**

NC A **midi system** is a small hi-fi system that is contained in a single unit, rather than in a number of separate units.

Midlands /mɪdləndz/

N PROP The **Midlands** is the region or area in the central part of a country, in particular the central part of England. *The largest falls in the unemployment rate were in the North, the Midlands and Wales... The play is set in a small Midlands village... The East Midlands has been chosen as the venue for the project.*

midnight /mɪdnaɪt/

1 NU **Midnight** is twelve o'clock in the middle of the night. *The accident happened shortly after midnight local time... Campaigning for tomorrow's elections ends officially at midnight tonight.*
2 N+N **Midnight** is used to describe something that happens at midnight or in the middle of the night. *About a thousand people attended midnight mass... She had had a midnight visit from police telling her to leave.*

midpoint /mɪdpɔɪnt/ **midpoints**

1 NC The **midpoint** of something long such as a line is the point on it that is the same distance from both ends. *At the midpoint of the bridge he stopped.*
2 NC The **midpoint** of an event is the time halfway between the beginning and the end of it. *The negotiations are taking place at the midpoint of the*

current four-year round of talks.

midriff /mɪdrɪf/ **midriffs**

NC Your **midriff** is the middle of your body, especially your waist and the area just above it. *He was up to his midriff in hot water.*

midst /mɪdst/; a formal word.

● **Midst** is used in these phrases. ● If you are **in the midst** of a group of people, you are among them or surrounded by them. *He had suddenly appeared in the midst of the many journalists. ...the determination of the whole community to stand up against the evil in its midst.* ● If something happens **in the midst of** an event, it happens during that event. *He came to office a year ago in the midst of the most serious economic and social crisis in the country's history.* ● If you are **in the midst of** doing something, you are doing it at the moment. *Argentina is in the midst of a presidential campaign... Brody was in the midst of swallowing a bite of egg salad sandwich.*

midstream /mɪdstriːm/

1 NU Someone or something that is in **midstream** is in the middle of a river, where the current is strongest. *He unlocked the boat and they were soon in midstream.*
2 If someone who has been speaking for a while stops or pauses **in midstream**, they stop speaking, often before continuing. *Cogg stopped in midstream to look round.*

midsummer /mɪdsʌmə/

NU **Midsummer** is the period in the middle of the summer. *...a hot midsummer day... The magazine also predicts increasing midsummer airport delays.*

Midsummer Day or **Midsummer's Day**, **Midsummer Days** or **Midsummer's Days**

N PROP **Midsummer Day** is the 24th of June. *Midsummer Day lay only a few weeks in the future.*

midway /mɪdweɪ/

1 ADV If something is **midway** between two places, it is between them and the same distance from each of them. *St Germain is midway between Cherbourg and Granville.*
2 ADV If something happens **midway** through a period of time, it happens during the middle part of it. *She arrived midway through the afternoon.*

midweek /mɪdwiːk/

ADV or ADJ ATTRIB If you do something **midweek**, you do it in the middle of the week. *Secretary Baker will leave midweek and travel first to Saudi Arabia... He was expected to make an appearance in a midweek reserve game.*

Midwest /mɪdwest/

N PROP The **Midwest** is the central part of the USA. *...retired farmers from the Midwest. ...Midwest grassland.*

Midwestern /mɪdwestən/

ADJ Something that is **Midwestern** belongs to or involves the Midwest. *...the Midwestern states of North America.*

midwife /mɪdwaɪf/ **midwives**

NC A **midwife** is a nurse who advises pregnant women and helps them to give birth. *I believe you have trained nurses or midwives in most clinics.*

midwifery /mɪdwɪfəri/

NU **Midwifery** is the work of a midwife and the skills it involves. *Nurses may go on to specialise in areas such as midwifery.*

midwinter /mɪdwɪntə/

NU **Midwinter** is the period in the middle of the winter. *It is a depressing place in midwinter. ...a lovely midwinter morning.*

mien /miːn/

N SING Someone's **mien** is their general appearance and manner, especially the expression on their face, which shows what they are feeling or thinking; a literary word. *There was assurance in his mien... His gentle mien reminded me of his mother.*

miffed /mɪft/

ADJ PRED If you are **miffed**, you are slightly annoyed and hurt because of something which someone has said or done to you; an informal word. *She sounded miffed... Many union workers were miffed at his coolness.*

might/maɪt, maɪt/. **Might** is sometimes considered to be the past tense of **may**, but in this dictionary the two words are dealt with separately.
1 MODAL If you say that something **might** happen, you mean that it is possible that it will happen. If you say that something **might** be true, you mean that it is possible that it is true. *I might even lose my job... I might go to a concert tonight... Many of them might still be alive.*
2 MODAL If you say that something **might** have happened, you mean that it is possible that it happened. *He might well have said that. I just don't remember... There are some clues, however, as to what might have happened... Some of you might have found it a bit difficult.*
3 MODAL You can also say that something **might** have happened when it was possible for it to have happened, although it did not in fact happen. *A lot of men died who might have been saved... Think of how different things might have been had they lived a decade or two later.*
4 MODAL You can use **might** in very polite and formal requests. *Might I inquire if you are the owner?... She asked the man's wife if she might borrow a pen.*
5 MODAL You can also use **might** when you are making suggestions. *The other thing you might find out is who owns the land.*
6 NU **Might** is power or strength; a literary use. *I tied the rope around the tree and heaved with all my might... Does he stay in power only because of military might?*
mightily/maɪtɪli/
ADV **Mightily** means to a great extent or degree; an old-fashioned word. *Things have changed mightily since then.*
mightn't/maɪtnt/
Mightn't is a spoken form of 'might not'. *It mightn't be true at all.*
might've/maɪtəv, maɪtəv/
Might've is a spoken form of 'might have', especially when 'have' is an auxiliary verb. *Someone might've written you a cheque.*
mighty/maɪti/ **mightier, mightiest**
1 ADJ **Mighty** means very large or powerful; a literary use. *...this mighty nation. ...two of Asia's mightiest rivers, the Ganges and the Brahmaputra... We're dealing with forces that are mightier than ourselves.*
2 SUBMOD In American English, **mighty** is also used in front of adjectives in order to emphasize them. *It's going to be mighty embarrassing... It's been mighty dry for about two months.*
migraine/miːgreɪn/ **migraines**
NU or NC **Migraine** is a painful headache that makes you feel very ill. *Do you suffer from migraine?... The experience had brought on one of her migraines.*
migrant/maɪgrənt/ **migrants**
NC A **migrant** is a person who moves from one place to another, especially in order to find work. *...migrants looking for a place to live... They're classified as illegal economic migrants, not entitled to refugee status... The problems of labour shortages and migrant workers are not confined to Europe.*
migrate/maɪgreɪt/ **migrates, migrating, migrated**
1 V When people **migrate**, they move from one place to another, especially in order to find work. *Millions have migrated to the cities.* ◆ **migration**,/maɪgreɪʃn/ **migrations** NU or NC *Migration for work is accelerating in the Third World. ...the vast Greek migrations into Asia and Egypt.*
2 V When birds or animals **migrate**, they go and live in a different area for part of the year, in order to breed or to find food. *Every spring they migrate towards the coast.* ◆ **migration** NU or NC *Swallows begin their migration south in early autumn. ...the migrations of the reindeer.*
mike/maɪk/ **mikes**
NC A **mike** is the same as a **microphone**; an informal word. *Is the mike turned on?*
mild/maɪld/ **milder, mildest**
1 ADJ Something that is **mild** is not strong and does not have any powerful effects. *...a mild detergent... He has suffered from mild Parkinson's disease.*

◆ **mildly** SUBMOD *The skin may become mildly infected.*
2 ADJ **Mild** people are gentle and do not get angry. *...my wife's mild nature. ...the moderate, mild approach of the government.* ◆ **mildly** ADV *'No need to shout,' he said mildly.* ◆ **mildness** NU *The Colonel spoke with great mildness.*
3 ADJ **Mild** weather is less cold than usual. *Milder weather is forecast for today... The increase in rats was caused by a mild winter last year.*
4 ADJ **Mild** also means not very great or extreme. *...a combination of mild curiosity and friendliness... Everyone I asked reacted with mild surprise.* ◆ **mildly** SUBMOD *It was mildly amusing.*
mildew/mɪldjuː/
NU **Mildew** is a soft white fungus that grows in warm and damp places. *The smell is overwhelming—a combination of human waste, sweat and mildew.*
mild-mannered
ADJ A **mild-mannered** person is gentle, polite, and avoids using rude language. *The attacks roused the normally mild-mannered and non-confrontational speaker... He was regarded more as a mild-mannered academic than a political heavyweight.*
mile/maɪl/ **miles**
NC A **mile** is a unit of distance equal to 1760 yards or approximately 1.6 kilometres. *The island is 16 miles wide. ...a small port a few miles south of the Irish border.*
mileage/maɪlɪdʒ/
NU **Mileage** refers to a distance that is travelled, measured in miles. *The approximate mileage for the journey is 200 miles.*
milestone/maɪlstəʊn/ **milestones**
1 NC+SUPP A **milestone** is an important event in the history or development of something. *The conference was a milestone in the history of the party... The decision is seen as a milestone in relations between the two nations.*
2 NC A **milestone** is also a stone by the side of the road showing the distances to particular places.
milieu/miːljɜː/ **milieux** or **milieus**
NC The **milieu** in which you live or work is the group of people that you live or work among; a formal word. *I was born in a social milieu where education was a luxury. ...a very different cultural milieu.*
militancy/mɪlɪtənsi/
NU **Militancy** is the behaviour and attitudes of people who are very active in trying to bring about political change, often in ways that some people find unacceptable. *The unions themselves have lost much of their former militancy... The new militancy was also a reaction to the government's decision.*
militant/mɪlɪtənt/ **militants**
1 ADJ Someone who is **militant** is very active in trying to bring about political change, often in ways that some people find unacceptable. *The farmers are a traditionally vocal and militant pressure group... The population is not in a militant mood. ...militant trade unionists... It started when a militant group ambushed a security patrol just before midnight.*
◆ **militantly** ADV or SUBMOD *...this failure to act militantly... Hogarth was the most militantly patriotic of artists.*
2 NC A **militant** is a someone who is very active in trying to bring about political change, often in ways that some people find unacceptable. *...a number of well-known militants... Mr Kinnock is at pains to show that Labour is not in the hands of trade union bosses or left-wing militants.*
militarism/mɪlɪtərɪzəm/
NU **Militarism** is the desire to strengthen and use the armed forces of your country in order to make it more powerful; used showing disapproval. *...the militarism which led to the First World War... The country slipped into a dangerous mixture of nationalism and militarism.*
militarist/mɪlɪtərɪst/ **militarists**; used showing disapproval.
1 NC A **militarist** is someone who is eager to strengthen and use the armed forces of their country in order to make it more powerful. *They believed this*

was essential to prevent militarists and dictators from taking over.
2 ADJ **Militarist** strategies are based on a desire to strengthen and use the armed forces of a particular country in order to make it more powerful. ...*the militarist strategies pursued by this government... What they do not want is the emergence of an authoritarian militarist regime which might be tempted to lash out in foreign adventures in order to relieve internal tensions.*

military /mɪlɪtəˀri/
1 ADJ ATTRIB **Military** means relating to or involving a country's armed forces. *He still hoped for a diplomatic rather than a military outcome. ...military leaders. ...direct military action.* ◆ **militarily** ADV *The IRA could not be defeated militarily.*
2 N COLL The **military** are the armed forces of a country, especially the officers of high rank. *The politicians and the military will do nothing... He retired from the military in 1975.*

military police
N PL The **military police** are part of an army, navy, or air force, and act as its police force. *Military police arrested the human rights activist as he stepped off the plane... The government has said it will reform the military police.*

military service
N U **Military service** is a period of compulsory service in the armed forces of a country. *An increasing number are resisting military service on political grounds.*

militate /mɪlɪteɪt/ **militates, militating, militated**
V+against If something **militates** against something else, it makes it less likely to happen or succeed; a formal word. *Various factors militated against the Party's success... The brevity of the two leaders' meeting—they will have only two and a half hours of discussions—also militates against a breakthrough.*

militia /məlɪʃə/ **militias**
N C A **militia** is an organization that operates like an army but whose members are not professional soldiers. ...*a building guarded by the local police and militia... The local militia had been asked to patrol the streets.*

militiaman /məlɪʃəmən/ **militiamen** /məlɪʃəmən/
N C A **militiaman** is a member of a militia. *Following the attack, militiamen closed the road leading to the camps. ...rival militiamen.*

milk /mɪlk/ **milks, milking, milked**
1 N U **Milk** is the white liquid produced by cows and goats, which people drink and make into butter, cheese, and yoghurt. *He only drinks milk in tea or coffee. ...a glass of milk. ...essential products such as milk, salt and sugar.* ● See also **condensed milk, skimmed milk**
2 V Oor V When someone **milks** a cow or goat, they get milk from it by pulling its udders. *The men had milked the cows in the early morning... Most farmers start milking at dawn.* ◆ **milking** N U *He used to help the farmer with his milking... I had to install milking equipment.*
3 N U **Milk** is also the white liquid from a woman's breasts which babies drink. *New-born babies are given temporary immunity from disease by antibodies passed on in their mother's milk.*
4 V Oor V O A If you **milk** something such as an organization or situation, or if you **milk** money or benefit from it, you selfishly get as much money or benefit as you can from it. *He's just milking the company dry... Forty-five thousand pounds was milked from her account.*

milk float, milk floats
N C In Britain, a **milk float** is a small van with a roof and no sides which is used to deliver milk to people's houses. *Milk floats usually have an electric motor.*

milkmaid /mɪlkmeɪd/ **milkmaids**
N C In former times, a **milkmaid** was a woman who milked cows and made butter and cheese. *The milkmaid and the cowherd have officially disappeared from British rural life.*

milkman /mɪlkmən/ **milkmen** /mɪlkmən/
N C A **milkman** is a person who delivers milk to

people's homes. *I worked as a milkman for a Canadian-owned dairy.*

milk-shake, milk-shakes
N Cor N U A **milk-shake** is a cold drink made by mixing milk with flavouring, and sometimes ice-cream, and then whisking it. ...*a strawberry milkshake.*

milk tooth, milk teeth
N C Your **milk teeth** are the first teeth that grow in your mouth, which later fall out and are replaced by a second set. *They were at that engaging stage of losing their front milk teeth, and their gappy smiles emphasized their tender years.*

milky /mɪlki/
1 ADJ Something that is **milky** in colour is pale white. ...*clouds of milky smoke.*
2 ADJ **Milky** food or drink contains a lot of milk. *We always had milky coffee at lunchtime.*

Milky Way
N PROP The **Milky Way** is the pale strip of light consisting of many stars that you can see stretching across the sky at night. *The Milky Way is a spiral galaxy.*

mill /mɪl/ **mills, milling, milled**
1 N C A **mill** is a building where grain is crushed to make flour. *He sends his crop to a large mill instead of grinding it himself.*
2 N C+SUPP A **mill** is also a factory used for making and processing materials such as steel, wool, or cotton. *He had worked in a steel mill... One of his thirty businesses is a wood mill.*
3 See also **run-of-the-mill.**

mill about or **mill around** PHRASAL VERB When a crowd of people **mill about** or **mill around**, they move around in a disorganized way. *Crowds of anxious and dispirited people mill about outside... More than 1000 people were milling around inside the airport terminal.*

millennium /mɪlɛniəm/ **millennia** or **millenniums**
N C A **millennium** is a thousand years; a formal word. *The threat of fossil fuels running out sometime into the next millennium looks ever greater. ...a landscape that had remained unchanged for millennia.*

millet /mɪlɪt/
N U **Millet** is a tall grass that is cultivated for its seeds or for hay. *He's developed his fields from scratch, planting clover, millet and wheat.*

milligram /mɪlɪgræm/ **milligrams**; also spelt **milligramme.**
N C A **milligram** is a unit of weight equal to one thousandth of a gram. ...*0.3 milligrams of mercury.*

millilitre /mɪlɪliːtə/ **millilitres**; spelt **milliliter** in American English.
N C A **millilitre** is a unit of volume for liquids and gases, equal to one thousandth of a litre. ...*45 millilitres of alcohol.*

millimetre /mɪlɪmiːtə/ **millimetres**; spelt **millimeter** in American English.
N C A **millimetre** is a unit of length equal to one tenth of a centimetre. ...*a silicon chip less than a millimetre thick.*

milliner /mɪlɪnə/ **milliners**
N C A **milliner** is a person whose job is making or selling women's hats.

millinery /mɪlɪnəˀri/
N U **Millinery** is used to refer to hats made or sold by a milliner. ...*a millinery display in a shop window.*

milling /mɪlɪŋ/
ADJ ATTRIB The people in a **milling** crowd move around in a disorganized way. *She escaped unnoticed into the milling crowds.*

million /mɪljən/ **millions**
1 A **million** is the number 1,000,000. ...*30 million dollars... Over six million Californians are without health insurance.*
2 QUANT You can use **millions** to refer to a very large number. ...*millions of mosquitoes... Her books still give pleasure to millions.*

millionaire /mɪljəneə/ **millionaires**
N C A **millionaire** is a rich person who has money or property worth at least a million pounds or dollars. *Hammer was a millionaire by the time he graduated from medical school at age 23. ...a millionaire Texas oilman.*

millionth /mɪljənθ/ **millionths**

1 NC A **millionth** is one of a million equal parts of something. ...*cut to an accuracy of one millionth of a second.*

2 ADJ The **millionth** item in a series is the one that you count as number one million. *This past week, the nation's five millionth patent was awarded.*

millipede /mɪlɪpiːd/ **millipedes**

NC A **millipede** is a very small creature with a long, narrow body made of many small segments, each segment with two pairs of legs.

millstone /mɪlstəʊn/ **millstones**

1 If you describe something as **a millstone round** your neck, you mean that it is a very unpleasant problem or responsibility that you cannot escape from. *The debt becomes an even bigger millstone round the poor man's neck.*

2 NC A **millstone** is one of two large flat round stones used, especially in former times, to grind grain into flour. *Grain could be ground on a large scale here because each water wheel powered its own set of millstones.*

mime /maɪm/ **mimes, miming, mimed**

1 NUorNC **Mime** is the use of movements and gestures to express something or tell a story without using speech. ...*the re-telling of legends in mime and song... He sought to improvise new mimes.*

2 V,VO,orV-REPORT If you **mime** something, you describe or express it using mime rather than speech. *If he can dance and he can mime alright, the show should be alright... We were told he was miming the god Shiva coming down from heaven... They all vigorously mimed I should speak as quietly as they did.*

3 VorVO If you **mime**, you pretend to be singing or playing an instrument, although the music is in fact coming from a record or cassette. *The majority of the people won't know if he's miming or not... In concerts, the group mime their songs.*

mimetic /mɪmɛtɪk/

ADJ **Mimetic** movements or actions are ones in which you imitate something; a technical term. *They perform their mimetic movements... She went through the mimetic actions of hearing a moan in the dark.*

mimic /mɪmɪk/ **mimics, mimicking, mimicked**

1 VO If you **mimic** someone's actions or voice, you imitate them in an amusing or entertaining way. *I can mimic Cockney speech reasonably well. ...a street kid who learns to mimic the behavior of the upper class.*

2 NC A **mimic** is a person who is able to mimic people. *One of my brothers is a wonderful mimic.*

mimicry /mɪmɪkri/

NU **Mimicry** is the action of mimicking someone or something. ...*his fine talent for mimicry.*

min.

Min. is a written abbreviation for 'minute' or 'minutes'. ...*an easy 10 min. run.*

minaret /mɪnərɛt/ **minarets**

NC A **minaret** is a tall, thin tower which is part of a mosque. *A muezzin calls the faithful to prayer from a minaret. ...the soaring minarets of a hundred mosques.*

mince /mɪns/ **minces, mincing, minced**

1 NU **Mince** is meat cut into very small pieces. ...*the nutritional value of mince.*

2 VO If you **mince** meat, you cut it into very small pieces. *Mince the lean meat finely.* ◆ **minced** ADJ ATTRIB *We've taken some finely minced beef.*

3 V To **mince** means to walk with quick small steps in an affected or effeminate way. *Off they minced to see the old lady.*

4 If you **do not mince your words**, you do not try to be polite or to avoid offending people when you tell them something unpleasant. *He did not mince his words and accused the State Governor and the police force of a massacre.*

mincemeat /mɪnsmiːt/

1 NU **Mincemeat** is a sticky mixture of small pieces of dried fruit. It is usually cooked in pastry to make mince pies.

2 NU **Mincemeat** is also meat such as beef or lamb

which has been minced; used in American English.

mince pie, mince pies

NC A **mince pie** is a small pie which contains a sticky mixture of small pieces of dried fruit. Mince pies are usually eaten at Christmas. *The dinner is the traditional one of turkey and mince pies.*

mincer /mɪnsə/ **mincers**

NC A **mincer** is a machine which cuts meat into very small pieces. *Mince the meat finely, putting it through the mincer a couple of times.*

mincing /mɪnsɪŋ/

ADJ A **mincing** walk consists of quick small steps and looks very affected or effeminate. ...*mincing steps.* ◆ **mincingly** ADV *Rudolph had to walk delicately, almost mincingly, to keep from slipping.*

mind /maɪnd/ **minds, minding, minded**

1 NC Your **mind** is your ability to think. *Television, he feels, stimulates their young minds... The emphasis throughout is on using nature to heal and refresh the mind, body and spirit. ...diseases of the nervous system and mind.*

2 VO,V+ING,V-REPORT,orV If you say that you do not **mind** something, you mean that you are not annoyed or bothered by it. *She doesn't mind the isolation... Does your family mind you being out here?... I don't mind walking... The Poles said they did not mind how the help was packaged... Do you mind if I stay here?... She said no, she didn't mind.*

3 VO You tell someone to **mind** something in order to warn them to be careful, so that they do not get hurt or damage something. *Mind the ice on the step as you go... Mind my specs!*

4 VO If you **mind** someone's child or **mind** their property, for example their shop or luggage, you look after the child or property for them for a while. *My mother is minding the office.*

● **Mind** is used in these phrases. ● If you **change** your **mind**, you change a decision that you have made or an opinion that you have had. *He'll come under further pressure to change his mind... The authorities might be changing their mind about the way they deal with signs of unrest.* ● If you tell someone to **bear** or **keep** something **in mind**, you are telling them to remember it because it is important or relevant. *Bear in mind that it was a basic research exercise... There are dangers to be borne in mind... I think that there are some guidelines that we should keep in mind.* ● When you **make** your **mind up**, you decide which of a number of possible things you will have or do. *He has a reputation for taking a long time to make up his mind... He made up his mind to do something that he believed could help.* ● If something **comes to mind**, you think of it without making any effort. *I just pick up whatever groceries come to mind.* ● If you **speak** your **mind**, you say exactly what you think, even if it may make other people angry. *He wants more freedom to speak his mind on policy. ...a man whose only offence had been to speak his mind.* ● If your **mind is on** something, you are thinking about it. *Her mind was not on the announcements she was making.* ● If something is **on your mind**, you are worried about it and think about it a lot. *He has one or two rather pressing domestic matters on his mind.* ● If you **have** something **in mind**, you intend to have it or do it. *He didn't make it clear what kind of dialogue he had in mind.* ● If you do something **with** a particular thing **in mind**, you do it for that reason or with that purpose. *Many will not be able to reach polling stations because of monsoon rains; the date of the election was fixed with that in mind... It's designed with the domestic market in mind.* ● You use **to my mind** to indicate that you are giving your own opinion. *That's an XK120, which to my mind is one of the most beautiful cars that Bill Lyons ever created.* ● If you have an **open mind**, you have not formed an opinion about a particular matter, and are waiting until you know all the facts. *The police say for the moment they're keeping an open mind... The government would enter the negotiations with an open mind and without preconditions.* ● Your **state of mind** is your mental state at a particular time. *She was in a fairly disturbed state of mind.* ● You use **mind you** when you are adding a further statement, especially one which contrasts with what you have just said. *Charles is fit and well. Not happy, mind you, just fit and well... Mind you, I have to be careful what I say.* ● If you say you **have a good mind** to do something, you mean that you would like to do it, although you will probably not do it. *I've a good mind to punish you for behaving so badly.* ● If you **put** your **mind** to something, you devote a lot of energy, effort, and attention to it. *You could get a job in London, if you put your mind to it.* ● If something **takes** your **mind off** a problem, it helps you to forget about it for a while. *Is there a way to take your mind off the situation?* ● If you are **in two minds** about something, you are uncertain whether or not to do it. *I was very much in two minds whether to apply for the Cambridge job.* ● If you see something **in** your **mind's eye**, you imagine it and have a clear picture of it in your mind. *In her mind's eye, she had pictured herself in the new house.* ● If you say that you **wouldn't mind** something, you mean that you would quite like it; an informal expression. *I wouldn't mind a Renault myself.* ● You say **never mind** to try and make someone feel better when they have suffered a minor disappointment. *Never mind, I'll be happy to buy it for you.* ● You also say **never mind** to indicate that something is not important, especially when someone is apologizing to you. *Some of their towels are soaking wet, but never mind.* ● You say **'Mind out'** as an urgent warning to someone that they are about to get hurt or to damage something. ● to **mind** your **own business**: see **business**. ● to **cross** your **mind**: see **cross**.

mind-blowing
ADJ Something that is **mind-blowing** is really astonishing; an informal word. *The effect was truly mind-blowing.*

mind-boggling
ADJ Something that is **mind-boggling** is so enormous or complicated that it is very hard to imagine; an informal word. *...mind-boggling wealth... The concept is mind-boggling.*

minded /maɪndɪd/
ADJ PRED If someone is **minded** to do something, they want or intend to do it; a formal word. *He can stop here if he is so minded.*

-minded /maɪndɪd/
1 SUFFIX **-minded** combines with adjectives to form new adjectives which describe the way a person thinks. *...some leading liberal-minded politicians... We look back at the life of this strong-minded individual.*
2 SUFFIX **-minded** combines with nouns to form adjectives that describe people who are interested in or concerned about a particular thing. *The incident gave him the opportunity to appoint reform-minded officers to top posts. ...two equally market-minded Prime Ministers.*

minder /maɪndə/ **minders**
1 NC+SUPP A **minder** is a person whose job is to look after someone, for example a child or an old person. *...a baby-minder. ...children looked after by child minders while their mothers worked.*
2 NC A **minder** is also a person whose job is to protect someone such as a businessman; an informal use. *...a host of bodyguards and minders. ...surrounded by a mob of burly minders.*
3 NC In some countries, a **minder** is a person assigned by the government to accompany or supervise foreign visitors. *Each of us was assigned a minder, someone who looked after visitors... I was able to get to people without the intervention of government minders.*

mindful /maɪndfl/
ADJ PRED If you are **mindful** of something, you remember it when taking action; a formal word. *Be mindful of the needs of others.*

mindless /maɪndləs/
1 ADJ ATTRIB **Mindless** actions are stupid and destructive. *...mindless violence. ...the mindless pollution of our cities.*
2 ADJ A **mindless** job or activity is so simple that you do not need to think about it. *...mindless routine tasks.*

mind reader, mind readers
NC A **mind reader** is a person who claims or seems to be able to know what people are thinking. *So in a sense—not being a mind reader—I'm not as knowledgeable as Mr Simmonds maybe thinks.*

mine /maɪn/ **mines, mining, mined**
1 PRON You use **mine** to indicate that something belongs or relates to you. *Margaret was a very old friend of mine... I took her hands in mine... He gave it to me, it's mine.*
2 NC A **mine** is a place where people dig deep holes or tunnels in order to obtain coal, diamonds, or other minerals. *...a coal mine... She found 673 retired miners who had worked in gold and uranium mines.*
3 VOorV To **mine** coal, diamonds, or other minerals means to obtain them from the ground by digging deep holes and tunnels. *They mine their own coal and ore. ... companies mining for gold.*
4 NC A **mine** is also a bomb hidden in the ground or floating on water which explodes when something touches it. *At least four people died when their jeep hit a land mine yesterday.*
5 See also **limpet mine, mining**.

minefield /maɪnfiːld/ **minefields**
1 NC A **minefield** is an area of land or water where explosive mines have been hidden. *The guerrillas had found it easy to lay minefields around its walls.*
2 NC If you describe a situation as a **minefield**, you mean that it is full of hidden dangers or problems. *Reform of local taxation in Britain has long been regarded as a political minefield which any sensible government should leave well alone.*

miner /maɪnə/ **miners**
NC A **miner** is a person who works underground in mines obtaining coal, diamonds, or other minerals. *My grandfather was a coal miner. ...last year's miners' strike.*

mineral /mɪnərəl/ **minerals**
1 NC A **mineral** is a substance such as tin, salt, uranium, or coal that is formed naturally in rocks and in the earth. *...a continent exceptionally wealthy in minerals. ...rich mineral deposits.*
2 NC **Minerals** are substances such as iron and sodium which are found in food and which your body needs. *Half the children took a daily tablet containing vitamins and minerals.*

mineralogy /mɪnərælədʒi/
NU **Mineralogy** is the scientific study of minerals such as tin, salt, uranium, or coal that are formed naturally in rocks and in the earth.

mineral water
N MASS **Mineral water** is water that comes out of the ground naturally and is often considered healthy to drink. *There are thousands of plastic bottles of mineral water. ...my favourite mineral water.*

minestrone /mɪnɪstrəʊni/
NU **Minestrone** or **minestrone soup** is a type of soup which is made from meat stock and contains small pieces of vegetables and pasta.

minesweeper /maɪnswiːpə/ **minesweepers**
NC A **minesweeper** is a ship that is used to clear away explosive mines in the sea. *French Navy minesweepers have found three mines, one floating on the surface.*

mingle /mɪŋgl/ **mingles, mingling, mingled**
1 V-RECIP When things **mingle**, they become mixed together. *Shops are open and smells and sounds mingle in the streets... His cries mingled with theirs... Sand and dust mingled with the blood.* ◆ **mingled** ADJ *John watched her with mingled dismay and pleasure.*
2 V If you **mingle**, you move among a group of people, chatting to different people. *Get out and mingle a bit... She invited me to drop in and mingle with the guests.*

mingy /mɪndʒi/ **mingier, mingiest**; an informal word.
1 ADJ Someone who is **mingy** is mean and unwilling to give or use very much of something. *She's rather mingy about food.*
2 ADJ Something that is **mingy** is smaller in size or amount than you expect or than you think is proper. *They gave us a mingy amount of cheese. ...a mingy profit.*

mini- /mɪni-/
PREFIX **Mini-** combines with nouns to form new nouns that refer to a smaller version of a particular thing. For example, a mini-computer is a computer which is smaller than a normal computer. *...the Chancellor's mini-budget.*

miniature /mɪnɪtʃə/ **miniatures**
1 ADJ ATTRIB A **miniature** thing is much smaller than other things of the same kind. *...tiny squares and miniature archways... They look like miniature sharks.*
2 If you describe one thing as another thing **in miniature**, you mean that it is much smaller than the other thing, but is otherwise exactly the same. *It was an Austrian chalet in miniature.*
3 NC A **miniature** is a very small detailed painting, often of a person. *I collect early English miniatures.*

miniaturize /mɪnɪtʃəraɪz/ **miniaturizes, miniaturizing, miniaturized**; also spelt **miniaturise.**
VO To **miniaturize** a machine means to produce a very small version of it. *We miniaturize spacecraft components.* ♦ **miniaturized** ADJ ATTRIB *...a miniaturized video recorder.* ♦ **miniaturization** /mɪnɪtʃəraɪzeɪʃn/ NU *...the miniaturization of electronic components.*

minibus /mɪnibʌs/ **minibuses**
NC A **minibus** is a van with seats in the back, which is used as a small bus. *We went to school by minibus.*

minicab /mɪnikæb/ **minicabs**
NC A **minicab** is a car which is used as a taxi but which is not specifically designed as one. Minicabs cannot be hailed in the street, but must be ordered by telephone or at the company's office. *...a minicab driver.*

minim /mɪnɪm/ **minims**
NC In music, a **minim** is a note that has a time value equal to two crotchets.

minimal /mɪnɪml/
ADJ Something that is **minimal** is very small in quantity or degree. *My knowledge of German was minimal... The United Nations has been bitterly criticised for its minimal involvement in the crisis so far.* ♦ **minimally** SUBMOD *His theories were only minimally more adequate than the ones they replaced.*

minimalism /mɪnɪməlɪzəm/
NU **Minimalism** is an artistic movement and philosophy whose followers try to show everything in as simple a form as possible. *...the minimalism of Philip Glass.*

minimalist /mɪnɪməlɪst/ **minimalists**
ADJ **Minimalist** art, music, or ideas attempt to show things in as simple and uncomplicated way as possible. *...in these days of minimalist aesthetics. ...a more minimalist approach.*

minimize /mɪnɪmaɪz/ **minimizes, minimizing, minimized**; also spelt **minimise.**
1 VO To **minimize** something means to reduce it to the lowest amount or degree possible, or prevent it increasing beyond that amount or degree. *Our aim must be to minimize the risks... Crop rotations will help to minimise disease.*
2 VO To **minimize** something also means to make it seem smaller or less important than it really is. *He was careful to minimise his role in these proceedings... It would be foolhardy to minimise or ignore the problems that existed.*

minimum /mɪnɪməm/
1 ADJ ATTRIB The **minimum** amount of something is the smallest that is possible or necessary. *You need a minimum deposit of $20,000. ...the minimum wage in industry.*
2 N SING The **minimum** is the smallest amount of something that is possible. *Two hundred pounds is the bare minimum... Practise each day for a minimum of twenty minutes... Nelson Mandela was welcomed at Nairobi with the minimum of fuss.*

mining /maɪnɪŋ/
NU **Mining** is the industry and activities connected with getting coal, diamonds, or other minerals from the ground. *...coal mining... The mining industry has suffered large-scale redundancies over the past year.*

minion /mɪnjən/ **minions**
NC A **minion** is a person who has a very unimportant job, especially one who carries out someone else's orders; a formal word. *He was brutal in dealing with his minions. ...the President's minions.*

mini-series /mɪnisɪəriːz/; **mini-series** is both the singular and the plural form.
NC A **mini-series** is a televised drama in three or four parts that is shown on consecutive days or weeks. *The mini-series and TV movies they produce generate much more income on foreign markets.*

mini-skirt /mɪniskɜːt/ **mini-skirts**
NC A **mini-skirt** is a very short skirt. Mini-skirts first became popular in the late 1960s. *Patterned pantyhose, tinted hair, mini-skirts, long nails and flashy jewelry are out.*

minister /mɪnɪstə/ **ministers, ministering, ministered**
1 NC A **minister** is a person in charge of a government department. *...the Minister for Scottish affairs... Each department will nominate a minister responsible for environmental policies.* ● See also **Prime Minister.**
2 NC A **minister** in a church, especially a Protestant church, is a member of the clergy. *...two methodist ministers. ...minister Richard Berneault, pastor of the Jubilee Christian Center in San José.*

minister to PHRASAL VERB If you **minister to** people or to their needs, you make sure that they have everything they need or want; a formal expression. *Think of a hospital, and I expect you see an image of cool, trim nurses in starched aprons, tenderly ministering to the sick.*

ministerial /mɪnɪstɪəriəl/
ADJ ATTRIB **Ministerial** means relating to a government minister or ministry. *We cannot afford a ministerial crisis... The options should be discussed at a future ministerial meeting planned by the two sides.*

ministrations /mɪnɪstreɪʃnz/
N PL | POSS A person's **ministrations** are the things that they do to help or care for someone in a particular situation, especially someone who is weak or ill; a formal word. *I thanked him for his spiritual ministrations.*

ministry /mɪnɪstri/ **ministries**
1 NC A **ministry** is a government department. *...the Ministry of Energy... The ministry will have no alternative but to cut its expenditure.*
2 NC The **ministry** of a religious person is the work that they do that is based on or inspired by their religious beliefs. *A remarkable old Irish priest whose ministry was the hospital... The central message of Christ's ministry was the concept of grace.*
3 N SING Members of the clergy belonging to some branches of the Christian church are referred to as the **ministry**. *Michael had intended to join the ministry.*

mink /mɪŋk/; **mink** is both the singular and the plural form.
1 NC **Mink** are small animals with short legs. Mink are bred for their beautiful fur. *It is fed to mink on fur farms.*
2 NU **Mink** is a very expensive fur used to make coats or hats. *...a woman in a mink coat.*

minnow /mɪnəʊ/ **minnows**
1 NC A **minnow** is a very small freshwater fish. *There seem to be some minnows and some duckweed.*
2 NC A **minnow** is also a small or insignificant person or thing. *Malta will be the smallest addition to the Community, tinier even than the current minnow of the European family, Luxembourg.*

minor /maɪnə/ **minors**
1 ADJ You use **minor** to describe something that is not as important, serious, or significant as other things. *For certain relatively minor offences, a term in prison can be commuted to a fine... Three police officers were treated for minor injuries. ...a rather minor artist.*
2 ADJ In European music, a **minor** scale is one in which the third note is three semitones higher than the first. *...Chopin's Scherzo in B flat minor.*
3 NC A **minor** is a person who is still legally a child. In Britain, people are minors until they reach the age of eighteen; a formal use. *...better methods to identify minors so they can't so easily buy alcohol... No unaccompanied minors allowed.*

minority /mɪnɒrəti/ **minorities**
1 N SING A **minority** of people or things in a group is

less than half of the whole group. *Only a small minority of children get a chance to benefit from this system.* ● If a group is **in a minority** or **in the minority**, they form less than half of a larger group. *Artistic people are in a tiny minority in this country.*
2 NC A **minority** is a group of people of a particular race or religion who live in a place where most of the people are of another race or religion. *Seventy percent of the children at the school come from ethnic minorities... Little has happened to justify the fears of the minorities.*

Minsk /mɪnsk/
Minsk is the capital of Byelorussia and its largest city. In 1991 it became the capital of the Commonwealth of Independent States. Population: 1,612,000 (1989).

minstrel /mɪnstrəl/ **minstrels**
NC In medieval times, a **minstrel** was a singer and musician who used to travel around and perform to noble families. *Minstrels would go from town to town producing, in essence, variety shows.*

mint /mɪnt/ **mints, minting, minted**
1 NU **Mint** is a type of herb used in cooking. *...a sprig of mint. ...mint tea.*
2 NC A **mint** is a sweet with a peppermint flavour. *...a packet of mints.*
3 N SING The place where a country's official coins are made is called its **mint**. *The Mint has decided to issue the new coins next year.*
4 VO When coins or medals **are minted**, they are made in a mint. *One of the coins, dated 1693, was minted in Portuguese Africa.*
5 If something is **in mint condition**, it is in very good condition, as if it was new. *Discovered only recently, it was in mint condition, packed in its original box.*

mint julep /mɪnt dʒuːlɪp/ **mint juleps**
NC A **mint julep** is an alcoholic drink made from rye whiskey, sugar, ice, and mint leaves. *We made mint juleps and drank them in the garden.*

mint sauce
NU **Mint sauce** is a sauce made from vinegar, mint leaves, and sugar. It is often eaten with lamb.

minus /maɪnəs/
1 PREP You use **minus** to show that one number is being subtracted from another, for example 'five minus three'. In arithmetic, you represent this in figures as '5 - 3'. *Gilbert's compensation is $1 million, minus $5,000 in fines.*
2 ADJ ATTRIB **Minus** is also used to indicate that a number is less than zero. For example, a temperature of **minus** four is four degrees below zero. *Temperatures there are colder than minus 20°C.*
3 **plus or minus**: see plus.

minuscule /mɪnəskjuːl/
ADJ Something that is **minuscule** is very small indeed. *There is minuscule danger to population centres... The numbers returning by this particular route are of course minuscule.*

minus sign, minus signs
NC A **minus sign** is the sign (-) which is put between two numbers to show that the second number is being subtracted from the first, or which is put in front of a number that is less than zero.

minute, minutes; pronounced /mɪnɪt/ when it is a noun and /maɪnjuːt/ when it is an adjective.
1 NC A **minute** is one of the sixty equal parts of an hour. *Davis was ten minutes late... An accident had taken place only a few minutes before.*
2 N PL The **minutes** of a meeting are the written records of what is said or decided. *You must learn how to take minutes.*
3 ADJ Something that is **minute** is extremely small. *...a substance that occurs naturally in our bodies in minute quantities... I had remembered in minute detail everything that had happened.*
4 ADJ ATTRIB A **minute** examination or study is very careful, with great attention paid to every detail. *They will have to carry out a minute examination of the debris.*
● **Minute** is used in these phrases. ● A **minute** is often used to mean a short time. *Will you excuse me if I sit down for a minute?... Wait there a minute.* ● If you do something **the minute** something else happens, you do

it as soon as the other thing happens. *Ask for help the minute you're stuck.* ● If you say that something must be done **this minute**, you mean that it must be done immediately. *She doesn't have to make a decision this minute.* ● If you say that something will happen at **any minute**, you mean that it is likely to happen very soon. *Mrs Curry was going to cry any minute.* ● **at the last minute**: see last-minute.

minutely /maɪnjuːtli/
1 ADV If you examine something **minutely**, you examine it very carefully, paying attention to every detail. *She began examining it minutely from all angles.*
2 ADV **Minutely** also means very slightly. *His fingers trembled minutely.*

minutiae /maɪnjuːʃiiː/
N PL **Minutiae** are small, unimportant details; a formal word. *He has little time for the minutiae of the game.*

miracle /mɪrəkl/ **miracles**
1 NC A **miracle** is a surprising and fortunate event, discovery, or invention. *His policies created the climate for the economic miracle. ...the miracle of modern communications.*
2 NC A **miracle** is also a wonderful and surprising event that is believed to be caused by God. *Millions of pilgrims want to believe in the miracle.*

miraculous /mɪrækjuləs/
1 ADJ **Miraculous** means very surprising and fortunate. *I had been expecting some miraculous change to occur.* ◆ **miraculously** ADV or ADV SEN *The door miraculously opened... It seemed, miraculously, that everyone was satisfied.*
2 ADJ **Miraculous** is also used to describe wonderful events that are believed to be caused by God. *...the miraculous powers of the saint.*

mirage /mɪrɑːʒ/ **mirages**
1 NC A **mirage** is an image which you see in the distance or in the air in very hot weather, but which does not actually exist. *...a mirage vibrating on the horizon.*
2 NC A **mirage** is also something in the future that you look forward to, but that never actually happens. *The promised land turns out to be a mirage... Maybe it was only a mirage of peace.*

mire /maɪə/
N SING+SUPP You can refer to an unpleasant or difficult situation as a **mire**; a literary word. *...the mire of militarism, tension, and war... Nothing he could do would stop the country sliding ever deeper into an economic mire.*

mirror /mɪrə/ **mirrors, mirroring, mirrored**
1 NC A **mirror** is a flat piece of glass which reflects light, so that you can see yourself in it. *She stared at herself in the mirror.*
2 VO If you see something reflected in water, you can say that the water **mirrors** it; a literary use. *The clear water mirrored the blue sky.*
3 VO To **mirror** something also means to have similar features to it and therefore to seem like a copy of it; a formal use. *The clash in personalities is mirrored by their very different chess styles... The success of her writing career was not mirrored in her private life.*

mirror image, mirror images
NC If one thing is a **mirror image** of another thing, it is like a reflection of it, either because it is exactly the same or because it is the same but reversed. *Here I would say the situation is a mirror image of that in the West... The room beyond proved to be a mirror image of the first room.*

mirth /mɜːθ/
NU **Mirth** is amusement and laughter; a literary word. *His anger gave place to mirth.*

mis- /mɪs-/
PREFIX **Mis-** combines with verbs and nouns to form new verbs and nouns which indicate that something is done badly or wrongly. For example, if you mismanage something, you manage it badly. *He had misjudged the situation. ...the misuse of psychiatry.*

misadventure /mɪsədvɛntʃə/ **misadventures**
N C or NU A **misadventure** is an unfortunate incident; a formal word. *...a funny story about a friend's*

misadventure. ...a verdict of death by misadventure.

misanthrope /mɪsnθrəʊp/ **misanthropes**
NC A **misanthrope** is a person who does not like other people; a formal word. *I have a dread of being thought a misanthrope.*

misanthropic /mɪsnθrɒpɪk/
ADJ **Misanthropic** behaviour is behaviour which shows that a person does not like other people; a formal word. *...some gruff and misanthropic authority figure.*

misanthropy /mɪsænθrəpi/
NU **Misanthropy** is dislike of other people; a formal word. *He felt himself plunging into misanthropy.*

misapprehend /mɪsæprɪhɛnd/ **misapprehends, misapprehending, misapprehended**
VO If you **misapprehend** something, you understand it wrongly; a formal word. *It is all too easy to misapprehend its nature.*

misapprehension /mɪsæprɪhɛnʃn/ **misapprehensions**
NCorNU A **misapprehension** is a wrong idea or impression. *I was still under a misapprehension as to the threat contained in the letter... It would give rise to immediate misapprehension.*

misappropriate /mɪsəprəʊprieɪt/ **misappropriates, misappropriating, misappropriated**
VO If someone **misappropriates** money or other valuable things which are not theirs, they take them and use them for their own purposes; a formal word. *I took no money for personal use and have not misappropriated any funds whatsoever... Vehicles and drugs have been misappropriated by government officials.* ◆ **misappropriation** /mɪsəprəʊprieɪʃn/ NU *He had been held responsible for the misappropriation of certain funds.*

misbehave /mɪsbɪheɪv/ **misbehaves, misbehaving, misbehaved**
V If someone, especially a child, **misbehaves**, they behave in a way that is not acceptable to other people. *When children misbehave, their parents shouldn't become angry.*

misbehaviour /mɪsbɪheɪvjə/; spelt **misbehavior** in American English.
NU **Misbehaviour** is behaviour that is not acceptable to other people. *They don't feel they can complain to a mother about her child's misbehaviour.*

miscalculate /mɪskælkjʊleɪt/ **miscalculates, miscalculating, miscalculated**
VorVO If you **miscalculate**, you make a mistake in judging a situation. *The paper suggests he has miscalculated... She had badly miscalculated the public's mood.*

miscalculation /mɪskælkjʊleɪʃn/ **miscalculations**
NCorNU A **miscalculation** is a mistake in judging a situation. *These miscalculations had serious consequences. ...the risks of miscalculation.*

miscarriage /mɪskærɪdʒ/ **miscarriages**
NC If a woman has a **miscarriage**, she gives birth to a foetus before it is properly formed and it dies. *She runs the risk of having a miscarriage or of bearing a child with mental and physical handicaps.*

miscarriage of justice, miscarriages of justice
NC A **miscarriage of justice** is a wrong decision made by a court, which has the result that an innocent person is punished. *Amnesty described the death sentences as a gross miscarriage of justice. ...one of the greatest miscarriages of justice in British legal history.*

miscarry /mɪskæri/ **miscarries, miscarrying, miscarried**
1 V If a woman **miscarries**, she has a miscarriage. *The hormone DES was given to two and a half million women in an effort to keep them from miscarrying.*
2 V If a plan **miscarries**, it goes wrong and fails. *Our scheme had miscarried.*

miscast /mɪskɑːst/
ADJ If someone who is acting in a play is **miscast**, the role that they have is not suitable for them. *Jose Garcia also seemed somewhat miscast as Roger.*

miscellaneous /mɪsəleɪnɪəs/
ADJ A **miscellaneous** group consists of people or things that are very different from each other. *...miscellaneous enemies of authority. ...a miscellaneous collection of tools.*

miscellany /mɪsɛləni/ **miscellanies**
NCorNU A **miscellany** is a collection or group of things that are very different from each other; a formal word. *The room was filled with a miscellany of objects. ...four pages of miscellany.*

mischance /mɪstʃɑːns/ **mischances**; a formal word.
1 NU **Mischance** is bad luck. *This might have been the merest mischance.*
2 NC A **mischance** is something that happens to you that is unlucky for you. *Deprivation is a common mischance. ...a series of mischances.*

mischief /mɪstʃɪf/
1 NU **Mischief** is eagerness to have fun, especially by embarrassing people or by playing tricks. *Her face was kind, her eyes full of mischief... There was about him an air of mischief.*
2 NU **Mischief** is also naughty behaviour by children. *He was old enough to get into mischief.*
3 NU **Mischief** is also behaviour that is intended to cause trouble between people. *The author's fanatical anti-communism coupled with his apparent desire to create mischief mean that his book should be read with caution.*

mischief-maker, mischief-makers
NC A **mischief-maker** is a person who says or does things which are intended to cause trouble between people. *She dismissed Sorel as a muddle-headed mischief-maker... The worst mischief-makers had been transferred elsewhere.*

mischievous /mɪstʃɪvəs/
1 ADJ A **mischievous** person is eager to have fun, especially by embarrassing people or by playing tricks. *She laughed and looked mischievous. ...a mischievous smile.* ◆ **mischievously** ADV *Kitty winked mischievously.*
2 ADJ A **mischievous** child or animal is often naughty. *At forty he still has the air of a mischievous schoolboy. ...a mischievous but lovable child.*
3 ADJ You also use **mischievous** to describe a person who intends to cause trouble between people, or to describe something such as a report or plan which is intended to cause trouble. *...an idle, mischievous woman... Mr Kinnock described the report as 'mischievous fiction'.*

misconceived /mɪskənsiːvd/
ADJ A **misconceived** plan or method is the wrong one for a particular situation and is therefore not likely to succeed. *Their whole approach was misconceived.*

misconception /mɪskənsɛpʃn/ **misconceptions**
NC A **misconception** is an idea that is not correct or that has been misunderstood. *Another misconception is that cancer is infectious. ...a popular misconception.*

misconduct /mɪskɒndʌkt/
NU **Misconduct** is bad or unacceptable behaviour, especially by a professional person. *They were victims of government misconduct... There was insufficient evidence to discipline the two doctors for incompetence or professional misconduct.*

misconstruction /mɪskənstrʌkʃn/ **misconstructions**
NCorNU A **misconstruction** is a wrong interpretation of something that happens or something that is said; a formal word. *There may be some error or misconstruction... The last scene is open to misconstruction.*

misconstrue /mɪskənstruː/ **misconstrues, misconstruing, misconstrued**
VO If you **misconstrue** something that happens or something that is said, you interpret it wrongly; a formal word. *I said something that might have been misconstrued as an apology... You know how things get misconstrued in a small community.*

misdeed /mɪsdiːd/ **misdeeds**
NC A **misdeed** is a bad or evil act; a formal word. *They had profited by his misdeeds... They tend to blame society for individual misdeeds.*

misdemeanour /mɪsdɪmiːnə/ **misdemeanours**; spelt **misdemeanor** in American English.
1 NC A **misdemeanour** is an act that people consider to be shocking or unacceptable; a formal use. *They listened to accounts of his misdemeanours.*
2 NC In countries where the legal system distinguishes between very serious crimes and less serious ones, a

misdemeanour is a less serious crime; a legal use. *He was charged with two misdemeanors; assaulting a police officer and resisting arrest... Under Greek law this means they're classified as misdemeanours and not under the more serious category of felonies.*

misdirect /mɪsdərɛkt/ **misdirects, misdirecting, misdirected**
1 vo If someone's energy or qualities **are misdirected**, they are used wrongly or inappropriately; a formal use. *Those qualities of leadership could be misdirected.* ◆ **misdirected** ADJ ATTRIB *This replacement of the mother's breast by the multinationals' tin can is one of the saddest examples of misdirected 'modernization'.*
2 vo If you **misdirect** someone, you send them to the wrong place. *Passengers for half a dozen flights had been misdirected to the same gate.*

miser /maɪzə/ **misers**
NC A **miser** is a person who enjoys saving money and hates spending it; used showing disapproval. *She had married a miser.*

miserable /mɪzə⁰rəbl/
1 ADJ If you are **miserable**, you are very unhappy. *Rudolph felt depressed and miserable... They all had miserable faces.* ◆ **miserably** ADV *He looked up miserably.*
2 ADJ A **miserable** place or situation makes you feel depressed. *Being without a grant is really miserable... They are trapped in miserable conditions.*
3 ADJ You say the weather is **miserable** when it is raining or dull. *...a miserable Monday morning... It was a wet miserable day.*

miserly /maɪzəli/
ADJ **Miserly** people are very mean and hate spending money. *...a miserly old lady.*

misery /mɪzə⁰ri/ **miseries**
NUorNC **Misery** is great unhappiness. *They have personal experience of the human misery caused by massive earthquakes... Droughts and cyclones have periodically hit the island adding to its miseries.*

misfire /mɪsfaɪə/ **misfires, misfiring, misfired**
v If a plan **misfires**, it goes wrong. *The use of force in support of their demands had misfired.*

misfit /mɪsfɪt/ **misfits**
NC A **misfit** is a person who is not easily accepted by other people, often because their behaviour is very different from everyone else's. *In such societies there have always been misfits.*

misfortune /mɪsfɔːtʃuːn/ **misfortunes**
NCorNU A **misfortune** is something very undesirable that happens to you. *The father suffered two misfortunes: at roughly the same time, he lost his money and his eyesight... They had suffered their share of misfortune.*

misgiving /mɪsgɪvɪŋ/ **misgivings**
N PLorNU If you have **misgivings** about something, or if you do it with **misgivings** or with **misgiving**, you are worried or unhappy about it. *Many of them do indeed have serious misgivings... The legislation was approved despite deep misgivings at the Pentagon... I was filled with misgiving about the whole venture.*

misguided /mɪsgaɪdɪd/
ADJ **Misguided** opinions and attitudes are wrong, because they are based on wrong information or beliefs. *...Sir Terence's view was misguided. ...misguided idealism.*

mishandle /mɪshændl/ **mishandles, mishandling, mishandled**
vo If you **mishandle** something, you deal with it badly or inefficiently. *The Koreans felt the referee had mishandled the whole match... The government badly mishandled an opposition rally in July.* ◆ **mishandling** NU *...his mishandling of the relief aid.*

mishap /mɪshæp/ **mishaps**
NCorNU A **mishap** is an unfortunate but not very serious event that happens to you. *The selection process ensures that no mishaps can occur... Tell your mother you have arrived here without mishap.*

mishear /mɪshɪə/ **mishears, mishearing, misheard** /mɪshɜːd/
vOorv If you **mishear** what someone says, you do not hear properly, so that you think they say something

different from what they really say. *I was sure I had misheard her question.*

misinform /mɪsɪnfɔːm/ **misinforms, misinforming, misinformed**
vo If you **are misinformed**, you are told something that is wrong or inaccurate. *Unfortunately we were misinformed about the purpose of the fund.*

misinformation /mɪsɪnfəmeɪʃn/
NU **Misinformation** is incorrect information which is deliberately given to people in order to deceive them. *He can give his account of the web of lies, misinformation and deception that has gone on there for many years.*

misinterpret /mɪsɪntɜːprɪt/ **misinterprets, misinterpreting, misinterpreted**
vo If you **misinterpret** something, you understand it wrongly. *He saw the smile and misinterpreted it as friendliness.* ◆ **misinterpretation**, /mɪsɪntɜːprɪteɪʃn/ **misinterpretations** NUorNC *The new version was less open to misinterpretation... The book was dismissed as 'a pot-pourri of maliciously selected misrepresentations, misinterpretations, fabrications and disinformation'.*

misjudge /mɪsdʒʌdʒ/ **misjudges, misjudging, misjudged**
vo If you **misjudge** someone or something, you form an incorrect idea or opinion about them, and often make a wrong decision about them as a result. *I had rather misjudged the timing... The companies seriously misjudged the market for plastics.*

misjudgement /mɪsdʒʌdʒmənt/ **misjudgements**; also spelt **misjudgment**.
NCorNU A **misjudgement** is the forming of an incorrect idea or opinion about someone or something, especially when you then make a wrong decision as a result. *Such expectations seem, however, to have been based on a misjudgement of the prevailing mood in the Islamic world... He admitted misjudgment and lack of action.*

mislay /mɪsleɪ/ **mislays, mislaying, mislaid**
vo If you **mislay** something, you lose it, because you put it somewhere and then forget where it is. *Vital documents have been mislaid. ...baggage previously missing or mislaid.*

mislead /mɪsliːd/ **misleads, misleading, misled** /mɪsled/
vo If you **mislead** someone, you make them believe something which is not true. *He accused the Prime Minister of deliberately misleading people about the Community... The public has been misled.* ◆ **misleading** ADJ *...misleading information... He said the comparisons were groundless and misleading.*

mismanage /mɪsmænɪdʒ/ **mismanages, mismanaging, mismanaged**
vo To **mismanage** something means to manage it badly. *The local people thought that education was being mismanaged.*

mismanagement /mɪsmænɪdʒmənt/
NU If there is **mismanagement** of something such as a system or organization, it is being organized or dealt with badly. *Economic mismanagement and corruption have taken their toll.*

misnamed /mɪsneɪmd/
ADJ Something that is **misnamed** has a name that describes it badly or incorrectly. *...the grotesquely misnamed National Government.*

misnomer /mɪsnəumə/ **misnomers**
NC A **misnomer** is a word or expression that describes something wrongly or inaccurately; a formal word. *A cave is perhaps a misnomer—they're really barrel-vaulted tunnels.*

misogynist /maɪsɒdʒənɪst/ **misogynists**
NC A **misogynist** is a man who hates women; a formal word. *He quickly gained the reputation of being a misogynist.*

misplaced /mɪspleɪst/
ADJ A **misplaced** feeling or action is inappropriate, or is directed towards the wrong thing or person. *...misplaced loyalties... The army says the objections are misplaced.*

misprint /mɪsprɪnt/ **misprints**
NC A **misprint** is a mistake in the way something is

printed, for example a spelling mistake.

mispronounce /mɪsprənaʊns/ **mispronounces, mispronouncing, mispronounced**
vo If you **mispronounce** a word, you pronounce it wrongly. *All babies start out mispronouncing most of the words that they use, and gradually improve.*

mispronunciation /mɪsprənʌnsɪeɪʃn/ **mispronunciations**
NCorNU A **mispronunciation** is a wrong pronunciation of a word. *Other mispronunciations seem to be due to quirks in the child's feelings.*

misquote /mɪskwəʊt/ **misquotes, misquoting, misquoted**
vo If you **misquote** someone or what someone has said or written, you repeat inaccurately what they have said or written. *He said that he had been misquoted and that Britain's position remained the same... The paper has often misrepresented or misquoted his statements on when a recovery is likely to occur... He began to misquote Shakespeare.*

misread, misreads, misreading. The form **misread** is used in the present tense, when it is pronounced /mɪsriːd/, and is also the past tense and past participle, when it is pronounced /mɪsred/.
1 vo If you **misread** a situation or someone's behaviour, you do not understand it properly. *Their behaviour was usually misread as indifference... He was unconsciously misreading their actions.*
2 vo If you **misread** something that has been written or printed, you look at it and think that it says something that it does not say. *She had misread a date in the Tour Book.*

misrepresent /mɪsreprɪzent/ **misrepresents, misrepresenting, misrepresented**
vo If you **misrepresent** someone, you give a wrong account of what they have said or written. *Witnesses claim to have been seriously misrepresented... He says that I have misrepresented his views.*
♦ **misrepresentation** /mɪsreprɪzenteɪʃn/ **misrepresentations** NUorNC *All political policies are open to misrepresentation... That's a complete misrepresentation.*

misrule /mɪsruːl/ **misrules, misruling, misruled**
vo To **misrule** a country means to govern it unfairly or inefficiently. *They misuse their powers and misrule our country.* ► Also NU ...*petty tyrants whose subjects groan under their misrule.*

miss /mɪs/ **misses, missing, missed**
1 TITLE You use **Miss** in front of the name of a girl or unmarried woman. *Good morning, Miss Haynes... Miss Garrison will now play the winners.*
2 vo If you **miss** something, you fail to notice it. *He doesn't miss much... You can't miss it, it's on the first floor.*
3 vOorV If you **miss** something, you fail to hit it. *He missed the ball at the first swipe... One bullet had narrowly missed his spinal chord... They expect the storm to miss the northern half of Britain... She had thrown her plate at his head and missed.*
4 NC A **miss** is a failure to hit something.
5 vo If you **miss** someone, you feel sad because they are no longer with you. If you **miss** something, you feel sad because you no longer have it or are no longer experiencing it. *I shall miss my colleagues very much... I knew I should miss living in the Transkei.*
6 vo If you **miss** a chance or opportunity, you fail to take advantage of it. *Liverpool missed their chance to go back to the top of the First Division, losing one-nil to Tottenham... People tried to make sure they didn't miss the opportunity of being allowed to travel abroad.*
7 vo If you **miss** a bus, plane, or train, you arrive too late to catch it. *She was going to miss her plane if her husband didn't hurry... A trainee flight attendant in Nancy missed the early morning flight because she overslept.*
8 vo If you **miss** something such as a meeting, you do not go to it. *I couldn't miss a departmental meeting... The injury means that Johnson will miss six races in Europe next month.*
9 If you **give** something **a miss**, you decide not to do it or not to go to it; an informal expression. *I'd advise you to give it a miss... Senator Gore deliberately gave*

Iowa a miss and campaigned only intermittently in New Hampshire.
10 See also **hit and miss, hit or miss, missing, near miss**.

miss out PHRASAL VERB 1 If you **miss out** something or someone, you do not include them. *You can miss out a surprising number of words and still be understood.* 2 If you **miss out** on something interesting or useful, you do not become involved in it or do not have it, when other people do. *Thailand does not want to miss out on any opportunities.*

misshapen /mɪsʃeɪpn/
ADJ Something that is **misshapen** does not have a normal or natural shape. *Her misshapen old fingers twitched at her beads.*

missile /mɪsaɪl/ **missiles**
1 NC A **missile** is a weapon that moves for long distances through the air and explodes when it reaches its target. ...*nuclear missiles... The two countries resumed missile attacks on each other's cities yesterday.*
2 NC Anything that is thrown as a weapon can be called a **missile**. *Demonstrators attacked police using sticks and assorted missiles.*

missing /mɪsɪŋ/
1 ADJ If someone or something is **missing**, they are not where you expect them to be, and you cannot find them. *The crew of the helicopter had been declared missing, presumed dead... I want to report a missing person... Some of her jewellery was missing.*
2 ADJ If a part of something is **missing**, it has been removed and has not been replaced. *The car was a wreck, with all its wheels missing.*

missing link, missing links
NC The **missing link** is the piece of information or evidence that you need in order to make your knowledge or understanding of something complete. *Suddenly, this week, the missing link fell into place.*

mission /mɪʃn/ **missions**
1 NC A **mission** is an important task that you are given to do, especially one that involves travelling to another country. ...*confidential missions to Berlin.*
2 NC A **mission** is also a group of people who have been sent to a foreign country to carry out an official task. *He became head of the Ugandan mission.*
3 NC A **mission** is also a special journey made by a military aeroplane or space rocket. ...*a bombing mission.*
4 N SINGorNU If you have a **mission**, there is something that you believe it is your duty to try to achieve. ...*one of those girls who had a mission in life... Her father's execution fuelled her sense of mission.*
5 NC A **mission** is also the activities of a group of Christians who have been sent to a place to teach people about Christianity. ...*evangelistic missions around Britain.*
6 NC A **mission** is also a building or group of buildings in which missionaries work or live. ...*Ombachi Mission... He was educated at a local mission school.*

missionary /mɪʃənəri/ **missionaries**
NC A **missionary** is a person who has been sent to a foreign country to teach people about his or her religion. *He had been educated by the missionaries... He was born in Tokyo to missionary parents.*

missive /mɪsɪv/ **missives**
NC A **missive** is a letter or other message that someone sends; a literary word. *I accepted this gloomy missive as gravely as I could.*

misspell /mɪsspel/ **misspells, misspelling, misspelled** or **misspelt** /mɪsspelt/
vo If you **misspell** a word, you spell it wrongly. *The name, she noticed, was misspelled... Each misspelt word should be put right immediately.*

misspend /mɪsspend/ **misspends, misspending, misspent** /mɪsspent/
vo If you say that someone has **misspent** time or money, you mean that they have wasted it or not used it properly. *I'll tell him about my misspent life... They have misspent their scarce funds on facilities that nobody needs.*

mist /mɪst/ **mists, misting, misted**
NUorNC **Mist** consists of many tiny drops of water in

the air. When there is a mist, you cannot see very far. *Everything was shrouded in mist. ...the mists of early morning.*

mist over or **mist up** PHRASAL VERB When a piece of glass **mists over** or **mists up**, it becomes covered with tiny drops of moisture, so that you cannot see through it easily. *His spectacles misted over.*

mistake /mɪsteɪk/ **mistakes, mistaking, mistook** /mɪstʊk/ **mistaken** /mɪsteɪkən/

1 NC If you make a **mistake**, you do something which you did not intend to do, or which produces a result that you do not want. *He had made a terrible mistake... The World Bank has clearly learned from past mistakes... They made the mistake of not giving them any land of their own. ...a spelling mistake.*

2 VO+*for* If you **mistake** one person or thing for another, you wrongly think that they are the other person or thing. *Members of an army patrol mistook him for the gunman... You mustn't mistake lack of formal education for lack of wisdom.*

3 VO If you **mistake** something such as a name or address, you are wrong about it. *At first he thought he had mistaken the address.*

● **Mistake** is used in these phrases. ● If you do something which you did not intend to do, you can say that you did it **by mistake**. *I opened the door into the library by mistake.* ● If you say **there is no mistaking** something, you mean that you cannot fail to recognize or understand it. *There was no mistaking the intense annoyance it caused him... Certainly there is no mistaking the firm message being sent by the international community.*

mistaken /mɪsteɪkən/

1 ADJ PRED If you are **mistaken** about something, you are wrong about it. *I told her she must be mistaken... How could she have been mistaken about a thing like this?... I had been mistaken in believing Nick was mad.*

2 ADJ A **mistaken** belief or opinion is incorrect. *I think this is a mistaken view... Labour's trade spokesman, Mr Gordon Brown, said the deficit was the result of what he called the mistaken policy of a failed government.* ◆ **mistakenly** ADV *The parents may mistakenly believe that they are to blame for their child's illness.*

3 When someone incorrectly thinks that they have found or recognized a person who they have been looking for or who they know, you refer to this as a case of **mistaken identity**. *Police are working on the theory that the shooting was a case of mistaken identity.*

mister /mɪstə/. See **Mr**.

mistime /mɪstaɪm/ **mistimes, mistiming, mistimed**

VO If you **mistime** something, you do it at the wrong time, so that it is not successful. *He had mistimed his operations... There are disastrous results if the farmer mistimes the planting of his crops.*

mistletoe /mɪsltəʊ/

NU **Mistletoe** is an evergreen plant which grows as a parasite on many types of trees. It has white berries and is used in Britain as a Christmas decoration. *...the tradition of kissing under the mistletoe... Holly, like ivy and mistletoe, is an evergreen.*

mistook /mɪstʊk/

Mistook is the past tense of **mistake**.

mistreat /mɪstriːt/ **mistreats, mistreating, mistreated**

VO If you **mistreat** a person or an animal, you treat them badly, especially by making them suffer physically. *He claimed to have been mistreated while in police custody... No animal was killed or mistreated for the purpose of making this film.*

mistress /mɪstrəs/ **mistresses**

1 NC A married man's **mistress** is a woman other than his wife with whom he is having a sexual relationship. *He was accompanied everywhere by a young mistress half his age. ...the husband's mistress.*

2 NC A **mistress** in a school is a female schoolteacher. *...the French mistress.*

mistrust /mɪstrʌst/ **mistrusts, mistrusting, mistrusted**

1 NU **Mistrust** is the feeling that you have towards someone who you do not trust. *She gazed on me with*

a sudden fear and mistrust... *These events, of course, will only increase mistrust of the authorities.*

2 VO If you **mistrust** someone or something, you do not trust them. *Marshall deeply mistrusted Jefferson... The child soon learns to mistrust offers of affection.*

mistrustful /mɪstrʌstfl/

ADJ If you are **mistrustful** of someone or their actions, you do not trust them. *He was innately mistrustful of everyone and everything.*

misty /mɪsti/

ADJ If it is **misty**, there is a lot of mist in the air. *The night was cold and misty.*

misunderstand /mɪsʌndəstænd/ **misunderstands, misunderstanding, misunderstood** /mɪsʌndəstʊd/

VOorV If you **misunderstand** someone, you do not understand properly what they say or write. *Mr Lawson insisted that he'd been misunderstood by the journalists... She misunderstood my question... You have completely misunderstood.*

misunderstanding /mɪsʌndəstændɪŋ/ **misunderstandings**

1 NCorNU A **misunderstanding** is a failure to understand something. *This was a minor misunderstanding which could be instantly cleared up. ...a source of suspicion and misunderstanding.*

2 NC If two people have a **misunderstanding**, they have a disagreement or a slight quarrel. *They usually sort out their misunderstandings.*

misuse, misuses, misusing, misused; pronounced /mɪsjuːs/ when it is a noun and /mɪsjuːz/ when it is a verb.

1 NUorNC The **misuse** of something is incorrect, careless, or dishonest use of it. *...the misuse of company funds... She cared deeply about words, and hated their misuse. ...a special ministerial group looking at alcohol misuse.*

2 VO If you **misuse** something, you use it incorrectly, carelessly, or dishonestly. *In some cases, pesticides are deliberately misused. ...accusations that government ministers had misused agricultural funds... He campaigned against officials misusing diplomatic privilege for espionage purposes.*

Mitchell, James /dʒeɪmz mɪtʃəl/

James Mitchell became Prime Minister of St Vincent and the Grenadines in 1984. He is the founder of the New Democratic Party (NDP). He became an MP in 1966. He served as Minister of Trade, Agriculture, Labour, and Tourism from 1967 to 1972, and was Premier of St Vincent from 1972 to 1974. Born: 1931.

mite /maɪt/ **mites**

1 N SING A **mite** of something is a very small amount of it; an old-fashioned use. *Anybody with a mite of common sense could see how useless it was... The old lady won't be a mite of trouble.* ● If someone or something is **a mite** old, **a mite** too big, and so on, they are rather old, rather too big, and so on; an old-fashioned, informal expression. *I admit to feeling a mite sentimental as she crossed the threshold... I have a bed a mite softer than this one.*

2 NC **Mites** are very tiny creatures that live on plants or animals. *As its name implies the house dust mite lives in the dust in houses. ...red spider mites.*

3 NC You can also refer to a small child, especially one that you feel sorry for, as a **mite**; an informal use. *It's cruel on the poor little mite.*

mitigate /mɪtɪgeɪt/ **mitigates, mitigating, mitigated**

VO To **mitigate** something means to make it less unpleasant, serious, or painful; a formal word. *They should endeavour to mitigate distress... They have worked on ways of mitigating the worst effects of the drought... The government attempted to mitigate the petrol increases by raising salaries.*

mitigating /mɪtɪgeɪtɪŋ/

ADJ ATTRIB **Mitigating** circumstances are reasons that explain why a crime was committed, which are told to a court in the hope that the person who committed the crime will receive a lighter punishment; a legal term. *They may deny the offence or plead mitigating circumstances.*

mitigation /mɪtɪgeɪʃn/

1 If a court is told something **in mitigation**, it is told

something that makes a crime easier to understand and excuse, usually in the hope that the person who committed the crime will receive a lighter punishment; a legal expression. *In mitigation, she could offer evidence of a deprived childhood... Mr Bertram tendered a plea in mitigation.*
2 NU **Mitigation** is a reduction in the unpleasantness, seriousness, or painfulness of something; a formal use. *Some partial mitigation had occurred, but the situation was still regarded as critical. ...earthquake mitigation measures.*

mitre /maɪtə/ **mitres**; also spelt **miter** in American English.
NC A **mitre** is a tall pointed hat that is worn by bishops and archbishops on ceremonial occasions. *He was wearing an impressive new cope and mitre.*

Mitsotakis, Konstantinos /kɒnstændiːnɒs miːtsəutækɪs/
Konstantinos Mitsotakis became Prime Minister of Greece in 1990. He was MP for Chania from 1946 to 1974, and was re-elected in 1977. He served as Minister for Economic Co-ordination from 1978 to 1980, and for Foreign Affairs from 1980 to 1981. He became the leader of the New Democracy Party (ND) in 1984. Born: 1918.

mitt /mɪt/ **mitts**
1 NC **Mitts** are the same as **mittens**; an informal use.
2 NC You can refer to a person's hands as their **mitts**; an informal use. *Keep your mitts off it!*
3 NC In baseball, a **mitt** is a glove that players wear to help them catch the ball. *I love this mitt—it's lasted me eight years... He catches fly balls with a casual flick of his mitt.*

mitten /mɪtn/ **mittens**
NC **Mittens** are gloves which have one section that covers your thumb and another section for all your fingers. *...mittens and scarves.*

Mitterrand, François /frɒnˤswa: miːtərɒnˤ/
François Mitterrand became President of France in 1981. He was active in the French Resistance in the Second World War and served as the Deputy for Nièvre in the National Assembly from 1946 to 1958 and from 1962 to 1981. He is a member of the Socialist Party (PS). He was Minister of the Interior from 1954 to 1955, and for Justice from 1956 to 1957. Born: 1916.

mix /mɪks/ **mixes, mixing, mixed**
1 V-ERG or V-RECIP If you **mix** two substances, you stir or shake them together. *The mug had been used for mixing flour and water... They drink whisky mixed with beer... Oil and water don't mix... You've got two ingredients inside the shell which mix together only when the shell is being fired.*
2 VO If you **mix** something, you make it by stirring or shaking substances together. *He carefully mixed the cement... He visited just as the nurse was mixing a fortified milk drink.*
3 N MASS+SUPP A **mix** is a powder containing all the substances that you need in order to make something, to which you add liquid. *She bought a packet of cement mix. ...cake mixes.*
4 NC A **mix** is also two or more things combined together. *We should try and keep a broad mix of subjects in our schools... I find the mix of politics and literature very interesting. ...the extraordinary ethnic mix of New York City.*
5 V If you **mix** with other people, you meet them and talk to them at a social event. *He was making no effort to mix... They arrested male and female guests for drinking alcoholic beverages and mixing with members of the opposite sex.*

mix up PHRASAL VERB 1 If you **mix up** two things or people, you confuse them, so that you think that one of them is the other one. *People even mix us up and greet us by each other's names... The company that made the medicine accidentally mixed up the chemicals... You've got politics and psychology mixed up here.* 2 If you **mix up** a number of things, you put them all together in a random way so that they are not in any particular order. *I'll be mixing up a couple of poems for you to guess which writers they come from.* 3 If you **mix up** a solution or a mixture, you make it by combining different things together. *It's*

got cocoa powder and milk in it, and you just mix it up a little at a time and then shake it. 4 See also **mixed up, mix-up.**

mix up with PHRASAL VERB If one thing is **mixed up with** another, the two things are combined so that they can no longer be identified separately. *When the water arrives through cracked pipes, mixed up with sewage, it can be lethal... The bags, in spite of the security, had inexplicably become mixed up with ordinary passenger luggage... No-one has yet produced a pure sample of the new material, as it always remains mixed up with a slightly different combination of the two elements.*

mixed /mɪkst/
1 ADJ You can use **mixed** to describe feelings, reactions, or opinions which consist of both some good and some bad things. *He has mixed feelings towards his wife... Reaction has been mixed to Pong Ofjon's acquittal... The song received mixed reviews from other writers... Veterans of Vietnam watched the film with mixed emotions.*
2 ADJ ATTRIB **Mixed** is used to describe something which includes or consists of different things of the same general kind. *...a mixed salad... The cashews had been removed from the mixed nuts. ...mixed media sculptural pieces.*
3 ADJ ATTRIB **Mixed** also means involving people from two or more different races. *He is of mixed parentage: half English, half Dutch. ...a mixed marriage. ...a town where there were many mixed couples.*
4 ADJ **Mixed** education or accommodation is intended for both males and females. *...a mixed school. ...the gradual introduction of mixed classes, on the grounds of lack of teaching personnel.*

mixed ability
ADJ ATTRIB A **mixed ability** class or teaching system is one in which pupils are taught together in the same class, even though some are more intelligent or better at a particular subject than others. *Despite the arguments in favour of a mixed ability education, the parents of many gifted children have given up on state schools. ...mixed ability teaching.*

mixed bag
N SING A **mixed bag** is something that contains a mixture of things or people of many different kinds, some good and some bad. *The front pages are a mixed bag of international and domestic stories... The beginning of the Christmas shopping season was a mixed bag for retailers—some reported good weekend sales, others did not... The rebels seem to be a mixed bag of exiles united mainly by their dislike of President Doe.*

mixed blessing, mixed blessings
NC If you describe someone or something as a **mixed blessing**, you mean that they may be helpful or enjoyable in some ways, but cause problems in other ways. *Children can be a mixed blessing!... Even oil is proving a mixed blessing these days.*

mixed doubles
NU **Mixed doubles** is a match in some sports, especially tennis and badminton, in which a man and a woman play as partners against another man and woman. *Cash teamed up with Hana Mandlikova to beat Bates and Sarah Loosemore in the mixed doubles.*

mixed economy, mixed economies
NC A **mixed economy** is an economic system in a country in which some companies are owned by the state and some are owned privately. *He sees Labour moving in the direction of a mixed economy with more emphasis on private ownership. ...their plans for a mixed economy and for political pluralism.*

mixed farming
NU **Mixed farming** is a system of farming that involves growing crops and keeping animals on the same farm. *Small farmers with about 100 acres, 50 acres, with mixed farming of both animals and crops.*

mixed grill, mixed grills
NC A **mixed grill** is a meal of grilled food, often including bacon, liver, chops, sausages, tomatoes, and mushrooms.

mixed up

1 ADJ If you are **mixed up**, you are confused. *I got mixed up and forgot which one I'd gone to first... Tim was in a strange mixed-up frame of mind.*

2 ADJ PRED If you are **mixed up** in a crime or a scandal, you are involved in it. *I wasn't mixed up in it myself.*

3 ADJ PRED If things get **mixed up**, they get out of order. *The letters had got too mixed up to be sorted out easily.*

mixer /mɪksə/ **mixers**

NC+SUPP A **mixer** is a machine used for mixing things together. *A reconditioned mixer churned up the ingredients for a fruit cake. ...a couple of cement mixers. ...a commercial mixer which is easy to clean and lasts for years.*

mixing bowl, mixing bowls

NC A **mixing bowl** is a large bowl used for mixing ingredients when cooking. *She adds the sugar to the yeast and milk and eggs in her mixing bowl.*

mixture /mɪkstʃə/ **mixtures**

1 N SING A **mixture** of things consists of several different things together. *I swallowed a mixture of pills... She stared at the cold green soup in a mixture of disgust and hunger.*

2 NC A **mixture** is a substance that consists of other substances which have been stirred or shaken together. *...a mixture of water and household bleach.*

mix-up, mix-ups

NC A **mix-up** is a mistake in something that was planned; an informal word. *Due to some administrative mix-up the letters had not been sent... Because of an administrative mix-up, the award was given to Embury instead.*

Miyazawa, Kiichi /kiːtʃi miːjəzɑːwə/

Kiichi Miyazawa became Prime Minister of Japan and leader of the Liberal Democratic Party (LDP) in 1991. He was elected to the House of Representatives in 1967. He served as Minister of International Trade and Industry from 1970 to 1971, for Foreign Affairs from 1974 to 1976, and of Finance from 1986 to 1988. He was Deputy Prime Minister from 1987 to 1988. Born: 1919.

ml

ml is a written abbreviation for 'millilitre' or 'millilitres'. *...180ml of water.*

mm

mm is a written abbreviation for 'millimetre' or 'millimetres'. *...35mm film.*

mmm /m/

Mmm or **mm** is used to represent a sound that you make when someone is talking, to indicate that you are listening to them, that you agree with them, or that you are preparing to say something. *'That's what you said, isn't it?'—'Mm, yes. I suppose so.'*

mnemonic /nɪmɒnɪk/ **mnemonics**

NC A **mnemonic** is a word, short poem, or sentence that is intended to help you remember something such as a scientific rule or a spelling rule. For example, 'i before e, except after c' is a mnemonic to help people remember how to spell words like 'believe' and 'receive'. *That's the mnemonic I learned from an American friend of mine... These codes need to have some mnemonic value.*

moan /məʊn/ **moans, moaning, moaned**

1 V If you **moan**, you make a low, miserable sound because you are unhappy or in pain. *Otto moaned from the pain... He was sitting in a corner, sort of moaning and shaking with the pain.* ▶ Also NC *Each time she moved her leg she let out a moan. ...the sound of struggling bodies, grunts and moans.*

2 V-REPORT, V-QUOTE, V, or V+about To **moan** also means to complain or to speak in a way which shows that you are very unhappy. *'What am I going to do?' she moaned... They're all moaning that Gorbachev has betrayed his revolution... Theatre, he said, should stop moaning and make itself more appealing to popular audiences... My brother's moaning about money again.*

moat /məʊt/ **moats**

NC A **moat** is a deep, wide ditch dug round a hill or castle for protection. *His enormous walled palace is filled with paintings and sculptures and is surrounded by a moat.*

mob /mɒb/ **mobs, mobbing, mobbed**

1 NC A **mob** is a large, disorganized, and often violent crowd of people. *The police faced a mob throwing bricks and petrol bombs... The two soldiers were dragged from their car by a mob, beaten, stripped and shot... Troops opened fire on what they described as an armed mob.*

2 VO If a crowd of people **mob** a person, they gather round the person and express their feelings in a disorderly and often threatening way. *As he emerged, he was mobbed by a crowd of well-wishers... Hundreds of grieving fans and supporters mobbed the hospital when news spread of his death.*

mobile /məʊbaɪl/ **mobiles**

1 ADJ Something or someone that is **mobile** is able to move or be moved easily. *Most antelopes are fully mobile as soon as they are born... The squadron was protected by a highly mobile air defence.* ◆ **mobility** /məʊbɪləti/ NU *Belongings take up space and restrict mobility... Bicycles are said to have been banned, to prevent mobility... Despite his restricted mobility due to old age and ill-health, he visited Sindh last year.*

2 ADJ PRED If you are socially **mobile**, you are able to move to a different social class. *...socially mobile business leaders... The young upwardly mobile professionals like to keep their credit cards in expensive wallets.* ◆ **mobility** NU *...growing affluence, opportunity, and social mobility... Prostitution and gambling are perhaps the side effect of a new social freedom and mobility.*

3 ADJ ATTRIB **Mobile** is used to describe facilities such as hospitals or libraries that are based in a van or caravan so that they can be driven around different parts of a country. *The Germans are planning to bring in a mobile field hospital with 200 beds... The agency has a mobile office touring Wales and giving commercial advice. ...a mobile Post Office Service that tours remote villages.*

4 NC A **mobile** is a light structure which hangs from a ceiling as a decoration and moves gently in the air.

mobile home, mobile homes

NC A **mobile home** is a large caravan that people live in and that usually remains in the same place, but which can be pulled to another place using a car or van. *Many of the homeless families have been accommodated in hostels, mobile homes and special bed-and-breakfast hotels. ...residents of a mobile home park.*

mobility allowance, mobility allowances

NC or NU In Britain, a **mobility allowance** is a sum of money which the government pays to a person who is physically handicapped, in order to help them with the extra transport expenses that they have. *They have to be virtually unable to walk before being able to qualify for a mobility allowance... The disability income group welcomed his decision to extend the age limit for mobility allowance from 75 to 80.*

mobilize /məʊbəlaɪz/ **mobilizes, mobilizing, mobilized**; also spelt **mobilise**.

1 VO If you **mobilize** a group of people, you gather them together in one place so that they can begin a particular activity. *They have mobilized thousands of workers to take over the factories... Now the authorities are struggling to mobilize transport to transfer food from the more prosperous south to the north.* ◆ **mobilization** /məʊbəlaɪzeɪʃn/ NU *The building of the canal required the mobilization of large masses of labour.*

2 VO If you **mobilize** support, opinion, or a political movement, you succeed in encouraging people to take action against or in support of a particular thing. *The Trade Union Congress is prepared to mobilize the whole movement to defeat the bill... Following Chernobyl, public opinion has been mobilized against the expansion of the nuclear industry.* ◆ **mobilization** NU *...anti-Americanism as an instrument of mobilisation and propaganda... The party was only the political expression of this massive mobilization of people.*

3 VO or V If a country **mobilizes** or **mobilizes** its armed forces, it prepares for war; a formal use. *On Friday morning Croatia announced that it was mobilizing its*

*militia reserves... General Aoun called on the
population in the area to mobilize against a possible
invasion.* ◆ **mobilization** NU *Defence chiefs urged
mobilization at once... I can see the point that
mobilisation and manoeuvres are not the same.*

mobster /mɒbstə/ **mobsters**
NC A **mobster** is a member of an organized group of
violent criminals; used in American English. *What's
alleged is that there was a pattern of diversion of
funds and payments to mobsters... They started a
protection racket in 1950s London and became mobster
nightclub owners.*

Mobutu Sese Seko /mɒbuːtu: seɪseɪ seɪkəʊ/
Marshal Mobutu Sese Seko became President of Zaïre
in 1965 when it was still called the Belgian Congo. He
was Secretary of State for National Defence and Chief
of Staff of the Congo Army in 1960 when he took power
for three months and suspended political activities,
before appointing a governing council. He was
Commander-in-Chief of Congolese forces from 1961 to
1965. He became President of the Popular Movement
of the Revolution (MPR) in 1967. Born: 1930.

moccasin /mɒkəsɪn/ **moccasins**
NC **Moccasins** are soft leather shoes with a raised
seam at the front. *...buffalo fur moccasins.*

mock /mɒk/ **mocks, mocking, mocked**
1 V or V-QUOTE If you **mock** someone, you say
something unkind or scornful about them, or imitate
them in an unkind way. *No child in this school would
mock a stutterer. ...an unsympathetic teacher who had
mocked her domestic ambitions... 'She wants me to
go away with her.'—'To Australia?' Lynn mocked.*
◆ **mocking** ADJ *...the boys' mocking laughter... The
tone of the statement was mocking, repeatedly
demeaning the President.*
2 ADJ ATTRIB You use **mock** to describe something
which is not genuine. *Robert squealed in mock
terror... The military staged mock battles.*

mockery /mɒkəri/
1 NU **Mockery** is words, behaviour, or opinions that
are unkind and scornful. *He had ignored Helen's
mockery... There was a tone of mockery in his voice.*
2 N SING If you describe an event or situation as a
mockery, you mean that it seems unsuccessful and
worthless. *The examination was a mockery... The
strikers were making a mockery of our efforts to build
up employment.*

mock-up, mock-ups
NC A **mock-up** of a structure is a model of it. *Here's a
mock-up of the central section of the submarine.*

mod /mɒd/ **mods**
NC **Mods** are people who wear a special kind of
clothes, ride motor-scooters, and like a particular kind
of pop music. Many young people were mods in the
early 1960s. *This was the era of teddy boys and mods
and rockers.*

MoD /eməʊdiː/
N PROP **MoD** is an abbreviation for 'Ministry of
Defence', the government department that deals with
matters affecting the defence of the United Kingdom.
*The MoD and Foreign Office sources confirm that the
decision has been taken to pull back the troops... An
MoD spokesman said the boats would stay out at sea.*

modal /məʊdl/ **modals**
NC In grammar, a **modal** or a **modal verb** is a word
such as 'can' or 'would' which is used in a verbal
group and which expresses ideas such as possibility,
intention, or necessity.

modality /məʊdælətɪ/ **modalities**
NC The **modalities** of a political process or event, for
example, an election or peace conference, are all the
detailed arrangements that have to be agreed before it
can take place. *There may be further protracted
bargaining over modalities and conditions... The two
sides signed a memorandum outlining the principle
and practical modalities of returning the prisoners.*

mod cons /mɒd kɒnz/
N PL If a house has all **mod cons**, it has all the
facilities such as hot water and heating that make it
pleasant to live in; an informal expression. *His two
daughters were well set up; reasonable husbands,
houses, all mod cons.*

mode /məʊd/ **modes**
NC+SUPP A **mode** of life or behaviour is a particular
way of living or behaving; a formal word.
*...conventionally acceptable modes of life... She always
chose this mode of transport... They were acting in a
purely defensive mode.*

model /mɒdl/ **models, modelling, modelled**; spelt
modeling, modeled in American English.
1 NC A **model** is a three-dimensional copy of an
object, usually one that is smaller than the object.
*...scale models of well known Navy ships. ...a model
theatre.*
2 NC If a system is used as a **model**, people copy it in
order to achieve similar results; a formal use. *This
system seemed a relevant model for the new Africa.
...the 'stalinist' model of government... Using the
invasion of Panama as a model, General Thurman has
thought up a new strategy for the drugs war.*
3 NC+of Something that is a **model** of clarity or a
model of fairness, for example, is extremely clear or
extremely fair. *Your reporting has been a model of
professionalism and patriotism... People singing
together are a model of the perfect human
community... But the union's methods are a model of
coherence compared with the government's actions.*
4 ADJ ATTRIB A **model** wife or a **model** teacher, for
example, is an excellent wife or an excellent teacher.
*They are model students... Cape Town was seen as a
model black territory... He was every inch the model
citizen until the day he abandoned his job and just
disappeared.*
5 V-REFL or VO If you **model** yourself on someone, or if
you **model** something on their behaviour or methods,
you copy the way that they do things, because you
admire them. *Cliff Richard had modelled himself on
his teenage hero, Elvis Presley... Cash was first and
foremost an editorialist who modelled himself after
H.L. Mencken... He explicitly rejected an agreement
modelled on the non-nuclear proliferation treaty...
Many of Picasso's paintings were modelled after
Guillot, although they weren't formal portraits.*
6 NC A particular **model** of a machine is a version of
it. *The Granada is the most popular model... Medivac
1000—that's the standard model—costs £174 in the UK.*
7 VO If you **model** an object, you make it out of a
substance such as clay. *...a statue of a boy that she
had modelled in wax... Their faces are modelled by
expert sculptors, who also match the colour of their
eyes and hair.*
8 NC An artist's **model** is someone who poses for an
artist. *She was one of Rossetti's favourite models...
He still works with carefully-posed models but the
results are more naturalistic.*
9 NC A fashion **model** is someone whose job is to
display clothes by wearing them. *...revelations about
his affair with a former model.*
10 VO If you **model** clothes, you display them by
wearing them. *He models cardigans in knitting
books... She modelled many of her own creations
herself.* ◆ **modelling** NU *She's not to do modelling
while she's still at school.*

moderate, moderates, moderating, moderated;
pronounced /mɒdərət/ when it is an adjective or noun
and /mɒdəreɪt/ when it is a verb.
1 ADJ **Moderate** political opinions or policies are not
extreme. *The movement drew its support from
moderate conservatives. ...moving forward in an
encouraging way to a more moderate attitude.*
2 NC A **moderate** is a person whose political opinions
and activities are not extreme. *The moderates have
plenty to be anxious about... He quotes Sayed Ahmed
Gailani, a leading moderate, as suggesting that the UN
could call a meeting of all parties.*
3 ADJ A **moderate** amount is neither large nor small.
*The sun's rays, in moderate quantities, are important
for health. ...her moderate income.*
4 V-ERG If you **moderate** something, or if it **moderates**,
it becomes less extreme or violent and more
acceptable; a formal use. *She had been given
instructions to moderate her tone... The bad weather
had moderated.*

moderately /mɒdəᵊrətli/
SUBMOD **Moderately** means to a medium degree. *Her handwriting was moderately good. ...even if oil prices remain moderately high. ...a moderately bright spring day.*

moderation /mɒdəreɪʃn/
1 NU **Moderation** is self-control and restraint. *He has not displayed the same moderation in his political behaviour as in his private life... The Israelis are likely to respond with diplomatic moderation.*
2 If you do something **in moderation**, you do not do it too much. *Already the messages for pregnant women are clear—avoid smoking altogether, drink in moderation, and watch your weight.*

moderator /mɒdəreɪtə/ **moderators**
1 NC A **moderator** is a member of the protestant clergy who is in charge at large and important church meetings. *...the moderator of the General Synod of the Dutch Reformed Church.*
2 NC A **moderator** is also someone who tries to help settle disputes between different groups of people. *According to the UN moderator, both sides have agreed that all negotiations will be held as face-to-face discussions... His main role in the government was that of moderator.*

modern /mɒdn/
1 ADJ ATTRIB **Modern** means relating to the present time, for example, the present decade or present century. *The social problems in modern society are mounting. ...one of the most fascinating aspects of modern French politics... He has been called the father of modern Burma.*
2 ADJ **Modern** things are new, or of a new kind. *...modern architecture. ...modern methods of production.* ◆ **modernity** /mɒdɜːnəti/ NU *...industries half way between tradition and modernity.*

modern-day
ADJ ATTRIB You use **modern-day** to describe something in the present that is very similar to something that happened or existed in the past. *We can see how language changes by comparing modern-day English, for example, with the writings of Shakespeare... He was convinced that he was a modern-day Messiah.*

modernise /mɒdənaɪz/. See **modernize**.

modernism /mɒdənɪzəm/
NU **Modernism** is the ideas and methods of modern art, especially when they are contrasted with earlier ideas and methods; a technical term. *...that moment when modernism first discovered itself. ...American Late Modernism.*

modernist /mɒdənɪst/ **modernists**; a technical term.
1 ADJ ATTRIB **Modernist** means relating to the ideas and methods of modern art. *The market in modernist work failed to boom. ...Late Modernist formalism.*
2 NC A **modernist** is an artist who uses the ideas and methods of modern art. *...the work of two of the greatest European modernists. ...the Late Modernists.*

modernistic /mɒdənɪstɪk/
ADJ A **modernistic** building, piece of furniture, and so on, has been designed and constructed in a noticeably modern way. *There are plans to build a gleaming, modernistic business centre. ...shiny tables in modernistic designs.*

modernize /mɒdənaɪz/ **modernizes, modernizing, modernized**; also spelt **modernise**.
VO To **modernize** a system or a factory means to introduce new methods or equipment. *...a twenty year programme to modernise Britain's transport system... Some weapons may be removed, others may be modernised... He has praised Salinas for his progress in modernizing Mexico's economy.* ◆ **modernization** /mɒdənaɪzeɪʃn/ NU *...plans for modernisation of the Post Office. ...a country that teeters between modernization and religious conservatism.*

modern languages
N PL If you study **modern languages**, you study modern European languages such as French, German, and Russian. *After three years at Cambridge studying modern languages, he travelled extensively around Europe.*

modest /mɒdɪst/
1 ADJ Something that is **modest** is quite small in size

or amount. *He moved from his hotel suite into a modest flat. ...a small theatre with a modest budget.* ◆ **modestly** ADV *More modestly, Japan Air Lines plans to ban smoking on only three internal flights... These modestly encouraging figures helped to check a nervous start to the Stock Exchange.*
2 ADJ Someone who is **modest** does not talk much about their abilities, achievements, or possessions; used showing approval. *He's got a drawer full of medals but he's too modest to wear them... Away from the board, she's as charming, modest and giggly as any normal schoolgirl.* ◆ **modestly** ADV *He talks quietly and modestly about his farm... Hubbard modestly described himself as an average runner.*
3 ADJ You can also say that someone is **modest** when they are easily embarrassed by things such as nudity. *...the Islamic ideal of women as modest and submissive.* ◆ **modestly** ADV *They slipped out of their garments modestly.*

modesty /mɒdɪsti/
1 NU Someone who shows **modesty** does not talk much about their abilities, achievements, or possessions; used showing approval. *His response was a nicely judged combination of gentlemanly modesty and boyish pride... Modesty was never Dali's strong point.*
2 NU **Modesty** is also the fact of being easily embarrassed by things such as nudity. *The mother wears a wig, to show modesty in the tradition of married Orthodox women.*

modicum /mɒdɪkəm/
N SING A **modicum** of something is a small amount of it; a formal word. *...a designer with a modicum of good taste. ...if the Soviet troops can leave with a modicum of dignity.*

modifier /mɒdɪfaɪə/ **modifiers**
NC In grammar, a **modifier** is a noun or an adjective which comes before a noun in a noun group and affects the meaning of the noun.

modify /mɒdɪfaɪ/ **modifies, modifying, modified**
VO If you **modify** something, you change it slightly, often in order to improve it. *The present Government has modified this approach... No permission has been given in order to modify these weapons... Are you saying that the treaty can't last and must be modified?* ◆ **modification** /mɒdɪfɪkeɪʃn/ **modifications** NCorNU *The engine was pulled apart for modifications... I said I thought the idea might need modification.*

modish /məʊdɪʃ/
ADJ Something that is **modish** is fashionable; a literary word. *Our modish outfits lay in a heap on the floor. ...modish magazines.*

modular /mɒdjʊlə/; a technical term.
1 ADJ In building, **modular** means relating to the construction of buildings in parts called modules. *Even many supposedly 'permanent' buildings today are constructed on a modular plan.*
2 ADJ **Modular** also means relating to the teaching of courses at college or university in units called modules. *Does the modular system work in the 3rd year as well?*

modulate /mɒdjʊleɪt/ **modulates, modulating, modulated**
1 VO If you **modulate** your voice, you change or vary the way that it sounds, for example its loudness, pitch, or tone, according to the effect you are trying to create. *Sam was so excited that he did not modulate his voice as he greeted her. ...a voice modulated to hold the attention of the audience.* ◆ **modulated** ADJ *...her beautifully modulated voice... He continued in his carefully modulated actor's tones.*
2 VO To **modulate** an activity or process means to alter or adjust it in order to make it more suitable for a particular set of circumstances; a formal use. *Attacks on industrial capital were modulated to attacks on monopoly and speculators... This calcium binding protein modulates the activity of the enzyme.* ◆ **modulation** /mɒdjʊleɪʃn/ **modulations** NCorNU *...all the modulations necessary to a decision-making process... It's the sort of modulation you could do electronically.*

module /mɒdjuːl/ **modules**
1 NC+SUPP A **module** is one part of something that can

be combined with other parts, for example, in order to make or build something, or to perform a particular task. *It takes about six weeks to put up a dormitory module... The other team checks that each module of the computer program obeys its specification... We ended up with a three module bridge spanning the 98 metres... Altogether these three cooker modules can serve about 150 to 300 children.*
2 NC A **module** is a part of a spacecraft which can operate independently of the other parts, often away from the spacecraft. *From lunar orbit, the rocket was to release a lunar module which would take the two men to the moon's surface... This is the living module where the astronauts will sleep, eat and relax.*
3 NC A **module** is also one of the units of a course taught at a college or university. *Most teachers approach each module with a concern for balance... We have a syllabus which says that they do 10 modules.*

modus operandi /məʊdəs ɒpərændi:/
N SING A **modus operandi** is a particular way of doing something; a formal expression. *The modus operandi of the crime resembles techniques used by Medellin drug traffickers.*

modus vivendi /məʊdəs vɪvendi:/
N SING A **modus vivendi** is an arrangement which allows people who have different attitudes to live or work together; a formal expression. *The managers and workers have to find some modus vivendi... They are trying to achieve some kind of modus vivendi between the opposition and the authorities.*

Mogadishu /mɒgədɪʃu:/
Mogadishu is the capital of Somalia and its largest city. Population: 500,000 (1981).

moggy /mɒgi/ **moggies**; also spelt **moggie**.
NC A **moggy** is the same as a **cat**; an informal word. *I've seen that cat before. It's the moggy that lives at the Prince of Denmark pub.*

mogul /məʊgl/ **moguls**
1 NC A **Mogul** was a Muslim ruler in India in the sixteenth to eighteenth centuries. *The Moguls had been the military enemies of the British. ...the Mogul empire.*
2 NC A **mogul** is an important, rich, and powerful businessman, especially one in the film or television industry. *He's a magnate, a movie mogul. ...a television mogul determined to win.*

mohair /məʊheə/
NU **Mohair** is a kind of very soft wool. *...a mohair coat.*

Moi, Daniel T arap /dænjəl ti: ærəp mɔɪ/
Daniel T arap Moi became President of Kenya in 1978, at the death of Jomo Kenyatta. He is a member of the Kenya African National Union (KANU). He was elected to the House of Representatives in 1961. He served as Minister of Education from 1961 to 1962, for Local Government from 1962 to 1964, and for Home Affairs from 1964 to 1967. He was Vice President from 1967 to 1978. Born: 1924.

moist /mɔɪst/ **moister, moistest**
ADJ Something that is moist is slightly wet. *...moist black earth... His eyes grew moist... They were advised not to leave the house without a moist cloth over their mouths.*

moisten /mɔɪsn/ **moistens, moistening, moistened**
VO To **moisten** something means to make it slightly wet. *The girl moistened her lips... Early rain had moistened the track, and the surface changed rapidly.*

moisture /mɔɪstʃə/
NU **Moisture** is tiny drops of water that are present somewhere. *The kitchen's stone floor was shiny with moisture... Trees have enormous roots that can reach out for moisture far below the surface. ...grain with a moisture content of over 30 per cent.*

molar /məʊlə/ **molars**
NC Your **molars** are the large, flat teeth you use for chewing food. *...molars and incisors... This is a series of models of molar teeth.*

molasses /məlæsɪz/
NU **Molasses** is a sweet, thick, dark brown syrup which is produced when sugar is refined. It is used in cooking. *He poured milk and molasses into a bowl.*

mold /məʊld/. See **mould**.

Moldavia /mɒldeɪviə/
The **Moldavian Republic**, also called Moldova, became independent of the USSR in 1991. It is located in the south-west of the former USSR, to the east of Romania. Two-thirds of the population are ethnic Romanians. Mircea Snegur, a nationalist, became President in 1990. Moldavia produces tractors and other machinery, sunflower seeds, and other agricultural products. In 1991 it joined the Commonwealth of Independent States. ◆ **Moldavian** /mɒldeɪviən/ N, ADJ
■ *per capita GNP:* US$3,830 ■ *religion:* Christianity
■ *language:* Moldavian (Romanian) ■ *currency:* rouble
■ *capital:* Kishinev ■ *population:* 4 million (1989) ■ *size:* 33,700 square kilometres.

Moldova /mɒldəʊvə/. See **Moldavia**.

moldy /məʊldi/. See **mouldy**.

mole /məʊl/ **moles**
1 NC A **mole** is a natural dark spot on someone's skin. *He had a little mole between his left ear and his sideburn.*
2 NC A **mole** is also a small animal with black fur that lives underground. *...predators that feed mainly on mice and moles.*
3 NC A member of an organization who secretly reveals confidential information to the press or to a rival organization is also called a **mole**. *There is some gossip in Westminster that there is a mole in the Thatcher cabinet.*

molecular /məlekjʊlə/
ADJ ATTRIB **Molecular** means relating to or involving molecules. *...molecular biology. ...molecular techniques used to develop vaccines.*

molecule /mɒlɪkju:l/ **molecules**
NC A **molecule** is the smallest amount of a chemical substance which can exist. *The haemoglobin molecule contains only four atoms of iron.*

molehill /məʊlhɪl/ **molehills**
1 NC A **molehill** is a small pile of earth resulting from a mole digging a tunnel. *I planted spurge, and in 15 years I have never had another molehill in my garden.*
2 If someone is **making a mountain out of a molehill**, they are treating an unimportant difficulty as if it were very serious. *Foreign reporters usually like to exaggerate, and make a mountain out of a molehill.*

molest /məlest/ **molests, molesting, molested**; a formal word.
1 VO Someone who **molests** women or children touches them in a sexual way against their will. *Homes have been burnt down, women have been molested, and all major towns have been placed under curfew... Don't you care about little children being molested and raped by these men?* ◆ **molestation** /məʊlesteɪʃn/ NU *...child molestation.*
2 VO If someone **molests** you, they threaten you or prevent you from doing something. *They feared they would be molested by the angry crowd.*

molester /məlestə/ **molesters**
NC A **molester** is a person who touches women or children in a sexual way against their will. *...the judge who jailed a child molester for life yesterday.*

moll /mɒl/ **molls**
NC A gangster's **moll** is a woman who lives with him and has a sexual relationship with him; an old-fashioned word. *...his association with a woman who was a moll of the Chicago mob.*

mollify /mɒlɪfaɪ/ **mollifies, mollifying, mollified**
VO If you **mollify** someone, you make them less upset or angry; a formal word. *Mrs Pringle allowed herself to be mollified... They hope that this will mollify critics of Syria's record on human rights and terrorism.* ◆ **mollified** ADJ PRED *She appeared slightly mollified.*

mollusc /mɒləsk/ **molluscs**
NC A **mollusc** is an animal such as a snail, slug, clam, or octopus, which has a soft body and no backbone. Many types of mollusc have hard shells to protect them. *...a small freshwater mollusc... Dead fish, molluscs and crustaceans clutter the shoreline and the sea bed.*

mollycoddle /mɒlikɒdl/ **mollycoddles, mollycoddling, mollycoddled**
VO If you **mollycoddle** someone, you do too many things for them and you protect them from unpleasant experiences; used showing disapproval. *A man must not allow himself to be mollycoddled.*

Molotov cocktail /mɒlətɒf kɒkteɪl/ **Molotov cocktails**
NC A **Molotov cocktail** is a bomb made by putting petrol in a bottle and sealing it with a cloth in the top. *The rioters were throwing Molotov cocktails... The government says that Molotov cocktails, munitions and drugs were found on the premises.*

molt /məʊlt/. See **moult**.

molten /məʊltən/
ADJ **Molten** rock or metal has been heated until it is a thick liquid. *...a great mass of molten rock.*

mom /mɒm/ **moms**
VOCATIVE or NC Someone's **mom** is their mother; used in American English. *Mom, one of these days, I'm going to own my own business... All I had to do to feel better was call my mom.*

moment /məʊmənt/ **moments**
NC A **moment** is a very short period of time. *She hesitated for only a moment... A few moments later he heard footsteps... At that precise moment, Miss Pulteney came into the office. ...the moment of death.* ● **Moment** is used in these phrases. ● A situation that exists **at the moment** exists now. *The biggest problem at the moment is unemployment... At the moment, the politicians are not taking the possibility of action seriously enough.* ● If you do something at **the last moment**, you do it at the latest possible time. *We escaped from Saigon at the last moment... Delegates were not able to debate it because at the last moment, the organisers realised there were not enough copies of the report... Until the last moment, the time and venue of the congress was kept a closely-guarded secret.* ● If you cannot do something **for the moment**, you cannot do it now, but you may be able to do it later. *I don't want to discuss this for the moment... They do not believe, for the moment at least, that there is any need to evacuate them.* ● If something happens **the moment** something else happens, it happens as soon as the other thing happens. *The moment I saw this, it appealed to me... The moment one starts to treat sex offenders, one becomes aware of how they use pornography to justify their actions.*

momentarily /məʊməntəʳəli, məʊməntɛərəli/
1 ADV If something happens **momentarily**, it only happens for a short time. *I had momentarily forgotten... 'I can work any shift' said Eddie, but that seemed to only momentarily please the interviewer.*
2 ADV In American English, **momentarily** is also used to say that something will happen very soon. *We are expecting a statement from the presidential spokesman momentarily... Trading is expected to resume momentarily.*

momentary /məʊməntəʳri/
ADJ Something that is **momentary** lasts for only a very short time. *There was a momentary pause... One of the greatest pleasures of writing fiction is the momentary feeling of being someone else.*

moment of truth, moments of truth
NC A **moment of truth** is an important time when you must make a decision quickly and whatever you decide will have important consequences in the future. *The moment of truth came when she got to the airport... It all amounts, the paper says, to the moment of truth for the Soviet President.*

momentous /məmentəs/
ADJ A **momentous** event is very important. *There was no doubt it would be a momentous occasion... She became caught up in the momentous events recalled in this book.*

momentum /məmentəm/
1 NU **Momentum** is the ability that something has to keep developing. *It was necessary to crush the rebel movement before it had a chance to gather momentum... He denies the independence struggle has lost momentum.*
2 NU **Momentum** is also the ability that an object has to continue moving, because of its mass and speed.

...the momentum of the rocket.

momma /mɒmə/ **mommas**. The forms **mommy** /mɒmi/, **mommies** are also used.
VOCATIVE or NC Some people address or refer to their mother as **momma** or **mommy**; used in informal American English. *Mommy, do you know what I want for Christmas?... My momma had six girls... God bless Mommy and Daddy.*

Momoh, Joseph Saidu /dʒəʊzɪf saɪiːdu: mɒməʊ/
Major-General Joseph Saidu Momoh became President of Sierra Leone in 1985. He was an MP from 1973 to 1985. He is a member of the All-People's Congress (APC), which was the only legal party until opposition parties were legalized in 1991. Born: 1937.

Mon.
Mon. is a written abbreviation for 'Monday'. *...Mon. Feb. 26.*

Monaco /mɒnəkəʊ/
The **Principality of Monaco** is a country in south-east France, in western Europe. It has the highest population density of any independent country in the world. The house of Grimaldi has ruled Monaco since 1297. In 1861 it became an independent country under the protection of France. Monaco was occupied by Italy in 1940 and by Germany in 1943. Prince Rainier III succeeded to the throne in 1949. Tourism and banking are important industries. ◆ **Monégasque** /mɒnɪɡæsk/ N, ADJ
▪ *religion:* Christianity (mainly Roman Catholic) ▪ *language:* French (official), Monégasque, Italian, English ▪ *currency:* French franc ▪ *population:* 30,000 (1990) ▪ *size:* 2 square kilometres.

monarch /mɒnək/ **monarchs**
NC A **monarch** is a king or queen who reigns over a country. *Both monarchs are great-great-grandchildren of Queen Victoria.*

monarchical /mɒnɑːkɪkl/
ADJ ATTRIB **Monarchical** means relating to a monarch or monarchs. *...the monarchical principle. ...monarchical and feudal institutions.*

monarchist /mɒnəkɪst/ **monarchists**
NC A **monarchist** is a person who believes that their country should have a monarch. *He shares the feelings of the monarchists that the czar should be restored. ...a staunch monarchist.*

monarchy /mɒnəki/ **monarchies**
1 NC A **monarchy** is a system in which a country has a king or queen. *We want to abolish the monarchy... He added that Lesotho would remain a constitutional monarchy.*
2 NC The **monarchy** is used to refer to the king and queen of a country, and their immediate family. *...the need to modernize the Japanese monarchy, bringing them in closer touch with the people.*

monastery /mɒnəstri/ **monasteries**
NC A **monastery** is a building or collection of buildings in which monks live. *...a monastery run by Benedictine monks. ...a monk at the country's only functioning Buddhist monastery.*

monastic /mənæstɪk/
1 ADJ **Monastic** means relating to monks or to a monastery. *...monastic buildings.*
2 ADJ If you live a **monastic** life, you live simply, without any luxuries. *...my austere, monastic life. ...monastic frugality.*

Monday /mʌndeɪ, mʌndi/ **Mondays**
N U or NC **Monday** is the day after Sunday and before Tuesday. *Today is Monday April 22nd... The bellringers at the church hold a practice session every Monday evening... The accident happened last Monday when a train carrying the chemicals was derailed.*

monetarism /mʌnɪtərɪzəm/
N U **Monetarism** is the control of a country's economy by regulating the total amount of money that is available and in use at any one time; a technical term in economics. *She can't claim that monetarism has worked as it was meant to. ...the prevailing world trend towards monetarism.*

monetarist /mʌnɪtəʳrɪst/ **monetarists**; a technical term in economics.
1 ADJ **Monetarist** means relating to monetarism. *He is the main advocate of a more radical monetarist*

course... *Mr Wapenhans praised the Polish government's tough monetarist policy, which has brought down inflation. ...Mrs Thatcher's monetarist government.*
2 NC A **monetarist** is someone who believes that their country's economy should be controlled by regulating the total amount of money that is available and in use at any one time. *The ministers in charge of economic policy are all convinced monetarists... The monetarists are at least partly right.*

monetary /mɒnɪtəºri/
ADJ ATTRIB **Monetary** means relating to money, especially the money in a country; a formal word. *The CDU in the East is keen to introduce monetary and economic union as quickly as possible... Eventually member states' budgets, as well as their monetary policy, would be affected.*

money /mʌni/
NU **Money** is the coins or bank notes that you use to buy things, or the sum that you have in a bank account. *I spent all my money on sweets... They may not accept English money.* ● See also **blood money**, **easy money**.
● **Money** is used in these phrases. ● If you **make money**, you obtain money by earning it or by making a profit. *To make money you've got to take chances.* ● If you get your **money's worth**, you get good value for the money that you spend. *I always insist on getting my money's worth.*

money-box, **money-boxes**
NC A **money-box** is a small box with an opening at the top, into which a child puts coins as a way of saving money. *I took five dollars and twenty cents out of my money-box.*

money market, **money markets**
NC A country's **money market** consists of all the institutions such as the government and commercial banks that deal with short-term loans, capital, and foreign exchange. *There has been a steady drop in the value of the dollar on international money markets over the last twenty-four hours... This morning, the bank raised the rate at which it lends to the London money market by just over half of one percent.*

money order, **money orders**
NC A **money order** is the same as a **postal order**; used in American English. *You can pay your bills by cash or money order at no extra cost.*

-monger /-mʌŋgə/ **-mongers**
SUFFIX **-monger** is added to nouns which refer to people who start or encourage trouble between other people. For example, a 'war-monger' encourages people to start a war. *...scandal-monger. ...rumour-mongers. ...scare-mongers.*

Mongolia /mɒŋgəʊliə/
The State of **Mongolia** is a country in central Asia. It was ruled by China from 1691 until 1911. Between 1911 and 1924, when the People's Republic of Mongolia was proclaimed, Russia and China struggled for control. The USSR became the dominant influence. The Mongolian People's Revolutionary Party (MPRP) was the sole legal party from 1924 to 1990, when political parties were legalized. Punsalmaagiyn Ochirbat became the first President of Mongolia in 1990. He resigned from the MPRP in 1991, when all senior officials were required to resign from political parties. Dashiyn Byambasüren was appointed Prime Minister in 1990. Mongolia exports coal, copper, timber, and hides. ◆ **Mongol, Mongolian** /mɒŋgəl, mɒŋgəʊliən/ N, ADJ
■ *per capita GNP:* US$660 ■ *religion:* Tibetan Buddhism ■ *language:* Khalkha Mongolian ■ *currency:* tughrik ■ *capital:* Ulaanbaatar ■ *population:* 2 million (1991) ■ *size:* 1,565,000 square kilometres.

mongolism /mɒŋgəlɪzəm/
NU **Mongolism** is an offensive term for **Down's syndrome**.

mongoose /mɒŋguːs/ **mongooses**
NC A **mongoose** is a small furry animal with a long tail that lives in hot countries. *In Fiji, the mongoose has made 26 species of birds extinct.*

mongrel /mʌŋgrəl/ **mongrels**
NC A **mongrel** is a dog with parents of different breeds. *No mongrels are allowed to take part in Crufts—this is strictly a show for the aristocrats of the dog world.*

monitor /mɒnɪtə/ **monitors, monitoring, monitored**
1 VO If you **monitor** something, you regularly check its development or progress. *The child's progress is being monitored... The work will be monitored by a cabinet committee, headed by the Prime Minister.*
◆ **monitoring** NU *...such issues as price monitoring, employment, food, and consumption. ...careful monitoring.*
2 NC A **monitor** is a machine used to check or record things. *The patient was connected to the monitor.*
3 NC You can also refer to a person who checks that something is done correctly, or that it is fair, as a **monitor**. *During the election period, the mission personnel would be augmented by eighty election monitors. ...a journalist and human rights monitor.*

monk /mʌŋk/ **monks**
NC A **monk** is a member of a male religious community that is separated from the outside world. *The crowd was led by a man in saffron robes, the clothes of a Buddhist monk... Thousands of priests, monks and nuns were sent to prison camps and every aspect of religious life subjected to strict state control.*

monkey /mʌŋki/ **monkeys**
NC A **monkey** is an animal with a long tail which lives in hot countries. Monkeys climb trees, and belong to the same family as gorillas and chimpanzees. *...the sound of howler monkeys in the tropical forest.*

monkey business
NU **Monkey business** is slightly unacceptable, dishonest, or illegal behaviour; an informal expression. *I knew there had been some monkey business going on.*

monkey nut, monkey nuts
NC A **monkey nut** is the same as a **peanut**; an informal expression.

mono /mɒnəʊ/
NU **Mono** is used to describe a record or a system of playing music in which all the sound is directed through one speaker only. *Most of his recordings were made in mono, and so you don't really hear his music today as it originally was.*

mono- /mɒnəʊ-/
PREFIX **Mono-** is used in nouns and adjectives that have 'one' or 'single' as part of their meaning. *Improved understanding of wing design enabled designers to switch to the monoplanes that are almost universal now... There is little incentive for farmers to reduce the cotton monoculture.*

monochrome /mɒnəkrəʊm/; a technical term.
1 ADJ A **monochrome** painting is painted using only one colour in various shades. *I did a monochrome painting.*
2 ADJ Films, photographs, or televisions that are **monochrome** show black, white, and shades of grey, but no other colours. *...negatives, colour and monochrome transparencies.*

monocle /mɒnəkl/ **monocles**
NC A **monocle** is a glass lens which people used to wear in front of one of their eyes to improve their ability to see with that eye. *He had wavy white hair and a monocle dangling from a ribbon.*

monogamous /mənɒgəməs/
ADJ **Monogamous** means having only one husband, wife, or mate. *Those least at risk of sexual disease were couples in long-term, monogamous relationships... The birds are monogamous.*

monogamy /mənɒgəmi/
NU **Monogamy** is the custom of being married to only one person at a time. *Lifelong monogamy has other drawbacks... It should be made clear to them that monogamy is the ideal relationship between husband and wife.*

monogram /mɒnəgræm/ **monograms**
NC A **monogram** is a design based on someone's initials which is used to mark the things they own such as a cigarette case, stationery, or clothing. *I picked up the lighter and examined it. There was a monogram on it.*

monogrammed /mɒnəgræmd/
ADJ Something that is **monogrammed** is marked with
a design that includes a person's initials. ...*his
monogrammed hair brushes.*

monograph /mɒnəgrɑːf/ **monographs**
NC A **monograph** is a book which is a detailed study of
only one subject. *Rainer Crone published a
monograph on Warhol.*

monolith /mɒnəlɪθ/ **monoliths**
NC A **monolith** is a very large, upright piece of stone.
Some monoliths were erected in ancient times. *He
stumbled towards the huge, solitary monolith which
had attracted his attention... There is magnetism
emanating from these prehistoric monoliths.*

monolithic /mɒnəlɪθɪk/
ADJ A **monolithic** organization or system is very large
and seems unlikely to change. ...*the monolithic
character of the main political parties.*

monologue /mɒnəlɒg/ **monologues**
NC A **monologue** is a long speech by one person. *He
went into a long monologue... These ballads are
dramatic monologues.*

monopolize /mənɒpəlaɪz/ **monopolizes, monopolizing,
monopolized**; also spelt **monopolise**.
VO To **monopolize** something means to control it
completely and prevent other people having a share in
it. *The Dutch wanted to monopolize the profitable
spice trade from the East... They accused the
Socialists of trying to monopolize supplies of printing
ink and paper.*

monopoly /mənɒpəli/ **monopolies**
NCorNU A **monopoly** is the control or possession of a
particular thing by only one person or group. *Many
local papers are prosperous because they enjoy a
virtual monopoly... The days of trade by monopoly
were over. ...the ending of the Communist Party's
monopoly of power... The company will be referred to
the Mergers and Monopolies Commission.*

monorail /mɒnəʊreɪl/ **monorails**
NC A **monorail** is a system of transport in which trains
travel along a single rail which is usually high above
the ground. *Monorail systems could help ease traffic
congestion.*

monosyllabic /mɒnəʊsɪlæbɪk/
ADJ If you speak in a **monosyllabic** way, you use
words with only one syllable, for example, 'yes' and
'no'. *She said she'd be along in an hour, to which I
grunted something monosyllabic.*

monosyllable /mɒnəʊsɪləbl/ **monosyllables**
NC If someone speaks in **monosyllables**, they speak
using words with only one syllable, for example 'yes'
and 'no'. *He was answering only in monosyllables.*

monotone /mɒnətəʊn/
N SING A **monotone** is a sound which does not vary at
all and is boring to listen to. *He droned on in a steady
monotone.*

monotonous /mənɒtənəs/
ADJ Something that is **monotonous** never changes and
is boring. ...*people who have monotonous jobs... A
recent article spoke of them living monotonous,
poverty-stricken lives... Constitutional crises followed
one another with monotonous regularity.*

monotony /mənɒtəni/
N U The **monotony** of something is the fact that it
never changes and is boring. ...*the monotony of work
on the assembly line... This breaks the monotony of
what they're doing, takes their minds off it a bit.*

Monrovia /mɒnrəʊviə/
Monrovia is the capital of Liberia and its largest city.
Population: 421,000 (1984).

Monsignor /mɒnsiːnjɔː/ **Monsignors** or **Monsignori**
/mɒnsɪnjɔːri/
NC **Monsignor** is the title of a priest of high rank in
the Catholic Church. ...*Monsignor Glemp, Poland's
new Primate.*

monsoon /mɒnsuːn/ **monsoons**
NC The **monsoon** is the season of very heavy rain in
Southern Asia. *Even during the monsoons the
afternoons were warm and clear.*

monster /mɒnstə/ **monsters**
1 NC A **monster** is a large imaginary creature that is
very frightening. ...*hairy white monsters... They have

offered £250,000 for proof of the existence of the Loch
Ness monster.*
2 ADJ ATTRIB **Monster** means extremely large. ...*the
monster Piccadilly Hotel.*

monstrosity /mɒnstrɒsəti/ **monstrosities**
NC A **monstrosity** is something that is large and
extremely ugly. ...*a monstrosity of a house.*

monstrous /mɒnstrəs/
1 ADJ If you describe a situation or event as
monstrous, you mean that it is very shocking or
unfair. *The court's judgement was absolutely
monstrous... The assassination has been described as a
monstrous crime.*
2 ADJ Something that is **monstrous** is very large and
rather ugly or shocking. ...*a heavy man in a
monstrous mustard-coloured sweater.*

montage /mɒntɑːʒ/ **montages**
NC A **montage** is a picture, film, or piece of music,
which consists of several different items that are put
together, often in an unusual combination or sequence;
a technical term. ...*a montage of variegated scraps of
paper... I merged all these colours together in a kind
of montage.*

Monteiro, Antonio Mascarenhas
/əntɒnjuː məʃkərenjəs mʊnteɪruː/
Antonio Mascarenhas Monteiro became Cape Verde's
first freely elected President in 1991. He was a
Supreme Court judge from 1980 to 1990. He is an
independent, supported by the Movement for
Democracy (MPD). Born: 1944.

Montevideo /mɒntɪvɪdeɪəʊ/
Montevideo is the capital of Uruguay and its largest
city. Population: 1,252,000 (1985).

month /mʌnθ/ **months**
1 NC A **month** is one of the twelve periods of time that
a year is divided into, for example January or
February. *It's happened three times this month... The
pay will be five hundred pounds a month.*
2 NC A **month** is also a period of about four weeks.
He was kidnapped just over a month ago.

monthly /mʌnθli/
ADJ ATTRIBor ADV You use **monthly** to describe
something that happens every month. ...*a monthly
meeting... Our staff are paid monthly.*

Montserrat /mɒntsəræt/
Montserrat is a territory of the United Kingdom in the
Caribbean. It is one of the Leeward Islands. It was
colonized by Britain from 1632. Montserrat exports
electrical components, cotton, and fruit. It is an
important data processing centre. Tourism and
banking are important industries.
■ *per capita GNP:* US$4,030 ■ *religion:* Christianity
■ *language:* English (official) ■ *currency:* East
Caribbean dollar ■ *capital:* Plymouth ■ *population:*
12,000 (1989) ■ *size:* 102 square kilometres.

monument /mɒnjʊmənt/ **monuments**
1 NC A **monument** is a large stone structure built to
remind people of a person or event. ...*a monument to
F D Roosevelt. ...a monument built in honour of three
Brazilian steelworkers shot dead during an industrial
dispute.*
2 NC A **monument** is also something such as a castle
or bridge that was built a long time ago and that is
thought to be an important part of a country's history.
*For many years cultural and historic monuments have
been destroyed. ...the ancient monument of
Stonehenge.*

monumental /mɒnjʊmentl/
1 ADJ ATTRIB A **monumental** building or work of art is
very large and impressive. ...*the monumental facade
of the Royal School.*
2 ADJ **Monumental** also means very great or extreme.
...*a monumental hailstorm... He described the decision
as a monumental blunder.*

moo /muː/ **moos, mooing, mooed**
V When a cow **moos**, it makes the noise that cows
typically make.

mooch /muːtʃ/ **mooches, mooching, mooched**
mooch about or **mooch around** PHRASAL VERB If you
mooch about or **mooch around**, you walk around
slowly with no particular purpose; an informal
expression. *He mooched about the house in his

pyjamas... He was mooching around, unshaven and grumpy.

mood /muːd/ **moods**
1 NC Your **mood** is the state of your emotions at a particular time. *He was always in a good mood... I wasn't in the mood for helping.*
2 NC If you are in a **mood**, you are angry and impatient. *When Chris was in one of his moods, he was unpleasant to everyone.*
3 N SING The **mood** of a group of people is their general feeling or attitude. *The debate took place amid a mood of growing political despair... The mood of this week's meeting has been one of cautious optimism.*

moody /muːdi/
1 ADJ Someone who is **moody** is depressed and does not want to talk. *He's only moody because things aren't working out.* ◆ **moodily** ADV *She drank her coffee moodily.*
2 ADJ **Moody** people have feelings which change frequently. *He was moody and unpredictable.*

moon /muːn/ **moons**
1 N SING The **moon** is the object which appears in the sky at night as a circle or part of a circle. *...television pictures of a man walking on the moon.*
2 NC A **moon** is a natural object that travels round a planet. *...one of Mars's two moons.*

moonbeam /muːnbiːm/ **moonbeams**
NC A **moonbeam** is a ray of light from the moon. *In the story, the boy travels on a moonbeam.*

moonless /muːnləs/
ADJ A **moonless** sky or night is dark because there is no moon in the sky. *The attack came on a moonless night in November.*

moonlight /muːnlaɪt/ **moonlights, moonlighting, moonlighted**
1 NU **Moonlight** is the light that comes from the moon at night. *The field looked like water in the moonlight... Our meeting took place by moonlight.*
2 V If you **moonlight**, you have a second job in addition to your main job, often without informing your main employers or the tax office. *She moonlighted as a waitress.*

moonlit /muːnlɪt/
ADJ Something that is **moonlit** is lit by moonlight. *...a moonlit night.*

moony /muːni/
ADJ If you say a person has **moony** eyes, you mean their eyes are big and round and make the person seem vague or dreamy.

moor /mɔː, mʊə/ **moors, mooring, moored**
1 NC A **moor** is a high area of open land covered mainly with rough grass and heather. *The mists had vanished from the moor... He used to go for long walks on the moors.*
2 VO If a boat is **moored**, it is on the water but is attached to the land with a rope. *Boats were moored on both sides of the river.*

moorhen /mɔːhen, mʊəhen/ **moorhens**
NC A **moorhen** is a medium-sized black bird that lives near water. *The birds live by the reedbeds, feeding on voles and moorhens.*

mooring /mɔːrɪŋ, mʊərɪŋ/ **moorings**
NC A **mooring** is a place where a boat that is on the water can be attached to the land with a rope. *During the storm, boats were torn from their moorings.*

moorland /mɔːlənd, mʊələnd/ **moorlands**
N U or N PL **Moorland** is land which consists of moors. *...forty-eight square miles of pinewood, moorland and mountain. ...the beauty of Britain's moorlands.*

moose /muːs/; **moose** is both the singular and the plural form.
NC A **moose** is a large North American deer with flat antlers. *...Canadian forests thick with deer, bears and moose.*

mooted /muːtɪd/
V-PASS If something is **mooted**, it is suggested or introduced as a subject that you want people to discuss; a formal word. *A holiday in France had been mooted earlier in the term.*

moot point /muːt pɔɪnt/ **moot points**
NC A **moot point** is a statement or idea that may or may not be true, or that people cannot agree about. *...how serious he was about this is a moot point... It is a moot point which issue is most important.*

mop /mɒp/ **mops, mopping, mopped**
1 NC A **mop** is a tool for washing floors. It consists of a sponge or many pieces of string attached to a long handle. *She was helpless with a mop and hopeless with a broom.*
2 VO If you **mop** a floor, you clean it with a mop. *Maintenance crews mop the floors and wipe the walls, but nothing can disguise the stench.*
3 VO If you **mop** a liquid from a surface or if you **mop** the surface, you wipe the surface with a dry cloth in order to remove the liquid. *He mopped the sweat from his face... Mop it with a tissue... He mopped his sweating brow.*
4 NC A **mop** of hair is a large amount of loose or untidy hair. *...a coarse mop of black hair.*

mop up PHRASAL VERB 1 If you **mop up** a liquid from a surface, you clean it up and get rid of it. *Mother started mopping up the oil... Firemen were called to Stanstead airport to mop up forty gallons of detergent... Inside, the Browns were busy mopping up the water blowing through the seams of the closed windows.* ◆ **mopping up** N U or N+N *Mopping up and repair work is under way in several countries after another violent storm... A large-scale mopping-up operation has continued today in the area affected by last week's floods.* 2 If you **mop up** something that you think is undesirable or dangerous, you remove it or deal with it so that it is no longer a problem. *The Soviet News Agency 'Tass' reported that loyal troops had mopped up the main pockets of resistance... If it takes off, this initiative will help to mop up excess savings and will take some of the pressure off the budget.* ◆ **mopping up** N U or N+N *This mopping up of liquidity is expected to act as a strong control on consumer demand... Government forces were involved in mopping-up operations to capture dissidents still at large.*

mope /məʊp/ **mopes, moping, moped** /məʊpt/
V If you **mope**, you feel miserable and are not interested in anything. *He just sits about, moping in an armchair.*

moped /məʊped/ **mopeds**
NC A **moped** is a small motorcycle. *He was making his way home on his moped.*

moral /mɒrəl/ **morals**
1 N PL **Morals** are principles and beliefs concerning right and wrong behaviour. *Business morals nowadays are very low... Films like this are a danger to public morals.*
2 ADJ ATTRIB **Moral** means concerned with right or wrong behaviour. *I have noticed a fall in moral standards... It is our moral duty to stay.* ◆ **morally** SUBMOD *It is morally wrong not to do more to help the poor.*
3 ADJ Someone who is **moral** behaves in a way that they believe is right. *If parents see themselves honest and moral, their children will be too.* ◆ **morally** ADV *I try to live morally.*
4 ADJ If you give someone **moral** support, you encourage them in what they are doing by expressing approval. *I looked across to give moral support to my colleagues.*
5 N SING The **moral** of a story or event is what you learn from it about how you should or should not behave. *The moral is clear: you must never marry for money.*

morale /mərɑːl/
NU **Morale** is the amount of confidence and optimism that people have. *The morale of the men was good.*

moral fibre; spelt **moral fiber** in American English.
NU **Moral fibre** is the quality of being determined to do what you think is right. *We have something of that same kind of amorality and lack of moral fibre. ...our belief in their having a very high moral fibre.*

moralise /mɒrəlaɪz/. See moralize.

moralist /mɒrəlɪst/ **moralists**
NC A **moralist** is someone with strong ideas about right and wrong behaviour. *My grandfather was a stern moralist.*

moralistic /mɒrəlɪstɪk/

ADJ Someone who is **moralistic** has harsh or extreme ideas about what is right and wrong, and tries to force other people to accept those ideas. *She had rebuked David for his moralistic attitude.*

morality /məræləti/ **moralities**

1 NUorNC **Morality** is the belief that some behaviour is right and acceptable and that other behaviour is wrong. *...the decline in traditional morality... Conflicts must arise between the two moralities.*

2 NU The **morality** of something is how right or acceptable it is. *...arguments concerning the morality of taking part in a war.*

moralize /mɒrəlaɪz/ **moralizes, moralizing, moralized;** also spelt **moralise.**

v If someone **moralizes,** they tell people what they think is right or wrong; used showing disapproval. *...moralizing about the dangers of drink.*

moral victory

N SING If you say that someone has won a **moral victory,** you mean that although they have officially lost a contest or dispute, you think that they have succeeded in showing they are right about something, or that they have better qualities or skills than someone else. *Despite their eventual and inevitable defeat, they felt they had achieved a kind of moral victory... She said her party had won a moral victory, and accused the caretaker government of massive and blatant fraud.*

morass /məræs/

N SING You use **morass** to refer to something that it is extremely complicated and confused. *These men are usually bogged down in a morass of paperwork. ...a state finding its way out of the political and economic morass.*

moratorium /mɒrətɔːriəm/ **moratoriums**

NC If there is a **moratorium** on a particular activity, it is officially stopped for a period of time; a formal word. *The meeting did agree to extend the moratorium on the building of new warships.*

morbid /mɔːbɪd/

ADJ If a person or their behaviour is **morbid,** they have too great an interest in unpleasant things, especially in death. *It's morbid to dwell on cemeteries and suchlike. ...morbid imaginations.*

mordant /mɔːdnt/

ADJ **Mordant** humour or wit is very sarcastic and sharply critical; a literary word. *The book sparkles with mordant humour... The mordant Ambrose Bierce was forty-five.*

more /mɔː/

1 DETorQUANT **More** means a greater number or amount than before or than something else. *Do you spend more time teaching, or doing research?... Better management may enable one man to milk more cows... He saw more than 800 children dying of starvation... There are more of them seeking jobs than there are jobs available.*

2 ADV **More** also means to a greater extent. *The books that are true to life will attract them more... They were more amused than concerned.*

3 ADV If you do something some **more,** you continue doing it. *They talked a bit more... I apologized and thought no more about it.*

4 DETorPRON **More** is also used to refer to an additional thing or amount. *In the next hour he found two more diamonds... Have some more coffee, Vicar... I wanted to find out more about her.*

5 SUBMOD **More** is used in front of adjectives or adverbs to form comparatives. *Your child's health is more important than the doctor's feelings... Next time, I will choose more carefully.*

● **More** is used in these phrases. ● If something is not the case **any more,** it has stopped being the case. *The employers don't want quality work any more... They're not here any more... He did not feel like working any more.* ● If something is **more than** a particular thing, it has greater value or importance than this thing. *This is more than a hunter's job... It wasn't much more than a formality.* ● You can also use **more than** to emphasize that something is true to a greater degree than is necessary or than is said.

You'll have more than enough money for any equipment you need... This was a more than generous arrangement. ● If something is **more or less** true, it is true in a general way, but is not completely true. *Brian more or less implied that we were lying.* ● You use **what's more** to introduce an additional piece of information which supports or emphasizes the point you are making. *What's more, he adds, there are no signs of a change.*

moreover /mɔːrəʊvə/

ADV SEN **Moreover** is used to introduce a piece of information that adds to or supports the previous statement; a formal word. *They have accused the Government of corruption. Moreover, they have named names.*

mores /mɔːreɪz/

N PL The **mores** of a particular group of people are the customs and habits that they typically have; a formal word. *The last thirty years have seen great changes in social mores... What do we learn of the manners and mores of the New Zealand people from this film?*

morgue /mɔːg/ **morgues**

NC A **morgue** is a building where dead bodies are kept before they are cremated or buried. *...the city morgue.*

moribund /mɒrɪbʌnd/

ADJ Something that is **moribund** is about to come to an end because it no longer performs a worthwhile function; a formal word. *The moribund Post Office Advisory Board was replaced. ...moribund industries.*

Mormon /mɔːmən/ **Mormons**

NC A **Mormon** is a person who belongs to the religious group called the Church of Jesus Christ of Latter-Day Saints. *In June, the government froze the activities of Mormons and Jehovah's witnesses, and banned three local Christian sects. ...the Mormon Church in Britain.*

morning /mɔːnɪŋ/ **mornings**

1 NCorNU The **morning** is the part of a day between the time that people wake up and lunchtime. *This morning she visited the Florence Nightingale Museum... A small truck leaves early each morning to buy any supplies it can... I was reading the morning paper.*

2 NC The part of a day between midnight and noon is also called the **morning.** *She died in the very early hours of this morning... It was five o'clock in the morning.*

morning coat, morning coats

NC A **morning coat** is a man's coat, usually black or grey, that is longer at the back than at the front and is worn as part of morning dress.

morning dress

NU **Morning dress** is a suit of clothes in black or grey that is worn with a white shirt, a grey tie, and a top hat by men on very formal occasions such as weddings. *He also added to the sense of theatre by wearing morning dress.*

morning room, morning rooms

NC A **morning room** is a sitting-room in a large, old-fashioned house, which is designed to get the sun in the mornings.

morning sickness

NU **Morning sickness** is a feeling of sickness that some women have when they are pregnant. *In the 1950s thalidomide was prescribed to thousands of pregnant women to reduce morning sickness.*

Morocco /mərɒkəʊ/

The **Kingdom of Morocco** is a country in north-west Africa. It was a French colony from 1912 until independence in 1956, when it was reunited with a small northern area which had been a Spanish protectorate. King Hassan II succeeded his father in 1961. Spain ceded the territory of Spanish Sahara (now called Western Sahara) to Morocco and Mauritania in 1976. Morocco's attempts to annex the area were opposed by the Polisario Front, a group fighting to establish an independent Western Sahara. Morocco resigned from the Organization of African Unity in 1985, after Western Sahara was admitted as a member. Dr Azzedine Laraki (independent) became Prime Minister in 1986. Morocco is a member of the Arab League. It is the world's largest exporter of phosphate rock. Tourism is an important industry. Large foreign debts are a serious economic problem. ◆ **Moroccan** /mərɒkən/ N, ADJ ▪ *per capita GNP:* US$750 ▪ *religion:* Islam (mainly Sunni) ▪ *language:* Arabic (official), Berber ▪ *currency:* dirham ▪ *capital:* Rabat ▪ *largest city:* Casablanca ▪ *population:* 25 million (1989) ▪ *size:* 458,730 square kilometres.

moron /mɔːrɒn/ **morons**
NC If you describe someone as a **moron**, you mean that they are very stupid; an informal word. *He expressed contempt for those he described as Militant's mindless morons.*

Moroni /mərəuni/
Moroni is the capital of the Comoros and its largest town. Population: 17,000 (1980).

moronic /mərɒnɪk/
ADJ **Moronic** means very stupid; an informal word. *It can be seen in the current moronic Building Society television campaign.*

morose /mərəus/
ADJ Someone who is **morose** is miserable, bad-tempered, and refuses to say very much. *He was morose and silent... His morose expression couldn't disguise a fiercely competitive edge.* ◆ **morosely** ADV *The man followed me morosely round the museum.*

morphia /mɔːfiə/
NU **Morphia** is the same as **morphine**; an old-fashioned word. *Anthony gasped at the pain. 'Morphia?'—'No, I can cope.'*

morphine /mɔːfiːn/
NU **Morphine** is a drug used to relieve pain. *We sometimes use morphine for these babies, which helps with pain relief and also sedates the baby.*

morris dancer /mɒrɪs dɑːnsə/ **morris dancers**
NC A **morris dancer** is a person who takes part in morris dancing. *Open air concerts and live displays will take place, including brass bands, folk singers, morris dancers and a daily Festival parade.*

morris dancing /mɒrɪs dɑːnsɪŋ/
NU **Morris dancing** is a type of old English country dancing which is performed by people who wear a special costume. *It may be the month for morris dancing, but Somerset were left feeling anything but merry yesterday.*

morse code /mɔːs kəud/
NU **Morse code** or **morse** is an international code which is used for sending messages. It uses a system of written dots and dashes, or short and long sounds, to represent each letter of the alphabet. *It takes only a few hours to become reasonably proficient in morse code... He tapped out his initials in morse.*

morsel /mɔːsl/ **morsels**
NC A **morsel** of something, especially food, is a very small piece or amount of it. *He cannot swallow—even a morsel of food... She said her husband had but a morsel of land, one cow and a poor little horse.*

mortal /mɔːtl/ **mortals**
1 ADJ When you describe people as **mortal**, you are referring to the fact that they have to die and cannot live forever. *Remember that you are mortal... He will be the first Emperor to ascend the throne as an ordinary mortal, not as a divine figure.*
2 NC You can refer to ordinary people as **mortals** when contrasting them with someone very powerful or successful; often used humorously. *He passed first time, something which we mortals couldn't manage... He might ease up a bit, just as we mere mortals have to as we reach forty.*
3 ADJ ATTRIB A **mortal** enemy, danger, threat, and so on is one which may cause you severe harm. *They regard the police as their mortal enemies... We are all in mortal danger... The loss of Juba would be a mortal blow to the government... They were locked in mortal combat.*

mortality /mɔːtæləti/
1 NU **Mortality** is the fact that all people must die and cannot live forever. *...man contemplating his own mortality... The experience did make her more aware of her human mortality.*
2 NU The **mortality** in a particular place or situation is the number of people who die. *Infant mortality on*

the island has been reported at 200 per 1,000 births. ...variations in hospital mortality rates.

mortally /mɔːtəli/
ADV Someone who is **mortally** wounded or **mortally** ill is going to die as a result of their wound or illness. *The authorities believe his captors shot and mortally wounded him... The group has denied reports that its founder and leader had been mortally wounded.*

mortar /mɔːtə/ **mortars**
1 NC A **mortar** is a short cannon which fires missiles high into the air for a short distance. *We returned fire with mortars and machine-guns... The building, which has been besieged for two weeks, is now under heavy mortar attack.*
2 NU **Mortar** is a mixture of sand, water, and cement which is used to hold bricks firmly together. *He built the delicate spires from steel and mortar.*

mortarboard /mɔːtəbɔːd/ **mortarboards**
NC A **mortarboard** is a stiff black cap with a flat, square top and a tassel hanging from it. Mortarboards are sometimes worn on formal occasions by university students and teachers. *It was unlike the four-cornered mortarboards being carried by the gentlemen.*

mortgage /mɔːgɪdʒ/ **mortgages, mortgaging, mortgaged**
1 NC A **mortgage** is a loan of money which you get from a bank or building society in order to buy a house. *We can't get a mortgage. ...mortgage repayments.*
2 VO If you **mortgage** your house or land, you use it as a guarantee to a company in order to borrow money from them. *He will have to mortgage his land for a loan.*

mortician /mɔːtɪʃn/ **morticians**
NC A **mortician** is a person whose job is to look after the bodies of people who have died, and to arrange their funerals; used in American English. *You get teased a lot if you're a mortician.*

mortify /mɔːtɪfaɪ/ **mortifies, mortifying, mortified**
VO If you **are mortified**, you feel very offended, ashamed, or embarrassed. *She was deeply mortified at this rebuff... The rest of us were just totally mortified—this guy had a new idea every day.* ◆ **mortifying** ADJ *There were some mortifying setbacks.* ◆ **mortification** /mɔːtɪfɪkeɪʃn/ NU *Dave was hiding his head in mortification.*

mortise lock /mɔːtɪs lɒk/ **mortise locks**
NC A **mortise lock** is a type of lock which fits into a hole cut into the edge of a door rather than being fixed to one side of it. The lock cannot be seen or unscrewed when the door is closed. *A simple mortise lock is no match for an officer carrying a plastic credit card and his set of private keys.*

mortuary /mɔːtjuəri/ **mortuaries**
NC A **mortuary** is a building or a room, for example in a hospital, where dead bodies are kept before they are buried or cremated. *All the people at the mortuary can think about is their grief and revenge... US officials confirmed that they're expecting to receive the remains at a military mortuary in Saudi Arabia.*

mosaic /məuzeɪɪk/ **mosaics**
1 NC A **mosaic** is a design made of small pieces of coloured stone or glass set in concrete or plaster. *...a Roman mosaic. ...walls covered with mosaics... A small area of mosaic flooring made from marble.*
2 NC You can use **mosaic** to refer to something that consists of many different things that are of the same general type. *O'Brien's novel gives us a mosaic of characters—local Indians, barmaids, cowgirls, businessmen and farmhands... All of these things are consistent with the mosaic of economic data that suggests we are coming out of the recession.*

Moscow /mɒskəu/
Moscow is the capital of Russia and its largest city. It was formerly the capital of the USSR. Population: 8,967,000 (1989).

mosey /məuzi/ **moseys, moseying, moseyed**
VA If you **mosey** somewhere, you go there slowly, often without any particular purpose except to see what is there; used in informal American English. *I think I'll mosey down to the shops.* ▶ Also N SING *I've just had a mosey round the garden.*

Moslem /mɒzləm, muzlım/. See **Muslim.**

mosque /mɒsk/ **mosques**
NC A **mosque** is a building where Muslims go to worship. *...prayers at Jerusalem's most holy mosque. ...even holy places such as shrines and mosques had been hit.*

mosquito /məskiːtəʊ/ **mosquitoes** or **mosquitos**
NC **Mosquitoes** are small flying insects which bite people in order to suck their blood. *The presence of mosquitos is one of the main worries of the over-worked medical staff. ...the failure of spraying programmes to control the mosquitos that transmit malaria.*

mosquito net, mosquito nets
NC A **mosquito net** is a curtain made of very fine cloth which is hung round a bed in order to keep mosquitoes and other insects away from a person who is sleeping. *Mosquito nets soaked in insecticide are more effective at keeping away malaria attacks than drugs.*

moss /mɒs/ **mosses**
N MASS **Moss** is a very small soft green plant which grows on damp soil, or on wood or stone. *The bark was covered with moss. ...non-flowering plants such as mosses and fungi.*

mossy /mɒsi/
ADJ Something that is **mossy** is covered with moss. *...a flight of mossy stone steps.*

most /məʊst/
1 QUANT or DET You can use **most** to refer to the majority of a group of things or people or the largest part of something. *I saw most of the early Shirley Temple films... He used to spend most of his time in the library... Most Arabic speakers understand Egyptian Arabic.*
2 ADJ or PRON The **most** means a larger amount than anyone or anything else, or the largest amount possible. *This is the area that attracts the most attention... The most I could learn was that Lithgow had been sacked... More exercise is needed by fat people whose bodies make the most efficient use of food.*
3 ADV You can use **most** or the **most** to indicate that something is true or happens to a greater degree or extent than anything else. *What he most feared was being left alone... Which do you value most—wealth or health?... I liked him the most.*
4 SUBMOD **Most** is used in front of adjectives or adverbs to form superlatives. *It was one of the most important discoveries ever made... These are the works I respond to most strongly. ...Britain's most famous aviation pioneer, Sir Thomas Sopwith.*
5 SUBMOD You can use **most** to emphasize an adjective or adverb. For example, if you say that something is **most** interesting, you mean that it is very interesting; a formal use. *The trading results show a most encouraging trend... He always acted most graciously.* ● **Most** is used in these phrases. ● You use **at most** or **at the most** to emphasize that a number or amount that you have mentioned is the maximum number that is possible or likely. *There would be at most a hundred people listening... I only have fifteen minutes or twenty minutes at the most... The police estimate was a thousand at the most.* ● If you **make the most of** something, you get the maximum use or advantage from it. *Governments should face up to the situation and make the most of it.*

-most /-məʊst/
SUFFIX **-most** is added to adjectives to form other adjectives that describe something as being further in a particular direction than other things of the same kind. For example, the northernmost part of a country is the part that is farthest to the north. *...the innermost room of the castle. ...the topmost branches of a tree.*

most favoured nation
N+N If one country grants another **most favoured nation** status, it agrees to apply low rates of tariff when trading with it. *Most favoured nation status reduces tariffs in US-China trade to the lowest possible levels... The State Department official said there was no question of Bulgaria being given most favoured nation treatment on tariffs and quotas.*

mostly /məʊstli/
ADV or ADV SEN **Mostly** is used to indicate that a statement is generally true, for example true about the majority of a group of things or people, or true most of the time. *The men at the party were mostly fairly young... Mostly, I think, it showed that the days of Communist supremacy were numbered... A rattlesnake hunts mostly at night.*

MOT /emaʊtiː/ **MOTs**
NC In Britain an **MOT** is a test which is made each year on all road vehicles that are more than 3 years old, in order to check that they are safe to drive. *Our ageing minibus failed its MOT.*

motel /məʊtel/ **motels**
NC A **motel** is a hotel intended for people who are travelling by car. *It was part of the experience—winding up in those motels and eating that kind of food that I had to eat on the road... They installed us in a sort of seedy motel for the night.*

moth /mɒθ/ **moths**
NC A **moth** is an insect like a butterfly, which usually flies about at night. *It is a very pretty moth with a two inch wingspan and comes from upland South Africa... The caterpillars of the Garden Pebble Moth eat cabbages.*

mothball /mɒθbɔːl/ **mothballs, mothballing, mothballed**
1 VO If something such as a piece of equipment or a plan **is mothballed**, you stop using it or decide not to continue with it for a while. *Navy spokesmen say the ship is being mothballed because of defense cuts... They want to see the city mothball the project for at least two years... He says the production facility should be mothballed.* ◆ **mothballed** ADJ ATTRIB *They are leasing barren land where they hope to park about 30 mothballed planes... Some of the mothballed jets will make it back into the air.* ◆ **mothballing** NU *'The Times' says the mothballing of NATO's power is surely the most welcome challenge the West has ever faced.*
2 If something is **in mothballs**, it is not being used or worked on. If you take something **out of mothballs**, you start using it or working on it again after it has been in disuse for a while. *The space agency spent more than a billion dollars on research before plans were put in mothballs... The navy says the ship can be pulled out of mothballs in three to five months if it's needed for active duty... Nobody would be happier than the military, to see ships of this kind go back into mothballs.*
3 NC **Mothballs** are small white balls made of a special chemical, which you can put amongst clothes or blankets in order to keep moths away. *The room even has a small fridge that smells of mothballs.*

moth-eaten
ADJ **Moth-eaten** clothes look very old and ragged. *...moth-eaten sweaters and worn-out shoes.*

mother /mʌðə/ **mothers, mothering, mothered**
1 NC or VOCATIVE Your **mother** is the woman who gave birth to you. *I always did everything my mother told me... You are looking wonderful, Mother.*
2 VO The way that a mother **mothers** her children is the way that she looks after them and brings them up. *Female monkeys who were badly mothered became bad mothers themselves.*
3 VO If someone **mothers** you, they treat you with great affection, and often spoil you. *Both the other senior typists tended to mother me.*

mother country, mother countries
1 NC Someone's **mother country** is the country where they were born or where their ancestors originally came from, and to which they still feel emotionally linked, wherever they might live. *Our wish is to go back and be part of Armenia, because that is our mother country... He expressed hopes that they would safeguard their cultural traditions and maintain contact with their mother countries.*
2 NC The **mother country** of a particular state or country is the very powerful country that used to control its affairs. *Of major importance to the poorer West African states will be their future relationship with their mother country, France... Australia is no*

longer a collection of colonies with a strong bond of allegiance to the Queen and the mother country, Britain.

mother figure, mother figures
NC If you consider a woman as a **mother figure**, you think of her as a person to whom you can turn for help, advice, or support. *The new measures include recruiting mature women to act as mother figures to assist young recruits.*

motherhood /mʌðəhʊd/
NU **Motherhood** is the state of being a mother. *...girls preparing for motherhood.*

Mothering Sunday
NU **Mothering Sunday** is the same as **Mother's Day**; an old-fashioned expression. *Mothering Sunday, as it used to be known in Britain, grew out of a Christian festival.*

mother-in-law, mothers-in-law
NC Your **mother-in-law** is the mother of your husband or wife. *She did in fact marry last year, but her mother-in-law discovered her background and the marriage was declared void.*

motherland /mʌðəlænd/ **motherlands**
NC Someone's **motherland** is the country where they were born or where their ancestors originally came from, and to which they still feel emotionally linked, wherever they might live. *There can be no sacrifice greater than that made for the unity of the motherland.*

motherless /mʌðələs/
ADJ You describe children as **motherless** when their mother has died or does not live with them. *Left motherless at four, she was brought up in North Dakota by a step-mother.*

motherly /mʌðəli/
ADJ A **motherly** woman is warm, kind, and protective. *...a plump, motherly woman.*

Mother Nature
NU **Mother Nature** is sometimes used to refer to nature, especially when it is being considered as a force that affects human beings; a literary expression. *We cannot control the caprices of Mother Nature.*

mother-of-pearl
NU **Mother-of-pearl** is the shining layer on the inside of some shells. It is used to make buttons or to decorate things. *Its walls are studded with mother-of-pearl and semi-precious stones.*

Mother's Day
NU **Mother's Day** is a special day in some countries on which mothers receive gifts and cards from their children. *Happy Mother's Day!... If anyone asks me what I want for Mother's Day this year, I will say I want my sons home.*

Mother Superior, Mother Superiors
NC A **Mother Superior** is a nun who is in charge of the other nuns in a convent. *Officials delivered a notice this morning to the Mother Superior, saying they would return.*

mother-to-be, mothers-to-be
NC A **mother-to-be** is a woman who is pregnant, especially for the first time. *A healthy mother-to-be spending just two hours a day in a smoke-filled atmosphere doubles the risk of giving birth to a baby of low weight.*

mother tongue, mother tongues
NC Your **mother tongue** is the language you learned from your parents when you were a child. *Generous minority rights have included access to newspapers, information, and educational facilities in the mother tongue. ...the refugees, mainly of Hungarian mother tongue, who have fled to Hungary from Romania.*

motif /məʊtiːf/ **motifs**
NC A **motif** is a design used as a decoration. *There were white curtains with black and red motifs on them.*

motion /məʊʃn/ **motions, motioning, motioned**
1 NU **Motion** is the process of continually changing position or moving from one place to another. *The bed swayed with the motion of the ship... Just keep moving, stay in motion. ...Newton's three laws of motion.* ● See also **slow motion**.

2 NC A **motion** is an action, gesture, or movement. *He made stabbing motions with his spear... With a quick motion of her hands, she did her hair up in a knot.*
3 NC A **motion** in a meeting or debate is a proposal which is discussed and voted on. *He proposed the motion that 'the Public Schools of England should be abolished'... He has tabled a motion, to be debated this evening, to suspend Mr Brown... Eighty-five MPs have already signed the motion.*
4 V or VO If you **motion** to someone, you make a movement with your hand in order to show them what they should do. *Boylan motioned to Rudolph to sit down... He motioned Tom to follow him.*
● **Motion** is used in these phrases. ● If you **go through the motions**, you say or do something that is expected of you, without being very sincere or serious about it. *Major Hawks went through the motions of advising me to quit.* ● A process or event that is **in motion** is happening already. *The changes are already in motion.*

motionless /məʊʃnləs/
ADJ Someone or something that is **motionless** is not moving at all. *Rudolph sat motionless. ...queues of motionless cars.*

motion picture, motion pictures
NC A **motion picture** is the same as a film in the cinema; used in formal American English. *The series was used as the basis for a motion picture. ...the motion-picture industry.*

motivate /məʊtɪveɪt/ **motivates, motivating, motivated**
1 VO If you **are motivated** by something, especially an emotion, it causes you to behave in a particular way. *...people motivated by envy and the lust for power... My decision to make this trip was motivated by a desire to leave the country... They are motivated, he says, by stark fear... The killing might be politically motivated.* ◆ **motivation** /məʊtɪveɪʃn/ **motivations** NC or NU *Their main motivations were hatred and revenge... The US government comes into the talks with more straightforward motivation.*
2 VO If you **motivate** someone, you make them feel determined to do something. *You have first got to motivate the children and then to teach them... I just couldn't get her motivated... All our energy seems to go into preaching to the converted, rather than motivating and encouraging those who don't agree with us.* ◆ **motivated** ADJ *...highly motivated and enthusiastic people... The Confederate troops were better motivated and, under Robert Lee, better led.* ◆ **motivation** NU *She insists her success is due to motivation rather than brilliance... Lack of sleep can undermine your motivation.*

motive /məʊtɪv/ **motives**
NC Your **motive** for doing something is your reason for doing it. *I urge you to question his motives... The police say it is too early to identify a motive for the murder... It seems that the motive behind the attack was probably political.*

motley /mɒtli/
ADJ ATTRIB A **motley** collection or group consists of people or things that are all different, so that the group seems rather odd; used showing disapproval. *Their weapons are a motley collection of everything from single barrel shotguns to heavy automatics. ...a motley group of independent MPs.*

motor /məʊtə/ **motors, motoring, motored**
1 NC A **motor** is a part of a machine or vehicle that uses electricity or fuel to produce movement or provide the power that makes the machine or vehicle work. *He got into the car and started the motor. ...an electric motor.*
2 ADJ ATTRIB **Motor** means relating to vehicles with a petrol or diesel engine. *...the decline of the motor industry. ...a motor mechanic.*
3 V If you **are motoring** somewhere, you are travelling there by car; an old-fashioned use. *They spent a week motoring through Italy.* ● See also **motoring**.

motor- /məʊtə-/
PREFIX **Motor-** is used before other nouns to form words that describe things or events that use motor powered vehicles. *...motor-scooters. ...motor-rally.*

motorbike /mɔ͟utəbaɪk/ **motorbikes**

NC A **motorbike** is a two wheeled vehicle with an engine. *...youths riding up and down on powerful motorbikes.*

motorboat /mɔ͟utəbəʊt/ **motorboats**

NC A **motorboat** is a boat that is driven by an engine. *...smuggling by high speed motorboat.*

motorcade /mɔ͟utəkeɪd/ **motorcades**

NC A **motorcade** is a line of slowly-moving cars carrying important people, usually as part of a public ceremony. *The president was in an open car at the head of a long motorcade.*

motor car, motor cars

NC A **motor car** is the same as a **car**; a formal word. *There can be few people who have not heard the name 'Ford' associated with the motor car.*

motorcycle /mɔ͟utəsaɪkl/ **motorcycles**

NC A **motorcycle** is the same as a **motorbike**. *...cars and motorcycles for hire.*

motorcyclist /mɔ͟utəsaɪklɪst/ **motorcyclists**

NC A **motorcyclist** is someone who rides a motorcycle. *...police motorcyclists.*

motoring /mɔ͟utərɪŋ/

ADJ ATTRIB **Motoring** means relating to cars and to driving. *...motoring offences. ...the motoring organisation, the RAC.*

motorised /mɔ͟utəraɪzd/. See **motorized**.

motorist /mɔ͟utərɪst/ **motorists**

NC A **motorist** is someone who drives a car. *Any motorist convicted of driving under the influence of alcohol will be banned for at least a year.*

motorized /mɔ͟utəraɪzd/; also spelt **motorised**.

ADJ **Motorized** vehicles have engines. *...a motorised tricycle.*

motorway /mɔ͟utəweɪ/ **motorways**

NC A **motorway** is a wide road that has been specially built for fast travel over long distance. *...Britain's most heavily used motorway, the M25.*

mottled /mɒ̱tld/

ADJ Something that is **mottled** has areas of different colours that do not have a regular pattern. *...a mottled camouflage jacket.*

motto /mɒ̱təʊ/ **mottoes** or **mottos**

NC A **motto** is a short sentence or phrase that expresses a rule for good or sensible behaviour. *...the BBC's motto: 'Nation shall speak peace unto Nation'.*

mould /mo͟uld/ **moulds, moulding, moulded**; also spelt **mold** in American English.

1 VO To **mould** someone or something means to change or influence them over a period of time so that they develop in a particular way. *...the desire to mould the child into a disciplined creature... Television plays a dominant role in moulding public opinion.*

2 VO If you **mould** plastic or clay, you make it into a particular shape. *...clay moulded into pots.*

3 NC A **mould** is a container that is used to make substances such as metal into a particular shape. You pour a liquid into the mould, and when it becomes solid you take it out. *Vibrations ensure the concrete mix settles well into the mould producing a professional finish.*

4 N MASS **Mould** is a soft grey, green, or blue substance that sometimes forms on old food or on damp walls or clothes. *...nasty green mould... Peanuts, when they go bad, produce a mould.*

mouldy /mo͟uldi/; also spelt **moldy** in American English.

ADJ Something that is **mouldy** is covered with mould. *...mouldy fruit.*

moult /mo͟ult/ **moults, moulting, moulted**; also spelt **molt** in American English.

V When an animal or bird **moults**, it loses its coat or feathers so that a new coat or feathers can grow. *The carrion crows are moulting and the fields are scattered with their long black flight-feathers.*

mound /ma͟und/ **mounds**

1 NC A **mound** is a pile of earth like a very small hill. *This is the graveyard and there are mounds of earth everywhere.*

2 NC A **mound** is also a large, untidy pile of things. *He lay in his bunk under a mound of blankets.*

mount /ma͟und/ **mounts, mounting, mounted**

1 VO To **mount** a campaign or event means to organize it and make it take place. *No rescue operations could be mounted... We mounted an exhibition of recent books.*

2 V If something is **mounting** or if it **mounts** up, it is increasing in size, scope, or degree. *Social problems in modern society are mounting... The temperature mounted rapidly... The soil becomes more and more acidic as pollution mounts up.* ◆ **mounting** ADJ ATTRIB *...mounting unemployment.*

3 VO To **mount** something means to go to the top of it; a formal use. *Walter mounted the steps and pressed the bell.*

4 VOorV If you **mount** a horse, you climb on to its back. *The brothers watched as she mounted the mare.* ● See also **mounted**.

5 VO If you **mount** an object in a particular place, you fix it there. *The sword was mounted in a mahogany case.*

6 **Mount** is used as part of the name of a mountain. *...Mount Erebus.*

7 If you **mount guard** or if you **mount a guard** over something, you guard it or get someone to guard it. *She had been asked to mount guard over a number of dogs... Bird lovers are mounting a twenty four-hour guard over the nest of England's only nesting eagles.*

mountain /ma͟untɪn/ **mountains**

1 NC A **mountain** is a very high area of land with steep sides. *Mount Kilimanjaro, Africa's highest mountain, lies close to the border with Kenya... They returned to their homes in nearby mountain villages... In Guatemala, a bus has crashed on a mountain road near the capital. ...an earthquake in the southern Santa Cruz mountains.*

2 NC A **mountain** of something is a very large amount of it. *They had a mountain of used clothing... The Prime Minister faces a mountain of problems... The issue attracts mountains of mail to parliament.*

3 to **make a mountain out of a molehill**: see **molehill**.

mountaineer /ma͟untɪnɪ͟ə/ **mountaineers**

NC A **mountaineer** is a person who climbs mountains as a hobby or a sport. *Local mountaineers say conditions are dangerous, particularly in the gulleys.*

mountaineering /ma͟untɪnɪ͟ərɪŋ/

NU **Mountaineering** is the activity of climbing mountains as a hobby or sport. *The incident was one of the worst disasters in the history of mountaineering... Two six-man mountaineering expeditions are making assaults on Mount Everest this week.*

mountainous /ma͟untɪnəs/

ADJ A **mountainous** area has a lot of mountains. *...a remote and mountainous area... It's a mountainous territory, dominated by the beautiful Pamir range.*

mountain range, mountain ranges

NC A **mountain range** or **range of mountains** is a row of mountains that were formed at the same time in the earth's history. *We could just see beyond the next mountain range.*

mountainside /ma͟untɪnsaɪd/ **mountainsides**

NC A **mountainside** is one of the steep sides of a mountain. *A slab of hard packed snow crashed down the mountainside.*

mountebank /ma͟untɪbæŋk/ **mountebanks**

NC A **mountebank** is a person who tries to deceive people by claiming to be able to do wonderful things; a literary word. *The nation was led astray by a mountebank... You get fakes, cheats and mountebanks the world over.*

mounted /ma͟untɪd/

ADJ ATTRIB **Mounted** police or soldiers ride horses when they are on duty. *...the Royal Canadian Mounted Police. ...a contingent of mounted police.*

mourn /mɔ͟ːn/ **mourns, mourning, mourned**

1 VOorV+for If you **mourn** someone who has died or **mourn** for them, you are very sad and think about them a lot. *I remained to mourn him in Chicago... I shall always love Guy and mourn for him.*

2 VOorV+for If you **mourn** something or **mourn** for it, you are very sad about something that has happened. *Armenians gathered in Moscow to mourn the recent*

inter-communal clashes in the Azerbaijani city of Sumgait... I mourned for the loss of my beauty.
3 See also **mourning**.
mourner /mɔːnə/ **mourners**
NC A **mourner** is a person who attends a funeral. *The mourners gathered around the grave.*
mournful /mɔːnfl/; a literary word.
1 ADJ If you are **mournful**, you are very sad. *Tomorrow should be quite a send off, not at all sad and mournful.* ◆ **mournfully** ADV *He shook his head mournfully.*
2 ADJ A **mournful** sound seems very sad. *The little train kept up its mournful howl.*
mourning /mɔːnɪŋ/
1 NU **Mourning** is behaviour in which you show sadness about a person's death. *Many people are taking part in a day of mourning... Beards were shaved off as a sign of mourning.*
2 If you are **in mourning**, you are wearing special clothes or behaving in a special way because a member of your family has died. *He was in mourning for his wife... Malaysia has been in mourning after the death of its founding father Tunku Abdul Rahman.*
mouse /maʊs/ **mice** or mouses. The plural form is **mice** for the meaning in paragraph 1 and either **mouses** or **mice** for the meaning in paragraph 2.
1 NC A **mouse** is a small furry animal with a long tail. *The cat was there to keep the mice out of the kitchen.*
2 NC A **mouse** is a hand-held device that you use with a computer system. By moving it over a flat surface and pressing its buttons, you can move the cursor around the screen and perform certain operations without using the keyboard. *Put the computer mouse on the part of the screen labeled 'Help'.*
mousetrap /maʊstræp/ **mousetraps**
NC A **mousetrap** is a small device that catches or kills mice.
mousey /maʊsi/. See **mousy**.
moussaka /muːsɑːkə/ **moussakas**
N MASS **Moussaka** is a cooked dish consisting of layers of meat and aubergines.
mousse /muːs/ **mousses**
N MASS **Mousse** is a sweet, light food made from eggs and cream. *...the last mouthful of chocolate mousse.*
moustache /məstɑːʃ/ **moustaches**; also spelt **mustache**.
NC A man's **moustache** is the hair that grows on his upper lip. *...a tall man with a moustache.*
mousy /maʊsi/
ADJ **Mousy** hair is a dull, light brown colour. *Her mousy hair had been cheaply permed.*
mouth, mouths, mouthing, mouthed. The noun is pronounced /maʊθ/ in the singular and /maʊðz/ in the plural. The verb is pronounced /maʊð/.
1 NC Your **mouth** is your lips, or the space behind your lips where your teeth and tongue are. *She opened her mouth to say something, then closed it.*
2 NC The **mouth** of a cave, hole, or bottle is its entrance or opening. *There was a vicious snarling in the mouth of the shelter.*
3 NC The **mouth** of a river is the place where it flows into the sea. *We lived near the mouth of the Bashee River.*
4 V Oor V-QUOTE If you **mouth** something, you form words with your lips without making any sound. *She mouthed the word 'no'... They mouth the words 'Hi, Mom' whenever a TV camera is turned on them.*
5 **shut your mouth**: see **shut**. See also **hand-to-mouth**, **loud-mouthed**, **open-mouthed**, **word of mouth**.
mouthful /maʊθfʊl/ **mouthfuls**
NC A **mouthful** of food or drink is an amount that you put or have in your mouth. *He took another mouthful of whisky... 'Don't you like me?' she asked between mouthfuls.*
mouth organ, **mouth organs**
NC A **mouth organ** is a small musical instrument which you play by blowing and sucking air through it.
mouthpiece /maʊθpiːs/ **mouthpieces**
1 NC The **mouthpiece** of a telephone is the part that you speak into. *She had her hand over the mouthpiece.*

2 NC The **mouthpiece** of a musical instrument is the part that you blow into. *The tuba is heavy to carry and the mouthpiece leaves big red marks on your lips.*
3 NC The **mouthpiece** of a person or organization is someone who informs other people of the opinions and policies of that person or organization. *He became the official mouthpiece of the leadership.*
mouthwash /maʊθwɒʃ/ **mouthwashes**
N MASS **Mouthwash** is a liquid that you rinse your mouth with, in order to clean and freshen it. *She brushed her teeth and gargled with mouthwash.*
mouth-watering
ADJ **Mouth-watering** food looks or smells extremely delicious. *Ceviche is a mouth-watering dish of uncooked fish marinated in a mixture of lemon juice, chilli and onion.*
movable /muːvəbl/; also spelt **moveable**.
ADJ Something that is **movable** can be moved from one place or position to another. *Damage can be avoided if moveable objects are tied down... It's a vinyl doll with movable arms and legs. ...movable screens.*
move /muːv/ **moves, moving, moved**
1 V-ERG When something **moves** or when you **move** something, it changes its position. *The curtains began to move... I'll have to move the car... The sea is moving the boat.*
2 V When you **move**, you change your position or go to a different place. *I was so scared I couldn't move... He moved eagerly towards the door to welcome his visitors.* ▶ Also N SING *Neither she nor any of the others made a move.*
3 V or V O If you **move** or if you **move house**, you go to live in a different house, taking all your belongings with you. *My parents moved from Hyde to Stepney... Somebody phoned the editor at home but he had recently moved house.* ▶ Also NC *I wrecked a good stereo on my last move.*
4 V-ERG If you **move** or if somebody **moves** you from one place or job to another, you go from one place or job to another. *He'd moved to the BBC from publishing... Executives are being moved around from one company to another.* ▶ Also NC *Regular moves for junior executives are a company policy.*
5 V A If you **move** towards a particular state or opinion, you start to be in that state or have that opinion. *We are moving rapidly into the nuclear age.* ▶ Also N SING *This was the first step in his move away from the Labour party.*
6 V If a situation is **moving**, it is developing or progressing. *Events now moved swiftly... A writer must keep the story moving.*
7 V O+*to*-INF If something **moves** you to do something, it causes you to do it; a formal use. *What has moved the President to take this step?*
8 V O If something **moves** you, it causes you to feel a deep emotion, usually sadness or sympathy. *The whole incident had moved her profoundly.* ◆ **moved** ADJ *He was too moved to speak.*
9 V O If you **move** a motion or amendment at a meeting, you propose it so that people can vote for or against it. *The conference gave overwhelming support to a motion moved by John MacDonald demanding a written constitution.*
10 NC A **move** is also an action that you take in order to achieve something. *Accepting this job was a very good move... For six days neither side made a move.*
11 NC In a game such as chess, a **move** is the act of putting a counter or chess piece in a different position on the board. *Whose move is it?*
12 See also **moving**.
● **Move** is used in these phrases. ● If you are **on the move**, you are going from one place to another. *Billie Jean is constantly on the move.* ● If you tell someone to **get a move on**, you are telling them to hurry; an informal expression. *Get a move on, you two.*
move down PHRASAL VERB If you **move down**, you go to a lower level, grade, or class. *When they fail their mathematics exams they move down a year.*
move in PHRASAL VERB 1 If you **move in** somewhere, you begin to live in a different house or place. *He moved in with Mrs Camish.* 2 If soldiers or police

move in, they go towards a place or person in order to attack them or deal with them. *They were under orders to move in from France.*

move off PHRASAL VERB When vehicles or people **move off**, they start moving away from a place. *The gleaming fleet of cars prepared to move off.*

move on PHRASAL VERB When you **move on**, you leave a place or activity and go somewhere else or do something else. *After three weeks in Hong Kong, we moved on to Japan... Can we move on to the second question?*

move out PHRASAL VERB If you **move out**, you leave the house or place where you have been living, and go and live somewhere else. *They want to move out of their little room... He says there are many people living in the bush, too frightened as yet to move out.*

move up PHRASAL VERB If you **move up**, you go to a higher level, grade, or class. *The Vice-President should move up into the Presidency.*

moveable /mu:vəbl/. See movable.

movement /mu:vmənt/ movements
1 N U or N C **Movement** involves changing position or going from one place to another. *He heard movement in the hut. ...the movement of oil cargoes... Tom lit a cigarette with quick, jerky movements.*
2 N U or N C **Movement** is also a gradual change in an attitude, opinion, or policy. *The new Soviet Minister of Defence has called for a gradual movement away from conscription... There was a movement towards a revival of conscription.*
3 N PL Your **movements** are everything which you do or plan to do during a period of time. *I don't know why you have any interest in my movements.*
4 N C A **movement** is also a group of people who share the same beliefs, ideas, or aims. *...the Trade Union Movement. ...the successful movement to abolish child labour.*
5 N C A **movement** of a piece of classical music is one of its major sections. *There is an immensely long first movement.*

movie /mu:vi/ movies
1 N C A **movie** is a film that is shown in the cinema or sold in video shops. *...a war movie... I went to a movie.*
2 N PL The cinema is sometimes called the **movies**. *Let's go to the movies.*

moviegoer /mu:vigəʊə/ moviegoers
N C A **moviegoer** is a person who often goes to the cinema; used in American English. *Films like 'M*A*S*H' changed the way moviegoers viewed war.*

movie theater, movie theaters
N C A **movie theater** is the same as a cinema; used in American English. *The closest movie theater is 23 miles away.*

moving /mu:vɪŋ/
1 ADJ Something that is **moving** causes you to feel a deep emotion, usually sadness or sympathy. *There is a moving account of his father's death.* ◆ **movingly** ADV *Her childhood is movingly described.*
2 ADJ ATTRIB A **moving** model or part of a machine is able to move. *These devices have no moving parts.*

moving picture, moving pictures
N C A **moving picture** is a film; an old-fashioned expression.

mow /maʊ/ mows, mowing, mowed or mown
V O or V If you **mow** an area of grass, you cut it using a lawnmower. *He was still hard at work, sweeping the cuttings from the section he'd mown.*

mow down PHRASAL VERB If a large number of people are **mown down**, they are all killed violently at one time. *The victims were mown down by machine gun fire.*

mower /maʊə/ mowers
N C A **mower** is a machine for cutting grass, corn, or wheat. *...rotary and hover mowers.*

Mozambique /məʊzæmbi:k/
The **Republic of Mozambique** is a country in south-eastern Africa. Mozambique became a Portuguese colony in the 19th century. A war to achieve independence lasted from 1964 to 1974. Samora Machel, leader of Frelimo (Front for the Liberation of Mozambique), became the first President of

independent Mozambique in 1975. Frelimo was opposed by Renamo, also known as the MNR (Mozambique National Resistance), which was initially supported by Rhodesia and subsequently by South Africa. The economy has been completely disrupted by the civil war and over one million refugees have fled to Malawi or South Africa. Samora Machel died in 1986 in a plane crash and Joaquim Alberto Chissano became President. Frelimo was the only party until 1990, when political parties were legalized. Mozambique exports shrimps and prawns, cashew nuts, and sugar. Large foreign debts and high inflation are major economic problems. It is a member of the Organization of African Unity. ◆ **Mozambican** /məʊzæmbi:kən/ N, ADJ ▪ *per capita GNP:* US$100 ▪ *religion:* Christianity, Islam ▪ *language:* Portuguese (official), Ronga, Shangaan, Muchope ▪ *currency:* metical ▪ *capital:* Maputo ▪ *population:* 15 million (1989) ▪ *size:* 799,380 square kilometres.

MP /empi:/ MPs
N C An **MP** is a person who has been elected to represent people in a country's parliament. **MP** is an abbreviation for 'Member of Parliament'. *...the MP for South East Bristol.*

mpg /empi:dʒi:/
mpg is an abbreviation for 'miles per gallon'; used especially after a number to indicate how far a vehicle can travel using one gallon of fuel. *It does 20 mpg.*

mph /empi:eɪtʃ/
mph is an abbreviation for 'miles per hour'; used after a number to indicate the speed of a vehicle. *These cars are reasonably economical at a steady 56 mph.*

Mr /mɪstə/
1 TITLE **Mr** is used before a man's name when you are speaking or referring to him. *...Mr Jenkins.*
2 TITLE **Mr** is sometimes used before titles such as 'President' or 'chairman' when you are addressing the person who holds that position. *...Mr Ambassador.*

Mrs /mɪsɪz/
TITLE **Mrs** is used before the name of a married woman when you are speaking or referring to her. *...Mrs Carstairs.*

MS /emes/
N U **MS** is an abbreviation for 'multiple sclerosis'. *They have developed this new experimental treatment for MS... About 95% of MS patients remain only moderately disabled for at least 30 years.*

Ms /mɪz, məz/
TITLE **Ms** is used before the name of a single or married woman when you are speaking or referring to her. *...Ms Harman.*

ms., mss.
N C **ms.** is a written abbreviation for 'manuscript'.

MSc /emesi:/ MScs
N C An **MSc** is a higher degree in a scientific subject. **MSc** is an abbreviation for 'Master of Science'. *He holds a BSc in engineering and studied for an MSc in the United States.*

Mswati III, King /mswɑ:ti/
Mswati III became King of Swaziland in 1986. He is the son of King Sobhuza II, who died in 1982. Born: 1968.

Mt, Mts
1 **Mt** is a written abbreviation for 'mount'; used as part of the name of a particular mountain. *...Mt Etna.*
2 **Mt** is also an abbreviation for 'mountain'; used as part of the name of a particular mountain or range or mountains. *...Holyhead Mt. ...the Rocky Mts.*

Mubarak, Muhammad Hosni /muhæmɪd husni mubɑ:rək/
Lieutenant-General Muhammad Hosni Mubarak became President of Egypt in 1981, when President Anwar Sadat was assassinated. He was Air Force Chief of Staff from 1969 to 1972, and Commander-in-Chief from 1972 to 1975. He was Vice President of Egypt from 1975 to 1981, and Prime Minister from 1981 to 1982. He became Chairman of the National Democratic Party in 1982. Born: 1928.

much /mʌtʃ/. For the meanings in paragraphs 1, 2, and 4, the comparative is **more** and the superlative is **most**: see the separate entries for these words.
1 ADV You use **much** to emphasize that something is

true to a great extent. *Myra and I are looking forward very much to the party... Now I feel much more confident.*
2 ADV If something does not happen **much**, it does not happen very often. *She doesn't talk about them much.*
3 ADV If two things are **much** the same, they are very similar. *The landscape was then much as it is today... The two poems convey much the same emotional tone.*
4 QUANT You also use **much** to refer to a large amount or proportion of something. *Much of the recent trouble has come from outside... There wasn't much to do... She had endured so much... We hadn't got much money.*
5 QUANT You also use **much** when you ask for or give information about an amount. *How much did he tell you?... He's done as much as I have... I doubt if she sees as much of him as you do... How much money have you got left?*
● **Much** is used in these phrases. ● If something is **not so much** one thing as another, it is more like the second thing than the first. *It was not so much an argument as a monologue.* ● If you say **so much for** a particular thing, you mean that it has not been successful or helpful. *So much for the experts and their learning.* ● **Nothing much** means an amount that is so small that it is not important. *There's nothing much left.* ● If a situation or action is **too much for** you, you cannot cope with it. *The long journey each day might prove too much for him.* ● If you describe something as **not much of** a particular type of thing, you mean that it is small or of poor quality. *It wasn't much of a garden.* ● You say '**I thought as much**' after you have just been told something that you had expected or guessed. *'I'm afraid he never arrived.'—'Yes, I thought as much.'* ● **a bit much**: see bit. ● **not up to much**: see up.

muchness /mˈʌtʃnəs/
If two or more things are **much of a muchness**, they are very similar; an informal expression. *In general appearance the men were all much of a muchness.*

muck /mʌk/ **mucks, mucking, mucked**
NU **Muck** is dirt or manure; an informal word. *There was muck everywhere. ...a muck heap.*
muck about PHRASAL VERB If you **muck about** or **muck around**, you behave in a stupid way and waste time; an informal expression. *She was mucking about with a jug of flowers on the table... They're not interested in intellectual pursuits: they just want to muck around outside.*
muck around PHRASAL VERB See **muck about**.
muck out PHRASAL VERB If you **muck out** a stable, pigsty, or cow shed, you clean it. *You wouldn't want to go and muck out a 200 cow dairy.*
muck up PHRASAL VERB If you **muck** something **up**, you do it very badly or fail when you try to do it; an informal expression. *'How was the exam?'—'I mucked it up.'*

muck-raking
NU **Muck-raking** is the act of finding and spreading scandal relating to public figures. *He brushed off allegations levelled against him in the latest round of political muck-raking.*

mucky /mˈʌki/; an informal word.
1 ADJ Something that is **mucky** is very dirty. *...mucky fields.*
2 ADJ A **mucky** book or film describes or shows a lot of sex; used showing disapproval.

mucus /mjuːkəs/
NU **Mucus** is a slimy liquid that is produced in some parts of your body, for example the inside of your nose; a formal word. *...mucus streaming from his nostrils.*

mud /mʌd/
NU **Mud** is a sticky mixture of earth and water. *She was covered in mud.*

muddle /mˈʌdl/ **muddles, muddling, muddled**
1 NCorNU A **muddle** is a confused state or situation. *I have got into a muddle. ...the worsening muddle of her finances. ...years of muddle and incompetence.*
2 VO If you **muddle** things or if you **muddle** them **up**, you mix them up or get them in the wrong order. *I wish you wouldn't muddle my books and drawings...*

Later they may muddle up your names with those of your cousins. ◆ **muddled** ADJ *He gets his facts rather muddled.*
3 VO If you **muddle** someone, you confuse them. *Don't muddle her with too many suggestions.* ◆ **muddled** ADJ *I'm sorry. I'm getting muddled.*
muddle along PHRASAL VERB If you **muddle along**, you live or exist without a proper plan or purpose in your life. *The church has lost its way, muddling along from Sunday to Sunday.*
muddle through PHRASAL VERB If you **muddle through**, you manage to do something even though you do not really know how to do it properly. *The children are left to muddle through on their own.*

muddle-headed
ADJ If you are **muddle-headed**, you are confused or incapable of thinking clearly about something. *He was dismissed as a muddle-headed mischief-maker.*

muddy /mˈʌdi/ **muddier, muddiest; muddies, muddying, muddied**
1 ADJ Something that is **muddy** contains or is covered in mud. *...a muddy ditch. ...the muddy floor.*
2 ADJ A **muddy** colour is dull and brownish. *The landscape turns a mottled, muddy brown.*
3 VO If you **muddy** a situation or issue, you make it harder to understand. *The issue has been muddied by allegations of bribery.*

mudflat /mˈʌdflæt/ **mudflats**
NC A **mudflat** is an area of flat empty coastal land which is covered by the sea only when the tide is in. *...on the salt marsh and mudflats of Wigtown Bay.*

mudguard /mˈʌdɡɑːd/ **mudguards**
NC The **mudguards** on a bicycle or other vehicle are the metal or plastic parts above the tyres, which stop the rider or vehicle from being splashed with mud.

muesli /mjuːzli/
NU **Muesli** is a mixture of nuts, dried fruit, and grains that you eat for breakfast with milk or yoghurt.

muezzin /mu̱ɛzɪn/ **muezzins**
NC In a mosque, a **muezzin** is an official who calls from its tower when it is time for Muslims to say their prayers. *A muezzin calls the faithful to prayer from a minaret.*

muff /mʌf/ **muffs, muffing, muffed**
1 VO If you **muff** something, you do it badly or you make a mistake while you are doing it; an informal use. *I muffed a catch at cricket.*
2 NC A **muff** is a piece of fur or thick cloth shaped like a short hollow cylinder that you wear on your hands to keep them warm in cold weather. *I used to clench my hands inside the muff.*

muffin /mˈʌfɪn/ **muffins**
1 NC A **muffin** is a type of small cake, usually with fruit or some other kind of flavouring in it. *...bran muffins.*
2 NC A **muffin** is also a type of small, round bread roll which you eat hot; an old-fashioned use.

muffle /mˈʌfl/ **muffles, muffling, muffled**
VO If something **muffles** a sound, it makes it quieter and more difficult to hear. *The snow muffled the sound of our footsteps... The sound of the children had been muffled by brick walls.*

muffled /mˈʌfld/
1 ADJ A **muffled** sound is quiet, dull, or difficult to hear. *'I don't know,' he said in a muffled voice. ...a muffled explosion.*
2 ADJ PRED If you are **muffled** or **muffled up**, you are wearing thick, warm clothes which hide most of your body or face. *He was heavily muffled in a black overcoat. ...a boy muffled up in a blue scarf.*

muffler /mˈʌflə/ **mufflers**; used in American English.
1 NC A **muffler** is a scarf. *...with a long, knitted muffler around her neck.*
2 NC A **muffler** is the part of a car or motorcycle's exhaust system that makes it quieter. *...motorcycles with special mufflers to keep the vehicles quiet.*

mug /mʌɡ/ **mugs, mugging, mugged**
1 NC A **mug** is a large, deep cup with straight sides. *...a chipped mug.*
2 NC You can use **mug** to refer to a mug and its contents, or to the contents only. *He sipped at his mug of coffee.*

3 VO If someone **mugs** you, they attack you when you are in the street and steal your money; an informal use. *They lurk in dark side streets and mug passers-by.* ◆ **mugging, muggings** N C or N U *There has been a great increase in vandalism and muggings... Mugging in the street, even in broad daylight, was not uncommon.*
4 NC If you call someone a **mug**, you mean that you think they are stupid and easily deceived; an informal use. *'All right,' he said, like the mug he was, 'I won't say anything.'*

Mugabe, Robert /rɒbət mugɑːbi/
Robert Mugabe was Prime Minister of Zimbabwe from 1980 to 1987, and became President in 1987. He co-founded ZANU (Zimbabwe African National Union) in 1963 and became its leader in 1975. Born: 1924.

mugger /mʌgə/ **muggers**
NC A **mugger** is a person who attacks someone in the street and steals their money; an informal word. *Gangs of teenage muggers roam the streets.*

muggins /mʌgɪnz/
NU If you refer to yourself as **muggins**, you mean that you have been stupid and people have taken advantage of you.

muggy /mʌgi/
ADJ **Muggy** weather is unpleasantly warm and damp. *We've had warm and muggy weather, but now it's getting a little chilly.*

mug shot, mug shots
NC A **mug shot** is a photograph taken by the police of a person who has been charged with a crime; an informal expression. *Many hours passed before the mug shots and fingerprints were finally taken.*

mulberry /mʌlbəⁱri/ **mulberries**
1 NC A **mulberry** is a tree. It has small edible berries, and leaves which are used to feed silkworms. *He planted a mulberry tree to replace the one put there by his great-great grandfather.*
2 NC **Mulberries** are the small edible purple berries that grow on mulberry trees.

mulch /mʌltʃ/ **mulches**
NC A **mulch** is a mixture of rotting leaves and twigs which you put round the base of plants in order to protect them and to help them to grow. *A good, nourishing annual mulch is a great help.*

mule /mjuːl/ **mules**
NC A **mule** is an animal that is produced when a female horse mates with a male donkey. *Peasants on foot trundled along behind wagons and mules.*

mulish /mjuːlɪʃ/
ADJ Someone who is **mulish** is unwilling to change their attitude or to do what other people tell them to do. *He's a very headstrong and mulish person most of the time, but underneath I think he's quite vulnerable.*

mull /mʌl/ **mulls, mulling, mulled**
mull over PHRASAL VERB If you **mull** something **over**, you think about it for a long time before deciding what to do. *I sat there and tried to mull things over in my mind.*

mulled /mʌld/
ADJ ATTRIB **Mulled** wine has sugar and spice added, and is served warm. *They ordered mulled wine.*

mullet /mʌlɪt/; **mullet** is both the singular and the plural form.
NC A **mullet** is a small sea fish that people cook and eat. *...smoked mullet.*

Mulroney, Brian /braɪən mʌruːni/
Brian Mulroney became Prime Minister of Canada in 1984. He became a Member of Parliament and leader of the Progressive Conservative Party in 1983. Born: 1939.

multi- /mʌlti-/
PREFIX **Multi-** is used to form adjectives indicating that something has many things of a particular kind. *...multi-cultural societies. ...multi-faceted. ...multi-purpose.*

multi-coloured /mʌltikʌləd/; also spelt **multicoloured**.
ADJ Something that is **multi-coloured** has many different colours. *In the middle are multicoloured paving stones.*

multifarious /mʌltifɛəriəs/
ADJ **Multifarious** things are many in number or of many different kinds; a formal word. *...pursuing their multifarious hobbies and interests.*

multilateral /mʌltilætəⁱrəl/
ADJ Something that is **multilateral** involves more than two different countries or groups of people. *...multilateral nuclear disarmament.*

multilingual /mʌltilɪŋgwəl/
1 ADJ Something that is **multilingual** is written or said in several different languages. *...a multilingual pamphlet.*
2 ADJ Someone who is **multilingual** is able to speak more than two languages very well. *In Amnesty's headquarters, a multilingual staff of 260 compile reports on human rights abuses.*

multi-millionaire, multi-millionaires
NC A **multi-millionaire** is a very rich person who has money or property worth several million pounds or dollars. *Mr Virani, who is now a multi-millionaire, has built up one of Britain's top companies.*

multinational /mʌltinæʃənəl/ **multinationals**
1 ADJ A **multinational** company has branches in many different countries. *Many of the West's large multinational companies have operations in Africa.* ▶ Also NC *Trade in bananas is dominated by three huge food multinationals.*
2 ADJ **Multinational** also describes something that involves several different countries. *...the multinational forces deployed under the treaty.*

multiple /mʌltɪpl/
ADJ ATTRIB You use **multiple** to describe things that consist of many parts, involve many people, or have many uses. *...multiple locks on the doors... There have been several multiple collisions in fog this winter.*

multiple-choice
ADJ When you do a **multiple-choice** test, you have to select the correct answer from several possible choices. *Guessing usually boosts scores in multiple-choice tests.*

multiple sclerosis /mʌltɪpl sklərəʊsɪs/
NU **Multiple sclerosis** is a serious disease of the nervous system, which gradually makes a person weaker, and sometimes affects their sight or speech. *Her husband became seriously ill from multiple sclerosis.*

multiplication /mʌltɪplɪkeɪʃn/
1 NU **Multiplication** is the process of calculating the result of one number multiplied by another. *...an understanding of numbers—including addition, subtraction, multiplication and division.*
2 NU+SUPP The **multiplication** of things of a particular kind is a large increase in the number or amount of them. *...the multiplication of universities.*

multiplication sign, multiplication signs
NC A **multiplication sign** is the sign (×) which is put between two numbers to show that they are being multiplied.

multiplication table, multiplication tables
NC A **multiplication table** is a list of the multiplications of numbers between one and twelve. Children often have to learn multiplication tables at school. *You needed a command of the multiplication tables, and the ability to spell.*

multiplicity /mʌltɪplɪsəti/
N SING+of A **multiplicity** of things is a large number or large variety of them; a formal word. *...the multiplicity of languages spoken in Africa.*

multiply /mʌltɪplaɪ/ **multiplies, multiplying, multiplied**
1 V-ERG When something **multiplies** or when you **multiply** it, it increases greatly in number or amount. *The shops began to multiply, eventually springing up in almost every town in the area... With the experimental solar furnaces, they've multiplied the sun's power nearly 60,000 times.*
2 V When animals **multiply**, they produce large numbers of young. *The creatures began to multiply very rapidly.*
3 VO If you **multiply** one number by another, you calculate the total which you get when you add the number to itself a particular number of times. For example, 2 multiplied by 3 is equal to 2 plus 2 plus 2,

which equals 6. *Multiply this figure by the number of years you have worked.*

multiracial /mʌltıreıʃl/
ADJ Something that is **multiracial** consists of or involves people of many different nationalities and cultures. *We live in a multiracial society... The handbook also became more multiracial in content as well as in ideology.*

multi-storey
ADJ ATTRIB A **multi-storey** building or car park has several floors at different levels above the ground. *They are cut off from the rest of the world in a flat in a multi-storey block. ...a multi-storey car park.*

multitude /mʌltıtjuːd/ **multitudes**
NC A **multitude** of things or people is a very large number of them; a formal word. *It didn't work out quite like I intended it to, for a multitude of reasons... 'We are keeping our options open,' he had told the assembled multitude.*

mum /mʌm/ **mums**
NC or VOCATIVE Your **mum** is your mother; an informal word. *My mum used to live here... I've been put in the special class, Mum.*

mumble /mʌmbl/ **mumbles, mumbling, mumbled**
V, V-QUOTE, or V-REPORT If you **mumble**, you speak in a very quiet and indistinct way. *Stop mumbling... He took my hand and mumbled, 'Don't worry.'... I mumbled something about having an appointment.*

mumbo jumbo /mʌmbəʊ dʒʌmbəʊ/
NU If something is **mumbo jumbo**, it does not make any sense at all to you; an informal expression. *The order of the alphabet is mumbo jumbo to a child who cannot write his name... It was all mumbo jumbo and I didn't understand a word.*

mummified /mʌmıfaıd/
ADJ A **mummified** dead body has stayed preserved for a long time, especially because special oils were rubbed into it. *...the mummified bodies of a dynasty of pharaohs.*

mummy /mʌmi/ **mummies**
1 NC or VOCATIVE **Mummy** means mother; an informal word. *Mummy put me on the train at Victoria.*
2 NC A **mummy** is a dead body which was preserved long ago by being rubbed with oils and wrapped in cloth. *The display case will have a controlled atmosphere to preserve the mummy inside.*

mumps /mʌmps/
NU **Mumps** is a disease that causes a mild fever and painful swelling of the glands in the neck. *A triple vaccine to fight measles, mumps and rubella was to be launched in the autumn.*

munch /mʌntʃ/ **munches, munching, munched**
VO or V If you **munch** food, you chew it steadily and thoroughly. *The father and son sat there, munching bread and butter. ...snack packs of things to munch.*

mundane /mʌndeın/
ADJ Something that is **mundane** is ordinary and not interesting. *...mundane tasks such as washing up.*

municipal /mjuːnısıpl/
ADJ ATTRIB **Municipal** means associated with or belonging to a city or town that has its own local government. *...a big municipal housing scheme. ...the municipal gardens.*

municipality /mjuːnısıpæləti/ **municipalities**
NC A **municipality** is a city or town which has the authority to appoint a local council and local officials to administer its internal affairs; used also to refer to the local government of the city or town. A formal word. *It was a big park, and the municipality did not have enough money to keep it tidy.*

munificent /mjuːnıfısənt/
ADJ A **munificent** person is very generous; a formal word.

munitions /mjuːnıʃnz/
N PL **Munitions** are military equipment such as bombs, guns, or supplies. *The rebels were dropping their demands to be resupplied with munitions during the ceasefire. ...a one hundred million dollar munitions stockpile.*

mural /mjuərəl/ **murals**
NC A **mural** is a picture which is painted on a wall. *The mural is meant to depict the excesses of Wall Street. ...painted landscapes and vast historical murals.*

murder /mɜːdə/ **murders, murdering, murdered**
1 NU or NC **Murder** is the crime of deliberately killing a person. *...attempted murder. ...the rising number of murders in San Francisco.*
2 VO To **murder** someone means to commit the crime of killing them deliberately. *The IRA said they murdered him... His father, mother, and sister were all murdered by the terrorists.*
3 If someone **gets away with murder,** they do whatever they like and nobody punishes them; an informal expression. *They thought they could get away with murder because they weren't regulated.*

murderer /mɜːdərə/ **murderers**
NC A **murderer** is someone who commits the crime of deliberately killing another person. *I want to track down the murderers of my son.*

murderous /mɜːdərəs/
1 ADJ Someone who is **murderous** is likely to murder someone and may already be guilty of such a crime. *...this murderous gang of known criminals... The girl might have murderous tendencies.*
2 ADJ A **murderous** attack or other action results in the death of many people. *...murderous guerrilla raids.*

murk /mɜːk/
N SING **Murk** refers to darkness or thick mist that you cannot see through very well. *Through the murk the dull red sun was visible.*

murky /mɜːki/
1 ADJ **Murky** places are dark and rather unpleasant. *We looked out into the murky streets.*
2 ADJ **Murky** water is so dark and dirty that you cannot see through it. *...murky ponds.*
3 ADJ **Murky** is also used to describe something that you suspect is dishonest or morally wrong; a literary use. *...murky goings-on in a local gallery. ...the murky world of Nigeria's drug barons.*

murmur /mɜːmə/ **murmurs, murmuring, murmured**
1 VO, V-QUOTE, V-REPORT, or V If you **murmur** something, you say it very quietly. *They murmured agreement... 'Darling,' she murmured... He murmured what sounded like yes but Brigit could not be sure.*
2 NC A **murmur** is something that someone says which can hardly be heard. *There were murmurs of sympathy.*
3 N SING+SUPP A **murmur** is also a continuous, quiet, indistinct sound. *...the murmur of waves on a beach.*

Muscat /mʌskət/
Muscat is the capital of Oman and its largest city. Population: 50,000 (1981).

muscle /mʌsl/ **muscles, muscling, muscled**
1 NC or NU A **muscle** is a piece of tissue inside your body which is able to become smaller and to get bigger again. Your muscles enable you to move. *The boys couldn't help admiring their bulging muscles... Your mouth is mainly composed of muscle.*
2 NU If someone has **muscle**, they have strength and power, which enables them to do difficult things; an informal use. *The campaign was valueless without the muscle of an organisation behind it.* ● to **flex** one's **muscle**: see **flex**.

muscle in PHRASAL VERB If you **muscle in** on something, you force your way into a situation when you are not welcome. *They resent the way you are muscling in on their territory.*

muscular /mʌskjulə/
1 ADJ ATTRIB **Muscular** means involving or affecting your muscles. *Great muscular effort is needed. ...muscular pains.*
2 ADJ A **muscular** person has strong, firm muscles. *...a short but muscular man. ...his muscular arms.*

muscular dystrophy /mʌskjulə dıstrəfi/
NU **Muscular dystrophy** is a serious disease in which your muscles gradually weaken. *Medical science has reported an advance in the study of treating muscular dystrophy.*

muse /mjuːz/ **muses, musing, mused**
1 V, VA, or V-QUOTE If you **muse**, you think about something slowly and carefully; a literary use. *She lay musing for a while... Mr Brady mused on why*

Moscow should not get a Western loan... 'I can't see him as a family man,' she mused.
2 NC A **muse** is an imaginary force which is believed to give people inspiration and creative ideas, especially for poetry or music; a literary use. *...the muse of music.*

museum /mjuːzi̱əm/ **museums**
NC A **museum** is a building where interesting and valuable objects are kept and displayed to the public. *...classical sculpture in the British Museum.*

museum piece, museum pieces
NC A **museum piece** is an object or building which is very old and unusual. *The gun was a museum piece. It hadn't been fired for years... The house is now something of a museum piece.*

Museveni, Yoweri /jəʊwe̱ri muːse̱vəni/
Yoweri Museveni became President of Uganda in 1986. He served as Minister of Defence in 1980. He was the leader of the National Resistance Army (NRA), which fought against Milton Obote from 1980 until 1986. He is a member of the ruling National Resistance Movement (NRM). Born: 1944.

mush /mʌ̱ʃ/
NU or N SING **Mush** is a substance that is like a thick soft paste; an informal word. *Apples are ground into mush... He gulped down the tasteless mush.*

mushroom /mʌ̱ʃrʊm/ **mushrooms, mushrooming, mushroomed**
1 NC A **mushroom** is a fungus which often has a short stem and a round top. You can eat some kinds of mushrooms. *I liked helping to pick mushrooms.*
2 V If something **mushrooms**, it grows or appears very quickly. *The organization quickly mushroomed into a mass movement.*

mushroom cloud, mushroom clouds
NC A **mushroom** cloud is a large cloud of dust which rises into the sky after a nuclear explosion. *The blast sent a huge mushroom cloud of toxic gas into the air.*

mushy /mʌ̱ʃi/
1 ADJ Vegetables and fruit that are **mushy** have become too soft. *All the entrees were served with a baked potato and somewhat mushy green beans.*
2 ADJ **Mushy** stories are very sentimental; used showing disapproval. *The film is a mushy, but strangely moving story of young love.*

music /mju̱ːzɪk/
1 NU **Music** is the pattern of sounds performed by people singing or playing instruments. *...dance music. ...the music of Irving Berlin.*
2 NU **Music** is also the symbols written on paper that represent musical sounds. *Not one of them could read a note of music.*

musical /mju̱ːzɪkl/ **musicals**
1 ADJ ATTRIB **Musical** describes things that are concerned with playing or studying music. *...a musical career. ...one of London's most important musical events.* ◆ **musically** ADV *There is a lot going on musically every night in London.*
2 ADJ Someone who is **musical** has a natural ability and interest in music. *He came from a musical family.*
3 ADJ **Musical** sounds are tuneful and pleasant. *A musical bell softly sounded somewhere in the passageway.*
4 NC A **musical** is a play or film that uses singing and dancing in the story. *She appeared in the musical 'Oklahoma'.*

musical box, musical boxes
NC A **musical box** is a box that contains a clockwork mechanism which plays a tune when you open the lid. *...Christmas trees fitted with musical boxes that played Christmas carols.*

musical chairs
1 NU **Musical chairs** is a game in which children run around a row of chairs while music is played and try to sit down on them when the music stops. *The world's biggest game of musical chairs took place on Weymouth beach in Dorset, using 6,500 deckchairs.*
2 NU You can also use the term **musical chairs** to describe a situation in which people exchange jobs or positions very often. *It was time for political musical chairs again in the country... The premiership at this*

time was a prize in a game of musical chairs.

musical instrument, musical instruments
NC A **musical instrument** is an object such as a piano, guitar, or violin which you play in order to produce music. *More than half of all children learn a musical instrument between the ages of six and ten.*

music hall, music halls
1 NC A **music hall** was a theatre that presented shows consisting of a series of performances by comedians, singers, and dancers. *It was the only time I have ever appeared in a music hall.*
2 NU **Music hall** was a popular form of entertainment in the theatre during the early part of the twentieth century, and consisted of a series of performances by comedians, singers, and dancers. *She went to France and became a star of the Parisian music hall.*

musician /mjuːzɪ̱ʃn/ **musicians**
NC A **musician** is a person who plays a musical instrument as their job or hobby. *New Orleans, where many black American jazz musicians won their fame, has a unique musical character.*

music stand, music stands
NC A **music stand** is a device that holds pages of music in position while you play a musical instrument. *If you're going to take up the violin, I suppose we'll have to get you a music stand.*

musk /mʌ̱sk/
NU **Musk** is a substance with a strong, sweet smell which is used to make perfume. *The new fragrance contains essence of jasmine, rose and carnation, with musk and sandalwood.*

musket /mʌ̱skɪt/ **muskets**
NC A **musket** was an early type of rifle with a very long barrel. *...illustrations showing a full range of weaponry in use, from bows and arrows to cannons and muskets.*

musky /mʌ̱ski/
ADJ **Musky** means smelling like musk. *...a sweet musky perfume.*

Muslim /mʊ̱zlɪm/ **Muslims**; also spelt **Moslem**.
NC A **Muslim** is a person who believes in Islam and lives according to its rules. *...a pious Muslim on his way to Mecca.* ▶ Also ADJ *...the medieval Muslim philosophers.*

muslin /mʌ̱zlɪn/
NU **Muslin** is a very thin cotton material. *...women in white muslin dresses.*

mussel /mʌ̱sl/ **mussels**
NC A **mussel** is a kind of shellfish. *...fresh-water mussels.*

must /məst, mʌst, mʌ̱st/
1 MODAL If something **must** happen, it is very important or necessary that it happens. If something **must** not happen, it is very important or necessary that it does not happen. *Mr Major insisted that the European Community must welcome new members... These standards must apply at all times... They must not be allowed to succeed... Things must change.*
2 MODAL You also use **must** to express intentions or to make suggestions; an informal use. *I must come over and see you when he's away... You must play at the ship's concert... You must come and visit me.*
3 MODAL You ask why someone **must** do something when you are angry or upset about it and do not understand why they are doing it. *Why must she be so nasty to me?*
4 MODAL If you say that something **must** be true or **must** have happened, you mean that it is very likely to be the case. *The result must have been a disappointment... Everything is green at the moment. We must have had some rain pretty recently... This must be a cause for celebration... We must have taken the wrong road.*
5 You say **'if you must'** when you cannot stop someone from doing something that you think is wrong or stupid. *Write and ask them yourself if you must.*
6 N SING If something is a **must**, it is absolutely necessary; an informal use. *For almost all Chinese youngsters, marriage is still a must.*

mustache /mʌ̱stæʃ, məstɑ̱ːʃ/. See **moustache**.

mustard /mʌ̱stəd/
NU **Mustard** is a yellow or brown spicy paste that is

made from the seeds of the mustard plant, and which is used to flavour food. *...a dash of French mustard.*

mustard gas, mustard gasses

NUorNC **Mustard gas** is a highly poisonous chemical liquid which is used in the production of chemical weapons. *Soldiers suffering from the after effects of mustard gas have been brought to Britain for treatment... Mustard gasses were banned in the 1925 Geneva Protocol.*

muster /mʌstə/ **musters, mustering, mustered**

1 VO If you **muster** something such as strength or energy, you gather as much of it as you can in order to do something. *I hit him with all the force I could muster... The group cannot muster sufficient working class support.*

2 V-ERG When soldiers **muster** or when someone **musters** them, they gather in one place in order to take part in a military action. *An enormous convoy mustered in the city... The US would have to muster a force of 3 million troops.*

mustn't /mʌsnt/

Mustn't is the usual spoken form of 'must not'. *They can't hold meetings outside and mustn't distribute leaflets in the street.*

must've /mʌstəv, mʌstəv/

Must've is a spoken form of 'must have', when 'have' is an auxiliary verb. *A stranger must've done it.*

musty /mʌsti/

ADJ Something that is **musty** smells stale and damp. *...musty old books.*

mutant /mjuːtnt/ **mutants**

NC A **mutant** is an animal or plant that is physically different from others of the same species as the result of a change in its genetic structure. *Biologists noticed certain mutant fruitflies had interesting mottled eye colour.*

mutate /mjuːteɪt/ **mutates, mutating, mutated**

V If an animal or plant **mutates**, it develops different characteristics as the result of a change in its genes. *We're getting an insight into just how easy it is for the parasite to mutate and become resistant to the drug.* ◆ **mutated** ADJ *...a mutated flu virus.*

mutation /mjuːteɪʃn/ **mutations**

NC A **mutation** is a change in the genetic structure of an animal or plant which causes a new sort of animal or plant to develop. *The rate at which mutations occur is fairly regular.*

mute /mjuːt/ **mutes, muting, muted**; a literary word.

1 ADJ Someone who is **mute** does not speak. *Sally was staring at him, mute and awestruck... Fanny clasped her hands in mute protest.* ● See also **deaf-mute**.

2 VO If you **mute** a noise or sound, you make it quieter. *She had closed all the windows to mute the sounds from the town.*

muted /mjuːtɪd/

1 ADJ **Muted** colours or sounds are soft and gentle. *...a muted colour scheme of cream and white... People spoke in muted voices.*

2 ADJ If a reaction is **muted**, it is not very strong. *On the whole, criticism was muted. ...muted enthusiasm.*

mutilate /mjuːtɪleɪt/ **mutilates, mutilating, mutilated**

1 VO If someone is **mutilated**, their body is damaged very severely. *They tortured and mutilated their victims... Both bodies had been mutilated.* ◆ **mutilation** /mjuːtɪleɪʃn/ **mutilations** NUorNC *...the death or mutilation of innocent men and women. ...permanent mutilations of the skin.*

2 VO If you **mutilate** something, you deliberately damage it and spoil it. *Almost every book had been mutilated.*

mutilated /mjuːtɪleɪtɪd/

ADJ ATTRIB A **mutilated** body has been violently and severely damaged. *They were arrested after the mutilated bodies of two small boys were found on a riverbank near the city.*

mutineer /mjuːtɪnɪə/ **mutineers**

NC A **mutineer** is a person who takes part in a mutiny. *The three day revolt is over and the mutineers have agreed to lay down their arms.*

mutinous /mjuːtɪnəs/

ADJ A person who is **mutinous** is likely to disobey or rebel against the people in authority; a formal word.

The crew were restive and mutinous.

mutiny /mjuːtəni/ **mutinies**

NCorNU A **mutiny** is a rebellion by a group of people against a person in authority, especially a rebellion by members of the armed forces. *The mutiny was the sixth attempt to overthrow the government of President Corazon Aquino... The charge of mutiny levelled against Colonel Rico is one of the most serious in Argentina's military code of justice.*

mutt /mʌt/ **mutts**

NC A **mutt** is the same as a **mongrel**.

mutter /mʌtə/ **mutters, muttering, muttered**

V, V-QUOTE, or V-REPORT If you **mutter**, you speak very quietly so that you cannot easily be heard. *Denis could be heard muttering to himself about my stupidity... 'Sorry,' he muttered... When it's over the victor rises and the loser's left muttering what might have been.* ▶ Also N SING *...a quick low mutter.*

mutton /mʌtn/

NU **Mutton** is meat from an adult sheep; an old-fashioned word. *...a leg of mutton.*

mutual /mjuːtʃuəl/

1 ADJ You use **mutual** to describe something that two or more people do to each other or for each other, or a feeling that they have towards each other. *They are in danger of mutual destruction... I didn't like him and I was sure the feeling was mutual.*

2 ADJ You also use **mutual** to describe something such as an interest which two or more people share. *They had discovered a mutual interest in rugby football... He sent a mutual friend to ask me.*

mutual fund, mutual funds

NC A **mutual fund** is the same as a **unit trust**; used in American English. *...allowing banking companies to get into new lines of business such as selling stocks, mutual funds and insurance.*

mutually /mjuːtʃuəli/

1 SUBMOD You use **mutually** when describing a situation in which two or more people feel the same way about each other. *He enjoyed a mutually respectful relationship with them.*

2 If two things are **mutually** exclusive or **mutually** contradictory, they cannot both be true or both exist together. *There was also a feeling that conservation and development were mutually exclusive... The principles on which it is based are mutually contradictory.*

Muzak /mjuːzæk/

NU **Muzak** is recorded music that is played as background music in shops, restaurants, etc; **Muzak** is a trademark. *Muzak seems to be catching on in a big way.*

muzzle /mʌzl/ **muzzles, muzzling, muzzled**

1 NC The **muzzle** of an animal such as a dog or a wolf is its nose and mouth. *The dog laid his muzzle on Mr Halliday's knee.*

2 NC A **muzzle** is also a device that is put over a dog's nose and mouth so that it cannot bite people or bark. *They have recently made it mandatory for Pitbulls to wear muzzles while being exercised.*

3 VO If you **muzzle** a dog, you put a muzzle over its nose and mouth. *One possibility is to require the owners of certain breeds to muzzle their dogs in public places.*

4 VO If someone **muzzles** another person or group of people, they stop them expressing their views. *The journalists say the government's move is a crude attempt to muzzle press freedom.*

5 NC The **muzzle** of a gun is the end where the bullets come out when it is fired. *I annoyed him, and he responded by swinging the muzzle of his gun in the direction of my face.*

muzzy /mʌzi/

1 ADJ Someone who feels **muzzy** is unable to think clearly, because they are ill or tired, or have drunk a lot of alcohol. *I'm feeling a bit muzzy in the head.*

2 ADJ Something that is **muzzy** is blurred and unclear. *...looking through the muzzy green of the holly bushes.*

MW

1 **MW** is a written abbreviation for 'medium wave'; written on radios to help you find a particular radio

station which is broadcast on medium wave.
2 **MW** is also a written abbreviation for 'mega watts'.
...a 100 MW power station.

Mwinyi, Ali Hassan /ˈæli hæsən mwiːnji/
Ali Hassan Mwinyi became President of Tanzania in
1985, succeeding Julius Nyerere. He was Vice
President from 1984 to 1985. He is a member of the
Revolutionary Party of Tanzania (CCM). Born: 1925.

my /maɪ/
DET A speaker or writer uses **my** to indicate that
something belongs or relates to himself or herself. *My
name is Alan Jones... I closed my eyes.*

Myanmar /mjænmɑː/. See **Burma**.

myopia /maɪˈəʊpiə/
NU **Myopia** is the inability to see clearly things which
are far away from you; a formal word. *If the eye is
too long, the result is short-sightedness or myopia.*

myopic /maɪˈɒpɪk/
ADJ Someone who is **myopic** cannot see distant things;
a formal word. *...adults who are already myopic.*

myriad /mɪriəd/ **myriads**
QUANT A **myriad** of people or things is a very large
number of them; a literary word. *...a myriad of
political action groups. ...myriads of tiny yellow
flowers.* ▶ Also ADJ *...myriad pots of paint.*

myself /maɪsɛlf/
1 PRON REFL A speaker or writer uses **myself** as the
object of a verb or preposition in a clause where 'I' is
the subject or 'me' is a previous object. *If you do not
help me, I will kill myself... I was thoroughly ashamed
of myself... I poured myself a small drink.*
2 PRON REFL **Myself** is also used to emphasize the
subject or object of a clause. *I myself feel that Muriel
Spark is very underrated... I find it a bit odd myself.*
3 PRON REFL A speaker or writer also uses **myself** in
expressions such as 'I did it myself' in order to say
that they did something without any help or
interference from anyone else. *I dealt with it myself.*

mysterious /mɪstɪəriəs/
1 ADJ Something that is **mysterious** is strange and is
not known about or understood. *Their grandson died
of a mysterious illness. ...an investigation to try and
discover what is causing a mysterious phenomenon
known as corn circles.* ◆ **mysteriously** ADV *The
American had mysteriously disappeared.*
2 ADJ If you are **mysterious** about something, you
deliberately do not talk about it, usually because you
want people to be curious about it. *Stop being so
mysterious.* ◆ **mysteriously** ADV *They smiled
mysteriously and said nothing.*

mystery /mɪstəri/ **mysteries**
1 NC A **mystery** is something that is not understood or
known about. *These two deaths have remained a
mystery.*
2 NU If you talk about the **mystery** of someone or
something, you are talking about how difficult they are
to understand or to know about. *The place continues
to fascinate visitors, cloaked in its mystery. ...the
mystery of God.*
3 ADJ ATTRIB A **mystery** person or thing is one whose

identity or nature is not known. *...the mystery voice.
...a mystery tour.*

mystic /mɪstɪk/ **mystics**
1 NC A **mystic** is a person who practises or believes in
religious mysticism. *...the shrine of the sixteenth
century Muslim mystic, Khwaja Moinuddin Chisti.*
2 ADJ ATTRIB **Mystic** means the same as **mystical**. *...a
performer in a mystic rite.*

mystical /mɪstɪkl/
ADJ ATTRIB Something that is **mystical** involves
spiritual powers and influences that most people do not
understand. *...religious and mystical experiences.*

mysticism /mɪstɪsɪzəm/
NU **Mysticism** is a religious practice in which people
search for truth, knowledge, and unity with God
through meditation and prayer. *There are those who
advocate personal fulfilment through mysticism,
spiritual healing and astrology... People here practice
a mixture of mysticism and Roman Catholicism.*

mystify /mɪstɪfaɪ/ **mystifies, mystifying, mystified**
VO Something that **mystifies** you is impossible to
explain or understand. *They say that they are
mystified by the decision.* ◆ **mystified** ADJ *I felt a bit
mystified.*

mystique /mɪstiːk/
NU **Mystique** is an atmosphere of mystery and
importance or difficulty which is associated with a
particular person or thing; a literary word. *...the
mystique surrounding doctors.*

myth /mɪθ/ **myths**
1 NC A **myth** is an untrue belief or explanation; used
showing disapproval. *...myths about the causes of
cancer. ...the myth of love at first sight.*
2 NCorNU A **myth** is also a story which has been made
up in the past to explain natural events or to justify
religious beliefs. *...the Greek myth of Orpheus.
...queens in history, legend, and myth.*

mythic /mɪθɪk/
ADJ ATTRIB Something that is **mythic** exists in a myth
or is like something in a myth; a formal word. *My
husband has none of the attributes of a mythic lover.*

mythical /mɪθɪkl/
1 ADJ Something that is **mythical** is imaginary and
only exists in myths. *...mythical figures such as Count
Dracula or Robin Hood.*
2 ADJ **Mythical** is also used to describe something
which is untrue or does not exist. *They trekked out to
the west coast in search of the mythical opportunities
there.*

mythology /mɪθɒlədʒi/
1 NU **Mythology** refers to stories that have been made
up in the past to explain natural events or to justify
religious beliefs. *Prometheus in Greek mythology
brought fire to man.* ◆ **mythological** ADJ ATTRIB
*Jupiter was the Roman mythological king of the
heavens.*
2 NU You can also use **mythology** to refer to beliefs
that people have about something which is incorrect or
untrue. *The whole mythology of national greatness
needs to be questioned.*

N n

N, n /ɛn/ **N's, n's**
1 NC **N** is the fourteenth letter of the English alphabet.
2 **N** is also a written abbreviation for 'north'.

N.A.; also written **n/a.**
You write **N.A.** on a form that you are filling in when a question or category is not relevant to you. **N.A.** is an abbreviation for 'not applicable'.

nab /næb/ **nabs, nabbing, nabbed**
VO If you **nab** someone, you catch them doing something wrong or arrest them; an informal word. *It was the CID who'd nabbed Peters.*

Nabiyev, Rakhmon /rəxmɑːn nəbiːəf/
Rakhmon Nabiyev became President of Tadjikistan in 1991. He was the Tadjik Minister of Agriculture from 1971 to 1973, and Chairman of the Tadjik Council of Ministers and Minister of Foreign Affairs from 1973 to 1982. He was Deputy Chairman of the USSR Council of Ministers from 1973 to 1982. He served as First Secretary of the Tadjik Communist Party, now renamed the Socialist Party of Tadjikistan, from 1982 to 1985. Born: 1930.

nadir /neɪdɪə/
N SING The **nadir** of something is its lowest point; a literary word. *The government was at the nadir of its unpopularity.*

naff /næf/; an informal word.
1 ADJ If you find something **naff**, you do not like it because it is boring or in bad taste. *...a boring plot followed by a pretty naff ending... The film last night was really naff.*
2 If you tell someone to **naff off**, you are telling them to go away. *She told the newspapermen to naff off.*

nag /næg/ **nags, nagging, nagged**
1 VOorV If someone **nags** you, they keep complaining to you. *He used to nag me endlessly about money. ...having nagged for an invitation.*
2 V+at If a doubt or suspicion **nags** at you, it worries you a lot. *Something that she had said had been nagging at him.* ◆ **nagging** ADJ ATTRIB *She had a nagging sense of inadequacy. ...the nagging question remains.*

Nahayan, Shaikh Zaid bin Sultan al- /ʃeɪk zɑːjɪd bɪn sʊltɑːn əl næhəjæn/
Shaikh Zaid bin Sultan al-Nahayan became Ruler of Abu Dhabi in 1966, when he deposed his brother. In 1971 he became the first President of the United Arab Emirates. Born: 1918.

nail /neɪl/ **nails, nailing, nailed**
1 NC A **nail** is a small piece of metal with a sharp end which you hit with a hammer in order to push it into something. *...the mirror that hung from a nail on the wall.*
2 VOA If you **nail** something somewhere, you attach it there using a nail. *They nail plastic sheets over their windows... There were signs nailed to the trees.*
3 NC Your **nails** are the thin hard areas covering the ends of your fingers and toes. *He keeps biting his nails.*
4 If you say that someone has **hit the nail on the head**, you mean that what they have said is exactly right. *You've hit the nail on the head with that particular comment.*

5 a **nail in** something's **coffin**: see **coffin.**

nail down PHRASAL VERB 1 If you **nail** something **down,** you fasten it securely to something underneath it using nails. *If it won't stay there we'll have to nail it down.* 2 If you **nail** someone **down,** you force them to state clearly their opinions and intentions. *He said that he'd travelled to Africa to nail down the Angolan government's commitment... US officials would like to get the START treaty nailed down before the summit.*

nail up PHRASAL VERB If you **nail** something **up,** you fix it to a vertical surface using nails. *...the warning notice that he had nailed up on the pole.*

nail brush, nail brushes
NC A **nail brush** is a small brush that you use for cleaning your nails.

nail file, nail files
NC A **nail file** is a small strip of metal that you rub on the end of your nails to make them smooth and give them a rounded shape.

nail polish
NU **Nail polish** is the same as **nail varnish.** *...toenails painted with red nail polish.*

nail scissors
N PL **Nail scissors** are small scissors that you use for cutting your nails.

nail varnish
NU **Nail varnish** is a thick liquid that women paint on their nails.

Nairobi /naɪrəʊbi/
Nairobi is the capital of Kenya and its largest city. Population: 1,162,000 (1985).

naive /naɪiːv/; also spelt **naïve.**
1 ADJ A **naive** person believes that things are much simpler and less complex than they really are. *You're surely not so naive as to think that this will change anything... The British companies involved in the visit are hardly naive newcomers to the East European scene.* ◆ **naively** ADV *They naively assume that things can only get better.*
2 ADJ If something such as an offer or plan is **naive,** it has little chance of success because it does not take into consideration the complexity of a situation. *Mr Baker described this plan as naive and counter-productive... From a distance of only two decades, the optimism and protest can seem naive, even irrelevant.*

naivety /naɪiːvəti/; also spelt **naïvety** or **naïveté.**
NU **Naivety** is behaviour which shows that a person thinks that things are much less difficult than they really are. *In this he showed political naivety.*

Najibullah Ahmadzai /nædʒiːbʊlɑː æxmædzaɪ/
Dr Najibullah Ahmadzai became President of Afghanistan in 1987. He is a member of the Homeland Party (formerly PDPA) and became General Secretary of the PDPA Central Committee in 1986. He was head of the State Information Service (KHAD) from 1979 to 1986. Born: 1947.

naked /neɪkɪd/
1 ADJ Someone who is **naked** is not wearing any clothes. *He was naked except for a pair of underpants. ...the men's naked bodies.* ◆ **nakedness**
NU *They seized towels to hide their nakedness.*
2 ADJ ATTRIB You can describe objects as **naked** when

they are not covered. ...*naked light bulbs*... *Never look for a gas leak with a naked flame.*

3 ADJ ATTRIB You can also use **naked** to describe actions, behaviour, or emotions which are not disguised or hidden in any way. *The home employment offered to housewives is naked exploitation*... *His face broke into an expression of naked anxiety.*

4 ADJ ATTRIB If you can see something with the **naked** eye, you can see it without using specialist equipment such as binoculars, a telescope, or a microscope. *Body heat is invisible to the naked eye.* ...*the five thousand or so stars that can be seen with the naked eye.*

Namaliu, Sir Rabbie /rǽbi nəmɑːli/
Sir Rabbie Namaliu became Prime Minister of Papua New Guinea in 1988. He was elected MP in 1982. He served as Minister for Foreign Affairs and Trade from 1982 to 1984, and for Primary Industry from 1984 to 1985. He was Deputy Leader of the Pangu Party from 1985 to 1988, and became the Leader in 1988. Born: 1947.

namby-pamby /nǽmbi pǽmbi/
ADJ If you refer to someone as **namby-pamby**, you think they are very sentimental or prim; an informal word. *He was rather a namby-pamby sort of young man, I thought.*

name /neɪm/ **names, naming, named**
1 NC The **name** of a person, thing, or place is the word or words that you use to identify them. *His name is Richard Arnason*... *He refused to give the name of his informant*... *Pulsars, as their name implies, give up pulses of radiation*... *The region, given the name Bosanska Krajina, had been declared an inseparable part of federal Yugoslavia.*

2 VOC If you **name** someone or something, you give them a name. *She wanted to name the baby Colleen.* ...*a supersonic aeroplane, eventually named the Concorde.*

3 VO To **name** someone or something also means to identify them by saying their name. ...*a Minister, whom he did not name.* ...*various flowers: roses, tulips and snapdragons, to name only a few.* ● See also **named.**

4 VO+*after* If you **name** someone or something after a person or thing, you give them the same name as that person or thing. *The College in Holborn is named after her.* ...*the Baker Plan—named after James Baker.*

5 VO If you **name** something, for example a date for a meeting or the price of something, you say what you want it to be. *He named a price he thought would scare me off.*

6 NC You can refer to someone's or something's reputation as their **name.** *He'd only returned to Britain to clear his name*... *They were giving the country a bad name.* ...*allergic reactions that can get drugs a bad name.*

7 NC+SUPP You can say that someone is a big **name**, a famous **name**, and so on when they are well-known in their particular field. *This album features a host of famous names*... *Some of the top names in West Indian cricket were in London recently to take part in a charity match.*

8 See also **assumed name, brand name, Christian name, household name, maiden name.**
● **Name** is used in these phrases. ● If you refer to or mention someone or something by **name**, you say their name rather than referring to them indirectly. *He repeatedly referred to Israel by name*... *Its leader is not mentioned by name in the statement.* ● If you **call** someone **names**, you insult or offend them by using unpleasant words to describe them. *Some of the soldiers called us names, and we were afraid.* ● You use by the **name of** to say what someone or something is called, especially when you are talking to someone about them for the first time. *This mechanism goes by the name of the Higgs mechanism.* ● If something is registered in your **name**, it officially belongs to you or has been reserved for you. *The room was reserved in the name of Peters.* ● If you do something in the **name of** an ideal, a person, or a group of people, you

do it because you believe in the ideal or represent the person or people. *The group claims to speak in the name of 'the simple people of the country'*... *The Foreign Minister thanked Syria in the name of the Chancellor*... *The public have a right to know what is being done in their name in the courts.* ● If you **make a name for yourself,** for example as a writer or singer, or if you **make your name** in a particular field, you become well-known and admired for what you do. *Eliot had already made a name for herself as a writer*... *She made her name as an actress.* ● You use the expression the **name of the game** to describe a particular activity or idea that is the most important in a particular situation. *Political self-preservation is now the name of the game.*

named /neɪmd/
ADJ PRED When you say what a person, thing, or place is **named**, you give their name. ...*a lecturer named Harold Levy.*

name-dropping
NU **Name-dropping** is the habit of referring to famous people as though they were your friends, in order to impress people; showing disapproval. *There was a good deal of academic name-dropping*... *All book reviews with any pretensions should contain at least one example of name-dropping.*

nameless /neɪmləs/
ADJ ATTRIB You describe people and things as **nameless** when you do not know their name or when they have not been given a name. ...*a new and nameless disease.* ...*nameless, faceless bureaucrats*... *He asked that he remain nameless to avoid retribution.*

namely /neɪmli/
ADV SEN You use **namely** to introduce detailed information about what you have just said. ...*three famous physicists, namely Simon, Kurte and Mendelssohn.*

name plate, name plates
NC A **name plate** is a small sign on or next to a door, showing the name of the person or organization that works in the building. ...*the shining new name plate on the wall of the building.*

namesake /neɪmseɪk/ **namesakes**
NC+POSS Your **namesake** is someone with the same name as you. *Smith's namesake, and fellow-Scot, John Smith MP, is the Shadow Chancellor of the Exchequer.*

Namibia /nəmɪbiə/
The **Republic of Namibia**, formerly known as South West Africa, is a country in southern Africa. It was a German colony from 1884 until the First World War, when it came under South African rule through a League of Nations mandate. In 1966 the United Nations revoked the mandate and recognized the country of Namibia, but South Africa refused to relinquish control. In 1966 SWAPO (South West African People's Organization), led by Sam Nujoma, began an insurrection against South African rule. In 1990 Namibia achieved independence, with Sam Nujoma as the first President. Hage Geingob was appointed Prime Minister. Namibia is a member of the Organization of African Unity and the Commonwealth. It exports diamonds and uranium. ◆ **Namibian** /nəmɪbiən/ N, ADJ
■ *per capita GNP:* US$1,060 ■ *religion:* Christianity, animism ■ *language:* English (official) ■ *currency:* South African rand ■ *capital:* Windhoek ■ *population:* 1 million (1989) ■ *size:* 824,292 square kilometres.

nanny /nǽni/ **nannies**
NC A **nanny** is a woman who is paid by parents to look after their children. *He was brought up in the English manner by a formidable British nanny.*

nanny goat, nanny goats
NC A **nanny goat** is a female goat.

nap /nǽp/ **naps, napping, napped**
1 NC A **nap** is a short sleep during the day. *It was time for her to take a nap.* ...*my childhood naps.*

2 V If you **nap**, you fall asleep for a short time during the day. ...*a tendency to nap in the afternoon*... *The former manager sometimes napped on the bench in the late innings.*

3 If someone is **caught napping**, something happens to them when they are not prepared for it. *They don't want to be caught napping in case the army moves in again.*

napalm /ˈneɪpɑːm/ **napalms, napalming, napalmed**
1 NU **Napalm** is a substance containing petrol which is used to make bombs that burn and destroy people and plants. *Weapons such as fragmentation bombs and napalm should be banned... He said the air force had dropped napalm bombs on civilian homes.*
2 VO If people **napalm** other people or places, they attack and burn them using napalm. *They can be napalmed and starved into retreat... Some areas have been napalmed from the air.*

nape /neɪp/ **napes**
NC The **nape** of your neck is the back of it. *He saw a soldier point a gun at the nape of the man's neck and shoot.*

napkin /ˈnæpkɪn/ **napkins**
NC A **napkin** is a small piece of cloth or paper used to protect your clothes when you are eating. *...tables with linen tablecloths and napkins... I wiped my nose on a napkin and got on my feet.*

nappy /ˈnæpi/ **nappies**
NC A **nappy** is a piece of thick cloth or paper which is fastened round a baby's bottom in order to soak up its urine and faeces. *I seem to spend all day changing nappies.*

narcissi /nɑːˈsɪsaɪ/
Narcissi is a plural form of **narcissus**.

narcissism /ˈnɑːsɪsɪzəm/
NU **Narcissism** is the habit of always thinking about and admiring yourself instead of thinking about other people; a formal word. *His poetry shows evidence of narcissism.*

narcissistic /ˌnɑːsɪˈsɪstɪk/
ADJ **Narcissistic** people think about themselves a lot and admire themselves greatly; a formal word. *There is a strong narcissistic element in your work.*

narcissus /nɑːˈsɪsəs/ **narcissi** The plural form can be either **narcissi** or **narcissus**.
NC A **narcissus** is a yellow, white, or orange flower that looks like a daffodil.

narcotic /nɑːˈkɒtɪk/ **narcotics**
NC **Narcotics** are addictive drugs such as opium or morphine which make you sleepy and unable to feel pain. *The foreign ministers have also announced plans to intensify campaigns to combat international narcotics trafficking.*

narrate /nəˈreɪt/ **narrates, narrating, narrated**
1 VO If you **narrate** a story, you tell it in your own words; a literary word. *He narrated this tale with great effect.* ♦ **narration** /nəˈreɪʃn/ NU *...the narration of the story... The narration is crisp and clear with delightful touches of humour from our narrator.*
2 VO If someone **narrates** a documentary film or programme, they make a spoken commentary on it to accompany and explain the pictures. *The programme was narrated by Trinidadian-born Saul.* ♦ **narration** NU *...a taped narration to a slide show.*

narrative /ˈnærətɪv/ **narratives**
NC A **narrative** is a story or an account of events. *...the narrative of her battle against depression.*

narrator /nəˈreɪtə/ **narrators**
1 NC A **narrator** is someone who is telling a story, especially in a book. *In Salinger's classic novel about alienated youth, the 17 year-old narrator Holden Caulfield describes his expulsion from boarding school.*
2 NC In a documentary film or broadcast, the **narrator** is the person who accompanies and explains the pictures with a spoken commentary. *What emerges is, in the words of narrator David Jessel, a sinister blend of Germany in the thirties and Stalinist Russia of the fifties.*

narrow /ˈnærəʊ/ **narrower, narrowest; narrows, narrowing, narrowed**
1 ADJ Something that is **narrow** has a very small distance from one side to the other. *We turned into a narrow lane... The stream became narrower.* ♦ **narrowness** NU *...the narrowness of the tunnels.*
2 V If something **narrows**, it becomes less wide. *The river narrowed and curved sharply to the left.*

3 V-ERG If you **narrow** your eyes or if your eyes **narrow**, you almost close them. *'I want you back here in five minutes,' he growled, narrowing his eyes... The boy's eyes narrowed with suspicion.*
4 V-ERG If you **narrow** the difference between two things or if they **narrow**, it becomes smaller. *...South Africa's efforts to narrow differences with neighbouring states... The gap between the rich and the poor is narrowing.* ♦ **narrowing** NU+SUPP *...the narrowing of the individual's field of choice.*
5 ADJ If you have a **narrow** victory, you just succeed in winning. *Pete Wilson defeated the former San Francisco Mayor Dianne Feinstein by a narrow margin... The margin of victory was narrow.* ♦ **narrowly** ADV *The motion was narrowly defeated.*
6 ADJ ATTRIB If you have a **narrow** escape, something unpleasant nearly happens to you. *One man had a narrow escape as he was driving along the road seconds before the crash. ...narrow misses.* ♦ **narrowly** ADV *He narrowly escaped being run over.*
7 ADJ If someone's ideas or beliefs are **narrow**, they are concerned with only a few aspects of a situation and ignore other aspects. *I think you are taking too narrow a view.* ♦ **narrowness** NU *...the narrowness of the range of opinion represented.*
narrow down PHRASAL VERB If you **narrow** something **down**, you reduce it to a smaller number. *They had narrowed the choice down to a dozen sites... It does narrow down the options.*

narrow-minded
ADJ If someone is **narrow-minded**, they are unwilling to consider new ideas or opinions. *How narrow-minded he had become. ...a narrow-minded approach to broadcasting.*

NASA /ˈnæsə/
N PROP **NASA** is an American government organization which is concerned with developing the exploration of space. **NASA** is an abbreviation for 'National Aeronautics and Space Administration'. *Recently NASA has announced plans to make a return to Mars in the next few years.*

nasal /ˈneɪzl/
1 ADJ You produce **nasal** sounds when air passes through your nose and mouth when you speak. *He spoke in a nasal voice... The voice was always distinctive—slightly harsh and nasal.*
2 ADJ ATTRIB **Nasal** also means relating to your nose. *...nasal discharge.*

nascent /ˈnæsənt/
ADJ ATTRIB **Nascent** things or processes are just beginning, and are expected to become stronger or to grow bigger; a formal word. *...nascent industries and old traditional ones.*

Nassau /ˈnæsɔː/
Nassau is the capital of the Bahamas and its largest city. Population: 154,000 (1985).

nasturtium /nəˈstɜːʃəm/ **nasturtiums**
NC A **nasturtium** is a brightly-coloured garden flower.

nasty /ˈnɑːsti/ **nastier, nastiest; nasties**
1 ADJ Something that is **nasty** is very unpleasant. *This place has a nasty smell... I got a nasty feeling that I was being followed.*
2 ADJ You can also describe things as **nasty** when you think that they are unattractive or in bad taste. *It's a tacky, nasty little movie.*
3 ADJ A **nasty** problem or question is a difficult one. *This presented a nasty problem to Mayor Lindsay.*
4 ADJ You describe a disease or injury as **nasty** when it is serious or looks very unpleasant. *Rats carry very nasty diseases... A nasty bruise rose where the handbag had landed.*
5 ADJ You describe someone's behaviour as **nasty** when they behave in an unkind and unpleasant way. *Why must she be so nasty to me?* ♦ **nastily** ADV *He was staring at them nastily.*
6 NC A **nasty** is a dangerous or destructive element or example of something. *Neuroscientists can use the molecular nasties in venoms... Our machine has a filter on it which will trap and retain these nasties.*
● See also **video nasty**.

nation /ˈneɪʃn/ **nations**
1 NC A **nation** is a country, together with its social

and political structures. *...the leaders of the seven main industrialised nations... Debt problems in developing nations remained unresolved... The Easter Uprising of 1916 was the birth of Ireland as a nation.*
2 N SING The people who live in a country are sometimes referred to as the **nation**. *He appealed to the nation for self-restraint... She will address the nation on its one-hundred and twenty-third birthday.*
3 See also **most favoured nation**

national /næʃ^ənəl/ **nationals**
1 ADJ **National** means relating to the whole of a country, rather than to part of it. *A national day of mourning was declared... The document must be approved by parliament and a national referendum. ...the Israeli national airline... It made the headlines in the national newspapers.* ♦ **nationally** ADV *Should housing policy be decided nationally or locally?*
2 ADJ ATTRIB **National** is also used to describe things that are typical of the people of a particular country. *Common sense is a national characteristic. ...national dress.*
3 NC+SUPP A **national** of a country is a citizen of that country. *Only nationals of Egypt, Jordan and Yemen are exempt. ...a German national.* ● See also **foreign national**.

national anthem, national anthems
NC A country's **national anthem** is its official song. *The crowd listened to speeches and sang the national anthem before dispersing peacefully.*

national government, national governments
N COLL A **national government** is a coalition government, especially one that is formed during a crisis. *The Sudanese parliament has overwhelmingly endorsed proposals for a broad-based national government.*

National Health Service
N PROP In Britain, the **National Health Service** is a system providing medical care that is free or inexpensive. *...a campaign to urge the government to spend more money on the National Health Service.*

national insurance
NU **National insurance** is the system by which a government collects money regularly from employers and employees. This money is paid to people who are ill, unemployed, or retired. *They may not pay National Insurance or tax contributions for the workers.*

nationalise /næʃ^ənəlaɪz/. See **nationalize**.

nationalism /næʃ^ənəlɪzəm/
1 NU **Nationalism** is the desire for political independence by people who have the same religion, language, or culture. *...nineteenth-century Czech nationalism.*
2 NU **Nationalism** is also a great love for your country which is often associated with the belief that it is better than other countries. *They fear the resurgence of an assertive nationalism in Japan.*

nationalist /næʃ^ənəlɪst/ **nationalists**
1 ADJ ATTRIB **Nationalist** ideas or movements are connected with attempts to obtain political independence for a particular group of people. *...the nationalist movements of French West Africa... The main nationalist group has failed to win enough seats to push through its independence programme.*
2 NC A **nationalist** is a person with nationalist beliefs. *...a great Indonesian nationalist... There were demonstrations by Ukrainian nationalists demanding full independence... They desecrated a monument to a nineteenth century nationalist hero.*

nationalistic /næʃ^ənəlɪstɪk/
ADJ Someone who is **nationalistic** is very proud of their country and believes that it is better than other countries. *...an attempt to arouse nationalistic passions.*

nationality /næʃənæləti/ **nationalities**
NU or NC You can use **nationality** to refer to the country that people belong to, because they were born there or have been legally accepted by it. For example, someone with British **nationality** is legally a British citizen. *...an identity card proving Belgian nationality. ...scientists of different nationalities.*

nationalize /næʃ^ənəlaɪz/ **nationalizes, nationalizing, nationalized**; also spelt **nationalise**.
VO If a government **nationalizes** a private industry, the industry becomes owned by the state. *The revolutionary government has nationalized the mines... The coffee industry was nationalized at the time of independence.* ♦ **nationalized** ADJ *...nationalized industries.* ♦ **nationalization** /næʃ^ənəlaɪzeɪʃn/ NU *He argued for nationalisation on grounds of efficiency.*

national park, national parks
NC A **national park** is a large area of land protected by the government of a country because of its natural beauty, its plants, or its wildlife. National parks are usually open for the public to visit. *The Ramblers Association accuses the government of not doing enough to safeguard Britain's National Parks.*

national service
NU **National service** is a period of compulsory service in a country's armed forces. *Some NATO countries, like America and Britain, do not have compulsory national service at all.*

nationhood /neɪʃnhʊd/
NU A country's **nationhood** is its status as a nation. *In June of that year Seychelles achieved independent nationhood. ...a strong sense of nationhood. ...a long struggle for nationhood.*

nation-state, nation-states
NC A **nation-state** is an independent state which is composed exclusively of people from a single national group. *Lithuania, in its modern form as a small nation-state, emerged during the First World War.*

nationwide /neɪʃnwaɪd/
ADJ ATTRIB A **nationwide** activity happens in all parts of a country. *...a nationwide address on radio and TV. ...a nationwide campaign to recruit women into trade unions.* ► Also ADV *She had lectured nationwide to various organizations.*

native /neɪtɪv/ **natives**
1 ADJ ATTRIB Your **native** country is the one where you were born. *She made her way home to her native Russia.*
2 NC+SUPP A **native** of a country or region is someone who was born there. *...John Magee, a native of Northern Ireland.* ► Also ADJ ATTRIB *...native Britons.*
3 NC A **native** is someone who was born or lives in a non-Western country and who belongs to the race or tribe that forms the majority of its inhabitants. *They used force to banish the natives from the more fertile land.*
4 ADJ ATTRIB Your **native** language is the language that you learned to speak as a child. *He read a poem in his native Hungarian.*
5 ADJ Animals or plants that are **native** to a region grow there naturally and have not been brought there; a formal use. *These are the only lilies native to Great Britain.*

Native American, Native Americans
NC **Native Americans** are people from any one of the many tribes which were already living in North America before Europeans arrived there. *The Association on Native Indian Affairs has researched the portrayal of Native Americans in textbooks.*

native speaker, native speakers
NC A **native speaker** of a language is someone who speaks that language as their first language rather than having learnt it as a foreign language. *Could a well-meaning native-speaker understand what the pupil is trying to say? ...a native speaker of English.*

Nativity /nətɪvəti/
N SING The **Nativity** is the birth of Jesus, which is celebrated by Christians at Christmas. *...like a child hearing the story of the Nativity.*

nativity play, nativity plays
NC A **nativity play** is a play about the birth of Jesus, usually performed by children at Christmas time.

NATO (North Atlantic Treaty Organization) /neɪtəʊ/
NATO was founded in 1949 as an organization for collective defence. An attack on one member country would be regarded as an attack on all. The headquarters are in Brussels. The members of NATO

are: Belgium, Canada, Denmark, France, Germany, Greece, Iceland, Italy, Luxembourg, Netherlands, Norway, Portugal, Spain, Turkey, United Kingdom, and United States.

natter /nætə/ natters, nattering, nattered
v When people **natter**, they talk casually for a long time about unimportant things; an informal word. *We just want to natter together about old times.* ▸ Also N SING *They like to have a bit of a natter.*

natty /næti/ nattier, nattiest; an informal word.
1 ADJ **Natty** people and clothes are smart and neat in appearance. *He's a very natty dresser. ...natty headgear.*
2 ADJ Something that is **natty** is smart and cleverly designed. *...a natty metal tool box.*

natural /nætʃərəl/ naturals
1 ADJ If you say that something is **natural**, you mean that it is normal and expected. *She's upset. It's natural, isn't it? Today's the funeral... It is natural for trade unions to adopt an aggressive posture.*
2 ADJ You also say that someone's behaviour is **natural** when they are not trying to hide anything. *...walking in a relaxed, natural manner... There was something not quite natural about her behaviour.*
♦ **naturalness** NU *I was impressed by their ease and naturalness.*
3 ADJ ATTRIB Someone with a **natural** ability was born with that ability and did not have to learn it. *He had a natural gift for making things work... Follow your own natural inclinations... She was a natural organizer.*
4 NC If you describe someone as a **natural**, you mean that they were born with the ability to do something well; an informal use. *He is a great craftsman, a natural.*
5 ADJ ATTRIB **Natural** is used to describe things that exist in nature and were not made or caused by people. *Numerous natural disasters which have affected countries around the world this year... Scientists have found synthetic substitutes for natural materials.*
6 If someone died of **natural causes**, they died because they were ill and not because they committed suicide or were killed. *The post-mortem showed that death was due to natural causes.*
7 ADJ ATTRIB Someone's **natural** mother or father is their real mother or father, rather than someone who has adopted them. *She claimed Prince Yousoupoff as her natural father.*
8 ADJ after N A **natural** is note in music that is not a sharp or a flat. *...B natural.*

natural childbirth
NU **Natural childbirth** is a method of childbirth in which the mother is given no anaesthetics but uses special breathing and relaxation exercises. *More and more women want to have their babies by natural childbirth.*

natural gas
NU **Natural gas** is gas which is found underground or under the sea. It is collected and stored, and piped into people's houses to be used for cooking and heating. *The agency said Iran was also anxious to resume sales of natural gas to the Soviet Union.*

natural history
1 NU **Natural history** is the study of animals, plants, and other living things. *He is professor of natural history at Edinburgh University.*
2 NU The **natural history** of a place, plant, or animal species is its evolution and its habits and conditions of existence. *Sediments in the mud of rivers hold a wealth of information about the natural history of an area. ...the details of the dinosaurs' natural history.*

naturalise /nætʃərəlaɪz/. See naturalize.

naturalised /nætʃərəlaɪzd/. See naturalized.

naturalism /nætʃərəlɪzəm/
NU **Naturalism** is a theory in art and literature which states that people and objects should be shown as they actually are, rather than in an idealistic or unnatural way. *Within one scene you can go from absolute naturalism to high flown verse.*

naturalist /nætʃərəlɪst/ naturalists
NC A **naturalist** is a person who studies plants,

animals, and other living things. *For years, naturalists have argued that Yosemite is losing its wilderness character... Sixteen swans were rescued by naturalists and taken to a wildlife sanctuary.*

naturalistic /nætʃərəlɪstɪk/
1 ADJ ATTRIB **Naturalistic** describes something that simulates the effects or characteristics of nature. *Exposure to naturalistic twilights has a very profound effect on the body's time keeping mechanism.*
2 ADJ ATTRIB **Naturalistic** artists and writers believe in and practise the theory of naturalism in art and literature. *You think of Hogarth as a naturalistic artist drawing the world as he thought it really was.*

naturalize /nætʃərəlaɪz/ naturalizes, naturalizing, naturalized; also spelt naturalise.
v O If someone is **naturalized**, they become a citizen of a country which they were not born in. *All persons born or naturalized in the United States are entitled to vote.*

naturalized /nætʃərəlaɪzd/; also spelt naturalised.
ADJ ATTRIB A **naturalized** citizen has legally become a citizen of a country that they were not born in. *...a naturalized British subject.*

naturally /nætʃərəli/
1 ADV SEN You use **naturally** to indicate that something is obvious and not surprising. *Dena was crying, so naturally Hannah was upset... 'Do you propose to take account of that?'—'Naturally.'*
2 ADV If one thing develops **naturally** from another, it develops as a normal result of it. *This leads us fairly naturally into what career advisers call careers counselling.*
3 ADV Something that happens or exists **naturally** happens or exists in nature and was not made or caused by people. *They tried to reproduce artificially what they had observed to happen naturally.*
4 ADV You say that someone is behaving **naturally** when they are not trying to hide anything or pretend in any way. *The children were too frightened to behave naturally.*
5 SUBMOD You can also use **naturally** to talk about qualities that people were born with, rather than those that were learned later. *...people who are naturally brilliant... She had a naturally cheerful and serene expression.*
6 If something **comes naturally** to you, you can do it easily. *Politics came naturally to Tony.*

natural resources
N PL **Natural resources** are all the land, forests, minerals, and sources of energy that occur naturally. *They plan to open up the region with its wealth of natural resources... The businesses involved are largely concerned with exploiting Vietnam's natural resources.*

natural selection
NU **Natural selection** is a process which results in animal and plant species that are best adapted to their environment surviving and reproducing, while those that are less well adapted die out. *Natural selection is producing strains that will happily live in these harsher environments. ...Darwin's theory of natural selection.*

nature /neɪtʃə/ natures
1 NU **Nature** is all the animals, plants, and other things in the world that are not made by people, and all the events and processes that are not caused by people. *A sunset is one of the most beautiful sights in nature... The influence of society is so great and so damaging on the life supporting systems of nature.*
2 NU+SUPP The **nature** of something is its basic quality or character. *The Vatican condemned the overtly political nature of some of the 'Liberation Theologians' teaching and work... Both protest and strikes are basically symbolic in nature... Such a situation is by nature painful... The report defines sexual harassment as persistent offensive behaviour of a sexual nature.*
3 NC+SUPP Someone's **nature** is their character, which they show by their behaviour. *Rob had a very sweet nature. ...a woman with a wildly passionate nature.*
● **Nature** is used in these phrases. ● Someone's **better nature** is their feelings of kindness and helpfulness. *...to manipulate people by appeals to their better*

nature. ● If a way of behaving is **second nature** to you, you behave like that without thinking because you have done it so often. *The 20 foot climb is second nature to Alphonso: he scampers up the rope ladder with an agility that belies his 67 years.* ● See also **human nature.**

nature trail, nature trails
NC A **nature trail** is a route which is signposted through an area of countryside, pointing out interesting animals, plants, and rocks. *The trust will also be creating nature trails and helping with the Chelsea Flower Show.*

naturism /ˈneɪtʃərɪzəm/
NU **Naturism** is the practice of not wearing clothes because you believe that this is a good thing. *In some countries naturism is against the law.* ◆ **naturist, naturists** NC *There are two swimming pools, one for naturists.*

naught /nɔːt/. See **nought.**

naughty /ˈnɔːti/ **naughtier,naughtiest**
1 ADJ You say that small children are **naughty** when they behave badly. *Don't be a naughty boy.*
2 ADJ **Naughty** books, pictures, or words are slightly rude or indecent. *...little boys who use naughty words... It's rather a naughty play.*

Nauru /naʊˈruː/
The **Republic of Nauru** is a country in the Pacific Ocean. It was administered by Australia from 1914. From 1942 to 1945, Nauru was occupied by Japan. It was then administered by Australia until independence in 1968. Bernard Dowiyogo, of the Nauru Party, became President in 1989. Nauru is a member of the Commonwealth. Its wealth derives from the world's richest phosphate deposits, which will be exhausted by 1995. ◆ **Nauruan** /naʊˈruːən/ N, ADJ
▪ *per capita GNP:* approximately US$8,070 ▪ *religion:* Christianity (mainly Nauruan Protestant Church) ▪ *language:* Nauruan ▪ *currency:* Australian dollar ▪ *capital:* none ▪ *population:* 9,000 (1989) ▪ *size:* 21 square kilometres.

nausea /ˈnɔːziə/
NU **Nausea** is a feeling of sickness and dizziness. *I cut into the meat and felt a sudden twinge of nausea.*

nauseam /ˈnɔːziæm/. See **ad nauseam.**

nauseate /ˈnɔːzieɪt/ **nauseates, nauseating, nauseated**
1 VO If something **nauseates** you, it makes you feel as if you are going to vomit. *The thought of food nauseated him.* ◆ **nauseating** ADJ *...a nauseating candy bar.*
2 VO Something that **nauseates** you, cause you to feel disgust or dislike towards it because it is very unpleasant. *The idea of Uncle Harold outside Nicola's door nauseated him.* ◆ **nauseating** ADJ *They are responsible for the most nauseating murders.*

nauseous /ˈnɔːziəs/
1 ADJ PRED If you feel **nauseous**, you feel sick and as if you are likely to vomit. *I felt dizzy and nauseous.*
2 ADJ Something that is **nauseous** is unpleasant and causes you to feel strong feelings of disgust or dislike. *...the nauseous ugliness of the nightmare.*

nautical /ˈnɔːtɪkl/
ADJ ATTRIB **Nautical** people and things are related to ships and the sea. *...a nautical uniform.*

nautical mile, nautical miles
NC A **nautical mile** is a unit of measurement used at sea. It is equal to 1852 metres. *The accident occurred about 370 nautical miles south of Cape Race.*

naval /ˈneɪvl/
ADJ ATTRIB **Naval** means connected with or belonging to a country's navy. *Both countries already have substantial naval forces in the area... Another American naval vessel was on its way to offer assistance.*

nave /neɪv/ **naves**
NC The **nave** of a church or cathedral is the long central part where the congregation sits. *...the long nave of Westminster Abbey.*

navel /ˈneɪvl/ **navels**
NC Your **navel** is the small hollow in the middle of the front of your body. *An arrow of pubic hair ran down his firm stomach to his navel.*

navigable /ˈnævɪɡəbl/
ADJ A **navigable** river or waterway is wide enough or deep enough for a boat to travel safely. *Settlements were scattered along the banks of navigable rivers.*

navigate /ˈnævɪɡeɪt/ **navigates, navigating, navigated**
1 V-ERG When someone **navigates** a ship or when a ship is **navigated**, it goes or is directed in the right direction. *Fishermen could navigate a boat without a compass and without light... The Vietnamese boat was unseaworthy and unable to navigate... The resolution appeared to limit the freedom of ships to navigate in international waters.* ◆ **navigation** /ˌnævɪˈɡeɪʃn/ NU *You can't teach navigation in the middle of a storm.*
2 VA When fish or animals **navigate**, they find a direction to go in. *The salmon navigate over the vast distances to and from their oceanic feeding grounds... Bats navigate by ultrasound.*
3 VOorVA If you **navigate** a dangerous or difficult place, or **navigate** round an obstacle, you travel carefully in order to avoid the danger or difficulty. *Until then no ship had been large enough to navigate the Atlantic... The ship is trying to navigate round the anchor chain, but without power that's proving very difficult.*
4 VA If someone **navigates** in or through a difficult or complicated situation, they deal with it carefully or diplomatically. *He said Britain would like to navigate through existing difficulties back to reasonable and regular relations.*

navigator /ˈnævɪɡeɪtə/ **navigators**
NC A **navigator** is someone who works out the direction in which a ship, aeroplane, or a car should go. *The pilot and his navigator ejected from the plane when it developed problems. ...the famous Portuguese navigator, Vasco de Gama.*

navvy /ˈnævi/ **navvies**
NC A **navvy** is a person who is employed to do hard physical work, for example building roads or canals; an old-fashioned word. *...a colonel who had once been a navvy.*

navy /ˈneɪvi/ **navies**
1 N COLL A country's **navy** is the part of its armed forces that is trained to fight at sea; also used to refer to the ships and equipment they use. *My father's in the Navy... Why does the US Navy maintain a fleet in the Mediterranean?... There are no plans to alter the size of the Royal Navy patrol in the area.*
2 ADJ Something that is **navy** or **navy-blue** is dark blue. *He wore navy-blue pinstripe trousers.*

nay /neɪ/
1 **Nay** means no; an old-fashioned use.
2 ADV SEN You use **nay** in front of a stronger word or phrase which you feel is more appropriate than the one you have just used; a formal use. *It also enabled, nay, compelled me to pass through Portsmouth... Restriction of freedom begins with birth. Nay, it begins long before birth.*

Nazarbayev, Nursultan /nʊəsʊltɑːn næzəbaɪəf/
Nursultan Nazarbayev became President of Kazakhstan in 1990. He was Secretary of the Central Committee of the Kazakh Communist Party from 1979 to 1984, and First Secretary of the Kazakh Communist Party from 1989 to 1991. Born: 1940.

NB /ˌenˈbiː/
You write **NB** to draw someone's attention to what you are going to write next. *NB The root of the plant is poisonous.*

NCO /ˌensiːˈəʊ/ **NCO's**
NC An **NCO** is a soldier who has a rank such as sergeant or corporal. **NCO** is an abbreviation for 'non-commissioned officer'. *He had a minute staff of four officers, one NCO and eight men.*

-nd
SUFFIX **-nd** is added to most numbers written in figures and ending in 2 in order to form ordinal numbers. 2nd is pronounced the same as 'second'. *...2nd October 1957. ...42nd Street.*

N'Djaména /ndʒəˈmeɪnə/
N'Djaména, formerly known as Fort-Lamy, is the capital of Chad and its largest city. Population: 594,000 (1988).

NE
NE is a written abbreviation for 'north-east'.

Neanderthal /niˈændətɑːl/
ADJ ATTRIB **Neanderthal** people lived in Europe between 35 and 70,000 years ago. ...*a long-standing controversy over the importance of Neanderthal Man in the ascent of Modern Man.*

near /nɪə/ **nearer, nearest; nears, nearing, neared**
1 PREP, ADV, or ADJ If something is **near** a place or thing or **near to** it, it is a short distance from it. *He stood near the door. ...a small town near the border with Pakistan... I wish I lived nearer London... I looked at the books nearest to where I stood... The sounds of battle gradually came nearer again... The nearest police station is Al-Duthman.*
2 PREP If someone or something is **near** a particular state or **near to** it, they have almost reached it. *Her father was angry, her mother near tears... The air traffic system was near breaking point... I was very near to giving in to their demands... The paper says farm reform seems no nearer a solution than when the last summit broke up in December... Independent observers have put the figure nearer one per cent.*
3 PREP If something happens **near** a particular time or **near to** it, it happens just before or just after that time. ...*near the beginning of the play... The attack came near the end of a big funeral procession... He came to Baghdad on January 12th, which the US says is too near to the January 15th deadline.*
4 ADV or ADJ If a time or event is **near**, it will happen very soon. ...*as her wedding day drew near... They heard Mr Mandela say that victory over apartheid was near.*
5 ADJ ATTRIB Your **near** relatives are your closest relatives, for example your parents and grandparents. *Those with information need to ensure that the nearest relatives are told before any lists are issued to the press and media.*
6 ADJ ATTRIB In a contest, your **nearest** rival or challenger is the one that is most likely to defeat you. *He defeated his nearest rival for the Republican nomination... In 1987, the Conservatives got twice as many votes here as their nearest challenger.*
7 ADJ ATTRIB You say that someone or something is the **nearest** thing or the **nearest** equivalent to another person or thing when they are the most similar. *The Express says Mother Teresa may be the nearest thing to a living saint... The Spanish are the nearest thing to an ally that Cuba has in Western Europe... In Moscow the supreme soviet, the nearest equivalent to a national parliament, has supported Mr Gorbachev's plans.*
8 ADJ ATTRIB or SUBMOD You can also use **near** to say that something almost has a particular quality or almost happens. ...*a state of near chaos. ...our near catastrophic economic troubles... There's been another near collision between two airliners over South East England.*
9 VO If someone or something is **nearing** a particular place or stage in its development, they are approaching it. *As they neared the harbour, it began to rain. ...the factory now nearing completion will be capable of manufacturing chemical weapons.*
10 V-ERG When you **near** a particular date or point in time, or when the date or time **nears**, it comes closer. ...*a great and original Australian writer, nearing 80, Christina Stead. ...when the time neared for the prayer.*
● **Near** is used in these phrases. ● The expressions **near enough** and **as near as makes no difference** mean that something is almost true; an informal expression. *He paid £100, or as near as makes no difference.* ● If you say that something will happen in the **near future**, you mean that it will happen quite soon. *They expected her release to take place in the near future... He thought it unlikely that the state of emergency would be lifted in the near future.* ● You say 'it was a **near thing**', when you are describing a situation that nearly ended in an unpleasant or disastrous way. *I lived—but it was a near thing.*
● **nowhere near**: see **nowhere**.

near- /nɪə-/
PREFIX **near-** combines with nouns and adjectives to express the idea that something has almost all of the qualities usually associated with the original noun or adjective. *Thousands of examples of near-death experiences have now been recorded from round the world... A near-riot erupted. ...a near-bankrupt national economy... The space-station was to be built in near-earth orbit.*

nearby /nɪəbaɪ/
ADJ or ADV **Nearby** things and places are only a short distance away. *A woman was held in the nearby town of Amesbury... There was a river nearby... Reports say the President was not hurt but a soldier standing nearby was wounded.*

Near East
N PROP The **Near East** is the same as the **Middle East**.

nearly /nɪəli/
1 ADV **Nearly** means not completely or not exactly. *It was nearly dark... I can nearly swim a mile... She was nearly as tall as he was... It involves an investment of nearly two and a half million dollars... The dollar fell by nearly two yen.*
2 You use **not nearly** to emphasize that something is not the case. For example, if something is 'not nearly big enough', it is much too small. ...*but then the food situation was not nearly so bad as it is now... I haven't spent nearly long enough here... They don't have nearly so many foods to choose from as we do.*

near miss, near misses
1 NC A **near miss** is also a situation where you nearly had an accident or disaster. *Most aircraft accidents or near misses are caused by pilot error. ...another near miss by two airliners.*
2 NC A **near miss** is a bomb or shot which just misses the target.
3 NC An attempt to do something which nearly succeeds, but just fails to do so, is also called a **near miss**. *There was another near miss for Britain in the showjumping when David Broom completed two rounds with only four faults in each.*

nearside /nɪəsaɪd/
N SING The **nearside** of a vehicle is the side that is nearest to the edge of the road when the vehicle is being driven normally. ...*a dent on the nearside... The mini had just touched the offside of this truck with its nearside wing.*

near-sighted
ADJ Someone who is **near-sighted** cannot see things properly when they are far away. *He was near-sighted and wore glasses.*

neat /niːt/ **neater, neatest**
1 ADJ Something that is **neat** is tidy and smart. *His clothes were neat. ...small, neat writing.* ◆ **neatly** ADV *Mother's clothes hung neatly in a row.*
◆ **neatness** NU *Their desks are models of neatness... I was pleased at the neatness of the stitches.*
2 ADJ Someone who is **neat** is careful and tidy in their appearance and behaviour. *The Brigadier is a trim, neat man.*
3 ADJ If you drink an alcoholic drink **neat**, you drink it without adding anything such as water or tonic. *She takes her whisky neat... He gulped the neat brandy down in one draught.*

nebulous /nebjʊləs/
ADJ **Nebulous** ideas are vague and not precise; a formal word. *I had a nebulous notion of a life after death.*

necessarily /nesəsəˈrɪli, nesəsrəli/
1 ADV If something is not **necessarily** the case, it is not always the case. *Fleas are not necessarily associated with dirt... Documentaries don't necessarily need interviewers... His resignation does not necessarily mean he will find himself in the political wilderness.*
2 ADV If something **necessarily** happens in particular circumstances, it must happen in those circumstances; a formal use. *Growth has necessarily levelled off... It's true that the process of army training is necessarily tough.*

necessary /nesəsəˈri/
1 ADJ Something that is **necessary** is needed in order

to get a particular result or effect. *Are we teaching undergraduates the necessary skills?... Make a soft dough, using a little more water if necessary... I don't want to stay longer than necessary... The two leaders agreed that all necessary measures would be taken to resolve the problem... Military officials don't seem to believe an air blockade is necessary for sanctions to succeed.*
2 ADJ ATTRIB A **necessary** factor or quality is one that must be present in a particular situation; a formal use. *There is no necessary connection between industrial democracy and productivity.*

necessitate /nəsɛsɪteɪt/ **necessitates, necessitating, necessitated**
V 0 or V+ING If something **necessitates** a particular course of action, it makes it necessary; a formal word. *The Government's action had necessitated a by-election... This job would necessitate working with his hands.*

necessity /nəsɛsəti/ **necessities**
1 NU **Necessity** is the need to do something. *She went to work not out of choice but necessity.*
2 NC **Necessities** are things that you must have in order to live. *They were supplied with all the necessities of life... People queue for hours for the most basic necessities.*

neck /nɛk/ **necks**
1 NC Your **neck** is the part of your body which joins your head to the rest of your body. *She threw her arms around his neck... There was a bad nick at the base of his neck from a recent haircut.*
2 NC The **neck** of a dress or shirt is the part which is round your neck or just below it. *...a dress with a lace neck... His shirt was open at the neck.*
3 NC The **neck** of something such as a bottle or a musical instrument is the long narrow part at the top. *He picked up the violin carefully by the neck.*
● **Neck** is used in these phrases. ● If two competitors are **neck and neck**, they are level with each other and appear to have an equal chance of succeeding or winning. *The two main contenders are running neck and neck... It was neck and neck to the finish.* ● If you are **up to** your **neck** in problems, you are deeply involved in them. *You were up to your neck in trouble with the press.* ● If someone is **breathing down** your **neck**, they are watching and checking everything you do very carefully; an informal expression. ● If you **risk** your **neck**, you do something very dangerous to achieve something or to help someone. *I thanked him for risking his neck for me.* ● If you **stick** your **neck out**, you do something that makes you likely to be criticized or harmed; an informal expression. *Let someone else stick their neck out and take responsibility.* ● Someone or something that is from your **neck of the woods** is from the same part of the country as you are. *There's a caller on the line, actually from almost your neck of the woods, on Route 9 in Massachusetts.* ● **by the scruff of** your **neck**: see scruff.

neckerchief /nɛkətʃiːf/ **neckerchiefs**
NC A **neckerchief** is a piece of cloth folded diagonally to form a triangle, which people can wear round their necks. *The brightly coloured silk neckerchief completed the effect.*

necklace /nɛkləs/ **necklaces**
NC A **necklace** is a piece of jewellery such as a chain or string of beads which a woman wears round her neck. *Yesterday, a necklace worth over seven hundred thousand pounds was stolen.*

neckline /nɛklaɪn/ **necklines**
NC The **neckline** of a dress or blouse is the top edge at the front. *...a mini-dress with a plunging neckline.*

necktie /nɛktaɪ/ **neckties**
NC A **necktie** is a long narrow piece of cloth worn under someone's shirt collar and tied in a knot at the front; used in American English. *He started wearing a necktie with a Mickey Mouse motif to faculty meetings.*

necromancy /nɛkrəmænsi/
NU **Necromancy** is black magic or witchcraft; a formal word.

nectar /nɛktə/
NU **Nectar** is a sweet liquid produced by flowers, which bees and other insects collect. *...bees spending the summer collecting nectar and turning it into honey.*

nectarine /nɛktərɪn/ **nectarines**
NC A **nectarine** is a kind of peach which has a smooth skin. *...the sliced nectarines and red onions on a blue plate with the tuna steaks on top.*

née /neɪ/
née is used before a name to indicate that it was a woman's surname before she got married; a formal word. *...Jane Carmichael, née Byers.*

need /niːd/ **needs, needing, needed**
1 V 0 or V+to-INF If you **need** something or **need** to do it, it is necessary for you to have it or to do it. *These animals need food throughout the winter... The country badly needs a period of sustained, coherent government... Children need to feel they matter to someone... Before we answer this question, we need to look briefly at the world environment.*
2 SEMI-MODAL If you say that something **need not** happen, or that someone **need not** do something, you are saying that there is no good reason for it to happen. *You needn't worry... It needn't cost very much... People died of diseases that need not have proved fatal.*
3 V 0, V+ING, or V+to-INF If something **needs** a particular action or if an action **needs** doing, this action is necessary. *The shed needs a good clean out... The Official Secrets Act needs reform... Keep a list of all the jobs that need doing... The top rim needs to be cut off.*
4 N PL+POSS Your **needs** are the things you need for a satisfactory or comfortable life. *She learned how to provide for her own needs... The government would find it hard to meet people's basic needs.*
5 N SING+SUPP A **need** is also a strong feeling that you must have or do something. *I began to feel the need of somewhere to retreat. ...Yugoslavia's need for a new credit or bridging loan... Ministers agreed that there was a need to make progress... She felt no need to speak.*
● **Need** is used in these phrases. ● You use **if need be** to say that an action will be carried out if it is necessary. *He said if need be Australia would send more help... She said she would stay with me for months and years if need be.* ● If someone or something is **in need of** something, they need it. *I am badly in need of advice... More than three million people in Angola are in need of emergency food aid... The hospital was in need of decorating.* ● People **in need** do not have enough money, or require help of some kind. *State aid will go to those most in need.*

needful /niːdfl/
ADJ **Needful** means necessary; an old-fashioned word. *...to provide the food, clothing, and shelter needful for the maintenance of health.*

needle /niːdl/ **needles, needling, needled**
1 NC A **needle** is a small piece of polished metal with a hole at one end which is used for sewing. *Then we get a needle and cotton and sew up the hole.*
2 NC You can refer to knitting needles as **needles**. *...a room full of old ladies knitting away with steel needles.*
3 NC The **needle** in a record player is the small pointed instrument that touches the record and picks up the sound signals. *Her mother covered her up, took the needle off the record, and turned the lights out. ...a standard phonograph needle.*
4 NC A **needle** is also the sharp piece of hollow metal which is attached to a syringe and which is used to give injections. *If that person doesn't share his or her needle, then he is very unlikely to get infected.*
5 NC On an instrument measuring speed, weight, electricity, and so on, the **needle** is the thin piece of metal or plastic which moves backwards and forwards and shows the measurement. *It doesn't look like a compass to me because it hasn't got a needle... A scanning tunnelling microscope employs a needle that floats above the material it is studying.*
6 NC The **needles** of a fir or pine tree are its thin

pointed leaves. *There was nothing on the ground except a thick layer of pine needles.*
7 VO If someone **needles** you, they annoy you by criticizing you repeatedly; an informal use. *She was needling me about Doris.*
8 **a needle in a haystack**: see **haystack**. See also **pins and needles**.

needless /niːdləs/
1 ADJ Something that is **needless** is completely unnecessary. *It was a needless risk to run.* ◆ **needlessly** ADV *This may upset a mother needlessly.*
2 You say **needless to say** to emphasize that what you are saying is obvious. *I left college in disgrace (needless to say without my Diploma).*

needlewoman /niːdlwʊmən/ **needlewomen**
NC A **needlewoman** is a woman who does a lot of sewing; an old-fashioned word.

needlework /niːdlwɜːk/
1 NU **Needlework** is sewing or embroidery that is done by hand. *...the basket in which she kept her needlework.*
2 NU **Needlework** is also the activity of sewing or embroidering. *The girls spend much time doing needlework.*

needn't /niːdnt/
Needn't is the usual spoken form of 'need not'.

needy /niːdi/ **needier, neediest**
1 ADJ A **needy** person is very poor. *The concessions are aimed at helping pensioners, the disabled and other needy people... They are among the neediest children in Britain.*
2 N PL **Needy** people are sometimes referred to as the **needy**. *It is important to serve everybody, not just the needy. ...favouring the rich at the expense of the needy.*

nefarious /nɪfeəriəs/
ADJ Something that is **nefarious** is wicked and immoral; a literary word. *...a nefarious system erected to exploit people... They maintain that they are engaged in nothing secret or nefarious.*

negate /nɪgeɪt/ **negates, negating, negated**
VO If you **negate** something that someone has done, you cause it to have no value or effect; a formal word. *The denial of the importance of minorities negates all our efforts on their behalf.*

negation /nɪgeɪʃn/; a formal word.
1 NU **Negation** is a person's disagreement with someone or refusal of something. *The office shook with the impresario's negation of whatever was under discussion.*
2 NU **Negation** is also the act of saying that something does not exist. *...the negation by the State authority of the rights of its citizens.*
3 N SING+*of* The **negation** of a quality or ideal is its complete opposite or its complete absence. *The very possibility of divorce is the negation of Christian marriage. ...the very negation of the spirit of kindness.*

negative /negətɪv/ **negatives**
1 ADJ **Negative** is used to describe statements that mean 'no'. *We expected to receive a negative answer.* ◆ **negatively** ADV *The public responded negatively.*
2 If an answer is **in the negative**, it is 'no'. *This question had been answered in the negative.*
3 ADJ If someone is **negative** or has a **negative** attitude, they consider only the bad aspects of a situation, rather than the good ones. *He was especially negative about my written work... No one else I met ever had such a negative view of Alice Springs... According to this document, negative attitudes to foreign languages start at school.*
4 ADJ If a medical or other scientific test is **negative**, it shows that something has not happened or is not present. *...a negative pregnancy test.*
5 NC A **negative** is the image that is first produced when you take a photograph. *The original negatives had mysteriously vanished.*
6 ADJ A **negative** number is less than zero.

neglect /nɪglekt/ **neglects, neglecting, neglected**
1 VO If you **neglect** someone or something, you do not look after them properly. *...the farmer who neglects his crops... The report says politicians have neglected*

old people when drawing up policies. ◆ **neglected** ADJ *The child looked neglected, scruffy and unloved.*
2 V+*to*-INF or VO If you **neglect** to do something, you fail to do it. *I neglected to bring a gift... I feel I'm neglecting my duty.*
3 NU **Neglect** is failure to look after someone or something properly. *...estates suffering from vandalism and neglect... The present crisis is rooted in the years of neglect of black education in South Africa.*

neglectful /nɪglektfl/
ADJ If someone is **neglectful** of someone or something, they do not look after them properly or give them the attention they deserve. *He had been neglectful of his duties. ...a neglectful father.*

negligee /neglɪʒeɪ/ **negligees**; also spelt **négligée**.
NC A woman's **negligee** is a dressing gown made of very thin material. *All the actresses in the film wear revealing negligees and low-cut gowns.*

negligence /neglɪdʒəns/
NU **Negligence** is failure to do something that you ought to do. *The chairman of the Party had been dismissed for negligence.*

negligent /neglɪdʒənt/
ADJ When someone is **negligent**, they fail to do something that they should do. *The law suit charged that the government was negligent in the design of the plant. ...inadequate safety procedures, and negligent management.* ◆ **negligently** ADV *They may act foolishly or negligently.*

negligible /neglɪdʒəbl/
ADJ Something that is **negligible** is so small or unimportant that it is not worth considering. *The cost in human life had been negligible... This would have a negligible effect on the temperature.*

negotiable /nɪgəʊʃəbl/
ADJ Something that is **negotiable** can be changed or agreed by means of discussion. *The price is negotiable.*

negotiate /nɪgəʊʃieɪt/ **negotiates, negotiating, negotiated**
1 V-RECIP If a person or group **negotiates** with another, or if two people or groups **negotiate**, they talk about a problem or situation on which they have different opinions in order to find a solution. *They called off the action to make it easier for union leaders and employers to negotiate... His government was prepared to negotiate directly with any of the parties involved in the conflict.*
2 V-RECIP If a person or group **negotiates** an agreement with another, or if two people or groups **negotiate** an agreement, they obtain it through discussion. *He negotiated a trade agreement with Brazil... They have negotiated an amnesty agreement under which the Prime Minister will resign and an election will be called.* ◆ **negotiated** ADJ ATTRIB *He would continue his efforts to find a negotiated settlement.*
3 V+*for* If you **negotiate** for something, you try to obtain it by discussing it with other people. *Paul is negotiating for a job worth £18,000... He called on the Chinese to negotiate for a solution.*
4 VO If you **negotiate** an obstacle, you succeed in moving around it. *Patrick is not sure whether he can negotiate the turn at the bottom.*

negotiating table
N SING If you say that people are at the **negotiating table**, you mean that they are having serious discussions about something on which they disagree, and that they are trying to reach an agreement. *The Russians and the Americans have come to the negotiating table.*

negotiation /nɪgəʊʃieɪʃn/ **negotiations**
NC **Negotiations** are discussions that take place between people with different interests, in which they try to reach an agreement. *The early stages of their negotiations with the Government were unsuccessful... The strikers have asked for direct negotiations with the Deputy Prime Minister.* ► Also NU *We need to allow more time for negotiation.*

negotiator /nɪgəʊʃieɪtə/ **negotiators**
NC **Negotiators** are people who take part in negotiations in business, politics, or international

affairs. *They acted as negotiators in all dealings with other villages. ...Pakistan's chief negotiator at the Geneva talks.*

Negro /niːgrəʊ/ **Negroes**
NC A **Negro** is someone with black skin; some people find this word offensive. *In Atlanta there were more than 200,000 Negroes.*

neigh /neɪ/ **neighs, neighing, neighed**
V When a horse **neighs**, it makes the loud sound that is typical of horses. *It galloped away neighing.* ▸ Also NC *The horse gave a loud neigh.*

neighbour /neɪbə/ **neighbours**; spelt **neighbor** in American English.
1 NC Your **neighbours** are the people who live near you, especially the people who live in the house or flat next to you. *Don't be afraid of what the neighbours will think.*
2 NC+POSS Your **neighbour** is also the person who is standing or sitting next to you. *Rudolph turned his head towards his neighbour.*
3 NC+POSS A country's **neighbours** are the countries that are next to it. *Papua New Guinea achieved independence from its large southern neighbour as recently as 1975.*
4 NC+POSS You can refer to something which is near or next to something else of the same kind as its **neighbour**. *The young plant risks being overshadowed by its neighbours.*

neighbourhood /neɪbəhʊd/ **neighbourhoods**; spelt **neighborhood** in American English.
1 NC A **neighbourhood** is a part of a town where people live. *She'd just moved into the neighbourhood. ...a wealthy neighbourhood.*
2 If something is **in the neighbourhood** of a place, it is near to it. *We were heading for a destination in the neighbourhood of the Lofoten Islands.*

neighbouring /neɪbərɪŋ/; spelt **neighboring** in American English.
ADJ ATTRIB **Neighbouring** describes the places and things that are near to the place or thing that you are talking about. *Families came from neighbouring villages to look at her... The Algerian leader has arrived in neighbouring Tunisia.*

neighbourly /neɪbəli/; spelt **neighborly** in American English.
ADJ If people living near you are **neighbourly**, they are kind, friendly, and helpful. *That's a neighbourly thing to do.*

neither /naɪðə, niːðə/
1 CONJ You use **neither** in front of the first of two or more words or expressions when you are saying that two or more things are not true or do not happen. The other things are introduced by 'nor'. *He spoke neither English nor French... She neither drinks, smokes, nor eats meat... The Englishman was neither gratified nor displeased.*
2 PRON or DET You also use **neither** to refer to both of two things or people, when you are making a negative statement about both of them. *Neither of us was having any luck... Neither was suffering pain... Militarily, neither side can win.*
3 CONJ If you say that one thing is not the case and **neither** is another, you mean that the second thing is also not the case. *'I don't normally drink at lunch.'— 'Neither do I.'*

nemesis /neməsɪs/
N SING The **nemesis** of something such as a society is a disastrous period in its history that may be considered a just punishment for something that is wrong or immoral about it; a literary word. *Every civilization seems to have its nemesis.*

neo- /niːəʊ-/
PREFIX **Neo-** is used to form nouns and adjectives that refer to modern versions of ideologies and styles that existed in the past. *...neo-imperialism. ...neo-Fascist groups.*

neoclassical /niːəʊklæsɪkl/; also spelt **neo-classical**.
ADJ **Neoclassical** architecture or art dates from the late 18th century and uses designs and motifs drawn from Roman and Greek architecture and art. *...a neo-classical church.*

neo-colonialism
NU **Neo-colonialism** is economic control or political influence that one country has over another country, especially by having control of its businesses or financial institutions. *President Mengistu regards this attitude as a form of neo-colonialism.*

neolithic /niːəlɪθɪk/
ADJ **Neolithic** means belonging to the period when people first started farming but still used stone weapons and tools. *...in neolithic times. ...neolithic weapons. ...neolithic settlements.*

neologism /niɒlədʒɪzəm/ **neologisms**
NC A **neologism** is a new word or expression in a language, or a familiar word or expression that is now being used with a new meaning; a formal word. *I refuse to use the hideous neologism 'nicemanship'.*

neon /niːɒn/
NU or N+N **Neon** is a gas which exists in very small amounts in the atmosphere. It is used in glass tubes to make bright lights and signs. *...gases like carbon dioxide, helium or neon... At eleven all neon lighting will have to be switched off. ...neon signs on banks, shops and hoardings.*

neophyte /niːəfaɪt/ **neophytes**
NC A **neophyte** is someone who is new to a particular activity; a formal word. *America was a neophyte on the world stage. ...a political neophyte.*

Nepal /nɪpɔːl/
The **Kingdom of Nepal** is a country in southern Asia, north-east of India. Until 1951 Nepal was ruled by the king in conjunction with a hereditary Prime Minister from the Rana family. Until 1990 there was a one-party system with an absolute monarchy. King Birendra Bir Bikram Shah Dev became head of state in 1972. Girija Prasad Koirala of the Nepali Congress Party (NCP) was elected Prime Minister in 1991. Nepal produces rice, jute, sugar, clothing, carpets, and leather goods. Cannabis is illegally exported. Tourism is an important industry. ◆ **Nepalese** /nepəliːz/ N, ADJ
▪ *per capita GNP:* US$110 ▪ *religion:* Hinduism
▪ *language:* Nepali (official), Maithir, Bhojpuri
▪ *currency:* rupee ▪ *capital:* Kāthmāndu ▪ *population:* 19 million (1989) ▪ *size:* 147,181 square kilometres.

nephew /nefjuː, nevjuː/ **nephews**
NC Your **nephew** is the son of your sister, brother, sister-in-law, or brother-in-law. *He had two nephews... Mr Sope is the nephew of the former president Sokomanu.*

nepotism /nepətɪzəm/
NU If someone uses their power or authority to get jobs or other benefits for members of their family, you refer to this action as **nepotism**. *...the nepotism and corruption of their civil service.*

nerd /nɜːd/ **nerds**
NC If you refer to someone as a **nerd**, you mean that you think they behave in a stupid way; an informal word. *...the shame of being labelled a nerd... I felt a total nerd.*

Nerette, Joseph /ʒəʊzef nerɛt/
Joseph Nerette was appointed interim President of Haiti, following a coup in 1991. He was formerly a senior High Court judge.

nerve /nɜːv/ **nerves**
1 NC A **nerve** is a long, thin fibre that transmits messages between your brain and other parts of your body. *...the vital substance responsible for carrying instructions from nerves to muscles... Light entering the eyes stimulates the optic nerves.*
2 N PL If you talk about someone's **nerves**, you are referring to how able they are to remain calm and not become worried in a stressful situation. *They claimed that cigarettes helped to calm their nerves... We have quite strong nerves... She displayed no nerves.* ● See also **war of nerves**.
3 NU **Nerve** is the courage you need to do something difficult or dangerous. *Nobody had the nerve to remind him that he was several hours late... His nerve began to crack.*
● **Nerve** is used in these phrases. ● If someone or something **gets on** your **nerves**, they annoy or irritate you very much; an informal expression. *The children get on her nerves.* ● If you say that someone **had a**

nerve or **had the nerve** to do something, you mean that they made you angry by doing something rude or disrespectful; used in informal English. *He had the nerve to say Fleet Street was corrupting me.*

nerve centre, nerve centres
NC The **nerve centre** of an organization is the place from where the activities of the organization are controlled and where the leaders of the organization meet. *This office is the union's nerve centre.*

nerve gas, nerve gases
N MASS **Nerve gas** is a poisonous gas that is used in war to paralyse people and even kill them. *They described the appalling effects of nerve gas on the local population.*

nerveless /nɜːvləs/
1 ADJ ATTRIB **Nerveless** fingers and hands are numb and do not have any strength because of cold, fear, tiredness, etc. *Plate after plate dropped from his nerveless fingers and smashed on the tiles.*
2 ADJ Someone who is **nerveless** is extremely brave and shows no fear at all. *A few men, nerveless and cool, slept soundly.*

nerve-racking
ADJ Something that is **nerve-racking** makes you tense and worried. *It was a nerve-racking period for us all.*

nervous /nɜːvəs/
1 ADJ If you are **nervous**, you are worried and frightened, and show this in your behaviour. *Both actors were exceedingly nervous on the day of the performance.* ◆ **nervously** ADV *He laughed nervously.*
◆ **nervousness** NU *'Pa,' Rudolph began, trying to conquer his nervousness.*
2 ADJ ATTRIB A **nervous** person is very tense and easily upset. *She was a particularly nervous woman.*
3 ADJ PRED If you are **nervous** about something, you feel rather afraid or worried about it. *He's nervous of thieves in that little shop of his.*
4 ADJ ATTRIB A **nervous** illness or condition affects your mental state. *She had suffered a lot of nervous strain.*

nervous breakdown, nervous breakdowns
NC A **nervous breakdown** is an illness in which someone suffers from deep depression and needs psychiatric treatment. *You'll give yourself a nervous breakdown going on working like this.*

nervous system, nervous systems
NC Your **nervous system** is all the nerves in your body together with your brain and spinal cord, which control your movements and feelings. *When we feel pain, our hand, through our nervous system, responds to that pain. ...a disease of the brain and nervous system called 'scrapie'.*

nervous wreck, nervous wrecks
NC If someone is a **nervous wreck**, they are extremely nervous or worried; an informal expression. *I waited so long that by the time my turn came I was a nervous wreck.*

nervy /nɜːvi/
ADJ Someone who is **nervy** tends to be very tense, anxious, and easily upset. *She never recovered from it, and she was very nervy afterwards.*

-ness /-nəs/ **-nesses**
SUFFIX **-ness** combines with adjectives to form nouns that refer to a state or quality described by the adjective. Nouns of this kind are usually not defined but are treated with the related adjectives. *The aim of life is happiness. ...the smallness of the school.*

nest /nest/ **nests, nesting, nested**
1 NC A **nest** is a place that birds, insects, and some other animals make to lay eggs in or give birth to their young in. *We had a wasp's nest in the roof.*
2 V When a bird **nests** somewhere, it builds a nest and settles there to lay its eggs. *Hornbills nest in holes in trees.*

nest egg, nest eggs
NC A **nest egg** is a sum of money that you are saving for a particular purpose; an informal expression. *They squandered their little nest egg.*

nestle /nesl/ **nestles, nestling, nestled**
1 VA If you **nestle** somewhere, you move into a comfortable position, often by pressing against someone or something soft. *They nestled together on*

the sofa... *The baby may just want to nestle and cuddle up to its mother.*
2 VA If a house or village **nestles** somewhere, it is in that place or position and seems safe or sheltered. *A village nestled in the hills to their right.*

nestling /nesəlɪŋ/ **nestlings**
NC A **nestling** is a young bird that has not yet learnt to fly. *...the male passes food to his mate and nestlings.*

net /net/ **nets, netting, netted**; also spelt **nett** in for the meanings in paragraphs 4 and 5.
1 NU **Net** is a cloth which you can see through. It is made of very fine threads woven together so that there are small spaces between them. *The bride wore a veil of white net... All the windows have net curtains.*
● See also **netting**.
2 NC A **net** is a piece of netting of a particular shape which you use, for example, to protect something or to catch fish. *...a net to cover the plants. ...a butterfly trapped in a net.*
3 NC **Nets** are also used to divide the two halves of a tennis or badminton court, or to form the back of a goal in football. *He lobbed the ball over the head of the goal-keeper into the back of the net.*
4 VO If you **net** something, you manage to get it, often by using skill. *He was netting his largest fortune.*
5 ADJ ATTRIB or ADJ after N A **net** result or amount is one that is final, when everything necessary has been considered or included. *That gave him a net profit of just over 23%... The net result is a massive labour surplus... Last year he made a profit of £20,000 net.*
6 ADJ ATTRIB or ADJ after N The **net** weight of something is its weight without its container or wrapping. *If you look at the label, you'll see it says 450g net.*

netball /netbɔːl/
NU **Netball** is a game played by two teams of seven players, usually women or girls. Each team tries to score goals by throwing a ball through a net which is at the top of a pole at each end of the court. *Most pupils also played traditional games like football, cricket, netball and tennis.*

nether /neðə/
ADJ ATTRIB **Nether** is used to describe the lower part of a thing or place; a literary word. *Her parents retreated into the nether regions of the house.*

Netherlands /neðələndz/
The **Kingdom of the Netherlands** is a country in north-west Europe. It was occupied by Germany from 1940 to 1945. Queen Beatrix became head of state in 1980. Rudolph Lubbers, of the Christian Democratic Appeal (CDA), became Prime Minister in 1982. The Netherlands is a member of NATO and the European Community. It exports agricultural products and chemicals. ◆ **Dutchman, Dutchwoman** /dʌtʃmən, dʌtʃwumən/ N **Dutch** /dʌtʃ/ ADJ, N PL
▪ *per capita GNP:* US$14,530 ▪ *religion:* Christianity
▪ *language:* Dutch ▪ *currency:* guilder (gulden)
▪ *capital:* Amsterdam (the seat of government is The Hague) ▪ *population:* 15 million (1989) ▪ *size:* 33,933 square kilometres.

Netherlands Antilles /neðələndz æntɪliːz/
The **Netherlands Antilles** is a self-governing territory of the Netherlands in the Caribbean. The principal islands are Curaçao, Bonaire, St Eustatius, Saba, and St Maarten. Curaçao became a Dutch colony in 1634. It exports oil. Aruba was part of the Netherlands Antilles until it was accorded separate status in 1986. Tourism and banking are important industries. ◆ **Netherlands Antillean** /neðələndz æntɪliən/ N, ADJ
▪ *per capita GNP:* US$6,110 ▪ *religion:* Christianity
▪ *language:* Dutch and English (official), Papiamento
▪ *currency:* guilder ▪ *capital:* Willemstad ▪ *population:* 191,000 (1989) ▪ *size:* 800 square kilometres.

nett /net/. See **net**.

netting /netɪŋ/
NU **Netting** is material made of threads or metal wires woven or knotted together so that there are equal spaces between them. *...wire netting on the windows.*

nettle /netl/ **nettles**
1 NC A **nettle** is a wild plant with leaves that sting. *In the far corner there, we've got thistles, nettles and general weeds growing. ...reactions very similar to stinging nettle reactions.*

2 If you **grasp the nettle**, you deal with a problem, or do something that is unpleasant or difficult, in a determined way. *It remains to be seen whether they will be bold enough to grasp the nettle of price reform... They will have to wait and see if the Kremlin grasps what is a very delicate nettle.*

nettled /nɛtld/
ADJ If you are **nettled**, you are annoyed or offended. *Judy was a bit nettled.*

nettle rash
NU **Nettle rash** is a rash of small itchy red or white lumps on a person's skin which are usually caused by a stinging nettle.

network /nɛtwɜːk/ **networks**
1 NC A **network** is a large number of roads, veins, or other things which look like lines, which cross each other or meet at many points. *...the network of back streets in the Latin Quarter. ...a network of tiny red veins running over her white skin.*
2 NC A **network** is a large number of people or organizations that have a connection with each other and work together as a system. *...a criminal network based in Karachi. ...a network of clinics.*
3 NC A radio or television **network** is a company or group of companies that usually broadcasts the same programmes at the same time in different parts of the country. *She gave an interview on a national television network.*

neural /njʊərəl/
ADJ ATTRIB **Neural** is used to describe things relating to a nerve or to the nervous system; a technical term. *There is evidence of the existence of a specific neural mechanism that carries out this function. ...the neural system.*

neuralgia /njʊərældʒə/
NU **Neuralgia** is very severe pain along the whole length of a nerve; a medical term. *I suffer from very painful facial neuralgia.*

neurological /njʊərəlɒdʒɪkl/
ADJ ATTRIB **Neurological** is used to describe things relating to the nervous system; a medical term. *...a progressive neurological disease.*

neurology /njʊərɒlədʒi/
NU **Neurology** is the study of the structure, function, and diseases of the nervous system; a medical term. *...the Midlands Centre for Neurosurgery and Neurology in Smethwick.* ◆ **neurologist** /njʊərɒlədʒɪst/ **neurologists** NC *Finally my doctor advised me to see a neurologist and I agreed.*

neuron /njʊərɒn/ **neurons**
NC A **neuron** is a cell that is part of the nervous system and that conducts messages to and from the brain; a technical term. *...looking in detail at the way the neurons respond to the stimuli.*

neurone /njʊərəʊn/ **neurones**
NC A **neurone** is the same as a **neuron**. *The human brain consists of neurones, blood cells and chemical elements.*

neurosis /njʊərəʊsɪs/ **neuroses** /njʊərəʊsiːz/
NU or NC **Neurosis** is a mental illness which causes people to have continual and unreasonable fears and worries. *Such problems can distort personality and lead to neurosis. ...a victim of Mark's neuroses.*

neurotic /njʊərɒtɪk/
ADJ If someone is **neurotic**, they continually show a lot of unreasonable anxiety about something. *They are becoming neurotic about their careers.*

neuter /njuːtə/ **neuters, neutering, neutered**
1 ADJ In the grammar of some languages, words that are **neuter** have sets of inflections which are different from those of masculine and feminine words.
2 VO When an animal is **neutered**, its reproductive organs are removed. *The RSPCA is to neuter every cat or dog it sends to a new home, in an effort to reduce the number of unwanted animals in Britain.*

neutral /njuːtrəl/
1 ADJ A **neutral** country or person does not support either side in a disagreement or war. *Because I was neutral in the conflict I was a welcome visitor... Thailand would prefer the talks to be held in a neutral country... Presidents Mobutu and Neto met on neutral ground in the Congo capital, Brazzaville.* ◆ **neutrality**

/njuːtræləti/ NU *We have a tradition of political neutrality.*
2 ADJ If someone is **neutral** or if something that they do is **neutral**, they do not show any emotions or opinions. *I waited, but her eyes were neutral... 'Look,' she said in a neutral voice.*
3 NU **Neutral** is the position between the gears of a vehicle, in which the gears are not connected to the engine. *I pushed the handle into neutral.*
4 ADJ The **neutral** wire in an electric plug is the wire that is not earth or live and that is needed to complete the electrical circuit. *Cut back the the covers of the neutral and live wires about one inch.*

neutralize /njuːtrəlaɪz/ **neutralizes, neutralizing, neutralized**; also spelt **neutralise**.
VO To **neutralize** something means to prevent it from having any effect or from working properly. *Their aim is to neutralize the Council's campaign.* ◆ **neutralization** /njuːtrəlaɪzeɪʃn/ NU *...what the union radicals see as a neutralization of their movement.*

neutron /njuːtrɒn/ **neutrons**
NC A **neutron** is an atomic particle that has no electrical charge. *The neutrons pass through the aluminium walls of the tube.*

neutron bomb, neutron bombs
NC A **neutron bomb** is a nuclear weapon that is designed to kill people and animals without a large explosion and without destroying buildings. *The Prime Minister was asked whether France should manufacture neutron bombs. ...an accident on the eve of a neutron bomb test in 1979.*

never /nɛvə/
1 ADV **Never** means at no time in the past or future. *I've never been to Europe... I shall never forget this day... I never eat breakfast on Sundays.*
2 ADV **Never** means not in any circumstances at all. *What is morally wrong can never be politically right.*
3 **Never ever** is an emphatic expression for 'never'; an informal use. *She never ever wears a hat.*
4 ADV You use **never** with the simple past tense to mean 'did not'; an informal use. *My bus never arrived... Good gracious! I never knew that.* ● **never mind**: see **mind**.

never-ending
ADJ If something is **never-ending**, it lasts a very long time, and seems as if it will never end. *...the never-ending flow of refugees.*

never-never
If you buy something **on the never-never**, you buy it by hire purchase or on credit; an old-fashioned, informal word, used showing disapproval. *He bought the car on the never-never.*

never-never land
NU **Never-never land** is an imaginary land where everything is nice and pleasant; an informal expression. *They are back in the real world after a spell in never-never land.*

nevertheless /nɛvəðəlɛs/
ADV SEN **Nevertheless** means in spite of what has just been said; a formal word. *She saw Clarissa immediately, but nevertheless pretended to look around for her.*

new /njuː/ **newer, newest; news.** New is an adjective and news is a noun.
1 ADJ Something that is **new** has been recently made or created, or is in the process of being made or created. *...smart new houses. ...a new type of bandage that stops minor bleeding almost immediately.* ● See also **brand-new**.
2 ADJ You also use **new** to say that something has not been used or owned by anyone else. *There was another sign advertising new and used tractors... They cost over twenty dollars new.*
3 ADJ ATTRIB **New** also means different from what you have had, used, done, or experienced before. *Not long after that, he got a new job... The villagers were suspicious of anything new.* ◆ **newness** NU *...the newness and strangeness of her surroundings.*
4 ADJ ATTRIB You can describe something that has only recently been discovered as **new**. *In 1781 William Herschel discovered a new planet.*
5 ADJ ATTRIB A **new** period of time is just about to

begin. ...*on the eve of a new era... A new phase was about to start.*

6 ADJ ATTRIB **New** is also used to show that something has only just happened. For example, a **new** parent has only recently become a parent. *Thousands were there to hear the new party leader.* ● See also **newly-**.

7 ADJ PRED If you are **new** to a situation or place or if the situation or place is **new** to you, you have not experienced it or seen it before. ...*a person who's new to the job of teaching.* ...*a part of England completely new to him.*

8 N U or N SING **News** is information about a recent event or a recently changed situation. *I've got some good news for you.* ...*after receiving the news of my acceptance.*

9 N U or N SING **News** is also information that is given in newspapers and on radio and television about recent events in the country or the world. ...*a half hour of world and domestic news... It was on the news at 9.30.*
10 new blood: see **blood**. **to turn over a new leaf**: see **leaf**.

new- /njuː-/
PREFIX **New-** combines with the past participle of some verbs to make words or expressions which indicate that an action has been done or completed very recently. ...*a lovely smell, like new-cut grass.* ...*thousands of new-made graves.*

newborn /njuːbɔːn/
ADJ A **newborn** baby is one that has been born recently. ...*the medical care of newborn babies.* ...*vaccination of newborn children.*

new broom, new brooms
N C You can refer to a person who has just started a new job and who intends to make a lot of changes as a **new broom**; an informal expression. *'Daintry,' the Brigadier explained, 'is our new broom.'*

New Caledonia /nju: kælɪdəʊniə/
New Caledonia and Dependencies is a territory of France in the South Pacific, east of Australia. The principal islands are New Caledonia or Grande Terre, the Loyalty Islands, and the Chesterfield Islands. They were annexed by France in 1853. Agitation for independence from France has been a source of civil unrest. New Caledonia has the world's largest known nickel deposits. Tourism is an important industry.
♦ **New Caledonian** /nju: kælɪdəʊniən/ N, ADJ
■ *per capita GNP:* US$6,541 ■ *religion:* Christianity (mainly Roman Catholic) ■ *language:* French (official), Polynesian, Melanesian ■ *currency:* Pacific franc ■ *capital:* Nouméa ■ *population:* 164,000 (1989) ■ *size:* 19,103 square kilometres.

newcomer /njuːkʌmə/ **newcomers**
N C A **newcomer** is a person who has recently arrived to live in a place, joined an organization, or started a job. ...*newcomers to the neighbourhood.*

newel /njuːəl/ **newels**
N C A **newel** or a **newel post** is the thick post at the top or bottom of a staircase, supporting the hand rail. *The main staircases were usually of stone, and turned in broad flights round a square stone newel.*

new face, new faces
N C You can refer to someone who is new to an organization where you work or an area where you live, and who you do not recognize, as a **new face**. *New faces will accompany new policies... The new government that will help him achieve this includes fourteen new faces out of a cabinet of twenty-two.*

new-fangled
ADJ ATTRIB Older people sometimes describe new ideas or pieces of machinery as **new-fangled**, often when they think they are unnecessary or too complicated; an informal word. ...*a new-fangled Japanese camera.*

new-found
ADJ ATTRIB A **new-found** quality, ability, or person is one that you have discovered recently. ...*this new-found confidence.*

Ne Win, U /neɪ wɪn/
General U Ne Win came to power in Burma in a coup in 1962. He had served as Deputy Prime Minister from 1949 to 1950, and had been a caretaker Prime Minister from 1958 to 1960. He was Chief of Staff from 1962 to 1972, Prime Minister from 1962 to 1963 and from 1965

to 1974, and President from 1974 to 1981. He outlawed all political parties except the Burma Socialist Programme Party (BSPP) in 1964. He was Chairman of the BSPP from 1973 to 1988, when he resigned after nationwide protests. In the early 1990s, although he held no official post, he remained an important political figure. Born: 1911.

new-laid
ADJ ATTRIB **New-laid** eggs are very fresh because they have been laid very recently.

newly- /njuːli/
ADV **Newly-** combines with past participles to indicate that an action is very recent. ...*the newly-appointed American Defence Secretary.* ...*the newly-opened Finnish consulate in Tallinn.*

newlyweds /njuːliwedz/
N PL You can refer to a man and woman who have just got married as **newlyweds**. ...*Britain's royal newlyweds on their honeymoon cruise.*

new moon, new moons
N C The moon is a **new moon** when it is a thin crescent shape at the start of its four-week cycle of appearing to become larger and then smaller. *Clouds shrouded the new moon.*

news. See **new**.

news agency, news agencies
N C A **news agency** is an organization which collects news stories from all over the world and sells them to newspapers and television and radio stations. *Mr Wu accused foreign news agencies of distortions and exaggeration in their coverage of the recent unrest.*

newsagent /njuːzeɪdʒənt/ **newsagents**
N C A **newsagent** or **newsagent's** is a shop which sells newspapers, magazines, sweets, and cigarettes. *It costs 50 pence and is on sale in all the major newsagents.*

newscast /njuːzkɑːst/ **newscasts**
N C A **newscast** is a programme on radio or television that gives information about recent events in the world; used in American English. *Coming up after the newscast, a discussion of the week's major events.*

newscaster /njuːzkɑːstə/ **newscasters**
N C A **newscaster** is a person who reads the news on television or radio. ...*Dan Rather, the CBS newscaster.*

news conference, news conferences
N C A **news conference** is the same as a **press conference**; used in American English. *The Senator called a news conference to deny the CBS report.*

newscopy /njuːzkɒpi/
N U **Newscopy** is a report or reports provided by journalists to be printed in a newspaper or broadcast on a radio or television news programme. *The newsroom will not be using this newscopy from Stephen Fleay.*

newsflash /njuːzflæʃ/ **newsflashes**
N C A **newsflash** is an interruption that is made to a radio or television programme to announce an important piece of news. ...*a newsflash announcing the dissolution of Malaysia's parliament.*

newsletter /njuːzletə/ **newsletters**
N C A **newsletter** is a printed sheet or small magazine containing information about an organization that is sent regularly to its members. *Members receive a newsletter three times a year.*

newsman /njuːzmən/ **newsmen** /njuːzmən/
N C A **newsman** is a reporter for a newspaper or a television or radio news programme. *Sharp-eyed newsmen had spotted it.*

newspaper /njuːspeɪpə/ **newspapers**
1 N C A **newspaper** is a number of large sheets of folded paper on which news, articles, advertisements, and other information are printed. Some newspapers are produced every day from Monday to Saturday, and others once a week. ...*copies of France's leading daily newspaper Le Figaro.* ...*a weekly newspaper.*
2 N C A **newspaper** is also the organization that produces a newspaper. *I work for a newspaper.*
3 N U **Newspaper** consists of pieces of old newspapers, especially when they are being used for another purpose such as wrapping things up. *Wedge it with a wad of newspaper.*

newspaperman /njuːspeɪpəmæn/ **newspapermen**
NC A **newspaperman** is a reporter or a photographer
who works for a newspaper. *Hearst mingled with
newspapermen day and night... What wouldn't a
newspaperman give to get a picture of that!*

newsprint /njuːzprɪnt/
NU **Newsprint** is the cheap paper on which newspapers
are printed. *...bales of newsprint.*

newsreader /njuːzriːdə/ **newsreaders**
NC A **newsreader** is the same as a **newscaster**. *The
newsreader continued reading the news headlines.
...the newsreader's calm tones.*

newsreel /njuːzriːl/ **newsreels**
NC A **newsreel** is a short film which gives an account
of recent events in a country or the world, made
especially for showing in cinemas. *Contemporary
newsreel recorded the advent of independence... She
had spent hours viewing newsreel footage of Princess
Anne.*

newsroom /njuːzruːm, njuːzrʊm/ **newsrooms**
1 NC A **newsroom** is a radio or television studio where
news reports are prepared and broadcast. *From the
BBC World Service newsroom in London this is
Michael Powles and Julian Potter with Newsdesk...
Valerie Jones reports from our Belfast Newsroom.*
2 NC A **newsroom** is also an office at a newspaper
where news reports are written and edited before they
are printed. *Leaving his office I peeped into the
newsroom, where the reporters were clattering on
typewriters.*

news-stand, news-stands
NC A **news-stand** is a movable stand or stall in the
street or at a railway station from which newspapers
are sold. *She went to the news-stand at the end of the
platform and bought a paper.*

newsworthy /njuːzwɜːði/
ADJ Something that is **newsworthy** is sufficiently
interesting to be reported as news on the radio or
television or in the newspapers. *...their selection of
newsworthy events and interpretations.*

newsy /njuːzi/
ADJ A **newsy** letter is full of interesting news about
yourself, your family, and your friends; an informal
word. *After dinner, he wrote a newsy note to Andrew
and Madge Wentworth.*

newt /njuːt/ **newts**
NC A **newt** is a small animal with a moist skin, short
legs, and a long tail. Newts live partly on land and
partly in water. *...some sort of salamander or newt.*

New Testament
N PROP The **New Testament** is the part of the Bible
that deals with the life of Jesus Christ and with
Christianity in the early Church. *The New Testament,
covering Jesus' life and teachings, was originally
written mainly in ancient Greek.*

new town, new towns
NC A **new town** is a town that has been planned and
built as a whole, including shops, houses, and
factories, rather than one that has developed
gradually. *Almost fourteen hundred families have
gone to the new town which is expanding daily.*

new wave, new waves
NC A **new wave** is a movement in art, music, or film,
which introduces new ideas instead of following
traditional ones. *...the new wave of British music...
Here we hear him singing an arrangement of another
new wave musician, Dany Silva.*

New World
N PROP The American continent is sometimes referred
to as the **New World**, especially when talking about the
discovery of this continent by Europeans. *...the great
voyages of discovery to the New World.*

New Year
N U or N SING **New Year** or the **New Year** is the time
when people celebrate the start of a year. *We had a
marvellous time over New Year... Happy New Year!*

New Year's Day
NU **New Year's Day** is the first day of a year. In
Western countries this is January 1st. *From New
Year's Day the European Community will ban imports
of any meat that has been treated with growth
hormones.*

New Year's Eve
NU **New Year's Eve** is the last day of the year. *New
Year's Eve is the traditional day for giving presents in
the Soviet Union.*

New York City /njuː jɔːk sɪti/
New York City is the largest city in the United States.
Population: 7,353,000 (1988).

New Zealand /njuː ziːlənd/
The **Dominion of New Zealand** is a country in the
Pacific, south-east of Australia. It consists of two main
islands, North and South. It was a British colony from
1840 to 1947. Jim Bolger, of the National Party,
became Prime Minister in 1990. New Zealand is a
member of the Commonwealth. Its membership of
ANZUS was suspended in 1986, after it refused to allow
nuclear ships from the US to use its ports. New
Zealand exports wool, lamb, beef, butter, and cheese.
Tourism is an important industry. ◆ **New Zealander**
/njuː ziːləndə/ N
▪ *per capita GNP:* US$9,620 ▪ *religion:* Christianity
▪ *language:* English (official), Maori ▪ *currency:* dollar
▪ *capital:* Wellington ▪ *largest city:* Auckland
▪ *population:* 3 million (1989) ▪ *size:* 267,844 square
kilometres.

next /nekst/
1 ADJ The **next** period of time, event, person, or thing
is the one that comes immediately after the present
one or after the one you have just mentioned. *The
next five years are of vital importance... The next day,
I left better prepared... I may vote for her at the next
election... I am going to be the next President of the
United States... My next question is, 'What is art?'...
What's next on the agenda?*
2 ADJ The **next** place or person is also the one nearest
to you or the first one that you come to. *The telephone
was ringing in the next room... Pull into the next lay-
by... He whispered the words to the next man.*
3 ADV The thing that happens **next** is the thing that
happens immediately after something else. *The
audience does not know what is going to happen next...
Next, I'd like to show you some pictures.*
4 ADV When you **next** do something, you do it for the
first time since you last did it. *It was some years
later when I next saw her.*
5 ADV You use **next** to say that something has more of
a quality than all other things except one. For
example, the thing that is **next** best is the one that is
best except for one other thing. *The next best team is
Nottingham Forest with 61 points... Most Bangladeshis
are Muslims. The next largest group is Hindus.*
6 PREP If one thing is **next to** another thing, it is at
the side of it. *She went and sat next to him... There
was a bowl of goldfish next to the bed.*
● **Next** is used in these phrases. ● You use **after next**
in expressions such as 'the week after next' to refer to
a period of time after the next one. For example,
when it is May, the month after next is July. *He had
to go there the week after next.* ● You can use **next to**
in front of an adjective, especially a negative adjective
such as 'nothing', to mean almost. *I knew next to
nothing about him... The photographs were next to
useless but they were all we had.*

next door
1 ADV or ADJ If a house or flat is **next door** to the one
you live in, or **next door**, there are no other houses or
flats between that one and the one you live in. *Next
door to her house there were two shacks which were
rented out to different people... She lived next door to
the Wilsons... I'm going next door to tell them to be
quiet. ...our next-door neighbour, Joan.*
2 ADV or ADJ If one building or place is **next door** to
another, or **next door**, there are no other buildings or
places between them. *...the town of Paisley, next door
to Scotland's largest city, Glasgow. ...the policy of
building new nuclear power stations next door to
existing ones... He said the envoy was being held
captive in the same apartment block in Beirut, in the
room next door.*

next of kin
N PL or N SING Your **next of kin** are your closest
relatives; a formal expression. *Next of kin are being
informed of the incident... The man's next of kin have*

been notified... *The only next of kin seems to be a cousin in Droitwich.*

nexus /nɛksəs/. Nexus is both the singular and the plural form.
NC+SUPP A **nexus** is a connection or a series of connections and links within a particular situation or system; a formal word. *The cash nexus cast its net to cover the world... They have gradually been sucked into this nexus of non-opposition.*

Nguza Karl-I-Bond. See Karl-I-Bond, Nguza.

NHS /ɛneɪtʃɛs/
N PROP **NHS** is an abbreviation for 'National Health Service'. *Workers in the transfusion service are amongst the lowest paid in the NHS.*

NI /ɛnaɪ/
NU **NI** is an abbreviation for 'national insurance'. *You don't have to pay NI contributions while you are out of work.*

Niamey /njɑːmeɪ/
Niamey is the capital of Niger and its largest city. Population: 399,000 (1983).

nib /nɪb/ **nibs**
NC The **nib** on a pen is the small pointed piece of metal at the end, where the ink comes out as you write. *...a fountain pen with a gold nib.*

nibble /nɪbl/ **nibbles, nibbling, nibbled**
1 VOorV If you **nibble** something, or **nibble** at it, you eat it slowly by taking small bites out of it. *Just nibble a piece of bread... She nibbled at her food.*
2 VOorV When a mouse or other small animal **nibbles** something, it takes small bites out of it quickly and repeatedly. *It was nibbling the end of a leaf.*
3 NC A **nibble** is a gentle or quick bite of something.

Nicaragua /nɪkərægjuə/
The **Republic of Nicaragua** is a country in Central America. It was a Spanish colony from the 16th century until 1821. US troops were stationed in Nicaragua from 1912 until 1933, during which time the Somoza family came to power, as leader of the National Guard and the National Liberal Party (PLN). General Anastasio Somoza was deposed by the Sandinista National Liberation Front (FSLN) in 1979 after a civil war which began in the early 1970s. Daniel Ortega Saavedra became the Nicaraguan leader. He was elected President in 1984. Armed opposition to the Sandinista government was led by the Contras, who originally were the remnants of Somoza's National Guard, and were supported by the US. In 1990 Violeta Barrios de Chamorro, of the National Opposition Union (UNO), was elected President. Nicaragua is a member of the Organization of American States. It exports coffee, cotton, and bananas. Nicaragua's economy was severely disrupted by the civil war. Large foreign debts and high inflation are serious economic problems. ◆ **Nicaraguan** /nɪkərægjuən/ N, ADJ
▪ *per capita GNP:* US$830 ▪ *religion:* Christianity (mainly Roman Catholic) ▪ *language:* Spanish (official) ▪ *currency:* córdoba ▪ *capital:* Managua ▪ *population:* 4 million (1990) ▪ *size:* 120,254 square kilometres.

nice /naɪs/ **nicer, nicest**
1 ADJ If you say that something is **nice**, you mean that you find it enjoyable, pleasant, or attractive. *It would be nice to see you... Did you have a nice time at the party?... How nice you look.* ◆ **nicely** ADV *I always think Bessie dresses very nicely.*
2 ADJ If someone does or says something **nice**, they are being kind and thoughtful. *It's nice of you to say that... How nice of you to come... He said some very nice things about my poetry.*
3 ADJ If someone is **nice**, they are friendly and pleasant. *He's a genuinely nice person who takes an enormous amount of trouble with people... The people here are very nice.*
4 ADJ PRED If you are **nice** to someone, you behave in a friendly, pleasant or polite way towards them. *I wish I'd been nicer to him... Promise you'll be nice to her when she comes.* ◆ **nicely** ADV *You may go if you ask nicely.*
5 ADJ PRED If you say that something is, for example, **nice** and small, you mean that it is nice because it is small. *You can keep yourself nice and warm... It's*

nice and peaceful here.

nicely /naɪsli/
ADV Something that is happening or working **nicely** is working in a satisfactory way. *He thought he could manage quite nicely without them.*

nicety /naɪsəti/ **niceties**
NC **Niceties** are small details, especially concerning polite behaviour. *Here the niceties of etiquette must be observed.*

niche /niːʃ/ **niches**
1 NC A **niche** is a hollow area in a wall, or a natural hollow part in a cliff. *...the little statue of the saint in his niche near the pulpit.*
2 NC If you say that you have found your **niche** in life, you mean that you have a job or position which is exactly right for you. *You can then find your own niche in public life.*

nick /nɪk/ **nicks, nicking, nicked**
1 VOorV-REFL If you **nick** something, you make a small cut into the surface of it. *She prepared meat every day, often nicking her fingers... He shaved badly, nicking himself in a couple of places.*
2 NC A **nick** is a small cut made in the surface of something. *...with a nick out of the rear edge each side of the tail. ...little nicks and scratches.*
3 VO If someone **nicks** something, they steal it; an informal word. *My typewriter had been nicked.*
4 If something is achieved **in the nick of time**, it is achieved successfully, but at the last possible moment; an informal expression. *We got there in the nick of time... In the nick of time the fortunes of the Peronist Party have made a remarkable recovery.*

nickel /nɪkl/ **nickels**
1 NU **Nickel** is a silver-coloured metal that is used in making steel. *New, lightweight coins will be minted containing less nickel and copper.*
2 NC In the United States and Canada, a **nickel** is a coin worth five cents. *None of the coins were nickels. ...a pencil that was selling for a nickel in the United States.*

nickname /nɪkneɪm/ **nicknames, nicknaming, nicknamed**
1 NC A **nickname** is an informal name for someone. *...Graham Rathbone, whose nickname was Raffy.*
2 VOC If you **nickname** someone or something, you give them a nickname. *For a brief while, Mrs Thatcher was nicknamed 'Tina'.*

Nicosia /nɪkəsiːə/
Nicosia is the capital of Cyprus and its largest city. The 1974 invasion of Cyprus by Turkey led to the partition of Nicosia into a northern, Turkish Cypriot sector and a southern, Greek Cypriot sector. Population (excluding the Turkish Cypriot sector): 149,000 (1982).

nicotine /nɪkətiːn/
NU **Nicotine** is an addictive substance in tobacco. *...teeth browned by nicotine.*

niece /niːs/ **nieces**
NC Your **niece** is the daughter of your sister, brother, sister-in-law, or brother-in-law. *...a poem for his eight year old niece.*

nifty /nɪfti/ **niftier, niftiest**
ADJ Something that is **nifty** is neat and pleasing or cleverly done; an informal word. *That was a nifty piece of work. ...a nifty station wagon.*

Niger /niːʒeə/
The **Republic of Niger** is a country in western Africa. Over two-thirds of its territory is desert. It was a French colony, part of French West Africa, from 1901 until independence in 1960. Major-General Seyni Kountché came to power in a coup in 1974, suspended the constitution, and outlawed all political parties. He died in 1987 and was succeeded by Brigadier Ali Saibou. From 1974 until 1991, when political parties were legalized, the sole party was the National Movement for a Development Society (MNSD). A conference on constitutional reform in 1991 stripped Saibou of executive powers and appointed Amadou Cheffou Prime Minister. Niger is a member of the Organization of African Unity. It exports uranium. Large foreign debts are a serious economic problem. ◆ **Nigerien** /niːʒeəriən/ N, ADJ

▪ *per capita GNP:* US$290 ▪ *religion:* Islam, animism ▪ *language:* French (official), Hausa, Tuareg, Djerma, Fulani ▪ *currency:* CFA franc ▪ *capital:* Niamey ▪ *population:* 7 million (1988) ▪ *size:* 1,267,000 square kilometres.

Nigeria /naɪdʒɪəriə/
The **Federal Republic of Nigeria** is a country in western Africa. It is the most populous country in Africa. The main ethnic groups include Hausa, Yoruba, Ibo, and Fulani. Nigeria was a British colony from the 19th century until it became independent in 1960. From 1967 to 1970 there was a civil war caused by the secession of Biafra in eastern Nigeria. The war ended with Biafra's surrender and the reunification of the country. There has been a military government since 1983 and in 1984 political parties were banned. Major-General Ibrahim Babangida became President in 1985. There are two legal parties, created by the government in 1989: the Social Democratic Party (SDP) and the National Republican Convention (NRC). Nigeria is a member of the Commonwealth, OPEC, and the Organization of African Unity. It exports oil, cocoa, and rubber. Cannabis is illegally produced. Large foreign debts and high inflation are major economic problems. ◆ **Nigerian** /naɪdʒɪəriən/ N, ADJ
▪ *per capita GNP:* US$290 ▪ *religion:* Islam, Christianity ▪ *language:* English (official), Hausa, Yoruba, Ibo ▪ *currency:* naira ▪ *capital:* Abuja (some government offices remain in Lagos) ▪ *largest city:* Lagos ▪ *population:* 89 million (1991) ▪ *size:* 923,768 square kilometres.

niggardly /nɪɡədli/
ADJ Someone who is **niggardly** is not very generous, either with money or with praise. *I don't want to seem niggardly.*

nigger /nɪɡə/ **niggers**
NC **Nigger** is an extremely offensive word for a black person, especially someone who comes from Africa or whose ancestors come from Africa. *He was threatened, punched and called a 'nigger'.*

niggle /nɪɡl/ **niggles, niggling, niggled**
1 V or VO If something **niggles** you, it makes you worry slightly over a long time. *The question niggled at the back of his mind.* ◆ **niggling** ADJ ATTRIB *...little niggling doubts.*
2 NC A **niggle** is a small worry that you keep thinking about. *...a series of relatively minor niggles.*

nigh /naɪ/
ADV If someone says that an event is **nigh**, they mean that it will happen very soon; an old-fashioned word. *He declared that the end of the world was nigh.*
● **Nigh** is used in these phrases. ● You use **well nigh** in front of an adjective, especially a negative one such as 'impossible', to mean nearly or almost. *It's extremely difficult, well nigh impossible to choose between them... The otter is well-nigh extinct in Britain.* ● **Nigh on** an amount, number, or age, means almost that amount, number, or age; an old-fashioned expression. *He is nigh on forty but he doesn't think about getting married at all.*

night /naɪt/ **nights**
1 NC or NU The **night** is the part of each period of twenty-four hours when it is dark outside, especially the time when most people are sleeping. *The weather is unusually cool for early September and the nights are chilly... The embassy could help by finding them a safe place to sleep at night... I smoke. I drink. I stay up all night.*
2 NC or NU You also use **night** to refer to the period of time between the end of the afternoon and the time when you go to bed. *They go out on Friday nights... It was on the news last night.... Mr Gorbachev went on television last night to defend his reform programmes... They came at around eight at night.*
● **Night** is used in these phrases. ● If something happens **day and night** or **night and day**, it happens all the time without stopping. *They were being guarded night and day.* ● If you **have an early night**, you go to bed early. If you **have a late night**, you go to bed late. *She'll be getting an early night in readiness for her four day visit to Africa... A heavy legislative*

programme means late nights and long hours for both peers and MPs.

nightcap /naɪtkæp/ **nightcaps**
1 NC A **nightcap** is a drink that you have just before you go to bed. *What about a nightcap?*
2 NC A **nightcap** is also a kind of hat that people used to wear in bed. *He pulled his nightcap well over his ears.*

nightclothes /naɪtkləʊðz/
N PL **Nightclothes** are clothes that you wear in bed, such as pyjamas or nightdresses. *Some people fled from their homes in their nightclothes.*

nightclub /naɪtklʌb/ **nightclubs**
NC A **nightclub** is a place where people go late in the evening to drink and to dance or see a show. *The same thing happened when they went to nightclubs for an evening out. ...a city centre nightclub.*

nightdress /naɪtdres/ **nightdresses**
NC A **nightdress** is a sort of dress that women or girls wear in bed. *With only her nightdress to wear, she was frozen.*

nightfall /naɪtfɔːl/
NU **Nightfall** is the time of day when it starts to get dark. *We wanted to get out before nightfall.*

nightgown /naɪtɡaʊn/ **nightgowns**
NC A **nightgown** is the same as a **nightdress**; an old-fashioned word. *She put on her nightgown and climbed into bed.*

nightie /naɪti/ **nighties**
NC A **nightie** is a nightdress; an informal word. *She was sitting at her dressing table in her nightie, brushing her hair.*

nightingale /naɪtɪŋɡeɪl/ **nightingales**
NC A **nightingale** is a small brown European bird. The male nightingale is famous for singing beautifully at night. *...a garden where nightingales sing.*

nightlife /naɪtlaɪf/
NU **Nightlife** is the entertainment available at night in towns, such as nightclubs, theatres, and bars. *...the exotic nightlife of Montmartre.*

nightlight /naɪtlaɪt/ **nightlights**
NC A **nightlight** is a very dim light that can be left on at night in a bedroom.

nightly /naɪtli/
ADJ ATTRIB or ADV A **nightly** event happens every night. *I watched the nightly television news... My mother prayed nightly.*

nightmare /naɪtmeə/ **nightmares**
1 NC A **nightmare** is a very frightening dream. *He rushed to her room when she had nightmares and comforted her.*
2 NC A **nightmare** is also a very frightening or unpleasant situation or time. *The first day was a nightmare.*

nightmarish /naɪtmeərɪʃ/
ADJ If you describe a situation as **nightmarish**, you mean that it is extremely frightening. *I had nightmarish visions of what could go wrong.*

night owl, night owls
NC A **night owl** is someone who regularly stays up late at night, or who prefers to work at night; an informal expression. *...people who don't come to life until later in the day—the night owls.*

night porter, night porters
NC A **night porter** is a person whose job is to be on duty at the main reception desk of a hotel throughout the night. *He has found himself a live-in job as a night porter in a sleazy hotel.*

night school, night schools
NU or NC **Night school** is a place where adults can go to educational courses in the evenings. *Go to night school after work and learn another language.*

night shift, night shifts; also spelt **night-shift**.
NC or NU A **night shift** is a period of work that is done regularly at night as part of a job, for example in a hospital or factory. *They will be paid more for working night shifts. ...seventy seven men who'd been on night shift at one particular mine... He started off as a night-shift worker in a factory.*

nightshirt /naɪtʃɜːt/ **nightshirts**
NC A **nightshirt** is a long, loose shirt that men and boys can wear in bed.

nightstick /naɪtstɪk/ **nightsticks**
NC A **nightstick** is a type of truncheon carried by American police officers. *...two officers wielding their nightsticks.*

night-time
NU or N+N **Night-time** is the part of the day between the time when it gets dark and the time when it gets light again. *She toured the streets of London at night-time... Thirty-one people have been killed in a series of night-time attacks.*

night-watchman, night-watchmen
NC A **night-watchman** is a person whose job is to guard buildings at night. *He advised that she should hire a night-watchman.*

nightwear /naɪtweə/
NU **Nightwear** is clothing that you wear in bed, such as pyjamas or nightdresses; a formal word. *Children's nylon or synthetic nightwear is now made flame-proof.*

nihilism /naɪɪlɪzəm/
NU **Nihilism** is a belief which rejects all political and religious authorities or institutions. *The energy and idealism that is common to the young is diverted into paths of nihilism and violence.* ◆ **nihilist** /naɪɪlɪst/ **nihilists** NC *It was enough to turn you into a nihilist.*

Nikkei average /nɪkeɪ ævrɪdʒ/
N SING The **Nikkei average** or the **Nikkei index** is an index of share prices which is based on the average price of shares in 225 Japanese companies on the Japanese Stock Exchange. It is used by shareholders and investors to check general changes in share prices. *Panic selling drove the Nikkei average to its lowest close in three years... The Nikkei average fell more than eleven hundred points.*

nil /nɪl/
1 **Nil** means the same as **nought**; used especially in the scores of sports games. *Wales beat England three nil.*
2 If you say that something is **nil**, you mean that it does not exist at all. *You can reduce the danger to almost nil... The prospects for a new centre party are nil.*

nimble /nɪmbl/ **nimbler, nimblest**
1 ADJ Someone who is **nimble** is able to move their fingers, hands, or legs quickly and easily. *By now, he was quite nimble on his wooden leg.* ◆ **nimbly** ADV *Harold got out of his seat nimbly.*
2 ADJ Someone who has a **nimble** mind is very quick and clever in the way they think.

nimbus /nɪmbəs/ **nimbuses**
NC A **nimbus** is a large dark grey cloud that brings rain or snow; a technical term.

nincompoop /nɪŋkəmpuːp/ **nincompoops**
NC If you refer to someone as a **nincompoop,** you mean that you think they are rather silly; an informal word. *I felt such a nincompoop!*

nine /naɪn/ **nines**
Nine is the number 9. *He had been vice-president for nine years.*

nineteen /naɪntiːn/ **nineteens**
Nineteen is the number 19. *Nineteen people are still missing.*

nineteenth /naɪntiːnθ/
ADJ The **nineteenth** item in a series is the one that you count as number nineteen. *The presidential elections are scheduled for the nineteenth of March.*

ninetieth /naɪntiəθ/
ADJ The **ninetieth** item in a series is the one that you count as number ninety. *...celebrations to mark the ninetieth birthday of Queen Elizabeth, the Queen Mother.*

ninety /naɪnti/ **nineties**
Ninety is the number 90. *The court took ninety minutes to reach their verdict.*

ninny /nɪni/ **ninnies**
NC If you refer to someone as a **ninny,** you mean that you think they are rather silly; an informal word. *That was the one good result of our son marrying a rich ninny.*

ninth /naɪnθ/ **ninths**
1 ADJ The **ninth** item in a series is the one that you count as number nine. *...the ninth floor of the Hotel.*
2 NC A **ninth** is one of nine equal parts of something. *In exchange for this work they get one ninth of the crop.*

nip /nɪp/ **nips, nipping, nipped**
1 VA If you **nip** somewhere, usually somewhere nearby, you go there quickly or for a short time; an informal use. *I'll just nip out and post these letters.*
2 VO If you **nip** someone, you pinch or bite them lightly. *The horse nipped me on the back of the head.*

nipper /nɪpə/ **nippers**
NC A **nipper** is a child; an old-fashioned, informal word. *He's known the place since he was a nipper.*

nipple /nɪpl/ **nipples**
NC Your **nipples** are the two small pieces of slightly hard flesh on your chest. Babies suck milk through the nipples on their mothers' breasts. *...the repeated stimulus of the nipple by the sucking baby.*

nippy /nɪpi/; an informal word.
1 ADJ If you say that the weather is **nippy,** you mean that it is rather cold. *The air was nippy outside.*
2 ADJ Someone or something that is **nippy** moves very quickly. *You'll catch him if you're nippy.*

nirvana /nɪəvɑːnə/ **nirvanas**
1 NU **Nirvana** is the ultimate state of spiritual enlightenment which Hindus and Buddhists believe can be achieved. *...spiritual progress towards nirvana.*
2 NU or NC **Nirvana** also refers to a state of complete happiness and peace. *They would live in a Nirvana of perpetual happiness.*

nit /nɪt/ **nits**
NC **Nits** are the eggs of a kind of louse that sometimes lives in people's hair. *The school doctor looks to see if you have nits in your hair.*

nitpicking /nɪtpɪkɪŋ/
NU If you refer to someone's **nitpicking,** you mean that they find fault with small and unimportant details; used showing disapproval. *I'm sick of all this nitpicking.* ▸ Also ADJ *...a legal process which is long, laborious, and nitpicking.*

nitrate /naɪtreɪt/ **nitrates**
NC or NU A **nitrate** is a chemical compound that includes nitrogen and oxygen. **Nitrates** are used as fertilizers. *....huge quantities of nutrients such as nitrates and phosphorous... The problem is caused by too much nitrate in most of Britain's water... Nitrate fertilizers are taken up very rapidly by the crops.*

nitrogen /naɪtrədʒən/
NU **Nitrogen** is a colourless element that has no smell and usually occurs as a gas. *By far the greatest part of the air we breathe is nitrogen, 78% in fact.*

nitty-gritty /nɪtigrɪti/; also spelt **nitty gritty.**
N SING The **nitty-gritty** of a matter, situation, or activity, is the most basic and important aspects or parts of it. *We had to set out the nitty gritty of our aims. ...complex negotiations over these nitty-gritty issues.*

nitwit /nɪtwɪt/ **nitwits**
NC If you call someone a **nitwit** you mean that you think they are stupid or silly; an informal word. *They're a bunch of nitwits.*

Niue /njuːi/
Niue is a self-governing territory, in free association with New Zealand, in the South Pacific, east of Australia. Britain claimed it in 1900 and in 1901 it was annexed to New Zealand. It entered a compact of free association with New Zealand in 1974. Emigration from Niue to New Zealand has caused serious social and economic problems. Honey and tropical fruit are exported. ◆ **Niuean** /njuːiən/ N, ADJ
▪ *religion:* Christianity (mainly Niuean Church)
▪ *language:* English, Niuean ▪ *currency:* New Zealand dollar ▪ *capital:* Alofi ▪ *population:* 2,000 (1989) ▪ *size:* 263 square kilometres.

Nixon, Richard /rɪtʃəd nɪksn/
Richard Nixon was President of the United States from 1969 to 1974. He is a member of the Republican Party. He served in the House of Representatives from 1947 to 1951 and the Senate from 1951 to 1953. He was Vice President from 1953 to 1961 and was defeated by John F Kennedy in the 1960 Presidential election. Nixon was the first President of the United States to resign from office. He faced impeachment following

the Watergate scandal. Born: 1913.

Niyazov, Saparmurad /sǝpǝmuɑːt niɑːzǝf/
Saparmurad Niyazov became President of
Turkmenistan in 1990. He was Chairman of the Council
of Ministers of the Turkmen Soviet Socialist Republic
in 1985, and First Secretary of the Central Committee
of the Turkmen Communist Party from 1985 to 1989.
He became President of the Turkmen Supreme Soviet
in 1990. Born: 1940.

no /nǝu/
1 You use **no** to give a negative answer to a question,
to say that something is not true, to refuse an offer, or
to refuse permission. *'Did you see that programme
last night?'—'No, I didn't.'... 'They go round kissing
one another when they meet.'—'No they don't.'... 'Do
you want a biscuit?'—'No thanks.'... 'Can I come
too?'—'No.'*
2 You use **no** to say that you agree with a negative
statement that someone else has made. *'It's not
difficult, you see.'—'No, it must be quite easy when
you know how.'*
3 You also use **no** to express shock or disappointment
at something. *'Michael's fallen off his bike.'—'Oh no,
not again.'*
4 ADV SEN You use **no** as a way of introducing a
correction to what you have just said. *...500 grams,
no, a little less than that.*
5 DET **No** indicates that there is not even one thing of
a particular kind or not even a small amount of a
particular thing. For example, if someone has no job
or no money, they do not have a job or do not have
any money. *I do it all on my own. I have no help at
all... The general knew he had no chance of winning.*
6 DET You use **no** to emphasize that someone or
something is not a particular kind of person or thing.
For example, if you say that someone is no fool, you
mean that they are definitely not a fool. *She is no
friend of mine.*
7 SUBMOD You use **no** when emphasizing that
something does not exceed a particular amount or
number, or does not have more of a particular quality
than something else. For example, something that is
no bigger than a fingernail is not bigger than a
fingernail. *The whole gun was no longer than eighteen
inches... Winners will be notified by post no later than
31st August. ...a job that was no better than a common
labourer's.*
8 DET **No** is also used, especially on notices, to say
that a particular thing is forbidden. *No smoking... No
talking once we're inside.*
● **No** is used in these phrases. ● If you say **there is no**
doing a particular thing, you mean that it is
impossible to do that thing. *There's no arguing with
my father.* ● **no comment**: see **comment**; ● **no matter**:
see **matter**; ● **no mean**: see **mean**; ● **by no means**:
see **mean**.

No., Nos.
No. is a written abbreviation for 'number'. *He lives at
No. 14 Sumatra Road.*

nob /nɒb/ **nobs**
NC A **nob** is a person who is rich or who comes from a
much higher social class than you; an old-fashioned,
informal word. *...the nobs attending the royal
wedding.*

no ball, no balls
NC A **no ball** is a ball that is bowled in cricket or
rounders in a way that is not allowed by the rules.

nobble /nɒbl/ **nobbles, nobbling, nobbled**; an informal
word.
1 VO If you **nobble** someone, you get their attention so
that you can talk to them.
2 VO To **nobble** someone or something also means to
try and make them do whatever you want, or to make
what you want happen, for example by bribing or
threatening them.

nobility /nǝubɪlǝti/
1 NU **Nobility** is the quality of being noble. *He had
nobility in defeat... He followed his principles with
nobility.*
2 N COLL The **nobility** of a society are all the people
who have titles and high social rank. *He is descended
from Spanish nobility. ...the palaces of the nobility.*

noble /nǝubl/ **nobler, noblest; nobles**
1 ADJ Someone who is **noble** is honest, brave, and
unselfish, and deserves admiration and respect.
*Among them were some of the greatest and noblest
men in our history. ...a man of noble character.*
◆ **nobly** ADV *She had nobly served the cause of
Christianity.*
2 ADJ If someone is **noble** they belong to a high social
class and have a title. *...young men of noble birth.*
► Also NC *Every noble in the land wanted to marry
the king's daughter.*
3 ADJ Something that is **noble** is very impressive in
quality or appearance. *...an old man with a noble
head and a bristling moustache.*

nobleman /nǝublmǝn/ **noblemen** /nǝublmǝn/
NC A **nobleman** is a man who is a member of the
nobility. *The silver had been put up for auction by a
British nobleman, the Marquess of Northampton.*

noblewoman /nǝublwumǝn/ **noblewomen**
NC A **noblewoman** is a woman who is a member of the
nobility. *...a noblewoman close to the court of the last
Dalai Lama.*

nobody /nǝubǝdi, nǝubɒdi/ **nobodies**
1 PRON INDEF **Nobody** means not a single person.
*Nobody seems to notice... There was nobody on the
bridge at all.* ● See also **no-one**.
2 NC If you say that someone is a **nobody**, you mean
that they are not at all important. *Miss Watkins was
a nobody; no family, no close friends.*

no-confidence
NU In politics, a vote of **no-confidence** in a person or
party that is in power is a vote to decide whether they
should continue to hold office, especially when they
have failed to deal with or solve particular problems.
*The Thai Prime Minister has easily defeated an
opposition vote of no-confidence in his government.
...the tabling of a no-confidence motion.*

nocturnal /nɒktɜːnl/
1 ADJ **Nocturnal** events happen during the night.
...your nocturnal sightseeing tour of our city.
2 ADJ An animal that is **nocturnal** is active mostly at
night. *Their nocturnal habits make long-eared owls
hard to see.*

nocturne /nɒktɜːn/ **nocturnes**
NC A **nocturne** is a short gentle piece of music, often
one written to be played on the piano. *...Chopin's
Nocturne in D flat.*

nod /nɒd/ **nods, nodding, nodded**
1 V or VO If you **nod**, you move your head down and up
to show that you are answering 'yes' to a question, or
to show agreement, understanding, or approval. *He
listened to the conditions laid down for his release and
nodded... He nodded his head.*
2 VA To **nod** also means to bend your head once in a
particular direction in order to indicate something.
'Ask him,' said Ringbaum, nodding towards Philip.
3 V or VO To **nod** also means to bend your head once, as
a way of saying hello or goodbye. *I nodded to the
ladies and sat down... They all nodded a final
goodnight.*
4 NC A **nod** is a quick movement of your head down
and up. *From time to time, he gave him an
encouraging nod.*

nod off PHRASAL VERB If you **nod off**, you fall asleep,
especially when you had not intended to; an informal
expression. *His remarks left delegates nodding off.*

noddle /nɒdl/ **noddles**
NC Your **noddle** is your head; an informal word.

node /nǝud/ **nodes**
1 NC A **node** is the place on the stem of a plant from
which a branch or leaf grows; a technical term in
biology. *Take the shoots and cut them into single node
pieces—that means with one leaf and the piece of
associated stem.*
2 NC A **node** is also a place on a diagram where two
lines or branches meet.

nodule /nɒdjuːl/ **nodules**
NC A **nodule** is a small round lump on something,
often on the root of a plant. *...bacteria in the root
nodules of beans.*

Noel /nǝuel/
N PROP **Noel** means Christmas, especially in greetings

and on cards that you send to people at Christmas.

noggin /nɒgɪn/ **noggins**

NC A **noggin** is a small amount of an alcoholic drink; an old-fashioned word. *Meantime we might as well have a noggin.*

no-go area, no-go areas

NC A **no-go area** is a place which is controlled by a group of people who use force to prevent other people from entering it. *Parts of the main town were effectively made no-go areas by barricades of rubble and burning tyres.*

noise /nɔɪz/ **noises**

1 NCorNU A **noise** is a sound that someone or something makes. *A sudden noise made Brody jump... Our washing machine is making a terrible noise... One of them heard noises downstairs... The noise of bombs and guns was incessant... Try not to make so much noise... Noise is often a problem in offices.*

2 N PL+SUPP You can use **noises** to talk about the way that someone appears to be intending to act. For example, if someone is making encouraging **noises**, they are behaving in a way which suggests they will respond positively to a particular suggestion. *The US did far more than make encouraging noises in support of talks... Czechoslovakia has been making noises about sending a consular delegation to Israel soon... In spite of optimistic noises from the NATO side, the Soviet side still refuses to concede the main point.*

noiseless /nɔɪzləs/

ADJ Something that is **noiseless** does not make any sound. *...a totally noiseless fan.*

noisome /nɔɪsəm/

ADJ Someone or something that is **noisome** is offensive and extremely unpleasant; a formal word. *...the most noisome politicians of this or any other century. ...noisome vapours.*

noisy /nɔɪzi/ **noisier, noisiest**

1 ADJ Someone or something that is **noisy** makes a lot of loud or unpleasant noise. *The audience was large and noisy.* ◆ **noisily** ADV *My sister was crying noisily.*

2 ADJ A place that is **noisy** is full of loud or unpleasant noise. *They complained that Canton was hot and noisy.*

nomad /nəʊmæd/ **nomads**

NC A **nomad** is a member of a tribe which travels from place to place rather than living in one place all the time. *...the life of a nomad, riding out into the desert by day and sleeping under the stars by night... By tradition they are a nomad people who consider themselves at one with the land.*

nomadic /nəʊmædɪk/

ADJ **Nomadic** people travel from place to place rather than living in one place all the time. *These tribes have a nomadic way of life.*

no-man's land

NU **No-man's land** is land that is not owned or controlled by anyone, for example the land between two boundaries. *...the no-man's land between Iraq and Jordan.*

nom de plume /nɒm də pluːm/ **noms de plume**. The singular and the plural are pronounced in the same way.

NC A **nom de plume** is the name that an author uses instead of his or her real name; a formal expression. *Why would a lady choose a nom de plume such as George Eliot?... He intended to use a nom de plume in case our English friends disliked his views.*

nomenclature /nəmenklətʃə/

NU The **nomenclature** of a particular set of things is the system of naming those things; a formal word. *...scientific nomenclature.*

nominal /nɒmɪnl/

1 ADJ You use **nominal** to describe a position or characteristic which someone or something is supposed to have but which it does not have in reality. *We were directing the operation, though under the nominal leadership of a guerrilla general.*

◆ **nominally** ADV *Dad, nominally a Methodist, entered churches only for weddings and funerals.*

2 ADJ ATTRIB A **nominal** price or sum of money is very small in comparison with the real cost or value of the thing you are buying or selling. *At a nominal price,*

the settlers got the rest of the land.

nominate /nɒmɪneɪt/ **nominates, nominating, nominated**

VO If you **nominate** someone for a job, you suggest them as a candidate or formally choose them to hold that job. *I've been nominated for a Senior Lectureship... Trade unions nominate representatives to public bodies.*

nomination /nɒmɪneɪʃn/ **nominations**

1 NC A **nomination** is an official suggestion of someone as a candidate in an election or for a job. *...a list of nominations for senior lectureships.*

2 NUorNC The **nomination** of someone to a job or position is their appointment to that job or position. *Dr Hromadka returned from Rome to announce the nomination of two new bishops and an archbishop. ...Judge O'Connor's nomination to the Supreme Court.*

nominative /nɒmənətɪv/ **nominatives**

ADJ In the grammar of some languages, for example Latin, the **nominative** case is the form of a noun or pronoun that shows that the noun or pronoun is the subject of a verb. ► Also N SING *It's in the nominative.*

nominee /nɒmɪniː/ **nominees**

NC A **nominee** is someone who is nominated for something. *Dave is this year's nominee for the Exchange scheme.*

non- /nɒn-/

1 PREFIX **Non-** combines with nouns and adjectives to form new nouns and adjectives. Words formed in this way indicate that something does not have a particular quality or characteristic. *The children of smoking parents are nearly twice as likely to get lung cancer as the children of non-smokers... It may still be possible to take direct, non-violent action.*

2 PREFIX **Non-** also combines with nouns that refer to a particular type of action to form new nouns which indicate that a particular action has not been taken or that it will not be taken. *...a 10 year period of non-withdrawal.*

non-aggression

NU **Non-aggression** is the idea or plan that countries should not attack, fight, or try to harm each other in any way. *He met top Soviet leaders, which led to a non-aggression pact between the two countries.*

non-alcoholic

ADJ A **non-alcoholic** drink does not contain alcohol. *The British still love drinking tea more than any other non-alcoholic beverage.*

non-aligned

ADJ A country that is **non-aligned** does not support or is not part of any politically linked group of countries. *...a policy of friendship toward the developing and non-aligned countries.*

non-alignment

NU **Non-alignment** is the state or policy of being non-aligned. *No change in our position of non-alignment is contemplated.*

nonchalance /nɒnʃələns/

NU **Nonchalance** is the quality of being very calm and of seeming not to worry or care very much about things. *Clem leaned up against the wall with an effort at world-weary nonchalance.*

nonchalant /nɒnʃələnt/

ADJ Someone who is **nonchalant** behaves calmly and appears not to care much about things. *He tried to sound cheerful and nonchalant.* ◆ **nonchalantly** ADV *The officer waved a hand nonchalantly.*

non-combatant, non-combatants

NC A **non-combatant** is someone who does not actually fight in a war, although they may be in the armed forces or involved in the war in some way. *...violence against unarmed civilian non-combatants... All were non-combatant military personnel, including three women.*

non-commissioned officer, non-commissioned officers

NC A **non-commissioned officer** is a person who holds a military rank such as sergeant or corporal and who was promoted from the lower ranks. *Just under two hundred officers and non-commissioned officers had been killed in fighting with the security police.*

noncommittal /nɒŋkəmɪtl/
ADJ If someone is **noncommittal**, they do not express their opinion or decision firmly. *I received a noncommittal letter in return.*

non compos mentis /nɒn kɒmpəs mɛntɪs/
ADJ PRED If someone is **non compos mentis**, they are unable to understand what they are doing, for example because they are mentally ill, and are therefore not legally responsible for their actions; a legal expression.

nonconformist /nɒŋkənfɔːmɪst/ **nonconformists**
NC A **nonconformist** is someone whose behaviour or beliefs are unusual. *...the persecution of nonconformists and minorities.* ▶ Also ADJ *I've got rather nonconformist ideas on this.*

nonconformity /nɒŋkənfɔːməti/
NU **Nonconformity** is unusual behaviour or beliefs. *...the product of middle-class nonconformity and dissent.*

non-cooperation
NU **Non-cooperation** is a way of protesting in which you do not do any work apart from the work that you are officially required to do. *They adopted a policy of non-cooperation with management.*

nondescript /nɒndɪskrɪpt/
ADJ Something that is **nondescript** is dull and uninteresting in appearance or design. *...a complex of nondescript buildings... The women were dressed in nondescript clothes.*

none /nʌn/
1 PRON **None** means not a single thing or person, or not even a small amount of a particular thing. *None of these suggestions is very helpful... None of us were allowed to go... I have answered every single question. My opponent has answered none... 'You had no difficulty in finding it?'—'None at all.'*
2 You use **none too** to mean 'not at all'. *We're none too sure what we're arguing about... He hauled her none too gently to her feet.*

nonentity /nɒnɛntəti/ **nonentities**
NC If you refer to someone as a **nonentity**, you mean that they are not special or important in any way; used showing disapproval. *Grant came from a family of nonentities.*

nonetheless /nʌnðəlɛs/
ADV SEN **Nonetheless** means in spite of what has just been said; a formal word. *She couldn't act at all. Nonetheless she was a big box office attraction... It was not an impossible task, but they failed nonetheless.*

non-event, non-events
NC If you describe something that happens as a **non-event**, you mean that it is not at all interesting or exciting. *The congress may turn out to be something of a non-event... The crash of last October had turned out to be the economic non-event of 1987.*

non-existent /nɒnɪgzɪstənt/
ADJ Something that is **non-existent** does not exist in a place or does not exist at all. *Medical facilities are non-existent in most rural areas... Photographs showed the wrong beach and hotel descriptions listed non-existent facilities.*

non-fiction
NU **Non-fiction** is writing that gives information or describes real events, rather than telling a story. *...works of non-fiction. ...number six among the best-selling non-fiction books in Britain.*

non-flammable
ADJ If a fabric or substance is **non-flammable**, it will not catch fire. *They are non-flammable, odourless and chemically unreactive.*

non-human
ADJ **Non-human** means not human or not coming from humans. *...the non-human primates—chimpanzees and the like... Whether a baby is breast-fed or fed with a non-human milk formula is now known to be significant.*

non-iron
ADJ **Non-iron** clothes do not need to be ironed because they are made of fabrics that do not crease. *Without polyester, drip-dry non-iron clothes might not have happened.*

non-member, non-members
NC A **non-member** of a particular club or organization is someone who is not a member of it; used for example of someone who visits the club with a member and has to pay a different entrance fee. *Norway is a non-member of OPEC but supports limiting production to stabilise prices.*

non-nuclear
ADJ ATTRIB **Non-nuclear** means not using or involving nuclear weapons or nuclear power. *...the deployment of non-nuclear weapons... Dr Penman agrees that the use of non-nuclear energy sources also has its drawbacks.*

no-no
N SING If something is a **no-no**, it is considered undesirable or unacceptable; an informal word. *We all know that cheating on our income taxes is a no-no... He didn't quite grasp why photos were a no-no.*

no-nonsense
ADJ ATTRIB A **no-nonsense** person or attitude is firm and efficient. *I liked his no-nonsense approach to the whole matter... His no-nonsense, decisive leadership style is credited with giving Malaysia political stability.*

non-payment
NU **Non-payment** is a failure to pay a sum of money that is owed. *Joy's stepfather was in prison for non-payment of fines.*

nonplussed /nɒnplʌst/
ADJ If you are **nonplussed** when something happens, you are surprised and unsure how to react; a literary word. *'I've heard nothing about this,' he said, nonplussed.*

non-profit-making.
ADJ An organization or charity that is **non-profit-making** is not run with the intention of making a profit. *...a non-profit-making charitable organization. ...a non-profit-making hospital.*

non-resident, non-residents
NC A **non-resident** is someone who is not living in a particular place such as a country or not staying in a particular building such as a hotel. *Is the hotel bar open to non-residents?*

nonsense /nɒnsəns/
1 NU You use **nonsense** to refer to words or to combinations of words that do not mean anything. *Let's take a nonsense word. I'll say the word 'moof'... Edward Lear was the 19th century English author of nonsense rhymes.*
2 NU If you say that something spoken or written is **nonsense**, you mean that it is untrue or silly. *A lot of nonsense is talked about the temperature of wine... Stop this nonsense, Louisa, for God's sake... 'I am her father.'—'Nonsense,' he said. 'You are not.'*
3 To **make nonsense of** something means to make it seem ridiculous or pointless. *The rest of his policies made nonsense of his call for moderation.*

nonsensical /nɒnsɛnsɪkl/
ADJ Something that is **nonsensical** is stupid or ridiculous. *This attitude seemed nonsensical to the general public.*

non sequitur /nɒn sɛkwɪtə/ **non sequiturs**
NC A **non sequitur** is a statement, remark, or conclusion that does not follow naturally or logically from what has just been said; a formal expression. *This is a complete non sequitur from what's been going on.*

non-shrink
ADJ Fabric that is **non-shrink** has been specially treated so that it does not shrink when it is washed.

non-smoker, non-smokers
NC A **non-smoker** is someone who does not smoke. *For many years non-smokers were ridiculed for objecting to tobacco.*

non-smoking
ADJ A **non-smoking** area in a public place such as a train or cinema is an area in which people are not allowed to smoke. *Do you prefer the smoking or non-smoking section?*

non-starter, non-starters
NC If you say that a plan or idea is a **non-starter**, you mean that it has no chance of success; an informal

word. *Such a policy is really a complete non-starter... At least one Israeli Minister has already dismissed this as a non-starter.*

non-stick
ADJ A **non-stick** saucepan, frying-pan, or baking tin has a layer of a special substance on its inside which prevents food from sticking to it. *Teflon came from the USA in 1943, and a Frenchman coated it onto non-stick cooking pans in 1954.*

non-stop
ADJ or ADV A **non-stop** activity continues without any pauses or breaks. *They keep up a non-stop conversation... Carter laughed non-stop for several minutes.*

non-verbal
ADJ **Non-verbal** communication does not involve the use of words. *Art, like gesture, is a form of non-verbal expression... Children's ability was measured by verbal and non-verbal reasoning tests.*

non-violence
NU **Non-violence** is the use of peaceful methods to try to bring about change. *The churchmen repeated their commitment to non-violence.*

non-violent
ADJ **Non-violent** methods of bringing about change do not involve hurting people or causing damage. *It is to be a peaceful, non-violent protest... We wished to indicate that it is still possible to take direct non-violent action.*

non-white, non-whites
ADJ Someone who is **non-white** belongs to a race of people who are not of European origin. *...the non-white majority in South Africa... She was Britain's first non-white woman magistrate.* ▶ Also NC *Such economic policies are hurting non-whites badly.*

noodles /ˈnuːdlz/
NC **Noodles** are long, thin pieces of pasta which usually contain egg. Noodles are often used in Chinese cookery. *...instant hot noodles.*

nook /nʊk/ **nooks**
You use **every nook and cranny** or **nooks and crannies** to emphasize that you are talking about every part of a place. *Toddlers poke into every nook and cranny... We've been forcing wildlife into the remaining nooks and crannies of natural lands.*

noon /nuːn/
NU **Noon** is twelve o'clock in the middle of the day. *The visitor turned up at noon.* ● See also **high noon.**

noonday /ˈnuːndeɪ/
ADJ ATTRIB **Noonday** means happening in the middle part of the day; a literary word. *...a flash brighter than the noonday sun.*

no-one; also spelt **no one.**
PRON INDEF **No-one** means not anyone. *They had seen no-one else all afternoon... Sorry, there's no-one here called Nikki... No-one, it declared, should try to discredit action to save human lives... The fighting benefited no-one.* ● See also **nobody.**

noose /nuːs/ **nooses**
1 NC A **noose** is a loop at the end of a piece of rope, especially one used to hang someone. *A hangman fits the noose around the neck of another murderer.*
2 You can say that someone **is tightening the noose** or that **the noose is tightening,** when they deliberately make a difficult situation worse in order to force another person to agree to something. *He said his forces were tightening the noose around the capital... He felt the noose tightening as wild accusations against him appeared in the papers.*

nope /nəʊp/
Nope is sometimes used instead of 'no' as a response in informal English. *'Can you start tomorrow?'—'Nope. Monday's the earliest.'*

nor /nɔː/
1 CONJ You use **nor** after 'neither' to introduce the second thing that a negative statement applies to. *The reports have been neither confirmed nor denied... He said there was neither the time nor the money to industrialise the whole country... Neither Margaret nor John was there... My father could neither read nor write.*
2 CONJ You also use **nor** after a negative statement in

order to add something else that the negative statement applies to. *Melanie was not to be found not that day—nor the next day, nor the day after that... I could not afford to eat in restaurants and nor could anyone I knew.*

Nordic /ˈnɔːdɪk/
1 ADJ **Nordic** means relating to the countries Norway, Sweden, Denmark, Iceland, and Finland. *He considers that the British political landscape resembles that of the Nordic countries... The speech was welcomed by Nordic leaders—although cautiously by Norway.*
2 ADJ Someone who looks **Nordic** has blond hair, blue eyes, and a fair skin, and is fairly tall. *The colonel was a handsome man, with his strong Nordic face and white-blond hair.*

Norfolk Island /ˈnɔːfək aɪlənd/
Norfolk Island is a territory of Australia in the South Pacific, east of Australia. It was used as a penal colony until 1855, and then was settled by Pitcairn Islanders, the descendants of the Bounty mutineers. Tourism is an important industry. ◆ **Norfolk Islander** /ˈnɔːfək aɪləndə/ N
■ *religion:* Christianity ■ *language:* English (official), Norfolk ■ *currency:* Australian dollar ■ *capital:* Kingston ■ *population:* 2,000 (1989) ■ *size:* 35 square kilometres.

norm /nɔːm/ **norms**
1 N SING If you say that a situation is the **norm,** you mean that it is usual and expected. *In Russia, working wives have been the norm for many years.*
2 NC A **norm** is an official standard or level of achievement that a person or organization is expected to reach or conform to. *Radiation levels were still above the permissible norm.*
3 N PL **Norms** are ways of behaving that are considered normal in a particular society. *...the conventional norms of polite European society.*

normal /ˈnɔːml/
ADJ Something that is **normal** is usual and ordinary, and what people expect. *Under normal circumstances only a small fraction of the population is affected... Washington must first lift economic sanctions and restore normal relations... This is a perfectly normal baby.*

normalcy /ˈnɔːmlsi/
NU **Normalcy** is the same as **normality;** a formal word. *Elsewhere in the East the government says normalcy is being restored.*

normality /nɔːˈmæləti/
NU **Normality** is a situation in which everything is normal. *People have a longing for normality... Residents are taking the first steps to restore normality to their town.*

normalize /ˈnɔːməlaɪz/ **normalizes, normalizing, normalized;** also spelt **normalise.**
VO When one country or group **normalizes** relations with another country or group or when they **normalize** a situation, they make their relations or the situation normal again after a period of tension or conflict. *American officials describe the occasion as a step towards normalising relations... The Prime Minister said he expected that Sino-Vietnamese ties would be normalised in the near future.* ◆ **normalization** /ˌnɔːməlaɪˈzeɪʃn/ NU *There were also some signs of normalisation and return to civilian government.*

normally /ˈnɔːməli/
1 ADV SEN If something **normally** happens, it happens most of the time or as part of a routine. *Meetings are normally held three or four times a year... I don't normally drink at lunch... Normally, offices close at 4.30 p.m.*
2 ADV If you do something **normally,** you do it in the usual or conventional way. *The important thing is that she's eating normally... When social institutions cannot function normally, emergency measures are required.*

Norman /ˈnɔːmən/ **Normans**
1 NC The **Normans** were the people who came from Northern France to England in 1066, or their descendants. *...repeated invasions by the Romans, by the Saxon English and by the Norman French.*
2 ADJ **Norman** is also used to refer to the period of

British history from 1066 until around 1300, and in particular to the architecture of that period.

normative /nɔːmətɪv/

ADJ **Normative** means making or stating rules of behaviour or standards to be followed. *We must provide some normative guidelines. ...a normative judgment about equality.*

north /nɔːθ/

1 N SING The **north** is the direction on your left when you are looking towards the place where the sun rises. *The land to the north was low-lying.*

2 N SING The **north** of a place is the part which is towards the north. *...a man from somewhere in the north of England... There is still no news on when voting is expected to take place in the troubled north and east.* ► Also ADJ ATTRIB *...a flat in north London... It is unclear whether he will resume his North African tour.*

3 ADV **North** means towards the north, or to the north of a place or thing. *They were heading north... It's 150 miles north of Salisbury.*

4 ADJ ATTRIB A **north** wind blows from the north.

North America /nɔːθ əmerɪkə/

North America is the third largest continent in the world and has approximately one-twelfth of the world's population. It is 24 million square kilometres and in 1981 had a population of 376 million. One eighth of the land area is arable. Major river systems are the Columbia, Delaware, Hudson, Mackenzie, Mississippi, Missouri, Potomac, Rio Grande, and St Lawrence. Mount McKinley (6,193 metres) in Alaska is the highest point in North America.

North Atlantic Treaty Organization See **NATO**

northbound /nɔːθbaʊnd/

ADJ **Northbound** roads, cars, trains, etc lead or are travelling towards the north. *An accident has closed the northbound section of the Dartford Tunnel. ...platform 1 northbound, platform 2 southbound.*

north-east

1 N SING The **north-east** is the direction halfway between north and east. *We attack from the north-east.*

2 N SING The **north-east** of a place is the part which is towards the north-east. *...the north-east of England... Large parts of the country seem to have been unaffected, including the North-East and the South-West.* ► Also ADJ ATTRIB *...north-east Brazil.*

3 ADV **North-east** means towards the north-east, or to the north-east of a place or thing. *Turn left and go north-east towards the station... It's a small town about fifteen kilometers north-east of Uppsala.*

4 ADJ ATTRIB A **north-east** wind blows from the north-east.

north-easterly

1 ADJ A **north-easterly** point, region, or direction is to the north-east or towards the north-east. *All the streams were flowing in a north-easterly direction to the coast.*

2 ADJ A **north-easterly** wind blows from the north-east. *Cyclones occur where north easterly winds from Asia meet south westerlies from the Indian Ocean.*

north-eastern

ADJ ATTRIB **North-eastern** means in or from the north-east of a region or country. *...floods in north-eastern India.*

northerly /nɔːðəli/

1 ADJ **Northerly** means towards the north. *...the wet, northerly slopes... We proceeded along a more northerly route.*

2 ADJ A **northerly** wind blows from the north. *...with a northerly wind of between 10 and 20 knots affecting the smaller boats.*

northern /nɔːðn/

ADJ ATTRIB **Northern** means in or from the north of a region or country. *...the Northern Hemisphere. ...the high mountains of northern Japan... Northern businessmen firmly believe that their southern neighbours earn more than they do.*

northerner /nɔːðənə/ **northerners**

N C A **northerner** is a person who was born in or who lives in the north of a country. *More civil service posts and contracts would be likely to go to*

Northerners under these proposals.

Northern Ireland /nɔːðən aɪələnd/

Northern Ireland, also known as **Ulster,** is a province of the United Kingdom. It was established in 1921 when Ireland was divided, and consists of the six counties of Antrim, Armagh, Down, Fermanagh, Londonderry, and Tyrone. It is 14,153 square kilometres. Northern Ireland had a population of 2 million in 1990, of which approximately two-thirds were Protestant and one-third were Roman Catholic. Historically, most Protestants were Unionists, favouring the continuation of links with the United Kingdom, while some Catholics favoured a re-united Ireland. Since the 1960s conflict between Catholics and Protestants has been a source of civil disorder. The capital of Northern Ireland is Belfast.

Northern Mariana Islands
/nɔːðən mærɪænə aɪləndz/

The **Commonwealth of the Northern Mariana Islands** is a self-governing territory of the United States in the Pacific. It includes all the Mariana Islands except Guam. The three main islands are Saipan, Tinian, and Rota. The islands were claimed by Spain in 1521, and were a colony from 1688 until they were sold to Germany in 1899. Japan controlled the islands from the First World War until 1944, when they were taken by US troops. Clothing, vegetables, and meat are exported. Tourism is an important industry.
■ *religion:* Christianity (mainly Roman Catholic)
■ *language:* English (official), Chamorro, Carolinian, Japanese ■ *currency:* US dollar ■ *capital:* Saipan
■ *population:* 30,000 (1988) ■ *size:* 457 square kilometres.

northernmost /nɔːðnməʊst/

ADJ ATTRIB The **northernmost** thing or part of an area is the one that is farther towards the north than any other. *That was only possible in his country on its northernmost island, Hokkaido.*

North Korea /nɔːθ kəriːə/

The **Democratic People's Republic of Korea** is a country which occupies the northern portion of the Korean peninsula in east Asia. The Korean peninsula was occupied by Japan from 1905 until 1945, when northern Korea was occupied by Soviet troops and southern Korea was occupied by US troops. In 1948 the two areas were formally divided into North Korea and South Korea. North Korean forces crossed the 38th parallel in 1950, beginning the Korean War, which ended in 1953. Marshal Kim Il Sung, who led the Korean People's Revolutionary Army against Japan and commanded the North Korean army during the Korean War, founded the Korean Workers' Party (KWP) in 1945. He has led North Korea since 1946, assuming the title of President in 1972. His son, Kim Jong Il, became an important government leader in the 1980s. Yon Hyong Muk became Premier in 1988. The KWP is the sole legal party. North Korea exports coal, minerals, and metals. ◆ **North Korean** /nɔːθ kəriən/ N, ADJ
■ *per capita GNP:* approximately US$987 ■ *religion:* Buddhism, Christianity, Chundo Kyo ■ *language:* Korean ■ *currency:* won ■ *capital:* P'yŏngyang
■ *population:* 22 million (1988) ■ *size:* 120,538 square kilometres.

North Pole

N PROP The **North Pole** is the place on the earth which is farthest north. *It was the second time Sir Ranulph had attempted to reach the North Pole on foot.*

northward /nɔːθwəd/ or **northwards**

1 ADV **Northward** or **northwards** means towards the north. *Children were put on ponies and sent racing northward... They had fled northwards towards Kurnal.*

2 ADJ **Northward** is used to describe things which are moving towards the north or which face towards the north. *...the northward drift of the massive Himalayan chain.*

north-west

1 N SING The **north-west** is the direction halfway between north and west. *At the bridge the lake curves to the north-west.*

2 N SING The **north-west** of a place is the part which is

towards the north-west. ...*a hilly area in the north-west.* ► Also ADJ ATTRIB ...*a Roman settlement in north-west England.*
3 ADV **North-west** means towards the north-west, or to the north-west of a place or thing. *Some 300 miles north-west of Kampala there is an abandoned village.*
4 ADJ ATTRIB A **north-west** wind blows from the north-west.

north-westerly
1 ADJ A **north-westerly** point, region, or direction is to the north-west or towards the north-west. *We took the more picturesque north-westerly route.*
2 ADJ A **north-westerly** wind blows from the north-west.

north-western
ADJ **North-western** means in or from the north-west of a region or country. ...*a cattle station in North-western Australia.*

Norway /nɔːweɪ/
The **Kingdom of Norway** is a country in northern Europe. Norway became independent from Sweden in 1905 and was occupied by Germany from 1940 to 1945. It is a member of NATO. King Harald V succeeded his father in 1991. Gro Harlem Brundtland, of the Norwegian Labour Party (DNA), became Prime Minister in 1990. Norway exports oil. ♦ **Norwegian** /nɔːwiːdʒən/ N, ADJ
▪ *per capita GNP:* US$20,020 ▪ *religion:* Christianity (mainly Evangelical Lutheran) ▪ *language:* Norwegian ▪ *currency:* krone ▪ *capital:* Oslo ▪ *population:* 4 million (1990) ▪ *size:* 323,877 square kilometres.

nose /nəʊz/ **noses, nosing, nosed**
1 NC Your **nose** is the part of your face which you use for smelling. *Johnny punched me in the nose. ...ear, nose and throat irritations.*
2 NC The **nose** of a plane is its front part. *A huge crane lifted both the nose and tail sections of the plane from the embankment where it crashed.*
● **Nose** is used in these phrases. ● If something is happening **under** your **nose**, it is happening in front of you and it should be obvious to you. *Cheating was going on under the teacher's nose... They carried out protest marches under the nose of the army.* ● To **poke** your **nose into** something means to interfere in it; an informal expression. *He had been sent to poke his nose into their business.* ● If you **pay through the nose** for something, you pay a very high price for it; an informal expression. *Country people have to pay through the nose for their goods.*

nose about PHRASAL VERB See **nose around**.
nose around PHRASAL VERB If you **nose around** or **nose about**, you look around a place to see if you can find something interesting; used in informal English. *Stay outside the door and see that no one comes nosing around... He nosed about among the boilers.*

nosebag /nəʊzbæg/ **nosebags**
NC A **nosebag** is a bag containing food for a horse, which is hung over the horse's head.

nosebleed /nəʊzbliːd/ **nosebleeds**
NC If you have a **nosebleed**, blood comes out from inside your nose, sometimes because it has been hit. *What should we have done about the nosebleeds?*

nosedive /nəʊzdaɪv/ **nosedives, nosediving, nosedived**
NC If a plane does a **nosedive**, it flies very fast towards the ground, pointing downwards. *The plane went into a deliberate nosedive.* ► Also V *Suddenly, it nosedived towards the roof of a school.*

nosey /nəʊzi/. See **nosy**.

nosey-parker /nəʊzipɑːkə/ **nosey-parkers**
NC A **nosey-parker** is someone who is interested in things which do not concern them; used in informal English, showing disapproval. *'Do you think I'm a terrible nosey-parker?'*

nosh /nɒʃ/
N U or N SING **Nosh** is food that is ready to eat; an informal word. *Here's Ruth with the nosh.*

nostalgia /nɒstældʒə/
N U **Nostalgia** is an affectionate feeling for things you have experienced in the past. ...*nostalgia for the good old days... Much of her appeal today lies in the popular nostalgia for that earlier period.*

nostalgic /nɒstældʒɪk/
ADJ If you feel **nostalgic**, you think affectionately about experiences you have had in the past. *He was full of memories, nostalgic for the past.* ♦ **nostalgically** ADV ...*talking nostalgically of the good old days.*

nostril /nɒstrəl/ **nostrils**
NC Your **nostrils** are the two openings at the end of your nose. ...*with the smell of smoke in my nostrils.*

nosy /nəʊzi/ **nosier, nosiest**; also spelt **nosey**.
ADJ Someone who is **nosy** tries to find out about things which do not concern them; used showing disapproval. *'Who was it?'—'Don't be so nosy.'*

not /nɒt/. You use **not** to make sentences, clauses, or particular words negative. In speech, **not** is usually shortened to **-n't**.
1 If the verb group contains an auxiliary or modal auxiliary, you put **not** between the auxiliary and the main verb. *I haven't tried to telephone him... She couldn't hear the orchestra properly.*
2 If the verb does not already have an auxiliary, you add 'do' in front of **not**. *I don't agree with everything he says... She did not answer.*
3 If the main verb is 'be', you use **not** without an auxiliary. *There wasn't enough room for everybody.*
4 When **not** is used with verbs such as 'think', 'want', and 'seem', the negative effect of **not** belongs to the clause or infinitive that follows the verb. For example, 'I don't think she's here' means 'I think she's not here'. *I don't want to talk about it... The book doesn't seem to be here.*
5 You use **not** in question tags after a positive statement. *That's a new one, isn't it?... You've seen this, haven't you?*
6 You use **not** in questions, for example when you are expressing surprise or annoyance. *Don't they realize it's against the law?*
7 You use **not** to represent the negative or opposite of a word, group, or clause that has just been used. *'Do you know how much it is?'—'I'm afraid not.'... They'd know if it was all right or not.*
8 You use **not** before 'all', 'every', or 'always' to say that there are exceptions to something that is generally true. *Not all scientists are honest... Not everyone agrees with me.*
● **Not** is used in these phrases. ● You use the structure **not...but** when you are contrasting something that is untrue with something that is true. *We wept, not because we were frightened but because we were ashamed.* ● You use **not that** to introduce a negative clause that decreases the importance of the previous statement. *Bob helped him. Not that it was difficult.* ● **Not at all** is an emphatic way of saying 'No' or of agreeing that the answer to a question is 'No'. *'Does that seem nonsense to you?'—'Not at all.'... 'Would you mind?'—'Not at all.'* ● **Not at all** is also a formal way of acknowledging thanks. *'Thanks.'—'Not at all.'* ● **if not**: see **if**. ● **nothing if not**: see **nothing**.

notable /nəʊtəbl/ **notables**
1 ADJ Something or someone that is **notable** is important or interesting. *With a few notable exceptions this trend has continued... Watermouth is notable for experimental forms of teaching.*
2 N PL You can refer to people who have an important position in public life as **notables**. *A peace committee has to be set up from among Afghan intellectuals, experienced politicians and notables.*

notably /nəʊtəbli/
ADV You use **notably** before mentioning the most important example of the thing you are talking about. *Some people, notably his business associates, had begun to distrust him.*

notary /nəʊtəri/ **notaries**
NC A **notary** is a person, usually a lawyer, who has legal authority to witness the signing of documents in order to make them legally valid. *The document was not witnessed by a notary.*

notation /nəʊteɪʃn/ **notations**
NC A **notation** is a set of written symbols used in a system such as music or mathematics. *He invented a system of notation, a system of symbols and signs that could describe the engine.*

notch /nɒtʃ/ notches, notching, notched
  NC A **notch** is a small V-shaped cut in the surface or edge of something. *Carve notches at either end of a stick and wind the thread round them.*
  notch up PHRASAL VERB If you **notch up** a score or total, you achieve it. *The Tory candidate had notched up eleven hundred votes.*

note /nəʊt/ notes, noting, noted
  1 NC A **note** is a short letter. *She left a note saying she would see us again.*
  2 NC A **note** is also something that you write down to remind you about something. *I'll make a note of that... I took notes at the lecture.*
  3 NC In a book or article, a **note** is a short piece of additional information. *Yugoslavia is a different matter (see note on the Yugoslav situation, below).*
  4 NC In music, a **note** is a sound of a particular pitch, or a written symbol representing this sound. *The first notes of the concerto sounded softly in the room... Not one of them could read a note of music.*
  5 NC A **note** is also a banknote. *...a five pound note.*
  6 N SING+SUPP You can use **note** to refer to a quality in someone's voice that shows how they feel. *There was a note of triumph in her voice.*
  7 N SING+SUPP You can also use **note** to refer to a particular feeling, impression, or atmosphere that is produced and that everyone is aware of. *The first day ended on a positive note... On a lighter note, the Telegraph reports on a new novel by John Le Carré.*
  8 V O or V-REPORT If you **note** a fact, you become aware of it. *He noted the change in her expression... Note that the report does not carry any form of official recommendation... His audience, I noted with regret, were looking bored.* ● See also **noted**.
  ● **Note** is used in these phrases. ● If something that someone says **strikes** or **sounds** a particular **note**, it produces a particular feeling, impression, or atmosphere. *His words struck a slightly false note for me... Mr Kinnock, too, sounded an optimistic note about foreign affairs.* ● If you **take note** of something, you pay attention to it because you think it is important. *I had to start taking some note of political developments.* ● If you **make a mental note** of something, you try to remember it, because it will be important or useful later. *He made a mental note to tell Lamin later who these men were.* ● If you **compare notes** with someone, you talk to them and find out whether they have the same opinion, information, or experiences as yourself. *There are a few things we might compare notes on.*
  note down PHRASAL VERB If you **note** something **down**, you write it down so that you have a record of it. *I'll give you time to note down where to send them.*

notebook /nəʊtbʊk/ notebooks
  NC A **notebook** is a small book for writing notes in. *...my old notebook with the once familiar names and telephone numbers.*

noted /nəʊtɪd/
  ADJ Someone who is **noted** for something they do or have is well-known and admired for it; a formal word. *...a Scottish family noted for its intellect. ...a noted American writer.*

notepad /nəʊtpæd/ notepads
  NC A **notepad** is a pad of paper that you write notes on. *...a diary, notepad and address book.*

notepaper /nəʊtpeɪpə/
  NU **Notepaper** is paper that you write letters on. *It was written on the headed notepaper of the Foreign Ministry.*

noteworthy /nəʊtwɜːði/
  ADJ A **noteworthy** fact or event is interesting or significant; a formal word. *It was noteworthy that the Count was the only person there. ...one of the most noteworthy features of the conference.*

nothing /nʌθɪŋ/
  1 PRON INDEF You use **nothing** when you are referring to an absence of things of a particular kind, for example objects, events, or ideas. *She shook the bottle over the glass; nothing came out... There's nothing to worry about... But nothing more was heard from the kidnappers.*

  2 PRON INDEF **Nothing** can also be used to mean that something or someone is very unimportant or uninteresting. *In those days time was nothing. Now it is everything... I hate you. You're disgusting. You're nothing.*
  3 PRON INDEF You can also use **nothing** in front of an adjective, to refer to a situation, event, or activity and to say that it does not have the particular quality mentioned. *This is nothing new to them... There was nothing unusual or illegal about the tactic.*
  ● **Nothing** is used in these phrases. ● If you say 'It's **nothing**', you are saying that something is not as important, serious, or significant as other people might think. *'What's the matter with you?' Claud asked. 'It's nothing,' he gasped.* ● **Nothing** but a particular thing means only that thing. *She could see nothing but his head. ...thirty years of nothing but war.* ● You say **nothing of the sort** to emphasize a refusal or a negative statement. *You will do nothing of the sort... Nothing of the sort occurred.* ● You say **nothing if not** to emphasize that someone or something has a lot of a quality. For example, if you say that someone is **nothing if not** considerate, you mean that they are very considerate; a formal expression. ● If you say that **there is nothing for it** but to do something, you mean that it is the only possible thing to do. *There was nothing for it now except to go straight ahead with the plan.* ● to **come to nothing**: see **nought**. ● **nothing like**: see **like**.

notice /nəʊtɪs/ notices, noticing, noticed
  1 V O or V-REPORT If you **notice** something, you become aware of it. *I suddenly noticed a friend in the front row... Ralph noticed a rapid tapping noise... She noticed him scratching his head... I've noticed that computers never go wrong in my favour.*
  2 NC A **notice** is a written announcement in a place where everyone can read it. *At the main entrance, there was a large notice which said 'Visitors welcome at any time'... The request is published in notices in today's national newspapers.*
  3 NU If you give **notice** of something that is going to happen, you warn people about it. *The union was to give 8 days' notice of strikes... She could have done it if she'd had a bit more notice.*
  ● **Notice** is used in these phrases. ● If you **take notice** of what someone says or does, you pay attention to it. *I hope the heads of schools will take notice of my comments.* ● If you **take no notice** of someone, you ignore them. *Take no notice of him. He's always rude to people.* ● If something **comes to** your **notice** or is **brought to** your **notice**, you become aware of it. *Many cases have come to my notice... We bring to the notice of the committee things that ought to be done.* ● If something **escapes** your **notice**, you fail to notice it. *It did not escape her notice that he kept glancing at her.* ● If something is done at **short notice** or at a **moment's notice**, you are told about it only a short time before it needs to be done. *It's going to be difficult to fix things at such short notice... It is there ready to be switched on at a moment's notice.* ● If a situation will exist **until further notice**, it will continue until someone changes it. *The beaches are closed until further notice.* ● If your employer **gives** you **notice**, he or she tells you that you must leave within a fixed period of time. *She had been given two weeks' notice at the Works.* ● If you **hand in** your **notice**, you tell your employer that you intend to leave after a fixed period of time.

noticeable /nəʊtɪsəbl/
  ADJ Something that is **noticeable** is very obvious, so that it is easy to see or recognize. *It did not have any noticeable effect upon the rate of economic growth... There was also a noticeable increase in press freedom.*
  ◆ **noticeably** SUBMOD or ADV *The air became noticeably cooler... As always, the Princess relaxed noticeably in the company of children.*

noticeboard /nəʊtɪsbɔːd/ noticeboards
  NC A **noticeboard** is a board on a wall, which people pin notices to. *Scores of students gathered today in front of a campus noticeboard.*

notifiable /nəʊtɪfaɪəbl/
  ADJ A **notifiable** disease is one that must be reported

to the authorities whenever it occurs, because it is extremely dangerous. *Rabies is a notifiable disease in this country.*

notification /nəʊtɪfɪkeɪʃn/
NU If you are given **notification** of something, you are officially informed of it. *You will be sent notification of the results of your interview by post... They received advance notification of his military actions.*

notify /nəʊtɪfaɪ/ **notifies, notifying, notified**
V Oor V O-REPORT If you **notify** someone of something, you officially inform them of it. *The Housing Department is notified of all planning applications... He wrote to notify me that the cheque had arrived.*

notion /nəʊʃn/ **notions**
NC A **notion** is a belief or idea. *The notion that only foreigners could distribute aid was both racist and out of date, he said... He had only the vaguest notion of what it was about.*

notional /nəʊʃəⁿəl/
ADJ Something that is **notional** exists only in theory or as an idea, but not in reality. *The boundaries between high and popular art are purely notional.* ◆ **notionally** ADV *Many of its leaders notionally represent constituencies on the mainland.*

notoriety /nəʊtəraɪəti/
NU To achieve **notoriety** means to become well known for something bad. *...terrorists who acquired international notoriety for the kidnapping of government figures.*

notorious /nəʊtɔːriəs/
ADJ Someone or something that is **notorious** is well known for something bad. *...the behaviour of the now notorious English football hooligans... The area was notorious for murders... They have become notorious for cheating on quotas.* ◆ **notoriously** SUBMOD *Predicting the weather is a notoriously difficult business.*

notwithstanding /nɒtwɪðstændɪŋ/
PREP If something is true **notwithstanding** something else, it is true in spite of that other thing; a formal word. *Computing remains a growth area in which, notwithstanding economic recessions, the outlook looks bright.*

Nouakchott /nwækʃɒt/
Nouakchott is the capital of Mauritania and its largest city. Population: 350,000 (1984).

nougat /nuːgɑː/
NU **Nougat** is a kind of hard, chewy sweet, containing nuts and sometimes fruit.

nought /nɔːt/ **noughts**
1 **Nought** is the number 0. *In 1987, growth was only nought point two percent up on the 1986 level.*
2 If you try to do something but your efforts are not successful, you can say that your efforts **come to nought** or **come to nothing**; a formal expression. *Six weeks of peace talks almost came to nought when last minute differences arose... So far their attempts have come to nothing.*

noughts and crosses
NU **Noughts and crosses** is a game played on a piece of paper which has a square divided into nine smaller squares. Two players compete to fill a row of three crosses or of three noughts in the spaces.

Nouméa /nuːmeɪə/
Nouméa is the capital of New Caledonia and its largest city. Population: 65,000 (1989).

noun /naʊn/ **nouns**
NC In grammar, a **noun** is a word used to refer to a person, a thing, or an abstract idea such as a feeling or quality.

noun group, noun groups
NC In grammar, a **noun group** is a word or a group of words which can be the subject, object, or complement of a clause, or the object of a preposition. In the sentence, 'There was a note of satisfaction in his voice', 'a note of satisfaction' and 'his voice' are both noun groups.

nourish /nʌrɪʃ/ **nourishes, nourishing, nourished**
1 VO To **nourish** people or animals means to provide them with food. *It is much better to nourish schoolchildren by feeding them good food than by giving them pills... A great variety of animals nourish

themselves on the vegetable foods provided by the world's forests.* ◆ **nourished** ADJ *Some of the children are clearly not well nourished.*
2 VO If you **nourish** a feeling or belief, you allow it to grow or you encourage it to grow; a literary use. *She had nourished dreams of escape.*

nourishing /nʌrɪʃɪŋ/
ADJ **Nourishing** food makes you strong and healthy. *Ham sandwiches are nourishing and filling. ...a nourishing diet.*

nourishment /nʌrɪʃmənt/
NU **Nourishment** is the food that people and animals need to grow and remain healthy. *The seeds are full of nourishment.*

nous /naʊs/
NU **Nous** is common sense; an old-fashioned, informal word. *He has a certain amount of social nous.*

nouveau-riche /nuːvəʊriːʃ/ **nouveaux-riches.** /nuːvəʊriːʃ/
NC A **nouveau-riche** is someone who has only recently become rich, but who comes from a lower social class than other rich people and has tastes, manners, or a lifestyle that others consider vulgar. *...the number of nouveaux-riches who appeared on the scene.*

Nov.
Nov. is a written abbreviation for 'November'. *...Sunday Nov. 11th.*

novel /nɒvl/ **novels**
1 NC A **novel** is a long story written about imaginary events. *...a novel by Henry James... Agatha Christie's first crime novel was rejected by six publishers.*
2 ADJ Something that is **novel** is unlike anything else that has been done or made before. *...a novel experience. ...novel teaching methods... It has come up with the novel idea of forming a company with the residents.*

novelette /nɒvəlet/ **novelettes**
NC A **novelette** is a short novel, usually about a subject that is not very serious. *...television soap operas and cheap novelettes.*

novelist /nɒvəlɪst/ **novelists**
NC A **novelist** is a person who writes novels. *As well as being a best selling novelist, Robert Elegant is also a very experienced journalist.*

novelty /nɒvlti/ **novelties**
1 NU **Novelty** is the quality of being different and unusual. *He became interested because of the novelty of the problem.*
2 NC A **novelty** is something that is new and therefore interesting. *The car was still a novelty at that time.*
3 NC A **novelty** is also a cheap, unusual object sold as a gift or as a souvenir. *...novelty jewellery.*

November /nəʊvembə/
NU **November** is the eleventh month of the year in the Western calendar. *He said that by the end of November two thousand five hundred people would have left... The party failed to win any seats in last November's general election.*

novice /nɒvɪs/ **novices**
1 NC A **novice** is someone who is not experienced at the job or activity that they are doing. *He's still a novice as far as film acting is concerned. ...novice riders.*
2 NC In a monastery or convent, a **novice** is a person who is preparing to become a monk or nun. *He's looking back to those events in the Abbey when, as a novice, he accompanied his master on a mission.*

now /naʊ/
1 ADV You use **now** to refer to the present time, often in contrast to the past or the future. *It is now just after one o'clock... She has three children now... Now is the time to find out... From now on, you are free to do what you like... It now seems certain that unions can expect new legislation.*
2 CONJ You also use **now** or **now that** when you are talking about the effect of an event or change. *I like him a lot now he's older... Now that she's found him, she'll never let him go.*
3 ADV **Now** also means as a result of what recently happened. *I was hoping to see you tomorrow. Now that won't be possible.*

4 ADV In stories, you can use **now** to contrast a situation with an earlier one. *They were walking more slowly now... By now the country had changed dramatically.*

5 ADV SEN You can also use **now** in stories to introduce important or surprising information. *I ran downstairs. Now this was something the intruder had not expected.* ● **Now** is used in these phrases. ● If you say that something will happen **any day now** or **any time now**, you mean that it will happen very soon. *Any day now, the local authority is going to close it down.* ● **Just now** means a very short time ago. *I was talking to him just now.* ● If something happens **now and then**, **every now and then**, or **now and again**, it happens occasionally, but not often or regularly. *Every now and then there is a confrontation... I used to let him play with us now and again.*

nowadays /ˈnaʊədeɪz/
ADV **Nowadays** means at the present time, in contrast with the past. *Nowadays most babies in this country are born in a hospital... Why don't we ever see Jim nowadays?*

nowhere /ˈnəʊweə/
ADV You use **nowhere** to say that there is no place where something can happen or did happen. *There was nowhere to hide... She had nowhere else to go... Nowhere have I seen any mention of this.* ● **Nowhere** is used in these phrases. ● If you say that someone or something appears **from nowhere** or **out of nowhere**, you mean that they appear suddenly and unexpectedly. *A ping-pong table suddenly appeared from nowhere... Coming from nowhere they polled seven-and-a-half percent in elections in West Berlin.* ● If you say that a place is **in the middle of nowhere**, you mean that it is a long way from other places; an informal expression. *I spent hours waiting for a bus in the middle of nowhere.* ● If you say that you are **getting nowhere** or that something **is getting** you **nowhere**, you mean that you are not achieving anything or having any success. *Talks in Europe on nuclear and conventional arms reductions were getting nowhere... Calling me names will get you nowhere.* ● You can use **nowhere near** instead of 'not' to emphasize that something is far from being the case. *Lions are nowhere near as fast as cheetahs... It was nowhere near enough to meet London's needs.*

noxious /ˈnɒkʃəs/
ADJ A **noxious** gas or substance is harmful or poisonous; a formal word. *...a cloud of noxious paraffin vapour.*

nozzle /ˈnɒzl/ **nozzles**
NC A **nozzle** is a narrow end piece fitted to a hose or pipe to control the flow of a liquid or air coming out of it. *The water shoots out of the nozzle in a powerful jet.*

NPR /ˌenpiːˈɑː/
N PROP **NPR** is an American organization which broadcasts radio programmes throughout the United States. **NPR** is an abbreviation for 'National Public Radio'. *Alan Tomlinson is also in Jordan for NPR and is hoping to get into Baghdad.*

nr
Nr is a written abbreviation for 'near'; used especially as part of an address. *Offchurch, nr Leamington Spa, Warwicks.*

nth /enθ/
ADJ The **nth** item in a series is the highest or latest item, used when you do not know how many other items there are. **Nth** is often used to suggest that something has happened or been done a lot of times. *...smoking his nth cigarette... She had to repeat for the nth time the details of her conversation.*

nuance /ˈnjuːɑːns/ **nuances**
NCorNU A **nuance** is a small difference in sound, appearance, feeling, or meaning. *It can listen to a CD and memorise every nuance of volume change throughout the disc... They are pondering the implications and studying the nuances of the American statement... The experts have detected changes in nuance and emphasis.*

nub /nʌb/ **nubs**
N SING The **nub** of a situation, problem, or argument is

the central and most basic part of it. *We ought to get down to the nub of the matter... It reduces her case to its legal nub.*

nubile /ˈnjuːbaɪl/
ADJ A woman who is **nubile** is young, physically mature, and sexually attractive; often used humorously. *...a nubile Hollywood actress.*

nuclear /ˈnjuːklɪə/
1 ADJ ATTRIB **Nuclear** means relating to the nuclei of atoms, or to the energy produced when these nuclei are split or combined. *...nuclear physics. ...nuclear energy.*
2 ADJ ATTRIB **Nuclear** also means relating to weapons that explode by using the energy released by atoms. *...nuclear weapons. ...nuclear war... This would have an important bearing on the nuclear arms race as well... Britain would still have its own nuclear deterrent.*

nuclear family, nuclear families
NC A **nuclear family** is a family group including only parents and their children, not more distant relatives. *...her reaction against the nuclear family.*

nuclear-free
ADJ ATTRIB A **nuclear-free** place is a place where nuclear weapons and nuclear energy are forbidden. *...if Europe becomes a nuclear-free zone... He wants to press on towards his vision of a nuclear-free world.*

nuclear reactor, nuclear reactors
NC A **nuclear reactor** is a machine which produces nuclear energy. *Today's nuclear reactors are too large and uneconomic.*

nuclear winter
NUorN SING **Nuclear winter** refers to the possible effects on the environment of a war in which large numbers of nuclear weapons were used. It is thought that there would be very low temperatures and very little light during a nuclear winter. *Doctors and scientists jointly stress the perils of nuclear winter... This research has lead Professor Robock to suggest that a nuclear winter would be more severe than estimated by earlier calculations. ...the threat of nuclear winter.*

nucleus /ˈnjuːklɪəs/ **nuclei** /ˈnjuːklɪaɪ/
1 NC The **nucleus** of an atom or cell is the central part of it. *...the electrical forces between electrons and atomic nuclei... This gene has a very general effect on the nucleus of the cell.*
2 NC The most important and dedicated people in a group can be referred to as its **nucleus**. *These people formed the nucleus of the American Vegetarian Movement.*

nude /njuːd/ **nudes**
1 ADJ Someone who is **nude** is not wearing any clothes. *They lay nude on the beach.* ● Someone who is **in the nude** is nude. *He wanted to paint me in the nude.*
2 NC A **nude** is a picture or statue of a nude person. *...a Reubens painting or some sort of Dutch nude.*

nudge /nʌdʒ/ **nudges, nudging, nudged**
1 VO If you **nudge** someone, you push them gently with your elbow, in order to draw their attention to something or to make them move. *The girls grinned and nudged each other.*
2 NC If you give someone a **nudge**, you nudge them. *Nods and winks and nudges from Dad mean something different every time.*

nudism /ˈnjuːdɪzəm/
NU **Nudism** is the practice of not wearing any clothes, often because of a belief that this is a healthy way of life. *In some countries nudism is against the law.* ◆ **nudist, nudists** NC *The beach was reserved for nudists. ...a nudist club.*

nudity /ˈnjuːdəti/
NU **Nudity** is the state of wearing no clothes. *The boys treated nudity as a natural thing.*

nugget /ˈnʌgɪt/ **nuggets**
NC A **nugget** of information is an interesting or useful piece of information. *Where had he picked up that little nugget?*

nuisance /ˈnjuːsns/ **nuisances**
NC If you say that someone or something is a **nuisance**, you mean that they annoy you or cause you

problems. *It was a nuisance for them to have all these visitors sitting around... I'm sorry to be such a nuisance.* ● If you **make a nuisance of** yourself, you behave in a way that annoys people; an informal expression. *They generally made a nuisance of themselves and they were pretty successful.*

Nujoma, Sam /sæm nuːjəʊmə/
Sam Nujoma became the first President of Namibia in 1990. In 1959, he founded SWAPO (South West African People's Organization, originally called the Ovamboland People's Organization) and led SWAPO in the war against South African rule of Namibia. Born: 1929.

nuke /njuːk/ **nukes, nuking, nuked**; an informal word.
1 NC A **nuke** is a nuclear weapon. *No more nukes!... They have nukes, and if they're sufficiently pushed, they'll use them.*
2 VO If one country **nukes** another, it bombs it using nuclear weapons. *They've been nuked.*

Nuku'alofa /nuːkuːəlɒfə/
Nuku'alofa is the capital of Tonga and its largest city. Population: 21,000 (1986).

null /nʌl/
If a contract or agreement is **null and void**, it is not legally valid. *The contract was declared null and void... The authorities declared voting in some areas null and void.*

nullify /nʌlɪfaɪ/ **nullifies, nullifying, nullified**
1 VO To **nullify** something means to make it ineffective; a formal use. *This had the effect of nullifying our original advantage... It not only caused deterioration but nullified the benefits of expensive conservation work already carried out.*
2 VO To **nullify** a legal decision or procedure means to declare it not legally valid; a legal use. *Each state had the right to nullify the federal government's laws.*

numb /nʌm/ **numbs, numbing, numbed**
1 ADJ If a part of your body is **numb**, you cannot feel anything there. *My shoulder was completely numb.*
2 ADJ If you are **numb** with shock or fear, you are so shocked or frightened that you cannot think clearly or feel any emotion. *I didn't feel it any longer. I was numb.*
3 VO If a blow or cold weather **numbs** a part of your body, you can no longer feel anything in it. *A stone numbed his shoulder... Her fingers were numbed by the frost.*
4 VO If an experience **numbs** you, you can no longer think clearly or feel any emotion. *We are numbed by repeated disappointments.* ◆ **numbed** ADJ *He stood there in a numbed daze.*

number /nʌmbə/ **numbers, numbering, numbered**
1 NC A **number** is a word such as 'two', 'nine', or 'eleven', or a symbol such as 1, 3, or 47. You use numbers to say how many things you are referring to or where something comes in a series. *Your licence number is here... He lives at number 19 New King Street.*
2 In sport, you can say how someone is ranked in the world or in a particular competition by referring to them as the **number** one, the **number** two, and so on. *The overwhelming favourite for the title is now the number two, Gabriela Sabatini... He now meets the world number six, Brett Martin.*
3 NC Someone's **number** is the series of digits that you dial when you telephone them. *Ring me tomorrow. Here's my number.*
4 NC+SUPP You use **number** with words such as 'large' or 'small' to say approximately how many things or people there are. *...cities with large numbers of children in care... They were produced in vast numbers... A surprising number of men never marry... A record number of countries—161—has agreed to participate.*
5 VC If a group of people or things **numbers** a particular amount, there are that many of them. *The force numbered almost a quarter of a million men.*
6 VO If you **number** something, you give it a number in a series and write the number on it. *I haven't numbered the pages yet.*
7 See also **opposite number**.
● **Number** is used in these phrases. ● **A number of**

things means several things. *A number of people disagreed.* ● **Any number of** things means a lot of things. *The work can be done in any number of ways.*

numberless /nʌmbələs/
ADJ **Numberless** means too many to be counted; a literary word. *He had had bad digestion, fevers and numberless other illnesses.*

number one
ADJ ATTRIB **Number one** means better, more important, or more popular than anything else of its kind; an informal expression. *They regard unemployment as their number one priority.*

number plate, number plates
NC A vehicle's **number plates** are the signs on the front and back that show its registration number. *We're standing next to a car with a Californian number plate.*

Number Ten
N PROP **Number Ten** is often used to refer to 10 Downing Street, London, the official home of the British Prime Minister. It is also used with reference to political activity there. *There has been no response from Number Ten.*

numbskull /nʌmskʌl/. See **numskull**.

numeracy /njuːmərəsi/
NU **Numeracy** is the ability to do arithmetic. *...numeracy problems... He also urged employers to introduce literacy and numeracy classes during working hours.*

numeral /njuːmərəl/ **numerals**
NC A **numeral** is a symbol used to represent a number; a formal word. *My clock has Roman numerals.*

numerate /njuːmərət/
ADJ Someone who is **numerate** is able to do arithmetic. *'The need to be numerate is of paramount importance,' he emphasised.*

numerical /njuːmerɪkl/
ADJ **Numerical** means expressed in numbers or relating to numbers. *...numerical data.* ◆ **numerically** ADV *...a numerically small group.*

numerous /njuːmərəs/
1 QUANT **Numerous** things or people means a lot of them. *He has been seen in public on numerous occasions... Numerous residents of the town had been affected.*
2 ADJ If people or things are **numerous**, there are a lot of them. *Small enterprises have become more numerous.*

numinous /njuːmɪnəs/
ADJ **Numinous** means holy, awe-inspiring, and mysterious; a literary word. *The numinous power of the rock shook him.*

numskull /nʌmskʌl/ **numskulls**; also spelt **numbskull**.
NC A **numskull** is a silly or stupid person; an old-fashioned, informal word.

nun /nʌn/ **nuns**
NC A **nun** is a member of a female religious community. *...Mother Teresa of Calcutta, the Roman Catholic nun renowned for her work with the poor.*

nunnery /nʌnəri/ **nunneries**
NC A **nunnery** is the same as a **convent**; an old-fashioned word. *She refused marriage and entered a nunnery.*

nuptial /nʌpʃl/ **nuptials**; an old-fashioned word.
1 ADJ ATTRIB **Nuptial** means relating to a wedding or to marriage. *...nuptial bliss.*
2 N PL Someone's **nuptials** are their wedding celebrations. *Naturally I watched the nuptials of the Prince and Princess of Wales.*

nurse /nɜːs/ **nurses, nursing, nursed**
1 NC A **nurse** is a person whose job is to care for people who are ill. *...a trained nurse... He was working as a male nurse in a Baghdad hospital.*
2 VO If you **nurse** someone, you care for them while they are ill. *I took her home and nursed her for three months until she died... He's been nursed back to full fitness by his trainer.*
3 VO If you **nurse** an illness or injury, you allow it to get better by resting. *He is nursing a minor gunshot wound. ...Gascoigne, who's nursing a serious knee injury.*

4 VO If you **nurse** an emotion or an ambition, you feel it strongly for a long time. *Wilson had long nursed a desire to build his own yacht. ...Michael Heseltine, who has long nursed the ambition to replace Mrs Thatcher.*
5 See also **nursing**.

nursemaid /nɜːsmeɪd/ **nursemaids**
NC A **nursemaid** is a woman or girl who is paid to look after young children. *He decided to hire the girl as a nursemaid for his two small children.*

nursery /nɜːsəʳri/ **nurseries**
1 NC A **nursery** is a place where very young children can be looked after while their parents are at work. *They take their children to nurseries or day-care centres.*
2 ADJ ATTRIB **Nursery** education is the education of children who are between three and five years old. *...the noise and bustle of a nursery class.*
3 NC A **nursery** is also a place where plants are grown in order to be sold. *Go out to your local garden centre or tree nursery and try to buy one like that.*

nursery nurse, nursery nurses
NC A **nursery nurse** is a person who has been trained to look after very young children. *She is assisted by nursery nurses who have trained for two years.*

nursery rhyme, nursery rhymes
NC A **nursery rhyme** is a poem or song for young children, especially one that is old or well-known. *...songs and nursery rhymes we learn as infants.*

nursery school, nursery schools
NCorNU A **nursery school** is a school for children who are between three and five years old. *In Spain, state-financed nursery schools already look after two thirds of all 3-5 year olds... There is 11 years of compulsory education and all children go to nursery school.*

nursery slopes
N PL **Nursery slopes** are the gentle slopes on a mountain that are used by people who are learning to ski. *There was hardly any snow at all on the nursery slopes this year.*

nursing /nɜːsɪŋ/
1 NU **Nursing** is the profession or activity of looking after people who are ill. *They're calling for improved education to make nursing more attractive to young people... Before that most nursing had been done by untrained nuns... Delays have been blamed on shortages of trained nursing staff.*
2 ADJ ATTRIB A **nursing** mother feeds her baby with milk from her breasts. *The UN remained very concerned about the effects of cold and lack of food on children, the elderly, the sick and nursing mothers.*

nursing home, nursing homes
NC A **nursing home** is a private hospital, especially one for old people. *One of Britain's best known actors, Sir John Clements, has died in a nursing home in Sussex.*

nurture /nɜːtʃəʳ/ **nurtures, nurturing, nurtured**; a formal word.
1 VO If you **nurture** a young child or a young plant, you care for it while it is growing and developing. *...a mother's duty to nurture her children.*
2 VO If you **nurture** plans, ideas, or people, you encourage their development and success. *After spending two years nurturing this project, Bains came to England.*

nut /nʌt/ **nuts**
1 NC **Nuts** grow on trees. They have hard shells and firm insides that can be eaten. *The report says that Britons crunched their way through two hundred and twenty-five tons of snacks, crisps and nuts last year.*
2 NC A **nut** is also a small piece of metal with a hole in it which a bolt screws into. Nuts and bolts are used to fasten things together. *Take your spanner and tighten the nut.*

nutcase /nʌtkeɪs/ **nutcases**
NC If you say that someone is a **nutcase**, you mean that they are mad or foolish; an informal word.

nutcracker /nʌtkrækəʳ/ **nutcrackers**
NC A **nutcracker** is a tool for cracking the shell of a nut to get to the part you can eat inside. *The*

Toughnut nutcracker has been designed to crack nuts perfectly, using the minimum of effort.

nuthouse /nʌthaʊs/ **nuthouses**
NC A **nuthouse** is a psychiatric hospital; an offensive word.

nutmeg /nʌtmeg/
NU **Nutmeg** is a spice that you can grate into food.

nutrient /njuːtriənt/ **nutrients**
NC **Nutrients** are substances that help plants and animals to grow; a technical word. *Excessive rainfall washes out valuable minerals and nutrients from the soil.*

nutriment /njuːtrɪmənt/ **nutriments**
NUorNC **Nutriment** is the nourishment that all living things need in order to grow and remain healthy; a formal word. *There were other sources of nutriment. ...drying out the soil, extracting nutriments.*

nutrition /njuːtrɪʃn/
NU **Nutrition** is the process of taking and absorbing nutrients from food; a formal word. *...improvements in nutrition... They have launched a new scheme to teach mothers more about nutrition.*

nutritional /njuːtrɪʃəʰnəl/
ADJ ATTRIB **Nutritional** means involving or relating to the food that you eat and to the nutrients in the food that help you to remain healthy; a formal word. *...the nutritional value of steak.*

nutritionist /njuːtrɪʃənɪst/ **nutritionists**
NC A **nutritionist** is a person who studies different foods and gives advice on what you should eat in order to stay healthy. *Nutritionists are encouraging people to eat more vegetables.*

nutritious /njuːtrɪʃəs/
ADJ Food that is **nutritious** helps your body to be healthy; a formal word. *Milk is one of the most nutritious foods available. ...a nutritious diet.*

nutritive /njuːtrətɪv/
ADJ ATTRIB **Nutritive** means concerning the food that you eat and the proteins, vitamins, and minerals in it which help you to remain healthy; a technical word. *Their vegetable food was poor in nutritive value.*

nutshell /nʌtʃel/
You use **in a nutshell** to indicate that you are saying something in the briefest way possible. *That, in a nutshell, is what we're trying to do here.*

nutter /nʌtəʳ/ **nutters**
NC If you call someone a **nutter**, you mean that they are mad or very foolish; an offensive word.

nutty /nʌti/ **nuttier, nuttiest**
1 ADJ If you describe someone or something as **nutty**, you mean that they are very foolish; an informal use. *...this nutty idea he has.*
2 ADJ Food that has a **nutty** taste has the taste of nuts. *...rice with a pleasantly nutty taste.*

Nuuk /nuːk/
Nuuk, also known as Godthab, is the capital of Greenland and its largest town. Population: 12,000 (1990).

nuzzle /nʌzl/ **nuzzles, nuzzling, nuzzled**
VOorVA If you **nuzzle** someone, you gently rub your nose and mouth against them to show affection. *'Ellen,' he said, nuzzling her neck... The dog began to nuzzle at his coat.*

NW
NW is a written abbreviation for 'north-west'.

nylon /naɪlɒn/
NU **Nylon** is a strong type of artificial fibre. *...synthetic upholstery materials such as nylon and acrylic. ...nylon stockings.*

nymph /nɪmf/ **nymphs**
NC In Greek and Roman mythology and in popular legend, **nymphs** were spirits of nature who took the form of young women. *...Burne Jones's painting of the magician Merlin being betrayed by a seductive nymph.*

nymphomaniac /nɪmfəmeɪniæk/ **nymphomaniacs**
NC If someone calls a woman a **nymphomaniac**, they mean that she has sex or wants to have sex much more often than they consider normal; used showing disapproval.

O o

O, o /əʊ/ **O's, o's**
1 NC **O** is the fifteenth letter of the English alphabet.
2 **O** is used in exclamations, especially when you are expressing strong feelings. *O God, I want to go home... O the joy of those Saturday afternoons... 'He's not the Chancellor now.'—'O yes, he is.'* ● See also **oh**.

o' /ə/
PREP In written English, **o'** is used to represent the word 'of', when it is spoken very quickly. *...a cup o' tea. ...a lot o' money. ...one o' them.*

oaf /əʊf/ **oafs**
NC If you call someone an **oaf**, you mean that you think they are clumsy and stupid. *Paul, you are a big oaf!*

oak /əʊk/ **oaks**
NCorNU An **oak** or an **oak tree** is a large tree. The wood from oak trees, which is strong and hard, is also called **oak**. *The mature oaks will be enclosed in railings... They appear to have been made of oak covered with paper and cloth... Seven mature oak trees are to be planted today.*

oaken /əʊkən/
ADJ **Oaken** means made of wood that comes from an oak tree; a literary word. *...the heavy oaken door.*

OAP /əʊeɪpiː/ **OAPs**
NC An **OAP** is a man over the age of 65 or a woman over the age of 60. **OAP** is an abbreviation for 'old-age pensioner'.

oar /ɔː/ **oars**
NCorNU **Oars** are long poles with a wide, flat blade at one end which are used for rowing a boat. *...sitting almost on the side of the ship with their oars supported by outriggers... Both fleets were taken into battle by oar.*

oarsman /ɔːzmən/ **oarsmen** /ɔːzmən/
NC An **oarsman** is someone who rows, especially in a racing boat. *...the Cambridge University oarsman, Ian Clarke, who's confident of victory in the boat race tomorrow.*

OAS /əʊeɪes/. See **Organization of American States**.

oasis /əʊeɪsɪs/ **oases** /əʊeɪsiːz/
1 NC In a desert, an **oasis** is a small area where water and plants are found. *Ancient oases like Chinguetti had their palm groves almost completely destroyed and many nomad families lost their entire herd.*
2 NC+SUPP You can refer to any pleasant place or situation as an **oasis** when it is surrounded by unpleasant ones. *The town was an oasis of prosperity in a desert of poverty... It's also a tranquil oasis of some charm in the centre of an otherwise drab city.*

oat /əʊt/ **oats**
NC **Oats** are a cereal crop or its grains, used for making porridge or feeding animals. *...hundreds of varieties of cereals, wheat, oats, and spring and winter barleys. ...oats eaten as porridge.*

oath /əʊθ/ **oaths** /əʊðz/
1 NC An **oath** is a formal promise. *...an oath of allegiance.* ● If someone is **on oath** or **under oath**, they have made a promise to tell the truth in a court of law. *It is the first time that such officials have been called to testify under oath before parliament.*
2 NC An **oath** is also a swear-word; an old-fashioned

use. *He was answered with a torrent of French oaths.*

oatmeal /əʊtmiːl/
1 NU **Oatmeal** is a coarse flour made by crushing oats. *...oatmeal biscuits.*
2 ADJ Something that is **oatmeal** in colour is very pale creamy brown. *...an oatmeal coat.*

OAU /əʊeɪjuː/. See **Organization of African Unity**.

obduracy /ɒbdjʊrəsi/
NU **Obduracy** is stubborn behaviour or determination not to change your mind about something; a formal word, used showing disapproval. *...the obduracy of his silence. ...his obduracy over China.*

obdurate /ɒbdjʊrət/
ADJ If someone is **obdurate**, they are stubborn and determined not to change their mind about something; a formal word, used showing disapproval. *The headman remained obdurate. ...her obdurate leadership.* ◆ **obdurately** ADV *She waited obdurately for a taxi.*

obedience /əbiːdiəns/
NU **Obedience** is your behaviour when you do what someone in authority asks or tells you to do, especially something that you may not want to do. *She failed to show proper obedience and respect to the elders... He did it in obedience to her wishes... Membership of the party also meant blind obedience to the party.*

obedient /əbiːdiənt/
ADJ Someone who is **obedient** does what they are told to do. *She was an obedient little girl.* ◆ **obediently** ADV *'Try it,' Clem ordered. Obediently I picked up the cup.*

obeisance /əʊbeɪsns/ **obeisances**; a formal word.
1 NU **Obeisance** is respect or obedience for someone or something. *...the obeisance of subordinates... While paying obeisance to general principles, it left the decision to its individual members.*
2 NUorNC **Obeisance** is a physical gesture, especially a bow, that you make in order to show your respect for someone or something. *The emperor made obeisance to this image... Making a very low obeisance, she received a kiss from him.*

obelisk /ɒbəlɪsk/ **obelisks**
NC An **obelisk** is a tall stone pillar that has been built in honour of a person or an important event. *...a granite obelisk commemorating the battle. ...an Egyptian obelisk.*

obese /əbiːs/
ADJ Someone who is **obese** is very fat; a formal word. *Researchers investigated babies from both thin and obese mothers.* ◆ **obesity** /əbiːsəti/ NU *Obesity is a health hazard.*

obey /əbeɪ/ **obeys, obeying, obeyed**
VOorV If you **obey** a person, a command, or an instruction, you do what you are told to do. *The troops were reluctant to obey orders... They obeyed me without question... Don't question anything, just obey!*

obituary /əbɪtʃuəri/ **obituaries**
NC An **obituary** is a piece of writing about someone who has just died. *I read Sewell's obituary in the Daily News.*

obj.
Obj. is a written abbreviation for 'object'.

object, objects, objecting, objected; pronounced /ˈɒbdʒɪkt/ when it is a noun and /əbˈdʒɛkt/ when it is a verb.

1 NC An **object** is anything that has a fixed shape and is not alive. *...the shabby, black object he was carrying. ...mats, bowls, and other objects... Refugees smashed equipment and pelted the police with any objects they could lay their hands on.*

2 NC Someone's **object** or the **object** of what they are doing is their aim or purpose. *The minder's object is to keep the child asleep... She would journey for months with the sole object of filming a rare creature.*

3 NC The **object** of a feeling, a wish, or a kind of behaviour is the thing or person that it is directed towards. *She became an object of worship... The Prime Minister is also the object of severe criticism in Serbia. ...an object of ridicule.*

4 NC In grammar, the **object** of a clause is a noun group, other than the subject, which refers to a person or thing that is involved in or affected by the action of the verb. In the sentence 'She married a young engineer', 'a young engineer' is the object. In the sentence 'She gave me a lovely present', 'a lovely present' is the direct object and 'me' is the indirect object.

5 V, V+*to*, or V-REPORT If you **object** to something, you do not approve of it or you say that you do not approve of it. *The men objected and the women supported them... Students have objected to new arrangements for the allocation of university places... You may object that the system makes boys effeminate.*

objection /əbˈdʒɛkʃn/ **objections**

1 NC If you make or raise an **objection** to something, you say that you do not approve of it. *They raised objections to Seagram's bid... The objection that he had no experience was ignored.*

2 If you **have no objection to** something, you do not disapprove of it. *He had no real objection to drinking.*

objectionable /əbˈdʒɛkʃənəbl/

ADJ Someone or something that is **objectionable** is offensive and unacceptable; a formal word. *...politicians whose views he found objectionable.*

objective /əbˈdʒɛktɪv/ **objectives**

1 NC Your **objective** is what you are trying to achieve. *Mobil's primary objective is to win.*

2 ADJ **Objective** information is based on facts. *There is no objective evidence.*

3 ADJ If someone is **objective**, they base their opinions on facts, rather than on their feelings. *...a book on communism written by an astonishingly objective author.* ♦ **objectively** ADV *It was desirable to view these things objectively.* ♦ **objectivity** /ˌɒbdʒɛkˈtɪvəti/ NU *Historians strive after objectivity.*

object lesson, object lessons

NC An **object lesson** in something is an action, event, or situation that demonstrates the best way to do something, or that demonstrates the truth or wisdom of a particular principle. *Thank you, that was an object lesson in how to handle a difficult customer!*

objector /əbˈdʒɛktə/ **objectors**

NC An **objector** is someone who states or shows that they oppose or disapprove of something. *...the inquiry for which the objectors had asked.* ● See also **conscientious objector.**

objet d'art /ˌɒbʒeɪ ˈdɑː/ **objets d'art** /ˌɒbʒeɪ ˈdɑː/

NC An **objet d'art** is a small ornament or object that is thought to have artistic merit.

obligated /ˈɒblɪɡeɪtɪd/; used in American English.

1 ADJ PRED If you feel **obligated** to do something, you feel that it is your duty to do it. *No one is obligated to attend.*

2 ADJ PRED If you feel **obligated** to someone, you feel that you owe them something, usually because you are grateful to them for some reason. *She was here first, so I kind of feel obligated to her.*

obligation /ˌɒblɪˈɡeɪʃn/ **obligations**

NCorNU An **obligation** is a duty to do something. *He had to go home because of family obligations... The cricket union had a moral and legal obligation to honour the contracts. ...freedom from obligation.*

obligatory /əˈblɪɡətₒºri/

1 ADJ If something is **obligatory**, you must do it,

because there is a rule or law about it. *It is not obligatory to answer... They must undergo an obligatory test for the AIDS virus.*

2 ADJ **Obligatory** can also refer to things which are always done in certain situations. *She is adept at using the obligatory photo-opportunities at any Royal function to her own advantage.*

oblige /əˈblaɪdʒ/ **obliges, obliging, obliged**; a formal word.

1 VO+*to*-INF If something **obliges** you to do something, it makes you feel that you must do it. *Politeness obliged me to go on with the conversation... The ruling obliged them to meet new standards within ten years.* ♦ **obliged** ADJ PRED+*to*-INF *I felt obliged to invite him into the parlour.*

2 VorVO If you **oblige** someone, you help them by doing what they have asked you to do. *'Who did you ask?'—'Charlie. He's only too glad to oblige.'... They obliged him by giving the Socialists a massive majority.*

obliging /əˈblaɪdʒɪŋ/

ADJ Someone who is **obliging** is willing to do helpful things. *...an obliging doorman who helps people struggling with their drinks and coffee.*

oblique /əˈbliːk/

1 ADJ An **oblique** statement or comment is indirect and therefore difficult to understand. *...an oblique compliment.*

2 ADJ An **oblique** line is a sloping line. *It smashed into the earth at an oblique angle.*

obliterate /əˈblɪtəreɪt/ **obliterates, obliterating, obliterated**

VO To **obliterate** something means to destroy it completely. *I watched bombs obliterate the villages.*

oblivion /əˈblɪviən/

1 NU **Oblivion** is the state of not being aware of what is happening around you, because you are asleep, unconscious, or dead. *Cal still slept, deep in oblivion... He couldn't paint without drinking; he boozed himself into oblivion almost every night.*

2 NU **Oblivion** is the state of having been forgotten. *The affair should not sink into oblivion... This art faded into oblivion years ago. ...political oblivion.*

oblivious /əˈblɪviəs/

ADJ PRED If you are **oblivious** of something or to something, you are not aware of it. *She seemed oblivious of the attention she was drawing to herself... She remained oblivious to criticism.*

oblong /ˈɒblɒŋ/ **oblongs**

NC An **oblong** is a shape with two long sides and two short sides at right angles to each other. *...a small oblong of silver.* ▶ Also ADJ *...an oblong table.*

obnoxious /əbˈnɒkʃəs/

ADJ Someone who is **obnoxious** is very unpleasant and bad-mannered. *They were rude and obnoxious.*

oboe /ˈəʊbəʊ/ **oboes**

NC An **oboe** is a woodwind instrument with a double reed in its mouthpiece. *...a concerto for oboe and strings. ...the man who did more than anyone else to bring the oboe to prominence as a solo instrument.*

oboist /ˈəʊbəʊɪst/ **oboists**

NC An **oboist** is someone who plays the oboe. *...Leon Goossens, one of the world's finest oboists.*

obscene /əbˈsiːn/

ADJ Something that is **obscene** shocks and offends people, usually because it relates to sex. *...obscene pictures.*

obscenity /əbˈsɛnəti/ **obscenities**

1 NU **Obscenity** is behaviour that relates to sex and shocks and offends people. *Existing laws on obscenity are to be tightened.*

2 NC An **obscenity** is a very rude word or expression. *They started yelling obscenities.*

obscurantism /ˌɒbskjʊˈræntɪzəm/

NU **Obscurantism** is the practice or policy of deliberately making something vague and difficult to understand, especially in order to stop people finding out the truth. *Indeed, obscurantism had become the official policy.*

obscure /əbˈskjʊə/ **obscurer, obscurest; obscures, obscuring, obscured**

1 ADJ Something that is **obscure** is known by only a

few people. *...experts in obscure subjects.*
2 ADJ **Obscure** also means difficult to understand or see. *...obscure points of theology... He saw the hideous, obscure shape rise slowly to the surface.*
3 VO To **obscure** something means to make it difficult to understand, see, or hear. *Words that obscure the truth must be discarded... Some areas were obscured by fog.*

obscurity /əbskjʊərəti/
1 NU **Obscurity** is the state of being known to very few people. *Today he is retired and continues to live in virtual obscurity... He came from obscurity to finish a surprising second in the initial round of elections last month.*
2 NU **Obscurity** is also the quality of being very difficult to understand. *Dixon didn't mind the obscurity of the reference. ...the obscurity of the language.*

obsequious /əbsiːkwiəs/
ADJ Someone who is **obsequious** is very eager to help or agree with people who they think are important; used showing disapproval. *...obsequious shop assistants.*

observable /əbzɜːvəbl/
ADJ Something that is **observable** can be seen. *It is an action that is observable in almost all countries in the world.*

observance /əbzɜːvəns/
NU+SUPP The **observance** of a law or custom is the practice of obeying or following it. *Most of them are not orthodox in their religious observance. ...observance of speed limits.*

observant /əbzɜːvənt/
1 ADJ Someone who is **observant** notices things that are not usually noticed. *He was not an especially observant man.*
2 ADJ ATTRIB An **observant** follower of a religion performs all the duties that his or her religion requires. *Observant Moslems don't eat in daylight hours of the twenty-eight days of Ramadan... Isaac Bashevis Singer considered himself a believer in God although not an observant Jew.*

observation /ɒbzəveɪʃn/ observations
1 NU or N PL **Observation** involves carefully watching someone or something. *...information gathered by observation or experiment... She was put under observation in a nursing home... Scientists have been monitoring the spread of the ash cloud using observations from the ground and satellite imagery.*
2 NC An **observation** is something that you have learned by seeing or watching something and thinking about it. *Looking around the animal world today we can make a number of general observations about how animals move. ...clinical observations.*
3 NC An **observation** is also a remark or comment. *We listened to Mama's tearful observations on the subject.*
4 NU **Observation** is also the ability to notice things that are not usually noticed. *...keen powers of observation.*

observational /ɒbzəveɪʃənəl/; a formal word.
1 ADJ **Observational** means relating to people's ability to notice things. *...your observational faculties.*
2 ADJ **Observational** also means relating to the watching of something in order to learn new things. *As an observational device, it is primitive. ...observational surveys by astronomers.*

observatory /əbzɜːvətri/ observatories
NC An **observatory** is a special building with telescopes that scientists use to study the sun, the moon, the planets, and the stars. *...an observatory for studying the stars and tracking space probes.*

observe /əbzɜːv/ observes, observing, observed
1 VO If you **observe** someone or something, you watch them carefully. *By observing your boss's moods, you will soon discover when to talk and when to keep quiet.*
2 VO To **observe** someone or something also means to see or notice them; a formal use. *They observed a key in the bedroom door.*
3 V-QUOTE or V-REPORT To **observe** also means to make a remark or comment related to something that has

happened; a formal use. *'People aren't interested in spiritual things,' observed the actress... A spokesman observed that Son Sann had probably been misquoted.*
4 VO If you **observe** something such as a law or custom, you obey it or follow it. *'Laws have to be observed by all', he said... Parliament has long observed this convention.*

observer /əbzɜːvə/ observers
1 NC An **observer** is someone who studies the latest news about a situation. *...political observers... One observer says we may be on the road to peace.*
2 NC An **observer** is also someone who sees or notices something. *A casual observer may get the wrong impression.*
3 NC An **observer** is a member of a group of people who are sent to a particular country to watch an event such as an election or the withdrawal of troops, and to report on whether it is carried out in a fair way. *Mr Baker again called for American observers to be allowed to monitor them. ...the eagerly awaited reports of the international observer mission.*

obsess /əbses/ obsesses, obsessing, obsessed
VO If you **are obsessed** with something or someone, you think about them all the time; used showing disapproval. *He became obsessed with a girl reporter.*

obsession /əbseʃn/ obsessions
NC If you have an **obsession** about something, you think about it all the time or regard it as very important; used showing disapproval. *Taylor's fascination with bees developed into an obsession.*

obsessional /əbseʃənəl/
ADJ **Obsessional** means the same as **obsessive**; used showing disapproval. *...an obsessional need to win.*

obsessive /əbsesɪv/
ADJ If someone's behaviour is **obsessive**, they cannot stop doing something or thinking about something; used showing disapproval. *Obsessive tidiness in the office is a bad sign.* ◆ **obsessively** ADV *At intervals, he obsessively read Conrad.*

obsolescence /ɒbsəlesns/
NU **Obsolescence** is the state of being no longer needed because something newer or more efficient has been invented. *...an educational system whose obsolescence becomes more evident every day.*

obsolescent /ɒbsəlesnt/
ADJ Something that is **obsolescent** is nearly obsolete or becoming obsolete. *The missile is increasingly obsolescent and ineffective.*

obsolete /ɒbsəliːt/
ADJ Something that is **obsolete** is no longer needed because a better thing now exists. *The Falcon missile was now obsolete.*

obstacle /ɒbstəkl/ obstacles
NC An **obstacle** is something which makes it difficult for you to go forward or do something. *Bats can sense obstacles in their path. ...the bureaucratic obstacles to getting her son over from Jamaica.*

obstetric /əbstetrɪk/ obstetrics; a medical term.
1 NU **Obstetrics** is the branch of medicine that is concerned with pregnancy and childbirth. *By this time I had decided that my future lay in obstetrics and gynaecology.*
2 ADJ ATTRIB **Obstetric** means concerned with obstetrics. *...obstetric nurses.*

obstetrician /ɒbstətrɪʃn/ obstetricians
NC An **obstetrician** is a doctor who is specially trained to help with childbirth and the care of pregnant women. *They chose a young obstetrician to attend the birth.*

obstinacy /ɒbstɪnəsi/
NU **Obstinacy** is obstinate behaviour. *Both sides have accused each other of arrogance and obstinacy.*

obstinate /ɒbstɪnət/
ADJ Someone who is **obstinate** refuses to do what they do not want to do or to change their opinions; used showing disapproval. *...an obstinate, rebellious child.*

obstreperous /əbstrepərəs/
ADJ Someone who is **obstreperous** is noisy and difficult to control. *Drunks were rarely charged unless they became obstreperous.*

obstruct /əbstrʌkt/ obstructs, obstructing, obstructed
1 VO If something **obstructs** a road or path, it blocks

it, so that people or vehicles cannot get past. *The crash obstructed the road for several hours... Normally, police move in as soon as protestors obstruct traffic.*
2 vo If someone **obstructs** something such as justice or progress, they prevent it from happening, developing, or being carried out. *It is a crime for the President to obstruct justice... The government, he said, was obstructing the peace process.*

obstruction /əbstrʌkʃn/ **obstructions**
1 NC An **obstruction** is something that blocks a road or path. *The obstructions could take weeks to clear... The vehicle crashed into a concrete obstruction.*
2 NCorNU An **obstruction** is also something that blocks a passage in your body. *The boy was suffering from a bowel obstruction and he died... These tumours develop in the lining of the airways and once again they cause obstruction.*
3 NU **Obstruction** is the act of deliberately preventing something from happening. *The unions faced legal obstruction... I hope that no obstruction will be allowed to block this great humanitarian effort.*

obstructionism /əbstrʌkʃənɪzəm/
NU **Obstructionism** is the practice or policy of deliberately delaying or preventing legal, business, or parliamentary operations. *The era of international bickering and cold war obstructionism has finally ended.*

obstructionist /əbstrʌkʃənɪst/
ADJ If a country or other group or organization adopts **obstructionist** policies, they deliberately try to delay or prevent things happening or being achieved. *Both leaders deplored what they called the obstructionist approach of certain forces.*

obstructive /əbstrʌktɪv/
ADJ Someone who is **obstructive** deliberately causes difficulties for other people. *...hoping to bypass possibly obstructive bureaucrats... The authorities have denied reports that they're being obstructive.*

obtain /əbteɪn/ **obtains, obtaining, obtained**
vo If you **obtain** something, you get it or achieve it; a formal word. *These books can be obtained from the Public Library... She obtained her degree in 1951.*

obtainable /əbteɪnəbl/
ADJ Something that is **obtainable** can be obtained. *...the best cognac obtainable... Credit had become too easily obtainable.*

obtrude /əbtruːd/ **obtrudes, obtruding, obtruded**
1 V-ERG When something **obtrudes** or when you **obtrude** it, it becomes noticeable in an undesirable way; a formal use. *Those measures obtruded on his privacy... Gertrude now clearly felt that she had obtruded her sorrow.*
2 v If an object **obtrudes**, it sticks out.

obtrusive /əbtruːsɪv/
ADJ Something that is **obtrusive** is noticeable in an unpleasant way. *Equally obtrusive was the graffiti that had started to appear.* ♦ **obtrusively** ADV *Hawke got up and walked obtrusively out of the building.*

obtuse /əbtjuːs/
1 ADJ Someone who is **obtuse** has difficulty understanding things, or makes no effort to understand them; a formal use. *Are you normally stupid or just being deliberately obtuse?* ♦ **obtuseness** NU *...the cowardly obtuseness of white liberals.*
2 ADJ An **obtuse** angle is between 90° and 180°; a technical term in mathematics.

obverse /ɒbvɜːs/
N SING The **obverse** of an opinion, situation, or argument is the same question looked at from the opposite point of view; a formal word. *The obverse of expansion at the top was contraction at the bottom. ...the obverse side of that question.*

obviate /ɒbvieɪt/ **obviates, obviating, obviated**
vo To **obviate** something such as a problem or a need means to remove it or make it unnecessary; a formal word. *Energy conservation obviates the need for further generating capacity... He destroyed the letter to obviate any suspicion that might fall on him.*

obvious /ɒbviəs/
ADJ If something is **obvious**, you can easily see it or understand it. *It was painfully obvious that I knew*

very little about it. *...obvious similarities.* ♦ **obviously**
ADV SEN or ADV *Obviously I don't need to say how important this project is... The soldier was obviously badly hurt.*

occasion /əkeɪʒn/ **occasions, occasioning, occasioned**
1 NC An **occasion** is a time when something happens. *I met him only on one occasion... One the last occasion when the matter was debated in the House of Commons, the majority of MPs against was 123.*
2 NC An **occasion** is also an important event, ceremony, or celebration. *They have the date fixed for the big occasion.*
3 N SING+SUPP or NU+to-INF An **occasion** for doing something is an opportunity for doing it; a formal use. *For the girls, nature study was an occasion for lazy walks and idle picnics... He had never had occasion to use his gun.*
4 If something happens **on occasion** or **on occasions**, it happens sometimes, but not very often; a formal expression. *You have on occasions surprised people.*
5 vo To **occasion** something means to cause it; a formal use. *...deaths occasioned by police activity.*

occasional /əkeɪʒəⁿnəl/
ADJ ATTRIB **Occasional** means happening sometimes, but not regularly or often. *...an occasional trip as far as Aberdeen... Occasional gunfire has been heard during the day in the centre of the city.* ♦ **occasionally**
ADV *Friends visit them occasionally.*

occidental /ɒksɪdentl/
ADJ **Occidental** means relating to the countries of Europe and America; a formal word. *...all religions, oriental and occidental.*

occult /ɒkʌlt, ɒkʌlt/
N SING The **occult** means supernatural or magical forces. *...enthusiasm for astrology and the occult.*
► Also ADJ ATTRIB *...the fantastic occult powers that he was said to possess.*

occupancy /ɒkjupənsi/
NU **Occupancy** is the fact of living or working in a room or building, especially for a fixed period of time; a formal word. *Another publishing firm had taken over the occupancy. ...on the first evening of his occupancy.*

occupant /ɒkjupənt/ **occupants**
NC The **occupants** of a building or room are the people there. *The room's sole occupants were the boy and a dog.*

occupation /ɒkjupeɪʃn/ **occupations**
1 NC Your **occupation** is your job or profession. *...a poorly paid occupation... More women should be encouraged to take up science and engineering occupations.*
2 NC An **occupation** is also something that you do for pleasure or as part of your daily life. *Riding was her favourite occupation.*
3 NU+SUPP The **occupation** of a country is its invasion and control by a foreign army. *...the French occupation of North Africa... Holland came under German occupation.*

occupational /ɒkjupeɪʃəⁿnəl/
ADJ ATTRIB **Occupational** means relating to a person's job or profession. *...occupational or personal pensions.*

occupational hazard, occupational hazards
NC An **occupational hazard** is something unpleasant that you may suffer or experience in the course of doing your job, hobby, or another activity. *...occupational hazards like dusts which harm the lungs. ...the occupational hazards of motorcycle riding.*

occupational therapy
NU **Occupational therapy** is a way of helping people who have been ill or injured to develop or regain skills by giving them things to do. *In hospital he read, wrote poetry and participated in occupational therapy.*

occupier /ɒkjupaɪə/ **occupiers**
NC The **occupier** of a house, flat, or piece of land is the person who lives or works there; a formal word. *The occupier of the premises has applied for planning permission.*

occupy /ɒkjupaɪ/ **occupies, occupying, occupied**
1 vo The people who **occupy** a building are the people who live or work there. *Houses occupied by the aged must be centrally heated.*

2 VO If something **occupies** a particular area or place, it fills or covers it or exists there. *Dry lands occupy a third of the world's surface.*
3 V-PASS If something such as a seat **is occupied**, someone is using it, so that it is not available for anyone else to use. *20 percent of the orthopaedic beds in Britain's hospitals are occupied by such cases.*
4 VO When people **occupy** a place or a country, they move into it and gain control of it. *The students occupied the Administration Block... Radio Mozambique says the Mozambican army has occupied the town of Lalaua after driving out Renamo rebels.*
5 VO If something **occupies** a particular place in a system, process, or plan, it has that place. *The demonstration occupies a central place in their campaign.*
6 V-REFLorVO If you **occupy** yourself in doing something, you are busy doing it. *They were occupying themselves in growing their own food... How do you occupy your time?*
7 VO If something **occupies** you, it requires your efforts, attention, or time. *I'm occupied with official business.*

occur /əkɜ:/ **occurs, occurring, occurred**
1 V When an event **occurs**, it happens. *Both incidents occurred in the city of Srinagar... The attack occurred six days ago.*
2 V To **occur** also means to exist or be present. *Racism and sexism occur in all institutions.*
3 V+to If a thought or idea **occurs** to you, you suddenly think of it or realize it. *It had never occurred to her that he might insist on paying. ...the first question that occurred to me.*

occurrence /əkʌrəns/ **occurrences**; a formal word.
1 NC An **occurrence** is something that happens. *...weeks before the tragic occurrence.*
2 NU+SUPP The **occurrence** of something is the fact that it happens or exists. *We may reduce the occurrence of cancer by fifty per cent.*

ocean /əʊʃn/ **oceans**
1 N SING Some people refer to the sea as the **ocean**. *...in the depths of the ocean. ...an exposed rocky face overlooking the ocean.*
2 NC **Ocean** is part of the name of five very large areas of sea. *...the Atlantic Ocean.*

oceanic /əʊʃiænɪk/
ADJ ATTRIB **Oceanic** means belonging or relating to an ocean or to the sea. *...oceanic currents. ...oceanic life forms.*

oceanography /əʊʃənɒgrəfi/
NU **Oceanography** is the scientific study of the sea, sea currents, the rocks on the sea bed, and the fish and animals that live in the sea. *...oceanography and oil prospecting.* ◆ **oceanographer, oceanographers** NC *...an oceanographer on a diving expedition.*
◆ **oceanographic** /əʊʃəʳnəgræfɪk/ ADJ ATTRIB *It will help in weather forecasting and oceanographic research.*

Ochirbat, Punsalmaagiyn /pʊnsælmɑ:gɪn ɒtʃɪəbæt/
Punsalmaagiyn Ochirbat became the first President of Mongolia in 1990. He became a member of the Central Committee of the Mongolian People's Revolutionary Party (MPRP) in 1976 and served as Chairman of the Presidium of the People's Great Hural in 1990. In 1991 he resigned from the MPRP. Born: 1942.

ochre /əʊkə/; also spelt **ocher** in American English.
1 NU **Ochre** is coloured earth, usually red or yellow, that is used to make dyes and paints. *They used red ochre to stain their blankets.*
2 ADJ Something that is **ochre** in colour is yellowish orange. *...a plateau of red and ochre. ...green tiles, ochre paint, red wood.*

o'clock /əklɒk/
You use **o'clock** after numbers from one to twelve to refer to a time that is exactly at an hour, not before it or after it. *...at two o'clock in the morning.*

Oct.
Oct. is a written abbreviation for 'October'. *...Oct. 24 to 26.*

octagon /ɒktəgən/ **octagons**
NC An **octagon** is a flat geometrical shape that has eight straight sides.

octagonal /ɒktægənl/
ADJ Something that is **octagonal** has eight sides. *...the octagonal tower.*

octane /ɒkteɪn/
NU **Octane** is a chemical substance that exists in petrol and that is used to measure and describe the quality of petrol. *This petrol has a lower octane value, which means a drop in engine efficiency. ...high octane petrol.*

octave /ɒktɪv/ **octaves**
NC An **octave** is the musical interval between the first note and the eighth note of a scale. *Taylor has a classical music training and this is reputed to give her a three octave vocal range.*

October /ɒktəʊbə/
NU **October** is the tenth month of the year in the Western calendar. *...the reintroduction of quotas in October 1987.*

octogenarian /ɒktəʊdʒɪneəriən/ **octogenarians**
NC An **octogenarian** is a person who is between eighty and eighty-nine years old. *...Peng Zhen, another octogenarian veteran of the Long March.*

octopus /ɒktəpəs/ **octopuses**
NC An **octopus** is a sea creature with eight tentacles. *...substantial cuts in European catches of squid and octopus.*

oculist /ɒkjʊlɪst/ **oculists**
NC An **oculist** is an optician; used in American English.

odd /ɒd/ **odder, oddest; odds**
1 ADJ If you say that someone or something is **odd**, you mean that they are strange or unusual. *There's something odd about its shape... It was odd that she still lived at home.* ◆ **oddly** ADV *The drug made him behave quite oddly.* ◆ **oddness** NU *...the slightest oddness in her voice.*
2 ADJ ATTRIB **Odd** is used before a noun to indicate that the type or size of something is random or not important. *You can add bones, the odd vegetable, and herbs... You just need some odd scraps of wood and some material... I read the odd poem.*
3 ADJ ATTRIB You say that two things are **odd** when they do not belong to the same set or pair. *...odd socks.*
4 ADJ ATTRIB **Odd** numbers, such as 3, 17, and 129, cannot be divided exactly by the number two. *Put even numbers on one side, odd numbers on the other.*
5 ADV You use **odd** after a number to indicate that it is approximate; an informal use. *We first met twenty odd years ago.*
6 N PL You refer to the probability of something happening as the **odds** that it will happen. *The odds are that they will succeed... The odds are against children learning in this environment.*
● **Odd** is used in these phrases. ● In a group of people or things, the **odd** one out is the one that is different from all the others. *I was the odd one out; all my friends were in couples.* ● If you are at **odds** with someone, you are disagreeing or quarrelling with them. *She is at odds with her boss.* ● See also **oddly, odds and ends.**

oddball /ɒdbɔ:l/ **oddballs**
NC An **oddball** is a person who behaves in a way which most people find unusual or peculiar; an informal word. *...an oddball who painted rocks on the sea shore.*

oddity /ɒdəti/ **oddities**
1 NC An **oddity** is someone or something strange. *A career woman is still regarded as something of an oddity.*
2 NU The **oddity** of something is the fact that it is strange. *...the oddity of her behaviour.*

odd-job man, odd-job men
NC An **odd-job man** is a man who is paid to do various manual jobs, usually in somebody's home, for example clearing drains or cleaning windows.

oddly /ɒdli/
SUBMOD If you say that something is **oddly** true, you mean that it is true but that it is not what you expected. *...Hendrix's flamboyant and oddly romantic image... The mechanism of terror was oddly legalistic.*
● You use **oddly enough** to emphasize that what you

are saying is surprising. *Oddly enough, problems more often occur in the afternoon than the morning.*
● See also **odd**.

oddment /ˈɒdmənt/ **oddments**
NC **Oddments** are unimportant things of various kinds. *...old postcards and scraps, all sorts of oddments.*

odds and ends
N PL You can refer to a disorganized group of things of various kinds as **odds and ends**; an informal expression. *I had a trunk filled with various odds and ends that I would need for camping.*

odds-on
ADJ If there is an **odds-on** chance that something will happen, it is very likely that it will happen. *It was odds-on that there was no killer... Calderwood is the odds-on favourite to win.*

Oddsson, Davíd /ˈdɔːvɪd ˈɒdsɒn/
David Oddsson became Prime Minister of Iceland and Chairman of the Independence Party (IP) in 1991. He was formerly Mayor of Reykjavík. Born: 1948.

ode /əʊd/ **odes**
NC An **ode** is a poem, usually one that is written in praise of a particular person, thing, or event. *There are some poems that are almost loving odes to work while there are others that give a very bleak, very desperate view of working class life.*

odious /ˈəʊdiəs/
ADJ Someone or something that is **odious** is extremely unpleasant; a formal word. *The judge described the crime as odious. ...a pointless and odious infringement of civil rights.*

odium /ˈəʊdiəm/
NU **Odium** is dislike, disapproval, or hatred that people feel for a particular person, usually because of something that the person has done; a literary word. *Everyone who is involved was named and held up to public odium and ridicule.*

odor /ˈəʊdə/. See **odour**.

odorous /ˈəʊdərəs/
ADJ Something that is **odorous** has a particular smell, especially a pleasant one; a literary word. *...the sweetly odorous premises of big stores.*

odour /ˈəʊdə/ **odours**; spelt **odor** in American English.
NC An **odour** is a smell; a formal word. *...the warm odour of freshly-baked scones.*

odyssey /ˈɒdəsi/ **odysseys**
NC An **odyssey** is a long exciting journey in which a lot of things happen. *...dream holidays and youthful odysseys.*

oesophagus /iːˈsɒfəgəs/ **oesophaguses**; also spelt **esophagus**.
NC A person or animal's **oesophagus** is the part of their body that carries the food from their throat to their stomach. *...blood vessels in the oesophagus.*

oestrogen /ˈiːstrədʒən/; also spelt **estrogen**.
NU **Oestrogen** is a hormone produced in the ovaries of female humans and animals. Oestrogen controls the reproductive cycle and prepares the body for pregnancy. *...a sudden loss of oestrogen production brought on by the menopause.*

of /əv, ɒv/
1 PREP You use **of** after nouns referring to quantities, groups, amounts, or containers to show what kind of thing or substance is involved. *...a collection of essays. ...25 gallons of hot water. ...a big piece of apple pie. ...a cup of tea.*
2 PREP You use **of** to indicate what group something belongs to or what thing a part belongs to. *...the first of his many historic meetings with Winston Churchill... Many of the students come from other countries... Some of her jewellery was missing. ...the corners of a triangle.*
3 PREP You use **of** to indicate who or what something belongs to or is connected with. *...the religious beliefs of the peasant communities. ...the size of the crowd. ...the Mayor of Moscow... Imagine a child of yours doing that.*
4 PREP You use **of** to indicate what something relates to or concerns. *...their hopes of a reconciliation. ...the cause of the infection. ...cancer of the stomach. ...a map of Sweden. ...the Department of Employment.*

5 PREP You use **of** with some verbs to indicate something else involved in the action, especially when the action involves thinking, having a quality, or removal. *I couldn't think of any practical alternatives... He reminded me of my brother... The towel smelled of lavender... His body was secretly disposed of.*
6 PREP You use **of** with some adjectives to indicate the thing that a feeling or quality relates to. *I'm frightened of machines... He is capable of doing much better... I'm not wholly devoid of imagination.*
7 PREP You use **of** to indicate a person or thing involved in an action, as the performer or the thing or person affected. *...the murder of a British soldier. ...protection of the environment. ...the failure of the talks.*
8 PREP You use **of** to indicate what someone creates, affects, or has a particular attitude towards. *...the organizers of the conference.*
9 PREP You also use **of** to indicate a characteristic or quality that something has. *...men of matchless honesty... She helped him to a gin and tonic of giant proportions.*
10 PREP You use **of** to indicate a person's age. *...a boy of nineteen.*
11 PREP You use **of** to indicate the material that forms something. *...a disc of steel.*
12 PREP You also use **of** after a noun to give more exact information about it. *...strong feelings of jealousy. ...gifts of olive oil. ...the village of Fairwater Green. ...a price increase of 2%.*
13 PREP You also use **of** when mentioning a date, to indicate what month a day occurs in. *...the 17th of June.*
14 PREP You use **of** in front of dates and periods of time to indicate when something happened. *...the recession of 1974-75. ...the great conflicts of the past ten years.*
15 PREP You use **of** after words referring to the time that an event occurred to indicate what the event was. *...on the day of his inauguration. ...at the time of the earthquake.*
16 PREP If you say that it is a certain number of minutes of an hour, you mean that the time is that number of minutes before that hour; used in American English. *...at about quarter of seven Eastern time this evening... She turned her clock three hours ahead. It read two minutes of midnight.*
17 PREP You also use **of** to say what caused someone's death. *She died of pneumonia... The man later died of his injuries.*
18 PREP You also use **of** to indicate the person who performs an action when giving your opinion of it. *It was kind of her to take me in... That was nasty of him!*

of course. See **course**.

off /ɒf/
1 PREP or ADV When something is taken **off** something else or when it moves or comes **off**, it is removed or it moves away so that it is no longer on the other thing. *He took his hand off her arm... He was wiping sweat off his face... The paint was peeling off... He took off his jacket.*
2 PREP or ADV When you get **off** a bus, train, or plane, you get out of it. *The train stopped and people got off. ...when you got off the train at Kirkcaldy.*
3 ADV When you go **off**, you leave the place where you were. *He started the motor and drove off abruptly... When are you off to America?*
4 PREP If you keep **off** a street or piece of land, you do not go onto it. *I kept off the main roads.*
5 ADV A or ADV+ING You can say that someone is **off** somewhere or **off** doing something when they are in a different place from yourself. *She's off in Florida at some labour conference... A lot of men were off fighting.*
6 PREP If something is **off** a larger or more important place, it is near it. *...two islands off the mainland of China. ...a hotel just off the Via Condotti.*
7 ADV If an area of land is walled **off** or fenced **off**, it has a wall or fence around it or in front of it. *The area surrounding the office had been cordoned off.*

8 ADV If you fight something **off** or keep it **off**, you make it go away or prevent it. *I could no longer ward off thoughts of my imprisonment.*
9 ADV If you have some time **off**, you do not go to work for a period of time. *I would love to have a year off.* • If you are **off** work, you are not working because you are ill.
10 PREP or ADV If an amount of money is taken **off** the price of an item, the price is reduced by that amount. *Ford Motor Company has announced that it's cutting up to £2000 off the retail price of its cars... You can get 10 percent off with a student card.*
11 ADJ PRED or ADV If something such as a machine or an electric light is **off**, it is not functioning at the time you are talking about. *All the lights were off... Boylan switched off the headlights... He turned the radio off.*
12 ADJ PRED If an agreement or an arranged event is **off**, it has been cancelled. *I presume the deal is off.*
13 ADJ PRED If food or drink is **off**, it tastes and smells unpleasant because it is going bad. *The wine was off.*
14 PREP If you are **off** something, you have stopped using it or liking it; an informal use. *My father was off alcohol... He's gone off liberty.*
15 ADV If something is a long time **off**, it will not happen for a long time. *Control over the mind is not as far off as we think.*
16 **on and off**: see **on**.

offal /ɒfl/
NU **Offal** is the liver, kidneys, and other internal organs of animals, which are eaten by people or pets. *...beef offal from the brain and spinal cord.*

off-balance
1 ADV or ADJ PRED If someone is **off-balance**, they are not standing firmly and can easily fall or be knocked over. *She was running, off-balance, with her feet wrongly positioned... He was thrown off-balance.*
2 ADJ PRED or ADV You can also say someone is **off-balance** when they are not expecting a particular event or piece of news and are extremely surprised or upset by it. *He was pleased but still slightly off-balance and unable to capitalize on the new situation... Her casual announcement caught me completely off-balance.*

offbeat /ɒfbiːt/
ADJ Something that is **offbeat** is unusual and often humorous; an informal word. *We'll have no more offbeat dialogue.*

off-centre
ADJ or ADV If something is **off-centre**, it is not exactly in the middle of a space or surface. *The assembly can be mounted slightly off-centre so that it swings aside.*

off-chance
If you do something **on the off-chance**, you do it because you hope that it will succeed or be useful, although you think that this is unlikely. *He collected an enormous amount of information on the off-chance that he might later have a use for it.*

off-colour
ADJ PRED If you are **off-colour**, you are slightly ill. *He's been a bit off-colour for two days.*

off-day, off-days
NC If you have an **off-day**, you do not work or perform as well as usual. *We all have our off-days, of course.*

off duty
ADJ When someone who works unusual hours, such as a nurse, is **off duty**, they are not working. *What do you do when you're off duty? ...an off-duty policeman.*

offence /əfɛns/ **offences**; spelt **offense** in American English.
1 NC An **offence** is a crime; a formal use. *The illegal use of force is a criminal offence... They were arrested for drug offences.*
2 NU If you give **offence**, you upset or embarrass someone. *The play is liable to give offence to many people... That will cause further offence and resentment.*
3 If you **take offence**, you are upset by something that someone says or does. *He was always so quick to take offence... The feminists took offence.*

offend /əfɛnd/ **offends, offending, offended**
1 VO If you **offend** someone, you upset or embarrass them. *I'm sorry if I offended you... Mr Rushdie's book*

offended many Muslims. ◆ **offended** ADJ PRED *Clarissa looked offended.*
2 V O or V+*against* If something **offends** a law, rule, or principle, it breaks it; a formal use. *This process offends every known natural law... It would offend against her conventions.*
3 V To **offend** also means to commit a crime; a formal use. *...criminals who offend again when they're released.*

offender /əfɛndə/ **offenders**
1 NC An **offender** is a person who has committed a crime; a formal use. *In 1965, 42% of convicted offenders ended up in prison. ...thieves, vandals, sex offenders and muggers. ...the harsh treatment of young offenders.*
2 NC You can refer to one of a number of people or things that cause a particular kind of harm as an **offender**. *Television is the worst offender of the lot.*

offending /əfɛndɪŋ/
ADJ ATTRIB You use **offending** to describe something that is causing a problem. *He tapped the offending bulge with a pencil... He has employed a company to fit wheelclamps on offending vehicles.*

offense /əfɛns/. See **offence**.

offensive /əfɛnsɪv/ **offensives**
1 ADJ Something that is **offensive** upsets or embarrasses people because it is rude or insulting. *That was an extremely offensive remark.* ◆ **offensively** ADV *The examiners were often offensively rude.*
2 NC An **offensive** is a strong attack. *...the enemy's air offensive. ...a propaganda offensive against the government.* ▶ Also ADJ *We took immediate offensive action.*

offer /ɒfə/ **offers, offering, offered**
1 V O+*to* or V O O If you **offer** something to someone, you ask them if they would like to have it or to use it. *Japan has offered two million dollars worth of aid. ...an apple which he offered to his friend... I was offered a place at Harvard University... Leeds offered £1.5 million for the players.*
2 V+*to*-INF or V-QUOTE If you **offer** to do something, you say that you are willing to do it. *Gopal offered to take us to Mysore... 'We could take it for you,' offered Dolly.*
3 NC An **offer** is something that someone says they will give you or do for you if you want them to. *She accepted the offer of a cigarette. ...Kirk's offer to take me to the clinic.* • If someone **makes an offer** for something, they offer to buy it at a particular price. *Terry Venables has confirmed that his consortium have made an offer for the club.*
4 V O or V O O If you **offer** someone information, advice, or praise, you give it to them. *They didn't ask Liebermann's name and Liebermann didn't offer it. ...offering him advice about accommodation... Kunta offered her no explanation for his behaviour.*
5 V O or V O O If something **offers** a service, opportunity, or product, it provides it. *The new car plant offers the prospect of 5,000 jobs. ...the facilities and equipment offered by the playgroup... It offers the listening public a rare example of what they want.*
6 NC+SUPP An **offer** in a shop is a specially low price for a product, or something extra that you get by buying the product. *...cut price offers. ...special offers.*
7 If something is **on offer**, it is available to be used or bought. *...the weird and wonderful range of gear on offer.*

offering /ɒfəʳrɪŋ/ **offerings**
1 NC You can refer to something that has been specially provided as an **offering**. *...last week's offerings of caviar and smoked salmon.*
2 NC An **offering** is also something that is offered to a god as a sacrifice. *Whenever they have to go to worship a divinity, they produce an offering of coca leaves.*

off-guard
ADV or ADJ If someone is caught **off-guard**, they are not expecting a surprise or danger that suddenly occurs. *...the near disaster when the country was caught off-guard at the start of the Middle East War... It is easy to be taken off-guard.*

off-hand

1 ADJ If someone behaves in an **off-hand** way, they are not friendly or polite, and show little interest. *...the off-hand contempt with which she treated most men.*
2 ADV SEN or ADJ **Off-hand** means without needing to think very hard. *Off-hand, I can think of three examples. ...an off-hand remark at a social gathering.*

office /ɒfɪs/ **offices**

1 NC An **office** is a room or a part of a building where people work sitting at desks. *You didn't go to the office today?... On the wall of his office was a large map.*
2 NC An **office** is also a department of an organization, especially the government, where people deal with a particular kind of administrative work. *...your local education office. ...the tax office.*
3 NC An **office** is also a small building or room where people can go for information, tickets, or a service of some kind. *...the ticket office. ...the enquiry office.*
4 NU Someone who holds **office** has an important job or a position of authority in government or in an organization. *The President of the BMA holds office for one year. ...Baldwin's second term of office as Premier.*
5 NC A doctor's **office** is the room or house where he or she works; used in American English. *I walked into the doctor's office.*

office automation

NU **Office automation** is used to describe all the electronic equipment used in an office, for example computers, printers, and word processors.

office-holder, office-holders

NC An **office-holder** is a person who has an important official position in an organization; a formal word. *...a former office-holder in the Oxford Union... The two principal office-holders wield enormous power.*

officer /ɒfɪsə/ **officers**

1 NC In the armed forces, an **officer** is a person in a position of authority. *...a retired army officer.*
2 NC People with responsible positions in organizations, especially government organizations, are also referred to as **officers**. *...a Careers Officer. ...prison officers.*
3 NC or VOCATIVE Members of the police force are sometimes referred to as **officers**. *Inspector Darroway was the officer in charge of the investigation... Listen, Officer, why do you need all this information?*

official /əfɪʃl/ **officials**

1 ADJ Something that is **official** is approved by the government or by someone else in authority. *The official figures were published in January... Arabic is the official language of Morocco. ...the official opening of the new bridge.* ◆ **officially** ADV *The war officially ended the following year.*
2 ADJ ATTRIB **Official** is used to describe things which are done or used by people in authority as part of their job or position. *...an official visit to Tanzania. ...the Prime Minister's official residence.*
3 ADJ ATTRIB The **official** reason or explanation for a particular thing is something that is probably incorrect but that people are told because the truth is embarrassing. *The announcement came that he was to retire; the official explanation was 'for health reasons'... Visiting his aunt was only the official motive.* ◆ **officially** ADV SEN *Officially she shares a flat with some girlfriend.*
4 NC An **official** is a person who holds a position of authority in an organization. *...government officials. ...trade union officials.*

officialdom /əfɪʃldəm/

NU You use **officialdom** to refer to officials in government and other organizations, especially when you think they are very slow and unhelpful, or when you disapprove of their rules and regulations. *This leaves the individual at the mercy of officialdom.*

official receiver

N SING The **official receiver** is the person appointed by the government to deal with the affairs of a person or company after they have gone bankrupt. *Investors crammed into the hall to hear the official receiver set out how much money is available to meet their claims.*

officiate /əfɪʃieɪt/ **officiates, officiating, officiated**

V When someone **officiates** at a ceremony or formal occasion, he or she is in charge and performs the official part of the ceremony. *Who officiated at your wedding?*

officious /əfɪʃəs/

ADJ Someone who is **officious** is too eager to tell people what to do. *He stepped forward, stern and officious. ...officious interference by managers.*

offing /ɒfɪŋ/

If you say that something is **in the offing**, you mean that it is likely to happen soon. *War was already in the offing.*

off-key

ADJ If you say that music is **off-key**, you mean that it is not in tune. *Sheila was singing loudly in an off-key soprano.*

off-licence, off-licences

NC An **off-licence** is a shop which sells alcoholic drinks. *...buying a bottle of wine at an off-licence.*

off line

ADJ A part of a computer system that is **off line** is not connected directly to the central processing unit of the computer for a time.

offload /ɒfləʊd/ **offloads, offloading, offloaded**

1 VO If you **offload** something that you do not want, you get rid of it, especially by giving it to someone else; an informal use. *They use export subsidies to help offload their excess food, cut-price, in world markets.*
2 V-PASS When goods **are offloaded** from a container or vehicle, they are removed from it, usually after being transported somewhere. *The cargo was offloaded in the Dutch port of Vlaardingen... A boatload of guns was offloaded in Jamaica just before Christmas... The oil is offloaded into foreign tankers.*

off-peak

ADJ ATTRIB **Off-peak** things are available at a time when there is little demand for them, so that they are cheaper than usual. *...those who travel in off-peak hours and for short journeys. ...off-peak electricity.*

off-putting

ADJ You describe someone as **off-putting** when you find them rather unpleasant and do not want to know them better. *She has a rather off-putting manner... His behaviour is deliberately intended to be off-putting.*

off season

N SING or N+N The **off season** is the part of the year when not many people go on holiday and when things such as hotels and plane tickets are often cheaper. *We like to go there in the off season... Off-season tickets are a lot cheaper.*

offset /ɒfsɛt/ **offsets, offsetting.** The form **offset** is used in the present tense and is also the past tense and past participle.

VO If one thing is **offset** by another, its effect is reduced by the other thing, so there is no great advantage or disadvantage as a result. *They argued that their wage increases would be offset by higher prices.*

offshoot /ɒfʃuːt/ **offshoots**

NC+SUPP If one thing is an **offshoot** of another thing, it has developed from the other thing. *It's called Accelerated Learning and it's an offshoot of an idea that began in Bulgaria... Afrikaans is an offshoot of Dutch.*

offshore /ɒfʃɔː/

ADJ or ADV Something that is **offshore** is situated in the sea near to the coast. *...offshore oil terminals... The boats waited offshore.*

offside /ɒfsaɪd/

1 ADJ or ADV If a player in a game of football or hockey is **offside**, they have broken the rules by moving too far forward. *Tim Breacher found a way through the offside trap with a long ball to Stein... Attacking players in line with the last outfield player will no longer be ruled offside.*
2 N SING The **offside** of a vehicle is the side farthest from the edge of the road when you are driving normally. *He leant across to roll down his offside window... The mini had touched the offside of the truck with its nearside wing.*

offspring /ˈɒfsprɪŋ/; **offspring** is both the singular and the plural form.
NC Your **offspring** are your children; a formal word. *How do parents pass genes on to their offspring?*

offstage /ɒfˈsteɪdʒ/
1 ADJ ATTRIB or ADV **Offstage** describes the sounds in a play that happen in the part of a theatre that the audience cannot see but can hear. *...off-stage thunder... There were tremendous roars off stage.*
2 ADV or ADJ **Offstage** also describes the behaviour of actors and actresses in real life, when they are not acting in a play or film. *Offstage she is direct, honest, and forceful. ...Ernest's off-stage voice.*

off-the-cuff
ADJ An **off-the-cuff** remark is spoken without being planned or practised in advance. *His off-the-cuff replies convulsed the audience.*

off-the-peg
ADJ or ADV **Off-the-peg** clothes are bought in a shop and not made especially for a particular person. *This street is notable for off-the-peg gents' clothing... Hilary bought a wedding dress off the peg at C & A, and flew out to join him.*

off-the-record
ADJ ATTRIB or ADV **Off-the-record** remarks and statements are made unofficially and are not intended to be made public. *...an off-the-record chat. ...an off-the-record briefing to the press... Senior officials have talked, off the record, of a 'messy compromise'.*

off-white
ADJ Something that is **off-white** is not pure white, but slightly grey or yellow. *...a tatty off-white dress.*

oft /ɒft/
ADV **Oft** means the same as 'often' and is usually used in compounds such as 'oft-repeated,' or 'oft-heard'; a formal word. *...the oft-quoted statement that 'numbers always lie'.*

often /ˈɒfn, ˈɒftən/
1 ADV If something happens **often**, it happens many times or much of the time. *We often get very wet cold winters here... It's not often you meet someone who's really interested.*
2 How **often** is used to ask questions about how frequently something happens. *How often do you need to weigh the baby?*
3 If you say that something happens **every so often**, you mean that it happens occasionally. *Every so often, she spends a weekend in London.*

ogle /ˈəʊgl/ **ogles, ogling, ogled**
VO If someone **ogles** someone else, they stare at them, especially in a way that indicates a sexual interest; used showing disapproval. *The men ogled her lasciviously. ...the ladies ogling their hero.*

ogre /ˈəʊgə/ **ogres**
1 NC An **ogre** is a character in fairy stories who is large, cruel, and frightening. *...a horrible tale about an ogre who hangs his human meat up in his cellar.*
2 NC An **ogre** is also a person or situation that you find very frightening. *I grew up believing my father was an ogre.*

oh /əʊ/
1 You use **oh** to introduce a response or a comment on something that has just been said. *'How's your brother then?'—'Oh, he's fine.'... 'I have a flat in London.'—'Oh yes, whereabouts?'*
2 You also use **oh** to express a feeling such as surprise, pain, annoyance, or joy. *'He wants to see you immediately,' I said. 'Oh!' she said. Her smile vanished.* ● See also **o**.

ohm /əʊm/ **ohms**
NC An **ohm** is a unit which is used to measure electrical resistance; a technical term in physics. *...a resistance of forty ohms.*

O.H.M.S. /ˌəʊ eɪtʃ em ˈes/
O.H.M.S. is an abbreviation for 'On Her Majesty's Service' or 'On His Majesty's Service'. It is used on official letters from British or Commonwealth government offices.

oil /ɔɪl/ **oils, oiling, oiled**
1 NU **Oil** is a smooth, thick, sticky liquid used as a fuel and for lubricating machines. Oil is found underground. *They are trying to increase energy efficiency and reduce their dependence on oil... The picture is further complicated by uncertainties over the oil price and the prospect of higher US interest rates.*
2 VO If you **oil** a machine, you put oil into it in order to make it work smoothly. *He has to oil and wind the clock.*
3 NU **Oil** is also a smooth, thick, sticky liquid made from plants or animals. Some oils are used for cooking. *...cooking oil. ...olive oil.*
4 N PL **Oils** are oil paintings or oil paints. *...an exhibition of watercolours and oils by Turner. ...trying to capture the scene in oils.*

oilcloth /ˈɔɪlklɒθ/
NU **Oilcloth** is a cotton fabric with a shiny waterproof surface, formerly used for tablecloths or other covers. *He wrapped the painting in a big square of oilcloth.*

oilfield /ˈɔɪlfiːld/ **oilfields**
NC An **oilfield** is an area of land or part of the seabed where oil is found and from which it is removed. *Those oilfields are still out of production... They also attacked installations in an oilfield.*

oil-fired
ADJ Things that are **oil-fired**, for example radiators or central heating systems, use oil as a fuel. *...back-up coal and oil-fired power stations were brought into operation.*

oil paint, oil paints
N U or N PL **Oil paint** is a thick paint used by artists. It is made from a coloured powder and an oil called linseed oil. *He developed a technique for working rapidly in oil paint, on paper, in the open air. ...a box of oil paints and easel.*

oil painting, oil paintings
NC An **oil painting** is a painting that has been painted using oil paint. *...the theft of a valuable oil painting by the French Impressionist Edouard Manet.*

oil platform, oil platforms
NC An **oil platform** is a structure in the sea that people use as a base when drilling for or extracting oil. *...helicopters operating from an offshore oil platform.*

oilrig /ˈɔɪlrɪg/ **oilrigs**
NC An **oilrig** is a structure on land or in the sea that people use as a base when drilling for or extracting oil. *Most of the oilrig crew were winched to safety by helicopter.*

oilseed rape /ˌɔɪlsiːd ˈreɪp/
NU **Oilseed rape** is a plant with bright yellow flowers whose seeds are crushed to make oil for cooking. *Oilseed rape in Europe is a relatively important oil crop grown on 2 million hectares.*

oilskin /ˈɔɪlskɪn/ **oilskins**
NC An **oilskin** is a coat, pair of trousers, or other piece of clothing that is made from thick waterproof cotton. *...sea boots and oilskins.*

oil slick, oil slicks
NC An **oil slick** is a layer of oil that is floating on top of the sea or a lake because oil has accidentally come out of a ship or container. *Emergency services are fighting to contain an oil slick sixteen miles long.*

oil tanker, oil tankers
NC An **oil tanker** is a ship, lorry, or other vehicle that is used for transporting oil. *...oil tankers and other merchant vessels.*

oil well, oil wells
NC An **oil well** is a hole which is drilled into the ground or the seabed in order to remove the oil which lies underground. *Once an oil well has been drilled it pays to keep the production going regardless.*

oily /ˈɔɪli/
1 ADJ Something that is **oily** is covered with oil or contains oil. *...oily rags... Oily chemicals produced by the intense heat could poison local water supplies... Eat plenty of fish, preferably oily fish such as mackerel.*
2 ADJ An **oily** substance looks or feels like oil. *There was an oily streak on her stocking.*
3 ADJ Someone who is **oily** is unpleasant because they flatter people or behave in an excessively polite way. *...an oily smile.*

oink /ɔɪŋk/
Oink is used in writing to represent the sound that a pig utters.

ointment /ɔɪntmənt/ **ointments**
N MASS An **ointment** is a smooth thick substance that is put on sore skin or a wound to help it heal. ...*eye ointments.* ...*a tube of sunburn ointment.*

OK /əʊkeɪ/. See **okay**.

okay /əʊkeɪ/; also spelt **OK**; an informal word.
1 ADJ or ADV If you say that something is **okay**, you mean that it is acceptable. *I'll have another coffee and then I'll be going, if that's okay... She wanted to know if the trip was OK with the government... I asked Jenny how she thought it all went. 'Okay,' she said.*
2 ADJ PRED If you say that someone is **okay**, you mean that they are safe and well. *'Where's Jane?'—'Just back there. She's okay. Just shocked.'*
3 You can say **okay** when you are agreeing to something or checking whether someone else understands or agrees. *'I'll be back at a quarter past one.'—'OK. I'll see you then.'... I'll be back in fifteen minutes. OK?*
4 You can also use **okay** to indicate to someone that you want to start talking about something else or doing something else. *Okay, do you mind if we speak a bit of German now?*

okra /əʊkrə/
NU **Okra** is a vegetable that consists of long green pods. ...*growing tomatoes, aubergine, okra and other vegetables.*

old /əʊld/ **older, oldest**
1 ADJ Someone who is **old** has lived for many years. ...*his old mother... He thought he'd be too old for the job.*
2 ADJ **Old** is also used in questions or statements about age. *How old are you?... She is twenty-one years old today... She was a couple of years older than me.*
3 N PL You can refer to people who are old as the **old**. ...*the particular needs of the old and infirm.*
4 ADJ Something that is **old** has existed for a long time, and is perhaps in bad condition. ...*a massive old building of crumbling red brick. ...an old joke. ...wardrobes full of old clothes.*
5 ADJ ATTRIB **Old** is also used of things which are no longer used or which have been replaced by something else. *I was directed into the old dining room. ...his old job at the publishing company.*
6 ADJ ATTRIB If someone is an **old** friend of yours, they have been your friend for a long time. ...*an old friend, military classmate, and political ally... He particularly defended an old friend of twenty years.*
7 ADJ ATTRIB You can use **old** to express affection or familiarity when talking to or about someone you know; an informal use. *I got a letter from good old Lewis.*
● **Old** is used in these phrases. ● **In the old days** means many years ago, before things changed. *Hong Kong was a shopper's paradise in the old days.* ● You use **any old** to emphasize that the quality or type of something is not important; an informal expression. *Any old board will do.*

old-age pensioner, old-age pensioners
NC An **old-age pensioner** is the same as an OAP. ...*a scheme to help poorer old-age pensioners.*

old boy, old boys
1 NC An **old boy** of a particular school or college is a man who used to be a pupil there. ...*an old boy's club.*
● The **old-boy network** is the informal arrangement in which people who knew each other at public school or university use their positions of influence to help each other; used showing disapproval. *He arrived on the board through the old-boy network.*
2 NC An **old boy** is also any old or middle-aged man; an old-fashioned, informal use. *She can twist the old boy round her little finger... Some of the old boys simply have long memories.*

olden /əʊldən/
In the olden days means long ago in the past. *In the olden days children were spanked a lot, and nobody thought much about it.*

old-fashioned
1 ADJ Something that is **old-fashioned** is no longer considered appropriate in style or design, because it has been replaced by something more modern. ...*old-fashioned plastic-rimmed glasses.*
2 ADJ If someone is **old-fashioned**, their behaviour and beliefs are those which were common or accepted in the past, but are no longer common. *He was a kind, gentle, old-fashioned romantic. ...an old-fashioned and very puritanical view of what science is. ...old-fashioned authoritarian methods.*

old flame, old flames
NC An **old flame** is someone who you once had a romantic relationship with. ...*an old flame of Charlotte's.*

old girl, old girls
1 NC An **old girl** of a particular school or college is a woman who used to be a pupil there.
2 NC An **old girl** is also any old or middle-aged woman; an old-fashioned, informal use. *The old girl is slightly dotty.*

old guard
N COLL When people talk about the **old guard**, they are referring to a group of people who have worked together for a long time and who they think are rather old-fashioned. *Tensions began to arise between the old guard and some of their newer members.*

old hand, old hands
NC An **old hand** is a person who is very skilled at something because they have a lot of experience. ...*a few old hands in the press corps.*

old hat. See **hat**.

old maid, old maids
NC People sometimes refer to an old or middle-aged woman as an **old maid** when they think she has never been married or had a sexual relationship, and want to show that they disapprove of that fact; an offensive expression. *The worst fate in the world, she thinks, is to become an old maid, always on the sidelines of life.*

old man
N SING Someone's **old man** is their father or their husband; an informal expression. *The first letter I got from my old man told me how proud he was of me.*

old master, old masters
NC An **old master** is a painting by a famous painter of the past. *Wealthy individuals and institutions looked on works of art, particularly old masters, as valuable assets.*

old school tie
NU **Old school tie** refers to the situation in which people who knew each other at public school or university use their positions of influence to help each other; used showing disapproval.

old-style
ADJ ATTRIB **Old-style** means relating to a previous time or way of doing things. ...*a return to old-style family values... President Gorbachev has spoken of the defeat of old-style communism in the Soviet Union.*

Old Testament
N PROP The **Old Testament** is the first part of the Christian Bible. ...*what happened to Adam and Eve in the Old Testament. ...Old Testament prophets.*

old-timer, old-timers; used in informal American English.
1 NC An **old-timer** is someone who has been in a particular place or job for a long time. *The real problem is how to gracefully remove the old-timers from positions of political power.*
2 **Old-timer** is also used to refer to an old man. ...*a grizzled old-timer.*

old wives' tale, old wives' tales
NC An **old wives' tale** is a traditional idea which is believed by many people but is usually incorrect.

old woman, old women
NC If you call someone, especially a man, an **old woman**, you mean that they are very fussy; an old-fashioned expression. *He's a bit of an old woman.*

oleander /əʊliændə/ **oleanders**
NC An **oleander** is an evergreen tree or shrub. It has white, pink, or purple flowers.

O level /əʊ levl/ **O levels**
NC An **O level** is an educational qualification in a

particular subject which used to be taken by some British schoolchildren at the age of 15 or 16. O levels were replaced by GCSEs in Britain in 1988. *...O level and CSE exams.*

olfactory /ɒlfæktəᵒri/
ADJ ATTRIB **Olfactory** means concerned with the sense of smell; a technical term in biology. *...delicate olfactory nerves... It arouses their olfactory sense.*

oligarchy /ɒlɪgɑːki/ **oligarchies**
1 NC An **oligarchy** is a small group of people who control and run a particular country or organization. *...the ageing oligarchy that constitutes its leadership.*
2 NU **Oligarchy** is a situation in which a country or organization is run by an oligarchy. *The attack, a statement said, was a protest against imperialism and oligarchy in the region.*

olive /ɒlɪv/ **olives**
1 NC An **olive** is a small green or black fruit with a bitter taste. *Officials are concerned by the fall-off in the country's exports of olives... There has been damage to olive trees in Tunisia.*
2 ADJ Something that is **olive** or **olive green** is yellowish-green. *They are now housed in olive green tents.*

olive branch
N SING If you offer an **olive branch** to someone, you say or do something in order to show that you want to end a disagreement or quarrel; a formal expression. *They conceded the point, accepting his olive branch, and we all shook hands... I shall extend the olive branch to that poor misguided child.*

olive oil
NU **Olive oil** is oil obtained by pressing olives. It is put on salads or used for cooking. *...their traditional exports, wine, olive oil and citrus fruits.*

-ological /-əlɒdʒɪkl/
SUFFIX **-ological** is used to replace '-ology' at the end of nouns in order to form adjectives that describe something as relating to a particular science or subject. In this dictionary, adjectives of this kind are not usually defined but are treated with the related nouns. *...a geological survey. ...the Zoological Society.*

-ologist /-ɒlədʒɪst/ **-ologists**
SUFFIX **-ologist** is used to replace '-ology' at the end of nouns in order to form other nouns that refer to people concerned with a particular science or subject. In this dictionary, nouns of this kind are not usually defined but are treated with the nouns ending in '-ology'. *...a well known anthropologist. ...amateur geologists.*

Olszewski, Jan /jæn ɒlʃɛfski/
Jan Olszewski became Prime Minister of Poland in 1991. He was a member of the Central Committee of the Polish United Workers' Party (PZPR) from 1986 to 1989, and is now a member of the Centre Alliance.

Olympic /əlɪmpɪk/
ADJ ATTRIB **Olympic** means relating to the Olympic Games. *...an Olympic finalist... He is to join the British Olympic Association as their new technical advisory officer.*

Olympic Games
N PL The **Olympic Games** or the **Olympics** are a set of international sports competitions which take place every four years, each time in a different country. *The City of Manchester was nominated as the British Bid to host the 1996 Olympic Games... He won six gold medals at the Munich Olympics in 1972.*

Oman /əʊmɑːn/
The **Sultanate of Oman** is a country on the Arabian Peninsula. It became independent of Britain in 1951 and was known as Muscat and Oman until 1970. There are no political parties. Qaboos bin Said became Sultan and Prime Minister in 1970. Oman is a member of the Arab League and the Gulf Co-operation Council. It exports oil. ◆ **Omani** /əʊmɑːni/ N, ADJ
▪ *per capita GNP:* US$5,070 ▪ *religion:* Islam (mainly Ibadi), Hinduism ▪ *language:* Arabic (official) ▪ *currency:* rial ▪ *capital:* Muscat ▪ *population:* 1 million (1989) ▪ *size:* 300,000 square kilometres.

ombudsman /ɒmbʊdzmən/ **ombudsmen** /ɒmbʊdzmən/
NC An **ombudsman** is an official who is appointed by a government or other large organization to investigate

complaints that people make against them. *There should be perhaps an international ombudsman, or some sort of human rights tribunal.*

omelette /ɒmlət/ **omelettes**; spelt **omelet** in American English.
NC An **omelette** is a food made by beating eggs and cooking them in a flat pan. *He received steak and omelettes to eat.*

omen /əʊmen/ **omens**
NC An **omen** is something that is thought to indicate what is going to happen in the future. *An eclipse of the sun is the worst of bad omens.*

ominous /ɒmɪnəs/
ADJ Something that is **ominous** is worrying or frightening because it makes you think that something unpleasant is going to happen. *There was an ominous silence.* ◆ **ominously** ADV *Black clouds were piling up ominously.*

omission /əmɪʃn/ **omissions**
NCorNU An **omission** is the act of not including something or not doing something. *The reports were full of errors and omissions... There is one notable omission from Mr Major's cabinet. ...the omission of women from these studies.*

omit /əmɪt/ **omits, omitting, omitted**; a formal word.
1 VO If you **omit** something, you do not include it. *Two groups were omitted from the survey—the old and women... He deliberately omitted them from the list.*
2 V+to-INF If you **omit** to do something, you do not do it. *He omitted to say whether the men were armed.*

omnibus /ɒmnɪbəs/ **omnibuses**
1 NC An **omnibus** is a written document such as a book which contains a large collection of stories or articles, often by the same person or about the same subject. *...the Sherlock Holmes omnibus. ...an omnibus trade bill which contains strong measures against countries practising unfair trade.*
2 NC An **omnibus** is also a radio or television broadcast which contains two or more similar programmes that were originally broadcast separately. *...the omnibus edition of 'The Archers'.*
3 NC An **omnibus** is the same as a **bus**; an old-fashioned use. *In front of the City Hotel an omnibus was stopped.*

omnipotence /ɒmnɪpətəns/
NU **Omnipotence** is the state of having total authority or power; a formal word. *...God's omnipotence. ...the omnipotence of the army.*

omnipotent /ɒmnɪpətənt/
ADJ Someone or something that is **omnipotent** has complete power over things or people; a formal word. *...an omnipotent central committee. ...an omnipotent and perfect deity.*

omnipresent /ɒmnɪprɛznt/
ADJ Something that is **omnipresent** is present everywhere or affects everyone at the same time; a formal word. *The fear of failure was omnipresent. ...the omnipresent coal dust.*

omniscient /ɒmnɪsiənt/
ADJ Someone who is **omniscient** knows or seems to know everything; a formal word. *...faith in an omniscient God.*

omnivorous /ɒmnɪvəᵒrəs/
ADJ An **omnivorous** person or animal eats both meat and plants; a technical term in biology. *...an omnivorous diet.*

on /ɒn, ɒn/
1 PREP If you are standing or resting **on** something, it is underneath you and is supporting your weight. *They were sitting on chairs. ...a cow grazing on a hill... Put the tray on the bed, please.*
2 PREP If you are **on** a bus, train, or plane, you are travelling in it. *Afterwards they got on a bus and went to the cinema... The freed men were put on a plane to take them to their homes.*
3 PREP If something is **on** a surface or object, it is stuck to it or attached to it. *...the posters on the walls. ...the light on the ceiling. ...the buttons on a shirt.*
4 PREP If there is something **on** a piece of paper, it has been written or printed there. *...the table on the*

back page of the book... She wrote it down on a piece of paper. ...a card with his name on.
5 ADV When you put **on** a piece of clothing, you place it over a part of your body in order to wear it. *She put her shoes on... She had her coat on.*
6 PREP You can say that you have something **on** you if you are carrying it in your pocket or in a bag. *...a political leaflet from a Kurdish exile group was found on him... I didn't have any money on me.*
7 PREP If a building is **on** a road, it is next to it. *The house is on Pacific Avenue.*
8 PREP You can use **on** when mentioning the area of land where someone works or lives. *My father worked on a farm.*
9 PREP If you hurt yourself **on** something, you hurt yourself by accidentally hitting it with a part of your body. *He cut himself on the gatepost.*
10 PREP If something happens **on** a particular day or date, that is when it happens. *...on the first day of term. ...on Thursday night... Caro was born on April 10th.*
11 PREP You use **on** when mentioning an event that was followed by another one; a formal use. *'It's so unfair,' Clarissa said on her return... On being called 'young lady', she laughed.*
12 PREP If something is done on an instrument, machine, or system, it is done using that instrument, machine, or system. *...waltzes played on the violin... His first film was shown on television yesterday... They work on a rota system.*
13 ADV If something such as a machine or an electric light is **on**, it is being used or ready to be used. *A tap had been left on... The television set remained on.*
14 PREP Books, discussions, remarks, or thoughts **on** a particular subject are concerned with that subject. *...books on philosophy, art, and religion... They occasionally commented on how good her work was. ...brooding on the events that had taken place.*
15 PREP If something affects you, you can say that it has an effect **on** you. *The effect on the environment could be considerable.*
16 PREP Taxes or profits that are obtained from something are referred to as taxes or profits **on** it. *...a new sales tax on luxury goods... Profits on books will be down... You pay interest on your mortgage.*
17 PREP To spend money on something means to buy it or to pay for repairs to it. *...the amount of money he spent on clothes... Why waste money on them?*
18 PREP To spend time **on** something means to spend time doing it or making it. *I spent a lot of time on this picture.*
19 PREP You use **on** with some verbs when mentioning something else involved in the action, especially when the action involves attacking, relying, or using. *The dog turned on her and bit her... Never rely on your memory... Beveridge's calculations were all based on 1938 prices.*
20 ADV You use **on** to indicate that someone or something continues, progresses, or moves forward. *I read on... He urged them on as they charged up Sayer Street.*
21 PREP If you are **on** a council or committee, you are a member of it. *Although Hong Kong is on the committee, its representatives are in a minority.*
22 PREP Someone who is **on** a drug or who lives **on** a particular kind of food regularly consumes it. *She was on pills of various kinds.*
23 PREP If you are **on** a particular kind of income, that is the kind of income you have. *...people on a low income.*
24 ADV If an event is **on**, it is happening. *The war was on then... What's on at the Odeon?*
25 PREP When you pay for something that someone else receives, you can say that it is **on** you; an informal use. *The drinks were always on him.*
26 ADV If you say that someone goes **on** at you or **on** about something, you mean they are talking to you in an irritating or boring way; an informal use. *He's always on at me about the way I dress... He's always on about yoga... What are you on about?*
● **On** is used in these phrases. ● If you **have a lot on**, you are very busy. If you **do not have much on**, you

are not busy; an informal expression. *I asked her to do it but she's got such a lot on that she won't have time.* ● If you say that something happens **on and off**, you mean that it happens occasionally. *...almost six years of talks on and off.* ● If you say that something is **not on**, you mean that it is not acceptable and should not happen. *That sort of writing just isn't on.*
● **and so on**: see so.

once /wʌns/
1 ADV If something happens **once**, it happens one time only, or one time within a particular period of time. *I've been out with him once, that's all... Some trees only bear fruit once every twenty-five years.*
2 ADV If something was **once** true, it was true at some time in the past, but is no longer true. *Texas was once ruled by Mexico.*
3 CONJ If something happens **once** another thing has happened, it happens immediately afterwards. *Once inside her flat, she glanced at the clock... Once the sun had set, the air turned cold.*
● **Once** is used in these phrases. ● If you do something **at once**, you do it immediately. *I knew at once that something was wrong.* ● If several things happen **at once** or **all at once**, they all happen at the same time. *Everybody is talking at once.* ● If something happens **once again** or **once more**, it happens again. *Companies are once again queueing to join the scheme... She wanted to see him once more before she died.* ● If you have done something **once or twice**, you have done it before, but not very often. *She had been to London once or twice before.* ● If something happens **once in a while**, it happens occasionally. *Once in a while she'd give me some lilacs to take home.* ● If you say that something happened **for once**, you are emphasizing that it does not usually happen. *For once Castle went without his lunch.* ● If something happens **once and for all**, it happens completely or finally. *They had to be defeated once and for all.*
● **Once upon a time** is used to indicate that something happened or existed a long time ago; used especially at the beginning of children's stories. *Once upon a time there were three princes.*

once-over
If you **give** someone or something **the once-over**, you quickly look at or inspect them; an informal expression. *I'll give it the once-over when you've finished.*

oncoming /ˈɒnkʌmɪŋ/
ADJ ATTRIB **Oncoming** means moving towards you. *...oncoming traffic. ...an oncoming cyclone.*

one /wʌn/ **ones**
1 **One** is the number 1. *...one hundred miles... Of these four suggestions, only one is correct... The two friends share one job... The road goes from one side of the town to the other.*
2 PRON You also use **one** to refer to a particular thing or person. *These trousers aren't as tight as the other ones... buying old houses and building new ones... Oh, that's a difficult one to answer, isn't it?*
3 DET You can use **one** when referring to a time in the past or the future. For example, if you say that you did something **one** day, you mean that you did it on a day in the past. If you say that you will do something **one** day, you mean that you will do it on a day in the future. *One evening, I had a visit from Henry Cox... One day you and I must have a long talk together.*
4 PRON You can use **one** to refer to people in general; a formal use. *One can eat well here... The law should guard one against this sort of thing... One's never quite sure exactly how things are going to turn out.*
5 PRON **One** is also used by a speaker or writer to refer to himself or herself; a formal use. *Naturally, one wanted only the best for one's children.*
● **One** is used in these phrases. ● **One or two** means a very few. *One or two of the girls help in the kitchen.* ● If you are **one up on** someone, or have **one up on** them, you have an advantage over them; an informal expression. *She'd got one up on me.* ● **A hundred and one** or **a thousand and one** means a great many. *There must be a thousand and one books of this sort on the market.* ● **one another**: see another.

one-armed bandit, one-armed bandits
NC A **one-armed bandit** is the same as a **fruit machine**. *They play roulette and take on the one-armed bandits.*

one-horse
1 ADJ ATTRIB A **one-horse** town is a very small, dull, and old-fashioned town. *...a little one-horse town miles from anywhere.*
2 ADJ ATTRIB A **one-horse** vehicle is a vehicle that is drawn by one horse. *...the one-horse bus that travelled between the villages.*

One-hundred Share Index
N SING The **One-hundred Share Index** is the same as the **Financial Times Stock Exchange 100 Index**. *Not surprisingly, the One-hundred Share Index slipped 7.6 to 1750.2.*

one-liner, one-liners
NC A **one-liner** is a funny remark or a joke told in one sentence, for example in a play or comedy programme; an informal word. *There were some good one-liners.*

one-man
1 ADJ ATTRIB A **one-man** performance is given by one man, rather than by several people. *...a one-man show.*
2 ADJ ATTRIB A **one-man** organization such as a business or type of government is controlled by one man, rather than by several people. *Some banks are better for the small business, and will happily deal with a one-man firm... He was a shrewd politician who saw that this would provide a cloak of legitimacy for one-man military rule.*

one-man band, one-man bands
NC A **one-man band** is a street entertainer who wears and plays a lot of different instruments at the same time, for example drums, cymbals, and the mouth organ.

one-night stand, one-night stands
1 NC A **one-night stand** is a very brief sexual relationship, usually involving having sex with a particular person on only one occasion. *I'm tired of one-night stands.*
2 NC A **one-night stand** is also a performance that is given in a particular place on only one evening, rather than on several evenings in a row. *I played a few one-night stands around the country.*

one-off, one-offs
NC A **one-off** is something that happens or is made only once; an informal word. *'A one-off,' he said. 'A tailor-made gun.'* ► Also ADJ ATTRIB *...one-off projects.*

one-parent family, one-parent families
NC A **one-parent family** consists of a child or children living with only one of their parents. *There is a large number of one-parent families where the mother brings up the children alone.*

one-piece
ADJ ATTRIB **One-piece** is used to describe clothing, for example a swimming costume, which consists of only one piece, rather than two or more separate parts. *Both wore one-piece swimsuits.*

onerous /ˈəʊnərəs/
ADJ **Onerous** work is difficult and unpleasant; a formal word. *...the onerous duties of postal delivery.*

oneself /wʌnˈsɛlf/
1 PRON REFL A speaker or writer uses **oneself** as the object of a verb or preposition in a clause where 'one' is the subject or a previous object. *One must keep such interests to oneself.*
2 PRON REFL **Oneself** is also used to emphasize the subject or object of a clause. *Others might find odd what one finds perfectly normal oneself.*

one-sided
1 ADJ In a **one-sided** activity or relationship, one of the people involved does much more or is much stronger than the other. *...one-sided conversations... She won the most one-sided French Open in history 6-1 6-1.*
2 ADJ Someone or something that is **one-sided** considers only some of the relevant facts of a particular, issue, or event; used showing disapproval. *The report is one-sided in its interpretation of the evidence.*

one-time
ADJ ATTRIB You use **one-time** to indicate that someone used to have a particular job, position, or role. *...Fred Dunn, a onetime farm worker.*

one-to-one
ADJ ATTRIB In a **one-to-one** relationship, you deal with only one other person. *...one-to-one tuition.*

one-track mind, one-track minds
NC Someone who has a **one-track mind** thinks about and is interested in only one thing. *...fanatical men of action with one-track minds who are narrow-minded to the point of genius.*

one-upmanship /wʌnˈʌpmənʃɪp/
NU **One-upmanship** is the practice of trying to appear better than someone else and make them feel inferior. *A commentary rejected what it called their cheap one-upmanship.*

one-way
1 ADJ ATTRIB **One-way** streets are streets along which vehicles can drive in only one direction. *The robbers sped off up a one-way street in the wrong direction.*
2 ADJ ATTRIB A **one-way** ticket is one which you can use to travel to a place, but not to travel back again. *...a one-way ticket to Jersey.*

one-woman
ADJ ATTRIB A **one-woman** performance is given by one woman, rather than by several people. *The Best Actress was Pauline Collins in the one-woman show 'Shirley Valentine' by Willy Russell.*

ongoing /ˈɒŋɡəʊɪŋ/
ADJ ATTRIB An **ongoing** situation is continuing to happen. *...an ongoing economic crisis.*

onion /ˈʌnjən/ **onions**
N COR NU An **onion** is a small round vegetable. It is white with a brown skin, and has a strong smell and taste. *...fresh vegetables such as onions and lettuce. ...two tablespoons of oil, one finely chopped onion and one cup of celery.*

on line
ADJ OR ADV A part of a computer system that is **on line** is directly connected to and controlled by the central processing unit of the computer. *Almost all these chemical analyses we're able to do now on line. ...a system for the on-line, automated screening of cervical smears. ...going on line to search a remote computer.*

onlooker /ˈɒnlʊkə/ **onlookers**
NC An **onlooker** is someone who is watching an event. *She blew a kiss to the shivering onlookers.*

only /ˈəʊnli/. In written English, 'only' is usually placed immediately before the word it qualifies. In spoken English, you can use stress to indicate what 'only' qualifies, so its position is not so important.
1 ADV You use **only** to indicate the one thing that is involved or that happens in a particular situation. *He read only paperbacks... I'm only interested in facts... Only Mother knows... The video is to be used for teaching purposes only.*
2 ADJ ATTRIB If you talk about the **only** thing involved in a particular situation, you mean that there are no others. *I was the only one smoking... It was the only way out.*
3 ADJ ATTRIB An **only** child has no brothers or sisters. *He was an only child, relentlessly driven by his ambitious mother.*
4 ADV You can use **only** to emphasize that something is unimportant or small. *It was only a squirrel... I was only joking... We only paid £26.*
5 ADV You can use **only** to emphasize how recently something happened. *I've only just arrived.*
6 ADV You can also use **only** to emphasize a wish or hope. *I only wish I had the money.*
7 CONJ You can use **only** to add a comment which slightly changes or corrects what you have just said; an informal use. *Snake is just like chicken, only tougher.*
8 CONJ You can use **only** to introduce the reason why something is not done; an informal use. *'That's what I'm trying to do,' said Mrs Oliver, 'only I can't get near enough.'*
9 ADV+to-INF You can use **only** in front of a 'to'-infinitive to introduce an event which happens immediately after the previous one, and which is

rather surprising or unfortunate. *He broke off, only to resume almost at once... I had tried this years before, only to receive a polite refusal.*
10 SUBMOD You can use **only** to emphasize that you think a course of action or type of behaviour is reasonable in a particular situation. *It is only natural that she will have mixed feelings about your promotion.*
● **Only** is used in these phrases. ● You say that one thing will happen **only if** another thing happens when you want to indicate that it will not happen unless the other thing happens. *These snakes only attack if they feel cornered or threatened.* ● You say that something is **only just** the case to emphasize that it is very nearly not the case. *He could only just hear them... The heat was only just bearable.* ● You use **not only** to introduce the first of two linked statements when the second is even more surprising or extreme than the first. *Chimpanzees not only use tools but make them.* ● If you say that someone **has only** to do one thing in order to achieve or prove another, you are emphasizing how easily or quickly it can be done. *You've only got to read the newspapers to see what can happen to hitch-hikers.* ● You use **only too** to emphasize that something happens to a greater extent than is expected or wanted. *He is only too pleased to help... She remembered that night only too clearly.*
● **if only**: see **if**.

o.n.o.
o.n.o. is written after a price in an advertisement to indicate that the person who is selling something is willing to accept slightly less money than the sum they have mentioned. o.n.o. is an abbreviation for 'or near offer'. ...*£600 o.n.o.*

onomatopoeia /ɒnəmætəpiːə/
N U **Onomatopoeia** is the formation and use of words which sound like the noise they are describing or referring to. 'Hiss,' 'buzz,' and 'rat-a-tat-tat' are examples of onomatopoeia.

onomatopoeic /ɒnəmætəpiːɪk/
ADJ Language that is **onomatopoeic** uses onomatopoeia.

onrush /ɒnrʌʃ/
N SING+of You say that there is an **onrush** of a feeling or emotion when it develops suddenly and quickly; a literary word. ...*the onrush of her tears. ...an onrush of pain.*

on-screen
ADJ Something that is **on-screen** is displayed on a screen, for example on the screen of a word processor, computer terminal, or television. ...*commercial television companies which finance their broadcasting by on-screen advertising.*

onset /ɒnset/
N SING The **onset** of something unpleasant is the beginning of it. ...*the onset of war.*

onshore /ɒnʃɔː/
1 ADJ or ADV **Onshore** means happening or moving towards the land. ...*a light onshore breeze.*
2 ADJ or ADV **Onshore** also means happening on or near land, rather than at sea. ...*the largest onshore oilfield in Western Europe... The ship will be built onshore in dry dock.*

onslaught /ɒnslɔːt/ **onslaughts**
N C+SUPP An **onslaught** is an extremely forceful physical or verbal attack on someone or something. ...*a co-ordinated onslaught on enemy airfields. ...a resolution condemning Iraq for its military onslaught against its Kurdish minority... The Transport Secretary will face a sustained onslaught from opposition MPs in the Commons.*

on-the-job
ADJ ATTRIB **On-the-job** training or experience is training or experience which you are given or gain while you are working. ...*official plans to begin on-the-job training for unqualified staff.*

on-the-spot
ADJ ATTRIB **On-the-spot** is used to describe something that happens in a place where other things have already happened or are happening, especially when there is not time for a great deal of preparation. ...*on-the-spot field work. ...on-the-spot investigations.*

onto /ɒntə, ɒntuː/; also spelt **on to**.
1 PREP If someone or something moves **onto** an object or is put **onto** it, the object is then underneath them and supporting them. *I got onto the bed... She spooned a portion of potato onto his plate... I ran out onto the porch.*
2 PREP When you get **onto** a bus, train, or plane, you get into it. *About 200 students got onto a bus for Cotonou.*
3 PREP If you fasten one thing **onto** another, you fasten the first thing to the second one. *I bent a pin and tied it onto a piece of string.*
4 PREP If you hold **onto** something, you hold it firmly. ...*clinging onto his shirt.*
5 PREP If people who are talking get **onto** a different subject, they begin talking about it. *Let's move onto another question.*

onus /əʊnəs/
N SING If you say that the **onus** is on someone to do something, you mean that it is their duty or responsibility to do it; a formal word. *The onus was on me to earn enough to support the family.*

onward /ɒnwəd/ **onwards**. In normal British English, **onwards** is an adverb and **onward** is an adjective. In formal British English and in American English, **onward** is both an adjective and an adverb.
1 ADV If something happens from a particular time **onwards** or **onward**, it begins to happen at that time and continues to happen. *From 1968 onwards the situation began to change... From that time onward he had never spoken to her again.*
2 ADV or ADJ ATTRIB If someone or something moves **onwards** or **onward**, they continue travelling or moving forward. *We travelled from China to India, and onwards to East Africa. ...the onward motion of the boat.*
3 ADV or ADJ ATTRIB You can say that things move **onwards** or **onward** when they continue to develop or progress. ...*a tremendous self-confidence that the country is moving onwards and upwards. ...this onward march of the Labour movement.*

onyx /ɒnɪks/
N U **Onyx** is a semi-precious stone which can be various colours. It is used for making ornaments and jewellery. ...*an onyx and silver trophy.*

oodles /uːdlz/
N PL **Oodles** of something means a very large quantity of it; an informal word. ...*corn on the cob with oodles of butter.*

ooh /uː/
People say **ooh** when they are surprised or when something pleasant or unpleasant suddenly happens. *Ooh, you are awful... Ooh, that feels nice.*

oomph /ʊmf/
N U If a person or thing has **oomph**, they are forceful, energetic or lively; an informal word. *They want to show that Jamaica's got oomph... He gave it all the extra oomph he could.*

oops /ʊps, uːps/
You say **oops** to show that there has been a slight accident or mistake. *Oops, sorry... Oops! He's fallen down.*

ooze /uːz/ **oozes, oozing, oozed**
1 V-ERG When a thick, sticky liquid **oozes** from an object or when the object **oozes** it, the liquid flows slowly from the object. ...*blood oozing from his wounds... His sandals oozed black slime.*
2 VO or V+with If someone **oozes** a quality or feeling, they show it very strongly, often when they do not really feel it. *His letter, oozing remorse, appeared in all the newspapers... Her voice oozed with politeness.*

opacity /əʊpæsəti/; a formal word.
1 NU **Opacity** is the quality of being difficult to see through. ...*the opacity of the paper.*
2 NU **Opacity** is also the quality of being difficult to understand. ...*Coleridge's opacity.*

opal /əʊpl/ **opals**
N C An **opal** is a semi-precious stone that is usually milky white in colour. ...*the discovery of huge reserves of opals in New South Wales.*

opalescent /əʊpəlesnt/
ADJ **Opalescent** means colourless or milky white like

an opal, or changing colour like an opal. ...*an opalescent veil... The sky was covered with an opalescent vapour.*

opaque /əʊpeɪk/

1 ADJ An object or substance that is **opaque** has enough thickness or colour to prevent you seeing through it. ...*the opaque windows of the jail. ...the opaque water.*

2 ADJ If someone or something is **opaque**, it is difficult to understand; a formal use. *Germany's post-war status and the re-unification debate are likely to remain, quite deliberately, opaque.*

op. cit. /ɒp sɪt/

op. cit. is used in writing, especially in footnotes, to refer to a book which has already been mentioned. *op. cit. p. 326.*

OPEC (Organization of Petroleum Exporting Countries) /əʊpek/

OPEC was founded in 1960 to co-ordinate the petroleum policies of major petroleum producing countries. The headquarters of OPEC are in Vienna. OPEC members possess an estimated 77 per cent of the world's known petroleum reserves. The members of OPEC are: Algeria, Ecuador, Gabon, Indonesia, Iran, Iraq, Kuwait, Libya, Nigeria, Qatar, Saudi Arabia, United Arab Emirates, and Venezuela.

open /əʊpən/ **opens, opening, opened**

1 V-ERG When you **open** something such as a door or the lid of a box, or when it **opens**, you move it so that it no longer covers a hole or gap. *Elizabeth opened the door and went in... The door opened almost before Brody had finished knocking.* ▶ Also ADJ ...*the open window.*

2 VO When you **open** a cupboard, container, or letter, you move, remove, or cut part of it so that you can take out what is inside. *Open the tool-box... I opened a can of beans.* ▶ Also ADV *He tore open the envelope.*

3 VO When you **open** a book, you move its covers apart in order to read or write on the pages inside. *He opened the book at random.* ▶ Also ADJ ...*the open Bible.*

4 V-ERG When you **open** your mouth, or when it **opens**, you move your lips and teeth apart. *She opened her mouth to say something, then closed it... 'Open wide and point to the tooth that hurts.'* ▶ Also ADJ *Angelica looked at me with her mouth open.*

5 V-ERG When you **open** your eyes, or when they **open**, you move your eyelids upwards so that you can see. *She opened her eyes and looked at me... The child's eyes opened and they could see she was alive.* ▶ Also ADJ ...*lying with his eyes wide open.*

6 ADJ If you have an **open** mind or are **open** to ideas or suggestions, you are prepared to consider any ideas or suggestions. *Let's proceed with caution, with vigilance and with an open mind... Investigators are maintaining an open mind about the two possible explanations... He has usually shown himself open to new ideas.*

7 ADJ An **open** person is honest and does not try to hide anything. *They looked at her with open curiosity.* ◆ **openness** NU ...*Mikhail Gorbachev's policies of restructuring and openness. ...their relaxed openness.*

8 ADJ PRED+to If you say that a person, idea, or system is **open** to something such as criticism or blame, you mean they could be treated in the way indicated. *The proposals were certainly open to criticism.*

9 V-ERG When you **open** a shop, office, or public building, or when it **opens**, its doors are unlocked and the people in it start working. *One man who attempted to open his shop during the curfew was forced to close it... Some banks opened their doors but there was no transaction... When does the library open?* ▶ Also ADJ *The Tate Gallery is open 10 a.m.—6 p.m.*

10 VO When someone important **opens** a building or a public area, they declare officially in a public ceremony that it is ready to be used or to start operating. *The Queen Mother opened the High Technology Unit in 1987.* ▶ Also ADJ PRED *Lord Shawcross declared the hotel open.* ◆ **opening** NU+SUPP ...*the opening of the new theatre.*

11 V When an event such as a conference or a play **opens**, it begins to take place or to be performed. *The UN General Assembly opens in New York later this month.* ◆ **opening** NU ...*the opening of 'Nicholas Nickleby' on Broadway.*

12 VO The person who **opens** an event is the first to speak or do something. *Senator Denton opened the hearing by reminding us of our duty.*

13 VO If you **open** an account with a bank, you begin to use their services by giving them some of your money to look after or invest. *I'm opening an account to save up for a new car.*

14 VA On the stock exchange, the price that a currency, shares, or a commodity such as gold or oil **opens** at is its value at the start of that day's trading. *In Frankfurt the dollar opened at half a cent lower at 1 mark 5175... Prices opened lower on the New York stock exchange this morning.*

15 VA If a room or door **opens** into or onto a place, you can go straight to that place from the room or through the door. *These rooms have doors opening directly onto the garden.*

16 V When flowers **open**, their petals spread out. *Roses opened and fell within a day.*

17 ADJ If an item of clothing is **open**, it is not fastened. ...*an open black raincoat. ...an open-necked shirt.*

18 ADJ ATTRIB An **open** area of land or sea is a large area with few things such as buildings or islands in it. *The road stretched across open country... The drivers started to prepare again for the open road. ...secret and dangerous journeys on the open sea by boat.* ◆ **openness** NU ...*the openness of Vincent Square.*

19 ADJ ATTRIB You can use **open** to describe something that is not covered or enclosed. ...*an open car... Never dry clothes in front of an open fire.*

20 ADJ PRED+to If a course of action is **open** to you, it is possible for you to do it. *We should use the opportunities now open to us.*

21 ADJ An **open** meeting, competition, or invitation is one which anyone can take part in or accept. *Most Council meetings are open to the public. ...the Women's Open Golf Championship.*

22 ADJ If you describe a situation or topic as **open**, you mean that no decision has been made about it yet. *I let joining the Party remain an open question... They had left their options open... The coroner recorded an open verdict.*

23 See also **opening, openly.**

● **Open** is used in these phrases. ● If you do something **in the open**, you do it out of doors. *The children enjoyed sleeping out in the open.* ● If a situation is brought out **into the open**, people are told about it and it is no longer a secret. *The Noriega scandal is going to bring out into the open unsavoury stories about alleged international crime and CIA dirty tricks... This debate has now come out into the open.* ● to **welcome** something **with open arms**: see **arm.**

open out PHRASAL VERB If a road or passage **opens out**, it gradually becomes larger or wider. *At the mouth of the valley, the mountains finally opened out into the plain.*

open up PHRASAL VERB 1 When an opportunity **opens up** or is **opened up**, it is given to you. *All sorts of possibilities began to open up.* 2 If a place **opens up** or is **opened up**, people can then get to it or trade with it more easily. ...*his vision of Alaska as a frontier that needs to be opened up and developed.* 3 If someone with a gun **opens up**, they start shooting. *As many as two dozen officers opened up, shooting into a crowd of unarmed students.* 4 When someone **opens up** a building or **opens up**, they unlock the door so that people can get in. *'Open up! It's snowing out here.'*

open air

N SING If you are in the **open air**, you are outside. *Dry clothes in the open air, if possible. ...open-air swimming pools.*

open-and-shut

ADJ A problem, legal matter, or dispute that is **open-and-shut** is easily decided or solved because the facts are very clear. *An open-and-shut murder case.*

open-cast

ADJ An **open-cast** mine is a mine in which the coal or other minerals are near the surface and underground passages are not needed. *The Kuzbass produces the cheapest coal in the Soviet Union, because much of it comes from open-cast mines. ...the world's largest open-cast copper operation.*

open day, open days

NC An **open day** is a special day when the public are allowed to visit a particular school or other institution. *You can meet the teacher on open days.*

open-ended

ADJ An **open-ended** discussion or activity is started without the intention of achieving a particular decision or result. *The research has become practically open-ended... He is no longer in favour of open-ended negotiations.*

open house

NU **Open house** is used to refer to an arrangement in which people allow friends or visitors to come to their house whenever they want to. *It was open house to a fairly closed circle of friends... They keep open house.*

opening /ˈəʊpənɪŋ/ **openings**

1 ADJ ATTRIB The **opening** item or part of something is the first one. *...his opening remarks.*
2 N SING The **opening** of a book or film is the first part of it. *The main characters are established in the opening of the book.*
3 NC An **opening** is a hole or empty space through which things can pass. *We slid through the opening into the field.*
4 NC An **opening** is also an opportunity to do something, for example to get a job that is available or to talk about a particular subject. *Charlotte herself provided me with an opening... This is a real good opening that everyone should seize... He believed there was an opening for economic relations between Israel and the Soviet Union.*
5 See also **open**.

opening hours

N PL The **opening hours** of a shop, bank, library, or pub are the times when it is open for business. *Banks often have very short opening hours.*

opening night, opening nights

NC The **opening night** of something such as a play or opera, is the first night on which a particular production of it is performed. *I was at the opening night with my parents.*

opening time

NU **Opening time** is the time that a shop, bank, library, or pub opens for business. *Men would be hanging around the pub doors at opening time.*

open letter, open letters

NC An **open letter** is a letter that is published in a newspaper or magazine and is written by one famous person to another, usually in order to protest or complain about something. *...an article headed 'Open Letter to Dr. Verwoerd'... They organized an open letter to the Labour movement.*

openly /ˈəʊpənli/

ADV If you do something **openly**, you do it without trying to hide anything. *His mother wept openly.*

open market

N SING The **open market** is used to refer to the normal process of buying and selling goods, in which the goods are advertised and sold publicly and not privately; compare **black market**. *He was able to sell his work in the open market... You won't get a picture as good as this on the open market.*

open-minded

ADJ Someone who is **open-minded** is willing to listen to other people's ideas and consider them. *...an intelligent, open-minded man. ...an open-minded approach to new techniques.*

open-mouthed

ADJ If someone is looking **open-mouthed** at something, their mouth is open because they are very surprised. *She was staring open-mouthed at a picture of her father.*

open-necked

ADJ ATTRIB If you are wearing an **open-necked** shirt or blouse, you are wearing a shirt or blouse with the top button unfastened and no tie. *...dressed in open-necked shirt and shorts.*

open-plan

ADJ An **open-plan** building has just one large area on each storey, rather than several separate rooms. *...an open-plan office.*

open prison, open prisons

NC An **open prison** is a prison where the prisoners are allowed to do more activities and to have a greater degree of freedom than in other prisons. *No prisoner was sent to an open prison unless he was deemed suitable. ...the dangers of using an open prison to house prisoners convicted of violence or drugs offences.*

open secret, open secrets

NC An **open secret** is something which is supposed to be a secret, but that many people know about. *It is an open secret that he has just become engaged.*

Open University

N PROP The **Open University** is a university in Britain that runs degree courses on the radio and television for students who do not have the proper qualifications and want to study part-time or mainly at home. Students send their work by post to their tutors. *After two years she had four of the six credits needed for her B.A. at the Open University.*

opera /ˈɒpərə/ **operas**

NCorNU An **opera** is a musical entertainment. It is like a play, but most of the words are sung. *...choruses from Verdi's operas. ...a book on Italian opera.*

operate /ˈɒpəreɪt/ **operates, operating, operated**

1 V-ERG If you **operate** a business or organization, or if a business or organization **operates** in a place, it carries out its work there. *He operates an Afghan news service. ...the multinational companies which operate in their country.* ◆ **operation** /ˌɒpəˈreɪʃn/ NU *...our first year of operation.*
2 V The way that something **operates** is the way that it works or has an effect. *We discussed how language operates... Laws of the same kind operate in nature.*
3 V-ERG When you **operate** a machine or device, or when it **operates**, you make it work. *...how to operate the safety equipment. ...the way the calculators operated.* ◆ **operation** NU *...instructions for the operation of machinery.*
4 V When surgeons **operate** on a patient, they cut open the patient's body in order to remove, replace, or repair a diseased or damaged part. *They operated but it was too late... His knees have been operated on three times.*
5 See also **operation**.

operatic /ˌɒpəˈrætɪk/

ADJ **Operatic** means relating to opera. *...the local operatic society.*

operating room, operating rooms

NC An **operating room** is the same as an **operating theatre**; used in American English. *Most of the surgeons are satisfied with the operating room.*

operating system, operating systems

NC The **operating system** of a computer is its most basic program, which deals with such things as the functions of the keyboard, screen, printer, and disks. Without it the computer could not function. *The term 'software' means an internal operating system.*

operating theatre, operating theatres

NC An **operating theatre** is a room in a hospital where surgeons carry out operations. *...equipped with a full medical unit, including an operating theatre and a one-hundred bed hospital.*

operation /ˌɒpəˈreɪʃn/ **operations**

1 NC An **operation** is a planned activity that involves many complicated actions. *...military operations in Europe. ...a rescue operation.*
2 NC Businesses or companies are sometimes referred to as **operations**. *...Multiponics, a large-scale farming operation.*
3 NC If a patient has an **operation**, a surgeon cuts open the patient's body in order to remove, replace, or repair a diseased or damaged part. *Her mother was about to undergo a major operation. ...heart operations.*
4 If something is in **operation**, it is working or being

used. ...*gas drilling rigs in operation in the USA... The plans were put into operation at once.*
5 See also **operate.**

operational /ɒpərˈeɪʃəⁿəl/
1 ADJ A machine or piece of equipment that is **operational** is working or able to be used. ...*fifty operational warships... The system is not yet operational.*
2 ADJ ATTRIB **Operational** is used to describe actions, situations, or problems that occur when a plan or system is being carried out. ...*operational positions... Ten-million dollars were needed to cover operational costs.*

operative /ɒpəˈrətɪv/ **operatives**
1 ADJ Something that is **operative** is working or having an effect. *The scheme was fully operative by 1975.*
2 NC An **operative** is a worker, especially one that does manual work; a formal use. ...*each operative on a production line.*
3 NC An **operative** is also someone who works for a government agency, especially the intelligence service; used in American English. *He doesn't seem to have supporters among Republican political operatives. ...the CIA operative who tried to publish his memoirs.*

operator /ɒpəˈreɪtə/ **operators**
1 NC An **operator** is a person who works at a telephone exchange or on the switchboard of an office or hotel. *He dialled the operator. ...telephone operators.*
2 NC+SUPP An **operator** is also someone who is employed to operate or control a machine. ...*computer operators.*
3 NC+SUPP An **operator** is also someone who runs a business. ...*tour operators. ...casino operators.*

operetta /ɒpəˈretə/ **operettas**
NCorNU An **operetta** is a type of opera which is light-hearted and often comic and has some of the words spoken rather than sung. ...*a comedy of errors equivalent to a Gilbert and Sullivan operetta... The operetta isn't dead of course; there are always revivals of works by Lehar, Strauss, Offenbach and Gilbert and Sullivan.*

ophthalmic /ɒfˈθælmɪk/
ADJ ATTRIB **Ophthalmic** means relating to or concerned with the medical care of your eyes; a medical term. ...*an ophthalmic optician.*

opiate /ˈəʊpiət/ **opiates**; a formal word.
1 NC An **opiate** is a drug that contains opium. Opiates can reduce pain or cause you to sleep. ...*repeated doses of opiates.*
2 NC If you say something is an **opiate,** you mean it makes people think less or spend less time on things which are important. *They rejected the cinema as a mindless opiate that would destroy good conversation. ...the Marxist view of religion as the opiate of the poor.*

opinion /əˈpɪnjən/ **opinions**
1 NC Your **opinion** of something is what you think about it. *The students were eager to express their opinions... Information of this nature was valuable, in his opinion... We have a high opinion of you.*
2 If someone **is of the opinion** that something is the case, they think that it is the case; a formal expression. *He is of the opinion that money is not important.*
3 NU People's **opinion** is the beliefs or views that they have. ...*changes in public opinion... Difficulties arise where there's a difference of opinion.*

opinionated /əˈpɪnjəneɪtɪd/
ADJ Someone who is **opinionated** has firm opinions and refuses to accept that they may be wrong; used showing disapproval. ...*this inexperienced but opinionated newcomer.*

opinion poll, opinion polls
NC An **opinion poll** involves asking people for their opinion on a particular subject, especially one concerning politics. *The latest opinion poll puts Mr Bush seventeen percentage points ahead.*

opium /ˈəʊpiəm/
NU **Opium** is a drug made from the seeds of a type of poppy. Opium is illegal in many countries. ...*large scale seizures of heroin and opium. ...a centre for opium smuggling by British and other European traders.*

opossum /əˈpɒsəm/ **opossums**
NC An **opossum** is a small animal that lives in America. It carries its young in a pouch on its body, and has thick fur and a long tail.

opp.
Opp. is a written abbreviation for 'opposite' or 'opposition'. ...*recalling NATO opp. to Moscow's plans... The Interior Ministry for the first time acknowledged the sizable Opp: fifty-three percent against forty-four.*

opponent /əˈpəʊnənt/ **opponents**
1 NC A politician's **opponents** are other politicians who belong to a different party or have different aims or policies. *The papers note that Mrs Thatcher was also criticised by her political opponents... Miss Bhutto's opponents are campaigning seriously against her return to power.*
2 NC In a game, your **opponent** is the person who is playing against you. *He beat his opponent three sets to love.*
3 NC The **opponents** of an idea or policy do not agree with it. ...*a leading opponent of the budget cuts.*

opportune /ˈɒpətjuːn/
ADJ **Opportune** means happening at a convenient time; a formal word. *It was most opportune that Mrs Davenport should arrive... The call came at an opportune moment.*

opportunism /ˈɒpətjuːnɪzəm/
NU If you refer to someone's behaviour as **opportunism,** you mean they take advantage of any situation that will help them personally, without thinking about whether their actions are right or wrong; a formal word. ...*a piece of cheap, cynical opportunism.* ♦ **opportunist** /ˈɒpətjuːnɪst/ **opportunists** NC ...*the intrigues of a business opportunist.*

opportunistic /ˌɒpətjuːˈnɪstɪk/
ADJ If you describe someone's behaviour as **opportunistic,** you mean that they take advantage of any situation that will help them personally, without thinking about whether their actions are right or wrong; a formal word. ...*an opportunistic foreign policy.*

opportunity /ˌɒpətjuːnəti/ **opportunities**
NCorNU An **opportunity** is a situation in which it is possible for you to do something that you want to do. *It will give you an opportunity to meet all kinds of people... They would return to power at the first opportunity. ...equality of opportunity.*

oppose /əˈpəʊz/ **opposes, opposing, opposed**
VO If you **oppose** someone or **oppose** what they want to do, you disagree with what they want to do and try to prevent them from doing it. *Your father opposed your wish to become a sculptor.*

opposed /əˈpəʊzd/
1 ADJ PRED If you are **opposed** to something, you disagree with it or disapprove of it. *They were violently opposed to the idea... I am opposed to capital punishment.*
2 ADJ You say that two ideas or systems are **opposed** when they are opposite to each other or very different from each other. ...*two bitterly opposed schools of socialist thought. ...a strategy which is diametrically opposed to that of the previous government.*
3 You use **as opposed to** when you want to make it clear that you are talking about a particular thing and not something else. *There's a need for technical colleges as opposed to universities.*

opposing /əˈpəʊzɪŋ/
ADJ ATTRIB **Opposing** ideas or tendencies are totally different from each other. *We held opposing points of view.*

opposite /ˈɒpəzɪt/ **opposites**
1 PREP or ADV If one thing is **opposite** another, it is facing it. *The hotel is opposite a railway station... Lynn was sitting opposite him.*
2 ADJ The **opposite** side or part of something is the one that is farthest away from you. ...*on the opposite side of the street.*

3 ADJ ATTRIB **Opposite** is used to describe things of the same kind which are as different as possible in a particular way. For example, north and south are opposite directions, and winning and losing are opposite results in a game. *I wanted to impress them but probably had the opposite effect... Paul turned and walked in the opposite direction.*
4 NC If two things of the same kind are completely different in a particular way, you can say that one is the **opposite** of the other. *My interpretation was the absolute opposite of Olivier's... My brother is just the opposite. He loves sport.*

opposite number, opposite numbers
NC+POSS Your **opposite number** is a person who does the same job as you, but works in a different department, firm, or organization. *My opposite numbers in industry don't have this problem.*

opposition /ɒpəzɪʃn/
1 NU When there is **opposition** to a plan or proposal, people disapprove of it and try to prevent it being carried out. *It was only built after much opposition from the planners.*
2 N COLL The **opposition** refers to the politicians or political parties that form part of a country's parliament but are not in the government. *...the leader of the Opposition. ...two new opposition parties.*
3 N COLL The **opposition** is also the people who are against you in an argument or sports contest. *The opposition consisted of chiefs and elders... One player broke through the opposition's defence.*

oppositionist /ɒpəzɪʃənɪst/ **oppositionists**
NC An **oppositionist** is a person who is politically opposed to the government of a particular country, especially where official political opposition is not allowed. *Negotiations will resume in mid-March when the oppositionists hold their congress. ...hundreds of left-wing oppositionists have been sent to the firing squads.*

oppress /əprɛs/ **oppresses, oppressing, oppressed**
1 VO To **oppress** someone means to treat them cruelly or unfairly. *...institutions that oppress women.* ◆ **oppressed** ADJ *...the sufferings of oppressed people everywhere.*
2 VO If something **oppresses** you, it makes you feel depressed and uncomfortable. *Somehow the room oppressed him.*

oppression /əprɛʃn/
1 NU **Oppression** is the cruel or unfair treatment of a group of people. *...the oppression of the weak and defenceless.*
2 NU **Oppression** is also a feeling of depression, especially one caused by a place or situation. *Passing the place, my sense of oppression increased.*

oppressive /əprɛsɪv/
1 ADJ You can say that the weather is **oppressive** when it is hot and humid. *...the oppressive heat of the plains.* ◆ **oppressively** SUBMOD *The room was oppressively hot.*
2 ADJ An **oppressive** situation makes you feel depressed or uncomfortable. *The silence became oppressive.*
3 ADJ **Oppressive** laws, societies, and customs treat people cruelly and unfairly. *...an oppressive bureaucracy.*

oppressor /əprɛsə/ **oppressors**
NC An **oppressor** is someone who treats other people cruelly or unfairly. *They didn't have the will to stand up against their foreign oppressors.*

opprobrious /əprəʊbrɪəs/
ADJ **Opprobrious** language expresses scorn or contempt for someone or something; a formal word. *The term 'native' lost its dictionary definition and became an opprobrious word, signifying an inferior race.*

opprobrium /əprəʊbrɪəm/
NU **Opprobrium** is someone's dislike and disapproval of you because of something you have done; a formal word. *The opprobrium and enmity he incurred were caused by his outspoken brashness... France's activities in the Pacific have earned her the opprobrium of surrounding states.*

opt /ɒpt/ **opts, opting, opted**
V+*for* or V+*to*-INF If you **opt** for something, you choose it. If you **opt** to do something, you choose to do it. *My father left the choice of career to me, and I opted for law. ...those who opt to cooperate with the regime.*
opt out PHRASAL VERB If you **opt out** of something, you choose not to be involved in it. *He tried to opt out of political decision-making.*

optic /ɒptɪk/ **optics.**
1 ADJ ATTRIB **Optic** means relating to eyes or to sight. *...the optic nerves.*
2 NU **Optics** is the branch of science concerned with vision, sight, and light. *Newton published his first work on optics.*

optical /ɒptɪkl/
1 ADJ ATTRIB **Optical** instruments, devices, or processes involve or relate to vision or light. *...an optical microscope.*
2 ADJ ATTRIB **Optical** means relating to the way that things appear to people. *A small child is turned on to textures, colour contrasts and optical effects.*

optical illusion, optical illusions
NC An **optical illusion** is something such as an object or design that deceives your eyes and causes you to think you see something different from what is really there. *The science behind it is based on the psychology and physics of optical illusion... It was merely a clever optical illusion.*

optician /ɒptɪʃn/ **opticians**
NC An **optician** is someone whose job involves testing people's eyesight or providing glasses and contact lenses.

optimism /ɒptɪmɪzəm/
NU **Optimism** is the feeling of being hopeful about the future. *I felt cheerful and full of optimism.* ◆ **optimist** /ɒptɪmɪst/ **optimists** NC *I'm an optimist by nature.*

optimistic /ɒptɪmɪstɪk/
ADJ Someone who is **optimistic** is hopeful about the future. *...an optimistic estimate.* ◆ **optimistically** ADV *It might work, she thought optimistically.*

optimum /ɒptɪməm/
ADJ ATTRIB **Optimum** means the best that is possible; a formal word. *The optimum feeding time is around dawn.*

option /ɒpʃn/ **options**
1 NC An **option** is a choice between two or more things. *He had, I would say, two options. ...the option of another referendum.*
2 N SING If you have the **option** to do something, you can choose whether to do it or not. *He was given the option: give them up or lose your job. ...mothers who have no option but to work.*
3 NC An **option** is also a subject which a student can choose to study as part of his or her course. *I did a special option in phonetics.*

optional /ɒpʃənəl/
ADJ If something is **optional**, you can choose whether you do it or not. *Games are optional at this school.*

opulence /ɒpjʊləns/
NU **Opulence** refers to great wealth or to things that suggest someone has great wealth; a formal word. *His eyes had never beheld such opulence.*

opulent /ɒpjʊlənt/
ADJ **Opulent** things look grand and expensive; a formal word. *...the magnificently opulent marble altar.*

opus /əʊpəs, ɒpəs/ **opuses**
1 NC An **opus** is a musical composition, for example a symphony or concerto. 'Opus' is usually used with a number to indicate when the composition was written. *Brahms' Variations on a Hungarian Song, Opus 21 No 2.*
2 NC An **opus** is also a great artistic work, such as a piece of writing or a painting; often used humorously. *I had after all a learned opus to write.*

or /ə, ɔː/
1 CONJ You use **or** to link alternatives. *Do you want your drink up there or do you want to come down for it?... Have you any brothers or sisters?*
2 CONJ **Or** is used to give a second alternative, when the first alternative is introduced by 'either' or 'whether'. *Most aircraft accidents occur at either*

*take-off or landing... He didn't know whether to laugh
or cry.*
3 CONJ **Or** is also used between two numbers to
indicate that you are giving an approximate amount.
*You are supposed to polish your car three or four
times a year.*
4 CONJ You also use **or** to introduce a comment which
corrects or modifies what you have just said. *The
company is paying the rent or at least contributing to
it.*
5 CONJ You use **or** when you are telling someone what
will happen if they do not follow your instructions or
advice. *Don't put anything plastic in the oven or it
will probably start melting.*
6 CONJ You can also use **or** to introduce an
explanation or justification for what you have just
said. *He can't be that bad, can he, or they wouldn't
have allowed him home.*
7 **or else**: see **else. or other**: see **other. or so**: see **so.**
-or /-ə/ **-ors**
SUFFIX **-or** is added to some verbs to form nouns
referring to people who do a particular thing. For
example, a supervisor is someone who supervises
people. In this dictionary, nouns of this kind are
sometimes not defined but are treated with the related
verbs. *He worked as a translator. ...the conquerors of
Peru.*
oracle /prəkl/ **oracles**
1 NC An **oracle** was a priest or priestess in ancient
Greece, who made predictions about the future or told
people the truth about a particular situation. *Socrates
had been told by the Delphic oracle that he was the
wisest of men.*
2 NC An **oracle** is also a prophecy or other statement
made by an oracle. *The past must give way to
modernity but the belief in the power of oracles and
mysticism does not give way.*
oracular /prækjulə/
ADJ Something that is **oracular** comes from or is
related to an oracle; a formal word. *...oracular
guidance for the future.*
oral /ɔːrəl/ **orals**
1 ADJ ATTRIB **Oral** is used to describe things that
involve speaking rather than writing. *...an oral test in
German.* ♦ **orally** ADV *The candidate will be
examined orally.*
2 NC An **oral** is an oral test or examination. *The oral
follows a written paper.*
3 ADJ **Oral** medicines are ones that you swallow. *...an
oral vaccine.* ♦ **orally** ADV *...a pill taken orally.*
orange /prɪndʒ/ **oranges**
1 ADJ Something that is **orange** is of a colour between
red and yellow. *...an orange silk scarf.*
2 NC An **orange** is a round orange fruit that is juicy
and sweet. *...a truck-load of oranges. ...oranges,
lemons and bananas. ...a glass of orange juice.*
orangeade /prɪndʒeɪd/
NU **Orangeade** is a sweet orange-coloured drink that
tastes of oranges. Orangeade is sometimes fizzy, and
sometimes mixed with water. *She asked us if we'd
like some orangeade.*
orange blossom
NU **Orange blossom** consists of the white flowers of an
orange tree. Orange blossom is sweetly scented and
traditionally carried by European and American
brides at their wedding.
orangery /prɪndʒəᵒri/ **orangeries**
NC An **orangery** is a conservatory or greenhouse in
which orange trees are grown.
orang-outang /ərænguːtæn/ **orang-outangs**; also spelt
orang-utan.
NC An **orang-outang** is a large ape with long arms that
comes from the rain forests of Borneo and Sumatra.
*The orang-outang, an Asian ape, presumably evolved
along a family tree that split off before this time.*
Oranjestad /ɔːrɑːnjəstɑːt/
Oranjestad is the capital of Aruba and its largest city.
Population: 20,000 (1980).
oration /əreɪʃn/ **orations**
NC An **oration** is a formal public speech; a formal
word. *...a funeral oration.*

orator /prətə/ **orators**
NC An **orator** is someone who is skilled at making
speeches; a formal word. *His skills as an orator and
his flair for publicity attracted the international
media... A persuasive orator, Malcolm X expressed
the anger that other blacks dared not express.*
oratorical /prətɒrɪkl/
ADJ ATTRIB **Oratorical** means relating to or using
oratory; a formal word. *...oratorical skills. ...a long
oratorical speech.*
oratorio /prətɔːriəʊ/ **oratorios**
NC An **oratorio** is a piece of music that has a religious
subject and is written for singers and an orchestra.
*...a dramatic oratorio such as Bach's 'St Matthew
Passion'.*
oratory /prətəᵒri/
NU **Oratory** is the art of making formal speeches; a
formal word. *He roused the troops with his oratory.*
orb /ɔːb/ **orbs**
1 NC An **orb** is something that is shaped like a ball,
for example the sun or moon; a literary use. *...that
great red orb, now sinking down towards the Bristol
Channel. ...the dusty yellow orbs of street lamps.*
2 NC An **orb** is also a small, ornamental ball with a
cross on top that is carried by a king or queen in
important ceremonies, for example when they are
being crowned.
orbit /ɔːbɪt/ **orbits, orbiting, orbited**
1 NCorNU An **orbit** is the curved path followed by an
object going round a planet, a moon, or the sun. *...the
orbit of Mercury... How much does it cost to put a
satellite into orbit?*
2 VOorV If something such as a satellite **orbits** a
planet, a moon, or the sun, it goes round and round it.
*The shuttle orbited the earth twice before being
brought down for a perfect landing. ...the first
American astronaut to orbit in space.*
orbital /ɔːbɪtl/
ADJ ATTRIB An **orbital** road goes all the way round a
large city. *...the orbital motorway round London, the
M25.*
orbiter /ɔːbɪtə/ **orbiters**
NC An **orbiter** is a spacecraft or satellite that goes
round a planet, moon, or sun without ever landing on
it. *The orbiter was designed to circle Venus at
varying heights above the planet's atmosphere... The
orbiter will continue to explore Saturn and its moons
for four more years.*
orchard /ɔːtʃəd/ **orchards**
NC An **orchard** is an area of land on which fruit trees
are grown. *...rich farmland and abundant fruit
orchards. ...neat little gardens and orchards.*
orchestra /ɔːkɪstrə/ **orchestras**
NC An **orchestra** is a large group of musicians who
play a variety of different instruments together. *She
taught the college orchestra Tippett's Fourth
Symphony. ...a 19-piece orchestra.*
orchestral /ɔːkestrəl/
ADJ ATTRIB **Orchestral** means consisting of or relating
to the music played by an orchestra. *...Mozart's
orchestral pieces.*
orchestra pit, orchestra pits
NC The **orchestra pit** in a theatre is the space
reserved for the musicians, immediately in front of or
under the stage. *The theatre had an enormously wide
orchestra pit between auditorium and stage.*
orchestrate /ɔːkɪstreɪt/ **orchestrates, orchestrating,
orchestrated**
1 VO If you **orchestrate** something, you organize it
very carefully in order to produce a particular result
or situation. *He personally orchestrated that entire
evening.* ♦ **orchestrated** ADJ ATTRIB *...a brilliantly
orchestrated campaign of persuasion and protest.*
2 VO If you **orchestrate** a piece of music, you rewrite
it so that it can be played by an orchestra. *Mulligan's
gone on to orchestrate jazz for concert bands and
symphony orchestras.*
orchestration /ɔːkɪstreɪʃn/ **orchestrations**
NC An **orchestration** is a piece of music that has been
rewritten so that it can be played by an orchestra.
...his orchestrations of Bach, Handel, and Brahms.

orchid /ˈɔːkɪd/ **orchids**
NC An **orchid** is a plant with beautiful and unusual flowers. *...growing an endangered orchid.*

ordain /ɔːˈdeɪn/ **ordains, ordaining, ordained**
1 VO When someone **is ordained**, they are made a member of the clergy in a religious ceremony. *When I was first ordained, I served as a hospital chaplain.*
2 VOor V-REPORT If someone in authority **ordains** something, they order that it shall happen; a formal use. *Lady Sackville ordained complete discretion... The law ordained that she should be executed.*

ordeal /ɔːˈdiːl/ **ordeals**
NC An **ordeal** is an extremely unpleasant and difficult experience. *He described the rest of his terrible ordeal.*

order /ˈɔːdə/ **orders, ordering, ordered**
1 NC If someone in authority gives you an **order**, they tell you to do something. *George went away to carry out this order... He had received orders that morning to continue with the work... An official inquiry was set up on the orders of the Minister of Health.*
2 VO, V-REPORT, V QUOTE, or VO+to-INF If someone in authority **orders** people to do something or **orders** something to be done, they tell people to do it. *Sherman ordered an investigation into her husband's death... The Captain ordered the ship's masts to be cut down... 'Sit down!' he ordered... He ordered me to fetch the books... The prime minister ordered that they be taken to prison.*
3 NC An **order** is something that you ask to be brought or sent to you, and that you are going to pay for. *A waiter came to take their order... We will continue to deal with overseas orders.*
4 VOor V When you **order** something that you are going to pay for, you ask for it to be brought or sent to you. *She ordered an extra delivery of coal... I'll order now.*
5 NU If a set of things are arranged or done in a particular **order**, one thing is put first or done first, another thing second, another thing third, and so on. *The names are not in alphabetical order.*
6 NU **Order** is the situation that exists when everything is in the correct place or is done at the correct time. *I felt it would create some order in our lives... Gretchen combed her hair into some sort of order.*
7 NU **Order** is also the situation that exists when people live together peacefully rather than fighting or causing trouble. *...the task of restoring order. ...anyone considered to be a threat to public order.*
8 N SING+SUPP When people talk about a particular **order**, they mean the way society is organized at a particular time. *They don't accept the existing order... The society has been set up with the aim of defending the socialist order.*
9 NC An **order** is also a group of monks or nuns who live according to certain rules. *She came from a very strict religious order.*
10 N SING+SUPP If you refer to something of a particular **order**, you mean something of a particular quality, amount, or degree; a formal use. *...a thinker of the highest order.*
● **Order** is used in these phrases. ● If you do something **in order to** achieve a particular thing, you do it because you want to achieve that thing. *He had to hurry in order to reach the next place on his schedule... Rose trod with care, in order not to spread the dirt... They are learning English in order to study engineering.* ● If you are **under orders** to do something, you have been told to do it by someone in authority. *They were apparently under orders to avoid the area... We're under orders not to take pictures.* ● Something that is **on order**, for example at a shop, has been asked for but has not yet been supplied. *All the aircraft on order will be powered by Rolls Royce engines.* ● If a set of things are done, arranged, or dealt with **in order**, they are done, arranged, or dealt with according to the correct sequence. *It's only human to want to pay your debts in order.* ● If you **keep order** or **keep people in order**, you prevent people from behaving in an excited or violent way. *Troops could be sent in to keep order... At first the police kept well back and the stewards*

tried to keep order. ● A machine or device that is **in working order** is functioning properly and is not broken. *...cars in good working order.* ● A machine or device that is **out of order** is broken and does not work. *...public telephones which are out of order.* ● If you tell someone to put their **house in order**, you tell them that they should organize their own affairs and solve their own problems before telling anyone else how to solve theirs. *The Southern African states would have no hope unless they got their house in order.* ● You use **in the order of** or **of the order of** when giving an approximate figure; a formal expression. *Britain's contribution is something in the order of 5 per cent.* ● **a tall order**: see **tall**. ● See also **law and order, mail order, postal order, standing order.**

order about PHRASAL VERB If you **order** someone **about** or **order** them **around**, you always tell them what to do, in an unsympathetic way. *Don't try and order them about... It was intolerable that those two fat slobs should order her around.*

order around PHRASAL VERB See **order about.**

ordered /ˈɔːdəd/
ADJ An **ordered** society or system is well organized or arranged. *In Mrs Kaul's house everything was well ordered.*

orderly /ˈɔːdəli/ **orderlies**
1 ADJ Something that is **orderly** is well organized or arranged. *...a system of orderly government.*
♦ **orderliness** NU *We pride ourselves on the orderliness of our way of life.*
2 NC An **orderly** is a hospital attendant. *I sat at the end of the ward with the orderly.*

ordinal number /ˈɔːdɪnl nʌmbə/ **ordinal numbers**
NC An **ordinal number**, or an **ordinal**, is a number that is used to say what position something has in a list or set, such as 1st, 3rd, and 10th; compare **cardinal number.**

ordinance /ˈɔːdɪnəns/ **ordinances**
NC An **ordinance** is an official rule or order; a formal word. *In 1972 the city passed an ordinance compelling all outdoor lighting to be switched off at 9.00 p.m.*

ordinand /ˈɔːdɪnænd/ **ordinands**
NC An **ordinand** is someone who is being trained to be a priest.

ordinarily /ˈɔːdənərəli/
ADV or ADV SEN If something **ordinarily** happens, it usually happens. *This room was ordinarily used by the doctor... Ordinarily, of course, we would use the telephone.*

ordinary /ˈɔːdənri/
1 ADJ Something that is **ordinary** is not special or different in any way. *...ordinary everyday objects... What do ordinary people really think about universities?... She is likeable enough, but very ordinary.*
2 Something that is **out of the ordinary** is unusual or different. *I'd like to bring her something a little out of the ordinary.*

ordination /ˌɔːdɪˈneɪʃn/ **ordinations**
NC or NU When someone's **ordination** takes place, they are made a member of the Christian clergy in a special ceremony. *...his ordination in the magnificent York Minster. ...the ordination of women.*

ordnance /ˈɔːdnəns/
NU **Ordnance** consists of military supplies, especially weapons. *...Royal Ordnance Factories.*

Ordnance Survey
N PROP The **Ordnance Survey** is the British government organization that produces detailed maps of Britain and Ireland.

ordure /ˈɔːdjʊə/
NU **Ordure** is excrement; a formal word. *...a bucketful of ordure.*

ore /ɔː/ **ores**
N MASS **Ore** is rock or earth from which metal can be obtained. *...the mining of iron ore.*

oregano /ˌɒrɪˈɡɑːnəʊ/
NU **Oregano** is a plant that is used as a herb in cooking. *Season with a little salt, oregano, and soy sauce.*

organ /ˈɔːgən/ **organs**
1 NC An **organ** is a part of your body that has a particular purpose or function, for example your heart or your lungs. *Children's bones and organs are very sensitive to radiation.*
2 NC An **organ** is also a large musical instrument with pipes of different lengths through which air is forced. You play the organ rather like a piano. *...the great cathedral organ. ...a mixture of organ music, hymns, sermons and meditations.* ◆ **organist** /ˈɔːgənɪst/ **organists** NC *He is a very fine organist.*
3 NC+SUPP You refer to a newspaper as an **organ** of a particular organization when the organization uses it as a means of giving information or influencing people. *They decided to close the newspaper and launch it again as a government organ.*

organdie /ˈɔːgəndi/; also spelt **organdy** in American English.
NU **Organdie** is a fine, slightly stiff cotton fabric that is used for making dresses. *...a white organdie blouse.*

organ-grinder, organ-grinders
NC An **organ-grinder** is an entertainer who plays a barrel organ in the streets. *The men take their simple pleasures dancing a clog dance in the street, or listening to an organ-grinder.*

organic /ɔːˈgænɪk/
1 ADJ Something that is **organic** is produced by or found in plants or animals. *The rocks were carefully searched for organic remains.*
2 ADJ ATTRIB **Organic** is used to refer to methods of gardening or farming that use only natural animal and plant products to fertilize the land and control pests, rather than using chemicals. *...organic farming in Africa and Britain... He said there was increasing consumer demand for organic produce.* ◆ **organically** ADV *...organically grown vegetables.*

organisation /ˌɔːgənaɪˈzeɪʃn/. See **organization**.
organisational /ˌɔːgənaɪˈzeɪʃ⁰nəl/. See **organizational**.
organise /ˈɔːgənaɪz/. See **organize**.
organiser /ˈɔːgənaɪzə/. See **organizer**.
organism /ˈɔːgənɪzəm/ **organisms**
NC An **organism** is an animal or plant, especially one that is so small that you cannot see it without a microscope. *These creatures are descended from simpler organisms like corals.*

organization /ˌɔːgənaɪˈzeɪʃn/ **organizations**; also spelt **organisation**.
1 NC An **organization** is a group of people who do something together regularly in an organized way. Businesses and clubs are organizations. *...student organizations. ...the World Health Organisation.*
2 NU The **organization** of a system is the way in which its different parts are related and how they work together. *There has been a total change in the organization of society.*
3 NU The **organization** of an activity or public event involves making all the arrangements for it. *I don't want to get involved in the actual organisation of things.*

organizational /ˌɔːgənaɪˈzeɪʃ⁰nəl/; also spelt **organisational**.
1 ADJ ATTRIB **Organizational** means relating to the way that things are planned and arranged. *...an organizational genius named Alfred P. Sloan.*
2 ADJ ATTRIB **Organizational** also means relating to organizations. *The group has no political or organisational links with the terrorists.*

Organization of African Unity (OAU)
The **Organization of African Unity** was founded in 1963 to promote co-operation and unity among African countries. The headquarters are in Addis Ababa. Western Sahara was admitted in 1982, but its membership is disputed. Morocco withdrew from the OAU in 1985 over the issue of Western Sahara. The members of the OAU are: Algeria, Angola, Benin, Botswana, Burkina Faso, Burundi, Cameroon, Cape Verde, Central African Republic, Chad, Comoros, Congo, Côte d'Ivoire, Djibouti, Egypt, Equatorial Guinea, Ethiopia, Gabon, Gambia, Ghana, Guinea, Guinea-Bissau, Kenya, Lesotho, Liberia, Libya, Madagascar, Malawi, Mali, Mauritania, Mauritius, Mozambique, Namibia, Niger, Nigeria, Rwanda, São

Tomé and Príncipe, Senegal, Seychelles, Sierra Leone, Somalia, Sudan, Swaziland, Tanzania, Togo, Tunisia, Uganda, Zaïre, Zambia, and Zimbabwe.

Organization of American States (OAS)
The **Organization of American States** was founded in 1948 to promote collective security and co-operation among countries of the Western Hemisphere. In recent years it has become concerned with economic and social development in Central and South America. The headquarters of the OAS are in Washington, DC. Cuba was suspended in 1962. Members of the OAS are: Antigua and Barbuda, Argentina, Bahamas, Barbados, Belize, Bolivia, Brazil, Canada, Chile, Colombia, Costa Rica, Dominica, Dominican Republic, Ecuador, El Salvador, Grenada, Guatemala, Guyana, Haiti, Honduras, Jamaica, Mexico, Nicaragua, Panama, Paraguay, Peru, St Christopher and Nevis, St Lucia, St Vincent and the Grenadines, Surinam, Trinidad and Tobago, United States of America, Uruguay, and Venezuela.

Organization of Petroleum Exporting Countries See **OPEC**

organize /ˈɔːgənaɪz/ **organizes, organizing, organized**; also spelt **organise**.
1 VO If you **organize** an activity or event, you make all the arrangements for it. *We organized a concert in the village hall.*
2 VO If you **organize** things, you put them into order. *He's better able now to organise his thoughts... Papers are organized in enormous filing cabinets.*
3 V When workers or employees **organize**, they form themselves into a group such as a trade union in order to have more power. *Their poverty prevents them from organizing effectively to improve their wages.*

organized /ˈɔːgənaɪzd/; also spelt **organised**.
1 ADJ ATTRIB **Organized** activities are planned and controlled. *...an organized holiday. ...organized crime.*
2 ADJ People who are **organized** work in an efficient and effective way. *How organised you are!*

organizer /ˈɔːgənaɪzə/ **organizers**; also spelt **organiser**.
NC An **organizer** is the person who makes all the arrangements for an activity or event and makes sure that it happens as planned. *...the organizers of the conference... The organisers include refugee agencies and the human rights organisation, Amnesty International... They accused the strike organisers of breaking the law.*

orgasm /ˈɔːgæzəm/ **orgasms**
NC An **orgasm** is the moment of greatest pleasure and excitement during sexual activity. *Of course this tension is sexualized, is itself part of the rhythmic build to orgasm.*

orgasmic /ɔːˈgæzmɪk/
1 ADJ **Orgasmic** means relating to a sexual orgasm; a formal use. *...orgasmic homosexual and heterosexual orgies.*
2 ADJ **Orgasmic** also means very enjoyable or exciting; an informal use. *The war was the orgasmic experience of his newspaper career.*

orgiastic /ˌɔːdʒiˈæstɪk/
ADJ **Orgiastic** means involving extreme pleasure; a literary word. *...moods of orgiastic intoxication.*

orgy /ˈɔːdʒi/ **orgies**
1 NC An **orgy** is a party in which people behave in a very uncontrolled way, especially involving sexual activity. *...lurid stories of sex orgies.*
2 NC+SUPP You can refer to any activity that is done to an excessive extent as an **orgy** of that activity; used showing disapproval. *...an orgy of destruction. ...a destructive orgy of drink and drugs. ...an orgy of grief.*

orient /ˈɔːriənt/ **orients, orienting, oriented**
V-REFL If you **orient** yourself to a new situation, you learn about it and prepare to deal with it; a formal word. *The raw newcomer has to orient himself.* ● See also **oriented**.

oriental /ˌɔːriˈentl/
ADJ Something that is **oriental** comes from or is associated with eastern and south-eastern Asia. *...Oriental philosophy. ...her oriental features.*

orientate /ˈɔːriənteɪt/ **orientates, orientating, orientated**
V-REFL When you **orientate** yourself, you discover where you are by looking at a map, or by searching for familiar places or objects. *...trying to orientate myself on the map.*
orientated /ˈɔːriənteɪtɪd/
ADJ **Orientated** means the same as **oriented**. *...an industry orientated towards quick, easy profits.*
orientation /ˌɔːriənˈteɪʃn/
NU+SUPP You can refer to the activities and aims of an organization as its **orientation**. *...the party's revolutionary orientation.*
oriented /ˈɔːriəntɪd/
ADJ You use **oriented** to indicate what someone or something is interested in or concerned with. For example, if someone is politically **oriented**, they are interested in politics. *...a society oriented towards information... The motive was racially oriented.*
orienteering /ˌɔːriənˈtɪərɪŋ/
NU **Orienteering** is a sport in which people run from one place to another, using a compass and a map to guide them between points that are marked along the route.
orifice /ˈɒrɪfɪs/ **orifices**
NC An **orifice** is an opening or hole, especially one in your body such as your mouth; a formal word, often used humorously. *An endless flow of words streamed from the same orifice. ...the building's orifices.*
origin /ˈɒrɪdʒɪn/ **origins**
1 NCorNU You can refer to the beginning or cause of something as its **origin** or its **origins**. *The unrest has its origins in economic problems. ...the origin of the universe. ...a word of recent origin.*
2 NCorNU When you talk about a person's **origin** or **origins**, you are referring to the country, race, or social class of their parents or ancestors. *...a woman of Pakistani origin... His origins were humble.*
original /əˈrɪdʒɑⁿəl/ **originals**
1 ADJ ATTRIB You use **original** to refer to the characteristics or appearance that something had when it first existed or when it was first made or thought of. *They will restore the house to its original state... The original idea came from Dr Ball.*
♦ **originally** ADV *It was originally a toy factory.*
2 NC You refer to a work of art or a document as an **original** when it is genuine and not a copy. *The original is in the British Museum.* ► Also ADJ *...working on original documents.*
3 ADJ An **original** piece of writing or music was written recently and has not been published or performed before. *...her first collection of short stories, some original, some reprinted.*
4 ADJ If you describe someone, their ideas, or their work as **original**, you mean that they are very imaginative and clever. *...a daring and original idea.*
♦ **originality** /əˌrɪdʒəˈnælɪti/ NU *...a sculptor of genius and great originality.*
originate /əˈrɪdʒəneɪt/ **originates, originating, originated**
V-ERG When something **originates** or when someone **originates** it, it begins to happen or exist. *He originated the Norplant birth control device... We are the country that originated the concept of self-determination... These beliefs originated in the 19th century... The epidemic is believed to have originated from contaminated seafood.*
originator /əˈrɪdʒəneɪtə/ **originators**
NC The **originator** of something such as an idea or scheme is the person who first thought of it or began it. *The originator of the idea was a young professor.*
ornament /ˈɔːnəmənt/ **ornaments**
1 NC An **ornament** is a small object that you display in your home because it is attractive. *...painted china ornaments.*
2 NU **Ornament** refers to decorations and designs on a building or piece of furniture. *...different styles of ornament.*
ornamental /ˌɔːnəˈmentl/
ADJ Something that is **ornamental** is intended to be attractive rather than useful. *...an ornamental pond.*

ornamented /ˈɔːnəmentɪd/
ADJ If something is **ornamented** with attractive objects or patterns, it is decorated with them. *The sand was ornamented with shells and seaweed.*
ornate /ɔːˈneɪt/
ADJ Something that is **ornate** has a lot of decoration on it. *...ornate necklaces.*
ornithology /ˌɔːnɪˈθɒlədʒi/
NU **Ornithology** is the study of birds; a formal word. *The census was commissioned from the British Trust for Ornithology because of the concern about farming methods on bird life.*
orphan /ˈɔːfn/ **orphans, orphaned**
1 NC An **orphan** is a child whose parents are dead. *She became an orphan at twelve.*
2 V-PASS If a child **is orphaned**, its parents die. *We adopted the twins when they were orphaned.*
orphanage /ˈɔːfənɪdʒ/ **orphanages**
NC An **orphanage** is a place where orphans are looked after. *...a special programme to help children in orphanages and children's homes.*
orthodox /ˈɔːθədɒks/
1 ADJ ATTRIB **Orthodox** beliefs, methods, or systems are the ones that most people have or use. *...orthodox medicine.*
2 ADJ People who are **orthodox** believe in the older and more traditional ideas of their religion or political party. *...Orthodox Jews. ...a fairly orthodox socialist.*
orthodoxy /ˈɔːθədɒksi/ **orthodoxies**
1 NC An **orthodoxy** is an accepted view about something. *...the prevailing orthodoxy on this problem.*
2 NU+SUPP **Orthodoxy** is traditional and accepted beliefs. *...Islamic orthodoxy. ...Marxist orthodoxy.*
3 NU+SUPP **Orthodoxy** is the degree to which a person believes in and supports the ideas of their religion or political party. *It portrays itself as the guardian of communist orthodoxy. ...the rigid orthodoxy of Mr Mzali.*
orthography /ɔːˈθɒɡrəfi/
NU **Orthography** means the way words are spelt or should be spelt; a formal word. *They were written down without any standardisation of orthography.*
orthopaedic /ˌɔːθəˈpiːdɪk/; also spelt **orthopedic**.
ADJ ATTRIB **Orthopaedic** means concerning the medical care of the bones in the bodies of humans and animals, especially the treatment or prevention of injuries or defects; a medical term. *...the Orthopaedic Hospital. ...orthopaedic patients. ...orthopaedic boots.*
OS
1 ADJ **OS** is a written abbreviation for 'outsize'; used especially on labels on clothes, or in advertising clothes for sale.
2 N+N **OS** is also a written abbreviation for 'Ordnance Survey'. *...OS maps.*
oscillate /ˈɒsɪleɪt/ **oscillates, oscillating, oscillated**; a formal word.
1 V If something **oscillates**, it moves repeatedly from one position to another and back again. *Its wings oscillate up and down.*
2 V+between If you **oscillate** between two moods, attitudes, or types of behaviour, you keep changing from one to the other and back again. *His mood oscillated between co-operation and aggression.*
oscillation /ˌɒsɪˈleɪʃn/ **oscillations**
NC An **oscillation** is an increase or decrease in an amount that happens frequently or regularly. *...the short-term oscillation of the share index.*
Oslo /ˈɒzləʊ/
Oslo is the capital of Norway and its largest city. Population: 458,000 (1990).
osmosis /ɒzˈməʊsɪs/
1 NU **Osmosis** is the process by which a liquid passes through a thin piece of solid substance such as the roots of a plant; a technical use. *From this reverse osmosis filtering machine we get water as pure as distilled water.*
2 NU **Osmosis** is also the way in which people or ideas influence each other gradually and without any obvious signs. *...a kind of sisterly osmosis.*
ossify /ˈɒsɪfaɪ/ **ossifies, ossifying, ossified**
V-ERG If you say that an idea, system, or organization

ossifies, or something **ossifies** it, you mean that it becomes fixed and difficult to change; a formal word, used showing disapproval. *These social customs and complexities have ossified... The State ossifies class relationships.* ◆ **ossified** ADJ *...a large, bureaucratic and ossified system... Things became ossified in the late 17th century.* ◆ **ossification** /ɒsɪfɪkeɪʃn/ NU *...social ossification and the denial of individual rights.*

ostensible /ɒstɛnsəbl/
ADJ ATTRIB **Ostensible** is used to refer to things that seem or are said to be the case, but which you think are probably not the case; a formal word. *...the ostensible purpose of his excursion.* ◆ **ostensibly** ADV *Rose left the room, ostensibly to explain about dinner to the cook.*

ostentation /ɒstenteɪʃn/
NU You say that someone's behaviour is **ostentation** when they do things in order to impress other people with their wealth or importance; a formal word. *More than two telephones is pure ostentation.*

ostentatious /ɒstenteɪʃəs/; a formal word, used showing disapproval.
1 ADJ Something that is **ostentatious** is very expensive and is intended to impress people. *...a magnificent and ostentatious palace.*
2 ADJ People who are **ostentatious** try to impress other people with their wealth or importance. *...allegations that the country's wealth has been milked off by a rich and ostentatious elite.* ◆ **ostentatiously** ADV *They were never ostentatiously dressed.*
3 ADJ An **ostentatious** action is done in an exaggerated way in order to attract people's attention. *...an ostentatious gesture.* ◆ **ostentatiously** ADV *...ostentatiously smiling.*

osteopath /ɒstiəpæθ/ **osteopaths**
NC An **osteopath** is a person who treats illnesses by massaging people's bodies and bending them in different ways, especially in order to reduce pain or stiffness. *He went to an osteopath; one crack and never a twinge of pain since.*

ostracism /ɒstrəsɪzəm/
NU **Ostracism** is the state of being ostracized or the act of ostracizing someone; a formal word. *The mothers of these children feared social ostracism... They faced hostility, contempt, ostracism.*

ostracize /ɒstrəsaɪz/ **ostracizes, ostracizing, ostracized**; also spelt **ostracise**.
VO If you **are ostracized**, people deliberately behave in an unfriendly way towards you and do not allow you to take part in their social activities; a formal word. *Their children were ostracized by teachers and pupils alike.*

ostrich /ɒstrɪtʃ/ **ostriches**
NC An **ostrich** is a large African bird that cannot fly. *The meat of an ostrich is not really palatable to the human.*

other /ʌðə/ **others**. When **other** is used after the determiner 'an', it is written as one word. See **another**.
1 ADJ ATTRIB or PRON **Other** people or things are not the people or things that you have just mentioned or have just been talking about, but are different things. *There were some other people in the compartment... There was no other way to do it... Results in other countries are impressive... Some projects are shorter than others.*
2 ADJ ATTRIB or PRON When you have mentioned the first of two things, you refer to the second one as the **other** one. *He had his papers in one hand, his hat in the other... They have two daughters, one a baby, the other a girl of twelve.*
3 ADJ ATTRIB or N PL The **other** people or things in a group are the rest of them. *...the other members of the class... I shall wait until the others come back... Nine of the occupants died in the bar and others in hospital.*
4 ADJ ATTRIB or N PL You refer to **other** people or **others** when you are talking about people in general, but not including yourself. *One ought not to inflict one's problems on other people... Working for others can be most fulfilling.*
5 ADJ ATTRIB You use **other** with words such as 'day' or 'week' when you want to say that something

happened recently but you are not saying exactly when. *I saw Davis the other day.*
● **Other** is used in these phrases. ● You use **among other things** or **among others** to say there are several more facts, things, people, and so on that are like the ones you are talking about, but you are not going to discuss them in detail. *Among other things, he opened a new superstore that has only recently been permitted to operate in Japan... Amongst others, he defended the Communist leader Braam Fisher, the activist Govan Mbeki, and Steve Biko.* ● You use **other than** after a negative in order to introduce an exception to what you have said, or to introduce something that is the only thing possible in the situation. *She never discussed it with anyone other than Derek... There's no choice other than to reopen his case... There is no evidence that he's suffering anything other than gastric flu.* ● You use **every other** when talking about the intervals at which something occurs. For example, if something happens **every other** day, it could happen on the 1st, 3rd, 5th, and so on of a particular month. *Their local committees are usually held every other month.* ● You say **or other** after words such as 'some', 'something', or 'somehow' in order to show that you are not being precise about the information you are giving. *For some reason or other your name was omitted... Somehow or other, he reached the Alps.* ● You use **one or other** to refer to one or more things or people in a group, when it does not matter which one is thought of or chosen. *One or other current must be altered.* ● **each other**: see **each**.
● **in other words**: see **word**.

otherwise /ʌðəwaɪz/
1 ADV SEN You use **otherwise** after stating a situation or fact, to say what the result or consequence would be if this situation or fact was not the case. *It's perfectly harmless, otherwise I wouldn't have done it... Ministers should be providing opportunities, otherwise we will carry the burden of the unemployed for a very long time.*
2 ADV SEN or SUBMOD You use **otherwise** when stating the general condition or quality of something after you have mentioned an exception to this general condition or quality. *The cement is slightly cracked but otherwise in good condition... That was a sudden outbreak in an otherwise blameless career.*
3 SUBMOD You use **otherwise** known as, when you give another and often better known name to something or someone you have just mentioned. *...the International Bank for Reconstruction and Development, otherwise known as the World Bank. ...teenage car thieves, otherwise known as joy-riders.*
4 ADV **Otherwise** is also used to refer to the opposite of something, or something very different from what was previously stated; a formal use. *They say he died, but until proved otherwise, Israel assumes all prisoners are alive... Stiff and formal, the man was incapable of acting otherwise.*
5 You use the expression **or otherwise** to refer to the opposite of the preceding word, especially in cases where either of them might be correct. *He insisted there would never be any support, military or otherwise, for the Khmer Rouge... His release may depend on the success or otherwise of John McCarthy's diplomatic mission.*

other-worldly
ADJ **Other-worldly** means more concerned with spiritual matters than with daily life. *They encourage an image of Tibet as an other-worldly sort of place. ...other-worldly, unrealistic people.*

Ottawa /ɒtəwə/
Ottawa is the capital of Canada and its fourth largest city. Population: 819,000 (1986).

otter /ɒtə/ **otters**
NC An **otter** is a small animal with a long tail. Otters swim well and eat fish. *Some studies have involved seal pups, otters and ducks.*

Ouagadougou /wægədʊːguː/
Ouagadougou is the capital of Burkina Faso and its largest city. Population: 442,000 (1985).

ouch /aʊtʃ/
People say **'Ouch!'** when they suddenly feel pain. *One*

car dealer, asked what the previous 6 months had been like, answered with a single word—ouch.

ought /ɔːt, ɔːt/

1 MODAL If you say that someone **ought** to do something, or **ought** to have done it, you mean that it is the right thing to do, or that it would have been the right thing to do. *She ought to see the doctor... 'I don't care,' he said. 'Well, you ought to,' she said... I ought to have said yes... I ought not to have come here.*

2 MODAL If you say that something **ought** to be true, you mean that you expect it to be true. *It ought to be quite easy... He ought to be out of jail by now.*

oughtn't /ɔːtnt/

Oughtn't is a spoken form of 'ought not'. *That's just the position the President oughtn't to allow.*

ounce /aʊns/ **ounces**

1 NC An **ounce** is a unit of weight equal to approximately 28.35 grams. *...an ounce of tobacco... The baby gains 6 to 8 ounces a week.* ● See also **fluid ounce**.

2 N SING You can also refer to a very small amount of a quality or characteristic as an **ounce**. *...using every ounce of strength he possessed. ...anyone with an ounce of intelligence.*

our /ɑː, aʊə/

DET A speaker or writer uses **our** to refer to something that belongs or relates to a group of people which includes himself or herself. *...our children... This could change our lives... Our Moscow correspondent reports.*

ours /aʊəz, ɑːz/

PRON A speaker or writer uses **ours** to refer to something that belongs or relates to a group of people which includes himself or herself. *It is a very different country from ours.*

ourselves /ɑːsɛlvz, aʊəsɛlvz/

1 PRON REFL A speaker or writer uses **ourselves** as the object of a verb or preposition in a clause where 'we' is the subject or 'us' is a previous object. *We almost made ourselves ill... In 1968 we built ourselves a new surgery.*

2 PRON REFL **Ourselves** is also used to emphasize the subject or object of a clause. *In teaching, we ourselves have to do a lot of learning.*

3 PRON REFL A speaker or writer also uses **ourselves** in expressions such as 'we did it ourselves' in order to say that a group of people which included himself or herself did something without any help or interference from anyone else. *Should we not be doing it ourselves without the Communists?*

oust /aʊst/ **ousts, ousting, ousted**

VO If you **oust** someone from a job or a place, you force them to leave it. *...the coup which ousted the President. ...Mr Zhivkov, who was ousted from power last November... It's alleged they planned to oust the President.* ◆ **ousted** ADJ ATTRIB *...the ousted military leader.* ◆ **ousting** N SING+of *The biggest talking point has been the ousting of one of the country's most outspoken members of parliament.*

out /aʊt/ **outs, outing, outed**

1 ADV When you go **out** of a place or get **out** of something such as a vehicle, you leave it, so that you are no longer inside it. *She rushed out of the house... She's just got out of bed. ...Vietnamese troops who are due to be pulled out of Kampuchea by next Wednesday.*

2 ADV If you are **out**, you are not at home or not at your usual place of work. *He came when I was out... Joe is out looking for her... I've been out in the city all day. ...an evening out.*

3 ADV If you look **out** of a window, you look through it at things that are outside. *She stared out at the rain... I was standing looking out over the view.*

4 ADV You can use **out** to indicate that something is happening outside a building rather than inside it. *Many people were sleeping out... It's hot out.*

5 ADV If you say that someone is **out** in a particular place, you are referring to the fact that they are in a different place from the one you are speaking from. *He's out in the Cambridgeshire countryside.*

6 ADV If you take something **out** of a container or

place, you remove it from the container or place. *She opened a box and took out a cigarette... He got out a book and read.*

7 ADV You can use **out** to say that someone is leaving an institution or has left it. *I had been out of university a year.*

8 ADV If you keep someone or something **out** of a place, or throw them **out** of it, you prevent them from going in there, or remove them from it. *It's designed to keep out intruders.*

9 ADV If a light or fire is **out**, it is no longer shining or burning. *The lights went out... He helped to put the fire out.*

10 ADJ PRED If flowers are **out**, their petals have opened. *The daffodils were out.*

11 ADJ PRED If something such as a book or record is **out**, it is available for people to buy. *..a debut LP is due out soon.*

12 ADV You use **out** to say that a number of things are distributed to several places or in several different directions. *We sent out a leaflet to every household.*

13 ADJ PRED If workers are **out**, they are on strike; an informal use. *The men stayed out for nearly a month.*

14 ADJ PRED In a game or sport, if someone is **out**, they can no longer take part either because they are unable to or because they have been eliminated. *If he's out, his place is likely to be taken by Patrick Serriere... Pakistan were restricted to 177 all out.*

15 ADJ PRED If you say that a proposal or suggestion is **out**, you mean that it is unacceptable; an informal use. *That's right out, I'm afraid.*

16 ADJ PRED If a particular fashion or method is **out**, it is no longer fashionable; an informal use. *Romance is making a comeback. Reality is out.*

17 ADV When the sea or tide goes **out**, the sea moves away from the shore.

18 ADJ PRED If a calculation or measurement is **out**, it is incorrect. *It's only a couple of degrees out.*

19 ADJ PRED If someone is **out** to do something, they intend to do it; an informal use. *They're out to use your house as a free hotel. ...the selfish interests of a few people who were out to plunge the country into chaos.*

20 PREP You use **out of** to say what causes someone to do something. For example, if you do something **out of** pity, you do it because you pity someone. *He wrote that review out of pure spite... Jan Palach committed suicide in 1969 out of despair.*

21 PREP If you get pleasure or an advantage **out of** something, you get it because you were involved in that thing. *But what does he get out of behaving like that?*

22 PREP If you are **out of** something, you no longer have it or any of it. *We're out of paper... Thousands of printers who once manned the presses are out of a job.*

23 PREP If something is made **out of** a particular material, it is made from it. *You can make petroleum out of coal.*

24 PREP You use **out of** to indicate what proportion of a group of things something is true of. *Four out of five transplant patients now have their donor kidney working after a year.*

25 VO If a group of people **out** a public figure or famous person, they reveal that person's homosexuality against their wishes. *One of the men he recently outed was a US Congressman, whom he met in a gay bar... Attempts to out her stem from complaints that gay men get a bad reputation in the film.* ◆ **outing** NU *I think that time will prove that outing was a correct and necessary tactic to use... The posters represent the first British example of the outing campaign.*

26 See also **outing**.

out- /aʊt-/

PREFIX **Out-** is used to form verbs that describe one person doing something better than another. For example, if you can outswim someone, you can swim farther or faster than they can. *She managed to outrun them... Prices rose through the year as demand outpaced supply... Crops grown from hybrid seeds will typically outyield the crops grown from what we call* *inbred seeds... He outsprinted the pack to win the first stage of the race.*

outage /ˈaʊtreɪdʒ/ outages
NC An **outage** is the same as a **power failure**; used in American English. *The exact cause of the outage is unknown... Severe winter weather has caused power outages and road closures.*

out-and-out
ADJ ATTRIB You use **out-and-out** to emphasize that someone or something has all the characteristics of a particular type of person or thing. *He's an out-and-out villain. ...an out-and-out triumph.*

outback /ˈaʊtbæk/
N SING The parts of Australia where very few people live are referred to as the **outback**. *In the Australian outback, farmers are facing the worst economic crisis in living memory.*

outbid /aʊtˈbɪd/ outbids, outbidding, outbidded. The past tense and past participle can be either **outbidded** or **outbid**.
VO If you **outbid** someone, you offer more money than they do for something that you want to buy. *We'll be outbid at every auction... They are outbidding other potential buyers.*

outboard motor /aʊtbɔːd ˈmaʊtə/ outboard motors
NC An **outboard motor** is a motor with a propeller that you can fix to the back of a small boat. *...a solidly-built rowing boat, powered by an outboard motor.*

outbound /ˈaʊtbaʊnd/
ADJ A plane that is **outbound** is leaving or is due to leave its place of departure. *Luggage from the 727 outbound from Frankfurt was loaded directly in a sealed container. ... a British Caledonian 1-11, outbound for Amsterdam.*

outbreak /ˈaʊtbreɪk/ outbreaks
NC+SUPP An **outbreak** of something unpleasant is a sudden occurrence of it. *...the outbreak of war. ...outbreaks of disease... The victims are also having to contend with outbreaks of malaria and hepatitis... Five people have been killed in the latest outbreak of fighting between rival black political groups.*

outbuilding /ˈaʊtbɪldɪŋ/ outbuildings
NC **Outbuildings** are small buildings such as barns or stables that are part of a larger property. *Military officials say fierce fighting is continuing in outbuildings around the fort.*

outburst /ˈaʊtbɜːst/ outbursts
1 NC An **outburst** is a sudden and strong expression of anger or other strong emotion. *I apologize for my outburst just now... When he discovered that the leaders of the uprising were executed, he found a huge outburst of emotion, of national feeling.*
2 NC+SUPP An **outburst** of violent activity is a sudden period of it. *There followed an outburst of shooting. ...the worst outburst of violence since the strike began.*

outcast /ˈaʊtkɑːst/ outcasts
NC An **outcast** is someone who is rejected by a group of people. *They are treated as outcasts... It should mean that Peru, so long an outcast from the international community, will be able to re-establish relations with the industrial world.*

outclass /aʊtˈklɑːs/ outclasses, outclassing, outclassed
VO If you **outclass** someone, you show that you are a lot better than they are at a particular activity. *He was totally outclassed... The twenty-four year old Thobela outclassed Antonio Rivera to record his twenty-sixth win.*

outcome /ˈaʊtkʌm/ outcomes
NC The **outcome** of an action or process is the result of it. *Nobody dared predict the outcome of the election... He has expressed his optimism at the prospect of a successful outcome to the talks.*

outcrop /ˈaʊtkrɒp/ outcrops
NC An **outcrop** is a large area of rock sticking out of the ground. *...a massive outcrop of granite.*

outcry /ˈaʊtkraɪ/ outcries
NC An **outcry** is a strong reaction of disapproval or anger by many people. *The experiments continued, despite the public outcry against them... There's been an international outcry over the case... The deaths have caused a public outcry.*

outdated /aʊtˈdeɪtɪd/
ADJ Something that is **outdated** is old-fashioned and no longer useful. *...outdated methods of management.*

outdid /aʊtˈdɪd/
Outdid is the past tense of **outdo**.

outdistance /aʊtˈdɪstəns/ outdistances, outdistancing, outdistanced
1 VO If you **outdistance** someone, you are a lot better and more successful than they are at a particular activity. *He easily outdistanced men like Castle, who was of an older generation... They have outdistanced Peking in the field of political change.*
2 VO If you **outdistance** your opponents in a race or in an election, you beat them easily. *She outdistanced all the opposition... He enters the campaign as the firm favourite to outdistance both of the chief candidates of the right.*

outdo /aʊtˈduː/ outdoes, outdoing, outdid, outdone
1 VO If you **outdo** someone, you are more successful than they are at a particular activity. *A heavy person can outdo a lighter one in such jobs.*
2 You use the expression **not to be outdone** to say that someone does something because they want to prove that they are better than or just as good as someone else. *The British ambassador offered a toast to England. Not to be outdone, the French ambassador toasted 'To France, the delight of all nations'... With one million men under arms, Iraq is a bigger threat, but perhaps the Libyan leader is not to be outdone.*

outdoor /aʊtˈdɔː/
ADJ ATTRIB **Outdoor** activities or clothes take place or are used in the open air, rather than in a building. *...outdoor work... He was fully dressed in his outdoor clothes.*

outdoors /aʊtˈdɔːz/
ADV If something exists or happens **outdoors**, it exists or happens in the open air, rather than in a building. *School classes were held outdoors... Let them go outdoors and play.*

outer /ˈaʊtə/
ADJ ATTRIB The **outer** parts of something are the parts which contain or enclose the other parts, and which are farthest from the centre. *Peel off the outer plastic cover of the flex.*

outermost /ˈaʊtəməʊst/
ADJ ATTRIB The **outermost** thing in a group of things is the one that is farthest from the centre. *...the outermost wall... The outermost tail feathers are slightly longer in the male.*

outer space
NU **Outer space** refers to the area outside the Earth's atmosphere. *The first forms of life on earth could have come from outer space in meteorite showers.*

outfit /ˈaʊtfɪt/ outfits
1 NC An **outfit** is a set of clothes. *I can't afford a new evening outfit.*
2 NC You can refer to an organization as an **outfit**; an informal use. *I joined this outfit hoping to go abroad. ...a couple of guys from a security outfit.*

outfitter /ˈaʊtfɪtə/ outfitters
NC An **outfitter** or **outfitters** is a shop that sells men's clothes; an old-fashioned word. *...a gentleman's outfitter.*

outflank /aʊtˈflæŋk/ outflanks, outflanking, outflanked
1 VO If one army **outflanks** another, it succeeds in getting round the side of it in order to attack it. *...an attempt to outflank the main force... I don't share your optimism about the campaign to outflank forces in Kuwait.*
2 VO If you **outflank** someone, you succeed in getting into a position where you can defeat them, for example in an argument. *He found himself outflanked over incomes policy... There is talk of outflanking the Democrats and launching a war against poverty and unemployment.*

outflow /ˈaʊtfləʊ/ outflows
NC When there is an **outflow** of something such as money or people, a large quantity of it or them moves from one place to another. *... the net outflow of resources from Latin America... What measures are Albania's communist authorities taking to stem the outflow of refugees?*

outfox /aʊtfɒks/ outfoxes, outfoxing, outfoxed
vo If you **outfox** someone, you are a lot more clever or cunning than they are and so defeat them in some way. *We managed to outfox him... Almadovar made a worldwide name outfoxing France's censors in the 60s and 70s and filming 'Flamenco Ballet' in the 80s... On the face of it, Mr Gandhi has been outfoxed.*

outgassing /aʊtgæsɪŋ/
NU or NC **Outgassing** is the release of chemical gases into the atmosphere by factories and chemical plants. *He calculated the total emission rate for the outgassing of carbon... That would cause an outgassing of dioxide from the reservoirs... We have reason to believe that the outgassing rate may have been several times higher.*

outgoing /aʊtgəʊɪŋ/ outgoing
1 ADJ ATTRIB You use **outgoing** to describe someone or something that is leaving a place or position. *...the outgoing president in his last days of office... He began his inaugural address by paying tribute to the outgoing President. ...outgoing mail. ...incoming and outgoing passengers.*
2 ADJ An **outgoing** person is very friendly and likes meeting people. *Adler was an outgoing, sociable kind of man.*
3 N PL Your **outgoings** are the amounts of money which you spend. *Try to reduce as many outgoings as possible.*

outgrow /aʊtgrəʊ/ outgrows, outgrowing, outgrew, outgrown
1 vo If you **outgrow** a piece of clothing, you get bigger and can no longer wear it. *Small children outgrow their shoes at a fast rate.*
2 vo If you **outgrow** a particular way of behaving or thinking, you become more mature so that you no longer behave or think in that way. *Dr Adang says that this sort of behaviour is usually outgrown by the age of 20... Many Westerners concluded that the Soviet Union had outgrown its Communist roots.*

outgrowth /aʊtgrəʊθ/
N SING Something that is an **outgrowth** of another thing has developed naturally as a result of the first thing. *Clearly, their trial is the outgrowth of the drug trafficking scandal... Her first book is a natural outgrowth of an art project she began in 1988.*

outhouse /aʊthaʊs/ outhouses
NC An **outhouse** is a small building attached to a house or in its garden. *They have had to develop an outhouse in the compound for toilet facilities.*

outing /aʊtɪŋ/ outings
1 NC An **outing** is an occasion on which you leave your house, school, or place of work, usually for an enjoyable activity. *...family outings on the River Thames... A pleasure boat carrying people on a works outing was swamped by heavy seas.*
2 NC You can also use **outing** to refer to an occasion when someone in a sport or contest competes in a particular competition. *His last outing was in the Liege-Bastogne-Liege Classic five months ago... Davies, now a Rugby League player, completed his first full outing for Widnes Reserves last night.*
3 See also **out**.

outlandish /aʊtlændɪʃ/
ADJ Something that is **outlandish**, is very unusual or strange; used showing disapproval. *He was ashamed of his father's outlandish looks. ...an outlandish idea.*

outlast /aʊtlɑːst/ outlasts, outlasting, outlasted
vo If one thing **outlasts** another, it lives or exists longer than the other thing. *Even those trees would outlast him... She had not yet outlasted her usefulness.*

outlaw /aʊtlɔː/ outlaws, outlawing, outlawed
1 vo When something is **outlawed**, it is made illegal. *The use of poison gas was outlawed. ...legislation which will outlaw this system... The document outlaws arbitrary arrests, detention or exile and torture.* ◆ **outlawed** ADJ ATTRIB *A judge has detained four leading members of the outlawed Communist party.*
2 NC An **outlaw** is a criminal who is hiding from the authorities; an old-fashioned use. *...a band of outlaws.*

outlay /aʊtleɪ/ outlays
NC An **outlay** is an amount of money that is invested

in a project or business; a formal word. *...an initial outlay for clothing and books. ...a total outlay of £72,550.*

outlet /aʊtlet/ outlets
1 NC An **outlet** is an activity which allows you to express your feelings or ideas. *They can find no outlet for their grievances... Competitiveness can find an outlet in sport... They argue that pornography provides a natural and harmless outlet for sexual excitement.*
2 NC An **outlet** is also a hole or pipe through which water or air can flow away. *...the sewage outlet. ...the only existing sea outlet to the Gulf.*

outline /aʊtlaɪn/ outlines, outlining, outlined
1 vo If you **outline** an idea or plan, you explain it in a general way. *I outlined my reasons. ...a set of measures which would outline Britain's approach to environmental issues... A Libyan envoy has arrived in Abu Dhabi to outline a plan to resolve the Gulf crisis.*
2 N SING An **outline** is a general explanation or description of something. *...a brief outline of European art... An outline of the new document has been made public today.*
3 vo You say that an object is **outlined** when you can see its general shape because there is a light behind it. *He was clearly outlined in the light of a lamp.*
4 N SING An **outline** of something is also its general shape, especially when it cannot be clearly seen. *He saw the outline of a house against the sky.*

outlive /aʊtlɪv/ outlives, outliving, outlived
vo If one person or a thing **outlives** another, they are still alive or still exist after the second person or thing has died or no longer exists. *Olivia outlived Pepita by eighteen years... The organization had outlived its usefulness.*

outlook /aʊtlʊk/
1 NU+SUPP Your **outlook** is your general attitude towards life. *My whole outlook had changed... They are European in outlook.*
2 N SING+SUPP The **outlook** of a situation is the way it is likely to develop. *It is somewhat depressing to read the latest world economic outlook prepared by the IMF staff... This year's trade deficit outlook is better than last year's.*

outlying /aʊtlaɪɪŋ/
ADJ ATTRIB **Outlying** places are far away from the main cities of a country. *...teachers from outlying villages.*

outmanoeuvre /aʊtmənuːvə/ outmanoeuvres, outmanoeuvring, outmanoeuvred; spelt outmaneuver in American English.
vo To **outmanoeuvre** someone means to gain an advantage over them in a particular situation by behaving in a clever or skilful way. *With the ANC hampered by internal discord, the government has outmanoeuvred them in the negotiations... The truth is that the opposition as a whole has been consistently outmanoeuvred by the President.*

outmoded /aʊtməʊdɪd/
ADJ Something that is **outmoded** is old-fashioned and no longer useful. *...outmoded techniques... The country has become weakened by discord and an outmoded electoral system.*

outnumber /aʊtnʌmbə/ outnumbers, outnumbering, outnumbered
vo If one group of people or things **outnumbers** another, it has more people or things in it than the other group. *The men outnumbered the women by four to one... The black residents of New Orleans are outnumbered by the white residents in the city.*

out-of- /aʊtəv-/
PREFIX **Out-of-** combines with nouns to form adjectives that indicate that something occurs or is done outside its normal context or location. *NATO is at the moment unwilling to take a role in out-of-area problems... I'd love to have hidden powers or have out-of-body experiences. ..a reduction in out-of-school activities.*

out of court
ADV or ADJ ATTRIB When you settle **out of court**, or you make an **out-of-court** settlement, you end a disagreement or dispute without going to a court of law. *He said that by settling out of court, the state*

had admitted its guilt... His party would fight any move to make an out-of-court settlement.

out of date

ADJ Something that is **out of date** is old-fashioned and no longer useful, correct, or relevant. *It wasn't published until 1972, by which time it was out of date... This is rather an out-of-date concept.*

out of doors

ADV **Out of doors** means outside a building rather than inside it. *Hunting dogs should be kept out of doors... We sat out of doors beneath the trees.*

out-of-the-way

ADJ **Out-of-the-way** places are difficult to reach and are therefore not often visited. *Our expeditions have been to some out-of-the-way places.*

out of touch

ADJ PRED Someone who is **out of touch** is not aware of a new situation and recent trends. *They claim the government is out of touch with the public.*

out of work

ADJ Someone who is **out of work** does not have a job. *The number of people out of work has dropped by more than seventy thousand. ...out-of-work actors.*

out-patient, out-patients

NC An **out-patient** is someone who receives treatment at a hospital but does not stay there overnight. *The psychiatrists dealt with her as an out-patient. ...an out-patient clinic.*

outpost /aʊtpəʊst/ **outposts**

NC An **outpost** is a small settlement in a foreign country or in a distant area. *...a trading outpost. ...the furthest US outpost on the road to Basra.*

outpouring /aʊtpɔːrɪŋ/ **outpourings**

1 NC+SUPP An **outpouring** of something is a large amount of it that is produced very rapidly. *...a prolific outpouring of ideas and energy. ...an outpouring of wild rumours... I've never seen such an outpouring of excellent baseball books.*

2 N PL+SUPP **Outpourings** are strong feelings that are expressed in an uncontrolled way. *...the hysterical outpourings of fanatics... There have been rallies, and huge outpourings of sympathy for the chief.*

output /aʊtpʊt/ **outputs**

1 NU or NC You use **output** to refer to the amount of something that a person or thing produces. *The party maintains a constant output of pamphlets... Their total industrial output grew at an annual rate of 7%.*

2 NU or NC The **output** of a computer is the information that it displays on a screen or prints on paper as a result of a particular program. *The computer can display the output on each strip.*

outrage /aʊtreɪdʒ/ **outrages, outraging, outraged;** also pronounced /aʊtreɪdʒ/ in paragraph 1.

1 VO If something **outrages** you, it makes you extremely shocked and angry. *The idea outraged me... One woman was outraged by this response... They were appalled and outraged that the guardsmen were released on bail.* ◆ **outraged** ADJ *...the expression of outraged dignity on his face.*

2 NU **Outrage** is a strong feeling of anger and shock. *Benn shared this sense of outrage... Moral outrage was expressed by Mr Kinnock.*

3 NC An **outrage** is an act or event which people find very shocking. *There have been more reports of bomb outrages in Falmouth... Such an outrage against foreigners would attract wider publicity.*

outrageous /aʊtreɪdʒəs/

ADJ If something is **outrageous**, it is very shocking. *She used to say some outrageous things. ...outrageous crimes... It was an outrageous suggestion.* ◆ **outrageously** ADV *He was behaving outrageously... The jokes were of the outrageously vulgar kind so loved by the British.*

outran /aʊtræn/

Outran is the past tense of **outrun**.

outré /uːtreɪ/

ADJ Something or someone that is **outré** is very unusual, and rather shocking; a formal word. *...Thelma's style garb. ...some of the more outré members of Parliament.*

outrider /aʊtraɪdə/ **outriders**

NC An **outrider** is a policeman or policewoman on a

motorcycle or a horse, who escorts and protects people in an official vehicle. *Eight police outriders escorted the minister's car.*

outright; pronounced /aʊtraɪt/ when it is an adjective and /aʊtraɪt/ when it is an adverb.

1 ADJ ATTRIB or ADV You use **outright** to describe actions and behaviour that are open and direct, rather than indirect. *...an outright refusal... If I ask outright I get nowhere.* ◆ **outrightly** ADV *He has held back from outrightly rejecting the proposals.*

2 ADJ ATTRIB or ADV **Outright** also means complete and total. *...an outright victory... He again made clear his outright opposition to abortion... He stressed that the peace proposals had not been rejected outright.*

● If someone is **killed outright**, they die immediately, for example in an accident. *Two of the men with me were killed outright.*

outrun /aʊtrʌn/ **outruns, outrunning, outran**

1 VO If you **outrun** someone, you run faster than they do in order to escape from them, or to arrive somewhere before they do. *She managed to outrun them.*

2 VO If one thing **outruns** another thing, it develops faster than the other thing. *City growth far outran the population boom... I think they suddenly found that expenditure outran income.*

outsell /aʊtsel/ **outsells, outselling, outsold**

VO If a product **outsells** another product, it is sold faster or in larger quantities than the other product. *In some places American skis are outselling Scandinavian, Swiss, and Austrian ones... The Boeing 737 is the most important commercial aircraft in the world, outselling all its major competitors.*

outset /aʊtset/

If something happens **at the outset** of an event, process, or period of time, it happens at the very beginning of it. *You should explain this to him at the outset... The police had participated from the outset.*

outshine /aʊtʃaɪn/ **outshines, outshining, outshone**

VO If you **outshine** someone at a particular activity, you are much better than they are at it. *He felt sure he could outshine them all... The United States golfers have been outshone by Europeans over the last 12 months.*

outside /aʊtsaɪd/ **outsides**

1 NC or ADJ ATTRIB The **outside** of a container or building is the part which surrounds or encloses the rest of it. *...the outside of the bottle... Examine the property closely from the outside. ...a wooden shed that stood against the outside wall.*

2 ADV, PREP, or ADJ ATTRIB If you are **outside** a building, place, or country, you are not in it. *Let's go outside... It was dark outside... He's on the landing outside. ...a small village just outside Birmingham. ...an outside lavatory.*

3 ADJ When you talk about the **outside** world, you are referring to things that happen or exist in places other than your own home or community. *They don't want to go out into the outside world... He reaffirmed their commitment to opening up to the outside world... Is life outside really as dangerous as that?*

4 ADJ ATTRIB On a wide road, the **outside** lane is the right-hand lane in countries where you drive on the left, and the left-hand lane in countries where you drive on the right.

5 PREP or ADJ ATTRIB People or things that are **outside** a group, range, or organization are not included in it. *The bill was supported by a mass movement outside Parliament... The pipeline was outside his range of responsibility... Since 1974, no outside body has questioned the advice.*

6 PREP Something that happens **outside** a particular period of time does not happen during that time. *You'll have to do it outside office hours.*

outside broadcast, outside broadcasts

NC An **outside broadcast** is a radio or television programme that is not recorded or filmed in a studio, but in another building or in the open air. *...the problems of doing an outside broadcast... Police say a cable connecting the BBC outside broadcast unit with the British Telecom system was cut deliberately.*

outside of; used in American English.
1 PREP If you are **outside of** a place, area, or country, you are not in it. *Many of the young men waited in the rain and prayed outside of Bellvue hospital. ...a small industrial town just outside of Chicago.*
2 PREP **Outside of** is used to introduce the only thing or person that prevents your main statement from being completely true. *That's the only thing, outside of my wife, that keeps me going... Our ethnic heritage is different, but outside of that, we're no different.*

outsider /aʊtsaɪdə/ **outsiders**
NC An **outsider** is someone who is not involved in a particular group, or is not accepted by that group. *...an independent committee of seven outsiders. ...the sense of being out of place, of being an outsider.*

outsize /aʊtsaɪz/
ADJ ATTRIB **Outsize** or **outsized** things are much larger than usual. *...a blonde with outsize spectacles. ...an outsized envelope.*

outskirts /aʊtskɜːts/
N PL The **outskirts** of a city or town are the parts that are farthest from its centre. *The garage was on the outskirts of town.*

outsmart /aʊtsmɑːt/ **outsmarts, outsmarting, outsmarted**
VO If you **outsmart** someone, you cleverly defeat them or gain an advantage over them. *The council outsmarted us by releasing their own press statement.*

outspoken /aʊtspəʊkən/
1 ADJ If you are **outspoken**, you give your opinions about things openly, even if they shock people. *You are younger and more outspoken than they are... He was an outspoken advocate of greater democracy.*
♦ **outspokenly** ADV *...criticizing the Party more outspokenly than ever before.* ♦ **outspokenness** NU *He has lost none of the outspokenness which led to his sacking.*
2 ADJ An **outspoken** remark or criticism is open and direct and may shock some people. *The authorities are trying to silence their outspoken criticism of the government... There was an outspoken attack on her by some black political leaders. ...clear, outspoken statements.* ♦ **outspokenly** SUBMOD *...the most outspokenly pro-reform Soviet paper. ..outspokenly critical views.*

outspread /aʊtspred/
ADJ If something is **outspread**, it is stretched or spread out as far as possible. *...supporting himself on his outspread fingers. ...perched on a crag, its wings outspread. ...the outspread newspaper.*

outstanding /aʊtstændɪŋ/
1 ADJ If you describe a person or their work as **outstanding**, you mean that they are very good and impressive. *She would never be an outstanding actress... His war record was outstanding. ...in recognition of his outstanding contribution.*
♦ **outstandingly** SUBMOD *...an outstandingly successful director.*
2 ADJ ATTRIB **Outstanding** also means very obvious or important. *There are significant exceptions, of which oil is the outstanding example.*
3 ADJ ATTRIB An **outstanding** issue or problem is one that has not yet been resolved. *They had a fairly brief exchange over the outstanding bilateral issues. ...Baghdad's recent unexpected gesture in conceding to Tehran's outstanding claims... Ministers have been unable to resolve outstanding differences on other topics.*
4 ADJ Money that is **outstanding** is still owed to someone. *There is fifty pounds outstanding. ...£280 in outstanding fines. ...failure to pay outstanding debts.*

outstay /aʊsteɪ/ **outstays, outstaying, outstayed**
If you **outstay** your welcome, you stay somewhere, for example at someone's house or party, longer than they want you to or expect you to. *He decided to leave before he outstayed his welcome.*

outstretched /aʊtstretʃt/
ADJ If your arms or hands are **outstretched**, they are stretched out as far as possible. *...balancing himself with outstretched arms... He sat there, hand outstretched in greeting.*

outstrip /aʊtstrɪp/ **outstrips, outstripping, outstripped**
VO If one thing **outstrips** another, it becomes larger in amount or more successful than the second thing. *His wealth far outstripped Northcliffe's.*

out tray, out trays
NC An **out tray** is a tray or shallow basket used in offices to put letters and documents in before they are sent out of the office. *Check Malcolm's diary with him, and empty his out tray.*

outvote /aʊtvəʊt/ **outvotes, outvoting, outvoted**
VO If you **are outvoted**, more people vote against what you are proposing than vote for it, so that your proposal is defeated. *Shop stewards recommending strike action have been outvoted... I have a lot of confidence in him — but I was outvoted.*

outward /aʊtwəd/ **outwards**. In normal British English, **outwards** is an adverb and **outward** is an adjective. In formal British English and in American English, **outward** is both an adjective and an adverb.
1 ADV If something moves or faces **outwards** or **outward**, it moves or faces away from the place you are in or the place you are talking about. *He swam outwards into the bay... The door opened outwards... When a nerve is severed, the part of it leading outwards to the surface of the body dies.*
2 ADJ ATTRIBor ADV An **outward** journey is a journey that you make away from a place that you are intending to return to later. *It was time to begin the outward trek... Our journey outwards was delayed at the airport.*
3 ADJ ATTRIB The **outward** feelings or qualities are the ones people appear to have, rather than the ones they actually have. *I said it with what I hoped was outward calm... This outward show of unity conceals serious differences within NATO.* ♦ **outwardly** ADV *He is seething, but outwardly he remains composed... As they try to establish a firm democratic structure, an outwardly small event can be taken very seriously.*
4 ADJ ATTRIB The **outward** features of something are the ones that you can see from the outside. *...the outward and visible signs of the disease... Its outward appearances, the vodka looks and smells like normal vodka.*
5 ADV **Outwards** is used to indicate that a person's actions concern or affect people other than themselves, or the country or group that they belong to. *He was willing to initiate reforms, to change old ways and look outwards... We're searching more within our own culture than looking outwards.*

outward-looking
ADJ Someone or something that is **outward-looking** is interested in other people and things and would like greater involvement with them. *Britain should play a constructive role in an outward-looking European Community. ...a more outward-looking foreign policy.*

outweigh /aʊtweɪ/ **outweighs, outweighing, outweighed**
VO If you say that the advantages of something **outweigh** the disadvantages, you mean that the advantages are more important than the disadvantages; a formal word. *The benefits from the medicine outweigh the risks of treatment.*

outwit /aʊtwɪt/ **outwits, outwitting, outwitted**
VO If you **outwit** someone, you cleverly defeat them or gain an advantage over them. *They managed to outwit Bill and get inside... If a machine can outwit a human player, it would suggest they are intelligent and can learn to think... Scientists are developing new ways to outwit pests and diseases.*

outworn /aʊtwɔːn/
ADJ An **outworn** idea or method is old-fashioned and no longer useful; a formal word. *...an editorial denouncing what it calls the outworn creed of President Fidel Castro.*

ouzo /uːzəʊ/
N MASS **Ouzo** is a strong, aniseed-flavoured alcoholic drink that is made in Greece. *There will also be trade protection for ouzo from Greece and grappa from Italy.*

ova /əʊvə/
NC **Ova** is the plural of **ovum**.

oval /ˈəʊvl/ **ovals**
NC An **oval** is a round shape which is similar to a circle, but is wider in one direction than the other. *...an oval mirror... The amphitheatre would have been oval in shape.*

ovarian /əʊˈvɛəriən/
ADJ ATTRIB **Ovarian** means relating to or coming from the ovaries; a technical term. *Ultra sound screening can detect ovarian cancer at its very early stages... Foetal ovarian tissue can be used to produce donor eggs.*

ovary /ˈəʊvəri/ **ovaries**
NC A woman's **ovaries** are the two organs in her body that produce eggs. *The ovaries may be hard to locate in young girls.*

ovation /əʊˈveɪʃn/ **ovations**
NC An **ovation** is a long burst of applause; a formal word. *Mr Haughey got a prolonged ovation from some five thousand delegates.* ● See also **standing ovation.**

oven /ˈʌvn/ **ovens**
NC An **oven** is a cooker or part of a cooker that is like a box with a door. You cook food inside an oven. *These were baked by the local baker in a clay oven.*

ovenproof /ˈʌvnpruːf/
ADJ An **ovenproof** dish is one that has been specially made to be used in an oven without being damaged by the heat.

over /ˈəʊvə/
1 PREP If one thing is **over** another thing, it is directly above it, either resting on it, or with a space between them. *I had reached the little bridge over the stream. ...the monument over the west door... Leave it to dry over the back of the sofa.*
2 PREP You can also say that one thing is **over** another when the first thing covers the second. *Place a piece of blotting paper over the stain... Students were spraying paint over each other.*
3 PREP If you look or talk **over** an object, you look or talk across the top of it. *The ponies would come and look over the wall... She was watching him over the rim of her cup.*
4 PREP If you look **over** a piece of writing or a group of things, you quickly look at all the writing or all the things. *He ran his eye over one particular paragraph.*
5 PREP If a window has a view **over** a piece of land, you can see the land through the window. *The windows look out over a park.*
6 ADV If you go **over** to a place, you go there. *The doctor walked over to the door... I've got some friends coming over tonight... Liz, come over here.*
7 PREP If someone or something goes **over** a boundary of some kind, such as a river or bridge, or if they go **over** an area of land, they cross it and get to the other side. *His pen moved rapidly over the paper. ...on the way back over the Channel... Castle stepped over the dog... They throw their rubbish over the fence into the neighbour's garden.*
8 PREP or ADV A You can use **over** to indicate a particular position or place away from you. *Eastwards over the Severn lie the hills... Mr Stryker was standing over by the window.*
9 ADV **Over** is used to say that someone or something falls towards or onto the ground or the floor, often suddenly or violently. *She fell over in the mud... He slumped over in his seat... He was knocked over by a bus.*
10 ADV or PREP If you lean **over**, you bend your body in a particular direction. *Pat leaned over and picked it up... He crouched over a typewriter.*
11 ADV If something rolls **over** or is turned **over**, its position changes so that it is facing in another direction. *He flicked over the page... She tipped the pan over.*
12 PREP or ADV If something is **over** a particular amount or measurement it is more than that amount or measurement. *They paid out over 3 million pounds. ...people aged 80 or over... She did it for over a week.*
13 ADV If an activity, event, or situation is **over** or all **over**, it is completely finished. *Rodin's search was over... Why worry her when it's all over?*
14 PREP If someone has control or influence **over** other people, they are able to control or influence them.

...his authority over them.
15 PREP You also use **over** to indicate the cause of a disagreement or action. *...disagreements over administrative policies... They were always quarrelling over women... He had been suspended over allegations of misconduct... The local administration has also come in for criticism over allegations of corruption.*
16 PREP If something happens **over** a period of time, it happens during that time. *He'd had flu over Christmas. ...a process developed over many decades.*
17 NC In cricket, an **over** consists of six correctly bowled balls. *Australia scored 215 for five off the 48 overs bowled.*
● **Over** is used in these phrases. ● **All over** a place means in every part of it. *I've been all over Austria... They come from all over the world.* ● **Over there** means in a place away from you, or in another country. **Over here** means near you, or in the country you are in. *Who's the woman over there?... Are you over here on a trip?* ● If you say that something is happening **all over again**, you mean that it is happening again, and that it is tiring, boring, or unpleasant. *The whole thing began all over again.* ● If you say that something happened **over and over** or **over and over again**, you mean that it happened many times. *Over and over, the same stories kept cropping up... I read it over and over again.*

over- /ˈəʊvə-/
PREFIX **Over-** is used to form words that indicate that a quality or thing exists or an action is done to too great an extent. For example, if you say that someone is being over-cautious, you mean that they are being too cautious. *...an over-confident young man... Money was largely wasted through over-staffing and poor planning. ...the alleged over-booking of hotels... There is a substantial over-capacity in European defence industries.*

overact /ˌəʊvərˈækt/ **overacts, overacting, overacted**
V If you **overact**, you exaggerate your emotions and gestures, especially when acting in a play; used showing disapproval. *I knew I had been overacting... It's true they've been discriminated against, but I think they overacted.*

overall, overalls; pronounced /ˌəʊvərˈɔːl/ when it is an adjective or an adverb and /ˈəʊvərɔːl/ when it is a noun.
1 ADJ ATTRIB You use **overall** to indicate that you are talking about a situation in general or considering it as a whole. *...the overall pattern of his life... The overall impression was of a smoky industrial city... He retained his overall lead in the Paris to Nice race.* ▶ Also ADV SEN *Overall, imports account for half of our stock.*
2 N PL **Overalls** are a piece of clothing that combine trousers and a jacket which you wear over your clothes to protect them while you are working. *Witnesses had seen a man in blue overalls going into the machine room.*
3 N PL **Overalls** are also the same as **dungarees**; used in American English. *He would have been more comfortable in his overalls than his uniform.*
4 NC An **overall** is a type of coat that you wear over your clothes to protect them while you are working. *Wear an overall, not an apron.*

overall majority, overall majorities
NC If a political party wins an **overall majority** in an election or vote, they get more votes or seats than the total number of votes or seats gained by their opponents. *No political party appears to have the slightest chance of winning an overall majority... Her party failed to gain an overall majority in the recent elections.*

overarm /ˈəʊvərɑːm/
ADV or ADJ **Overarm** is used to describe actions that you do, such as throwing a ball, in which you stretch your arm over your shoulder. *She would throw overarm. ...his strong overarm strokes.*

overawe /ˌəʊvərˈɔː/ **overawes, overawing, overawed**
V O If you **are overawed** by something, you are very impressed by it and a little afraid of it. *Don't be overawed by what the experts say... Britain's newest*

young player refused to be overawed by the world's number four.

overbalance /ˌəʊvəbæləns/ **overbalances, overbalancing, overbalanced**
v If you **overbalance**, you fall over because you are not in a steady position. *He flung an arm in the direction of the church and nearly overbalanced.*

overbearing /ˌəʊvəbeərɪŋ/
ADJ An **overbearing** person tries to make other people do what he or she wants in an unpleasant and forceful way. *...her jealous, overbearing mother-in-law... He's admired for his outspokenness and energy, although some say he's too overbearing and ambitious.*

overboard /ˈəʊvəbɔːd/
ADV If you fall **overboard**, you fall over the side of a ship into the water. *He had to hang on to avoid being washed overboard... The captain was then stabbed and thrown overboard.*

overburdened /ˌəʊvəbɜːdnd/
ADJ If you are **overburdened** with something such as work or problems, you have more of it than you can cope with. *You're not overburdened with work just now?... She did not want to trouble relatives already overburdened with stress.*

overcame /ˌəʊvəkeɪm/
Overcame is the past tense of **overcome**.

overcast /ˌəʊvəkɑːst/
ADJ If it is **overcast**, there are a lot of clouds in the sky. *It was a warm day, but overcast. ...the habitually overcast, drizzly skies.*

overcharge /ˌəʊvətʃɑːdʒ/ **overcharges, overcharging, overcharged**
V O or V If someone **overcharges** you, they charge you too much money for their goods or services. *The taxi-driver tried to overcharge her. ...tough action against contractors who overcharge or defraud.*
♦ **overcharging** NU *Severe penalties may be imposed on companies guilty of overcharging and fraud... More than one thousand one hundred contracts have involved overcharging in the past fourteen years.*

overcoat /ˈəʊvəkəʊt/ **overcoats**
NC An **overcoat** is a thick, warm coat. *...an expensive navy blue Kashmir overcoat.*

overcome /ˌəʊvəkʌm/ **overcomes, overcoming, overcame** The form **overcome** is used in the present tense and is also the past participle.
1 V O If you **overcome** a problem or a feeling, you successfully deal with it or control it. *I was still trying to overcome my fear of the dark... We tried to overcome their objections to the plan.*
2 V O If you **are overcome** by a feeling, you feel it very strongly. *I was overcome by a sense of failure... He was overcome with astonishment.*

overcrowded /ˌəʊvəkraʊdɪd/
ADJ If a place is **overcrowded**, there are too many things or people in it. *...overcrowded cities... They live in overcrowded, airless conditions.*

overcrowding /ˌəʊvəkraʊdɪŋ/
NU If there is **overcrowding** in a place, there is not enough room for all the people living there. *There is serious overcrowding in our prisons. ...the stress caused by overcrowding and time-wasting on the Underground.*

overdo /ˌəʊvəduː/ **overdoes, overdoing, overdid, overdone**
1 V O If someone **overdoes** something, they behave in an exaggerated way. *Wish them luck, but don't overdo it or they may become suspicious.*
2 V O If you **overdo** an activity, you try to do more than you can physically manage. *Don't overdo it. It's very hot in the sun.*

overdone /ˌəʊvədʌn/
ADJ PRED If food is **overdone**, it has been cooked for too long.

overdose /ˈəʊvədəʊs/ **overdoses**
NC If someone takes an **overdose**, they take more of a drug than it is safe to do, and may lose consciousness and die. *Alice took an overdose after a row with her mother.*

overdraft /ˈəʊvədrɑːft/ **overdrafts**
NC An **overdraft** is an arrangement with a bank that allows you to spend more money than you have in

your account. *She asked for a fifty-pound overdraft.*

overdrawn /ˌəʊvədrɔːn/
ADJ If a person is **overdrawn** or if their bank account is **overdrawn**, they have spent more money than they have in their account. *I'm overdrawn this month, but it should balance out next month. ...interest charged on overdrawn accounts.*

overdressed /ˌəʊvədrest/
ADJ You say that someone is **overdressed** when you think that they are wearing too many clothes or clothes which are too formal for a particular occasion. *He's sort of, I'd say, overdressed for the weather.*

overdue /ˌəʊvədjuː/
1 ADJ If a person, bus, or train is **overdue**, they are late in arriving somewhere. *They're half an hour overdue. I wish they'd come.*
2 ADJ If a change or an event is **overdue**, it should have happened before the present time. *Reform in all these areas is long overdue... A less austere attitude to lending rates is now overdue.*
3 ADJ If something borrowed or due to be paid is **overdue**, it is now later than the date when it should have been returned or paid. *The rent on his apartment was three weeks overdue. ...overdue library books.*

overeat /ˌəʊvəriːt/ **overeats, overeating, overate, overeaten**
v If you **overeat**, you eat more than you need to or more than is healthy. *She has a tendency to overeat... People are inclined to be irritable with indigestion after overeating.* ♦ **overeating** NU *Obesity is mainly caused by overeating. ...a disease he ascribes to overworking, overeating, and overdrinking.*

overemphasis /ˌəʊvəremfəsɪs/ **overemphases**
NU or NC **Overemphasis** on something is the fact that too much importance or attention is given to it. *...development that can no longer permit undue overemphasis on economic parochialism... The human rights debate was unbalanced by an overemphasis on political dissidents.*

overemphasize /ˌəʊvəremfəsaɪz/ **overemphasizes, overemphasizing, overemphasized**; also spelt **overemphasise**.
V O or V-REPORT If you **overemphasize** something, you give it more importance than it deserves or than is considered appropriate. *I hope nobody will overemphasize the importance of these little essays... I cannot overemphasize how delicate this business is... They believe Soviet aid should not be overemphasized.*

overestimate /ˌəʊvərestɪmeɪt/ **overestimates, overestimating, overestimated**
V O If you **overestimate** someone or something, you think that they are better, bigger, or more important than they really are. *We greatly overestimated the time this would take... Her confidence drained away and he knew he had overestimated her.*

overflight /ˈəʊvəflaɪt/ **overflights**
NC An **overflight** is the passage of an aircraft from one country over another country's territory. *Chad accuses the Libyan airforce of repeated overflights of its territory.*

overflow, overflows, overflowing, overflowed; pronounced /ˌəʊvəˈfləʊ/ when it is a verb and /ˈəʊvəfləʊ/ when it is a noun.
1 V or V-ERG If a liquid or a river **overflows**, it flows over the edges of the container it is in or the place where it is. *He was careful to see that the jar did not overflow... Rivers often overflow their banks.*
2 V+*with* If something **is overflowing** with things, it is too full of them. *The table was overflowing with clothes... Schools and churches said to be overflowing with refugees... Polytechnics are reported to be overflowing with new student intakes.* ● If you describe a place as full **to overflowing**, you mean that it is extremely full, so that no more things or people can fit in it. *The rally took place in the cathedral, which was full to overflowing... He was one of the teachers who always filled lecture halls to overflowing.*
3 V If someone **is overflowing** with a feeling, they are experiencing it very strongly and show this in their behaviour. *...a nurse overflowing with love.*

4 NC An **overflow** is a hole or pipe through which liquid can flow out of a container when it gets too full. ...*the sink overflow.* ...*overflow pipes.*

over-flying
ADJ ATTRIB **Over-flying** rights are the rights an airline company has to fly over a country's territory. *I don't think there is any attempt at present to interfere with over-flying rights.*

overgrown /əʊvəgrəʊn/
ADJ If a place is **overgrown**, it is thickly covered with plants because it has not been looked after. ...*a large house, overgrown with brambles.* ...*the overgrown path.*

overhang, overhangs, overhanging, overhung; pronounced /əʊvəhæŋ/ when it is a verb and /əʊvəhæŋ/ when it is a noun.
1 V O or V If one thing **overhangs** another, it sticks out sideways above it. ...*a tree which overhung the lake.* ...*the shadow of an overhanging rock.* ...*wet clothes overhang the tub.*
2 N SING If there is an **overhang** of money, there is more of it than was expected and this can be or must be used in some way. *The starting point of his analysis is the vast overhang of private savings... Unless we cope with the debt overhang, it's going to be that much more difficult to cope with other problems.*

overhaul, overhauls, overhauling, overhauled; pronounced /əʊvəhɔːl/ when it is a verb and /əʊvəhɔːl/ when it is a noun.
1 V O If you **overhaul** a piece of equipment, you clean and check it, and repair it if necessary. *The engines were overhauled before our departure.*
2 V O If you **overhaul** a system or method, you examine it carefully and change it in order to improve it. *The company needs to overhaul its techniques and methods.* ▶ Also NC ...*a major overhaul of the country's educational system.*

overhead, overheads; pronounced /əʊvəhed/ when it is an adverb or a predicative adjective and /əʊvəhed/ when it is a noun or an attributive adjective.
1 ADV or ADJ If something is **overhead**, it is above you or above the place you are talking about. *Seagulls were circling overhead... The guard switched on an overhead light.*
2 NC The **overheads** of a business are its regular and essential expenses, such as rent or telephone charges. ...*reducing expenditure on overheads.*

overhear /əʊvəhɪə/ **overhears, overhearing, overheard**
V O If you **overhear** someone, you hear what they are saying when they are not talking to you and do not know that you are listening. *Judy overheard him telling the children about it... I was too far away to overhear their conversation.*

overheat /əʊvəhiːt/ **overheats, overheating, overheated**
1 V-ERG If a machine **overheats** or if you **overheat** it, it becomes hotter than it should, usually because there is a fault in it. *The appliances might overheat and catch fire... You are running a serious risk of overheating the appliance.*
2 V If the economic system in a country is **overheating**, it grows so rapidly that inflation and interest rates rise very quickly. ...*plans to cut back on imports and prevent the economy from overheating... With increases in the borrowing rate, we ask if the economy is beginning to overheat.*

overhung /əʊvəhʌŋ/
Overhung is the past tense and past participle of **overhang**.

overjoyed /əʊvədʒɔɪd/
ADJ PRED If you are **overjoyed**, you are extremely pleased about something. *Francis was overjoyed to see him... They were overjoyed at this treatment.*

overkill /əʊvəkɪl/
N U You say that there is **overkill** when something is spoiled by being done to a much greater extent than is necessary. *So this overkill in negative propaganda resulted in an upsurge of interest.* ...*the media's overkill coverage.*

overladen /əʊvəleɪdn/
ADJ PRED When one thing is **overladen** with another, it is covered and obscured by it. *The planet has no water at all and is overladen with a dense carbon dioxide atmosphere... The issue has been overladen with Middle East politics.*

overland /əʊvəlænd/
ADJ or ADV An **overland** journey is made across land rather than on water or by air. *They rely on overland transport routes between the Mediterranean and the Black Sea... You travelled overland to India?*

overlap, overlaps, overlapping, overlapped; pronounced /əʊvəlæp/ when it is a verb and /əʊvəlæp/ when it is a noun.
1 V-RECIP If one thing **overlaps** another or if two things **overlap**, one part of one thing covers a part of the other thing. *The circles overlap... A quilt must overlap the sides of the bed.*
2 V-RECIP If two ideas or activities **overlap**, they involve some of the same subjects, people, or periods of time. *The two theories obviously overlap... The work of the inspectors overlaps with that of the internal auditors... We worked overlapping shifts so there were always two of us on duty.* ▶ Also NU or NC *There is no overlap between our material and that of Lipset.*

overlay, overlays, overlaying, overlaid; pronounced /əʊvəleɪ/ when it is a verb and /əʊvəleɪ/ when it is a noun.
1 V O If something is **overlaid** with something else, it is covered by it. *Silt from the rivers will overlay the ground.* ...*broken slabs overlaid with rubble.*
2 V O If one type of behaviour, attitude, or idea is **overlaid** by another, the first one is added to the other. *The ancient teachings have been overlaid by so many layers of interpretation and social custom... These feelings were overlaid by the child's need for a father.* ▶ Also N SING *It was said with an overlay of good humour.*
3 See also **overladen**.

overleaf /əʊvəliːf/
ADV **Overleaf** is used in books and magazines to say that something is on the next page. *Some of the animals are illustrated overleaf.*

overload /əʊvələʊd/ **overloads, overloading, overloaded**
1 V O If a vehicle is **overloaded**, there is not enough room for the things or people in it. ...*little boats overloaded with desperate people.*
2 V O If you **overload** an electrical system, you use too many appliances and damage it. *Your fuse has blown because you have overloaded the circuit.*
3 V O If you **overload** someone with work or problems, you give them more than they can manage. *Medical services were overloaded with casualties.*

overlook /əʊvəlʊk/ **overlooks, overlooking, overlooked**
1 V O If a building or window **overlooks** a place, you can see the place from the building or window. ...*a room which overlooked the garden.*
2 V O If you **overlook** a fact or problem, you ignore it, do not notice it, or do not realize its importance. *They overlook the enormous risks involved.*
3 V O If you **overlook** someone's faults or bad behaviour, you forgive them and do not criticize them. *Many of those taking part in the Arab Summit chose to overlook if not forgive Egypt's peace treaty with Israel.*

overlord /əʊvəlɔːd/ **overlords**
NC An **overlord** was a person in former times who had power over many people. ...*an excellent overlord, who protected his people from bandits.*

overly /əʊvəli/
SUBMOD **Overly** means more than is normal, necessary, or reasonable. *He did not get an overly enthusiastic response from British officials... The statements turned out to be overly enthusiastic... I'm not overly keen on him.*

overmanned /əʊvəmænd/
ADJ If a place or particular type of work is **overmanned**, there are too many people working there or doing the work. *The industry is not only heavily*

overmanned but also in financial difficulties.

overmanning /ˌəʊvəˈmænɪŋ/

NU If there is **overmanning** in a place or type of work, there are too many people working there or doing the work. *The ministries are notorious for overmanning, inefficiency, sloth and the constant passing on of responsibility.*

overmuch /ˌəʊvəˈmʌtʃ/

ADV If something happens **overmuch**, it happens too much or very much; a formal word. *The rumours she heard did not bother her overmuch.* ▶ Also ADJ ATTRIB *He had done her a disservice by showing overmuch affection.*

overnight /ˌəʊvəˈnaɪt/

1 ADV or ADJ ATTRIB **Overnight** means during all of the night. *Soak the raisins overnight in water. ...an overnight stay.*
2 ADJ ATTRIB **Overnight** cases or clothes are ones that you take when you go and stay somewhere for one or two nights. *He packed a little overnight bag.*
3 ADV You say that something happens **overnight** when it happens quickly and unexpectedly. *The colonel became a hero overnight... You can't expect these problems to be solved overnight.*

overpaid /ˌəʊvəˈpeɪd/

ADJ If you say that someone is **overpaid** or that their job is **overpaid**, you mean that they are paid too much for the work that they do. *He was grossly overpaid... In most countries such jobs are overpaid in relation to the average income.*

overpass /ˈəʊvəpɑːs/ **overpasses**

NC An **overpass** is the same as a **flyover**; used in American English. *Every day, on average, 28,950 vehicles will pass safely under this overpass.*

overplay /ˌəʊvəˈpleɪ/ **overplays, overplaying, overplayed**

1 VO If you **overplay** something, you make it seem more important than it really is. *He's been overplaying his promotion a bit.*
2 If you **overplay** your **hand**, you believe that you are in a stronger position than you actually are and, as a result, act too confidently. *The right may now have overplayed its hand, because Gorbachev has made a sudden lurch towards the left.*

overpopulated /ˌəʊvəˈpɒpjʊleɪtɪd/

ADJ A city or country that is **overpopulated** has too many people living in it. *The President has himself described his country as 'small, overpopulated and on the list of the world's poorest countries'.*

overpopulation /ˌəʊvəpɒpjʊˈleɪʃn/

NU If there is **overpopulation** in a place, there are too many people living there. *...poverty and overpopulation... They encourage family planning to avoid overpopulation.*

overpower /ˌəʊvəˈpaʊə/ **overpowers, overpowering, overpowered**

1 VO If you **overpower** someone, you seize them despite their struggles because you are stronger than they are. *They easily overpowered her and dragged her inside.*
2 VO In a match or sports game, if one team or player **overpowers** another, they play much better than them and defeat them easily. *The Sri Lanka B team completely overpowered a Zimbabwe side in a fifty over match.*
3 VO If an emotion or sensation **overpowers** you, it affects you very strongly. *Occasionally this desire overpowers me and leads me to be cruel.*
♦ **overpowering** ADJ *...an overpowering feeling of failure.*

overpriced /ˌəʊvəˈpraɪst/

ADJ You say that goods are **overpriced** when you think that they are too expensive. *He spent his money on overpriced and tasteless clothes.*

overran /ˌəʊvəˈræn/

Overran is the past tense of **overrun**.

overrate /ˌəʊvəˈreɪt/ **overrates, overrating, overrated**

VO If you **overrate** something, you think it is better or more important than it really is. *They overrate the extent of political freedom in England... I think the notion of a pluralistic democracy is overrated.*

overreach /ˌəʊvəˈriːtʃ/ **overreaches, overreaching, overreached**

V-REFL If you **overreach** yourself, you fail by trying to be too clever or by trying to do more than you can. *'It isn't wise to be too clever,' I said. 'Sometimes you overreach yourself.'... Is the media overreaching itself, prying too deeply into the private lives of the candidates.*

overreact /ˌəʊvəriˈækt/ **overreacts, overreacting, overreacted**

V If someone **overreacts** to something that happens, they react to it by being more angry, upset, afraid, and so on, than they need to be. *People tend to overreact when they hear about a shark attack.*

override /ˌəʊvəˈraɪd/ **overrides, overriding, overrode, overridden**

1 VO If something **overrides** other things, it is more important than these things. *The day-to-day struggle for survival overrode all other things... Commercial interests override everything else at this level of international football.*
2 VO If you **override** an automatic machine, you operate it manually, for example because it would be unsafe to allow it to operate automatically. *If the fault happened again, the crew would override the automatic system and bring the space capsule down manually.*
3 VO If you **override** a person or their decisions, you cancel their decisions because you have more authority than they have. *Will they dare override what the people decide?... He has appointed a new body which can override the veto of the Council of Guardians.*
4 NC An **override** is an attempt to cancel someone's decisions by using your authority over them or by gaining more votes than them in an election or contest; used in American English. *An override is considered unlikely... The 66 to 34 vote was one short of the number needed for an override... This is the first override of a governor's veto in this century.*

overriding /ˌəʊvəˈraɪdɪŋ/

ADJ ATTRIB **Overriding** means more important than anything else. *The overriding need in the world is to promote peace... He said that his overriding concern was not to interfere in the activities of the courts.*

overrule /ˌəʊvəˈruːl/ **overrules, overruling, overruled**

VO If someone in authority **overrules** a person or their decisions, they officially decide that their decisions are incorrect or not valid. *The judgement was overruled by the Supreme Court... Frank was overruled by the planners in Berlin.*

overrun /ˌəʊvəˈrʌn/ **overruns, overrunning, overran**

The form **overrun** is used in the present tense and is also the past participle.

1 VO If an army **overruns** a country or an area, it succeeds in occupying it quickly. *The north was overrun by the advancing troops... A group of rebels overran the port area.*
2 VO If a place **is overrun** with animals or plants, there are too many of them there. *The city is overrun by rodents.*
3 V or VO If an event or meeting **overruns**, it continues for a longer time than it should have. *I think we've overrun our time, haven't we?*

oversaw /ˌəʊvəˈsɔː/

Oversaw is the past tense of **oversee**.

overseas /ˌəʊvəˈsiːz/

1 ADJ ATTRIB or ADV You use **overseas** to describe things that happen or exist in countries that you must cross the sea to get to. *There is a vast overseas market for our goods... Roughly 4 million Americans travel overseas each year.*
2 ADJ ATTRIB An **overseas** student or visitor comes from a foreign country that you must cross the sea to get to. *Overseas students in Britain now pay much more in fees than they used to.*

oversee /ˌəʊvəˈsiː/ **oversees, overseeing, oversaw, overseen**

VO If someone in authority **oversees** a job or an activity, they make sure that it is done properly. *We need a guy to oversee our operations in Guyana... General Jaruzelski was also the man who oversaw*

Poland's transition to a non-communist state in 1989.

overseer /ˈəʊvəsɪə/ **overseers**

NC An **overseer** is someone whose job is to make sure that employees are working properly or that a project is being carried out correctly. *An official journal has attacked Stalin's one-time cultural overseer Zhdanov as a murderer of culture.*

oversell /ˈəʊvəsel/ **oversells, overselling, oversold**

VO If you **oversell** something or someone, you exaggerate their merits or abilities. *It would be foolish to oversell yourself.*

oversexed /ˈəʊvəsekst/

ADJ If you describe someone as **oversexed**, you mean that they are more interested in sex or more involved in sexual activities than you think they should be. *...a tough, oversexed, working-class kid.*

overshadow /ˈəʊvəʃædəʊ/ **overshadows, overshadowing, overshadowed**

1 VO If a building, tree, or large structure **overshadows** another, it stands near it and is taller than it. *...the elm trees overshadowing the school.*
2 VO If someone or something is **overshadowed**, they are seen to be less successful, important, or impressive by someone or something else. *She was sometimes overshadowed by the more talkative members... How far was your meeting overshadowed or possibly dominated by what you saw?* *...overshadowing the whole summit will be the meeting between Miss Bhutto and Mr Gandhi.*
3 VO If an unpleasant event or situation **overshadows** another event or situation, it makes it seem less of an achievement or less enjoyable. *The polling has already been overshadowed by one serious incident.*

overshoe /ˈəʊvəʃuː/ **overshoes**

NC An **overshoe** is a large shoe, often made of rubber or plastic, that you wear over an ordinary shoe in order to protect it. *...old fashioned rubber overshoes worn in wet weather.*

overshoot /ˈəʊvəʃuːt/ **overshoots, overshooting, overshot**

VO If you **overshoot** a place that you want to get to, you go past it by mistake. *Natalie's glider overshot the landing zone and crashed into a field... The aeroplane in which they were travelling overshot the runway at Yonago airport and crashed into the sea.*

oversight /ˈəʊvəsaɪt/ **oversights**

NCorNU An **oversight** is something which you should have done but did not. *My oversight was in not remembering to inform the authorities.*

oversimplify /ˈəʊvəsɪmplɪfaɪ/ **oversimplifies, oversimplifying, oversimplified**

VO If you **oversimplify** something, you explain it so simply that what you say is no longer true or reasonable. *We may have oversimplified the discussion by ignoring this.* ♦ **oversimplified** ADJ *...an oversimplified view of the world.* ♦ **oversimplification** /ˈəʊvəsɪmplɪfɪkeɪʃn/ N SING *It was not an oversimplification to talk of 'reformists' and 'conservatives' as two cohesive and competing groups. ...a gross oversimplification.*

oversize /ˈəʊvəsaɪz/

ADJ **Oversize** or **oversized** things are too big, or bigger than usual. *...a girl in an oversize pair of slacks. ...an oversized tent.*

oversleep /ˈəʊvəsliːp/ **oversleeps, oversleeping, overslept**

V If you **oversleep**, you sleep longer than you intended to. *Some mornings I oversleep and miss breakfast.*

overspill /ˈəʊvəspɪl/

NUorN+N **Overspill** is an arrangement by which people are moved from an overcrowded city and are accommodated in new houses or flats in smaller towns. *...towns built to accommodate overspill from nearby big cities. ...London overspill towns. ...London overspill plans... These flats are an overspill development.*

overstaffed /ˈəʊvəstɑːft/

ADJ You say that a place is **overstaffed** when there are too many people working there. *...the overstaffed kitchen... The train company is overstaffed and notoriously inefficient.*

overstate /ˈəʊvəsteɪt/ **overstates, overstating, overstated**

VO If you **overstate** something, you describe it in a way that exaggerates its importance or a quality that it has. *Its effect on history cannot be overstated... That fear may be a bit overstated... This second problem is difficult to overstate.*

overstatement /ˈəʊvəsteɪtmənt/ **overstatements**

NCorNU An **overstatement** is a way of describing something that makes it seem more important or serious than it really is. *'Vast' proved to be something of an overstatement... It is not an overstatement to use the word 'massacre' in describing this incident.*

overstay /ˈəʊvəsteɪ/ **overstays, overstaying, overstayed**

VO If you **overstay** your time or your welcome, you stay somewhere longer than people want you to. *I'd already overstayed my time by a week.*

overstep /ˈəʊvəstep/ **oversteps, overstepping, overstepped**

1 VO If you **overstep** something such as the rules of a system or the limits of a situation, you go beyond what is permissible or acceptable. *He accused UN forces of overstepping their mandate... He was told he had been overstepping the boundaries of his job.*
2 If you **overstep the mark**, you behave in an unacceptable way. *Last week he overstepped the mark and there will be trouble.*

overstretch /ˈəʊvəstretʃ/ **overstretches, overstretching, overstretched**

VO If you **overstretch** something or someone, you force them to go beyond their normal capacity and may do them harm as a result. *Do not overstretch the insides of the legs... Do not try to overstretch the child's natural instincts.*

overstretched /ˈəʊvəstretʃt/

ADJ If a system or organization is **overstretched**, it is being forced to work more than it is supposed to do. *The whole air control system is overstretched. ...new problems for the government's already overstretched consular services.*

overt /əʊvɜːt/

ADJ An **overt** action or attitude is done or shown in an open and obvious way. *...overt hostility. ...overt acts of violence.* ♦ **overtly** ADV *His jokes got more overtly malicious.*

overtake /ˈəʊvəteɪk/ **overtakes, overtaking, overtook, overtaken**

1 VorVO If you **overtake** a moving vehicle or person, you pass them because you are moving faster than they are. *Within seconds, Senna in his McLaren tried to overtake... The truck had overtaken us. ...people waiting to overtake.*
2 VO If an event **overtakes** you, it happens unexpectedly or suddenly, before you are ready for it. *...all the changes that have overtaken Shetland recently.*

overtax /ˈəʊvətæks/ **overtaxes, overtaxing, overtaxed**

1 V-REFLorVO If you **overtax** yourself, or are **overtaxed**, you are physically or mentally exhausted. *I was afraid that he would overtax himself... They were dangerously overtaxed... My overtaxed brain rebelled, and everything went blank.*
2 VO If a government **overtaxes** a country or its people, it makes them pay too much tax. *They believed that Britain was overtaxed.*

overthrow, overthrows, overthrowing, overthrew, overthrown; pronounced /ˈəʊvəθrəʊ/ when it is a verb and /ˈəʊvəθrəʊ/ when it is a noun.

1 VO When a government or a leader is **overthrown**, they are removed by force. *He was arrested for attempting to overthrow the regime. ...the man who led the revolution and overthrew the dictator.* ► Also NC *...the overthrow of the dictator. ...the overthrow of 3000 years of imperial rule.*
2 VO If an idea, value, or standard is **overthrown**, it is replaced by another one. *Laws are openly violated, standards of behaviour are overthrown.*

overtime /ˈəʊvətaɪm/

1 NU **Overtime** is time that you spend at your job in addition to your normal working hours. *During the dispute, they have been refusing to work overtime at*

weekends... They have given him a red Mercedes, which they built for him during unpaid overtime. ...an overtime ban.

2 You can say that someone is **working overtime** when they use a lot of energy, effort, or enthusiasm in doing something; an informal expression. *Neil Kinnock and the team around him have been working overtime to improve Labour's image... Ministers have been working overtime in an attempt to persuade party rebels to tow the line.*

3 NU **Overtime** is the same as **extra time**; used in American English. *They won the first game of the season, beating the Boston Bruins 3-2 in overtime.*

overtone /ˈəʊvətəʊn/ **overtones**
NC If something has **overtones** of a particular quality, it has a small amount of that quality but does not openly express it. *The play has heavy political overtones. ...a pleasure that carried no overtones of fear.*

overtook /ˌəʊvəˈtʊk/
Overtook is the past tense of **overtake**.

overture /ˈəʊvətjʊə/ **overtures**
1 NC An **overture** is a piece of music used as the introduction to an opera or play. *...Elgar's 'Cockaigne' Overture.*
2 N PL If you make **overtures** to someone, you start to behave in a friendly or romantic way towards them. *Mrs Thorne had made overtures of friendship... He feared they would reject his overtures.*

overturn /ˌəʊvəˈtɜːn/ **overturns, overturning, overturned**
1 V-ERG If something **overturns** or if you **overturn** it, it turns upside down or on its side. *She overturned the chairs and hurled the cushions about... His car crashed into a tree and overturned.*
2 VO If someone with more authority than you **overturns** your decision, they change it. *If they persist in their attitude he can't overturn their decision... The Court of Appeal rejected a plea by the government to overturn a decision by the High Court... Its lawyers have advised that a court would be unlikely to overturn the ban.*
3 VO To **overturn** a government or system means to remove or destroy it. *The unrest might have overturned the military rulers.*

overvalue /ˌəʊvəˈvæljuː/ **overvalues, overvaluing, overvalued**
VO If you **overvalue** someone or something, you think that they are much more important or valuable than they really are. *We generally tend to overvalue money and undervalue art.*

overview /ˈəʊvəvjuː/ **overviews**
NC An **overview** of a situation is a general understanding or description of it. *...a short report giving a useful overview of recent developments.*

overweening /ˌəʊvəˈwiːnɪŋ/
ADJ ATTRIB **Overweening** pride, arrogance, and so on is very great pride, arrogance, and so on; a formal word, used showing disapproval. *This was merely the outcome of her overweening pride. ...his overweening impatience.*

overweight /ˌəʊvəˈweɪt/
ADJ Someone who is **overweight** is too fat. *Nearly half the people in this country are overweight. ...an overweight schoolgirl.*

overwhelm /ˌəʊvəˈwelm/ **overwhelms, overwhelming, overwhelmed**
1 VO If you **are overwhelmed** by a feeling or event, it affects you very strongly and you find it difficult to deal with. *He was overwhelmed by the intensity of her love... The horror of it all had overwhelmed me.*
2 VO If a group of people **overwhelm** a place or another group, they gain control of them. *Their mission was to seize the bridges and overwhelm the garrison.*

overwhelming /ˌəʊvəˈwelmɪŋ/
1 ADJ Something that is **overwhelming** affects you very strongly. *...an overwhelming sense of powerlessness.* ◆ **overwhelmingly** ADV *They had been overwhelmingly appreciative.*
2 ADJ You can use **overwhelming** to emphasize that one part of something is much greater than the rest of

it. *An overwhelming majority of people are in favour of this plan... The Soviet Parliament has given overwhelming backing to President's Gorbachov's revised plan.* ◆ **overwhelmingly** SUBMOD or ADV *It is still an overwhelmingly rural country... A month later the Parliament voted overwhelmingly for building to go ahead.*

overwork /ˌəʊvəˈwɜːk/ **overworks, overworking, overworked**
1 V-ERG If you **are overworking** or **are overworked**, you are working too hard. *You look tired. Have you been overworking?... They were overworked and poorly paid.* ► Also NU *...a body made weak through undernourishment and overwork.*
2 VO If you **overwork** something, you use it too much. *Farmers have overworked the soil.* ◆ **overworked** ADJ *'Crisis' has become one of the most overworked words of modern politics.*

overwrought /ˌəʊvəˈrɔːt/
ADJ Someone who is **overwrought** is upset and uncontrolled in their behaviour. *During the first few days, I was so tired and overwrought that I wasn't capable of taking much in... Whatever you may think, the camp is not just a collection of emotionally overwrought females.*

ovulate /ˈɒvjʊleɪt/ **ovulates, ovulating, ovulated**
V When a woman or female animal **ovulates**, she produces ova from her ovary; a technical term in biology. *For instance, when a woman ovulates, she may release the eggs but they may fail to be fertilized.* ◆ **ovulation** /ˌɒvjʊˈleɪʃn/ NU *These hormones appear in highest concentration around the time of ovulation.*

ovum /ˈəʊvəm/ **ova** /ˈəʊvə/
NC An **ovum** is one of the reproductive cells of a woman, or female animal. It is fertilized by a male sperm to produce young; a technical term in biology. *Scientists have been going to abattoirs to collect ova from slaughtered cows.*

ow /aʊ/
People say **'Ow!'** when they suddenly feel pain. *Ow! You're hurting me!*

owe /əʊ/ **owes, owing, owed**
1 VO or VOO If you **owe** money to someone, they have lent you money and you have not yet paid it to them. *I still owe you seven pounds... I paid Gower what I owed him.*
2 VO+to If you **owe** a quality or ability to someone or something, they are responsible for your having it. *She owed her technique entirely to his teaching.*
3 VOO or VO+to If you say that you **owe** gratitude, respect, or loyalty to someone, you mean that they deserve it from you; a formal use. *We owe you our thanks, Dr Marlowe... Neither he nor Melanie owe me any explanation.*
4 PREP You use **owing to** to introduce the reason for something. *I missed my flight owing to a traffic hold-up.*

owl /aʊl/ **owls**
NC An **owl** is a bird with large eyes which hunts small animals at night. *The habitat of two endangered species—an owl and an eagle—lay in the disputed islands.*

owlish /ˈaʊlɪʃ/
ADJ Someone who is **owlish** looks rather like an owl and seems to be very serious and clever. *Jimmie was almost owlish in his earnest solemnity.* ◆ **owlishly** ADV *Patrick peered owlishly at us through his horn-rimmed glasses.*

own /əʊn/ **owns, owning, owned**
1 ADJ ATTRIB You use **own** to emphasize that something belongs to, or is typical of the person or thing mentioned. *She'd killed her own children... Each city has its own peculiarities... We have information from our own people out there.* ► Also PRON *His background was similar to my own.*
2 ADJ You also use **own** to emphasize that someone does something without any help. *They are expected to make their own beds.* ► Also PRON *I said 'What about lunch?' and he said, 'Oh, get your own.'*
3 VO If you **own** something, it is your property. *...a huge old house owned by an Irish doctor.*

● **Own** is used in these phrases. ● When you are **on** your **own**, you are alone. *She lived on her own. ...sitting on his own.* ● If you do something **on** your **own**, you do it without any help. *We want to write a book on our own.* ● If you get your **own back**, you harm or trick someone who has harmed or tricked you; an informal expression. *At last he was getting his own back.* ● to hold your **own**: see **hold**.
own up PHRASAL VERB If you **own up** to something wrong that you have done, you admit that you did it. *They don't want to own up to this.*

-owned /-əʊnd/
SUFFIX **-owned** combines with other words, like nouns and adverbs, to form adjectives that indicate who something belongs to. *He ordered Zaire's state-owned companies to relocate elsewhere in Europe. ...the Zambian government-owned Daily Mail newspaper... It has campaigned on a pledge to promote new locally-owned businesses.*

owner /ˈəʊnə/ **owners**
NC The **owner** of something is the person to whom it belongs. *The average car owner drives 10,000 miles per year... Shop owners are refusing credit cards and cheques... The owners say that if no buyer is found, they will close the factory down.*

owner-driver, owner-drivers
NC An **owner-driver** is a person who owns the car or lorry that they drive. *A British owner-driver had the cab of his lorry set on fire.*

owner-occupier, owner-occupiers
NC An **owner-occupier** is a person who owns the house or flat that they live in. *Most of the grants had been taken up by owner-occupiers.*

ownership /ˈəʊnəʃɪp/
NU **Ownership** is the state of owning something. *...public ownership of land. ...the desire for home ownership. ...a referendum to be held on the controversial issue of the private ownership of land.*

own goal, own goals
1 NC In sport, if someone scores an **own goal**, they accidentally score a goal for the team they are playing against. *Liverpool captain Alan Hansen scored an own goal in the 24th minute.*
2 NC If someone's plan or a project has a bad effect on them, you can refer to it as an **own goal**. *She described it as an own goal scored by the human race against itself.*

ox /ɒks/ **oxen** /ɒksn/
NC An **ox** is a castrated bull. *...a plough pulled by two oxen.*

Oxbridge /ˈɒksbrɪdʒ/
N PROP **Oxbridge** is used to refer to the universities of Oxford and Cambridge together, rather than the other British universities. *...Oxbridge graduates.*

oxidation /ɒksɪˈdeɪʃn/
NU **Oxidation** is a process in which a chemical substance changes because of the addition of oxygen, for example when something rusts; a technical term in chemistry. *The ease of oxidation varies according to the metal.*

oxide /ˈɒksaɪd/ **oxides**
NC or NU An **oxide** is a compound of oxygen and another chemical element. *...oxides of nitrogen. ...iron oxide.*

oxidize /ˈɒksɪdaɪz/ **oxidizes, oxidizing, oxidized**; also spelt **oxidise**.
V-ERG When a substance **oxidizes** or is **oxidized**, it

changes chemically because of the effect of oxygen on it. For example, when a metal **oxidizes**, it becomes rusty. *Aluminium doesn't oxidise in wet weather.*

oxtail /ˈɒksteɪl/
NC **Oxtail** is the tail of an cow which is used as meat or in making soup. *Steve is as much at home with oxtail and carrots as he is with fillet of beef. ...oxtail soup.*

oxyacetylene /ˌɒksiəˈsetəliːn/
NU **Oxyacetylene** is a mixture of two gases, oxygen and acetylene, that burns with a very hot, bright flame. *You can cut anything open with an oxyacetylene flame.*

oxygen /ˈɒksɪdʒən/
NU **Oxygen** is a colourless gas in the air which is needed by all living things. *Scientists think that restriction of the oxygen supply to the ears could be responsible for damage to hearing.*

oxygenate /ˈɒksɪdʒəneɪt/ **oxygenates, oxygenating, oxygenated**
VO To **oxygenate** something means to mix or dissolve oxygen into it. *The heart-lung machine oxygenates the blood and pumps it round.* ◆ **oxygenated** ADJ *...oxygenated water.*

oxygen mask, oxygen masks
NC An **oxygen mask** is placed over a patient's nose and mouth so that they can be given more oxygen and can therefore breathe more easily. *She was breathing using an oxygen mask.*

oxygen tent, oxygen tents
NC An **oxygen tent** is a clear tent that is put over a patient who is very ill in hospital and filled with pure oxygen to help them breathe. *...children in oxygen tents.*

oyster /ˈɔɪstə/ **oysters**
NC An **oyster** is a large, flat shellfish. Some oysters can be eaten and others produce pearls. *They have warned inhabitants not to eat oysters or shellfish taken from the affected area... The whole town is strewn with oyster shells.*

oyster bed, oyster beds
NC An **oyster bed** is a place where oysters live or are kept, so that they can be used as food or for producing pearls. *We started off down the long dyke, through the oyster beds.*

oz.
oz is a written abbreviation for 'ounce' or 'ounces'.

Özal, Turgut /ˈtuəgut ˈ3ːzæl/
Turgut Özal became President of Turkey in 1989. He founded the Motherland Party (ANAP) in 1983 and became Chairman in 1988. He was Deputy Prime Minister from 1980 to 1982 and Prime Minister from 1983 to 1989. Born: 1927.

ozone /ˈəʊzəʊn/
NU **Ozone** is a form of oxygen. There is a layer of ozone high above the Earth's surface. *Scientists can't predict how continued ozone depletion will affect world food production... There has been intensive research in the ozone hole.*

ozone layer
N SING The **ozone layer** is the part of the Earth's atmosphere that has the highest number of ozone molecules, and which protects living things from the harmful radiation of the sun. *British scientists found evidence that the ozone layer over the Antarctic was beginning to thin... Any diminution in the ozone layer is therefore very serious.*

P p

P, p /piː/ **P's, p's**
1 NC **P** is the sixteenth letter of the English alphabet.
2 **p** is an abbreviation for 'pence' or 'penny'. *It's only 10p. ...a 50p piece.*
3 You write **p.** in front of a number as an abbreviation for 'page'. The plural form is 'pp.' *See p.72. ...Tables I and II on pp.40-43.*

pa /pɑː/ **pas**
VOCATIVE or NC Some people address or refer to their father as **pa**; an old-fashioned, informal word. *'Pa,' Gretchen said, 'be serious.'... Pa won't be pleased if you miss evening prayers.*

PA /piː eɪ/ **PAs**
1 NC **PA** is an abbreviation for 'personal assistant'. *He needs a PA rather than a secretary.*
2 N SING **PA** is also an abbreviation for 'public address': see **public address system**. *I heard the bark of the PA system.*

p.a.
p.a. is a written abbreviation for 'per annum'. *I shall be paid £12,000 p.a.*

pace /peɪs/ **paces, pacing, paced**
1 NU The **pace** of something is the speed at which it happens or is done. *...the pace of change... The sale resumed at a brisk pace.*
2 N SING Your **pace** is the speed at which you walk. *He proceeds at a leisurely pace... He quickened his pace.*
3 NC A **pace** is the distance you move when you take one step. *He took two quick paces forward... He stopped when he was a few paces away.*
4 VA or VO If you **pace** up and down, you keep walking up and down, because you are anxious or impatient. *Harold paced nervously up and down the platform... She paced the room angrily.*
● **Pace** is used in these phrases. ● To **keep pace** with something that is changing means to change quickly in response to it. *Earnings have not kept pace with inflation.* ● If you do something **at your own pace**, you do it at a speed that is comfortable for you.

pacemaker /peɪsmeɪkə/ **pacemakers**
1 NC A **pacemaker** is a device that is put next to someone's heart, usually under their skin, in order to make their heart beat in the right way. *He had had a pacemaker fitted the year before.*
2 NC A **pacemaker** is also a competitor who is in front of other competitors during part of a race and who therefore causes that part of the race to be run at a particular speed.
3 NC A **pacemaker** is also the same as a **pace-setter**.

pace-setter, pace-setters
NC If someone or something is a **pace-setter** for other people or things, they are the first to achieve something and they therefore encourage others to do the same as them. *He is among the pace-setters at the Bay Hill Golf Classic in the United States... Ford have now agreed on a pay deal which is bound to be seen as a pace-setter for the rest of the industry.*

pachyderm /pækidɜːm/ **pachyderms**
NC A **pachyderm** is a large thick-skinned animal such as an elephant or rhinoceros; a technical term in biology.

pacific /pəsɪfɪk/
1 N PROP The **Pacific** or the **Pacific Ocean** is a very large area of sea to the west of North and South America, and to the east of Asia and Australia. *The Soviet military is nervous that their access to the Pacific Ocean will be impeded if the islands are returned to Japan.*
2 ADJ ATTRIB **Pacific** is used to describe things that are in or that relate to the Pacific Ocean. *...Pacific islands... He has issued specific policy initiatives directed at the Pacific countries.*
3 ADJ Something that is **pacific** is peaceful or intended to result in peace; a formal use. *...their pacific intentions.*

pacifier /pæsɪfaɪə/ **pacifiers**
NC A **pacifier** is a child's dummy; used in American English. *His grandson was toddling around with a pacifier in his mouth.*

pacifism /pæsɪfɪzəm/
NU **Pacifism** is the belief that war and violence are always wrong. *...a state committed after the Second World War to total pacifism.* ◆ **pacifist, pacifists** NC *I was accused of being a pacifist.*

pacify /pæsɪfaɪ/ **pacifies, pacifying, pacified**
1 VO If you **pacify** someone who is angry or upset, you succeed in making them calm. *The manager was trying hard to pacify our clients.* ◆ **pacification** /pæsɪfɪkeɪʃn/ NU *In this crisis he's made some contribution to pacification.*
2 VO If the army or the police **pacify** a group of people, they use force to overcome their resistance or protests. *The streets were full of tear gas as the riot police sought to pacify hundreds of furious farmers... He accused them of using extreme violence in their attempts to pacify villages in the province.*
◆ **pacification** NU *...a pacification campaign similar to what the Americans used in Vietnam.*

pack /pæk/ **packs, packing, packed**
1 V or VO When you **pack**, you put your belongings into a bag, because you are leaving. *While the bill was being prepared he went upstairs to pack... He packed his bags and left.* ◆ **packing** NU *Have you started your packing?*
2 VO When goods **are packed**, they are put into containers or parcels so that they can be transported. *...the wooden boxes in which the eggs were packed.*
3 V-ERG A If people or things **are packed** into a place, there are so many of them that the place is full. *About 300 of us were packed into a half-built mansion... Thirty thousand people packed into the stadium to hear him.*
4 VO To **pack** a gun means to carry it; used in informal American English. *...the individual's right to pack a gun.*
5 NC A **pack** is a rucksack. *He pulled a plastic bag out of his pack.*
6 NC A **pack** of things is a packet of them; used in American English. *...a pack of cigarettes.*
7 NC A **pack** of playing cards is a complete set of them. *...a pack of cards.*
8 NC A **pack** of wolves or dogs is a group of them hunting together. *...a cunning fox which was trying to*

escape from a pack of baying hounds and horn-blowing huntsmen.

9 See also **packed, packing case.**

pack in PHRASAL VERB If you **pack** something **in**, you stop doing it; an informal expression. *It's a good job. I don't think he'd pack it in.*

pack into PHRASAL VERB If someone **packs** a lot of work or activities **into** a period of time, they do a lot of work or activities during that time; an informal expression. *Mrs Thatcher is packing as much as she can into her three days in Poland.*

pack off PHRASAL VERB If you **pack** someone **off** somewhere, you send them there; an informal expression. *They pack their sons off to boarding school.*

pack up PHRASAL VERB If you **pack up** your belongings, you put them in a case or bag, because you are leaving. *We packed up the things I had accumulated... Once term finishes we all pack up and go home.*

package /ˈpækɪdʒ/ packages, packaging, packaged
1 NC A **package** is a small parcel. *...a small package wrapped in tissue paper.*
2 VO When something is **packaged**, it is put into packets to be sold. *The cereal is packaged in plain boxes.* ◆ **packaging** NU *Some seventy per cent of China's exports to the U.S. go first to Hong Kong, for packaging and shipping.*
3 NC+SUPP You also use **package** to refer to a set of offers, proposals, or arrangements that is made by a government or organization. *He promised a $200 million aid package to help make up the losses caused by sanctions. ...the announcement of a fresh package of spending cuts... He said that almost the entire package of arrangements had already been agreed in the talks.*
4 See also **packaging.**

package deal, package deals
NC A **package deal** is a set of offers, proposals, or arrangements which is made by a government or organization and which must be accepted or rejected as a whole. *They rejected the package deal put forward by the management... Mr Baker spoke of a package deal; the Soviet Union would not be able to accept only parts of it.*

package holiday, package holidays
NC A **package holiday** or a **package tour** is a holiday arranged by a travel company in which your travel and accommodation are booked for you. *...the rapid growth in foreign package holidays.*

packaging /ˈpækɪdʒɪŋ/
1 NU The paper, plastic, or box that something is sold in is called its **packaging**. *...extra warnings should be put on the packaging of contraceptive pills... These packaging materials are on the increase and they will pose growing problems for recycling.*
2 See also **packaging.**

pack animal, pack animals
NC A **pack animal** is an animal such as a horse or donkey that is used to carry things on journeys. *They could take up to three weeks walking with pack animals over difficult mountain terrain.*

packed /pækt/
1 ADJ A **packed** place is very crowded. *The theatre was packed. ...a packed courtroom.*
2 ADJ PRED Something that is **packed** with things contains a very large number of them. *The book is packed full of information.*

packed lunch, packed lunches
NC A **packed lunch** is food, for example sandwiches, which you take to work, to school, or on an outing and eat as your lunch.

packed out
ADJ PRED If a place is **packed out**, it is completely full of people; an informal expression. *The cinema was packed out.*

packer /ˈpækə/ packers
NC A **packer** is a person whose job is to pack things into containers.

packet /ˈpækɪt/ packets
1 NC A **packet** is a small box, bag, or envelope in which a quantity of something is sold. *Check the*

washing instructions on the packet.
2 NC You can use **packet** to refer to a packet and its contents, or to the contents only. *...a packet of cigarettes. ...a packet of crisps.*

pack ice
NU **Pack ice** is an area of ice that is floating on the sea. It is made up of pieces of ice that have been pushed together. *The pack ice is beginning to thaw.*

packing case, packing cases
NC A **packing case** is a large wooden box in which things are stored or taken somewhere.

pact /pækt/ pacts
NC A **pact** is a formal agreement between two or more governments, organizations, or people to do a particular thing or to help each other. *A pact was signed banning all military activity... That probably rules out an electoral pact between the two main opposition groups at next year's parliamentary elections.*

pad /pæd/ pads
1 NC A **pad** is a thick, flat piece of a material such as cloth or foam rubber. Pads are used, for example, to clean things or for protection. *...a cotton wool pad soaked in antiseptic... Elbow pads and knee pads are essential on a skateboard.*
2 NC A **pad** is also a number of pieces of paper fixed together along one side, so that each piece can be torn off when it has been used. *He took a pad and pencil from his pocket.*
3 NC A helicopter **pad** is an area of flat, hard ground where helicopters can land and take off.
4 NC A launch **pad** is a place where missiles and rockets can be fired from. *The European Space Agency has successfully launched an Ariane rocket from its launch pad in French Guiana... Reports that Iraq had set up missile pads in northern Sudan to threaten Egypt provoked an angry response from the President.*
5 NC A cat's or dog's **pads** are the soft parts on the bottom of its paws.

padded /ˈpædɪd/
ADJ Something that is **padded** has soft material on it or inside it which makes it less hard, protects it, or gives it a different shape. *The steering wheel is padded with real leather.*

padded cell, padded cells
NC A **padded cell** is a small room with padded walls in a psychiatric hospital, where patients can be put if it is thought that they might hurt themselves in an ordinary room.

padding /ˈpædɪŋ/
NU **Padding** is soft material on the outside or inside of something which makes it less hard, protects it, or gives it a different shape. *...a jacket with padding at the shoulders.*

paddle /ˈpædl/ paddles, paddling, paddled
1 NC A **paddle** is a short pole with a wide, flat part at one end or at both ends, which you use as an oar to move a small boat through water. *In the kayak races, the canoeists use paddles with blades at each end.*
2 V When people **paddle**, they walk or stand in shallow water at the edge of the sea, for pleasure. *It was too cold for paddling.*

paddle boat, paddle boats
NC A **paddle boat** or a **paddle steamer** is a large boat that is pushed through the water by the movement of large wheels that are attached to its sides. *...one of the last paddle steamers operating in Britain.*

paddling pool, paddling pools
NC A **paddling pool** is a shallow artificial pool for children to paddle in.

paddock /ˈpædək/ paddocks
1 NC A **paddock** is a small field where horses are kept.
2 NC At a race course, the **paddock** is the place where the horses walk about before each race.

paddy /ˈpædi/ paddies
NC A **paddy** or a **paddy field** is a flooded field that is used for growing rice. *...the rice paddies shining bright green, almost ready for harvest.*

padlock /ˈpædlɒk/ padlocks, padlocking, padlocked
1 NC A **padlock** is a lock with a U-shaped bar attached to it. One end of this bar is released when the padlock

is unlocked. *A big padlock was seen hanging at the main gate.*
2 VO If you **padlock** something, you lock it or fasten it to something else using a padlock. *Staff arrived at the office one morning to find that during the night someone had padlocked it shut.*

padre /pɑːdreɪ/ **padres**
N C or VOCATIVE A **padre** is a Christian priest, especially a chaplain to the armed forces; an informal word. *The padre never used that prayer again... Good evening, Padre.*

paean /piːən/ **paeans**
NC A **paean** is a piece of music, writing, or film that expresses praise, admiration, or joy; a literary word. *The film is a paean to nature.*

paediatrician /piːdiətrɪʃn/ **paediatricians**; also spelt **pediatrician**.
NC A **paediatrician** is a doctor who specializes in treating sick children. *... a consultant paediatrician at London's Great Ormond Street Hospital.*

paediatrics /piːdiætrɪks/; also spelt **pediatrics**.
NU **Paediatrics** is the area of medicine that is concerned with children's illnesses and their treatment. *They will specialise for a similar period in fields such as maternity, geriatrics and paediatrics.*

paedophile /piːdəfaɪl/ **paedophiles**; also spelt **pedophile**.
NC A **paedophile** is someone who is sexually attracted to children. *This obscene material is being produced and distributed by rings of paedophiles.*

paedophilia /piːdəfɪliə/; also spelt **pedophilia**.
NU **Paedophilia** is sexual attraction to children. *It's vital to understand how pornography fits into the network of paedophilia.*

paella /paɪelə/
NU **Paella** is a dish cooked especially in Spain which consists of rice mixed with small pieces of vegetables, fish, and chicken.

Paeniu, Bikenibeu /bɪkənɪbjuː paːenjuː/
Bikenibeu Paeniu became Prime Minister of Tuvalu in 1989. Born: 1956.

paeony /piːəni/. See **peony**.

pagan /peɪɡən/ **pagans**
1 ADJ **Pagan** is used to describe religious beliefs and practices that do not belong to any of the main religions of the world. *...an ancient pagan festival. ...pagan gods.*
2 NC A **pagan** is a person who has pagan beliefs or who takes part in pagan practices. *He says that paganism has been lurking underneath the Christian facade ever since Christians first came to convert the pagans.*

paganism /peɪɡənɪzəm/
NU **Paganism** is the state of having pagan beliefs or practices. *Beliefs and practices clearly rooted in ancient paganism continued to flourish secretly for a very long time.*

page /peɪdʒ/ **pages, paging, paged**
1 NC A **page** is a side of one of the pieces of paper in a book, magazine, or newspaper. *The story appeared on the front page of the Daily Mail... For details of pensions, see page 16.*
2 NC The **pages** of a book, magazine, or newspaper are the pieces of paper it consists of. *When they recovered their passports from the officer, they discovered that pages had been torn from each of them.*
3 VO To **page** someone in an airport, hotel, or large shop means to ask them over a loudspeaker to come and receive a message or help someone. *At East London airport I was paged to take a telephone call.*

pageant /pædʒənt/ **pageants**
NC A **pageant** is a show, often performed out of doors, which is made up of historical or literary scenes. *The organisers hope the pageant will raise at least a quarter of a million pounds for charity.*

pageantry /pædʒəntri/
NU You can refer to grand and colourful ceremonies as **pageantry**. *The week was crammed with festivities and pageantry.*

pageboy /peɪdʒbɔɪ/ **pageboys**
1 NC A **pageboy** is a small boy who is one of the

bride's attendants at a wedding.
2 NC A **pageboy** is a medium-length hairstyle in which all the hair is smooth and the ends are curled under, framing the face.

page three
ADJ ATTRIB **Page three** girls are young women who pose with their breasts showing for photographs which appear in certain popular British newspapers. The photographs are intended to be sexually appealing. *She introduced a Bill in Parliament to ban page three girls... He compared page three photographs with nudes in famous paintings.*

pagination /pædʒɪneɪʃn/
NU The **pagination** of a book, magazine, or document is the way that the pages have been numbered; a formal word. *The pagination is wrong—there's no page 56.*

pagoda /pəɡəʊdə/ **pagodas**
NC A **pagoda** is a tall, ornately decorated building which is used for religious purposes, especially by Buddhists, in China, Japan, and South-East Asia. *In Mandalay, the main pagoda is heavily guarded and worshippers are being prevented by the army from approaching the main Buddha image.*

Pago Pago /pæŋəʊ pæŋəʊ/
Pago Pago, on Tutuila island, is the capital of American Samoa and its largest town. Population: 3,000 (1980).

paid /peɪd/
1 **Paid** is the past tense and past participle of **pay**.
2 ADJ If you are well **paid**, you receive a lot of money for your work. If you are badly **paid**, you do not receive much money for it. *Secretaries are pretty well paid these days. ...low paid jobs.*
3 ADJ ATTRIB If you have **paid** holiday, you receive your pay even when you are on holiday. *Many have given their employees a day's paid leave.*

paid-up
ADJ ATTRIB If you are a **paid-up** member of a group, you have paid the money required to be a member. *Over three million people in Britain are paid-up members of conservation groups.*

pail /peɪl/ **pails**
NC A **pail** is a bucket made of metal or wood; an old-fashioned word. *...a pail of water.*

pain /peɪn/ **pains, paining, pained**
1 NU or NC **Pain** is an unpleasant feeling in a part of your body that is caused by illness or an injury. *He was in pain... She complained of severe pains in her chest.*
2 NU **Pain** is also the unhappiness that you feel when something very upsetting happens. *...the pain of realizing that she had failed.*
3 VO If something **pains** you, it makes you feel upset or unhappy. *It pained him that his father talked like that.*
● **Pain** is used in these phrases. ● If you say that someone is a **pain** or a **pain in the neck**, you mean they are very annoying or irritating; used in informal English. ● If you **take pains** to do something, you try hard to do it successfully. *She took great pains to conceal this from her parents... She always took great pains with her make-up.*

pained /peɪnd/
ADJ Someone who looks or sounds **pained** seems upset or offended. *She raised her eyebrows and looked pained. ...a pained expression.*

painful /peɪnfl/
1 ADJ If a part of your body is **painful**, it hurts. *My back is so painful that I cannot stand upright.*
2 ADJ You say that things are **painful** when they cause you physical pain. *My boots are still painful. ...a long and painful illness.* ◆ **painfully** ADV *She struck him, quite painfully, with the ruler.*
3 ADJ A **painful** experience is upsetting or difficult. *...the painful process of growing up... It was painful to admit that I was wrong.* ◆ **painfully** SUBMOD *I was always painfully aware of my shortcomings.*

painkiller /peɪnkɪlə/ **painkillers**
NC A **painkiller** is a pill or other form of drug which reduces or stops physical pain. *There are painkillers to relieve their suffering.*

painless /peɪnləs/
1 ADJ When something is **painless**, it does not cause physical pain. ...*painless childbirth.* ♦ **painlessly** ADV *My tooth came out quite painlessly.*
2 ADJ A **painless** way of achieving something does not involve much trouble. ...*the painless way to learn German.* ♦ **painlessly** ADV *Industrialization in western countries was achieved painlessly.*
painstaking /peɪnsteɪkɪŋ/
ADJ Someone who is **painstaking** does things extremely thoroughly. *The picture had been cleaned with painstaking care.* ♦ **painstakingly** ADV *He painstakingly records details of every race.*
paint /peɪnt/ **paints, painting, painted**
1 N MASS **Paint** is a coloured liquid that you put on a wall or other surface with a brush. ...*a tin of pink paint.* ...*non-drip paints.*
2 N MASS **Paint** is also a coloured liquid or thick paste that is used to make a picture. *He combines ink, charcoal and paint in his drawings.* ...*oil paints.*
3 VOorV When you **paint** something or **paint** a picture of it, you make a picture of it using paint. *Whistler painted his mother in a rocking chair... Could this type of research help to spot which pictures were painted by Rembrandt and which were not?... Hopper painted in a 'realist' style.*
4 VO When you **paint** something such as a wall or piece of furniture, you cover it with paint. *The rooms were painted green.* ♦ **painted** ADJ ...*painted furniture.* ...*white-painted passages.*
paintbox /peɪntbɒks/ **paintboxes**
NC A **paintbox** is a small flat tin containing a number of little blocks of paint which can be made wet and used to paint a picture.
paintbrush /peɪntbrʌʃ/ **paintbrushes**
NC A **paintbrush** is a brush which you use for putting paint onto something.
painter /peɪntə/ **painters**
1 NC A **painter** is an artist who paints pictures. ...*a landscape painter.*
2 NC A **painter** is also someone whose job is painting parts of buildings. *This man, a painter and decorator by trade, doesn't want to be named.*
painting /peɪntɪŋ/ **paintings**
1 NC A **painting** is a picture that is produced using paint. ...*a painting of a horse... A valuable painting has been stolen from the National Gallery in Prague.*
2 NU **Painting** is the activity of painting pictures. ...*the unique nature of Elizabethan painting.*
3 NU+SUPP You also use **painting** to refer to the pictures painted by a particular artist or group of artists, and to the style in which they are painted. ...*an exhibition of Italian painting at the National Gallery.*
4 NU **Painting** is also the activity of painting walls, furniture, and so on. *They might do the wallpapering and the painting.*
paint stripper
NU **Paint stripper** is a substance, usually a thick liquid, which you use in order to remove the old paint from things such as doors or pieces of furniture.
paintwork /peɪntwɜːk/
NU The **paintwork** of a building or vehicle is the paint on it. *Use warm water and detergent to wash paintwork.*
pair /peə/ **pairs, pairing, paired**
1 NC You refer to two things as a **pair** when they are the same size and shape and are intended to be used together. ...*a pair of boots... Dragonflies have two pairs of wings.*
2 NC You also use **pair** when you are referring to certain objects which have two main parts of the same size and shape. ...*a pair of trousers.* ...*a pair of scissors.*
3 N COLL You can refer to two people as a **pair** when they are standing or walking together or when they have some kind of relationship with each other. *They'd always been a devoted pair... The pair have become famous for their attempts to expose corruption... When the pair was arrested soon afterwards, they were carrying Soviet and British-made weapons.*

4 See also **au pair.**
pair off PHRASAL VERB When people **pair off** or are **paired off**, they become grouped in pairs. *People are paired off according to their level of competence.*
paisley /peɪzli/
NU **Paisley** is a special pattern of curving shapes and colours, used especially on fabric. *Yuppies even had a uniform—striped shirt, brightly coloured braces, paisley or spotted tie.*
pajamas /pədʒɑːməz/. See **pyjamas.**
Pakistan /pɑːkɪstɑːn/
The **Islamic Republic of Pakistan** is a country in southern Asia, north-west of India, formerly known as West Pakistan. It was part of British India until the Partition of 1947, when East and West Pakistan were separated from India to form a Muslim state. East Pakistan declared itself independent in 1971, causing civil war and the creation of the separate state of Bangladesh. Over three million refugees from Afghanistan have fled into Pakistan. Ghulam Ishaq Khan became President in 1988. Mian Mohammad Nawaz Sharif, of the Islamic Democratic Alliance (IJI), was elected Prime Minister in 1990. Pakistan is a member of the Commonwealth. It exports cotton and textiles. Opium and cannabis are illegally produced. Large foreign debts are a major economic problem.
♦ **Pakistani** /pɑːkɪstɑːni/ N, ADJ
▪ *per capita GNP:* US$350 ▪ *religion:* Islam (mainly Sunni) ▪ *language:* Urdu (official), English, Punjabi, Pushto, Sindhi ▪ *currency:* rupee ▪ *capital:* Islāmābād ▪ *largest city:* Karāchi ▪ *population:* 110 million (1989) ▪ *size:* 803,943 square kilometres.
pal /pæl/ **pals**
NC Your **pal** is your friend; an old-fashioned, informal word. *Is he a pal of yours?*
palace /pæləs/ **palaces**
NC A **palace** is a very large, grand house, especially one which is the home of a king, queen, or president. ...*Buckingham Palace.*
palaeontology /pæliɒntɒlədʒi/
NU **Palaeontology** is the study of the fossils of extinct animals and plants. ...*Dr Stringer of the Department of Palaeontology at the British Museum.*
♦ **palaeontologist, palaeontologists** NC *The announcement has caused a great deal of interest among palaeontologists.*
palatable /pælətəbl/; a formal word.
1 ADJ If you describe food or drink as **palatable**, you mean that it tastes quite pleasant. *The food looked quite palatable.* ♦ **palatability** /pælətəbɪləti/ NU *But it is still a wild plant, and it has factors causing low palatability both for humans and for livestock.*
2 ADJ If you describe something such as an idea as **palatable**, you mean that it is easy to accept. *The truth is not always palatable.*
palate /pælət/ **palates**
1 NC Your **palate** is the top part of the inside of your mouth. ...*children born with cleft lips and palates.*
2 NC You can also refer to someone's ability to judge good food and wine as their **palate**. *All that junk food must have ruined my palate.*
palatial /pəleɪʃl/
ADJ If a house is **palatial**, it is very large and splendid. *He received me in his palatial governor's mansion overlooking the Dal Lake.*
Palau /pəlaʊ/. See **Belau.**
palaver /pəlɑːvə/
NU **Palaver** is unnecessary fuss and bother about the way something is done; an informal word. *What a palaver it was!*
pale /peɪl/ **paler, palest**
1 ADJ Something that is **pale** is not strong or bright in colour. *The house is built of pale stone... He had on a pale blue shirt.*
2 ADJ If someone looks **pale**, their face is a lighter colour than usual, because they are ill, frightened, or shocked. *You look awfully pale: are you all right?*
♦ **paleness** NU *Symptoms are unusual paleness and tiredness.*
Palestine /pæləstaɪn/
Palestine is an area in the eastern Mediterranean, parts of which lie in Israel and Jordan. The number of

Palestinians worldwide is estimated at between five and six million. Palestine was part of the Ottoman Empire from 1517 to 1918. After the First World War it became a British mandate and European Jews began to immigrate in large numbers. The state of Israel was created in 1948. War between Israel and Arab armies, including Palestinian troops, followed, with about 780,000 Palestinians becoming refugees. The PLO (Palestine Liberation Organization) was founded in 1964, with the aim of establishing a state of Palestine. In 1967 Israel occupied the West Bank and Gaza Strip. The intifada (uprising) by Palestinians living in the West Bank and Gaza Strip began in 1987. In 1988 the PNC (Palestine National Council) in exile declared an independent state of Palestine, with Jerusalem as its capital and Yasser Arafat as its President. It is a member of the Arab League and is recognized by most Arab states. The PLO has observer status at the UN and has diplomatic missions in some European and other capitals. ♦ **Palestinian** /pælǝstɪnɪǝn/ N, ADJ

palette /pælǝt/ **palettes**
1 NC A **palette** is a flat piece of wood or plastic on which an artist mixes paints.
2 NC A **palette** is also the range of colours that are characteristic of a particular artist or school of painting. *The lighter palette of the impressionists suited her femininity.*

palette knife, palette knives
NC A **palette knife** is an instrument with a broad, flat, flexible blade, used in cookery and in oil painting.

Palikir /pɑːlɪkɪǝ/
Palikir, on the island of Pohnpei, is the capital of Micronesia.

palindrome /pælɪndrǝʊm/ **palindromes**
NC A **palindrome** is a word, phrase, or number that is the same whether you read it backwards or forwards, for example the word 'refer'.

palings /peɪlɪŋz/
N PL **Palings** are a fence that is made of a series of long, thin, pointed, upright pieces of wood or metal. *Mrs Burt stuck her head over the palings wearing her husband's hat.*

palisade /pælɪseɪd/ **palisades**
NC A **palisade** is a fence of wooden posts which are driven into the ground in order to protect people from attack.

pall /pɔːl/ **palls, palling, palled**
1 V If something **palls**, it becomes less interesting or less enjoyable. *George's jokes were beginning to pall.*
2 NC+SUPP A **pall** of smoke is a thick cloud of it; a literary use. *A pall of smoke hung over the entire area.*

pallbearer /pɔːlbeǝrǝ/ **pallbearers**
NC A **pallbearer** is a person who helps to carry the coffin or walks beside it at a funeral. *The bier was carried by seventy-six pallbearers dressed in white.*

pallet /pælǝt/ **pallets**
1 NC A **pallet** is a flat wooden platform on which goods are stacked so that they can be lifted and moved using a fork-lift truck.
2 NC A luggage **pallet** is a metal platform on which luggage is stacked and transported in an aeroplane. *Two parts of the frame of the plane's metal luggage pallet show evidence of a detonating high explosive.*
3 NC A **pallet** is also a narrow mattress filled with straw which is put on the floor for someone to sleep on. *I lay on a pallet on the floor of a dim, white room.*
4 NC A **pallet** is also a hard, narrow bed.

palliative /pælɪǝtɪv/ **palliatives**
1 NC A drug or medical treatment that is a **palliative** is one which relieves suffering without treating the cause of the suffering. *...its effectiveness as a cure or palliative for so many ailments.*
2 NC An action that is a **palliative** is intended to make someone feel less angry or concerned about a problem, but does not actually solve the problem. *They are not going to be fobbed off with something, a palliative of some sort... This can be seen as an official palliative to the evident inequity of the system.* ▶ Also ADJ *...the application of palliative methods. ...palliative words.*

pallid /pælɪd/
ADJ **Pallid** means unnaturally pale; a literary word. *...his pallid face.*

pallor /pælǝ/
N SING Someone's **pallor** is an unhealthy paleness in their face; a literary word. *I was struck by her pallor.*

pally /pæli/
ADJ If you are **pally** with someone, you are friendly with them; an informal word. *He was certainly not a man to be pally with.*

palm /pɑːm/ **palms**
1 NC A **palm** or a **palm tree** is a type of tree. It has long leaves at the top and no branches. *He sat in the shade beneath the palms.*
2 NC+POSS The **palm** of your hand is the flat surface which your fingers can bend towards. *She placed the money in his palm.*

palmistry /pɑːmɪstri/
NU **Palmistry** is the practice and art of telling what people are like and what will happen in their future life by examining the lines on the palms of their hands. *Palmistry first emerged in India some three thousand years ago.*

Palm Sunday
NU **Palm Sunday** is the Sunday before Easter. *In Jerusalem, the traditional Palm Sunday procession was cancelled.*

palomino /pælǝmiːnǝʊ/ **palominos**
NC A **palomino** is a horse which is golden or cream in colour and has a white mane and tail.

palpable /pælpǝbl/
ADJ Something that is **palpable** is very obvious; a formal word. *...a palpable lie.* ♦ **palpably** ADV *Gorbachev has palpably succeeded in one of his main aims in dynamising society... It was palpably unjust.*

palpitate /pælpɪteɪt/ **palpitates, palpitating, palpitated**
1 V If someone's heart **palpitates**, it beats very fast and irregularly because they are frightened or anxious.
2 V If something **palpitates**, it trembles or moves quickly backwards and forwards, or seems to move in this way; a literary use. *Inside the crowded courtroom, the silence palpitated with the frustration of people powerless to do anything.*

palpitation /pælpɪteɪʃn/ **palpitations**
N PLorNU If you have **palpitations**, your heart beats very fast and with an irregular beat, usually because you are suffering from stress or are afraid. *I got palpitations when I read the name... It must be a long time since so many Americans have awaited the outcome of a court case with such palpitation of the heart.*

palsied /pɔːlzid/
ADJ Someone who is **palsied** is unable to control their muscles because of illness, and often their limbs shake uncontrollably as a result. *...problems of paraplegic, spastic and palsied children. ...brass padlocks that a blind and palsied thief could have opened.*

palsy /pɔːlzi/
NU **Palsy** is an illness which results in paralysis. There are several kinds of palsy. *...an affliction of the elderly which he called very graphically 'the shaking palsy'.* ● See also **cerebral palsy**.

paltry /pɔːltri/
ADJ A **paltry** sum of money or amount is very small and of not much use or value; a literary word. *The deal cost him a paltry £100... He works unofficially as a taxi driver to supplement his paltry pension... The response was paltry, with only two hundred people signing up.*

pampas /pæmpǝs/
N SING The **pampas** is the large areas of flat, grassy land in South America where no trees grow. *Puig was born in 1932 in the small town of General Villegas on the barren pampas land of Argentina.*

pampas grass
NU **Pampas grass** is a tall plant which has large, feathery, cream-coloured flower heads on the end of long stalks.

pamper /pǽmpə/ **pampers, pampering, pampered**
vo If you **pamper** someone, you treat them too kindly
and do too much for them. *His mother pampered him.*

pamphlet /pǽmflət/ **pamphlets**
NC A **pamphlet** is a very thin book with a paper cover,
which is produced to tell people about a particular
subject. *Amnesty International has also issued a
pamphlet dealing with the abuse of children around
the world.*

pamphleteer /pæmflətɪə/ **pamphleteers**
NC A **pamphleteer** is a person who writes pamphlets,
especially about political subjects. *...the political
thinker and pamphleteer Adam Michnik.*

pan /pæn/ **pans**
NC A **pan** is a round metal container with a long
handle, which is used for cooking things, usually on
top of a cooker. *...food cooked in aluminium pans.*

pan- /pæn-/
PREFIX **Pan-** combines with adjectives in order to form
new adjectives that describe something as connected
with the whole of a nation, area, or group of people.
For example, a 'pan-African' project involves the
whole of Africa. *...Pan-American Airways. ...the Pan-
African Congress.*

panacea /pænəsɪə/ **panaceas**
NC A **panacea** is something that is supposed to be a
cure for any problem or illness. *...an obsession with
technology as a panacea for life's ills.*

panache /pənǽʃ/
NU If you do something with **panache**, you do it in a
confident and stylish way. *He made his final speech
with more panache than ever before.*

Panama /pǽnəmɑː/
The **Republic of Panama** is a country in Central
America. It was a Spanish colony from the 16th
century until 1821. It was part of Colombia until 1903,
when it became independent with the support of the
United States. A treaty in 1903 gave the United States
the right to build the Panama Canal and control over
the Canal Zone. The Panama Canal, which connects
the Atlantic and Pacific oceans, was completed in 1914.
In 1979 Panama regained control of the Canal Zone,
which was abolished, and the canal became jointly
controlled by Panama and the United States. General
Manuel Noriega, the commander of the National
Defence Force, came to power in 1983. He was
overthrown in a military intervention by the United
States and was taken to the United States to stand
trial. Guillermo Endara Galimany, of the Democratic
Civic Opposition Alliance (ADOC), became President
in 1989, following the overthrow of Manuel Noriega.
Panama is a member of the Organization of American
States. It exports bananas, shrimp, and sugar. The
canal is an important source of revenue. Banking and
shipping are important industries. Large foreign debts
are a serious economic problem. ◆ **Panamanian**
/pænəmeɪnɪən/ N, ADJ
▪ *per capita GNP:* US$1,780 ▪ *religion:* Christianity
(mainly Roman Catholic) ▪ *language:* Spanish (official)
▪ *currency:* balboa ▪ *capital:* Panama City
▪ *population:* 2.5 million (1991) ▪ *size:* 75,517 square
kilometres.

Panama City /pænəmɑː sɪti/
Panama City is the capital of Panama and its largest
city. Population: 424,000 (1984).

panama hat /pænəmɑː hæt/ **panama hats**
NC A **panama hat** or a **panama** is a straw hat, worn
especially by men, that has a rounded crown and quite
a wide brim. *He presented a summery appearance in
his pale grey flannel suit and panama hat.*

panatella /pænətélə/ **panatellas**; also spelt **panatela**.
NC A **panatella** is a long thin cigar.

pancake /pǽŋkeɪk/ **pancakes**
NC A **pancake** is a thin, flat, circular piece of cooked
batter. Pancakes are usually folded and eaten hot with
a sweet or savoury filling. *...the tradition of tossing
pancakes.*

Pancake Day
NU **Pancake Day** is the Tuesday before Ash
Wednesday. People traditionally eat pancakes on
Pancake Day; an informal expression. *Today is
Shrove Tuesday—or Pancake Day—in Britain.*

pancake roll, pancake rolls
NC A **pancake roll** is a small pancake that is filled
with Chinese-style vegetables and sometimes meat,
and then rolled up.

pancreas /pǽŋkrɪəs/ **pancreases**
NC Your **pancreas** is an organ in your body that is
situated behind your stomach. It produces insulin, and
enzymes which help in the digestion of food. *Very
little is known about the prime causes of diabetes, and
why the cells which make insulin in the pancreas
become damaged.*

pancreatic /pæŋkrɪǽtɪk/
ADJ ATTRIB **Pancreatic** means relating to or involving
the pancreas. *...a medical drug originally developed
to treat pancreatic disease. ...pancreatic researchers
in Universities and institutes throughout the world.*

panda /pǽndə/ **pandas**
NC A **panda** or **giant panda** is a large animal with
black and white fur which lives in China. *The panda
is a protected animal in China... A large part of the
money raised to help save the giant panda from
extinction has been wasted.*

panda car, panda cars
NC A **panda car** is a small police patrol car. *Two
police officers in a panda car gave chase.*

pandemic /pændémɪk/ **pandemics**
NC A **pandemic** is a disease or problem that affects
everybody over a very wide area; a formal word. *As
well as the tragic personal implications of these
figures, the AIDS pandemic will have a huge impact
on health and social services... Children are now
suffering an epidemic, even a pandemic, of low-grade
intoxication.* ▶ Also ADJ *Racial prejudice was
discovered to be pandemic.*

pandemonium /pændəmáʊnɪəm/
NU If there is **pandemonium** in a place, the people
there are behaving in a very noisy and confused way.
*When the spectators heard about this, pandemonium
broke loose.*

pander /pǽndə/ **panders, pandering, pandered**
V+to If you **pander** to someone, you do everything they
want; used showing disapproval. *They pander to their
children's slightest whim.*

pandit /pʌ́ndɪt, pǽndɪt/ **pandits**
TITLE or NC A **pandit** is a wise man, especially in India.
*Pandit Dayanand formed this association... The Pandit
said that the Buddhists depended on tourism.*

p & p
NU **p & p** is a written abbreviation for 'postage and
packing'; used when stating the cost of packing goods
in a parcel and sending them through the post to a
customer. *...cost £4.50 + p & p. ...£20 p & p incl.*

pane /peɪn/ **panes**
NC A **pane** is a flat sheet of glass in a window or
door. *He then made his escape, but not before
replacing the window pane he had removed to get into
the house in the first place.*

panegyric /pænədʒírɪk/ **panegyrics**
NC A **panegyric** is a formal speech or piece of writing
that praises someone or something; a formal word.
He breaks into a lengthy panegyric on English culture.

panel /pǽnl/ **panels**
1 N COLL A **panel** is a small group of people who are
chosen to do something, for example to discuss
something in public or to make a decision. *...questions
answered by a panel of experts... The advisory panel
includes some of the top names from previous
administrations.*
2 NC A **panel** is also a flat, rectangular piece of wood
or other material that forms part of a larger object
such as a door. *There were glass panels in the front
door.*
3 NC+SUPP A control **panel** or instrument **panel** is a
board containing switches and controls. *The
instrument panel is just forward of the wheel.*

panelled /pǽnld/; spelt **paneled** in American English.
ADJ A **panelled** room has decorative wooden panels
covering its walls. *His office was panelled in dark
wood.*

panelling /pǽnəlɪŋ/; spelt **paneling** in American
English.
NU **Panelling** consists of boards or strips of wood

covering a wall inside a building. *...wooden panelling.*

panellist /pǽnəlɪst/ **panellists**
NC A **panellist** is a person who sits on a panel and speaks in public, especially on a radio or television programme.

pang /pǽŋ/ **pangs**
NC+SUPP A **pang** is a sudden, strong feeling, for example of sadness or pain. *She felt a sudden pang of regret. ...hunger pangs.*

panhandle /pǽnhændl/ **panhandles, panhandling, panhandled**; used in American English.
1 NC A **panhandle** is a narrow strip of land which extends from one state into another. *...the Texas Panhandle.*
2 V or VO To **panhandle** means to stop people in the street and ask them for money or food; an informal use. *They were refusing to allow the poor to panhandle... You see the same people day after day and you're panhandled, you're harassed. ...rice and vegetables bought with such money as he can panhandle.*

panhandler /pǽnhændəʰlə/ **panhandlers**
NC A **panhandler** is a person who stops other people in the street and asks them for money or food, because he or she is poor; used in informal American English. *The word 'homeless' generally conjures up images of the city: busy streets dotted with panhandlers, bus stops serving as bedrooms.*

panic /pǽnɪk/ **panics, panicking, panicked**
1 NU **Panic** is a strong feeling of anxiety or fear that makes you act without thinking sensibly. *Sandy was close to panic.*
2 NC A **panic** is a situation in which there is panic. *We don't want to start a panic.*
3 V If you **panic**, you become anxious or afraid, and act without thinking sensibly. *She panicked as his hand closed on her wrist.*

panic buying
NU If there is **panic buying**, people buy large quantities of goods because they fear that there are going to be shortages, for example because of a crisis such as a strike or because large price increases have been announced. *There was panic buying at all the shops as people stocked up for what could prove to be a long protest... The rises had been widely expected and caused a wave of panic buying on Friday and Saturday.*

panicky /pǽnɪki/
ADJ A **panicky** feeling or **panicky** behaviour is characterized by panic. *...a panicky feeling that lasts for a moment before each exam. ...a panicky reaction.*

panic-stricken
ADJ Someone who is **panic-stricken** is so anxious or afraid that they are acting without thinking sensibly. *...a panic-stricken crowd.*

pannier /pǽnɪə/ **panniers**
1 NC A **pannier** is one of two bags or boxes for carrying things which are fixed on each side of the wheel of a bicycle or motorbike, usually at the back. *Within moments, there are people with panniers on the backs of their bicycles pedalling off.*
2 NC A **pannier** is also a large basket, especially one of two that are put over an animal used for carrying loads. *The lane was so narrow that a donkey with panniers could hardly have scraped its way through.*

panoply /pǽnəpli/
NU A **panoply** of things or people is an impressive collection or display of them, especially associated with a particular ceremonial event; a formal word. *Their wedding had been formal and formidable, with a full panoply of relatives. ...the entire panoply of courtly love.*

panorama /pænərɑ́ːmə/ **panoramas**
NC A **panorama** is a view in which you can see a long way over a wide area of land. *...every bend in the road revealing fresh panoramas of empty beaches.*

panoramic /pænərǽmɪk/
ADJ If you have a **panoramic** view, you can see a long way over a wide area. *...a panoramic view of the valley.*

panpipes /pǽnpaɪps/
N PL **Panpipes** are a musical instrument made of a number of short wooden pipes of different lengths that you blow.

pansy /pǽnzi/ **pansies**
NC A **pansy** is a small garden flower with large, round petals.

pant /pǽnt/ **pants, panting, panted**
1 N PL **Pants** are a piece of underwear with two holes to put your legs through and elastic around the top. *...a pair of pants.*
2 N PL In American English, trousers are referred to as **pants**. *She's wearing tennis shoes, khaki pants and a white T-shirt... He fumbled in his pants pocket for his whistle.*
3 V or V-QUOTE If you **pant**, you breathe quickly and loudly, because you have been doing something energetic. *We lugged the branch along, panting and puffing... 'Morris!' he panted. 'Glad I caught you.'*

pantaloons /pæntəlúːnz/
N PL **Pantaloons** are long trousers with very wide legs, gathered at the ankle. *...a man with a traditional Cossack pigtail and red silk pantaloons.*

pantechnicon /pæntéknɪkən/ **pantechnicons**
NC A **pantechnicon** is a large covered lorry, especially one that is used for moving equipment or furniture about from one place to another; a formal word.

pantheism /pǽnθiːɪzəm/
1 NU **Pantheism** is the religious belief that God is in everything in nature and the universe.
2 NU **Pantheism** is also a willingness to worship and believe in all gods.

pantheistic /pænθiːɪstɪk/
ADJ A **pantheistic** religion or belief is based on the idea that God is in everything in nature and the universe. *His religion was pantheistic and humanist. ...a certain mystical, pantheistic idealism.*

pantheon /pǽnθiən/ **pantheons**
1 NC A **pantheon** is a building which is erected to honour all the gods or dead heroes of a nation. *...the most famous ancient building in Rome, the Pantheon.*
2 NC+SUPP You can also use **pantheon** to refer to a group of important or distinguished people; a formal use. *...his place in the pantheon of national artists. ...the rise and fall of this saint of the Stalinist pantheon.*

panther /pǽnθə/ **panthers**
NC A **panther** is a large wild animal that belongs to the cat family. Panthers are usually black.

panties /pǽntiz/
N PL **Panties** are pants worn by women or girls.

panto /pǽntəʊ/ **pantos**
NC A **panto** is a pantomime; an informal word. *This is his first panto role.*

pantomime /pǽntəmaɪm/ **pantomimes**
NC A **pantomime** is a funny musical play for children. Pantomimes are usually performed at Christmas. *The pantomime started in the middle of winter, the day after Christmas.*

pantry /pǽntri/ **pantries**
NC A **pantry** is a small room where food is kept. *Go into your pantry and pull out a can of tuna fish.*

panty hose /pǽnti həʊz/
NU **Panty hose** is nylon tights worn by women; an old-fashioned expression.

pap /pǽp/
1 NU If you describe something such as information or entertainment as **pap**, you mean that you consider it to be of no worth, value, or serious interest. *Students today are unwilling to go on being fed the pap that the schools dispense so readily.*
2 NU **Pap** is also any soft or liquid food, especially food that is intended for babies or people who are ill; an old-fashioned use. *In Victorian England the poor survived mainly on a diet of pap—that is, bread and water.*

papa /pəpɑ́ː/ **papas**
N C or VOCATIVE Someone's **papa** is their father; an old-fashioned word. *How are your papa and mama?... Papa, over here, Papa!*

papacy /péɪpəsi/
N SING The **papacy** is the position, power, and authority of the Pope; a formal word. *One of the first acts of Pope Paul's papacy was the appointment of*

this commission... There was strong pressure for the papacy to be returned to Rome.

papal /ˈpeɪpl/
ADJ ATTRIB **Papal** is used to describe things relating to the Pope. *They do not exclude the possibility of a papal visit some time in the future. ...a papal election.*

papaya /pəˈpaɪə/ **papayas**
N COR NU A **papaya** is a fruit with a green skin, sweet yellow flesh, and hard, round, black seeds.

Papeete /pɑːˈpeɪteɪ/
Papeete, on the island of Tahiti, is the capital of French Polynesia and its largest city. Population: 23,000 (1992).

paper /ˈpeɪpə/ **papers, papering, papered**
1 NU **Paper** is a material that you write on or wrap things with. The pages of this book are made of paper. *Rudolph picked up the piece of paper and gave it to her. ...a paper bag.*
2 NC A **paper** is a newspaper. *I read about the riots in the papers... The three articles appeared in British papers last week.*
3 N PL **Papers** are sheets of paper with information on them. *He consulted the papers on his knee.*
4 N PL Your **papers** are your official documents, for example your passport or identity card. *One of the men had no papers.*
5 NC A **paper** is also part of a written examination. *He failed the history paper... You have two hours for each paper.*
6 NC A **paper** is also a long essay on an academic subject. *...a paper on linguistics and literary criticism.*
7 If you put your thoughts down **on paper**, you write them down. *He had put his suggestions down on paper.*
8 VO If you **paper** a wall, you put wallpaper on it. *The lounge was papered and painted.*
paper over PHRASAL VERB If you **paper over** a difficulty, you try to hide it by giving the impression that things are going well. *The rift between the two men appears to have been papered over... There is no papering over the fact that basic disputes exist.*

paperback /ˈpeɪpəbæk/ **paperbacks**
NC A **paperback** is a book with a paper cover. *From then on he read only paperbacks.* ● If a book is available **in paperback**, you can buy a paperback copy of it.

paper boy, paper boys
NC A **paper boy** is a boy who delivers newspapers to people's homes.

paper clip, paper clips
NC A **paper clip** is a small piece of bent wire that is used to fasten papers together. *The international news agency has banned paper clips in its offices.*

paper-knife, paper-knives
NC A **paper-knife** is a blunt knife-shaped object which is used for opening envelopes.

paper money
NU **Paper money** is money which is made of paper. *A church in New York blocked a transfer of ten million dollars of paper money to Panama.*

paper round, paper rounds
NC A **paper round** is a job of delivering newspapers to houses along a certain route. *Andrew does a paper round on Saturday mornings.*

paper shop, paper shops
NC A **paper shop** is the same as a newsagent.

paper tiger, paper tigers
NC A **paper tiger** is a country, institution, or person that seems powerful but is not so in reality. *If the group cannot control events, it will be seen as a paper tiger.*

paperweight /ˈpeɪpəweɪt/ **paperweights**
NC A **paperweight** is a small, heavy object that is placed on papers to prevent them from being blown away.

paperwork /ˈpeɪpəwɜːk/
NU **Paperwork** is the routine part of a job which involves dealing with letters, reports, and records. *They had not completed the necessary paperwork at the American Embassy in Managua. ...a backlog of paperwork.*

papery /ˈpeɪpəri/
ADJ Something that is **papery** is thin and dry like paper. *...papery leaves.*

papier-mâché /ˌpæpieɪˈmæʃeɪ/
NU **Papier-mâché** is a mixture of pieces of paper and glue, which is used to make objects such as bowls, ornaments, and models. *...papier-mâché boxes lacquered with flowers.*

paprika /ˈpæprɪkə, pəˈpriːkə/
NU **Paprika** is a red powder that is made from a type of pepper. It is used for flavouring food. *Pile the mixture back into the skins and sprinkle with a little paprika.*

Papua New Guinea /ˌpæpjuə njuː ˈgɪni/
The **Independent State of Papua New Guinea** is a country in the Pacific Ocean. It comprises the eastern half of New Guinea and 600 other islands. The Territory of Papua was ruled by Australia from 1906 and the Trust Territory of New Guinea, a former German possession, was ruled by Australia from 1914. Both territories were occupied in part by the Japanese from 1942 to 1945, and were merged in 1949. Papua New Guinea became independent in 1975. Sir Rabbie Namaliu, of the Pangu Party, became Prime Minister in 1988. The Bougainville Revolutionary Army (BRA) wants to achieve independence for Bougainville Island. Papua New Guinea is a member of the Commonwealth. It exports copper, gold, coffee, and timber. ◆ **Papua New Guinean** /ˌpæpjuə njuː ˈgɪniən/
N, ADJ
▪ *per capita GNP:* US$770 ▪ *religion:* animism, Christianity ▪ *language:* Pidgin, English, and Motu (all official) ▪ *currency:* kina ▪ *capital:* Port Moresby
▪ *population:* 4 million (1988) ▪ *size:* 462,840 square kilometres.

papyrus /pəˈpaɪrəs/ **papyruses** or **papyri** /pəˈpaɪraɪ/
1 NU **Papyrus** is a tall water plant that grows in Africa.
2 NU **Papyrus** is also a type of paper made from papyrus stems that was used in ancient Egypt, Rome, and Greece. *...thin overlapping orange cross-sections using the same laminating technique as papyrus.*
3 NC A **papyrus** is an ancient document written on papyrus.

par /pɑː/
If one thing is **on a par** with another, the two things are equally good or equally bad. *Forcing a child to learn is on a par with forcing a man to adopt a religion.*

para /ˈpærə/ **paras**
NC A **para** is a paratrooper; an informal word. *The First Colonial Paras were in the mutiny almost to a man.*

parable /ˈpærəbl/ **parables**
NC A **parable** is a short story which makes a moral or religious point. *The story is a parable of the compromises many people made with the Communist regime.*

parabola /pəˈræbələ/ **parabolas**
NC A **parabola** is a type of curve that is like the path of something that is thrown up into the air and comes down in a different place. *These aircraft fly in a parabola.*

parachute /ˈpærəʃuːt/ **parachutes, parachuting, parachuted**
1 NC A **parachute** is a device which enables a person or a thing to float to the ground from an aircraft. It consists of a large circle of thin cloth attached to the body or to the object by strings. *His parachute had failed to open... The Americans won't be sending supplies by parachute.*
2 VA If someone **parachutes** somewhere, they jump from an aircraft using a parachute. *At the moment I am told that no-one will be parachuting into Honduras... Police are currently being trained to parachute into trouble areas.*
3 VOA If someone **parachutes** a person or thing somewhere, they drop that person or thing there from an aircraft with a parachute attached. *The crew are arguing fiercely about whether to parachute an injured colleague out of the plane.*

parachutist /pærəʃuːtɪst/ **parachutists**
NC A **parachutist** is a person who jumps from an aircraft using a parachute. *Parachutists have landed east of the Orne... The plane was carrying a group of sport parachutists.*

parade /pəreɪd/ **parades, parading, paraded**
1 NC A **parade** is a line of people or vehicles moving together, for example through the streets of a town, to celebrate a special event. *When the war was over there was a parade in London.*
2 VA When soldiers or other people **parade** somewhere, they march or walk there together in a formal group so that people can see them. *The army paraded round the square... The troops paraded to the sound of a military band... After the one thousand seven hundred competitors had paraded round, the Olympic flame was lit.*
3 When soldiers are **on parade**, they are standing or marching together on a formal occasion. *The number of countries in the world where you can see and hear the British Army on parade has diminished rapidly since the end of the Second World War.*
4 VO If you **parade** something, you show it to people or make it obvious in order to make an impression on people. *They paraded banners outside the headquarters of the World Bank... She seldom paraded this knowledge.*
5 VOA In some countries, when criminals **are paraded** through the streets, they are driven around or are forced to walk around in public, where other people can see them. *The local district officer paraded him through the town of Njabini in handcuffs.*

parade ground, parade grounds
NC A **parade ground** is an area of ground where soldiers practise marching and where they hold parades. *...as efficiently drilled as their performance on the parade ground. ...more than seven hundred Peking University students showing off parade ground skills.*

paradigm /pærədaɪm/ **paradigms**
1 NC A **paradigm** is a model for something which explains it or shows how it can be produced; a technical use. *...particular models or paradigms of society and how it functions.*
2 NC A **paradigm** is also a clear and typical example of something. *This episode may serve as a paradigm of industry's problems.*

paradise /pærədaɪs/
1 N PROP According to some religions, **Paradise** is a wonderful place where good people go after they die. *...the firm conviction that they would ascend to Paradise.*
2 NUorN SING You can refer to a place or situation that seems perfect as **paradise**. *'That must have been interesting.'—'For me it was paradise.' ...the palm-fringed paradise of Mauritius. ...a choice between a world transformed either into a paradise or into a disaster area.*

paradox /pærədɒks/ **paradoxes**
NC You refer to a situation as a **paradox** when it involves two facts, and you would not expect it to be possible for both of them to be true. *It was crowded and yet at the same time peaceful. This was a paradox she often remarked on.*

paradoxical /pærədɒksɪkl/
ADJ You describe a situation as **paradoxical** when it involves two facts, and you would not expect it to be possible for both of them to be true. *It's paradoxical that the loneliest people live in the most crowded places.* ♦ **paradoxically** ADV SEN *Paradoxically, he represented both escape and safety.*

paraffin /pærəfɪn/
NU **Paraffin** is a strong-smelling liquid which is used as a fuel in heaters, lamps, and engines. *Zimbabwe has just gone from being a petrol engine to being a paraffin engine market.*

paragon /pærəgən/ **paragons**
NC If you describe someone as a **paragon**, you mean that their behaviour is perfect. *He was a paragon of honesty.*

paragraph /pærəgrɑːf/ **paragraphs**
NC A **paragraph** is a section of a piece of writing. A paragraph always begins on a new line and consists of at least one sentence. *Please correct the final sentence of the first paragraph of this despatch. ...the paragraph which has aroused most comment.*

Paraguay /pærəgwaɪ/
The **Republic of Paraguay** is a country in central South America. It was a Spanish colony from the 16th century to 1811. The Colorado Party (PC) has ruled since 1947. General Alfredo Stroessner ruled from 1954 to 1989. General Andrés Rodríguez came to power in a coup in 1989. Paraguay produces cotton, soya beans, and beef. Cannabis is illegally exported. Large foreign debts and high inflation are major economic problems. It is a member of the Organization of American States. ♦ **Paraguayan** /pærəgwaɪən/ N, ADJ
▪ *per capita GNP:* US$1,180 ▪ *religion:* Christianity (mainly Roman Catholic) ▪ *language:* Spanish (official), Guaraní ▪ *currency:* guaraní ▪ *capital:* Asunción ▪ *population:* 4 million (1988) ▪ *size:* 406,752 square kilometres.

parakeet /pæraki:t/ **parakeets**
NC A **parakeet** is a small parrot with a long tail.

parallel /pærəlel/ **parallels, paralleling, paralleled**; also spelt **paralleling, parallelled** in British English.
1 NC A **parallel** is something that is very similar to something else, but exists or happens in a different place or at a different time. *It is not difficult to find a living parallel for these prehistoric creatures. ...a book which has no parallel in the English language.*
2 NC If there are **parallels** between two things, they are similar in some ways. *There are curious parallels between medicine and law... His career and attitudes have interesting parallels with Potter's.*
3 VO If something **parallels** something else, it is as good as that thing, or it is similar to it. *...computers with intellects paralleling Man's.*
4 ADJ ATTRIB A **parallel** event or situation is one that happens at the same time as another, or one that is similar to another. *The Sandinistas are holding parallel talks in Managua with fourteen opposition groups... They may feel that already the notion of parallel realities is too far-fetched.*
5 ADJ If two lines or two long objects are **parallel**, they are the same distance apart all along their length. *The boys were marching in two parallel lines... Vanderhoff Street ran parallel to Broadway.*

parallelogram /pærəleləgræm/ **parallelograms**
NC A **parallelogram** is a four-sided geometrical figure in which every side is parallel to the side opposite it.

paralyse /pærəlaɪz/ **paralyses, paralysing, paralysed**; spelt **paralyze** in American English.
1 VO If something **paralyses** you, it causes you to have no feeling in your body, and to be unable to move. *A stroke paralysed half his face.* ♦ **paralysed** ADJ *...a person paralysed from the neck down.*
2 VO If people, places, or organizations **are paralysed** by something, they are unable to act or function properly. *Great cities are paralysed by strikes and power failures.*

paralysis /pəræləsɪs/
NU **Paralysis** is loss of feeling in your body and inability to move. *One drop of this poison would be enough to induce paralysis and blindness.*

paralytic /pærəlɪtɪk/ **paralytics**
1 NC A **paralytic** is a person whose body, or part of it, is paralysed.
2 ADJ Someone who is **paralytic** is extremely drunk, often so drunk that they can hardly walk; an informal use.

Paramaribo /pærəmærɪbəʊ/
Paramaribo is the capital of Suriname and its largest city. Population: 68,000 (1980).

paramedic /pærəmedɪk/ **paramedics**
NC A **paramedic** is a person whose job is to do medical work, for example as a member of the ambulance service, but who is not a doctor or nurse. *He managed to resuscitate his father before the paramedics (the ambulance service) arrived.*

parameter /pəræmɪtə/ **parameters**
NC **Parameters** are factors or limits which affect the way something can be done or made; a formal word. *It is necessary to be aware of all the parameters that*

have a bearing on the design process.

paramilitary /pærəmɪlɪtəᵊri/, **paramilitaries**
1 ADJ ATTRIB A **paramilitary** organization is one that has a military structure and performs either military or civil functions in a country. *French troops and paramilitary police have begun a military crackdown in three trouble spots in the country.*
2 ADJ ATTRIB A **paramilitary** organization is also an illegal group that is organized like an army and operates against an established power. *Lawyers involved in the investigation have been threatened by paramilitary groups. ...a paramilitary terrorist group.*
3 N PL **Paramilitaries** are the members of a paramilitary organization. *There is a good deal of evidence of collaboration between elements of the armed forces and the paramilitaries. ...the Communist Party's armed paramilitaries.*

paramount /pærəmaʊnt/
ADJ Something that is **paramount** is more important than anything else. *The interests of the child are paramount.*

paranoia /pærənɔɪə/
1 NU If you say that someone suffers from **paranoia**, you mean that they are very suspicious, distrustful, and afraid of other people. *...this acute sense of insecurity that sometimes seems to amount to paranoia... He also accused the government of paranoia against the BBC and commercial broadcasting.*
2 NU **Paranoia** is also a mental condition in which someone wrongly believes that other people are trying to harm them, or that they are much more important than they really are; a technical use in psychology.

paranoid /pærənɔɪd/
ADJ **Paranoid** people are very suspicious, distrustful, and afraid of other people. *You're getting paranoid.*

paranormal /pærənɔːml/
1 ADJ A **paranormal** event or power, for example the appearance of a ghost, is one that does not seem to be in accordance with scientific laws and is thought to involve strange, unknown forces. *...paranormal phenomena.*
2 N SING You can refer to paranormal events and matters as the **paranormal**. *Even in the West, interest in the paranormal and scientifically inexplicable phenomena has grown.*

parapet /pærəpɪt/ **parapets**
NC A **parapet** is a low wall along the edge of a bridge, roof, or balcony. *There was a gap of about three feet across to a concrete parapet.*

paraphernalia /pærəfəneɪliə/
NU You can refer to a large number of belongings or pieces of equipment as **paraphernalia**. *The girls gathered together their hockey sticks, satchels, and other paraphernalia.*

paraphrase /pærəfreɪz/ **paraphrases, paraphrasing, paraphrased**
1 NC A **paraphrase** of something that is written or spoken is the same thing expressed in a different way. *This article was a close paraphrase of Dixon's own original article.*
2 VO If you **paraphrase** someone, you express what they have said or written in a different way. *We must, to paraphrase Socrates, bring out the knowledge that people have inside them.*

paraplegia /pærəpliːdʒə/
NU **Paraplegia** is paralysis of the lower half of the body. *...a patient with paraplegia who's got a spinal nerve lesion.*

paraplegic /pærəpliːdʒɪk/ **paraplegics**
NC A **paraplegic** is someone whose lower body is paralysed, for example as a result of an injury to their spine. *...equipment that turns book pages, switches TV channels and dials the telephone for paraplegics.*

parapsychology /pærəsaɪkɒlədʒi/
NU **Parapsychology** is the study of strange mental abilities which seem to exist but which are impossible according to accepted scientific theories. *He has written books on history and more recently fringe medicine and parapsychology.*

parasite /pærəsaɪt/ **parasites**
1 NC A **parasite** is a small animal, plant, or organism that lives on or inside a larger animal, plant, or organism and gets its food from it. *This is the first time that scientists have been able to grow the parasite outside the human body.*
2 NC If you call someone a **parasite**, you mean that they get money or other things from people without doing anything in return. *He said too many organisations are living like parasites off the state budget.*

parasitic /pærəsɪtɪk/
1 ADJ **Parasitic** animals or plants live on or inside larger animals or plants and get their food from them. *...tiny parasitic insects.*
2 ADJ **Parasitic** diseases are caused by parasites. *...vaccines against tropical parasitic diseases.*
3 ADJ A **parasitic** person or organization gets money or other things from people without doing anything in return. *...their parasitic exploitation of the masses.*

parasol /pærəsɒl/ **parasols**
NC A **parasol** is an umbrella that provides shade from the sun. *The bride is holding a parasol.*

paratrooper /pærətruːpə/ **paratroopers**
NC A **paratrooper** is a soldier who is a member of a group of paratroops. *They have threatened to kill their prisoners if French paratroopers attempt a rescue operation.*

paratroops /pærətruːps/. The form **paratroop** is used as a noun modifier.
N PL **Paratroops** are soldiers who are dropped by parachute. *...elite paratroops in their red berets. ...paratroop attacks.. Belgium sent more than five hundred paratroops to Rwanda after the invasion to protect its nationals.*

parboil /pɑːbɔɪl/ **parboils, parboiling, parboiled**
VO If you **parboil** vegetables, you boil them until they are partly cooked.

parcel /pɑːsl/ **parcels**
NC A **parcel** is something that is wrapped in paper. *He started undoing a little parcel tied with string... Charities sent parcels of clothes.* ● **part and parcel**: see **part**.

parcel bomb, parcel bombs
NC A **parcel bomb** is a small bomb which is sent in a parcel through the post and which is designed to explode when the parcel is opened. *Anti-terrorist police officers have defused a parcel bomb that was sent to the embassy... Two people were killed in a parcel bomb explosion in Rangoon.*

parch /pɑːtʃ/ **parches, parching, parched**
VO If the sun **parches** something, especially the ground or plants, it makes it completely dry. *The hot sun parched the bare earth below.*

parched /pɑːtʃt/
1 ADJ If the ground is **parched**, it is very dry, because there has been no rain. *...the parched plains of India.*
2 ADJ If your mouth, throat, or lips are **parched**, they are unpleasantly dry. *She touched her wet fingertips to her parched lips.*
3 ADJ PRED If you are **parched**, you are very thirsty; an informal use. *I'm parched.*

parchment /pɑːtʃmənt/
NU In former times, **parchment** was the skin of a sheep or goat that was used for writing on. *...his efforts to look after the old parchment.*

pardon /pɑːdn/ **pardons, pardoning, pardoned**
1 You say '**Pardon?**' or, in American English, '**Pardon me?**' when you want someone to repeat what they have just said. *'How old is she?'—'Pardon?'—'I said how old is she?'... 'Whatever you do, don't give him the other guy's number.'—'Pardon me?'—'Don't give him the first guy's number.'*
2 You can also say '**I beg your pardon**' when you want someone to repeat what they have just said; a formal use. *'Did they have a dog?'—'I beg your pardon?'—'I said did they have a dog?'*
3 You also say '**I beg your pardon**' when you want to apologize because you have done something slightly embarrassing; a formal use.
4 NC If someone who has been found guilty of a crime is given a **pardon**, they are officially allowed to go free and are not punished. *Mr Walesa said he would be seeking a pardon for the two men when he met*

President Pinochet... President Campaore has granted a pardon to all political detainees to mark the sixth anniversary of his coming to power.
5 vo If someone who has been found guilty of a crime is **pardoned**, they are officially allowed to go free and are not punished. *The Spanish government has pardoned an army general who was one of the leaders of a failed coup attempt in 1981.*

pardonable /pɑːdəⁿnəbl/
ADJ You describe a bad action or attitude as **pardonable** when you can understand why someone did it or has it and think that they can be forgiven for it in the circumstances. *It was an exaggeration, but a pardonable one, I thought.*

pare /peə/ pares, paring, pared
vo When you **pare** something, you cut off its skin or its outer layer. *Mother was paring apples.*
pare down PHRASAL VERB 1 If you **pare** something **down**, you make it smaller by cutting thin pieces off it. *He noticed her pared-down fingernails.* 2 To **pare** something **down** also means to reduce it. *I had pared my possessions down to almost nothing.*

parent /peərənt/ parents
NC Your **parents** are your father and mother. *Her parents are well-off. ...the bond between parents and children.*

parentage /peərəntɪdʒ/
NU Your **parentage** is the facts about the identity and origins of your parents. *They still did not know her place of birth or her parentage... The children in the village school were of racially mixed parentage.*

parental /pərentl/
ADJ ATTRIB **Parental** is used to describe something that relates to parents in general, or that relates to one or both of the parents of a particular child. *...lack of parental control.*

parenthesis /pərenθəsɪs/ parentheses /pərenθəsiːz/
1 NC A **parenthesis** is a remark or extra part that is put into a sentence. *His reply was so full of clauses and parentheses it was difficult to understand.* ● If you say something in **parenthesis** while you are talking, you interrupt yourself to say it and then go on with what you were saying before.
2 NC In writing, **parentheses** are a pair of brackets or dashes that are put round a word or sentence; a technical use. *This material in parentheses is not to be broadcast.*

parenthetical /pærən0etɪkl/
ADJ A **parenthetical** remark or section is put into something that is written or spoken, but is not an essential part of it; a formal word. *There is a parenthetical section in the middle of the poem.*
♦ **parenthetically** ADV *She mentioned parenthetically that her mother had been ill.*

parenthood /peərənthʊd/
NU **Parenthood** is the state of being a parent. *...the responsibility of parenthood.*

parenting /peərəntɪŋ/
NU **Parenting** is the activity of bringing up and looking after your child. *...the effects of bad parenting.*

parent-teacher association, parent-teacher associations
NC A **parent-teacher association** is an organization where the parents and teachers of children at a particular school can discuss school matters that affect the children. *We are thinking of forming a parent-teacher association.*

par excellence /pɑːr eksəlɑːns/
ADJ after N You say **par excellence** when you want to emphasize that something is the best possible example of a particular thing; a formal expression. *She was strongly committed to her job, a policewoman par excellence... This is the chicken and egg situation par excellence.*

pariah /pəraɪə/ pariahs
NC A person who is a **pariah** is disliked so much by other people that they refuse to associate with him or her; a formal word. *From then on, he was treated as a pariah by all his former friends.*

paring /peərɪŋ/ parings
NC A **paring** is a thin piece that has been cut off something, especially a fingernail or fruit or

vegetable. *...a fingernail paring. ...potato parings.*
Paris /pærɪs/
Paris is the capital of France and its largest city. Population: 2,189,000 (1982).

parish /pærɪʃ/ parishes
1 NCorN+N A **parish** is the area served by an Anglican or Catholic church. *...the parish of St Mark's, Sambourne Fishley. ...the parish church.*
2 NCorN+N A **parish** is also a small country area with its own elected council. *Stroud parish has a population of 20,000. ...a parish councillor.*

parishioner /pərɪʃəⁿnə/ parishioners
NC A clergyman's **parishioners** are the people in his parish. *He was greatly loved by his parishioners.*

parity /pærəti/
NU If there is **parity** between two things, they have equal power, status, or value; a formal word. *...the theoretical parity in powers between the two Houses of Parliament... Woman are making progress towards parity in many parts of India's society.*

park /pɑːk/ parks, parking, parked
1 NC A **park** is a public area of land with grass and trees where people can go to relax and enjoy themselves. *She took her children for a walk in the park. ...Hyde Park.*
2 NC In Britain, a **park** is also a private area of grass and trees around a large country house. *The stream divides Lord Upminster's park from the agricultural land.*
3 VOorV When you **park** a vehicle, you drive it into a position where it can be left. *He parked his car in the open, rather than a lock-up garage... She parked in front of the library.* ♦ **parked** ADJ *We could see the lights of a parked car.* ♦ **parking** NU *...a 'No parking' sign.*
4 See also **car park, national park**.

parka /pɑːkə/ parkas
NC A **parka** is a jacket or coat which has a quilted lining and a hood with fur round the edge. *She was wearing full winter regalia, with a parka jacket and a scarf and rubber boots.*

parking lot, parking lots
NC A **parking lot** is the same as a **car park**; used in American English. *A number of cars in the hotel parking lot were also engulfed in flames.*

parking meter, parking meters
NC A **parking meter** is a device next to a parking space which you have to put money into when you park there. *Motorists manipulate parking meters with bent paper clips.*

parking ticket, parking tickets
NC A **parking ticket** is a piece of paper with instructions to pay a fine, which a traffic warden puts on your car when you have parked somewhere illegally. *The city claims that the embassy's 250 vehicles receive up to 100 parking tickets a day.*

Parkinson's disease /pɑːkɪnsənz dɪziːz/
NU **Parkinson's disease** is a disease which causes a person's limbs to shake and become uncontrollable. *The same research breakthrough could also be used to improve the treatment of Parkinson's disease.*

Parkinson's Law /pɑːkɪnsənz lɔː/
NU **Parkinson's Law** is the belief or fact that work expands to fill the amount of time you have to do it in.

parkland /pɑːklænd/
NU **Parkland** is land with grass and trees on it, especially around a country house. *...twenty-five acres of parkland.*

parky /pɑːki/
ADJ If you say it is **parky**, you mean it is rather cold; an informal word.

parlance /pɑːləns/
You use **parlance** in phrases such as 'in common parlance' or 'in medical parlance' when you want to indicate what kind of people normally use an expression that you are using; a formal word. *...the National Economic Development Council ('Neddy' in popular parlance)... The British Newspaper, the Mail on Sunday, has achieved, in newspaper parlance, a scoop.*

parley /pɑːli/ parleys, parleying, parleyed
NUorNC **Parley** or a **parley** is a discussion, especially

between two people or groups that are opposed to each other but that want to come to an agreement; an old-fashioned word. *The man started the car without further parley... One of the warring families wanted to make peace and arrange a parley.* ▶ Also v *Whatever the reason, Mathews refused to parley.*

parliament /pɑːləmənt/ **parliaments**
NCorNU The **parliament** of a country is the group of people who make or change its laws. *...the creation of Welsh and Scottish parliaments... He was the second farm-worker to get into Parliament.* ● See also **Member of Parliament.**

parliamentarian /pɑːləmentɛərɪən/ **parliamentarians**
1 NC **Parliamentarians** are Members of Parliament; used especially to refer to a group of Members of Parliament who are dealing with a particular task. *The only movement in the last few months has been discussions between parliamentarians on both sides... It was the first visit to Indonesia by Australian parliamentarians for more than five years.*
2 NC A **parliamentarian** is a Member of Parliament who is an expert on the rules and procedures of Parliament and takes an active part in debates. *It was during this time that he made his reputation as a parliamentarian.*
3 NC In the English Civil War, the **Parliamentarians** were the people who supported Parliament and opposed the King. *People were either Parliamentarians or Royalists.*

parliamentary /pɑːləmentəʳri/
ADJ ATTRIB **Parliamentary** means relating to the parliament of a country. *...the start of each parliamentary session... A parliamentary committee has accused the government of complacency in its approach.*

parlour /pɑːlə/ **parlours**; spelt **parlor** in American English.
1 NC A **parlour** is a sitting-room; an old-fashioned use. *It was in the whitewashed parlour of a rancher's house.*
2 NC+SUPP **Parlour** is used in the names of some types of shops which provide a service, rather than selling goods. *He calls his operation a massage parlor. ...a funeral parlour.*

parlour game, parlour games
NC A **parlour game** is a game that is played indoors by families or at parties, for example a guessing game or word game.

parlourmaid /pɑːləmeɪd/ **parlourmaids**
NC A **parlourmaid** was, in former times, a female servant whose job involved waiting at table.

parlous /pɑːləs/
ADJ Something that is in a **parlous** state is in a bad or dangerous situation or condition; an old-fashioned word. *The economy has been in a parlous state for some years. ...the parlous state of the roof.*

parochial /pərəʊkɪəl/
ADJ Someone who is **parochial** is too concerned with their own local affairs and interests; used showing disapproval. *This is a narrow and parochial view.*

parochialism /pərəʊkɪəlɪzəm/
NU **Parochialism** is the quality of being parochial; used showing disapproval. *...their parochialism contrasting poorly with the Vatican's universality and authority. ...economic parochialism.*

parody /pærədi/ **parodies**
NCorNU A **parody** is an amusing imitation of the style of an author or of a familiar situation. *...a parody of American life. ...real modern verse, not parody.*

parole /pərəʊl/ **paroles, paroling, paroled**
1 NU When prisoners are given **parole**, they are released before their sentences are due to end, on condition that they behave well. *He will be eligible for parole in six years.* ● Prisoners who are **on parole** have been given parole. *The authorities released him on parole in 1985.*
2 VO If prisoners **are paroled**, they are released before their sentences are due to end, on condition that they behave well. *The paper says he could be paroled after serving twelve years of his sentence... The government paroled 470 prisoners today in a special pardon marking Christmas.*

paroxysm /pærəksɪzəm/ **paroxysms**
NC+of A **paroxysm** of anger or jealousy is a very strong feeling of it. *In a sudden paroxysm of rage, Wilt hurled the vase across the room.*

parquet /pɑːkeɪ/
NU **Parquet** is a floor covering made of small rectangular blocks of wood fitted together. *...the highly polished parquet floor.*

parricide /pærɪsaɪd/ **parricides**; a formal word.
1 NC A **parricide** is someone who has killed one of their parents.
2 NU **Parricide** is the crime of killing one of your parents.

parrot /pærət/ **parrots, parroting, parroted**
1 NC A **parrot** is a tropical bird with a curved beak and brightly-coloured or grey feathers. Parrots can be kept as pets and sometimes copy what people say. *His first priority will be to buy a pet parrot for a friend.*
2 VO If you **parrot** what someone else has said, you repeat it without really understanding what it means. *Most journalists had attracted similar scorn themselves by simply parroting outdated ideology.*
3 If you repeat something **parrot fashion**, you do it accurately but without really understanding what it means. *Pupils often had to stand to attention and repeat lessons parrot fashion.*

parry /pæri/ **parries, parrying, parried**
1 VOorV+with If you **parry** an argument or question, you cleverly avoid dealing with it or answering it. *He parried the arguments put to him by saying that he could not comment until the report was published... Instead of answering he parried with another question.*
2 VO If you **parry** a blow, you push aside your attacker's arm or weapon so that you are not hurt.

parse /pɑːz/ **parses, parsing, parsed**
VO In grammar, if you **parse** a sentence, you examine each word and clause in order to work out what grammatical type each one is.

parsimonious /pɑːsɪməʊnɪəs/
ADJ Someone who is **parsimonious** is very unwilling to spend money; a formal word, used showing disapproval. *The government is clearly sensitive to mounting criticism of its parsimonious treatment of areas such as the National Health Service.*

parsimony /pɑːsɪməni/
NU **Parsimony** is extreme unwillingness to spend money; a formal word, used showing disapproval. *His parsimony was legendary throughout the film world.*

parsley /pɑːsli/
NU **Parsley** is a small plant with curly leaves that is used for flavouring or decorating savoury food. *...parsley sauce.*

parsnip /pɑːsnɪp/ **parsnips**
NCorNU A **parsnip** is a long, thick, pale cream vegetable that grows under the ground. *After the first frost has touched parsnips is the time to start eating them.*

parson /pɑːsn/ **parsons**
NC A **parson** is a vicar or other clergyman; an old-fashioned word. *...the days when every country parish had its parson.*

parsonage /pɑːsəⁿnɪdʒ/ **parsonages**
NC A **parsonage** is the house where a parson lives; an old-fashioned word.

parson's nose
N SING The **parson's nose** of a cooked bird is the fatty piece of flesh at the tail end.

part /pɑːt/ **parts, parting, parted**
1 NCorNU If one thing is a **part** of another thing or part of it, the first thing is one of the pieces, sections, or elements that the second thing consists of. *The head is the most sensitive part of the body... I don't know this part of London very well... The first part of that statement is a lie... Economic measures must form part of any solution to this crisis.*
2 ADJ ATTRIB A **part** thing or state is not whole or complete. *The part payment of wages did not end a strike by public employees.*
3 NC You can use **part** when you are talking about the proportions of substances in a mixture. *Mix together equal parts of salt and soda crystals... Wipe the skin with one part spirits to five parts water.*

4 NC A **part** in a play or film is one of the roles in it. *She plays the part of the witch.*

5 N SING Your **part** in something that happens is your involvement in it. *He was arrested for his part in the demonstrations.*

6 NC The **part** in someone's hair is the line along their head where their hair has been combed in different directions; used in American English. *...her waved, thick hair, with the part in the middle.*

7 V-ERG If things which are touching **part** or are **parted**, they move away from each other. *Ralph's lips parted in a delighted smile... Rudolph parted the curtains.*

8 V-RECIP When people **part**, they leave each other; a formal use. *A year ago they had parted for ever... I parted from them on excellent terms.*

9 VO If people are **parted**, they are prevented from being together. *The women and children have been parted from their menfolk.*

10 VO If your hair is **parted**, it is combed in two different directions so that there is a straight line across your head. *She has thin black hair parted in the middle.*

11 See also **parting, partly.**

● **Part** is used in these phrases. ● If you **take part** in an activity, you are one of the people involved in it. *I asked her if she'd take part in a discussion about the uprising.* ● If you **play** a large or important **part** in something, you are very involved in it and have an important effect on what happens. *Men should play a bigger part in children's upbringing.* ● You can refer to what someone feels or does as a feeling or action **on** their **part**; a formal expression. *I consider this a gross oversight on your part.* ● **For the most part** means mostly. *The forest is, for the most part, dark and wet.* ● **In part** means partly. *The improvement was brought about in part by the Trade Union Movement.* ● If you say that one thing is **part and parcel** of another, you are emphasizing that it is involved or included in it. *These things are part and parcel of my everyday life... This is part and parcel of the Moscow-inspired process of glasnost.* ● If something happened for **the best part** of or **the better part** of a period of time, it happened for most of that time. *The men stayed for the best part of a year.* ● When two people who have been working together to achieve something **part company**, they stop working together, usually because they disagree about something. *The Prime Minister has parted company with one of his closest advisers.* ● You also say that two people **part company** when they go in different directions after they have been going in the same direction together; a formal use. *We parted company at the bottom of the street.*

part with PHRASAL VERB If you **part with** something that you would prefer to keep, you give it or sell it to someone else. *She didn't want to part with the money.*

partake /pɑːˈteɪk/ **partakes, partaking, partook, partaken;** an formal word.

1 V+of If you **partake** of food or drink, you eat or drink some of it. *He refused to partake of the meal Serafina had prepared.*

2 V+in If you **partake** in an activity, you take part in it. *...people deprived of the right to partake in social decision-making.*

3 V+of If something **partakes** of a particular quality, it has that quality to some extent. *Here the process of education partakes of the nature of discovery.*

partial /ˈpɑːʃl/

1 ADJ A **partial** action, state, or quality is not complete or whole. *There had been no indication that he was considering even a partial withdrawal from Kuwait... I could give it only partial support. ...a partial solution to the crisis.*

2 ADJ PRED+to If you are **partial** to something, you like it very much. *The vicar is very partial to roast pheasant.*

partially /ˈpɑːʃəli/

ADV or SUBMOD **Partially** means to some extent, but not completely. *The United States is reported to have partially lifted its ban on arms sales to Argentina. ...a horse partially hidden by the trees.*

participant /pɑːˈtɪsɪpənt/ **participants**

NC A **participant** in an activity is someone who takes part in it. *She was a willing participant in these campaigns.*

participate /pɑːˈtɪsɪpeɪt/ **participates, participating, participated**

V+in or V If you **participate** in an activity, you take part in it. *We asked high school students to participate in an anti-drugs campaign... Eighty-four countries are expected to participate.* ◆ **participating** ADJ ATTRIB *The Foreign Ministers of all participating countries arrive in Vienna on January 17th.* ◆ **participation** /pɑːˌtɪsɪˈpeɪʃn/ NU *The success of the festival depended upon the participation of the whole community.*

participatory /pɑːˌtɪsɪˈpeɪtəri/

ADJ A **participatory** system, activity, or role involves a person or group of people taking part in it; a formal word. *...participatory democracy.*

participial /pɑːtɪˈsɪpiəl/

ADJ ATTRIB In grammar, **participial** means relating to a participle.

participle /ˈpɑːtɪsɪpl/ **participles**

NC In grammar, a **participle** is a form of a verb that can be used in compound tenses. English verbs have a past participle, which usually ends in '-ed', and a present participle, which ends in '-ing'.

particle /ˈpɑːtɪkl/ **particles**

1 NC A **particle** of something is a very small piece or amount of it. *...particles of metal. ...food particles.*

2 NC In physics, a **particle** is piece of matter smaller than an atom, for example, an electron or a proton. *These particles can only be revealed by smashing atomic nuclei into smaller pieces.*

3 NC In grammar, a **particle** is a word which has a function rather than a meaning. In the sentence 'Alice put the book on my desk', the preposition 'on' is a particle.

particle physics

NU **Particle physics** is the study of the qualities of atoms and molecules and the way they behave and react. *...the mystery of sub-atomic particle physics. ...the European particle physics laboratory in Geneva.*

particular /pəˈtɪkjʊlə/ **particulars**

1 ADJ ATTRIB If you refer to a **particular** thing, you are referring only to that thing, rather than to other things of that type. *Let me ask you about one particular artist... In this particular infection the parasite lives in the blood... Cotton is the most suitable crop in that particular area.*

2 ADJ ATTRIB If a person or thing has a **particular** quality or possession, it belongs only to them. *It is important to discuss a child's particular problems and interests... Each species has its own particular place on the reef.*

3 You use **in particular** to indicate that what you are saying applies especially to one thing, person, or group. *He mentioned in particular electronics, chemicals and tourism... Joan Greenwood in particular I thought was wonderful. ...Africans, and in particular African women.*

4 ADJ ATTRIB You can use **particular** to emphasize that something is greater or more intense than usual. *The shortage of airfields gave particular concern.*

5 N PL **Particulars** are facts or details, especially ones that are written down; a formal use. *Renshaw jotted down a few particulars in his notebook.*

6 ADJ PRED Someone who is **particular** has very high standards and is not easily satisfied. *They're quite particular about their personnel.*

particularize /pəˈtɪkjʊləraɪz/ **particularizes, particularizing, particularized;** also spelt **particularise.**

V or VO If you **particularize** something you have been talking about in a general way, you give details or specific examples of it. *Restaurants, in a survey as broad as this, are perilous to particularise.*

particularly /pəˈtɪkjʊləli/

1 ADV You use **particularly** to indicate that what you are saying applies especially to one situation, person, or thing. *It was hard for children, particularly when they were ill... He was challenged by a number of workers, particularly Gibson. ...starchy foods,*

particularly white flour.
2 SUBMOD **Particularly** also means more than usually or more than normally. *She was looking particularly attractive today... This is not particularly difficult to do.*

parting /pɑːtɪŋ/ **partings**
1 NU or NC **Parting** is the act or process of leaving a particular person or place. *She felt unable to bear the strain of parting... George said no more until their final parting... We'll be hearing the parting words from Washington's man in Afghanistan.*
2 NC The **parting** in someone's hair is the line along their head where their hair has been combed in different directions.

parting shot, parting shots
NC A **parting shot** is a remark, usually an unpleasant one, that you make at the end of a conversation, just before leaving. *Lionel paused to deliver a parting shot at the door.*

partisan /pɑːtɪzæn/ **partisans**
1 ADJ Someone who is **partisan** strongly supports a particular person or cause, often without fair consideration of the facts and circumstances; a formal use. *He desires to be seen as President of a whole nation, rather than appearing a partisan figure... The caretaker government was widely regarded as partisan... 'The minister owes the country an explanation for this partisan behaviour,' she declared.*
2 NC If you are a **partisan** of someone, you support them; a formal use. *He was a partisan of General Jackson.*
3 NC **Partisans** are ordinary people, rather than soldiers, who join together to fight enemy soldiers who are occupying their country. *...those who fought in the hills as partisans.*

partisanship /pɑːtɪzænʃɪp/
NU **Partisanship** is support for a person or group without fair consideration of the facts and circumstances. *...accusations of political partisanship. ...an opportunity to demonstrate to the electorate that he can rise above partisanship to consider great issues.*

partition /pɑːtɪʃn/ **partitions, partitioning, partitioned**
1 NC A **partition** is a wall or screen separating one part of a room or vehicle from another. *In one corner behind a partition was a lavatory... David tapped on the glass partition and the car stopped.*
2 VO If you **partition** a room, you separate one part of it from another by means of a partition. *They had partitioned the inside into offices.*
3 VO To **partition** a country means to divide it into two or more independent countries. *One plan involved partitioning the country.* ▶ Also NU *...the partition of India in 1947.*

partitive /pɑːtətɪv/ **partitives**
NC or N+N In grammar, a **partitive** is a word or expression that comes before a noun and indicates that you are referring to a particular amount of something. *In the sentence 'Would you like a piece of cake?', 'piece of' is a partitive expression.*

partly /pɑːtli/
ADV or SUBMOD **Partly** means to some extent, but not completely. *This is partly a political and partly a legal question... They suffered bad harvests partly due to unavoidable natural circumstances... He held him partly responsible.*

partner /pɑːtnə/ **partners, partnering, partnered**
1 NC Your **partner** is the person you are married to or are having a sexual relationship with. *A marriage is likely to last if you and your partner are similar in personality.*
2 NC Your **partner** is the person you are doing something with, for example if you are dancing together, or if you are playing a game against another pair of people. *He's joined by his long-standing partner Michael Lynagh, the world record points scorer.*
3 NC+SUPP The **partner** of a country or organization is another country or organization with which they have an alliance or agreement. *Japan and West Germany will remain important trading partners. ...the growing*

political crisis between the two main coalition partners in government.
4 NC The **partners** in a business are the people who share the ownership of it. *She was a partner in a firm of solicitors.*
5 VO If you **partner** someone, you are their partner in a game or in a social occasion. *He will be partnered by another American.*

partnership /pɑːtnəʃɪp/ **partnerships**
NU or NC **Partnership** is a relationship in which people or organizations work together in an equal and co-operative way. *In partnership with local authorities and private investors, the government has sponsored the events... We have partnerships with some local non-government organisations or foundations.*

part of speech, parts of speech
NC A **part of speech** is a grammatical word class, for example noun, adjective, or verb.

partook /pɑːtʊk/
Partook is the past tense of **partake.**

partridge /pɑːtrɪdʒ/ **partridges**
NC A **partridge** is a wild bird with a round body and a short tail. *Birds like pheasants and partridges can be reared in captivity.*

part-singing
NU **Part-singing** is the singing of songs in which several tunes that go together are sung at the same time.

part-time
ADJ If someone is a **part-time** worker or has a **part-time** job, they work for only a part of each day or week. *We employ five part-time receptionists. ...a part-time member of the security services.* ▶ Also ADV *40 per cent of women work part-time.*

part-timer, part-timers
NC A **part-timer** is a person who works part-time. *It was decided that the duties of part-timers should be reduced.*

part way; also spelt **partway** /pɑːtweɪ/
ADV **Part way** means part of the way or partly; an informal expression. *Part way through the meal she became suspicious... The window was partway open.*

party /pɑːti/ **parties**
1 NC A **party** is a social event at which people enjoy themselves doing things such as eating, drinking, dancing, talking, or playing games. *...a birthday party... They gave a farewell party for her.* ● See also **garden party.**
2 NC A political **party** is an organization that tries to get its members elected to parliament. *He's a member of the Labour Party... He will now begin a round of consultations with the various party leaders. ...the three main opposition parties.*
3 NC A **party** of people is a group of them doing something together. *...a party of Americans on a tour. ...rescue parties.*
4 NC+SUPP One of the people involved in a legal agreement or dispute can be referred to as a particular **party;** a formal use. *I believe that eventually the guilty party will be identified.* ● See also **third party.**
5 If you **are a party to** an action or agreement, you are involved in it, and are therefore partly responsible for it; a formal expression. *They wouldn't be a party to such a ridiculous enterprise.*

partying /pɑːtiɪŋ/
NU **Partying** is the activity of going to parties; an informal word. *...not everyone was in the mood for partying.*

party line, party lines
1 N SING The **party line** on a particular issue is the official view taken by a political party, which its members are expected to support. *A number of MPs defied their party line. ...an attempt to persuade the Tory rebels to toe the party line in tomorrow's vote.*
2 NC A **party line** is a telephone line shared by two or more houses or offices.

party piece, party pieces
NC Someone's **party piece** is something that they often do to entertain people, especially at parties, for example singing a particular song or saying a particular poem; an informal expression.

party political
ADJ ATTRIB **Party political** matters relate to political parties and their internal affairs. *He has described the proposal as a party political manoeuvre. ... a free vote—that means that MPs do not vote on party political lines.*

party political broadcast, party political broadcasts
NC A **party political broadcast** is a short broadcast on radio or television made by a political party, especially before an election. *He's presenting a party political broadcast for the Scottish National Party.*

party politics
NU When politicians take part in **party politics**, they are involved in the internal affairs of their party or in the attitude of their party towards other parties rather than acting for the good of the country. *The papers are devoting a lot of space to the internal party politics of both Labour and the Conservatives... Spokesmen have accused them of irresponsibility and playing party politics.*

party wall, party walls
NC A **party wall** is a wall between two houses or other buildings that are joined together.

parvenu /pɑːvənjuː/ **parvenus**
NC You refer to someone as a **parvenu** when they have suddenly acquired wealth or an important position, but you think they are not very cultured or well-educated; a formal word, used showing disapproval. *...a political parvenu.*

pass /pɑːs/ **passes, passing, passed**
1 VOorV If you **pass** someone or something, you go past them. *We passed the New Hotel... Please let us pass... Nigel drove fast and well, passing cars only when it was safe.*
2 VA To **pass** in a particular direction means to move or go in that direction. *They passed through an arched gateway... The pipe passed under the city sewer... The eye of the hurricane passed over the city of Charleston.*
3 VOA If you **pass** something such as a rope through something, over it, or round it, you put one end of it through, over, or round that thing. *Pass the string under the hook.*
4 VOorVOO If you **pass** an object to someone, you give it to them. *Pass the sugar, please... She passed me her glass.*
5 V+to If something **passes** from one person to another, the second person then has it instead of the first. *Her property passes to her next of kin.*
6 VAorVOA In sport, if you **pass** to someone else in your team, you kick, hit, or throw the ball to them. *Robson passed to Lineker on the right wing.* ▶ Also NC *Hughes intercepted a pass by Jones.*
7 V When a period of time or an event **passes**, it happens and finishes. *The time seems to have passed so quickly... The crisis passed.*
8 VOAorVO+ING If you **pass** a period of time in a particular way, you spend it in that way. *Am I to pass all my life abroad?... Men pass their lives farming their small plots of land.*
9 VOorV If someone or something **passes** a test or is **passed**, they are considered to be of an acceptable standard. *I passed my driving test in Holland... This drug has been passed by the US Food and Drug Administration... You have to get 120 marks out of 200 to pass.*
10 VO When people in authority **pass** a new law or a proposal, they formally agree to it or approve it. *Many of the laws passed by Parliament are never enforced... There was every chance that the meeting might break up without any resolution being passed at all.*
11 When a judge **passes sentence** on someone, he or she says what their punishment will be. *A court in Sudan has postponed for another month passing sentence on five Palestinians.*
12 V+for or V+as To **pass** for or as a particular thing means to be accepted as that thing, in spite of not having all the right qualities. *...that brief period that passes for summer in those regions... A strip of space 4 feet wide passed as a kitchen.*

13 VAorVC If something **passes** without comment or reaction or **passes** unnoticed, nobody comments on it, reacts to it, or notices it. *Events in western Europe do not pass without comment... Social change was so slow that it passed unnoticed.*
14 NC A **pass** in an examination or test is a successful result in it. *She got a grade A pass in physics.*
15 NC A **pass** is also a document that allows you to do something, for example, to visit a particular place, or to travel on a train or bus without paying. *I have a pass to go from New York to East Hampton... A registration charge of a pound is made when you first purchase a bus pass.*
16 NC A **pass** in a mountainous area is a narrow way between two mountains. *...the Khyber Pass.*
17 to **pass judgement**: see **judgement**. to **pass the time**: see **time**. to **pass water**: see **water**. See also **passing**.

pass along PHRASAL VERB 1 If things such as stories, traditions, or characteristics are **passed along**, they are told, taught, or given to someone who belongs to a younger generation; used in American English. *They were able to preserve rituals and music and pass them along from generation to generation.* 2 If you **pass along** a message or a piece of information that you have been given, you give it to someone else. *Those people reported it to friends and family who passed it along to still others... Mr Baker passed along a message from President George Bush.* 3 If you **pass** something that you have used **along**, you give it to someone else because you do not need it or want it any more. *When you've finished reading it you can pass it along.* 4 If a company **passes along** costs or savings to their customers, they raise or lower their prices to take account of changes in production costs; used in American English. *This tax will cost him close to $100,000, a cost he will pass along to his customers... Should we expect to hear some announcements from the banks that they are lowering their rates and passing these savings along?*

pass around PHRASAL VERB See **pass round**.

pass away PHRASAL VERB If someone **passes away**, they die; an old-fashioned use. *He passed away in his sleep at his home in Sussex.*

pass by PHRASAL VERB If you **pass by** something, you go past it. *I was just passing by and I saw your car. ...a car that passed by his house.*

pass down PHRASAL VERB 1 If things such as stories, traditions or characteristics are **passed down**, they are told, taught or given to someone who belongs to a younger generation. *The knowledge has been passed down from father to son... There is a genetic component that gets passed down.* 2 If you **pass** something **down**, you give it to someone who is standing or sitting below you or next to you in a row. *Can you pass the receipts down, Pat?* 3 If an organization such as a parliament **passes down** a law or a decision, they decide that it is to come into effect. *...a law passed down in the Iranian parliament... The military council endorsed the death sentences passed down by the military tribunal.*

pass off PHRASAL VERB 1 If an event **passes off** well, it happens successfully and without any unpleasant incidents. *Today's demonstration passed off peacefully... The match itself passed off without crowd trouble.* 2 If you **pass** one thing **off** as another, you convince people that it is the other thing. *The man who made the cabinet passed it off as an antique... Investigators discovered that Yugoslav corn was passed off as Greek.*

pass on PHRASAL VERB 1 If you **pass on** something that you have been given, you give it to someone else. *He handed a sheet to Lee to pass on to me.* 2 If you **pass on** a message or a piece of information that you have been given, you give it to someone else. *An official was in Teheran in order to pass on a message from Dr Kohl... Mr Balaoui had agreed to pass on Mr Pelletreau's views to the PLO chairman, Mr Arafat.* 3 If a company **passes on** costs or savings to their customers, they raise or lower their prices to take account of changes in production costs. *Governments have tried to stop firms from passing on cost* *increases... Any such saving will automatically be passed on to clients.*

pass out PHRASAL VERB If you **pass out**, you faint or collapse. *Four people passed out on the opening night of 'Titus Andronicus'.*

pass over PHRASAL VERB 1 If something or someone is **passed over**, they are forgotten, ignored, or not mentioned. *...two issues that seem to have been passed over during the meeting... He passed over the events of that week... Was she just frustrated at being passed over for promotion?* 2 If someone **passes** something **over**, they give it to someone else, especially in secret. *The former sergeant passed over documents of high secrecy.*

pass round or **pass around** PHRASAL VERB If a group of people **pass** something **round** or **pass** it **around**, they each take it and then give it to the next person. *The men pass round the sweet palm wine.*

pass up PHRASAL VERB If you **pass up** an opportunity, you do not take advantage of it. *I wouldn't have passed up the chance for a million dollars.*

passable /ˈpɑːsəbl/
1 ADJ Something that is **passable** is satisfactory in quality. *...some passable small restaurants.* 2 ADJ PRED If a road or path is **passable**, it is not completely blocked. *Many of these roads are not passable in bad weather.*

passage /ˈpæsɪdʒ/ **passages**
1 NC A **passage** is a long, narrow space between walls or fences connecting one room or place with another. *At the end of the narrow passage was a bathroom... We went along a little passage to the garden.* 2 NC A **passage** in a book, speech, or piece of music is a section of it. *The flute and oboe have long solo passages. ...a key passage in the interview.* 3 NU The **passage** of someone or something is their movement or progress from one place or stage to another. *The wind of the train's passage ruffled his hair. ...the moment of passage from one state to the next.* 4 NC A **passage** is also a journey by ship. *The passage across to Belfast was very rough.*

passageway /ˈpæsɪdʒweɪ/ **passageways**
NC A **passageway** is a long, narrow space between walls or fences connecting one room or place with another. *At the end of that passageway is the home of a journal called 'Freedom'.*

passant /ˈpæsɒnt/. See en passant.

passé /ˈpɑːseɪ, ˈpæseɪ/
ADJ Something that is **passé** is no longer regarded as fashionable. *It was fashionable in the sixties, okay in the seventies but definitely passé in the eighties.*

passenger /ˈpæsɪndʒə/ **passengers**
NC A **passenger** is a person who is travelling in a vehicle, aircraft, or ship but is not controlling it or working on it. *The ferry service handles 400 passengers a week... A morning passenger train was derailed about thirty miles west of Copenhagen.*

passer-by /ˌpɑːsəˈbaɪ/ **passers-by**
NC A **passer-by** is a person who is walking past someone or something. *One of the boys stopped a passer-by and asked him to phone an ambulance.*

passim /ˈpæsɪm/
In the indexes and notes of a book, **passim** is used to indicate that a particular name or subject occurs frequently throughout a piece of writing or section of a book; a technical term. *...Johnson, S: pp. 102-114 passim.*

passing /ˈpɑːsɪŋ/
1 ADJ ATTRIB A **passing** state, feeling, or activity lasts for only a short period of time. *He described the dispute as a passing crisis. ...the passing whims of her mother.* 2 If you mention something **in passing**, you mention it briefly while you are talking or writing about something else. *We can note, in passing, the rapid expansion of private security organisations.*

passion /ˈpæʃn/ **passions**
1 NU or N PL **Passion** is a very strong feeling or belief. *The violence which erupted in Khartoum is a symptom of the passion aroused by the peace agreement. ...their attempt to arouse nationalistic passions.*

2 NU or NC You can refer to a very strong feelings of sexual desire for someone as **passion**. *The King's passion for Anne soon waned... Flirtations often develop into passions.* 3 NC+SUPP If you have a **passion** for something, you like it very much. *She had developed a passion for gardens... Biology is their great passion.*

passionate /ˈpæʃənət/
1 ADJ A **passionate** person has very strong feelings or beliefs. *Einstein was also a passionate believer in social justice.* ◆ **passionately** ADV *People care deeply and passionately about this issue.* 2 ADJ ATTRIB A **passionate** feeling or statement is very intense and may be intended to persuade someone or make them feel strongly about something. *In a final passionate appeal today he insisted that the court had made a big mistake... Many delegates may not have agreed with his passionate defence of liberal values— but at least they admired his speech.* 3 ADJ You can also use **passionate** to describe a person who has strong sexual or romantic feelings, or to describe behaviour which expresses these feelings. *She says she is very passionate... I am a passionate and lonely woman. ...a passionate kiss.* ◆ **passionately** ADV *She is passionately in love with him.*

passion fruit; **passion fruit** is both the singular and the plural form.
N C or N U A **passion fruit** is a small egg-shaped fruit that is produced by a plant which grows in hot countries. *...exporters of passion fruit to the UK market.*

passion play, **passion plays**
NC A **passion play** is a play which tells the story of the suffering and death of Jesus Christ.

passive /ˈpæsɪv/ **passives**
1 ADJ Someone who is **passive** does not react or show their feelings when things are said or done to them. *She was so enraged that she could remain passive no longer.* ◆ **passively** ADV *They accept passively every law that is passed.* ◆ **passivity** /pæˈsɪvəti/ NU *There are now influential voices saying that his passivity in the face of the report is unacceptable.* 2 NC In grammar, the **passive** consists of a verb group made up of the auxiliary verb 'be' and the past participle of a main verb. For example, in 'She was asked to wait', the verb 'ask' is in the passive.

passive smoking
NU **Passive smoking** is breathing in tobacco smoke from people who are smoking nearby you when you are not smoking yourself. *We asked him how much passive smoking could increase the risks of lung cancer. ...a report on passive smoking just published in the United States.*

Passover /ˈpɑːsəʊvə/
N PROP **Passover** is a Jewish festival that begins in late March or early April and lasts for eight days. *This weekend, Jews all over the world will be celebrating Passover.*

passport /ˈpɑːspɔːt/ **passports**
1 NC A **passport** is an official document containing your name, photograph, and personal details, which you need to show when you enter or leave a country. *My husband has a British passport.* 2 NC+SUPP If you say that something is a **passport** to something that you want, you mean that it enables you to get it. *The right contacts were the only passports to success.*

passport-holder, **passport-holders**
NC If you describe someone as a **passport-holder** of a particular country, you mean that they have the nationality of that country. *US passport-holders coming this way have long been able to travel visa-free. ...more than one-hundred foreign passport-holders stranded on the northern Jaffna peninsula.*

password /ˈpɑːswɜːd/ **passwords**
NC A **password** is a secret word or phrase that enables you to enter a place or use a computer system. *The caller's identity, password and telephone number are requested.*

past /pɑːst/
1 N SING The **past** is the period of time before the present, and the things that happened in that period.

He was highly praised in the past as head of the National Security Agency. ...the traditional values of the past... He never discussed his past.
2 ADJ ATTRIB You use **past** to describe things that happened or existed before the present time. *He refused to answer questions about his past business dealings... They criticised past Governments for spending £3,500m on military aid.*
3 ADJ ATTRIB You use **past** to describe a period of time immediately before the present time. *I've spent the past eight years at sea.*
4 PREP or ADV You use **past** when you are telling the time. For example, if it is twenty **past** six, it is twenty minutes after six o'clock. *It's ten past eleven... It's quarter past.*
5 PREP or ADV If you go **past** something, you go near it and then continue moving in a straight line until you are away from it. *He drove straight past me... People ran past laughing.*
6 PREP If something is **past** a particular place, it is further away from you than that place. *Past Doctor Ford's surgery was the grocer's... The body was carried to the burying place, not far past the village.*
7 If someone or something is **past** a particular condition or stage of development, they are no longer in that condition or at that stage. *The machines were long past their prime... She is past her peak.*
8 If you say that someone is **past** it, you mean that they no longer have the skill or energy to do something; an informal expression. *Theatregoers who feared that the he might be past it were quickly reassured.*

pasta /pæstə/
NU **Pasta** is a type of food made from a mixture of flour, eggs, and water that is formed into different shapes. Spaghetti and macaroni are types of pasta. *The menu was pasta, roast veal and a sweet followed by a glass of sparkling white wine.*

paste /peɪst/ **pastes, pasting, pasted**
1 NU or NC **Paste** is a soft, often sticky mixture of a substance and a liquid, which can be spread easily. *...tomato paste... Mix together the flour and the water to form a paste.*
2 VOA If you **paste** something on a surface, you stick it to the surface with glue. *The children were busy pasting gold stars on a chart.*

pastel /pæstl/
ADJ ATTRIB **Pastel** colours are pale. *...pastel shades of pink, blue, and brown.*

pasteurization /pɑːstʃəraɪzeɪʃn/; also spelt **pasteurisation.**
NU **Pasteurization** is the removal of bacteria from milk, cream, or fruit juice by a special process of heating. *These bacteria wouldn't survive the pasteurisation process.*

pasteurized /pɑːstʃəraɪzd/; also spelt **pasteurised.**
ADJ **Pasteurized** milk or cream has had bacteria removed from it by means of a special heating process. *There is not much taste to pasteurised milk.*

pastiche /pæstiːʃ/ **pastiches**
NC A **pastiche** is a piece of writing or music, or a picture, in which the style is copied from someone or something else; a formal word. *Ashton's 'Ondine' can be seen as a pastiche on the 19th century romantic ballets.*

pastille /pæstl/ **pastilles**
NC A **pastille** is a small, round sweet, often with a fruit flavour. Some pastilles contain medicine and you can suck them if you have a sore throat or a cough. *...a strawberry fruit pastille.*

pastime /pɑːstaɪm/ **pastimes**
NC A **pastime** is something that you do in your spare time because you enjoy it. *...leisurely pastimes, like gardening, woodwork, music and toy-making.*

past master, past masters
NC If you are a **past master** at something, you are very skilful at it because you have had a lot of experience of doing it. *General Prem was a past master at balancing the often conflicting financial demands of his cabinet.*

pastor /pɑːstə/ **pastors**
NC A **pastor** is a member of the clergy in some Protestant churches. *There was also criticism of some protestant pastors for backing the activists.*

pastoral /pɑːstɔ⁰rəl/
1 ADJ ATTRIB The **pastoral** activities of clergy relate to the general needs of people, rather than just their religious needs. *Pope John Paul will carry out pastoral visits in Alsace-Lorraine, and on Tuesday he addresses the European Parliament.*
2 ADJ ATTRIB **Pastoral** also means relating to peaceful country life. *...a pastoral scene with little lambs and yellow flowers.*

past participle, past participles
NC In grammar, the **past participle** of a verb is a form which usually ends in '-ed' or '-en'. For example, the past participle of 'wait' is 'waited'; the past participle of 'mistake' is 'mistaken'. Past participles are used to form perfect tenses and passives, and to modify nouns.

past perfect
N SING You use the **past perfect** tense of a verb when you are describing an action that took place before another action. It is formed by the auxiliary 'had' and the past participle of a verb. In the sentence 'Jenny had gone home', 'had gone' is the past perfect tense.

pastrami /pəstrɑːmi/
NU **Pastrami** is strongly seasoned smoked beef.

pastry /peɪstri/ **pastries**
1 N MASS **Pastry** is a food made of flour, fat, and water mixed into a dough and then rolled flat. It is used for making pies and flans. *Cover the pie with wholemeal pastry and bake in a preheated oven for 30 minutes.*
2 NC A **pastry** is a small cake made with sweet pastry. *The surly waitresses offer weak, instant coffee, two kinds of pastries, and little else.*

past tense
N SING In grammar, the **past tense** is used to refer to things that happened or existed before the time when you are speaking or writing.

pasture /pɑːstʃə/ **pastures**
NU or NC **Pasture** is an area of grass on which farm animals graze. *...five acres of pasture. ...the lush green pastures of Ireland. ...an over-grazed pasture.*

pasty /peɪsti/ **pasties**
1 ADJ If you look **pasty**, you look pale and unhealthy. *...pasty skin.*
2 NC A **pasty** is a small pie which consists of pastry folded around a savoury filling. *...Cornish pasties.*

pat /pæt/ **pats, patting, patted**
VO If you **pat** something, you touch it lightly with your hand held flat. *He patted the tree trunk softly.* ► Also NC *...a friendly pat on the shoulder.*

patch /pætʃ/ **patches, patching, patched**
1 NC A **patch** is a piece of material used to cover a hole in something. *I mended holes in the sheets by sewing on square patches.*
2 VO If you **patch** something that has a hole in it, you mend it by fixing a patch over the hole. *They patched the leaking roof... Anne sat by the fire, patching a pair of jeans.*
3 NC An eye **patch** is a small piece of material which you wear to cover an injured eye. *He appeared wearing dark glasses and an eye patch.*
4 NC+SUPP A **patch** on a surface is a part of it which is different in appearance from the area around it. *...the damp patch at the corner of the ceiling. ...patches of snow.*
5 NC+SUPP You can refer to a period of difficulties or problems as a bad **patch**. *I had a fairly bad patch for a few years when my luck seemed to have run out... Relations between Britain and Iraq had been going through a very difficult patch.*

patch over PHRASAL VERB 1 If people **patch over** their differences, they decide not to give them too much importance when coming to an agreement. *France and Germany attempted to patch over differences over the pace of European monetary union... There are few signs that the five have been able to patch over their major differences on Cambodia.* 2 If someone **patches over** a problem, they try to hide it or make it seem less important than it is. *They tried to patch over their current domestic problems.*

patch together PHRASAL VERB If something is **patched together**, it is formed from a number of parts in a hurried or careless way. *A new government was patched together with the help of the military.*

patch up PHRASAL VERB 1 If you **patch up** something which is damaged, you mend it. *They have to patch up the mud walls that the rains have battered.* 2 If you **patch up** a quarrel or a difference with someone, you end it. *They tried to patch things up... It could now be possible to start making progress in patching up the differences between them.* 3 If you **patch up** an agreement with someone, you decide on a compromise after a difficult discussion. *The presidents have been seeking to patch up an agreement.*

patchwork /pǽtʃwɜːk/
1 ADJ ATTRIB A **patchwork** quilt or dress has been made by sewing together small pieces of material of different colours. *...an immense patchwork quilt.*
2 N SING+*of* If you describe something as a **patchwork** of things, you mean that it is composed of a variety of different elements. *Afghanistan is a patchwork of ethnic, linguistic and tribal communities. ...the complex patchwork of grievances.*

patchy /pǽtʃi/ **patchier, patchiest**
1 ADJ Something that is **patchy** is not spread evenly, but exists in different quantities in different places. *If you dye clothes in too small a pan, the colour will be patchy... The general strike received solid support across the country after an initially patchy response.*
2 ADJ If you describe information or knowledge as **patchy**, you mean that it is incomplete. *The evidence is a bit patchy.*

pâté /pǽteɪ/ **pâtés**
N MASS **Pâté** is meat, fish, or vegetables mashed into a fairly soft mass. It is usually spread on bread or toast. *...products such as liver pâté.*

patella /pətélə/ **patellae** /pətéliː/
NC Your **patella** is your kneecap; a medical term.

patent /péɪtnt/ **patents, patenting, patented**; also pronounced /pǽtnt/ for the meanings in paragraphs 1 and 2.
1 NC A **patent** is an official right to be the only person or company to make and sell a new product. *The first English patent for a typewriter was issued in 1714.*
2 VO If you **patent** something, you obtain a patent for it. *I never attempted to patent the idea.*
3 ADJ ATTRIB **Patent** means obvious; a formal use. *This is patent nonsense. ...the patent honesty of Butler.*
◆ **patently** ADV *Anne was patently annoyed.*

patent leather
NU **Patent leather** is leather or plastic with a special shiny surface. *...a pair of black patent leather shoes.*

patent medicine, patent medicines
1 NC A **patent medicine** is a medicine that is supposed to have secret ingredients which will cure you. **Patent medicines** are sold by people who have no medical knowledge. *They should spend their money on food instead of on patent medicines.*
2 NC A **Patent medicine** is also a medicine or drug that is produced and patented by one particular firm.

paterfamilias /péɪtəfəmíliæs/
N SING When you refer to a man as a **paterfamilias**, you are referring to him in his role as a father and head of a family; an old-fashioned word. *He was a natural paterfamilias.*

paternal /pətɜːnl/
1 ADJ ATTRIB **Paternal** is used to describe the feelings or behaviour that a father typically shows towards his child. *...lack of paternal love. ...sensitivity and paternal concern for individuals... They had a sort of paternal relationship.*
2 ADJ ATTRIB **Paternal** is also used to indicate that someone is related to you through your father rather than your mother; a formal use. *...our paternal grandmother.*

paternalism /pətɜːnəlɪzəm/
NU **Paternalism** is an attitude which is shown by a government or other authority that makes all the decisions for people instead of giving them any personal responsibility. *...a philosophy flavoured with paternalism.* ◆ **paternalist** /pətɜːnəlɪst/ ADJ *...a paternalist state.*

paternalistic /pətɜːnəlɪstɪk/
ADJ **Paternalistic** systems or beliefs have the qualities of paternalism. *...a paternalistic society. ...paternalistic attitudes.*

paternity /pətɜːnəti/
NU **Paternity** is the state or fact of being the father of a particular child. *He acknowledged his paternity of Pepita's three daughters.*

paternity leave
NU If a man has **paternity leave**, his employer allows him some time off work because the man's child has just been born. *Fathers-to-be have been given five days' paternity leave.*

paternity suit, paternity suits
NC If a woman starts or takes out a **paternity suit**, she asks a law court to help her to prove that a particular man is the father of her child, often in order to claim financial support from him.

paternoster /pǽtənɒstə/ **paternosters**
1 NC A **paternoster** is a type of lift which consists of a chain of open compartments that move slowly in a loop up and down inside a building without stopping.
2 N SING The Lord's Prayer is sometimes called the **Paternoster**, especially by Catholics and especially when the prayer is said in Latin.

path /pɑːθ/ **paths**
1 NC A **path** is a strip of ground that people walk along to get somewhere. *He went up the path to his front door.*
2 NC+POSS Your **path** is the space ahead of you as you move along. *On arrival he found his path barred... It moves forward taking anything in its path.*
3 NC+POSS The **path** of something is the line which it moves along in a particular direction. *The flight path of the 747 carried it directly overhead.*
4 NC+SUPP A **path** that you take is a particular course of action or way of doing something. *He saw public ownership as one of many paths to achieving a socialist society.*

pathetic /pəθétɪk/
1 ADJ Someone or something that is **pathetic** is sad and weak or helpless, and makes you feel pity and sadness. *It was pathetic to see a man to whom reading meant so much become almost totally blind. ...a pathetic figure.* ◆ **pathetically** ADV *He looked pathetically defenceless.*
2 ADJ You can also describe someone or something as **pathetic** when they are so bad or weak that they make you feel impatient or angry. *Our efforts so far have been rather pathetic. ...pathetic accusations of petty corruption.*

pathfinder /pɑːθfaɪndə/ **pathfinders**
NC A **pathfinder** is someone whose job is to find routes across areas.

pathogen /pǽθədʒən/ **pathogens**
NC A **pathogen** is an organism that causes disease; a technical term. *Once the pathogens get into the plant there is no way to stop them... However, these wouldn't be as effective in controlling the pathogens.*

pathological /pǽθəlɒdʒɪkl/
1 ADJ If you describe a person or their behaviour as **pathological**, you mean that he or she behaves in an extreme way, and is unable to control himself or herself. *...a pathological liar. ...a pathological fear of being late.* ◆ **pathologically** SUBMOD *His wife is almost pathologically shy.*
2 ADJ ATTRIB **Pathological** also means relating to diseases and illnesses; a medical use. *...pathological changes in the nervous system.*

pathologist /pəθɒlədʒɪst/ **pathologists**
NC A **pathologist** is someone who studies diseases and illnesses, especially by examining dead bodies in order to find out the cause of death. *...a pathologist who carried out the post mortem.*

pathology /pəθɒlədʒi/; a medical term.
1 NU **Pathology** is the study of diseases and illnesses. *...the Pathology Department of St Mary's Hospital in London.*
2 N SING The **pathology** of a disease or illness is its causes and development in the body. *...the characteristic pathology of this family of diseases.*

pathos /ˈpeɪθɒs/
NU **Pathos** is a quality in a situation that makes people feel sadness and pity; a literary word. ...*the pathos of his situation.* ...*a scene of real pathos.*

pathway /ˈpɑːθweɪ/ **pathways**
NC A **pathway** is a path which you can walk along or a route which you can take. *Marsha could make out a possible pathway through the wire.*

patience /ˈpeɪʃns/
1 NU If you have **patience**, you are able to stay calm and not get annoyed, for example when you are waiting for something. *Paul was waiting his turn with patience... I've lost all patience with him and his excuses.*
2 If you **try** someone's **patience**, you annoy them so much that it is very difficult for them to stay calm. *I tried her patience to the limit.*
3 NU **Patience** is also a card game for only one player.

patient /ˈpeɪʃnt/ **patients**
1 ADJ If you are **patient**, you are able to stay calm and not get annoyed, for example when you are waiting for something. *He was very patient with me.*
◆ **patiently** ADV *James waited patiently for her to finish.*
2 NC A **patient** is a person who is receiving medical treatment, or who is registered with a particular doctor. ...*a consultant who treats kidney patients.*

patina /ˈpætɪnə/; a formal word.
1 N SING+SUPP A **patina** of a particular substance is a fine layer of it that forms or appears on the surface of something. *The directories were piled high, with a patina of grey-brown grease.*
2 N SING+SUPP The **patina** on an antique or other old object is a soft shine that develops on its surface as it grows older. ...*the patina of age.*

patio /ˈpætɪəʊ/ **patios**
NC A **patio** is a paved area at the back of a house, where people can sit and relax. *She was sitting in a deck chair on the patio.*

patio doors
N PL **Patio doors** are glass doors that lead onto a patio.

patisserie /pəˈtiːsəri/ **patisseries**
NC A **patisserie** is a shop where you can buy cakes and pastries. ...*Lisbon's best known and best loved cafés and patisseries.*

patois /ˈpætwɑː/; the plural is both the singular and the plural form. The plural is pronounced /ˈpætwɑːz/.
NCorNU A **patois** is a form of a language that is spoken by the ordinary people in a particular area of a country. It has different pronunciations, words, and grammar from more formal varieties of the language. *Mouriere works methodically, chatting freely in patois.*

patriarch /ˈpeɪtriɑːk/ **patriarchs**
1 NC A **patriarch** is the male head of a family, group, or tribe. *Each family of gorillas is led by a great silver-backed patriarch.*
2 NC A **patriarch** is also the head of one of a number of Eastern Christian Churches. ...*Pope Shenauda III, patriarch of the Coptic Church.*

patriarchal /ˌpeɪtriˈɑːkl/
1 ADJ ATTRIB A **patriarchal** society, family, or system is one in which men have all or most of the power and importance. *We live in a patriarchal society... Some men still try and re-create their traditional, patriarchal role.*
2 ADJ ATTRIB A **patriarchal** man is quite old and looks impressive and powerful. *He was a large and splendidly patriarchal figure with piercing blue eyes and a white beard.*

patriarchy /ˈpeɪtriɑːki/ **patriarchies**
1 NU **Patriarchy** is a system in which men rather than women have all or most of the power and importance in a society or group. ...*the dawn of 'civilisation' and patriarchy.*
2 NC A **patriarchy** is a patriarchal society.

patrician /pəˈtrɪʃn/ **patricians**
NC A **patrician** is a person who comes from a family of high social rank, or looks or behaves as if he or she does; a formal word. *The new President is a curious mixture of New England patrician and Texas oil executive.* ...*local magnates and patrician families.*

patricide /ˈpætrɪsaɪd/ **patricides**
1 NU **Patricide** is the crime of killing your father.
2 NC A **patricide** is someone who has killed their father.

patrimony /ˈpætrɪməni/ **patrimonies**; a formal word.
1 NC Someone's **patrimony** is the possessions that they have inherited from their father or ancestors.
2 NC A country's **patrimony** is its national treasures and works of art. ...*three centuries of neglect of the national patrimony.*

patriot /ˈpætriət, ˈpeɪtriət/ **patriots**
NC A **patriot** is someone who loves their country and feels very loyal towards it. *An official obituary described him as a great patriot.*

patriotic /ˌpætriˈɒtɪk, ˌpeɪtriˈɒtɪk/
ADJ A **patriotic** person or **patriotic** behaviour shows love for a country and loyalty towards it. *He said it was his duty as a patriotic Cambodian to return to his beloved country... They will be able to present themselves as more patriotic and more hardline than Mr Le Pen... We marched and sang patriotic songs... He tried to make his position sound more patriotic.*

patriotism /ˈpætriətɪzəm, ˈpeɪtriətɪzəm/
NU **Patriotism** is love for your country and loyalty towards it. *He campaigned on a policy of nationalism and a new sense of patriotism.*

patrol /pəˈtrəʊl/ **patrols, patrolling, patrolled**
1 VOorVA When soldiers, police, or guards **patrol** an area or building, they move around it in order to make sure that there is no trouble. *I saw men patrolling the streets with rifles on their backs.* ...*the policeman who is patrolling in a dangerous area.* ▶ Also NC *An entire platoon was ambushed during a patrol.*
2 If someone is **on patrol**, they are patrolling an area. *Two policemen on patrol saw the boy running away.*
3 NC A **patrol** is a group of soldiers or vehicles that are patrolling an area. *The bomb went off near a joint army and police patrol.*

patrol boat, patrol boats
NC A **patrol boat** is a small boat used by the navy for patrolling the coast or for small naval operations. *He was killed when a patrol boat opened fire on his vessel... It was intercepted on Saturday by an Australian patrol boat.*

patrol car, patrol cars
NC A **patrol car** is a police car used for patrolling streets and motorways. *The police came in a black unmarked patrol car.*

patrolman /pəˈtrəʊlmən/ **patrolmen** /pəˈtrəʊlmən/
1 NC In American English, a **patrolman** is a uniformed policeman who patrols a particular area. *One of the patrolmen shone his flashlight into Joe's face.* ...*Patrolman Len Hendricks.*
2 NC In British English, a **patrolman** is a person employed by a motorists' association to assist motorists when their cars break down. *The AA patrolman is now believed to have been discharged from hospital.*

patron /ˈpeɪtrən/ **patrons**
1 NC A **patron** is a person who supports artists, writers, or musicians by giving them money. ...*a patron of the arts.*
2 NC The **patron** of a charity, group, or campaign is an important person who is interested in it and who allows his or her name to be used for publicity. *Our Chamber Music Society has the Lord Mayor as its patron.*
3 NC The **patrons** of a particular shop, pub, or other place are its customers; a formal use. *Patrons are requested to wear neat attire.*

patronage /ˈpætrənɪdʒ/
NU **Patronage** is the support and money given by someone to a person or a group such as a charity. ...*public patronage of the arts.*

patronize /ˈpætrənaɪz/ **patronizes, patronizing, patronized**; also spelt **patronise**.
1 VO If someone **patronizes** you, they speak or behave towards you in a way which seems friendly, but which shows that they think they are superior to you; used showing disapproval. *Don't patronize me!... He argued that Mrs Thatcher now wanted to patronize Mr Haughey.*

2 vo If you **patronize** a shop, pub, or other place, you are one of its customers; a formal use. *The bar is patronized mainly by black people.*
3 vo If you **patronize** something, you encourage its development and give it support. *...moral and ideological qualities which ardent supporters have sought to foster and patronize. ...opposing factions within the party who try to patronize certain newspapers.*

patronizing /pǽtrənaɪzɪŋ/; also spelt **patronising**.
ADJ If someone is **patronizing**, they speak or behave towards you in a way which seems friendly, but which shows that they think that they are superior to you; used showing disapproval. *This remark angered the Opposition, who condemned the Minister for being patronizing. ...a patronizing attitude.* ◆ **patronizingly**
ADV *He added patronizingly that this fact was apparent to anyone capable of thinking.*

patron saint, patron saints
NC+SUPP The **patron saint** of a place or a group of people is a saint who is believed to give them special help and protection. *...St Hubert, patron saint of hunters.*

patter /pǽtə/ **patters, pattering, pattered**
1 VA If something **patters** on a surface, it makes light tapping sounds as it hits it. *Spots of rain pattered on the window... I heard her feet pattering about upstairs.*
▶ Also N SING *They heard a patter of paws as the dog came to meet them.*
2 NC The **patter** of an entertainer or salesman is the series of things that they say quickly and easily, because they have learnt them in advance. *He gave the usual patter about watertight boxes.*

pattern /pǽtn/ **patterns**
1 NC A **pattern** is an arrangement on a surface of lines, colours, or shapes, especially one which is repeated at regular intervals. *Jack was drawing a pattern in the sand with his forefinger.*
2 NC A **pattern** is a particular way in which something is usually done or occurs, or the way something is organized. *Over the next few months their work pattern changed. ...behaviour patterns. ...a genetic pattern... These incidents do fit into a pattern.*
3 NC A **pattern** is also a diagram or shape that you can use as a guide when you are making something such as a model or a piece of clothing. *I have been searching out old sewing patterns.*

patterned /pǽtnd/
ADJ Something that is **patterned** is covered with a pattern or design. *...patterned carpets.*

patterning /pǽtəⁿnɪŋ/
1 NU **Patterning** is the forming of fixed ways of behaving or doing things, by constantly repeating them or copying them; a formal use. *...social patterning.*
2 NU Lines, spots, and other patterns, for example on the body of an animal, are referred to as **patterning**.

Patterson, P.J. /píː dʒéɪ pǽtəsən/
P.J. Patterson became Prime Minister of Jamaica and leader of the People's National Party (PNP) in 1992, when Michael Manley resigned. He was elected to Parliament in 1970 and was formerly Minister of Industry and Tourism, Foreign Minister, Deputy Prime Minister, and Finance Minister. Born: 1936.

patty /pǽti/ **patties**
NC A **patty** is a small, round, meat pie; used in American English.

paucity /pɔ́ːsəti/
N SING+of If you say that there is a **paucity** of something, you mean that there is not enough of it; a formal word. *There is a paucity of academic work on 'fringe' political groups... The very paucity of evidence tells a tale.*

paunch /pɔ́ːntʃ/ **paunches**
NC If a man has a **paunch**, he has a fat stomach. *...dark, well-cut suits which remarkably disguise his growing paunch.*

pauper /pɔ́ːpə/ **paupers**
NC A **pauper** is a very poor person; an old-fashioned word. *He died a pauper and is buried in an unmarked grave.*

pauperism /pɔ́ːpərɪzəm/
NU **Pauperism** is the state of being very poor; an old-fashioned word.

pauperize /pɔ́ːpəraɪz/ **pauperizes, pauperizing, pauperized**; also spelt **pauperise**.
vo If something **pauperizes** a group of people, it causes them to become very poor; a formal word. *Smallholders are being pauperized and turned into landless labourers... This imperialism pauperized an entire nation.*

pause /pɔ́ːz/ **pauses, pausing, paused**
v If you **pause** while you are speaking or doing something, you stop for a short time. *He paused and then went on in a low voice... He does not pause for breath until he reaches the top floor.* ▶ Also NC *She continued after a pause.*

pave /péɪv/ **paves, paving, paved**
1 vo When an area of ground is **paved**, it is covered with blocks of stone, bricks, or concrete. *The vacant lot had been fenced in and paved.* ◆ **paved** ADJ *...a small paved path.*
2 If one thing **paves the way** for another, it makes it possible for the other thing to happen. *His work paved the way for Burkitt's theories. ...a factor which helped pave the way for a ceasefire.*
pave over PHRASAL VERB When an area of ground is **paved over**, it is covered with blocks of stone, bricks, or concrete so that it is suitable for walking on.

pavement /péɪvmənt/ **pavements**
NC A **pavement** is a path with a hard surface by the side of a road. *He was standing on the pavement.*

pavement artist, pavement artists
NC A **pavement artist** is a person who draws pictures on the pavement with coloured chalks in order to get money from passers-by.

pavilion /pəvɪ́liən/ **pavilions**
1 NC A **pavilion** is a building on the edge of a sports field where players can change their clothes and wash. *Only one ball was bowled before the players retired to the pavilion.*
2 NC A **pavilion** is also a temporary structure, especially a large tent, which is used at an outdoor public event, for example an exhibition. *...an opportunity to exhibit its consumer goods altogether in one pavilion.*

paving /péɪvɪŋ/
NU **Paving** is a paved area or surface. *...a little rectangle of brick paving... His suede shoes slap lightly on the paving.* ● See also **crazy paving**.

paving stone, paving stones
NC **Paving stones** are flat pieces of stone, usually square or rectangular, that are used for making pavements. *...the laying of paving stones.*

paw /pɔ́ː/ **paws, pawing, pawed**
1 NC The **paws** of an animal such as a cat, dog, or bear are its feet. *...a black cat with white paws.*
2 Voor V+at If an animal **paws** something or **paws** at it, it draws its paw or hoof over it. *...bulls pawing the earth... The dog pawed at the door again.*

pawn /pɔ́ːn/ **pawns, pawning, pawned**
1 vo If you **pawn** something that you own, you leave it with a pawnbroker, who gives you money for it and who can sell it if you do not pay back the money before a certain time. *Brian didn't have a watch—he had pawned it some years ago.*
2 NC In chess, a **pawn** is the smallest and least valuable playing piece.
3 NC If you say that someone is using you as a **pawn**, you mean that they are using you for their own advantage. *We are simply pawns in the hands of larger powers.*

pawnbroker /pɔ́ːnbrəʊkə/ **pawnbrokers**
NC A **pawnbroker** is a person who lends you money if you give them something that you own. The pawnbroker can sell that thing if you do not pay back the money before a certain time. *...the reappearance of the pawnbroker in the British High Street.*

pawn shop, pawn shops
NC A **pawn shop** is a pawnbroker's shop. *He used a handgun he'd bought in a Dallas pawn shop.*

pawpaw /pɔ́ːpɔ́ː/ **pawpaws**
NCorNU A **pawpaw** is the same as a **papaya**. *Patches*

of soil are used to plant the odd pawpaw tree.

pay /peɪ/ **pays, paying, paid**

1 V A, V O, V O O, V O A, or V When you **pay** for something, you give money to someone who is selling you something or who is providing you with a service. *Willie paid for the drinks... I'll pay by cheque... I've left you some money to pay the window cleaner... Pay me five pounds... He had paid £5,000 for the boat... She admitted to allowing customers to take goods without paying.*

2 V O, V O O, V A, or V O A When your employers **pay** you, they give you your wages or salary. *...a protest by several hundred teachers who had not been paid... She was being paid sixty dollars a week... The company pays well... They are reasonably well paid.*

3 N U Someone's **pay** is the money that they receive as their wages or salary. *She lost three weeks' pay. ...a pay rise of £20 a week. They pick up their pay cheques on Thursday afternoons.*

4 V O or V A If a job, deal, or investment **pays** a particular amount of money, it brings you that amount as a result of it. *A day's work pays £2,500... She complained about her job and how poorly it paid.*

5 V If a course of action **pays**, it results in some advantage or benefit for you. *It pays to keep on the right side of your boss.*

6 V A or V O If you **pay** for an action or an attitude, you suffer as a result. *He paid dearly for his mistake... You failed, and you must pay the penalty.*

7 V O You use **pay** with some nouns to indicate that something is given or done. *It would be nice if you paid me a visit... I paid little attention to what I heard... It was probably the greatest compliment I could have paid her.*

8 If you **pay** your **way**, you pay for things that you need rather than letting other people pay for them.

9 See also **paid**.

pay back PHRASAL VERB 1 If you **pay back** money that you have borrowed from someone, you give it back to them at a later time. *I'll pay you back next week.* 2 If you **pay** someone **back** for doing something unpleasant to you, you make them suffer in some way by doing something that they do not like. *'What if Joseph still hates us and plans to pay us back for all the harm we did to him?'*

pay off PHRASAL VERB 1 If you **pay off** a debt, you give someone all the money that you owe them. *He had used the firm's money to pay off gambling debts.* 2 If an action **pays off**, it is successful. *It was a risk and it paid off.* 3 See also **payoff**.

pay out PHRASAL VERB If you **pay out** money, usually a large amount, you spend it on a particular thing. *He had paid out good money to educate Julie.* ● See also **payout**.

pay up PHRASAL VERB If you **pay up**, you give someone the money that you owe them unwillingly or after a delay. *Come on, pay up.*

payable /peɪəbl/

1 ADJ PRED If an amount of money is **payable**, it has to be paid or it can be paid. *The interest payable on these loans was vast.*

2 ADJ PRED+to If a cheque is made **payable** to you, it has your name written on it to indicate that you are the person who will receive the money. *Cheques should be made payable to Trans Euro Travel Ltd.*

pay award, pay awards

N C A **pay award** is an increase in pay for a particular group of people, especially people who work for the government or for local authorities. *The strike is being held in protest at this year's average pay award for teachers of just under eight percent.*

pay bargaining

N U **Pay bargaining** is the discussions between workers and their employers about wage increases. *...the dispute over how future pay bargaining should be conducted.*

pay-bed, pay-beds

N C In Britain, a **pay-bed** is a bed in an N.H.S. hospital that is used by a patient who is paying for treatment.

pay-day, pay-days

N C **Pay-day** is the day on which a worker is paid his or her salary or wages. *Can you lend me £5 till*

pay-day? Pay-day is Thursday here.

PAYE /piːeɪwaɪiː/

N U In Britain, **PAYE** is a system of paying income tax in which your employer subtracts your tax from your salary or wages and then pays it directly to the government. **PAYE** is an abbreviation for 'pay as you earn'.

payee /peɪiː/ **payees**

N C The **payee** of a cheque or banker's order is the person who is to be given the money; a technical term.

paying guest, paying guests

N C A **paying guest** is a person who pays to stay in someone's home, usually for a short period of time.

paying-in book, paying-in books

N C A **paying-in book** is a book of paying-in slips. *You can request a cheque book or a paying-in book.*

paying-in slip, paying-in slips

N C A **paying-in slip** is a form that you fill in when you pay cash or cheques into a bank account.

payload /peɪləʊd/ **payloads**

1 N C or N U The **payload** of an aircraft or other form of transport is the amount of things or people that it can carry. *It was to be the first supersonic airliner that would fly with a commercial payload... The shuttle will touch down while carrying its heaviest-ever payload—a ten and a half ton satellite.*

2 N C The **payload** of a missile is the quantity of explosives it contains. *They produced a longer-range version of the missile by adding a supplementary fuel tank and reducing the payload.*

paymaster /peɪmɑːstə/ **paymasters**

N C A **paymaster** is a person or organization that pays for an activity or project to be carried out, and therefore has some control over it. *He's rejected allegations that he's acted as a paymaster and arms dealer for them.*

payment /peɪmənt/ **payments**

1 N U **Payment** is the act of paying money to someone or of being paid. *...the payment of rent... When can I expect payment?*

2 N C A **payment** is an amount of money that is paid to someone. *Some said that social security payments were too high.*

payoff /peɪɒf/ **payoffs**

N C A **payoff** is an advantage or benefit that results from an action. *Some carry out research and hope that there could be a practical payoff... It's clear he expects a political payoff too.*

payout /peɪaʊt/ **payouts**

N C A **payout** is the amount of money an organization spends or gives as a result of an agreement, contract, or competition. *...this year's total record payout of £52 million. ...small payouts.*

pay packet, pay packets

1 N C Your **pay packet** is the envelope containing your wages or the money in the envelope, which you usually receive at the end of each month. *...pieces of torn pay packets outside the factory gates.*

2 N C You can refer to someone's wages or salary as their **pay packet**. *Trade unions said workers' pay packets were already hit by inflation.*

payphone /peɪfəʊn/ **payphones**

N C A **payphone** is a coin-operated telephone, usually in a public place such as a restaurant or theatre. *The company recently lost its monopoly on public payphones.*

payroll /peɪrəʊl/

N SING If you are on an organization's **payroll**, you are employed and paid by that organization. *He strongly denied that he was on the CIA payroll.*

payslip /peɪslɪp/ **payslips**

N C A **payslip** is a piece of paper given to an employee at the end of each week or month, which states how much money he or she has earned and how much money has been deducted for things like pensions, tax, or national insurance.

Paz Zamora, Jaime /xaɪmeɪ pæs sæmɔːrə/

Jaime Paz Zamora became President of Bolivia in 1989. He was Vice President from 1982 to 1984. He is a founder of the Movement of the Revolutionary Left (MIR). Born: 1939.

PC /piːsiː/ **PCs**
1 TITLE In Britain, PC is used in front of the name of a male police officer of the lowest rank; PC is an abbreviation for 'Police Constable'. ...*PC Cooper*.
2 NC A PC is a small computer that is usually used by one person in a small business, a school, or in their home. PC is an abbreviation for 'personal computer'. *The pocket PC has a plug-in memory chip rather like a credit card.*

pcm
pcm is the written abbreviation for 'per calendar month' which is used especially in advertisements for flats when indicating how much the rent is. ...*£130 pcm.*

PE /piː iː/
NU PE is a lesson in school in which children do physical exercises or take part in physical games or sports. PE is an abbreviation for 'physical education'. *We had two lessons of PE a week.*

pea /piː/ **peas**
NC Peas are small, round, green seeds which grow in pods and are eaten as a vegetable. ...*frozen peas.*

peace /piːs/
1 NU Peace is a state of undisturbed quiet and calm. *Go away and leave us in peace... He returned to the peace of his village.*
2 NU When there is peace in a country it is not involved in a war. *Their activities threaten world peace. ...a political solution to try to bring lasting peace. ...the prospects for peace initiatives in the Middle East.*
3 NU If there is peace among a group of people, they live or work together in a friendly way and do not quarrel. *She had done it for the sake of peace in the family.*

peaceable /piːsəbl/
ADJ Someone who is peaceable tries to avoid quarrelling or fighting with other people. ...*peaceable citizens.*

Peace Corps
N PROP In the United States, the Peace Corps is an organization that sends young people as volunteers to help with projects in developing countries. *The guerrillas are still holding a US Peace Corps volunteer.*

peace dividend
N SING The peace dividend is the money that is no longer being spent on defence because of the disarmament process which began in the late 1980s. *The trade unions are anxious to spend the peace dividend on job creation and social services.*

peaceful /piːsfl/
1 ADJ If a place or time is peaceful, it is quiet, calm, and undisturbed. ...*peaceful parks and gardens... It was a peaceful Christmas... So far, it's all been peaceful.* ◆ **peacefully** ADV *They lived there peacefully, happily.*
2 ADJ PRED Someone who feels or looks peaceful is calm and not at all worried. *He looked peaceful as he lay there.* ◆ **peacefully** ADV *That night he slept peacefully.*
3 ADJ Peaceful people are not violent and try to avoid quarrelling or fighting with other people. ...*the most peaceful nation on earth. ...peaceful demonstrations.*
4 ADJ ATTRIB A peaceful solution or settlement to a problem is one that results from discussion rather than from violence or armed conflict. *Both say that they would like to negotiate a peaceful solution. ...the basis for a durable, peaceful solution to the conflict.*

peacekeeper /piːskiːpə/ **peacekeepers**; also spelt **peace-keeper**.
1 NC A peacekeeper is an organization that intervenes in a violent conflict to try to prevent more fighting. *The Secretary General noted that over the past year the United Nations had again assumed an important role as peacekeeper... This latest plan gives the role of peacekeeper to the federal police.*
2 N PL Peacekeepers are members of an organization that intervenes in a violent conflict to try to prevent more fighting. *They would welcome Soviet and American peacekeepers to police a potential ceasefire.*

peace-keeping
ADJ Peace-keeping forces or activities are ones that try to prevent violence in a country where there is war or fighting. *He has recommended a substantial cut in the United Nations peace-keeping force to be sent to Namibia. ...its most expensive peace-keeping operation to date.*

peace-loving
ADJ A person or country that is peace-loving avoids using violence to solve problems or obtain what they want. ...*his image as a peace-loving sovereign... A senior representative of the Dalai Lama said that Tibetans were peace-loving people.*

peacemaker /piːsmeɪkə/ **peacemakers**
NC A peacemaker is a person who tries to stop people or countries from quarrelling or fighting by talking to the people concerned. *He is widely regarded as a potential peacemaker in the war.*

peacemaking /piːsmeɪkɪŋ/
NU Peacemaking is the activity of trying to stop people quarrelling and fighting in order to make them talk about the problem they have. *She said the pace of peacemaking had quickened over the past year. ...Arab-Israeli peacemaking. ...the UN's peacemaking function.*

peace offering, peace offerings
NC A peace offering is something that is given or said to someone as a way of apologizing to them or ending a quarrel with them. *I bought Mum some flowers as a peace offering.*

peacetime /piːstaɪm/
NU Peacetime is a period of time during which a country is not at war. ...*the party which had freed the nation from military conscription in peacetime. ...peacetime exercises and training.*

peach /piːtʃ/ **peaches**
NC A peach is a soft, round, juicy fruit with sweet yellow flesh and pinky-yellow skin. ...*a kilo of peaches.*

peach melba /piːtʃ melbə/ **peach melbas**
NU or NC Peach melba is a dessert made from peaches, ice cream, and raspberry sauce.

peacock /piːkɒk/ **peacocks**
NC A peacock is a large bird. The male has a very long tail with large blue and green spots which it can spread out like a fan. *Two abandoned peacocks perch in a nearby tree.*

pea-green
ADJ Something that is pea-green is bright green in colour, like the colour of peas.

peahen /piːhen/ **peahens**
NC A peahen is a female peacock.

peak /piːk/ **peaks, peaking, peaked**
1 NC The peak of a process or activity, or the peak period or time for a process or activity, is the point at which it is greatest, most successful, or most fully developed. *They were trained to a peak of physical fitness... Computer technology has not yet reached its peak.*
2 V When something or someone peaks, they reach their highest value or highest level of success. *The annual workload peaks at harvest time... Inflation is now down to single figures after peaking at around thirty per cent... His career peaked during the 1970's.*
3 ADJ ATTRIB The peak level or value of something is its highest level or value. ...*the peak period for holiday travel. ...an interview on peak time TV. ...a peak output of 165 cars per day.*
4 NC A peak is also a mountain, or the top of a mountain. *It is one of the highest peaks in the Alps.*
5 NC The peak of a cap is the part at the front that sticks out above your eyes. *He wore a brown cloth cap with the peak pulled down low over his eyes.*

peaked /piːkt/
ADJ ATTRIB A peaked cap has a part at the front that sticks out above your eyes. ...*a man in a blue-grey uniform and peaked cap.*

peaky /piːki/ **peakier, peakiest**
ADJ If someone looks peaky, they look pale and rather ill; an informal word. *He said that I looked a bit peaky to him, and suggested that I had a lie down.*

peal /piːl/ **peals, pealing, pealed**
1 v When bells **peal**, they ring one after the other, making a musical sound. *Nearby church bells pealed across the quiet city.* ▸ Also NC *The peals can be overwhelming for people living nearby.*
2 NC+SUPP A **peal** of laughter or thunder consists of a long, loud series of sounds. *...bursting into peals of laughter.*

peanut /piːnʌt/ **peanuts**
1 NC **Peanuts** are small nuts often eaten as a snack, usually after they have been roasted and salted. *...a bag of peanuts.*
2 N PL You can refer to a very small sum of money as **peanuts**; an informal use. *It said that Arab oil was being sold for peanuts... She's a canteen assistant and is paid peanuts.*

peanut butter
NU **Peanut butter** is a brown paste made out of crushed peanuts, which you can spread on bread and eat. *...peanut butter sandwiches.*

pear /peə/ **pears**
NC A **pear** is a juicy fruit which is narrow at the top and wider at the bottom. It has white flesh and green or yellow skin.

pearl /pɜːl/ **pearls**
NC A **pearl** is a hard, shiny white ball which grows inside the shell of some oysters. Pearls are used for making jewellery. *She was wearing a string of pearls.*
● See also **mother-of-pearl**.

pearl barley
NU **Pearl barley** is small grains of barley which have been ground smooth and which are often used in making soups.

pearl-grey
ADJ Something that is **pearl-grey** in colour is pale bluish-grey. *...a pattern of navy-blue flowers set on a pearl-grey background.*

pearly /pɜːli/
ADJ Something that is **pearly** shines softly like a pearl. *...pearly teeth.*

peasant /pɛznt/ **peasants**
NC A **peasant** is a person who works on the land, especially in a poor country. *The international community must also provide outlets for the produce of peasant farmers. ...leader of the national peasant union.*

peasantry /pɛzntri/
N COLL The peasants in a country can be referred to as the **peasantry**; an old-fashioned word. *...giving back plots of land to the peasantry.*

peashooter /piːʃuːtə/ **peashooters**
NC A **peashooter** is a tube used by children as a weapon for blowing small objects such as dried peas at people.

pea-souper /piːsuːpə/ **pea-soupers**
NC A **pea-souper** or a **pea-soup** fog is a very thick, dirty fog; an informal word.

peat /piːt/
NU **Peat** is dark decaying plant material which is found in some cool, wet regions. **Peat** is added to soil to improve it or is used as fuel. *Two scientists were analysing peat taken from an ancient bog in Cheshire.*

peaty /piːti/
ADJ **Peaty** soil or land contains a large quantity of peat.

pebble /pɛbl/ **pebbles**
NC A **pebble** is a smooth, round stone. *...the pebbles on the beach.*

pebbledash /pɛbldæʃ/
NU **Pebbledash** is a covering for the outside walls of a house which is made of small stones set in plaster.

pebbly /pɛbəli/
ADJ A **pebbly** beach or river bed is covered in pebbles. *I prefer sandy beaches to pebbly ones.*

pecan /piːkən, pɪkæn/ **pecans**
NC A **pecan** is a nut with a thin, smooth shell that grows on trees in the southern United States. Pecans can be eaten.

peccadillo /pɛkədɪləʊ/ **peccadillos** or **peccadilloes**
NC A **peccadillo** is a small sin or bad action that you consider to be unimportant; an old-fashioned word. *She could easily forgive these little peccadilloes.*

peck /pɛk/ **pecks, pecking, pecked**
1 V O or V A If a bird **pecks** something, it moves its beak forward quickly and bites at it. *...a plump brown hen, pecking around for grains of corn.* ▸ Also N SING *It hopped over and made a quick peck at the ground.*
2 V O If you **peck** someone on the cheek, you give them a quick, light kiss. *She pecked his cheek.* ▸ Also N SING *She gave him a peck on the cheek.*

pecker /pɛkə/
If you tell someone to **keep their pecker up**, you are encouraging them to be cheerful in a difficult situation; an informal expression.

pecking order
N SING The **pecking order** in a group is the order of seniority or power within the group. *He didn't like being at the bottom of the pecking order.*

peckish /pɛkɪʃ/
ADJ PRED If you say that you are feeling **peckish**, you mean that you are fairly hungry; an informal word. *Well, children, I expect you're feeling rather peckish.*

pectin /pɛktɪn/
NU **Pectin** is a substance that is found in ripe fruit. It is used in the manufacture of jam to help it set. *We know from jam-making that pectin leads to stiffening in liquids.*

pectoral /pɛktərəl/ **pectorals**
1 NC Your **pectorals** or **pectoral** muscles are the large chest muscles that help you to move your shoulders and your arms. *...strong women with bulging pectorals. ...flexing the biceps and pectoral muscles he's developed from years of shovelling snow.*
2 NC A **pectoral** is also a pectoral fin.

pectoral fin, pectoral fins
NC The **pectoral fin** of a fish is a fin that is just behind its head and that helps it to control the direction in which it moves.

peculiar /pɪkjuːliə/
1 ADJ Someone or something that is **peculiar** is strange and sometimes rather unpleasant. *He was wearing a peculiar suit... She gave him a peculiar look.* ◆ **peculiarly** ADV *Molly is behaving rather peculiarly these days.*
2 ADJ PRED If you feel **peculiar**, you feel slightly ill or dizzy. *Seeing blood makes me feel a bit peculiar inside.*
3 ADJ PRED+to If something is **peculiar** to a particular thing or person, it belongs or relates only to that thing or person. *...the style of decoration peculiar to the late 1920s... This change is not peculiar to London but is national.* ◆ **peculiarly** ADV *It's an idiom that people recognise as peculiarly English.*

peculiarity /pɪkjuːliærəti/ **peculiarities**
1 NC A **peculiarity** that someone or something has is an individual characteristic or habit, especially an unusual one. *Each city has its own peculiarities, its own history and character.*
2 NU **Peculiarity** is the quality of being strange and sometimes rather unpleasant. *...the peculiarity of his eyes.*

pecuniary /pɪkjuːniəri/
ADJ **Pecuniary** means concerning or involving money; a formal word. *There can be few places in the world where pecuniary self-interest is pursued more diligently.*

pedagogic /pɛdəgɒdʒɪk/
ADJ **Pedagogic** or **pedagogical** means concerning the methods and theory of teaching; a formal word. *...pedagogic and paediatric authorities.*

pedagogue /pɛdəgɒg/ **pedagogues**
NC A **pedagogue** is a teacher; an old-fashioned word. *...a conservative and dictatorial pedagogue.*

pedagogy /pɛdəgɒdʒi/
NU **Pedagogy** is the study and theory of the methods and principles of teaching; a formal word.

pedal /pɛdl/ **pedals, pedalling, pedalled;** spelt **pedaling, pedaled** in American English.
1 NC The **pedals** on a bicycle are the two parts that you push with your feet in order to make the bicycle move. *Bicycle chains make the pedals drive the wheels round.*
2 V or V O When you **pedal** a bicycle, you push the pedals around with your feet to make it move. *His*

legs were aching from pedalling too fast.
3 NC A **pedal** is also a lever that you press with your foot in order to control a car or machine. *...a new lathe he's thought up, operated by a foot pedal.*

pedal bin, pedal bins
NC A **pedal bin** is a waste bin that has a lid controlled by a pedal.

pedant /pɛdnt/ **pedants**
NC If you say that someone is a **pedant**, you mean that they are too concerned with unimportant details or traditional rules; used showing disapproval. *...some pedant muttering something about 'only canvas would be used by real artists.'*

pedantic /pədæntɪk/
ADJ Someone who is **pedantic** is too concerned with unimportant details or traditional rules; used showing disapproval. *...a fussy and pedantic middle-aged clerk.*

pedantry /pɛdntri/
NU **Pedantry** is behaviour or actions which show unnecessarily great attention to details or rules; used showing disapproval. *...an exercise in diplomatic pedantry.*

peddle /pɛdl/ **peddles, peddling, peddled**
1 VO Someone who **peddles** something, such as secrets or drugs, sells them illegally. *He peddled American and British secrets.* ◆ **peddling** NU *...the latest coup in the war against drug peddling.*
2 VO You can say that someone **peddles** something to indicate that you do not approve of their goods or of their way of selling them. *You can see them peddling their jewellery all over the streets of Europe... The weapons industry peddled its wares at a trade show.*
3 VO If someone **peddles** an idea or piece of information, they try hard to get people to accept it; used showing disapproval. *...those who peddled this solution.*

peddler /pɛdlə/ **peddlers**
1 NC+SUPP A **peddler** of drugs or arms sells them illegally. *Foreigners in Peking have recently been approached by drug peddlers... This latest proposal would discourage the biggest peddlers of arms.*
2 NC A **peddler** is someone who goes from place to place in order to sell something. *Peddlers stood outside the courtyard offering maps of Israel.*

pedestal /pɛdɪstl/ **pedestals**
1 NC A **pedestal** is the base on which a statue or a column stands. *The statue has been put back on a pedestal. ...a pedestal five feet wide.*
2 NC If you put someone on a **pedestal**, you admire them very much and think that they cannot be criticized. If someone falls from a **pedestal**, people cease to admire them. *...putting women on a pedestal... He falls off his lofty pedestal... She finds it difficult to come down from the pedestal where she had placed herself.*

pedestrian /pədɛstriən/ **pedestrians**
1 NC A **pedestrian** is a person who is walking, especially in a town or city, rather than travelling in a vehicle. *Pedestrians jostled them on the pavement.*
2 ADJ Someone or something that is **pedestrian** is dull and ordinary; a formal use. *Baker brings a touch of style to a government whose members are pretty pedestrian.*

pedestrian crossing, pedestrian crossings
NC A **pedestrian crossing** is a place on a street where motorists have to stop when pedestrians want to cross. In Britain, pedestrian crossings are indicated by black and white stripes painted across a section of the street, or by special traffic lights which are operated by pedestrians pressing a control button. *Engineers have designed a pedestrian crossing that uses pressure sensors and infra-red detectors to reduce risks to pedestrians.*

pedestrianize /pədɛstriənaɪz/ **pedestrianizes, pedestrianizing, pedestrianized; also spelt pedestrianise.**
VO To **pedestrianize** a street or shopping area means to make it into an area that is intended mainly for pedestrians and not for vehicles. *They have decided to pedestrianise the centre of Plymouth.* ◆ **pedestrianized**
ADJ ATTRIB *Bollards are often used to stop drivers*

driving into pedestrianised areas.

pedestrian precinct, pedestrian precincts
NC A **pedestrian precinct** is a street or part of a town that is used only by pedestrians and where vehicles are not usually allowed to go. *Parliament Square might even become a pedestrian precinct.*

pediatrician /piːdiətrɪʃn/. See **paediatrician**.
pediatrics /piːdiætrɪks/. See **paediatrics**.

pedicure /pɛdɪkjʊə/ **pedicures**
NU or NC **Pedicure** is treatment and care of the feet, either by a medical expert or by a beautician.

pedigree /pɛdɪgriː/ **pedigrees**
1 ADJ ATTRIB A **pedigree** animal is descended from animals which have all been of a particular breed and is therefore considered to be of good quality. *...a pedigree cat.*
2 NC If an animal has a **pedigree**, its ancestors are known and recorded. *...fine dogs with pedigrees.*
3 NC+SUPP Someone's **pedigree** is their background or ancestry. *His political pedigree stretches back to the second world war... He had a criminal pedigree.*

pediment /pɛdɪmənt/ **pediments**
NC A **pediment** is a triangular piece of stone or wood that is built over a doorway or window as a decoration. *...the Marco Polo building, which mixes classical motifs like pillars and pediments with the use of high-tech material.*

pedlar /pɛdlə/ **pedlars**
1 NC A **pedlar** is someone who sells small objects, especially by taking them round from house to house; an old-fashioned use. *The family had given shelter to an old pedlar.*
2 NC+of A **pedlar** of particular ideas is someone who frequently expresses such ideas to other people; used showing disapproval. *...a pedlar of gloom and despondency. ...a pedlar of dreams.*

pedophile /piːdəfaɪl/. See **paedophile**.
pedophilia /piːdəfɪliə/. See **paedophilia**.

pee /piː/ **pees, peeing, peed**
V When someone **pees**, they urinate; an informal word which some people find offensive. *The little boys looked anxiously around for somewhere to pee.*

peek /piːk/ **peeks, peeking, peeked**
VA If you **peek** at something or someone, you have a quick look at them, often secretly; an informal word. *He peeked through the door.* ▸ Also N SING *I took a peek at the list.*

peel /piːl/ **peels, peeling, peeled**
1 NU The **peel** of a fruit such as a lemon or apple is its skin. *...grated lemon peel.*
2 VO When you **peel** fruit or vegetables, you remove their skins. *I found Jane peeling potatoes.*
3 V A or V If paint is **peeling** off a surface or if the surface is **peeling**, the paint is coming off. *The paint was peeling off the woodwork... The walls are peeling through neglect.* ▸ Also ADJ ATTRIB *...peeling yellow walls.*
4 V If you **are peeling**, small pieces of skin are coming off your body, usually because you are sunburnt. *Her nose was peeling.*
peel off PHRASAL VERB 1 If you **peel** something **off** a surface, you pull it off gently in one piece. *I peeled some moss off the wood... Peel off the outer plastic cover.* 2 If you **peel off** a piece of clothing that is tight or wet, you take it off with difficulty, often with the result that you have to turn it inside out. *She peeled off her sweater.*

peeler /piːlə/ **peelers**
NC A **peeler** is a special knife used for removing the skin from fruit and vegetables. *He's still got my potato peeler.*

peelings /piːlɪŋz/
N PL+SUPP **Peelings** are pieces of skin that have been peeled from fruit or vegetables. *Potato peelings, cabbage stalks and so on are used to make compost. ...well-known insect-repellants—lemon grass, orange leaves and orange peelings.*

peep /piːp/ **peeps, peeping, peeped**
1 VA If you **peep** at something, you have a quick look at it, often secretly. *They crept up to the glass doors and peeped inside.* ▸ Also N SING *I was allowed in to have a peep at the painting.*

2 VA If something **peeps** out from somewhere, a small part of it is visible; a literary use. *The sun was just peeping over the horizon.*

peephole /piːphəʊl/ **peepholes**
NC A **peephole** is a small hole in a door or wall through which you can look secretly at what is happening on the other side. *We were able just to see—through a small peephole at first—the people on the other side.*

Peeping Tom, Peeping Toms
NC A **Peeping Tom** is a man who habitually and secretly watches women who are undressing or are in the nude.

peepshow /piːpʃəʊ/ **peepshows**
NC A **peepshow** is a box containing moving pictures which you can look at through a small hole. In former times, peepshows were a form of entertainment at fairs.

peer /pɪə/ **peers, peering, peered**
1 VA If you **peer** at something, you look at it very hard, usually because it is difficult to see clearly. *He peered at his reflection... Howard sat peering through the windscreen.*
2 NC A **peer** is a member of the nobility, either by being the child of aristocratic parents, or by being appointed by a King or Queen. *...Lord Caradon (or Sir Hugh Foot as he was known before he was made a Peer). ...Conservative peers.* ● See also **life peer**.
3 N PL Your **peers** are people of the same age or status as you; a formal use. *...comparing students with their peers outside university.*

peerage /pɪərɪdʒ/ **peerages**
1 NC If someone has a **peerage**, they have the rank of a peer. *...an heir to a peerage... Sir Robert Armstrong was given a life peerage.*
2 N SING The peers of a country are referred to as the **peerage**. *...his elevation to the peerage.*

peeress /pɪərɛs/ **peeresses**
NC A **peeress** is a woman who is a member of the nobility. *The introduction of life peers and peeresses has transformed the House of Lords. ...the Conservative Peeress, Baroness Lane-Fox.*

peer group, peer groups
NC Your **peer group** is the group of people who are of the same age or status as yourself; a formal expression. *They discuss how they can resist the pressures of their peer group... She must be given the opportunity to integrate freely with her peer group.*

peerless /pɪələs/
ADJ Something that is **peerless** is so beautiful or wonderful that you feel that nothing can equal it; a literary word. *It was another peerless day.*

peer of the realm, peers of the realm
NC In Britain, a **peer of the realm** is a member of the nobility who has the right to sit in the House of Lords. *...the peers of the realm in their red robes trimmed with white ermine fur.*

peeved /piːvd/
ADJ If you are **peeved** about something, you are annoyed about it; an informal word. *He was rather peeved to discover that they had gone.*

peevish /piːvɪʃ/
ADJ Someone who is **peevish** is irritated and bad-tempered. *Patty was peevish because the cousins took little notice of her.* ◆ **peevishly** ADV *'Where have you been?' she asked peevishly.*

peewit /piːwɪt/ **peewits**
NC A **peewit** is the same as a **lapwing**.

peg /pɛg/ **pegs, pegging, pegged**
1 NC A **peg** is a small hook or knob on a wall or door which is used for hanging things on. *He takes his coat from the peg. ...keys hanging on pegs.*
2 NC A **peg** is also a wooden or plastic object used to fix things in a particular place, for example to attach washing to a clothes line. *It will anchor itself, you don't need pegs or anything else. ...two-foot long metal tent pegs.*
3 VOAorVO If you **peg** the value of something at a particular figure, you fix it at that figure and try to prevent it changing. *...to peg inflation to twenty-five per cent... They have continued to peg their currencies to the dollar... The government has pegged the amount*

of money paid to parents.
● **Peg** is used in these phrases. ● If you say that someone should **be brought down a peg or two** or **taken down a peg or two**, you mean that they should be made to realize that they are not as important or wonderful as they think they are. *Few people abroad would mourn if Britain was taken down a peg or two.*
● If you say that something is a **peg** on which to **hang** something else, you mean that the first thing can be used to explain the second or that it can be used as a way of trying to achieve the second thing. *Some issues may be merely pegs on which to hang individual hostilities... It is a total mistake to think that a second rate story can be hung on such a topical peg.*

peg-leg, peg-legs
NC A **peg-leg** is an artificial leg made out of wood; an old-fashioned, informal word.

pejorative /pədʒɒrətɪv/
ADJ A **pejorative** word or expression is one which expresses criticism of someone or something; a formal word. *He sued because of pejorative comments made about him in a book... He is a born political schemer. And I don't mean that in a pejorative sense.*

pekinese /piːkɪniːz/ **pekineses**; also spelt **pekingese**.
NC A **pekinese** is a small dog with long hair, short legs, and a short, flat nose. *...flat-faced breeds like Pekinese and Pugs.*

Peking /piːkɪŋ/
Peking, also called Beijing, is the capital of China and its second largest city. Population: 6,800,000 (1988).

pelican /pɛlɪkən/ **pelicans**
NC A **pelican** is a large water bird. It catches fish and keeps them in the lower part of its beak until it eats them or feeds them to its young. *Pelicans and seagulls have made their home on the banks.*

pelican crossing, pelican crossings
NC A **pelican crossing** is a place where pedestrians can cross a road by pressing a button which operates traffic lights to stop the traffic.

pellagra /pəlægrə/
NU **Pellagra** is a disease caused by poor diet and which is characterized by tiredness and disorders of the skin and the central nervous system.

pellet /pɛlɪt/ **pellets**
NC A **pellet** is a small ball of paper, mud, lead, or other material. *...a pellet of mud. ...shotgun pellets.*

pell-mell /pɛlmɛl/
ADV If you run **pell-mell** somewhere, you move there in a hurried and disorderly way. *I dashed pell-mell into the drawing room.*

pellucid /pəluːsɪd/
ADJ Something that is **pellucid** is extremely clear; a literary word. *Startled crows shrieked and wheeled in the warm pellucid air.*

pelmet /pɛlmɪt/ **pelmets**
NC A **pelmet** is a long, narrow piece of wood or fabric which is fixed at the top of a window for decoration and to hide the curtain rail.

pelt /pɛlt/ **pelts, pelting, pelted**
1 VO+with If you **pelt** someone with things, you throw things at them. *He was pelted with eggs... The crowd replied by pelting the police with stones.*
2 VA If it is **pelting** with rain or if it is **pelting** down with rain, it is raining very hard; an informal use. *It's pelting with rain out there!... The rain pelted down outside.* ◆ **pelting** ADJ *...grey skies, mist, and pelting rain.*

pelvic /pɛlvɪk/
ADJ ATTRIB **Pelvic** means close to your pelvis or relating to it. *...a serious pelvic injury. ...to increase bloodflow to the pelvic region.*

pelvis /pɛlvɪs/ **pelvises**
NC Your **pelvis** is the wide, curved group of bones at the level of your hips. *...injuries including a fractured skull and broken pelvis. ...no signs of arthritic disease in the spine or pelvis.*

pen /pɛn/ **pens, penning, penned**
1 NC A **pen** is a long thin object which you use to write in ink. *The soldier with a note-book and a pen asked many questions. ...a few strokes of the pen.*
2 VO If someone **pens** something such as a letter,

article, book, or song, they write it; a literary use. *Infuriated, he penned a blistering reply... This song is unusual in that it was penned by Liverpool striker Craig Johnson.* ♦ **penned** ADJ *...an article penned by Alexander Bovin. ...six poorly penned signatures.*
3 If you **put pen to paper**, you write something; a formal use. *The Utah Governor put on his glasses and put pen to paper... As for many writers of his generation, it became dangerous even to put pen to paper.*
4 NC A **pen** is also a small fenced area in which animals are kept for a short time, for example on a farm. *There was a nice black heifer in one pen... Once the animals are caught, they are kept in special pens for a month.*
5 VOA If people or animals **are penned** in a place or if they are **penned** up in a place, they are forced to remain there, often in difficult and uncomfortable conditions. *The government forces were penned in the city itself. ...endless hours penned up in a hot and dusty railway carriage... These cattle were penned in for hours at a time.*

penal /piːnl/
ADJ ATTRIB **Penal** means relating to the punishment of criminals. *...the British penal system.*

penal code, penal codes
NC The **penal code** in a country consists of all its laws that are concerned with crime and punishment; a formal expression. *Conspiracy and racketeering are not covered by the Swiss penal code.*

penalize /piːnəlaɪz/ **penalizes, penalizing, penalized**; also spelt **penalise**.
VOorVO+*for* If someone is **penalized** for something, they are made to suffer some disadvantage because of it. *It would be unfair to penalise those without a job. ...the government's plan to penalise fathers who desert their children... They are being penalised for expressing their views.*

penal servitude
NU **Penal servitude** is the punishment of being sent to prison and forced to do hard physical work; a formal expression. *In 1922 he was sentenced to seven years' penal servitude.*

penalty /penlti/ **penalties**
1 NC A **penalty** is a punishment that someone is given for doing something which is against a law or rule. *There are now stiffer penalties for drunken drivers... There is growing pressure for tougher penalties against army rebels. ...a maximum penalty of seven years in jail.* ● See also **death penalty.**
2 If you **pay the penalty** for a wrong action or a bad decision, you suffer the effects of it. *The last budget was a mistake, and he's having to pay the penalty... They are paying the penalty for failing to unite.*
3 NC In sports such as football, hockey, and rugby, a **penalty** is a free kick or hit at goal, which is given to the attacking team if the defending team commit a foul near their own goal. *He scored both goals, the first a penalty after 23 minutes... Villa missed a penalty... The full-back Bianchi kicked his third penalty.* ● In football, if someone scores **from the penalty spot**, they score when they have been awarded a penalty. *He scored from the penalty spot in the 58th minute... Peter Weir equalized from the penalty spot.*
● In football, if a game that ends in a draw is decided **on penalties**, each team takes penalty kicks until one of them misses and loses the game. *...a match which was decided on penalties... Nigeria beat Algeria on penalties.* ● See also **penalty shoot-out.**

penalty area, penalty areas
NC The **penalty area** is a rectangular area on a football pitch in front of the goal. Inside this area, the goalkeeper is allowed to handle the ball, and a penalty is given if a foul is committed by the defending team. *...a shot from outside the penalty area... Voeller broke through and went tumbling in the penalty area.*

penalty box, penalty boxes
1 NC The **penalty box** in football is the same as the **penalty area;** an informal use. *He drove the ball past the goalkeeper from just inside the penalty box.*
2 NC The **penalty box** in ice hockey is an area in which players who have been penalized have to sit for

the period of time of their penalty. *They'll make you pay for it while you're in the penalty box.*

penalty clause, penalty clauses
NC A **penalty clause** in a contract is a clause which states what the penalty is for breaking the agreement, for example how much money must be paid; a legal term. *Surprisingly he did not insert a penalty clause. ...stringent penalty clauses in the agreement with Czechoslovakia.*

penalty shoot-out, penalty shoot-outs
NC In football, a **penalty shoot-out** is a way of deciding the result of a game that has ended in a draw. Each team takes penalty kicks until one of them misses and loses the game. *Iran beat China three-nil in a penalty shoot-out. ...the universally unpopular penalty shoot-outs which decided both semi-finals.*

penance /penəns/
NU If you do **penance** for something wrong that you have done, you do something that you find unpleasant to show you are sorry. *He went into retreat in a voluntary gesture of penance for abuses committed during his eight years as president. ...penance for sins of the past and present.*

pen-and-ink
ADJ ATTRIB A **pen-and-ink** drawing is done using a pen rather than a pencil. *...a pen-and-ink drawing of Zinoviev.*

pence /pens/
Pence is a plural form of **penny.** *They would be asked to pay fifty pence a day. ...petrol price rises of five and a half pence per gallon. ...a cut in the basic rate of tax to twenty-five pence in the pound.*

penchant /pɒnⁿʃɒnⁿ/
N SING+*for* If someone has a **penchant** for something, they have a special liking for it or tendency to do it; a formal word. *The Americans, he considered, had a penchant for being disconcertingly frank.*

pencil /pensl/ **pencils, pencilling, pencilled**
1 NC A **pencil** is a thin wooden piece of wood with graphite down the centre which is used for writing or drawing. *...that pencil on the table. ...forging the ballot papers using pencils, felt-tip pens and ballpoints.*
2 VO If you **pencil** something, you write it using a pencil. *He pencilled his initials at the end... The unions pencilled their signatures to an agreement.*
♦ **pencilled** ADJ *...a pencilled note.*
pencil in PHRASAL VERB If an event or appointment is **pencilled in**, it has been agreed that it should take place, but it will have to be confirmed later. *The meeting is now being pencilled in for the end of this month. ...four games pencilled in for early June... We had a series of dates pencilled in.*

pendant /pendənt/ **pendants**
NC A **pendant** is an ornament on a chain worn round your neck. *Dimitri wears a silver pendant... The alarm can be worn around the neck as a pendant.*

pending /pendɪn/; a formal word.
1 ADJ Something that is **pending** is going to happen or be dealt with soon. *He knew my examination was pending. ...a pending lawsuit... Charges are still pending against a number of other dissidents.*
2 PREP If something is done **pending** a future event, it is done before that event happens, when the situation may change. *An interim government is to be set up, pending elections... He was released on bail pending further inquiries... Two others remain in custody pending trial... The pilot had been suspended pending an investigation.*

pendulous /pendjʊləs/
ADJ Something that is **pendulous** hangs downwards and swings freely, especially in an unattractive way; a literary word. *His stomach was distended and pendulous.*

pendulum /pendjʊləm/ **pendulums**
1 NC The **pendulum** of a clock is a rod with a weight at the end which swings from side to side in order to make the clock work. *Any pendulum is highly sensitive to its environment.*
2 N SING People use the word **pendulum** as a way of talking about regular changes in a situation or in people's opinions. *...the pendulum of fashion... The political pendulum is slowly swinging back towards the*

Conservatives... This shows how far the pendulum has swung in favour of the pro-reform forces.

penetrate /pɛnɪtreɪt/ **penetrates, penetrating, penetrated**
1 VOorVA If someone or something **penetrates** a physical object or an area, they succeed in getting into it or through it. *The sun was not high enough yet to penetrate the thick foliage overhead... This new weapon is powerful enough to penetrate armoured vehicles... They penetrated into territory where no man had ever gone before... No light penetrates to the ocean floor.* ◆ **penetration** /pɛnɪtreɪʃn/ NU *It can deflect a missile or shell and prevent penetration. ...the penetration of hostile defences.*
2 VO If someone or something **penetrates** an organization, a group, or a profession, they succeed in entering it although it is difficult to do so. *The legal profession has been difficult for Blacks and Asians to penetrate... Will these new directives penetrate the French Stock Exchange?*
3 VO If someone **penetrates** an enemy group or organization, they succeed in joining it in order to gather secret information about it or cause trouble in it. *...the only man of the Cambridge spy ring to penetrate the code breaking section of British intelligence. ...the loss of a KGB spy who penetrated American intelligence.*
4 VO If a company or country **penetrates** a market or area, they succeed in selling their products there. *...agricultural producers seeking to penetrate the EC market. ...nervousness about letting any outsiders penetrate its highly protected rice market.*
◆ **penetration** NU *...its powerful economic penetration of the region. ...bitter over East Asian penetration of their markets.*

penetrating /pɛnɪtreɪtɪŋ/
1 ADJ A **penetrating** sound is loud and clear. *...his penetrating voice... It's a very penetrating tone that you get.*
2 ADJ Something such as a remark or an argument that is **penetrating** shows deep understanding. *...a penetrating question. ...a penetrating study of democracy.*

pen-friend, pen-friends
NC A **pen-friend** is someone to whom you regularly write friendly personal letters, although the two of you may never have met.

penguin /pɛŋgwɪn/ **penguins**
NC A **penguin** is a black and white bird found mainly in the Antarctic. Penguins cannot fly. *...creatures such as the penguins which are its natural inhabitants... The airstrip poses a threat to penguin colonies.*

penicillin /pɛnəsɪlɪn/
NU **Penicillin** is an antibiotic. *...the greatest medical discovery since penicillin... Over ninety percent of the cases were cured by penicillin.*

penile /piːnaɪl/
ADJ ATTRIB **Penile** means relating to a penis; a medical term. *...penile cancer.*

peninsula /pənɪnsjʊlə/ **peninsulas**
NC A **peninsula** is a long narrow piece of land that is almost completely surrounded by water but that is joined to the mainland. *...the defence of the Korean peninsula. ...air attacks on two villages in the peninsula.*

penis /piːnɪs/ **penises**
NC A man's **penis** is the part of his body that he uses when urinating and when having sex. *...a virus that can cause cancer of the penis.*

penitence /pɛnɪtəns/
NU **Penitence** is sincere regret for wrong or evil things that you have done. *The spirit of penitence was in the air.*

penitent /pɛnɪtənt/
ADJ Someone who is **penitent** is very sorry for doing something wrong; a literary word. *The General faced the military tribunal in penitent mood.*

penitential /pɛnɪtɛnʃl/
ADJ **Penitential** means expressing deep sorrow and regret at having done something wrong; a formal word. *...a penitential pilgrimage.*

penitentiary /pɛnɪtɛnʃəri/ **penitentiaries**
NC A **penitentiary** is a prison; used in American English. *He was led from the court building back to his cell at the national penitentiary. ...prisoners at the maximum security State Penitentiary.*

penknife /pɛnnaɪf/ **penknives**
NC A **penknife** is a small knife with a blade that folds back into the handle.

penmanship /pɛnmənʃɪp/
NU **Penmanship** is the art and skill of writing by hand; a formal word. *...kids like sweet, quiet little Olivia, who has perfect penmanship.*

pen-name, pen-names
NC A writer's **pen-name** is the name that he or she uses on books and articles instead of his or her real name. *...an Englishwoman writing under the pen-name of Natalya Lowndes... Simenon had written more than 200 novels under 16 pen-names.*

pennant /pɛnənt/ **pennants**
1 NC A **pennant** is a long, narrow, triangular flag. *...a big boat flying the Australian pennant... The horsemen swept past, spears raised and pennants flying.*
2 N SING In baseball, a **pennant** is a flag that is given to the team that wins a league championship; used in American English. *They last won the National League pennant in 1945.*

penniless /pɛnɪləs/
ADJ Someone who is **penniless** does not have any money. *He says he's penniless. ...young people, penniless and stranded in London without anywhere to live. ...miserable, penniless refugees.*

penny /pɛni/ **pennies** or **pence**. The plural form is **pennies** for the meaning in paragraph 1 and **pence** for the meaning in paragraph 2.
1 NC A **penny** is a British coin worth one hundredth of a pound.
2 NC A **penny** is also the amount of money that a penny is worth. *...a ten pence coin... They only cost a few pence.*

penny farthing, penny farthings
NC A **penny farthing** is an old-fashioned bicycle that had a very large front wheel and a small back wheel.

penny-pinching
NU **Penny-pinching** is the practice of spending very little money; used showing disapproval. *Good preventive health care means we cannot allow penny-pinching... The answer doesn't lie in penny-pinching.*
▶ Also ADJ *...penny-pinching miserly old men... They accused the government of being mean and penny-pinching.*

penny whistle, penny whistles
NC A **penny whistle** is a simple musical instrument, consisting of a metal tube with holes in it and a mouthpiece that you blow into.

pennyworth /pɛniwəθ, pɛnəθ//
N SING A **pennyworth** of something is the amount of it that can be bought for a penny; an old-fashioned word. *...a pennyworth of mustard pickle. ...the common things that people buy by the pennyworth.*

pen pal, pen pals
NC A **pen pal** is the same as a **pen-friend**; an informal word. *...letters written by Anne and Margot to pen pals in Iowa in 1940... I have lots of pen pals.*

penpusher /pɛnpʊʃə/ **penpushers**
NC A **penpusher** is a person whose work consists of a lot of boring, repetitive jobs that involve writing.

pension /pɛnʃn/ **pensions, pensioning, pensioned**
NC A **pension** is a regular sum of money paid to someone who is old, retired, widowed, or disabled. *She and her disabled husband are currently living off a pension of just £100 a week. ...an old age pension.*
pension off PHRASAL VERB If someone **is pensioned off**, they are made to retire from work and are given a pension. *We were pensioned off at the age of fifty.*

pensionable /pɛnʃənəbl/
ADJ **Pensionable** means relating to someone's entitlement to receive a pension. *...anybody over pensionable age... The poor have no savings and no cushy, pensionable positions.*

pension book, pension books
NC In Britain, a **pension book** is a small booklet

containing payment slips, which is issued to pensioners by the government. The slips can be exchanged for money at a Post Office each week. *People in residential homes may be given pocket money by staff, instead of retaining their own pension books.*

pensioned /pɛnʃnd/
ADJ ATTRIB **Pensioned** means receiving a pension. *...the pensioned professionals.*

pensioner /pɛnʃəⁿnə/ **pensioners**
NC A **pensioner** is a person who receives a pension, especially an old or retired person. *...a seventy-four-year old pensioner. ...one pensioner, a retired engineer... Old age pensioners, children and needy families will be worse off.*

pension scheme, pension schemes
NC A **pension scheme** is a scheme which enables people to receive a pension after contributing to the scheme for a certain period. *...a health and pension scheme for farmers. ...compulsory pension schemes in all EEC countries.*

pensive /pɛnsɪv/
ADJ Someone who is **pensive** is thinking deeply about something. *Jefferson looked pensive. 'What's wrong?' asked Tyler.* ♦ **pensively** ADV *He gazed pensively at the water.*

pentagon /pɛntəgən/ **pentagons**
1 N PROP The US Defense Department is often referred to by journalists and politicians as the **Pentagon.** *The Pentagon says an investigation is under way... James Webb joined the Pentagon in nineteen-eighty-four... Pentagon spokesman Bob Hall says that the number isn't unusually high.*
2 N PROP The **Pentagon** is the building in Washington that is the headquarters of the US Defense Department. *Defense Secretary Dick Cheney told reporters at the Pentagon that all briefings had been suspended. ...the total chaos inside the Pentagon at the time.*
3 NC A **pentagon** is a shape which has five sides and five angles. *The common soccer ball is actually composed of a pattern of hexagons and pentagons.*

pentameter /pɛntæmɪtə/ **pentameters**
NCorNU A **pentameter** is a line of poetry that has five strong beats in it; a technical term. *The iambic pentameter follows the natural rhythm of English speech.*

pentathlon /pɛntæθlən/ **pentathlons**
NC A **pentathlon** is an athletics competition in which each person must compete in five different events. *The French modern pentathlon team are leading Poland and Austria after the first day. ...1972 Olympic women's pentathlon gold medallist Mary Peters.*

Pentecost /pɛntɪkɒst/
1 NU In the Jewish religion, **Pentecost** is a festival that takes place 50 days after Passover, and that celebrates the harvest.
2 NU In the Christian religion, **Pentecost** is a festival that celebrates the sending of the Holy Spirit to the first apostles. *The Frankfurt market was closed yesterday for the Pentecost holiday.*

penthouse /pɛnthaʊs/ **penthouses**
NCorN+N A **penthouse** or a **penthouse** apartment or suite is a luxurious set of rooms at the top of a tall building. *It's like a penthouse compared to where I was living. ...Ali al-Husseini's sixth-floor penthouse apartment in Beirut.*

pent-up /pɛntʌp/
ADJ ATTRIB **Pent-up** emotions or energies have been held back and not expressed or released. *...pent-up frustrations.*

penultimate /pɛnʌltɪmət/
ADJ The **penultimate** thing in a series is the last but one; a formal word. *...the penultimate paragraph of the letter. ...on the penultimate day of the Asian Games. ...the penultimate stage of the Paris to Dakar rally.*

penurious /pənjʊəriəs/
ADJ Someone who is **penurious** is very poor indeed; a formal word. *...left-overs from the table of their equally penurious next-door neighbours.*

penury /pɛnjʊri/
NU **Penury** is extreme poverty; a formal word. *They would face penury unless they could secure employment very soon.*

peony /piːəni/ **peonies**; also spelt **paeony.**
NC A **peony** is a medium-sized garden plant that has large round flowers, usually pink, crimson, or white in colour. *Peonies, aren't they gorgeous?*

people /piːpl/ **peoples, peopling, peopled**
1 N PL **People** are men, women, and children. *The amount of potatoes and bread people buy has dropped... We'll talk to the people concerned and see how they feel... He spent a long time on that explanation and I think people got rather bored.*
2 N PL The **people** are ordinary men and women, as opposed to the upper classes or the government. *I don't think MPs really represent the people as such... Power to the people!*
3 NC A **people** consists of all the men, women, and children of a particular country or race. *...the beliefs of various peoples across the world.*
4 VO If a place is **peopled** by a particular group of people, those people live there; a formal use. *...Istanbul, now peopled by 4 million Turks.*

-people
SUFFIX **-people** combines with nouns to form new nouns which refer to people who live in a particular place, or who are involved in a particular activity. *...the Scottish townspeople whose homes had been destroyed in the crash... The tribespeople of Bomvanaland lived on hills and in valleys... Only 16% of UK businesspeople had heard of the Single Market.*

pep /pɛp/ **peps, pepping, pepped**; an informal word.
NU **Pep** is liveliness and energy. *It puts colour in the cheeks and gives more pep to humans of all ages.*
pep up PHRASAL VERB 1 If you try to **pep** something **up,** you try to make it more lively or interesting. *He realized that the conference needed pepping up a bit... The company is trying to pep up its product line.* 2 If you give someone something to **pep** them **up,** you give them something that will give them more energy. *I gave him an extra dose of glucose to pep him up.*

pepper /pɛpə/ **peppers, peppering, peppered**
1 NU **Pepper** is a hot-tasting powder used to flavour food. *...salt and pepper.*
2 NC A **pepper** is a hollow green, red, or yellow vegetable. *...a salad of green peppers.*
3 VO If something is **peppered** with small objects, they hit it or are scattered over it. *I felt my fingers being peppered with small, hot fragments.*

pepper-and-salt. See **salt-and-pepper.**

peppercorn /pɛpəkɔːn/ **peppercorns**
NC A **peppercorn** is a small, dried berry which comes from a pepper plant, and which is crushed in order to produce pepper.

peppered /pɛpəd/
1 ADJ Food that is **peppered** has had pepper added to it to give it a spicy flavour. *That night's pot of soup was heavily peppered and spiced.*
2 ADJ PRED Something that is **peppered** with things has many of them all over its surface, or contains a lot of them. *We can reasonably assume that the universe is peppered with these planets... His French is heavily peppered with Americanisms.*

peppermint /pɛpəmɪnt/ **peppermints**
1 NU **Peppermint** is a strong sharp flavouring that is used especially to flavour sweets. *...a very strong smell of peppermint. ...peppermint candy.*
2 NC A **peppermint** is a peppermint-flavoured sweet. *He had to suck peppermints in case they smelt the alcohol on his breath. ...an American brand of peppermint.*

pepperoni /pɛpərəʊni/
NU **Pepperoni** is a kind of spicy sausage, usually eaten in thin slices on top of pizzas. *Twelve large cheese and green pepper pizzas with pepperoni, no broccoli. ...a pepperoni pizza.*

pepperpot /pɛpəpɒt/ **pepperpots**
NC A **pepperpot** is a container for pepper, which is used during meals. A pepperpot usually has a lot of holes in the top for shaking out the pepper.

peppery /pɛpəri/
1 ADJ Food that is **peppery** has a strong taste of pepper.

2 ADJ If you describe someone as **peppery**, you mean that they are irritable and bad-tempered. ...*the familiar type of the peppery old colonel.*

pep pill, pep pills
NC A **pep pill** is a pill that people take to make themselves feel happier or more active; an old-fashioned expression.

pep talk, pep talks
NC A **pep talk** is a speech intended to encourage a group of people to make more effort; an informal expression. *Mrs Thatcher has given her customary end of term pep talk to back-bench Conservative MPs. ...a last-minute pep talk from head coach Bud Carson... Powell delivered a series of pep talks to the troops.*

peptic ulcer /pɛptɪk ʌlsə/ **peptic ulcers**
NC A **peptic ulcer** is an ulcer that occurs in the digestive system of people or animals. ...*patients suffering from peptic ulcers... They have been used as drugs to treat peptic ulcers for many years.*

per /pə, pɜː/
PREP You use **per** to express rates and ratios. For example, if something costs £50 **per** year, you must pay £50 each year for it. If a vehicle is travelling at 40 miles **per** hour, it travels 40 miles each hour. ...*an income of less than £1000 per person. ...oil prices fell below $10 per barrel... The airport already deals with seven-hundred-and-fifty flights per day.*

perambulate /pəræmbjʊleɪt/ **perambulates, perambulating, perambulated**
V When someone **perambulates**, they walk about for pleasure; an old-fashioned word. ◆ **perambulation** /pəræmbjʊleɪʃn/ NU *Hyde Park has always been a place for a promenade, for perambulation.*

perambulator /pəræmbjʊleɪtə/ **perambulators**
NC A **perambulator** is a pram; an old-fashioned word. *Children are pushed in a perambulator.*

per annum /pər ænəm/
ADV A particular amount **per annum** means that amount each year. *It costs £125 per annum.*

per capita /pə kæpɪtə/
ADJ ATTRIB or ADV When you are talking about the distribution of money, land, or other resources, if you state an amount **per capita**, you are stating the average amount for each person in the country or area. *Per capita incomes have grown... What is the average wage per capita?*

perceive /pəsiːv/ **perceives, perceiving, perceived**
1 V O or V-REPORT If you **perceive** something, especially something that is not obvious, you see, notice, or realize it. *Many insects can perceive colours that are invisible to us... They failed to perceive that this was what I objected to.*
2 V O A If you **perceive** someone or something as being or doing a particular thing, you think you have understood what they are or what they are doing. *It is important that the president be perceived as moving the country forward. ...the truth as I perceive it.*

per cent /pə sɛnt/
You use **per cent** to talk about fractions. For example, if an amount is 10 **per cent** of a larger amount, it is equal to 10 hundredths of the larger amount. **Per cent** is often written %. *45 per cent of Americans were against it.*

percentage /pəsɛntɪdʒ/ **percentages**
NC A **percentage** is a fraction expressed as a particular number of hundredths. *What is the percentage of nitrogen in air? ...areas with a high percentage of immigrants.*

percentage point, percentage points
NC If a rate changes by one **percentage point**, it increases or decreases by one per cent; a technical term. *Interest rates are to be cut by one percentage point... The latest opinion poll gives Labour a lead over the government of ten percentage points.*

perceptible /pəsɛptəbl/
ADJ Something that is **perceptible** can only just be seen. *There was a barely perceptible flicker of light.*

perception /pəsɛpʃn/ **perceptions**
1 NU **Perception** is the recognition of things by using your senses, especially the sense of sight. ...*visual perception.*

2 NU Someone who has **perception** realizes or notices things that are not obvious. ...*a person of extraordinary perception.*
3 NC A **perception** is an opinion that you have about someone or something. *My perception of her had changed.*

perceptive /pəsɛptɪv/
ADJ Someone who is **perceptive** realizes or notices things that are not obvious. ...*a perceptive critic.*

perch /pɜːtʃ/ **perches, perching, perched**
1 V A If you **perch** on something, you sit lightly on the edge or tip of it. *Dr Quilty perched on the corner of his desk... The police and soldiers perched on the roofs overlooking the square.* ◆ **perched** ADJ PRED ...*two drummers and a trumpeter, perched on top of the gateway.*
2 V-ERG A If one thing **perches** on another, or you **perch** it there, it is on the top or edge of the other thing, and looks as if it might fall off. *The building perches precariously within a few feet of a sudden drop... The monument weighs several tons and is perched on a granite base.* ◆ **perched** ADJ PRED ...*a predominantly Catholic town perched on the border with the Irish Republic.*
3 V A or V When a bird **perches** somewhere, for example on a branch or a wall, it stands there. *Two peacocks perch in a nearby tree... There's nowhere for the birds to perch.*
4 NC A **perch** is a place where a bird stands, especially a short rod in a cage where a pet bird stands. *Then it will sit on a perch and wait for the other birds to catch up... These are the perches where they stay overnight.*

perchance /pətʃɑːns/
ADV SEN **Perchance** means perhaps; a literary word. *She asked me if I were Swiss perchance. ...even if I should perchance be punished.*

percipient /pəsɪpiənt/
ADJ Someone who is **percipient** notices or realizes things quickly, often things that other people do not notice or realize; a formal word. ...*a very percipient author. ...as the more percipient local residents may have realized.*

percolate /pɜːkəleɪt/ **percolates, percolating, percolated**
1 V A If something **percolates** somewhere, it passes slowly through something that has very small holes or gaps in it. ...*mysterious light percolating through stained-glass windows... The heated sea water percolating downwards becomes very corrosive... Nitrates tend to percolate slowly through the soil.*
2 V When coffee is being made in a percolator and it **percolates**, it passes through the filter and becomes ready to drink. *While the coffee was percolating, he glanced round for the telephone.*
3 V A If an idea, information, or feeling **percolates** through a group of people, it spreads slowly through the group. *The news percolates through the city, spread by bands of motorcycle messengers.*

percolator /pɜːkəleɪtə/ **percolators**
NC A **percolator** is a special piece of equipment for making and serving coffee.

percussion /pəkʌʃn/
NU or N+N **Percussion** instruments are musical instruments that you hit, such as drums and cymbals. *We had Dailey on percussion, and Flannery on the clarinet.*

percussion cap, percussion caps
NC A **percussion cap** is a small device containing explosive powder that is used as a detonator in guns and bombs. *He carefully fitted a bullet, until only the brass percussion caps showed to view.*

percussionist /pəkʌʃənɪst/ **percussionists**
NC A **percussionist** is a person who plays percussion instruments such as drums. *We could always hire professional percussionists. ...a master percussionist from South India.*

perdition /pədɪʃn/
NU **Perdition** is the state of never-ending punishment after death; a literary word. ...*one more step down the road to perdition.*

peregrination /pɛrəgrɪneɪʃn/ **peregrinations**
NC A **peregrination** is a long journey which involves
wandering about from place to place; a formal word.
*I often think of Boswell's peregrinations through
darkest London... Strictly speaking, my peregrinations
were unnecessary.*

peregrine falcon /pɛrəgrɪn fɔːlkən/ **peregrine
falcons**
NC A **peregrine falcon** or a **peregrine** is a large bird of
prey, which has a dark-coloured back and is lighter
coloured underneath. *...a number of rare birds,
including peregrine falcons.*

peremptory /pərɛmptəⁿri/
ADJ Someone who does something in a **peremptory**
way shows that they expect to be obeyed immediately;
a formal word. *...the hijackers' peremptory demands
for fuel... Our conversation was interrupted by a
peremptory thudding at the door... Some of them
thought the ultimatum too peremptory.* ◆ **peremptorily**
ADV *Come! he said peremptorily.*

perennial /pərɛniəl/ **perennials**
1 ADJ ATTRIB A **perennial** situation is one that keeps
occurring or always remains the same. *...perennial
problems. ...a perennial feature of British politics. ...a
classic piece of pop music, and a perennial favourite.*
2 NC A **perennial** is a plant that lives for several
years. *Daffodils, tulips, and snowdrops are what we
call perennials. ...perennial grass abundant in the
Sudanic zone.*

perestroika /pɛrɪstrɔɪkə/
NU **Perestroika** is a term used to describe the
changing of the political and social structure in the
former Soviet Union during the late 1980s. *...groups
opposed to perestroika... All 100,000 members are in
support of perestroika. ...Mr Gorbachev's perestroika
programme.*

Pérez Rodriguez, Carlos Andrés
/kɑːləʊs ændreɪs pɛres rɒdriːges/
Carlos Andrés Pérez Rodriguez became President of
Venezuela in 1989. He was a member of the Chamber
of Deputies from 1947 to 1948, and from 1958 to 1974.
He was Minister of the Interior from 1963 to 1964, and
had previously served as President from 1974 to 1979.
He is a member of the Democratic Action Party (AD).
Born: 1922.

perfect, perfects, perfecting, perfected; pronounced
/pɜːfɪkt/ when it is an adjective, and /pəfɛkt/ when it is
a verb.
1 ADJ Something that is **perfect** is as good as it can
possibly be. *She speaks perfect English... I've got the
perfect solution.* ◆ **perfectly** ADV *The plan worked
perfectly.*
2 ADJ ATTRIB You can use **perfect** for emphasis. *They
may be perfect strangers... I have a perfect right to
be here.* ◆ **perfectly** SUBMOD *It's a perfectly
reasonable question... I knew perfectly well it was a
trap.*
3 VO If you **perfect** something, you make it as good as
it can possibly be. *She hoped to perfect her
technique... If this system could be perfected, the
patient could live a relatively normal life.*
4 ADJ ATTRIB In grammar, the **perfect** tenses of a verb
are the tenses formed with the auxiliary 'have' and
the past participle of the verb; a technical term in
linguistics.

perfection /pəfɛkʃn/
NU **Perfection** is the quality of being perfect.
...gardens of incredible perfection.

perfectionism /pəfɛkʃənɪzəm/
NU **Perfectionism** is the state or quality of being a
perfectionist. *It was a blow to Phoebe's pride and
perfectionism.*

perfectionist /pəfɛkʃənɪst/ **perfectionists**
NC Someone who is a **perfectionist** refuses to do or
accept anything that is not perfect. *She is a great
performer, a true professional. A perfectionist... He
had a reputation for being a perfectionist, a brilliant
student. ...a perfectionist attitude.*

perfect pitch
NU Someone who has **perfect pitch** is able to identify
any musical note with total accuracy without using an
instrument or a tuning fork. *Musicians have argued*

*for decades about the nature of perfect pitch. ...a
pianist with perfect pitch.*

perfidious /pəfɪdiəs/
ADJ Someone who is **perfidious** is treacherous or
untrustworthy; a literary word. *The government has
accused the Prince of perfidious manoeuvres... Their
feet will trample on the dead bodies of their perfidious
aggressors.*

perforate /pɜːfəreɪt/ **perforates, perforating,
perforated**
VO If something **perforates** something else, it pierces
it or causes it to have holes in it. *His eardrum had
been perforated by a blow struck by a detective.
...exhausts which pump out lead poison human beings,
but don't perforate the stratosphere.* ◆ **perforated** ADJ
*He suffered broken ribs, a perforated lung, and kidney
damage. ...a transparent cone with a red plastic
perforated top.* ◆ **perforation** /pɜːfəreɪʃn/ **perforations**
NC *The insects get into the trap through the
perforations. ...the perforations on the sides of stamps.*

perforce /pəfɔːs/
ADV SEN **Perforce** is used to say that something
happens or is the case because it is inevitable in a
particular situation, rather than because it is intended
or desired; an old-fashioned word. *This freedom at
last gave back a voice to those who had perforce been
silent for so long... Much of what is said about the
behaviour of ancient man is, perforce, guesswork.*

perform /pəfɔːm/ **performs, performing, performed**
1 VO To **perform** a task, action, or service means to
do it. *About 200 heart operations a year are
performed at the Brook Hospital... Their organization
performs a vital service.*
2 VA If something **performs** well or badly, it works or
functions well or badly. *...the difficulty of finding a
rifle which will perform satisfactorily under those
conditions.*
3 VOorV If you **perform** a play, a piece of music, or a
dance, you do it in front of an audience. *He
performed for them a dance of his native Samoa... We
had to perform on stage.*

performance /pəfɔːməns/ **performances**
1 NC A **performance** is the acting of a play or the
playing or singing of a piece of music in front of an
audience. *...an amateur performance of 'Macbeth'.*
2 NU Your **performance** is how well you do
something. *...Britain's poor economic performance.
...a disappointing performance in the semi-final.*
3 N SING The **performance** of a task or action is the
doing of it. *...the performance of his Presidential
duties.*

performer /pəfɔːmə/ **performers**
1 NC A **performer** is a person who does something to
entertain an audience, for example acting, singing, or
playing an instrument. *...a gifted performer... He
earned a useful living as a night club performer.*
2 NC+SUPP Someone who is a particular kind of
performer does a particular thing in the way indicated
or to the standard indicated. *He was the most
impressive performer at the Grand Prix meeting at
Koblenz in Germany... His supporters are all
wondering why he is such a rotten performer on
television when he is such a brilliant speaker in
parliament.*

performing arts
N PL Dance, drama, music, and other forms of
entertainment that are usually performed live in front
of an audience are referred to as the **performing arts**.
*...his stimulating approach to the theatre and the
performing arts. ...the John F Kennedy Center for the
Performing Arts.*

perfume /pɜːfjuːm/ **perfumes**
1 N MASS **Perfume** is a pleasant-smelling liquid which
you put on your body. *...a bottle of perfume. ...an
expensive perfume.*
2 NC A **perfume** is a pleasant smell. *The familiar
perfumes of wild flowers filled her nostrils.*

perfumed /pɜːfjuːmd/
ADJ Something that is **perfumed** has a pleasant smell.
...the perfumed air.

perfunctory /pəfʌŋktəⁿri/
ADJ A **perfunctory** action is done quickly and

carelessly; a formal word. *Max gave his wife a perfunctory kiss.*

pergola /pɜːgələ/ **pergolas**
NC A **pergola** is an arch or roofed structure in a garden, which consists of a framework over which climbing plants can be grown.

perhaps /pəhæps/
ADV SEN You use **perhaps** to indicate that you are not sure whether something is true, possible, or likely. *Perhaps Andrew is right after all... Perhaps I'll come. Perhaps not... There are perhaps fifty women here.*

per head
ADV If a group of people have, give, or receive a particular amount of something **per head**, that is the average amount for each person. *Meals were being subsidized by up to £16 per head... So the average amount of land per head is declining.*

peril /pɛrəl/ **perils**
NUorNC **Peril** is great danger; a formal word. *They placed themselves in great peril by openly opposing him. ...the perils of being a fugitive.* • If you warn someone or say that they do something **at their peril**, you mean that it is dangerous and likely to result in harm for them. *They ignore the environment at their peril... We underestimate AIDS at our peril... They will do so at their own peril.*

perilous /pɛrələs/
ADJ Something that is **perilous** is very dangerous; a formal word. *The perilous journey was over.*
◆ **perilously** SUBMOD or ADV *It came perilously close to destruction... You then rather perilously climb onto the plank.*

perimeter /pərɪmɪtə/ **perimeters**
NCorN+N The **perimeter** of an area of land is its outer edge or boundary. *...the perimeter of the clearing... Guards keep watch on its perimeter. ...the perimeter wall of the maximum security jail.*

period /pɪəriəd/ **periods**
1 NC A particular **period** is a particular length of time. *...over a period of several months. ...a short period of time. ...long periods of rain. ...in the Edwardian period. ...in the period before the introduction of martial law.*
2 ADJ ATTRIB **Period** costumes, objects, and houses were made at an earlier time in history, or look as if they were made then. *...period furniture.*
3 NC A woman's **period** is the bleeding from her womb that happens each month. *...women who've had painful or long or irregular periods. ...ten days or more after the woman has missed her last period.*
4 NC A **period** is also a full stop; used in American English.
5 People sometimes say '**period**' at the end of a statement to emphasize that they think it is a totally accurate summary of a situation, and no more can be said about it; used in American English. *He says there will be no change in the status of Jerusalem, period... When you're dealing with that kind of animal, you don't rationalize, period.*

periodic /pɪəriɒdɪk/
ADJ ATTRIB A **periodic** event or situation happens occasionally, at fairly regular intervals. *...periodic droughts. ...making periodic attempts to clear his name.*

periodical /pɪəriɒdɪkl/ **periodicals**
1 NC A **periodical** is a magazine, especially a serious or academic one. *...an authoritative American periodical... Official groups are allowed to publish newspapers and periodicals.*
2 ADJ ATTRIB **Periodical** means the same as periodic. *These mood shifts are periodical and recurring.*
◆ **periodically** /pɪəriɒdɪkli/ ADV *We met them periodically during the summer break.*

periodic table
N SING The **periodic table** is a table showing the chemical elements arranged according to their atomic numbers; a technical term in chemistry. *They tried silicon, which of course comes under carbon in the periodic table.*

peripatetic /pɛrɪpətɛtɪk/
ADJ ATTRIB **Peripatetic** workers have jobs which require them to work for short periods of time in different places; a technical term. *...the son of a peripatetic engineer.*

peripheral /pərɪfərəl/; a formal word.
1 ADJ A **peripheral** thing or part of something is not very important compared with other things or parts. *...the peripheral features of religion.*
2 ADJ **Peripheral** also means on or relating to the edge of an area. *This gives greater peripheral vision.*

periphery /pərɪfəri/ **peripheries**
NC The **periphery** of an area is the edge of it; a formal word. *The cost of land on the periphery of Calcutta went up.*

periscope /pɛrɪskəup/ **periscopes**
NC A **periscope** is a vertical tube through which people in a submarine can see above the surface of the water. *...looking through the periscope... Conventional periscopes rely on a complex set of lenses and mirrors... 'Standard surface attack—Down Periscope!'*

perish /pɛrɪʃ/ **perishes, perishing, perished**
1 V To **perish** means to die or be destroyed; a formal use. *All the passengers and crew members perished... The old religion is perishing.*
2 V If rubber, leather, or a fabric **perishes**, it starts to fall to pieces. *The material perishes if left too long exposed to air.*

perishable /pɛrɪʃəbl/
ADJ If something is **perishable**, it goes rotten or becomes unusable quite quickly. *...lorries carrying perishable goods... Ripe tomatoes are highly perishable... Perishable foods requiring refrigeration went rotten... It's very perishable information.*

perisher /pɛrɪʃə/ **perishers**
NC You can refer to a child as a **perisher** when you are annoyed with it or feel sorry for it; an old-fashioned, informal word. *The poor little perisher died in my arms.*

perishing /pɛrɪʃɪŋ/
1 ADJ If the weather is **perishing** or **perishing cold**, it is extremely cold. *I was up in Minnesota during its perishing winter... It's perishing cold this morning.*
2 ADJ ATTRIB You can use **perishing** to emphasize something when you dislike it or are annoyed; an informal use. *'Why don't you throw that thing out?'— 'What thing, dear?'—'That perishing clock.'*

peritonitis /pɛrɪtənaɪtɪs/
NU If you have **peritonitis**, the inside wall of your abdomen is inflamed and very painful; a medical term.

periwinkle /pɛrɪwɪŋkl/ **periwinkles**
1 NC A **periwinkle** is an evergreen plant that grows along the ground and has blue flowers. *The rosy periwinkle provides the drugs which are used in the treatment of leukaemia.*
2 NC A **periwinkle** is also an edible creature like a snail that lives in or near the sea.

perjure /pɜːdʒə/ **perjures, perjuring, perjured**
V-REFL If you **perjure** yourself in a court of law, you lie although you have taken an oath to tell the truth; a legal term. *You can't expect me to perjure myself in the witness-box.*

perjury /pɜːdʒəri/
NU If someone who has taken an oath in a court of law commits **perjury** while giving evidence, they lie; a legal term. *She was charged with perjury.*

perk /pɜːk/ **perks, perking, perked**
NC A **perk** is something extra that employees get in addition to their salaries. *It's just another perk of the job. ...company cars, interest-free loans, all executive perks... Top directors will probably have all their private telephone bills paid by the company, as a perk.*

perk up PHRASAL VERB When someone **perks up**, they become more cheerful. *John was being a misery. He perked up when we got there, though.*

perky /pɜːki/ **perkier, perkiest**
ADJ If someone is **perky**, they are cheerful, lively, and enthusiastic. *The paper comments that President Bush had not looked so perky since his inauguration. ...a perky school-leaver from Donnington. ...one of the perkiest people at the Conference.*

perm /pɜːm/ **perms, perming, permed**
NC If you have a **perm**, your hair is treated with chemicals and then curled so that the curls last for several months. ► Also VO *She had her hair permed.*

permafrost /pɜːməfrɒst/
NU **Permafrost** is land that is permanently frozen to a great depth, even though the surface may thaw slightly in the summer. *...the permafrost of the North.*

permanence /pɜːmənəns/
NU If something has **permanence**, it remains the same for a long time or for ever. *The fight had to be led by a party with more permanence in its membership and structure. ...people have a need for permanence.*

permanency /pɜːmənənsi/ **permanencies**
1 NC A **permanency** is someone or something that is always present or always the same. *He seems to have become a permanency in her life.*
2 NU **Permanency** also means the same as **permanence**. *...an air of permanency.*

permanent /pɜːmənənt/
ADJ Something that is **permanent** lasts for ever or is present all the time. *Some drugs taken in large quantities cause permanent brain damage. ...the only permanent water supply. ...the five permanent members of the United Nations Security Council.*
♦ **permanently** ADV *The doors were kept permanently locked.*

permeable /pɜːmiəbl/
ADJ If something is **permeable**, liquids are able to pass through its surface; a formal word. *The insect's skin is permeable.*

permeate /pɜːmieɪt/ **permeates, permeating, permeated**; a formal word.
1 VO If something such as an idea or attitude **permeates** something, it affects every part of it. *Racist attitudes permeate our establishments from top to bottom. ...the extent to which secrecy permeates every part of our society... Changes in civilian life have not yet begun to permeate the army.*
2 VOorV+through If a liquid, smell, or flavour **permeates** something, it spreads through it. *Damp can easily permeate the wood... Chemicals may permeate through the soil into rivers.*

permissible /pəmɪsəbl/
ADJ Something that is **permissible** is allowed; a formal word. *...the maximum permissible levels of radiation.*

permission /pəmɪʃn/
NU If you give someone **permission** to do something, you say that they are allowed to do it. *It is not clear how many of them have been given permission to leave... I have permission to tell you... He refused permission for Biddle to enter Britain... You can't go without permission.*

permissive /pəmɪsɪv/
ADJ A **permissive** society allows people a lot of freedom, especially in sexual behaviour, despite the objection of certain parts of that society. *...the frequency of divorce within the permissive society. ...a permissive attitude towards abortion.*
♦ **permissiveness** NU *...those who argue for a return to old moral values after the permissiveness of the 1960's. ...sexual permissiveness.*

permit, permits, permitting, permitted; pronounced /pəmɪt/ when it is a verb and /pɜːmɪt/ when it is a noun.
1 VO If you **permit** something, you allow it; a formal use. *Visits are permitted only once a month... Her father would not permit her to eat sweets... The doctor has permitted him only two meals a day.*
2 VOorV If something **permits** a particular thing, it makes it possible for that thing to happen; a formal use. *The timetable permits teams only a few weeks for preparation... Had time permitted, we would have stayed longer.*
3 NC A **permit** is an official document which says that you may do something. *She could not get in without a permit. ...work permits.*

permutation /pɜːmjuːteɪʃn/ **permutations**
NC A **permutation** is one of the ways in which a set or group of things can be arranged; a formal word. *The possible permutations were endless.*

pernicious /pənɪʃəs/
ADJ Something that is **pernicious** is very harmful; a formal word. *This had a pernicious influence on countless generations.*

pernickety /pənɪkəti/
ADJ Someone who is **pernickety** worries too much about small details that are not important; an informal word. *You can't be so pernickety about everything!*

peroration /perəreɪʃn/ **perorations**
NC A **peroration** is the last part of a speech, particularly the part where the speaker summarizes his or her main points; a formal word.

peroxide /pərɒksaɪd/
NU **Peroxide** or **hydrogen peroxide** is a chemical that exists naturally in the air and in living creatures. It is also made artificially and used for bleaching hair or as an antiseptic. *...the minute amounts of ozone and hydrogen peroxide that are normally present in the atmosphere... One truck carried organic peroxide.*

perpendicular /pɜːpəndɪkjulə/
ADJ Something that is **perpendicular** points straight up, instead of sloping; a formal word. *...the perpendicular cliff-face.*

perpetrate /pɜːpətreɪt/ **perpetrates, perpetrating, perpetrated**
VO If someone **perpetrates** a crime or a harmful or immoral act, they do it; a formal word. *They are known to be capable of perpetrating such a crime. ...a fraud perpetrated by lawyers. ...perpetrating acts of terror and violence.*

perpetrator /pɜːpətreɪtə/ **perpetrators**
NC The **perpetrator** of a crime or act of violence is a person who has committed that crime or act; a formal word. *He condemned the shooting and said the perpetrators would be brought to justice... Perpetrators of violence would be firmly dealt with.*

perpetual /pəpetʃuəl/
ADJ ATTRIB **Perpetual** means never ending or changing. *These bats live in deep caves in perpetual darkness... She had me in perpetual fear.*
♦ **perpetually** ADV *The younger children seemed to be perpetually hungry.*

perpetuate /pəpetʃueɪt/ **perpetuates, perpetuating, perpetuated**
VO If someone or something **perpetuates** a situation or belief, they cause it to continue; a formal word. *...an education system that perpetuates inequality.*

perpetuity /pɜːpɪtjuːəti/
If something is done in **perpetuity** or **for perpetuity**, it is intended to last for ever; a formal expression. *The plots where they were buried were dedicated in perpetuity to the United States.*

perplexed /pəplekst/
ADJ If you are **perplexed**, you are puzzled or do not know what to do. *She frowned a little, as if perplexed.*

perplexing /pəpleksɪŋ/
ADJ If something is **perplexing**, you do not understand it or do not know how to deal with it. *...a perplexing and difficult problem.*

perplexity /pəpleksəti/
NU **Perplexity** is the state of being perplexed. *She looked at us in some perplexity.*

perquisite /pɜːkwɪzɪt/ **perquisites**
NC A **perquisite** is the same as a **perk**; a formal word. *They are rewarded in pay, power and perquisites.*

per se /pɜː seɪ/
ADV **Per se** is added after mentioning something, to say that you are considering only that thing by itself and not other things that it may be connected with; a formal expression. *Most people know very little about the educational process per se... The White House is not opposed to sanctions per se... Anything socially practical is good per se.*

persecute /pɜːsɪkjuːt/ **persecutes, persecuting, persecuted**
VO If someone **persecutes** you, they treat you cruelly and unfairly over a long period of time. *Members of these sects are ruthlessly persecuted... The new government has made it clear that it is not going to persecute the refugees.* ♦ **persecution** /pɜːsɪkjuːʃn/ NU

...*the persecution of minorities.*

persecutor /pɜːsɪkjuːtə/ **persecutors**
NC A **persecutor** is someone who treats a person or group unfairly and cruelly, especially because of their political or religious beliefs. *He vowed to take his revenge on his persecutors.*

perseverance /pɜːsɪvɪərəns/
NU **Perseverance** is the fact of continuing with something difficult, rather than giving up. *I underestimated his perseverance.*

persevere /pɜːsɪvɪə/ **perseveres, persevering, persevered**
V or V+*with* If you **persevere** with something difficult, you continue doing it and do not give up. *Confidence is needed both to start and to persevere... They still believe it's worth persevering with the initiative.*

Persian /pɜːʒn/
1 ADJ Something that is **Persian** belongs or relates to the ancient kingdom of Persia, or sometimes to the modern state of Iran. *...agreements that go back 400 years to the Ottoman and Persian Empires. ...a procession through the town to mark Nowruz or Persian New Year.*
2 ADJ **Persian** carpets and rugs are from Persia or Iran. They have geometric patterns in rich colours and are made by hand from silk or wool.
3 NU **Persian** is the language that is spoken by people in Iran, and was spoken in ancient Persia. *...a fluent Persian speaker. ...the BBC Persian Service.*

Persian cat, Persian cats
NC A **Persian cat** is a type of cat that has long thin hair and a round face. *Persian cats are very popular amongst Western cat lovers.*

Persian Gulf
N PROP In American English, the area of sea between Saudi Arabia and Iran is referred to as **Persian Gulf**. *...vital areas like the Persian Gulf... The USS Vincennes was one of the navy ships sent to the Persian Gulf.*

persist /pəsɪst/ **persists, persisting, persisted**
1 V If something undesirable **persists**, it continues to exist. *Political differences still persist... The pain persisted until the morning.*
2 V A If you **persist** in doing something, you continue to do it, even though it is difficult or other people oppose you. *People still persist in thinking that standards are going down... He persisted with his policy of conciliation.*

persistence /pəsɪstəns/
1 NU The **persistence** of something is the fact of its continuing to exist for a long time. *Because of the suddenness and persistence of the depression I saw my doctor... This persistence of ties with the countryside is not uncommon.*
2 NU If you have **persistence**, you continue to do something with determination, even though it is difficult or other people are against it. *She managed it by persistence and ambition.*

persistent /pəsɪstənt/
1 ADJ Something that is **persistent** continues to exist or happen for a long time. *How do you get rid of a persistent nasty smell? ...persistent reports of widespread killing of civilians by government troops.*
♦ **persistently** ADV *...persistently rattling window frames.*
2 ADJ Someone who is **persistent** continues trying to do something, even though it is difficult or other people oppose them. *I think you have to be persistent if people say no to you.* ♦ **persistently** ADV *...policemen who tried persistently to force their way into his house.*

person /pɜːsn/ **persons**. The form **persons** is only used in formal or legal language. **People** is normally used instead to refer to more than one person: see **people**.
1 NC A **person** is a man or a woman. *I want to see the person responsible for dealing with accounts... She was a charming person... He had learned through official channels that four persons were killed in the clashes.*
2 NC+SUPP In grammar, the first **person** means the speaker, or the speaker and someone else, the second **person** means the person or people being spoken to,

and the third **person** means someone or something else.
● **Person** occurs in these phrases. ● If you do something **in person**, you do it yourself, rather than someone else doing it for you. *He wished he had gone to the house in person... He would be allowed to collect the prize in person.* ● If you hear or see someone **in person**, you hear or see them directly, rather than on radio or television. *Many actually saw him in person. ...wanting to see Mr Botha in person.*

-person
1 SUFFIX **-person** combines with nouns to form new nouns which refer to someone who carries out a particular role or has a particular job. **-person** is often used instead of '-man' or '-woman' in order to avoid specifying what sex somebody is. *...a spokesperson for the Hungarian delegation... The Istanbul branch of the Party tried to elect a chairperson last month.*
2 SUFFIX **-person** also combines with numbers to form words which describe how many people a particular object or activity is intended for. *The report speaks of thousands of prisoners being two or three to a one-person cell. ...the remaining twenty-one seats on the 60-person Council. ...the 700-person workforce.*

persona /pəsəunə/ **personas** or **personae** /pəsəuniː/
NC Your **persona** is the aspect of your character or nature that you present to other people, perhaps in contrast to your real character or nature; a formal word. *He decided to adopt an entirely new persona.*

personable /pɜːsənəbl/
ADJ Someone who is **personable** has a pleasant appearance and character; an old-fashioned word. *...a personable young man.*

personage /pɜːsənɪdʒ/ **personages**
NC A **personage** is a famous or important person; a formal word. *...a distinguished personage.*

personal /pɜːsnəl/
1 ADJ ATTRIB A **personal** opinion, quality, or thing belongs or relates to a particular person. *My personal view is that he should resign... I can vouch for that from personal experience. ...his personal belongings.*
2 ADJ ATTRIB If you give something your **personal** attention, you deal with it yourself rather than letting someone else deal with it. *The book was translated under the personal supervision of the author... The mine was only re-opened after the personal intervention of the Prime Minister. ...delivering a personal message from the Turkish Prime Minister.*
3 ADJ **Personal** matters relate to your feelings, relationships, and health. *...the most intimate details of their personal lives. ...personal problems... Her personal life was turbulent, too.*
4 ADJ **Personal** comments refer to someone's appearance or character in an offensive way. *I think we're getting too personal.*

personal assistant, personal assistants
NC A **personal assistant** is a person who does secretarial and administrative work for someone. *Rykov was his personal assistant... He was personal assistant to Prince Saddrudin.*

personal column, personal columns
NC The **personal column** in a newspaper is a column which contains messages for individual people or advertisements of a private nature. *...advertisements placed in the personal columns of national newspapers... I put an ad in the Daily News, in the personal column, and he answered it.*

personal computer, personal computers
NC A **personal computer** is a fairly small computer that is used mainly by people at home rather than by large businesses or organizations. *We will be able to run this software on a personal computer at home... He expects them to capture half of the personal computer market.*

personality /pɜːsənælətɪ/ **personalities**
1 NC+SUPP or NU Your **personality** is your whole character and nature. *He has a wonderful personality... He lacks the personality to overcome these misfortunes... He was no judge of personality.*
2 NC You can refer to a famous entertainer, broadcaster, or sports player as a **personality**. *...a television personality.*

personalized /pɜːsəⁿnəlaɪzd/; also spelt **personalised.**
1 ADJ A **personalized** object has its owner's initials or name on it. *...personalized pens. ...a car with a personalised number plate.*
2 ADJ **Personalized** also means designed for or aimed at one particular person. *...personalized counseling services... Political power was exercised in a very personalised fashion. ...a highly personalised attack by the Prime Minister.*

personally /pɜːsəⁿnəli/
1 ADV SEN You use **personally** to emphasize that you are giving your own opinion. *Well, personally, I feel that this is very difficult.*
2 ADV If you do something **personally**, you do it yourself rather than letting someone else do it. *Since then I have undertaken all the enquiries personally.*
3 ADV or SUBMOD Something that affects you **personally** affects you rather than other people. *I wasn't referring to you personally... They would be held personally responsible for the horrors taking place there.*

personal pronoun, personal pronouns
NC In grammar, **personal pronouns** are pronouns such as 'I, me, you, she, it, we, us, they, them', which refer to the speaker, the person or people being spoken to, or other people or things which have already been mentioned.

personal stereo, personal stereos
NC A **personal stereo** is a small cassette player with very light headphones, which people carry around so that they can listen to music while they are doing something else. *Eventually it will be small enough to wear on a belt rather like a personal stereo.*

persona non grata /pəsəʊnə nɒn grɑːtə/
If you declare someone **persona non grata**, they become unwelcome or unacceptable because they have done something which you disapprove of. *The Brigadier had been declared persona non grata... He was prohibited from entering the country and is, in Austria, persona non grata.*

personify /pəsɒnɪfaɪ/ **personifies, personifying, personified**
VO If someone **personifies** a particular quality, they seem to have that quality to a very large degree. *He seemed to personify the evil that was in the world.*

personnel /pɜːsənel/
N PL The **personnel** of an organization are the people who work for it. *...international companies and diplomatic missions who send personnel abroad... Eight people were wounded, including both military personnel and civilians. ...a number of personnel changes in the Czechoslovak leadership.*

perspective /pəspektɪv/ **perspectives**
1 NC A **perspective** is a particular way of thinking about something. *He wanted to leave the country in order to get a better perspective on things.*
2 If you put something **in perspective** or **into perspective**, you are able to judge its importance or value more correctly by relating it to other things. *It will help to put in perspective the vast gulf that separates existing groups... We have to get it into perspective.*
3 NU In art, **perspective** is the method by which artists are able to make some objects or people look further away than others. *...the illusions created by light and shade and by the tricks of perspective... Leonardo used perspective drawings to capture a mood, an idea, a detail.*

Perspex /pɜːspeks/
NU **Perspex** is a strong, clear plastic which is sometimes used instead of glass; **Perspex** is a trademark. *...a model of a dam, made of Perspex... And there's another small Perspex box here with a handle on it.*

perspicacious /pɜːspɪkeɪʃəs/
ADJ Someone who is **perspicacious** notices, realizes, and understands things quickly; a formal word. *Even the most perspicacious of students of human nature may fail to notice this trait in his character.*

perspicacity /pɜːspɪkæsəti/
NU **Perspicacity** is the quality of being perspicacious; a formal word. *The Moscow News talks of his 'remarkable depth and perspicacity'. ...the taste and perspicacity of great directors.*

perspiration /pɜːspəreɪʃn/
NU **Perspiration** is the same as **sweat**; a formal word. *There were beads of perspiration on his upper lip.*

perspire /pəspaɪə/ **perspires, perspiring, perspired**
V When you **perspire**, sweat comes out onto your skin; a formal word. *Hot and perspiring, John toiled up the dusty ascent.*

persuade /pəsweɪd/ **persuades, persuading, persuaded**
1 VO+*to*-INF If someone or something **persuades** you to do a particular thing, they cause you to do it by giving you a good reason for doing it. *Marsha was trying to persuade Posy to change her mind. ...as the threat of unemployment persuades workers to moderate their pay demands. ...if Gorbachev can persuade the military to accept this.*
2 VO-REPORT or VO+*of* If someone **persuades** you that something is true, they say things that eventually make you believe that it is true. *We worked hard to persuade them that we were genuinely interested... Persuade him of your seriousness about this.*
◆ **persuaded** ADJ PRED *Few of them are persuaded of the benefits of the shop.*

persuasion /pəsweɪʒn/ **persuasions**
1 NU **Persuasion** is the act of persuading someone to do something or to believe that something is true. *They didn't need much persuasion.*
2 NC+SUPP If you are of a particular **persuasion**, you have a particular set of beliefs; a formal use. *...people of different political persuasions... The Salvation Front is led by former Communists—albeit of a reformist persuasion.*

persuasive /pəsweɪsɪv/
ADJ Someone or something that is **persuasive** is likely to persuade you to do or believe a particular thing. *...a very persuasive argument.*

pert /pɜːt/
ADJ If you talk about a **pert** young woman or her **pert** appearance or behaviour, you mean that she is lively and cheeky; a literary word. *She looked totally different, pert and secretarial. ...blonde hair round a pert face... The voice was pert, almost coquettish now.*

pertain /pəteɪn/ **pertains, pertaining, pertained**
V+*to* Something that **pertains** to something else belongs or relates to it; a formal word. *...documents pertaining to the suspects.*

pertinent /pɜːtɪnənt/
ADJ Something that is **pertinent** is relevant; a formal word. *I asked him a lot of pertinent questions about the original production.*

perturbation /pɜːtəbeɪʃn/ **perturbations**
1 NU **Perturbation** is anxiety and worry; a formal word. *They had been pressing for a tight incomes policy, to the growing perturbation of the unions.*
2 NC **Perturbations** are small changes in something that is mostly regular, such as a movement or a force; a technical use. *...the likely effects of tiny perturbations of gravity on the flight... It would explain some odd perturbations in the orbits of the planets.*

perturbed /pətɜːbd/
ADJ PRED Someone who is **perturbed** is worried; a formal word. *She was perturbed about a rash which had come out on her face.*

Peru /pəruː/
The **Republic of Peru** is a country in western South America. It was a Spanish colony from the 16th century to 1826. In recent years the guerrilla activities of a Maoist group, Sendero Luminoso (Shining Path), and other armed factions, have threatened public order. Large parts of the country are under a state of emergency. In 1989 approximately 3,200 people died in political violence. Alberto Keinyo Fujimori, of Change 90, became President in 1990. Peru is the world's largest exporter of fishmeal. It also produces copper, lead, zinc, cotton, sugar, and coffee. Cocaine is illegally produced. High inflation and large foreign debts are major economic problems. Peru is a member of the Organization of American States.

◆ **Peruvian** /pəru:viən/ N, ADJ
▪ *per capita GNP:* approximately US$1,440 ▪ *religion:*
Christianity (mainly Roman Catholic) ▪ *language:*
Spanish, Quechua, Aymara ▪ *currency:* inti ▪ *capital:*
Lima ▪ *population:* 21 million (1988) ▪ *size:* 1,280,000
square kilometres.

perusal /pəru:zl/
NU **Perusal** is the act of reading a piece of writing
fairly quickly, without concentrating very hard on it; a
formal word. *Clare handed it over for my perusal... A
perusal of the White Paper suggests otherwise.*

peruse /pəru:z/ **peruses, perusing, perused**
VO If you **peruse** a piece of writing, you read it; a
formal word. *Having perused its contents, he flung
down the paper.*

pervade /pəveɪd/ **pervades, pervading, pervaded**
VO If something **pervades** a place or thing, it is
present or noticed throughout that place or thing; a
formal word. *An atmosphere of contentment pervades
the school.*

pervasive /pəveɪsɪv/
ADJ Something that is **pervasive** is present or noticed
throughout a place or thing; a formal word. *He said it
was a very pervasive form of advertising and difficult
to avoid. ...in a country where the problem of
unemployment is pervasive. ...demonstrations against
the pervasive influence of the army in national life.*
◆ **pervasiveness** NU *...the size of its economy and the
pervasiveness of its culture. ...the pervasiveness of
English in India.*

perverse /pəvɜːs/
ADJ Someone who is **perverse** deliberately does things
that are unreasonable. *He takes a perverse delight in
irritating people.* ◆ **perversely** ADV *They persisted,
perversely, in trying to grow grain.*

perversion /pəvɜːʃn/ **perversions**
1 NCorNU A **perversion** is a sexual desire or action
that is considered abnormal and unacceptable. *Overt
sexuality was described as a Western perversion.*
2 NU+SUPPorNC+SUPP The **perversion** of something is
the changing of it so that it is no longer what it should
be. *...the systematic perversion of the truth... Mrs
Suzman said the sentence imposed by the judge was a
gross perversion of justice.*

perversity /pəvɜːsəti/
NU Someone who shows **perversity** deliberately does
things that are unreasonable. *...her perversity as a
child.*

pervert, perverts, perverting, perverted;
pronounced /pəvɜːt/ when it is a verb and /pɜːvɜːt/
when it is a noun.
1 VO If you **pervert** something, for example a process
or society, you interfere with it so that it is not what it
used to be or should be; a formal word. *Traditional
ceremonies were perverted into meaningless rituals.*
2 NC A **pervert** is a person whose behaviour,
especially sexual behaviour, is considered abnormal or
unacceptable. *...a speech in which he called them
perverts... They portrayed him as a murderer, a
sexual pervert and a madman.*

perverted /pəvɜːtɪd/
1 ADJ Someone who is **perverted** is considered to have
abnormal behaviour or ideas, especially sexual ones.
*...an obscenity committed by depraved and perverted
people.*
2 ADJ Something that is **perverted** is wrong, unnatural,
or harmful. *...a perverted form of love. ...a perverted
way of thinking... It's sick, it's perverted, it's foul.*

pessary /pesəri/ **pessaries**
1 NC A **pessary** is a solid medicine for curing
infections. A woman puts it into her vagina and it
dissolves there. *Many of us remember our
grandmothers having these rather strange vaginal
pessaries.*
2 NC A **pessary** is also a contraceptive device which
looks rather like a pill and contains a chemical which
kills sperm. A woman puts it into her vagina and it
dissolves there.

pessimism /pesɪmɪzəm/
NU **Pessimism** is the belief that bad things are going
to happen. *His pessimism was unjustified.* ◆ **pessimist**
/pesɪmɪst/ **pessimists** NC *Pessimists tell us that the*
family is doomed.

pessimistic /pesɪmɪstɪk/
ADJ Someone who is **pessimistic** thinks that bad things
are going to happen, or that progress will be slow.
*Success now seemed very remote and Mick felt
pessimistic... The Commission is now more pessimistic
about Europe's growth prospects this year... The
engineers are taking a pessimistic view of what might
happen.* ◆ **pessimistically** ADV *'Well, let's get it over
with,' he said pessimistically.*

pest /pest/ **pests**
1 NC A **pest** is an insect or small animal which
damages crops or food supplies and can be a threat to
health and safety. *A spokesman said pigeons—like
rats—were pests and had to be controlled... Some
remarkable work is going on in pest control in
mangoes.*
2 NC Someone who is a **pest** keeps bothering you; an
informal use. *She can't stand him, see, because he's a
pest.*

pester /pestə/ **pesters, pestering, pestered**
VO If you **pester** someone, you keep bothering them or
asking them to do something. *Desiree had been
pestering him to take her to Europe.*

pesticide /pestɪsaɪd/ **pesticides**
N MASS **Pesticides** are chemicals which farmers put on
their crops to kill harmful insects. *...shortages of
fertiliser and pesticide. ...polluting the environment
with chemical pesticides.*

pestilence /pestɪləns/ **pestilences**
NUorN SING **Pestilence** or a **pestilence** is a disease that
spreads quickly and kills large numbers of people; a
formal word. *According to the experts, drought and
pestilence are bound to increase... Britain should join
the United States in endeavouring to tackle this
pestilence.*

pestle /pesl/ **pestles**
NC A **pestle** is a short stick made of wood or stone,
with a thick, round end. It is used for crushing herbs,
grain, or other substances in a bowl called a mortar.
*The women were using a traditional pestle and
mortar.*

pet /pet/ **pets, petting, petted**
1 NCorN+N A **pet** is an animal that you keep in your
home to give you company and pleasure. *It is against
the rules to keep pets. ...his pet dog. ...importing
meat for pet food.*
2 ADJ ATTRIB Someone's **pet** theory or subject is one
that they particularly support or like. *We were
listening to a gardener with his pet theories.*
3 VO If you **pet** a person or animal, you pat or stroke
them affectionately. *...being cuddled and petted and
getting attention... He spends his time relaxing by the
pool or petting his horse, Rising Sun.*

petal /petl/ **petals**
NC The **petals** of a flower are the thin coloured outer
parts. *...rose petals.*

petard /petɑːd/
If someone who has planned to harm someone else is
hoist with their own petard, their plan in fact results
in harm to themselves. *They are slowly and
agonizingly being hoist with their own petard.*

peter /piːtə/ **peters, petering, petered**
peter out PHRASAL VERB If something **peters out**, it
gradually comes to an end. *The tracks petered out a
mile later... The strikes earlier this month appear to
have petered out... This dialogue soon petered out.*

petite /pətiːt/
ADJ A woman who is **petite** is small and slim. *...his
petite bride.*

petit-four /petɪfɔː/ **petit-fours** or **petits-fours**
NC A **petit-four** is a very small sweet cake or biscuit,
often made of marzipan. *'Have a petit-four.'—'Thank
you,' said Mrs Oliver.*

petition /pətɪʃn/ **petitions, petitioning, petitioned**
1 NC A **petition** is a document signed by a lot of
people which asks for some official action to be taken.
*He presented a petition signed by 10,357 electors...
Forty minutes went by as petitions against his bill
were presented. ...a petition calling for greater
religious freedom.*
2 NC A **petition** is also an application to a court of law

for some specific legal action to be taken; a legal use. *She has filed a petition for divorce.*
3 VO+*to*-INF or V+*for* If you **petition** someone in authority to do something, you make a formal request to them to do it; a formal use. *It is my duty to petition the court to declare this action illegal. ...organizations that have petitioned for experimental TV coverage.*

petitioner /pəˈtɪʃəʰnə/ **petitioners**
1 NC A **petitioner** is a person who presents or signs a petition. *There was much coming and going of petitioners.*
2 NC A **petitioner** is also a person who brings a legal case to a court of law. *...the petitioner who originally filed the allegations. ...the character, fitness and position of the petitioner. ...the petitioners in this case.*
3 NC In Britain, a **petitioner** is someone who goes to a court of law to obtain a divorce.

pet name, pet names
NC A **pet name** is a special name that you use to address a close friend or a member of your family. *Teddy was her pet name for him.*

petrify /ˈpetrɪfaɪ/ **petrifies, petrifying, petrified**
1 VO If something **petrifies** you, it makes you feel very frightened indeed, perhaps so frightened that you cannot move. *The warning whistle started to blow. The sound petrified him.* ◆ **petrified** ADJ PRED *They're petrified of failure.*
2 V When something that is dead **petrifies**, it gradually changes into stone. ◆ **petrified** ADJ ATTRIB *The mountain range loomed menacingly like some petrified prehistoric monster. ...as she sits on this petrified log.*
3 V-ERG If a society or institution **petrifies** or if something **petrifies** it, it ceases to change and develop; a formal use. *There is always the danger that civilization may wither or petrify... Militarism and xenophobia petrified the social order.* ◆ **petrification** /ˌpetrɪfɪˈkeɪʃn/ NU *These statements, taken too literally, lead to the petrification of meaning.*

petrochemical /ˌpetrəʊˈkemɪkl/ **petrochemicals**
NC A **petrochemical** is a chemical that is obtained from petroleum or natural gas. *...at least 15 major employers, including manufacturers of petrochemicals. ...the export of petrochemicals to Europe. ...the petrochemical industry.*

petrodollars /ˈpetrəʊdɒləz/. The form **petrodollar** is used as a noun modifier.
N PL **Petrodollars** are a unit of money used to calculate how much a country has earned by exporting petroleum. They are equivalent in value to American dollars. *...the importance of Iraq's oil and petrodollars. ...their declining petrodollar income.*

petrol /ˈpetrəl/
NU **Petrol** is a liquid used as a fuel for motor vehicles. *...motorists waiting to buy petrol... Petrol prices will rise by over eighty per cent... Petrol rationing will end on January the first.*

petrol bomb, petrol bombs
NC A **petrol bomb** is a simple bomb consisting of a bottle full of petrol with a cloth in it that is lit just before the bottle is thrown. *They were found guilty of possessing petrol bombs and assaulting police. ...gangs of youths throwing petrol bombs.*

petroleum /pəˈtrəʊliəm/
NU **Petroleum** is oil which is found underground or under the sea bed. Petrol and paraffin are obtained from petroleum. *...the country's petroleum and natural gas reserves... The Soviet Union started importing refined petroleum. ...the trade in petroleum products.*

petroleum jelly
NU **Petroleum jelly** is a soft, clear, jelly-like substance which is obtained from petroleum. It is used to make ointments for your skin or to grease surfaces. *For relief of sunburn, you can apply plain cold cream or petroleum jelly.*

petrol station, petrol stations
NC A **petrol station** is a garage where petrol is sold and put into vehicles. *There are long queues at all petrol stations in the city... Some petrol stations and bread shops were forced to close.*

petticoat /ˈpetikəʊt/ **petticoats**
NC A **petticoat** is an item of women's underwear like a thin skirt which is worn under a dress or skirt. *...girls wearing petticoats and dresses. ...women in their pantaloons and petticoats.*

pettifogging /ˈpetifɒgɪŋ/
ADJ Someone who is **pettifogging** pays unnecessary attention to unimportant, boring details; an old-fashioned word. *They were small men with the low suspiciousness of pettifogging attorneys.*

pettish /ˈpetɪʃ/
ADJ Someone who is **pettish** shows childish irritation and anger over something that is not really important; an old-fashioned word. *He was getting more and more pettish and hysterical.*

petty /ˈpeti/
1 ADJ **Petty** things are small and unimportant. *...petty details. ...petty problems. ...in cases of petty theft, such as shoplifting. ...petty criminals.*
2 ADJ If someone is **petty**, they care too much about unimportant things and are perhaps selfish and unkind. *...petty jealousies.*

petty cash
NU **Petty cash** is money kept in an office for making small payments. *Have you been buying ashtrays for your office out of the petty cash? ...answering mail, handling the petty cash, organising the maintenance of the building.*

petty larceny
NU **Petty larceny** is the theft of property that is not very valuable; a legal term.

petty officer, petty officers
N C or TITLE A **petty officer** is a non-commissioned officer in the navy. *...a former Royal Navy petty officer. ...a petty officer in charge of administration... Petty Officer Diane Avery is a nurse.*

petulance /ˈpetjʊləns/
NU **Petulance** is unreasonable, childish bad temper over something unimportant. *...an exhibition of petulance and arrogance.*

petulant /ˈpetjʊlənt/
ADJ Someone who is **petulant** is angry and upset in a childish way; a literary word. *With a petulant snarl, I pushed the door.* ◆ **petulantly** ADV *'Oh, why do you say that?' I cried petulantly.*

petunia /pəˈtjuːniə/ **petunias**
NC A **petunia** is a garden plant with pink, white, or purple trumpet-shaped flowers. *...an area planted with geraniums, marigolds, and petunias.*

pew /pjuː/ **pews**
NC A **pew** is a long wooden seat for people in church. *Late-comers were standing in the aisles because every pew was taken. ...sitting on hard church pews.*

pewter /ˈpjuːtə/
NU **Pewter** is a grey metal made by mixing tin and lead. *...pewter plates.*

pH /piː ˈeɪtʃ/
N SING or NU The **pH** of a solution indicates whether it is an acid or alkali. A pH of less than 7 indicates that it is an acid, and a pH of more than 7 indicates that it is an alkali. *Lowering the pH to below 7 is the method of dealing with this. ...the pH of sea water. ...a slight increase in pH.*

phalanx /ˈfælæŋks/ **phalanxes** or **phalanges** /fəˈlændʒiːz/; a formal word.
1 NC A **phalanx** is a group of soldiers or police who are standing or marching close together in order to fight. *...a phalanx of infantrymen. ...a phalanx of about 10,000 riot police have stormed the shipyard.*
2 NC+SUPP A **phalanx** of people is a large group who are brought together for a particular purpose. *There wasn't the usual phalanx of lawyers and advisers around her. ...a phalanx of politicians.*

phallic /ˈfælɪk/
ADJ Something that is **phallic** is shaped like a penis or refers to male sexual powers. *...the great stone pillar that rose like a phallic symbol from the earth.*

phallus /ˈfæləs/ **phalli** /ˈfælaɪ/ or **phalluses**
1 NC A **phallus** is a model of a penis, especially one used as a symbol in ancient religions.
2 NC A **phallus** is also a penis; a technical use in psychology. *Small boys are often ashamed of the size*

of their phallus.

phantasmagoria /fæntæzməgɔːriə/ **phantasmagorias**
NC A **phantasmagoria** is a series of confused images of real or imaginary things; a literary word. *...a technicoloured phantasmagoria of carpets, bicycles, laurel bushes... There hovered round the body in the coffin a phantasmagoria of dream-like thoughts.*

phantom /fæntəm/ **phantoms**
1 NC A **phantom** is a ghost; a literary use. *He was found lying in a Baltimore street, delirious and babbling to phantoms. ...a phantom presence.*
2 ADJ ATTRIB **Phantom** is used to describe business organizations, agreements, or goods which do not really exist, but which someone pretends do exist in order to cheat people. *...false customers, phantom contracts... Phantom investment companies had been set up. ...dealing in anything from phantom ships to stolen oil.*

pharaoh /feərəʊ/ **pharaohs**
NC A **pharaoh** was a king of ancient Egypt. *...Thutmose III, an Egyptian pharaoh of the XVIII dynasty.*

Pharisee /færɪsiː/ **Pharisees**
NC The **Pharisees** were a group of Jews, mentioned in the Bible, that believed in strictly obeying the laws of Judaism.

pharmaceutical /fɑːməsjʰuːtɪkl/ **pharmaceuticals**
1 ADJ ATTRIB **Pharmaceutical** means connected with the industrial production of medicines and medical products. *...the world's largest pharmaceutical company.*
2 N PL **Pharmaceuticals** are medicines. *...the sale of pharmaceuticals... The factory will produce only pharmaceuticals.*

pharmacist /fɑːməsɪst/ **pharmacists**
NC A **pharmacist** is a person who is qualified to prepare and sell medicines. *...a pharmacist who worked in a government hospital. ...its new advisory service to pharmacists.*

pharmacology /fɑːməkɒlədʒi/
NU **Pharmacology** is the branch of science relating to drugs and medicines. *...Professor of Clinical Pharmacology at Liverpool University. ...one of the major breakthroughs in pharmacology.*

pharmacy /fɑːməsi/ **pharmacies**
NC A **pharmacy** is a shop where medicines are sold. *The patients go off and buy the drugs from the private pharmacy next door. ...when you walk into a chemist or a pharmacy in the United States.*

phase /feɪz/ **phases, phasing, phased**
1 NC A **phase** is a particular stage in a process or in the development of something. *We have moved into a new phase in European history. ...cameras set to record every phase of the eclipse.*
2 VO If you **phase** a change over a period of time, you cause it to happen in stages. *The reduction in nuclear weapons would be phased over ten years.* ◆ **phased** ADJ ATTRIB *...a phased withdrawal of troops. ...a phased withdrawal from its bases in the Philippines. ...a phased reduction of their armed forces.*

phase in PHRASAL VERB If you **phase in** something new, you introduce it gradually. *...a plan to phase in equal pay.*

phase out PHRASAL VERB If you **phase** something **out**, you gradually stop using it or doing it. *This type of weapon was now being finally phased out. ...if nuclear power were phased out over the next twenty years. ...phasing out tax relief on mortgages.*

phase-out
N SING A **phase-out** is the process of gradually stopping an action or ending a situation. *They're calling for a complete phase-out of these gases by the year 2000. ...to propose a 10-year phase-out for US forces.*

PhD /piːeɪtʃ diː/ **PhDs**
NC A **PhD** is a degree awarded to people who have done advanced research. Someone who has a PhD has the title 'Doctor'. *He had a PhD in physics. ...if I finish my PhD. ...a young PhD student at Cambridge.*

pheasant /feznt/ **pheasants**. The plural form can be either **pheasants** or **pheasant**.
NC A **pheasant** is a bird with a long tail, sometimes shot for sport and then eaten. *Is this a good habitat*

for pheasants? ...enjoying some pheasant shooting... Martin ate some of the white pheasant meat.

phenomena /fənɒmɪnə/
Phenomena is the plural of **phenomenon**.

phenomenal /fənɒmɪnl/
ADJ Something that is **phenomenal** is extraordinarily great or good. *It was a phenomenal success.*
◆ **phenomenally** SUBMOD *It's phenomenally expensive.*

phenomenon /fənɒmɪnən/ **phenomena** /fənɒmɪnə/
NC A **phenomenon** is something that is observed to happen or exist. *...animals and plants and other natural phenomena... Is this concern about energy a recent phenomenon?*

pheromone /ferəməʊn/ **pheromones**
NC **Pheromones** are chemicals that some living creatures produce, which affect other creatures of the same species, for example attracting them sexually. *...the sex pheromones... The females produce the pheromones in a specialised gland.*

phew /fjuː/
Phew is used to represent the sound that you make when you breathe out quickly, for example when you are very hot or when you are relieved. *'Phew,' she said, 'it's hot out.'*

phial /faɪəl/ **phials**
NC A **phial** is a small tube-shaped glass bottle, usually containing liquid medicines used in injections. *...a package which contained two phials. ...a little glass phial.*

philanderer /fɪlændəʰrə/ **philanderers**
NC A **philanderer** is a man who flirts a lot or has a lot of casual love affairs with women; an old-fashioned word, used showing disapproval. *...a sleazy philanderer, who's loved and idolised by four different women.*

philanthropic /fɪlənθrɒpɪk/
ADJ A **philanthropic** person or organization is mainly concerned with helping people, often by giving them money, without wanting anything in return. *...a private philanthropic trust.*

philanthropist /fɪlænθrəpɪst/ **philanthropists**
NC A **philanthropist** is someone whose main concern is to help people, often by giving them money, without wanting anything in return. *...wealthy philanthropists.*

philanthropy /fɪlænθrəpi/
NU **Philanthropy** is the activity of doing helpful actions for other people, often involving giving them money, without wanting anything in return. *...an organization noted for its philanthropy. ...acts of philanthropy or affection.*

philatelist /fɪlætəlɪst/ **philatelists**
NC A **philatelist** is a person who collects and studies postage stamps; a formal word. *King George V was a keen philatelist. ...the encouragement given to philatelists by the great international stamp exhibition.*

philately /fɪlætəli/
NU **Philately** is the hobby of collecting and learning about postage stamps; a formal word. *Half the joy of philately is to show to others the treasures that you have collected. ...a hobby, like beekeeping or philately.*

Philip, Prince /fɪlɪp/
Prince Philip, Duke of Edinburgh, is the husband of Queen Elizabeth II of Great Britain and Northern Ireland. He is the son of Prince Andrew of Greece and Denmark. In 1947, at his marriage, he renounced his succession to the Greek and Danish thrones and adopted his mother's surname of Mountbatten. Born: 1921.

Philippines /fɪlɪpiːnz/
The **Republic of the Philippines** is a country in the western Pacific. It consists of over 7,000 islands, including Luzon and Mindanao. The Philippines were a Spanish colony from the 16th century until 1898, when they were occupied by the United States. They were occupied by Japan from 1941 to 1945 and became independent in 1946. Ferdinand Marcos was President from 1965 to 1986, when Corazon Aquino, widow of the opposition leader Benigno Aquino, became President. She is a member of UNIDO (United Nationalist Democratic Organization). Armed opposition organizations are a serious threat to public order: on Luzon the New People's Army (NPA), a Maoist group,

and on Mindanao, the Moro National Liberation Front (MNLF), a Muslim separatist group. The Philippines are a member of the Association of South East Asian Nations. They produce fruit, copper, metals, wood, clothing, and electrical goods. Cannabis is illegally produced. Large foreign debts and high inflation are major economic problems. ◆ **Filipino, Filipina** /fɪlɪpiːnəʊ, fɪlɪpiːnə/ N, ADJ **Philippine** /fɪlɪpiːn/ ADJ ▪ *per capita GNP:* US$630 ▪ *religion:* Christianity (mainly Roman Catholic), Muslim ▪ *language:* Filipino, English ▪ *currency:* peso ▪ *capital:* Manila ▪ *population:* 60 million (1989) ▪ *size:* 300,000 square kilometres.

philistine /fɪlɪstaɪn/ **philistines**
NC If you say that someone is a **philistine**, you mean that they do not like or care about art, music, or literature; used showing disapproval. *What does a little philistine like you know about it?* ▶ Also ADJ *He raged at a philistine public.*

philistinism /fɪlɪstɪnɪzəm/
NU **Philistinism** is the attitude or fact of not liking or caring about art, music, or literature; used showing disapproval. *She wrote an article lamenting the philistinism of an egalitarian culture.*

philology /fɪlɒlədʒi/
NU **Philology** is the study of words, especially the history and development of the words in a particular language or group of languages. *...those wishing to specialize in Slavonic philology.*

philosopher /fɪlɒsəfə/ **philosophers**
NC A **philosopher** is a person who creates or studies theories about basic things such as the nature of existence or how people should live. *...the Greek philosopher Thales.*

philosophic /fɪləsɒfɪk/
ADJ **Philosophic** means the same as **philosophical**; an old-fashioned or formal word.

philosophical /fɪləsɒfɪkl/
1 ADJ ATTRIB **Philosophical** or **philosophic** means concerned with or relating to philosophy. *They used to have long philosophical conversations. ...the religious and philosophic wisdom of our ancestors.*
2 ADJ Someone who is **philosophical** or has a **philosophic** attitude does not get upset when disappointing or disturbing things happen. *He was a placid boy with a philosophical approach to life... The government kept a certain philosophic detachment.*
◆ **philosophically** ADV *He accepted their conclusion philosophically.*

philosophize /fɪlɒsəfaɪz/ **philosophizes, philosophizing, philosophized**; also spelt **philosophise**.
V Someone who **philosophizes** talks about important subjects such as life, often in a boring, pretentious way. *Academics are indulging in an old Russian pastime—philosophising about things outside their experience.*

philosophy /fɪlɒsəfi/ **philosophies**
1 NU **Philosophy** is the study or creation of theories about subjects such as the nature of existence and knowledge or how people should live. *...an expert on Eastern philosophy.*
2 NC+SUPP A **philosophy** is a particular set of theories or beliefs. *...the political philosophies of the West. ...new philosophies of child rearing.*

phlegm /flem/
NU **Phlegm** is the thick yellowish substance that develops in your throat when you have a cold. *Are you coughing up any phlegm?*

phlegmatic /flegmætɪk/
ADJ Someone who is **phlegmatic** stays calm even when upsetting or exciting things happen; a formal word. *He was a phlegmatic, rather unemotional, certainly undemonstrative man.*

Phnom Penh /pnɒm pen/
Phnom Penh is the capital of Cambodia and its largest city. Population: 800,000 (1989).

phobia /fəʊbiə/ **phobias**
NC A **phobia** is an irrational fear or hatred of something. *I've got a phobia about spiders.*

phobic /fəʊbɪk/ **phobics**
1 ADJ ATTRIB A **phobic** feeling, reaction, and so on results from or is related to a strong, irrational fear or

hatred of something. *...phobic anxieties about going out.*
2 ADJ Someone who is **phobic** has a strong, irrational fear or hatred of something. *There is a general feeling that to be phobic is to be an incomplete person.* ▶ Also NC *...school phobics.*

phoenix /fiːnɪks/ **phoenixes**
NC A **phoenix** is an imaginary bird which, according to ancient myths, burns itself to ashes every five hundred years and is then born again. *Religion, like a phoenix, has been resurrected from the ashes of the revolution.*

Phomvihane, Kaysone /kaɪsɒn pəʊmviːhɑːn/
Kaysone Phomvihane became Prime Minister of Laos in 1975 and President in 1991. He was Commander-in-Chief of Pathet Lao forces from 1954 to 1957. He was General Secretary of the Lao People's Revolutionary Party (LPRP) from 1982 to 1991, and became Chairman in 1991. Born: 1920.

phone /fəʊn/ **phones, phoning, phoned**
1 N SING or NU The **phone** is an electronic system of communication that makes it possible to talk to someone in another place who also has a phone, by dialling a number on a piece of equipment and speaking into it. *Most of the work is carried out over the phone... The Dutch Ambassador told ITN by phone that the Government of President Ceausescu had collapsed.*
2 NC A **phone** is the piece of equipment that you use when you talk to someone by phone. *I'm scared to answer the phone... The phone rang. ...cellular phones.*
3 V OorV When you **phone** someone, you dial their phone number and speak to them by phone. *I went to phone Jenny... Harland phoned to tell me what time the bus was due.*
● **Phone** is used in these phrases. ● If you are **on the phone**, you are speaking to someone by phone. *I spent an hour on the phone trying to sort things out.* ● You also say that you are **on the phone** when you have a phone in your home. *Are you on the phone?*
phone up PHRASAL VERB When you **phone** someone **up**, you dial their number and speak to them by phone. *I must phone her up tonight.*

phone book, phone books
NC A **phone book** is a book containing an alphabetical list of the names, addresses, and telephone numbers of the people in a town or area. *His number was listed in the phone book.*

phone booth, phone booths
NC A **phone booth** is a place in a public building where there is a telephone that can be used by the public. *A phone book hanging in a corner phone booth lists the businesses.*

phone box, phone boxes
NC A **phone box** is the same as a **telephone box**. *Every phone box in Selly Oak had been vandalized.*

phone call, phone calls
NC When you make a **phone call**, you phone someone. *I must go and make a phone call... Newspapers have been receiving phone calls from people trying to get more information about the incident.*

phone-in, phone-ins
NC A **phone-in** is a radio or television programme in which people telephone the broadcasting company with questions or opinions and their calls are broadcast. *Paul McCartney went on a live phone-in to the Soviet Union via the BBC Russian Service. ...a radio phone-in programme.*

phone tapping
NU **Phone tapping** is the activity of attaching a special device to someone's telephone line in order to listen secretly to their phone conversations. In most cases phone tapping is illegal. *Today's report is a yearly statement on the extent of official phone tapping.*

phonetic /fənetɪk/ **phonetics**; a technical term.
1 NU **Phonetics** is the study of speech sounds. *He studied acoustic theory and phonetics.*
2 ADJ ATTRIB **Phonetic** means relating to the sound of a word or to the sounds that are used in languages. *Phonetic methods stressing the learning of individual letters are decried as merely instilling 'decoding skills'.*
3 ADJ ATTRIB A **phonetic** system of spelling is one in

which a sound is represented by one written symbol
and each written symbol represents only one sound.
*Japanese word-processors usually operate with
phonetic typing on a Western keyboard.* ◆ **phonetically**
/fənetıkəˈli/ *We have a twenty thousand word
dictionary which you can look up phonetically.* ● See
also **IPA**.

phoney /ˈfəuni/ **phoneys**; also spelt **phony**. An informal
word.
1 ADJ Something that is **phoney** is false. *The
accounting, they claim, is phoney... At least $17
million were transferred to a phoney insurance
company in the Bahamas.*
2 ADJ Someone who is **phoney** is insincere or
pretentious. *He thought all grown-ups were phony.*
▶ Also NC *I suddenly realized what a phoney he is.*

phonograph /ˈfəunəgrɑːf/ **phonographs**
NC A **phonograph** is the same as a **record player**; an
old-fashioned word. *We played cards and listened to
the phonograph.*

phonology /fəˈnɒlədʒi/
NU **Phonology** is the study of the speech sounds in a
particular language; a technical term in linguistics.
*...a two term course in phonology, language origin,
and linguistic change.* ◆ **phonological** /ˌfəunəˈlɒdʒıkl/
ADJ ATTRIB *...important phonological distinctions.*

phony /ˈfəuni/. See **phoney**.

phosphate /ˈfɒsfeɪt/ **phosphates**
NCorNU A **phosphate** is a chemical compound that
contains phosphorus. Phosphates are often used in
fertilizers. *...detergents containing phosphates. ...the
state-owned phosphate mining company.*

phosphorescence /ˌfɒsfəˈresns/
NU **Phosphorescence** is a glow or brightness which is
produced without using heat; a literary word.
...letters that shine with a fearful phosphorescence.

phosphorescent /ˌfɒsfəˈresnt/
ADJ Something that is **phosphorescent** glows with a
soft light but gives out little or no heat; a formal
word. *...a phosphorescent gas.*

phosphorus /ˈfɒsfərəs/
NU **Phosphorus** is a poisonous whitish substance that
glows faintly and that burns when it is in contact with
air. *The Kurds accused the army of using napalm and
phosphorus... The explosion was caused by a
phosphorus bomb.*

photo /ˈfəutəu/ **photos**
NC A **photo** is the same as a **photograph**; an informal
word. *I took a magnificent photo of him.*

photo- /ˈfəutəu-, fəutɒ-/
PREFIX **Photo-** is added to nouns and adjectives in
order to form other nouns and adjectives which refer
or relate to photography. *...photo-journalism.
...photomontage. ...photoengraving.*

photocopier /ˈfəutəukɒpiə/ **photocopiers**
NC A **photocopier** is a machine which quickly copies
documents by photographing them. *In most offices the
photocopier is one of the most needed and most hated
things there is.*

photocopy /ˈfəutəukɒpi/ **photocopies, photocopying,
photocopied**
1 NC A **photocopy** is a copy of a document made using
a photocopier. *He made a photocopy of the telegram.*
2 VO If you **photocopy** a document, you make a copy
of it using a photocopier. *Workers can photocopy their
work histories and make telephone calls for new jobs.*
◆ **photocopied** ADJ ATTRIB *Her classroom is cluttered
with borrowed and photocopied books, pamphlets, and
articles.*

photo finish
N SING If a race ends in a **photo finish**, two or more
competitors cross the finishing line so close together
that a photograph has to be examined to find out who
has won. *He won the 400 metres on a photo finish.*

Photofit /ˈfəutəufɪt/
N+N A **photofit** picture is a picture of someone wanted
by the police that has been made up from several
photographs of different facial features; **Photofit** is a
trademark. *They issued a photofit picture of a man
they want to question.*

photogenic /ˌfəutəˈdʒenɪk/
ADJ Someone who is **photogenic** looks attractive in

photographs. *Photogenic girls were sought for a series
of adverts.*

photograph /ˈfəutəgrɑːf/ **photographs, photographing,
photographed**
1 NC A **photograph** is a picture that is made using a
camera. *They contacted the police after seeing his
photograph in a newspaper.*
2 VO When you **photograph** someone or something, you
use a camera to obtain a picture of them. *She
photographed the pigeons in Trafalgar Square.*

photographer /fəˈtɒgrəfə/ **photographers**
NC A **photographer** is someone who takes photographs,
especially as their job. *...a press photographer. ...a
keen amateur photographer.*

photographic /ˌfəutəˈgræfɪk/
1 ADJ ATTRIB **Photographic** means connected with
photography. *...expensive photographic equipment.*
2 ADJ ATTRIB If you have a **photographic** memory, you
can remember things in great detail after seeing them
once. *People memorise dates by using regularities in
the calendar, and don't rely simply on a photographic
memory.*

photography /fəˈtɒgrəfi/
NU **Photography** is the skill, job, or process of
producing photographs. *Fox-Talbot was a pioneer of
photography.*

photo session, photo sessions
NC A **photo session** is a short period of time during
which a famous person or people allow journalists or
professional photographers to take photographs of
them. *Mr Gorbachev rejected the rumours during a
photo session before talks with the President.*

Photostat /ˈfəutəstæt/ **Photostats**
NC A **photostat** is a particular type of photocopy;
Photostat is a trademark. *...a photostat of the report.*

phrasal verb, phrasal verbs
NC A **phrasal verb** is a combination of a verb and an
adverb or preposition, used together to have a
particular meaning. 'Give up' and 'set out' are phrasal
verbs.

phrase /freɪz/ **phrases, phrasing, phrased**
1 NC A **phrase** is a group of words which forms a unit,
either on its own or within a sentence. *...a key phrase
in the White Paper.*
2 NC A **phrase** is also a short group of words that are
used as a unit and whose meaning is not obvious from
the words contained in it. *People still use the phrase
'doctor's orders'.*
3 VOA If you **phrase** something in a particular way,
the words you speak or write express it in that way.
*The moment I'd said it, I could see that I'd phrased it
wrong.*
4 A **turn of phrase** is a particular way of expressing
something in words. *You have a nice turn of phrase.*

phrase book, phrase books
NC A **phrase book** is a book for travellers with lists of
useful words and expressions in a foreign language,
together with the translation of each word or
expression. *A phrase book might come in handy.*

phraseology /ˌfreɪziˈɒlədʒi/
NU+SUPP If something is expressed using a particular
phraseology, it is expressed in words and expressions
of that type; a formal word. *...the sort of phraseology
used by some journalists.*

phrasing /ˈfreɪzɪŋ/
1 NU The **phrasing** of something that is said is the
exact words that are used to say it. *...the careful
phrasing of the Minister's statement.*
2 NU The **phrasing** of someone who is singing, playing
a piece of music, acting, or reading poetry is the way
in which they divide up the work that they are
performing by pausing slightly in appropriate places.
Her phrasing was faultless.

phrenology /frəˈnɒlədʒi/
NU **Phrenology** is the science of finding out what
people's characters and abilities are by examining the
shape and size of their skulls. *In the new science of
phrenology, apparently all the secrets of character are
revealed by the bumps on the head.*

physical /ˈfɪzɪkl/
1 ADJ ATTRIB **Physical** qualities, actions, or things are
connected with a person's body, rather than with their

mind. *All his physical and emotional needs would be attended to.* ♦ **physically** ADV *He looked physically fit... She didn't attract me physically.*
2 ADJ ATTRIB **Physical** also refers to things that can be touched or seen, especially with regard to their size or shape. *...the physical characteristics of the earth. ...the physical size of a computer. ...piecing together all the physical evidence from the scene.* ♦ **physically** ADV *They cause water vapour and nitrogen compounds to be physically removed from the atmosphere... Soldiers have been sent to physically wipe out the cocaine laboratories.*
3 ADJ ATTRIB You can refer to things connected with physics as **physical**. *...basic physical laws.*

physical education
NU **Physical education** consists of the lessons in school in which children do physical exercises or take part in physical games or sports. Physical education is often abbreviated to 'PE'. *...a timetable for physical education. ...a trained physical education instructor.*

physical jerks
N PL **Physical jerks** are physical exercises that people do to keep fit; an old-fashioned expression.

physical science, physical sciences
NCorNU The **physical sciences** are sciences such as physics, chemistry, and geology that are concerned with non-living things and natural forces. *...the life sciences and the physical sciences. ...the division of physical science into chemistry and physics.*

physical training
NU **Physical training** is the same as **physical education**; an old-fashioned expression. *They have regular parades and do physical training together.*

physician /fɪzɪʃn/ **physicians**
NC A **physician** is a doctor; used in American English. *...the chief physician on the ward.*

physicist /fɪzɪsɪst/ **physicists**
NC A **physicist** is a person who studies physics. *...a well-known nuclear physicist.*

physics /fɪzɪks/
NU **Physics** is the scientific study of forces and qualities such as heat, light, sound, pressure, gravity, and electricity. *According to our present ideas of physics, nothing can travel faster than light. ...nuclear physics. ...the study of the mathematical laws that explain quantum physics.*

physio /fɪziəʊ/ **physios**; an informal word.
1 NU **Physio** is the same as **physiotherapy**. *When we talk about physio and physiotherapy it's how to exercise the limbs isn't it?*
2 NC A **physio** is also the same as a **physiotherapist**. *The referee sensed something was wrong because he called on the Tottenham physio immediately.*

physiognomy /fɪziɒnəmi/ **physiognomies**; a formal word.
1 NC Your **physiognomy** is your face; used especially when your face is considered to show your character. *He kept his eyes fixed upon the benign physiognomy of Mr Didlington.*
2 N SING The **physiognomy** of an area of countryside is its shape and the geographical features in it, such as hills and rivers.

physiologically /fɪziəlɒdʒɪkəʰli/
ADV **Physiologically** means relating to the body. *...the ability to survive physiologically.*

physiologist /fɪziɒlədʒɪst/ **physiologists**
NC A **physiologist** is a person who studies human and animal bodies and how they work.

physiology /fɪziɒlədʒi/
1 NU **Physiology** is the scientific study of how people, animals, and plants function. *...the International Centre for Insect Physiology.*
2 N SING+POSS The **physiology** of an animal or plant is the way that it functions. *He was interested in the physiology of bulls.* ♦ **physiological** /fɪziəlɒdʒɪkl/ ADJ *...physiological changes.*

physiotherapist /fɪziəʊθerəpɪst/ **physiotherapists**
NC A **physiotherapist** is a person whose job is doing physiotherapy. *They start to regain their strength and mobility in the gym, under the guidance of a physiotherapist.*

physiotherapy /fɪziəʊθerəpi/
NU **Physiotherapy** is medical treatment given to people who cannot move a part of their body and involves exercise, massage, or heat treatment. *He'll need intensive physiotherapy to counter any long term effects.*

physique /fɪziːk/ **physiques**
NCorNU Someone's **physique** is the shape and size of their body. *...a good-looking lad with a fine physique.*

pi /paɪ/
Pi is a number, approximately 3.142, which is equal to the circumference of a circle divided by its diameter. It is usually represented by the Greek letter π.

pianist /pɪənɪst/ **pianists**
NC A **pianist** is a person who plays the piano. *He was outstanding as a concert pianist.*

piano /pɪænəʊ/ **pianos**
NC A **piano** is a large musical instrument with a row of black and white keys. You strike the keys with your fingers in order to make a sound. *I was invited to play piano in a jazz band.* ● See also **grand piano**.

pianoforte /pɪænəʊfɔːti/ **pianofortes**
NCorNU A **pianoforte** is the same as a **piano**; a formal or old-fashioned word.

picaresque /pɪkəresk/
ADJ A **picaresque** story is one in which a dishonest but likeable hero travels around and has lots of exciting adventures; a literary word. *...adventures as picaresque and unlikely as those of any hero of romance.*

piccalilli /pɪkəlɪli/
NU **Piccalilli** is a sharp-tasting yellow sauce made from chopped and pickled vegetables.

piccolo /pɪkələʊ/ **piccolos**
NC A **piccolo** is a very small musical instrument that is shaped like a flute but produces higher notes.

pick /pɪk/ **picks, picking, picked**
1 VO If you **pick** a particular person or thing, you choose that one. *Next time let's pick somebody else... I could not have picked a better way to travel.*
2 VO When you **pick** flowers, fruit, or leaves, you break them off the plant and collect them. *...the woods where we picked blackberries.*
3 VOA If you **pick** something from a place, you remove it from there with your fingers. *...the teacher who picks imaginary pieces of fluff from his jacket.*
4 VO If you **pick** an argument with someone, you deliberately cause one. *He had ceased to pick quarrels with her.*
5 VO If someone **picks** a lock, they open it without using a key, for example by using a piece of wire.
6 VO If you **pick** a musical instrument such as a guitar or banjo, you play it by quickly pulling the individual strings.
7 If you **pick** your **way** across an area, you walk across it carefully, avoiding any obstacles. *He began to pick his way over the rocks.*
8 NC A **pick** is a **pickaxe**. *I got torn and bleeding hands working with a pick and shovel.*
9 to **pick** someone's **brains**: see **brain**. to **pick holes in** something: see **hole**. to **pick** someone's **pocket**: see **pocket**. See also **hand-picked**.

pick at PHRASAL VERB If you **pick at** the food you are eating, you eat only very small amounts of it. *Laing was picking morosely at his salad.*

pick off PHRASAL VERB If someone **picks off** people or things, they kill or destroy them one by one. *Troops escorted him everywhere he went, evidently afraid that he could be picked off by sniper fire... The government's tactics are now clearly to pick off the smaller strikes around the country.*

pick on PHRASAL VERB If you **pick on** someone, you criticize them unfairly or are unkind to them; an informal expression. *Why are you always picking on me?*

pick out PHRASAL VERB 1 If you **pick out** someone or something, you recognize them when it is difficult to see them. *Ralph picked out Jack easily, even at that distance.* 2 If you **pick out** someone or something from a group of people or things, you choose them. *I think there are two stories we could pick out of our book.*

pick up PHRASAL VERB 1 When you **pick** an object **up**, you lift it up. *He stooped down to pick up the two pebbles.* 2 When you **pick** yourself **up** after you have fallen or been knocked down, you stand up rather slowly. *He picked himself up and walked away.* 3 When you **pick up** something or someone, you collect them from somewhere. *I might get my brother to come and pick me up.* 4 If someone is **picked up** by the police, they are arrested. *I don't want you to be picked up for drunkenness.* 5 If you **pick up** a skill or an idea, you acquire it without effort; an informal use. *Did you pick up any Swedish?... I may pick up a couple of useful ideas for my book.* 6 If you **pick up** someone you do not know, you talk to them and try to start a sexual relationship with them; an informal use. *I doubt whether Tony ever picked up a woman in his life.* 7 If a piece of equipment **picks up** a signal or sound, it receives it or detects it. *It was easier to pick up Radio Luxembourg than the Light Programme.* 8 If you **pick up** something, such as a feature or pattern, you discover or identify it. *We believe we've been able to pick up a particular feature.* 9 If someone **picks up** a point or topic that has already been mentioned, or if they **pick up on** it, they refer to it or develop it. *Can I pick up your point about Mr Milosevic?... Two of the papers pick up on the latest controversy in the elections.* 10 If something such as the trade or the economy of a country **picks up**, it improves or increases. *The economy is picking up... Interest in Russia is already beginning to pick up.* 11 If someone **picks up**, or their health **picks up**, they get better. *A good dose of tonic will help you to pick up.* 12 If you **pick up the pieces** after a disaster, you do what you can to get the situation back to normal again or to make it better. *What we've got to do now is try and pick up the pieces and get on with the business.* 13 See also **pick-up**.

pickaxe /pɪkæks/ **pickaxes**; spelt **pickax** in American English.
NC A **pickaxe** is a tool consisting of a curved, pointed piece of metal with a long handle joined to the middle. Pickaxes are used for breaking up rocks or the ground. *...a farmer, wielding a pickaxe... The police found a number of weapons including knives and pickaxe handles.*

picker /pɪkə/ **pickers**
NC+SUPP A fruit **picker** or cotton **picker** is a person who picks fruit or cotton, usually for money. *...strawberry pickers.*

picket /pɪkɪt/ **pickets, picketing, picketed**
1 VOorVA When a group of workers who are on strike **picket** a place of work, they stand outside it as a protest and try to prevent other workers going into the building. *The plan was to picket docks and power stations... 100 union members picketed outside.* ▸ Also NC *...the historic picket at Saltley coke depot.*
♦ **picketing** NU *...before the mass picketing and its consequent mass arrests began.*
2 NC **Pickets** are people who are picketing a place of work. *We could hear the chanting of the pickets.*

picket line, picket lines
NC A **picket line** is a group of pickets outside a place of work. *The engineering union have joined them on the picket line.*

pickings /pɪkɪŋz/
N PL+SUPP You can refer to the money that can be made easily in a particular place, enterprise, or area of activity as the **pickings**. *Others found rich pickings in the field of insurance... You think you can find easier pickings here.*

pickle /pɪkl/ **pickles, pickling, pickled**
1 NCorNU **Pickles** are vegetables or fruit which have been kept in vinegar or salt water for a long time to give them a strong sharp taste. *...a jar of pickles... You can make pickle from them.*
2 VO When you **pickle** food, you preserve it by keeping it in vinegar or salt water. *To pickle herring, soak the fish in salted water.*

pickled /pɪkld/
1 ADJ ATTRIB **Pickled** vegetables, meat, and so on have been kept in vinegar or salt water to preserve them. *His breath smelled of beer and pickled onions. ...pickled herring.*

2 ADJ PRED Someone who is **pickled** is drunk; an informal use.

pick-me-up, pick-me-ups
NC A **pick-me-up** is a drink that you have in order to make you feel healthier and more energetic; an informal word. *Tea is a good pick-me-up.*

pickpocket /pɪkpɒkɪt/ **pickpockets**
NC A **pickpocket** is a person who steals things from people's pockets or handbags. *They were prey to pickpockets and other criminals.*

pick-up, pick-ups
1 NC A **pick-up** or a **pick-up** truck is a small truck with low sides that can be easily loaded and unloaded. *The pick-up then sped off... They were driven off on a pick-up truck.*
2 NC+in A **pick-up** in trade or in a country's economy is an improvement in it. *...the pick-up in economic activity. ...a more modest pick-up in export.*
3 NC When a **pick-up** takes place, someone talks to another person in a friendly way in the hope of having a casual sexual relationship with them; an informal use. *The practice of 'cottaging', hanging around public lavatories in the hope of a pick-up, was hazardous, particularly for an MP.*
4 NC A **pick-up**, is a device that turns vibrations into sound, for example on a telephone or an electric guitar. *...a pick-up lead attached to the handset.*

picky /pɪki/ **pickier, pickiest**
ADJ Someone who is **picky** is difficult to please and only likes a small range of things; an informal word. *Let's not be too picky!... Sinatra is picky about what he sings.*

picnic /pɪknɪk/ **picnics, picnicking, picnicked**
1 NC When people have a **picnic**, they eat a meal in the open air. *They often went on picnics.*
2 VorVA When people **picnic**, they eat a picnic somewhere. *The woods might be full of people picnicking... The Somme is visited by thousands of sightseers every year, some of whom picnic in the trenches.*

picnicker /pɪknɪkə/ **picnickers**
NC A **picnicker** is someone who is having a picnic. *In October, picnickers were unlikely.*

pictorial /pɪktɔːrɪəl/
ADJ ATTRIB **Pictorial** means relating to or using pictures. *...pictorial conventions. ...pictorial skills.*

picture /pɪktʃə/ **pictures, picturing, pictured**
1 NC A **picture** is a drawing or painting. *...the most important picture Picasso ever painted... He picked up a book to look at the pictures.*
2 NC A **picture** is also a photograph. *We all had our pictures taken.*
3 VO If someone or something is **pictured** in a newspaper or magazine, they appear in a photograph in it. *Murray was pictured in The Times.*
4 NC You can refer to the image you see on a television screen as a **picture**. *We have all seen television news pictures of their forces in action.*
5 NC You can also refer to a film that is shown in the cinema as a **picture**. *We worked together in the last picture I made.*
6 N PL The **pictures** is another word for the cinema. *She met him at the pictures.*
7 NC If you have a **picture** of something, you have an idea or impression of it in your mind. *A picture flashed through Kunta's mind of the panther springing at him... He already has a clear picture of the sort of people that he wants.*
8 VO If you **picture** something in your mind, you have a clear mental image of what it is like or what it would be like. *He could picture all too easily the consequences of being caught.*
9 NC If you give a **picture** of what something is like, you describe it. *Mr Hamilton gives a most interesting picture of Monty's family background.*
10 N SING When you refer to the **picture** in a particular place or with regard to a particular thing or group, you are referring to the situation in that place or in regard to that thing or group. *In Nigeria, the picture appears to be different... The economic picture is far from good.*
11 If you **put** someone **in the picture**, you give them

the details of a situation. *Let me put you in the picture about the situation there.*

picture rail, picture rails
NC A **picture rail** is a narrow piece of wood which is fixed to the walls of a room just below the ceiling that pictures can be hung from.

picturesque /pɪktʃəˈresk/
ADJ A **picturesque** place is attractive, interesting, and unspoiled. *...a small hotel overlooking the picturesque fishing harbour of Zeebrugge... While their family lifestyle is picturesque, it's the exception.*

piddle /ˈpɪdl/ **piddles, piddling, piddled**
V When someone **piddles**, they urinate; an informal word.

piddling /ˈpɪdəʰlɪŋ/
ADJ **Piddling** means small or not important; an informal word. *...piddling little jobs... They gave her a piddling sum by way of compensation.*

pidgin /ˈpɪdʒɪn/ **pidgins**
NCorNU A **pidgin** is a language which is a mixture of two other languages. A pidgin is not usually anyone's native language but is used when people who speak different languages communicate with each other. ► Also ADJ ATTRIB *They spoke pidgin English.*

pie /paɪ/ **pies**
NCorNU A **pie** consists of meat, vegetables, or fruit, baked in pastry. *...chicken pie. ...a piece of apple pie.*

piebald /ˈpaɪbɔːld/
ADJ Something, especially an animal, that is **piebald** has patches of two different colours on it, usually black and white. *...a thin piebald pony.*

piece /piːs/ **pieces, piecing, pieced**
1 NC A **piece** of something is a portion, part, or section of it. *He came back dragging a great big piece of a tree... He tore both letters into small pieces... She cut the cake and gave me a piece.*
2 NC A **piece** of something is also an individual item of it. *The only piece of clothing she bought was a jumper. ...the most important piece of apparatus.*
3 N SING You use **piece** to refer to an individual group of facts or an individual action or product. *...a valuable piece of information. ...a thoughtful piece of research. ...this piece of advice.*
4 NC A **piece** is also something that is written or created, such as an article, work of art, or musical composition. *...a thoughtful piece about President Roosevelt... It was a classic piece called Forever Is For Us.*
5 NC+SUPP You can refer to specific coins as **pieces**. For example, a 10p **piece** is a coin that is worth 10p. *...a lighter that was no bigger than a 50p piece.*
6 NC In a board game, the **pieces** are the objects which you move around the board. *...two chess pieces in the shape of elephants.*
● **Piece** is used in these phrases. ● If someone or something is still **in one piece** after a dangerous experience, they are not damaged or hurt. *Surprisingly, most of the crockery was in one piece.* ● If you **go to pieces**, you lose control of yourself because you are nervous or upset; an informal expression. *He did not go to pieces as I feared he might.* ● If someone **tears** you **to pieces** or **pulls** your work **to pieces**, they criticize you or your work very severely; an informal expression. *He never praised you and he never tore you to pieces... I explained my theory and he just pulled it to pieces.* ● **a piece of cake**: see **cake**.

piece together PHRASAL VERB 1 If you **piece together** the truth about something, you gradually discover it. *She had not yet been able to piece together exactly what had happened.* 2 If you **piece** something **together**, you gradually make it complete by joining its parts together. *She pieced together the torn-up drawing.*

-piece /-piːs/
SUFFIX **-piece** combines with numbers to indicate that a set of things contains a particular number of items or members. *...this four-piece all-female band. ...men in dark, three-piece suits.*

pièce de résistance /piˌes də reɪˈzɪstɒnॱs/
N SING The **pièce de résistance** of a group or series of things is the most important or impressive item in it. *This was the pièce de résistance of her performance.*

piecemeal /ˈpiːsmiːl/
ADJorADV A **piecemeal** process happens gradually, usually at irregular intervals. *...the piecemeal accumulation of land... Films are financed piecemeal; the distributor doles out money little by little.*

piecework /ˈpiːswɜːk/
NU If you do **piecework**, you are paid for the amount of work you do rather than the length of time you work. *Because piecework forces an even faster rate of work, it reduces the quality of work produced.*

pied-à-terre /piˌeɪdætˈeə/ **pieds-à-terre**. The plural is pronounced in the same way as the singular.
NC A **pied-à-terre** is a small house or flat, especially in a town, which you own but only use occasionally.

pie-eyed
ADJ Someone who is **pie-eyed** is drunk; an informal word.

pier /pɪə/ **piers**
NC A **pier** is a large platform which sticks out into the sea and which people can walk along. *The Authority has granted a licence for a pier and moorings.*

pierce /pɪəs/ **pierces, piercing, pierced**
VOorVA If you **pierce** something with a sharp object, the object goes into it and makes a hole. *When the snake's fangs pierce its victim's flesh, the venom is injected... The pointed end of the stick pierced through its throat into its mouth.*

pierced /pɪəst/
ADJ A **pierced** object has had holes made in it deliberately. *...pierced wooden screens. ...pierced ears.*

piercing /ˈpɪəsɪŋ/
1 ADJ A **piercing** sound is high-pitched and sharp in an unpleasant way. *I was jolted out of my exhaustion by piercing screams.*
2 ADJ Someone with **piercing** eyes has bright eyes which seem to look at you very intensely. *He had piercing blue eyes.*
3 ADJ A **piercing** wind is very cold. *I was trembling in a piercing draught.*

pierrot /ˈpɪərəʊ/ **pierrots**
NC A **pierrot** is a clown or entertainer who wears a white costume and a white pointed hat and whose face is covered with white make-up.

piety /ˈpaɪəti/
NU **Piety** is strong religious belief, or religious behaviour. *...men of true piety. ...this period of fasting and religious piety.*

piffle /ˈpɪfl/
NU If you describe what someone says as **piffle**, you mean that you think that it is nonsense; an informal word.

piffling /ˈpɪfəʰlɪŋ/
ADJ Something that is **piffling** is small or unimportant, and ridiculous; an informal word. *The steps taken are so piffling in the face of the enormity of the problem.*

pig /pɪg/ **pigs**
1 NC A **pig** is a farm animal which is bred for its meat. *It is the first recorded case of a pig getting the disease.*
2 NC If you call someone a **pig**, you mean that you think they are greedy, unkind, or unpleasant in some way; an offensive use. *I couldn't just say, 'Oh, you pig,' and push him over and walk away.*
3 If you **make a pig of** yourself, you eat too much; an informal expression. *Make a right pig of yourself, eat them all at once, and enjoy it.*

pigeon /ˈpɪdʒɪn/ **pigeons**
NC A **pigeon** is a grey bird which is often seen in towns. *...huge flocks of pigeons.*

pigeon-hole, pigeon-holes
NC A **pigeon-hole** is one of the sections in a frame on a wall where letters and messages can be left. *Howard strolled over to the rows of pigeon-holes to collect his mail.*

piggery /ˈpɪgəri/ **piggeries**
NC A **piggery** is a farm or a part of a farm where pigs are kept. *...the effluent from the piggery.*

piggy /ˈpɪgi/ **piggies**; an informal word.
1 NC Young children often refer to a pig as a **piggy**.
2 ADJ Someone who is **piggy** is greedy or selfish; used by children.

3 ADJ ATTRIB If someone has **piggy** eyes, their eyes are small and unattractive.

piggyback /pɪgibæk/ **piggybacks**
NC If you give someone a **piggyback**, you carry them high on your back, supporting them under their knees.

piggybank /pɪgibæŋk/ **piggybanks**
NC A **piggybank** is a small container shaped like a pig, with a slot in it to put coins in. Children use piggybanks to save money in. *A boy opened up his piggybank where he found 100 coins totalling exactly $5.*

piggy in the middle
1 NU **Piggy in the middle** or **pig in the middle** is a game in which two children throw a ball to each other while a third child stands between them and tries to catch it.
2 If someone **is piggy in the middle** or **is pig in the middle**, they are unwillingly involved in or affected by a quarrel between two other people or groups. *I'm sick of being piggy in the middle all the time!*

pig-headed
ADJ Someone who is **pig-headed** refuses to change their mind about things; used showing disapproval. *...sheer pig-headed determination.*

piglet /pɪglət/ **piglets**
NC A **piglet** is a young pig. *The moment came to round up the piglets.*

pigment /pɪgmənt/ **pigments**
NCorNU A **pigment** is a substance that gives something a particular colour; a formal word. *It forms part of the red pigment of blood... I persisted with brush, pigment, and canvas.*

pigmentation /pɪgmenteɪʃn/
NU The **pigmentation** of a person, animal, or plant is the natural colouring it has; a formal word. *...the dark skin pigmentation of people living near the equator.*

pigmy /pɪgmi/. See **pygmy**.

pigpen /pɪgpen/ **pigpens**
NC A **pigpen** is the same as a **pigsty**; used in American English.

pigskin /pɪgskɪn/
NUorN+N **Pigskin** is a fine leather made from the skin of pigs. *She had a new pigskin case.*

pigsty /pɪgstaɪ/ **pigsties**
NC A **pigsty** is a hut with a yard where pigs are kept.

pigtail /pɪgteɪl/ **pigtails**
NC A **pigtail** is a length of plaited hair. *...a girl with a blonde pigtail down her back.*

pike /paɪk/; **pike** is both the singular and the plural form.
NC A **pike** is a large river fish that catches other fish. *A species known as Nile pike lives in murky water.*

pikestaff /paɪkstɑːf/
If something is **as plain as a pikestaff**, it is very obvious or easy to see; an old-fashioned expression. *There it was in black and white, as plain as a pikestaff: 'No pets allowed'.*

pilchard /pɪltʃəd/ **pilchards**
NC A **pilchard** is a small fish that lives in the sea. *...tins of pilchards.*

pile /paɪl/ **piles, piling, piled**
1 NC+SUPP A **pile** of things is a quantity of them lying on top of one another. *There in front of me was a great pile of old tin cans. ...a pile of sand... He lifted a pile of books from the bedside table.*
2 VOA If you **pile** a quantity of things somewhere, you put them there so that they form a pile. *Brody piled the heap of papers on top of a radiator.*
3 VO If something **is piled** with things, or **is piled** high with them, it is covered with piles of them. *His desk was piled with papers. ...the streets of the city were piled high with overturned cars and wreckage.*
4 NC A **pile** or **piles** of something is a large amount of it; an informal use. *He's got an enormous pile of money stashed away.*
5 VA If people **pile** into or out of a place, they all go into it or out of it in a disorganized way. *The troops piled into the coaches.*
6 NPL **Piles** are painful swellings in the veins inside a person's anus.
7 NU The **pile** of a carpet is its soft surface, which

consists of lots of little threads standing on end. *...a luxurious deep pile carpet.*

pile up PHRASAL VERB **1** If you **pile** things **up**, you gather them together in a pile. *Her hair had been piled up on top of her head... The papers she was meant to be reading piled up on her desk.* **2** If things **pile up**, or if you **pile up** things, more and more of them happen or are acquired. *All these disasters piled up on the unfortunate villagers... Last year the company piled up losses totalling £4 billion.*

pile-up, pile-ups
NC A **pile-up** is a road accident involving several vehicles. *Nearly two-hundred cars and trucks were involved in the pile-up, which happened in thick fog.*

pilfer /pɪlfə/ **pilfers, pilfering, pilfered**
VorVO If someone **pilfers** things, usually inexpensive things, they steal them. *He habitually pilfered from supermarkets... They are pilfering car stereos.*
♦ **pilfering** NU *There is remarkably little pilfering.*

pilgrim /pɪlgrɪm/ **pilgrims**
NC A **pilgrim** is a person who makes a journey to a holy place. *...an influx of around two million pilgrims. ...a gathering of Muslim pilgrims.*

pilgrimage /pɪlgrɪmɪdʒ/ **pilgrimages**
NCorNU A **pilgrimage** is a journey that someone makes to a holy place. *She made the pilgrimage to Lourdes. ...a place of pilgrimage.*

pill /pɪl/ **pills**
1 NC A **pill** is a small, round mass of medicine that you swallow. *I took a sleeping pill.*
2 N SING The **pill** is a type of drug that women can take regularly to prevent pregnancy. *I'm not on the pill.*
3 If you describe an event or situation as a **bitter pill**, or say that it is a **bitter pill to swallow**, you mean that it is very disappointing or unpleasant. *It will be a bitter pill for the General... The paper says the participants would have some bitter pills to swallow in return for peace.*

pillage /pɪlɪdʒ/ **pillages, pillaging, pillaged**
VO If a group of people **pillage** a place, they steal property from it in a violent way; a formal word. *They pillaged and looted every house in the village.*
► Also NU *...looting and pillage by people searching for food.* ♦ **pillaging** NU *...the pillaging of the French ambassador's residence.*

pillar /pɪlə/ **pillars**
1 NC A **pillar** is a tall, narrow, solid structure, which is used to support part of a building. *I fell asleep leaning against a pillar on someone's porch.*
2 NC+SUPP Someone who is a **pillar** of a particular group is an active and important member of it. *I thought you had to be a pillar of the community to foster children. ...pillars of society.*

pillar box, pillar boxes
NC A **pillar box** is a red box in the street in which you put letters that you are sending by post; an old-fashioned word.

pillared /pɪləd/
ADJ A **pillared** building or part of a building has pillars supporting it. *...under the pillared arcade.*

pillbox /pɪlbɒks/ **pillboxes**
NC A **pillbox** is a tiny tin or box which you can use to carry pills in. *She groped in her handbag for her pillbox.*

pillion /pɪljən/
ADVorADJ If you ride **pillion** on a motorcycle, or if you are a **pillion** passenger, you sit behind the person who is controlling it. *... a youth riding pillion on a scooter... His pillion passenger was thrown off and into a car.*

pillory /pɪləri/ **pillories, pillorying, pilloried**
1 VO If someone is **pilloried**, they are criticized severely, especially in newspapers or on radio and television; a formal use. *He was pilloried in the newspapers and his resignation was demanded... The attempts to pillory him backfired.*
2 NC In Europe in the Middle Ages, a **pillory** was a wooden frame with holes for the head and hands where criminals were locked for a period of time as a punishment.

pillow /pɪləʊ/ **pillows**
NC A **pillow** is a rectangular cushion which you rest your head on when you are in bed. *She pulled the covers over him and straightened his pillow.*

pillowcase /pɪləʊkeɪs/ **pillowcases**
NC A **pillowcase** is a cover for a pillow.

pillowslip /pɪləʊslɪp/ **pillowslips**
NC A **pillowslip** is the same as a **pillowcase**; an old-fashioned word.

pillow talk
NU The intimate conversations that people have when they are in bed together can be referred to as **pillow talk**.

pilot /paɪlət/ **pilots, piloting, piloted**
1 NC A **pilot** is a person who flies an aircraft as a job. *The pilot of the plane was forced to fly to San Jose airport.*
2 NC A **pilot** is also someone who steers a ship through a difficult stretch of water such as the entrance to a harbour. *As the ship eases towards the dock, the pilot guides the captain around the partly sunken patrol boats.*
3 VO When someone **pilots** an aircraft or a ship, they act as its pilot. *...the replica of the fighter plane Mr Bush piloted during the Second World War.*
4 VO If you **pilot** a new law or scheme, you introduce it. *He was keen to see through the Bill which John Silkin was piloting.*
5 ADJ ATTRIB **Pilot** is used to describe something, such as a scheme or project, which is done as a test on a small scale in order to see whether it will be successful. *This year we are trying a pilot scheme whereby the university leases one or two houses for students... A pilot plant will be built and field trials will begin.*

pilotless /paɪlətləs/
ADJ ATTRIB A **pilotless** aircraft is one that can fly without a pilot. *...the successful maiden flight of a pilotless aircraft.*

pilot light, pilot lights
NC A **pilot light** is a small gas flame in a cooker, boiler, or heater which burns all the time and lights the main large flame when the gas is turned fully on. *Don't leave your oven with the pilot light on.*

pimento /pɪmentəʊ/ **pimentos**
NC A **pimento** is a mild-tasting red pepper.

pimp /pɪmp/ **pimps**
NC A **pimp** is a man who finds clients for prostitutes and takes a large part of their earnings; an informal word. *...an influx of prostitutes protected by pimps.*

pimple /pɪmpl/ **pimples**
NC **Pimples** are small red spots, especially on your face. *He knew that eating sweets causes pimples.*

pimply /pɪmpli/
ADJ Someone who is **pimply** has a lot of pimples. *He was an ugly, pimply little boy.*

pin /pɪn/ **pins, pinning, pinned**
1 NC A **pin** is a very small, thin, pointed piece of metal that is used to fasten pieces of cloth together.
● See also **drawing pin, safety pin**.
2 NC A **pin** is also an ornamental badge that you can wear on your clothes; used in American English. *Nineteen-year-old Alexa Markowski wears a lapel pin with a color portrait of Nicholas II.*
3 VOA If you **pin** something somewhere, you fasten it there with a pin, a drawing pin, or a safety pin. *She wore a white rose pinned to her blouse.*
4 VOA If someone **pins** you in a particular position, they hold you down firmly so that you cannot move. *He pinned Miss Patrick against a van.*
5 VO+on or upon If someone **pins** the blame for something on you, they say that you did it or caused it; an informal use. *You can't pin that on me.*
6 VO+on or upon If you **pin** your hopes on something, you rely on it to be successful. *He pinned his hopes on the prospect of a split in the opposition party.*

pin down PHRASAL VERB 1 If you try to **pin down** something which is hard to describe, you try to say exactly what it is or what it is like. *The courts have found obscenity impossible to pin down as a punishable offence.* 2 If you **pin** someone **down**, you force them to make a definite statement. *He was*

anxious to **pin** the Minister **down** to some definite commitment.

pin up PHRASAL VERB 1 If you **pin up** a poster or a notice, you pin it to a wall. *It was common practice for security circulars to be pinned up.* 2 If you **pin up** part of a piece of clothing, you pin the bottom of it to a higher position. *The hem was pinned up.* 3 See also **pin-up**.

pinafore /pɪnəfɔː/ **pinafores**
NC A **pinafore** is a type of sleeveless dress that can be worn over a blouse or sweater, or over another dress to protect it.

pinball /pɪnbɔːl/
NU **Pinball** is a game in which a player tries to keep a small ball from rolling to the bottom of a pin-table, by getting it to bounce off obstructions on the surface of the pin-table.

pinball machine, pinball machines
NC A **pinball machine** is the same as a **pin-table**. *The pool tables and pinball machines stood idle.*

pince-nez /pæⁿsneɪ/
N PL **Pince-nez** are old-fashioned spectacles which consist of two lenses in a frame that fits tightly onto the top of the nose. *He was the only man I'd ever seen wearing pince-nez.*

pincer /pɪnsə/ **pincers**
1 N PL **Pincers** are a tool consisting of two pieces of metal that are hinged in the middle. Pincers are used for gripping things tightly. *...a pair of pincers.*
2 NC The **pincers** of an insect such as an ant or an animal such as a crab are its front claws. *Each ant clamped its pincers into the flesh... Some sea scorpions grew to a length of two metres and were armed with immense pincers.*

pincer movement, pincer movements
NC A **pincer movement** is an attack by an army or other group in which they attack their enemies from two different directions at once with the aim of surrounding them. *...the pincer movement on the capital.*

pinch /pɪntʃ/ **pinches, pinching, pinched**
1 VO If you **pinch** someone, you squeeze a small piece of their flesh between your thumb and first finger. *Dr. Hochstadt pinched Judy's cheek as she passed.* ► Also NC *She gave my wrist a little pinch.*
2 N SING A **pinch** of something is the amount of it that you can hold between your thumb and your first finger. *Season with salt and a pinch of cinnamon.*
3 VO If someone **pinches** something, they steal it; an informal use. *I pinched fourpence from the box.*
● **Pinch** is used in these phrases. ● If you are prepared to do something **at a pinch**, you will do it if it is absolutely necessary and if there is no alternative; an informal expression. *At a pinch the new doctor would do.* ● If you **are feeling the pinch**, you do not have as much money as you used to, and cannot buy all the things that you want. *The big fashion establishments have been feeling the pinch lately.* ● to take something **with a pinch of** salt: see **salt**.

pinched /pɪntʃt/
ADJ If someone's face is **pinched**, it looks thin and pale, usually because they are ill or cold. *He lay on his bed, looking pinched and worn.*

pincushion /pɪnkʊʃn/ **pincushions**
NC A **pincushion** is a very small cushion that you stick pins and needles into so that you can get them easily when you need them.

Pindling, Sir Lynden O. /lɪndən əʊ pɪndlɪŋ/
Sir Lynden O. **Pindling** became Prime Minister of the Bahamas in 1969. He was Premier from 1967 to 1969. He became the leader of the Progressive Liberal Party (PLP) in 1963. Born: 1930.

pine /paɪn/ **pines, pining, pined**
1 NC or NU A **pine** or a **pine tree** is a tall evergreen tree. It has long thin leaves, brown cones, and a fresh smell. The tree's pale-coloured wood, which is used for making furniture, is also called **pine**. *...a walk among the pine trees. ...nut trees like oak and pine.*
2 V+for or V+to-INF If you **are pining** for something, you feel sad because you cannot have it. *Helen pines for you... Most of them were pining to be recognized and admitted as citizens.*

pine away PHRASAL VERB If someone **pines away**, they gradually become weaker and die because they are very unhappy. *I believe she actually pined away—lost her will to live.*

pineapple /paɪnæpl/ **pineapples**
N Cor NU A **pineapple** is a large oval fruit with sweet juicy flesh and a thick, brownish, hard skin. *...a slice of pineapple.*

pinecone /paɪnkəʊn/ **pinecones**
NC A **pinecone** is a small oval seed case that is produced by a pine tree.

pine-needle, pine-needles
NC **Pine-needles** are long, thin, sharp leaves that grow on pine trees. *...sulphur dioxide pollution was helping to trap and stick the ammonia to the pine-needles.*

pinewood /paɪnwʊd/ **pinewoods**
1 NC A **pinewood** is a wood which consists of pine trees. *They planted a 1 500-tree pinewood.*
2 NU **Pinewood** is wood that has come from a pine tree.

ping /pɪŋ/ **pings, pinging, pinged**
1 NC A **ping** is a short, high-pitched, metallic sound. *There is a loud ping from the alarm clock.*
2 V If something such as a bell **pings**, it makes a short high-pitched noise. *The bell pings; the lift doors open.*

ping-pong /pɪŋpɒŋ/
NU **Ping-pong** is the same as **table tennis**; an informal word. *A lot of them played ping-pong.*

pinhead /pɪnhed/ **pinheads**
1 NC A **pinhead** is a small metal or plastic ball on the end of a pin. *Imagine a computer the size of a pinhead.*
2 NC If you refer to someone as a **pinhead**, you think that they are stupid; an informal use. *...the question some pinhead had asked him.*

pinion /pɪnjən/ **pinions, pinioning, pinioned**
VO If you **pinion** someone, you prevent them from moving or escaping, especially by holding their arms. *Pinioned by the press of men around them, they were unable to move.*

pink /pɪŋk/ **pinker, pinkest**
1 ADJ Something that is **pink** is of the colour between red and white. *...the white and pink blossom of orchard apples.*
2 ADJ If someone goes **pink**, their face goes slightly red because they are embarrassed or angry. *He went very pink, and looked away.*

pinking shears
N PL **Pinking shears** are special scissors that give zigzag edges to anything that they cut. They are used especially to cut cloth.

pinkish /pɪŋkɪʃ/
ADJ **Pinkish** means slightly pink. *...a faint pinkish glow.*

pin money
NU **Pin money** is a small amount of extra money that someone earns in order to buy things that they want but that they do not really need. *The Treasury's attitude is almost that women work for pin money to pay for the work they've left behind at home.*

pinnacle /pɪnəkl/ **pinnacles**
1 NC A **pinnacle** is a tall pointed piece of a building or a mountain. *...the pinnacles of St John's Church. ...the white pinnacles of the distant mountains.*
2 NC+SUPP The **pinnacle** of something is the best or highest level of it. *These newspapers were regarded as the pinnacle of journalism.*

pinny /pɪni/ **pinnies**
NC A **pinny** is an apron that you wear over the top of your normal clothes to prevent them from getting dirty, for example when you are cooking; an old-fashioned word.

pinpoint /pɪnpɔɪnt/ **pinpoints, pinpointing, pinpointed**
1 VO If you **pinpoint** something, you discover or explain exactly what it is. *In their book, Jackson and Marsden pinpointed the difference.*
2 VO If you **pinpoint** the position of something, you indicate its exact position. *'Just here,' he said, pinpointing it on the map.*

pinprick /pɪnprɪk/ **pinpricks**
1 NC A **pinprick** is something that annoys you for a short time. *...the daily pinpricks of family life.*

2 NC+SUPP A **pinprick** of light is a very small spot of light.

pins and needles
1 N PL If you get **pins and needles**, you feel sharp tingling pains for a while because you have been in an awkward or uncomfortable position. *If he has been bitten by a dog, he might get a funny sensation like pins and needles.*
2 If you are **on pins and needles**, you are anxious or nervous about something that is about to happen; used in American English. *I was on pins and needles saying, 'I hope they like it'.*

pin-stripe
ADJ ATTRIB A **pin-stripe** suit or a **pin-striped** suit is made of dark cloth that has very narrow vertical stripes. *The boys wear straw hats, stiff collars and pin-stripe trousers.*

pint /paɪnt/ **pints**
1 NC In Britain, a **pint** is a unit of volume for liquids equal to one-eighth of an imperial gallon or approximately 568 cubic centimetres. *...one pint of milk.*
2 NC In the United States, a **pint** is a unit of volume for liquids equal to one-eighth of an American gallon or approximately 473 cubic centimetres.
3 NC In Britain, a **pint** is also a pint of beer. *He likes having a couple of pints with his lunch.*

pin-table, pin-tables
NC A **pin-table** is a sloping surface with pins and other obstructions on it, on which the game of pinball is played.

pint-size
ADJ Someone or something that is described as **pint-size** or **pint-sized** is very small. *...a pint-sized powerhouse of musical talent.*

pin-up, pin-ups
NC A **pin-up** is a picture of an attractive woman or man, usually a famous actor or pop-singer, or a model wearing very few clothes. *...pin-ups of film stars.*

pioneer /paɪənɪə/ **pioneers, pioneering, pioneered**
1 NC A **pioneer** in a particular activity is one of the first people to be involved in it and develop it. *He was a pioneer of photography.*
2 VO Someone who **pioneers** a new activity, invention, or process is one of the first people to do it or use it. *...a hospital which pioneered open heart surgery in this country.*
3 NC A **pioneer** is also one of the first people to live or farm in a particular place. *...a tribute to pioneers who started a new life in the isolation and loneliness of the bush.*

pioneering
ADJ ATTRIB **Pioneering** means doing something that has not been done before, for example using new methods or techniques, or belonging to a new political movement. *...a pioneering and innovative banker. ...a founder member of the pioneering opposition group, New Forum.*

pious /paɪəs/
1 ADJ A **pious** person is very religious and moral. *...the pious little Portuguese princess.*
2 ADJ ATTRIB A **pious** action or declaration is religious and moral and appears to be very sincere. *...carrying out pious duties. ...pious declarations of unity.*
♦ **piously** ADV *'No', I said piously, 'it belongs to God.'*
3 ADJ ATTRIB A **pious** hope is unlikely to come true. *...the rather pious hope that many of the people will come to realise that rational land use is better.*

pip /pɪp/ **pips, pipping, pipped**
1 NC A **pip** is one of the small hard seeds in a fruit such as an apple, orange, or pear. *The pips and the skin are actually fermented with the alcohol.*
2 NC On the radio, the **pips** are a series of short, high-pitched sounds that are used as a time signal. *...the Greenwich Time Signal Pips.*
3 NC The **pips** on the shoulder of a soldier's uniform are an emblem which shows his rank; an informal use. *...three pips on his shoulder and a pistol at his hip.*
4 VO+to If you **pip** someone to something, such as a prize or an award, you narrowly defeat them in a game or competition. *...it was pipped to the title of*

best film... The Samoan team pipped Oxford last weekend. ● If you **pip** someone **to the post**, you narrowly defeat them in a game or competition. *Alongside him is another of the world's great players, Tom Watson, who could pip him to the post.*

pipe /paɪp/ **pipes, piping, piped**
1 NC A **pipe** is a long, round, hollow object through which a liquid or gas can flow. *...hot water pipes.*
2 VO To **pipe** a liquid or gas somewhere means to transfer it from one place to another through a pipe. *Hot water is piped to all the rooms.*
3 NC A **pipe** is also an object which is used for smoking tobacco. It consists of a hollow cup-shaped bowl for holding the tobacco, and a tube through which you inhale the smoke. *He was sitting in his armchair, smoking a pipe and reading the paper.*
4 See also **piping, piping hot.**

pipe cleaner, pipe cleaners
NC A **pipe cleaner** is a piece of wire covered with a soft woolly substance which is used for cleaning a tobacco pipe. *She made camels and hippopotamuses out of coloured pipe cleaners.*

piped music
NU **Piped music** is music which is played through loudspeakers in public places. *I could hear the piped music from the swimming pool.*

pipe dream, pipe dreams
NC A **pipe dream** is a hope or plan which you know will never really happen. *You could waste your whole life on a pipe dream.*

pipeline /paɪplaɪn/ **pipelines**
1 NC A **pipeline** is a large pipe through which oil or gas flow over a long distance. *...a vital oil pipeline.*
2 If something is **in the pipeline**, it has already been planned or begun. *More improvements were in the pipeline. ...another billion dollars in the pipeline.*

piper /paɪpə/ **pipers**
NC A **piper** is a musician who plays the bagpipes. *...a Scottish piper.*

pipette /pɪpet/ **pipettes**
NC A **pipette** is a thin glass tube which is used in scientific experiments for carrying or measuring small amounts of liquid. *It's done by using a fine-tipped pipette to inject the solution of the DNA into the embryos.*

pipework /paɪpwɜːk/
NU **Pipework** consists of the pipes that are part of a machine or construction. *This pipework is separate from the reactor. ...exposed pieces of pipework.*

piping /paɪpɪŋ/
1 NU **Piping** consists of lengths of pipe or tube made from metal or plastic. *...a length of steel piping.*
2 ADJ ATTRIB A **piping** voice is high-pitched and shrill. *In a piping voice she ordered me to sit down.*

piping hot
ADJ Food or water that is **piping hot** is very hot. *...mugs of piping hot coffee.*

pipsqueak /pɪpskwiːk/ **pipsqueaks**
NC If you refer to someone as a **pipsqueak**, you are showing contempt for them by saying that they are unimportant; an informal word.

piquancy /piːkənsi/
1 NU If something adds **piquancy** to a situation, it adds interest and excitement; a formal use. *Argument adds piquancy to the contest.*
2 NU **Piquancy** is also a pleasantly spicy taste. *...using herbs or spices to give variety and piquancy.*

piquant /piːkənt/
1 ADJ Something that is **piquant** is interesting and exciting; a formal use. *...a piquant face with large appealing dark-blue eyes.*
2 ADJ **Piquant** food has a pleasantly spicy taste. *...a piquant sauce.*

pique /piːk/
NU **Pique** is the feeling of resentment you have when your pride is hurt. *He withdrew from the contest in a fit of pique.*

piqued /piːkt/
ADJ PRED If someone is **piqued**, they are angry and resentful because their pride has been hurt. *They have also been piqued by the suddenness of the American policy change.*

piracy /paɪrəsi/
1 NU **Piracy** is robbery carried out by pirates. *There have been almost 50 reports of piracy involving boat people in the waters of South East Asia.*
2 NU You can also refer to the illegal copying and selling of computer software, music, or books as **piracy**. *...software piracy.*

piranha /pɪrɑːnə/ **piranhas**
NC A **piranha** is a small, fierce fish from South America that can eat human and animal flesh.

pirate /paɪrət/ **pirates, pirating, pirated**
1 NC **Pirates** are sailors who attack and rob other ships. *Seventy Vietnamese boat people are missing after being attacked by pirates off the coast of Malaysia.*
2 VO Someone who **pirates** electronic, recorded, or printed material copies and sells it illegally. *New advertisers were pirating his paintings.* ◆ **pirated** ADJ *There were a lot of pirated editions.*
3 ADJ ATTRIB A **pirate** version of something is an illegal copy of it. *Pirate copies of novels and video films are freely available.*

pirate radio, pirate radios
NU or NC **Pirate radio** is the broadcasting of radio programmes illegally, for example by transmitting from a ship in the sea. *There was evidence of pirate radios interfering with shipping. ...a pirate radio station.*

pirouette /pɪruet/ **pirouettes**
NC In ballet, a **pirouette** is a fast turn of the dancer's body while standing. *Think of the control of a ballet dancer performing a pirouette on a point.*

piss /pɪs/ **pisses, pissing, pissed**; an informal or rude word which some people find offensive.
1 V To **piss** means to urinate.
2 N SING If someone has a **piss**, they urinate.
3 NU **Piss** is urine.

piss down PHRASAL VERB If it is **pissing down**, it is raining hard; an informal or rude expression which some people find offensive.

piss off PHRASAL VERB 1 If someone tells a person to **piss off**, they are telling the person to go away; a rude and offensive expression which you should avoid using.
2 If someone is **pissed off** with something or someone, they feel bored and irritated by them; an informal or rude expression which some people find offensive.

pissed /pɪst/
ADJ PRED Someone who is **pissed** is drunk; an informal or rude word which some people find offensive.

pistol /pɪstl/ **pistols**
NC A **pistol** is a small hand gun. *The guard on duty drew his pistol and held it as we spoke.*

piston /pɪstən/ **pistons**
NC A **piston** is a cylinder or metal disc in an engine. Pistons slide up and down inside tubes to make parts of the engine move. *...the effort required to push the piston through the oil.*

pit /pɪt/ **pits, pitting, pitted**
1 NC A **pit** is a hole in the ground. *The pit was stacked with ammunition.*
2 NC A **pit** is also a small, shallow hole in the surface of something. *...scratches and pits on the enamel.*
3 NC You can refer to a coal mine as a **pit**. *...the men coming home from the pit.*
4 N PL In motor racing, the **pits** are the areas where drivers stop for fuel and repairs during races. *Track marshals signalled drivers to return to the pits while the track was cleared.*
5 See also **pitted.**
● **Pit** is used in these phrases. ● If you have a feeling **in the pit of your stomach**, you have an unpleasant feeling inside your body because you are afraid or anxious. *The ache in the pit of her stomach was no worse than the one in her heart.* ● If you describe someone or something as **the pits**, you mean that they are the worst of their kind; an informal expression. *That first week is the pits, isn't it?* ● If you **pit** your **wits against** someone, you compete with them in a test of knowledge or intelligence. *Messrs Reagan and Gorbachev actually enjoy pitting their wits against one another.*

pitapat /ˈpɪtəpæt/
N SING or ADV **Pitapat** is a way of referring to a sound that consists of a series of short, light taps, like the sound of raindrops falling on a surface.

pitch /pɪtʃ/ **pitches, pitching, pitched**
1 NC A **pitch** is an area of ground that is marked out and used for playing a game such as football, cricket, or hockey. ...*one of the few teams who beat Liverpool on their own home pitch.*
2 VO If you **pitch** an object somewhere, you throw it forcefully but aiming carefully. *He was pitching a penny at a crack in the sidewalk.*
3 VA If someone or something **pitches** to the ground, they suddenly fall forwards. *He suddenly pitched headlong to the ground.*
4 NU The **pitch** of a sound is how high or low it is. *Her voice dropped to a lower pitch.*
5 N SING+SUPP If a feeling reaches a high **pitch**, it reaches a high level or degree. *Excitement is now at fever pitch... Her frustration mounted to such a pitch of anger that she could no longer keep silent.*
6 VOA If you **pitch** something such as an argument or explanation at a particular level, you set it at that level. *Her lectures are pitched directly at the level of the students... I think people thought we'd pitched the argument about right... That is perhaps why they have pitched their demands so high, including a demand for a non-Communist Interior Minister.*
7 VO If you **pitch** a tent, you erect it. *They continue to pitch tents for the new arrivals.*
pitch in PHRASAL VERB If you **pitch in**, you join in an activity; an informal expression. *They will be expected to pitch in and make their own beds.*

pitch-black
ADJ If a place or the night is **pitch-black**, it is completely dark. ...*a pitch-black cavern.*

pitched /pɪtʃt/
ADJ A **pitched** roof is one that slopes quite steeply as opposed to one that is flat. ...*steeply pitched roofs and tall gables.*

pitched battle, pitched battles
NC A **pitched battle** is a very fierce, violent fight. *Police fought a pitched battle with about 40 youths.*

pitcher /ˈpɪtʃə/ **pitchers**
1 NC A **pitcher** is a jug; an old-fashioned word. ...*a pitcher of water.*
2 NC In baseball, the **pitcher** is the person who throws the ball to the person who is batting; used in American English. *He was a very dominating pitcher.*

pitchfork /ˈpɪtʃfɔːk/ **pitchforks**
NC A **pitchfork** is a large fork with a long handle and two prongs that is used for lifting hay or grass.

piteous /ˈpɪtiəs/; a literary word.
1 ADJ Something that is **piteous** is so sad that you feel great pity. *There were piteous sounds of suffering and pain.*
2 ADJ **Piteous** is also used to describe something that is unimportant and poor in quality or degree. *They still make only a piteous showing on the graph.*

pitfall /ˈpɪtfɔːl/ **pitfalls**
NC The **pitfalls** of a particular activity or situation are the things that may go wrong or may cause problems later. ...*the pitfalls of pursuing such a drastic policy.*

pith /pɪθ/
NU The **pith** of a citrus fruit such as an orange is the white substance underneath the peel.

pithead /ˈpɪthed/ **pitheads**
NC The **pithead** at a coal mine is all the buildings, machinery, and so on which are above the ground. *He was accosted by his men at the pithead... It was agreed that there would be a pithead ballot.*

pithy /ˈpɪθi/
ADJ A comment or piece of writing that is **pithy** is short, direct, and memorable. ...*pithy, ironic observations. ...pithy working-class humour.*

pitiable /ˈpɪtiəbl/
ADJ Someone who is **pitiable** is in such a sad or weak situation that you feel pity for them. *She was in a pitiable plight.*

pitiful /ˈpɪtɪfl/
1 ADJ Someone or something that is **pitiful** is so sad, weak, or small that you feel pity for them. ...*his thin,*

bony legs and his pitiful arms. ...the pitiful sound of a human being in pain. ◆ **pitifully** ADV *He looks pitifully thin.*
2 ADJ If you describe something as **pitiful**, you mean that it is inadequate; used showing disapproval. *They described the rises to cover inflation as pitiful.*

pitiless /ˈpɪtɪləs/
ADJ Someone or something that is **pitiless** shows no feelings of pity or mercy. *His face was cool and pitiless.*

pittance /ˈpɪtns/
N SING If you receive a **pittance**, you receive only a very small amount of money. *They are tired of working for a pittance.*

pitted /ˈpɪtɪd/
ADJ If the surface of something is **pitted**, it is covered with a lot of small shallow holes. *The walls were pitted with bullet holes.*

pitter-patter /ˈpɪtəpætə/
N SING or ADV **Pitter-patter** is a way of referring to a sound that consists of a series of short, light taps like the sound of raindrops falling on a surface. ...*the pitter-patter of tiny feet.*

pituitary /pɪˈtjuːɪtəri/ **pituitaries**
NC The **pituitary** or **pituitary gland** is a gland that is attached to the base of the brain; a technical term. ...*a substance produced by the pituitary gland.*

pity /ˈpɪti/ **pities, pitying, pitied**
1 NU If you feel **pity** for someone, you feel very sorry for them. *I feel pity rather than anger for these men. ...Mother Teresa's pity and concern for the homeless.*
2 VO If you **pity** someone, you feel very sorry for them. *She pitied him with her whole heart.*
3 N SING You say that it is a **pity** that something is the case when you are expressing disappointment or regret. *I think that's a great pity after all she's done... It's a pity they're scared to move.*
4 If you **take pity on** someone, you feel sorry for them and help them. *A man who spoke English took pity on us and it was all sorted out.*

pitying /ˈpɪtiɪŋ/
ADJ ATTRIB A **pitying** look shows that someone feels pity and perhaps slight contempt. *Angelica gave me a pitying smile.* ◆ **pityingly** ADV *He shook his head pityingly.*

pivot /ˈpɪvət/ **pivots, pivoting, pivoted**
1 NC A **pivot** is the pin or central point on which something balances or turns. *The compass needle swung round on its pivot.*
2 V To **pivot** means to balance or turn on a central point. *There's a pedal on the back that pivots on the end.*
3 NC The **pivot** in a situation is the most important thing around which everything else is based or arranged. *Their daughter was the pivot of their lives.*

pivotal /ˈpɪvətl/
ADJ A **pivotal** point, factor, or role in something is one that is very important and affects the success or development of that thing. *This scene is probably the pivotal point of the whole book... It is often observed that Syria plays a pivotal role.*

pixie /ˈpɪksi/ **pixies**
NC A **pixie** is an imaginary little creature like a fairy which has pointed ears and a pointed hat. *International aid workers, dressed up as pixies, drove a truck around the capital.*

pixie hat, pixie hats
NC A **pixie hat** is a pointed woollen hat.

pizza /ˈpiːtsə/ **pizzas**
NC or NU A **pizza** is a flat piece of dough covered with tomatoes, cheese, and other savoury food, which is baked in an oven. ...*twelve large cheese and green pepper pizzas... Dieters could still go on eating ice cream, cakes and pizzas so long as they were low fat versions. ...a plate of pizza.*

pizzazz /pəˈzæz/
NU Someone or something that has **pizzazz** is very exciting or attractive; an informal word. *The polls showed that the candidate was thought to have no charisma, no pizzazz, no passion.*

pl
pl is a written abbreviation for 'plural'.

placard /plækɑːd/ **placards**
NC A **placard** is a large notice that is carried in a march or demonstration. *Many of them carried placards demanding the right to emigrate.*

placate /pləkeɪt/ **placates, placating, placated**
VO If you **placate** someone, you try to stop them feeling angry or resentful by doing things that will please them. *...the desire of politicians to placate the public.*

placatory /pləkeɪtəri/
ADJ A **placatory** remark or action is intended to stop someone feeling angry or resentful by doing or saying things that will please them. *The President's speech seemed astonishingly placatory... They were making placatory gestures.*

place /pleɪs/ **places, placing, placed**
1 NC A **place** is any building, area, town, or country. *The cellar was a very dark place. ...photographs of places taken during his travels abroad. ...a meeting place... There are nightclubs and parties but they're not ideal places to meet people.*
2 NC+SUPP You can refer to the position where something belongs as its **place**. *She put the book back in its place on the shelf.*
3 NC A **place** within a larger area is a specific point or area within that larger area. *In some places it is quite a bit warmer than normal... In several places the police beat back the crowds.*
4 N SING **Place** can be used after 'any', 'no', 'some', or 'every' to mean 'anywhere', 'nowhere', 'somewhere', or 'everywhere'; used in informal American English. *You are not going any place... He had no place else to go.*
5 NC Your **place** is the house or flat where you live; an informal use. *What sort of place do they have?*
6 NC A **place** is also somewhere that provides a service, such as a hotel, pub, or institution; an informal use. *...corner stores and bed-and-breakfast places... I was writing off to various places in Britain asking about courses.*
7 NC Your **place** at a table or in a classroom, for example, is a seat that is intended for you to use or that you normally use. *She had to leave her place and go to the back of the room.*
8 NC A **place** at a table is also a space with a knife, fork, and other things arranged on it, so that one person can sit down and eat. *Every day 12 places are laid for dinner.*
9 NC If you have a **place** on a committee or at a college, for example, you are a member of the committee or are accepted by the college as a student. *Harper failed to win a place on the committee... I got a place at a teachers' training college. ...job offers and invitations to take up college places.*
10 NC+SUPP Your **place** in a society, system, or situation is your position or role in relation to other people. *...Britain's place in the world... Frank felt it was not his place to raise any objection... The demonstration occupies a central place in their political campaign.*
11 NC Your **place** in a competition or on a scale is your position at the end or at a particular stage of the competition or on the scale. First place is the winning or top position. *The US leapt from sixth place to second.*
12 NC+POSS Your **place** in a book or speech is the point that you have reached in it. *He lost his place in his notes.*
13 VOA If you **place** something somewhere, you put it there neatly or carefully. *She placed the music on the piano and sat down... Chairs had been placed in rows all down the room.*
14 VO+on or upon If you **place** responsibility, pressure, or a restriction on someone, you cause them to have it or be affected by it. *The responsibility placed upon us is too heavy to bear... They have issued a statement expressing their concern at restrictions placed by the government on their travel.*
15 VO+on or upon If you **place** emphasis or blame on something, you emphasize or blame it. *The New Left placed much emphasis on the role of culture.*

16 VO If you **place** an order for goods, or if you **place** an advertisement in a newspaper, you ask a company to send you the goods or you ask the newspaper to publish the advertisement. *Dad placed the order... The organisers have placed advertisements in newspapers.*
17 VO If you cannot **place** someone, you cannot remember exactly who they are or where you have met them before. *She was looking at me as if she could not quite place me.*
18 NC If you say how many decimal **places** there are in a number, you are saying how many numbers there are to the right of the decimal point. *It will calculate to thirty decimal places.*
● **Place** is used in these phrases. ● If something is in **place**, it is in its correct or usual position. *He held the handle in place while the glue set.* ● You say **in the first place** when you are talking about the beginning of a situation. *Nobody can remember what was agreed in the first place.* ● You say **in the first place** and **in the second place** to introduce the first and second in a series of points. *...information that, in the first place, would have been very difficult for me to obtain and, in the second place, would have been useless anyhow.* ● If something or someone is **out of place**, they do not fit in with their surroundings. *Although dignified, Mr Havel looked slightly out of place surrounded by the pomp and circumstance of a Soviet military parade.* ● When something **takes place**, it happens. *The next attack took place four hours later... The talks will take place in Vienna.* ● If one thing or person is used or included **in place of** another, or if they **take the place of** the other thing or person, they replace the other thing or person. *This task is carried out by robots in place of human workers... McNeill takes the place of Philip Danaher.* ● If you **put** someone **in their place**, you show them that they are less important or clever than they think they are; an informal expression. *The ambitious ministers seem to have been firmly put in their place by the President's decision.*

placebo /pləsiːbəʊ/ **placebos**
1 NC A **placebo** is a harmless, inactive substance that a doctor gives to a patient instead of a drug, for example when testing a new drug, or when the patient has imagined their illness. *Some will get the new drug while others receive an inert placebo. ...a placebo vaccine.*
2 NC You can refer to something that is done, said, or given to a person who feels discontented or depressed in order to please or comfort them as a **placebo**; a literary use.

placed /pleɪst/
ADJ PRED If someone is well **placed**, they have more advantages or resources than other people. *How well are we placed with regard to America?... As for finance, we're better placed than people think... The BBC World Service is uniquely placed to provide a link between Britain and those caught up in the Gulf crisis.*

placement /pleɪsmənt/ **placements**
1 NU+SUPP The **placement** of someone or something is the act or process of putting them in a particular place or position. *I spent a week directing the placement of the boulders.*
2 NC If someone gets a **placement**, they get a job for a period of time which will give them experience in the work they are training for. *Amongst other placements, he spent some months at the Children's Hospital.*

placement office, placement offices
NC A **placement office** is an office in a college or university that helps its students to find jobs, especially after they have finished their course; used in American English. *...second-semester seniors going to placement offices and saying, 'Find me a job'.*

placenta /pləsentə/ **placentas**
NC The **placenta** is the mass of veins and tissue inside the womb of a pregnant woman or animal, which the foetus is attached to. *The other test is done on a sample taken from the placenta.*

place setting, place settings
NC A **place setting** is a complete set of equipment including knives, forks, spoons, and glasses, that is

arranged on a table for one person to use at a meal.

placid /plæsɪd/
ADJ A **placid** person or situation is calm and does not create any excitement. *With the outcome of Sunday's voting certain, the general mood is placid. ...one of the more prosperous and placid corners of West Africa.*

plagiarism /pleɪdʒərɪzəm/
NU **Plagiarism** is the practice of using or copying someone else's idea or work and pretending that you thought of it or created it; used showing disapproval. *It was a shameless piece of plagiarism.* ♦ **plagiarist**, **plagiarists** NC *One would be dealing with the work of a forger or plagiarist.*

plagiarize /pleɪdʒəraɪz/ **plagiarizes, plagiarizing, plagiarized**; also spelt **plagiarise**.
VOorV If someone **plagiarizes** another person's idea or work, they use it or copy it and pretend that they thought of it or created it; used showing disapproval. *He's constantly plagiarizing other people's research... She said she plagiarized the phrase from 'Lady Chatterley's Lover'... They also plagiarized incessantly.*

plague /pleɪg/ **plagues, plaguing, plagued**
1 NCorNU A **plague** is a very infectious disease that spreads quickly and kills large numbers of people or animals. *The last major plague to affect seals was in 1988 in Northern Europe. ...analyses of the impact of directly transmitted infections such as smallpox and bubonic plague.*
2 NC+of A **plague** of unpleasant things is a large number of them that arrive or happen at the same time. *...a plague of locusts... President Reagan seems to be in a serene mood, despite the plague of scandals now affecting his administration.*
3 VO If unpleasant things **plague** you, they keep happening and cause you a lot of trouble. *The system is plagued by technical faults... He suffered severe back injuries, which plague him to this day.*
4 VO If you **plague** someone, you keep bothering them or asking them for something. *The readers were urged to plague their MP with letters of protest.*

plaice /pleɪs/; **plaice** is both the singular and the plural form.
NCorNU A **plaice** is a kind of flat sea fish. *...a whole fillet of plaice... Serve the plaice with the broccoli.*

plaid /plæd/ **plaids**
1 N MASS **Plaid** is material with a tartan or other check design on it, or the design itself; used in American English. *She wore a plaid shirt and blue jeans. ...their fondness for plaids and checks.*
2 NC A **plaid** is a long piece of tartan material which is worn over the shoulder as part of Scottish Highland national dress.

plain /pleɪn/ **plains; plainer, plainest**
1 ADJ ATTRIB A **plain** object or surface is entirely in one colour and has no pattern, design, or writing on it. *They are set against a plain background with carefully controlled lighting.*
2 ADJ **Plain** things are very simple in style. *She felt ashamed of her plain dress... I enjoy good plain food; nothing fancy.*
3 ADJ If a fact, situation or statement is **plain**, it is easy to recognize or understand. *It was plain that Eddie wanted to get back to sleep. ...a plain statement of fact.*
4 ADJ ATTRIBorSUBMOD **Plain** can be used for emphasis before a noun or an adjective. *Petty is the wrong word—It's plain meanness... Logical judgment can also be just plain wrong.*
5 ADJ A **plain** woman or girl is not at all beautiful. *...a plain plump girl with pigtails.*
6 NC A **plain** is a large, flat area of land with very few trees on it. *...vast plains covered in yellow grasses.*

plain chocolate
NU **Plain chocolate** is dark brown chocolate that has a stronger and less sweet taste than milk chocolate.

plain-clothes
ADJ ATTRIB **Plain-clothes** police officers wear ordinary clothes instead of a uniform. *Lebel ordered a plain-clothes detective to check into the hotel.*

plain flour
NU **Plain flour** is flour that does not have chemicals

added to it that make cakes increase in size when they are cooked.

plainly /pleɪnli/
1 ADV SEN If something is **plainly** the case, it is obviously the case. *He was plainly angry.*
2 ADV If you can see, hear, or smell something **plainly**, you can see, hear, or smell it easily. *You could see the oysters quite plainly, lying all over the sea-bed.*
3 ADV If you say something **plainly**, it is easy to understand and cannot be mistaken. *The judge said that quite plainly.*

plainsong /pleɪnsɒŋ/
NU **Plainsong** is a type of church music in which a group of people sing one tune together, without having musical instruments played at the same time. *Musical purists would have preferred the ancient plainsong.*

plain speaking
NU **Plain speaking** means saying exactly what you think, even when you know that what you say may not please other people. *She maintained her reputation for plain speaking... There had, he said, been some plain speaking between the two leaders, but their talks had been good-humoured.*

plainspoken /pleɪnspəʊkən/
ADJ Someone who is **plainspoken** says exactly what they think, even when they know that what they say may not please other people.

plaint /pleɪnt/ **plaints**
NC A **plaint** is a complaint or a sad cry; a literary word. *...the moans and plaints of their children.*

plaintiff /pleɪntɪf/ **plaintiffs**
NC A **plaintiff** is a person who brings a legal case against someone; a legal term. *The plaintiffs are suing for assault and wrongful arrest.*

plaintive /pleɪntɪv/
ADJ A **plaintive** sound or voice is sad and high-pitched. *...a plaintive wail.*

plait /plæt/ **plaits, plaiting, plaited**
1 VO If you **plait** three or more lengths of hair or rope together, you twist them over and under each other to make one thick length. *Her thick brown hair was plaited in a single braid down her back.* ♦ **plaited** ADJ ATTRIB *...long ropes of plaited rushes.*
2 NC A **plait** is a length of hair that has been plaited. *...her long gold plaits.*

plan /plæn/ **plans, planning, planned**
1 NC A **plan** is a method of achieving something that you have worked out carefully in advance. *I told them of my plan. ...a plan to give women more power... He also announced plans to help Czechoslovakia privatise its economy. ...a new Middle East peace plan.*
2 VOorV+for If you **plan** what you are going to do, you decide in detail what you are going to do. *At breakfast I planned my day... We must plan for the future.*
3 V+to-INForVO If you **plan** to do something, you intend to do it. *What do you plan to do after college?... I was planning a career in law... A meeting was originally planned for last night.* ♦ **planned** ADJ ATTRIB *...news of the planned sale of 50,000 acres of state forests.*
4 N PL If you have **plans**, you intend to do a particular thing. *The gales forced him to change his plans.*
5 VO When you **plan** something that you are going to make, build, or create, you decide what the main parts of it will be and how they will be arranged. *How do you plan a book? ...the art of planning gardens.*
6 NC A **plan** of something that is going to be built or made is a detailed diagram or drawing of it. *...the plan and overall design of the building... Make a neat plan of your new home.*
7 A **plan of action** or a **plan of campaign** is a series of actions that you have decided to take in order to achieve something. *She proposes a three-point plan of action to improve the UN response at an operational level... His plan of campaign is to cycle into town and collect the money personally.*
8 See also **planning**.

plan on PHRASAL VERB If you **plan on** doing something, you intend to do it. *I plan on staying in London.*
plan out PHRASAL VERB If you **plan out** what you are

going to do, you decide in detail what you are going to do. *I hadn't even planned out the route yet.*

plane /pleɪn/ **planes, planing, planed**
1 NC A **plane** is a vehicle with wings and engines which can fly. *We went by plane... We bought the cigarettes on the plane. ...a military transport plane... He was killed in a plane crash.*
2 NC A **plane** is also a flat surface; a technical use. *...an elaborate structure of coloured planes.*
3 NC+SUPP You can refer to a particular level of something as a particular **plane**; a literary use. *She tried to lift the conversation onto a more elevated plane.*
4 NC A **plane** is also a tool that has a flat bottom with a sharp blade in it. You move the plane over a piece of wood to remove thin pieces of its surface. ▶ Also VO *It's simply a few planks taken down to a workshop to be planed down.*

planet /plænɪt/ **planets**
NC A **planet** is a large, round object in space that moves around a star. The Earth is a planet. *...the orbit of the planet Mars... It's big compared with the Earth, but much smaller than some of the planets in our own solar system.*

planetarium /plænɪteərɪəm/ **planetariums**
NC A **planetarium** is a building where lights are shone on the ceiling to represent the planets and the stars and to show how they appear to move. *The meteorite is on display at the Hayden Planetarium.*

planetary /plænɪtəri/
ADJ ATTRIB **Planetary** means relating to or belonging to planets. *...the planetary exploration programme.*

plane tree, plane tree
NC A **plane tree** is a large tree with broad leaves that often grows in towns.

plank /plæŋk/ **planks**
1 NC A **plank** is a long rectangular piece of wood. *One officer required stitches after being hit on the jaw by a plank of wood.*
2 NC+SUPP The main **plank** of a political campaign is the main principle on which the campaign is based. *The main plank of his election campaign had been trade policy... The central plank of Mr Gorbachev's agrarian reform is the fifty-year land lease.*

planking /plæŋkɪŋ/
NU **Planking** is wood which has been cut into planks. *He felt an odd vibration from the hard rough planking he lay on.*

plankton /plæŋktən/
NU **Plankton** are very small animals and plants that live near the surface of the sea. *Plankton, infected with cholera bacteria, could then have poisoned fish and seafood that ended up being eaten by humans.*

planned economy, planned economies
NC In a **planned economy** prices and business activities are controlled by the government, rather than by individual companies. *The transition to a market economy, and the phasing out of a planned economy, will lead at first to instability... Inflation is not supposed to happen in a centrally planned economy.*

planner /plænə/ **planners**
1 NC The **planners** in local government are the people who decide how land should be used and what new buildings should be built. *...architects and planners.*
2 NC A **planner** is a person who works out in detail what is going to be done in the future. *...TV programme planners... By the late 1970's US military planners faced a problem.*

planning /plænɪŋ/
1 NU **Planning** is the process of deciding in detail how to do something before you actually start to do it. *A draft plan calls for a four-stage switch to a market economy after six decades of central planning... The project is still in the planning stage.*
2 NU **Planning** is also control by the local government of the way that land is used and of what new buildings are built. *...the concrete deserts created by modern planning at its worst.*
3 See also **family planning**.

planning permission
NU **Planning permission** is official permission that you must get from the local authority before you can build a house or make an extension to an existing building. *The occupier of the above premises has applied for planning permission.*

plant /plɑːnt/ **plants, planting, planted**
1 NC A **plant** is a living thing that grows in the earth and has a stem, leaves, and roots. *...a tall banana plant... Many plants and animals will become extinct.*
2 VO When you **plant** a seed, plant, or young tree, you put it into the ground to grow. *Each autumn we planted primroses in the garden.*
3 VO When someone **plants** land with a particular type of plant or crop, they put plants or seeds into the land to grow. *...small front gardens planted with rose trees.*
4 NC A **plant** is also a factory, or a place where power is generated. *Ninety per cent of the six thousand workers at the plant took part in the ballot. ...the re-opening of a nuclear plant after an accident.*
5 NU **Plant** is large machinery used in industrial processes; a technical use. *The company plans to spend nearly £1 billion on new plant and equipment.*
6 VOA If you **plant** something somewhere, you put it there. *I planted my deckchair beside hers... They had planted the bomb beneath the house.*
7 VO If you **plant** something such as a weapon or drugs on someone, you put it amongst their belongings so that they will be wrongly accused of a crime. *I'm convinced the evidence was planted in John's flat.*

plant out PHRASAL VERB When you **plant out** young plants, you plant them outside in the ground where they are to be left to grow. *We had to rear it in a nursery and plant it out.*

plantain /plæntɪn/ **plantains**
1 NC A **plantain** is a large tree that grows in tropical areas of the world.
2 NC **Plantains** are large green bananas that grow on a plantain tree. *The aroma of sweet plantains and rice and beans fills the air.*
3 NC A **plantain** is also a wild plant with broad leaves and a head of tiny green flowers on a long stem.

plantation /plɑːnteɪʃn/ **plantations**
1 NC A **plantation** is a large piece of land where crops such as cotton, tea, or sugar are grown. *...rubber plantations.*
2 NC A **plantation** is also a large number of trees planted together. *...conifer plantations.*

planter /plɑːntə/ **planters**
NC+SUPP A **planter** is a person who owns or manages a plantation in a tropical country. *...Indian tea planters.*

plant pot, plant pots
NC A **plant pot** is a round pot, usually made of clay or plastic, that you fill with earth in order to grow plants in it. *...an ordinary brown plastic plant pot.*

plaque /plæk, plɑːk/ **plaques**
1 NC A **plaque** is a flat piece of metal or wood, which is fixed to a wall or monument in memory of a person or event. *...a memorial plaque at the crematorium... A plaque marks the site of Chippendale's workshops.*
2 NU **Plaque** is a substance that forms on the surface of your teeth. It consists of saliva, bacteria, and food. *It also releases anti-bacterial agents that attack the plaque.*

plasma /plæzmə/
NU **Plasma** is the clear fluid part of blood. *Supplies of high protein foods, medicines, blood plasma, tents, warm clothes and blankets are on their way to the earthquake zone.*

plaster /plɑːstə/ **plasters, plastering, plastered**
1 NU **Plaster** is a smooth paste made of sand, lime, and water, used to cover walls and ceilings inside buildings. *The walls were in a dreadful condition—the plaster was peeling off.*
2 VO If you **plaster** a wall or ceiling, you cover it with a layer of plaster. *...a wall that was poorly plastered.*
3 NC A **plaster** is a strip of sticky material with a small pad, used for covering small cuts or sores on your body. *I dabbed the cut and applied a plaster.*
4 If your leg or arm is in **plaster**, it has a plaster cast on it to protect a broken bone. *His arm will remain in plaster for at least two months.*

plasterboard /plɑ:stəbɔːd/
NU **Plasterboard** is thin rectangular boards in the form of sheets of cardboard held together with plaster. It can be used to cover walls and ceilings inside a building.

plaster cast, plaster casts
NC A **plaster cast** is a hard case made of plaster of Paris, used for protecting broken bones by keeping part of the body rigid. *Botham is expected to be in hospital for at least three weeks and will be immobilised in a plaster cast.*

plastered /plɑːstəd/
1 ADJ PRED+*to* If something is **plastered** to a surface, it is sticking to the surface. *His wet hair was plastered to his forehead.*
2 ADJ PRED+*with* If a surface is **plastered** with something, it is covered with it. *Her back was thickly plastered with suntan oil... The walls of his tiny shop were plastered with pictures of actors.*

plasterer /plɑːstərə/ **plasterers**
NC A **plasterer** is a person whose job it is to cover walls and ceilings with plaster. *You need a plasterer to do that job properly.*

plaster of Paris
NU **Plaster of Paris** is a type of plaster made from a white powder and water which is used to make plaster casts. *The stones at the opening of the chamber were found to be sealed with a mortar that's rather like plaster of Paris.*

plastic /plæstɪk/ **plastics**
NUorNC **Plastic** is a light material produced by a chemical process. It can be moulded when soft and used to make objects. *The roofs are covered in winter by sheets of plastic... What's special about this new type of plastic?... It's used in making some paints and plastics. ...a plastic bag.*

plastic bomb, plastic bombs
NC A **plastic bomb** is a small bomb which contains plastic explosive. *...the wave of plastic bombs exploding in cinemas and cafés.*

plastic bullet, plastic bullets
NC A **plastic bullet** is a bullet made of plastic, which is intended to injure people rather than kill them, and is therefore used by police or soldiers to control crowds in riots. *Police used tear gas and plastic bullets to break up demonstrations in three towns... A woman was hit at close range by a plastic bullet.*

plastic explosive, plastic explosives
NCorNU **Plastic explosive** is a soft material which explodes. It can be pressed into different shapes and is used to make bombs. *Spanish police found one hundred kilograms of plastic explosive in the boot... Commandos using plastic explosives have taken control of the whole of the building except the basement.*

Plasticine /plæstəsiːn/
NU **Plasticine** is a soft coloured substance like clay which children use for making little models; **Plasticine** is a trademark.

plastic surgery
NU **Plastic surgery** is the practice of performing operations to repair damaged skin, or to improve people's appearance by changing their features. *One of the survivors needed plastic surgery.*

plat du jour /plɑː duː ʒʊə/ **plats du jour.** The plural is pronounced in the same way as the singular.
NC The **plat du jour** in a restaurant is the dish which has been specially prepared on a particular day.

plate /pleɪt/ **plates, plating, plated**
1 NC A **plate** is a round or oval flat dish used to hold food. *He looked at the food on his plate.*
2 NC You can use **plate** to refer to a plate and its contents, or to the contents only. *She pushed her plate of boiled fish away... He greedily ate up a plate of food that he did not want.*
3 NC A **plate** is also a flat piece of metal, especially on machinery or a building. *We got into the cellar through a round hole covered by a metal plate.*
4 NU **Plate** consists of dishes, bowls, and cups made of silver or gold. *We would prefer church plate and other treasures to be stored in bank vaults.*
5 NC A **plate** in a book is a picture or photograph

which takes up a whole page.
6 NC A dental **plate** is a piece of shaped plastic with a set of false teeth attached to it. *He would first provide me with provisional plates until the gums settled.*
7 If you have a lot **on** your **plate**, you have a lot of work to do or a lot of things to deal with; an informal expression. *As if they didn't have enough problems on their plate already!... Yeltsin has plenty on his plate developing Russia as a new nation state.*
8 See also **license plate, number plate.**

plateau /plætəʊ/ **plateaus** or **plateaux**
1 NC A **plateau** is a large area of high, flat land. *After about half an hour's flying we landed on a high plateau, overlooking a river valley.*
2 N SING If an activity or process has reached a **plateau**, it has reached a stage where there is no further change or development. *The US space programme seemed to have reached a plateau of development.*

plated /pleɪtɪd/
ADJ Metal that is **plated** is covered with a thin layer of another kind of metal. *It's made in solid brass and chrome plated. ...gold-plated brooches.*

plateful /pleɪtfʊl/ **platefuls**
NC A **plateful** of food is an amount of food that is on a plate and fills it. *...a plateful of sandwiches.*

plate glass
NU **Plate glass** is thick glass made in large, flat pieces, used to make large windows and doors. *Bricks started flying through the windows and there was plate glass all over the place. ...a new plate-glass window.*

platform /plætfɔːm/ **platforms**
1 NC A **platform** is a flat raised structure, on which someone or something can stand. *The speaker mounted the platform. ...loading platforms... Iranian rockets had destroyed an Iraqi missile platform near Tib. ...a raised platform area for sleeping.*
2 NC A **platform** is also a structure built for people to work on when drilling for oil or gas at sea, or when extracting it. *...one of the four platforms pumping oil from Britain's biggest offshore reserve. ...the accident in the North Sea that closed three production platforms... The blaze started on an oil platform on Sunday when leaking gas exploded.*
3 NC A **platform** in a railway station is the raised area beside the rails where you wait for or get off a train. *Jordache paced nervously up and down the platform.*
4 NC If someone has a **platform**, they have an opportunity to tell people what they think or want. *It provides a platform for the consumer's viewpoint... Tirana has frequently condemned such meetings as providing a platform for the two superpowers to extend their powers over states.*
5 NC⫽SUPP The **platform** of a political party is what they say they will do if they are elected. *He campaigned on a socialist platform... What is now needed is a strong political platform and adequate people to carry it out.*

plating /pleɪtɪŋ/
NU **Plating** is a thin layer of metal on something, or a covering of metal plates. *The security force are worried that the new weapon can penetrate the armour plating now fitted to Land-Rovers and other vehicles.*

platinum /plætɪnəm/
1 NU **Platinum** is a valuable, silvery-grey metal often used for making jewellery. *Both platinum and gold have been found in Antarctica.*
2 ADJ **Platinum** blonde hair is very fair, almost white. *...a platinum blonde.*

platitude /plætɪtjuːd/ **platitudes**
NC A **platitude** is a statement considered to be meaningless because it has been made many times before in similar situations; a formal word. *...empty platitudes about democracy.*

platitudinous /plætɪtjuːdɪnəs/
ADJ A **platitudinous** remark or speech is boring and not original; a formal word. *...a platitudinous statement affirming 'the right of the individual to live freely'.*

platonic /plətɒnɪk/
ADJ **Platonic** relationships or feelings do not involve

sex. *Her interest in him was entirely platonic.*

platoon /plətuːn/ **platoons**
N COLL A **platoon** is a small group of soldiers commanded by a lieutenant. *In his platoon he had thirty-two men.*

platter /plætə/ **platters**
NC A **platter** is a large serving dish; an old-fashioned word. *There are steaming platters of rice and meat. ...a silver platter.*

plaudits /plɔːdɪts/
N PL If a person or thing receives **plaudits** from a group of people, those people express their admiration for or approval of that person or thing; a formal word. *The building won immediate plaudits from architects and laymen alike.*

plausible /plɔːzəbl/
ADJ An explanation that is **plausible** seems likely to be true or valid. *Such a theory seems very plausible. ...a plausible answer.*

play /pleɪ/ **plays, playing, played**
1 V When children **play**, they spend time with their toys or taking part in games. *The kids went off to play on the swings... I played with the children all day.* ▶ Also NU *The very uselessness of play is its greatest asset. ...special educational play.*
2 V Oor V When you **play** a sport, game, or match, you take part in it. *Do you play chess?... I used to play for the village cricket team.*
3 V Oor V+against When one person or team **plays** another, they compete against them in a sport or game. *In the semi-finals, Celtic will play Dundee United at Hampden Park on September 25th... I saw Australia play against England at Lords.*
4 NU **Play** is the playing of a game or match for a period of time. *Bad light stopped play for some time on this fourth day... The noise reached a crescendo before each point, then dropped to an expectant hush as play began.*
5 VO If you **play** a joke or a trick on someone, you deceive or surprise them in a way that you think is funny, but may annoy them. *I presumed someone was playing a rather silly joke.*
6 VC You can use **play** to say how someone behaves. For example, if someone **plays** the innocent, they pretend to be innocent; an informal use. *Don't you play the wise old professor with me, Franz.*
7 NC A **play** is a piece of writing performed in a theatre, on the radio, or on television. *Wesker has written four major plays since then.*
8 VOor V A If an actor **plays** a character in a play or film, he or she performs the part of that character. *Brutus was played by James Mason... I was asked to play in a revival of 'Ghosts'.*
9 VOor V When you **play** a musical instrument or **play** a tune on it, you produce music from it. *Out on the balcony, a man stood playing a trombone... The child played him a tune... Doesn't he play beautifully?*
10 VO If you **play** a record or tape, you put it on a machine so you can listen to it. *I'll play you the tape.*
11 See also **fair play, foul play.**
● **Play** is used in these phrases. ● If something or someone **plays a part** or **plays a role** in a situation, they are involved in it and have an effect on it. *Examinations seem to play a large part in education... In recent years, China has been keen to play a bigger role in the Middle East.* ● If someone **plays it safe,** they do not take risks. *Should I play it safe and follow the judge's order?* ● If you **play for time,** you try to delay something happening, so that you can prepare for it or prevent it from happening. *She was playing for time, half hoping that he would forget all about it.* ● to **play host:** see host.

play along PHRASAL VERB If you **play along** with a person you agree with them and do what they want, even though you are not sure whether they are right. *I'll play along with them for the moment.*

play at PHRASAL VERB 1 If you **play at** an activity, you do it casually and without any real effort. *I realized that I had only been playing at politics at University.* 2 If someone, especially a child, **plays at** being a particular kind of person or being in a particular situation, they pretend to be that person or

in that situation, usually as a game. *They played at being huntsmen.* 3 If you ask **what** someone **is playing at,** you are angry because you think that they are doing something stupid or wrong; an informal expression. *What do you think you're playing at?*

play back PHRASAL VERB When you **play back** a tape or film, you listen to the sounds or watch the pictures after recording them. *If you make a tape recording and you hear your voice played back, you'll say, 'That doesn't sound like me.'*

play down PHRASAL VERB If you **play down** a fact or feature, you try to make people think that it is not particularly important. *He played down his recent promotion.*

play off against PHRASAL VERB If you **play** people **off against** each other, you make them compete or argue, so that you gain some advantage. *Annie played one parent off against the other.*

play on PHRASAL VERB If you **play on** or **play upon** people's weaknesses or faults, you deliberately use them in order to achieve what you want. *He used to play on their prejudices and their fears... He found himself in a position to play upon the fears of his colleagues.*

play up PHRASAL VERB 1 If you **play up** a fact or feature, you emphasize it and try to make people think that it is more important than it really is. *Many Poles wonder whether Walesa will not be tempted to play up popular discontent over the effects of the government's harsh economic reforms... This increase in crime is definitely being played up by the media.* 2 If something such as a machine or a part of your body is **playing up** or is **playing** you **up,** it is not working properly. *Our phone is playing up again... Is your leg still playing you up?* 3 When children **are playing up,** they are being naughty and are difficult to control; an informal use. *The kids are playing up again.*

play upon PHRASAL VERB See **play on.**

play-act, play-acts, play-acting, play-acted
V Someone who is **play-acting** is pretending to have feelings or attitudes that they do not really have. *I wasn't really hurt—I was just play-acting.*

playback /pleɪbæk/
NU The **playback** of a tape is the operation of the machine it is in so that you can listen to the sound recorded on it or watch the pictures recorded on it. *You're listening to an instantaneous playback of the tape... Then all you have to do is press the playback button.*

playbill /pleɪbɪl/ **playbills**
NC A **playbill** is a piece of paper which tells the public when and where a play will be performed.

playboy /pleɪbɔɪ/ **playboys**
NC A **playboy** is a rich man who spends most of his time enjoying himself. *He was a playboy with a liking for fast cars.*

player /pleɪə/ **players**
1 NC A **player** in a sport or game is a person who takes part. *The top woman player is Li Lingwei, winner of this year's World Cup in Bangkok. ...international football's highest paid player.*
2 NC You can refer to a musician as a **player.** For example, a piano **player** is someone who plays the piano. *He's one of the most original guitar players in jazz. ...another well-known bass player.*
3 NC A **player** is also a person, group, or country that takes part in a process. *The key player is Germany, whose role in Europe has been brought sharply into focus by the Yugoslav crisis... Mr Outtara is also an important player in the Ivorian economic crisis.*
4 See also **cassette player, CD player, record player.**

playful /pleɪfl/
1 ADJ Someone who is **playful** is friendly and likes to have fun. *She gave Philip's hand a little playful squeeze.* ◆ **playfully** ADV *Elaine kissed Harold playfully on the cheek.*
2 ADJ An animal that is **playful** is lively and friendly. *...a playful kitten.*

playground /pleɪgraund/ **playgrounds**
NC A **playground** is a piece of land where children can play. *An investigation has found that two out of three playgrounds are unsafe.*

playgroup /ˈpleɪgruːp/ **playgroups**
N or NU A **playgroup** is an informal kind of school for very young children where they learn by playing. *The government is setting up a committee to look into the provision of nursery education in both schools and playgroups. ...while the children are at playgroup.*

playhouse /ˈpleɪhaʊs/ **playhouses**
NC A **playhouse** is a theatre; an old-fashioned word. *...London playhouses.*

playing card, playing cards
NC **Playing cards** are thin pieces of card with numbers and pictures on them that are used to play various games. *...a pack of playing cards.*

playing field, playing fields
1 NC A **playing field** is a large area of grass where people play games such as hockey and football. *State law requires high schools to be built on at least 17 acres, with plenty of room for playing fields.*
2 N SING You talk about a level **playing field** when you want to refer to a situation that is fair, because the opponents in it have equal advantages. *We will challenge unfair trade practices of other countries in order to achieve a level playing field for American industries... David Boren argues that spending limits would actually level the playing field and help challengers.*

playmate /ˈpleɪmeɪt/ **playmates**
NC A child's **playmates** are other children who often play with him or her. *My playmates were my cousins.*

playoff /ˈpleɪɒf/ **playoffs**
NC A **playoff** is an extra game to decide the final positions of the competitors when two or more of them have the same score or have reached the same stage in a competition. *India beat Kenya 4-nil, and in a playoff for fifth place, Poland beat Malaysia 4-3... It was the local boy Larry Mize who won after a playoff against Norman and Ballesteros.*

play on words
N SING A **play on words** is a clever and amusing use of a word with more than one meaning, or a word that sounds like another word, so that what you say has two different meanings. *It is a play on words that works on several levels.*

playpen /ˈpleɪpen/ **playpens**
NC A **playpen** is a small structure which is designed for a baby or young child to play safely in. It has bars or a net round the sides and is open at the top. *In good weather they can sit safely in the playpen on the porch.*

playroom /ˈpleɪruːm, ˈpleɪrʊm/ **playrooms**
NC A **playroom** is a room in a house for children to play in.

plaything /ˈpleɪθɪŋ/ **playthings**; a formal word.
1 NC A **plaything** is a toy that a child plays with. *I used to get them new playthings to keep them quiet.*
2 NC You can refer to a person or thing that someone uses carelessly for their own pleasure or for some other purpose as a **plaything**. *Mr Zhivkov said that he would not allow anyone to make him into a political plaything for their own ends... Cocaine ceased to be merely a plaything for the rich.*

playtime /ˈpleɪtaɪm/
NU **Playtime** is a period of time between lessons at school when children can play outside. *I waited for the children to settle down after playtime.*

playwright /ˈpleɪraɪt/ **playwrights**
NC A **playwright** is a person who writes plays. *Jennifer Davidson is a novelist and playwright who lives in Washington.*

plc /ˌpiːelˈsiː/
plc is an abbreviation for 'public limited company'. It is used after the name of a company whose shares can be bought by the public. *...National Westminster Bank plc.*

plea /pliː/ **pleas**
1 NC A **plea** is an intense, emotional request for something. *She at last responded to his pleas for help.*
2 NC In a court of law, a **plea** is the answer which someone gives when they say whether they are guilty or not; a legal use. *I agreed to enter a plea of guilty.*

plead /pliːd/ **pleads, pleading, pleaded.** The form **pled** can also be used for the past tense and past participle

in American English.
1 V A, V-QUOTE, or V-REPORT If you **plead** with someone to do something, you ask them in an intense, emotional way to do it. *He was pleading with her to control herself... He was pleading for support from the outside world... 'Take me with you,' he pleaded.*
2 N or VA If someone, especially a lawyer, **pleads** someone else's case or cause, they speak in support or defence of that person; a formal use. *Of course his mother does her best to plead his case... Who will plead for us?*
3 V or V-REPORT If you **plead** a particular thing, you give it as your reason or excuse for not doing something. *The only surviving ex-president not in attendance was Jimmy Carter, who pleaded a prior engagement... The soldiers pleaded that they shouldn't have to pay the tax because they didn't receive local services... I pleaded that I felt ill.*
4 V C or V When someone who is charged with a crime **pleads** guilty in a court of law, they officially state that they are guilty of the crime. If they **plead** not guilty, they state that they are not guilty. *All four pleaded guilty to the smuggling charges... 'How do you plead?'—'Not guilty.'... A not guilty plea was entered for the seventh, who refused to plead.*

pleading /ˈpliːdɪŋ/ **pleadings**
1 ADJ ATTRIB A **pleading** expression or gesture shows that you want something very much and is intended to persuade someone to give it to you. *Then he saw his brother's pleading expression and his heart softened.*
2 NU or N PL **Pleading** is asking someone in an intense, emotional way to do something. *After days of tearful pleading and sulking, she stayed... It was hard to resist his daughter's pleadings.*

pleasant /ˈpleznt/ **pleasanter, pleasantest**
1 ADJ Something that is **pleasant** is enjoyable or attractive. *...a pleasant chat... It was pleasant to sit under the apple tree.* ◆ **pleasantly** ADV *I was pleasantly surprised. ...a pleasantly nutty taste.*
2 ADJ Someone who is **pleasant** is friendly and likeable. *They were pleasant lads.* ◆ **pleasantly** ADV *'Please come in,' she said pleasantly.*

pleasantry /ˈplezntri/ **pleasantries**
NC **Pleasantries** are casual, friendly remarks which you say in order to be polite; a formal word. *We stood exchanging a few pleasantries.*

please /pliːz/ **pleases, pleasing, pleased**
1 You say **please** to show politeness when you ask someone to do something or ask them for something. *'Follow me, please,' the guide said... Could I speak to Sue, please?*
2 You use **please** when you are accepting something politely. *'Do you want some milk?'—'Yes please.'*
3 V O or V If someone or something **pleases** you, they make you feel happy and satisfied. *Neither idea pleased me... He seemed eager to please.*
4 V You use **please** in phrases such as 'as she pleases' and 'whatever you please' to indicate that someone can do or have whatever they want. *Judy had a right to come and go as she pleased... He can get anyone he pleases to work with him.*
5 You say '**please yourself**' to indicate in a rude way that you do not mind or care whether the person you are talking to does a particular thing or not; an informal expression. *'Do you mind if I wait?' I asked. Melanie shrugged: 'Please yourself.'*

pleased /pliːzd/
1 ADJ PRED If you are **pleased**, you are happy about something or satisfied with it. *She seemed very pleased that he had come... He was pleased with my progress.*
2 You say '**Pleased to meet you**' as a polite way of greeting someone you are meeting for the first time. *'Pleased to meet you. I'm glad you came.'*

pleasing /ˈpliːzɪŋ/
ADJ Something that is **pleasing** gives you pleasure and satisfaction; a formal word. *...a pleasing piece of news... It has a pleasing smell.*

pleasurable /ˈpleʒərəbl/
ADJ Something that is **pleasurable** is pleasant and enjoyable; a formal word. *...a pleasurable sensation.*

pleasure /plɛʒə/ **pleasures**
1 NU **Pleasure** is a feeling of happiness, satisfaction,
or enjoyment. *McPherson could scarcely conceal his
pleasure at my resignation. ...giving pleasure to all
rose lovers.*
2 NU **Pleasure** is also the activity of enjoying yourself
rather than working. *She is a disciplined creature who
will put duty before pleasure... The important thing to
realise was that this was not a pleasure trip.*
3 NC A **pleasure** is an activity or experience that you
find very enjoyable and satisfying. *...the pleasures of
choral singing.*
● **Pleasure** is used in these phrases. ● You can say
'**It's a pleasure**' or '**My pleasure**' as a polite way of
replying to someone who has just thanked you for
doing something. *'Thank you for talking to us about
your research.'—'It's a pleasure.'... 'Thanks very
much for speaking with us.'—'My pleasure.'* ● You
can say '**With pleasure**' as a polite way of saying that
you are very willing to do something; a formal
expression. *'Could you help?'—'With pleasure.'*

pleat /pliːt/ **pleats**
NC A **pleat** in a piece of clothing is a permanent fold
made in the cloth.

pleated /pliːtɪd/
ADJ A **pleated** piece of clothing has pleats in it. *...a
brown pleated skirt.*

pleb /plɛb/ **plebs**
NC A **pleb** is the same as a **plebeian**; an informal
word.

plebeian /pləbiːən/ **plebeians**; an offensive word.
1 NC A **plebeian** is a member of the lower social
classes. *...his dislike of what he called the plebeians.*
2 ADJ Something that is **plebeian** is connected with, or
typical of, the lower social classes. *He had gone back
to his rather plebeian job... He had a rather thick,
short, plebeian neck.*

plebiscite /plɛbɪsaɪt/ **plebiscites**
NC A **plebiscite** is a vote in which all the people in a
country or region are asked whether they agree or
disagree with a particular policy, for example a policy
of unification with another country. *They've been
calling for a plebiscite to allow Kashmiris the right to
decide if they want to remain in India or join the
Islamic state of Pakistan.*

plectrum /plɛktrəm/ **plectrums**
NC A **plectrum** is a small thin piece of plastic, wood,
or metal that is held between the finger and thumb
and used for plucking the strings of a guitar, banjo, or
mandolin. *The band's guitarist, Robbie Krieger,
played his electric instrument without a plectrum.*

pled /plɛd/
In American English, **pled** is a past tense and past
participle of **plead**.

pledge /plɛdʒ/ **pledges, pledging, pledged**
1 NC A **pledge** is a solemn promise to do something.
*The Government should fulfil its 1979 Manifesto
pledge... He gave a pledge to handle the affair in a
friendly manner.*
2 VO, V+to-INF, or V-REPORT If you **pledge** something, you
promise solemnly that you will do it or give it. *The
Japanese have pledged support in general terms for
America's lead... They will pledge $1 million to fund
the project... The government pledged to reduce the
level of imports... He has pledged that the ban will be
lifted after two years.*
3 V-REFL If you **pledge** yourself to something, you
promise to follow a particular course of action or to
support a particular person, group, or idea. *The new
organization pledged itself to the revolutionary
overthrow of the dictator.*

plenary /pliːnəri/ **plenaries**
ADJ ATTRIB A **plenary** session or meeting is attended
by all the members of a committee or all of the
participants at a conference; a formal word. *Later,
all the ministers taking part in the summit were
holding a plenary session... A plenary meeting was
called for.* ▶ Also NC *The plenary petered out after
half an hour.*

plenipotentiary /plɛnɪpətɛnʃəri/ **plenipotentiaries**
NC A **plenipotentiary** is someone who has full power
and authority to act as a representative of a country

or organization; a formal word. *One of the
plenipotentiaries actually refused to sign the treaty.*
▶ Also ADJ *...plenipotentiary powers.*

plentiful /plɛntɪfl/
ADJ Something that is **plentiful** exists in large
amounts. *Food became more plentiful each day... The
Soviet Union has its own oil in plentiful supply.*

plenty /plɛnti/
QUANT If there is **plenty** of something, there is more
than enough of it. If there are **plenty** of things, there
are more than enough of them. *We've got plenty of
time... There are always plenty of jobs... There was
plenty to discuss... A fiver should be plenty.*

plenum /pliːnəm/ **plenums**
NC A **plenum** is a session or meeting that is attended
by all the members of a committee or all of the
participants at a conference; a formal word. *...a two-
day plenum of the Bulgarian Communist Party Central
Committee.*

plethora /plɛθərə/
N SING+of A **plethora** of something is an amount of it
that is much greater than you want or need; a formal
word. *He stood there, surrounded by that plethora of
microphones, amplifiers, speakers, and reporters.*

pleurisy /plʊərəsi/
NU **Pleurisy** is a serious illness in which a person's
lungs are inflamed and breathing is difficult. *The test
will help most with early diagnosis of tuberculosis,
meningitis and pleurisy... I had not completely
recovered from my attack of pleurisy.*

pliable /plaɪəbl/
1 ADJ If something is **pliable**, it bends easily without
breaking. *...light, pliable materials such as wood,
matting and paper.*
2 ADJ Someone who is **pliable** can be easily influenced
and controlled. *...a pliable leader of the opposition...
He wanted the two sides to try to adopt a more pliable
attitude.*

pliant /plaɪənt/
1 ADJ Someone who is **pliant** can be easily influenced
and controlled by other people. *They want to be able
to replace union workers with a more pliant non-union
workforce... She was pliant and docile.*
2 ADJ If something is **pliant**, you can bend it easily
without breaking it.

pliers /plaɪəz/
N PL **Pliers** are a tool used for holding or pulling out
things such as nails, or for bending or cutting wire.
Use a pair of pliers.

plight /plaɪt/
N SING+POSS Someone's **plight** is the difficult or
dangerous situation that they are in; a formal word.
*...the plight of the mentally handicapped... He had
heard of my plight through an acquaintance... East
Germany's economic plight is far worse than had been
expected.*

plimsoll /plɪmsəl/ **plimsolls**
NC **Plimsolls** are shoes made of canvas with flat
rubber soles worn for sports and leisure. *He was in
yachtsman's trousers, striped towelling shirt and
plimsolls.*

Plimsoll line, Plimsoll lines
NC The **Plimsoll line** on a ship is a line painted on the
outside which marks how deep the ship can lie in the
water when loaded, before it becomes unsafe.
...loading a ship using the Plimsoll line.

plinth /plɪnθ/ **plinths**
NC A **plinth** is a square block made of stone on which
a statue or a pillar stands. *The statue was to have
stood on a tall plinth in the town of Katowice on the
old Polish-German border.*

plod /plɒd/ **plods, plodding, plodded**
1 V If someone **plods** along, they walk slowly and
heavily. *He plodded along the road.*
2 VA If someone **plods** on or **plods** along with a job,
they work slowly and without enthusiasm. *He plodded
on in the Board of Trade.*

plonk /plɒŋk/ **plonks, plonking, plonked**
VOA If you **plonk** something in a place, you put it or
drop it there heavily and carelessly; an informal
word. *Bottles of beer were plonked on the wooden
table. ...plonking himself down in the middle.*

plop /plɒp/ **plops, plopping, plopped**
1 NC A **plop** is a soft gentle sound, like the sound made by something light dropping into water. *My hat landed with a plop in the bucket.*
2 VA If something **plops** into a liquid, it drops into it with a soft gentle sound. *Great big tears plopped into her soup.*

plot /plɒt/ **plots, plotting, plotted**
1 NC A **plot** is a secret plan by a group of people to do something illegal or wrong. *Another plot to assassinate the General was uncovered... He denies taking part in this alleged plot.*
2 VO, V+to-INF, or V If people **plot** something or **plot** to do something illegal or wrong, they plan secretly to do it. *He was always plotting strikes... They were accused of plotting to assassinate the President... Anyone convicted of plotting against the king will be executed.*
3 NC The **plot** of a film, novel, or play is the story and the way in which it develops. *They were having some difficulty in following the plot.*
4 NC A **plot** is a small piece of land. *His land is split up into several widely scattered plots.*
5 VO When someone **plots** the position or course of a plane or ship, they mark it on a map or chart. *They plotted the new positions of each vessel.*
6 VO When you are drawing a graph, you **plot** the points on it by marking them at the correct places to form the graph. *Most studies of the relationship between alcohol and cardiovascular disease have shown, when plotted on a graph, a U-shaped curve.*

plotter /plɒtə/ **plotters**
1 NC A **plotter** is a person who secretly plans with others to do something that is illegal or wrong, usually against a person or a government. *The arrest of the plotters soon followed... The coup plotters' only chance of success would have been to silence Yeltsin.*
2 NC A **plotter** is a person or instrument that marks the position of something, for example a ship or plane, on a map or chart.

plough /plaʊ/ **ploughs, ploughing, ploughed**; spelt **plow** in American English.
1 NC A **plough** is a large farming tool with sharp blades that is pulled across the soil to turn it over, usually before seeds are planted. *...a man behind the plough with his donkey.*
2 VOorV When someone **ploughs** an area of land, they turn over the soil using a plough. *A small tractor can plough an acre in six to nine hours... The big population demands more firewood and more space to plough.*

plough back PHRASAL VERB If you **plough** profits **back** into a business, you spend the profits on things that will improve the business so that you can make more money in the long term. *The profits we make are constantly ploughed back because there are opportunities in all directions.*

plough into PHRASAL VERB 1 If one thing **ploughs** into another, it crashes into it. *The car wavered crazily before ploughing into the bank... After hitting the ground, the plane ploughed into electricity cables and exploded.* 2 If someone **ploughs** money **into** a business or organization, they invest large sums of money in it. *...the huge sums of money which were ploughed into computing... He went on to say that his ministry was ploughing money into the trade union movement.*

plough on PHRASAL VERB If you **plough on**, you continue with a task even though it is difficult or unpleasant. *Under Brezhnev, they would have ploughed on, undoubtedly, but under Gorbachev they are pulling out... The fighters ploughed on to their destination airfields.*

plough through PHRASAL VERB 1 If you **plough through** a meal or a piece of work, you eat it all or do it all, although it is difficult because there is a lot of it. *I can't quite imagine ploughing through three bowls of porridge oats every day, even for the sake of my heart.* 2 To **plough through** something means to move through it with a great deal of force. *The plane ploughed through houses at the end of the runway and came to rest in a marsh.*

plough up PHRASAL VERB If an area of grassland is **ploughed up**, the soil is turned over using a plough, so

that crops can be grown there. *Golf courses were ploughed up for use as agricultural land.*

ploughman /plaʊmən/ **ploughmen** /plaʊmən/; spelt **plowman** in American English.
NC A **ploughman** is a person whose job is to plough the land, especially using a plough pulled by animals. *He was forced to leave and work long hard hours as a ploughman.*

ploughman's lunch, ploughman's lunches
NC A **ploughman's lunch** or a **ploughman's** is a snack consisting of bread, cheese and pickles. It is usually bought and eaten in a pub.

ploughshare /plaʊʃeə/ **ploughshares**; spelt **plowshare** in American English.
If you talk about people **turning swords into ploughshares**, you are talking about people who have been fighting or quarrelling making peace with each other. *It is time to turn swords into ploughshares.*

plover /plʌvə/ **plovers**
NC A **plover** is a bird with long wings and a short straight beak that lives mainly on the seashore.

plow /plaʊ/. See **plough.**

ploy /plɔɪ/ **ploys**
NC A **ploy** is a way of behaving that you have planned carefully in order to achieve a secret purpose or advantage for yourself. *This headache was clearly a delaying ploy.*

pluck /plʌk/ **plucks, plucking, plucked**
1 VO If you **pluck** something from somewhere, you take hold of it and pull it with a sharp movement. *He plucked a tomato and offered it to Hilda... He laughed and plucked the paper from my hand.*
2 VO If you **pluck** someone from an unpleasant or dangerous situation, you rescue them. *A lifeboat managed to pluck the rest of the party to safety... Many were plucked from the rooftops of their homes.*
3 VO If you **pluck** a chicken or other dead bird, you pull its feathers out to prepare it for cooking.
4 VOorVA If you **pluck** a guitar or other stringed musical instrument, you use your fingers to pull the strings and let them go, so that they make a sound. *The guitarists plucked out a little melody.*
5 If you **pluck up** the **courage** to do something frightening, you make a great effort so that you are brave enough to do it. *I eventually plucked up enough courage to go in... The tax is a mistake and the Prime Minister should pluck up courage and admit it.*

plucky /plʌki/ **pluckier, pluckiest**
ADJ A **plucky** person has courage; an old-fashioned word. *This schoolgirl story featured a plucky heroine.*

plug /plʌg/ **plugs, plugging, plugged**
1 NC A **plug** is a small plastic object with metal pieces which fit into the holes in a socket and connect a piece of electrical equipment to the electricity supply. *This lamp doesn't have a plug.*
2 NC A **plug** is also a socket in the wall of a room that is a source of electricity; an informal use. *...electricity from a plug in the garage.*
3 NC A **plug** is also a thick, circular piece of rubber or plastic used to block the hole in a bath or sink when it is filled with water. *It was like emptying a bath—you pull out the plug and the water runs away.*
4 VO If you **plug** a hole, you block it with something. *Have you plugged all the leaks?*
5 VO If someone **plugs** a book or film, they praise it to encourage people to buy it or see it because they have an interest in it doing well; an informal use. *The radio stations are plugging the record like mad.* ▶ Also NC *Can I quickly give our new show a plug?*

plug in PHRASAL VERB If you **plug in** a piece of electrical equipment, you push its plug into an electric socket. *I plugged in the kettle.*

plugged /plʌgd/
ADJ If a part of your body such as your nose is **plugged**, it is blocked by mucus or other substance, usually because you are ill. *...a plugged tear duct.*

plughole /plʌghəʊl/ **plugholes**
NC A **plughole** is a hole in a bath or sink which allows the water to flow away. *...the water going down a plughole in a bathtub.*

plum /plʌm/ **plums**
1 NC A **plum** is a small, sweet fruit with a smooth red

or yellow skin and a stone in the middle. ...*ripe plums... The plum trees were already in bloom.*
2 ADJ ATTRIB A **plum** job is a very good job that a lot of people would like. ...*plum ministerial posts... Fort Multry had long been considered a plum assignment.*

plumage /ˈpluːmɪdʒ/
NU A bird's **plumage** is all its feathers. *Its plumage had turned grey.*

plumb /plʌm/ **plumbs, plumbing, plumbed**
If someone **plumbs the depths** of an unpleasant emotion, they experience it to an extreme degree. *The story shows how she plumbs the depths of humiliation.*

plumber /ˈplʌmə/ **plumbers**
NC A **plumber** is a person who connects and repairs things such as water and drainage pipes, baths, and toilets. *The plumbers came to mend the pipes.*

plumbing /ˈplʌmɪŋ/
1 NU The **plumbing** in a building consists of the water and drainage pipes, baths, and toilets. *Will it need new wiring and plumbing?*
2 NU **Plumbing** is the work of connecting and repairing water and drainage pipes, baths, and toilets. ...*minor plumbing repairs.*

plumb line, plumb lines
NC A **plumb line** is a piece of string with a weight attached to the end, which is used to check that something such as a wall is vertical or slopes at the correct angle.

plume /pluːm/ **plumes**
1 NC A **plume** is a large, often brightly coloured bird's feather; a formal use. ...*an ostrich plume.*
2 NC+of A **plume** of smoke is a small column of it rising into the air. *The last plume of blue smoke curled away.*

plumed /pluːmd/
ADJ **Plumed** means decorated with a plume or plumes, or shaped like a plume; a literary word. ...*his plumed helmet.* ...*brightly plumed pheasants.* ...*a slow sway of his plumed tail.*

plummet /ˈplʌmɪt/ **plummets, plummeting, plummeted**
1 VA If something **plummets** downwards, it falls very quickly. *The explosion sent the aircraft plummeting towards the sea.*
2 V If an amount, rate, or price **plummets**, it decreases quickly and suddenly. *The price of paper plummeted.*

plummy /ˈplʌmi/ **plummier, plummiest**
1 ADJ If you say that someone has a **plummy** voice or accent, you mean that they speak in a rather old-fashioned, upper-class English way.
2 ADJ Something that is **plummy** is dark red in colour; a literary use. *The peaks were turning a plummy maroon.*

plump /plʌmp/ **plumper, plumpest; plumps, plumping, plumped**
ADJ Someone who is **plump** is rather fat. ...*a plump, red-faced man.*
plump for PHRASAL VERB If you **plump for** someone or something, you choose them after hesitating and thinking. *She plumped for the éclair.*
plump up PHRASAL VERB When you **plump up** a cushion or pillow, you squeeze and shake it back into a rounded shape. *He plumped up the cushions and switched on the lamp.*

plum pudding, plum puddings
NCorNU A **plum pudding** is a special pudding that is eaten at Christmas, made with dried fruit, spices, and suet; an old-fashioned expression. ...*generous slices of a great spherical plum pudding.* ...*their standard feast—roast goose and plum pudding.*

plunder /ˈplʌndə/ **plunders, plundering, plundered**
1 VOorV If someone **plunders** a place or **plunders** things from a place, they steal things from it using force; a literary use. *Imperialist governments plunder the weaker nations... Houses have been set alight, property stolen and livestock plundered... Instead he chose to plunder and kill.*
2 NUorN SING **Plunder** is the activity of stealing property from places or people. ...*the savage burning and plunder of the commercial centre of town.*
3 NU **Plunder** is also stolen property; a literary use.

He escaped with his plunder.

plunge /plʌndʒ/ **plunges, plunging, plunged**
1 VA If something **plunges** in a particular direction, it falls in that direction. *The car plunged into the river... They plunged into the pool together.* ► Also N SING *They were relying on the plunge into icy waters to kill me.*
2 VOA If you **plunge** an object into something, you push it quickly or violently into it. *She plunged her hands into her coat pockets... He plunged the knife into her breast.*
3 V-ERGA To **plunge** someone or something into a state means to cause them suddenly to be in that state. ...*the danger of plunging society into chaos and anarchy... The hall was plunged into darkness... The country would plunge into a constitutional crisis.*
4 V+into If you **plunge** into an activity, you suddenly get very involved in it. *She plunged bravely into the debate.*
5 V If an amount or rate **plunges**, it decreases quickly and suddenly. *Sales have plunged by 24%... Oil output plunged by ten percent over the last six months.*
6 If you **take the plunge**, you decide to do something that you consider difficult or risky. *Take the plunge and start your own firm.*

plunger /ˈplʌndʒə/ **plungers**
NC A **plunger** is a device for unblocking pipes and sinks. It consists of a rubber cup on the end of a stick. You press it up and down over the pipe or the hole in the sink, and the suction moves the blockage. ...*a sink plunger.*

plunging /ˈplʌndʒɪŋ/
ADJ ATTRIB A **plunging** neckline on a woman's dress is one that is cut very low down with a steep V-shape. ...*a long sparkly dress with a deeply plunging neckline.*

pluperfect /pluːˈpɜːfɪkt/
N SING In grammar, the **pluperfect** is the tense of a verb describing actions that were completed before another event in the past happened. In English it is formed using 'had' followed by the past participle of the verb. In the sentences 'I had gone by then' and 'She'd eaten them before I arrived' the verbs 'go' and 'eat' are in the pluperfect. The **pluperfect** is often called the past perfect.

plural /ˈpluərəl/
1 N SINGorN+N In grammar, **plural** is the term used for a noun, pronoun, determiner, or verb when it refers to two or more people, things, or groups. See also **singular**.
2 ADJ ATTRIB **Plural** also means consisting of more than one person or thing or different kinds of people or things; a formal use. *We need a plural system of education.*

pluralism /ˈpluərəlɪzəm/; a formal word.
1 NU **Pluralism** is the existence of a variety of different opinions or principles within the same society, system, or philosophy. *He asked whether it was possible to have political pluralism within a Communist system.* ...*the pluralism and complexity of the real issues.*
2 NU **Pluralism** is also the belief that it is good for a society, system, or philosophy to have a variety of different people, opinions, or principles. ...*a one-system world whose opposite is pluralism, a chaos of opinions... The same push towards pluralism is evident in painting, too.*

pluralist /ˈpluərəlɪst/ **pluralists**
1 ADJ A **pluralist** society, system, or philosophy is one that is made up of a variety of different people, opinions, or principles. ...*a pluralist political system.* ...*a society that was increasingly pluralist.*
2 NC A **pluralist** is someone who believes that it is good for a society, system, or philosophy to have a variety of different people, opinions, or principles. *'Are you a pluralist, then?'—'I'm a kind of anarchist, I suppose.'* ...*the promotion of humane pluralist values.*

pluralistic /ˌpluərəˈlɪstɪk/
ADJ A **pluralistic** society, system, or philosophy consists of a variety of different people, opinions, or principles. ...*a pluralistic power structure.* ...*a complex, pluralistic society.* ...*a pluralistic approach to leisure.*

plurality /plʊəræləti/ **pluralities**
1 NU **Plurality** is the existence of more than one person or thing, or different kinds of people or things; a formal use. *He now believes in a mixed economy and political plurality.*
2 NC If a person or party has a **plurality** in an election, they have more votes than any other person or party, but they do not have a majority; used in American English. *They hoped to increase that plurality, if not actually get a majority.*

plus /plʌs/
1 PREP You use **plus** to show that one number is being added to another, for example, 'five plus three'. You represent this in figures as '5+3'. *What's seventeen plus nine?... It costs £29 a bottle plus VAT... They only cost $10.95 plus $2.50 postage and handling.*
2 ADJ after N You use **plus** to show that the actual number or quantity is greater than the one mentioned; an informal use. *Patients tend to be relatively old—60 plus... They take the exams at 13 plus.*
3 PREP or CONJ You can also use **plus** to add an item to one or more that you have already mentioned. *Now five people, plus Val, are missing... He wore strange scarves and beads, plus he was English.*
4 N SING A **plus** is an advantage or benefit. *The net effect, in some cases, is a plus and in others a minus for the farmer... It's a plus to the business traveller.*
5 You use **plus or minus** to give the amount by which a particular number may vary. *It might be possible to track it down to within plus or minus a kilometre or two... The margin of error is plus or minus three percent.*

plush /plʌʃ/
ADJ Something that is **plush** is smart, comfortable, and expensive. *...his plush car with reclining seats.*

plushy /plʌʃi/ **plushier, plushiest**
ADJ Something that is **plushy** is very smart, comfortable, and expensive; an informal word. *...plushy interiors.*

plus sign, plus signs
NC A **plus sign** is the sign (+) which is put between two numbers to show that the second number is being added to the first one.

plutocracy /pluːtɒkrəsi/ **plutocracies**
NU or NC **Plutocracy** is the political system in which a country is ruled by its wealthiest people. It is also used to refer to the country or the people who rule it; a formal word. *Newspapers are the organs of plutocracy.*

plutocrat /pluːtəkræt/ **plutocrats**
NC A **plutocrat** is someone who is powerful only because they are rich; a formal word, used showing disapproval. *You're nothing but a plutocrat... Bureaucrats and plutocrats thrive in every European capital.*

plutonium /pluːtəʊniəm/
NU **Plutonium** is a radioactive element used especially as a fuel in nuclear power stations, and in nuclear weapons. *The new reactor was apparently designed to produce plutonium for nuclear weapons.*

ply /plaɪ/ **plies, plying, plied**
1 VO+*with* If you **ply** someone with food or drink, you keep giving them more of it. *Dolly plied me with sweets.*
2 VO+*with* If you **ply** someone with questions, you keep asking them questions. *I plied him with questions about his novel.*
3 NU **Ply** is the thickness of wool, thread, or rope measured by the number of strands it is made from. *...four-ply wool.*

Plymouth /plɪməθ/
Plymouth is the capital of Montserrat and its largest town. Population: 1,400 (1980).

plywood /plaɪwʊd/
NU **Plywood** consists of several thin layers of wood stuck together to make a board. *He used a huge sheet of plywood. ...the flimsy plywood door.*

p.m. /piː em/
p.m. after a number indicates that the number refers to a particular time between noon and midnight. *He was confined to his home from 6 p.m. to 6 a.m.*

PM /piː em/
N PROP **PM** is an abbreviation for 'Prime Minister'; an informal word. *...the PM's speech to the conference.*

pneumatic /njuːmætɪk/
1 ADJ ATTRIB **Pneumatic** machines are operated by using the power of compressed air. *This will leave five or six metres of rock that will be removed using mechanical diggers and manually operated pneumatic drills. ...pneumatic hammers.*
2 ADJ ATTRIB Pneumatic tyres are filled with air rather than being solid. *In those days, pneumatic tyres had not yet been heard of and the roads were appalling.*

pneumonia /njuːməʊniə/
NU **Pneumonia** is a serious disease which affects your lungs and makes breathing difficult. *She nearly died of pneumonia.*

PO /piː əʊ/
PO is an abbreviation for 'Post Office'.

poach /pəʊtʃ/ **poaches, poaching, poached**
1 V Oor V If someone **poaches** animals, they catch them illegally on someone else's property. *He had been poaching deer... If you aren't mobile the poachers are going to go on poaching and getting away with it.*
2 VO If someone **poaches** an idea, they dishonestly use the idea. *The design had even been poached by manufacturers of washing powder.*
3 VO If you **poach** food such as fish or eggs, you cook it gently in boiling water or milk. *...poached eggs and beans. ...poached salmon.*

poacher /pəʊtʃə/ **poachers**
NC A **poacher** is someone who illegally catches animals on someone else's property. *Africa's war against wildlife poachers has intensified over the past few years.*

PO Box /piː əʊ bɒks/
PO Box is used followed by a number as part of an address. The Post Office keeps the letters for collection by the customer. *...PO Box 48... It left a PO box number to write to.*

pock /pɒk/ **pocks**
NC **Pocks** are small hollows on the surface of someone's skin, which have been caused by disease.

pocked /pɒkt/
ADJ Something that is **pocked** has small irregular holes all over its surface. *Building after building is pocked with bullet holes.*

pocket /pɒkɪt/ **pockets, pocketing, pocketed**
1 NC A **pocket** is a small bag or pouch that forms part of a piece of clothing. *She put her hand in her coat pocket.*
2 N+N You use **pocket** to describe something that is small enough to fit into a pocket. *...pocket phones. ...pocket calculators.*
3 NC+POSS If you say that something will affect someone's **pocket**, you mean that it will affect the amount of money that they have. *Tax cuts have put more money in the pockets of working people... Staff sometimes have to buy medicine out of their own pockets.*
4 NC A **pocket** of something is a small area where something is happening or which has a particular quality, in contrast to surrounding areas. *Action was still being taken against isolated pockets of resistance... There are pockets of great wealth in the North... We sat in the pocket of warmth by the fire.*
5 VO If you **pocket** something, you put it in your pocket. *I locked the door and pocketed the key.*
6 VO If someone **pockets** money or something that is valuable, they take it, especially when they do not have the right to do so; an informal use. *The men pocketed the cash handed over by motorists. ...servants who pocketed household funds for their own use.*
7 See also **air pocket**.
● **Pocket** is used in these phrases. ● If someone **picks** your **pocket**, they steal something from it or from something you are carrying. ● If you are **out of pocket**, you have less money than you should have, usually because you have paid for something for someone else. *I don't want you to end up out of pocket. ...social security reforms which have left some needy families out of pocket.* ● If people **line** their

pockets, they make money in an unacceptable or dishonest way. *Officials have been lining their pockets.*

pocketbook /pɒkɪtbʊk/ **pocketbooks**
1 NC A **pocketbook** is a wallet or small case used for carrying money and papers; used in American English. *I hunted through my pocketbook and discovered twenty-three cents.*
2 NC You can talk about your **pocketbook** to refer to your personal finances; used in American English. *All over the world people still vote with their pocketbooks... They worry about how reform will affect their pocketbooks.*
3 NC A **pocketbook** is a small book or notebook.

pocket calculator, pocket calculators
NC A **pocket calculator** is a small and inexpensive electronic machine which does arithmetic calculations. *Many children these days use pocket calculators in school.*

pocketful /pɒkɪtfʊl/ **pocketfuls**
1 NC A **pocketful** of something is about the amount that a pocket will hold. *I collected two pocketfuls of shells from the beach.*
2 NC You can refer to a large amount of something, especially money, as **pocketfuls** of it; an informal use. *He must make pocketfuls of money in that job.*

pocket handkerchief, pocket handkerchiefs
NC A **pocket handkerchief** is a small handkerchief; an old-fashioned expression.

pocket knife, pocket knives
NC A **pocket knife** is the same as a penknife. *The American soldiers who searched him overlooked a small pocket knife.*

pocket money
1 NU **Pocket money** is money which some parents give their children each week. *Fifty pence may well be too much for the average child's pocket money... Thirteen-year-olds are spending their pocket money on fruit machines.*
2 NU **Pocket money** is also small amounts of money that you carry with you for everyday personal expenses; used in American English. *Stories abound of people trying to survive on pocket money and small businesses unable to pay employees.*

pocket-sized
ADJ ATTRIB Something that is **pocket-sized** is smaller than the usual size. *...the world's first pocket-sized IBM-compatible computer... This explains why two pocket-sized nations are at war.*

pockmark /pɒkmɑːk/ **pockmarks**
NC **Pockmarks** are small hollows on the surface of something, usually caused by violence. *...the pockmarks left by the gunplay that Sunday evening.*

pockmarked /pɒkmɑːkt/
ADJ If the surface of something is **pockmarked**, it has small hollow marks covering it. *The plane was making its approach to the pockmarked landing strip.*

pod /pɒd/ **pods**
NC A **pod** is a seed container that grows on some plants such as peas or beans. *...beans and lentils and peas—anything in a pod. ...the seed pod.*

podgy /pɒdʒi/
ADJ Someone who is **podgy** is fairly fat; an informal word. *...a small, podgy girl.*

podium /pəʊdiəm/ **podiums**
NC A **podium** is a small platform on which someone stands in order to give a lecture or conduct an orchestra. *He was allowed to address the meeting from the podium.*

poem /pəʊɪm/ **poems**
NC A **poem** is a piece of writing in which the words are chosen for their beauty and sound and are carefully arranged, often in short lines which rhyme. *His first poems were published when he was nineteen. ...Victorian love poems.*

poet /pəʊɪt/ **poets**
NC A **poet** is a person who writes poems. *Octavio Paz is considered by many to be Latin America's finest living poet... He's a poet, novelist and academic.*

poetic /pəʊetɪk/
1 ADJ Something that is **poetic** is very beautiful, expressive, and sensitive. *...a poetic and beautiful*

picture of the landscape. ...a story of poetic brilliance. ♦ **poetically** ADV *Theology uses language poetically to describe things that cannot be measured.*
2 ADJ ATTRIB **Poetic** also means relating to poetry. *...a poetic tradition older than writing.*

poetical /pəʊetɪkl/
ADJ **Poetical** means the same as poetic. *No man of poetical temperament can avoid strong passions. ...a distinguished poetical tradition.*

poetic justice
NU If you describe something that happens to someone as **poetic justice**, you mean that you consider it to be perfectly suitable or deserved, because of the things that that person has done. *It was maybe poetic justice that I should now be on the receiving end.*

poetic licence
NU **Poetic licence** is freedom from the normal rules of language and truth, such as is found in poetry and fiction. *We have to allow him a bit of poetic licence.*

poet laureate /pəʊɪt lɒriət/. The plural form can be either **poet laureates** or, in formal English, **poets laureate**.
NC The **poet laureate** is the poet who is chosen and paid by the monarch or government for the rest of the poet's lifetime, or, in the United States, for a fixed term, and who writes poems for special occasions. *...such poets as Ted Hughes, now Britain's Poet Laureate. ...Mark Strand, who's about to conclude his term as poet laureate of the United States.*

poetry /pəʊətri/
NU You use **poetry** to refer to poems, especially when considered as a form of literature. *...a book of poetry. ...some of the world's greatest drama and poetry.*

pogo stick /pəʊɡəʊ stɪk/ **pogo sticks**
NC A **pogo stick** is a toy consisting of a long metal pole with a spring in the lower end and a bar on which a child can stand and jump up and down.

pogrom /pɒɡrəm/ **pogroms**
NC A **pogrom** is an organized, official persecution, for racial or religious reasons, which usually leads to mass killing of a group of people. *...immigrants fleeing from poverty and pogroms in eastern Europe... This horrific pogrom is said to have been instigated by the secret police.*

poignancy /pɔɪnjənsi/
NU **Poignancy** is the quality that something has when it affects you deeply and makes you feel very sad; a formal word. *It was a moment of extraordinary poignancy... Her appeal this year for faith in the organisation has special poignancy.*

poignant /pɔɪnjənt/
ADJ Something that is **poignant** affects you deeply and makes you feel very sad. *This makes the incident especially poignant. ...poignant moments.* ♦ **poignantly** ADV *He poignantly describes poverty as it existed in his own childhood.*

poinsettia /pɔɪnsetiə/ **poinsettias**
NC A **poinsettia** is a plant with groups of bright red or pink leaves that grows naturally in Central America and is popular as a houseplant. *I want a nice poinsettia for the hall.*

point /pɔɪnt/ **points, pointing, pointed**
1 NC A **point** is something that you say or write which expresses a particular fact, idea, or opinion. *I want to make several quick points... That's a point we'll come back to in a few minutes... Let me tell you a little story to illustrate my point.*
2 NC If you say that someone has a **point**, you mean that you accept that what they have said is worth considering. *You've got a point there... He has a point.*
3 N SING The **point** of what you are saying or discussing is the most important part that provides a reason or explanation for the rest. *The point was that Dick could not walk... You've all missed the point... I may as well come straight to the point.*
4 N SING You use **point** in expressions such as 'I don't see the point of it', 'What's the point?', and 'There's no point' in order to say that a particular action has no purpose or would not be useful. *I didn't see the point of boring you with all this... There was not much point in thinking about it.*

5 NC+SUPP A **point** is also a detail, aspect, or quality of something or someone. *The two books have some interesting points in common... Your strong points are your speed and accuracy.*
6 NC A **point** is also a particular place or position where something happens. *We were nearing the point where the lane curved round to the right... The circle passes through those two points.*
7 N SING+SUPP You also use **point** to refer to a particular time or moment, or a particular stage in the development of something. *At one point, I was dreadfully rude... The strikers brought the economy to crisis point... I exercised to the point of exhaustion.*
8 V+to If something **points** to a particular situation, it suggests that the situation exists or is likely to occur. *The two major parties were both able to point to successes... This activity points to the likelihood that an armed revolution is imminent.*
9 V A If something **points** to a place or **points** in a particular direction, it shows where that place is or faces in that direction. *...a street sign that pointed down towards the cemetery... One of its toes pointed backwards.*
10 NC+SUPP The **points** of a compass are the marks on it that show the directions, especially North, South, East, and West.
11 NC The **point** of something such as a pin, needle, or knife is the thin, sharp end of it. *...tapping with the point of the pencil at a place on the diagram.*
12 NC On a railway track, the **points** are the levers and rails which enable a train to move from one track to another. *The rear coach of the train was de-railed as it went over points.*
13 NC The decimal **point** in a number is the dot that separates the whole numbers from the fractions. *Unemployment rose for the third month in succession to stand at five point seven per cent.*
14 NC In some competitions and studies a **point** is one of the single marks that are counted to measure or compare different people and events. *The panel of judges gave him the highest points. ...an earthquake measuring seven points on the Richter Scale.*
15 NC A **point** is also an electric socket. *The room has a wash-basin and an electric shaver point.*
16 V A or V O A If you **point** at something, you hold out your finger or an object such as a stick to show someone where it is or to make them notice it. *'Over there,' she said and pointed to the door... He pointed a finger at my friend and hissed with rage.*
17 V O A If you **point** something at someone, you aim the tip or end of it towards them. *They grabbed my neck and pointed a gun at the back of my head.*
● **Point** is used in these phrases. ● If something is **beside the point**, it is not relevant to the subject that you are discussing. *The fact that their poems, paintings and philosophical ramblings are pretty mediocre is beside the point.* ● If you **make a point** of doing something, you do it in a very obvious way and do not miss a chance to do it. *The United Sates has made a point of condemning such deportations... He made it a point to try to keep in touch.* ● If you are **on the point** of doing something, you are just about to do it. *The Chinese army is on the point of intervening... When they saw that the world economy was not on the point of collapse, their confidence increased.* ● If something is true **up to a point**, it is partly, but not completely, true. *He is right, but only up to a point... This has been effective up to a point.* ● to be a **case in point**: see case. ● **in point of fact**: see fact. ● to **point the finger at** someone: see finger. ● a **sore point**: see sore. ● See also **focal point, vantage point**.
point out PHRASAL VERB **1** If you **point out** an object or place, you make people look at it or show them where it is. *On car journeys we all used to shout and point out lovely places along the way.* **2** If you **point out** a fact or mistake, you tell someone about it. *They point out that it was only written in 1983... She pointed out that he was wrong.*
point-blank
1 ADV or ADJ ATTRIB If you say something **point-blank**, you say it very directly, without explaining or apologizing. *She asked him point-blank if I was with*

him on Saturday. ...a point-blank refusal to discuss the matter.
2 ADV or ADJ ATTRIB To shoot someone or something **point-blank** means to shoot them when the gun is touching them or very close to them. *He shot him in the brain, point-blank... One of them was shot dead at point-blank range.*
pointed /ˈpɔɪntɪd/
1 ADJ Something that is **pointed** has a point at one end. *...a little black dog with pointed ears. ...a pointed stick which is used to make the hole in the ground.*
2 ADJ **Pointed** comments or behaviour express criticism or warning in an obvious and often unpleasant way. *The general ended with a pointed warning... She made two pointed comments.*
◆ **pointedly** ADV *'How old is he?' Freya asked pointedly.*
pointer /ˈpɔɪntə/ **pointers**
1 NC A **pointer** is a piece of advice or information which helps you to understand a situation or solve a problem. *...a list of things that seemed to be pointers to the truth of what happened... Sir Geoffrey expects his visit to be a useful pointer to the possibility of progress on arms control.*
2 NC A **pointer** is also a long, thin stick that you use to point at things such as charts. *A pointer leant against the blackboard.*
3 NC The **pointer** on a measuring instrument is the long, thin piece of metal that points to the numbers.
pointing /ˈpɔɪntɪŋ/
1 NU **Pointing** is a way of repairing the outside of a building by filling in the holes between the bricks or stones. *...the way people do pointing on stonework.*
2 NU **Pointing** also refers to the cement between bricks or stones in a wall. *We've got leaking drainpipes and worn pointing.*
pointless /ˈpɔɪntləs/
ADJ Something that is **pointless** has no sense or purpose. *...pointless violence... It was pointless to protest.* ◆ **pointlessly** ADV *He had pointlessly hurt her.*
point of order, points of order
NC A **point of order** is an objection that someone makes in a formal debate because the proper rules of behaviour or organization have been broken. *On a point of order from the chairman, the constitution was amended.*
point of reference, points of reference
NC A **point of reference** is something which you use to help you understand a situation or to communicate with someone. *We have nothing in common to talk about, no points of reference.*
point of view, points of view
1 NC Your **point of view** is your opinion about something or your attitude towards it. *We understand your point of view.*
2 If you consider something **from a** particular **point of view**, you are using just one aspect of a situation to judge the whole situation. *From the commercial point of view, they have little to lose.*
poise /pɔɪz/
NU If you behave with **poise**, you behave in a calm and dignified manner. *She received me with incredible poise for one so young.*
poised /pɔɪzd/
1 ADJ PRED If a part of your body is **poised**, it is completely still but ready to move at any moment. *I saw her hand poised to strike.*
2 ADJ PRED If you are **poised** to do something, you are ready to take action at any moment. *His party seems poised to return to power. ...powerful military forces, poised for invasion.*
3 ADJ PRED If you are **poised**, you are calm and dignified. *She was poised and diplomatic on the telephone.*
poison /ˈpɔɪzn/ **poisons, poisoning, poisoned**
1 N MASS **Poison** is a substance that harms or kills people or animals if they swallow or absorb it. *Lead is a powerful poison of particular danger to small children. ...rat poison.*
2 V O If someone **poisons** another person or an animal, they kill the person or animal or make them ill by

means of poison. *He had been poisoned with strychnine... A rare golden eagle has been found dead, apparently poisoned.* ◆ **poisoning** NU *Police in France are investigating the poisoning of ninety-four sheep.*
3 VO If you **are poisoned** by a substance, it makes you very ill. *You can be poisoned by agricultural and industrial wastes.* ◆ **poisoning** NU *There are up to 200 reported cases of pesticide poisoning every year. ...food poisoning.*
4 V-PASS If something such as food or the atmosphere **is poisoned**, it has poison or other harmful substances added to it by accident or deliberately. *New scientific evidence shows that the North Sea is being poisoned by toxic waste... The yoghurt drink must have been poisoned.* ◆ **poisoned** ADJ *...a poisoned whisky bottle.*

poisoner /pɔɪzəⁿnə/ **poisoners**
NC A **poisoner** is someone who has killed or harmed another person or other people by using poison. *Arsenic, of course, is a very well-known poison used by poisoners throughout the centuries.*

poison gas
NU **Poison gas** is a gas that is poisonous and usually used to kill people, for example in war or to execute criminals. *The use of poison gas was outlawed by international convention.*

poisonous /pɔɪzəⁿnəs/
1 ADJ **Poisonous** substances will kill you or make you ill if you swallow or absorb them. *She ate some poisonous mushrooms... They are highly poisonous and have killed hundreds of seabirds.*
2 ADJ A **poisonous** animal produces a poison that will kill you or make you ill if the animal bites you. *They are fending off disease, starvation and poisonous snakes.*

poison-pen letter, poison-pen letters
NC A **poison-pen letter** is a letter which is sent in order to upset someone or to cause trouble. It says unpleasant things about the receiver or about someone close to him or her. *Imagine receiving a poison-pen letter or an obscene telephone call... Poison-pen letters are not illegal at the moment.*

poke /pəuk/ **pokes, poking, poked**
1 VO If you **poke** someone or something, you quickly push them with your finger or a sharp object. *People poked the students with their umbrellas... Ralph began to poke little holes in the sand.* ▶ Also NC *Len gave him an affectionate poke.*
2 VOA If you **poke** one thing into another, you push the first thing into the second thing. *Never poke scissors into an electric socket.*
3 VA If something **pokes** out of or through another thing, you can see part of it appearing from behind or underneath the other thing. *...cotton wool poking out of his ear... Blades of grass poked up between the paving stones.*
4 VOA If you **poke** your head through an opening, you push it through, often so that you can see something more easily. *The driver slowed down and poked his head out of the window.*
5 to **poke fun at**: see **fun**.

poke about or **poke around** PHRASAL VERB If you **poke about** or **poke around** for something, you search for it, usually by moving lots of objects around; used in informal English. *He was lying flat on his stomach, poking around under the bed with his arm.*

poke at PHRASAL VERB If you **poke at** something, you make lots of little pushing movements at it with a sharp object. *The chef poked at his little pile of ashes.*

poker /pəukə/ **pokers**
1 NU **Poker** is a card game that people play, usually in order to win money. *...a professional poker player... He lost it to his wife at poker.*
2 NC A **poker** is a metal bar which you use to move coal or wood in a fire so that air can circulate. *...a poker and tongs.*

poker face
N SING A **poker face** is an expression on your face that does not show your feelings; an informal expression. *Keep calm, keep a poker face and proceed methodically.*

poker-faced
ADJ If you are **poker-faced**, you have an expression on

your face that does not show your feelings; an informal word.

poky /pəuki/ **pokier, pokiest**
ADJ A room or house that is **poky** is small and uncomfortable; an informal word. *Her flat has three poky little rooms.*

Poland /pəulənd/
The **Republic of Poland** is a country in eastern Europe. It was a member of the former Warsaw Pact. It was occupied by Germany from 1939 to 1945. A Communist government was established in 1947. In 1980 Solidarity, an independent trade union, was formed under the leadership of Lech Wałęsa, a Gdańsk shipyard electrician. Solidarity was suppressed and martial law declared in 1981 by General Wojciech Jaruzelski. Solidarity was legalized and elections were held in 1989. Solidarity became the ruling party. Lech Wałęsa became President in 1990. Jan Olszewski, of the Centre Alliance, became Prime Minister in 1991. Poland exports coal, clothing, and iron and steel. High inflation and large foreign debts are serious economic problems. ◆ **Pole** /pəul/ N **Polish** /pəulɪʃ/ ADJ
■ *per capita GNP:* US$1,850 ■ *religion:* Christianity (mainly Roman Catholic) ■ *language:* Polish
■ *currency:* zloty ■ *capital:* Warsaw (Warszawa)
■ *population:* 38 million (1989) ■ *size:* 312,683 square kilometres.

polar /pəulə/
ADJ ATTRIB **Polar** refers to the area around the North and South Poles. *...the melting of the polar ice caps... There are other differences between the two polar regions.*

polar bear, polar bears
NC A **polar bear** is a large white bear which lives near the North Pole. *Polar bears fit into the Arctic scene because they are born with thick white fur.*

polarise /pəuləraɪz/. See **polarize**.

polarity /pəulærəti/ **polarities**
NU or NC If two people, ideas, or things have completely opposite qualities or opinions, you can refer to this difference as **polarity** between them. *The cathedrals represent the polarity of the two communities. ...the polarities of good and evil.*

polarize /pəuləraɪz/ **polarizes, polarizing, polarized**; also spelt **polarise**.
V-ERG If people **are polarized**, they form into two separate groups with opposite opinions or positions. *In Britain the political debate is polarized between two major parties... Do we now polarize into two groups?* ◆ **polarization** /pəuləraɪzeɪʃn/ NU *...a growing polarization between rich and poor countries... There is a process of political polarization at work.*

Polaroid /pəulərɔɪd/ **Polaroids**; **Polaroid** is a trademark.
1 NC A **Polaroid** is a photograph taken with a Polaroid camera. *...the polaroids which I work from myself... His pictures are huge, crystal-clear, surreal, yet he starts out taking everyday Polaroids.*
2 NU **Polaroid** is a special substance that is used to treat glass, so that the amount of glare shining through the glass from bright light is reduced. *...Polaroid glasses.*
3 N PL **Polaroids** are sunglasses which have been treated with Polaroid in order to reduce the glare of the sun. *I must get myself a new pair of Polaroids for the holiday.*

Polaroid camera, Polaroid cameras
NC A **Polaroid camera** is a small camera that can take, develop, and print a photograph in a few seconds; **Polaroid** is a trademark. *A Polaroid camera can be extremely useful at times.*

pole /pəul/ **poles**
1 NC A **pole** is a long, thin piece of wood or metal, used especially for supporting things. *...tent poles... We'll need poles and blankets to make a stretcher.*
2 NC+SUPP The earth's **poles** are the two opposite ends of its axis. *This plane will not be able to fly over the North Pole itself.*
3 If you say that two people are **poles apart**, you mean that they have completely different beliefs and opinions. *On broader political questions, the two sides remain poles apart.*

polecat /pəʊlkæt/ **polecats**
NC A **polecat** is a small, fierce, wild animal rather like a weasel, which lives in Europe, Asia, and North Africa. Polecats have a very unpleasant smell.

polemic /pəlemɪk/ **polemics;** a formal word.
1 NCorNU A **polemic** is a fierce written or spoken attack on, or defence of, a particular belief or opinion. *Williams wrote a splendid polemic in my favour. ...Sartre's great polemics against his friends. ...an endless swirl of discussion, debate, and polemic.*
2 NU **Polemics** is the skill or practice of arguing passionately for or against a doctrine, belief, or opinion. *This could lead to less polemics and a more practical attitude towards talks.*

polemical /pəlemɪkl/
ADJ **Polemical** means arguing fiercely and passionately for or against a belief or opinion; a formal word. *...a polemical book arguing the case for better adult education in Britain... When I made that statement I was being polemical.*

polemicist /pəlemɪsɪst/ **polemicists**
NC A **polemicist** is someone who is skilled at arguing passionately for or against a doctrine, opinion, or belief; a formal word. *...Chomsky, the distinguished American linguist and anti-establishment polemicist.*

Pole Star
N SING The **Pole Star** is the star that is nearest to the North Pole in the Northern hemisphere.

pole vault, pole vaults
NC A **pole vault** is a very high jump which athletes make over a high bar, using a long, flexible pole to help lift themselves up. *Rodion Gataullin has become the first man to clear six metres at the indoor pole vault.*

police /pəliːs/ **polices, policing, policed**
1 N PL The **police** are the official organization that is responsible for making sure that people obey the law, or the people who are members of this organization. *Police believe the bomb was planted by the IRA... They were detained by the police.*
2 VO To **police** a place means to preserve law and order in it by means of the police or the army. *The terrain in that area is extremely difficult to police... UN officials say the soldiers in the north are not policing the region.*

police constable, police constables
NC A **police constable** is a policeman or policewoman of the lowest rank. *...Police Constable Jones. ...a uniformed police constable.*

police force, police forces
NC A **police force** is the police organization in a particular country or area. *...the local police force.*

policeman /pəliːsmən/ **policemen** /pəliːsmən/
NC A **policeman** is a man who is a member of the police force. *The injured policeman was taken to hospital... Fire fighters and about 10,000 policemen are on full alert.*

police officer, police officers
NC A **police officer** is a policeman or policewoman. *Nearly seven thousand police officers have been assigned to traffic and security duty.*

police state, police states
NC A **police state** is a state or country in which the government controls people's freedom by means of the police, especially secret police; used showing disapproval. *...the lasting legacy of the former police state... He described the government's action as 'police-state tactics'.*

police station, police stations
NC A **police station** is the local office of the police force in a particular area. *He is being taken to a local police station for questioning.*

policewoman /pəliːswʊmən/ **policewomen**
NC A **policewoman** is a woman who is a member of the police force. *The suspect lunged at the policewoman with a knife as she was trying to arrest him.*

policing /pəliːsɪŋ/
NU **Policing** is the system used by the police to preserve law and order in a particular place. *...an outburst of resentment at methods of policing. ...neighborhood policing programmes.*

policy /pɒləsi/ **policies**
1 NCorNU A **policy** is a set of plans that is used as a basis for making decisions, especially in politics, economics, or business. *She was known for her strong criticism of the government's economic policies... He insisted there would be no change of policy... They have urged bishops to issue a clear policy statement on homosexuality.*
2 NC An insurance **policy** is a document which shows the agreement that you have made with an insurance company. *...a life assurance policy... This service is free to policy holders.*

policy-making
NU **Policy-making** is the process of deciding new policy. *Policy-making and administration will be split apart in many ministries... They still hope some of their ideas will be fed into future policy-making... This has caused difficulties in the policy-making process.*

polio /pəʊliəʊ/
NU **Polio** is a serious infectious disease which often causes paralysis. *You are far more likely to get polio if you don't take the vaccine. ...the polio virus.*

poliomyelitis /pəʊliəʊmaɪəlaɪtɪs/
NU **Poliomyelitis** is the same as **polio;** a medical term. *...vaccinations for poliomyelitis and tetanus.*

polish, polishes, polishing, polished; pronounced /pɒlɪʃ/ for the meanings in paragraphs 1 to 3, and /pəʊlɪʃ/ for the meanings in paragraphs 4 and 5.
1 NU **Polish** is a substance that you put on the surface of something to clean it and make it shine. *Use wax polish on wooden furniture. ...shoe polish.*
2 VO If you **polish** something, you put polish on it and then rub it with a cloth in order to make it shine. *Leather needs polishing with good quality cream... I had the watch cleaned and polished.* ◆ **polished** ADJ *She slipped on the polished wooden floor. ...a piece of polished stone.*
3 VO To **polish** something also means to rub it with a cloth in order to make it shine. *I polished my glasses with a handkerchief.*
4 ADJ **Polish** means belonging to or relating to Poland. *...the Polish government. ...a Polish newspaper.*
5 NU **Polish** is the language spoken by people who live in Poland. *He speaks Polish with a Canadian accent.*

polish off PHRASAL VERB If you **polish** something **off,** you finish it completely and quickly; an informal expression. *I had no trouble polishing off the pudding.*

polished /pɒlɪʃt/
1 ADJ Someone who is **polished** shows confidence and sophistication. *He had the most polished, sophisticated manner.*
2 ADJ If you describe an ability, skill, or piece of work as **polished,** you mean that it is sophisticated and of a high standard. *The play is less polished than the later works... My German was not very polished.*

Politburo /pɒlɪtbjʊərəʊ/ **Politburos**
NC The **Politburo** in a communist country is the chief committee that makes policies and decisions. *He was sacked from the Politburo.*

polite /pəlaɪt/ **politer, politest**
ADJ A **polite** person has good manners and is not rude to other people. *He was very polite to his superiors. ...a polite refusal.* ◆ **politely** ADV *He thanked me politely.* ◆ **politeness** NU *I do expect reasonable politeness.*

politic /pɒlɪtɪk/
1 ADJ If you say that something is **politic,** you mean that you think it is the most sensible thing to do, usually because it will help you to gain an advantage or to avoid a problem; a formal word. *It might be more politic to tell him yourself than let him find out from someone else.*
2 See also **politics.**

political /pəlɪtɪkl/
1 ADJ **Political** means relating to politics. *...the major political parties. ...its ambitious programme of economic and political reform.* ◆ **politically** ADV *Most of the killings were politically motivated.*
2 ADJ A **political** person is interested in politics and holds strong beliefs about it. *He was always very political.*

political asylum
NU **Political asylum** is the protection given by a government to people who have been forced to leave or escape from their own country for political reasons. *Around half of them were seeking political asylum in the West... She asked for political asylum in this country and was refused.*

political economy
NU **Political economy** is the study of the way in which a government influences or organizes a nation's wealth. *...a professor of political economy at Harvard University.*

political prisoner, political prisoners
NC A **political prisoner** is someone who has been imprisoned because they have expressed views which disagree with those of their government. *Among its demands was an unconditional amnesty for political prisoners.*

political science
NU **Political science** is the study of the ways in which power is acquired and used in a country, especially by those who govern the country. *He has agreed to give guest lectures in political science at ten different colleges this year.*

political scientist, political scientists
NC A **political scientist** is someone who studies and lectures on political science. *One political scientist I talked to says this shows a measure of desperation.*

politician /pɒlɪtɪʃn/ **politicians**
NC A **politician** is a person whose job is in politics, especially a member of parliament. *...a well known local politician.*

politicize /pəlɪtəsaɪz/ **politicizes, politicizing, politicized**; also spelt **politicise**. A formal word.
1 VO To **politicize** someone means to make them more interested in or aware of politics. *The British people were politicized by their wartime experiences.* ◆ **politicized** ADJ *...a highly politicised army.* ◆ **politicization** /pəlɪtəsaɪzeɪʃn/ NU *...the increasing politicization of the country.*
2 VO To **politicize** an event, situation, or activity means to turn it into a political issue. *The people of East Timor are angry at attempts by the Indonesian authorities to politicize the Pope's visit.* ◆ **politicized** ADJ *...the most politicized industrial dispute since the miners' strike.* ◆ **politicization** NU *Such politicization detracts from the important technical work of these organizations.*

politicking /pɒlɪtɪkɪŋ/
NU **Politicking** is political activity that people take part in, usually to gain votes or for their own personal advantage; used showing disapproval. *There was little in his frenetic politicking which gave any hint of future statesmanship.*

politico /pəlɪtɪkəʊ/ **politicos**
NC A **politico** is a politician; used showing disapproval. *I was accused by a visiting politico of being a bourgeois individualist.*

politics /pɒlɪtɪks/
1 N SING **Politics** is the actions or activities which people use to achieve power in a country, society, or organization. *Politics is a tough business... The bitterness will cast a shadow over Irish politics for the foreseeable future... He was active in Liberal politics. ...office politics.*
2 N PL Your **politics** are your beliefs about how a country should be governed. *I have no politics... Her politics could be described as radical... They are divided by politics as well as geography.*
3 NU **Politics** is the study of the ways in which a country is governed. *...a lecturer in politics.*
4 See also **politic**.

polity /pɒlɪti/ **polities**
NC A **polity** is an organized society, for example a nation, city, or church, together with its government and administration; a formal word. *...the classic conservative yearning for an ordered polity. ...geographical India, consolidated into a polity by Britain.*

polka /pɒlkə/ **polkas**
1 NC A **polka** is a fast, lively dance that was popular in the nineteenth century and at the beginning of the

twentieth century.
2 NC A **polka** is also a piece of music that has the rhythm of this dance. *The kind of repertoire they would play would be polkas, light classical, and some ragtime things.*

polka dot, polka dots
NC **Polka dots** are lots of spots printed on a piece of cloth, especially when the cloth is part of a person's clothing. *...a pattern of black polka dots.*

poll /pəʊl/ **polls, polling, polled**
1 NC A **poll** is a survey in which people are asked their opinions about something. *Last year the polls gave the President a 10 to 15 point lead.* ● See also **exit poll, opinion poll.**
2 N PL The **polls** are a political election. *The party won a convincing victory at the polls.*
3 VO If a political party or candidate **polls** a certain number of votes, they get that number of votes in an election. *Labour polled just over two thousand votes.*

pollarded /pɒlədɪd/
ADJ ATTRIB A **pollarded** tree has had its top branches cut off so that its growth is more bushy; a technical term. *A hawk was hovering in the air above some pollarded willows.*

pollen /pɒlən/
NU **Pollen** is the fine powder which flowers produce in order to fertilize other flowers of the same species. *In summertime there's a lot of pollen from grasses in the air.*

pollen count, pollen counts
NC A **pollen count** is a measurement of the amount of pollen in the air at a particular place and time. *We can expect a high pollen count over the next week or so.*

pollinate /pɒləneɪt/ **pollinates, pollinating, pollinated**
VO To **pollinate** a plant or tree means to fertilize it with pollen. *The plant may pollinate itself.* ◆ **pollination** /pɒləneɪʃn/ NU *Planting trees in groups helps pollination.*

polling /pəʊlɪŋ/
NU **Polling** is the act of voting in an election. *The result of the polling will be known tomorrow morning... The polling has taken place to schedule.*

polling day
NU **Polling day** is the day on which people vote in an election. *In France it's illegal to publish opinion polls for a week before polling day.*

polling station, polling stations
NC A **polling station** is a place where people go to vote at an election. It is often a school or other public building. *Queues formed before polling stations opened.*

pollster /pəʊlstə/ **pollsters**
NC **Pollsters** are people or organizations that conduct opinion polls and try to make predictions from their results. *The pollsters think this could favour the Congress.*

poll tax
1 N SING or NU In Britain, the **poll tax** is the same as the **community charge**; an informal use. *...a demonstration against the poll tax. ...an average poll tax bill of about three hundred and eighty pounds.*
2 N SING A **poll tax** is a tax that every adult in a country must pay. *He warned against the idea of a poll tax.*

pollutant /pəluːtənt/ **pollutants**
NC A **pollutant** is a substance that pollutes water, the air, or the environment. *The most obvious indoor pollutant is tobacco smoke. ...industrial pollutants.*

pollute /pəluːt/ **pollutes, polluting, polluted**
VO To **pollute** water, the air, or the environment means to make it dirty and dangerous to use or live in. *The report says that Britain's rivers are being polluted at a faster rate than at any time since national records began.*

polluter /pəluːtə/ **polluters**
NC A **polluter** is a company or factory whose processes cause pollution. *Many of the old inefficient plants now being closed are among the worst polluters.*

pollution /pəluːʃn/
1 NU **Pollution** is the process of polluting water, the air, or the environment. *...changes in the climate due*

to pollution of the atmosphere by industrial waste.
2 NU **Pollution** is also the unpleasant substances that pollute water, the air, or the environment. *Industrialisation generates waste and pollution. ...levels of pollution.*

polo /pəʊləʊ/
NU **Polo** is a game played between two teams of players. The players ride horses and use wooden hammers with long handles to hit a ball.

polo-necked
ADJ ATTRIB A **polo-necked** sweater has a thick fold of material at the top which covers most of a person's neck. *I was wearing a polo-necked jumper and sports jacket.*

poltergeist /pɒltəgaɪst/ **poltergeists**
NC A **poltergeist** is an invisible force which is believed to move furniture or throw objects around, and which is often thought of as a type of ghost. *The building is apparently haunted by a poltergeist.*

poly /pɒli/ **polys**
NC A **poly** is the same as a **polytechnic**; an informal word. *...a poly student.*

polyester /pɒliestə/
NU **Polyester** is a type of artificial fibre or cloth that is used especially to make clothes. *Bob wore a black 100% polyester suit.*

polyethylene /pɒlieθəliːn/
NU **Polyethylene** is the same as **polythene**; used in American English. *...a waterproof material such as polyethylene.*

polygamy /pəlɪgəmi/
NU **Polygamy** is the custom of having more than one wife at the same time. *Polygamy is becoming more widespread in their country.*

polyglot /pɒliglɒt/ **polyglots**; a formal word.
1 ADJ **Polyglot** is used to describe something such as a book or society in which several different languages are used. *...a polyglot culture.*
2 NC A **polyglot** is a person who speaks or understands several different languages.

polygon /pɒligən/ **polygons**
NC A **polygon** is a shape made by three or more straight lines or sides; a technical term in mathematics.

polygraph /pɒligrɑːf/ **polygraphs**
NC A **polygraph** is an instrument which records physical signals such as a person's pulse rate and skin temperature. Polygraphs are usually used to find out whether someone is telling the truth. *The government has abandoned plans for the possible use of the polygraph—or lie detector... We've gone through psychological evaluations and polygraph tests.*

polymath /pɒlimæθ/ **polymaths**
NC A **polymath** is a person who is very knowledgeable in many different subjects; a formal word. *Grove was something of a polymath. He was a distinguished lawyer and judge as well as a good researcher.*

polymer /pɒlimə/ **polymers**
NC A **polymer** is a chemical compound with large molecules made of many smaller molecules of the same kind; a technical term in chemistry. *Most modern paints are based on polymers... This work involves binding suitable drugs to non-soluble polymers.*

polyp /pɒlip/ **polyps**
1 NCorNU A **polyp** is a small animal that lives in the sea. It has a hollow body like a tube and tentacles around its mouth. *...coral polyps. ...strange growths of coral, polyp, and weed.*
2 NC A **polyp** is also a small, unhealthy growth on a surface inside your body, especially inside your nose. Polyps are not usually dangerous. *The chances of such a polyp actually turning cancerous are quite small.*

polyphony /pəlɪfəni/
NU **Polyphony** is the playing of several different melodies or the singing of different lines of a song at the same time in a piece of music; a technical term. *...rhythmic polyphony. ...twelve-part polyphony.*

polystyrene /pɒlistaɪriːn/
NU **Polystyrene** is a very light, plastic substance that is used especially to make containers or as insulating

material. *The polystyrene packages account for nearly 75 percent of the chain's foam use.*

polysyllable /pɒlisɪləbl/ **polysyllables**
NC A **polysyllable** is a word that has more than two syllables; a technical term in linguistics.

polytechnic /pɒliteknɪk/ **polytechnics**
NC A **polytechnic** is a college in Britain where you can go to study for a degree or vocational qualification after leaving school. *...a course in drama at Manchester Polytechnic... It wants to end the divide between universities and polytechnics.*

polythene /pɒliθiːn/
NU **Polythene** is a type of plastic that is made into thin sheets or bags and used especially to keep food fresh. *It was wrapped in polythene. ...polythene bags.*

polyunsaturated /pɒliʌnsætʃʊreɪtɪd/
ADJ **Polyunsaturated** oils and margarine are made mainly from vegetable fats and are considered healthier than those made from animal fats. *Their diet is high in saturated fat, it's low in unsaturated fats and polyunsaturated fats.*

polyurethane /pɒlijʊərəθeɪn/
NU **Polyurethane** is a plastic material that is used especially to make paint or types of foam and rubber which prevent water or heat from passing through them. *...polyurethane paints.*

pom /pɒm/ **poms**
NC A **pom** is the same as a **pommy**.

pomegranate /pɒmɪɡrænət/ **pomegranates**
NC A **pomegranate** is a round fruit with a thick, reddish skin. It contains lots of small seeds with juicy flesh around them.

pommel /pɒml/ **pommels**
1 NC A **pommel** is the knob on the end of the handle of a sword. *...ceremonial daggers with their metal hilts, gem encrusted pommels and slender blades.*
2 NC A **pommel** is also the part of a saddle that rises up at the front, or a knob that is fixed there.

pommy /pɒmi/ **pommies**; also spelt **pommie**.
NC Some Australian people use **pommy** in informal speech to refer to an English person. *Despite the much-talked-of rivalry between 'Aussies' and 'Pommies', we tend to like each other.*

pomp /pɒmp/
NU **Pomp** is the use of a lot of ceremony, fine clothes, and decorations, especially on a special occasion. *...coming ashore with pomp and ceremony.*

pom-pom /pɒmpɒm/ **pom-poms**
NC A **pom-pom** is a small ball of wool or other material that is used to decorate something such as a cap or furniture. *...a black knitted cap with a red pom-pom.*

pomposity /pɒmpɒsəti/
NU **Pomposity** is very serious behaviour or speech which shows that you think you are more important than you really are; a formal word, used showing disapproval. *He hated grandeur and pomposity.*

pompous /pɒmpəs/
1 ADJ Someone who is **pompous** behaves in a very serious way because they think they are more important than they really are; used showing disapproval. *...a pompous and conceited old fool. ...a pompous document of over 500 pages.* ♦ **pompously** ADV *The men stood at the bar, puffing pompously at fat German cigars.*
2 ADJ A **pompous** building or ceremony is very grand and elaborate. *...a pompous celebration.*

ponce /pɒns/ **ponces, poncing, ponced**; an informal word, used showing disapproval.
1 NC A **ponce** is the same as a **pimp**. *She gave all the money to her ponce.* ► Also V *If you walk down the road with a boyfriend, he's accused of poncing.*
2 NC If you call a man a **ponce**, you are insulting him because you think that he is too fussy in the way he dresses and in his manners. *Get out of my way, you little ponce!*
3 VA If you say that someone is **poncing** about or is **poncing** around, you mean that they are not doing something properly, quickly, or seriously.

poncho /pɒntʃəʊ/ **ponchos**
NC A **poncho** is a piece of clothing that consists of a long piece of material, usually wool, with a hole cut in

the middle which you put your head through. ...*a Peruvian wool poncho.*

pond /pɒnd/ **ponds**
NC A **pond** is an area of water that is smaller than a lake, often one which has been artificially created. ...*an ornamental pond in the garden.*

ponder /pɒndə/ **ponders, pondering, pondered**
VO, VA, V-REPORT, or V If you **ponder** something, you think about it slowly and carefully. *For centuries poets, philosophers and scientists have pondered the nature of time... The Prime Minister pondered on when to go to the polls... He was kept under house arrest while the authorities pondered how to react... As the activity heightened, Aage began to ponder.*

ponderous /pɒndə⁰rəs/; a literary word.
1 ADJ **Ponderous** speech or writing is dull, lengthy, and serious. *He spoke in a slow, ponderous way.*
◆ **ponderously** ADV *She nodded ponderously.*
2 ADJ A **ponderous** person or object is large and heavy. *He was overweight, ponderous, his blond hair almost white. ...ponderous royal tombs.*
3 ADJ A **ponderous** action is slow or clumsy. ...*taking a ponderous swing at the ball.* ◆ **ponderously** ADV *Slowly, ponderously, the vehicle shifted a few inches.*

pong /pɒŋ/ **pongs, ponging, ponged**; an informal word.
1 NC A **pong** is an unpleasant smell. *There was a pong in the room... Kitchen or bathroom pongs can be extracted with an electric fan.*
2 V If you say that something **pongs**, you mean that it has an unpleasant smell. *Take that thing away! It pongs!*

pontiff /pɒntɪf/ **pontiffs**
N PROP or NC The **pontiff** is the Pope; a formal word. *The pontiff spoke with pilgrims and tourists in St.Peter's Square.*

pontifical /pɒntɪfɪkl/
ADJ If someone behaves in a **pontifical** way, they behave as if they have complete authority; a formal word, used showing disapproval. *'Mrs Waites,' said Mr Willet, in his pontifical manner, 'is well-meaning, but ignorant.'... The lawyer, with pontifical gravity, sat on a high chair.*

pontificate, pontificates, pontificating, pontificated; pronounced /pɒntɪfɪkeɪt/ when it is a verb and /pɒntɪfɪkət/ when it is a noun. A formal word.
1 V or V-REPORT If someone **pontificates**, they state their opinions as if they are the only correct ones. *While the United Nations pontificates, the people of Cambodia live in fear of sudden death... A man pontificated that 'all good ideas are worked out at boring committee meetings'.*
2 NC+POSS The **pontificate** of a pope is the period of time during which he is pope. ...*the sadly brief pontificate of Pope John Paul I.*

pontoon /pɒntuːn/ **pontoons**
NC A **pontoon** is a floating platform, often one used to support a bridge. *They would have a difficult time getting tanks over pontoon bridges.*

pony /pəʊni/ **ponies**
NC A **pony** is a small horse. *Two girls rode up on small ponies.*

ponytail /pəʊniteɪl/ **ponytails**
NC If someone has their hair in a **ponytail**, it is tied up at the back of their head so that it hangs down like a tail. *I brush my teeth for fifteen minutes and then put my hair in a ponytail.*

poodle /puːdl/ **poodles**
NC A **poodle** is a type of dog with thick curly hair. *One French lady brought her poodle.*

poof /puf/ **poofs**; also spelt **pouf**.
1 NC A **poof** is a homosexual man; an offensive use.
2 **Poof** is used in writing to represent a sound that some people make to indicate that something happened very suddenly, or to express scorn, disbelief, or impatience.

pooh /puː/
You say '**Pooh**' to express your disgust at an unpleasant smell. *Pooh! It really stinks in here!*

pooh-pooh /puːpuː/ **pooh-poohs, pooh-poohing, pooh-poohed**
VO If someone **pooh-poohs** an idea or suggestion, they show that they consider it foolish, impractical, or

unnecessary; an informal word. *He pooh-poohed Thomas's anxieties about it... Sally pooh-poohed the idea that you need three meals a day.*

pool /puːl/ **pools, pooling, pooled**
1 NC A **pool** is a small area of still water. ...*long stretches of sand with rocks and pools.*
2 NC A **pool** is also a swimming pool. *She went swimming in the hotel pool.*
3 NC+of A **pool** of liquid or light is a small area of it. ...*a pool of blood... A spotlight threw a pool of violet light onto the stage.*
4 NC+SUPP A **pool** of people, money, or things is a number of them that are used or shared by several people or organizations, or by the whole community. ...*car pools... The new proposal would create a reserve pool of cash... Successful sophisticated economies are built on a well-educated, well-trained pool of workers.*
5 VO If a group of people or organizations **pool** their money, knowledge, or equipment, they allow it to be used or shared by everyone in the group. *We pooled our money, bought a van, and travelled... Several member countries are now ready to pool their efforts in defence and security.*
6 NU **Pool** is a game in which players use long, thin sticks to hit coloured balls into holes around the edges of a table. *We just sit around and look at TV or play pool. ...a pool table.*
7 N PL If you do the **pools** or the football **pools**, you take part in a gambling competition in which people try to win money by guessing correctly the results of football matches. *An unemployed waiter has won a million pounds on the pools.*

poop /puːp/ **poops**
NC The **poop** of an old-fashioned sailing ship is the raised structure at the back end of it.

poor /pɔː, pʊə/ **poorer, poorest**
1 ADJ Someone who is **poor** has very little money or few possessions. *I was a student then, and very poor. ...a poor family... He was now one thousand pounds poorer.*
2 N PL The **poor** are poor people. *That program will double the amount of money available in many states to help the poor... The poor still have hope in the justice of the revolution.*
3 ADJ A **poor** country or area is inhabited by people with very little money or few possessions. ...*aid to the poorer countries. ...a shop in a poor part of Stratford.*
4 ADJ ATTRIB You use **poor** to express sympathy for someone. *Poor old Dennis, he can't do a thing right... What on earth are you doing to this poor child?*
5 ADJ If you describe something as **poor**, you mean that it is of a low quality or standard. *In spite of poor health, I was able to continue working... Rescue workers have been hampered by lack of equipment and poor communications... The pay was poor.*
◆ **poorly** ADV ...*poorly designed equipment.*
6 ADJ ATTRIB You also use **poor** to describe someone who is not very skilful in a particular activity. *She was a very poor swimmer.* ◆ **poorly** ADV *I spoke Spanish so poorly.*
7 ADJ PRED+in If something is **poor** in a particular quality or substance, it contains very little of the quality or substance. *The water was poor in oxygen.*

poorhouse /pɔːhaʊs, pʊəhaʊs/ **poorhouses**
NC In former times in Britain, a **poorhouse** was an institution in which poor people could live if they had nowhere else to go. *My mother said I would die in the poorhouse, which is where she is, poor thing. ...the poorhouses and orphanages of England.*

poorly /pɔːli, pʊəli/
ADJ PRED If someone is **poorly**, they are ill; an informal word. *Your brother's had an operation and he's quite poorly.*

poor relation, poor relations
NC If you describe one thing as a **poor relation** of another, you mean that it is similar to or part of the other thing but inferior to it. ...*community care, the poor relation of the health service.*

pop /pɒp/ **pops, popping, popped**
1 NU or N+N **Pop** is modern music that usually has a strong rhythm and uses electronic equipment. ...*pop music. ...pop concerts. ...pop and rock stars.*

2 N MASS You can refer to fizzy drinks such as lemonade as **pop**; an informal use. *...soda pop and candy bars.*
3 NC **Pop** is used to represent a short sharp sound such as the sound made by bursting a balloon or by pulling a cork out of a bottle. *The cork came out with a loud pop.*
4 V If something **pops**, it makes a short sharp sound. *The cork popped and flew out of the bottle.*
5 V If your eyes **pop**, you look very surprised or excited; an informal use. *His mouth hung open and his eyes popped.*
6 V OA If you **pop** something somewhere, you put it there; an informal use. *He popped a piece of gum into his mouth... I popped a note through her letter box.*
7 V A If you **pop** somewhere, you go there; an informal use. *I'm just popping out for a haircut.*
8 VOCATIVE or NC **Pop** is used to address or talk about your father; used in informal American English. *This goose is great, Pop... Pop would tell the kids to take their little swimming suits.*

pop in PHRASAL VERB If you **pop in** somewhere, you go in for a short time, informally. *I think we should just pop in very quickly... Why don't you pop in for a coffee?*
pop up PHRASAL VERB If someone or something **pops up**, they appear in a place or situation unexpectedly. *He's one of those rare types who pops up every so often.*

pop art
N U **Pop art** is a style of modern art which began in the 1960's. It uses bright colours and takes a lot of its techniques and subject matter from everyday, popular sources. *Most people probably remember Andy Warhol as the artist who produced the famous pop art images of Marilyn Monroe.*

popcorn /pɒpkɔːn/
N U **Popcorn** is grains of maize that have been heated until they burst and become large and light. *We had to keep going out and getting popcorn and ice cream and Coca Colas.*

Pope /pəʊp/ **Popes**
N PROP, TITLE, or NC The **Pope** is the head of the Roman Catholic Church. *The Pope has celebrated midnight mass on Christmas Eve before thousands of worshippers in Saint Peter's Basilica in Rome. ...Pope John Paul II... He is only stating the teaching of the Catholic Church, as have all the hundreds of Popes before him.*

pop-eyed
ADJ ATTRIB If you say that someone is **pop-eyed**, you mean that their eyes are wide open because they are surprised or excited; an informal word. *...sauntering, pop-eyed tourists.*

popish /pəʊpɪʃ/
ADJ ATTRIB **Popish** is used to describe the beliefs, practices, and teachings of Roman Catholics by people who are opposed to them.

poplar /pɒplə/ **poplars**
NC A **poplar** is a tall, thin tree with triangular-shaped leaves. *Just behind the statue are three poplar trees, almost leafless except for the top branches.*

poplin /pɒplɪn/
N U **Poplin** is a type of cotton material used to make clothes. *...a dress of striped poplin. ...a poplin blouse.*

poppa /pɒpə/ **poppas**
VOCATIVE or NC Your **poppa** is your father; used in informal American English. *Sabrina's momma and poppa live in the house next to her.*

popper /pɒpə/ **poppers**
NC A **popper** is a device for fastening clothes. It consists of two pieces of plastic or metal which you press together.

poppet /pɒpɪt/ **poppets**
VOCATIVE or NC **Poppet** is used to address or refer to a child or someone you are very fond of; an informal word. *Whatever you say, poppet.*

poppy /pɒpi/ **poppies**
NC A **poppy** is a plant with large, delicate, usually red flowers. *...dark blue corn flowers with a bright red poppy in the centre.*

poppycock /pɒpikɒk/
N U You can use **poppycock** to refer to something which you think is nonsense; an old-fashioned, informal word. *You're talking utter poppycock.*

Poppy Day
N U **Poppy Day** is the day in Britain on which people remember those who died in the two world wars. *...the Queen laying her Poppy Day wreath.*

populace /pɒpjʊləs/
N SING The **populace** of a country is its people; a formal word. *They represented only a fraction of the general populace... Are these remedies for a starving and desperate populace?*

popular /pɒpjʊlə/
1 ADJ Someone or something that is **popular** is liked or enjoyed by a lot of people. *The song was written for the tremendously popular TV series 'Neighbours'... It was more popular among boys than girls.* ◆ **popularity** /pɒpjʊlærəti/ N U *The government's popularity has fallen dramatically.*
2 ADJ ATTRIB **Popular** ideas or attitudes are held or approved of by most people. *Contrary to popular belief, science does not offer us certainties... Governments of the region are clearly aware of the popular mood... He lacks popular appeal.*
3 ADJ ATTRIB **Popular** newspapers and television programmes are aimed at the widest possible audience and not at specialists in a particular subject. *The popular press is obsessed with the Royal Family.*
4 ADJ ATTRIB **Popular** is used to describe political activities which involve everyone, and not just members of political parties. *...popular democracy.*

popularize /pɒpjʊləraɪz/ **popularizes, popularizing, popularized**; also spelt **popularise**.
1 V O To **popularize** something means to make a lot of people interested in it and able to enjoy it. *Television has done a great deal to popularize snooker.*
2 V O To **popularize** an academic subject or idea means to make it more easily understandable to ordinary people; a formal use. *Scientific notions soon become inaccurate when they are popularized.*

popularly /pɒpjʊləli/
1 ADV You use **popularly** to indicate that a name is used by most people, although it is not the official one. *This theory was popularly called the Big Bang.*
2 ADV You also use **popularly** to indicate that an idea is believed by most people, although it may not be true. *It is popularly believed that eating carrots makes you see better in the dark.*

populate /pɒpjʊleɪt/ **populates, populating, populated**
V O If an area is **populated** by people or animals, those people or animals live there. *...an oil-rich province of Iraq that's populated by Kurds.* ◆ **populated** ADJ *Britain is a densely populated island.*

population /pɒpjʊleɪʃn/ **populations**
1 NC or N U The **population** of a place is all the people who live in it. *Kandahar has a population of 230,000... He also drew attention to the ever-growing world population... The country is unable to feed its population... Economic growth failed to match the increase in population.*
2 NC+SUPP You also use **population** to refer to all the people or animals of a particular type in a place. *...the civilian population. ...a prison population of 44,000... American links with the Catholic population here are strong.*

populism /pɒpjʊlɪzəm/
N U **Populism** refers to political activities or ideas that are based on the interests, opinions, and prejudices of ordinary people; a formal word. *...the party's abandonment of populism and its surrender to the socialists... It was a short step from populism to racism.*

populist /pɒpjʊlɪst/ **populists**; a formal word.
1 ADJ **Populist** ideas or **populist** politicians appeal to ordinary people because they reflect their interests, opinions, and prejudices. *Its ideology was more populist than bourgeois... He has shown himself to be a highly effective populist campaigner, able to capitalize on his appeal to the public.*
2 NC A politician who is a **populist** appeals to ordinary people by showing that he or she has the same

interests, opinions, and prejudices. *His challenger is a populist with mainly regional appeal.*

populous /pɒpjuləs/
ADJ A **populous** country or area has a lot of people living in it; a formal word. *...India and China, the two most populous countries in the world. ...the less populous areas of London.*

pop-up
1 ADJ ATTRIB A **pop-up** book, usually a children's book, has pictures that stand up when you open the pages. *They created gimmicks for children with pop-up books, games and puzzles.*
2 ADJ ATTRIB A **pop-up** toaster has a mechanism that pushes slices of bread up when they are toasted.

porcelain /pɔːsəˀlɪn/
NU **Porcelain** is a hard, shiny substance that is made by heating clay. It is used to make cups, plates, and ornaments. *...antique pottery and porcelain. ...a fourteenth century Ming porcelain vase.*

porch /pɔːtʃ/ **porches**
1 NC A **porch** is a sheltered area at the entrance to a building. It has a roof and sometimes walls. *...a big house with a glass porch.*
2 NC A **porch** is also a raised platform built along the outside wall of a house and often covered with a roof; used in American English. *Homer was not in his usual chair on the porch. ...an iron railing on the porch.*

porcine /pɔːsaɪn/
ADJ If you describe someone as **porcine**, you mean that you think they look like a pig; a literary word. *...a bald porcine old man... She had faintly porcine features.*

porcupine /pɔːkjʊpaɪn/ **porcupines**
NC A **porcupine** is an animal with many long, thin, spines on its back. *Sometimes a porcupine scuttled across the road or a wild pig could be heard.*

pore /pɔː/ **pores, poring, pored**
1 NC The **pores** in your skin or on the surface of a plant are the very small holes which allow moisture to pass through. *...the pores round his nose. ...mushrooms with minute yellow pores.*
2 NC **Pores** in rocks or soil are tiny gaps or cracks. *...water trapped in pores in rocks.*
pore over PHRASAL VERB If you **pore over** a book or information, you look at it and study it very carefully. *We pored over our maps.*

pork /pɔːk/
NU **Pork** is meat from a pig, usually fresh and not smoked or salted. *...pork chops.*

pork pie, pork pies
NCorNU A **pork pie** is a deep, round pie with cooked pork inside the pastry. *...pork pies and sausage rolls. ...a good thick wedge of pork pie.*

porn /pɔːn/
NU **Porn** is pornography; an informal word. *...porn shops.*

pornographic /pɔːnəgræfɪk/
ADJ Something that is **pornographic** is designed to cause sexual excitement by showing people involved in sexual activity; used showing disapproval. *...pornographic films and magazines.*

pornography /pɔːnɒgrəfi/
NU **Pornography** refers to books, magazines, and films that are designed to cause sexual excitement by showing people involved in sexual activity; used showing disapproval. *The government is to make it an offence to possess child pornography... They would like to see more effective legislation, banning pornography.*

porous /pɔːrəs/
ADJ Something that is **porous** has many small holes in it, which water and air can pass through. *The volcanic rocks are porous... It's even effective on porous surfaces.*

porpoise /pɔːpəs/ **porpoises**
NC A **porpoise** is a sea animal that looks similar to a dolphin. *Whales, porpoises, dolphins and sea turtles are regularly killed in drift net operations.*

porridge /pɒrɪdʒ/
NU **Porridge** is a thick, sticky food made from oats cooked in water. *As well as being a tasty and satisfying breakfast dish, porridge actually is good for you.*

port /pɔːt/ **ports**
1 NC A **port** is a town by the sea or on a river, which has a harbour. *...a fishing port. ...the port city of Limassol in Cyprus.*
2 NC A **port** is also a harbour area with docks and warehouses, where ships load or unload goods or passengers. *The ferry was towed into the port... At the Channel ports many sailings have continued normally.*
3 ADJ ATTRIB The **port** side of a ship is the left side when you are facing the front. *He stands in the wheel house calling out rudder commands, port for left, starboard for right.*
4 N MASS **Port** is a type of strong, sweet red wine. *...a glass of port.*

portable /pɔːtəbl/
ADJ A **portable** machine or device is designed to be easily carried. *...a portable computer for the businessman... It's portable but not terribly light.*

portal /pɔːtl/ **portals**
NC A **portal** is a large, impressive entrance to a building; a literary word. *...villas with huge marble portals.*

Port-au-Prince /pɔːtəʊprɪns/
Port-au-Prince is the capital of Haiti and its largest city. Population: 738,000 (1984).

portcullis /pɔːtkʌlɪs/ **portcullises**
NC A **portcullis** is a strong gate above an entrance to a castle or fort which used to be lowered to the ground in order to keep out enemies. *The Portcullis leads us into the Queen's Square.*

portend /pɔːtend/ **portends, portending, portended**
VO If something **portends** something, it indicates what is likely to happen in the future; a formal word. *The berries on your hedge portend an early and severe winter. ...an omen portending our future victory... What do these changes portend for food production?*

portent /pɔːtent/ **portents**
NC A **portent** is something that indicates what is likely to happen in the future; a formal word. *Are dreams a portent of things to come?*

portentous /pɔːtentəs/
ADJ Something that is **portentous** is important in indicating or affecting future events; a formal word. *Its consequences were historically portentous.*

porter /pɔːtə/ **porters**
1 NC A **porter** is a person whose job is to be in charge of the entrance of a building such as a hotel. *...a hotel porter.*
2 NC A **porter** is also a person whose job is to carry things, for example passengers' luggage at a railway station. *...railway porters. ...a thirty-five year old hospital porter from North London.*

portfolio /pɔːtfəʊliəʊ/ **portfolios**
1 NC A government minister's **portfolio** is the area of government for which he or she has particular responsibility. *...the defence portfolio... Andrew Bennett has resigned his education portfolio.* ● A minister **without portfolio** does not have particular responsibility for any one area of government. *He'll remain in the cabinet as a minister without portfolio.*
2 NC If a person or company has a collection of stocks and shares in different businesses, you can refer to this collection of stocks and shares as a **portfolio**. *Already, people are jittery about spending because their houses and their stock portfolios are worth less. ...an estimated $100 billion portfolio of foreign holdings.*
3 NC A **portfolio** is a thin, flat case for carrying papers or drawings. *Both of us were carrying portfolios and we unzipped and compared drawings.*
4 A **portfolio** is also a set of drawings or paintings that represent an artist's work. *...a portfolio of photographs.*

porthole /pɔːθəʊl/ **portholes**
NC A **porthole** is a small round window in a ship or aircraft. *I tried to break the porthole but with no success.*

portico /pɔːtɪkəʊ/ **porticos** or **porticoes**
NC A **portico** is a large, covered area at the entrance to a building, with pillars supporting the roof; a formal word. *St. Anne's needs the money to restore*

the interior, roof, portico and church surrounds.

portion /pɔːʃn/ **portions, portioning, portioned**

1 NC A **portion** of something is a part of it. *Divide the cake into eight portions... A large portion of this money would come to her... A considerable portion of the fund has not been properly accounted for.*

2 NC A **portion** is the amount of food that is given to one person at a meal. *...a small portion.*

portion out PHRASAL VERB If you **portion out** something, you give a share of it to each person in a group. *The presents were then further portioned out.*

Port Louis /pɔːt luːi/
Port Louis is the capital of Mauritius and its largest city. Population: 136,000 (1985).

portly /pɔːtli/
ADJ **Portly** people are rather fat; an old-fashioned word. *...portly middle-aged gentlemen.*

portmanteau /pɔːtmæntəʊ/ **portmanteaus** or **portmanteaux** /pɔːtmæntəʊz/

1 NC A **portmanteau** is a large travelling case which opens out into two equal compartments; an old-fashioned use. *...stuffing shirts into his portmanteau.*

2 ADJ ATTRIB **Portmanteau** is used to describe a word that combines parts of the forms and meanings of two other words. For example, 'brunch' is formed from 'breakfast' and 'lunch' and means a meal that is eaten in the middle of the morning; a technical use.

3 ADJ ATTRIB **Portmanteau** is also used to describe someone or something that combines many different features or uses; a formal use. *...a portmanteau title, embracing in its scope such things as clocks and Chelsea porcelain.*

Port Moresby /pɔːt mɔːzbi/
Port Moresby is the capital of Papua New Guinea and its largest city. Population: 145,000 (1987).

port of call, ports of call

1 NC A **port of call** is a place where a ship stops during a journey. *Our next port of call was Cyprus.*

2 NC A **port of call** is also any place where you stop for a short time, especially during a day when you visit several places or people; an informal use. *His last port of call was the chemist's.*

Port of Spain /pɔːt əv speɪn/
Port of Spain, on Trinidad, is the capital of Trinidad and Tobago and its largest city. Population: 59,000 (1988).

Porto-Novo /pɔːtəʊnəʊvəʊ/
Porto-Novo is the capital of Benin and its second largest city. Population: 208,000 (1992).

portrait /pɔːtrət, pɔːtreɪt/ **portraits**
NC A **portrait** is a painting, drawing, or photograph of a person. *...the portrait of George Washington.*

portraiture /pɔːtrətʃə/
NU **Portraiture** is the art of painting or drawing portraits; a technical term. *...a master of portraiture.*

portray /pɔːtreɪ/ **portrays, portraying, portrayed**

1 VO When an actor or actress **portrays** someone, he or she plays that person in a play or film. *In her final sketch she portrayed a temperamental countess.*

2 VOA To **portray** someone or something in a particular way means to represent them in that way, for example in a book or film. *Advertising tends to portray women in a very traditional role.*

portrayal /pɔːtreɪəl/ **portrayals**
NC A **portrayal** of someone is a representation of them in a play, film, or book. *...his portrayal of Willy Loman in 'Death of a Salesman'.*

Portugal /pɔːtʃʊgəl/
The Republic of Portugal is a country in south-west Europe. It is a member of NATO and the European Community. António de Oliveira Salazar was the Prime Minister from 1932 to 1968. Gradual liberalization took place following an army coup in 1974. Dr Mário Lopes Soares, of the Socialist Party (PS), became President in 1986. Aníbal Cavaço Silva, of the Social Democratic Party (PSD), became Prime Minister in 1985. Portugal exports cotton, textiles and clothing, cork, fish, and wine. Tourism is an important industry. ◆ **Portuguese** /pɔːtʃəgiːz/ N, N PL, ADJ
■ *per capita GNP:* US$3,670 ■ *religion:* Christianity (mainly Roman Catholic) ■ *language:* Portuguese
■ *currency:* escudo ■ *capital:* Lisbon (Lisboa)

■ *population:* 10 million (1988) ■ *size:* 91,949 square kilometres.

Port Vila /pɔːt viːlə/
Port Vila, on Éfaté Island, is the capital of Vanuatu and its largest town. Population: 19,000 (1989).

pos.
Pos. is a written abbreviation for 'positive'.

pose /pəʊz/ **poses, posing, posed**

1 VO If something **poses** a problem or danger, it is the cause of it; a formal use. *Rain has been falling recently, posing problems for those sleeping out in the open... He said the experiment posed absolutely no threat to safety.*

2 VO If you **pose** a question, you ask it; a formal use. *This brings me back to the question you posed earlier... The authorities' handling of the affair poses serious questions.*

3 V+as If you **pose** as someone, you pretend to be that person in order to deceive people. *...an agent posing as a telephone engineer.*

4 V If someone **is posing**, they are behaving in a particular way in order to impress people or deceive them; used showing disapproval. *You're always posing.*

5 V If you **pose** for a photograph or painting, you stay in a particular position so that someone can photograph or paint you. *The bride and groom posed for the photograph.*

6 NC+SUPP Your **pose** is the way you stand, sit, or lie when you are being painted or photographed. *...hundreds of photographs in various poses.*

poser /pəʊzə/ **posers**

1 NC If you call someone a **poser**, you mean that they are behaving in a particular way in order to impress people or deceive them; used showing disapproval. *I think he's something of a poser.*

2 NC A **poser** is also a difficult problem or puzzle. *Mr Seljmani gave an ambivalent answer to this poser... I remember putting the familiar poser to my father.*

poseur /pəʊzɜː/ **poseurs**
NC A **poseur** is the same as a **poser**; a literary word. *...a hypocritical poseur.*

posh /pɒʃ/ **posher, poshest**; an informal word.

1 ADJ **Posh** means smart, fashionable, and expensive. *She had stayed in posh hotels.*

2 ADJ If you describe a person as **posh**, you mean that they belong to a high social class. *...your posh friends.*

position /pəzɪʃn/ **positions, positioning, positioned**

1 NCorNU The **position** of someone or something is the place where they are. *They tell the time by the position of the sun... He had shifted position from the front to the back of the room.* ● If someone or something is in **position**, they are in their correct or usual place. *By 8.05 the groups were in position.*

2 NC+SUPP When someone or something is in a particular **position**, they are sitting, lying, or arranged in that way. *I helped her to a sitting position... Hold it in an upright position.*

3 VOorV-REFL If you **position** something somewhere, you put it there carefully. *Mel positioned his car alongside the foreman's... The boy positioned himself near the door.*

4 NC+SUPP Your **position** in society is your status in it. *Women hold a strong position in Aboriginal society. ...people in positions of power and influence.*

5 NC Someone's **position** in a company or organization is their job; a formal use. *...top management positions... Thorn lost his position as steward.*

6 NC+SUPP Your **position** in a race or competition is your place among the winners, or your place at some time during the event. *The world motor rally champion Carlos Sainz has moved into third position.*

7 NC+SUPP You can describe your situation at a particular time by saying that you are in a particular **position**. *It puts me in a rather difficult position... You are in the fortunate position of having no responsibilities.*

8 NC+SUPP Your **position** on a particular matter is your attitude towards it; a formal use. *What is their position on the proposed sale of aircraft?*

9 If you are **in a position to** do something, you are able to do it because you have enough authority,

money, or time. *The EPRDF will be in a position to wield considerable power... Asked about compensation for the families, he said he was not in a position to make that decision.*

positive /pɒzətɪv/
1 ADJ People who are **positive** are hopeful and confident. *I began to feel more positive... They had come to the talks with an open and positive attitude.*
2 ADJ A **positive** action is done in very deliberate or forceful way that is likely to have good results. *They want to make a positive gesture towards peace... We need positive help from the West to allow us to make the necessary economic changes.*
3 ADJ A **positive** development or achievement is considered to be good or useful. *In the past few month's the region has seen some positive developments... The peace talks are producing positive results... He hopes the meeting will achieve something positive.*
4 ADJ A **positive** response shows agreement, approval, or encouragement. *Public response was positive... The reaction from Swiss investors had been positive.*
5 ADJ ATTRIB You can use **positive** to emphasize that something is the case. *Life in a town brings positive advantages to children. ...positive health benefits.*
6 ADJ PRED If you are **positive** about something, you are completely sure about it. *He was positive that he had seen it in the newspaper.*
7 ADJ ATTRIB **Positive** evidence gives definite proof of something. *I was looking for some positive evidence that Barney came to the flat.*
8 ADJ If a scientific test is **positive**, it shows that something has happened or is present. *...a positive pregnancy test... A blue dot means that the test was positive.*
9 ADJ A **positive** number is greater than zero. *If (x) is positive, (y) must be negative.*

positive discrimination
NU **Positive discrimination** is the policy of deliberately treating one group of people better than others because they have previously been treated unfairly. *...the need for positive discrimination to help minorities. ...positive discrimination in favour of female employees.*

positively /pɒzətɪvli/
SUBMOD or ADV SEN You use **positively** to emphasize that something is the case. *Her friends had been positively abusive... It's quite positively the last time that you'll see me.*

positive vetting
NU **Positive vetting** is the thorough checking of a person by a government before they are trusted with official secrets. *I'm not so happy about Davis, in spite of the positive vetting.*

positivism /pɒzətɪvɪzəm/
NU **Positivism** is a philosophical system which accepts only things that can be seen or proved. *...religious mysticism and scientific positivism.* ◆ **positivist, positivists** NC *...a logical positivist. ...the positivist approach.*

poss /pɒs/
Poss is an abbreviation for 'possible'; used in informal speech. *I'll do it as soon as poss.*

posse /pɒsi/ **posses**
1 NC In former times, a **posse** was a group of men brought together by an American sheriff to help him chase and capture a criminal. *...the outlaw Jesse James, pursued by a posse.*
2 N SING+SUPP A **posse** of people is a group with the same job or purpose. *...a large posse of Afghan troops. ...a vicious posse of neo-Nazis.*

possess /pəzɛs/ **possesses, possessing, possessed;** a formal word.
1 VO If you **possess** something, you have it or own it. *How I longed to possess a suit like that... They were found guilty of possessing petrol bombs.*
2 VO To **possess** a quality, ability, or feature means to have it. *He possessed the qualities of a war leader... They were felt to possess magical properties.*

possession /pəzɛʃn/ **possessions**
1 NU The **possession** of something is the fact of having it or owning it; a formal use. *Freedom depended on*

the possession of land... The possession of a degree does not guarantee you a job.
2 If something is in your **possession**, or if you are in **possession** of it, you have it; a formal expression. *I had in my possession a portion of the money... The document came into the possession of the Daily Mail... MacDonald has been in possession of the letter for some weeks.*
3 NC Your **possessions** are the things that you own or have with you. *He had few possessions... Check your possessions on arrival.*

possessive /pəzɛsɪv/ **possessives**
1 ADJ Someone who is **possessive** about another person wants all that person's love and attention. *She was very possessive about Rod.* ◆ **possessiveness** NU *...a child's possessiveness towards its mother.*
2 ADJ When people are **possessive** about things that they own, they do not like other people to use them. *I am possessive about my car.*
3 NC or N+N In grammar, the **possessive** is the form of a noun or pronoun used to indicate possession. For example, 'George's', 'her', and 'mine' are possessives.

possessor /pəzɛsə/ **possessors**
NC The **possessor** of something is the person who has it or owns it; a formal word. *He is the possessor of an unusually innovative mind.*

possibility /pɒsəbɪləti/ **possibilities**
1 NC If there is a **possibility** of something happening or being true, it might happen or might be true. *We must accept the possibility that we might be wrong... There is at least the possibility that this drought is going to continue for many decades.*
2 NC A **possibility** is also one of several different things that could be done. *One possibility would be to issue public invitations to the peace conference... Real possibilities existed for avoiding war and initiating a dialogue.*

possible /pɒsəbl/
1 ADJ If it is **possible** to do something, it can be done. *It is possible for us to measure his progress... They are doing everything possible to take care of you... Whenever possible, loads were flown in... 'When do you want to go?'—'This weekend, if possible.'*
2 ADJ If you do something as soon as **possible**, you do it as soon as you can. If you get as much as **possible** of something, you get as much as you can. *Go as soon as possible... I like to know as much as possible about my patients... He sat as far away from the others as possible.*
3 ADJ You use **possible** with superlative adjectives to emphasize that something has more or less of a quality than anything else of its kind. *We provide the best possible accommodation for our students. ...the harshest possible conditions.*
4 ADJ If it is **possible** that something is true or correct, it might be true or correct. *It is possible that he said these things.*
5 ADJ A **possible** event is one that might happen. *His staff warned him of the possible consequences.*
6 ADJ ATTRIB If you describe someone as, for example, a **possible** Prime Minister, you mean that he or she may become the Prime Minister. *America and Russia were both possible financiers of the dam.*
7 You add **if possible** to a wish or intention to show that although this is what you really want, you may have to accept something less or slightly different. *Hungary would indeed like these negotiations to succeed and finish soon, if possible within the next month.*

possibly /pɒsəbli/
1 ADV SEN You use **possibly** to indicate that you are not sure whether something is true or will happen. *Television is possibly to blame for this... We could possibly get some money by going to my parents.*
2 ADV You use **possibly** to emphasize that you are surprised or puzzled. *How could it possibly accomplish anything?... I wondered what he could possibly be doing it for.*
3 ADV You use **possibly** in front of 'can' or 'could' to emphasize that something is done as well or as soon as it can be done. *He will do everything he possibly can to aid you... I have made myself as comfortable*

as I possibly can... He planned to come back as soon as he possibly could.

4 ADV You use **possibly** with a 'cannot' or 'could not' to emphasize that something cannot happen or cannot be done. *I can't possibly stay in all the weekend... Nobody could possibly tell the difference.*

possum /pɒsəm/ **possums**

1 NC A **possum** is the same as an **opossum**; used in informal American English. *The raccoons and possums got a lot of them.*

2 If you **play possum**, you pretend that you are asleep or that you do not know something in order to deceive someone; an informal expression. *She's just playing possum.*

post /pəʊst/ **posts, posting, posted**

1 N SING or NU The **post** is the public service by which letters and parcels are collected and delivered. *There is a cheque for you in the post... Winners will be notified by post.*

2 NU You can refer to letters and parcels delivered to you as your **post**. *There is some post for you... Rose was reluctant to answer her post.*

3 VO If you **post** a letter or parcel, you send it to someone by putting it in a post-box or by taking it to a post office. *I'm going to post a letter... I'll be glad to post you details.*

4 If you **keep** someone **posted**, you inform them immediately of any changes or developments in a situation. *David promised to keep them posted.*

5 NC A **post** is an upright pole fixed into the ground. *A dog sat chained to a post.*

6 NC A **post** in an organization is a job or official position in it; a formal use. *She is well qualified for the post.*

7 VOA If you **are posted** somewhere, you are sent there by the organization you work for. *I have been posted to Paris.*

8 See also **posting**.

post- /pəʊst-/

PREFIX **Post-** combines with nouns, adjectives, and dates to form words that describe something as taking place after a particular date or event. *...the post-1918 period. ...a post-election survey.*

postage /pəʊstɪdʒ/

NU **Postage** is the money that you pay for sending letters and parcels by post. *Send 25p extra for postage and packing.*

postage stamp, postage stamps

NC A **postage stamp** is a small piece of paper that you have to buy and stick on an envelope or parcel before you post it; a formal expression. *It is possible to buy postage stamps from at least 35,000 shops throughout the country.*

postal /pəʊstl/

ADJ ATTRIB **Postal** is used to describe things connected with the service of collecting and delivering letters and parcels. *...increases in postal charges. ...the postal service.*

postal order, postal orders

NC If you want to send money to someone through the post, you can send a **postal order**. This is a piece of paper representing a sum of money which you buy at a post office. *The writer, who didn't give his name, enclosed postal orders worth a total of £100.*

postbag /pəʊstbæg/ **postbags**

1 NC A **postbag** is a bag in which a postman carries letters and parcels.

2 N SING The letters that are received by an important person, an organization, or a newspaper or magazine are sometimes referred to as the **postbag**, especially when they represent public opinion on a particular subject. *The statement brought Rodgers his biggest postbag to date... The power of the postbag must never be underestimated.*

post-box, post-boxes

NC A **post-box** is a large container in the street where you post letters. *Marion, run down to the post-box with this letter.*

postcard /pəʊstkɑːd/ **postcards**

NC A **postcard** is a piece of card, often with a picture on one side, which you can write on and post to someone without using an envelope. *We received a*

postcard from Leonard Fass in Stockton, California... Thank you for your postcard.

postcode /pəʊstkəʊd/ **postcodes**

NC Your **postcode** is a short sequence of numbers and letters at the end of your address, which helps the post office to sort the mail. *Our postcode is ST7, showing that letters come via Stoke-on-Trent.*

postdate /pəʊstdeɪt/ **postdates, postdating, postdated**

VO If you **postdate** a document such as a cheque or letter, you write a date on it that is later than the date when you actually write it. You do this in order to allow yourself a period of time before it becomes valid.

poster /pəʊstə/ **posters**

NC A **poster** is a large notice, advertisement, or picture that you stick on a wall or noticeboard. *The election is only nine weeks away and campaign posters are already going up around the country... Dr Sherr has been measuring the effects of posters and TV advertising on two particular groups of people in Britain.*

poste restante /pəʊst restɒnt/

NU **Poste restante** is a service operated by post offices by which letters and parcels that are sent to you are kept at a particular post office until you collect them. *...the clerk at the poste restante counter. ...a poste restante address.* ▶ Also ADV *You'd better send it poste restante.*

posterior /pɒstɪərɪə/ **posteriors**

1 NC Someone's buttocks can be referred to as their **posterior**; often used humorously. *He paused a moment to raise his posterior from the chair.*

2 ADJ ATTRIB **Posterior** describes something that is situated at the back of something else; a technical use. *...the posterior muscles.*

posterity /pɒstɛrɪti/

NU You can refer to everyone who will be alive in the future as **posterity**; a formal word. *This fine building should be preserved for posterity.*

poster paint, poster paints

NC or NU **Poster paint** is a type of paint similar to watercolour paint. *...tins of poster paints... I had a jar of red poster paint sitting on my drawing table.*

postgraduate /pəʊstgrædʒuət/ **postgraduates**

1 NC A **postgraduate** is a student with a first degree who is studying or doing research at a more advanced level. *In the universities, the majority of LIS students are postgraduates. ...postgraduate students.*

2 ADJ ATTRIB **Postgraduate** work or research is done by a student who has a first degree and is studying or doing research at a higher level. *Many students go on and do postgraduate work.*

posthumous /pɒstjʊməs/

ADJ **Posthumous** is used to describe something that happens after someone's death; a formal word. *A posthumous George Medal was awarded to Mr Michael Skippern.* ◆ **posthumously** ADV *One of the awards is made posthumously to Constable Michael Todd.*

post-industrial

ADJ ATTRIB **Post-industrial** is used to describe the present state of many Western societies, referring especially to the changes in types of industry, methods of manufacture, and people's lifestyles. *...the post-industrial computer age. ...the merits of a post-industrial leisure society.*

posting /pəʊstɪŋ/ **postings**

NC A **posting** is a job that you are given which involves going to a different town or country. *I've been given an overseas posting to Japan.*

postman /pəʊstmən/ **postmen** /pəʊstmən/

NC A **postman** is a man whose job is to collect and deliver letters and parcels that are sent by post. *Postmen are refusing to make any more deliveries.*

postmark /pəʊstmɑːk/ **postmarks**

NC A **postmark** is a mark printed on letters and parcels at a post office. It shows the time and place at which they are sorted. *The first thing she looks for is the postmark. ...special postmarks used on envelopes and cards.*

postmaster /pəʊstmɑːstə/ **postmasters**

NC A **postmaster** is a man in charge of a post office; an old-fashioned word. *The three armed and masked* *men were waiting upstairs when the postmaster and his wife arrived to open up the shop.*

postmistress /pəʊstmɪstrəs/ **postmistresses**
NC A **postmistress** is a woman in charge of a post office; an old-fashioned word. *The postmistress was a widow.*

post-mortem /pəʊstmɔːtəm/ **post-mortems**
NC A **post-mortem** is a medical examination of a dead person's body to find out how they died. *The post-mortem revealed acute pneumonia and damage to the intestines... A second post-mortem examination is being performed on the body.*

post-natal /pəʊstneɪtl/
ADJ ATTRIB **Post-natal** means happening after the birth of a baby. *...post-natal care... Mothers may suffer from post-natal depression.*

post office, post offices
1 N SING The **Post Office** is the national organization responsible for postal services. *The Post Office has issued a special set of stamps to mark the occasion... I worked for the Post Office for twenty-five years.*
2 NC A **post office** is a building where you can buy stamps, post letters and parcels, and use other services provided by the national postal service. *The gang were trying to rob a post office.*

postpone /pəspəʊn/ **postpones, postponing, postponed**
VO If you **postpone** an event, you arrange for it to take place later. *Could you postpone your departure for five minutes?... The flight had been postponed until eleven o'clock.*

postponement /pəspəʊnmənt/ **postponements**
NCorNU The **postponement** of an event is the act of arranging for it to take place later. *The incident led to the postponement of peace talks between the government and the ANC. ...the costs of cancellation or postponement.*

postscript /pəʊstskrɪpt/ **postscripts**
1 NC A **postscript** is a message written at the end of a letter after you have signed your name. You write 'PS' in front of it. *He sent a copy of his letter to President Bush with a postscript telling him, 'I'm with you all the way'.*
2 NC You can refer to an addition to a finished account, statement, or event as a **postscript**. *A postscript to the controversy is published in today's Daily Telegraph... There is a postscript: Anderson was hailed as a hero in the North.*

postulate, postulates, postulating, postulated; a formal word, pronounced /pɒstjʊleɪt/ when it is a verb and /pɒstjʊlət/ when it is a noun.
1 VOorV-REPORT If you **postulate** something, you suggest it as the basis for a theory, argument, or calculation, or assume that it is the basis. *They postulate excessive increases in population... This is consistent with the sort of infective process we're postulating... Most historians postulate that a clear distinction lay between Trotsky and Lenin on most issues.*
2 NC A **postulate** is an idea that is suggested as or assumed to be the basis for a theory, argument, or calculation. *Is this a reasonable postulate? ...the postulates of Marxism.*

posture /pɒstʃə/ **postures, posturing, postured**
1 NU Your **posture** is the position or manner in which you stand or sit. *...his stiff, upright posture... Maintain a good posture when working at the VDU.*
2 NC+SUPP Your **posture** is also your attitude towards a particular matter. *They are trying to adopt a more co-operative posture.*
3 V If someone is **posturing**, they are behaving in an exaggerated or insincere way in order to get attention, or because they want people to have a particular impression of them. *He said the ANC was not posturing.* ► Also NU *His remarks were dismissed as political posturing.*

post-war
ADJ ATTRIB **Post-war** is used to describe things that happen, exist, or are made in the period immediately after a war, especially the Second World War. *...the most influential politician in post-war Austria. ...the collapse of Italy's forty-seventh post-war government.*

posy /pəʊzi/ **posies**
NC A **posy** is a small bunch of flowers. *She presented a posy to the Queen Mother.*

pot /pɒt/ **pots, potting, potted**
1 NC A **pot** is a deep, round container used for cooking, or a round container for paint or some other thick liquid. *An old woman was filling pots with water... Dishes and pots are stacked on a shelf. ...huge pots of ketchup and mayonnaise.*
2 NC A **pot** is also a round container, usually made of earthenware or plastic, which is used for growing plants in. *Pots of geraniums stood on the window-sill. ...a huge plastic plant pot.*
3 NC You can use **pot** to refer to a pot and its contents, or to the contents only. *How long would it take you to bring a pot of water to boiling point? ...a pot of cream.*
4 NC You can also use **pot** to refer to a teapot or coffee pot, with or without its contents, or to the contents only. *I'll go and make a fresh pot of tea.*
5 VO If you **pot** a plant, you put it into a flowerpot filled with earth, so that it can grow there. *I was helping him pot the cuttings.*
6 NU **Pot** is the same as **cannabis**; an informal use. *What connection could there be between the smoking of pot and the development of these symptoms?*
7 See also **potted, chamber pot, chimney pot, lobster pot, melting pot, pot belly, pot plant, pot roast.**

potash /pɒtæʃ/
NU **Potash** is a white powdery substance, obtained from the ashes of burnt wood. It is used especially as a fertilizer. *It has a nitrogen value of 3 percent, 1 percent phosphate and 3 percent potash.*

potassium /pətæsiəm/
NU **Potassium** is a soft silvery-white chemical element, which occurs mainly in compounds. These compounds are used especially in making glass, soap, detergents, and fertilizers. *...chemicals which protect the heart from high concentrations of potassium. ...potassium cyanide.*

potato /pəteɪtəʊ/ **potatoes**
1 NCorNU A **potato** is a round white vegetable with a brown or red skin. Potatoes grow underground. *They had been working in the fields for days collecting potatoes. ...a commercial variety of potato... They were eating cold pork pie, pickles, and potato salad.*
2 See also **hot potato.**

potato chip, potato chips
NC **Potato chips** are the same as **crisps**; used in American English. *...sour cream flavored potato chips.*

pot-bellied /pɒtbelid/
ADJ Someone who is **pot-bellied** has got a pot belly.

pot belly, pot bellies
NC Someone who has a **pot belly** has a round, fat stomach which sticks out. *People with big bottoms seem to have fewer heart attacks than people with pot bellies.*

pot-boiler, pot-boilers
NC A **pot-boiler** is a piece of writing, music, or other work which a writer, musician, or other artist has created in order to earn money quickly rather than as a work of artistic merit. *These short stories were written as pot-boilers to get him out of debt.*

pot-bound
ADJ A plant that is **pot-bound** is growing in a pot which is too small for it, so that the roots cannot continue to grow.

potency /pəʊtnsi/
1 NU **Potency** is the power and influence that a person, action, or idea has to affect people's lives or beliefs. *The play conjures up the potency of evil... Princess Ida's spell lost its potency.*
2 NU The **potency** of a drug, poison, or other chemical is its strength. *These drugs are of unknown potency... The potency of some of the insecticides being sprayed has caused concern for their effect on fruit and crops.*
3 NU **Potency** is also a man's capability to have sex. *This can be seen as an insult to a man's sexual potency.*

potent /pəʊtnt/
1 ADJ Something that is **potent** is effective and

powerful. *Potent new weapons will shortly be available... This is a very potent argument in the current climate.*
2 ADJ A man who is **potent** is capable of having sex. *In early adulthood you are at your most potent.*

potentate /pəʊtnteɪt/ **potentates**
NC A **potentate** is a ruler who has direct power over his people; a formal word. *...these magnificent foreign potentates.*

potential /pətenʃl/
1 ADJ ATTRIB You use **potential** to describe something as capable of becoming a particular kind of thing. *The East European countries are no longer seen as the potential enemy of the West... Indonesia is facing a potential food crisis... They are looking for potential foreign investors.* ◆ **potentially** SUBMOD *Electricity is potentially dangerous.*
2 NU If something has **potential**, it is capable of being useful or successful in the future. *The land has great strategic potential.*
3 NU+SUPP If something has a particular **potential**, it is possible that it may develop in the way mentioned. *The two leaders agreed that there was potential for greater trade between the two countries... Many feel the potential for trouble is still there.*
4 N SING Your **potential** is the range of abilities which you have, even if you are not actually using them. *Many children do not achieve their potential.*

potentiality /pətenʃiæləti/ **potentialities**
N PLorNU If something has **potentialities** or **potentiality**, it is capable of being used or developed; a formal word. *...the potentialities of motoring and flight. ...the realization of human potentiality.*

pothole /pɒthəʊl/ **potholes**
NC A **pothole** is a large hole in the surface of a road, caused by traffic and bad weather. *...a rough road, pitted in parts with potholes.*

potholer /pɒthəʊlə/ **potholers**
NC A **potholer** is someone who explores underground caves as a sport. *Five potholers who went missing overnight in a cave in north Yorkshire have been rescued.*

potholing /pɒthəʊlɪŋ/
NU **Potholing** is the sport of exploring underground caves. *He kept himself fit with exercises and he loved climbing and potholing.*

potion /pəʊʃn/ **potions**
NC A **potion** is a drink containing medicine, poison, or something that is supposed to have magic powers. *He believed he had been given a poisonous potion.*

pot plant, pot plants
NC A **pot plant** is a plant which is grown indoors in a flowerpot. *There are pictures on the walls, and pot plants in the lounge.*

potpourri /pəʊpʊəri/ **potpourris**
1 NCorNU A **potpourri** is a mixture of dried petals and leaves from different flowers in a bowl. Potpourris are used to make rooms smell pleasant.
2 NC A **potpourri** is also a collection of various different items which were not originally intended to form a group. *...a whole potpourri of useless gadgets.*

pot roast, pot roasts
NCorNU A **pot roast** is a piece of meat that is cooked very slowly with a small amount of liquid in a covered pot.

pot-shot, pot-shots
NC If you take a **pot-shot** at something or someone, you shoot at them without taking the time to aim carefully; an informal word. *It was very dark and I felt sure someone would take a pot-shot at me.*

potted /pɒtɪd/
1 ADJ ATTRIB **Potted** meat or fish has been cooked and put into a small sealed container. *...cocktail snails potted in garlic butter.*
2 ADJ ATTRIB A **potted** biography or history contains the main facts in a simplified form. *...a potted history of fifties pop music.*

potter /pɒtə/ **potters, pottering, pottered**
NC A **potter** is someone who makes pottery. *Centring the ball of clay is the first major hurdle for any potter.*
potter about PHRASAL VERB If you **potter about** or **potter around**, you pass the time in an unhurried way,

doing pleasant things. *He loved to potter around in the garden.*

pottery /pɒtəʳri/
1 NU **Pottery** is pots, dishes, and other objects made from clay. *...a sale of antique pottery.*
2 NU **Pottery** is also the craft or activity of making pottery. *My hobbies are pottery and basket-weaving.*

potting compost /pɒtɪŋ kɒmpɒst/
NU **Potting compost** is soil that is specially prepared to help young plants to grow. *We use as much peat as potting compost.*

potting shed, potting sheds
NC A **potting shed** is a shed in a garden, in which you can keep things such as seeds and garden tools.

potty /pɒti/ **potties**
1 NC A **potty** is a deep bowl which a small child uses as a toilet. *I would empty the potty and flush the lavatory.*
2 ADJ Someone who is **potty** is crazy or foolish; an informal use. *They thought she was potty... I think it's a potty idea.*

potty-trained
ADJ When a small child is **potty-trained**, it is able to use a potty and therefore does not need to wear nappies any more.

potty-training
NU **Potty-training** is the process of teaching a small child to use a potty, so that it will not need to wear nappies any more.

pouch /paʊtʃ/ **pouches**
1 NC A **pouch** is a flexible container like a small bag. *...a tobacco pouch.*
2 NC A kangaroo's **pouch** is a pocket of skin on its stomach in which its baby grows.

pouf /puf/. See **poof**.

pouffe /puːf/ **pouffes**
NC A **pouffe** is a low, soft piece of furniture which is used for sitting on or for resting your feet on.

poultice /pəʊltɪs/ **poultices**
NC A **poultice** is a bandage containing a mixture of soft, heated ointments. It is put over a swollen or painful part of someone's body. *...a poultice for inflamed eyes... She treated the swelling with poultices of herbs.*

poultry /pəʊltri/
1 N PL **Poultry** can refer to chickens, ducks, and other birds kept for their eggs and meat as **poultry**. *They keep poultry.*
2 NU You can also refer to the meat of these birds as **poultry**. *They sell cooked and fresh poultry.*

pounce /paʊns/ **pounces, pouncing, pounced**
1 V When an animal or bird **pounces** on something, it leaps on it and grabs it. *He had seen leopards pouncing on young baboons.*
2 V If you **pounce** on something such as a mistake, you draw attention to it. *Local politicians are quick to pounce on any trouble.*

pound /paʊnd/ **pounds, pounding, pounded**
1 NC A **pound** is a unit of money in Britain, equal to one hundred pence. Many other countries use a unit of money called a **pound**. *The project will last five years and cost almost two and a half million pounds.*
2 NC A **pound** is also a unit of weight equal to 16 ounces or approximately 0.454 kilograms. *...one pound of rice... He weighs about 140 pounds.*
3 VOorVA If you **pound** something or **pound** on it, you hit it loudly and repeatedly with your fists. *In frustration she would pound the dining-room table... They began pounding on the walls.* ◆ **pounding** NU *The pounding of the drums grew louder.*
4 VO To **pound** something also means to crush it into a paste or powder, or into very small pieces. *The women of the village pounded grain in their mortars.*
5 V If your heart is **pounding**, it is beating with a strong, fast rhythm. *My heart pounded with joy.* ◆ **pounding** NU *I felt only the pounding of my heart.*

pour /pɔː/ **pours, pouring, poured**
1 VO If you **pour** a liquid or other substance, you make it flow steadily out of a container by holding the container at an angle. *The waiter poured the wine into her glass. ...a machine that poured grain into sacks.*

2 VOO or VO+*for* If you **pour** someone a drink, you fill a cup or glass with it so that they can drink it. *He poured Ellen a glass of wine... She poured a drink for herself.*
3 VA When a liquid or other substance **pours** somewhere, it flows there quickly and in large quantities. *The rain poured through a hole in the roof.*
4 V When it is **pouring**, it is raining heavily. *In London it poured all the time... It was absolutely pouring with rain.* ◆ **pouring** ADJ ATTRIB *Don't go out in the pouring rain.*
5 VA When people **pour** into a place, they go into it in large numbers. *Refugees are now pouring into this country... Thousands of people poured out onto the streets.*
6 VO+*into* When someone **pours** money into an activity or organization, they spend a lot of money on it. *The government poured money into its space programme.*
7 If someone **pours cold water** on an idea or plan, they say that it is completely impossible. *The British have also poured cold water on the ideas.*
8 **pour scorn**; see **scorn**.
pour out PHRASAL VERB If you **pour out** a drink, you fill a cup or glass with it. *Castle poured out two glasses of whisky.*

pout /paʊt/ **pouts, pouting, pouted**
V If you **pout**, you stick out your lips as a way of showing that you are annoyed. *She tossed back her hair and pouted.* ◆ **pouting** ADJ ATTRIB *...a moody look, with pouting lips and dark greasy hair.*

poverty /pɒvəti/
NU **Poverty** is the state of being very poor. *Homelessness and poverty are on the increase there... Overall, a third of the total population of the world are living in abject poverty.*

poverty-stricken
ADJ **Poverty-stricken** people or places are extremely poor. *They are desperate to leave their repressive and poverty-stricken country.*

POW /piːəʊdʌbljuː/ **POWs**
POW is an abbreviation for 'prisoner of war'. *They welcomed the announcement that two hundred and fifty five sick and wounded POWs would be released. ...a POW camp.*

powder /paʊdə/ **powders, powdering, powdered**
1 N MASS **Powder** consists of many tiny particles of a solid substance. *Put a small amount of the powder in a container and mix with water... Aerosol cans were one of the most convenient methods for dispensing liquids and powders.*
2 V-REFL or VO If you **powder** yourself, you cover parts of your body with scented powder. *After her bath, she powdered herself and brushed her teeth... She lightly powdered her face.*

powdered /paʊdəd/
ADJ ATTRIB A **powdered** substance is in the form of a powder. *The Red Cross is appealing for powdered milk and baby's bottles. ...the healing powers of powdered rhinoceros horn.*

powder keg, powder kegs
NC If you describe a situation or an area as a **powder keg**, you mean that it is very dangerous and could become violent at any time. *He said the region will remain a powder keg, which could blow up the whole world... Inmates were dispersed to other jails which were already packed and potential powder kegs.*

powder puff, powder puffs
NC A **powder puff** is a round piece of soft, thick material which women use to put powder on their faces.

powder room, powder rooms
NC A **powder room** is a room for women in public buildings such as hotels, where they can use the toilet, have a wash, or do their hair and make-up.

powdery /paʊdəri/
ADJ Something that is **powdery** looks or feels like powder. *...fresh, cold, powdery snow. ...black, powdery graphite.*

power /paʊə/ **powers, powering, powered**
1 NU Someone who has **power** has control over people and activities. *...his yearning for power... It gave the President too much power... The military authorities are refusing to hand over power.*
2 NU If a person or a group of people takes **power**, or comes to **power**, they take charge of a country's affairs. *The armed forces took power in 1976... This is one of the most serious setbacks since she came to power. ...the unsuccessful attempt by hardliners to seize power.*
3 NC+SUPP You can also use **power** to refer to a country that is very rich or important, or has strong military forces. *Heads of seven industrial powers gather in London next week. ...the western powers.*
4 NU+SUPP Your **power** to do something is your ability to do it. *They lose the power to walk... They did not have the power of speech.*
5 N PL+SUPP or NU+SUPP If someone in authority has the **power** to do something, they have the legal right to do it. *The law will give the government special powers to control prices and wages... The court still has the power to send those convicted to prison.*
6 NU+SUPP The **power** of something is its physical strength. *I underestimated the power of the explosion.*
7 NU **Power** is energy obtained, for example, by burning fuel or by using the wind or the sun. *The plant is capable of supplying a cheap source of power to local industry... At present nuclear power is responsible for about fifteen to twenty percent of Britain's electricity.*
8 NU Electricity is often referred to as **power**. *A hydro-electric scheme would generate 300 megawatts of power.*
9 VO To **power** a machine means to provide the energy that makes it work. *Its radar equipment was powered by a nuclear reactor.*
10 See also **power of attorney**.
● **Power** is used in these phrases. ● If someone is in **power**, they are in charge of a country's affairs. *The President of Paraguay has been in power for thirty-four years.* ● If something is within or in your **power**, you are able to do it. *It may not be within their power to help... I did everything in my power to console her.*

powerboat /paʊəbəʊt/ **powerboats**
NC A **powerboat** is a very fast, powerful motorboat. *Her husband was killed in a powerboat accident.*

power cut, power cuts
NC A **power cut** is a period of time when the electricity supply to a particular building or area is interrupted, sometimes deliberately. *Rescue work is being hampered by blocked roads and power cuts.*

power failure, power failures
NC or NU A **power failure** is a period of time when the electricity supply to a particular building or area is interrupted, for example because of damage to the cables. *Power failures have been recorded in Kent and Sussex. ...in the event of power failure.*

powerful /paʊəfl/
1 ADJ A **powerful** person or organization is able to control or influence people and events. *Until his illness, President Botha was by far the most powerful and popular figure in white South African politics... Our correspondent says the Tigers are still by far the most powerful Tamil organisation.*
2 ADJ If someone's body is **powerful**, it is physically strong. *He had broad shoulders and powerful arms.* ◆ **powerfully** ADV *They were young, powerfully built men.*
3 ADJ A **powerful** smell is strong and unpleasant. *...the powerful odour of horse manure.* ◆ **powerfully** ADV *...a room smelling powerfully of cats.*
4 ADJ A **powerful** voice is loud and easily heard.
5 ADJ A **powerful** speech or work of art has a strong effect on people's feelings. *He produced a series of extraordinarily powerful paintings.*

power game, power games
NC When you refer to the **power game**, you are referring to a situation in which different people or groups are competing for power. *...the provincial power game being played out in Baluchistan.*

powerhouse /paʊəhaʊs/ **powerhouses**
1 NC A **powerhouse** is a country or organization that has a lot of power or influence. *No longer is West Germany the economic powerhouse of Europe... Mr Gorbachev has lessened the influence of the*

Politburo—the traditional powerhouse of the country.
2 NC You can refer to someone who is very energetic as a **powerhouse**; an informal use. *Mel was a powerhouse of disciplined energy.*

powerless /paʊələs/
1 ADJ Someone who is **powerless** is unable to control or influence events. *Without the support of the party, the Cabinet is powerless... She fought to defend the poor and the powerless.* ◆ **powerlessness** NU *She experienced an overwhelming sense of powerlessness.*
2 ADJ PRED+*to*-INF If you are **powerless** to do something, you are unable to do it. *The government appears powerless to stop this spiral of violence... The judge said the court was powerless to direct the case to proceed.*

power line, power lines
NC A **power line** is a cable, especially above ground, along which electricity is conveyed to an area or building. *The winds brought down power lines, leaving thousands of homes without electricity.*

power of attorney
NU **Power of attorney** is a legal document which allows you to appoint someone, for example a solicitor, to act on your behalf in specified matters. *He has signed a power of attorney over his family's assets in favour of the Prime Minister.*

power plant, power plants
NC A **power plant** is a place where electricity is generated. *The company made plans to build a huge power plant able to cater for the needs of the growing community.*

power point, power points
NC A **power point** is a device that is connected to an electricity supply and fitted into a wall. If a plug is pushed into it, electricity can pass through the plug and into another device such as a television or an electric fire. *At the top it has power points for plugging in your electric drill.*

power-sharing
NU **Power-sharing** is a system in which people who would not normally take part in activities such as the government of their country or the management of their factory are allowed to do so. *...the demand for power-sharing from the unions.*

power station, power stations
NC A **power station** is a place where electricity is generated. *Taiwan has contracted to buy Indonesian natural gas to help fuel its power stations.*

power worker, power workers
NC A **power worker** is someone who works at a power station. *A strike by power workers began yesterday.*

pox /pɒks/
N SING The **pox** is syphilis; an informal word. ● See also **chickenpox, smallpox.**

pp.
pp. is the plural of 'p.' and means 'pages'.

PR /piː aː/
1 **PR** is an abbreviation for 'public relations'. *Arrangements had been made by his PR man and aide.*
2 **PR** is also an abbreviation for 'proportional representation'. *Labour's shadow health spokesman, Robin Cook, is a leading advocate of PR.*

practicable /præktɪkəbl/
ADJ If a task or plan is **practicable**, it is capable of being carried out; a formal word. *He privately expressed doubts, saying that the scheme was too vague to be practicable.*

practical /præktɪkl/ **practicals**
1 ADJ ATTRIB **Practical** means involving real situations, rather than ideas and theories. *The Party faces practical difficulties of organization and finance... Practical experience of broadcasting would be valuable.*
2 ADJ **Practical** people deal with problems sensibly and effectively. *The situation is urgent and he is a practical man... He was quite practical always in what he was writing.*
3 ADJ **Practical** ideas and methods are able to be carried out successfully. *Their ideas are too opposed to our way of thinking to be considered practical... How long will it be before nuclear fusion becomes*

practical? ...a practical alternative.
4 ADJ **Practical** clothes and things in your house are useful rather than fashionable or attractive. *Ceramic tiles are very hard on the feet, though practical.*
5 NC A **practical** is an examination or lesson in which you make things or do experiments rather than simply write. *I use that book for writing up physics practicals.*
6 See also **practically**.

practicality /præktɪkælətɪ/ **practicalities**
N PL The **practicalities** of a situation are the aspects of it which are concerned with real events rather than with ideas or theories. *He turned out to know very little about the practicalities of teaching.*

practical joke, practical jokes
NC A **practical joke** is a trick that is intended to make someone look ridiculous. *April the first is traditionally the day in Britain for playing practical jokes.*

practically /præktɪklɪ/
1 ADV **Practically** means almost. *The town was practically deserted... He knew practically no English.*
2 ADV You also use **practically** to describe something which involves real actions or events rather than ideas or theories. *So how can it be put to use practically?... These two problems had prevented high temperature superconductors being used practically.*

practice /præktɪs/ **practices**
1 NC You can refer to something that people do regularly, or to the way in which they do it, as a **practice**. *The practice of irradiating food is growing... An MP said the practice should be halted on the grounds of cruelty to the sheep... They are campaigning against new working practices.*
2 NU or NC **Practice** is regular training or exercise in something, or the period of time you spend doing this. *I help them with their music practice... Skating's just a matter of practice... The coach ended the day's practice early... In Friday's final practice he averaged over 174 kilometres per hour.*
3 NU+SUPP People's religious activities are referred to as the **practice** of their religion. *They said the free practice of religion was hindered by the authorities.*
4 NC A doctor's or lawyer's **practice** is his or her business, often shared with other doctors or lawyers. *...a doctor with a private practice.*
● **Practice** is used in these phrases. ● If you **put** an idea or method **into practice**, you make use of it. *He had not yet attempted to put his principles into practice... I'm not sure how effective these methods will be when put into practice.* ● What happens **in practice** is what really happens, in contrast to what is supposed to happen. *In practice, he exerted little influence over the others... What it means in practice is that he does twice the work for half the money.* ● If you are **out of practice** at doing something, you have not done it recently. *Gower will be back, although he admits he's out of practice.*

practise /præktɪs/ **practises, practising, practised;** spelt **practice, practices, practicing, practiced** in American English.
1 V O or V If you **practise** something, you keep doing it regularly in order to do it better. *I played the piece I had been practising for months... The baseball team was practising in the park.*
2 V O To **practise** something such as a custom, craft, or religion means to take part in the activities associated with it. *These crafts were practised by many early cultures... They have managed to practise their religion for years.*
3 V O Someone who **practises** medicine or law works as a doctor or lawyer; a formal use. *He's in Hull practising medicine now.* ◆ **practising** ADJ ATTRIB *...a practising doctor.*

practised /præktɪst/
ADJ Someone who is **practised** at something is good at it because they have had a lot of experience of it. *A practised burglar rarely leaves any trace of his presence.*

practitioner /præktɪʃə⁹nə/ **practitioners**
NC Doctors are sometimes referred to as **practitioners**; a formal word. *It brings a number of advantages both to the practitioner and to the patient.*

...*Professor Anton Jayasuriya, Sri Lanka's leading practitioner of acupuncture and homeopathy.*

praesidium. See presidium.

pragmatic /prægmˈætɪk/
ADJ A **pragmatic** way of dealing with something is based on practical considerations, rather than theoretical ones. *He argued the case for increased state intervention on wholly pragmatic grounds.* ◆ **pragmatically** ADV *We have to be ready to tackle situations pragmatically.*

pragmatism /prˈægmətɪzəm/
NU **Pragmatism** is a way of thinking or of dealing with problems in a practical way, rather than by using theory or abstract principles; a formal word. *He was widely praised for his diplomatic skill and pragmatism... The paper welcomes the economic pragmatism of the country's new leaders.*

Prague /prɑːg/
Prague is the capital of Czechoslovakia and its largest city. Population: 1,215,000 (1989).

prairie /prˈeəri/ **prairies**
NCorNU A **prairie** is a large area of flat, grassy land in North America. *...days of travel across the prairies. ...acres of rolling prairie.*

praise /prˈeɪz/ **praises, praising, praised**
1 VO If you **praise** someone or something, you express approval for their achievements or qualities. *Sylvia had a stern father who never praised her... They praised his speech for its clarity and humour.*
2 NU **Praise** is what you say or write about someone when you are praising them. *Three entrants were singled out for special praise... She finds it hard to give praise.*
3 To sing someone's **praises** means to praise them in an enthusiastic way. *He'd always been the first to sing the President's praises.*

praiseworthy /prˈeɪzwɜːðɪ/
ADJ If you say that something is **praiseworthy**, you mean that it is very good and deserves to be praised; a formal word. *...a praiseworthy action.*

pram /præm/ **prams**
NC A **pram** is a baby's cot which has wheels so that you can push it along when you want to take a small baby somewhere. *The child's father was pushing the pram past the car.*

prance /prɑːns/ **prances, prancing, pranced**
1 VA If someone **prances** around, they walk with exaggerated movements. *He prances about on high-heeled shoes.*
2 V When a horse **prances**, it moves with quick, high steps.

prank /præŋk/ **pranks**
NC A **prank** is a childish trick; an old-fashioned word. *It all started with his wild pranks at school.*

prankster /prˈæŋkstə/ **pranksters**
NC A **prankster** is someone who plays tricks and practical jokes on people; an old-fashioned word. *Student pranksters welcomed the new president by removing his office door and hiding it.*

prat /præt/ **prats**
NC If you call someone a **prat**, you mean that they are very stupid or foolish; an informal word which some people find offensive.

prattle /prˈætl/ **prattles, prattling, prattled**
V If someone **prattles** on about something, they talk a great deal without saying anything important; an informal word. *Brigadier Tomlinson prattled on.* ▶ Also NU *He was impervious to her laughter and prattle.*

prawn /prɔːn/ **prawns**
NC A **prawn** is a small shellfish, similar to a shrimp. *...frozen prawns. ...fresh water prawns.*

prawn cocktail, prawn cocktails
NCorNU A **prawn cocktail** is a dish that consists of prawns, salad, and a sauce. It is usually eaten at the beginning of a meal.

pray /prˈeɪ/ **prays, praying, prayed**
VorV-REPORT When people **pray**, they speak to God in order to give thanks or to ask for help. *He kneeled down and prayed to Allah... She prayed that God would send her strength.*

prayer /prˈeə/ **prayers**
1 NU **Prayer** is the activity of praying to God. *Her eyes were shut and her lips were moving in prayer.*
2 When people say their **prayers**, they pray. *He and his wife were saying their prayers.*
3 NC A **prayer** is the words that someone says when they pray. *I made a brief prayer for her recovery... There were prayers for the dead and their families.*

prayer book, prayer books
NC A **prayer book** is a book which contains the prayers which are used in church or at home. *...familiar words in the prayer book.*

pre- /priː-/
PREFIX **Pre-** is used to form words that describe something as taking place before a particular date or event. *He's used eye-witness accounts from the pre-1945 period... This concluded two days of pre-summit talks in Moscow... The shops are bursting with goods as the pre-Christmas spending spree gets into its stride.*

preach /priːtʃ/ **preaches, preaching, preached** ·
1 VorVO When someone, especially a member of the clergy, **preaches**, he or she gives a talk on a religious or moral subject as part of a church service. *The chaplain preached to a packed church... Two leading anti-apartheid churchmen have preached Easter messages to their followers.*
2 VO To **preach** a set of ideas means to try to persuade people to accept them. *He used to go round the villages preaching Socialism.*

preacher /priːtʃə/ **preachers**
NC A **preacher** is a person, usually a member of the clergy, who preaches sermons as part of a church service. *The preacher is Father Herbert McCabe from Blackfriars in Oxford.*

preamble /priːæmbl, priːæmbl/ **preambles**
NCorNU A **preamble** is an introduction to something you say or write; a formal word. *...an intensely long preamble... Philip said quickly without preamble, 'Somebody shot your father'.*

prearranged /priːərˈeɪndʒd/
ADJ Something that is **prearranged** has been planned or arranged before the time when it actually happens. *They were certain the riot couldn't have been prearranged. ...a prearranged signal.*

precarious /prɪkˈeəriəs/
1 ADJ If your situation is **precarious**, you might fail at any time in what you are doing. *The management was in a precarious position.* ◆ **precariously** ADV *I found myself living, somewhat precariously, from one assignment to another.*
2 ADJ If something is **precarious**, it is not securely held in place and seems likely to fall. *...precarious piles of books.* ◆ **precariously** ADV *I sat precariously on the roof of the cabin.*

precaution /prɪkˈɔːʃn/ **precautions**
NC A **precaution** is an action that is intended to prevent something dangerous or unpleasant from happening. *I had taken the precaution of swallowing two seasickness tablets. ...fire precautions.*

precautionary /prɪkˈɔːʃənəri/
ADJ **Precautionary** actions are intended to prevent something dangerous or unpleasant from happening. *Precautionary measures were unnecessary.*

precede /prɪsˈiːd/ **precedes, preceding, preceded;** a formal word.
1 VO If one event or period of time **precedes** another, it happens before it. *Today's discussions precede the summit meeting in Addis Ababa... The ceremony was preceded by a moment of silence.* ◆ **preceding** ADJ ATTRIB *...the activities we discussed in the preceding chapter.*
2 VO If you **precede** someone somewhere, you go in front of them. *She preceded him across the hallway... We were preceded by a huge man called Teddy Brown.*

precedence /prˈesɪdəns/
If one thing **takes precedence** over another, the first thing is regarded as more important than the second one; a formal expression. *The peaceful ordering of society takes precedence over every other consideration.*

precedent /prɛsɪdənt/ **precedents**; a formal word.
1 NC If an action or decision is regarded as a
precedent, people refer to it as a reason for taking a
similar action or decision at a later time. *The
Supreme Court had already set a precedent... The
British government has involved itself in negotiations
before—there are precedents.*
2 NCorNU If there has been a **precedent** for something,
something similar to it has happened before. *There
was no precedent for the riots... He broke with
precedent by making his maiden speech on a
controversial subject.*

precept /priːsept/ **precepts**
NC A **precept** is a general rule that helps you to decide
how you should behave in particular circumstances; a
formal word. *They would have to abide by the human
rights precepts laid down in the Helsinki accords.*

precinct /priːsɪŋkt/ **precincts**
1 NC A shopping **precinct** or a pedestrian **precinct** is a
specially built shopping area in the centre of a town,
in which cars are not allowed. *...the main Belfast
shopping precinct... There were some rowdy scenes
when she went for a walk in a pedestrian precinct in
Melbourne.*
2 NC In the United States, a **precinct** is a part of a
city which has its own police force and fire service.
...police at work patrolling the 12th precinct.
3 N PL The **precincts** of an institution are its buildings
and land; a formal use. *Gambling is prohibited within
the precincts of the University.*

precious /prɛʃəs/
1 ADJ If you say that something such as time is
precious, you mean that it is valuable and should not
be wasted. *They have lost precious working time...
The one resource more precious than any other was
land.*
2 ADJ **Precious** objects and materials are worth a lot
of money because they are rare. *Most of the precious
objects in the city's museums have now been removed
for safekeeping.*
3 ADJ If a possession is **precious** to you, you regard it
as important and do not want to lose it. *The women
and the children, clutching their precious teddy bears
and other toys, were told to take water and food with
them.*
4 ADJ ATTRIB People sometimes use **precious** to
express their dislike for things which other people
think are important; an informal use. *I'm sick and
tired of your precious brother-in-law.*
5 ADJ If you describe someone as **precious**, you mean
that they behave in a formal and unnatural way.
*...that rather precious young man... He has a slightly
precious prose style.*
6 **Precious little** of something means very little of it;
used showing disapproval. *Precious little is being
done to encourage migration northwards.*

precious metal, precious metals
NC A **precious metal** is a valuable metal such as gold
or silver. *Its platinum mines accounted for about one
third of global production of the precious metal two
years ago... The Soviet Union has reserves of this
precious metal.*

precious stone, precious stones
NC **Precious stones** are valuable stones such as
diamonds, rubies, and sapphires that are used for
making jewellery. *...sumptuous pieces of gold and
silver work encrusted with precious stones.*

precipice /prɛsəpɪs/ **precipices**
NC A **precipice** is a very steep cliff on a mountain; a
literary word. *They fell over a rocky precipice.*

precipitate /prəsɪpəteɪt/ **precipitates, precipitating,
precipitated**
VO If something **precipitates** a new event or situation,
it causes it to happen suddenly; a formal word. *The
situation in Croatia threatened to precipitate a
national crisis in Yugoslavia.*

precipitation /prəsɪpəteɪʃn/
1 NU **Precipitation** is a process in a chemical reaction
which causes solid particles to become separated from
a liquid; a technical use in chemistry. *Clogging is
also due to the precipitation of chemicals.*
2 NU **Precipitation** is also rain, snow, or hail that falls

as water or ice after it condenses in the atmosphere; a
technical use. *The warming atmosphere may actually
give rise to an increase in precipitation, and therefore
a reduction in sea level.*
3 NU **Precipitation** is also extreme haste in the way
you carry out an action; a formal use.

precipitous /prəsɪpɪtəs/
ADJ **Precipitous** means very steep; a formal word.
*Roads have been driven through shifting sands, across
salt marshes, and down the precipitous slopes of rocky
mountains.*

précis /preɪsiː/; **précis** is both the singular and the
plural form. The plural is pronounced /preɪsiːz/.
NC A **précis** is a short piece of writing which contains
the main points of a book or report, but not the
details. *...a comprehensive précis of the main points
of the case.*

precise /prəsaɪs/
1 ADJ ATTRIB You use **precise** to emphasize that you
are describing something correctly and exactly. *At
that precise moment we were interrupted by the
telephone... The precise nature of the disease has not
yet been established.* ◆ **precisely** ADV SEN *He was
furious, precisely because he had not been consulted.*
2 ADJ Something that is **precise** is exact and
accurate. *Mr Jones gave him precise instructions...
The timing had to be very precise.* ◆ **precisely** ADV
He made the knots precisely, losing no time.

precision /prəsɪʒn/
1 NU If you do something with **precision**, you do it
exactly as it should be done. *He had established a
reputation for unfailing precision in his job.*
2 N+N **Precision** equipment is carefully made so that it
is very accurate. *A key design feature of the laser is
its precision guidance system.*

preclude /prɪkluːd/ **precludes, precluding, precluded**
VO If something **precludes** an event or action, it
prevents it from happening; a formal word. *This
should not preclude a search for a better hypothesis.*

precocious /prɪkəʊʃəs/
ADJ **Precocious** children do or say things that seem
very advanced for their age. *I have a brilliant,
precocious pupil in my class. ...Shirley's precocious
talents as a singer and dancer.* ◆ **precociously** ADV
...his precociously articulate children.

precocity /prɪkɒsəti/
NU **Precocity** is the quality or state of being very
advanced in your behaviour; a formal word.
*Impressed by my precocity, the General offered me a
place on his staff.*

preconceived /priːkənsiːvd/
ADJ ATTRIB If you have **preconceived** ideas about
something, you have already formed an opinion about
it before you have had enough information or
experience. *Did you have any preconceived ideas
about what you might find?*

preconception /priːkənsepʃn/ **preconceptions**
NC Your **preconceptions** about something are beliefs
formed about it before you have had enough
information or experience. *I don't like southerners
generally because of my preconceptions about what
they are like.*

precondition /priːkəndɪʃn/ **preconditions**
NC If one thing is a **precondition** for another, it must
happen or be done before the second thing can
happen; a formal word. *He made the unconditional
withdrawal of all troops a precondition for peace... He
repeated his view that all hostages should be released
without preconditions.*

pre-cooked
ADJ **Pre-cooked** food has been prepared and cooked in
advance so that it can be heated quickly before you
eat it. *One in three microwave ovens on the British
market failed to heat pre-cooked food to a safe
temperature.*

precursor /priːkɜːsə/ **precursors**
NC A **precursor** of something is a similar thing that
happened or existed before; a formal word. *...the
precursors of man.*

predate /priːdeɪt/ **predates, predating, predated**
VO If you say that one thing **predated** another, you
mean that the first thing happened or existed some

time before the second thing; a formal word. *The building of the Nansera airfield predated the building of the Shiraz by several years.*

predator /prɛdətə/ **predators**
NC A **predator** is an animal that kills and eats other animals. *The whiting is a major predator on smaller fish.*

predatory /prɛdətə°ri/
1 ADJ ATTRIB **Predatory** animals kill and eat other animals. *When did our ancestors start using fire for warding off predatory animals?*
2 ADJ ATTRIB **Predatory** people or organizations are eager to take advantage of someone else's weakness or suffering. *...a rich state surrounded by powerful and predatory neighbours. ...the predatory activities of greedy politicians.*

predecessor /priːdɪsesə/ **predecessors**
1 NC+POSS Someone's **predecessor** is the person who had their job or role before them. *The pictures showed Mr Bush shaking hands with his predecessor, Ronald Reagan... He made it clear he has no intention of abandoning his predecessor's strategy.*
2 NC+POSS The **predecessor** of an object or machine is the object or machine that it replaced. *The latest model is more refined than its predecessor.*

predestination /priːdestɪneɪʃn/
NU **Predestination** is the belief that people have no control over events because the events have already been decided by God or by fate. *...as irreconcilable as notions of predestination and free will.*

predestined /priːdestɪnd/
ADJ If you say something was **predestined** to happen, you mean that it could not have been prevented because it had already been decided by God or by fate. *I was predestined to be a slave.*

predetermined /priːdɪtɜːmɪnd/
ADJ If something is **predetermined**, its form or nature was decided by previous events or by people rather than by chance; a formal word. *It has a memory module which can be told to take a reading at predetermined intervals... The government insists that it only launches attacks on predetermined targets.*

predeterminer /priːdɪtɜːmɪnə/ **predeterminers**
NC In grammar, a **predeterminer** is a word that is used before a determiner, and that gives you more information about the noun in the noun group. For example, 'all' in 'all the time', 'both' in 'both our children', and 'half' in 'half an hour' are predeterminers.

predicament /prɪdɪkəmənt/ **predicaments**
NC If you are in a **predicament**, you are in a difficult situation. *His predicament is very serious... He believed that the country's current predicament was due to its misguided economic policies.*

predicate, predicates, predicating, predicated.
pronounced /prɛdɪkət/ when it is a noun and /prɛdɪkeɪt/ when it is a verb.
1 NC In grammar, the **predicate** of a sentence or clause is the part of it that is not the subject. In the sentence: 'I decided what to do', 'decided what to do' is the predicate.
2 V-REPORT If you **predicate** that something is the case, you state that you believe that it is true; a formal use. *It has been predicated that a seismic shock was the cause of these phenomena.*
3 VO+on or upon If you say that one idea or situation is **predicated** on another, you mean that the first idea or situation can be true or real only if the second one is true or real; a formal use. *Other points raised in the proposals are predicated on a major role for the United Nations... Treatment of the sick and injured should not be predicated upon money.*

predicative /prɛdɪkətɪv/
ADJ ATTRIB In grammar, if an adjective is in **predicative** position, it comes after a verb such as 'be' or 'seem'. In the sentence 'The house is white', 'white' is in the predicative position.

predict /prɪdɪkt/ **predicts, predicting, predicted**
V or V-REPORT If you **predict** an event, you say that it will happen. *Many economists predict a recession... The World Health Organisation has predicted that up to 40 million people will be infected with the AIDS virus by the end of the century.*

predictable /prɪdɪktəbl/
ADJ Something that is **predictable** can be known about in advance. *The result was predictable... They claimed that everything that happened yesterday was predictable.* ◆ **predictably** ADV SEN or ADV *Predictably, the affair went hopelessly wrong. ...situations where everyone behaves predictably.* ◆ **predictability** /prɪdɪktəbɪlətɪ/ NU *It happened month by month, with boring predictability.*

prediction /prɪdɪkʃn/ **predictions**
NC or NU If you make a **prediction**, you say what you think will happen. *Computer predictions indicate that they will get just under 50 per cent of the vote nationwide. ...a prediction of the likely outcome of the next election. ...methods of prediction.*

predictive /prɪdɪktɪv/
ADJ Speech, writing, or tests that are **predictive** are concerned with information about future events; a formal word. *The predictive power of science is becoming much greater than anyone expected. ...a predictive test for cancer.*

predilection /priːdɪlekʃn/ **predilections**
NC If you have a **predilection** for something, you have a strong liking for it; a formal word. *...the American predilection for salads with every meal.*

predispose /priːdɪspəʊz/ **predisposes, predisposing, predisposed**
VO+to-INF If something **predisposes** you to think or behave in a particular way, it makes it likely that you will think or behave in that way; a formal word. *Their experiences predisposed them to accept extremist policies.* ◆ **predisposed** ADJ PRED+to-INF *She was predisposed to be critical.*

predisposition /priːdɪspəzɪʃn/ **predispositions**
NC If you have a **predisposition** to behave in a particular way, you tend to behave like that because of the kind of person that you are; a formal word. *He had a predisposition to depression.*

predominance /prɪdɒmɪnəns/
NU If there is a **predominance** of one type of person or thing, there are many more of that type than any other; a formal word. *...the predominance of businessmen in the party's ranks.*

predominant /prɪdɒmɪnənt/
ADJ If something is **predominant**, it is more important or noticeable than other things of the same kind; a formal word. *Italian opera became predominant at the end of the 17th century... The predominant mood among policy-makers is one of despair.* ◆ **predominantly** ADV *The debates were predominantly about international affairs.*

predominate /prɪdɒmɪneɪt/ **predominates, predominating, predominated**
V If one type of person or thing **predominates** in a group, there are more of that type than any other; a formal word. *In most churches, women predominate in the congregations... Although the Chinese predominate, the Malay, Indian and Eurasian communities play an important role in Singapore.*

pre-eminence /priːemɪnəns/
NU **Pre-eminence** is the quality of being more important, powerful, or capable than other people or things in a group; a formal word. *No one disputed his claim to pre-eminence. ...the pre-eminence of the Communist Party.*

pre-eminent /priːemɪnənt/
ADJ If someone or something is **pre-eminent** in a group, they are more important, powerful, or capable than other people or things in the group; a formal word. *For the next thirty years Bryce was the pre-eminent figure in Canadian economic policy... Rajiv Gandhi's family had been pre-eminent in Indian politics since independence from Britain.*

pre-eminently /priːemɪnəntli/
ADV **Pre-eminently** means to a very great extent. *This attitude is at the same time pre-eminently political.*

pre-empt /priːempt/ **pre-empts, pre-empting, pre-empted,** a formal word.
1 VO If you **pre-empt** an action, you prevent it from happening by doing something which makes it pointless or impossible. *The army sent reinforcements*

into the area to try to pre-empt any trouble...
Supporters pre-empted Sunday's vote by organising
their own elections.
2 VO If you **pre-empt** something, you take possession
of it in a way that prevents anyone else from having
it. *The Soviet Union pre-empted many of Vietnam's*
exports.

pre-emptive /priːˈɛmptɪv/
ADJ ATTRIB A **pre-emptive** strike or action is intended
to weaken an enemy or opponent, for example by
destroying their weapons so that they can no longer
cause damage or trouble. *Neither side has the ability*
to launch a pre-emptive strike... He said they were
taking pre-emptive action to forestall violent unrest.

preen /priːn/ **preens, preening, preened**
1 V-REFL When people **preen** themselves, they spend
time making themselves look neat and attractive;
often used humorously. *He preened himself in front of*
the mirror.
2 V or VO When birds **preen** their feathers, they clean
and arrange them with their beaks. *A peacock pecked*
and preened on the lawn.

prefab /ˈpriːfæb/ **prefabs**
NC A **prefab** is a house built with parts which have
been made in a factory and then quickly put together.
...a wartime prefab.

prefabricated /priːˈfæbrɪkeɪtɪd/
ADJ ATTRIB **Prefabricated** buildings are built from
large parts which can be easily put together.
Thousands of people were still homeless and living in
tents and prefabricated huts.

preface /ˈprefəs/ **prefaces, prefacing, prefaced**
1 NC A **preface** is an introduction at the beginning of a
book. *The book had a preface by the President.*
2 VO+*with* or VO+*by* If you **preface** an action or speech
with something else, you do or say this other thing
first; a formal use. *The speech was prefaced with*
verses from the Koran... The French President
prefaced his remarks by emphasising the friendship
which united France and Germany.

prefect /ˈpriːfekt/ **prefects**
1 NC In some countries, a **prefect** is the chief
administrator of a particular government department
or region. *They were told by one local prefect that the*
murders were no matter for concern.
2 NC In some schools, a **prefect** is an older pupil who
has special duties.

prefer /prɪˈfɜː/ **prefers, preferring, preferred**
VO, VO+*to*-INF, V+*to*-INF, or V-REPORT If you **prefer** one
thing to another, you like the first thing better. *I*
prefer Barber to his deputy... The Head Master
prefers them to act plays they have written
themselves... They prefer to suffer deprivation rather
than claim legal aid... We prefer that they are also
present in the talks.

preferable /ˈprefərəbl/
ADJ If one thing is **preferable** to another, it is more
desirable or suitable. *Gradual change is preferable to*
sudden, large-scale change... Many people find this
method immensely preferable. ♦ **preferably** ADV SEN
They need care, preferably in quiet surroundings.

preference /ˈprefərəns/ **preferences**
1 NC or NU If you have a **preference** for something, you
would like to have or do it rather than something else.
Each of us has personal preferences for certain types
of entertainment... I took the non-stop flight to London,
in preference to the two-stage journey via New York.
2 NU If you give **preference** to someone, you choose
them rather than someone else. *Preference was given*
to those who had overseas experience.

preferential /ˌprefəˈrenʃl/
ADJ ATTRIB If you get **preferential** treatment, you are
treated better than other people. *Disabled people at*
work should have preferential treatment.

preferment /prɪˈfɜːmənt/
NU **Preferment** is promotion to a better and more
influential job; a formal word. *...a man whose sole*
claim to preferment was his wealth.

prefigure /priːˈfɪɡə/ **prefigures, prefiguring,**
prefigured
VO If something **prefigures** something else, it is a first
indication which suggests or determines that the

second thing will happen. *The communist-built wall*
through Berlin was finally ruptured, prefiguring the
disintegration of East Germany.

prefix /ˈpriːfɪks/ **prefixes**
NC A **prefix** is a letter or group of letters added to the
beginning of a word in order to make a new word with
a different meaning. For example, 're' is a prefix.

pregnancy /ˈpreɡnənsi/ **pregnancies**
NU or NC **Pregnancy** is the condition of being pregnant,
or the period of time during which a female is
pregnant. *The breasts enlarge during pregnancy... She*
has had fifteen pregnancies.

pregnancy test, pregnancy tests
NC A **pregnancy test** is a medical test which women
have in order to find out whether they have become
pregnant. *Wait until six weeks after your last period*
and get a pregnancy test.

pregnant /ˈpreɡnənt/
ADJ If a woman or female animal is **pregnant**, a baby
is developing in her body. *She was three months*
pregnant... My mother was pregnant with me at the
time.

preheat /priːˈhiːt/ **preheats, preheating, preheated**
VO If you **preheat** an oven, you switch it on and allow
it to reach a certain temperature before you put food
inside it. *Preheat the oven to gas mark 4.* ▶ Also
ADJ ATTRIB *Bake in a preheated oven at 375°F.*

prehensile /prɪˈhensaɪl/
ADJ A part of an animal's body that is **prehensile** is
able to curl round objects and grip them; a technical
term. *...the African monkey's prehensile tail.*

prehistoric /ˌpriːhɪˈstɒrɪk/
ADJ ATTRIB **Prehistoric** people and things existed
before information was written down. *At the side of*
that country road was a prehistoric burial ground.

prehistory /priːˈhɪstəri/
NU **Prehistory** is the time in history before any
information was written down. *...the prehistory of the*
solar system. ...archaeologists who have studied the
prehistory of man.

pre-industrial
ADJ ATTRIB **Pre-industrial** refers to the time before
machines were introduced to produce goods on a large
scale. *The pre-industrial family was a self-sufficient*
unit. ...the transformation of pre-industrial into
advanced industrial societies.

prejudge /priːˈdʒʌdʒ/ **prejudges, prejudging,**
prejudged
VO or V If you **prejudge** a situation, you form an opinion
about it before you know all the facts; a formal word.
We should try not to prejudge the issue.

prejudice /ˈpredʒʊdɪs/ **prejudices**
1 NU or NC **Prejudice** is an unreasonable dislike of
someone or something. *Community leaders would like*
to see more effective action in combating racial
prejudice... He told the party leaders to abandon their
prejudice against a market economy... Barber was a
man of strong prejudices.
2 NU If you show **prejudice** in favour of someone, you
treat them better than other people. If you show
prejudice against someone, you treat them worse than
other people. *There was some regrettable prejudice in*
favour of middle class children... They're urging
governments to take action to end prejudice against
AIDS and HIV sufferers.

prejudiced /ˈpredʒʊdɪst/
ADJ A person who is **prejudiced** against someone has
an unreasonable dislike of them. A person who is
prejudiced in favour of someone has an unreasonable
preference for them. *People were prejudiced against*
her... We all know how difficult it is to reason with a
prejudiced person.

prejudicial /ˌpredʒʊˈdɪʃl/
ADJ PRED **Prejudicial** actions or situations are harmful,
especially to people's health, their safety, or their way
of life; a formal word. *Such actions were clearly*
prejudicial to the health and safety of the public.

prelate /ˈprelət/ **prelates**
NC A **prelate** is a clergyman of high rank, for example
a bishop or an archbishop; a formal word. *The Pope*
has appointed a Vietnamese prelate as one of his two
personal secretaries.

preliminary /prəlɪmɪnə⁰ri/ **preliminaries**
ADJ ATTRIB **Preliminary** activities happen at the beginning of a series of events, often as a form of preparation. *In February, Kenya held its preliminary elections to select candidates for the general election... He visited the holy places to make preliminary arrangements for the pilgrims. ...the preliminary draft of a resolution.* ▸ Also NC *He spent a long time on polite preliminaries.*

prelude /prɛljuːd/ **preludes**
NC You describe an event as a **prelude** to a more important event when it happens before it and acts as an introduction to it. *This speech has been hailed by his friends as the prelude to his return to office.*

Premadasa, Ranasinghe /rɑnəsɪŋhə preɪmədɑːsə/
Ranasinghe Premadasa became President of Sri Lanka in 1989. He was elected to the National State Assembly in 1977. He was Local Government Minister from 1968 to 1970, and in 1977. He served as Prime Minister from 1978 to 1989. He became Deputy Leader of the United National Party (UNP) in 1976. Born: 1924.

premarital /priːmærɪtl/
ADJ ATTRIB **Premarital** means relating to the time before people get married, especially when they are intending to get married soon. *...premarital sex. ...gossip about the latest premarital pregnancies.*

premature /prɛmətʃə, prɛmətʃuə/
1 ADJ Something that is **premature** happens too early or earlier than expected. *This disease produces premature ageing. ...the premature departure of the visitors.* ◆ **prematurely** ADV *The warden retired prematurely with a nervous disorder.*
2 ADJ A **premature** baby is born before the date when it was due to be born. *...a study of 400 premature babies at two British hospitals.*

premeditated /priːmɛdɪteɪtɪd/
ADJ A **premeditated** action is carefully planned or thought about before it is carried out. *...a premeditated act of murder.*

premeditation /priːmɛdɪteɪʃn/
NU **Premeditation** is thinking about something or planning it before you actually do it; a formal word. *The door of his study was open, and without premeditation he turned into it.*

premier /prɛmiə/ **premiers**
1 NC or TITLE A **premier** is a prime minister who is the leader of a country's government. *...the French premier... The Chinese Premier Li Peng has ended his two day visit to Tehrän.*
2 ADJ ATTRIB **Premier** is used to describe something that is considered to be the best or most important thing of its kind. *The article referred to Hull as Europe's premier port. ...the Premier Division of the Scottish League.*

premiere /prɛmiə/ **premieres, premiering, premiered**
1 NC The **premiere** of a new play or film is its first public performance. *The film had its world premiere at San Sebastian.*
2 VO When a new production of something such as a play or film is **premiered**, it is shown to an audience for the first time. *The play was premiered last year in Johannesburg... Fox television and NBC are premiering new series and running new episodes of old series.*

premiership /prɛmiəʃɪp/
N SING or NU **Premiership** is the position of being the leader of a government, or the time during which someone holds this position. *He should never have been considered for the premiership... Mr Mikulic is facing a mid-term review of his premiership.*

premise /prɛmɪs/ **premises, premised**; also spelt **premiss** for the meaning in paragraph 2.
1 N PL The **premises** of a business are all the buildings and land that it occupies. *In 1971 the firm moved to new premises in Bethnal Green.*
2 NC A **premise** is something that you suppose is true and therefore use as a basis for an idea; a formal use. *I'm questioning whether the whole premise is correct.*
3 V-PASS If a theory is **premised** on an idea or belief,

that idea or belief is assumed to be correct and has been used as the basis for the theory; a formal use. *The agreement was premised on the continuing presence of Vietnamese troops in Kampuchea.*

premium /priːmiəm/ **premiums**
1 NC A **premium** is an extra sum of money which is paid in addition to the normal cost of something. *Investors were willing to pay a premium for companies that offered such a potential for growth.*
2 NC A **premium** is also a sum of money that you pay regularly to an insurance company for an insurance policy. *...tax relief on life insurance premiums.*
3 If something is **at a premium** or if it is sold **at a premium**, it is wanted but is hard to obtain or has been sold at a high price because it is in short supply. *Water is at a premium, so every effort has to be made to save it... Those who make their money pumping oil from the ground get away with selling it at a premium.*

premium bond, premium bonds
NC **Premium bonds** are numbered bonds that are sold by the government in Britain. Each month, a computer randomly selects several numbers, and the people whose tickets have those numbers win prize money.

premonition /prɛmənɪʃn/ **premonitions**
NC+SUPP If you have a **premonition**, you have a feeling that something is going to happen, often something which is unpleasant. *He had a sudden terrible premonition that she had run away.*

premonitory /prɪmɒnɪtə⁰ri/
ADJ **Premonitory** feelings or events make you think that something unpleasant is about to happen; a formal word. *Daniel felt a premonitory anxiety just watching the crowd gather.*

prenatal /priːneɪtl/
ADJ ATTRIB **Prenatal** is used to describe things that relate to the medical care of pregnant women. *...prenatal classes for expectant mothers.*

preoccupation /priːɒkjupeɪʃn/ **preoccupations**
NU or NC If you have a **preoccupation** with something, you keep thinking about it, because it is important to you. *He was capable of total preoccupation... Virginia Woolf started a day-to-day diary to record her activities, observations and preoccupations.*

preoccupied /priːɒkjupaɪd/
ADJ PRED Someone who is **preoccupied** is thinking a lot about one particular thing, and seems to hardly notice other things. *His wife becomes more and more preoccupied with the children... She seemed rather preoccupied and distant.*

preoccupy /priːɒkjupaɪ/ **preoccupies, preoccupying, preoccupied**
VO If something **preoccupies** you, you think about it a great deal, so that it takes up a lot of your time. *This is a question which increasingly preoccupies me... The situation in the Gulf is preoccupying many of the delegates.*

preordained /priːɔːdeɪnd/
ADJ Something that is **preordained** is believed to be happening in the way that has been decided by God or fate; a formal word. *Certain people are preordained to a higher status by an omniscient God... What is preordained for her will certainly befall her.*

pre-packed /priːpækt/
ADJ **Pre-packed** goods are packed or wrapped before they are sent to the shop where they are going to be sold. *...pre-packed cooked food on sale in supermarkets.*

prepaid /priːpeɪd/
ADJ ATTRIB **Prepaid** items are paid for in advance. *Prepaid postcards had been provided.*

preparation /prɛpəreɪʃn/ **preparations**
1 NU The **preparation** of something is the activity of getting it ready. *Benn was involved in the preparation of Labour's manifesto. ...food preparation.*
2 N PL **Preparations** are the particular arrangements that are made for a future event. *He'll have to make preparations for the funeral... In addition to military preparations for an attack, diplomatic preparations must be made.*

3 NC A **preparation** is a mixture that has been prepared for use as food, medicine, or a cosmetic; a formal use. *North American Indians used preparations from the seeds of this plant to treat skin diseases.*

preparatory /prəpǽrətəⁱri/
ADJ ATTRIB **Preparatory** actions are done in preparation for something else; a formal word. *...a preparatory report. ...preparatory language courses.*

preparatory school, preparatory schools
NCorNU A **preparatory school** is the same as a **prep school**; a formal expression. *Their first visit was to a preparatory school in County Down... He was only eight or nine—at preparatory school.*

prepare /prɪpɛ́ə/ **prepares, preparing, prepared**
1 VO If you **prepare** someone or something, you make them ready for something that is going to happen in the future. *Schools have to prepare children for life in the community... A room has been prepared for you.*
2 VorV-REFL If you **prepare** for an event, action, or situation, you get ready for it. *The guests prepared for their departure... Prepare yourself for a shock... I was not really prepared for her fits of boredom.*
3 VO When you **prepare** food, you get it ready to be eaten, for example by cooking or cleaning it; a formal use. *He had spent all morning preparing the meal.*

prepared /prɪpɛ́əd/
1 ADJ PRED+to-INF If you are **prepared** to do something, you are willing to do it. *I'm prepared to say I was wrong... Many countries seem prepared to consider nuclear energy... The Federal Reserve may not be prepared to cut interest rates.*
2 ADJ PRED If you are **prepared** for something that may happen, you are ready for it, and it does not surprise you. *Be prepared for power cuts by buying lots of candles... If they agree to the plan, Britain should be able to send teams that are better prepared.*
3 ADJ Something that is **prepared** has been done or made beforehand. *He read out a prepared statement.*

preparedness /prɪpɛ́əridnəs/
NU **Preparedness** is the state of being ready for something to happen; used especially when referring to events such as a war or a disaster of some kind. *The coalition of allies have made clear their military preparedness... The Soviet media have criticized the lack of preparedness for the earthquake disaster.*

preponderance /prɪpɒ́ndə⁰rəns/
NU If there is a **preponderance** of one type of person or thing in a group, there are more of that type than of any other; a formal word. *There is a definite preponderance of women among those who study English Literature.*

preponderant /prɪpɒ́ndə⁰rənt/
ADJ If a particular type of person or thing is **preponderant**, that type is in the majority, or is more important than the others in its group; a formal word. *...a group among whom Germans would be preponderant.* ◆ **preponderantly** ADV *Its supporters remain preponderantly students rather than workers.*

preposition /prɛpəzɪ́ʃn/ **prepositions**
NC In grammar, a **preposition** is a word such as 'by', 'for', 'into', or 'with', which is always followed by a noun group or a clause built around the '-ing' form of a verb. *...noun, verb, adjective, preposition and every other grammatical part.*

prepositional /prɛpəzɪ́ʃə⁰nəl/
ADJ ATTRIB **Prepositional** means including or relating to a preposition. *...prepositional phrases.*

prepossessing /prɪːpəzɛ́sɪŋ/
ADJ Someone or something that is **prepossessing** is attractive or impressive in appearance. *The description that's been given of her is not exactly prepossessing.*

preposterous /prɪpɒ́stə⁰rəs/
ADJ If you describe something as **preposterous**, you mean that you think it is extremely unreasonable, unlikely, and foolish. *A spokesman described the allegations as preposterous and completely untrue.*

prep school /prɛ́p skuːl/ **prep schools**
1 NCorNU A **prep school** is a private school for children up to 11 or 13. *Their daughter goes to prep school.*

2 NCorNU In the United States, a **prep school** is a private secondary school to prepare students to enter college. *He writes to her from his prep school... These boys don't look much like prep school students.*

Pre-Raphaelite /prɪːrǽfəlaɪt/ **Pre-Raphaelites**
1 NC The **Pre-Raphaelites** were a group of British artists in the nineteenth century who concentrated on themes from medieval history, romantic myth, and folklore. *She had been a great idol of the Pre-Raphaelites. ...a whole section on Pre-Raphaelite landscape.*
2 ADJ If you describe a woman as **Pre-Raphaelite**, you mean that she looks like a character in a Pre-Raphaelite picture, for example because she has long wavy hair and a young delicate face.

pre-recorded /prɪːrɪkɔ́ːdɪd/
ADJ Something that is **pre-recorded** has been recorded in advance so that it can be broadcast or played later. *These programmes are pre-recorded and then relayed to Brighton.*

prerequisite /prɪːrɛ́kwəzɪt/ **prerequisites**
NC If one thing is a **prerequisite** for another, it must happen or exist before the second thing is possible; a formal word. *Confidence is a prerequisite for mastering other skills.*

prerogative /prɪrɒ́gətɪv/ **prerogatives**
NC Something that is the **prerogative** of a particular person or group is a privilege or right that only they have; a formal word. *...luxuries which were considered the prerogative of the rich.*

presage /prɛ́sɪdʒ/ **presages, presaging, presaged**
VO If something **presages** a situation or event, it is considered to be a warning or sign of what is about to happen; a formal word. *The drive for equality often presages chaos, disruption, and unhappiness.*

presbytery /prɛ́zbɪtə⁰ri/ **presbyteries**
NC A **presbytery** is the house in which a Roman Catholic priest lives. *...the building of new churches and presbyteries.*

pre-school /prɪːskuːl/
ADJ ATTRIB **Pre-school** is used to describe things relating to the care and education of children before they reach the age when they have to go to school. *...a pre-school playgroup. ...private nursery schools for pre-school children.*

prescience /prɛ́sɪəns/
NU **Prescience** is the ability to see what is likely to happen in the future and to take appropriate action; a formal word. *I believe that we can solve this problem—we have the resources, the skills and the moral prescience.*

prescient /prɛ́sɪənt/
ADJ If you say that someone or something was **prescient**, you mean that they were able to know or predict what was going to happen in the future; a formal word. *It was a prescient film about what later happened in Three Mile Island.*

prescribe /prɪskraɪb/ **prescribes, prescribing, prescribed**
1 VO If a doctor **prescribes** treatment or medicine for you when you are ill, they tell you what medicine or treatment you should have, and write a prescription for you if necessary. *Her doctor prescribed a sedative.*
2 VO If someone **prescribes** an action or duty, they state formally that it must be done; a formal use. *The factory laws prescribed a heavy fine for contravention of this rule.* ◆ **prescribed** ADJ ATTRIB *The list of prescribed duties has been drawn up by the federation.*

prescription /prɪskrɪ́pʃn/ **prescriptions**
1 NC A **prescription** is a medicine which a doctor has told you to take, or the form on which the doctor has written the details of that medicine. *...a prescription for sleeping tablets.*
2 A medicine that is available **on prescription** is available from a chemist if you have a prescription for it. *GLA (in the form of capsules called Epogam) is now available on prescription from doctors.*
3 NCorNU A **prescription** is also an instruction or plan which states what must be done in a particular situation; a formal use. *Mrs Chalker said it was not for outsiders to offer prescriptions for economic ills...*

He has been in hiding since the movement was forced underground by government prescription.

prescriptive /prɪskrɪptɪv/

ADJ Something that is **prescriptive** sets down rules and states what should and should not happen in certain circumstances; a formal word. *He is a man free of prescriptive social norms... His account was descriptive rather than prescriptive.*

presence /prɛzns/

1 NU+POSS Someone's **presence** in a place is the fact that they are there. *He tried to justify his presence in Belfast... He had to cope with the presence of her family.*

2 If you are **in** someone's **presence**, you are in the same place as they are. *I felt comfortable in her presence... Haldane repeated his statement in the presence of the chairman.*

3 NU If someone has **presence**, they have an impressive appearance and manner. *He had tremendous physical presence.*

presence of mind

NU **Presence of mind** is the ability to act quickly and sensibly in a difficult situation. *Richard had the presence of mind to step forward and pick it up.*

present, presents, presenting, presented;

pronounced /prɛznt/ when it is an adjective or a noun, and /prɪzɛnt/ when it is a verb.

1 ADJ ATTRIB You use **present** to describe people and things that exist now, rather than in the past or the future. *The present chairperson is a woman... Economic planning cannot succeed in present conditions... They are prepared to form a coalition government with members of the present regime in Kabul.*

2 N SING The **present** is the period of time that is taking place now and the things that are happening now. *...the present versus the future.* ● See also **present-day.**

3 ADJ PRED If someone is **present** at an event, they are there. *He had been present at the dance... There was a photographer present.*

4 NC A **present** is something that you give to someone, for example on their birthday or Christmas. *I gave him an atlas as a birthday present.*

5 V-REFL A If you **present** yourself somewhere, you announce that you have arrived; a formal use. *The next morning I presented myself at their offices.*

6 VO If you **present** someone to an important person, you officially introduce them; a formal use. *May I present Mr Rudolph Wallace.*

7 VO If you **present** someone with something, you formally give it to them. *He presented her with a signed copy of his book... One of his constituents presented a petition to Parliament.*

8 VO If you **present** people with information, you give it to them. *...a way of presenting new material... Our teachers were trying to present us with an accurate picture of history.*

9 VO Something that **presents** a difficulty or a challenge causes or provides it. *The tornado presented the island with severe problems.*

10 VOA If you **present** someone or something in a particular way, you describe them in that way. *Her lawyer wanted to present her in the most favourable light... They present the British as the colonialist oppressor.*

11 VO Someone who **presents** a programme on television or radio introduces each part of it or each person on it. *...'University Link', compiled and presented by Dr Brian Smith.*

● **Present** is used in these phrases. ● If something is happening **at present** or **at the present time**, it is happening now. *He is at present serving a life sentence... The two sides were unwilling to discuss a ceasefire in the war at the present time.* ● If a situation exists **for the present**, it exists now but is likely to change. *For the present she continues with the antibiotics.* ● The **present day** is the period of history that is taking place now. *This tradition has continued till the present day.*

presentable /prɪzɛntəbl/

ADJ If someone or something is **presentable**, they are

quite attractive and are suitable for other people to see. *She looked quite presentable. ...some of his more presentable pictures.*

presentation /prɛznt̪eɪʃn/ **presentations**

1 NU The **presentation** of information is the process of giving it to people. *...the collection and presentation of statistical data.*

2 NU **Presentation** is the appearance of something and the impression that it gives to people. *Presentation is very important in cooking.*

3 NC A **presentation** is a formal event at which someone is given something such as a prize. *I said I would not be able to attend the presentation.*

4 NC+SUPP A **presentation** is also something such as a play or a lecture that is presented before an audience; a formal use. *Darwin was urged to deliver a presentation on the subject.*

present-day

ADJ ATTRIB You use **present-day** to describe people and things that exist now rather than in the past. *...present-day Japanese children. ...social conditions in present-day India.*

presenter /prɪzɛntə/ **presenters**

NC A **presenter** is a person who introduces a television or radio programme, especially a programme that gives news or information. *...a sports presenter from one of Sydney's commercial radio stations.*

presentiment /prɪzɛntɪmənt/ **presentiments**

NC A **presentiment** is a feeling that a particular event, for example someone's death, will soon take place; a formal word. *Mel had not forgotten the vague unease, the presentiment of danger he had felt while on the plane.*

presently /prɛzntli/

1 ADV You use **presently** to indicate that something happened quite a short time after another thing that you have just mentioned; an old-fashioned use. *Presently I got the whole story.*

2 ADV If you say that something will happen **presently**, you mean that it will happen quite soon; an old-fashioned use. *He will be here presently.*

3 ADV If something is **presently** happening, it is happening at the time you are speaking or writing. *...the oil rigs that are presently in operation.*

present participle, present participles

NC The **present participle** of an English verb is the form that ends in '-ing'. It is used to form continuous tenses, and to form adjectives and nouns from a verb.

present perfect

N SING In grammar, the **present perfect** tense of an English verb is the tense that is formed with the present tense of the auxiliary 'have' and the past participle of the main verb.

present tense

N SING In grammar, the **present tense** of a verb is used mainly to talk about things that happen or exist at the time of speaking or writing.

preservative /prɪzɜ:vətɪv/ **preservatives**

N MASS A **preservative** is a chemical that prevents things from decaying. Some preservatives are added to food, and others are used to treat wood or metal. *This yoghurt is free from artificial preservatives... One preservative liquid stops the paint clinging to the bristles.*

preserve /prɪzɜ:v/ **preserves, preserving, preserved**

1 VO If you **preserve** a situation or condition, you make sure that it stays as it is. *We are interested in preserving world peace... I stood there, determined to preserve my dignity.* ◆ **preservation** /prɛzəveɪʃn/ NU *...the preservation of democracy.*

2 VO If you **preserve** something, you take action to save it or protect it from damage or decay. *...a big house which had been preserved as a museum.*

3 VO If you **preserve** food, you treat it in a way that prevents it from decaying. *Deep freezing is the simplest way of preserving food.*

4 NC+SUPP A particular **preserve** is an area of life or an activity that is restricted to a chosen person or group of people. *Medicine tends to be a male preserve... Permission to spend hard currency has in the past been the preserve of the privileged few in the Soviet Union.*

5 N MASS **Preserves** are foods such as jam or chutney that are made by cooking them with sugar, salt or vinegar so that they can be stored for a long time.

preserved /prɪzɜːvd/
ADJ Something that is well **preserved** is in good condition or has not changed even though it is very old. *There are some excellently preserved fossilized tree stumps.*

pre-set, pre-sets, pre-setting. The form **pre-set** is used in the present tense and is also the past tense and past participle of the verb.
VO If you **pre-set** a piece of equipment, you set the controls in advance of the time when you want it to work. *She pre-set the video recorder before she went out.* ♦ **pre-set** ADJ ATTRIB *Bake in a pre-set oven for 45 minutes.*

preside /prɪzaɪd/ **presides, presiding, presided**
V A If you **preside** over a formal meeting or event, you are in charge or act as the chairperson; a formal word. *Their complaint concerns the behaviour of the judge who presided over the trial... The Cardinal presided at talks between the two sides...* ♦ **presiding** ADJ ATTRIB *The special prosecutor has asked the presiding judge to drop the charges.*

presidency /prɛzɪdənsi/
N SING The **presidency** is the position or function of being the president of a country. *He is to be nominated for the presidency.*

president /prɛzɪdənt/ **presidents**
1 N C or TITLE The **president** of a country which is a republic is the person with the highest political position or who is the head of state. *The French president arrived in the United States this week. ...the assassination of President Kennedy.*
2 NC The **president** of an organization is the person with the highest position in it. *Phillips' President, Geffen Gill, thinks consumers are ready for the product. ...the former President of the Royal Academy.*

president-elect, president-elects
NC The **president-elect** is the person who has been elected as the next president but who has not yet started work as president. *The leader of the coloured parliament in South Africa is to attend the inauguration of President-elect Bush.*

presidential /prɛzɪdɛnʃl/
ADJ ATTRIB **Presidential** activities or things relate or belong to a president. *...the next presidential election.*

presidium /prɪzɪdiəm/; also spelt **praesidium.**
N SING In Communist countries, a **presidium** is a committee which takes policy decisions on behalf of a larger group such as a parliament. *...the Presidium of the USSR's Supreme Soviet.*

press /prɛs/ **presses, pressing, pressed**
1 V O A If you **press** one thing against another, you push the first thing against the second. *Stroganov pressed his hand to his heart... The animal presses itself against a tree trunk.*
2 VO If you **press** a button or switch, you push it with your finger to make it work. *Mrs Carstairs pressed an electric bell.* ▶ Also NC *All this can be called up at the press of a button.*
3 V A or VO If you **press** on something or **press** it, you push it with your hand or foot. *She pressed down upon the velvet cloth. ...pressing the mattress with his fingers.*
4 VO If you **press** clothes, you remove any creases by ironing them. *He always pressed his trousers before wearing them.*
5 V+*for* If you **press** for something, you try hard to persuade someone to give it to you. *Britain has been pressing for a worldwide ban on chemical weapons for a long time... He's clashed with the Chancellor in pressing for higher taxation to curb inflation.*
6 VO If you **press** someone, you try hard to persuade them to do or say something. *He pressed me to have a cup of coffee with him.*
7 VO+*on or upon* If you **press** something on someone, you insist that they take it. *His aunt was pressing upon him cups of tea and cookies.*
8 VO If you **press** charges against someone, you make an official accusation which has to be settled in a court

of law. *A police spokesman said there was insufficient evidence to press charges.*
9 N COLL The **Press** refers to newspapers, or to the journalists who write them. *...an amusing story in the press... I got to know a lot of the American press.*
10 N SING If someone or something gets a good **press**, they are praised, especially in the newspapers, on television, or on radio. If someone or something gets a bad **press**, they are criticized, especially in the newspapers, on television, or on radio. *Hypnotherapy hasn't always enjoyed a good press over the years... The IMF is conscious of the bad press it has received.*
11 NC A printing **press** is a machine used for printing books, newspapers, and leaflets. *The building houses a printing press where many pro-independence newspapers are produced.*
12 See also **pressed, pressing.**
press ahead PHRASAL VERB If you **press ahead** with a task or activity, you begin or continue doing it in a determined way, knowing that it may take a lot of time and effort. *The government is determined to press ahead with the price rises.*
press on PHRASAL VERB If you **press on**, you continue doing something in spite of difficulties. *They courageously pressed on with their vital repair work.*

press box, press boxes
NC A **press box** is a room at a sports ground which is reserved for journalists to watch sporting events. *In the press box at Mile High Stadium, Frank Harroway keeps the official score for minor-league games.*

press conference, press conferences
NC A **press conference** is a meeting held by a famous or important person in which they answer questions asked by journalists. *He called a press conference to brief the media on developments in Iran.*

press corps
N COLL The **press corps** is a group of reporters who are all working in the same place; used in American English. *I had friends in the press corps... I attached myself to the White House press corps.*

press cutting, press cuttings
NC A **press cutting** is a report that you cut out of a newspaper and keep, usually because it refers to you or to someone you know or admire. *She took an old crumpled press cutting out of her bag.*

pressed /prɛst/
ADJ PRED If you are **pressed** for money or time, you do not have enough money or time. *When pressed for funds, they will find it hard to resist external seductions.*

press-gang /prɛsɡæŋ/ **press-gangs, press-ganging, press-ganged;** also spelt **press gang** when it is a noun.
1 N COLL A **press-gang** is a group of men who capture men and boys and force them to join the navy or army. *...the growing threat of press gangs forcibly drafting resistors.*
2 V O A If you **are press-ganged** into doing something, you are made to do it, even though you do not really want to. *A couple of months later, I found myself press-ganged into standing at the election.*

pressing /prɛsɪŋ/
ADJ Something that is **pressing** needs to be dealt with immediately. *...a pressing appointment with the doctor.*

pressman /prɛsmæn/ **pressmen**
NC A **pressman** is a reporter, especially a man, who works for a newspaper or magazine. *He passed on Mr Thompson's reply to waiting pressmen.*

press officer, press officers
NC A **press officer** is a person who is employed by an organization to give information about the organization to the press. *The park's chief press officer says Alton Towers is designed to offer something for everyone. ...a Ministry of Defence press officer.*

press release, press releases
NC A **press release** is a written statement about a matter of public interest which is given to the press by an organization that is directly concerned with the matter. *We considered issuing some sort of press release afterwards.*

press-up, press-ups

NC **Press-ups** are exercises to strengthen arm and chest muscles. They are done by lying with your face towards the floor and pushing with your hands to raise your body off the floor until your arms are straight. *In that three hours he must have done 600 press-ups.*

pressure /preʃə/ **pressures, pressuring, pressured**

1 NU **Pressure** is the force produced when you press hard on something. *He disliked the pressure of her hand... It bent when pressure was put upon it.*
2 NU+SUPP **Pressure** is also the force that a quantity of gas or liquid has on a surface that it touches. *I'll just check the tyre pressure.*
3 NU If someone puts **pressure** on you, they try to persuade you to do something. *For a long time he's been trying to put pressure on us to go... They were under pressure from feminists.*
4 VO If you **pressure** someone to do something, you try to persuade them forcefully to do it. *The children are not pressured to eat... Some young people are pressured into staying on at school.*
5 NU or N PL If you feel **pressure**, you feel that you have too much to do and not enough time to do it. *We do our best work under pressure. ...the pressures of public life.*
6 See also **blood pressure**.

pressure cooker, pressure cookers

NC A **pressure cooker** is a large saucepan with a lid that fits tightly, in which you can cook food quickly using steam at high pressure. *If you use a pressure cooker, you can make water get to a higher temperature than its normal boiling point.*

pressure group, pressure groups

NC A **pressure group** is an organization that campaigns to make a government or other authority take a particular course of action. *There followed six years of campaigning by pressure groups... The environment pressure group, Greenpeace, is urging shoppers to boycott a supermarket chain.*

pressurize /preʃəraɪz/ **pressurizes, pressurizing, pressurized**; also spelt **pressurise**.

VO+to-INF or VO+into If you **pressurize** someone to do something, you try hard to persuade or force them to do it. *It was a move designed to pressurise workers to return earlier... There are signs that Pakistan would be willing to pressurize the Mujaheddin into accepting a coalition government.*

pressurized /preʃəraɪzd/; also spelt **pressurised**.

ADJ In a **pressurized** container or area, the pressure inside is different from the pressure outside. *...the pressurized cabin of a Boeing 707.*

prestige /prestiːʒ/

NU If you have **prestige**, other people admire you because of your position or the quality of your work. *...a job with some prestige attached to it.*

prestigious /prestɪdʒəs/

ADJ Something that is **prestigious** is important and admired by people. *...one of the most prestigious universities in the country.*

pre-stressed concrete

NU **Pre-stressed concrete** is concrete that has steel wires inside it to strengthen it. *It is constructed from pre-stressed concrete... The pre-stressed concrete pressure vessel surrounds the whole of the primary circuit of the reactor.*

presumably /prɪzjuːməbli/

ADV SEN If you say that something is **presumably** the case, you mean that you think it is the case, although you are not certain. *Presumably they're a bit more expensive... The bomb was presumably intended to go off while the meeting was in progress.*

presume /prɪzjuːm/ **presumes, presuming, presumed**

1 V-REPORT If you **presume** that something is the case, you think that it is the case, but you are not certain. *If you do not come, I shall presume the deal is off... You are married, I presume?... It is presumed that only 10 to 15% of the drugs being smuggled are actually caught by Customs officers.*
2 VO+to-INF or VO C If something **is presumed** to be the case, people believe that it is the case, although they are not certain. *He is presumed to be living in Spain... Two of its foreign staff workers are missing,*

presumed kidnapped, in south Lebanon. ...Larry Burrows, missing and presumed dead since 1971.

presumption /prɪzʌmpʃn/ **presumptions**

NC A **presumption** is something that is believed to be true but has not been proved. *...the presumption that heaven exists. ...a continued presumption by the privileged that they are a cut above the rest.*

presumptive /prɪzʌmptɪv/

ADJ ATTRIB or ADJ after N **Presumptive** is used to describe things that are based on presumptions about what is probably true, rather than on certainty. *...a presumptive diagnosis of thrombosis.*

presumptuous /prɪzʌmptʃuəs/

ADJ If someone is **presumptuous**, they do things that they have no right to do. *It is dangerous and presumptuous to interfere between parents and children.*

presuppose /priːsəpəuz/ **presupposes, presupposing, presupposed**

VO or V-REPORT If one thing **presupposes** another, the first thing cannot be true or exist unless the second is true or exists; a formal word. *This deficit presupposes an increase in government revenue... Such a question presupposes that the reform was a coherent plan... The myth of the Ascension presupposes there is a Heaven.*

presupposition /priːsʌpəzɪʃn/ **presuppositions**

NC A **presupposition** is something that you assume to be true, especially something which you must assume is true in order to continue with what you are saying or thinking; a formal word. *People can be persuaded to believe things which contradict their former presuppositions.*

pretence /prɪtens/ **pretences**; spelt **pretense** in American English.

1 NC or NU A **pretence** is behaviour that is intended to deceive people and make them believe something that is not true. *She leapt up with a pretence of eagerness... The industry has abandoned any pretence of restraint.*
2 If you do something **under false pretences**, you do it when people do not know the truth about you and your intentions. *I felt that I was taking money under false pretences.*

pretend /prɪtend/ **pretends, pretending, pretended**

V-REPORT or V+to-INF If you **pretend** that something is the case, you try to make people believe that it is the case, although it is not. *Her father tried to pretend that nothing unusual had happened... He pretended to fall over.*

pretender /prɪtendə/ **pretenders**

NC A **pretender** is someone who claims the right to a particular position which they do not have, when their claim is disputed by other people. *...the pretender to the Yugoslav throne, King Peter's son Alexander. ...the 100 metres world champion Carl Lewis loses out to the young pretender Leroy Burrell.*

pretension /prɪtenʃn/ **pretensions**

N PL or NU Someone with **pretensions** pretends that they are better or more important than they really are. *He has pretensions to greatness... He is evidently a person of some social pretension.*

pretentious /prɪtenʃəs/

ADJ Someone or something that is **pretentious** tries to appear more important or significant than they really are. *In Wyoming, you're considered pretentious if you drive anything fancier than a Ford Bronco. ...one of the most pretentious films of all time.*

preternatural /priːtənætʃərəl/

ADJ **Preternatural** is used to describe something that is unusual or exceptional in a way that might make you believe that superhuman forces are involved; a formal word. *...his drive towards a preternatural clarity.* ◆ **preternaturally** SUBMOD *She was preternaturally calm.*

pretext /priːtekst/ **pretexts**

NC A **pretext** is a reason which you pretend has caused you to do something. *The Government invented a 'plot' as a pretext for arresting opposition leaders.*

Pretoria /prɪtɔːriə/

Pretoria is the administrative capital of South Africa

and its fourth largest city. It is the capital of the
Transvaal. Population: 823,000 (1985).

pretty /prɪti/ **prettier, prettiest**
1 ADJ **Pretty** means attractive or charming in a
delicate way. *Who's that pretty little girl?... The
wallpaper was very pretty, covered in roses.* ♦ **prettily**
ADV *She smiled prettily... The living room itself was
prettily decorated.* ♦ **prettiness** NU *...the fairy-tale
prettiness of the town.*
2 SUBMOD You can use **pretty** before an adjective or
adverb to mean 'quite' or 'rather'; an informal use. *I
thought it was pretty good... I'm pretty certain she
enjoys it.*
3 **Pretty much** or **pretty well** means almost; an
informal expression. *She hated pretty well all of
them... I felt pretty much the same.*

prevail /prɪveɪl/ **prevails, prevailing, prevailed**
1 VA If a custom or belief **prevails** at a particular
place or time, it is normal or generally accepted at
that place or time. *...the traditions that have
prevailed in Britain since the 17th century.*
♦ **prevailing** ADJ ATTRIB *The prevailing view shifted
still further.*
2 V If a proposal or a principle **prevails**, it gains
influence or is accepted after a period of argument. *In
the end, common sense prevailed... Political
arguments had prevailed over economic sense.*

prevalence /prevələns/
N SING The **prevalence** of something is the fact that it
is widespread and occurs commonly. *...the prevalence
of snobbery in Britain.*

prevalent /prevələnt/
ADJ If something such as a condition, belief, or action
is **prevalent**, it exists or occurs very commonly.
*Police manpower and resources are to be concentrated
where violent crimes are prevalent... He took the
opportunity to attack some of the prevalent myths
about the Labour party.*

prevaricate /prɪværɪkeɪt/ **prevaricates,
prevaricating, prevaricated**
V If you **prevaricate**, you avoid doing something that
you should do, or you avoid giving a direct answer or
a firm decision about something. *The doctors
prevaricated, arguing the need for additional tests.*

prevent /prɪvent/ **prevents, preventing, prevented**
1 VO+*from* or VO+ING If you **prevent** someone from doing
something, you do not allow them to start doing it.
*My only idea was to prevent him from speaking...
Their foreign minister says that the US is preventing
him from attending the UN General Assembly
meetings... The border has been sealed off to prevent
Rwandans re-entering Uganda.*
2 VO To **prevent** something from happening means to
ensure that it does not happen. *It was not enough to
prevent war... It was thought that only the ship was
preventing the bridge from falling into the river.
...calls for urgent action to prevent a famine in Sudan.*

preventative /prɪventətɪv/
ADJ ATTRIB **Preventative** means the same as
preventive.

prevention /prɪvenʃn/
N U **Prevention** is action that prevents something from
happening. *...the prevention of cruelty to animals.
...fire prevention.*

preventive /prɪventɪv/
ADJ ATTRIB **Preventive** actions are intended to stop
things such as disease or crime from happening.
*Preventive measures are essential. ...preventive
medicine.*

preverbal /priːvɜːbl/
ADJ ATTRIB The **preverbal** stage in a child's life is the
one before he or she can speak; a technical term in
psychology. *She sank at times into a preverbal baby
stammer.*

preview /priːvjuː/ **previews**
NC A **preview** of something such as a film or
exhibition is an opportunity to see it before it opens to
the general public. *Welcome to the press preview of
the Seyer Street exhibition.*

previous /priːviəs/
ADJ ATTRIB A **previous** event or thing is one that
occurred before the one you are talking about.

*...children from a previous marriage... They had
arrived the previous night.*

previously /priːviəsli/
1 ADV **Previously** means at some time before the
period that you are talking about. *He was previously
British consul in Atlanta.*
2 ADV You can use **previously** to say how much earlier
one event was than another. *They had retired ten
years previously.*

pre-war /priːwɔː/
ADJ ATTRIB **Pre-war** things existed before a war,
especially the Second World War. *...the pre-war
telephone network.*

prey /preɪ/ **preys, preying, preyed**
NU+POSS An animal's **prey** are the creatures that it
hunts and eats in order to live. *The mole seeks its
prey entirely underground.*

prey on PHRASAL VERB 1 If one animal **preys on**
another, it lives by catching and eating the second
animal. *The amphibians were hunters, preying on
worms and insects.* 2 If something **preys on** your
mind, you cannot stop worrying about it. *Barton
agreed, but the decision preyed on his mind.*

price /praɪs/ **prices, pricing, priced**
1 NCorNU The **price** of something is the amount of
money that you must pay to buy it. *The price of
firewood has risen steeply... Petrol will continue to
drop in price.*
2 N SING+SUPP The **price** that you pay for something is
an unpleasant thing you have to do in order to get it.
*This was the price that had to be paid for progress...
This is a small price to pay for freedom.*
3 VO If something **is priced** at a particular amount, it
costs that amount. *The least expensive will be priced
at £7,000. ...reasonably priced accommodation.*
4 See also **cut-price**.

Price, George /dʒɔːdʒ praɪs/
George Price became Prime Minister of Belize in 1989.
He was a founder member of the People's United
Party (PUP) in 1950 and became its leader in 1956. He
was Mayor of Belize City from 1956 to 1962. From 1954
to 1965 he was a member of the Legislative Assembly
and from 1965 to 1984 he was a member of the House
of Representatives. He served as First Minister from
1961 to 1963, and Premier from 1964 to 1981. He was
previously Prime Minister from 1981 to 1984. Born:
1919.

priceless /praɪsləs/
1 ADJ Something such as a work of art or a rare jewel
that is **priceless** is extremely valuable. *Art experts
are restoring the cartoon of the Virgin by Leonardo da
Vinci, one of the most priceless works of art in
existence. ...a beautiful priceless sapphire.*
2 ADJ You can also describe something such as a
characteristic or an asset as **priceless** when it is
extremely useful. *This priceless asset has enabled
him to win innumerable tournaments... Late in the
second half, Wim Keift gave Eindhoven that priceless
away goal.*

pricey /praɪsi/
ADJ If you say that something is **pricey**, you mean that
you think it is too expensive; an informal word. *The
book was a bit pricey.*

prick /prɪk/ **pricks, pricking, pricked**
1 VO If you **prick** something, you make a small hole in
it with a sharp object such as a pin. *Prick the apples
all over, using the prongs of a fork... He pricked
himself with the needle.*
2 VO If something sharp **pricks** you, it sticks into your
skin. *Sharp thorns pricked his knees.* ► Also NC *...the
sharp pricks as the pellets struck his hands.*

prick up PHRASAL VERB 1 If an animal **pricks up** its
ears, or if its ears **prick up**, its ears suddenly point
straight up because it has heard a noise. *Desert
Orchid loves crowds, always pricking up his ears when
he hears people cheering him on... He would prick his
ears and whine at the sound of my voice.* 2 If you
prick up your ears, or if your ears **prick up**, you
suddenly listen eagerly when you hear something
interesting or important. *He pricked up his ears at
the sound of his father's voice.*

prickle /prɪkl/ **prickles, prickling, prickled**
1 NC **Prickles** are small, sharp points that stick out from leaves or the stalks of plants. *The prickles and tough outer peel are removed and the stalks are then used in salads.*
2 V If your skin **prickles**, it feels as if a lot of small, sharp points are being stuck into it. *The shirt I was wearing made my skin prickle... My skin prickled with fear.* ► Also NC *I felt a prickle of pleasure.*

prickly /prɪkᵊli/
1 ADJ A **prickly** plant has a lot of sharp points sticking out from it. *...prickly thorn bushes.*
2 ADJ Someone who is **prickly** loses their temper very easily. *...a prickly and tiresome man.*

prickly heat
NU **Prickly heat** is a condition caused by very hot weather, in which your skin becomes hot and itchy and is covered with lots of tiny bumps. *Prickly heat usually starts round the neck.*

prickly pear, prickly pears. The plural form can be either **prickly pears** or **prickly pear.**
NC A **prickly pear** is a kind of cactus that has round fruit with prickles on; also used of the fruit itself, which you can eat. *The trail winds up and down through fields of dry grass and prickly pear cactus.*

pride /praɪd/ **prides, priding, prided**
1 NU **Pride** is a feeling of satisfaction which you have because you or people close to you have done something good or possess something good. *His mother looked at him with affection and pride... She pointed with pride to the fine horses she had trained.*
2 NU **Pride** is also a feeling of dignity and self-respect that you have about yourself. *My pride did not allow me to complain too often... Pride alone prevented her from giving up.*
3 NU You can also use refer to a feeling of being superior to other people as **pride**. *...a show of masculine pride.*
4 V-REFL+on If you **pride** yourself on a quality or skill, you are very proud of having it. *Mrs Hochstadt prided herself on her intelligence... They pride themselves on being impatient.*
● **Pride** is used in these phrases. ● If you **take pride** in something that you have or do, you feel pleased and happy because of it. *I take great pride in the success of my children.* ● If you **swallow** your **pride**, you decide that you must do something that you are rather ashamed of in order to get something that is very important to you. *He swallowed his pride and accepted the money.* ● If something in a group has **pride of place**, it is the most important thing there. *Musical compositions take pride of place in the festivities.*

priest /priːst/ **priests**
1 NC A **priest** is a member of the clergy in the Catholic or Orthodox church, and in some Protestant churches. *...an Anglican priest... In prayers, the parish priest commended the souls of the family to God.*
2 NC A **priest** is also a man in many non-Christian religions with particular duties and responsibilities in a place where people worship. *...a Buddhist priest.*

priestess /priːstes/ **priestesses**
NC A **priestess** is a woman in a non-Christian religion with particular duties and responsibilities in a place where people worship. *Her mother was a 'sangoma'—a Xhosa priestess and healer.*

priesthood /priːsthʊd/
1 N SING The **priesthood** is the position and office of being a priest. *...the responsibilities of the priesthood.*
2 N SING You can refer to all the members of the Christian clergy as the **priesthood**. *It was this strong sense of vocation and discipline that led John Wesley to enter the Church of England priesthood.*

priestly /priːstli/
ADJ ATTRIB **Priestly** refers to things belonging or relating to a priest. *...priestly duties.*

prig /prɪg/ **prigs**
NC If you refer to someone as a **prig**, you mean that they are irritating because they behave very correctly and disapprove of other people's behaviour; an old-fashioned word.

priggish /prɪgɪʃ/
ADJ If you describe someone as **priggish**, you mean that they are irritating because they behave in a very moral and disapproving way.

prim /prɪm/
ADJ Someone who is **prim** is easily shocked by anything that is rude or improper; used showing disapproval. *...a prim, severe woman.* ◆ **primly** ADV *His sister sat primly with her legs together.*

prima ballerina /priːmə bæləriːnə/ **prima ballerinas**
NC A **prima ballerina** is the most important female dancer in a ballet or a ballet company. *...the Bolshoi's prima ballerina.*

primacy /praɪməsi/
NU Something that has **primacy** in a particular situation is the most important or most powerful thing in that situation; a formal word. *America should give greater recognition to Indian primacy in South Asia. ...the primacy of the Third World in liberation theology.*

prima donna /priːmə dɒnə/ **prima donnas**
1 NC A **prima donna** is the main female singer in an opera. *Her great talent and virtuoso were confirmed when she produced an album called 'The Art of the Prima Donna'.*
2 NC If you describe someone as a **prima donna**, you mean that they are difficult to deal with because their moods change suddenly. *Bob was a prima donna who played heartily at office politics.*

primaeval /praɪmiːvl/. See **primeval.**

prima facie /praɪmə feɪʃi/
ADJ ATTRIB or ADV SEN **Prima facie** is used to describe something which seems to be true when you consider it for the first time; a formal expression. *There is indeed some prima facie evidence to support such a thesis... Six antique chairs would prima facie constitute a set. ...a prima facie case of murder.*

primal /praɪml/
ADJ ATTRIB **Primal** is used to describe something that relates to the causes or origins of things; a formal word. *...the primal cause of all life.*

primarily /praɪmᵊrəli, praɪmerəli/
ADV You use **primarily** to indicate the most important feature of something or the reason for something. *These linguists were concerned primarily with the structure of languages.*

primary /praɪməri/ **primaries**
1 ADJ The **primary** one of a group of things is the most important one or the thing that must be dealt with first. *One of Europe's primary requirements was minerals... She gets her primary satisfaction from her career... President Hrawi's primary task would be to incorporate all Lebanese leaders into the decision-making process.*
2 ADJ ATTRIB **Primary** education is for pupils between the ages of 5 and 11. *Up to 100 million children in the world have no access to primary education.*
3 NC In the United States, a **primary** is a vote in a particular state that is taken by the local members of a political party to elect a candidate for a political office. *If he wins the New York primary, will he be assured of the Democratic nomination?.. He was defeated in the Republican primary, and he has only a few more weeks to serve in Congress.*

primary colour, primary colours
NC The **primary colours** are red, yellow, and blue. They can be mixed together in different ways to make all other colours. *...a garish petrol logo, plastic and in bright, primary colours.*

primary school, primary schools
NC or NU A **primary school** is a school for young children who are between the ages of 5 and 11. *...plans to improve the standard of science teaching in primary schools... One third of Bangladeshi children never have the chance to attend primary school.*

primate, primates; pronounced /praɪmət/ for the meaning in paragraph 1 and /praɪmeɪt/ for the meaning in paragraph 2.
1 NC The **Primate** of a particular country or region is the archbishop of that country or region. *The report now goes to the Archbishop of Canterbury and later to all the Anglican Primates. ...the Roman Catholic*

Primate of Ireland, Cardinal Thomas O'Fiaich.
2 NC A **primate** is a member of the group of mammals which includes humans, monkeys, and apes. *The Madagascar government has agreed to protect its virgin forests—the natural habitat for many plants and primates.*

prime /praɪm/ **primes, priming, primed**
1 ADJ ATTRIB You use **prime** to describe something that is the most important in a situation. *What was said was of prime importance... Maths is no longer a prime requirement for a career in accountancy.*
2 ADJ ATTRIB **Prime** is also used to describe something that is of the best possible quality. *He wants his herd delivered in prime condition.*
3 ADJ ATTRIB A **prime** example of something is a typical example of it. *...a prime example of the power of the press.*
4 N SING+POSS Your **prime** is the stage in your life when you are most active or most successful. *I had been a good player in my prime.*
5 VO If you **prime** someone, you give them information about something before it happens, so that they are prepared for it. *I had primed him for this meeting.*

Prime Minister, Prime Ministers
N PROP or NC The leader of the government in some countries is called the **Prime Minister**. *...the Dutch Prime Minister, Mr Lubbers... Miss Bhutto may be the first woman prime minister of an Islamic state.*

prime mover, prime movers
NC Someone or something that is the **prime mover** in a plan, idea, or situation has an important influence in starting it. *They were prime movers in the enterprise... For the Europeans, profit was usually the prime mover.*

prime number, prime numbers
NC A **prime number** is a whole number greater than 1 that cannot be divided exactly by any whole number except itself and the number 1; a technical term in mathematics. *2, 3, 7, and 11 are prime numbers.*

primer /praɪmə/ **primers**
1 N MASS **Primer** is a type of paint that is put onto wood in order to prepare it for the main layer of paint. *Use primer before applying the main coat.*
2 NC A **primer** is a book containing basic facts about a subject, which is used by someone who is beginning to study that subject. *...Longman Green's basic English Primer... The IRRI published a simple guide to their major crop—'A Farmer's Primer on Growing Rice'.*

prime time
ADJ **Prime time** television or radio programmes are broadcast when the most viewers and listeners are watching television or listening to the radio. *Mayor Dinkins took his plea to the airwaves in a prime time TV and radio address to the city. ...prime time evening television.* ► Also NU *Audience share has plummeted to a point where even in prime time we are barely breaking 50 per cent of the audience.*

primeval /praɪmiːvl/; also spelt **primaeval.**
ADJ ATTRIB **Primeval** is used to describe things belonging or relating to a very early period in the history of the world. *...primeval forests. ...our primeval ancestors.*

primitive /prɪmətɪv/
1 ADJ In **primitive** societies, people live in a simple way, usually without industries or a writing system. *...primitive tribes.*
2 ADJ Something that is **primitive** is of an early type and is therefore not well developed. *...primitive insect-eating mammals. ...primitive microprocessors.*
3 ADJ If you describe something as **primitive**, you mean that it is very basic or old-fashioned. *The sleeping accommodation is somewhat primitive.*

primordial /praɪmɔːdiəl/
ADJ ATTRIB **Primordial** is used to describe things that have existed from a very early period of time or since the beginning of the world; a formal word. *...the primordial moment when everything began. ...a wild, haunting, primordial sound.*

primrose /prɪmrəʊz/ **primroses**
NC A **primrose** is a wild plant with pale yellow flowers.

primula /prɪmjʊlə/ **primulae** /prɪmjʊliː/ or **primulas**
NC A **primula** is a type of primrose with brightly coloured flowers. *...lilies, primulas and convolvulus in profusion.*

Primus /praɪməs/ **Primuses**
NC A **Primus** or a **Primus stove** is a small cooker that burns paraffin and is often used in camping; a trademark. *The kettle was steaming away on the Primus stove.*

prince /prɪns/ **princes**
N C or TITLE A **prince** is a male member of a royal family, especially the son of a king or queen. *...the Japanese tradition of imperial princes choosing their brides from the aristocracy. ...Prince Charles.*

princely /prɪnsli/
1 ADJ Something that is **princely** belongs to a prince or is suitable for a prince. *...the princely courts of Asia.*
2 ADJ ATTRIB A **princely** sum of money is a large sum of money. *We're managing to sell them at a princely £25 a time.*

Prince of Wales
N PROP The **Prince of Wales** is the eldest son of the British monarch. He is the person who will be the next king. *Edward VII lived here for years as Prince of Wales... A new museum has been opened in London by the Prince of Wales.*

princess /prɪnsɛs/ **princesses**
N C or TITLE A **princess** is a female member of a royal family, especially the daughter of a king or queen or the wife of a prince. *She was an invaluable source of advice for the two new princesses. ...Princess Mary.*

principal /prɪnsəpl/ **principals**
1 ADJ ATTRIB The **principal** person or thing is the main or most important one. *...the principal character in James Bernard Fagan's play.*
2 NC The **principal** of a school or college is the person in charge of it. *He has taught at a number of colleges, becoming Principal of Trinity College Bristol in 1982.*

principality /prɪnsəpæləti/ **principalities**
NC A **principality** is a country that is ruled by a prince. *...the principality of Liechtenstein.*

principally /prɪnsəpəˀli/
ADV **Principally** means more than anything else. *He dealt principally with Ethiopia. ...a protein which occurs principally in wheat.*

principle /prɪnsəpl/ **principles**
1 N C or NU A **principle** is a belief that you have about the way you should behave. *...a man of high principles... Our party remains a party of principle.*
2 NC+SUPP A **principle** is also a general rule or scientific law about how something happens or works. *...the principles of formal logic. ...the principle of acceleration.*
● **Principle** is used in these phrases. ● If you do something **on principle**, you do it because of a particular belief that you have. *I had to vote for him, of course, on principle.* ● If you agree with something **in principle**, you agree with the idea but may be unable or unwilling to support it in practice. *We are willing, in principle, to look afresh at the 1921 constitution.*

principled /prɪnsəpld/
ADJ **Principled** behaviour is based on the moral principles that guide the way people act. *...the principled stand we have taken on matters of contemporary concern.*

print /prɪnt/ **prints, printing, printed**
1 VO If someone **prints** a book, newspaper, or leaflet, they produce it in large quantities by a mechanical process. *I asked him for an estimate to print a weekly paper for me.* ◆ **printing** NU *...the invention of printing.*
2 VO If someone **prints** a speech or a piece of writing, they include it in a newspaper, magazine, or book. *The paper printed a story about Margaret Thatcher.*
3 NU The letters and numbers on a page of a book or newspaper are the **print**. *The print is rather poor.*
● See also **fine print.**
4 NC A **print** is one of the photographs from a film that has been developed. *...simple black and white prints.*

5 NC A **print** is also a picture that is copied from a painting by photography or made mechanically from specially prepared surfaces. *The art world is now flooded with fake Dali prints. ...restoring damaged prints and drawings.*
6 VO If you **print** a pattern on cloth, you reproduce it on the cloth using dye and special equipment. *...a pattern which is printed onto the fabric by hand.*
7 NC **Prints** are footprints or fingerprints. *His feet left prints in the soft soil.*
8 V or VO If you **print**, you write in letters that are not joined together. *As long as you print clearly, you don't have to type... There was an envelope on her desk with her name printed on it.*
● **Print** is used in these phrases. ● If something appears **in print**, it appears in a book or newspaper. *He admitted it in print... Although he has begun writing articles again, none have appeared in print.*
● If a book is **in print**, it is available from bookshops. If a book is **out of print**, it is no longer available. *The vast majority of her books are still in print... Most of his books are now out of print.*
print out PHRASAL VERB When information from a computer is **printed out**, it is reproduced on paper. *It's not necessary to print out the whole disc to find out what is on it.*
printable /ˈprɪntəbl/
ADJ If something that someone says is not **printable**, it is likely to offend people, and is therefore not suitable for printing in a newspaper or a magazine. *I doubt if my views on the Loch Ness monster were printable... They translated his notions into printable editorials.*
printer /ˈprɪntə/ **printers**
1 NC A **printer** is a person or firm that prints books, newspapers, or leaflets. *Three journalists and a printer were arrested, having tried to launch an anti-Ceausescu manifesto... I've come from Hanover with 13,000 copies of 'Der Spiegel', which I got from the printers.*
2 NC A **printer** is also a machine used for printing information from a computer. *The price for the high resolution printer is now below $600.*
printing press, **printing presses**
NC A **printing press** is a machine that is used for printing. *This six-colour printing press comes from Japan.*
printout /ˈprɪntaʊt/ **printouts**
NC or NU A **printout** is a piece of paper on which information from a computer has been printed. *Make twenty copies of the printout and hand them over to whoever seems to want them... A hard copy printout is available if required.*
prior /ˈpraɪə/; a formal word.
1 PREP If something happens **prior to** a particular time or event, it happens before that time or event. *It occurred in Dallas, just prior to President Kennedy's assassination.*
2 ADJ ATTRIB You use **prior** to describe something that has happened or been planned earlier. *No prior knowledge should be required... I have a prior engagement.*
3 ADJ ATTRIB A **prior** claim or duty is more important than other claims or duties. *He feels a prior obligation to his job as a journalist.*
prioritize /praɪˈɒrɪtaɪz/ **prioritizes, prioritizing, prioritized**; also spelt **prioritise**.
VO If you **prioritize** several tasks or if you **prioritize** one task out of several, you decide how important each task is, and then arrange them so that you do the most important one first and the least important one last. *The scientists are going to have to prioritize the experiments that they want to do first.*
priority /praɪˈɒrɪti/ **priorities**
1 NC+SUPP Something that is a **priority** must be done or dealt with as soon as possible. *Getting food was the main priority... Factories seemed to be China's highest priority.* ▶ Also ADJ ATTRIB *The waiting list contains a thousand priority cases.*
2 N PL Someone's **priorities** are the tasks or things they consider to be the most important. *We must find out the priorities of the public... He had his priorities right.*

3 NU If someone or something has **priority** over other things, they are considered to be more important than other things and are therefore dealt with first. *These children are given priority when day nursery places are allocated.*
priory /ˈpraɪəri/ **priories**
NC A **priory** is a place where a small group of monks live and work together. *...the ruins of the Cluniac Priory of Stansgate.*
prise /praɪz/ **prises, prising, prised**; also spelt **prize**.
VOA If you **prise** one thing away from another, you use force to remove it from the other thing. *He prised the lid off a tin of paint.*
prism /ˈprɪzəm/ **prisms**
NC A **prism** is an object made of clear glass with many straight sides and angles. When light passes through it, the light waves separate and form a rainbow.
prison /ˈprɪzn/ **prisons**
NC or NU A **prison** is a building where criminals are kept. *I had never before been inside a prison... He was sent to prison for two years.*
prison camp, **prison camps**
NC A **prison camp** is a guarded camp where prisoners of war or political prisoners are kept. *...soldiers who have recently been released from prison camps.*
prisoner /ˈprɪzənə/ **prisoners**
NC A **prisoner** is a person who is kept in a prison as a punishment or because they have been captured by an enemy. *The prisoner had been sentenced to death for the murder of a woman... Bobby Sands became the first IRA prisoner to die on hunger strike.*
prisoner of war, **prisoners of war**
NC A **prisoner of war** is a soldier who is captured by the enemy during a war and is kept as a prisoner until the end of the war. *Under the terms of the Geneva Convention, he had to be treated as a prisoner of war.*
prissy /ˈprɪsi/
ADJ If you describe someone as **prissy**, you think that they always behave very correctly in a fussy way and are easily shocked by anything rude or improper; an informal word. *She had a prissy way of talking.*
pristine /ˈprɪstiːn, ˈprɪstaɪn/
ADJ Something that is **pristine** is new or as good as new because it is in an extremely clean condition; a formal word. *He wiped his fingers on his pristine handkerchief.*
privacy /ˈprɪvəsi, ˈpraɪvəsi/
NU **Privacy** is the state of being alone, so that you can do things without being seen or disturbed. *...the privacy of your own home... Take it home and read it in privacy.*
private /ˈpraɪvət/ **privates**
1 ADJ If something is **private**, it is for the use of one person or group only, rather than for the general public. *All rooms have got private bath and WC. ...private property.*
2 ADJ ATTRIB **Private** discussions take place between a small group of people and are kept secret from others. *...a private interview.* ◆ **privately** ADV *The notion was discussed privately between the two men at lunch.*
3 If you do something **in private**, you do it on your own or with only a few other people being present, usually because you want to keep it secret. *Because these preliminary hearings are held in private, no details are being disclosed... Greetings took place in private, away from the media spotlight.*
4 If you say something **in private**, you say it to one person or small group rather than to the general public. *He has still made no official request, but has been talking in private to other leaders about the extreme need for aid... So far he has remained loyal in public but in private he's scathing about her arguments.*
5 ADJ ATTRIB **Private** activities and belongings are connected with your personal life rather than with your work or business. *Officials insist that the private quarrel between them is not related to the diplomatic feud between the two countries. ...private cars causing traffic jams that nearly brought Vienna to a standstill.*
6 ADJ ATTRIB Your **private** thoughts are personal and

you do not discuss them with other people. *He was engaged in a private quest of his own.* ◆ **privately**
ADV *Privately Ben felt close to despair.*
7 ADJ A **private** place is quiet and secluded from other people. *...a private place of meditation.*
8 ADJ A **private** person is very quiet and does not share their thoughts and feelings with other people. *Away from the glare of publicity he becomes an intensely private man.*
9 ADJ ATTRIB **Private** is used to describe services or industries that are owned by an individual person or group, rather than being controlled by the state. *...private education. ...private health insurance.*
◆ **privately** ADV *...privately owned firms.*
10 NCorTITLE A **private** is a soldier of the lowest rank. *They talked to the generals as well as the privates about the makeup of the military force... Four hundred people packed the church for the funeral of Private Jason Winter.*

private detective, private detectives
NC A **private detective** is a detective who works alone rather than in the police force and who you can hire to carry out investigations for you. *He hired a private detective to go out and make enquiries.*

private enterprise
NU **Private enterprise** is industry and business which is owned by an individual person or group and is not supported financially by the government. *...rich societies organized along private enterprise lines.*

private eye, private eyes
NC A **private eye** is the same as a **private detective**; used in informal American English. *...Edmond Pankel, a former IRS investigator and Houston private eye specializing in white collar crime.*

private member's bill, private member's bills or **private members' bills**
NC A **private member's bill** is a law that is proposed by a member of parliament acting as an individual rather than as a member of his or her political party. *...her successful private member's bill... He was one of six to sponsor Sydney Silverman's Private Member's Bill.*

private parts
N PL If you talk about someone's **private parts**, you are referring to the outer sex organs on their body in a polite way. *Even the women's private parts were inspected.*

private school, private schools
NC A **private school** is a school which is not supported financially by the government and which parents have to pay for their children to go to. *John Major did not go to an expensive private school, as most of the other Conservative cabinet ministers did. ...fees for the children who are at private school.*

private sector
N SING The **private sector** is the part of a country's economy which is not controlled or supported financially by the government. *In the private sector, urban salaried workers have been able to obtain higher incomes.*

privation /praɪveɪʃn/ **privations**
NUorNC If you suffer **privation**, you are deprived of the basic things you need to live a normal life; a formal word. *Life was riddled with privation. ...the privations of frontier life.*

privatize /praɪvətaɪz/ **privatizes, privatizing, privatized**; also spelt **privatise.**
VO If an organization that is owned by the state is **privatized**, the government sells it by offering shares in it to private individuals or groups. *The nuclear industry was to be privatized.* ◆ **privatization**
/praɪvətaɪzeɪʃn/ NU *...the privatisation of the telephone service.*

privet /prɪvɪt/
NU **Privet** is a type of bush with small leaves that stay green all year round. It is often grown in gardens to form hedges. *...houses separated by privet hedges.*

privilege /prɪvəlɪdʒ/ **privileges**
NCorNU A **privilege** is a special right or advantage that puts one person or group in a better position than other people. *The children would resent any special privileges given to the staff. ...the power and privilege*

which they had once enjoyed. *...the Cambridge atmosphere of privilege and intellectualism.*

privileged /prɪvəlɪdʒd/
ADJ Someone who is **privileged** has an advantage or opportunity that most other people do not have. *It was expensive and available only to the privileged few.*

privy /prɪvi/
ADJ PRED+to If you are **privy** to something secret, you know about it; a formal word. *Very few of them were privy to the details of the conspiracy.*

Privy Council /prɪvi kaunsl/
N COLL The **Privy Council** is a group of people who are appointed to advise the king or queen on political affairs. *The President of the Privy Council, together with a number of supporting officials, were summoned to a meeting at the palace.*

prize /praɪz/ **prizes, prizing, prized**
1 NC A **prize** is something of value, such as money or a trophy, that is given to the winner of a game, competition, or contest. *I entered two competitions and won prizes. ...Nobel Prize winners.*
2 ADJ ATTRIB You use **prize** to describe things that are of a very high quality. *...prize carnations.*
3 VO Something that is **prized** is wanted and admired because it is of good quality. *These fish are highly prized for their excellent flavour.*
4 See also **prise.**

prize-fighter, prize-fighters
NC A **prize-fighter** is a boxer who fights to win money. *Prize-fighters present themselves as being in the peak of condition and fitness. ...a punch-drunk prize-fighter.*

prize-giving, prize-givings
NCorNU A **prize-giving** is a ceremony where people are given prizes, for example because they have won a competition or done good work. *Steve McCormack was at the prize-giving. ...a school prize-giving. ...a prize-giving ceremony at an athletics meeting.*

pro /prəʊ/ **pros**
1 NC A **pro** is someone who does something to earn money rather than as a hobby; an informal use. *He's a pro and I'm only an amateur.*
2 The **pros and cons** of something are its advantages and disadvantages. *The World Service Science Unit explores some of the pros and cons of incinerating toxic waste in this way.*

pro- /prəʊ-/
PREFIX **Pro-** is used to form adjectives that describe people or organizations as supporting something such as a country, a group of people, or an activity. *...the pro-Iranian group, Islamic Jihad. ...pro-government newspapers. ...the pro-nuclear lobby.*

pro-active
ADJ Policies and actions that are **pro-active** are intended to cause things to happen rather than waiting to react to outside events. *Holliman says the idea of a pro-active national organization is still young in Japan... There has been a very passive approach to marketing; we must be more pro-active in this area.*

probability /prɒbəbɪləti/ **probabilities**
1 NCorNU The **probability** of something happening is how likely it is to happen, sometimes expressed as a fraction or a percentage. *Many people prefer mathematical probabilities to inspired guesses. ...a triumph of determination against all probability... The probability of the former is four-fifths times five-sixths times one-seventh.*
2 NCorNU The **probability** that something will happen is the fact that it is very likely to happen. *The real source of his gloom was the probability that Kathy would not come... The probability is that they will find themselves in debt.*

probable /prɒbəbl/
ADJ Something that is **probable** is very likely to be true or likely to happen. *It seems very probable that they are descended from a single ancestor... The Belgians face a probable general election this autumn.*

probably /prɒbəbli/
ADV SEN If something is **probably** the case, it is very likely to be the case. *He probably kept your examination papers... The owner is probably a salesman.*

probation /prəbeɪʃn/
1 During a criminal's period of **probation**, they are not sent to prison but instead have to report regularly to the official in charge of their case. *In addition to his term in prison, he will have to serve fifteen years of probation... I gave him probation for 12 months.* ● If someone is **on probation**, they are serving part of their prison sentence under the supervision of an official rather than staying at a prison. *I wondered whether Daniel would be let off on probation.*
2 NU **Probation** is a period of time during which someone's work is assessed before they are given a permanent job. *Probation is more or less a formality.*

probationary /prəbeɪʃənⁿri/
1 ADJ ATTRIB **Probationary** is used to describe someone who has finished their training in a particular job or profession, but who is still being assessed to see if they will be allowed to continue. *...the probationary teachers in our school.*
2 ADJ ATTRIB **Probationary** is also used to describe the time during which someone is assessed at the beginning of their career before they are allowed to continue. *You can become a qualified teacher and then do a probationary year. ...a six-month probationary period.*

probationer /prəbeɪʃənⁿə/ **probationers**
1 NC A **probationer** is someone such as a nurse or a police officer who is still being trained.
2 NC A **probationer** is also someone who has committed a crime and who is on probation rather than in prison.

probation officer, probation officers
NC A **probation officer** is a person whose job is to supervise and help people who have committed crimes but who are not serving a prison sentence for them. *Probation officers are expressing concern that many women with children are being jailed for minor and non-violent offences.*

probe /prəʊb/ **probes, probing, probed**
1 V or VO If you **probe**, you try to find out about something, for example by asking a lot of questions. *She had learnt not to probe too far. ...attempting to probe the mysteries of the universe... Indian newspapers probed into the details of the Bofors deal.*
2 NC A **probe** is the process of trying to find out about something, for example by asking a lot of questions. *Opposition leaders have demanded a judicial probe into atrocities on citizens after last Thursday's incident. ...a probe into suspected drug dealing in Florida.*
3 NC A **probe** is a long thin metal instrument that is used by someone such as a doctor or a scientist to examine someone or something. *The microscope has a probe, a very fine tungsten needle... This movement of electricity gives off new signals which the probe detects.*
4 NC A **probe** is also the same as a **space probe**. *After the space shuttle 3 lifts Ulysses into orbit, three rockets will fire to propel the probe towards Jupiter.*

probity /prəʊbəti/
NU **Probity** is a high standard of correct moral behaviour; a formal word. *The situation has not been handled with your customary thoroughness and probity.*

problem /prɒbləm/ **problems**
1 NC A **problem** is an unsatisfactory situation that causes difficulties for people. *They have financial problems. ...to help solve the problem of racism... It is often a problem drying freshly-washed clothes, especially in winter.*
2 NC A **problem** is also a puzzle that requires logical thought or a mathematical process to solve it. *Lucinda had been unable to do simple mathematical problems.*

problematic /prɒbləmætɪk/
ADJ Something that is **problematic** involves problems and difficulties; a formal word. *...the problematic nature of the relationship... This piece seems far less problematic than Mahler's later symphonies.*

problematical /prɒbləmætɪkl/
ADJ **Problematical** means the same as **problematic**; a formal word.

problem-solving
NU **Problem-solving** is the activity of finding solutions to problems, especially in your job or work. *Energetic diplomacy has become one of the hallmarks of Mr Gorbachov's approach to problem-solving... You've got to spend money on training if you want people to have problem-solving skills.*

proboscis /prəbɒsɪs/ **proboscises**; a technical term in biology.
1 NC A **proboscis** is a long flexible tube that some kinds of insects have, and use to pierce the skin of other animals or to suck food. *The parasite is carried in the mosquito's gut, until it is discharged through the proboscis into the bloodstream.*
2 NC A **proboscis** is also an elephant's trunk.

procedural /prəsiːdʒəⁿrəl/
ADJ **Procedural** means involving a formal procedure; a formal word. *The meeting was bogged down in procedural problems... Mr Shamir's objections are essentially procedural.*

procedure /prəsiːdʒə/ **procedures**
NCorNU A **procedure** is a way of doing something, especially the accepted or correct way. *...the proper procedure to be followed in decision-making... This was not standard procedure.*

proceed, **proceeds**, **proceeding**, **proceeded**; pronounced /prəsiːd/ when it is a verb and /prəʊsiːdz/ when it is a noun.
1 V+to-INF If you **proceed** to do something, you do it after doing something else. *He proceeded to explain... He horrified the guards by going up to one of his own canvases and calmly proceeding to paint on it.*
2 V If you **proceed** with a course of action, you continue with it; a formal use. *It is necessary to examine this claim before we proceed any further... There are strong reasons for proceeding with caution.*
3 V If an activity, process, or event **proceeds**, it continues as planned; a formal use. *Preparations were proceeding on schedule... The council have now reopened the account and payment is proceeding normally.*
4 VA If you **proceed** in a particular direction, you go in that direction; a formal use. *...as we were proceeding along Chiswick High Street.*
5 NPL The **proceeds** of an event or activity are the money that has been obtained from it. *The proceeds will be given away to a deserving charity.*

proceeding /prəsiːdɪŋ/ **proceedings**; a formal word.
1 NPL You can refer to an organized series of events that happen in a place as the **proceedings**. *Millions of people watched the proceedings on television.*
2 NC Legal **proceedings** are legal actions that are taken against a person. *At a separate court proceeding, an injunction prevented him from using his machine... I shall institute proceedings against you for unfair dismissal.*

process /prəʊses/ **processes, processing, processed**
1 NC A **process** is a series of actions or events which have a particular result. *It has been a long process getting this information. ...industrial processes.*
2 VO When raw materials or foods **are processed**, they are changed in a chemical or industrial process in order to make them suitable for a particular purpose. *What matters with caviar is the care and skill with which it has been processed... Everything from battery fluid to tyres will be processed and re-used... The guide includes lightly processed food, such as dairy products and bacon.* ◆ **processing** NU *...the processing and storing of radioactive materials. ...proposals for the construction of a sugar processing plant.*
3 VO To **process** information means to deal with it. *Ten computers are processing the data... Your application will take a few weeks to process.* ● See also **word processing**.
● **Process** is used in these phrases. ● If you are **in the process of** doing something, you are doing it. *She is still in the painful process of growing up.* ● If you are doing something and you do something else **in the process**, you do the second thing as a result of doing the first thing. *I got him out, but overbalanced in the process and fell... The Cunard line had dominated*

transatlantic sea-crossings, and in the process had carved out a place for themselves in marine history.

procession /prəseʃn/ **processions**
NC A **procession** is a group of people who are walking, riding, or driving in a line as part of a public event. *Lady Branwell led the procession through the village.*

processional /prəseʃənəl/
ADJ ATTRIB **Processional** means used for or taking part in a ceremonial procession. *Thousands of people lined the processional route.*

proclaim /prəkleɪm/ **proclaims, proclaiming, proclaimed**
VO, V-QUOTE or V-REPORT To **proclaim** something means to announce it; a formal word. *The Government proclaimed a state of emergency... The demonstrators held signs written in English, French, and German proclaiming 'Death to America'... Governor Wilkinson proclaimed that Kentucky's education reform would make history.*

proclamation /prɒkləmeɪʃn/ **proclamations**
NC A **proclamation** is a public announcement about something important. *The king issued a proclamation outlawing the rebels... The Council have annulled the proclamation of sovereignty by Abkhazia.*

proclivity /prəklɪvəti/ **proclivities**
NC+SUPP or NU+SUPP A **proclivity** for a particular kind of behaviour is a tendency to behave in that way; a formal word. *He then goes on, for 90-odd pages, to analyze our sexual proclivities... She interviewed hundreds of men and women about their proclivity for suppressing or expressing anger.*

procrastinate /prəʊkræstɪneɪt/ **procrastinates, procrastinating, procrastinated**
V If you **procrastinate**, you are very slow to do something, because you keep leaving it until later; a formal word. *...if you can honestly admit that you are procrastinating about doing something unpleasant.*
♦ **procrastination** /prəʊkræstɪneɪʃn/ NU *There was now little cause for procrastination.*

procreate /prəʊkrieɪt/ **procreates, procreating, procreated**
V When animals or people **procreate**, they produce young animals or babies; a formal word. *Although transsexuals cannot procreate, they can often consummate sex.*

procreation /prəʊkrieɪʃn/
NU **Procreation** is the producing of babies or young; a formal word. *The most basic human instinct, after survival, is the procreation and nurturing of children.*

procurator /prɒkjʊreɪtə/ **procurators**
NC In some countries, and also in the Roman Catholic Church or the ancient Roman Empire, a **procurator** is an administrative official with legal powers. *A military procurator told viewers that he had gone willingly into the army.*

procurator fiscal, procurators fiscal
NC In Scotland, the **procurator fiscal** is a legal officer who performs the functions of a public prosecutor. *A report was being sent to the procurator fiscal.*

procure /prəkjʊə/ **procures, procuring, procured**
VO If you **procure** something, especially something that is difficult to get, you obtain it; a formal word. *It would be necessary to procure more grain.*

procurement /prəkjʊəmənt/
NU **Procurement** is the act of buying or obtaining something, especially supplies for a large organization such as the army; a formal word. *The Council will handle arms control weapon procurement, and other questions of military cooperation... They have long been angered by low procurement prices.*

prod /prɒd/ **prods, prodding, prodded**
1 VO If you **prod** someone or something, you give them a quick push with your finger or with a pointed object. *She prodded a bean with her fork... Woodlice curl up into a ball if you prod them.* ▶ Also NC *Mrs Travers gave her a prod.*
2 VOA If you **prod** someone into doing something, you remind them or urge them to do it. *...companies who prod the ministry into action every now and again... They are trying to prod the Bush administration into doing more for the Kurds.*
3 NC A **prod** or a cattle prod is a long, pointed, metal

stick which can be used to poke people or animals as a way of making them move along. *The prods, which administer a painful electric shock, are widely used by the security services for riot control... Police, armed with truncheons and cattle prods, went into the crowd.*

prodigal /prɒdɪgl/
ADJ ATTRIB Someone who behaves in a **prodigal** way spends a lot of money carelessly or is wasteful, and does not think about what will happen when they have nothing left; a literary word. *...prodigal expenses on clothes... The prodigal son returned home to put his trial behind him and seek forgiveness from his people.*
▶ Also N SING *Alice had dreamed sentimentally that the prodigal would return.*

prodigious /prədɪdʒəs/
ADJ Something that is **prodigious** is so large in size or amount that it amazes people; a formal word. *...prodigious amounts of food... What emerged from the gimmickry was a man of prodigious talent and enormous arrogance.*

prodigy /prɒdədʒi/ **prodigies**
1 NC A **prodigy** is a person with an unusually great natural ability for something such as music or mathematics, which shows itself at an early age. *Musical prodigies are unfathomable and irrational... I was something of a child prodigy, in a small-time way.*
2 NC A **prodigy** is also something amazing and wonderful; a literary use. *His vacation was a reward for the prodigies he had already achieved.*

produce, produces, producing, produced;
pronounced /prədjuːs/ when it is a verb and /prɒdjuːs/ when it is a noun.
1 VO To **produce** something means to make it, create it, or cause it. *...factories producing electrical goods... Parents are responsible for the offspring they produce... This drug has produced terrible effects on children.*
2 VO If you **produce** evidence or an argument, you show it or explain it to people. *The US may have been involved, although so far no evidence has been produced... He also produced a photograph of a man, said to be a monk, setting fire to a car.*
3 VO If you **produce** an object from somewhere, you bring it out so that it can be seen. *Poirot produced the letter from his pocket... He proposed, and immediately produced a diamond ring.*
4 VO If someone **produces** a play, film, programme, or record, they organize it and decide how it should be done. *The film was directed, written and produced by Mel Brooks... The programme is by Christopher Martin, who produced the controversial 'Vision of Britain' documentary.*
5 NU **Produce** is food or other things grown in large quantities to be sold. *They go to market to buy supplies and sell their produce.*

producer /prədjuːsə/ **producers**
1 NC A **producer** is a person whose job is organizing plays, films, programmes, or records. *Her husband was a friend of Australian theatre producer Liz Bliss.*
2 NC+SUPP A **producer** of a food or material is a company or country that grows or provides a large amount of it. *...producers of consumer goods... The Soviet Union is the world's leading crude oil producer.*

product /prɒdʌkt/ **products**
1 NC A **product** is something that a company makes and sells, often in large quantities. *The research has not yet led to a commercial product. ...the use of animals in testing cosmetics and other products.*
2 NC+SUPP Something or someone that is a **product** of a particular situation or process has been caused by that situation or process. *The uniformity of the dancers was the product of hours of training... She is a product of the 1970s.*

production /prədʌkʃn/ **productions**
1 NU **Production** is the process of manufacturing or growing something in large quantities. *...more efficient methods of production... The two countries have agreed to cooperate on car production.*
2 NU You can also use **production** to refer to the amount of goods that is manufactured or grown by a company or country. *Industrial production has fallen by 20% over two years... The South African platinum*

mines account for one third of global production.
...EEC production quotas.
3 NU+SUPP The **production** of something is its
creation. *...the production of electricity... The illegal*
production of alcoholic drink has exceeded state
production.
4 NC A **production** is a particular performed version of
a play, opera, or other show. *The new production has*
a strong cast, led by the tenor Philip Langridge. ...The
Royal Shakespeare Company's production of 'Titus
Andronicus'.

production line, production lines
NC A **production line** is a system in a factory in which
individual machines make one part of the product
before passing it on to the next machine. *...cars*
coming off the production line.

productive /prədʌktɪv/
1 ADJ Something or someone that is **productive**
produces a lot of goods or does a lot of work.
...industrial policies designed to make companies more
productive... He's in a very clear and productive
period in his writing... Part-time workers have less job
commitment and are less likely to be productive or
efficient.
2 ADJ If a meeting or a relationship is **productive**,
good or useful things happen as a result of it. *Their*
relationship was a long, warm, and productive one...
James Baker said he'd had productive and useful talks
with King Hussein.

productivity /prɒdəktɪvəti/
NU **Productivity** is the rate at which goods are
produced, or the amount of goods produced by each
worker. *...increases in agricultural productivity...*
Union rules on safety can reduce stress, but doesn't
that slow down productivity?

Prof. /prɒf/
Prof. is a written abbreviation for 'Professor'. *...Prof.*
Brewer.

profane /prəfeɪn/
1 ADJ **Profane** means showing disrespect for religion
or religious things. *It said illustrating the Koran with*
profane pictures constituted sacrilege and heresy... His
language was often extremely coarse and profane, but
he could also charm and flatter. ◆ **profanity** /prəfænəti/
NU *...shocking acts of profanity.*
2 ADJ You can also use **profane** to refer to everyday
life rather than spiritual or religious things. *Cardinal*
Daly has said that churches should not be used for
profane or secular purposes.

profess /prəfes/ **professes, professing, professed**
V+to-INF or VO If you **profess** to do or have something,
you claim that you do it or have it; a formal word.
Nell didn't like her, or professed not to... Many have
professed disgust at the use of such weapons.
◆ **professed** ADJ ATTRIB *...the assassination of*
McKinley by a professed anarchist. ...a professed love
of everything about that country.

profession /prəfeʃn/ **professions**
1 NC A **profession** is a type of job that requires
advanced education or training. *She decided on law or*
journalism as her profession.
2 N COLL You use **profession** to refer to all the people
who have the same profession. *The medical profession*
are doing a difficult job.

professional /prəfeʃənəl/ **professionals**
1 ADJ ATTRIB **Professional** means relating to the work
of someone who is qualified for a particular job,
especially work that requires special training. *The*
professional association representing accountants has
also demanded extra money... Try to reduce the
baby's temperature, then seek professional help.
◆ **professionally** ADV *They are all professionally*
qualified.
2 ADJ ATTRIB You use **professional** to describe people
who do a particular thing to earn money rather than
as a hobby. *...a professional athlete... At present,*
there are not many professional cat breeders in Iran...
He said it was the work of highly professional killers.
◆ **professionally** ADV *...someone who's never acted*
professionally.
3 ADJ ATTRIB **Professional** is also used to refer to the
games or activities that are played by sportsmen and

women as a way of earning a living rather than as a
hobby. *Huge crowds were going to watch professional*
football of a highly accomplished level... After the
success of the first professional tennis tournament at
the weekend, the Soviet Union is poised to bring golf to
its citizens.
4 ADJ ATTRIB **Professional** people have jobs that
require advanced education or training. *The flat is*
ideal for the professional single person.
5 ADJ If something that someone does is **professional**,
it is done well, and is of a very high standard. *He had*
typed the whole scheme out in a very professional
manner.
6 NC A **professional** is someone who does something to
earn money rather than as a hobby. *He has 17*
championship victories as a professional plus two
amateur titles... Harvey Smith is the first Olympic
showjumper to be granted a change of status from
professional to competitor.
7 NC A **professional** is also someone who has a job
that requires special training and has a fairly high
status. *...nurses, doctors, social workers, and other*
professionals.

professionalism /prəfeʃⁿəlɪzəm/
NU **Professionalism** is skill at doing a job. *The paper*
was produced with incredible professionalism.

professor /prəfesə/ **professors**
1 NCor TITLE A **professor** in a British university is the
most senior teacher in a department. *...the Professor*
of English at Strathclyde University. ...Professor Cole.
2 NC A **professor** in an American or Canadian
university or college is a teacher there. *From*
obscurity as a law professor, he surged to prominence
as a leading reformer.

professorial /prɒfəsɔːriəl/; a formal word.
1 ADJ **Professorial** means looking or behaving like a
person who has great authority. *They were*
professorial with me, telling me God was
incomprehensible.
2 ADJ **Professorial** means relating to the work of a
professor. *She will be there in her professorial*
capacity.

professorship /prəfesəʃɪp/ **professorships**
NC A **professorship** is the post of professor in a
university. *He was offered the professorship, but*
turned it down.

proffer /prɒfə/ **proffers, proffering, proffered**
VO If you **proffer** something to someone, you offer it to
them; a formal word. *He put down his luggage and*
proffered his passport... She had already proffered her
resignation.

proficiency /prəfɪʃnsi/
NU **Proficiency** is the ability to do something well.
They were segregated according to their proficiency in
standard English... Over the years, he acquired
proficiency and command over the Tamil language.
...a test of the proficiency of our military units.

proficient /prəfɪʃnt/
ADJ If you are **proficient** in something, you can do it
well. *They were all proficient in needlework. ...a*
proficient swimmer.

profile /prəʊfaɪl/ **profiles, profiling, profiled**
1 NC Your **profile** is the outline of your face seen from
the side. *She glanced at his haughty profile.*
2 NC+SUPP A **profile** of someone is a short article or
programme describing their life and character. *She*
wanted to write profiles of the founders of the Party.
3 VO If someone such as a reporter **profiles** someone,
they write an account of that person's life and work.
Writer Mark Cohen profiled Weinberg for a Baltimore
magazine... Joe Homeless is the pen name of a writer
we profiled on this show last fall.
4 If you keep a **low profile**, you deliberately avoid
people because you do not want to attract attention to
yourself. *The police maintained a low profile and the*
demonstrators dispersed peacefully... It is likely he
will try and keep as low a profile as possible.

profit /prɒfɪt/ **profits, profiting, profited**
1 NCor NU A **profit** is an amount of money that you
gain when you are paid more for something than it
cost you. *The cassette can be copied countless times*
and sold for a massive profit... British Telecom are

heading for substantial profits, and could afford to keep prices low... She sells it on many occasions with a very small margin of profit.
2 V+from or by If you **profit** from something, you benefit or gain from it; a formal use. There is some evidence that he and his wife profited by the organisation's operations... Seven officials are accused of profiting from the refugee programme... Politicians should not profit from manipulating the release of hostages to suit their campaign schedules.

profitable /prɒfɪtəbl/
1 ADJ A **profitable** organization or practice makes a profit. The farm is a highly profitable business... It was more profitable to export the crops. ♦ **profitably** ADV Can the motor vehicle industry operate profitably? ♦ **profitability** /prɒfɪtəbɪləti/ NU ...a decline in the profitability of public transport.
2 ADJ Something that is **profitable** results in some benefit for you. He certainly made profitable use of the lessons he had learnt. ♦ **profitably** ADV There was little I could profitably do sitting at my desk.

profiteer /prɒfɪtɪə/ **profiteers**
NC A **profiteer** is a person who makes large profits by charging high prices for goods that are hard to get; used showing disapproval. The Government has blamed profiteers among the bazaar merchants.

profiteering /prɒfɪtɪərɪŋ/
NU **Profiteering** is the activity of making large profits by charging high prices for goods that are hard to get; used showing disapproval. He appeared in court on charges of drug profiteering. ...stiffer penalties for profiteering.

profit-making
NU **Profit-making** is the activity or fact of making a profit. Businesses were scientific about profit-making... Laws introduced by Mr Gorbachov will allow profit-making. ▶ Also ADJ ...a profit-making industry.

profit margin, profit margins
NC A **profit margin** is the difference between the selling price of a product and the cost of producing and marketing it. There were so many buyer incentives that the profit margin per car was virtually eliminated.

profit-sharing
NU **Profit-sharing** is a system by which all the people who work in a company have a share in its profits. He spoke of the need to allow workers to participate in ownership, and to introduce profit-sharing.

profit-taking
NU **Profit-taking** is the selling of stocks and shares at a profit after their value has risen or just before their value falls. Analysts say there was some profit-taking, but most traders were waiting for the results of today's meeting.

profligacy /prɒflɪgəsi/
NU **Profligacy** is extravagance and being wasteful; a formal word. The US government often criticised the United Nations for profligacy and what it saw as political irresponsibility.

profligate /prɒflɪgət/
ADJ **Profligate** means extravagant and wasteful; a formal word. ...our profligate use of resources... The word 'liberal' came to symbolise a soft line on law and order and profligate government spending.

profound /prəfaʊnd/
1 ADJ You use **profound** to emphasize how great or how intense something is. The war was to have a profound effect on all our lives... Peter recalled examples of the prisoners' interest in religion, whether superficial or profound... Soviet military thinking is undergoing a profound change. ♦ **profoundly** ADV I found the film profoundly moving.
2 ADJ A **profound** idea or work shows great intellectual understanding. This research brings up deeper, more profound questions about the creation of galaxies... So is Agatha Christie a more profound and moralistic writer than we give her credit for?

profundity /prəfʌndəti/ **profundities**; a formal word.
1 NU **Profundity** is great intellectual depth and understanding. ...their profundity in arguing socialist theory... Horowitz was criticised for displaying a preference for superficial works, over those that demanded profundity or cerebral effort.
2 NU If you refer to the **profundity** of a feeling, experience, change, or so on, you mean that it is deep, powerful, or serious. ...the speed and profundity of the changes around us... For me, these tales fell short of the profundity of the 'Indian experience'.
3 NC A **profundity** is a remark that shows great intellectual depth and understanding. ...a robed and beaded mystic, muttering profundities about love.

profuse /prəfjuːs/
ADJ **Profuse** is used to indicate that a quantity of something is very large; a formal word. There were profuse apologies for its absence... He criticised the act for showing profuse generosity to the rich and petty meanness to everyone else. ♦ **profusely** ADV He was bleeding profusely.

profusion /prəfjuːʒn/
N SING or NU If there is a **profusion** of something or if it occurs in **profusion**, there is a very large quantity of it; a formal word. ...a garden filled with a profusion of flowering shrubs... The economy was deliberately slowed down and bank notes were not printed in such profusion.

progenitor /prəʊdʒenɪtə/ **progenitors**; a formal word.
1 NC Someone's **progenitors** are their direct ancestors. For 100,000 years, their progenitors inhabited the river valley.
2 NC The **progenitor** of an idea is the person who first thought of it. He was one of the progenitors of the revolution, who was executed later.

progeny /prɒdʒəni/; a formal word.
1 N PL The **progeny** of animals or people are the young animals or babies that they produce. These crossbreeds are the progeny of local goats and imported goats from England.
2 N PL The **progeny** of a particular thing are the things that develop from it. ...these computers and their even faster, even smaller progeny.

prognosis /prɒgnəʊsɪs/ **prognoses** /prɒgnəʊsiːz/
NC A **prognosis** is a prediction about the future of someone or something, especially someone who is ill; a formal word. It was a serious heart defect; the prognosis was poor, even with treatment... Unforeseen factors such as the recession could hinder the favourable economic prognosis.

prognostication /prɒgnɒstɪkeɪʃn/ **prognostications**
NU or NC A **prognostication** is a prediction about something; a formal word. Success could not be guaranteed, but there were not grounds for such gloomy prognostication... Jonathan Fryer examines whether such hopeful prognostications are more than wishful thinking.

program /prəʊgræm/ **programs, programming, programmed**
1 NC A **program** is a set of instructions that a computer follows. Now to do this efficiently, you need a computer program.
2 VO When you **program** a computer, you give it a set of instructions to make it able to perform a particular task. Can computers be programmed to hold intelligent conversations?... The pilot said he had done most of his work programming the computers before the aircraft left the ground. ♦ **programming** NU He accused the government of using fraudulent computer programming to rig the election.
3 **Program** is also the American spelling for **programme**.

programme /prəʊgræm/ **programmes, programming, programmed**; spelt **program** in American English.
1 NC A **programme** is a series of actions or events that are planned to be done. ...a programme of modernization... They have embarked on an ambitious energy programme... There's been a busy programme of matches in the three European club competitions.
2 NC A television or radio **programme** is something that is broadcast on television or radio. ...the last programme in our series on education. ...gardening programmes.
3 NC A theatre or concert **programme** is a booklet giving information about the play or concert you are attending.

4 vo When you **programme** a machine or system, you set its controls so that it will work in a particular way. *The radiators are programmed to come on at six every morning.*

programmer /prəʊgræmə/ **programmers**
NC A computer **programmer** is a person whose job involves writing programs for computers. *A disgruntled programmer might think of revenge by stopping or delaying his manager's pay on the computer.*

progress, progresses, progressing, progressed; pronounced /prəʊgres/ when it is a noun and /prəgres/ when it is a verb.
1 NU **Progress** is the process of gradually improving or getting nearer to achieving or completing something. *She is making good progress with her German. ...technological progress.*
2 N SING The **progress** of an activity is the way in which it develops. *He followed the progress of hostilities with impatience... He has asked for a further progress report from the Airport Authorities.*
3 If something is **in progress**, it is happening. *The battle was still in progress... Crisis talks have been in progress for months.*
4 v To **progress** means to improve or to become more advanced or higher in rank. *You're not progressing quickly enough... Technology did not progress any further for centuries.*
5 v If events **progress**, they continue to happen gradually over a period of time. *My impressions changed as the trip progressed... As the debate progressed, it became apparent that the opposition was beginning to crumble.*
6 v+to If you **progress** to something new, better, or more advanced, you start doing it or having it. *From there we progressed to a discussion on politics... The top two seeds, Edberg and Becker, both progressed to the third round.*

progression /prəgreʃn/ **progressions**
NC+SUPP A **progression** is a gradual development from one state to another. *The progression from one extreme to the other is gradual... The new single is really a musical progression for the band.*

progressive /prəgresɪv/
1 ADJ Someone who is **progressive** has modern ideas and opinions and is eager to change the existing way of doing things. *Some young parents are eager to be progressive. ...Bulgaria's progressive Marxist traditions.*
2 ADJ A **progressive** change happens gradually. *...the progressive industrialization of our society.*
♦ **progressively** ADV *It became progressively easier to see.*

prohibit /prəhɪbɪt/ **prohibits, prohibiting, prohibited**
vo If someone **prohibits** something, they forbid it or make it illegal. *She believes that nuclear weapons should be totally prohibited... The country has a law prohibiting employees from striking.* ♦ **prohibition** /prəʊɪbɪʃn/ **prohibitions** NU or NC *...the prohibition of strikes. ...a prohibition on nuclear weapons.*

prohibitive /prəhɪbətɪv/
ADJ If the cost of something is **prohibitive**, it is so high that you cannot afford it. *...the prohibitive price of domestic labour... The old machines are not being manufactured anymore, and the cost of manufacturing a new one is prohibitive.*

project, projects, projecting, projected; pronounced /prɒdʒekt/ when it is a noun and /prədʒekt/ when it is a verb.
1 NC A **project** is a large-scale attempt to do something. *...the cancellation of the Blue Streak Missile project... He supported the BBC's project for satellite television.*
2 NC A **project** is also a detailed study of a subject by a pupil or student. *It has meant a considerable amount of project work for pupils... If you have a good, well written-out project, you ought to be confident.*
3 vo If something is **projected**, it is planned or expected. *The population of Calcutta is projected to rise to seventy million people... Profits are currently projected at £84 million.* ♦ **projected** ADJ ATTRIB

There were demonstrations against the projected visit... With a projected $220 million deficit, the city is on the verge of bankruptcy.
4 vo If you **project** a film or picture onto a screen or wall, you make it appear there. *A picture of each dress was projected on one huge screen... Skilfully projected video images of mice and rabbits make it look like rodents are scurrying all over the stage.*
5 vo The way that someone or something **is projected** is the way that they are made to seem. *In 1988, Mr Reagan and Mr Gorbachov projected a new image of detente... Dr Vranitski was projected to the electorate as a 'Mr Clean'.*
6 v If something **projects**, it sticks out beyond a surface or edge. *He could see the end of a spear projecting over the rock.*
7 vo If you **project** your voice, you speak loudly and clearly so that your voice can be heard at a distance. *It was a demanding play but the actors projected their voices magnificently.*
8 vo+on or upon If you **project** your feelings upon other people, you imagine that other people have the same feelings as you. *She easily projects her own anxieties and insecurity upon other people.*

projectile /prədʒektaɪl/ **projectiles**
NC A **projectile** is an object that is fired from a gun or other weapon; a formal word. *The projectile damaged the third floor facade and smashed several windows.*

projection /prədʒekʃn/ **projections**
1 NC A **projection** is an estimate of a future amount. *The company made projections of sales of 3000 aircraft.*
2 NC A **projection** is also a part of something that sticks out; a formal use. *...the projection on the mantelpiece.*
3 NU **Projection** is the act of projecting light or a film onto a wall or screen, using a projector. *We use small format video, slide projection and tape recordings. ...a portable projection screen.*

projectionist /prədʒekʃənɪst/ **projectionists**
NC A **projectionist** is someone whose job is to work a projector, for example at a cinema. *At five in the morning, the projectionist there would sneak in and show a film for you.*

projector /prədʒektə/ **projectors**
NC A **projector** is a machine that projects films or slides onto a screen or wall. *...a 35mm slide projector.*

proletarian /prəʊləteəriən/
ADJ ATTRIB **Proletarian** means relating to the proletariat; a formal word. *He argued that the intellectuals had set out to weaken the traditions of proletarian literature. ...the theory of proletarian revolution.*

proletariat /prəʊləteəriət/
N COLL Working-class people, especially industrial workers, are sometimes referred to as the **proletariat**; a formal word. *Progress was achieved by one class, the proletariat struggling against the interests of the bourgeoisie.*

proliferate /prəlɪfəreɪt/ **proliferates, proliferating, proliferated**
v If things **proliferate**, they quickly increase in number; a formal word. *Polytechnics proliferated all over the country... Following a period of warm, wet weather, the eggs have hatched and the locust larvae are proliferating.* ♦ **proliferation** /prəlɪfəreɪʃn/ NU *Cell proliferation in the bone marrow is regulated by cells with a limited capacity to divide. ...the Nuclear Non-Proliferation Treaty.*

prolific /prəlɪfɪk/
ADJ A **prolific** writer, artist, or composer produces a large number of works. *He became renowned for his prolific output... Her performance enabled her to develop a prolific recording career.*

prolix /prəʊlɪks/
ADJ A piece of writing that is **prolix** is longer than necessary; a formal word. *Obscure points of theology presage schisms which ripple across the world in a prolix scholasticism.*

prologue /prəʊlɒg/ **prologues**
1 NC A **prologue** is a speech or section that introduces a play or book. *One result of the workshop was the*

addition of a prologue to help present the play in the context of its time.

2 NC In a racing event, a **prologue** is a preliminary race which is held as a way of deciding the starting order for the main race. *Jose Recio, winner of the prologue on Tuesday, slipped to second place overall... He suffered a twenty-one minute penalty for turning up late for the prologue stage.*

prolong /prəlɒŋ/ **prolongs, prolonging, prolonged**
VO If you **prolong** something you make it last longer. *All the time people are seeking to prolong life... Japan does not want to be seen to be prolonging a cold war mentality.*

prolonged /prəlɒŋd/
ADJ A **prolonged** event or situation continues for a long time. *...a prolonged period of uncertainty... Any legal battle that ensues is likely to be prolonged and expensive.*

prom /prɒm/ **proms**; an informal word.
1 NC A **prom** is one of a series of promenade concerts, especially those held in the Royal Albert Hall in London. *The last night of the proms will be performed as advertised... The Prom began with Sir Charles conducting a performance of Mozart's 'Prague' Symphony.*
2 NC In the United States, a **prom** is a formal dance that is held for students at a high school or college. *When she mentioned that she had no date for the prom, he offered to escort her.*
3 NC At a seaside town, the **prom** is the **promenade**.

promenade /prɒmənɑːd/ **promenades**
1 NC At a seaside town, the **promenade** is a road or path next to the sea. *Two hotels on the seafront promenade were evacuated after a fire broke out.*
2 ADJ ATTRIB A **promenade** concert or theatre performance is one at which some of the audience stand rather than sit. *This year's promenade concerts will have an Austrian flavour... At Regent's Park, the audience is seated, whereas here the plays are given as promenade productions.*

prominence /prɒmɪnəns/
NU If someone or something is in a position of **prominence**, they are important and are well-known or very noticeable. *Alan Travers had risen to prominence in his wife's organisation... Two stories vie for prominence on the front pages today... Several newspapers give prominence in their editorials to the recent unrest in Armenia.*

prominent /prɒmɪnənt/
1 ADJ Someone who is **prominent** is important and well-known. *...US Senators and other prominent American personalities... One of the most prominent speakers, Chandra Muzaffar, described the political atmosphere as unhealthy.*
2 ADJ Something that is **prominent** is very noticeable or important. *There were two prominent landmarks... Quite simply, it would be the most prominent advertisement in the newspaper.* ♦ **prominently** ADV *...a large photograph prominently displayed in her front room... Although there is no set agenda, arms control is expected to feature prominently.*

promiscuity /prɒmɪskjuːəti/
NU **Promiscuity** is the behaviour of someone who has sex with many different people; used showing disapproval. *They argued that the greater availability of condoms would lead to greater promiscuity among young people.*

promiscuous /prəmɪskjuəs/
ADJ Someone who is **promiscuous** has sex with many different people; used showing disapproval. *His outlook on life is that of a promiscuous gentleman.*

promise /prɒmɪs/ **promises, promising, promised**
1 V-REPORT, V O-REPORT, V-QUOTE, or V+to-INF If you **promise** that you will do something, you say that you will definitely do it. *He promised that further measures would follow once he had read the report... I promised your father that you should never know he had been in prison... Last night he promised 'You haven't seen the last of me. I shall return.'... I promised to take the children to the fair... The rebels have promised not to move into the capital before the peace talks are scheduled.*

2 V O O or V O If you **promise** someone something, you tell them that you will definitely give it to them or make sure that they have it. *I promised him a canary for his birthday... The President met student leaders today and promised them a plan... Japan has promised $386,000 for earthquake victims.*
3 NC A **promise** is a statement which you make to someone in which you say that you will definitely do something or give them something. *They tried to break the promises made in negotiations... They fulfilled their promise to revive trade.*
4 V+to-INF If a situation or event **promises** to be a particular thing or have a particular quality, it shows signs that it will be that thing or have that quality. *The debate promises to be lively... Today's transfer promises to put the mines under Yeltsin's government.*
5 NU If someone or something shows **promise**, they seem likely to be very good or successful. *She showed considerable promise as a tennis player... Another natural plant extract is showing promise at stabilising AIDS patients.*

promising /prɒmɪsɪŋ/
ADJ Someone or something that is **promising** seems likely to be very good or successful. *...a most promising new actress... The menu looked promising.*

promissory note /prɒmɪsəri nəʊt/ **promissory notes**
NC A **promissory note** is an official document which promises to pay someone a certain amount of money on a certain date. *These promissory notes were written at a fixed rate of interest... He has resigned amid a scandal involving false promissory notes valued at $500 million.*

promontory /prɒməntəri/ **promontories**
NC A **promontory** is a cliff that stretches out into the sea. *The mansion was on a promontory, high over the Pacific.*

promote /prəməʊt/ **promotes, promoting, promoted**
1 VO If people **promote** something, they help or encourage it to develop or succeed. *The government could do more to promote economic growth... Did writers like Wilde and Britten promote homosexuality?... She founded Les Ballets Africains in 1952 to promote African dance and culture.*
2 VO If a firm **promotes** a product, it tries to increase the sales or popularity of that product. *The advertisements will promote Pepsi Cola and will be similar to those shown in the States... The new town was vigorously promoted as an ideal place to settle.*
3 VO If someone **is promoted**, they are given a more important job. *He had recently been promoted to captain.*
4 VO When a football team **is promoted**, they play in the division above their present one for the next season because they have scored more points than the other teams in their division. *Middlesborough have been promoted to the First Division, while Chelsea have lost their First Division status.*
5 See also **promotion**.

promoter /prəməʊtə/ **promoters**
1 NC A **promoter** is a person who helps organize and finance a public event. *One of Britain's leading boxing promoters, Henry Levene, has died at the age of 93... The Tennis Association will require tournament promoters to pay the bulk of the prize money.*
2 NC The **promoter** of something is someone who tries to make it become popular. *Alan is the organiser of the Carnival, and a tireless promoter of Afro-Caribbean culture.*

promotion /prəməʊʃn/ **promotions**
1 NU or NC The **promotion** of a product is the way a firm tries to increase its sales or popularity, often by advertising. *There are government controls on the promotion of cigarettes... Many stores are trying various promotions including giveaways and sales.*
2 NU or NC If you are given **promotion** in your job, you are given more important things to do and you are paid more money. *Further years of hard and dedicated work may mean promotion to the rank of ward sister... Hispanic employees had been deliberately denied promotions.*

promotional /prəməʊʃənəl/
ADJ ATTRIB **Promotional** events or ideas are designed

to increase the sales of a product or service. *Her first success came after a series of promotional appearances at large UK shopping centres... For today's ceremony, they've produced a promotional video.*

prompt /prɒmpt/ **prompts, prompting, prompted**
1 VO If something **prompts** someone to do something, it makes them decide to do it. *The protests have prompted the President to call a state of siege... The inquiry was prompted by a series of claims that there were a number of such war criminals in Britain... Mrs Currie's statement led to a fall in egg sales, and prompted calls for her resignation.*
2 V-QUOTE or VO If you **prompt** someone when they stop speaking, you encourage or help them to continue. *'Yes?' Morris prompted, after a pause... He doesn't speak English, but his crew members would prompt him.*
3 ADJ A **prompt** action is done without any delay. *...a prompt reply... She requires prompt medical attention.* ● See also **promptly**.

prompter /prɒmptə/ **prompters**
NC A **prompter** is the person whose job is to remind actors of words that they have forgotten during a performance.

prompting /prɒmptɪŋ/ **promptings**
NU or NC **Prompting** is the act of saying something in order to cause someone to do something. *She did it without any prompting. ...Mummy's constant promptings to be 'a nice, clever, boy like your brother'.*

promptly /prɒmptli/
1 ADV If you do something **promptly**, you do it immediately. *He slapped her and she promptly burst into tears... Firemen arrived on the scene promptly.*
2 ADV **Promptly** also means at exactly the time that has been arranged. *I arrived at the gates promptly at six o'clock.*

promulgate /prɒmlgeɪt/ **promulgates, promulgating, promulgated**
VO If people **promulgate** a new law or idea, they announce it publicly; a formal word. *The President has promulgated a decree making the dumping of harmful waste punishable by life imprisonment... He must immediately fashion and promulgate a clear view of how his new administration will be conducted.* ◆ **promulgation** /prɒmlgeɪʃn/ NU *...awaiting the date of promulgation... The next step is the promulgation of a new constitution.*

prone /prəʊn/
1 ADJ PRED If you are **prone** to something, you have a tendency to be affected by it or to do it. *He was prone to indigestion. ...a psychologist prone to drunken self-indulgent confessions.*
2 ADJ If you are lying **prone**, you are lying flat, facing downwards; a formal use. *I will now lie on the ground prone, and pretend to be unconscious.*

prong /prɒŋ/ **prongs**
NC The **prongs** of a fork are the long, thin pointed parts.

-pronged /-prɒŋd/
SUFFIX **-pronged** is used with numbers above one to say that an action is divided into a particular number of parts. For example, a 'two-pronged attack' is an attack consisting of two separate parts. *Guerrillas launched a two-pronged assault on the city... It's really in some senses a three-pronged approach... The report announced a two-pronged strategy for poverty reduction.*

pronominal /prəʊnɒmɪnl/
ADJ **Pronominal** means relating to a pronoun.

pronoun /prəʊnaʊn/ **pronouns**
NC In grammar, a **pronoun** is a word which is used instead of a noun or noun group to refer to someone or something. 'He', 'she', 'them', and 'something' are pronouns.

pronounce /prənaʊns/ **pronounces, pronouncing, pronounced**
1 VO To **pronounce** a word means to say it. *I can't pronounce his name. ...the town of Ixtlan, pronounced East-lon.*
2 VOC or V-REFLC If you **pronounce** something to be

true, you state that it is true; a formal use. *The victim was pronounced dead on arrival at the hospital... The doctors examined the prince after breakfast and pronounced him fit to leave... She pronounced herself pleased at what she called the greatly improved situation.*
3 VO, V-QUOTE or V-REPORT If someone **pronounces** a verdict or opinion on something, they give their verdict or opinion of it; a formal use. *'Are the people ready to pronounce their verdict?'—'Guilty.'... 'Not bad,' he pronounced... Fourteen hundred people have died, but the King pronounced that it had been God's will.*

pronounced /prənaʊnst/
ADJ Something that is **pronounced** is very noticeable. *...walking with a pronounced limp... He spoke with a pronounced English accent... The atmosphere of mistrust is now less pronounced.*

pronouncement /prənaʊnsmənt/ **pronouncements**
NC A **pronouncement** is a public or official statement on an important topic; a formal word. *...official pronouncements made by politicians.*

pronto /prɒntəʊ/
ADV If something must be done **pronto**, it must be done quickly; an informal word. *Let's get out of here pronto.*

pronunciation /prənʌnsieɪʃn/ **pronunciations**
NU or NC The **pronunciation** of a word or language is the way in which it is pronounced. *...the recommended American pronunciation... He tried to correct François's pronunciation.*

proof /pruːf/ **proofs**
1 NU or NC **Proof** is a fact or a piece of evidence which shows that something is true or exists. *Do you have any proof of that allegation?... Unless the proof against her is watertight, the plan may backfire... Henry is said to have cried when given proofs of her infidelity.*
2 NC A **proof** is a first printed copy of something such as a book. It is produced so that mistakes can be corrected before more copies are printed. *He worked from home, correcting proofs.*
3 ADJ **Proof** is used after a number to show the alcoholic strength of a drink such as whisky or brandy. *It is 65% proof instead of the usual 70%.*

-proof /-pruːf/
SUFFIX **-proof** combines with nouns to form adjectives which indicate that something cannot be damaged by a particular thing or person. *This building's supposed to be earthquake-proof... The water heater has been designed to be very tough and it's virtually vandal-proof.*

proofread, proofreads, proofreading. The form **proofread** is used in the present tense, pronounced /pruːfriːd/, and is also the past tense and past participle, pronounced /pruːfred/.
V or VO When someone **proofreads** a text that is going to be printed, they read it and mark any mistakes that need to be corrected by the printer. *A group of volunteers are proofreading for the society... They rely on a network of educated people to supply examples and proofread the entries.*

proofreader /pruːfriːdə/ **proofreaders**
NC A **proofreader** is a person whose job is to proofread texts that are going to be sent to a printer.

prop /prɒp/ **props, propping, propped**
1 VOA If you **prop** an object on something, you place it so that it is supported by that thing. *She propped her chin on her hand... His gun lay propped against the wall.*
2 NC A **prop** is a stick or other object used to support something. *We need a clothes prop for the washing line.*
3 NC The **props** in a play or film are the objects and furniture used in it. *They are known for their use of masks, plastic sheeting and rubber tubing as props.*
prop up PHRASAL VERB 1 To **prop** something **up** means to support it in an upright or raised position. *...timbers used to prop a building up during alterations... His feet were propped up on the coffee table.* 2 If a government or group of people **props up** an organization that is unlikely to survive on its own,

they support it and help it to survive. *The Government does not intend to prop up declining industries... After all, it is overseas aid that props up their ailing economy.*

propaganda /prɒpəgændə/
NU **Propaganda** is information, often inaccurate or biased information, which an organization publishes or broadcasts in order to influence people. *He faces charges of incitement and spreading anti-revolutionary propaganda... The government have described the claims as blatant propaganda.*

propagandist /prɒpəgændɪst/ **propagandists**
NC A **propagandist** is a person who tries to persuade people to support a particular idea or group, often by giving them false, misleading, or biased information. *...gay rights propagandists... Journalists can unwittingly become propagandists.*

propagate /prɒpəgeɪt/ **propagates, propagating, propagated**
1 VO If people **propagate** an idea or some information, they spread it; a formal use. *The group is doing what it can to propagate the rumour... All three agencies had been accused of propagating Christianity.*
2 VorVO If you **propagate** plants, you grow more of them from the original ones; a technical use in biology. *The yucca plant has many applications as food, and it is easily propagated... I asked Professor Kauppinen why he needed to propagate birch trees.*

propane /prəʊpeɪn/
NU **Propane** is a gas that comes from petroleum and is used for cooking and heating. *Shop owners would need at least one kilogram of propane, and that would worry the safety authorities. ...propane gas cylinders.*

propel /prəpɛl/ **propels, propelling, propelled**
VO To **propel** something means to cause it to move along. *The bullet is propelled out of the chamber... You can see I'm propelling myself along by simply rocking backwards and forwards.*

propellant /prəpɛlənt/ **propellants**
1 N MASS A **propellant** is something, for example a motor, chemical, or fuel, that causes an object to move forwards. *The plant, at Pavlograd, makes rocket propellant for the newest long-range nuclear missiles... The fuel is a solid propellant, a mixture of aluminium and acid.*
2 N MASS A **propellant** is also a gas that is used in aerosol cans that forces the contents out when the button is pressed. *...chemicals released into the air by aerosol propellants... The propellant in these cans is nitrous oxide, which is possibly worse than the CFCs normally used.*

propeller /prəpɛlə/ **propellers**
NC A **propeller** on a boat or aircraft is a device with blades which rotates and causes the boat or aircraft to move. *He got into difficulties when a rope caught around the propeller.*

propelling pencil, propelling pencils
NC A **propelling pencil** is a type of pencil in which the lead can be moved down as it is needed by turning the top of the pencil. *He wrote the note with a small gold propelling pencil.*

propensity /prəpɛnsəti/ **propensities**
NC+SUPP A **propensity** to behave in a particular way is a natural tendency to behave in that way; a formal word. *There was no evidence of any propensity to act violently towards others. ...the patient's propensity for socially dangerous behaviour.*

proper /prɒpə/
1 ADJ ATTRIB You use **proper** to describe things that you consider to be real and satisfactory. *He's never had a proper job... Lack of proper funding is making our job more difficult... We consulted all the proper authorities.*
2 ADJ ATTRIB The **proper** thing is the one that is correct or most suitable. *Everything was in its proper place... What's the proper word for those things? ...a moral framework for proper behaviour.*
3 ADJ PRED If you say that a way of behaving is **proper**, you mean that it is the accepted way of behaving according to the standards or conventions of a particular group or society. *It wasn't proper for a man to show his emotions.*

4 ADJ after N You can add **proper** after a word to emphasize that you are referring to the main, central, and most important part of a place, event, or object in order to distinguish it from other things which are not regarded as being important or central to it. *By the time I got to the village proper everyone was out to meet me... His visit to Washington will mark the start of the election campaign proper.*

properly /prɒpəli/
ADV If something is done **properly**, it is done correctly and satisfactorily. *We must see that the children are properly fed... The reviewers aren't doing their job properly.*

proper noun, proper nouns
NC In grammar, a **proper noun** is a noun which refers to a particular person, place, or institution. Proper nouns begin with a capital letter.

property /prɒpəti/ **properties**
1 NU Someone's **property** is all the things that belong to them, or something that belongs to them. *Their job is to protect private property... They have requested the confiscation of millions of dollar's worth of property.*
2 NC A **property** is a building and the land belonging to it. *He arranged to rent the property... The family owns cattle ranches and other properties in the Amazon. ...the world's biggest commercial property development.*
3 NC The **properties** of a substance or object are the ways in which it behaves in particular conditions; a technical use. *Powdered rhino horn is rumoured to have aphrodisiac properties... Besides having nitrogen-fixing properties, trees can be used as a source of fuel.*

prophecy /prɒfəsi/ **prophecies**
NCorNU A **prophecy** is a statement that something will happen or will become true in the future. *Perhaps he never lost hope that his own prophecy might yet come to be fulfilled... The worry is that the gloomy forecasts are in danger of becoming a self-fulfilling prophecy... There's been a revival of interest in prophecy lately.*

prophesy /prɒfəsaɪ/ **prophesies, prophesying, prophesied**
V-REPORT, V O, or V-QUOTE If you **prophesy** something, you say that you believe it will happen. *At the ceremony, one speaker prophesied that the system would be the pioneer for many others... He wept over the city as he prophesied its forthcoming destruction... In only five year's time, Professor Cantor prophesied, it will be possible to look at genes under the microscope.*

prophet /prɒfɪt/ **prophets**
NC A **prophet** is a person believed to be chosen by God to say the things that God wants to tell people. *He regards these laws as a corruption of the prophet's teachings. ...the story of the prophet Joseph and his brothers.*

prophetic /prəfɛtɪk/
ADJ Something that is **prophetic** describes or predicts things that eventually happen or come true. *If the conflict does become a holy war, David Smith's book could prove grimly prophetic. ...more than fifty years after she wrote those prophetic words.*

prophylactic /prɒfɪlæktɪk/ **prophylactics**; a medical term.
ADJ A **prophylactic** drug or type of treatment is concerned with preventing, rather than curing, disease. *These substances can be used initially for prophylactic purposes... Which is better against malaria, a mosquito net or prophylactic drugs?*

propinquity /prəpɪŋkwəti/
NU **Propinquity** is nearness to someone, either because you live near to them or because you are closely related to them; a formal word. *They value their friends because of their residential propinquity.*

propitiate /prəpɪʃieɪt/ **propitiates, propitiating, propitiated**
VO If you **propitiate** a person or a god, you try to please them because they are angry or impatient; a formal word. *There was a new favourite to be flattered and propitiated by those who desire favour.*

propitious /prəpɪʃəs/
ADJ If something is **propitious**, it is likely to lead to

success; a formal word. *It was hardly a propitious time to join one of those newspapers... In more propitious circumstances, the two sides might have found it possible to co-exist.*

proponent /prəpəʊnənt/ **proponents**
N C The **proponent** of a particular idea or course of action is someone who actively supports it; a formal word. *M. Chirac and M. Mitterrand are the two most redoubtable proponents of nuclear power... He is seen as the chief proponent of radical thinking in the Politburo.*

proportion /prəpɔːʃn/ **proportions**
1 N C A **proportion** of an amount or group is a part of it. *Courts are now sending a smaller proportion of offenders to prison... The government have not yet decided what proportion will be sold to the private sector.*
2 NC+SUPP The **proportion** of one part of a group is its size in relation to the whole group or to another part of it. *The proportion of workers to employers was large... Usually men outnumber women, but we have about equal proportions at Sussex.*
3 N PL+SUPP You can refer to the size of something as its **proportions**. *...a gin and tonic of giant proportions.*
● **Proportion** is used in these phrases. ● If one thing is small or large **in proportion to** another thing, it is small or large when you compare it with the other thing. *Babies have big heads in proportion to their bodies... The risk for each individual increases in direct proportion to the length of time for which they are overweight.* ● If something is **out of proportion** or **out of all proportion** to something else, it is far greater or more serious than it should be. *He said the Prince's remarks had been taken out of context and blown up out of proportion... Every small event was magnified out of all proportion to its importance.* ● If someone has a **sense of proportion**, they know what is really important and what is not. *The paper urges a sense of proportion and says an exaggerated fear of crime is almost as damaging as the real thing.*

proportional /prəpɔːʃənəl/
ADJ If one amount is **proportional** to another, it always remains the same fraction of the other. *As a rule the suicide rates are proportional to the size of the city.*
♦ **proportionally** ADV *In all these meals the amount of vegetables is proportionally too small.*

proportional representation
N U **Proportional representation** is a system of voting in elections in which each political party is represented in parliament in proportion to the number of people who voted for it. *...allocating seats on the basis of proportional representation.*

proportionate /prəpɔːʃənət/
ADJ **Proportionate** means the same as **proportional**. *After a run, your recovery time is proportionate to your fitness.* ♦ **proportionately** ADV *Britain spent proportionately more on research than its competitors.*

proposal /prəpəʊzl/ **proposals**
1 N C A **proposal** is a suggestion or plan, often a written one, which is put forward for people to discuss and decide upon. *There is controversy about a proposal to build a new nuclear power station. ...proposals for cheaper flights to the United States... There is not much enthusiasm for the American proposal that there should be an international arms embargo.*
2 N C A **proposal** is also a request that someone makes to another person to marry them. *...the second proposal of marriage which she received... By tradition, a man refusing a marriage proposal must pay the woman a £1 fine.*

propose /prəpəʊz/ **proposes, proposing, proposed**
1 V-REPORT or V O If you **propose** a plan or idea, you suggest it to people for them to think about and decide upon. *I proposed that the culprits should be fined... The scientists propose that boys and girls should be injected with the vaccine before puberty... He is likely to propose a major shift in military strategy.*
♦ **proposed** ADJ ATTRIB *...the proposed alliance.*
2 V+to-INF If you **propose** to do something, you intend to do it. *I do not propose to discuss this matter... The government does now propose to enhance security at*

the Temple... How do you propose to get there?
3 V O If someone **proposes** a motion in a debate, they introduce it and say why people should agree with it. *Webb proposed the motion 'That this House has no confidence in the Government'.*
4 V O If you **propose** someone in an election or vote, you suggest their name as a candidate for that election or vote. *Egypt proposed Dr Boutros Ghali for the Secretary Generalship of UNESCO three years ago... According to the constitution, it is the President who will propose a candidate for Prime Minister... He intends to propose the candidacy of Shcharansky.*
5 V O If you **propose** a toast to someone or something, you ask people to drink a toast to them. *He proposed a toast to the friendship between American and Georgian people.*
6 V If you **propose** to someone, you ask them to marry you. *He had known her for two years before he proposed. ...women who see it as perfectly natural to propose to their men.*

proposition /prɒpəzɪʃn/ **propositions, propositioning, propositioned**
1 N C A **proposition** is a statement expressing a theory or opinion. *I had plenty of evidence to support the proposition that man was basically selfish.*
2 N C A **proposition** is also an offer or suggestion. *He came to me one day with an extraordinary proposition.*
3 V O If you **proposition** someone who you are not married to or having a relationship with, you ask them to have sex with you. *The gunner's mate had propositioned another sailor and been rejected... Women have suffered unwanted sexual attention: being insulted, threatened and propositioned by men.*

propound /prəpaʊnd/ **propounds, propounding, propounded**
V O If you **propound** an argument, idea, or point of view, you put it forward forcefully for people to consider; a formal word. *This line of argument is propounded largely by the more influential US commentators... They will wait to see what policies he propounds before deciding how to vote.*

proprietary /prəpraɪətəri/
ADJ ATTRIB **Proprietary** substances are ones sold under a trade name; a formal word. *...a proprietary dry cleaner.*

proprietor /prəpraɪətə/ **proprietors**
N C The **proprietor** of a hotel, shop, or newspaper is the person who owns it. *They refused to prosecute the proprietor of the newspaper... Mr Morritt is asking proprietors of hotels, holiday flats, and guest houses to cooperate.*

proprietorial /prəpraɪətɔːriəl/; a formal word.
1 ADJ ATTRIB **Proprietorial** means belonging to or relating to a proprietor. *...the abuse of proprietorial power.*
2 ADJ **Proprietorial** behaviour indicates that someone is, or thinks they are, the owner of something; used showing disapproval. *She had a proprietorial attitude towards the children... The Foreign Ministry has adopted an aggressively proprietorial tone.*

proprietress /prəpraɪətrəs/ **proprietresses**
N C The **proprietress** is a woman who is the owner of a business such as a hotel, shop, or newspaper; an old-fashioned word. *The grey haired proprietress of the restuarant was entertaining them with a dance.*

propriety /prəpraɪəti/
N U **Propriety** is the quality of being socially or morally acceptable; a formal word. *I doubt the propriety of receiving a lady this late at night... He was concerned by the propriety of TV interviewing of witnesses and trial by television.*

propulsion /prəpʌlʃn/
N U **Propulsion** is the power that moves something, especially a vehicle, in a forward direction. *...jet propulsion... Propulsion was derived from an internal combustion engine.*

pro rata /prəʊ rɑːtə/
ADV or ADJ ATTRIB To pay someone for something **pro rata** means to pay them according to how much of a facility has been used or received; a formal expression. *Computer time is paid for pro rata... The*

orchestra is paid on a pro rata basis for concertos.

prosaic /prəzeɪɪk/
ADJ Something that is **prosaic** is dull and uninteresting. *The job sounds prosaic on the surface... He changed his name from the prosaic Reg Dwight, and became a master of skilful self-promotion.*

proscenium /prəsiːniəm/ **prosceniums**
NC A **proscenium** or a **proscenium arch** in a theatre is the part of the auditorium with an arch which separates the stage from the audience; a technical term. *At this point, I go beyond the proscenium... The main opera house has a proscenium arch and upwards of 2,000 seats.*

proscribe /prəskraɪb/ **proscribes, proscribing, proscribed**
VO If people in authority **proscribe** something, they publicly state that the existence or the use of that thing is forbidden; a formal word. *The State might proscribe private education altogether... The party was proscribed in 1983 when it was blamed for inciting riots.*

proscription /prəskrɪpʃn/
NU The **proscription** of something is the act of stating that its existence or use is forbidden; a formal word. *...the lifting of the proscription... They have asked for immediate proscription of the political wing of the IRA.*

prose /prəʊz/
NU **Prose** is ordinary written language, in contrast to poetry. *...an edition of A.E.Housman's poetry and prose... Both the prose and drama awards were withheld because entries failed to reach the required standard.*

prosecute /prɒsɪkjuːt/ **prosecutes, prosecuting, prosecuted**
1 VOorV If you **prosecute** someone, you bring criminal charges against them, and they go on trial. *The campaigner Mary Whitehouse successfully prosecuted the editor of Gay News... His critics say he should have been prosecuted under the Official Secrets Act... They are threatening to prosecute.*
2 V The person who **prosecutes** in a trial tries to prove that the person who has been accused of a crime is guilty. *David Jeffreys, prosecuting, said that no seafaring experience was needed to appreciate the obvious danger of sailing with the bow doors open... Mr Woodly always defends, he never prosecutes.*

prosecution /prɒsɪkjuːʃn/ **prosecutions**
1 NUorNC **Prosecution** is the action of charging someone with a crime and putting them on trial. *He could face criminal prosecution... The Smiths brought a prosecution against the organizers.*
2 N SING The lawyers who try to prove that a person on trial is guilty are called the **prosecution**. *Today he will be questioned by the prosecution... For the prosecution, Josephine Sivaratnam said the trial judge had been right to discount duress... The main prosecution witness has withdrawn his evidence.*

prosecutor /prɒsɪkjuːtə/ **prosecutors**
NC A **prosecutor** is a lawyer or official who brings charges against someone or tries to prove in a trial that they are guilty. *The prosecutor also demanded fifteen years in a labour camp for the co-defendant.*

proselytize /prɒsəlɪtaɪz/ **proselytizes, proselytizing, proselytized**; also spelt **proselytise**.
V If you **proselytize**, you try very hard to persuade someone to leave their religious faith, political party, or so on, and to join yours; a formal word. *You're a lost cause. I'm not going to waste my time proselytizing on you. ...the usual incidents involving party workers proselytising too close to the polling booths.*

prospect, prospects, prospecting, prospected; pronounced /prɒspekt/ when it is a noun and /prəspekt/ when it is a verb.
1 NCorNU If there is a **prospect** of something happening, there is a possibility that it will happen. *She did not relish the prospect of climbing another flight of stairs... Any prospects for an early settlement were dashed from the outset... There was little prospect of significant military aid.*
2 N PL Someone's **prospects** are their chances of being

successful. *Success or failure here would be crucial to his future prospects... The Government remained optimistic about Britain's prospects.*
3 V If people **prospect** for a valuable substance such as oil or gold, they look for it in the ground or under the sea. *In fact, the oil companies are already prospecting not far from here.*

prospective /prəspektɪv/
ADJ ATTRIB You use **prospective** to describe a person who wants to be the thing mentioned. *...the controversial practice of vetting prospective employees... Current and prospective England players must decide if it is worth risking a winter in South Africa.*

prospector /prəspektə/ **prospectors**
NC A **prospector** is a person who looks for a valuable substance such as oil or gold. *About 5 million prospectors are panning for gold dust in the Amazonian rain forest.*

prospectus /prəspektəs/ **prospectuses**
NC A **prospectus** is a document produced by a college, school, or company which gives details about it. *The 1989 prospectus is a glossy 128 pages full of colour photographs.*

prosper /prɒspə/ **prospers, prospering, prospered**
V If people or businesses **prosper**, they are successful and do well financially. *He moved to London, where his business prospered... The best companies will survive and prosper in the new Europe.*

prosperity /prɒsperəti/
NU **Prosperity** is a condition in which a person or community is doing well financially. *Economic prosperity depends critically on an open world trading policy. ...democracy as an instrument that would bring peace and prosperity.*

prosperous /prɒspərəs/
ADJ A town, business, or person who is **prosperous** is wealthy and successful. *The president's home village is a prosperous little place set in good farmland... He has a prosperous legal practice in Panama City... He was born sixty-four years ago to a prosperous family.*

prostate /prɒsteɪt/ **prostates**
NC The **prostate** or **prostate gland** is an organ situated at the neck of the bladder in male mammals which produces a liquid which forms part of the semen. *Certain cancers, of the kidney and the prostate, had a lower death rate... He had radiology treatment for a prostate gland disorder.*

prostitute /prɒstɪtjuːt/ **prostitutes**
NC A **prostitute** is a person, usually a woman, who has sex with men in exchange for money. *The tribal girls who go to Thailand work as prostitutes there... It was alleged that he'd had sex with a homosexual prostitute.*

prostitution /prɒstɪtjuːʃn/
NU **Prostitution** involves having sex in exchange for money. *Almost all young women who turn to prostitution do so as a means of survival. ...problems such as child prostitution.*

prostrate, prostrates, prostrating, prostrated; pronounced /prɒstreɪt/ when it is a verb and /prɒstreɪt/ when it is an adjective.
1 V-REFL If you **prostrate** yourself, you lie flat on the ground with your face downwards. *I watched the pilgrims prostrate themselves in a slow procession round the Temple.*
2 ADJ If you are **prostrate**, you are lying flat on the ground with your face downwards. *I saw a man lying prostrate and motionless on his back near the tree... He collapsed, and was prostrate with ankle ligament injuries.*

protagonist /prətægənɪst/ **protagonists**; a formal word.
1 NC A **protagonist** in a play, novel, or event is one of the main people in it. *The main protagonist is a woman who wants to be Joan of Arc... He'll be a protagonist in negotiations with the government.*
2 NC A **protagonist** of an idea or movement is a supporter of it. *She was a vehement protagonist of sexual equality.*

protect /prətekt/ **protects, protecting, protected**
VO To **protect** someone or something means to prevent

them from being harmed or damaged. *She had his umbrella to protect her from the rain... Babies are protected against diseases like measles by their mothers' milk.*

protection /prətɛkʃn/
NU If something gives **protection** against something unpleasant, it prevents people or things from being harmed or damaged by it. *The mud walls of these huts offer little protection against rats... We need protection from the sun's rays.*

protectionism /prətɛkʃənizəm/
NU **Protectionism** is the policy some countries have of helping its own industries by putting a large tax on imported goods. *He was asked whether US protectionism might jeopardize the agreement... He says he will maintain his opposition to the Bill unless provisions calling for protectionism are removed.*

protectionist /prətɛkʃənist/ **protectionists**
1 NC A **protectionist** is someone who agrees with and supports protectionism. *He is one of the strongest protectionists in the Senate.*
2 ADJ **Protectionist** policies, laws, agreements, and so on, are based on protectionism, or help to create or support it. *The Bill is filled with scores of provisions that are protectionist and defeatist... The President accepted a protectionist compromise.*

protective /prətɛktɪv/
1 ADJ ATTRIB A **protective** object or action is intended to protect something or someone from harm. *British troops put on a demonstration of protective clothing and gas masks... The boy was taken into protective custody after he had been assaulted by his father. ...protective measures to reduce X-ray exposure.*
2 ADJ If someone is **protective** towards you, they show a strong desire to keep you safe. *She felt very protective towards her sister.* ◆ **protectively** ADV *She cradles the baby tenderly, protectively.*

protector /prətɛktə/ **protectors**
NC A **protector** of someone or something is a person or device that prevents them from being harmed or damaged. *...ecologists and protectors of wildlife... He called the soldiers particularly brave and the protectors of democracy.*

protectorate /prətɛktərət/ **protectorates**
NC A **protectorate** is a country that is controlled and protected by a more powerful country. *The Republic of the Maldives was a British protectorate until 1965.*

protégé /prɒtɪʒeɪ/ **protégés**; also spelt **protégée** when referring to a woman.
NC+POSS Someone's **protégé** is a person that they help and guide over a period of time. *She was a painter and a protégée of Duncan Grant.*

protein /prəutiːn/ **proteins**
NCorNU **Protein** is a substance that is found, for example, in meat, eggs, and milk and that is needed for growth. *Similar proteins to these are found in normal cells... These discoveries concern the three main ingredients of our food—protein, fat, and carbohydrate. ...protein deficiency.*

pro tem /prəu tɛm/
ADJ If someone has a particular position or job **pro tem**, they have it temporarily. *I'm president pro tem of the California State Senate... The pro tem committee for the new party includes Tunku Abdul Rahman as president.*

protest, protests, protesting, protested; pronounced /prətɛst/ when it is a verb and /prəutɛst/ when it is a noun.
1 V A or V If you **protest** about something, you say or show publicly that you do not approve of it. *Some local labourers were protesting about police corruption... They have been holding hunger strikes to protest against social conditions... They forced him into the car, pushing away his wife who protested vigorously... When the Ministers protested, they were told they were 'free to leave the government'.*
2 V-REPORT, V-QUOTE, or V O If you **protest** that something is the case, you insist that it is the case, when other people think that it may not be. *They protested that they had never heard of him... 'You're wrong,' I protested... The mother protested her innocence.*
3 NC or NU A **protest** is the act of saying or showing

publicly that you do not approve of something. *They joined in the protests against the government's proposals... There was a wave of student riots, in protest at university conditions.*

Protestant /prɒtɪstənt/ **Protestants**
NC A **Protestant** is a member of one of the Christian churches which separated from the Roman Catholic Church. *...bringing Catholics and Protestants together. ...Protestant clergymen.*

Protestantism /prɒtɪstəntizəm/
NU **Protestantism** is the set of Christian beliefs that are held by Protestants. *This doctrine distinguishes it from mainstream Protestantism.*

protestation /prɒtɪsteɪʃn/ **protestations**
NC A **protestation** is a strong declaration; a formal word. *...his protestations of innocence.*

protester /prətɛstə/ **protesters**
NC A **protester** is a person who protests publicly about something, for example by taking part in a demonstration. *The protesters surrendered to the police after about an hour.*

protocol /prəutəkɒl/ **protocols**
1 NU **Protocol** is a system of rules about the correct way to act in formal situations. *Mr Gandhi broke protocol, speaking a few initial sentences of his address in Italian.*
2 NC A **protocol** is a written record of a treaty or agreement that has been made by two or more countries. *They appeared to be inching closer towards a signing of the protocol. ...the 1988 Bilateral Trade protocol.*

proton /prəutɒn/ **protons**
NC A **proton** is an atomic particle that has a positive electrical charge. *We need to investigate whether there are even smaller particles inside the proton.*

protoplasm /prəutəplæzəm/
NU **Protoplasm** is the living substance inside the cells of animals and plants; a technical term in biology. *Mycelium is really a system of fine branching tubes full of protoplasm.*

prototype /prəutətaɪp/ **prototypes**
NC A **prototype** is the first model that is made of something new. *Funds for testing of the prototypes ran out.*

protracted /prətræktɪd/
ADJ Something that is **protracted** lasts a long time, especially longer than usual or longer than expected. *...exploring ways to end Angola's protracted civil war... Although the negotiations have been protracted, there's been no indication of what the outcome will be.*

protractor /prətræktə/ **protractors**
NC A **protractor** is a flat, semicircular piece of plastic or metal which is used for measuring angles.

protrude /prətruːd/ **protrudes, protruding, protruded**
V A or V If something **protrudes** from somewhere, it sticks out; a formal word. *He tripped over a pair of boots protruding from under the table... They were weak and emaciated, their bones protruding through their skins... Suckling can make the teeth protrude.* ◆ **protruding** ADJ ATTRIB *Each cube has a protruding tooth that slots into a corresponding notch.*

protrusion /prətruːʒn/ **protrusions**
NC A **protrusion** is something that sticks out from somewhere; a formal word. *...a jumble of spikes and jagged protrusions.*

protuberance /prətjuːbərəns/ **protuberances**
NC A **protuberance** is a rounded part that sticks out from the surface of something; a formal word. *The rhino's horn is a protuberance of compressed hair.*

protuberant /prətjuːbərənt/
ADJ Something that is **protuberant** sticks out from a surface; a formal word. *...his rather protuberant ears.*

proud /praud/ **prouder, proudest**
1 ADJ If you feel **proud**, you feel pleasure and satisfaction at something that you own, have done, or are connected with. *They seemed proud of what they had accomplished... It makes me proud to be an American.* ◆ **proudly** ADV *He was grinning proudly, delighted with his achievement.*
2 ADJ Someone who is **proud** has dignity and self-respect. *He was a poor but very proud old man.*

3 ADJ You can also use **proud** to describe someone who feels that they are superior to other people. *She was too proud to apologize.*

provable /pruːvəbl/
ADJ Statements and theories that are **provable** can be proved to be true or correct. *...a mathematically provable law.*

prove /pruːv/ **proves, proving, proved, proven.** The past participle can be either **proved** or **proven**.
1 V-REPORT, V O, V O C, or V O+to-INF To **prove** that something is true means to show definitely that it is true. *He was able to prove that he was an American... He is going to have to prove his innocence... The case against the six men has not been proven... She has to be proved wrong... I have proved it to be sound.*
2 V+to-INF or V C If someone or something **proves** to have a particular quality, they are found to have that quality. *I proved to be hopeless as a teacher... This information has proved useful.*

proven /pruːvn/
ADJ ATTRIB Something that is **proven** has been definitely shown to be true. *This man is a proven liar... Their proven links with death squad activities and opposition to reform have made them unpopular.*

provenance /prɒvənəns/
NU The **provenance** of someone or something is the place from which it originated; a formal word. *Despite these differences in provenance and production, Bordeaux wines are still worth buying. ...a burly male guard of East German provenance.*

provender /prɒvɪndə/
NU **Provender** is food for animals, especially corn and hay; an old-fashioned word.

proverb /prɒvɜːb/ **proverbs**
NC A **proverb** is a short sentence that people often quote, which gives advice or comments on life. *Consider the African proverb, which says that the only thing gained from feeding a crocodile is a bigger crocodile.*

proverbial /prəvɜːbiəl/
1 ADJ ATTRIB You use **proverbial** to emphasize that what you are saying is part of a proverb or well-known expression. *It is rather like looking for the needle in the proverbial haystack.*
2 ADJ Something that is **proverbial** is very well-known by a lot of people. *Dealers said the market was suffering from the proverbial Christmas blues.*

provide /prəvaɪd/ **provides, providing, provided**
1 V O or V O A If you **provide** something that someone needs or wants, you give it to them or make it available to them. *Meals are being provided by the WRVS... Most animals provide food for their young... The government cannot provide all young people with a job.*
2 V O If something **provides** a useful or desirable feature or quality, it has or gives that feature or quality and people can benefit from it. *There are jobs on the farm to which the machine provides no real answer... Kenya provides an example of the trend towards democratic government in Africa.*
3 V-REPORT If a law or decision **provides** that something will happen, it states that it will happen. *The draft legislation provides that parliament may vote public funds to help pay running costs... The agreement provides that no additional members of the military will be stationed in Peru.*
provide for PHRASAL VERB 1 If you **provide for** someone, you give them the things that they need. *Parents are expected to provide for their children.* 2 If you **provide for** a possible future event, you make arrangements to deal with it; a formal use. *Should the law provide for these cases?*

provided /prəvaɪdɪd/
CONJ If something will happen **provided** or **providing** something else happens, the first thing will happen only if the second thing also happens. *Children were permitted into the hall, provided they sat at the back... It would be pleasant living in Glasgow providing you were living in a nice flat.*

providence /prɒvɪdəns/
NU **Providence** is God, or a force which is believed to arrange the things that happen to us; a literary word.

The money lender proposed that they let providence decide the matter.

providential /prɒvɪdenʃl/
ADJ An event that is **providential** is lucky; a formal word. *...his providential deliverance from danger... It was providential that it started in front of the reform church.*

provider /prəvaɪdə/ **providers**
NC A **provider** is someone or something that gives people the things that they need or want. *...her duties as a provider of food... As the provider of medical services, the government has a moral duty to its citizens.*

providing /prəvaɪdɪŋ/. See **provide, provided.**

province /prɒvɪns/ **provinces**
1 NC A **province** is a large section of a country, with its own administration. *...rallies in Zimbabwe's five provinces. ...the Thai province of Chiang Rai.*
2 N PL The **provinces** are the parts of a country outside the area of the capital. *...teenage life in the provinces... He has a string of public appearances in the provinces.*
3 N SING+POSS If you say that a subject or activity is the **province** of a particular person, that person has a special interest in it, knowledge about it, or responsibility for it. *That's a question that will be outside the province of my office... This will always be the province of the specialist.*

provincial /prəvɪnʃl/
1 ADJ ATTRIB **Provincial** means connected with the parts of a country outside the capital. *This isn't the first time they've won a provincial election... His comments were published in a French provincial newspaper.*
2 ADJ Someone or something that is **provincial** is narrow-minded or unsophisticated. *Supporters of modernism called his work provincial and escapist... He was a plain, even provincial man, who imprinted his name on a large part of American history.*

provincialism /prəvɪnʃəlɪzəm/
NU **Provincialism** is a narrow outlook and lack of cultural sophistication. *Quite honestly, with the provincialism of some American audiences, there's never going to be a foreign film that's a real hit over here.*

provision /prəvɪʒn/ **provisions**
1 NU The **provision** of something is the act of giving it or making it available. *...helping needy people by the provision of food, clothing, and shelter.*
2 NU If you make **provision** for a future need, you make arrangements to ensure that it is dealt with. *She did not make any provision for her children.*
3 NC A **provision** in an agreement or law is an arrangement included in it. *The Government had still to agree on the provisions of the Bill.*
4 N PL **Provisions** are supplies of food. *We set out with enough provisions for the long trip.*

provisional /prəvɪʒ⁰nəl/
ADJ Something that is **provisional** has been arranged or appointed for the present time, but may be changed in the future. *...a provisional government. ...a provisional diagnosis of schizophrenia.*

proviso /prəvaɪzəʊ/ **provisos**
NC A **proviso** is a condition in an agreement. *At last she consented, with the proviso that he should repay her as soon as he could... Certain legal provisos can be used to deny dissidents their travelling rights.*

provocation /prɒvəkeɪʃn/ **provocations**
NU or NC **Provocation** is a deliberate attempt to make someone react angrily. *She has a tantrum at the least provocation... They must not react to this provocation.*

provocative /prəvɒkətɪv/
1 ADJ Something that is **provocative** is intended to make people react angrily. *He wrote a provocative article on 'Anti-racialism'.*
2 ADJ **Provocative** behaviour is intended to make someone feel sexual desire. *...a provocative dance.*

provoke /prəvəʊk/ **provokes, provoking, provoked**
1 V O If you **provoke** someone, you deliberately annoy them and try to make them behave in an aggressive way. *Ray was trying to provoke them into fighting... The police claim they were provoked.*

2 vo If something **provokes** a violent or unpleasant reaction, it causes it. *The petition provoked a storm of criticism... The name Richard Branson provokes a curious mixture of feelings in the minds of the British public.*

provost /prɒvəst/ **provosts**
1 NCorTITLE A **provost** is the head of certain university colleges in Britain and the United States. *...Lord Briggs, the provost of Worcester College... Bowsa Wilson, acting Provost of John Jay College, disagrees.*
2 NCorTITLE In Scotland, a **provost** is the chief magistrate of a borough. *...the Provost of Clydebank, Robert Fleming.*
3 NCorTITLE In the Catholic and Anglican Churches, a **provost** is the person who is in charge of the administration of a cathedral. *'You're the provost? You own the cathedral?—'No, it belongs to God.'*

prow /praʊ/ **prows**
NC The **prow** of a ship or boat is the front part of it. *...a famous photo of the Queen, standing motionless in the prow of a ship.*

prowess /praʊes/
NU Someone's **prowess** is their great ability at doing something; a literary word. *There are legends about his prowess as a jockey... They believe that social deprivation breeds sporting prowess.*

prowl /praʊl/ **prowls, prowling, prowled**
VAorVO When animals or people **prowl** around, they move around quietly, for example when they are hunting. *I found four foxes prowling round my flock one night... Gangs of youths prowl the streets.* ▶ Also NC+SUPP *They set out on their nightly prowl.*

prowl car, prowl cars
NC A **prowl car** is a car that the police use for patrolling an area; used in American English.

prowler /praʊlə/ **prowlers**
NC A **prowler** is someone who creeps around houses at night, usually because they intend to rob or harm the people living there. *...unwanted prowlers.*

proximity /prɒksɪməti/
NU+to **Proximity** to something or someone is the fact of being near them; a formal word. *...the town's proximity to the northern cape of Japan... They were in close proximity to the principle earthquake region. ...an uneasy feeling that continual proximity to violence can be addictive.*

proxy /prɒksi/
If you do something **by proxy**, you arrange for someone else to do it for you. *They have the right to vote by proxy in France itself or at their local embassy.*

prude /pruːd/ **prudes**
NC Someone who is a **prude** is easily shocked by things relating to nudity or sex; used showing disapproval. *I hardly consider myself a prude, but I was a bit taken aback by Daniel's story.*

prudence /pruːdns/
NU **Prudence** is care and wisdom that someone shows when they are making decisions. *Her eagerness had overcome her prudence... His watchwords are caution and prudence... It is likely, therefore, that prudence dictated her decision.*

prudent /pruːdnt/
ADJ Someone who is **prudent** is sensible and careful. *He now considered it prudent to carry a revolver.*
♦ **prudently** ADV *Fanny prudently resolved to keep silent.*

prudish /pruːdɪʃ/
ADJ A **prudish** person is easily shocked by things relating to nudity or sex; used showing disapproval. *...four aunts, religious and prudish... He is strangely prudish about sex.*

prune /pruːn/ **prunes, pruning, pruned**
1 NC A **prune** is a dried plum. *What's so special about hot prunes in sauce?*
2 VO When you **prune** a tree or bush, you cut off some of the branches. *It takes several hours to prune a tree in the traditional way.*
3 VO If you **prune** something such as a piece of writing, you make it shorter by removing parts of it. *What he said was passed down and pruned even*

further into a more concise expression.
4 VO To **prune** an organization, its expenditure, or the jobs it provides means to make it smaller by reducing it in size, or by reducing the amount of money it spends. *He tried to prune the party of apparatchiks and hard-liners... He's currently engaged on an attempt to prune back the defence budget... The big companies are getting ready to prune another 40,000 jobs before Christmas.*

pruning hook, pruning hooks
NC A **pruning hook** is a tool that is used for pruning trees and shrubs.

prurient /prʊəriənt/
ADJ Someone who is **prurient** shows a strong interest in sexual matters; a formal word, used showing disapproval. *The girls were ogled by prurient officials.*

prussic acid /prʌsɪk æsɪd/
NU **Prussic acid** is an extremely poisonous acid. *He discovered a wasp's nest, which he intended to destroy using prussic acid.*

pry /praɪ/ **pries, prying, pried**
1 V When someone **pries**, they try to find out about someone else's private affairs. *Don't go prying into my affairs or you'll get hurt.*
2 VOA If you **pry** something open or **pry** it away from a surface, you force it open or force it to come away from the surface; used in American English. *These bottles are very hard to pry open... A small group of men were hunched over the ambulance, trying to pry off the compressor... We made various attempts to pry the bus out.*

PS /piː es/
You write **PS** to introduce a further message at the end of a letter after you have signed it. *With love from us both, Dad. PS Mum asks me to remind you to bring back her duvet.*

psalm /sɑːm/ **psalms**
NC The **Psalms** are the 150 songs, poems, and prayers which together form the Book of Psalms in the Bible. *A Rabbi led the audience in an impressive round of prayers and psalms.*

pseud /sjuːd/ **pseuds**
NC If you say that someone is a **pseud**, you mean that they are trying to appear very well-educated or artistic, in a false or pretentious way; an informal word. *In Kundera's work, the human race emerges as a bunch of pseuds, all surface and no substance.*

pseudo- /sjuːdəʊ-/
PREFIX **Pseudo-** is used to form nouns and adjectives that refer to or describe things that are not really what they seem or claim to be. For example, if you describe a country as a pseudo-democracy, you mean that it is not really a democracy, although its government claims that it is. *...pseudo-scientific ideas. ...pseudo-liberals.*

pseudonym /sjuːdənɪm/ **pseudonyms**
NC A **pseudonym** is a name used by a writer instead of his or her real name. *Many journalists wrote under pseudonyms.*

psych /saɪk/ **psychs, psyching, psyched**; also spelt **psyche, psyches.**
VOA If you **psych** yourself up, for example before a contest, or **psych** yourself into doing something difficult, you prepare yourself mentally, especially by telling yourself that you can win or succeed. *They won't need any psyching up for this one... He had to psych himself into writing the book.*

psyche /saɪki/ **psyches**
1 NC Your **psyche** is your mind and your deepest feelings and attitudes. *It is easy to understand how a person's psyche can be damaged by such experiences... By the time we've finished, we know a lot about their psyches.*
2 See also **psych**.

psychedelic /saɪkədelɪk/
1 ADJ ATTRIB **Psychedelic** drugs are drugs such as LSD, which affect your mind and make you imagine that you are seeing strange things. *...the use of drugs in the pursuit of psychedelic experience.*
2 ADJ **Psychedelic** art has bright colours and strange patterns. *...psychedelic posters.*

psychiatric /saɪkiˈætrɪk/
ADJ ATTRIB **Psychiatric** means relating to psychiatry or involving mental illness. ...*a psychiatric hospital.* ...*a mother with psychiatric problems.*

psychiatrist /saɪkaɪətrɪst/ **psychiatrists**
NC A **psychiatrist** is a doctor who treats people suffering from mental illness. *In counselling sessions with psychiatrists patients talk about their short-term and long-term problems and worries.*

psychiatry /saɪkaɪətri/
NU **Psychiatry** is the branch of medicine concerned with the treatment of mental illness. ...*nurses in specialist areas such as psychiatry and intensive care.*

psychic /saɪkɪk/
1 ADJ Someone who is **psychic** has unusual mental powers, such as being able to read the minds of other people or to see into the future. *The boy is the seventh son of a seventh son which, according to gypsy tradition, endows him with certain psychic powers.*
2 ADJ **Psychic** means relating to the mind rather than the body; a formal use. *Most of the psychic damage to a child is done in the first five years of its life.*

psychical /saɪkɪkl/
ADJ **Psychical** means the same as **psychic**; a formal word. ...*the Society for Psychical Research.*

psycho /saɪkəʊ/ **psychos**
NC A **psycho** is the same as a **psychopath**; an informal word. ...*a raving psycho who kills just for kicks.*

psychoanalyse /saɪkəʊˈænəlaɪz/ **psychoanalyses, psychoanalysing, psychoanalysed**; spelt **psychoanalyze** in American English.
VO When a psychiatrist or psychotherapist **psychoanalyses** someone who is disturbed or has a mental problem, he or she examines or treats them using the method of psychoanalysis. *The movie sees Burton psychoanalysing Firth to cure him of his depression.*

psychoanalysis /saɪkəʊəˈnæləsɪs/
NU **Psychoanalysis** is the method of treating someone who is disturbed or has a mental problem by asking them about their feelings and their past in order to discover what may be causing their condition. ...*the sense of psychoanalysis enabling people to understand themselves better.* ...*ideas of psychoanalysis and sexual psychology.*

psychoanalyst /saɪkəʊˈænəlɪst/ **psychoanalysts**
NC A **psychoanalyst** is someone who is trained in psychoanalysis to treat people who are disturbed or have a mental problem. ...*a psychoanalyst with experience of dealing with the reactions of children to the death of a parent.* ...*the great Austrian psychoanalyst, Sigmund Freud.*

psychoanalytic /saɪkəʊænəˈlɪtɪk/
ADJ **Psychoanalytic** means relating to psychoanalysis. *This is consistent with psychoanalytic theory.*

psychoanalyze /saɪkəʊˈænəlaɪz/. See **psychoanalyse**.

psychological /saɪkəˈlɒdʒɪkl/
1 ADJ **Psychological** means concerned with people's minds and thoughts. *Are there important psychological differences between the two sexes?... The psychological abuse suffered by prisoners was just as difficult to bear... Post-traumatic stress is a psychological disturbance that afflicts thousands of Vietnam veterans.* ◆ **psychologically** ADV *She was tough, both physically and psychologically.*
2 ADJ ATTRIB **Psychological** also means relating to psychology. ...*psychological tests.* ...*the American Psychological Association.*

psychological warfare
NU **Psychological warfare** consists of attempts to make your enemy lose confidence, give up hope, or feel afraid, so that you can win. ...*an effective campaign of psychological warfare aimed at undermining Mrs Aquino... It was psychological warfare and you really felt emotionally drained most of the time.*

psychology /saɪkɒlədʒi/
1 NU **Psychology** is the scientific study of the human mind and the reasons for people's behaviour. *John Wilson calls for practical applications for the discoveries in psychology.* ...*Jung's most important*

contribution to human psychology. ◆ **psychologist** /saɪkɒlədʒɪst/ **psychologists** NC ...*child psychologists.*
2 N SING If you refer to someone's **psychology**, you mean the kind of mind that they have, which makes them think or behave in a particular way. ...*the psychology of the travelling salesman.*

psychopath /saɪkəʊpæθ/ **psychopaths**
NC A **psychopath** is someone who has a severe personality disorder which makes them do violent and anti-social things, such as attacking or killing people. *Neil Kinnock described the shooting as the work of a psychopath.* ...*a violent psychopath.*

psychopathic /saɪkəʊˈpæθɪk/
ADJ ATTRIB Someone who is **psychopathic** is a psychopath. ...*a psychopathic murderer.* ...*psychopathic acts.*

psychosis /saɪkəʊsɪs/
NU **Psychosis** is a kind of severe mental illness; a medical term. ...*acute psychosis following the birth of her first child.*

psychosomatic /saɪkəʊsəˈmætɪk/
ADJ If you describe someone's illness as **psychosomatic**, you mean that you think their symptoms are caused by feeling worried or unhappy rather than by a physical problem. *Doctors haven't always been very sympathetic, some dismissing it as purely psychosomatic... The condition she suffered from was eventually recognised as a real disease, not psychosomatic or a form of malingering.*

psychotherapy /saɪkəʊˈθerəpi/
NU **Psychotherapy** is the use of psychological methods to treat people who are mentally ill, rather than physical methods such as drugs or surgery. *Psychotherapy has helped me enormously.* ◆ **psychotherapist** /saɪkəʊˈθerəpɪst/ **psychotherapists** NC ...*a psychotherapist who has treated many suicidal young women.*

psychotic /saɪkɒtɪk/
ADJ Someone who is **psychotic** has a severe mental illness; a medical term. ...*a psychotic patient.*

PT /piːtiː/
NU **PT** is a physical education lesson given during schooltime. **PT** is an abbreviation for 'physical training'. ...*a PT instructor.*

pt, pts. The plural form can be either **pts** or **pt**.
pt is a written abbreviation for 'pint'; a unit of liquid measurement. ...*1 pt warm water.*

PTA /piːtiːˈeɪ/ **PTA's**
NC A **PTA** is a school association run jointly by the teachers and some of the pupils' parents to monitor the school's academic progress and organize its social events. **PTA** is an abbreviation for 'parent-teacher association'. *We've even joined the PTA.*

pterodactyl /ˌterəˈdæktɪl/ **pterodactyls**
NC A **pterodactyl** was a flying reptile that existed in prehistoric times. ...*the prehistoric pterodactyl, with a wing span of 9 metres.*

PTO /piːtiːˈəʊ/
PTO is a written abbreviation for 'please turn over', and is written at the bottom of a page to indicate that there is more writing on the other side.

pub /pʌb/ **pubs**
NC In Britain, a **pub** is a building where people can have drinks, especially alcoholic drinks, and talk to their friends. *They celebrated with much drinking and merry-making at a pub in central London... The future of the British pub is threatened by an increase in the number of off-licences and licensed clubs.*

pub crawl, pub crawls
NC A **pub crawl** is an activity in which someone goes from one pub to another having drinks in each one; an informal expression. *I used to go on pub crawls with him every weekend.*

puberty /pjuːbəti/
NU **Puberty** is the stage in someone's life when they start to change physically from a child to an adult. ...*a boy who has reached the age of puberty.*

pubescent /pjuːbesnt/
ADJ ATTRIB A **pubescent** girl or boy has reached the stage in their life when they are changing physically from a child to an adult; a formal word. *She played Iris, the pubescent prostitute in 'Taxi Driver'.*

pubic /pjuːbɪk/
ADJ ATTRIB **Pubic** means relating to the area just above a person's genitals. *...pubic hair.*

public /pʌblɪk/
1 N COLL You can refer to people in general as the **public**. *All members of the public are welcome... The gardens are open to the public.*
2 ADJ ATTRIB **Public** means relating to or concerning all the people in a country or community. *These fumes are a hazard to public health. ...the running of everyday public affairs.*
3 ADJ ATTRIB **Public** spending is money spent by a government to provide services for its people. *The government is reducing public spending.*
4 ADJ ATTRIB **Public** buildings and services are provided for everyone to use. *Both of these books can be obtained from the Public Library. ...public transport.*
5 ADJ ATTRIB A **public** figure or a person in **public** life is known about by many people. *...famous and highly respected public figures... Well-known people from all sections of public life gave the scheme their support.*
6 ADJ ATTRIB **Public** statements, actions, and events are made or done in such a way that everyone can see them or be aware of them. *No public announcement had yet been made. ...public meetings. ...a group pressing for a full public inquiry into the disaster.*
◆ **publicly** ADV *I am going to say what I think of him openly and publicly... The Soviet Union has admitted publicly that its state budget is in the red.*
7 If you say or do something **in public**, you say or do it when a group of other people are present. *He repeated in public what he had said in private.*
8 ADJ PRED If a fact is made **public** or you go **public** about it, it becomes known to everyone rather than being kept secret. *The cause of death was not made public... Colonel Diaz went public with allegations of serious corruption.*
9 ADJ A **public** place is one where people can go about freely and where you can easily be seen and heard. *This is a very public place. Can we talk somewhere else?*

public address system, public address systems
NC A **public address system** is an electrical system including a microphone, amplifier, and loudspeakers which is used so that someone's voice, or music, can be heard by everyone in a large area such as a building or ship. *The captain spoke to the passengers over the public address system.*

publican /pʌblɪkən/ **publicans**
NC A **publican** is a person who owns or manages a pub; a formal word. *Publicans who sell drinks to drivers they know to be over the legal limit should be liable to prosecution.*

publication /pʌblɪkeɪʃn/ **publications**
1 NU The **publication** of a book or magazine is the act of printing it and making it available. *Several of her articles have already been accepted for publication.*
2 NC A **publication** is a book, magazine, or article that has been published. *...journalists from the French publications La Croix and Le Point... Three publications have now been banned since the President declared a state of emergency last month.*

public bar, public bars
NC A **public bar** is a room in a British pub where the furniture is plain and the drinks are cheaper than in the other bars; a formal expression. *The public bar was crowded; a darts match was in progress.*

public company, public companies
NC A **public company** is a company whose shares can be bought by the general public. *The Abbey National has announced that it plans to become a public company.*

public convenience, public conveniences
NC A **public convenience** is a toilet provided in a public place for anyone to use; a formal expression. *His colleagues wondered how long it would be before he was arrested in a public convenience.*

public enterprise
NU **Public enterprise** is the ownership and management of industries and companies by the state rather than by individual people. *They are also*

looking to privatize public enterprise and encourage private investment.

public holiday, public holidays
NC A **public holiday** is a day which is a holiday for everyone in the whole of a particular country. *A traditional destination on these public holidays is the seaside resort... Monday is a public holiday in the United States.*

public house, public houses
NC A **public house** is the same as a **pub**; a formal word. *...a bill extending drinking hours at public houses. ...a disturbance at a public house.*

publicise /pʌblɪsaɪz/. See **publicize**.

publicist /pʌblɪsɪst/ **publicists**
NC A **publicist** is a person who publicizes things, especially as part of a job in advertising or journalism. *The commercials were described by the Coca-Cola publicists as combining old-world charm with the stark background of New York City.*

publicity /pʌblɪsəti/
1 NU **Publicity** is advertising, information, or actions intended to attract the public's attention to someone or something. *There was some advance publicity for the book... So far the Government has funded two major publicity campaigns, with adverts in all the media.*
2 NU When newspapers and television pay a lot of attention to something, you can say that it is receiving **publicity**. *Feminism has attracted a lot of publicity... The organisers blamed bad publicity for the low turnout.*

publicity agent, publicity agents
NC A **publicity agent** is a person whose job is to make sure that as many people as possible know about a person or thing such as an actor or show so that the actor or show is successful. *The 'Yorkshire Post' feels that NATO ought to devote itself to real problems, instead of acting as a publicity agent for Mr Gorbachev.*

publicize /pʌblɪsaɪz/ **publicizes, publicizing, publicized**; also spelt **publicise**.
VO If you **publicize** a fact or event, you make it widely known to the public. *His programme for reform was well publicised in his newspapers.*

public nuisance, public nuisances
1 N SING If someone causes a **public nuisance**, they do something that harms or disturbs members of the public and is illegal; a legal term. *...citizens who are behaving abnormally or causing a public nuisance.*
2 NC You say that a person or thing is a **public nuisance** when they annoy and bother other people. *One of the present day curses is chewing gum; it's difficult to remove and adheres to clothing, becoming a public nuisance.*

public opinion
NU **Public opinion** is the opinion or attitude of the public regarding a particular matter. *The politicians have to respond to public opinion... Public opinion polls showed Grant trailing Murray.*

public prosecutor, public prosecutors
NC A **public prosecutor** is an official who carries out criminal prosecutions on behalf of the government and people of a particular country. *The police have passed the case to the public prosecutor. ...top officials from the public prosecutor's office... The public prosecutor announced that the charges have been altered.*

public relations
1 NU **Public relations** is the part of an organization's work that is concerned with obtaining the public's approval for what it does. *Public relations is a function of management. ...running a large public relations department.*
2 N PL **Public relations** is also the state of the relationship between an organization and the public. *It's good for public relations.*

public relations officer, public relations officers
NC A **public relations officer** is a person who is employed by an organization to try to make the public approve of what the organization does. *He's a public relations officer for the firm.*

public school, public schools
1 NCorNU In Britain, a **public school** is a private school that provides secondary education. Parents

have to pay fees to send their children to a public
school. *He went to one of Britain's top public schools,
and then to Cambridge University... I didn't go to
public school, or anything like that. ...this English
public school ethos.*
2 NCorNU In the United States, Australia, and some
other countries, a **public school** is a school that is
supported financially by the government. *Students can
have the choice to go from a public school to a private
school... 89 percent of the young people in the United
States still depend on the public schools system...
Laura is seventeen, black, and Mexican and has just
graduated from public school.*

public sector
N SING The **public sector** is the part of a country's
economy which is controlled or supported financially
by the government. *...the giant institutions of the
private and public sector.*

public-spirited
ADJ Someone who is **public-spirited** tries to help the
community that they belong to. *She's a public-spirited
woman who takes part in politics.*

public works
N PL **Public works** are buildings, roads, and so on that
are built by the government for the public. *...by
providing employment in public works projects.*

publish /pʌblɪʃ/ **publishes, publishing, published**
1 VO When a company **publishes** a book or magazine,
it prints copies of it, which are sent to shops and sold.
*White's first novel, 'The Aunt's Story', was published
in 1948... The first children's newspaper to be
published in Britain in thirty years is to go on sale
later this morning.*
2 VO When a piece of writing or information is
published in a newspaper, magazine, or document, it
is included and printed there. *The Times would never
publish any letter I sent in... Full details of the report
are to be published in a few days time... An interview
with her has been published in The Times newspaper
in Britain.*
3 VO If someone **publishes** a book or an article that
they have written, they arrange to have it published.
He has published quite a lot of articles.

publisher /pʌblɪʃə/ **publishers**
NC A **publisher** is a person or company that publishes
books. *My book is being considered by a publisher,
and things look promising.*

publishing /pʌblɪʃɪŋ/
NU **Publishing** is the business of publishing books.
*...the Third World Foundation which has interests in
publishing. ...a report on Australia's book publishing
industry.*

publishing house, publishing houses
NC A **publishing house** is a company which publishes
books. *...one of the world's most famous publishing
houses, Oxford University Press. ...a printer at
Romania's largest publishing house, Casa Scinteii.*

puce /pjuːs/
ADJ Something that is **puce** in colour is dark purple.
...his puce complexion.

puck /pʌk/ **pucks**
NC The **puck** in the game of ice hockey is the small
rubber disc that is used instead of a ball. *...hockey
pucks.*

pucker /pʌkə/ **puckers, puckering, puckered**
V-ERG When a part of your face **puckers** or is
puckered, it becomes wrinkled because you are
frowning or trying not to cry. *His face puckered, the
tears leapt from his eyes... Her face was puckered by
the wind.*

puckish /pʌkɪʃ/
ADJ Someone who is **puckish** is mischievous and enjoys
playing tricks on people; an old-fashioned word. *One
glimpsed the almost puckish spirit of someone who
was never a respecter of persons.*

pud /pʊd/ **puds**
NCorNU **Pud** is the same as **pudding**; an informal
word. *What's for pud today?... After the lamb with
mint sauce came the pud.*

pudding /pʊdɪŋ/ **puddings**
NCorNU A **pudding** is a cooked sweet food made with
flour, fat, and eggs, and usually served hot as the

sweet course of a meal. *They want vanilla pudding.
...rich and fatty pastries and puddings.*

pudding basin, pudding basins
NC A **pudding basin** is a deep round bowl that is used
in the kitchen, especially for mixing or for cooking
puddings. *Stretch the fabric over a pudding basin and
keep it in position with a rubber band.*

puddle /pʌdl/ **puddles**
NC A **puddle** is a small, shallow pool of liquid on the
ground. *The road was filled with puddles from the
rain. ...a puddle of blood.*

puerile /pjʊəraɪl/
ADJ You describe behaviour as **puerile** when it is silly
and childish. *She had me doing things I thought were
puerile and degrading... His newspapers mounted a
puerile campaign against him.*

Puerto Rico /pweətəʊ riːkəʊ/
The **Commonwealth of Puerto Rico** is a territory of the
United States in the Caribbean. It was a Spanish
colony from the 16th century until 1898, when it was
occupied by the United States. Puerto Ricans were
granted United States citizenship in 1917 and it became
a Commonwealth in 1952. Puerto Rico exports
pharmaceutical products and electronic goods.
Tourism is an important industry. ♦ **Puerto Rican**
/pweətəʊ riːkən/ N, ADJ
▪ *per capita GNP:* approximately US$5,540 ▪ *religion:*
Christianity (mainly Roman Catholic) ▪ *language:*
Spanish, English ▪ *currency:* US dollar ▪ *capital:* San
Juan ▪ *population:* 3 million (1989) ▪ *size:* 8,959 square
kilometres.

puff /pʌf/ **puffs, puffing, puffed**
1 VorVO If someone **puffs** a cigarette or pipe or if they
puff at it, they smoke it. *He puffed his pipe for
several moments... She puffed on the cigarette.* ► Also
NC *She raised the cigarette to her lips, intending to
take a puff.*
2 V If you **are puffing**, you are breathing loudly and
quickly because you are out of breath after a lot of
physical effort. *We lugged the branch underneath,
panting and puffing.* ► Also NC *Her breath came in
puffs and gasps.*
3 NC A **puff** of air or smoke is a small amount of it
that is blown out from somewhere. *You can see the
puff of smoke on the other side of the valley.*

puff out PHRASAL VERB To **puff** something **out** means
to make it larger and rounder by filling it with air.
*Their chests were puffed out like angry swans... They
puffed out their cheeks.*

puff up PHRASAL VERB If part of your body **puffs up** as
the result of an injury or allergy, it becomes swollen.
Small areas on their arms or legs would puff up. ● See
also **puffed.**

puffball /pʌfbɔːl/ **puffballs**
1 NC A **puffball** is a large round fungus which bursts
to release a cloud of spores when it is ripe. *The larger
edible fungi can do no harm; puffballs, blewitts and
parasol mushrooms.*
2 ADJ ATTRIB A **puffball** skirt is short and flared, and is
often decorated with frills. *She developed her 'look'—
taffeta puffball skirts and neat grosgrain jackets.*

puffed /pʌft/
1 ADJ PRED If a part of your body is **puffed** or **puffed
up**, it is swollen because of an injury. *...his scarred,
puffed face... Her left eye is all puffed up.*
2 ADJ PRED If you are **puffed** or **puffed out**, you are
breathing with difficulty because you have been using
a lot of energy; an informal use. *By the time I got to
the top I was pretty well puffed out.*

puffed up
ADJ Someone who is **puffed up** is very proud of
themselves because they think that they are very
important. *I was expecting that he would return all
puffed up with himself... We had to listen to puffed-up
males telling their stories of bravery.*

puffin /pʌfɪn/ **puffins**
NC A **puffin** is a black and white bird with a large,
brightly-coloured beak that nests near the sea. *The
puffin is one of Britain's favourite sea birds... Other
species are also at risk, including kittiwakes, puffins,
and arctic skuas.*

puff pastry

NU **Puff pastry** is a type of pastry which is very light, airy, and flaky. *...puff pastry filled with cream.*

puffy /pʌfi/

ADJ Something that is **puffy** has a round, swollen appearance. *One eye was a slit in his puffy cheek.*

pug /pʌg/ **pugs**

NC A **pug** is a small, fat dog with short hair and a flat nose. *...flat-faced breeds like the Pekinese and Pugs.*

pugnacious /pʌgneɪʃəs/

ADJ Someone who is **pugnacious** is always ready to quarrel or start a fight; a formal word. *I got punched in the face by a pugnacious apprentice.*

puke /pjuːk/ **pukes, puking, puked**

V When someone **pukes**, they vomit; an informal word. *The baby puked a couple more times.*

pull /pʊl/ **pulls, pulling, pulled**

1 VOorV When you **pull** something, you hold it firmly and move it towards you. *She pulled Paul's hair so hard that he yelled... I shut my eyes when I pulled the trigger... He hoisted the rope over the branch and pulled with all his strength.*
2 VO When a vehicle, animal, or person **pulls** a cart or piece of machinery, they are attached to it or hold it, so that it moves along behind them when they move forward. *I would have thought a heavy horse could have pulled a bigger dung spreader than that.*
3 VOA If you **pull** a part of your body in a particular direction, you move it forcefully in that direction. *'Let go of me,' she said, and pulled her arm savagely out of his grasp.*
4 V-REFL A If you **pull** yourself out of a place, you hold onto something and use effort to move your body out of the place. *Ralph pulled himself out of the water.*
5 VO When you **pull** a curtain or blind, you move it across a window in order to cover or uncover it. *She closed the window and pulled the blind.*
6 VOA If you **pull** something apart or **pull** it to pieces, you break it or take it apart without much care. *If you pull apart one of the calculators, you won't get it back together again... Try and stop the cat pulling the Christmas tree to bits.*
7 VO To **pull** people means to attract their support or interest; an informal use. *He was interested in the number of voters she would pull.*
8 VO If you **pull** a muscle, you injure it by stretching it too much or too suddenly. *The nineteen year-old Adams pulled a back muscle during the warm-up period.*
9 NC A **pull** is a strong physical force which is difficult to resist and which causes things to move in a particular direction. *...the earth's gravitational pull. ...the pull of the sun and the moon. ...the closer to the centre of the Earth, the stronger the pull.*
10 NC Something's **pull** is its quality of being influential or attractive. *Armenia, by contrast, has no equivalent pull. ...the pull of the prize money. ...the pull of the family.*

pull ahead PHRASAL VERB 1 If you **pull ahead** of something that is travelling in front of you, you manage to pass them. *Haakinen pulled ahead as Brabham remained stationary, trying to select first gear.* 2 If you **pull ahead** in a race or competition, you start to do better than your opponents. *Senator Pete Wilson, a Republican, has pulled ahead of the former mayor of San Francisco.*

pull apart PHRASAL VERB If you **pull** people or animals **apart** when they are fighting, you separate them using force. *I rushed in and tried to pull the dogs apart.*

pull at PHRASAL VERB If you **pull at** something, you hold it and move it towards you and then let it go again. *'Come home now, Jim,' she said, pulling at his sleeve.*

pull away PHRASAL VERB 1 When a vehicle **pulls away**, it starts moving forward. *As the lights changed, I pulled away.* 2 If you **pull away** from someone who is holding you, you suddenly move away from them. *He tried to kiss her, but she pulled away fiercely.*

pull back PHRASAL VERB When an army **pulls back** from an area or country, they withdraw from it. *Both sides are preparing to pull back their forces. ...pulling back its troops, agents and armed police from the no-go zone.*

pull down PHRASAL VERB When a building **is pulled down**, it is deliberately destroyed, often in order to build a new one. *Why did they pull those houses down?*

pull in PHRASAL VERB When a vehicle **pulls in** somewhere, it stops there. *The London train pulled in to the station.*

pull off PHRASAL VERB 1 When you **pull off** your clothes, you take them off quickly. *He pulled off his shirt.* 2 If someone has succeeded in doing something very difficult, you can say that they **have pulled** it **off**; an informal expression. *Mr Heath has pulled off a diplomatic coup... He has already taken massive political risks, but once again, he seems to have pulled it off.*

pull on PHRASAL VERB When you **pull on** your clothes, you put them on quickly. *He started to pull on his shorts.*

pull out PHRASAL VERB 1 When a vehicle **pulls out** from a place, it moves out of the place. *The train pulled out of the station.* 2 If you **pull out** of an activity or agreement, you decide not to continue it. *You pay a 10% deposit which you lose if you pull out before completion... He pulled his party out of the coalition.* 3 If an army **pulls out** of a place, it leaves it. *Troops had begun to pull out of the area... The Prime Minister intended to pull them out soon.*

pull over PHRASAL VERB When a vehicle **pulls over**, it moves closer to the side of the road. *Pull over, Oliver. Stop the car.*

pull through PHRASAL VERB If you are seriously ill and you **pull through** or if someone **pulls** you **through**, you recover. *I think she'll pull through... I can't thank the nurses enough for pulling her through.*

pull together PHRASAL VERB 1 If people **pull together**, they co-operate with each other. *We all pulled together during the war.* 2 If someone tells you to **pull** yourself **together** when you are upset or angry, they are telling you to control your feelings. *But Becker pulled himself together and took the fourth set to win in three hours.*

pull up PHRASAL VERB 1 When a vehicle **pulls up**, it slows down and stops. *The rain stopped as we pulled up at the hotel.* 2 If you **pull up** a chair, you move it closer to something or someone. *I pulled up a chair and sat down to watch the news.*

pull-back, pull-backs

NC A **pull-back** is a withdrawal by an army from a particular area or country. *The purpose of the talks was to arrange a ceasefire and pull-back by both armies. ...a substantial pull-back from the front lines. ...troop withdrawals and pull-backs.*

pullet /pʊlɪt/ **pullets**

NC A **pullet** is a hen that is less than one year old. *The women clucked like starved pullets.*

pulley /pʊli/ **pulleys**

NC A **pulley** is a device used for lifting or lowering heavy weights. It consists of a rope stretched over the rim of a wheel which is attached at one end to the weight. You pull or gradually release the other end of the rope to lift or lower the weight. *...using pedals connected via levers and pulleys to ropes attached to the wings. ...people walking up and down a ladder with a load on their shoulders, or using pulleys.*

pull-in, pull-ins

NC A **pull-in** is a place beside a road where there is a cafe or other services where you can stop and park for a while. *We followed the dirt road past some trees to a camper's pull-in.*

Pullman /pʊlmən/ **Pullmans**

NC A **Pullman** is a type of train or a carriage on this type of train which is extremely comfortable and luxurious. *He plays a black Pullman porter with five children.*

pull-out, pull-outs

1 NC+SUPP The **pull-out** of a group of people such as an army is their departure from the area or country that they are in. *The wholesale pull-out of all civilian staff has begun in earnest. ...the regional peace*

agreement governing the Cuban pull-out. ...a pull-out of all foreign forces.
2 NC A **pull-out** is a section of a magazine, usually in the middle, which you can remove easily and keep. *Peter Watson's new book, 'Landscape of Lies', comes complete with a coloured pull-out... On Cup Final day, the popular papers carry pull-out sections with profiles of the main players.*

pullover /pʊləʊvə/ **pullovers**
NC A **pullover** is a woollen piece of clothing that covers the upper part of your body and your arms. *He was wearing a blue anorak, a pullover and casual trousers.*

pulmonary /pʌlmənəᵒri/
ADJ ATTRIB **Pulmonary** means relating to your lungs; a medical term. *...pulmonary tuberculosis.*

pulp /pʌlp/
NUorN SING If something is turned into **pulp**, it is crushed or beaten until it is soft, smooth, and moist. *We squashed the berries into a pulp. ...wood pulp.*

pulpit /pʊlpɪt/ **pulpits**
NC A **pulpit** is a small raised platform in a church with a rail or barrier around it, where a member of the clergy stands to preach. *A young priest appealed from the pulpit for the cathedral to be returned to the church... The Reverend Frank Chikane read from the pulpit.*

pulpy /pʌlpi/
ADJ Something that is **pulpy** is soft, smooth, and wet, often because it has been crushed or beaten. *Her lips felt pulpy and tender.*

pulsate /pʌlseɪt/ **pulsates, pulsating, pulsated**
V If something **pulsates**, it moves in and out or shakes with strong, regular movements. *The creature has no heart, only a number of pulsating arteries.*

pulse /pʌls/ **pulses, pulsing, pulsed**
1 NC Your **pulse** is the regular beat you can feel when you touch particular parts of your body such as your wrist or neck, which is caused by blood being pumped through your body by your heart. *Her pulse started to race.* ● When a doctor or nurse takes your **pulse**, they finds out how often your heart beats by feeling the pulse in your wrist. *He moves quickly from patient to patient, taking a pulse or a temperature and scribbling notes on a card.*
2 NC Some seeds which can be cooked and eaten are called **pulses**, for example the seeds of peas, beans, and lentils. *...a variety of pulses and grains. ...carbohydrates such as rice, potatoes, pulses and bread.*
3 V If something **pulses**, it moves or shakes with strong, regular movements. *...a soft rhythmic pulsing sound.*

pulverize /pʌlvəraɪz/ **pulverizes, pulverizing, pulverized**; also spelt **pulverise**.
VO To **pulverize** something means to crush it into a powder. *The processes involved pulverising the nuts.*

puma /pjuːmə/ **pumas**
NC A **puma** is a large wild animal that is a member of the cat family. **Pumas** have brownish-grey fur and live in mountain regions of North and South America. *Of course, big cats, such as lynxes, panthers and pumas, are native to some countries.*

pumice /pʌmɪs/
NU **Pumice** or **pumice stone** is a kind of grey stone that is very light in weight. You can use it to clean surfaces, or you can rub it on your skin in order to soften it. *He used pumice stone to smooth the maplewood.*

pummel /pʌml/ **pummels, pummelling, pummelled**; spelt **pummeling, pummeled** in American English.
VO If you **pummel** someone or something, you hit them repeatedly with your fists. *He could only lean helplessly against the ropes as Lalonde pummelled him mercilessly.*

pump /pʌmp/ **pumps, pumping, pumped**
1 NC A **pump** is a machine or device used to force a liquid or gas to flow in a particular direction. *...a continuous infusion pump like that used for insulin by some diabetics.*
2 NC A **pump** is also a device for bringing water to the surface from below the ground. *We scrubbed*

ourselves under the pump.
3 NC A **pump** is also a device that you use to force air into something, especially into the tyre of a vehicle. *...a bicycle pump.*
4 NC A petrol **pump** is a machine with a hose attached to it from which you can fill a car with petrol. *...faulty fuel pumps... I'm not talking about the crude oil price; I'm talking strictly about the retail price at the pump.*
5 NC **Pumps** are canvas shoes with flat rubber soles which people wear for sports and leisure. *...a ten-year old in bright red patent pumps.*
6 VOA To **pump** a liquid or gas in a particular direction means to force it to flow in that direction, using a pump. *We can use the electricity to pump water back into a dam or a reservoir.*
7 VO To **pump** water, oil, or gas means to get a supply of it from below the ground, using a pump. *John went to a cast-iron pump and started pumping water to drink.*
8 VO+into If you **pump** money or energy into something, you put a lot of money or energy into it; an informal use. *Most governments have pumped all available funds into large-scale modern technological projects.*
9 VO If you **pump** someone about something, you keep asking them questions in order to get information; an informal use. *I pumped him discreetly about his past.*
pump out PHRASAL VERB 1 To **pump** a liquid or gas **out** means to remove it from a place by forcing it to flow in a particular direction, using a pump. *...steam engines, developed originally to pump water out of the mines.* 2 If a doctor **pumps out** someone's stomach, he or she removes the contents of the stomach using a pump, because the person has swallowed poison or taken an overdose of drugs. *I became conscious again as they pumped out my stomach.* 3 To **pump** things **out** means to produce or supply them continually in large amounts; an informal use. *...a radio station pumping out pop music.*
pump up PHRASAL VERB If you **pump up** something such as a tyre, you fill it with air, using a pump. *You can pump up the tyre using a foot pump.*

pumpkin /pʌmpkɪn/ **pumpkins**
NCorNU A **pumpkin** is a large, round, orange vegetable with a thick skin. *Seeds of pumpkin have a lot of protein... We wanted to start growing eggplants, zucchinis and pumpkins... He had just eaten a bowl of pumpkin soup.*

pun /pʌn/ **puns**
NC A **pun** is a clever and amusing use of words which have more than one meaning, or which have the same sound, so that what you say has two different meanings. *I think agriculture remains, if you'll pardon the pun, a growth industry.*

punch /pʌntʃ/ **punches, punching, punched**
1 VO If you **punch** someone, you hit them hard with your fist. *Boylan punched him hard on the nose... I was punched in the stomach... It was she who had begun the violence, by repeatedly punching him.* ▶ Also NC *...aiming a slow punch at my jaw.*
2 VO If you **punch** something such as the buttons on a computer or typewriter keyboard, you press them quite hard. If you **punch** information into a computer, you press the keys on the keyboard in order to enter the information into the computer. *A portly staff sergeant sits punching an adding machine... All you have to do is punch in a daily access code to use it.*
3 NC A **punch** is a tool used for making holes in something. *He made a small hole in the belt with a leather punch.*
4 VO If you **punch** holes in something, you make holes in it by pushing or pressing it with something sharp. *Edward was punching holes in a can... I shortened the strap and punched a new hole.*
5 N MASS **Punch** is a drink usually made from wine or spirits mixed with sugar, fruit, and spices. *...hot rum punch.*
6 NU If you say that something has **punch**, you mean that it has a special force or power that makes it effective and interesting. *The movie has no momentum, and it has no punch, you can predict it.*

● **Punch** is used in these phrases. ● If you **throw a punch**, you try to hit someone hard with your fist. *Fighting is not just throwing punches, there's brain work involved too... He started throwing karate punches into thin air.* ● If you do not **pull punches** when you are criticizing someone, you say exactly what you think, without softening your criticism in any way. *They don't pull any punches, often providing graphic photographs of conditions to the world's press... He denies that the campaign is pulling its punches now.*

Punch and Judy show /pʌntʃ ən dʒuːdi ʃəʊ/ **Punch and Judy shows**
NC A **Punch and Judy show** is a comic puppet show for children, in which Punch, a small, hook-nosed puppet, fights with his wife Judy. These shows are usually performed in a small booth at fairs or at the seaside. *The actors pretend to be glove puppets, popping up on an enlarged Punch and Judy stage.*

punchbag /pʌntʃbæg/ **punchbags**
NC A **punchbag** is a heavy leather bag, stuffed with horsehair or other material and hanging on a rope, which is punched hard by boxers and other sportsmen for training and exercise. *The front of the room is taken up by a single boxing ring; in the middle of the room are the punchbags.*

punchball /pʌntʃbɔːl/ **punchballs**
NC A **punchball** is a large leather ball fixed on a spring, which is punched rapidly by boxers and other sportsmen for training and exercise.

punchbowl /pʌntʃbəʊl/ **punchbowls**
NC A **punchbowl** is a large bowl in which drinks, especially punch, are mixed and served.

punch-drunk
1 ADJ In sport, boxers who are **punch-drunk** show signs of brain damage, such as unsteadiness and the inability to think clearly because they have suffered many blows to the head. *...tangles in the brain-nerves similar to those in the brains of punch-drunk boxers.*
2 ADJ You can also use **punch-drunk** to refer to someone who is dazed and confused, for example because they have been working too hard or doing something very intensely, so that they feel their brain can no longer absorb anything. *They're delighting in having got me punch-drunk with talk.*

punching bag, punching bags
NC A **punching bag** is the same as a **punchbag**; used in American English.

punch-line, punch-lines
NC The **punch-line** of a joke or funny story is its last sentence or phrase, which gives it its humour. *The feature could end here, or what about closing music or some sort of punch-line?*

punch-up, punch-ups
NC A **punch-up** is a fight in which people hit each other; an informal word. *'Looks as though you've been in a real punch-up,' says the barmaid.*

punchy /pʌntʃi/ **punchier, punchiest**
ADJ If you describe a piece of writing as **punchy**, you mean that it is effective and forceful, because points are made clearly, briefly, and decisively. *...a punchy little leaflet.*

punctilious /pʌŋktɪliəs/
ADJ You say that someone is **punctilious** when they are very careful to behave correctly; a formal word. *You are the most punctilious person I ever met... In public he was punctilious about such things.* ◆ **punctiliously** ADV *He thanked her punctiliously.*

punctual /pʌŋktʃuəl/
ADJ PRED If you are **punctual**, you arrive or do something at the arranged time. *I expect my guests to be punctual for breakfast.* ◆ **punctually** ADV *Mary arrived punctually at ten o'clock.*

punctuate /pʌŋktʃueɪt/ **punctuates, punctuating, punctuated**
VO If an activity is **punctuated** by something, it is regularly interrupted by it. *The old lady's words were punctuated by noise from outside... The afternoon was quiet, after a morning punctuated with regular volleys of gunfire.*

punctuation /pʌŋktʃueɪʃn/
NU **Punctuation** is the system of marks such as full

stops, commas, and question marks that you use in writing to divide words into sentences and clauses. *...punctuation and spelling mistakes.*

punctuation mark, punctuation marks
NC A **punctuation mark** is a sign such as a full stop, comma, or question mark. *Put in a punctuation mark.*

puncture /pʌŋktʃə/ **punctures, puncturing, punctured**
1 NC A **puncture** is a small hole in a car or bicycle tyre that has been made by a sharp object. *One of the wheels has a puncture.*
2 VO To **puncture** something means to make a small hole in it. *...the use of needles to puncture the skin... The rioters threw nails onto the street to puncture the tyres of cars.*

pundit /pʌndɪt/ **pundits**
NC A **pundit** is a person who knows a lot about a subject and is asked to give information or opinions about it. *This is the time when political pundits try to predict what is likely to happen... It was one of those events which confounds the pundits as well as the politicians.*

pungency /pʌndʒənsi/
1 NU If something has **pungency**, it has a strong, sharp smell or taste. *...the pungency of burning peat.*
2 NU If speech or writing has **pungency**, it uses words and ideas that have a direct, powerful effect and often cleverly criticize something; a formal use. *She writes with relentless pungency.*

pungent /pʌndʒənt/
1 ADJ Something that is **pungent** has a strong, unpleasant smell or taste. *The pungent, choking smell of sulphur filled the air.*
2 ADJ **Pungent** speech or writing is direct, powerful, and often critical; a formal use. *...producing often pungent analyses of what it calls the predicament of mankind.*

punish /pʌnɪʃ/ **punishes, punishing, punished**
1 VO To **punish** someone means to make them suffer in some way because they have done something wrong. *The defence ministry has ordered an inquiry, and it says some soldiers could be punished... They discovered his crime and punished him for it... He was caught and punished for using cocaine three times... She will go down in history as the Prime Minister who rewarded the rich and punished the poor.*
2 VO To **punish** a crime means to fine, imprison or, in some countries, execute anyone who commits that crime. *They punished adultery with death... Criticism of socialism was punished, sometimes with school expulsion.*

punishable /pʌnɪʃəbl/
ADJ If a crime is **punishable** in a particular way, anyone who commits it can be punished in that way. *Possession of drugs is punishable by prison... They will be in violation of the law, which is punishable as a felony.*

punishing /pʌnɪʃɪŋ/
ADJ ATTRIB A **punishing** experience makes you very weak or helpless. *The purpose was to inflict a punishing defeat on the enemy.*

punishment /pʌnɪʃmənt/ **punishments**
1 NU **Punishment** is the act of punishing someone. *Punishment and prison sentences cannot reform the hardened criminal.*
2 NC A **punishment** is a particular way of punishing someone. *He maintained that the only true punishment for murder was death.*
3 NU **Punishment** is also severe physical treatment of any kind. *The crew were in no condition to withstand any further punishment from the sea.*
4 See also **capital punishment, corporal punishment**.

punitive /pjuːnətɪv/
ADJ **Punitive** actions are intended to punish people; a formal word. *We will take no punitive action against those who have broken the rules.*

punk /pʌŋk/ **punks**
1 ADJ ATTRIB **Punk** is used to describe a style of music, fashion, art, and so on that was popular in the late 1970s, and which is typically bold, aggressive, and expresses a protest against conventional ideas and ways of behaving. *For a decade, X were the prominent punk band... Coe aligned himself with the*

punk movement which rejected English society's class consciousness... The origin of the punk hairdos you see around is actually Africa. ...punk rockers.
2 NC A **punk** is a young person who behaves in an unruly, aggressive, or anti-social manner; used in American English. *He had a punk kid working there who had been tagged for stealing stamps... He's fast getting a reputation for being a punk, but there's time for him to change.*

punnet /pʌnɪt/ **punnets**
NC A **punnet** is a small, light, square box in which soft fruits such as strawberries or raspberries are often sold. *...punnets of strawberries.*

punt, punts, punting, punted; pronounced /pʌnt/ for the meanings in paragraphs 1 and 2, and /pʊnt/ for the meaning in paragraph 3.
1 NC A **punt** is a long boat with a flat bottom. You move the boat along by standing at one end and pushing a long pole down against the bottom of the river. *A young man, an undergraduate, was poling the punt upstream.*
2 VO When a ball is **punted** in games such as football or rugby, it is kicked a long way. *The goal was the result of a long ball punted astutely upfield by Thorn.*
▶ Also NC *Taylor unleashed a long punt which flew at least 50 yards.*
3 NC A **punt** is a unit of money used in the Irish Republic. *...the strength of the pound against the weak punt.*

punter /pʌntə/ **punters**; an informal word.
1 NC A **punter** is a person who bets money, especially on horse races. *...an unnamed punter must be ecstatic; he won £212,000.*
2 NC People sometimes refer to their customers or clients as the **punters**. *The punters buy tickets from places like record shops.*

puny /pjuːni/
ADJ **Puny** means very small or weak. *...a puny old man. ...her puny efforts.*

pup /pʌp/ **pups**
NC A **pup** is a young dog. Some other young animals are also called **pups**. *...a cocker spaniel pup. ...a seal pup.*

pupa /pjuːpə/ **pupae** /pjuːpiː/
NC A **pupa** is an insect that is in the stage of development between a larva and a fully grown adult. It has a protective covering and does not move; a technical term in biology. *...a butterfly pupa.*

pupil /pjuːpl/ **pupils**
1 NC The **pupils** of a school are the children who go to it. *...a school with more than 1300 pupils.*
2 NC+POSS A **pupil** of a painter, musician, or other expert is someone who studies with them to learn their skills. *The Library attracted academics and intellectuals from all over the Mediterranean, including several pupils of Aristotle... As they became acquainted, Lenin realised the potential of his faithful pupil.*
3 NC The **pupils** of your eyes are the small, round, black centres of them. *...the contraction of the pupil that occurs with the use of opiates. ...a study which had shown that these eyedrops could dilate the pupils of drug addicts.*

puppet /pʌpɪt/ **puppets**
1 NC A **puppet** is a doll that you can move, either by pulling strings which are attached to it, or by putting your hand inside its body and moving your fingers. *...the Cairo Puppet Theatre... The play's about a puppet who comes to life.*
2 NC You can refer to people or countries as **puppets** when their actions are controlled by more powerful people or countries, even though they appear to be independent. *...puppet governments... They accuse him of being a puppet of the South African government... A legitimate government must be restored to replace the puppet regime.*

puppeteer /pʌpɪtɪə/ **puppeteers**
NC A **puppeteer** is a person who gives shows using puppets. *A crèche has been laid on for young children and entertainment provided by a puppeteer.*

puppy /pʌpi/ **puppies**
NC A **puppy** is a young dog. *...the deaths of seventy-nine Beagle puppies. ...a kitten, a young rabbit, a duckling and a puppy.*

puppy fat
NU **Puppy fat** is fat that some children have on their bodies when they are young but that disappears when they grow older and taller. *She had a lot of puppy fat then.*

puppy love
NU **Puppy love** is the romantic and usually not very lasting love that an adolescent feels for someone. *It's only puppy love.*

purchase /pɜːtʃəs/ **purchases, purchasing, purchased**; a formal word.
1 VO When you **purchase** something, you buy it. *He sold the house he had purchased only two years before.*
2 NU **Purchase** is the act of buying something. *We need to know the exact day of purchase.*
3 NC A **purchase** is something that you buy. *Among his purchases were several books.*

purchaser /pɜːtʃəsə/ **purchasers**
NC A **purchaser** is a person who buys something; a formal word. *Four bids have been received from prospective purchasers... The present property laws place most of the burden on the purchaser.*

purchase tax
NU **Purchase tax** is a tax that you pay when you buy something which is included in the price. *The programme includes progressive price increases, a new purchase tax and no more wage increases this year.*

purchasing power
1 NU The **purchasing power** of an individual or a community is the amount of money that they have available in order to buy goods. *The value of the country's currency declined along with the purchasing power of its inhabitants... A rise in incomes will create increased purchasing power.*
2 NU+POSS The **purchasing power** of a currency is its value in terms of how much can be bought with it at any one time. *...the purchasing power of the pound.*

purdah /pɜːdə/
NU **Purdah** is a custom practised in some Muslim and Hindu societies, in which women keep apart from male strangers, for example by staying in a special part of a house or by covering their faces and the whole of their bodies to avoid being seen. *Kabul women admit privately that they fear they will be forced back into the tyranny of purdah... I said that I did not agree with purdah... He kept her in purdah.*

pure /pjuə, pjɔː/ **purer, purest**
1 ADJ ATTRIB **Pure** means not mixed with anything else or not spoiled by anything. *...a dress of pure silk. ...pure white.* ◆ **purity** /pjuərəti/ NU *...their claim to ideological purity.*
2 ADJ Something that is **pure** is clean, healthy, and does not contain any harmful substances. *...the pure, dry desert air.* ◆ **purity** NU *...the importance of purity in the water supply.*
3 ADJ People who are **pure** have not done anything bad or sinful; a literary use. *...pure in mind and body.* ◆ **purity** NU *...the forces of virtue and purity.*
4 ADJ A **pure** sound is clear and pleasant to hear. *The singer's voice remained pure and clear throughout the evening.*
5 ADJ ATTRIB **Pure** science or research is concerned only with theory and not with how this theory can be used in practical ways. *...pure maths. ...chemistry, both pure and applied.*
6 ADJ ATTRIB **Pure** also means complete and total. *I came on the idea by pure chance. ...pure bliss.*

puree /pjuəreɪ/ **purees, pureeing, pureed**
1 N MASS A **puree** is food which has been mashed or blended so that it forms a thick, smooth sauce. *An electric blender rapidly makes soups, purees, and puddings. ...tomato puree.*
2 VO If you **puree** food, you make it into a puree. *I use a blender to puree cooked meats, vegetables, and fruits.*

purely /pjuəli/
1 ADV **Purely** means involving only one feature or characteristic and not including anything else.

...something purely practical like mending a washing machine... There's nothing personal in this. Purely a routine check.
2 You use **purely and simply** to emphasize that a particular thing is the only thing involved. *It is done through ignorance purely and simply.*

purgative /pɜːgətɪv/ **purgatives**
NC A **purgative** is a medicine that causes you to defecate and so to get rid of unwanted substances from your body; an old-fashioned word. *Purgatives and internal cleansers have been used for centuries.*

purgatory /pɜːgətri/
1 N PROP **Purgatory** is the place where Roman Catholics believe the spirits of dead people are sent to suffer for their sins before they can go to heaven. *Do you believe in purgatory?*
2 NU You can refer to a very unpleasant experience as **purgatory**. *It was a sort of purgatory that had to be endured. ...four or five years of economic purgatory, strikes, and poor wages.*

purge /pɜːdʒ/ **purges, purging, purged**
1 VO To **purge** an organization of its unacceptable members means to remove them from it. You can also talk about **purging** people from an organization. *...to purge the government of Latimer's supporters... They had done their best to purge extremists from the party.* ▸ Also NC *They discovered that there were infiltrators inside the party. A purge began... When the purges at Central TV began this year, the first targets were not the established figures.*
2 VOorV-REFL When you **purge** something of undesirable things, you get rid of them. *I tried desperately to purge myself of these dangerous desires... They brought pails and pumps to purge the dirty water.*

purify /pjʊərɪfaɪ/ **purifies, purifying, purified**
VO If you **purify** a substance, you make it pure by removing any harmful, dirty, or inferior substances from it. *...specially purified water.*

purist /pjʊərɪst/ **purists**
NC A **purist** is a person who believes in absolute correctness. *Musical purists were outraged at this innovation.*

puritan /pjʊərɪtən/ **puritans**
NC You refer to someone as a **puritan** when they live according to strict moral or religious principles, especially by avoiding physical pleasures. *...an austere old puritan.* ▸ Also ADJ *...puritan morality.*

puritanical /pjʊərɪtænɪkl/
ADJ Someone who is **puritanical** behaves according to strict moral or religious principles, especially by avoiding physical pleasures. *...a puritanical distaste for alcohol.*

puritanism /pjʊərɪtənɪzəm/
NU **Puritanism** is behaviour or beliefs that are based on strict moral or religious principles, especially the principle that people should avoid physical pleasures. *I had felt that puritanism and sexual repression were essentially political... They have cultivated an image of working class puritanism.*

purl /pɜːl/ **purls, purling, purled**
1 NUorN+N **Purl** is a stitch in knitting in which you put the needle into the back rather than the front of the stitch on the other needle. *...a row of purl. ...a purl jumper.*
2 VO When you **purl** a stitch in knitting, you make it using a purl stitch. *...knit one, purl one.*

purlieus /pɜːljuːz/
N PL The **purlieus** of a place are the areas immediately surrounding it; a literary word. *...exploring the overgrown purlieus of the temple.*

purloin /pɜːlɔɪn/ **purloins, purloining, purloined**
VO If you **purloin** something, you steal it or borrow it without asking permission; a formal word, often used humorously. *I purloined his discarded newspaper after he left the room.*

purple /pɜːpl/
ADJ Something that is **purple** in colour is reddish-blue. *...a most sumptuous gown of purple velvet... They used water cannon to spray the demonstrators with purple dye.*

purple heart, purple hearts
1 NC The **Purple Heart** is a medal that is given to members of US Armed Forces who have been wounded during battle. *Heatherman received a Purple Heart for his service in Vietnam.*
2 NC **Purple hearts** are small, purple coloured, heart shaped pills containing amphetamine. *We'd trade pills like sweets—'I'll give you six greenies for eight purple hearts'.*

purplish /pɜːpəlɪʃ/
ADJ Something that is **purplish** is slightly purple. *What's that purplish spot on your neck?*

purport /pəpɔːt/ **purports, purporting, purported**
V+to-INF If something **purports** to do or be a particular thing, it is claimed to do or be that thing; a formal word. *...advertisements for cosmetics purporting to delay the development of wrinkles.*

purpose /pɜːpəs/ **purposes**
1 NC The **purpose** of something is the reason for which it is made or done. *The purpose of the meeting was to discuss the committee's report... The buildings are now used as a prison, but they weren't built for that purpose.*
2 NC Your **purpose** is the thing that you want to achieve. *Her only purpose in life was to get rich.*
3 NU **Purpose** is the feeling of having a definite aim and of being determined to achieve it. *She has given them a sense of purpose.*
● **Purpose** is used in these phrases. ● If you do something **on purpose**, you do it deliberately. *He had gone there on purpose, to see what happened.* ● You use the phrase **for all practical purposes** to suggest that a situation is not exactly as you describe it but the effect is the same as if it were. *The rest are now, for all practical purposes, useless.* ● If you say that an action was done to **no purpose**, you mean that it achieved nothing. If you say that it was done to **good purpose**, you mean that it achieved something. *The ultimate tragedy for the bereaved is that it is all to no purpose... He used his past experience to good purpose.* ● **to all intents and purposes**: see **intent**.

purpose-built
ADJ Something that has been **purpose-built** has been specially designed and built for a particular use. *...a purpose-built nursery school.*

purposeful /pɜːpəsfl/
ADJ If someone is **purposeful**, they show that they have a definite aim and a strong desire to achieve it. *They were striving to bring about change in a purposeful way.* ◆ **purposefully** ADV *She began walking slowly but purposefully towards the bridge.*

purposeless /pɜːpəsləs/
ADJ If an action is **purposeless**, it does not seem to have a sensible purpose. *...casual, unprovoked and purposeless violence.*

purposely /pɜːpəsli/
ADV If you do something **purposely**, you do it deliberately. *She purposely sat in the outside seat.*

purr /pɜː/ **purrs, purring, purred**
1 V When a cat **purrs**, it makes a low vibrating sound in its throat. *Anne stroked Perkins who was now purring contentedly.*
2 V When an engine or machine **purrs**, it makes a quiet, continuous, vibrating sound. *I heard cars purr in the distance... VDU machines purr in the background as reporters put the finishing touches to their stories.* ▸ Also N SING *I could hear the gentle purr of a movie projector.*

purse /pɜːs/ **purses, pursing, pursed**
1 NC A **purse** is a very small bag that people, especially women, keep their money in. *She began hunting in her purse for some coins.*
2 NC A **purse** is also the same as a **handbag**; used in American English. *She strolled along, swinging her old white purse.*
3 VO If you **purse** your lips, you move them into a small, rounded shape. *He pursed his lips in distaste.*

purser /pɜːsə/ **pursers**
1 NC The **purser** on a ship is an officer who deals with the accounts and official papers. *The news bulletins were typed up by the purser and delivered to the first-class smoking room.*

2 NC On a passenger ship or aeroplane, the **purser** is also responsible for the welfare of the passengers. *The chief purser came through the aircraft and told the passengers something was going to happen.*

purse strings

N PL If you say that someone holds or controls the **purse strings**, you mean that they control the way money is spent for example in a particular family, group, or country. *Implementing foreign policy requires money, and Congress holds the purse strings... The vastly important job of controlling Britain's purse strings belongs to the Chancellor of the Exchequer... Saudi Arabia has begun to tighten its purse strings, too.*

pursuance /pəsjuːəns/

If you do something **in pursuance of** a particular activity, you do it as part of that activity; a formal expression. *It was all done in pursuance of his duties.*

pursue /pəsjuː/ **pursues, pursuing, pursued**; a formal word.

1 VO If you **pursue** an activity, interest, or plan, you do it or carry it out. *Lyttleton pursued a policy of peace and order... His wealth enabled him to pursue his passionate interest in art.*

2 VO If you **pursue** a particular aim or result, you make efforts to achieve it, often over a long period of time. *Economic growth must not be pursued at the expense of environmental pollution.*

3 VO If you **pursue** a particular topic, you try to find out more about it. *I don't want to pursue that question now.*

4 VO If you **pursue** someone or something, you follow them, usually in order to catch them. *The police pursued the wrong car.*

pursuer /pəsjuːə/ **pursuers**

NC Your **pursuers** are people who are chasing or searching for you; a formal word. *He managed to give his pursuers the slip.*

pursuit /pəsjuːt/ **pursuits**; a formal word.

1 NU+*of* Your **pursuit** of something that you want consists of your attempts at achieving it. *...the pursuit of happiness... How far should any of us go in pursuit of what we want?*

2 NU+*of* The **pursuit** of an activity, interest, or plan consists of all the things that you do when you are carrying it out. *...some of the risks inherent in the pursuit of these policies.*

3 NU The **pursuit** of someone or something is the act of chasing them. *...a gamekeeper in pursuit of a poacher.* ● If you are **in hot pursuit**, you are chasing after someone with great determination. *He started running—with all the others in hot pursuit.*

4 NC **Pursuits** are activities, especially ones that you do for enjoyment. *Games like chess are rather intellectual pursuits.*

purvey /pəveɪ/ **purveys, purveying, purveyed**; a formal word.

1 VO If you **purvey** something such as information, you tell it to people. *...the editor's comment that he was in business to purvey news... Such women, he said, were purveying ideas not suitable for Algerians.*

2 VO If someone **purveys** goods or services, they provide them. *...an enterprising young actress purveying nosegays to the tourists.*

purveyor /pəveɪə/ **purveyors**; a formal word.

1 NC+*of* A **purveyor** of information is someone who tells people the information. *...the vocal testimony which refutes these purveyors of lies.*

2 NC+SUPP A **purveyor** of goods or services is a person or company that provides them. *...purveyors of commodities. ...purveyors of revolving bow ties.*

pus /pʌs/

NU **Pus** is a thick yellowish liquid that forms in wounds when they are infected. *Dead cells and other debris may ooze from the wound in the form of pus.*

push /pʊʃ/ **pushes, pushing, pushed**

1 VOorV When you **push** something, you press it with force, often in order to move it. *She pushed the button that locked the door... I pushed open the door... Castle pushed his bicycle up King's Road.* ▶ Also NC *The gate slid open at the push of a button.*

2 VOAorVA If you **push** through things that are

blocking your way or **push** your way through them, you use force in order to be able to move past them. *I pushed my way through the people... Ralph pushed between them to get a better view.*

3 VOA To **push** a value or amount up or down means to cause it to increase or decrease. *The oil boom will push the inflation rate up to higher levels.*

4 VO If you **push** someone into doing something, you urge or force them to do it. *No one pushed me into this; I decided to do it of my own accord... The government was pushed to desperate extremes.*

5 V+*for* If you **push** for something, you try very hard to achieve it. *He is pushing for secret balloting in Party elections.* ▶ Also N SING *India led the non-aligned nations in a push for sanctions.*

6 VO To **push** something also means to try to increase its popularity or to attract people to it; an informal use. *...huge adverts pushing slimming drugs.*

7 VO If you **push** a particular subject, idea, or belief that you have, you try to make people listen to you, agree with you, or support you. *I'm sure you understand what I mean without me having to push the point.*

8 VO When someone **pushes** drugs, they sell them illegally; an informal use. *She was jailed for pushing heroin.*

9 If someone **gives** you **the push**, they say they no longer want you; an informal expression. *Another forty workers have been given the push.*

10 See also **pushed**.

push ahead PHRASAL VERB If you **push ahead** with something, you continue to make progress with it. *They have pushed ahead with an optimistic development strategy.*

push around PHRASAL VERB If someone **pushes** you **around**, they give you orders in a rude and insulting way. *We're not going to let them push us around.*

push back PHRASAL VERB If a group of people or an army is **pushed back**, they are forced to move backwards. *In the end, reinforcements arrived, and the crowd was pushed back... The rebels were pushed back to their strongholds in the mountains.*

push in PHRASAL VERB When someone **pushes in**, they come into a queue in front of other people, often in a rough or rude way. *Felicity pushed in next to Howard.*

push off PHRASAL VERB When you **push off**, you leave a place; an informal use. *Push off. You're not wanted.*

push on PHRASAL VERB When you **push on**, you continue travelling somewhere or doing something. *I felt restless, and wanted to push on.*

push over PHRASAL VERB If you **push** someone or something **over**, you push them so that they fall onto the ground. *The children were pushing each other over on the sand.*

push through PHRASAL VERB If you **push through** a proposal, you succeed in getting it accepted, often with difficulty. *I'll see that the scheme is pushed through at the earliest date.*

push bike, push bikes

NC People sometimes refer to a bicycle as a **push bike**; an old-fashioned expression. *She used to do her rounds on an old push bike.*

push-button

ADJ ATTRIB A **push-button** machine or process is controlled by means of buttons or switches. *...push-button telephones.*

pushcart /pʊʃkɑːt/ **pushcarts**

NC A **pushcart** is a small cart with a long handle for carrying small things; used in American English. *They were heaping garbage onto ramshackle pushcarts.*

pushchair /pʊʃtʃeə/ **pushchairs**

NC A **pushchair** is a small chair on wheels, in which a small child can sit and be wheeled around. *You can make very simple seats, trolleys, little pushchairs.*

pushed /pʊʃt/

ADJ PRED If you are **pushed** for time or space, you do not have very much time or space in which to do things; an informal use. *Interest rates are still high, and Baker may be pushed for time.*

pusher /pʊʃə/ **pushers**
NC A **pusher** is a person who sells illegal drugs; an informal word. *He also tracked down the pusher and exposed a fairly large drug ring... In the city you walk past dope pushers and muggers.*

pushing /pʊʃɪŋ/
PREP If you say that someone is **pushing** a particular age, you mean that they are nearly that age; an informal use. *Until a man is pushing sixty-five, he doesn't usually think about retirement.*

pushover /pʊʃəʊvə/
N SING You say that something or someone is a **pushover** when it is easy to obtain what you want from them; an informal word. *Although his tone was conciliatory, the President made it clear he was going to be anything but a pushover in the battles that still lie ahead... From a British point of view, it sounds like a pushover.*

push-up, push-ups
NC A **push-up** is the same as a **press-up**; used in American English. *Rebel soldiers were ordered to do push-ups in public as a punishment.*

pushy /pʊʃi/ **pushier, pushiest**
ADJ A **pushy** person behaves in a forceful way to get things done, often because they want to do better or get more than anyone else; an informal word. *I have to be pushy in my job or I get nowhere at all... I don't think I would have been a pushy, fighting type.*

pusillanimous /pjuːsɪlænɪməs/
ADJ If you describe someone as **pusillanimous**, you mean that you think they are too timid and too scared to take risks; a formal word. *The General accused the ambassador of 'pusillanimous and petulant behaviour'... Labour, said Mr Ashdown, had been pusillanimous on the issue.*

puss /pʊs/
VOCATIVE People sometimes call a cat by saying 'Puss'. *'Puss! Puss!' he called.*

pussy /pʊsi/ **pussies**
NC You can refer to a cat as a **pussy** or a **pussy cat**; an informal word. *I thought I saw a pussy cat in that tree.*

pussyfooting /pʊsifʊtɪŋ/
V or V A If you say that someone is **pussyfooting**, or is **pussyfooting** around, you mean that they are being too cautious because they are unsure what to do and are afraid to commit themselves; an informal word. *Stop pussyfooting and get on with it... One member accused the government of pussyfooting around rather than pushing for the changes needed.* ► Also NU *The 'News of the World' agrees, saying the pussyfooting has to stop... The judge said the time for pussyfooting was over.*

pussy-willow, pussy-willows
NC A **pussy-willow** is a willow tree which has long, thin, furry white flowers in the spring. *The growth patterns of the pussy willow have led a student to develop a new seed-planting tool.*

put /pʊt/ **puts, putting.** The form **put** is used in the present tense and is also the past tense and past participle.
1 V O A When you **put** something in a particular place or position, you move it into that place or position. *She put her hand on his arm... I put her suitcase on the table... Marsha put her cup down... The women put a garland round her neck.*
2 V O A If you **put** someone somewhere, you cause them to go there and to stay there. *They had to put him into an asylum... I have to put the kids to bed.*
3 V O A When you **put** an idea or remark in a particular way, you express it in that way. *They cannot put their feelings into words... To put it briefly, the man is mad and may become dangerous.*
4 V O+to When you **put** a question or suggestion to someone, you ask them the question or make the suggestion. *I put this question to Dr Leslie Cook... I put it to him that, in fact, he was losing a good worker.*
5 V O A To **put** a person or thing in a particular state or situation means to cause them to be in that state or situation. *It puts me in a rather difficult position... The company closed several months ago, putting 120*

people out of a job... This would put the party into power.
6 V O+on or upon To **put** something on people or things means to cause them to have it or be affected by it. *It puts a tremendous responsibility on us... We put pressure on our children to learn to read. ...a plan to put a tax on children's clothes.*
7 V O If you **put** written information somewhere, you write or type it there. *Put all the details on the card... For 'profession' he put down simply 'businessman'.*
● **Put** is used in these phrases. ● If you **put** something **right**, you try and correct something that you think is wrong. *The technology does not yet exist to put the problem right. ...put right any mistakes made in the earlier process.* ● to **stay put**: see **stay**.

put across PHRASAL VERB When you **put** something **across** or **put** it **over**, you succeed in describing or explaining it to someone. *You need the skill to put your ideas across... It is difficult for her to put over her own thoughts.*

put aside PHRASAL VERB 1 If you **put** something **aside**, you keep it to be dealt with or used at a later time. *Your best plan is to put aside funds to cover these bills.* 2 If you **put** a problem **aside**, you deliberately do not think about it and try to forget about it. *The summit has been an occasion for old enemies to put aside their past differences.*

put at PHRASAL VERB If the cost, age, or value of something **is put at** a particular amount, it is estimated to be that amount. *The pipeline's cost is now put at 2.7 billion pounds.*

put away PHRASAL VERB 1 If you **put** something **away**, you put it into the place where it is normally kept. *Right—put your books away.* 2 If someone is **put away**, they are sent to prison or to a mental hospital; an informal use. *The doctor wanted to have him put away.*

put back PHRASAL VERB To **put** something **back** means to delay or postpone it. *The meeting's been put back till Monday... This will put production back at least a month.*

put by PHRASAL VERB If you **put** money **by**, you keep it so that you can use it at a later time. *I've got a bit put by.*

put down PHRASAL VERB 1 When soldiers, police, or the government **put down** a riot or rebellion, they stop it by using force. *These riots were put down by the local police.* 2 If you **put** someone **down**, you criticize them or make them appear foolish; an informal use. *...her infuriating habit of putting people down in small ways.* ● See also **put-down.** 3 When an animal is **put down**, it is killed because it is dangerous or very ill. *We had to have the cat put down.*

put down to PHRASAL VERB If you **put** something **down to** a particular thing, you believe that it is caused by that thing. *I put it down to arthritis.*

put forward PHRASAL VERB If you **put forward** something or someone, you suggest that they should be considered or chosen for a particular purpose or job. *They rejected every proposal put forward.*

put in PHRASAL VERB 1 If you **put in** an amount of time or effort doing something, you spend that time or effort doing it. *I put in fifteen hours of work daily... You've put in a lot of work.* 2 If you **put in** a request or **put in** for something, you make a formal request or application for it. *I put in a request for an interview... After the gamekeeper died, Father put in for his job.* 3 to **put in a word** for someone: see **word**.

put into PHRASAL VERB 1 If you **put** time, strength, or energy **into** an activity, you use it in doing that activity. *She put all her energy into tidying the place up.* 2 If you **put** money **into** a business or project, you invest the money in it. *Capitalists are encouraged to put their wealth into productive enterprises.*

put off PHRASAL VERB 1 If you **put** something **off**, you delay doing it. *Don't put it off till tomorrow.* 2 If you **put** someone **off**, you cause them to stop trying to get or do what they had planned. *Nothing would put her off once she had made up her mind.* 3 To **put** someone **off** something means to cause them to dislike it. *I had seen enough to put me off farm work.*

put on PHRASAL VERB 1 When you **put on** a piece of

clothing, you place it on your body in order to wear it. *I put on my jacket.* 2 When people **put on** a show, exhibition, or service, they perform it, arrange it, or organize it. *A French company has put on 'Peter Grimes'... They're putting on a special train service.* 3 If someone **puts on** weight, they become heavier. *She had put on over a stone since I last saw her.* 4 If you **put on** a piece of equipment or a device, you make it start working. *He put on the light... She put the radio on.* 5 If you **put on** a record, tape, or video, you place it on a record player or in a tape machine so you can listen to it or watch it. *We put on a record called 'Laughing Gas'.* 6 If you **put** food **on**, you begin to cook it. *She often forgets to put the dinner on before she goes to collect the children.* 7 If you **put on** a way of behaving, you behave in a way that is not natural to you or that does not express your real feelings. *She put on that look of not caring... I don't see why you have to put on a phoney English accent.*

put onto PHRASAL VERB If you **put** someone **onto** something, you tell them about something that could benefit them. *One of his friends put him on to Voluntary Service Overseas.*

put out PHRASAL VERB 1 If you **put out** an announcement or story, you make it known to a lot of people. *He put out a statement denouncing the commission's conclusions.* 2 If you **put out** something that is burning, you make it stop burning. *He helped to put the fire out.* 3 If you **put out** an electric light, you make it stop shining by pressing a switch. *She put out the light.* 4 If you **put out** things that will be needed, you place them somewhere ready to be used. *I put clean clothes out for you on the bed.* 5 If you **put out** your hand, you move it forward, away from your body, often in order to greet someone. *I walked over to one young woman and put out my hand.* 6 If you **are put out** by something, you are rather annoyed or upset by it. *I was somewhat put out when the audience laughed loudly.* 7 If you **put** yourself **out** for someone, you do something for them even though it requires a lot of effort or causes you problems. *He was putting himself out to please her.*

put over PHRASAL VERB See **put across**.

put through PHRASAL VERB 1 When someone **puts through** a telephone call or a caller, they make the connection that allows the caller to speak to the person they are phoning. *'Data Room, please.'—'I'll put you through.'* 2 If someone **puts** you **through** an unpleasant experience, they make you experience it. *I'm sorry to put you through this again.*

put together PHRASAL VERB 1 If you **put** something **together**, you join its different parts to each other so that it can be used. *He started to put his fishing rod together.* 2 If you **put** an event **together**, you organize or arrange it. *The agency has put together the biggest ever campaign for a new car.* 3 You say that one person or thing is better or greater than a group of other people or things **put together** when you are emphasizing how much better or greater they are. *He is smarter than all your colonels put together.*

put up PHRASAL VERB 1 If people **put up** a wall or a building, they construct it. *We shall have to put up a fence.* 2 If you **put up** something such as an umbrella or hood, you unfold it or raise it so that it covers you. *Why don't you put the hood up?* 3 If you **put up** a poster or notice, you fix it to a wall or board. *These posters were put up all over the place.* 4 If you **put up** a resistance or opposition to something, you resist or oppose it and try to stop it happening. *America has put up so much resistance to Concorde... We had put up a fierce struggle.* 5 If you **put up** the money for something, you provide the money that is needed to pay for it. *The National Council for the Arts put up half the cost.* 6 To **put up** the price of something means to cause it to increase. *This is what happens when they put up prices too far.* 7 If someone **puts** you **up**, you stay at their home. *I offered to put him up for the night.*

put up to PHRASAL VERB If you **put** someone **up to** something wrong or foolish, you encourage them to do it. *Julie herself had probably put them up to it.*

put up with PHRASAL VERB If you **put up with**

something, you tolerate or accept it, even though you find it unpleasant or unsatisfactory. *The natives have to put up with gaping tourists... I can't think why I put up with it.*

putative /pjuːtətɪv/
ADJ ATTRIB If you describe someone or something as **putative**, you mean that they are thought to be, but are not definitely the particular thing mentioned; a formal word. *...the putative father of her child.*

put-down, put-downs
NC A **put-down** is a remark or action which makes someone appear foolish; an informal word. *The ultimate put-down is to be given a pat on the head.*

putrefy /pjuːtrɪfaɪ/ putrefies, putrefying, putrefied
V When something **putrefies**, it rots and produces a disgusting smell; a formal word. *Thousands of bodies were decomposing and putrefying.*

putrescent /pjuːtrɛsnt/
ADJ Something that is **putrescent** is beginning to rot and produce a disgusting smell; a formal word. *...a putrescent corpse.*

putrid /pjuːtrɪd/
ADJ Something that is **putrid** is rotten and beginning to smell disgusting; a formal word. *...a rotted and putrid mess.*

putsch /pʊtʃ/ putsches
NC A **putsch** is an organized attempt to overthrow a government. *They are continuing to deny that a putsch is being planned... It was his role in crushing that putsch that brought him to power.*

putt /pʌt/ putts, putting, putted
NC A **putt** is a stroke in golf that you make with a special club when the ball has reached the green. *I managed to miss a three-foot putt.* ▸ Also V or VO *He usually putted well with that club... He putted his second shot into the water.*

putter /pʌtə/ putters, puttering, puttered
1 NC A **putter** is a club used for hitting a golf ball when it has reached the green. *Blaine McAllister is a golf winner in Florida after a hot streak with the putter... Both put their putters to good use to return scores of five under par 67s.* 2 V When a boat or vehicle **putters**, its engine makes a slow throbbing sound as it moves. *A few fishing boats puttered past.* 3 V To **putter** also means the same as to **potter about**; used in American English. *He spent his days puttering in his rose garden.*

putting green, putting greens
NC A **putting green** is a very small golf course on which the grass is kept short and on which there are no obstacles. *He was irritated by squirrels scratching up his putting green.*

putty /pʌti/
NU **Putty** is a kind of stiff paste, often used to fix glass panes into frames and to fill cracks or holes. *...as soft as putty. ...dental putty used for taking impressions.*

put-up
If something is a **put-up job**, it has been arranged beforehand in order to deceive someone; an informal expression. *...an agent provocateur, taking part in a put-up job.*

put-upon
ADJ If you are **put-upon**, you have been treated badly by someone who has taken advantage of your willingness to help them; an informal expression. *I felt cheated and put-upon.*

puzzle /pʌzl/ puzzles, puzzling, puzzled
1 VO If something **puzzles** you, it makes you feel confused because you do not understand it. *There was one sentence which puzzled me deeply.* ♦ **puzzling** ADJ *I find this rather puzzling. ...one of the most puzzling aspects of the Gulf war.* 2 VA If you **puzzle** over something, you try hard to think of the answer or the explanation for it. *Astronomers had puzzled over these white ovals for some time.* 3 NC A **puzzle** is a question, game, or toy which you have to think about carefully in order to answer it correctly or put it together properly. *Her husband settled down to do a crossword puzzle. ...numerical puzzles.*

4 N SING You can describe anything that is hard to understand as a **puzzle**. *The motives of the film-makers remain a puzzle.*

puzzle out PHRASAL VERB If you **puzzle out** a problem, you find the answer to it by thinking hard about it. *She sat down and tried to puzzle out the reports.*

puzzled /pʌzld/
ADJ If you are **puzzled**, you are confused because you do not understand something. *The police are also puzzled; they believe the culprit may be deranged... His remark was greeted with puzzled silence.*

puzzlement /pʌzlmənt/
NU **Puzzlement** is confusion that you feel when you do not understand something. *I looked at him in puzzlement.*

PVC /piːviːsiː/
NU **PVC** is a plastic material which is used for making things such as clothing, pipes, and tiles. **PVC** is an abbreviation for 'polyvinyl chloride'. *...steel which has been coated with hard-wearing PVC. ...a tough, plastic PVC tube.*

pw
pw is a written abbreviation for 'per week'. It is used especially when stating the weekly cost of something. *...rent—£25 pw.*

pygmy /pɪgmi/ **pygmies**; also spelt **pigmy**.
1 N+N **Pygmy** is used to refer to a species of animal which is the smallest of a group of related species; a technical use. *The pygmy marmoset has a body length of only ten centimetres.*
2 NC A **pygmy** is a very small person, especially a person who comes from a racial group in which the people are all small. *...the pygmies of the Amazon jungle.*

pyjamas /pədʒɑːməz/; spelt **pajamas** in American English. The forms **pyjama** and **pajama** are used as noun modifiers.
N PL A pair of **pyjamas** consists of loose trousers and a loose jacket that people, especially men, wear in bed. *He had been taken to the prison in his pyjamas. ...dressed only in pyjamas. ...pyjama trousers.*

pylon /paɪlən/ **pylons**
NC **Pylons** are tall metal structures which hold electric cables high above the ground so that electricity can be transmitted over long distances. *...high-voltage electricity pylons... 674 more pylons on the transmission lines have been sabotaged.*

P'yŏngyang /pjɒnjæn/
P'yŏngyang is the capital of North Korea and its largest city. Population: 2 million (1986).

pyramid /pɪrəmɪd/ **pyramids**
NC A **pyramid** is a three-dimensional shape with a flat base and flat triangular sides which slope upwards to a point. *...the Egyptian pyramids. ...an eight hundred foot sky-scraper topped off by a pyramid... The canopies have a pyramid shape which is the strongest of all structural shapes.*

pyre /paɪə/ **pyres**
NC A **pyre** is a high pile of wood which is built outside in order to ceremonially burn dead bodies or religious offerings. *...a funeral pyre... They built pyres and made burnt offerings to their god.*

Pyrex /paɪreks/
NU **Pyrex** is a type of strong glass which is used for making bowls and dishes that do not break when you cook things in them; **Pyrex** is a trademark. *...Pyrex dishes.*

pyrotechnics /paɪrətekniks/
NU **Pyrotechnics** is the making or displaying of fireworks. *...his tremendous mix of cleverly crafted electronic music, lasers and pyrotechnics.*

python /paɪθn/ **pythons**
NC A **python** is a large snake that kills animals by squeezing them with its body. *The thieves smashed down the doors to the reptile house and took a number of pythons.*

Q q

Q, q /kjuː/ **Q's, q's**
NC **Q** is the seventeenth letter of the English alphabet.

Qaboos bin Said, Sultan /kəbuːs bɪn sɑːiːd/
Qaboos bin Said became Sultan and Prime Minister of Oman in 1970, when his father, Said bin Taimur, was deposed. Born: 1940.

Qatar /kʌtɑː/
The **State of Qatar** is a country in the Gulf. It was a British protectorate from 1916 until independence in 1971. Shaikh Khalifa bin Hamad al-Thani became Amir and Prime Minister in 1972. There are no political parties. It is a member of the Arab League, OPEC, and the Gulf Co-operation Council. Qatar exports oil.
◆ **Qatari** /kætɑːri/ N, ADJ
■ *per capita GNP:* US$11,610 ■ *religion:* Islam (mainly Wahhabi) ■ *language:* Arabic (official), English ■ *currency:* riyal ■ *capital:* Doha ■ *population:* 341,000 (1988) (approximately 70% are foreign workers) ■ *size:* 11,437 square kilometres.

QC /kjuːsiː/ **QCs**
A **QC** is a senior barrister in Britain. **QC** is an abbreviation for 'Queen's Counsel'. ...*Lord Gifford, QC. ...a leading QC.*

Q.E.D. /kjuː iː diː/
1 In mathematics, **Q.E.D.** is used to say that you have proved what you originally set out to prove.
2 **Q.E.D.** is also used to indicate that something which has just been said or done is the answer to a question; an informal use.

qua /kweɪ, kwɑː/
PREP **Qua** is used to indicate that you are talking about something as an ideal or as an abstract idea; a formal word. *It's the bourgeoisie he's after, not the English qua English.*

quack /kwæk/ **quacks, quacking, quacked**
1 V When a duck **quacks,** it makes the noise that ducks typically make. ...*wild duck quacking on the river.*
2 NC A **quack** is a person who pretends to be a doctor and makes money by selling medicine, but who has no medical qualifications; used showing disapproval. *The idea of curing baldness with preparations known as 'hair restorer' has long been associated with quacks... It will always be tempting to follow the quacks when the experts don't have all the answers.*

quad /kwɒd/ **quads**
NC **Quads** are the same as **quadruplets.** *The quads— three boys and a girl—had been born less than twelve hours earlier.*

quadrangle /kwɒdræŋgl/ **quadrangles**
NC A **quadrangle** is an open square area with buildings round it. *We were in this little room looking out on the quadrangle.*

quadrilateral /kwɒdrɪlætəʳrəl/ **quadrilaterals**
NC A **quadrilateral** is a geometrical shape that has four straight sides joined together.

quadrille /kwədrɪl/ **quadrilles**
NC A **quadrille** is an old-fashioned dance for four or more couples. ...*19th century dances with such exotic names as the mazurka, the galop and the quadrille.*

quadripartite /kwɒdrɪpɑːtaɪt/
ADJ ATTRIB A **quadripartite** organization or agreement consists of or involves four parts. *They want a quadripartite government of all the Kampuchean factions.*

quadruped /kwɒdrʊped/ **quadrupeds**
NC A **quadruped** is any animal with four legs; a formal word. ...*true quadrupeds like cats and dogs.*

quadruple /kwɒdrʊpl, kwɒdruːpl/ **quadruples, quadrupling, quadrupled**
V When an amount or number **quadruples,** it becomes four times as large. *Wheat production has almost quadrupled.*

quadruplet /kwɒdrʊplət, kwɒdruːplət/ **quadruplets**
NC **Quadruplets** are four children who are born to the same mother at the same time. *Test tube quintuplets and test tube quadruplets have been born on the same day at the same hospital in Australia.*

quaff /kwɒf/ **quaffs, quaffing, quaffed**
V O If you **quaff** a drink, you drink it quickly; an old-fashioned word. *He quaffed half the contents of his glass in one gulp.*

quagmire /kwægmaɪə, kwɒgmaɪə/ **quagmires**
1 NC A **quagmire** is a soft, wet area of land, especially one which you sink into if you try to walk on it. ...*the winter rains come, turning the ground into a quagmire.*
2 NC A **quagmire** is also an awkward, complicated, or embarrassing situation. *The only way out of this political quagmire is to call fresh elections.*

quail /kweɪl/ **quails.** The plural form can be either **quails** or **quail.**
NC **Quails** are small birds which people sometimes shoot and eat. ...*using small partridge-like birds called quails... She's an adventurous and exciting cook and we've feasted on doves, turkeys and quail.*

quaint /kweɪnt/
ADJ Something that is **quaint** is attractive because it is unusual and rather old-fashioned. ...*a quaint fishing village.*

quake /kweɪk/ **quakes, quaking, quaked**
1 V If you **quake,** you tremble or shake because you are afraid. *I stood there quaking with fear... Businessmen were quaking at the thought of what socialism might do to their investments.*
2 NC A **quake** is the same as an **earthquake;** an informal use. *The quake was also felt in north-western Iran and Turkey... Nearly one third of buildings in the area had been destroyed by the quake.*

Quaker /kweɪkə/ **Quakers**
NC A **Quaker** is a person who belongs to a Christian group called the Society of Friends which started in the 17th century. *The Rowntrees, like all Quakers, abstained from alcohol... Joan Baez's family background as a Quaker gave her a strong moral awareness.*

qualification /kwɒlɪfɪkeɪʃn/ **qualifications**
1 NC Your **qualifications** are the examinations that you have passed. *I haven't got any qualifications in English Literature.*
2 NU **Qualification** is the act of passing the examinations that you need to pass in order to work in a particular profession. *Even after qualification, jobs were hard to find.*

3 NC The **qualifications** needed for a particular activity or task are the qualities and skills that you need in order to do it. *One of the qualifications you need in advertising is a fertile mind... A knowledge of Welsh is an additional qualification for all posts.*
4 NCorNU A **qualification** is also something that you add to a statement to make it less strong or less generalized. *Two qualifications need to be made... The government has also conceded, almost without qualification.*

qualified /kwɒlɪfaɪd/
1 ADJ Someone who is **qualified** has passed the examinations that they need in order to work in a particular profession. *A qualified engineer was on board. ...a shortage of qualified nurses... Increasing numbers of French employers want more qualified personnel.*
2 ADJ PRED If you are **qualified** to do something, you have the qualities, knowledge, or skills necessary to do it. *He is as qualified as any man could be for this task... As a former jockey himself, Dick Francis is particularly well qualified in this subject.*
3 ADJ **Qualified** agreement or praise is not total and suggests that you have doubts. *The most likely outcome is a cautious and qualified approval. ...qualified optimism.*

qualifier /kwɒlɪfaɪə/ **qualifiers**
1 NC A **qualifier** is a person or thing that qualifies for something, especially a person who is successful in the first part of a competition and qualifies for the main competition or the next round. *Jansher beat the British qualifier Phil Whitlock 9-3, 9-3, 9-2... Another Kenyan, Joseph Gikonyo, led the qualifiers for the 100-metres final.*
2 NC A **qualifier** is a race or competition that entrants must win or do well in so that they can progress to a more important race or competition. *There was no First Division football today due to England's European Championship qualifier on Wednesday against Poland. ...as they prepare for tomorrow's crucial World Cup qualifier in Spain.*

qualify /kwɒlɪfaɪ/ **qualifies, qualifying, qualified**
1 V When someone **qualifies**, they pass the examinations that they need to pass in order to work in a particular profession. *He studied at the London School of Economics and afterwards qualified as a lawyer.*
2 VO If you **qualify** a statement, you add a detail or explanation to it to make it less strong or less generalized. *Mr Neeman qualified his earlier remarks... It does qualify its findings by saying that there may be 'exceptional circumstances'.*
3 V+for If someone **qualifies** for something, they have the right to have it. *They were being interviewed to see if they qualified for refugee status... They can't afford the premiums and don't qualify for help... Anyone who takes up his offer will qualify for a free night's stay at the hotel.*
4 V If you **qualify** in a competition, you are successful in one part of it and go on to the next stage. *Australia have qualified for the final of the World Cup cricket series... Nigeria qualified with a two-nil win against Algeria after extra time.* ◆ **qualifying** ADJ ATTRIB *There are two other qualifying matches tonight.*

qualitative /kwɒlɪtətɪv/
ADJ ATTRIB **Qualitative** means relating to the quality of something. *...qualitative improvements. ...a qualitative change.* ◆ **qualitatively** ADV *...qualitatively and quantitatively... That will be a different and qualitatively new step.*

quality /kwɒlɪti/ **qualities**
1 NU+SUPP The **quality** of something is how good or bad it is. *The quality of the grasses there is poor... There was seldom food available, and if there was, it was of low quality. ...extra congestion on poor quality roads.*
2 NU **Quality** also means of a high standard. *...a programme of quality... Many are difficult to store without loss of taste or quality.* ▶ Also ADJ ATTRIB *The employers don't want quality work any more.*
3 NC Your **qualities** are your good characteristics. *Her great quality is patience... Gorbachev showed not*

only wit and warmth but the qualities of true leadership.
4 NC The **qualities** of a substance or object are its physical characteristics. *The skin on the baby's face had a pearly translucent quality.*
5 ADJ ATTRIB The **quality** newspapers are generally considered to write seriously and thoughtfully about issues of importance. *'Lidove Noviny' used to be the most popular quality newspaper published in the Czech language.*

quality control
NU **Quality control** is the activity of checking that products are all of a satisfactory standard and quality, usually by testing samples of them. *They were trained in better management, quality control and marketing... Quality control procedures are of paramount importance.*

quality of life
NU You can use **quality of life** when you refer to how much you are able to enjoy your life and spend your time in an interesting or useful way. *They tend to believe that the quality of life in the North is better. ...treatments that have improved the quality of life for millions.*

qualm /kwɑːm/ **qualms**
NC If you have **qualms** about what you are doing, you are worried that it may not be right. *Social security minister Nicholas Scott has no qualms about the plans... He used treacherous promises which he had no qualms about breaking.*

quandary /kwɒnd°ri/ **quandaries**
NC If you are in a **quandary**, you cannot decide what to do. *Several Latin American countries are in a quandary as to how to proceed.*

quanta /kwɒntə/
Quanta is the plural of **quantum**.

quantifiable /kwɒntɪfaɪəbl/
ADJ If something is **quantifiable**, it can be measured in objective terms. *There was little quantifiable improvement... There is also a value which arises out of that which is not quantifiable.*

quantify /kwɒntɪfaɪ/ **quantifies, quantifying, quantified**
VO If you **quantify** something, you represent it as an amount or number so that it can be counted, measured, or compared to other things. *It's hard to quantify the benefits to Britain of such links but it is generally thought to be good for trade.*

quantitative /kwɒntɪtətɪv/
ADJ **Quantitative** means relating to the size or amount of something. *...a quantitative assessment of the effectiveness of our investment.* ◆ **quantitatively** ADV *You wanted to measure it quantitatively.*

quantity /kwɒntəti/ **quantities**
1 NC A **quantity** of something is an amount that you can measure or count. *You only need a very small quantity. ...a quantity of leaves... Huge quantities of oil are imported to prepare for winter.*
2 NU **Quantity** is the amount of something that there is. It is often contrasted with that thing's quality. *People still really go for the quality as well as the quantity... These could not compare with the exports of other countries either in quality or in quantity.*
● **Quantity** is used in these phrases. ● If something is done **in quantity**, it is done in large amounts. *They can afford to import basic food stuffs and raw materials in quantity.* ● You can say that someone or something is an **unknown quantity** when you do not know anything about them. *Mr Taylor remains something of an unknown quantity to most outsiders.*
● You can say that someone or something is a **known quantity** when you know something about them and feel you understand and can predict their behaviour. *He is a known quantity, a familiar face.*

quantity surveyor, quantity surveyors
NC A **quantity surveyor** is a person who works with builders and architects and whose job is to calculate how long pieces of work will take and how much they will cost. *I started off wanting to be a quantity surveyor.*

quantum /kwɒntəm/ **quanta**
1 NC A **quantum** is a quantity of something, especially

a very small quantity; a formal use. *He supplies a quantum of effort or of energy which could as well be supplied by almost anyone else.*
2 NC **Quantum** is used to describe theories in physics and mathematics which are concerned with atomic particles; a technical use. *...the quanta of gravitational radiation. ...the laws of quantum mechanics.*

quantum leap, quantum leaps
NC A **quantum leap** or a **quantum jump** is a very great change, increase, or advance. *...a quantum leap in growth... This visit represents a quantum jump in the relationship.*

quarantine /kwɒrəntiːn/ **quarantines, quarantining, quarantined**
1 NU If a person or animal is in **quarantine**, they are kept separate from other people or animals for a certain period in case they have an infectious disease. *We used to put people in quarantine for the measles. ...quarantine restrictions on the movement of animals.*
2 VO To **quarantine** a person or animal means to keep them separate from others for a certain period in case they have an infectious disease. *It has been quarantined following an outbreak of foot and mouth disease.*

quark /kwɑːk/ **quarks**
NC A **quark** is one of at least five particles, smaller than an atom, with an electrical charge of one third or two thirds of an electron; a technical term in physics. *Physicists' theories about the nature of subatomic particles predict that there are six types of quark... The top quark must weigh more than about 40 proton masses.*

quarrel /kwɒrəl/ **quarrels, quarrelling, quarrelled**; spelt **quarreling, quarreled** in American English.
1 NC A **quarrel** is an angry argument between two or more people. *I don't think we should enter into a family quarrel... There wasn't any evidence of quarrels between them.*
2 V-RECIP When two or more people **quarrel**, they have an angry argument. *I don't want to quarrel with you... They quarrelled quite often.*
3 N SING If you say that you have no **quarrel** with something, you mean that you do not object to it. *I wouldn't have any quarrel with this proposal myself.*

quarrelsome /kwɒrəlsəm/
ADJ People who are **quarrelsome** are always having angry arguments. *...the prime minister's divided and quarrelsome party.*

quarry /kwɒri/ **quarries, quarrying, quarried.** The form **quarry** is both the singular and the plural of the noun in paragraph 3.
1 NC A **quarry** is a place where large quantities of stone, slate, or minerals are dug out of the ground. *Kesiria's father worked in an Indian stone quarry.*
2 VO To **quarry** a stone or mineral means to remove it from a quarry by digging, drilling, or blasting. *Limestone has been quarried for centuries.*
3 NC A person's or animal's **quarry** is the animal that they are hunting; a formal use. *Move slowly, or you will startle your quarry.*

quart /kwɔːt/ **quarts**
NC A **quart** is a unit of volume that is equal to two pints. *...a quart of milk.*

quarter /kwɔːtə/ **quarters**
1 NC A **quarter** is one of four equal parts of something. *It would mean a reduction of about a quarter in the defence budget... A quarter of the workforce is now unemployed... Two-thirds to three-quarters of patients improve.* ▶ Also ADJ ATTRIB *He will have completed a quarter century in power... The pound was up one and a quarter cents against the dollar at one dollar eighty-three.*
2 NU or N SING If it is a **quarter** to a particular hour, it is fifteen minutes before that hour. If it is a **quarter** past a particular hour, it is fifteen minutes past that hour. *It went off at quarter to six in the morning, local time. ...at about a quarter past five.*
3 NC A **quarter** is also a period of three months. *The rate of inflation was eleven percent in the first quarter of this year... We update that once a quarter.*
4 NC In the United States and Canada, a **quarter** is a

coin worth 25 cents. *These are all American coins—by that I mean penny, dime, quarter, half-dollar and dollar... What kind of lunch can you give me for four quarters?*
5 NC+SUPP You can refer to the area in a town where a particular group of people live or work as a particular **quarter**. *...the Versailles restaurant in the heart of Miami's Cuban quarter. ...a residential quarter.*
6 NC+SUPP When you refer to the feeling or reaction in certain **quarters** or from a particular **quarter**, you are referring in general terms to the feeling or reaction of a particular person or group. *It had been criticised in some quarters as unnecessary... The threat of violence from this quarter has increased sharply.*
7 N PL+SUPP You can refer to the room or rooms provided for a person such as a soldier to live in as that person's **quarters**. *A fire started in the engine room and accommodation quarters... They made their way through the prison's married quarters.*
8 If you see someone at close **quarters**, you see them from a place that is very close to them. *The Red Cross emblem is distinctive at close quarters.*

quarterback /kwɔːtəbæk/ **quarterbacks**
NC In American football, a **quarterback** is a player who tells the other players in his team how and where to direct their attack. *New York has a new quarterback, Jeff Hostetler, who has led his team to three consecutive victories.*

quarterdeck /kwɔːtədek/ **quarterdecks**
NC The **quarterdeck** on a ship is the highest part of the deck, which is near the back of the ship. *Drenching spray now and then splashed over the quarterdeck.*

quarter-final /kwɔːtəfaɪnl/ **quarter-finals**
NC A **quarter-final** is one of the four matches in a competition which decides which four players or teams will compete in the semi-final. *The Chinese team was expected to do well in their quarter-final against Thailand.*

quarterly /kwɔːtəli/
ADV or ADJ ATTRIB If something happens **quarterly**, it happens regularly four times a year, at intervals of three months. *The floppy discs will be issued quarterly. ...the latest quarterly survey published by the main employers' organisation.*

quartermaster /kwɔːtəmɑːstə/ **quartermasters**
NC A **quartermaster** is an army officer who is responsible for accommodation, food, and equipment. *...a former quartermaster in the Mozambican army.*

quartet /kwɔːtet/ **quartets**
1 NC A **quartet** is a group of four people who play musical instruments or sing together. *The White House's favourite jazz quartet will perform at Tuesday's dinner.*
2 NC A **quartet** is also a piece of music for four instruments or four singers. *I wrote something like twelve piano sonatas, four or five string quartets and dozens of songs.*

quarto /kwɔːtəʊ/ **quartos**
1 NU **Quarto** is a size of paper which is about 20 centimetres by 26 centimetres in size.
2 NC A **quarto** is a book which has pages which are quarto size.

quartz /kwɔːts/
NU **Quartz** is a kind of hard, shiny crystal, used in making electronic equipment and very accurate watches and clocks. *He straps on his cheap quartz wristwatch.*

quasar /kweɪzɑː/ **quasars**
NC A **quasar** is an object in outer space which is like a star and which produces powerful radio waves and other forms of energy; a technical term. *There's even a theory that active galaxies have a quasar at their centre.*

quash /kwɒʃ/ **quashes, quashing, quashed**
1 VO If someone in authority **quashes** a decision or judgement, they officially reject it so that it is no longer legally valid. *Their prison sentences were quashed... He would now refer the case to the Court of Appeal, which has the power to quash the convictions.*
2 VO If someone in authority **quashes** something such

as a movement of resistance or a rumour, they destroy it or end it firmly. *In recent months the military government has moved convincingly to quash all internal opposition... He supported the Prime Minister's prompt action to quash further speculation.*

quasi- /kwˈeɪzaɪ-/
PREFIX **quasi-** is used to form adjectives that describe something as being very like something else, without actually being that thing. **Quasi-** occasionally combines in this way with nouns. *This quasi-colonial approach breeds resentment. ...quasi-military groups. ...a quasi-religious experience... They have turned their countries into quasi-republics.*

quatrain /kwˈɒtreɪn/ **quatrains**
NC A **quatrain** is a verse of poetry that has four lines; a technical term.

quaver /kwˈeɪvə/ **quavers, quavering, quavered**
1 V-QUOTE If someone's voice **quavers**, it sounds unsteady, for example because they are nervous or uncertain. *'Am I safe?' he quavered.* ♦ **quavering** ADJ ATTRIB *That quivering voice of his had the ring of another century.*
2 NC In music, a **quaver** is a note that has a time value equivalent to half a crotchet.

quay /kiː/ **quays**
NC A **quay** is a long platform beside the sea or a river where boats can be tied up and loaded or unloaded. *...the quays where the ferries are expected to dock.*

quayside /kiːsaɪd/
N SING The **quayside** is the area at the edge of a quay. *A hundred and fifty lorry drivers met at the quayside at Dover's Eastern Docks. ...food piled on the quayside.*

queasy /kwˈiːzi/
ADJ If you feel **queasy**, you feel rather sick. *She felt a little queasy on the boat.*

queen /kwiːn/ **queens**
1 NC or TITLE A **queen** is a woman who rules a country as its monarch, or a woman who is married to a king. *The Queen has sent a message of sympathy to relatives.*
2 NC A **queen** or a **queen bee** is a large female bee which lays eggs. *It separates the queen bee from the honey.*
3 NC In chess, the **queen** is the most powerful piece, which can be moved in any direction. *A good chess-player avoids exposing his queen.*
4 NC A **queen** is also a playing card with a picture of a queen on it. *...the queen of spades.*

queenly /kwˈiːnli/
ADJ Someone or something that is **queenly** is like a queen, or is considered to be suitable for a queen. *...Dante Gabriel Rossetti's queenly portraits of women... Rose's status was not exactly queenly.*

Queen Mother, Queen Mothers
NC or TITLE The **Queen Mother** is the mother of a ruling king or queen. *The Queen Mother has been celebrating her ninety-first birthday. ...a tribute to Queen Elizabeth the Queen Mother.*

Queen's speech, Queen's speeches
NC The **Queen's speech** is a speech that the Queen reads at the opening session of parliament in Britain. It is written by the government and it summarizes the laws and policies of the government for that session of parliament. *...legislation which is expected to be included in the Queen's speech to parliament next month... It depends on how Mrs Thatcher performs in the Queen's speech debate.*

queer /kwˈɪə/ **queerer, queerest**
ADJ **Queer** means strange or peculiar. *...a queer sensation.*

quell /kwˈel/ **quells, quelling, quelled**
1 VO To **quell** opposition or violent behaviour means to stop it by using persuasion or force. *The army sent in reinforcements to quell the unrest.*
2 VO If you **quell** feelings such as fear or grief, you stop yourself having these feelings. *I was trying to quell a growing unease.*

quench /kwˈentʃ/ **quenches, quenching, quenched**
VO You **quench** your thirst when you are thirsty by having a drink. *You can quench your thirst with local beer.*

querulous /kwˈerʊləs/
ADJ Someone who is **querulous** often complains about things; a formal word. *The president is beginning to look less like a conquering hero, more like a querulous, somewhat defensive wimp.*

query /kwˈɪəri/ **queries, querying, queried**
1 NC or NU A **query** is a question about a particular point. *If you have any queries, please don't hesitate to write... The assistant accepted my cheque without query.*
2 V-QUOTE You can use **query** to say that someone asks a question. *'How much do I owe you?' I queried.*
3 VO or V-REPORT If you **query** something, you ask about it because you doubt that it is correct or accurate. *Your expenses have been queried by the tax man... It's not just the more conservative governments in the industrialised world which are now querying the viability of a rescue package for Africa... He queried whether it was in the vital interests of the United States.*

quest /kwˈest/ **quests**
NC A **quest** is a long and difficult search for something; a literary word. *The quest for peace must go on... What are we to make of Yeats' spiritual quest?*

question /kwˈestʃən/ **questions, questioning, questioned**
1 NC A **question** is something which you say or write in order to ask about a particular matter. *The survey did not ask any question about political views... We put the question first to British Labour politician, Gerald Kaufman... A panel of experts will answer questions on education.*
2 VO If you **question** someone, you ask them a lot of questions about something. *They will question five thousand people between 16 and 21 from a variety of communities and backgrounds... Road blocks are in position while drivers and pedestrians are questioned.*
3 VO If you **question** something, you express your doubts about whether it is true, genuine, reasonable, or worthwhile. *He questioned the need for a three year wait... His honesty is being questioned again.*
4 NU+SUPP If there is **question** about a particular matter, there is doubt or uncertainty about it. *There's some question of where the president stands in all of this... There was absolutely no question about the diagnosis.*
5 NC+SUPP A **question** is also a problem or point which needs to be discussed. *The question of cancelling debt is not raised in the report... He tackles the central question of the struggle for land.*
6 NC In an examination, a **question** is a problem which is set in order to test your knowledge or ability. *You have to answer four questions in two hours.*
● **Question** is used in these phrases. ● If something is **beyond question**, there is no doubt at all about it. *She knew beyond question that I was a person who could be trusted.* ● If you **call** something **into question**, you express serious doubts about it. *Are you calling my professional competence into question?... Their methods were called into question.* ● If something is **open to question**, it is not certain and people may disagree about it. *The EC's continued involvement in the peace process is open to question.* ● If something is **out of the question**, it is impossible. *Mr Yegor Ligachov dismissed such ideas as out of the question.* ● If **there is no question** of something, it is impossible. *With so much happening there was no question of getting a full night's sleep.* ● If something is true **without question**, there can be no doubt that it is true. *The hardliners represent, without question, the most serious challenge just at the moment.* ● If you do something **without question**, you do it without arguing or asking why it is necessary. *In their present mood, deputies would agree to any decisive changes without question.* ● The time, place, person, or thing **in question** is the time, place, person, or thing you have just been talking about. *The army had demolished about half of the buildings in question.* ● If something is **in question**, there is some doubt about it. *The situation was difficult, but safety at the airport was not in question.*

questionable /kwɛstʃənəbl/
ADJ If you say that something is **questionable**, you mean that it is not certain or reliable because you think there is something wrong with it. *The wisdom of such a move is highly questionable. ...a very questionable argument... It must remain questionable whether the admission was given voluntarily.*

questioner /kwɛstʃənə/ **questioners**
NC A **questioner** is a person who is asking a question. *There doesn't seem to be an immediate answer to this questioner's problem.*

questioning /kwɛstʃənɪŋ/
1 ADJ ATTRIB If someone has a **questioning** expression on their face, they look as if they are expecting to hear an answer to a question. *He looked at her with a questioning expression.* ◆ **questioningly** ADV *We pointed to the bag and raised our eyebrows questioningly.*
2 NU **Questioning** is a process in which someone is asked a lot of questions. *The three men were taken to the police station for questioning... They are being held for further questioning.*

question mark, question marks
1 NC A **question mark** is the punctuation mark (?).
2 NC A **question mark** can also mean a doubt or uncertainty over something or someone. *A big question mark hangs over the future of Britain's biggest education authority... The big question mark around the Geneva talks remains.*

question-master, question-masters
NC A **question-master** is the person who asks the questions in a game or a quiz on the television or radio.

questionnaire /kwɛstʃəneə/ **questionnaires**
NC A **questionnaire** is a written list of questions which are answered by a number of people in order to provide information for a report or survey. *The woman fills in a questionnaire which gives us her medical history. ...sociological methods, such as personal interviews and questionnaires.*

question tag, question tags
NC A **question tag** is a very short clause at the end of a statement which can change the statement into a question. For example, in 'She said half price, didn't she?', the words 'didn't she' are a question tag.

queue /kjuː/ **queues, queueing** or **queuing, queued**
1 NC A **queue** is a line of people or vehicles that are waiting for something. *Long queues built up around London... Queues have formed for petrol... Customers at the back of the queue looked nervous.*
2 NC+*of* If you say that there is a **queue** of people or organizations, you mean that they are all waiting for a particular opportunity. *There is still a queue of merchant banks waiting for seats on the Tokyo exchange... The government says it will not join the queue of developing countries seeking to reschedule their foreign debt.*
3 V or VA When people **queue** they stand in a line waiting for something. *Hundreds of people queued before the banks opened... Shoppers queued for the same goods which two months ago no-one wanted to buy.*
queue up PHRASAL VERB To **queue up** means the same as to **queue**. *By first light today, hundreds of motorists were already queueing up.*

quibble /kwɪbl/ **quibbles, quibbling, quibbled**
1 V, V+*over*, or V+*about* When people **quibble**, they argue about a small matter which is not important. *It ought to trust the evidence and not quibble about minor legal points... The Senate has been quibbling over how much money each state receives.*
2 NC A **quibble** is a minor objection to something. *Mr Gorbachev will not let a quibble over spies damage the relationship between the two countries.*

quiche /kiːʃ/ **quiches**
NC A **quiche** is a tart filled with a savoury mixture of eggs, cheese, and other things. Quiches can be eaten either hot or cold.

quick /kwɪk/ **quicker, quickest**
1 ADJ **Quick** means moving or doing things with speed. *She was precise and quick in her movements... Her hands were quick and strong.* ◆ **quickly** ADV

Towards the end of the year inflation began to rise quite quickly.
2 ADJ Something that is **quick** takes or lasts only a short time. *Let's just have a quick look at that. ...a quick visit.* ◆ **quickly** ADV *They embraced quickly.*
3 ADJ **Quick** also means happening with very little delay. *You're likely to get a quicker reply if you telephone... John was quick to help him.* ◆ **quickly** ADV *Such cases should be dealt with as quickly as possible.*
4 **quick off the mark:** see **mark. quick on the uptake:** see **uptake.**

quicken /kwɪkən/ **quickens, quickening, quickened**
V-ERG If something **quickens** or is **quickened**, it moves at a greater speed. *They will definitely quicken progress toward a cease-fire... This thought made him quicken his pace... Our correspondent says the pace of the negotiations appears to be quickening.*

quickening /kwɪkənɪŋ/
1 ADJ ATTRIB A **quickening** pace, speed, or development is getting faster. *...the quickening pace of democracy. ...a quickening inflation rate.*
2 N SING+SUPP A **quickening** of interest or enthusiasm is a rapid increase in it. *There is a quickening of interest in the French presidential elections here.*

quick fix, quick fixes
NC A **quick fix** is a quick but probably not permanent solution to a problem; used showing disapproval. *He said there could be no easy solution or quick fix to the refugee problem... A quick fix agreement would be worse than useless.*

quickie /kwɪki/ **quickies**
NC A **quickie** is something that only takes a short time to do or deal with, for example a drink or a question; an informal word. *We've just got time for one more question, so let's have a quickie.*

quicklime /kwɪklaɪm/
NU **Quicklime** is a white substance made by heating limestone. It is used, for example, for making cement.

quicksand /kwɪksænd/
NU **Quicksand** is deep, wet sand that you sink into when you try to walk on it. *Dealing with problems like this is rather like walking on quicksand.*

quicksilver /kwɪksɪlvə/
NU **Quicksilver** is mercury; an old-fashioned word.

quickstep /kwɪkstɛp/
N SING The **quickstep** is a ballroom dance with a lot of quick steps. It can also refer to the music it is danced to. *...the strains of the waltz, quickstep and tango.*

quid /kwɪd/; **quid** is both the singular and the plural form.
NC A **quid** is a pound in money; an informal word. *To produce your first CD to sell, it's going to cost you well over a million quid.*

quid pro quo /kwɪd prəʊ kwəʊ/ **quid pro quos**
NC A **quid pro quo** is a gift or advantage that is given to someone in return for something they have done; a formal expression. *His promotion may be regarded as the quid pro quo for his support.*

quiescent /kwiɛsnt/
ADJ Something that is **quiescent** is quiet and inactive; a literary word. *...careful portraits of quiescent animals... Once quiescent minorities are asserting their rights again.*

quiet /kwaɪət/ **quieter, quietest; quiets, quieting, quieted**
1 ADJ Something or someone that is **quiet** makes only a small amount of noise. *Hal said in a quiet voice, 'I have resigned.'... The trains are extremely fast, quiet and non-polluting.* ◆ **quietly** ADV *'I'm going to do it,' I said quietly.*
2 ADJ If a place is **quiet**, there is very little noise there. *It was very quiet in there; you could just hear the wind moving the trees.* ◆ **quietness** NU *Winter brings a strange quietness to the seashore.*
3 NU **Quiet** is silence. *They wanted as much peace and quiet as possible.*
4 ADJ PRED If you are **quiet**, you do not say anything. *Mr Hughes was twice told to be quiet.* ◆ **quietly** ADV *We lay quietly.*
5 ADJ You also say that a place is **quiet** when nothing exciting or important happens there. *...a quiet*

residential area of the city... In London, the Stock Market had another quiet day.

6 ADJ You describe activities as **quiet** when they happen in secret or in such a way that people do not notice. He conducted some quiet diplomacy for the president during his world tour. ◆ **quietly** The government has quietly renewed martial law for a further month.

7 ADJ You describe colours or clothes as **quiet** when they are not bright or noticeable.

● **Quiet** is used in these phrases. ● If something is done **on the quiet**, it is done secretly, or so that people do not notice; used showing disapproval. ...an attempt to sell oil on the quiet. ● If you **keep quiet** about something, you do not say anything about it. A generation ago, most people would have kept quiet about borrowing money.

quiet down PHRASAL VERB To **quiet down** means to become less noisy, less active, or calmer; used in American English. Things will just quiet down in Turkey... Have the earthquakes quieted down?

quieten /ˈkwaɪətn/ **quietens, quietening, quietened**
V-ERG If you **quieten** a person or situation or if they **quieten**, they become less noisy or less tense. Can you do anything to quieten those children a bit?... All efforts should be made now to open negotiations and quieten the tension... The mayhem has continued for over an hour, although in the last few minutes it has quietened slightly.

quieten down PHRASAL VERB To **quieten down** means to become less noisy, less active, or calmer. To **quieten** someone **down** means to make them less noisy or active. Things have quietened down sufficiently for the patrol to resume its normal activities... Parents and neighbours threw stones before police managed to quieten them down.

quietism /ˈkwaɪətɪzəm/
NU **Quietism** is the belief that you must calmly accept what happens and not try to change things; a formal word.

quill /kwɪl/ **quills**
1 NC A **quill** is a pen made from a bird's feather. Quills are not used very much now. ...quill pens.
2 NC A bird's **quills** are the large, stiff feathers on its wings and tail.
3 NC A porcupine's **quills** are the long, stiff, sharp points on its body.

quilt /kwɪlt/ **quilts**
NC A **quilt** is a bed covering filled with feathers or other warm, soft material. ...feathers for bed quilts and pillows.

quilted /ˈkwɪltɪd/
ADJ **Quilted** clothes or coverings consist of two layers of fabric with a layer of thick material between them. ...a quilted jacket.

quin /kwɪn/ **quins**
NC A **quin** is the same as a **quintuplet**.

quince /kwɪns/ **quinces**
NC A **quince** is a hard fruit with an acid taste that is used for making jelly and marmalade. ...quince marmalade.

quinine /kwɪˈniːn, ˈkwɪniːn/
NU **Quinine** is a drug used to treat and prevent fevers such as malaria. Doctors had to fall back on the old treatment of using intravenous quinine.

quintessence /kwɪnˈtesns/; a formal word.
1 N SING+of The **quintessence** of something is the aspect of it which seems to represent its central nature. That surely is the quintessence of possession... He was the personified quintessence of the nation.
2 N SING+of The **quintessence** of something is also the most perfect or typical example of it. She is the quintessence of sweetness. ...with his slick hair and gleaming smile, the very quintessence of style.

quintessential /ˌkwɪntɪˈsenʃl/
ADJ **Quintessential** means seeming to represent the central nature of something in a pure, concentrated form; a formal word. ...the quintessential early Renaissance man.

quintet /kwɪnˈtet/ **quintets**
1 NC A **quintet** is a group of five singers or musicians singing or playing together. The Quintet was a great

success, playing in fashionable Parisian clubs and winning international fame.
2 NC A **quintet** is also a piece of music written for five instruments or five singers. ...this new disc of Mozart String Quintets.

quintuplet /kwɪntˈjuːplət, kwɪntjuːˈplət/ **quintuplets**
NC A **quintuplet** is one of five children who are born to the same mother at the same time. The quintuplets— four girls and a boy—were delivered by caesarian at the King Edward Memorial Hospital in Perth.

quip /kwɪp/ **quips, quipping, quipped**
1 NC A **quip** is an amusing or clever remark; an old-fashioned word. He can charm away criticism by the combination of a simple quip and a winning smile.
2 V-QUOTE or V-REPORT If you **quip**, you say something funny or clever in order to amuse people. 'Denis on the rocks again,' he quipped... Some lawmakers quip that the latest version has been designed by congressional committees.

quirk /kwɜːk/ **quirks**
1 NC A **quirk** is a strange occurrence that is difficult to explain. By one of those strange quirks of fate, both had died within a few days of each other.
2 NC A **quirk** is also a habit or aspect of a person's character, or of people in general, which is odd or unusual. It is a strange quirk of human nature that often the funniest situations to the onlooker are the most physically painful to the victim.

quirky /ˈkwɜːki/ **quirkier, quirkiest**
ADJ Something or someone that is **quirky** is rather odd in their behaviour, character, or appearance. They are known for their quirky and humorous work, performed in silence... The car they produced was quirky to say the least.

quisling /ˈkwɪzlɪŋ/ **quislings**
NC A **quisling** is a traitor who helps the enemy army that has invaded his or her own country; an old-fashioned word. Quislings in villages who've informed on villagers are liable to have their throats slit.

quit /kwɪt/ **quits, quitting**. The form quit is used in the present tense and is also the past tense and past participle of the verb.
1 V, VO, or V+ING If you **quit** doing something, you stop doing it. He gave no reason for his sudden decision to quit... They are sometimes forced to quit their jobs... It's time to quit talking about this stuff and make the commitment to do it.
2 V or VO If you **quit** a place, you leave it; an old-fashioned use. ...putting the British Raj on notice that it must quit Indian Shores.
3 If people who are arguing or fighting **call it quits**, they agree to stop their argument or fight; an informal expression. We decided to call it quits.

quite /kwaɪt/
1 SUBMOD, PREDET, or ADV You use **quite** to indicate that something is the case to a fairly great extent but not to a very great extent. It sounds quite complicated... The economy is slowing down quite sharply... We sell quite a few of them... I quite enjoy looking round museums.
2 ADV or SUBMOD You also use **quite** to emphasize that something is completely the case or very much the case. Oh I quite agree... Quite clearly, the strength of the pound helps to limit inflation... I stood quite still.
3 ADV You use **quite** after a negative to reduce the force of the negative, and to express uncertainty or politeness. I didn't quite understand what it was all about... I don't know quite where to go... It's not quite big enough.
4 You use **quite a** to emphasize that something is unusual, impressive, or significant. It was quite a sight... They have quite a problem.
5 You can say **'quite'** to express your agreement with someone; a formal use. 'It does a lot for public relations.'—'Quite.'

Quito /ˈkiːtəʊ/
Quito is the capital of Ecuador and its second largest city. Population: 1,282,000 (1990).

quitter /ˈkwɪtə/ **quitters**
NC A **quitter** is a person who gives up easily instead of finishing something that they have started. I don't believe you're a quitter.

quiver /kwɪvə/ quivers, quivering, quivered
v If something **quivers**, it shakes or trembles. *His fingers quivered uncontrollably.* ▸ Also N SING *Her whole body gave a slight quiver.*

quixotic /kwɪksɒtɪk/
ADJ **Quixotic** means having romantic and unrealistic ideas of things that are impossible or impractical; a literary word. *It's a play which often defies adequate production by its very poetic and quixotic nature. ...a quixotic mixture of generosity and brutal discipline.*

quiz /kwɪz/ quizzes
NC A **quiz** is a game or competition in which someone tests your knowledge by asking you questions. *...musical quizzes on TV.*

quizmaster /kwɪzmɑːstə/ quizmasters
NC A **quizmaster** is the same as a **question-master.**

quizzical /kwɪzɪkl/
ADJ If you give someone a **quizzical** look, you look at them in a way that shows that you question their behaviour or that you are amused by it. *She had a real quizzical look on her face, didn't she?*
♦ **quizzically** ADV *The dogs looked quizzically at me. ...his quizzically humorous observations on life in Britain.*

quoit /kɔɪt/ quoits
1 NU **Quoits** is a game in which rings are thrown over a small post.
2 NC A **quoit** is a ring that is used in the game of quoits.

quorum /kwɔːrəm/
N SING A **quorum** is the smallest number of members of a group, committee, or organization, that is officially necessary before a meeting is allowed to begin. *The council needs thirty-two of its ninety-five members to make a quorum... We now have a quorum, so we can begin.*

quota /kwəʊtə/ quotas
1 NC A **quota** is the required quantity of something, such as goods produced or imported. *Various promises were made concerning import quotas... That still represents less than half of this year's quota.*
2 NC A **quota** is also a fixed proportion of people from certain groups who are permitted to do something such as enter a university or work for the government. *The quotas should be based on economic need... It would encourage employers to adopt a quota system for recruiting staff.*

quotation /kwəʊteɪʃn/ quotations
1 NC A **quotation** is a passage or phrase from a book, poem, or play. *...a quotation from a novel by Somerset Maugham.*
2 NC When someone gives you a **quotation**, they tell you how much they will charge to do a particular piece of work. *They submitted quotations and agreed*

prices for the work on the house.

quotation mark, quotation marks
NC **Quotation marks** are punctuation marks used in writing to show where speech or a quotation begins and ends. They are usually written or printed as (' ') or (" ").

quote /kwəʊt/ quotes, quoting, quoted
1 VO, VA, or V-QUOTE If you **quote** someone or something, you repeat the exact words that they have written or said. *It quoted a government spokesman as saying all aspects of the incident would be investigated... Police sources are quoted as saying five people were killed... She quoted from the Bible... 'Words are loaded pistols,' he quoted. 'We use them at our peril.'*
2 VO If you **quote** something such as a law or a fact, you state it because it supports what you are saying. *They quote figures to compare the costs of adult education in different countries... The British government has quoted these views in support of its own opposition to the ban.*
3 NC A **quote** from a book, poem, play, or speech is a passage or phrase from it. *At the front of the book there's a quote from Lawrence's teenage girlfriend, Jessie Chambers... The other quote is from Mrs Thatcher.*
4 NC A **quote** for a piece of work is the price that someone says they will charge you to do the work. *Get a quote from a caterer for a big party.*
5 N PL **Quotes** are the same as **quotation marks;** an informal use.

quoth /kwəʊθ/
V-QUOTE **Quoth** means 'said'. It is only used in the past tense, usually as a third person singular; an old-fashioned word, often used humorously. *'Would it bore you very much,' quoth Hazel, 'to come with us tomorrow for a swim?'*

quotidian /kwəʊtɪdiən/
ADJ **Quotidian** activities are normal, everyday activities; a formal word.

quotient /kwəʊʃnt/ quotients
1 N SING+SUPP The **quotient** of a particular thing is its amount or degree. *This job has a high stress quotient... Your vulnerability quotient was extremely high.* ● **intelligence quotient:** see **IQ.**
2 NC A **quotient** is the number you get when you divide one number into another; a technical use in mathematics.

Qur'an /kɔːrɑːn/; also spelt **Koran.**
N PROP The **Qur'an** is the sacred book on which the religion of Islam is based. *...the Holy Qur'an.*

Quranic /kɔːrænɪk/; also spelt **Koranic.**
ADJ ATTRIB **Quranic** is used to describe something which belongs or relates to the Qur'an. *They said it could even ignore Quranic injunctions.*

R r

R, r /ɑː/ **R's, r's**
NC **R** is the eighteenth letter of the English alphabet.

Rabat /rəbæt/
Rabat is the capital of Morocco and its second largest city. Population: 1,287,000 (1987).

rabbi /ræbaɪ/ **rabbis**
TITLE or NC A **rabbi** is a Jewish religious leader. *Rabbi Mark Schneier is the first foreign rabbi to be allowed to conduct such a service... Ten years later he was invited to become Chief Rabbi of Ireland.*

rabbit /ræbɪt/ **rabbits**
NC A **rabbit** is a small, furry animal with long ears. Rabbits are kept as pets, or live wild in holes in the ground. *The dog disappeared on a mountainside while hunting rabbits.*

rabble /ræbl/
N SING A **rabble** is a crowd of noisy, disorderly people. *...a rabble of boys and girls of all ages.*

rabble-rouser, rabble-rousers
NC A **rabble-rouser** is a clever speaker who can persuade people to be violent or unruly, often for his or her own political advantage. *Poland, Mr Mazowiecki continued, did not need rabble-rousers.*

rabble-rousing
NU **Rabble-rousing** is encouragement that a person gives to other people to be violent or unruly, often for his or her own political advantage. *He deplored such rabble-rousing.* ▶ Also ADJ ATTRIB *...a rabble-rousing newspaper.*

rabid /ræbɪd, reɪbɪd/
1 ADJ ATTRIB You use **rabid** to describe someone who you think has very strong and unreasonable opinions. *...a rabid feminist.*
2 ADJ A **rabid** animal is infected with rabies. *...a rabid dog.*

rabies /reɪbiːz/
NU **Rabies** is a serious infectious disease which causes people and animals to go mad and die. *...a campaign to get dog owners to vaccinate their dogs against rabies.*

RAC /ɑːreɪsiː/
N PROP The **RAC** is a British motoring association that helps members when their cars break down. **RAC** is an abbreviation for 'Royal Automobile Club'. *The RAC said traffic in most parts of the country was flowing smoothly.*

raccoon /rəkuːn/ **raccoons**; also spelt **racoon**.
NC A **raccoon** is a small animal with dark-coloured fur, black stripes on its face, and a long striped tail. Raccoons live in forests in North and Central America and the West Indies. *Raccoons are capable of making some extraordinary noises when they're angry.*

race /reɪs/ **races, racing, raced**
1 NC A **race** is a competition to see who is the fastest, for example in running or driving. *She came second in the race... The race is run through the streets of London.*
2 N SING+SUPP A **race** for power or control is a situation in which people compete for power or control. *The race for the White House is now on. ...the arms race.*
3 V OorV A If you **race** someone or **race** against them,

you compete with them in a race. *They would often race one another to the bus stop... She has raced against some of the best runners in the country.* ● See also **racing**.
4 V A If you **race** somewhere, you go there as quickly as possible. *She raced down the stairs... We had to race across London to get the train.*
5 V If your heart **races**, it beats very quickly. *His heart raced as he saw the plane coming in to land.*
6 NC or NU A **race** is also one of the major groups which human beings can be divided into according to their physical features, such as their skin colour. *The Scouts are a worldwide movement embracing all faiths and all races. ...discrimination on the grounds of colour or race.*
7 If you describe a situation as **a race against time**, you mean you have to work very fast to get something done before a particular time. *His legal team has had a race against time to get him out of jail before the weekend.*
8 See also **human race, rat race**.

racecourse /reɪskɔːs/ **racecourses**
NC A **racecourse** is a track on which horses race. *More than sixty thousand people turned out at the Aintree racecourse to watch the Grand National.*

racehorse /reɪshɔːs/ **racehorses**
NC A **racehorse** is a horse that is trained to run in races. *...Britain's most famous racehorse, Desert Orchid. ...the racehorse trainer, Dermot Browne.*

race meeting, race meetings
NC A **race meeting** is an occasion when a series of horse races are held at the same racecourse, often during a period of several days. *His best performance was in finishing second at a race meeting in Leicester.*

racer /reɪsə/ **racers**
1 NC You can refer to a person or animal that takes part in races as a **racer**. *The Australian Motor Cycle racer Kevin Magee was seriously injured at the Laguna Seca track in California earlier this year... She said her horse was not a racer.*
2 NC A **racer** is also a vehicle, especially a car or bicycle, that is designed to be very fast and used in races.

race relations
N PL **Race relations** are the ways in which people of different races behave towards each other. *...efforts to improve race relations.*

racetrack /reɪstræk/ **racetracks**
1 NC A **racetrack** is a track for races, especially between cars or bicycles. *He spends a week getting to know a racetrack before he lines up for a Grand Prix.*
2 NC A **racetrack** is the same as a **racecourse**; used in American English. *Futo is Vietnam's only racetrack.*

racial /reɪʃl/
ADJ **Racial** describes things relating to people's race. *...a vigorous commitment to defeat racial discrimination. ...victims of racial attacks. ...racial harmony. ...people of all racial backgrounds.*
◆ **racially** ADV *There are seventy thousand racially motivated attacks each year. ...a racially segregated society.*

racialism /reɪʃəlɪzəm/
NU **Racialism** is the same as **racism**. *She is an enemy of apartheid, and all kinds of racialism.*

racialist /reɪʃəlɪst/ **racialists**
NCorN+N **Racialist** means the same as **racist**; an old-fashioned word. *These racialist groups were getting more organized and there was a lot of ill-will.*

racing /reɪsɪŋ/
NU **Racing** refers to races between animals, especially horses, or vehicles. *It's been a day for record breakers in racing and cricket... She is a great lover of horse racing. ...one of the world's most famous names in motor racing. ...Britain's leading racing driver, Nigel Mansell. ...a racing car.*

racism /reɪsɪzəm/
NU **Racism** is the belief that people of particular races are inferior to others, and behaviour which is a result of this belief; used showing disapproval. *...subtle forms of racism. ...a struggle against racism.*

racist /reɪsɪst/ **racists**; used showing disapproval.
1 ADJ **Racist** things, people, or behaviour are influenced by the belief that some people are inferior because they belong to a particular race. *...a clear demonstration of the racist nature of their justice... He went round sticking racist posters on the wall.*
2 NC A **racist** is a person who believes that some people are inferior because they belong to a particular race. *He's a racist and a sexist.*

rack /ræk/ **racks, racking, racked**; the verb is also spelt **wrack** in American English.
1 NC A **rack** is a piece of equipment, usually with bars, hooks, or pegs, used for holding things or hanging things on. *He rinsed the plates and put them on the rack to drain.*
2 VO If someone is **racked** by something, it causes them great suffering or pain; a literary use. *She stood there, racked by indecision, and began to cry.* ● See also **racking**.
3 to **rack** your **brains**: see **brain**.

racket /rækɪt/ **rackets**; also spelt **racquet** for the meaning in paragraph 3.
1 N SING A **racket** is a loud unpleasant noise. *...the non-stop racket that a healthy baby makes.*
2 NC You can refer to an illegal activity used to make money as a **racket**. *He was involved in an insurance racket... They suspect that the gangs are operating a new smuggling racket.*
3 NC A **racket** is also a bat in the shape of an oval with strings across it which is used in games such as tennis and badminton. *I bought her a new tennis racket.*

racketeer /rækətɪə/ **racketeers**
NC A **racketeer** is someone who makes money by threatening people or by selling them worthless, illegal, or immoral goods or services. *His killing may have been ordered by drugs racketeers.*

racketeering /rækətɪərɪŋ/
NU **Racketeering** is making money by threatening people or by selling them worthless, illegal, or immoral goods or services. *He was taken into custody accused of murder and racketeering.*

racking /rækɪŋ/
ADJ ATTRIB A **racking** pain or emotion is one which you feel very strongly. *She burst into terrible racking sobs.*

raconteur /rækɒntɜː/ **raconteurs**
NC A **raconteur** is someone who can tell stories in an interesting or amusing way. *Kazan is a great raconteur.*

racoon /rəkuːn/. See **raccoon**.

racquet /rækɪt/. See **racket**.

racy /reɪsi/
ADJ **Racy** writing or behaviour is lively, amusing, and slightly shocking. *...a racy, romantic historical novel.*

radar /reɪdɑː/
NU **Radar** is a way of using radio signals to discover the position or speed of objects such as aircraft or ships when they cannot be seen. *His speed was checked by radar. ...air defence equipment and radar systems.*

radar trap, radar traps
NC A **radar trap** is a device which is used by the police to measure how fast motorists are driving. *She was reported for speeding after police had set up a radar trap.*

radial /reɪdiəl/ **radials**
1 ADJ **Radial** is used to describe things that form the kind of pattern that you get when straight lines are drawn from the centre of a circle to a number of points round the edge. *...one of the radial streets leading out from the market square. ...radial roads.*
2 NC A **radial** is a tyre which is strengthened on the inside by cords that point towards the centre of the wheel. Radials look softer and are less likely to skid than other tyres.

radiance /reɪdiəns/
1 NU **Radiance** is great happiness which is shown in someone's face. *...the radiance of her features... Hilary lost a little of her radiance.*
2 NU **Radiance** is also a glowing light shining from something. *The candle's light threw a faint radiance on the sleeping girl.*

radiant /reɪdiənt/
1 ADJ Someone who is **radiant** is so happy that their joy shows in their face. *Charlotte, you look radiant.*
◆ **radiantly** ADV *Jane smiled radiantly.*
2 ADJ Something that is **radiant** glows brightly. *...a morning of radiant light.*

radiate /reɪdieɪt/ **radiates, radiating, radiated**
1 V If things **radiate** from a place, they form a pattern that spreads out like lines drawn from the centre of a circle. *...roads that radiated before us... Rods radiate outwards from the centre.*
2 VOorV+from If you **radiate** an emotion or quality, or if it **radiates** from you, people can see it very clearly in your face and in your behaviour. *Mr Reagan radiated optimism... There was a tenderness that radiated from her.*

radiation /reɪdieɪʃn/
1 NU **Radiation** is very small particles of a radioactive substance that can cause illness and death. *Those exposed to a very large amount of radiation experience internal bleeding.*
2 NU **Radiation** is also energy, especially heat, that comes from a particular source. *Solar radiation warms up the air.*

radiation sickness
NU **Radiation sickness** is an illness that is caused by a person being exposed to too much radiation. *You would probably start to show the first signs of radiation sickness within two hours.*

radiator /reɪdieɪtə/ **radiators**
1 NC A **radiator** is a hollow metal device which is connected to a central heating system and used to heat a room. *She spent her nights huddled close to a radiator.*
2 NC A car **radiator** is the part of the engine which is used to cool the engine. *His car had a punctured radiator.*

radical /rædɪkl/ **radicals**
1 ADJ **Radical** refers to things that affect or relate to the most important, basic qualities of a situation or thing. *...a radical disagreement over fundamentals... They hope to bring radical changes to Afghan society. ...the need for radical economic reform.* ◆ **radically** ADV *Attitudes towards education will have to change radically.*
2 ADJ Someone who is **radical** believes that there should be great changes in society and tries to bring about these changes. *...Mr Gorbachev's leading radical opponent, Mr Boris Yeltsin... The League had become too radical.* ▶ Also NC *...a new group of radicals who turned against the established social order.*

radicalism /rædɪkəlɪzəm/
NU **Radicalism** is radical beliefs, ideas, or behaviour. *...the radicalism of the Government. ...the traditions of radicalism and dissent.*

radii /reɪdiaɪ/
Radii is the plural of **radius**.

radio /reɪdiəʊ/ **radios, radioing, radioed**
1 N SINGorNU **Radio** is the broadcasting of programmes for the public to listen to, by sending out signals from a transmitter. *...one of those plays that*

are the stuff of radio. ...a local radio station.
2 If you hear something **on the radio,** you hear it when
it is being broadcast by radio. *I heard the news on the
radio half an hour ago.*
3 NC A **radio** is also the piece of equipment used to
listen to radio programmes. *She switched on the
radio.*
4 NU **Radio** is the system of sending sound over a
distance by transmitting electrical signals. *...radio
waves... We managed to establish radio
communication with them.*
5 VOorV If you **radio** someone, you send a message to
them using radio. *I had radioed Rick and arranged to
have a car waiting for me... The captain had radioed
ahead and the security guards were waiting.*
radioactive /reɪdɪəʊæktɪv/
  ADJ Something that is **radioactive** contains a substance
  that produces energy in the form of powerful and
  harmful rays. *...highly radioactive waste.*
radioactivity /reɪdɪəʊæktɪvəti/
  NU **Radioactivity** is radioactive energy. *...a serious
  leak of radioactivity.*
radiocarbon /reɪdɪəʊkɑːbən/
  NU **Radiocarbon** is a type of carbon which is
  radioactive, and which therefore breaks up slowly at a
  steady rate. The amount of radiocarbon in an object
  can be measured in order to indicate the object's age.
  ...radiocarbon dating.
radio-controlled
  ADJ A **radio-controlled** device works by receiving radio
  signals which operate it. *I once made a radio-
  controlled plane from a kit.*
radiogram /reɪdɪəʊɡræm/ **radiograms**
  NC A **radiogram** is a piece of equipment consisting of
  a cabinet that contains a record-player and a radio.
  Radiograms are now quite rare. *By then the
  radiogram had become an indispensable item in
  almost every home in Europe.*
radiograph /reɪdɪəʊɡrɑːf/ **radiographs**
  NC A **radiograph** is a picture of the inside of your
  body, which is made by sending X-rays through it, and
  is used by doctors to check the condition of your bones
  or organs; an old-fashioned word. *The radiographer
  will go outside the room and will take a radiograph.*
radiographer /reɪdɪɒɡrəfə/ **radiographers**
  NC A **radiographer** is a person who is trained to take
  X-rays.
radiography /reɪdɪɒɡrəfi/
  NU **Radiography** is the process of taking X-rays.
radiologist /reɪdɪɒlədʒɪst/ **radiologists**
  NC A **radiologist** is a doctor who is trained in
  radiology. *A consultant radiologist said that the
  benefits of X-rays far outweigh the risk of having
  them.*
radiology /reɪdɪɒlədʒi/
  NU **Radiology** is the branch of medical science that
  uses radioactivity. *He has been receiving radiology
  treatment over the past four years.*
radio-telephone, radio-telephones
  NC A **radio-telephone** is a telephone which carries
  sound by sending radio signals rather than by using
  wires, and which is often used in cars. *The hospital is
  out in the bush and can only be reached by radio-
  telephone.*
radio telescope, radio telescopes
  NC A **radio telescope** is an instrument that receives
  radio waves from space and finds the position of stars
  and other objects in space. *...a network of radio
  telescopes across Britain, connected by microwave
  communications links.*
radiotherapist /reɪdɪəʊθerəpɪst/ **radiotherapists**
  NC A **radiotherapist** is a person who is trained in the
  treatment of diseases by radiation. *Radiotherapists
  plan the treatment very carefully.*
radiotherapy /reɪdɪəʊθerəpi/
  NU **Radiotherapy** is the treatment of diseases such as
  cancer using radiation. *Approximately the same
  number of women had had radiotherapy and
  chemotherapy.*
radish /rædɪʃ/ **radishes**
  NC A **radish** is a small red or white root vegetable
  which is eaten raw in salads.

radium /reɪdɪəm/
  NU **Radium** is a radioactive element which is used in
  the treatment of cancer and other serious diseases.
  ...radium therapy.
radius /reɪdɪəs/ **radii** /reɪdiaɪ/
  1 NC The **radius** of a circle is the distance from its
  centre to its outside edge.
  2 N SING+SUPP **Radius** also refers to the distance in
  any direction from a particular point. *The missile
  landed within a half-mile radius of its target.*
RAF /ɑːreɪef, ræf/
  RAF is an abbreviation for 'Royal Air Force'; the air
  force of the United Kingdom. *The second plane
  crashed, killing the two RAF pilots on board.*
raffia /ræfiə/
  NU **Raffia** is a fibre made from palm leaves. It is used
  to make mats and baskets. *...coarse raffia string.*
raffish /ræfɪʃ/
  ADJ A **raffish** person is someone who behaves in a way
  that is not considered correct, but who does so in a
  stylish or daring way which you find amusing or
  likeable; an old-fashioned word. *...a raffish but
  dedicated young politician... His raffish charm
  appealed to audiences throughout the world.*
  ◆ **raffishness** NU *He had a raffishness that women
  found rather charming.*
raffle /ræfl/ **raffles**
  NC A **raffle** is a competition in which you buy
  numbered tickets. If your ticket is chosen, you win a
  prize. *A group of students organised a raffle and the
  proceeds went to the Book Fund in Jamaica.*
Rafsanjani, Hojatoleslam Hashemi Ali Akbar
  /hɑːʃemiː æliː ækbɑː ræfsændʒɑːniː/
  Hojatoleslam Hashemi Ali Akbar Rafsanjani became
  President of Iran in 1989. He was Acting Commander-
  in-Chief of the Armed Forces from 1988 to 1989, and
  was Speaker of the Islamic Consultative Assembly
  from 1980 to 1989. He was a founder of the now defunct
  Islamic Republican Party and served on its Central
  Committee from 1983 to 1987. Born: 1934.
raft /rɑːft/ **rafts**
  NC A **raft** is a floating platform made from large
  pieces of wood tied together. *After about two weeks in
  the raft, Mr Gyani was washed ashore.*
rafter /rɑːftə/ **rafters**
  NC **Rafters** are the sloping pieces of wood that support
  a roof. *Most of these houses still have their original
  rafters.*
rag /ræɡ/ **rags**
  1 NCorNU A **rag** is a piece of old cloth which you can
  use to clean or wipe things. *Wiping his hands on a
  rag, he went out to the car. ...a crumpled piece of rag.*
  2 N PL **Rags** are old, torn clothes. *They were thin and
  hungry, dressed in rags.*
  3 NC People refer to a newspaper as a **rag** when have
  a low opinion of it; an informal use. *...the local rag.*
ragamuffin /ræɡəmʌfɪn/ **ragamuffins**
  NC A **ragamuffin** is a child who is dirty and wears torn
  clothes; an old-fashioned word. *He didn't want his
  boys to come in looking like ragamuffins.*
rag-and-bone man, rag-and-bone men
  NC A **rag-and-bone man** is a person who goes from
  street to street with a horse and cart or a van trying
  to buy and sell things such as old clothes and
  furniture.
ragbag /ræɡbæɡ/ **ragbags**
  NC+SUPP A **ragbag** of things is a group of things which
  do not have much in common with each other, but
  which are being considered together at the same time;
  an informal word. *...that complicated cultural ragbag
  of people's values.*
rag doll, rag dolls
  NC A **rag doll** is a soft doll made from pieces of cloth.
rage /reɪdʒ/ **rages, raging, raged**
  1 NUorNC **Rage** is strong, uncontrollable anger. *She
  was trembling with rage... I stormed out of the room
  in a rage.*
  2 VorV-QUOTE If you **rage** about something, you speak
  or think very angrily about it. *There were moments
  when I raged at my captors... 'How do you mean, you
  can't tell me?' he raged.*
  3 V If something **rages,** it continues with great force

or violence. *There was a monsoon raging outside...*
The debate raged throughout the whole day.
4 If something is **all the rage**, it is very popular and
fashionable; an informal expression. *Board games are
all the rage.*

ragged /rægɪd/
1 ADJ Someone who is **ragged** is wearing clothes that
are old and torn. *...a ragged, skinny man of about
fifty.*
2 ADJ **Ragged** clothes are old and torn. *...ragged
cotton garments.*
3 ADJ A **ragged** line or edge is uneven or rough.
*There were four ragged screw holes where the handle
should have been.*

raging /reɪdʒɪŋ/
ADJ ATTRIB **Raging** feelings or desires are very intense
and severe. *...a raging thirst.*

ragtime /rægtaɪm/
NU **Ragtime** is a kind of jazz music that became
popular in America in the early 1900s. *He played
ragtime and blues music in Californian clubs.*

rag trade
N SING The **rag trade** is the business and industry of
making and selling clothes, especially women's
clothes; an informal expression. *Forty years she
spent in the rag trade.*

rag week
NU In Britain, **rag week** is an annual event lasting a
week, during which students raise money for charity
in a variety of ways. *In rag week students try all
sorts of pranks to raise money for charity.*

raid /reɪd/ **raids, raiding, raided**
1 VO When soldiers, the police, or criminals **raid** a
place, they enter it by force to attack it, or to look for
someone or something. *Blanco's supporters are still
raiding villages along the border... Their headquarters
in London were raided by the police.* ▸ Also NC
...police raids. ...a series of bank raids.
2 See also **air raid**.

raider /reɪdə/ **raiders**
NC **Raiders** are people who take part in a raid. *Three
masked raiders attacked their sub-post office. ...armed
cattle raiders from the north.*

rail /reɪl/ **rails**
1 NC A **rail** is a horizontal bar which is fixed to
something and used as a fence or as a support for
hanging things on. *Holding on to the rail with one
hand, he pulled himself up. ...picture rails. ...a towel
rail.*
2 NC The steel bars which trains run on are called
rails. *The train came off the rails in a mountainous
area some two hundred miles from the capital.*
3 NU If you travel or send something by **rail**, you
travel on or send it in a train. *I usually go by rail.
...proposals for improving the rail network.*
4 If something such as a plan, discussion, or
agreement is **back on the rails**, it continues after a
period when it almost failed. *Anglo-Irish relations
were back on the rails.*

railcard /reɪlkɑːd/ **railcards**
NC A **railcard** is an identity card that allows people to
buy train tickets cheaply. *...a Senior Citizens
Railcard.*

railing /reɪlɪŋ/ **railings**
N PLorNC A fence made from metal bars is called
railings or a **railing**. *I peered through the railings into
the courtyard... This railing should be cleaned.*

raillery /reɪləri/
NU **Raillery** is behaviour that involves friendly jokes
and teasing remarks; a literary word. *There was a
certain amount of raillery at Basil's expense.*

railroad /reɪlrəʊd/ **railroads**
NC A **railroad** is the same as a **railway**; used in
American English. *China would help Iran to rebuild
factories, dams and railroads.*

railway /reɪlweɪ/ **railways**
1 NC A **railway** is a route along which trains travel on
steel rails. *...the railway to Addis Ababa. ...the early
days of railways. ...the main railway station.*
2 NC A **railway** is also a company or organization that
operates railway routes. *...the Great Western
Railway.*

railway line, railway lines
1 NC A **railway line** is a route along which trains
travel on steel rails. *...the railway line from London
to Brighton.*
2 NC A **railway line** is also the steel rails on which
trains travel. *...a new railway line for high speed
trains.*

railwayman /reɪlweɪmən/ **railwaymen** /reɪlweɪmən/
NC **Railwaymen** are men who work for the railway.
*Two railwaymen have been killed in an accident
during engineering work.*

railway track, railway tracks
NC A **railway track** is a specially prepared strip of
ground with metal rails on it that trains travel on.
*...just outside Ramsdale, between the railway tracks
and Lakeview Hill.*

raiment /reɪmənt/
NU **Raiment** is clothing; an old-fashioned word. *He
put on the sober black raiment which was his usual
wear.*

rain /reɪn/ **rains, raining, rained**
1 NU **Rain** is water that falls from the clouds in small
drops. *You can't go home in this rain... A light rain
had begun to fall.*
2 N PL In countries where rain only falls in certain
seasons, this rain is referred to as the **rains**. *The
rains end this month... Relief workers have warned of
serious shortages because of poor rains.*
3 V When rain falls, you can say that it **is raining**. *It
had started to rain... It's still raining heavily.*
4 V-ERG A If things such as bullets **rain** from above,
they fall rapidly in large quantities. *Ash rained from
the sky... Syrian and Druze gunners rained rockets
and mortars on Christian areas.*
rain down PHRASAL VERB If things such as bullets
rain down, they fall rapidly in large quantities.
*Mortar shells rained down... They aren't alone in
occasionally raining down nuclear debris on us.*
rain off PHRASAL VERB If a sports match is **rained off**,
it cannot take place because of the rain. *The Men's
Open was rained off before the leaders played their
second round.*

rainbow /reɪnbəʊ/ **rainbows**
NC A **rainbow** is the arch of different colours that you
sometimes see in the sky when it is raining.
...thousands of birds, in every colour of the rainbow.

rain check
If you say that you will **take a rain check** on an offer
or a suggestion, you mean that you do not want to
accept it straight away, but you might accept it later;
an informal expression, used in American English.

raincoat /reɪnkəʊt/ **raincoats**
NC A **raincoat** is a waterproof coat. *Most people have
turned up with umbrellas and raincoats after forecasts
of rain.*

raindrop /reɪndrɒp/ **raindrops**
NC A **raindrop** is a single drop of rain. *Large
raindrops splashed onto the newly fallen tree.*

rainfall /reɪnfɔːl/
NU **Rainfall** is the amount of rain that falls in a place
during a particular period of time. *...the average
monthly rainfall of London.*

rainforest /reɪnfɒrɪst/ **rainforests**
NCorNU A **rainforest** is a thick forest of tall trees
found in tropical areas where there is a lot of rain.
*Mr Mendes won a number of awards for his work to
save the rainforest. ...100 hectares of virgin rainforest.*

Rainier III, Prince of Monaco /reɪnjeɪ/
Rainier III became Prince of Monaco in 1949,
succeeding his grandfather, Prince Louis II. Born:
1923.

rainstorm /reɪnstɔːm/ **rainstorms**
NC A **rainstorm** is a heavy fall of rain. *Heavy
rainstorms created treacherous driving conditions and
caused dozens of accidents.*

rainwater /reɪnwɔːtə/
NU **Rainwater** is water that has fallen as rain.
Rainwater had leaked through the roof.

rainy /reɪni/
1 ADJ If it is **rainy**, it is raining a lot. *Most tropical
areas have rainy and dry seasons. ...a rainy Sunday
afternoon.*

2 If you are saving something **for a rainy day,** you are saving it until a time when you might need it. *They put part of the money in the bank for a rainy day.*

raise /reɪz/ **raises, raising, raised**

1 vo If you **raise** something, you move it to a higher position. *He tried to raise the window, but the sash cord was broken... She raised her eyebrows in surprise.*

2 vo If you **raise** the rate or level of something, you increase it. *The maximum speed was raised to seventy miles per hour... Corporate tax has been raised from 40 per cent to 45 per cent.*

3 vo To **raise** the standard of something means to improve it. *Putting teachers in day nurseries would raise standards.*

4 vo If you **raise** your voice, you speak more loudly. *Raising his voice, he warned that he would not tolerate efforts to undermine national stability.*

5 nc A **raise** is an increase in your wages or salary; used in American English. *He hopes to get a raise.*

6 vo To **raise** money for a charity or a cause means to get people to donate money towards it. *He raised £300 to finance it... A marathon television programme has raised more than £10 million for charity.*

7 vo To **raise** a child means to look after it until it is grown up. *It was no place to raise a child.*

8 vo To **raise** a particular type of animal or crop means to breed the animal or grow the crop. *He moved to Petaluma to raise chickens.*

9 vo If you **raise** a subject, objection, or question, you mention it or bring it to someone's attention. *You would have to raise that with Mr Gerran personally.*

raised /reɪzd/

ADJ A flat object or area that is **raised** is higher than its surrounding surface. *...a raised jetty four feet high... On her shoulder was a raised purple-pink swelling.*

raisin /reɪzn/ **raisins**

nc **Raisins** are dried grapes.

raison d'être /reɪzɒnⁿ detrə/

n sing A person or organization's **raison d'être** is the most important reason for them existing in the way that they do; a formal expression. *Selling, after all, is their raison d'être.*

rake /reɪk/ **rakes, raking, raked**

1 nc A **rake** is a garden tool consisting of a row of metal teeth attached to a long handle. *Any gardener knows that a rake is an essential tool.*

2 vo To **rake** leaves or soil means to use a rake to gather the leaves or make the soil smooth. *Jeremy had raked the fallen leaves into a pile... The field had been raked.*

rake in PHRASAL VERB If someone is **raking in** money, they are earning a lot of it fairly easily; an informal expression. *He had been raking in millions of dollars for himself in illicit international deals.*

rake up PHRASAL VERB If you **rake up** something unpleasant or embarrassing from the past, you talk about it and remind people of it. *He accused them of unnecessarily raking up controversies.*

raked /reɪkt/

ADJ If a surface such as the stage in a theatre is **raked,** it slopes up towards the back, for example so that all the audience can see clearly. *The stage is raked steeply upwards.*

rake-off

n sing A **rake-off** is an illegal share in profits that is taken by someone who has helped to arrange a business deal; an informal word.

rakish /reɪkɪʃ/

1 ADJ If a man is described as **rakish,** he is considered to be rather immoral and irresponsible; an old-fashioned use. *There was little she had not heard about his rakish, wandering existence.* ◆ **rakishly** ADV *He grinned rakishly.*

2 ADJ If you wear a hat at a **rakish** angle, it is pulled down at one side in a way that is intended to seem casual and confident. *...a beret worn at a rakish angle.* ◆ **rakishly** ADV *...a round white cap rakishly tilted over her left ear.*

rally /ræli/ **rallies, rallying, rallied**

1 nc A **rally** is a large public meeting held in support of something such as a political party, or to protest against something. *...a big anti-government rally in Hyde Park... Both those who support and those who oppose the bill are planning mass rallies in London.*

2 nc A **rally** is also a competition in which vehicles are driven in timed stages over public roads. *The Paris-Dakar Rally will go through Libya for the first time.*

3 nc A **rally** in a game of tennis, badminton, or squash, is a continuous series of shots that the players exchange without stopping. *Rallies on grass courts tend to be shorter than on clay.*

4 v-ERG When people **rally** to something, they unite to support it. *Mr Gorbachev's supporters rallied to his defence... They made a final effort to rally their supporters.*

5 v When someone **rallies,** they become stronger again, for example during a sports match or when ill. *Martin dropped the first game but rallied to beat his opponent 7-15, 15-8, 15-9, 15-4... The President rallied, but then died from his wounds nine days later.*

6 v When share prices or currencies that have declined in value **rally,** their value increases again. *Both share prices and the pound have rallied slightly.*

rally round PHRASAL VERB When people **rally round,** they work as a group in order to support a person or organization at a difficult time. *Conservative MPs have rallied round in support... The People's Daily called on workers to rally round the party.*

rallying /rælɪɪŋ/

nu Motor **rallying** is a sport in which cars are driven in timed stages over public roads. *The third event in the world motor rallying calendar goes into its first full day tomorrow.*

rallying cry, rallying cries

1 nc A **rallying cry** or **rallying call** is a slogan or a short speech which is intended to inspire people to unite in support of a political group or ideal. *'I'm on your side' is his new rallying cry... The Prime Minister issued a rallying call for all Malays to unite around him.*

2 nc A **rallying cry** or **rallying call** is also something such as an event, ideal, or belief that inspires people to unite in support of a political group or ideal. *The emotive imagery of the suffering of children served as a powerful rallying cry. ...the potential power of the Palestinian issue as a rallying call.*

rallying point, rallying points

1 nc A **rallying point** is a place, event, or person that people are attracted to as a symbol of a political group or ideal. *The violence occurred in front of the Johcang Temple, a traditional rallying point for anti-Chinese protests... The former king is still regarded as a rallying point by moderate Afghanis.*

2 nc A **rallying point** is also a place where people gather at the start or finish of a political demonstration. *Only about a hundred people gathered at the rallying point for the lunchtime march.*

ram /ræm/ **rams, ramming, rammed**

1 vo If one vehicle **rams** another, it crashes into it with a lot of force. *The ship had been rammed by a British destroyer.*

2 voA If you **ram** something somewhere, you push it there with great force. *I rammed the bolt back across the door.*

3 nc A **ram** is an adult male sheep. *We fatten the rams and sell them to supermarkets and so forth.*

Ramadan /ræmədæn/

nu **Ramadan** is the ninth month of the Muslim year, during which Muslims must fast from sunrise to sunset. *It's the Sultan who sees the moon and declares the start and the end of Ramadan.*

Ramaema, Elias Phisoana

/ɪlaɪəs pɪswaːnə raːməeɪmə/

Colonel **Elias Phisoana Ramaema** became Chairman of the Military Council of Lesotho following a coup in 1991. He was Head of Planning, Economic Affairs and Manpower Development, Information and Broadcasting, Public Service and Employment, Social Welfare and Pensions from 1986 to 1991. Born: 1933.

ramble /ræmbl/ **rambles, rambling, rambled**

1 nc A **ramble** is a long walk in the countryside. *We*

were out on a country ramble. ▸ Also V A ...*rambling over the Yorkshire hills.*

2 v If someone **rambles**, they talk for a long time in a confused way. *He often rambled and said strange things.*

ramble on PHRASAL VERB If someone **rambles on**, they talk for a long time in a confused way. ...*listening to Miriam as she rambled on.*

rambler /ˈræmblə/ **ramblers**
N C A **rambler** is a person who goes for long walks in the countryside, usually as part of an organized group. *The ramblers believe private landowners should open up more of their property for the enjoyment of the public.*

rambling /ˈræmblɪŋ/
1 ADJ A **rambling** building is big and old with an irregular shape. *We bought a rambling old house near the village.*
2 ADJ **Rambling** speech or writing is very long and confused. *She wrote me a long rambling letter.*

ramification /ˌræmɪfɪˈkeɪʃn/ **ramifications**
N C The **ramifications** of a decision, idea, or plan are all its consequences and effects, especially ones which were not obvious at first; a formal word. *Not many people actually understand the ramifications of these guidelines.*

ramp /ræmp/ **ramps**
1 N C A **ramp** is a sloping surface between two places that are at different levels. *It was driven up a ramp and straight on to the train.*
2 N C In American English, a **ramp** is also a road which leads onto or off a freeway. *We went to the next off ramp and turned around.*

rampage /ˈræmpeɪdʒ/ **rampages, rampaging, rampaged**
1 V A When people or animals **rampage** through a place, they rush about there in a wild or violent way, causing damage or destruction. *Angry demonstrators rampaged through the main business district.* ...*elephants rampaging through the bush.*
2 If people **go on the rampage**, they rush about in a wild or violent way, causing damage or destruction. *A section of the crowd broke loose and went on the rampage.*

rampant /ˈræmpənt/
ADJ If a something such as a crime or disease is **rampant**, it is growing or spreading in an uncontrolled way. ...*the abuses now rampant in the American legal system.* ...*rampant inflation...* *The tests were carried out on volunteers from Zaire, where the disease is rampant.*

ramparts /ˈræmpɑːts/
N PL The **ramparts** of a fort, castle, or city are the earth bank, often with a wall on top, that used to be built around it for protection. ...*photographs of the two leaders standing under the ramparts of an ancient castle.*

ramrod /ˈræmrɒd/ **ramrods**
1 N C A **ramrod** is a long thin rod that is used for cleaning the barrel of a gun or for forcing gunpowder down the barrel.
2 If someone sits or stands as **stiff as a ramrod** or as **straight as a ramrod**, they sit or stand in a very stiff and upright way. *She sat there stiff as a ramrod.*
3 ADJ ATTRIB or ADV **Ramrod** is used to describe someone who is holding their body very straight and upright. *The small cortege swept past the ramrod guards... They stand ramrod straight.*

ramshackle /ˈræmʃækl/
ADJ ATTRIB A **ramshackle** building is badly made or in a very bad condition. ...*a ramshackle cottage.*

ran /ræn/
Ran is the past tense of **run**.

ranch /rɑːntʃ/ **ranches**
N C A **ranch** is a large farm, especially one used for breeding farm animals. ...*the remote cattle ranch in Panama where she raises prize animals.*

rancher /ˈrɑːntʃə/ **ranchers**
N C A **rancher** is someone who owns or manages a ranch. *Those forests are being cut down at a terrifying rate by cattle ranchers.*

ranching /ˈrɑːntʃɪŋ/
N U **Ranching** is the activity of running a ranch. ...*beef and sheep ranching.*

rancid /ˈrænsɪd/
ADJ If butter, bacon, or other fatty foods are **rancid**, they have gone bad and taste unpleasant. *We have been using antioxidants to make sure that those fats don't go rancid.*

rancorous /ˈræŋkərəs/
ADJ Someone who is **rancorous** feels deep and bitter hatred; a formal word. *He had been incredibly rancorous toward McKinley.*

rancour /ˈræŋkə/; spelt **rancor** in American English.
N U **Rancour** is a feeling of deep and bitter hatred; a formal word. *He was shaken by rage and rancour.*

random /ˈrændəm/
1 ADJ Something that is done in a **random** way is done without a definite plan or pattern. *The way the books were arranged seemed completely random.* ...*a random selection...* *Police officers supported the introduction of random breath tests.* ◆ **randomly** ADV *Ink had been randomly squirted on the floor and walls.*
2 If something is done **at random**, it is done without a definite plan or pattern. *He opened the book at random... I let my thoughts come at random.*

randy /ˈrændi/
ADJ Someone who is **randy** is eager to have sexual intercourse; an informal word. *The heat made them both randy.*

rang /ræŋ/
Rang is the past tense of some meanings of **ring**.

range /reɪndʒ/ **ranges, ranging, ranged**
1 N C+SUPP The **range** of something is the maximum area within which it can reach things or detect things. *What is the range of their transmitters? ...medium range ballistic missiles.*
2 N SING+SUPP A **range** of things is a number of different things of the same general kind. ...*a wide range of electrical goods.* ...*the range of research activities in the university.*
3 N C+SUPP A **range** is the complete group that is included between two points on a scale of measurement or quality. *The age range is from six months to forty-seven years.*
4 V A When things **range** between two points or **range** from one point to another, they vary within these points on a scale of measurement or quality. *Their politics ranged from liberal to radical... They were offered increases ranging from £6.71 to £16.31 a week.*
5 V A A piece of writing or speech that **ranges** over a group of topics includes all those topics. *The book ranges historically as far back as the Renaissance... The conversation ranged widely.*
6 N C+SUPP A **range** of mountains or hills is a line of them. ...*the proposed railway project through the Caucasus mountain range.*
7 N C In American English, a **range** is a large area of open grassy land where cattle or animals feed.
8 N C A rifle **range** or a firing **range** is a place where people can practise shooting at targets. ...*staff employed to search firing ranges for unexploded shells.*
● **Range** is used in these phrases. ● If something is **within range**, it is near enough to be reached or detected. If it is **out of range**, it is too far away to be reached or detected. *The whole of the waterway is also within range of Iraqi war planes... We managed to keep out of range.* ● If you shoot something at **close range**, you are very close to it when you shoot it. *A masked gunman shot him four or five times at close range.*

rangefinder /ˈreɪndʒfaɪndə/ **rangefinders**
N C A **rangefinder** is an instrument that is used for measuring how far away from you something that you are shooting at or photographing is. *The tank has a high velocity 125 mm gun and laser rangefinder.*

ranger /ˈreɪndʒə/ **rangers**
N C A **ranger** is a person whose job is to look after a forest or park. *He ordered his game rangers to shoot poachers on sight.*

Rangoon /ræŋˈguːn/
Rangoon, also known as Yangon, is the capital of

Burma and its largest city. Population: 2,513,000 (1983).

rank /ræŋk/ **ranks, ranking, ranked**
1 N C or N U Someone's **rank** is their position or grade in an organization, for example in the armed forces or the police. *A prisoner of war must only reveal his name, rank, and serial number... She achieved the rank of professor at the age of 31... He wasn't getting the salary to which he was entitled by rank.*
2 V-ERG A When you say how something **ranks** or is **ranked**, you state its position on a scale. *The island ranks as one of the poorest of the whole region... They are ranked according to the quality of things they make.*
3 N PL The **ranks** are the ordinary members of an organization, especially of the armed forces. *...a senior officer who had risen from the ranks.*
4 N PL+SUPP When you become a member of a large group of people, you can say that you are joining its **ranks**. *This morning many people joined the ranks of protesters outside the news agency. ...the growing ranks of the unemployed.*
5 ADJ ATTRIB You use **rank** to describe a very bad or undesirable quality; a formal use. *...rank corruption. ...rank favouritism.*
6 ADJ You can describe something with a strong and unpleasant smell as **rank**; a formal use. *He trudged heavily up the steps, rank with the sweat of his night's work.*
● **Rank** is used in these phrases. ● If someone **pulls rank**, they make unfair use of the authority that they have in an organization. *She usually gets her own way without needing to pull rank.* ● When the members of a group **close ranks**, they support each other in a united way to oppose any attack or criticism; used showing disapproval. *Mr Heath's outburst might actually encourage dissenters from Mrs Thatcher's line to close ranks behind her out of loyalty.*

rank and file
N COLL The **rank and file** are the ordinary members of an organization rather than the leaders or officers. *...political differences between the leadership and the rank and file... Mr Scargill retains the loyalty of many rank and file union members.*

ranking /ræŋkɪŋ/
ADJ You use **ranking** after a word such as 'high' to describe someone's position or grade in an organization. *President Ershad will be accompanied by high ranking trade officials... There is concern about the attitude of the middle ranking military officers.*

rankle /ræŋkl/ **rankles, rankling, rankled**
v If something **rankles**, it makes you feel angry or bitter. *The argument with Sam earlier on still rankled.*

rank outsider, rank outsiders
NC A **rank outsider** is someone in a contest, vote, or competition who is not expected to win. *The opening match produced an astonishing result—rank outsiders Cameroon beat Argentina by one goal to nil... Until the election campaign started, Tyminski was an unknown rank outsider.*

ransack /rænsæk/ **ransacks, ransacking, ransacked**
v o If you **ransack** a building or a room, you disturb everything in it and leave it in a mess, because you are looking for something. *Detectives ransacked the house.*

ransom /rænsəm/ **ransoms**
1 NC A **ransom** is an amount of money that is demanded for the release of a person who has been kidnapped. *The family paid a ransom of £50,000 for the child's release.*
2 If someone **holds** a person **to ransom** or **holds** them **ransom**, they keep that person as a prisoner until money is paid for them to be set free. *They were accused of kidnapping a Brazilian businessman and holding him to ransom... A bus-load of schoolchildren were held ransom.*
3 To **hold** a government or group of people **to ransom** means to try to force them to agree to something. *Union leaders held the nation to ransom.*

rant /rænt/ **rants, ranting, ranted**
v If someone **rants**, they talk in a loud, excited, and angry way. *He would rant like this till she could not bear it any more.* ◆ **ranting, rantings** N C *...the rantings and ravings of these lunatics.*

Rao, P V Narasimha /piː viː nærəsɪmhə rauː/
P V Narasimha Rao became Prime Minister of India in 1991. He is a member of the Congress (I) Party and became leader of the party when Rajiv Gandhi was assassinated in 1991. He has held many Cabinet posts, including Health and Family Welfare from 1986 to 1988, and External Affairs from 1988 to 1989. Born: 1921.

rap /ræp/ **raps, rapping, rapped**
1 V A or V O A If you **rap** on something or if you **rap** it, you hit it with a series of quick blows. *He rapped on the table and called for silence... Breslow walked across to the wall and rapped his knuckles against the marble.*
2 NC A **rap** is a quick hit or knock against something. *A light rap sounded at the door.*
3 NU **Rap** is a style of pop music in which someone talks rhythmically to a musical backing. *Rap is perhaps the most important development in popular music in the past decade... De La Soul have established themselves as one of the most successful rap bands.*
● **Rap** is used in these phrases. ● If you receive **a rap over the knuckles**, you receive a warning or criticism. *She rejected suggestions that the United States was merely giving Mr Shamir a small rap over the knuckles for his remarks.* ● If you **take the rap**, you are blamed or punished for something, even if it is not your fault; an informal expression. *Lloyd will have to take the rap.*
rap out PHRASAL VERB If you **rap out** an order or a question, you say it quickly and sharply. *'Is that the truth?' he suddenly rapped out.*

rapacious /rəpeɪʃəs/
ADJ A **rapacious** person is extremely greedy for money; a formal word. *...rapacious businessmen.*

rapacity /rəpæsəti/
NU **Rapacity** is extreme greed, especially for money; a formal word. *...the rapacity of humans.*

rape /reɪp/ **rapes, raping, raped**
v o When a man **rapes** a woman, he has sex with her by force, against her will. *...an organization to help women who have been raped.* ▶ Also N U or N C *She had to testify to his attempts at rape. ...the riots, rapes, and muggings in our streets and parks.*

rapid /ræpɪd/ **rapids**
1 ADJ Something that is **rapid** happens or moves very quickly. *...a time of rapid economic growth... He took a few rapid steps towards the beach.* ◆ **rapidly** ADV *The situation had rapidly deteriorated.* ◆ **rapidity** /rəpɪdəti/ NU *The film shows the rapidity of the changes in this area of medicine.*
2 N PL **Rapids** are parts of a river where the water moves very fast. *Further down the river is another stretch of rapids.*

rapier /reɪpiə/ **rapiers**
NC A **rapier** is a long, thin, pointed sword.

rapist /reɪpɪst/ **rapists**
NC A **rapist** is a man who has raped a woman. *...the police's failure to apprehend the rapists.*

rapport /ræpɔː/
NU **Rapport** is a feeling of understanding and sympathy which two or more people share. *There is insufficient rapport between hospitals and family doctors.*

rapprochement /rəprɒʃmɒŋ/
NU If there is a **rapprochement** between two countries, groups, or individuals, they start to become friendly again after a period of disagreement; a formal word. *The first steps towards a rapprochement between Egypt and Jordan have already been taken... Many Americans called for a rapprochement with Latin America... A period of rapprochement is necessary before re-unification is considered.*

rapt /ræpt/
ADJ Someone who is **rapt** is so interested in or fascinated by something that they cannot think about

anything else. *Claud was staring at me, rapt... My audience listened in rapt silence.*

rapture /ˈræptʃə/ **raptures**
N U or N PL **Rapture** is an overpowering feeling of delight; a literary word. *...his face shining with rapture. ...the first raptures of their honeymoon.*

rapturous /ˈræptʃəʳrəs/
ADJ A **rapturous** feeling or reaction is one of great happiness or enthusiasm. *...a rapturous reception from their supporters.*

rare /reə/ **rarer, rarest**
1 ADJ Something that is **rare** is not common or does not happen very often, and is therefore interesting, valuable, or unusual. *Diane's hobby is collecting rare books... Cases of smallpox are extremely rare.*
2 ADJ **Rare** meat is very lightly cooked. *...a rare beef steak.*

rarebit /ˈreəbɪt/
N U **Rarebit** is the same as **Welsh rarebit.**

rarefied /ˈreərɪfaɪd/; also spelt **rarified.**
ADJ You use **rarefied** to describe people or situations that do not seem to be connected with ordinary life, because of their high social standing or academic nature; used showing disapproval. *...the rarefied world of the very rich. ...the rather rarefied atmosphere of university life.*

rarely /ˈreəli/
ADV **Rarely** means not very often. *We rarely quarrel.*

raring /ˈreərɪŋ/
ADJ PRED+to-INF If you are **raring** to do something, you are very eager to do it. *They were raring to fight for more victories.* ● If you are **raring to go**, you are very eager to start something; an informal expression. *We're all raring to go.*

rarity /ˈreərəti/ **rarities**
1 NC A **rarity** is something that is interesting or valuable because it is so unusual. *Blue marble was a rarity anywhere.*
2 NU The **rarity** of something is the fact that it is very uncommon. *Many animals are endangered by their rarity and beauty.*

rascal /ˈrɑːskl/ **rascals**
NC If you refer to a man or a child as a **rascal**, you mean that they behave badly or dishonestly, but in a way which does not really make you angry. *He's a nice old rascal.*

rascally /ˈrɑːskəli/
ADJ Someone who is **rascally** behaves badly or dishonestly, but in a way which does not really make you angry.

rash /ræʃ/ **rashes**
1 ADJ If someone's behaviour is **rash**, they do foolish things because they act without thinking carefully first. *Don't do anything rash... Some rash promises were made.* ◆ **rashly** ADV *I'm not a man who does things rashly.*
2 NC A **rash** is an area of red spots on your skin which appear when you are ill or have an allergy. *...a man with a rash on one side of his neck.*
3 N SING A **rash** of events is a large number of them that all happen within a short period of time. *No one wishes to see a rash of strikes.*

rasher /ˈræʃə/ **rashers**
NC A **rasher** of bacon is a thin slice of it.

rasp /rɑːsp/ **rasps, rasping, rasped**
V or V-QUOTE To **rasp** means to make a harsh unpleasant sound. *Crickets rasped loudly... 'It's frightful,' she rasped.* ► Also N SING *...the rasp of sandpaper on wood.* ◆ **rasping** ADJ *...a dry rasping voice.*

raspberry /ˈrɑːzbəʳri/ **raspberries**
1 NC A **raspberry** is a small, soft, red fruit that grows on bushes. *...raspberry jam.*
2 If someone blows a **raspberry**, they make a sound by putting their tongue out and blowing, in order to insult someone or to make fun of them. *He then blew a lengthy raspberry.*

Rasta /ˈræstə/ **Rastas**
NC **Rasta** means the same as **Rastafarian**; an informal word. *...Haile Selassie, the figure who represents God to Rastas.*

Rastafarian /ˌræstəˈfeəriən/ **Rastafarians**
NC A **Rastafarian** is a believer in a religion that originated in Jamaica. Rastafarians worship a former emperor of Ethiopia, Haile Selassie, as God. *It could lead to Rastafarians being given official status as an ethnic group.* ► Also ADJ *Reggae groups tended to sing about the Rastafarian religion.*

rat /ræt/ **rats**
1 NC A **rat** is an animal which has a long tail and looks like a large mouse. *The sewers are swarming with rats. ...rat poison.*
2 NC You call someone a **rat** when you are angry with them because they have done something unpleasant; an informal use. *Oh, you rat... They're all rats in our business.*
3 See also **rat race.**

rat-a-tat /ˌrætəˈtæt/
N SING **Rat-a-tat** or rat-a-tat-tat is used in writing to represent a repeated knocking or tapping sound. *There was a knock at the door. Rat-a-tat-tat. ...the continual rat-a-tat of machine-gun fire.*

ratchet /ˈrætʃɪt/ **ratchets**
NC A **ratchet** is a wheel or bar with sloping teeth that is only able to turn in one direction because a piece of metal prevents the teeth from moving backwards. *...a mechanical toy with a broken ratchet. ...ratchet wrenches.*

rate /reɪt/ **rates, rating, rated**
1 NC+SUPP The **rate** at which something happens is the speed or frequency at which it happens. *...the rapid rate of change which the industrial world is facing... The divorce rate is fantastically high. ...a rising rate of unemployment.*
2 NC+SUPP The **rate** of taxation or interest is its level, expressed as a percentage. *This money is taxed at the rate of 59%. ...a good rate of interest... The Chancellor defended the latest rise in interest rates.*
● See also **exchange rate.**
3 N PL Until 1990, **rates** were a local tax in Britain paid by people who owned buildings or who rented unfurnished buildings. *The Bill aims to replace the rates with a community charge or poll tax.*
4 VOA, VOC, or VC You use **rate** to talk about your opinion of someone or something. For example, if someone **is rated** as brilliant, people consider them to be brilliant. *Leontiev rated socialism highly... Ballesteros is still rated the best golfer in the world... On a scale of one to ten, it probably rated number seven.*
5 See also **rating.**
● **Rate** is used in these phrases. ● If you say that at **this rate** a particular thing will happen, you mean that it will happen if the present situation continues. *At this rate we'll be millionaires by Christmas!* ● You use **at any rate** to indicate that the important thing is what you are going to say now and not what has just been said. *I don't think there's been an edition since 1977; at any rate that's the one I'll be referring to.*

rateable value /ˌreɪtəbl ˈvæljuː/ **rateable values**
NC In Britain, the **rateable value** of a building was a theoretical value based on its size and facilities. It was used to calculate how much the owner had to pay in rates: see **rate 3**. *The rateable values of properties in London have soared during the past sixteen years.*

ratepayer /ˈreɪtpeɪə/ **ratepayers**
NC In Britain, a **ratepayer** was a person who had to pay rates: see **rate 3**. *Councillors estimate it will cost about twelve thousand pounds of ratepayers' money each week.*

rather /ˈrɑːðə/
1 SUBMOD or PREDET You use **rather** to say that something is the case to a slight extent. *I'm rather puzzled by this question... It was rather a struggle.*
2 SUBMOD or PREDET You also use **rather** to say that something is the case to a large or surprising extent. *The company thought I did rather well... That seems rather a long way away at the moment.*
3 SUBMOD or ADV **Rather** is often used to make a criticism sound less severe, or to avoid making a statement that sounds rude or abrupt. *This is getting rather complicated... It's just a rather crude reproduction, I'm afraid... The whole thing sounds*

rather childish... I rather think it was three hundred and fifty pounds.
4 If you say that you **would rather** do a particular thing, you mean that you would prefer to do that thing. *'What was all that about?'—'I'm sorry, I'd rather not say.'*
5 PREP or CONJ You use **rather than** to introduce a statement saying what is not done, to contrast this with a statement saying what actually is done. *I have used familiar English names rather than scientific Latin ones.*
6 ADV SEN You also use **rather** to introduce a correction or contrast to what you have just said. *This was no matter for congratulation, but rather a matter for vengeance.*

ratification /rætɪfɪkeɪʃn/
NU **Ratification** of an agreement or proposal occurs when it is formally approved and adopted by a government or organization; a formal word. *Senators have postponed a debate on the ratification of the treaty... American objections prevented ratification of the proposals.*

ratify /rætɪfaɪ/ **ratifies, ratifying, ratified**
VO When a government or organization **ratifies** an agreement or proposal, it formally approves and adopts it; a formal word. *Over 90 countries ratified an agreement to ban the use of these chemicals... The merger still has to be ratified by the Social Democrats.*

rating /reɪtɪŋ/ **ratings**
1 NC+SUPP The popularity **rating** of a government, political party, or public figure is the extent of their popularity, reflected in the opinion polls. *President Bush's popularity rating is still very high... Their opinion poll rating is below 10 per cent.*
2 NC+SUPP A **rating** is a score or assessment based on how much of a particular quality someone or something has. *...jobs which are assigned a low rating on the economic scale... Brazil's credit rating has been cut because of its failure to honour outstanding commitments.*
3 N PL The **ratings** are the statistics published each week which show how many people watch each television programme. *Political broadcasts are always at the bottom end of the ratings because of their boring, one-sided nature.*

ratio /reɪʃɪəʊ/ **ratios**
NC A **ratio** is a relationship between two numbers, amounts, or measurements, which show how much greater one is than the other. For example, if there are two boys and six girls in a room, the ratio of boys to girls is one to three. *...a high teacher/pupil ratio... The Commons voted by a ratio of two to one that courts should not be able to sentence convicted murderers to death.*

ration /ræʃn/ **rations, rationing, rationed**
1 NC When something is scarce, your **ration** of it is the amount that you are allowed to have. *...monthly meat rations.*
2 VO When something is **rationed**, you are only allowed to have a limited amount of it. *Meat, flour and sugar were all rationed.* ◆ **rationing** NU *...food and petrol rationing during the war.*
3 N PL **Rations** are the food which is supplied to a soldier or a member of an expedition each day. *They had two days' rations.*

rational /ræʃəⁿnəl/
ADJ A **rational** person is able to make decisions and judgements based on reason rather than emotion. *Let's talk about this like two rational people... Panic destroys rational thought.* ◆ **rationally** /ræʃəⁿnəli/ ADV *Let's discuss this rationally.* ◆ **rationality** /ræʃənæləti/ NU *The debate soon lost all semblance of rationality.*

rationale /ræʃənɑːl/
N SING The **rationale** for a course of action, practice, or belief is the set of reasons on which it is based. *We discussed the rationale for taking city kids into the country.*

rationalism /ræʃəⁿnəlɪzəm/
NU **Rationalism** is the belief that your life should be based on reason and not on emotions or religious beliefs. *...the great divide which separates rationalism*

from superstition. ◆ **rationalist, rationalists** NC *Lavrov was a thorough rationalist.*

rationalize /ræʃəⁿnəlaɪz/, **rationalizes, rationalizing, rationalized**; also spelt **rationalise.**
1 VO If you **rationalize** something that you are unhappy or unsure about, you think of reasons to justify it or explain it. *I rationalise my decision by saying that I need the money.* ◆ **rationalization,** /ræʃəⁿnəlaɪzeɪʃn/ **rationalizations** NC or NU *They devise elaborate rationalizations for their behaviour. ...periodic attempts at rationalization.*
2 VO When a company, system, or industry is **rationalized**, it is made more efficient, especially by getting rid of staff and equipment. *The government also intended to rationalise and restructure state enterprises.* ◆ **rationalization** NU *...the continuing rationalization of the armed forces.*

rat race
N SING If you describe a job or way of life as a **rat race**, you mean that the people in it are all competing fiercely with each other; used showing disapproval. *I was determined to get out of the rat race.*

Ratsiraka, Didier /diːdjeɪ rætsɪərək/
Admiral Didier Ratsiraka became President of the Supreme Council of the Revolution in 1975 and President of Madagascar in 1976. He served as Minister of Foreign Affairs from 1972 to 1975. He became Secretary General of the Vanguard of the Malagasy Revolution (AREMA) in 1976. Born: 1936.

rat-tat /rættæt/
N SING **Rat-tat** or **rat-tat-tat** means the same as **rat-a-tat.** *There was a rat-tat at the door.*

ratter /rætə/ **ratters**
NC A **ratter** is a dog or cat that catches and kills rats.

rattle /rætl/ **rattles, rattling, rattled**
1 V-ERG When something **rattles** or is **rattled,** it makes a series of short, regular knocking sounds because it is being shaken or it is hitting against something hard. *The explosive and batteries were not fixed, and would rattle... A cold November wind rattled the windows.* ▸ Also NC *The rattle of the engine became louder.*
2 NC A **rattle** is a baby's toy with loose bits inside which make a noise when it is shaken.
3 VO If something **rattles** you, it makes you worried or annoyed. *His questions obviously rattled her.*

rattle off PHRASAL VERB If you **rattle** something **off,** you say it or do it quickly and without much effort. *She rattled off a few names that I tried to write down.*

rattle on PHRASAL VERB When someone **rattles on** about something, they talk about it for a long time in a way that annoys you. *Some of the women would rattle on about sex.*

rattle through PHRASAL VERB If you **rattle through** something, you deal with it quickly in order to finish it. *They rattled through the rest of the meeting.*

rattler /rætələ/ **rattlers**
NC A **rattler** is the same as a **rattlesnake**; used in informal American English.

rattlesnake /rætlsneɪk/ **rattlesnakes**
NC A **rattlesnake** is a poisonous American snake with a tail that makes a rattling noise. *...a rattlesnake sleeping on a warm rock.*

rattling /rætⁿlɪŋ/
SUBMOD **Rattling** is used to emphasize how good or pleasant something is; an old-fashioned, informal word. *...a rattling good story.*

ratty /ræti/ **rattier, rattiest**
ADJ If someone is **ratty,** they are very irritable; an informal word. *All right, don't get ratty... The pain makes you ratty.*

raucous /rɔːkəs/
ADJ A **raucous** voice is loud and harsh. *...raucous laughter.*

raunchy /rɔːntʃi/, **raunchier, raunchiest**
ADJ Someone who is **raunchy** looks or sounds as though they have a strong and aggressive desire for sex; an informal word. *...some of the most brazen, raunchy people in the world... She has one of the raunchiest voices in rock music.*

ravage /rævɪdʒ/ **ravages, ravaging, ravaged**
1 VO To **ravage** something means to harm or damage it so that it is almost destroyed. *...the diseases which*

ravage Aboriginal populations. ...a country ravaged by war.

2 N PL The **ravages** of the weather, time, or war are the bad effects these things have. *He could help Angola to recover from the ravages of a long and bitter war.*

rave /reɪv/ **raves, raving, raved**
1 V If someone **raves**, they talk in an excited and uncontrolled way. *He started raving about the horror and brutality of war.*
2 V+*about*, V-QUOTE, or V-REPORT If you **rave** about something, you speak or write about it very enthusiastically; an informal use. *People were raving about his fantastic course... One newspaper raved: 'the most exciting play I have ever seen'.*
3 N+N A **rave** review is a very enthusiastic one; an informal use. *Stoppard's new play has received rave reviews.*
4 N C A **rave** is a secretly organized event at which people dance to electronic music and take illegal drugs. *All night raves have become a widespread attraction in little over two years.*
5 See also **raving**.

raven /reɪvn/ **ravens**
1 N C A **raven** is a large black bird with a deep harsh call. *The only sound was the cawing of ravens.*
2 ADJ **Raven** hair is shiny and black; a literary use. *...the raven blackness of those curls.*

ravenous /rævənəs/
ADJ If you are **ravenous**, you are very hungry indeed. *By that time I was ravenous... Most infants have a ravenous appetite.* ◆ **ravenously** ADV or SUBMOD *He looked ravenously at the table to see what they were having for dinner... I was ravenously hungry.*

raver /reɪvə/ **ravers**
N C A **raver** is a person who is very lively and has an exciting social life; an informal word. *He's a bit of a raver.*

rave-up, rave-ups
N C A **rave-up** is a very lively party; an informal word. *We are looking for more friends to have a rave-up with tonight.*

ravine /rəviːn/ **ravines**
N C A **ravine** is a very deep, narrow valley with steep sides. *The bus went off the road and plunged into a deep ravine.*

raving /reɪvɪŋ/
ADJ If you describe someone as **raving** or **raving mad**, you mean that you think they are completely mad; an informal word. *You're all raving lunatics... He went raving mad.*

ravioli /rævioʊli/
NU **Ravioli** is an Italian food made from small squares of pasta which are filled with meat and served with a sauce.

ravish /rævɪʃ/ **ravishes, ravishing, ravished**
V O If you **are ravished** by something that is very beautiful, it gives you great pleasure and delight; a literary word. *...ravished by the beauty of the language.*

ravishing /rævɪʃɪŋ/
ADJ Someone or something that is **ravishing** is very beautiful. *...a ravishing blonde.*

raw /rɔː/
1 ADJ **Raw** food is uncooked. *...a piece of raw meat. ...a raw carrot.*
2 ADJ ATTRIB A **raw** substance is in its natural state before being processed. *...exports of raw cotton. ...raw rubber from Malaysia.*
3 ADJ If a part of your body is **raw**, it is sore because the skin has been damaged. *Every boy's feet had big raw blisters on them.*
4 ADJ If you describe someone as **raw**, you mean that they are too inexperienced to know how to behave properly. *He's just a raw kid.*
5 If you have been given a **raw deal**, you have been treated unfairly; an informal expression. *Ordinary people are getting a raw deal.*

raw-boned
ADJ Someone who is **raw-boned** is very thin. *...the tall raw-boned youth.*

rawhide /rɔːhaɪd/ **rawhides**; used in American English.
1 NU **Rawhide** is untreated leather made from the skin of a cow. *...a rawhide belt.*
2 N C A **rawhide** is a whip that is made of rawhide.

Rawlings, Jerry /dʒeri rɔːlɪŋz/
Flight-Lieutenant **Jerry Rawlings** became Chairman of the Provisional National Defence Council (PNDC) of Ghana in a coup in 1981. He previously led a coup in 1979 and was head of state for four months. Born: 1947.

raw material, raw materials
N C or NU **Raw materials** are the natural substances used to make something, for example in an industrial process. *...coal, oil, gas, and other raw materials.*

ray /reɪ/ **rays**
1 N C A **ray** is a beam of heat or light. *...the rays of the sun. ...ultraviolet rays.*
2 N SING You can refer to something that makes a bad situation seem better as a **ray** of hope or comfort. *The peace talks provide a ray of hope in the appalling cycle of violence in Central America.*

rayon /reɪɒn/
NU **Rayon** is a smooth fabric made from cotton, wool, or synthetic fibres. *The only synthetic fabric was 'artificial silk' or rayon.*

Razanamasy, Guy Willy /giː vɪli rɑːzənəmɑːs/
Guy Willy Razanamasy was appointed Prime Minister of Madagascar in 1991. He was formerly Mayor of Antananarivo.

raze /reɪz/ **razes, razing, razed**
V O If people **raze** a building, town, or forest, they completely destroy it. *Many villages were razed to the ground.*

razor /reɪzə/ **razors**
N C A **razor** is a tool used for shaving. *...an electric razor.*

razor blade, razor blades
N C A **razor blade** is a small, thin, sharp piece of metal that you fix to a razor and use for shaving. *Some of them had razor blades hidden in their pockets.*

razzle /ræzl/
If you go **on the razzle**, you go out and enjoy yourself in a lively and noisy way, for example by going to pubs or night clubs; an informal expression. *We're off on the razzle again tonight.*

RC /ɑːsiː/ **RCs**
RC is an abbreviation for 'Roman Catholic'. *Some are RC, some Eastern Orthodox, some Muslim.*

Rd
Rd is a written abbreviation for 'road'. *...49 St Johns Rd.*

-rd
SUFFIX **-rd** is added to most numbers written in figures and ending in 3 in order to form ordinal numbers. 3rd is pronounced the same as 'third'. *...3rd November 1972.*

re /riː/
PREP **Re** is used in formal written English to introduce a subject which is going to be discussed or referred to in detail. *Re your letter of 16th July, I am pleased to inform you that you will soon receive a cheque for £16.50 in settlement of your claim.*

re- /riː-, rɪ-/
PREFIX **Re-** combines with verbs and nouns to form new verbs and nouns that refer to the repeating of an action or process. For example, to re-read something means to read it again. *She was re-arrested late on Monday night having been released on Sunday... I would like to see him stand for re-election.*

-'re /-ə/
SUFFIX **-'re** is a short form of 'are' used in spoken English and informal written English. *You're quite right... What're you waiting for?*

R.E. /ɑːr iː/
NU **R.E.** is the lessons in school which deal with religion. R.E. is an abbreviation for 'Religious Education'. *The content of R.E. syllabuses will be drawn up at local level.*

reach /riːtʃ/ **reaches, reaching, reached**
1 V O When someone or something **reaches** a place, they arrive there. *It was dark by the time I reached*

their house... *It took three days for the letter to reach me.*

2 VAorVOA If you **reach** in a particular direction, you stretch out your arm to do something or to get something. *He reached into his inside pocket and produced a pen... I reached out a hand and caught the ball.*

3 VOorV If you say that you can **reach** something, you mean that you can touch it by stretching out your arm and hand. *I can't reach that shelf unless I stand on a chair... I can just reach.*

4 VO You can say that you **reach** someone when you succeed in contacting them by telephone. *Where can I reach you?*

5 VOorVA If something **reaches** a particular place, point, or level, it gets as far or as high as that place, point, or level. *Rumours of an enemy invasion began to reach the capital... When the water reached his waist, he had to start swimming... She wore a long blue skirt reaching down to the ground.*

6 VO If someone or something **reaches** a particular stage, condition, or level, they get to it. *Most children stay at home until they reach school age... Unemployment has reached a very high level.*

7 VO When people **reach** an agreement, decision, or result, they succeed in achieving it. *They managed to reach an agreement on rates of pay.*

8 N PL+SUPP You use **reaches** to talk about a large section of a river or a large area of land or space. For example, the furthest **reaches** of a place are the furthest part of it. *...the upper reaches of the Amazon. ...the planet Jupiter, in the outer reaches of the solar system.*

react /riˈækt/ **reacts, reacting, reacted**
1 V When you **react** to something that has happened to you, you behave in a particular way because of it. *She tends to react strongly if he lights a cigarette... Dr Merwe said he found it quite understandable that Mrs Thatcher would react like this.*

2 V+against If you **react** against the way other people behave, you deliberately behave in a different way. *They reacted against the formality of their predecessors... The church had not been vigilant enough in reacting against anti-Semitism.*

3 V When someone **reacts** to a drug, they are made ill by it. *We were alarmed at the way in which Katie reacted to the drug.*

4 V-RECIP When one chemical substance **reacts** with another, it combines with it chemically to form another substance. *The sulphur dioxide reacts with the hydrogen peroxide to form sulphuric acid... Nitrogen and oxygen can react together in a variety of ways.*

reaction /riˈækʃn/ **reactions**
1 NC+SUPPorNU+SUPP Your **reaction** to something is what you feel, say, or do because of it. *My immediate reaction was one of revulsion... The Bulgarian media have said very little about local reaction... There's been no official reaction to the results of the Pakistan elections.*

2 NC+against A **reaction** against something is a way of behaving or doing something that is deliberately different from what has been done before. *My work has never been a reaction against Abstract Expressionism.*

3 NC+against If there is a **reaction** against something, it becomes unpopular. *This led to a reaction against public expenditure.*

4 N PL Your **reactions** are your ability to move quickly in response to something, for example when you are in danger. *...a computer game designed to time their reactions.*

5 NC A chemical **reaction** is a process in which two substances combine together chemically to form another substance. *It might be possible to block the reaction, and so to stop the disease progressing.*

6 See also **chain reaction**.

reactionary /riˈækʃənəri/ **reactionaries**
ADJ Someone who is **reactionary** tries to prevent social or political changes; used showing disapproval. *...reactionary forces.* ▶ Also NC *...political reactionaries.*

reactivate /riˈæktɪveɪt/ **reactivates, reactivating, reactivated**
VO If people **reactivate** a system or organization, they make it work again after it has not been working for a while. *The western allies were continuing their efforts to reactivate the Office of Strategic Services.*

reactive /riˈæktɪv/
ADJ Something that is **reactive** is able to react chemically with a lot of different substances. *...these sensitive and highly reactive compounds.*

reactor /riˈæktə/ **reactors**
NC A **reactor** is the same as a **nuclear reactor**. *The design of reactors has been modified since the Chernobyl disaster.*

read, reads, reading. The form **read** is used in the present tense, pronounced /riːd/, and is also the past tense and past participle, pronounced /red/.
1 VorVO When you **read** something that is written down, you look at written words or symbols and understand them. *More than a quarter of the world adult population are unable to read and write... I remember reading about it in the paper... Have you read that article?... I have never been able to read music.*

2 VO,V+to,VOO,orVO+to To **read** something that is written down also means to say it aloud. *Some learn them by heart, others read them aloud... Shall I read to you?... We read you that despatch from Mark Tully... Children everywhere love to have stories read to them.*

3 V A If you refer to how a piece of writing **reads**, you are referring to its style. *It read like a translation from the Latin.*

4 VC You can use **read** to say what is written somewhere. For example, if a notice **reads** 'Exit', the word 'Exit' is written on it. *'The Times' headline reads: 'Gadaffi vows revenge on the United States'. ...banners which read, 'No peace and no surrender'.*

5 VO If you **read** someone's moods or mind, you succeed in guessing their feelings or thoughts. *He so often reads my thoughts.*

6 VO When you **read** a meter or gauge, you look at it and record the figure on it. *We'd better read the gas meter.*

7 VC If a measuring device **reads** a particular amount, it shows that amount. *The thermometers are reading 108 degrees in the shade.*

8 VO If you **read** a subject at university, you study it. *He read law at the prestigious Georgetown University Law School.*

9 See also **reading**.

● **Read** is used in these phrases. ● If you **read between the lines**, you understand what someone really means, or what is really happening in a situation, even though it is not said openly. *Those who read between the lines deduce that the Vice-President is under attack.* ● If a book or magazine is **a good read**, it is very enjoyable to read. *His book is £12.95 and a jolly good read.*

read into PHRASAL VERB If you **read** a meaning **into** something, you think the meaning is there although it may not be. *Some people read sex into the most innocent story... Analysts are not reading too much into the figures.*

read out PHRASAL VERB If you **read** a piece of writing **out**, you say it aloud. *Could you just read out this next paragraph?*

read up on PHRASAL VERB If you **read up on** a subject, you read as much as you can about it so that you get to know more about it. *I'll have to read up on this particular case.*

readable /riːdəbl/
ADJ A book or article that is **readable** is interesting and worth reading. *...an attempt to provide a readable introduction for the non-specialist.*

reader /riːdə/ **readers**
NC The **readers** of a newspaper, magazine, or book are the people who read it. *The paper is gathering one thousand new readers a week. ...a stodgy style that sends the reader to sleep.*

readership /riːdəʃɪp/
N SING+SUPP The **readership** of a newspaper, magazine,

or book is all the people who read it. ...*a readership of about ten million people.*

readily /rédɪli/
1 ADV If you do something **readily**, you do it in a way which shows that you are willing to do it. *He readily accepted an invitation to dinner.*
2 ADV You also use **readily** to say that something can be done or obtained quickly and easily. *Personal computers are readily available these days.*

readiness /rédɪnəs/
1 NU **Readiness** is the state of being prepared for something. *He faces it with calm readiness and resolute determination.*
2 NU+*to*-INF Your **readiness** to do something is your willingness to do it. *They appear to be combining toughness with a readiness to negotiate on pay demands.*

reading /ríːdɪŋ/ **readings**
1 NU **Reading** is the activity of reading books. *I don't do a lot of reading.*
2 NC+SUPP A poetry **reading** is a social event at which poetry is read to an audience. *This year's event consisted of readings, lectures and workshops.*
3 NC The **reading** on a meter or gauge is the figure or measurement that it shows. *The crew are getting erratic pressure readings from one of the fuel gauges.*

reading lamp, reading lamps
NC A **reading lamp** is a small lamp that you keep on a desk or table. It can be adjusted to direct the light to where you need it.

reading room, reading rooms
NC A **reading room** is a quiet room in a library or museum where you can read and study. *He went down to the reading room of the British Museum.*

readjust /ríːədʒʌst/ **readjusts, readjusting, readjusted**
1 V or V-REFL If you **readjust** or **readjust** yourself, you adapt to a new situation. *It is difficult to readjust to changing environments... The applicants readjust themselves to meet the availability of university places.*
2 VO If you **readjust** something, you alter the position it is in. *He readjusted the saddle before getting on.*

readjustment /ríːədʒʌstmənt/ **readjustments**
1 NU or NC **Readjustment** is adapting to a new situation. *...a period of readjustment... The launch requires great readjustments on all sides.*
2 NC or NU A **readjustment** of something is an alteration of it so that it functions in a different way. *Most schools now face a readjustment of their timetables... The organization denies that it is seeking any readjustment of state borders.*

ready /rédi/ **readies, readying, readied**
1 ADJ PRED If someone or something is **ready**, they are properly prepared for something, or they now have the right qualities for something. *Are you ready? I'll drive you back to your flat... You're nowhere near ready for such a job.*
2 ADJ PRED If something is **ready**, it is able to be used, taken, or bought after a period of preparation. *Lunch is ready... Their crops would soon be ready for harvesting.*
3 ADJ PRED+*to*-INF If you are **ready** to do something, you are willing to do it or are about to do it. *...couples who are ready to move house in order to get work... I was ready to cry.*
4 ADJ PRED+*for* If you are **ready** for something, you need it or want it. *We were all ready for sleep.*
5 ADJ ATTRIB **Ready** money or **ready** cash is in the form of notes or coins rather than cheques or credit cards, and so it can be used immediately. *...ready cash.*
6 V O or V-REFL When you **ready** something, you prepare it for a particular purpose; a formal use. *The satellite would be readied with all possible haste. ...as Peking readies itself for an influx of foreigners for the Asian Games.*

ready-made
1 ADJ ATTRIB or ADV If something that you buy is **ready-made**, you can use it immediately. *...the convenience of ready-made meals... You can buy your greenhouse ready-made.*

2 ADJ If you have a **ready-made** reply to a question, you can answer it immediately. *He had no ready-made answers.*

reaffirm /ríːəfɜ́ːm/ **reaffirms, reaffirming, reaffirmed**
V-REPORT If you **reaffirm** something, you state it again; a formal word. *The ministers reaffirmed their intention not to surrender... She reaffirmed that the laws would be changed.*

Reagan, Ronald /rɒnəld réɪgən/
Ronald Reagan was the President of the United States from 1981 to 1989. He was a film actor before serving as Governor of California from 1967 to 1974. He is a member of the Republican Party. Born: 1911.

real /rɪəl/
1 ADJ Something that is **real** actually exists and is not imagined, invented, or theoretical. *You must know the difference between what's real and make-believe. ...real or imagined feelings of inferiority... There was a real possibility of success.*
2 ADJ **Real** also means genuine and not artificial or an imitation. *...real leather. ...fancy chocolates with real liqueurs inside.*
3 ADJ ATTRIB You also use **real** to say that something has all the characteristics or qualities that such a thing typically has. *...the only real accident that I've ever had... I used to tell him he wasn't a real Christian.*
4 ADJ ATTRIB **Real** can also mean that something is the true or original thing of its kind, in contrast to one that people may wrongly believe to be true or original. *That is the real reason for the muddle... My real home is in Tshabo.*
5 SUBMOD In American English, **real** is sometimes used instead of 'very'. *You and I must have lunch together real soon.*
● **Real** is used in these phrases. ● You use **for real** to emphasize that something is actually happening or being done; an informal expression. *Mr. Gorbachev is ready to take some crucial measures to show that his efforts at restructuring Soviet society are for real.*
● You use **in real terms** to talk about the actual value or cost of something. For example, if your salary rises by 5% but prices rise by 10%, your salary has fallen **in real terms**. *Funding has increased by forty per cent in real terms.*

real estate
NU **Real estate** is property in the form of buildings and land; used in American English. *He acquired a bit of real estate. ...real estate agents.*

realign /ríːəláɪn/ **realigns, realigning, realigned**
VOA If you **realign** one thing with another, you change it so that it corresponds to the other thing; a formal word. *Its aim is to realign Western military strategy to the political changes in Eastern Europe. ...realigning prices with actual costs.*

realignment /ríːəláɪnmənt/ **realignments**
NC+*of* A **realignment** of the way something is organized is a new arrangement of it; a formal word. *We believe that the need for a realignment of British politics must now be faced.*

realise /rɪəlaɪz/. See **realize**.

realism /rɪəlɪzəm/
1 NU When people show **realism** in their behaviour, they recognize and accept the true nature of a situation and try to deal with it in a practical way. *He marvelled at his father's lack of realism.*
2 NU In painting, novels, and films, **realism** is the representing of things and people in a way that is like real life. *It is perhaps this gritty realism which gives her books their special appeal.*

realist /rɪəlɪst/ **realists**
NC A **realist** is someone who accepts the true nature of a situation and tries to deal with it practically. *I am a realist and know that all this cannot last.*

realistic /rɪəlístɪk/
1 ADJ If you are **realistic** about a situation, you recognize and accept its true nature and try to deal with it practically. *They were more realistic about its long term commercial prospects. ...a realistic attempt to solve problems.* ◆ **realistically** ADV *She accepted the position realistically.*
2 ADJ A **realistic** painting, story, or film attempts to

represent things and people in a way that is like real
life. ...*a 19th century realistic novel.*

reality /rɪˈælətɪ/ **realities**
1 NU **Reality** is the real nature of everything, rather
than the way someone imagines it to be. *He is out of
touch with reality... It is often hard to distinguish
fantasy from reality.*
2 NC+SUPP The **reality** of a situation is the truth about
it, especially when it is unpleasant. *...the harsh
reality of daily life.*
3 NCorNU If something becomes a **reality**, it actually
exists or is actually happening. *The Channel Tunnel is
becoming a reality... For many the dream has failed
to become reality.*
4 You can use **in reality** to state the real nature of
something, when it contrasts with something that is
incorrect or imaginary. *They imagined that they
made the rules but, in reality, they were mere
puppets.*

realizable /rɪəˈlaɪzəbl/
1 ADJ Something, such as an idea or project, that is
realizable, can be achieved or carried out because the
necessary knowledge, equipment, or money is
available. *Most of it is technically realizable at this
moment.*
2 ADJ In finance and commerce, something that is
realizable can be carried out, sold, or made profitable
easily, for example without any legal problems or
official waiting period; a technical use. *...realizable
assets.*

realize /rɪəlaɪz/ **realizes, realizing, realized**; also
spelt **realise.**
1 V-REPORTorVO If you **realize** something, you become
aware of it. *I realized that this man wasn't going to
hurt me... She realized the significance of what he was
trying to do.* ◆ **realization** /rɪəlaɪzeɪʃn/ N SING *This
realization was shattering for all of us. ...a growing
realization of the damage that this whole episode is
doing.*
2 VO When someone **realizes** a design or an idea, they
put it into a physical form, for example by painting a
picture or building a machine; a formal use. *No
design is too sophisticated for him to realize.*
3 VO If your hopes, desires, or fears **are realized**, the
things that you hope for, desire, or fear actually
happen; a formal use. *My worst fears were realized.*
◆ **realization** N SING *...the realization of a lifelong
dream.*

reallocate /riːˈæləkeɪt/ **reallocates, reallocating,
reallocated**
VO If you **reallocate** something, such as money or aid,
you decide that it should be used for a different
purpose or that it should be given to a different person
from the one you originally intended it for. *...an anti-
drug aid package, due to go to Peru, might be
reallocated by Congress to Bolivia and Colombia.*

really /rɪəlɪ/
1 ADVorSUBMOD You can use **really** to emphasize what
you are saying. *I really ought to go... It really was
very sudden... It was really good... You know they are
really violent.*
2 ADV You use **really** to mention the real facts about
something, as opposed to something that is incorrect.
*I want to know what really happened... He's not really
going for a bath; he's going to sit in the garden.*
3 ADV People use **really** in questions when they want
you to answer 'no'; used in speech. *Do you really
think they bother to listen to us?... Is there really
anything new to say about him?... Do you really want
this?*
4 ADV You can add **really** to negative statements to
avoid seeming impolite. *I'm not really in favour of
that... 'Any more problems?'—'Not really, no.'*
5 You can say '**Really?**' to express great interest,
surprise, or disbelief. *'It was quite close to the
airport.'—'Really?'... 'Inflation's dropped faster than it
did under Labour.'—'Has it really?'*

realm /rɛlm/ **realms**; a formal word.
1 NC+SUPP You can refer to any area of activity or
thought as a **realm**. *Changes would not be confined to
the technical realm. ...the realm of imagination rather
than historical fact.*

2 NC A **realm** is also a country with a king or queen.
...the established church of the realm.

realpolitik /reɪˈælpɒlɪtiːk, reɪˈælpɒlɪtiːk/
NU **Realpolitik** is a way of dealing with political issues
that is practical and realistic rather than idealistic or
moralistic. *It is realpolitik and national politics that
will determine their reaction. ...the new realpolitik in
the Middle East.*

real time; a technical expression, spelt **real-time** for
the meaning in paragraph 2.
1 NU If you do something in **real time,** there is no
noticeable delay between your action and its effect or
consequences. *...manipulate structures of chemicals
on screen and in real time... We are actually shooting
in real time.*
2 ADJ ATTRIB **Real-time** processing is a type of
computer programming or data processing in which
the information received is processed by the computer
almost immediately. *...real-time processing.*

realtor /rɪəltə/ **realtors**
NC A **realtor** is an estate agent; used in American
English. *A realtor helped them find a place to live.*

real world
N SING If you talk about the **real world**, you are
referring to the world and life in general, usually in
contrast to a particular person's own life or ideas
when these seem untypical or unrealistic. *How do you
manage to keep your students in touch with the real
world?... We get worried about what is going on in the
real world. ...real-world knowledge.*

reams /riːmz/
N PL If you say that there are **reams** of something,
especially writing, you mean that there is a large
amount of it; an informal word. *She's written reams
of poetry.*

reap /riːp/ **reaps, reaping, reaped**
1 VO When people **reap** a crop such as corn, they cut
and gather it. *This year's harvest, which is just
beginning to be reaped, should total around 1.3 million
tons.*
2 VO If you **reap** a benefit or a reward, you obtain
something useful because of a helpful situation or
because of preparations that you have made. *A love
of reading needs to be nurtured at a very early age in
order to reap its benefits later on.*

reaper /riːpə/ **reapers**
1 NC A **reaper** is a machine that is used to cut and
gather crops. *A rabbit got caught in the blades of the
reaper.*
2 NC A person who cuts and gathers crops by hand is
also called a **reaper.**

reappear /riːəpɪə/ **reappears, reappearing,
reappeared**
V When people or things **reappear**, you can see them
again, because they have returned from another place
or because they are being used again. *The waiter
reappeared with a loaded tray... The Bill was quietly
dropped, but the subject has since reappeared on the
agenda.*

reappearance /riːəpɪərəns/ **reappearances**
NC+SUPP The **reappearance** of someone or something
that has previously disappeared or been away is their
appearance again. *He wanted to know the reason for
my sudden reappearance. ...the reappearance of left-
wing urban guerrilla action.*

reappraisal /riːəpreɪzl/ **reappraisals**
NCorNU A **reappraisal** of something such as a policy is
the process of thinking carefully about it and deciding
whether or not to change it; a formal word. *...a
reappraisal of U.S. policy toward South Asia. ...a
period of necessary reappraisal.*

reappraise /riːəpreɪz/ **reappraises, reappraising,
reappraised**
VO If you **reappraise** something such as an idea, you
carefully consider it in order to decide whether to
change what you think about it; a formal word. *They
have obliged politicians of all parties to reappraise the
role of small businesses.*

rear /rɪə/ **rears, rearing, reared**
1 N SING The **rear** of something such as a building or
vehicle is the part at the back of it. *He walked toward
the rear of the house.* ▸ Also ADJ ATTRIB *I got out and*

examined the right rear wheel.
2 VO If you **rear** children, you bring them up until they are old enough to look after themselves. *Geraldo has adopted and reared four children.*
3 V When a horse **rears** or **rears** up, it stands on its hind legs. *Most horses would have been terrified, they would have reared and thrown their riders.*
4 N SING If you are at the **rear** of a queue or line of people, you are the last person in it.
● **Rear** is used in these phrases. ● If you **bring up the rear**, you are the last person in a moving line of people. ● If something unpleasant **rears** its **ugly head**, it happens or appears. *Jealousy might so easily have reared its ugly head... The trade deficit rears its ugly head again.*

rear admiral, rear admirals
NC A **rear admiral** is an officer in the navy who is under a vice admiral in rank. *...commander of the formidable Soviet Northern fleet, rear admiral Vasily Yeremin.*

rearguard /rɪəgɑːd/
1 N SING The **rearguard** is the group of soldiers who protect the back part of an army in a battle, especially when the army is retreating.
2 If someone **fights a rearguard action**, they make a determined effort to prevent something happening which they disapprove of, although it is probably too late for them to succeed. *The President is fighting a rearguard action against rebels of the National Patriotic Front.*

rearm /riːɑːm/ **rearms, rearming, rearmed**
V-ERG When a country **rearms**, it starts to build up a stock of military weapons again. *Both sides were regrouping and rearming... There have been reports going back to last summer that Iraq has been rearming the Christian Maronite militias in Lebanon.*

rearmament /riːɑːməmənt/
NU **Rearmament** is the process of building up a new stock of military weapons. *...the pace of conventional rearmament. ...the biggest US rearmament programme in peacetime history.*

rearmost /rɪəməʊst/
ADJ ATTRIB The **rearmost** thing in a line is the one that is nearest to the back of the line. *They jumped on to the rearmost carriages.*

rearrange /riːəreɪndʒ/ **rearranges, rearranging, rearranged**
VO If you **rearrange** something, you organize or arrange it in a different way. *She rearranged the furniture... It was later announced that President Bush had rearranged a very tight schedule in order to meet them.*

rearrangement /riːəreɪndʒmənt/ **rearrangements**
NCorNU A **rearrangement** is a change in the way that something is arranged or organized. *The Tate Gallery in London has reopened after a rearrangement of the entire collection of paintings and sculptures... Our editorial workers were spread over three floors and it was feasible with some rearrangement to bring them all on to one floor.*

rear-view mirror, rear-view mirrors
NC A **rear-view mirror** is a mirror inside a car which enables you to see the traffic behind you while you are driving. *I glanced in the rear-view mirror.*

reason /riːzn/ **reasons, reasoning, reasoned**
1 NC The **reason** for something is the fact or situation which explains why it happens or exists. *I asked the reason for the decision. ...the main reasons for setting up the Anglo-Irish agreement.*
2 NU You use **reason** to say that you believe or feel something and that there are definite facts or situations which cause you to believe it or feel it. *I have reason to believe that you are concealing something... I'm getting annoyed, and with reason.*
3 NU **Reason** is also the ability people have to think and make judgements. *He had to rely less on reason than on emotion.*
4 If you get someone to **listen to reason**, you persuade them to listen to sensible arguments and be influenced by them. *The man refused to listen to reason.*
5 V-REPORT If you **reason** that something is the case, you decide after careful and logical thought that it is

the case. *Copernicus reasoned that the earth revolved around the sun.*
6 **without rhyme or reason**: see **rhyme**. See also **reasoned, reasoning.**
reason with PHRASAL VERB If you **reason with** someone, you try to convince them of something using logical arguments. *The Dalai Lama stayed for ten years, trying to reason with the Chinese.*

reasonable /riːzənəbl/
1 ADJ If someone is being **reasonable**, they are behaving in a fair and sensible way. *I can't do that, Morris. Be reasonable... The rally leaders have appealed to people to be calm and reasonable.*
◆ **reasonableness** NU *The landlords responded with great reasonableness.*
2 ADJ If a decision or explanation is **reasonable**, there are good reasons for thinking that it is correct. *There was no reasonable explanation for her decision... It was quite reasonable to suppose that he wanted the money too.*
3 ADJ A **reasonable** amount of something is a fairly large amount. *...a reasonable amount of luck... A reasonable number of students are involved.*
4 ADJ If the price of something is **reasonable**, it is fair and not too high. *The first priority should be reasonable prices and better service... The problem is accessing the product and getting it to the consumer at a reasonable price.*

reasonably /riːzənəbli/
1 SUBMOD **Reasonably** means to quite a good or great degree. *I'm reasonably broad across the shoulders. ...a reasonably well-known writer.*
2 ADV If someone is behaving **reasonably**, they are behaving in a fair and sensible way. *It was said that the Home Office had acted reasonably and properly.*

reasoned /riːznd/
ADJ ATTRIB A **reasoned** argument or explanation is based on sensible reasons, rather than on feelings. *We must counter their propaganda with reasoned argument.*

reasoning /riːzənɪŋ/
NU **Reasoning** is the process by which you reach a conclusion after considering all the facts. *I'm puzzled by his reasoning.*

reassemble /riːəsembl/ **reassembles, reassembling, reassembled**
VO If you **reassemble** something, you put it back together after it has been taken apart. *He reassembled an entire engine.*

reassembly /riːəsembli/
1 NU **Reassembly** is the gathering together again of a group of people; a formal word. *...the reassembly of Parliament in the New Year.*
2 NU **Reassembly** is also the putting together of something such as a machine after it has been taken apart. *...instructions for reassembly of the rifle.*

reassert /riːəsɜːt/ **reasserts, reasserting, reasserted**
1 VO If you **reassert** a claim or demand, you make it again firmly and forcefully. *China responded quickly reasserting its claim to the islands... Mr Bush moved quickly to reassert his demand that they must withdraw immediately.*
2 VO If you **reassert** your power, authority, or other qualities, you make it clear that you have them again. *He made efforts to reassert his authority over them... President Alfonsin also wants to reassert his credibility among the civilian population.*
3 V-REFL If you **reassert** yourself, you speak and act in a forceful way so that people pay attention to you and your opinions again. *Mr Gorbachev, however, appears to be reasserting himself against his opponents.*
4 V-REFL If an idea or habit **reasserts** itself, it becomes noticeable again. *The urge to survive reasserted itself.*

reassess /riːəses/ **reassesses, reassessing, reassessed**
VO If you **reassess** something, you consider it and decide whether it still has the same value or importance as you thought previously. *He was reassessing his political position... One of his main aims is to reassess American policy on Afghanistan.*

reassessment /riːəsesmənt/ **reassessments**
NCorNU If you make a **reassessment** of something, you

think about it and decide whether it still has the same value or importance. ...*a radical reassessment of Britain's military requirements... The approach to planning, and the reasons for planning, need reassessment if you're setting out towards improving quality.*

reassurance /riːəˈʃɔːrəns/ **reassurances**
NCorNU **Reassurances** are things you say to stop someone worrying. *Reassurances were given that investigations would proceed... Parents in this city are worried and they may require a lot more reassurance that their children are safe.*

reassure /riːəˈʃɔː/ **reassures, reassuring, reassured**
VO-REPORT If you **reassure** someone, you say or do things to stop them worrying. *I was trying to reassure her that things weren't as bad as she thought... The President reassured his listeners that they had nothing to fear.*

reassuring /riːəˈʃɔːrɪŋ/
ADJ Someone or something that is **reassuring** helps you not to worry. *The woman smiled at him in a reassuring manner... It's very reassuring and very encouraging.* ♦ **reassuringly** ADV *She looked at me reassuringly.*

rebate /ˈriːbeɪt/ **rebates**
NC A **rebate** is an amount of money which is paid back to you because you have paid too much tax or rent. *Those on the lowest incomes qualify for an eighty per cent rebate on their community charge.*

rebel, rebels, rebelling, rebelled; pronounced /ˈrebl/ when it is a noun and /rɪˈbel/ when it is a verb.
1 NC **Rebels** are people who are fighting against their own country's army in order to change the political system. ...*the conflict with anti-government rebels in the north.* ...*rebel forces in Northern Somalia.*
2 V When people **rebel**, they fight against their own country's army in order to change the political system. *The Hungarians rebelled against communist rule in 1956... The Duke of Monmouth rebelled against James II in 1685.*
3 NC You also describe someone as a **rebel** when they behave differently from other people, having rejected their society's values. *She was too individualistic; too much of a rebel... He is a rebel at heart.*
4 V You can say that someone **rebels** when they behave differently from other people because they have rejected their society's or parents' values. ...*adolescents who rebel and demand freedom and independence.*

rebellion /rɪˈbeliən/ **rebellions**
1 NCorNU A **rebellion** is a violent, organized action by a large group of people who are trying to change their country's political system. *Last month the military commander in the region said the armed rebellion had been crushed... He is unlikely to forgive them for rising up in rebellion against him during the Gulf War.*
2 NCorNU Opposition to the leaders of an organization by members of the organization itself can also be referred to as a **rebellion**. *He faces a growing rebellion from the left wing of his party... The proposal to make people pay for dental check-ups produced an even bigger Conservative rebellion.*

rebellious /rɪˈbeliəs/
1 ADJ A **rebellious** person does not want to behave in the way that other people think they should. ...*an obstinate, rebellious child with a violent temper... Young people in Britain have become more materialistic and fashion-conscious and less rebellious than their parents' generation.* ♦ **rebelliously** ADV *'Nonsense,' said my assistant rebelliously.*
♦ **rebelliousness** NU ...*teenage rebelliousness.*
2 ADJ People who oppose the decisions of their leaders can be referred to as **rebellious**. *Only hours before, the rebellious officer had rejected terms offered by the government.*

rebirth /riːˈbɜːθ/
N SING+SUPP The **rebirth** of something such as a political movement that was popular or important in the past is the fact that it becomes popular or important again. ...*the rebirth of nationalism.*

reborn /riːˈbɔːn/
ADJ If you say that someone or something is or has

been **reborn**, you mean that they have now become active again after a period of inactivity. *Hatred of the system had been reborn in him.*

rebound, rebounds, rebounding, rebounded; pronounced /rɪˈbaʊnd/ when it is a verb and /ˈriːbaʊnd/ when it is a noun.
1 VAorV If something **rebounds**, it bounces or springs back after hitting a solid surface such as the floor or a wall. *A shot from Stevens rebounded from the crossbar... When the ball rebounded, the Chinese goalkeeper, Hong Ping Ding, was penalized for obstruction.*
2 VorVA If something **rebounds**, it becomes active again or gets better after a difficult or disappointing period. ...*allowing investment and consumer spending to rebound... Last year revenues rebounded to their highest level since 1985.* ▶ Also NC *Retail sales rose eight tenths of a per cent last month due to a rebound in auto sales.*
3 If you say that someone is **on the rebound**, you mean that they have just ended a close personal relationship with a person who has rejected them, and are already beginning a new relationship with someone else. *She married him on the rebound.*
4 V+onoragainst If an action or situation **rebounds** on or against you, it has an unpleasant effect some time after it originally happened. *The deal rebounded on him when the Department of Trade and Industry began its investigation... Economic chaos will rebound against the General and force him to leave the country.*

rebuff /rɪˈbʌf/ **rebuffs, rebuffing, rebuffed**
VO If you **rebuff** someone's suggestion or advice, you respond in an unfriendly way and refuse to accept it. *He tried to question the girl and got rebuffed... The Chinese government has rebuffed a formal complaint from foreign journalists.* ▶ Also NC *Her rebuff had hurt him.*

rebuild /riːˈbɪld/ **rebuilds, rebuilding, rebuilt**
1 VO If people **rebuild** a town or building, they build it again after it has been damaged or destroyed. *The men must stay to rebuild their shattered towns and cities.*
2 VO When an organization is **rebuilt**, it is developed again after it has stopped or become ineffective. ...*help him to rebuild his nation's shattered economy.*

rebuke /rɪˈbjuːk/ **rebukes, rebuking, rebuked**
VO If you **rebuke** someone, you speak severely to them because they have said or done something that you do not approve of; a formal word. *She often rebuked David for his authoritarian attitude... He has publicly rebuked the Foreign Ministry for the way it has treated foreign aid.* ▶ Also NCorNU *He received a stern rebuke from his superiors... The team now returns to face rebuke from the Athlete's Association.*

rebut /rɪˈbʌt/ **rebuts, rebutting, rebutted**
VO If you **rebut** a charge or criticism that is made against you, you say or write something which proves that it is not true; a formal word. *I am writing this letter to rebut the suggestion that I have failed in my duty.*

rebuttal /rɪˈbʌtl/ **rebuttals**
NC A **rebuttal** is a statement which proves that a charge or a criticism that has been made against you is not true; a formal word. *It was a complete rebuttal of the charges against him... Pakistan has still not offered an official rebuttal to the latest Indian statements.*

recalcitrance /rɪˈkælsɪtrəns/
NU **Recalcitrance** is a stubborn unwillingness to obey orders or to co-operate; a formal word. *In the end their recalcitrance was too much for him.*

recalcitrant /rɪˈkælsɪtrənt/
ADJ Someone or something that is **recalcitrant** is stubbornly unwilling to obey orders or to co-operate; a formal word. ...*dealing with a recalcitrant boy in his classroom.*

recall, recalls, recalling, recalled; pronounced /rɪˈkɔːl/ when it is a verb, and /ˈriːkɔːl/ when it is a noun.
1 V-REPORT, VO, or V-QUOTE When you **recall** something, you remember it. *I recalled that my blankets had been taken away... I started to recall the years after*

the War... Deirdre recalled seeing a poster on his wall... 'I ran outside to look for my children,' recalled Miriam.
2 NU Your **recall** is your ability to remember things. *In order to assist your recall even further you can use linking and review techniques.*
3 VOorV-REPORT If one person **recalls** an incident or another person's words while they are making a speech, they remind their audience of it. *The Pope recalled with pleasure the two meetings he had had with President Gorbachev... Mr Singh recalled that thousands of such attacks were reported each year.*
4 VO If you **are recalled** to a place, you are ordered to return there. *Eighteen months ago they recalled him to Mozambique... Army troops were recalled to their barracks.*

recant /rɪkænt/ **recants, recanting, recanted**
VorVO If you **recant**, you say in public that you no longer have a particular set of beliefs; a formal word. *He was brought before the Inquisition on charges of heresy, and forced to recant... Under threat of death, men recanted their religion before the altar.*

recap /riːkæp/ **recaps, recapping, recapped**
VorV When you **recap**, you repeat the main points of an explanation, description, or argument. *Just to recap; these are substances that don't kill cancer cells, they reform them... It was necessary to recap briefly the events of the period.* ▸ Also NC *Here is a recap of these suggestions.*

recapitulate /riːkəpɪtjʊleɪt/ **recapitulates, recapitulating, recapitulated**
VOorV When you **recapitulate**, you repeat the main points of an explanation, description, or argument, as a summary of it; a formal word. *These points will recapitulate what has been established so far.*

recapitulation /riːkəpɪtjʊleɪʃn/ **recapitulations**
NCorNU A **recapitulation** is a summary of an explanation, description, or argument; a formal word. *The next lesson will be a quick recapitulation of what we've done so far.*

recapture /riːkæptʃə/ **recaptures, recapturing, recaptured**
1 VO When prisoners **are recaptured**, they are caught after they have escaped. *A convicted murderer, who escaped from a prison near Bristol, has been recaptured in Cardiff, Wales... Armed police have raided a flat in London and recaptured a man.*
2 VO When soldiers **recapture** a place, they capture it from the people who had taken it from them. *Saudi Arabia says its troops have recaptured the border town of Khafji.* ▸ Also N SING *...the recapture of the lost territories.*
3 VO When you **recapture** a pleasant feeling, you experience it again. *She failed to recapture her earlier mood.*

recast /riːkɑːst/ **recasts, recasting.** The form **recast** is used in the present tense and is also the past tense and past participle.
1 VO If you **recast** something, you change it by organizing it in a different way; a formal use. *...recasting the subsidy system... The text had been recast into language comprehensible only to legal experts.*
2 VO If a part in a play or film **is recast**, it is given to a different actor or actress. *To everyone's surprise the part of Claudius had been recast.*

recede /rɪsiːd/ **recedes, receding, receded**
1 V If something **recedes**, it moves away into the distance. *Now and then cars passed me, their tail-lights receding.*
2 V You also say that something **recedes** when it decreases in clarity, brightness, or amount. *Already the memory was receding... The floods caused by two days of storms receded over the weekend.*

receipt /rɪsiːt/ **receipts**
1 NC A **receipt** is a piece of paper that confirms that money or goods have been received. *Give students a written receipt for each payment.*
2 N PL Money received in a shop or a theatre is often referred to as the **receipts**. *The receipts from admission fees fell sharply.*
3 NU The **receipt** of something is the act of receiving

it; a formal use. You have to sign here and acknowledge receipt.

receive /rɪsiːv/ **receives, receiving, received**
1 VO When you **receive** something, someone gives it to you, or it arrives after it has been sent to you. *Did they receive money for their work?... Northcliffe received a letter from his brother... He has not received a reply.*
2 VO You can use **receive** to say that certain kinds of things happen to you. *...the criticism he received in England... She received a tremendous ovation.* ● If you **are on the receiving end** of something unpleasant, you are the person that it happens to. *We've been on the receiving end of most political violence... She found out what it was like to be on the receiving end.*
3 VO When you **receive** a visitor or guest, you welcome them; a formal use. *Fass received Lieber in his office.*
4 VOA If something **is received** in a particular way, people react to it in that way. *Her latest novel has been very well received.*

received /rɪsiːvd/
ADJ ATTRIB The **received** opinion or method is the one that is generally accepted as correct; a formal word. *...received ideas. ...received religion.*

Received Pronunciation
NU **Received Pronunciation** is a standard accent of British English that is considered to have no regional features. *The attitudes towards regional accents versus Received Pronunciation are discussed.*

receiver /rɪsiːvə/ **receivers**
1 NC A **receiver** is the part of a telephone that you hold near to your ear and speak into. *He replaced the receiver.*
2 NC A **receiver** is also a radio or television set; a technical use. *The bomb was hidden in a radio receiver.*
3 See also **official receiver**.

receivership /rɪsiːvəʃɪp/
NU **Receivership** is the state of being bankrupt and in the charge of the official receivers. *The company will go into receivership.*

recent /riːsnt/
ADJ A **recent** event or period of time happened a short time ago. *...their recent trip to Africa... Few sights have become more familiar in recent times... This has caused growing concern in recent years.*

recently /riːsntli/
ADV If something happened **recently**, it happened only a short time ago. *Recently, I lectured to seven hundred Swedes... The problem has been ignored until very recently.*

recently- /riːsntli-/
PREFIX **Recently-** combines with past participles to form adjectives which indicate that something was done a short time ago. *...her recently-published autobiography. ...recently-formed opposition groups. ...the recently-appointed director. ...recently-elected members of parliament.*

receptacle /rɪseptəkl/ **receptacles**
NC A **receptacle** is an object which you use to put or keep things in; a formal word. *Please put your cigarette ends into the receptacle provided.*

reception /rɪsepʃn/ **receptions**
1 NU In a hotel, office, or hospital, **reception** is the place where reservations, appointments, and enquiries are dealt with. *I signed in at reception. ...the reception desk.*
2 NC A **reception** is a formal party which is given to welcome someone or to celebrate a special event such as a wedding. *The reception was held in the Albany... The bill for the reception includes flowers and catering and the traditional wedding cake.*
3 NC+SUPP If something or someone has a particular kind of reception, that is the way people react to them. *I wrote to George about the enthusiastic reception of his book... Butler received a hostile reception in Bristol.*
4 N SING The **reception** of guests is the act of formally welcoming them; a formal use. *...a room which was kept for the reception of visitors.*
5 NU If you get good **reception** from your radio or

television, the sound or picture is clear. *Radio reception kept fading.*

reception centre, reception centres
NC A **reception centre** is a place which provides temporary accommodation for people who have nowhere else to live. *The Department for Family Welfare set up reception centres.*

reception class, reception classes
NC A **reception class** in an infant school is the first class that children go into when they start school.

receptionist /rɪsɛpʃəʰnɪst/ **receptionists**
NC The **receptionist** in a hotel, office, or doctor's surgery is the person whose job is to deal with people when they first arrive, to answer the telephone, and to arrange reservations or appointments. *He finally chose a 19-year-old receptionist from Brisbane.*

reception room, reception rooms
NC A **reception room** is a room in a house where people can sit together, for example a living room or a dining room; used especially in advertisements of houses for sale. *The small front reception room was decorated with a Christmas tree.*

receptive /rɪsɛptɪv/
ADJ A **receptive** person is willing to consider and accept new ideas and suggestions. *America has proved more receptive to Anna Freud's ideas.*

receptor /rɪsɛptə/ **receptors**
NC A **receptor** is a nerve ending or a cell that is stimulated by external contact or signals; a technical term. *...a receptor on the surface of the cells of the baby's gut.*

recess /riːsɛs/ **recesses**
1 NUorNC A **recess** is a holiday period between the sessions of a committee or parliament. *The committee is going into recess for a couple of weeks... The congress was recalled from its summer recess.*
2 NU **Recess** is the time between lessons when children play in the school grounds; used in American English. *A number of schoolchildren on recess came over.*
3 NC In a room, a **recess** is a small area created when one part of a wall is built farther back than the rest. *...the arched window recess.*
4 NC+SUPP The **recesses** of something are its deep or hidden parts. *I pushed the problem down into the dim recesses of my mind.*

recession /rɪsɛʃn/ **recessions**
NCorNU A **recession** is a period when the economy of a country is not very successful, for example because industry is producing less and more people are becoming unemployed. *...new prosperity and Britain's emergence from the recession... Some analysts predict only a slow-down in economic growth rather than a recession. ...the combination of recession and record unemployment.*

recharge /riːtʃɑːdʒ/ **recharges, recharging, recharged**
VO To **recharge** a battery means to fill it with electricity again after it has been used, by connecting it to a special piece of electrical equipment. *Does your battery need recharging?*

rechargeable /riːtʃɑːdʒəbl/
ADJ A battery that is **rechargeable** can be recharged so that it can be used again. *'How long will the batteries last?'—'Several months, but they are rechargeable.'*

recherché /rəʃɛəʃeɪ/
ADJ Something that is **recherché** is known or understood by only a few clever people or experts; a formal word. *...a very recherché sort of film.*

recidivist /rɪsɪdɪvɪst/ **recidivists**
NC A **recidivist** is someone who repeatedly commits crimes although they have already been punished or sent to prison. *Dawn was a hopeless recidivist.*

recipe /rɛsəpi/ **recipes**
1 NC A **recipe** is a list of ingredients and a set of instructions telling you how to cook something. *...a recipe for beetroot soup... There are lots of recipe books which give advice on how to do that.*
2 N SING+for If something is a **recipe** for disaster or a **recipe** for success, you mean that it is likely to result in disaster or success. *He warned that the ANC did*

not have a recipe for instant success. ... a recipe for chaos.

recipient /rɪsɪpiənt/ **recipients**
NC The **recipient** is the person or thing that receives something; a formal word. *...letters kept by the recipients. ...a recipient of American aid... The recipient cells would then start to make the protein.*

reciprocal /rɪsɪprəkl/
ADJ **Reciprocal** actions or arrangements involve two people or groups who do the same thing to each other or who agree to help each other in a similar way; a formal word. *Their social security system is linked to Britain's by a reciprocal agreement.*

reciprocate /rɪsɪprəkeɪt/ **reciprocates, reciprocating, reciprocated**
VOorV If you **reciprocate** someone's feelings or behaviour towards you, you share the same feelings or behave in the same way towards them; a formal word. *This hostile attitude is reciprocated by potential employers... Maybe one day it will occur to you to reciprocate.*

reciprocity /rɛsɪprɒsəti/
NU **Reciprocity** is behaviour between two people or groups of people in which each gives or concedes a lot to the other; a formal word. *Many writers have sought to establish a relationship of real reciprocity and equality with their readers.*

recital /rɪsaɪtl/ **recitals**
NC A **recital** is a solo performance of music or poetry. *She had been asked to give a piano recital.*

recitation /rɛsɪteɪʃn/ **recitations**
NC When someone gives a **recitation**, they say aloud a piece of poetry or other writing that they have learned. *The transmission began with a recitation from the Koran.*

recite /rɪsaɪt/ **recites, reciting, recited**
1 VO If you **recite** a piece of writing, you read or say it aloud after you have learned it. *She recited a speech from 'As You Like It'.*
2 VO If you **recite** a list of things, you say it aloud. *Mrs Zapp recited a catalogue of her husband's sins.*

reckless /rɛkləs/
ADJ A **reckless** person shows a lack of care about danger or about the results of their actions. *I don't like the way he drives. He's reckless... They denounced the government for its reckless squandering of public funds.* ♦ **recklessly** ADV *He accelerated recklessly round a blind corner.* ♦ **recklessness** NU *...the recklessness of the attack.*

reckon /rɛkən/ **reckons, reckoning, reckoned**
1 V-REPORT If you **reckon** that something is true, you think it is true; an informal use. *She reckoned that there was a risk... What do you reckon?*
2 VO+to-INF If something is **reckoned** to be true, people generally think that it is true. *About 40 per cent of the country is reckoned to be illiterate.*
3 VO When you **reckon** an amount, you calculate it. *The number of days lost through unemployment can be reckoned at 146 million.*

reckon on PHRASAL VERB If you **reckon on** something, you feel certain that it will happen and you make your plans accordingly. *He reckoned on a large reward if he succeeded.*

reckon with PHRASAL VERB 1 If you say that someone or something is **to be reckoned with**, you mean that you have to deal with them and it is difficult. *Now they have to reckon with a much more resolute leader... They are a force to be reckoned with.* 2 If you had not **reckoned with** something, you had not expected it and so were not ready for it. *She had not reckoned with a surprise of this sort.*

reckon without PHRASAL VERB If you say that you had **reckoned without** something, you mean that you had not expected it and so were not prepared for it. *They reckoned without Margaret's determination.*

reckoning /rɛkəʰnɪŋ/ **reckonings**
1 NCorNU A **reckoning** is something that you think about and work out, often mathematically. *It's only a rough reckoning... By his own reckoning, he had taken five hours to get there... Output fell by one per cent in the three summer months, by some reckoning the sharpest contraction in production for a decade.*

2 Someone's **day of reckoning** is the time when they pay or are punished for the things they have done wrong. *It was amazing that BCCI's day of reckoning had not come sooner.*

reclaim /rɪkleɪm/ **reclaims, reclaiming, reclaimed**
1 VO If you **reclaim** something that you have lost or had taken away from you, you succeed in getting it back. *The Asians should have the right to reclaim the houses and the businesses which were seized from them... You must present this ticket when you reclaim your luggage.*
2 VO When people **reclaim** land, they make it suitable for use by draining or irrigating it. *Lowland bogs have been reclaimed.* ♦ **reclaimed** ADJ *...reclaimed land.*
3 VO If people **reclaim** a substance, they extract it from rubbish or waste materials so that it can be used again. *Aluminium is hard to separate, but economically there's a very good case for reclaiming it... The plastic will be recovered or reclaimed.*

reclamation /rekləmeɪʃn/; a formal word.
1 NU **Reclamation** is the successful attempt to make desert, marshland, or other unusable land suitable for farming or building. *...the reclamation of marginal lands.*
2 NU **Reclamation** is also the recovery of a substance found in rubbish, used products, or waste materials so that it can be used again. *We should encourage reclamation and recycling.*

recline /rɪklaɪn/ **reclines, reclining, reclined**
V If you **recline**, you sit or lie with the upper part of your body supported at an angle; a formal word. *She was reclining comfortably in her chair.*

reclining /rɪklaɪnɪŋ/
ADJ ATTRIB A **reclining** chair or seat is designed so that you can lie down or sit with the upper part of your body supported at an angle.

recluse /rɪkluːs/ **recluses**
NC A **recluse** is a person who lives alone and deliberately avoids other people. *He now lives as a recluse in the squalor of his London flat.*

reclusive /rɪkluːsɪv/
ADJ Someone who is **reclusive** lives alone and deliberately avoids other people; a formal word. *His estranged wife, Becky, had become increasingly reclusive.*

recognise /rekəgnaɪz/. See **recognize**.

recognition /rekəgnɪʃn/
1 NU **Recognition** is the experience of recognizing someone or something. *She walked past me without so much as a glance of recognition.*
2 NU+SUPP When there is **recognition** of something, people realize or accept that it exists or that it is true. *There has been insufficient recognition of the magnitude of the problem. ...a recognition of their importance.*
3 If something is done **in recognition of** someone's achievements, it is done as a way of showing official appreciation of them. *He was awarded a knighthood in recognition of his great contribution to the British cinema.*
4 NU When a country or organization receives **recognition**, another country officially accepts its existence and is prepared to work with it. *He has for three years tried to win diplomatic recognition.*

recognizable /rekəgnaɪzəbl/; also spelt **recognisable**.
ADJ Something that is **recognizable** is easy to recognize or identify. *...a recognizable voice. ...an old statue barely recognisable as Charles II.*
♦ **recognizably** ADV *Its arrangement is recognizably based on what existed before.*

recognize /rekəgnaɪz/ **recognizes, recognizing, recognized**; also spelt **recognise**.
1 VO If you **recognize** someone or something, you know who or what they are, because you have seen or heard them before or because they have been described to you. *They are trained to recognize the symptoms of radiation-sickness... The postmistress recognised her as Mrs Pennington's daughter.*
2 VOorV-REPORT You also say that you **recognize** something when you realize or accept that it exists or that it is true. *Governments are beginning to*

recognize the problem... *We recognise this as a genuine need... They refused to recognise that a wrong decision had been made.*
3 VO You say that something is **recognized** when it is officially accepted or approved. *Are qualifications gained in Britain recognized in other European countries?... The new regime was at once recognized by China.*
4 VO When an achievement is **recognized**, people officially show their appreciation of it. *The nation recognized her efforts by making her property a historical site.*

recognized /rekəgnaɪzd/; also spelt **recognised**.
ADJ **Recognized** means generally approved or accepted as having a particular quality or position. *There are several recognized techniques for dealing with this... She's a recognized authority on artificial intelligence.*

recoil /rɪkɔɪl/ **recoils, recoiling, recoiled**
1 V If you **recoil** from something, you feel afraid or disgusted by it. *He recoiled in horror from the savagery which he witnessed... Parents may recoil at this kind of behaviour.*
2 V You also say that someone **recoils** when they move part of their body away from something because it gives them an unpleasant feeling. *When he touched the man's arm, he recoiled in horror, for it was cold and rigid.*

recollect /rekəlekt/ **recollects, recollecting, recollected**
VOorV-REPORT If you **recollect** something, you remember it; a formal word. *He was unable to recollect the names... He does not recollect how long they were in the house.*

recollection /rekəlekʃn/ **recollections**
NCorNU If you have a **recollection** of something, you remember it. *I have a vivid recollection of the house where I was born. ...a flash of recollection.*

recommend /rekəmend/ **recommends, recommending, recommended**
1 VOorVOO If someone **recommends** something to you, they suggest that you should have it or use it, because it is good or useful. *...a fine novel which I'd strongly recommend... Perhaps you could recommend me a solicitor.*
2 VOorV-REPORT If you **recommend** an action, you suggest that it should be done. *He recommends cycling as a good form of exercise... The Committee recommended that shareholders should vote against the offer.*

recommendation /rekəmendeɪʃn/ **recommendations**
1 NC A **recommendation** is advice about the best thing to do. *...recommendations for training. ...President Bush's recommendation that Egypt's military debt be waived.*
2 NCorNU If you make a **recommendation**, you suggest that someone should have something or use something, because it is good or useful. *...recommendations of people who've seen and admire their work... The best way to find a gardener is through personal recommendation.*

recompense /rekəmpens/ **recompenses, recompensing, recompensed**
1 NU **Recompense** is something, usually money, that you give to someone to thank them for helping you or to pay for any damage that you have done. *Would you accept this as a little recompense for all the trouble you have taken?... The boatman asked for recompense for the damage done.*
2 VO+for If you **recompense** someone for something, you give them something, usually money, to thank them for helping you or to pay for any damage that you have done. *We had to recompense the peasants for the loss of their goats.*

reconcile /rekənsaɪl/ **reconciles, reconciling, reconciled**
1 VO If you **reconcile** two opposing beliefs, you find a way in which both of them can be held by the same person at the same time. *I asked how he would reconcile apartheid with Christianity.*
2 VO If you are **reconciled** with someone, you become friendly with them again after a disagreement. *They had been reconciled with their families.*

◆ **reconciliation** /rɛkənsɪlieɪʃn/ NU ...*hopes of reconciliation in Western Europe.* ...*the process of national reconciliation.*
3 V-REFL If you **reconcile** yourself to an unpleasant situation, you accept it. *He told them to reconcile themselves to their misery on earth.*

reconciled /rɛkənsaɪld/
ADJ PRED+*to* If you are **reconciled** to something, you agree to accept it although it is unpleasant. *After a while he grew reconciled to the situation.*

recondite /rɛkəndaɪt/
ADJ Something that is **recondite** is not known about by many people and is therefore difficult to understand; a formal word. ...*an expert in a recondite branch of knowledge.*

recondition /riːkəndɪʃn/ **reconditions, reconditioning, reconditioned**
VO To **recondition** a machine or piece of equipment means to repair or replace all the parts that are worn or broken. *This one's new, but the others have only been reconditioned.* ◆ **reconditioned** ADJ ...*a reconditioned cooker.*

reconnaissance /rɪkɒnɪsəns/
NU **Reconnaissance** is the process of obtaining military information about the size and position of an army or about the geographical features of an area using soldiers, planes, or satellites; a technical term. *They decided to step up reconnaissance of enemy naval movements.*

reconnoitre /rɛkənɔɪtə/ **reconnoitres, reconnoitring, reconnoitred;** spelt **reconnoiter** in American English.
VOorV To **reconnoitre** means to obtain information about the size and position of an army or about the geographical features of an area, using soldiers, planes, or satellites; a technical term. *Small armoured task forces had reconnoitred the area... The site itself was being reconnoitred by radar.*

reconsider /riːkənsɪdə/ **reconsiders, reconsidering, reconsidered**
VO,V,orV-REPORT If you **reconsider** a decision or method, you think about it and try to decide whether it should be changed. *He asked me to reconsider my decision... I asked them to reconsider but they refused... We must constantly reconsider how this principle can best be implemented.* ◆ **reconsideration** /riːkənsɪdəreɪʃn/ NU *This would allow time for reconsideration.*

reconstitute /riːkɒnstɪtjuːt/ **reconstitutes, reconstituting, reconstituted**
1 VO To **reconstitute** an organization means to form it again in a different way. *The group was reconstituted after 26 March.* ◆ **reconstituted** ADJ ATTRIB ...*the reconstituted provisional government.*
2 VO If you **reconstitute** a food that is dried, you change it back to its original form by adding water to it. *Use warm water to reconstitute dried yeast.*

reconstruct /riːkənstrʌkt/ **reconstructs, reconstructing, reconstructed**
1 VO If you **reconstruct** a building or a town that has been destroyed or badly damaged, you build it again. ...*international assistance to help reconstruct the war-damaged towns of the north.*
2 VO When a system or policy is **reconstructed**, it is replaced with one that works differently. ...*an attempt to reconstruct race relations policy.*
3 VO If you **reconstruct** a past event, you obtain a complete description of it by combining a lot of small pieces of information. *The scheme uses television and newspapers to reconstruct crimes.*

reconstruction /riːkənstrʌkʃn/ **reconstructions**
1 NU **Reconstruction** is the process of making a country normal again after a war, for example by replacing buildings that have been damaged or destroyed. ...*the reconstruction of post-war Britain.* ...*the huge programme of emergency aid and reconstruction assistance needed in Afghanistan.*
2 NU When the **reconstruction** of a building takes place, it is built again after it has been damaged or destroyed. ...*the start of building work on a reconstruction of Shakespeare's Globe Theatre.*
3 NC+SUPP A **reconstruction** of an event such as a crime is an attempt to act it out again using all the

information about it that is available, to help people to understand how it happened or remember details that they have forgotten. *Federal police staged a reconstruction but discovered nothing, so they decided to wait until the stolen money appeared in circulation.* ...*a reconstruction of the trial of King Louis just held on French television.*

reconvene /riːkənviːn/ **reconvenes, reconvening, reconvened;** a formal word.
1 VO If you **reconvene** a meeting or group of people, you ask them to come back to discuss something. *The two leaders did reconvene the media yesterday.*
2 V If an official group of people **reconvene**, they come together again for a meeting. *The assembly may reconvene to discuss the matter next week.*

record, records, recording, recorded; pronounced /rɛkɔːd/ when it is a noun or an adjective and /rɪkɔːd/ when it is a verb.
1 NC If you keep a **record** of something, you keep a written account of it or store information about it in a computer. *Keep a record of any repair bills.* ...*medical records.*
2 VO If you **record** something, you write it down, film it, or put it into a computer so that it can be referred to later. *All the details could be recorded on a computer... Their every action was recorded by concealed cameras.*
3 NC A **record** is a round, flat piece of black plastic on which sound, especially music, is stored. *She sold more records than any other British female artist.*
4 NC A **record** is also the music or other sounds that are on a record when you listen to it. *Several old records became Top Twenty hits again in 1988.*
5 VO When music or speech is **recorded**, it is put onto a tape or a record, so that it can be heard again later. *This song was first recorded by Gene Pitney back in 1967... They recorded acoustic versions of their songs... She recorded dozens of interviews.*
6 NC A **record** is also the time, distance, or number of victories that is the best that has been achieved in a particular sport or other activity. *He held the record for the mile... He has set the world record for the men's 50 metres backstroke... Kieran Perkins broke the 800-metres freestyle world record.*
7 ADJ ATTRIB You use **record** to say that something is higher, lower, or better than has ever been achieved before. *Unemployment was at a record high.*
8 NC+SUPP Your **record** is all the facts that are known about your achievements or character. *Mr Gerran has a very distinguished record... There will be new checks on the criminal records of potential jurors.*
9 See also **recording, track record, off-the-record.**
● **Record** is used in these phrases. ● If you **set** or **put** the **record straight**, you show that something which has been regarded as true is in fact not true. *Harold Begbie wrote a book to put the record straight.* ● You use **on record** to say that something is, for example, the best, worst, or largest thing of its kind that has been noticed or recorded in writing. *1990 was the hottest year on record.* ● If you are **on record** as saying something, you have said it publicly or officially and people will remember it. *People are on record as saying that nothing useful will ever grow here again.*

record-breaker, record-breakers
NC A **record-breaker** is someone who beats the previous record for a particular performance or achievement, especially in sport. *I don't think we'll see any record-breakers today.*

record-breaking
ADJ ATTRIB Something that is **record-breaking** is better than the previous record for a particular performance or achievement. *The play enjoyed a record-breaking Christmas season.* ...*a record-breaking stay in space.*

recorded delivery
NU In Britain, if you send a letter or parcel by **recorded delivery**, the Post Office gives you an official record of the fact that the letter or parcel has been posted. When the letter or parcel arrives, the person who receives it has to sign to say they have received it. *The biggest increases in customer dissatisfaction involved recorded delivery.*

recorder /rɪkɔːdə/ **recorders**
1 NC You can refer to a cassette recorder, a tape recorder, or a video recorder as a **recorder**. *Many people today have cassette recorders of reasonable quality at home or in the office... He switched the recorder off.*
2 NC A **recorder** is also a hollow musical instrument that you play by blowing down one end and covering a series of holes with your fingers. *Mostly children tend to swap their recorders for flutes or clarinets... Our seven year-old daughter Elizabeth had had her weekly recorder lesson.*

recording /rɪkɔːdɪŋ/ **recordings**
1 NC A recording of something is a record, tape, or video of it. *...a new recording of Puccini's tragic opera 'Madame Butterfly'.*
2 NU **Recording** is the process of making records, tapes, or videos. *...a recording engineer... I went up to the big recording studio in Maida Vale.*

record library, record libraries
NC A **record library** is a library from which you can borrow records and cassettes with music on them. *The copy we keep in our record library is badly scratched.*

record player, record players
NC A **record player** is a machine on which you play records. *There's a tape-recorder and an old record player which also serves as their amplifier.*

recount, recounts, recounting, recounted;
pronounced /rɪkaʊnt/ when it is a verb and /riːkaʊnt/ when it is a noun.
1 VO If you **recount** a story or event, you tell it to people; a formal use. *I let Henry recount the incident in his own words.*
2 NC A **recount** is a second count of votes in an election when the result is very close. *Mr Baltasar Corrada, from the New Progressive Party, at first demanded a recount but later conceded defeat.*

recoup /rɪkuːp/ **recoups, recouping, recouped**
VO If you **recoup** a sum of money that you have spent or lost, you get it back. *I recouped the initial cost within two years.*

recourse /rɪkɔːs/
NU If you have **recourse** to something, you use it to help you in a difficult situation; a formal word. *We need never have recourse to violence.*

recover /rɪkʌvə/ **recovers, recovering, recovered**
1 V When you **recover** from an illness or an injury, you become well again. *It was weeks before he fully recovered. ...a wound from which he did not recover.*
2 V If you **recover** from an unhappy or unpleasant experience, you stop being upset by it. *They took a long time to recover from this shock.*
3 VO If you **recover** something that has been lost or stolen, you get it back. *I would do my best to recover these documents... They recovered her body from the old mine-shaft.*
4 VO If you **recover** your former mental or physical state or **recover** the ability to do something, you get it back. *He died without recovering consciousness... He was beginning to recover the use of his voice.*

recoverable /rɪkʌv⁰rəbl/
ADJ If something is **recoverable**, it is possible for you to get it back. *...forgotten but still recoverable knowledge.*

recovered /rɪkʌvəd/
ADJ PRED If you are **recovered**, you are well again after you have been ill. *Stay at home until you are fully recovered.*

recovery /rɪkʌvə⁰ri/ **recoveries**
1 N SING or NU If a sick person makes a **recovery**, he or she becomes well again. *He made a good recovery from his stroke... The shock of the operation delayed his recovery... Their prospects of recovery, even with first-class medical assistance, were negligible.*
2 NU or NC When there is a **recovery** in a country's economy, it improves after being in a bad state. *His advisers insisted that economic recovery was in sight. ...an economic recovery programme. ...last minute recoveries despite two decades of steady decline.*
3 N SING or NU The **recovery** of something that was lost or stolen is the fact of getting it back; a formal use.

...the recovery of the treasure... It can be left for later recovery by stronger lifting gear.
4 N SING or NU The **recovery** of someone's physical or mental state is their return to this state; a formal use. *The news was sufficient to bring about the recovery of his equanimity.*

recreate /riːkrieɪt/ **recreates, recreating, recreated**
VO If you **recreate** something, you succeed in making it happen or exist again. *The opportunity could not be recreated... In his book, he recreates a way of life that disappeared before the Second World War.*

recreation /rɛkrieɪʃn/ **recreations**
NU or NC **Recreation** consists of things that you do to exercise your body or mind when you are not working or studying. *Sport and recreation have always been part of university life... The library was reserved for quieter recreations.*

recreational /rɛkrieɪʃnl/
ADJ **Recreational** means relating to recreation. *...recreational facilities.*

recreation ground, recreation grounds
NC A **recreation ground** is a piece of public land, usually in a town, where people can go to play sport and games. *The ban will affect such areas as streets, shopping centres, parks and recreation grounds.*

recrimination /rɪkrɪmɪneɪʃn/ **recriminations**
N PL or NU **Recriminations** are accusations that two people or groups make about each other. *There will be recriminations, no doubt. ...prolonged bouts of recrimination.*

recriminatory /rɪkrɪmɪnətə⁰ri/
ADJ If something that you say or do is **recriminatory**, it involves you accusing someone of something. *...recriminatory arguments.*

recruit /rɪkruːt/ **recruits, recruiting, recruited**
1 VO or V If you **recruit** people for an organization, you get them to join it or work for it. *Extra staff were recruited... I am recruiting for the Union.* ♦ **recruiting** NU *Other organizations reported sharp rises in recruiting.*
2 NC A **recruit** is a person who has recently joined an organization or army. *He joined the firm as a young recruit more than thirty years ago.*
3 VO If you **recruit** someone for a particular purpose, you get them to do something for you. *Men from the villages were recruited to carry stores... The Royal Navy announced last month that women would be recruited to serve on its warships at sea.*

recruitment /rɪkruːtmənt/
NU When **recruitment** takes place, people are persuaded to join an organization or an army. *...the mass recruitment of volunteer teachers.*

rectangle /rɛktæŋgl/ **rectangles**
NC A **rectangle** is a shape with four sides whose angles are all right angles. Each side of a rectangle is the same length as the one opposite to it. *...a large rectangle of white marble.*

rectangular /rɛktæŋgjʊlə/
ADJ Something that is **rectangular** is shaped like a rectangle. *...a rectangular flower-bed.*

rectify /rɛktɪfaɪ/ **rectifies, rectifying, rectified**
VO If you **rectify** something that is damaged or that is causing problems, you change it so that it becomes correct or satisfactory. *The tenant will be held responsible for rectifying any damage... Armed forces were sent in to rectify the situation.*

rectilinear /rɛktɪlɪnɪə/
ADJ Something that is **rectilinear** consists of straight lines or forms a pattern of straight lines; a formal word. *...rectilinear streets.*

rectitude /rɛktɪtjuːd/
NU **Rectitude** is a quality or attitude that makes people behave honestly and virtuously according to accepted standards; a literary word. *...striving for rectitude and righteousness.*

rector /rɛktə/ **rectors**
1 NC A **rector** is a Church of England priest in charge of a parish. *He was rector of All Hallows Church in Wellingborough.*
2 NC A **rector** is also a high-ranking official in some universities. *...the rector of the Sorbonne.*

rectory /rɛktə⁰ri/ **rectories**
NC A **rectory** is a house in which a priest of the Church of England lives. *Lawton Hall was an old rectory.*

rectum /rɛktəm/ **rectums**
NC Your **rectum** is the bottom end of the tube down which waste food passes out of your body; a medical term. *If a smuggler has inserted drug packets directly into his rectum, physical examination should reveal them.*

recumbent /rɪkʌmbənt/
ADJ If you are **recumbent**, you are lying down; a literary word. *I nodded towards the recumbent occupant of the other bed.*

recuperate /rɪkuːpəreɪt/ **recuperates, recuperating, recuperated**
V If you **recuperate**, you recover your health or strength after you have been ill or injured; a formal word. *I was recuperating from an accident in the gym.* ♦ **recuperation** /rɪkuːpəreɪʃn/ NU *My mother has gone to Bath for rest and recuperation.*

recuperative /rɪkuːpə⁰rətɪv/
ADJ Something that is **recuperative** helps you to recover after you have been ill; a formal word. *His recuperative powers were quite remarkable.*

recur /rɪkɜː/ **recurs, recurring, recurred**
V If something **recurs**, it happens again, either once or many times; a formal word. *It was probable that the same circumstances would now recur... It was a phrase that was to recur again and again.*

recurrence /rɪkʌrəns/ **recurrences**
NCorNU If there is a **recurrence** of something that is unpleasant or bad, it happens again; a formal word. *There were minor recurrences of her eye trouble. ...the principle of eternal recurrence.*

recurrent /rɪkʌrənt/
ADJ ATTRIB **Recurrent** means the same as **recurring**; a formal word. *The recurrent problem is one of discipline.*

recurring /rɪkɜːrɪŋ/
ADJ ATTRIB **Recurring** things happen many times. *Food scarcity will be a recurring problem in the future.*

recycle /riːsaɪkl/ **recycles, recycling, recycled**
VO If you **recycle** things that have already been used, such as bottles or sheets of paper, you process them so that they can be used again. *Plastic bottles can easily be recycled.* ♦ **recycled** ADJ *...recycled paper.*

red /rɛd/ **redder, reddest; reds**
1 ADJ Something that is **red** is the colour of blood or of a ripe tomato. *...a bunch of red roses... They are thought to have escaped in a red car.* ► Also NU *...a colourful and flamboyant figure who dresses in red or pink.*
2 ADJ If someone goes **red**, their face becomes redder than normal, because they are embarrassed or angry. *Ralph clenched his fist and went very red.*
3 ADJ **Red** hair is between red and brown in colour. *His bristly red hair was standing on end.*
4 NC If you call someone a **red**, you mean that they support left-wing ideas such as communism; used showing disapproval. *The song goes, 'El Salvador will be the tomb where the reds finish up'.*
● **Red** is used in these phrases. ● If you are **in the red**, you have spent more money than you have in your account and therefore you owe money to the bank. You can also say that a company's accounts or a country's economy is **in the red** when that company or that country is not earning enough money to cover expenditure; an informal expression. *The club is millions of dollars in the red... Yesterday's announcement showed Britain's trade more than two billion pounds in the red.* ● If you **see red**, you become very angry.

red alert, red alerts
NCorNU A **red alert** is a warning about an emergency that is given to hospitals and other organizations so that they can be ready to deal with it. *A red alert has been sounded... The military remained on red alert amid rumours of a coup attempt.*

red-blooded /rɛdblʌdɪd/
ADJ Someone who is **red-blooded** has lots of energy and interest in sex; an informal word, used showing approval. *'I'm a red-blooded, normal American boy,'* Thomas said.

redbrick /rɛdbrɪk/
ADJ ATTRIB A **redbrick** university is one of the British universities that were established in large cities outside London in the late 19th and early 20th centuries, as opposed to much older universities such as Oxford and Cambridge.

red carpet
N SING The **red carpet** is special treatment that is given to important or honoured visitors, for example the laying of a strip of red carpet for them to walk on. *We shall have to roll out the red carpet when he comes.*

Red Crescent
N PROP The **Red Crescent** is an organization in Muslim countries that helps people who are suffering because of war, famine, or natural disaster. *The operation has been organized by the Turkish Red Crescent.*

Red Cross
N PROP The **Red Cross** is an international organization that helps people who are suffering because of war, famine, or natural disaster. *The Red Cross reports that 750 civilians have been hurt in recent days. ...the internationally-recognized Red Cross flag.*

redcurrant /rɛdkʌrənt/ **redcurrants**
NC A **redcurrant** is a small, bright red fruit that grows in bunches on a bush; used also of the bush itself.

redden /rɛdn/ **reddens, reddening, reddened**
1 V If you **redden** or if your face **reddens**, your face becomes redder in colour, usually because of a strong emotion that you are feeling. *I saw him redden with pleasure... The soldier's face reddened in anger.*
2 VO To **redden** something means to cause it to become red or more red in colour. *Was the liquid really blood or merely water reddened with betel juice?*

reddish /rɛdɪʃ/
ADJ Something that is **reddish** is slightly red. *The giant reddish mass advances ominously.*

redecorate /riːdɛkəreɪt/ **redecorates, redecorating, redecorated**
VO To **redecorate** a building or a room means to paint it again or put new wallpaper on the walls. *The lounge had been redecorated since his last visit.*

redeem /rɪdiːm/ **redeems, redeeming, redeemed**
1 VO When something **redeems** a bad thing or situation, it prevents it from being completely bad. *Swallow was doing his best to redeem what could be a disastrous dinner.* ♦ **redeeming** ADJ ATTRIB *...a book with no redeeming qualities.*
2 V-REFL If you **redeem** yourself, you do something that gives people a good opinion of you again after you have behaved badly. *He was trying to redeem himself for his earlier failure.*
3 VO If you **redeem** something, you get it back from someone by repaying them money that you have borrowed from them; a technical use. *They came to redeem their jewellery.*

redeemable /rɪdiːməbl/
ADJ If something is **redeemable**, it can be exchanged for a particular sum of money or for goods worth a particular sum. *...inexpensive gift certificates redeemable at local stores.*

redeemer /rɪdiːmə/ **redeemers**
1 N PROP In Christianity, the **Redeemer** is Jesus Christ, who is believed to have freed people from the consequences of sin and evil. *The statue of Christ the Redeemer towers over the city of Rio de Janeiro.*
2 NC A **redeemer** is any person who saves someone from a difficult or dangerous situation; an old-fashioned use. *Was it possible that Italy had found her redeemer?*

redefine /riːdɪfaɪn/ **redefines, redefining, redefined**
VO If you **redefine** something, you give it a different function, role, or structure from the one it had previously. *...the new treaty which redefines the relationship between Moscow and the Soviet republics... NATO has comprehensively redefined its military strategy.*

redefinition /riːdefɪnɪʃn/
N SING A **redefinition** of something is a modification of its function, role, or structure. *...a significant redefinition of the party's role. ...the redefinition of the Western alliance.*

redemption /rɪdempʃn/
N U **Redemption** is freedom from the consequences of sin and evil which Christians believe was made possible by Christ's death. *...her belief that Christianity is concerned with spiritual redemption.*

redemptive /rɪdemptɪv/
ADJ In Christianity, something that is **redemptive** leads to freedom from the consequences of sin and evil, a formal word. *Christ's redemptive sacrifice.*

red ensign, red ensigns
N C A **red ensign** is a flag that is flown by ships of the British Merchant Navy. It is a red flag with a Union Jack in the top corner.

redeploy /riːdɪplɔɪ/ **redeploys, redeploying, redeployed**
V O To **redeploy** troops or forces means to distribute them in a different way so that they are ready for use or action. *The reconnaissance Tornados were redeployed to the south.*

redeployment /riːdɪplɔɪmənt/
N U **Redeployment** is the redistribution of troops, weapons, or resources so that they are ready for use or action. *There was a southward redeployment of Allied forces... Agreements can be reached on voluntary redundancy or redeployment.*

redevelop /riːdɪveləp/ **redevelops, redeveloping, redeveloped**
V O To **redevelop** an area means to change it by removing existing buildings and roads, and by building new ones. *The whole of the city centre has now been redeveloped.*

redevelopment /riːdɪveləpmənt/ **redevelopments**
N U or N C When **redevelopment** takes place, old buildings in a part of a town are replaced by new ones. *The area is undergoing redevelopment... The city council is planning an ambitious redevelopment of the vast shopping centre.*

red-faced
1 ADJ Someone who is **red-faced** has a face that appears red, for example because they drink a lot. *Everyone knew Tinker, a burly, red-faced man.*
2 ADJ If people are **red-faced**, they are embarrassed because they have done something wrong or foolish and realize that other people have noticed their mistake. *Several companies, though, are very red-faced over this.*

red-handed
If you **catch** someone **red-handed**, you catch them while they are in the act of doing something wrong. *A woman had been caught red-handed passing information to the West German intelligence service.*

redhead /redhed/ **redheads**
N C A **redhead** is a person whose hair is a colour that is between red and brown.

redheaded /redhedɪd/
ADJ Someone who is **redheaded** is a redhead. *...a redheaded young man.*

red herring, red herrings
N C A **red herring** is something which is irrelevant and takes people's attention away from the main subject they are considering. *They were using the issue as a red herring.*

red-hot
1 ADJ Something that is **red-hot** is so hot that it turns red. *...screens which are continually sprayed with water to cut down on the heat from the red-hot metal surrounding them.*
2 ADJ ATTRIB People or situations that are **red-hot** are full of very strong feelings; an informal use. *...a red-hot revolutionary. ...red-hot patriotism.*

Red Indian, Red Indians
N C A **Red Indian** is a native North American Indian; an old-fashioned, offensive expression.

redirect /riːdərekt/ **redirects, redirecting, redirected**
1 V O If you **redirect** your energy, resources, or ability, you begin to work in a different way because your aims have changed. *I needed to redirect my*

energies... *Most industries were redirected to the needs of a wartime economy.*
2 V O To **redirect** something such as traffic means to change the course or direction that it has to follow. *All traffic is being redirected to avoid this stretch of the motorway.*
3 V O If you **redirect** someone's post, you send it to their new address after it has been delivered to an address where they no longer live. *Please redirect all letters to the following address.*

redistribute /riːdɪstrɪbjuːt/ **redistributes, redistributing, redistributed**
V O When money or goods **are redistributed**, they are shared among people or organizations in a different way from the way that they were previously shared. *Money would be redistributed from the traditional arts institutions.* ◆ **redistribution** /riːdɪstrɪbjuːʃn/ **redistributions** N U or N C *We do not envisage any redistribution of wealth and power. ...a redistribution of land.*

red light, red lights
1 N C A **red light** is a traffic signal which shines red to indicate that drivers must stop. *...driving madly through red lights and down one-way streets.*
2 N SING People also refer to a decision or a situation that prevents them from doing something as a **red light**. *White House officials insist Moscow's extreme caution does not amount to a permanent red light.*
3 ADJ ATTRIB The **red-light** district of a city is the area where prostitutes work. *...the heart of Paris's red-light district. ...the naval base, with its red-light district and good-time girls.*

red meat
N U **Red meat** is meat such as beef or lamb, which is dark brown in colour after it has been cooked. *...the swing away from red meat and dairy products in consumer demand.*

redo /riːduː/ **redoes, redoing, redid, redone**
V O If you **redo** a piece of work, you do it again in order to improve it or change it. *I had to redo the stitching twice before I was satisfied.*

redolent /redələnt/; a literary word.
1 ADJ PRED+of If something is **redolent** of something else, it has features that make you think of that other thing. *It was written in language redolent of the Lakeland Poets.*
2 ADJ PRED+of To be **redolent** of something else also means to have a strong smell of that other thing. *Her colour was high and her breath redolent of gin.*

redouble /riːdʌbl/ **redoubles, redoubling, redoubled**
V O If you **redouble** your efforts, you try much harder to achieve something. *She redoubled her efforts to attract his curiosity... Mr Mitterrand has redoubled his efforts in the past week.*

redoubtable /rɪdautəbl/
ADJ Someone who is **redoubtable** has a very strong character, which makes people respect and slightly fear them; a formal word. *She realised that the redoubtable Marie Tempest was coming her way.*

red pepper, red peppers
1 N C A **red pepper** is a ripe pepper that is used in cooking and can be eaten raw in salads.
2 N U **Red pepper** is a hot-tasting red powder that is made from red peppers and used to flavour food.

redraw /riːdrɔː/ **redraws, redrawing, redrew, redrawn**
V O If you **redraw** the borders or the boundaries of a country or region, you change them so that the country or region covers a slightly different, greater, or smaller area from the one it previously covered. *They also claim that regional boundaries have been redrawn to favour the European voters... The deputies had proposed to redraw Yugoslavia's internal borders.* ◆ **redrawing** N SING *...a complete redrawing of the internal frontiers.*

redress /rɪdres/ **redresses, redressing, redressed**; a formal word.
1 V O If you **redress** something such as a wrong or a grievance, you do something to correct it or to improve things for the person who has been badly treated. *He did all that he could to redress these wrongs.*

2 NU **Redress** is compensation for something wrong that has been done. *Your claims for redress may yet succeed.*
3 If you **redress the balance** between two unequal things, you make them equal again. *We were refused the pay increase needed to redress the balance.*

redskin /rɛdskɪn/ **redskins**
NC A **redskin** is a native North American Indian; an old-fashioned, extremely offensive word.

red tape
NU or N SING You refer to official rules and procedures as **red tape** when they seem unnecessary and cause delay. *...a minimum of red tape. ...as he struggles to cut the red tape and bureaucracy.*

reduce /rɪdjuːs/ **reduces, reducing, reduced**
1 VO If you **reduce** something, you make it smaller. *They have promised to reduce public expenditure... The work-force would have to be reduced from 13,000 to 7,500.* ◆ **reduced** ADJ *...a reduced rate of production.*
2 VO+*to* If you say that someone **is reduced** to a weaker or inferior state, you mean that they change to this state as a result of something that happens to them. *He was reduced to tears... Her mother was reduced to infantile dependence.*
3 VO+*to* If someone **is reduced** to doing something, they have to do it, although it is unpleasant or humiliating. *They are reduced to begging in the streets.*

reduction /rɪdʌkʃn/ **reductions**
NU or NC When there is a **reduction** in something, it is made smaller. *They're talking about arms reduction all over Europe... The unions will be demanding a reduction in working hours.*

redundancy /rɪdʌndənsi/ **redundancies**
1 NC When there are **redundancies**, an organization tells some of its employees that they can no longer work there because their jobs are no longer necessary or because the organization can no longer afford to pay them. *The trade unions accepted 3500 redundancies.*
2 NU **Redundancy** is the state of no longer having a job because you have been made redundant. *The possibility of redundancy was present in their minds.*

redundant /rɪdʌndənt/
1 ADJ If you are made **redundant**, you lose your job because it is no longer necessary or because your employer cannot afford to keep paying you. *Alumetal Ltd will be making 250 workers redundant next year.*
2 ADJ Something that is **redundant** is no longer needed because it has been replaced by something else. *...skills which have been made redundant by technological advance. ...redundant machinery from the tobacco industry.*

redwood /rɛdwʊd/ **redwoods**
NC or NU A **redwood** is a very tall tree that grows in northern California and southern Oregon. Its leaves are shaped like needles, and the wood that comes from it is also called **redwood**. *Reprocessed, the redwood fetches closer to $600 per ton. ...ancient redwood forests.*

reed /riːd/ **reeds**
NC **Reeds** are tall plants that grow in shallow water or wet ground. *Reeds aren't the only plants that like growing on sewage.*

re-educate, re-educates, re-educating, re-educated
VO If you say that a government is **re-educating** people, you mean that it is encouraging or trying to force them to adopt new attitudes which it considers to be politically correct. *China had already set up sixty-eight centres to re-educate prostitutes... 770 people have already been re-educated.*

re-education
NU **Re-education** is the activity of encouraging or trying to force people to adopt new attitudes which are considered to be politically correct. *The system had failed in its declared aim of correction and re-education... He said that all prisoners being held in re-education camps in the country will be freed soon.*

reedy /riːdi/ **reedier, reediest**
1 ADJ A place that is **reedy** has reeds growing all over it. *...a house by the reedy banks of Whitelake River.*

2 ADJ If you describe a voice as **reedy**, you mean that it has a high and unpleasant sound. *Richard, in his thin, reedy voice, made a painfully dull ninety-minute speech.*

reef /riːf/ **reefs**
NC A **reef** is a long line of rocks or sand lying close to the surface of the sea. *The country's main attraction is its barrier reef.*

reefer /riːfə/ **reefers**
1 NC A **reefer** or **reefer jacket** is a short thick coat which is often worn by sailors.
2 NC A **reefer** is also a cigarette which is made with marijuana and tobacco; an old-fashioned, informal use.

reef knot, reef knots
NC A **reef knot** is a type of double knot that will not come undone easily.

reek /riːk/ **reeks, reeking, reeked**
1 V If someone or something **reeks** of a particular thing, they smell very strongly of it. *...reeking of brandy.*
2 V If you say that a situation **reeks** of an unpleasant quality, you mean that this quality seems to be present. *The ruling reeked of double standards and in protest she began her hunger strike.*
3 N SING+*of* A **reek** of something is a strong, unpleasant smell of it. *...the sickening reek of blood.*

reel /riːl/ **reels, reeling, reeled**
1 NC A **reel** is a cylindrical object around which you wrap something such as thread or cinema film. *...a reel of white string.*
2 NC The **reel** on a fishing rod is a round device used to control the length of the fishing line. *He always seemed to have a fishing reel in his hand.*
3 V If someone **reels** somewhere, they move there unsteadily as if they were going to fall. *I reeled back into the room.*
4 V A If someone or something **reels** from an unpleasant experience, they are deeply affected by it. *The Times says President Bush was reeling from his embarrassing defeat... The economy reeled under the blow.*
5 V If your brain or your mind is **reeling**, you are very confused because you have too much to think about. *His mind was dazed and reeling with all that he had seen and heard.*

reel in PHRASAL VERB If you **reel in** a fish, you pull it towards you by turning the handle on the reel and shortening the line. *You could throw a bare hook into the water and reel it in, and more often than not you'd catch a fish.*

reel off PHRASAL VERB If you **reel off** information, you repeat it from memory quickly and easily. *Mrs Thatcher reeled off a string of statistics.*

re-elect, re-elects, re-electing, re-elected
VO When someone such as an MP or a trade union official is **re-elected**, they win a new election and are therefore able to continue in their position as MP or union official. *I was re-elected with a majority of over 4,300... Most of the papers predict that Mr Mitterrand will be re-elected... The Council re-elected him President.* ◆ **re-election** NU *He stood for re-election. ...his re-election to the leadership.*

reel-to-reel
ADJ ATTRIB **Reel-to-reel** tape is magnetic tape that goes from one reel of a tape recorder or computer to another and is not enclosed in a cassette. *Conventional data systems use reel-to-reel tape to record their data.*

re-enact, re-enacts, re-enacting, re-enacted
VO If you **re-enact** a scene or incident, you repeat the movements that were made during the original scene or incident. *They used to re-enact this play, endlessly, in the playground.*

re-entry
1 NU **Re-entry** is the act of returning to a place that you have left, especially a country. *He said that they would back Egypt's re-entry into the Arab League... You should apply for a re-entry visa before you leave the country.*
2 NU or N SING **Re-entry** is also used to refer to the moment when a spacecraft comes back into the

Earth's atmosphere after being in space. *The station would burn up on re-entry into the earth's atmosphere... One of the great advantages of the shuttle is that it's a relatively painless re-entry.*

re-examine, re-examines, re-examining, re-examined

VO If you **re-examine** your ideas or beliefs, you think about them carefully because you are no longer sure if they are correct. *This forced researchers to re-examine their assumptions about man's early evolution... In view of the complaints, the government is re-examining the changes.* ◆ **re-examination, re-examinations** NCorNU *...a re-examination of the purposes of education in modern Britain. ...a book that brings you to attentive and reflective re-examination.*

ref /rɛf/ **refs**

NC A **ref** is the official who controls a game such as football or boxing; an informal word.

ref.

Ref. is an abbreviation for 'reference'; written in front of a code at the top of business letters so that the letter can be filed. *Ref. ESB/33593/64.*

refectory /rɪfɛktəʳri/ **refectories**

NC In a university or a monastery, the **refectory** is the dining hall.

refer /rɪfɜːʳ/ **refers, referring, referred**

1 V+to If you **refer to** a particular subject or person, you talk about them or mention them. *In his letters he rarely referred to political events... I am not allowed to describe the officers or refer to them by name.*

2 V+to If you **refer** to someone or something by a particular name, you call them this name. *This kind of art is often referred to as 'minimal art'. ...the men who Mr Gorbachev called adventurists and Mr Yeltsin referred to as scum.*

3 V+to If a word or expression **refers** to something, it is used as a name for it. *In the 18th century, 'antique' referred specifically to Greek and Roman antiquities.*

4 V+to If you **refer to** a book or other source of information, you look at it in order to find something out. *She could make a new dish without referring to a cookery book.*

5 VOAorVO If you **refer** a task or problem to a person or an organization, you formally request that they deal with it. *She referred the matter to the European Court of Justice... They can refer a bid of this sort to the Monopolies Commission... The takeover has been referred because of the possible implications.*

referee /rɛfəriː/ **referees, refereeing, refereed**

1 NC The **referee** is the official who controls a game such as football or boxing. *The referee stopped the fight in the fourth round.* ▶ Also VO *The World Cup final will be refereed by a Mexican doctor.*

2 NC A person who acts as your **referee** when you are applying for a job gives you a reference describing your character and abilities. *Applicants are asked to give the names of three referees.*

reference /rɛfəʳrəns/ **references**

1 NUorNC If you make a **reference** to someone or something, you talk about them or mention them; a formal use. *The charter lacks any reference to freedom of information... He made no reference on his arrival to the latest developments in South Africa. ...a passing reference.*

2 NU **Reference** is also the act of referring to someone or something for information. *They acted without reference to the police committee.*

3 NC A **reference** is something such as a number or a name that tells you where you can obtain information. *...the two page references that I gave you.*

4 N+N **Reference** materials, works, or libraries are ones which you consult when you need specific information about a particular subject. *...a valuable reference document.*

5 You use **'with reference to'** to indicate who or what you are referring to; a formal expression. *Dear Sir, With reference to your recent communication, the following points may be of interest to you.*

6 NC A **reference** is a letter written by someone who knows you, which describes your character and

abilities, and that you need in order to be able to do something, such as apply for a job. *They need to get references from their employers and from the local administration.*

reference book, reference books

NC A **reference book** is a book such as a dictionary or encyclopedia which contains detailed information, often about a particular subject. *...a list of reference books on his subject.*

referendum /rɛfərɛndəm/ **referenda** /rɛfərɛndə/ or **referendums**

NC A **referendum** is a vote in which all the people in a country are asked whether they agree or disagree with a particular policy. *He will hold a referendum on the issue.*

referral /rɪfɜːrəl/ **referrals**

NCorNU The **referral** of something or someone to another person or organization is the act of sending them to a person or organization that is authorized or better qualified to deal with them. *The unit has closed its doors to emergency referrals. ...the ruling is subject to referral to higher authorities.*

refill /riːfɪl/ **refills, refilling, refilled**

VO If you **refill** something, you fill it again after it has been emptied. *Sue refilled Jennifer's glass.*

refinance /riːfaɪnæns/ **refinances, refinancing, refinanced**

VO If a country **refinances** its debt, it borrows more money and creates a second debt in order to pay the first one. *Algeria was seeking help from banks to refinance part of its heavy foreign debt.* ▶ Also NU *...the necessary refinancing had been pledged.*

refine /rɪfaɪn/ **refines, refining, refined**

1 VO When a substance **is refined**, it is made pure by the removal of other substances from it. *...men who tested and refined gold.* ◆ **refining** NU *...the refining of petroleum.*

2 VO If you **refine** something such as a theory or an idea, you improve it by making small alterations to it. *I used these meetings to refine my ideas.*

refined /rɪfaɪnd/

1 ADJ **Refined** people are very polite and well-mannered. *...a thin, refined man in a bow tie.*

2 ADJ A machine or process that is **refined** has been carefully developed to be made very efficient. *The new model was larger, faster, and more refined than its predecessor.*

3 ADJ A **refined** substance has been made pure by having other substances removed from it. *...refined oil.*

refinement /rɪfaɪnmənt/ **refinements**

1 NCorNU **Refinements** are small alterations that you make to something in order to improve it. *...refinements of the system... The British company Celltech have just opened a lab at Slough for the refinement and manufacture of these antibodies.*

2 NU **Refinement** is politeness and good manners; a formal use. *Mr Willet's tone changed to one of genteel refinement.*

refiner /rɪfaɪnə/ **refiners**

NC A **refiner** is a person or organization that refines a substance, such as oil, in order to sell it. *Governments authorised oil companies and refiners to draw on their abundant stockpiles. ...refiners of drugs.*

refinery /rɪfaɪnəri/ **refineries**

NC A **refinery** is a factory where substances such as oil or sugar are refined. *A British-led consortium is to build an oil refinery in West Java... The refinery will have a capacity of 125,000 barrels a day.*

refit /riːfɪt/ **refits, refitting, refitted**

VO To **refit** a ship means to repair it or fit new parts to it, or to adapt it for a different purpose. *...where Royal Navy nuclear submarines are refitted... After the war it was refitted into a luxury liner.*

reflag /riːflæg/ **reflags, reflagging, reflagged**

VO If a ship or tanker is **reflagged**, it begins to carry the flag of a powerful nation in order to be entitled to protection from that country's navy in case of attack. *The Americans agreed to reflag the Kuwaiti tankers.* ◆ **reflagged** ADJ ATTRIB *The Defence Department has denied reports that it is suspending its naval escort for reflagged tankers.*

reflate /riːˈfleɪt/ reflates, reflating, reflated
vo To **reflate** a country's economy means to increase the amount of money that is available for use in order to encourage more economic activity; a technical term in economics. ...*government measures to reflate the economy.* ♦ **reflation** /riːˈfleɪʃn/ NU *The experiment of reflation could hardly come at a worse time.*

reflationary /riːˈfleɪʃənəᵊri/
ADJ ATTRIB **Reflationary** economic activities cause an increase in the amount of money that is in circulation in a country; a technical term. ...*a major reflationary programme... We must avoid any risky reflationary exercise.*

reflect /rɪˈflekt/ reflects, reflecting, reflected
1 vo If something **reflects** someone's attitude or a situation, it indicates that the attitude or situation exists. *The choice of school reflected Dad's hopes for us. ...a concern that was also reflected in a speech by British Foreign Secretary Douglas Hurd.*
2 vo When something **reflects** light or heat, the light or heat is sent back from it and does not pass through it. *Unlike a normal fabric, it reflects heat back into the room.*
3 vo When something **is reflected** in a mirror or in water, you can see its image in the mirror or water. *I saw street lamps mistily reflected in black water.*
4 v When you **reflect** on something or **reflect** over it, you think deeply about it. *Rodin reflected long over Casson's argument.*
5 V-QUOTE or V-REPORT If you **reflect**, you make a comment that expresses your thoughts. *'Well,' I reflected, 'I couldn't say I hadn't been warned.'... He reflected that some community members favoured an air blockade.*

reflection /rɪˈflekʃn/ reflections
1 NC+*of* If something is a **reflection** of a person's attitude or a situation, it indicates that the attitude or situation exists. *Their behaviour was a reflection of their very different personalities... It is a reflection of current political uncertainty.*
2 N SING+*on* A **reflection** on something is also a situation or event which has the effect of making people aware of a particular aspect of someone or something. *This is a very sad reflection on the state of the Labour Party.*
3 NC A **reflection** is an image that you can see in a mirror or in water. *She was standing there looking at her reflection in the mirror.*
4 NU **Reflection** is the process by which light and heat are sent back from a surface and do not pass through it; a technical use. ...*the laws of reflection of light.*
5 NU or NC **Reflection** is thought. You can refer to your thoughts about something as your **reflections**. *On reflection, he says, he very much regrets the comments he made... 'You ought to take it,' she said, after a moment's reflection... It is not a time for triumphalism, but rather for candid reflections.*

reflective /rɪˈflektɪv/
ADJ If you are **reflective**, you are thinking deeply about something. *He studied the statement in the same reflective way he always studied things... There was a long reflective silence.* ♦ **reflectively** ADV *Barney scratched his chin reflectively.*

reflector /rɪˈflektə/ reflectors
1 NC A **reflector** is a small piece of specially patterned glass or plastic which is fitted to the back of a bicycle or car or to a post beside the road, and which glows when light shines on it. ...*road sign reflectors.*
2 NC A **reflector** is also a type of telescope which has a spherical mirror; a technical use. *He made an excellent 18 inch reflector with a focal length of 20 feet.*

reflex /ˈriːfleks/ reflexes
1 NC A **reflex** or a **reflex action** is a sudden, uncontrollable movement made by a part of your body as a result of pressure or a blow. ...*the reflex that makes the baby kick.*
2 N PL If you have good **reflexes**, you can respond quickly to an unexpected event, for example while you are driving a car. *She had incredible reflexes.*

reflexive /rɪˈfleksɪv/
ADJ An action or movement that is **reflexive** is done immediately as a result of something happening. *It was a purely reflexive move on his part.* ♦ **reflexively** ADV *Reflexively, he stepped backwards.*

reflexive pronoun, reflexive pronouns
NC In grammar, a **reflexive pronoun** is one which refers back to the subject of a sentence or clause. In the sentence 'you'll just have to do it yourself', 'yourself' is a reflexive pronoun.

reflexive verb, reflexive verbs
NC In grammar, a **reflexive verb** is a transitive verb which describes actions in which the subject and the object are the same. The object is always a reflexive pronoun. In the sentence 'She introduced herself', 'introduced' is a reflexive verb.

refloat /riːˈfləʊt/ refloats, refloating, refloated
1 vo If you **refloat** a ship, you bring it up from the bottom of the sea where it sank. *Tugs refloated the ship on the high tide after about two hours.*
2 vo To **refloat** an economy or the financial situation of an organization means to make it better again after a period of great difficulty. *He wants to try and refloat the country's economy.*

reforest /riːˈfɒrɪst/ reforests, reforesting, reforested
vo To **reforest** an area that no longer has any trees on it means to plant trees there in order to make a forest. *The government is making strenuous efforts to reforest the hills.* ♦ **reforestation** /riːfɒrɪsteɪʃn/ NU *Independent landowners took decisive steps towards reforestation.*

reform /rɪˈfɔːm/ reforms, reforming, reformed
1 NU or NC **Reform** consists of changes and improvements to a law, social system, or institution. *There was an urgent need for reform... He called for the reform of the divorce laws. ...the task of carrying through the necessary reforms.*
2 vo To **reform** something such as a law, a social system, or an institution means to improve it by making changes. ...*proposals to reform the Labour Party... He said the 1988 Education Act had changed everything, but reformed nothing.*
3 V-ERG When someone **reforms**, or something **reforms** them, they stop doing something that society does not approve of such as drinking too much alcohol or stealing. *You have had every chance to reform... Prison sentences cannot reform the criminal.* ♦ **reformed** ADJ ...*a reformed alcoholic.*

reformatory /rɪˈfɔːmətəᵊri/ reformatories
NC A **reformatory** is a special school where young people who have committed an offence against the law live and receive training. *He became principal of a reformatory for black delinquents. ...a juvenile reformatory.*

reformer /rɪˈfɔːmə/ reformers
NC A **reformer** is someone who tries to improve laws or social conditions. *The new prime minister is a reformer at heart.*

reformist /rɪˈfɔːmɪst/ reformists
NC A **reformist** is someone who is trying to introduce reforms into an organization or situation. ...*the most outspoken reformist in the leadership. ...the Government's adoption of reformist policies... The reformist element is a minority within the party.*

refract /rɪˈfrækt/ refracts, refracting, refracted
V-ERG When something **refracts** a ray of light or a sound wave or when it **refracts**, the path it follows bends at a particular point, for example where it enters water or glass. ...*its ability to refract rays of light. ...a soft flow of reflected and refracted light.* ♦ **refraction** /rɪˈfrækʃn/ NU *The colours are separated by refraction.*

refractory /rɪˈfræktəᵊri/
ADJ Someone who is **refractory** is stubborn and very difficult to work with or control; a formal word. *The whole enterprise revolves round a refractory individual genius like Frank.*

refrain /rɪˈfreɪn/ refrains, refraining, refrained; a formal word.
1 V A If you **refrain** from doing something, you deliberately do not do it. *I carefully refrained from looking at him.*
2 NC A **refrain** is a short, simple part of a song which you repeat several times. *I still remember the refrain*

of one of the most popular ballads of that day.
3 NC A **refrain** is a slogan or a simple idea that
someone often repeats. *... a familiar refrain of hopes
for closer economic ties.*
refresh /rɪfrɛʃ/ **refreshes, refreshing, refreshed**
1 VO If something **refreshes** when you are hot or
tired, it makes you feel cooler or more energetic. *I
hoped that sleep would refresh me.* ◆ **refreshed** ADJ
...feeling positively refreshed.
2 If someone **refreshes** your **memory**, they tell you
something you have forgotten. *He asked her to begin
by refreshing our memories.*
refresher course, refresher courses
NC A **refresher course** is a training course in which
people improve their knowledge or skills and learn
about new developments relating to the job that they
do. *I had two brief refresher courses just before the
flight.*
refreshing /rɪfrɛʃɪŋ/
1 ADJ If something is **refreshing**, it is pleasantly
different from what you are used to. *It was a
refreshing change for her to meet a woman
executive... The change will be refreshing.*
◆ **refreshingly** ADV *The plot is refreshingly intelligent
and original.*
2 ADJ ATTRIB A **refreshing** bath or drink makes you
feel better after you have been uncomfortably tired or
hot. *He enjoyed the refreshing swims in the nearby
creek... It also makes a very refreshing drink.*
refreshment /rɪfrɛʃmənt/ **refreshments**
N PL or N U **Refreshments** are drinks and small amounts
of food that are provided, for example, during a
meeting or journey. *Refreshments have been sent on
board... Many passengers complained they were left
stranded without transport, refreshment or lavatories.*
refrigerate /rɪfrɪdʒəreɪt/ **refrigerates, refrigerating,
refrigerated**
VO If you **refrigerate** food, you make it very cold in
order to preserve it. *Milk can be kept 3 days if it is
well refrigerated.* ◆ **refrigeration** /rɪfrɪdʒəreɪʃn/ N U
They had no air-conditioning and no refrigeration.
refrigerator /rɪfrɪdʒəreɪtə/ **refrigerators**
NC A **refrigerator** is a large container which is kept
cool inside, usually by electricity, so that the food and
drink in it stays fresh. *...the retail cost of a
refrigerator.*
refuel /riːfjuːəl/ **refuels, refuelling, refuelled;** spelt
refueling, refueled in American English.
1 V-ERG When an aircraft **refuels** or is **refuelled**, it is
filled with more fuel so that it can continue its
journey. *Concorde needs to refuel on flights of above
3,500 miles... The aircraft are being refuelled in flight
every hour.* ◆ **refuelling** N U *...a transport plane
capable of providing in-flight refuelling.*
2 VO If something **refuels** your feelings or emotions, it
makes them stronger. *Their shares inexplicably
jumped 10p to 114p, refuelling speculation of a possible
takeover.*
refuge /rɛfjuːdʒ/ **refuges**
1 NU When you seek or take **refuge**, you try to protect
yourself from unhappiness or an unpleasant situation
by behaving or thinking in a particular way. *He seeks
refuge in silence.*
2 NU To take **refuge** also means to try and avoid
physical harm by hiding somewhere. *People have
taken refuge on railway embankments and rooftops...
Most of the townspeople sought refuge underground in
cellars and air-raid shelters.*
3 NC A **refuge** is a place where you go for safety and
protection. *A small cave was the only refuge from the
cold.*
refugee /rɛfjuːdʒiː/ **refugees**
NC **Refugees** are people who have been forced to leave
their country because there is a war there or because
of their political or religious beliefs. *...emergency aid
to refugees. ...the wretched conditions in the refugee
camps.*
refund, refunds, refunding, refunded; pronounced
/riːfʌnd/ when it is a noun and /rɪfʌnd/ when it is a
verb.
1 NC A **refund** is a sum of money which is returned to
you, for example because you have paid too much for

goods, or have returned them to a shop. *The revenue
service had never been known to give a refund.*
2 VO If you **refund** money to someone, you return it to
them, for example because they have paid you too
much for something. *Three-quarters of the cost is
refunded to the patient.*
refurbish /riːfɜːbɪʃ/ **refurbishes, refurbishing,
refurbished**
1 VO If you **refurbish** something, you clean it and re-
equip it to make it more attractive or more modern; a
formal word. *The city's museum was being
refurbished. ...more money to refurbish state-run
schools and improve standards.*
2 VO If you **refurbish** the image of something or
someone, you improve it in order to make it more
popular. *The leadership is hoping it will help to
refurbish its image after last year's anti-government
protests. ...refurbish the image of the Soviet army.*
refurbishment /riːfɜːbɪʃmənt/
NU The **refurbishment** of a place or thing is its re-
equipping and redecoration. *The guard-post was due
for simple refurbishment. ...refurbishment for the
Royal Australian Navy.*
refusal /rɪfjuːzl/ **refusals**
NC You describe someone's behaviour as a **refusal**
when they say firmly that they will not do, allow, give,
or accept something. *Her husband was receiving
harsh treatment in prison because of his refusal to
change his views. ...his refusal of medical treatment...
I made many applications and had many refusals.*
refuse, refuses, refusing, refused; pronounced
/rɪfjuːz/ when it is a verb and /rɛfjuːs/ when it is a
noun.
1 V+to-INF If you **refuse** to do something, you
deliberately do not do it, or say firmly that you will
not do it. *He refused to accept this advice... Their
bosses refuse to allow them any responsibility.*
2 VO If someone **refuses** you something, they do not
allow you to have it. *Only the president could refuse
him a loan... The Council refused permission for them
to live together.*
3 VO If you **refuse** something that is offered to you,
you do not accept it. *I offered him wine but he
refused it.*
4 NU **Refuse** consists of the rubbish and unwanted
things in a house, shop, or factory, that are regularly
thrown away; a formal use. *...a dump for refuse.
...refuse collection.*
refusenik /rɪfjuːznɪk/ **refuseniks;** also spelt **refusnik**.
NC **Refuseniks** were Jewish people who were not
allowed to emigrate from the former Soviet Union.
*...the family of another prominent refusenik. ...the
problem of refusenik emigrants.*
refute /rɪfjuːt/ **refutes, refuting, refuted;** a formal
word.
1 VO If you **refute** something such as an allegation,
theory or argument, you prove that it is false or
wrong. *This piece of evidence would have refuted the
charge of his main accuser.* ◆ **refutation** /rɛfjuːteɪʃn/
refutations N C or N U *That report came out last year
and there haven't been any confirmations nor
refutations of that yet... The bolder our hypotheses,
the more vulnerable they are to refutation.*
2 VO To **refute** an allegation also means to deny it
without providing any evidence. Some users of English
believe that it is not correct to use **refute** with this
meaning. *We refute this charge with the utmost
vigour.* ◆ **refutation, refutations** N C or N U *This can be
seen as an implicit refutation of the official Polish
Communist assertion.*
regain /rɪgeɪn/ **regains, regaining, regained**
VO If you **regain** something that you have lost, you get
it back again. *He might be able to regain his old job.*
regal /riːgl/
ADJ Something that is **regal** is very impressive. *...a
regal staircase leading into a vast reception hall.*
regale /rɪgeɪl/ **regales, regaling, regaled**
VO+with If someone **regales** you with stories or jokes,
they tell you a lot of them, whether you want to hear
them or not. *After the ceremony, he regaled the
reporters with stories.*

regalia /rɪɡeɪliə/
NU **Regalia** refers to all the traditional clothes and items which someone such as a king or a judge wears or carries on official occasions; a formal word. *...a Judge of the Supreme Court in full regalia.*

regard /rɪgɑːd/ **regards, regarding, regarded**
1 VOorV-REFL If you **regard** someone or something as being a particular thing or as having a particular quality, you believe that they are that thing or have that quality. *I regard it as one of my masterpieces... He always regarded himself simply as an entertainer.*
2 VO If you **regard** something or someone with a particular feeling, you have that feeling about them. *He is regarded with some suspicion by the country's leaders.*
3 N SING If you have a high **regard** for someone, you have a lot of respect for them. *I have a high regard for Mike... My regard for him grew day by day.*
4 N PL **Regards** is used in expressions like 'best regards' and 'with warm regards' as a way of expressing friendly feelings towards someone. *Give my regards to your daughter.*
5 You can say **as regards**, **with regard to**, or **in regard to** when indicating what you are referring to; used in formal English. *As regards the car, I put an advertisement in the paper... With regard to the gas fire, we hardly use it... My upbringing was fairly strict in regard to obedience and truthfulness.*

regarding /rɪgɑːdɪŋ/
PREP You can use **regarding** to indicate what you are referring to; a formal word. *There was always some question regarding education.*

regardless /rɪgɑːdləs/
1 If something happens **regardless of** something else, it happens in spite of it. *If they are determined to strike, they will do so regardless of what the law says.*
2 ADV If someone did something **regardless**, they did it even though there were problems that could have stopped them. *Mrs Hochstadt walked on regardless.*

regatta /rɪgætə/ **regattas**
NC A **regatta** is a sports event consisting of races between yachts or rowing boats. *The prestigious regatta is held there every year.*

regency /riːdʒənsi/ **regencies**
1 ADJ **Regency** is used to refer to the period in Britain at the beginning of the nineteenth century and to the style of architecture, literature, and so on, that was popular at the time. *The house itself was full of family portraits and Regency furniture.*
2 NC **Regency** is the position or function of being a regent. *The Queen Regent, Dzeliwe, assumed the regency in 1982.*

regenerate /rɪdʒenəreɪt/ **regenerates, regenerating, regenerated**
VO To **regenerate** a place or a system means to develop and improve it and make it more active, successful, or important, especially after a period when it has been declining; a formal word. *We are looking for ways in which community development could help regenerate the inner cities.* ◆ **regeneration** /rɪdʒenəreɪʃn/ NU *...the goal of economic regeneration. ...a regeneration of local democracy.*

regenerative /rɪdʒenərətɪv/
ADJ **Regenerative** actions, processes, and so on, cause something to become more active, successful, or important again; a formal word. *The defeat might provide a regenerative process for the party. ...the regenerative powers of the earth. ...regenerative farming techniques.*

regent /riːdʒənt/ **regents**
NCorTITLE A **regent** is a person who rules a country when the king or queen is unable to rule, for example because they are too young or too ill. *She visited the Regent of Hungary. ...an estate designed for the Prince Regent.*

reggae /regeɪ/
NU **Reggae** is a kind of West Indian popular music with a very strong beat. *What brought reggae out of Jamaica and onto the world stage was, quite frankly, Bob Marley.*

regicide /redʒɪsaɪd/ **regicides**; a formal word.
1 NC A **regicide** is a person who kills a king.

...Cromwell and his fellow regicides.
2 NU **Regicide** is the act of killing a king.

regime /reɪʒiːm/ **regimes**; also spelt **régime**.
1 NC A **regime** is a group of people who rule a country; used showing disapproval. *...the corrupt regime that had ruled since 1921... They say they were unfairly convicted under the former communist regime.*
2 NC A **regime** is also a system or method of government; used showing disapproval. *Conscription is perhaps the most hated aspect of the present regime... He might be persuaded to move towards a more democratic regime.*
3 NC A **regime** is also a system or method of achieving something; a formal use. *The Nicaraguan government has announced a series of drastic economic reforms, including a new regime of prices and wages.*
4 NC A **regime** is also the same as a **regimen**.

regimen /redʒɪmən/ **regimens**
NC A **regimen** is a set of rules about food and exercise that some people follow in order to stay healthy; an old-fashioned word. *He kept to his prescribed regimen.*

regiment /redʒɪmənt/ **regiments**
NC A **regiment** is a large group of soldiers commanded by a colonel. *He was the sixth member of the regiment to be killed this year. ...the Ulster Defence Regiment.*

regimental /redʒɪmentl/
ADJ ATTRIB **Regimental** means belonging to a particular regiment. *...the regimental commander.*

regimentation /redʒɪmenteɪʃn/
NU **Regimentation** is very strict control over a group of people; a formal word. *He detested every aspect of public school: the regimentation, the monotony, and the lack of privacy.*

regimented /redʒɪmentɪd/
ADJ Something that is **regimented** is very strictly controlled; used showing disapproval. *...the tightly regimented life of the prison.*

region /riːdʒən/ **regions**
1 NC A **region** is an area of a country or of the world. *The country has nine autonomous regions... We cannot accept its ambitions to become the predominant power in the region. ...desert regions.*
2 You say **in the region of** to indicate that you are mentioning an approximate amount. *Temperatures would be in the region of 500 degrees centigrade.*

regional /riːdʒəⁿnəl/
ADJ **Regional** means relating to or belonging to a particular region. *...regional health authorities... They concluded that superpower intervention in regional conflicts must be brought to an end... It should not divert attention from their own schemes for regional co-operation.* ◆ **regionally** ADV *That is going to affect the climate both on a global scale and regionally.*

regionalism /riːdʒəⁿnəlɪzəm/
NU **Regionalism** is a strong feeling of pride or loyalty that people in a region have for that region, often including a desire to govern themselves; a formal word. *A new threat to national unity has emerged with the outbreak of regionalism.*

register /redʒɪstə/ **registers, registering, registered**
1 NC A **register** is an official list or record of names, objects, events, and so on. *...the register of births, marriages, and deaths.*
2 VA If you **register** for something, you put your name on an official list. *You must register for work at the employment agency... They're coming to register as students on the English course.* ◆ **registered** ADJ ATTRIB *...a registered drug addict.*
3 VO If you **register** something, you cause information about it to be recorded on an official list. *One of the cars was registered in my name.* ◆ **registered** ADJ ATTRIB *The GAIA Foundation is a registered charity.*
4 V-ERG When an amount or measurement **registers** or when something **registers** it, it is shown on a scale or measuring instrument. *The earthquake registered 5.2 on the Richter scale... The inflation index registered a*

modest 7.8% annual rate... When so many cars are using the circuit, how can you be certain that it's your transmitter that's registering the lap time?
5 VO If you **register** a feeling or opinion that you have, you make it clear to other people. He stared at me for a moment, his face registering disbelief... Thousands joined the march to register their opposition to the cuts in education.
6 VO If you **register** a letter or parcel, you send it by a special form of postal service, for which you pay an extra amount to insure it against not being delivered. If you're sending it through the post, it would be a good idea to register it. ◆ **registered** ADJ ATTRIB Amateur players need only inform their association by registered letter and are then free to play elsewhere.

register office, register offices
NC In Britain, a **register office** is the same as a **registry office**. Nearly half of all marriages in Britain now take place in register offices.

registrar /rɛdʒɪstrɑː/ **registrars**
1 NC A **registrar** is a person whose job is to keep official records, especially of births, marriages, and deaths. Registrars would be able to offer marriages in glamorous settings, such as luxury hotels.
2 NC A **registrar** is also a senior administrative official in a college or university. The registrar of the University of Nigeria said he had closed the campuses on the advice of the military government.

registration /rɛdʒɪstreɪʃn/
NU The **registration** of something is the recording of it in an official list. ...a certificate of registration of death.

registration number, registration numbers
NC A car or other vehicle's **registration number** is the series of letters and numbers that is displayed on a metal or plastic plate at the front and back. The proposed changes also include a distinctive typeface to make registration numbers clearer to read.

registry /rɛdʒɪstri/ **registries**
NC A **registry** is a place where official records are kept. He is in charge of a classified document registry at divisional headquarters. ...the National Bone Marrow Registry.

registry office, registry offices
NC A **registry office** is a place where births, marriages, and deaths are officially recorded, and where people can get married. Registry office weddings appeal more to couples marrying for the second time.

regress /rɪgrɛs/ **regresses, regressing, regressed**
V If someone or something **regresses**, they return to a worse condition; a formal word. Since 1976 many rivers have regressed from being clean to being grossly polluted. ◆ **regression** /rɪgrɛʃn/ NU ...moral and social regression.

regressive /rɪgrɛsɪv/
1 ADJ In a system of **regressive** taxation, the rate of taxation becomes lower as the amount of money to be taxed increases; a technical term. This fee has been criticized as a regressive tax... The problem is that you end up with all of the taxes being regressive, affecting the poor more than the rich.
2 ADJ Something that is **regressive** involves a return to a worse condition; a formal word. Mr Kinnock accused the government of a regressive attitude in the wake of the INF treaty signed in Washington in December.

regret /rɪgrɛt/ **regrets, regretting, regretted**
1 VO, V-REPORT, or V+ING If you **regret** something that you have done, you wish that you had not done it. I immediately regretted my decision... It made me regret that I had left home... Afterwards he regretted having spoken to them. ▶ Also NU or NC ...pangs of regret... The President had only one regret, and that was that the economic deficit was so large... Linda has no regrets at having become a banker.
2 VO or V-REPORT You can say that you **regret** something as a polite way of saying that you are sorry about it; a formal use. London Transport regrets any inconvenience caused by these delays... The Prime Minister regrets that he is unable to reconsider your case. ▶ Also NU We informed them with regret of our

decision... Mr Bush expressed regret at the hardship being caused.
3 You can use expressions such as '**I regret to say**' or '**I regret to inform you**' to show that you are sorry about something; a formal use. The food and service, I regret to say, were disappointing... 'I regret to have to inform you that it was a friend of mine.'

regretful /rɪgrɛtfl/
ADJ If you are **regretful**, you feel sorry about something. Michael gave me a sad regretful smile. ◆ **regretfully** /rɪgrɛtfəli/ ADV He shook his head regretfully.

regrettable /rɪgrɛtəbl/
ADJ Something that is **regrettable** is unfortunate and undesirable. His tiredness caused him to make a regrettable error. ◆ **regrettably** SUBMOD or ADV SEN /rɪgrɛtəbli/ Regrettably few of them have gone to university... Regrettably, it is not an easy plant to grow in this country.

regroup /riːgruːp/ **regroups, regrouping, regrouped**
V-ERG When soldiers **regroup** or when someone **regroups** them, they form into an organized group again, in order to continue fighting. They are now regrouping and intend to launch an attack later today... The rest will be regrouped in the north of the country... They have used ceasefires in the past to regroup their fighters before beginning another offensive.

regular /rɛgjʊlə/ **regulars**
1 ADJ **Regular** things happen at equal intervals, or involve things happening at equal intervals. They give regular Sunday afternoon concerts... You need to take regular exercise... The doctor examined the baby at regular intervals. ◆ **regularly** ADV The members meet regularly in one another's homes.
2 ADJ **Regular** events happen often, usually over a long period of time. ...one of the regular bombings. ◆ **regularly** ADV Children are regularly abandoned.
3 ADJ ATTRIB **Regular** is also used to describe people who often go to a particular place. ...our regular customers. ▶ Also NC He's one of the regulars at the village pub.
4 ADJ ATTRIB You can use **regular** to refer to times, places, conditions, and so on that are considered normal or usual. It's past his regular bedtime... You can get in touch with a psychiatrist through your regular doctor.
5 ADJ In American English, you use **regular** to describe things that are normal and ordinary. The AAA says the average price of regular gasoline went up last week... He was only obliged to reimburse the Air Force the cost of a regular airline ticket. ...the National Football League's regular season.
6 ADJ If an object is **regular**, it has parts of equal size or is symmetrical and well-balanced in appearance. His face was sun-tanned, with regular features. ...a regular shape.
7 ADJ A **regular** verb, noun, or adjective inflects in the same way as most other verbs, nouns, or adjectives in the language.
8 ADJ ATTRIB **Regular** soldiers or troops have a career in the armed forces, in contrast with people who are doing their military service or have volunteered to fight during a war. It could be a long and bloody fight, even for a regular army... He said the morale of both regular and volunteer reserve troops was high.

regularity /rɛgjʊlærəti/ **regularities**
1 NU If something happens with **regularity**, it happens repeatedly, often according to a definite plan. The same exam questions cropped up with unfailing regularity.
2 NC **Regularities** are similar features which you notice in several different things and which may have the same cause or explanation. ...regularities in nature.

regularize /rɛgjʊləraɪz/ **regularizes, regularizing, regularized**; also spelt **regularise**.
VO To **regularize** something means to cause it to have a regular pattern or arrangement, often so that it can be given official approval or recognition. Their status and area of work is thereby regularized. ...a team to regularize state finances. ...diplomacy aimed at

regularizing relations between Israel and several key Arab states.

regulate /rɛgjʊleɪt/ **regulates, regulating, regulated**
1 VO To **regulate** an activity or process means to control it, usually by means of rules. *The Government has a responsibility to regulate this kind of technology.* ◆ **regulated** ADJ *His life was too well regulated to be affected by affairs of the heart.*
2 VO If you **regulate** a machine or device, you adjust it to control the way it operates. *Do you know how to regulate the boiler?*

regulation /rɛgjʊleɪʃn/ **regulations**
1 NC **Regulations** are rules made by a government or other authority. *The South African government has lifted emergency regulations imposed on black townships around Johannesburg... There are specific regulations governing these types of machines.* ► Also ADJ ATTRIB *He had the short regulation haircut of a policeman.*
2 NU **Regulation** is the controlling of an activity or process, usually by means of rules. *...strict regulation over toxic waste disposal.*

regulator /rɛgjʊleɪtə/ **regulators**
NC A **regulator** is a device that automatically controls something such as the temperature or humidity in a room. *He used this knowledge to design new plant growth regulators.*

regulatory /rɛgjʊleɪtəri/
ADJ ATTRIB **Regulatory** authorities or measures are intended to control the activities of companies and other organizations, usually by means of rules. *The project is to be examined in detail by the regulatory bodies in both Britain and the European Community... They're not subject to any regulatory control.*

regurgitate /rɪgɜːdʒɪteɪt/ **regurgitates, regurgitating, regurgitated**
1 VO If you **regurgitate** food, you bring it back up from your stomach; a formal word. *Female wolves feed their young by regurgitating food.*
2 VO If you **regurgitate** ideas or facts, you repeat them without thinking about them or understanding them. *Regurgitating all the earlier constitutional arguments would impose a strain on the country... The student is expected to regurgitate an answer to the teacher.*

rehabilitate /riːəbɪlɪteɪt/ **rehabilitates, rehabilitating, rehabilitated**
1 VO To **rehabilitate** someone who has been ill or in prison means to help them to live a normal life again. *He used exercise programmes to rehabilitate heart-attack victims... Probation officers have been concerned not to damage their chances of rehabilitating offenders.* ◆ **rehabilitation** /riːəbɪlɪteɪʃn/ NU *...the rehabilitation of drug addicts... I work in the rehabilitation centre for blind people.*
2 VO If a government **rehabilitates** someone, it begins to consider them acceptable again after a period during which it has rejected them or severely criticized them. *The leading Bolshevik leaders Bukharin and Rykov, both executed by Stalin in the '30s, have been officially rehabilitated.* ◆ **rehabilitation** NU *Mr de Klerk's tour represents a further step in South Africa's international political rehabilitation.*
3 VO To **rehabilitate** something such as a building or area means to improve its condition so that it can be used again; a formal use. *The money would be used to rehabilitate basic utilities such as roads, hospitals and schools.* ◆ **rehabilitation** NU *The Save the Children Fund is helping to finance the rehabilitation of the hospital.*

rehash, rehashes, rehashing, rehashed; pronounced /riːhæʃ/ when it is a noun and /riːhæʃ/ when it is a verb. Used showing disapproval.
1 NC A **rehash** is something that you write or say using old ideas or facts, often rearranging them so that they appear to be new. *His new book seems to be just a rehash of one of his earlier ones.*
2 VO If you **rehash** ideas or facts, you use them again but in a slightly different way so that your work appears to be original. *Later writers have rehashed Fort's material.*

rehearsal /rɪhɜːsl/ **rehearsals**
NCorNU A **rehearsal** of a play, dance, or piece of music is a practice of it in preparation for a public performance. *I develop a part during rehearsals with the company... In rehearsal he was meticulous and efficient.*

rehearse /rɪhɜːs/ **rehearses, rehearsing, rehearsed**
VOorV When people **rehearse** a play, dance, or piece of music, they practise it in preparation for a public performance. *The actors began to rehearse a few scenes... Stay and hear the orchestra rehearse... Tens of thousands of people have been rehearsing for the opening ceremony in the workers' stadium.*

rehouse /riːhaʊz/ **rehouses, rehousing, rehoused**
VO If someone is **rehoused**, they are provided with a different house to live in. *Thirty inmates were rehoused by the local social services department... Her solution: demolish the flats and rehouse the residents.*

Reig, Oscar Ribas /ɒskɑː riːbæs reɪtʃ/
Oscar Ribas Reig became Head of Government in Andorra in 1990. He was previously Head of Government from 1982 to 1984.

reign /reɪn/ **reigns, reigning, reigned**
1 V When a king or queen **reigns**, he or she is the leader of the country. *The emperor Chia Ching reigned from 1522 to 1566.*
2 NC+POSS The **reign** of a king or queen is the period during which he or she is the leader of the country. *...George III's long reign.*
3 V You can say that something **reigns** when it is the strongest or most noticeable feature of a situation or period of time; a literary use. *In the kitchen, chaos reigned.*

reigning /reɪnɪŋ/
ADJ ATTRIB The **reigning** champion of a contest or competition is the most recent winner of it, or the winner of it at the specific time that you are talking about. *John McEnroe, the reigning champion, was beaten in the first round.*

reimburse /riːɪmbɜːs/ **reimburses, reimbursing, reimbursed**
VOAorVO If you **reimburse** someone for something, or if you **reimburse** their money, you pay them back the money that they have spent or lost while doing something for you or because of something you have done; a formal word. *I promised to reimburse her for the damage to her car... The money will be reimbursed by the central government.*

reimbursement /riːɪmbɜːsmənt/ **reimbursements**
NUorNC **Reimbursement** is the repayment to someone of money that they have spent or lost while doing something for you or because of something you have done; a formal word. *The Soviets want reimbursement for the properties they left behind... Depositors claiming reimbursements of more than one million rupees must produce their tax returns.*

rein /reɪn/ **reins**
N PL **Reins** are the leather straps which are attached to a horse's bridle. They are used for controlling the horse. *He pulled at the reins.*
● **Rein** is used in these phrases. ● If you **give free rein** to someone, or to your feelings or thoughts, you give them a lot of freedom. *They were encouraged to give free rein to their feelings.* ● If you **keep a tight rein on** someone or something, you control them firmly. *Both governments are trying to keep a tight rein on wage increases.*

reincarnated /riːɪnkɑːneɪtɪd, riːɪnkɑːneɪtɪd/
V-PASS If people believe that they will **be reincarnated** when they die, they believe that their spirit will be born again and will live in the body of another person or animal. *What good is it then to be reincarnated?* ► Also ADJ ATTRIBorADJafterN *The Dalai Lama is the reincarnated spirit of Buddha's compassion... At one time I thought I was Michelangelo reincarnated.*

reincarnation /riːɪnkɑːneɪʃn/ **reincarnations**
1 NU **Reincarnation** is a belief that after death the soul of a person passes into the body of another living creature. *We Buddhists believe in reincarnation.*
2 NC A **reincarnation** is a person or animal who is believed to be a dead person born again. *...reincarnations of their ancestors.*

reindeer /ˈreɪndɪə/; **reindeer** is both the singular and the plural form.
NC A **reindeer** is a deer with large antlers that lives in northern areas of Europe, Asia, and North America. *The fires have forced herds of reindeer to leave their grazing areas.*

reinforce /riːɪnˈfɔːs/ **reinforces, reinforcing, reinforced**
1 VO If something **reinforces** a feeling, situation, or process, it strengthens it. *This sort of experience reinforces their feelings of worthlessness.*
2 VO If something **reinforces** an idea or point of view, it provides more evidence or support for it. *This report reinforces practically everything that has been said.*
3 VO To **reinforce** an object means to make it stronger or harder. *I had not thought of reinforcing the handles with leather.* ◆ **reinforced** ADJ *...reinforced plastics.*

reinforced concrete
NU **Reinforced concrete** is concrete that is made with pieces of metal inside it to make it stronger. *The old bridge was replaced by a new structure of reinforced concrete.*

reinforcement /riːɪnˈfɔːsmənt/ **reinforcements**
1 N PL **Reinforcements** are soldiers or police who are sent to join an army or group of police in order to make it stronger. *Defence ministry officials say reinforcements are on their way... Police reinforcements had to be brought in.*
2 NU **Reinforcement** is the strengthening of something such as an attitude or a feeling. *...the reinforcement of existing systems.*

reinstate /riːɪnˈsteɪt/ **reinstates, reinstating, reinstated**
1 VO If you **reinstate** someone, you give them back a job or position which has been taken from them. *Two months later all charges against him were dropped and he was reinstated... A union official said efforts would be made to reinstate men sacked during the dispute.*
2 VO To **reinstate** something means to allow it to exist again. *The trip reinstated my faith in myself... Shelter called on the Government to reinstate the full state benefits for young people.*

reinstatement /riːɪnˈsteɪtmənt/
1 NU **Reinstatement** is the act of giving someone back a job or position which has been taken away from them. *The National Football League today approved Manley's reinstatement one year after he was suspended.*
2 NU **Reinstatement** is also the act of allowing something to exist again. *The United States has warned General Namphy that the reinstatement of aid depends on the credibility of the new election.*

reissue /riːˈɪʃjuː/ **reissues, reissuing, reissued**
1 NC A **reissue** is something such as a book or a record that is published or produced again after it has not been available for some time. *The group's songs on the RCA reissue were recorded in 1937.*
2 VO To **reissue** something such as a book or record means to publish or produce it again after it has not been available for some time. *The writings of Jean Rhys have recently been reissued.*

reiterate /riːˈɪtəreɪt/ **reiterates, reiterating, reiterated**
VO or V-REPORT If you **reiterate** something, you say it again; a formal word. *He reiterated this advice several more times during the meeting... The spokesman reiterated that Pakistan is against any interference in the internal affairs of other countries.* ◆ **reiteration** /riːˌɪtəˈreɪʃn/ **reiterations** NU or NC *The resolution passed at the end of the meeting was merely a reiteration of the government's old stand... It always took three or four explanations and reiterations before she acknowledged an understanding.*

reject, rejects, rejecting, rejected; pronounced /rɪˈdʒekt/ when it is a verb and /ˈriːdʒekt/ when it is a noun.
1 VO If you **reject** something such as a proposal or request, you do not accept it or agree to it. *I rejected his offer... The amendment was rejected by 207 votes to 143... South African police have rejected allegations that they were involved in yesterday's attack... Mr*

Bush forcefully rejected any compromise. ◆ **rejection** /rɪˈdʒekʃn/ **rejections** NC or NU *...his rejection of repeated requests for military action... An attempt to introduce new working rotas met with flat rejection.*
2 VO If you **reject** a belief or a political system, you decide that you do not believe in it or want to support it. *It was hard for me to reject my family's religious beliefs.* ◆ **rejection** NU+SUPP *There is a rejection of conventional social values. ...rejection of racial discrimination.*
3 VO If an employer **rejects** a person who has applied for a job, he or she does not offer that person the job. *Many candidates were rejected.* ◆ **rejection, rejections** NU or NC *...in the face of repeated rejection. ...a succession of rejections.*
4 VO If the work that someone such as a writer or designer produces is **rejected**, the prospective buyer does not accept it. *His first novel was rejected... Les had taken his design for a solid body guitar to the Gibson company and been rejected.*
5 VO If someone **rejects** another person who expects affection from them, they are cruel or hostile towards them. *She rejected her lover with a forcefulness that made him whinge. ...children rejected by their natural parents.* ◆ **rejection** NU *The performance demands of the school sends these children on the road to rejection.*
6 NC A **reject** is a product that is sold cheaply, or not sold at all, because there is something wrong with it. *They have found that what they think is for the reject pile is frequently picked up avidly by some customer or other.*

rejoice /rɪˈdʒɔɪs/ **rejoices, rejoicing, rejoiced**
V If you **rejoice**, you are very pleased about something; a literary word. *All his friends gathered to rejoice in his freedom.*

rejoicing /rɪˈdʒɔɪsɪŋ/ **rejoicings**
NU or N PL **Rejoicing** is behaviour in which a lot of people show great delight about something, usually in a noisy way; a literary word. *It is a time for great rejoicing... There were terrific rejoicings on the day war ended.*

rejoin, rejoins, rejoining, rejoined; pronounced /riːˈdʒɔɪn/ for the meanings in paragraphs 1 and 2, and /rɪˈdʒɔɪn/ for the meaning in paragraph 3.
1 VO If you **rejoin** someone, you go back to them after having left them for a short time. *Instead of rejoining his friends, he went off to sit by himself.*
2 VO If you **rejoin** a group or club, you become a member of it again after not being a member for a period of time. *He was determined to rejoin the RAF.*
3 V-QUOTE If you **rejoin**, you make a quick reply to something that someone has said, usually in a witty or critical manner; a formal use. *'That is a matter that will be dealt with in due time,' I rejoined.*

rejoinder /rɪˈdʒɔɪndə/ **rejoinders**
NC A **rejoinder** is a reply to a question or remark, especially a quick, witty, or critical one; a literary word. *This brought a somewhat sharp rejoinder from Mr Harper.*

rejuvenate /rɪˈdʒuːvəneɪt/ **rejuvenates, rejuvenating, rejuvenated**
1 VO If something **rejuvenates** you, it makes you feel or look young again. *I think we were rejuvenated by the experience.* ◆ **rejuvenating** ADJ *...rejuvenating cosmetics.*
2 VO If you **rejuvenate** an organization or system, you make it more lively and more efficient. *The aim is to rejuvenate inner city areas.* ◆ **rejuvenation** /rɪˌdʒuːvəˈneɪʃn/ NU *The policy is seen as a rejuvenation of America's space programme.*

rekindle /riːˈkɪndl/ **rekindles, rekindling, rekindled**
VO If something **rekindles** an interest, feeling, or thought that you used to have, it makes you think about it or feel it again; a literary word. *We hoped we could rekindle his enthusiasm for cricket... My maternal longings were rekindled.*

relapse, relapses, relapsing, relapsed; pronounced /rɪˈlæps/ when it is a verb and /rɪlæps/ or /ˈriːlæps/ when it is a noun.
1 V If someone **relapses** into undesirable behaviour, they start to behave that way again. *She relapsed into*

depression. ► Also NC *...India's relapse into chaos and anarchy.*

2 NC If a sick person has a **relapse**, their health suddenly gets worse after it had been improving. *A hospital spokesman said Matthew suffered a relapse overnight.*

relate /rɪleɪt/ **relates, relating, related**

1 V+*to* If something **relates** to a particular subject, it concerns that subject. *I want to ask you a question that relates to electricity.*

2 V-RECIP The way that two things **relate**, or the way that one thing **relates** to another, is the sort of connection that exists between them. *How the two agreements related is unimportant... Let us examine the way that the words in a sentence relate to each other.*

3 VO+*to* If you **relate** one thing to another, you see or say what connection there is between them. *It enables students to relate their theory to the real world.*

4 V-RECIP The way that one person **relates** to another, is the way that they communicate with each other and behave towards each other. *Children need to learn to relate to other children.*

5 VO If you **relate** a story, you tell it; a literary use. *Davis related the experience of three Cuban girls.*

related /rɪleɪtɪd/

1 ADJ If two or more things are **related**, there is a connection between them. *...two important and closely related questions... Physics is closely related to mathematics.*

2 ADJ PRED People who are **related** belong to the same family. *...four people closely related to each other.*

relating /rɪleɪtɪŋ/

PREP **Relating to** a particular subject means concerning that subject or with reference to it. *They passed a law relating to noise... They meet weekly for discussion on matters relating to home-making in all its aspects.*

relation /rɪleɪʃn/ **relations**

1 N PL+SUPP **Relations** between people, groups, or countries are contacts between them and the way they behave towards each other. *He's trying to improve relations with the military... The unions should have close relations with management... The Philippines and South Korea have agreed to establish diplomatic relations this year... The European Community indicated it's interested in restoring normal relations with Iran.* ● See also **industrial relations**.

2 N U The **relation** of one thing to another is the connection between them. *She argued that literature has no relation to reality.*

3 When you are comparing one thing with another, you can use **in relation to** as a way of introducing the second thing. *Wages are very low in relation to the cost of living.*

4 NC Your **relations** are the members of your family. *I was a distant relation of her husband.*

relationship /rɪleɪʃnʃɪp/ **relationships**

1 NC+SUPP The **relationship** between two people, groups, or countries is the way they feel and behave towards each other. *The special relationship between Belgium and Zaire was at an end... He described his relationship with Mr Kadar as one of mutual respect.* ● See also **love-hate relationship**.

2 NC A **relationship** is also a close friendship between two people, especially one involving romantic or sexual feelings. *...putting your partner and your relationship first... He withdrew from the campaign after allegations involving a sexual relationship with a young model.*

3 NC The **relationship** between two things is the way in which they are connected. *What is the relationship between language and thought? ...the relationship between population and environment.*

relative /relətɪv/ **relatives**

1 ADJ ATTRIB You use **relative** to indicate that the accuracy of your description of something is based on a comparison with other things. *The head of the department is a relative newcomer... He chose to return to the relative peace of his childhood village.* ◆ **relatively** SUBMOD *A relatively small number of people disagreed.*

2 ADJ ATTRIB You also use **relative** when you are referring to a comparison of the size or nature of two things. *There was a discussion on the relative naval strengths of the two countries.*

3 ADJ PRED If you say that something is **relative**, you mean that it needs to be considered and judged in relation to other things. *All human values are relative.*

4 **Relative to** something means in comparison with it; a formal use. *There is a shortage of labour relative to the demand for it.*

5 NC Your **relatives** are the members of your family. *His exact whereabouts were not known but a close relative said it was a secure place.*

relative clause, relative clauses

NC In grammar, a **relative clause** is a subordinate clause relating to a noun group, which is introduced by a relative pronoun such as 'who', or by a relative conjunction such as 'where'.

relative conjunction, relative conjunctions

NC In grammar, a **relative conjunction** is a conjunction such as 'when' or 'where' that is being used to introduce a relative clause.

relative pronoun, relative pronouns

NC In grammar, a **relative pronoun** is a pronoun such as 'who' that is used to introduce a relative clause.

relativity /relətɪvəti/

NU The theory of **relativity** is Einstein's theory concerning space, time, and motion; a technical term in physics. *Quantum mechanics and the theory of relativity challenge the mind with incredible wonders.*

relax /rɪlæks/ **relaxes, relaxing, relaxed**

1 V-ERG If you **relax** or if something **relaxes** you, you feel calmer and less worried or tense. *He saw that nothing was wrong, and relaxed... Running relaxes you.* ◆ **relaxing** ADJ *It is a delightful, relaxing place for a holiday.*

2 V When your body or a part of it **relaxes**, it becomes less stiff, firm, or tense. *All his facial muscles relaxed.*

3 V-ERG If you **relax** your grip on something or if your grip **relaxes**, you hold the thing less tightly than before. *He relaxed his grip on her arm... His hands relaxed on the mike switch.*

4 VO If you **relax** rules or controls, you make them less strict. *The time had probably come to start relaxing the ban on loans to China... Officials say there is no possibility of relaxing the curfew.*

relaxation /riːlækseɪʃn/

NU **Relaxation** refers to ways of spending time that are pleasant and restful. *It is so necessary for the mother to have some rest and relaxation.*

relaxed /rɪlækst/

1 ADJ If you are **relaxed**, you are not at all worried or anxious. *She gave the impression of being quite relaxed.*

2 ADJ A situation that is **relaxed** is calm and peaceful, and does not involve any hostility. *...a relaxed and informal discussion... Negotiations have been conducted in a more relaxed atmosphere.*

relay, relays, relaying, relayed; pronounced /riːleɪ/ when it is a noun and /rɪleɪ/ or /rɪleɪ/ when it is a verb.

1 NC A **relay** or a **relay race** is a race between teams in which each member of the team runs or swims one section of the race. *China won both the men's and women's 4 x 100m relays... The Nigerians won all four relay races to finish with ten gold medals.*

2 If people do something **in relays**, they do it in small groups at different times, usually following one after another. *The children at our school have to be fed in two relays.*

3 VO To **relay** television or radio signals means to send them on or broadcast them. *The Sunday Concert will be relayed live on Radio Three.*

4 VO If you **relay** something that has been said to you, you repeat it to another person. *McKenzie relayed the question to me.*

release /rɪliːs/ **releases, releasing, released**

1 VO To **release** someone means to set them free. *They had just been released from prison... This failure released him from any obligation to take further exams.* ► Also NU *Nearly a year after his release he*

was still unable to sleep properly.
2 VO To **release** something such as a statement or record means to issue it or make it available. *...in a statement released at 8 a.m... Last week they released their latest album, 'Cloudland'.* ▶ Also NU *...the release of their debut album.*
3 VO If something such as gas or water is **released**, it is let out of an enclosed space. *It came quite close to releasing radioactivity into the environment.* ▶ Also NU+SUPP *...a great release of explosive energy. ...the controlled release of water from the reservoir.*
4 VO If you **release** something, you stop holding it; a formal use. *He quickly released her hand.*
5 VO If you **release** a catch or brake, you move it so that it stops holding something.
6 NC+SUPP A press **release** or publicity **release** is an official written statement that is given to reporters. *According to a press release, his next movie will be 'Venice, Venice'.*
7 NC+SUPP A new **release** is a new record, video, or film that has just become available for people to buy or see. *Their new release is called 'Tattoo You'.*

relegate /rɛlɪgeɪt/ **relegates, relegating, relegated**
VO If you **relegate** someone or something, you give them a less important position or status. *The management had relegated Mr Pelker to the role of part-time consultant.*

relent /rɪlɛnt/ **relents, relenting, relented**
V If you **relent**, you allow someone to do something that you did not allow them to do before. *Sometimes our parents would relent and permit us to meet.*

relentless /rɪlɛntləs/; a literary word.
1 ADJ Something that is **relentless** never stops or never becomes less intense. *...the relentless beating of the sun on the roofs.* ◆ **relentlessly** ADV *The chase relentlessly continues.*
2 ADJ Someone who is **relentless** is determined to do something and refuses to give up. *He could be a relentless enemy.* ◆ **relentlessly** ADV *...a relentlessly ambitious politician.*

relevance /rɛləvəns/
NU The **relevance** that something has to whatever is being talked or written about is the connection between them. *She did not understand the relevance of his remarks.*

relevant /rɛləvənt/
1 ADJ If something is **relevant**, it is connected with what you are talking or writing about. *This is not strictly relevant to what I'll be saying... Police officials are to be present so that all relevant information can be made available.*
2 ADJ ATTRIB The **relevant** thing of a particular kind is the one that is appropriate. *They are made to conform with the relevant British Standards.*

reliable /rɪlaɪəbl/
1 ADJ People or things that are **reliable** can be trusted to work well or to behave in the way that you want them to. *She is a charming and reliable person... The diesel engine is long-lasting and extremely reliable.*
◆ **reliably** ADV *They worked reliably under battle conditions.* ◆ **reliability** /rɪlaɪəbɪləti/ NU *These machines have always been noted for reliability.*
2 ADJ **Reliable** information is very likely to be correct. *...information from a reliable source.*
◆ **reliably** ADV *We are reliably informed that her new record will be released in the autumn.*

reliance /rɪlaɪəns/
NU **Reliance** on someone or something is the state of needing them in order to live or work properly. *...the student's reliance on the teacher. ...complete reliance on drugs.*

reliant /rɪlaɪənt/
ADJ PRED+on or upon Someone who is **reliant** on something needs it and often cannot live or work without it. *We have become reliant on mechanical equipment... This left them completely reliant upon the Soviet Union for assistance.*

relic /rɛlɪk/ **relics**
1 NC Something that is a **relic** has survived from an earlier time. *...a museum with relics of great explorers.*
2 NC A religious **relic** is part of the body of a saint, or

an object associated with a saint. *The relics include fragments of what is said to be the cross on which Jesus was crucified.*

relief /rɪliːf/
1 NU or N SING If you feel **relief**, you feel glad because something unpleasant has not happened or has stopped. *I breathed a sigh of relief... It was such a relief to be free of disguises and pretence... To my relief, he found the suggestion acceptable.*
2 NU **Relief** is also money, food, or clothing that is provided for people who are very poor or hungry. *She outlined what was being done to provide relief... A massive US relief operation is under way in northern Iraq. ...relief workers.*

relieve /rɪliːv/ **relieves, relieving, relieved**
1 VO If something **relieves** an unpleasant feeling, it makes it less unpleasant. *The passengers in the plane swallow to relieve the pressure on their eardrums.*
2 VO+of If someone or something **relieves** you of an unpleasant feeling or a difficulty, they take it away from you. *The news relieved him of some of his embarrassment.*
3 VO+of If you **relieve** someone of something that is heavy or they want to get rid of, you take it away from them; a formal use. *He relieved her of the plates she was holding... Let me relieve you of your coat.*
4 VO If an army **relieves** a town, it frees it after it has been surrounded by an enemy force. *Troops moved into the town relieving the garrison which had been besieged for more than a month.*
5 VO If you **relieve** someone, you take their place and continue doing the job or duty that they were doing. *The last American troops left Iraq today after they were relieved by a UN peacekeeping force.*
6 If someone is **relieved** of their **duties** or **relieved** of their **post**, they are dismissed from their job; used in formal English. *A US helicopter commander has been relieved of his duties after firing on two US armed vehicles... He was relieved of his post and asked to admit his mistakes.*

relieved /rɪliːvd/
ADJ If you are **relieved**, you feel glad because something unpleasant has not happened or has stopped. *I am relieved to hear that this isn't true... Most MEPs seem relieved that a deal was reached at the summit... The photographs show the smiling, relieved faces of the hostages who were released yesterday.*

religion /rɪlɪdʒən/ **religions**
NU or NC **Religion** is belief in a god or gods and the activities connected with this belief. *The school placed strong emphasis on religion. ...the Christian religion.*

religious /rɪlɪdʒəs/
1 ADJ ATTRIB You use **religious** to describe things connected with religion. *All religious activities were suppressed... Mr Yao said the religious beliefs of Tibetans would be respected. ...a religious festival.*
2 ADJ Someone who is **religious** has a strong belief in a god or gods. *The Muslims of Bangladesh are deeply religious.*

religious education
NU **Religious education** is the lessons in school which deal with religion. Its abbreviation is 'R.E.' *The government is to place greater emphasis on the role of religious education in the school curriculum.*

religiously /rɪlɪdʒəsli/
ADV If you do something **religiously**, you do it very regularly because you regard it as necessary or as a duty. *The ornaments were all religiously dusted by Gertrude.*

relinquish /rɪlɪŋkwɪʃ/ **relinquishes, relinquishing, relinquished**
VO If you **relinquish** something such as authority or responsibility, you give it up; a formal word. *She relinquished the editorship of the newspaper.*

reliquary /rɛlɪkwəri/ **reliquaries**
NC A **reliquary** is a box in which a relic of a saint is kept. *The artefacts include ninth century manuscripts, a silver reliquary and various crucifixes.*

relish /rɛlɪʃ/ **relishes, relishing, relished**
1 VO If you **relish** something, you get a lot of

enjoyment from it. *He relishes the challenge of competition.* ▶ Also NU *In his book he exposed with relish all the evils of our present day.*
2 VO If you **relish** the idea or prospect of something, you are looking forward to that thing very much. *She didn't relish the idea of going on her own.*
3 N MASS **Relish** is a sauce or pickle that you can add to food in order to give it more flavour. *...red-onion relish.*

relive /riːˈlɪv/ **relives, reliving, relived**
VO If you **relive** something that has happened to you in the past, you remember it and imagine that you are experiencing it again. *I'm reliving my childhood with my kids... They're starting to wonder whether they're about to relive the trauma they underwent in 1975.*

reload /riːˈləʊd/ **reloads, reloading, reloaded**
V or VO When you **reload** a gun, you load it again by putting in more bullets or explosive. *The captain stopped to reload... Someone else was responsible for reloading the gun and making it safe.*

relocate /riːləʊˈkeɪt/ **relocates, relocating, relocated**
V-ERG If people or businesses **relocate** or if someone **relocates** them, they move to a different place. *Semi-skilled workers find themselves compelled to relocate... In the United States, families have been relocated because toxic waste had been dumped in their region... They relocated me in another building.*
◆ **relocation** /riːləʊˈkeɪʃn/ NU *Priority must be given to the relocation of industry.*

reluctance /rɪˈlʌktəns/
NU **Reluctance** to do something is unwillingness to do it. *...the reluctance of the banks to allow credit.*

reluctant /rɪˈlʌktənt/
ADJ If you are **reluctant** to do something, you are unwilling to do it. *He is reluctant to be photographed.*
◆ **reluctantly** ADV *A wage increase of 21% was reluctantly conceded.*

rely /rɪˈlaɪ/ **relies, relying, relied**
1 V+on or upon If you **rely** on someone or something, you need them in order to live or work properly. *Some industries rely heavily on government for finance... Many of the generals, upon whom Mr Gorbachev is relying to spread his message of radical reform, have personal experience of Afghanistan.*
2 V+on or upon If you can **rely** on someone to work well or behave as you want them to, you can trust them to do this. *One could always rely on him to be polite... His troops could not be relied upon to obey orders.*

remade /riːˈmeɪd/
Remade is the past tense and past participle of **remake**.

remain /rɪˈmeɪn/ **remains, remaining, remained**
1 V C or V A To **remain** in a particular state means to stay in that state and not change. *Oliver remained silent... The results of these experiments remain a secret... Support for Labour remains at forty-six per cent.*
2 V A or V If you **remain** in a place, you stay there and do not move away. *Congressman Tauke remained in Washington for budget negotiations... I was allowed to remain at home.*
3 V If something **remains**, it still exists. *Even today remnants of this practice remain... The fact remains that they mean to destroy us... But obstacles still remain.* ◆ **remaining** ADJ ATTRIB *...the demise of her last remaining relatives.*
4 V+to-INF If something **remains** to be done, it has not yet been done. *One hazard remained to be overcome.*
5 If you say that something **remains to be seen**, you mean that it is not at all certain what will happen. *It remains to be seen what the long term effects will be... How effective this will be remains to be seen.*
6 N PL The **remains** of something are the parts of it that are left after most of it has been used up, taken away, or destroyed. *The remains of the meat sat on the kitchen table... They discovered the remains of a huge dinosaur... They did uncover what appeared to be human remains.*
7 N PL **Remains** are objects and parts of buildings from an earlier period of history, usually found in the ground. *...Roman remains.*

remainder /rɪˈmeɪndə/
N SING The **remainder** of something is the part of it that remains after the other parts have gone or been dealt with. *She went to Brighton where she lived for the remainder of her life... I will pay you a hundred pounds deposit and the remainder on delivery.*

remake /riːˈmeɪk/ **remakes, remaking, remade**
VO If you **remake** something, you make it again, especially in a better way. *Ask what the price is for remaking old mattresses.*

remand /rɪˈmɑːnd/ **remands, remanding, remanded**
1 VO If someone who is accused of a crime is **remanded** by a judge, they are ordered to come back for their trial at a later date. *He was refused bail and was remanded in custody to Crumlin Road prison... The men were remanded on bail until November.*
2 If someone is **on remand**, they have appeared in court and are waiting for their trial to take place. *The government has been urged not to send boys under the age of seventeen into adult prisons if they are being held on remand.*
3 NU **Remand** is the period of time that someone spends on remand. *About fifty suspects are in detention and are facing a police request to have their remand extended... There are no remand prisoners being held in police cells.*

remand centre, remand centres
NC A **remand centre** is an institution where young people who have been accused of a crime are sent until their trial begins or while a decision about their punishment is being made. *Magistrates sent him to a remand centre and the case was adjourned for seven days.*

remark /rɪˈmɑːk/ **remarks, remarking, remarked**
1 V-REPORT, V-QUOTE, or V+on If you **remark** that something is the case, you say that it is the case. *He remarked that the lighting was not very good... He remarked, 'Is this a crazy town or what?'... His friends remarked on his failure to arrive.*
2 NC A **remark** is something that you say, often in a casual way. *At school some of the children used to make unkind remarks about my clothes... He wants the minister to resign for racially insensitive remarks made last month in Tokyo.*

remarkable /rɪˈmɑːkəbl/
ADJ Someone or something that is **remarkable** is very impressive or unusual. *He prepared the dinner with remarkable speed and efficiency... Their most remarkable feature is their hind legs.* ◆ **remarkably** SUBMOD or ADV SEN *He has recovered from the accident remarkably well... Remarkably, Egypt became the first Arab nation to establish diplomatic relations with Israel.*

remarriage /riːˈmærɪdʒ/ **remarriages**
NU or NC **Remarriage** is the act of remarrying. *The equivalent figures among women also show a decrease in remarriage.*

remarry /riːˈmæri/ **remarries, remarrying, remarried**
V or VO If you **remarry**, you marry again after you and your previous husband or wife have obtained a divorce, or after your previous husband or wife has died. *His wife divorced him many years ago and remarried... At the age of seventy-eight, he remarried a thirty-two year old Spanish woman, Carmen Llera.*

remedial /rɪˈmiːdiəl/
1 ADJ ATTRIB **Remedial** measures are intended to correct something that is considered to be wrong or harmful. *...the government's reluctance to take remedial action against unfair trade practices.*
2 ADJ ATTRIB **Remedial** activities are intended to improve someone's ability to read, write, and so on when they have had difficulty learning to do these things. *The children who were falling behind in reading were given special remedial help.*
3 ADJ ATTRIB You also use **remedial** to describe activities which are intended to improve someone's health when they are ill. *...remedial exercises for handicapped children.*

remedy /ˈremədi/ **remedies, remedying, remedied**
1 NC A **remedy** is a successful way of dealing with a problem. *...a drastic remedy for lawlessness and disorder.*

2 NC A **remedy** is also something that is intended to stop illness or pain. *Home-made remedies can often lessen the pain.*
3 VO If you **remedy** something that is wrong or harmful, you correct it. *Technicians laboriously tried to find and remedy faults.*

remember /rɪmɛmbə/ **remembers, remembering, remembered**
1 VO, V-REPORT, V+ING, or V If you **remember** people or events from the past, your mind still has an impression of them and you are able to think about them. *The Passover asks Jews to remember their days as slaves... I remember him falling down the steps... I also remembered that the shop was on the way to Muswell Hill... I remember being very sore... Sure, we all remember.*
2 VO, V-REPORT, V+ING, or V If you can **remember** something, you are able to bring it back into your mind by making an effort to do so. *I'm trying to remember the things I have to do... There was something else, but she could not remember what it was... He can't remember now whether he ever had anything to do with it... I remember meeting her for the first time in 1983, somewhere in the Sahara... I can't really remember.*
3 V+to-INF or V If you **remember** to do something, you think of it and do it at the right time. *Remember to go to the bank... She gave me a list of things to remember.*
4 VO+to If you ask someone to **remember** you to a person who you have not seen for a long time, you are asking them to pass your greetings to that person. *Remember me to your Grandma.*

remembrance /rɪmɛmbrəns/
NU If you do something in **remembrance** of a dead person, you do it as a way of showing that you remember them and respect them; a formal word. *We stood in silence for two minutes in remembrance of the dead.*

Remembrance Day
NU **Remembrance Day** is the Sunday nearest to November 11 when people in Britain honour the memory of the people who died in the two World Wars. *The bomb exploded as crowds gathered at the town cenotaph on Remembrance Day.*

remind /rɪmaɪnd/ **reminds, reminding, reminded**
1 VO+of or about, VO-REPORT, or V+to-INF If someone **reminds** you of a fact or event that you already know about, they deliberately say something which makes you think about it. *Miss Lemon reminded him of two appointments... He would remind us about Indonesia and what it was like... She had to remind him that he had a wife... Remind me to speak to you about Davis.*
2 VO+of If someone or something **reminds** you of another person or thing, they are similar to the other person or thing and they make you think about them. *Your son reminds me of you at his age... Reading his book reminded me of something.*

reminder /rɪmaɪndə/ **reminders**
1 NC If one thing is a **reminder** of another, the first thing makes you think about the second. *Seeing her again was a painful reminder of how different things had been five years ago... A wave of industrial disputes in several key areas has brought a sharp reminder of times past.*
2 NC A **reminder** is also a letter that is sent to tell you that you have not done something such as pay a bill or return library books. *I've had another reminder from the library.*

reminisce /rɛmɪnɪs/ **reminisces, reminiscing, reminisced**
V If you **reminisce** about something from your past, you remember it, and write or talk about it, often with pleasure. *He reminisced about the 'old days'.*

reminiscence /rɛmɪnɪsəns/ **reminiscences**
NC or NU Someone's **reminiscences** are things which they remember from the past, and which they talk or write about. *It's not merely a collection of reminiscences... The newspapers have been full of articles of personal reminiscence and of critical comment from historians.*

reminiscent /rɛmɪnɪsənt/
ADJ PRED If one thing is **reminiscent** of another, the first thing reminds you of the second; a formal word. *There was a sweet smell, vaguely reminiscent of coffee.*

remiss /rɪmɪs/
ADJ PRED If someone is **remiss**, they neglect to do things which ought to be done; a formal word. *Unfortunately, sociologists have been remiss in countering such misconceptions.*

remission /rɪmɪʃn/
NU If someone in prison gets **remission**, their prison sentence is reduced, usually because they have behaved well. *I got four months' remission for good conduct.*

remit, remits, remitting, remitted; pronounced /rɪmɪt/ when it is a verb and /riːmɪt/ when it is a noun. A formal word.
1 VO or V If you **remit** money to someone, you send it to them as payment for something. *I promised to remit the balance, plus interest, in monthly instalments... The travel bureau was asking me to remit promptly.*
2 N SING The **remit** of a person, an official committee, a piece of research, and so on is the area of activity or information that they are expected to deal with or that they have authority to deal with. *Lord Scarman's remit for the second phase of his inquiry is still confined to Brixton.*

remittance /rɪmɪtəns/ **remittances**
NC A **remittance** is a sum of money that you send as payment for something; a formal word. *Post the form with the remittance to the appropriate passport office.*

remnant /rɛmnənt/ **remnants**
NC A **remnant** of something is a small part of it that is left when the main part has disappeared or been destroyed. *The remains are the only known remnants of an Elizabethan theatre.*

remodel /riːmɒdl/ **remodels, remodelling, remodelled**; spelt **remodeling, remodeled** in American English.
VO If someone **remodels** a building or room, they give it a different form or shape. *The Kirks had remodelled their house... The building has been much altered and remodelled.*

remonstrance /rɪmɒnstrəns/
NU **Remonstrance** is protest about a situation or a person's behaviour that you are trying to change or stop; a formal word. *She had abandoned all attempts at remonstrance with Thomas.*

remonstrate /rɛmənstreɪt/ **remonstrates, remonstrating, remonstrated**
V+with or V If you **remonstrate** with someone, you protest to them about a situation or about their behaviour and try to get it changed or stopped; a formal word. *She remonstrated with the porter... He had gone to the manager to remonstrate.*

remorse /rɪmɔːs/
NU **Remorse** is a strong feeling of regret and guilt about something wrong that you have done; a formal word. *I had been filled with remorse over hurting her.*

remorseful /rɪmɔːsfl/
ADJ Someone who is **remorseful** has strong feelings of regret and guilt about something that they have done; a formal word. *There he stood, looking sad and remorseful, agreeing with every word.*

remorseless /rɪmɔːsləs/; a formal word.
1 ADJ Someone who is **remorseless** continually behaves in a very unkind way towards other people, and has no pity for them or regret about this behaviour. *...the remorseless teacher at school, insisting that all the work must be done again.* ♦ **remorselessly** ADV *The Press still pursued their victim remorselessly.*
2 ADJ Something that is **remorseless** continues in an unpleasant and persistent way. *...the frightful, remorseless noise of the engines.* ♦ **remorselessly** ADV *I was woken before six by the rain hammering remorselessly against the bedroom window.*

remote /rɪməʊt/ **remoter, remotest**
1 ADJ **Remote** areas are far away from places where people live. *The drawback is that in this remote area communications are bad... They operate in small*

groups in remote villages. ◆ **remoteness** NU *Because of the remoteness of the area, it will not be possible for rescue teams to reach the site until tomorrow.*
2 ADJ If something happened in the **remote** past, it happened a very long time ago. *Influences from the remote past are at the bottom of his troubles.*
3 ADJ PRED If something is **remote** from ordinary people or life, it is not very relevant to it because it is so different. *His stories are too remote from everyday life.*
4 ADJ If someone is **remote**, they are not friendly and do not get closely involved with other people. *She was a silent girl, cool and remote.* ◆ **remoteness** NU *He criticised the remoteness of public authorities.*
5 ADJ If the possibility of something happening is **remote**, it is very unlikely that it will happen. *Geoffrey Kemp talks about a peaceful settlement as if it is only a remote possibility.*
6 If you **do not have the remotest idea** about something, you know absolutely nothing about it. *I hadn't the remotest idea what Rock Springs would be like, but it was an alluring name.*

remote control
NU **Remote control** is a system of controlling a machine or vehicle from a distance by using radio or electronic signals. *The missile is guided by remote control.*

remote-controlled
ADJ Something that is **remote-controlled** is controlled from a distance by the use of radio or electronic signals. *...remote-controlled unmanned aircraft.*

remotely /rɪməʊtli/
SUBMOD You use **remotely** to emphasize a negative statement. *Agreement did not seem remotely possible at the time... I've never seen anything remotely like it.*

remould, remoulds, remoulding, remoulded;
pronounced /riːməʊld/ when it is a noun and /riːməʊld/ when it is a verb.
1 NC A **remould** is an old tyre which has been given a new surface so that it can be used again.
2 VO To **remould** something such as a way of thinking means to change it so that it has a new structure or is based on different principles; a formal use. *The post-war constitution imposed on Japan by the US had the stated aim of remoulding Japanese society into a peaceful democracy.*

remount /riːmaʊnt/ **remounts, remounting, remounted**
VorVO When you **remount** a bicycle or horse, you get back on it after you have got off it or fallen off it. *Why didn't you remount and ride back instead of just sitting there?... The children remounted their ponies and trotted off.*

removal /rɪmuːvl/
1 NU The **removal** of something is the act of removing it. *He consented to the removal of the flags.*
2 N+N A **removal** company transports furniture from one building to another, for example when people move house. *...removal men.*

remove /rɪmuːv/ **removes, removing, removed**
1 VO If you **remove** something from a place, you take it away. *The servants came in to remove the cups... He removed his hand from the man's collar.*
2 VO When you **remove** clothing, you take it off. *Will you remove your shoes before you go in, please?*
3 VO If you **remove** a stain from something, you treat it with a chemical or wash it and make the stain disappear. *This is a fluid to remove gum from fabrics. ...the difficult job of removing graffiti from the walls of apartment buildings.*
4 VO When you **remove** something undesirable, you get rid of it. *Instant publication would have removed suspicion.*
5 VO If people **remove** someone from a group such as a committee, they stop them being a member of that group, usually against their wishes. *They made an attempt to remove her from the General Council. ...former party leader Nikita Khrushchev, who was removed from office in 1964.*

removed /rɪmuːvd/
ADJ PRED If an idea or situation is far **removed** from something, it is very different from it. *His ideas on*

foreign policy were far removed from those of the Government.

remover /rɪmuːvə/ **removers**
N MASS A **remover** is a substance that you use for removing unwanted stains, marks, and so on. *Have we any stain remover?*

remuneration /rɪmjuːnəreɪʃn/ **remunerations**
NUorNC **Remuneration** is the payment that is made to someone for work they have done; a formal word. *...the introduction of remuneration for councillors... A small remuneration and expenses are paid.*

remunerative /rɪmjuːnəˈrətɪv/
ADJ A **remunerative** job or task is one which you are paid for; a formal word. *He is prepared to accept any remunerative chore, however demeaning.*

renaissance /rɪneɪsns, rənəsɒns/
1 N PROP The **Renaissance** was the period in Europe during the 14th, 15th, and 16th centuries during which there was a great revival of interest in art, literature, and learning. *At the time of the Renaissance there was no division separating Art from Science. ...Renaissance art.*
2 N SING When there is a **renaissance**, there is a revival of interest in a particular type of activity, especially in the arts. *...the renaissance of the British theatre in the late 1950s. ...the Harlem renaissance.*

renal /riːnl/
ADJ **Renal** means concerning or relating to the kidneys; a medical term. *...an experiment on the renal circulation.*

rename /riːneɪm/ **renames, renaming, renamed**
VO If you **rename** something, you give it a different name. *Mr Haq has taken over the Carousel Cafe and renamed it The Pearl of India.*

rend /rend/ **rends, rending, rent**; a literary word.
1 VO When a loud noise **rends** the air, it occurs very suddenly and violently. *The air was rent with their grunts and whistles. ...people who rent the night with the sound of drums and trumpets.*
2 VO If you **rend** something, you tear or rip it apart violently. *Women rent their clothes and tore their hair in grief... The bitter debate is likely to continue rending the country.* ◆ **rending** ADJ ATTRIB *There was a sound of rending metal.*

render /rendə/ **renders, rendering, rendered**; a formal word.
1 VOC You can use **render** to say that someone or something is changed. For example, if you **render** something harmless, you make it harmless. *Frank was rendered speechless by her reply... The vaccine would then be rendered useless by the antibodies already present.*
2 VO+toorVO If you **render** help or assistance to someone, you help them. *Dr Lister Smith rendered vital first aid to Commander Bond... He said the US would render any humanitarian assistance it could.*

rendering /rendəˈrɪŋ/ **renderings**
NC Someone's **rendering** of a play, poem, or piece of music is the way they perform it; a formal word. *...a rendering of the hymn 'Onward Christian Soldiers'.*

rendezvous /rɒndeɪvuː/; **rendezvous** is both the singular and plural form. The plural is pronounced /rɒndeɪvuːz/.
1 NC A **rendezvous** is a meeting, often a secret one, that you have arranged with someone for a particular time and place. *We made a dawn rendezvous.*
2 NC A **rendezvous** is also a place where you have arranged to meet someone. *I met him at a secret rendezvous outside the city.*

rendition /rendɪʃn/ **renditions**
NC A **rendition** of a play, poem, or piece of music is a performance of it; a formal word. *...a rendition of 'The Four Seasons'.*

René, France Albert /frɒnˈs ælbeə rəneɪ/
France Albert René became President of the Seychelles in a coup in 1977. He was elected MP in 1965. He served as Minister of Works and Land Development from 1975 to 1977, and was Prime Minister from 1976 to 1977. He founded and became the leader of the Seychelles People's United Party (now the Seychelles People's Progressive Front (SPPF)), in 1964. Born: 1935.

renegade /rɛnɪgeɪd/ **renegades**
NC A **renegade** is a person who abandons their former group and joins an opposing or different group; a formal word. *He was a traitor and renegade.* *...renegade supporters of the deposed king.*

renege /rɪniːg/ **reneges, reneging, reneged**
V+on If someone **reneges** on an agreement or promise that they have made, they do not keep to it; a formal word. *They had to return £400,000 because they had reneged on the deal. ...those who renege on their responsibilities.*

renew /rɪnjuː/ **renews, renewing, renewed**
1 VO If you **renew** an activity or relationship, you begin it again. *She at once renewed her attack on Judy... They will renew cargo flights to South Africa... I hoped that we might renew our friendship.*
2 VO When you **renew** something such as a licence or a contract, you extend the period of time for which it is valid. *It may soon be possible to renew your motor vehicle registration by telephone.*
3 VO If something that has been destroyed or lost is **renewed**, it comes again or is replaced. *My strength was renewed.*

renewable /rɪnjuːəbl/
ADJ A **renewable** source of energy is one which is naturally replaced when it is used, rather than being destroyed. *Wind power is another renewable source of electricity.*

renewal /rɪnjuːəl/ **renewals**
1 NU+of If there is a **renewal** of an activity, it starts again. *He rejected a request by Nicaragua for a renewal of direct talks... Renewal of hostility with neighbouring countries seemed likely.*
2 NUorNC The **renewal** of a document such as a licence or a contract is an official extension of the time for which it remains valid. *Some licences need yearly renewal. ...passport applications and renewals.*
3 NU+SUPP Urban **renewal** is the process of replacing or improving old buildings in an area near the centre of a town, in order to provide new housing and facilities. *What we've ended up with in Dublin is a situation where the areas of the city which least needed urban renewal were the ones that got it. ...inner city renewal schemes.*

renewed /rɪnjuːd/
ADJ ATTRIB **Renewed** activities or attitudes have begun to happen or exist again after a period when they did not happen or exist. *...renewed efforts to recruit more members... Renewed violence in South Africa claimed the lives of six people in Soweto earlier today... He looked at me with renewed interest.*

rennet /rɛnɪt/
NU **Rennet** is a substance which causes milk to become thick and sour, and which is used in making yoghurt and cheese.

renounce /rɪnaʊns/ **renounces, renouncing, renounced**
VO If you **renounce** a belief or a way of behaving, you decide to stop having that belief or behaving in that way. *The Bishop has always refused to renounce his allegiance to Rome... The ANC renounced the use of violence. ...a joint statement renouncing hostility.*

renovate /rɛnəveɪt/ **renovates, renovating, renovated**
VO If someone **renovates** an old building or machine, they repair it and get it back into good condition. *The house had been renovated three years earlier.*
♦ **renovation** /rɛnəveɪʃn/ **renovations** NUorNC *...the renovation of old buildings... Many of the homes still need extensive renovations.*

renown /rɪnaʊn/
NU **Renown** is the state of being well known or famous, usually for doing something good; a literary word. *He was a scholar of great renown... Birmingham has already won renown for its City of Birmingham Symphony Orchestra.*

renowned /rɪnaʊnd/
ADJ Someone who is **renowned** is famous or well-known. *The locals are renowned for their hospitality. ...the renowned tailors of Savile Row.*

rent /rɛnt/ **rents, renting, rented**
1 VO If you **rent** something, you regularly pay its owner a sum of money for using it. *They rented a villa not far from Rome... He rented a colour TV soon after moving in.* ♦ **rented** ADJ *...a rented flat.*
2 VO In American English, to **rent** something also means to allow it to be used in return for payment. *Most will probably rent their land to the cooperative now working on it.*
3 NCorNU The **rent** is the amount of money that you pay regularly for the use of a house, flat, or piece of land. *He made enough money to pay the rent... Rents might have to be increased by another thirty per cent. ...twenty thousand council tenants who currently pay them rent.*

rent out PHRASAL VERB If you **rent out** something such as a room or a car, you allow it to be used in return for payment. *Income from tenants was so low that landlords were deterred from renting out accommodation.*

rental /rɛntl/
1 ADJ ATTRIB **Rental** means connected with the renting out of goods. *...a computer rental service.*
2 N SING The **rental** is the amount of money that you have to pay when you rent something such as a television or a car. *The quarterly rental will be £35.*

rent book, rent books
NC A **rent book** is a small book which is used to record the date and amount of rent paid by a tenant.

rent-free
ADJorADV **Rent-free** accommodation is available for use without paying any rent. *...rent-free housing... The other three houses were given rent-free to retired friends.*

rent strike, rent strikes
NUorNC If people go on **rent strike**, they refuse to pay their rent, as a form of protest. *New York has seen a lot of rent strikes, but seldom on 5th Avenue.*

renunciation /rɪnʌnsieɪʃn/
NU The **renunciation** of a belief or way of behaving is a decision to stop having that belief or behaving in that way; a formal word. *...the renunciation of revolution.*

reopen /riːəʊpən/ **reopens, reopening, reopened**
1 V-ERG If you **reopen** a shop, bar, restaurant, or so on, or if it **reopens**, you open it again after it has been closed for some time. *They temporarily reopened the airport to allow military aircraft already there to leave... When the pub reopened, everything was new and gleaming.*
2 VO If someone **reopens** something such as a discussion or a legal case, they start it again after it has stopped or been closed. *...a clear commitment to reopen disarmament talks... We can reopen the case and make a new decision.*
3 VO To **reopen** a border or a route means to allow people and goods to cross it or go along it after a period during which it has been closed. *Israel reopened the West Bank and Gaza Strip today.*
4 V-ERG If a wound **reopens** or if you **reopen** it, it breaks open again after the skin has begun to heal. *Vaca's suspect eye reopened and Honeyghan exploited the advantage, hammering him with head and body punches... With the dressing on, he could go through thorn and scrub without fear of reopening the wound.*
5 V-ERG If old arguments or disagreements between people **reopen** or if someone or something **reopens** them, they start again after being over for a long time. *The party's leadership crisis could soon be reopened... The comments have reopened a controversy that began five years ago... The incident has reopened old wounds at just the wrong time.*

reorganize /riːɔːgənaɪz/ **reorganizes, reorganizing, reorganized**; also spelt **reorganise**.
VOorV If you **reorganize** something, you organize it in a new way. *The manufacturers were reorganising the soap industry... We simply decided to stop right now and to reorganize.* ♦ **reorganization** /riːɔːgənaɪzeɪʃn/ **reorganizations** NUorNC *...the reorganization of the health system. ...a special conference to discuss the reorganisation.*

rep /rɛp/ **reps**
1 NC A **rep** is a person who travels round selling their company's products or services to other companies or to shops; an informal word. *...a sales rep.*

2 NU When actors are working in **rep**, they are working for a repertory company; also used to refer to theatres where these companies perform. *He spent 5 years in rep in Nottingham and Sheffield... His stage debut came in 1924 with the Liverpool rep... As a teenager he joined a local rep.*

Rep.
1 **Rep.** is a written abbreviation for 'Representative'. It is written in front of someone's name to indicate that they are a member of the House of Representatives in the USA. *...Rep. Barber B. Conable.*
2 **Rep.** is also a written abbreviation for 'Republican' or 'Republic'. *...England v Rep. of Ireland.*

repaid /rɪpeɪd/
Repaid is the past tense and past participle of **repay**.

repair /rɪpeə/ **repairs, repairing, repaired**
1 NCorNU A **repair** is something that you do to mend an item that is damaged or is not working properly. *He had left his car for repairs in the garage... The chairs are in need of repair.*
2 VO If you **repair** something that is damaged or is not working properly, you mend it. *No one knew how to repair the engine.*
3 If something such as a building is **in good repair**, it is in good condition. If it is in **bad repair**, it is in bad condition; a formal use. *It's worth keeping in good repair... Soldiers report low morale and equipment in bad repair.*
4 VO If you **repair** an undesirable action or situation, you do something to correct it; a formal use. *I'll repair the omission.*

reparation /repəreɪʃn/ **reparations**
1 NU **Reparation** is the act of giving someone money or doing something for them because you have caused them to suffer in the past; a formal use. *They are still trying to make some sort of atonement and reparation.*
2 NC **Reparations** are sums of money that are paid after a war by the defeated country for damage and injuries it caused. *The proceeds could then be used to pay war reparations. ...reparation debts.*

repartee /repɑːtiː/
NU **Repartee** is conversation that consists of quick, witty comments and replies. *...his constant chatter and repartee with the spectators.*

repast /rɪpɑːst/ **repasts**
NC A **repast** is a meal such as breakfast, lunch or dinner, or the food that you have at a meal; a literary word. *...elegantly prepared repasts at the family mansion... This repast was accompanied by a mug of tea.*

repatriate /riːpætrɪeɪt/ **repatriates, repatriating, repatriated**
VO If someone is **repatriated**, they are sent back to their own country. *Some fifty thousand of the refugees who fled to Rwanda have been repatriated.*

repatriation /riːpætrɪeɪʃn/ **repatriations**
NUorNC **Repatriation** is the act or process of sending people back to their own country. *Many more Iraqi prisoners await repatriation... Vietnam refused to accept any more forcible repatriations. ...emergency repatriation flights for tourists.*

repay /rɪpeɪ/ **repays, repaying, repaid**
1 VO If you **repay** money, you give it back to the person you borrowed it from or took it from. *He plans to repay most of that debt... He ordered the President to repay the money to the State.*
2 VO If you **repay** a favour that someone did for you, you do something or give them something in return. *We hope we can repay you for the pleasure you have given us.*

repayable /rɪpeɪəbl/
ADJ PRED A loan that is **repayable** within a particular period of time must be paid back within that time. *The loan is repayable in ten years.*

repayment /rɪpeɪmənt/ **repayments**
1 NC **Repayments** are amounts of money which you pay at regular intervals to a person or organization in order to repay a debt over a period of time. *Debt repayments are already an enormous burden on the economies of countries like Brazil and Peru.*

2 NU The **repayment** of money is the process of paying it back to the person you owe it to. *...repayment of international debts.*

repeal /rɪpiːl/ **repeals, repealing, repealed**
VO If the government **repeals** a law, it officially ends it; a legal term. *Nine countries repealed their anti-discrimination laws last year.* ▶ Also NU *...a campaign for the repeal of incomes legislation.*

repeat /rɪpiːt/ **repeats, repeating, repeated**
1 VO, V-REPORT,or V-QUOTE If you **repeat** something, you say or write it again. *Haldane repeated his statement in the presence of the Prime Minister... Afterwards, the chief repeated that he will not resign... 'We need half a million dollars,' Monty kept repeating.*
2 VO, V-REPORT,or V-QUOTE If you **repeat** something that someone else has said or written, you say or write the same thing. *He repeated appeals for more international assistance... Ballin repeated what he had been told by Haldane... He's likely to have repeated what his superior said recently... 'I love you,' he says, and she repeats, 'I love you.'*
3 V-REFL If you **repeat** yourself, you say something which you have said before, without meaning to. *People tend to repeat themselves a lot in conversation.*
4 VO If you **repeat** an action, you do it again. *I decided not to repeat the mistake of my first marriage.*
5 VO If a television or radio programme **is repeated**, it is broadcast again. *Most letters asked for the series to be repeated.*
6 NC A **repeat** is a television or radio broadcast which has been seen or heard before. *'Any Questions' can be heard at 8, with a repeat on Monday afternoon... They're all old films or repeats.*
7 NC A **repeat** is also something which is done again or which happens again. *He didn't want a repeat of yesterday's scene with Hooper. ...a repeat performance.*

repeated /rɪpiːtɪd/
ADJ ATTRIB **Repeated** actions or events are ones which happen many times. *After repeated attempts, the manager finally managed to call the police.*

repeatedly /rɪpiːtɪdli/
ADV If you do something **repeatedly**, you do it many times. *The child learns to read by seeing the words repeatedly... Keating has repeatedly denied the charges.*

repel /rɪpel/ **repels, repelling, repelled**
VO If something **repels** you, you find it horrible and disgusting. *Any deformity frightened and repelled her.*

repellent /rɪpelənt/ **repellents**
1 ADJ If you find something **repellent**, you find it horrible and disgusting. *The idea of eating meat has become repellent to me.*
2 N MASS A **repellent** is a chemical which is used to keep insects or other creatures away. *...a bottle of insect repellent.*

repent /rɪpent/ **repents, repenting, repented**
VorVO If you **repent**, you feel sorry for wrong or evil things that you have done; a formal word. *He may repent of his sins... He said those political prisoners who have not repented their past mistakes will not be freed.*

repentance /rɪpentəns/
NU **Repentance** is sorrow that you feel for wrong or evil things that you have done; a formal word. *...the need for repentance.*

repentant /rɪpentənt/
ADJ Someone who is **repentant** feels sorry for bad or evil things that they have done; a formal word. *...repentant sinners.*

repercussions /riːpəkʌʃnz/
N PL The **repercussions** of an event are the effects that it has at a later time; a formal word. *They cannot foresee the complex repercussions of these changes... What happened had enormous repercussions on my family... There'd be long-term political repercussions.*

repertoire /repətwɑː/
1 N SING+SUPP A performer's **repertoire** is all the pieces of music or parts in plays he or she has learned and can perform. *It was wonderful to be able to extend my song repertoire.*

2 N SING+SUPP The **repertoire** of a person or thing is all the things that person or thing is capable of doing. *It's a tough operation calling for all the skills in the cosmetic surgeon's repertoire... This computer is capable of only a limited repertoire of activities.*

repertory /rɛpətⁿri/
NU **Repertory** is the practice of performing a small number of plays in a theatre during a period of time, using the same actors in every play. *He appeared in repertory at Stratford-upon-Avon... He went on tour with a repertory company.*

repetition /rɛpətɪʃn/ **repetitions**
N CorNU If there is a **repetition** of something that has happened before, it happens again. *He didn't want a repetition of the scene with his mother... Music relies on repetition, because that gives us a sense of perspective and expectation.*

repetitious /rɛpətɪʃəs/
ADJ **Repetitious** means the same as **repetitive**. *...repetitious jobs.*

repetitive /rɪpɛtətɪv/
ADJ Something that is **repetitive** is repeated many times; used especially to refer to something which contains unnecessary repetition, and is therefore boring. *The dance was performed to a powerful repetitive beat of Philip Glass's music... His job consists of dull, repetitive work.*

rephrase /riːfreɪz/ **rephrases, rephrasing, rephrased**
VO If you **rephrase** a question or statement, you ask it or say it again in a different way. *I guess you could rephrase it and say, 'Would air power alone get the job done?'*

replace /rɪpleɪs/ **replaces, replacing, replaced**
1 VO When one thing or person **replaces** another, the first one takes the place of the second one. *Thomas bought a new sweater to replace the one he lost... He replaces Mr Shin Hasegawa, who has stepped down because of ill health.*
2 VO If you **replace** something that is damaged, lost, or old-fashioned, you get a new thing which will perform the same function. *The books that have been stolen will have to be replaced... The airline is currently replacing its DC10s with Boeing 747s.*
3 VO To **replace** something also means to put it back in the place where it was before. *She replaced the receiver.*

replacement /rɪpleɪsmənt/ **replacements**
1 NU The **replacement** of someone or something happens when they are replaced by another person or thing. *...the replacement of steam by diesel.*
2 NC A **replacement** is a person or thing that takes the place of another. *The Colonel's replacement was due any day now.*

replay, replays, replaying, replayed; pronounced /riːpleɪ/ when it is a verb and /riːpleɪ/ when it is a noun.
1 VO If two sports teams **replay** a match in a competition, they play it again because the previous match between them was a draw. *The match will be replayed on Saturday.* ► Also NC *Who won the replay?*
2 VO If you **replay** something that you have recorded on tape or film, you play it in order to listen to it or look at it. *His remarks were captured on video tape and replayed by the opposition during last month's election campaign.*

replenish /rɪplɛnɪʃ/ **replenishes, replenishing, replenished**
VO To **replenish** something means to make it full or complete again by adding a quantity of a substance that has gone; a formal word. *We have to import an extra 4 million tons of wheat to replenish our reserves... Mr Jones replenished his glass.*

replete /rɪpliːt/; a formal word.
1 ADJ If you are **replete**, you are pleasantly full of food and drink so that you do not want to eat or drink anything else. *No more for me, thanks. I'm quite replete... Replete and drowsy, Gretchen lay on the couch.*
2 ADJ PRED+*with* If something is **replete** with something, it is fully supplied with it. *The battleships of the US North Atlantic Squadron were replete with fuel and ammunition.*

replica /rɛplɪkə/ **replicas**
NC A **replica** of something such as a statue, machine, or building is an accurate copy of it. *They've built a human-sized replica of the Statue of Liberty... His gun was later found to be a replica.*

replicate /rɛplɪkeɪt/ **replicates, replicating, replicated**
VOor V-REFL To **replicate** something means to repeat it in exactly the same way or to make an exact copy of it; a formal word. *The study has been replicated over and over again... DNA has the capacity to replicate itself.*

reply /rɪplaɪ/ **replies, replying, replied**
1 V+*to*, V-QUOTE, V, or V-REPORT When you **reply** to something that someone has said or written to you, you say or write something as an answer. *He gave me no chance to reply to his question... 'Did you have a nice journey?'—'Yes,' Jenny replied... I sent you a letter, and you never replied... He replied that there was no need to worry about Egypt's stand.*
2 NC A **reply** is something that you say or write when you reply to someone. *He called 'Sarah', but there was no reply... I received about a dozen replies to my enquiry... The decision was announced in a Commons written reply by the Transport Secretary, Mr Paul Channon.*
3 If you say or do something **in reply** to what someone else has said or done, you say or do it as a response to them. *I have nothing to say in reply to your question.*

repoint /riːpɔɪnt/ **repoints, repointing, repointed**
VO If you **repoint** brickwork, you put new mortar between the bricks. *The portion of the brickwork which had not been repointed was crumbling.*

report /rɪpɔːt/ **reports, reporting, reported**
1 VOor V-REPORT If a person, newspaper, or news programme **reports** something, they tell people you that it has happened or that it is thought to be true. *Accidents must be reported to the police within twenty-four hours... The papers reported that Southern England was 'paralysed' by snow. ...the right of the press to report allegations of scandal in government... At least seven people are reported to have been killed.*
♦ **reported** ADJ ATTRIB *They have expressed concern about the reported human rights violations. ...the last reported position of the hurricane.*
2 V+*on* or V+*to* If you **report** on an event or subject, you tell people what you have found out about it because it is your job or duty to do so. *It is now incumbent on them to investigate and report on the complaint... The committee should report to Parliament by early May.*
3 VO If you **report** someone to a person in authority, you tell the person in authority about something wrong that the other person has done. *You should have reported them to the police.*
4 V If you **report** to a person or place, you go to them and say that you are ready to start work. *The next morning he reported for duty at Jack Starke's office... I told him to report to me after the job was completed.*
5 NC A **report** is a written or spoken account of something that has happened, for example in a newspaper. *So far, there have been no reports of bomb attacks in the area... Unconfirmed reports say that well over a dozen people have been killed in the riot... According to eyewitness reports by western correspondents, the police drove into the demonstrators, using truncheons and tear-gas sprays.*
6 NC A **report** is also an official document that discusses a particular subject. *A report on Britain's magistrates courts says that many are misusing the law to protect well-known defendants from publicity.*
7 NC A school **report** is a written account of how well or badly a pupil has done during the term that has just finished. *My daughter got a very bad report last term.*

report back PHRASAL VERB If you **report back** to someone, you tell them about something that it was your job to find out about. *She was sent to attend the meeting and then to report back on its discussions.*

reportage /rɪpɔːtɪdʒ/
NU **Reportage** is the act or the technique of reporting news; a formal word. *President Habyarimana has*

reacted angrily to such reports, dismissing much of
the reportage of the three week old conflict as
'systematic and diabolical' lies. ...the rules of
parliamentary reportage.

report card, report cards
NC A **report card** is a written or spoken account of
how well or badly someone is doing, especially an
account that describes a child's progress at school;
used in American English. *If you're happy with your
child's report card, say so... Last week, the federal
government issued its report card on the nation's
health.*

reportedly /rɪpɔːtɪdli/
ADV If something is **reportedly** true, someone has said
that it is true; a formal word. *The rebels reportedly
captured an army post at the weekend at the town of
Kakata... He has reportedly instructed his family not
to interfere if he tries to kill himself.*

reported speech
NU In grammar, **reported speech** gives an account of
something that someone has said, but without quoting
their actual words. The sentence 'He said that he was
tired', contains reported speech.

reporter /rɪpɔːtə/ **reporters**
NC A **reporter** is someone who writes news articles or
broadcasts news reports. *...a reporter from a Chicago
newspaper.*

reporting /rɪpɔːtɪŋ/
NU **Reporting** is the presenting of news in newspapers
or on radio or television. *The magazine was asked to
be less selective in its reporting.*

repose /rɪpəʊz/
NU **Repose** is a state in which you are resting and feel
calm; a literary word. *Her face was lovely in repose.*

repository /rɪpɒzɪtəˀri/ **repositories**
NC+SUPP A **repository** is a place where something is
kept safely; a formal word. *The Foreign Office was
regarded as the repository of all relevant
information... The museum was the main repository
for the country's antiquities.*

repossess /riːpəzes/ **repossess, repossessing,
repossessed**
VO If someone **repossesses** something, especially
something that has not been paid for, they take it
back; a formal word. *They wanted to repossess the
building... In the first half of this year, there was an
increase of a third in the number of houses
repossessed because the loans were not being repaid.*

repot /riːpɒt/ **repots, repotting, repotted**
VO If you **repot** a plant, you plant it in a bigger pot
because it has grown too big for the one that it is in.

reprehensible /reprɪhensəbl/
ADJ **Reprehensible** behaviour is morally wrong; a
formal word. *He said the US would regard any
retaliation as 'totally reprehensible and unjustified'...
The Senate denounced him for what it called
reprehensible conduct.*

represent /reprɪzent/ **represents, representing,
represented**
1 VO If someone **represents** you, they act on your
behalf, for example in a court of law or in
parliament. *...lawyers representing relatives of the
victims... The Council represents all major Christian
groups in Ghana except the Roman Catholic church...
Thirty one nations are now represented at the
Disarmament Conference.*
2 VO If someone **represents** a group of people, they
are considered to be a typical member of that group.
*Thirteen years younger than his colleague, John Major
represents a different generation of Tories.*
3 V-PASS If a group of people is well **represented** at a
particular place, there are a lot of them present or a
lot of examples of their work. *Japanese firms are
already well represented in the North East... All these
artists are well represented at the exhibition.*
4 VO If you say that an action or event **represents**
something, you mean that it is that thing; a formal
use. *The passage of Security Council Resolution 678
represents an unprecedented step for the United
Nations... The planned general strike represents an
important economic challenge to the government.*
5 VO If you **represent** something in a particular way,

you describe it in that way. *The evacuation of our
forces was represented as a triumphant success... It
was represented as an attempt to gain money and to
gain publicity.*
6 VO If a sign or symbol **represents** something, it is
accepted as meaning that thing. *The word 'love' was
represented by a small heart.*

representation /reprɪzenteɪʃn/ **representations**
1 NU **Representation** is the state of being represented
by someone, for example in a parliament or on a
committee. *They're campaigning for student
representation on the university's governing bodies.*
● See also proportional representation.
2 NC You can describe a picture or statue of someone
as a **representation** of them; a formal use. *...crude
representations of angels.*
3 N PL **Representations** are formal requests,
complaints, or statements made to a government or
other official group. *...representations made by a
group of local residents.*

representational /reprɪzenteɪʃəˀnəl/
ADJ **Representational** art attempts to show things as
they actually look; a formal word. *...representational
styles of medieval manuscript illumination.
...representational images.*

representative /reprɪzentətɪv/ **representatives**
1 NC A **representative** is a person who acts on behalf
of another person or group of people. *The Consumer
Congress is made up of representatives of a wide
range of organizations. ...union representatives... The
rebels say they will not take part in proposed peace
talks with government representatives.*
2 ADJ ATTRIB A **representative** group acts on behalf of
a larger group. *The government consists of two
representative assemblies.*
3 ADJ If something is **representative** of a group, it is
typical of that group. *...a representative cross-section
of the public.*

repress /rɪpres/ **represses, repressing, repressed**
1 VO If you **repress** a feeling, you succeed in not
having it or not showing it. *Freud's belief that
children have strong sexual feelings which they learn
to repress was central to his work... It was all I could
do to repress my laughter.*
2 VO To **repress** a group of people means to restrict
their freedom and control them by force. *The officers
would help to repress their own people... Police
repressed the demonstrations using batons and tear-
gas... While the authorities are determined to repress
human rights dissidents, they are not keen on putting
them on trial.*

repressed /rɪprest/
1 ADJ **Repressed** people try to stop themselves having
natural feelings and desires, especially sexual ones.
In her next film she played a repressed governess.
2 ADJ A person's **repressed** feelings are the ones they
do not allow themselves to know about consciously.
...the child's repressed hate of his mother.

repression /rɪpreʃn/
NU **Repression** is the use of force to restrict and
control a group of people. *They wanted to fight all
forms of injustice and repression... They have accused
the authorities there of brutal repression in their
handling of the disturbances... The repression of pro-
democracy activists continues.*

repressive /rɪpresɪv/
ADJ **Repressive** governments use force and unjust laws
to restrict and control their people. *...the leader of a
repressive regime. ...a repressive society. ...Noriega's
corrupt and repressive rule.*

reprieve /rɪpriːv/ **reprieves, reprieving, reprieved**
1 VO If someone who has been sentenced to death is
reprieved, their sentence is changed and they are not
executed. *90 were condemned to death—most were
reprieved, but 15 did go to the firing squad.*
2 NC A **reprieve** is an official order cancelling a death
sentence. *Harris obtained a last-minute reprieve, and
his case remains on appeal... In Taiwan, three men
have been executed for kidnapping the son of the
country's richest businessman, despite appeals for a
reprieve.*
3 NC A **reprieve** is also an unexpected delay before

something unpleasant happens. *The finding of oil represents a colossal reprieve for the islanders... Last night, the paper's owner announced a reprieve for the daily, which he had threatened to shut down.*

reprimand /rɛprɪmɑːnd/ **reprimands, reprimanding, reprimanded**
vo If someone in authority **reprimands** you, they tell you officially that you have done something wrong; a formal word. *He was called to the office of a superior to be reprimanded.* ▶ Also NC ...*a gentle reprimand.*

reprint, reprints, reprinting, reprinted; pronounced /riːprɪnt/ when it is a verb and /riːprɪnt/ when it is a noun.
1 vo When something such as a book is **reprinted**, further copies of it are printed, for example after all the other ones have been sold. *They said it was up to individual publishing houses to decide whether to reprint works by Solzhenitsyn which were banned in the Brezhnev era.*
2 NC A **reprint** is a copy of something such as a book or newspaper article which has been reprinted. ...*reprints of official statements from the Romanian and Hungarian sides.* ...*a scaled down reprint of the offending front page.*

reprisal /rɪpraɪzl/ **reprisals**
NCorNU **Reprisals** are violent actions taken by a group of people against another group who have harmed them. *They engaged in brutal reprisals against those who had fought them... This latest wave of violence may be a reprisal for recent raids on drug warehouses.* ...*threats of reprisal.*

reproach /rɪprəʊtʃ/ **reproaches, reproaching, reproached;** a formal word.
1 NUorNC If you express **reproach**, you indicate to someone that you are sad and disappointed about something they have done. *She was still staring at him in shocked and silent reproach... She responded submissively to his reproaches.*
2 VOorV-REFL If you **reproach** someone, you tell them sadly they have done something wrong. *He used to reproach her mother for not being nice enough to her... He had bitterly reproached himself for his complacency.*
3 If someone is **beyond reproach** or **above reproach**, their behaviour has been so good that they cannot be criticized. *They will field no candidate whose private and public life is not beyond reproach.*

reproachful /rɪprəʊtʃfl/
ADJ **Reproachful** looks or remarks show sadness and disappointment about something that someone has done. *They kept sending us reproachful messages.*
◆ **reproachfully** ADV *Morris looked at her reproachfully.*

reprobate /rɛprəbeɪt/ **reprobates**
NCorN+N A **reprobate** is a person who behaves in a way that you do not approve of, for example by getting drunk regularly or by gambling; an old-fashioned word. *It is time this reprobate was removed from office.* ...*that reprobate, gambling aristocrat.*

reprocess /riːprəʊses/ **reprocesses, reprocessing, reprocessed**
vo To **reprocess** a material or substance that has already been used, especially one that is toxic, means to treat it in order to make it safe, or so that it can be used again. *The form which the item will take after being reprocessed may be similar or markedly dissimilar... The plant reprocesses waste paper into paper pulp for the nearby Bridgewater Paper Mill.*

reproduce /riːprədjuːs/ **reproduces, reproducing, reproduced**
1 vo If you **reproduce** something, you produce a copy of it. *This painting has never been reproduced anywhere.*
2 VorV-REFL When people, animals, or plants **reproduce** or **reproduce** themselves, they produce more of their own species. *Bacteria reproduce by splitting into two... the mechanism by which human cells reproduce themselves.*

reproduction /riːprədʌkʃn/ **reproductions**
1 NC A **reproduction** is a modern copy of a painting or piece of furniture. ...*reproductions of Impressionist paintings.*

2 NU The **reproduction** of sound, art, or writing is the copying of it. *The Controller has no objection to the reproduction of the Report... Sound recorded on compact discs has given a more faithful reproduction of live concerts.*
3 NU **Reproduction** is the process by which living things produce more of their own species. *Genes that interfere with the reproduction of the malaria parasite itself would be very useful.* ...*plant reproduction.*

reproductive /riːprədʌktɪv/
ADJ ATTRIB **Reproductive** means relating to the reproduction of living things. ...*a worm's digestive and reproductive systems.*

reproof /rɪpruːf/ **reproofs**
NCorNU A **reproof** is something that you say to someone to show that you disapprove of what they have done; a formal word. *This reproof was ignored... Discipline and reproof are out of fashion.*

reprove /rɪpruːv/ **reproves, reproving, reproved**
vo If you **reprove** someone, you tell them that they have behaved wrongly or foolishly; a formal word. *He constantly reproved Sonny for his outbursts of temper.*
◆ **reproving** ADJ *She received a reproving look from her Aunt Agnes.*

reptile /rɛptaɪl/ **reptiles**
NC A **reptile** is a scaly animal which lays eggs. Snakes, lizards, and crocodiles are reptiles. ...*heathlands that are home for some of Britain's rarest species of birds and reptiles.* ...*reptiles such as the sand lizard and the smooth snake.*

reptilian /rɛptɪlɪən/
ADJ ATTRIB **Reptilian** means characteristic of reptiles or like a reptile. *Scientists now realise that dinosaurs were much more bird-like than reptilian.*

republic /rɪpʌblɪk/ **republics**
NC A **republic** is a country which has a president and is governed by elected representatives. *Cuba became an independent republic.* ...*the Republic of Ireland... the three Baltic republics.*

Republican /rɪpʌblɪkən/ **Republicans**
1 NC In the United States, a **Republican** is a person who belongs to or supports the Republican Party. *Eisenhower, in many ways, is a model for George Bush as a sort of moderate Republican... Webster was a lifelong Republican.* ...*Republican voters.*
2 NC A **Republican** is also a person who believes that Northern Ireland should not be ruled by Britain but should become part of the Republic of Ireland. *In Northern Ireland, Republicans have held a series of marches and parades to mark the anniversary of the 1916 Easter uprising against British rule.* ...*the struggle between anti-British Catholic Republicans and pro-British Protestants.* ...*a man of strong Republican views.*

republicanism /rɪpʌblɪkənɪzəm/
1 NU **Republicanism** is the belief that the best system of government for a country is a republic. *In England, republicanism was never the remotest threat—English royalty lived on, triumphantly.*
2 NU **Republicanism** is also support for the idea that Northern Ireland should become part of the Republic of Ireland. *He was particularly touchy about Irish republicanism and the Ulster question.*
3 NU In the United States, **Republicanism** is membership of the Republican Party in the United States. *He was converted from his respectable Republicanism by President Roosevelt.*

repudiate /rɪpjuːdieɪt/ **repudiates, repudiating, repudiated**
vo If you **repudiate** something, you say that you will not accept it or have anything to do with it; a formal word. *He repudiated the authority of the Church.*
◆ **repudiation** /rɪpjuːdieɪʃn/ NU+SUPP *Most condemned the pact and called for its official repudiation.* ...*his repudiation of the evidence.*

repugnance /rɪpʌgnəns/
NU **Repugnance** is a feeling of very strong dislike and disgust that you feel towards someone or something; a formal word. *He screwed up his face in an expression of utter repugnance.*

repugnant /rɪpʌgnənt/
ADJ If something is **repugnant** to you, you think that it

is horrible and disgusting; a formal word. *The majority of British people find this sort of souvenir repugnant.*

repulse /rɪpʌls/ **repulses, repulsing, repulsed**
1 vo If something **repulses** you, you find it horrible and disgusting, and you want to avoid it. *Like all the great war photographers he is at once repulsed by what he sees and drawn to it.*
2 vo If an army or other group of people **repulses** an enemy force, they fight it and force it to retreat. *The raid was swiftly repulsed.*

repulsion /rɪpʌlʃn/
NU **Repulsion** is a strong feeling of dislike and disgust; a formal word. *She shivered with repulsion.*

repulsive /rɪpʌlsɪv/
ADJ **Repulsive** means horrible and disgusting. *It's a repulsive idea... His behaviour was absolutely repulsive... They were seen as something subhuman and repulsive.*

reputable /repjʊtəbl/
ADJ A **reputable** company or person is known to be good and reliable. *All reputable companies give a guarantee.*

reputation /repjʊteɪʃn/ **reputations**
NC Your **reputation** is the opinion that people have of you. *She had a reputation as a very good writer. ...his reputation for integrity.*

repute /rɪpjuːt/; a formal word.
1 Something or someone of **repute** is respected and known to be honest and trustworthy. *This story was published by two journals of repute... There was an unsuccessful search for a witness of repute.*
2 If something is held **in repute**, it is respected and considered to be of high quality. *Her work was held in high repute by many critics. ...the task of bringing football back into repute.*

reputed /rɪpjuːtɪd/
ADJ If something is **reputed** to be true or to exist, some people say that it is true or that it exists. *The buildings were reputed to be haunted. ...their reputed beauty.* ◆ **reputedly** ADV *...events that reputedly took place thousands of years ago.*

request /rɪkwest/ **requests, requesting, requested**
1 VO, VO+to-INF, or V-REPORT To **request** something means to ask for it formally. *The President requested an emergency session of the United Nations... France has formally requested the Soviet Union to use its influence to secure the release of a French journalist... India has requested that a ship should be allowed through the blockade.*
2 NC If you make a **request** for something, you ask for it. *I made repeated requests for money.* ● **Request** is used in these phrases. ● If something is done **on request**, it is done when you ask for it. *A booklet on this subject will be sent on request.* ● If you do something at someone's **request**, you do it because they ask you to. *He returned on a jet chartered at Sununu's request... That meeting had been scheduled for today but was postponed at Iraq's request.*

request stop, request stops
NC A **request stop** is a bus stop at which a bus will stop only if someone makes a signal for it to do so.

requiem /rekwiem/ **requiems**
1 NC A **requiem** or a **requiem mass** is a mass celebrated in remembrance of someone who has recently died. *There will be a requiem mass for him at St Joseph's Church on the 15th.*
2 NC A **requiem** is a piece of music for singers and musicians that can be performed either as a celebration of a requiem mass or as part of a concert. *The concert will end with a performance of Verdi's Requiem.*

require /rɪkwaɪə/ **requires, requiring, required**; a formal word.
1 vo To **require** something means to need it. *Is there anything you require?... Parliamentary approval would be required for it... Clothing, blankets and tents are also required.*
2 vo If you **are required** to do something, you have to do it, for example because of a rule or law. *All the boys were required to study religion... Connecticut law requires Bridgeport to submit a balanced budget to a*

review board... *He was doing what was required of him.* ◆ **required** ADJ *Check that the machines meet required standards.*

requirement /rɪkwaɪəmənt/ **requirements**
1 NC A **requirement** is something that you must have or do in order to do what you want. *Maths is no longer the most important requirement for a career in accounting.*
2 NC Your **requirements** are the things that you need. *Mexico imported half her grain requirements in 1940.*

requisite /rekwɪzɪt/
ADJ ATTRIB **Requisite** means necessary for a particular purpose; a formal word. *They needed time to establish the requisite number of prisons.*

requisition /rekwɪzɪʃn/ **requisitions, requisitioning, requisitioned**
vo When people, especially soldiers, **requisition** something, they take it for their own use. *Transport was being requisitioned by the army.*

requite /rɪkwaɪt/ **requites, requiting, requited**
vo If a desire or feeling is **requited**, it is satisfied; a literary word. *No matter what desires are requited, they are always replaced by others... He had seen her flushed with requited love.*

re-route, re-routes, re-routing, re-routed
vo If something such as traffic is **re-routed**, it is directed along different roads, for example because a road is blocked. *The main bridge over the Euphrates is down and traffic is re-routed to a pontoon bridge... Michael McCooe has been campaigning for years to have the march re-routed.*

re-run, re-runs, re-running, re-ran; pronounced /riːrʌn/ when it is a noun and /riːrʌn/ when it is a verb. The form **re-run** is used in the present tense and is also the past participle of the verb.
1 V-PASS If an election is **re-run**, it is held again, for example because the correct procedures were not followed or because no candidate obtained an overall majority. *The ballot had to be re-run because of a breach of security... Elections will have to be re-run in a third of the hundred and forty one seats.* ► Also NC *The election is a re-run of the one held last December... In most constituencies, there'll have to be re-runs in two weeks time.*
2 vo If a process or event is **re-run**, it is done or held again. *Using a computer, we re-ran the program with the expansion stopped and then re-calculated the intensity... In 1912, the race had to be stopped and re-run after both crews sank.* ► Also NC *Budd earned £90,000 for a re-run with Decker, where she was again left trailing.*
3 N SING+SUPP If you say that something is a **re-run** of a particular event or experience, you mean that what is done or what happens now is very similar to what was done or what happened in the past. *The present fighting is a re-run of battles between the two groups a year ago... This morning, COHSE said it wasn't interested in a re-run of Tuesday when the unions walked out.*
4 vo If a theatre company or cinema **re-runs** a play or a film, it shows or puts it on again. *In honour of Jane Fonda's visit, the Cubans re-ran one of her films at the cinema and another two on television.*
5 NC A **re-run** is a film, play, or programme, that is broadcast or put on again. *They put on a re-run of 'The Government Inspector' with Alan Howard. ...a wearisome re-run of an old film... I grew up watching re-runs of 'Mr Smith goes to Washington'.*

reschedule /riːʃedjuːl, riːskedjuːl/ **reschedules, rescheduling, rescheduled**
1 vo If an event is **rescheduled**, arrangements are made for it to take place because it did not take place when it was originally supposed to happen. *The elections were rescheduled after those last November were cancelled in a wave of violence... The match had been delayed and rescheduled due to rain yesterday.*
2 vo If a debt is **rescheduled**, the country or banks that lent the money agree that it can be paid back to them less quickly. *Moscow has already agreed to reschedule Egypt's massive and long-outstanding military debt... Even after restricting imports and rescheduling debts, Nigeria is expected to have a big*

balance of payments gap. ♦ **rescheduling** N SING or NU *Panama has run into heavy arrears and has had to ask the private banks for a rescheduling... He tried for some time to persuade the foreign banks to accept a new kind of debt rescheduling.*

rescind /rɪsɪnd/ **rescinds, rescinding, rescinded**
VO If a government or group of people in power **rescind** a law or agreement, they officially withdraw it and state that it is no longer valid; a formal word. *This law was later rescinded... They had to summon a second conference and rescind the previous motion.*

rescue /reskjuː/ **rescues, rescuing, rescued**
1 VO If you **rescue** someone, you get them out of a dangerous or difficult situation. *He was rescued from the sinking aircraft by a passing ship... The Cabinet decided not to rescue the company... Most of the crew have been rescued.*
2 NU or NC **Rescue** is help which gets someone out of a dangerous or difficult situation. *Rescue was at hand... The coastguard may be working on as many as 20 rescues at any one time... Mountain rescue teams in north-west Scotland are searching for two hikers missing in bad weather conditions.*
3 If you **come to** someone's **rescue**, you help them when they are in danger or difficulty. *There is widespread disappointment that the United States has not come to the country's rescue... An army patrol came to the rescue of the trapped motorists.*

rescuer /reskjuːə/ **rescuers**
NC A **rescuer** is a person who rescues or tries to rescue someone else. *Rescuers found her dead... The man's shouts could not be heard by the rescuers.*

research /rɪsɜːtʃ/ **researches, researching, researched**
1 NU or N PL **Research** is work that involves studying something and trying to discover facts about it. *More research is also needed to look at health care policies and strategies... Research has shown that many abusers continue to inject drugs in prison... Soon after, Faraday began his researches into electricity.*
2 VO or V If you **research** something, you try to discover facts about it. *She spent two years here researching her documentary... I spent some time researching abroad... The historical background to the play had been very carefully researched.*

researcher /rɪsɜːtʃə/ **researchers**
NC A **researcher** is someone who does research into a subject. *A team of Canadian researchers, at McMaster University, has provided the missing evidence. ...the increasingly complicated treatments discovered by medical researchers.*

reseat /riːsiːt/ **reseats, reseating, reseated**
V-REFL If you **reseat** yourself, you sit down again. *Mary and Sam came slowly back and reseated themselves by his side.*

resell /riːsel/ **resells, reselling, resold**
VO or V If you **resell** something, you sell it again after you have bought it. *The price went up, and coffee was resold for large profits... You may not resell, or at any rate not at a capital gain.*

resemblance /rɪzembləns/
N SING or NU If there is a **resemblance** between two people or things, they are similar to each other. *She bore a striking resemblance to his wife... The situation bears some resemblance to that of Germany during the rampant inflation of the early twenties.*

resemble /rɪzembl/ **resembles, resembling, resembled**
VO If one thing or person **resembles** another, they are similar to each other. *The situation closely resembles that of Europe in 1940.*

resent /rɪzent/ **resents, resenting, resented**
VO If you **resent** something, you feel bitter and angry about it. *I resented his attitude... They resent being treated as common criminals.*

resentful /rɪzentfl/
ADJ If you are **resentful**, you feel resentment. *He was resentful at the way he had been treated.*

resentment /rɪzentmənt/
NU **Resentment** is a feeling of bitterness and anger. *He was filled with resentment... I felt no resentment against Keith.*

reservation /rezəveɪʃn/ **reservations**
1 NC or NU If you have **reservations** about something, you are not sure that it is entirely good or right. *I have reservations about the desirability of such a change... They accepted the plan without reservation... There are strong reservations about the way the situation is being handled.*
2 NC If you make a **reservation**, you arrange for something such as a table in a restaurant or a room in a hotel to be kept for you. *I will make the reservation for seven thirty.*

reserve /rɪzɜːv/ **reserves, reserving, reserved**
1 VO If something **is reserved** for a particular person or purpose, it is kept specially for that person or purpose. *The garden is reserved for those who work in the museum... St Faith's Chapel is reserved for private prayer... An agreed number of places for lorries will be reserved on ships to Dover... Thirty parliamentary seats will be reserved for women.*
2 NC A **reserve** is a supply of something that is available for use when needed. *We have large coal reserves. ...a seemingly endless reserve of energy... He was able to draw on vast reserves of talent and enthusiasm.*
3 If you have something **in reserve**, you have it available for use when needed. *I kept some tranquillizers in reserve in case I became agitated... They have been warned that funds should be held in reserve for unpredicted future events... The police were out in force with hundreds more in reserve.*
4 NC In sport, a **reserve** is someone who is available to compete or play for a particular team if one of its members cannot take part. *The technically brilliant Adriana Dunavska is a reserve... Jose Diurrin takes over as reserve goalkeeper from Juan Carlos Ablanedo who is injured.*
5 NC A nature **reserve** is an area of land where animals, birds, and plants are officially protected. *Over the past 30 years Swaziland has been carefully building up the wildlife stocks in the country's game reserves. ...a gang hunting rare giant pandas in a nature reserve.*
6 NU If someone shows **reserve**, they keep their feelings hidden. *His tone had lost the cautious reserve it had previously had.*
7 to **reserve judgement**: see **judgement**.

reserved /rɪzɜːvd/
ADJ Someone who is **reserved** keeps their feelings hidden. *He is reserved and cautious, never making a swift decision.*

reservist /rɪzɜːvɪst/ **reservists**
NC A **reservist** is a soldier who belongs to a country's reserve army. *Army reservists were being replaced by professional soldiers. ...the drafting of recruits and reservists into the Red Army.*

reservoir /rezəvwɑː/ **reservoirs**
1 NC A **reservoir** is a lake used for storing water before it is supplied to people. *Dam building projects also produce victims—those whose lands are submerged beneath the waters of the new reservoirs... From the 1930s to the 1950s farmers drilled wells and built dozens of small reservoirs like this to irrigate crops.*
2 NC A **reservoir** is also a large amount of something that is available for use when needed, even though you may not always know that it exists. *One way of finding underground water in the desert would be to drill holes at random and hope that you hit a reservoir. ...reservoirs of nitrogen gas... Bankers don't have a reservoir of public goodwill to draw on now that they're facing hard times.*

reset /riːset/ **resets, resetting.** The form **reset** is used in the present tense and is also the past participle.
1 VO If you **reset** a machine or device, you set it again so that it is ready to work again or ready to perform a particular function. *He reset the alarm and climbed back into bed.*
2 VO If someone **resets** a bone, they put it back into its correct position after it has been broken. *He underwent an operation to reset the bone... His nose had been broken and reset.*

resettle /riːsɛtl/ resettles, resettling, resettled
V-ERG If a government or other organization **resettles** people, or if people **resettle**, they move to a different place to live because they are no longer able or allowed to stay in the area where they live at the moment. *The programme to resettle black families on better land still had a long way to go, the President admitted... These people began to resettle in London... The refugees themselves do not want to be resettled.*

resettlement /riːsɛtlmənt/
NU **Resettlement** is the process of moving people to a different place to live, because they are no longer allowed to stay in the area where they live at the moment. *The UN hopes to encourage people to return by offering them 3,300 rupees to help with transportation costs and initial resettlement. ...a massive programme of resettlement.*

reshuffle, reshuffles, reshuffling, reshuffled;
pronounced /riːʃʌfl/ when it is a noun and /riːʃʌfl/ when it is a verb.
1 NC A **reshuffle** is a reorganization of people or things, especially of jobs within a government. *The move is expected to pave the way for a reshuffle of the party leadership. ...a wide-ranging cabinet reshuffle in which more than two thirds of the ministers were replaced.*
2 VOorV If the manager or leader of a group of workers, especially government ministers, **reshuffles** them, he or she changes their jobs around so that they have different responsibilities. *He felt it was time to reshuffle the team... In Peru, President Alan Garcia has again reshuffled his cabinet... Those things are happening, of course, as they reshuffle.*

reside /rɪzaɪd/ resides, residing, resided
V If a quality **resides** in something, it is in that thing; a formal word. *Real power now resides in the workshop... The value of his sculptures resides in their simplicity.*

residence /rɛzɪdəns/ residences; a formal word.
1 NC Someone's **residence** is their house. *...the Prime Minister's official residence.*
2 NU Your place of **residence** is the place where you live. *The hotel is heavily used by visiting journalists and officials, as a place of residence, a headquarters, and a communication centre.*
3 See also **hall of residence**.
● **Residence** is used in these phrases. ● If you **take up residence** somewhere, you start living there. *Mrs Thatcher first took up residence at 10 Downing Street in 1979. ...the many homeless people who have taken up residence in the subways.* ● If someone is **in residence** in a place, they are living there. *Considering more than 500 adolescent boys are in residence here, it's unbelievably quiet.*

residency /rɛzɪdənsi/
NU Someone's **residency** in a particular place, especially a country, is the fact that they live there or that they are officially allowed to live there. *German law grants residency to anyone who can prove he or she is of German descent... He has applied for United States residency along with his wife and two daughters.*

resident /rɛzɪdənt/ residents
1 NC The **residents** of an area are the people who live there. *The local residents complained... He's been a resident of Papua New Guinea for more than forty years.*
2 ADJ Someone who is **resident** in a country or town lives there; a formal use. *...students resident in England... Other foreigners resident in the town were evacuated last week.*
3 ADJ **Resident** is used to describe people who live in the place where they work. *...a resident chaplain.*
4 NC A **resident** is also a doctor who has already qualified but who is doing more training in order to learn how to treat a specific kind of illness or medical problem; used in American English. *They started out in medicine together as residents at a Boston hospital... This extra money subsidizes medical education—it pays for residents and interns to treat patients.*

residential /rɛzɪdɛnʃl/
1 ADJ ATTRIB A **residential** area contains houses rather than offices or factories. *...a densely populated residential area. ...fashionable residential suburbs.*
2 ADJ ATTRIB A **residential** institution is one where you can live while you are studying or being cared for there. *Sean now lives in a residential home run by a Christian charity. ...residential colleges.*

residents' association, residents' associations
N COLL A **residents' association** is a group of people who live in an area and who try to encourage their local authority to make that area more pleasant to live in. *The local residents' association has been campaigning for a full independent enquiry. ...a meeting called this morning by the residents' association.*

residual /rɪzɪdjuəl/
ADJ ATTRIB **Residual** is used to describe what remains of something when most of it has gone; a formal word. *...the residual prejudices of the past.*

residue /rɛzɪdjuː/ residues
NC A **residue** of something is a small amount that remains after most of it has gone; a formal word. *Residues of pesticides can build up in the soil.*

resign /rɪzaɪn/ resigns, resigning, resigned
1 V If you **resign** from a job or position, you formally announce that you are leaving it. *Mrs Thatcher has announced her intention to resign... She resigned from the Government... Lloyd George was threatening to resign.*
2 V-REFL+to If you **resign** yourself to an unpleasant situation or fact, you accept it because you cannot change it. *Many retailers have resigned themselves to the fact that the most important thing is to empty their shelves... You're a widow now, Mrs Pearl. I think you must resign yourself to that fact.*

resignation /rɛzɪgneɪʃn/ resignations
1 NCorNU Your **resignation** is a formal statement of your intention to leave a job or position. *Mr McPherson has accepted my resignation. ...her letter of resignation... Hardline Communists from several regions have said they will call for his resignation as General Secretary.*
2 NU **Resignation** is the acceptance of an unpleasant situation or fact because you cannot change it. *She spoke with quiet resignation... There's a mood of resignation among some delegates here.*

resigned /rɪzaɪnd/
ADJ If you are **resigned** to an unpleasant situation or fact, you accept it because you cannot change it. *They feel resigned to losing their money.* ◆ **resignedly** /rɪzaɪnɪdli/ ADV *'He will come,' said Joe resignedly.*

resilience /rɪzɪliəns/
1 NUorN SING **Resilience** is the ability that a person or institution has to recover quickly from a setback or misfortune. *The chairman has shown remarkable resilience... Democratic political structures have a remarkable resilience. ...their resilience, courage and character.*
2 NUorN SING **Resilience** is also the quality that something has of being strong and not damaged easily, for example by being hit, stretched, or squeezed. *It makes the road surface tougher because it has a sort of resilience... He was bouncing on the mattress to demonstrate its resilience.*

resilient /rɪzɪliənt/
ADJ People who are **resilient** are able to recover quickly from unpleasant things that happen to them. *He's bright, resilient, and ambitious.*

resin /rɛzɪn/ resins
1 N MASS **Resin** is a sticky substance produced by some trees. *...the native Indians who have traditionally farmed the forest for resins, rubber, and medicinal plant extracts. ...resin from pine trees.*
2 N MASS **Resin** is also a chemically produced substance used to make plastics. *...the chemical used only in the production of paints and resins... Another company has suspended a shipment of resin to the Soviet Union.*

resinous /rɛzɪnəs/
ADJ ATTRIB **Resinous** means like resin or containing resin. *...their sweet, resinous smell.*

resist /rɪzɪst/ resists, resisting, resisted
1 VO If you **resist** something such as a change, you refuse to accept it and try to prevent it. *Our trade union has resisted the introduction of automation... The Japanese Government has resisted calls to scrap the treaty.*
2 VOorV To **resist** an attack means to fight back. *Any attack will be resisted with force if necessary... They then tried to kidnap a twenty-year-old woman but when she resisted they stabbed her to death.*
3 VOorV+ING If you **resist** the temptation to do something, you do not do it. *I resisted the temptation to get very drunk... I can't resist teasing him.*

resistance /rɪzɪstəns/
1 NU **Resistance** to something such as a change or a new idea is a refusal to accept it. *There will be fierce resistance if this is attempted. ...resistance to bureaucratic controls.*
2 NU When there is **resistance** to an attack, people fight back. *The advancing army met with no resistance. ...the Warsaw uprising when thousands of Polish resistance fighters took to the streets against German occupation.*
3 NU **Resistance** is also opposition to the flow of an electrical current through a circuit. Resistance is measured in ohms; a technical term in physics. *Ceramics at normal room temperatures have a very high resistance to the flow of electric current.*

resistant /rɪzɪstənt/; a formal word.
1 ADJ PRED People who are **resistant** to something are opposed to it and want to prevent it. *They are extremely resistant to change... Most of the population is Muslim and highly resistant to assimilation into the Soviet mainstream.*
2 ADJ If something is **resistant** to something else, it is not harmed by it. *This type of plastic is highly resistant to steam... The most virulent form of malaria became resistant to the drug chloroquine in the 1960s.*

resister /rɪzɪstə/ resisters
NC A **resister** is someone who tries to avoid serving in the armed forces when they have been ordered to do so. *Support for the resisters comes from an organization called the End Conscription Campaign... The three war resisters reject the argument that they're cowards.*

resistor /rɪzɪstə/ resistors
NC A **resistor** is a device which is designed to increase the resistance in an electrical circuit; a technical term. *The devices were in fact ordinary capacitors and resistors used in a range of domestic appliances.*

resolute /rɛzəluːt/
ADJ Someone who is **resolute** refuses to change their mind or to give up a course of action; a formal word. *We urged him to be resolute. ...their resolute refusal to make any real concessions.* ♦ **resolutely** ADV *She had resolutely refused to speak to me.*

resolution /rɛzəluːʃn/ resolutions
1 NC A **resolution** is a formal decision taken at a meeting by means of a vote. *Congress passed a resolution accepting his services... A resolution calling for sanctions was vetoed by Britain and the United States yesterday.*
2 NC If you make a **resolution** to do something, you decide to try hard to do it. *I'm always making resolutions, like giving up smoking.*
3 NU **Resolution** is determination to do something or not do something. *A note of resolution entered his voice.*
4 NU The **resolution** of a problem or difficulty is the solving of it; a formal use. *British officials are hoping that a resolution of the airport controversy might emerge from the trip. ...a resolution of conflicting financial claims.*

resolve /rɪzɒlv/ resolves, resolving, resolved; a formal word.
1 V+to-INF or V-REPORT If you **resolve** to do something, you make a firm decision to do it. *They resolved to take action... I resolved to tell the truth... He had already resolved that Kitchener should be appointed.*
2 NU **Resolve** is determination to do something. *We must be firm in our resolve to oppose them... It is no use governments adopting great declarations and commitments about fighting terrorism if they lack the resolve to put them into practice.*
3 VO To **resolve** a problem, argument, or difficulty means to deal with it successfully. *The Cabinet met to resolve the crisis... A number of issues raised at the Vienna conference still remain to be resolved... They objected to the use of violence to resolve a dispute that they think should be solved through negotiations.*

resolved /rɪzɒlvd/
ADJ PRED If you are **resolved** to do something, you are determined to do it. *I was firmly resolved to speak to her.*

resonance /rɛzənəns/ resonances
1 NCorNU If something has a **resonance** for someone, it has a special meaning or is particularly important to them, for example because they agree with it, or because it is similar in some way to something else. *They are calling for freedom, but also for justice—a concept which has a deep resonance in the Romanian mind... The revolution had been, he said, an event of universal resonance for the world.*
2 NU **Resonance** is the quality that a sound has of being deep, clear, and echoing. *His voice suddenly took on a new resonance.*
3 NCorNU A **resonance** is the sound which is produced in one object when it vibrates at the same rate as the sound waves from another object.

resonant /rɛzənənt/
1 ADJ **Resonant** sounds are deep and strong. *Theatrical colleagues remember his considerable acting talent, and above all, his wonderful, resonant voice... The bigger, resonant booms of rifles and shotguns are unmistakable.*
2 ADJ Something that is **resonant** has a special meaning or is particularly important to people usually because they agree with it or because it is similar to something else; a literary use. *The storming of the Bastille in Paris remains one of the most resonant of revolutionary acts. ...a speech resonant with historical echoes.*

resonate /rɛzəneɪt/ resonates, resonating, resonated; a literary word.
1 V If something **resonates**, it vibrates and produces a deep, strong sound. *His laughter resonated among the rocks... Prayers resonate from a loudspeaker.*
2 V You also say that something **resonates** when it has a special meaning or is very important to a particular person or thing. *...the themes of motherhood and family that resonate through the book... Charles Johnson wants each one of his sentences to resonate with echoes of other literature, history and philosophy.*

resort /rɪzɔːt/ resorts, resorting, resorted
1 V+to If you **resort** to methods that you disapprove of, you use them because you cannot see any other way of achieving what you want. *They had not so far chosen to resort to violence... After the boom, the economy overheated and the Government resorted to interest rates to dampen it down.*
2 If you do something **as a last resort**, you do it to solve a problem after trying all other ways of solving it. *He assured parliament the workforce intended to use strikes only as a last resort... As a last resort he went to the British Library.*
3 NC+SUPP A **resort** is a place where many people spend their holidays. *A traditional destination on public holidays is the seaside resort. ...the Swiss ski resort of Klosters.*

resound /rɪzaʊnd/ resounds, resounding, resounded; a literary word.
1 V When a noise **resounds**, it is heard loudly and clearly. *His steps resounded in the courtyard.*
2 V If a place **resounds** with noise, it is filled with it. *The room began to resound with that powerful voice.*

resounding /rɪzaʊndɪŋ/
1 ADJ ATTRIB A **resounding** noise is loud and echoing. *The tile sprang from the wall with a resounding crack.*
2 ADJ ATTRIB A **resounding** success is a very great success. *British officials regard the summit as a resounding success for the British Prime Minister... The Liberal Democrats won a resounding victory in the Eastbourne By-Election.*

resource /rɪzɔːs, rɪsɔːs/ **resources**
NC The **resources** of a country, organization, or person are the things they have and can use. *...Britain's energy resources... Julius had invested all his resources in a restaurant... Disarmament should lead to resources being switched to peaceful economic development.*

resourceful /rɪzɔːsfl, rɪsɔːsfl/
ADJ Someone who is **resourceful** is good at finding ways of dealing with problems. *...an able, resourceful politician... They are tough, resourceful and intelligent.* ◆ **resourcefulness** NU *They faced misfortune with resourcefulness and courage.*

respect /rɪspɛkt/ **respects, respecting, respected**
1 VO If you **respect** someone, you have a good opinion of their character or ideas. *The French actually respect intellectuals... He was particularly respected for his integrity... He is a professional soldier and is widely respected amongst his troops.*
2 NU Your **respect** for someone is your good opinion of them. *He enjoys a great deal of respect and goodwill in these countries... Mr Kinnock hopes that being received with respect in the Oval Office will improve his standing both at home and abroad.*
3 VO If you **respect** someone's wishes, rights, or customs, you avoid doing things that they would dislike or regard as wrong. *She respected his need for peace and quiet... We must respect the practices of cultures different from our own.*
4 NU If you show **respect** for someone's wishes, rights, or customs, you avoid doing anything they would dislike or regard as wrong. *Douglas Hurd, at a press conference in Saudi Arabia, stressed their respect for Islam... They've suspended the search until Friday out of respect for a Jewish festival. ...respect for the rights of the minority.*
5 VO If you **respect** a law or a moral principle, you agree not to break it. *They would, he said, respect Croatia's existing borders... The government had promised to respect and guarantee trade union rights.*
● **Respect** is used in these formal phrases. ● You say **with respect** when you are politely disagreeing with someone. *But Mr Hume, with respect, that wouldn't work.* ● You say **with respect to** to indicate what something relates to. *He informed me about my rights with respect to the forthcoming extradition.* ● You say **in this respect** to indicate that what you are saying applies to the thing you have just mentioned. *We are lagging behind in this respect.* ● **In many respects** means in many different ways. *He is different from the people around him in many respects.*

respectable /rɪspɛktəbl/
1 ADJ Someone or something that is **respectable** is approved of by society and considered to be morally correct. *...a respectable businessman. ...young people from respectable homes... He was brought up in a flat in a terraced house in poor, but respectable, Brixton.* ◆ **respectability** /rɪspɛktəbɪləti/ NU *...a statesman of great eminence and respectability.*
2 ADJ **Respectable** also means adequate or acceptable. *He had begun to earn a very respectable income... The West Indies finished with a very respectable score of 311 for five.*

respected /rɪspɛktɪd/
ADJ Someone or something that is **respected** is admired and considered to be important by many people. *...a highly respected scholar... He is respected abroad for both his diplomacy and his liberal, flexible attitudes.*

respecter /rɪspɛktə/ **respecters**
1 NC+of If you describe someone as a **respecter** of something such as a belief or idea, you mean that they behave in a way which shows that they have a high opinion of it. *The President is pre-eminently a respecter of this tradition.*
2 If you say that someone or something is **no respecter of** something such as a rule or tradition, you mean that the rule or tradition is not important to them. *Pollution is no respecter of international borders... Chris Evert gives nothing away and is no respecter of reputations.*

respectful /rɪspɛktfl/
ADJ If you are **respectful**, you show respect for someone. *The woman kept a respectful silence... The tone of his letter is distinctly more respectful than earlier messages sent to Moscow.* ◆ **respectfully** ADV *He expected them to stand respectfully when he entered the room.*

respective /rɪspɛktɪv/
ADJ ATTRIB **Respective** means relating separately to the people you have just mentioned. *He drove them both to their respective homes.*

respectively /rɪspɛktɪvli/
ADV **Respectively** means in the same order as the items you have just mentioned. *Harvard University and MIT are respectively the fourth and fifth largest employers in the area.*

respiration /rɛspəreɪʃn/
NU Your **respiration** is your breathing; a medical term. *Children, if their circulation or respiration is disturbed, get very cold. ...a specialist in the physiology of respiration.*

respirator /rɛspəreɪtə/ **respirators**
1 NC A **respirator** is a device you wear over your mouth and nose in order to be able to breathe when you are surrounded by smoke or poisonous gas. *To combat this threat they are working on better respirators and protective clothing.*
2 NC A **respirator** is also a device that allows people to breathe when they cannot breathe naturally, for example because they are ill or have been injured. *Doctors say she will never come out of a coma, and hospital officials want to disconnect the respirator that keeps her alive.*

respiratory /rɛspərətri, rɪspɪrətəʊri/
ADJ ATTRIB **Respiratory** means relating to breathing; a medical term. *Doctors have kept him on a respiratory machine. ...respiratory infections. ...the respiratory system.*

respire /rɪspaɪə/ **respires, respiring, respired**
V To **respire** means to breathe; a formal word. *You respire approximately 21,666 times a day.*

respite /rɛspaɪt, rɛspɪt/
NUorN SING **Respite** is a short period of rest from something unpleasant; a formal word. *She was interrogated without respite for twenty-four hours... For them and their children at least there'll be a respite from the fear and tension.*

resplendent /rɪsplɛndənt/
ADJ If someone is **resplendent**, their appearance is very impressive; a formal word. *Miss Jackson, resplendent in a new red suit, watched the ceremony. ...resplendent jewels.*

respond /rɪspɒnd/ **responds, responding, responded**
V When you **respond** to something that is done or said, you react by doing or saying something yourself in reply. *The government has responded to pressure by moving towards reform... The crowd waved and the liner responded with a blast on its siren... He did not respond to repeated calls from the crowd for a general strike.*

respondent /rɪspɒndənt/ **respondents**
NC A **respondent** is a person who answers a questionnaire or a request for information of some kind. *In 1959, 43 per cent of Gallup's respondents thought the trade unions 'too powerful'.*

response /rɪspɒns/ **responses**
1 NC Your **response** to an event, action, or statement is what you do or say as a reaction or reply to it. *The Government's response to the riots was firm... Even though some European countries have said they're willing to help, there's been no favourable response from the United States.*
2 If you do or say something **in response** to an event, action, or statement, you do it or say it as a reaction or reply to it. *Will waved his hand in response... In response to requests for more time to meet this demand, the British gave them three years to sell their shares.*

responsibility /rɪspɒnsəbɪləti/ **responsibilities**
1 NU If you have **responsibility** for something or if it is your **responsibility**, it is your duty to deal with it and make decisions relating to it. *She took over the*

responsibility for the project.
2 NU If you accept **responsibility** for something that has happened, you agree that you were to blame for it. *No group has admitted responsibility for the attack... I made a mistake and I will assume responsibility for it.*
3 NC Your **responsibilities** are the duties that you have because of your job or position. *One of our primary responsibilities is to make such materials more widely available. ...the responsibilities of citizenship.*
4 NC If you have a **responsibility** to someone, you have a duty to help them or to look after them. *I presume you take your responsibility to your students seriously?*

responsible /rɪspɒnsəbl/
1 ADJ PRED If you are **responsible** for something, it is your job or duty to deal with it. *...the minister responsible for civil defence... Managers have been made directly responsible for their companies' performance... They are responsible for their own defence.*
2 ADJ PRED If you are **responsible** for something bad that has happened, it is your fault. *I hold you personally responsible for all this... Those responsible for the violence should be severely punished... Increased acid is responsible for ulcers in the duodenum.*
3 ADJ PRED If you are **responsible** to a person or group, you are controlled by them and have to report to them about what you have done. *We're responsible to a development committee... The government will be responsible to the President alone.*
4 ADJ **Responsible** people behave properly without needing to be controlled by anyone else. *...responsible members of the local community.* ◆ **responsibly** ADV *You are doing your job conscientiously and responsibly.*
5 ADJ ATTRIB **Responsible** jobs involve making important decisions or carrying out important actions. *...a difficult, responsible job.*

responsive /rɪspɒnsɪv/
1 ADJ Someone who is **responsive** is quick to show emotions such as pleasure and affection. *The children were the most responsive members of the audience.*
2 ADJ PRED If you are **responsive** to people or to things that happen, you take notice of them and react in an appropriate way. *Broadcasters should be responsive to public opinion... Industry is highly responsive to consumer demand.*

rest /rest/ **rests, resting, rested**
1 N SING The **rest** of something is all that remains of it. *He spent the rest of his life in prison... She has been told that she must use birth control for the rest of her childbearing years... It was happening not only in America but also throughout the rest of the world.*
2 N SING When you have been talking about one member of a group of things or people, you can refer to all the other members as the **rest**. *It was just another grave like all the rest... The rest of us were allowed to go home.*
3 V or VO If you **rest**, you do not do anything active for a period of time. *Go back to bed and rest... Stop to relax and rest your muscles.*
4 NU or NC If you get some **rest** or have a **rest**, you sit or lie down and do not do anything active. *Try to get some rest... They wanted a rest.*
5 V+on or V+upon If something such as an idea **rests** on a particular thing, it depends on that thing; a formal use. *I believe that the future of civilization rests on that decision... Deterrence ultimately rests upon the threat of massive nuclear retaliation.*
6 V+with If a responsibility or duty **rests** with you, you have that responsibility or duty; a formal use. *Final authority on all matters rests with him... Responsibility for the crimes rests with the leadership.*
7 V-ERG A If something **rests** somewhere, its weight is supported there. *He let her shoulders rest against his knees. ...a tub with a wide edge to rest your arm on.*
8 V+on or V+upon If your eyes **rest** on something, you stop looking round you and look at that thing; a literary use. *Her eyes travelled slowly upward and rested on his hands.*

9 NC+SUPP A **rest** is also an object used to support something. *Put your chin on the chin rest, please. ...a head rest.*
● **Rest** is used in these phrases. ● When a moving object **comes to rest**, it stops. *...Mount Ararat, where Noah's Ark is supposed to have come to rest after the flood... The front portion of the plane is intact—it's come to rest at the base of a tree.* ● If you put someone's **mind at rest** or set their **mind at rest**, you say something that stops them worrying. *...a development to put some of these people's fears at rest... They could set their minds at rest, he said—it was state policy that co-operation with foreign countries would continue.*

restate /riːsteɪt/ **restates, restating, restated**
VO If you **restate** something, you say it again in words or writing, usually in a new way; a formal word. *I restated our readiness to resume negotiations... The government took the opportunity to restate its basic policies.*

restatement /riːsteɪtmənt/ **restatements**
NC The **restatement** of a policy or idea is the expression of it in words or writing, usually in a new way; a formal word. *The speech was a restatement of democratic principles and his belief in the need for drastic change. ...a strong restatement of the Irish Government's position.*

restaurant /restəᵊrɒnt, restəᵊrɒnᵊ/ **restaurants**
NC A **restaurant** is a place where you can buy and eat a meal. *...a meal in a Chinese restaurant... For ten years he worked as a chef and a waiter in an Indian restaurant... Shops and restaurants were open all day.*

restaurateur /restəᵊrətɜː/ **restaurateurs**
NC A **restaurateur** is a person who owns and runs a restaurant; a formal word. *The Roux brothers of France are the only restaurateurs to be awarded the three star grading by the new guide. ...a restaurateur in Manchester who's producing heart-shaped pizzas.*

rested /restɪd/
ADJ If you feel **rested**, you feel less tired than you did before because you have had a rest. *They looked as if they were rested and fit.*

restful /restfl/
ADJ Something that is **restful** helps you to feel calm and relaxed. *The lighting is restful... He has had a quiet, restful day.*

rest-home, rest-homes
NC A **rest-home** is a place in which old people live and are looked after. *...a rest-home in Bournemouth.*

resting place, resting places
1 NC A **resting place** is a place where you can stay and rest, usually for a short period of time. *At least for the moment they have a resting place and a home.*
2 NC You can refer to someone's grave as their **resting place**. *...his final, private resting place in a shaded corner of the churchyard.*

restitution /restɪtjuːʃn/
NU **Restitution** is the act of giving back to a person something that was lost or stolen, or of paying them money for the loss; a formal word. *The former owners of factories, shops and real estate have only been promised partial compensation instead of full restitution of their property. ...its promise to make some restitution to the banks.*

restive /restɪv/
ADJ If you are **restive**, you are impatient, bored, or dissatisfied; a formal word. *The crew were restive and mutinous... The Communist regime struggled to retain control over an increasingly restive population.*

restless /restləs/
1 ADJ If you are **restless**, you are bored or dissatisfied, and want to do something else. *I knew that within a fortnight I should feel restless again.* ◆ **restlessness** NU *They are showing some signs of restlessness.*
2 ADJ You also say that someone is **restless** when they keep moving around because they find it difficult to keep still. *She was restless and fidgety.* ◆ **restlessly** ADV *He walked restlessly around the room.*

restock /riːstɒk/ **restocks, restocking, restocked**
1 V O or V When you **restock**, you buy a lot of food or other goods to replace things that you have used or sold. *I have to restock the freezer... Over the past*

four weeks, the garrison has been restocked with twenty-one thousand tons of supplies... Turkey allowed the ship to dock temporarily at Istanbul to restock.
2 VOorV To **restock** a park, lake, or woodlands means to put an additional number of animals or fish in it, or to plant more trees in it because there are very few left. *The Forestry Commission will use the gift to restock the damaged woodlands of South-East England.*

restorative /rɪstɔːrətɪv/ **restoratives**
1 ADJ Something that is **restorative** is likely to make you feel better or more cheerful after you have been feeling tired or miserable. *...a hot bath scented with restorative powders.*
2 NC A **restorative** is a drink, especially an alcoholic one, that you feel you need in order to feel better or more refreshed; often used humorously. *Captain Imrie poured himself his first restorative of the morning.*

restore /rɪstɔː/ **restores, restoring, restored**
1 VO To **restore** something means to cause it to exist again or to start being active again. *Troop reinforcements have been sent in to restore order... Diplomatic ties were restored last year... Engineers and soldiers are working to restore electricity and telephone lines to thousands of homes.* ◆ **restoration** /restəreɪʃn/ NU *Their greatest accomplishment would be the restoration of democracy. ...the restoration of law and order.*
2 VO+to To **restore** someone or something to a previous state or condition means to cause them to return to that state or condition. *The Tories were restored to power.*
3 VO When someone **restores** something such as an old building, painting, or piece of furniture, they repair and clean it, so that it returns to its original condition. *They are restoring the grave and bust of Karl Marx in London's Highgate cemetery... It's taken four and a half years to restore the south transept after the fire.* ◆ **restoration** NU *...the restoration of ancient halls and manors.*
4 VO If you **restore** something that was lost or stolen to someone, you return it to them; a formal use. *The measures will also restore church property confiscated after the war.*

restorer /rɪstɔːrə/ **restorers**
NC A **restorer** is someone whose job is to repair houses, furniture, or pictures which have got into a bad condition because they are very old. *The restorers took eight years to carry out the cleaning. ...a craftsman who trained as a picture restorer at the Victoria and Albert Museum in London.*

restrain /rɪstreɪn/ **restrains, restraining, restrained**
1 VOorV-REFL To **restrain** someone means to stop them doing what they were going to do. *Another rescuer had to be restrained from going in to the burning plane... He had been unable to restrain himself from telling Gertrude.*
2 VO To **restrain** something that is growing or increasing means to prevent it from getting too large. *The newspaper warns of a rise in food prices, and called on people to restrain consumption. ...the efforts of governments to restrain inflation... Wage rises should be restrained.*

restrained /rɪstreɪnd/
1 ADJ Someone who is **restrained** is calm and unemotional. *He was polite and restrained. ...the usually rather restrained Mr de Klerk.*
2 ADJ If a speech or piece of writing is **restrained**, it argues its points less forcefully than people might have expected. *Although the message was upbeat, Mrs Thatcher's delivery was fairly restrained... The Times also features the story prominently, but is more restrained.*

restraint /rɪstreɪnt/ **restraints**
1 NCorNU **Restraints** are rules or conditions that limit or restrict someone or something. *The king suffered few restraints on his freedom of action. ...an agreed policy of income and price restraint.*
2 NU **Restraint** is calm, controlled, and unemotional behaviour. *'Dear me,' he said with splendid restraint.*

restrict /rɪstrɪkt/ **restricts, restricting, restricted**
1 VO If you **restrict** something, you put a limit on it to stop it becoming too large. *A third possibility would be to restrict wage increases... The Saudis restricted the number of Iranian pilgrims to 50,000.*
2 VOorV-REFL To **restrict** people or animals means to limit their movements or actions. *...an international agreement to restrict the making and sales of chemical and biological weapons... The device is designed to give patients greater mobility and not restrict them to hospital beds... Some manufacturers were not prepared to restrict themselves voluntarily.*
3 VO+to If you **restrict** someone's activities to one thing, you ensure that they can only do or deal with that thing. *The State should restrict its activities to the maintenance of law and order... I will restrict myself to countries where English is the main language.*
4 VO+to If something **is restricted** to a particular group, only that group can have it or do it. *Membership is restricted to men.*

restricted /rɪstrɪktɪd/
1 ADJ Something that is **restricted** is quite small or limited. *The range of choices is not as restricted as this. ...the restricted field of vision provided by the camera... They spend their day in a restricted space.*
2 ADJ **Restricted** documents can only be read by people who have special permission to do so. *A restricted document has disappeared from an Ulster Defence Regiment base in County Down... He was sacked for passing a restricted document to a journalist.*
3 ADJ A **restricted** place or area is one that is very dangerous or that the authorities wish to keep secret. Only people with special permission are allowed to visit a restricted area. *The town is now a restricted area barred to journalists without special authorization... Diplomats from a number of foreign missions are to have their passes to restricted areas revoked.*
4 See also **restrict**.

restriction /rɪstrɪkʃn/ **restrictions**
1 NCorNU A **restriction** is an official rule that limits what you can do or that limits the amount or size of something. *The government placed restrictions on sales of weapons. ...one large market, where people and goods would move freely without restriction... There is no restriction on filming in the area.*
2 NC You can refer to anything that limits what you can do as a **restriction**. *...small salaries which placed restrictions on our social life.*

restrictive /rɪstrɪktɪv/
ADJ Something that is **restrictive** makes it difficult for you to do what you want to do. *...teenagers eager to escape restrictive home environments.*

rest room, rest rooms
NC A **rest room** is a toilet in a public place such as a restaurant or theatre; used in American English. *Theatergoers needing the rest rooms had to go next door to the Hastings Law School.*

restructure /riːstrʌktʃə/ **restructures, restructuring, restructured**
VO To **restructure** an organization or system means to change the way it is organized. *Mr Bilak also said the journal should be restructured—he said it should reflect a broad range of ideas, and should not avoid topical issues. ...the drive to restructure, democratize and renew all parts of Soviet society.* ◆ **restructuring** NUorN SING *Mr Zhivkov said that it was going to be difficult to implement Bulgaria's programme of restructuring... The pay award will be linked to a radical restructuring of the profession.*

result /rɪzʌlt/ **results, resulting, resulted**
1 NC A **result** is something that happens or exists because of something else that has happened. *I nearly missed the flight as a result of going to Havana... Twice he followed his own advice, with disastrous results... His new politics were the direct result of his experience as Minister of Technology.*
2 V+in If something **results** in a particular situation or event, it causes that situation or event to happen. *Thursday's local elections in much of Britain resulted*

in sweeping gains for the opposition Labour Party...
Trouble in the ambulance and prison services last
year had resulted in huge overtime bills... The use of
such techniques could result in disastrous ecological
changes.
3 v If something **results** from a particular event or
action, it is caused by that event or action. *Four-fifths*
of the damage resulted from bombing. ...the parched
landscape, which has resulted from several years of
drought.
4 NC A **result** is also the situation that exists at the
end of a contest. *The final total of those who voted*
won't be known until the election results are declared.
...the result of the Warrington by-election. ...football
results.
5 NC A **result** is also the number that you get when
you do a calculation. *The result should be calculated*
to three decimal places.
6 NC Your **results** are the marks or grades that you
get for examinations. *You need good A-level results...*
Their exam results are due out in two weeks time.

resultant /rɪzʌltənt/
ADJ ATTRIB **Resultant** means caused by the event just
mentioned; a formal use. *The resultant improvement*
in health totally justified the treatment.

resume /rɪzjuːm/ **resumes, resuming, resumed**; a
formal word.
1 V-ERG If you **resume** an activity or if it **resumes**, it
begins again. *She was ready to resume her duties...*
The music would stop at intervals, then resume after a
while.
2 vo If you **resume** your former place or position, you
return to it. *He resumed his seat.*

résumé /rɛzjumeɪ/ **résumés**; also spelt **resumé**.
1 NC A **résumé** is a short account of something that
somebody has said or written. *Later we received*
further résumés of what she had said.
2 NC A **résumé** is the same as a **curriculum vitae**;
used in American English. *They are able to read the*
résumé to see what their qualifications are... I'm going
to quit tomorrow and go out and get my résumé and
look for a job.

resumption /rɪzʌmpʃn/
NU+SUPP When there is a **resumption** of an activity, it
begins again; a formal word. *A key factor would be*
the resumption of British diplomatic relations with
Iran and Syria. ...a quick resumption of arms
negotiations... They still cherish hopes for a
resumption of US military aid.

resurface /riːsɜːfɪs/ **resurfaces, resurfacing,**
resurfaced
1 vo To **resurface** something such as a road means to
put a new surface on it. *The M6 motorway near*
Coventry is having to be resurfaced because of
damage caused by accidents and fires... The normal
runway at Gatwick is being resurfaced so the
emergency runway was being used in its place.
2 v If something such as an idea or problem
resurfaces, it becomes important or noticeable again.
Traditional resentments and prejudices have
resurfaced. ...a problem that is going to resurface
again and again... This idea was forgotten and
ignored for a period of almost twenty years but
suddenly it's resurfaced again.
3 v If someone **resurfaces** after they have been absent
or busy for a time, they return or start to become
socially active again; an informal use. *She then*
escaped from Lusaka and resurfaced in Zimbabwe... I
had resurfaced in Harvard.
4 v If someone or something that has been under
water **resurfaces**, they come back to the surface of the
water again.

resurgence /rɪsɜːdʒəns/
N SING or NU If there is a **resurgence** of an attitude or
activity, it reappears and grows; a formal word.
There has been a resurgence of small scale guerrilla
activity. ...a period of economic resurgence. ...the
resurgence of democracy throughout the world.

resurgent /rɪsɜːdʒənt/
ADJ Something that is **resurgent** is becoming stronger
and more popular again after a period of decline; a
formal word. *...the resurgent African states... A*

resurgent, more united Labour Party opposition might
not be such a pushover in the next general election.

resurrect /rɛzərɛkt/ **resurrects, resurrecting,**
resurrected
vo When you **resurrect** something that has ended, you
cause it to exist again. *There is not the remotest*
possibility of the government ever resurrecting the
Maplin project.

resurrection /rɛzərɛkʃn/
1 NU The **resurrection** of something that has ended is
the act of making it exist or become active again.
...the resurrection of nationalism. ...the resurrection of
English football as something the nation can feel
proud of.
2 N PROP In Christianity, the **Resurrection** is the event
in which Jesus Christ is believed to have come alive
again three days after he was killed. *He urged*
Christians never to forget that God had triumphed
through the resurrection of Christ.

resuscitate /rɪsʌsɪteɪt/ **resuscitates, resuscitating,**
resuscitated
1 vo If you **resuscitate** someone who has lost
consciousness, for example because they are ill or
have been injured, you cause them to become
conscious again. *Firemen attempted to resuscitate all*
four of the victims but only the woman responded...
He managed to resuscitate his father before the
ambulance service arrived. ◆ **resuscitation** /rɪsʌsɪteɪʃn/
NU *He was given mouth-to-mouth and cardiac*
resuscitation treatment but did not respond.
2 vo If you **resuscitate** something, you make it
become active or successful again. *They promised to*
resuscitate one of the state's most impoverished and
worst performing school systems. ...part of a
programme intended to eliminate subsidies and
resuscitate a moribund economy. ◆ **resuscitation** NU
...the resuscitation of the old political parties in
Eastern Europe.

retail /riːteɪl/
N+N **Retail** is the activity of selling goods to the
public. *We have opened a retail department... The*
original retail price was $80... Retail sales have been
acutely affected by slower consumer spending.

retailer /riːteɪlə/ **retailers**
NC A **retailer** is a person or business that sells goods
to the public. *B and Q and several other big retailers*
have been campaigning for some time to be allowed to
sell general goods on Sundays. ...a well-known High
Street retailer.

retail price index
N SING The **retail price index** is a list of prices of
typical goods which shows how much the cost of living
changes from one month to the next. *The retail price*
index announced on Friday showed inflation up by
0.6% in September.

retain /rɪteɪn/ **retains, retaining, retained**; a formal
word.
1 vo If you **retain** something, you keep it. *He has*
retained close links with that country ever since... We
are fighting to retain some independence.
2 vo If an object or substance **retains** heat or a liquid,
it continues to contain it. *Water retains heat much*
longer than air.

retainer /rɪteɪnə/ **retainers**
1 NC A **retainer** is a fee that you pay someone in
order to make sure that they will be available to do
work for you if you need them to. *The offer of a*
retainer from Biancone was too good to refuse. ...a one
hundred dollar retainer agreement.
2 NC A **retainer** is also a reduced rent that you pay
for a rented room or flat while you are away, in order
to make sure that you can use it in the future. *A*
retainer may be charged for keeping the student's
room over the vacation.
3 NC A servant who has been with one family for a
long time can be referred to as a **retainer**. *Her*
arrival had just been announced by the faithful
retainer. ...family retainers.

retake, retakes, retaking, retook, retaken;
pronounced /riːteɪk/ when it is a verb and /riːteɪk/ when
it is a noun.
1 vo When a military force **retakes** a place or

building which it has lost in a war or battle, it captures it again. *The last village had just been retaken... Government troops have attacked and retaken a hotel which was taken over by rebel soldiers.*
2 NC A **retake** is a scene in a film that has been photographed again because it needed to be changed or improved. *We all had to go back and do a retake.*
3 VO If you **retake** an exam, you take it again because you failed it the first time. *Children who do badly will not have to retake the examination, the education department said.* ▶ Also NC *Limits will be placed on the number of exam retakes students can sit. ...'A' level and 'O' level retakes.*

retaliate /rɪtælieɪt/ **retaliates, retaliating, retaliated**
V If you **retaliate** when someone harms you, you harm them in return. *...the ability to retaliate during an attack... They retaliated by changing the venue for the meeting.* ◆ **retaliation** /rɪtælieɪʃn/ NU *It was agreed that immediate retaliation was necessary.*

retaliatory /rɪtæliətəri/
ADJ If you take **retaliatory** action, you try to harm someone who has harmed you; a formal word. *At the back of Mr Hurd's mind must be the risk of retaliatory action. ...a large retaliatory air and land attack.*

retard /rɪtɑːd/ **retards, retarding, retarded**
VO If something **retards** a process or development, it makes it happen more slowly. *The children's emotional development had been retarded by traumatic experiences.*

retardation /riːtɑːdeɪʃn/
NU **Retardation** is the process of making something happen or develop more slowly; a formal word. *The women in their trial were known to be at risk of foetal growth retardation from previous pregnancies. ...the possibility of economic retardation for generations to come.*

retarded /rɪtɑːdɪd/
ADJ **Retarded** people are less advanced mentally than most people of their age. *Her younger daughter was mentally retarded... They know they aren't retarded— they just can't read very well.*

retch /retʃ/ **retches, retching, retched**
V If you **retch**, your stomach moves and you make a noise as if you are vomiting. *The thought made him retch.*

retd
ADJ after N **Retd** is a written abbreviation for 'retired'. It is used after someone's name to indicate that they have retired from the army, navy, or air force. *Maj Gen George Grantham, retd.*

retell /riːtel/ **retells, retelling, retold**
VO If you **retell** a story, you write it, tell it, or present it again, often in a different way from its original form. *Why did Pinter choose this very curious way of retelling John Fowles's novel?... The tale has been told and retold many times before.*

retention /rɪtenʃn/
NU The **retention** of something is the keeping of it; a formal word. *They voted in favour of the retention of capital punishment... Mr Hussey admitted they had a problem concerning recruitment and retention of staff in some areas... Each blanket gives 90% heat retention.*

retentive /rɪtentɪv/
ADJ If you have a **retentive** memory or mind, you are able to remember things very well and keep a lot of facts in your mind. *...his extraordinarily retentive memory for verse.*

rethink /riːθɪŋk/ **rethinks, rethinking, rethought**
VO, V, or V-REPORT If you **rethink** something such as a plan or a policy, you think about it again and change it. *This forced us to rethink all of our plans... You'll have a chance to rethink and to reinvest in three months... Today's impasse may cause some members to rethink whether they should support drilling for more oil.*

reticence /retɪsəns/
NU **Reticence** is unwillingness to talk about what you know or what you feel; a formal word. *He broke out of his normal reticence and told me the whole story.*

reticent /retɪsənt/
ADJ If you are **reticent** about something, you do not talk about it. *She was always extremely reticent about her colleagues.*

reticule /retɪkjuːl/ **reticules**
NC A **reticule** is a type of small handbag; an old-fashioned word.

retina /retɪnə/. The plural form can be **retinae** /retɪniː/ or **retinas**.
NC Your **retina** is the part of your eye at the back of your eyeball. It receives the image that you see and then sends the image to your brain. *Jackson recently suffered a detached retina but he's reported to have been given medical clearance to box again.*

retinal /retɪnl/
ADJ ATTRIB **Retinal** is used to refer to the condition, treatment, or function of a person or animal's retina; a technical term. *Many of them suffered retinal burns. ...the retinal image.*

retinue /retɪnjuː/ **retinues**
NC A **retinue** of people is the group of servants, friends, or assistants who travel with an important or powerful person. *He strode past with his retinue of aides. ...the tight security surrounding the Emir and his retinue.*

retire /rɪtaɪə/ **retires, retiring, retired**
1 V When older people **retire**, they leave their job and stop working. *Women, unlike men, retire at sixty... They had decided to retire from farming.*
2 V To **retire** also means to go to bed; a formal use. *She retired early with a good book.*

retired /rɪtaɪəd/
ADJ A **retired** person is an older person who has left his or her job and has stopped working. *...a retired Army officer.*

retiree /rɪtaɪəriː/ **retirees**
NC A **retiree** is someone who has left their job and has stopped working; used in American English. *Many of the residents are retirees on fixed incomes worrying about the growing cost of living... Chrysler has roughly one retiree for each active worker.*

retirement /rɪtaɪəmənt/
1 NU **Retirement** is the time when a worker retires. *Since my retirement, I have felt more energetic.*
2 NU **Retirement** is also the period in a person's life after they have retired. *...the house that he had bought for his retirement.*

retiring /rɪtaɪərɪŋ/
ADJ Someone who is **retiring** is shy and avoids meeting other people. *She was a shy, retiring girl.*

retold /riːtəʊld/
Retold is the past tense and past participle of **retell**.

retook /riːtʊk/
Retook is the past tense of **retake**.

retort /rɪtɔːt/ **retorts, retorting, retorted**
V-REPORT, V-QUOTE, or V To **retort** means to reply angrily; used in written English. *Lady Sackville retorted that if they came, she would leave... An obviously angry Mr Shultz retorted, 'To have you consider my country to be untrustworthy and unreliable is going further than I would like to go.'... Mrs Thatcher retorted with a staunch defence of the measures.* ▶ Also NC *...a sharp retort.*

retouch /riːtʌtʃ/ **retouches, retouching, retouched**
VO If you **retouch** something such as a painting or photograph, you restore or improve it by painting over parts of it. *He said the photographs had been retouched to include a sign.*

retrace /rɪtreɪs/ **retraces, retracing, retraced**
VO If you **retrace** your steps or **retrace** your way, you use the same route to return to where you started from. *Stella retraced her steps toward the entrance.*

retract /rɪtrækt/ **retracts, retracting, retracted**; a formal word.
1 VO If you **retract** something that you have said or written, you say publicly that you did not mean it. *At his trial, he retracted his confession... The US adviser has since retracted his testimony.*
2 V-ERG If a part of a machine **retracts** or **is retracted**, it is moved inwards so that it no longer sticks out. *The lift-off was abandoned with less than a minute to go when part of the launch tower failed to retract*

properly... *A needle carrying thread is pushed through, and the thread is caught on the other side of the fold when the needle is retracted.*

retractable /rɪtræktəbl/
ADJ **Retractable** parts of a machine can be moved back into a different place or position. *All the planes had retractable undercarriages... The watering can has a retractable spout.*

retraction /rɪtrækʃn/ **retractions**
NC A **retraction** is a statement that you make when you want to say that you no longer mean what you said earlier. *His retraction was published in several newspapers... A federal judge ordered the organization to mail a retraction to everyone who had received the original pamphlet.*

retread /riːtred/ **retreads**
NC A **retread** is a tyre that is made from an old tyre which has been given a new outer surface.

retreat /rɪtriːt/ **retreats, retreating, retreated**
1 V If you **retreat** from someone or something, you move away from them; a literary use. *Betsy and I retreated to the edge of the field.*
2 V When an army **retreats**, it moves away from an enemy in order to avoid fighting. *They retreated a few kilometres... Reports from the area say that the army appears to have retreated.* ▸ Also NCorNU *It appears that the retreat began a few hours after the bombing raid... They can be starved into retreat.*
3 NC A **retreat** is a quiet place where you go to rest or to do something in private. *They met at a woodland retreat.*

retrial /riːtraɪəl/ **retrials**
NC A **retrial** is a second trial that someone has, because the jury at the first trial could not reach a decision or because the first trial was not properly conducted. *Judges may sometimes be reluctant to believe that fellow judges could possibly have made a mistake, and so refuse to order a retrial—however strong the evidence.*

retribution /retrɪbjuːʃn/
NU **Retribution** is punishment for a crime; a literary word. *...the fear of retribution... The Phillipine's Consul General has hailed the legal initiative as a long awaited chance to exact full retribution for decades of alleged criminal activity.*

retributive /rɪtrɪbjʊtɪv/
ADJ ATTRIB **Retributive** actions or powers involve punishing people; a formal word. *There is concern that there could be retributive violence against conservative whites by blacks angry at Mr Lubowski's death. ...a lifelong retributive vendetta.*

retrieval /rɪtriːvl/
1 NU The **retrieval** of information from a computer is the process of getting it back. *...data retrieval... It can be linked to a printer or computer, allowing long-term storage of readings for retrieval and analysis at a later date.*
2 NU The **retrieval** of something is the process of getting it back from a particular place, especially from a place where it should not be. *The mission will deal with the retrieval of equipment abandoned in Venezuela... The intensity of the fighting has prevented the retrieval of bodies from the centre of the battle zone.*

retrieve /rɪtriːv/ **retrieves, retrieving, retrieved**; a formal word.
1 VO If you **retrieve** something, you get it back from a particular place, especially from a place where it should not be. *I ran back to my room and retrieved my bag... Part of a cargo door that came off a jet last year has been found and retrieved from the floor of the ocean.*
2 VO If you **retrieve** a situation, you bring it back into a more acceptable state. *Mediators are still trying to retrieve the situation, but the latest ceasefire lasted barely two hours.*
3 VO To **retrieve** information from a computer means to get it back. *It stores this data within its memory, where it can be retrieved and analysed at any time... It is possible to retrieve information that has been previously stored in the network.*

retriever /rɪtriːvə/ **retrievers**
NC A **retriever** is a dog that is often trained and used by hunters to bring back birds and animals which have been shot. *Nancy Kelly lives in San Mateo and breeds golden retrievers.*

retroactive /retrəʊæktɪv/
ADJ If a decision or action is **retroactive**, it is intended to take effect from a date in the past; a formal word. *...a fifty per cent increase in salaries retroactive to the beginning of August.*

retrograde /retrəgreɪd/
ADJ You describe an action as **retrograde** when you think that it makes a situation worse rather than better; a formal word. *The move was held to be an economically retrograde step.*

retrogress /retrəgres/ **retrogresses, retrogressing, retrogressed**
V If an organization or process **retrogresses**, it goes back to an earlier and less efficient stage in its development; a formal word. *Civilization remained static or retrogressed instead of sustaining the original impetus.*

retrogressive /retrəgresɪv/
ADJ If an action or idea is **retrogressive**, it returns to old ideas or beliefs and does not take advantage of recent progress; a formal word. *...a fundamental and retrogressive change in the whole basis of industrial relations.*

retrospect /retrəspekt/
When you consider something in **retrospect**, you think about it some time after it has happened when you may be able to understand it more clearly. *In retrospect, what I had done was clearly unjustifiable.*

retrospective /retrəspektɪv/
1 ADJ **Retrospective** feelings or opinions concern things that happened in the past. *...a retrospective view of what went wrong.*
2 ADJ **Retrospective** laws or legislation take effect from a date earlier than the date when the law or legislation was passed. *I don't think we've ever had retrospective legislation of this sort before... The decision will apply from next April, and will not be retrospective.* ◆ **retrospectively** ADV *He argued in Cabinet for the change in personal savings limits to be applied retrospectively.*
3 NCorN+N A **retrospective** is an exhibition of work done by an artist over many years, rather than his or her most recent work. *David Hockney was 50 last July, and 1988 sees a major retrospective of his work now showing in Los Angeles... The occasion is being marked by a major retrospective exhibition of his work.*

return /rɪtɜːn/ **returns, returning, returned**
1 V When you **return** to a place, you go back there. *He returned home several hours later... Her husband left for work one morning and did not return.*
2 NU+POSS Your **return** is your arrival back at a place. *On his return Haldane reported to the Cabinet.*
3 VO If you **return** something that you have taken or borrowed, you put it back or give it back. *We returned the books to the shelf... He borrowed my best suit and didn't return it.*
4 NU You can refer to the giving back of something as its **return**. *Greece will be offered the return of these treasures as a goodwill gift.*
5 VO If you **return** something such as a smile, you smile back at someone who has smiled at you. If you **return** someone's feelings, you feel the same way towards them as they feel towards you. *He didn't return their greetings... She was looking for somebody to return her affection.*
6 VO If someone such as a soldier **returns** fire, they shoot at someone who has already begun firing at them. *Demonstrators fired shots at police, forcing them to return fire... He said the helicopters would only return fire if shot at.*
7 V If a feeling or situation **returns**, it happens again. *If the pain returns, the treatment is repeated... After nine months, the rains returned.*
8 N SING+SUPP You can refer to the reappearance of a feeling or situation as its **return**. *...the return of better times.*

9 V+*to* If you **return** to a subject, you start talking about it again. If you **return** to an activity, you start doing it again. *We shall return to this theme in Chapter 7... After lunch, Edward returned to his gardening.*
10 V+*to* If you **return** to a state you were in before, you start being in that state again. *...the groans of wounded men returning to consciousness.*
11 N SING+*to* You can refer to a change back to a former state as a **return** to that state. *He referred to the Party's hopes for a return to power.*
12 VO When a judge or jury **returns** a verdict, they announce whether a person is guilty or not; a legal use. *The jury took only six minutes to return a guilty verdict... The Coroner has urged the jury to return a verdict of accidental death.*
13 NC A **return** is also the same as a **return ticket**. *The first-class return is about £74.*
14 NCorNU The **return** on an investment is the profit you get from it. *Companies seek higher returns by investing in other corporations... With the return on any share investment likely to be less than the rate of inflation, there is little encouragement for the small investor.*
● **Return** is used in these phrases. ● If you do something **in return** for what someone has done for you, you do it because of what they did. *They had nothing to give in return.* ● You say '**many happy returns**' to wish someone a happy birthday. ● If you have reached **the point of no return**, you have to continue with what you are doing and it is too late to stop. *When the Wall did come down, Europe passed the point of no return, and no-one could doubt that a political revolution was under way.*

returnee /rɪtɜːniː/ **returnees**
NC A **returnee** is a person who returns to the country where they were born, usually after they have been away for a long time. *In South Africa, a formal repatriation of political exiles begins with a planeload of returnees arriving today from Zambia.*

returning officer, returning officers
NC A **returning officer** is an official who is responsible for arranging an election in a particular town or district and who formally announces the result. *Apply for nomination papers to your local returning officer.*

return match, return matches
NC A **return match** is the second of two matches that are played between two sports teams. *France has made three changes to the team which was beaten at Avignon last month for the return match at Leeds on Sunday.*

return ticket, return tickets
NC A **return ticket** is a ticket for a train, bus, or aeroplane that allows you to travel to a particular place and then back again. *He exchanged his return ticket to Vienna for one to Dusseldorf.*

reunion /riːjuːniən/ **reunions**
1 NC A **reunion** is a party attended by members of the same family, school, or other group who have not seen each other for a long time. *A few years later, there was a class reunion. ...a family reunion... He had a reunion with veterans of the aircraft carrier he served on during World War II.*
2 NC A **reunion** is also a meeting of people who have been separated from each other. *It was an incredible reunion—his family hadn't seen him since before the invasion... There was an emotional reunion with relatives.*

Réunion /riːjuːniən/
Réunion is a territory of France in the Indian Ocean, between Madagascar and Mauritius. It was declared a French possession in 1642. Réunion exports sugar, rum, and oil of geranium. Tourism is an important industry. ◆ **Réunionnais, Réunionese** /reɪuːniɒneɪ, riːjuːniəniːz/ N, ADJ
▪ *religion:* Christianity (mainly Roman Catholic)
▪ *language:* French (official), Creole ▪ *currency:* French franc ▪ *capital:* Saint-Denis ▪ *population:* 597,000 (1990) ▪ *size:* 2,512 square kilometres.

reunite /riːjuːnaɪt/ **reunites, reuniting, reunited**
1 VO If you **are reunited** with your family or friends, you meet them again after being separated from

them. *For the hundreds who were reunited with their families, it was an emotional homecoming... Mr Smith was reunited with his wife and two daughters at Heathrow airport.*
2 VO To **reunite** a divided organization or country means to cause it to be united again. *Both men are committed to reopening negotiations with the Turkish Cypriot community on reuniting the divided land... He worked to reunite the Labour movement.*

re-use, re-uses, re-using, re-used; pronounced /riːjuːs/ when it is a noun and /riːjuːz/ when it is a verb.
1 NU The **re-use** of materials involves using them again after they have already been used once, rather than throwing them away. *It can be sterilized ready for re-use... A large number of babies have been infected by the re-use of contaminated hypodermic needles.*
2 VO When you **re-use** something, you use it again instead of throwing it away. *Much of the stone has been re-used in rebuilding.*

rev /rev/ **revs, revving, revved**
V-ERG When you **rev** the engine of a stationary vehicle or when it **revs**, you increase the engine speed by pressing the accelerator. *He revved the motor and then roared off... I heard the sound of an engine revving up.*

Rev /rev/
Rev is a written abbreviation for 'Reverend'. *...the Rev David Drew.*

revalue /riːvæljuː/ **revalues, revaluing, revalued**
1 VO To **revalue** a price or payment means to increase its amount so that its value stays roughly the same in comparison with other things, even if there is inflation. *Your earnings are revalued to keep pace with the general rise in earnings nationally. ...the debt would be revalued each year in line with inflation... The government revalued the old assets.* ◆ **revaluation** /riːvæljueɪʃn/ NU *...the consolidation and revaluation of their holdings.*
2 VO When a country **revalues** its currency, it increases its value so that it can buy more foreign currency than before. *The Israeli government has revalued the country's currency for the second time in a week.* ◆ **revaluation** NU *Adjustments are needed—they have to have revaluation and devaluation from time to time. ...the progressive revaluation of the dollar.*
3 VO If you **revalue** something, you examine it again and decide what you think is good or bad about it. *They have been trying to encourage people to revalue natural medicines. ...an inability to revalue what one sees because of commitment to previous methods.* ◆ **revaluation, revaluations** NU+SUPP or NC+SUPP *...the cultural revaluation of decorative arts. ...a revaluation by China of its policy towards Tibet.*

revamp /riːvæmp/ **revamps, revamping, revamped**
VO If someone **revamps** a system, group, or organization, they make changes to it in order to try and improve it; an informal word. *The system has been revamped considerably.* ◆ **revamped** ADJ ATTRIB *The revamped management has been trying to sort out the mess.* ◆ **revamping** N SING+SUPP *They were concerned with the revamping of their social frameworks.*

revanchism /rɪvænt∫ɪzəm/
NU **Revanchism** is a country's policy of trying to regain land that it previously lost control of; a formal word. *Romania emerged from the 1914-18 war twice as large as before, but felt threatened by Hungarian and Soviet revanchism.*

Revd
Revd is a written abbreviation for 'Reverend'. *In his sermon the rector, the Revd Alan Brooksbank, paid tribute to the fortitude of the boy's parents.*

reveal /rɪviːl/ **reveals, revealing, revealed**
1 VOorV-REPORT To **reveal** something means to make people aware of it. *They were not ready to reveal any details of the arrest... A newspaper had once revealed that he'd wanted to marry his cousin.*
2 VO If you **reveal** something that has been out of sight, you uncover it so that people can see it. *She drew the curtains aside to reveal beautiful gardens...*

The morning fog cleared to reveal a deserted city.
revealing /rɪviːlɪŋ/
1 ADJ A **revealing** action or statement tells you something that you were not aware of. *He had nothing very revealing to say... How we use words and language can be very revealing.*
2 ADJ **Revealing** clothes show a lot of your body. *All the actresses in the Spanish film wear unbelievably revealing negligées and low-cut gowns.*

reveille /rɪvælɪ/
NU or N SING **Reveille** is the time when soldiers have to get up in the morning. In military camps, a short tune is played on trumpets or drums to wake them up. *Several minutes before the usual five-thirty reveille, the whistle sounded... The drummer had sounded the reveille.*

revel /rɛvl/ **revels, revelling, revelled;** spelt **reveling, reveled** in American English.
v If you **revel** in a situation or experience, you enjoy it very much. *She seemed to revel in her success... The Labour Party, revelling in the government's discomfiture, has come up with its own compromise.*

revelation /rɛvəleɪʃn/ **revelations**
1 NC **Revelations** are interesting facts that are made known to people. *His book offers no illuminating personal revelations... Tax inspectors have been investigating the club's finances following revelations in a Sunday newspaper last year.*
2 N SING If an experience is a **revelation** to you, it makes you aware of something that you did not know before. *The whole episode was a revelation to him of how poor the family had been.*

reveller /rɛvələ/ **revellers;** spelt **reveler** in American English.
NC **Revellers** are people who are enjoying themselves in a noisy and often drunken way; an old-fashioned word. *The town stays packed with revellers most of the night.*

revelry /rɛvəlri/
NU **Revelry** is noisy and often drunken enjoyment; an old-fashioned word. *...all this drinking and merriment and high-spirited revelry.*

revenge /rɪvɛndʒ/ **revenges, revenging, revenged**
1 NU **Revenge** involves hurting someone who has hurt you. *They had taken their revenge by blowing up his house... It's thought the killings could have been revenge attacks following the murder of a migrant worker on Sunday.*
2 V-REFL If you **revenge** yourself on someone who has hurt you, you hurt them in return; a formal use. *She will revenge herself on those who helped him to escape... Tory MPs were clearly shaken by Mr Lawson's intervention and by the extent of his willingness to revenge himself on Mrs Thatcher.*

revengeful /rɪvɛndʒfl/
ADJ Someone who is **revengeful** wants to take their revenge on someone who has hurt or harmed them. *He looked angry now, almost revengeful.*
◆ **revengefully** ADV *He tore up her photograph savagely, revengefully.*

revenue /rɛvənjuː/ **revenues**
1 NU or N PL **Revenue** is the money that a government or organization receives from people. *The editor was concerned at the drop in advertising revenue... A recession would reduce government tax revenues... Oil revenues are vital to both countries.*
2 See also **Inland Revenue**.

reverberate /rɪvɜːbəreɪt/ **reverberates, reverberating, reverberated**
1 v When a loud sound **reverberates**, it echoes through a place; a literary word. *Several miles outside Kabul the mountainous region reverberated with sounds of heavy artillery and rockets... The roar of another explosion reverberated in the sky.*
2 v If actions, events, or ideas **reverberate**, they have a powerful, far-reaching effect which lasts a long time. *The consequences are still reverberating on the internal political scene... The thrust of the court's decision will reverberate beyond the United States.*

reverberation /rɪvɜːbəreɪʃn/ **reverberations;** a formal word.
1 NC A **reverberation** is a serious effect that follows a sudden, dramatic event. *His action was not a self-contained incident; its reverberations would affect us all. ...the enormous reverberation of his downfall.*
2 N PL **Reverberations** are the shaking and echoing effect that you hear after a loud sound has been made. *The reverberations could be heard for miles.*

revere /rɪvɪə/ **reveres, revering, revered**
VO If you **revere** someone, you respect and admire them greatly; a formal word. *...her dead mother, whose memory she revered.* ◆ **revered** ADJ *He was a revered figure with a national reputation.*

reverence /rɛvərəns/
NU **Reverence** is a feeling of great respect for someone or something. *The sect teaches reverence for all life.*

Reverend /rɛvərənd/
Reverend is a title used before the name of a member of the clergy. *...the Reverend John Lamb.*

reverent /rɛvərənt/
ADJ If your behaviour is **reverent**, you show great respect for someone or something. *We filed past the tomb in a reverent manner.* ◆ **reverently** ADV *She laid the book reverently on the desk.*

reverential /rɛvərɛnʃl/
ADJ If someone's feelings or actions are **reverential**, they feel respect, admiration, and awe for someone or something else; a formal word. *He uttered the name with the most reverential respect... Their mood was reverential. ...a reverential atmosphere.*

reverie /rɛvəri/ **reveries**
NC or NU A **reverie** is a kind of daydream in which you think about pleasant things or events; a literary word. *The Colonel snapped out of his reverie. ...sitting on a train and rocked into reverie by the rhythm of the wheels.*

reversal /rɪvɜːsl/ **reversals**
NC When there is a **reversal** of a process or policy, it is changed to the opposite process or policy. *Fortunately there was a reversal of this tendency. ...a reversal of the country's former policy of self-sufficiency.*

reverse /rɪvɜːs/ **reverses, reversing, reversed**
1 VO To **reverse** a process, decision, or policy means to change it to its opposite. *By then it may be too late to take effective measures to reverse the greenhouse effect... They put pressure on British Steel and the government to reverse the decision... The farmers want to see this trend reversed.*
2 VO If you **reverse** the order of a set of things, you arrange them in the opposite order, so that the first thing comes last. *You could reverse the order—start with the Z and work back towards the A.*
3 VO If you **reverse** the positions or functions of two things, you change them so that each thing has the position or function that the other one had. *In this play the traditional sex roles are reversed.*
4 V-ERG When a car **reverses** or when you **reverse** it, you drive it backwards. *The street was so narrow that cars which entered it had to reverse out again... As he started to reverse the car into a workbay, the bomb exploded.*
5 NU If your car is in **reverse**, you have changed gear so that you can drive it backwards. *I threw the truck into reverse... The car went into reverse and came back down towards everybody.*
6 ADJ ATTRIB **Reverse** means opposite to what has just been described. *In the past ten years I think we've seen the reverse process... British scientists argue that the reverse problem in the lower atmosphere— the creation of ozone by human activity—could be just as serious.*
7 N SING The **reverse** is the opposite of what has just been mentioned. *You may think we have been making a profit. In fact the reverse is true... Couples should be offered tax advantages if they have children, not the reverse.*
8 If you **reverse the charges** when you make a telephone call, the person you are calling pays for the call. *Ring me up when you get there—reverse the charges if you like.*

reverse gear, reverse gears
NU or NC A vehicle's **reverse gear** is the gear which you

use in order to make the vehicle go backwards. *I found it difficult to get into reverse gear... The van had two reverse gears.*

reversible /rɪvɜːsəbl/
1 ADJ If a process or decision is **reversible**, it can be stopped or changed at any time. *These decisions are reversible under favourable circumstances... Is vasectomy reversible?*
2 ADJ Clothing that is **reversible** has been made so that it can be worn with either side on the outside. *I was wearing a reversible winter jacket.*

reversing light, reversing lights
NC A **reversing light** is a white light on the back of a motor vehicle which shines when the vehicle is being driven backwards. *Very few cars had reversing lights in those days.*

reversion /rɪvɜːʃn/
NU+*to* **Reversion** to a former state, system, or kind of behaviour is a change back to it; a formal word. *...this reversion to pre-scientific attitudes. ...Hong Kong's reversion to Chinese rule in 1997.*

revert /rɪvɜːt/ **reverts, reverting, reverted**
V+*to* When people or things **revert** to a former state, system, or type of behaviour, they go back to it; a formal word. *He was reverting rapidly to adolescence... Areas cleared for farming sometimes revert to forest later.*

review /rɪvjuː/ **reviews, reviewing, reviewed**
1 NC A **review** is an article in a newspaper or magazine, or an item on television or radio, in which someone gives their opinion of something such as a new book or play. *...a review of Lord Harewood's autobiography. ...book reviews.*
2 VO When someone **reviews** something such as a new book or play, they write an article or give a talk on television or radio in which they express their opinion of it. *His autobiography has just been published in Britain, and here to review it is Martin Haslett... His book about Afghanistan is reviewed here by Anthony Hyman, a writer on the region.*
3 NCorNU When there is a **review** of a situation or system, it is formally examined in order to decide whether changes are needed. *According to the International Press Institute's annual review, 1988 was a bleak year for freedom of the press. ...a review of public expenditure... In three years time the treaty is due for review.*
4 VO When a situation or system **is reviewed**, it is formally examined in order to decide whether changes are needed. *By law, state pensions must be reviewed once a year... There were many things that would have to be reviewed and evaluated.*
5 When something **comes up for review**, the time arrives for it to be formally examined to see whether changes are needed. When it is **under review**, it is being examined in this way. *The present extradition act comes up for review in parliament on Tuesday... He said that security arrangements were under review.*
6 VO If you **review** a situation, you consider it carefully. *Some of the nurses at St Thomas's in London are calling on the Royal College of Nursing to review its prohibition of strike action... The government has been urged to review its level of support for low-income families.*

reviewer /rɪvjuːə/ **reviewers**
NC A **reviewer** is a person who reviews books, plays, art exhibitions, and so on. *Maeve Binchy was our reviewer of 'The Temptation of Eileen Hughes'.*

revile /rɪvaɪl/ **reviles, reviling, reviled**
VO If you **revile** someone or something, you insult them because you hate and despise them; a formal word. *They had been reviled and misunderstood by almost everyone.*

revise /rɪvaɪz/ **revises, revising, revised**
1 VO If you **revise** something, you alter it in order to make it better or more correct. *The judges may revise their selection process... He said he knew about the article before it was published, and had revised and corrected it... The government has revised its estimate of the cost of rebuilding the devastated areas.*
2 VorVO When you **revise** for an examination, you

read things again in order to learn them thoroughly. *I've been revising for the last three days... I was revising Dickens last night.*

revision /rɪvɪʒn/ **revisions**
1 NCorNU When there is a **revision** of something, it is altered in order to improve it. *They're discussing a complete revision of the timetable... The Shops Act is in need of revision.*
2 NU When you do **revision**, you read things again in order to learn them for an examination. *I've got to do some revision.*

revisionism /rɪvɪʒənɪzəm/
NU **Revisionism** refers to something such as a political theory or religious belief which has developed from but is different from an earlier theory or belief. Revisionism is often thought to be wrong and dangerous by the people who support the original theory or belief. *For some more conservative elements in Moscow, calls for economic independence smack of heresy and revisionism... There are also worrying signs of revisionism in the affair.*
♦ **revisionist, revisionists** NC *On the one hand there are traditionalists, on the other there are revisionists who want the Church to adapt to the modern world.*

revisit /riːvɪzɪt/ **revisits, revisiting, revisited**
VOorV If you **revisit** a place, you go back there after you have been away for a long time. *As many people head home for the holidays, we revisit scenes of childhood memories to find out how they've changed... A 'Times' reporter, revisiting Moscow, says that although the city looks exactly the same as five years ago, one has only to open the newspapers and everything has changed.*

revitalization /riːvaɪtəlaɪzeɪʃn/; also spelt **revitalisation**.
NU The **revitalization** of something is the act or process of making it more active, lively, or successful. *Venezuela again underlined its support for what it called the revitalization of Panamanian democracy. ...a programme of economic revitalization through a free trade agreement.*

revitalize /riːvaɪtəlaɪz/ **revitalizes, revitalizing, revitalized**; also spelt **revitalise**.
VO To **revitalize** something means to make it more active, lively, or successful; a formal word. *...its plan to revitalise the economy... Bulgaria is making a second attempt to revitalize large rural areas of its territory which have become depopulated.*

revival /rɪvaɪvl/ **revivals**
NUorNC When there is a **revival** of something, it becomes active again. *Inflation may start to rise with the revival of trade. ...a revival of interest in the supernatural.*

revivalism /rɪvaɪvəlɪzəm/
NU **Revivalism** is a movement that tries to make a particular religion more popular and more influential. *By this time, militant Hindu revivalism had become more than a creed.*

revivalist /rɪvaɪvəlɪst/ **revivalists**
NC A **revivalist** is a person who tries to make a particular religion more popular and more influential. *Hindu revivalists want to pull the mosque down and replace it with a Hindu temple.* ▶ Also ADJ ATTRIB *...the religious revivalist movements. ...a revivalist ministry.*

revive /rɪvaɪv/ **revives, reviving, revived**
1 V-ERG When something such as a feeling or a practice **revives** or **is revived**, it becomes active or successful again. *My spirits revived as we drove out into the countryside... They failed to fulfil their promises to revive the economy.*
2 V-ERG When you **revive** someone or when they **revive**, they become conscious again after they have fainted or been unconscious. *They had difficulty in reviving him... He slowly began to revive.*

revivify /riːvɪvɪfaɪ/ **revivifies, revivifying, revivified**
VO To **revivify** a situation, event, or activity means to make it become more active, lively, or efficient; a formal word. *Sport would play a major role in helping to revivify the nation.*

revocation /revəkeɪʃn/
NU+SUPP **Revocation** is the cancelling of an

agreement, law, or title so that it is no longer legal or official; a legal term. *Mr Ghising has demanded the immediate withdrawal of paramilitary troops and the revocation of the anti-terrorist laws. ...a revocation of his agreement to attend the talks.*

revoke /rɪvəʊk/ **revokes, revoking, revoked**
vo When someone in authority **revokes** something such as an order, they cancel it; a formal word. *Pretoria was given a United Nations mandate to administer the territory but refused to hand over power when the mandate was revoked... Any companies which do not comply will have their contracts suspended or revoked.*

revolt /rɪvəʊlt/ **revolts, revolting, revolted**
1 NCorNU A **revolt** is a violent attempt by a group of people to change their country's political system. *...the Peasants' Revolt of 1381... BBC correspondents say the city appears to be in revolt.*
2 v When people **revolt**, they use violence to try to change a country's political system. *Large sections of the army revolted against the civil government.*

revolting /rɪvəʊltɪŋ/
ADJ Something that is **revolting** is horrible and disgusting. *The smell was quite revolting... It's revolting, it's disgusting, it's cruel and it's got to stop!*

revolution /rɛvəluːʃn/ **revolutions**
1 NCorNU A **revolution** is an attempt by a large group of people to change their country's political system, often by using force. *Our leaders realised soon after the East European revolutions that it was their turn. ...the fiftieth anniversary of the Russian revolution... France seemed to be on the verge of revolution.*
2 NC+SUPP A **revolution** is also an important change in a particular area of human activity. *...the Industrial Revolution. ...the revolution in communications.*

revolutionary /rɛvəluːʃənəʳri/ **revolutionaries**
1 ADJ **Revolutionary** activities are intended to cause a political revolution. *They had fled as a result of their revolutionary activities... He was once more on trial, this time on charges of sabotage and conspiracy to overthrow the government by revolutionary means.*
2 NC A **revolutionary** is a person who tries to cause a revolution or who takes part in one. *...subversive revolutionaries... The revolutionaries who took over the centres of power were unable to set up a creditable committee to represent them.*
3 ADJ **Revolutionary** ideas and developments involve great changes in the way something is done or made. *They have succeeded where other scientists have always failed, by adopting a revolutionary new approach to the problem. ...a revolutionary change in the way cars are manufactured.*

revolutionize /rɛvəluːʃənaɪz/ **revolutionizes, revolutionizing, revolutionized**; also spelt **revolutionise.**
vo When something **revolutionizes** an activity, it causes great changes in the way it is done. *Our ideas will revolutionize the film industry.*

revolve /rɪvɒlv/ **revolves, revolving, revolved**
1 V+around or V+round If you say that someone's life **revolves** around something, you mean that that thing is the main feature of their life. *Rural life revolved around agriculture. ...a home background which revolves round a completely different language and culture.*
2 V+around or V+round If a discussion **revolves** around a particular topic, it is mainly about that topic. *Ultimately the debate revolved around the respective rights of the president and the congress to regulate US foreign trade... The discussion revolved round three topics.*
3 v When something **revolves**, it moves or turns in a circle around a central point or line. *...the discovery that the earth revolved around the sun.* ◆ **revolving** ADJ ATTRIB *They were watering the ground with big revolving sprinklers.*

revolver /rɪvɒlvəʳ/ **revolvers**
NC A **revolver** is a kind of gun that you hold in your hand. *A shot was fired from a police-issue revolver, injuring a man in the stomach... They were armed with a revolver and shotgun.*

revolving door, revolving doors
1 NC A **revolving door** consists of four glass doors which turn together around a vertical post. *The manager locked up the two large revolving doors at the front a couple of hours before the usual closing time.*
2 N SING A **revolving door** is also a situation in which people in a particular organization or institution leave and are replaced very quickly or in which two things or people are exchanged very easily. *It was a revolving door—they'd bring in players on Tuesday and they'd be starting on Sunday.*

revue /rɪvjuː/ **revues**
NC A **revue** is a light theatrical entertainment consisting of songs, dances, and jokes about recent events. *I was asked to arrange a Christmas revue.*

revulsion /rɪvʌlʃn/
NU **Revulsion** is a strong feeling of disgust or disapproval. *Germ warfare has always been regarded with revulsion.*

reward /rɪwɔːd/ **rewards, rewarding, rewarded**
1 NCorNU A **reward** is something that you are given because you have done something useful or good. *...a reward for outstanding service... They work with no thought of reward.*
2 VO To **reward** someone means to give them something because they have done something useful or good. *People should be rewarded for special effort... They rewarded the winners with gifts of fruit and flowers.*

rewarding /rɪwɔːdɪŋ/
ADJ Something that is **rewarding** gives you a lot of satisfaction. *...rewarding jobs.*

rewind /riːwaɪnd/ **rewinds, rewinding, rewound**
VOorV When you **rewind** the tape on a tape recorder or a video recorder, you make the tape go backwards so that you can play it again. *He rewound the tape and settled back to see 'Psycho' once more... Only one tape recorder will be storing information and each time it stops to rewind, scientists will lose some observations.*

rewire /riːwaɪəʳ/ **rewires, rewiring, rewired**
VO To **rewire** a building or electrical device means to put a new system of electrical wiring into it. *Since the place had to be rewired, they took out all the central lights... To change a program, one literally had to rewire part of the machine.*

rework /riːwɜːk/ **reworks, reworking, reworked**
VO If you **rework** something such as an idea or a piece of writing, you think about it again and make changes to it in order to improve it or bring it up to date. *He reworked the income schedules... Eleven year old timetables may have to be taken out of dusty covers and reworked before the flights actually restart.*

rewrite, rewrites, rewriting, rewrote, rewritten; pronounced /riːraɪt/ when it is a verb and /riːraɪt/ when it is a noun.
VO If you **rewrite** a piece of writing, you write it again in a different way in order to try and improve it. *The historians were busy rewriting the textbook based on the basis of all the new revelations that were coming out... Matura has rewritten the play and retitled it 'The Trinidadian Sisters'.* ▶ Also NC *This is the first major rewrite of the immigration laws in 66 years... All speeches have to be submitted seven days in advance, which means that rewrites are not possible.*

Reykjavík /reɪkjəviːk/
Reykjavík is the capital of Iceland and its largest city. Population: 97,000 (1989).

Reynolds, Albert /ælbət renəldz/
Albert Reynolds became Prime Minister of Ireland and leader of Fianna Fáil in 1992, following the resignation of Charles Haughey. He was elected to the Irish Parliament in 1977. He was Minister for Posts and Telegraphs and Transport from 1979 to 1981, for Industry and Energy in 1982, for Industry and Commerce from 1987 to 1988, and for Finance from 1988 to 1991. Born: 1932.

rhapsodize /ræpsədaɪz/ **rhapsodizes, rhapsodizing, rhapsodized;** also spelt **rhapsodise.**
VorV-QUOTE If you **rhapsodize** about someone or something, you express great delight or enthusiasm

about them; a literary word. *It is bad to rhapsodize about a child when he or she is present... 'You've got wonderful hair,' he kept rhapsodizing.*

rhapsody /ˈræpsədi/ **rhapsodies**
NC A **rhapsody** is a piece of music which is irregular in form, but very passionate and flowing. *...Liszt's Second Hungarian Rhapsody.*

rhesus /ˈriːsəs/ **rhesuses**
NC A **rhesus** or **rhesus monkey** is a small short-tailed monkey from Northern India which is often used in scientific experiments. *The studies so far have been limited to a primate—the rhesus monkey.*

rhetoric /ˈretərɪk/
NU **Rhetoric** is speech or writing that is meant to convince and impress people. *North Korea has reserved some of its harshest rhetoric for what they see as a blatant betrayal by a member of the communist world... Militant rhetoric both from the right and from the left is hampering the chances of peace in South Africa.*

rhetorical /rɪˈtɒrɪkl/
1 ADJ A **rhetorical** question is used in order to make a statement rather than to get an answer. *He asked whether the party was capable of preventing society slipping into chaos. It was of course a rhetorical question.* ◆ **rhetorically** ADV *'What,' asked Mr Shultz rhetorically, 'would be the effect of that decision?'*
2 ADJ **Rhetorical** language is intended to be grand and impressive. *He described the speech as a rhetorical success but a diplomatic failure. ...rhetorical exchanges between the superpowers.*

rhetorician /ˌretəˈrɪʃn/ **rhetoricians**
NC A **rhetorician** is a person who is good at public speaking or who is trained in the art of rhetoric. *He was an ancient Greek—a rhetorician.*

rheumatic /ruːˈmætɪk/
ADJ **Rheumatic** diseases and pains are caused by rheumatism. *...the inflammation that is found in the joints of patients with rheumatic diseases.*

rheumatic fever
NU **Rheumatic fever** is a serious disease which causes fever, a sore throat, and swelling and pain in your joints. *He had been seriously ill with rheumatic fever and could no longer travel easily.*

rheumaticky /ruːˈmætɪki/
ADJ Someone who is **rheumaticky** suffers from rheumatism; an informal word. *Only now he realized how rheumaticky he was becoming. ...his rheumaticky fingers.*

rheumatism /ˈruːmətɪzəm/
NU **Rheumatism** is an illness that makes your joints or muscles stiff and painful. *Arthritis and rheumatism are two of the oldest diseases known.*

rheumatoid arthritis /ˈruːmətɔɪd ɑːˈθraɪtɪs/
NU **Rheumatoid arthritis** is a chronic disease that causes your joints to swell up and become painful. *It is in cases where rheumatoid arthritis has attacked the elbow that joint replacement is most often useful.*

rheumy /ˈruːmi/
ADJ If someone has **rheumy** eyes, their eyes are moist and watery, usually because they are very ill or old; a literary word. *'I got on well with my Ma', she said, her rheumy eyes weeping a little.*

rhinestone /ˈraɪnstəʊn/ **rhinestones**
NC A **rhinestone** is a very bright, colourless stone that is used in cheap jewellery and ornaments. *She wore dark glasses that had rhinestones on their frame. ...rhinestone earrings.*

rhino /ˈraɪnəʊ/ **rhinos**. The plural form can be either **rhinos** or **rhino**.
NC A **rhino** is the same as a **rhinoceros**. *...a survey to find out how many rhino were left in the country.*

rhinoceros /raɪˈnɒsərəs/ **rhinoceroses**. The plural form can be either **rhinoceroses** or **rhinoceros**.
NC A **rhinoceros** is a large animal from Africa or Asia with one or two horns on its nose. *Poachers are said to have killed three rhinoceroses, an elephant and a lion.*

rhododendron /ˌrəʊdəˈdendrən/ **rhododendrons**
NC A **rhododendron** is a bush with large pink or purple flowers. *These days, flowers like lilies and rhododendrons are often found in gardens.*

rhombus /ˈrɒmbəs/ **rhombuses**
NC A **rhombus** is a geometrical shape which has four equal sides but is not a square; a technical term in mathematics. *The watering can is shaped something like a rhombus, a slanted rectangular shape, leaning towards the pouring end.*

rhubarb /ˈruːbɑːb/
NU **Rhubarb** is a plant with long red stems which can be cooked and eaten. *I had rhubarb tart with loads of cream.*

rhyme /raɪm/ **rhymes, rhyming, rhymed**
1 V-RECIP If one word **rhymes** with another or if two words **rhyme**, they have a very similar sound. *She called him Guppy, to rhyme with puppy. ...ten-syllable lines whose last syllables rhyme.*
2 NC A **rhyme** is a word which has a similar sound to another word. *...two words he could not find a rhyme for.*
3 NC A **rhyme** is also a short poem with rhyming words at the ends of its lines. *...children's games and rhymes.* ● See also **nursery rhyme**.
4 NU **Rhyme** is the use of rhyming words as a technique in poetry. *She had a gift for rhythm and rhyme.*
5 If you say that something happens **without rhyme or reason**, you mean that it happens even though there seems to be no sensible reason for it. *I think that people who can do things like that without rhyme or reason are not good people.*

rhymed /raɪmd/
ADJ ATTRIB **Rhymed** poems or pieces of text contain lines or words which rhyme with each other. *...an enormous poem in rhymed couplets. ...rhymed sayings.*

rhyming slang
NU **Rhyming slang** is a colloquial form of language in which you do not use the normal word for something, but say a word or phrase that rhymes with it instead. For example, in Cockney rhyming slang 'apples and pears' means 'stairs'.

rhythm /ˈrɪðəm/ **rhythms**
1 NCorNU A **rhythm** is a regular movement or beat. *...the rhythm of the drums... J J Cale uses rhythm for the opposite effect in his music... the effects of shift work or jet lag on body rhythms.*
2 NC A **rhythm** is also a regular pattern of changes, for example changes in the seasons or the tides. *These biological rhythms of plants are very much tied in with the timing of flowering.*

rhythm-and-blues
NU **Rhythm-and-blues** is a popular musical style developed in the 1940s from blues music, but using electrically amplified instruments. *She started as a rhythm-and-blues singer in small clubs in St. Louis in the late 1950s.*

rhythmic /ˈrɪðmɪk/
ADJ If a movement or sound is **rhythmic**, it is repeated at regular intervals, forming a regular pattern or beat. *The machine made a soft rhythmic sound.* ◆ **rhythmically** /ˈrɪðmɪkli/ ADV *The cradle rocked rhythmically to and fro.*

rhythm method
N SING The **rhythm method**, is a form of contraception where a couple try to prevent pregnancy by having sex only at times when the woman is not likely to become pregnant. *As you know, there are several forms of birth control: contraceptives, the rhythm method, and also sterilisation.*

rib /rɪb/ **ribs, ribbing, ribbed**
1 NC Your **ribs** are the curved bones that go from your backbone to your chest. *One officer was treated for cracked ribs... Bodzianowski was troubled by a rib injury.*
2 NC A **rib** is a long, curved piece of wood or metal that is part of the structure of a building, a boat, or an aeroplane and that makes the structure strong. *Experts believe that some of these steel ribs may have been taken out and replaced with explosives.*
3 VO If you **rib** someone, you tease them in a friendly way; an informal use. *I had been ribbing him about something he had written for our local newspaper.* ◆ **ribbing** NU *This assumption is the source of some*

good-natured ribbing from his clientele.
4 See also **ribbed**.

ribald /ˈrɪbld/
ADJ **Ribald** remarks are rather rude and refer to sex in a humorous way; an old-fashioned word. *Pioneers such as Gillray and Cruikshank turned the cartoon into a rude and ribald form of political expression. ...ribald laughter.*

ribaldry /ˈrɪbldri/
NU **Ribaldry** is humour that is considered to be rather rude because it refers to sex; an old-fashioned word. *He was roused to laughter by her ribaldry.*

riband /ˈrɪbənd/ **ribands**; also spelt **ribband**.
NC A **riband** is a ribbon used for fastening things, or for decoration; an old-fashioned word.

ribbed /ˈrɪbd/
ADJ Something such as material that is **ribbed** has a raised pattern of parallel lines on it. *...ribbed black stockings. ...ribbed jumpers.*

ribbon /ˈrɪbən/ **ribbons**
1 NCorNU A **ribbon** is a long, narrow piece of cloth used for fastening things or for decoration. *The cross hangs from a dark red ribbon. ...a piece of ribbon.*
2 NCorNU A typewriter **ribbon** is the long, narrow piece of cloth containing ink that is used in a typewriter to make typed letters visible. *... a machine which re-inks ribbons used in printers, word processors and typewriters.*

rib-cage, **rib-cages**
NC Your **rib-cage** is the structure of ribs in your chest. *Instead he shows them how to produce deep breathing from much lower down in the rib-cage.*

riboflavin /ˌraɪbəʊˈfleɪvɪn/
NU **Riboflavin** is a vitamin that occurs in green vegetables, milk, fish, eggs, liver, and kidney.

rib-tickler /ˈrɪb ˌtɪkᵊlə/ **rib-ticklers**
NC A **rib-tickler** is a very funny joke or story; an old-fashioned, informal word.

rice /raɪs/
NU **Rice** is a food consisting of white or brown grains which you cook and eat. The plant from which rice is taken is also called **rice**. *Stocks of rice, the staple food, are now exhausted... The storm may have severely damaged Bangladesh's winter rice crop.*

rice paper
NU **Rice paper** is very thin paper made from the straw of rice plants. Cakes can be baked on it and it can be eaten. *Line a baking sheet with rice paper.*

rice pudding, **rice puddings**
NUorNC **Rice pudding** is a food made by baking rice in milk and sugar. It is usually eaten as a dessert.

rich /rɪtʃ/ **richer**, **richest**; **riches**
1 ADJ A **rich** person has a lot of money or valuable possessions. *She was extremely rich... Our father was a very rich man.*
2 N PL The **rich** are rich people. *Robin Hood is a popular folk hero who used to rob the rich to feed the poor... Action is needed to make sure that it's not only the rich who benefit from the country's booming economy.*
3 ADJ A **rich** country has a strong economy and therefore many of the people who live there have a high standard of living. *I think the government is partly to blame for encouraging consumerism before the country was rich enough to handle the situation... There is hunger in many parts of the world, even in rich countries... He is a staunch advocate of making the rich countries look after the poor more effectively.*
4 N PL **Riches** are valuable possessions or large amounts of money. *I can give up riches and pleasure. ...US comic book heroes who rose from rags to riches.*
5 ADJ PRED+in If something is **rich** in a desirable substance or quality, it has a lot of it. *The sea bed is rich in buried minerals... The story is rich in comic and dramatic detail.* ◆ **richness** NU *...the richness of Asian culture.*
6 ADJ ATTRIB A **rich** deposit of a mineral or other substance consists of a large amount of it. *Rich deposits of lignite have been discovered in the north-west of Belfast.*
7 ADJ **Rich** soil contains large amounts of substances that make it good for growing crops or flowers in. *It*

was one of Mozambique's most fertile areas—the soil is rich and well watered.
8 ADJ **Rich** food contains a lot of fat or oil. *He was prone to indigestion after rich restaurant meals.*
9 ADJ If a place has a **rich** history, its history is very interesting. *The town has a rich social history.*

richly /ˈrɪtʃli/
1 ADV You use **richly** to say that someone deserves or has been given something valuable for what they have done. *It was a richly deserved honour... I had seldom been so richly rewarded.*
2 ADV You also use **richly** to say that a place or thing has a large amount of elaborate or valuable things. *These libraries are richly equipped with games and books. ...the richly carved wooden screen.*

Richter Scale /ˈrɪktə skeɪl/
N SING The **Richter Scale** is a scale from 0 to 8 which is used for measuring how severe earthquakes are. *The quake registered more than six on the Richter Scale.*

rick /rɪk/ **ricks**, **ricking**, **ricked**
1 NC A **rick** is a large pile of hay or straw that is built in a regular shape and usually has a thatched top. *Some ricks were nine yards long by five yards wide.*
2 VO If you **rick** your neck or your back, you hurt it by pulling or twisting it in an unusual way. *I ricked my neck and missed a game.*

rickets /ˈrɪkɪts/
NU **Rickets** is a disease that children sometimes get when their food does not contain enough Vitamin D. It makes their bones soft and causes their liver and spleen to become too large. *...a child who is suffering from rickets.*

rickety /ˈrɪkəti/
ADJ A **rickety** building, machine, or piece of furniture is likely to collapse or break; an informal word. *Everyone had a bike of some kind, usually a rickety old thing.*

rickshaw /ˈrɪkʃɔː/ **rickshaws**
NC A **rickshaw** is a cart, often pulled by hand, that is used in parts of Asia for carrying passengers. *I took a rickshaw back to Hong Ku.*

ricochet /ˈrɪkəʃeɪ/ **ricochets**, **ricocheting**, **ricocheted**
V When a bullet **ricochets**, it hits a surface and bounces away from it. *Reporters were injured by bullets ricocheting off the hotel.*

rid /rɪd/ **rids**, **ridding**. The form **rid** is used in the present tense and is also the past tense and past participle of the verb.
1 When you **get rid** of something or someone that you do not want, you take action so that you no longer have them. *She bathed thoroughly to get rid of the last traces of make-up... NATO is being pressed to get rid of more nuclear weapons... We had to get rid of the director.*
2 VO+of If you **rid** a place or yourself of something unpleasant or annoying, you take action so that it no longer exists, or no longer affects you; a formal use. *We must rid the country of this wickedness... He had rid himself of his illusions.*
3 ADJ PRED+of If you are **rid** of someone or something unpleasant or annoying, they are no longer with you or affecting you. *Eric was glad to be rid of him.*

riddance /ˈrɪdns/
You say **good riddance** to indicate that you are glad that someone has left; an informal expression. *One paper carried a picture of a senior United Nations official on his departure from Thailand, with the caption 'Good riddance'.*

ridden /ˈrɪdn/
Ridden is the past participle of **ride**.

riddle /ˈrɪdl/ **riddles**
1 NC A **riddle** is a puzzle in which you ask a question that seems to be nonsense but which has a clever or amusing answer. An example is 'Why do you never get hungry in the desert? Because of the sandwiches (sand which is) there.'
2 NC You can describe something that is puzzling as a **riddle**. *One of the investigators told the BBC that now the only riddle remaining to be solved is: who was behind the murder?*

riddled /rɪdld/
1 ADJ PRED+*with* If something is **riddled** with holes, it is full of them. *A few vehicles escaped without a scratch, but hundreds were riddled with the deadly little holes that cluster bombs make... Clay along the sides of the canal is riddled with natural cracks and fissures.*
2 ADJ PRED+*with* If something is **riddled** with bullets, a lot of bullets have been fired into it. *Afterwards the car was riddled with bullets.*
3 ADJ PRED+*with* If something is **riddled** with undesirable qualities or features, it is full of them. *The Lord Chief Justice said the evidence in the case was riddled with inconsistencies. ...a country riddled with prejudices against the handicapped.*

ride /raɪd/ rides, riding, rode, ridden
1 V Oor V When you **ride** a horse, you sit on it and control its movements. *Every morning he used to ride his mare across the fields... I rode in the Grand National.*
2 V Oor V A When you **ride** a bicycle or motorcycle, you control it and travel along on it. *Two men riding a motorcycle threw two hand grenades at an army checkpoint... He rode round the campus on a bicycle.*
3 V A When you **ride** in a vehicle such as a car, you travel in it. *That afternoon he rode in a jeep to the village.*
4 NC A **ride** is a journey on a horse or bicycle, or in a vehicle. *...the bus ride to Worcester.*
5 N SING+SUPP If someone has a rough **ride**, they do not find it easy to do something, because they face opposition. If they have an easy **ride**, they find it fairly easy to do something, because they do not face much opposition. *The government is likely to face a rough ride in parliament... Analysts say neither state can expect an easy ride in the months and years to come.*
6 If someone **has taken** you **for a ride**, they have deceived or cheated you; an informal expression. *They think he's taken the British for a ride.*

ride out PHRASAL VERB If a government, leader, or company **rides out** a crisis, they manage to survive it without suffering serious harm. *For the moment, the government hopes to ride out the international storm over the killing of the men.*

ride up PHRASAL VERB If a skirt or dress **rides up**, it moves upwards, out of its proper position. *This skirt always rides up when I'm sitting down.*

rider /raɪdə/ riders
NC A **rider** is someone who is riding a horse, a bicycle, or a motorcycle. *The line of floats, bands and horseback riders stretches on for three miles.*

ridge /rɪdʒ/ ridges
1 NC A **ridge** is a long, narrow piece of raised land. *We drove up a hillside and finally stopped on a high ridge.*
2 NC A **ridge** is also a raised line on a flat surface. *He was counting the ridges in the wet sand.*

ridged /rɪdʒd/
ADJ Something that is **ridged** has raised lines on its surface. *His forehead was ridged in concentration. ...muscles ridged like rope.*

ridicule /rɪdɪkjuːl/ ridicules, ridiculing, ridiculed
V O If you **ridicule** someone, you make fun of them in an unkind way. *He is liable to be teased and ridiculed.* ▸ Also NU *His prophecy was greeted with a good deal of ridicule.*

ridiculous /rɪdɪkjʊləs/
ADJ Something that is **ridiculous** is very foolish. *It would be ridiculous to pretend that there were no difficulties... They charge you a ridiculous price.*
◆ **ridiculously** SUBMOD *He let out his house at a ridiculously low rent.*

riding habit, riding habits
NC A **riding habit** is a long dress with a full skirt, or a jacket and long skirt, that women used to wear when they were riding horses.

rife /raɪf/
ADJ PRED If something bad or unpleasant is **rife**, it is happening very frequently; a formal word. *Bribery and corruption in the government service were rife.*

riffle /rɪfl/ riffles, riffling, riffled
V+*through* or V O If you **riffle** through the pages of a book, or **riffle** them, you turn them over quickly, without reading all that is written on them. *He opened the book at random and riffled through the pages... He opened Hamilton's work and riffled the pages.*

riffraff /rɪfræf/
NU or N SING If someone refers to a group of people as **riffraff**, they mean that they think they are worthless and disreputable; an old-fashioned word. *...poets, painters, and other such riffraff.*

rifle /raɪfl/ rifles, rifling, rifled
1 NC A **rifle** is a gun with a long barrel. *The pillion passenger pulled out an automatic rifle and shot him in the head.*
2 V O When someone **rifles** a place, they steal everything they want from it. *He rifled the dead man's wallet.*
3 V+*through* If you **rifle** through things, you make a quick search among them. *The doctor rifled through the papers.*

rifleman /raɪflmən/ riflemen /raɪflmən/
NC A **rifleman** is someone, especially a soldier, who is skilled in the use of a rifle. *The photograph shows a lone rifleman racing out of an open door. ...the Cape Mounted Riflemen.*

rifle range, rifle ranges
NC A **rifle range** is a place where you can practise shooting with a rifle. *We would run a few miles down to the rifle range and receive instructions in using a rifle.*

rift /rɪft/ rifts
1 NC A **rift** between friends or colleagues is something such as a difference of opinion, which stops them from having a good relationship. *One view is that he was driven to suicide because of a serious rift with his father... There have been signs of a growing rift between the President and the Prime Minister.*
2 NC A **rift** is also a split that appears in the ground. *The Jemez Mountains face Santa Fe across the rift.*

rig /rɪg/ rigs, rigging, rigged
1 V O If someone **rigs** something such as an election, they dishonestly arrange it so that they achieve the result that they want. *Opposition parties claimed the vote was rigged.*
2 NC A **rig** is a large structure that is used when drilling for or extracting oil or gas from the ground or the sea bed. *The valves have already been fitted to a high percentage of the 160 rigs in the area... The report contains 106 recommendations on improving the safety of offshore oil rigs.*

rig up PHRASAL VERB If you **rig** something **up**, you make it and fix it in place using any available materials. *He had rigged up a listening device.*

Riga /riːgə/
Riga is the capital of Latvia and its largest city. Population: 915,000 (1989).

rigging /rɪgɪŋ/
1 NU **Rigging** is the act or process of dishonestly arranging something such as an election so that you achieve the result that you want. *She told a news conference that rigging had occurred in some forty to fifty constituencies... Allegations of ballot rigging are frequent.*
2 NU The ropes which support a ship's masts and sails are referred to as the **rigging**. *...light which hangs in the rigging of a boat.*

right /raɪt/ rights, righting, righted
1 ADJ or ADV If something is **right**, it is correct and in accordance with the facts. *You get full marks for getting the right answer... You are French, is that right?... I hope I'm pronouncing the name right.*
2 ADJ PRED If someone is **right** about something, they are correct in what they say or think about it. *Lally was right about the repairs which the cottage needed.*
◆ **rightly** ADV *The arts are, as Geoffrey rightly said, underfinanced.*
3 ADJ If something such as a choice, action, or decision is the **right** one, it is the best or most suitable one. *I thought it was the right thing to do... Clare is obviously the right person to talk to about it.*
4 ADJ PRED If a situation isn't **right**, there is something unsatisfactory about it. *She sensed that things weren't right between us.*

5 ADJ PRED If someone is **right** to do something, they are morally justified in doing it. *We were right to insist on certain reforms... I don't think it's right to leave children alone in a house.* ♦ **rightly** ADV *Many people are rightly indignant.*

6 NU **Right** is used to refer to actions that are considered to be morally good and acceptable. *One must have some principles, some sense of right and wrong.*

7 ADJ ATTRIB If you refer to the **right** people or places, you are referring to people and places that are socially admired. *He knew all the right people... She liked to be seen in all the right places.*

8 ADJ ATTRIB The **right** side of a piece of material is the side that is intended to be seen when it is made into clothes or furnishings.

9 ADV SEN You say **'Right'** in order to attract someone's attention. *Right, open your mouth, let's have a look.*

10 NC If you have a **right** to do or have something, you are morally or legally entitled to do it or have it. *...the right to strike... They will fight for their rights... It is a constitutional right.*

11 N SING The **right** is one of two opposite directions, sides, or positions. In the word 'to', the 'o' is to the right of the 't'. *On my left was Tony Heard and on my right Allister Sparks.* ▶ Also ADV or ADJ ATTRIB *Turn right off Broadway into Caxton Street... Her right hand was covered in blood.*

12 N COLL In politics, the **Right** is used to refer to the people or groups who support capitalism and conservatism rather than socialism. *The extreme Right is not a newcomer to the French political scene. ...the resurgence of the far Right in Europe.*

13 ADV A **Right** is used to emphasize the precise place or distance that you are talking about. *Our hotel was right on the beach... Stay right here... We took the lift right down to the basement.*

14 ADJ ATTRIB **Right** is also used to emphasize a noun referring to something bad; an informal use. *They've made a right mess of that, haven't they?*

15 ADV A **Right** also means immediately. *I'll be right back... The Music Hall is going to close down right after Easter.*

16 V-REFL If something that has fallen over **rights** itself, it returns to its normal position. *The ship righted itself.*

17 VO To **right** a wrong means to correct it or compensate for it. *We've made progress in righting the wrongs of the past.*

● **Right** is used in these phrases. ● If you **get** something **right**, you do it correctly. *Get the spelling right this time.* ● **Right away** means immediately. *He had written down a list of things to do right away.* ● If you are **in the right**, what you are doing is morally or legally correct. *This was a clear-cut case of the original landowner being in the right.* ● If something should be the case **by rights**, it should be the case, but it is not. *I should by rights speak German—my mother's German—but I only know a few words.* ● If you have a position, title, or claim to something **in your own right**, you have it because of what you are yourself rather than because of other people. *He had emerged as a leader in his own right.* ● to **serve** someone **right**: see serve. ● **on the right side of** someone: see side. ● See also **all right, civil rights, human rights.**

right-about turn, right-about turns
NC A **right-about turn** is a movement that you make that leaves you facing in the opposite direction to the one you started from.

right angle, right angles
1 NC A **right angle** is an angle of 90°. *I'm having trouble visualizing a house that does not have any right angles at all.*
2 If two things are **at right angles**, they form an angle of 90° where they touch. *...four corridors at right angles to each other.*

right-angled
1 ADJ A **right-angled** triangle has one angle which is a right angle.
2 ADJ A **right-angled** bend is a sharp bend that turns

through approximately ninety degrees.

righteous /ˈraɪtʃəs/
ADJ **Righteous** people behave in a way that is morally good and admirable; a formal word. *...a just and righteous king. ...righteous anger.* ♦ **righteousness** NU *Some of us strive for righteousness.* ● See also **self-righteous.**

rightful /ˈraɪtfl/
ADJ ATTRIB Someone's **rightful** possession, place, or role is one which they have a legal or moral right to have; a formal word. *They had been deprived of their rightful share of the property.*

right-hand
ADJ ATTRIB **Right-hand** refers to something which is on the right side. *...a biggish house on the right-hand side of the road.*

right-hand drive
ADJ ATTRIB A **right-hand drive** car, van, or lorry has the steering wheel on the right side, and is designed to be used in countries such as Britain where people drive on the left side of the road. *Even with local number plates, British right-hand drive cars could still be conspicuous.*

right-handed
ADJ **Right-handed** people use their right hand rather than their left hand for activities such as writing or throwing a ball. *There is a larger number of people who are right-handed than left.*

right-hander, right-handers
NC A **right-hander** is someone who uses their right hand rather than their left hand for activities such as writing and painting.

right-hand man, right-hand men
NC If you refer to a man as your **right-hand man**, you mean that he is the person who helps you most in your work. *I'm counting on you being my right-hand man.*

rightist /ˈraɪtɪst/ **rightists**
1 NC A **rightist** is someone who is politically conservative and traditional and supports the ideas of capitalism. *He was able to bring back some of the rightists who had been dismissed.*
2 ADJ ATTRIB **Rightist** ideals, activities, and people are politically conservative and traditional and support or believe in the ideas of capitalism. *The main opposition group is the rightist movement.*

right-minded
ADJ You describe someone as **right-minded** when you think that their opinions or beliefs are correct. *This is something perfectly forgivable by any right-minded person.*

righto /ˈraɪtəʊ/; also spelt **right-ho.**
You say **'righto'** to show that you have heard what someone has said and are willing to do what they want or to do something to please them; used in informal English. *'Drive on,' Mary cried. 'Righto,' he said.*

right-of-centre
ADJ **Right-of-centre** people or political parties support political ideas which are closer to conservatism and a market economy than to socialism. *Some of its nominees suffered clear defeats against right-of-centre candidates.*

right of way, rights of way
1 NU When a car or other vehicle has **right of way**, other traffic must stop for it at a junction or roundabout. *Who has right of way here?*
2 NC A **right of way** is a public path across private land. *Are there any rights of way across the property?*

right-thinking
ADJ ATTRIB **Right-thinking** means the same as **right-minded.** *Every right-thinking young person is going to agree.*

right-wing; spelt **right wing** for the meaning in paragraph 2.
1 ADJ **Right-wing** people support the political ideals of conservatism and capitalism. *...the election of a right-wing government... They are very right-wing... The attack was carried out by right-wing extremists.*
2 N SING The **right wing** of a political party consists of the members who are most strongly in favour of conservatism and capitalism. *...the right wing of the Republican party.*

right-winger, right-wingers
NC A **right-winger** is a person whose political beliefs are closer to conservatism and capitalism than those of other people in the same party. *Despite being denounced by some as a right-winger, he has stuck with Labour through thick and thin.*

rigid /rɪdʒɪd/
1 ADJ **Rigid** laws or systems cannot be changed or varied, and are therefore considered to be rather severe. *Some mothers resented the rigid controls.* ◆ **rigidity** /rɪdʒɪdəti/ NU *...the rigidity of Victorian marriage.*
2 ADJ A **rigid** person cannot or will not change their attitudes, opinions, or behaviour; used showing disapproval. *...the rigid attitude of the Foreign Secretary.*
3 ADJ A **rigid** substance or object is stiff and does not bend easily. *...with permed hair in rigid waves.* ◆ **rigidity** NU *The function of bones is largely to give rigidity.*

rigidly /rɪdʒɪdli/
1 ADV If you stay **rigidly** in one position, you do not move. *I looked rigidly ahead... My features stayed rigidly fixed in the same expression.*
2 ADV If you do something **rigidly**, you do it in a strict way with no possibility of variation or change. *These suggestions must not be interpreted too rigidly.*

rigmarole /rɪgmərəʊl/ **rigmaroles**; an informal word.
1 NC A **rigmarole** is a complicated series of actions that have to be done in a particular activity. *I don't imagine you want to go through all that rigmarole.*
2 NC A **rigmarole** is also a series of pointless or misleading statements. *She told me some rigmarole about the insurance.*

rigor /rɪgə/. See **rigour**.

rigor mortis /rɪgə mɔːtɪs/
NU **Rigor mortis** is stiffness of the joints and muscles in the body of a dead person or animal. *Within a few hours rigor mortis would set in.*

rigorous /rɪgərəs/
ADJ **Rigorous** is used to describe things that are done or carried out thoroughly. *...rigorous controls... We go through rigorous selection procedures.* ◆ **rigorously** ADV *These methods have been rigorously tested over many years.*

rigour /rɪgə/ **rigours**; spelt **rigor** in American English. A formal word.
1 N PL The **rigours** of a situation or way of life are the features that make it unpleasant. *...the rigours of a city winter.*
2 NU **Rigour** is strictness in something such as law or a punishment. *This could change if the Bankruptcy Law is enforced with greater rigour... Trouble makers will be treated with the full rigour of the law... He didn't approach his work with academic rigour.*

rig-out, rig-outs
NC A **rig-out** is a set of clothes, especially clothes that you would not usually wear; an old-fashioned, informal word. *She'd got herself a whole new rig-out for the trip.*

rile /raɪl/ **riles, riling, riled**
VO If someone **riles** you, they make you angry; an informal word. *There are some things he does that really rile me... I don't see any reason why either of us should get riled.*

rim /rɪm/ **rims**
NC The **rim** of a container or round object is its top edge or its outside edge. *...the rim of his glass... Muller's glasses had gold rims.*

rimless /rɪmləs/
ADJ ATTRIB **Rimless** spectacles do not have frames around the lenses. *With his solemn, intelligent face and rimless spectacles he looked just right for the role of distinguished professor.*

rimmed /rɪmd/
ADJ PRED+*with* If something is **rimmed** with a particular colour, it has a border or edge of that colour. *They stood there exhausted, their eyes rimmed with red from the fatigue... I saw my father's thick finger, its nail rimmed with black.*

rind /raɪnd/ **rinds**
1 NCorNU The **rind** of a fruit such as a lemon is its thick outer skin. *...fruit with tough rinds. ...grated lemon rind.*
2 NCorNU The **rind** of cheese or bacon is the hard outer edge. *He never cut the rinds off the rashers. ...cheese rind.*

ring /rɪŋ/ **rings, ringing, rang, rung**. For the meanings in paragraphs 9 and 10, the past tense and past participle is **ringed**.
1 VOorV If you **ring** someone, you phone them. *You must ring the hospital at once... He may ring again.*
2 V-ERG When you **ring** a bell or when a bell **rings**, it makes a sound. *He had to ring the bell several times... In the distance a church bell was ringing.*
3 NC A **ring** is the sound made by a bell. *There was a ring at the door.*
4 V If a place **rings** with a sound, the sound there is very loud; a literary use. *The barn rang with the cries of geese and turkeys.* ● See also **ringing**.
5 N SING You can use **ring** after an adjective to say that something that is mentioned seems to you to have a particular quality. *The books he mentioned had a familiar ring about them... The name had an unpleasant ring to it.*
6 NC A **ring** is also a small circle of metal worn on your finger as an ornament or to show that you are married or engaged. *...a rare gold ring... She still wears the wedding ring he gave her.*
7 NC An object or group of things with the shape of a circle can be referred to as a **ring**. *They formed a ring round him. ...a ring of excited faces.*
8 NC A **ring** is also the enclosed space with seats round it where a boxing match, show jumping contest, or circus performance takes place. *Tonight's contest is his first appearance as a professional boxer in a British ring.*
9 VO If you **ring** something, you draw a circle round it. *I got a map and ringed all the likely villages.*
10 V-PASS If a place is **ringed** with something, it is surrounded by that thing. *...a valley ringed with mountains... The yard has been ringed by riot police.*
11 NC A **ring** is also a group of people who do something illegal together, such as selling drugs or controlling the sale of art or antiques. *Police say they have smashed a drugs ring which specialised in supplying cocaine.*
● **Ring** is used in these phrases. ● If you **give** someone a **ring**, you telephone them; an informal expression. *Give me a ring if you need me.* ● If a statement **rings true**, it seems likely to be true. *The bishop's answers so often ring true.*

ring back PHRASAL VERB If someone phones you and you **ring** them **back**, you then phone them. *He asked if you'd ring him back when you got in.*

ring off PHRASAL VERB If you **ring off** when you are using the phone, you put down your receiver. *The girl laughed and rang off.*

ring out PHRASAL VERB If a sound **rings out**, it is heard loudly and clearly. *The old stable clock rings out ten o' clock.*

ring up PHRASAL VERB If you **ring** someone **up**, you phone them. *He's used the telephone, ringing up at least one different country's leader every day... They are warned of the cost when they ring up.*

ring binder, ring binders
NC A **ring binder** is a document folder made of thick cardboard and often covered in plastic, with metal rings inside which clip open and shut. *Designed around a ring binder in the style of a personal organiser, each Newspack contains over two hundred pages of information.*

ringer /rɪŋə/ **ringers**
1 NC A **ringer** is a person who rings church bells or hand bells, especially as a hobby. *...fellow ringers at St Botolph's Church in the village of Newbold on Avon... There are 40,000 amateur bell ringers in England.*
2 If you say that someone is a **dead ringer** for someone else, you mean that they look exactly like the other person; an informal expression. *He's a dead ringer for the young Sigmund Freud.*
3 NC Someone or something that is entered into a competition under false pretences, especially an

athlete or an animal, is known as a **ringer**. *His horse lost the Derby to a ringer.*

ring finger, ring fingers
NC Your **ring finger** is the third finger of either your left or your right hand. It is the finger on which people wear a wedding ring or engagement ring. *Charlotte rapped on the door with her ring finger.*

ringing /rɪŋɪŋ/
ADJ ATTRIB A **ringing** sound can be heard very clearly. *...clear ringing tones.*

ringleader /rɪŋliːdə/ **ringleaders**
NC The **ringleader** of a group of people who are causing trouble is the person who is leading them. *...the army major who's accused of being the ringleader of this operation.*

ringlet /rɪŋlət/ **ringlets**
NC **Ringlets** are long, loose curls of hair that hang down. *...a solemn little girl in high-buttoned boots and ringlets.*

ringmaster /rɪŋmɑːstə/ **ringmasters**
NC The **ringmaster** in a circus is the person who introduces the different acts. *Some in the circus may resent his success, but the ringmaster says the clown is extraordinary.*

ring road, ring roads
NC A **ring road** is a road that goes round the edge of a town and avoids the centre of it. *The main project will be a ring road linking the new airport with an industrial area on the coast.*

ringside /rɪŋsaɪd/
1 N SING The **ringside** is the area immediately around an area such as a circus ring or a boxing ring. *An usher led them to their seats three rows from the ringside.*
2 ADJ ATTRIB If you have a **ringside** seat or a **ringside** view, you have a clear and uninterrupted view of an event. *We got a ringside view of the procession.*

ringway /rɪŋweɪ/ **ringways**
NC A **ringway** is the same as a **ring road**.

ringworm /rɪŋwɜːm/
NU **Ringworm** is a disease that causes red patches on a person's or animal's skin. *...ointment for a boy who has ringworm.*

rink /rɪŋk/ **rinks**
NC A **rink** is a large area, usually indoors, where people go to skate. *There's a good ice rink in Leeds.*

rinse /rɪns/ **rinses, rinsing, rinsed**
1 VO When you **rinse** something that you have washed, you use clean water to get rid of the soap. *Gordon was washing the glasses in a bowl of soapy water and rinsing them at the sink... Rinse the equipment again with cold water.*
2 VO When you **rinse** something, you wash it quickly, often without using soap. *He rinsed his hands under the tap.* ► Also NC *Just give these a quick rinse.*
rinse out PHRASAL VERB 1 When you **rinse out** something that you have washed, you use clean water to get rid of the soap. *She left them in detergent overnight, then rinsed them out the next morning.*
2 When you **rinse** something **out**, you wash it quickly, often without using soap. *He rinses the container out at the end of the day to be reused.*

riot /raɪət/ **riots, rioting, rioted**
1 NC When there is a **riot**, a crowd of people behave violently in a public place. *In May 1968 there was a wave of student riots... Several people have been killed recently in race riots in suburban areas... Riots are reported to have broken out in the provincial capital.*
2 V When a crowd of people **riot**, they behave violently in a public place. *If food prices are put up too far, the people will riot.* ◆ **rioting** NU *This was followed by days of violent rioting in which over ten people were killed.*

rioter /raɪətə/ **rioters**
NC A **rioter** is someone who takes part in a riot. *Courts dealt with rioters quickly and harshly.*

riot gear
NU **Riot gear** is the special clothing and equipment that is worn or carried by the police when they are trying to control violent crowds. *They were blocked by police in riot gear.*

riotous /raɪətəs/
1 ADJ ATTRIB **Riotous** behaviour is violent and uncontrolled. *He was found guilty of riotous behaviour. ...a riotous mob.*
2 ADJ You can also describe people's behaviour as **riotous** when they do things very enthusiastically. *Both children would come rushing out in a riotous welcome.*

riot police
N PL **Riot police** are police in riot gear who are trying to control violent crowds. *They were eventually driven off by riot police using tear gas.*

rip /rɪp/ **rips, ripping, ripped**
1 V-ERG When something **rips** or **is ripped**, it is torn violently. *The canvas bags had ripped... The poster had been ripped to pieces.*
2 VOA If you **rip** something away, you remove it quickly and violently. *I ripped the phone from her hand... He ripped his shirt off.*
3 NC A **rip** is a long cut or split in something made of cloth or paper. *He had seen the rip in the book.*
rip off PHRASAL VERB If someone **rips** you **off**, they cheat you by charging too much for goods or services; an informal expression. *The local shopkeepers were all trying to rip off the tourists.* ● See also **rip-off**.
rip up PHRASAL VERB If you **rip** something **up**, you tear it into small pieces. *It turned into complete uproar as the opposition members ripped up their ballot papers.*

ripcord /rɪpkɔːd/ **ripcords**
NC A **ripcord** is the cord that you pull in order to open a parachute. *On a couple of occasions—such as when he pulled the wrong ripcord while parachuting—he almost lost his life.*

ripe /raɪp/ **riper, ripest**
1 ADJ **Ripe** fruit or grain is fully grown and ready to be harvested or eaten. *The pears are heavy and ripe.*
2 ADJ PRED+*for* If something is **ripe** for something such as a change, it is ready for it. *Our people are ripe for freedom... The nation was ripe for collapse.*
● **Ripe** is used in these phrases. ● If you say **the time is ripe**, you mean that a suitable time has arrived for something to happen. *The time was ripe to break his silence.* ● If someone lives to a **ripe old age**, they live to be very old. *Most of us live to a ripe old age without getting Alzheimer's disease.*

ripen /raɪpən/ **ripens, ripening, ripened**
V-ERG When crops **ripen** or when the sun **ripens** them, they become ripe. *Genetically engineered crops could ripen quicker. ...a lack of sunshine to ripen crops.*

rip-off, rip-offs
NC If you say that something that you bought was a **rip-off**, you mean that you were charged too much for it; an informal word. *Most motorists think that the new tax is a rip-off.*

riposte /rɪpɒst/ **ripostes, riposting, riposted;** a literary word.
1 NC A **riposte** is a quick response to something that someone has said or done to you. *Lutz Stavenhagen, one of Chancellor Kohl's closest advisors, gave a sharp riposte... They thus threaten a devastating riposte against an aggressor.*
2 V or V-QUOTE If you **riposte**, you respond quickly to something that someone has said or done to you. *Walesa and his supporters riposte by saying they're more in touch with people than the intellectuals of Warsaw are... Plessey had riposted with a plan to take over GEC in a consortium that included America's General Electric... Mrs Thatcher riposted, 'Well, you had better make it one-and-a-half million immediately.'*

ripple /rɪpl/ **ripples, rippling, rippled**
1 NC **Ripples** are small waves on the surface of water caused by the wind or by an object dropping into the water. *...sending out patterns of ripples.*
2 V-ERG When the surface of an area of water **ripples**, a number of small waves appear on it. *...the pond rippling where the wind ruffled through the grass... A gentle breeze rippled the surface of the sea.*
3 N SING+*of* A **ripple** of laughter or applause is a short, quiet burst of it. *...a ripple of amused applause.*

rise /raɪz/ rises, rising, rose, risen
1 v If something **rises**, it moves upwards. *We saw the black smoke rising over the barbed wire... Clouds of birds rose from the tree-tops.*
2 v When you **rise**, you stand up; a formal use. *Dr Willoughby rose to greet him.*
3 v To **rise** also means to get out of bed; a formal use. *They had risen at dawn.*
4 v When the sun or moon rises, it appears from below the horizon. *At this time of year the sun never rises.*
5 v If land **rises**, it slopes upwards. *He followed Jack towards the castle where the ground rose slightly.*
♦ **rising** ADJ ATTRIB *The house was built on rising ground.*
6 v If a sound **rises**, it becomes louder or higher. *His voice rose to a shriek.*
7 v If a sound **rises** from a group of people, it comes from them. *A loud gasp rose from the boys.*
8 v If an amount **rises**, it increases. *Prices rose by more than 10%... The number of complaints has risen sharply... The temperature began to rise.* ♦ **rising** ADJ ATTRIB *...the rising rate of inflation.*
9 NC+SUPP A **rise** in the amount of something is an increase in it. *...the rise in crime. ...price rises. ...a pay rise of about £20 a week.*
10 V+to If you **rise** to a challenge or remark, you respond to it, rather than ignoring it. *He called on Japan to rise to the challenge of the yen's increased weight in the global economy.*
11 v When the people in a country **rise**, they start fighting the people in authority there. *The settlers rose in revolt.* ♦ **rising**, risings NC *...a big peasant rising.*
12 VA If someone **rises** to a higher position or status, they become more important, successful, or powerful. *Bergson rose rapidly to fame.*
13 N SING Someone's **rise** is the process by which they become more important, successful, or powerful. *...the decline of the Liberal Party and the rise of Labour. ...his rise to fame.*
14 If something gives **rise** to an event or situation, it causes it. *This breakthrough could give rise to ethical problems.*
rise above PHRASAL VERB If you **rise above** a problem, you do not allow it to affect you. *She was in continual pain, but rose above it.*
rise up PHRASAL VERB 1 If something **rises up**, it moves upwards. *He could see the smoke from his bonfire rising up in a white column.* 2 When the people in a country **rise up**, they start fighting the people in authority there. *He ended his address with a message to those in Burma who had risen up against the government in 1988.* ● See also **uprising**.
risen /rɪzn/
Risen is the past participle of **rise**.
riser /raɪzə/ risers
1 NC+SUPP An early **riser** is someone who likes to get up early in the morning. A late **riser** is someone who likes to get up late. *I've been an early riser all my life.*
2 NC A **riser** is the flat vertical part of a step or stair.
risible /rɪzəbl/
ADJ If you say that something is **risible**, you are showing contempt for it because you think it is obviously untrue or bad; a formal word. *He said the Minister's denial of any government negligence was risible.*
rising damp
NU If a building has **rising damp**, moisture is getting into the bricks from the outside and is moving upwards, causing damage to the wall. *The basement is badly afflicted by rising damp.*
rising star, rising stars
NC You can refer to someone who is good at their job and who is expected to become successful and well-known in the future as a **rising star**. *At thirty-eight, David Mellor is a rising star on the British political scene.*
risk /rɪsk/ risks, risking, risked
1 NCorNU If there is a **risk** of something unpleasant, there is a possibility that it will happen. *...the risk*

that their men might disappear without trace... There is very little risk of infection. ...a gigantic and costly experiment with a high risk of failure.
2 N SING If something is a **risk**, it might have dangerous or unpleasant results. *Such a response would be an irrational risk... Your television is a fire risk if left plugged in overnight... The rats are becoming a major health risk.*
3 V0orV+ING If you **risk** something unpleasant, you do something knowing that the unpleasant thing might happen as a result. *If it turns down the offer, Pakistan risks an indefinite continuation of the war... They were willing to risk losing their jobs.*
4 V+INGorVO If you **risk** doing something, you do it, even though you know that it might have undesirable consequences. *If you have an expensive rug, don't risk washing it yourself... His bid for freedom was not well planned. He simply decided to risk it.*
5 VO If you **risk** someone's life, you put them in a dangerous position. *She had risked her life to help save mine.*
● **Risk** is used in these phrases. ● To be **at risk** means to be in a situation where something unpleasant or dangerous might happen. *Tens of thousands of Sudanese are at risk of starvation... You're putting my career at risk.* ● If you are doing something **at your own risk**, it will be your own responsibility if you are harmed. *They would interfere at their own risk.* ● If you **run the risk** of doing or experiencing something undesirable or dangerous, you do something knowing that this thing might happen as a result. *We run the risk of confusing the voters.* ● If you **take a risk**, you do something which you know might be dangerous. *I am taking a tremendous risk.*
risky /rɪski/ riskier, riskiest
ADJ If an activity or action is **risky**, it is dangerous or likely to fail. *The whole thing has become too risky... Investing in shares can be a risky business.*
risotto /rɪzɒtəʊ/ risottos
N MASS **Risotto** is an Italian dish of rice cooked with other ingredients such as tomatoes, cheese, and chicken. *I've made a risotto... Would you like some risotto?*
risqué /rɪskeɪ/
ADJ **Risqué** jokes, stories, or actions might be considered slightly rude or offensive because they refer to sex, or make you think about sex. *Madonna's show will be showy, lively, full of risqué dance routines.*
rissole /rɪsəʊl/ rissoles
NC **Rissoles** are round flat pieces of a mixture containing chopped meat or vegetables. Rissoles are cooked in hot fat. *Fry the rissoles in hot oil for six minutes each side until golden brown.*
rite /raɪt/ rites
NC A **rite** is a traditional ceremony carried out by a particular group. *...the rite of circumcision. ...fertility rites.*
ritual /rɪtʃuəl/ rituals
1 NCorNU A **ritual** is a series of actions which are traditionally carried out in a particular situation. *Our society has many rituals of greeting, farewell, and celebration. ...the veil of mystery and ritual which characterizes the Japanese Imperial Household.*
2 ADJ ATTRIB **Ritual** activities happen as part of a ritual or tradition. *...the practice of ritual murder. ...the ritual slaughter of livestock.* ♦ **ritually** ADV *The door of the Commons is ritually slammed in his face before it is opened to summon MPs into the House of Lords.*
ritualistic /rɪtʃuəlɪstɪk/
1 ADJ **Ritualistic** activities or words follow the same pattern every time they are used. *He came out with some ritualistic nonsense about 'the challenge of change'.*
2 ADJ **Ritualistic** activities are a regular and fixed part of a religious service or other ceremony. *...ritualistic words of prayer.*
rival /raɪvl/ rivals, rivalling, rivalled; spelt rivaling, rivaled in American English.
1 NC Your **rival** is someone who you are competing with. *His newspaper outstripped its rivals in*

circulation... *He has built up a considerable lead over his main rival.* ► Also ADJ ATTRIB *Fighting broke out between rival groups... He was beaten up by supporters of a rival candidate.*
2 VO If one thing **rivals** another, they are both of the same standard or quality. *Of all the flowers in the garden few can rival the lily... They found luxuries and opulence rivalling many of the great buildings of Europe.*

rivalry /ˈraɪvlri/ **rivalries**
NCorNU **Rivalry** is active competition between people. *...the intense rivalries between groups and personalities... Burr's rivalry with Hamilton began in those days.*

riven /ˈrɪvn/
ADJ Something that is **riven** has been divided or split and is therefore weaker than it was; a formal word. *...a country riven by deep divisions of race and ideology.*

river /ˈrɪvə/ **rivers**
NC A **river** is a large amount of fresh water flowing continuously in a long line across land. *The river is a vital waterway for the entire region... There will also be a raft race on the river Thames... The Jordan River runs through the center of this no-man's land.*

river bank, river banks
NC A **river bank** is the land along the edge of a river. *We walked along the river bank... They followed the river bank downstream.*

river bed, river beds
NC A **river bed** is the ground which a river flows over. *Their waste flows openly through the dry river beds of this town.*

river blindness
NU **River blindness** is a serious disease which causes inflammation and sometimes blindness. It is found in parts of Africa and tropical America. *Millions of people have lost their sight through river blindness caused by the bite of a river-breeding fly.*

riverside /ˈrɪvəsaɪd/
N SINGorN+N The **riverside** is the area of land by the banks of a river. *The cutting down of trees in riverside areas has led to the silting up of the rivers.*

rivet /ˈrɪvɪt/ **rivets, riveting, riveted**
1 VO If you **are riveted** by something, it fascinates you. *I was riveted by his presentation.* ♦ **riveting** ADJ *...a riveting television documentary.*
2 NC A **rivet** is a type of bolt used for holding pieces of metal together. *Since the accident all the plane's rivets have been tested using electronic equipment.*

rivulet /ˈrɪvjʊlət/ **rivulets**
NC A **rivulet** is a small stream; a literary word. *A small group of youths is said to have crossed the small bridge spanning the rivulet.*

Riyadh /riːˈjɑːd/
Riyadh is the capital of Saudi Arabia. It is the headquarters of the Gulf Co-operation Council. Population: 500,000 (1988).

RN
RN is a written abbreviation for 'Royal Navy'; the navy of the United Kingdom.

roach /rəʊtʃ/ **roaches**
NC A **roach** is the same as a **cockroach**; used in American English. *He found his brother in a seedy, roach-infested apartment in Denver.*

road /rəʊd/ **roads**
1 NC A **road** is a long piece of hard ground built between two places so that people can drive or ride easily from one place to the other. *...the road from Belfast to Londonderry... The ruins were accessible by road. ...Tottenham Court Road... Miles from the nearest main road, it's a picturesque hilltop village.*
2 NC+SUPP The **road** to a particular result is a means of achieving it. *The road to capitalism could be particularly bumpy... The only road to peace is through direct face-to-face negotiations... The road is still long, but this is a step in the right direction.* ● If you are **on the road to** a particular result, you are acting in a way which makes it likely that you will achieve it. *One observer says we may be on the road to peace... We're on the road to catastrophe.*

road block, road blocks
NC A **road block** is a barrier which is put across a road to prevent people or traffic going along the road. *The IRA men were shot at a police road block in County Armagh... Police will set up dozens of road blocks on main roads.*

roadhog /ˈrəʊdhɒg/ **roadhogs**
NC A **roadhog** is someone who drives in an inconsiderate fashion, often in a way that causes danger to other drivers; an informal word.

roadhouse /ˈrəʊdhaʊs/ **roadhouses**
NC A **roadhouse** is a pub or restaurant on a road outside a city, whose customers are usually people who are on a long journey; used in American English. *We had a few drinks in a roadhouse off the main highway.*

road sense
NU **Road sense** is the ability to make good judgements and decisions about how you walk or drive through traffic, so that you do not cause any accidents to yourself or to others.

roadside /ˈrəʊdsaɪd/ **roadsides**
NC The **roadside** is the area at the edge of a road. *Women dipped buckets into muddy puddles at the roadside to get drinking water for their children.*

roadster /ˈrəʊdstə/ **roadsters**
NC A **roadster** is a car with no roof and only two seats; an old-fashioned word. *On this day in 1927 the Model A roadster was introduced as the successor to the Model T.*

Road Town /rəʊd taʊn/
Road Town, on Tortola Island, is the capital of the British Virgin Islands and its largest town. Population: 2,500 (1987).

roadway /ˈrəʊdweɪ/ **roadways**
NC People sometimes refer to a road or track as a **roadway** when they are considering it as a means of getting somewhere. *The roadways are completely inadequate for the 500,000 or 600,000 people you get moving through a city from the Olympics... The men were working in an underground roadway when they were trapped by falling rocks.*

roadworks /ˈrəʊdwɜːks/
N PL **Roadworks** are repairs or other work being done on the road. *Around roadworks there'll be mandatory speed limits and lorries will have to keep to the nearside lane.*

roadworthy /ˈrəʊdwɜːði/
ADJ PRED If a car is considered to be **roadworthy**, it is considered to be in quite good condition and unlikely to have any sudden mechanical problems or breakdowns. *I will only drive the car after he has made it roadworthy.*

roam /rəʊm/ **roams, roaming, roamed**
VOorVA If you **roam** an area or **roam** around it, you wander around it without having a particular purpose. *He roamed the streets at night... They roam over the hills and plains.*

roan /rəʊn/ **roans**
NC A **roan** is a horse that is brown or black with some white hairs mixed in.

roar /rɔː/ **roars, roaring, roared**
1 V If something **roars**, it makes a very loud noise. *The wind roared in the forest... The sea roared along the length of the shore.* ► Also N SING *I could hear the roar of traffic outside.*
2 V, VO, or V-QUOTE If someone **roars**, they shout very loudly. *He used to kick and scream and roar if he didn't get what he wanted... The crowd roared its approval... 'Forward with the Revolution,' the crowd roared back.*
3 V When a lion **roars**, it makes the loud sound typical of a lion. *The lion was roaring triumphantly.* ► Also NC *The lion let out one of its roars.*

roaring /ˈrɔːrɪŋ/
1 ADJ ATTRIB **Roaring** means making a very loud noise. *He sat on the terrace a few feet from the roaring traffic... A roaring explosion ripped through his home.*
2 ADJ ATTRIB A **roaring** fire is one which is very hot with large flames. *We washed up the tea things and settled thankfully one on each side of the roaring fire.*

3 If someone is **doing a roaring trade**, they are selling a lot of goods very quickly; an informal expression. *The sellers in Cotonou market were doing a roaring trade.*

4 ADJ ATTRIB If something is a **roaring** success, it is very successful indeed. *I certainly don't expect to tell you next week that this treatment is a roaring success.*

roast /rəʊst/ **roasts, roasting, roasted**
1 V-ERG When you **roast** meat or other food, you cook it using dry heat in an oven or over a fire. *...roast the nuts for twenty minutes... The stake burnt more quickly than the pig roasted.* ▸ Also ADJ ATTRIB *...roast beef.*
2 NCorNU A **roast** is a piece of meat that has been roasted. *...taking the roast out of the oven. ...a thick slab of roast.*

roasting /rəʊstɪŋ/ **roastings**
NC If someone gives you a **roasting**, they criticize you severely about something in a way that shows that they are very annoyed with you; an informal word. *The boss gave me a real roasting this morning.*

rob /rɒb/ **robs, robbing, robbed**
1 VO If a person is **robbed**, money or property is stolen from them, often by means of force or threats. *They told the police that they'd been robbed... Police in San Francisco are searching for a gang who have robbed at least ten motorists.*
2 VO If a place that contains a lot of money or valuable objects is **robbed**, some of the money or valuable objects are stolen, often by means of force or threats. *A train travelling from Brighton to London has been robbed by a gang of men... The men were trying to rob a betting shop.*
3 VO+of If you **rob** someone of something that they should have or that they deserve, you take it away from them or stop them from having it. *He tried to rob her of her share... You robbed me of my moment of glory... The National Peasant Party was robbed of victory by the Communists.*

robber /rɒbə/ **robbers**
NC A **robber** is someone who steals money or property from a place such as a bank, shop, or train, often by using force. *The robber knocked out a warden before stripping the portraits from their frames.*

robbery /rɒbəri/ **robberies**
NUorNC **Robbery** is the crime of stealing money or property, often by using force or threats. *He was arrested on charges of armed robbery... The robbery occurred at the Gardner Museum, which houses one of the finest art collections in the country.*

robe /rəʊb/ **robes**
NC A **robe** is a loose piece of clothing which reaches the ground. *...ceremonial robes.*

robin /rɒbɪn/ **robins**
1 NC A **robin** is a small brown bird. Male robins have a red breast. *The British robin is a traditional symbol of Christmas.*
2 See also **round-robin**.

Robinson, Mary /meəri rɒbɪnsən/
Mary Robinson became President of Ireland in 1990. She is an independent, supported by the Labour Party and the Workers' Party. Born: 1944.

robot /rəʊbɒt/ **robots**
NC A **robot** is a machine which moves and performs certain tasks automatically. *Industry is making increasing use of robots.*

robotic /rəʊbɒtɪk/ **robotics**
1 NU **Robotics** is the science of designing and building robots; a technical use. *During this visit we signed a five-year collaborative agreement in the field of robotics and control.*
2 ADJ ATTRIB **Robotic** activities are carried out by using robots. *Today, robotic surgery seems revolutionary.*
3 ADJ If you describe someone or something's movements as **robotic**, you mean that they move in a quick, jerky way, like a robot.

robust /rəʊbʌst/
1 ADJ Someone or something that is **robust** is strong and healthy. *She has four robust daughters... The once robust economy now lies in ruins.*
2 ADJ **Robust** views or opinions are strongly held and

firmly expressed. *Mr Baker was unapologetic and gave a robust and forthright defence of America's views... He devoted the bulk of his hour-long speech to a robust and often angry attack on his conservative critics.* ◆ **robustly** ADV *Mr Gould robustly rejected the notion that State industries were by definition less efficient than private enterprise.*

rock /rɒk/ **rocks, rocking, rocked**
1 NU **Rock** is the hard substance which the Earth is made of. *Large masses of rock are constantly falling into the sea.*
2 NC A **rock** is a piece of stone sticking out of the ground or the sea, or one that has broken away from a mountain or cliff. *I sat down on a rock.*
3 V-ERG When something **rocks**, it moves slowly and regularly backwards and forwards or from side to side. *She sat there, rocking gently... Our parents cuddle and hug us, and rock us gently back and forth.*
4 VO If something **rocks** people, it shocks and horrifies them; used in written English. *France was rocked by an outbreak of violent crime.*
5 NU **Rock** is also the same as **rock music**.
6 NU **Rock** is also a sweet made in long, hard sticks which are often sold at seaside towns.
● **Rock** is used in these phrases. ● An alcoholic drink that is **on the rocks** is served with ice. *...whisky on the rocks.* ● If a relationship is **on the rocks**, it is unsuccessful and is likely to end soon. *Both men were anxious to head off speculation that the superpower relationship might be on the rocks.* ● to **rock the boat**: see **boat**.

rock and roll
NU **Rock and roll** is a kind of music developed in the 1950s which has a strong beat and is played by small groups. *The music is a bit like rock and roll... He is a great admirer of the rock and roll star, Elvis Presley.*

rock-bottom
1 ADJ ATTRIB A **rock-bottom** price or level is a very low one. *You can get black-and-white television sets at rock-bottom prices.*
2 NU If someone reaches **rock-bottom**, they become extremely poor or extremely depressed. *Until they reach rock-bottom, it is difficult for people to get financial help.*

rock-climber, rock-climbers
NC A **rock-climber** is a person whose hobby or sport is climbing rocks, cliffs, or mountains.

rock-climbing
NU **Rock-climbing** is the activity of climbing rocks, cliffs, or mountains as a hobby or sport. *...dangerous pastimes such as rock-climbing and boxing.*

rocker /rɒkə/ **rockers**
1 NC A **rocker** is the same as a **rocking chair**; used in American English. *...sitting in his wicker rocker.*
2 If you say that someone is **off** their **rocker**, you mean that they are mad; an informal expression. *His landlady appeared to be slightly off her rocker.*

rockery /rɒkəri/ **rockeries**
NC A **rockery** is a raised part of a garden which is built of stones and soil, in which small plants are grown. *The stone figures decorate the rockery in the garden of a cottage in Aysgarth.*

rocket /rɒkɪt/ **rockets, rocketing, rocketed**
1 NC A **rocket** is a space vehicle shaped like a long tube. *...a space rocket.*
2 NC A **rocket** is also a missile that contains explosive and which is powered by gas. *There were about ten casualties on Tuesday when the rebels fired rockets into the city. ...anti-tank rockets... It is working on ways to protect its civilians against rocket attacks.*
3 V If prices or profits **rocket**, they increase very quickly and suddenly; an informal use. *Water is scarce and prices are rocketing... Land sales rocketed.*

rocket launcher /rɒkɪt lɔːntʃə/ **rocket launchers**
NC A **rocket launcher** is a cylindrical device that can be carried and used by soldiers for firing rockets. *He carried an antitank rocket launcher.*

rock garden, rock gardens
NC A **rock garden** is a garden of rocks and soil, in which small plants are grown. *It's a big rock garden enclosed by skyscrapers.*

rock-hard
 ADJ Something that is **rock-hard** is extremely hard indeed. ...*the rock-hard earth.*

rocking chair, rocking chairs
 NC A **rocking chair** is a chair that is built on two curved pieces of wood so that you can rock yourself backwards and forwards when you are sitting in it.

rocking horse, rocking horses
 NC A **rocking horse** is a toy horse on which a child can sit and rock backwards and forwards. *Hamleys also report selling a lot of hand-made wooden toys, including rocking horses.*

rock-like
 ADJ Something that is **rock-like** is very strong or firm and unlikely to change. ...*the rock-like quality of the old religion.*

rock music
 NU **Rock music** is loud music with a strong beat that is usually played and sung by a small group of people using a variety of instruments including electric guitars and drums. *Roy Orbison was a much-loved figure in rock music. ...a new album by a superstar of rock music.*

rock'n'roll
 NU **Rock'n'roll** is the same as **rock and roll**; used in informal written English. *The record is a medley of rock'n'roll classics.*

rock pool, rock pools
 NC A **rock pool** is a small pool between rocks on the seashore. *He dived into a dangerous rock pool and bumped his head.*

rock salt
 NU **Rock salt** is salt that is formed in the ground. It is removed by mining. *Sea salt is considered to be more natural, and therefore healthier, than common rock salt.*

rocky /rɒki/
 ADJ A **rocky** place is covered with rocks. *She drives carefully up the rocky lane.*

rococo /rəkəʊkəʊ/
 ADJ **Rococo** buildings, furniture, and works of art are in the style that existed in Europe in the eighteenth century. The rococo style is characterized by complicated curly decoration. ...*a rococo shop front that dates from 1760.*

rod /rɒd/ **rods**
 NC A **rod** is a long, thin metal or wooden bar. *The aluminium rod that held the seats broke.*

rode /rəʊd/
 Rode is the past tense of **ride**.

rodent /rəʊdnt/ **rodents**
 NC A **rodent** is a small mammal with sharp front teeth. Rats, mice, and squirrels are rodents. *Some of the crop may be eaten up by insects or rodents.*

rodeo /rəʊdiəʊ, rəʊdeɪəʊ/ **rodeos**
 NC In the United States, a **rodeo** is a public entertainment in which cowboys show different skills, including riding wild horses and catching calves with ropes. *He used to be a rodeo rider in Iowa.*

Rodríguez, Andrés /ændreɪs rɒdriːges/
 General **Andrés Rodríguez** came to power in a coup in Paraguay in 1989, in which he overthrew his father-in-law, General Alfredo Stroessner. He is a member of the Colorado Party (PC). Born: 1924.

roe /rəʊ/
 NU **Roe** is the eggs or sperm of a fish, which is eaten as food. *Vitamin B1 is found in yeast, cod's roe, nuts, peas, and also in small amounts in many other foods.*

rogue /rəʊg/ **rogues**
 NC A **rogue** is a man who behaves in a dishonest way. *He suggests that the forces of law and order strangely resemble the rogues they pursue.*

roguery /rəʊgəri/
 NU **Roguery** is dishonest or immoral behaviour; an old-fashioned word. *There's corruption and roguery everywhere!*

roguish /rəʊgɪʃ/
 ADJ A **roguish** expression on your face shows that you are amused, often because you are about to do something mischievous. ...*a roguish smile... He has a most disconcerting, roguish laugh.* ◆ **roguishly** ADV *He winked at me roguishly.*

Roh Tae Woo /nəʊ teɪ uː/
 Roh Tae Woo became President of South Korea in 1988. He retired from the Army as a four-star general in 1981. He served as Minister for National Security and Foreign Affairs from 1981 to 1982, of Sports in 1982, and of Home Affairs from 1982 to 1983. He was Chairman of the Democratic Justice Party from 1985 to 1987 and President from 1987 to 1990. In 1990 he became joint President of the Democratic Liberal Party (DLP). Born: 1932.

role /rəʊl/ **roles**
 1 NC+SUPP Your **role** is your position and function in a situation or society. *What is the role of the University in modern society?... He had played a major role in the formation of the United Nations... Nato now says it will seek a greater political role.*
 2 NC A **role** is one of the characters that an actor or singer plays in a film, play, or opera. *She played the leading role in The Winter's Tale.*

role play
 NU **Role play** is the act of imitating the character and behaviour of a type of person who is very different from yourself. Role play is usually used as a training exercise. ...*using role play as our revision method.*

role-playing
 NU **Role-playing** is the act of imitating the character and behaviour of a type of person who is very different from yourself, either deliberately, for example as a training exercise, or without knowing it. *I've got a general idea of using role-playing in the course... We all indulge in unconscious role-playing.*

roll /rəʊl/ **rolls, rolling, rolled**
 1 V-ERG When something **rolls**, it moves along a surface, turning over many times. *The bucket rolled and clattered down the path... He rolled a boulder down the slope.*
 2 VA When vehicles **roll** along, they move along. *Trucks with loudspeakers rolled through the streets.*
 3 VA If drops of liquid **roll** down a surface, they move quickly down it. *He stood in a corner with tears rolling down his face... The sweat rolled down my neck.*
 4 VOA If you **roll** something into a cylinder or a ball, or if you **roll** it up, you form it into a cylinder or a ball by wrapping it several times around itself or by shaping it between your hands. *She went on sorting the socks, rolling them into neat little bundles.* ◆ **rolled** ADJ ATTRIB ...*a rolled newspaper. ...a rolled umbrella.*
 5 NC A **roll** of paper or cloth is a long piece of it that has been wrapped many times around itself or around a tube. ...*a roll of film. ...a roll of metal foil.*
 6 NC A **roll** is a small circular loaf of bread. *Bread will be rationed at 80 grams per person daily—about the weight of two small rolls.*
 7 NC+SUPP A **roll** is also an official list of people's names. ...*the roll of members.*
 8 NC A **roll** of drums is a long rumbling sound made by drums, especially as part of an official ceremony. *It was towed out of a hanger to the accompaniment of a drum roll from a military band.*
 9 See also **rolling, rock and roll, sausage roll, toilet roll.**
 ● **Roll** is used in these phrases. ● If something is several things **rolled into one**, it combines the main features of those things. *A good musical is a new play, a new opera and a new ballet all rolled into one.*
 ● to **start the ball rolling:** see **ball.**

roll back PHRASAL VERB 1 To **roll back** a situation or action means to do something so that it no longer exists or no longer has any effect. *Thatcher was determined to roll back what she felt was a dangerous trend towards socialism... The administration is accused of attempting to roll back the reforms of the 1960s and 1970s.* 2 If a government or company **rolls back** taxes or prices, or **rolls back** increases in them, it reduces the taxes or prices, often to a previous level; used in American English. *Exxon says it's rolling back wholesale gasoline prices by five cents a gallon... Hungarian officials avoided a general strike today, agreeing to roll back a 65% hike in gasoline prices.*

roll in PHRASAL VERB If money or profits **are rolling**

in, they are being received in large quantities; an informal expression. *Large amounts of money are rolling in.*

roll over PHRASAL VERB 1 If someone who is lying down rolls over, they move so that a different part of them is facing upwards. *I rolled over on my stomach.* 2 When a vehicle rolls over, it falls sideways and rolls so that it lands on its roof. *Senna's car rolled over— apparently after a tyre was punctured.*

roll up PHRASAL VERB 1 If you roll up something flexible, you wrap it several times around itself until it is shaped like a cylinder or a ball. *You sort out the tent while I roll up the sleeping bags.* 2 If you roll up your sleeves or trouser legs, you fold the edges over several times to make them shorter. *Men are asked to roll up their shirt sleeves to display any distinguishing marks.*

roll-call, roll-calls
NC If you take a **roll-call**, you check which of the members of a group are present by reading out their names. *The deaths were discovered when the three men failed to report for this morning's roll-call.*

rolled-up
1 ADJ ATTRIB **Rolled-up** describes things that are folded or wrapped into a cylindrical shape, for example a newspaper. *He lunged at the wasp with a rolled-up newspaper... Another man carries a rolled-up stretcher.* 2 ADJ **Rolled-up** also describes pieces of clothing that are made shorter by being folded over at the edge. *...her rolled-up jeans.*

roller /rəʊlə/ **rollers**
1 NC A **roller** is a cylinder that turns round in a machine or device. *She pulled the sheet of paper out of the roller.* 2 NC **Rollers** are hollow tubes that women use in their hair to make it curly. *...pink hair rollers.*

roller-coaster, roller-coasters
NC At a fairground, a **roller-coaster** is a small railway that goes up and down steep slopes and which people ride on for pleasure. *The more daring queue to ride on the roller-coaster, whose twisting track can be seen from many parts of the city.*

roller-skate, roller-skates, roller-skating, roller-skated
1 NC **Roller-skates** are shoes with four small wheels on the bottom. *She tightened the strap of her roller-skate.* 2 V If you **roller-skate**, you move over a flat surface wearing roller-skates. *As a child I once roller-skated down the Mall.* ♦ **roller-skating** NU *She continues with her favourite hobbies, roller-skating and disco dancing.*

rolling /rəʊlɪŋ/
1 ADJ ATTRIB **Rolling** hills are small with gentle slopes that extend a long way into the distance. *...the rolling countryside west of Detroit.* 2 ADJ ATTRIB A **rolling** walk is slow and swaying, usually because the person is drunk or very fat.

rolling pin, rolling pins
NC A **rolling pin** is a cylinder that you roll over pastry to make it flat. *...rolling the dough with a wooden rolling pin.*

rolling stock
NU **Rolling stock** is the engines, carriages, and wagons that are used on a railway. *British Rail defends these fare rises by pointing to the introduction of new rolling stock giving a better standard of service.*

roll of honour, rolls of honour
NC A **roll of honour** is a list of the names of people who are admired or respected for something that they have done, such as the people who have died while they were fighting for their country. *The names of the dead women were inscribed in the journal's Roll of Honour... You won't find him in the encyclopedias or the Nobel roll of honour.*

roll-on/roll-off
ADJ A **roll-on/roll-off** ship is designed so that cars and lorries can drive in at one end before the ship sails, and then drive out at the other end after the voyage. *Hundreds of roll-on/roll-off car ferries cross the English Channel carrying millions of passengers each year.*

roly-poly /rəʊlipəʊli/
ADJ ATTRIB **Roly-poly** people are pleasantly fat and round. *...a roly-poly toddler.*

Roman /rəʊmən/ **Romans**
1 ADJ **Roman** means related to or connected with Rome and its empire in ancient times. *...the Roman Empire. ...the remarkably well-preserved remains of a Roman amphitheatre. ...a Roman centurion.* 2 ADJ **Roman** also means also related to or connected with modern Rome. *...Roman hotels.* 3 NC A **Roman** was a citizen of Rome or the Roman Empire in ancient times. *The Romans left Britain in 410.* 4 NC A **Roman** is also someone who lives or was born in the city of Rome. *...Dr Carlo Spagnolli, a 32-year-old Roman.* 5 NU **Roman** is the most common style of printing in books and magazines. It consists of small upright letters. The definitions in this dictionary are printed in roman type.

Roman alphabet
N SING The **Roman alphabet** is the alphabet which was used by the Romans in ancient times and which is used for writing most western European languages, including English. *Arabic script was replaced by the Roman alphabet in official documents.*

Roman Catholic, Roman Catholics
NC A **Roman Catholic** is the same as a **Catholic**. *I was a Roman Catholic... Aristide is a Roman Catholic priest.*

Roman Catholicism
NU **Roman Catholicism** is the same as **Catholicism**. *Roman Catholicism is the predominant religion in Panama.*

romance /rəmæns, rəʊmæns/ **romances**
1 NC A **romance** is a relationship in which two people love each other in a sexual way. *...a wartime romance... Mick Jagger finally married model Jerry Hall, 15 years after the start of their much publicised romance.* 2 NU **Romance** refers to the actions or behaviour of two people who are in love with each other, especially when their actions or behaviour are very thoughtful, impulsive, or extravagant. *Young people are re-discovering romance and passion.* 3 NU You can refer to the pleasure and excitement of doing something new or exciting as **romance**. *There is romance to be found in life on the river.* 4 NC A **romance** is also a novel about a love affair. *...historical romances.*

Romania /rumeɪnɪə/
The **Republic of Romania** is a country in south-eastern Europe. It was a member of the former Warsaw Pact. After the Second World War the Romanian People's Republic was declared and the Romanian Communist Party became the only legal party. Nicolae Ceauşescu ruled from 1965 until the popular uprising of 1989. He and his wife, Elena, were executed on Christmas Day 1989. In multi-party elections in 1990, the National Salvation Front (NSF) came to power and Ion Iliescu became President. Teodor Stolojan was appointed Prime Minister in 1991. Romania produces machinery, coal, and metals. ♦ **Romanian** /rumeɪnɪən/ N, ADJ
▪ *religion:* Christianity (mainly Romanian Orthodox)
▪ *language:* Romanian ▪ *currency:* leu ▪ *capital:* Bucharest (Bucureşti) ▪ *population:* 23 million (1989)
▪ *size:* 229,077 square kilometres.

Roman law
NU **Roman law** is the system of laws which was used in Rome in ancient times and which is the basis of many western legal systems. *Concepts of private property derived from Roman law.*

Roman numeral, Roman numerals
NC **Roman numerals** are the letters used by the ancient Romans to write numbers. For example, I, IV, XL, and C are used to represent 1, 4, 40, and 100.

romantic /rəmæntɪk/ **romantics**
1 ADJ A **romantic** person has a lot of unrealistic ideas, especially about love. *She's as romantic as a child of sixteen.* ▶ Also NC *Cedric's a great romantic.* 2 ADJ ATTRIB **Romantic** means connected with sexual love. *No woman needs a romantic attachment.*

3 ADJ ATTRIB A **romantic** play, film, or story describes or represents a love affair. *...a charming romantic comedy starring Audrey Hepburn.*
4 ADJ Something that is **romantic** is beautiful in a way that strongly affects your feelings. *...a romantic moonlight ride.* ♦ **romantically** ADV *Her long hair was spread romantically over the pillow.*

romanticism /rəmæntɪsɪzəm/
1 NU **Romanticism** is thoughts and feelings which are idealistic and romantic, rather than realistic. *We present this tribute to the actress whose youthful romanticism went on even into old age.*
2 NU **Romanticism** is also the artistic movement of the eighteenth and nineteenth centuries which was concerned with the expression of feelings and emotions; a technical use. *Like romanticism, existentialism emphasises the idea that people are free to choose their own destiny.*

romanticize /rəmæntɪsaɪz/ **romanticizes, romanticizing, romanticized**; also spelt **romanticise**.
VO If you **romanticize** someone or something, you imagine them to be better than they really are. *Perhaps he romanticized the onward march of the people somewhat.*

Romany /rɒmənɪ, rɑumənɪ/ **Romanies**
1 NC A **Romany** is a gypsy. *With two million Hungarians, two million Romanies, and half a dozen other national minorities, Romania is not an ethnically homogeneous state.*
2 NU **Romany** is the language spoken by many gypsies.

Rome /rɑum/
Rome is the capital of Italy and its largest city. Population: 2,816,000 (1988).

romp /rɒmp/ **romps, romping, romped**
V When children **romp** around, they play and move around in a noisy, happy way. *They romped with their dogs.*

rompers /rɒmpəz/
N PL **Rompers** are a piece of clothing worn by babies or young children. **Rompers** consist of loose trousers and a top that are joined together. *Doesn't he look sweet in those rompers?*

rondo /rɒndəu/ **rondos**
NC A **rondo** is a piece of classical music in which the main tune is repeated several times, often as part of a sonata or concerto. **Rondo** is a technical term. *...the Rondo from the Duo for Violin and Cello by Martinu.*

roof /ruːf/ **roofs** /ruːvz, ruːfs/
1 NC The **roof** of a building or car is the covering on top of it. *...a slate roof... I fixed a leak in the roof of her shed.*
2 NC The **roof** of your mouth is the highest part of it. *His tongue seemed stuck to the roof of his mouth.*
3 NC The **roof** of an underground space such as a cave is the highest part of it.
● **Roof** is used in these phrases. ● If you have a **roof over your head**, you have somewhere to live. *She was without money and with no real roof over her head.*
● If you **hit the roof**, you are very angry indeed, and usually show your anger by shouting at someone or speaking very harshly to them; an informal expression. *Its headline says 'Thatcher hit the roof' over her predecessor's intention to mediate with Saddam Hussein.*

roofed /ruːft, ruːvd/
ADJ You can use **roofed** to say what kind of roof a building has. *...houses roofed with reddish-brown tiles. ...red-roofed farmhouses.*

roofing /ruːfɪŋ/
NU **Roofing** is material used for making or covering roofs. *He sells bundles of rushes for roofing... Slate is the very best roofing material.*

roof-rack, roof-racks
NC A **roof-rack** is a metal frame that is fixed on top of a car and used for carrying large objects.

rooftop /ruːftɒp/ **rooftops**
NC **Rooftops** are the outside parts of roofs. *...a view over the rooftops.*

rook /ruk/ **rooks**
1 NC A **rook** is a large black bird. *The birds that we have most at Gatwick are gulls, rooks and lapwings.*

2 NC In chess, a **rook** is a piece which can move forwards, backwards, or sideways. A **rook** is also called a castle.

rookery /rukərɪ/ **rookeries**
NC A **rookery** is a place, usually a group of trees, where a lot of rooks have their nests.

rookie /rukɪ/ **rookies**
NC A **rookie** is a new recruit without much experience, especially a recruit in the army or police force; used in informal American English. *He was a rookie policeman.*

room /ruːm, rum/ **rooms**
1 NC A **room** is one of the separate sections in a building, which has its own walls, ceiling, floor, and door. *The room contained a couch and a glass cabinet.*
2 NU If there is **room** for something, there is enough space for it. *There wasn't enough room for everybody.*
3 NU If there is **room** for a particular kind of behaviour, people are able to behave in that way. *There ought to be room for differences of opinion... There is room for much more research.*
4 See also **common room, consulting room, dining room, double room, drawing room, dressing room, ladies' room, leg room, living room, locker room, men's room, morning room, powder room, reading room, reception room, rest room, spare room, standing room.**

roomful /ruːmful, rumful/ **roomfuls**
NC If you talk about a **roomful** of things or people, you mean a room that is full of them. *...a roomful of old ladies. ...a roomful of furniture.*

rooming house, rooming houses
NC A **rooming house** is a building that is divided into small flats or single rooms which people rent to live in; used in American English. *The big old homes were now rooming houses.*

roommate /ruːmmeɪt, rummeɪt/ **roommates**
NC Your **roommate** is the person who you share a rented room or house with. *We want to meet your roommate and all your friends.*

room service
NU **Room service** is a service in a hotel by which meals or drinks are provided for guests in their rooms. *I spent the rest of the day in my suite, reading and ordering things from room service.*

roomy /ruːmɪ/ **roomier, roomiest**
ADJ A **roomy** place has plenty of space. *...a ground floor apartment which was roomy but sparsely furnished.*

roost /ruːst/ **roosts, roosting, roosted**
1 NC A **roost** is a place where birds rest or build nests. *The gulls were returning to their roosts among the rocks.*
2 V When birds **roost**, they settle in somewhere for the night. *The chickens roost there all winter.*

rooster /ruːstə/ **roosters**
NC A **rooster** is an adult male chicken. *We've got a few roosters and chickens under the house.*

root /ruːt/ **roots, rooting, rooted**
1 NC The **roots** of a plant are the parts that grow underground. *These trees have large, spreading roots.*
2 NC The **root** of a hair or tooth is the part beneath the skin. *They pulled her hair out by the roots.*
3 N PL Your **roots** are the place or culture that you or your family grew up in, which you have now left. *People are searching again for their roots.*
4 NC The **root** of something is its original cause or basis. *Perhaps the root of the tragedy was here.*
▶ Also ADJ ATTRIB *...the root causes of poverty.*
5 V A If you **root** through things, you search through them thoroughly. *Meadows rooted around in his bag and pulled out a map.*
6 See also **grass roots, square root.**
● **Root** is used in these phrases. ● To **take root** means to start to grow or develop. *The seedlings of bushes and trees might take root there. ...the ideas that were to take root in a new land.* ● If you **put down roots** in a place, you begin to feel that you belong there, for example because you take part in activities there and have made a lot of friends, so that eventually you

think of the place as your home. *He says he's already been here for fifteen years, and so has put down roots.*
root for PHRASAL VERB If you **root for** someone or something, you support them and hope that they succeed in what they are trying to do. *This is where the World Cup will be played, and naturally I'll be rooting for Italy.*
root out PHRASAL VERB If you **root** someone or something **out**, you find them and remove them from a place. *He's in there somewhere. Let's go and root him out.*

root beer, root beers
N MASS **Root beer** is a sweet fizzy drink flavoured with extracts from roots and herbs. *This calls for ice-cold root beer all around.*

root crop, root crops
NC **Root crops** are plants such as potatoes or turnips that are grown in large quantities so that their roots can be eaten; a technical term. *Normally their diets are very deficient in protein and highly dependent on one or two staple root crops.*

rooted /ruːtɪd/
1 ADJ PRED+*in* If one thing is **rooted** in another, it is strongly influenced by that thing or has developed from it. *...attitudes deeply rooted in history... The traditional songs are all rooted in the subject matter of everyday life.*
2 ADJ ATTRIB A **rooted** opinion is a firm one that is unlikely to change. *He had a rooted objection to British drivers.* ● See also **deep-rooted**.

rootless /ruːtləs/
ADJ Someone who is **rootless** does not belong to any particular community or country. *...a rootless vagabond.*

rope /rəʊp/ **ropes, roping, roped**
1 NCorNU A **rope** is a long piece of very thick string, made by twisting together several thinner pieces of string or several bunches of fibres. *They should be tied together with a rope. ...a piece of rope.*
2 VOA If you **rope** one thing to another, you tie them together with a rope. *His body was roped to a hospital bed... The wagons were roped together.*
3 If you **are learning the ropes**, you are learning how a particular task or job is done. If you **know the ropes**, you know how a particular task or job should be done; an informal expression. *He had also spent three years at the Moscow Party School learning the ropes in the fifties... I think it takes experience to know the ropes in state government.*
rope in PHRASAL VERB If you **rope** someone **in** to do something, you persuade them to help you; an informal expression. *I wouldn't be surprised if JVP are roped in by Premadasa to a kind of coalition government.*
rope off PHRASAL VERB If you **rope off** an area, you tie ropes between posts around its edges to keep people away from it. *The quay was roped off and the spectators were pushed back.*

rope ladder, rope ladders
NC A **rope ladder** is a ladder made of two long ropes connected by short pieces of rope or by pieces of wood or metal. *He escaped from prison using a rope ladder.*

ropey /rəʊpi/ **ropier, ropiest**; an informal word.
1 ADJ If you say that something is **ropey**, you mean that its quality is poor or unsatisfactory. *The food was a bit ropey... I thought it was a ropey performance.*
2 ADJ If you feel **ropey**, you feel ill.

rosary /rəʊzəri/ **rosaries**
NC A **rosary** is a string of beads that members of some religions such as Christians or Hindus use when they are praying. It is also used of the prayers that are said by Christians when they are using a rosary. *They held up crucifixes and rosaries, sang hymns and recited Hail Marys... They say the rosary and have devotions to the Blessed Virgin.*

rose /rəʊz/ **roses**
1 NC A **rose** is a flower which has a pleasant smell and grows on a bush with thorns. *...three red roses surrounded by deep green foliage.*
2 If you say that something is not **a bed of roses**, you mean that it has some unpleasant aspects to it as well as some good ones. *No one's life is a bed of roses.*

3 **Rose** is also the past tense of **rise**.

rosé /rəʊzeɪ/
NU **Rosé** is a wine that is pink in colour.

roseate /rəʊziət/
ADJ Something that is **roseate** is reddish-pink in colour; a literary word. *Alexander sipped tea from roseate china.*

Roseau /rəʊzəʊ/
Roseau is the capital of Dominica and its largest town. Population: 20,000 (1992).

rosebud /rəʊzbʌd/ **rosebuds**
NC A **rosebud** is a young rose that is still rolled up and has not yet opened out fully.

rose hip, rose hips
NC A **rose hip** is a bright red or orange fruit that grows on some kinds of rose bushes.

rosemary /rəʊzmə⁰ri/
NU **Rosemary** is a plant with small spiky greyish-green leaves that are used as a herb in cooking. It is used also to refer to the actual leaves or to the herb itself. *...chicken livers with rosemary.*

rosette /rəʊzet/ **rosettes**
NC A **rosette** is a large, circular badge made from coloured ribbons. You wear a rosette as a prize or to show support for a sports team or political party.

rosewood /rəʊzwʊd/
NU **Rosewood** is a hard dark-coloured wood that is used for making furniture. *...a rosewood table.*

roster /rɒstə/ **rosters**
NC A **roster** is a list of people. It is used to show who does a particular job at a particular time. *They are involved in a dispute over pay and conditions and over new work rosters... The theatre roster became filled with the names of stars.*

rostrum /rɒstrəm/ **rostrums** or **rostra** /rɒstrə/
NC A **rostrum** is a raised platform on which someone stands when they are speaking to an audience, or conducting an orchestra, or receiving a prize. *A delegate from Latvia walked to the rostrum and addressed the assembly... Also on the winners' rostrum was the Commonwealth Games champion Linford Christie.*

rosy /rəʊzi/
1 ADJ Something that is **rosy** is pink. *...her bright eyes and rosy cheeks.*
2 ADJ If a situation seems **rosy**, it seems likely to be good. *The President painted a very rosy picture of economic prosperity.*

rot /rɒt/ **rots, rotting, rotted**
1 V-ERG When food, wood, or other substances **rot** or when something **rots** them, they decay and fall apart. *Her teeth were rotting... Bleach might not the fibres. ...the smell of rotting vegetables.* ▶ Also NU *Destroy any bulbs with rot and buy healthy ones.*
2 You can say that **the rot sets in** when a situation begins to get worse and nothing can prevent this from happening. *It was at the last summit that the rot that finally toppled Mrs Thatcher from power set in.*
rot away PHRASAL VERB When something made of a natural material **rots away**, it slowly decays until none of it remains. *The shack rotted away.*

rota /rəʊtə/ **rotas**
NC A **rota** is a list of people who take turns to do a particular job. *The strike is in protest at planned job cuts and changes in working rotas.*

rotary /rəʊtəri/
ADJ ATTRIB **Rotary** movement goes round in circles. *...a rotary mower.*

rotate /rəʊteɪt/ **rotates, rotating, rotated**
1 V-ERG When something **rotates** or when you **rotate** it, it turns with a circular movement. *...two drums rotating in opposite directions... He rotated the camera.* ◆ **rotation** /rəʊteɪʃn/ **rotations** NUorNC *...the earth's rotation. ...the rotations of the ceiling fan.*
2 V-ERG If things or people **rotate**, they each carry out a particular task or function in turn and then begin with the first one again. *...the arrangement whereby the premiership rotated between the two groups... The programme calls for the post of president to be rotated.* ◆ **rotation** NUorNC *She did everything in strict rotation.*
3 VO When farmers **rotate** their crops, they use fields

for different crops each year in order to avoid using up all the goodness in the soil. *The more advanced farmers will apply manure and even rotate their crops.* ◆ **rotation** NU *An integrated farming system includes crop rotation and integration of livestock... It's often sown in rotation with cereals like wheat or barley.*

rote /rəʊt/
1 ADJ ATTRIB **Rote** means arrived at by routine or habit rather than by careful thought. *The company sought nothing more than rote agreement. ...rote learning.*
2 If you learn something **by rote**, you learn it by memorizing it and not by thinking about it or trying to understand it. *He learned the work by rote.*

rotor /rəʊtə/ **rotors**
NC The **rotors** or **rotor blades** of a helicopter are the four long pieces of metal on top of it which go round and lift it off the ground. *Wires strong enough to wreck a helicopter's rotor blades are to be installed above prison exercise yards.*

rotten /rɒtn/
1 ADJ If food, wood, or other substances are **rotten**, they have become bad or they have fallen apart through decay, and can no longer be used. *Health Ministry officials have continued destroying spoiled or rotten food-stuffs. ...rotten fruit.*
2 ADJ If you say that something is **rotten**, you mean that it is bad, unpleasant, or unfair; an informal use. *...a rotten novel... They're having a rotten deal.*
3 ADJ PRED If you feel **rotten**, you feel ill; an informal use.

rotter /rɒtə/ **rotters**
NC If you call someone a **rotter**, you mean that they have behaved in a very unkind or selfish way; an old-fashioned, informal word.

rotund /rəʊtʌnd/
ADJ Something or someone that is **rotund** is round and fat; a formal word, often used humorously. *He turned and patted his rotund stomach.*

rotunda /rəʊtʌndə/ **rotundas**
NC A **rotunda** is a round building or room, especially one with a dome. *...the huge rotunda of the Albert Hall.*

rouble /ruːbl/ **roubles**
NC A **rouble** is a unit of money that was used in the former Soviet Union. It is still a unit of currency in some of the republics that form the Commonwealth of Independent States. *One decree calls for the commercial rate of the rouble to be devalued.*

roué /ruːeɪ/ **roués**
NC A **roué** is a man who is regarded as behaving in a rather immoral way, for example by gambling, drinking, or having sexual relationships with many women; an old-fashioned word. *Anyone can see that he is nothing but a roué and not to be trusted.*

rouge /ruːʒ/
NU **Rouge** is a red cosmetic powder which some women and actors put on their cheeks in order to give them more colour. *They wore lipstick and rouge.*

rouged /ruːʒd/
ADJ If a woman's or actor's cheeks are **rouged**, they look red because they are covered in rouge. *...an elderly lady with rouged cheeks.*

rough /rʌf/ **rougher, roughest; roughs, roughing, roughed**
1 ADJ If a surface is **rough**, it is uneven and not smooth. *...rough roads... By now the sea was really rough.* ◆ **roughness** NU *Roughness of the skin can be caused by bad diet.*
2 ADJ If someone is having a **rough** time, they are experiencing some unpleasantness or some having difficulty with what they are doing; an informal use. *Both brothers seem to have had a rough time in prison... With the American economy in a slump, car dealers are having a particularly rough time.*
3 ADJ A **rough** calculation, description, or drawing is approximate rather than exact or detailed. *Multiply the weekly amount by fifty-two to get the rough annual cost. ...a rough outline of the proposals.* ◆ **roughly** ADV *...a woman of roughly her own age... Could you tell us roughly what is required?*

4 ADJ You can describe something as **rough** when it is not well made. *...a rough shelter of branches and leaves.* ◆ **roughly** ADV *The pieces were then roughly cobbled together.*
5 ADJ You say that people are **rough** when they use too much force. *...complaints of rough handling.* ◆ **roughly** ADV *He shoved the boy roughly aside.*
6 ADJ If a town or district is **rough**, there is a lot of crime or violence there. *...one of the roughest towns in America.*
7 When people **sleep rough**, they sleep out of doors, usually because they have no home. *They were laying out their cardboard boxes, preparing for another night sleeping rough.*

rough out PHRASAL VERB If you **rough out** a drawing or an idea, you draw or write down its main features before you do the final version in detail. *I've roughed out a scene for my new play.*

rough up PHRASAL VERB If someone **roughs** you **up**, they attack you and beat you; an informal expression. *They roughed me up a bit and then left me.*

roughage /rʌfɪdʒ/
NU **Roughage** refers to substances in food such as bran or fibre that make digestion easier and help your bowels to work properly. *One is told to increase one's roughage intake to prevent constipation.*

rough and ready
ADJ If you describe something as **rough and ready**, you mean that it has been made, done, or arranged in a hurry and may not be totally satisfactory. *...a rough and ready calculation. ...rough and ready treatments... The accommodation was a bit rough and ready.*

rough and tumble
NU If you refer to the **rough and tumble** of a situation, you mean that the people involved try hard to get what they want, and do not worry about upsetting or harming others. *...the rough and tumble of world politics.*

roughcast /rʌfkɑːst/
NU **Roughcast** is a mixture of plaster and small stones used for covering the outside walls of buildings.

roughen /rʌfn/ **roughens, roughening, roughened**
VO To **roughen** something or to **roughen** its surface means to make its surface less smooth. *The harsh climate had roughened her skin.*

rough-hewn
ADJ **Rough-hewn** wood or stone has been cut into a shape but has not yet been smoothed or finished off. *...a wall of rough-hewn blocks of grey stone.*

roughshod /rʌfʃɒd/
If you **ride roughshod over** someone or their ideas, you completely ignore their suggestions and use your authority to promote your own interests. *The government has ridden roughshod over the recommendations made by the committee of enquiry.*

roulette /ruːlet/
NU **Roulette** is a gambling game in which a ball is dropped onto a revolving wheel with numbered holes in it. The players bet on which hole the ball will fall into. *A percentage of the profits from the spins of the roulette wheel go to the government as gaming tax.*

round /raʊnd/ **rounder, roundest; rounds, rounding, rounded;** pronounced /raʊnd/ when it is a preposition. The form **around** can be used instead of **round** when it is a preposition or an adverb.
1 ADJ Something that is **round** is shaped like a ball or a circle. *...heavy round stones... Shanti had a round face.*
2 ADJ **Round** also means curved. *...the round bulge of the girl's belly.*
3 PREP or ADV If something or a group of things is **round** or **around** something else, it is situated on every side of it. *She was wearing a scarf round her head... We were sitting round a table eating and drinking... There was a wall all the way round.*
4 PREP or ADV If one thing moves **round** or **around** another, the first thing keeps moving in a circle, with the second thing at the centre of the circle. *The Shuttle crew in orbit round the earth will be measuring the effects of atomic oxygen... Bruce circled round him barking.*
5 If something is going **round and round**, it is spinning

or moving in circles. *A swallow flew frantically round and round.*

6 ADV If you turn or look **round** or **around**, you turn so that you are facing in a different direction. *He swung round and faced the window.*

7 PREP or ADV If you go **round** or **around** something, you move in a curve past it. *They sailed round the Cape... The boys had disappeared around a corner... Hogan walked round to the driver's side.*

8 VO When you **round** something, you move in a curve past it. *...as he rounded the corner at the top of the stairs.*

9 PREP If something happens or exists in many parts of a place, you can say that it happens or exists **round** or **around** that place. *Think of what's happening politically round the world.*

10 PREP or ADV If you go **round** or **around** a place, you go to several different parts of it. *You do not have to walk all the way round the edge... He has already been round the country three times in the past year... I wandered around the orchard.*

11 ADV When you ask people **round** or when someone comes **round**, they visit your house to see you. *I'd like to ask him round for dinner.*

12 NC+SUPP A **round** of events is a series of connected events that is part of a longer series. *And the issue continues to threaten the next round of peace talks which are due to open in Washington next week... The second round of voting is due to take place on January 16th.*

13 NC+SUPP A **round** of a competition is a set of games or turns within it. *The two top seeds are through to the third round of the United States Open squash tournament.*

14 NC A **round** of golf is one game. *He shot a 7 under par round of 65.*

15 NC In a boxing match or a wrestling match, a **round** is one of the periods during which the boxers or wrestlers fight. *Tyson remains the firm favourite to win the fight over 10 rounds.*

16 NC If you buy a **round** of drinks, you buy a drink for each member of the group of people that you are with. *Whose round is it?*

17 NC A **round** of ammunition is the bullet or bullets that are released when a gun is fired. *Three people have been arrested and rifles, a handgun and 163 rounds of ammunition were recovered.*

18 NC When people such as doctors go on their **rounds**, they make a series of visits as part of their job. *The doctor's on his rounds.*

round off PHRASAL VERB If something has been **rounded off** or if you **round** something **off**, it has been completed in a satisfactory way. *Mary Thompson rounded off an excellent competition by adding a further win to her impressive haul... We round off this chapter with a summary profile of it.*

round on PHRASAL VERB If you **round on** someone who is criticizing you, attacking you, or causing you difficulties, you respond angrily by criticizing or attacking that person yourself. *He rounded on the reporter in a schoolmasterly fashion, accusing him of being obsessed with the issue... One man carrying a pro-Iraqi banner was rounded on by several demonstrators.*

round up PHRASAL VERB If you **round up** animals or people, you gather them together. *They had rounded up people at gunpoint.* ● See also **roundup**.

roundabout /ˈraʊndəbaʊt/ **roundabouts**

1 NC A **roundabout** is a circular traffic junction that controls the flow of traffic at a place where several roads meet. You drive round it until you come to the road that you want. *Take the first exit from the roundabout... An oil tank truck exploded after overturning at a roundabout.*

2 NC In a fair or playground, a **roundabout** is a large, circular platform with seats which goes round and round. *...ice-creams, roundabouts and bouncy castles.*

3 ADJ ATTRIB If you do something in a **roundabout** way, you do not do it in the simplest or most direct way. *They drove back to Glasgow by a long roundabout route... He told me this in a rather gentle, roundabout way.*

rounded /ˈraʊndɪd/

ADJ Something that is **rounded** is curved rather than pointed or sharp. *Its teeth are small and rounded.*

rounders /ˈraʊndəz/

NU **Rounders** is a game played by two teams, in which a player scores points by hitting a ball thrown by a member of the other team and running round all four sides of a square.

round-eyed

ADJ You describe someone as **round-eyed** when their eyes are open very wide, usually because they are surprised or afraid. *Suddenly they looked like twins, both of them round-eyed.*

roundly /ˈraʊndli/

1 ADV If you **roundly** condemn or criticize someone or something, you condemn them or criticize them very forcefully. *Britain was roundly condemned for selling arms to the rebels... The President has roundly attacked radical critics.*

2 ADV If you **roundly** defeat someone, you defeat them very easily. *It is now clear that the governing Christian Democrats have been roundly defeated.*

round-robin

ADJ ATTRIB A **round-robin** sporting event is a tournament where each player or team competing in it plays all the other players or teams in turn. *Pakistan are top of the table at the halfway stage of the round-robin competition.*

round-shouldered

ADJ Someone who is **round-shouldered** bends forward when they sit or stand, and their shoulders are curved rather than straight; used showing disapproval. *He's very round-shouldered.*

round-the-clock

ADJ ATTRIB or ADV **Round-the-clock** activities happen all day and all night. *...keeping the hotel under round-the-clock surveillance... Factories are working round-the-clock.*

round trip, round trips; written **round-trip** when it is an adjective.

1 NC If you make a **round trip,** you travel to a place and then travel back again. *Three days a week she makes the 50-mile round trip between the restaurant and her home.*

2 ADJ ATTRIB A **round-trip** fare or ticket is one that includes the journey to and from a place; used in American English. *They were offering round-trip fares to Europe. ...cheaper round-trip tickets between Los Angeles and cities in Mexico.*

roundup /ˈraʊndʌp/ **roundups**

NC On television or radio, a **roundup** of the information contained in the news is a summary of it. *With a roundup of the other stories that have been making the news, here's John Newell... Sports Roundup will bring reports from the games throughout their two week duration.*

rouse /raʊz/ **rouses, rousing, roused**

1 VO If you **rouse** someone, you wake them up from their sleep; a formal use. *He was roused from his sleep in the early hours of the morning by a knock on the door.*

2 V-REFL+to-INF If you **rouse** yourself to do something, you make yourself get up and do it. *He roused himself to talk to Christine.*

3 VO If something **rouses** you, it makes you very emotional or excited. *He roused the troops with his oratory.*

4 VO If something **rouses** an emotion in you, it causes you to feel it. *The proposal roused fears among the public... The case has roused widespread international concern.*

rousing /ˈraʊzɪŋ/

ADJ Something that is **rousing** makes you feel very emotional or excited and ready to take action. *...that rousing patriotic hymn, 'Jerusalem'... Cuban troops were given a rousing send-off by thousands of Angolans.*

rout /raʊt/ **routs, routing, routed**

VO If an army or a sports team **routs** its opponents, it defeats them very easily. *Spain could not muster sufficient resources to rout the Cubans... The South American champions ended their tournament by* *routing Huracan Buceo 5 nil.* ▶ Also NCorNU *The retreat turned into a rout... The terrified army fled in rout.*

route /ruːt/ **routes, routing, routed**
1 NC A **route** is a way that leads from one place to another. It is used especially to describe a well known direction that is marked on a map. *I took the route through Beechwood. ...the main route out of London to the west.* ● See also **en route.**
2 NC+SUPP You can refer to a way of achieving something as a **route**. *Another route is by active participation in a trade union... The top clubs see the new league as a route to greater income.*
3 VO When vehicles **are routed** past a place or through it, they are made to travel past it or through it. *Flights were being routed around the trouble area.*

route march, route marches
NC A **route march** is a long, difficult, and tiring walk, especially one done by soldiers as a training exercise. *His recruits had to endure 74 kilometre route marches without sleep.*

routine /ruːtiːn/ **routines**
1 ADJ **Routine** activities are done regularly as a normal part of your job, rather than for a special reason. *The reactor is out of service for routine maintenance. ...a routine training exercise. ...a routine exchange of information.* ◆ **routinely** ADV *This information is routinely collected and published.*
2 NCorNU A **routine** is the set of things that is usually done in a particular way, so that tasks can be organized more efficiently or productively. *...his daily routine. ...the nine to five routine... The report says that they should give health education advice as a matter of routine.*

rove /rəʊv/ **roves, roving, roved**
VOorVA Someone who **roves** an area wanders around it; a literary word. *...the thugs who rove the streets at night. ...his old habits of roving round the rubbish tips.* ◆ **roving** ADJ ATTRIB *Small roving bands of rebel fighters may continue to harass government forces... He became a roving troubleshooter for the authorities.*

row, rows, rowing, rowed; pronounced /rəʊ/ for the meanings in paragraphs 1 to 3, and /raʊ/ for the meanings in paragraphs 4 and 5.
1 NC A **row** of things or people is a number of them arranged in a line. *...a large hall filled with rows of desks... They were standing neatly in a row.*
2 If the same thing happens several times **in a row**, it happens that number of times without interruption. *He was elected president three times in a row.*
3 VorVO When you **row** a boat, you make it move through the water by using oars. *We rowed slowly towards the centre of the river... The man who rows the boat doesn't generally rock it.* ▶ Also N SING *...a row on the lake.*
4 NC If there is a **row** between people, there is a quarrel or argument between them. *A furious row has developed within the Alliance over the controversial policy statement.*
5 N SING If someone or something is making a **row**, they are making a loud, unpleasant noise. *What a row they're making next door!*

rowboat /rəʊbəʊt/ **rowboats**
NC A **rowboat** is the same as a **rowing boat**; used in American English. *They are arriving on all sorts of vessels: fishing boats, trawlers and even rowboats.*

rowdy /raʊdi/
ADJ If people, their behaviour, or events are **rowdy**, they are noisy, rough, and likely to cause trouble. *People were more worried in areas where there were graffiti, rowdy teenagers and drunks... There was a rowdy confrontation and a shot was fired.* ◆ **rowdiness** NU *...getting into trouble with fighting, rowdiness on the street and conflicts with the police.*

rower /rəʊə/ **rowers**
NC A **rower** is a person who rows a boat, especially in the sport of rowing. *...long-distance rowers.*

rowing /rəʊɪŋ/
NU **Rowing** is a sport in which people or teams race against each other in special rowing boats. *Gold medals are at stake in rowing, gymnastics, swimming and wrestling. ...a rowing club.*

rowing boat, rowing boats
NC A **rowing boat** is a small boat that you move through the water by using oars. *...a boat yard with rowing boats and sailing dinghies.*

rowlock /rɒlək/ **rowlocks**
NC **Rowlocks** are the U-shaped pieces of metal on the sides of a rowing boat that are used to hold the oars in position as you move them backwards and forwards. *He took the oars from the rowlocks and laid them side by side.*

royal /rɔɪəl/
1 ADJ ATTRIB **Royal** means related or belonging to a king, a queen, or a member of their family. *...the royal family. ...the royal wedding.*
2 ADJ ATTRIB **Royal** is used in the names of organizations that are officially appointed or supported by a member of a royal family. *...the Royal Navy.*

royal blue
ADJ Something that is **royal blue** in colour is deep blue. *The police say they're looking for a man dressed in a royal blue and white striped shirt.*

Royal Highness, Royal Highnesses
TITLE **Your Royal Highness, His** or **Her Royal Highness,** or **Their Royal Highnesses** are used to address or refer to members of royal families who are not kings or queens. *...Her Royal Highness Princess Alexandra.*

royalist /rɔɪəlɪst/ **royalists**
NC A **royalist** is someone who approves of their country having a royal family. *...troops sent to fight for the Republican forces against the then Royalist government.*

royalty /rɔɪəlti/ **royalties**
1 NU The members of a royal family are sometimes referred to as **royalty**. *...an official visit by royalty. ...traditional names used by royalty and the aristocracy for generations.*
2 NC **Royalties** are payments made to authors and musicians which are linked to the sales of their books or records, or to performances of their works. *...all the royalties from my next play. ...hundreds of millions of dollars a year in lost royalties.*

RP /ɑːpiː/
NU **RP** is a standard accent of British English that is considered to have no regional features. **RP** is an abbreviation for 'received pronunciation'.

rpm /ɑːpiːem/
rpm is an abbreviation for 'revolutions per minute'. It is used to indicate the speed of something by saying how many times it will go round in a circle in one minute. *Electricity generation requires speeds of several thousand rpm.*

RSVP /ɑːresviːpiː/
RSVP is written at the end of invitations and means 'please reply'. **RSVP** is an abbreviation for the French expression 'répondez s'il vous plaît'.

Rt. Hon. /raɪt ɒn/
In Britain, **Rt. Hon.** is used as part of the formal title of members of the Privy Council and some judges. **Rt.Hon.** is a written abbreviation for 'Right Honourable'. *...the Rt. Hon. Roy Jenkins.*

rub /rʌb/ **rubs, rubbing, rubbed**
1 VOorVA If you **rub** something, you move your hand or a cloth backwards and forwards over it while pressing firmly. *He groaned and rubbed his eyes... He rubbed at his throat. ...plant extracts, which after diluting, are rubbed and stroked into the skin.*
2 VOA If you **rub** a part of your body against a surface, you move it backwards and forwards while pressing it against the surface. *She rubbed her cheek against my temple.*
3 VOA If you **rub** a substance onto a surface, you spread it over the surface using your hand. *The ointment he rubbed into the wound made it feel better.*
4 V-ERG If two things **rub** together or if you **rub** them together, they move backwards and forwards, pressing against each other. *The brake pads are rubbing against the rotor... He rubbed his hands and laughed.*
● **Rub** is used in these phrases. ● If someone draws attention to something that involves you and that you find embarrassing or unpleasant, you can say that they are **rubbing it in**; an informal expression. *'How old*

are you? Forty?'—'All right, no need to rub it in.'
● **to rub salt into** someone's **wounds**: see **salt**. ● **to rub shoulders with** someone: see **shoulder**.
rub off PHRASAL VERB 1 If you **rub** something **off** a surface, you remove it by wiping the surface with something such as a cloth. *She rubbed off the dirt with her hand.* 2 If someone's habits or characteristics **rub off** on you, you develop the same habits or characteristics after spending time with them; an informal expression. *They hoped that some of his prowess might rub off on them.*
rub out PHRASAL VERB If you **rub out** something written on paper or on a blackboard, you remove it by rubbing it with a rubber or a cloth.
rubber /rʌbə/ **rubbers**
1 NU **Rubber** is a strong, waterproof, elastic substance made from the sap of a tropical tree. It can also be produced chemically. Rubber can be used for making products such as tyres and waterproof boots. *...a rubber ball. ...rubber gloves.*
2 NC A **rubber** is a small piece of rubber used for rubbing out writing.
rubber band, rubber bands
NC A **rubber band** is a thin circle of rubber that you put around things to hold them together. *The rubber band's been stretched.*
rubber bullet, rubber bullets
NC A **rubber bullet** is a bullet made of a metal ball coated with rubber. It is intended to injure people rather than kill them, and is used by police or soldiers to control crowds during a riot. *The police in Switzerland are reported to have used rubber bullets to break up a demonstration in the northern city of Winterthur... Riot police used teargas and rubber bullets to disperse the protesters.*
rubber plant, rubber plants
NC A **rubber plant** is a type of plant with shiny leaves. It grows naturally in Asia, but is also grown in pots indoors in other parts of the world.
rubber-stamp, rubber-stamps, rubber-stamping, rubber-stamped; also written **rubber stamp** when it is a noun.
1 NC A **rubber stamp** is a small device with something such as a name or a date on it. You press it on to an ink pad and then on to a document in order to show that the document has been officially dealt with. *Each voter has to use quite a large rubber stamp to make a mark in quite a small empty box.*
2 VO When someone in authority **rubber-stamps** something, they agree to it without thinking about it or discussing it; used showing disapproval. *The Council merely rubber-stamp decisions taken by him and his office.*
rubbery /rʌbəri/
ADJ Something that is **rubbery** is soft or stretchable like rubber. *...a long, rubbery piece of seaweed.*
rubbing /rʌbɪŋ/ **rubbings**
NC A **rubbing** is a picture that you make by putting a piece of paper over a carved surface and rubbing wax or charcoal over it to obtain an impression. *...rubbings of the tombstones.* ● See also **rub**.
rubbish /rʌbɪʃ/
1 NU **Rubbish** consists of unwanted things or waste material such as used paper or tins. *That old shed is full of rubbish. ...a rubbish dump.*
2 NU You can refer to something as **rubbish** when you think that it is of very poor quality. *He has described the story as rubbish... There is so much rubbish on TV.*
3 NU You can describe an idea or a statement as **rubbish** if you think that it is foolish or wrong; an informal use. *Don't talk rubbish... 'I suppose he has a right to be angry.'—'Rubbish!'*
rubbishy /rʌbɪʃi/
ADJ If you describe something as **rubbishy**, you mean that you think it is very poor quality; an informal word. *...food that they believe to be rubbishy. ...rooms which he thought rubbishy.*
rubble /rʌbl/
NU **Rubble** consists of the bricks or pieces of stone or concrete which result when a building is destroyed. *Every building was reduced to rubble.*

rubella /ruːbɛlə/
NU **Rubella** is a disease that is similar to measles. It causes you to have a cough, a sore throat, and red spots on your skin; a medical term. *Girls between 11 and 13 are given rubella vaccine.*
rubicund /ruːbɪkənd/
ADJ Someone who is **rubicund** has a red, shiny face; an old-fashioned, literary word. *Crowe smiled, benign and rubicund. ...a rubicund sea-captain.*
rubric /ruːbrɪk/ **rubrics**
NC A **rubric** is a set of rules or instructions, such as the instructions at the beginning of an examination paper; a formal word. *They want the process to go forward under some kind of UN rubric.*
ruby /ruːbi/ **rubies**
NC A **ruby** is a dark red jewel. *...a necklace of pearls, diamonds, emeralds and rubies.*
ruck /rʌk/ **rucks, rucking, rucked**
1 NC A **ruck** is a group of struggling people, for example in a fight or a game such as rugby; an old-fashioned or technical use. *...when a player has been tackled and a ruck has been formed.*
2 NC A **ruck** is also a fold or crease in cloth or clothing. *...a ruck of grey blanket... His sleeves were pushed back to the elbows in heavy rucks.*
3 N SING The **ruck** is used to refer to ordinary people or ordinary life; used showing disapproval. *Byron lifted him out of the ruck.*
rucksack /rʌksæk/ **rucksacks**
NC A **rucksack** is a bag, often on a frame, used for carrying things on your back, for example when you are climbing. *This compact water purifier can be carried in your rucksack on holiday.*
ruction /rʌkʃn/ **ructions**
NC **Ructions** are strong protests, quarrels, or other trouble; an informal word. *There'll be ructions when your mother hears about that!*
rudder /rʌdə/ **rudders**
NC A **rudder** is a vertical piece of wood or metal at the back of a boat or plane which is moved to make the boat or plane turn. *Coast guard officials who boarded the vessel at sea found that its rudder was broken.*
ruddy /rʌdi/
ADJ Something that is **ruddy** is reddish in colour; a literary word. *...a square ruddy face.*
rude /ruːd/ **ruder, rudest**
1 ADJ If someone is **rude**, they behave in a way that is not polite. *I was rather rude to a young nurse... It's rude to stare. ...rude remarks.* ◆ **rudeness** NU *He seemed not to notice their rudeness.*
2 ADJ **Rude** words and behaviour are likely to embarrass or offend people, because they relate to sex or other bodily functions. *...a rude gesture. ...a rude joke.*
3 ADJ ATTRIB **Rude** is also used to describe events that are unexpected and unpleasant. *...a rude awakening to the realization that he had been robbed.* ◆ **rudely** ADV *My belief in the future was rudely shattered.*
rudimentary /ruːdɪmɛntəri/
ADJ Something that is **rudimentary** is very basic and undeveloped or incomplete; a formal word. *Many do not even receive the most rudimentary education.*
rudiments /ruːdɪmənts/
N PL The **rudiments** of something are the simplest and most important things about it which you need to know in order to understand it. *Spain acquired many of the rudiments of modern science from their Arab neighbours.*
rue /ruː/ **rues, ruing, rued**
VO If you **rue** something that you have done, you are sorry that you did it, because it has had unpleasant results; a literary word. *I had ample cause to rue that decision.*
rueful /ruːfl/
ADJ If someone is **rueful**, they feel or express regret or sorrow in a quiet and gentle way; a literary word. *She managed a rueful little smile.* ◆ **ruefully** ADV *She smiled ruefully.*
ruff /rʌf/ **ruffs**
1 NC A **ruff** is a stiff strip of cloth or other material with many small folds in it, which was worn round the

neck in former times. *...a ruff of lace.*
2 NC A **ruff** is also a thick band of feathers or fur round the neck of a bird or animal. *...a deep brown ruff beneath the beak.*

ruffian /rʌfiən/ **ruffians**
NC A **ruffian** is a man who behaves in a bad mannered or violent way; an old-fashioned word. *The report said only a few ruffians were involved in the rebellion... He is a ruffian, always brawling, always in trouble at school.*

ruffle /rʌfl/ **ruffles, ruffling, ruffled**
1 VO If you **ruffle** someone's hair, you move your hand quickly and fairly roughly over their head as a way of showing affection. *He tingled wonderfully as she ruffled his hair.*
2 NC **Ruffles** are small, decorative folds of material. *...this season no puffs, ruffles, bows or pleats on the basis that they were too severe.*

ruffled /rʌfld/
1 ADJ Something that is **ruffled** is no longer smooth or neat. *...the ruffled bedclothes.*
2 ADJ **Ruffled** clothes are decorated with small folds of material. *...a ruffled white blouse.*
3 ADJ If someone is **ruffled,** they are confused or annoyed. *'Why don't you come back later?' said Alex, mildly ruffled.*

rug /rʌg/ **rugs**
1 NC A **rug** is a small piece of carpet material that you put on the floor. *...Oriental rugs.*
2 NC A **rug** is also a small blanket which you use to cover your shoulders or your knees. *...deck chairs in which you recline with a rug over your legs.*

rugby /rʌgbi/
NU **Rugby** is an outdoor game played between two teams who attempt to score by getting an oval ball behind their opponents' goal line. *Phil Davies is retiring from international rugby after being left out of the Welsh side... England's rugby union selectors have named their squad for the tour of Australia.*

rugged /rʌgɪd/
1 ADJ A **rugged** area of land is rocky and difficult to travel across, and is usually far away from where people live. *The coastline is wild and rugged... The separatists fight in rugged, mountainous countryside.*
2 ADJ If you describe a man as **rugged,** you mean that his physique or his facial features are strong or rough. *He was rugged and handsome.*

rugger /rʌgə/
NU **Rugger** is the same as **rugby**; an informal word. *A schoolboy was severely disabled on the rugger field.*

ruin /ruːɪn/ **ruins, ruining, ruined**
1 VO To **ruin** something means to severely harm, damage, or spoil it. *You are ruining your health... India's textile industry was ruined.*
2 NC A **ruin** is a building that has been partly destroyed. *It was splendid once, but it is a ruin now. ...the ruins of an old tower.*
3 If something is **in ruins,** it has been completely or almost completely destroyed. *The castle, partly in ruins, stands on a crag... Their once robust economy lies in ruins.*
4 N PL+*of* The **ruins** of something are the parts of it that remain after it has been severely damaged or weakened. *The Progressive Party was founded on the ruins of our Federal Party... The new state which will emerge from the ruins of the old will be an alliance.*
5 VO To **ruin** a person, an organization, or a country means to cause them no longer to have any money. *The contract would certainly have ruined him... The pressures this will place on an already unhealthy economy could ruin the country.* ◆ **ruined** ADJ ATTRIB *The German Unity Fund is designed to raise money to reconstruct the ruined East German economy.*
6 NU **Ruin** is the state of no longer having any money. *Crow was heading for ruin.*

ruination /ruːɪneɪʃn/
NU **Ruination** is the act of ruining something or the process of being ruined. *...the ruination of fields and crops by chemical sprays... He muttered wildly about the ruination of his life.*

ruined /ruːɪnd/
ADJ ATTRIB A **ruined** building has been badly damaged

or has fallen apart from disuse. *A radio report said that twenty-five thousand people were buried underneath the ruined buildings. ...a ruined mediaeval tower in the West of Ireland.*

ruinous /ruːɪnəs/
1 ADJ If something is **ruinous,** it costs far more money than you can afford or than is reasonable. *...the ruinous expense of a funeral... Militarisation is wasteful for any country and can be ruinous when taken to extremes.*
2 ADJ ATTRIB A **ruinous** state or condition is one in which a person, an organization, or a country has no more money. *They blame the President for the ruinous state of the country... These have all contributed to the airway's ruinous condition.*

rule /ruːl/ **rules, ruling, ruled**
1 NC **Rules** are instructions that tell you what you are allowed to do and what you are not allowed to do. *...the rules of chess... It is against the rules to keep pets... If she breaks the rules, she will be punished.*
2 N SING If something is the **rule,** it is the normal state of affairs. *Short haircuts became the rule.*
3 VOor V+*over* When someone **rules** a country, they control its affairs. *The National Liberation Front has ruled Algeria since its independence from France... At this time Denmark ruled over Southern Sweden.* ▶ Also NU+SUPP *...the days of British rule.*
4 V+*on* or V-REPORT When someone in authority **rules** on a particular matter, they give an official decision about it; a formal use. *I was asked to rule on the case of a British seaman... The Supreme Court ruled that there was no federal offence involved.*
5 See also **ruling, ground rules, majority rule, work-to-rule.**
● **Rule** is used in these phrases. ● If you say that a particular thing happens **as a rule,** you mean that it usually happens. *Doctors are not as a rule trained in child rearing.* ● If someone in authority **bends the rules,** they allow you to do something, even though it is against the rules. *A State Department spokesman welcomed the decision to bend the rules, which he said would avoid cutting off aid to Egypt.*

rule out PHRASAL VERB 1 If you **rule out** an idea or course of action, you reject it because it is impossible or unsuitable. *The Chadian president did not rule out a summit meeting with the Libyan leader... The United Nations has not ruled out the use of force to free Kuwait.* 2 If one thing **rules out** another, it prevents it from happening or from being possible. *The radio was on, effectively ruling out conversation.*

rule book, rule books
NC A **rule book** contains the official rules for a particular job, organization, and so on. *He relied on his own initiative, instead of on the rule book... The rule book said he should be provided with protective clothing.* ● If someone does something **by the rule book,** they do it in the way that is considered to be correct or reasonable in a particular situation; an informal expression. *They aren't fighting by the rule book, so why should we?*

ruled /ruːld/
ADJ ATTRIB **Ruled** paper has thin, straight lines printed across it. *She began to write on the ruled paper.*

rule of law
N SING The **rule of law** refers to the situation in which people obey their society's laws and enable that social system to function properly; a formal expression. *A free society depends on the rule of law... It was essential to uphold the rule of law.*

ruler /ruːlə/ **rulers**
1 NC A **ruler** is a person such as a president or a prime minister who governs a country. *Caesar was then ruler of Persia.*
2 NC A **ruler** is also a long, flat object with straight edges marked in inches or centimetres, which is used for measuring things or for drawing straight lines. *...your compass, pencil and ruler.*

ruling /ruːlɪŋ/ **rulings**
1 ADJ ATTRIB The **ruling** group of people in an organization or country is the group that controls its affairs. *...the Church's ruling body.*
2 NC A **ruling** is an official decision made by a judge

or a court. *The judge gave his ruling.*

rum /rʌm/

NU **Rum** is an alcoholic drink made from sugar cane juice. *Only spirit made from sugar cane can be called rum.*

rumble /rʌmbl/ **rumbles, rumbling, rumbled**

V If something **rumbles**, it makes a low, continuous noise, often while moving slowly. *...tanks and military trucks rumbling through the streets. ...the rumbling noise of barrels being rolled down the ramp.* ▶ Also NC *...a menacing rumble of distant thunder.*

rumble on PHRASAL VERB 1 If an argument, a discussion, or a process **rumbles on**, it continues happening for a long time in a way that does not attract a lot of attention. *The dispute rumbled on for over a century. ...as the legal arguments and submissions rumble on.* 2 If someone **rumbles on**, they continue speaking in a boring way for a long time. *He rumbled on in this vein for some time.*

rumbling /rʌmblɪŋ/ **rumblings**

1 NC A **rumbling** is a low, continuous noise. *...the rumbling of thunder.*

2 NC **Rumblings** are signs that a bad situation is developing. *...rumblings of discontent.*

ruminate /ruːmɪneɪt/ **ruminates, ruminating, ruminated**

V A or V If you **ruminate** about something, you think about it very carefully; a literary word. *He ruminated about the Bush-Dukakis campaign... MPs of all parties ruminated yesterday on the crisis facing Mrs Margaret Thatcher... She ruminated a bit longer.*

rumination /ruːmɪneɪʃn/ **ruminations**

NC Your **ruminations** are your careful thoughts about something; a literary word. *...their inspector's ruminations. ...the ruminations of my disciples.*

ruminative /ruːmɪnətɪv/

ADJ If you are **ruminative**, you are thinking very deeply and carefully about something; a literary word. *...a ruminative twenty minutes.* ◆ **ruminatively** ADV *He stares into it ruminatively... He drove back ruminatively to the school.*

rummage /rʌmɪdʒ/ **rummages, rummaging, rummaged**

V A If you **rummage** in a place, you search for something there by moving things in a hurried or careless way. *He rummaged around in his drawer... He begins rummaging in his bag... They are less willing to rummage through the garbage.*

rummy /rʌmi/

NU **Rummy** is a card game in which players try to collect cards of the same value or cards in a sequence. *I had to play rummy with Dr Lutz.*

rumour /ruːmə/ **rumours, rumoured**; spelt **rumor** in American English.

1 NC A **rumour** is a piece of information that may or may not be true, but that people are talking about. *There's a rumour that five army Commanders have committed suicide. ...rumours of street fighting and violence.*

2 V-PASS If something is **rumoured** to be true, people are suggesting that it is true, but they do not know for certain. *He was rumoured to be living in Detroit... It was rumoured that the body had been removed.*

rump /rʌmp/ **rumps**

1 NC An animal's **rump** is its rear end. *They are large thrushes with a chestnut back and a grey head and rump.*

2 NC Someone's **rump** is their buttocks; often used humorously. *I remember as a child watching my aunt's wide rump disappear into the marsh grass.*

3 N SING The **rump** of a group or organization consists of the members who remain in it or who are loyal to it after it has lost its importance or its power. *Rover is the new name for what is in effect the rump of Britain's one time proud motor manufacturing industry... The prospect will open up a formal split in the Arab League, with the majority moving to Cairo and a rump remaining in Tunis.*

rumple /rʌmpl/ **rumples, rumpling, rumpled**

V O If you **rumple** something, you cause it to be untidy or creased. *He rumpled her hair.* ◆ **rumpled** ADJ *...a rumpled grey suit.*

rumpus /rʌmpəs/

N SING A **rumpus** is a lot of noise or an argument. *They caused a rumpus in the House of Commons... An enquiry had been launched to find out who was involved in the rumpus.*

run /rʌn/ **runs, running, ran.** The form run is used in the present tense and is also the past participle of the verb.

1 V or V O When you **run**, or **run** a particular distance, you move quickly, leaving the ground during each stride. *I ran downstairs to open the door... He ran the mile in just over four minutes.* ▶ Also NC *We had to go for a cross-country run every weekend... He found himself breaking into a run.*

2 V A You say that something long, such as a road, **runs** in a particular direction when you are describing its course or position. *The reef runs parallel to the coast. ...a tunnel running from the Mediterranean into the Black Sea.*

3 V O A If you **run** an object or your hand over something, you move the object or your hand over it. *She ran her finger down a list of names.*

4 V A In an election, if someone **runs** for political office, they take part as a candidate; used in American English. *He ran for Governor... He ran for Vice President on the democratic ticket.*

5 V O If you **run** an organization or an activity, you are in charge of it or you organize it. *She ran the office as a captain runs a ship... We run a course for local teachers.*

6 V O If you **run** an experiment, computer program, or tape, you start it and let it continue. *Check everything and run the whole test again... We've run it through the computer a dozen times.*

7 V O If you **run** a car or piece of equipment, you have it and use it. *My mother runs her own car... A freezer doesn't cost much to run.*

8 V When a machine is **running**, it is switched on and operating. *The engine was running.*

9 V-ERG If a machine **runs** on or off a particular source of energy or if you **run** a machine on or off a particular source of energy, you use that source of energy to make it work. *The heater ran on half-price electricity... You can run the entire system off a mains plug.*

10 V If a train or bus **runs** somewhere, it travels there on a regular route at set times. *No buses have been running in the town for the past week... The train was running from Pakistan to India.*

11 V O A If you **run** someone somewhere in a car, you drive them there. *Would you mind running me to the station?*

12 V A If a liquid **runs** in a particular direction, it flows in that direction. *Tears were running down his face... The river ran past our house.*

13 V O If you **run** water or if you **run** a tap, you cause water to flow from the tap. *She was running hot water into the tub... Run my bath now!*

14 V If the colour in a piece of clothing **runs**, it comes out when the clothing is washed. *The colours had faded and run.*

15 V A If a play, event, or legal contract **runs** for a particular period of time, it lasts for that period of time. *'Chu-Chin-Chow' ran for years... The monsoons had six weeks more to run.*

16 NC+SUPP In the theatre, a **run** is the period of time during which the production of a play, opera, or ballet is regularly performed. *The play ended its six-week run at the Regent.*

17 NC+SUPP A **run** of success or failure is a series of successes or failures. *This policy has had an unending run of success in Africa... Leeds United had a run of wins in December.*

18 NC In cricket or baseball, a **run** is a score of one, which is made by players running between marked places on the pitch after hitting the ball. *They had beaten England by seventeen runs.*

19 See also **running, trial run.**

● **Run** is used in these phrases. ● If someone is **on the run**, they are trying to escape or hide from someone such as the police or an enemy. *He is on the run after being arrested on drugs charges.* ● If you **make a run** for it or if you **run for it**, you go somewhere quickly in order to escape from something. *It was still raining hard, but we made a run for it... We'll just have to run for it.* ● If you talk about what will happen **in the long run**, you are saying what you think will happen over a long period of time in the future. If you talk about what will happen **in the short run**, you are saying what you think will happen in the near future. *Their policy would prove very costly in the long run... The President in the short run was preparing himself for 1993.* ● If someone or something **runs late**, they have taken more time than had been planned. *I'm in a rush this morning, I'm running late for my train... In the women's event, the defending champion received a reprieve when play ran late.* ● If a river or well **runs dry**, it ceases to have any water in it. *Their only source of water, a reservoir in the mountains, will probably run dry before the end of the year.* ● If people's feelings are **running high**, they are very angry, concerned, or excited. *Public indignation was running high.* ● to **make** your **blood run cold**: see blood. ● to **run its course**: see course. ● to **run** someone or something **to ground**: see ground. ● to **run the risk**: see risk. ● to **run wild**: see wild.

run across PHRASAL VERB If you **run across** someone, you meet them unexpectedly. *I keep running across my old students.*

run along PHRASAL VERB If you tell a child to **run along**, you mean that you want them to go away; an informal expression. *Run along up to bed now, Sam.*

run away PHRASAL VERB 1 If you **run away** from a place, you leave it because you are unhappy there. *He had run away from home at the age of thirteen.* 2 See also **runaway**.

run away with PHRASAL VERB If you let your emotions **run away with** you, you fail to control them. *They did not allow their enthusiasm to run away with them.*

run down PHRASAL VERB 1 If you **run down** people or things, you criticize them strongly. *She was not used to people running down their own families.* 2 See also **run-down**.

run into PHRASAL VERB 1 If you **run into** problems or difficulties, you unexpectedly begin to experience them. *The firm ran into foreign exchange problems.* 2 If you **run into** someone, you meet them unexpectedly. *I ran into him in a gay bar.* 3 If a vehicle **runs into** something, it accidentally hits it. *It crashed into a car which in turn collided with a truck which ran into a third car... A diesel engine ran into the back of another train.* 4 You use **run into** to say that something costs a lot of money. *...exports running into billions of dollars.*

run off PHRASAL VERB 1 If you **run off** with someone, you secretly go away with them in order to live with them or marry them. *His wife ran off with another man.* 2 If you **run off** copies of a piece of writing, you produce them using a machine. *Could you run me off five copies of this article, please?*

run on PHRASAL VERB If something **runs on**, it continues for longer than expected. *Donleavy tends to let his jokes run on too long.*

run out PHRASAL VERB 1 If you **run out** of something or if it **runs out**, you have no more of it left. *We were rapidly running out of money... Time is running out fast.* ● to **run out of steam**: see steam. 2 When a legal document **runs out**, it stops being valid. *My passport's run out.*

run over PHRASAL VERB If a vehicle **runs over** someone or something, it knocks them down. *Rosamund nearly got run over last night.*

run through PHRASAL VERB 1 If you **run through** something, you rehearse it or practise it. *You could hear the performers running through the whole programme in the background.* 2 If you **run through** a list of items, you read or mention all the items quickly. *He ran through what were expected to be the main items of discussion.* 3 See also **run-through**.

run to PHRASAL VERB 1 If you **run to** someone, you go to them for help or to tell them something. *I didn't think he'd run to you with the story.* 2 If something **runs to** a particular amount or size, it is that amount

or size; a formal expression. *The transcript runs to 1,200 pages.*

run up PHRASAL VERB 1 If someone **runs up** bills or debts, they acquire them by buying a lot of things or borrowing money. *Many countries ran up huge foreign debts in the boom years of the 1970s.* 2 See also **run-up**.

run up against PHRASAL VERB If you **run up against** problems, you suddenly begin to experience them. *Each peace keeping force ran up against the hostility between Syria and Iraq... The investigation ran up against a number of obstacles.*

runabout /rʌnəbaʊt/ **runabouts**
NC A **runabout** is a small car used mainly for short journeys; an informal word. *Sabine pulled up in her little runabout.*

runaround /rʌnəraʊnd/
If someone **gives** you **the runaround**, they deliberately do not give you all the information or help that you want; an informal expression. *Everybody I ask gives me the runaround.*

runaway /rʌnəweɪ/
1 ADJ ATTRIB You use **runaway** to describe someone who has left their home secretly. *...a runaway slave.*
2 ADJ ATTRIB A **runaway** vehicle is moving and its driver has lost control of it. *...a runaway bulldozer.*
3 ADJ ATTRIB You also use **runaway** to describe situations which happen unexpectedly and cannot be controlled. *...the runaway success of 'Nicholas Nickleby'.*

run-down
1 ADJ PRED If someone is **run-down**, they are tired or ill; an informal use. *If you start to feel run-down, then cut down on your training and rest.*
2 ADJ A **run-down** building or organization is in very poor condition. *...two small rooms in a run-down building. ...run-down public services.*
3 N SING If you give someone the **run-down** on a situation or subject, you tell them the important facts about it; an informal use. *Now, first, give us a quick rundown on what these taxes and spending cuts are.*

rung /rʌŋ/ **rungs**
1 NC The **rungs** of a ladder are the wooden or metal bars that form the steps. *I had my foot on the first rung when she grabbed my arm.*
2 NC+SUPP If you reach a particular **rung** in an organization, you reach that level in it. *...the lower rungs of management.*
3 **Rung** is also the past participle of some meanings of **ring**.

run-in, run-ins
1 NC If you have a **run-in** with someone, you argue or quarrel with them; an informal use. *He's probably had a run-in at work with Ted. ...a minor run-in with Eldridge over the money.*
2 NC A **run-in** is also a violent struggle or a short armed conflict. *After several run-ins, they formed their own gangs for protection. ...those early spring run-ins with the enemy when we began talking about chemical weapons.*
3 NC A **run-in** is also a rehearsal which takes place just before the actual performance or just before a more important performance. *We'd done it for two weeks in Birmingham as a run-in for the main season.*
4 NC The **run-in** to an event is the period of time or the journey before it. *The situation looks set to remain tense during the run-in to that meeting.*

runner /rʌnə/ **runners**
1 NC A **runner** is a person who runs, especially for sport or pleasure. *...a long-distance runner... Not being a fast runner, I was glad I was close to the hall.*
2 NC+SUPP A drugs **runner** or gun **runner** is someone who illegally takes drugs or guns into a country. *Questioning of the drug runner led to the present investigation.*
3 NC **Runners** are thin strips of wood or metal underneath something which help it to move smoothly. *...sledge runners.*

runner bean, runner beans
NC **Runner beans** are the long green pods of a climbing plant which are eaten as a vegetable.

runner-up, runners-up

NC A **runner-up** is a person or team that finishes in second place in a race or competition. In some competitions, many people can be runners-up. *He had once been a runner-up for the King's Cup... One hundred runners-up will all receive a sweatshirt.*

running /rʌnɪŋ/

1 NU **Running** is the activity of running, especially as a sport. *...running the Boston marathon... Two gunmen were seen running from the scene of the crime.*

2 NU+SUPP The **running** of an organization, company, and so on is the activity of managing or organizing it. *...the day-to-day running of the school... The United Nations itself will shortly take over the running of the refugee camps.*

3 ADJ ATTRIB You can also use **running** to describe things such as disputes that are continuous. *...a running battle between architects and planners. ...an attempt to defuse the running confrontation between the township youths and the police.*

4 ADJ after N You also use **running** to say that something happens repeatedly. For example, if something has happened every day for five days, you can say that it has happened for five days running, or that it has happened for the fifth day running. *For three days running he had left the sandwiches at home.*

5 ADJ ATTRIB **Running** water is flowing rather than standing still. *...the sound of running water.*

● **Running** is used in these phrases. ● If someone **makes the running** in a situation, they take the initiative or advantage because they are more active than the other people involved. *Women made all the running in the demands for change.* ● If someone is **in the running** for something, they have a good chance of winning or obtaining it. If they are **out of the running**, they have no chance of winning or obtaining it. *He's still in the running for the leadership of the Labour Party... This may have put him out of the running for the coveted title.*

running commentary, running commentaries

NC A **running commentary** is a detailed, continuous description of an event, especially a sporting event, that is spoken or broadcast while the event is taking place. *...a running commentary on the match against Brazil... She gave him an exhaustive tour of the shrine and a running commentary.*

running costs

N PL The **running costs** of a company or an organization are the money it spends on day-to-day administration, rather than on expansion or development. *The party did not rely on official grants to meet its running costs. ...an attempt to reduce running costs.*

running mate, running mates

NC In an election campaign, someone's **running mate** is the person that they choose to be the candidate for a political post that is the next lower in rank to the post for which they are trying to be elected; used in American English. *...McGovern's vice presidential running mate... Wallace had asked him to be his running mate.*

runny /rʌni/

1 ADJ Something that is **runny** is more liquid than usual or than was intended. *They had runny eggs for breakfast.*

2 ADJ If someone's nose or eyes are **runny**, liquid is flowing from them. *They developed symptoms like sore eyes, runny noses and problems with breathing.*

run-off, run-offs

NCorN+N A **run-off** is an extra race or contest which is held at the end of a competition in order to decide the winner, because two people or teams have got the same number of points, votes, and so on. *...school memories of run-off races which I always lost... The run-off elections in the remaining three constituencies will be held this weekend.*

run-of-the-mill

ADJ If you describe someone or something as **run-of-the-mill**, you mean that person or thing is very ordinary in ability or quality, with no interesting

features. *...a run-of-the-mill engineer. ...run-of-the-mill stories.*

runt /rʌnt/ **runts**

NC If you call a small person a **runt**, you are expressing your dislike for them because you think they are small or unimportant. *Pegler was a skinny little runt.*

run-through, run-throughs

NC A **run-through** of a play or event is a rehearsal of it or practice for it. *The operation was just a preliminary run-through.*

run-up

N SING The **run-up** to an event is the period of time just before it. *...the run-up to the election.*

runway /rʌnweɪ/ **runways**

NC A **runway** is a long strip of ground with a hard surface which is used by aeroplanes when they are taking off or landing. *The plane has taxied down to the end of the runway.*

rupee /ruːpiː/ **rupees**

NC A **rupee** is a unit of money that is used in India, Pakistan, and some other countries. *Gunmen stole more than twelve-million rupees from the government treasury at Anantnag.*

rupture /rʌptʃə/ **ruptures, rupturing, ruptured**

1 V-ERG or V-REFL If you **rupture** a part of your body or if part of your body **ruptures**, it tears or bursts open. *An abscess had ruptured... He ruptured himself playing football. ...the Mayor's ruptured appendix.*

2 NC A **rupture** is a severe injury in which a part of your body tears or bursts open. Ruptures occur especially in the wall between the bowel and the abdomen. *He has suffered a rupture to the aorta, the main artery leading from the heart.*

3 NC When there is a **rupture** between people, their relationship ends; a formal use. *The two countries restored diplomatic relations in 1986, after a 21-year rupture.*

rural /rʊərəl/

ADJ ATTRIB **Rural** means relating to country areas as opposed to large towns. *...small rural schools... The grants are to be used to improve water supplies in rural areas.*

ruse /ruːz/ **ruses**

NC A **ruse** is an action or plan which is intended to deceive someone; a formal word. *The offer was just a ruse to gain time.*

rush /rʌʃ/ **rushes, rushing, rushed**

1 VA To **rush** somewhere means to go there quickly. *When they saw us, they rushed forward... Please don't rush off... Police rushed to the spot.*

2 V+to-INF or V+to When people **rush** to do something, they do it without delay, because they are very eager to do it. *People were rushing to buy the newspaper... Her friends rushed to her aid.*

3 VO If a group of people such as police or soldiers **rush** a person or a place, they attack them suddenly in order to take control of them. *His officers had rushed the prisoners on the roof... A group of students rushed the heavily guarded front fence of the U.S. embassy.*

4 VO If you **rush** something, you do it in a hurry. *I rushed my lunch... Stop rushing it!* ◆ **rushed** ADJ ATTRIB *It'll be a bit of a rushed job, I'm afraid.*

5 VOA If you **rush** someone or something to a place, you take them there quickly. *Barnett was rushed to hospital with a broken back... The victim of the attack was rushed to the nearby Royal Victoria Hospital.*

6 VO If you **rush** someone into doing something, you make them do it without allowing them enough time to think about it. *Do not be rushed into parting with goods before taking legal advice.*

7 If there is **no rush** to do something, there is no need to do it quickly. *There is no rush to fill the vacancy... I'm not in any rush... He decided that there was no rush for him to declare his own candidacy.*

8 N SING+SUPP If there is a **rush** for something or a **rush** to do something, there is a sudden increase in people's attempts to get it or do it. *There had been a rush for tickets. ...a rush to find the treasure.*

9 VA If air or liquid **rushes** somewhere, it flows there suddenly and quickly. *The water rushed in over the top of his boots.* ► Also N SING *There was a little rush*

of air. ◆ **rushing** ADJ ATTRIB *They were carried along in the rushing stream.*
10 N SING+*of* If you experience a **rush** of a feeling, you suddenly experience it very strongly. *She felt a rush of pity for the boy... He felt a rush of nausea and dizziness.*
11 N PL The **rushes** of a film are the parts that have been filmed but have not yet been edited; a technical term. *We had never been allowed to see any of the rushes, nor had any of the bosses at RKO.*
12 NC **Rushes** are plants that grow near water and have long, thin stems.
rush in PHRASAL VERB If you **rush in** or **rush into** something, you do or decide something too quickly, without thinking about it carefully enough. *It doesn't help us to rush in and then spoil the opportunity that has been given to us... Don't rush into marriage.*

rush-hour
N SING The **rush-hour** is the period during the morning and the evening when most people are travelling to or from work. *I had to start in the morning rush-hour.*

rusk /rʌsk/ **rusks**
NC A **rusk** is a hard, dry biscuit, especially one that is given to babies. *At six months, they can hold their own rusk. ...salads and slimming rusks.*

russet /rʌsɪt/
ADJ **Russet** means reddish-brown in colour; a literary word. *She had russet curls. ...golden-brown and russet leaves.*

Russia /rʌʃə/
The Federation of **Russia** is the largest and most populous of the former republics of the USSR. It extends from the Arctic Ocean and Baltic Sea in the north and west, across all of northern Asia to the Pacific Ocean, and to the borders of Mongolia and China in the south and east. Boris Yeltsin was elected President in 1991. Russia produces machinery, iron and steel, chemicals, and timber. It joined the Commonwealth of Independent States in 1991.
◆ **Russian** /rʌʃn/ N, ADJ
▪ *per capita GNP:* US$5,810 ▪ *religion:* Christianity ▪ *language:* Russian ▪ *currency:* rouble ▪ *capital:* Moscow ▪ *population:* 147 million ▪ *size:* 17 million square kilometres.

rust /rʌst/ **rusts, rusting, rusted**
1 NU **Rust** is a brown substance that forms on iron or steel which has been in contact with water and which is in the process of gradually decaying. *Air with moisture in it can cause rust.*
2 V When a metal object **rusts**, it becomes covered in rust. *She pushed it out into the yard and left it to rust.* ◆ **rusted** ADJ *...kicking some rusted tins.*

rustic /rʌstɪk/
ADJ ATTRIB **Rustic** things are simple, often in a way that is typical of the countryside; a literary word. *...rustic comfort and good food. ...rustic benches.*

rustle /rʌsl/ **rustles, rustling, rustled**
1 V-ERG When something **rustles** or when you **rustle** it, it makes soft sounds as it moves. *They could hear mice rustling about... He rustled his papers.* ◆ **rustling, rustlings** NCorNU *Jim heard some furtive rustlings among the bushes.*
2 NCorNU A **rustle** is a soft sound made by something moving gently. *She heard a rustle behind her and turned. ...the rustle of chocolate wrappers.*
rustle up PHRASAL VERB If you **rustle up** a meal, you cook it quickly using whatever food you have available. *I'll rustle something up... We could rustle up an omelette.*

rustler /rʌslə/ **rustlers**
NC A **rustler** is someone who steals other people's animals. *Mr Kitele says the rustlers came from just across the border.*

rusty /rʌsti/
1 ADJ Something that is **rusty** is affected by rust. *...a heap of rusty tins.*

2 ADJ If someone's skill or knowledge is **rusty**, it is not as good as it was before, because they have not used it for a long time; an informal use. *My German's pretty rusty.*

rut /rʌt/ **ruts**
1 NC A **rut** is a deep, narrow mark made in the ground by the wheels of vehicles. *We bumped over the ruts.*
2 NC If someone is in a **rut**, they have become fixed in their way of thinking and doing things which makes them feel dissatisfied or prevents them from making progress. *We tend to get into a rut... The crisis was brought on by errors of leadership, which got the country into a rut.*
3 N SING The **rut** is the period of the year when some animals such as deer are sexually active, and the males fight for leadership of the herd. *Stags stop feeding during the rut, and can only hold hinds for three or four weeks.*

ruthless /ruːθləs/
ADJ Someone who is **ruthless** is very harsh or determined, and will do anything that is necessary to achieve their aim. *Political power was in the hands of a few ruthless men. ...a ruthless investigation.*
◆ **ruthlessly** ADV *Napoleon acted swiftly and ruthlessly.* ◆ **ruthlessness** NU *He often operated with extreme ruthlessness.*

rutted /rʌtɪd/
ADJ A road or surface that is **rutted** is very uneven because it has a lot of ruts in it. *We turned off down a little rutted lane... The road was narrow and deeply rutted by the passage of numerous heavy vehicles.*

Rüütel, Arnold /ɔːnɒld ruːtel/
Arnold Rüütel became President of Estonia in 1990. He was Secretary of the Central Committee of the Estonian Communist Party from 1977 to 1979, First Deputy President of the Council of Ministers from 1979 to 1983, and President of the Presidium of the Supreme Soviet of Estonia from 1983 to 1984. He was Deputy President of the Presidium of the Supreme Soviet of the USSR from 1984 to 1990, and President from 1990 to 1991. Born: 1928.

Rwanda /ruː̈ændə/
The **Republic of Rwanda** is a country in central Africa, which is the most densely populated in Africa. It was part of German East Africa from 1899 until the First World War, when Belgium was granted a United Nations mandate to govern it. Rwanda became independent in 1962. Major-General Juvénal Habyarimana became President in a coup in 1973. He established the National Revolutionary Movement for Development (MRND) as the sole legal party in 1975. Political parties were legalized in 1991, when the MRND was renamed the National Republican Movement for Democracy and Development. Ethnic violence between Hutu and Tutsi has been a source of civil disorder. The Rwandan Patriotic Front (FRP) is a guerrilla group, which aims to overthrow the government and return Tutsi refugees who have fled Rwanda during periods of ethnic violence. Rwanda exports coffee, tea, and tin. It is a member of the Organization of African Unity. ◆ **Rwandan** /ruː̈ændən/ N, ADJ
▪ *per capita GNP:* US$310 ▪ *religion:* animism, Christianity (mainly Roman Catholic) ▪ *language:* French and Kinyarwanda (official), Kiswahili ▪ *currency:* franc ▪ *capital:* Kigali ▪ *population:* 7 million (1989) ▪ *size:* 26,338 square kilometres.

rye /raɪ/
NU **Rye** is a type of cereal grass that is grown in cold countries for animals to eat, and for making some types of bread and whisky. *Rye and barley contain more soluble fibre than wheat.*

rye whiskey
NU **Rye whiskey** is whisky made from rye. *...several barrels of rye whiskey.*

S s

S, s /ɛs/ **S's, s's**
1 NC **S** is the nineteenth letter of the English alphabet.
2 **s** was a written form of 'shilling' or 'shillings' in Britain before decimal currency was introduced in 1971.
3 **S** is a written abbreviation for 'south'.

-s; also spelt **-es**. The ending **-s** is pronounced /-s/ when it follows the consonant sounds /p, t, k, f/ or /θ/ and pronounced /-z/ when it follows a vowel sound and pronounced /-ɪz/ otherwise.
1 SUFFIX **-s** and **-es** are added to nouns to form plurals. ...*dogs, cats, and rabbits*. ...*ancient palaces*. ...*profits and losses*.
2 SUFFIX **-s** and **-es** are added to verbs to form the third person singular of the present tense. *The lift stops at the fifth floor... He realizes what he has done... He pushes the button.*

-'s; pronounced /-s/ after the consonant sounds /p, t, k, f/ or /θ/ and /-ɪz/ after the consonant sounds /s, z, ʃ, ʒ, tʃ/ or /dʒ/. In all other cases **-'s** is pronounced /-z/.
1 SUFFIX **-'s** is added to singular nouns or names, and plural nouns that do not end in 's', to form possessives. With a plural noun ending in 's', you form the possessive by just adding '. ...*Ralph's voice... The girl's name was Pam. ...women's rights. ...students' interests.*
2 SUFFIX **-'s** is a short form of 'is' or 'has', especially when 'has' is an auxiliary verb; used in speech and in informal written English. *It's fantastic... She's gone home.*
3 SUFFIX **-'s** is added to letters, numbers, and abbreviations to form plurals. ...*a row of q's. ...the 1870's.*

Sabah, Sheikh Jaber al-Ahmad al-
/dʒɑːbə əl ɑːxməd əsəbɑːx/
Sheikh Jaber al-Ahmad al-Sabah became Amir of Kuwait in 1977, when he succeeded his uncle. He was Prime Minister from 1965 to 1967, and Crown Prince from 1966 to 1977. Born: 1928.

Sabah, Sheikh Saad al-Abdullah al-Salem al-
/sɑːd əl æbdʊlə əsɑliːm əsəbɑːx/
Sheikh Saad al-Abdullah al-Salem al-Sabah became Crown Prince and Prime Minister of Kuwait in 1978. Born: 1930.

Sabbath /sæbəθ/
N PROP The **Sabbath** is the day of the week which members of some religious groups, especially Jews and Christians, devote to religious worship. Jews celebrate the Sabbath on Saturdays and Christians celebrate it on Sundays. *The subject of sport on the Sabbath is still an emotive one.*

sabbatical /səbætɪkl/ **sabbaticals**
NC A **sabbatical** is a period of time during which a teacher or university lecturer can leave their normal teaching duties so that they can travel or study. *The contract allows you to take a sabbatical every seven years... Professor Steel, currently on sabbatical in London, is doing research for a new book.*

saber /seɪbə/. See **sabre**.

sable /seɪbl/ **sables**; **sable** can be the plural form for the meaning in paragraph 2.
1 NU **Sable** is a very expensive fur that is used to make things such as coats and hats. *The only furs I like are sable and mink. ...a sable jacket.*
2 NC A **sable** is a wild animal that lives in northern Europe and northern Asia, from which sable is obtained. ...*a sister group of animals such as oryx, sable and roan antelope.*

sabotage /sæbətɑːʒ/ **sabotages, sabotaging, sabotaged**
1 VO If something is **sabotaged**, it is deliberately damaged or destroyed. *The power station had been sabotaged by anti-government guerrillas... Rebels say they sabotaged the oil pipeline.* ▶ Also NU ...*widespread sabotage and the disruption of rail communications. ...several failed attempts to carry out sabotage attacks.*
2 VO If you **sabotage** a plan or activity, you deliberately prevent it from being successful. *I don't wish to be accused of sabotaging the President's programme.*

saboteur /sæbətɜː/ **saboteurs**
NC A **saboteur** is a person who deliberately damages or destroys things such as machines, railway lines, and bridges in order to weaken an enemy or as a protest. *Orders were given to root out the saboteurs.*

sabre /seɪbə/ **sabres**; also spelt **saber** in American English.
1 NC A **sabre** is a heavy sword with a curved blade, that was formerly used by soldiers on horseback. *A soldier came up to her with a drawn sabre.*
2 NC A **sabre** is also a light sword used in fencing. ...*the men's sabre team.*

sabre-rattling
NU **Sabre-rattling** is an aggressive show of force, usually in a military context, which is intended to intimidate the enemy or the opponent. *The inevitable showdown finally happened after weeks of sabre-rattling... The threats are mere sabre-rattling.*

sac /sæk/ **sacs**
NC A **sac** is a small part of an animal's body, shaped like a little bag. It contains air, liquid or some other substance; a technical term in biology. ...*the nectar that a bee can bring back in its honey sac. ...an extra amount of fluid in the sac that surrounds the testicle.*

saccharine; also spelt **saccharin**. **Saccharine** is usually pronounced /sækəʰrɪn/ when it is a noun and /sækəriːn/ when it is an adjective.
1 NU **Saccharine** is a sweet chemical substance, sometimes used instead of sugar.
2 ADJ If you describe someone or something as **saccharine**, you mean that they are too sentimental. *He has been mocked for being saccharine. ...saccharine portrayals of the elderly.*

sachet /sæʃeɪ/ **sachets**
NC A **sachet** is a small closed plastic or paper packet, containing a small quantity of something. *Cut the top off the sachet. ...a large shampoo sachet.*

sack /sæk/ **sacks, sacking, sacked**
1 NC A **sack** is a large bag made of rough material. Sacks are used to carry or store goods. ...*sacks of flour.*
2 NC A **sack** is also a large bag made of strong brown

paper that people carry their food shopping in when they leave a shop or market; used in American English. *They couldn't find a sack in the market.*
3 VO If your employers **sack** you from your job, they say that you can no longer work for them, often because your work is not good enough. *Three railwaymen were sacked because they would not join a union.* ● See also **sacking**.
4 If you **get the sack** or **are given the sack**, your employer sacks you. *One thousand employees have been given the sack... They are going to get the sack.*
5 VO If an army or other group of people **sacks** a building or town, they destroy it and take away anything of value. *Rebels took over a state-owned supermarket and sacked it... They have taken to murdering officials and sacking villages.*

sackcloth /ˈsækklɒθ/
1 NU **Sackcloth** is rough woven material that is used to make sacks. *...saris wrapped in sackcloth to protect them.*
2 NU If you talk about **sackcloth** or **sackcloth and ashes**, you are referring to someone's exaggerated attempt to apologize or to compensate for something they have done wrong; an old-fashioned use. *They would long ago have repented in sackcloth and ashes.*

sacking /ˈsækɪŋ/ **sackings**
1 NC The **sacking** of someone is their dismissal from their job. *...the sacking of thousands of civil servants... The news of his sacking was greeted with consternation. ...a wave of sackings.*
2 N SING The **sacking** of a place is its destruction, especially by an invading army. *...the sacking of Kuwait. ...the sacking of churches by the Communists in the early thirties.*
3 NU **Sacking** is rough woven material that is used to make sacks. *The Belgian produced several rolls of hessian sacking and laid them on the desk. ...little huts patched together out of mud and old boards and pieces of sacking.*

Sacko, Soumana /suːmɑːnɑː ˈsækəʊ/
Soumana Sacko was appointed Prime Minister of Mali in 1991. He served as Minister of Finance in 1987. He is a member of the Transition Committee for the Salvation of the People (CTSP).

sacrament /ˈsækrəmənt/ **sacraments**
NC A **sacrament** is an important Christian religious ceremony such as communion, baptism, or marriage. *This doctrine of the Eucharist is the key sacrament.*

sacred /ˈseɪkrɪd/
1 ADJ Something that is **sacred** is believed to be holy. *They entered the sacred mosque.* ◆ **sacredness** NU *The sacredness of the shrine had been violated.*
2 ADJ ATTRIB **Sacred** also means connected with religion or used in religious ceremonies. *...sacred music.*
3 ADJ You can describe something as **sacred** when you regard it as too important to be changed or interfered with. *In their search for a good news story, nothing was sacred.* ◆ **sacredness** NU *...the sacredness of private property.*

sacred cow, sacred cows
NC You can describe a belief, custom, or institution as a **sacred cow** when you think that people regard it with too much respect and never criticize it or question it. *The need for secrecy has become a kind of sacred cow... Politically speaking, the National Health Service has been a sacred cow.*

sacrifice /ˈsækrɪfaɪs/ **sacrifices, sacrificing, sacrificed**
1 VO To **sacrifice** an animal means to kill it as an offering to God or to a god. *White animals were sacrificed by white-robed priests.* ► Also NCorNU *...a ritual sacrifice. ...human sacrifice.*
2 VO If you **sacrifice** something valuable or important, you give it up, often in order to do something for another person. *...women who have sacrificed career and marriage to care for elderly relatives.* ► Also NCorNU *...a mother's sacrifices for her children. ...a story of bravery and sacrifice.*

sacrificial /ˌsækrɪˈfɪʃl/
ADJ ATTRIB **Sacrificial** means connected with or used in a religious sacrifice. *...sacrificial victims.*

sacrilege /ˈsækrɪlɪdʒ/
1 NU **Sacrilege** is disrespectful behaviour towards something holy. *The Archbishop called it an act of desecration and sacrilege.*
2 NU You can also use **sacrilege** to refer to disrespect that is shown towards a person or thing you admire or believe in. *Air Marshals reject the idea as sacrilege.*

sacrilegious /ˌsækrɪˈlɪdʒəs/
ADJ If your behaviour is **sacrilegious**, you show disrespect towards something holy or towards something that should be respected. *It would have been sacrilegious to speak.*

sacrosanct /ˈsækrəsæŋkt/
ADJ Something that is **sacrosanct** is considered to be so important or special that it must not be criticized or changed. *He seems to think there's something sacrosanct about his annual fishing trip... The League of Communists remains sacrosanct in Serbia.*

sad /sæd/ **sadder, saddest**
1 ADJ If you are **sad**, you are not happy, usually because something upleasant has happened. *She looked sad... He was sad to see her go. ...a sad face.* ◆ **sadly** ADV *He shook his head sadly.* ◆ **sadness** NU *The news filled him with sadness.*
2 ADJ Something that is **sad** makes you feel sad. *She told Susan there was some sad news for her.* ◆ **sadness** NU *...the indescribable sadness of those final pages.*
3 ADJ ATTRIB You also use **sad** to describe an unfortunate situation. *The sad fact is that full employment may never be regained... It's a sad day for world cricket. ...one of the saddest elements of the crisis.* ◆ **sadly** ADVorADV SEN *One aspect of education today has been sadly neglected... Sadly, we don't appear to have much chance of getting the contract.*

sadden /ˈsædn/ **saddens, saddening, saddened**
VO If something **saddens** you, it makes you feel sad. *I'm saddened by the fact that so many people died for nothing.*

saddle /ˈsædl/ **saddles, saddling, saddled**
1 NC A **saddle** is a leather seat that you sit on when you ride a horse or other animal. *Jennifer swung herself into the saddle.*
2 NC A **saddle** is also a seat on a bicycle. *He made a living selling insurance policies from the saddle of his bicycle.*
3 VO If you **saddle** a horse or pony, you put a saddle on it. *My father often saddled his horse and rode to Madwaleni to visit the family.*
4 VO In horse racing, you can say that someone **saddles** a horse when he or she is the trainer of that horse and decides when it should race. *Pipe became the first trainer to saddle one hundred winners before the New Year... Owen O'Neill saddles Mole Board for the Sun Alliance Hurdles on Wednesday.*
● **Saddle** is used in these phrases. ● To be **in the saddle** means to be riding a horse or bicycle, usually in a race. *He will be in the saddle for next month's Tour of the Americas.* ● To be **in the saddle** also means to be in a position of power or control. *The reformist leader is back in the saddle and looking a great deal stronger... The same commanders remained in the saddle.*

saddle up PHRASAL VERB If you **saddle up**, you put a saddle on a horse or pony. *I saddled up and rode off... He went out to saddle up his horse.*

saddle with PHRASAL VERB If you **saddle** someone **with** something unpleasant or difficult, you put them in a position where they have to deal with it. *The last thing I want is to saddle myself with a second mortgage... This 'old-fashioned' view of socialism is something the Labour Party today shouldn't be saddled with.*

saddlebag /ˈsædlbæɡ/ **saddlebags**
NC A **saddlebag** is a bag attached to the saddle of a horse, bicycle, or motorcycle. *The books could have fallen from somebody's saddlebags as they were riding through the town.*

sadism /ˈseɪdɪzəm/
NU **Sadism** is behaviour in which a person gets pleasure from hurting other people and making them suffer. *He teased her with malicious sadism.* ◆ **sadist, sadists** NC *...sadists and bullies.*

sadistic /sədɪstɪk/
ADJ Someone who is **sadistic**, or whose behaviour is sadistic, gets pleasure from hurting other people and making them suffer. ...*scenes of sadistic cruelty.*
♦ **sadistically** /sədɪstɪkəᵊli/ ADV *He was sadistically cruel in his interrogations.*

sado-masochism /seɪdəʊmæsəkɪzəm/
NU **Sado-masochism** is sexual activity between two people in which one of them has a sadistic role and the other one has a masochistic role. *The judge went on to characterize the photographs as portraying sado-masochism.*

sado-masochistic /seɪdəʊmæsəkɪstɪk/
ADJ **Sado-masochistic** is used to describe a person, a thing, or an activity that involves sado-masochism. *They were forced to take part in sado-masochistic or bestial fantasies.*

s.a.e. /es eɪ iː/ **s.a.e.s**
NC An **s.a.e.** is an envelope on which you have stuck a stamp and written your own name and address. You send it to someone so that they can send you something back in it. s.a.e. is an abbreviation for 'stamped addressed envelope'. *Send an s.a.e. for a list of qualified aromatherapists.*

safari /səfɑːri/ **safaris**
NC A **safari** is an expedition for hunting or observing wild animals, especially in Africa. *The prince left to go on a five-day safari in Tanzania.*

safari park, safari parks
NC A **safari park** is a large enclosed area of land where wild animals, such as lions and elephants, live and move around freely. The animals can be watched by people who drive through the area. *They preferred to see wild animals in safari parks, where they felt safer.*

safe /seɪf/ **safer, safest; safes**
1 ADJ Something that is **safe** does not cause harm or danger. *This powder is not safe for babies... It isn't safe to swim here... Keep your passport in a safe place.* ♦ **safely** ADV *Most food can safely be frozen for months.*
2 ADJ PRED If you are **safe**, you are not in any danger. *We're safe now. They've gone... They were safe from attack.*
3 ADJ ATTRIB A **safe** journey or arrival is one in which you arrive somewhere without being harmed. ...*the safe delivery of essential equipment.* ♦ **safely** ADV *I sent a telegram to my mother saying I had arrived safely.*
4 ADJ ATTRIB If you keep at a **safe** distance from someone or something, you stay far enough away from them to avoid danger or collision. *The vehicle behind is at a safe distance... He wanted to be absolutely sure of keeping a safe distance between them.*
5 ADJ If it is **safe** to say something, you can say it with little risk of being wrong. *These practices, it is safe to say, are no longer common.* ♦ **safely** ADV *These creatures, we can safely say, have been dead a long time.*
6 ADJ PRED If a secret is **safe** with you, you will not tell it to anyone. *They knew their secrets would be safe with him.*
7 NC A **safe** is a strong metal cupboard with special locks, in which you keep money, jewellery, and other valuable things. ...*the contents of the safe were left by an elderly Russian lady.*
8 ADJ ATTRIB You can refer to a parliamentary seat as a **safe** seat when it has been won by a particular party or candidate and you think it is unlikely to be lost by them in a future election. *He was elected to the safe Labour seat of Bootle... Half the safe seats defended by the government since 1979 had been lost.*
● **Safe** is used in these phrases. ● You say that someone is **safe and sound** when they are unharmed after being in danger. *I'm glad to see you home safe and sound.* ● If you **play safe**, you do not take unnecessary risks. *Play safe and always wear goggles.* ● If you say that you are doing something to **be on the safe side**, you mean that you are doing it as a precaution, in case something unexpected or unpleasant happens. *I'll repeat it, just to be on the safe side.* ● If someone or something is **in safe hands**,

they are being looked after by a reliable person and will not be harmed. *Don't worry, she's in safe hands at the hospital.*

safe bet, safe bets
NC You can say that an action or event is a **safe bet** when it does not involve a lot of risks. *A safe bet for the organizers was the production of Verdi's popular opera... It seems a safe bet that the brand new, cheap housing units will not remain empty for long.*

safe conduct, safe conducts; also spelt **safe-conduct.**
1 NU **Safe conduct** is official permission to travel through a place, for example during a war, with an assurance that you will not be harmed or arrested while you are travelling. *He returned to India on an assurance of safe conduct.*
2 NC A **safe-conduct** is also the document on which the permission to travel safely through a place is written. *Both journalists were issued with a safe-conduct valid for thirty six hours.*

safeguard /seɪfgɑːd/ **safeguards, safeguarding, safeguarded**
1 VO To **safeguard** something means to prevent it from being harmed. *They have to fight to safeguard their future... France and Belgium say they have sent troops purely to safeguard their own citizens.*
2 NC A **safeguard** is a law or rule that is intended to prevent someone or something from being harmed in some way. *This clause was inserted as a safeguard against possible exploitation... They have called for a freer flow of information as a safeguard for human rights.*

safekeeping /seɪfkiːpɪŋ/
NU If something is given to you for **safekeeping**, it is given to you so that you will make sure that it is not harmed or stolen. *It had been placed in a Paris museum for safekeeping. ...the people entrusted with its safekeeping.*

safe passage
NU or N SING If someone is given **safe passage**, they are allowed to leave a place safely, without being attacked or arrested, in order to go to another place. *The demonstrators were calling for the General to be allowed safe passage to France... He could negotiate a safe passage for the troops to withdraw. ...a guarantee of safe passage.*

safe sex. The form **safer sex** is also used.
NU **Safe sex** is sexual intercourse between two people who use protection, such as condoms, in order to avoid spreading such diseases as AIDS. *The Chief Medical Officer said it was vital for people to practise safe sex. ...campaigns to eliminate AIDS and to promote safer sex.*

safety /seɪfti/
1 NU **Safety** is the state of being safe from harm or danger. *He was assured of his daughter's safety... They swam to the safety of a small, rocky island. ...ensure public safety against criminals.*
2 N SING+of If you are concerned about the **safety** of something, you are concerned that it might be harmful or dangerous. *People worry about the safety of nuclear energy. ...the safety of cross-channel ferries.*
3 N+N **Safety** features are intended to make something less dangerous. *The report calls for improved safety measures... Every car will come with built-in safety features... It incorporates all the latest safety devices.*

safety belt, safety belts
NC A **safety belt** is a strap that you fasten across your body for safety when travelling in a car or aeroplane. See also **seat-belt.** *I told them to return to their seats and fasten their safety belts.*

safety catch, safety catches
NC The **safety catch** on a gun is a device that stops you firing the gun accidentally. *I carefully loaded my pistol, and made sure the safety catch was on.*

safety net, safety nets
1 NC A **safety net** is a large net that is placed somewhere where it is thought people might have an accident, especially by falling, in order to catch them and try to prevent them being injured. *Marc Giradelli suffered severe bruising after crashing into the safety net at the finish of the downhill course... Initial indications are that its brakes failed—it hit the*

arresting gear, but then slammed into the safety net.
2 NC A **safety net** is also something that you can rely
on to help you if you get into a difficult situation. *The
new law will act as a safety net. ...a political safety
net for Japan's regional economic interests.*

safety pin, safety pins
NC A **safety pin** is a bent metal pin, used for fastening
things together. The point of the pin has a cover. *She
wore a tartan shirt with a stainless steel safety pin in
it.*

safety-valve, safety-valves
1 NC A **safety-valve** is a piece of equipment in a
machine that allows liquids or gases to escape when
the pressure inside the machine becomes too great.
*The blast was caused by a gas leak after a safety-
valve had been removed for maintenance.*
2 N SING You can use **safety-valve** to refer to
something that allows you to express strong feelings
without harming other people. *...a safety-valve for the
harmless release of rebellious feelings.*

saffron /sæfrən/
1 NU **Saffron** is a yellowish-orange substance that is
obtained from a flower. It is used to add flavour and
colouring to some foods. *Toss a pinch of saffron into
the rice while it is cooking.*
2 ADJ **Saffron** is also a yellowish-orange colour.
*Desiree's red plaits flamed against the saffron pillows
of the huge bed. ...a saffron robe.*

sag /sæg/ **sags, sagging, sagged**
v When something **sags**, it hangs down loosely or sinks
downwards in the middle. *The bed sagged in the
middle.*

saga /sɑːɡə/ **sagas**
1 NC A **saga** is a long and often complicated sequence
of events. *The past six decades have been an
unedifying saga of military coups, repression and war.
...another twist to the saga. ...the latest development
in this long-running saga.*
2 NC A **saga** is also a type of long story, novel,
television series, or film that covers a period of many
years and often several generations of a family. *This
saga about two feuding Texas oil dynasties was seen
in eighty-five countries. ...the haunting lines of
Beowulf's saga... He is the author of seven acclaimed
books of fiction, including his saga of the Hudson River
Valley, 'World's End'.*

sagacious /səɡeɪʃəs/
ADJ A **sagacious** person is intelligent and has the
ability to make good judgements and decisions; a
formal word. *He's proved himself quite a wise and
sagacious leader... They nodded wisely to each other
and exchanged sagacious remarks.*

sage /seɪdʒ/ **sages**
1 NC A **sage** is a person who is regarded as being
wise; a literary use. *His writings have the requisite
aura of inaccessible wisdom appropriate to a sage.
...the great poet and sage, Matthew Arnold.*
2 ADJ A **sage** person is wise and knowledgeable,
usually because they are old and have had a lot of
experience; a literary use. *...sage parents anxious to
dispense their wisdom. ...the sage and serious poet,
Spenser.* ◆ **sagely** ADV *He nodded his head sagely.*
3 NU **Sage** is a plant that grows in warm countries. Its
leaves are used for flavouring in cooking. *Sage, dried
and made into a stuffing, goes well with chicken.*

sago /seɪɡəʊ/
NCorNU A **sago** is a type of palm tree. Its trunk
produces an edible starch which is also called **sago**
that is used for making certain types of food such as
puddings and for thickening sauces. *The swamp is
where the sago grows. ...a factory to process sago into
flour. ...sago pudding.*

Saharan Arab Democratic Republic
/səhɑːrən ærəb deməkrætɪk rɪpʌblɪk/ See **Western
Sahara.**

sahib /sɑːb, sɑːhɪb/ **sahibs**
NCorTITLE Some people in India use **sahib** when they
are referring to or speaking to a man in a position of
authority, especially a white government official
during the period of British rule. *She remembered the
old race of British Sahibs and Memsahibs... Dinner for
tonight, Sahib.*

Saibou, Ali /æli seɪbuː/
Brigadier Ali Saibou became President of Niger in
1987. He served as Minister of Rural Economy in 1974,
and was Army Chief of Staff from 1974 to 1987. He
became President of the National Movement for a
Development Society (MNSD) in 1989. Born: 1940.

said /sed/
Said is the past tense and past participle of **say.**

sail /seɪl/ **sails, sailing, sailed**
1 NC A **sail** is a large piece of material attached to the
mast of a boat. The wind blows against the sail and
moves the boat along. *...the white sails of the yacht.*
2 VorV-ERG If you **sail** somewhere, or if you **sail** a boat
or ship somewhere, you travel across water in a boat
or ship. *He's sailed twice round the world... The
tanker sailed out of the Gulf. ...the officers and men
who actually sailed the ships.*
3 When a ship **sets sail**, it leaves a port. *It's not clear
when the two vessels will be setting sail. ...an Indian
ship which is due to set sail for the Gulf.*
4 VA If someone or something **sails** somewhere, they
move there steadily and fairly quickly. *I watched the
ball as it went sailing over the bushes.*

sail through PHRASAL VERB If you **sail through** a
difficult situation or experience, you deal with it easily
and successfully. *She was expecting to sail through
her exams... The budget sailed through the National
Assembly.*

sailboat /seɪlbəʊt/ **sailboats**
NC A **sailboat** is the same as a **sailing boat**; used in
American English. *426 refugees were jammed aboard
two small sailboats.*

sailing /seɪlɪŋ/ **sailings**
1 NC A **sailing** is a voyage made by a ship carrying
passengers. *...regular sailings from Portsmouth...
The company has now had to cancel five of its ferry
sailings.*
2 NU **Sailing** is the activity or sport of sailing boats.
...the traditional Royal sailing week in August.
3 You can say that something, such as a course of
action or an event, is **plain sailing** when it presents no
problems or obstacles. *It hasn't all been plain sailing
for the Prime Minister... The future looked pretty
plain sailing for the Conservative Party.*

sailing boat, sailing boats
NC A **sailing boat** is a boat with sails. *The sunshine
was sparkling on the white sailing boats.*

sailing ship, sailing ships
NC A **sailing ship** is a large ship with sails, especially
of the kind that was used in the past to carry
passengers or cargo. *A fleet of sailing ships has
arrived in Botany Bay.*

sailor /seɪlə/ **sailors**
NC A **sailor** is a person who works on a ship as a
member of its crew. *He had been a sailor in the
Italian navy.*

saint /seɪnt/ **saints;** usually pronounced /sənt/ when it is
a title.
1 NCorTITLE A **saint** is a dead person who is officially
recognized and honoured by the Christian church
because his or her life was a perfect example of the
way Christians should live. *Later the Pope attended
Mass at which he canonized Paraguay's first saint, a
Jesuit missionary who was killed by Indians in 1628.
...the church of Saint Francis.*
2 NC If you describe someone as a **saint**, you mean
that you think they are very kind, patient and
unselfish. *He said he thought Mr Thatcher had been a
saint to put up with eleven years in Number Ten
Downing Street... In Mr Craxi's words, he was 'neither
a saint nor a hero'.*

Saint Christopher and Nevis
/sənt krɪstəfə ən niːvɪs/
The **Federation of Saint Christopher and Nevis** is a
country in the Caribbean. Its usual written form is **St
Christopher and Nevis,** often shortened to **St Kitts.** It
was a British colony from the 17th century until
independence in 1983. Dr Kennedy Alphonse
Simmonds, of the People's Action Movement (PAM),
became Premier in 1980 and Prime Minister in 1983.
Saint Christopher and Nevis is a member of the
Commonwealth and the Organization of American

States. Sugar is exported and tourism is an important industry. ◆ **Kittian, Nevisian** /kɪtsiən, nəvɪʒən/ N, ADJ ▪ *per capita GNP:* US$2,770 ▪ *religion:* Christianity (mainly Anglican) ▪ *language:* English (official) ▪ *currency:* East Caribbean dollar ▪ *capital:* Basseterre ▪ *population:* 41,000 (1989) ▪ *size:* 262 square kilometres.

Saint-Denis /sænⁿ dəniː/
Saint-Denis is the capital of Réunion and its largest city. Population: 122,000 (1990).

sainted /seɪntɪd/
ADJ ATTRIB A **sainted** person has the qualities of a saint; an old-fashioned word. *Your sainted father would agree.*

Saint George's /sənt dʒɔːdʒɪz/
Saint George's is the capital of Grenada and its largest town. Its usual written form is **St George's**. Population: 7,500 (1980).

Saint Helena /sənt həliːnə/
Saint Helena and Dependencies is a territory of the United Kingdom in the South Atlantic, roughly midway between Africa and South America. It consists of the widely separated islands of Saint Helena, Ascension, and Tristan da Cunha. Saint Helena was settled by Britain in the 17th century and Ascension in the 19th century. Napoleon spent the last years of his life in exile on Saint Helena after his defeat at Waterloo in 1815. Fishing is a major industry. Ascension is an important communications and military centre.
▪ *religion:* Christianity (mainly Anglican) ▪ *language:* English ▪ *currency:* pound ▪ *capital:* Jamestown ▪ *population:* 7,000 (1989) ▪ *size:* 350 square kilometres.

Saint John's /sənt dʒɒnz/
Saint John's is the capital of Antigua and Barbuda and its largest city. Its usual written form is **St John's**. Population: 36,000 (1986).

Saint Lucia /sənt luːʃə/
Saint Lucia is a country in the Caribbean. Its usual written form is **St Lucia**. It is a member of the Commonwealth and the Organization of American States. St Lucia became a French colony in the 17th century and changed hands many times before becoming a British colony in 1814. It became independent in 1979. John Compton, of the United Workers' Party (UWP), became Prime Minister in 1982. Saint Lucia exports bananas and tourism is an important industry. ◆ **Saint Lucian, St Lucian** /sənt luːʃən/ N, ADJ
▪ *per capita GNP:* US$1,540 ▪ *religion:* Christianity (mainly Roman Catholic) ▪ *language:* English (official), French patois ▪ *currency:* East Caribbean dollar ▪ *capital:* Castries ▪ *population:* 147,000 (1989) ▪ *size:* 616 square kilometres.

saintly /seɪntli/
ADJ A **saintly** person behaves in a very good or holy way. *...his saintly brother King Richard.*

Saint-Pierre /sænⁿ pjeə/
Saint-Pierre is the capital of Saint Pierre and Miquelon and its largest town.

Saint Pierre and Miquelon
/sænⁿ pjeər ənd miːkəlɒnⁿ/
The **Territorial Collectivity of Saint Pierre and Miquelon** is a possession of France in the North Atlantic, off the coast of eastern Canada. The islands were settled by France in 1604, and were administered by Britain from 1713 to 1763 and from 1794 to 1816, when they reverted to French control. Fishing and the provision of ships' supplies are important industries.
▪ *religion:* Christianity (mainly Roman Catholic) ▪ *language:* French ▪ *currency:* French franc ▪ *capital:* Saint-Pierre ▪ *population:* 6,000 (1990) ▪ *size:* 242 square kilometres.

Saint Vincent and the Grenadines
/sənt vɪnsnt ənd ðə grenədiːnz/
Saint Vincent and the Grenadines is a country in the Caribbean. Its usual written form is **St Vincent and the Grenadines**. It was a British colony from the 18th century until independence in 1979. James Mitchell, of the New Democratic Party (NDP), became Prime Minister in 1984. It is a member of the Commonwealth and the Organization of American States. Saint Vincent and the Grenadines exports bananas and is

the world's largest producer of arrowroot starch. Tourism is an important industry. ◆ **Saint Vincentian** /sənt vɪnsenʃən/ N, ADJ
▪ *per capita GNP:* US$1,100 ▪ *religion:* Christianity ▪ *language:* English (official) ▪ *currency:* East Caribbean dollar ▪ *capital:* Kingstown ▪ *population:* 114,000 (1989) ▪ *size:* 389 square kilometres.

Saipan /saɪpæn/
Saipan is the capital of the Northern Mariana Islands and its largest island. Population: 19,000 (1988).

sake /seɪk/ **sakes**
● **Sake** is used in these phrases. ● If you do something **for the sake of** a particular thing, you do it for that purpose or in order to achieve that result. *I usually check from time to time, just for safety's sake... Let us assume, for the sake of argument, that the level of unemployment does not fall.* ● If you do something **for its own sake**, you do it because you enjoy it, and not for any other reason. *I'm studying the subject for its own sake.* ● When you do something **for** someone's **sake**, you do it in order to help them. *We moved out to the country for the children's sake.* ● Some people say **'for God's sake'** or **'for heaven's sake'** in order to express annoyance or impatience, or to add force to a question or request. *For God's sake, don't betray two centuries of struggle!*

salaam /səlɑːm/ **salaams, salaaming, salaamed**
1 V To **salaam** means to bow with your right hand on your forehead as a formal and respectful way of greeting someone. People sometimes greet each other like this in India and in Muslim countries. *He looked from one to the other of them, then salaamed and left.*
▶ Also NC *She finally left with many salaams and apologies.*
2 Muslims also say **'Salaam'** as a way of greeting people. *Awal Shah stepped out of the shadows and brought his hand up to a salute, 'Salaam Sahib', he said.*

salacious /səleɪʃəs/
ADJ If you describe something such as a book, joke, or film as **salacious**, you mean that you think it deals with sexual matters in an unnecessarily detailed way; a formal word, used showing disapproval. *It is a theme which commonly gets salacious treatment in the media. ...a salacious novel. ...Sheila's salacious wit.*

salad /sæləd/ **salads**
N MASS A **salad** is a mixture of uncooked vegetables or of cooked vegetables that are eaten cold. *...a tin of potato salad.*

salad dressing, salad dressings
N MASS **Salad dressing** is a mixture of oil, vinegar or lemon juice, and other flavourings, which you pour on salads. *...the sort of salad dressing they enjoy.*

salami /səlɑːmi/
NU **Salami** is a type of sausage made from chopped meat and spices. *...a thin stick of salami.*

salaried /sælərɪd/
ADJ ATTRIB **Salaried** people receive a salary.
...salaried employees of the Israeli administration.

salary /sæləri/ **salaries**
NCorNU A **salary** is the money that someone is paid for their job each month, especially when they have a professional job. *She earns a high salary as an accountant. ...the difference in salary between an instructor and a lecturer.*

sale /seɪl/ **sales**
1 N SING The **sale** of goods is the selling of them for money. *...new laws to control the sale of guns.*
2 N PL The **sales** of a product are the quantity that is sold. *Car sales are 5 per cent down... Sales of the magazine are declining... The administration wants to increase arms sales abroad.*
3 N PL The part of a company that deals with **sales** deals with selling the company's products. *...a sales executive.*
4 NC A **sale** is an occasion when a shop sells things at less than their normal price. *They're having a clearance sale.*
5 NC A **sale** is also an event at which goods are sold to the person who offers the highest price. *...the quarterly cattle sale.*

● Sale is used in these phrases. ● If something is for sale or up for sale, its owner is trying to sell it. *Their house is up for sale.* ● Products that are on sale can be bought in shops. *The only English newspaper on sale was the Morning Star.* ● See also jumble sale.

Saleh, Ali Abdullah /ˈæli æbˈdʊlə ˈsɑːli/
Lieutenant-General Ali Abdullah Saleh became President of the newly united Yemen in 1990. He was Deputy Commander-in-Chief of the North Yemen Armed Forces in 1978, and Commander-in-Chief from 1978 to 1990. He was President of North Yemen from 1978 to 1990. He became Secretary General of the People's Congress in 1982. Born: 1942.

sales clerk, sales clerks
NC A sales clerk is a shop assistant; used in American English. *...a sales clerk sitting by the cash register.*

salesgirl /ˈseɪlzɡɜːl/ **salesgirls**
NC A salesgirl is a young woman who serves customers in a shop. *The paper points to the polite and smiling salesgirls and the lack of queues in Marks and Spencer's shops.*

salesman /ˈseɪlzmən/ **salesmen** /ˈseɪlzmən/
NC A salesman is a man whose job is selling things, especially directly to shops or other businesses. *A salesman cannot afford to bore a sceptical client.*

salesmanship /ˈseɪlzmənʃɪp/
NU Salesmanship is skill that a person has in persuading people to buy things. *...a two-day course on methods of salesmanship.*

salesperson /ˈseɪlzpɜːsn/ **salespeople** or **salespersons**
NC A salesperson is a person whose job is to sell things, either in a shop or directly to customers. *We have a vacancy for an experienced salesperson.*

sales talk
NU Sales talk is all the things that a salesperson says when they are trying to persuade a customer to buy something. *I didn't believe all that sales talk about it cutting your heating bills in half.*

saleswoman /ˈseɪlzwʊmən/ **saleswomen**
NC A saleswoman is a woman whose job is to sell things, especially in a shop. *He hired his first saleswoman four years ago.*

salient /ˈseɪliənt/
1 ADJ The salient points or facts of a situation are the most important and relevant ones; a formal word. *The report contained very salient points... The issue is taking an awful long time to become politically salient... The salient fact is that the reshuffle marked the end of tooth and claw Thatcherism.*
2 NC A salient is a narrow area of land where an army has pushed its front line forward into enemy territory. *Further enemy attacks had opened up a salient on the left of our Corps. ...the Sejra salient, a finger of land which extends ten miles into India.*

Salinas de Gortari, Carlos /kɑːˈlɒʊs sælˈiːnæs deɪ ɡɔːˈtɑːri/
Carlos Salinas de Gortari became President of Mexico in 1988. He served as Minister of Planning and Federal Budget from 1982 to 1987. He is a member of the Institutional Revolutionary Party (PRI). Born: 1948.

saline /ˈseɪlaɪn/
ADJ A saline substance or liquid contains salt; a formal word. *The water in the basin has now become too saline to support fish. ...a saline solution.*

saliva /səˈlaɪvə/
NU Saliva is the watery liquid that forms in your mouth. *These chemicals are also secreted in our saliva.*

salivate /ˈsælɪveɪt/ **salivates, salivating, salivated**
V If you salivate, you produce a lot of saliva in your mouth, often as a result of seeing or smelling food; a formal word. *The mere thought of food made me start to salivate.*

sallow /ˈsæləʊ/
ADJ If someone is sallow, their skin has a pale yellowish colour and looks unhealthy.

sally /ˈsæli/ **sallies**
NC Sallies are clever and amusing remarks; a literary word. *The laughter with which his sallies were greeted excited him.*

sally forth PHRASAL VERB If someone sallies forth, they go to a place quickly or energetically; a literary expression. *Boldly they sallied forth to meet them.*

sally out PHRASAL VERB If someone sallies out, they leave a place in order to go somewhere; a literary expression. *He sallied out into the raw London night.*

salmon /ˈsæmən/; salmon is both the singular and the plural form.
1 NC A salmon is a large silver-coloured fish that can be eaten. *The fishermen were held on charges of illegally fishing for salmon.*
2 NU Salmon is also the edible flesh of the fish. *...smoked salmon sandwiches.*

salmonella /ˌsælməˈnelə/
NU Salmonella is a kind of bacteria which can cause severe food poisoning. *...the controversy over salmonella in eggs... A nine year old boy has died in hospital from salmonella poisoning.*

salon /ˈsælɒn/ **salons**
1 NC A salon is a place where hairdressers or beauticians work. *...a nail salon which provides much more than a basic manicure. ...the salon where she used to have her hair cut as a child. ...a beauty salon.*
2 NC A salon is also a shop where smart, expensive clothes are sold. *She is dressed by Dior, whose salon is located across the street.*

saloon /səˈluːn/ **saloons**
1 NC A saloon is a car with seats for four or more people, a fixed roof, and a boot that is separated from the rear seats. *...a bright red Mercedes saloon... The couple were driven off in a large saloon car.*
2 NC In the United States, a saloon is a place where alcoholic drinks are sold and drunk. *This is a family saloon where you can go and get a beer.*
3 NC In Britain, the saloon or saloon bar in a pub or hotel is a comfortable bar where the drinks are more expensive than in the other bars. *The small saloon bar is already full.*

salt /sɔːlt, sɒlt/ **salts, salting, salted**
1 NU Salt is a substance in the form of white powder or crystals, used to improve the flavour of food or to preserve it. Salt occurs naturally in sea water. *...a quarter of a teaspoonful of salt.*
2 VO When you salt food, you add salt to it. *The potatoes should be lightly salted.* ◆ salted ADJ *...salted peanuts.*
● Salt is used in these phrases. ● If something or someone rubs salt into your wounds, they make the unpleasant situation that you are in even worse, often by reminding you of your failures or faults. *For many French Communist Party officials, the commentary was simply rubbing salt into the wound.* ● If you take something with a pinch of salt, you do not believe that it is completely accurate or true; an informal expression. *He says he takes the news with a pinch of salt... The official explanation is being taken with a large pinch of salt.*

SALT /sɔːlt, sɒlt/
N PROP SALT is an abbreviation for 'Strategic Arms Limitation Talks'; a series of discussions that were held between the United States and the former Soviet Union on how the number of nuclear weapons they possessed could be limited or reduced. *I hoped the American Congress would ratify SALT II. ...the beginning of the SALT talks.*

salt-and-pepper
ADJ Salt-and-pepper or pepper-and-salt is used to describe things such as cloth or hair that have small dark and white specks of colour. *In 1959 his hair and beard were black, then they became salt-and-pepper, and now he is totally grey. ...the salt-and-pepper beard he has now.*

salt cellar, salt cellars
NC A salt cellar is a small container for salt, used at mealtimes.

saltpetre /ˌsɔːltˈpiːtə, ˌsɒltˈpiːtə/; spelt saltpeter in American English.
NU Saltpetre is potassium nitrate, a substance that is used in making gunpowder, matches, and fertilizers, and in preserving meat. *One of the substances the Chinese alchemist experimented with was saltpetre.*

salty /ˈsɔːlti, ˈsɒlti/ **saltier, saltiest**
ADJ Salty things contain salt or taste of salt. *...salty water.*

salubrious /səˈluːbriəs/

ADJ A place that is **salubrious** is pleasant and healthy; a formal word. *By 1800, the wealthy residents had left the area for more salubrious parts of London... He was presented with the award in more salubrious surroundings—the Savoy Hotel in London.*

salutary /ˈsæljutəʳri/

ADJ A **salutary** experience is good for you, even though it may seem difficult or unpleasant; a formal word. *The defeat was a deserved punishment, but also a salutary shock.*

salutation /ˌsæljuˈteɪʃn/ **salutations**; a formal word.

1 NUorNC **Salutation** or a **salutation** is a greeting to someone. *They heard her voice raised in lively salutation... Mr Raim addresses us with the salutation, 'Gentlepersons'... She threw a kiss as a salutation.*
2 NC A **salutation** in a letter is the phrase that is used at the beginning of the letter, for example 'Dear Sir' or 'Dear Jim'.

salute /səˈluːt/ **salutes, saluting, saluted**

1 VO If you **salute** someone, you greet them or show your respect with a formal sign. Soldiers salute officers by raising their right hand so that their fingers touch their forehead. *He stood as if he were saluting the flag.* ▶ Also NC *He greeted King Edward VIII with the customary salute.* ● When a head of state or a military leader **takes the salute** at a military parade, they watch as troops salute them to show their loyalty. *The Queen will take the salute from the balcony of Buckingham Palace.*
2 VO To **salute** a person or an achievement means to publicly show or state your admiration for them. *He saluted those who had fought for freedom. ...festivals in Spain that salute the independence of the Spanish character.* ▶ Also NC *...a salute to America.*

salvage /ˈsælvɪdʒ/ **salvages, salvaging, salvaged**

1 VO When you **salvage** things, you manage to save them, for example from a ship that has sunk, or from a building that has been destroyed. *...a finely decorated window salvaged from an old chemist's shop.*
2 NU **Salvage** from wrecked ships or destroyed buildings consists of the things that are saved from them. *The insurers are entitled to take the wreck as salvage. ...a salvage operation.*
3 VO If you **salvage** something from a difficult situation, you manage to get something useful from it so that it is not a complete failure. *They were salvaging what they could from the present unhappy state of affairs. ...a make-or-break attempt to salvage a new world trade agreement.*

salvation /sælˈveɪʃn/

1 NU In Christianity, the **salvation** of a person is the fact that Christ has saved them from evil. *...a rejection of the idea that religion is simply a matter of personal salvation.*
2 NU The **salvation** of someone or something is the act of saving them from harm. *The country's salvation was of immense importance.*
3 N SING+POSS If someone or something is your **salvation**, they are responsible for saving you from harm or from an unpleasant situation. *Small industries will be the salvation of many areas now in decline... Their children were their only salvation.*

Salvation Army

N PROP The **Salvation Army** is a Christian religious organization that is structured like an army and that tries to help people in need. *Members of the Salvation Army supply them with food and clothing... The service was conducted by Anglican and Roman Catholic clergymen with a Salvation Army Major... The Salvation Army are getting more and more involved with care of the elderly.*

salve /sælv/ **salves, salving, salved**

If you **salve** your **conscience** by doing something, it makes you feel less guilty or worried. *We give money to charities, and thus salve our consciences.*

salver /ˈsælvə/ **salvers**

NC A **salver** is a tray or large plate, usually made of silver and finely decorated. *A maid brought in a salver on which were glasses, a bottle of wine and a dish of sweetmeats... Thomas will receive an inscribed*

silver salver and a cheque for £250.

salvo /ˈsælvəu/ **salvoes**

1 NC A **salvo** is the firing of several guns or missiles at the same time in a battle or as part of a ceremony. *The centre of London resounded with the triumphant salvoes. ...two attacks, each consisting of salvoes of four missiles.*
2 NC A **salvo** is also a sudden outburst of a particular activity, often in a situation of conflict or opposition between two forces. *The latest salvo in the debate suggests frustration on the part of the reform movement. ...his wish to avoid a further salvo of intimate questions. ...salvoes of raucous laughter.*

Samaritan /səˈmærɪtən/ **Samaritans**

NC You can refer to someone as a **Samaritan** or as a good **Samaritan** if they help you when you are in difficulty. *This good Samaritan took me all the way there in his car... Whenever there's illness, who's there but our friend Mary Stuart—she's a kind of Samaritan.*

samba /ˈsæmbə/ **sambas**

NC A **samba** is a lively Brazilian dance. *...music from a live samba band.*

same /seɪm/

1 ADJ ATTRIBorPRON If two things are the **same** or if one thing is the **same** as another, the two are exactly like each other in some way. *They both wore the same overcoats... He did exactly the same as John did.*
2 ADJ ATTRIB If two things have the **same** quality, they both have that quality. *He and Tom were exactly the same age... It was the same colour as the wall.*
3 ADJ ATTRIB You use **same** to indicate that you are referring to only one thing, and not to different ones. *We come from the same place... The attack happened on the same day as one at Vienna airport... It was possible to work while watching TV at the same time.*
4 PRONorADJ ATTRIB Something that is still the **same** has not changed in any way. *The village stayed the same... He will never be the same again... It wouldn't improve me, I'd be the same person I was before I saw it.*
5 ADJ ATTRIBorPRON You also use **same** to refer to something that has already been mentioned. *For the same reason, the United States lodged a formal protest... It's the same with teenage fashions.*
● **Same** is used in these phrases. ● You say **all the same** or **just the same** to indicate that a situation or your opinion has not changed, in spite of what has happened or been said. *The glass in the windows was still shattered, but the meeting was held just the same... All the same, the courses are very popular.*
● **thanks all the same**: see **thank**.

sameness /ˈseɪmnəs/

NU The **sameness** of something is its lack of variety. *I was struck by the sameness of clothing among the villagers.*

Samoa, American /əˈmerɪkən sɑːˈməuə/

The **Territory of American Samoa** is a possession of the United States in the South Pacific. The United States in 1878 was granted the right to establish a naval base at Pago Pago on Tutuila. Eastern Samoa became known as American Samoa in 1911 and was administered by the US Navy until 1951. American Samoa exports tuna. ◆ **American Samoan** /əˈmerɪkən sɑːˈməuən/ N, ADJ
▪ *per capita GNP:* US$5,410 ▪ *religion:* Christianity (mainly Christian Congregational) ▪ *language:* Samoan, English ▪ *currency:* US dollar ▪ *capital:* Pago Pago ▪ *population:* 38,000 (1989) ▪ *size:* 195 square kilometres.

Samoa, Western /ˈwestən sɑːˈməuə/

The **Independent State of Western Samoa** is a country in the South Pacific. The two largest islands are Upolu and Savai'i. New Zealand annexed Western Samoa in 1914 and administered it until 1962, when it became an independent country and a member of the Commonwealth. Malietoa Tanumafili II became head of state in 1962. Tofilau Eti Alesana, of the Human Rights Protection Party (HRPP), became Prime Minister in 1988. Western Samoa exports cocoa, coconuts, bananas, taro, and yams. Tourism is an

important industry. ◆ **Western Samoan** /ˌwɛstən
saːˈməuən/ N, ADJ
▪ *per capita GNP:* US$580 ▪ *religion:* Christianity
▪ *language:* English, Samoan ▪ *currency:* tala ▪ *capital:*
Apia ▪ *population:* 168,000 (1988) ▪ *size:* 2,831 square
kilometres.

sample /ˈsɑːmpl/ **samples, sampling, sampled**
1 NC A **sample** of a substance or product is a small
quantity of it that shows you what it is like. *...free
samples of shampoo.*
2 NC A **sample** of a substance is also a small amount
of it that is examined and analysed scientifically. *I'll
take water samples here and in East Hampton. ...tests
that will use a blood sample.*
3 NC A **sample** of people or things is a number of
them chosen out of a larger group and then used in
tests or used to provide information about the whole
group. *...a random sample of 10,000 adult civilians.*
4 VO If you **sample** food or drink, you taste a small
amount of it in order to find out if you like it. *Next he
sampled the roast beef.*
5 VO If you **sample** a place or situation, you
experience it for a short time in order to find out about
it. *They can learn the language and sample the
British way of life.*

sampler /ˈsɑːmplə/ **samplers**
1 NC A **sampler** is a piece of cloth embroidered with
various patterns, which is intended to show the skill of
the person who made it. *Twice a week she
embroidered a sampler she wasn't remotely interested
in. ...a sampler worked by Lily and Enid when they
were children.*
2 NC A **sampler** is also a piece of electronic equipment
that is used for taking samples of something.
*...cervical smears that have been taken using the
sampler. ...a portable air pollution sampler.*

San'aa /sɑːˈnɑː/
San'aa is the capital of Yemen and its largest city.
Population: 500,000 (1990).

sanatorium /ˌsænəˈtɔːriəm/ **sanatoriums** or **sanatoria**
/ˌsænəˈtɔːriə/; spelt **sanitarium** /ˌsænɪˈtɛəriəm/ in
American English.
NC A **sanatorium** is an institution that provides
medical treatment and rest for people who suffer from
long illnesses. *...the sanatorium where Cubans who
are HIV positive are held.*

sanctify /ˈsæŋktɪfaɪ/ **sanctifies, sanctifying, sanctified**
1 VO If the Church or a holy person **sanctifies**
something, they officially bless it or approve of it. *St
Francis wanted to sanctify poverty, not to abolish it.*
2 VO If someone **sanctifies** an idea, practice, or
situation, they approve of it, support it, and want it to
stay the same. *...to protect and sanctify the power
that was so ruthlessly being used.*

sanctimonious /ˌsæŋktɪˈməuniəs/
ADJ Someone who is **sanctimonious** tries to appear
deeply religious or virtuous; used showing
disapproval. *...a sanctimonious hypocrite.*

sanction /ˈsæŋkʃn/ **sanctions, sanctioning, sanctioned**
1 VO If someone in authority **sanctions** an action or
practice, they officially approve of it and allow it to be
done. *...the law of 1856 which sanctioned the
remarriage of widows.* ▶ Also NU+SUPP *Some months
later our proposal was given official sanction.*
◆ **sanctioning** NU *The ANC's sanctioning of such an
approach would mark a significant shift in its policy.*
2 NC A **sanction** is a severe course of action which is
intended to make people obey the law. *The ultimate
sanction of the government is the withdrawal of funds.*
3 N PL **Sanctions** are measures taken by countries to
restrict trade and official contact with a country that
has broken international law. *The UN would impose
economic sanctions against the offending nation... The
international community reacted with trade sanctions.*

sanctions-busting
NU **Sanctions-busting** is the breaking of sanctions
imposed on a country that has broken international
law. *It instructs all countries to detain ships
suspected of sanctions-busting.*

sanctity /ˈsæŋktəti/
NU If you talk about the **sanctity** of something, you
mean that it is important and should be respected.

...the sanctity of human life.

sanctuary /ˈsæŋktjuəri/ **sanctuaries**
1 NCorNU A **sanctuary** is a place of safety. *It was
Clement's island and his sanctuary... This would give
him sanctuary in the British Embassy... Some forces
sought sanctuary in neighbouring Angola.*
2 NC A wildlife **sanctuary** is a place where birds or
animals are protected and allowed to live freely. *...a
vast wildlife sanctuary in Alaska. ...a bird sanctuary.*

sand /sænd/ **sands, sanding, sanded**
1 NU **Sand** is a powder-like substance that consists of
extremely small pieces of stone. Most deserts and
beaches are made of sand. *The children played in the
sand at the water's edge. ...grains of sand.*
2 N PL **Sands** are a large area of sand, for example a
beach or desert. *...miles of empty sands.*
3 VO If you **sand** an object, you rub sandpaper over it
in order to make it smooth or clean. *A scratched item
of furniture can be professionally sanded.*

sandal /ˈsændl/ **sandals**
NC **Sandals** are light shoes that have straps instead of
a solid part over the top of your foot. *...a pair of
plastic sandals.*

sandalwood /ˈsændlwud/
1 NCorNU A **sandalwood** is a tree that grows mainly in
South Asia and Australia. It has a sweet-smelling wood
that is also called **sandalwood**. *...a funeral pyre of
sandalwood logs.*
2 NU **Sandalwood** is also an oil that is extracted from
sandalwood and used to make perfume. *The new
fragrance contains essence of jasmine, rose and
carnation with musk and sandalwood.*

sandbag /ˈsændbæg/ **sandbags, sandbagging,
sandbagged**
1 NC A **sandbag** is a sack filled with sand which is
used, for example, to build walls as a protection
against floods or explosions. *They've built a wall of
sandbags across the road.*
2 VO To **sandbag** something means to protect or
strengthen it by means of sandbags. *The water tank
had been sandbagged.*

sandbank /ˈsændbæŋk/ **sandbanks**
NC A **sandbank** is a bank of sand below the surface of
the sea or a river. *The ship was thought to have hit a
sandbank.*

sandbox /ˈsændbɒks/ **sandboxes**
NC A **sandbox** is the same as a **sandpit**; used in
American English. *There is a sandbox in the almost
non-existent front yard.*

sand castle, sand castles
NC A **sand castle** is a model that children make out of
sand in the shape of a castle when they are playing on
the beach. *Lally was helping us with our sand castle,
which had a tower at each corner and a moat all
round.*

Sandiford, Erskine /ˈɜːskɪn ˈsændɪfəd/
Erskine Sandiford became Prime Minister of Barbados
in 1987. He was a member of the Senate from 1967 to
1971, and was elected to the House of Assembly in
1971. He served as Minister of Education from 1967 to
1975, and of Health and Welfare from 1975 to 1976. He
was Deputy Prime Minister from 1986 to 1987. He is a
member of the Democratic Labour Party (DLP), and
was President of the DLP from 1974 to 1975. Born:
1937.

sandpaper /ˈsændpeɪpə/
NU **Sandpaper** is strong paper that has a coating of
sand on it. It is used for rubbing surfaces to make
them smoother. *The way we smoothed the edges of
the bottles was to use wet and dry sandpaper.*

sandpit /ˈsændpɪt/ **sandpits**
NC A **sandpit** is a shallow hole or box in the ground
with sand in it where small children can play. *They
found him waving a loaded pistol in a children's
sandpit.*

sandstone /ˈsændstəun/
NU **Sandstone** is a type of rock that contains a lot of
sand and is often used in building. *...a long sandstone
cliff.*

sandstorm /ˈsændstɔːm/ **sandstorms**
NC A **sandstorm** is a strong wind in a desert area,
which creates large moving clouds of sand. *The start*

*of the twelfth stage of the rally was delayed after a
sandstorm developed this morning.*
sandwich /sǽnwɪdʒ, sǽnwɪtʃ/ **sandwiches,
sandwiched**
1 NC A **sandwich** consists of two slices of bread with a
layer of food such as cheese or meat between them.
...a bacon, lettuce, and tomato sandwich.
2 V-PASSA When something is **sandwiched** between two
other things, it occupies a small or narrow space
between them. *Wooden shacks are sandwiched
between modern blocks of flats... The Tibetans are a
small nation, sandwiched between the vast human
masses of China and India.*
3 VO You can also say that something is **sandwiched**
between two other things when it is done or happens in
a very short period of time between them. *The
meeting is sandwiched between two sessions of the
Warsaw Pact's disarmament commission... He flew in
and out on Concorde, sandwiching his one-day trip
between important meetings in Britain.*
sandwich board, sandwich boards
NC A **sandwich board** is a pair of two connected
boards which are hung over a person's shoulders, and
which display advertisements or other messages in
front and behind. *The man walked around Moscow
with a sandwich board attacking the President.*
sandwich course, sandwich courses
NC A **sandwich course** is an educational course in
which you have periods of study in between periods of
work in industry or business. *Most are doing part-
time or sandwich courses.*
sandy /sǽndi/
1 ADJ A **sandy** area is made up of or contains sand.
*...the long sandy beach... His farm has sandy, acidic
soil.*
2 ADJ **Sandy** hair is light orange-brown.
*...DiAugustino, a small man in his 60s with sandy grey
hair.*
sane /seɪn/ **saner, sanest**
1 ADJ Someone who is **sane** is able to think and
behave normally and reasonably, and is not mentally
ill. *She appeared to be completely sane.*
2 ADJ If you describe an action or idea as **sane**, you
mean that it is reasonable and sensible. *It is the only
sane thing to do.*
sang /sæŋ/
Sang is the past tense of **sing**.
sang-froid /sɒnfrwɑ́ː/
NU A person's **sang-froid** is their ability to remain
calm in a dangerous or difficult situation; a formal
word. *He faced the attack with amazing sang-froid.*
sanguine /sǽŋgwɪn/
ADJ If you are **sanguine** about something, you are
cheerful and confident that things will happen as you
want them to; a formal word. *He was not sanguine
about Bill's probable reactions.*
sanitarium /sǽnɪtɛə́riəm/. See **sanatorium**.
sanitary /sǽnɪtəʳri/; a formal word.
1 ADJ If you say that a place is not **sanitary**, you
mean that it is not very clean. *...a small and not very
sanitary café in Soho.*
2 ADJ ATTRIB **Sanitary** also means concerned with
keeping things clean and hygienic. *Sanitary conditions
in the hospitals had deteriorated rapidly. ...a sanitary
inspector.*
sanitary napkin, sanitary napkins
NC A **sanitary napkin** is the same as a **sanitary towel**;
used in American English.
sanitary towel, sanitary towels
NC A **sanitary towel** is a pad of thick soft material
which some women use when they have periods. *The
first disposable sanitary towel was marketed in 1880.*
sanitation /sǽnɪteɪʃn/
NU **Sanitation** is the process of keeping places clean
and hygienic, especially by providing a sewage system
and a clean water supply. *...the lack of sanitation and
adequate health care.*
sanity /sǽnəti/
1 NU A person's **sanity** is their ability to think and
behave in a normal and reasonable way. *It's a
wonder really that so many cope and retain their
sanity. ...doubts about Wilt's sanity.*

2 NU **Sanity** is also the quality of having a purpose
and a regular pattern, rather than being confusing and
worrying. *They give some point and sanity to daily
life.*
San José /sæn xɒséɪ/
San José is the capital of Costa Rica and its largest
city. Population: 285,000 (1989).
San Juan /sæn hwɑ́ːn/
San Juan is the capital of Puerto Rico and its largest
city. Population: 435,000 (1980).
sank /sæŋk/
Sank is the past tense of **sink**.
San Marino /sæn mərí:nəʊ/
The Republic of San Marino lies within the borders of
Italy. It is the only survivor of the many small states
which existed in Italy before unification in 1861. It
shares economic union with Italy. San Marino's heads
of state and government are two Captains-Regent,
elected every six months by the legislature from its
membership. Tourism is an important industry.
■ *religion:* Christianity (mainly Roman Catholic)
■ *language:* Italian ■ *currency:* Italian lira ■ *capital:*
San Marino ■ *population:* 23,000 (1990) ■ *size:* 61 square
kilometres.
San Salvador /sæn sǽlvədɔː/
San Salvador is the capital of El Salvador and its
largest city. Population: 463,000 (1985).
Sanskrit /sǽnskrɪt/
NU **Sanskrit** is a very old language which used to be
spoken in India and which is now used only in
religious writings and ceremonies. *The play is based
on an ancient Sanskrit poem.*
Santa Claus /sǽntə klɔ́ːz/
N PROP **Santa Claus** is another name for Father
Christmas. *'Michelle, it's Christmas Eve, it's 11:30—
go to bed and get ready for Santa Claus!'... The crowd
of parents and children welcomed Santa Claus at a
Christmas party.*
Santa Fé de Bogotá /sæntæ feɪ deɪ bɒgɒtɑ́ː/
Santa Fé de Bogotá is the official name for **Bogotá**, the
capital of Colombia.
Santer, Jacques /ʒæk sɒnˠteɪ/
Jacques Santer became Prime Minister of
Luxembourg in 1984. He was Secretary of State for
Cultural and Social Affairs from 1972 to 1974, and
served in the Chamber of Deputies from 1974 to 1979.
He was a member of the European Parliament from
1975 to 1979, and Vice President from 1975 to 1977. In
1991 he was President of the European Community.
From 1979 to 1984 he was Minister of Finance, Labour,
and Social Security. He was Secretary General of the
Christian Social Party (PCS) from 1972 to 1974, and
President from 1974 to 1982. Born: 1937.
Santiago /sæntiɑ́ːgəʊ/
Santiago is the capital of Chile and its largest city.
Population: 4,385,000 (1990).
Santo Domingo /sæntəʊ dəmíŋgəʊ/
Santo Domingo is the capital of the Dominican
Republic and its largest city. Population: 1,313,000
(1981).
São Paulo /saʊ paʊ́ləʊ/
São Paulo is the largest city in Brazil. Population:
10,998,000 (1989).
São Tomé /saʊ təméɪ/
São Tomé is the capital of São Tomé and Príncipe and
its largest city. Population: 35,000 (1984).
São Tomé and Príncipe /saʊ təméɪ ən príːnˠsɪpə/
The Democratic Republic of São Tomé and Príncipe is
a country in the Gulf of Guinea, off the west coast of
Africa. São Tomé was colonized by Portugal in the
15th century. It became independent in 1975, with Dr
Manuel Pinto da Costa as its first President. He
established the Movement for the Liberation of São
Tomé and Príncipe (MLSTP) as the sole legal party.
Following the first multi-party elections in 1991, Miguel
Trovoada, an independent supported by the
Democratic Convergence Party - Reflexion Group
(PDC-GR), became President after ten years in exile.
Major Daniel Lima dos Santos Daio (PDC-GR)
became Prime Minister. São Tomé and Príncipe
exports cocoa. It is a member of the Organization of
African Unity. Large foreign debts and high inflation

are serious economic problems.
■ *per capita GNP:* US$360 ■ *religion:* Christianity
(mainly Roman Catholic) ■ *language:* Portuguese
(official), Crioulo ■ *currency:* dobra ■ *capital:* São
Tomé ■ *population:* 122,000 (1989) ■ *size:* 964 square
kilometres.

sap /sæp/ saps, sapping, sapped
1 vo If something **saps** your strength or confidence, it
gradually weakens or destroys it over a period of
time. *The constant tension at work was sapping my
energy.*
2 NU **Sap** is the watery liquid in plants and trees. *The
sap was rising in the maples.*

sapling /sæplɪŋ/ saplings
NC A **sapling** is a young tree. *Vandals damaged
saplings which were planted shortly after the storm.*

sapper /sæpə/ sappers
1 NCorTITLE A **sapper** is a soldier of the Royal
Engineers in the British Army. *Sapper John Wright
has been awarded the Queen's Gallantry Medal.*
2 NC A **sapper** is also a soldier of any army whose job
is to dig trenches and prepare minefields. *Their
sappers have been mining the border area.*

sapphire /sæfaɪə/ sapphires
NC A **sapphire** is a blue precious stone. *...the rising
price of rubies and sapphires.*

sarcasm /sɑːkæzəm/
NU **Sarcasm** is speech or writing which is intended to
mock or insult someone and which seems to say one
thing but actually means the opposite. See also **irony**.
*'Oh yeah,' said Jenny with broad sarcasm, 'I notice
how you hate getting paid.'... He tinges his bitterness
with sarcasm.*

sarcastic /sɑːkæstɪk/
ADJ If you are **sarcastic**, you mock or insult someone,
often saying one thing but actually meaning the
opposite. *She seemed her usual sarcastic self at
dinner. ...a sarcastic smile.* ◆ **sarcastically** ADV
*Brady became the seventh player to be cautioned for
sarcastically applauding the referee.*

sarcophagus /sɑːkɒfəgəs/ sarcophagi or
sarcophaguses
NC A **sarcophagus** is a large decorated stone coffin
that was used in ancient times. *...a Roman
sarcophagus with a Saxon lid.*

sardine /sɑːdiːn/ sardines
NC A **sardine** is a small sea fish that can be eaten.
*...tins of sardines. ...lorry loads of herrings and
sardines.*

sardonic /sɑːdɒnɪk/
ADJ A **sardonic** person is mocking or scornful in their
behaviour. *...a sardonic young man who never joined
in the fun. ...a sardonic chuckle.* ◆ **sardonically** ADV
She smiled sardonically.

sari /sɑːri/ saris
NC A **sari** is a piece of clothing worn especially by
Indian women. It consists of a long piece of thin
material that is wrapped around the body. *...women
in brightly-coloured saris.*

sartorial /sɑːtɔːriəl/
ADJ ATTRIB **Sartorial** means relating to clothes and to
the way they are made or worn; a formal word.
People's sartorial habits have changed.

SAS /eseɪes/
N PROP The **SAS** is a group of highly trained British
soldiers who work on secret or very difficult military
operations. **SAS** is an abbreviation for 'Special Air
Service'. *...a brilliantly successful SAS attack.*

sash /sæʃ/ sashes
NC A **sash** is a long piece of cloth which people wear
round their waist or over one shoulder, especially with
formal or official clothes. *...a tunic tied at the waist
with a sash. ...the presidential sash of office.*

sash cord, sash cords
NC A **sash cord** is a strong piece of thin rope which
connects a weight to the sliding half of a sash
window. *He tried to raise the window, but the sash
cord was broken.*

sash window, sash windows
NC A **sash window** is a window which consists of two
frames placed one above the other. The window can be
opened by sliding one frame over the other.

Sassou-Nguesso, Denis /dəniː sæsuː gesəu/
General Denis Sassou-Nguesso became President of
Congo in 1979. He was a member of the Council of
State from 1976 to 1977, and Minister of Defence and
National Security from 1977 to 1980. He became
Chairman of the Congolese Party of Labour (PCT) in
1979. He lost most of his power after a national
conference was held in 1991. Born: 1943.

sat /sæt/
Sat is the past tense and past participle of **sit**.

Sat.
Sat. is a written abbreviation for 'Saturday'.

Satan /seɪtn/
N PROP **Satan** is a name given to the Devil in the
Jewish, Christian, and Muslim religions. *...a clear
message about hell and Satan.*

satanic /sətænɪk/
ADJ Something that is **satanic** is considered to be
caused by or influenced by Satan. *...allegations of
satanic rituals.*

satanism /seɪtənɪzəm/
NU **Satanism** is the worship of Satan. *Many people
have called for a ban on all forms of satanism.*

satchel /sætʃəl/ satchels
NC A **satchel** is a bag made from leather or cloth and
which has a shoulder strap. *Men carrying satchels of
grenades stood guard. ...uniforms, hockey sticks,
satchels and other paraphernalia.*

sated /seɪtɪd/
ADJ If you are **sated** with something, you have had
more of it than you can enjoy; a formal word. *They
were sated with fresh air and hard exercise.*

satellite /sætəlaɪt/ satellites
1 NC A **satellite** is an object which has been sent into
space in order to collect information or to be part of a
communications system. Satellites move continually
round the earth or other planets. *Each rocket is
capable of putting two communications satellites into
orbit... The pictures were transmitted by satellite... He
made the pledge in an address broadcast to Europe by
satellite television.*
2 NC A **satellite** is also a natural object in space that
moves round a planet or star. *The last great impacts
which hit the moon around this period must have been
due to satellites of the moon. ...Jupiter's satellite Io.*
3 NC **Satellite** countries, places, and organizations
have very little power of their own, but are dependent
on a larger and more powerful country or
organization. *Many of these problems are shared by
the former satellite countries. ...countries which were
previously satellites of the Soviet Union. ...the capital
city of Lima and its surrounding satellite towns.*

satiate /seɪʃieɪt/ satiates, satiating, satiated
vo If something such as food or pleasure **satiates** you,
you have so much of it that you become tired of it; a
formal word. *There is usually enough fruit on one
apple tree to satiate several children... During the
week of the royal wedding there were enough
festivities to satiate most people.*

satin /sætɪn/
NU **Satin** is a smooth and shiny type of cloth. *The
bride was dressed in white satin.*

satire /sætaɪə/ satires
1 NU **Satire** is humour and exaggeration that is used
to show how foolish or wrong something is.
...exquisite touches of irony and satire.
2 NC A **satire** is a play or piece of writing that uses
satire to criticize something. *...a brilliant political
satire. ...a satire on existing society.*

satirical /sətɪrɪkl/
ADJ **Satirical** drawings, writings, or performances use
satire to criticize something. *...satirical cartoons. ...a
satirical fortnightly magazine.*

satirist /sætərɪst/ satirists
NC A **satirist** is a person who uses satire in their
writing in order to express their feelings about people
or society. *...a political satirist.*

satirize /sætəraɪz/ satirizes, satirizing, satirized; also
spelt **satirise**.
vo If you **satirize** a person or group of people, you
criticize them or make fun of them through the use of
satire in something such as a play, novel, or poem.

They satirized the way wealthy capitalists behaved...
These characteristics were often used by caricaturists
to satirize feminists.
satisfaction /sætɪsfækʃn/
1 NU **Satisfaction** is the pleasure you feel when you do
something that you wanted or needed to do or when
you have done something well. *She read what she had*
written with satisfaction... Both sides have expressed
satisfaction at the progress made in the discussions.
...a sense of satisfaction.
2 NU If you get **satisfaction** from someone, you get
money or an apology from them because of some
harm or injustice which has been done to you.
Consumers who have been unable to get satisfaction
from their local branch should write direct to the
Chairman.
3 If something is done to your **satisfaction**, you are
happy with the way it has been done. *Every detail*
was worked out to everyone's satisfaction.
satisfactory /sætɪsfæktəˀri/
ADJ If something is **satisfactory**, it is acceptable to
you or fulfils a particular need or purpose. *His doctor*
described his general state of health as fairly
satisfactory... The arrangement sounded satisfactory.
♦ **satisfactorily** ADV *She was not recovering*
satisfactorily.
satisfied /sætɪsfaɪd/
1 ADJ If you are **satisfied** with something, you are
pleased because you have got what you wanted. *He*
was well satisfied with the success of the aircraft.
...satisfied customers who had bought the car.
2 ADJ PRED If you are **satisfied** that something is true
or has been done properly, you are convinced about
this after checking it. *We can be satisfied that we've*
missed nothing important.
satisfy /sætɪsfaɪ/ **satisfies, satisfying, satisfied**
1 VO If someone or something **satisfies** you, they give
you enough of what you want to make you pleased or
contented. *More frequent feeding will usually help to*
satisfy a baby... He had not even been able to satisfy
her simple needs.
2 VOorV-REFL If someone **satisfies** you that something
is true or has been done properly, they convince you
by giving you more information or by showing you
what has been done. *He would need to satisfy the*
authorities that he had paid tax for the previous three
years... I glanced around, satisfied myself that the last
diner had left, and turned off the lights.
3 VO If you **satisfy** the requirements for something,
you are good enough or suitable to fulfil these
requirements. *There is some doubt whether they can*
satisfy our entrance requirements.
satisfying /sætɪsfaɪɪŋ/
ADJ Something that is **satisfying** gives you a feeling of
pleasure and fulfilment. *There's nothing more*
satisfying than doing the work you love.
satsuma /sætsuːmə/ **satsumas**
NC A **satsuma** is a type of small orange.
saturate /sætʃəreɪt/ **saturates, saturating, saturated**
1 VO If a place is **saturated** with things, it is so full of
those things that no more can be added. *The next*
morning, teams saturated the community with
literature about the attack. ♦ **saturation** /sætʃəreɪʃn/
NU *Even when the market reaches saturation, the*
process doesn't stop.
2 VO If someone or something is **saturated**, they
become extremely wet. *Philip was totally saturated.*
saturated fat, saturated fats
NUorN PL **Saturated fat** is a type of fat that contains a
lot of fatty acids. It produces cholesterol in the body
and can be a cause of heart disease and cancer. *The*
first thing you've got to do is cut down on saturated
fat... Urgent steps are needed to reduce the intake of
saturated fats in people's diets.
Saturday /sætədeɪ, sætədi/ **Saturdays**
NUorNC **Saturday** is the day after Friday and before
Sunday. *...marches due to take place on Saturday.*
saturnine /sætənaɪn/
ADJ Someone who is **saturnine** is gloomy and
unfriendly; a literary word. *A saturnine customs*
officer looked through our baggage.

satyr /sætə/ **satyrs**
NC If you refer to a man as a **satyr**, you mean that he
has excessively strong sexual desires; a literary
word. *He was a bit of a satyr, really—I wondered*
where he got the energy... With a flourish, the aged
satyr kissed her hand.
sauce /sɔːs/ **sauces**
N MASS A **sauce** is a thick liquid which is served with
other food. *...tomato sauce... Make a sauce to go with*
the fish.
sauce-boat, sauce-boats
NC A **sauce-boat** is a long shallow jug in which sauce
is served. *A pouring sauce should be thinner and flow*
easily from a sauce-boat.
saucepan /sɔːspən/ **saucepans**
NC A **saucepan** is a deep metal cooking pot, usually
with a long handle and a lid. *Put the chicken in a*
large saucepan with the onion.
saucer /sɔːsə/ **saucers**
NC A **saucer** is a small curved plate on which you
stand a cup. *...her best cup and saucer.* ● See also
flying saucer.
saucy /sɔːsi/
ADJ Someone or something that is **saucy** is rather rude
or cheeky, especially in a light-hearted or amusing
way; an informal word. *Don't be saucy with me... It's*
so saucy it heads Britain's bestseller list.
Saudi Arabia /saudi əreɪbiə/
The **Kingdom of Saudi Arabia** is a country on the
Arabian Peninsula. Abd al-Aziz (known as Ibn Sa'ud)
proclaimed the Kingdom of Saudi Arabia in 1932,
restoring the Sa'ud dynasty, which had ruled in Arabia
in the 19th century. Ibn Sa'ud died in 1953 and his sons
have ruled Saudi Arabia since. King Fahd ibn Abdul
Aziz succeeded in 1982. Oil was discovered in 1938. It
has the largest petroleum reserves and is the largest
exporter of petroleum in the world. Saudi Arabia is a
member of OPEC, the Arab League, and the Gulf Co-
operation Council. Approximately one million pilgrims
visit Mecca, the birthplace of Muhammad, every year.
♦ **Saudi** /saudi/ N, ADJ **Saudi Arabian** /saudi əreɪbiən/
N, ADJ
■ *per capita GNP:* US$6,170 ■ *religion:* Islam (mainly
Sunni) ■ *language:* Arabic ■ *currency:* riyal ■ *capital:*
Riyadh (royal capital), Jeddah (administrative
capital) ■ *population:* 14 million (1989) ■ *size:* 2,149,690
square kilometres.
sauerkraut /sauəkraut/
NU **Sauerkraut** is cabbage that has been cut into very
small slices and pickled. It is eaten mainly in
Germany. *...a layer of aromatic sauerkraut on black*
bread.
sauna /sɔːnə/ **saunas**
1 NC A **sauna** is a hot steam bath. *It's traditional to*
jump in the water after a sauna, isn't it?... The
humidity makes it feel like living in a sauna.
2 NC A **sauna** is also the room or building where you
have a sauna. *We have a swimming pool, solarium*
and sauna. ...a health spa with gymnasium and sauna.
saunter /sɔːntə/ **saunters, sauntering, sauntered**
VA If you **saunter** somewhere, you walk there in a
slow, casual way. *He sauntered up and down, looking*
at the shops and the people.
sausage /sɒsɪdʒ/ **sausages**
1 NU **Sausage** is finely minced meat which is mixed
with other ingredients and put into a thin casing like a
tube. *We lunched on garlic sausage and bread.*
2 NC A **sausage** is a tube-shaped piece of minced
meat. *...bacon, eggs, and sausages for breakfast.*
sausage dog, sausage dogs
NC A **sausage dog** is the same as a **dachshund**; an
informal expression.
sausage roll, sausage rolls
NC A **sausage roll** is a small amount of sausage or
minced meat which is covered with pastry and
cooked. *She makes very good sausage rolls.*
sauté /sauteɪ/ **sautés, sautéing, sautéed**
VO When you **sauté** food, you fry it quickly in hot oil
or butter. *Sauté the chicken breasts until they are*
golden brown. ♦ **sautéed** ADJ *...sautéed potatoes.*
savage /sævɪdʒ/ **savages, savaging, savaged**
1 ADJ Something that is **savage** is extremely fierce or

violent. *Mr Haughey condemned the attacks as savage and futile. ...a savage dog, half crazy with the smell of blood. ...two weeks of savage rioting.*
◆ **savagely** ADV *The dog began to bark savagely.*
2 ADJ **Savage** remarks and actions are cruel and nasty. *...savage remarks about the futility of life. ...his keen insight and sometimes savage wit.*
◆ **savagely** ADV *...the report he has so savagely denounced.*
3 NC If you call someone a **savage**, you mean that they are cruel, violent, or uncivilized. *The paper describes the men as 'savages'... We cannot call ourselves civilized—merely dangerously clever savages.*
4 VO If an animal, such as a dog, **savages** you, it attacks you violently. *A 3-year-old girl was savaged to death this afternoon by a pitbull terrier.*
5 VO If you **savage** someone or **savage** something they have done, you criticize them severely. *An opposition spokesman savaged the Government's housing programme... Delegates from Croatia and Slovenia savaged the economic record of Prime Minister Branko Mikulic.*

savagery /sǽvɪdʒri/
NU **Savagery** is cruel and violent behaviour. *...the savagery of the attack.*

savannah /səvǽnə/ **savannahs**; also spelt **savanna**.
NCorNU A **savannah** is an open, flat stretch of grassland, usually in Africa. *During the wet season they will move out into the savannah area.*

save /seɪv/ **saves, saving, saved**
1 VO If you **save** someone or something, you help them to avoid harm or to escape from a dangerous or unpleasant situation. *An artificial heart could save his life... She saved him from drowning.*
2 VOorV If you **save** money, you gradually collect it by spending less than you get, often in order to buy something you want. *They had managed to save enough to buy a house... She told him that she was saving with a building society.*
3 VO,VOO,orV If you **save** time or money, you prevent the loss or waste of it. *The government's real motive is to save money... It can save time for both patient and doctor... This measure would save the government £185 million... It's an attempt to save on labour costs.*
4 VOorVOO If you **save** something, you keep it because it will be needed later. *Always save business letters, bills, and receipts... Will you save him a place at your table?*
5 VO+*from*orV I ING If someone or something **saves** you from doing something, they do it for you or change the situation so that you do not have to do it. *Well, that saves me from denying it... Using electronic circuit boards saves wiring up thousands of individual transistors.*
6 V-REFLO If you **save** yourself something difficult or unpleasant, you find a way of avoiding it. *He could have saved himself a considerable amount of trouble if he'd been more open... You could save yourself a lot of work if you used a computer.*
7 VO If a goalkeeper **saves** a shot, he or she prevents the ball from going into the goal. *The shot was saved by Buller.* ▶ Also NC *He made a brilliant save.*
8 PREP You can use **save** or **save for** to introduce an exception to your main statement; a formal use. *No visitors are allowed save in the most exceptional cases... The stage was empty save for a few pieces of furniture.*
save up PHRASAL VERB If you **save up** for something, you collect money by spending less than you get, in order to buy it. *It took me a year to save up for a new coat... The main purpose is to save up enough money for a bicycle.*

saving /seɪvɪŋ/ **savings**
1 NC A **saving** is a reduction in the amount of time or money that is used or needed. *...a very great saving in cost... The new management had achieved even bigger savings.*
2 N PL Your **savings** are the money that you have saved, especially in a bank or a building society. *She drew out all her savings. ...a savings account.*

-saving
1 SUFFIX **-saving** combines with nouns to form adjectives that describe things as preventing something such as time or energy being wasted. *...the latest labour-saving gadgetry. ...research on the most efficient designs and energy-saving schemes for hospitals. ...low-cost or even cost-saving options.*
2 SUFFIX **-saving** also combines with nouns to form adjectives that describe things as intended to prevent something being lost or destroyed. *The hospitals are in dire need of what he calls life-saving drugs... Not all the ideas are exactly world-saving, though... Sight-saving vitamin A is available from vegetables and green leaves.*

saving grace
N SING A **saving grace** is a good quality in a person or thing that prevents them from being completely bad or worthless. *The play's only saving grace was the high standard of acting.*

saviour /seɪvjə/ **saviours**
1 NC A **saviour** is a person who saves people from danger; a literary use. *Many people regarded Churchill as the saviour of the country.*
2 N PROP In Christianity, the **Saviour** is Jesus Christ. *Last year I came to know Jesus Christ personally as my Lord and Saviour.*

savoir-faire /sǽvwɑːfeə/
NU **Savoir-faire** is the confidence to say and do the appropriate thing in a social situation; a formal word. *I was impressed with her savoir-faire and social skills.*

savour /seɪvə/ **savours, savouring, savoured**; spelt **savor** in American English.
1 VO If you **savour** food or drink, you eat or drink it slowly in order to taste its full flavour and to enjoy it properly. *Meadows took a bite of meat, savoured it, and said, 'Fantastic'.*
2 VO If you **savour** an experience, you take great pleasure and delight in it, enjoying it as much as you can. *He leaned back into his seat, savouring the comfort.*

savoury /seɪvəri/; spelt **savory** in American English.
1 ADJ **Savoury** food has a salty or spicy flavour rather than a sweet one. *...crisps—the British public's favourite savoury snack.*
2 ADJ Something that is not very **savoury** is not very pleasant or morally acceptable. *...the less savoury episodes in her past.*

savvy /sǽvi/ **savvier, savviest**
ADJ Someone who is **savvy** has practical knowledge and ability; used in informal American English. *Savvy consumers can get real deals... They're surrounded by some of the savviest players.* ▶ Also NU *...long-term vision and political savvy.*

saw /sɔː/ **saws, sawing, sawed, sawn**
1 **Saw** is the past tense of **see**.
2 NC A **saw** is a tool for cutting wood, which has a blade with sharp teeth along one edge. *...an hydraulic power source for drills, saws and water pumps.*
3 VO If you **saw** something, you cut it with a saw. *I started sawing the branches off the main trunk.*

sawdust /sɔːdʌst/
NU **Sawdust** is the very fine fragments of wood which are produced when you saw wood. *He was covered with sawdust.*

Saw Maung /sɔː maʊŋ/
Senior General **Saw Maung** became Chairman of the State Law and Order Restoration Council (SLORC) and Prime Minister of Burma following a coup in 1988. In 1985 he became Commander-in-Chief of Defence Services.

sawmill /sɔːmɪl/ **sawmills**
NC A **sawmill** is a factory in which wood is sawn up into planks, using a power-driven saw. *The forests are cut and the wood goes to a sawmill 20 miles away.*

sawn /sɔːn/
Sawn is the past participle of **saw**.

sawn-off shotgun, sawn-off shotguns
NC A **sawn-off shotgun** is a shotgun on which the barrel has been cut short. Criminals use sawn-off shotguns because they can hide them more easily than complete shotguns. *...hijackers armed with two sawn-off shotguns.*

Sawyer, Dr Amos /ˈsɔːjə/
Dr Amos Sawyer became interim President of Liberia in 1990, when the government of Samuel Doe collapsed and Doe was killed. He became Chairman of the Liberian People's Party (LPP) in 1984.

sax /sæks/ **saxes**
N C or N U A **sax** is the same as a **saxophone**; an informal word. *There was one kid who played sax. ...a tenor sax.*

Saxon /ˈsæksn/
ADJ Something that is **Saxon** relates to, or is characteristic of, the ancient Saxons, the Anglo-Saxons, or their descendants. *Parts of the arch and clock-tower date back to Saxon times.*

saxophone /ˈsæksəfəʊn/ **saxophones**
N C A **saxophone** is a musical wind instrument. It is made of metal in a curved shape, and is often played in jazz bands. *That was Charlie Parker himself playing the saxophone on his own composition.*

saxophonist /sækˈsɒfənɪst/ **saxophonists**
N C A **saxophonist** is someone who plays a saxophone. *...a personal tribute to the great US jazz saxophonist, Stan Getz.*

say /seɪ/ **says, saying, said**
1 V-REPORT, VO, or V-QUOTE When you **say** something, you speak words. *He said it was an accident... He had said nothing to me about his meeting... 'Please come in,' she said.*
2 V-REPORT or VO You use **say** to introduce an opinion or comment. *I just want to say how pleased I am to be here... One thing you have to say about Americans: they love drama... It's hard for me to say what his attitude is.*
3 V-REPORT or V-QUOTE If you **say** something in a letter or a book, for example, you express it in writing. *She wrote to say she wanted to meet me in London... There were stickers all over the crate saying: 'Glass—Handle with Care'.*
4 V-REPORT or V-QUOTE If something such as a clock or map **says** a particular thing, it gives you information when you look at it. *The clock says that it is six o'clock... The road was not where the map said it should be.*
5 VO To **say** something about a person, situation, or thing means to reveal something about them. *Their glances seemed to be saying something about their relationship... The title says it all... Your clothes say a lot about you.*
6 You can use **say** when you mention something as an example or when you mention an approximate amount or time. *Compare, say, a Michelangelo painting with a Van Gogh. ...in the next, say, ten years.*
7 N SING If you have a **say** in something, you have the right to give your opinion and influence decisions. *People want a much greater say in how the country should be governed... Teachers have had little say in the new curriculum.*
● **Say** is used in these phrases. ● If you **say** something to yourself, you think it without speaking it aloud. *I began to say to myself, 'What about becoming an actor?'* ● You use expressions such as **just say** and **let's say** when you want to discuss something that might possibly happen or be true. *Just say you found treasure in your garden. Would you sell it?* ● You use **to say the least** to suggest that a situation is actually much more serious, shocking, or extreme than you say it is. *She lacked tact (to say the least) in expressing her views.* ● You use **that is** to say to indicate that you are about to express the same idea more clearly; a formal expression. *The Romans left Britain in 410 AD—that is to say, England was under Roman rule for nearly 500 years.* ● You use **to say nothing of** when you add something which gives even more strength to the point you are making. *The effort required is immense, to say nothing of the cost.* ● If something **goes without saying**, it is obvious or is bound to be true. *It goes without saying that I am grateful for all your help.* ● If something **has a lot to be said for it**, it has a lot of good qualities. *It's her first full-scale novel and I think that there's a lot to be said for it.*

saying /ˈseɪɪŋ/ **sayings**
N C A **saying** is a traditional sentence that people often

say and that gives advice or information about life. *There is a saying that 'man shall not live by bread alone'.*

say-so
N SING+POSS If you do something on someone's **say-so**, they tell you to do it or they give you permission to do it; an informal word. *Daniel had already left, on his father's say-so... No luggage can go into the aircraft without his say-so.*

scab /skæb/ **scabs**
1 N C A **scab** is a hard, dry covering that forms over the surface of a wound. *A great scab had formed on his right knee.*
2 N C If someone who is on strike calls another person a **scab**, they are accusing them of breaking the strike by continuing to work; an offensive use. *The lorry drove straight through to the dockside to cries of 'Scab'. ...scab labour.*

scabbard /ˈskæbəd/ **scabbards**
N C A **scabbard** is a holder for a sword or knife, especially one that hangs from a belt. *Nearly all these daggers had one or more leather thongs dangling from the scabbard—each thong denoting a man killed.*

scabby /ˈskæbi/ **scabbier, scabbiest**
ADJ If your skin is **scabby**, it is covered with scabs. *...the freckled, scabby hands of the old men.*

scabies /ˈskeɪbiːz/
N U **Scabies** is a very infectious skin disease caused by a parasite, which makes you want to scratch a lot; a medical term. *One of the mothers started complaining about that fact that her child had scabies.*

scaffold /ˈskæfəʊld/ **scaffolds**
N C A **scaffold** is a platform on which criminals used to be executed. *Guy Fawkes died on the scaffold.*

scaffolding /ˈskæfəldɪŋ/
N U **Scaffolding** is a temporary framework of poles and boards, used by workmen while they are constructing, repairing, or painting the outside walls of a tall building. *The incident occurred when scaffolding outside the building collapsed.*

scald /skɔːld/ **scalds, scalding, scalded**
1 V-REFL or VO If you **scald** yourself, you burn yourself with very hot liquid or steam. *When it was cool enough not to scald my lips, I swallowed the coffee and asked for more.*
2 N C A **scald** is a burn caused by very hot liquid or steam. *...burns and scalds.*

scalding /ˈskɔːldɪŋ/
ADJ Something that is **scalding** is very hot. *...scalding coffee.*

scale /skeɪl/ **scales, scaling, scaled**
1 N SING+SUPP If you refer to the **scale** of something, you are referring to its size, especially when it is big. *The scale of change is so enormous. ...the sheer scale of the United States.*
2 N U You use **scale** in expressions such as 'large scale' and 'on a small scale' when you are indicating the size, extent, or degree of one thing as compared to other similar things. *The district grew peas on a large scale... The plan was never very grand in scale. ...small scale methods of getting energy. ...a full scale confrontation between the students and the police.*
3 N C A **scale** is a set of levels or numbers which are used in a particular system of measuring things or comparing things. *...the scale by which we measure the severity of earthquakes. ...a temperature scale. ...the pay scale.*
4 N SING The **scale** of a map, plan, or model is the relationship between its measurements and those of the thing in the real world that it represents. *...a map with a scale of 1:50,000.* ● If a map, plan, or model is **to scale**, it is accurately drawn or made according to the scale being used. *She makes the initial drawing to scale.*
5 N C A **scale** is also a sequence of musical notes that are played or sung in an upward or downward order. *...the scale of C.*
6 N C The **scales** of fish or reptiles are the small, flat pieces of hard skin that cover their bodies. *The scales are only loosely attached to the underlying soft tissue.*
7 N PL **Scales** are a piece of equipment for weighing things. *...a pair of scales.*

8 VO If you **scale** something high or steep, you climb up or over it. *She scaled the barrier like a commando.*
scale down PHRASAL VERB If something is **scaled down**, it is made smaller in size or amount than it used to be. *The operations were scaled down.*
scale up PHRASAL VERB If you **scale up** an activity, you intensify it or make it bigger. *Trade union leaders have threatened to scale up strike action... This new product will allow industry to scale up its operations.*

scaled-down
ADJ ATTRIB **Scaled-down** is used to describe things that have been made smaller than they originally were, although they still have the same proportions as the original thing. *...scaled-down multi-national NATO units. ...a scaled-down chorus of eighty professional singers.*

scallop /skɒləp/ **scallops**
1 NC **Scallops** are shellfish that have two flat fan-shaped shells, and can be eaten. *It was his first Chinese meal—he even tried scallops. ...frozen shrimps and scallops.*
2 NC **Scallops** are also a series of small curves that form an ornamental border on things such as clothes, tablecloths, or handkerchiefs. *That season no pleats, ruffles, bows, scallops, or darts were too extreme.*

scalloped /skɒləpt/
ADJ ATTRIB **Scalloped** objects are decorated with a series of small curves along the edges. *...a blue and green scalloped design.*

scalp /skælp/ **scalps**
NC Your **scalp** is the skin under the hair on your head. *...rubbing his sore scalp.*

scalpel /skælpl/ **scalpels**
NC A **scalpel** is a knife with a short, thin, sharp blade. Scalpels are used by surgeons during operations. *...cancerous cells the surgeon's scalpel may have missed.*

scaly /skeɪli/
ADJ Something that is **scaly** is covered in small, stiff patches of hard skin. *Psoriasis is a scaly red skin rash.*

scam /skæm/ **scams**
NC A **scam** is an illegal or dishonest scheme for making money; used in American English. *Typical scams include promises of jobs for people who ring expensive 900-numbers... Federal prosecutors in New Jersey say it's becoming a big-time scam. ...a new scam being used by sophisticated con artists.*

scamp /skæmp/ **scamps**
NC If you call a child a **scamp**, you mean that they are very naughty but you like them, so you find it difficult to be angry with them; an informal word. *...that lovely scamp, Liam... What have you been up to, you young scamp?*

scamper /skæmpə/ **scampers, scampering, scampered**
VA When children or small animals **scamper** somewhere, they move with small, quick, bouncing steps. *The squirrels scamper along the twigs.*

scampi /skæmpi/
N PL **Scampi** are large prawns that are often fried in batter and eaten. *...shellfish such as crab, lobster, prawns and scampi.*

scan /skæn/ **scans, scanning, scanned**
1 VO When you **scan** an area, group of things, or piece of writing, you look at it carefully, but often fairly quickly, usually because you are looking for something in particular. *Anxiously Carol scanned their faces to see who she might know. ...lifeguards scanning the sea for shark fins.*
2 VO If a machine **scans** something, it examines it quickly, for example by moving a beam of light or X-rays over it. *The reconnaissance plane's job was to scan the oceans with its radar... Its radar scans the sky.* ► Also NC *A liver scan was performed.*
◆ **scanning** NU *...ultrasonic scanning for looking at soft tissue in the body. ...sophisticated scanning equipment.*

scandal /skændl/ **scandals**
1 NC A **scandal** is a situation or event that a lot of

people think is shocking and immoral. *We can't afford another scandal in the firm. ...a series of political and financial scandals.*
2 NU **Scandal** is talk about people's shocking and immoral behaviour. *Someone must have been spreading scandal.*
3 N SING You can refer to something as a **scandal** when you are angry about it. *The defences were a scandal.*

scandalize /skændəlaɪz/ **scandalizes, scandalizing, scandalized**; also spelt **scandalise.**
VO If you **are scandalized**, you are shocked and offended. *He was uncertain whether to laugh or be scandalized.*

scandalmonger /skændlmʌngə/ **scandalmongers**
NC A **scandalmonger** is someone who deliberately spreads stories that emphasize the shocking or immoral qualities of particular people; used showing disapproval.

scandalous /skændələs/
1 ADJ Something that is **scandalous** is considered immoral and shocking. *There were some scandalous stories about her.*
2 ADJ You can describe something as **scandalous** when it makes you very angry. *It is scandalous that the public should be treated in this way.* ◆ **scandalously** SUBMOD *...schemes offering scandalously large tax advantages.*

Scandinavia /skændɪneɪviə/
N PROP **Scandinavia** is the region in northern Europe that contains the countries of Norway, Sweden, Denmark, Finland, Iceland, and the Faroe Islands. *Acid rain is known to have caused severe damage to trees and lakes in Scandinavia and Germany. ...discussions about making Scandinavia and its surrounding seas into a nuclear-free zone.*

Scandinavian /skændɪneɪviən/ **Scandinavians**
1 ADJ Something that is **Scandinavian** belongs or relates to Scandinavia, or to its countries, peoples, or languages. *...the Netherlands, Austria and the Scandinavian countries.*
2 NC A **Scandinavian** is a person who comes from Scandinavia. *At the present time we have five Scandinavians and one German in our class.*

scanner /skænə/ **scanners**
NC A **scanner** is a machine which is used to examine things, for example by moving a beam of light or X-rays over them. Scanners are used in places such as hospitals, airports, and research laboratories. *...brain and body scanners using radio waves to probe the structures inside us.*

scant /skænt/
ADJ ATTRIB **Scant** is used to indicate that there is only a very small amount of something and to say that this is not enough. *The campaign was conducted with scant regard for truth. ...scant resources... The media gave the conference scant coverage.*

scanty /skænti/ **scantier, scantiest**
ADJ You describe something as **scanty** when it is smaller in quantity or size than you think it should be. *...a rather scanty but enthusiastic audience. ...waitresses wearing scanty black bathing suits... She had only the scantiest education.* ◆ **scantily** ADV *The bedroom was scantily furnished.*

scapegoat /skeɪpgəʊt/ **scapegoats**
NC If someone is made a **scapegoat**, they are blamed for something that they were not fully responsible for because other people want to protect themselves. *He said he did not intend to be made a scapegoat. ...a convenient scapegoat.*

scapula /skæpjʊlə/ **scapulas**
NC Your **scapula** is your shoulder blade; a medical term. *The shoulder girdle is composed of the scapula and clavicle.*

scar /skɑː/ **scars, scarring, scarred**
1 NC A **scar** is a mark on the skin which is left after a wound has healed. *There was a scar on her arm.*
2 VO If your skin is **scarred**, it is badly marked as a result of a wound. *They will be scarred for life.*
3 ADJ If an object is **scarred**, it is damaged and there are ugly marks on it. *...the scarred tree trunk.*
4 NC A **scar** is also a permanent effect on someone's

mind that results from an unpleasant experience.
...the scars of poverty.
5 VO If an unpleasant experience scars you, it has a
permanent effect on you, and influences the way you
think and behave. *...the violence of the attack that
scarred my mind.*

scarce /skeəs/ **scarcer, scarcest**
ADJ If something is scarce, there is not much of it.
...an environment where water is scarce.

scarcely /skeəsli/
1 ADV You use scarcely to say that something is only
just true. *I can scarcely remember what we ate...
They were scarcely ever apart. ...a very young man,
scarcely more than a boy.*
2 ADV You can use scarcely in an ironic way to
emphasize that something is certainly not true. *There
could scarcely be a less promising environment for
children.*
3 ADV If you say scarcely had one thing happened
when something else happened, you mean that the first
event was followed immediately by the second.
*Scarcely had the car drawn to a halt when armed
police surrounded it.*

scarcity /skeəsəti/ **scarcities**
NCorNU If there is a scarcity of something, there is
not enough of it; a formal word. *A scarcity of safe
water is helping the disease to spread. ...the
combination of rigid economic control and scarcity.
...shortages and scarcities.*

scare /skeə/ **scares, scaring, scared**
1 VO When people or things scare you, they frighten
you or make you feel very worried. *I didn't mean to
scare you... The Minister said America could not scare
Pakistan with aid cuts.*
2 NC If something gives you a scare, it frightens you
or makes you feel very worried. *That night I had an
even worse scare. ...a scare about the spread of
Muslim fundamentalism.*
3 NC If there is a scare about something, a lot of
people are worried or frightened by it. *Since none of
the fragments picked up was radioactive, the scare
died down... A bomb scare delayed horse racing at
Newbury for almost one and a half hours yesterday.*
scare away or **scare off** PHRASAL VERB 1 If you
scare animals or people **away** or if you scare them **off**,
you frighten them so that they go away. *The least
shadow or movement would scare the fish away... I
thought of scaring them off with a few shotgun pellets.*
2 If you scare someone **away** or if you scare them **off**,
you make them so nervous that they decide not to do
something that they were planning to do. *Foreign
investors would be scared away by political
instability... No doubt the party is anxious not to
needlessly scare off any aid donors.*

scarecrow /skeəkrəʊ/ **scarecrows**
NC A scarecrow is an object in the shape of a person.
It is put in a field to frighten birds away from crops.
*...traditional hay-stuffed scarecrows with stalks
spilling from their sleeves.*

scared /skeəd/
1 ADJ PRED If you are scared of someone or
something, you are frightened of them. *Everybody's
scared of him... She was terribly scared but not
injured... People are too scared to apply for travel
documents.*
2 ADJ PRED If you are scared that something
unpleasant might happen, you are nervous and worried
because you think that it might happen. *I'm scared
that these will turn out to be the wrong ones... They're
scared of making a fool of themselves.*

scaremonger /skeəmʌŋgə/ **scaremongers**
NC A scaremonger is someone who deliberately
spreads worrying stories to try and frighten people.
*Some people are calling them irresponsible
scaremongers.*

scaremongering /skeəmʌŋgərɪŋ/
NU Scaremongering is the activity of deliberately
spreading worrying stories to try and frighten people.
*The government dismisses the talk of recession as
dangerous scaremongering... The leader of the
National Union of Teachers has been accused of
scaremongering.*

scare story, scare stories
NC A scare story is something that is said or written
to make people think that a situation is more
frightening or dangerous than it really is. *If you
believe every scare story about the causes of cancer,
you'll end up leading a very restricted lifestyle.*

scarf /skɑːf/ **scarfs** or **scarves**
NC A scarf is a piece of cloth that you wear round
your neck or head, usually to keep yourself warm.
*...woolly socks, hats and scarves... The Princess was
wearing a white silk dress with a navy and white
scarf.*

scarlet /skɑːlət/
ADJ Something that is scarlet is bright red. *...a
scarlet handkerchief.*

scarlet fever
NU Scarlet fever is an infectious disease that gives
you a sore throat, high temperature, and red rash. *He
died of scarlet fever when he was four.*

scarper /skɑːpə/ **scarpers, scarpering, scarpered**
V If someone scarpers, they go away from a place
quickly; an informal word. *Go on, scarper!... I had to
scarper when I heard you at the door.*

scarves /skɑːvz/
Scarves is a plural of scarf.

scary /skeəri/
ADJ Scary things are frightening; an informal word.
It was a scary moment.

scathing /skeɪðɪŋ/
ADJ If you are scathing about something, you criticize
it harshly and scornfully. *Miss Jackson was scathing
about our efforts... The proposals came under scathing
attack from the Labour spokesman.* ♦ **scathingly** ADV
He refers scathingly to these superstitions.

scatter /skætə/ **scatters, scattering, scattered**
1 V-ERG If things are scattered over an area or if you
scatter them there, they are thrown or dropped so that
they spread all over the area. *The papers had been
scattered all over the floor... Parrots scatter their food
about and make a mess... Debris scattered for miles.*
2 V-ERG If a group of people scatter or if they are
scattered, they suddenly separate and move in
different directions. *The students scattered and
regrouped around the intersection... Police opened fire
with tear-gas, scattering the crowd of protestors.*

scatterbrain /skætəbreɪn/ **scatterbrains**
NC Someone who is a scatterbrain often forgets things
and seems unable to think sensibly about anything; an
informal word.

scatterbrained /skætəbreɪnd/
ADJ Someone who is scatterbrained often forgets
things and seems unable to think sensibly about
anything; an informal word.

scattered /skætəd/
1 ADJ Things that are scattered are spread over an
area and are a long way from each other. *The old
people could not visit their scattered families...
Resistance was scattered, but increasing.*
2 ADJ PRED+with If something is scattered with a lot of
small things, they are spread all over it. *Her hair was
scattered with pollen.*

scattering /skætəʳrɪŋ/
N SING A scattering of things is a number of them
spread over a large area; a literary word. *...the blue
night sky with its scattering of stars.*

scatty /skæti/ **scattier, scattiest**
ADJ Someone who is scatty often forgets things and
behaves in a silly way; an informal word. *She's a
scatty but charming girl.*

scavenge /skævɪndʒ/ **scavenges, scavenging,
scavenged**
V+fororVO If someone scavenges for food or other
things or scavenges them, they collect them by
searching among waste and unwanted objects. *It it
thought they were trying to scavenge for military
equipment... He had to scavenge information from
newspapers and journals... I had no resources at all,
except what I could scavenge or beg.*

scavenger /skævɪndʒə/ **scavengers**
NC A scavenger is a person, bird, or animal that
collects food or other things by searching among waste
and unwanted objects. *...a scavenger living from the*

dustbins behind restaurants. ...scavengers like the vulture.

scenario /sɪnɑːriəʊ/ **scenarios**

1 NC If you talk about a likely or possible **scenario**, you are talking about the way in which a situation may develop. *Such a scenario may not be just a bad dream for the bankers... Early estimates were probably little more than worst-case scenarios.*
2 NC The **scenario** of a film is a piece of writing that gives an outline of the story; a technical use.

scene /siːn/ **scenes**

1 NC A **scene** is one of the parts of a play, film, or book in which a series of events happen in the same place. *...the balcony scene from 'Romeo and Juliet'... Act III, scene ii... It was like some scene from a Victorian novel.*
2 NC+SUPP Paintings and drawings of places are sometimes called **scenes**. *...the harbour scenes that he drew as a teenager.*
3 NC+SUPP You can describe something that you see as a **scene** of a particular kind. *The moon rose over a scene of extraordinary destruction. ...a scene of domestic tranquillity.*
4 NC The **scene** of an accident or crime is the place where it happened. *Two men carrying shotguns were seen running away from the scene of the crime. ...Mrs Thatcher's visit to the scene of the disaster... A helicopter is circling the scene at the moment.*
5 N SING+SUPP You can refer to an area of activity as a particular **scene**. *...the business scene. ...the German political scene.*
6 NC If you make a **scene**, you embarrass people by publicly showing your anger about something. *There was a scene, and Father called Christopher a liar.*
● **Scene** is used in these phrases. ● If something is done **behind the scenes**, it is done so that the general public is not aware of it. *Officials working behind the scenes urged them to avoid further confrontation. ...their usual skilful behind-the-scene diplomacy.*
● When someone appears **on the scene**, they arrive. *...representatives of the International Red Cross, who arrived on the scene within hours of the earthquake.*
● You also say that something or someone appears **on the scene** when they become widely known or used. *Lenny came on the scene in the autumn of 1989 with his first album.* ● Something that **sets the scene** for a particular event to happen creates the conditions in which the event is likely to happen. *That could have set the scene for a confrontation with the US.*

scenery /siːnəri/

1 N SING or NU You can refer to everything you see around you as the **scenery**, especially when you are in the countryside. *As we neared the border, the scenery became lush and spectacular. ...the steady change of scenery as the author and his friend trudge up and down Bangladesh.*
2 N SING or NU In a theatre, the **scenery** is the painted cloth and boards at the back of the stage. *Who designed the scenery?... The production uses a minimum of scenery.*

scene-shifter /siːnʃɪftə/ **scene-shifters**

NC A **scene-shifter** is a person who works in a theatre and moves scenery on and off the stage. *...scene hands, scene shifters and carpenters.*

scenic /siːnɪk/

ADJ ATTRIB A **scenic** place or route is attractive and has nice views. *The island has a scenic coastline. ...a scenic railway.*

scent /sɛnt/ **scents, scenting, scented**

1 NC A **scent** is a pleasant smell. *...the overpowering scent of English garden flowers.*
2 N MASS **Scent** is a liquid that women put on their skin in order to smell nice. *She walked in smelling of French scent.*
3 NC or NU An animal's **scent** is the smell that it gives off. *The queen bee produces a scent which attracts the other bees... They mark their territories with scent from glands in their groin.*
4 VO When an animal **scents** something, it becomes aware of it by smelling it. *If it scents its prey it swings its head from side to side.*
5 VO If you **scent** something, you feel that it is going

to happen or that it is possibly the case; a literary use. *They scent the real possibility of independence... The paper scents a hint of desperation in the killings.*

scented /sɛntɪd/

ADJ Something that is **scented** has a pleasant smell. *...scented soap. ...a sweet-scented variety of rose.*

scepter /sɛptə/. See **sceptre**.

sceptic /skɛptɪk/ **sceptics**; spelt **skeptic** in American English.

NC A **sceptic** is a person who has doubts about things that other people believe. *Sceptics have been quick to dismiss these moves... He's a sceptic on European Monetary Union.*

sceptical /skɛptɪkl/; spelt **skeptical** in American English.

ADJ If you are **sceptical** about something, you have doubts about it. *Robert's father was sceptical about hypnotism... Mrs Swallow gave a sceptical grunt.*
◆ **sceptically** ADV *I listened sceptically to the broadcast.*

scepticism /skɛptɪsɪzəm/; spelt **skepticism** in American English.

NU **Scepticism** is doubt about something. *There was widespread scepticism about these proposals.*

sceptre /sɛptə/ **sceptres**; spelt **scepter** in American English.

NC A **sceptre** is an ornamental rod that a king or queen carries as a symbol of his or her power on some ceremonial occasions. *...the British Royal Sceptre.*

schedule /ʃɛdjuːl, skɛdjuːl/ **schedules, scheduling, scheduled**

1 NC A **schedule** is a plan that gives a list of events or tasks, together with the times at which each thing should happen or be done. *The president even found time in a busy schedule to buy silk at the capital's best-known department store. ...the daily schedule of classes.*
2 VO If something is **scheduled** to happen at a particular time, arrangements have been made for it to happen then. *He was scheduled to leave Plymouth yesterday... A meeting had been scheduled for that day.*
3 NC A **schedule** is also a written list of things, for example a list of prices, details, or conditions; a formal use. *During the first half of December the January export schedules will be prepared.*
4 NC A **schedule** is also a timetable for trains, buses, and aeroplanes; used in American English. *American Airlines say it will cut back its flight schedule and lay off employees.*
● **Schedule** is used in these phrases. ● If something happens **ahead of schedule**, it happens earlier than the time planned. *It's reached its forty-two million pound target a year ahead of schedule.* ● If you are **behind schedule**, you are doing things later than the times planned. *The airliner resumed its flight several hours behind schedule.* ● If something happens **on schedule**, it happens at the time planned. *The Presidential plane arrived precisely on schedule.* ● If something is done **to schedule** or **according to schedule**, it is done at the times that were planned in advance. *The operations have been carried out according to schedule.*

scheduled /ʃɛdjuːld, skɛdjuːld/

ADJ ATTRIB A **scheduled** flight or aircraft is part of a regular service, not specially chartered by an individual person or group. *Many airlines have cancelled scheduled flights because of the action.*

schema /skiːmə/ **schemata** /skiːmɑːtə, skiːmətə/

NC A **schema** is an outline of a plan or theory; a formal word. *I condensed this into the following schema... This is, of course, a highly simplified schema.*

schematic /skiːmætɪk/

ADJ A **schematic** representation is a drawing or diagram showing how something works in a simplified way; a technical term. *...our schematic representation of the design process. ...a schematic diagram of a hydraulic ram.* ◆ **schematically** ADV *Here I can do no more than indicate the process schematically.*

scheme /skiːm/ **schemes, scheming, schemed**

1 NC A **scheme** is a plan produced by one person as a

way of achieving something. *He had a crazy scheme to corner the champagne market. ...some scheme for perfecting the world.*
2 NC A **scheme** is also a large-scale plan produced by a government or by an organization. *...the State Pension scheme. ...a 5.6 million pound scheme to build 63 houses and a motel.*
3 V When people **scheme**, they make secret plans; used showing disapproval. *He schemed against her... She schemed on her daughter's behalf.* ◆ **scheming** ADJ ATTRIB *...a ruthless, scheming man.*
4 **The scheme of things** is the way that everything in the world or in a particular situation seems to be organized. *Man needed to understand his place in the scheme of things... He will be seeking assurances about the future of his militia in the future scheme of things.*

schemer /skiːmə/ **schemers**
NC A **schemer** is a person who schemes; used showing disapproval. *...a political schemer or agitator.*

schism /skɪzəm, sɪzəm/ **schisms**
NU or NC When **schism** or a **schism** happens, a group or organization divides into two groups as a result of differences in thinking and beliefs; a formal word. *The problems are not those of class war, but of schism and separatism. ...ideological schisms.*

schizophrenia /skɪtsəfriːniə/
NU **Schizophrenia** is a serious mental illness that prevents people from relating their thoughts and feelings to what is happening around them. *About two per cent of the population suffers from either schizophrenia or manic depression.*

schizophrenic /skɪtsəfrɛnɪk/ **schizophrenics**
NC A **schizophrenic** is a person who is suffering from schizophrenia. *...a paranoid schizophrenic.* ▶ Also ADJ *...a schizophrenic patient.*

Schlüter, Poul /paʊl ʃluːtə/
Poul Schlüter became Prime Minister of Denmark in 1982. He became a member of the Folketing (Danish parliament) in 1964 and Chairman of the Conservative People's Party (KF) in 1974. Born: 1929.

scholar /skɒlə/ **scholars**
1 NC A **scholar** is a person who studies an academic subject and knows a lot about it. *...Benjamin Jowett, the theologian and Greek scholar.*
2 NC A **scholar** is also a pupil or student who has a scholarship. *...an Eton scholar.*

scholarly /skɒləli/
1 ADJ A **scholarly** piece of writing or a **scholarly** discussion is serious and careful and is usually written by an academic at a university. *...scholarly research... It combines scholarly information with practical tips for the traveller.*
2 ADJ A **scholarly** person spends a lot of time studying and knows a lot about academic subjects. *...his father, a scholarly and cultured man.*

scholarship /skɒləʃɪp/ **scholarships**
1 NC If you get a **scholarship** to a school or university, you get money for your studies from the school or university or some other organization. *I applied for a scholarship to study philosophy at Oxford.*
2 NU **Scholarship** is serious academic study and the knowledge that is obtained from it. *...the Islamic tradition of scholarship.*

scholastic /skəlæstɪk/
ADJ ATTRIB Your **scholastic** ability is your ability to study and learn things at school; a formal word. *He was more involved in sports than in scholastic achievements.*

school /skuːl/ **schools**
1 NU or NC **School** or a **school** is a place where children are educated. *He left to take his children to school... I was late for school. ...the school holidays... The youngsters themselves do their very best to get into the best possible school.* ● See also **schooling**.
2 NC **School** is also used to refer to the pupils or teachers at a school. *She gave a talk to the school... He persuaded the school to take her back the following academic year.*
3 NC+SUPP University departments and colleges are sometimes called **schools**. *David Dyker, of the School of European Studies, University of Sussex, examines*

the background. *...London's School of Oriental and African Studies.*
4 NU In America, university is often referred to as **school**; an informal use. *She had recently graduated from law school... What do you get out of graduate school?*
5 NC A **school** is a group of people such as artists, writers, or thinkers, whose work, opinions, or theories are similar. *This school might loosely be described as 'the alternative defence theorists'... It also saw the emergence of the Impressionist school of painting.*
6 NC A **school** of whales, dolphins, or fish is a large group of them. *...a school of whales... His life was saved by a school of dolphins which chased the shark away from the beach.*
● **School** is used in these phrases. ● Someone who is part of the **old school**, has qualities or opinions that are less common now than they were in the past. *Ian Gow was seen as one of the few remaining Tories of the old school.* ● A **school of thought** is a theory or an opinion shared by a group of people. *One school of thought led by Britain prefers an Atlantic solution.*

school age
NU When a child reaches **school age**, he or she is old enough to go to school. People of **school age** are aged between 5 and 16. *...children under school age.* ▶ Also ADJ *...a school-age child.*

schoolboy /skuːlbɔɪ/ **schoolboys**
NC A **schoolboy** is a boy who goes to school. *...a group of primary schoolboys on a football holiday.*

schoolchild /skuːltʃaɪld/ **schoolchildren**
NC **Schoolchildren** are children who go to school. *Dozens of holiday coaches, many of them carrying schoolchildren, are facing long delays at Dover... Half of all schoolchildren now have school lunches.*

schooldays /skuːldeɪz/
N PL Your **schooldays** are the period of your life when you are at school. *Prince Charles, who spent part of his schooldays here, looks particularly relaxed... Since my own schooldays, I cannot remember ever having been on a group trip.*

schooled /skuːld/
ADJ PRED If you are **schooled** in something, you know a lot about it as a result of training or experience. *...two heroes schooled in the old methods... Our officers are well schooled.*

school friend, school friends
NC Your **school friends** are the people who are, or were, your friends while you are, or were, at school. *They were used to bringing school friends home. ...a postcard sent to me by an old school friend.*

schoolgirl /skuːlɡɜːl/ **schoolgirls**
NC A **schoolgirl** is a girl who goes to school. *She is charming, modest and giggly like any normal schoolgirl. ...a group of thirty-five schoolgirls and their teachers.*

schoolhouse /skuːlhaʊs/ **schoolhouses**
NC A **schoolhouse** is a building that is used as a school; used in American English. *Sachs went to tiny one-room schoolhouses such as the one in McCloud, North Dakota.*

schooling /skuːlɪŋ/
NU Your **schooling** is the education that you receive at school. *Many of the workers had no schooling at all.*

school-leaver /skuːlliːvə/ **school-leavers**
NC **School-leavers** are young people who have just left school and who are looking for their first job or going on to higher education. *Each year more than 20,000 school-leavers join the hunt for jobs.*

schoolmaster /skuːlmɑːstə/ **schoolmasters**
NC A **schoolmaster** is a man who teaches children in a school; an old-fashioned word. *He didn't believe any blame could be directed at the schoolmaster in charge of the boys.*

schoolmate /skuːlmeɪt/ **schoolmates**
NC Your **schoolmates** are your school friends; an old-fashioned word. *He met an old schoolmate of his from Umtata.*

schoolmistress /skuːlmɪstrəs/ **schoolmistresses**
NC A **schoolmistress** is a woman who teaches children in a school; an old-fashioned word. *...the village schoolmistress.*

schoolroom /skuːlruːm, skuːlrʊm/ **schoolrooms**
NC A **schoolroom** is a classroom, especially when it is the only classroom in a small school; an old-fashioned word. *Every schoolroom and every office had a portrait or bust of Lenin.*

schoolteacher /skuːltiːtʃə/ **schoolteachers**
NC A **schoolteacher** is a teacher in a school. *He called for extra pay and status for schoolteachers around the world.*

schoolteaching /skuːltiːtʃɪŋ/
NU **Schoolteaching** is the work that schoolteachers do; an old-fashioned word. *I was thinking of going in for schoolteaching.*

schoolwork /skuːlwɜːk/
NU **Schoolwork** is the work that a child does at school or as homework. *When they have children, they find that they want to read stories to them and help them with schoolwork.*

schoolyard /skuːljɑːd/ **schoolyards**
NC A **schoolyard** is an area of land next to the school buildings where pupils can play between lessons; used in American English. *In the schoolyard of Brooklyn's Junior High School 51 it is lunchtime.*

schooner /skuːnə/ **schooners**
1 NC A **schooner** is a sailing ship. *...two and three masted schooners in the harbour at Camden.*
2 NC A **schooner** is also a large glass which you use for sherry. *You've already drunk three schooners of sherry.*

sciatica /saɪætɪkə/
NU **Sciatica** is a severe pain in the nerve in your legs or the lower part of your back; a medical term. *He has been troubled by sciatica for most of the season.*

science /saɪəns/ **sciences**
1 NU **Science** is the study of the nature and behaviour of natural things and the knowledge that we obtain about them. *Not everything can be explained by science or reason... Seven year olds in Britain will take part in national tests in mathematics, English and science next May.*
2 NCorNU A **science** is a particular branch of science, for example physics or biology. *...the shortage of teachers, especially in maths, the sciences and modern languages... So far, medical science has not been able to come up with a vaccine that offers long-term protection against the disease.*
3 See also **social science**.

science fiction
NU **Science fiction** consists of stories and films about events that take place in the future or in other parts of the universe. *Science may once again follow the path of science fiction... Science fiction writer Arthur C. Clark used it in one of his early stories.*

scientific /saɪəntɪfɪk/
1 ADJ ATTRIB **Scientific** is used to describe things that relate to science or to a particular science. *In this programme we look at the latest scientific developments... The early projects are of major scientific importance... The aim of this policy is to establish a scientific base on the Moon.* ◆ **scientifically** ADV *...a scientifically advanced civilisation.*
2 ADJ If you do something in a **scientific** way, you do it systematically, using experiments or tests. *Training structures allowed the discovery and encouragement of swimming talent in a scientific way.* ◆ **scientifically** ADV *The firm insists the survey was carried out scientifically... It will be very hard to prove scientifically.*

scientist /saɪəntɪst/ **scientists**
NC A **scientist** is an expert who does work in one of the sciences. *Scientists in the United States say they have discovered the real source of hair growth... More than 150 scientists and technicians are at work on the Maraca Rainforest Project.*

sci-fi /saɪfaɪ/
NU **Sci-fi** is science fiction; an informal word. *...sci-fi novels.*

scintillating /sɪntɪleɪtɪŋ/
ADJ Conversation, humour, or a performance that is **scintillating** is very lively, skilful and amusing. *...her scintillating wit. ...scintillating personalities.*

scion /saɪən/ **scions**
NC+SUPP A **scion** of a rich or famous family is one of its younger or more recent members; a literary word. *...the scion of a distinguished family. ...the scions of the wealthy.*

scissors /sɪzəz/
N PL **Scissors** are a small tool with two sharp blades which are screwed together. You use scissors for cutting things such as paper and cloth. *She took a pair of scissors and cut his hair.*

sclerosis /sklərəʊsɪs/
NU **Sclerosis** is a disease in which the tissue in a part of your body becomes abnormally hard; a medical term. *...people suffering from sclerosis.* ● See also **multiple sclerosis**.

scoff /skɒf/ **scoffs, scoffing, scoffed**
V+at, V-QUOTE, or V If you **scoff**, you speak in a scornful, mocking way about someone or something. *The United States delegation at the Manila talks scoffed at the suggestion... They scoff at the idea that he will retire next year... 'Women's movement!' they scoffed. 'There isn't one.'... I'm not scoffing!*

scold /skəʊld/ **scolds, scolding, scolded**
V OorV-QUOTE If you **scold** someone, you speak angrily to them because they have done something wrong. *He scolded his daughter for keeping them waiting... 'Where have you been?' scolded Mary.* ◆ **scolding** NC *I sometimes get a scolding from my parents.*

scone /skɒn, skəʊn/ **scones**
NC **Scones** are small cakes made from flour and fat. They are usually eaten with butter.

scoop /skuːp/ **scoops, scooping, scooped**
1 V OorV OA If you **scoop** something somewhere, you pick it up with your hands or arms or with something such as a spoon and take it from one place to another. *I scooped the child in my arms and carried her up the stairs... He scooped some instant coffee into a cup.*
2 NC A **scoop** is an object like a large spoon which is used for picking up a quantity of a food such as ice cream or flour. *...an ice-cream scoop.*
3 VO To **scoop** something also means to obtain it as a result of skill or luck. *They recently scooped all the major awards at a UK ceremony... He publishes the results as fast as possible, before anyone else can scoop the idea.*
4 NC A **scoop** is also an exciting news story which is reported in one newspaper before it appears anywhere else. *He was just a reporter after a scoop. ...a worldwide scoop.*

scoop out PHRASAL VERB If you **scoop** something **out**, you remove it using a spoon or other tool. *Scoop out the flesh of the melon with a teaspoon... We found the cave and began to scoop the earth out.*

scoop up PHRASAL VERB If you **scoop** something **up**, you lift it in a quick movement by putting your hands under it or using a tool that takes hold of it from underneath. *The boys began to scoop up handfuls of water... I had to scoop it up with my fingers. ...recovery vessels which will be used to scoop up the remaining oil.*

scoot /skuːt/ **scoots, scooting, scooted**
V If you **scoot**, you leave quickly; an informal word. *I'd better scoot. Bye.*

scooter /skuːtə/ **scooters**
1 NC A **scooter** is a small, lightweight motorcycle with a low seat. *The attackers are said to have fled on motor scooters.*
2 NC A **scooter** is also a type of child's bicycle which has two wheels joined by a board and a handle on a long pole attached to the front wheel. The child makes it move by having one foot on the board and the other pushing against the ground. *At Selfridges the surprise best-sellers are scooters for very young children.*

scope /skəʊp/
1 NU If there is **scope** for a particular kind of behaviour, you have the opportunity to act in this way. *There is not much scope for originality.*
2 NU The **scope** of an activity or piece of work is the area which it deals with or includes. *Lack of time limited the scope of the course... It seemed out of place in a book so limited in scope.*

scorch /skɔːtʃ/ **scorches, scorching, scorched**
vo If something **is scorched**, it is burned slightly or
damaged by heat. *I once scorched a beautiful pink
suit while ironing it... The lawn was scorched and the
soil was baked hard.*

scorched-earth policy, scorched-earth policies
NC A **scorched-earth policy** is the deliberate burning,
destruction, and removal by an army of everything
that could be useful to an enemy in a particular area.
*Relief agency sources fear that the government may
be adopting a scorched-earth policy against northern
rebels.*

scorcher /skɔːtʃə/ **scorchers**
NC A **scorcher** is a very hot day; an informal word.
Today's going to be a scorcher.

scorching /skɔːtʃɪŋ/
ADJ **Scorching** weather is very hot; an informal word.
...a scorching day.

score /skɔː/ **scores, scoring, scored**
1 VOorV If someone **scores** in a game, they get a goal,
run, or point. *Trevor Christie scored Walsall's first
goal... Southampton's Colin Clark scored after 71
minutes.*
2 VO If someone **scores** a particular number of goals,
runs, or points, that is the total they get in a game.
He scored 69 as India finished the day at 211 for four.
3 NC The **score** in a game is the number of goals,
runs, or points obtained by the teams or players.
*'What's the score?'—'Two nil.'... Here are the
lunchtime scores.*
4 VO If you **score** a success, victory, or hit, you are
successful in what you are doing. *The Reverend Jesse
Jackson has scored an important victory in Michigan.*
5 VAorVO If you **score** over someone or **score** a point,
you gain an advantage over them or defeat them in
some way. *The Government was anxious to score
over the opposition in the education debate... Gareth
grinned, as if he had scored an important point.*
6 N PL **Scores** of things or people means a large
number of them. *The demonstration was just one of
scores held in cities throughout Britain and Northern
Ireland... Police made scores of arrests during and
after the game.*
7 VO If something sharp **scores** a surface, it cuts a
line into it; a formal use. *Each stone is scored with
very thin grooves.*
8 NC The **score** of a piece of music is the written
version of it. *His scores for various films included
some of the best selling songs of the period.*
9 **On this score** or **on that score** means in relation to
the thing already mentioned. *There was no need for
concern on that score.*

scoreboard /skɔːbɔːd/ **scoreboards**
NC A **scoreboard** is a large board which shows how
many goals, runs, or points have been obtained in a
match or competition. *We were standing around
looking up at the scoreboard, trying to see who was
winning.*

scorecard /skɔːkɑːd/ **scorecards**
1 NC A **scorecard** is a printed card which tells you
who is playing in a match or race, and on which you
can record the scores the players get.
2 NC A **scorecard** is also a card on which players
record the scores they make in various games,
especially golf.

scoreline /skɔːlaɪn/ **scorelines**
NC The **scoreline** is the score or the final result of a
game or match. *India beat Kenya 2-1 and that was
also the winning scoreline for Malaysia over Spain...
Majed Abdullah levelled the scoreline twenty minutes
from the end.*

scorer /skɔːrə/ **scorers**
1 NC A **scorer** is a player who scores a goal, run, or
points in a match. *Who were the scorers?... Gower
was the highest scorer in the match.*
2 NC A **scorer** is also the official who writes down the
score of a match or competition as it is being played.

scorn /skɔːn/ **scorns, scorning, scorned**
1 NU If you treat someone or something with **scorn**,
you show contempt for them. *This suggestion was
greeted with scorn... She had nothing but scorn for
those who got themselves into debt.* ● If you **pour

scorn** on someone or something, you criticize them
very harshly and say that they are stupid or
worthless. *The government has consistently poured
scorn on the economic sanctions imposed last June.*
2 VO If you **scorn** someone or something, you feel or
show contempt for them. *She scorned the girls who
worshipped football heroes... What is now admired as
art was then scorned as vulgar extravagance.*
3 VO If you **scorn** something, you refuse to accept it
because you think it is not good enough or suitable for
you; a formal use. *Although his hearing was not good,
he scorned a deaf aid.*

scornful /skɔːnfl/
ADJ If you are **scornful**, you show contempt for
someone or something. *She is openly scornful of the
idea that girls are weaker than men. ...scornful
laughter.* ◆ **scornfully** ADV *She looked at him
scornfully.*

scorpion /skɔːpiən/ **scorpions**
NC A **scorpion** is a small tropical animal that has a
long tail with a poisonous sting on the end. *He saw a
woman and two children recovering from scorpion
bites.*

Scot /skɒt/ **Scots**
1 NC A **Scot** is a person who comes from Scotland.
*Another Scot, Yvonne Murray was a popular winner of
the 3,000 metres. ...Mr Rifkind, who is himself a Scot.*
2 NU **Scots** is a dialect of the English language that is
spoken in Scotland. *He speaks broad Scots.*
3 ADJ ATTRIB **Scots** also means the same as **Scottish**.
He spoke with a Scots accent.

scotch /skɒtʃ/ **scotches**
1 NU **Scotch** or **scotch whisky** is whisky made in
Scotland. *They are already filling supermarket
shelves with half-price Scotch. ...a bottle of Scotch.*
2 NC A **scotch** is a glass of scotch. *He fixed two more
scotches.*
3 VO If you **scotch** something such as a rumour or an
idea, you stop it before it can develop any further.
*He's scotched rumours of another price freeze... He
has scotched speculation that he's about to leave
politics.*

Scotch egg, Scotch eggs
NC A **Scotch egg** is a hard-boiled egg which is covered
with sausage meat and then fried in oil. *'What's for
lunch today?'—'Scotch eggs, pancake rolls and chips.'*

Scotch tape
NU In the United States, **Scotch tape** is a transparent
sticky tape that you use for sticking together things
such as paper and cardboard; **Scotch** is a trademark.
The Scotch tape has been pulled away and replaced.

scot-free
ADV If you get away **scot-free**, you manage not to be
punished at all for something you have done. *The
hi-jackers had apparently been allowed to get away
scot-free... I'm not letting you off scot-free.*

Scotland /skɒtlənd/
Scotland is a country of the United Kingdom of Great
Britain and Northern Ireland. It is approximately
79,000 square kilometres, which is about one-third of
the island of Great Britain. Scotland became part of
the United Kingdom through the Act of Union in 1707.
The population of Scotland in 1986 was 5 million. The
capital is Edinburgh.

Scotsman /skɒtsmən/ **Scotsmen** /skɒtsmən/
NC A **Scotsman** is a man who comes from Scotland.
*The prize was shared between two Americans and a
Scotsman... Miller will become the third Scotsman to
have played sixty times for his country.*

Scotswoman /skɒtswʊmən/ **Scotswomen**
NC A **Scotswoman** is a woman who comes from
Scotland.

Scotticism /skɒtɪsɪzəm/ **Scotticisms**
NC A **Scotticism** is a Scottish word or expression. *His
speech was full of Scotticisms.*

Scottish /skɒtɪʃ/
ADJ **Scottish** means belonging or relating to Scotland.
...the Scottish mountains. ...the Scottish legal system.

scoundrel /skaʊndrəl/ **scoundrels**
NC A **scoundrel** is someone who cheats and deceives
people; an old-fashioned word. *...a scoundrel and a
liar.*

scour /skaʊə/ scours, scouring, scoured
1 VO If you **scour** a place for something, you make a thorough search there for it. *Traders were scouring the villages for family treasures.*
2 VO If you **scour** something like a pan or a floor, you clean it by rubbing it hard with something rough. *She insisted on scouring her kitchen floor every week.*

scourer /skaʊərə/ scourers
NC A **scourer** is a small, rough ball made of plastic or wire net, which is used for cleaning kitchen pans.

scourge /skɜːdʒ/
N SING When something causes a lot of trouble or suffering to a group of people, you can refer to it as a **scourge**. *Smallpox was the scourge of the Western world.*

scout /skaʊt/ scouts, scouting, scouted
1 NC A **scout** or a **boy scout** is a member of the Scout Association. Scouts are encouraged to be disciplined and to learn practical skills. In the United States, girls can be scouts as well. *Anyone who's been a scout will remember the hours of fun they had. ...boy scouts and girl guides. ...the Boy and Girl Scouts of America.*
2 NC A **scout** is also a person who is sent somewhere to find out the position of an enemy army. *The scouts reported that the enemy was advancing.*
3 VA If you **scout** around for something, you search for it in different places. *We'll scout around to see if anyone is here.*

scoutmaster /skaʊtmɑːstə/ scoutmasters
NC A **scoutmaster** is a man who is in charge of a troop of boy scouts.

scowl /skaʊl/ scowls, scowling, scowled
V+at or V If you **scowl**, you frown because you are angry. *I scowled at him... Stone-faced youths scowled from street corners.* ▶ Also NC *Her grin changed to a scowl.*

scrabble /skræbl/ scrabbles, scrabbling, scrabbled
1 VA If you **scrabble** at something, you scrape at it with your fingers or feet. *The woman scrabbled at the side of the boat... I hung there, scrabbling with my feet to find a foothold.*
2 VA If you **scrabble** somewhere or **scrabble** around, you move your hands or feet about in order to find something that you cannot see. *She scrabbled in her handbag... I scrabbled around on the floor and eventually found my ring.*
3 NU **Scrabble** is a word game played with letters on a board; **Scrabble** is a trademark. *Traditional board games are doing extremely well, for example Scrabble and Monopoly.*

scraggly /skrægəli/ scragglier, scraggliest
ADJ Hair or plants that are **scraggly** are unevenly grown and untidy; used in American English. *...a scraggly bearded man.*

scraggy /skrægi/ scraggier, scraggiest
ADJ **Scraggy** people are unpleasantly thin and bony. *The vest made Pa look even scraggier... He examined the large watch which ornamented his scraggy wrist.*

scram /skræm/ scrams
V If you **scram**, you leave a place quickly; an informal word. *Maybe we both should scram... Scram!*

scramble /skræmbl/ scrambles, scrambling, scrambled
1 VA If you **scramble** over rough or difficult ground, you move quickly over it using your hands to help you. *John scrambled up the bank... They scrambled away over the rocks and fled.*
2 VA To **scramble** also means to move somewhere in a hurried, undignified way. *He scrambled to his feet... Sightseers had scrambled for the best position.*
3 N SING If there is a **scramble** for something, people rush to get it. *There may be a world-wide scramble for oil.*
4 VO If you **scramble** a radio or telephone message, you interfere with the sound so that the message can only be understood by someone who has special equipment. *These devices can be used to scramble conversation.*
5 VO When fighter aeroplanes **are scrambled**, their pilots get them into the air quickly in order to attack enemy aeroplanes. *...two F-5 fighters which were*

scrambled *when the helicopters came across the border.*

scrambled egg, scrambled eggs
N U or N PL **Scrambled egg** or **scrambled eggs** is a dish made of eggs and milk, and cooked in a pan. *She'd had scrambled egg on toast—and enjoyed it.*

scrambler /skræmblə/ scramblers
NC A **scrambler** is an electronic device which alters the sound of a radio or telephone message so that it can only be understood by someone who has special equipment; a technical term. *...the nearest phone with a scrambler.*

scrap /skræp/ scraps, scrapping, scrapped
1 NC A **scrap** of something is a very small piece or amount of it. *It is little more than a scrap of paper torn from a larger document. ...a rug made of scraps of old clothes... They will put together every scrap of evidence they can obtain.*
2 N PL **Scraps** are pieces of unwanted food which are thrown away or given to animals. *...a tame puppy, begging for scraps.*
3 VO If you **scrap** something, you get rid of it or cancel it. *They want the government to scrap pay controls as well... More than 800 helicopters and aircraft will be scrapped.*
4 ADJ ATTRIB **Scrap** metal or paper is metal or paper that is no longer wanted for its original purpose, but which may have some other use. *Her father had made a fortune in scrap metal. ...women who pick up scrap papers from the street.*
5 NU **Scrap** is metal from old or damaged machinery or vehicles that is melted down so that it can be used again. *Some private collectors will pay up to twenty thousand pounds for a T-55 tank—around ten times their value as scrap.*
6 NC A **scrap** is also a fight; an informal use. *...an unruly scrap.*

scrapbook /skræpbʊk/ scrapbooks
NC A **scrapbook** is a book with blank pages where people stick things such as pictures or newspaper articles. *My hobby was cutting out pictures of cars and airplanes from magazines and pasting them in a scrapbook.*

scrape /skreɪp/ scrapes, scraping, scraped
1 VOA If you **scrape** something from a surface or **scrape** it off, you remove it by pulling a knife or other object over it. *She scraped the mud off her boots.*
2 VO If you **scrape** something, you remove its skin or surface by pulling a knife over it. *The nuts can be eaten raw once they have been scraped.*
3 VOA If you **scrape** one thing against another, you rub the first thing against the second, causing slight damage. *He scraped his hand painfully on a rock.*
4 VO or VA If something **scrapes** something else or **scrapes** against it, it rubs against it and damages it slightly or makes a harsh noise. *In winter, the branches tapped and scraped the glass... His beard scraped against her skin.* ▶ Also N SING *...the clink and scrape of knives and forks.*
5 V You say that people **scrape** when they spend as little money as possible in order to have enough money to buy things that they want or need. *He did not want his kids to have to scrape to get through college.*

scrape through PHRASAL VERB If you **scrape through** a competition or examination, you only just succeed in winning or passing it. *England scraped through to the World Cup semi-final.*

scrape together PHRASAL VERB If you **scrape together** an amount of money or a number of things you need, you succeed with difficulty in obtaining them. *If we could scrape together a dozen people, we could hire a minibus.*

scrape up PHRASAL VERB If you **scrape up** an amount of money, you succeed with difficulty to get the money you need. *He scraped up the money to start a restaurant.*

scrap-heap, scrap-heaps
If you **throw** someone or something **on the scrap-heap**, you dismiss them or get rid of them completely because they are no longer of any use to you. *The aircraft was ingloriously consigned to the scrap-heap*

in the mid-1970s... He found himself thrown on the political scrap-heap.

scrapie /skreɪpi/
NU **Scrapie** is a serious viral disease of sheep and goats which affects their central nervous system and may be related to a similar disease in cows, called BSE. *One of the herd was found to have the disease scrapie... Scrapie is endemic in many European countries.*

scrappy /skræpi/ **scrappier, scrappiest**
ADJ If you describe something as **scrappy** you mean that it is does not seem to be well organized. *...a scrappy education. ...the play's somewhat scrappy structure.*

scratch /skrætʃ/ **scratches, scratching, scratched**
1 VO If a sharp object **scratches** you, it rubs against your skin, cutting you slightly. *I got scratched by a rose bush... His knees were scratched by thorns.*
2 VO If you **scratch** an object, you accidentally make small cuts on it. *It is completely covered to protect it so it won't get scratched.*
3 NC **Scratches** on someone or something are small cuts or marks. *The driver of the bus jumped clear at the last moment and escaped with only a few scratches... White shoe polish can hide scratches on white woodwork.*
4 VO, V-REFL, or V If you **scratch** a part of your body or **scratch** yourself, you rub your fingernails against your skin because it is itching. *The cook began scratching the rash on his neck... Jackson was sleepily scratching himself... We are scratching because we itch.*
5 V-ERG If someone **scratches** from a race in which they had been entered or if they **are scratched** from it, they do not take part in it. *Last years' winners scratched from the event 24 hours from the start... The horse was scratched from Saturday's Doncaster Handicap... She was forced to scratch after pulling a calf muscle.*
● **Scratch** is used in these phrases. ● If you say that someone **is scratching** their **head**, you mean that they are thinking hard and trying to solve a problem. *Frankly, we are still scratching our heads, wondering why they did this.* ● If you do something **from scratch**, you do it without making use of anything that has been done before. *A new register will have to be created from scratch... It will be necessary to build the town from scratch.* ● If something is **not up to scratch**, it is not good enough. *The reason the cattle die is that the management is not up to scratch.* ● If you only **scratch the surface** of a problem or subject, you deal with it in some way, but not enough to solve or understand it fully. *Some anti-apartheid campaigners fear that such measures will only scratch the surface of the problem.*

scratch pad, scratch pads
NC A **scratch pad** is a small book or pad for writing rough notes and ideas. *Purchases are totalled with a pencil and a scratch pad.*

scrawl /skrɔːl/ **scrawls, scrawling, scrawled**
1 VO If you **scrawl** something, you write it carelessly and untidily. *Someone had scrawled 'What does it all mean?' across the cover.*
2 NU **Scrawl** is writing that looks careless and untidy. *I did my best to write neatly instead of with my usual scrawl.*

scrawny /skrɔːni/ **scrawnier, scrawniest**
ADJ A **scrawny** person or animal is unpleasantly thin and bony. *...a scrawny youth. ...scrawny cattle.*

scream /skriːm/ **screams, screaming, screamed**
1 V When someone **screams**, they make a loud, high-pitched cry, usually because they are in pain or frightened. *Kunta screamed as a whip struck his back.* ► Also NC *He was awakened by the sound of screams.*
2 V When something makes a loud, high-pitched noise, you can say that it **screams**. *The jets screamed overhead.*
3 V, V-QUOTE, or VO If you **scream** something, you shout it in a loud, high-pitched voice. *People were shouting and screaming... 'Get out of there,' I screamed... She stood there screaming abuse at me.*
4 N SING If someone or something is a **scream**, they

are very funny; an informal use. *Do you know Sheila? She's a scream.*

scree /skriː/ **screes**
NU or NC **Scree** or a **scree** is a mass of loose stones on the side of a mountain. *...boulders and scree washed down by the floods... They made their way over screes of sharp stone.*

screech /skriːtʃ/ **screeches, screeching, screeched**
1 V or V-QUOTE When a person or an animal **screeches**, they make an unpleasant, loud, high-pitched cry. *The parrots screeched in the trees... 'You'll be sorry you did that!' she screeched.* ► Also NC *The parrot gave a loud screech.*
2 V If a vehicle **screeches**, its tyres make an unpleasant high-pitched noise on the road. *The bus came screeching to a stop.* ► Also N SING *I heard a screech of tyres.*

screen /skriːn/ **screens, screening, screened**
1 NC A **screen** is the flat, vertical surface of a television or computer or in the cinema on which pictures or words are shown. *...a student sitting in front of a computer screen... They are very similar to those which we see on our television screens today.* ● See also **flat-screen**.
2 N SING The films that are shown in cinemas are sometimes referred to as the **screen** or the big **screen**. *...Greta Garbo and other stars of the screen... Mickey Mouse had already appeared in more than a hundred cartoons on the big screen.*
3 VO When a film or a television programme is **screened**, it is shown in the cinema or broadcast on television. *They tried to prevent the programme being screened.* ◆ **screening, screenings** NU or NC *They called for a reduction in the screening of violent films on television... Screenings of the new movies took place at midnight.*
4 VO To **screen** people for a disease means to examine them to make sure that they do not have it. *A simple test could screen for individuals at risk of heart attack.* ◆ **screening, screenings** NU or NC *It recommends that breast cancer screening should be restricted to women over fifty. ...symptoms that occur between screenings.*
5 VO When a country or an organization **screens** people, they investigate them to make sure that they can enter the country or join the organization and that they are not likely to be dangerous or disloyal. *The Secret Service screens several hundred people every week.* ◆ **screening** NU *Members of the civilian intelligence agency are already undergoing similar screening... Screening had shown that none was a genuine political refugee.*
6 VO If someone **screens** luggage, they check it to make sure it does not contain a weapon or bomb. *The airline had not been searching unaccompanied baggage by hand, but only screening it on X-ray machines.*
7 VO If you **screen** someone, you stand in front of them or place something in front of them, in order to prevent them from being seen or hurt. *I moved in front of her trying to screen her.*
8 NC A **screen** is also a vertical panel that is used to separate different parts of a room or to stop people from seeing something behind it. *He got up and walked behind the screen... Any sightseers would have been discouraged by a large screen that's been erected around the crash site.*

screen off PHRASAL VERB If you **screen off** part of a room, you make it into a separate area, using a screen. *It was one long room that had a sleeping area screened off.*

screenplay /skriːnpleɪ/ **screenplays**
NC The **screenplay** of a film is the script. *'The French Lieutenant's Woman' has a screenplay by Harold Pinter.*

screenwriter /skriːnraɪtə/ **screenwriters**
NC A **screenwriter** is a person who writes screenplays. *Rada Bardwarsh is the screenwriter and director of 'Closet Land'.*

screw /skruː/ **screws, screwing, screwed**
1 NC A **screw** is a small, sharp piece of metal with a spiral groove, which is used to fix one thing to

another. *Tighten the tiny screw on the side of the tap.*
2 V-ERG A If you **screw** one thing to another or if it
screws there, it is fixed there by means of a screw or
screws. *I'm going to screw some handles onto the
bathroom cabinet... The curtains are attached to
special clips which screw to the window-frame.*
3 V-ERG A To **screw** something also means to fasten or
fix it by twisting it round and round. *He screwed the
lid tightly onto the top of the jar. ...hollow tubes which
screw together.*
4 If you **tighten the screws**, you put severe and
increasing pressure on someone, often to make them
do what you want them to. *Opposition leaders say the
screws are being tightened still further... With the aid
workers out of the way, the government can tighten
the screws of force and hunger.*
screw up PHRASAL VERB **1** If you **screw up** your face
or something flexible, you twist it or squeeze it so that
it no longer has its natural shape. *She screwed up her
eyes as she faced the sun... She screwed up the paper
and tossed it in the bin.* **2** If you **screw** something **up**,
you make it fail or get it badly wrong and cause
disorder; an informal expression. *He can't do that;
that screws up all my arrangements... The car broke
down, so that screwed up our holiday.* **3** Something
that **screws** you **up** makes you unhappy and unable to
deal with life; an informal expression. *...the dangers
of using a drug which is going to screw them up.*
screwdriver /ˈskruːdraɪvə/ **screwdrivers**
N C A **screwdriver** is a tool for fixing screws into
place. *With only a screwdriver and a pair of pliers, a
good car thief can force open a car door. ...items of
equipment including insulating tape and electrical
screwdrivers.*
screwed-up
1 ADJ ATTRIB If something such as a piece of paper or
a face is **screwed-up**, it has been twisted so that it is
creased and no longer in its natural shape. *...a ball of
screwed-up paper... Snow blew into our screwed-up
eyes.*
2 ADJ Someone who is **screwed-up** is very unhappy and
unable to deal with life; an informal expression. *He's
really screwed-up about these exams.*
screw-top, screw-tops
ADJ ATTRIB A **screw-top** bottle or jar has a lid or top
that is fastened by being tightly twisted. *It will keep
for one week in a screwtop jar in the fridge.* ▶ Also
N C *...bottles with screw-tops.*
screwy /ˈskruːi/ **screwier, screwiest**
ADJ If you say that someone is **screwy**, you mean that
they are slightly mad or eccentric; an informal word.
*The neighbours are a screwy lot... He's got some
pretty screwy ideas.*
scribble /ˈskrɪbl/ **scribbles, scribbling, scribbled**
1 V O or V If you **scribble** something, you write it
quickly and untidily. *She was scribbling a letter to
her mother... We were scribbling away furiously.*
2 V A To **scribble** also means to make meaningless
marks or untidy drawings using a pencil or pen.
Someone's scribbled all over the wall.
3 N U or N C **Scribble** or a **scribble** is something that has
been written or drawn quickly and untidily. *She was
looking at my scribble, trying to work out what it
said... There are scribbles on the lift wall.*
scribe /skraɪb/ **scribes**
N C A **scribe** was a person who wrote copies of things
such as letters or documents, especially before
printing was invented. *These palace records were
copied out three and a half thousand years ago by an
Egyptian scribe.*
scrimmage /ˈskrɪmɪdʒ/ **scrimmages**
N C A **scrimmage** is a rough, disorganized fight or
struggle. *There were howls and screams, rocks were
thrown, and out of the scrimmage the police came
running.*
scrimp /skrɪmp/ **scrimps, scrimping, scrimped**
If you **scrimp and save**, you live cheaply and spend as
little money as possible. *I was scrimping and saving
to buy necessities.*
script /skrɪpt/ **scripts**
1 N C The **script** of a play, film, or television
programme is the written version of it. *You can't*

have good acting without a decent script.
2 N C or N U A **script** is a particular system of writing.
...the Arabic script.
scripted /ˈskrɪptɪd/
ADJ If a speech is **scripted**, it has been written in
advance, although the speaker may try to pretend that
it is spoken without preparation. *If the patient asked,
the doctor was to follow a scripted speech.*
scripture /ˈskrɪptʃə/ **scriptures**
N U or N C You use **scripture** or **scriptures** to refer to
writings that are regarded as sacred in a particular
religion. *The scripture says, 'Man cannot live on
bread alone.'... They invoked Hindu scripture to justify
their position.*
scriptwriter /ˈskrɪptraɪtə/ **scriptwriters**
N C A **scriptwriter** is a person who writes scripts for
films or for radio or television programmes.
...Hollywood scriptwriters.
scroll /skrəʊl/ **scrolls**
N C A **scroll** is a long roll of paper, parchment, or
other material with writing on it. *...an ancient
Chinese scroll.*
scrotum /ˈskrəʊtəm/ **scrotums** or **scrota** /ˈskrəʊtə/
N C A man's **scrotum** is the bag of skin that contains
his testicles; a medical term.
scrounge /skraʊndʒ/ **scrounges, scrounging,
scrounged**
V O, V+for, or V If you **scrounge** something such as food or
money, you get it by asking someone for it, rather
than by buying it or earning it; an informal word,
used showing disapproval. *He had come over to
scrounge a few cans of food... They still had to
scrounge for food and water... She was always
scrounging.*
scrounger /ˈskraʊndʒə/ **scroungers**
N C If you call someone a **scrounger**, you mean that
they try to get things such as money or food without
working for them; an informal word. *They have the
reputation of being scroungers.*
scrub /skrʌb/ **scrubs, scrubbing, scrubbed**
1 V O If you **scrub** something, you rub it hard in order
to clean it, using a stiff brush and water. *They scrub
the kitchen floor every day... He scrubbed his hands at
the sink.* ▶ Also N SING *That floor needs a good scrub.*
2 V O A If you **scrub** dirt off something, you remove it
by rubbing hard. *There was a stain on the collar and
he tried to scrub it off.*
3 N U **Scrub** consists of low trees and bushes in an area
that has very little rain. *The country is flat, grassy,
and covered in scrub.*
scrubby /ˈskrʌbi/
ADJ **Scrubby** land is rough and dry and covered with
scrub. *...the scrubby slopes of the hills.*
scrubland /ˈskrʌblænd/
N U **Scrubland** is land that is covered with low trees
and bushes. *Most of the country is desert and
scrubland.*
scruff /skrʌf/
1 If someone holds you **by the scruff of** your **neck**,
they hold the back of your neck or collar. *They're
getting hold of them by the scruff of the neck.*
2 If you **take** a problem or a situation **by the scruff of
the neck**, you deal with it in a forceful way. *Mrs
Thatcher had been right to take the country by the
scruff of the neck and shake it.*
scruffy /ˈskrʌfi/ **scruffier, scruffiest**
ADJ Someone or something that is **scruffy** is dirty and
untidy. *We looked scruffy. ...scruffy trousers.*
scrum /skrʌm/ **scrums**
1 N C In the game of rugby, a **scrum** is a formation in
which players form a tight group and push against
each other with their heads down in an attempt to get
the ball. *They won a scrum 25 yards out... Most
injuries today take place outside the scrum, during
tackling.*
2 N SING A **scrum** of people is a crowd who are
pushing against each other; an informal use. *...a
scrum of photographers.*
scrumptious /ˈskrʌmpʃəs/
ADJ If you describe food as **scrumptious**, you mean
that it is delicious; an informal word. *Her cakes are
scrumptious.*

scrunch /skrʌntʃ/ **scrunches, scrunching, scrunched**
1 V-ERG If you **scrunch** something or if it **scrunches**,
you press it or crush it noisily. ...*scrunching the
pebbles as we walked across the beach... Just scrunch
the bag... The gravel scrunched and there was a knock
at the door.*
2 NC A **scrunch** is a noise made by pressing or
crushing something, for example when you are
walking or driving over loose stones. *And with a
scrunch and a skid we drove off.*
scrunch up PHRASAL VERB If you **scrunch** something
up, you squeeze it, crush it, or bend it so that it is no
longer in its natural shape. *She started to read it,
then scrunched it up and threw it away.*
scruples /skruːplz/
N PL **Scruples** are moral principles that make you
unwilling to do something that seems wrong. *He had
no scruples about borrowing money. ...religious
scruples.*
scrupulous /skruːpjʊləs/
1 ADJ A **scrupulous** person or organization takes great
care to do what is fair, honest, or morally right. *The
paper was not entirely scrupulous in setting out its
assumptions.* ♦ **scrupulously** ADV ...*the pressure on
manufacturers to behave scrupulously.*
2 ADJ **Scrupulous** also means thorough, exact, and
careful about details. *They pay scrupulous attention
to style.* ♦ **scrupulously** ADV *Everything was
scrupulously clean.*
scrutinize /skruːtɪnaɪz/ **scrutinizes, scrutinizing,
scrutinized**; also spelt **scrutinise**.
V O If you **scrutinize** something, you examine it very
carefully. *Bank examiners scrutinized the books of 600
financial institutions... He began to scrutinize the faces
in the compartment.*
scrutiny /skruːtɪni/
NU If something is under **scrutiny**, it is being studied
or observed very carefully. *At these visits the whole
college comes under scrutiny. ...close scrutiny by
explosives experts.*
scuba diving /skuːbə daɪvɪŋ/
NU **Scuba diving** is the activity of swimming under the
surface of the sea using special breathing equipment.
scud /skʌd/ **scuds, scudding, scudded**
1 V A If something **scuds**, it moves quickly and
smoothly along; a literary word. ...*clouds scudding
across the sky. ...children scudding downhill on their
sledges.*
2 NC A **Scud** is a type of surface to surface missile
that has a range of 300 kilometres or more. *The same
sources said that at least nine Scuds had been
launched eastward... On occasions, Scud missiles had
been used.*
scuff /skʌf/ **scuffs, scuffing, scuffed**
V O If you **scuff** your feet, you drag them along the
ground when you walk. *My sister was scuffing her
feet as we walked down the road.*
scuffed /skʌft/
ADJ **Scuffed** shoes have been damaged by being
scraped against things. ...*a man in a baggy suit and
scuffed shoes.*
scuffle /skʌfl/ **scuffles, scuffling, scuffled**
NC A **scuffle** is a short fight or struggle. *There was a
scuffle in which one of the soldiers fired into the
crowd.* ▶ Also V *Young people in Cameroon scuffled
with the police.*
scull /skʌl/ **sculls, sculling, sculled**
1 NC **Sculls** are small oars which are held by one
person and are used to move a boat through water.
2 V To **scull** means to move a boat through water
using sculls. *We went sculling on the river.*
3 N SING **Sculls** is a race between small boats, each
moved by one person using short oars. ...*Thomas
Lange, Germany's Olympic and world single sculls
champion.*
scullery /skʌləri/ **sculleries**
NC A **scullery** is a small room next to a kitchen where
washing is done; an old-fashioned word. *He was
walking down the passage to the scullery.*
sculpt /skʌlpt/ **sculpts, sculpting, sculpted**
V O If an artist **sculpts** something, they carve and
shape it out of stone or wood, a formal word. ...*a nude

woman, sculpted in marble.*
sculptor /skʌlptə/ **sculptors**
NC A **sculptor** is someone who makes sculptures.
...*Henry Moore, the English sculptor.*
sculpture /skʌlptʃə/ **sculptures**
1 NCorNU A **sculpture** is a work of art that is
produced by carving or shaping stone, clay, or
other materials. ...*Aztec sculptures. ...an exhibition
of 20th century sculpture.*
2 NU **Sculpture** is the art of making sculptures. *The
college offers classes in sculpture.*
sculptured /skʌlptʃəd/
ADJ **Sculptured** objects have been carved or shaped
from something. ...*sculptured heads of civic
dignitaries.*
scum /skʌm/
1 N SINGorNU **Scum** is a layer of an unpleasant-looking
substance on the surface of a liquid. *There was green
scum over the pond.*
2 N PL If you call people **scum**, you are expressing
your feelings of dislike and disgust for them. ...*the
men Mr Gorbachev called adventurists and Mr Yeltsin
referred to as scum.*
scupper /skʌpə/ **scuppers, scuppering, scuppered**
1 V O To **scupper** a plan or an attempt means to
completely spoil it. *It failed to kill anyone but
succeeded in completely scuppering the peace
process... There's still no guarantee that the whole
deal won't be scuppered at the last minute.*
2 NC A **scupper** is an opening in the side of a boat that
allows water to flow off the deck into the sea.
scurrilous /skʌrələs/
ADJ If someone says or writes something **scurrilous**,
they criticize someone unfairly or untruthfully in a
way that may damage that person's reputation; a
formal word. ...*a scurrilous weekly magazine.*
scurry /skʌri/ **scurries, scurrying, scurried**
V A To **scurry** somewhere means to run there quickly,
like a small animal that is frightened. *A mouse
scurried across the floor... Everyone scurried for
cover.*
scuttle /skʌtl/ **scuttles, scuttling, scuttled**
1 V O To **scuttle** a ship means to sink it by making
holes in the bottom, especially when this is done
deliberately in order to prevent someone else from
capturing it. *The captain gave orders that the ship
should be scuttled.*
2 V O If someone or something **scuttles** a plan or a
proposal, they make it fail or they cause it to stop.
*Such threats could scuttle the peace conference... A
new urban operation was underway but has now been
scuttled.*
3 V A To **scuttle** somewhere means to run there with
short, quick steps. *A porcupine scuttled across the
road.*
scythe /saɪð/ **scythes**
NC A **scythe** is a tool with a long handle and a long
curved blade, used for cutting grass or grain. *We
have to go over it manually with scythes to clear the
weeds in the areas that the grasscutter doesn't reach.
...peasants armed with scythes.*
SDP /esdiːpiː/
N PROP **SDP** is an abbreviation for 'Social Democratic
Party'. The SDP was a British political party. *Both
the SDP and the Liberals regard themselves as
moderate, reforming forces... The SDP conference
takes place at Sheffield next weekend.*
SE
SE is a written abbreviation for 'south-east'. ...*SE
London. ...SE Asia.*
sea /siː/ **seas**
1 NCorNU The **sea** is the salty water that covers much
of the earth's surface. *I watched the children running
into the sea. ...a wrecked ship at the bottom of the
sea. ...calm seas. ...a bit of blue sea.*
2 NC A **sea** is a large area of salty water. It can be
part of an ocean or be surrounded by land. ...*the
North Sea. ...the Caspian Sea.*
3 N SING+of A **sea** of people or things is a very large
number of them; a literary use. ...*a sea of white
faces. ...a sea of troubles.*
● **Sea** is used in these phrases. ● **At sea** means on or

under the sea, far away from land. *...a storm at sea... Submarines can stay at sea for weeks.* ● If someone is **at sea** or if they are **all at sea**, they are in a state of confusion. ● If you travel or send something **by sea**, you travel or you send it in a ship. *They were said to have been trying to infiltrate Israel by sea.*

sea air
NU The **sea air** is the air at the seaside, which is sometimes regarded as being good for people's health. *She took a deep breath of sea air.*

seabed /síːbed/
N SING The **seabed** is the ground under the sea. *They measure the time it takes to be reflected back from the seabed directly beneath the ship. ...oil resources in the surrounding seabed.*

seabird /síːbɜːd/ **seabirds**
NC **Seabirds** are birds that live near the sea and get their food from it. *Leakages have killed thousands of seabirds off the coasts of Europe and North America.*

seaboard /síːbɔːd/ **seaboards**
NC+SUPP A **seaboard** is the part of a country that is next to the sea; a formal word. *...the eastern seaboard of the United States. ...Sydney, on the Pacific Ocean seaboard.*

sea breeze, sea breezes
NC A **sea breeze** is a wind blowing from the sea towards the land.

seafarer /síːfeərə/ **seafarers**
NC A **seafarer** is someone who works at sea; an old-fashioned word. *...a nation of traders and seafarers... Only experienced seafarers were employed.*

seafaring /síːfeərɪŋ/
ADJ ATTRIB **Seafaring** means working as a sailor or travelling regularly on the sea; an old-fashioned word. *Britain has always been a seafaring nation.*

seafood /síːfuːd/
NU **Seafood** refers to sea creatures that you can eat, especially shellfish such as lobsters, mussels, or crabs. *They cooked three kinds of seafood for us. ...fish and seafood from open air markets.*

seafront /síːfrʌnt/ **seafronts**
NC The **seafront** is the part of a seaside town that is next to the sea. It usually consists of a road with buildings facing the sea. *I walked along the seafront.*

sea-going
ADJ ATTRIB **Sea-going** boats and ships are designed for travelling on the sea, rather than on lakes, rivers, or canals. *In sea-going car ferries, passengers have to leave their cars for the duration of the crossing.*

seagull /síːgʌl/ **seagulls**
NC A **seagull** is a type of bird with long wings and a white and grey body. *...flocks of thousands of seagulls.*

seahorse /síːhɔːs/ **seahorses**
NC A **seahorse** is a type of small fish whose head looks something like the head of a horse.

seal /siːl/ **seals, sealing, sealed**
1 NC A **seal** is something fixed to a letter or container, especially a food container, that must be broken before it can be opened. *I noticed that the seals of the packet had been broken... The French protestors banged on the sides of the lorry and broke customs seals on the doors.*
2 VO If you **seal** an opening, you fill or cover it to prevent air, gas, or a liquid getting in or out. *Small cracks can be sealed with this compound. ...a thin tube sealed at one end.*
3 VO If you **seal** an envelope, you stick down the flap. *Mrs Slesers sealed the envelopes and left them on her desk.* ◆ **sealed** ADJ *He took a sealed envelope from the folder on his desk.*
4 NC A **seal** is also an official mark on a document which shows that it is genuine. *...the minister's seal of office. ...a great parchment document with its official red seals.*
5 NC A **seal** is also a large, shiny animal with flippers, which eats fish and lives partly on land and partly in the sea. *Periods of warmer weather encourage seals to leave the water... The Canadian government has banned the commercial hunting of seals.*
● Seal is used in these phrases. ● If someone **gives** something their **seal of approval** or if they **put** their **seal of approval on** something, they say officially that

they approve of it. *There is little doubt that the Party Congress in January will give them its seal of approval... The cabinet had put its seal of approval on the budget. ...foods that qualify for the Institute's seal of approval.* ● If something **puts** or **sets the seal on** something, it makes it definite or confirms how it is going to be. *Neil Kinnock sees this conference as one to put the final seal on the dramatic changes in policy... They have met in Damascus to set the seal on a reconciliation after five years of bitter rivalry.*
seal off PHRASAL VERB If you **seal** a place **off**, you block all the entrances so that nobody can get in or out. *It will not be possible to completely seal off the border.*

sea lane, sea lanes
NC A **sea lane** is a particular route that is regularly used by ships when crossing a sea or ocean. *It was vital for America to keep these sea lanes open.*

sea legs
If you **get** or **find** your **sea legs**, you become used to the movement of a ship at sea, so that you do not feel seasick. *We didn't get bad weather until we were about a week out, and most people had got their sea legs by then.*

sea level
1 NU If you are at **sea level**, you are at the same level as the surface of the sea. *...very low lying land generally less than one metre above sea level... Some of the islands are said to be below sea level.*
2 NU The **sea level** is the surface of the sea. *The sea level in the Mediterranean has risen.*

sealing wax
NU **Sealing wax** is a hard, usually red, substance that melts quickly and is used for putting seals on documents, certificates, or letters.

sea lion, sea lions
NC A **sea lion** is a type of large seal. *We've seen seals and sea lions out there you know.*

seam /siːm/ **seams**
1 NC A **seam** is a line of stitches joining two pieces of cloth together. *If you break one thread in the seam you can pull it apart.*
2 NC A **seam** of coal is a long, narrow layer of it beneath the ground. *...the traditional method of pick and shovel to extract coal from seams.*
● Seam is used in these phrases. ● If something is **bursting at the seams**, it is very full. *The action came at a time when the camps were bursting at the seams... The embassies began to burst at the seams.*
● If something is **coming apart at the seams**, its parts are no longer working properly together, and it may soon be totally ineffective. *The pressure grew so intense that at times I felt that the government itself might come apart at its seams... The arrangement came apart at the seams.*

seaman /síːmən/ **seamen** /síːmən/
NC A **seaman** is a sailor. *A seaman was drowned in the Atlantic after being swept off the deck of a tanker.*

seamanship /síːmənʃɪp/
NU **Seamanship** is skill in managing a boat and controlling its movement through the sea. *The journey round Cape Horn demanded a high degree of seamanship.*

seamed /síːmd/
ADJ If something is **seamed**, it has long, thin lines on its surface; a literary word. *His brown face was seamed and wrinkled.*

seamless /síːmləs/
1 ADJ A **seamless** piece of clothing has no seams.
2 ADJ If you describe something as **seamless**, you mean that you cannot see where the different parts of it join together; used showing approval. *The gardens make a seamless whole with Hyde Park on the east.*

seamstress /síːmstrəs, sémstrəs/ **seamstresses**
NC A **seamstress** is a woman who sews and makes clothes as her job.

seamy /síːmi/ **seamier, seamiest**
ADJ Something that is **seamy** is unpleasant, especially because it involves aspects of life such as crime, sex, or violence. *He was involved in a particularly seamy divorce case. ...the seamy side of life.*

séance /seɪɑːns/ **séances**; also spelt **seance**.
NC A **séance** is a meeting in which people try to speak to people who are dead. *Miss Martin communes with the dead—but not through séances. She simply holds conversations with them.*

seaplane /siːpleɪn/ **seaplanes**
NC A **seaplane** is a type of aeroplane that can take off or land on water.

seaport /siːpɔːt/ **seaports**
NC A **seaport** is a harbour or port, or a town containing one, that sea-going ships can use. *They have offered assurances that the seaports are open.*

sear /sɪə/ **sears, searing, seared**
1 VO To **sear** something means to burn its surface with a sudden intense heat. *Sear the meat for one minute, then reduce the heat and cook slowly.*
2 VO If something **sears** a part of your body, it causes a painful burning feeling there; a literary use. *The pungent, choking smell of sulphur and burnt sand seared our nostrils.*
3 See also **searing**.

search /sɜːtʃ/ **searches, searching, searched**
1 VOorVA If you **search** a place, you look carefully for something or someone there. *Police say they are now searching an area of a hundred square miles... Private homes of business managers and employees were also searched... He searched through the drawer and eventually found the photo.*
2 V+for If you **search** for something or someone, you look carefully for them. *Hundreds of police and members of the public have been searching for the boy since he disappeared. ...searching for ways to end the dispute.*
3 VO If the police or someone else in authority **searches** you, they examine your clothing for hidden objects. *The police can also search people on arrival in Britain if they suspect them of involvement in terrorism... The airport has responsibility for searching passengers and their baggage.*
4 NC A **search** is an attempt to find a person or thing by looking for them carefully. *Their search for gold has taken some of them to the Catrimani River... The search has resumed for two climbers who are believed buried in the snow. ...an air and sea search.* • If you go **in search of** something, you try to find it. *...people leaving the countryside in search of food... There is one positive sign for those in search of peace.*
search out PHRASAL VERB If you **search** something **out**, you keep looking for it until you find it. *I have been searching out old sewing patterns.*

searcher /sɜːtʃə/ **searchers**
NC A **searcher** is a person who is employed or has volunteered to look for someone or something that is missing. *Heavy rain during the morning made the searchers' task more difficult and unpleasant... Searchers and rescue dogs have uncovered the bodies of nine skiers who died last night.*

searching /sɜːtʃɪŋ/
ADJ A **searching** question or look is intended to discover the truth about something. *Although support for the President has been strong, searching questions will now be asked... He gave the girl a quick, searching look.* • **searchingly** ADV *She was looking at me searchingly.*

searchlight /sɜːtʃlaɪt/ **searchlights**
NCorNU A **searchlight** is a large powerful light that can be turned to shine for a long way in any direction. *During the night I saw searchlights sweep the temple and the buildings surrounding it... Rescue workers worked by searchlight digging people out of the rubble.*

search party, search parties
NC A **search party** is an organized group of people who are looking for someone or something. *The search parties have now located four engines.*

search warrant, search warrants
NC A **search warrant** is an official document that gives the police permission to search a building, for example when they are looking for drugs or stolen goods. *Their search warrant indicated they were looking for arms and ammunition.*

searing /sɪərɪŋ/
1 ADJ ATTRIB A **searing** pain is very sharp. *He felt a searing pain in his left arm.*
2 ADJ ATTRIB A **searing** speech or piece of writing is very critical. *...a searing exposure of modern America.*

seascape /siːskeɪp/ **seascapes**
NC A **seascape** is a painting of the sea. *Nassee turned to still-lifes of flowers and seascapes with sail-boats and bright skies.*

seashell /siːʃel/ **seashells**
NC A **seashell** is the empty shell of a small sea creature. *A seaside pub will decorate its bar with fishing nets and seashells.*

seashore /siːʃɔː/ **seashores**
NC The **seashore** is the part of a coast where the land slopes down into the sea. *...a walk along the seashore.*

seasick /siːsɪk/
ADJ If you are **seasick** when you are in a boat, the movement of the boat causes you to vomit or feel sick. *He felt seasick.* • **seasickness** NU *He suffers from seasickness.*

seaside /siːsaɪd/
N SING The **seaside** is a place next to the sea, especially one where people go for their holidays. *We spent the weekend at the seaside. ...a seaside resort.*

season /siːzn/ **seasons, seasoning, seasoned**
1 NC The **seasons** are the periods into which a year is divided, because there is different weather in each period. *Autumn is my favourite season... Most transportation is done by small boats, especially during the rainy season.*
2 NC A **season** is also a period during each year when something usually happens. *...the beginning of the football season... Most fruit have a short growing season... The West Indian captain, Viv Richards, could be playing for Yorkshire next season... Hotel rooms are available even at the height of the season.*
3 NC+SUPP A **season** of films, plays, or concerts is several of them shown as a series because they are connected in some way. *...a season of Clint Eastwood movies.*
4 VO If you **season** food, you add salt, pepper, or spices to it. *...tuna fish seasoned with salt.*
• **Season** is used in these phrases. • If fruit or vegetables are **in season**, it is the time of year when they are ready for eating and are widely available. *Raspberries are in season now.* • If you go to a place **out of season**, you go there when it is not the busy holiday period. *We've often been there out of season, and it's much quieter.*

seasonable /siːzənəbl/
1 ADJ **Seasonable** weather conditions are the kind that is expected or usual at a particular time of year. *...seasonable March winds.*
2 ADJ Something that is **seasonable** comes or happens at just the right time. *This seasonable advice was just what we needed.*

seasonal /siːzənəl/
ADJ Something that is **seasonal** happens during one particular time of the year. *People found seasonal work on farms.* • **seasonally** ADV *People there are employed seasonally. ...the seasonally adjusted unemployment figures.*

seasoned /siːznd/
ADJ ATTRIB **Seasoned** means having a lot of experience of something. For example, a seasoned traveller is someone who has travelled a lot. *...seasoned troops.*

seasoning /siːzənɪŋ/
NU **Seasoning** is salt, pepper, or spices that are added to food. *We've taken some finely minced beef and added to that some coriander-based seasoning.*

season ticket, season tickets
NC A **season ticket** is a ticket that you can use repeatedly over a certain period without having to pay each time. *...a monthly season ticket... This entrance is reserved for season ticket holders.*

seat /siːt/ **seats, seating, seated**
1 NC A **seat** is an object that you can sit on, for example a chair. *Roger sat down carefully, using the edge of the crate as a seat. ...the back seat of the car... I rang the theatre to see if I could get seats for*

the show... Come in, take a seat.

2 NC The **seat** of a chair is the part that you sit on. *There was a cushion on the seat of the chair.*

3 V-REFL A If you **seat** yourself somewhere, you sit down; a formal use. *'Thank you,' she said, seating herself on the sofa.* ◆ **seated** ADJ PRED *General Tomkins was seated behind his desk.*

4 VO A building or vehicle that **seats** a particular number of people has enough seats for that number. *The church seats more than a thousand.*

5 NC When someone is elected to parliament, you can say that they or their party have won a **seat**. *He won the seat at the last election with a majority of four thousand three hundred... Mr Smith says he will resign his seat at the next general election.* ● See also **safe seat**.

6 NC+SUPP The **seat** of an organization or wealthy family is where they have their base. *...Strasbourg, the seat of the European parliament. ...a single building on the main square which is the seat of all local power. ...the country seat of the Earls of Shrewsbury.*

7 NC+SUPP The **seat** of a movement or activity is the place where it originates. *Several hundred people were moved away from a poor district close to the seat of the rebellion. ...Esztergom, the ancient seat of Hungarian Christianity.*

8 If you **take a back seat**, you allow other people to have all the power and to make all the decisions. *I think in the longer term the President would probably have to take more of a back seat in French politics.*

seat-belt, seat-belts
NC A **seat-belt** is a strap that you fasten across your body for safety when travelling in a car or aeroplane. *The coach was not fitted with passenger seat-belts.*

seating /siːtɪŋ/
NU The **seating** in a place is the seats there. *The plastic seating was uncomfortable.*

sea urchin, sea urchins
NC A **sea urchin** is a small round sea creature that has a hard shell covered with sharp points.

seaweed /siːwiːd/ **seaweeds**
N MASS **Seaweed** is a plant that grows in the sea. *It's his job to clear the sand of seaweed, shells and trash.*

sec /sek/ **secs**
NC If you ask someone to wait a **sec**, you are asking them to wait for a very short time; an informal expression. *Hang on a sec, let me have a look... I'll join you in a sec.*

secateurs /sekətəz, sekətɜːz/
N PL A pair of **secateurs** is a gardening tool that looks like a pair of strong, heavy scissors and is used for cutting the stems of plants. *Secateurs are very useful for pruning.*

secede /sɪsiːd/ **secedes, seceding, seceded**
V or V+*from* If a group or region **secedes** from a larger group or country to which it belongs, it formally ends its membership of the group and forms an independent group or country; a formal word. *...the democratically expressed desire of all three Republics to secede... Some would like the South to secede from France, to be an independent country.*

secession /sɪseʃn/
NU The **secession** of a group or region from a larger group or country to which it belongs is its formal separation from the group or country; a formal word. *The constitution provided for the secession of the constituent republics. ...the secession of a small group of MPs to form a new party.*

secessionist /sɪseʃənɪst/ **secessionists**
NC **Secessionists** are people who want their group or region to become independent from a larger group or country which it is part of. *The government's main task was to crush terrorism and isolate secessionists. ...the leaders of a secessionist movement.*

secluded /sɪkluːdɪd/
ADJ A **secluded** place is quiet, private, and undisturbed. *...secluded beaches.*

seclusion /sɪkluːʒn/
NU If you are living in **seclusion**, you are in a quiet place away from other people. *She was reared in seclusion.*

second, seconds, seconding, seconded; pronounced /sekənd/, for the meanings in paragraphs 1 to 5, 7, and in the phrases, and /sɪkɒnd/ for the meaning in paragraph 6.

1 NC A **second** is one of the sixty parts that a minute is divided into. *The rocket was rising at the rate of 300 feet per second... Per Eklund is in third place, 2 minutes 51 seconds behind the leader.*

2 NC A **second** or **seconds** is also used to mean a very short time. *Could I see your book for a second?... The explosion came seconds after he had driven past.*

3 ADJ The **second** item in a series is the one that you count as number two. *...his father's second marriage. ...the second of February. ...Iraq's second city, Basra... The British came second and the Germans third.*

4 NC **Seconds** are goods that are sold cheaply because they are slightly faulty. *Some of the articles you see are seconds.*

5 VO If you **second** a proposal in a meeting or debate, you formally agree with it so that it can then be discussed or voted on. *I seconded Gene's nomination.*

6 VO If you **are seconded** somewhere, you are moved there temporarily in order to do special duties. *He was for a time seconded to the army.*

7 second nature: see **nature**.
● **Second** is used in these phrases. ● You can say that someone or something is **second only to** one other person or thing when this other person or thing is the only one better or more important than they are. *San Francisco is second only to New York as the tourist city of the States.* ● If you say that someone or something is **second to none**, you mean that they are better than anyone else or anything else at a particular activity or in a particular category. *As a physician he is second to none.* ● If you experience something at **second hand**, you are told about it by other people rather than experiencing it yourself. *I knew nothing about Judith except what I'd heard at second hand.* ● See also **second-hand.**

secondary /sekəndərɪ/
1 ADJ **Secondary** means less important than something else. *Many older people still believe that men's careers come first and women's careers are secondary.*

2 ADJ ATTRIB **Secondary** education is for pupils between the ages of 11 and 18. *...the quality of our elementary and secondary education system.*

secondary action
NU **Secondary action** is action such as secondary picketing and sympathy strikes taken by workers in order to make their strike more effective or in order to support other workers who are on strike. *...the right to stage sympathy strikes and other forms of secondary action.*

secondary modern, secondary moderns
NC A **secondary modern** is a school which existed until recently in Britain for pupils aged between about eleven and sixteen, where more attention was paid to practical skills and less to academic study than in a grammar school. *If they didn't get through the exam they went to Framlingham Secondary Modern.*

secondary picketing
NU **Secondary picketing** happens when people who are on strike demonstrate outside a factory or company that supplies or buys from their employers, or that provides the same service as them. It is illegal in Great Britain. *Sealink's services have been affected by secondary picketing in support of P&O workers. ...restrictions on secondary picketing.*

secondary school, secondary schools
N C or NU In Britain, a **secondary school** is a school for pupils between the ages of 11 and 18. *They'd got 140 applicants including people qualified from secondary school... These two boys from a North London secondary school are at the beginning of their second year of Spanish.*

second-best
ADJ or N SING Something that is **second-best** is not as good as the best thing of its kind but is better than all the other things of that kind. *...businessmen in their second-best suits... Hiring professionals is impractical,*

so as a second-best, we will use unpaid amateurs.

second childhood
N SING If you say that an old person is in their **second childhood**, you mean that they are losing their mental powers and becoming like a small child in their behaviour. *The poor old dear's in her second childhood and doesn't know what she's saying.*

second-class
1 ADJ ATTRIB **Second-class** things are regarded as less valuable or less important than others of the same kind. *It accused party leaders of trying to treat non-party members as second-class citizens.*
2 ADJ or ADV **Second-class** refers to the ordinary accommodation on a train, aircraft, or ship rather than the first-class or luxury accommodation. *...a second-class carriage... He travels second-class.*
3 ADJ or ADV **Second-class** postage is a cheaper type of postage. **Second-class** letters and parcels take longer to arrive than first-class ones.
4 ADJ ATTRIB A **second-class** degree is a good or average university degree.

second cousin, second cousins
NC Your **second cousins** are the children of your parents' cousins.

second-guess, second-guesses, second-guessing, second-guessed
VO If you **second-guess** someone, you think of different ways they could have done something after the event. *He says this was a decision that historians are going to second-guess forever.*

second hand, second hands
NC A **second hand** is the hand that marks the seconds on a clock or a watch.

second-hand
1 ADJ or ADV Something that is **second-hand** has been owned by someone else. *It costs £550; enough to buy a second-hand car. ...a book he bought second-hand.*
2 ADJ ATTRIB A **second-hand** shop sells second-hand goods. *He personally enjoyed looking for bargains in second-hand clothes markets.*
3 ADV or ADJ If you hear a story **second-hand,** you hear it from someone who has heard it from someone else. *I heard about it secondhand. ...a second-hand report.*

second language
N SING Someone's **second language** is a language which is not their native language but which they use at work or at school. *...learners of English as a second language.*

secondly /sɛkəndli/
ADV SEN You say **secondly** when you want to make a second point or give a second reason for something. *Firstly, the energy already exists in the ground. Secondly, there's plenty of it.*

secondment /sɪkɒndmənt/ **secondments**
NU or NC If you are sent on **secondment**, you are sent away from your job for a short time to do a particular job or special duties somewhere else. *He's on secondment to the Ministry of Defence.*

second nature
NU If something is **second nature** to you, you have done it so much that you no longer think about it, and it seems as if it is part of your character. *Diplomacy was second nature to Jonathan.*

second person
N SING In grammar, the **second person** is the person who is addressed in speech or writing. In modern English it is the word 'you'. *...the second person plural 'you' form.*

second-rate
ADJ Something that is **second-rate** is of poor quality. *...second-rate ideas. ...second-rate students.*

second sight
NU If you say that someone has **second sight**, you mean that they are, or seem to be, able to see or know about things happening in another place or in the future.

second thoughts
N PL If you have **second thoughts** about a decision, you have doubts and begin to wonder if it was wise. *There are growing signs that some whites are having second thoughts about returning to the days of hardline apartheid.* • You say **on second thoughts** when you

suddenly change your mind about something. *Tell me more about America. No, on second thoughts, tell me more about your family.*

second wind
N SING If a person or an activity gets a **second wind**, they are able to continue after a difficult or strenuous period. *Now it seems negotiations have a second wind.*

Second World War
N PROP The **Second World War** or the **Second War** is the major war that was fought between 1939 and 1945. *After the Second World War he entered the Diplomatic Service.*

secrecy /siːkrəsi/
NU **Secrecy** is the fact or state of keeping something secret. *She stressed the necessity of absolute secrecy... The meeting took place in secrecy.*

secret /siːkrət/ **secrets**
1 ADJ Something that is **secret** is known about by only a small number of people, and is not told or shown to anyone else. *The details are secret... Directors of the companies have been holding regular secret meetings.* ◆ **secretly** ADV *Their work had to be done secretly.*
2 ADJ ATTRIB You use **secret** to describe someone who does something that they do not tell other people about. *She had become a secret drinker.* ◆ **secretly** ADV or ADV SEN *He secretly hoped I would one day change my mind... Secretly, perhaps, some of them were also a little scared.*
3 If you do something **in secret**, you do it without anyone else knowing. *The talks took place in secret... These illegal practices continue to flourish in secret.*
4 NC A **secret** is a fact that is known by only a small number of people, and is not told to anyone else. *The venue and the timing of the meeting are being kept a secret... The trial was supposed to be a secret.*
5 N SING If a way of behaving is the **secret** of achieving something, it is the best way or the only way to achieve it, and it is only known by a few people. *The powerful man died, and with him died the secret of making so much money.*
6 See also **open secret**.

secret agent, secret agents
NC A **secret agent** is a person employed by a government to find out the secrets of other governments, or to do secret work against organizations which threaten their government. *...one of the two secret agents responsible for blowing up the ship.*

secretarial /sɛkrəteəriəl/
ADJ ATTRIB **Secretarial** means involving or relating to the work of a secretary. *They offered more money for lower paid clerical and secretarial staff.*

secretariat /sɛkrəteəriət/ **secretariats**
NC A **secretariat** is a department responsible for the administration of an international political organization or of a legislative body. *...a senior member of the U.N. Secretariat.*

secretary /sɛkrətəʰri/ **secretaries**
1 NC+SUPP In Britain, **Secretary** is used in the titles of ministers who are in charge of one of the main government departments. *The conference will be addressed by the Environment Secretary, Mr Ron Howard.*
2 NC+SUPP In the United States, **Secretary** is used in the titles of the heads of main government departments, appointed by the President. *...the former American Defense Secretary, Caspar Weinberger. ...this follows a first meeting between Secretary Baker and the Vietnamese Foreign Minister.*
3 NC A **secretary** is a person whose job is to type letters, answer phone calls and do other office work. *The business employs three secretaries.*
4 NC The **secretary** of a club is the person whose job involves keeping records and writing letters. *If you want to join the cricket club, write to the secretary.*

Secretary-General, Secretary-Generals
NC A **Secretary-General** is the person in charge of the administration of an international political organization. *The UN Secretary-General, Mr Javier Perez de Cuellar, has expressed his distress at the renewed violence.*

Secretary of State, Secretaries of State
1 NC A **Secretary of State** is a government minister in Britain. *...the Secretary of State for Northern Ireland. ...a meeting with the Secretary of State.*
2 NC In the United States, the **Secretary of State** is the head of the government department that deals with foreign affairs. *Secretary of State Baker held talks in Damascus last Saturday... Deputy Secretary of State Lawrence Eagleburger defended the administration's handling of the proposed sale.*

secrete /sɪkriːt/ **secretes, secreting, secreted**
1 VO If part of a plant or animal **secretes** a liquid, it produces it. *The skin pores enlarge and secrete more oil.* ◆ **secretion** /sɪkriːʃn/ **secretions** NCorNU *Scientists in Canada have analysed secretions from the queen bee's mandible glands... The effect is to increase the rate of secretion.*
2 VO If you **secrete** something somewhere, you hide it there; a formal use. *...clothes that she had secreted in her basket.*

secretive /siːkrətɪv/
ADJ If you are **secretive**, you keep your feelings, intentions, or activities hidden from other people. *They have remained secretive about the talks. ...the secretive world of Hollywood.*

secret police
N PL The **secret police** is a police force, especially in a non-democratic country, that works secretly and is concerned with political crimes. *Several politicians have been forced to resign because of their connections with the secret police.*

secret service, secret services
NC A country's **secret service** is a government department that is responsible for the security of a country, and whose job is to find out enemy secrets and to prevent its own government's secrets from being discovered. *He continued working for the Secret Service right up to the time of his defection. ...the memoirs of a former secret service agent.*

sect /sekt/ **sects**
NC A **sect** is a group of people that has separated from a larger group and has a particular set of religious or political beliefs. *...an extremist Protestant sect.*

sectarian /sektɛəriən/; a formal word.
1 ADJ ATTRIB **Sectarian** means resulting from the differences between sects. *The conference had collapsed in sectarian squabbles... Police are treating the attack as sectarian.*
2 ADJ Someone who is **sectarian** strongly supports a particular sect; used showing disapproval. *This group is frequently attacked as sectarian and fanatical.*

sectarianism /sektɛəriənɪzm/
NU **Sectarianism** is strong support for a particular sect and its beliefs, often in a narrow-minded way. *The political scene there is dominated by uncompromising sectarianism.*

section /sekʃn/ **sections**
NC A **section** of something is one of the separate parts that it is divided into. *The paper now comes in two sections. ...the canal's narrowest and most dangerous section. ...the underprivileged section of British society... Refer to Section Sixty-One of the new draft constitution.* ● See also **cross-section.**

sectional /sekʃəⁿnəl/
ADJ ATTRIB **Sectional** interests or objectives are those of a particular group within a community or country. *Broadcasting must not become an instrument of narrow sectional interests... The People's Army used to be the only organization that could rise above national and sectional interests.*

sector /sektə/ **sectors**
1 NC+SUPP A **sector** of a country's economy is a particular part of it. A particular **sector** consists of all the companies which are involved in a particular area of work or all the companies that are run according to a particular system. *The agricultural sector has responded quite well to the adjustment... Public sector companies lost around $4,000 million last year alone.*
2 NC+SUPP A **sector** is also one group or area which is part of another, larger one. *No sector of the government will be affected... Workers in the*

Norwegian sector of the North Sea oil fields have gone on strike.

secular /sekjulə/
ADJ You use **secular** to describe things that have no connection with religion. *It is a largely secular country... The choir sings both sacred and secular music.*

secularism /sekjulərɪzəm/
NU **Secularism** is the belief that religion should have no influence on or connection with the running of a country, for example in the educational or political system. *Secularism is a very strong current in the structure and ideology of this country... Secularism does have broad public sympathy, and an increased stress on Islam will not be popular.* ◆ **secularist, secularists** NC *As a well-known secularist, Mr Giray may have been upset about the debate on whether women students should wear Islamic headscarves on campus... They have complained that what they call secularists are often favoured for employment.*

secularize /sekjulᵊraɪz/ **secularizes, secularizing, secularized**; also spelt **secularise.**
VO To **secularize** a system such as society or education means to change it so it is no longer under the control or influence of religion. *...ideas about how to secularize Muslim Turkey... In our century, these biblical visions rapidly became secularized and transposed into revolutionary theory.*

secure /sɪkjuə/ **secures, securing, secured**
1 ADJ Something that is **secure** is safe and certain to remain and not be lost. *You've got a secure job... His place in history is secure.* ◆ **securely** ADV *The strike was securely under the union's control.*
2 VO If you **secure** something such as a position, result, or something you really want, you get it after a lot of effort; a formal use. *I did everything possible to secure him a posting... He secured only 526 votes... They are doing all they can to secure his release.*
3 ADJ If a building is **secure**, it is tightly locked or well protected. *Try and make your house as secure as you can... They are worried that Brixton prison is not secure enough for high-risk prisoners.*
4 VO If you **secure** a place, you make it safe from harm or attack; a formal use. *They endeavoured to secure the bridge from the threat of attack... Yugoslavia's frontiers must be secured. ...a non-aggression treaty aimed at securing the Western border.*
5 ADJ If an object is **secure**, it is fixed firmly in position. *Check that the leads to the battery are in good condition and secure.* ◆ **securely** ADV *The chain seemed to be securely fastened.*
6 VO If you **secure** an object, you fasten it firmly to another object. *A plastic box was secured to the wall by screws.*
7 ADJ If you feel **secure**, you feel safe and happy and are not worried about life. *We feel financially secure... All in all, the road to a secure future is strewn with awkward obstacles... They are trying to create a secure atmosphere.*

security /sɪkjuərᵊti/ **securities**
1 NU **Security** refers to all the precautions that are taken to protect a place. *...a threat to national security. ...new developments in airport safety and security... Seoul has responded to these fears by tightening security.*
2 NU+SUPP **Security** is legal protection against possible harm or loss. *He hasn't got security of employment... The tenants are exploited and have no security of tenure.*
3 NU A feeling of **security** is a feeling of being safe. *Children count on their parents for love and security.*
4 NUorNC If you give something valuable to someone as **security**, you promise to give it to them if you fail to pay back some money that you owe them. *The bank may ask for security if you want an overdraft. ...disputes over security guarantees.*
5 NC **Securities** are stocks, shares, bonds, or other certificates bought as an investment; a technical use. *Foreigners helped finance the budget deficit by buying government securities.*
6 See also **social security.**

security risk, security risks
NC If you describe someone or something as a security risk, you mean that they may be a threat to the safety of a country or organization. *His work on the nuclear weapons programme made him a security risk... He described the demonstrations as a security risk.*

sedan /sɪdæn/ **sedans**
NC A sedan is the same as a saloon car; used in American English. *He pulled up in a white sedan.*

sedan chair, sedan chairs
NC A sedan chair is a special carriage for one person which was carried on two poles by two men, one in front and one behind. Sedan chairs were used in the 17th and 18th centuries. *He crossed the Alps on foot in 1680 because he could not afford a sedan chair.*

sedate /sɪdeɪt/ **sedates, sedating, sedated**
1 ADJ A sedate person is quiet, calm, and rather dignified. *Irene was graver and more sedate... This fascinating rabble was followed by a group of very sedate ladies in black lace jackets and traditional sarongs.* ◆ **sedately** ADV *He walked sedately down the lane.*
2 ADJ Something that is sedate is slow, peaceful, and not very active or exciting. *The Independent reports on a controversy in the sedate town of Tunbridge Wells. ...Egypt, traditionally the home of more sedate and elaborate Oriental music.*
3 VO If a person or animal is sedated, they are given a drug to calm them or to make them sleep. *They had been sedated to calm them during the voyage... The patient is lightly sedated and will feel no pain while this is being done.*

sedation /sɪdeɪʃn/
NU Sedation is the use of drugs in order to calm someone or to make them sleep. *The disease is very difficult to treat, except by permanent sedation... Freddie was still under sedation.*

sedative /sedətɪv/ **sedatives**
NC A sedative is a drug that calms you or makes you sleep. *People infected with rabies should be given sedatives to reduce anxiety and pain.*

sedentary /sedəntəˀri/
ADJ A sedentary occupation or way of life involves a lot of sitting down and not much exercise. *Textile workers spend hours in a sedentary occupation... Black Rhinos are by nature sedentary.*

sedge /sedʒ/ **sedges**
N MASS Sedge is a grass-like plant that grows in wet, marshy ground. *...birds slipping invisibly through the sedge and brambles.*

sediment /sedɪmənt/ **sediments**
NU or NC Sediment is solid material that settles at the bottom of a liquid. *We take cores of sediment from the lake... What have your latest studies of these sediments told you?*

sedimentary /sedɪmentəˀri/
ADJ Sedimentary rocks, deposits, and so on are formed from sediment left by water, ice, or wind. *...fossils in ancient sedimentary rocks.*

sedition /sɪdɪʃn/
NU Sedition is speech, writing, or behaviour intended to encourage rebellion or resistance against the government. *They were charged with sedition... The government has called the march an act of sedition.*

seditious /sɪdɪʃəs/
ADJ Something that is seditious encourages rebellion or resistance against the government. *He was convicted of seditious activities... He was charged with publishing a seditious magazine.*

seduce /sɪdjuːs/ **seduces, seducing, seduced**
1 VO If something seduces you, it is so attractive that it tempts you to do something that you would not normally approve of. *He was seduced into saying that he would do it... The game of soccer has seduced the American public for decades.*
2 VO If someone seduces another person, they persuade that person to have sex with them; used showing disapproval. *He used to seduce all the maids.* ◆ **seduction** /sɪdʌkʃn/ **seductions** NC or NU *The girl's seduction is an important part of the story. ...a subtle form of seduction.*

seductive /sɪdʌktɪv/
1 ADJ Something that is seductive is very attractive or tempting, but possibly harmful or dangerous. *These are seductive arguments... Anton Kara's seductive music for the film was played on the zither... Much of the campaign has been a seductive mixture of religion and nationalism.*
2 ADJ A seductive person is sexually attractive. *...a sophisticated and seductive woman... Africa is imagined in the likeness of a gorgeous, infinitely seductive woman's body.* ◆ **seductively** ADV *She plays a woman who got drunk in a bar and danced seductively before being gang-raped.*

see /siː/ **sees, seeing, saw, seen**
1 V O or V When you see, you notice or recognize something or someone, using your eyes. *I saw him glance at his watch... Some animals have the ability to see in very dim light.*
2 VO When you see something, you look at it because you are interested in it. *Did you see 'The Doctor's Dilemma' on telly last night?... He went to India to see the Taj Mahal.*
3 VO If you go to see someone, you visit them or meet them. *Perhaps she did not wish to come and see me... It would be a good idea for you to see a doctor for a checkup.*
4 V O A If you see someone to a particular place, you accompany them to make sure that they get there safely. *I went down to see her safely to her car.*
5 V-REPORT or VO If you see that something is true or exists, you realize that it is true or exists, by carefully observing it or thinking about it. *They saw that the system was wrong... He failed to see that changes were necessary... Economic problems forced the Maghreb countries to see the necessity for regional co-operation.*
6 V-REPORT, VO, or V If you see why something happens or see what someone means, you understand why it happens or what they mean. *'Yes,' she said. 'I see what you mean.'... I can see why Mr Smith is worried... It's hard to see how these protests can be stamped out.*
7 V-REPORT If you say that you will see what is happening or what the situation is, you mean you intend to find out. *I'd better go and see what he wants... I must phone her up and see if she can come tonight... Let's see if you can manage without us.*
8 V-REPORT If you see that something is done, you make sure that it is done. *If they go out they have to see that everything's locked up.*
9 VO If you see a situation or someone's behaviour in a particular way, you regard it in that way. *So Professor, you don't see this as a major problem?... I did not see his determination as a defect.*
10 VO If a person or a period of time sees a particular change or event, the change or event takes place while that person is alive or during that period of time. *In recent years we have seen a huge split develop between rich and poor nations... Last week saw a drop in the bond market... Recent years have seen the acceptance of a greater degree of foreign investment.*
11 V O A If you see something happening in the future, you imagine it, or predict that it will happen. *They assumed he saw himself as chairman... Can you see women going into combat carrying forty-pound guns?*
12 VO See is used in books to indicate to readers where they should look for more information. *Reference to this problem is made elsewhere (see Chapter 14).*
● See is used in these phrases. ● If you say that you will see if you can do something, you mean that you will try to do it. *See if you can find my birthday book anywhere.* ● When someone asks you for help, if you say that you will 'see what you can do', or 'see what can be done', you mean that you will try to help them. *He promised to see what could be done.*
● People say 'I'll see' or 'We'll see' to indicate that they do not intend to make a decision immediately, and will decide later. *'Will you write to me?' she asked. 'I'll see,' he said.* ● People say 'let me see' or 'let's see' when they are trying to remember something, or are trying to find something. *I think*

I've got her name somewhere. Now let me see. ● You say '**I see**' to indicate that you understand what someone is telling you. *Oh I see, you went to the cinema.* ● You can use '**seeing that**' or '**seeing as**' to introduce the reason for what you are doing or saying; an informal use. *Seeing that you're the guest on this little trip, you can decide where we're going.* ● '**See you**' and '**see you later**' are informal ways of saying goodbye when you expect to meet someone again soon.

see about PHRASAL VERB 1 When you **see about** something, you arrange for it to be done or provided. *Rudolph went into the station to see about Thomas's ticket.* 2 If someone says that they will do something, and you say '**We'll see about that**', you mean that you intend to prevent them from doing it. *'We're moving'—'We'll see about that.'*

see in PHRASAL VERB If you ask what someone sees **in** a particular person, you want to know what they find attractive about that person. *'What can she see in him?'*

see off PHRASAL VERB 1 When you **see** someone **off**, you go with them to a station, airport, or port that they are leaving from, and say goodbye to them there. *Are you seeing someone off too?... The two men turned out at the airport to see Prince Charles off.* 2 To **see** someone or something **off** means to force them to leave a place. *I saw off those children that were hanging around the sheds.* 3 In a game or competition, if you **see off** your opponents, you succeed in improving your position so that you win. *Algeria saw off the challenge of Senegal two-one in their match in Algiers.*

see through PHRASAL VERB 1 If you **see through** someone or **see through** what they are doing, you realize what their intentions are, even though they are trying to hide them. *She had learned to see through him... The jailers saw through my scheme.* 2 If someone or something **sees** you **through** a problem or a difficult time, they support you and help you to cope with it. *He gave thanks for her help in seeing the union through eight hard years of imprisonment and underground existence.*

see to PHRASAL VERB If you **see to** something that needs attention, you deal with it. *Don't you worry about that. I'll see to that... He went out to see to the chickens.*

seed /siːd/ **seeds, seeding, seeded**
1 NCorNU A **seed** is the small, hard part of a plant from which a new plant grows. *Each flower produces thousands of seeds. ...a packet of seed.*
2 VO If you **seed** a piece of land, you plant seeds in it. *All of us neighbours got together and ploughed, harrowed, and seeded it all in one day.* ◆ **seeded** ADJ ATTRIB *They are reported to have driven across newly seeded athletic fields.*
3 N PL+SUPP The **seeds** of something are its beginnings or origins; a literary use. *The seeds of doubt had been sown.*
4 NC In a knockout tournament, the **seeds** are the strongest players or teams who are kept apart in the early stages of the tournament. *The top seeds Jimmy Connors and Amos Mansdorf are safely through to the third round... Second seed Lendl won in straight sets.*
5 V-PASS In a knockout tournament, when sports players or teams **are seeded** at a particular level, they are ranked according to their ability to play the game. *The Canadian Helen Kelesi, seeded fourth, beat Catherine Tanvier of France... Florida State Seminoles are seeded number one.* ◆ **seeded** ADJ ATTRIB *He caused an upset in the Spanish Open by defeating the seeded Australian, Ross Thorne.*

seedless /siːdləs/
ADJ A **seedless** fruit has no seeds in it. *...seedless grapes. ...seedless oranges.*

seedling /siːdlɪŋ/ **seedlings**
NC A **seedling** is a young plant grown from a seed. *The diseases cause seedlings to collapse before they reach maturity.*

seedy /siːdi/
ADJ A **seedy** person or place is untidy, shabby, and unpleasant. *...a seedy character with a cigarette between his lips. ...a seedy and rundown*

photographer's studio.

seek /siːk/ **seeks, seeking, sought;** a formal word.
1 VOorV+for If you **are seeking** something, you are trying to find and obtain it. *Thousands of people were seeking food and shelter... I was seeking the help of someone who spoke French... Books are eagerly sought for and sold on the streets.*
2 VO If someone **seeks** something such as peace, revenge, or the solution to a problem, they try to obtain it. *Thousands of Somalis sought refuge in neighbouring Ethiopia... The Home Office has unveiled plans to help victims of crime seek compensation... They declared that the two sides would seek a mutually acceptable solution... More than 139,000 people sought political asylum in Germany in 1990.*
3 V+to-INF If you **seek** to do something, you try or intend to do it. *Power stations are seeking to reduce their use of oil.*

seek out PHRASAL VERB If you **seek out** someone or something, you keep looking for them until you find them. *He vowed to seek out and punish the bombers... We're going to seek out all the information we can.*

seem /siːm/ **seems, seeming, seemed**
1 V+to-INF, V A, or V-REPORT If something **seems** to happen or if a particular state of affairs **seems** to exist, you get the impression that it happens or that it exists. *The experiments seem to prove that sugar is not good for you... There don't seem to be many people here today... He seemed to be in good health, although he was clearly exhausted... To the spectators, it seemed as if the horse tried to jump a fence that wasn't there... It seemed that everybody smoked cigarettes.*
2 VC, V A, or V+to-INF You use **seem** to say that someone or something gives the impression of having a particular quality or feature, although you are not completely sure that you are correct. *Even minor problems seem important... It seemed like a good idea... The Prince seemed a little hoarse at times, but paid tribute to the crowd... At the end of the year, Dr Mahathir's position seemed to be more secure than ever... I seem to remember that he was a fiction writer.*
3 VC, V A, or V-REPORT **Seem** is used when you are giving your opinion or attitude about something, or asking for someone else's opinion or attitude. *That would seem a sensible thing to do... Does that seem nonsense to you?... It doesn't seem as if he has much of a political future on the national level... It did seem to me that she was far too romantic.*
4 V+to-INF If you say that you cannot **seem** to do something, you mean that you have tried to do it and are unable to do it. *I can't seem to get to sleep... The Republicans and Democrats can't seem to agree... We can't seem to be able to educate our young.*

seeming /siːmɪŋ/
ADJ ATTRIB Someone's **seeming** willingness or **seeming** interest means that they appear to be willing or interested, but you are not sure whether they really are. *...his seeming willingness to participate... The cosmonaut appeared in seeming good health at a press conference.* ◆ **seemingly** SUBMODor ADV SEN *...their seemingly limitless resources... Seemingly they don't have any problems.*

seemly /siːmli/
ADJ **Seemly** behaviour, dress, and so on is appropriate in the particular circumstances, and is usually quiet and dignified; an old-fashioned word. *The italic font looks most seemly on the page. ...seemly conduct... Our task is to see that divorces are conducted in a fair and seemly fashion.*

seen /siːn/
Seen is the past participle of **see**.

seep /siːp/ **seeps, seeping, seeped**
V A If a liquid or gas **seeps** through something, it passes through it very slowly. *I used to lie awake at night watching the rain seep through the cracks.*

seer /sɪə/ **seers**
NC A **seer** is a person who tells people what will happen in the future; an old-fashioned word. *He was considered a seer and a prophet... Ignatius sees himself as a seer and philosopher.*

see-saw /ˈsiːsɔː/ **see-saws, see-sawing, see-sawed**
1 NC A **see-saw** is a playground toy for children. It consists of a long board which is balanced on a fixed part in the middle. Children play on see-saws by making the plank tilt up and down when one child sits on each end. *There is a paddling pool, a sand pit, a see-saw, and swings.*
2 V A If a situation **see-saws** from one state to another, it continually changes from one state to the other. *Over the last two months, the Gulf crisis has see-sawed between hopes of peace and fears of war... Control of territory in northern Kurdish Iraq continues to see-saw back and forth... The match see-sawed as the two players took it in turns to break each other's serve.*

seethe /siːð/ **seethes, seething, seethed**
1 V If you **are seething**, you are very angry but do not express your feelings. *I seethed with secret rage... By now David was seething... Meanwhile, lawmakers continue to seethe over the United Air's refusal to send a representative to testify.*
2 V+with If a place is **seething** with people or animals, there are a lot of them moving about in a disorganized fashion. *The streets of London seethed with a marching, cheering crowd... Beneath them was dead, dry sand seething with crabs and nematodes.*
♦ **seething** ADJ ATTRIB *...a seething mass of maggots.*

see-through
ADJ ATTRIB **See-through** clothes are made of thin cloth, so that you can see a person's body or underclothes through them. *...a see-through blouse. ...the beige see-through dress.*

segment /ˈsegmənt/ **segments**
1 NC A **segment** of something is one part of it which is considered separately from the rest. *This affects large segments of the population... The English segment of the footpath would cover five-hundred miles. ...insects with anterior head segments.*
2 NC A **segment** of a fruit such as an orange, lemon, or grapefruit is one of the sections into which it can easily be divided. *He began to batter the lemon segment with his spoon.*

segregate /ˈsegrɪgeɪt/ **segregates, segregating, segregated**
VO To **segregate** two groups or types of things means to keep them apart. *They tried to segregate pedestrians and vehicles... It's more difficult on warships to segregate combat duties... Supporters will not automatically be segregated during next year's finals.*

segregated /ˈsegrɪgeɪtɪd/
1 ADJ A **segregated** group of people is kept apart from other people belonging to a different sex, race, or religion. *He refused to play before segregated audiences.*
2 ADJ **Segregated** facilities such as schools, hospitals, transport, and so on are provided for the use of one group of people who are of the same sex, race, or religion, and no other group is allowed to use them. *...the sensitive issue of segregated beaches... A number of Asian politicians have chosen to take part in the segregated parliament. ...protests against last Wednesday's segregated elections.*

segregation /ˌsegrɪˈgeɪʃn/
NU **Segregation** is the practice of keeping apart people of different sexes, races, or religious groups. *There was a very strict system of segregation.*

Seignoret, Sir Clarence Augustus
/ˈklærəns ɔːˈgʌstəs senjəreɪ/
Sir Clarence Augustus Seignoret became President of Dominica in 1983. He was Secretary to the Cabinet from 1967 to 1977, and served as Acting President on eight occasions between 1966 and 1983. Born: 1919.

seismic /ˈsaɪzmɪk/
ADJ ATTRIB **Seismic** events happen as part of an earthquake, or as the result of an earthquake; a technical term. *A seismic shock caused the formation of a huge tidal wave. ...seismic activity... There's no adequate seismic data to determine whether more pressure is building up around the earth's crust.*

seismograph /ˈsaɪzməgrɑːf/ **seismographs**
NC A **seismograph** is an instrument for recording and measuring the strength of earthquakes. *There were several small shocks, which have been monitored by seismographs.*

seismology /saɪzˈmɒlədʒi/
NU **Seismology** is the scientific study of earthquakes; a technical term. *...using seismology to investigate the ocean floor.* ♦ **seismologist, seismologists** NC *To the seismologists, a prediction requires a clear statement of when, where, and how big the earthquake will be.*

seize /siːz/ **seizes, seizing, seized**
1 VO If you **seize** something, you take hold of it quickly and firmly. *I seized him by the collar.*
2 VO When a group of people **seize** a place, or **seize** control of it, they take control of it quickly and suddenly, using force. *The airfield had been seized by US troops... The rebels had seized control of the town.*
3 VO When someone is **seized**, they are arrested or captured. *A university professor was seized on Wednesday by three armed men.*
4 VO If you **seize** an opportunity, you take advantage of it, and do something that you want to do. *Derrick seized the chance and went to Spain.*

seize on or **seize upon** PHRASAL VERB If you **seize on** something or **seize upon** it, you show great interest in it, often because it is useful to you. *This was one of the points that I seized upon with some force. ...seizing on it as an excuse for a rest period.*

seize up PHRASAL VERB 1 If a part of your body **seizes up**, it suddenly becomes too painful to move, because you have strained it. *Your back may seize up.* 2 You can also say something such as an engine, machine, or system **seizes up** when it stops working altogether. *The wheel bearings may seize up, and then I'd have to fix it... Jordan continues to import oil from Iraq, without which its own economy would seize up.*

seize upon PHRASAL VERB See **seize on.**

seizure /ˈsiːʒə/ **seizures**
1 NC If there is a **seizure** of drugs, weapons, or stolen goods, they are taken away by the authorities. *...the seizure at Tilbury docks of three and a half tons of cannabis... It was the second arms seizure this week.*
2 NC If there is a **seizure** of power in a place, a group of people suddenly take control of the place, using force. *...the seizure of factories by the workers.*
3 NU If someone has a **seizure**, they have a sudden violent attack of illness, especially a heart attack or an epileptic fit. *...malformed blood vessels that might give rise to strokes or seizures.*

seldom /ˈseldəm/
ADV If something **seldom** happens, it happens only occasionally. *He seldom gives interviews.*

select /sɪˈlekt/ **selects, selecting, selected**
1 VO If you **select** something, you choose it. *So which products did you select?... They've selected February the 25th for the contest in Las Vegas.* ♦ **selected** ADJ ATTRIB *We were shown carefully selected places during our visit.*
2 ADJ **Select** means considered to be among the best of its kind. *They are members of a select band of professional athletes.*

selection /sɪˈlekʃn/ **selections**
1 NU **Selection** is the act of choosing one or more things or people from a group for a particular purpose. *The selection has begun of about five thousand delegates to next month's special conference... She stood little chance of selection.*
2 NC A **selection** of people or things is a set of them chosen from a larger group. *The orchestra was playing a selection of tunes from the Merry Widow.*
3 N SING The **selection** of goods in a shop is the range of goods available. *...London's largest selection of office furniture.*

selective /sɪˈlektɪv/
1 ADJ ATTRIB A **selective** process involves choosing particular people or things. *...the selective education of the most talented children... This has been achieved without selective breeding.* ♦ **selectively** ADV *Trees are felled selectively.*
2 ADJ When someone is **selective**, they choose very carefully what they do, say, or buy. *They are particularly selective in their television watching...*

There's a lot of money, and they're going to have to be selective... The Church must be careful not to fall into the trap of selective moralising. ♦ **selectively** ADV A film crew was selectively filming broken windows of shops owned by white people.

selector /sɪlɛktə/ **selectors**

1 NC A **selector** is one of a group of people who choose the members of a sports team. The selectors chose to leave him out... I consulted the other selectors for their views.

2 NC A **selector** is also a device that enables you to choose something, or that chooses it for you. In Germany, TV sets have selectors for thirteen different channels.

self /sɛlf/ **selves**

1 NC+POSS Your **self** is your basic personality or nature, considered in terms of what you are like as a person. By evening she was her normal self again... She cut herself off forever from her true self.

2 N SING or NU A person's **self** is the essential part of their nature which makes them different from other people; a formal use. Within each person there are two people, the conscious self and the unconscious self. ...Freud's theory of self.

self- /sɛlf-/

PREFIX **Self-** combines with nouns to form new nouns or with past and present participles to form adjectives. Words formed in this way describe something that people or things do to or by themselves. For example, 'self-government' is the government of a country by its own people rather than by another country. With self-management more people really take part... He's a very successful self-publicist.

self-addressed

ADJ A **self-addressed** envelope is one that you write your address on and send to someone in another envelope with your letter so that they can send something back to you. I enclose a stamped self-addressed envelope for your reply.

self-adhesive

ADJ Something that is **self-adhesive** is covered on one side with a sticky substance like glue, so that it will stick to surfaces. ...the self-adhesive backing sticks firmly to skin.

self-appointed

ADJ A **self-appointed** leader or ruler has assumed the position of leader or ruler without anyone else asking them or choosing them to have it. ...the self appointed leader of the Nationalist Movement. ...the self-appointed spokesperson for the whole of Africa.

self-assurance

NU Someone who has **self-assurance** shows confidence in the things that they say and do because they are sure of their abilities and they are not afraid. His monumental self-assurance was based upon his complete faith in his own ability.

self-assured

ADJ Someone who is **self-assured** shows confidence in what they say and do. The Prime Minister appeared less self-assured than usual.

self-catering

N+N **Self-catering** accommodation is intended for people who provide their own food. ...self-catering flats for students.

self-centred

ADJ Someone who is **self-centred** is only concerned with their own wants and needs. He was much too self-centred to notice her.

self-confessed

ADJ ATTRIB **Self-confessed** is used to describe someone who admits openly that they have a particular characteristic which is considered to be bad. ...a self-confessed mass-murderer.

self-confidence

NU If you have **self-confidence**, you behave confidently because you feel sure of your abilities or worth. We began to lose our self-confidence... The ruling party is exuding self-confidence.

self-confident

ADJ Someone who is **self-confident** behaves confidently because they feel sure of their abilities or worth. She

was remarkably self-confident for her age.

self-conscious

ADJ Someone who is **self-conscious** is easily embarrassed and worried about what other people think of them. I stood there, feeling self-conscious. Was my hair out of place?

self-contained

1 ADJ Something that is **self-contained** is complete and separate and does not need help or resources from outside. ...a society of immense power, self-contained and well organized... Each group of species has its own self-contained eco-system... The mobile clinic is self-contained, so we don't actually have to be connected to the towing vehicle.

2 ADJ A **self-contained** flat has all its own facilities including a kitchen and bathroom. Her accommodation was a self-contained flat, and it was clear that she and her son were the only occupants.

self-control

NU Your **self-control** is your ability to control your feelings and appear calm, even when you feel angry or afraid. He lost his self-control and cried aloud.

self-controlled

ADJ Someone who is **self-controlled** is able to control their feelings so that they appear calm, even when they feel very angry or afraid. She appeared calm and self-controlled in the face of the disaster.

self-defeating

ADJ A plan or action that is **self-defeating** is likely to cause problems or difficulties instead of producing any useful results. He denounced the campaign as destructive and self-defeating... The paper describes the takeover as short-sighted and self-defeating.

self-defence; spelt **self-defense** in American English.

1 NU **Self-defence** is the use of violence or special physical skills to protect yourself against someone who attacks you. He had struck her in self-defence.

2 If you say something **in self-defence**, you give reasons for your behaviour to someone who thinks you have behaved wrongly. 'I didn't want to go anyway,' he grumbled in self-defence.

self-denial

NU **Self denial** is the habit of refusing to do or have things that you would like, either because you cannot afford them or because you believe it is morally good for you not to do them or have them. They were urged to dedicate Friday as a day of fasting and self-denial.

self-determination

1 NU **Self-determination** is the right of a country to be independent instead of being controlled by a foreign country, and to choose its own form of government. Only national self-determination within a framework of parliamentary democracy would be acceptable.

2 NU **Self-determination** also refers to the power of individuals to make important decisions themselves without being influenced by others. He believed in the self-determination, natural equality and freedom of individuals.

self-discipline

NU **Self-discipline** is the ability to control yourself and to make yourself work hard or behave in a particular way without needing anyone else to tell you what to do. They approve of the independence and self-discipline which develops within a large family.

self-drive

ADJ ATTRIB A **self-drive** car or van is one which you hire and drive yourself. He called in to order a self-drive hire car for the following morning.

self-educated

ADJ People who are **self-educated** have learnt a skill by themselves rather than being taught it formally by someone else such as a teacher at school. For a self-educated writer I think his work shows remarkable talent.

self-effacing

ADJ If you are **self-effacing**, you are modest and do not like talking about yourself or drawing attention to yourself. Gielgud is also generous and self-effacing with his fellow actors.

self-employed

ADJ If you are **self-employed**, you organize your own

work, pay, and taxes, rather than being employed by
someone who pays you regularly. ...*a self-employed
builder and decorator.*

self-esteem
NU If you have **self-esteem**, you feel that you are a
good, worthwhile person, and so you behave
confidently. *He wanted to regain his self-esteem.*

self-evident
ADJ A fact or situation that is **self-evident** is so obvious
that there is no need for proof or explanation. *The
answers to moral problems are not self-evident.*

self-explanatory
ADJ Something that is **self-explanatory** is clear and
easy to understand without needing any extra
information or explanation. *That phrase is self-
explanatory.*

self-expression
NU A person's **self-expression** is the expression of their
own personality, feelings, or opinions, for example
through a creative activity such as drawing or
dancing. *I do so admire your superb gift of self-
expression. ...opportunities for political self-expression.*

self-financing
ADJ A plan, project, or business that is **self-financing** is
not dependent on anyone else to provide money for it.
*He has told factories to be self-financing, drawing their
profits from sales... The project will be entirely self-
financing—if it fails to generate money, the authorities
will not help out.*

self-governing
ADJ A **self-governing** country or organization is
governed or run by its own members rather than by
another country or organization. *They talked of
establishing a self-governing Commonwealth... The
Government says hospitals should become self-
governing.*

self-government
NU **Self-government** is government of a country by its
own people rather than by others. *In Parliament he
called for the democratic self-government of the
colonies.*

self-help
NU **Self-help** consists of people providing support and
help for each other in an informal way, rather than
relying on the authorities or other official
organizations. *Small groups coming together for self-
help have enabled people to avoid becoming
institutionalized... Single parents join self-help groups
for social life and mutual help.*

self-important
ADJ Someone who is **self-important** behaves in a way
which shows that they believe they are more
important than other people. *He coughed and
hummed in a self-important way.*

self-imposed
ADJ A **self-imposed** task, responsibility, or situation is
one that you have deliberately accepted for yourself.
*...troubles that were largely self-imposed... He is living
in self-imposed exile.*

self-indulgence
NU **Self-indulgence** is the act of allowing yourself to
have or do the things that you enjoy; used showing
disapproval. *Temptations to self-indulgence should be
resisted.*

self-indulgent
ADJ If you are **self-indulgent**, you allow yourself to
have or do things that you enjoy very much; used
showing disapproval. *We are, by and large, idle, self-
indulgent and lacking in public spirit.*

self-inflicted
ADJ A **self-inflicted** wound or injury is one that you
cause to yourself deliberately. *Another six people are
said to have died from self-inflicted injuries.*

self-interest
NU **Self-interest** is the attitude of always wanting to do
what is best for yourself. *Are they influenced by duty
or self-interest?*

self-interested
ADJ If you are **self-interested**, you always want to do
what is best for yourself rather than for anyone else.
*They've managed to agree on the ceasefire for self-
interested reasons on either side.*

selfish /sɛlfɪʃ/
ADJ If you are **selfish**, you care only about yourself,
and do not want to share things with other people.
*Many people think the British are more selfish and
less happy than they used to be. ...a totally selfish
attitude.* ◆ **selfishly** ADV *Why is he acting so
selfishly?* ◆ **selfishness** NU *He felt ashamed of his
selfishness.*

selfless /sɛlfləs/
ADJ A **selfless** person considers other people's needs
rather than their own. *It was impossible to repay
years of selfless devotion.*

self-made
ADJ ATTRIB **Self-made** people have become successful
and rich through their own efforts. *...a self-made
woman who has risen entirely on her own merits.*

self-opinionated
ADJ Someone who is **self-opinionated** believes firmly
that their own opinions and ideas are always right,
and refuses to admit that they might be wrong.
*Certainly an aggressive or self-opinionated boy will
need to be able to stick up for himself.*

self-perpetuating
ADJ A **self-perpetuating** system or organization is
organized or structured so that it can continue to
function or exist, even when people try to change it.
*The judiciary must rid itself of its image as a self-
perpetuating club of elderly men... For two millennia,
China was ruled by a self-perpetuating elite of civil
servants... The system eventually became self-
perpetuating, the means gradually predominating over
the end towards which they were directed.*

self-pity
NU **Self-pity** is a feeling of unhappiness and depression
that you have about yourself and your problems,
which is often unnecessary or greatly exaggerated.
*She should do something to help instead of indulging in
all that self-pity... She writes of her time in the
concentration camp without self-pity.*

self-portrait, self-portraits
NC A **self-portrait** is a drawing, painting, or written
description that you do of yourself. *...an exhibition of
Rembrandt's self-portraits.*

self-possessed
ADJ If you are **self-possessed**, you are calm and
confident and in control of your emotions. *Anne is a
pleasant, self-possessed girl of eighteen.*

self-possession
NU **Self-possession** is the quality of being calm and
confident and in control of your emotions. *She acted
with the most extraordinary self-possession.*

self-preservation
NU **Self-preservation** is the instinctive behaviour that
makes you keep yourself safe from injury or death in
a dangerous situation. *I have a strong instinct for
self-preservation.*

self-raising flour
NU **Self-raising flour** is flour that contains baking
powder to make it rise easily. You use self-raising
flour for baking cakes. *...4 oz. self-raising flour sifted
with a pinch of salt.*

self-reliance
NU **Self-reliance** is the ability to do things and make
decisions by yourself, without needing other people to
help you. *One needed an unusual degree of self-
reliance to cope... The Prime Minister called for more
economic self-reliance.*

self-respect
NU **Self-respect** is a feeling of confidence and pride in
your own ability and worth. *I'd lost all my self-
respect... Any man with self-respect would have
resigned.*

self-respecting
1 ADJ A **self-respecting** person has self-respect. *...a
mature, self-respecting citizen.*
2 ADJ ATTRIB **Self-respecting** is used to describe a
particular type of person when you are saying that
something must definitely be done or owned by people
who want to be considered as this type of person. *All
self-respecting feminists have seen this film... No self-
respecting oil tycoon has fewer than two helicopters.*

self-righteous

ADJ Someone who is **self-righteous** is convinced that they are right in their beliefs and attitudes and that other people are wrong. *Few of us, I suspect, can afford to feel self-righteous.* ◆ **self-righteousness** NU *...a strong note of self-righteousness in his voice.*

self-sacrifice

NU **Self-sacrifice** is the giving up of what you want so that other people can have what they need. *The children's education demanded effort and self-sacrifice.*

self-sacrificing

ADJ Someone or something that is **self-sacrificing** shows self-sacrifice. *The opera puts the spotlight on the self-sacrificing heroic peasant.*

self-same

ADJ ATTRIB You use **self-same** when you want to emphasize that the person or thing mentioned is exactly the same as the one mentioned previously. *This was the self-same woman I'd met on the train.*

self-satisfaction

NU **Self-satisfaction** is the feeling you have when you are self-satisfied. *His expression of self-satisfaction was almost grotesque.*

self-satisfied

ADJ If someone is **self-satisfied**, they are so pleased about their achievements or their situation that they do not feel there is any need to do anything more. *...a self-satisfied political elite.*

self-seeking

1 ADJ If you are **self-seeking**, you are interested only in doing things which give you an advantage over other people. *Most of her colleagues are intolerant, self-seeking and shallow.*
2 NU **Self-seeking** is behaviour which shows you are interested only in doing things which give you an advantage over other people. *He is driven by ambition and self-seeking.*

self-service

ADJ A **self-service** shop, restaurant, garage, and so on is one where you serve yourself. *The price at the self-service pumps went up to almost 1.25 dollars a gallon.*

self-starter, self-starters

1 NC A **self-starter** is an electric device that starts a car engine. *They climbed into the car, and Antony pressed the self-starter. Nothing happened.*
2 NC A **self-starter** is someone who is prepared to work hard without much supervision, especially in business or commerce. *Here's an advert for 'an ambitious young self-starter'.*

self-styled

ADJ ATTRIB **Self-styled** is used to describe someone who claims to have a particular title but does not actually have any right to this title. *He is the self-styled president of the island.*

self-sufficiency

NU **Self-sufficiency** is the state of being self-sufficient. *We have achieved self-sufficiency in coal and gas.*

self-sufficient

ADJ If a country, group, or person is **self-sufficient**, they are able to produce or make everything that they need. *This country is self-sufficient in energy supplies.*

self-supporting

ADJ A **self-supporting** company, scheme, and so on earns enough money to continue without needing financial help from anyone else. *The plan was for British Rail to become self-supporting.*

self-taught

ADJ If you are **self-taught**, you have learnt a skill by yourself rather than being taught it formally by someone else such as a teacher at school. *The mathematician, a poor clerk from Madras, was entirely self-taught.*

self-willed

ADJ If you are **self-willed**, you are determined to do the things that you want to do and will not take advice from other people; used showing disapproval. *Young Tony, like so many children, was self-willed and quick to anger.*

sell /sɛl/ sells, selling, sold

1 VOO If you **sell** something, you let someone have it in return for money. *I hope to sell the house for £60,000... He is going to sell me his car.*
2 VO If a shop **sells** a particular thing, it has it available for people to buy. *Do you sell flowers?*
3 V+*for* or *at* If something **sells** for a particular price, or **sells** at that price, it is offered for sale at that price. *These little books sell for 95p each. ...a pocket calculator selling at the same price.*
4 V If something **sells**, it is bought in fairly large quantities. *Their revolutionary jet did not sell well.*
5 VO Something that **sells** a product makes people want to buy the product. *Scandal and gossip is what sells newspapers.*
6 V-REFL If you **sell yourself**, you present yourself in a way which makes people have confidence in you and your abilities. *You've got to sell yourself in the interview.*

sell off PHRASAL VERB If you **sell** something **off**, you get rid of it by selling it, usually because you need the money. *He had to sell his cattle off at derisory prices.*

sell out PHRASAL VERB 1 If a shop is **sold out** of something or **has sold out** of it, it has sold it all and there is none left. *They've sold out of bread.* 2 If a performance of a play, film, or other entertainment is **sold out**, all the tickets have been sold. *Their American tour is already sold out.*

sell up PHRASAL VERB If you **sell up**, you sell everything that you have, such as your house or your business, because you need the money. *It was littered with debris, like a vacant shop when the owners have sold up and gone.*

sell-by date, sell-by dates

1 NC The **sell-by date** of a food product is a date marked on the package. The food must be sold by that date to make sure that it will still be fresh and safe to eat when it is bought. *Some of the eggs had been in stock for a long time and were well past any sell-by date.*
2 Someone or something that is **past their sell-by date** is old, and no longer interesting, important, or relevant; an informal expression. *Many biographies are about minor royals, wrinkly media stars and politicians past their sell-by dates... Once women have decided a relationship is past its sell-by date, they are capable of ending it without further ado.*

seller /sɛlə/ sellers

NC A **seller** is a person or business that sells something. *...street traders and cigarette sellers.*
● See also best-seller.

selling point, selling points

NC A **selling point** is a quality or feature that something or someone has which makes it likely that people will want to buy it or employ them. *The car's main selling point is its originality... Your experience of teaching is certainly a selling point.*

sellotape /sɛlə(ʊ)teɪp/ sellotapes, sellotaping, sellotaped

1 NU **Sellotape** is a transparent sticky tape that is sold in rolls and is used for sticking together things such as paper and cardboard; **Sellotape** is a trademark. *I tried to stick the sign back on with Sellotape.*
2 VO If you **sellotape** something, you mend, fasten, or stick it together using sellotape. *I sellotaped the note to his door.*

sell-out, sell-outs

1 N SING If a play, film, or sports event is a **sell-out**, all the tickets for it have been sold. *Their concert was a sell-out.*
2 NC If you describe someone's behaviour as a **sell-out**, you mean that they have betrayed you, especially in order to gain an advantage or benefit; an informal use. *The agreement was seen as sell-out.*

selves /sɛlvz/

Selves is the plural of **self**.

semantic /sɪmæntɪk/ semantics

1 ADJ **Semantic** is used to describe something which concerns the meaning of words and sentences; a formal use. *...semantic confusions... This argument is largely a semantic one.*
2 NU **Semantics** is the branch of linguistics that deals with meaning in language; a technical use in linguistics. *My first lecture was on 'Syntax and Semantics'.*

semaphore /sɛməfɔː/
NU **Semaphore** is a system of sending messages by using two flags. One flag is held in each hand and the arms are moved to various positions representing different letters of the alphabet. *The information was sent by semaphore.*

semblance /sɛmbləns/
N SING+*of* If there is a **semblance** of a particular condition or quality, it appears to exist, even though this may be a false impression; a formal word. *By this time some semblance of order had been established.*

semen /siːmən/
NU **Semen** is the liquid containing sperm produced by the sex organs of men or male animals. *There's a feeling that all bodily products are impure, and this includes urine, blood, semen, and defecation. ...canisters labelled 'bull semen'.*

semester /sɪmɛstə/ **semesters**
NC In colleges and universities in the United States, a **semester** is one of the two periods into which the year is divided. *At the end of the semester, she withdrew from college... I completely flunked the first semester of fourth grade.*

semi /sɛmi/ **semis**
NC A **semi** is the same as a **semi-detached** house; an informal word. *We have a semi in Acton.*

semi- /sɛmi-/
PREFIX **Semi-** combines with nouns and adjectives to form new nouns and adjectives that describe someone or something as being partly, but not completely, in a particular state. *We sat in the semi-darkness. ...semi-skilled workers.*

semibreve /sɛmibriːv/ **semibreves**
NC In music, a **semibreve** is a note that has a time value equal to four crotchets.

semicircle /sɛmisɜːkl/ **semicircles**
NC A **semicircle** is one half of a circle. *We sat in a big semicircle round Hunter's desk.*

semicircular /sɛmisɜːkjʊlə/
ADJ Something that is **semicircular** has the shape of a semicircle. *...the inner ear bones, near what's known as the semi-circular canals... The design uses a semicircular arc of light.*

semi-colon /sɛmi-kəʊlən/ **semi-colons**
NC A **semi-colon** is the sign (;) which is used in writing to separate parts of a sentence or to indicate a pause. *I once had an argument over putting a semi-colon into one of his long sentences.*

semiconductor /sɛmikəndʌktə/ **semiconductors**
NC A **semiconductor** is a substance used in electronics whose ability to conduct electricity increases with greater heat. *It is vital now for scientists to learn all they can about the new carbon-based semiconductors.*

semi-conscious
ADJ If someone is **semi-conscious**, they are not fully conscious. *For the last weeks of his illness, he has been in a semi-conscious state.*

semi-detached
ADJ A **semi-detached** house is a house joined to another house on one side by a shared wall. *...his small semi-detached house in King's Road.* ► Also N SING *They have a small semi-detached.*

semi-final, semi-finals
NC A **semi-final** is one of the two matches in a competition played to decide who will compete in the final. *He lost in the semi-final to Todd Nelson... Argentina beat Italy in the World Cup semi-finals.*

semi-finalist, semi-finalists
NC A **semi-finalist** is a player or team who is competing in a semi-final. *The Wimbledon semi-finalist Goran Ivanisevic defeated Marc Rosset in five sets.*

semi-modal, semi-modals
NC The **semi-modals** are the verbs 'dare', 'need', and 'used to'. They can be used like the modal verbs, in which case they do not inflect and are followed by the base form of the verb. 'Dare', and 'need' can also be used as ordinary verbs.

seminal /sɛmɪnl/
ADJ A **seminal** book, work, film, and so on is one that has a great influence in a particular field; a formal

word. *Anthony Crosland's 'The Future of Socialism' in 1956 was seminal... This experience was to have a seminal influence on his own political development.*

seminar /sɛmɪnɑː/ **seminars**
1 NC A **seminar** is a meeting where a group of people discuss a problem or topic. *He was speaking at a seminar devoted to disarmament questions.*
2 NC A **seminar** is also a class at a university in which the teacher and a small group of students discuss a topic. *I read a few passages out in our seminar, and everyone laughed. ...nightly seminars.*

seminary /sɛmɪnəri/ **seminaries**
NC A **seminary** is a college where priests are trained. *...his early education at a French seminary.*

semiotics /sɛmiɒtɪks/
NU **Semiotics** is the study of human communication, especially communication using signs and symbols; a technical term in linguistics. *Readers unfamiliar with post-Sassurian semiotics may want to skip this chapter.*

semi-precious
ADJ ATTRIB **Semi-precious** stones are stones such as opals and turquoises that are used in jewellery. They are less valuable than precious stones such as diamonds and sapphires. *The walls were studded with semi-precious stones.*

semiquaver /sɛmikweɪvə/ **semiquavers**
NC In music, a **semiquaver** is a note that has a time value equal to a quarter of a crotchet. *The symphony is in quaver and semiquaver beats.*

Semitic /səmɪtɪk/
1 ADJ ATTRIB The **Semitic** languages are a group of languages that include Arabic and Hebrew. *...the root structure of the Semitic languages. ...Comparative Semitic Grammar.*
2 ADJ **Semitic** people belong to one of the groups of people who speak a Semitic language. *...people of Semitic origin. ...the Semitic Phoenicians.*
3 ADJ **Semitic** is sometimes used to mean Jewish. *I came to the conclusion that her beauty was seen through Semitic eyes.* ● See also **anti-Semitic**.

semitone /sɛmitəʊn/ **semitones**
NC A **semitone** is the smallest interval between two notes in Western music. Twelve semitones are equal to one octave. *...moving down the scale in semitones.*

semolina /sɛməliːnə/
NU **Semolina** consists of small hard grains of wheat that are used for making foods such as spaghetti and macaroni and for making sweet puddings with milk. *Supplies of basics such as flour and semolina are available in the shops. ...semolina pudding.*

Senate /sɛnət/
N PROP The **Senate** is the smaller and more important of the two councils in the government of some countries, such as the United States of America. *This proposal was approved by both the House and the Senate.*

senator /sɛnətə/ **senators**
NC or TITLE A **senator** is a member of a Senate. *The letter was signed by sixty-six senators. ...Senator Edward Kennedy.*

send /sɛnd/ **sends, sending, sent**
1 VOA, VOO, or VO When you **send** something to a person or place, you arrange for it to be taken and delivered to that person or place, for example by post. *The Queen has sent messages of sympathy to their families... A lot of the food is put into containers and sent abroad... I promised I would send her the money... The letter was sent on Wednesday night.*
2 VOA or VO If you **send** someone somewhere, they go there because you have told them or arranged for them to go. *Could you send someone round to fix the washing machine?... The Foreign Minister was sent to Brussels... They have said that they will send troops as part of a UN force... The neighbouring republic of Georgia has also sent medical teams.*
3 VOA or VO+ING If something **sends** things or people in a particular direction, it causes them to move in that direction. *The floods and landslides sent raging torrents of mud and water into the city area... The noise sent them racing towards the bush.*
4 VO If you **send** an electronic signal or message, you

cause it to go to a place by means of radio waves or some other electronic system. *An American warship was heard sending a radio message to the Sassan oilfield... The satellites send us back cloud pictures.*
send for PHRASAL VERB 1 If you **send for** someone, you ask them to come and see you, by sending them a message. *She sent for a doctor... We'd better send for the police.* 2 If you **send for** something or **send off for** it, you write and ask for it to be sent to you. *Send for the nomination forms before it's too late... I'll send off for them next week.*
send in PHRASAL VERB If you **send in** a report or an application, you send it to a place where it will be officially dealt with. *I was expected to send in a written report every two months.*
send off PHRASAL VERB 1 If you **send off** a letter or parcel, you send it somewhere by post. *You fill in both parts of the form, then send it off.* 2 If a player is **sent off** in a game of football, he or she is made to leave the field as a punishment for seriously breaking the rules. *He was sent off for using foul language in a match last Sunday.*
send off for PHRASAL VERB See **send for.**
send out PHRASAL VERB 1 If you **send out** something such as letters or leaflets, copies of them are delivered to several different people. *We sent out a leaflet to every household. ...sending out questionnaires to 34,000 doctors.* 2 If a machine **sends out** sound or light, it causes sound or light to travel in a particular direction. *...a small but powerful searchlight capable of sending out a flashing beam... An automatic radio beacon capable of sending out a continuous signal was to be switched on.*
send up PHRASAL VERB If you **send** someone or something **up**, you imitate them in a way that makes them appear foolish; an informal expression. *He walked behind me to send me up for the amusement of the passers-by.* ● See also **send-up.**
sender /sendə/ **senders**
NC The **sender** of a letter, parcel, and so on is the person who sent it. *The sender's name and address should be written on the back.*
sending-off, sending-offs
NC A **sending-off** in a game of football occurs when a player is made to leave the field as a punishment for seriously breaking the rules. *A.C. Milan were clearly hampered by the sending-off of their key striker Pier Paolo Virdis.*
send-off, send-offs
NC A **send-off** is an occasion when people come together to say goodbye to someone who is starting a journey or going away to live in another place; an informal word. *They were given a rousing send-off by thousands of Angolans as they flew out of the capital.*
send-up, send-ups
NC A **send-up** is a piece of writing or acting in which a person or practice is imitated in a way that makes them appear foolish in order to amuse other people; an informal word. *The final episode is a send-up of the film 'It's a Wonderful Life'... He made a name for himself with his comic send-ups of girls' school stories.*
Senegal /senɪgɔːl/
The **Republic of Senegal** is a country in western Africa. It was a French colony from the 17th century to 1960. Abdou Diouf, of the Socialist Party (PS), became President in 1981. Habib Thiam (PS) became Prime Minister in 1991. Senegal exports fish, groundnuts, sugar cane, cotton, phosphates, and salt. Poor recent harvests have contributed to worsening social and economic conditions. Large foreign debts are a major economic problem. Senegal is a member of the Organization of African Unity. ◆ **Senegalese** /senɪgəliːz/ N, ADJ
▪ *per capita GNP:* US$630 ▪ *religion:* Islam (mainly Sunni) ▪ *language:* French (official) ▪ *currency:* CFA franc ▪ *capital:* Dakar ▪ *population:* 7 million (1988) ▪ *size:* 196,722 square kilometres.
senile /siːnaɪl/
ADJ If old people become **senile**, they become confused or mentally ill and are unable to look after themselves. *The old lady was now half blind and nearly senile.* ◆ **senility** /sənɪləti/ NU *Sheila became*

increasingly affected by senility.
senior /siːniə/ **seniors**
1 ADJ The **senior** people in an organization have the highest and most important jobs in it. *Britain's senior police officers have rejected the idea of setting up a national riot squad... The Defence Minister and his senior staff met to discuss the events of the past few days.* ▶ Also NC *His seniors, however, were not amused.*
2 N SING+POSS Someone who is your **senior** is older than you are. *She was at least fifteen years his senior.*
3 NC In the United States, a **senior** is a student in the last year of a high school or university course. *The seniors are writing research papers.*
4 ADJ In the United States, a student's **senior** year is the final year of their high school or university course. *...the end of his senior year in high school.*
5 See also **Snr.**
senior citizen, senior citizens
NC A **senior citizen** is a person who is old enough to receive an old-age pension. *...free bus travel for senior citizens.*
seniority /siːnɪɒrəti/
NU A person's **seniority** in an organization is their degree of importance and power compared to other people. *The report listed their names in order of seniority.*
sensation /senseɪʃn/ **sensations**
1 NU+SUPP **Sensation** is your ability to feel things physically, especially through your sense of touch. *The finger lost all sensation... I had severed the nerves and therefore had no sensation.*
2 NC+SUPP A **sensation** is a physical feeling. *It produces a mild burning sensation in the mouth.*
3 NC You can use **sensation** to refer to the general feeling caused by a particular experience. *It was a strange sensation to return to the school again after so long.*
4 NC If an event or situation is a **sensation**, it causes great excitement or interest. *The discovery was hailed as the scientific sensation of the century.*
sensational /senseɪʃənəl/
1 ADJ Something that is **sensational** is remarkable and causes great excitement and interest. *...the most sensational result of any election since the war.*
2 ADJ A newspaper report or television or radio broadcast that is **sensational** presents the facts in a way that is intended to produce strong feelings of shock, anger, or excitement; used showing disapproval. *He described media reports of the famine as 'sensational' and 'without foundation'... He also outlines his own technique for buying sensational stories.*
3 ADJ You can describe something as **sensational** when you think that it is extremely good. *That was a sensational evening.* ◆ **sensationally** SUBMOD *Edith Evans was sensationally good.*
sensationalism /senseɪʃənəlɪzəm/
NU **Sensationalism** is the presentation of facts in a way that is intended to produce strong feelings of shock, anger, or excitement; used showing disapproval. *Many people were affronted by the Post's resort to sensationalism and scandal... She rejected what she called 'vulgar tabloid sensationalism'... He accused him of being a spy, lying, and sensationalism.*
sensationalist /senseɪʃənəlɪst/ **sensationalists;** used showing disapproval.
1 NC A **sensationalist** is someone who makes a situation seem more shocking or worse than it really is. *He was a sensationalist and a showman.*
2 ADJ **Sensationalist** news reports and television and radio programmes present the facts in a way that make them seem more shocking or worse than they really are. *He blames sensationalist press reports for exaggerating the country's problems... A spokesman described Pretoria's move as sensationalist.*
sensationalize /senseɪʃənəlaɪz/ **sensationalizes, sensationalizing, sensationalized**
VO If someone **sensationalizes** a situation, they make it seem more shocking or worse than it really is; used showing disapproval. *The abortive rebellion was*

sensationalized in press reports... The media now has to defend itself from the charge that it sensationalised the whole affair... The erotic scenes are well handled and not sensationalized.

sense /sɛns/ **senses, sensing, sensed**

1 NC Your **senses** are the physical abilities of sight, smell, hearing, touch, and taste. *They all have an excellent sense of smell... The seals become lethargic and lose their sense of direction... All knowledge comes to us through our senses.*

2 VO or V-REPORT If you **sense** something, you become aware of it, although it is not very obvious. *Doctors often sense uneasiness in people... He sensed that she did not want to talk to him.*

3 N SING If you have a **sense** that something is happening or that something is true, you believe as a result of your experiences that it is happening or is true. *There's a growing sense that the power struggle in China is over... There is a sense too of wanting to see progress in the protracted debt crisis.*

4 N SING+of If you have a **sense** of something such as duty or justice, you can recognize it and you believe that it is important. *She has a strong sense of justice... The process would need careful preparation and a sense of responsibility on all sides.*

5 N SING+of You can use **sense** to say that you have a particular feeling such as freedom, guilt, excitement, and so on. *Living away from home had given her a sense of independence... I was overcome by a sense of failure. ...the sense of adventure.*

6 N SING+SUPP Someone who has a **sense** of something, for example timing or style, has a natural ability for timing or style. *A good sense of timing is important for an actor... He hasn't got much dress sense.*

7 NU **Sense** is the ability to make good judgements and to behave sensibly. *She had the good sense to realize that the plan would never work... He has excellent news sense, talking to Western correspondents as no other Soviet leader has done before... He said he hoped good sense would prevail.* ● See also **common sense**.

8 NC A **sense** of a word or expression is one of its possible meanings. *I don't like the Washington climate—in all senses of the word... There's no censorship now, at least not in the strict sense of the word... Well, it depends in what sense you mean 'a crisis'.*

● **Sense** is used in these phrases. ● If something **makes sense** or you can **make sense** of it, you can understand it. *I looked at the page but the words made no sense... You had to read it six times to make any sense of it.* ● If a course of action **makes sense**, it seems sensible. *Under these conditions it made sense to adopt labour-saving methods.* ● If you say that someone **talks sense**, you mean that what they say is sensible. *On defence matters he talked a great deal of sense.* ● If someone **has come to their senses** or **has been brought to** their **senses**, they have stopped being foolish and are being sensible again. *The country was facing its last chance to come to its senses and avoid catastrophe.* ● If you say that something is true **in a sense**, you mean that it is partly true. You say **in no sense** in order to emphasize that something is not true at all. *In a sense, I still love him... The government, in a sense, recognizes that today has been a special day... They are in no sense losers, in no way diminished... The administration has a specific purpose, and is in no sense a compromise.*

senseless /sɛnsləs/

1 ADJ A **senseless** action seems to have no meaning or purpose. *The White House called the killings a senseless act of terror.*

2 ADJ If someone is **senseless**, they are unconscious. *A heavy blow with a club knocked him senseless.*

sense of humour

1 N SING Someone who has a **sense of humour** often finds things amusing, rather than being serious all the time; used showing approval. *He lacked any sense of humour.*

2 NU Someone's **sense of humour** is the way that they are amused by certain things but not by others. *I see your sense of humour hasn't changed.*

sensibility /sɛnsəbɪləti/ **sensibilities**

1 NU or NC Someone's **sensibility** is their ability to experience deep feelings; a formal word. *...a writer of high sensibility and intelligence. ...his extraordinary sensibility to music.*

2 NC or NU **Sensibility** is a tendency that people have to be influenced or offended by the things that other people say or do. *Out of deference to Islamic sensibilities, Christmas celebrations were subdued... The article offends on the grounds of taste, morality, and religious sensibility.*

sensible /sɛnsəbl/

ADJ A **sensible** person is able to make good decisions and judgements based on reason. *It seemed sensible to move to a bigger house... I think it is a very sensible decision.* ◆ **sensibly** ADV *They sensibly concluded that this wouldn't be a good idea.*

sensitise /sɛnsətaɪz/. See **sensitize**.

sensitive /sɛnsətɪv/

1 ADJ If you are **sensitive** to other people's problems and feelings, you understand and are aware of them. *We're trying to make people more sensitive to the difficulties faced by working mothers.* ◆ **sensitively** ADV *...this well acted, sensitively directed play.*

2 ADJ If you are **sensitive** about something, it worries or upsets you. *You really must stop being so sensitive about your accent... He's very sensitive to criticism.*

3 ADJ A **sensitive** subject or issue needs to be dealt with carefully because it is likely to cause disagreement or make people upset. *This is one of the most sensitive issues that the government faces.*

4 ADJ Something that is **sensitive** to a physical force, substance, or condition is easily affected or harmed by it. *Children's bones are very sensitive to radiation. ...people with sensitive skin.*

5 ADJ A **sensitive** piece of scientific equipment is capable of measuring or recording very small changes. *...highly sensitive electronic cameras.*

sensitivity /sɛnsətɪvəti/ **sensitivities**

1 NU **Sensitivity** is the state or quality of being sensitive to other people's feelings or problems. *Her remarks showed a lack of sensitivity.*

2 NU **Sensitivity** is also the state or quality of being sensitive to a physical force, substance, or condition. *...the sensitivity of the lining of the nasal cavity.*

3 N PL A person's **sensitivities** are subjects or issues that need to be dealt with carefully because they are likely to cause disagreement or make that person upset. *Mr Bush is no stranger to the sensitivities of this particular ally... They are yet to come to an agreement because of the political sensitivities involved.*

sensitize /sɛnsətaɪz/ **sensitizes, sensitizing, sensitized**; also spelt **sensitise**.

1 VO If you **sensitize** people to a particular problem or situation, you make them aware of it; a formal use. *Hinkle has worked for years to sensitize the medical profession to the importance of this.*

2 VO If a material is **sensitized** to a physical effect such as light or touch, it is made sensitive to it. *...writing on a sensitised electronic pad.*

sensor /sɛnsə/ **sensors**

NC A **sensor** is an instrument which reacts to certain physical conditions or impressions such as heat or light, and which is used to provide information. *Some buildings are equipped with sensors to detect tremors.*

sensory /sɛnsəⁿri/

ADJ ATTRIB **Sensory** means relating to the physical senses. *With these two highly developed sensory organs it hunts at night for insects.*

sensual /sɛnsjuəl/

1 ADJ A **sensual** person shows or suggests a great liking for physical pleasures, especially sexual pleasures. *...an extravagantly sensual woman.* ◆ **sensuality** /sɛnsjuæləti/ NU *Her body shone through the cloth with sheer sensuality.*

2 ADJ Something that is **sensual** gives pleasure to your physical senses rather than to your mind. *...the subtle, sensual rhythms of the drums.* ◆ **sensuality** NU *...African gardens of strangeness and sensuality.*

sensuous /sɛnsjuəs/

ADJ Something that is **sensuous** gives pleasure to the

mind or body through the senses. *...fresh peaches, sweet, cool, and sensuous.* ◆ **sensuously** ADV *Her fingers sensuously stroked his neck.*

sent /sɛnt/
Sent is the past tense and past participle of **send**.

sentence /sɛntəns/ **sentences, sentencing, sentenced**
1 NCorNU In a law court, a **sentence** is the punishment that a person receives after they have been found guilty. *He is serving a life sentence for murder. ...offenders who misbehave during their sentence... She had been found guilty, but sentence had not yet been passed.*
2 VO When judges **sentence** someone, they state in court what their punishment will be. *Griffiths was sentenced to four years' imprisonment.*
3 NC A **sentence** is a group of words which, when they are written down, begin with a capital letter and end with a full stop. *...the opening sentence of the report... He put the phone down before she could finish the sentence.*

sentence adverb, sentence adverbs
NC In grammar, a **sentence adverb** is an adverb which comments on the whole clause or sentence rather than on a single word. Sentence adverbs usually express the speaker's or writer's personal opinion.

sententious /sɛntɛnʃəs/
ADJ Someone who is **sententious** tries to say things that sound wise and often makes judgements about moral questions; a formal word, used showing disapproval. *...sententious remarks.* ◆ **sententiously** ADV *'Well, you must persevere,' said Fanny sententiously.*

sentient /sɛntiənt, sɛnʃnt/
ADJ Something that is **sentient** is capable of experiencing sensations through the physical senses; a formal word. *...sentient creatures.*

sentiment /sɛntɪmənt/ **sentiments**
1 NUorNC A **sentiment** is an attitude, feeling, or opinion. *...anti-imperialist sentiment... These sentiments were generally echoed by other speakers at the meeting.*
2 NU **Sentiment** is an emotion such as tenderness, romance, or sadness, which influences a person's behaviour. *I'm worried that you might be doing it out of sentiment. Out of affection for me.*

sentimental /sɛntɪmɛntl/
1 ADJ A **sentimental** person or thing feels or arouses emotions such as tenderness, romance, or sadness, sometimes to an extent which is considered exaggerated or foolish. *...sentimental songs... People have become sentimental about the passing of ways and customs.* ◆ **sentimentality** /sɛntɪmɛntælətɪ/ NU *...her sentimentality about animals.*
2 ADJ **Sentimental** means relating to a person's emotions. *The ring had been her mother's and she wore it for sentimental reasons.* ◆ **sentimentally** ADV *He had become sentimentally attached to a student.*

sentinel /sɛntɪnəl/ **sentinels**
NC A **sentinel** is the same as a **sentry**; a formal word. *Sentinels were placed at all the approaches to the farm. ...sentinel duties.*

sentry /sɛntri/ **sentries**
NC A **sentry** is a soldier who guards a camp or a building. *...look-out posts where sentries kept watch.*

sentry box, sentry boxes
NC A **sentry box** is a narrow shelter with an open front in which a sentry can stand while on duty. *In the twin sentry boxes, the two troopers of the Household Regiment stand guard.*

Seoul /səʊl/
Seoul is the capital of South Korea and its largest city. Population: 9,639,000 (1985).

separable /sɛpə⁰rəbl/
ADJ If things are **separable**, they can be separated from each other. *There may be some parts which seem separable from the whole.*

separate, separates, separating, separated;
pronounced /sɛpə⁰rət/ when it is an adjective and /sɛpəreɪt/ when it is a verb.
1 ADJ If one thing is **separate** from another, the two things are apart and are not connected. *Rosa had remained separate from us, asking for a room by*

herself... *Two masses can be kept separate inside the bomb casing... These issues need to be kept separate.* ◆ **separately** ADV *What we achieve together is more important than what we can do separately.*
2 ADJ **Separate** things are individual and distinct from each other. *The sunlight caught each tiny separate hair and made it shine.* ◆ **separately** ADV *Wash each pile separately.*
3 V-RECIP If you **separate** people, things, or ideas, or if they **separate**, they are kept apart or considered individually. *In any angry discussion he would separate the opponents and soothe them... It is important to separate learning English orally from learning English by reading books... What would happen to the people if these republics started to separate?*
4 V-RECIP If something **separates** two or more people or things, or if they **separate**, they are prevented from having contact with each other. *A fence at the back of the garden separated us from the neighbours... Racial prejudice separates the two main ethnic groups... Many of the families that survived were separated... Eventually, Alaska and Antartica separated.*
5 VO A detail that **separates** one thing from another thing shows that the two things are different from each other. *Higher living standards separate the older generation from their children.*
6 VOorVOA If you **separate** a group of things, or if you **separate** it out, you divide it into different parts. *The latest work consisted of separating a sample of rats into two groups... Most schools decide to separate out their pupils into different groups according to age.*
7 V-RECIP If two or more people or things **separate**, they move away from each other after being together or connected for a time. *They talked by the gate, unwilling to separate... The two pipes separated from each other.*
8 V If a married couple **separate**, they decide to live apart. *...new laws to make it harder for couples to separate.*

separated /sɛpəreɪtɪd/
ADJ PRED Someone who is **separated** from their wife or husband lives apart from them, but is not divorced. *My wife and I are separated.*

separation /sɛpəreɪʃn/ **separations**
1 NU+SUPP The **separation** of two or more people or things is their movement away from each other or their state of being kept apart. *...the needless separation of children from their parents... The republic rejected an offer of separation from the State.*
2 NC A **separation** between two or more people is a period of time that they spend apart from each other. *Children recover remarkably quickly from a brief separation from their parents.*
3 NCorNU If a married couple have a **separation**, they decide to live apart. *Last night we talked about a separation. ...marital disruption, caused by separation.*

sepia /siːpiə/
ADJ Something that is **sepia** in colour is deep brown, like the colour of very old photographs. *On the walls of the office are turn-of-the-century sepia photographs. ...all shades of skin from black to brown to sepia to pink.*

Sept.
Sept. is a written abbreviation for 'September'. *...Wed. 19 Sept. 1990.*

September /sɛptɛmbə/
NU **September** is the ninth month of the year in the Western calendar. *...17th September 1990.*

septic /sɛptɪk/
ADJ If part of your body or a wound becomes **septic**, it becomes infected by harmful bacteria. *Cellulitis is only going to get worse without medical attention, and eventually could become septic.*

septic tank, septic tanks
NC A **septic tank** is an underground tank where faeces, urine, and other waste matter is made harmless by using a bacteria that breaks it down and decomposes it. *...effluent from septic tanks.*

sepulchre /sɛplkə/ **sepulchres;** spelt **sepulcher** in American English.
NC A **sepulchre** is a large tomb in which a dead

person is buried; a literary word. *The Church of the Holy Sepulchre is the traditional site of Christ's burial.*

sequel /siːkwəl/ **sequels**

1 NC The **sequel** to a book or film is another one which continues the story. *He starred in 'The Godfather' and in its sequel, 'The Godfather II'.*

2 NC The **sequel** to an event is something that happened after it or because of it. *There was an amusing sequel to this incident.*

sequence /siːkwəns/ **sequences**

1 NC+SUPP A **sequence** of events or things is a number of them that come one after another in a particular order. *...the strange sequence of events that led up to the murder.*

2 NCorNU A particular **sequence** is the order in which things happen or are arranged. *The paintings are exhibited in a chronological sequence... These recordings are in sequence and continuous.*

3 NC A film **sequence** is a short part of a film that shows one event or one set of actions. *What did you think of that ghastly sequence at the end?*

sequential /sɪkwenʃl/

ADJ Something that is **sequential** follows a fixed order and thus forms a pattern; a formal word. *...sequential mental processes... She wanted to find some sequential link.*

sequin /siːkwɪn/ **sequins**

NC **Sequins** are small, shiny discs that are sewn on clothes to decorate them. *...a gown made of sequins and ostrich feathers. ...sequin dresses.*

sera /sɪərə/

Sera is a plural of **serum**.

seraph /serəf/ **seraphs** or **seraphim** /serəfɪm/

NC According to the Bible, a **seraph** is one of the angels that guard God's throne.

Serekunda /serɪkʊndə/

Serekunda is the largest city in Gambia. Population: 68,000 (1983).

serenade /serəneɪd/ **serenades, serenading, serenaded**

1 VO If you **serenade** someone, you sing or play a piece of music for them. People sometimes do this outside the window of the person they love. *He serenaded her in the moonlight... We cuddled each other on the porch, serenaded by the dawn chorus of a thousand birds.*

2 NC A **serenade** is a song or piece of music that is performed outside in the evening, especially by a man under the window of a woman he loves. *He composed a serenade to a woman called Felicity.*

3 NC A **serenade** is also a piece of classical music in several parts, written for a small orchestra. *...Tchaikovsky's nostalgic 'Serenade for Strings'.*

serendipity /serəndɪpəti/

NU **Serendipity** is the natural talent that some people have for finding interesting or valuable things by chance; a formal word. *Friendship has got to be found, and it won't be found by serendipity. It has to be worked at.*

serene /səriːn/

ADJ **Serene** means calm, quiet and peaceful. *She had a naturally cheerful and serene expression. ...a serene mountain landscape.* ◆ **serenely** ADV *Her blue eyes gazed serenely into space.* ◆ **serenity** /sərenəti/ NU *I was moved by her serenity and confidence.*

serf /sɜːf/ **serfs**

NC **Serfs** were a class of people in medieval Europe who had to work on their master's land and could not leave without his permission. *He was not prepared to be treated as a serf paying homage to his lord.*

serge /sɜːdʒ/

NU **Serge** is a type of strong woollen cloth which is used to make coats, suits, trousers, or other clothes. *...dark blue serge.*

sergeant /sɑːdʒənt/ **sergeants**

1 NCorTITLE A **sergeant** is a non-commissioned officer of middle rank in the army or air force. *A class of 212 military sergeants will graduate from Fort Dix at the end of the month... The citation praises Sergeant Horne for his courageous action.*

2 NC A police **sergeant** is a police officer of the next to lowest rank. *The police team, a sergeant, a constable*

and a woman from the anti-drug squad are on patrol in the Oktober district of Moscow.

sergeant major, sergeant majors

NCorTITLE A **sergeant major** is a non-commissioned army officer of the highest rank. *...the regimental sergeant major. ...Sergeant Major Ken Harley.*

serial /sɪərɪəl/ **serials**

1 NC A **serial** is a story which is broadcast or published in a number of parts over a period of time. *They were watching the last episode of the most popular serial ever shown on Indian television.*

2 ADJ ATTRIB **Serial** killings are a number of murders that are committed by the same person at different times. *The novel is about a serial killer in Manhattan... He has worked on a number of serial murder cases.*

serialize /sɪərɪəlaɪz/ **serializes, serializing, serialized**; also spelt **serialise.**

VO If a book is **serialized**, it is broadcast or published in a number of parts. *Orwell's modern classic, '1984', has been serialized in the mass-circulation Zagreb daily.*

serial number, serial numbers

NC The **serial number** of an object is the number on it which identifies it. *...the serial number of the cheque card.*

series /sɪəriːz/; **series** is both the singular and the plural form.

1 NC A **series** of things or events is a number of them that come one after the other. *He was arrested in connection with a series of armed bank robberies. ...a series of lectures on American politics... The England batsmen made a solid start to the Test series against New Zealand.* ● See also **World Series.**

2 NC A radio or television **series** is a set of related programmes with the same title. *David Lynch's TV series 'Twin Peaks' is the front runner at tonight's Emmy Awards ceremony. ...the 1960s' TV puppet series 'Thunderbirds'.*

serious /sɪərɪəs/

1 ADJ **Serious** problems or situations are very bad and cause people to be worried. *Bad housing is one of the most serious problems in the inner cities. ...a serious illness.* ◆ **seriously** ADV *She was seriously ill.* ◆ **seriousness** NU *...the seriousness of the problem.*

2 ADJ **Serious** matters are important enough to deserve careful consideration. *It's time to get down to the serious business of the meeting... She is a serious candidate for the presidency.*

3 ADJ ATTRIB When important matters are dealt with in a **serious** way, they are given a lot of thought or consideration because they are important or difficult to understand. *The programme is a forum for serious political discussion. ...a serious newspaper.*

4 ADJ If you are **serious** about something, you are sincere about it, and not joking. *You can't be serious!... I knew that he was serious about the struggle.* ◆ **seriously** ADV *I'm seriously thinking of retiring.* ◆ **seriousness** NU *I see no reason, in all seriousness, why women should not become priests.*

5 ADJ **Serious** people are thoughtful, quiet, and slightly humourless. *She was a rather serious girl.* ◆ **seriously** ADV *He talked very seriously and solemnly about theoretical matters.*

seriously /sɪərɪəsli/

1 ADV SEN You use **seriously** when you want the person you are talking to to realize that you are not joking and that you mean what you say. *What I do think is important, quite seriously, is that people should know the facts.*

2 ADV SEN You also use **seriously** when you are surprised by what someone has said and you want to ask them if they really mean it. *You haven't seriously locked the door?*

3 If you **take** someone or something **seriously**, you believe that they are important and deserve attention. *His work was not taken seriously.*

sermon /sɜːmən/ **sermons**

NC A **sermon** is a talk on a religious or moral subject given during a church service. *The vicar preached a sermon on the importance of humility... The theme of hope dominated the Archbishop of Canterbury's* *sermon in Canterbury Cathedral.*

sermonizing /sɜmənaɪzɪŋ/; also spelt **sermonising**.
NU **Sermonizing** is the activity of giving people advice about how they should behave and what is right and wrong, although they usually do not want the advice and are annoyed or bored by it. *He has warned that there must be no interference or sermonising from others.*

serpent /sɜːpənt/ **serpents**
NC A **serpent** is a snake; a literary word. *He tells the students to open their Bibles and read with him the story of Adam and the serpent.*

serpentine /sɜːpəntaɪn/
ADJ Something that is **serpentine** is curving and winding in shape, like a snake when it moves; a literary word. *...a serpentine stream.*

Serrano Elías, Jorge /xɔːxeɪ serɑːnəʊ eliːæs/
Jorge Serrano Elías became President of Guatemala in 1991. He was President of the Council of State from 1982 to 1983. He founded the Solidarity and Action Movement (MAS) in 1986. Born: 1945.

serrated /səreɪtɪd/
ADJ ATTRIB A **serrated** blade has a row of V-shaped points along the edge, like a saw. *...serrated scissors. ...blades a foot long with serrated edges.*

serried /serɪd/
ADJ **Serried** means closely crowded together in a regular arrangement; a literary word. *The soldiers marched in serried ranks towards the depot. ...the serried red plumes of the Guards.*

serum /sɪərəm/ **serums** or **sera**
1 NCorNU A **serum** is a liquid that is taken from an animal which has become immune to a disease. It is injected into someone's blood to protect them against that disease or as an antidote to poison. *This serum was most effective against snake poison. ...an antidote of serum.*
2 NU **Serum** is the pale, watery part of your blood that contains protein. *If you spin blood, the red blood cells go to the bottom, and the clear straw-coloured liquid on the top is the serum.*

servant /sɜːvnt/ **servants**
NC A **servant** is someone who is employed to work in another person's house, for example as a cleaner or a gardener. *...a luxurious home with servants and chauffeurs... She treated her servants like slaves.*
● See also **civil servant**.

serve /sɜːv/ **serves**, **serving**, **served**
1 VOorVA If you **serve** your country, an organization, or a person, you do useful work for them. *For over thirty years, she has served the company loyally and well... He served with the army in France.*
2 VA, V+to-INF, orVO If something **serves** as a particular thing or **serves** a particular purpose, that is its use or function. *There was a long, grey building that served as a cafeteria... His refusal to answer only serves to increase our suspicions... I failed to see what purpose this could serve.*
3 VO If something **serves** people or an area, it provides them with something that they need. *There were five water taps to serve all thirty camps. ...work which will serve the community.*
4 VOorVOO If you **serve** people or if you **serve** food and drink, you give people food and drink. *When everybody had been served, the meal began... He was serving coffee... I served the children their meal.*
5 VOorV If someone **serves** customers in a shop or a bar, they provide them with what they want to buy. *Are you being served?... She spent six months serving in a shop.*
6 VO When a court **serves** a legal order on someone or **serves** them with it, it sends the order to them; a legal use. *Lonrho has served a writ on the House of Fraser... It has already served High Court writs over the handling of the money by its president.*
7 VO If you **serve** a prison sentence, you spend a period of time in jail. *He is now serving a life sentence in an Italian jail... More than three-hundred people are serving sentences for political crimes.*
8 VorVO When you **serve** in games such as tennis and badminton, you throw the ball up and hit it in order to start play. *It's my turn to serve... In his 7-6, 7-5*

victory, Dickson served 11 aces. ► Also NC *Her second serve went into the net.*
9 If you say that it **serves** someone **right** when something unpleasant happens to them, you mean that it is their own fault and you have no sympathy for them. *Western experts took an attitude of 'serves them right for stealing our technology'.*
10 See also **serving**.

serve out PHRASAL VERB When you **serve out** food, you give it to people at the beginning of a meal, or during it. *Miss Clare and I served out slices of cold meat.*

serve up PHRASAL VERB When you **serve up** food, you give it to people at the beginning of a meal. *When you want them to try something new, serve it up casually.*

service /sɜːvɪs/ **services**, **servicing**, **serviced**
1 NC+SUPP A **service** is an organization or system that provides something for the public. *I think the train service is better than it used to be. ...the postal service.*
2 NC Some government organizations are called **services**. *...the diplomatic service. ...the British intelligence service.*
3 N PL **Services** are things such as schools, hospitals, and roads that are paid for from people's taxes. *...fire, police and medical services. ...the social services.*
4 NC+SUPP A **service** is also a job that an organization or business can do for you. *The fee for this service is £6... It boosts demand for goods and services. ...service industries such as banking and finance.*
5 N PL The **services** are the army, navy, and air force. *Young people are being encouraged to join the services.*
6 N PL+POSS Your **services** are the work that you can do for people. *They will be very happy to give their services free of charge.*
7 NU **Service** is the state or activity of working for a particular person or organization. *Conscription would be limited to a maximum of six months' service.*
8 NU **Service** is also the process of being served in a shop or restaurant. *He hammered the table for immediate service... Service is not included on the bill.*
9 NU If a machine or vehicle is in **service**, it is being used or is able to be used. If it is out of **service**, it is not being used or is not able to be used. *The American tank is already in service with the US army... The reactor is currently out of service for routine maintenance... It is planned that of the 7,000 Soviet tanks to be withdrawn from service this year, 5,000 will be destroyed.*
10 VO To **service** a machine or vehicle means to examine, adjust, and clean it so that it will keep working efficiently and safely. *Gas appliances should be serviced regularly.* ► Also NC *The car needs a service.*
11 NC A **service** is also a religious ceremony, especially a Christian one. *...the Sunday evening service.*
12 NC A dinner **service** or a tea **service** is a complete set of dishes, plates, and other crockery.
13 NC A **services** is a place on a motorway where there is a garage, restaurant, shop, and toilets. The form **services** is both the singular and the plural.
14 See also **Civil Service**, **National Health Service**, **national service**.

serviceable /sɜːvɪsəbl/
ADJ Something that is **serviceable** performs its function effectively; a formal word. *I wore serviceable boots.*

service charge
N SING A **service charge** is an amount added to your restaurant bill to pay for the work of the waiter or waitress. *Prices will have to include tax and restaurants will not be allowed to spring an unmentioned service charge on customers.*

serviceman /sɜːvɪsmən/ **servicemen** /sɜːvɪsmən/
NC A **serviceman** is a man who is in the army, navy, or air force. *A United States serviceman was wounded in a bomb attack on a nightclub in Panama City.*

service station, service stations
1 NC A **service station** is a garage that sells petrol, oil, spare parts, and so on. *The price of petrol is being cut from midnight tomorrow at Jet service stations.*
2 NC A **service station** is also a place where you can stop on the motorway and where there is a garage, restaurant, shop, and toilets. *...customers at a busy motorway service station.*

service woman, service women
NC A **service woman** is a woman who is in the army, navy, or air force. *The Army and Navy are urgently considering what wider opportunities can be given to service women.*

serviette /sɜːvi̯et/ **serviettes**
NC A **serviette** is a square of cloth or paper that you use to protect your clothes or to wipe your mouth when you are eating.

servile /sɜːvaɪl/
ADJ A **servile** person is too eager to do things for someone and shows them too much respect; a formal word, used showing disapproval. *The recipients of aid should not become servile but maintain their dignity.*

serving /sɜːvɪŋ/ **servings**
1 NC A **serving** is an amount of food given to one person at a meal. *His mother was spooning out servings of tuna fish casserole.*
2 ADJ ATTRIB A **serving** spoon or dish is used for serving food. *...stacks of dinner plates and serving dishes.*

servitude /sɜːvɪtjuːd/
NU **Servitude** is the condition of being a slave or of being completely under the control of someone else; a formal word. *Workers were tricked into servitude by plantation owners.* ● See also **penal servitude**.

session /seʃn/ **sessions**
1 NCorNU A **session** is a single meeting of an official group or organization. *...an emergency session of the United Nations Security Council... The court was in session.*
2 NCorNU A **session** is also a period during which the meetings of an official group or organization are regularly held. *In the last Parliamentary session, the main government measure encountered strong opposition from some Conservative backbenchers... Every session of Parliament gets off to a frantic start as the government's plans for legislation are first announced... The five person panel will remain in session for a further month.*
3 NC+SUPP A **session** of a particular activity is a period of that activity. *When the two leaders emerged for a photo session they were smiling but refused to answer questions. ...a tough bargaining session... The police say there was a brawl following a drinking session.*
4 NCorNU A **session** is also a school or university year, or one of the terms into which it is divided; a formal use. *...disruption of academic sessions. ...now that school is back in session.*

session musician, session musicians
NC A **session musician** is a professional musician who does not belong to a particular group, but who plays for different performers at different times, especially in a recording studio. *At the time of that recording, the 21-year old trumpeter had already established himself as a leading session musician.*

set /set/ **sets, setting.** The form **set** is used in the present tense and is also the past tense and past participle of the verb.
1 NC+SUPP A **set** of things is a number of them that are considered as a group. *...a set of encyclopaedias. ...a chess set... We soon encountered a new set of problems.*
2 VOA If you **set** something somewhere, you put it there, especially in a careful or deliberate way. *He filled the kettle and set it on the stove.*
3 V-PASS-A If something is **set** in a particular place or position, it is in that place or position. *The house is set back from the road... His eyes were set close together.*
4 VO+*into*or*in* If something is **set** into a surface, it is fixed in and does not stick out. *There was one tiny*

window set into the stone wall. ...nine large panels set in a rich framework.
5 VOA,VOC,orVO+ING You can use **set** to say that a person or thing causes something to happen. *Let me set your mind at rest... One prisoner had been set free... Two further pieces of information set me questioning it all again.*
6 V When the sun **sets**, it goes below the horizon. *As the sun set, the convoy of trucks crossed the bridge over the River Tigris.*
7 VO To **set** a trap means to make it ready for use. *The Drug Enforcement Agency was allowing certain shipments to get through in order to set a trap for a drug organization.*
8 VO If you **set** the table, you put the plates and cutlery on it ready for a meal. *It's almost evening and only three tables have been set for dinner.*
9 VO If you **set** a clock or control, you adjust it to a particular point or level. *His alarm clock was set for four a.m... Set the control to the coldest setting.*
10 VO If you **set** a time, price, or level, you decide what it will be. *They haven't set a date for the wedding... The government set a minimum price of £1.15.*
11 ADJ ATTRIB You use **set** to describe something which is fixed and does not change. *We paid a set amount for the course... Her day usually followed a set pattern.*
12 VO If you **set** a precedent, standard, or example, you establish it for other people to copy or try to achieve. *Try and set the younger children a good example... They tended to follow the trend set by the other banks.*
13 VOorVOO If someone **sets** you some work or **sets** a target, they say that you must do the work or reach the target. *Let me set you a little problem... It set a target for economic growth.*
14 ADJ PRED+*to*-INF If you are **set** to do something, you are ready or likely to do it. *The left-wing seem set to do very well in the general election.*
15 ADJ PRED+*on* If you are **set** on doing something, you are determined to do it. *She is set on regaining her title.*
16 V When glue, jelly, or cement **sets**, it becomes firm. *The cement had set hard.*
17 VO+*to* If someone **sets** a poem to music, they write music for it. *'Cats' has music by Andrew Lloyd Webber set to lighthearted poems by T S Eliot.*
18 NC A television **set** is a television. *We have a TV set in the living room.*
19 NC The **set** for a play or film is the scenery or furniture that is on the stage or in the studio when the play is being performed or the scene is being filmed. *The sets and costumes are designed by Tim Goodchild.*
20 VOA If a play, film, or story is **set** at a particular time or in a particular place, the events in it take place at that time or in that place. *The play is set in a small Midlands village.*
21 NC In tennis, a **set** is one of the groups of six or more games that form part of a match. *A crowd of 14,000 enjoyed the tennis match, which Lendl won in three sets.*
22 **set in your ways:** see **way.** **to set fire to something:** see **fire.** **to set foot:** see **foot.** **to set your heart on something:** see **heart.** **to set sail:** see **sail.** **to set the stage for:** see **stage.** See also **setting.**

set about PHRASAL VERB If you **set about** doing something, you start doing it. *The next morning they set about cleaning the house.*

set against PHRASAL VERB To **set** one person **against** another means to cause them to become enemies or rivals. *As a result of this war, parent had been set against child and child against parent.*

set apart PHRASAL VERB If a characteristic **sets** you **apart** from other people, it makes you noticeably different from the others. *His exceptional height set him apart from the rest of the men.*

set aside PHRASAL VERB 1 If you **set** something **aside** for a special use or purpose, you keep it available for that use or purpose. *Try and set aside time to do some mending jobs... The Milk Marketing Board have set aside over a million pounds to fund women's sports* *events.* 2 If you **set aside** a belief, principle, or feeling, you decide that you will not be influenced by it. *We must try and set aside our past hostilities... He called for political differences to be set aside in an effort to tackle worldwide problems.*

set back PHRASAL VERB 1 To **set** someone or something **back** means to delay them. *This has set back the whole programme of nuclear power in America... The unusual cold had set them back with the painting.* 2 If something **sets** you **back** a large amount of money, it costs you that much money; an informal use. *A meal for two here will set you back the equivalent of a Hungarian's monthly salary.* 3 See also **setback**.

set down PHRASAL VERB If you **set down** your thoughts or experiences, you write them down. *They were asked to set down a summary of their views... When he retired to Britain he set down the story of his career.*

set in PHRASAL VERB If something unpleasant **sets in**, it begins and seems likely to continue or develop. *A feeling of anti-climax set in... It must be treated quickly before infection sets in... The bad weather has set in for the winter.*

set off PHRASAL VERB 1 When you **set off**, you start a journey. *He set off on a trip to Mexico.* 2 If something **sets off** an event or a series of events, it causes it to start. *Any Iraqi attack on the Jewish state will set off a vigorous US response.* 3 If you **set off** a bomb or a firework, you cause it to explode. *The police say the bomb was set off by remote control... East Berlin people drank champagne, set off fireworks and tooted their car horns.*

set on PHRASAL VERB To **set** animals **on** or **upon** someone means to cause the animals to attack them. *We were afraid they might set the dogs on us... She set his own hounds upon him.*

set out PHRASAL VERB 1 When you **set out**, you start a journey. *They set out for Cuba.* 2 If you **set out** to do something, you start trying to do it. *They had failed in what they had set out to do.* 3 If you **set** things **out**, you arrange them for people to use or display them for people to see. *There were plenty of chairs set out for the guests.* 4 If you **set out** facts or opinions, you state them in a clear, organized way. *Darwin set out his theory in 'The Origin of Species'.*

set up PHRASAL VERB 1 If you **set** something **up**, you make the necessary preparations for it to be used or for it to work. *It took a long time to set up the experiment... The government were setting up an inquiry into the affair... An anti-terrorist squad was set up.* ♦ **setting up** N SING *...the setting up of a Northern Seas Environmental Control Agency.* 2 If you **set up** a structure, you place it or build it somewhere. *A fund was launched to set up a monument in memory of the dead men.* 3 If you **set up** somewhere, you establish yourself in a new home or business. *She left her parents' home and set up on her own... He used the money to set himself up in business.* 4 If someone **sets** you **up**, they make it seem that you have done something wrong when you have not; an informal use. *...complaining about the American police who set him up.* 5 See also **set-up**.

setback /sɛtbæk/ setbacks

NC A **setback** is an event that delays you or makes your position worse than before. *The by-election result is a serious setback for the government.*

set piece, set pieces

1 NC A **set piece** is a part of a play, piece of music, or novel which has a strong dramatic effect and which is often not an essential part of the main story. *There are some marvellous set pieces... He is at his best in the great set piece scenes, like the Hall of the Mountain King.* 2 NC A **set piece** is also a military operation or a move in a football match, that has been carefully planned and is carried out in an ordered way. *Both cities were targets for a set piece offensive.*

set square, set squares

NC A **set square** is a flat piece of plastic or metal in the shape of a right-angled triangle, which is used for drawing angles and lines.

settee /sɛtiː/ settees

NC A **settee** is a long comfortable seat which has a back and arms and which two or more people can sit on. *They came along to the staff-room, plonked themselves down on the settee, and announced their presence.*

setter /sɛtə/ setters

NC A **setter** is a type of long-haired dog that can be trained to show hunters where birds and animals are.

set theory

NU **Set theory** is the part of mathematics that deals with sets.

setting /sɛtɪŋ/ settings

1 NC+SUPP The **setting** for something is its surroundings or the circumstances in which it takes place. *The castle provided the perfect setting for a horror story... Children should be cared for in a home setting.* 2 NC The **settings** on a machine are the different positions to which the controls can be adjusted.

settle /sɛtl/ settles, settling, settled

1 VO When an argument or problem is **settled**, it has been ended because an agreement has been reached. *The strike went on for over a year before it was finally settled... Both sides should also pledge not to use force to settle their disputes.* 2 VO If something is **settled**, it has all been decided and arranged. *Two of the World Cup's quarter finals have been settled.* 3 VO If you **settle** a bill, you pay it. *Officials first learned of their departure when the Romanian delegation settled their bill on Monday morning.* 4 VA When people **settle** somewhere, they start living there permanently. *He had settled in England.* 5 V A or V-REFL If you **settle** yourself somewhere or **settle** somewhere, you sit down and make yourself comfortable. *Casson took off his raincoat and settled before the fire... He settled himself beside her in the car.* 6 V If something **settles**, it sinks slowly down and becomes still. *Asbestos dust has settled over a wide area... The hull of the boat slowly settled in the mud.* 7 VA When birds or insects **settle** on something, they land on it from above. *...flies and other insects that settle on plants growing on the banks.*

settle down PHRASAL VERB 1 If you **settle down** to something, you prepare to do it and concentrate on it. *...before they settle down to university work... He had settled down to watch a sports programme.* 2 When someone **settles down**, they start living a quiet life in one place, especially when they get married or buy a house. *The main reasons given for wanting to get married are the desires to settle down and to enter into a commitment... You should get a job and settle down.* 3 If people who are upset or noisy **settle down**, they become calm or quiet. *It took her some time to settle down.* 4 If a situation **settles down**, it becomes calmer and more stable. *During the course of next year things should settle down and price rises should be back under five per cent.*

settle for PHRASAL VERB If you **settle for** something, you choose or accept it, especially when it is not what you really want but there is nothing else available. *When in doubt he settled for hamburgers.*

settle in PHRASAL VERB If you are **settling in**, you are getting used to living in a new place or doing a new job. *And how are you settling in, Mr Swallow?*

settle on PHRASAL VERB If you **settle on** a particular thing, you choose it after considering other possible choices. *Have you settled on a name for him yet?*

settle up PHRASAL VERB When you **settle up**, you pay a bill or pay someone what you owe them. *As soon as the money arrived I was able to settle up with him.*

settled /sɛtld/

1 ADJ If you have a **settled** way of life, you stay in one place rather than travelling around. *It's time Humboldt led a more dignified settled life.* 2 ADJ A **settled** system stays the same all the time. *...an easy, rich, peaceful and settled social order.* 3 ADJ If you feel **settled**, you have been living or working in a place long enough to feel comfortable. *I felt as settled as I could in such circumstances.*

settlement /sɛtlmənt/ **settlements**
1 NC A **settlement** is an official agreement between two sides who have been involved in a conflict. *The chance for a peaceful political settlement has disappeared. ...enormous wage settlements.*
2 NC A **settlement** is also a place where people have come to live and build homes. *He lives in the jungle, in a settlement by a river. The US Marines are setting up protected refugee settlements inside the border.*

settler /sɛtˀlə/ **settlers**
NC **Settlers** are people who go to live in a new country. *The first white settlers in South Africa were Dutch.*

set-to, set-tos
NC A **set-to** is a fight, especially one in which people use their fists; an informal word. *There was a bit of a set-to outside the pub.*

set-up, set-ups
NC A particular **set-up** is a particular system or way of organizing something; an informal word. *I've only been here a couple of days and I don't quite know the set-up.* ● See also set **up**.

seven /sɛvn/ **sevens**
Seven is the number 7. *Most shops and businesses will close at seven pm.* ● at sixes and sevens: see six.

seventeen /sɛvntiːn/ **seventeens**
Seventeen is the number 17. *I was seventeen years old when I enlisted.*

seventeenth /sɛvntiːnθ/
ADJ The **seventeenth** item in a series is the one that you count as number seventeen. *...October the seventeenth.*

seventh /sɛvnθ/ **sevenths**
1 ADJ The **seventh** item in a series is the one that you count as number seven. *...the seventh century AD.*
2 NC A **seventh** is one of seven equal parts of something. *In Tibet, a million people are thought to have died—a seventh of the population.*

seventieth /sɛvntiəθ/
ADJ The **seventieth** item in a series is the one that you count as number seventy. *...celebrating the seventieth anniversary of women being granted the right to vote.*

seventy /sɛvnti/ **seventies**
Seventy is the number 70. *Seventy per cent of its budget goes on education.*

sever /sɛvə/ **severs, severing, severed**
1 VO To **sever** something means to cut right through it so that one part is completely separated from the rest. *A bulldozer had severed a gas pipe... The boy's legs were severed at the hip.*
2 VO If you **sever** a relationship or connection with someone, you end it completely. *She had to sever all ties with her parents... Syria, like most Arab countries, severed all contacts with Egypt after this country signed a peace treaty with Israel in 1979.*

several /sɛvrəl/
DET, QUANT, or PRON **Several** is used to refer in an imprecise way to a number of things or people, when the number is not large but is more than two. *He returned home several hours later... The selectors have included several new faces in their tour party for New Zealand... Several of the survivors have said that the tunnel became intolerably hot... The battle for power in Panama is the biggest foreign story in Wednesday's papers, and the lead in several.*

severance /sɛvəˀrəns/; a formal word.
1 NU+SUPP Your **severance** from other people or from a place is your separation from them so that you no longer have a relationship or connection with them. *The real severance from my father came later... The ruling council announced the severance of their new relationship with Egypt.*
2 N+N **Severance** pay is money that an organization pays its employees when they are told that they can no longer work there, either because their jobs are no longer necessary or because the organization can no longer afford to pay them. *Inside the envelopes were redundancy notices and details of severance pay... They would not cede to their main demand for higher severance payments.*

severe /sɪvɪə/ **severer, severest**
1 ADJ You use **severe** to describe something which is very bad or undesirable, and which is great in extent or degree. *...a severe shortage of food... The blast caused severe damage.* ♦ **severely** ADV *A fire had severely damaged the school.* ♦ **severity** /sɪvɛrəti/ NU *...the severity of the world-wide recession.*
2 ADJ A **severe** person is stern and treats people somewhat harshly. *I hope the magistrate has not been too severe with him... He said the measures were severe and certain to be unpopular.* ♦ **severely** ADV *They were severely punished.* ♦ **severity** NU *...prison sentences of excessive severity.*

sew /səu/ **sews, sewing, sewed, sewn**
VorVO When you **sew** things together, you join them using a needle and thread. *They teach the children to cook, sew, or knit. ...sewing buttons onto one of my shirts.*

sew up PHRASAL VERB 1 If you **sew up** a piece of cloth, you join two parts of it together using a needle and thread. *You tore it so you can sew it up!* 2 If something such as a deal is **sewn up**, you have arranged things so that you are certain to be successful; an informal use. *He has got the Republican Party's nomination virtually sewn up.*

sewage /suːɪdʒ/
NU **Sewage** is waste matter from homes and factories, which flows away through sewers. *...ensuring that food and water supplies can't be contaminated by sewage... Raw sewage from nearly six million people comes down those hills into the sea.*

sewage farm, sewage farms
NC A **sewage farm** is the same as a **sewage works**.

sewage works; **sewage works** is both the singular and the plural form.
NC A **sewage works** is a place where sewage is treated so that it can be used as manure or disposed of safely. *Three billion US dollars are needed to provide a sewage works alone.*

sewer /suːə/ **sewers**
NC A **sewer** is a large underground channel that carries waste matter and rain water away. *Public service workers digging sewers recently came upon a monumental archaeological find... The terrain is surrounded by a stinking open sewer.*

sewerage /suːərɪdʒ/
1 NU **Sewerage** refers to the system that is used to take away waste matter from homes and factories. *The government is spending large sums on providing better services such as water, electricity and sewerage. ...maintaining and repairing sewerage pipes.*
2 NU **Sewerage** is also the same as **sewage**. *...sea water contaminated by sewerage.*

sewing /səuɪŋ/
1 NU **Sewing** is the activity of making or mending things using a needle and thread. *All the children are taught sewing.*
2 NU **Sewing** is also things that are being sewn. *My aunt put aside her sewing.*

sewing machine, sewing machines
NC A **sewing machine** is a machine that you use for sewing, with a needle that is driven by an electric motor, or by movements of your hand or foot. *...scraps of denim piled beside each sewing machine.*

sewn /səun/
Sewn is the past participle of **sew**.

sex /sɛks/ **sexes**
1 NCorNU The **sexes** are the two groups, male and female, into which people and animals are divided according to the function they have in producing young. *...people of both sexes. ...a member of the opposite sex. ...tests to ascertain the sex of the baby before it was born. ...to prevent discrimination on the grounds of sex.*
2 NU **Sex** is the physical activity by which people and animals can produce young. *In general, condoms were not used by those engaging in casual sex... The council takes a tougher approach to the screening of explicit sex, violence, crime and bad language... They continue to have a good sex life.* ● If two people **have sex**, they perform the physical act of sex. *A prostitute claimed she was having sex with as many as 15 men a night.*

sex appeal

NU If you say that someone has **sex appeal**, you mean that they are sexually attractive. ...*a character of tremendous sex appeal... Is sex appeal just a matter of anatomy these days?*

sex education

NU **Sex education** is education in schools on the subject of sexual activity and sexual relationships. *Just how detailed should sex education be in elementary schools?*

sexism /sɛksɪzəm/

NU **Sexism** is discrimination against the members of one sex, usually women; used showing disapproval. *The independent weekly has been accused in the past of promoting racism and sexism.*

sexist /sɛksɪst/ sexists

1 ADJ Something that is **sexist** involves sexism. ...*sexist attitudes.* ...*sexist jokes.*

2 NC A **sexist** is a person, usually a man, who has sexist attitudes. *My control over that environment is totally shattered if a male sexist walks in and says, 'Hi Honey. How's it going?'*

sexless /sɛksləs/

ADJ If you describe a person as **sexless**, you mean that they have no sexual feelings. ...*nondescript middle-aged sexless couples.*

sex object, sex objects

NC If someone, especially a woman, is considered as a **sex object**, they are considered only in terms of their physical attractiveness and not their character or abilities. ...*people who have been brought up to view women as sex objects... I don't have any hankering to be looked upon as a male sex object.*

sex shop, sex shops

NC A **sex shop** is a shop that sells products that are connected with sexual pleasure, for example magazines, video films, and special clothing and equipment. *He owns seven porn magazines and a string of sex shops.*

sextet /sɛkstɛt/ sextets

NC A **sextet** is a group of six musicians or singers who play or sing together. *He plays the drums in a jazz sextet.*

sexton /sɛkstən/ sextons

NC A **sexton** is a person whose job is to look after a church and its graveyard.

sexual /sɛksjuəl/

1 ADJ **Sexual** feelings or activities are connected with the act of sex or with desire for sex. *They were not having a sexual relationship.* ...*sexual attraction.*
♦ **sexually** ADV *I find her sexually attractive.*

2 ADJ ATTRIB **Sexual** also means relating to the differences between men and women. ...*campaigning for non-discrimination and sexual equality.*

3 ADJ ATTRIB **Sexual** is also used to refer to the biological process by which people and animals produce young. ...*sexual reproduction.* ...*the sexual cycle of the elephant.*

sexual intercourse

NU **Sexual intercourse** is the physical act of sex between a man and a woman; a formal expression. *In Britain, it is an offence to have sexual intercourse with a girl under sixteen.*

sexuality /sɛksjuæləti/

1 NU **Sexuality** is the ability that people have to experience sexual feelings, or the sexual part of their nature. ...*a work by Sigmund Freud called 'Essays on the Psychology of Sexuality'... He shocked the older generation with his raw sexuality and the defiant energy of his music.*

2 NU+POSS You also refer to a person's **sexuality** when you are talking about whether they are heterosexual, homosexual, or bisexual. *The gay rights movement prompted many homosexuals not only to be open about their sexuality, but to take pride in it.*

sexual orientation

NU If you refer to a person's **sexual orientation**, you are talking about whether they are heterosexual, homosexual, or bisexual; a formal expression. *They signed an undertaking not to discriminate between people on the grounds of sex, race, nationality, marital status or sexual orientation.*

sexy /sɛksi/ sexier, sexiest

ADJ **Sexy** means sexually exciting or sexually attractive. ...*her sexy brown eyes.*

Seychelles /seɪʃɛlz/

The **Republic of the Seychelles** is a country in the Indian Ocean, consisting of over 100 islands. It was annexed by France in the 18th century and was ceded to Britain in 1814. It became independent in 1976. France Albert René became President in a coup in 1977, and established the Seychelles People's Progressive Front (SPPF) as the only party in 1979. It is a member of the Commonwealth and the Organization of African Unity. Fish and cinnamon are exported. Tourism is an important industry.
♦ **Seychellois** /seɪʃɛlwɑː/ N, ADJ
▪ *per capita GNP:* US$3,800 ▪ *religion:* Christianity (mainly Roman Catholic) ▪ *language:* Creole (official), English, French ▪ *currency:* rupee ▪ *capital:* Victoria ▪ *population:* 68,000 (1989) ▪ *size:* 454 square kilometres.

Sgt

Sgt is a written abbreviation for 'sergeant' when it is part of someone's title. ...*Sgt Tomkins.*

sh /ʃ/

Sh is used in writing to represent the noise that you make to tell someone to be quiet. *Sh! The boys are in bed.*

shabby /ʃæbi/ shabbier, shabbiest

1 ADJ Something that is **shabby** looks old and is in bad condition. ...*his shabby clothes.* ♦ **shabbily** ADV *They were shabbily dressed.*

2 ADJ A **shabby** person is wearing old, worn clothes. ...*shabby children in the streets.*

3 ADJ **Shabby** behaviour is unfair or unacceptable. ...*a series of shabby compromises.* ♦ **shabbily** ADV *Don't you think you've treated me a little shabbily?*

shack /ʃæk/ shacks

NC A **shack** is a small hut built from bits of wood or metal. *They live in a one-room plywood shack with no electricity and no running water.*

shackle /ʃækl/ shackles, shackling, shackled

1 N PL **Shackles** are two metal rings joined by a chain which are fastened around someone's wrists or ankles to prevent them from moving or escaping. *Five young Palestinians appeared in court in shackles.*

2 VO To **shackle** someone means to put shackles on them. *The guards shackled his wrists and ankles.*

3 N PL **Shackles** are also circumstances that prevent you from doing what you want to do; a literary use. *There are a few who have managed to throw off the shackles of the past.* ...*the shackles of racial tyranny.*

4 VO If you **are shackled** by something, it prevents you from doing what you want to do; a literary use. *He is shackled by domestic responsibilities.*

shade /ʃeɪd/ shades, shading, shaded

1 NU or N SING **Shade** is an area of darkness and coolness which the sun does not reach. *There are no trees or bushes to give shade.* ...*the shade of a large oak tree... The air is cool in the shade.*

2 VO If a place **is shaded** by something, that thing prevents light from falling on it. *The broad walks are shaded by chestnut trees.*

3 NC A **shade** is a lampshade. ...*a lamp with a thick silk shade.*

4 N PL **Shades** are the same as **sunglasses**; an informal use.

5 NC In American English, **shades** are also pieces of stiff cloth or paper which you pull down over windows to keep out the light. *He pulled down the thick green shades and darkness fell on the store.*

6 NC The **shades** of a particular colour are its different forms. For example, emerald green and olive green are shades of green. ...*jackets in shades of pink, blue, and brown.*

7 NC+SUPP The **shades** of something abstract are its different forms, especially when they are only slightly different from each other. *The phrase has many shades of meaning.* ...*various shades of socialist opinion.*

8 V+into When one thing **shades** into another, there is no clear division between them; a literary use. ...*reds shading into pinks.* ...*innocence shading into ignorance.*

9 If someone or something puts someone or something else **in the shade**, they are so impressive or significant that they make the other person or thing seem unimportant by comparison. *The Pope's visit to the largely Catholic territory will likely put the rest of his visit to Indonesia in the shade.*

shading /ˈʃeɪdɪŋ/ **shadings**
1 NU The **shading** in a drawing or painting is the dark parts of it, which often make objects in the picture look three-dimensional rather than flat. *...their complexity of detail and delicacy of shading.*
2 NC+SUPP **Shadings** are very small changes or differences between things. *There are many fine shadings of status through the social hierarchy... The gardens, hedges and ground were all in muted shadings of grey, black and white.*

shadow /ˈʃædəʊ/ **shadows**
1 NC A **shadow** is a dark shape made when something prevents light from reaching a surface. *...a car parked in the shadow of a tree.*
2 NU **Shadow** is darkness caused by light not reaching a place. *The whole canyon is in shadow.*
3 ADJ ATTRIB In Britain, the **Shadow** Cabinet consists of the leaders of the main opposition party. Each Shadow Cabinet member takes a special interest in matters of a particular kind. *He is Shadow Secretary for Trade and Industry.*
4 VO If someone or something **shadows** you, they follow you very closely. *I noticed a police car shadowing us... Allied warships have been shadowing maritime transport in the Gulf since the early days of the crisis.*
5 N SING If there is not a **shadow** of doubt about something, there is no doubt about it. *The Cubans say that without a shadow of a doubt, one of the men was the former Cuban intelligence agent. ...testing the equipment to prove beyond a shadow of doubt that it had been tampered with.*
6 If you say that someone or something is **a shadow of** their **former self**, you mean that they are much less strong or vigorous than they used to be. *Several smaller unions have either amalgamated or faded into a mere shadow of their former selves... The army is determined that it should not be reduced to a shadow of its former self.*

shadowy /ˈʃædəʊi/
1 ADJ A **shadowy** place is dark and full of shadows. *...a shadowy alcove.*
2 ADJ ATTRIB A **shadowy** figure or shape is difficult to see because there is not much light. *...the shadowy musicians in the background.*
3 ADJ You describe people and activities as **shadowy** when very little is known about them, and you think that they may be dishonest or dangerous. *Some of its shadowy membership may have been involved in the coup attempt. ...the shadowy world of espionage.*

shady /ˈʃeɪdi/
1 ADJ A **shady** place is sheltered from the sun by buildings or trees. *We found a shady spot in the park to have a rest. ...waiting under the palms in the shady courtyard of the French Cultural Centre.*
2 ADJ **Shady** trees produce a lot of shade. *It was a delightful walk, under cool and shady trees.*
3 ADJ **Shady** people and activities are slightly dishonest; an informal use. *Martin portrayed the shady detective J D LaRue in the series. ...black marketeering, smuggling and other shady dealings.*

shaft /ʃɑːft/ **shafts**
1 NC A **shaft** is a vertical passage, for example in a mine or a place where a lift goes up and down. *Rescuers are trying to locate the miner missing in number three shaft... He passed the main part of the foyer, where the lift shaft was.*
2 NC A **shaft** in a machine is a rod that turns round and round to transfer power or movement in the machine. *The generator is connected to the runner by a drive shaft... A crank shaft drives a piston in a cylinder.*
3 NC A **shaft** of light is a narrow beam of light. *She was awakened by a shaft of sunlight coming through the curtains.*

shag /ʃæɡ/ **shags, shagging, shagged**
1 NC A **shag** is a black seabird with a yellow beak. *...ocean-going seabirds like the shag and common tern.*
2 NU **Shag** is a strong tasting tobacco which has been cut into long thin pieces. *The air became thick with shag tobacco smoke.*
3 ADJ ATTRIB A **shag** carpet or rug is made of long thick woollen threads. *His alligator loafers sank deep into the ivory shag carpet.*
4 VO To **shag** someone means to have sex with them; an offensive use. *'Do you know he was shagging Barbara during the cabaret?' Alan said.*

shagged /ʃæɡd/
ADJ If you are **shagged** or **shagged out**, you are very tired and have no energy left; an informal expression which some people find offensive. *I'll bet you used to flog your shagged-out old body through terrible exercises.*

shaggy /ˈʃæɡi/
ADJ **Shaggy** hair or fur is long and untidy. *...his shaggy, unkempt beard. ...shaggy sheep.*

Shah /ʃɑː/ **Shahs**
NC The **Shah** of Iran was the hereditary ruler of Iran until the Islamic Revolution of 1979. *With the fall of the Shah of Iran, the US announced the stationing of a carrier task force in the Arabian Sea.*

Shah, Sultan Azlan Muhibbuddin
/ˌʌzlən muhɪbudiːn ʃɑː/
Sultan Azlan Muhibbuddin Shah became King of Malaysia in 1989, when he was elected by the nine hereditary Malay rulers. He became Sultan of Perak in 1984 and was Lord President of the Supreme Court of Malaysia from 1982 to 1984. Born: 1939.

shake /ʃeɪk/ **shakes, shaking, shook, shaken**
1 V-ERG If you **shake** someone or something or if they **shake**, they move quickly backwards and forwards or up and down. *He awakened to find himself being shaken roughly by his father... The wind shook white petals from the tree... The earth shook and the sky darkened.* ▶ Also NC *She gave her skirts a vigorous shake.*
2 V If someone is **shaking**, they are trembling and unable to control their movements, for example because they are afraid, upset, or ill. *He seemed very nervous, and his hands were shaking... Mrs Thatcher was shaking as she left the scene... As he went through withdrawal, he shook until his muscles went rigid... He was shaking with laughter.*
3 V If your voice is **shaking**, you cannot control it because you are nervous or angry. *His eyes were wild and his voice shook... His voice shook as he denied the allegations.*
4 VO If something **shakes** you, it makes you feel shocked and upset. *My mother's death had shaken him dreadfully.* ◆ **shaken** ADJ *I was badly shaken. I had never had a crash before.*
5 VO If something **shakes** your beliefs or ideas, it makes you feel less certain about them. *Their faith in his sincerity may have been shaken.*
● **Shake** is used in these phrases. ● If you **shake hands** with someone or **shake** their **hand**, you hold their right hand in your own when you are meeting them, saying goodbye, congratulating them, or showing friendship. *Elijah and I shook hands and said good night... Someone shook my hand.* ● If you **shake** your **head**, you move it from side to side in order to say 'no'. *He shook his head and said he didn't know a Miss Cavell.*
shake off PHRASAL VERB If you **shake off** someone or something that you do not want, you manage to get away from them or get rid of them. *It had taken Franklin several hours to shake off the police. ...as the nations of Eastern Europe shook off oppression.*
shake up PHRASAL VERB 1 If something bad, unexpected, or frightening **shakes** you **up**, it makes you feel very shocked or upset. *Did that lightning shake you up?... The other factor that shook up the market was the Labor Department's announcement about inflation.* 2 If you **shake up** something such as an organization, institution, or profession, you make major changes to it. *The government has announced its intention to shake up the legal profession in this country... Mr Gorbachov hopes to give his reforms*

fresh impetus, essentially by shaking up the party itself.

shake-out, shake-outs
N C If there is a **shake-out** in an organization, a number of its employees are told that they can no longer work there, because their jobs are no longer necessary or because the organization is trying to spend less money. *Analysts say the new laws will lead to a shake-out in over-staffed firms.*

Shaker, Sharif Zaid ibn /ʃəriːf zeɪd bɪn ʃækə/
Field Marshal Sharif Zaid ibn Shaker became Prime Minister of Jordan in 1991. He was Chief of Staff of Jordanian Armed Forces in 1972 and Commander-in-Chief from 1976 to 1988. He served as Minister of State, Chief of the Royal Court, and Adviser to King Hussein on Armed Forces Affairs from 1988 to 1991. He previously served as Prime Minister in 1989. Born: 1934.

shake-up, shake-ups
N C A **shake-up** is a major set of changes in an organization or system. *Only a few senior ministers held their jobs in the most substantial shake-up since the Labour Party was elected seven years ago... There's been a call for a radical shake-up in Britain's education system.*

shaky /ʃeɪki/ **shakier, shakiest**
1 ADJ If you are **shaky**, you are shaking or feeling weak because you are frightened, shocked, or ill. *I was nervous and a bit shaky... The Prince was said to be weepy and shaky after the incident.* ♦ **shakily** ADV *The man stood up shakily.*
2 ADJ Something that is described as **shaky** is rather weak or not very good. *After a shaky start the orchestra grew more confident. ...a company with very shaky financial prospects.*

shale /ʃeɪl/
N U **Shale** is smooth soft rock that breaks easily into thin layers. *They lay on the sand, stone and shale.*

shall /ʃəl, ʃæl, ʃæl/. The usual spoken form of 'shall not' is 'shan't'.
1 MODAL You use **shall** when you are referring to something that you intend to do or that will happen to you in the future. *I shall get angry in a moment... I shan't let you go... We probably shan't sleep much.*
2 MODAL If you say that something **shall** happen, you are saying that it must happen and therefore it will happen; a formal use. *It must be done and therefore it shall be done... You're here to enjoy yourself, and enjoy yourself you shall... No more drink shall be drunk tonight.*
3 MODAL You use **shall** in questions when you are asking for advice. *Whatever shall I do?... Where shall we go for our drink?*
4 MODAL You also use **shall** in questions when you are making a suggestion. *Shall I shut the door?... Shall we go and see a film?... We'll go forward a little more, shall we?*

shallot /ʃəlɒt/ **shallots**
N C A **shallot** is a small, round vegetable that grows underground and is similar to an onion.

shallow /ʃæləʊ/ **shallower, shallowest; shallows**
1 ADJ A **shallow** hole, container, or layer of something measures only a short distance from the top to the bottom. *...a shallow bowl... Bodies were laid in the ground in shallow graves. ...birds which wade in shallow water.*
2 ADJ A **shallow** person, idea, or activity does not show or involve serious or careful thought; used showing disapproval. *I was too young and shallow to understand love... This kind of life is shallow and trivial.* ♦ **shallowness** N U *...the shallowness of her social life.*
3 ADJ If your breathing is **shallow**, you take only a small amount of air into your lungs at each breath. *Her face was alabaster white and her breathing very shallow... Most of these breaths are a rapid shallow panting that fills about one-sixth of your lungs.*
4 N PL The **shallows** are the shallow part of an area of water. *Thousands of little fish swim in the shallows.*

sham /ʃæm/ **shams**
N C Something that is a **sham** is not what it seems to be; used showing disapproval. *Their independence is*

a sham... He was attacking what he saw as shams and hypocrisy in society. ► Also ADJ ATTRIB *Radicals will boycott what they consider to be sham elections.*

shamble /ʃæmbl/ **shambles, shambling, shambled**
1 N SING If a place, event, or situation is a **shambles**, everything is in confusion and disorder, often because it has not been organized properly; an informal use. *The rehearsal was a shambles... His campaign is a shambles with much squabbling amongst his leading aides.*
2 V A If you **shamble** somewhere, you walk clumsily, dragging your feet. *They got up and shambled out.*

shambolic /ʃæmbɒlɪk/
ADJ If you describe something as **shambolic**, you mean that it is very disorganized or chaotic; an informal word. *The prosecution procedure got off to what some observers have called a shambolic start.*

shame /ʃeɪm/ **shames, shaming, shamed**
1 N U **Shame** is an uncomfortable feeling that you have when you know that you have done something wrong or embarrassing, or when you know that someone close to you has. *The memory fills me with shame... Simon lowered his face in shame.*
2 N U If someone brings **shame** on you, they make other people lose their respect for you. *Don't bring shame on the family.*
3 V O If something **shames** you, it causes you to feel shame. *It shamed him to know that his father had behaved in such a way.*
4 V O A If you **shame** someone into doing something, you force them to do it by making them feel ashamed not to. *Father was shamed into helping them.*
5 N SING If you say that something is a **shame**, you mean that you are sorry or sad about it. *It's a shame he didn't come too... It's a shame to waste all this food.*

shamefaced /ʃeɪmfeɪst/
ADJ If you are **shamefaced**, you feel embarrassed because you have done something that you know you should not have done. *Henry stared at Howard with a slightly shamefaced, slightly baffled look.*

shameful /ʃeɪmfl/
ADJ **Shameful** behaviour is so bad that the people who behave in that way ought to be ashamed. *It shows a shameful lack of concern. ...a reminder of an earlier and shameful decade.* ♦ **shamefully** ADV *The government have shamefully neglected this area.*

shameless /ʃeɪmləs/
ADJ Someone who is **shameless** behaves very badly, but is not ashamed of their behaviour. *There are shameless people around who wouldn't think twice about searching through a man's possessions... It was a shameless piece of plagiarism.* ♦ **shamelessly** ADV *Matty flatters me shamelessly.*

Shamir, Yitzhak /jɪtshɑːk ʃæmɪə/
Yitzhak Shamir became the Prime Minister of Israel in 1986. He became a member of the Knesset (the Israeli Parliament) in 1973, and was Speaker of the Knesset from 1977 to 1980. He served as Minister of Foreign Affairs from 1980 to 1983, and from 1984 to 1986. He was Prime Minister from 1983 to 1984 and Deputy Prime Minister from 1984 to 1986. He is a member of Likud. Born: 1915.

shampoo /ʃæmpuː/ **shampoos**
N MASS **Shampoo** is a soapy liquid that you use for washing your hair. *The substance is used in a wide range of cosmetic products, including shampoo. ...a new range of hair shampoos made in West Germany.*

shamrock /ʃæmrɒk/ **shamrocks**
N C A **shamrock** is a plant with three round leaves on its stem. The shamrock is the national emblem of Ireland.

shandy /ʃændi/ **shandies**
N MASS **Shandy** is a drink which is made by mixing beer and lemonade. *They poured her a shandy... Gerald and I drank our shandies.*

Shanghai /ʃæŋhaɪ/
Shanghai is the largest city in China. Population: 7,330,000 (1988).

shan't /ʃɑːnt/
Shan't is the usual spoken form of 'shall not'. *'Ain't you finished yet?'—'Shan't be a minute.'*

shanty /ʃænti/ shanties

1 NC A **shanty** is a small rough hut which people live in, built from tin, cardboard, or another material that is not very strong. *They are concentrated in shanties on the outskirts of the city... A landslide destroyed a shanty area close to the city of Fez.*

2 NC A **shanty** is also a song which sailors used to sing while they were doing work on a ship such as pulling in ropes. *...a sea shanty.*

shanty town, shanty towns

NC A **shanty town** is a large collection of rough huts which people live in. *The floods and landslides swept through the shanty towns on the outskirts of the capital.*

shape /ʃeɪp/ shapes, shaping, shaped

1 NCorNU The **shape** of something is the form or pattern of its outline, for example whether it is round or square. *...pieces of wood of different sizes and shapes... You can spin-dry this sweater and it will still retain its shape. ...a huge animal the size and shape of a rhinoceros... Bear Island is triangular in shape.*

2 NC A **shape** is something which has a definite form, for example a circle, square, or triangle. *...patterns created from geometric shapes... The material can be moulded into the appropriate coiled shape.*

3 NC A **shape** is also an object or person that you cannot see clearly because it is too dark or too far away. *One could just distinguish a slim shape in a short white dress.*

4 N SING+POSS The **shape** of something such as a plan or organization is its structure and size. *...developments which may alter the future course and shape of industry.*

5 VO If you **shape** an object, you cause it to have a particular shape. *He began to shape the dough into rolls.*

6 VO To **shape** a thing or an activity means to cause it to develop in a particular way. *It was the Greeks who shaped the thinking of Western man.*

● **Shape** is used in these phrases. ● If someone or something is **in good shape**, they are in a good condition or state of health. If they are in **bad shape**, they are in a bad condition or state of health. *Keep yourself in good shape and do moderate exercise... Dale has lived on the street for years and she's in pretty bad shape... He warned that the nation's education system was in bad shape.* ● If you **get** someone or something that is in a poor condition **into shape** or if they **get into shape**, their condition improves so that it becomes satisfactory. *The Sri Lankan government wanted more time to try to get the economy into shape... The organisation will then be able to get into shape to contest the now inevitable multi-party elections.* ● If someone **licks** you **into shape**, they make you think, work, or behave in the way that they think you should. *He has licked the Labour Party into shape.* ● If you say that something comes in **all shapes and sizes**, you mean that there are many different types or designs of it, and that some types are very different to others. *Lasers come in all shapes and sizes. ...missiles and rockets of all shapes and sizes.* ● You use **in the shape of** before mentioning exactly what you are referring to, after referring to it in a general way. *He was convinced that the end of the world was at hand in the shape of a nuclear holocaust.* ● When something **takes shape**, it develops and starts to have a definite structure or shape. *So far, the joint force is no more than a controversial idea that's unlikely to take shape in the near future.* ● If you say that you will not accept or tolerate something **in any shape or form**, you are emphasizing that you will not accept or tolerate it at all. *There's no way people would accept the Khmer Rouge back in any shape or form.*

shape up PHRASAL VERB If someone or something is **shaping up** in a particular way, they are developing or progressing in that way. *The new recruits are shaping up quite well.*

shaped /ʃeɪpt/

ADJ Something that is **shaped** in a particular way has the shape indicated. *...a chair shaped like a saddle. ...weirdly shaped trees.*

-shaped /-ʃeɪpt/

SUFFIX **-shaped** is added to nouns to form adjectives that describe the shape of an object. *...an egg-shaped face. ...a star-shaped card.*

shapeless /ʃeɪpləs/

ADJ Something that is **shapeless** does not have a definite or attractive shape. *...shapeless pyjamas.*

shapely /ʃeɪpli/

ADJ A **shapely** person has an attractive figure. *She had a slim waist and shapely legs.*

shard /ʃɑːd/ shards

NC A **shard** is a piece of broken pottery, glass, or metal; a formal word. *...white porcelain shards from the early Yung Cheng period... It bounced twice and exploded, sending white-hot shards of shrapnel flying through the air.*

share /ʃeə/ shares, sharing, shared

1 V-RECIP If you **share** something with another person, you both use it or have some of it. *Ralph went upstairs to the room he shared with his brother... Workers shared plots of land for growing flowers and vegetables... Governor Xing said counter-revolutionaries shared the same cells as other prisoners... We've welcomed them and we've shared our food and resources.*

2 V-RECIPor V+in If people **share** a task or duty, they each do part of it or they do it together. *The US believes responsibility should be shared by other countries... France has shared the financing of the meeting with Canada... Both partners share in rearing their family.*

3 V-RECIP If you **share** an experience with someone else, you both have it, either at the same time or at a different time. *She will be a good parent, enthusiastically sharing activities with her child... Old age was something they would never be able to share... The Pact was a defensive alliance of countries which shared a common fate.* ◆ **shared** ADJ ATTRIB *...a solidarity based on shared experiences of imperialism, poverty and underdevelopment.*

4 V-RECIP If you **share** something personal such as a thought or piece of news with someone, you tell them about it. *He was so excited about his idea that he felt he had to share it with someone... She shared her thoughts with reporters... There are pictures of the two men sharing a joke.*

5 V-RECIP If two people or things **share** a particular quality, characteristic, or idea, they both have it. *I share your concern... He shared his father's anti-facist feelings... This was a taste which he shared with Guy... China and Japan share many characteristics.* ◆ **shared** ADJ ATTRIB *...shared hopes or shared fears.*

6 V-RECIP In a competition, if two or more people **share** the points or **share** a place, they finish on the same score or at the same time. *Dundee and Hearts shared the points in a 1-all draw... Third place went to Greg Norman, and four players shared fourth place... Craig Parry, on 284, shared third place with Katsunari Tahahashi and Hiroshi Makino.*

7 N SING If you have or do a **share** of something, you have or do part of it. *...a campaign for parents to have a share in discussing school policy... The Iranians had to take their share of the blame... An increasing share of the work is handed over to computers... The United States was willing to pay its fair share of the cost.*

8 NC The **shares** of a company are the equal parts into which its ownership is divided. People can buy shares in a company as an investment. *The firm's shares jumped 10p to 114p.*

share out PHRASAL VERB If you **share** something **out**, you give each person in a group an equal or fair part of it. *The farmers have 120 million dollars of government aid to share out between them.*

shareholder /ʃeəhəʊldə/ shareholders

NC A **shareholder** is a person who owns shares in a company. *Public companies often have hundreds of shareholders.*

share-out, share-outs

NC If there is a **share-out** of something, several people are given equal or fair parts of it. *...a share-out of the profits.*

Sharif, Mian Mohammad Nawaz
/miæn məuhæmɪd nəwɑːz ʃəriːf/
Mian Mohammad Nawaz Sharif became Prime Minister of Pakistan in 1990. He was Chief Minister of Punjab from 1985 to 1990. He became President of the Islamic Democratic Alliance (IJI) in 1988. Born: 1949.

shark /ʃɑːk/ **sharks**
1 NC A **shark** is a very large fish with sharp teeth. Sharks sometimes attack people. *It must have been a ferocious creature as its mouth was lined with large, jagged teeth, like a shark's.*
2 See also **loan shark**.

sharp /ʃɑːp/ **sharper, sharpest; sharps**
1 ADJ A **sharp** object has a very thin edge or a very pointed end and so it can easily cut or pierce things. *Cut it away with a sharp knife. ...small, sharp teeth.*
2 ADJ A **sharp** picture, outline, or distinction is clear and easy to see or understand. *...sharp, fresh footprints in the snow... We try to draw a sharp dividing line between Civil Service and Government.*
♦ **sharply** ADV *His clothes contrast sharply with Gaspar's.*
3 ADJ Someone who is **sharp** is quick to notice, hear, or understand things. *You've got to be sharp to get ahead... His sharp eyes would never miss it.*
4 ADJ A **sharp** change is sudden and very big. *...sharp food-price increases. ...a sharp drop in oil prices.*
♦ **sharply** ADV *Sales of the car have risen sharply in recent weeks.*
5 ADJ A **sharp** action or movement is quick and firm. *She received a sharp clout on the head... With his finger and thumb he gave it a sharp turn.* ♦ **sharply** ADV *Both birds turned their heads sharply at the sound.*
6 ADJ A **sharp** bend or turn is one that changes direction very quickly. *The car left the road on a sharp bend... All three failed to negotiate a sharp right-hand turn.*
7 ADJ If someone says something in a **sharp** way, they say it suddenly and rather firmly or angrily. *A sharp order came through his headphones... The nation came under sharp criticism for price increases.* ♦ **sharply** ADV *'Don't talk nonsense,' she said sharply.*
8 ADJ A **sharp** sound is very short, sudden, and quite loud. *...the sharp crack of a twig.*
9 ADJ **Sharp** pain or cold hurts a lot. *His blistered foot at that moment caused him a sharp pang.*
10 If you are at the **sharp** end of a problem, situation, or project, you are directly involved in it, and often are under the most pressure or have the most responsibility. *I want to focus at the moment on the sharp end of the problem, and make it unnecessary for people to sleep rough in central London. ...a leader who knows what it is to be at the sharp end of township violence.*
11 ADJ Food that has a **sharp** taste is slightly sour and refreshing. *...the sharp, pure taste of gooseberries.*
12 ADV If something happens at a certain time **sharp**, it happens at exactly that time. *His train came in at eight sharp.*
13 NC or ADJ after N In music, a **sharp** is the note a semitone higher than the note described by the same letter. It is usually represented by the symbol (♯) after the letter. *I have to play four sharps in this piece. ...C sharp.*
14 ADJ or ADV A **sharp** musical note or instrument is slightly higher in pitch than it should be. *The violin sounds a bit sharp... She sang sharp all the way through.*

sharpen /ʃɑːpən/ **sharpens, sharpening, sharpened**
1 VO If you **sharpen** an object, you make its edge very thin or you make its end pointed. *Roger sharpened a stick at both ends.*
2 V-ERG If your senses or abilities **sharpen** or if you **sharpen** them, you become quicker at thinking or at noticing things, or better at your particular skill. *His eyes and instincts sharpened as he saw the fort in the distance... Generations of urban living had sharpened their wits... Martinez does this exercise to sharpen her timing, to perfect her movements.*
3 V-ERG If disagreements or differences between people **sharpen** or if something **sharpens** them, they

increase; a formal use. *Political tension has sharpened after Wednesday's elections... The crisis in Egyptian-Sudanese relations has been sharpened considerably by the present drought.*
4 V-ERG If your voice **sharpens** or if you **sharpen** it, you begin to speak more angrily and quickly. *'Who told you?' Her voice had sharpened a little... Fear and urgency sharpened Sarah's voice.*
sharpen up PHRASAL VERB 1 If you **sharpen** a knife or other tool **up**, you make its edge thinner or make its end more pointed. *I was practical enough to sharpen up my knives... All you can hear at night is a grinding noise as makeshift weapons are sharpened up.* 2 If someone **sharpens up** their image, performance, or opinion, or if it **sharpens up**, it becomes better or more clearly defined. *Their memory and their ability to learn new things sharpened up while they were taking the drug... He has warned that the party must sharpen up its image.*

sharpener /ʃɑːpnə/ **sharpeners**
NC A pencil **sharpener** is a device for sharpening pencils.

sharpish /ʃɑːpɪʃ/
ADV **Sharpish** means quickly, without any delay; an informal word. *I've no doubt she'll want her supper sharpish after that long journey.*

sharp practice
NU If you describe something that someone does as **sharp practice**, you mean that it is clever but dishonest. *The committee has accused the government of sharp practice in the deal.*

shatter /ʃætə/ **shatters, shattering, shattered**
1 V-ERG If something **shatters**, it breaks into a lot of small pieces. *The vase fell from her hand and shattered on the floor... I shattered the glass.*
2 VO If something **shatters** your beliefs or hopes, it destroys them. *By 1974, relations looked decidedly hopeful, until the dramatic events that led to the island's division occurred, and shattered the prospects for reconciliation... Confidence in their good faith has been shattered.*
3 V-PASS If someone is **shattered** by an event, it shocks and upsets them. *My father was shattered by the news... Archbishop Desmond Tutu, who was in court when the convictions were announced, said he was shattered by the verdict.* ♦ **shattered** ADJ PRED *It was the first time I had seen them since my arrest, and they all looked shattered.*

shattered /ʃætəd/
ADJ PRED You can say that you are **shattered** when you are very tired; an informal use. *I was shattered from yesterday and took a rest.*

shattering /ʃætərɪŋ/
1 ADJ Something that is **shattering** shocks and upsets you. *The two leaders failed to address themselves to the shattering changes taking place in Europe. ...the shattering event of President Kennedy's assassination.*
2 ADJ You can also use **shattering** to describe something which makes you very tired. *Sunday had been a shattering day.*

shave /ʃeɪv/ **shaves, shaving, shaved**
1 V When a man **shaves**, he cuts hair from his face using a razor. *When he had shaved and dressed, he went down to the kitchen... He had shaved off his beard.* ► Also NC *He had a shave and a bath.*
2 VO When someone **shaves** a part of their body, they cut all the hair from it using a razor. *I have to shave my legs... A small patch of his hair was shaved off.*
3 If something was a **close shave**, there was nearly an accident or a disaster but it was avoided. *After several close shaves over the past few days, many are beginning to reconsider the wisdom of travelling... There was a close shave for top seed Mats Wilander who didn't win a single game in the first set, before recovering to take the next two sets 6-4.*

shaven /ʃeɪvn/
ADJ If a part of someone's body is **shaven**, it has been shaved. *His hair was very short, the back of his neck shaven... Devotees wear brightly-coloured Indian dress and have shaven heads.* ● See also **clean-shaven**.

shaver /ʃeɪvə/ **shavers**
NC A **shaver** is an electric tool used for shaving hair.

...a buzzing electric shaver.

shaving /ˈʃeɪvɪŋ/ **shavings**

1 N+N You use **shaving** to describe things that people use when they shave. *...a shaving brush.*
2 NC **Shavings** are small, very thin pieces cut from something such as wood. *...moist sawdust or wood shavings. ...metal shavings.*

shawl /ʃɔːl/ **shawls**

NC A **shawl** is a large piece of woollen cloth worn over a woman's shoulders or head, or wrapped around a baby to keep it warm. *She arrived swathed in shawls covering her body and hair. ...a baby, about a few weeks old, wrapped up in shawls.*

she /ʃi, ʃiː/. **She** is used as the subject of a verb.

1 PRON You use **she** to refer to a woman, girl, or female animal that has already been mentioned, or whose identity is known. *'So long,' Mary said as she passed Miss Saunders... She is a very active woman... Ask her if she can do something with them.*
2 PRON You can use **she** to refer to a nation. *Britain is a poor nation now, and she would do well to remember this.*
3 PRON You can also use **she** to refer to a ship, car, or other vehicle. *She does 0 to 60 in 10 seconds.*

sheaf /ʃiːf/ **sheaves**

1 NC A **sheaf** of papers is a bundle of them. *...a thick sheaf of letters.*
2 NC A **sheaf** of corn is a bundle of ripe corn plants tied together. *...wheat sheaves.*

shear /ʃɪə/ **shears, shearing, sheared, shorn.** The past participle of the verb can be either **sheared** or **shorn.**

1 VO To **shear** a sheep means to cut off its wool. *She loved watching them shear sheep... People living in the towns can come and see life in the countryside and watch animals being milked or sheared.*
2 N PL A pair of **shears** is a garden tool like a large pair of scissors. *...a pair of garden shears.*
3 See also **shorn.**

shear off PHRASAL VERB If something such as a piece of metal **shears off**, it breaks off because of pressure or old age. *Another bolt had sheared off.*

sheath /ʃiːθ/ **sheaths**

1 NC A **sheath** is a covering for the blade of a knife. *...a knife in its sheath.*
2 NC A **sheath** is also a rubber covering for a man's penis that is used as a contraceptive. *Preliminary results suggest that women prefer using the female condom to using the male sheath.*

sheathe /ʃiːð/ **sheathes, sheathing, sheathed**

VO When you **sheathe** a knife, you put it in its sheath.

sheath knife, sheath knives

NC A **sheath knife** is a knife that has a blade that is sharp on one side and has a heavy handle. Sheath knives are used outdoors, especially for cutting sticks or rope.

sheaves /ʃiːvz/

Sheaves is the plural of **sheaf.**

shed /ʃed/ **sheds, shedding.** The form **shed** is used in the present tense and is also the past tense and past participle of the verb.

1 NC A **shed** is a small building used for storing things. *...the coal shed.*
2 VO When an animal **sheds** hair or skin, some of its hair or skin drops off. When a tree **sheds** its leaves, its leaves fall off. *Have you ever seen a snake shedding its skin?... Many trees shed their leaves in winter.*
3 VO To **shed** something means to get rid of it. *I shed all my restraint... It has shed the Communist system in favour of multi-party democracy.*
4 VO If a company or organization **sheds** jobs, or **sheds** employees, it makes a number of its employees redundant. *A company making Irish whiskey was shedding jobs as sales of their products in Ireland declined... The security forces have shed hundreds of thousands of employees.*
5 VO If a lorry **sheds** its load, the goods it is carrying fall onto the road. *People living in Burton on Trent have been warned to stay indoors and keep their windows shut after a lorry shed its load of cyanide on a nearby road.*
● **Shed** is used in these phrases. ● To **shed tears** means to cry. *He became famous as a singer who*

shed tears during his performances... Many tears have been shed today in memory of the dead. ● If you say that someone does not **shed** any **tears** about a sad or disappointing event or situation, you mean that they are not at all upset by it. *Mrs Thatcher is unlikely to shed any tears at his retirement... Few tears have been shed about the fate of Ceausescu's henchmen.*
● To **shed blood** means to kill people in a violent way. *The troops that have been sent into the area over the past two weeks have shed a lot of blood... They accused us of shedding blood... He said there was no reason for shedding the blood of innocents.* ● To **shed light on** something such as a problem means to make it easier to understand. *Officials hope the voice recorder will shed light on the reasons for the crash. ...some recent discoveries that shed light on the current debate on the nature of evolution.*

she'd /ʃiːd, ʃid/

She'd is the usual spoken form of 'she had', especially when 'had' is an auxiliary verb. **She'd** is also a spoken form of 'she would'. *It was too late. She'd done it... She said she'd come by train.*

sheen /ʃiːn/

N SING+SUPP If the surface of something has a **sheen**, it has a smooth and gentle brightness. *...beautiful, long hair with a silky sheen.*

sheep /ʃiːp/; **sheep** is both the singular and the plural form.

NC A **sheep** is a farm animal with a thick woolly coat. Sheep are kept for their wool or meat. *...a flock of sheep.* ● See also **black sheep.**

sheepdog /ʃiːpdɒg/ **sheepdogs**

NC A **sheepdog** is a breed of dog. There are several different types of sheepdog. Some sheepdogs are used for controlling sheep. *On country walks he usually had a large sheepdog at his heels.*

sheepish /ʃiːpɪʃ/

ADJ If you look **sheepish**, you look embarrassed because you feel foolish. *He gave me a sheepish grin.*
◆ **sheepishly** ADV *Jo looked up at his father sheepishly.*

sheepskin /ʃiːpskɪn/

NU **Sheepskin** is the skin and wool of a sheep, used especially for coats and rugs. *...a sheepskin jacket.*

sheer /ʃɪə/

1 ADJ ATTRIB **Sheer** means complete and not mixed with anything else; often used to emphasize the word it describes. *The eighth floor of the hotel was sheer luxury... Many of the audience walked out through sheer boredom... On the road, breakdowns, road works, accidents, and the sheer number of vehicles led to many traffic jams.*
2 ADJ A **sheer** cliff or drop is completely vertical. *Thornhill fell more than three hundred feet as he climbed a three thousand foot sheer cliff face known as Trollvegen in Western Norway. ...a gorge with sheer rock sides.*
3 ADJ **Sheer** is used to describe silk or other material which is very thin and delicate. *...sheer stockings.*

sheet /ʃiːt/ **sheets**

1 NC A **sheet** is a large rectangular piece of cloth, used with blankets or a duvet on a bed. *...sales of household linen—sheets, towels and tablecloths. ...a weekly wash of mattress covers and bed sheets.*
2 NC A **sheet** of paper is a rectangular piece of it. *He handed a typewritten sheet to Karen... He found them written on a loose sheet of paper attached to the manuscript.*
3 NC A **sheet** of a solid material such as glass, metal, or wood, is a large, flat, thin piece of it. *Watch how you go, the pavement's like a sheet of ice. ...a sheet of polyester.*

sheet anchor, sheet anchors

1 NC A **sheet anchor** is an anchor which is much larger and stronger than an ordinary anchor and which is only used when a boat is in difficulties.
2 N SING You can refer to someone or something that helps you more than anything else when problems or difficulties occur as a **sheet anchor**. *Willy Whitelaw has been the fixer, the smoother, the sheet anchor, and the professional politician who held the party together... People put more stress on friendship as the*

sheet anchor of marriage.
sheet ice
NU **Sheet ice** is a solid layer of ice over a road or path. *The pavement was covered in sheet ice.*
sheeting /ʃiːtɪŋ/
NU+SUPP **Sheeting** is a material such as metal or plastic that is made into large, flat, and fairly thin pieces, usually in the shape of a square or rectangle. *...pieces of zinc sheeting... The homeless are currently sleeping in tents or under plastic sheeting.*
sheet music
NU **Sheet music** is printed music on single sheets of paper or on sheets that are fastened together without a hard cover. *I had got hold of the music—the original sheet music from 1928 or '29. ...the sheet music to 'Happy Days'.*
sheikh /ʃeɪk/ **sheikhs**; also spelt **sheik**.
NC A **sheikh** is an Arab chief or ruler. *...the ruler of the Gulf state of Sharjah, Sheikh Sultan Bin Mohammed al Qassimi. ...the style of the Gulf sheikhs with their elaborate and dignified Arab hospitality.*
shelf /ʃelf/ **shelves**
1 NC A **shelf** is a flat piece of wood, metal, or glass fixed to a wall or inside a cupboard. Shelves are used for keeping things on. *There were a lot of books on the shelves.*
2 NC A **shelf** is also a section of something such as a rock or a mountain that sticks out like a shelf.
shelf life
N SING+SUPP The **shelf life** of a product, especially food, is the length of time that it can be kept in a shop before it becomes too old to sell. *The typical shelf life of fully ripe tomatoes is about four to five days... Packaging already used to give meat a longer shelf life could be modified for apples and tomatoes.*
shell /ʃel/ **shells, shelling, shelled**
1 NC The **shell** of an egg or nut is the hard covering which surrounds it. *...coconut shells.*
2 NC The **shell** of a tortoise, snail, or crab is the hard, protective covering on its back. *Lobsters moult their shells at frequent intervals.*
3 NC A **shell** is also a hard covering which surrounds, or used to surround, a small, soft sea creature. *...a handkerchief full of shells which my sister had collected. ...oyster shells.*
4 VO If you **shell** peas or nuts, you remove their covering. *Can you help me shell these peas?*
5 NC You can refer to the frame of a building as a **shell**. *...the burned-out shell that had once been their home.*
6 NC A **shell** is also a metal container filled with explosives that is fired from a large gun. *Arnold had his leg smashed when a shell hit the truck he was driving.*
7 VO To **shell** a place means to fire explosive shells at it. *They continued to shell towns on the northern coast... The oil platform was shelled and set ablaze by warships of the American fleet.* ◆ **shelling** NU *Reports say fighting has flared up again after a night of sporadic shooting and shelling... The city has come under heavy shelling and air attack.*
shell out PHRASAL VERB If you **shell out** for something, you spend money on it, often more than you intended to; an informal expression. *I shelled out sixty quid on that carpet.*
she'll /ʃiːl, ʃɪl/
She'll is the usual spoken form of 'she will'. *I hope she'll be all right.*
shellfish /ʃelfɪʃ/; **shellfish** is both the singular and the plural form.
NC A **shellfish** is a small creature with a shell that lives in the sea. *They are looking at the way toxic compounds collect in the bodies of shellfish, especially mussels and oysters... Scientists have, in the past, been intrigued by the way shellfish construct their shells.*
shell-shock
NC **Shell-shock** is an illness affecting the mind or the nerves, caused by the frightening experiences that happen to soldiers during a war. *The army has known about the effects of shell-shock since the First World War.*

shell-shocked
1 ADJ A soldier who is **shell-shocked** is suffering from shell-shock.
2 ADJ If you feel **shell-shocked**, you feel very tired and under stress because of something you have just experienced; an informal use. *I was feeling shell-shocked after the interview.*
shell suit, shell suits
NC A **shell suit** is a loose casual suit consisting of trousers and a top, made of a special light, slightly shiny material. *Our top quality shell suit is only £29.99.*
shelter /ʃeltə/ **shelters, sheltering, sheltered**
1 NC A **shelter** is a small building or covered place constructed to protect people from bad weather or danger. *Many of them went to a storm shelter... Many people are forced to sleep in makeshift shelters... It was used as a civilian bomb shelter.*
2 NU If a place provides **shelter**, it provides protection from bad weather or danger. *He found shelter in caves. ...areas where people can sleep, and above all, take shelter if they come under fire... We waited in the shelter of the trees.*
3 V If you **shelter** in a place, you stay there and are protected from bad weather or danger. *A lot of people's lives were saved because they were able to shelter there. ...people sheltering inside bunkers... It is natural to shelter from a storm.*
4 VO If a place or thing is **sheltered** by something, it is protected by it from wind and rain. *This wide alley is sheltered by plane trees.*
5 VO If you **shelter** someone, you hide them when people are looking for them. *Some villagers are prepared to shelter wanted men.*
sheltered /ʃeltəd/
1 ADJ A **sheltered** place is protected from wind and rain. *I lay down in the warmest and most sheltered spot I could find.*
2 ADJ If you have a **sheltered** life, you do not experience things which other people experience, especially unpleasant things. *We lived a sheltered life in our Irish village.*
3 ADJ ATTRIB **Sheltered** accommodation is designed for old or handicapped people. It allows them to be independent but also provides care when they need it. *...a sheltered housing scheme.*
shelve /ʃelv/ **shelves, shelving, shelved**
1 VO If you **shelve** a plan, you decide not to continue with it for a while. *The project seems to have been shelved for the moment.*
2 **Shelves** is the plural of **shelf**.
shelving /ʃelvɪŋ/
NU **Shelving** is a set of shelves. *...layers of glass shelving.*
shepherd /ʃepəd/ **shepherds, shepherding, shepherded**
1 NC A **shepherd** is a person whose job is to look after sheep or goats. *Why did the shepherds let the sheep drink from the wells? ...the little shepherd girl chasing her goats down the mountainside.*
2 VO If you **shepherd** someone somewhere, you accompany them there to make sure that they go to the right place. *I shepherded them towards the lobby.*
shepherdess /ʃepədes/ **shepherdesses**
NC A **shepherdess** is a woman or girl whose job is looking after sheep. *One local resident said young shepherdesses had been chased in the fields.*
shepherd's pie, shepherd's pies
NUorNC **Shepherd's pie** is a dish consisting of minced meat covered with a layer of mashed potato.
sherbet /ʃɜːbət/ **sherbets**
1 NU **Sherbet** is a sweet dry powder that tastes fizzy and is eaten as a sweet or used to make a drink.
2 NUorNC In American English, **sherbet** is the same as sorbet.
sheriff /ʃerɪf/ **sheriffs**
NC In the United States, a **sheriff** is a person who is elected to make sure that the law is obeyed in a particular county. *As Los Angeles County sheriff Sherman Block puts it, murder is increasingly a random, even casual event. ...two detectives from the*

Broward County Sheriff's Department.

sherry /ʃɛri/ **sherries**

N MASS **Sherry** is a strong alcoholic drink made from grapes. It is usually drunk before a meal. *The consumption of wines, including sherry and port, has more than doubled in the past seven years... The oldest wine in the collection is a Spanish sherry of the 1775 vintage.*

she's /ʃiːz, ʃiz/

She's is the usual spoken form of 'she is' or 'she has', especially when 'has' is an auxiliary verb. *She's Swedish... She's gone back to Montrose.*

Shetland pony /ʃɛtlənd pəʊni/ **Shetland ponies**

NC A **Shetland pony** is a small pony with long, shaggy hair.

Shevardnadze, Eduard /ɛdvɑːd ʃɛvədnædzə/

Eduard Shevardnadze became President of the State Council of Georgia in 1992. He was First Secretary of the Central Committee of the Georgian Communist Party from 1972 to 1985. From 1985 to 1990, and again briefly in 1991, he was the Soviet Foreign Minister. Born: 1928.

shibboleth /ʃɪbəlɛθ/ **shibboleths**

NC A **shibboleth** is an old idea or practice which is no longer thought to be important; a formal word. *He has never sought to hide his contempt for 'outworn shibboleths' like discipline and examinations.*

shield /ʃiːld/ **shields, shielding, shielded**

1 NC A **shield** is a large piece of a strong material such as metal which soldiers or other people likely to become involved in fighting carry to protect their bodies. *...the treasures of the Anglo-Saxon King Redwald—his shield, sword, and magnificent iron helmet... West German riot police closed in on the crowd with shields, water cannons, and tear gas.*
2 NC Something which is a **shield** against a particular danger provides protection against it. *The virus forms a sort of protective shield against infection... He believes the material can provide an effective shield from the heat generated by the oil fires.*
3 VO To **shield** someone from danger means to protect them by being between them and the danger. *She was hurried away shielded by her bodyguards... The ozone layer shields all living things against harmful ultra-violet rays from the sun.*

shift /ʃɪft/ **shifts, shifting, shifted**

1 V-ERG If you **shift** something somewhere, you move it there. *He shifted the chair closer to the bed... Muller's eyes shifted to the telephone.*
2 NC+SUPP A **shift** in a situation or in someone's opinion is a slight change. *You may detect a shift of emphasis. ...a radical shift in public opinion.*
3 V-ERG If a situation or opinion **shifts**, it changes slightly. *The talk shifted to our neighbour's land. ...shifting the balance of financial control.*
4 VO If you **shift** blame or responsibility onto someone, you transfer it to them. *Each airport has been trying to shift the blame on to the other. ...the plan to shift responsibility for training from the state to private business.*
5 NC A **shift** is also one of the set periods of time during which people work, for example in a factory. *He had chosen the midnight to 8 shift. ...a dispute over a new shift work system.*

shifting /ʃɪftɪŋ/

ADJ ATTRIB **Shifting** is used to describe things which are made up of different parts that continuously move and change position in relation to each other. *He drifted into the shifting crowd... The Congo still remains divided between shifting coalitions of the various political parties.*

shift key, shift keys

NC A **shift key** on a typewriter or computer keyboard is the button which you press so that the next letter that you type is a capital.

shiftless /ʃɪftləs/

ADJ Someone who is **shiftless** has no interest in doing anything and no desire to achieve anything. *He's lazy and shiftless.*

shifty /ʃɪfti/

ADJ Someone who looks **shifty** gives the impression of being deceitful. *...a man with small shifty eyes.*

shilling /ʃɪlɪŋ/ **shillings**

1 NC A **shilling** was a unit of money equivalent to 5p which was used in Britain until 1971. *The company was founded in 1923 with a top dividend of two pounds and twelve shillings.*
2 NC A **shilling** is also a unit of money that is used in Kenya, Tanzania, Uganda, and Somalia. One shilling is divided into one hundred cents. *...a job with a salary of 48,000 Kenyan shillings a month... Tanzania's currency will be devalued by a further 21%—the US dollar will now sell at 120 Tanzanian shillings.*

shilly-shally /ʃɪliʃæli/ **shilly-shallies, shilly-shallying, shilly-shallied**

V If you say that someone is **shilly-shallying**, you mean that you think they are being too slow about something, for example if they are hesitating when they should be making a decision; an informal word. *For goodness sake stop shilly-shallying and get a move on!*

shimmer /ʃɪmə/ **shimmers, shimmering, shimmered**

V If something **shimmers**, it shines with a faint, unsteady light. *I sat looking at the sea shimmering in the moonlight.*

shin /ʃɪn/ **shins, shinning, shinned**

NC Your **shin** is the front part of your leg between your knee and ankle. *England captain Will Carling has confirmed that he won't be fit to play because of the stress fracture in his left shin.*

shin up PHRASAL VERB If you **shin up** a tree or a pole, you climb it quickly and easily. *I shinned up a lamp post to get a better view.*

shindig /ʃɪndɪg/ **shindigs**

NC A **shindig** is a large, noisy, enjoyable party; an informal word. *'When are you planning this shindig for?'—'I was thinking about tomorrow night.'*

shine /ʃaɪn/ **shines, shining, shone**

1 V When the sun or a light **shines**, it gives out bright light. *The skies were blue and the sun was shining... A few miles from the compound, car headlights shine on army buses and a soldier directing traffic.*
2 VO If you **shine** a torch or lamp somewhere, you point its light there. *I asked him to shine the headlight on the door... One of the tanks shines its searchlight and points its guns at the crowd.*
3 V Something that **shines** is very bright, usually because it is reflecting light. *We cross wet rice paddies shining in the sun like mirrors... The leaves shine like knife blades in the beam of his flashlight... Everything shines when it's wet.* ♦ **shining** ADJ *...rows of shining glasses.*
4 V If someone's eyes **shine**, their eyes show that they are very happy and excited.
5 V Someone who **shines** at a skill or activity does it very well. *He shines at amateur theatricals.*
6 If something **takes the shine off** a victory or success, it makes it seem less impressive or enjoyable. *They risk the political hurly burly of a new session taking the shine off Mr Major's summer success.*

shingle /ʃɪŋgl/ **shingles**

1 NU **Shingle** consists of small stones on the shore of a sea or river. *The beach is a mixture of sand and shingle.*
2 NC A **shingle** is a small thin tile, usually made of wood, which is used to cover a roof or a wall. *...scales that overlap like shingles on a roof.*
3 NU **Shingles** is a disease that causes a rash of painful red spots which spreads in a band around a person's body, especially around their waist. *He has been suffering from shingles.*

shiny /ʃaɪni/

ADJ **Shiny** things are bright and reflect light. *...shiny black shoes. ...shiny cars.*

ship /ʃɪp/ **ships, shipping, shipped**

1 NC A **ship** is a large boat which carries passengers or cargo. *The ship was due to sail the following morning... They were sent home by ship.*
2 VOA If people or things **are shipped** somewhere, they are sent there by ship or by some other means of transport. *They will build thousands of cars to be shipped to Siberia.*

shipbuilding /ʃɪpbɪldɪŋ/

NU **Shipbuilding** is the industry or activity of making

ships. *...the Chinese shipbuilding industry... The government has announced the closure of a big state-owned shipbuilding yard.*

shipment /ˈʃɪpmənt/ **shipments**
1 NC A **shipment** is a quantity of a particular kind of cargo that is sent somewhere, especially to another country, for example, on a ship, train, or aeroplane. *They sent him a shipment of tobacco... The blockade prevented shipments of foreign food from reaching our shores.*
2 NU The **shipment** of a cargo somewhere is the activity or process of sending it there, for example, by ship, train, or aeroplane. *The dispute has seriously disrupted shipment of aluminium to Japan since July... He will arrange for shipment from Britain.*

shipping /ˈʃɪpɪŋ/
NU **Shipping** refers to ships in general or to a group of ships. *Nearly a fifth of the shipping had been sunk.*

shipshape /ˈʃɪpʃeɪp/
ADJ Something that is **shipshape** is tidy and neat with everything in its proper place. *I got the house all shipshape while she was away.*

shipwreck /ˈʃɪprek/ **shipwrecks, shipwrecked**
1 NC When there is a **shipwreck**, a ship is destroyed in an accident at sea. *The whole family perished in a shipwreck.*
2 NC A **shipwreck** is also a ship which has been destroyed in a shipwreck. *Treasure has sometimes been found in shipwrecks.*
3 V-PASS When someone **is shipwrecked**, their ship is destroyed but they survive and reach land. *He was shipwrecked off the lonely island of Iona.*

shipyard /ˈʃɪpjɑːd/ **shipyards**
NC A **shipyard** is a place where ships are built and repaired. *In their heyday, shipyards on the Clyde river in Scotland produced 70 percent of the world's ships.*

shire /ʃaɪə/ **shires**
1 NC A **shire** is a county; an old-fashioned use. *...the shire of Peebles.*
2 N PL The **Shires** or **shire counties** are the counties in the central part of England which are mainly rural. *He spent his time in the Shires riding, hunting, and shooting... This proposal should go down well in the shire counties.*
3 NC A **shire** or **shire horse** is a large heavy horse used for pulling loads. *There will be shire horses pulling a wagon laden with beer barrels.*

shirk /ʃɜːk/ **shirks, shirking, shirked**
V OR V If someone **shirks** something such as a job or task that they are supposed to do, they avoid doing it; used showing disapproval. *It was a job everyone shirked whenever possible... We in Congress have our role to play and we can't shirk our responsibilities... He worked as he had always done, never shirking and never complaining.*

shirt /ʃɜːt/ **shirts**
NC A **shirt** is a piece of clothing worn on the upper part of your body. Shirts usually have a collar, sleeves, and buttons down the front. *He was dressed in a light blue shirt and grey trousers... He was wearing a light coloured shirt and a white sun hat.*

shirtsleeves /ˈʃɜːtsliːvz/
If a man is in his **shirtsleeves**, he is wearing a shirt but not a jacket. *I lay on the bed in my shirtsleeves.*

shirt-tail, shirt-tails
NC A man's **shirt-tails** are the long parts of his shirt below the waist, which are normally tucked into his trousers. *His shirt-tails were hanging out at the back.*

shirty /ˈʃɜːti/
ADJ If you describe someone as **shirty**, you mean that they are behaving in a bad-tempered and rude way; an informal word. *Sorry if I was a little shirty just now.*

shit /ʃɪt/ **shits, shitting, shat;** a very rude word used in informal English.
1 NU **Shit** is waste matter from the body of a human being or an animal.
2 V To **shit** means to get rid of faeces from the body.
3 NU People sometimes refer to things that they do not like as **shit**.
4 NC People sometimes refer to a person who they do

not like as a **shit**; an offensive use.
5 **Shit** is used to express anger, impatience or disgust.
6 NU The **shits** is diarrhoea.

shitty /ˈʃɪti/
ADJ If someone describes a thing or person as **shitty**, they mean that they dislike them or think they are unpleasant; a very rude word used in informal English.

shiver /ˈʃɪvə/ **shivers, shivering, shivered**
V When you **shiver**, your body shakes slightly because you are cold or frightened. *I stood shivering with cold on the doorstep.* ▸ Also NC *I could not repress a shiver whenever I thought of him.*

shivery /ˈʃɪvəri/
ADJ If you are **shivery**, you are trembling because you are cold, frightened, or unwell; an informal word.

shoal /ʃəʊl/ **shoals**
NC A **shoal** of fish is a large group of them swimming together. *...shoals of giant jellyfish. ...a small shoal of exotic fish.*

shock /ʃɒk/ **shocks, shocking, shocked**
1 NC If you have a **shock**, you suddenly have an unpleasant or surprising experience. *She got such a shock that she dropped the milk... I recovered gradually from the shock of her death... It was a shock to discover that they were English.*
2 NU **Shock** is a person's emotional and physical condition when something frightening or upsetting has happened to them. *Numb with shock, she stood watching as they took his body away.*
3 NU In medicine, **shock** is a serious physical condition in which your blood cannot circulate properly, for example because you have had a bad injury. *She was taken to hospital suffering from shock.*
4 NC OR NU A **shock** is also a slight movement in something when it is hit by something else. *This padding should absorb any sudden shocks... It also has springs in the heel and toe so you don't get all the shock going up into your back.*
5 NC A **shock** is also the same as an **electric shock**. *I got a nasty shock from the electric iron.*
6 VO If something **shocks** you, it makes you feel very upset. *She was deeply shocked by her husband's death.*
7 V OR V You can also say that something **shocks** you when it upsets or offends you because you think it is rude or morally wrong. *Are you easily shocked?... The killings have shocked and angered people here... Many of those who take up these attitudes and symbols do it merely to shock.* ◆ **shocked** ADJ *Don't look so shocked.*
8 NC A **shock** of hair is a thick mass of it; a literary use. *He was tall and handsome with a shock of hair falling over his forehead.*

shock absorber, shock absorbers
NC A **shock absorber** is a device that is designed to reduce the effect of a force or shock; used especially of devices that are fitted to cars or other vehicles in order to make travelling over bumpy surfaces feel smoother. *Shock absorbers reduce the uncomfortable and wearing effects of driving on a rough or bumpy road. ...front and rear shock absorbers.*

shocker /ˈʃɒkə/ **shockers**
NC A **shocker** is something such as a story, a piece of news, or a film, that shocks people or that is intended to shock them; an informal word, often used humorously. *We watched a late-night shocker called 'Tales of Terror'... The last shocker was the discovery that the judge had been taking bribes.*

shocking /ˈʃɒkɪŋ/
1 ADJ Something that is **shocking** makes people upset or angry, because they think it is morally wrong. *It was shocking how badly paid these young girls were. ...the most shocking book of its time.*
2 ADJ **Shocking** also means very bad; an informal use. *The paintwork was really shocking... I'm shocking at spelling.*

shockproof /ˈʃɒkpruːf/
ADJ A **shockproof** watch is not easily damaged if you knock it or drop it.

shock tactics

N PL If you use **shock tactics**, you do something violently or suddenly in order to surprise and defeat an opponent. *It remains to be seen whether shock tactics can produce any change in policy.*

shock therapy

1 NU **Shock therapy** or **shock treatment** is a way of treating mental illness by passing an electric current through a patient's brain. *Many homes for the mentally ill used sedatives, seclusion, shock therapy, and restraints... In cases of severe depression, electric shock treatment is administered.*

2 NU You can refer to the use of extreme policies or actions to solve a particular problem, especially to solve it quickly, as **shock therapy** or **shock treatment**. *...the shock therapy required to revive the East European economies... Mr Lawson has told a committee of MPs the British economy did not need the kind of shock treatment that was administered in 1979.*

shock wave, shock waves

1 NC A **shock wave** is an area of intense heat and high pressure moving through the air. Shock waves can be caused by an explosion, earthquake, or by an object travelling faster than sound. *The shock wave from a one megaton bomb could devastate a whole city.*

2 NC A **shock wave** is also the effect of something such as a piece of news or a new type of activity that causes strong reactions when it spreads through a place. *When the news was broadcast, shock waves spread through voters from Land's End to John o' Groats. ...the difficulties of absorbing the shock waves of change.*

shod /ʃɒd/

Shod is the past tense and past participle of **shoe**.

shoddy /ʃɒdi/

ADJ Something that is **shoddy** has been done or made carelessly or badly. *It is up to the teacher not to accept shoddy work. ...shoddy goods.*

shoe /ʃuː/ **shoes, shoeing, shod**

1 NC **Shoes** are objects worn on your feet, usually over socks or stockings. **Shoes** cover most of your foot but not your ankle. *She needs a new pair of shoes.*

2 VO To **shoe** a horse means to fix horseshoes onto its hooves. *I was shoeing an average of eight horses a day.*

3 If you **step into** someone's **shoes**, or fill someone's **shoe's**, you take their place by doing the job that they were doing. *Can the army produce a new leader to step into General Zia's shoes?... He is trying to prevent the possibility of Michael Heseltine filling Mrs Thatcher's shoes.*

shoehorn /ʃuːhɔːn/ **shoehorns**

NC A **shoehorn** is a piece of metal or plastic with a slight curve that you hold in the back of your shoe to help you put the shoe on more easily.

shoelace /ʃuːleɪs/ **shoelaces**

NC **Shoelaces** are long, narrow cords used to fasten shoes. *He stopped to tie up his shoelace.*

shoestring /ʃuːstrɪŋ/

If something is done **on a shoestring**, it is done using very little money. *...budgeting for a family on a shoestring.*

shone /ʃɒn/

Shone is the past tense and past participle of **shine**.

shoo /ʃuː/ **shoos, shooing, shooed**; an informal word.

1 VOA If you **shoo** an animal or a person somewhere, you make them go there by waving your hands or arms at them. *She shooed the birds in the direction of the open window... They'd clap their hands to shoo the camels away.*

2 You say '**Shoo!**' to an animal to make it go away. *'Go away!' we shouted. 'Shoo!'*

shook /ʃʊk/

Shook is the past tense of **shake**.

shoot /ʃuːt/ **shoots, shooting, shot**

1 V or V A To **shoot** means to fire a bullet from a gun. *The men were armed and ready to shoot... 'Don't shoot', he shouted... We were told to shoot first and ask questions later... We suddenly realised we were being shot at.*

2 VO or V-REFL To **shoot** a person or animal means to kill or injure them by firing a gun at them. *Two police officers have been shot and seriously wounded in Belfast. ...criminal poachers who shoot elephants to sell their ivory... He shot his wife and then shot himself.*

3 VO If you **shoot** an arrow, you fire it from a bow. *The kids are dancing round shooting arrows at them.*

4 V-ERG A To **shoot** in a particular direction means to move in that direction quickly and suddenly. *She shot back into the room... He shot out his hand and stopped the child from falling.*

5 VOA If you **shoot** a glance at someone, you look at them quickly and briefly; a literary use. *He shot a suspicious glare at me.*

6 VO When a film is **shot**, it is photographed using film cameras. *Most of the film was shot in Spain.*

7 V When someone **shoots** in a game such as football or hockey, they try to score by suddenly sending the ball towards the goal. *He missed a great opportunity to shoot at goal... 'Shoot!', yelled the crowd.*

8 NC A **shoot** is also a plant that is beginning to grow, or a new part growing from a plant or tree. *A few tender shoots had started to appear.*

9 See also **shot**. to **shoot on sight**: see **sight**.

shoot down PHRASAL VERB If someone **shoots down** an aeroplane or helicopter, they make it fall to the ground by hitting it with a bullet or missile. *Angola's UNITA rebels say they have shot down a cargo plane and killed nineteen government soldiers in the past week... It's been unofficially confirmed that a fighter bomber was shot down after intruding in Pakistani air space.*

shoot up PHRASAL VERB If something **shoots up**, it grows or increases very quickly. *The inflation rate shot up from 30% to 48%.*

shooting /ʃuːtɪŋ/ **shootings**

1 NC When there is a **shooting**, someone is killed or injured by being shot with a gun. *The police arrived fifteen minutes after the shooting... He has also been involved in planning bombings and shootings.*

2 NU **Shooting** is the sport of hunting birds or animals with a gun. *'You care for nothing but shooting, dogs, and rat-catching.' ...the start of the grouse shooting season on the moors of Scotland and Northern England.*

shooting gallery, shooting galleries

NC A **shooting gallery** is a place where people use rifles to shoot at targets, especially in order to win prizes, for example at a fair. *...wild rides, shooting galleries and loud music.*

shooting star, shooting stars

NC A **shooting star** is a piece of rock or metal that burns very brightly when it enters the earth's atmosphere from space, and is seen from earth as a bright star travelling very fast across the sky. *I was amazed to see a brilliant streak of light cutting across the sky—it was a shooting star. ...marvellous showers of shooting stars.*

shooting stick, shooting sticks

NC A **shooting stick** is a strong stick with a sharp point at one end and a flat piece at the other end. You stick the point into the ground and sit on the flat end.

shoot-out, shoot-outs

NC A **shoot-out** is a fight in which people shoot at each other with guns. *He was wounded during a shoot-out with the police.*

shop /ʃɒp/ **shops, shopping, shopped**

1 NC A **shop** is a building or part of a building where things are sold. *Two customers came into the shop. ...a shoe shop.*

2 V When you **shop**, you go to shops and buy things. *We allow the older girls to shop in the village without an escort... They tend to shop at the supermarket.*

3 NC+SUPP A **shop** is also a place where a particular kind of thing is made. *...metalwork shops.*

4 See also **shopping**.

shop around PHRASAL VERB If you **shop around**, you go to different shops and compare prices and quality before buying something. *Shop around for the best price for petrol that you can find... Consumers can always get a better deal simply by shopping around.*

shop assistant, shop assistants
NC A **shop assistant** is a person who works in a shop selling things to customers. *The department store, Woolworths, has allowed a shop assistant to keep her job after first suspending her for refusing to work on the cigarette counter... Shop assistants spend their whole day marking up prices.*

shop floor
N SING The **shop floor** refers to all the workers in a factory, especially in contrast to the management. *There should be participation in decisions made on the shop floor.*

shop front, shop fronts
NC A **shop front** is the outside part of a shop which faces the street, including the door and windows. *Quite a few of the shop-fronts were still boarded up.*

shopkeeper /ˈʃɒpkiːpə/ **shopkeepers**
NC A **shopkeeper** is a person who owns a small shop. *More than one in two shopkeepers are illegally selling cigarettes and other tobacco products to children under 16. ...shopkeepers and small business.*

shoplifter /ˈʃɒplɪftə/ **shoplifters**
NC A **shoplifter** is a person who steals things from a shop by shoplifting. *...the technology used in department stores to discourage shoplifters.*

shoplifting /ˈʃɒplɪftɪŋ/
NU **Shoplifting** is stealing from a shop by walking round the shop and hiding things in your bag or clothes. *The grocer accused her of shoplifting and demanded to look in her bag... Some months ago she was involved in an alleged shoplifting offence.*

shopper /ˈʃɒpə/ **shoppers**
NC A **shopper** is someone who is shopping. *The city centre was crowded with shoppers.*

shopping /ˈʃɒpɪŋ/
1 NU **Shopping** is the activity of going to shops to buy something. *They went shopping after lunch... An estimated 62 per cent of shopping is done in supermarkets.*
2 NU Your **shopping** consists of things that you have just bought from shops. *She put her shopping away in the kitchen.*

shopping centre, shopping centres
NC A **shopping centre** is an area in a town where a lot of shops have been built close together. *...a plan to build an underground car park at a nearby shopping centre. ...the city's busiest shopping centre.*

shopping list, shopping lists
NC A **shopping list** is a written list of the things that you want to buy when you go shopping. *Make a shopping list and try to keep to it.*

shopping mall, shopping malls
NC A **shopping mall** is an area where a lot of shops have been built close together and where cars are not allowed. *In the shopping mall some businesses are closed. Others are holding going-out-of-business sales... He asked where he could go to buy a newspaper. They pointed him in the direction of a shopping mall.*

shop-soiled
ADJ **Shop-soiled** goods are slightly dirty or damaged, and are therefore sold at a lower price. *...a shop-soiled dress.*

shop steward, shop stewards
NC A **shop steward** is a trade union member who has been elected to represent other members. *Shop stewards have decided to hold a ballot on whether workers should end their month-long strike over pay... The deal had been recommended by the union negotiators but the stop stewards advised their members to reject it.*

shopworn /ˈʃɒpwɔːn/
ADJ **Shopworn** means the same as **shop-soiled**; used in American English.

shore /ʃɔː/ **shores, shoring, shored**
1 NC The **shore** of a sea, lake, or wide river is the land along the edge of it. *We could see the trees on the other shore.*
2 Someone who is **on shore** is on the land rather than on a ship. *They say at this stage there is no need for people on shore to be concerned about the oil spillage.*
shore up PHRASAL VERB If you **shore up** something which is becoming weak, you strengthen it. *Action is*

needed to shore up economic links with American suppliers.

shoreline /ˈʃɔːlaɪn/ **shorelines**
NCorNU The **shoreline** is the edge of a sea, lake, or wide river. *Traces of the blue-green algae have been found on the shoreline of Rutland Water... The oil tanker ran aground in the Gulf of Alaska and polluted more than twelve hundred miles of shoreline.*

shorn /ʃɔːn/
1 **Shorn** is a past participle of **shear**.
2 ADJ **Shorn** grass or hair has been cut very short. *...shorn blades of grass. ...his shorn head.*
3 If you are **shorn of** something that is important to you, it is taken away from you. *...demoralized people shorn of personal initiative... Weddings and burials were shorn of their customary festivities.*

short /ʃɔːt/ **shorter, shortest; shorts**
1 ADJ If something lasts for a **short** time, it does not last very long. *...a short holiday... He died last week after a short illness... He uttered a short cry of surprise.*
2 ADJ **Short** speeches, letters, or books do not have many words or pages. *He made a short speech expressing solidarity with the Hungarian people... The short play 'Mountain Language' was inspired by a visit he made to Turkey in 1985... She spoke in short sentences.*
3 ADJ A **short** person is not as tall as most people. *...a short, fat man.*
4 ADJ A **short** object measures only a small amount from one end to the other. *...a short flight of steps... Her hair was cut short.*
5 ADJ PRED+*with* If you are **short** with someone, you speak impatiently and crossly to them. *I'm sorry I was so short with you.*
6 ADJ If you have a **short** temper, you get angry easily. *His critics recall him as a reactionary with a short temper.*
7 N PL **Shorts** are trousers with short legs. *He was wearing a white sun hat and tennis shorts.*
8 ADJ PRED If you are **short** of something or if it is **short**, you do not have enough of it. *We're dreadfully short of staff at present... When money is short, we stick to a very careful budget.*
9 See also **shortly**.
● **Short** is used in these phrases. ● If something is **short of** a place or amount, it has not quite reached it. *He drove up the hill and stopped the car just short of the summit... He was only a year short of fifty.* ● If something **is running short**, or you **are running short** of it, you have almost used up your supply of it. *Food is running short because the floodwaters have disrupted transport... He has denied reports that they're running short of arms and ammunition.* ● If something **is cut short**, it is stopped before it has finished. *The war cut short his education.* ● To **fall short** of a target means to fail to reach it. *The grenade fell short of the vehicle and the officers were unhurt... The agreement falls short of full diplomatic ties.* ● If you **stop short** or if something **stops** you **short**, you suddenly stop what you are doing, for example because something has surprised you. *The soldier took a few steps and then stopped short... His disapproval stopped her short.* ● If someone **stops short of** doing something, they nearly do it but do not actually do it. *He just stopped short of calling her a murderer.* ● If you are called something **for short**, it is a short version of your name. You can also say that a short version of your name is **short for** your name. *Her name was Madeleine but Celia always called her 'Maddy' for short... People usually call me 'Ferdy'. It's short for 'Ferdinand'.* ● You use the expression **in short** when you are summarizing what you have just said. *I was packing, arranging the trip, cleaning the house, and saying countless goodbyes. In short, it was a hectic week.* ● **at short notice**: see notice. ● **in short supply**: see supply.

shortage /ˈʃɔːtɪdʒ/ **shortages**
NC If there is a **shortage** of something, there is not enough of it. *He said conditions were now improving, though there was still an acute food shortage. ...a world shortage of fuel. ...the housing shortage.*

shortbread /ʃɔːtbred/
NU **Shortbread** is a kind of biscuit made from flour, sugar, and butter.

shortcake /ʃɔːtkeɪk/
NU **Shortcake** is the same as **shortbread**.

short-change, short-changes, short-changing, short-changed
1 VO If someone **short-changes** you, they cheat you by not giving you enough change when you have bought something from them. *That's the second time I've been short-changed in that shop.*
2 VO You can also say that someone **short-changes** you if they behave unfairly or dishonestly towards you, for example by treating you badly or giving you less than they should; an informal use. *We have been short-changed by the government... These kids knew they were not getting an education, and they knew they were being short-changed... I think this short-changes students—I think it deprives them of the opportunity to read anything of significance.*

short-circuit, short-circuits
NC If there is a **short-circuit** in an electrical system, there is a wrong connection or a damaged wire, so that electricity travels along the wrong route and damages the system or device. *The electrical wiring was inadequately insulated, which resulted in a short-circuit... This aluminium strip had been incorporated by mistake into the chip's wiring pattern and was causing a short-circuit to a vital part.*

shortcoming /ʃɔːtkʌmɪŋ/ **shortcomings**
NC The **shortcomings** of a person, organization, or system are its faults or weaknesses. *You've got to realize your own shortcomings... He criticized shortcomings in the quality and quantity of supplies of consumer goods.*

shortcrust /ʃɔːtkrʌst/
ADJ ATTRIB **Shortcrust** pastry is a simple kind of pastry that is quick and easy to make and that crumbles very easily.

short cut, short cuts
1 NC A **short cut** is a way of getting somewhere that is quicker than the usual route. *Will you show me that short cut to Wirral Hill?*
2 NC A **short cut** is also a quicker way of achieving something than if you use the usual methods. *Short cuts at this stage can be costly... Parents of twins simply have to find short-cuts in housework.*

shorten /ʃɔːtn/ **shortens, shortening, shortened**
1 VO If you **shorten** an event or the length of time that something lasts, it does not last as long as it would otherwise have done. *The colonel had a plan to shorten the war.*
2 V-ERG If an object **shortens** or if you **shorten** it, it becomes smaller in length. *The back muscles contract and shorten as your leg lifts... She wondered if she could have the sleeves shortened.*

shortfall /ʃɔːtfɔːl/ **shortfalls**
NC If there is a **shortfall** of something, there is less of it than you need. *There were serious shortfalls in the planned production of oil and coal. ...a shortfall of energy supplies.*

shorthand /ʃɔːthænd/
1 NU **Shorthand** is a quick way of writing which uses signs to represent words or syllables. *...people who can write shorthand at amazingly fast speeds... It was written in 1914 in longhand and shorthand, on pages torn from a notebook.*
2 NU If one phrase or explanation is **shorthand** for another, more complicated phrase or explanation, it is a quick and easy way of referring to it. *The disease is commonly known as Mad Cow Disease, shorthand for Bovine Spongiform Encephalopathy.*

short-handed
ADJ If a firm or company is **short-handed**, it does not have enough people to work on a particular job. *These volunteers would staff military health facilities that are short-handed because of the war.*

shorthand typist, shorthand typists
NC A **shorthand typist** is a person whose job is to type and do shorthand, usually in an office.

short-haul
ADJ ATTRIB **Short-haul** is used to describe things that

involve transporting goods or passengers over short distances. *Her family owned three small trucks and did a short-haul business... The employees prepare meals for short-haul jets.*

short-list, short-lists, short-listing, short-listed
1 NC If someone or something is on a **short-list** for a job or prize, they are one of a small group chosen from a larger group. The small group is judged again and a final decision is made about which of them is the best. *The short-list for Britain's most prestigious award for literary fiction, the Booker Prize, has just been announced... In future, members of Labour's National Executive will draw up a short-list of suitable candidates.*
2 VO If someone or something is **short-listed**, they are put on a short-list. *Her novel has been short-listed for the Booker Prize... Sanyo considered several countries in Europe and short-listed the United Kingdom and France.*

short-lived
ADJ Something that is **short-lived** does not last very long. *His joy and relief were short-lived.*

shortly /ʃɔːtli/
1 ADV If something is going to happen **shortly**, it is going to happen soon. If something happened **shortly** after something else, it happened soon after it. *She's going to London shortly... She died in an accident shortly afterwards... Shortly before dawn he had an idea.*
2 ADV If you speak to someone **shortly**, you speak in a cross or impatient way. *'You ought to be in bed,' I said shortly.*

short-range
ADJ Something that is **short-range** reaches or covers only a short distance or time. *Short-range weapons were carried on smaller missiles.*

short-sighted
1 ADJ If you are **short-sighted**, you cannot see things properly when they are far away. *He is very short-sighted... Being comparatively short-sighted they can only see a meal up to five or ten centimetres away.*
2 ADJ A **short-sighted** decision does not take account of the way things may develop in the future; used showing disapproval. *Environmentalists fear that this is a short-sighted approach to the problem of global warming... He's being very short-sighted about this.*

short-staffed
ADJ A company that is **short-staffed** does not have enough people working for it. *They're rather short-staffed at the moment.*

short story, short stories
NC A **short story** is a piece of prose fiction that is much shorter than a conventional novel. *Bierce was a journalist, poet, and writer of short stories. ...a collection of Scott Fitzgerald's short stories.*

short-tempered
ADJ **Short-tempered** people get angry very easily. *Mr Rokowski has a reputation for being short-tempered.*

short-term
1 ADJ Something such as a problem or solution that is **short-term** lasts for only a short time. *For many, the problems are more than short-term... The artificial heart is designed only for short-term use.*
2 ADJ **Short-term** effects or developments will happen soon, rather than happening more gradually over a period of time. *The effects of the computer revolution will be felt in the short-term future.*

short-wave
N+N **Short-wave** is a range of radio waves used for broadcasting. *The only communication with the mainland was by short-wave radio.*

shot /ʃɒt/ **shots**
1 **Shot** is the past tense and past participle of **shoot**.
2 NC If you fire a **shot**, you fire a gun once. *One of them fired several shots at Ward.*
3 NC Someone who is a good **shot** can shoot well. *He's an excellent shot.*
4 NC In sport, a **shot** is the act of kicking or hitting a ball, especially in an attempt to score. *Try to hit the green with your first shot... Oh, good shot.*
5 NC A **shot** is also a photograph. *I got some great shots of you.*

6 NC A **shot** of a drug is an injection of it. *The doctor gave her a shot of Librium.*
● **Shot** is used in these phrases. ● If you **have a shot** at something, you try to do it; an informal expression. *We must have a shot at saying how large or small it is.* ● If you do something **like a shot**, you do it without any delay; an informal expression. *I told him to bring her at once. He was off like a shot.* ● If you describe something as a **shot in the arm**, you mean that it provides help and encouragement, and is likely to cause an improvement. *The removal of these restrictions brought economic growth and proved a shot in the arm for international trade.* ● If you describe a guess as a **shot in the dark**, you mean that it is a complete guess because you really have no idea what the answer is. *It was a complete shot in the dark, but it turned out to be the right answer.*

shotgun /ʃɒtgʌn/ **shotguns**
NC A **shotgun** is a gun designed for shooting birds and animals which fires a lot of small metal balls at one time. *Californian law requires a 15-day waiting period and background check for the purchase of all guns, including rifles and shotguns... He'd been hit in the back with shotgun pellets.*

shot put
N SING In athletics, the **shot put** is a competition in which the contestants throw a heavy metal ball as far as possible. *In the last Turner National Gymnastics Competition, Al Grossman competed in the parallel bars, the shot put, and the long jump... East Germany's Ulf Timmerman took the shot put title.*

shot putter, **shot putters**
NC A **shot putter** is an athlete who takes part in the shot put. *There were other English golds for the women's 400 metres relay team and for shot putter Simon Williams.*

should /ʃəd, ʃʊd, ʃʊd/. **Should** is sometimes considered to be the past tense of **shall**, but in this dictionary the two words are dealt with separately.
1 MODAL If you say that something **should** happen, you mean that it will probably happen. *We should be there by dinner time... There shouldn't be any difficulties.*
2 MODAL You also say that something **should** happen when you think that it is right or a good idea. *Crimes should be punished... These birds shouldn't be in a cage... Should we remain in the EC?*
3 MODAL You use **should** in questions when you are asking for advice, permission, or information. *Where should I meet you tonight?... Should I turn the light on?*
4 MODAL You use 'I **should**' when you are giving advice. *If you have anything really confidential I should install a safe... I shouldn't bother to copy these down.*
5 MODAL If you say that something **should have** happened, you mean that it did not happen, although it was expected to happen. *Muskie should have won by a huge margin.*
6 MODAL If you say that something **should have** happened by now, you mean that it has probably happened by now. *Dear Mom, you should have heard by now that I'm O.K... The first vessel, the Tipu Sultan, should have already arrived there.*
7 MODAL You say that you **should** have done something when you realize that a mistake has been made and you are suggesting how it could have been avoided. *'Common sense tells you this should have been investigated,' he said.*
8 MODAL If you say that you **should** think something is true, you mean that you think it is true but you are not sure. *I should think it was about twelve years ago... He weighs, I should say, about 140 pounds.*
9 MODAL You also use **should** to say politely that you would like to have something or do something. *I should like a large cutlet, please... I should like to say something about my new novel.*
10 MODAL You also use **should** in 'that' clauses after some verbs and adjectives. *It was arranged that Celia should come to Switzerland... It's strange that you should come today.*
11 MODAL Some people use **should** in conditional clauses when they are talking about things that might

happen; a formal use. *If we should be seen arriving together, they would get suspicious... Should agreement on aid be reached, then the other difficulties will be swept aside.*

shoulder /ʃəʊldə/ **shoulders**, **shouldering**, **shouldered**
1 NC Your **shoulders** are the two parts of your body between your neck and the tops of your arms. *Sally patted me on the shoulder... He stopped and looked over his shoulder.*
2 VO If you **shoulder** something heavy, you put it across one of your shoulders so that you can carry it more easily. *He shouldered his bundle again and set off.*
3 VO If you **shoulder** the responsibility or blame for something, you accept it. *The government is expected to shoulder the responsibility for financing the project.*
4 N PL You can say that a person's problems or responsibilities are on that person's **shoulders**; a literary use. *The burden of decision is placed on the shoulders of the individual.*
5 NCorNU A **shoulder** is also a joint of meat from the upper part of the front leg of an animal. *...a shoulder of lamb.*
6 See also **hard shoulder**.
● **Shoulder** is used in these phrases. ● If two people who are different from each other in some way **rub shoulders**, or if they **rub shoulders** with each other, they are both present in the same place, often meeting and talking to each other there; an informal expression. *Patrolling soldiers and sullen residents rub shoulders uneasily... Over the past 5 years we have had 110 nationalities represented on our campus, rubbing shoulders with students from the United Kingdom.* ● If one thing or person stands **head and shoulders above** another, they are a lot better than they are. *She is head and shoulders above anyone else... They continue to rise head and shoulders above the rest.*

shoulder-bag, **shoulder-bags**
NC A **shoulder-bag** is a bag that has a long strap so that it can be carried on a person's shoulder. *The Folding Flipstick can be assembled in seconds and fits neatly into a triangular shoulder-bag... The man, who was alone, was carrying a shoulder-bag.*

shoulder blade, **shoulder blades**
NC Your **shoulder blades** are the two large, flat, triangular bones in the upper part of your back, below your shoulders. *I received a sharp blow beneath my left shoulder blade.*

shoulder-length
ADJ **Shoulder-length** hair is long enough to reach your shoulders.

shouldn't /ʃʊdnt/
Shouldn't is the usual spoken form of 'should not'.

should've /ʃʊdəv, ʃʊdəv/
Should've is the usual spoken form of 'should have', especially when 'have' is an auxiliary verb.

shout /ʃaʊt/ **shouts**, **shouting**, **shouted**
1 NC A **shout** is a loud call or cry. *Excited shouts and laughter could be heard from the garden. ...a shout of victory... A shout went up from several thousand demonstrators as Lukanov announced his departure.*
2 V,VO,V-QUOTE,or V-REPORT If you **shout**, you speak as loudly as you can, so that you can be heard a long way away. *The people around him were shouting and screaming... The driver shouted a warning for people to clear the area... 'Stop it!' he shouted... The demonstrators shouted that the treaty had not been honoured.*
3 V+at or V If you **shout** at someone, you talk angrily to them in a loud voice. *The negotiators shouted at each other across the table... There's no need to shout.*
shout down PHRASAL VERB To **shout** someone **down** means to prevent them from being heard by shouting at them. *Mr Healey was shouted down at a meeting in Birmingham... One man stood up to praise Watson's courage and was quickly shouted down.*
shout out PHRASAL VERB If you **shout** something **out**, you suddenly shout it. *We began to shout out that we wanted our money back... The girl stood on the bank shouting out orders.*

shouting match, shouting matches

NC A **shouting match** is a very loud and angry argument between two or more people; an informal expression. *There were a few scuffles and then a prolonged shouting match began, with each faction hurling abuse at the other.*

shove /ʃʌv/ **shoves, shoving, shoved**

VOA If you **shove** someone or something, you give them a hard push. *They were pushed and shoved out of the area... He shoved the letter under her door.* ▶ Also NC *I gave him a shove in the direction of the street.*

shove off PHRASAL VERB If you tell someone to **shove off,** you are telling them angrily to go away; an informal expression. *You shove off, Eric. See?*

shovel /ʃʌvl/ **shovels, shovelling, shovelled;** spelt **shoveling, shoveled** in American English.

1 NC A **shovel** is a tool like a spade, used for lifting and moving substances such as earth, coal, or snow. *Groups of villagers with picks and shovels chip away at the earth in which their homes are buried... Two demonstrators with shovels were arrested for attempting to dig graves in a lawn outside the Pentagon.*

2 VO If you **shovel** earth, coal, or snow, you lift and move it with a shovel. *She helped us shovel the snow off the front path.*

3 VOA If you **shovel** something somewhere, you push a lot of it there quickly. *They were shovelling food into their mouths.*

show /ʃəʊ/ **shows, showing, showed, shown**

1 V,VO,orV REPORT If something **shows** that a state of affairs exists, it proves it or makes people aware of it. *As the statement showed, a great deal of pressure is being put on them... These figures show an 8.5 per cent increase in exports... The post-mortem shows that death was due to natural causes.*

2 VO If a picture **shows** something, it represents it. *The painting shows four athletes bathing... Television pictures showed buildings turned into piles of rubble and dazed residents wandering in the streets.*

3 VOorVOO If you **show** something to someone, you give it to them, take them to it, or point to it, so that they can see it. *Fetch that lovely drawing and show it to the vicar... I showed William what I had written... She showed me where to park the car.*

4 VOA If you **show** someone to a room or seat, you lead them to it. *I was shown into a large apartment.*

5 V-REPORT,VO,orVO-REPORT If you **show** someone how to do something, you do it yourself so that they can watch and learn how to do it. *The woman took the gun and showed how the cylinder slotted into the barrel... Show us a card game... He showed me how an airline pilot would prepare for a flight.*

6 V-ERG If something **shows,** it is visible or noticeable. *The stitching is so fine that it doesn't show at all... He had a strange fierce way of grinning that showed his teeth... Come out from there and show yourself.*

7 VO If something **shows** a quality or characteristic, you can see that it has it. *Prices began to show some signs of decline in 1974... The sketch shows a lot of talent.*

8 VOorV-REPORT If you **show** a particular attitude towards someone or something, people can see that you have it from the way you behave. *I had been taught to show respect towards my elders... He showed his gratitude by making a donation towards a new gallery... He dared not show that he was pleased.*

9 NC When you make a **show** or put on a **show** of having a feeling or attitude, you try to make people think that you have it. *...those who had made open shows of defiance... She put on a good show of looking interested.*

10 NC A **show** is an entertainment at the theatre or on television. *I'll never forget the first Broadway show I ever saw... A successful TV show can certainly make a lot of money.*

11 VO When a film or television programme is **shown,** it appears in a cinema or is broadcast on television. *One evening the school showed a cowboy film.*

12 NC A **show** is also an exhibition of things, often involving a competition to judge which of them is the best. *...a flower show.*

● **Show** is used in these phrases. ● If something is on **show,** it has been put in a place where it can be seen by the public. *The photographs are on show at the Museum until October.* ● When something is done for **show,** it is done just to give a good impression. *The openness of this parliament is partly for show... Is this all for show or is this proposal a serious one that might actually go somewhere?* ● If you say that something **goes to show** that a particular thing is the case, you mean it proves that it is the case. *This policy only goes to show that the US government has not abandoned its desire to try to topple the Contras.* ● What you **have to show for** your efforts is what you have achieved. *There is little to show for his years in leadership... There has been a lot of talking, with more to come, but there is still nothing to show for it.* ● A **show of hands** is a method of voting in which people raise their hands to be counted. *The Labour leadership opposed the motion which was decided on a show of hands... They were protesting at the ruling that the vote should be taken by a show of hands rather than a secret ballot.* ● You can say that someone **steals the show** if they get a lot of attention or praise, especially when you did not expect them to. *It was young Nicola Loud who won the competition and stole the show.*

show around PHRASAL VERB See **show round.**

show off PHRASAL VERB 1 When someone **shows off,** they try to impress people; used showing disapproval. *These young men proudly show off for the camera... Neil Kinnock said he thought televising the Commons would reduce the tendency of certain MPs to show off by acting irresponsibly.* 2 If you **show off** something that you are proud of, you show it to a lot of people. *He was eager to show off the new car... He usually goes around without a shirt to show off his rippling muscles.* 3 See also **show-off.**

show round PHRASAL VERB If you **show** someone **round** a place, or **show** them **around,** you go round it with them, pointing out its interesting features. *Mr Bush says he plans to show them around his new home personally... Maternity Services Manager Heather Cawthorne showed me round.*

show up PHRASAL VERB 1 To **show up** means to arrive; an informal expression. *He showed up at ten o'clock the next morning.* 2 If someone who is with you **shows you up,** they behave in public in a way that embarrasses you. *Behave yourself! You're showing me up!*

showbiz /ʃəʊbɪz/

NU **Showbiz** is show business; an informal word. *We do get some remarkable glimpses of showbiz life.*

show business

NU **Show business** is the entertainment industry of film, theatre, and television. *He began his career in show business as a musician and radio performer... He received the kind of reception usually given to show business celebrities rather than foreign parliamentarians.*

showcase /ʃəʊkeɪs/ **showcases, showcasing, showcased**

1 NC A **showcase** is a glass container used to display objects that are valuable, interesting, or important. *The first showcase in this exhibition contains a bizarre set of draughts... The masks are displayed prominently here in the store showcase window.*

2 N SING A **showcase** is also a particular situation, setting, or example of something in which something is displayed or presented to its best advantage. *The World Bank regards Ghana as something of a showcase, as a successful proponent of structural adjustment... The steel mill and the surrounding city were built in the 1950s as a showcase for Stalinist-style industrialization.* ▶ Also VO *This is where manufacturers showcase their new lines... In 1953 Vaughan Williams wrote a tuba concerto showcasing the instrument's capabilities.*

showdown /ʃəʊdaʊn/ **showdowns**

NC A **showdown** is a big argument or conflict which is intended to settle a dispute. *It's time for a showdown with your boss.*

shower /ʃauə/ **showers, showering, showered**
1 NC A **shower** is a device which sprays you with water so that you can wash yourself. *Something like a third of East German apartments don't even have showers and toilets. ...a shower room with hot and cold water.*
2 NC If you have a **shower**, you wash yourself by standing under a shower. *I want to brush my teeth and take a shower... A hot shower and a change of clothes would be wonderful.*
3 NC A **shower** is also a short period of rain. *...a week of scattered showers.*
4 NC You can refer to a lot of small objects that are falling as a **shower**. *...a shower of falling leaves.*
5 VOA If you **are showered** with a lot of small objects, they are scattered onto you from above. *Suddenly the lid came off and showered him with flakes of rust.*
6 VOA If you **shower** someone with presents or kisses, you give them a lot of them. *They showered each other with gifts at Christmas.*

showerproof /ʃauəpruːf/
ADJ A **showerproof** coat is one that will keep you dry in a small amount of rain but not in a lot of rain.

showery /ʃauəri/
ADJ If the weather is **showery**, there are showers of rain but it is not raining all the time. *A raincoat will keep you dry in showery weather.*

showing /ʃəuɪŋ/ **showings**
NC A **showing** of a film or exhibition is a presentation of it somewhere so that people can see it. *He had just been to a private showing of the film. ...Kung Fu films, now shown at special late night showings.*

show jumping
NU **Show jumping** is a sport in which horses are ridden in competitions to demonstrate their skill in jumping over walls and fences. *He secured the title in today's show jumping with a clear round... Todd looked destined to win but brought down the last fence in the show jumping section.*

showman /ʃəumən/ **showmen** /ʃəumən/
NC A **showman** is a person who is skilful at presenting or expressing something in an effective and entertaining way. *Mr Perkins, always the showman, arrived on the back of an elephant.*

showmanship /ʃəumənʃɪp/
NU **Showmanship** is a person's skill at presenting or expressing something in an effective and entertaining way. *This was a piece of calculated showmanship.*

shown /ʃəun/
Shown is the past participle of **show**.

show-off, show-offs
NC A **show-off** is someone who shows their skills or abilities in an obvious way in order to impress people; used showing disapproval. *Some people are apt to regard him as something of a show-off.*

showpiece /ʃəupiːs/ **showpieces**
1 NC A **showpiece** is something that is displayed or performed in public, and that is usually intended to show someone's skill at something. *Great harpsichord playing is by no means limited to brilliant showpieces like that.*
2 NC A **showpiece** is also something that is admired as a very good example of its type. *The cotton mills became the showpiece of their time... The package is the first of several aimed at making Bradford a showpiece of local authority enterprise.*

showplace /ʃəupleɪs/ **showplaces**
NC A **showplace** is a place or building that is very impressive, for example because it is beautifully designed or well equipped. *The factory was a showplace... Too much was spent on showplace terminals.*

showroom /ʃəuruːm, ʃəurum/ **showrooms**
NC A **showroom** is a shop in which goods such as cars, furniture, or electrical appliances are displayed for sale. *The new model will be in the showrooms in a fortnight's time.*

show trial, show trials
NC A **show trial** is a trial that is widely publicized and that is held, for example, in order to convince people that a problem is being dealt with, or to make it seem as if someone is guilty of a particular crime, usually when this is not actually the case. *The observers fear that the case will become a show trial to impress international opinion rather than the start of a real crackdown... After a show trial in 1938 he had Bukharin shot as a foreign spy.*

showy /ʃəui/
ADJ Something that is **showy** is very noticeable because it is large, colourful, or bright. *...a showy bracelet and earrings.*

shrank /ʃræŋk/
Shrank is the past tense of **shrink**.

shrapnel /ʃræpnl/
NU **Shrapnel** consists of small pieces of metal scattered from exploding bombs and shells. *...a piece of shrapnel.*

shred /ʃred/ **shreds, shredding, shredded**
1 VO If you **shred** something such as food or paper, you cut or tear it into very small pieces. *He still faces charges of obstructing inquiries by shredding documents and making false statements... Carrots taste delicious shredded in salad.*
2 NC A **shred** of material is a small piece of it that has been cut from a larger piece. *She took the letter and ripped it to shreds... One woman said she saw people with their clothes in shreds.*
3 NC A **shred** of something is a very small piece or amount of it. *He said there was not a shred of evidence to support such remarks... Failure will almost certainly cost them the last shreds of confidence of the US people and government.*

shredder /ʃredə/ **shredders**
NC A **shredder** is a machine which slices paper into very small pieces. *They're allegedly still consigning the compromising papers to the shredders and the incinerators... He picked up the agenda sheets and fed them into a shredder.*

shrew /ʃruː/ **shrews**
1 NC A **shrew** is an animal like a small mouse with a pointed nose. *...shrews and voles.*
2 NC If you refer to a woman as a **shrew**, you mean that you think she is very bad tempered or mean; an offensive use. *He found himself married to a vulgar shrew.*

shrewd /ʃruːd/ **shrewder, shrewdest**
ADJ **Shrewd** people are able to understand and judge situations quickly. *He is a shrewd and sometimes ruthless adversary.* ◆ **shrewdly** ADV *She looked at him shrewdly.*

shrewish /ʃruːɪʃ/
ADJ If you describe a woman as **shrewish**, you think that you think she is very bad-tempered or mean; an offensive word. *...mean-spirited and shrewish.*

shriek /ʃriːk/ **shrieks, shrieking, shrieked**
V If you **shriek**, you give a sudden loud, high-pitched scream. *She shrieked in alarm.* ► Also NC *...a shriek of laughter.*

shrill /ʃrɪl/ **shriller, shrillest**
ADJ A **shrill** sound is high-pitched, piercing, and unpleasant to listen to. *The boys broke into shrill, excited cheering.* ◆ **shrilly** ADV *Lewis whistled shrilly.*

shrimp /ʃrɪmp/ **shrimps**
NC A **shrimp** is a small shellfish with a long tail and many legs. *If you looked in a rockpool, you might see crabs and shrimps.*

shrine /ʃraɪn/ **shrines**
NC A **shrine** is a holy place associated with a sacred person or object. *...the shrine of St Foy.*

shrink /ʃrɪŋk/ **shrinks, shrinking, shrank, shrunk**
1 V-ERG When cloth **shrinks**, or if you **shrink** it, it becomes smaller as a result of being wet. *You should dry-clean curtains if possible, as they are likely to shrink... Do not allow your washing to boil, as you may shrink it.*
2 V-ERG If something **shrinks**, or if you **shrink** it, it becomes smaller. *By October last year some key sectors of industry were actually shrinking... Drug treatment has been used to shrink tumours as large as 10 centimetres in diameter to less than 3 centimetres in diameter.*
3 VA If you **shrink** away from something, you move away because you are frightened or horrified by it. *The boys shrank away in horror.*

4 V+*from* If you **shrink** from doing something, you are reluctant to do it because you find it unpleasant. *He shrank from giving Francis a direct answer.*
5 NC A **shrink** is a psychiatrist; an informal use.

shrinkage /ˈʃrɪŋkɪdʒ/
NU **Shrinkage** is a decrease in the size or amount of something. *This is the third straight month that consumer credit has declined and translates to an annual shrinkage of 3.7 percent. ...the steady shrinkage of the tropical forests.*

shrivel /ˈʃrɪvl/ **shrivels, shrivelling, shrivelled**; spelt **shriveling, shriveled** in American English.
V-ERG When something **shrivels** or when something **shrivels** it, it becomes dry and wrinkled. *Trees on the island shrivelled and died... Every year we have a long dry season that shrivels and scorches plants.*
shrivel up PHRASAL VERB When something **shrivels up**, it becomes dry and withered, usually because it has been overheated. *The seedlings had shrivelled up in the hot sun.*

shroud /ʃraʊd/ **shrouds, shrouding, shrouded**
1 NC A **shroud** is a cloth used for wrapping a dead body. *Workers had built an altar of sandalwood logs upon which the mourners placed the body, wrapped in a funeral shroud.*
2 VO If something **is shrouded** in darkness or fog, it is hidden by it; a literary use. *Everything was shrouded in mist... Mexico City was shrouded in dust from the collapsed buildings.*
3 VO If something **is shrouded** in mystery, very little is known about it. *Talks between the advisers continued today, shrouded in secrecy.*

shrub /ʃrʌb/ **shrubs**
NC A **shrub** is a plant like a small tree with several stems instead of a trunk. *Desert rocks, flowers, grasses, trees, shrubs, and cacti are arranged here to show that yards without lawns can be attractive.*

shrubbery /ˈʃrʌbəri/ **shrubberies**
1 NU You can refer to a lot of shrubs or to shrubs in general as **shrubbery**. *The area is remote and overgrown with shrubbery... The camel can eat the harshest shrubbery.*
2 NC In a garden, a **shrubbery** is an area where there are a lot of shrubs. *The voices seemed to be coming from the shrubbery.*

shrug /ʃrʌg/ **shrugs, shrugging, shrugged**
VorVO If you **shrug** your shoulders, you raise them to show that you are not interested in something or that you do not know or care about it. *'Do you mind if I wait?' I asked. Melanie shrugged. 'Please yourself.'... Many shrugged their shoulders when asked their political preference.* ▶ Also NC *The man nodded with a faint shrug of his shoulders.*
shrug off PHRASAL VERB If you **shrug** something **off**, you treat it as not important or serious. *The chairman shrugs off any criticism that their methods are not legal.*

shrunk /ʃrʌŋk/
Shrunk is the past participle of **shrink**.

shrunken /ˈʃrʌŋkən/
ADJ Something that is **shrunken** has become smaller. *...a shrunken old man.*

shucks /ʃʌks/
You can say **shucks** to express disappointment, annoyance, or embarrassment; used in informal American English. *'You made a fine speech.'— 'Shucks, it was nothing really.'*

shudder /ˈʃʌdə/ **shudders, shuddering, shuddered**
1 V If you **shudder**, you tremble with fear, horror, or disgust. *Robert shuddered with fear... The smell made her shudder.* ▶ Also NC *Max looked round him with a shudder.*
2 V If something such as a machine **shudders**, it shakes violently. *The tank braked and shuddered to a violent halt.*

shuffle /ˈʃʌfl/ **shuffles, shuffling, shuffled**
1 V If you **shuffle** somewhere, you walk without lifting your feet properly. *He shuffled out of the room... Patients become progressively more stiff and can often only shuffle painfully for short distances... They shuffle aimlessly about.* ▶ Also N SING *We recognized him by his distinctive walk, a kind of shuffle.*

2 VOorV If you **shuffle** when you are sitting or standing, you move your bottom or your feet about, because you are uncomfortable or embarrassed. *I shuffled my feet and mumbled... I was shuffling in my seat.*
3 VO If you **shuffle** a pack of cards, you mix them up before you begin a game. *Shuffle a pack of cards and the result, surprisingly, will be far from random.*

shun /ʃʌn/ **shuns, shunning, shunned**
VO If you **shun** something or someone, you deliberately avoid them. *These people shun publicity... He shunned reporters' questions on how loan rates would change... The same officials who shunned him as a criminal now treat him as a celebrity.*

shunt /ʃʌnt/ **shunts, shunting, shunted**
VO If people or objects **are shunted** somewhere, they are moved there, usually at someone's command; an informal word. *...the sound of heavy desks being shunted across the room... Colleen has spent years being shunted from one foster family to another.*

shush /ʃʊʃ/
You say **shush** when you are telling someone to be quiet.

Shushkevich, Stanislav /stænˈɪslɑːf ʃʊʃˈkjeɪvɪtʃ/
Stanislav **Shushkevich** became President of Byelorussia in 1991.

shut /ʃʌt/ **shuts, shutting. Shut** is used in the present tense and is also the past tense and past participle of the verb.
1 V-ERG If you **shut** something such as a door or window, or if it **shuts**, it closes. *They've shut the main door to stop the pigs getting out... He goes in and the door shuts behind him.* ▶ Also ADJ PRED *The windows were all shut... You have to hold the trigger to keep it shut.*
2 VO If you **shut** your eyes, you lower your eyelids so that you cannot see. *Mrs Kaul shut her eyes for a moment.* ▶ Also ADJ PRED *He lay with his eyes shut.*
3 VO If you **shut** your mouth, you place your lips close together. *Mr Boggis opened his mouth, then quickly shut it again.*
4 V-ERG When a shop or other business **shuts**, or when the owner **shuts** it, it is closed and you cannot go into it until it opens again. *'What time do the shops shut?'—'Half past five.'... The troops forced merchants to shut their shops.* ▶ Also ADJ PRED *I'm afraid all the pubs will be shut.*
shut away PHRASAL VERB If you **shut** something **away**, you keep it in a place where people cannot see it. *We have a small number of books which are shut away.*
shut down PHRASAL VERB 1 If a factory or business is **shut down**, it closes and stops working. *His department was shut down for lack of funds... The US has decided to shut down the embassy in Kabul because of the turmoil there.* 2 If an engine **shuts down** or if you **shut** it **down**, it stops working altogether, sometimes only for a short time. *The idea is to shut down the cooling system at the plant to prove that the station is safe... The engine apparently shut down eleven minutes after take-off.* 3 See also **shutdown**.
shut in PHRASAL VERB 1 If someone **shuts** you **in** a room or other confined space, they close the door so that you cannot leave. *He was shut in with an assortment of strangers.* 2 If you **shut** yourself **in** a room, you stay in there and make sure nobody else can get in. *She shut herself in the bathroom and wept.*
shut out PHRASAL VERB 1 If you **shut** someone or something **out**, you prevent them from getting into a place. *They had covered the holes to shut out the water.* 2 If you **shut out** a thought or a feeling, you stop yourself thinking about it or feeling it. *She found it impossible to shut out the pain... The best thing to do is to shut out the real world, and go on living in the past.*
shut up PHRASAL VERB an informal expression. 1 If you **shut up**, you stop talking. *Shut up and listen... Tell that girl to shut up.* 2 If someone **shuts** you **up**, they prevent you from talking. *Why do you have to shut me up when everyone else is allowed to sing?...*

Turn the television on. That usually shuts them up.
3 If you are **shut up** in a building, room, or other confined space, you are kept there and cannot get out. *Eight scientists are going to be shut up in a massive dome in the desert to see whether they can survive for two years... Hundreds of protesters were shut up in the Mosque of Al-Azhar.*

shutdown /ʃʌtdaʊn/ **shutdowns**
NC A **shutdown** is the closing of a factory, shop, or other business, usually for a short time. *...temporary shutdowns... Britain's biggest motor car company, Ford, is facing a complete shutdown tomorrow.*

shut-eye
NU **Shut-eye** is sleep; an old-fashioned, informal word. *You'd better get some shut-eye.*

shutter /ʃʌtə/ **shutters**
1 NC **Shutters** are wooden or metal covers fitted to a window. *...an old brick house with green shutters... Thousands of flags were out and shop-owners pulled down their shutters.*
2 NC The **shutter** in a camera is the part which opens to allow light through the lens when a photograph is taken. *The instrument measures the light signal, then the shutter closes.*

shuttered /ʃʌtəd/
ADJ A **shuttered** window or door has its shutters closed. *All doors were locked and the windows closed and shuttered... Markets and shops across the city were barred and shuttered.*

shuttle /ʃʌtl/ **shuttles, shuttling, shuttled**
1 ADJ ATTRIB A **shuttle** service is an air, bus, or train service which makes frequent journeys between two places. *...technical problems on a shuttle flight from Edinburgh.* ▶ Also NC *He caught the nine o'clock shuttle to New York.*
2 NC A **shuttle** is also the same as a **space shuttle**. *The Americans have not put a shuttle into orbit since the Challenger exploded two years ago.*
3 VA If you **shuttle** between two places, you make frequent journeys between them. *The UN envoy had to shuttle between the Pakistani and Afghan camps... They had to appoint a special negotiator to shuttle back and forth between the two countries.*

shuttlecock /ʃʌtlkɒk/ **shuttlecocks**
NC A **shuttlecock** is the small, feathered object that you hit over the net in a game of badminton.

shuttle diplomacy
NU **Shuttle diplomacy** is the movement of a diplomat between countries whose leaders refuse to talk directly to each other, in order to mediate between them. *The UN Special Mediator has just finished a three-week period of shuttle diplomacy between Islamabad and Kabul.*

shy /ʃaɪ/ **shyer, shyest; shies, shying, shied**
1 ADJ A **shy** person is nervous and uncomfortable with other people. *Helen was too shy to say a word in class. ...a shy smile... Akihito takes after his father in being a shy, retiring man.* ◆ **shyly** ADV *They giggled, and turned away shyly.* ◆ **shyness** NU *I tried to overcome my shyness... He showed a mixture of shyness and humour.*
2 ADJ Animals that are **shy** avoid humans and are easily frightened by them. *The black rhino is a very shy animal, with poor vision.*
3 ADJ PRED+of If you are **shy** of doing something, you are unwilling to do it because you are afraid of what might happen. *Don't be shy of telling them what you think... My parents taught me not to be shy of my ideas, and what I wanted to do with them.*
4 V When a horse **shies**, it moves suddenly because it is frightened. *You must have complete control of him should he decide to shy.*
5 PREP If one thing or number is **shy of** another, it is almost at the same level or amount, but not quite. *Singer Jimmy McPartland died early today just shy of his 84th birthday... The vote was 273-185, a good 17 votes shy of a majority.*
6 to **fight shy** of something: see **fight**. See also **work-shy**.

shy away from PHRASAL VERB If you **shy away from** doing something, you avoid doing it, often because you are afraid or not confident enough. *He warned them*

that the Soviet Union would not shy away from imposing even stricter sanctions... Are you going to grasp these opportunities or shy away from them? ...the sort of decisions he has until recently shied away from.

SI /esaɪ/
NU **SI** is the international standard for units of measurement. *SI was introduced when I was at school.*

Siamese cat /saɪəmiːz kæt/ **Siamese cats**
NC A **Siamese cat** is a type of cat with short cream or brown fur, blue eyes, dark ears, and a dark tail. *She was cradling two Siamese cats.*

Siamese twins /saɪəmiːz twɪnz/
N PL **Siamese twins** are twins who are born joined to each other by a part of their bodies. *Doctors have performed further surgery on one of the Siamese twins who were separated at birth.*

sibilant /sɪbɪlənt/
ADJ Something that is **sibilant** makes a soft, hissing sound; a literary word. *There was a little sibilant whispering.*

sibling /sɪblɪŋ/ **siblings**
NC Your **siblings** are your brothers and sisters; a formal word. *Taun lost his parents and his only sibling, a sister, in the war. ...sibling rivalry.*

sic /sɪk/
You write **sic** in brackets after a word or expression to show that it really was spelt or written in the way that you have spelt or written it, even though it is, or seems to be, incorrect. *...No Smokeing (sic). ...February Fun Raising (sic).*

sick /sɪk/ **sicker, sickest**
1 ADJ If you are **sick**, you have a disease or illness. *Thirty-three sick and elderly hostages arrived back in Britain this morning. ...sick and wounded prisoners of war... The sick pig was killed and its brain examined... Two psychiatric doctors refused to endorse the report that he was mentally sick.*
2 ADJ PRED If you feel **sick**, you feel as if the food you have eaten is going come up from your stomach and out of your mouth. If you are **sick**, the food does come up through your mouth. *Flying always makes me feel sick... I only had to look at a cigarette and my throat muscles would tighten, as if I was going to be sick.*
3 ADJ PRED+of If you are **sick** of something, you are annoyed or bored by it and want it to stop; an informal use. *We're sick of sitting around waiting for something to happen... It's denigrated who I am, and I'm sick of it and I'm not going to take it any longer... The population are reported to be heartily sick of these feuds.*
4 ADJ A **sick** story or joke deals with death or suffering in an unpleasantly frivolous way. *She made a rather sick joke.*
5 N PL The **sick** are people who are ill or who have a disease. *She tended the wounded, the sick, and the starving. ...the old, the sick and the handicapped.*
● **Sick** is used in these phrases. ● If you are **off sick**, you are absent from work or school because of illness. *At any one time in Britain 2,000 nurses are off sick with back injury.* ● If something or someone **makes** you **sick**, it makes you feel angry or disgusted; an informal expression. *It makes me sick the way they waste our money... How do you tell a man that he makes you sick?* ● If you are **worried sick**, you are extremely worried; an informal expression. *He was worried sick that the factory might close.* ● If you say that you are **sick and tired** of something, you mean that you are very annoyed by it and want it to stop; an informal expression. *He claimed that the people of this country were sick and tired of being lectured by Mrs Thatcher on what's good for them... They are sick and tired of what's been going on in Washington.*

sick bay, sick bays
NC A **sick bay** is an area, for example on a ship, where people can be given medical treatment and care. *The sick bay was generally empty.*

sickbed /sɪkbed/ **sickbeds**
NC Your **sickbed** is the bed that you are lying in while you are ill; an old-fashioned word. *I was able to watch television from my sickbed.*

sick building, sick buildings

NC You use **sick building** to refer to a modern building which makes people feel ill, tired, or unhappy because of the artificial lighting and air conditioning inside it. *In some sick buildings, they've seen productivity drop as much as 60 per cent... Sick Building Syndrome can manifest itself when levels of indoor pollution are seemingly below the present legal levels.*

sicken /sɪkən/ **sickens, sickening, sickened**

VO If you **are sickened** by something, it makes you feel disgusted or horrified. *I was sickened to see young, healthy men getting killed everyday... It sickens me to think that they are planning to hold this party so soon after my daughter has died.*

sickening /sɪkəⁿnɪŋ/

ADJ You describe something as **sickening** when it gives you feelings of horror and disgust, or makes you feel sick in your stomach. *...a horrifying and sickening murder... Spanish customs officials were alerted by a sickening stench... I had a sickening feeling before I even opened the envelope.*

sickle /sɪkl/ **sickles**

NC A **sickle** is a tool with a short handle and a curved blade that is used for cutting grass and grain crops. *...a red flag bearing a hammer and sickle.*

sick leave

NU **Sick leave** is the time that a person is officially allowed to spend away from work because of illness or injury. *...a job with paid holidays and sick leave... Mr Walesa is currently on sick leave.*

sickle-cell anaemia

NU **Sickle-cell anaemia** is a hereditary disease in which the red blood cells become sickle-shaped, causing jaundice, ulcers, and a high temperature. *Gene therapy could be tremendously useful in curing genetic diseases such as sickle-cell anaemia, diabetes, and schizophrenia... I later found out that Jimmy suffers from sickle-cell anaemia.*

sickly /sɪkli/ **sicklier, sickliest**

1 ADJ A **sickly** person is weak and often ill. *He was a sickly and ineffective man. ...a sickly infant.*

2 ADJ **Sickly** things are unpleasant to smell, taste, or look at. *...a musty, sickly smell... That sickly sweet grape juice always takes me back to my childhood.*

sickness /sɪknəs/ **sicknesses**

1 NU **Sickness** is the state of being ill or unhealthy. *...people who are not working because of sickness or unemployment... Initially the scheme will provide benefit payments only for injury, sickness and child birth.*

2 NU **Sickness** is also a condition in which you feel ill in your stomach and in which food that you have eaten is sent out through your mouth. *The disease causes sickness and diarrhoea... Side effects of taking the drugs included a feeling of sickness in some patients.*

3 NC A **sickness** is particular disease. *In the early 1980s news began to emerge of a deadly sickness that was sweeping through the villages of Uganda, known locally as 'slim'.*

4 See also **morning sickness**.

sickness benefit

NU **Sickness benefit** is money that you receive regularly from the government when you are unable to work because of illness. *...those who qualify for sickness benefit... The average Swede claims 25 days sickness benefit a year.*

sick note, sick notes

NC A **sick note** is a note, written by yourself or your doctor, which you give to your employer to inform him or her that you are, or have been, ill and unable to work. *If you can't sign on for work because you are ill, ask your doctor for a sick note.*

sick-out, sick-outs.

NC A **sick-out** is a protest in which all the workers in a factory or business report themselves sick and stay away from work at the same time; used in American English. *Leaders of the pilot unions have denied that there is a sick-out underway... They escalated their sick-out over the holiday period.*

sick pay

NU **Sick pay** is money that is paid to you by your employer while you are not able to work. *...very poor job security, with no holidays or sick pay... He has been on sick pay ever since.*

sickroom /sɪkruːm, sɪkrum/ **sickrooms**

NC A **sickroom** is a room in which a sick person is lying in bed. *They hustled him out of the sickroom.*

side /saɪd/ **sides, siding, sided**

1 NC The **side** of something is a position to the left or right of it. *A taxi bumped into us from the side... Standing on either side of him were two younger men... I sat down by her side... She was kneeling by the side of the bed.*

2 NC Something that is on one **side** of a boundary or barrier is in one of the two areas that the boundary or barrier separates. *We were told of threatening developments on the other side of the border... As they crossed the line, soldiers on both sides started jeering.*

3 NC Your **sides** are the parts of your body from your armpits down to your hips. *She lay on her side with her back to me.*

4 NC The **sides** of an object are the outside surfaces that are not the top or the bottom. *The box opens on this side... Hogan walked round to the side of the car and unlocked the door.* ▶ Also ADJ ATTRIB *Smithy left the side door open... A large stone was thrown through the driver's side window.*

5 NC The **sides** of an area or surface are its two halves or its edges. *Blood was streaming from one side of her face. ...the wrong side of the road... A hedge surrounds my garden on three sides.*

6 NC The **sides** of something flat, such as a piece of paper, are its two flat surfaces. *What does the leaflet say on the other side?... On one side you're listening to the live performance, and on the other there's a playback of the tape.*

7 NC The **sides** of a hill or valley are the sloping parts between its top and bottom. *We were driving up the side of a mountain... The eagles nest on the sides of the cliffs.*

8 ADJ ATTRIB A **side** road is a less important road leading off an important one. *The riot began on a quiet side street lined with houses... They should have diverted the train onto a side track.*

9 NC You can call the two groups of people involved in an argument, war, or game the two **sides** of that argument, war, or game. *The argument was settled to the satisfaction of both sides... Neither side would comment on the details of a tentative pact that was reached last night... She said she would fight on the side of the farmers.*

10 NC The two **sides** of an argument are the opposing points of view. *She only ever hears his side of things... I had a chance to tell some parts of my side of it.*

11 NC A particular **side** of something is one aspect of it. *The producers wanted to emphasize the political side of the play... There is something distasteful about this side of her character... The ambassador added that there was a sad side to the story.*

12 NC The two **sides** of your family are your mother's family and your father's family. *My grandparents on my father's side were both Polish.*

● **Side** is used in these phrases. ● If you put something **to one side**, you keep it separate from other things, so that you can deal with it later. *I'm going to leave to one side the factor that is most discussed, the military balance... Public opinion is unlikely to allow the government to set the problem to one side.* ● If two people or things are **side by side**, they are next to each other. *She and my brother would sit side by side on the couch staring at the presents... Our degree certificates hung side by side on the wall.* ● To move **from side to side** means to move repeatedly to the left and to the right. *In strong winds, the high buildings tended to wobble dangerously from side to side... When he talks, he rocks from side to side.* ● If someone stays **at your side** or **by your side**, they stay near you and support or comfort you. *On previous overseas trips, she has always been at the President's side... He wanted to live forever by her side.* ● If you **take sides** or **take someone's side**, you support someone who is involved in an argument. *In the first meeting, he was evidently anxious not to take sides... I*

wouldn't want anyone to take my side against Tom.
● If you are **on someone's side**, you are supporting
them in an argument or a war. *Whose side are you
on?... As a boy, he was always on his father's side of
course.* ● If you do something **on the side**, you do it in
addition to your main work. *If the farm prospers, we
could start a little business on the side.* ● You can use
side to give your opinion about the size or quality of
something. For example, if something is **on the** large
side, it is slightly too large. *The food is excellent
though on the expensive side.* ● If you keep **on the
right side** of someone, you try to please them and
avoid annoying them. If you get **on the wrong side of**
someone, you annoy them and make them dislike you.
*Britain is looking for a stable system in Hong Kong,
and that means keeping on the right side of Peking.*
● If you **look on the bright side**, you try to be cheerful
and optimistic about a difficult situation. *Look on the
bright side, if we're too young to see the movie, we
can go home and play.* ● to **err on the side of**
something: see **err**.
side against PHRASAL VERB If people **side against**
you, they join together in order to defeat you in an
argument. *Her opponents always seemed to side
against me.*
side with PHRASAL VERB If you **side with** someone,
you support them in an argument. *The daughters
sided with their mothers... The 'Today' newspaper is
the only one to side with Dr. Owen.*

sideboard /sˈaɪdbɔːd/ **sideboards**
1 NC A **sideboard** is a long, low cupboard, in which
plates and glasses are kept. *Castle went to the
sideboard and poured himself a whisky.*
2 N PL **Sideboards** are the same as **sideburns**; an old-
fashioned use. *He had a moustache and sideboards.*

sideburns /sˈaɪdbɜːnz/
N PL If a man has **sideburns**, he has a strip of hair
growing down the side of each cheek. *With his casual
clothes, collar-length hair and long sideburns, he looks
more like an ageing pop star.*

sidecar /sˈaɪdkɑː/ **sidecars**
NC A **sidecar** is a kind of box with wheels which you
can attach to the side of a motorbike so that you can
carry a passenger in it. *Colin Barrington is at the
controls of a 1939 BSA motor-cycle and sidecar.*

side-effect, side-effects
1 NC The **side-effects** of a drug are the effects, often
bad ones, that it has on you in addition to its function
of curing illness or pain. *This type of aspirin can have
appalling side-effects... The clinical trials may be
halted because of bad side-effects.*
2 NC The **side-effects** of a situation are the things that
happen in addition to the main consequences, without
being planned. *One side-effect of the crisis could be
that she loses her job... In Eastern Europe, one of the
side-effects of freedom appears to be crime.*

side issue, side issues
NC A **side issue** is an issue or subject that is not
considered to be as important as the main one. *I think
that's rather a side issue, don't you?*

sidekick /sˈaɪdkɪk/ **sidekicks**
NC+SUPP Someone's **sidekick** is a companion or
colleague who helps them with routine tasks, but who
is considered to be inferior to them. *When you were
at the Home Office, I was your sidekick... Bernard
specialised in playing weary police officers and
hapless sidekicks.*

sidelight /sˈaɪdlaɪt/ **sidelights**
1 NC A **sidelight** on a particular situation is an
interesting but minor aspect of it. *It is a curious
sidelight on these events that the word 'pogrom' is
hardly to be found in Soviet dictionaries... But a
puzzling sidelight is cast on the situation by the
statement she made to the police.*
2 NC The **sidelights** on a vehicle are the small lights
at the front that help other drivers to notice the
vehicle and judge its width.

sideline /sˈaɪdlaɪn/ **sidelines, sidelining, sidelined**
1 NC A **sideline** is an extra job you do in addition to
your main job. *Fishing is both a relaxing hobby and a
money-producing sideline... He considered music to be
a sideline.*

2 NC The **sidelines** of a tennis court or football pitch
are the lines marking the long sides. *Sometimes,
despite your best defence, some guy comes streaking
down the sideline and goes for a touchdown.*
3 N PL If you are on the **sidelines** in a situation, you
are not involved in it. *I prefer to stand on the
sidelines and watch... The army appeared to be
watching today's elections from the sidelines.*
4 VO If someone is **sidelined**, they are made to seem
unimportant and are no longer included in what other
people are doing. *It's clear that the Committee have
been skilfully sidelined from day to day decision-
making. ...his attempt to sideline the efforts of his old
conservative opponent, Yegor Ligachev.*
5 VO In sport, if a player is **sidelined**, they are not
able to play for a period of time. *He's already been
sidelined for three weeks this season after an
operation on his knee... Canada's Ben Johnson was
sidelined from the race with a pulled muscle.*

sidelong /sˈaɪdlɒŋ/
ADV or ADJ ATTRIB If you look at someone **sidelong** or if
you give them **sidelong** looks, you look at them out of
the corner of your eyes. *Ralph looked at him sidelong
and said nothing... Terry and I exchanged sidelong
glances.*

side-saddle
ADV or ADJ ATTRIB If a person, usually a woman, rides a
horse **side-saddle**, they sit with both their legs on one
side rather than one leg on each side of the horse.
*The horse became famous as the monarch rode him
side-saddle to the annual review each June.*

sideshow /sˈaɪdʃəʊ/ **sideshows**
1 NC **Sideshows** are the stalls at a fairground where
you can do things such as shooting and throwing
darts. *Hey look, there are sideshows on the other side
of the Rotunda.*
2 NC A **sideshow** is a less important or less significant
event or situation related to a larger, more important
one that is happening at the same time. *Alarming as
the American involvement is, it is a mere sideshow
compared with the real war on land... What's
happening in Moscow may only be a sideshow, but I
think we have to be awfully careful.*

side-splitting
ADJ Something that is **side-splitting** is very funny and
makes you laugh so much that you ache all over; an
old-fashioned, informal word. *Rather than using side-
splitting gags, he probes gently.*

sidestep /sˈaɪdstep/ **sidesteps, sidestepping,
sidestepped**
VO If you **sidestep** a problem, you avoid dealing with
it. *...a book that does not sidestep essential
questions... They have sidestepped rather than
resolved their disagreement.*

sideswipe /sˈaɪdswaɪp/ **sideswipes**
NC If you take a **sideswipe** at something, you make an
unexpected attack on it while discussing something
else. *The Prince of Wales yesterday opened his first
architecture summer school with a sideswipe at
existing training.*

sidetrack /sˈaɪdtræk/
VO If you **are sidetracked**, you forget what you are
supposed to be doing and start doing something else. *I
told him how I'd been sidetracked by Mr Starke...
They said they would not be sidetracked by the
growing election fever.*

sidewalk /sˈaɪdwɔːk/ **sidewalks**
NC A **sidewalk** is the same as a **pavement**; used in
American English. *He left his office and walked out
onto the sidewalk.*

sideways /sˈaɪdweɪz/
ADV or ADJ ATTRIB **Sideways** means from or to the side
of something or someone. *Flames blew out sideways
from the fire. He rubbed his chin, and shot me a
sideways glance.*

siding /sˈaɪdɪŋ/ **sidings**
1 NC A **siding** is a short railway track beside the main
tracks which is used for engines and carriages which
are not being used. *The government cannot afford to
allow hundreds of tons of food to rot in railway
sidings.*
2 NC A **siding** consists of wood or metal which has

been cut into strips and attached to the outside of a building to protect it from the weather; used in American English. *With its rippled metal siding, it looks like a huge gray warehouse... Because of the lack of building material, the houses were built out of clay and given a lapboard siding.*

sidle /saɪdl/ **sidles, sidling, sidled**
V A If you **sidle** somewhere, you walk there cautiously, as if you do not want to be noticed. *I turned sideways and began to sidle through the crowd... A woman sidled up to him.*

siege /siːdʒ/ **sieges**
N Cor NU A **siege** is a military or police operation in which an army or police force surrounds a place in order to force the people to come out. *He had been in London to report on the Embassy siege... Since the state of siege was declared, 55 people have been killed... The camp, at Elephant Pass, has been under siege for nearly three weeks.*
● **Siege** is used in these phrases. ● If an army or police force **lays siege** to a building or town, they surround it in order to force the people in it to surrender. *He ordered his army to lay siege to the enclave held by General Aoun... They have been laying siege to a military camp for three weeks.* ● A **state of siege** is a situation in which a government or other authority puts restrictions on the movement of people into or out of a country, town, or building. *The President reiterated his threat to declare a state of siege... The state of siege has been lifted, but leading left-wing politicians have been forced to leave the country.* ● If a building or town is **under siege**, it is surrounded, as a way of forcing the people inside to surrender. *They are trying to make sure that food and water reach people under siege in embassies in Kuwait... The Temple has been under siege by security forces.*

siege mentality
N SING If someone has a **siege mentality**, they refuse to co-operate or make concessions, because they think that other people are constantly trying to harm or defeat them. *The commission said the police officers had a siege mentality that isolated them from the people they served.*

Sierra Leone /sɪerə liəʊn/
The **Republic of Sierra Leone** is a country in western Africa. It was a British colony from the 19th century until independence in 1961. The All-People's Congress (APC) became the only party in 1978 and Major-General Joseph Saidu Momoh became President in 1985. After a referendum in 1991 opposition parties were legalized. Sierra Leone is a member of the Commonwealth and the Organization of African Unity. It exports rutile (titanium dioxide), diamonds, and bauxite. Large foreign debts and high inflation are serious economic problems. ◆ **Sierra Leonean** /sɪerə liəʊnɪən/ N, ADJ
▪ *per capita GNP:* US$240 ▪ *religion:* animism, Islam ▪ *language:* English (official), Mende, Limba, Temne ▪ *currency:* leone ▪ *capital:* Freetown ▪ *population:* 4 million (1989) ▪ *size:* 71,740 square kilometres.

siesta /siˈestə/ **siestas**
N Cor NU A **siesta** is a short sleep that people have in the early afternoon in hot countries. *Regular afternoon siestas, Mediterranean-style, certainly aren't institutional in Britain.*

sieve /sɪv/ **sieves, sieving, sieved**
1 NC A **sieve** is a tool consisting of a metal or plastic ring with a wire or plastic net attached to it. It is used for separating liquids from solids or larger pieces of something from smaller pieces. *Don't throw away the mixture that is left in the sieve.*
2 VO When you **sieve** a liquid or powder-like substance, you put it through a sieve. *Sieve the flour into a basin to remove all the lumps.*

sievert /siːvət/ **sieverts**
NC A **sievert** is a unit of measurement of exposure to radiation.

sift /sɪft/ **sifts, sifting, sifted**
1 VO If you **sift** a powder-like substance such as flour or sand, you put it through a sieve to remove large lumps. *Always sift icing sugar through a fine sieve.*

2 V+*through* or VO If you **sift through** something such as evidence, you examine it thoroughly. *There are archives and documents to be sifted through... He was accustomed to sifting evidence.*

sigh /saɪ/ **sighs, sighing, sighed**
V When you **sigh**, you let out a deep breath as a way of expressing feelings such as disappointment, tiredness, or pleasure. *She sighed and shook her head sadly... Sighing with relief, she took the money.* ► Also NC *With a sigh, he rose and walked away.*

sight /saɪt/ **sights, sighting, sighted**
1 NU **Sight** is the ability to see. *Her sight is failing. ...different senses such as sight, hearing, and touch.*
2 NC+SUPP A **sight** is something that you see, or the act of seeing it. *Beggars are a common sight, and most of them are teenagers... All manner of extraordinary sights could be seen here... The sight of continuing violence on the television has aroused the public's conscience.*
3 N PL The **sights** are interesting places that are often visited by tourists. *The president found time to see all the tourist sights, such as the Zimbabwe ruins... For ninety-nine pounds a head, visitors are taken on a tour of the northern country's sights.*
4 VO If someone or something **is sighted** somewhere, they are seen there briefly or suddenly. *The missing woman has been sighted in the Birmingham area... The bombers were sighted yesterday morning flying at high altitudes... An RAF helicopter sighted the wreckage on a hillside.*
5 NC The part of a gun that helps you to aim it more accurately is called the **sight** or the **sights**. *He surveys the surrounding hillsides through telescopic sights. ...the gun sights of allied artillery and aircraft.*
● **Sight** is used in these phrases. ● If someone or something appears to have certain characteristics at **first sight**, they appear to have them when you first meet them, although they may not actually be like that when you know them better. *The issue is at first sight a technical one... At first sight, tomorrow's Cup Final appears to be a match between David and Goliath.* ● If one thing is **a sight** better or **a sight** worse than a similar thing, it is very much better or very much worse; used in informal English. *It's a damn sight better than most of the places we've stayed in.* ● If something is **in sight**, you can see it. If it is **out of sight**, you cannot see it. *They were allowed to take over the precincts of the government, with hardly a policeman in sight... As soon as the car was out of sight, we relaxed.* ● If a result or a decision is **in sight**, it is likely to happen soon. *It seemed that an end to his agony was in sight... There seemed to be no clear winner in sight... The end of the war was in sight.* ● If you **catch sight** of someone, you see them suddenly or briefly. *She caught sight of her mother... From the ferry, Dave and Val caught sight of the island that could soon become their home.* ● If you **know** someone **by sight**, you can recognize them when you see them, but you have never spoken to them. *Jerry was his name, I knew him by sight, but I'd never spoken to him.* ● If someone is ordered to **shoot on sight**, they have to shoot someone as soon as they see them. *They used to shoot on sight in those days... They have orders to shoot on sight anyone seen in the Golden Temple complex.* ● If you **set your sights on** something, you are determined to have it. *We have set our sights on a bigger house... Her sights are still firmly fixed on a fifth Grand Slam title.* ● to **lose sight of something:** see lose.

sighted /saɪtɪd/
1 ADJ **Sighted** people are not blind. *The system allows blind operators to produce written text for sighted people. ...blind and partially sighted children.*
2 See also **far-sighted, long-sighted, short-sighted.**

sighting /saɪtɪŋ/ **sightings**
NC A **sighting** of something is an occasion on which it is seen, often only for a short time. *There had been four reports of shark sightings... The last known sighting of the priest was on Christmas Eve.*

sightless /saɪtləs/
ADJ Someone who is **sightless** is blind. *They train sightless workers who would otherwise have no jobs.*

sight-read, sight-reads, sight-reading. The form **sight-read** is used in the present tense, pronounced /saɪt riːd/, and is also the past tense and past participle, pronounced /saɪt red/.

V or VO Someone who can **sight-read** can read musical symbols and sing or play them immediately when they see them. *Symphony musicians cannot necessarily sight-read.*

sightseeing /saɪtsiːɪŋ/

NU If you go **sightseeing**, you travel around visiting the interesting places that tourists usually visit. *The queen is expected to do some sightseeing during the next two days.*

sightseer /saɪtsiːə/ **sightseers**

NC A **sightseer** is someone who travels to visit one or more places of interest. *...a large crowd of sightseers... Plain-clothed police mingled among the sightseers, but there was no sign of trouble.*

sign /saɪn/ **signs, signing, signed**

1 NC A **sign** is a mark or shape with a particular meaning, for example in mathematics or music. *...a minus sign... Look at the figures on either side of the equals sign.*

2 NC+SUPP If there is a **sign** of something, there is evidence that it exists or that it will happen soon. *The move is being seen as another sign of Turkey's good relations with Iran... There are now sure signs that intellectuals in the party are unhappy with the leadership... He told Friday prayers in Teheran that he saw no sign of a peaceful solution.*

3 NC A **sign** is a movement of your arms, hands, or head which is intended to have a particular meaning. *Through signs she communicated that she wanted the women to hide.*

4 NC A **sign** is also a piece of wood, metal, or plastic with words or pictures on it, giving information or instructions. *The exit sign is marked with an arrow... A sign saying 'Women's Centre' hung over the door. ...neon signs.*

5 VO or V If you **sign** a document, you put your signature on it. *Sign your name in the book... Sign here to acknowledge receipt.*

6 VO If a sports team **signs** a player, he or she joins that team after leaving another team. *The Lazio club have signed German midfielder Thomas Doll from Hamburg for $7million.*

7 If you say that something is **a sign of the times**, you mean that it is typical of the way people behave nowadays. *That such a character could ever emerge as a hero is surely a sign of the times.*

sign away PHRASAL VERB If you **sign** something away, you sign official documents to say that you no longer have a right to it. *Chiefs were encouraged to sign away land that appeared to be unoccupied... They signed away all their rights.*

sign for PHRASAL VERB If you **sign for** something, you officially state that you have received or accepted it, by signing a form. *When signing for any parcel, always add 'not inspected'.*

sign in PHRASAL VERB If you **sign in**, you indicate that you have arrived at a hotel or club by signing a book or form. *They signed in at the reception desk.*

sign on PHRASAL VERB 1 If you **sign on** for a job or course, or **sign up** for it, you officially agree to do it by signing a contract or form. *He signed on the next morning with the RAF... You could sign on for a course in word processing... He signed up as a painter on the Federal Art Project.* 2 If you **sign on**, you officially state that you are unemployed, so that you can receive money from the government in order to live. *You will have to go on calling at the office every fortnight to sign on while you are claiming benefit.*

sign out PHRASAL VERB If you **sign out**, you indicate that you have left a hotel or club by signing a book or form. *That Friday, I signed out for the weekend... Make sure people sign out, so we know where they are.*

sign up PHRASAL VERB See **sign on**.

signal /sɪɡnəl/ **signals, signalling, signalled**; spelt **signaling, signaled** in American English.

1 NC A **signal** is a gesture, sound, or action which is intended to send a particular message. *She saw a man blow a whistle as a signal to the gunmen... The alarm signals do alert medical staff... He said the nomination would be a reassuring signal to domestic and international finance markets.*

2 VO, V-REPORT, or V+to If you **signal** something, or if you **signal** to someone, you make a gesture or you say something, sometimes indirectly, in order to give a particular message to someone. *The Prime Minister has signalled Czechoslovakia's interest in closer economic co-operation... Recently, government ministers have signalled that a change is needed... The members have clearly signalled to British Coal that the NUM is no longer prepared to be pushed around. ...a parent signalling to a child in the distance.*

3 NC+SUPP If an event or action is a **signal** of something, it suggests that this thing exists or is going to happen. *This was the first signal that an attack was brewing... The dismissal of Yeltsin was a signal for many of them to jump into the Conservative camp.*

4 VO or V-REPORT If something **signals** an event, it suggests that the event is happening or is likely to happen. *The flame will be lit to signal the start of the Winter Olympics... The decline of the cult of Stalin signals a change in the political climate... The policies are designed to signal that Labour has learned from its election defeats.*

5 NC A **signal** is also a piece of equipment beside a railway, which tells train drivers whether to stop. *Railway staff were checking the signals on the line. ...confirmation by British Rail that a signal failure was responsible for the crash.*

6 NC A **signal** is also a series of sound or light waves which carry information. *Marconi finally succeeded in sending a signal across the Atlantic... The boat is not likely to reflect radar signals.*

7 ADJ ATTRIB A **signal** triumph or failure, is one that is significant and considered to be important or noticeable; a formal use. *The performance of the US dollar has been a signal triumph for the central banks... The paper sees the number of entrants as a signal victory for South Korea... Recent talks between the two countries were a signal failure.*

signal box, signal boxes

NC A **signal box** is a small building near a railway containing the switches used to control the signals. *Audible and visible alarms are triggered in the signal box.*

signatory /sɪɡnətə⁰ri/ **signatories**

NC The **signatories** of an official document are the people who sign it; a formal word. *...a signatory to the North Atlantic Treaty.*

signature /sɪɡnətʃə/ **signatures**

NC Your **signature** is your name, written in your own characteristic way, often at the end of a document to indicate that you wrote the document or that you agree with what it says. *He underlined his signature with a little flourish... He supported his argument with a petition containing 170 signatures.*

signature tune, signature tunes

NC A **signature tune** is the tune which is always played at the beginning or end of a particular television or radio programme. *The signature tune's been changed.*

signboard /saɪnbɔːd/ **signboards**

NC A **signboard** is a piece of wood which has written or painted on it information about a particular building or place. *A painted signboard has been erected, giving details of the meeting.*

signet ring /sɪɡnət rɪŋ/ **signet rings**

NC A **signet ring** is a ring which is engraved with an initial or other pattern. *His signet ring bore the emblem of a dagger.*

significance /sɪɡnɪfɪkəns/

NU The **significance** of something is its importance or special meaning. *A year later I found out the true significance of the name... The talks will take on added significance because of the forthcoming Toronto summit... It was a discovery of enormous significance... Dr. Najibullah said his visit was one of historic significance.*

significant /sɪɡnɪfɪkənt/

1 ADJ A **significant** amount is a large amount. *Lack of*

insulation can result in a significant amount of heat being lost... There's been a significant increase on spending levels. ◆ **significantly** ADV *Prices were significantly reduced.*
2 ADJ Something that is **significant** is important. *...a significant discovery... The arrests of senior officials were far more significant than was first thought.*
3 ADJ Something that is **significant** has a special meaning. *With a significant look at her husband, Mrs Hochstadt went out.* ◆ **significantly** ADV or ADV SEN *He cleared his throat significantly a few times... Significantly, there was no reference to Iran.*

signify /sɪgnɪfaɪ/ **signifies, signifying, signified**
VO or V-REPORT A sign, symbol, or gesture that **signifies** something has a particular meaning. *The resolution does not signify any change in US-Israeli relations... The representatives raised the flag in a symbolic ceremony, signifying that the UN will eventually assume control there.*

sign language, sign languages
NU or NC **Sign language** is a way of communicating using special movements of your hands and arms, rather than your voice. *My parents started learning sign language. ...the Deaf-and-Dumb sign language of hand signals.*

signpost /saɪnpəʊst/ **signposts**
1 NC A **signpost** is a sign beside a road with information on it such as the name of a town and how far away it is. *Yellow ribbons adorned neighbouring trees, signposts and front doors... There are no landmarks or signposts here, except a group of tents draped with camouflage nets.*
2 NC The **signpost** of a future event is a clear indication of it. *The outcome of tomorrow's elections will be studied carefully as a signpost of East German voter intentions... So what are the signposts for recovery?*

signposted /saɪnpəʊstɪd/
ADJ A road or route that is **signposted** has signposts beside the road to show the way. *The route is well signposted.*

Sihanouk, Prince Norodom /nɒrədɒm siːənuːk/
Prince Norodom Sihanouk returned to Cambodia in 1991 at the head of a government of national unity. He is the son of King Norodom Suramarit and became the ruler of independent Cambodia in 1953. He was deposed in 1970 and established the Royal Government of National Union of Cambodia (GRUNC) in exile. He was restored as head of state when GRUNC forces overthrew the Khmer Republic in 1975 and resigned in 1976. From 1982 to 1988 and from 1989 to 1991, he was the head of state in exile of the National Government of Kampuchea. Born: 1922.

Sikh /siːk/ **Sikhs**
NC A **Sikh** is a person who believes in the Indian religion of Sikhism. *The Sikhs pulled us out of the hole, and took us back to camp where supper was waiting... The Golden Temple is the Sikhs' most sacred shrine. ...Sikh separatists.*

Sikhism /siːkɪzəm/
NU **Sikhism** is an Indian religion which teaches that there is only one God. It was started in the early 16th century by Guru Nanak. *Bhindranwale established his headquarters in the Golden Temple and began preaching his form of Sikhism.*

silence /saɪləns/ **silences, silencing, silenced**
1 NU or NC If there is **silence**, it is completely quiet. *Thousands of people marched in silence through the streets... His report in Congress was met with stony silence... There was a shocked silence.*
2 NU+SUPP Someone's **silence** about something is their refusal to tell people anything about it. *Levy's silence on the subject was unnerving... He accused the major powers of a conspiracy of silence... He broke his virtual silence of 20 years with an article in the Italian Communist newspaper.*
3 VO If you **silence** someone or something, you stop them speaking or making a noise. *Rodin silenced him with a gesture... Butler's firm speech failed to silence opposition... When children are abused, pornography becomes a tool for blackmail to silence them.*

silencer /saɪlənsə/ **silencers**
NC A **silencer** is a device on a gun or a car exhaust which makes it quieter. *He then killed the general manager with a gun fitted with a silencer... Some of the cars will not be imported unless they are refitted with silencers.*

silent /saɪlənt/
1 ADJ Someone who is **silent** is not speaking. *The woman was silent for a moment... They had to remain silent to avoid giving away their position.* ◆ **silently** ADV *We finished breakfast silently... During the hearing, he stood silently in the dock.*
2 ADJ A **silent** person does not talk to people very much. *She was a silent girl, cool and aloof.*
3 ADJ PRED If you are **silent** about something, you do not tell people about it. *A number of suspects exercised their right to remain silent while being questioned... The Afghan government has been largely silent on the crisis.*
4 ADJ ATTRIB A **silent** action or emotion is one that happens or exists, but is not expressed in words to other people. *About two hundred people held a silent protest in the middle of the square... They stopped and stared in silent disbelief.*
5 ADJ You use **silent** to say that a place or thing that has previously been active or noisy is no longer lively or no longer noisy; a literary use. *The guns have fallen silent... The streets are empty, silent, and not particularly safe.*
6 ADJ ATTRIB A **silent** film has no sound or speech. *In 1924 I did my first silent film... In her early silent movies she was immediately successful as a femme fatale.*
7 ADJ A **silent** letter in a word is written but not pronounced. For example, the 'k' in the word 'know' is silent.

silhouette /sɪluːet/ **silhouettes**
NC A **silhouette** is the outline of a dark shape against a bright light or pale background. *The figure turned towards the sunrise, a tiny silhouette... The cataract shows up in silhouette, using reflected light.*

silhouetted /sɪluːetɪd/
ADJ PRED If something is **silhouetted** against a background, it can be seen as a silhouette. *The houses were silhouetted against a night sky. ...a tall man, silhouetted against the grass as the sun set.*

silica /sɪlɪkə/
NU **Silica** is a substance which is used to make glass. *...crystals of silica... The reflective surfaces contain silica sand.*

silicon /sɪlɪkən/
NU **Silicon** is an element that is used to make parts of computers and other electronic equipment. *Conventional semi-conductors are composed of silicon or galium arsenide. ...severe lung disease caused by exposure to silicon dust in the mines.*

silicon chip, silicon chips
NC A **silicon chip** is part of a circuit in a computer or transistor consisting of a tiny square of silicon with electronic components on it. *The silicon chip has certainly revolutionised our listening habits.*

silicone /sɪlɪkəʊn/
NU **Silicone** is a tough artificial substance made from silicon. *A boy who was born with only one ear was given a second one made from silicone.*

silk /sɪlk/ **silks**
N MASS **Silk** is a very smooth, fine cloth made from a substance that is produced by a kind of moth. *The bride looked radiant in a dress of ivory silk... She wore a fine woollen cloak over a thin silk shirt. ...delicate silks.*

silken /sɪlkən/
ADJ You use **silken** to describe things that are smooth and soft; a literary word. *...silken hair.*

silkworm /sɪlkwɜːm/ **silkworms**
NC A **silkworm** is a type of caterpillar that produces a substance used to make silk. *Silk is now produced by silkworms grown on synthetic food. ...silkworm farmers.*

silky /sɪlki/
ADJ Something that is **silky** is smooth and soft. *...fine silky skin.*

sill /sɪl/ sills
NC A **sill** is a ledge at the bottom of a window. *She sat with one elbow resting on the sill of the open window. ...the window sill.*

silly /sɪli/ sillier, silliest
ADJ Someone who is being **silly** is behaving in a foolish or childish way. *You're a silly little boy... It'd be silly of us not to take part in some sort of communication... What a silly question!*

silo /saɪləʊ/ silos
1 NC A **silo** is a tall round metal tower on a farm, in which grain or other materials are stored. *Police say a silo was blown across a state highway in the tornado... The site was being bulldozed to build grain storage silos.*
2 NC A **silo** is also a specially built place underground where a missile is kept ready to be launched. *...ballistic missiles in permanent silos.*

silt /sɪlt/ silts, silting, silted
NU **Silt** is fine sand or mud which is carried along by a river. *The problem is keeping the harbours free of silt... There's a very high silt content here.*
silt up PHRASAL VERB If a river or lake **silts up**, it becomes blocked with silt. *Forestry ruins the habitat, and promotes soil erosion which in turn silts up the rivers... The Shatt is now silted up and blocked by boats.*

silver /sɪlvə/ silvers
1 NU **Silver** is a valuable greyish-white, shiny metal used for making jewellery and ornaments. *...a little box made of solid silver... A maid passed cheese wafers on a tiny silver dish.*
2 NU **Silver** is also coins that look like silver. *...leaving five pounds in silver in case somebody needed change.*
3 NU In a house, the **silver** is the things that are made from silver, for example cutlery. *...a fine array of furniture, porcelain, silver, and clocks. ...a hoard of silver and jewels valued at forty million dollars.*
4 ADJ Something that is **silver** in colour is greyish-white. *...sparkling silver paint. ...a tall old man with long silver hair.*
5 NCorNU A **silver** is the same as a **silver medal**. *Light heavyweight Bai Chong Guang is expected to win at least a silver... Japan took silver in both events. ...a silver medallist.*
6 ADJ A **silver** anniversary, jubilee, or wedding is the 25th anniversary of an important event or of the wedding. *...the silver anniversary of the nation of Singapore. ...a silver jubilee concert... It's Annie Walker's silver wedding on Monday.*

silver birch, silver birches
NC A **silver birch** is a tree. It has a greyish-white trunk and branches, and its bark looks as if it is peeling off from the trunk. *The coffin, draped in red flags, was borne through silver birch and fir trees.*

silverfish /sɪlvəfɪʃ/; silverfish is both the singular and the plural form.
NC A **silverfish** is a small silvery-coloured insect without wings, which you find in houses. *...a service to rid the premises of ants, cockroaches, even things like silverfish.*

silver lining
N SING A **silver lining** is something good that comes out of a bad situation. *There's usually a silver lining if you look hard enough... There was certainly no silver lining for Labour, who were humiliated in the election.*

silver medal
NC A **silver medal** is a medal made of silver which is awarded as second prize in a contest or competition. *Jenkins won a silver medal at the 1972 Olympics.*

silver paper
NU **Silver paper** is thin paper covered with silver-covered foil. *After taking off their silver paper, she stuck the orchids in a vase.*

silver-plated
ADJ Something that is **silver-plated** is covered with a thin layer of silver. *...silver-plated forks.*

silversmith /sɪlvəsmɪθ/ silversmiths
NC A **silversmith** is a person who makes things out of silver. *For a long time, Sheffield has been the home of silversmiths, and above all, cutlers.*

silverware /sɪlvəweə/
1 NU **Silverware** is cutlery and dishes that are made from silver or from a metal that looks like silver. *They are hiring all the silverware for use at Tuesday's dinner.*
2 NU Sports trophies are sometimes referred to as **silverware**; an informal use. *Celtic's Billy McNeill pays the price for failing to bring any silverware to Parkhead.*

silvery /sɪlvəri/
ADJ Something that is **silvery** looks like silver. *...a silvery dress.*

simian /sɪmiən/
1 ADJ **Simian** is used to describe someone who looks like a monkey or ape; a literary use. *The man in the lift was a small simian creature. ...an ugly, simian face.*
2 ADJ **Simian** is also used to describe things relating to monkeys or apes; a technical use in biology. *...simian deficiency virus in primates.*

similar /sɪmɪlə/
ADJ If one thing is **similar** to another, they have features that are the same or are like each other. *My problems are very similar to yours... The four restaurants were all serving similar food at similar prices... The incident came just four days after a similar fire on a ferry.*

similarity /sɪmɪlærəti/ similarities
NUorNC If there is a **similarity** between two or more things, they share some features that are the same. *They deny any similarity, however plausible, with the reforms of twenty years ago... There is no similarity between the New Zealand situation and the Danish one... Most newspapers note the strong similarity between this hi-jack and the one of 1984. ...the similarities and differences between British and American English.*

similarly /sɪmɪləli/
ADVorADV SEN You use **similarly** to say that one thing is similar to another that you have just mentioned. *Other guests sat under similarly striped umbrellas... Similarly, savings certificates should be registered with the Post Office... Terrible casualties have been inflicted by aerial bombardments, but similarly, rebel attacks have taken their toll.*

simile /sɪmɪli/ similes
NC A **simile** is an expression which describes one person or thing as being similar to another. For example, the sentences 'She runs like a deer' and 'He's as white as a sheet' are similes. *The poems proceed by similes, symbols and allusions... The term 'greenhouse effect' is an unfortunate simile, really. ...a dictionary of similes.*

simmer /sɪmə/ simmers, simmering, simmered
1 V-ERG When you **simmer** food, or when it **simmers**, you cook it by keeping it just below boiling point. *Simmer the beans for four hours until tender... Bring it to the boil, then let it simmer for twenty minutes.*
2 V When a violent situation or quarrel is **simmering** over a period of time, it is not openly expressed, but is likely to break out suddenly. *The dispute between the two countries has been simmering ever since a brief border war... Social unrest is simmering just below the surface... The occupying troops were the focus of an anger that's been simmering and pent up for 17 years.* ◆ **simmering** ADJ *...an atmosphere of simmering violence. ...twenty years of a simmering trade war with Japan.*
simmer down PHRASAL VERB If you **simmer down**, you stop being angry about something; an informal expression. *I thought the trip might give me time to simmer down... While the audience are simmering down, I play a gospel tune.*

Simmonds, Dr Kennedy Alphonse
/kenədi ælfɒns sɪməndz/
Dr Kennedy Alphonse Simmonds was Premier of St Christopher and Nevis from 1980 to 1983, and became Prime Minister in 1983. He was elected to Parliament in 1979. He was a founder member of the People's Action Movement (PAM) in 1965 and became President in 1976. Born: 1936.

simper /sɪmpə/ **simpers, simpering, simpered**
V or V-QUOTE When someone **simpers**, they smile in a rather silly, self-conscious way which suggests that they are trying to make you like them. *The maid lowered her chin and simpered... We were trained to simper, not to think... 'Oh, Professor Swallow, Mr Boon left a note in your mailbox' she simpered.* ▶ Also N SING *'Thank you, doctor,' she said with a simper.*

simple /sɪmpl/ **simpler, simplest**
1 ADJ If something is **simple**, it is easy to understand or do. *The point I am making is a very simple one. ...a simple guide to the elections... It's a simple operation, you can do it in a lunch hour.*
2 ADJ **Simple** things are plain and not elaborate in style. *...a tall woman in a simple brown dress... It's a simple device, made of stainless steel and plastic.*
3 ADJ A **simple** way of life is uncomplicated and fairly basic. *Nature, the simple life, that's what I need.*
4 ADJ A **simple** plant or organism is a form of life that is not well-developed or advanced. *Many complex behaviour patterns are seen in simple animals such as sea gooseberries.*
5 ADJ ATTRIB You use **simple** to emphasize that the thing you are mentioning is the only important one. *Simple fear of death is often what turns people to religion... The simple fact that the North and South are at last negotiating is a step forward.*

simple interest
N U **Simple interest** is interest that is calculated on the sum of money that you originally invest and not on any interest that is added to it later: see also **compound interest**.

simple majority
N SING In a vote, if you only need a **simple majority** to win, you only need to gain more than half of the votes, rather than a higher percentage, in order to win. *A simple majority is sufficient, unlike other UN organisations which require a two-thirds majority to agree to membership.*

simple-minded
1 ADJ A **simple-minded** person interprets things in a way that is too simple, because they do not understand how complicated things are; used showing disapproval. *But he's far from being a simple-minded or stupid man—he's proved himself on occasions a very subtle politician. ...the simple-minded view that people have of robots.*
2 ADJ You can also refer to someone who is mentally slow or confused as **simple-minded**. *She became frail, simple-minded, and returned to her youth.*

simpleton /sɪmpltən/ **simpletons**
N C A **simpleton** is a person with very low intelligence; an old-fashioned, offensive word. *The other inhabitants took him for a simpleton... He had a simpleton for a sister.*

simplicity /sɪmplɪsəti/
1 N U The **simplicity** of something is the fact that it is uncomplicated and can be understood easily. *The advantage of the idea was its simplicity... I can see a certain simplicity and fairness in the government proposals.*
2 N U If there is **simplicity** in the way that someone does something, they do it in a simple and attractive way. *He dressed with elegant simplicity.*

simplification /sɪmplɪfɪkeɪʃn/ **simplifications**
1 N C A **simplification** is the thing that you produce when you make something simpler. *I see this proposal as a long overdue simplification.*
2 N U **Simplification** is also the act of making something simpler. *There will be calls for simplification of the budget system and better financial controls.*

simplify /sɪmplɪfaɪ/ **simplifies, simplifying, simplified**
V O If you **simplify** something, you make it easier to understand or do. *The subject is immensely complex, and hard to simplify... The landlord can cut costs by simplifying administration and maintenance.*
◆ **simplified** ADJ *...a simplified version of the model.*

simplistic /sɪmplɪstɪk/
ADJ A **simplistic** view or interpretation makes something seem much less complicated than it really is; used showing disapproval. *...a rather simplistic*

analysis of the situation... They have often been criticised for being musically simplistic.*

simply /sɪmpli/
1 ADV You use **simply** to emphasize that something consists of only one thing, happens for only one reason, or is done in only one way. *It's simply a question of hard work... It's hard to tell whether his offer of resignation is a serious one, or whether it's simply a tactical move... Is it simply a case of his having no choice?*
2 ADV You also use **simply** to emphasize what you are saying. *Wouldn't it be simply awful?... I simply can't believe it... People are storing potatoes at home because there's simply nothing in the shops.*
3 ADV If you say or write something **simply**, you do it in a way that makes it easy to understand or without giving unnecessary details. *'His life is finished,' he said simply... Put simply, that's just the way Terry lives.*

simulate /sɪmjʊleɪt/ **simulates, simulating, simulated**
1 V O To **simulate** an object, a substance, or a noise, you produce something that looks, feels, or sounds like it. *The wood is carved to simulate hair... The test will involve simulating a nuclear emergency... The voice procedures for take-off can of course be simulated.*
2 V O If you **simulate** a feeling or an action, you pretend that you are feeling it or doing it. *We used this trick in the Army to simulate illness.*

simulation /sɪmjʊleɪʃn/ **simulations**
1 N U or N C **Simulation** is the process or result of simulating something. *The viewer was unable to distinguish reality from simulation... Her remark had been greeted with a simulation of diffidence... We saw no actual pictures of the war, just video game simulations.*
2 N C or N U A **simulation** is also an attempt to solve a problem by representing it mathematically, often using a computer. *Computer modelling and simulation have been used as an aid to battle tactics... Investigators are now using computer simulations, focusing on weather problems.*

simulator /sɪmjʊleɪtə/ **simulators**
N C A **simulator** is a device which is designed to reproduce actual conditions, for example in order to train pilots or astronauts. *I spent months on the simulator flying the Mig-31... We were reviewing information on our mission simulator.*

simultaneous /sɪmlteɪnɪəs/
ADJ **Simultaneous** things or events happen or exist at the same time. *...the simultaneous failure of all the lifts in the building... Iran would attempt to make the withdrawal of troops simultaneous. ...transmitting by simultaneous translation.* ◆ **simultaneously** ADV *Privatisation and price reform must proceed simultaneously.*

sin /sɪn/ **sins, sinning, sinned**
1 N U or N C **Sin** is behaviour which is considered to be very bad and immoral. *They had no sense of sin... They believed they were being punished for their sins.*
2 V If you **sin**, you do something that is believed to be very bad and immoral. *I have sinned against you, Lord, and I beg your forgiveness.*

since /sɪns/
1 PREP, CONJ, or ADV If something has happened **since** a particular time or event, it has happened from then until the present time. *I've been here since twelve o'clock... I've been wearing glasses since I was three... I came here in 1972 and I have lived here ever since.*
2 ADV **Since** also means at some time after a particular time or event in the past. *He used to be an art student. He has since become a lawyer.*
3 CONJ You use **since** to introduce a reason, especially when the reason is already known by the person you are talking to. *Aircraft noise is a problem here since we're close to Heathrow Airport... Since it was Saturday, he stayed in bed an extra hour.*
4 PREP You use **since** after a noun that is modified by the superlative form of an adjective to show that the thing you are talking about is the most extreme example of its type so far. *Nearly a million people watched the biggest parade since the Queen's coronation in 1953... Last year, the number of refugees*

jumped to 8,000, the highest since 1981... This looks like being his biggest hit since 'Roses are Red'.
5 If something has **long since** happened, it happened a long time ago. *...ceremonies and rituals that have long since disappeared... The British had long since abandoned their boats.*

sincere /sɪnsɪə/
ADJ If you are **sincere**, you really mean the things you say. *He was decent, sincere, a good man... He described himself as 'a sincere admirer of the Prime Minister'... The talks were open, sincere and very positive.* ◆ **sincerity** /sɪnsɛrɪtɪ/ NU *The Head Master is a man of deep conviction and sincerity.*

sincerely /sɪnsɪəlɪ/
1 ADV If you say or feel something **sincerely**, you really mean it or feel it. *'I owe you an awful lot,' I said sincerely... The members said they sincerely believe in the furtherance of democracy.*
2 You write **Yours sincerely** before your signature at the end of a formal letter when you have addressed it to someone by their name. For example, if you begin a letter 'Dear Mrs Smith', you can end it 'Yours sincerely'. *Look forward to hearing from you soon, Yours sincerely, David Thomas, Production Controller.*

sinecure /sɪnɪkjʊə/ **sinecures**
NC A **sinecure** is a job for which you receive payment but which does not involve much work or responsibility. *This job's no sinecure, believe me... Being a trustee for a national collection is no longer a sinecure providing amusing adornments for fashionable dinner tables.*

sine qua non /sɪneɪ kwɑː nəʊn/
N SING A **sine qua non** is something that is essential if you want to achieve something or take part in something; a formal expression. *Affection and love— each is a sine qua non of parenting... Tracing history was a sine qua non when addressing this group of academics.*

sinew /sɪnjuː/ **sinews**
NCorNU A **sinew** is a cord in your body that connects a muscle to a bone. *The sinews of his arm were tense... One rarely feels that players are straining heart or sinew.*

sinewy /sɪnjuːɪ/
ADJ A **sinewy** person has a lean body with strong muscles. *...his sinewy brown arm... She was a tall, sinewy type.*

sinful /sɪnfl/
ADJ Someone or something that is **sinful** is considered to be wicked or immoral. *Good women have always saved sinful men in stories... She believed that eye-shadow was sinful.*

sing /sɪŋ/ **sings, singing, sang, sung**
1 V,V O,orV-QUOTE If you **sing**, you make musical sounds with your voice, usually producing words that fit a tune. *She sang, and did a little dance... The marchers sang songs and chanted slogans... The national anthem was sung at the end of the meeting... They carried a small cake with candles and sang 'Happy Birthday'.*
2 V When birds or insects **sing**, they make pleasant sounds. *I could hear birds singing in the trees.*
3 If you **sing** someone's **praises**, you enthusiastically praise them. *I understand that he's now singing the praises of McLeod.*

Singapore /sɪŋgəpɔː/
The **Republic of Singapore** is a country in south-east Asia. It became a British colony in the 19th century and was occupied by Japan from 1942 to 1945. Singapore became independent, and separate from the Federation of Malaysia, in 1965. The People's Action Party (PAP) has been the ruling party since 1959. Lee Kuan Yew was Prime Minister from 1959 until 1990. Wee Kim Wee became President in 1985 and Goh Chok Tong became Prime Minister in 1990. Singapore is a member of the Commonwealth and the Association of South East Asian Nations. It exports petrochemical, electrical, and other manufactured products. Banking, finance, and tourism are important industries.
◆ **Singaporean** /sɪŋgəpɔːrɪən/ N, ADJ
▪ *per capita GNP:* US$9,100 ▪ *religion:* Buddhism, Islam, Christianity ▪ *language:* Malay, Chinese, Tamil,

English (all official) ▪ *currency:* dollar ▪ *population:* 3 million (1989) ▪ *size:* 625 square kilometres.

singe /sɪndʒ/ **singes, singeing, singed**
V-ERG If something **singes**, or if you **singe** it, it burns very slightly so that it changes colour but does not catch fire. *I singed my hair over the fire... A grey cat nearly got its coat singed by the raging bonfire.*
◆ **singed** ADJ *A short distance away, singed pillows, lifejackets, and fragments of clothing lie scattered.*

singer /sɪŋə/ **singers**
NC A **singer** is a person who sings, especially as part of their job. *Anderson used to be the lead singer with an Australian rock band called Rose Tattoo... Joan Sutherland is regarded as one of the greatest singers of this century.*

singing /sɪŋɪŋ/
1 NU **Singing** is the activity of making musical sounds with your voice. *The dancing and singing ended at midnight. ...unison choral singing.*
2 NU **Singing** is also the art of being a singer. *Her natural exuberance, and joy in the singing, endeared her to audiences. ...singing lessons.*
3 NU The pleasant sounds made by birds can be referred to as **singing**. *...the singing of the blackbirds.*

single /sɪŋgl/ **singles, singling, singled**
1 ADJ ATTRIB A **single** thing is only one, and not more. *We heard a single shot... Thousands of them formed a single, solemn line as they entered the church... In each move, you pick up a single coin and move it one square to the left or right.*
2 ADJ ATTRIB You use **single** in front of a noun to emphasize that you are considering something on its own and separately from other things that are like it. *This is the most important single invention since the wheel... We went to the house every single day for six months... The US is the single biggest producer of carbon dioxide.*
3 ADJ If you are **single**, you are not married. *Many single women earn their living by working... All individuals, straight, gay, married, or single have a right to sexual gratification.* ▶ Also NC *Singles in their 20s and 30s are under a lot of pressure to settle down. ...casual sex among singles.*
4 ADJ ATTRIB **Singles** activities, places, or organizations are aimed at people who are not married. *She was trying to find someone new, and wasn't interested in hanging around in singles bars. ...singles holidays.*
5 ADJ ATTRIB You use **single** to describe something that has only one part or feature, rather than having two or more of them. *He was fined £15 for parking on a single yellow line... Single thicknesses of material will not be enough.*
6 NU **Singles** is a game of tennis or badminton for only two players. *The high serve is used a lot in singles. ...the US Open Women's Singles Championship.*
7 ADJ A **single** bed or room is intended for one person. *Hospitals should be able to offer extras, such as single rooms, for a fee... Single room prices range from £52.50 to £60 per night.*
8 ADJ ATTRIB A **single** ticket is for a journey from one place to another but not back again. *How much is the single fare to London?* ▶ Also NC *A single to Edinburgh, please.*
9 NC A **single** is a recording of one or two short pieces of music on a small record, CD, or cassette. *Her last single 'I Think We're Alone Now' was number one in the American charts.*
10 If people move or stand **in single file**, they move or stand in a line, one behind the other. *...a lot of foot soldiers moving in single file down the road.*
11 **in single figures:** see **figure**.

single out PHRASAL VERB If you **single** someone **out**, you choose them from a group for special attention or treatment. *Three other people were singled out for special praise... They single out targets such as judges, retired policemen or prosecutors.*

single-breasted
ADJ A **single-breasted** coat, jacket, or suit has coat fronts that meet in the middle of the chest and only one row of buttons.

single cream
  NU **Single cream** is thin cream that does not have a lot of fat in it.
single-decker
  ADJ ATTRIB A **single-decker** bus does not have an upstairs area. *Most of the children were crammed into a single-decker bus.*
single-handed
  ADV If you do something **single-handed**, you do it without any help. *He had rescued the girl single-handed... The government says it doesn't have the resources to cope with the disaster single-handed.*
single-minded
  ADJ A **single-minded** person has only one aim and is determined to achieve it. *...one of the most outstanding and single-minded journalists in Southern Africa, Willie Musarurwa. ...the single-minded pursuit of wealth.*
single parent, single parents
  NC A **single parent** is someone who is bringing up a child on their own, because the other parent is not living with them. *The new tax means that eighty per cent of pensioners and single parents will benefit... One and a half million children in Britain live in single parent families.*
single sex
  ADJ **Single sex** schools, clubs, or organizations allow only people of one sex to go there. *Girls in single sex schools achieve the highest public examination results... The men are living hundreds of miles away from their families, in single sex hostels. ...a single sex admissions policy.*
singlet /sɪŋglət/ **singlets**
  NC A **singlet** is a sleeveless shirt with no front opening; an old-fashioned word. *...images of shorts and singlets and work-outs.*
singly /sɪŋgli/
  ADV If people do something **singly**, they do it on their own or one by one. *The discs can be read singly or in combination... A vitamin bottle should dispense pills singly.*
sing-song, sing-songs
  1 ADJ ATTRIB A **sing-song** voice repeatedly rises and falls in pitch. *The dialect of the area has a sing-song intonation.*
  2 NC A **sing-song** is an occasion when a group of people sing songs together for pleasure; an informal use. *We had a sing-song after the match.*
singular /sɪŋgjʊlə/
  1 N SING or N+N In grammar, **singular** is the term used for a noun, pronoun, determiner, or verb when it refers to only one person, thing, or group. For example, the words 'chair', 'he', and 'is'. See also **plural.**
  2 ADJ Something that is **singular** is unusual and remarkable; a formal use. *...a lady of singular beauty.*
singularly /sɪŋgjʊləli/
  SUBMOD **Singularly** means to a remarkable or extraordinary degree; a formal word. *Then we did some singularly boring experiments... Her search for financial support has so far been singularly unsuccessful.*
sinister /sɪnɪstə/
  ADJ Something that is **sinister** seems evil or harmful. *...a rather sinister figure walking behind the bushes... He dismissed allegations of a sinister conspiracy against him.*
sink /sɪŋk/ **sinks, sinking, sank, sunk**
  1 NC A **sink** is a basin with taps that supply water, usually in a kitchen or a bathroom. *You can wash your hands in the sink in my garage.*
  2 V-ERG If a boat **sinks**, or if someone **sinks** it, it moves slowly downwards below the surface of the water. *At least 56 people were killed when a boat sank in a river estuary in the east of the country... The skipper sank one boat and damaged several others as he tried to take his ship out of the main harbour. ...people deliberately ramming and sinking refugee boats.* ◆ **sinking, sinkings** NU or NC *...responsibility for the sinking of two British warships in 1946.*

  3 V If something **sinks**, it moves slowly down to a lower level. *As the sun sinks behind the Blue Ridge Mountains, a handful of hikers stumble up the Appalachian trail... But unlike Venice, England is not sinking because of water extraction.*
  4 V A If you **sink** somewhere, you move or fall into a lower position. *She sank back in her chair and sipped her drink.*
  5 V O A If you **sink** something into the ground, you make a hole for it or push it into the ground. *They had the clever idea of sinking an electrode 400 metres down an old borehole. ...British Coal's proposals to sink a pit in open countryside.*
  6 V A If an amount or value **sinks**, it decreases by a large amount. *Wages have sunk so low in relation to the cost of living... Our saving rate is abysmally low, and our investment rate is sinking... The temperature can sink as low as forty degrees below zero.*
  7 V If your voice **sinks**, it becomes quieter or lower; a literary use. *His voice had sunk to a confidential whisper.*
  8 V If your heart **sinks**, you become depressed. *His heart sank at the thought that the exams were a week away... Don't let your heart sink.*
  9 V O In games such as golf and snooker, if you **sink** the ball or **sink** a shot, you successfully hit the ball into a hole or pocket. *Patty Sheehan sank a 20-foot birdie putt on the final hole.*
  10 See also **sunken.**
  sink in PHRASAL VERB When a statement or fact **sinks in**, you understand and realize it. *It took a moment or two for her words to sink in... It might be very easy to learn facts by rote, but they might not actually sink in... The surprise is that it's taken so long for the truth to sink in.*
  sink into PHRASAL VERB 1 If something sharp **sinks into** a solid object or if you **sink** it **into** the solid object, it pierces the surface of it and moves deeply into it. *She walked back to the grave, her high heels sinking into the grass... He sank his teeth into the apple.* 2 If you **sink into** an unpleasant or less active state, you pass gradually into it. *My father sank further into debt... He sank into ever deeper melancholy at the decay of his family and loss of his childhood home... I sank into a deep sleep.* 3 If you **sink** money **into** a business or project, you invest a lot of money in it in the hope of making more money. *They have already indicated their reluctance to sink billions of dollars into the collapsing Soviet economy... Senegal, Mauritania, and Mali have all sunk large sums of money into the dam project.*
sinker /sɪŋkə/ **sinkers**
  NC A **sinker** is a weight attached to a fishing line or net to keep it under the water.
sinner /sɪnə/ **sinners**
  NC A **sinner** is someone who has committed a sin. *Christ is inviting sinners to repentance.*
sinuous /sɪnjuəs/
  ADJ Something that is **sinuous** moves with smooth twists and turns; a literary word. *...an incredibly long sinuous muscular tail. ...the dazzling sinuous intricacy of the dancing.*
sinus /saɪnəs/ **sinuses**
  NC Your **sinuses** are the spaces in the bones of your skull just behind your nose. *...the same sort of operation as having your sinuses cleaned out.*
sip /sɪp/ **sips, sipping, sipped**
  V O or V A If you **sip** a drink, you drink a small amount at a time. *...munching chocolate bars and sipping hot drinks... He sipped from a bottle of orange.* ▶ Also NC *She took another sip from her glass. ...sips of water.*
Siphandone, Khamtay /kʌmtaɪ siːpændɒn/
  General Khamtay Siphandone became Prime Minister of Laos in 1991. He commanded the Pathet Lao in 1965. He was Deputy Prime Minister from 1975 to 1982 and Minister of National Defence from 1975 to 1991. He is a member of the Lao People's Revolutionary Party (LPRP).
siphon /saɪfn/ **siphons, siphoning, siphoned;** also spelt **syphon.**
  1 V O If you **siphon** a liquid from a container, you draw

it out of the container through a tube by using atmospheric pressure. *Water is being siphoned out of the canal area through the drainage system.*
2 NC A **siphon** is a tube used for siphoning liquid. *If the siphons go, do you repair them too?*
siphon off PHRASAL VERB 1 If you **siphon off** a liquid, you draw it out of a container through a tube by using atmospheric pressure. *Claude siphoned off a little petrol from his father's car... A large part of the river has been siphoned off into irrigation canals.* 2 If you **siphon off** money or resources, you cause them to be used for a purpose for which they were not intended. *They were assured that there was no risk of the European countries siphoning off funds from the least developed countries. ...reports that state-grown wheat was being siphoned off to the black market.*

sir /sɜː/
1 VOCATIVE People sometimes call a man **sir** when they are being formal and polite. 'Dear Sir' is often used at the beginning of official letters addressed to men. *What would you like, sir? Dear Sir, I am writing in response to your letter of the 25th.*
2 TITLE **Sir** is the title used in front of the name of a knight or baronet. *...Sir John Hargreaves.*

sire /saɪə/ **sires, siring, sired**
1 VO When a man **sires** a child, the child is born and the man is its father; an old-fashioned use. *The old man had sired a healthy boy child at the age of ninety.*
2 NC+POSS An animal's **sire** is its father; a technical term. *You then split the females up amongst fertile sires.* ▶ Also VO *Bought two years ago, he's already sired ten thousand calves. ...an English-bred chestnut sired by Blushing Groom.*

siren /saɪərən/ **sirens**
NC A **siren** is a warning device which makes a long, loud, wailing noise. *...the distant wail of police sirens... A spokesman said the vehicle flashed its lights and sounded sirens to try and stop the car.*

sirloin /sɜːlɔɪn/ **sirloins**
N MASS A **sirloin** is a piece of beef which is cut from the lower part of a cow's back. *...a sirloin of Scotch beef... You don't have to use fillet, rump or sirloin.*

sissy /sɪsɪ/ **sissies**; also spelt **cissy**.
NC When boys describe another boy as a **sissy**, they mean that they think he does not like physical activity and is afraid to do things that are slightly dangerous; an informal word. *You're a lot of cry-babies and sissies... And if you didn't join him up on stage, you'd look like a sissy, you know?*

sister /sɪstə/ **sisters**
1 NC Your **sister** is a girl or woman who has the same parents as you. *Have you got any brothers and sisters?... He was much influenced by his sister, who's a dancer.* ● See also **half-sister.**
2 NCorTITLE A **sister** is a female member of a religious order. *...the Missionary Sisters of Charity... Sister Katherine's death will be felt deeply.*
3 NC A senior female nurse who supervises a hospital ward used to be called a **sister**. *He has refused to meet nurses over the controversial issue of new pay grades for ward sisters.*
4 NC A woman sometimes refers to other women as her **sisters** when she shares the same beliefs or aims. *They would go to Paris and stay with feminist sisters there.*
5 ADJ ATTRIB You use **sister** to describe a second thing that is connected with or related to something that you have just mentioned. *Her sister ship was sunk by a torpedo... The zoo itself, and its sister zoo at Whipsnade, will be run by a private company... Earth and Venus are regarded as sister planets.* ▶ Also NC+POSS *The city shows every sign of outgrowing its sister.*

sister-in-law, sisters-in-law
NC Your **sister-in-law** is the sister of your husband or wife, or the woman who is married to your brother or to your wife's or husband's brother. *Haydn wrote this concerto for his sister-in-law.*

sisterly /sɪstəlɪ/
ADJ ATTRIB A woman's **sisterly** feelings are her feelings of warmth and affection towards her sister or brother. *...expressions of sisterly love.*

sit /sɪt/ **sits, sitting, sat**
1 V If you **are sitting** somewhere, your weight is supported by your buttocks rather than your feet. *She was sitting on the edge of the bed... Sit with your head between your legs... They sat silently in court while the judge read out the extradition request.*
2 V When you **sit**, you lower your body until you are sitting on something. *He came into the room and sat in his usual chair... Muscular dystrophy is not noticeable before the age of five—the children can sit and walk normally.*
3 V If you **sit** an examination, you take it. *Pupils at the schools run by Trafford Council sat the exam in November.*
4 V+on If you **sit** on a committee, you are a member of it. *Representatives of the workers should sit on the board of directors... Deputies from Karabakh now sit on the Armenian parliament.*
5 V When a parliament, law court, or other official body **sits**, it officially carries out its work. *Visitors are only allowed in on days when the Houses are not sitting... This will be the first day the courts sit after the outbreak of disorder... The Commons does quite often sit until the early hours of the morning.*
6 VA If a building or other object **sits** in a particular place, it is in that place. *The little parish church sits cosily in the middle of the village... The computer sits quite happily on an ordinary worktop.*
7 See also **sitting, baby-sit.**
● **Sit** is used in these phrases. ● If you **sit tight**, you remain where you are and do not take any action. *All they have to do is sit tight until the Republic recognises their claims... Although the government had to remain calm, it could not just sit tight and do nothing.* ● to **sit on the fence**: see **fence.**

sit about PHRASAL VERB See **sit around.**
sit around PHRASAL VERB If you **sit around** or **sit about**, you spend a lot of time doing nothing except sitting; used in informal English. *We were tired of sitting about waiting for something to happen... We sat around in the house for 12 hours.*
sit back PHRASAL VERB If you **sit back**, you relax and do not become involved in a situation; an informal expression. *He believes he has the right to sit back while others do the hard work... Meanwhile, the Labour leader is able to sit back and gloat.*
sit down PHRASAL VERB 1 When you **sit down** or **sit yourself down**, you lower your body until you are sitting on something. *He sat down on the edge of the bed... Let's sit down and discuss this... It means he can sit himself down and get into a comfortable position and concentrate.* 2 If you **sit** someone **down**, you help them into a sitting position, often because they cannot do it for themselves. *The first thing you do is sit your casualty down and lean them forward.*
sit in on PHRASAL VERB If you **sit in on** a meeting you are present at it but do not take part. *I was allowed to sit in on the deliberations of the board... He used to sit in on the Chief of Court's cases.*
sit out PHRASAL VERB If you **sit** something **out**, you wait for it to finish, without taking any action. *They would retire to their caves to sit out the winter... The Embassy is full of would-be emigrants, determined to sit it out.*
sit through PHRASAL VERB If you **sit through** something such as a concert or lecture, you stay until it is finished although you are not enjoying it. *I sat through all three performances but none of them was any good.*
sit up PHRASAL VERB 1 If you **sit up**, you bring yourself into a sitting position when you have been leaning back or lying down. *She sat up in bed when she saw him coming... He was now able to sit up in bed and breathe without the help of a ventilator.* 2 If you **sit up** all night, you do not go to bed. *Sometimes I sit up reading until three or four in the morning... Mr Bush had his advisors sitting up late at night reworking the text.* 3 If something makes you **sit up**, it makes you pay attention. *Chinese methods of diagnosis are making Western doctors sit up and take notice. ...a book that made me sit up and whistle in disbelief.*

sitar /sɪtɑː/ **sitars**

NC A **sitar** is a type of stringed Indian musical instrument. *...Indian ragas played on the sitar by Imrat Khan.*

sitcom /sɪtkɒm/ **sitcoms**

NC A **sitcom** is a television comedy series which shows the same set of characters in each episode, in amusing situations that are similar to everyday life. *The actor, Gorden Kaye, plays a leading role in a sitcom about the French Resistance.*

sit-down

1 N SING If you have a **sit-down**, you sit down and rest for a short time; an informal use. *When we got to the top we had a bit of a sit-down.*

2 ADJ ATTRIB A **sit-down** meal is served to people sitting at tables. *She wants a church wedding, with a sit-down dinner and dancing.*

3 ADJ ATTRIB A **sit-down** strike or protest is one in which the protestors refuse to move until they get what they are asking for. *Some of the hotel workers had staged a sit-down protest on the main road... He was arrested during a mass sit-down demonstration in London.*

site /saɪt/ **sites, siting, sited**

1 NC A **site** is a piece of ground that is or was used for a particular purpose. *Remains of the building were unearthed during excavations for a development site... It looks just like a building site... It is built on the site of the old Lion Tower.*

2 NC A **site** is also the place where a particular event took place. *...the site of the murder of the little princes in 1483... Rescuers are reported to have reached the crash site on a remote hillside.*

3 VOA If something **is sited** in a particular place or position, it is placed there. *The automatic gate needs no mains electricity, so it can be sited anywhere... They refused to have cruise missiles sited on their soil... The planners said that siting a gas treatment plant there would have an intolerable environmental impact.*

sit-in, sit-ins

NC A **sit-in** is a protest in which people sit in a public place and refuse to be moved. *They plan to resume classes which have been disrupted by the sit-in... Protests and sit-ins are reported to have taken place outside several government buildings.*

sitter /sɪtə/ **sitters**

NC A **sitter** is the same as a **baby-sitter**. *We can get a sitter for Roger... It's important for the sitter to be someone the children know and like.*

sitting /sɪtɪŋ/ **sittings**

1 NC A **sitting** is one of the times when a meal is served, when there is not enough space for everyone to eat at the same time. *The first sitting for breakfast is at 7.30.*

2 NC A **sitting** is also an occasion when an official body, such as a parliament or law court, has a meeting. *...the first sitting of the Senate since the election... A programme of tax reforms has been approved after an all-night sitting... Protests from the opposition led to a suspension of the sitting.*

sitting-room, sitting-rooms

NC A **sitting-room** is a room in a house where people sit and relax. *The fire is thought to have started in the family's sitting-room.*

sitting tenant, sitting tenants

NC A **sitting tenant** is a person who rents a house or flat as their home, and is legally entitled to stay there if the owner sells the house or flat. *If you're a sitting tenant, then you're protected by a number of laws.*

situate /sɪtjueɪt/ **situates, situating, situated**

VOA If you **situate** something such as an idea or fact, you relate it to a particular context, especially in order to understand it better; a formal use. *The dangers which press upon us must be situated in this context.*

situated /sɪtjueɪtɪd/

ADJ PRED If something is **situated** somewhere, it is in a particular place or position. *The control centre is situated many miles away... Their flat was most conveniently situated... Bisham Abbey is delightfully situated on the Thames near Marlow.*

situation /sɪtjueɪʃn/ **situations**

1 NC You use the word **situation** to refer generally to what is happening at a particular place and time. *The situation was beginning to frighten me... He said his soldiers faced an almost impossible situation in the occupied territories... They have their own domestic political situation to consider... We have to consider what to do in situations where there are many people involved.*

2 NC Your **situation** refers to your circumstances and the things that are happening to you. *He knew a lot about my father's situation. ...the seriousness of his situation... What makes his situation even more tragic is his continuing faith in Communism.*

3 NC The **situation** of a building or town is its surroundings; a formal use. *The city is in a beautiful situation... The best situations for windmills are where the wind is blowing strongest.*

4 The **Situations Vacant** column in a newspaper is a list of jobs that are being advertised.

situation comedy, situation comedies

NCor NU A **situation comedy** is the same as a **sitcom**. *Those who were watching got three hours of music videos, baseball, and an American situation comedy... Harry Worth was best known for his BBC situation comedy series.*

six /sɪks/ **sixes**

1 **Six** is the number 6. *There are still delays of six hours or more.*

2 If someone or something is at **sixes and sevens**, they are in a state of confusion or disorganization. *We had a few meetings but they were all at sixes and sevens.*

six-pack, six-packs

NC A **six-pack** is a set of six cans or bottles of a drink, usually beer; used in American English. *...a pepperoni pizza and a six-pack.*

sixpence /sɪkspəns/ **sixpences**

NC A **sixpence** is a small silver coin which was used in Britain before the decimal money system was introduced in 1971. It was worth six old pence. *I drew the large amount of two shillings and sixpence for ninety hours work.*

sixteen /sɪkstiːn/ **sixteens**

Sixteen is the number 16. *...children aged between eleven and sixteen.*

sixteenth /sɪkstiːnθ/

ADJ The **sixteenth** item in a series is the one that you count as number sixteen. *...the sixteenth century. ...their sixteenth annual economic summit.*

sixth /sɪksθ/ **sixths**

1 ADJ The **sixth** item in a series is the one that you count as number six. *Los Angeles is the sixth city that I've visited.*

2 NC A **sixth** is one of six equal parts of something. *In London, the dollar is stronger by a sixth of a cent.*

sixth form, sixth forms

NC In a British school, the **sixth form** is the class that pupils go into at the age of sixteen to study for 'A' Levels. Pupils normally spend two years in the sixth form. *Ours is a large comprehensive school with quite a big sixth form. ...foreign language courses in school sixth forms.*

sixth former, sixth formers

NC A **sixth former** is a pupil who is in the sixth form at a school in Britain. *Sir John was answering questions from sixth formers for the BBC Northern Ireland programme 'Up Front'.*

sixth sense

N SING You say that someone has a **sixth sense** when they somehow know, or seem to know, things although they do not have any direct evidence of them. *He had a sort of sixth sense for tracking down burglary suspects.*

sixtieth /sɪkstiəθ/

ADJ The **sixtieth** item in a series is the one that you count as number sixty. *...his sixtieth birthday.*

sixty /sɪksti/ **sixties**

Sixty is the number 60. *It started about sixty years ago.*

sizable /saɪzəbl/. See sizeable.

size /saɪz/ **sizes, sizing, sized**

1 NU The **size** of something is how big or small it is.

The company doubled its size in nine years... It's a huge river, the size of the Thames. ...a vast nature reserve about 1,200 square metres in size. 2 NU The **size** of something is also the fact that it is very large. *The Grand was the only hotel of any size in the town... The world overwhelms us by its sheer size.* 3 NC A **size** is one of a series of graded measurements, especially for things such as clothes or shoes. *What size do you take? ...a jacket three sizes too big.* 4 If you **cut** someone **down to size**, you embarrass or humiliate them in order to make them aware that they are not as important as they think they are. *Members of his own party have intervened to cut him down to size.*

size up PHRASAL VERB If you **size up** a person or situation, you carefully look at the person or think about the situation, so that you can decide how to act; an informal expression. *...people sizing each other up as if for a fight.*

sizeable /sáɪzəbl/; also spelt **sizable**. ADJ **Sizeable** means fairly large. *A sizeable proportion of the oil and gas is exported to the Soviet Union. ...a sizeable pay rise. ...any sizeable town or city.*

-sized /-saɪzd/ or **-size** /-saɪz/ SUFFIX You can add **-sized** or **-size** to nouns to form adjectives that describe the size of something. *He announced special credit facilities for small and medium-sized businesses... There were now thousands of family-sized shops and restaurants. ...a city-size population.*

sizzle /sɪzl/ sizzles, sizzling, sizzled V If something **sizzles**, it makes a hissing sound like the sound made by frying food. *The steak and kidney pudding sizzled deliciously on the stove.*

skate /skeɪt/ skates, skating, skated 1 NC A **skate** is an ice-skate or roller-skate. *...carrying skates, skis and other equipment.* 2 V To **skate** means to move over ice or a flat surface wearing skates. *Brian Orser skated brilliantly. ...skating across the frozen pond.* ◆ **skating** NU *The men's figure skating is the event to watch out for.*

skate around PHRASAL VERB To **skate around** means the same as to **skate over**.

skate over PHRASAL VERB If you **skate over** a difficult subject, you avoid dealing with it fully. *Interesting early biographical detail was too good to skate over.*

skate round PHRASAL VERB To **skate round** means the same as to **skate over**.

skateboard /skéɪtbɔːd/ skateboards NC A **skateboard** is a narrow board on wheels, which people stand on and ride for pleasure. *They don't mind risking their necks on skateboards.*

skateboarding /skéɪtbɔːdɪŋ/ NU **Skateboarding** is the activity of riding on a skateboard. *In the mid sixties skateboarding expanded in the USA, but it remained closely related to the 'surfing subculture'.*

skater /skéɪtə/ skaters NC A **skater** is someone who ice-skates or roller-skates, especially in races or competitions. *The Dutch skater, Leo Visser, was second.*

skein /skeɪn/ skeins NC A **skein** is a loosely coiled length of thread, especially wool or silk. *...a skein of wool.*

skeletal /skélɪtl/ 1 ADJ ATTRIB **Skeletal** means relating to skeletons. *...skeletal remains. ...their skeletal structure.* 2 ADJ A **skeletal** person is so thin that you can see their bones through their skin. *Her body was skeletal. ...harrowing photographs of skeletal children.*

skeleton /skélɪtən/ skeletons 1 NC The **skeleton** of a person or animal is the framework of bones in their body. *There are also twenty family graves with between twenty and thirty skeletons in each grave. ...the skeleton of a gigantic whale.* 2 If someone has a **skeleton in the cupboard** or a **skeleton in the closet**, they are keeping secret something that is scandalous or embarrassing. *Rumours circulated about about skeletons in the*

cupboard... *It has started dragging old skeletons out of the closet.* 3 N+N A **skeleton** staff is the smallest number of staff necessary to run an organization. A **skeleton** service is operated with the smallest number of staff possible. *Government offices and banks are operating with skeleton staffs... Rail travel in the central belt has been badly hit with only a skeleton service operating in the Glasgow area.*

skeleton key, skeleton keys NC A **skeleton key** is a key which has been specially made so that it will open many different locks. *My father has a skeleton key to all the classrooms.*

skeptic /sképtɪk/. See sceptic. **skeptical** /sképtɪkl/. See sceptical. **skepticism** /sképtɪsɪzəm/. See scepticism.

sketch /sketʃ/ sketches, sketching, sketched 1 NC A **sketch** is a quick, rough drawing that may be used as preparation for a painting. *Roach's paintings begin as sketches and notes... During his travels he produced many sketches and watercolours.* 2 VOorV If you **sketch** something, you make a quick, rough drawing of it. *A young man was sketching the pattern of large stones... You sketch and paint as well.* 3 NC A **sketch** of a situation or incident is a brief description of it without many details. *...a sketch of post-war history in Western Europe... I had a basic sketch of a plan.* 4 VO If you **sketch** a situation or incident, you give a brief description of it without many details. *His rise to power is briefly sketched in the first two chapters.* 5 NC A **sketch** is also a short humorous piece of acting, usually forming part of a comedy show. *I loved the sketch about the dead parrot.*

sketch in PHRASAL VERB If you **sketch in** details about something, you tell them to people as extra information to help them understand a situation. *I'm going to sketch in a bit of the background to the current crisis.*

sketch out PHRASAL VERB If you **sketch out** a situation or an incident, you give a short description of it, including only the most important facts. *Reginald Bartholomew sketched out the modest goals that the US hopes to achieve.*

sketchbook /skétʃbʊk/ sketchbooks NC A **sketchbook** is a book of blank pages for drawing on. *The picture could be straight out of the sketchbook of a 19th century traveler.*

sketchpad /skétʃpæd/ sketchpads NC A **sketchpad** is a pad of blank pages for drawing on.

sketchy /skétʃi/ sketchier, sketchiest ADJ **Sketchy** knowledge or accounts of something are not complete because they do not have many details. *Accounts of what happened are still sketchy... The police say they have only sketchy details.* ◆ **sketchily** ADV *More recent developments, such as Euro-Communism, are dealt with sketchily.*

skew /skjuː/ skews, skewing, skewed 1 V-PASS If something **is skewed**, its position is distorted, usually because it is placed in a slanting position when it would normally be straight. *Their vision is skewed by the distorting lenses.* 2 ADJ Something that is **skew** is in a slanting position when it should be vertical or horizontal. *The picture was skew.* ▶ Also ADV *The cupboard was hanging a bit skew.* 3 V-PASS If something **is skewed**, it is altered or distorted, so that people do not get an accurate view of what is happening. *Some of the results may have been skewed because people who were healthy were less likely to participate.* ◆ **skewed** ADJ *It wants to present a skewed view of history, particularly Watergate.* 4 VA If a vehicle **skews** in a particular direction, it turns aside sharply from the direction in which it should be going. *At that moment the boat skewed off course, heading straight for the rocks.*

skewer /skjúːə/ skewers, skewering, skewered 1 NC A **skewer** is a long metal pin which is used to hold pieces of food together during cooking. *...shrimp grilled on a skewer.*

2 VO If you **skewer** something, you push a long, thin, pointed object through it. *They skewered bits of meat on branches and held them in the flames.*

skew-whiff /skjuːˈwɪf/
ADJ PRED Something that is **skew-whiff** is in a slanting position when it should be vertical or horizontal; an informal word. *Your hat's skew-whiff.*

ski /skiː/ **skis, skiing, skied**
1 NC **Skis** are long, flat, narrow pieces of wood, metal, or plastic that are fastened to boots so that you can move easily over snow. ...*a pair of skis.*
2 V When people **ski**, they move over snow on skis. *They know the slopes well, having skied there many times before... Most people cross-country ski or hike.* ◆ **skiing** NU *He was very scared of skiing.* ...*downhill skiing.*
3 N+N **Ski** is used to refer to things that are concerned with skiing. ...*ski boots.* ...*a Swiss ski instructor.* ...*the popular ski resort of St Anton.*

skid /skɪd/ **skids, skidding, skidded**
1 V If a vehicle **skids**, it slides sideways or forwards in an uncontrolled way, for example because the road is wet or icy. *The accident happened as the bus skidded off the road in torrential rain... His car skidded and hit a tree in County Down.* ► Also NC *The car went into a skid.*
2 If something such as a plan or someone's career is **on the skids**, it is going badly wrong and about to fail; an informal expression. *My marriage was on the skids... It was David Capel who really put the Australian innings on the skids.*

skier /ˈskiːə/ **skiers**
NC A **skier** is a person who skis. *Hundreds of skiers were cleared from the slopes at Glen Shee after heavy snowfalls.*

ski jump, ski jumps
1 NC A **ski jump** is a specially-built steep slope covered in snow with one end curving upwards. People ski down it and jump into the air at the end. *He stood at the top of the steep icy slope leading down to the 90 metre ski jump.*
2 N SING The **ski jump** is a sporting event in which people ski down a steep slope and then jump as far as they can at the end. *The 70 metre ski jump was won by the favourite, Matti Nykaenen of Finland.*

skilful /ˈskɪlfl/; spelt **skillful** in American English.
ADJ Someone who is **skilful** at something does it very well. *The girl had grown more skilful with the sewing-machine.* ...*a skilful hunter.* ...*skilful manoeuvres.* ◆ **skilfully** ADV ...*a skilfully organized campaign.*

ski lift, ski lifts
NC A **ski lift** is a machine for taking people to the top of a ski slope. It consists of a series of seats hanging down from a moving wire. *People depend on winter sports for their livelihood, operating ski lifts and cable cars.*

skill /skɪl/ **skills**
1 NU **Skill** is the knowledge and ability that enables you to do something well. *Does it require a lot of skill or are people finding it easy?... He can still deliver a political message with great skill... No skill with computers is required.*
2 NC A **skill** is a type of work or craft which requires special training and knowledge. *Skills of every kind were needed... Weaving cloth is, of course, a very traditional skill.*

skilled /skɪld/
1 ADJ Someone who is **skilled** has the knowledge and ability to do something well. *Skilled professionals, such as doctors and lawyers, have been leaving... Mr Gorbachev has always been skilled at controlling large gatherings.*
2 ADJ ATTRIB **Skilled** work can only be done by people who have had some training. *The profession has grown more demanding and skilled over the years.* ...*a skilled job.*

skillet /ˈskɪlɪt/ **skillets**
NC A **skillet** is the same as a **frying pan**; used in American English. ...*a cast iron skillet.*

skillful /ˈskɪlfl/. See **skilful**.

skim /skɪm/ **skims, skimming, skimmed**
1 VOA If you **skim** something from the surface of a liquid, you remove it. *Skim off the cream... Rough seas are preventing specially equipped ships from skimming oil off the water's surface.*
2 VO If something **skims** a surface, it moves quickly along just above it. *The birds swoop in a breathtaking arc to skim the pond.*
3 V+through or VO If you **skim** a piece of writing, you read through it quickly. *I was skimming through the book the first day she gave it to me... I think it tends to induce people to skim the text that they are reading.*

skimmed milk
NU **Skimmed milk** is milk from which the cream has been removed. *The government have opted to import skimmed milk powder.*

skimp /skɪmp/ **skimps, skimping, skimped**
V If you **skimp** on something, you use less of it than you really need, usually because you are trying to save money. *Trade unions resent business executives who pay huge amounts for art while skimping on wages... They're beginning to skimp and cut.*

skimpy /ˈskɪmpi/
ADJ **Skimpy** means too small in size or quantity. ...*a blonde model in a skimpy bathing suit.* ...*long hours, unsafe working conditions and skimpy pay.*

skin /skɪn/ **skins, skinning, skinned**
1 NU or NC Your **skin** is the natural covering of your body. *The poison may be absorbed through the skin.* ...*the skin of the face... Those with fair skins are far more at risk from skin cancer than people with darker skins.*
2 NC or NU An animal **skin** is the natural covering of an animal's body together with its fur or hair, which has been removed from a dead animal in order to make things such as coats or rugs. ...*snake skins... A few coats hung in the closet, one of leopard skin... It sells squares of elephant skin for about 10 Zimbabwe dollars a pound.*
3 NC or NU The **skin** of a type of food is its outer layer or covering. *Cook the potatoes quickly with their skins on.* ...*sausage skins... The cassava is chipped with the skin on, which adds fibre.*
4 NC or NU If a **skin** forms on the surface of a liquid, a fairly solid layer forms on it. *The custard had a thick skin on it... Stir the paint well to get rid of any skin.*
5 VO If you **skin** a dead animal, you remove its skin. *The boys skinned and cleaned the day's game.*
6 VO If you **skin** part of your body, you accidentally scrape some of the skin off. *She skinned her knee.*
● **Skin** is used in these phrases. ● If you do something **by the skin of** your **teeth**, you only just manage to do it. *It has survived by the skin of its teeth.* ● If someone tries to **save** their own **skin** or **protect** their own **skin**, they try to save themselves from something dangerous or unpleasant, often without caring what happens to anyone else. ...*the testimony of ruthless individuals who would lie to save their own skin.*

skin deep
ADJ PRED If you say that something is only **skin deep**, you mean that it has no real importance when it is thought about deeply, although it may seem important. *Beauty is only skin deep... In an editorial, the paper suggests that the Romanian revolution was only skin deep... The reformists in Moscow see his contribution as only skin deep.*

skin-diver, skin-divers
NC A **skin-diver** is someone who goes skin-diving.

skin-diving
NU **Skin-diving** is the sport or activity of swimming underwater using only light breathing apparatus and without a special diving suit.

skinflint /ˈskɪnflɪnt/ **skinflints**
NC A **skinflint** is a very mean person who hates spending money; an informal word. *That twisted old skinflint won't pay us a penny.*

skinhead /ˈskɪnhɛd/ **skinheads**
NC A **skinhead** is a young person whose hair is shaved or cut very short. Skinheads are usually regarded as violent and aggressive. *I was attacked by a group of skinheads on the railway station.*

-skinned /-skɪnd/

SUFFIX You can use **-skinned** with other adjectives to indicate that someone has skin of the type that is mentioned. *...soft-skinned babies... Most of them are fair-skinned.*

skinny /skɪni/

ADJ A **skinny** person is very thin, especially in an unattractive way; an informal word. *He's tall and skinny.*

skint /skɪnt/

ADJ PRED If you are **skint**, you have no money; an informal word. *I could do with £10, I'm skint.*

skin-tight

ADJ **Skin-tight** clothes fit very tightly. *...skin-tight jeans.*

skip /skɪp/ skips, skipping, skipped

1 V If you **skip**, you move along with a series of little jumps from one foot to the other. *He skipped around the room.* ▶ Also NC *...taking little skips as they walked.*

2 V To **skip** also means to jump up and down over a rope which you or other people are holding at each end and turning round and round. *Three energetic little girls were skipping in the playground.*

3 VO If you **skip** something that you usually do or that you have been instructed to do, you deliberately do not do it; an informal use. *Most of the home-based players have skipped training... Her 15 year old son Michael had started skipping school... Four of her co-defendants in the trial have skipped bail and disappeared.*

4 VO If you **skip** something such as a section of a book that you are reading, you pass over it quickly or miss it out altogether. *I'd skip this chapter if I were you.*

5 NC A **skip** is a large metal container for holding rubbish, usually from building work. *Debris was being loaded into skips.*

skipper /skɪpə/ skippers, skippering, skippered; an informal word.

1 NC The **skipper** of a ship or a boat is its captain. *An RAF helicopter took three of the crew off but the skipper stayed on board.*

2 NC In sport, the captain of a team is sometimes referred to as the **skipper**. *Skipper Viv Richards scored 38.*

3 VO If someone **skippers** a boat or a team, they are in charge of taking the decisions about how it is run and give instructions to the other members of the crew or team. *In third place at that stage was another Australian yacht, Hammer of Queensland, skippered by Arthur Bloore... Graham Gooch skippered the side in the last test.*

skipping rope, skipping ropes

NC A **skipping rope** is a rope, usually with a handle at each end, that is used for skipping.

skirmish /skɜːmɪʃ/ skirmishes

1 NC A **skirmish** is a short battle which is not part of a planned war strategy. *They dismissed the action as a border skirmish.* ▶ Also V+with *They skirmished with the police.*

2 NC A **skirmish** is also a short, sharp argument that often takes place before an agreement is reached. *Senator Tim Worth predicted a major skirmish in Congress over this issue.*

skirt /skɜːt/ skirts, skirting, skirted

1 NC A **skirt** is a piece of clothing worn by women and girls. It fastens at the waist and hangs down around the legs. *The Princess was wearing a royal blue jacket and skirt.*

2 VO Something that **skirts** an area is situated around the edge of it. *...the path which skirted the house.*

3 VOorV If you **skirt** something, or **skirt** round it, you go around the edge of it. *As I walked through the lobby, I had to skirt a group of ladies... They skirted round a bus.*

4 VO If you **skirt** a problem or question, you avoid dealing with it, usually because it is difficult or controversial. *The President has skirted the issue.*

skirting /skɜːtɪŋ/ skirtings

NCorNU A **skirting** or a **skirting board** is a narrow length of wood which goes along the bottom of a wall in a room. *Gaps between floorboards and skirting*

should be filled.

skit /skɪt/ skits

NC A **skit** is a short performance in which actors make fun of people, events, or types of literature by imitating them. *Shaw wrote it as a skit on her real character.*

skittish /skɪtɪʃ/

1 ADJ Someone who is **skittish** is lively and does not concentrate for a long time on anything or take life very seriously. *I was too skittish to study it closely.*

2 ADJ An animal or person that is **skittish** is very excitable and easily frightened. *...a skittish filly... Profits remain so low that skittish investors are cancelling their plans.*

skittle /skɪtl/ skittles

1 NC A **skittle** is a wooden object used as a target in the game of skittles. *You just use your ball and see how many skittles you can bowl over with one throw.*

2 NU **Skittles** is a game in which players try to knock over as many skittles as they can out of a group of nine by throwing a ball at them. *They play skittles and ten-pin bowling.*

skive /skaɪv/ skives, skiving, skived

V If you **skive**, you avoid working, especially by staying away from a place; an informal word. *Were you skiving or were you really ill?... He's always skiving off.*

skulduggery /skʌldʌgəri/

NU **Skulduggery** is behaviour in which someone acts secretly in a dishonest way in order to achieve their aim; an old-fashioned word. *Living in Washington he became accustomed to intrigue and political skulduggery.*

skulk /skʌlk/ skulks, skulking, skulked

V A If you **skulk** somewhere, you stay there quietly because you do not want to be seen. *There were half a dozen foxes skulking in the undergrowth.*

skull /skʌl/ skulls

NC Your **skull** is the bony part of your head which encloses your brain. *He had two broken ribs and a fractured skull.*

skull and crossbones /skʌl ən krɒsbəʊnz/

N SING A **skull and crossbones** is a picture of a human skull above a pair of crossed bones that warns of death or danger. It used to appear on the flags flown by pirate ships and is now sometimes found on containers holding poisonous or toxic substances. *On the streets of Tabachinga, posters emblazoned with a red skull and crossbones proclaim 'You could fall ill from cholera'.*

skullcap /skʌlkæp/ skullcaps

NC A **skullcap** is a close-fitting cap worn on the top of the head by some people, for example by Catholic priests and Jewish men. *...four rabbis all wearing skull caps. ...a knitted skull cap pinned to his hair.*

skunk /skʌŋk/ skunks

NC A **skunk** is a small black and white animal which gives off an unpleasant smell if it is frightened.

sky /skaɪ/ skies

NC The **sky** is the space around the earth which you can see when you stand outside and look upwards. *It'll warm up as soon as the sun gets higher in the sky... There were little white clouds high in the blue sky. ...the night skies of London.*

skydiver /skaɪdaɪvə/ skydivers

NC A **skydiver** is someone who does skydiving. *A skydiver whose parachute failed to open plummeted nearly 10,000 feet and survived.*

skydiving /skaɪdaɪvɪŋ/

NU **Skydiving** is the sport of jumping out of an aeroplane and falling freely through the air for a period of time before opening your parachute.

sky-high

1 ADVorADJ If prices or wages go **sky-high**, they reach a very high level. *Land value has gone sky-high. ...sky-high property prices.*

2 If you blow something **sky-high**, you destroy it completely. *His argument has just been blown sky-high.*

skylark /skaɪlɑːk/ skylarks

NC A **skylark** is a small brown bird that has a pleasant song, which it usually sings while it is hovering high above the ground. *...flocks of skylarks.*

skylight /skaɪlaɪt/ **skylights**

NC A **skylight** is a window in a roof. *...skylights and mirrors make the room seem bigger.*

skyline /skaɪlaɪn/ **skylines**

NC The **skyline** is the line where the sky meets the land; used especially when referring to a city where you can see the shapes of buildings against the sky. *...the impressive Manhattan skyline.*

skyrocket /skaɪrɒkɪt/ **skyrockets, skyrocketing, skyrocketed**

V If the price or cost of something **skyrockets**, it rapidly increases over a short period of time. *In the last three years, real-estate values have skyrocketed, driving out many small businessmen... They expect the dollar to skyrocket if war breaks out.* ◆ **skyrocketing** ADJ ATTRIB *Those who own homes can't afford to pay the skyrocketing prices.*

skyscraper /skaɪskreɪpə/ **skyscrapers**

NC A **skyscraper** is a very tall building in a city. *...the towering skyscrapers of central Tokyo. ...the 38-storey skyscraper.*

skyward /skaɪwəd/ **skywards**

ADV If you look **skyward** or **skywards**, you look up towards the sky; a literary word. *He had a habit of looking skyward each time he made a pronouncement.*

slab /slæb/ **slabs**

NC A **slab** of something is a thick, flat piece of it. *...a great slab of rock. ...a concrete slab. ...a slab of cheese.*

slack /slæk/ **slacker, slackest; slacks**

1 ADJ **Slack** means loose and not firmly stretched or tightly in position. *...a slack rope. ...his slack and wrinkled skin.*
2 NU If there is **slack** in a rope, part of it is hanging loose. *Pass down the rope with the winch and take up any slack in the rope.*
3 ADJ A **slack** period is one in which there is not much activity. *Very few hotels offered work for the slack season.*
4 ADJ If you are **slack** in your work, you do not do it properly. *Security's got a bit slack.* ◆ **slackness** NU *She was dismissed for slackness.*
5 N PL **Slacks** are casual trousers; an old-fashioned use. *...a pair of golfing slacks.*
6 If you **cut** someone **some slack**, you are more relaxed in your attitude towards them and allow them more freedom in the things that they do; used in informal American English. *If they understood our thinking they might cut us all some slack and their attitude might soften... Clemens made a mistake, but I think the umpire should have cut him a little more slack.*

slacken /slækən/ **slackens, slackening, slackened**

1 V-ERG If something **slackens** or if you **slacken** it, it becomes slower, less active, or less intense. *The rain began to slacken... Overall world trade has slackened... She slackened her pace.* ◆ **slackening** N SING *There has been no slackening of interest in the controversy... International pressure on him shows no signs of slackening.*
2 V-ERG If your grip or your body **slackens** or if you **slacken** it, it becomes looser or more relaxed. *The grip on Casson's right wrist did not slacken... Slacken your legs and slowly lie back.*
slacken off PHRASAL VERB If something **slackens off**, it becomes slower, less active, or less intense. *The Depression slackened off and prosperity returned.*

slacker /slækə/ **slackers**

NC A **slacker** is someone who is lazy and does much less work than they should; an informal word.

slag /slæg/ **slags, slagging, slagged**

NU **Slag** is waste material, such as rock and mud, left over from mining. *While coal is transported away from the mining towns, the slag is dumped on the outskirts of the communities.*
slag off PHRASAL VERB If you **slag** someone **off**, you criticize them in an unpleasant way; an informal expression. *Mark's always slagging off his friends behind their backs.*

slag heap, slag heaps

NC A **slag heap** is a hill made of waste materials from mines and factories. *The slag heaps of Wales are a feature of the landscape.*

slain /sleɪn/

Slain is the past participle of **slay**.

slake /sleɪk/ **slakes, slaking, slaked**

VO If you **slake** your thirst, you drink something which takes your thirst away; a literary use. *We returned to the barn and slaked our thirst with tea.*

slalom /slɑːləm/ **slaloms**

NC A **slalom** is a race, on skis or in canoes, in which the competitors have to avoid a series of obstacles in a very twisting, difficult course. *He won the giant slalom at Schladming last season.*

slam /slæm/ **slams, slamming, slammed**

1 V-ERG If you **slam** a door or window or if it **slams**, it shuts noisily and with great force. *She went out, slamming the door behind her... I waited for the gate behind me to slam shut.*
2 VOA If you **slam** something down, you put it there quickly and with great force. *He slammed the money on the table.*
3 VO If someone **slams** someone or something, they criticize that person or thing very severely. *In his first address to the summit, he slammed African leaders, accusing them of hypocrisy. ...popular speeches slamming drugs, crime and taxes.*

slammer /slæmə/

N SING The **slammer** is prison; an informal word. *Community service is what white-collar criminals do instead of a long time in the slammer.*

slander /slɑːndə/ **slanders, slandering, slandered**

1 NCorNU A **slander** is an untrue spoken statement about someone which is intended to damage their reputation. *...lies and slanders... I'll sue her for slander. ...a new law which forbids slander against the President.*
2 VO If someone **slanders** you, they make untrue spoken statements about you in order to damage your reputation. *She slandered him behind his back... He had been accused of spreading false reports and slandering the state.*

slanderous /slɑːndəʳrəs/

ADJ A spoken statement that is **slanderous** is untrue and intended to damage the reputation of the person that it refers to. *This is a slanderous misrepresentation of our policy... He described the accusations as slanderous.*

slang /slæŋ/

NU Words, expressions, and meanings which are very informal are referred to as **slang**. *His English is peppered with American slang. ...military slang.* ▶ Also ADJ ATTRIB *...greenback, a slang term for a dollar bill.*

slanging match, slanging matches

NC A **slanging match** is an angry quarrel in which people insult each other; an informal expression. *A public slanging match would not be helpful... Eddy had an abusive slanging match with the café owner.*

slangy /slæŋi/

ADJ **Slangy** speech or writing has a lot of slang in it. *...slangy colloquial passages.*

slant /slɑːnt/ **slants, slanting, slanted**

1 V Something that **slants** is sloping, rather than horizontal or vertical. *The old wooden floor slanted a little.* ◆ **slanting** ADJ ATTRIB *He stretched out in the slanting sun. ...a slanting roof.*
2 N SING If something is on a **slant**, it is in a slanting position. *For some reason the shelf was set on a slant.*
3 VO If someone **slants** news or information, they present it in a way that shows favour towards a particular group or opinion. *No matter how he slanted the facts, he could not convince us that there had been no cover-up.* ◆ **slanted** ADJ *President Mugabe has criticised the BBC's coverage of the elections as slanted and lacking objectivity.*
4 N SING+SUPP A particular **slant** on a subject is a particular way of thinking about it, especially one that is biased or prejudiced. *...a leftist political slant.*

slap /slæp/ **slaps, slapping, slapped**

1 VO If you **slap** someone, you hit them with the palm of your hand. *He slapped her across the face... I slapped her hand.* ▶ Also NC *Give him a slap if he is*

too much of a pest.
2 VO If you **slap** someone on the back, you hit them in a friendly manner on their back. *I slapped him on the back and wished him the best of luck.* ▸ Also NC ...*a hefty slap on the back.*
3 VOA If you **slap** something onto a surface, you put it there quickly and carelessly. *We slapped some paint on the wall to brighten up the room... All you have to do is slap a bit of Sellotape across it... He slapped the report down on the table.*
● **Slap** is used in these phrases. ● If something that someone does is **a slap in the face**, it shocks or upsets you because you feel that it is not justified and seems like a betrayal. *The nationalists see failure to ratify the amendment as a slap in the face for French Canada.* ● A **slap on the wrist** is a warning or punishment that is not very severe. *The two hijackers may receive no more than a slap on the wrist from the court.*

slap-bang
Slap-bang is used in expressions such as 'slap-bang in the middle' or 'slap-bang in front of them', to mean exactly in that place; an informal word. *The Maidan is green land, slap-bang in the middle of Calcutta.*

slapdash /slæpdæʃ/
ADJ Something that is **slapdash** is done quickly and carelessly, without much thinking or planning; an informal word. *My cooking is rather slapdash.*

slapstick /slæpstɪk/
NU **Slapstick** is a type of comedy in which actors make people laugh by behaving in a foolish way such as falling over or throwing things around rather than by telling spoken jokes. *...some dreadful slapstick comedy.*

slap-up
ADJ ATTRIB A **slap-up** meal is a large enjoyable meal, especially one that you eat at a restaurant; an informal word. *Room service comes into its own when you order a slap-up meal to be brought to you.*

slash /slæʃ/ slashes, slashing, slashed
1 VO If you **slash** something, you make a long, deep cut in it. *Jack's face had been slashed with broken glass... It was clear that someone had tried to slash her throat.*
2 V+at If you **slash** at something, you swing at it wildly with quick cutting movements. *...children slashing at each other with plastic swords.*
3 VO To **slash** money or time means to reduce it greatly; an informal use. *...a plan to slash taxes.*
4 NCorNU A **slash** is a diagonal line that separates letters, words, or numbers. For example, you say the number 340/21/K as 'Three four zero, slash two one, slash K'; used in speech.

slash and burn
ADJ ATTRIB **Slash and burn** methods of farming involve clearing land by destroying and burning the natural vegetation on it. *Traditional slash and burn farming methods have exhausted the soil... Hopefully we will lessen the need for slash and burn agriculture.*

slat /slæt/ slats
NC **Slats** are the narrow pieces of wood, metal, or plastic in things such as Venetian blinds or cupboard doors. *There are slats going across them making a pattern... She pushed the slats of the shutter aside to inhale a little air.*

slate /sleɪt/ slates, slated
1 NU **Slate** is a dark grey rock that can be easily split into thin layers. Slate is often used for covering roofs. *In the nineteenth century slate was exploited commercially. ...a slate quarry.*
2 NC **Slates** are the small flat pieces of slate used for covering roofs. *That could be a slate falling off a building.*
3 NC A **slate** is a list of candidates, usually from the same party, for an election; used in American English. *They decided to run a single slate of candidates for upcoming elections... The priest's presence on the electoral slate may cause more violence.*
4 V-PASS If something **is slated**, it has been planned or intended to happen at a particular time or in a particular way; used in American English. *The trial*

has been slated to begin the first week of August... The United States has withdrawn a hundred and forty million dollars in aid that was slated for Sudanese development.
5 V-PASS If a person or group **is slated** to do something, other people have predicted that they will almost certainly do it; used in American English. *The right-wing alliance is slated to win the up-coming presidential elections.*
6 If you **wipe the slate clean**, you decide to forget previous mistakes, failures, debts, and so on and make a fresh start. *Caicos Islanders are hoping the elections will wipe the slate clean and give the colony a fresh start... They are still pressing for a presidential pardon that would wipe his slate clean.*

slatted /slætɪd/
ADJ Something that is **slatted** is made with slats. *...white slatted Venetian blinds.*

slaughter /slɔːtə/ slaughters, slaughtering, slaughtered
1 VO To **slaughter** a large number of people or animals means to kill them in a way that is especially cruel, unjust, or needless. *Innocent citizens are being slaughtered.*
2 NU You can describe the killing of large numbers of people or animals as **slaughter**, particularly when it seems very cruel and senseless. *...the needless annual slaughter on our roads. ...the slaughter of dolphins.*
3 VO To **slaughter** animals such as cows and sheep means to kill them for their meat. *...a freshly slaughtered bullock.*
4 NU **Slaughter** is also the killing of animals for their meat. *...animals going away to slaughter.*

slaughterhouse /slɔːtəhaʊs/ slaughterhouses
NC A **slaughterhouse** is a place where animals are killed for their meat. *All slaughterhouses use a humane killer for cattle.*

Slav /slɑːv/ Slavs
NC A **Slav** is a member of any of the peoples of Eastern Europe who speak a Slavonic language. *He had something of the Slav temperament.*

slave /sleɪv/ slaves, slaving, slaved
1 NC A **slave** is a person who is owned by another person and has to work for that person. *...a story about a slave who escapes and becomes a free man... But in fact everybody knew that the sugar was produced by slaves.*
2 NC+SUPP If you are a **slave** to something, you are very strongly influenced or controlled by it. *He's just become a slave to possessions and money... We don't want to become slaves to a timetable.*
3 V If you **slave away**, or **slave** for someone, you work very hard. *Why am I slaving away, running a house and family single-handed?*

slave driver, slave drivers
NC If you call someone a **slave driver**, you mean that they make people work very hard; an informal expression. *You guys out there are real slave drivers.*

slave labour; spelt slave labor in American English.
1 NU **Slave labour** refers to slaves or very badly-paid people who are used for doing very hard, unpleasant work. *The pyramids were mostly built by slave labour... These are volunteer workers—they're not slave labour.*
2 NU **Slave labour** is also work done by slaves or by people who have to work very hard for little money. *I'm not working there any more—it's just slave labour.*

slavery /sleɪvəri/
1 NU **Slavery** is the system by which people are owned by other people as slaves. *...the abolition of slavery.*
2 NU+SUPP You can also use **slavery** to refer to the state of not being free because you have to work very hard or because you are strongly influenced by something. *I had at last been freed from the slavery of a 9 to 5 job.*

slave trade
N SING The **slave trade** is the buying and selling of slaves; used especially to refer to the transportation of Black Africans to America and the Caribbean from the 16th to the 19th centuries. *The slave trade was abolished in Britain in 1807.*

slavish /sleɪvɪʃ/
1 ADJ You use **slavish** to describe things that copy or imitate something exactly, without any attempt to be original. ...*a slavish adherence to things of the past.*
♦ **slavishly** ADV *I don't expect you to slavishly copy this.*
2 ADJ You also use **slavish** to describe someone who always obeys other people; used showing disapproval. ...*a slavish figure, down on her knees polishing the floor.*

Slavonic /sləvɒnɪk/
1 ADJ Something that is **Slavonic** relates to the group of languages, including Czech, Polish, Russian, and Slovak, which are spoken in Eastern Europe. ...*speaking a Slavonic language closely related to Russian.*
2 ADJ You can also use **Slavonic** to describe something that relates to the people who speak these languages. *He had broad, Slavonic cheekbones.*

slay /sleɪ/ **slays, slaying, slew, slain**
VO To **slay** someone means to kill them; a literary word. *Samson performed incredible feats of strength such as slaying 1,000 Philistines with the jawbone of an ass... Two visitors were brutally slain yesterday.*
♦ **slaying, slayings** NC *He's the suspect in the slayings of five college students.*

sleazy /sliːzi/ **sleazier, sleaziest**
ADJ **Sleazy** places or activities are those which respectable people would not want to be connected with because they are dirty or dishonest. ...*a sleazy cafe... He described the whole incident as a sleazy operation... He said it is making the government's conduct appear increasingly sleazy.*

sled /sled/ **sleds**
NC A **sled** is the same as a **sledge**; used in American English. ...*a sled descending a snowy hill.*

sledge /sledʒ/ **sledges**
NC A **sledge** is a vehicle which is designed to travel on snow. It consists of a frame which is attached to narrow wood or metal strips which slide over the snow. *They were the first to cross the Antarctic using only skis and sledges pulled by dogs.*

sledgehammer /sledʒhæmə/ **sledgehammers**
NC A **sledgehammer** is a large heavy hammer with a long handle. *They were attacked and a police dog was hit with a sledgehammer.*

sleek /sliːk/ **sleeker, sleekest**
1 ADJ **Sleek** hair or fur is smooth and shiny. ...*her sleek black hair.*
2 ADJ A **sleek** person looks stylish and smart. *They were fat and sleek and too pleased with themselves.*
3 ADJ A **sleek** vehicle or animal has a smooth, graceful shape. ...*a sleek black Mercedes... Modern cars usually have smooth, sleek styling.*

sleep /sliːp/ **sleeps, sleeping, slept**
1 NU **Sleep** is the natural state of rest in which your eyes are closed and your mind and body are inactive and unconscious. *Some of them had worked for thirty-two hours without food or sleep... Now go to sleep and stop worrying.*
2 V When you **sleep**, you rest in a state of sleep. *She slept till ten in the morning... He was so excited he could hardly sleep.* ♦ **sleeping** ADJ ATTRIB *I glanced down at the sleeping figure... Our working and sleeping lives.*
3 N SING A **sleep** is a period of sleeping. *He hasn't lost a night's sleep through worry in his life... You'll feel better if you have a little sleep.*
4 VO If a house **sleeps** a particular number of people, it has beds for that number. *Each apartment sleeps up to five adults.*
5 to **sleep rough**: see **rough**.
● Sleep is used in these phrases. ● If a part of your body **goes to sleep**, you lose the sense of feeling in it. *His foot had gone to sleep.* ● If a sick or injured animal is **put to sleep**, it is painlessly killed. *Sheba had to be put to sleep.*

sleep around PHRASAL VERB If someone **sleeps around**, they have many different sexual relationships within a short time; an informal expression, used showing disapproval. *I did everything I could to hurt her, including sleeping around.*

sleep off PHRASAL VERB If you **sleep off** the effects of too much food or alcohol, you recover from them by sleeping. *We went back to our room to sleep it off.*
sleep through PHRASAL VERB If you **sleep through** a noise or disturbance, it does not wake you up. *He slept through his friends returning to the car.*
sleep together PHRASAL VERB If two people **sleep together**, they have a sexual relationship; used especially when they are not married to each other. *They are presumably sleeping together.*
sleep with PHRASAL VERB If you **sleep with** someone, you have a sexual relationship with them, especially when you are not married to them. *I discovered that the girl I was going to marry had been sleeping with my best friend.*

sleeper /sliːpə/ **sleepers**
1 NC+SUPP You can use **sleeper** to describe the way that someone sleeps, for example someone who is a sound or deep sleeper is not easily woken up. *She was a late sleeper and hated getting up.*
2 NC A **sleeper** is a bed on a train. *I booked a first-class sleeper.*
3 NC A train with beds for passengers is also called a **sleeper**. *I usually go up to London on the sleeper.*
4 NC Railway **sleepers** are the large, heavy beams that support the rails of a railway track. *Trains between Sydney and Melbourne were stopped when railway sleepers burst into flames.*

sleeping bag, sleeping bags
NC A **sleeping bag** is a large, warm bag for sleeping in, especially when you are camping. *Emergency supplies called for include medicine, tents, blankets and sleeping bags.*

sleeping car, sleeping cars
NC A **sleeping car** is a railway carriage that provides beds for passengers to sleep in. ...*the arrangement of sleeping cars on the Moscow-Petersburg express.*

sleeping partner, sleeping partners
NC A **sleeping partner** is a person who provides some of the capital for a business but who does not take an active part in managing the business. *The non-active underwriters at Lloyds, the Names themselves, are really sleeping partners.*

sleeping pill, sleeping pills
NC A **sleeping pill** or a **sleeping tablet** is a pill that you can take to help you sleep. *He said that he had taken a sleeping pill and now wanted to have a good night's rest.*

sleeping sickness
NU **Sleeping sickness** is an illness that is spread by certain types of insect and makes people feverish and extremely tired. *Over the same area, many people fell ill with sleeping sickness. ...the parasite that causes sleeping sickness.*

sleepless /sliːpləs/
1 ADJ A **sleepless** night is one during which you do not sleep at all, or sleep for only a short time. *He'd had a sleepless night.*
2 ADJ If you are **sleepless**, you cannot sleep. *Late in the night, sleepless and troubled, he went for a walk.*
♦ **sleeplessness** NU *I began to suffer from sleeplessness.*

sleepwalk /sliːpwɔːk/ **sleepwalks, sleepwalking, sleepwalked**
V If someone is **sleepwalking**, they are walking around while they are asleep. *She must have been sleepwalking.*

sleepwalker /sliːpwɔːkə/ **sleepwalkers**
NC A **sleepwalker** is someone who walks around while they are asleep. *Who is responsible, for example, if a sleepwalker has an accident or commits a crime?*

sleepy /sliːpi/ **sleepier, sleepiest**
1 ADJ If you are **sleepy**, you feel tired and ready to go to sleep. *She suddenly started to feel very sleepy. ...a sleepy yawn.* ♦ **sleepily** ADV *'Where have you been?' Rudolph asked sleepily.*
2 ADJ ATTRIB A **sleepy** place is very quiet and does not have much excitement. ...*sleepy villages.*

sleepyhead /sliːpihed/ **sleepyheads**
NC If you call someone, especially a child, a **sleepyhead**, you mean that they look sleepy or are not paying attention. *Wake up you sleepyheads!*

sleet /sliːt/ **sleets, sleeting, sleeted**

1 NU **Sleet** is partly frozen rain. *An icy sleet was beginning to fall.*
2 V If it **is sleeting**, sleet is falling. *It started to sleet.*

sleeve /sliːv/ **sleeves**

1 NC The **sleeves** of a garment are the parts that cover your arms. *...a yellow dress with short sleeves.*
2 NC A record **sleeve** is the stiff envelope in which a gramophone record is kept. *There's a characteristic photograph of him on the record sleeve.*
3 If you **have** something **up** your **sleeve**, you have an idea or plan which you have not told anyone about; an informal expression. *There was intense speculation about what Mr Lawson has up his sleeve.*

sleeveless /sliːvləs/

ADJ ATTRIB A **sleeveless** garment has no sleeves. *...a blue sleeveless dress.*

sleigh /sleɪ/ **sleighs**

NC A **sleigh** is the same as a **sledge**. *Children know him as a mysterious stranger who arrives on Christmas Eve in a sleigh pulled by reindeer.*

sleight of hand /slaɪt əv hænd/

1 NU If you do something by **sleight of hand**, you do it using quick skilful movements of your hands so that other people cannot see your actions. *He switched the watches by sleight of hand.*
2 NU **Sleight of hand** is also a skilful piece of deception. *With a little statistical sleight of hand we could make things look all right.*

slender /slendə/

1 ADJ A **slender** person is thin and graceful in an attractive way. *...the girl's slender waist... She crossed her slender legs.*
2 ADJ You use **slender** to describe something that is small in amount or degree when you would like it to be greater. *With such slender resources they cannot hope to achieve their aims. ...slender prospects of promotion.*

slept /slept/

Slept is the past tense and past participle of **sleep**.

sleuth /sluːθ/ **sleuths**

NC A **sleuth** is a detective; an old-fashioned word. *...a series about a lady sleuth.*

slew /sljuː/

1 N SING+of A **slew** of people or things is the same as a lot of them; used in informal American English. *...the kids and a whole slew of their friends... There are a slew of federal regulations today that didn't use to exist.*
2 **Slew** is the past tense of **slay**.

slice /slaɪs/ **slices, slicing, sliced**

1 NC A **slice** is a thin or flat piece of food that has been cut from a larger piece. *She cut him three large slices of bread... Anybody want a slice of pizza?*
2 VO If you **slice** food, you cut it into thin pieces. *I saw her slicing an apple.*
3 NC A **slice** of something is a part of it. *A significant slice of their income is from the private sector.*
4 V O or V+through To **slice** or **slice through** something means to cut or move through it quickly, like a knife. *They sliced the air with their knives... The shark's fin sliced through the water.*

sliced /slaɪst/

ADJ ATTRIB **Sliced** bread is bread that has been cut into slices before being wrapped up and sold. *...a large sliced loaf.*

slick /slɪk/ **slicks; slicker, slickest**

1 NC A **slick** is the same as an **oil slick**. *The slick contaminated beaches and killed thousands of birds and sea creatures.*
2 ADJ A **slick** book or film seems well-made and attractive, but may have little quality or sincerity; used showing disapproval. *Some people thought the broadcasts too slick.*
3 ADJ A **slick** person speaks easily and is persuasive, but may not always be sincere; used showing disapproval. *...a slick businessman.*
4 ADJ A **slick** action, thing, or person is professionally presented or appears smart and attractive. *The group are described as slick and classy... Presentation of the party's key ideas must be made slicker and simpler.*
5 ADJ A **slick** action is done quickly and smoothly,

without obvious effort. *...a relay race round London, with slick baton-changing.*

slide /slaɪd/ **slides, sliding, slid**

1 V-ERG When something **slides** or when you **slide** it, it moves smoothly over or against something else. *On a rowing machine, the seat slides backwards and forwards... The gate slid open at the push of a button... She slid the key into the keyhole.*
2 VA To **slide** somewhere means to move there smoothly and quietly. *An elderly lady slid into the seat... The black Mercedes slid away.*
3 VA If you **slide** into a particular attitude, you change to it gradually, without trying to stop yourself. *He felt himself sliding into obsession.*
4 V If something such as prices or a currency **slides**, it is slowly getting into a bad or worse condition, and efforts to control it are not working. *On the currency markets, the pound has continued to slide... The government cannot stop the country from sliding further into financial chaos... His own popularity was sliding with each passing week.* ▶ Also N SING *Nothing else has succeeded so far in preventing a slide into civil war... The slide in the dollar has gone far enough.*
5 NC+SUPP A mud **slide** or a rock **slide** happens when a large amount of mud or rock comes away from the ground and falls down a hillside. *Rescue workers continue digging for bodies in houses buried in mud slides during weekend storms... Three miners have been killed after a rock slide in a gold mine.*
6 NC A **slide** is a small piece of photographic film which is mounted in a frame. You project light through the slide in order to display the picture on a screen. *Blunt is giving a lecture, with slides, on a painting in the Queen's collection.*
7 NC A **slide** is also a piece of glass on which you put something that you want to examine through a microscope. *...prepared laboratory slides.*
8 NC A **slide** in a playground is a structure that has a steep slope for children to slide down. *There were a few slides and climbing frames.*
9 NC A **slide** is also a hair slide. *She wore glasses and a slide in her hair.*

slide rule, slide rules

NC A **slide rule** is an instrument for calculating numbers. It looks like a ruler and has a middle part which slides backwards and forwards. *You've got to learn to use a slide rule.*

sliding scale, sliding scales

NC A **sliding scale** is a system for calculating something such as wages or taxes, in which the amounts paid vary because other things vary; a technical term. *Other payments will be made on a sliding scale.*

slight /slaɪt/ **slighter, slightest; slights, slighting, slighted**

1 ADJ Something that is **slight** is very small in degree or quantity. *The government has made slight changes in the immigration rules... This means the police can react to the slightest hint of trouble... I haven't the slightest idea what you're talking about.* ◆ **slightly** ADV *White wine should be slightly chilled.*
2 You use **in the slightest** to emphasize a negative statement. *My tennis hadn't improved in the slightest.*
3 ADJ A **slight** person has a slim and delicate body. *I watched her slight figure cross the street.*
4 VO If you **slight** someone, you insult them by treating them as if they were unimportant; a literary use. *His fear of being slighted made him avoid people.* ▶ Also NC *It was a slight on a past award-winner, Stevenson.*

slim /slɪm/ **slimmer, slimmest; slims, slimming, slimmed**

1 ADJ Someone who is **slim** has a thin, attractive, well-shaped body. *...a tall, slim girl with long, straight hair... Some of the girls also believed that smoking would keep them slim.*
2 V If you **slim**, you try to make yourself thinner and lighter by eating less food or healthier food. *I may be slimming but I've no intentions of starving myself.* ◆ **slimming** NU *I mean to take slimming a little more seriously. ...slimming magazines.*
3 ADJ A **slim** object is thinner than usual. *...a slim*

booklet containing private telephone numbers.
4 ADJ If the chance of something happening is **slim**, it
is unlikely to happen. *Their chances of release are
slim... Couples may spend thousands of pounds in the
slim hope of having a baby.*

slime /slaɪm/
NU **Slime** is a thick, slippery substance which covers a
surface or comes from the bodies of animals such as
snails. *There was green slime around the edges of the
tub. ...a trail of slime.*

slimmer /slɪmə/ **slimmers**
NC A **slimmer** is someone who is trying to lose weight
by dieting and exercising. *...clubs for slimmers.*

slimy /slaɪmi/
1 ADJ A **slimy** thing is covered in slime. *We had to
wade through water, sinking a foot deep into slimy
mud... They lay on a pile of rags and the deck was
slimy beneath them.*
2 ADJ If you describe someone as **slimy**, you mean
that they act in a pleasant and friendly way, but are
insincere; used showing disapproval. *...a slimy
politician.*

sling /slɪŋ/ **slings, slinging, slung**
1 VOA If you **sling** something somewhere, you throw it
there. *She slung the book across the room.*
2 VOA If you **sling** something over your shoulder, over
a chair, or over a hook, you put it there quickly and
carelessly so that it hangs down. *Patrick gets his bag
and slings it over his shoulder... His few bits of
clothing were slung over a string on the wall.*
3 VOA If you **sling** something such as a rope between
two points, you attach it so that it hangs loosely
between them. *...a hammock that was slung between
two trees above a very small rockery.*
4 NC A **sling** is an object made of ropes, straps, or
cloth that is used for carrying things. *Mothers carry
their babies around with them in slings.*
5 NC A **sling** is also a piece of cloth which is tied
around someone's neck to support an injured arm. *He
left a little after breakfast this morning, his right arm
in a sling.*

slingshot /slɪŋʃɒt/ **slingshots**
NC A **slingshot** is a small stick shaped like the letter
'Y' with a piece of elastic stretched across the middle
that is used to shoot small stones; used in American
English. *...with a crowd of hundreds attacking them
with stones and slingshots.*

slink /slɪŋk/ **slinks, slinking, slunk**
VA If you **slink** somewhere, you move there in a slow
and secretive way because you do not want to be
seen. *I slunk away to my room, to brood.*

slinky /slɪŋki/ **slinkier, slinkiest**
ADJ **Slinky** clothes fit closely to a woman's body in a
way that makes her sexually attractive. *She browbeat
her parents into letting her wear a slinky dress.*

slip /slɪp/ **slips, slipping, slipped**
1 V If you **slip**, you accidentally slide and lose your
balance. *Another woman climbing in the mountains
broke a leg when she slipped and fell... Standing on a
ladder it's easy to slip.*
2 V If something **slips**, it slides out of place. *The knife
slipped and I cut my hand... She pulled up her sock
which had slipped down... It slipped from his fingers
and fell with a bump.*
3 VA If you **slip** somewhere, you go there quickly,
trying not to let other people see you. *Then he slipped
upstairs for a nap... Some students managed to slip
into the embassy compound.*
4 VOA If you **slip** something somewhere, you put it
there quickly and quietly. *He slipped it quickly into
his pocket... He heard a note being slipped under the
door.*
5 V If something **slips**, its standard or value drops a
little, usually in comparison to other things of its
kind. *The pound has slipped further against the mark
in early European trading. ...complaints by teachers
that their earnings have slipped behind other
'professionals'... He said standards generally had
slipped.*
6 VAorVOA If you **slip** into clothes or **slip** them on, you
put them on quickly and easily. If you **slip** out of
clothes or **slip** them off, you take them off quickly and

easily. *I slipped into my pyjamas... He slipped on his
shoes and went out... He slipped his black robe over
his tunic... She slipped off her dress.*
7 NC A **slip** is a small mistake. *I must have made a
slip somewhere.*
8 NC A **slip** of paper is a small piece of paper. *An
Interior Ministry official is stamping numbers on slips
of paper.*
● **Slip** is used in these phrases. ● If something **slips**
your **mind or slips** your **memory**, you forget about it.
*In the confusion it had completely slipped my mind
that her father was our garbage man.* ● If you **give**
someone **the slip**, you succeed in escaping from them;
an informal expression. *I tried to follow her but she
gave me the slip.* ● If you **let** something **slip**, you
accidentally tell someone something that you or
another person did not want them to know; an
informal expression. *He's let slip what the Treasury
have thought privately about the future of the welfare
state. ...stories like this one, which was conveniently
let slip to eager journalists.* ● If you **let** an opportunity
or a chance **slip**, you do not try to use it, so you miss
it. *Mr Haughey is too experienced a politician to let
slip such an opportunity to sell his policies.* ● **slip of
the tongue: see tongue.**

slip up PHRASAL VERB If you **slip up**, you make a
mistake. *We must have slipped up somewhere.* ● See
also **slip-up.**

slip-on, slip-ons
NC **Slip-ons** are shoes that have no laces and that can
be put on or taken off easily. *He had discarded his
combat boots for a pair of Italian slip-ons.*

slippage /slɪpɪdʒ/
NU **Slippage** is a failure to maintain a steady rate of
progress, so that a particular target or standard is not
achieved. *The encounter may have contributed to his
recent slippage in the polls... The economy continues
to show signs of slippage.*

slipped disc, slipped discs
NC If you have a **slipped disc**, one of the discs in your
spine has moved out of its proper position. *You'll risk
a slipped disc if your ironing board is too low and you
have to stoop.*

slipper /slɪpə/ **slippers**
NC **Slippers** are soft shoes that you wear in the house.
...bedroom slippers.

slippery /slɪpəʳri/
1 ADJ Something that is **slippery** is smooth, wet, or
greasy and is therefore difficult to hold or walk on.
*The soap was smooth and slippery. ...a slippery
pavement.*
2 ADJ A **slippery** person acts in a dishonest way and
cannot be trusted. *Since we know that he's a slippery
customer, why should we should have trusted him?...
He's rather a slippery customer.*
3 If someone is going **down** a **slippery slope** or is **on** a
slippery slope, they are in a situation that is quickly
getting worse and will probably lead to some serious
trouble. *The country is heading down a slippery slope
which could end in civil war.*

slippy /slɪpi/
ADJ A **slippy** surface is smooth, wet, or greasy and
therefore difficult for you to walk on without sliding.
Be careful. It's a bit slippy.

slip road, slip roads
NC A **slip road** is a road which cars use to drive onto
or off a motorway. *The interchange became known as
Spaghetti Junction because of its intricate lay-out of
slip roads.*

slipshod /slɪpʃɒd/
ADJ If something is done in a **slipshod** way, it is done
without care or thoroughly. *...a slipshod and
inaccurate piece of research. ...slipshod spelling... He
strongly denied that he'd been slipshod over the whole
security issue.*

slipstream /slɪpstriːm/
N SING The **slipstream** of a fast-moving object,
especially a car or plane, is the flow of air directly
behind it. *Police on motorcycles were riding in the
slipstream of the official cars.*

slip-up, slip-ups
NC A **slip-up** is a small or unimportant mistake. *This*

is the basis of many flaws and slip-ups.

slit /slɪt/ **slits, slitting.** The form **slit** is used in the present tense and is also the past tense and past participle of the verb.
1 vo If you **slit** something, you make a long narrow cut in it. *She got a knife and slit the envelope... He slit open the packet with his thumb nail.*
2 NC A **slit** is a long narrow cut. *We make a tiny slit in it with a razor blade.*
3 NC A **slit** is also a long narrow opening in something. *...neon light came through the slits in the blind.*

slither /slɪðə/ **slithers, slithering, slithered**
VA If you **slither** somewhere, you slide along, often in an uncontrolled way. *We slithered down the steep slope.*

sliver /slɪvə/ **slivers**
NC A **sliver** of something is a small thin piece of it. *...a sliver of soap.*

slob /slɒb/ **slobs**
NC If you say that someone is a **slob**, you think they are very lazy and untidy; an informal word. *He may look like a slob, but under that gross exterior there is a man of great intellectual resource.*

slobber /slɒbə/ **slobbers, slobbering, slobbered**
V If someone **slobbers**, they let liquid fall from their mouth, like babies do. *Sally was happily slobbering in her pram.*
slobber over PHRASAL VERB If someone **slobbers over** someone or something, they show their attraction to that person or liking for that thing in an excessive way; used showing disapproval. *The women understandably say they don't like being slobbered over.*

slobbery /slɒbəri/
ADJ A **slobbery** mouth or kiss is very wet.

sloe /sləʊ/ **sloes**
NC A **sloe** is a small sour fruit that has a dark purple skin. *Sloes make marvellous fruit wine.*

slog /slɒg/ **slogs, slogging, slogged;** an informal word.
1 VA If you **slog** at something, you work hard and steadily at it. *The children are slogging away at revision.* ► Also N SING *...the hard slog of trying to get views changed.*
2 VA If you **slog** somewhere, you make a long and tiring journey there. *Early settlers had slogged this way to the west over this pass... The huge convoy slogged on through to Jerusalem.* ► Also N SING *...his long slog home.*

slogan /sləʊgən/ **slogans**
NC **Slogans** are short, easily-remembered phrases, often used in advertising or by politicians. *The crowd shouted anti-government slogans and chanted 'freedom'.*

slop /slɒp/ **slops, slopping, slopped**
1 V-ERG If liquid **slops** or if you **slop** it, it spills over the edge of a container in a messy way. *Wine was slopped into a dusty glass... We carried the buckets, slopping water, back to the kitchen... He slopped a perfectly good port over the letter.*
2 NU or N PL Liquid waste that contains the remnants of food is referred to as **slop** or **slops**, especially food that is fed to animals. *I fed the slop to the pigs... You used to get people throwing the slops of teacups down on you.*

slope /sləʊp/ **slopes, sloping, sloped**
1 NC A **slope** is a flat surface that is at an angle, so that one end is higher than the other. *They were now reaching an upward slope of the road.*
2 NC A **slope** is also the side of a hill, mountain, or valley. *She rode up a grassy slope... Climbers have been warned to stay off the slopes until the snow has settled. ...the main ski slopes.*
3 V If a surface **slopes**, it is at an angle, so that one end is higher than the other. *The roof sloped down at the back.* ◆ **sloping** ADJ ATTRIB *...gently sloping hills. ...a sloping escape shaft.*
4 V If something **slopes**, it leans to the right or to the left rather than being upright. *My handwriting sloped to the left.* ◆ **sloping** ADJ ATTRIB *...sloping handwriting.*
5 N SING+SUPP The **slope** of something is the angle at

which it slopes. *...a slope of ten degrees.*
6 slippery slope: see **slippery.**

sloppy /slɒpi/
1 ADJ Something that is **sloppy** is messy and careless; an informal word. *...sloppy workmanship... They are accused of being sloppy and badly prepared for action.* ◆ **sloppily** ADV *...a sloppily run hospital.*
2 ADJ You can say that something is **sloppy** when you think it is extremely sentimental. *I got very bored with all his sloppy clichés... You'll write me sloppy letters.*

slosh /slɒʃ/ **sloshes, sloshing, sloshed**
V-ERG If a liquid **sloshes** or if you **slosh** it, it splashes or moves around in a messy way. *The whiskey sloshed over from his glass on to his hand... They sat out on the decks laughing and sloshing water everywhere.*

sloshed /slɒʃt/
ADJ PRED Someone who is **sloshed** is drunk; an informal word. *Once I was sloshed, the housework and the children were all quite bearable.*

slot /slɒt/ **slots, slotting, slotted**
1 NC A **slot** is a narrow opening in a machine or container, for example a hole that you put coins in to make a machine work. *He put money in the slot and the music started again.*
2 V-RECIP When something **slots** into something else or when you slot it in, you put it into a space where it fits. *They slot into each other to form a circle... The cylinder just slots into the barrel... I slotted my money in.*
3 NC A **slot** is also a place in a schedule, scheme, or organization. *There are only occasional television slots for rock music. ...the take-off and landing slots at Heathrow airport.*

sloth /sləʊθ/
1 NU **Sloth** is laziness; a literary word. *The ministries are renowned for inefficiency, sloth and the passing on of responsibility.*
2 NC A **sloth** is an animal that is found mainly in Central and South America. They live in trees and move very slowly. *The fastest land animal is the cheetah and the slowest the three-toed sloth.*

slot machine, slot machines
NC A **slot machine** is a machine from which you can get something such as food or drink, or on which you can gamble. You work it by putting coins into a slot in the machine. *The 28 slot machines he installed bring in a new kind of customer.*

slouch /slaʊtʃ/ **slouches, slouching, slouched**
1 V If you **slouch**, you sit or walk in a lazy or tired way with your shoulders and head drooping down. *Many children slouch because of lack of self-confidence.*
2 If you **are no slouch** at a particular activity, you are skilful at it or know a lot about it; an informal expression. *You're certainly no slouch in the kitchen... He is no slouch when it comes to classical music.*

slough /slaʊ/ **sloughs, sloughing, sloughed**
slough off PHRASAL VERB **1** When an animal such as a snake **sloughs off** its skin, its skin comes off naturally. *Some lizards have special cracks in their tail-bones so they can slough off their tails in a panic.*
2 VO If you **slough off** something that you no longer need, you get rid of it; a literary use. *Women are less willing than their husbands to slough off a friendship after a move.*

Slovenia /sləviːniə/
The **Republic of Slovenia** is a country in south-eastern Europe, formerly part of Yugoslavia. It declared its independence from Yugoslavia in 1991. Civil war followed and it achieved international recognition in 1992. Milan Kučan, of the Party of Democratic Reform, became President in 1990. Slovenia exports agricultural products and manufactured goods.
◆ **Slovenian** /sləviːniən/ N, ADJ
▪ *religion:* Christianity (mainly Roman Catholic)
▪ *language:* Slovenian ▪ *currency:* tolar ▪ *capital:* Ljubljana ▪ *population:* 2 million (1981) ▪ *size:* 20,251 square kilometres.

slovenly /slʌvnli/
ADJ A **slovenly** person is careless, untidy, or

inefficient. *His appearance was even more slovenly than usual.*

slow /sləʊ/ **slower, slowest; slows, slowing, slowed**
1 ADJ Slow means moving, acting, or happening without very much speed. *His movements were all deliberate and slow... They have slow reflexes... He still appears to be making slow progress.* ► Also ADV *You're going too slow.* ◆ **slowly** ADV *He nodded slowly and walked very sadly out of the door.* ◆ **slowness** NU *Time passed with agonizing slowness.*
2 V-ERG If something **slows** or if you **slow** it, it starts to move or happen more slowly. *He slowed to a walk. ...ways of slowing population growth.*
3 ADJ PRED A person who is **slow** takes a long time to understand something, usually because they are not very clever; an informal use. *It has given her the idea that I am slow and pig-headed.*
4 ADJ PRED If an activity, place, or story is **slow**, it is not very busy or exciting. *Business will be slow in the shop for another hour.*
5 ADJ If a clock or watch is **slow**, it shows a time that is earlier than the correct time. *That clock's half an hour slow.*
slow down PHRASAL VERB 1 If something **slows down** or if you **slow** it **down**, it starts to move or happen more slowly than before. *Economic growth has slowed down dramatically... We're helping people to slow down their body rhythms... Harold slowed the car down.* 2 If someone **slows down**, they become less active. *He needs to slow down a little or he'll get an ulcer.*
slow up PHRASAL VERB If something **slows up** or if you **slow** it **up**, it starts to move or happen more slowly. *She slowed up a little... The extra weight would have slowed me up considerably.*

slowcoach /sləʊkəʊtʃ/ **slowcoaches**
NC If you call someone a **slowcoach**, you mean that they are moving or doing something too slowly; an informal word.

slowdown /sləʊdaʊn/ **slowdowns**
1 NC A **slowdown** is a reduction in speed, activity, or growth. *...a marked economic slowdown. ...a slowdown in investment. ...the slowdown in the arms race.*
2 NC A **slowdown** is also a protest by workers in which they deliberately work slowly and cause problems for their employers; used in American English. *A federal judge has banned any actions contributing to a work slowdown by airline pilots.*

slow motion
NU **Slow motion** is movement which is much slower than normal, especially in a film or on television. *I dreamt I was falling off a cliff in slow motion.* ► Also ADV *...slow-motion film of people talking.*

slow-witted
ADJ Someone who is **slow-witted** is not very clever or takes a long time to understand things. *Youngsters constantly curse mature drivers for allegedly being slow-witted and incompetent... He's a charming but slightly slow-witted fellow.*

sludge /slʌdʒ/
NU **Sludge** is a mixture that is made up of liquid and solids such as thick mud or sewage. *I was covered in sludge and weeds.*

slug /slʌɡ/ **slugs, slugging, slugged**
1 NC A **slug** is a small, slow-moving creature with a long, slimy body, like a snail without a shell. *Slugs cause extensive damage to plants and vegetables.*
2 NC A **slug** is also a bullet; used in informal American English. *They found a 25 caliber slug indented in the radio Lee kept in the breast pocket of his jacket.*
3 NC You can refer to a large mouthful of a drink that you are going to swallow as a **slug**; an informal use. *I was offered a big slug of Scotch poured into a grubby glass.*
4 VO If you **slug** someone, you hit them hard with your fist; used in informal American English. *I raised a fist to slug Eddie.*
5 If two people **slug** it **out**, they fight or argue strongly about something; an informal expression. *...as the resistance groups slug it out... Two leading medical experts slug it out.*

sluggish /slʌɡɪʃ/
ADJ Something that is **sluggish** moves or works much more slowly than normal. *I feel very sluggish. ...black sluggish waters... Growth will continue to be sluggish.*

sluice /sluːs/ **sluices, sluicing, sluiced**
1 NC A **sluice** is a passage that carries a current of water. It has an opening called a sluice gate which can be opened and closed to control the flow of water. *The Sukkur Barrage in Pakistan provides irrigation water to a vast area through 60 sluice gates.*
2 VO If you **sluice** something or **sluice** out something, you wash it with a stream of water or some other liquid. *We sluiced out the trough.*

slum /slʌm/ **slums**
NC A **slum** is an area of a city where living conditions are very bad and where the houses are in a bad condition. *...shanty towns and slums. ...children from a slum area... Many people are living in slum dwellings.*

slumber /slʌmbə/ **slumbers, slumbering, slumbered**; a literary word.
1 NUorNC **Slumber** is sleep. *She fell into profound and dreamless slumber... Roused from his slumbers, O'Shea departed.*
2 V If you **slumber**, you sleep. *One old man slumbered over his newspaper.*

slummy /slʌmi/ **slummier, slummiest**
ADJ A **slummy** area of a town is one where the houses are in very bad condition and a large number of poor people live. *That part was once very slummy but is now very smart.*

slump /slʌmp/ **slumps, slumping, slumped**
1 V If something such as the value of something **slumps**, it falls suddenly and by a large amount. *Prices slumped as excess coffee flooded the markets... The farmers say sales have slumped by as much as sixty percent.* ► Also NC *...the worldwide slump in demand for ships.*
2 If an industry or a company is **in a slump**, they have a lot less business than usual. *The housing industry has been in a slump for two years because of high interest rates.*
3 NC A **slump** is also a time when a country's economy slows down greatly and there is a lot of unemployment and poverty. *The slump set in during the summer of 1921.*
4 VA If you **slump** somewhere, you fall or sit down there heavily, for example because you are very tired or you have fainted. *Sarah slumped against the wall.* ◆ **slumped** ADJ *When officials entered the property, they found a man slumped in a chair.*

slung /slʌŋ/
Slung is the past tense and past participle of **sling**.

slunk /slʌŋk/
Slunk is the past tense and past participle of **slink**.

slur /slɜː/ **slurs, slurring, slurred**
1 NC A **slur** is an insulting remark which could damage someone's reputation. *He got angry whenever anyone cast the slightest slur on the regiment.*
2 V If you **slur** your speech or if it **slurs**, you do not pronounce your words clearly, often because you are drunk. *He tended to slur words and hiccough... 'I'll sing for you,' he said, his voice slurring so that he could barely be understood.* ◆ **slurred** ADJ *His words were slurred and his breath smelled of wine.*

slurp /slɜːp/ **slurps, slurping, slurped**
VOorV If you **slurp** a liquid, you drink it noisily. *He slurped the soup greedily... Ginny lifted her cup and slurped.*

slurry /slʌri/
NU **Slurry** is a watery mixture of something such as mud, cement, or manure. *It rained—how it rained! The farm turned into slurry... The cow's slurry is then brought back to fertilize the land.*

slush /slʌʃ/
NU **Slush** is snow which has begun to melt. *Much of the snow on the roads is now turning to slush.*

slush fund, slush funds
NC A **slush fund** is a sum of money collected to finance an illegal activity, especially in politics or business. *The twin scandals of a government-sanctioned slush*

fund and dirty tricks operation have sent shock waves across the political arena.

slushy /slʌʃi/
1 ADJ Ground that is **slushy** is covered in wet snow. *A thaw had set in and the streets were slushy.*
2 ADJ A **slushy** story or idea is extremely romantic and sentimental; an informal use. *...a slushy film.*

slut /slʌt/ **sluts;** an offensive word.
1 NC A **slut** is a woman who is dirty and untidy.
2 NC People also refer to a woman as a **slut** when they consider her to be very immoral in her sexual behaviour.

sly /slaɪ/ **slyer** or **slier, slyest** or **sliest**
1 ADJ A **sly** look, expression, or remark shows that you know something that other people do not know. *...a slow sly smile.* ◆ **slyly** ADV *She glanced slyly at Madeleine.*
2 ADJ A **sly** person is clever at deceiving people. *They are suspicious and wary and sly.*
3 If someone does something **on the sly,** they do it in a secretive way, often because it is something they should not be doing; an informal expression. *The National Peasant Party accused the Front of trying to take over power on the sly... They're closing down the store tonight on the sly because they don't want any fuss.*

smack /smæk/ **smacks, smacking, smacked**
1 VO If you **smack** someone, you hit them with your hand. *He smacked her on the bottom... Ninety per cent of parents smack their children.* ▶ Also NC *I gave him a smack in the face.*
2 VOA If you **smack** something somewhere, you put it or throw it there so that it makes a loud, sharp noise. *He laughed, smacking the flat of his hand on the steering wheel.* ▶ Also N SING *She gave out the books, dropping them with a satisfying smack on each desk.*
3 V+*of* If one thing **smacks** of another thing, it reminds you of it or is like it; used showing disapproval. *A Western correspondent suggested that this smacked of dual standards.*
4 ADV Something that is **smack** in a particular place is in that exact place; an informal use. *Jordan is smack in the center of the Middle East... The New Bethel Baptist Church is smack in the centre of Detroit... He rushed through that door and ran smack into two more doors.*

small /smɔːl/ **smaller, smallest**
1 ADJ Someone or something that is **small** is not large in physical size. *She was rather small in stature... The male is smaller than the female... This is the smallest church in England.* ◆ **smallness** NU *The smallness of the courtroom exaggerated its height.*
2 ADJ A **small** group or amount consists of only a few things or of not much of something. *...small families. ...a relatively small number of people. ...a small amount of milk.*
3 ADJ A **small** child is a very young child. *She had two small children.*
4 ADJ You also use **small** to describe something that is not significant or great in degree. *Certain small changes resulted from my report. ...a matter of small importance.*
● **Small** is used in these phrases. ● The **small of** your **back** is the narrow part of your back where it curves inwards slightly. *She had a pain in the small of her back.* ● If something makes you **feel small** or **look small,** it makes you feel or look ridiculous and humiliates you. *Feeling small and childish, she crossed back over the bridge.* ● the **small hours:** see **hour.** ● **small wonder:** see **wonder.**

small ad, small ads
NC A **small ad** in a newspaper is a short advertisement in which you can advertise something such as an object for sale or a room to let. *The best place to look for accommodation is in the small ads section of your local newspaper.*

small arms
N PL **Small arms** are guns that are light and have a small calibre. *They became experts in fighting with small arms.*

small business, small businesses
N Cor NU A **small business** is a company or firm that

does not have many employees and does not belong to a larger company. *...raise the money needed to start a small business. ...to encourage the people to venture into small business.*

small businessman, small businessmen
NC A **small businessman** is a businessman who owns a small company or firm that does not have many employees. *Another small businessman had his successful business totally destroyed. ...schemes to help small businessmen with loans.*

small change
NU **Small change** is coins of low value. *I need some small change to make a phone call.*

small fry
N PL **Small fry** is used to refer to people who are considered unimportant. *Some of the small fry of the drugs world have been caught while the big fish have got away.*

smallholder /smɔːlhəʊldə/ **smallholders**
NC A **smallholder** is someone who has a smallholding. *All over Asia smallholders are being made poorer.*

smallholding /smɔːlhəʊldɪŋ/ **smallholdings**
NC A **smallholding** is a piece of land used for farming that is smaller than a small farm. *...smallholdings of one acre or less.*

smallish /smɔːlɪʃ/
ADJ **Smallish** means fairly small. *He was a smallish man.*

small-minded
ADJ Someone who is **small-minded** has fixed opinions and is unwilling to change them or to think about a wider range of subjects; used showing disapproval. *This is a very small-minded old-fashioned attitude.*

smallpox /smɔːlpɒks/
NU **Smallpox** is a serious infectious disease that causes a high fever and a rash. *No case of smallpox has been reported anywhere since 1978.*

small-scale
ADJ ATTRIB A **small-scale** activity or organization is small in size and limited in extent. *...small-scale industry.*

small screen
N SING The **small screen** is television, especially considered in contrast to the cinema. *Despite his film successes, he has achieved little on the small screen.*

small talk
NU **Small talk** is conversation at social occasions about unimportant things. *We stood around making small talk.*

small-time
ADJ ATTRIB **Small-time** workers, businesses, or crooks are not considered to be very important, because they operate only on a small scale. *...the small-time farmers and traders of the region... He began as a small-time New York hoodlum and graduated to organized crime.*

small-town
1 ADJ ATTRIB You use **small-town** to describe things that are typical of, or exist in small towns as opposed to cities. *We like to look at some small-town newspapers from time to time... Our small-town video stores have a very limited selection.*
2 ADJ ATTRIB You can also use **small-town** to describe things which have the values or characteristics associated with small towns as opposed to cities. *...small-town Western values... It may not have the same small-town feel it once did.*

smarmy /smɑːmi/
ADJ Someone who is **smarmy** is unpleasantly polite and flattering; an informal word. *...a nasty little man, smarmy and obsequious.*

smart /smɑːt/ **smarter, smartest; smarts, smarting, smarted**
1 ADJ A **smart** person is pleasantly neat and clean in appearance. *The boys looked smart in their school uniforms.* ◆ **smartly** ADV *He's well educated and dresses smartly.*
2 ADJ **Smart** also means clever; used in American English. *She's one of the smartest students in the whole school. ...a smart idea.*
3 ADJ A **smart** place or event is connected with wealthy and fashionable people. *We met at a very*

smart lunch party. ...one of Delhi's smart residential areas.

4 ADJ ATTRIB A **smart** movement or action is sharp and quick; a literary use. *...the smart crack of a whip. ...moving along at a smart trot.* ◆ **smartly** ADV *Grabbing the bottle, she hit him smartly on the head.*

5 V If a part of your body or a wound **smarts**, you feel a sharp stinging pain in it. *His eyes smarted from the smoke of the fire.*

6 V If you **are smarting** from criticism or unkind remarks, you are feeling upset about it. *They are still smarting from the comments he made... The Israelis are said to be still smarting over his remarks.*

smarten /smɑːtn/ **smartens, smartening, smartened**
smarten up PHRASAL VERB If you **smarten** something **up**, you make it look neater and tidier. *The New Electric Cinema has been smartened up.*

smash /smæʃ/ **smashes, smashing, smashed**

1 VO If you **smash** something, you break it into many pieces by hitting, throwing, or dropping it. *Shop and hotel windows have been smashed... I nearly smashed the TV set.*

2 V If something **smashes**, it breaks into many pieces when it falls and hits the ground. *A plate dropped from his fingers and smashed on the kitchen floor.*

3 VA If something **smashes** or is **smashed** into or against something solid, it moves with great force against it. *Eye witnesses said the bus had smashed into the train... The boat was tossed over two or three times before being smashed on the beach.*

4 VA or VOA If someone **smashes** through something such as a door or **smashes** their way through it, they hit it hard enough to make a space for them to pass through. *The lorry smashed through a steel barrier on the bridge... The police smashed their way into eleven homes.*

5 VO If people **smash** something such as a political system, they deliberately try to destroy it. *We are interested in transforming the system rather than smashing it... Officials in the United States say they've smashed a big network that's been smuggling computers.*

6 NC A song, play, or film that is a **smash** or a **smash hit** is very successful and popular. *Simon Climie wrote the song 'I knew you were waiting for me'... The show was a smash hit in London and New York.*

7 NC A **smash** is also a car crash. *She had a serious motor smash on the way up to Scotland.*

smash down PHRASAL VERB If someone **smashes** a door or a barrier **down**, they hit it so that it breaks into pieces and falls down. *One of the doors was smashed down.*

smash up PHRASAL VERB If you **smash** something **up**, you completely destroy it by breaking it into many pieces. *He started smashing up all the furniture.*

smash-and-grab
ADJ ATTRIB A **smash-and-grab** robbery is a way of stealing from a shop that happens very quickly. A thief smashes the shop window, seizes the things that are on display there, and rushes away with them. *...smash-and-grab raids at jewellers' shops.*

smashed /smæʃt/
ADJ PRED Someone who is **smashed** is extremely drunk or under the influence of a powerful drug; an informal word. *I spent that evening smashed out of my mind.*

smasher /smæʃə/ **smashers**
NC If you refer to someone as a **smasher**, you mean that you find them very pleasant or attractive; an informal word. *She's a real smasher.*

smashing /smæʃɪŋ/
ADJ If you say something is **smashing**, you mean that you like it very much; an informal word. *We had a smashing time.*

smattering /smætərɪŋ/
N SING A **smattering** of knowledge or information is a very small amount of it. *Jane spoke Spanish, and a smattering of Greek.*

smear /smɪə/ **smears, smearing, smeared**

1 NC A **smear** is a dirty or greasy mark caused by something rubbing against a surface. *...a smear of blue paint.*

2 VO To **smear** something means to make dirty or

greasy marks on it. *Soot smeared our faces... The windows were all smeared.*

3 VOA If you **smear** a surface with a substance or **smear** the substance onto the surface, you spread a layer of the substance over the surface. *Smear the baking tin with butter... She smeared this blood onto a slide.*

4 NC A **smear** is also an unpleasant and untrue rumour or accusation that is intended to damage someone's reputation. *Party leaders denounced the allegation as a right-wing smear.*

5 NC A **smear test** or a **smear** is a medical test in which a small sample of fluid from a woman's cervix is taken to test for cancer or other diseases. *It also urges women to examine their breasts regularly and have cervical smear tests.*

smear campaign, smear campaigns
NC A **smear campaign** is an attempt made by a group of people over a period of time to damage the reputation of someone or something by starting unpleasant rumours and telling untrue stories about them. *He accused the authorities of a smear campaign against them, and denied that his party had any links with illegal groups.*

smell /smel/ **smells, smelling, smelled or smelt**

1 NC The **smell** of something is a quality it has which you become aware of through your nose. *What's that smell?... She remembers the smell of fruit and flowers... Soon the whole area complained about the dreadful smell. ...cooking smells.*

2 V If something **smells**, it has a quality which you become aware of through your nose. *The fridge began to smell... The room smelled of cigars... Our kitchen smelt like a rubber factory... The papers smelt musty and stale... Dinner smells good.*

3 VO If you **smell** something, you become aware of it through your nose. *Don't strike a match if you smell gas.*

4 VO To **smell** something also means to put your nose near it and breathe in, in order to discover its smell. *She picked up the soap and smelled it.*

5 NU **Smell** is the ability that your nose has to detect things. *A loss of the sense of smell is a common symptom of the disease.*

6 VO If you **smell** something such as danger, you feel instinctively that it is likely to happen. *He's shrewd and can smell a successful project.* ● If you **smell a rat**, you become suspicious that there is something wrong; an informal expression. *Old Genco would never have fallen for it, he would have smelled a rat.*

-smelling /-smelɪŋ/
SUFFIX You can use **-smelling** with other adjectives such as 'sweet' or 'foul' to indicate that something has that particular type of smell. *...sweet-smelling roses.*

smelly /smeli/
ADJ Something that is **smelly** has an unpleasant smell. *...some rather smelly cheese... It may come as a surprise but pure methane isn't smelly.*

smelt /smelt/ **smelts, smelting, smelted**

1 **Smelt** is the past tense and past participle of **smell**.

2 VO To **smelt** a substance containing metal means to process it by heating it until it melts, so that the metal is extracted and changed chemically. *Fire provided a means of smelting ores.*

smelter /smeltə/ **smelters**
NC+SUPP A **smelter** is a furnace for smelting metal.

smile /smaɪl/ **smiles, smiling, smiled**

1 V When you **smile**, the corners of your mouth curve outwards and slightly upwards, for example because you are pleased or amused. *Hooper smiled and leaned back in his chair... Both he and his wife Raisa were smiling broadly.*

2 NC A **smile** is the expression that you have on your face when you smile. *Barber welcomed me with a smile... There were also flowers and smiles.* ◆ **smiling** ADJ ATTRIB *...the smiling face of Tibet's spiritual leader, the Dalai Lama.*

3 V O or V-QUOTE If you **smile** something, you express or say it with a smile. *She smiled her approval... 'That remains to be seen,' smiled Mrs Barrett.* ◆ **smilingly** ADV *He smilingly replied that he didn't speak English.*

smile on PHRASAL VERB If something such as luck, fate, the weather, and so on **smiles on** or **smiles upon** you, you are very fortunate. *The soccer gods smiled on the Blues when their goalkeeper saved a penalty... Fortune has smiled on us today.*

smirk /smɜːk/ **smirks, smirking, smirked**
v If you **smirk**, you smile in an unpleasant and superior way, often because you have gained an advantage over someone or know something they do not know. *'That's where you're wrong,' Ellen said, smirking.* ▶ Also NC *Mark detected a smirk on the clerk's face.*

smite /smaɪt/ **smites, smiting, smote, smitten**
VO If you **smite** something, you hit it hard; an old-fashioned word. *He smote the ball over my head... The sun smote their faces.* ● See also **smitten**.

smithereens /smɪðəˈriːnz/
If something is smashed **to smithereens**, it is smashed into many small pieces so that it is completely destroyed. *She dropped the vase and smashed it to smithereens.*

smithy /smɪði/ **smithies**
NC A **smithy** is a place where a blacksmith works. *...a village smithy.*

smitten /smɪtn/
1 ADJ PRED If you are **smitten**, you find someone so attractive that you are or seem to be in love with them. *I was smitten with her.*
2 ADJ PRED If you are **smitten** by something, you are very impressed and enthusiastic about it. *I was quite smitten by her luminous green eyes and gold curls... After his first visit to France he was smitten by the French.*
3 **Smitten** is the past participle of **smite**.

smock /smɒk/ **smocks**
NC A **smock** is a loose garment which is often worn over other clothes to protect them. *They may not notice a woman in her 40s who wears a light blue smock.*

smog /smɒɡ/
NU **Smog** is a mixture of fog and smoke which occurs in some industrial cities. *Black smog reduced visibility to about fifty yards.*

smoggy /smɒɡi/
ADJ **Smoggy** places or air have a lot of smog. *The elderly and those with respiratory and heart disease are urged to stay indoors and avoid smoggy areas. ...a statewide plan to clean up the state's smoggy air.*

smoke /sməʊk/ **smokes, smoking, smoked**
1 NU **Smoke** consists of gas and small bits of solid material that are sent into the air when something burns. *The room was full of smoke... Smoke from many fires could be seen rising. ...cigarette smoke.*
2 V If something is **smoking**, smoke is coming from it. *Down below in the valleys the chimneys were smoking.*
3 V or VO When someone **smokes** a cigarette, cigar, or pipe, they suck smoke from it into their mouth and blow it out again. *He sat and smoked and stared out of the window. ...a child who smokes just one cigarette.* ▶ Also N SING *I'm dying for a smoke.*
4 V If you **smoke**, you regularly smoke cigarettes, cigars, or a pipe. *Do you smoke?*
5 VO To **smoke** fish or meat means to hang it over burning wood so that the smoke will preserve and flavour it. ◆ **smoked** ADJ ATTRIB *...smoked salmon.*
6 If something **goes up in smoke**, it fails or ends without anything being achieved. *With just eight minutes to go Palace's dreams went up in smoke as Liverpool scored twice.*

smoked /sməʊkt/
ADJ ATTRIB **Smoked** glass is glass that has been made darker by being treated with smoke. *The windows were smoked glass.*

smokeless /sməʊkləs/
ADJ ATTRIB **Smokeless** fuel burns without producing smoke. *It has already designated six areas where only smokeless fuel can be used.*

smokeless zone, smokeless zones
NC A **smokeless zone** is an area, especially in a big city, in which the burning of any fuel that produces smoke is forbidden by law.

smoker /sməʊkə/ **smokers**
1 NC A **smoker** is someone who smokes cigarettes or other forms of tobacco. *One smoker in twenty will give up the habit permanently... He has always been a pipe smoker.*
2 NC A **smoker** is also a carriage in a train in which passengers are allowed to smoke.

smokescreen /sməʊkskriːn/
N SING If something that you do or say is a **smokescreen**, it is intended to hide the truth about your activities or intentions. *The Association says that the government's review is a smokescreen to hide the need for extra funding... These membership rules are a smokescreen.*

smokestack /sməʊkstæk/ **smokestacks**
1 NC A **smokestack** is a tall chimney which is used in heavy industry to carry smoke away from a factory. *Water vapour from the river could be attracted to the particles coming from the smokestack.*
2 N+N **Smokestack** industry is heavy industry. *...the smokestack cities of the industrialized Midwest and East.*

smoking /sməʊkɪŋ/
1 NU **Smoking** is the act or habit of smoking cigarettes, cigars, or a pipe. *Does smoking cause cancer?... I'm trying to give up smoking.*
2 ADJ ATTRIB A **smoking** section or compartment is intended for smokers. *Do you want to go in the smoking or non-smoking section?*

smoky /sməʊki/
1 ADJ A **smoky** place has a lot of smoke in the air. *...a smoky industrial scene of the 1930's.*
2 ADJ ATTRIB You can also use **smoky** to describe something that reminds you of smoke. *...a smoky-blue scarf. ...the smoky twilight.*

smolder /sməʊldə/. See **smoulder**.

smooch /smuːtʃ/ **smooches, smooching, smooched**; an informal word.
1 V-RECIP If two people **smooch**, they kiss and hold each other closely. *He was smooching with her in the car... They were smooching on the sofa.* ▶ Also N SING *We had yet another long smooch during the film.*
2 V-RECIP You also say that two people are **smooching** when they dance very slowly and closely together with their arms around each other. *The room was full of couples smooching around the floor. ...a good record to smooch to.*

smoochy /smuːtʃi/
ADJ A **smoochy** record or piece of music is slow and suitable for people to smooch to; an informal word. *Put on a smoochy record.*

smooth /smuːð/ **smoother, smoothest; smooths, smoothing, smoothed**
1 ADJ A **smooth** surface has no roughness or holes. *Your skin looks so smooth... The boulders were so smooth and slippery I couldn't get a grip.*
◆ **smoothness** NU *...the smoothness of his skin.*
2 ADJ A **smooth** liquid or mixture has no lumps in it. *Beat the cream with the eggs and cheese until the mixture is smooth. ...a smooth paste.*
3 VO If you **smooth** something, or **smooth** it out, you move your hands over its surface to make it smooth and flat. *Don't iron pyjamas. Just smooth and fold them... He turned his head and smoothed back the hair over one temple.*
4 ADJ A **smooth** movement or process happens or is done evenly and steadily with no sudden changes or breaks. *He walked with a long, smooth stride.*
◆ **smoothly** ADV *The snake glides smoothly towards it.*
5 ADJ A **smooth** ride, flight, and so on is comfortable because there are no bumps or jolts. *Did you have a smooth crossing?*
6 ADJ **Smooth** also means successful and without problems. *Co-operation is essential if you are going to lead a smooth existence in the office.* ◆ **smoothly** ADV *Life is running smoothly for them.*
7 ADJ A **smooth** man is extremely smart, confident, and polite, often in an unpleasant way.

smooth out PHRASAL VERB If you **smooth** something **out**, you move your hands over its surface to make it smooth and flat. *I started smoothing out the tablecloth.*

smooth over PHRASAL VERB If you **smooth over** a problem or difficulty, you make it less serious and easier to deal with, especially by talking to the people concerned. *I tried to smooth over the awkwardness of this first meeting.*

smoothie /smuːðɪ/ **smoothies**; also spelt **smoothy**.
NC A **smoothie** is a man who behaves so politely and looks so smart and confident that you feel suspicious that he may be doing this simply to impress you; an informal word, used showing disapproval. *He is suspected of being untrustworthy, a smoothie or a city slicker.*

smooth-talking
ADJ Someone who is **smooth-talking** is very confident and persuasive in the way they talk, but is perhaps not sincere or honest. *...a smooth-talking salesman.*

smoothy /smuːðɪ/. See **smoothie**.

smote /sməʊt/
Smote is the past tense of **smite**.

smother /smʌðə/ **smothers, smothering, smothered**
1 VO If you **smother** a fire, you cover it with something in order to put it out. *She grabbed a blanket to smother the flames.*
2 VO To **smother** someone means to kill them by covering their face so that they cannot breathe. *One of the women had been strangled and the other smothered.*
3 VO To **smother** someone also means to give them too much love and protection. *She should love them without smothering them with attention.*
4 V-PASS+*in* or *with* If something **is smothered** in or with things, it is completely covered with them. *The pear tree was smothered in ivy... One board in their classroom is smothered with photographs of mothers, fathers and other relatives.*

smoulder /sməʊldə/ **smoulders, smouldering, smouldered**; spelt **smolder** in American English.
V If something **smoulders**, it burns slowly, producing smoke but not flames. *The ruins are still smouldering.*

smudge /smʌdʒ/ **smudges, smudging, smudged**
1 NC A **smudge** is a dirty or blurred mark. *The wallpaper had smudges all over it.*
2 VO If you **smudge** something, you make it dirty or messy by touching it. *Her cheeks were smudged with tears.*

smudgy /smʌdʒɪ/ **smudgier, smudgiest**
1 ADJ Something that is **smudgy** is covered with dirty marks. *Her face was smudgy with tears.*
2 ADJ Something that is **smudgy** is also blurred so that it is messy and its outline or details are no longer clear. *...old smudgy photos.*

smug /smʌg/
ADJ Someone who is **smug** is very pleased with how good or clever they are; used showing disapproval. *They appeared smug and complacent. ...looks of smug satisfaction.* ◆ **smugly** ADV *'I know all that,' I said smugly.* ◆ **smugness** NU *For many it was an exercise in smugness and hypocrisy.*

smuggle /smʌgl/ **smuggles, smuggling, smuggled**
VO If someone **smuggles** things or people into a place or out of it, they take them there illegally or secretly. *She smuggled these diamond bracelets out. ...smuggling refugees into the country.* ◆ **smuggling** NU *The customs service says that cocaine smuggling from South America is their greatest worry.* ◆ **smuggled** ADJ ATTRIB *Last year the authorities seized five times more smuggled heroin than in 1988.*

smuggler /smʌglə/ **smugglers**
NC A **smuggler** is someone who takes goods into or out of a country illegally. *...drug smugglers.*

smut /smʌt/ **smuts**
1 NU If you refer to words or pictures as **smut**, you mean that they are related to nudity or sex, and that you think that they have been said or published just to excite or shock people, rather than for serious reasons. *I find the media's growing obsession with smut and sensation deplorable.*
2 NU or NC **Smut** or **smuts** is dirt such as soot which makes a dark mark on something. *...black floating smuts which play havoc with clothes and complexions.*

smutty /smʌtɪ/ **smuttier, smuttiest**
1 ADJ Words or pictures that are **smutty** shock and

offend some people because they are related to nudity or sex. *My daughter would never read smutty books.*
2 ADJ Something that is **smutty** is marked with dark smudges of dirt such as soot. *...smutty seats.*

snack /snæk/ **snacks**
NC A **snack** is a small, quick meal, or something eaten between meals. *You can cut it into pieces and eat it as a snack.*

snack bar, snack bars
NC A **snack bar** is a place where you can buy small meals such as sandwiches, and also drinks. *...an unbroken succession of souvenir shops, snack bars and tourist offices.*

snag /snæg/ **snags, snagging, snagged**
1 NC A **snag** is a small problem or disadvantage. *It cleans very effectively. The only snag is that it dissolves plastics.*
2 VOA If you **snag** part of your clothing on a sharp or rough object, it gets caught on it and tears. *I snagged my skirt on a bramble.*

snail /sneɪl/ **snails**
1 NC A **snail** is a small, slimy, slow-moving animal with a spiral-shaped shell. Some snails live on land and others live in water. *...a fresh-water snail... Three species of snail play a vital role in keeping the Negev desert in Israel alive.*
2 If you move or do something **at a snail's pace**, you move or do it very slowly. *On these joint ventures progress has been at a snail's pace... Vote counting has been at a snail's pace.*

snake /sneɪk/ **snakes, snaking, snaked**
1 NC A **snake** is a long, thin reptile with no legs. *He was bitten by a poisonous snake.*
2 VA Something that **snakes** along goes along in a series of curves; a literary use. *The procession snaked round the houses.*

snake charmer, snake charmers
NC A **snake charmer** is a person who entertains people by playing music and causing a snake to rise out of a basket and drop back in again.

snakes and ladders
NU **Snakes and ladders** is a children's game played with dice on a board which has squares, some of which are connected by drawings of snakes and ladders. As you play, you move up the board where there is a ladder and down it where there is a snake.

snap /snæp/ **snaps, snapping, snapped**
1 V-ERG If something **snaps**, it breaks suddenly, usually with a sharp sound. *The rope snapped... One of those kicks could snap you in half like a dry twig.* ► Also N SING *The snap of a twig broke the silence.*
2 V If someone **snaps**, or if their patience **snaps**, they suddenly stop being calm and become angry because the situation has become too tense or difficult for them. *Twice this week the normally placid tube travellers have snapped... He says that the people's patience had obviously snapped.*
3 V-ERG A If something **snaps** around or into something else, it moves quickly into position, with a sharp sound. *She snapped the silver chain around her neck... When you let go, it will snap back into the normal position.* ► Also N SING *The trap closes with a sudden snap.*
4 If you **snap your fingers**, you make a sharp sound by moving your middle finger quickly across your thumb in order to accompany music or to order someone to do something. *...the kids are only allowed to snap their fingers and sing along... The President is no longer the powerful person who snaps his or her fingers and gets things done.*
5 V If an animal **snaps** at you, it shuts its jaws quickly near you, as if it was going to bite you. *The dogs ran snapping and barking at his heels.*
6 V-QUOTE or V+*at* If someone **snaps** at you, they speak to you in a sharp, unfriendly way. *'Don't do that!' she snapped... 'What the hell is that to you?' I snapped at him. ...his abrasive manner and habit of snapping at everyone.*
7 ADJ ATTRIB A **snap** decision or action is taken suddenly, often without careful thought. *The snap reaction of the press was to welcome the change... Congress could persuade him to call a snap election.*

8 NC A **snap** is a photograph that is taken quickly and casually; an informal use. *We had to look through all their holiday snaps.*

snap up PHRASAL VERB If you **snap** something **up**, you buy it quickly because it is a bargain or because it is just what you want; an informal expression. *All these houses were snapped up as soon as they were offered for sale.*

snapdragon /snæpdrægən/ **snapdragons**
NC A **snapdragon** is a common garden plant with small colourful flowers that can open and shut like a mouth.

snappy /snæpi/ **snappier, snappiest**
1 ADJ Someone who is **snappy** wears smart, fashionable clothes. *He's such a snappy dresser.*
2 ADJ Speaking to someone in a **snappy** way means to speak to them in a sharp, unfriendly manner. *It was run by a peculiarly snappy and short-tempered woman.*
3 ADJ Something that is **snappy** is lively and energetic in style or performance. *The mood of the show is spirited, snappy, and young.*
4 If you tell someone to **make it snappy**, you tell them to do something quickly; an informal expression. *Look at the pamphlets and make it snappy.*

snapshot /snæpʃɒt/ **snapshots**
1 NC A **snapshot** is a photograph that is taken quickly and casually. *...family snapshots.*
2 NC+SUPP You can refer to something that gives you a brief idea of what a place or situation is like as a **snapshot** of that place or situation. *I'll leave you with a tiny snapshot of Paris this July... The government has published the twentieth edition of Social Trends, its annual snapshot of life in Britain.*

snare /sneə/ **snares**
NC A **snare** is a trap for catching birds or small animals. *...a rabbit snare.*

snarl /snɑːl/ **snarls, snarling, snarled**
1 V When an animal **snarls**, it makes a fierce, rough sound and shows its teeth. *...dogs snarling and snapping at the heels of sheep.* ▶ Also NC *The leopard gave a snarl of fury.*
2 V-QUOTE If someone **snarls** when they speak, they say something in a fierce and unpleasant way. *He snarled, 'Thanks for being so bloody enthusiastic.'*

snarl-up, snarl-ups
NC A **snarl-up** is a confused, disorganized situation in which things are unable to move or work as normal. *Bureaucratic snarl-ups may have been to blame.*

snatch /snætʃ/ **snatches, snatching, snatched**
1 VOorV+at If you **snatch** something, you take it or pull it away quickly. *He snatched the letter from the man's hand... He remembered snatching at his gun.*
2 VO If you **snatch** a small amount of time or an opportunity, you quickly make use of it. *I packed, then snatched four hours' sleep... I snatched the opportunity to tell them that I was leaving.*
3 VO If you **snatch** victory in a competition or election, you defeat your opponent or rival by a small amount or just before the end of the contest. *He snatched victory in a final sprint at the finish... Ireland might have snatched a dramatic victory... Electoral fraud snatched away victory by only a few thousand votes.*
4 NC A **snatch** of a conversation or a song is a very small piece of it. *Ella's narrative is riddled with snatches of songs, proverbs, and anecdotes.*

snazzy /snæzi/ **snazzier, snazziest**
ADJ Something that is **snazzy** is stylish and attractive, sometimes in a rather showy way; an informal word. *I like your outfit—very snazzy!... It was one of those snazzy adverts.*

sneak /sniːk/ **sneaks, sneaking, sneaked**
1 VA If you **sneak** somewhere, you go there quietly, trying to avoid being seen or heard. *They had sneaked into a side room to watch the match... Three men armed with automatic weapons sneaked across the border under cover of darkness.*
2 VOA If you **sneak** something somewhere, you take it there secretly. *Eugene would sneak food down to his room.*
3 VOA If you **sneak** a look at someone or something,

you secretly have a quick look at them. *He sneaked a look at her as she was passing by.*

sneak up on PHRASAL VERB If someone **sneaks up on** you, they try and approach you without being seen or heard, perhaps to surprise you or do you harm. *They wouldn't sneak up on you at night... He is trying to sneak up on two hippopotamuses on the lawn.*

sneaker /sniːkə/ **sneakers**
NC **Sneakers** are casual shoes with rubber soles. *...four pairs of sneakers. ...designer jeans and fancy sneakers.*

sneaking /sniːkɪŋ/
ADJ ATTRIB A **sneaking** feeling is a slight or vague feeling, especially one that you are unwilling to accept. *I have a sneaking suspicion you're right. ...a sneaking admiration for his commercialism.*

sneak preview, sneak previews
NC A **sneak preview** of something is an unofficial opportunity to look at it before it is officially published or shown to the public. *He showed me his latest masterpiece in a sneak preview.*

sneaky /sniːki/
ADJ Someone who is **sneaky** does things secretly or dishonestly; an informal word, used showing disapproval. *I had a sneaky glimpse at the list... Why did they allege then that you used secrecy, subterfuge and sneaky methods to publish this?*

sneer /snɪə/ **sneers, sneering, sneered**
V+at or V-QUOTE If you **sneer** at someone or something, you express your contempt for them either by your tone of voice or by the expression on your face. *His technique was to bully and sneer at the accused... She was afraid he would sneer at the idea... 'We could certainly get cheaper estimates,' sneered Casson.* ▶ Also NC *'Oh yes,' said McFee, a sneer flitting over his face.*

sneeze /sniːz/ **sneezes, sneezing, sneezed**
V When you **sneeze**, you suddenly and involuntarily take in your breath and then blow it down your nose noisily. People sneeze a lot when they have a cold. *He sneezed violently.* ▶ Also NC *...a highly contagious disease which is spread by coughs and sneezes.*

Snegur, Mircea /mɪətʃə snegʊə/
Mircea Snegur became President of Moldavia in 1990 with the support of nationalists. His position was confirmed after a referendum in 1991. In 1986 he was Secretary of the Moldavian Communist Party. He was Chairman of the Presidium of the Moldavian Supreme Soviet from 1989 to 1990. Born: 1939.

snicker /snɪkə/ **snickers, snickering, snickered**
V or V+at To **snicker** is the same as to **snigger**; used in American English. *This usually makes us snicker... We snicker at sexual things in our culture.*

snide /snaɪd/
1 ADJ ATTRIB A **snide** comment or remark criticizes someone nastily, often in an indirect way. *...snide little remarks about political patronage.*
2 ADJ A **snide** person is one who makes critical remarks in an unpleasant and indirect way. *...yet another snide reporter all too eager to take aim at an easy target.*

sniff /snɪf/ **sniffs, sniffing, sniffed**
1 V When you **sniff**, you breathe in air noisily through your nose, for example when you have a cold, or are trying not to cry. *Felicity said, sniffing, 'When will you see me again?'* ▶ Also NC *The classroom rang with coughs, sniffs, and sneezes.*
2 V O or V+at If you **sniff** something, you smell it by breathing in through your nose. *'What a revolting smell,' he said, sniffing the air... The dog sniffed at Marsha's bags.* ▶ Also NC *He took a cautious sniff.*
3 VO If someone **sniffs** a substance such as glue, they deliberately breathe it in order to feel the effects of it. *More than 1 in 8 eleven year olds had tried drugs or sniffed solvents.*
4 V-QUOTE You can use **sniff** to indicate that someone is saying something in a superior or contemptuous way. *'The judge seems to suggest,' sniffed the professor, 'that I do not know my subject.'*

sniff out PHRASAL VERB If you **sniff** something **out**, you discover it, often after a search or by guessing where it might be; an informal expression. *Gordon* *sniffed out some lovely little quiet beaches.*

sniffer dog, sniffer dogs
NC A **sniffer dog** is a dog used by the police or army to find explosives or drugs by sniffing their scent. *Bomb disposal experts and sniffer dogs searched the aircraft.*

sniffle /snɪfl/ **sniffles, sniffling, sniffled**
V If you **sniffle**, you keep sniffing, for example because you have a cold or because you are crying. *...a small child sniffling back tears.*

sniffy /snɪfi/
ADJ Someone who is **sniffy** has a scornful and contemptuous attitude about something; an informal word. *James got sniffy at what Bill had said.*

snigger /snɪgə/ **sniggers, sniggering, sniggered**
V If you **snigger**, you laugh quietly and in a disrespectful way. *What are you sniggering at?* ► Also NC *His sniggers became uncontrollable.*

snip /snɪp/ **snips, snipping, snipped**
V or VA If you **snip** something, or if you **snip** at or through something, you cut it using a sharp instrument in a single quick action. *The wire has been snipped... Brian snipped energetically at the hedge... Snip through the strands.*
snip off PHRASAL VERB If you **snip** part of something **off**, you remove it with a cutting instrument in a single quick action. *...snipping off the last two inches of his hair.*

snipe /snaɪp/ **snipes, sniping, sniped**
1 V+at If someone **snipes** at you, they criticize you; used showing disapproval. *The unions are an easy target to snipe at... Critics have been sniping at him over rising inflation.* ► Also NC *This appears to be a snipe at Mrs Planinc.* ◆ **sniping** NU *Environment Secretary Nicholas Ridley was the main target for sniping by Conservative backbenchers.*
2 V To **snipe** at someone also means to shoot at them from a hidden position. *Just then someone started sniping at us.*
3 NC A **snipe** is a bird with a very long beak which normally lives in marshy areas.

sniper /snaɪpə/ **snipers**
NC A **sniper** is someone who shoots at people from a hidden position. *Snipers opened fire from nearby hills... He is reported to have come under sniper fire as he arrived.*

snippet /snɪpɪt/ **snippets**
NC A **snippet** of information or news is a small piece of it; an informal word. *We've seen snippets on television... The TV ads even include a snippet of music from one of the all-time great Western scores.*

snitch /snɪtʃ/ **snitches, snitching, snitched**
V If you **snitch** or **snitch** on someone, you tell someone in authority that that person has done something naughty or wrong; an informal word, used showing disapproval.

snivel /snɪvl/ **snivels, snivelling, snivelled**; spelt **sniveling, sniveled** in American English.
V If someone is **snivelling**, they are crying and sniffing in an irritating way. *I know you're tired, but do stop snivelling.*

snob /snɒb/ **snobs**; used showing disapproval.
1 NC A **snob** is someone who admires upper-class people and despises lower-class people. *...an elitist and a snob who sneered at the common people.*
2 NC+SUPP An intellectual **snob** is someone who believes that they are superior to other people because of their intelligence or taste. *He is a dreadful intellectual snob.*

snobbery /snɒbəri/
NU **Snobbery** is the attitude of a snob; used showing disapproval. *Social snobbery reached a peak in the last century.*

snobbish /snɒbɪʃ/
ADJ Someone who is **snobbish** is too proud of their social status, intelligence, or taste; used showing disapproval. *People from the south are more likely to be ambitious but snobbish.*

snobby /snɒbi/ **snobbier, snobbiest**
ADJ **Snobby** means the same as **snobbish**; an informal word.

snog /snɒg/ **snogs, snogging, snogged**
V-RECIP When two people **snog**, they kiss and cuddle each other for a long time; an informal word. *...snogging in the dark.* ► Also N SING *They went outside for a quiet snog.*

snooker /snuːkə/
NU **Snooker** is a game in which two players use long sticks called cues to hit a white ball across a special table so that it knocks coloured balls into pockets at the side of the table. *Do you play snooker? ...the semi-finals of the World Snooker Championship.*

snoop /snuːp/ **snoops, snooping, snooped**
1 V Someone who is **snooping** is secretly looking round a place in order to find out things. *...journalists who've been trying to snoop around and find out what's really going on.*
2 V+on If you **snoop** on someone, you watch them secretly in order to find out things about their life. *...the secret police whose main function was to snoop on their fellow citizens.*

snooty /snuːti/
ADJ Someone who is **snooty** behaves as if they are superior to other people; an informal word, used showing disapproval. *Don't be so snooty... I got a very snooty letter from them rejecting my application.*

snooze /snuːz/ **snoozes, snoozing, snoozed**
V When you **snooze** you have a short, light sleep during the day; an informal word. *I lay on the sofa, snoozing.* ► Also N SING *I've just had a nice snooze.*

snore /snɔː/ **snores, snoring, snored**
V When someone who is asleep **snores**, they make a loud noise each time they breathe. *He snored loudly on the camp-bed.* ► Also NC *I could hear heavy snores coming from the bedroom.*

snorkel /snɔːkl/ **snorkels**
NC A **snorkel** is a tube through which a person swimming just under the surface of the sea can breathe. *He put on a wet suit and snorkel.*

snorkelling /snɔːkəlɪŋ/; spelt **snorkeling** in American English.
NU If you go **snorkelling**, you swim underwater using a snorkel. *We went snorkelling today.*

snort /snɔːt/ **snorts, snorting, snorted**
1 V or V-QUOTE When people or animals **snort**, they breathe air noisily out through their noses. People snort in order to express disapproval or amusement. *The pigs grunted and snorted... My sister snorted with laughter... 'Since the eighties?' he snorts, aghast.* ► Also NC *Clarissa gave a snort of disgust.*
2 VO To **snort** a drug, such as cocaine, means to breathe it in quickly through one nostril. *He died of cardiac arrest after snorting cocaine at a party.*

snot /snɒt/
NU **Snot** is the substance that is produced inside your nose; an informal word which some people find offensive.

snotty /snɒti/; an informal word.
1 ADJ Something that is **snotty** is covered with snot; an informal word which some people find offensive. *...a snotty handkerchief.*
2 ADJ Someone who is **snotty** has a very proud and superior attitude to other people; used showing disapproval.

snout /snaʊt/ **snouts**
NC The **snout** of an animal such as a pig is its nose. *...its ugly little pointed snout.*

snow /snəʊ/ **snows, snowing, snowed**
1 NU or N PL **Snow** is the soft white bits of frozen water that sometimes fall from the sky in cold weather. *Outside the snow lay thick on the ground. ...driving down from the snows of the Alps.*
2 V When it **snows**, snow falls from the sky. *It was snowing quite heavily.* ● See also **snowed in, snowed under.**

snowball /snəʊbɔːl/ **snowballs, snowballing, snowballed**
1 NC A **snowball** is a ball of snow. *...children throwing snowballs.*
2 V If something such as a campaign **snowballs**, it rapidly increases and grows. *The protests snowballed... The strike snowballed into a national strike.*

snowbound /snəʊbaʊnd/
ADJ If people or vehicles are **snowbound**, they can move only with difficulty because of heavy snow. If places or roads are **snowbound**, heavy snow makes it difficult to reach them or travel along them. *Trucks rumbled into the city today on the snowbound highway from the Soviet Union.*

snow-capped
ADJ ATTRIB A **snow-capped** mountain or hill is covered with snow at the top; a literary word. *...the snow-capped peaks of the Himalayas.*

snowdrift /snəʊdrɪft/ **snowdrifts**
NC A **snowdrift** is a deep pile of snow formed by the wind. *It took rescuers more than two hours to reach the survivors because of deep snowdrifts.*

snowdrop /snəʊdrɒp/ **snowdrops**
NC A **snowdrop** is a small white flower which appears in the early spring. *We've had snowdrops for a long time now.*

snowed in
ADJ PRED If you are **snowed in** or **snowed up**, you cannot go anywhere because of heavy snow. *I hope we don't get snowed in... We were snowed up for a week.*

snowed under
ADJ PRED If you are **snowed under**, you have too much work to deal with. *At present we are snowed under with work.*

snowed up. See **snowed in**.

snowfall /snəʊfɔːl/ **snowfalls**
1 NU The **snowfall** in an area or country is the amount of snow that falls there during a particular period. *What's the average snowfall in San Moritz?*
2 NC A **snowfall** is a fall of snow. *Heavy snowfalls were hampering the search for further casualties.*

snowflake /snəʊfleɪk/ **snowflakes**
NC A **snowflake** is one of the soft, white bits of frozen water that fall as snow. *There were snowflakes over Minnesota.*

snow goose, snow geese
NC A **snow goose** is a North American goose that has white feathers and black tips on the ends of its wings. *Large colonies of snow geese breed every summer around the lakes.*

snowline /snəʊlaɪn/
N SING The **snowline** is the height on a mountain or group of mountains above which there is snow all the time.

snowman /snəʊmæn/ **snowmen**
NC A **snowman** is a mass of snow formed roughly into the shape of a person. *Children enjoy building snowmen and decorating them to look as realistic as possible.*

snowplough /snəʊplaʊ/ **snowploughs**; spelt **snowplow** in American English.
NC A **snowplough** is a vehicle used to push snow off roads, airport runways, or railway lines.

snowstorm /snəʊstɔːm/ **snowstorms**
NC A **snowstorm** is a very heavy fall of snow, usually when there is a lot of wind blowing at the same time. *She rushed out of the house into a whirling snowstorm.*

snow-white
ADJ Something that is **snow-white** is of a brilliant white colour. *...his snow-white hair.*

snowy /snəʊi/
ADJ Something that is **snowy** has a lot of snow. *...two high snowy peaks.*

Snr
ADJ after N **Snr** is a written abbreviation for 'Senior'. In the United States, it is often used after someone's name to distinguish them from a younger member of the family who has the same name. *...Charles Parker Snr.*

snub /snʌb/ **snubs, snubbing, snubbed**
VO If you **snub** someone, you insult them by ignoring them or by behaving rudely. *Both she and her husband were snubbed by the intellectuals they knew.*
► Also NC *But George was impervious to snubs.*

snub-nosed
ADJ Someone who is **snub-nosed** has a short nose which points slightly upwards.

snuff /snʌf/ **snuffs, snuffing, snuffed**
1 NU **Snuff** is powdered tobacco which people take by sniffing it up their nose. *My father used to take snuff.*
2 ADJ ATTRIB A **snuff** movie is a pornographic film in which one of the participants is really killed at the climax. *...child snuff movies being investigated by the Metropolitan police... There are suggestions that the boys died in pornographic snuff videos.*

snuff out PHRASAL VERB 1 If you **snuff out** a flame or something that is burning, you put it out by covering it in some way so that it can no longer burn. *She snuffed out her third cigarette and walked away.* 2 If someone **snuffs out** something such as a rebellion or a disagreement, they stop it, usually in a forceful or sudden way. *The army has played a role snuffing out inter-ethnic flare-ups before they get out of control.*

snuffle /snʌfl/ **snuffles, snuffling, snuffled**
V If people or animals **snuffle**, they make sniffing noises. *Brian snuffled into his handkerchief. ...snuffling pigs.*

snug /snʌg/
1 ADJ If you are **snug**, you feel warm and comfortable. *We lit a big fire which made us feel very snug and safe.*
2 ADJ A **snug** place is small but warm and comfortable. *It was warm and dry in his snug studio.*
3 ADJ Something such as a piece of clothing that is **snug** fits very closely. *With cotton briefs you have to strike a balance between being too tight or not snug enough.* ◆ **snugly** ADV *The metal box fitted snugly into the bottom.*

snuggle /snʌgl/ **snuggles, snuggling, snuggled**
VA If you **snuggle** somewhere, you settle yourself into a warm, comfortable position, especially by moving closer to another person. *He turned over to snuggle close to her.*

so /səʊ, səʊ/
1 ADV You use **so** when you are referring back to something that has just been mentioned. *Do you enjoy romantic films? If so, you should watch the film on ITV tonight... 'Is there anything else you want to tell me about?'—'I don't think so.'... The issue is unresolved, and will remain so until the next SDP Congress... 'The phone isn't working.'—'So I see.'*
2 ADV SEN If one person or thing does something and **so** does another one, the other one does it too. *Etta laughed heartily and so did he... His shoes are brightly polished; so is his briefcase.*
3 CONJ You use **so** and **so that** to introduce the result of the situation you have just mentioned. *He speaks very little English, so I talked to him through an interpreter... The door was open, so that anyone passing could look in.*
4 CONJ You use **so that** and **so as** to introduce the reason for doing the thing you have just mentioned. *He has to earn lots of money so that he can buy his children nice food and clothes... They went on foot, so as not to be heard.*
5 ADV SEN You can use **so** in a discussion or talk when you are checking something, summarizing something, or moving on to a new stage. *So it wasn't just an accident?... And so for now, goodnight... So what are the advantages of nuclear energy?*
6 ADV You can also use **so** when you are saying that something is done or arranged in the way that you describe. *They have the eyes so located as to give a wide field of vision... The others are moving right to left, like so.*
7 ADV You can also use **so** to describe or emphasize the degree or extent of something. *I'm so glad you could come... Don't go so fast... The engine was so hot the air around it shimmered... Carrying the weight was not so difficult.*
8 ADV You can also use **so** before words such as 'much' and 'many' to indicate that there is a limit to something. *We will only pay so much, no more.*
● **So** is used in these phrases. ● If you say that a state of affairs is **so**, you mean that it is the way it has been described. *It is worth knowing just why this is so.*
● You use **and so on** or **and so forth** at the end of a list to indicate that there are other items that you could also mention. *You can program a computer to paint,*

play chess and so on. ● You use **or so** when you are
giving an approximate amount. *We arrived a month
or so ago.* ● You use the structures **as...so** and **just
as...so** to indicate that two events or situations are
alike in some way. *Just as one gesture can have
many different meanings, so many different gestures
can have the same meaning.* ● You use the structures
not so much and **not so much...as** to say that
something is one kind of thing rather than another
kind. *...a cry not so much of pain as of amazement.*
● You say **'So?'** and **'So what?'** to indicate that you
think that what someone has said is unimportant; an
informal use. *'Someone will see us.'—'So what?'*
● **ever so**: see **ever**. ● **so far**: see **far**. ● **so long, so
long as**: see **long**. ● **so much for**: see **much**. ● **every
so often**: see **often**. ● **so there**: see **there**.

soak /səʊk/ **soaks, soaking, soaked**
  1 V-ERG When you **soak** something, you put it into a
  liquid and leave it there. *Soak the material for
  several hours in cold water... 'Can I help you with the
  dishes?'—'Oh, I'll just leave them to soak.'*
  2 VO When a liquid **soaks** something, it makes it very
  wet. *A stream of water came in and soaked both
  sleeping bags.*
  3 VA When a liquid **soaks** through something, it passes
  through it. *The blood had soaked through the
  handkerchief.*
  soak up PHRASAL VERB When a soft or dry substance
  soaks up a liquid, the liquid goes into the substance.
  The soil soaked up a huge volume of water.

soaked /səʊkt/
  ADJ PRED If someone or something gets **soaked**, they
  get extremely wet. *It was pouring down and we all
  got soaked.*

soaking /səʊkɪŋ/
  ADJ If something is **soaking** or **soaking wet**, it is very
  wet. *My boots were soaking wet inside.*

so-and-so
  NU You use **so-and-so** instead of a name or word when
  talking generally rather than giving a specific
  example; an informal word. *What happens is that
  somebody will phone me and say, 'Mrs So-and-So
  would like a visit'.*

soap /səʊp/ **soaps, soaping, soaped**
  1 N MASS **Soap** is a substance used with water for
  washing. *...a bar of yellow soap.*
  2 V-REFL When you **soap** yourself, you rub soap on
  your body to wash yourself. *She soaped herself all
  over.*
  3 NC A **soap** is the same as a **soap opera**. *...the very
  last episode of the soap 'Dallas'... Do soap addicts
  really begin to confuse fact and fiction on the screen?*

soapbox /səʊpbɒks/ **soapboxes**
  1 NC A **soapbox** is a small temporary platform on
  which a person stands when he or she is making a
  speech outdoors to passers-by. *He was equally at
  home in a pulpit or on a soapbox. ...a soapbox orator.*
  2 NC A **soapbox** is also a box or crate for packing
  soap in. *I had made a cage for my pigeons out of a
  soapbox.*

soapflakes /səʊpfleɪks/
  N PL **Soapflakes** are very small, thin pieces of soap
  used for washing clothes. *...an advertisement for
  soapflakes.*

soap opera, soap operas
  NC A **soap opera** is a television drama serial about the
  daily lives of a group of people. *Brazilian soap operas
  were a wild success on Cuban television. ...a soap
  opera star.*

soapsuds /səʊpsʌdz/
  N PL **Soapsuds** are the same as **suds**. *...a soft cloth
  dipped in warm soapsuds.*

soapy /səʊpi/
  ADJ Something that is **soapy** is full of soap or covered
  with soap. *Wash your brushes in warm soapy water.*

soar /sɔː/ **soars, soaring, soared**
  1 V If an amount **soars**, it quickly increases by a large
  amount. *Property prices have soared... Central bank
  policy has caused interest rates to soar.* ◆ **soaring**
  ADJ ATTRIB *Brazil has been hit by soaring inflation.*
  2 V If something **soars** into the air, it goes quickly
  upwards. *Flames were soaring into the sky.*

3 VA Trees or buildings that **soar** upwards are very
tall. *Great trees soar above to cut out most of the
light.* ◆ **soaring** ADJ ATTRIB *...the soaring spire of St
Patrick's.*

Soares, Dr Mário Lopes /mærjuː lɒpɪʃ swɔːrɪʃ/
  Dr Mário Lopes Soares became President of Portugal
  in 1986. He founded the Socialist Party (PS) in 1973
  and was its Secretary General from 1973 to 1986. He
  returned to Portugal following the coup in 1974, having
  been in exile since 1968. He was Minister for Foreign
  Affairs from 1974 to 1975, and from 1977 to 1978. He
  served as Prime Minister three times between 1976
  and 1985. Born: 1924.

sob /sɒb/ **sobs, sobbing, sobbed**
  1 V or V-QUOTE When someone **sobs**, they cry in a noisy
  way, breathing in short breaths. *She was sobbing
  bitterly... 'I'm praying to you,' he sobs. 'Look in your
  heart.'* ◆ **sobbing** NU *The sobbing began again.*
  2 NC A **sob** is one of the noises that you make when
  you are crying. *...gasping, choking sobs.*

sober /səʊbə/ **sobers, sobering, sobered**
  1 ADJ When you are **sober**, you are not drunk.
  Rudolph knew he had to stay sober to drive home.
  2 ADJ A **sober** person is serious and thoughtful.
  ...sober and sensible attitudes. ◆ **soberly** ADV *'That's
  true,' Andy said soberly.*
  3 ADJ ATTRIB **Sober** colours and clothes are plain and
  rather dull. *...a pair of sober black walking shoes.*
  ◆ **soberly** ADV *...a soberly dressed office employee.*
  sober up PHRASAL VERB When someone **sobers up**,
  they become sober after being drunk. *Most of those
  detained have been held while they sober up... When
  you sober up, you may be ashamed of what you have
  done.*

sobering /səʊbərɪŋ/
  ADJ **Sobering** words, actions, or ideas make you
  become serious. *His words had a sobering effect on
  Freddie... There was a more sobering thought:
  perhaps we should not succeed.*

sobriety /səbraɪəti/
  NU **Sobriety** is serious and thoughtful behaviour; a
  formal word. *...his mood of sobriety.*

sobriquet /səʊbrɪkeɪ/ **sobriquets**; also spelt **soubriquet**.
  NC A **sobriquet** is an informal name given to someone
  or something. *...the affair which has earned the
  sobriquet 'Dublingate'... The Western press are never
  short of a handy sobriquet.*

sob story, sob stories
  NC If someone tells you a **sob story**, they tell you
  about something that has happened to them in order to
  make you feel sorry for them; used showing
  disapproval. *She'll tell you a sob story about the
  hours she had to work.*

Soc.
  Soc. is a written abbreviation for 'Society'; used when
  it is part of a name.

so-called
  1 ADJ ATTRIB You use **so-called** in front of a word to
  indicate that you think that the word is incorrect or
  misleading. *...her so-called friends. ...the so-called
  'moderate' opposition.*
  2 ADJ ATTRIB You can also use **so-called** to indicate
  that something is usually referred to in a particular
  way. *We're experiencing the so-called 'greenhouse
  effect', caused by emissions of gases like carbon
  dioxide, nitrogen oxides and methane.*

soccer /sɒkə/
  NU **Soccer** is the same as **football**. *...a successful
  return to European soccer for English clubs. ...the
  British government's plans to compel soccer fans to
  carry identity cards for entry to grounds.*

sociable /səʊʃəbl/
  ADJ **Sociable** people enjoy meeting and talking to other
  people. *Adler was an outgoing, sociable kind of man.*
  ◆ **sociability** /səʊʃəbɪləti/ NU *There was no doubt
  about his sociability.*

social /səʊʃl/
  1 ADJ ATTRIB **Social** means relating to society.
  *...demands for modernisation and social change.
  ...children from different social backgrounds.*
  ◆ **socially** ADV *They must behave in a way which will
  be socially acceptable.*

2 ADJ **Social** activities are leisure activities that involve meeting other people, as opposed to activities related to work. *We've met at social and business functions. ...their circle of social contacts.* ♦ **soci.lly** ADV *...the only people my father ever visited socially.*

social climber, social climbers
NC A **social climber** is a person who tries to make friends with people who belong to a higher social class in order to be regarded as a member of that class; used showing disapproval. *The social climbers started to mimic their dress and behaviour.*

social democracy, social democracies
1 NU **Social democracy** is a political system according to which social justice and equality can be achieved within the framework of a market economy. *The radicals demanded a declaration in favour of abandoning all traces of Marxism-Leninism for western-style social democracy.*
2 NC A **social democracy** is a country which has a government that follows the principles of social democracy. *He talked about Romania becoming a social democracy.*

social democrat, social democrats
NC A **social democrat** is a person who is a member or supporter of a social democratic party. *...the social democrats, who gained a single seat in the election.*

social democratic party, social democratic parties
NC A **social democratic party** is a political party whose principles are based on social democracy. *...the special relationship which trade unions tend to have with socialist or social democratic parties. ...the alliance between the Social Democratic Party and the Liberal Party.*

social drinking
NU **Social drinking** is the practice of drinking alcohol on social occasions and with friends rather than when you are on your own. *Heavy social drinking was no solution to their problems.*

social engineering
NU **Social engineering** is the attempt by a government to change how people behave in order to produce the type of society that it wants. *...the government's experiment in moral and social engineering... They are treating schools as laboratories to test out their social engineering theories.*

socialise /ˈsəʊʃəlaɪz/. See **socialize**.
socialism /ˈsəʊʃəlɪzəm/
NU **Socialism** is the belief that the state should own industries on behalf of the people and that everyone should be equal. *His contribution to the struggle for socialism is unquestionable. ...his dream of building socialism in one country. ...the cause of socialism.*

socialist /ˈsəʊʃəlɪst/ **socialists**
1 NC A **socialist** is someone who believes that the state should own industries on behalf of the people and that everyone should be equal. *...disillusionment among radicals and socialists... Early projections suggest the Socialists are set to do better than in the last municipal elections in 1983.*
2 ADJ ATTRIB You use **socialist** to refer to belief in socialism or to people who believe in socialism. **Socialist** is also used in the names of some political parties. *...the French Socialist Party. ...people who still remain loyal to socialist ideas.*

socialite /ˈsəʊʃəlaɪt/ **socialites**
NC A **socialite** is a person who attends many fashionable upper-class social events and who is well known because of this. *Sir Oswald was generally regarded as a socialite.*

socialize /ˈsəʊʃəlaɪz/ **socializes, socializing, socialized**; also spelt **socialise**.
1 V If you **socialize**, you meet other people socially. *I socialized with the philosophy students.* ♦ **socializing** NU *...people who do all their socializing in pubs.*
2 VO When people **are socialized**, they gradually learn to behave in a way that is acceptable in their society or culture; a technical use. *We are socialized and become familiar with our culture and ways of doing things... He claimed that television socialized children much more effectively than their parents could.*

social life, social lives
1 NU A country's **social life** is the way in which the relations between different social groups and classes are organized. *He has been advocating change in social life as well. ...everyday economic and social life.*
2 NCorNU Your **social life** consists of ways in which you spend time with your friends and acquaintances. *Hardworking Britons are finding less and less time for a social life. ...Soho's reputation for social life continued.*

social order, social orders
NC The **social order** in a place is the way that society is organized there. *...acquiescence in the established social order... They have striven to create a new social order.*

social science, social sciences
1 NU **Social science** is the scientific study of society. *...a 26-year-old social science graduate.*
2 NC The **social sciences** are the various branches of social science. *Economics is the oldest of the social sciences.*

social scientist, social scientists
NC A **social scientist** is a person who studies or teaches social science. *...an Oxford-educated social scientist from Calcutta... Historians and social scientists rely heavily on documentation.*

social security
1 NU In Britain, **social security** is a system by which the government pays money regularly to people who have no income or only a very small income. *...the clauses of the future constitution dealing with social security and welfare. ...the annual review of social security benefits.*
2 NU In the United States, **social security** is a system by which the government pays money regularly to people who have retired from work or to the family of a worker who has died. *...the current deduction scheme for social security.*

social services
N PL **Social services** are services provided by a local authority to help people who have social and financial problems. *...children taken into care by the social services.*

social skills
N PL A person's **social skills** are their manners and their ability to get on with other people. *Social skills depend on how you understand another human being... We don't really have many good social skills.*

social spending
NU **Social spending** is the payment of money by a government for social services and welfare. *They wanted higher taxes for the rich and smaller cuts in social spending.*

social studies
N PL **Social studies** is a subject taught in some British schools and colleges. It includes sociology, politics, and economics.

social work
NU **Social work** involves giving help and advice to people with serious personal, family, or financial problems. *He was engaged in voluntary social work in a deprived area of London.*

social worker, social workers
NC A **social worker** is a person whose job is to do social work. *They learnt from the social worker the importance of hygiene.*

society /səˈsaɪəti/ **societies**
1 NUorNC You can refer to the people in a country as its **society**. *...society's attitude towards the elderly... We live in a multi-racial society.*
2 NC A **society** is an organization for people who have the same interest or aim. *...the Royal Horticultural Society... The Mafia was not a secret society but a 'way of life'.*

socio- /ˈsəʊsiəʊ-/
PREFIX **Socio-** is added to some adjectives and nouns to form technical terms in the social sciences. *...socio-economic. ...socio-political. ...socio-biology.*

sociology /ˌsəʊsiˈɒlədʒi/
NU **Sociology** is the study of human societies. *...sociology students.* ♦ **sociological** /ˌsəʊsiəˈlɒdʒɪkl/

ADJ ATTRIB   ...*sociological studies of criminals.*
◆ **sociologist, sociologists** NC   *This is what sociologists have been saying for years. ...a study by two American sociologists.*

sock /sɒk/ **socks**
NC **Socks** are pieces of clothing which cover your foot and ankle and are worn inside shoes. ...*a pair of light-blue wool socks.*

socket /sɒkɪt/ **sockets**
1 NC A **socket** is a place on a wall or on a piece of electrical equipment into which you can put something such as a plug or bulb. *I plugged a light into the socket on my wall... It looks like a normal socket that the telephone plugs into.*
2 NC You can refer to any hollow part or opening in a structure which another part fits into as a **socket**. ...*deep eye sockets.*

sod /sɒd/ **sods**
1 NC Some people call someone a **sod** when they are angry with them or think that they are unpleasant; an informal word which some people find offensive. *Get going, you lazy little sod!*
2 Some people use **sod** before a word or expression in order to indicate that they think that it is not important or that they do not care about it; an informal word which some people find offensive. *Sod the lot of them!*
3 Some people say **sod it** when they are angry because something has gone wrong or when they want to indicate that something is unimportant and that they do not intend to deal with it; an informal word which some people find offensive. *Sod it! I don't want to know.*
4 N SING The **sod** is the surface of the ground, together with the grass and roots that are growing in it; a literary use. ...*the heavy plough that slices through the sod.*

soda /səʊdə/ **sodas**
1 N MASS In Britain, **soda** or **soda water** is fizzy water used for mixing with alcoholic drinks or fruit juice. ...*a whisky and soda... Give her a little white wine mixed with soda water—she likes that.*
2 N MASS In the United States, **soda** is a sweet, fizzy flavoured drink. ...*a can of soda... He got up, went into the kitchen, got a soda with a straw in it and handed it to her.*

soda fountain, soda fountains
NC In the United States, a **soda fountain** is a cafe or bar where sweet drinks and ice cream are sold.

soda siphon, soda siphons; also spelt **soda syphon**.
NC A **soda siphon** is a special bottle from which you can squirt soda water into a drink.

soda water
NU **Soda water** is fizzy water used for mixing with alcoholic drinks and fruit juice.

sodden /sɒdn/
ADJ Something that is **sodden** is extremely wet. *My coat was sodden from the rain.*

sodding /sɒdɪŋ/
ADJ ATTRIB or ADV **Sodding** is a swear word used by people who are very angry about something.

sodium /səʊdiəm/
1 NU **Sodium** is a silvery-white chemical element which combines with other chemicals. Salt is a sodium compound. ...*sodium bicarbonate. ...sodium chloride.*
2 N+N **Sodium** lighting gives out a strong orange light. *Out over the town the sodium lights were lit. ...a sodium streetlamp.*

sodomy /sɒdəmi/
NU **Sodomy** is anal sexual intercourse, especially between males. *The punishment for sodomy was death.*

sofa /səʊfə/ **sofas**
NC A **sofa** is a long, comfortable seat with a back and arms, which two or three people can sit on. *He was asleep on the sofa.*

sofa-bed, sofa-beds
NC A **sofa-bed** is a sofa which is made with a folding seat so that it can also be used as a bed.

Sofia /səʊfiə/
Sofia is the capital of Bulgaria and its largest city. Population: 1,137,000 (1988).

soft /sɒft/ **softer, softest**
1 ADJ Something that is **soft** changes shape easily when you press it and is not hard or stiff. ...*a soft bed... His feet left prints in the soft soil. ...soft black fur.* ◆ **softness** NU ...*the softness of her arms.*
2 ADJ **Soft** also means very gentle, with no force. ...*a soft breeze.* ◆ **softly** ADV   *Mike softly placed his hand on her shoulder.*
3 ADJ A **soft** sound or voice is quiet and not harsh. *She had a soft South German accent.* ◆ **softly** ADV *'Listen,' she said softly.*
4 ADJ A **soft** light or colour is pleasant and restful, not bright. ...*the soft glow of the evening light. ...walls in soft pink stone.*
5 ADJ If you say that someone is **soft** you mean that they are not being strict or severe enough. *They were not regarded as in any way soft... They felt that the World Bank was being too soft.*
6 ADJ ATTRIB If you take a **soft** line or approach to a situation or problem, you decide to be careful and diplomatic when dealing with it. ...*too soft a line on alleged Pakistani support for the separatists. ...the softer line of the Soviet Union towards the Yugoslav president. ...a new, softer approach to international diplomacy.*
7 ADJ **Soft** drugs are illegal drugs which are not considered to be very strong or harmful. *Italy has just made it a crime to be in possession of either soft or hard drugs.*
● **Soft** is used in these phrases. ● If you **have a soft spot for** someone, they are especially fond of them. *The President has a soft spot in his heart for China where he served as an envoy.* ● If you say that a person is **going soft on** someone or something, you mean that they are no longer as severe when dealing with them as they used to be; used showing disapproval. *Indonesia is not going soft on communism.*

softball /sɒftbɔːl/ **softballs**
1 NU **Softball** is a game similar to baseball, played with a larger, softer, ball. *They play softball in the back yard.*
2 NC A **softball** is the ball used to play softball. *Kids were playing with softballs.*

soft currency, soft currencies
NC or NU A **soft currency** is money that is considered to be of relatively little value on the international money market because it is produced by a country with a weak economy. ...*a big and useless soft currency surplus. ...government restrictions on soft currency exports.*

soft drink, soft drinks
NC A **soft drink** is a non-alcoholic drink such as lemonade or fruit juice. *Food and soft drinks are being sent to the plane regularly. ...the soft drinks industry.*

soften /sɒfn/ **softens, softening, softened**
1 V-ERG If you **soften** something or if it **softens**, it becomes less hard, stiff, or firm. *Fry the onions for about 10 minutes to soften them... I'm waiting for the ice-cream to soften.*
2 VO If something **softens** a shock or a damaging effect, it makes it seem less severe. *He had alcohol to soften the blow.*
3 V-ERG If you **soften**, you become more sympathetic and less hostile. *She gradually softened towards me... I refused to be softened.* ◆ **softening** N SING or NU ...*a softening in the Pakistani position on the issue... The leadership is not planning any softening of its policies.*
soften up PHRASAL VERB 1 If you **soften** someone **up**, you put them into a good mood before asking them to do something; an informal expression. *Mr Murphy was simply trying to soften up the Syrians by visiting Damascus first.* 2 When a military force **softens up** an opposing army, they attack the army from a distance in order to weaken it before they approach and fight at close range. *I think we'll see several weeks of an air campaign to soften up their troops.*

soft furnishings
N PL **Soft furnishings** are cushions, curtains, lampshades, and furniture covers. *The mites live mainly in soft furnishings and the seams of pillows.*

soft-hearted
ADJ Someone who is **soft-hearted** is sympathetic and kind.

softie /ˈsɒfti/. See softy.

soft loan, soft loans
NC A **soft loan** is a loan on which interest is not charged. ...*a six billion dollar package of soft loans... A new soft loan deal is to be signed between Britain and Indonesia.*

softly-softly
ADJ ATTRIB A **softly-softly** approach to something is one which is cautious and patient and avoids direct action or force. *The chances of him succeeding in his softly-softly approach are better than average.*

soft option, soft options
NC If you choose the **soft option** in a particular situation, you avoid taking action that would involve creating difficulties or provoking angry reactions, even though this action may in fact be the best one. *The Times suggests the Belgians chose the soft option... They are what the Prime Minister calls soft options.*

soft palate, soft palates
NC Your **soft palate** is the soft top part of the inside of your mouth, near your throat.

soft-pedal, soft-pedals, soft-pedalling, soft-pedalled; also spelt **soft-pedaling, soft-pedaled** in American English.
V or VO If you **soft-pedal**, you deliberately reduce the amount of activity or pressure that you have been using to get something done. *I think we'd better soft-pedal on that contract for a while... Anthony certainly soft-pedalled his views before this committee.*

soft porn
NU **Soft porn** is pornography that shows or mentions sexual acts, but not in a very explicit or violent way. ...*soft-porn photographs of nude girls cuddling kittens.*

soft sell
N SING A **soft sell** is a method of selling or advertising that involves gentle persuasion rather than putting a lot of pressure on people.

soft-soap, soft-soaps, soft-soaping, soft-soaped
VO If you **soft-soap** someone, you flatter them in order to try to persuade them to do something; an informal word. *He has a track record in soft-soaping the outside world.*

soft-spoken
ADJ Someone who is **soft-spoken** has a quiet, gentle voice. ...*a soft-spoken and imposing figure. ...a widely-travelled man who our correspondent describes as soft-spoken and scholarly.*

soft target, soft targets
NC A **soft target** is one that can be easily attacked and destroyed because it is not a military target and therefore is not defended. *The organization was avoiding what he called soft targets. ...a spate of soft target attacks.*

soft touch
N SING If you describe someone as a **soft touch**, you mean that they can easily be persuaded to lend you money or to do things for you; an informal expression. *Mr Ryzhkov is regarded by some as something of a soft touch.*

software /ˈsɒftweə/
NU Computer programs are referred to as **software**. *They are planning further improvements to their software. ...the computer software needed to run the system.*

softwood /ˈsɒftwʊd/ **softwoods**
N MASS **Softwood** is wood from trees, such as pines, that grow quickly and produce wood which can be easily sawn. *They are converting the softwood in these plantations into charcoal.*

softy /ˈsɒfti/ **softies**; also spelt **softie**. An informal word.
1 NC You call someone a **softy** if they react to being hurt by crying too easily or making too much fuss. *Get up, you big softy! You haven't really hurt yourself.*
2 NC You can also refer to someone as a **softy** if you think that they are easily made to feel sympathy or sadness, for example by a sad film or story. *I'm really a softie, you know... This mild and courteous man showed that he was no softy.*

soggy /ˈsɒgi/
ADJ Something that is **soggy** is unpleasantly wet. ...*soggy biscuits.*

Soglo, Nicéphore /niːseɪfɔː sɒʊgləʊ/
Nicéphore Soglo became President of Benin in 1991. He was a governor of the International Monetary Fund in 1964 and a World Bank executive from 1979 to 1986. He served as Minister of Finance and Economic Affairs from 1965 to 1966, and of Economy and Planning from 1966 to 1967. He was Prime Minister from 1990 to 1991. He is a member of the Union of the Forces of Progress (UFP). Born: 1934.

soil /sɔɪl/ **soils, soiling, soiled**
1 NU **Soil** is the substance on the land surface of the earth in which plants grow. *The soil here is very fertile.*
2 NU+SUPP You can use **soil** to refer to a country's territory. ...*if no foreign armies had invaded Russian soil.*
3 VO If you **soil** something, you make it dirty; a formal use. *Garments hanging in vehicles risk being soiled and damaged in transit.* ◆ **soiled** ADJ ...*a soiled handkerchief.*

soiree /ˈswɑːreɪ/ **soirees**; also spelt **soirée**.
NC A **soiree** is a social gathering in the evening; a formal word. *I was usually invited to the musical soirees they regularly held.*

sojourn /ˈsɒdʒən/ **sojourns**
NC A **sojourn** is a stay for a short time in a place that is not your home; a literary word. *His sojourn in France had provided him with a number of stories.*

solace /ˈsɒləs/; a formal word.
1 NU **Solace** is a feeling of comfort that makes you feel less sad. *He began to find solace in the Bible.*
2 N SING If something is a **solace** to you, it makes you feel less sad. *Her poetry has always been a solace to me.*

solar /ˈsəʊlə/
ADJ ATTRIB **Solar** means relating to the sun. ...*solar eclipses. ...the potential of solar energy.*

solar cell, solar cells
NC A **solar cell** is a device that produces electricity from the sun's rays. *On the top of the mast there was a solar cell.*

solarium /səʊˈleərɪəm/ **solariums**
NC A **solarium** is a place equipped with sun-lamps, where you can go to get a suntan artificially. *We have a swimming pool, a solarium and a sauna.*

solar panel, solar panels
NC A **solar panel** is a panel made of solar cells that collect sunlight and turn it into electric power. *They introduced solar panels to charge battery-powered pumps.*

solar plexus /ˈsəʊlə ˈpleksəs/
N SING Your **solar plexus** is the part of your stomach, below your ribs, where the nerves which control your abdominal organs are situated.

solar system
N SING The **solar system** is the sun and all the planets that go round it. *Those neutron stars are thought to lie relatively close to our solar system.*

solar wind, solar winds
NC **Solar winds** are streams of magnetic material that are released by the sun at very high speeds. *Variations in the solar wind are known to alter the Earth's magnetic field... Scientists believe that the solar wind that reaches the Earth is different from solar winds that blow in the other direction.*

sold /səʊld/
Sold is the past tense and past participle of sell.

solder /ˈsəʊldə/ **solders, soldering, soldered**
1 VO If you **solder** two pieces of metal together, you join them by melting a small piece of soft metal and putting it between them, so that it holds them together after it has cooled. ...*pieces of wire that can be soldered together. ...automated soldering of electronics equipment.*
2 NU **Solder** is the soft metal used for soldering.

soldering iron, soldering irons
NC A **soldering iron** is a tool used to solder things together.

soldier /ˈsəʊldʒə/ **soldiers**
NC A **soldier** is a person in an army. *A soldier standing nearby was wounded... Indonesian soldiers have stepped up security in the provincial capital.*
soldier on PHRASAL VERB If you **soldier on** at something, you continue to work hard at it, even though it is difficult or unpleasant. *They want the government to soldier on in the current tough economic conditions.*

sole /səʊl/ **soles**
1 ADJ ATTRIB The **sole** thing or person of a particular type is the only one of that type. *They went with the sole purpose of making a nuisance of themselves... In some families, the woman is the sole wage earner.*
2 ADJ ATTRIB If you have **sole** charge or ownership of something, you are the only person who is in charge of it or who owns it. *She has sole responsibility for bringing up the child.*
3 NC The **sole** of your foot or of a shoe or sock is the underneath surface of it. *With their air-cushioned sole, these boots were invented in Germany in 1945.*
4 NCorNU A **sole** is a kind of flat fish that you can eat. The plural is also 'sole'. *...fillet of sole.*

solecism /ˈsɒlɪsɪzəm/ **solecisms**
NC A **solecism** is a minor grammatical mistake in speech or writing; a formal word.

solely /ˈsəʊlli/
ADV If something involves **solely** one thing, it involves only this thing and no others. *This is solely a matter of money... The blame for this situation lies solely with the government.*

solemn /ˈsɒləm/
1 ADJ Someone or something that is **solemn** is very serious rather than cheerful or humorous. *...solemn and mournful music.* ◆ **solemnly** ADV *Ralph nodded solemnly.* ◆ **solemnity** /səˈlɛmnəti/ NU *...the solemnity of the occasion.*
2 ADJ ATTRIB A **solemn** promise or agreement is formal and sincere. *The government has solemn commitments and must honour them.* ◆ **solemnly** ADV *Jacob solemnly vowed to keep this promise.*

solicit /səˈlɪsɪt/ **solicits, soliciting, solicited**
1 VO If you **solicit** money, help, or an opinion from someone, you ask them for it; a formal use. *Roy solicited aid from a number of influential members.*
2 V When prostitutes **solicit**, they offer to have sex with people in return for money. ◆ **soliciting** NU *She's been fined £35 for soliciting.*

solicitor /səˈlɪsɪtə/ **solicitors**
NC A **solicitor** is a lawyer who gives legal advice and prepares legal documents and cases. *In a statement, the solicitor protested his client's innocence. ...a solicitor representing the union.*

Solicitor General, Solicitors General
NC In Britain, the **Solicitor General** is the second most important legal officer, next in rank to the attorney general. *...the Solicitor General of Scotland, Mr Ewan Stewart, Q.C.*

solicitous /səˈlɪsɪtəs/
ADJ Someone who is **solicitous** shows anxious concern for someone; a formal word. *The hotel personnel could not have been more solicitous.* ◆ **solicitously** ADV *'Now, Mr Gerran, you must take it easy,' I said solicitously.*

solicitude /səˈlɪsɪtjuːd/
NU **Solicitude** is anxious concern for someone; a formal word. *I was moved by their genuine kindness and solicitude for Karin.*

solid /ˈsɒlɪd/ **solids**
1 ADJ A substance or object that is **solid** is hard or firm, rather than being a liquid or a gas. *The canoe bumped hard against something solid and unyielding... Even the sea around them is frozen solid... You very often find yellow solid sulphur deposits around gas vents.*
2 NC A **solid** is a substance that is hard or firm. *You must at least know whether it's a solid or a liquid or a gas.*
3 ADJ A **solid** object or mass does not have a space inside it, or any holes or gaps in it. *...a solid-tyred bus... The car park was packed solid... They've cut the wells out of what looks like solid rock.*

4 ADJ ATTRIB An object made of **solid** gold or **solid** oak, for example, is made of gold or oak all the way through. *The Queen was presented with a solid gold nugget weighing about two ounces.*
5 ADJ ATTRIB An object that is a **solid** colour is only that colour. *The trees were solid green.*
6 ADJ A **solid** structure is strong and is not likely to collapse or fall over. *...solid Victorian houses.* ◆ **solidly** ADV *...large houses built solidly of wooden planks.* ◆ **solidity** /səˈlɪdəti/ NU *...their appearance of massive solidity.*
7 ADJ A **solid** citizen is respectable and reliable. *She regarded them as solid, good, dull people.* ◆ **solidly** ADV *...a solidly respectable family.*
8 ADJ If something is **solid**, it is reliable, strong, or large in amount. *...a veteran British Council worker, with solid experience in Asia and Africa... Solid evidence is needed... A solid relationship and mutual trust are only established over a number of years.* ◆ **solidly** ADV *They are solidly behind the proposal.* ◆ **solidity** NU *...giving an added strength and solidity to the state.*
9 ADJ If someone's support or their control over something is **solid**, it is strong and unlikely to be changed or removed. *Glasgow Central has always been a solid Labour stronghold.*
10 ADJ ATTRIBor ADJafterN If you do something for a **solid** period of time, you do it without any pause or interruption throughout that time. *I waited a solid hour... I read for two hours solid.* ◆ **solidly** ADV *If you work for ten weeks solidly you might stand more of a chance.*

solidarity /ˌsɒlɪˈdærəti/
NU If a group of people show **solidarity**, they show complete unity and support for each other. *...working-class solidarity.*

solid fuel
NU **Solid fuel** is fuel that is a solid rather than a liquid or gas, for example coal, wood, or peat. *The basic choices are gas, electricity, or solid fuel. ...a solid fuel cooker.*

solidify /səˈlɪdɪfaɪ/ **solidifies, solidifying, solidified**
1 V-ERG If you **solidify** a liquid or if it **solidifies**, it changes into a solid. *A method being developed especially for radioactive wastes is to solidify and stabilise liquid or semi-liquid materials... The silica melts and solidifies on cooling to form a coating of glass.*
2 V-ERG If a group of separate things **solidify**, or if you **solidify** them, you make them more unified and stronger. *There may be a tendency now for the vote to solidify behind Michael Dukakis... The question then is how to solidify the loose, ad hoc coalition of regional countries.*

solid-state
ADJ ATTRIB **Solid-state** electronic equipment is made using transistors, silicon chips, or other semi-conductors, instead of valves or mechanical parts; a technical term. *...solid-state microelectronics.*

soliloquy /səˈlɪləkwi/ **soliloquies**
1 NC A **soliloquy** is a speech in a play in which an actor or actress speaks to himself or herself and to the audience, rather than to another actor in the play. *He comes centre stage and begins a soliloquy, unburdening his heart and mind to the audience.*
2 NC A **soliloquy** is also something that you say to yourself; a formal use. *I again held my ritual soliloquy.*

solitaire /ˈsɒlɪteə/ **solitaires**
1 NU **Solitaire** is a game that one person plays alone by moving pegs to different positions on a board, with the aim of having one peg left in the middle at the end of the game.
2 NU **Solitaire** is also a card game for only one player; used in American English.
3 NC A **solitaire** is a diamond or other jewel that is set on its own in a ring or other piece of jewellery. *...a solitaire diamond of immense value.*

solitary /ˈsɒlɪtəˈri/
1 ADJ ATTRIB A **solitary** activity is one that you do alone. *He formed the habit of taking long solitary walks.*

2 ADJ A person or animal that is **solitary** spends a lot of time alone. *Tigers are solitary creatures.*
3 ADJ ATTRIB A **solitary** person or object is alone and has no others nearby. *Madeleine walked over to the solitary figure.*

solitary confinement
NU A prisoner who is in **solitary confinement** is being kept alone, away from all other prisoners. *He claimed that he was being mistreated in prison by being kept in solitary confinement.*

solitude /splɪtjuːd/
NU **Solitude** is the state of being alone. *One can study far better in solitude.*

solo /səʊləʊ/ **solos**
1 NC A **solo** is a piece of music played or sung by one person. *...a clarinet solo by Donizetti.*
2 ADJ ATTRIB A **solo** performance or activity is done by one person. *...her second solo album since she left the all-girl American rock outfit. ...a solo flight.* ▶ Also ADV *...the boat in which he sailed solo round the world.*

soloist /səʊləʊɪst/ **soloists**
NC A **soloist** is a person who plays a musical instrument alone or sings alone. *He was asked whether he preferred playing the horn as a soloist or as part of an orchestra.*

Solomon Islands /spləmən aɪləndz/
The **Solomon Islands** is a country in the south-west Pacific. It consists of several hundred islands, including Guadalcanal, Malaita, New Georgia, San Cristobal (now called Makira), Santa Isabel and Choiseul. The islands became a British colony in the 19th century. They were occupied in part by Japan from 1942 to 1943 and became independent in 1978. Solomon Mamaloni, of the People's Alliance Party (PAP), became Prime Minister in 1989. It is a member of the Commonwealth. Fish and timber are exported. ◆ **Solomon Islander** /spləmən aɪləndə/ N ▪ *per capita GNP:* US$430 ▪ *religion:* Christianity ▪ *language:* English (official), Pidgin ▪ *currency:* dollar ▪ *capital:* Honiara ▪ *population:* 304,000 (1988) ▪ *size:* 27,556 square kilometres.

solstice /splstɪs/ **solstices**
NC A **solstice** is one of the two times in the year when the sun is farthest away from the equator. In the northern hemisphere, the summer solstice is on June 21 or 22, and the winter solstice is on December 21 or 22. In the southern hemisphere, the winter solstice is in June, and the summer solstice is in December. *...astronomical phenomena like phases of the moon or the winter and summer solstice.*

soluble /spljʊbl/
1 ADJ A **soluble** substance will dissolve in a liquid. *The powder is soluble in water.*
2 ADJ A problem that is **soluble** can be solved; a formal use. *A whole range of problems which have previously been intractable have suddenly become soluble.*

solution /səluːʃn/ **solutions**
1 NC A **solution** is a way of dealing with or removing a difficulty. *It's a very neat little solution to our problem... The loan was only a temporary solution to the country's financial problems.*
2 NC The **solution** to a riddle or a puzzle is the answer. *...the crossword solution.*
3 NC A **solution** is also a liquid in which a solid substance has been dissolved; a technical term. *...a solution of detergent and water.*

solve /splv/ **solves, solving, solved**
VO If you **solve** a problem or a question, you find a solution or an answer to it. *...the failure of successive government policies to solve Britain's economic problems. ...solving crossword puzzles.*

solvency /splvənsi/
N SING A country or organization's **solvency** is its ability to pay back its debts; a formal word. *More can be exported to preserve Hungary's precarious solvency.*

solvent /splvənt/ **solvents**
1 ADJ If a person or a company is **solvent**, they have enough money to pay all their debts; a formal use. *He has been responsible for keeping the country solvent*

despite its guerrilla war.
2 NCorNU A **solvent** is a liquid that can dissolve other substances; a technical use. *...rubber solvents. ...grease solvent.*

solvent abuse
NU **Solvent abuse** is the dangerous practice of breathing in solvents such as glue in order to feel their effects. *The Acorn Street Clinic in Glasgow has achieved remarkable success in the battle to prevent solvent abuse. ...the growing problem of drug, alcohol and solvent abuse in schools.*

Somalia /səmɑːliə/
The **Somali Democratic Republic** is a country in eastern Africa. In 1960 Somalia became an independent country. There is no effective central government because Somalia is divided into a number of warring factions. In 1991, the north west of the country was proclaimed The Republic of Somaliland by the Somaliland National Movement, but it has received no diplomatic recognition. ◆ **Somali** /səmɑːli/ N, ADJ

sombre /spmbə/; spelt **somber** in American English. A literary word.
1 ADJ **Sombre** colours and places are dark and dull. *...two women dressed in sombre black.*
2 ADJ If someone is **sombre**, or if their mood or view is **sombre**, they are serious, sad, or pessimistic. *The President was noticeably more sombre than after Mr Schultz's last visit. ... a picture of Mr Gorbachev in sombre mood... Mr Morris took a more sombre view.* ◆ **sombrely** ADV *Mercer shook his head sombrely.*

sombrero /spmbreərəʊ/ **sombreros**
NC A **sombrero** is a man's hat with a very wide brim which is worn especially in Mexico. *...an Indian in a sombrero.*

some /səm, sʌm/
1 DETorPRON You use **some** to refer to an unspecified amount of something or to a number of people or things. *She had a piece of pie and some coffee... I've got some friends coming over... 'You'll need graph paper.'—'Yeah, I've got some at home.'*
2 DET You also use **some** to emphasize that an amount or number is fairly large. *They were having some difficulty in following the plot... I did not meet her again for some years.*
3 QUANTorDET **Some** is also used to refer to part of an amount or group. *She took some of the meat out... Some sports are very dangerous.*
4 DET If you refer to **some** person or thing, you are referring to that person or thing vaguely, without stating precisely which one you mean. *We found it lying in some ditch in the middle of the desert... At some stage in your career you may need my help.*
5 **Some** is also used to mean approximately; a formal use. *...a single layer of stone, some four metres thick.*

somebody /sʌmbədi/. See **someone**.

some day
ADV **Some day** or **someday** means at an unspecified date in the future. *I'd like to see it some day.*

somehow /sʌmhaʊ/
1 ADV You use **somehow** to indicate that you do not know how something was done or will be done. *...a boy who'd somehow broken his thumb... We'll manage somehow.*
2 ADV SEN You also use **somehow** to indicate that you do not know the reason for something. *Somehow it didn't seem important to him any more.*

someone /sʌmwʌn/
PRON INDEF You use **someone** or **somebody** to refer to a person without saying exactly who you mean. *There's someone coming upstairs... She wrote a book on somebody famous... It belongs to somebody else.*

someplace /sʌmpleɪs/
ADV **Someplace** means the same as **somewhere**; used in informal American English. *Why don't you boys go and sit someplace else?*

somersault /sʌməsɒlt/ **somersaults, somersaulting, somersaulted**
NC A **somersault** is a rapid movement in which a person or object turns over completely in the air. *My sister turned a somersault.* ▶ Also V *His speedboat somersaulted and crashed at high speed.*

something /sʌmθɪŋ/
1 PRON INDEF You use **something** to refer to an object, action, or quality without saying exactly what you mean. *Hendricks saw something ahead of him... Something terrible has happened.*
2 PRON INDEF If what you have or what has been done is **something**, it is useful, even if only in a small way. *Of course I've got my savings now, that's something.* ● **Something** is used in these phrases. ● If you say that a person or thing is **something of** a particular thing, you mean that they are that thing to a limited extent. *It is something of a mystery.* ● If you say that **there is something in** an idea or suggestion, you mean that it is quite good. *I believe there is something in having ballots in trade unions.* ● **something like:** see like.

sometime /sʌmtaɪm/
1 ADV **Sometime** means at a vague or unspecified time in the future or the past. *Can I come and see you sometime?... He saw Frieda Maloney sometime last week.*
2 ADJ ATTRIB You can also use **sometime** to indicate what job a person used to have; a formal use. *...Sir Alfred Munnings, sometime President of the Royal Academy.*

sometimes /sʌmtaɪmz/
ADV You use **sometimes** to say that something happens on some occasions. *Sometimes they just come for a term, sometimes six months.*

someway /sʌmweɪ/
ADV You use **someway** to indicate that you will do something or that something will happen in a way that you have not decided on yet; used in informal American English. *Someway, we're going to protect you... Hopefully, we could stop it someway.*

somewhat /sʌmwɒt/
ADV or SUBMOD **Somewhat** means to a fairly large, but not great, extent or degree; a formal word. *...a fine, though somewhat daunting, director... Communication has altered things somewhat.*

somewhere /sʌmweə/
1 ADV You use **somewhere** to refer to a place without saying exactly where you mean. *They lived somewhere near Bournemouth... There's an ashtray somewhere.*
2 ADV You also use **somewhere** when giving an approximate amount, number, or time. *This part of the church was built somewhere around 700 AD. ...somewhere between 55,000 and 60,000 men.*
3 If you say that you are **getting somewhere**, you mean that you are making progress. *Now we're getting somewhere... He thought he might get somewhere if he re-opened the case.*

somnolent /sɒmnələnt/
ADJ If you are **somnolent**, you are sleepy; a literary word. *'Have a glass of wine,' I said, feeling somnolent... I returned to collect my somnolent children.*

son /sʌn/ **sons**
1 NC Your **son** is your male child. *Don Culver is the son of an engineer... Tony was the second of four sons.*
2 NC+*of* You can also describe a man as the **son** of his nation, when he has discovered or done something important or significant that honours the nation; a formal use. *She'd come to honour the memory of one of the greatest sons of the Czechoslovak nation... He describes Solzhenitsyn as a remarkable son of Russia.*

sonar /səʊnɑː/
NU or N+N **Sonar** is equipment on a ship which can calculate the depth of the sea or the position of an underwater object using sound waves. *...sonar apparatus.*

sonata /sənɑːtə/ **sonatas**
NC A **sonata** is a piece of classical music written for one instrument or for a small group of instruments and usually consisting of three or four movements. *...the opening passage from Schubert's violin sonata in A major.*

son et lumière /sɒn eɪ luːmieə/
N SING **Son et lumière** is an entertainment which is held at night in an old building such as a castle. A person describes the history of the place, and at the same time different parts of the building are brightly lit and music is played.

song /sɒŋ/ **songs**
1 NC or NU A **song** consists of words and music sung together. *...a love song... We all burst into song.*
2 NC or NU A bird's **song**, or bird **song**, is the pleasant, musical sounds that a bird makes when it sings. *...the sweet song of the skylark. ...speaking against a background of bird song in his garden.*

song and dance
1 N+N A **song and dance** act is an act performed in a theatre in which a person or group of people both sing and dance. *John Mills started his career as a song and dance man. ...the Red Army Song and Dance Ensemble.*
2 N SING If you say that someone is making a **song and dance** about something, you mean that they are making an unnecessary fuss about it; an informal expression. *Her father made a great song and dance about her being late home.*

songbird /sɒŋbɜːd/ **songbirds**
NC A **songbird** is a bird that produces musical sounds which are like singing. There are many different kinds of songbird. *...species of migratory birds, including storks, golden eagles and small songbirds which are protected species in Britain.*

sonic /sɒnɪk/
ADJ ATTRIB **Sonic** is used to describe things related to sound; a technical term. *...sonic probes.*

sonic boom, sonic booms
NC or NU A **sonic boom** is the loud noise caused by something such as an aircraft when it travels faster than the speed of sound. *...popular anxiety about Concorde's sonic boom.*

son-in-law, sons-in-law
NC+POSS Your **son-in-law** is the husband of your daughter. *He appointed his son-in-law as editor.*

sonnet /sɒnɪt/ **sonnets**
NC A **sonnet** is a poem with 14 lines, in which some lines rhyme with others according to fixed patterns. *She was reading from a sonnet by William Wordsworth.*

sonny /sʌni/
VOCATIVE **Sonny** is sometimes used to address a young boy; an informal word. *Hallo, sonny.*

son of a bitch, sons of bitches
NC If you call a man **son of a bitch**, you are referring to them in a very rude way, usually because they have made you angry or upset; an offensive expression, used in American English. *What's that son of a bitch done this time?*

sonorous /sɒnərəs/; a literary word.
1 ADJ A sound that is **sonorous** is deep and rich. *...his deep sonorous voice. ...from the piping choirboys to the sonorous bass.*
2 ADJ Words that are **sonorous** sound important and impressive. *...the sonorous names of Betelgeuse and Aldebaran.*

soon /suːn/ **sooner, soonest**
ADV If something is going to happen **soon**, it will happen after a short time. If something happened **soon** after a particular time or event, it happened a short time after it. *It will soon be Christmas... He rented a TV soon after moving into his apartment... Why wasn't it done sooner?*
● **Soon** or **sooner** is used in these phrases. ● If you say that something will happen **as soon as** something else happens, you mean that it will happen immediately after the other thing. *I will go to see the President as soon as I have been released... As soon as we get the tickets we'll send them to you... Contact the police as soon as possible.* ● You say the **sooner the better** when you think something should be done as soon as possible. *The sooner fighting stops the better... It's a wonderful piece, and the sooner they do another production of it, the better.* ● If you say that something will happen **sooner or later**, you mean that it will certainly happen, even though it might take a long time. *They will have to be included sooner or later... Whoever did this will sooner or later be caught.*
● If you say that **no sooner** did one thing happen **than** another thing happened, you mean that the second

thing happened immediately after the first. *No sooner was the news made public than a spokesman denied it.* ● If you say that you **would sooner** do something, you mean that you would prefer to do it. *I would sooner read than watch television.*

soot /sʊt/
NU **Soot** is black powder which collects on the inside of chimneys and can be found in smoke from coal. *Factory chimneys belch out soot and dangerous wastes.*

soothe /suːð/ **soothes, soothing, soothed**
1 VO If you **soothe** someone who is angry or upset, you make them calmer. *He tried to soothe her by making conversation.* ◆ **soothing** ADJ *...soothing music. ...a few soothing words.*
2 VO Something that **soothes** pain makes it less severe. *...cream she put on to soothe her sunburn.*

sooty /sʊti/
ADJ Something that is **sooty** is covered with soot. *...his sooty hands.*

sop /sɒp/ **sops, sopping, sopped**
1 NC A **sop** is something small or unimportant that you offer to someone who is dissatisfied or discontented in order to prevent them from getting angry or causing trouble. *The only sop they throw in the direction of the OAPs is their free bus passes. ...a sop to international opinion.*
2 See also **sopping**.
sop up PHRASAL VERB Material that **sops** a liquid **up** soaks it up like a sponge; an informal expression. *My bandage would sop the blood up all right.*

sophisticated /səfɪstɪkeɪtɪd/
1 ADJ A **sophisticated** person knows about culture, fashion, and other matters that are considered socially important. *...a glossy magazine for today's sophisticated woman. ...a sophisticated lifestyle.*
2 ADJ A **sophisticated** machine, device, or method is more advanced or complex than others. *These planes are among the most sophisticated aircraft now being manufactured.*

sophistication /səfɪstɪkeɪʃn/
1 NU **Sophistication** is the quality of knowing about culture, fashion, and other matters that are considered socially important. *In spite of his sophistication and diplomatic expertise, he has antagonized important sections of the public.*
2 NU The **sophistication** of machines, devices, or methods is their quality of being more advanced or complex than others. *Genetic testing has reached new levels of sophistication.*

sophistry /sɒfɪstri/
NU **Sophistry** is the practice of using clever arguments that sound convincing but are in fact false; a formal word. *He used his powers of sophistry to invoke theological right on his side. ...Iago's satanic sophistry.*

sophomore /sɒfəmɔː/ **sophomores**
NC In the United States, a student in the second year of a high school or university course is called a **sophomore**. *He's a sophomore at Western Connecticut State University majoring in music.*

soporific /sɒpərɪfɪk/
ADJ Something that is **soporific** makes you feel sleepy. *I had to fight the soporific effect of the drug all day... I found his style of lecturing rather soporific.*

sopping /sɒpɪŋ/
ADJ or SUBMOD Something that is **sopping** or **sopping** wet is extremely wet; an informal word. *He held out a sopping handful of clothes... I was sopping wet when I got back.*

soppy /sɒpi/
ADJ If you describe someone or something as **soppy**, you mean that they are silly or foolishly sentimental; an informal word. *...the soppy expressions on their faces... Don't be soppy, Manfred.*

soprano /səprɑːnəʊ/ **sopranos**
NC A **soprano** is a woman, girl, or boy with a high singing voice. *American soprano Cheryl Studer makes her debut in the role of Elsa. ...her pure soprano voice.*

sorbet /sɔːbeɪ/ **sorbets**
N MASS **Sorbet** is a dessert made from frozen water,

flavoured with fruit. *...orange sorbet.*

sorcerer /sɔːsərə/ **sorcerers**
NC A **sorcerer** is a person who performs magic by using the power of evil spirits.

sorceress /sɔːsərɛs/ **sorceresses**
NC A **sorceress** is a woman who performs magic by using the power of evil spirits.

sorcery /sɔːsəri/
NU **Sorcery** is the practice of performing magic by using the power of evil spirits. *At that time most people believed in sorcery and witchcraft.*

sordid /sɔːdɪd/
ADJ You say that something is **sordid** when it involves dishonest or immoral behaviour. *...a rather sordid affair. ...the sordid story of English soccer hooliganism.*

sore /sɔː/ **sores**
1 ADJ If part of your body is **sore**, it causes you pain and discomfort. *Her throat was so sore she could not talk.*
2 NC A **sore** is a painful place on your body where the skin is infected. *He had a wound on his knee and multiple sores and ulcers.*
3 ADJ PRED If you are **sore** about something, you are angry and upset about it; used in American English. *Nobody believed him, and this made him sore as hell.* ● **Sore** is used in these phrases. ● If something is a **sore point**, you do not like to talk about it because it makes you angry or upset. *This could create another sore point in relations between the two countries.* ● If something **sticks out like a sore thumb**, it is very obvious or noticeable, usually because it is strange or inappropriate. *The distinctive number plates of British servicemen's cars abroad made them stick out like sore thumbs.*

sorely /sɔːli/
ADV You use **sorely** to emphasize that a feeling such as disappointment or need is very strong. *His talents were sorely missed in the current crisis... They were sorely in need of rest.*

sorrow /sɒrəʊ/ **sorrows**
1 NU **Sorrow** is a feeling of deep sadness. *She wrote to express her sorrow at the tragic death of their son.*
2 NC **Sorrows** are events or situations that cause sorrow. *...the sorrows that life brings.*

sorrowful /sɒrəʊfl/
ADJ **Sorrowful** means very sad; a literary word. *They kept giving me sorrowful looks.*

sorry /sɒri/ **sorrier, sorriest**
1 You say **'Sorry'** or **'I'm sorry'** as a way of apologizing for something you have done. *'You're giving me a headache with all that noise.'—'Sorry.'... Sorry about the coffee on your bedspread... I'm sorry I'm late... I'm sorry if I worried you.*
2 You use **sorry** when you are saying that you cannot help someone or when you are giving them bad news. *I'm sorry but there's no-one here called Nikki... I'm sorry to say that the experiment has failed.*
3 You also say **sorry** when you have not heard what someone has said and you want them to repeat it. *'Have you seen the guide book anywhere?'—'Sorry?'—'Seen the guide book?'*
4 ADV SEN You can use **sorry** to correct yourself when you have said something incorrect. *It's in the southeast, sorry, southwest corner of the USA.*
5 ADJ PRED+about or for If you are **sorry** about a situation, you feel sadness, disappointment, or regret about it. *He said he was sorry about what had happened... Sorry for any inconvenience caused!*
6 ADJ PRED+for If you are **sorry** for someone who is unhappy or in an unpleasant situation, you feel sympathy for them. *I knew they were having a rough time and I felt sorry for them.*
7 ADJ ATTRIB You also use **sorry** to describe people and things that are in a bad state; a formal use. *'We are in a sorry state,' she lamented.*

sort /sɔːt/ **sorts, sorting, sorted**
1 NC+SUPP A particular **sort** of something is one of its different kinds or types. *'What sort of iron did she get?' ...a rock plant of some sort... There were five different sorts of biscuits... When you are young you dream about all sorts of things.*

2 V Oor V A If you **sort** things, you arrange them into groups according to their common features or characteristics. *Minnie was in the office, sorting mail... They had got mixed up and needed to be sorted into three sets.* ● Sort is used in these phrases. ● You use **sort of** when you want to say that something can roughly be described in a particular way; an informal expression. *She was wearing a sort of velvet dress.* ● You use **of sorts** to indicate that something is not of very good quality. *...cleaning a carpet of sorts... Farlow was a lawyer of sorts.* ● If you feel **out of sorts**, you feel slightly unwell or discontented. *She sighed and complained of being out of sorts.*
sort out PHRASAL VERB **1** If you **sort out** a group of things, you organize or tidy them. *It took a while to sort out all our luggage.* **2** If you **sort out** a problem, you deal with it and find a solution to it. *They are determined to make another attempt once the legal problems have been sorted out.*

sortie /sɔːti/ **sorties**
1 NC If a military force makes a **sortie**, it makes an attack or raid by leaving its own position and going briefly into enemy territory. *Pilots are now flying eight sorties a day... Settlers had already embarked upon night-time sorties.*
2 NC A **sortie** is a brief trip away from your home or base, especially a trip to an unfamiliar place; a literary use. *Apart from his occasional sorties to Exeter he hardly ever left the farm... The maid kept darting out on little sorties.*

sorting office, sorting offices
NC A **sorting office** is a place where letters, packages, and so on are taken after posting and are sorted according to their delivery addresses. *The Birmingham sorting office is the largest in Europe.*

sort-out, sort-outs
NC If you have a **sort-out**, you tidy something such as a room or house by putting everything in the right place and throwing away unwanted items; an informal word. *I gave the bedroom a good sort-out.*

SOS /esəuɛs/
N SING An **SOS** is a signal which indicates to other people that you are in danger and need help quickly. *...an SOS from a private plane... The freighter sent out an urgent SOS call.*

so-so
ADJ or ADV If you say that something is **so-so**, you mean that it is neither good nor bad, but of average quality; an informal word. *Some of the food is very good, some of it's so-so... 'How did the meeting go?'—'So-so.'*

souffle /suːfleɪ/ **souffles**; also spelt **soufflé**.
N Cor N U A **souffle** is a light food made from a mixture of beaten egg whites and other ingredients that is baked in the oven. *...a cheese souffle.*

sought /sɔːt/
Sought is the past tense and past participle of **seek**.

sought-after
ADJ Something that is much **sought-after** is in great demand, usually because it is rare or of very good quality. *The slums of the past are becoming much sought-after residences. ...one of Hollywood's most sought-after actors.*

soul /səul/ **souls**
1 NC A person's **soul** is the spiritual part of them which is believed to continue existing after their body is dead. *They said a prayer for the souls of the men who had been drowned.*
2 NC Your **soul** is also your mind, character, thoughts, and feelings. *His soul was in turmoil.*
3 N SING The **soul** of a nation or a political movement is the special quality that it has that represents its basic character. *...the soul of the American people.*
4 N SING+SUPP A person can be referred to as a particular kind of **soul**; an old-fashioned use. *She was a kind soul... Poor soul!*
5 N SING You use **soul** in negative statements to mean nobody at all. *When I first went there I didn't know a single soul... I swear I will never tell a soul.*
6 See also **soul music**.

soul-destroying
ADJ **Soul-destroying** activities are boring and

depressing. *The job has its soul-destroying aspects.*
soulful /səulfl/
ADJ Something that is **soulful** expresses deep feelings. *...big, soulful eyes.*
soulless /səulləs/
ADJ Something that is **soulless** lacks human qualities and the ability to feel or produce deep feelings. *The place seemed soulless. ...a soulless routine job.*
soul music
NU **Soul music** or **soul** is a type of pop music performed mainly by black American musicians. It developed from gospel and blues music and often expresses deep emotions. *...styles ranging from gospel to contemporary soul music. ...a band who blend jazz, blues, and soul. ...a new soul band from Chicago.*
soul-searching
NU **Soul-searching** is long and careful examination of your thoughts and feelings, especially when you are trying to make a difficult moral decision. *After much soul-searching the union called off the strike.*
sound /saund/ **sounds, sounding, sounded; sounder, soundest**
1 NC A **sound** is a particular thing that you hear. *He heard the sound of footsteps in the hall... He opened the door without a sound... We have identified twenty different sounds that dolphins make.*
2 NU **Sound** is what you hear as a result of vibrations travelling through the air or water. *Sound travels better in water than in air. ...the speed of sound.*
3 N SING The **sound** on a television set is what you hear coming from the television set. Its loudness can be controlled. *When the news had finished Morris would turn down the sound and get out a book.*
4 N SING The **sound** of a singer, band, or style of music, is the distinctive quality of the music. *The group have their own unique sound... This was the beginning of what became known as the fusion sound, a mixture of experimental jazz, soul and funk.*
5 V-ERG When something such as a horn **sounds** or if you **sound** it, it makes a noise. *The intercom buzzer sounded... A car passed him at top speed, sounding its horn.*
6 V Cor V A When you are describing a noise, you can talk about the way it **sounds**. *The rustling of the woman's dress sounded alarmingly loud... Her footsteps sounded like pistol shots.*
7 V Cor V A When you talk about the way someone **sounds**, you are describing the impression you have of them when they speak. *'Ah,' Piper said. He sounded a little discouraged... You know, you sound just like an insurance salesman.*
8 V Cor V A You can also give your impression of something you have read or heard about by talking about the way it **sounds**. *'They've got a small farm down in Devon.'—'That sounds nice.'... It sounds to me as though he's just doing it to be awkward.*
9 N SING The **sound** of something that you have heard about is the impression you get of it. *I don't like the sound of linguistics.*
10 ADJ If something is **sound**, it is in good condition, strong, or healthy. *My heart is basically sound. ...a policy designed to squeeze out inflation and establish a sound basis for a Western market economy.*
11 ADJ If you say that something such as advice is **sound**, you mean that it is reliable and sensible and that you approve of it. *This would appear to be sound advice... We found that many of the proposals were very sound... Synthetics are somehow a more humane or sound alternative than natural fur.*
● Sound is used in these phrases. ● If you are **sound asleep**, you are sleeping deeply. *I was sound asleep when the police came and woke me up.* ● **safe and sound**: see safe. ● **to sound a note**: see note.
sound out PHRASAL VERB If you **sound** someone **out**, you question them to find out their opinion. *The Secretary of State will sound them out on how to step up pressure in the next phase.*
sound barrier
N SING The **sound barrier** is the sudden increase in the force of the air against an aircraft that occurs as it passes the speed of sound. *In a few minutes, ladies and gentlemen, we will be breaking the sound barrier.*

soundbite /saʊndbaɪt/ **soundbites**
NC A **soundbite** is a short sentence or phrase, usually from a politician's speech, which is broadcast during a news bulletin. *Network newsreels were awash with soundbites and clips of gunfire.*

sound effect, sound effects
NC **Sound effects** are sounds created artificially to make a play or film more realistic. *Music and sound effects play a central role in this production.*

sounding board, sounding boards
NC If you use someone as a **sounding board**, you discuss your ideas with them while you are working them out. *The council will be used by Mr Gorbachev as a sounding board which can express a wide variety of opinions.*

soundly /saʊndli/
1 ADV If you sleep **soundly**, you sleep deeply and do not wake. *I sleep very soundly at night.*
2 ADV If someone is **soundly** defeated, they are thoroughly and severely defeated. *The right-wing candidate was soundly defeated... Ligachev was soundly beaten in his bid to become Mr Gorbachev's deputy.*

soundproof /saʊndpruːf/
ADJ A **soundproof** room has been constructed so that sound cannot get in or out. *...a soundproof glass booth.*

sound system, sound systems
NC A **sound system** is electrical equipment used for playing amplified music, for example in a discotheque. *They hire out sound systems, lighting, visuals.*

soundtrack /saʊndtræk/ **soundtracks**
1 NC The **soundtrack** of a film is its sound, including both speech and music. *...the grainy images and deteriorating soundtrack of the mutilated 1940 version of the film.*
2 NC You can also use **soundtrack** to refer to the recorded music that accompanies a film. *Prince has been commissioned to write and play the soundtrack on the new Batman movie.*

sound wave, sound waves
NC A **sound wave** is a vibration through air or water on which sound is carried. *Radar employs radio waves whereas sonar uses sound waves.*

soup /suːp/ **soups**
N MASS **Soup** is liquid food made by cooking meat, fish, or vegetables in water. *...home-made pea soup.*

soupçon /suːpsɒnº/
N SING A **soupçon** of something is a very small amount of it; a literary word. *...a soupçon of coriander. ...a favourable review, but with just a soupçon of sarcasm.*

soup kitchen, soup kitchens
NC A **soup kitchen** is a place where food and drink are given to people who have no money or possessions. *...tramps in rags queueing for food from soup kitchens. ...a church organization running soup kitchens for the poor.*

sour /saʊə/ **sours, souring, soured**
1 ADJ Something that is **sour** has a sharp taste like the taste of a lemon or an apple that is not ripe. *Add enough sugar to keep it from tasting sour.*
2 ADJ **Sour** milk has an unpleasant taste because it is no longer fresh. *This milk's gone sour.*
3 ADJ **Sour** people are bad-tempered and unfriendly. *I received a sour look every time I passed her house.*
4 V-ERG If a friendship or attitude **sours** or if something **sours** it, it becomes less friendly or hopeful. *Detente has soured... These latest cuts might sour relations between the government and the military.*
5 If a situation or relationship **turns sour**, it is not pleasant or satisfactory anymore. *By spring, the relationship had turned sour, and both manager and artist had resorted to law... Her triumph turned sour when she was found guilty of electoral malpractice.*

source /sɔːs/ **sources**
1 NC The **source** of something is the person, place, or thing from which it comes or from which you obtain it. *...one of the world's main sources of uranium... Candidates are required to publish the sources of their campaign funds... Whatever the source, cholera has*

established a strong foothold in poorer communities.
2 NC The **source** of a difficulty is its cause. *They're trying to trace the source of the trouble.*
3 NC A **source** of information is a person or book that provides information for a book or for a piece of research. *Western diplomatic sources confirmed reports of fighting in the capital... The story was based on information from a 'reliable source'.*
4 N SING The **source** of a river or stream is the place where it begins. *We are following the creek to its source.*

south /saʊθ/
1 N SING The **south** is the direction on your right when you are looking towards the place where the sun rises. *...a place in the hills to the south of the little town.*
2 N SING The **south** of a place is the part which is towards the south. *...the South of France.* ▶ Also ADJ ATTRIB *...South Wales.*
3 ADV **South** means towards the south, or to the south of a place or thing. *I travelled south by bus through Philadelphia... I was living in a house just south of Market Street.*
4 ADJ ATTRIB A **south** wind blows from the south.
5 N SING Some people refer to the less developed countries of Africa, Asia, and Latin America as the **South**. *The South must be developed, but in an environmentally-conscious way.*

South Africa /saʊθ æfrɪkə/
The **Republic of South Africa** is a country in southern Africa, which became a British colony in the late 18th century. The National Party came to power in 1948. It developed the policy of apartheid, which aimed to keep the races of South Africa separate. South Africans of European extraction comprise less than 17% of the population, but the black majority has no political power. South Africa left the Commonwealth and became a republic in 1961 under the leadership of Dr Hendrik Verwoerd. The African National Congress was established in 1912 to campaign for equal rights for all races. It was outlawed in 1960 and its leader, Nelson Mandela, was imprisoned in 1963. F W de Klerk, of the National Party, became President in 1989. He began the process of ending apartheid, by legalizing the ANC and other anti-apartheid groups. Many ANC leaders were released from prison in 1990, most notably Nelson Mandela. South Africa is the world's leading producer of gold. It also exports other metals and fruit. ♦ **South African** /saʊθ æfrɪkən/ N, ADJ ▪ *per capita GNP:* US$2,290 ▪ *religion:* Christianity ▪ *language:* Afrikaans and English (official), Xhosa, Zulu, Sesotho ▪ *currency:* rand ▪ *capital:* Cape Town (legislative), Pretoria (administrative), Bloemfontein (judicial) ▪ *population:* 35 million (1989) ▪ *size:* 1,221,037 square kilometres.

South America /saʊθ əmɛrɪkə/
South America is the fourth largest continent. It is approximately 18 million square kilometres in area, which is about one-eighth of the world's land. The Andes are the world's second highest mountain chain, rising to 7,084 metres at Ojos del Salado. The Amazon is the world's largest river basin. Other major river systems are the Orinoco and Río de la Plata. More than half of South America is forested, notably by the Amazonian rain forest. The estimated population of South America in 1984 was 260 million.

southbound /saʊθbaʊnd/
ADJ **Southbound** roads, cars, trains, and so on lead or are travelling towards the south. *Southbound traffic is being diverted via Northampton. ...the southbound carriageway of the M1.*

south-east
1 N SING The **south-east** is the direction halfway between south and east. *To the south-east there is a plantation.*
2 N SING The **south-east** of a place is the part which is towards the south-east. *Wages are higher in the South-East. ...the south-east of England.* ▶ Also ADJ ATTRIB *...south-east London.*
3 ADV **South-east** means towards the south-east, or to the south-east of a place or thing. *If we proceed south-east we come to Eaton Place.*

4 ADJ ATTRIB A **south-east** wind blows from the south-east.

south-eastern
ADJ ATTRIB **South-eastern** means in or from the south-east of a region or country. ...*a military prison in south-eastern Turkey.*

southerly /sʌðəli/
1 ADJ **Southerly** means towards the south. *They headed in a southerly direction. ...the most southerly tip of Bear Island.*
2 ADJ A **southerly** wind blows from the south. *Southerly breezes of around eight to twelve knots are expected tomorrow.*

southern /sʌðn/
ADJ ATTRIB **Southern** means in or from the south of a region or country. ...*the Nowa Huta steelworks near the southern city of Krakow.*

southerner /sʌðənə/ **southerners**
NC A **southerner** is a person who was born in or who lives in the south of a country. *The survey shows that southerners eat more fresh fruit and vegetables than those in other parts of the country.*

South Korea /saυθ kəriə/
The **Republic of Korea** is a country which occupies the southern portion of the Korean peninsula in east Asia. The Korean peninsula was occupied by Japan from 1905 until 1945, when northern Korea was occupied by Soviet troops and southern Korea was occupied by US troops. In 1948 the two areas were formally divided into North Korea and South Korea. North Korean forces crossed the 38th parallel in 1950, beginning the Korean War, which ended in 1953. General Park Chung Hee ruled from a military coup in 1961 until his assassination in 1979. Roh Tae Woo became President in 1988. He is a member of the Democratic Liberal Party (DLP). Chung Won Shik, of the DLP, was appointed Prime Minister in 1991. South Korea exports electrical goods, transport equipment, and shoes.
♦ **South Korean** /saυθ kəriən/ N, ADJ
▪ *per capita GNP:* US\$4,400 ▪ *religion:* Buddhism, Christianity, Chundo Kyo ▪ *language:* Korean ▪ *currency:* won ▪ *capital:* Seoul ▪ *population:* 42 million (1989) ▪ *size:* 99,222 square kilometres.

South Pole
N PROP The **South Pole** is the place on the surface of the earth which is farthest towards the south. *The expedition was very nearly abandoned at the South Pole.*

southward /saυθwəd/ or **southwards**
1 ADV **Southward** or **southwards** means towards the south. *A level expanse of low-lying country extended southward.*
2 ADJ **Southward** is used to describe things which are moving towards the south or which face towards the south. *The shore was badly eaten away on its southward side.*

south-west
1 N SING The **south-west** is the direction halfway between south and west. *To the south-west lay the city.*
2 N SING The **south-west** of a place is the part which is towards the south-west. *The worst affected area is the South-West. ...the south-west of England.* ▸ Also ADJ ATTRIB ...*the Conservative Party agent for south-west Staffordshire.*
3 ADV **South-west** means towards the south-west, or to the south-west of a place or thing. *It flows south-west to the Atlantic Ocean.*
4 ADJ ATTRIB A **south-west** wind blows from the south-west.

south-western
ADJ **South-western** means in or from the south-west of a region or country. ...*the Basque region in south-western France.*

souvenir /suːvənɪə/ **souvenirs**
NC A **souvenir** is something which you buy or keep to remind you of a holiday, place, or event. *He kept a spoon as a souvenir of his journey. ...the souvenir shop.*

sou'wester /saυwεstə/ **sou'westers**
NC A **sou'wester** is a waterproof hat that is worn especially by sailors in stormy weather. It has a wide brim at the back to keep your neck dry.

sovereign /sɒvrɪn/ **sovereigns**
1 NC A **sovereign** is a king, queen, or other royal ruler. *This would be the first visit by a British sovereign since the Russian Revolution of 1917.*
2 ADJ ATTRIB A **sovereign** state or country is not under the authority of any other country. ...*the creation of an independent and sovereign nation free of foreign forces. ...the last stages of their struggle for a sovereign state.*
3 ADJ **Sovereign** is used to describe someone who has the highest power in a country; a formal use. *Parliament is sovereign... He will be given sovereign powers.*

sovereignty /sɒvrənti/
NU **Sovereignty** is the power that a country has to govern itself or to govern other countries. ...*a threat to national sovereignty. ...the end of British sovereignty over Gibraltar.*

Soviet /səυviət, sɒviət/ **Soviets**
1 ADJ **Soviet** is used to describe something that belonged or was related to the former Soviet Union, or to its people. ...*the Soviet bloc.*
2 N PL The **Soviets** were people who came from the former Soviet Union. *In 1957 the Soviets had put an astronaut into space.*
3 NC A **soviet** was an elected local, regional, or national council in the former Soviet Union. *Gorbachev and other leaders have talked about increasing the powers of the soviets.*

Soviet Union /səυviət juːniən/ See **Union of Soviet Socialist Republics.**

sow, sows, sowing, sowed, sown; pronounced /səυ/ when it is a verb and /saυ/ when it is a noun.
1 VO If you **sow** seeds or **sow** an area of land with seeds, you plant the seeds in the ground. *You can sow winter wheat in October... The land was cleared of weeds and sown with grass.*
2 VO If you **sow** an undesirable feeling among people, you cause them to have it; a literary use. *She attacked those who sow dismay and division in the party... The aim of the foreign powers was to sow discord.*
3 NC A **sow** is an adult female pig. *These sows are having about twenty-six piglets a year.*

sown /səυn/
Sown is the past participle of **sow.**

soya /sɔɪə/
NU **Soya** is the same as **soya beans.** ...*surpluses of crops such as wheat and soya. ...soya margarine. ...soya milk.*

soya bean, soya beans
NC **Soya beans** are a type of bean that can be eaten or used to make flour, oil, or soy sauce. *She was trying to cook some soya beans. ...one of the largest producers of soya bean oil in Brazil.*

soybean /sɔɪbiːn/ **soybeans**
NCorNU A **soybean** is the same as a **soya bean**; used in American English. *He also grows wheat and soybeans... He raises mostly soybean, wheat, and some sorghum.*

soy sauce /sɔɪ sɔːs/
NU **Soy sauce** is a dark brown liquid flavouring made from soya beans.

sozzled /sɒzld/
ADJ PRED Someone who is **sozzled** is very drunk; an old-fashioned, informal word. *He was sozzled when he arrived at the party.*

spa /spɑː/ **spas**
NC A **spa** is a place where water with minerals in it bubbles out of the ground. People drink the water or bathe in it to improve their health. *He was advised to immerse himself for many hours in the warm mineral waters of the spa. ...a spa town famous for its genteel atmosphere.*

space /speɪs/ **spaces, spacing, spaced**
1 NU **Space** is the area that is empty or available in a building or container. *He says that there is not enough space for all the troops... Belongings take up space. ...the luggage space at the back of the car.*
2 NC A **space** is a gap or empty place. *The door had spaces at the top and bottom. ...a big open space*

strewn with rubble... We spent half an hour looking
for a parking space... There is no official space for it
on the form.

3 N SING+of A **space** of time is a period of time. *He
should arrive in a very short space of time... It
happened three times in the space of five months.*

4 NU **Space** is the amount of a talk or piece of writing
that is available for a particular thing to be
discussed. *There is no space in this book to argue the
alternative viewpoint... I shall devote some space to
describing my own viewpoint.*

5 NU You can refer to the freedom which is made
available to someone in order to do something or
carry out an activity as **space**. *...the amount of
political space opposition groups are allowed.*

6 NU **Space** is also the area outside the Earth's
atmosphere. *This is the longest time any human being
has spent in space... The government said it would not
be increasing its funds for space research.*

7 VO If you **space** a series of things, you arrange them
so that they have gaps or periods of time between
them. *The lines were spaced well apart... I had to
space my enquiries carefully.*

space out PHRASAL VERB If you **space** things **out**, you
arrange them so that they have gaps or periods of
time between them. *These books should have large
print well spaced out on the page... Their tactics
appear to be to vary the nature of their attacks as
much as possible, and to space them out.*

space age

1 N SING The **space age** is the present period in the
history of the world, when travel in space has become
possible. *Since the dawn of the space age in 1957,
about 4,000 satellites have been put in orbit.*

2 ADJ ATTRIB You use **space-age** to describe something
which is very modern and makes you think of the
technology of the space age. *...a space-age kitchen.*

space capsule, space capsules

NC A **space capsule** is the part of a spacecraft in
which people travel in space and in which they return
to earth. *...a Soyuz space capsule bringing three
cosmonauts back to earth from orbit in space.*

spacecraft /speɪskrɑːft/; **spacecraft** is both the singular
and the plural form.

NC A **spacecraft** is a rocket or other vehicle that can
travel in space. *A Soviet spacecraft has begun
orbiting the planet Mars.*

spaced out

ADJ PRED Someone who is **spaced out** has taken drugs
that make them feel as if nothing around them is real;
an informal expression. *Most of them were spaced out
on drugs.*

Space Invaders

NU **Space Invaders** is a computer game in which
players use control buttons and levers to try to shoot
at and destroy spaceships that move and attack them
on a computer screen.

spaceman /speɪsmæn/ **spacemen**

NC A **spaceman** is a man who travels in space.
*Moscow radio said the two spacemen were feeling well
this morning.*

space probe, space probes

NC A **space probe** is a small spacecraft that is sent
into space in order to transmit information about what
space or other planets are like. *The American space
probe Magellan has begun its systematic mapping of
the planet Venus.*

spaceship /speɪsʃɪp/ **spaceships**

NC A **spaceship** is the same as a **spacecraft**. *...an
unmanned Soviet cargo spaceship.*

space shuttle, space shuttles

NC A **space shuttle** is a spacecraft that is designed to
travel into space and back to earth several times. *The
American space shuttle, Discovery, has been launched
from Cape Canaveral.*

space station, space stations

NC A **space station** is a spacecraft which is sent into
space and then goes round the earth, and which is
used as a base by people travelling in space or doing
research into space. *He had been on board the space
station for the last year.*

spacesuit /speɪssuːt/ **spacesuits**

NC A **spacesuit** is a special protective suit covering
the whole body that is worn by an astronaut.

spacing /speɪsɪŋ/

NU **Spacing** refers to the way that typing or printing is
arranged on a page, especially in relation to the
amount of space that is left between words or between
lines of printing and typing. *With its even spacing and
equal margins it was a work of art... The document
should be typed in double spacing.*

spacious /speɪʃəs/

ADJ A **spacious** building or vehicle is large and has
plenty of room in it. *...a spacious dining-room.*

spade /speɪd/ **spades**

1 NC A **spade** is a tool used for digging, with a flat
metal blade and a long handle. *...a scheme to share
tools like spades and forks.*

2 NU **Spades** is one of the four suits in a pack of
playing cards.

3 If you **call a spade a spade**, you speak frankly and
directly, often about an embarrassing or unpleasant
subject. *He has a readiness to speak out and call a
spade a spade.*

spadework /speɪdwɜːk/

NU **Spadework** is uninteresting work that has to be
done as preparation before you can start a project or
activity. *Writing this sort of article always involves a
certain amount of preliminary spadework.*

spaghetti /spəgeti/

NU **Spaghetti** is a type of pasta. It looks like long
pieces of string and is usually served with a sauce.

spaghetti western, spaghetti westerns

NC A **spaghetti western** is a film made in Europe by
an Italian director about life in the American Wild
West.

Spain /speɪn/

The **Kingdom of Spain** is a country in south-west
Europe. General Francisco Franco defeated the
Republican government in the Spanish Civil War of
1936 to 1939. He banned all opposition to his Falangist
Party and ruled until his death in 1975. King Juan
Carlos, Franco's chosen successor, initiated the
restoration of democracy and the first free elections
were held in 1977. Militant Basque separatist groups
(especially ETA) have posed a threat to public order
since the 1960s. Spain is a member of NATO and the
European Community. Felipe González Márquez, of
the Socialist Workers' Party (PSOE), became Prime
Minister in 1982. Tourism is an important industry.
Spain exports cars, machinery, and agricultural
products, including olive oil and wine. ♦ **Spaniard**
/spænjəd/ N **Spanish** /spænɪʃ/ ADJ,N PL
■ *per capita GNP:* US$7,740 ■ *religion:* Christianity
(mainly Roman Catholic) ■ *language:* Castilian
Spanish ■ *currency:* peseta ■ *capital:* Madrid
■ *population:* 39 million (1988) ■ *size:* 499,542 square
kilometres.

span /spæn/ **spans, spanning, spanned**

1 NC A **span** is a period of time. *...the forty-year span
from 1913 to 1953. ...in the short span that man has
been on earth.*

2 NC Your attention **span** or your concentration **span**
is the length of time you are able to concentrate on
something or be interested in it. *It has improved his
attention span... Like my concentration span, my
memory had shrunk to nothing.*

3 VO If something **spans** a period of time, it lasts
throughout that time. *At 79, Dame Flora can look
back at a career spanning more than half a century.*

4 NC The **span** of something is its total length,
especially when it is stretched out as far as possible.
*Some eagles have a wing span of one and a half
metres.*

5 VO A bridge that **spans** a river or valley stretches
right across it. *...a long lake spanned by a high,
arching iron bridge.*

spangle /spæŋgl/ **spangles**

NC **Spangles** are small pieces of metal or plastic
which sparkle brightly and are used to decorate
clothing or hair.

spangled /spæŋgld/

ADJ Something that is **spangled** is covered with small

sparkling objects. ...*spangled headdresses.* ...*the star-spangled night sky.*

spaniel /spænjəl/ **spaniels**
NC A **spaniel** is a type of dog with long drooping ears.

Spanish /spænɪʃ/
1 ADJ **Spanish** means belonging or relating to Spain. ...*the Spanish government.* ...*a Spanish port.*
2 NU **Spanish** is the main language spoken in Spain, and in many countries in South and Central America. *He speaks fluent Spanish.*
3 N PL The **Spanish** are the people who come from Spain. *The scheme was supported by the Spanish.*

spank /spæŋk/ **spanks, spanking, spanked**
VO If someone **spanks** a child, they punish it by hitting its bottom several times with their hand. ...*a spoilt brat whose father suddenly loses patience and wants to spank him.*

spanking /spæŋkɪŋ/ **spankings**
1 NC A **spanking** is a series of slaps that someone gives to a child with their hand, usually on its bottom, as a way of punishing it. *Andrea gave her son a sound spanking.*
2 ADJ ATTRIB You use **spanking** to describe something that is clean, bright, and in excellent condition; an informal use. *A coat of enamel paint will give your bath a spanking new look... The skins were in spanking condition.*
3 ADJ ATTRIB You also use **spanking** to describe something that is moving quickly; an informal use. *Despite its spanking pace, the ball was quite easy to return.*

spanner /spænə/ **spanners**
1 NC A **spanner** is a metal tool with a specially shaped end that you use for tightening a nut. ...*many jobs that used to be done by people with spanners are now the preserve of robots and lasers.*
2 If you say that someone or something **throws a spanner in the works** or if they **throw a spanner in** a situation, you mean that they stop an event or process from happening in the way planned by creating an obstacle or difficulty. *It's still possible that they could throw a spanner in the works at the last minute... This new list of demands is likely to throw a spanner in the peace process.*

spar /spɑː/ **spars, sparring, sparred**
1 V-RECIP or V If you **spar** with someone, you box using fairly gentle blows instead of hitting your opponent hard, either when you are training or when you want to test how quickly your opponent reacts. *Tyson was sparring with Greg Page when he was accidentally head-butted... He will start sparring next week.*
2 V-RECIP To **spar** with someone also means to argue with them, but not in an openly aggressive way. *The warring parties spar for power... She was invited to spar with William F. Buckley Jr. on his 'Firing Line' programme.* ◆ **sparring** NU ...*months of sparring between the two leaders over South Africa's future.* ...*his continual political sparring with Mikhail Gorbachev.*
3 NC A **spar** is a strong pole, especially one that a sail is attached to on a sailing ship. ...*sails rigged to rigid wooden spars.*

spare /speə/ **spares, sparing, spared**
1 ADJ You use **spare** to describe an extra object that is like the ones you are using, but that you do not need yet. *Keep a spare fuse handy by the fuse box... Take a spare shirt.*
2 NC You can refer to an extra object that you do not yet need as a **spare**. *There are some spares at the back if anyone wants more.*
3 ADJ You can also use **spare** to describe something that is not being used by anyone, and is therefore available for you to use. *We found a spare parking meter.*
4 VO If you **spare** something for a particular purpose, you make it available for that purpose. *More land is needed to grow food and less can be spared to graze cattle... I got to my feet, thanking him for sparing time to see me.*
5 VO When a person or place is not punished or not harmed by a danger, you can say that they **are spared**. *Thank God we were spared... The great cities of the Rhineland had not been spared.*
6 VOO If you **spare** someone an unpleasant experience, you prevent them from having it. *We telephoned, wishing to spare poor Charlotte two or three hours of suspense... At least I am spared the shame of the children knowing.*
● **Spare** is used in these phrases. ● If you have time or money **to spare**, you have some extra time or money which you do not need for anything in particular. *He often had money to spare nowadays... She caught her plane with a few minutes to spare.* ● If you **spare no expense** in doing something, you do it as well as possible, without trying to save money. *The Agency has spared no expense with the system for storage.*

spare part, spare parts
NC **Spare parts** are parts that you can buy separately to replace old or broken parts in a piece of equipment, usually parts that are designed to be easily removed or fitted. *The tractors are out of order and there are no spare parts to get them working again... The guarantee includes the cost of spare parts and labour.*

spare ribs
N PL **Spare ribs** are the ribs of a pig with most of the meat trimmed off which are served as a cut of meat. *The four had spare ribs for lunch today.*

spare room, spare rooms
NC A **spare room** is a bedroom which is kept especially for visitors to sleep in. *They can both sleep in the spare room.*

spare time
NU Your **spare time** is the time during which you do not have to work and you can do what you want. *I did a lot of drawing in my spare time.* ...*a spare-time occupation.*

spare tyre, spare tyres
1 NC A **spare tyre** is the same as a **spare wheel**. *Keep the spare tyre checked and maintained to its correct pressure.*
2 N SING If you describe someone as having a **spare tyre**, you mean that they have a bulging ring of fat round their waist; often used humorously.

spare wheel, spare wheels
NC A **spare wheel** is a complete wheel with a tyre already on it, which is kept in a vehicle in case one of the tyres is punctured. *Is the spare wheel in this car under the bonnet?*

sparing /speərɪŋ/
ADJ PRED If you are **sparing** with something, you use it or give it only in very small quantities. *She was sparing with heat and light.* ◆ **sparingly** ADV *Use hot water sparingly.*

spark /spɑːk/ **sparks, sparking, sparked**
1 NC A **spark** is a tiny, bright piece of burning material that flies up from a fire. *The fire sent smoke and sparks over the top of the fence.*
2 NC A **spark** is also a flash of light caused by electricity. *Sparks showered from the faulty left-hand engine.*
3 N SING+of A **spark** of feeling is a small but noticeable amount of it. *A faint spark of pleasure came into his eyes.*
4 VO If one thing **sparks** another, it causes it to start happening. *The trial might spark another round of demonstrations.*
spark off PHRASAL VERB If one thing **sparks off** another, it causes it to start happening. *This incident could spark off a new round of violence.*

sparking plug, sparking plugs
NC A **sparking plug** is the same as a **spark plug**.

sparkle /spɑːkl/ **sparkles, sparkling, sparkled**
1 V If something **sparkles**, it shines with a lot of small points of light. *They looked down to the sea, sparkling in the sun... The lawn was sparkling with frost.* ► Also NU *Her eyes had lost their sparkle.*
2 V Someone who **sparkles** shows a quality of liveliness, originality, or wit. *She sparkles so much, and has as much zest as a person half her age.*
3 NU **Sparkle** is a quality of liveliness, originality, or wit. *There was little sparkle in their performance.*
4 See also **sparkling**.

sparkler /spɑːklə/ **sparklers**
NC A **sparkler** is a small firework that you can hold alight in your hand. It looks like a piece of thick wire and burns with a lot of small, bright sparks. ...*Roman Candles giving out showers of coloured lights, screamers, sparklers and bangers.*

sparkling /spɑːklɪŋ/
1 ADJ **Sparkling** things shine brightly. ...*a sparkling necklace. ...sparkling eyes.*
2 ADJ You use **sparkling** to describe a person or performance that is very lively and entertaining. *Both of them were sparkling performers in the world cup.*

sparkling wine, sparkling wines
N MASS **Sparkling wine** is wine which is slightly fizzy and is sold in bottles where the cork is held in place with wire.

spark plug, spark plugs
NC A **spark plug** is a device in the engine of a motor vehicle, which produces electric sparks to ignite the fuel.

sparrow /spærəʊ/ **sparrows**
NC A **sparrow** is a very common small brown bird. *Studies have also found a seventy-five percent drop in the number of tree sparrows.*

sparse /spɑːs/
ADJ If something is **sparse**, there is little of it and it is spread out over an area. *The population was sparse. ...his sparse white hair. ...the sparse rainfall.*
♦ **sparsely** ADV ...*a sparsely populated region. ...a population spread sparsely across eleven islands.*

spartan /spɑːtn/
ADJ A **spartan** way of life is very simple with no luxuries. ...*the spartan lives of the islanders.*

spasm /spæzəm/ **spasms**
1 NCorNU A **spasm** is a sudden tightening of your muscles which you cannot control. *Spasms shook her lungs and chest... This may leave the muscle in spasm.*
2 N SING+of You can refer to an unpleasant feeling which lasts for a short time as a **spasm** of that feeling. ...*a spasm of anger.*

spasmodic /spæzmɒdɪk/
ADJ Something that is **spasmodic** happens for short periods of time at irregular intervals. *The survivors suffer spasmodic bouts of illness.* ♦ **spasmodically** ADV *The orchestra continued to play spasmodically.*

spastic /spæstɪk/ **spastics**
NC A **spastic** is a person who is born with a disability which makes it difficult for them to control their muscles. *He had six young children, one of them a spastic. ...the Spastics Society—a charity which helps children with cerebral palsy.*

spat /spæt/
Spat is the past tense and past participle of **spit**.

spate /speɪt/
N SING+of A **spate** of things is a lot of them happening or appearing within a short period of time. *The incident caused another spate of protests. ...a spate of new books.*

spatial /speɪʃl/
1 ADJ ATTRIB **Spatial** is used to describe things relating to size, area, or position; a formal word. *The first dimension to concentrate on is the spatial one. ...spatial and temporal variations.*
2 ADJ ATTRIB Your **spatial** ability is your ability to see and understand the relationships between shapes, spaces, and areas. *It has been suggested that men find it easier to develop their spatial abilities.*

spatter /spætə/ **spatters, spattering, spattered**
V-ERG If you **spatter** a liquid over a surface or if the liquid **spatters** the surface, it covers the surface with small drops. *He picked up his spoon so hurriedly that it spattered milk over his cardigan... Beer spattered the bedspread.* ♦ **spattered** ADJ *My goggles were spattered with mud.*

spatula /spætjʊlə/ **spatulas**
1 NC A **spatula** is a tool with a narrow handle and a wide flat blade, which is used in cooking. *Smooth the icing over the cake with a spatula.*
2 NC A **spatula** is also a long, flat, wooden instrument about the size of a pen, which is used by doctors. *The spatula is used when examining throats.*

spawn /spɔːn/ **spawns, spawning, spawned**
1 NU **Spawn** is a jelly-like substance containing the eggs of fish or frogs.
2 V When fish or frogs **spawn**, they lay eggs. *Most tuna are caught on their way north to spawn.*
3 VO To **spawn** something means to cause it to happen or be created; a literary use. *Poverty had spawned numerous religious movements. ...the electronic movement and the devices it has spawned.*

spay /speɪ/ **spays, spaying, spayed**
VO When a female animal, especially a cat or a dog, is **spayed**, it has its ovaries removed so that it cannot become pregnant. *All stray bitches are spayed before being found new homes.* ♦ **spaying** NU *Many people are against spaying and neutering.*

speak /spiːk/ **speaks, speaking, spoke, spoken**
1 V When you **speak**, you use your voice to say words. *He drove without speaking for a while... The man spoke with a strong Northern English accent.*
2 V+to or V+with When you **speak** to someone or **speak** with them, you have a conversation with them. *President Gorbachev spoke to journalists and delegates outside the debating chamber... He has already spoken with representatives of American industry.*
3 V+about or V+of If you **speak** about someone or something or **speak** of them, they are the subject of conversation when you are talking to other people. *She spoke about the effects of drugs on young people... The Prime Minister has spoken of Japan's commitment to create stability and prosperity in the Asian region.*
4 VO If you **speak** a foreign language, you know it and can use it. *They spoke fluent English.*
5 VA If you **speak** well or badly of someone, you say good or bad things about them. *The students spoke highly of their history lecturer.*
6 V+to When someone **speaks** to a group of people, they make a speech. *President Alfonsin plans to speak to Congress on the situation.* ♦ **speaking** NU *He had little experience of public speaking.*
7 See also **spoken**.
● **Speak** is used in these phrases. ● You use expressions such as **generally speaking** and **technically speaking** when you are defining the way that you are describing something. *America is still, generally speaking, the most technologically advanced... Roughly speaking, there are two possibilities.* ● You can say '**speaking as** a parent' or '**speaking as** a teacher', for example, to indicate that the opinion you are giving is based on your experience as a parent or as a teacher. *Speaking as a married woman, I consider it important to provide nursery schools for all children who need them.* ● You can say **speaking of** a thing that has just been mentioned as a way of introducing a new topic which has some connection with that thing. *If you'd like to know more about this, write to us at Science in Action. And speaking of writing to us, it's time to get your requests and questions in for the new series.* ● You say **so to speak** to indicate that what you are saying is not literally true, but is a colourful way of describing a situation. *They have been the big barrier to the opposition getting together and uniting, so to speak, against their common enemy.* ● **Nobody to speak of** or **nothing to speak of** means hardly anyone or anything, or only unimportant people or things. *'Did you find anything?'—'No, nothing to speak of.'* ● People who are not **on speaking terms** never speak to each other. *Griffiths says that he's no longer on speaking terms with his bosses.* ● If you **speak your mind** about something, you say exactly what you think. *This has not stopped her speaking her mind on some controversial issue.* ● If something **speaks for itself**, its meaning or qualities are obvious and do not need to be explained or pointed out. *The historians say simply that their report speaks for itself.*
speak for PHRASAL VERB If you **speak for** a group of people, you give their opinion on their behalf. *He said he was speaking for millions of people. ...a group which speaks for people who use the National Health Service.*

speak out PHRASAL VERB If you **speak out** in favour of something or against something, you say publicly that you think it is a good thing or a bad thing. *He spoke out against racial discrimination many times.*

speak up PHRASAL VERB 1 If you **speak up** about something, you say publicly what you believe, especially in support of a person or idea. *...a song urging women to speak up for their rights.* 2 If you ask someone to **speak up**, you are asking them to speak more loudly. *Could you please speak up! We can't hear you at the back.*

-speak /-spiːk/
SUFFIX **-speak** can be added to the name of a person, group, or organization in order to form a noun referring to the characteristic language that they use, especially to their use of particular words. *...the flourishing of a new language—Thatcher-speak... Euro-speak is also deliberately used by bureaucrats to hide problems.*

speaker /spiːkə/ **speakers**
1 NC You can refer to someone who is speaking as the **speaker**. *...the gap between the speaker and the listener.*
2 NC A **speaker** is also a person who makes a speech. *The chairman got up to introduce the speaker.*
3 NC or TITLE In parliamentary assemblies, the **Speaker** acts as chairperson and ensures that events proceed according to the constitution. *The Speaker refused to allow his question... Mr Speaker, I agree with almost every word that my honourable friend has put so ably in his question.*
4 NC+SUPP A **speaker** of a particular language is someone who can speak that language. *Some sounds are very difficult for French speakers of English. ...a long-time resident of Iran and fluent Farsi speaker.*
5 NC A **speaker** is also the piece of equipment, for example on a radio or hi-fi, through which the sound comes out. *The stereo effect works with only two speakers.*

spear /spɪə/ **spears, spearing, speared**
1 NC A **spear** is a weapon consisting of a long pole with a sharp point. *Many carried traditional spears, sticks, and shields.*
2 VO If you **spear** something, you push a pointed object into it. *Lally took her fork and speared an oyster from its shell.*

spearhead /spɪəhed/ **spearheads, spearheading, spearheaded**
VO To **spearhead** a campaign means to lead it. *Mr Tom Pendry is spearheading the parliamentary campaign against racism in football.*

spearmint /spɪəmɪnt/ **spearmints**
N U or NC **Spearmint** is a flavouring obtained from a plant. Sweets which have this flavouring are called **spearmints**.

spec /spek/ **specs;** an informal word.
1 N PL Someone's **specs** are their glasses. *I've been wearing specs since I was three.*
2 If you do something **on spec**, you do it hoping to get something that you want as a result, but without any certainty that you will get it. *They just turned up on spec.*

special /speʃl/
1 ADJ Something that is **special** is better or more important than other things of the same kind. *...china that was reserved for special occasions... Is there anything special you would like for dinner?... This year's parade was of special significance.*
2 ADJ **Special** also means different from normal. *We treat them as a special case... What's special about the new form of polymer plastic? ...a special ceremony marking the opening of a new session of the Russian congress.*
3 ADJ You can describe something that is of very high quality or something that you like or enjoy very much as **special**. *...the very delicate, very special French perfume. ...a special treat.*
4 ADJ ATTRIB You also use **special** to describe someone who is officially appointed or who has a particular function. *...the United Nations special envoy... He was a special adviser to Mrs Judith Hart at the Ministry.*
5 ADJ ATTRIB **Special** schools or institutions are for

people who have particular problems such as physical or mental handicaps. *...special schools for maladjusted children. ...special hospitals such as Broadmoor.*
6 ADJ ATTRIB You also use **special** to describe something that relates to one particular person, group, or place. *He spoke his own special variety of German... Hospital food seldom caters for the special needs of the aged.*
7 ADJ ATTRIB A **special** product, service, or performance is offered in addition to the normal ones, sometimes at reduced prices. *Some places do special offers in May... When we finish early there's a special bus. ...the chartering of special flights to fly illegal immigrants.*
8 NC A **special** is a product, programme or meal which is only available or shown at a certain time, or which is made for a special purpose. *Monday's special was chicken, Tuesday's lamb. ...a TV special.*

Special Branch
N PROP The **Special Branch** is the department of the British police that is concerned with political security and deals with problems such as terrorism, visits by foreign leaders, political refugees, and so on. *...members of the Special Branch. ...a maximum security check with the help of Special Branch.*

special delivery
N U **Special delivery** is a service offered by the Post Office by which, for an extra amount of money, letters or parcels are delivered at a time which is not a usual delivery time. *I'll have it sent down by special delivery.*

special effect, special effects
NC A **special effect** is something unusual in the pictures or in the sound track of a film that is achieved using special techniques. *The special effects are quite extraordinary.*

specialise /speʃəlaɪz/. See **specialize**.

specialism /speʃəlɪzəm/ **specialisms**
1 NC Someone's **specialism** is a particular subject or skill which they study and know a lot about. *He may get too committed to his specialism.*
2 NU **Specialism** in a particular subject is specialization in it. *...medical specialism.*

specialist /speʃəlɪst/ **specialists**
NC A **specialist** is a person who has a particular skill or knows a lot about a particular subject. *...an eye specialist... She is a specialist in Eastern European affairs. ...a specialist teacher of mathematics.*

speciality /speʃiælətɪ/ **specialities**
1 NC Someone's **speciality** is the kind of work they do best or the subject they know most about. *His medical speciality was tuberculosis... They enjoy talking about their own specialities.*
2 NC+SUPP A **speciality** of a place is something that is very well made there. *Chocolate gateau was a speciality of the Café de Rome.*

specialize /speʃəlaɪz/ **specializes, specializing, specialized;** also spelt **specialise.**
V+*in* If you **specialize** in something, you know a lot about it and concentrate a great deal of your time and resources on it, especially in your work or when you are studying or training. *Both men specialise in the affairs of Asia and the Pacific. ...a shop specializing in camping equipment.* ♦ **specialization** /speʃəlaɪzeɪʃn/
N U *...the increasing specialization of working life.*

specialized /speʃəlaɪzd/; also spelt **specialised.**
ADJ Someone or something that is **specialized** is trained or developed for a particular purpose. *...highly specialized staff. ...radar and specialised television systems.*

specially /speʃəlɪ/
1 ADV or SUBMOD If something has been done **specially** for a particular person or purpose, it has been done only for that person or purpose. *...free hotels run by the state specially for tourists... The rules were specially designed to protect travellers.*
2 SUBMOD You use **specially** with an adjective to emphasize a quality; an informal use. *...a pub where the beer was specially good.*

specialty /speʃltɪ/ **specialties**
NC A **specialty** is the same as a **speciality;** used in

American English. *His specialty is military health care. ...specialty food shops.*

species /spiːʃiːz/; **species** is both the singular and the plural form.
NC A **species** is a class of plants or animals whose members have the same main characteristics and are able to breed with each other. *There are two hundred and fifty species of shark.*

specific /spəsɪfɪk/ **specifics**
1 ADJ ATTRIB You use **specific** to emphasize that you are talking about a particular thing or subject. *Education should not be restricted to any one specific age group... On certain specific issues there may be changes of emphasis.*
2 ADJ If a description is **specific**, it is precise and exact. *It was a tooth, a tiger-shark tooth, to be more specific... Let me be more specific.*
3 ADJ Something that is **specific** to a particular thing is connected with that thing only. *This problem is not specific to football.*
4 N PL The **specifics** of a subject are its details. *Let us focus on the specifics of Bengal's life.*

specifically /spəsɪfɪkli/
1 ADV You use **specifically** to emphasize that a subject is being considered separately from other subjects. *It is Christianity with which we are specifically concerned.*
2 ADV You also use **specifically** to indicate that you are stating or describing something precisely. *...the peasant rising in the West of France, in Brittany specifically.*
3 SUBMOD **Specifically** can also be used to emphasize a particular way of describing something, often when you are contrasting this with other ways of describing it. *I don't think it's a specifically medical problem... He could be described as radical more than specifically socialist.*

specification /spɛsɪfɪkeɪʃn/ **specifications**
NC A **specification** is a requirement which is clearly stated, for example about the necessary features in the design of something. *...ships built to merchant ship specifications.*

specific gravity, specific gravities
NC The **specific gravity** of a substance is the ratio of the density of the substance to the density of water; a technical term in physics. *The specific gravity is 0.84.*

specify /spɛsɪfaɪ/ **specifies, specifying, specified**
V O or V-REPORT If you **specify** something, you state it precisely. *The report specified seven areas where the Government had a responsibility... The landlord can specify that rent should be paid in cash.*

specimen /spɛsəmən/ **specimens**
NC A **specimen** of something is an example or small amount of it which gives an idea of the whole. *The fins of fossil specimens are carefully dissected. ...an authentic specimen of the work of Carl André.*

specious /spiːʃəs/
ADJ Something that is **specious** appears to be true or to exist, but is in fact false or an illusion; a formal word. *Ralph had been deceived by the specious appearance of depth in a beach pool... The argument is a specious one.*

speck /spɛk/ **specks**
NC A **speck** is a very small stain, mark, or amount of something. *There was a speck of blood on his collar. ...a tiny speck of dust.*

speckled /spɛkld/
ADJ A **speckled** object or animal is covered with small marks or spots. *...a speckled sweater... It has black-and-white speckled feathers on its back.*

spectacle /spɛktəkl/ **spectacles**
1 N PL Someone's **spectacles** are their glasses; a formal use. *She carried a spare pair of spectacles in her pocket.*
2 NC A **spectacle** is a strange or interesting sight or scene. *She stood at the head of the stairs and surveyed the spectacle.*
3 NC A **spectacle** is also an impressive event or performance. *...a seven-hour spectacle consisting of songs, comedy acts, and acrobatics.*

spectacular /spɛktækjʊlə/ **spectaculars**
1 ADJ Something that is **spectacular** is very

impressive or noticeable. *The most spectacular of these extraordinary fossils can be seen in the museum... It was a spectacular jump. ...a spectacular rise in house prices.*
2 NC+SUPP A **spectacular** is a grand and impressive show or performance. *They are to hold a fashion spectacular on Friday with 100 models.*

spectator /spɛkteɪtə/ **spectators**
NC A **spectator** is a person who watches something, especially a sporting event. *The match began with few spectators at the ground... More than 2,000 spectators have gathered to watch the launch of the shuttle.*

spectator sport, spectator sports
NC A **spectator sport** is a sport that is very enjoyable to watch and that generally interests people as spectators more than as participants. *The game is doomed as a spectator sport unless violent behaviour is eradicated... These horse trials have become one of the most attractive spectator sports in the world.*

spectra /spɛktrə/
Spectra is a plural of **spectrum**.

spectre /spɛktə/ **spectres**; a literary word, spelt **specter** in American English.
1 NC A **spectre** is a ghost.
2 N SING+of You can also refer to a frightening image or idea as a **spectre**. *...the looming spectre of recession... That's also raised the spectre in the minds of US citizens of huge US casualties.*

spectrum /spɛktrəm/
1 N SING The **spectrum** is the range of different colours produced when light passes through a prism or through a drop of water. *Light of the different colours of the spectrum travels in waves of different frequencies.*
2 N SING+SUPP **Spectrum** is also used to refer to a range of a particular type of thing. *We have experienced together the whole spectrum of emotion... The plan also addresses a wide spectrum of the Middle East issues... They have support at both ends of the political spectrum.*

speculate /spɛkjʊleɪt/ **speculates, speculating, speculated**
1 V+about, V+on, or V-REPORT If you **speculate** about something, you guess about its nature or identity, or about what might happen. *He refused to speculate about the contents of the letter. ...long feature articles speculating on the political future of Rajiv Gandhi's widow Sonia... Several papers speculate the bomb may have been the work of animal rights activists... They speculated that the death toll would be even higher.*
♦ **speculation** /spɛkjʊleɪʃn/ NU *The papers are full of speculation about who is likely to be the next prime minister.*
2 V+on or V+in When people **speculate** financially, they buy property or shares in the hope of being able to sell them at a profit. *...fraudulent loans to a restaurant owner who used the money to speculate on the stock market... The company speculated heavily in real estate.* ♦ **speculation** NU *He was tried for currency speculation and ordered out of the country.*

speculative /spɛkjʊlətɪv/
1 ADJ **Speculative** statements are based on guesses rather than knowledge. *Budgets and profit forecasts were equally speculative... Many newspaper reports were speculative or inaccurate.*
2 ADJ **Speculative** financial deals involve buying or investing in something when it is cheap in the belief that it will soon become more valuable and therefore can be sold at a profit. *...a surge in speculative currency dealing.*

speculator /spɛkjʊleɪtə/ **speculators**
NC A **speculator** is a person who speculates financially. *...unscrupulous speculators buying up food stocks. ...foreign currency speculators.*

sped /spɛd/
Sped is a past tense and past participle of **speed**.

speech /spiːtʃ/ **speeches**
1 NU **Speech** is the ability to speak or the act of speaking. *She was so shocked that she lost her powers of speech.*
2 NU **Speech** is also spoken language.

...*communication through writing and speech... In ordinary speech we often shorten the word 'cannot' to 'can't'.*
3 NC A **speech** is a formal talk given to an audience. *He made a speech vigorously attacking those who were slowing the pace of reform.*
4 NC A **speech** is also a group of lines spoken by a character in a play. *She recited a speech from 'As You Like It'.*
5 NU+SUPP The **speech** of a particular place is the language or dialect spoken there. *He can mimic Cockney speech quite well.*

speechless /spiːtʃləs/
ADJ If you are **speechless**, you are temporarily unable to speak, because something has shocked or affected you very deeply. *They were speechless with rage... He had been so exhilarated to be home he'd been speechless.*

speech therapist, speech therapists
NC A **speech therapist** is a person whose job is to help people to overcome speech and language problems.

speech therapy
NU **Speech therapy** is the treatment of people who have speech and language problems. *He is also having speech therapy to regain his voice.*

speed /spiːd/ **speeds, speeding, sped**. For the phrasal verb, the past tense and past participle is **speeded**.
1 NU or NC The **speed** of something is the rate at which it moves or travels. *I drove at great speed to West Bank. ...capable of reaching speeds of over 110kph.*
2 NU or NC **Speed** is also the rate at which something happens or is done. *None of us grows at the same speed... Computer processing speeds have increased astronomically.*
3 NU **Speed** is very fast movement. *The car is travelling at speed.*
4 VA To **speed** somewhere means to move or travel there quickly. *They sped along Main Street towards the highway.*
5 V A motorist who **is speeding** is driving a vehicle faster than the legal speed limit. *The pile up was made worse by drivers speeding.* ◆ **speeding** NU *His driver's licence was suspended for speeding. ...in court on a speeding charge.*
speed up PHRASAL VERB When something **speeds up**, it moves, happens, or is done more quickly. *They're way ahead of us—speed up!... Warmth speeds up chemical reactions.*

speedboat /spiːdbəʊt/ **speedboats**
NC A **speedboat** is a boat that is propelled by an engine and can travel at high speed. *They had crossed to the southern shore in speedboats.*

speed limit, speed limits
NC The **speed limit** on a road is the maximum speed at which you can legally drive on it. *The road has a speed limit of sixty miles per hour.*

speedometer /spiːdɒmɪtə/ **speedometers**
NC A **speedometer** is an instrument in a vehicle which shows how fast the vehicle is moving. *The train's speed appears on the speedometer.*

speed trap, speed traps
NC A **speed trap** is a section of a road along which the police are checking whether vehicles are going faster than the speed limit allows. *The government is being urged to introduce more effective speed traps, in an effort to reduce the number of crashes on motorways.*

speedway /spiːdweɪ/
NU **Speedway** is the sport of racing lightweight motorcycles on special tracks. *...one of the men responsible for the development of speedway in Britain... Per Johnson is the new world speedway champion.*

speedy /spiːdi/
ADJ A **speedy** action happens or is done very quickly. *A speedy settlement of the strike is essential.*
◆ **speedily** ADV *Such doubts were now speedily removed.*

spell /spel/ **spells, spelling, spelled** or **spelt**
1 VO When you **spell** a word, you write or speak each letter in the word in the correct order. *'Qatar'—'How do you spell that?'—'Q-A-T-A-R'... Ninety per cent of the words were spelt wrong.* ● See also **spelling**.

2 VC If something **spells** a particular result, it would cause this. *Nuclear conflict would spell the end of life as we know it... Any discussion of politics would spell disaster.*
3 NC A **spell** of an activity or type of weather is a short period of it. *She had a spell as editor. ...a spell of good summer weather.*
4 NC In children's stories, a **spell** is a sequence of words used to perform magic or to create a situation in which events are controlled by a magical power. *The spell of the wicked fairy was broken.*
5 If you are **under** someone's **spell**, you are so fascinated by them that you are prepared to believe everything they say or to do anything they ask. *For a few years after Tito's death, Yugoslavs were still under his spell... He immediately fell to some extent under Hirohito's spell.*
spell out PHRASAL VERB If you **spell** something **out**, you explain it in detail and as clearly as possible. *Let me try and spell out what I mean by that.*

spellbinding /spelbaɪndɪŋ/
ADJ If you find something **spellbinding**, you find it so fascinating that you cannot think about anything else. *It was a spellbinding experience... I found his description of life in Ancient Rome absolutely spellbinding.*

spellbound /spelbaʊnd/
ADJ If you are **spellbound**, you are so fascinated by something that you cannot think about anything else. *We were all spellbound as we listened to her.*

spelling /spelɪŋ/ **spellings**
1 NC The **spelling** of a word is the correct sequence of letters in it. *Please note the spelling of the Afghan official's name... That piece of writing was full of spelling mistakes.*
2 NU **Spelling** is the ability to spell words in the correct way, or the way that words are spelt. *A quarter of all students admitted they had difficulty with spelling... In this language the pronunciation has changed over the centuries but the spelling has not.*

spelt /spelt/
Spelt is a past tense and past participle of **spell**.

spend /spend/ **spends, spending, spent**
1 VO When you **spend** money, you use it to pay for things. *We always spend a lot of money on parties... A report estimated that in 1986 China spent $12,000 million on its military forces... The buildings need a lot of money spent on them.*
2 VOA or VO+ING If you **spend** a period of time somewhere, you are there during that time. If you **spend** a period of time doing something, you are doing it during that time. *He spent most of his time in the library... She woke early, meaning to spend all day writing.*
3 See also **spending, spent**.

spender /spendə/ **spenders**
NC+SUPP You use **spender** to refer to someone who spends money, especially when you want to say how much they spend. For example, a high **spender** spends a lot of money. *It is the Labour authorities that are the high spenders... Experts are being called in to help new generation of young spenders cope with debt.*

spending /spendɪŋ/
NU **Spending** refers to the amount of money a government or other organization uses for buying or paying for things. *Departments must reduce their spending by £35 million before July 1st... He wants to introduce budget spending cuts and impose free market structures.*

spending money
NU **Spending money** is money that you have or that you are given to spend on personal things for pleasure, for example when you are on holiday. *They indulged all three children with plentiful spending money.*

spendthrift /spendθrɪft/ **spendthrifts**
NC A **spendthrift** is a person who spends money in a wasteful or extravagant way. *What a spendthrift! All the money he makes goes on new cars... This confirmed all his worst fears about her spendthrift habits.*

spent /spent/
1 **Spent** is a past tense and past participle of **spend**.

2 ADJ **Spent** is used to describe things that have already been used and cannot be used again. ...*spent matches.*

sperm /spɜːm/ **sperms.** The plural form can be either **sperms** or **sperm.**

NC A **sperm** is a cell produced in the sex organs of a male animal which can enter a female animal's egg and fertilize it. A sperm is usually in a liquid with lots of other sperm. *There was a risk that radiation levels at the plant might affect mens' sperm.*

spermatozoon /spɜːmətəzəʊɒn/ **spermatozoa** /spɜːmətəzəʊə/

NC A **spermatozoon** is a sperm; a technical term in biology.

sperm whale, sperm whales

NC A **sperm whale** is a large whale which has a cavity in its head that contains a large amount of oil. ...*the now highly endangered sperm whales.*

spew /spjuː/ **spews, spewing, spewed**

1 V-ERG When things **spew** from a place or if they **are spewed** from it, they come out in large quantities; a literary use. *It seems volcanic lava has spewed over the entire planet... Factories spewed dense dirty smoke... Buses go past spewing out smoke and fumes.*

2 V or V+*up* If someone **spews** or **spews up**, they vomit; an informal use.

sphere /sfɪə/ **spheres**

1 NC A **sphere** is a round three-dimensional shape like a ball. *A rotating sphere looks very much like a stationary sphere. ...a hollow ceramic sphere.*

2 NC+SUPP A **sphere** of activity or interest is a particular area of it. *He works in the sphere of race relations. ...their involvement in the medical sphere.*

3 NC+SUPP A **sphere** can also be a group of people who are similar in social status or who have the same interests. *She's used to mixing in an altogether different sphere. ...the academic sphere.*

4 A country's **sphere of influence** is an area of the world where it is the dominant power and where it can affect events and development. ...*Germany's efforts to create a sphere of influence in northern Yugoslavia. ...countries that wanted to avoid joining either the Western or Soviet sphere of influence.*

spherical /sfɛrɪkl/

ADJ Something that is **spherical** is shaped like a sphere. ...*serving themselves generous slices of a great spherical plum pudding.*

sphinx /sfɪŋks/ **sphinxes**

1 N PROP In Greek mythology, the **Sphinx** is a monster with a person's head and a lion's body famous for setting a riddle which the Greek hero Oedipus finally solved. There is a huge statue of the Sphinx near the pyramids in Egypt which was built by the ancient Egyptians.

2 NC You can refer to a person who is mysterious or puzzling as a **sphinx.** *She gave the radiant but ambiguous smile of an ecstatic sphinx... It's not for nothing that he's been called the Sphinx of French politics.*

spice /spaɪs/ **spices, spicing, spiced**

1 NCorNU **Spice** is a powder used to flavour food, for example pepper or ginger. It is made from seeds, bark, or roots. *The buns are flavoured with spices besides being baked.*

2 VO When you **spice** food, you add spice to it. *Take the peas and butter and spice them with nutmeg.*

♦ **spiced** ADJ *The soup was heavily spiced.*

3 VOA If you **spice** something that you do or say, you add excitement or liveliness to it. *He has recently been spicing his speeches with risqué political jokes.*

4 NU You can refer to something which makes an event or situation more lively or interesting as **spice.** *His tantrums and antics often provide the only spice there is at these assemblies.*

spice up PHRASAL VERB If you **spice up** something that you do or say, you add excitement or liveliness to it. *He thinks this theme was only used to spice up a standard cops and robbers film.*

spick-and-span /spɪknspæn/

ADJ PRED A place that is **spick-and-span** is very clean and tidy; an informal expression. *I must make everything spick-and-span before they arrive.*

spicy /spaɪsi/

ADJ **Spicy** food is strongly flavoured with spices. ...*a spicy sauce. ...a spicy Mexican meal with jalapenyo peppers.*

spider /spaɪdə/ **spiders**

NC A **spider** is a small creature with eight legs. Most spiders make webs. *Without the work of spiders, the damage done to crops by insects would be far worse than it is... 62% of men would not kill a spider in the bath—they would scoop it up and put it outside.*

spidery /spaɪdəri/

ADJ ATTRIB **Spidery** handwriting consists of thin, angular lines and is hard to read. ...*a folded sheet of paper with faded spidery writing that he could not read.*

spiel /ʃpiːl/

N SING A **spiel** is a speech that someone makes, usually one that they have made many times before and often one in which they try to persuade you to do something or buy something; used in informal English, showing disapproval. *Has he delivered his spiel yet?... I know that spiel. I've heard it often.*

spike /spaɪk/ **spikes**

1 NC A **spike** is a long piece of metal with a sharp point. ...*a wall topped with spikes.*

2 NC Any long, pointed object can be referred to as a **spike.** *The plant bears spikes of greenish flowers.*

spiked /spaɪkt/

ADJ **Spiked** things have spikes or a spike on them. ...*a spiked fence. ...spiked shoes.*

spiky /spaɪki/

ADJ ATTRIB Something that is **spiky** has sharp points. ...*a tiny man with spiky hair... The shrub has spiky green leaves.*

spill /spɪl/ **spills, spilling, spilled** or **spilt**

1 V-ERG If you **spill** a liquid, or if it **spills**, it accidentally flows over the edge of its container. *She carried the bucket without spilling a drop... One thousand tons of crude oil were spilt yesterday after a tanker collided with a trawler... Make sure the water doesn't spill over the floor.*

2 V A If people or things **spill** out of a place, they come out in large numbers. *Crowds started spilling out of bars.*

spill over PHRASAL VERB **1** If something in one place or situation **spills over** into another, it begins to happen or have an effect in the other place or situation. *The fighting spilled over into surrounding areas... Moral issues frequently spill over into politics.* **2** If one feeling or situation **spills over** into another, more serious one, the first feeling or situation causes the second one to exist. *The bitter rivalry in El Salvador's election campaign is already spilling over into violence. ...trying to prevent the war of words in the Gulf spilling over into armed conflict.*

spillage /spɪlɪdʒ/ **spillages**

NCorNU A **spillage** happens when a substance such as crude oil escapes from its container; also used to refer to the substance that escapes. *As a result of the oil spillage, southern Dutch beaches were fouled with oil and thousands of sea birds died... Water authorities are trying to prevent spillage spreading by using booms—huge floating sponges—to soak up the fuel.*

spilt /spɪlt/

Spilt is a past tense and past participle form of **spill.**

spin /spɪn/ **spins, spinning, spun**

1 V-ERG If something **spins** or if you **spin** it, it turns quickly around a central point. *The football went spinning into the canal... The ball spins very fast... He spun the chair round to face the desk.*

2 V If your head **is spinning**, you feel dizzy or confused. *His head was spinning from wine and liqueurs.*

3 V or VO When people **spin**, they make thread by twisting together pieces of fibre using a device or machine. *My mother taught me to spin... His wife was spinning wool.*

4 N SING If you put a certain **spin** on an event or situation, you interpret it and try to publicize it in a particular way; an informal use. *The White House is putting its own spin on public opinion polls. ...the optimistic spin he is putting on his visit.*

5 If something **spins out of control**, the people who should be able to control it are suddenly not able to do so, and the situation becomes dangerous or damaging. *The missile spun out of control and blew up four seconds after lift-off... Li Peng painted an alarming picture of an economy spinning out of control.*
spin out PHRASAL VERB If you **spin** something **out**, you make it last longer than it otherwise would. *I might be able to spin my talk out to three-quarters of an hour.*

spina bifida /spaɪnə bɪfɪdə/
NU **Spina bifida** is a condition of the spine that some people are born with. It often causes paralysis. *...victims of spina bifida.*

spinach /spɪnɪtʃ, spɪnɪdʒ/
NU **Spinach** is a vegetable with large green leaves that are often chopped into very small pieces and cooked. *Those are eggs Florentine—poached eggs on spinach.*

spinal /spaɪnl/
ADJ ATTRIB **Spinal** means relating to your spine. *...a spinal injury.*

spinal column, spinal columns
NC Your **spinal column** is your spine; a technical expression. *Primary brain cancers actually start in the brain itself, or in the spinal column.*

spinal cord, spinal cords
NC Your **spinal cord** is a bundle of nerves inside your spine which connects your brain to nerves in all parts of your body. *Meningitis, a viral disease which attacks the brain and spinal cord, can be fatal if not treated early.*

spindle /spɪndl/ **spindles**
1 NC A **spindle** is a rod in a machine, around which another part of the machine turns. *The magnetic fields pull and push the spindle of the motor round.*
2 NC A **spindle** is also a pointed rod which you use when you are spinning wool by hand. You twist the wool round the spindle and form it into a long thread.

spindly /spɪndli/
ADJ Something that is **spindly** is long, thin, and weak. *...spindly legs... The plant itself goes all thin and spindly.*

spin doctor, spin doctors
NC A **spin doctor** is someone who is skilled in public relations and who advises political parties on how to present their policies favourably; an informal expression. *Party spin doctors later argued that the coolness of the reception was not really due to hostility to the property tax.*

spin drier, spin driers; also spelt **spin dryer.**
NC A **spin drier** is a machine that gets the water out of washing by spinning it. *Try to get a spin drier, which leaves clothes damp-dry.*

spin-dry, spin-dries, spin-drying, spin-dried
VO When you **spin-dry** washing, you get the water out of it using a spin drier or a washing machine. *You can spin-dry this jumper and it'll keep its shape.*

spine /spaɪn/
1 NC Your **spine** is the row of bones down your back. *He is in a stable condition following lengthy surgery to remove a bullet from his spine.*
2 NC **Spines** are long, sharp points on an animal's body or on a plant. *...a cactus with red spines.*

spineless /spaɪnləs/
ADJ If you say that someone is **spineless**, you mean that they are cowardly. *He also described the Prime Minister as spineless.*

spinning wheel, spinning wheels
NC A **spinning wheel** is a wooden spinning machine used in people's homes, mainly in former times. It has a wheel which makes the spindle turn round. *...the whirr of the spinning wheel.*

spin-off, spin-offs
1 NC A **spin-off** is something useful that happens unexpectedly as a result of activities that were designed to achieve something else. *The Fund is essentially a spin-off of the 'Peace Forum' held in Moscow last February... Commercial spin-offs from this sort of research are only a few years away.*
2 NC A **spin-off** is also a book, film, or television series that is derived from a similar book, film or television series that has been very successful. *She appeared in the Colbys, a spin-off from Dynasty.*

spinster /spɪnstə/ **spinsters**
NC A **spinster** is a woman who has never married; an old-fashioned word. *A seventy-five year old spinster was burgled and assaulted by two boys aged no more than thirteen.*

spiny /spaɪni/
ADJ A **spiny** animal or plant is covered with long, sharp points. *...the spiny ant-eater. ...a spiny shrub. ...creatures with spiny skins.*

spiral /spaɪərəl/ **spirals, spiralling, spiralled;** spelt **spiraling, spiraled** in American English.
1 NC A **spiral** is a curved shape which winds round and round, with each curve above or outside the previous one. *The hole is shaped like a clockwise spiral... We know that our galaxy, the Milky Way, is a spiral galaxy.* ▶ Also ADJ ATTRIB *...a spiral staircase.*
2 VA If something **spirals**, it moves up or down in a spiral curve. *A small bird shot up, spiralling into the sky.*
3 V If an amount or level **spirals**, it rises quickly. *Military budgets had continued to spiral.* ◆ **spiralling** ADJ ATTRIB *...a series of drastic measures to try to curb spiralling inflation.*
4 If an amount or level **spirals downwards**, it falls quickly. *Costs started to spiral downwards.*
5 N SING+SUPP If you say that there is a **spiral** of something, you mean that it is increasing and it would be difficult to stop it. *What is frightening is that the spiral of death and injury is likely to continue. ...the spiral of poverty and environmental decline.*

spire /spaɪə/ **spires**
NC The **spire** of a church is a tall cone-shaped structure on top of a tower. *Churches are often built on high ground, with their spires visible for miles around.*

spirit /spɪrɪt/ **spirits, spiriting, spirited**
1 N SING Your **spirit** is the part of you that is not physical and that is connected with your deepest thoughts and feelings. *Fulfilment must be sought through the spirit, not the body or the mind.*
2 NC The **spirit** of a dead person is a non-physical part of them that is believed to remain alive after their death. *If they get good crops, it means the ancestral spirits approve.*
3 NC A **spirit** is also a supernatural being. *The charm is worn to ward off evil spirits.*
4 NU **Spirit** is enthusiasm, energy, and self-confidence. *...a performance full of spirit and originality.*
5 N SING+SUPP The **spirit** in which you do something is the attitude that you show when you are doing it. *He made the proposal in a spirit of rebellion... It's been quite evident that the spirit of compromise is just not there.*
6 N PL You can refer to your **spirits** when saying how happy or unhappy you are. For example, if your **spirits** are high, you are happy. *The children lifted my spirits with their laughter.* ● If you are **in high spirits** or **in good spirits**, you are happy. *The team was in high spirits after beating Indianapolis the night before... She was in remarkably good spirits given the circumstances.*
7 N SING The **spirit** of a law or an agreement is the way that it was intended to be interpreted or applied. *I think we'd be breaking the spirit of the agreement if we went ahead.*
8 N PL **Spirits** are strong alcoholic drinks such as whisky and gin. *Spirits (whisky, gin and vodka, for instance) are not advertised on British television.*
9 VOA If you **spirit** someone or something out of or into a place, you get them out or in quickly and secretly. *Somehow the Action Service had spirited him across the frontier.*
10 If you **enter into the spirit** of an event, you take part in it in an enthusiastic way. *Mark Laity joined one of the army units in Saudi Arabia to find out how they were entering into the spirit of Christmas.*

spirited /spɪrɪtɪd/
ADJ A **spirited** action shows energy and courage. *Despite spirited resistance by Republican forces, the town fell to the Nationalists.*

spirit level, spirit levels
NC A **spirit level** is a device for testing a surface to see if it is level. It consists of a piece of wood or metal containing a tube of liquid with a bubble of air in it. When the bubble is in the middle of the tube, the surface that the spirit level is on is level. *Conventional spirit levels measure both vertical and horizontal surfaces.*

spiritual /spɪrɪtʃuəl/
1 ADJ **Spiritual** means relating to people's deepest thoughts and beliefs, rather than to their bodies and physical surroundings. *...people's pursuit of material ends to the neglect of their spiritual needs.*
♦ **spiritually** ADV *...a spiritually sick society.*
♦ **spirituality** /spɪrɪtʃuælɪti/ NU *...the decline of spirituality in our time.*
2 ADJ **Spiritual** also means relating to people's religious beliefs. *The Tibetan spiritual leader, the Dalai Lama, has called for demonstrations against the Chinese to continue.*

spiritualism /spɪrɪtʃulɪzəm/
NU **Spiritualism** is the belief that people who are alive can communicate with the spirits of people who are dead, and the practice of attempting to do this. *He decided that spiritualism might have something to be said for it.*

spiritualist /spɪrɪtʃulɪst/ **spiritualists**
NC A **spiritualist** is someone who believes that people who are alive can communicate with the spirits of people who are dead, and who attempts to do this. *The same view is taken by modern spiritualists... My mother's a spiritualist.*

spit /spɪt/ **spits, spitting, spat** The form **spit** is used for the past tense of the verb in American English.
1 NU **Spit** is the watery liquid produced in your mouth. *...a big gob of spit.*
2 V When people **spit**, they force an amount of spit out of their mouth. *The driver spat contemptuously.*
3 VOA If you **spit** liquid or food somewhere, you force a small amount of it out of your mouth. *If I don't like it I can always spit it out.*
4 NC A **spit** is a rod which is pushed through a piece of meat so that it can be hung over an open fire and cooked. *It's traditional in Italy and Greece to roast the lamb on a spit.*
5 If someone is **the spitting image of** another person, they look very like that other person. *She was the spitting image of his mother.*

spite /spaɪt/
NU **Spite** is the desire to hurt or upset someone. *He wrote that review out of pure spite.*
● **Spite** is used in these phrases. ● If you do something nasty **to spite** someone, you do it deliberately in order to hurt, upset, or damage them. *They are being controversial to spite us.* ● You use **in spite of** to introduce information which makes your previous or next statement seem surprising. *The morning air was still clear and fresh, in spite of the traffic... Relations between the two countries are improving of spite of a number of recent disputes.* ● If you do something **in spite of** yourself, you do it although you did not really intend to or expect to. *Jane became edgy in spite of herself.*

spiteful /spaɪtfl/
ADJ Someone who is **spiteful** does nasty things to people they dislike. *...a spiteful act of revenge... She is spiteful, quarrelsome and dishonest.*

spittle /spɪtl/
NU **Spittle** is the watery liquid produced in your mouth; an old-fashioned word. *The dog left a trail of spittle on my trousers.*

splash /splæʃ/ **splashes, splashing, splashed**
1 VOorVA If you **splash** around in water, you disturb the water in a violent and noisy way, so that it flies up. *They proceeded to hurl themselves about, splashing everybody within sight... Ralph started to run, splashing through the shallow water.*
2 V-ERGAorVO If a liquid **splashes** on something, it scatters in a lot of small drops over it. *Drenching spray splashed over the deck... He stopped at a fountain to splash water over his face... They flinched as the cold rain splashed them.*

3 NC A **splash** is the sound made when something hits water. *She disappeared into the water with a splash.*
4 NC A **splash** of a liquid is a small quantity of it that has been spilt on something. *He wiped away the splash of gasoline on the near fender.*
5 NC A **splash** of colour is an area of a bright colour. *A large bouquet of tulips made a brilliant splash of yellow on the table.*

splash out PHRASAL VERB If you **splash out** on a luxury, you buy it even though it costs a lot of money; an informal expression. *We splashed out on a colour television.*

splashdown /splæʃdaʊn/ **splashdowns**
NC A **splashdown** is the landing of a spacecraft in the sea after a flight. *...only two months after the Apollo 11 splashdown.*

splatter /splætə/ **splatters, splattering, splattered**
V-ERGAorVO If a thick wet substance is **splattered** on something or **splatters** it, the substance is splashed or thrown over it. *Food was splattered all over the kitchen walls... That tomato juice splattering all over everything looked like blood... Another egg splattered the windscreen of her open Land Rover.*

splay /spleɪ/ **splays, splaying, splayed**
V-ERGA If two or more things **splay** out or **are splayed** out, their ends are spread out away from each other. *The brush's bristles were beginning to splay out. ...with his legs splayed out. ...her hands so elegant that she flaunted them, holding them against her cheek and splaying them on her hips.*

spleen /spliːn/ **spleens**
1 NC Your **spleen** is an organ near your stomach. It controls the quality of the blood. *It broke a number of ribs and ruptured her spleen.*
2 NU **Spleen** is violent and spiteful anger; a literary use. *In an unusual burst of spleen, Rob wrote me a furious letter... He had to vent his spleen on someone.*

splendid /splɛndɪd/; an old-fashioned word.
1 ADJ Something that is **splendid** is excellent. *I think it's a splendid idea.* ♦ **splendidly** ADV *She was caring for him splendidly.*
2 ADJ A **splendid** building or work of art is magnificent and impressive. *In the middle of Hull stands a splendid Victorian building.* ♦ **splendidly** ADV *...a splendidly furnished room.*

splendour /splɛndə/ **splendours**; spelt **splendor** in American English.
1 NU The **splendour** of something is its magnificent and impressive appearance. *...the splendour of Hyde Park Hotel... The room was decorated with great splendour.*
2 N PL The **splendours** of something are its beautiful and impressive features. *...the Elizabethan splendours of Watermouth Hall.*

splice /splaɪs/ **splices, splicing, spliced**
1 VO If you **splice** two pieces of rope, film, or tape together, you join them together neatly at the ends so that they make one long continuous piece. *The man who had cut my cord tried to splice the severed ends.*
2 When two people **get spliced**, they get married; an old-fashioned, informal expression, often used humorously. *John and Mary are getting spliced on Saturday.*

splint /splɪnt/ **splints**
NC A **splint** is a long piece of wood or metal fastened to a broken arm or leg to keep it still. *A doctor even gave him treatment, providing him with a makeshift splint for his broken arm.*

splinter /splɪntə/ **splinters, splintering, splintered**
1 NC A **splinter** is a very thin, sharp piece of wood or glass which has broken off from a larger piece. *...splinters of coloured glass... Sue was worried about splinters in her bare feet.*
2 V-ERG If something **splinters** or someone **splinters** it, it breaks into thin, sharp pieces. *When feeding dogs, avoid chicken, rabbit or fish bones, which can splinter... This wood needs to be splintered into kindling for the fire.*

splinter group, splinter groups
NC A **splinter group** is a group of people who decide to break away from a larger group and form a separate organization of their own because they no longer agree

with the views of the larger group. ...*a splinter group led by one of his former commanders.*

split /splɪt/ **splits, splitting.** The form **split** is used in the present tense and is also the past tense and past participle of the verb.

1 V-ERG or V A If something **splits** or is **split**, it is divided into two or more parts. *Three people died when their car split in two after hitting a tree... The atom was split in 1938... The first carriage hit a set of pillars alongside the track and the following four carriages then split away.*

2 V If something **splits**, a long crack or tear appears in it. *It was a very poor quality wood which had already split in many places... The jeans split the first time she wore them.* ▶ Also ADJ *Eric fingered his split lip.*

3 NC A **split** is a long crack or tear. *There's a split down the page of the atlas.*

4 V-ERG or V A If an organization **splits** or is **split**, one group of members disagrees strongly with the other members, and may form a group of their own. *The council split down the middle over the issue... A bitter leadership battle is threatening to split the ruling Christian Democratic party in El Salvador... The rebel organization Anyanya Two split away from the SPLA in 1984.*

5 NC A **split** in an organization is a disagreement between its members. *The last thing he wanted was a split in the party... There was a danger of a split because of a row about the official title of the state.*

6 N SING A **split** between two things is a division or difference between them. *...the split between 'rich' and 'poor'. ...the split between reality and the perception of it.*

7 VO If two or more people **split** something, they share it between them. *The profits are to be split fifty-fifty between the two of them.*

8 to **split hairs**: see **hair**.

split off PHRASAL VERB If part of something **splits off** or is **split off** from the main part of it, it breaks off or is broken or cut off. *A particle splits off from the nucleus... A block had been split off from the rock.*

split up PHRASAL VERB 1 If two people **split up**, they end their relationship or marriage. *...how children are affected when Mum and Dad split up... After he split up with his wife he went to Arizona.* 2 If a group of people **split up** or are **split up**, they go away in different directions. *In Hamburg the girls split up... Whole families have been split up by the fighting.* 3 If you **split** something **up**, you divide it into a number of separate sections. *You achieve more by splitting them up into groups.*

split infinitive, split infinitives

NC A **split infinitive** is a construction in English in which an adverb or adjunct is put between the infinitive marker 'to' and the infinitive verb itself. An example of a split infinitive is 'to boldly go'. Some speakers of English think that split infinitives are incorrect.

split-level

ADJ A **split-level** house or room has part of the ground floor at a different level from another part, usually because the house has been built on ground that slopes.

split personality

N SING If you say that someone has a **split personality**, you mean that their moods can change so much that they seem to have two different, separate personalities.

split-screen

1 ADJ ATTRIB **Split-screen** is used to describe a technique in making films and television programmes in which two different pieces of film are shown at the same time, one on the left half of the screen and one on the right. *There has been an obsession recently with split-screen movies.*

2 ADJ ATTRIB **Split-screen** is also used to describe a technique of using a computer or word-processor in which two different sets of information are shown at the same time, one at the top of the screen and one at the bottom.

split second

N SING A **split second** is a very short period of time. *For a split second nothing happened... She has to make split-second decisions.*

splitting /splɪtɪŋ/

ADJ ATTRIB A **splitting** headache is a very severe one. *Rita used to get skin rashes and splitting headaches.*

splodge /splɒdʒ/ **splodges**

NC A **splodge** is a large uneven mark or stain, especially one that has been caused by a liquid. *The painting consisted of two red and green splodges in a blue circle.*

splurge /splɜːdʒ/ **splurges, splurging, splurged;** an informal word.

1 V+on or VO+on If you **splurge** on something, you spend a lot of money extravagantly, especially on things that you do not need. *We used to have lunch in a restaurant and then perhaps splurge on a movie... I splurged the extra money on a silver cigarette box.*

2 N SING If you have a **splurge**, you spend a lot of money, usually on things that you do not need. *We had a bit of a splurge and bought a video.*

splutter /splʌtə/ **splutters, spluttering, spluttered**

1 V or V-QUOTE If someone **splutters**, they have difficulty speaking clearly and make spitting sounds as they are talking because they are angry, embarrassed, or surprised. *They spluttered with rage... 'I know them. They're my friends,' I was spluttering.* ▶ Also NC *'Of course not,' she said with a splutter of mirth.*

2 V If someone or something **splutters**, they make a series of short, sharp sounds. *The fumes make you cough and splutter... The spluttering two-stroke engine produces clouds of blue smoke.*

spoil /spɔɪl/ **spoils, spoiling, spoiled** or **spoilt**

1 VO If you **spoil** something, you prevent it from being successful or satisfactory. *She shouted at him for spoiling her lovely evening... Fine views, for instance, up the River Thames, will soon be spoilt by great sky-scrapers... The strike will spoil everybody's image of nursing as the ultimate caring profession.*

2 VO If you **spoil** children, you give them everything they want, which has a bad effect on their character. ♦ **spoilt** or **spoiled** ADJ *I think he's just a spoilt child... He's terribly spoiled.*

3 VO or V-REFL If you **spoil** someone, you give them something nice as a treat. *'Oh you are spoiling me, aren't you,' Clarissa said, 'First chocolates and now flowers!'... Go on, spoil yourself, buy a nice dress.*

4 VO If you **spoil** your ballot paper when you are voting, you mark it in such a way that it cannot be accepted as a vote. *Judging the success or otherwise of the boycott campaign is also difficult without knowing how many voters spoilt their ballot papers... The National Party won eighty-four per cent of the vote, with very few spoilt papers.*

5 N PL **Spoils** are things that people get as a result of winning a battle or of doing something else successfully; a literary use. *...the spoils of war. ...ambitious politicians, competing with each other for the spoils of office.*

spoil for PHRASAL VERB If you **are spoiling for** something such as trouble or a fight, you are very eager for it to happen. *The unions are spoiling for a fight about pay and conditions once again.*

spoilsport /spɔɪlspɔːt/ **spoilsports**

NC If you say that someone is a **spoilsport**, you mean that they are behaving in a way that ruins other people's pleasure or enjoyment; an informal word. *'Oh, Don, don't be a jealous spoilsport,' said Dolly.*

spoke /spəʊk/ **spokes**

1 **Spoke** is the past tense of **speak**.

2 NC The **spokes** of a wheel are the bars that connect the outer ring to the centre. *It can also be dangerous because children can get their hands in the spokes.*

spoken /spəʊkən/

1 **Spoken** is the past participle of **speak**.

2 ADJ ATTRIB **Spoken** means produced by speaking. *She is a master of both the spoken and the written word... Their understanding of spoken English is based largely on films and television. ...a robot capable of understanding spoken commands.*

3 See also **well-spoken**.

spokesman /spəʊksmən/ **spokesmen** /spəʊksmən/
NC A **spokesman** is a male spokesperson. *A government spokesman described the bombing as a terrorist attack... Military spokesmen refused to divulge key details of the attacks.*

spokesperson /spəʊkspɜːsn/ **spokespersons**
NC A **spokesperson** is a person who speaks as the representative of a group or organization. *...the spokesperson for the delegation.*

spokeswoman /spəʊkswʊmən/ **spokeswomen**
NC A **spokeswoman** is a female spokesperson. *A State Department spokeswoman has indicated that such a step is not yet contemplated... A spokeswoman for the controller said she could not comment on press reports.*

sponge /spʌndʒ/ **sponges, sponging, sponged**
1 NCorNU A **sponge** is a piece of a squashy, absorbent substance with lots of holes in it, used for cleaning things or washing your body. *Wipe the surface with a clean sponge... It contains plastic sponge to soak up the water. ...a sponge mop.*
2 VO If you **sponge** something, you wipe it with a wet sponge. *The fabric should then be sponged with warm water.*
3 NCorNU A **sponge** is also a light cake or pudding. *Whisked egg and sugar mixture for a sponge should be placed over a saucepan half-filled with hot water. ...baked apple with a layer of sponge on top.*

sponge off PHRASAL VERB See **sponge on.**

sponge on PHRASAL VERB Someone who **sponges on** other people or **sponges off** them regularly gets money from them without giving anything in return; an informal expression, used showing disapproval. *He sponged on his friends... The young unemployed are not simply layabouts who sponge off the Welfare State.*

spongebag /spʌndʒbæg/ **spongebags**
NC A **spongebag** is the same as a **toilet bag.**

sponge cake, sponge cakes
NCorNU A **sponge cake** is a very light cake made from flour, eggs, sugar, and sometimes fat. *People in the north still prefer traditional British dishes such as fish and chips, sponge cakes and soups... Mr Geard had his mouth full of sponge cake.*

spongy /spʌndʒi/
ADJ Something that is **spongy** is soft and squashy. *...spongy bread.*

sponsor /spɒnsə/ **sponsors, sponsoring, sponsored**
1 VO If an organization **sponsors** an event or someone's training, it pays some or all of the expenses connected with it, often in return for publicity. *The conference was sponsored by the Guardian... The BBC was one of the organizations which sponsored the award.*
2 VO If you **sponsor** a proposal, you officially put it forward and support it. *Two Liberal MPs sponsored the Bill.*
3 VO When an organization such as the United Nations **sponsors** negotiations between countries, it suggests holding the negotiations and organizes them. *A comprehensive settlement must be worked out at an international conference sponsored by the United Nations.*
4 VO If one country accuses another of **sponsoring** terrorism, they mean that the other country does not do anything to prevent it, and may even encourage it. *Both countries have been accused of sponsoring terrorism.*
5 VO If you **sponsor** someone who is doing something to raise money for charity, for example trying to walk a certain distance, you agree to give them a sum of money for the charity if they succeed in doing it. *Would you mind sponsoring me in this swim for cancer research?*
6 NC A **sponsor** is a person or organization that sponsors something or someone. *The bill's sponsor, Steven Day, said it was estimated that the measure would initially save fifty children a year from serious injury or death... All our European partners gave a firm undertaking not to make concessions to terrorists or their sponsors.*

sponsored /spɒnsəd/
1 **Sponsored** is used after an adjective or noun which refers to a country or to an organization such as the United Nations, to say that it sponsors something. *The American State Department has issued a new warning about what it says is the threat of Iraqi sponsored terrorism... Earlier, the Council rejected a Cuban sponsored resolution which would have allowed food in with virtually no restrictions... The upsurge in the conflict has led to renewed calls for a UN sponsored ceasefire.*
2 ADJ ATTRIB A **sponsored** event is an event in which the participants try to do something such as walk a certain distance in order to raise money for charity. *...a sponsored walk... The leading attraction is a sponsored open-air balloon race.*

sponsorship /spɒnsəʃɪp/
1 NU **Sponsorship** is financial support given by a sponsor. *...industrial sponsorship of the arts... The government hopes that increased sponsorship from private companies will compensate for the loss of local authority funding.*
2 NU+SUPP **Sponsorship** of something is the act of sponsoring it. *He said the Libyan leader had renewed his sponsorship of international terrorism... He has appealed to their leaders to join him in forging peace under the sponsorship of the United Nations.*

spontaneity /spɒntəneɪəti/
NU **Spontaneity** is spontaneous, natural behaviour. *...a child's spontaneity.*

spontaneous /spɒnteɪnɪəs/
1 ADJ **Spontaneous** acts are not planned, arranged, or forced, but are done because someone suddenly wants to do them. *...a spontaneous display of friendship and affection... These riots have been spontaneous outbursts of frustration and anger.* ◆ **spontaneously** ADV *Flo and I decided spontaneously to board a train for Geneva.*
2 ADJ A **spontaneous** event happens because of processes within something, rather than being caused by things outside it. *...spontaneous explosions... It is enormously powerful in reducing spontaneous cancers in mice and rats.* ◆ **spontaneously** ADV *In some people the disease clears up spontaneously... The fuel ignites spontaneously from the heat created by the compression.*

spoof /spuːf/ **spoofs**
NC A **spoof** is something such as an article or television programme that seems to be about a serious matter but is actually a joke. *The weather forecast seemed to be some kind of spoof, predicting every possible combination of weather.*

spook /spuːk/ **spooks, spooking, spooked;** an informal word.
1 NC A **spook** is a ghost that is thought to appear and haunt a place.
2 NC A **spook** is the same as a **spy;** used in American English. *This would make sure that the former communist spooks serve the interests of the democratic state.*
3 VO When something or someone **spooks** people, it frightens them or makes them very nervous; used in American English. *Escalating tension in the Middle East spooked traders all day long... He has an emotionless manner which sometimes spooks his colleagues.*
4 NC You can refer to a person whom you find strange and rather frightening as a **spook.**

spooky /spuːki/
ADJ A place or thing that is **spooky** is strange and frightening; an informal word. *The whole place has a slightly spooky atmosphere.*

spool /spuːl/ **spools**
NC A **spool** is a round object onto which thread, tape, or film can be wound. *A very useful invention of his is the mechanism called a flyer, for winding thread evenly on a spool.*

spoon /spuːn/ **spoons, spooning, spooned**
1 NC A **spoon** is an object used for eating, stirring, and serving food. It is shaped like a small shallow bowl with a long handle. *...a knife, fork, and spoon.*
2 NC You can use **spoon** to refer to the amount of a substance that a spoon can hold. *He takes six spoons of sugar in his tea.*

3 VO If you **spoon** food somewhere, you put it there using a spoon. *He spooned the vegetables onto the plates.*

spoon-feed, spoon-feeds, spoon-feeding, spoon-fed
1 VOorVOO If you **spoon-feed** someone, you do everything for them or tell them everything that they need to know, so that you prevent them from having to think or act for themselves. *There is a tendency to spoon-feed your pupils when you're teaching because it is quicker and easier... We can't spoon-feed every bit of information about the world to computers.*
2 VOorVOO If you **spoon-feed** a baby, you feed it using a spoon. *Many parents spoon-feed one baby while the other one takes the bottle.*

spoonful /spuːnfl/ The plural form can be **spoonfuls** or **spoonsful**.
NC A **spoonful** of a substance is the amount that a spoon can hold. *She put a spoonful of milk in each of the two cups.*

spoor /spuə, spɔː/
N SING The **spoor** of an animal is the visible trail that it leaves as it moves along, especially its footprints. *They were amazed to notice that the elephant spoor had vanished.*

sporadic /spərædɪk/
ADJ **Sporadic** events happen at irregular intervals. *Sporadic attacks continued throughout the night... Sporadic violence continued around the country following yesterday's assassination.* ◆ **sporadically**
ADV *Most families watch television sporadically.*

spore /spɔː/ **spores**
NC **Spores** are cells produced by bacteria and non-flowering plants such as fungi which develop into new bacteria or plants; a technical term. *Uncleared ducts and filters can support colonies of bacteria and fungi which release spores directly into the circulating air.*

sport /spɔːt/ **sports, sporting, sported**
1 NCorNU **Sports** are games and other competitive activities which need physical effort and skill. *My favourite sport is football... I was bad at sport. ...a sports stadium.*
2 VO If you **sport** something noticeable or unusual, you wear it. *One of them even sported an earring.*

sporting /spɔːtɪŋ/
ADJ ATTRIB **Sporting** means relating to sport or used for sport. *It was his 29th international sporting event.*

sports car, sports cars
NC A **sports car** is a low, fast car, usually for only two people. *Mr Healey was best known for his part in designing the Austin Healey range of sports cars.*

sportscast /spɔːtskɑːst/ **sportscasts**
NC A **sportscast** is a radio or television broadcast which consists of a sports commentary or sports news; used in American English.

sportscaster /spɔːtskɑːstə/ **sportscasters**
NC A **sportscaster** is a person who broadcasts a sports commentary or sports news; used in American English. *President Ronald Reagan made his first reputation as a sportscaster, working for a small radio station in Iowa.*

sports jacket, sports jackets
NC A **sports jacket** is a man's jacket, usually made of tweed.

sportsman /spɔːtsmən/ **sportsmen** /spɔːtsmən/
NC A **sportsman** is a man who takes part in sports. *South Africa has produced many outstanding sportsmen and women.*

sportsmanlike /spɔːtsmənlaɪk/
ADJ Behaviour that is **sportsmanlike** is fair and decent, as it should be when you are playing a game.

sportsmanship /spɔːtsmənʃɪp/
NU **Sportsmanship** is the behaviour and attitudes that a good sportsman is expected to have. *He believed in manners and decency and sportsmanship.*

sportswear /spɔːtsweə/
NU **Sportswear** is the special clothing that is worn for playing sports, or for informal leisure activities. *Instead of his usual army uniform, he wore casual sportswear.*

sportswoman /spɔːtswumən/ **sportswomen**
NC A **sportswoman** is a woman who takes part in sports. *She has just been voted International*

Sportswoman of the Year.

sporty /spɔːti/; an informal word.
1 ADJ If a small car is **sporty**, it is fast. *I like the car's sporty performance.*
2 ADJ A **sporty** person likes playing sports. *Andrew and Sarah both went to such schools, and were sporty rather than academic.*

spot /spɒt/ **spots, spotting, spotted**
1 NC **Spots** are small, round, coloured areas on a surface. *She was wearing a white blouse with red spots.*
2 NC **Spots** on a person's skin are small lumps or marks. *Their bites leave itching red spots on the skin... I was covered with spots for a week.*
3 NC A **spot** of a substance is a small amount of it. *I felt a few spots of rain.*
4 N SING A **spot** of something is a small amount of it; an old-fashioned, informal use. *What about a spot of lunch?*
5 NC You can refer to a particular place as a **spot**. *It's a lovely spot for a picnic... Four brass plates in the floor mark the spot where the throne stood.*
6 VO If you **spot** someone or something, you notice them. *I spotted you standing by your car at the gas station... Two men with rifles were spotted near the railway line.*
7 See also **beauty spot, black spot, blind spot, high spot, hot spot, spotted, trouble spot.**
● **Spot** is used in these phrases. ● If you are **on the spot**, you are at the actual place where something is happening. *Certain decisions had to be taken by the man on the spot.* ● If you do something **on the spot**, you do it immediately. *They dismissed him on the spot.* ● If you put someone **on the spot**, you put them in a situation where they have to make a difficult decision, usually publicly. *By raising the issue again so forcefully, the Poles are putting America, in particular, on the spot... I think even clever people, though, are not terribly clever when put on the spot.*
● to **have a soft spot for** someone: see **soft**.

spot check, spot checks
NC A **spot check** is a random inspection of one of a group of things. *...law enforcement officers who are doing spot checks on newspaper advertisements.*

spotless /spɒtləs/
ADJ Something that is **spotless** is perfectly clean. *...a spotless white shirt.*

spotlight /spɒtlaɪt/ **spotlights, spotlighting, spotlighted**
1 N SING Someone or something that is in the **spotlight** is receiving a great deal of public attention. *The drug issue is very much in the spotlight in this year's election campaign... Over the past few years the singer's private life has also come under the media spotlight... He's just written a book which turns the spotlight on missionary activity among native people.*
2 VO If something **spotlights** a particular situation or problem, it causes public attention to be directed towards it. *The fighting over how to reduce the national budget deficit has spotlighted weaknesses in the economy.*
3 NC A **spotlight** is a powerful light, often in a theatre, which can be directed so that it lights up a small area. *Their lead singer was blinded by the spotlights on stage.*

spotlit /spɒtlɪt/
ADJ A **spotlit** stage or building is brightly lit up by one or more spotlights. *...the spotlit spires of Notre Dame.*

spot-on
ADJ **Spot-on** means exactly correct or accurate; an informal word. *You can use this weapon at 130 metres with spot-on accuracy.*

spotted /spɒtɪd/
ADJ Something that is **spotted** has a pattern of spots on it. *...a red and white spotted handkerchief.*

spotty /spɒti/
1 ADJ Someone who is **spotty** has spots or pimples on their skin, especially on their face. *You don't have to stay pale and spotty for ever.*
2 ADJ **Spotty** also means irregular or inconsistent; used in American English. *Relief efforts so far are said to be spotty... Business is very spotty. It's good*

one day and bad the next day.

spouse /spaʊs/ **spouses**

N C Someone's **spouse** is their husband or wife; a formal word. *They receive free membership for themselves and their spouses.*

spout /spaʊt/ **spouts, spouting, spouted**

1 V-ERG When liquid or flame **spouts** out of something, it comes out fast in a long stream. *...jets of water spouting up from the basins below... Their tanks came on in hordes, spouting flames.*

2 VO If someone **spouts** something that they have learned, they speak without stopping or thinking. *Gorbachev is not simply spouting Lenin's words. ...reactionaries spouting extreme prejudices.*

3 N C The **spout** of a kettle, teapot, or other liquid container is the tube that the liquid comes out of. *The watering can has a retractable spout.*

sprain /spreɪn/ **sprains, spraining, sprained**

1 VO If you **sprain** your ankle or wrist, you accidentally damage it by twisting it, for example when you fall. *The rumor was that he might not do so well this year because he'd sprained his ankle in training.* ◆ **sprained** ADJ *Henri Leconte retired with a sprained ankle.*

2 N C A **sprain** is the injury caused by spraining a joint. *Providing he can overcome an ankle sprain, he'll be playing Peter Lundgren in today's final.*

sprang /spræŋ/

Sprang is the past tense of **spring**.

sprawl /sprɔːl/ **sprawls, sprawling, sprawled**

1 V If you **sprawl** somewhere, you sit or lie down with your legs and arms spread out in a careless way. *Segal sprawled out on the couch.*

2 VA A place that **sprawls** covers a large area of land. *The village sprawls along the coastline... The university sprawls across the Lenin Hills.* ◆ **sprawling** ADJ *...a large, sprawling villa. ...a sprawling city.*

3 NU+SUPP You can use **sprawl** to refer to an area where a city has expanded in an uncontrolled way. *...London's urban sprawl.*

sprawled /sprɔːld/

ADJ PRED A If you are **sprawled** somewhere, you are sitting or lying with your arms and legs stretched out in a careless way. *He lay sprawled in the chair with his legs stretched out.*

spray /spreɪ/ **sprays, spraying, sprayed**

1 NU **Spray** is a lot of small drops of water which are being splashed or forced into the air. *Many of them have taken to wearing visors to protect their eyes from the effects of sea spray.*

2 VO If you **spray** something with a liquid, you cover it with drops of the liquid, for example using a hose or an aerosol. *Spray the shelves with insecticide... He sprayed a little eau-de-cologne over himself.*

3 N MASS A **spray** is a liquid kept under pressure in a container, which you can force out in very small drops. *...chemical sprays. ...hair spray.*

4 N C A **spray** is also a piece of equipment for spraying water or another liquid on something. *They are to ban the sale of aerosol sprays containing chlorofluorocarbons, which are blamed for destroying the ozone layer... There's a fan system for dispersing smoke and an inert gas spray for putting out fires in machinery sections.*

5 N C A **spray** of flowers or leaves is a number of them on one stem or branch. *...great sprays of lilies.*

spray can, spray cans

N C A **spray can** is a can containing liquid under pressure which can be sprayed out. *Most of the aerosol makers are trying hard to eliminate CFCs from their spray cans.*

spread /spred/ **spreads, spreading.** The form **spread** is used in the present tense and is also the past tense and past participle of the verb.

1 VO If you **spread** something, you arrange it over a surface, so that all of it can be seen or used easily. *He took the envelope, tipped it open and spread the contents on the table.*

2 VO If you **spread** your hands, arms, or legs, you move them far apart. *He just shrugged and spread his hands.*

3 VO If you **spread** a substance on a surface, you put a thin layer of the substance over the surface. *Liz was spreading marmalade on a piece of toast... I love biscuits spread with butter.*

4 N MASS A **spread** is a soft food which is put on bread. *...cheese spread.*

5 V-ERG If something such as liquid, gas, or smoke **spreads** or **is spread**, it moves outwards in all directions so that it covers a larger area. *A stain was spreading on the bathroom ceiling... We've taken the water out of the river and spread it across the land. ...a nuclear fire, spreading deadly radioactive dust into the surrounding countryside.*

6 V-ERG If something such as fire or a disease **spreads**, or **is spread**, it starts affecting more and more of an area, or more and more people. *Extremely dry weather and temperatures in the 70s helped the fire spread rapidly... There has been one confirmed death from the disease, which is spread by mosquitos. ...the risk of spreading AIDS.* ► Also N SING *...the rapid spread of disease.*

7 V-ERG If something such as news, or an idea or feeling **spreads** or **is spread**, it becomes known or is shared by more and more people. *Word spread quickly through the international community... The controversy has spread far beyond Russia's borders... They were accused of spreading rumours which discredit the government.*

8 N SING The **spread** of something is its increasing presence or occurrence. *Girls have benefited more than boys from the spread of higher education.*

9 V-ERG+*over* If something **is spread** or **spreads** over a period of time, it takes place over that period. *The breeding season is spread over five months.*

10 N SING A **spread** of ideas, interests, or other things is a wide variety of them. *The IBA wants to have a broad spread of opinion represented on its board.*

spread out PHRASAL VERB 1 If people, animals, or vehicles **spread out** or **are spread out**, they move away from each other, or are far apart. *They followed him and spread out, nervously, in the forest... My family were spread out all over the countryside.* 2 If you **spread** something **out**, you arrange it over a surface, so that all of it can be seen or used easily. *I removed the tool kit and spread it out on the seat.*

spread-eagled /spredˈiːgld/

ADJ or ADV Someone who is **spread-eagled** somewhere is lying with their arms and legs spread out. *A crudely drawn stick figure lies spread-eagled, having just been run over... He lay spread-eagled.*

spreadsheet /spredʃiːt/ **spreadsheets**

N C A **spreadsheet** is a computer program that is used for entering and arranging both numerical data and texts. Spreadsheets are used especially for financial planning and budgeting. *The software includes a word processor, diary, notepad and address book, spreadsheet and communications.*

spree /spriː/ **sprees**

N C A **spree** is a short period of doing something enjoyable with a lot of energy, especially in an excessive way. *Tim was away on a shopping spree. ...an after-match drinking spree.*

sprig /sprɪg/ **sprigs**

N C A **sprig** of a plant is a small piece of stem with leaves on it. *...a sprig of holly.*

sprightly /spraɪtli/

ADJ Someone, especially an old person, who is **sprightly** is lively and active. *Now 72, a short but sprightly man with penetrating eyes and a clipped moustache, he looks every inch a soldier.*

spring /sprɪŋ/ **springs, springing, sprang, sprung**

The form **sprung** can also be used for the past tense of the verb in American English.

1 NU or NC **Spring** is the season between winter and summer. In the spring the weather starts to get warmer. *...the first day of spring... He left in the spring of 1956... We had an exceptionally wet spring.*

2 N C A **spring** is a coil of wire which returns to its original shape after it is pressed or pulled. *With the aid of springs the artificial foot mimics the flexing of the human foot.*

3 N C A **spring** is also a place where water comes up naturally through the ground. *At the back of the farm*

there are some hot sulphur springs.

4 v When a person or animal **springs**, they move suddenly upwards or forwards. *She sprang to her feet and faced him... The panther crouched, ready to spring.*

5 VA If something **springs** in a particular direction, it moves suddenly and quickly. *A man sprang from his seat in the first class cabin brandishing a pistol... Hands sprang up.*

6 VA If one thing **springs** from another, the first thing is the result of the second. *These problems spring from different causes... Its strength springs from its legitimacy.*

7 VO If you **spring** some news or an event on someone, you tell them about it unexpectedly, so that they are surprised. *You're springing this on me all of a sudden.*

● **Spring** is used in these phrases. ● If a boat, container, or roof **springs a leak**, a hole or crack appears in it and it starts leaking. *The wind has been against them and the yacht has sprung a leak in the hull... What happens when a pipe in a nuclear power station springs a leak?* ● If something **springs to mind**, you suddenly think of it or it is the first thing that you think of when a particular subject is mentioned. *We can also look at epidemics of infectious diseases; the one that springs to mind is meningitis.*

spring up PHRASAL VERB If something **springs up**, it suddenly appears or comes into existence. *Computer stores are springing up all over the place.*

springboard /sprɪŋbɔːd/ **springboards**

1 NC+SUPP If something is a **springboard** for an action or enterprise, it makes it possible for the action or enterprise to begin. *The campaign might well be the springboard for the launching of a new party.*

2 NC A **springboard** is also a flexible board which you jump on before performing a dive or a gymnastic movement. *Its heated pool is bright blue, with springboards, ladders and a tiled surround.*

spring-clean, spring-cleans, spring-cleaning, spring-cleaned

VorVO When you **spring-clean** a house, you thoroughly clean everything in it, including the things that you do not clean very often. ◆ **spring-cleaning** NU *Mrs Pringle came to give me a hand with the spring-cleaning.*

spring onion, spring onions

NC A **spring onion** is a small onion with long green leaves that is often eaten raw in salads. *Garnish with chives or spring onions and serve with plain boiled rice.*

spring roll, spring rolls

NC A **spring roll** is an item of Chinese food consisting of a small roll of thin pastry filled with vegetables and sometimes meat, and cooked in oil. *I was sitting in the central market in Ho Chi Minh City having a meal of Vietnamese spring rolls.*

springtime /sprɪŋtaɪm/

NU **Springtime** is the period of time during which spring lasts. *Something that the movie does perhaps better than the written word is convey the stunning visual quality of the mountains in springtime.*

springy /sprɪŋi/

ADJ If something is **springy**, it returns quickly to its original shape after you press it. *...a springy mattress... The grass was short and springy.*

sprinkle /sprɪŋkl/ **sprinkles, sprinkling, sprinkled**

VO If you **sprinkle** a liquid or powder over something, you scatter it over it, usually in small amounts. *Sprinkle the oil over the courgettes... She sprinkled the cakes with sugar.*

sprinkler /sprɪŋklə/ **sprinklers**

NC A **sprinkler** is a device used to spray water, in order to water lawns or put out fires in buildings. *The sprinklers can be turned on as often as necessary... A British company has designed a sprinkler system to fight fires on aircraft.*

sprinkling /sprɪŋklɪŋ/

N SING A **sprinkling** of things is a small quantity of them. *...a sprinkling of sightseers outside the palace.*

sprint /sprɪnt/ **sprints, sprinting, sprinted**

1 NC A **sprint** is a short fast race. *...a 100 metre*

sprint. ...her disappointing form in the individual sprints. ► Also v *He has won medals for sprinting and long-jumping.*

2 N SING A **sprint** is also the last part of a long-distance race, when the athletes or cyclists start to run or cycle more quickly. *I'm really a long-distance runner, but I do my best in the final sprint... He took over the lead from Olaf Ludwig, and won the stage in a sprint finish.* ► Also v *He sprinted to victory at the end of the 244.4 kilometres from Albacete to Toledo.*

3 v If you **sprint**, you run or cycle as fast as you can over a short distance because you are in a hurry. *She sprinted to her car.* ► Also N SING *Bessie had suddenly broken into a sprint.*

sprinter /sprɪntə/ **sprinters**

NC A **sprinter** is a person who takes part in short, fast races. *He confirmed his position as the top 100-metres sprinter in the world.*

sprite /spraɪt/ **sprites**

NC A **sprite** is a type of fairy; a literary word. *...some hidden world where wood sprites and fairies and little folk are said to live.*

spritzer /sprɪtsə/ **spritzers**

N MASS **Spritzer** is a drink consisting of white wine and soda water.

sprout /spraʊt/ **sprouts, sprouting, sprouted**

1 V-ERG When plants or vegetables **sprout** new shoots or leaves, they produce them. *Greenery sprouted between the white gravestones... Farmers were concerned that crops sprouting too early would be killed off by frost... You can put a twig into earth, it sprouts roots and becomes a new plant.*

2 V-ERG If things **sprout**, or if something **sprouts** them, they suddenly appear and spread rapidly. *Concrete hotels and tourist villages are sprouting along the desert shore... San Francisco has sprouted a rash of little theatres.*

3 NC **Sprouts** or **Brussels sprouts** are vegetables like very small cabbages. *Spring vegetables, like Brussels sprouts, kale and Chinese cabbage, have just been planted.*

spruce /spruːs/ **spruces, sprucing, spruced**

1 NC A **spruce** is an evergreen tree. It has needle-like leaves that grow in a triangular shape. *...the Spartan spruce, a different type of Christmas tree to that used traditionally in Britain.*

2 ADJ Someone who is **spruce** is very neat and smart. *The President, a burly but spruce forty-one year old in a dark blue suit, described it as an historic day.*

spruce up PHRASAL VERB If you **spruce** someone or something **up**, you improve their appearance. *Buildings are being spruced up for the tenth anniversary celebrations in January.*

sprung /sprʌŋ/

Sprung is the past participle of **spring**.

spry /spraɪ/

ADJ An old person who is **spry** is lively and active. *He is clearly not the spry, energetically cheerful man he was last year.*

spud /spʌd/ **spuds**

NCorNU **Spuds** are potatoes; an informal word. *We already have an abundance of spuds and cabbages... We are trying to produce a new variety of spud.*

spun /spʌn/

Spun is the past tense and past participle of **spin**.

spunk /spʌŋk/

NU **Spunk** is courage; an old-fashioned, informal word. *You've got to admire her spunk.*

spunky /spʌŋki/ **spunkier, spunkiest**

ADJ Someone who is **spunky** shows courage; an old-fashioned, informal word. *She's a spunky kid.*

spur /spɜː/ **spurs, spurring, spurred**

1 VO If something **spurs** you to do something, it encourages you to do it. *Martin's job offer spurred the others to do something themselves... The Labour authority admits that the government's housing bill spurred them to take such action.*

2 VO If something **spurs** a change or event, it makes it happen faster or sooner. *...a period of extremely rapid growth, spurred by the advent of the microprocessor... Riots last February failed to spur the authorities into any meaningful reforms.*

3 N SING Something that acts as a **spur** encourages someone to do something or makes something happen faster or sooner. *International competition was a spur to modernisation.*
4 If you do something **on the spur of the moment**, you do it suddenly, without planning it beforehand. *I just took the bus on the spur of the moment... The decision was not taken on the spur of the moment.*
5 NC **Spurs** are sharp metal points attached to the heels of a rider's boots and used to make the horse go faster. *Don't tug at the horse's mouth or kick him with your spurs.*
spur on PHRASAL VERB If something **spurs** you **on**, it makes you want to make progress or achieve something. *Companies might spur one another on.*
spurious /spjʊəriəs/
ADJ Something that is **spurious** is not genuine or real; a formal word. *...the spurious attractions of modernity... It's a spurious argument and it has no basis in science or fact.*
spurn /spɜːn/ **spurns, spurning, spurned**
VO If you **spurn** something, you refuse to accept it; a formal word. *You spurned my friendship.*
spur-of-the-moment
ADJ ATTRIB A **spur-of-the-moment** action or decision is sudden and has not been planned. *...spur-of-the-moment impulses.*
spurt /spɜːt/ **spurts, spurting, spurted**
1 V-ERG When a liquid or flame **spurts** or is **spurted** out of something, it comes out quickly in a thin, powerful stream. *...a blow that sent blood spurting from his mouth... My arm began to spurt blood.* ► Also NC *...a small, clear spurt of flame.*
2 NC A **spurt** of activity or emotion is a sudden, brief period of it. *Her feelings varied from tenderness to sudden spurts of genuine love.*
3 V If you **spurt** somewhere, you suddenly increase your speed for a short while. *With Claude driving they spurted through back streets.* ► Also NC *I put on a spurt and caught them up.*
sputter /spʌtə/ **sputters, sputtering, sputtered**
V If something **sputters**, it makes soft hissing and popping sounds. *The engine began sputtering.*
spy /spaɪ/ **spies, spying, spied**
1 NC A **spy** is a person whose job is to find out secret information about another country or organization. *A member of his staff was discovered to be a foreign spy.*
2 V Someone who **spies** for a country or organization tries to find out secret information about another country or organization. *He spied for Moscow while serving as a senior officer in British intelligence.*
3 V+on If you **spy** on someone, you watch them secretly. *...girls spying on their unfaithful lovers.*
4 VO If you **spy** something, you notice it; a literary use. *Suddenly Quint spied a shark.*
spying /spaɪɪŋ/
NU **Spying** is the activity of trying to find out secret information about one country or organization in order to give it to another country or organization. *He was convicted of spying for Russia... She was arrested last September on spying charges.*
sq
sq is a written abbreviation for 'square' when giving the measurement of an area. *...280,000 sq ft of space.*
squabble /skwɒbl/ **squabbles, squabbling, squabbled**
V When people **squabble**, they quarrel about something unimportant. *They're always squabbling over details.* ► Also NC *...squabbles between the children.*
squad /skwɒd/ **squads**
1 NC+SUPP A **squad** is a section of a police force that is responsible for dealing with a particular type of crime. *...the drugs squad... Bomb squad officers were called in.*
2 NC A **squad** of soldiers is a small group of them. *The army says a squad of troops came under a barrage of stones and responded with warning shots.*
3 NC A **squad** is also a group of players from which a sports team will be chosen. *Oti pulled out of the England squad with a leg muscle injury.*
4 See also **death squad, firing squad, flying squad, vice squad.**

squad car, squad cars
NC A **squad car** is a car used by the police.
squaddie /skwɒdi/ **squaddies**
NC A **squaddie** is a soldier of the lowest rank in the army; an informal word. *Most squaddies join their local regiment... British squaddies, guns at the ready, crouch at the street corner.*
squadron /skwɒdrən/ **squadrons**
NC A **squadron** is a section of one of the armed forces, especially the air force. *...a squadron of fighter planes.*
squadron leader, squadron leaders
TITLE or NC A **squadron leader** is an officer in the British air force who has a rank above that of flight lieutenant. *...Squadron Leader Philips.*
squalid /skwɒlɪd/
1 ADJ A **squalid** place is dirty, untidy, and in bad condition. *...our small, squalid flat.*
2 ADJ **Squalid** activities are unpleasant and often dishonest. *They're involved in a rather squalid battle as to who controls the party.*
squall /skwɔːl/ **squalls**
NC A **squall** is a brief storm. *Search efforts will be made difficult by rain squalls and winds gusting up to twenty-five knots.*
squalor /skwɒlə/
NU You can refer to squalid conditions or surroundings as **squalor**. *...poor people living in conditions of squalor.*
squander /skwɒndə/ **squanders, squandering, squandered**
VO If you **squander** resources, you use them in a wasteful way. *They destroyed democracy and squandered public funds... He squandered large quantities of cash on overpriced clothes.*
square /skweə/ **squares, squaring, squared**
1 NC A **square** is a shape with four sides of the same length and four corners that are all right angles. *I folded the newspaper neatly in a square and put it away... In the table in front of me are a number of squares of fabric and other materials.*
2 ADJ Something that is **square** has a shape similar to a square. *The post office was a small, square building... He had a square ruddy face.*
3 NC In a town or city, a **square** is a flat open place, often in the shape of a square. *...Trafalgar Square.*
4 ADJ ATTRIB **Square** is used in front of units of length to form units of area such as 'square metre' and 'square inch'. *...hundreds of square miles of pine forest... It may cover 150 square kilometres or more.*
5 ADJ after N **Square** is also used after units of length when you are giving the length of each side of something square. *...a silicon chip less than a centimetre square.*
6 VO If you **square** a number, you multiply it by itself. For example, 3 squared is 3 x 3, or 9. You usually write 3 squared as 3^2. *We take two, we square it, and we get four.*
7 NC The **square** of a number is another number that is produced by multiplying the first number by itself. For example, the square of 2 is 4. *The gravitational attraction between two objects, depends only on their mass and on the square of the distance between them.*
8 V-ERG+with If two different situations or things **square** with each other, they can be accepted together or seem compatible. *His interpretation is unlikely to square with the Committee's guidelines... How this can be squared with support for a market economy is not clear.*
9 If you are **back to square one**, you have to start dealing with something from the beginning again; an informal expression. *If he says 'No', you are back to square one.*
square away PHRASAL VERB If you **square** a problem or task **away**, you deal with it so that you can do something else; used in American English. *I'm sorry about the technical problems, but we've got that squared away now and here you are.*
square up PHRASAL VERB **1** If you **square up** with someone, you pay the bills or debts that you owe them; an informal use. *Do you want to square up now or later.* **2** If you **square up** to a problem, person, or

situation, you accept that you have to deal with it and take action to do so. *But she had squared up to him all right.*

square bracket, square brackets
NC A **square bracket** is a bracket that is shaped like half a square rather than being round. *The draft is full of square brackets around those areas where agreement has yet to be reached.*

square deal, square deals
NC If you are given a **square deal**, you are treated fairly and honestly. *We've got to give them a square deal.*

squarely /skweəli/
1 ADV **Squarely** means directly and in the middle, rather than indirectly or at an angle. *The television mast fell squarely onto a Methodist chapel.*
2 ADV If you face something **squarely**, you face it directly, without trying to avoid it. *This difficulty will have to be squarely faced.*

square meal, square meals
NC A **square meal** is a large, satisfying, and nourishing one. *He had gone without a square meal for nearly three days.*

square root, square roots
NC The **square root** of a number is another number which produces the first number when it is multiplied by itself. For example, 4 is the square root of 16.

squash /skwɒʃ/ **squashes, squashing, squashed.** The plural form for the noun in paragraph 5 can be either **squashes** or **squash.**
1 VO If you **squash** something, you press it, so that it becomes flat or loses its shape. *Drinks cans can be squashed to a fifth of their original size... Eleven cars and their occupants were squashed flat, and construction workers were among those killed.*
2 VO If a government **squashes** something that is causing them trouble, they stop it, often by using force. *His security men will probably be successful in squashing the current wave of dissent.*
3 NU **Squash** is a game in which two players hit a small rubber ball against the walls of a court using rackets. *...if you wanted to have a game of squash after work... Fierce competition on the squash circuit continues all through the year.*
4 N MASS **Squash** is also a drink made from fruit juice, sugar, and water. *...a glass of orange squash.*
5 NCorNU A **squash** is a marrow or any vegetable of the marrow family; used in American English. *...a bag brimming with cucumbers and rotund orange squash... Small farmers there are growing many new vegetable crops, such as baby squash.*

squashy /skwɒʃi/
ADJ Something that is **squashy** is soft and can be squashed easily. *...squashy tomatoes.*

squat /skwɒt/ **squats, squatting, squatted**
1 VA If you **squat** down, you crouch, balancing on your feet with your legs bent. *He told the boys to squat in a semicircle around him.*
2 ADJ Something or someone that is **squat** is short and thick or fat, often in an unattractive way. *...a squat, bald, plump man. ...squat wooden churches.*
3 V A person who **squats** in an unused building lives there without having a legal right to do so. *We were squatting in an empty house.*

squatter, squatters
1 NC **Squatters** are people who live in an unused building without having a legal right to do so. *The police evicted squatters who had occupied some empty council flats.*
2 NC **Squatters** are also people who occupy unused land, either to build homes on it or to farm it, without having a legal right to do so. *...precarious shacks made out of cardboard by squatters... Violence has again flared up in a big South African squatter camp near Cape Town.*

squaw /skwɔː/ **squaws**
NC A **squaw** is a North American Indian woman.

squawk /skwɔːk/ **squawks, squawking, squawked**
V When a bird **squawks**, it makes a loud sharp noise. *Scrawny chickens ran squawking around the village.*
▶ Also NC *...the sad squawks of the peacocks.*

squeak /skwiːk/ **squeaks, squeaking, squeaked**
V If something **squeaks**, it makes a short, high-pitched sound. *As the dusk deepened, small black bats began squeaking... A door squeaked open nearby.* ▶ Also NC *She let out a squeak.*

squeaky /skwiːki/
ADJ Something that is **squeaky** makes squeaking noises. *...a squeaky iron gate. ...a high, squeaky voice.*

squeaky clean
ADJ If someone such as a politician is **squeaky clean**, they are very honest, and there is nothing in their personal life that might embarrass them; an informal expression. *...saying that we're wholesome and squeaky clean... He has a squeaky clean image.*

squeal /skwiːl/ **squeals, squealing, squealed**
V If someone or something **squeals**, they make a long, high-pitched sound. *The boys scattered, squealing in horror.* ▶ Also NC *There was a squeal of brakes.*

squeamish /skwiːmɪʃ/
ADJ If you are **squeamish**, you are easily upset by unpleasant sights or situations. *I don't mind doing it if you're squeamish.*

squeeze /skwiːz/ **squeezes, squeezing, squeezed**
1 VO When you **squeeze** something soft or flexible, you press it firmly from two sides. *The children were squeezing the packets to find out what was inside.*
▶ Also NC *He gave her hand a squeeze.*
2 VA If you **squeeze** through or into a small space, you manage to get through it or into it, often with great effort. *We squeezed under the wire... The inhabitants have to squeeze into a tiny area of living space.*
3 N SING If getting a number of people into a small space is a **squeeze**, it is only just possible; an informal use. *We all got in the lift but it was a bit of a squeeze.*
4 VOA If you **squeeze** something out of someone, especially money, you get it from them by means of force, persuasion, or great effort. *...their campaign to squeeze concessions out of the Kuwaiti government... It took public transport employees just one day to squeeze a 63 per cent pay rise from local officials... He's squeezed higher profits out of companies whose previous owners had all but written them off.*
5 VO If someone **is being squeezed** by something, they are having problems, usually because of lack of money. *West Germany is already being squeezed by the costs of unification... Mr Major's room for manoeuvre has been squeezed by inflation and lower growth.*
6 VO To **squeeze** the amount of money available means to restrict or reduce it. *This has had the effect of squeezing the Green Party's funds... Living standards are being squeezed hard after years of apparent prosperity.*
7 N SING A **squeeze** is also a situation in which it is difficult to borrow money because of strict controls, usually imposed by the government in order to fight inflation. *The CBI hopes the squeeze on industry will also slow down the rate of inflation... Panama is in the grip of an economic squeeze applied by the United States.*
8 VOA If you **squeeze** something into a small amount of time, you manage to fit it in. *Do you think you can squeeze your lunch break in between the two meetings.*

squeeze out PHRASAL VERB 1 When you **squeeze** a liquid or a soft substance **out** of an object, or **squeeze** the object **out**, you get the liquid or soft substance out by pressing the object. *...the waste stuff left over from sugar cane once the sugar's been squeezed out... Squeeze all the water out of the cloth.* 2 To **squeeze** someone or something **out** of a situation or activity means to prevent them from having a part in it. *Rapidly increasing prices had tended to squeeze first time buyers out of the market... They will squeeze the smaller operators out of profits and out of business.*

squelch /skwɛltʃ/ **squelches, squelching, squelched**
V To **squelch** means to make a wet, sucking sound, usually by walking through muddy ground. *I squelched along by the water's edge.*

squib /skwɪb/ **squibs**
1 NC A **squib** is a small firework that makes a loud

bang; an old-fashioned use. *Little boys were throwing home-made squibs.*
2 You can describe something such as an event or a performance as a **damp squib** when it is expected to be interesting, exciting, or impressive, but is not. *The party turned out to be a bit of a damp squib.*

squid /skwɪd/ **squids**. The plural form can be either **squids** or **squid**.
NC A **squid** is a sea creature with a soft body and many tentacles. *Female giant squid can have a body as long as six metres with tentacles as long as twelve metres.*

squiggle /skwɪgl/ **squiggles**
NC A **squiggle** is a line that bends and curls in an irregular way. *Her signature was a series of inky squiggles.*

squint /skwɪnt/ **squints, squinting, squinted**
1 v If you **squint** at something, you look at it with your eyes partly closed. *I squinted up at the sky.*
2 NC If someone has a **squint**, there is something wrong with their eyes which makes each eye look in a different direction. *It was such a bad squint that he couldn't really see where he was going.*

squire /skwaɪə/ **squires**
NC The **squire** of an English village is a man who owns most of the land in it; an old-fashioned word. *The new squire has inherited the village from his great aunt.*

squirm /skwɜːm/ **squirms, squirming, squirmed**
1 v If you **squirm**, you wriggle, because you are nervous or uncomfortable. *Children do not necessarily sit quietly through a performance. They talk and cry and squirm.*
2 v You can also say that someone **squirms** when they are very embarrassed or ashamed. *He squirmed with embarrassment.*

squirrel /skwɪrəl/ **squirrels**
NC A **squirrel** is a small furry animal which has a long bushy tail and climbs trees. *The grey squirrel was introduced from America.*

squirt /skwɜːt/ **squirts, squirting, squirted**
V-ERG or VO If liquid **squirts** or if you **squirt** it somewhere, the liquid comes out of a narrow opening in a thin fast stream. *Squirt a little oil into the keyhole... Water squirted out of a hole in the pipe... One woman was squirting windows with water.*

Sr
Sr is a written abbreviation for 'Senior', and is written after a man's name. It is used, in order to distinguish the man from his son when they both have the same name. *...Charles Parker, Sr.*

Sri Jayawardenepura /sriː dʒaɪəwɔːdənəpuərə/
Sri Jayawardenepura became the seat of government of Sri Lanka in 1982 (the capital is Colombo). Population: 107,000 (1988).

Sri Lanka /sriː læŋkə/
The **Democratic Socialist Republic of Sri Lanka** is a country in the Indian Ocean, south-east of India. It was a British colony, called Ceylon, from the 19th century until independence in 1948. Ethnic conflict between the Tamils of the north, who are Hindu, and the Sinhalese of the south, who are Buddhist, has been a source of civil disorder. The Liberation Tigers of Tamil Eelam (LTTE), known as the Tamil Tigers, is the largest guerrilla army fighting for the creation of a separate Tamil state (Eelam). Ranasinghe Premadasa, of the United National Party (UNP), became President of Sri Lanka in 1989. Dingiri Banda Wijetunge (UNP) became Prime Minister in 1989. Sri Lanka is a member of the Commonwealth. Sri Lanka is the world's second largest exporter of tea. It also exports rubber and clothing. Ethnic conflict has seriously damaged the economy and has particularly affected tourism, formerly an important industry. ♦ **Sri Lankan** /sriː laŋkən/ N, ADJ ▪ *per capita GNP:* US$420 ▪ *religion:* Buddhism, Hinduism ▪ *language:* Sinhala and Tamil (official), English ▪ *currency:* rupee ▪ *capital:* Colombo (in 1982 Sri Jayawardenepura became the seat of government) ▪ *population:* 17 million (1989) ▪ *size:* 64,628 square kilometres.

St. The plural form for the meaning in paragraph 2 is SS.
1 St is a written abbreviation for 'Street'. *...22 Harley St, London W1.*
2 St is also a written abbreviation for 'Saint'. *...St Anselm. ...SS Peter and Paul.*

st
st is a written abbreviation for 'stone'. *She weighs 8st 6lb.*

-st /-st, -ɪst/
SUFFIX -st is added to most numbers written in figures and ending in 1 to form ordinal numbers. 1st is pronounced the same as 'first'. *...1st April 1982. ...21st Street.*

stab /stæb/ **stabs, stabbing, stabbed**
1 VO To **stab** someone means to push a knife into their body. *A man was stabbed to death as he left a London library.*
2 VOorVA If you **stab** something or **stab** at it, you push at it with your finger or with something pointed. *He stabbed the air with his index finger... She was typing in a fury, her fingers stabbing at the keys.*
3 NC If you have a **stab** at something, you try to do it; an informal use. *I'd like to have a stab at tap dancing.*
4 N SING+*of* You can refer to a sudden, unpleasant feeling as a **stab** of that feeling; a literary use. *Kitty felt a stab of dismay.*
5 If you say that someone **has stabbed** you **in the back**, you mean that they have done something very harmful to you when you thought that you could trust them. *Moldavians feel they have been stabbed in the back by the Gagauz.*

stabbing /stæbɪŋ/ **stabbings**
1 NC A **stabbing** is an incident in which someone stabs someone else. *There was an investigation into the stabbing.*
2 ADJ ATTRIB A **stabbing** pain is a sudden sharp pain.

stability /stəbɪləti/
NU **Stability** is the state of being stable. *...a period of economic growth and stability... The biggest problem facing the relief effort is the lack of political stability.*

stabilize /steɪbəlaɪz/ **stabilizes, stabilizing, stabilized**; also spelt **stabilise**.
V-ERG If something **stabilizes** or **is stabilized**, it becomes stable. *Eventually your weight will stabilise... The move is designed to stabilise oil prices.*
♦ **stabilization** /steɪbəlaɪzeɪʃn/ NU *This was one of the surest signs yet of the stabilization of Philippine politics.*

stabilizer /steɪbəlaɪzə/ **stabilizers**; also spelt **stabiliser**.
NC A **stabilizer** is a device that helps a ship, plane, or racing car to remain stable. *He managed to complete his first lap without stabilisers.*

stable /steɪbl/ **stables**
1 ADJ If something is **stable**, it is not likely to change or come to an end suddenly. *Oil prices are stable for the first time in years. ...a stable marriage... He has been admitted to hospital with leg injuries and is said to be in a stable condition.*
2 ADJ If an object is **stable**, it is not likely to move or fall. *A typist's chair should be stable.*
3 NC A **stable** is a building in which horses are kept. *...a photograph of Mr Piggot smiling as he strokes a horse at his stables. ...riding stables.*

stable-boy, stable-boys
NC A **stable-boy** or **stable-lad** is a man who works in a stable looking after the horses. *She was always kind to the stableboy or the chauffeur... He got a job as a stable-lad in a Long Island mansion.*

stab wound, stab wounds
NC A **stab wound** is a wound that is caused by stabbing with a knife. *She died from multiple stab wounds.*

staccato /stəkɑːtəʊ/
ADJ ATTRIB A **staccato** noise consists of a series of short, sharp, separate sounds; a literary word. *...the man's staccato Berlin accent. ...the staccato sound of guns.*

stack /stæk/ **stacks, stacking, stacked**
1 NC A **stack** of things is a neat pile of them. *On the sideboard was a stack of plates.*

2 vo If you **stack** a number of things, you arrange them in neat piles. *I started stacking the chairs.*
3 v-pass If a place or surface is **stacked** with objects, it is filled with piles of them. *The shed was stacked with old boxes.*
4 quant **Stacks** of something means a lot of it; an informal use. *They've got stacks of money.*
5 If you say that **the odds are stacked against** someone, or that something they are dealing with is **stacked against** them, you mean that they are unlikely to succeed in what they want to do, because the conditions are not favourable. *The odds are stacked against you... The odds are still stacked against an outright opposition victory. ...a legal system that is stacked against her.*
stack up PHRASAL VERB 1 If you **stack** things **up**, you arrange them in a tall pile. *We stacked up the plates and carried them to the sink... Crates of prefilled petrol bombs have been stacked up on the roofs of nearby buildings.* 2 If you ask how one person or thing **stacks up** against other people or things, you are asking how they compare with them; used in informal American English. *How does this room stack up against the great libraries of Europe?... World competitions, of course, tend to be seen as a stage to see how US kids stack up.*
stadium /stéɪdiəm/ The plural form can be either **stadiums** or **stadia**.
nc A **stadium** is a large sports ground with rows of seats all round it. *The city does not yet have a main sports stadium that could accommodate the Games... Two big new stadia have been built in Nairobi.*
staff /stɑːf/ **staffs, staffed**
1 n coll The **staff** of an organization are the people who work for it. *She was invited to join the staff of the BBC... There are two students to every member of staff... Hospital staff have begun a series of stoppages... They have already agreed to cut their staffs.*
2 v-pass If an organization is **staffed** by particular people, they are the people who work for it. *It was staffed and run by engineers.*
staffer /stɑːfə/ **staffers**
nc A **staffer** is a member of staff, especially in a government organization or a newspaper; used in American English. *He was greeted by very enthusiastic applause by White House staffers... Times staffers used to joke that the paper gave more attention to shipping news than to TV.*
staffing /stɑːfɪŋ/
nu **Staffing** refers to the number of workers employed to work somewhere. *...inadequate staffing... Councils should review staffing levels.*
staff nurse, staff nurses
nc A **staff nurse** is a hospital nurse whose rank is just below that of a sister or charge nurse. *...a staff nurse in the intensive care unit.*
stag /stæg/ **stags**
nc A **stag** is an adult male deer. *Stags roar repeatedly during the autumn breeding season.*
stage /steɪdʒ/ **stages, staging, staged**
1 nc A **stage** is a part of a process or activity. *In the early stages of learning to read, a child will usually need a lot of help. ...at this stage in my life. ...the first stage of an 800 mile expedition... Today the final stage of negotiations over a budget deal began.*
2 ncorNU In a theatre, the **stage** is the raised platform where actors or entertainers perform. *She stood alone on the enormous stage... She has been accused of being too flamboyant on stage.*
3 n sing You can refer to acting and the production of plays in a theatre as the **stage**. *She retired from the stage some years ago... He's adapted one of his novels for the stage.*
4 vo If someone **stages** a play or other show, they present a performance of it. *Last weekend saw one of the biggest rock shows to be staged in Britain.*
5 vo If you **stage** an event, you organize it and usually take part in it. *The women staged a demonstration... Bus drivers have staged peak-hour strikes almost every day for the past three weeks... The Games are the biggest international sporting*

event China has staged.
6 To **set the stage** for something means to make preparations so that it can happen. *I believe Mr Gorbachev wants to set the stage for a more far-reaching disarmament treaty... The stage would seem to be set for a potentially explosive confrontation.*
7 n sing+supp You can refer to a particular area of activity as a particular **stage**, especially when you are talking about politics. *Mitterrand is very aware that he is introducing a new star onto the French political stage. ...a newcomer on the international stage... President Castro has been on the world stage for three decades.*
stagecoach /stéɪdʒkəʊtʃ/ **stagecoaches**
nc **Stagecoaches** were large carriages pulled by horses which carried passengers and mail. *Once located along merchant paths and a stagecoach route, the town prospered in earlier times.*
stage door, stage doors
nc The **stage door** of a theatre is the entrance used by performers and by employees of the theatre. *Crowds mobbed me at the stage door.*
stage fright
nu **Stage fright** is a feeling of fear or nervousness that some people have just before they appear in front of an audience. *What he experienced was intense stage fright.*
stagehand /stéɪdʒhænd/ **stagehands**
nc A **stagehand** is a person whose job is to move the scenery and equipment on the stage in a theatre. *One of the stagehands was kind enough to compliment me after the performance.*
stage-manage, stage-manages, stage-managing, stage-managed
vo If an event is **stage-managed**, it is carefully organized and controlled by someone, rather than happening spontaneously. *He maintained that the affair had been stage-managed in an attempt to divert attention from public unrest.* ◆ **stage-managed** ADJ *It was very much a stage-managed occasion for the benefit of the foreign press.*
stage manager, stage managers
nc A **stage manager** is the person who is responsible for the scenery and lights and for the way that actors or other performers move about and use the stage during a performance in the theatre. *'Miss Jordache,' the stage manager said. 'We're ready when you are.'... She asked me to go on tour with her, as assistant stage manager.*
stage-struck
ADJ Someone who is **stage-struck** is fascinated by the theatre and wants to become an actor or actress. *He's been stage-struck ever since we took him to 'Peter Pan'.*
stage whisper, stage whispers
nc A **stage whisper** is a loud whisper that is meant to be heard by several people. *'That was terrific,' she told him in a stage whisper.*
stagger /stǽgə/ **staggers, staggering, staggered**
1 v If you **stagger**, you walk very unsteadily, for example because you are ill. *I staggered to the nearest chair.*
2 vo If something **staggers** you, it surprises you very much. *This fact staggered me.* ◆ **staggered** ADJ *We were staggered to learn they would not be returning.* ◆ **staggering** ADJ *Its estimated cost has climbed to a staggering £35 billion.*
3 vo If things such as people's holidays or hours of work are **staggered**, they are arranged so that they do not all happen at the same time. *About thirty military observers will monitor the withdrawals, which will be staggered over more than two years... Drivers are being asked to stagger their journeys or use the bus services, which are running normally.*
staging post, staging posts
nc A **staging post** is a place where people or things go, or are sent, on their way to another place, often so that preparations can be made for something. *They are using the remote western province as a staging post for attacks on his country... Turkey is also being used as a channel for aid by other countries, with flights from abroad using Ankara airport as a staging*

post... Several islands have become notorious staging posts for cocaine en route to the United States from Colombia.

stagnant /stǽgnənt/
1 ADJ If something such as a business or society is **stagnant**, there is little activity or change; used showing disapproval. *...stagnant economies.*
2 ADJ **Stagnant** water is not flowing or fresh, and is dirty and unhealthy. *Algae are the organisms which form that green slime you find on ponds and other stagnant water.*

stagnate /stægnéɪt/ **stagnates, stagnating, stagnated**
V If something such as a business or society **stagnates**, it becomes inactive or does not change; used showing disapproval. *The economy stagnated as a result of these tax measures.* ♦ **stagnating** ADJ ATTRIB *A stagnating economy and rising unemployment have sapped enthusiasm for costly military adventures.* ♦ **stagnation** /stægnéɪʃn/ NU *The debt problem had resulted in economic stagnation and social unrest.*

stag night, stag nights
NC A **stag night** or a **stag party** is a party for a man who is getting married the next day, to which only men are invited.

staid /stéɪd/
ADJ A **staid** person is serious, dull, and rather old-fashioned. *Its population tends to be elderly, staid, set in its ways.*

stain /stéɪn/ **stains, staining, stained**
1 NC A **stain** is a dirty mark on something that is difficult to remove. *Blood stains were found afterwards. ...grease stains.*
2 VO If a substance **stains** something, the thing becomes coloured or marked by the substance. *...the pink spots staining my new blue jacket.* ♦ **stained** ADJ *...a little man with stained teeth... His shirt was stained with blood.*

stained glass
NU **Stained glass** consists of pieces of coloured glass fixed together to make decorative windows or other objects. *Artists were drawn to the possibilities of using stained glass in their work. ...Victorian stained-glass windows.*

stainless steel /stéɪnləs stíːl/
NU **Stainless steel** is a metal made from steel and chromium which does not rust. *It's a simple device made of stainless steel and plastic. ...a stainless steel sink.*

stair /stéə/ **stairs**
1 N PL **Stairs** are a set of steps inside a building. *He ran up the stairs. ...another flight of stairs.*
2 NC A **stair** is one of the steps in a set of stairs. *Not a stair creaked as she made her way downstairs.*

staircase /stéəkeɪs/ **staircases**
NC A **staircase** is a set of stairs inside a building. *I wanted to climb the winding little staircase.*

stairway /stéəweɪ/ **stairways**
NC A **stairway** is a set of steps, inside or outside a building. *She spent her nights huddled close to a radiator on the public stairway of an apartment block.*

stairwell /stéəwel/ **stairwells**
NC A **stairwell** is the part of a building that contains a staircase. *He leaned over the balcony above the stairwell.*

stake /stéɪk/ **stakes, staking, staked**
1 If something is **at stake**, it is being risked and might be lost or damaged. *There's a great deal of money at stake... His political life is at stake.*
2 N PL The **stakes** involved in a risky action or a contest are the things that can be gained or lost. *I'm playing for high stakes.*
3 VO If you **stake** something such as your money or your reputation on the result of something, you risk your money or reputation on it. *He staked his reputation as a prophet on this assertion.*
4 NC If you have a **stake** in something, its success matters to you, for example because you own part of it. *...a substantial stake in the British textile industry.*
5 N PL+SUPP You can use **stakes** to refer to something that is considered as a contest. *...the Presidential stakes... This gives you an advantage in the promotion stakes.*

6 NC A **stake** is a pointed wooden post. *His boat was fastened by a chain to a stake in the ground.*
7 If you **stake** a claim, you say that you have a right to something. *Each group had staked its claim to its own territory.*

stake-out, stake-outs
NC If police officers are on a **stake-out**, they are secretly watching a building for evidence of criminal activity. *Hundreds of police were involved in stake-outs at cash dispensers... The stake-out was mounted after the discovery of a poaching ring.*

stalactite /stǽləktaɪt/ **stalactites**
NC A **stalactite** is a piece of rock which looks like a large icicle and which hangs down from the roof of a cave. It is formed by the dripping of water containing lime. *These caves are famous because of the beauty of their stalactite formations.*

stalagmite /stǽləgmaɪt/ **stalagmites**
NC A **stalagmite** is a long piece of rock which sticks up from the floor of a cave and is formed by water containing lime dripping from the roof.

stale /stéɪl/
1 ADJ When things such as food or tobacco are **stale**, they are old and no longer fresh or good to eat or use. *The hostages survived on a diet of rice and stale bread.*
2 ADJ Air or smoke that is **stale** has an unpleasant smell because it is not fresh. *Inside the flat was a musty smell of stale air. ...stale cigarette smoke.*
3 ADJ If you feel **stale**, you have no new ideas and are bored. *The SDP was something new and fresh on a rather stale political scene.*

stalemate /stéɪlmeɪt/
NU **Stalemate** is a situation in which neither side in an argument or contest can win or in which no progress is possible. *Five hours of talks between the two governments have failed to break the stalemate over Northern Ireland... The coalition ended the political stalemate caused by the election.*

stalk /stɔːk/ **stalks, stalking, stalked**
1 NC The **stalk** of a flower, leaf, or fruit is the thin part that joins it to the plant or tree. *Leaves are stripped off the stalk and dried in the sun... The corn stalks had been flattened overnight.*
2 VO If you **stalk** a person or a wild animal, you follow them quietly and secretly in order to catch them or observe them. *He moved like a tiger stalking its prey.*
3 VA If you **stalk** somewhere, you walk in a stiff, proud, or angry way. *She stalked into the living room.*

stall /stɔːl/ **stalls, stalling, stalled**
1 V-ERG If a process **stalls**, or if someone or something **stalls** it, the process stops, but may continue at a later time. *It looks as though the reforms have stalled. ...the negotiations which only a week ago appeared to have stalled... They do not want this issue to stall their current drive to improve relations with China... Progress has been stalled by differences over the future of the armed forces.* ♦ **stalled** ADJ *At the moment, negotiations to produce a peace settlement are stalled... His resignation had nothing to do with the stalled peace process.*
2 VO If you **stall** someone, you prevent them from doing something until later, so for example, you have more time to think or to do something else. *They have been stalling the hijackers with a number of different reasons why refuelling cannot be carried out... Perhaps I can stall him till Thursday or Friday.*
3 V If you **stall**, you try to avoid doing something until later. *The Soviet Union has accused Pakistan of stalling at the Geneva talks on Afghanistan... 'Well?' she said. Tom grinned at her, stalling for time.*
4 V-ERG When a vehicle **stalls** or when you accidentally **stall** it, the engine stops suddenly. *The rear engine stalled, and the plane plummeted 3,500 feet... I stalled at the traffic lights and then had to wait for ages.*
5 NC A **stall** is a large table on which you put goods that you want to sell or information that you want to give to people. *Demonstrators ransacked market stalls after food prices increased by over 300 per cent in a week... Campaign groups have hired stalls just*

outside the conference hall.
6 NC A **stall** is a small enclosed area in a room which is used for a particular purpose, for example for a shower; used in American English. *...a shower stall... He was found in a locked bathroom stall, shot in the head.*
7 N PL The **stalls** in a theatre or concert hall are the seats on the ground floor in front of the stage. *I suddenly noticed her in the front row of the stalls.*

stallholder /stɔːlhəʊldə/ **stallholders**
NC A **stallholder** is a person who sells goods at a stall in a market. *Stallholders offered everything from live squid to eat to Coca Cola to drink.*

stallion /stæljən/ **stallions**
NC A **stallion** is a male horse. *...white Arabian stallions.*

stalwart /stɔːlwət/ **stalwarts**
ADJ A **stalwart** worker or supporter of an organization is loyal and hard-working. *...the stalwart Somerset cricketer, Bill Andrews.* ▶ Also NC *They were all Government stalwarts.*

stamen /steɪmən/ **stamens**
NC The **stamens** of a flower are the small, delicate stalks which grow inside the blossom and produce pollen.

stamina /stæmɪnə/
NU **Stamina** is the physical or mental energy needed to do a tiring activity for a long time. *In an impressive display of stamina the ministers have stayed up all night.*

stammer /stæmə/ **stammers, stammering, stammered**
1 V or V-QUOTE If you **stammer**, you speak with difficulty, hesitating and repeating words or sounds. *Four times as many men as women stammer... 'But...but...that's impossible,' the youth stammered.*
2 NC Someone who has a **stammer** tends to stammer when they speak. *...a stammer he had never been able to control.*
stammer out PHRASAL VERB If you **stammer** something **out**, you say it with difficulty, hesitating and repeating words, because you are nervous or afraid. *Before he could stammer out his thanks, she walked away.*

stamp /stæmp/ **stamps, stamping, stamped**
1 NC A **stamp** or a **postage stamp** is a small piece of gummed paper which you stick on an envelope or parcel before you post it, to show that you have paid the appropriate fee. *The price of a first class stamp will go up. ...a special issue of postage stamps in honour of the Queen Mother's 90th birthday.*
2 NC A **stamp** is also a small block of wood or metal with words or a design on it. You press it onto an inky pad and then onto a document in order to produce a mark on the document. The mark is also called a **stamp**. *They had German passports with Brazilian entrance stamps.*
3 VO If you **stamp** a mark or word on an object, you press the mark or word onto the object using a stamp or other device. *Articles that conform with the relevant British Standards are stamped with a kite-shaped mark... Unless pots are stamped 'ovenproof' assume they are not.*
4 N SING+SUPP If something bears the **stamp** of a particular quality or person, it clearly has that quality or was done by that person. *His work hardly bore the stamp of maturity. ...a designer who has left his stamp on 20th century industry.*
5 VO If you **stamp** your foot, you put your foot down very hard on the ground because you are angry. *'Damn you, Edward!' she shouted, stamping her foot.*
6 V+on If you **stamp** on something, you put your foot down on it very hard. *I stamped heavily on her foot and muttered, 'Shut up'.*
stamp on PHRASAL VERB If someone **stamps on** a dishonest or undesirable activity, they stop it happening or spreading. *Sporadic outbreaks of violence have been swiftly stamped on by the large police presence in the city.*
stamp out PHRASAL VERB If you **stamp** something **out**, you put an end to it or destroy it completely. *They are determined to stamp out political extremism. ...an*

effort to stamp out corruption in high places.

stamped /stæmpt/
ADJ A **stamped** envelope or parcel has a stamp stuck on it.

stamped addressed envelope, stamped addressed envelopes
NC A **stamped addressed envelope** is an envelope on which you stick a stamp and write your own name and address. You send it to an organization or person so that they can send you something, for example information about something. *Write to them enclosing a stamped addressed envelope.*

stampede /stæmpiːd/ **stampedes, stampeding, stampeded**
1 V When a group of animals or people **stampede**, they run in a wild, uncontrolled way. *As the blaze spread, people stampeded through the narrow streets to escape.*
2 NC When there is a **stampede**, a group of animals or people run in a wild, uncontrolled way. *...a stampede of elephants... Her foot got trodden on in the general stampede to the exit.*

stance /stæns, stɑːns/ **stances**
1 NC+SUPP Your **stance** on a particular matter is your attitude to it. *The new government will adopt a much tougher stance on foreign debt. ...his courageous stance. ...critics of the government's stance.*
2 NC Your **stance** is also the way that you are standing; a formal use. *He altered his stance slightly and leaned against a tree.*

stand /stænd/ **stands, standing, stood**
1 V When you **are standing**, your body is upright, your legs are straight, and your weight is supported by your feet. *The teacher stands in front of the class and instructs the child... The crowd was so large that many had to stand outside in the snow... People stand in queues for hours on end.*
2 V When you **stand**, you change your position so that you are standing, rather than sitting; a formal use. *One by one, he asked each graduate to stand.*
3 VA If you **stand** aside or **stand** back, you move to a different place a short distance away. *Miss Darke told the girls to stand aside... He stood back and surveyed his handiwork.*
4 VA If you **stand** as or for a political position, you are a candidate in an election for that position. *Mr Taylor also said he would stand as president... Abdou Diouf is standing for a second term in office... Mr Mitterrand said he decided to stand because he believed that he could maintain unity in France.*
5 VA You can describe the position of something such as a building or a piece of furniture by saying that it **stands** in a particular place. *Along the south bank of the river Thames stands one of the capital's most significant buildings... An old piano stood in the corner of the room. ...a medieval town which stands at the foot of the Austrian Alps.*
6 V You sometimes say that a building **is standing** when it remains after other buildings have fallen down or been destroyed. *Only one of the houses is still standing.*
7 VOA If you **stand** something somewhere, you put it there in an upright position. *He stood the bottle on the bench beside him.*
8 V If you leave food or a mixture of something to **stand**, you leave it without disturbing it for some time.
9 V If a decision or offer **stands**, it is still valid. *Fifty years later, this Supreme Court ruling still stands.*
10 VA or VC You can use **stand** instead of 'is' to describe the state or condition of something, often to emphasize the temporary nature of the state or condition. *Inflation now stands at its lowest level for a year... The law, as it now stands, permits divorce if there has been an irretrievable breakdown in a marriage.*
11 VA or VC If you **stand** in a particular way, you have a particular attitude or take a particular action in a situation. *Prime Minister Hawke has harsh words for politicians who stand in the way of the changes... There was never any doubt about where he stood on the racial issue. ...Bonn's resolve to stand firm against international terrorism.*

12 N SING If you take a **stand** or make a **stand,** you resist attempts to defeat you or to make you change your mind. *He was proud of the stand the nurses had taken... The government needs to take a firm stand on this kind of thing.*
13 VO If something can **stand** a situation or a test, it is good enough or strong enough to cope with it. *The economy couldn't stand another rise in interest rates... Her arguments could hardly stand close inspection.*
14 VO If you cannot **stand** something, it irritates you so that you cannot tolerate it. *He kept on nagging until I couldn't stand it any longer... She can't stand children.*
15 V+to-INF If you **stand** to gain or to lose something, you are likely to gain or lose it. *Transplant patients stand to benefit... Many people would stand to lose by the change.*
16 NC+SUPP A **stand** is a small stall or shop at an exhibition or in the street. *One of the first stands he visited was that of F J Price and Co. ...a newspaper stand.*
17 NC A **stand** is also a large structure at a sports ground, where the spectators sit or stand to watch what is happening. *A fire has destroyed the main stand at the football ground.*
18 NC A **stand** is also an object or piece of furniture that is designed for holding a particular kind of thing. *...an umbrella stand. ...a music stand.*
19 See also **standing.**
• **Stand** is used in these phrases. • If you say that it **stands to reason** that something is true or possible, you mean that it is obvious; an informal expression. *If they keep doing that, it stands to reason that the police are going to get suspicious.* • When someone **stands trial,** they are tried in a court of law. *He must stand trial on criminal charges.* • When a witness **takes the stand** in a court of law, he or she answers questions. *Hearne had not yet taken the stand.* • to **stand on your own two feet:** see **foot.** • to **stand your ground:** see **ground.**

stand by PHRASAL VERB 1 If you **stand by,** you are ready to help or take action if it becomes necessary. *Rescue helicopters stood by... The army has been ordered to stand by.* 2 If you **stand by** and let something bad happen, you allow it to do anything to stop it. *We cannot stand by and watch while our allies are attacked.* 3 If you **stand by** someone, you support them when they are in trouble. *If they try to make you resign, we'll stand by you.* 4 If you **stand by** an earlier decision or agreement, you do not change it. *They are insisting that they will stand by their promise and make up the whole agreed amount.* 5 See also **standby.**

stand down PHRASAL VERB If someone **stands down,** they resign. *He is certain to stand down as leader... He is still resisting calls to stand down.*

stand for PHRASAL VERB 1 If a letter **stands for** a particular word, it is an abbreviation for that word. *FARM stands for Food and Agricultural Research Management.* 2 The ideas or attitudes that someone or something **stands for** are the ones that they support or represent. *What are the main parties and what do they stand for?... It is busily trying to give the impression that it alone stands for democracy.* 3 If you will not **stand for** something, you will not tolerate it. *The Army would not stand for it much longer.*

stand in PHRASAL VERB 1 If you **stand in** for someone, you take their place or do their job. *He was standing in for his younger brother... You will stand in for me, John?* 2 See also **stand-in.**

stand out PHRASAL VERB 1 If something **stands out,** it can be seen very clearly. *They don't stand out in a crowd.* 2 If an issue or achievement **stands out,** it is very different, much better or more important than other, similar things. *One issue stood out as especially important... What stands out for you from the nine years or so you've been there?*

stand up PHRASAL VERB 1 When you **stand up,** you change your position so that you are standing, rather than sitting. *A junior minister stood up to make the closing speech.* 2 If something **stands up** to rough treatment, it is not damaged or harmed by it. *This*

carpet stands up to the wear and tear of continual use. 3 If you **stand up** to someone or something, you defend yourself against their attacks or demands. *Mrs Thatcher has stood up to international pressure.* 4 If you **stand up** for someone or something that is being criticized or threatened, you defend them. *I'm glad to see that he's standing up for himself... Children are among the least able to stand up for their rights.* 5 If something such as a claim or a piece of evidence **stands up,** it is accepted as true or satisfactory. *...evidence that would stand up in a court of law.* 6 If you **are stood up** by someone, especially a boyfriend or girlfriend, they fail to keep an arrangement to meet you; an informal use. *He said he'd meet her outside the station, but he stood her up.*

standard /stændəd/ **standards**
1 NC+SUPP or NU+SUPP A **standard** is a level of quality or achievement, especially a level that is thought to be acceptable. *The goods they produce are of a higher standard... There's been a record number of complaints about the standard of service on Britain's state-run railways.*
2 NC+SUPP A **standard** is also something that you use in order to judge the quality of something else. *Democracy is the standard by which governments are measured... By any standard the work was good.*
3 NC **Standards** are moral principles which affect people's behaviour. *He spoke of declining moral standards, alcoholism and crime.*
4 ADJ You use **standard** to describe things which are usual and normal. *There is a standard procedure for recording drugs given to patients... Mrs Thatcher has drawn up plans to cut the standard rate of income tax.*
5 ADJ ATTRIB A **standard** work or text on a particular subject is one which is widely read and often recommended. *This is the standard work on British moths.*
6 See also **double standard.**

standard bearer, standard bearers
NC A **standard bearer** is a person who acts as a leader or public representative of a group who have the same aims or interests. *For more than a decade, Tony Benn has been regarded as the standard bearer of the radical left.*

standardize /stændədaɪz/ **standardizes, standardizing, standardized;** also spelt **standardise.**
VO To **standardize** things means to change them so that they share the same features. *Some people have criticized television for standardizing speech, habits, and tastes.* ◆ **standardized** ADJ *Equipment is going to become more standardized.*

standard lamp, standard lamps
NC A **standard lamp** is a tall electric light which stands on the floor in a living-room.

standard of living, standards of living
NC Your **standard of living** is the level of comfort and wealth which you have. *People are enjoying the highest standard of living they have ever known. ...a drop in the standard of living.*

standby /stændbaɪ/ **standbys**
1 NC A **standby** is something or someone that is always ready to be used if it is needed. *Eggs are a great standby in the kitchen... Mueller, a standby driver, had driven this route many times.*
2 If something or someone is **on standby,** they are ready to be used when they are needed. *It would be on permanent standby to go to the scene of any disaster... They've put their snow-making machines on standby.*
3 N+N A **standby** ticket for the theatre or a plane journey is a cheap ticket that is sometimes available just before the performance starts or the plane leaves.
4 N+N If a country is in great need of money, it can apply to the International Monetary Fund for access to funds which can be drawn on when necessary. This is called a **standby** arrangement or **standby** credit. *The fund had assured him that Peru would receive standby credit for October. ...a standby loan from the International Monetary Fund.*

stand-in, stand-ins
NC A **stand-in** is a person who takes someone else's place because the other person is ill or unavailable.

Mr Kaifu was meant to be a temporary stand-in.
▶ Also ADJ ATTRIB *Ravi Shastri, their stand-in captain, started well.*

standing /stændɪŋ/
1 ADJ ATTRIB You use **standing** to describe something which is permanently in existence. *...a standing committee made up of about a hundred members... This is a standing joke amongst psychologists.*
2 NU+SUPP Someone's **standing** is their status or reputation; a formal use. *She was an economist of considerable standing. ...with the aim of improving the party's standing among young people.*
3 NU You can refer to the number of percentage points a politician or a political party has in the opinion polls as their **standing** in the polls. *The party improved its standing in the opinion polls to almost twenty per cent... The party's standing is only about 7 per cent with the voters.*
4 NU+SUPP You use **standing** to say how long something has existed or how long it has had a particular function. *...a member of twenty-five years' standing... The present unrest has its origins in social ills of long standing.*

standing order, standing orders
NC A **standing order** is an instruction to your bank to pay someone a fixed amount of money regularly. *I pay their allowance by standing order.*

standing ovation, standing ovations
NC If an audience gives a speaker a **standing ovation**, they stand up while they are applauding, to show their appreciation. *When he finished speaking he was given a standing ovation.*

standing room
NU **Standing room** is space in a room or bus, where people can stand when all the seats have been taken. *Inside there was standing room only.*

stand-off, stand-offs; used in American English.
1 NC A **stand-off** is a situation in which neither of two opposing groups or forces will make a move until the other does something, so nothing can happen until one party gives way. *There was a stand-off for more than five hours... This stand-off between army and church is clearly troubling the authorities.*
2 ADJ ATTRIB **Stand-off** missiles or weapons are designed mainly to balance or neutralize the enemy's forces. *...NATO's plans for modernising its stand-off nuclear aircraft bombs.*

stand-offish /stændɒfɪʃ/
ADJ PRED If you say that someone is **stand-offish**, you mean that they behave in a formal and rather unfriendly way.

standpipe /stændpaɪp/ **standpipes**
NC A **standpipe** is a vertical pipe that is connected to a water supply and stands in a street or other public place. *The introduction of wholesale water restrictions, with standpipes in the streets is still some way off.*

standpoint /stændpɔɪnt/ **standpoints**
NC+SUPP Your **standpoint** is a particular way of looking at or thinking about an event, situation, or idea. *Up to now, we have only discussed the issue from a western standpoint.*

standstill /stændstɪl/
N SING If movement or an activity comes to a **standstill**, it stops completely. *All train services are at a standstill today in a dispute over pay... The economy has been brought to a virtual standstill.*

stand-up
1 ADJ ATTRIB **Stand-up** comedy is comedy in which a comedian stands up alone in front of an audience and tells jokes. *...a stand-up comedian.*
2 ADJ ATTRIB A **stand-up** fight or argument is one in which people stand up and hit or shout at each other in an unrestrained way. *It started as a quarrel but turned into a stand-up fight... These proposals caused a stand-up row in Parliament.*

stank /stæŋk/
Stank is the past tense of **stink**.

Stanley /stænli/
Stanley, on East Falkland Island, is the capital of the Falkland Islands and its largest town. Population: 1,700 (1991).

stanza /stænzə/ **stanzas**
NC A **stanza** is a verse of a poem; a technical term. *Read the last stanza aloud.*

staple /steɪpl/ **staples, stapling, stapled**
1 ADJ ATTRIB A **staple** meal, diet, or food is one that forms a basic part of your everyday diet. *Sugar is a staple food in Sudan. ...the dry bread which is their staple diet.* ▶ Also NC *Supermarkets have already run out of basic staples such as cooking oil, sugar and meat.*
2 NC **Staples** are small pieces of wire used for holding sheets of paper together. They are pushed through the paper using a special device called a stapler. *The library will no longer be able to supply pens, pencils, staples and paper clips.*
3 VOA If you **staple** something, you fix it in place using staples. *The letter was stapled to the other documents in the file.*

stapler /steɪplə/ **staplers**
NC A **stapler** is a special device used for putting staples into sheets of paper.

star /stɑː/ **stars, starring, starred**
1 NC Famous actors, musicians, and sports players are often referred to as **stars**. *...a beautiful movie star... This of course, is Bela Lugosi, star of the classic 1931 film 'Dracula'.*
2 V If an actor or actress **stars** in a play or film, they have one of the most important parts in it. *She'll be starring in a new play by Alan Bleasdale.*
3 VO If a play or film **stars** a famous actor or actress, they have one of the most important parts in it. *The last version of the movie starred John Garfield and Lana Turner.*
4 NC A **star** is a large ball of burning gas in space. You can see stars on clear nights as small points of light. *...the sun and the stars... I would slowly fall asleep at night under the stars.*
5 NC You can refer to a shape or an object as a **star** when it has four, five, or more points sticking out of it in a regular pattern. *He had two gold stars on his uniform. ...little star-shaped flowers.*
6 NC **Stars** are star-shaped marks printed against the name of something to indicate its quality. *...a four-star hotel.*
7 N PL The horoscope in a newspaper or magazine is sometimes referred to as the **stars**; an informal use. *What do the stars say for today?*
8 See also **rising star**.

starboard /stɑːbəd/
ADJ ATTRIB The **starboard** side of a ship is the right side when you are facing the front. *As the boat rounded a headland, it began to lean to starboard.*

starch /stɑːtʃ/ **starches**
1 N MASS **Starch** is a carbohydrate found in foods such as bread, potatoes, and rice. *Your doctor may recommend limiting the amount of fat and starch in your diet.*
2 NU **Starch** is also a substance used for stiffening cloth.

starched /stɑːtʃt/
ADJ **Starched** garments have been stiffened using starch. *They wore starched caps and white gloves.*

starchy /stɑːtʃi/
ADJ **Starchy** food contains a lot of starch. *Avoid starchy vegetables such as potato.*

stardom /stɑːdəm/
NU **Stardom** is the state of being a film star, rock star, etc. *It's difficult to explain her rise to stardom.*

stare /steə/ **stares, staring, stared**
1 VA If you **stare** at something, you look at it for a long time. *He stared at us in disbelief... She sat there quietly, staring out of the window.* ▶ Also NC *...a dreamy stare.*
2 If a situation or the answer to a problem is **staring** you **in the face**, it is very obvious although you may not be immediately aware of it. *The collapse of the system is staring Mr Gorbachev in the face... You can fail to see the real answer even when it's staring you right in the face.*

starfish /stɑːfɪʃ/; **starfish** is both the singular and the plural form.
NC A **starfish** is a flat, star-shaped creature with five

arms that lives in the sea.

stark /stɑːk/ **starker, starkest**

1 ADJ Something that is **stark** is noticeable because it is very bare and plain in appearance. ...*the stark black rocks and deserted beaches... The names were written in stark black print.* ◆ **starkly** ADV *The bare black trees stood out starkly against their grey background.*

2 ADJ ATTRIB **Stark** means harsh and unpleasant. *They are now faced with a stark choice... He gave a stark warning of the risk of such weapons.* ◆ **starkly** ADV *The country's dependence on a foreign labour force has been starkly exposed.*

3 ADJ ATTRIB A **stark** contrast is considerable in degree, and very obvious. *The BBC Environment correspondent says the conclusions are in stark contrast to most other reports.* ◆ **starkly** ADV *The Prime Minister's rating in the polls contrasts starkly with Mr Kinnock's.*

4 Someone who is **stark naked** is completely naked.

starkers /stɑːkəz/

ADJ PRED If someone is **starkers**, they are completely naked; an informal word, often used humorously. *One of the girls was starkers.*

starlight /stɑːlaɪt/

NU **Starlight** is the light that comes from the stars at night. *I enjoyed the view of the bay in the starlight.*

starling /stɑːlɪŋ/ **starlings**

NC A **starling** is a very common European bird with greenish-black feathers. ...*small birds, such as starlings and thrushes.*

starlit /stɑːlɪt/

ADJ ATTRIB A **starlit** night, sky, or sea is made lighter or brighter by the stars.

starry /stɑːri/

ADJ ATTRIB A **starry** night or sky is full of stars. *It was a cold, starry night.*

starry-eyed

ADJ If you are **starry-eyed**, you are so optimistic about things that you do not see how they really are. *We were all starry-eyed about visiting London.*

Stars and Stripes

N SING The **Stars and Stripes** is the name of the national flag of the United States of America. *The ship was flying the Stars and Stripes. ...a gold medal hanging around my neck and the Stars and Stripes waving overhead.*

star sign, star signs

NC Your **star sign** is the sign of the Zodiac under which you were born. *Her star sign was Libra, and therefore she already had a very balanced approach.*

star-studded

ADJ ATTRIB A **star-studded** show, film, or cast is one that includes a large number of famous performers. *Don't miss Sunday's star-studded performance.*

start /stɑːt/ **starts, starting, started**

1 V+*to*-INF, V+ING, V O, or V If you **start** to do something, you do something you were not doing before. *They started to wonder where all the money was coming from... We've already started taking orders for Christmas cakes... The Swiss authorities have started an investigation into the tragedy... Please ring me when you're ready to start.* ► Also N SING *We've not made a bad start.*

2 V-ERG If you **start** something or if it **starts**, it comes into existence. *It's not known how the fire started... We didn't want to start a panic.*

3 V-ERG When you **start** something or when it **starts**, it begins to happen. *The meeting starts at 7... Senior officials from both countries have started talks on ending the conflict.* ► Also NC ...*the start of negotiations.*

4 V+*by* or *with* If you **start** by doing something, or if you **start** with something, you do that thing first in a series of actions. *They started by throwing stones at the police... It will start with an overtime ban, followed on Monday by a twenty-four hour strike.*

5 V O If you **start** a business or organization, you create it or cause it to begin. *He scraped up the money to start a restaurant.*

6 V-ERG If you **start** an engine or car or if it **starts**, it begins to work. *They have to push it to start it... The*

engine just wouldn't start.

7 V If you **start**, your body jerks because you are surprised or frightened. *I sat down so quietly that she started.* ► Also NC *He awakened with a start.*

8 V A If you say that someone **started** as a particular kind of worker, you mean that that was their first job. *I started as a dishwasher and then I worked as a bus boy.*

9 You use **for a start** to introduce the first of a number of things that you are about to say. *We can't afford this house for a start.*

10 **in fits and starts**: see fit. See also **head start**.

start off PHRASAL VERB 1 When someone **starts off**, they begin going in a particular direction. *Before we could stop him, he had started off across the desert.* 2 If you say that someone **started off** as a particular kind of worker, you mean that that was their first job. *He started off as a shop steward for the builders' and engineering workers' union, and rose to become its president.* 3 If you **start off** by doing something or with something, you do it as the first part of an activity. *I started off by showing a slide of the diseased cell... Over half of the 400 richest people in Britain started off with nothing.* 4 To **start** something **off** means to cause it to start. *I know what started it all off.*

start on PHRASAL VERB If you **start on** something that needs to be done, you begin doing it. *She put the forks in a neat pile and started on the knives.*

start out PHRASAL VERB 1 If someone or something **starts out** as a particular thing, they are that thing at the beginning although they change later. *These areas started out as the private lands of settlers.* 2 If you **start out** by doing something, you do it at the beginning of an activity. *You started out by saying that this was the weapon they used.*

start over PHRASAL VERB If you **start over** or **start** something **over**, you start something again from the beginning; used in American English. *I would almost be willing to throw everything out and start over again.*

start up PHRASAL VERB 1 If you **start up** something such as a new business, you create it or cause it to start. *She wanted to start up a little country pub.* 2 If you **start up** an engine or car, you make it start to work. *The driver started up the car.*

START /stɑːt/

N PROP **START** is an abbreviation for 'Strategic Arms Reduction Treaty', a treaty signed between the United States and the former Soviet Union that limited the number of strategic nuclear weapons that each side was allowed to possess. *The START takes the process of nuclear arms control a step further.*

starter /stɑːtə/ **starters**

1 NC A **starter** is a small quantity of food served as the first course of a meal. *Serve noodles tossed in butter or cream as a starter.*

2 NC The **starter** of a car is a device that starts the engine. *That was why they put the automatic starter on the car.*

3 NC The **starters** in a race are the people or animals who take part at the beginning even if they do not finish. *Only 11 of the 29 starters completed the course... Reynolds has been confirmed as a definite starter in a special 400 metres invitation race.*

starting point, starting points

1 NC Your **starting point** on a journey is the place from which you start. *This is a good starting point for a car tour.*

2 NC A **starting point** is an idea, statement, or position that can be used to begin a conversation, argument, or process. *He takes the notebook of a dead man as the starting point for his latest novel... This is a very vulnerable starting point for a decisive thrust towards a market economy.*

startle /stɑːtl/ **startles, startling, startled**

V O If something sudden **startles** you, it surprises and frightens you. *Goodness, you startled me—I thought you were in the garden.* ◆ **startled** ADJ *We laughed at the startled expressions on their faces.*

startling /stɑːtəlɪŋ/

ADJ Something that is **startling** is so unexpected that

people are surprised by it. *The results were quite startling—a 77% increase in six months.*

starvation /stɑːˈveɪʃn/
NU **Starvation** is extreme suffering or death, caused by lack of food. *Between five and seven million people would die from starvation... Hundreds of thousands of people face possible starvation.*

starve /stɑːv/ **starves, starving, starved**
1 V If people **are starving**, they are suffering from a serious lack of food and are likely to die. *Many refugees are starving and some have died... Over the past month, 10 children have starved to death in the East alone.*
2 VOorV-REFL To **starve** someone means to not give them any food. *He'd been beaten and starved... Ten men starved themselves to death in prison last year.*
3 V If you say that you **are starving**, you mean that you are very hungry; an informal use. *I've got to have something to eat. I'm starving.*
4 VO+of If you **are starved** of something you need, you are suffering because you are not getting enough of it. *They seem to be starved of attention from adults. ...new legislation to starve terrorists of funds.*

Star Wars
NU **Star Wars** is a defence system being developed by the United States. It consists of satellites armed with lasers which can destroy enemy missiles in space. Its formal name is Strategic Defense Initiative. *Negotiators still want an agreement on Star Wars. ...the Star Wars project.*

stash /stæʃ/ **stashes, stashing, stashed**
VOA If you **stash** something valuable somewhere, you store it there to keep it safe; an informal word. *They had all that money stashed away in the loft.*

state /steɪt/ **states, stating, stated**
1 NC You can refer to countries as **states**, particularly when you are discussing politics. *The Latin American states maintained their independence... Before that, for a brief period, they had been independent states.*
2 NC Some countries are divided into smaller areas called **states**. *Haryana and Punjab were the fastest-developing states in India. ...the oil-producing states of Texas and Oklahoma.*
3 N PROP The USA is sometimes referred to informally as the **States**. *We're opening up an office in the States which is based in New York.*
4 N SING You can refer to the government of a country as the **state**. *He has been arrested and charged with crimes against the state. ...the conflict between the freedom of the individual and the security of the state. ...the state budget.*
5 N+N **State** schools, industries, or organizations are financed and organized by the government rather than private companies. *State schools are administered by local authorities.*
6 N+N A **state** occasion is a formal one involving the head of a country. *It will be the first state visit to a Western country for President Evren.*
7 NC+SUPP The **state** of someone or something refers to what condition they are in or what they are like at the moment. *She seemed in a very queer and nervous state... They are very concerned about the state of the churchyard. ...his poor state of health. ...the state of relations between the two countries.*
8 VOorV-REPORT If you **state** something, you say or write it so that people can take it as a formal record of your beliefs or intentions. *He has publicly stated his support for reforms... Each side stated their basic positions... She has already stated that her government doesn't intend to produce the bomb... The declaration stated that the federal army should withdraw.*
9 See also **head of state, welfare state**.
● **State** is used in these phrases. ● If you are **in a state**, you feel upset and nervous; an informal expression. *He used to get into an awful state as exams approached.* ● If someone is **not in a fit state** to do something, they are too upset or ill to do it. *The parent is in no fit state to help the children.* ● If the dead body of an important person **lies in state**, it is publicly displayed for a few days before it is buried. *His body will lie in state until the funeral.*

state- /steɪt-/
PREFIX **State-** is added to some past participles to form an adjective showing that something is owned or organized by the government. *State-controlled television and radio stations repeatedly broadcast warnings about the damage. ...state-funded health care. ...the state-owned airline, Air France.*

State Department
N PROP The **State Department** is the United States government department that is concerned with foreign affairs. *According to the American State Department, at least twenty people have been killed. ...a spokesman for the State Department.*

statehood /steɪthʊd/
1 NU **Statehood** is the condition of being an independent state. *51 per cent favour statehood, with 39 percent for retaining the island's commonwealth status. ...the country's road to statehood.*
2 NU In American English, **statehood** is also the condition of being one of the United States of America. *...a question of statehood for the District of Columbia.*

statehouse /steɪthaʊs/ **statehouses**
NC A **statehouse** is a building in which the legislature of one of the states of the United States of America is housed. *I hope that we can make an impact in Washington and the statehouses.*

stateless /steɪtləs/
ADJ A person who is **stateless** is not a citizen of any country and therefore has no nationality. *...people who have been made stateless.*

stately /steɪtli/
ADJ **Stately** things are impressive and dignified. *...strong and stately towers... Today's ceremony was a stately affair.*

stately home, stately homes
NC A **stately home** is a large old house which has belonged to an aristocratic family for a long time and which can sometimes nowadays be visited by the public. *...an English stately home, the country seat of the Earls of Shrewsbury.*

statement /steɪtmənt/ **statements**
1 NC A **statement** is something that you say or write in a formal and definite way, rather than just suggesting it. *I could not deny the truth of this statement... I thought at first that she said it as a statement, but it was a question.*
2 NC A **statement** is also an official or formal announcement that has been specially prepared for a particular occasion or situation. *...a government statement on defence spending... Mr Channon will make a statement to the House of Commons later today... They listened to a statement read by one of the hijackers.*
3 NC You can refer to the official account of events which a criminal or a witness gives to the police as a **statement**. *She was asked by the lawyer why some of her claims had not been contained in the statements made to Scotland Yard.*
4 NC A **statement** is also something that you do or make in a way that clearly expresses a particular opinion or idea that you have. *His sculpture can be seen as positive statement of general relevance to modern society.*
5 NC The printed document showing all the money paid into and taken out of a bank or building society account is also called a **statement**. *Computerized bank statements are always correct, right?*

state of affairs
N SING A **state of affairs** is the general situation and circumstances connected with someone or something. *What our present state of affairs demands is a firm leader.*

state of emergency
1 N SING If a government declares a **state of emergency**, it gives itself much stronger powers than usual to do things like censor reporting and imprison people without trial. It usually does this because of civil conflict. *A spokesman said the state of emergency must be lifted and all political prisoners freed... Today, under the state of emergency, reporting of such an incident would be banned.*

2 N SING A government can also declare a **state of emergency** in a part or whole of the country if there has been a major disaster and it wants to use all available resources to help. *Michigan Governor James Blanchard has declared a state of emergency and says more fire-fighting equipment is being flown in.*

state of mind, states of mind
NC Your **state of mind** is your mood at a particular time. *My sister was in a happier state of mind.*

state-of-the-art
ADJ ATTRIB **State-of-the-art** technology or production uses the most recently-developed methods, materials, or ideas. *It is due to be replaced by a computerised state-of-the-art signal box some time next year.*

statesman /steɪtsmən/ **statesmen** /steɪtsmən/
NC A **statesman** is an experienced and famous senior politician. *...the international statesman, traveling to all corners of the globe.*

statesmanship /steɪtsmənʃɪp/
NU **Statesmanship** is the skill and activities of a statesman. *Stanley Baldwin was the symbol of statesmanship. ...an act of supreme statesmanship.*

statewide /steɪtwaɪd/
ADJ or ADV **Statewide** means across or throughout the whole of one of the states of the United States. *The school band was scheduled to appear in a statewide competition... About 1200 homes have been evacuated statewide.*

static /stætɪk/
1 ADJ Something that is **static** does not move or change. *...a series of static images... The military situation appeared to be static.*
2 NU **Static** or **static electricity** is electricity which is caused by friction and which collects in things such as your body or metal objects. *The middle one is designed to discharge any static electricity.*
3 NU If there is **static** on the radio or television, you hear loud crackling noises. *The static from my receiver crackled like gunfire.*

station /steɪʃn/ **stations, stationing, stationed**
1 NC A **station** is a building by a railway line where a train stops. *The trains are moving again at the main railway station in Berlin.*
2 NC+SUPP A bus **station** or coach **station** is a place where a large number of buses or coaches start their journey. *I remember this girl I used to know meeting me at the Greyhound bus station in Seattle.*
3 NC If you talk about a radio **station**, you are referring to the programmes broadcast on a particular frequency by a particular radio company. *The radio was tuned permanently to his favourite station.*
4 V-PASS If people **are stationed** somewhere, they are sent there to do a job or to work for a period of time. *Two guards were stationed at the top of the stairs. ...the British forces stationed in Germany.*
5 See also **fire station, gas station, petrol station, police station.**

stationary /steɪʃənəʳri/
ADJ Something that is **stationary** is not moving. *...a stationary boat... The vehicle remained stationary.*

stationer /steɪʃənə/ **stationers**
NC A **stationer** is a person who sells paper, envelopes, and writing equipment.

stationery /steɪʃənəʳri/
1 NU **Stationery** is paper, envelopes, and writing equipment. *...a shipment of stationery.*
2 NU+SUPP **Stationery** is also used to refer to paper for writing letters that has been specially printed with a company, hotel, or manufacturer's name. *He sent us a lovely letter on Blue Ridge Parkway stationery.*

stationmaster /steɪʃnmɑːstə/ **stationmasters**
NC A **stationmaster** is the person in charge of a railway station.

station wagon, station wagons
NC A **station wagon** is the same as an **estate car**; used in American English. *My family traveled hot Mississippi backroads in a rusty, faded-blue station wagon.*

statistic /stətɪstɪk/ **statistics**
1 NC **Statistics** are facts obtained from analysing information that is expressed in numbers. *...divorce*

statistics... *Employment statistics show that there are jobs available... The Defence Ministry did not quarrel with that statistic.*
2 NU **Statistics** is a branch of mathematics concerned with the study of information that is expressed in numbers. *I teach statistics.*

statistical /stətɪstɪkl/
ADJ **Statistical** means relating to the use of statistics. *Statistical techniques are regularly employed.*
♦ **statistically** ADV *Statistically you have a one in six chance of succeeding... It cannot be proved statistically.*

statistician /stætɪstɪʃn/ **statisticians**
NC A **statistician** is a person who studies statistics or who works using statistics. *...a statistician in the Civil Service.*

statuary /stætjuəri/
NU You can refer to all the statues and sculptures in a place as the **statuary**; a formal word. *...some magnificent Roman statuary.*

statue /stætjuː/ **statues**
NC A **statue** is a large stone or metal sculpture of a person or an animal. *...a bronze statue of Charles I.*

statuesque /stætjuesk/
ADJ A woman who is **statuesque** is big and tall and looks rather like a Greek statue of a woman. *She was a beautiful, statuesque creature with pale blue eyes.*

statuette /stætjuet/ **statuettes**
NC A **statuette** is a very small statue. *...a statuette of a little girl.*

stature /stætʃə/
1 NU Someone's **stature** is their height and general size. *He is a grey haired man, short in stature and extremely talkative.*
2 NU Someone's **stature** is also their importance and reputation. *Success in settling the strike would increase his political stature.*

status /steɪtəs/
1 NU Your **status** is your position in society. *...the changing status of women. ...a report on the status of children and young people in Britain.*
2 NU You can refer to the prestige and importance that someone has in the eyes of other people as **status**. *He came in search of wealth, status, and power... At first he was not prepared to accept Boris Yeltsin's enhanced status.*
3 NU+SUPP **Status** is also an official classification which gives a person, organization, or country certain rights or advantages. *They appeared to have dropped their demand for status as political prisoners... Dozens of Western countries had already formally acknowledged the new status of the governments in Vilnius, Riga and Tallinn.*

status quo /steɪtəs kwəʊ/
N SING The **status quo** is the situation that exists at a particular time; a formal expression. *Military action might be needed to restore the status quo... Analysts say he's maintained the status quo.*

status symbol, status symbols
NC A **status symbol** is something that someone has and that shows their prestige and importance in society. *A personal chauffeur is undoubtedly a status symbol.*

statute /stætjuːt/ **statutes**
NC A **statute** is a formal rule or law. *There have been more than twenty statutes governing what can be published in newspapers.*

statute book
N SING The **statute book** is a collection of all the laws that are in force in a particular country. *This legislation is not on the statute book.*

statutory /stætjutəʳri/
ADJ **Statutory** means consisting of, or done because of, formal rules or laws; a formal word. *Doctors have a statutory duty to inform the authorities of the names of patients with HIV. ...a statutory minimum wage.*

staunch /stɔːntʃ/ **staunchest; staunches, staunching, staunched**
1 ADJ ATTRIB A **staunch** supporter is a very loyal one. *...a staunch supporter of Mrs Thatcher... He's known in particular as a staunch defender of the police.*
♦ **staunchly** ADV *This has been condemned by*

politicians of the right but staunchly defended by the Left. ...one of Belfast's most staunchly Protestant areas.

2 vo If you **staunch** blood, you stop it from flowing out of a wound; a formal use. *Sophia staunched the blood with a cloth.*

stave /steɪv/ **staves, staving, staved**

1 NC A **stave** is the five lines that music is written on.

2 NC A **stave** is a strong stick, normally used as a weapon. *...organised worker militias, armed with staves... They beat him with their thick bamboo staves.*

stave off PHRASAL VERB If you **stave off** something, you manage, with difficulty, to stop it from happening. *...an effort to stave off bankruptcy... The authorities only staved off an impending collapse by closing the stock market down for a week.*

stay /steɪ/ **stays, staying, stayed**

1 VA If you **stay** somewhere, you continue to be there and do not move away. *...women who stay at home to manage the family house... People have been warned to stay indoors... They all have visas allowing them to stay in Britain for six months.*

2 VA If you **stay** in a town, hotel, or at someone's house, you live there for a short time. *The Princess stayed overnight in the small town of Boroma... She was staying in a hotel as I was.* ► Also NC *...during his two week stay in New York... During their stay they will also be going to Melbourne.*

3 VCorVA If someone or something **stays** in a particular state or situation, they continue to be in it. *Mr Major said that inflation would stay high for some time... People don't want to stay poor, they want a better life... His allowance stays at twenty thousand pounds a year.*

4 VA If you **stay** away from a place, you do not go there. *This town is unsafe: stay away from here... Most students stayed away from school.*

5 VA If you **stay** out of something, you do not get involved in it. *We try to stay out of politics.*

6 If you **stay put**, you remain somewhere. *The General has stayed put... Once again, the refugees will stay put.*

stay in PHRASAL VERB If you **stay in**, you remain at home and do not go out. *We ought to have stayed in tonight.*

stay on PHRASAL VERB If you **stay on** somewhere, you remain there. *He had stayed on to have a drink... He decided to stay on in India.*

stay out PHRASAL VERB 1 If you **stay out**, you remain away from home. *She stayed out all night.* 2 If workers **stay out**, they remain on strike. *The strikers have been ordered to stay out.*

stay up PHRASAL VERB If you **stay up**, you remain out of bed at a later time than normal. *The ministers have stayed up all night... Willie liked to eat out in restaurants and stay up late.*

staying power

NU If you have **staying power**, you have the strength and stamina to keep going until you reach the end of what you are doing. *There is some doubt about the staying power of the new government. ...the secret of his staying power.*

stay of execution, stays of execution

NC If someone is given a **stay of execution**, they are legally allowed to delay obeying an order of a court of law, especially the death sentence; a legal expression. *He therefore granted a stay of execution for one month.*

STD /esti:di:/ **STDs**

1 NC **STDs** are diseases such as syphilis and AIDS that can be transmitted through sexual contact. **STD** is an abbreviation for 'sexually-transmitted disease'. *The rate of all STDs among gay men has now plummeted. ...STD clinics.*

2 NU **STD** is also a system of making a telephone call in which you dial a number yourself and do not have to ask the operator to get the number for you. **STD** is an abbreviation for 'subscriber trunk dialling'.

stead /sted/

If something will **stand you in good stead**, it will be useful to you in the future. *My school theatrical*

performances stood me in good stead in later years.

steadfast /stedfɑːst/

ADJ If you are **steadfast** in your beliefs or opinions, you are convinced that they are right and you refuse to change them; used showing approval. *The refugees remained steadfast. ...steadfast loyalty.* ◆ **steadfastly** ADV *Her father has steadfastly refused to take part in such activities.* ◆ **steadfastness** NU *He said the uprising must be continued with determination and steadfastness.*

steady /stedi/ **steadier, steadiest; steadies, steadying, steadied**

1 ADJ Something that is **steady** continues or develops gradually without any interruptions or sudden changes. *...seven years of steady economic growth... There is a steady stream of people making the journey.* ◆ **steadily** ADV *Unemployment has risen steadily.*

2 ADJ If an object is **steady**, it is firm and does not move about. *His hand was not quite steady.*

3 ADJ If a situation is **steady**, it is not likely to change quickly. *Retail prices have been steady.*

4 ADJ A **steady** look or voice is calm and controlled. *Her voice was faint but steady.* ◆ **steadily** ADV *Foster looked steadily at me for some moments.*

5 ADJ **Steady** work is certain to continue for a long time. *With my father working here, I knew it was a good steady job.*

6 ADJ A **steady** person is sensible and reliable. *I like Simon very much—he's a very steady boy.*

7 V-ERG When you **steady** something or when it **steadies**, it stops shaking or moving about. *His elbows were resting on his knees to steady the binoculars... The boat moved slightly, then steadied.*

8 V-REFL When you **steady** yourself, you control and calm yourself. *He drew a deep breath to steady himself.*

steak /steɪk/ **steaks**

1 N MASS **Steak** is beef without much fat on it. *Dinner this evening consisted of steak, salad, and mixed greens.*

2 NC A fish **steak** is a large piece of fish. *...four halibut steaks.*

steal /stiːl/ **steals, stealing, stole, stolen**

1 VOorV If you **steal** something, you take it away from someone without their permission and without intending to return it. *He stole knives and a gun... They stole twenty-six bags of mail before escaping in a third vehicle... Children often steal.* ◆ **stealing** NU *He had been expelled from his previous school for stealing.* ◆ **stolen** ADJ *...stolen credit cards.*

2 VA If you **steal** somewhere, you move there quietly and cautiously; a literary use. *Simon came stealing out of the shadows.*

stealth /stelθ/

NU If you do something with **stealth**, you do it in a slow, quiet, and secretive way. *Sometimes tigers rely on stealth, creeping towards their victims.*

stealth bomber, stealth bombers

NC A **stealth bomber** is a type of military aircraft which uses very advanced technology so that it is very difficult for enemy radar to see it. *Nearly 30,000 million dollars has already been spent on the stealth bomber. ...a new long-range stealth bomber.*

stealthy /stelθi/ **stealthier, stealthiest**

ADJ **Stealthy** actions or movements are performed in a slow, quiet, and secretive way. *I managed to get there by a series of stealthy movements.* ◆ **stealthily** ADV *I heard my landlady creeping stealthily up to my door.*

steam /stiːm/ **steams, steaming, steamed**

1 NU **Steam** is the hot mist formed when water boils. *The room was filled with steam... Steam hissed between the blocks of lava.*

2 ADJ ATTRIB **Steam** vehicles and machines are powered by steam. *The first steam locomotive was introduced in 1825.*

3 V If something **steams**, it gives off steam. *The kettle was steaming away on the stove... Lynn brought her a steaming cup of tea.*

4 VO If you **steam** food, you cook it in steam rather than in water. *Steam vegetables or cook them quickly*

with their skins on.
● **Steam** is used in these phrases. ● If you **let off steam**, you get rid of your energy or anger by behaving noisily or violently; an informal expression.
● If a project **runs out of steam**, it slowly stops working or being efficient, because the people involved feel discouraged or have lost interest; an informal expression. *Other international efforts to find peace have largely run out of steam.*
steam up PHRASAL VERB 1 If you are **steamed up** about something, you are very annoyed about it; an informal expression. *What was she getting so steamed up about?* 2 When glass **steams up**, it becomes covered with steam or mist. *Her spectacles had steamed up and she couldn't see.*
steamer /stiːmə/ **steamers**
NC A **steamer** is a ship that is powered by steam. *...a steamer to Baltimore... The steamer would go up the river into Sligo.*
steam iron, steam irons
NC A **steam iron** is an electric iron that produces steam from water that you put into it, which makes it easier to get the creases out of your clothes.
steamroller /stiːmrəʊlə/ **steamrollers, steamrollering, steamrollered**
1 NC A **steamroller** is a large, heavy vehicle with wide solid wheels which is used to flatten road surfaces.
2 VO If you **steamroller** someone, you force them to do something that they do not want to do by using your power or by putting a lot of pressure on them. *...the Prime Minister's attempt to steamroller the General into a job he did not want... He was swiftly steamrollered out of the way.*
steamy /stiːmi/ **steamier, steamiest**
1 ADJ A **steamy** place is hot and humid, usually because it is full of steam. *...a steamy and noisy kitchen.*
2 ADJ Books, films, or plays that are **steamy** are erotic; an informal use. *...a steamy tale of racist hypocrisy and sexual obsession.*
steed /stiːd/ **steeds**
NC A **steed** is a large strong horse used for riding; a literary word. *He rode in on a white Arab steed.*
steel /stiːl/ **steels, steeling, steeled**
1 NU **Steel** is a strong metal made mainly from iron which is used for making many things, for example bridges, buildings, vehicles, and cutlery. *...a modern tower made of concrete and steel. ...steel girders.*
● See also **stainless steel**.
2 NU **Steel** is also used to refer to the industry that produces steel and items made of steel. *...the subject of nationalising steel. ...the steel strike.*
3 NU You can refer to a person's great strength or courage as **steel**. *He held my arm with a grip of steel. ...nerves of steel.*
4 V-REFL If you **steel** yourself, you prepare to deal with something unpleasant. *You had better steel yourself for a shock... The army is currently trying to steel itself politically against what is seen as a hostile, anti-communist ideology.*
steel band, steel bands
NC A **steel band** is a band of people who play music on special metal drums. *...the sounds of jazz and steel bands.*
steel wool
NU **Steel wool** is a mass of fine steel threads twisted together into a small ball and used for cleaning surfaces. *Carefully remove stubborn stains with fine steel wool.*
steelworker /stiːlwɜːkə/ **steelworkers**
NC A **steelworker** is a person who works in a steelworks. *Thousands of steelworkers are expected to lose their jobs as a result.*
steelworks /stiːlwɜːks/; **steelworks** is both the singular and the plural form.
NC A **steelworks** is a factory where steel is made. *They were complaining about the heavy pollution the steelworks are inflicting on the environment.*
steely /stiːli/
1 ADJ You use **steely** to describe something that has a hard, greyish colour. *The blue sky had changed to a steely grey.*

2 ADJ ATTRIB **Steely** is also used to describe someone who is tough, strong, and determined. *There was shy modesty behind that steely determination.*
steep /stiːp/ **steeper, steepest**
1 ADJ A **steep** slope rises at a very sharp angle and is difficult to go up. *He reached the steepest part of the mountain.* ◆ **steeply** ADV *...mountains rising steeply on three sides.*
2 ADJ A **steep** increase is a very big increase. *There's likely to be a steep increase in unemployment.*
◆ **steeply** ADV *The costs of public services have risen steeply.*
3 ADJ If the price of something is a bit **steep**, it is expensive; an informal use. *Your fees are pretty steep.*
steeped /stiːpt/
ADJ PRED+*in* If a place or person is **steeped** in a quality or characteristic, they are deeply influenced by it. *The house is centuries old and steeped in history.*
steeple /stiːpl/ **steeples**
NC A **steeple** is a tall pointed structure on top of a church tower. *...the angular church steeple in the town square.*
steeplechase /stiːpltʃeɪs/ **steeplechases**
1 NC A **steeplechase** is a long horse race in which the horses have to jump over different obstacles such as hedges and water jumps. *Today is the day of the Grand National steeplechase at Aintree.*
2 NC A **steeplechase** is also a long race in which people jump over hurdles and water jumps round an athletics track. *Kiviat won the silver in the 1500 metres and the gold in the 3000 metres steeplechase.*
steeplejack /stiːpldʒæk/ **steeplejacks**
NC A **steeplejack** is a person who climbs up high parts of buildings, for example church steeples, in order to repair them or paint them.
steer /stɪə/ **steers, steering, steered**
1 V-ERG A or V When a car, boat, or plane **steers** or when it is **steered**, it is controlled so that it goes in the correct direction. *The freighter steered out of Santiago Bay that evening... He steered the car through the broad entrance... I was trying to steer.*
2 VOA If you **steer** someone in a particular direction, you guide them there. *He steered me to a table and sat me down in a chair.*
3 VOA If you **steer** a person or group towards a course of action or attitude, you try to lead them gently in that direction. *The summit is aimed at steering NATO towards a more political role.*
4 If you **steer clear** of something or someone, you deliberately avoid them; an informal expression. *The Oil Ministers have, publicly at least, steered clear of confrontation.*
steering /stɪərɪŋ/
1 NU The **steering** in a car or other vehicle is the mechanical parts of it which make it possible to steer. *They had terrible troubles with the steering and transmission.*
2 ADJ ATTRIB A **steering** committee or a **steering** group is a group of people that manages the early stages of a project, in particular the order and priority of business. *A steering committee of solicitors will probably be set up to coordinate claims... The official steering committee says it's already guaranteed the thirty-two million pounds needed. ...a spokesman for the steering group.*
steering wheel, steering wheels
NC The **steering wheel** in a car or lorry is the wheel held by the driver when he or she is driving. *This means drivers cannot keep both hands on the steering wheel.*
stellar /stɛlə/
ADJ ATTRIB **Stellar** is used to describe things connected with stars; a formal word. *...beyond the earth's atmosphere, beyond the whole stellar system.*
stem /stɛm/ **stems, stemming, stemmed**
1 VO If you **stem** something that is continuing, spreading, or increasing, you put a stop to it. *...stemming the flow of illegal drugs... This is seen as an attempt to stem inflation.*
2 V+*from* If a condition or problem **stems from** a particular situation, it started originally because of

this situation. *The business community's opposition to the bill stems more from a basic mistrust of government.*
3 NC The **stem** of a plant is the long, thin, central part of it which is above the ground and which the leaves are joined to. *Certain types of lentil have a very thick woody stem.*
4 NC The **stem** of a glass or vase is the long thin part of it connecting the bowl to the base.
5 NC The **stem** of a pipe is the long part of it through which smoke is sucked.

stench /stɛntʃ/ **stenches**
NC A **stench** is a strong, unpleasant smell. *...the unmistakable stench of rotting eggs.*

stencil /stɛnsl/ **stencils, stencilling, stencilled;** spelt **stenciling, stenciled** in American English.
1 NC A **stencil** is a piece of paper, plastic, or metal with a design cut out of it. You place the stencil on a surface and create a design by putting ink or paint over the cut area. *The stencils are lightweight plastic with a little rim.*
2 V or V If you **stencil** letters or designs, you print them using a stencil. *...a black helmet with the word 'Mexico' stencilled on it.*

stenographer /stənɒɡrəfə/ **stenographers**
NC A **stenographer** is a shorthand typist; used in American English.

stentorian /stɛntɔːriən/
ADJ A **stentorian** voice is very loud and strong; a literary word. *...the stentorian voices of the guides.*

step /stɛp/ **steps, stepping, stepped**
1 NC A **step** is the movement made by lifting your foot and putting it down in a different place. *She took a step back... I walked on with quick steps.*
2 V+on If you **step on** something, you put your foot on it. *He had stepped on a thorn.*
3 V A If you **step** in a particular direction, you walk in that direction. *Step over the wire... Tom stepped back.*
4 NC A **step** is also one of a series of actions or one of a series of stages that is necessary in order to achieve a particular goal or to arrive at a successful conclusion. *Today's announcement is a step in the right direction... Simmel carried this idea one step further.*
5 NC A **step** is also a raised flat surface, often one of a series, on which you put your feet in order to walk up or down to a different level. *She was sitting on the top step. ...a flight of steps.*
● **Step** is used in these phrases. ● If someone tells you to **watch your step**, they are warning you to be more careful about your behaviour so that you don't get into trouble. *I'm cleverer than you are, so watch your step.* ● If you do something **step by step**, you do it by progressing gradually from one stage to the next. *The proof is set out, step by step, on page 6.* ● If you **take steps** to achieve a particular goal, you do the things that are necessary to achieve it. *Steps may be taken to hold a national referendum on the issue.* ● If a group of people are walking **in step**, they are moving their feet forward at exactly the same time as each other. *...a party of boys marching in step.*
step aside PHRASAL VERB If you **step aside**, you allow someone else to do a job or an activity that you had intended to do. *He will have to be paid well to step aside for a Douglas-Tyson re-match.*
step back PHRASAL VERB If you **step back**, you think about a situation in a fresh and detached way. *It is tempting to step back and ask whether it is worth all the trouble.*
step down PHRASAL VERB If you **step down** or **step aside**, you resign from an important job or position. *He is also stepping down as head of his party... He says he has no intention of stepping down.*
step in PHRASAL VERB If you **step in**, you start to help in a difficult situation which you are not directly involved in. *The IMF is clearly wary of stepping in too quickly with new forms of assistance.*
step up PHRASAL VERB If you **step up** something, you intensify it or increase it. *The government is stepping up its anti-smoking campaign... The Conservative Party is stepping up its efforts to attract support from*

Britons living overseas.

stepbrother /stɛpbrʌðə/ **stepbrothers**
NC Your **stepbrother** is the son of your stepfather or stepmother.

step-by-step
ADJ ATTRIB or ADV **Step-by-step** movements or progress are slow and careful. *Is there one particular step-by-step manual that you would recommend to a beginner?... She said they would move step-by-step.*

stepchild /stɛptʃaɪld/ **stepchildren**
NC Your **stepchild** is the child of your husband or wife by an earlier marriage.

stepdaughter /stɛpdɔːtə/ **stepdaughters**
NC Your **stepdaughter** is the daughter of your husband or wife by an earlier marriage.

stepfather /stɛpfɑːðə/ **stepfathers**
NC Your **stepfather** is the man who has married your mother after the death or divorce of your father. *The stepfather always feels a little left-out here.*

stepladder /stɛplædə/ **stepladders**
NC A **stepladder** is a ladder consisting of two sloping parts that are hinged together at the top so that it will stand up on its own.

stepmother /stɛpmʌðə/ **stepmothers**
NC Your **stepmother** is the woman who has married your father after the death or divorce of your mother.

stepparent /stɛppeərənt/ **stepparents**
NC Someone's **stepparent** is their stepfather or stepmother; a formal word.

steppe /stɛp/ **steppes**
N PL **Steppes** are large areas of land with grass but no trees, usually used to refer to the area that stretches from Eastern Europe across the south of the former Soviet Union to Siberia. *...the harshness of their nomadic life on the steppes.*

stepped-up
ADJ ATTRIB **Stepped-up** is used to describe something which is done at a faster rate or to a greater extent than before. *They are already caught up in a new, stepped-up pace of life.*

stepping stone, stepping stones
1 NC A **stepping stone** is a job or event that helps you to make progress. *It has historically been a stepping stone to the presidency.*
2 NC **Stepping stones** are a line of stones which you can walk on in order to cross a shallow stream or river. *There were stepping stones in the water.*

stepsister /stɛpsɪstə/ **stepsisters**
NC Your **stepsister** is the daughter of your stepfather or stepmother. *Jason has a half sister and two stepsisters.*

stepson /stɛpsʌn/ **stepsons**
NC Your **stepson** is the son of your husband or wife by an earlier marriage.

stereo /stɛriəʊ/ **stereos**
1 NU or NC **Stereo** is used to describe a record or a system of playing music in which the sound is directed through two different speakers. *It sounds much better in stereo. ...buying stereo equipment.*
2 NC A **stereo** is a hi-fi or record player with two speakers; an informal use. *He turned on the stereo.*

stereophonic /stɛriəfɒnɪk/
ADJ **Stereophonic** equipment or sound is the same as stereo equipment or sound; an old-fashioned word. *...all this while listening to music on his personal stereophonic headphones.*

stereotype /stɛriətaɪp/ **stereotypes, stereotyping, stereotyped**
1 NC A **stereotype** is a fixed general image or set of characteristics that are considered to represent a particular type of person or thing; used showing disapproval. *The song perpetuates two racist stereotypes.*
2 VO If you **stereotype** someone, you form a fixed general idea of them and assume that they will behave in a particular way. *...a couple of the sub-groups that the media has chosen to pick out and stereotype over the last ten years.*

sterile /stɛraɪl/
1 ADJ Something that is **sterile** is completely clean and free of germs. *...rolls of sterile bandage.*
2 ADJ A **sterile** person or animal is unable to have or

produce babies. *He had learnt early in his marriage that he was sterile.* ◆ **sterility** /stə'rɪlətɪ/ NU ...*physical degeneration leading to sterility.*
3 ADJ A **sterile** situation is lacking in energy and new ideas. *The meeting degenerated into a sterile debate.* ◆ **sterility** NU ...*the ugly sterility of urban life.*

sterilize /'stɛrəlaɪz/ **sterilizes, sterilizing, sterilized**; also spelt **sterilise**.
1 VO If you **sterilize** a thing or place, you make it completely clean and free from germs. *All nearby brickwork must be sterilized with a blowlamp.*
2 VO If a person or an animal is **sterilized**, they have an operation that makes it impossible for them to have or produce babies. *By 1950, 16 per cent of women over twenty had been sterilized.* ◆ **sterilization** /stɛrəlaɪ'zeɪʃn/ NU ...*compulsory sterilization for parents of more than two children.*

sterling /'stɜːlɪŋ/
1 NU or ADJ after N **Sterling** is the money system of Great Britain. *Sterling has once again become one of the stronger currencies.* ...*a hundred and fifty pounds sterling.*
2 ADJ ATTRIB **Sterling** means excellent in quality; a formal use. *Their banking sector has never had a sterling image.* ...*a man of sterling character.*

stern /stɜːn/ **sterner, sternest**; **sterns**
1 ADJ A **stern** person is very serious and strict. *Sylvia had a stern father who never praised her.* ◆ **sternly** ADV *He walked over and said to him sternly, 'Give that to me'.*
2 NC The **stern** of a boat is the back part of it. *She seated herself in the stern.*

sternum /'stɜːnəm/ **sternums** or **sterna** /'stɜːnə/
NC Your **sternum** is the long flat bone which goes from your throat to the bottom of your ribs and to which your ribs are attached; a medical term. *Coretta had a fractured sternum.*

steroid /'stɪərɔɪd, 'stɜːrɔɪd/ **steroids**
NC A **steroid** is a type of chemical substance found in your body. Steroids can be artificially introduced into the bodies of sportsmen to improve their strength. *It was found that he was taking steroids.*

stertorous /'stɜːtərəs/
ADJ **Stertorous** breathing is very noisy, like snoring; a literary word. *Her breathing became loud and stertorous.*

stethoscope /'stɛθəskəʊp/ **stethoscopes**
NC A **stethoscope** is an instrument that a doctor uses to listen to your heart and breathing. It consists of a hollow tube with ear pieces connected to a small disc.

stetson /'stɛtsn/ **stetsons**
NC A **stetson** is a hat with a wide brim that is worn especially by cowboys. ...*white stetsons and cowboy outfits*... *She's in a bright red jumpsuit and a small stetson hat.*

stevedore /'stiːvədɔː/ **stevedores**
NC A **stevedore** is a person who loads and unloads ships; used in American English. *Right. Stevedores, to your stations!*

stew /stjuː/ **stews, stewing, stewed**
1 N MASS A **stew** is a meal made by cooking vegetables, and usually meat, in liquid at a low temperature. *We've got lamb stew tonight.*
2 VO If you **stew** meat, vegetables, or fruit, you cook them slowly in liquid in a closed dish. ...*stewed fruit.*
3 ADJ ATTRIB **Stewing** beef, steak, or lamb is meat that is intended to be stewed. ...*stewing steak.*

steward /'stjuːəd/ **stewards**
1 NC A **steward** is a man whose job is to look after passengers on a ship or plane. *A British Airways spokesman praised the quick action of the crew and the two stewards.*
2 NC A **steward** is also someone who helps to organize a race, march, or other public event. *They were spotted by stewards who were organising the security.*
3 See also **shop steward**.

stewardess /'stjuːədɛs/ **stewardesses**
NC A **stewardess** is a woman whose job is to look after passengers on a ship or plane. *On the airplane back home, the stewardess called my name.*

stewardship /'stjuːədʃɪp/
NU **Stewardship** is the responsibility of looking after

something; a formal word. *It is above all in the economic sphere that Dr Mahathir's stewardship of Malaysian politics has reaped rich rewards... He has the stewardship of the taxpayers' money.*

stick /stɪk/ **sticks, sticking, stuck**
1 NC A **stick** is a long, thin piece of wood, for example dead wood from a tree. *I gathered some sticks to start the fire.*
2 NC A **stick** is the same as a **walking-stick**. *She handed him his hat and stick.*
3 NC A **stick** of something is a long thin piece of it. ...*a stick of rock.* ...*sticks of dynamite.*
4 V-ERG A If a pointed object **sticks** in something or if you **stick** it in something, you push it in. *The pig had two spears sticking in her side... He stuck the knife right in... He stuck a cigar in his mouth.*
5 VOA If you **stick** one thing to another, you fix them together using something such as glue or sticky tape. *They went round sticking posters on walls... Someone has stuck a label on the crate.*
6 V A If something **sticks** somewhere, it becomes attached or fixed in one position and is difficult to move. ...*sand that sticks to your hair and skin... If your zip sticks, it might be because a thread has caught in it.*
7 V+in If something **sticks** in your mind, you remember it for a long time. *One lecture stuck in my mind.*
8 VOA If you **stick** something somewhere, you put it there in a rather casual way; an informal use. *She closed the bag and stuck it back on the shelf.*
● **Stick** is used in these phrases. ● If you **stick it** in a difficult situation, or if you **stick it out**, you do not leave or give up; used in informal English. *I don't know how I've stuck it. It's been hell... I stuck it out as long as I could.* ● If someone gets the **wrong end of the stick**, they completely misunderstand something; an informal expression. *How on earth could you get the wrong end of the stick?* ● to **stick your neck out**: see **neck**. ● See also **stuck**.

stick around PHRASAL VERB If you **stick around**, you stay where you are; an informal expression. *I'll stick around and keep an eye on the food.*

stick at PHRASAL VERB If you **stick at** a task or activity, you continue doing it even if it is difficult. *You must stick at it if you want to succeed.*

stick by PHRASAL VERB If you **stick by** someone, you continue to help or support them. ...*a good commanding officer who stuck by his men when they got into trouble.*

stick out PHRASAL VERB 1 If something **sticks out**, it extends beyond something else. *There was a little chimney sticking out of the roof.* 2 If you **stick** something **out**, you make it appear from inside or behind something else. *Lally stuck her head out of a window... Lynn stuck out her tongue.* 3 You can also say that something **sticks out** when it is very noticeable. *His accent made him stick out.*

stick out for PHRASAL VERB If you **stick out for** something you want, you keep demanding it and do not accept anything different or less. *He stuck out for twice the usual salary, and got it.*

stick to PHRASAL VERB 1 If you **stick to** someone or something when you are travelling, you stay close to them. *I went over the hill instead of sticking to the river.* 2 If you **stick to** something, you do not change to something else. *They are sticking to their present policy.* 3 If you **stick to** a promise or agreement, you do what you said you would do. *They stuck to the bargain.*

stick together PHRASAL VERB If people **stick together**, they stay with each other and support each other. *The boys learned to stick together.*

stick up PHRASAL VERB 1 If you **stick up** a picture or a notice, you fix it to a wall. *We have a painting stuck up on the wall.* 2 If something long **sticks up**, it points upwards. *These plants stick up vertically from the seabed.*

stick up for PHRASAL VERB If you **stick up for** someone or something, you support or defend them forcefully. *He thanked his father for sticking up for him... I was too scared to stick up for my rights.*

stick with PHRASAL VERB 1 If you **stick with** an activity or a subject, you keep doing the same activity or talking about the same subject, and do not change to something else. *I stuck with my staple diet: brown rice.* 2 If you **stick with** someone, you stay close to them. *Stick with me and you'll be OK.*

sticker /stɪkə/ **stickers**
NC A **sticker** is a small piece of paper or plastic, with writing or a picture on it. It has glue on one side so that you can stick it onto a surface. *They sell stickers and badges... On the rear window was a sticker saying 'Save the Whales'.*

sticking plaster, sticking plasters
NU or NC **Sticking plaster** is material that you can stick over a cut or sore to protect it.

sticking point, sticking points
NC A **sticking point** in a discussion or negotiations is a point on which speakers cannot agree, and which may delay or stop the talks. *The main sticking points have been over aircraft limits... Agriculture was the main sticking point this time.*

stick insect, stick insects
NC A **stick insect** is an insect with a long thin body and legs. It looks like a small stick.

stick-in-the-mud, stick-in-the-muds
NC If you describe someone as a **stick-in-the-mud**, you mean that they do not like doing anything that is new or fun; used in informal English, showing disapproval. *Don't be such a stick-in-the-mud.*

stickler /stɪklə/ **sticklers**
NC+*for* If you are a **stickler** for something, you always insist on it. *Kitty was a stickler for routine.*

stick-on
ADJ ATTRIB **Stick-on** is used to describe something such as a label which has an adhesive material on one side so that it will stick to surfaces. *...stick-on labels.*

stick shift, stick shifts
NC A **stick shift** is a **gear lever**; used in American English. *I'd get a rattle out of the stick shift.*

stick-up, stick-ups
NC A **stick-up** is a robbery of a shop, bank, or post-office in which the thieves use guns; an old-fashioned, informal word.

sticky /stɪki/
1 ADJ Something that is **sticky** is covered with a substance that can stick to other things and leave unpleasant marks. *Her hands were sticky from the ice cream. ...a sticky bottle of fruit juice.*
2 ADJ **Sticky** paper has glue on one side so that you can stick it to surfaces. *...sticky labels.*
3 ADJ **Sticky** weather is unpleasantly hot and damp. *...a hot, sticky, July afternoon.*
4 ADJ A **sticky** problem or situation is difficult or embarrassing; an informal use. *...a sticky tax problem... The reparations issue is a sticky one.*

stiff /stɪf/ **stiffer, stiffest**
1 ADJ Something that is **stiff** is severe, difficult, or harsh. *He will face stiff competition from other candidates in the south. ...stiffer penalties for drunken drivers... They face stiff opposition from the league champions.*
2 ADJ **Stiff** can also mean firm and not bending easily. *Use a stiff brush. ...stiff brown paper.*
3 ADJ If a drawer or door is **stiff**, it does not move as easily as it should. *...a stiff latch.*
4 ADJ If you are **stiff**, your muscles or joints ache when you move. *My arms were stiff... Parents should contact their GPs if children develop severe headaches, stiff necks or vomiting.* ◆ **stiffness** NU *She complained of stiffness in her knees.*
5 ADJ **Stiff** behaviour is rather formal and not relaxed. *...a stiff smile... The letter was stiff and formal.* ◆ **stiffly** ADV *'No, I haven't,' Rudolph said stiffly.* ◆ **stiffness** NU *Their stiffness and self-consciousness soon disappeared.*
6 ADJ ATTRIB A **stiff** drink contains a large amount of alcohol. *Morris fixed himself a stiff drink.*
7 ADJ A **stiff** breeze is one which is blowing quite strongly. *There's quite a stiff breeze up here.*
8 ADV If you are bored **stiff**, worried **stiff**, or scared **stiff**, you are extremely bored, worried, or scared; an informal use. *The subject bores them stiff... I've got*

to go to the dentist myself soon and I'm absolutely scared stiff.
9 If you say that someone has a **stiff upper lip**, you mean that they do not show their emotions easily, especially when they are sad or frightened; an informal expression. *Men are supposed to have a stiff upper lip... Many cultures admire those who keep their feelings hidden, maintain a stiff upper lip.*

stiffen /stɪfn/ **stiffens, stiffening, stiffened**
1 V If you **stiffen**, you stop moving and become very tense, for example because you are afraid or angry. *Tom suddenly stiffened with alarm... Her whole body stiffened.*
2 V If your muscles or joints **stiffen**, they become difficult to bend or move. *You are unlikely to be troubled with stiffening joints.*
3 V-ERG If you **stiffen** a person's attitudes or behaviour or if their attitudes or behaviour **stiffen**, these become stronger or more severe, and less flexible. *Resistance stiffened even further last week... You will only stiffen his resolve.*
4 VO When something such as cloth **is stiffened**, it is made firm. ◆ **stiffened** ADJ *...a dress of stiffened satin.*

stiffener /stɪfənə/ **stiffeners**
NC A **stiffener** is something used to make something less likely to bend if it is pressed. *...collar stiffeners.*

stiff-necked
ADJ Someone who is **stiff-necked** is proud and stubborn; used showing disapproval.

stifle /staɪfl/ **stifles, stifling, stifled**
1 VO If someone **stifles** something that is happening, they stop it from continuing. *An authoritarian leadership stifled internal debate.*
2 VO If you **stifle** a cry or a yawn, you prevent yourself from crying or yawning. *She placed a hand over her mouth to stifle a shriek of laughter.*
3 VO If the air or the atmosphere **stifles** you, it makes you feel as if you cannot breathe properly. *She was stifled by its scent.*

stifling /staɪfəʊlɪŋ/
ADJ If the air or atmosphere is **stifling**, it is so hot that you feel as if you cannot breathe properly. *It was stifling inside. ...a stifling night.*

stigma /stɪgmə/ **stigmas**
NC or NU If something has a **stigma** attached to it, people consider it to be unacceptable or a disgrace. *The stigma attached to mental illness will be removed in future years. ...cultures which previously attached no stigmas to being fat.*

stile /staɪl/ **stiles**
NC A **stile** is a step on either side of a fence or wall that enables you to climb over.

stiletto /stɪletəʊ/ **stilettos**
NC **Stilettos** or **stiletto heels** are women's shoes that have high, very narrow heels.

still /stɪl/ **stiller, stillest; stills**
1 ADV If a situation that existed previously **still** exists, it has continued and exists at the present time. *She still lives in London... She was still beautiful... I was still a schoolboy.*
2 ADV If something that has not yet happened could **still** happen, it is possible that it will happen. *She could still change her mind... There is still a chance that a few might survive.*
3 ADV You use **still** to emphasize that something remains the case or is true in spite of what you have just said. *Whatever they have done, they are still your parents.*
4 ADV If you say that there is **still** an amount of something left, you are emphasizing that there is that amount left. *There are ten weeks still to go... I've still got three left.*
5 ADV SEN You also use **still** when dismissing a problem or difficulty as not really worth worrying about. *...and that made me miss the last bus. Still, that's life, isn't it?*
6 ADV You can use **still** with 'better' or 'more' to indicate that something has even more of a quality than something else. *How about some Bach to begin with? Or, better still, Vivaldi... There is a still more sensitive issue.*

7 ADJ PRED or ADV If you stay **still**, you stay in the same position without moving. *We had to keep still for about four minutes... Stand still!*
8 ADJ If something is **still**, there is no movement or activity there. *...the still water of the lagoon... Around them the forest was very still.* ◆ **stillness** NU *The stillness of the fields was broken by the sound of a gunshot.*
9 NC A **still** is a photograph taken from a cinema film which is used for publicity purposes. *...set designs and film stills by the great early Soviet film-maker, Sergei Eisenstein.*

stillbirth /stɪlbɜːθ/ **stillbirths**
N C or N U A **stillbirth** is the birth of a dead baby. *Stillbirths have also increased dramatically.*

stillborn /stɪlbɔːn/
ADJ A **stillborn** baby is dead when it is born. *...the birth of a stillborn infant.*

still life, still lifes
N C or N U A **still life** is a painting or drawing of an arrangement of objects such as flowers or fruit. *He's done some lovely still lifes... Still life is much harder. ...Ben Nicholson's early still life paintings.*

stilt /stɪlt/ **stilts**
1 NC **Stilts** are long upright pieces of wood or metal used to support some buildings. *Thatched huts were raised high above the paddy fields on stilts.*
2 NC **Stilts** are also two long pieces of wood that a person such as a circus clown can stand on in order to walk high up above the ground. *He is walking on stilts.*

stilted /stɪltɪd/
ADJ **Stilted** conversation or behaviour is very formal and unnatural. *After some stilted efforts at conversation, he gave up and left... The music is not Mozart's best, and the story is stilted.*

stimulant /stɪmjʊlənt/ **stimulants**
NC A **stimulant** is a drug that increases your heart rate and makes you less likely to sleep. *...coffee in which the drug caffeine acts as a stimulant.*

stimulate /stɪmjʊleɪt/ **stimulates, stimulating, stimulated**
1 VO To **stimulate** something means to encourage it to begin or develop further. *Rising prices will stimulate demands for higher incomes... An outsider who may stimulate new ideas.*
2 VO If something **stimulates** you, it makes you feel full of ideas and enthusiasm. *The art course stimulated me.* ◆ **stimulating** ADJ *...a conversation which I found both stimulating and exciting.* ◆ **stimulation** /stɪmjʊleɪʃn/ NU *I find great intellectual stimulation in these surroundings.*
3 VO If something **stimulates** a part of a person's body, it causes it to move or function automatically; a technical use. *The optical system of the eye stimulates cells in the retina.*

stimulus /stɪmjʊləs/ **stimuli** /stɪmjʊlaɪ/
1 NC If something acts as a **stimulus**, it makes a process develop further or more quickly. *There would not have been the same stimulus to mechanize production so rapidly... Falling oil prices provided the needed stimulus.*
2 NU **Stimulus** is something which causes people to feel energetic and enthusiastic. *...all the stimulus and excitement that battle brought.*
3 NC A **stimulus** is something that causes a part of a person's body to move or function automatically; a technical use. *Different muscle fibres react differently to the stimulus from the nerve net.*

sting /stɪŋ/ **stings, stinging, stung**
1 V O or V If an insect, animal, or plant **stings** you, it causes you to feel a sharp pain by pricking your skin, usually with poison. *Bees do not normally sting without being provoked.*
2 NC The **sting** of an insect or animal is the part that stings you. *The researchers never found a surviving hornet with a sting... They paralyse their victims with their stings.*
3 V-ERG If a part of your body **stings** or if something **stings** it, you feel a sharp pain there. *My eyes were stinging... The fire smoked glumly and stung our eyes.* ▸ Also N SING *...the sting of ashes in his eyes.*

4 VO If someone's remarks **sting** you, they upset and annoy you. *I wondered why I'd said it, knowing it would really sting him.* ◆ **stinging** ADJ *He made a stinging attack on Taverne.*
5 If something **takes the sting out** of a situation, it makes it less painful or unpleasant. *He smiled to take the sting out of his words.*

stingy /stɪndʒi/
ADJ A **stingy** person is mean; an informal word. *The government was stingy and his salary was miserable.*

stink /stɪŋk/ **stinks, stinking, stank, stunk**
1 V Something that **stinks** smells extremely unpleasant. *The butcher's shop stank in hot weather.* ▸ Also N SING *...the stink of vomit.*
2 V If a place or situation **stinks**, it is extremely bad or unpleasant; an informal use. *'What do you think of the town?'—'I think it stinks.'* ◆ **stinking** ADJ ATTRIB *I've got a stinking cold... You couldn't hide anything in this stinking little town.*

stint /stɪnt/ **stints**
NC+SUPP A **stint** is a period of time spent doing a particular job or activity; an informal word. *I arrived at the University for a three month stint as a lecturer.*

stipend /staɪpend/ **stipends**
NC A **stipend** is a sum of money paid regularly to a person, especially a clergyman, as a salary or as living expenses. *This sum was nearly a third of his total stipend.*

stipendiary /staɪpendiəri/ **stipendiaries**
NC A **stipendiary** is a person, usually a clergyman or a magistrate, who receives a stipend. *The trend is towards more stipendiaries.* ▸ Also ADJ ATTRIB *...stipendiary magistrates. ...the full-time stipendiary parish priest.*

stippled /stɪpld/
ADJ A surface that is **stippled** is covered with dots. *...a stippled glaze on earthenware... The green moss is stippled with bright toadstools.*

stipulate /stɪpjʊleɪt/ **stipulates, stipulating, stipulated**
V O or V-REPORT If you **stipulate** that something must be done, you state clearly that it must be done; a formal word. *The accord stipulated the withdrawal of government troops from the regions... A contract is being drawn up to stipulate how many days Clough can work for Wales... The resolution stipulates that foodstuffs should be provided through the United Nations.* ◆ **stipulation** /stɪpjʊleɪʃn/ **stipulations** NC *Iraq laid down a number of conditions, including a stipulation that he should travel to Baghdad... These stipulations have been modified.*

stir /stɜː/ **stirs, stirring, stirred**
1 VO When you **stir** a liquid, you mix it inside a container using something such as a spoon. *The tourist was stirring his coffee and gazing at the buildings.*
2 V If you **stir**, you move slightly, for example because you are uncomfortable. *The boys stirred uneasily... Etta didn't stir, pretending to be asleep.*
3 VO If the wind **stirs** an object, it moves it gently. *A stray breath of wind stirred the stillness of the robes.*
4 V-REFL If you **stir** yourself, you move in order to do something. *Finally, one of the males stirred himself and took a step forward.*
5 VO If something **stirs** you, it makes you react with a strong emotion because it is very beautiful or moving. *There was a particular passage which always stirred him profoundly.*
6 N SING If an event causes a **stir**, it causes great excitement, shock, or anger. *Her speech created a huge stir.*
7 V or V A If a particular mood, feeling, or idea **stirs** in someone, they begin to feel it or think about it. *The debate was reopened and a new mood was stirring... Something seemed to stir within her.*
stir up PHRASAL VERB **1** If something **stirs up** dust or mud, it causes it to move around. *Some gentle winds stirred up the dust.* **2** If you **stir up** trouble or **stir up** a feeling, you cause trouble or cause people to have the feeling. *...a rally called to stir up popular support for nuclear disarmament.*

stir-fry, stir-fries, stir-frying, stir-fried
V or VO If you **stir-fry** vegetables or meat, you cook

small pieces of them quickly by stirring them in a small quantity of very hot oil. This method is often used in Chinese cookery.

stirrer /stɜːrə/ **stirrers**
NC If you refer to someone as a **stirrer**, you mean that they deliberately cause trouble whenever they can; an informal word. *English fans had allowed themselves to be provoked by trouble stirrers.*

stirring /stɜːrɪŋ/ **stirrings**
1 ADJ Something that is **stirring** makes people very excited or enthusiastic. *His production of the play is austere, stirring and tragic. ...one of the most stirring shots of the whole film... They must have been stirring times.*
2 NC When there is a **stirring** of emotion, people begin to feel it. *There was a slight stirring of interest among them. ...the first stirrings of student protest.*

stirrup /stɪrəp/ **stirrups**
NC **Stirrups** are the two metal loops attached to a horse's saddle which the rider places his or her feet in. *His stirrup leathers broke in the closing stages of the Doncaster race.*

stitch /stɪtʃ/ **stitches, stitching, stitched**
1 V Oor V When you **stitch** pieces of material together, you join them using a needle and thread. *They were cut out and stitched together... She picked up her embroidery and started stitching.*
2 NC A **stitch** is one of the short pieces of thread that can be seen on a piece of material that has been stitched. *...the little stitches in the canvas she was embroidering.*
3 NC A **stitch** is also a piece of thread that has been used to stitch a wound. *His wound required five stitches.*
4 N SING If you have a **stitch**, you feel a sharp pain at the side of your stomach, usually after running fast or laughing a lot. *I began to have a bad stitch.*
5 If you are **in stitches**, you cannot stop laughing; an informal expression.
stitch together PHRASAL VERB If you **stitch** something **together**, you form it from a number of different parts, usually in a hurried or careless way. *He was trying to stitch together a new security arrangement... At the last moment European Community leaders stitched together an agreement.*
stitch up PHRASAL VERB When doctors **stitch up** an open wound, they join the skin together so that it will heal. *The doctors cleaned my wounds and stitched up one finger.*

stoat /stəʊt/ **stoats**
NC A **stoat** is a small wild animal that has brown fur. Some stoats that live in northern Europe have fur that turns white in winter. *...predators such as mountain lions and stoats.*

stock /stɒk/ **stocks, stocking, stocked**
1 NC **Stocks** are shares in the ownership of a company, or investments on which a fixed amount of interest will be paid. *...heavy bidding for oil company stocks... The team from Wall Street explained what a stock was.*
2 VO A shop that **stocks** particular goods keeps a supply of them to sell. *Several shops in London stock large fittings.*
3 NU A shop's **stock** is the total amount of goods which it has available to sell. *...selling a week's worth of stock in a single day.*
4 VO If you **stock** a shelf or cupboard, you fill it with food or other things. *I found part-time work, stocking shelves in supermarkets... His locker was always stocked with screws.*
5 NC+SUPP A **stock** of things is a supply of them. *Keep a stock of fuses... They want to conserve coal stocks during the miners' strike.*
6 N SING+SUPP The **stock** that a person or animal comes from is the type of people or animals from which they are descended. *His mother was of Russian stock. ...more than 700,000 Germans or people of German stock.*
7 N COLL Animals kept on a farm are referred to as **stock**. *...a sale of dairy stock.*
8 NU **Stock** is a liquid made by boiling meat, bones, or vegetables in water.

9 ADJ ATTRIB A **stock** expression or way of doing something is one that is commonly used. *'Wild and wanton' was a stock phrase of the time.*
● **Stock** is used in these phrases. ● If goods are **in stock** in a shop, they are available to be sold. If they are **out of stock**, they have all been sold. *A manufacturer might keep a month's supply of spare parts in stock... Petrol has run out and gas canisters too are out of stock.* ● If you **take stock**, you pause and think about a situation before deciding what to do next. *After that, the Secretary of State will take stock and decide on the way forward... Britain has requested a summit to take stock of the fundamental changes in world order.* ● See also **laughing stock**.
stock up PHRASAL VERB If you **stock up** with something, you buy a large supply of it for the future. *Stock up with groceries and canned foods.*

stockade /stɒkeɪd/ **stockades**
NC A **stockade** is a wall of large wooden posts built round an area to keep out enemies or wild animals. *...huts protected by an enormous high stockade of wood interlaced with branches.*

stockbroker /stɒkbrəʊkə/ **stockbrokers**
NC A **stockbroker** is a person whose job is to buy and sell stocks and shares for people. *Stockbrokers were unsure how the market would respond. ...a partner in a firm of London stockbrokers.*

stockbroking /stɒkbrəʊkɪŋ/
ADJ ATTRIB A **stockbroking** firm or company is one that buys and sells stocks and shares for people. *An American-owned stockbroking firm has closed its government bond dealing department in London. ...one of Wall Street's largest and most respected stockbroking companies.*

stock-car, stock-cars
NC A **stock-car** is an old car which has had changes made to it to make it suitable for races in which the cars often collide. *At a racing circuit in Cornwall, a stock-car ploughed into the crowd, seriously injuring a two-year-old girl.*

stock exchange, stock exchanges
NC A **stock exchange** is a place where people buy and sell stocks and shares. *Industrialists are not worried by the fall in share prices in the stock exchange. ...the Tokyo Stock Exchange.*

stockholder /stɒkhəʊldə/ **stockholders**
NC A **stockholder** is a shareholder; used in American English. *Her father is the majority stockholder in an oil company... This would have realized more than $60 a share for stockholders.*

Stockholm /stɒkhəʊm/
Stockholm is the capital of Sweden and its largest city. Population: 674,000 (1990).

stocking /stɒkɪŋ/ **stockings**
NC **Stockings** are long garments made of a thin stretchy material that fit closely round a woman's feet and legs up to the top part of her thighs. *...a woman in a flowered skirt and black stockings and shoes.*

stockinged /stɒkɪŋd/
Someone who is in their **stockinged feet** is wearing socks, tights, or stockings, but no shoes. *I stood exactly five and a half feet tall in my stockinged feet.*

stock-in-trade
N SING+POSS Someone's **stock-in-trade** is a usual part of their behaviour or work. *Cynicism was his stock-in-trade... Complaints were a stock-in-trade of an airport manager's job.*

stockist /stɒkɪst/ **stockists**
NC A **stockist** of a particular brand or type of goods is someone who sells this brand or type in their shop. *Try your nearest Moulinex stockist.*

stock market, stock markets
NC The **stock market** is all the organizations and the activity involved in buying and selling stocks and shares. *Prices have risen sharply on the stock market... On the London stock market, trading was quiet.*

stockpile /stɒkpaɪl/ **stockpiles, stockpiling, stockpiled**
1 VO If people **stockpile** things, they store large quantities of them for future use. *The government has been stockpiling food against future emergencies. ...a million colour televisions have been stockpiled in*

warehouses. ◆ **stockpiling** NU *The Protocol did not ban either the production or stockpiling of toxic weapons.*
2 NC A **stockpile** is a large store of something. *...a stockpile of nuclear weapons. ...huge unwanted stockpiles of basic foodstuffs.*

stockroom /stɒkruːm, stɒkrʊm/ **stockrooms**
NC A **stockroom** is a room, for example in a shop or factory, where a stock of goods is kept. *...stockrooms and offices.*

stock-still
ADV If someone stands or sits **stock-still**, they do not move at all. *She stood stock-still, staring at him.*

stocktaking /stɒkteɪkɪŋ/
NU **Stocktaking** is the activity of counting and checking all the goods that a shop or business has.

stocky /stɒki/ **stockier, stockiest**
ADJ **Stocky** people are rather short, but look strong and solid. *...a short, stocky man with dark hair.*

stodge /stɒdʒ/
NU If you describe food such as suet pudding as **stodge**, you mean that you think it is too solid and not very healthy or appetizing, especially because it makes you feel very full when you eat it; an informal word. *It's pure stodge, that's why I'm putting on pounds... They need protein and vegetable food, not loads of stodge obtained from processed foods.*

stodgy /stɒdʒi/; an informal word.
1 ADJ **Stodgy** food is very solid and makes you feel very full. *If the mixture looks too stodgy, add a little more syrup. ...overcooked vegetables and stodgy puddings.*
2 ADJ **Stodgy** also means dull and uninteresting. *His friend Beale was stodgy and solemn. ...a turgid collection of unenlightening and stodgy theory.*

stoic /stəʊɪk/ or **stoical** /stəʊɪkl/
ADJ If you behave in a **stoic** or **stoical** way, you accept difficulties and suffering without complaining or getting upset; a formal word. *I admired her stoic patience... He knew how brave and stoical they had to be.* ◆ **stoically** ADV *Accept your punishment stoically.*

stoicism /stəʊɪsɪzəm/
NU **Stoicism** is stoical behaviour; a formal word. *He endured this treatment with stoicism.*

stoke /stəʊk/ **stokes, stoking, stoked**
1 VO If you **stoke** a fire, you make sure it is kept alight by poking it or putting more fuel onto it. *I suggested she stoke the fire.*
2 VO To **stoke** an emotion or conflict means to make it stronger or worse. *Similar schemes will only stoke the conflict.*
stoke up PHRASAL VERB 1 If you **stoke up** a fire, you add fuel to it in order to increase its strength. *I went back to my camp and stoked up the fire.* 2 If you **stoke up** something such as a feeling, idea or conflict, you make it stronger or more intense, or you make it worse. *He stoked up their anger with his insensitive remarks... The Chancellor has stoked up general election fever... The flow of arms is killing many civilians and stoking up huge problems for the future.*

stole /stəʊl/
Stole is the past tense of **steal**.

stolen /stəʊlən/
Stolen is the past participle of **steal**.

stolid /stɒlɪd/
ADJ **Stolid** people do not show much emotion. *He was slow to move, stolid, and dependable.* ◆ **stolidly** ADV *He may just be sitting up there stolidly.*

Stolojan, Teodor /teɪdɔː, stɒlɒʒɑːn/
Teodor Stolojan was appointed Prime Minister of Romania in September 1991. He briefly served as Minister of Finance in the first National Salvation Government set up in June 1990. He is an independent. Born: 1943.

stomach /stʌmək/ **stomachs, stomaching, stomached**
1 NC Your **stomach** is the organ inside your body where food is digested. *Foxes have small stomachs... His stomach was rumbling.*
2 NC You can also refer to the front part of your body below your waist as your **stomach**. *He lay down on his stomach.*
3 VO If you cannot **stomach** something, you strongly

dislike it and cannot accept it. *Rothermere was unable to stomach the idea... Industrialists are in effect already in revolt over their tax burden and will stomach no more.*
4 If you say that someone **does not have the stomach for** something, or that they **have no stomach for** something, you mean that they do not feel able to deal with it because they lack strength or courage. *He appears to believe they don't have the stomach for a full-scale conflict... They had no stomach for a battle over such demands.*

stomach-ache, stomach-aches
NCorNU If you have a **stomach-ache**, you have a pain in your stomach. *They fell ill with stomach-aches, fever and nausea... The leaves have been used to cure ailments such as stomach-ache.*

stomach pump, stomach pumps
NC A **stomach pump** is a pump with a long tube that is eased down someone's throat into their stomach so that the contents can be removed. Doctors use it when people have eaten poisonous substances or taken an overdose of pills. *...the ignominy of the stomach pump.*

stomp /stɒmp/ **stomps, stomping, stomped**
VA If you **stomp** around, you walk with heavy steps, often because you are angry. *I stomped back to the hotel.*

stone /stəʊn/ **stones, stoning, stoned**
1 NU **Stone** is a hard, solid substance found in the ground and often used for building. *The bits of stone are joined together with cement. ...the little stone bridge. ...a low stone wall.*
2 NC A **stone** is a small piece of rock. *Roger picked up a stone and threw it at Henry.*
3 NC You can refer to a jewel as a **stone**. *An expert commissioned to cut the diamond described it as a perfect blue-white coloured stone. ...reports of gold, diamonds, or other precious stones.*
4 NC The **stone** in a fruit such as a peach or plum is the large seed in the middle. *...plum stones.*
5 VO To **stone** someone or something means to throw stones at them. *They took the man outside and stoned him to death... Rioters had been stoning the Embassy.* ◆ **stoning** NU *There were incidents of stoning and six buses were set on fire. ...a man and a woman sentenced to death by stoning.*
6 NC A **stone** is also a unit of weight equal to 14 pounds or approximately 6.35 kilograms. The plural form is 'stone' or 'stones'. *She weighed twelve stone.* ● **Stone** is used in these phrases. ● If one place is **a stone's throw** from another, the places are close together. *They live within a stone's throw of the school.* ● **to kill two birds with one stone**: see **bird**. ● See also **cornerstone, paving stone, precious stone, stepping stone.**

Stone Age
N PROP The **Stone Age** is the earliest known period of human history, when people used tools and weapons made of stone. *So-called Stone Age Man travelled and settled throughout the Old World.*

stonebreaker /stəʊnbreɪkə/ **stonebreakers**
NC A **stonebreaker** is a machine which breaks large pieces of stone into smaller pieces so that they can be used for making roads.

stone-cold
ADJ Something that is **stone-cold** has become very cold, although it is normally warm. *...cups of stone-cold coffee.*

stoned /stəʊnd/
ADJ Someone who is **stoned** is affected by drugs or very drunk; an informal use. *...five boys hanging out and getting stoned.*

stone deaf
ADJ Someone who is **stone deaf** is completely deaf. *They were either stone deaf or very hard of hearing.*

stonewall /stəʊnwɔːl/ **stonewalls, stonewalling, stonewalled**
VOorV To **stonewall** means to try and prevent someone from doing something, or to try and prevent something from happening, for example by refusing to answer questions or by refusing to co-operate in some way. *Serbia, which is still Marxist, has been stonewalling*

attempts by Slovenia and Croatia to become
independent... All attempts to confirm the reports with
the authorities had been stonewalled... The indications
are that the Algerians will continue to stonewall.
▸ Also NU I can assure you there will be no
stonewalling, no playing for time.

stonework /stəʊnwɜːk/
NU **Stonework** is objects or parts of a building that are
made of stone. ...figures carved into the stonework.

stony /stəʊni/
1 ADJ **Stony** ground is rough and contains a lot of
stones. ...a stony plain between low, barren hills.
2 ADJ If someone's expression or behaviour is **stony**,
they show no friendliness or sympathy. She turned a
stony face on Lucas... Her voice was stony... The
announcement was received in stony silence.

stood /stʊd/
Stood is the past tense and past participle of **stand**.

stooge /stuːdʒ/ **stooges**
NC A **stooge** is someone who is used by another person
to do unpleasant or dishonest tasks; an informal
word. With the help of his stooges, he awarded
contracts to favoured firms.

stool /stuːl/ **stools**
NC A **stool** is a seat with legs but no back or arms.
He was sitting on a stool.

stoop /stuːp/ **stoops, stooping, stooped**
1 V If you **stoop**, you stand or walk with your
shoulders bent forwards. If your ironing board is too
low you have to stoop over it. ▸ Also N SING He walks
with a stoop.
2 V If you **stoop** or stoop down, you bend your body
forwards and downwards. She stooped to feel the
carpet... Bert stooped down and arranged them in a
row.
3 V+to or V+to-INF If you **stoop** to doing something, you
lower your usual standards of behaviour in order to do
it; used showing disapproval. Only once did he stoop
to the tactics of his opponents. ...never stooping to
indulge the audience.

stop /stɒp/ **stops, stopping, stopped**
1 V or V If you **stop** doing something, you no longer do
it. She stopped work to have her baby... Stop it!
You're hurting!... He couldn't stop crying... We all
stopped talking... She put the key in the keyhole,
began turning it, and then she stopped.
2 VO If you **stop** something, you prevent it from
happening or continuing. You're trying to stop my trip
to London... How do I stop a tap dripping?... Nothing
was going to stop Sandy from being a writer.
3 V If an activity or process **stops**, it comes to an
end. The music stopped abruptly... They were waiting
for the rain to stop.
4 V-ERG If a machine or device **stops** or if you stop it,
it no longer works or it is switched off. My watch has
stopped... Stop the recording now.
5 V-ERG When people or things that are moving **stop**,
or if you stop them, they no longer move. He followed
them for a few yards, and then stopped... Stop the car
and let me out... The train stopped at Watford... Stop
people in Oxford Street and ask them to answer these
questions.
6 N SING If something that is moving comes to a **stop**,
it no longer moves. The elevator came to a stop on
the main floor... Harris brought the plane to a stop.
7 NC A **stop** is a place where buses or trains regularly
stop so that people can get on and off. We'll get off at
the next stop.
8 V If you **stop** somewhere on a journey, you stay
there for a short while before continuing. She always
stopped at the market on her way home... Iraqi
Foreign Minister, Tariq Aziz, stopped in Iran
yesterday on his way to Moscow.
9 NC A **stop** during a journey is a time or place at
which you stop. The first stop was a hotel outside
Paris.
10 VO If you **stop** someone's pay or a cheque, you
prevent the money from being paid.
● **Stop** is used in these phrases. ● If you **pull out all
the stops**, or **pull all the stops out**, you do everything
you can to make something happen or be successful.
The government had pulled out all the stops to try and

ensure its own victory... His wife told him to pull out
all the stops and go for the record... We pulled all the
stops out for our daughter's 21st birthday party. ● If
you **put a stop to** something, you prevent it from
happening or continuing. We must put a stop to all
this nonsense. ● If someone will **stop at nothing** to get
or achieve something, they are prepared to do
anything in order to get or achieve it, even if it
involves doing something wrong or dangerous. His
opponents call him a sell-out—a man who will stop at
nothing in his pursuit of power... They stopped at
nothing, using manipulation, lies and forgeries against
him.

stop by PHRASAL VERB If you **stop by** somewhere, you
visit a place for a short time; used in American
English. The President stopped by the press room to
say Happy New Year... You can stop by and you can
see it.

stop off PHRASAL VERB If you **stop off** somewhere, you
stay there for a short time in the middle of a journey.
On the way home I stopped off in London... She had to
stop off at the supermarket on her way back to pick
up the children.

stop over PHRASAL VERB To **stop over** means the
same as to **stop off**. Mr Schultz will stop over in
Helsinki... The plane will stop over in London and
arrive in North Carolina.

stopcock /stɒpkɒk/ **stopcocks**
NC A **stopcock** is a tap on a pipe, which you turn in
order to allow something to pass through the pipe or to
stop it from passing through. I turned the stopcock on
the tank for a little gas.

stopgap /stɒpgæp/ **stopgaps**
NC A **stopgap** is something that serves a purpose for a
short time, but is replaced as soon as possible. It can
be used as a stopgap with patients who have lost a lot
of blood.

stop-go
ADJ ATTRIB **Stop-go** is used to describe processes in
which inaction and action alternate. It seems China is
set to renew the stop-go cycle that has characterized
its economy throughout the 1980s. ...the stop-go history
of Hungary's economic reforms.

stoplight /stɒplaɪt/ **stoplights**
NC A **stoplight** is the same as a **traffic light**; used in
American English. At each stoplight, his gaze would
light on someone.

stopover /stɒpəʊvə/ **stopovers**
NC A **stopover** is a short stay in a place between parts
of a journey. ...a five-week tour abroad with a three-
day stopover in the United States. ...a short stopover
visit to meet a group from the European parliament.

stoppage /stɒpɪdʒ/ **stoppages**
NC When there is a **stoppage**, people stop working
because of a disagreement with their employers. It
will be Ford's first national stoppage for more than ten
years. ...yesterday's decision by the union to continue
the stoppage. ...reports of sporadic work stoppages at
several factories.

stopper /stɒpə/ **stoppers**
NC A **stopper** is a piece of glass, plastic, or cork that
fits into the top of a bottle or jar. I put the stopper in
the bottle.

stop press
N SING The **stop press** is the most recent news, which
is inserted into a special space on the front or back
page of a newspaper after the rest of the newspaper
has been printed. ...stop press for the bank crisis...
The evening papers will also carry stop press
announcements.

stopwatch /stɒpwɒtʃ/ **stopwatches**
NC A **stopwatch** is a watch that can be started and
stopped by pressing buttons in order to time the length
of a race or event. ...watching events with a
stopwatch in your hand.

storage /stɔːrɪdʒ/
1 NU **Storage** is the keeping of something in a special
place until it is needed. A quarter of the crop may be
lost in storage... You haven't got much storage space.
2 NU **Storage** is also the process of storing data in a
computer. ...information storage and retrieval
systems.

store /stɔː/ stores, storing, stored

1 NC A **store** is a shop. ...*a health-food store.* ...*a store that sells Western products.* ● See also **chain store**.

2 VO When you **store** things, you put or keep them somewhere until they are needed. *The tool kit is stored under the seat.* ...*storing water for use in the dry season.* ...*storing and transmitting electricity.*

3 NC A **store** is also a supply of something that you keep somewhere until you need it. ...*the village's store of grain.* ...*emergency stores of food and medical equipment.*

4 NCorNU A **store** is also a place where things are kept while they are not being used. ...*weapon stores in which nuclear warheads were kept... Goods in store will be insured for loss or damage.*

5 VO When you **store** information, you keep it in your memory, a file, or a computer. ...*stored as images in the minds of people.* ...*pocket calculators which can store telephone numbers.*

● Store is used in these phrases. ● Something that is **in store** for you is going to happen to you in the future. *He would have been even more astonished had he known what was in store for him... You never know what the next few months have got in store.* ● If you **set great store** or **put great store** on or by something, you think that it is extremely important or necessary; a formal expression. *He set the greatest store on carrying out his decision... The government is putting great store by Mrs Thatcher's meeting with Mr Mandela tomorrow.*

store up PHRASAL VERB 1 If you **store** something **up**, you keep it until you think that the time is right to use it. *She had some sausage carefully stored up for the occasion.* 2 If you **store up** trouble for yourself, you do something or behave in a way that is likely to cause you problems in the future. *There's concern that America is currently storing up trouble for itself in the future... They point to the troubles in Poland as a harbinger of the difficulties that China is storing up for itself.*

storehouse /stɔːhaʊs/ storehouses

1 NC A **storehouse** is a warehouse; used in American English. *Food was still plentiful in the storehouses.*

2 NC When a lot of things can be found together in one place, you can refer to this place as a **storehouse**. ...*Egypt, the great storehouse of archaeology.* ...*a storehouse of memories.*

storekeeper /stɔːkiːpə/ storekeepers

NC A **storekeeper** is a shopkeeper; used in American English. *Many storekeepers expect shoppers to browse and not buy.*

store-room, store-rooms

NC A **store-room** is a room in which you keep things until they are needed. ...*a store-room for coffins... I brought cases and cartons from the store-room.*

storey /stɔːri/ storeys; spelt **story**, **stories** in American English.

NC The **storeys** of a building are its different floors or levels. *The house was three storeys high.* ...*a multi-storey car park.*

stork /stɔːk/ storks

NC A **stork** is a large bird with a long beak and long legs, which lives near water. *One stork can eat as many as a thousand locusts in one day.*

storm /stɔːm/ storms, storming, stormed

1 NC A **storm** is very bad weather, with heavy rain, strong winds, and often thunder and lightning. *Wait until the storm passes over.*

2 NC+SUPP A **storm** is also an angry or excited reaction from a large number of people. *The decision provoked a storm of criticism from Conservative MPs... The veto was greeted by a storm of protest in Congress... The Government plans to stand by the minister in spite of the political storm that now lies ahead.*

3 VA If you **storm** into or out of a place, you enter or leave it quickly and noisily, because you are angry. *I stormed into the room in a rage... The Chancellor stormed out of the government last October... A party official stormed off the platform in a huff.*

4 V-QUOTEorV To **storm** means to say something very

loudly and angrily; a literary use. *'You misled us,' the professor stormed... No matter how I pleaded or stormed, I could never make her understand.*

5 VOorVA If people **storm** a place, they attack it. *The mob stormed the church... The infantry stormed through the walls of the Imperial Palace.* ◆ **storming** NU+of *The storming of the embassy contravened international law.*

6 If someone or something **takes** a place **by storm**, they are very successful in that place. *The President has taken the country by storm.* ...*the tragic love story which took Broadway by storm in 1957.*

storm cloud, storm clouds

1 NC **Storm clouds** are the dark clouds which are seen before a storm. *I looked up at the storm clouds.*

2 NC You can also use **storm clouds** to refer to a sign that something violent is going to happen; a formal expression. *The storm clouds of war gathered over Europe.*

stormy /stɔːmi/ stormier, stormiest

1 ADJ If the weather is **stormy**, there is a strong wind and heavy rain. ...*that stormy autumn evening.*

2 ADJ A **stormy** situation involves a lot of angry argument or criticism. *There was a stormy debate over it.* ...*the stormy relations between George and his mother.*

story /stɔːri/ stories

1 NC A **story** is a description of imaginary people and events, which is written or told in order to entertain people. *Tell me a story.* ...*a story about a foolish hunter.* ...*ghost stories.*

2 NC A **story** is also a description or account of things that have happened. *The story of the firm begins in 1820.* ...*her life story.* ● See also **tall story**.

3 NC In journalism, a **story** is a report or article on a particular subject. *For most papers, however, today's main story is Mr Bush's address to the United Nations.* ...*the front-page story in today's edition.*

4 See also **storey**.

● Story is used in these phrases. ● If you say that something is **not the whole story**, or is **only part of the story**, you mean that a particular situation cannot be fully understood because not enough is known about it. *As usual, statistics really don't tell the whole story... The face Moscow presents to the outside world is only part of the story.* ● You use **to cut** or **to make a long story short** to indicate that you are going to give the final result of an event or series of events, rather than give a lot of unnecessary details. *To cut a long story short it turns out that they solve their problems in a very similar way to us... And to make a long story short, we spent about eight hours together that day.*

storybook /stɔːribʊk/

N+N A **storybook** relationship, situation, or life is one that seems to be perfect and ends happily, in the way that many fairy stories do. *His was, as they say, a storybook life—a life from out of the movies... Tracy Austin's return to big-time tennis failed to have a storybook ending.* ...*a storybook romance.*

storyteller /stɔːritelə/ storytellers

NC A **storyteller** is a person who tells or writes stories, usually as a job. ...*her reputation as one of the greatest Caribbean storytellers.*

stout /staʊt/ stouter, stoutest

1 ADJ A **stout** person is rather fat. ...*a short, stout man.*

2 ADJ Something that is **stout** is thick and strong. *He broke a stout branch from a bush.* ...*stout black shoes.*

3 ADJ ATTRIB **Stout** actions or beliefs are firm and strong. ...*the stoutest possible resistance.* ◆ **stoutly** ADV *Chris stoutly denied Eva's accusations.*

stout-hearted

ADJ Someone who is **stout-hearted** is brave and determined; a literary word. ...*a loyal and stout-hearted servant.*

stove /stəʊv/ stoves

NC A **stove** is a piece of equipment for heating a room or cooking. *She left the sausages on the stove.* ...*a gas stove.*

stow /stəʊ/ stows, stowing, stowed

VOA If you **stow** something somewhere or **stow** it

away, you put it carefully somewhere until it is needed. *She stowed the bags in two baskets... His baggage was safely stowed away in the plane.*

stowaway /ˈstəʊəweɪ/ **stowaways**
NC A **stowaway** is a person who hides in a ship, plane, or other vehicle in order to make a journey without paying. *They arrived in Liverpool as stowaways on a Greek cargo ship.*

straddle /ˈstrædl/ **straddles, straddling, straddled**
1 VO If you **straddle** something, you sit or stand with one leg on each side of it. *He straddled a chair and began fiddling with the keys.*
2 VO If something **straddles** a place, it crosses it or links different parts of it together. *A viaduct straddles the river Wye. ...a communications net that straddles the globe.*

strafe /streɪf, strɑːf/ **strafes, strafing, strafed**
VO To **strafe** an enemy means to attack them by scattering bullets or bombs on them from a low-flying aircraft. *They strafed the invasion beaches and headlands.*

straggle /ˈstrægl/ **straggles, straggling, straggled**
1 VA If people **straggle** somewhere, they move there slowly in irregular, disorganized groups. *The players straggled across the field.*
2 VA When things **straggle** over an area, they cover it untidily. *The shacks straggle along the dirt road. ...her hair straggling down over her eyes.*

straggler /ˈstræɡələ/ **stragglers**
NC The **stragglers** are the people in a group who are moving more slowly or making less progress than the others. *...waiting until the last stragglers came in.*

straggly /ˈstræɡəli/
ADJ Something that is **straggly** grows or spreads out in different directions, in an untidy way. *...a few straggly trees. ...a straggly beard.*

straight /streɪt/ **straighter, straightest**
1 ADJ or ADV If something is **straight**, it continues in one direction and does not bend or curve. *...a straight line. ...a long straight road... I saw the car coming straight at me... She was staring straight ahead... Police cars drove straight at the crowd.*
2 ADJ or ADV A **straight** position is one that is upright or level, rather than sloping or bent. *Make sure it's straight... Keep your knees bent and your back straight... Check that all the pictures hang straight.*
3 N SING On a running track, the **straight** is the last 100 metres in a race after the last bend and before the finish. *Into the straight, he can't close the gap.*
4 ADV If you go **straight** to a place, you go there immediately without stopping on the way. *The doctor told me to go straight to bed.*
5 ADJ ATTRIB **Straight** also means simple, definite, or clear-cut. *I asked why he'd chosen to write the story as a novel rather than as straight history... He finds a marked bias both in straight news stories and in editorials... The Alliance has emerged as the clear winner but without a straight majority.*
6 ADJ If you are **straight** with someone, you speak to them honestly and frankly. *I don't think she's being completely straight with us... We couldn't give you a straight answer now.*
7 ADJ ATTRIB A **straight** choice or a **straight** fight involves only two people or things. *The voters have a straight choice between the two candidates.*
8 ADJ A **straight** person is heterosexual rather than homosexual. A **straight** relationship is a sexual one between a man and a woman; an informal use. *I was having sex with straight friends. ...gay and straight relationships.*
9 ADJ ATTRIB **Straight** also means following one after the other. *...four straight sessions... They won the championship in four straight games.*
● **Straight** is used in these phrases. ● If you **get** something **straight**, you make sure that you understand it properly. *Now, let me get this straight.* ● If someone who was a criminal is **going straight**, they are no longer involved in crime. *In all their time in Canada, he went straight.* ● If you **keep a straight face** in a funny situation, you manage not to laugh. *I found it hard to keep a straight face.* ● If you **set** or **put the record straight**, or if you **set** or **put matters**

straight, you remove any misunderstanding or confusion from a situation by what you say or do. *Will you feel the need to put the record straight on this particular point?... She put matters straight with a clear win. ...determined to set the record straight.*

straight away
ADV If you do something **straight away**, you do it immediately. *You might not recognize it straight away... We went to work straight away... Let me assure you straight away.*

straighten /ˈstreɪtn/ **straightens, straightening, straightened**
1 VO If you **straighten** something, you make it tidy or put it in its proper position. *I'll just straighten the bed... Straightening his tie, he knocked on the door.*
2 V or V+up If you are bending and you then **straighten** or **straighten** up, you make your body straight and upright. *The man straightened and looked him in the face... He straightens up, combs his hair, and walks into the meeting.*
straighten out PHRASAL VERB If you **straighten out** a confused situation, you succeed in dealing with it or getting it properly organized. *It'll take six weeks to get things straightened out.*

straight-faced
ADJ or ADV Someone who is **straight-faced** shows no sign of amusement in a funny situation, even though they really think that it is very amusing. *It was a brilliant joke and she told it completely straight-faced.*

straightforward /ˌstreɪtˈfɔːwəd/
1 ADJ Something that is **straightforward** is easy to do or understand. *...a very straightforward set of instructions in simple English... The conditions are stated in straightforward, unambiguous terms.*
2 ADJ If your behaviour is **straightforward**, you are honest and frank. *...the only Senator to speak with straightforward contempt.*

straightlaced /ˌstreɪtˈleɪst/. See straitlaced.

straight sets
N PL In tennis, if you win a match in **straight sets**, you defeat your opponent without losing a set. *The number three seed won in straight sets... He had a straight sets win over another American.*

strain /streɪn/ **strains, straining, strained**
1 NU or NC If there is a **strain** on something, it has to hold more or do more than normal, and may therefore break or become inefficient. *The additional supports will help to take some of the strain off the original structure... The existing military alliance in Western Europe is under some strain... This policy puts a greater strain on the economic system than it can bear.*
2 VO To **strain** something means to use it beyond normal or reasonable limits. *The oil-price increases have strained the resources of the poorer countries.*
3 V+to-INF or VO+to-INF If you **strain** to do something, you make a great effort to do it. *He was straining to hear what the speaker was saying... He strained his eyes to catch a glimpse of the President.*
4 NU or NC **Strain** is a state of worry and tension. *Many people doing this sort of job suffer from strain... I found it a strain being totally responsible for her. ...severe mental strains.*
5 VO If you **strain** a muscle, you injure it by using it suddenly or too much. *He limped off the field after straining a groin muscle.*
6 NU **Strain** is also a muscle injury. *...back strain.*
7 VO When you **strain** food, you pour the liquid off it. *I'll just strain the potatoes.*
8 NC+SUPP A **strain** of a plant is a variety of it. *...high-yielding strains of wheat.*
9 N PL+SUPP If you hear **strains** of music, you hear music being played; a literary use. *The strains of Chopin drifted in from the music room.*

strained /streɪnd/
1 ADJ If you are **strained**, you are worried and nervous. *She looked strained and tired... Her voice was strained.*
2 ADJ If relations between people are **strained**, they are unfriendly and do not trust each other. *Relations between the two families had become increasingly strained.*

strainer /streɪnə/ **strainers**
NC A **strainer** is a tool used for separating liquids from solids. It has a lot of small holes at the bottom through which liquid can pass but solid substances cannot. ...*a tea strainer*.

strait /streɪt/ **straits**
1 NC You can refer to a narrow strip of sea which joins two large areas of sea as a **strait** or the **straits**. *...the Strait of Hormuz. ...the Straits of Gibraltar.*
2 N PL+SUPP You use **straits** to say that someone is in a difficult situation. *The family was in difficult straits... The company was now in dire financial straits.*

straitened /streɪtnd/
ADJ If someone is living in **straitened** circumstances, they do not have as much money as they used to, and are finding it very hard to buy or pay for everything that they need; a formal word. *How long have they been in such straitened circumstances?... In that busy, straitened household they were too hard worked to have time for talking. ...hard pressed and financially straitened.*

strait jacket, strait jackets
1 NC A **strait jacket** is a special jacket used to tie the arms of a violent person tightly around his or her body. *They had lashed him in a strait jacket and locked him in Bellevue.*
2 NC If you say that an idea or situation is a **strait jacket**, you mean that it is very limited and restricting. *The attempt to save money had placed the company in a strait jacket that stifled its natural development. ...the ideological strait jacket that had bound the Chinese people.*

straitlaced /streɪtleɪst/; also spelt **straightlaced**.
ADJ If you describe someone as **straitlaced**, you mean that they have a very strict and severe attitude towards questions of morality. *Aunt Josephine is very straitlaced—she doesn't approve of Martin at all.*

strand /strænd/ **strands**
1 NC A **strand** of thread, wire, or hair is a single piece of it. *...a strand of silk... Make sure that there are no loose strands of wire... A strand of hair fell over her eyes.*
2 NC A **strand** of a situation or idea is one part of it. *...these two strands of industrial policy... Several strands in Kate's life seemed to be pulled together.*

stranded /strændɪd/
ADJ If someone or something is **stranded** somewhere, they are stuck there and cannot leave. *...the stranded holidaymakers... The boat was stranded in the mud... Hundreds of lorries are likely to be stranded for two days.*

strange /streɪndʒ/ **stranger, strangest**
1 ADJ **Strange** means odd, unfamiliar, or unexpected. *I had a strange dream last night... It was strange to hear her voice again... Her husband had become strange and distant.* ◆ **strangeness** NU *I was overwhelmed with a sense of strangeness.*
2 ADJ A **strange** person or place is one that you do not know. *I don't like strange people coming into my house... Never get in a strange car... Ipswich is really quite strange to me.*

strangely /streɪndʒli/
1 ADV or SUBMOD You use **strangely** to indicate that an action or quality is odd, unfamiliar, or unexpected. *They had acted strangely as he went by... He answered in a strangely calm voice.*
2 ADV SEN You use **strangely** or **strangely enough** to emphasize that what you are saying is surprising. *It has, strangely, only recently been discovered... 'Are students interested in religion these days?'—'Strangely enough, they are.'*

stranger /streɪndʒə/ **strangers**
1 NC A **stranger** is someone you have not met before. *Antonio was a stranger to all of us. ...a room full of strangers.*
2 NC Someone who is a **stranger** in a place has not been there before. *They are strangers in the village and lost their way in the fog.*
3 NC Someone who is a **stranger** to a situation has not experienced it before. *I was a stranger to this kind of gathering.*

strangle /stræŋgl/ **strangles, strangling, strangled**
1 VO To **strangle** someone means to kill them by squeezing their throat. *He was strangled in his bed.*
2 VO To **strangle** something means to prevent it from succeeding or developing. *Such policies were strangling economic development.*

strangled /stræŋgld/
ADJ A **strangled** sound is unclear and muffled. *...a strangled cry of amazement.*

stranglehold /stræŋglhəʊld/ **strangleholds**
NC To have a **stranglehold** on something means to have control over it and prevent it from developing. *The unions have a stranglehold on the country.*

strangulation /stræŋgjʊleɪʃn/
1 NU **Strangulation** is the act of killing someone by putting pressure on their throat, and so preventing them from breathing. *The victims died of slow strangulation.*
2 NU Economic **strangulation** is the act of preventing the growth of a country's economy, usually through a blockade or sanctions. *He told correspondents his country faced economic strangulation.*

strap /stræp/ **straps, strapping, strapped**
1 NC A **strap** is a narrow piece of leather or cloth, used to carry things or fasten them together. *I undid the straps, and opened the case. ...high-heeled shoes, with straps above the ankle.*
2 VOA If you **strap** something somewhere, you fasten it there with a strap. *Children should be strapped into a special car seat... He straps on his watch.*

strapless /stræpləs/
ADJ A **strapless** dress or bra does not have the usual narrow bands of material over the shoulders. *Miss Ryan was wearing a low strapless dress that hugged her curves.*

strapped /stræpt/
ADJ If someone is **strapped**, they do not have enough money. *The family is strapped for cash. ...placing special demands on financially strapped school systems.*

strapping /stræpɪŋ/
ADJ A **strapping** person is tall, strong, and healthy-looking. *...a strapping boy of eighteen.*

strata /strɑːtə/
Strata is the plural of **stratum**.

stratagem /strætədʒəm/ **stratagems**
NC A **stratagem** is a plan or tactic; a formal word. *...a cunning stratagem to quieten the rebellious peasants.*

strategic /strətiːdʒɪk/
1 ADJ A **strategic** plan or position is one which helps you to achieve something or to gain an advantage over other people. *I took up a strategic position near the exit. ...civil servants providing strategic advice to ministers.*
2 ADJ **Strategic** is also used to describe something that gives a country or an army a military advantage. *Militiamen blew up a strategic bridge... His country had made the same strategic error. ...Syria, Iran's strategic ally.* ◆ **strategically** ADV *The islands were strategically important to Venice.*
3 ADJ ATTRIB **Strategic** arms and weapons are aimed at places of military or economic importance in a potentially enemy country and are ready to be fired if a war starts. *...a 50 per cent reduction in both sides' strategic arms. ...a treaty on strategic nuclear weapons. ...long-range strategic missiles.*

strategist /strætədʒɪst/ **strategists**
NC A **strategist** is someone who is skilled in planning the best way to achieve something, especially in war. *He distinguished himself as a brave soldier and a bold strategist. ...the greatest political strategist in the country.*

strategy /strætədʒi/ **strategies**
1 NC A **strategy** is a plan. *He adopted a strategy of massive deflation. ...a strategy for world economic growth. ...Britain's defence strategy.*
2 NU **Strategy** is the art of planning the best way to achieve something, especially in war. *...a major exercise in military strategy. ...the debate over strategy.*

stratosphere /strætəsfɪə/
N SING The **stratosphere** is the layer of the earth's atmosphere which lies between 10 and 50 kilometres above the earth. *...gases that affect the ozone layer in the stratosphere.*

stratum /strɑːtəm/ **strata** /strɑːtə/
1 NC A **stratum** of society is a group of people in it who are similar in their education, income, or social class; a formal use. *Our military leaders have always been drawn from the upper strata of society... Intellectuals are the only social stratum which could come to terms with the revolution in computers.*
2 NC The **strata** in the earth's surface are the different layers of rock; a technical use. *...the underlying rock strata.*

straw /strɔː/ **straws**
1 NU **Straw** is the dried, yellowish stalks from crops such as wheat or barley. *The eggs were packed in straw.*
2 NC A **straw** is a thin tube of paper or plastic, which you drink through. *Fiona was drinking a milk shake through a straw.*
3 If you are **clutching at straws**, you are trying unusual or desperate methods to achieve something, often because other methods have failed. *Frustrated golfers clutch at every straw in search of that little extra that means so much.*
4 If something is **the last straw**, it is the latest in a series of bad events, and makes you feel that you cannot bear any more. *The Soviet move was the last straw to the Americans... The wage increases promised to government employees proved the last straw for many Sudanese.*

strawberry /strɔːbəri/ **strawberries**
NC A **strawberry** is a small red fruit with tiny seeds in its skin. *...strawberries and cream. ...a strawberry farmer from near Cheddar.*

strawberry mark, strawberry marks
NC A **strawberry mark** is a reddish mark on someone's skin which has been there since birth. *The physical resemblance was striking, complete with strawberry mark on his forehead.*

straw poll, straw polls
NC A **straw poll** or **straw vote** is the unofficial questioning of a group of people to find out their opinion about something. *We took a straw poll of voters outside the polling stations.*

stray /streɪ/ **strays, straying, strayed**
1 V If people or animals **stray**, they wander away from where they should be. *Children had strayed on to an airport runway... All too often, gates are left open and animals stray.*
2 ADJ ATTRIB A **stray** animal such as a cat or dog lives in the wild and is not looked after by anyone, for example because it wandered away from its owner's home and became lost. *About a dozen stray dogs in metal cages are awaiting adoption. ...stray cats.*
► Also NC *The dog, which had been picked up as a stray in Zambia, was being kept in quarantine. ...the fee would pay for dog wardens to patrol the streets and deal with strays.*
3 ADJ ATTRIB A **stray** bullet is one that hits someone, although it was not aimed at them. *His wife was injured by a stray bullet... A number of people were struck by stray bullets.*
4 ADJ ATTRIB **Stray** things have become separated from other similar things. *A hen was pecking around for stray grains of corn.*
5 V If your thoughts **stray**, you stop concentrating on a particular thing. *He let his thoughts stray for five minutes... He does not stray from facts.*

streak /striːk/ **streaks, streaking, streaked**
1 NC A **streak** is a long mark on or in something. *The table was smeared with streaks of paint... Her hair had a grey streak in it.*
2 VO If something is **streaked** with a colour, it has lines of the colour in it. *His moustache was streaked with grey... The sun is streaking the sea with long lines of gold.*
3 NC+SUPP If someone has a particular **streak**, they have a particular quality in their character. *Children have a streak of cruelty. I had always been aware of*

the possessive streak in her.
4 NC+SUPP A winning **streak** or a losing **streak** is a series of victories or defeats, usually in sport. *The New Zealand All-Blacks continue their winning streak... It looks as though he could be on another one of his winning streaks.*
5 V A To **streak** somewhere means to move there very quickly. *The fish streaked away.*

streaky /striːki/ **streakier, streakiest**
ADJ Something that is **streaky** is marked with streaks. *...horrible streaky wallpaper... The light made a streaky pattern on the carpet.*

streaky bacon
NU **Streaky bacon** is bacon which has stripes of fat between stripes of meat. *...a sausage, or a tiny bit of streaky bacon.*

stream /striːm/ **streams, streaming, streamed**
1 NC A **stream** is a small, narrow river. *He led us along the bank of the stream.*
2 NC You can refer to a regular flow of people or things as a **stream**. *A steady stream of workers left the factory. ...streams of tracer bullets in the skies. ...a stream of smoke... The stream of insults continues.* • See also **bloodstream**.
3 V A If people, vehicles, or liquids **stream** somewhere, large numbers or amounts of them move there in a steady flow. *The doors opened and the audience began to stream out... The cars are streaming by at sixty miles an hour... She stood in the doorway, tears streaming down her face.*
4 V A When light **streams** into a place, it shines into it strongly. *The sun was streaming in through the windows.*
5 NC+SUPP A **stream** in a school is a group of children of the same age and ability who are taught together. *...pupils in the top streams.*
6 VO To **stream** pupils means to teach them in groups according to their ability. ♦ **streaming** NU *Our new headmaster says he's going to end streaming.*

streamer /striːmə/ **streamers**
NC A **streamer** is a long narrow strip of coloured paper used as a decoration. *The little village of Whitsbury in Hampshire was festooned with balloons and streamers.*

streaming /striːmɪŋ/
ADJ ATTRIB If someone has **streaming** eyes or a **streaming** nose, their eyes or nose let out a lot of liquid, usually because of an illness. *...an allergic reaction in the form of streaming eyes and a wheezy chest. ...people with streaming eyes and noses when there's a lot of pollen about.*

streamline /striːmlaɪn/ **streamlines, streamlining, streamlined**
1 VO To **streamline** a vehicle or object means to improve its shape so that it moves more quickly and efficiently.
2 VO To **streamline** an organization or process means to make it more efficient by removing parts of it that are considered to be unnecessary. *He aimed to streamline the Post Office. ...an attempt to streamline timber production.*

streamlined /striːmlaɪnd/
1 ADJ Something that is **streamlined** has a shape that allows it to move quickly or efficiently through air or through water. *Mackerel have most marvellously streamlined bodies.*
2 ADJ Something that has been **streamlined** has been altered to make it more effective, useful, or efficient. *It's likely that the OAU will emerge as a more streamlined, efficient organization. ...a streamlined version of the old Communist Party.*

street /striːt/ **streets**
1 NC A **street** is a road in a town or village, usually with buildings along it. *The two men walked slowly down the street... She lives in Seyer Street.*
2 NC You can use **street** when talking about activities that happen out of doors in a town. *We've got to keep youngsters off the streets... We don't usually embrace friends in the street. ...street theatre.*
3 See also **high street**.
• **Street** is used in these phrases. • If you talk about **the man in the street**, you mean ordinary people in

general. *The man in the street was unlikely ever to have seen a ghost.* ● If something such as a subject or activity is **up** or **right up** your **street**, you like it a lot, are very interested in it, or know a lot about it; an informal expression. *Shakespeare and Congreve were not really up his street... Today's longer distance and softer going will be right up his street... That's very much up your street, of course.*

streetcar /ˈstriːtkɑː/ **streetcars**
NC A **streetcar** is a tram; used in American English. *He caught the next streetcar home.*

street credibility
NU If someone says that you have **street credibility** or **street cred**, they mean that ordinary young people would approve of you and consider you to be part of their culture, usually because you share their views or their sense of fashion; an informal expression. *Wearing that will do nothing for your street credibility!... When the band became more successful, I felt they rather lost their street credibility.*

street value
N SING The **street value** of a drug such as heroin is the price that is paid for it when it is sold illegally to drug users. *Police at Heathrow Airport have seized drugs with a street value of half a million pounds.*

streetwise /ˈstriːtwaɪz/
ADJ Someone who is **streetwise** knows how to cope with and be successful in difficult or dangerous situations, especially in big cities; an informal word. *You're streetwise, smart, clever—or at least that's how you'd like to be seen. ...a streetwise gang of runaways.*

strength /streŋθ/ **strengths**
1 NU Your **strength** is your physical energy and ability. *He pulled with all his strength. ...recovering their strength before trying again.*
2 NU **Strength** is also courage or determination. *This gave us the strength to resist further temptation... With unshakable strength of character she stayed on after the crisis.*
3 NU You can also refer to power or influence as **strength**. *...the enormous strength and influence of the unions... His critics question the benefits of increased military strength.*
4 NCorNU Your **strengths** are your good qualities and abilities. *Each firm has its particular strengths and weaknesses.*
5 NU The **strength** of an object is its ability to withstand rough treatment or heavy weights. *...the development of a number of high strength stainless steels.*
6 NU The **strength** of a feeling or opinion is the degree to which people have it. *The Government had clearly underestimated the strength of popular feeling. ...the strength of Jordanian public opinion.*
7 NU The **strength** of an argument or story is the extent to which it is likely to be true. *He continued to deny it, despite the growing strength of the argument.*
8 NU The **strength** of a relationship is its degree of closeness and the length of time it seems likely to continue for. *This leads to bonds of deceptive strength being formed with the company.*
9 NU The **strength** of a group of people is the total number of people in it. *Their forces were growing in strength.*
● **Strength** is used in these phrases. ● If something or someone **goes from strength to strength**, they gradually become more successful. *Trade with the West has been going from strength to strength.* ● If a group is at **full strength**, it has all it's members present or available. *At full strength, the mission should include 70 military observers and about 20 civilian support personnel... New Zealand's cricket side plans to be at full strength for today's one-day fixture against England.* ● If a group is present or exists **in strength**, it consists of a large number of people. *The army has been deployed in strength throughout the country... Miss Bhutto called on voters and party workers to turn out in strength... Troops are patrolling the streets in strength.* ● If you act **on the strength of** a fact or situation, this provides the basis or reason for your action. *The Cabinet agreed to a*

grant of £4m on the strength of the Company's projections of sales.

strengthen /ˈstreŋθn/ **strengthens, strengthening, strengthened**
1 VO If a number of people **strengthen** a group, they make it more powerful by joining it. *The new peers will strengthen the Labour Party in the Upper House.*
2 VO If something **strengthens** an argument or opinion, it provides more reasons or evidence to support it. *The uncertainty about the railways strengthened the argument for planning.*
3 V-ERG If a feeling or attitude **strengthens** or if someone or something **strengthens** it, it becomes more intense and has greater influence. *During the prolonged depression of the seventies, racialism strengthened. ...countless little cruelties that only strengthened my resolve not to give in.*
4 VO If a relationship is **strengthened**, it becomes closer and is more likely to continue in the future. *He strengthened US relations with its principle ally in the Far East... We want to strengthen our ties with the United States.*
5 V-ERG If a particular currency **strengthens** or is **strengthened**, its value increases in relation to the currency of one or more other countries. *Share prices in London rose sharply, and the pound strengthened, moving up four cents against the dollar... Dealers there said the dollar was strengthened on expectations that Japanese interest rates would be cut.*
6 VO If something **strengthens** you, it increases your courage and determination. *It is designed to strengthen you against the hostile world.*
7 VO If something **strengthens** an object, it makes it able to withstand rough treatment or heavy weights. *...struts designed to strengthen the wings of aeroplanes.*

strenuous /ˈstrenjuəs/
ADJ A **strenuous** action or activity involves a lot of effort or energy. *Alf made strenuous efforts to improve his reading. ...a strenuous twenty minute walk... The campaign trail is strenuous.* ◆ **strenuously** ADV *He strenuously denied that his airline was in any danger.*

stress /stres/ **stresses, stressing, stressed**
1 V-REPORT, VO, or V-QUOTE If you **stress** a point, you emphasize it because you think it is important. *I ought to stress that this was not a trial but an enquiry... He stressed the importance of better public relations... 'We deal with governments,' he stressed.* ▶ Also NU+*on* *...this stress on community values.*
2 NUorNC If you feel or are under **stress**, you feel tense and worried about something. *...parents under stress. ...the stress of examinations... Too many stresses are being placed on the family. ...the stresses and strains of growing up.*
3 NCorNU **Stresses** are strong physical pressures applied to an object. *Earthquakes can result from stresses in the earth's crust... It has stood up to tests under extreme heat and stress.*
4 NUorNC **Stress** is the emphasis that you put on a word or part of a word when you say it, so that it sounds slightly louder.
5 VO If you **stress** a word or part of a word when you say it, you put emphasis on it. *You should stress the second syllable in 'computer'.*

stressed /strest/
1 ADJ If you are **stressed**, you feel tension and anxiety because of difficulties in your life. *This has not stopped adults feeling stressed and anxious.*
2 ADJ An object that is **stressed** is affected because strong physical pressure has been applied to it; a technical term in physics.

stressful /ˈstresfl/
ADJ A **stressful** situation or experience causes someone to feel stress. *Life with several children is hard and stressful.*

stretch /stretʃ/ **stretches, stretching, stretched**
1 VA Something that **stretches** over a particular area or distance is present or exists in that area or for the distance specified. *A line of cars nearly a mile long stretched along the road from the airport. ...the belt of flat land which stretches from the capital up to York...*

Ranks of unmanned computer terminals stretch down the empty hall... The forest will stretch over four counties—Staffordshire, Derbyshire, Warwickshire, and Leicestershire.
2 NC+SUPP A **stretch** of land or water is an area of it. *The northern and western stretches controlled by guerillas are suffering from this year's drought and food shortage. ...the five-hundred mile stretch of desert that makes up the border between Saudi Arabia and Iraq.*
3 V or VO When you **stretch**, you hold your arms or legs out straight and tighten your muscles. *Thomas yawned and stretched... I just grunted and stretched my limbs.*
4 NC A **stretch** of time is a period of time. *Any job carries with it daily stretches of boredom.* ● *If* something happens or you do something for a particular length of time **at a stretch**, it happens or you do it for that length of time without stopping. *In recent years, he has often failed to appear in public for many weeks at a stretch. ...legislation restricting the number of hours doctors may work at a stretch.*
5 V-ERG When something soft or elastic **stretches** or is **stretched**, it is pulled until it becomes tight. *Nylon stretches... The skin of her face was stretched very tightly over the bones.*
6 ADJ ATTRIB **Stretch** material can be stretched. *...stretch covers on armchairs.*
7 VO If someone's money or resources **are stretched**, they have hardly enough for their needs. *The nation's resources were already stretched to their limits.* ◆ **stretched** ADJ ATTRIB *...stretched NHS budgets. ...its stretched oil economy.*
8 VO If a job or task **stretches** you, it makes you use all your energy or skills. *He said that pupils needed to be stretched more.*
9 If you say that something is not true or possible by **any stretch of the imagination**, you mean that you think it is completely untrue or absolutely impossible. *It could by no stretch of the imagination be seen as a victory.*
stretch out PHRASAL VERB 1 If you **stretch out** or if you **stretch** yourself **out** somewhere, you lie there with your legs and body in a straight line. *I just want to stretch out in my own bed.* 2 If you **stretch out** a part of your body, you hold it out straight. *He stretched out a thin arm and took our hands.*
stretcher /strɛtʃə/ **stretchers**
NC A **stretcher** is a long piece of canvas with a pole along each side, used to carry an injured person. *He was carried into the clinic on a stretcher.*
stretcher-bearer, stretcher-bearers
NC A **stretcher-bearer** is a person who helps to carry a stretcher. *An ambulance pulled up and two stretcher-bearers jumped out.*
stretchy /strɛtʃi/ **stretchier, stretchiest**
ADJ **Stretchy** material is slightly elastic and able to stretch easily. *That material's a bit stretchy for a shirt.*
strew /struː/ **strews, strewing, strewed, strewn** /struːn/
1 VO If things **are strewn** somewhere, they are scattered there untidily. *His clothes were strewn all over the room... Broken glass was strewn across the street corner.*
2 VO If things **strew** a place, they lie scattered there. *Books and cushions strewed the floor... The carpet is strewn with broken glass.*
stricken /strɪkn/
ADJ If someone is **stricken** by something unpleasant, they are severely affected by it. *Madeleine was stricken by fear... Stricken with arthritis, she lay in bed for many years... Food relief to the stricken areas has been disrupted.*
strict /strɪkt/ **stricter, strictest**
1 ADJ A **strict** person does not tolerate impolite or disobedient behaviour. *Parents were strict in Victorian times. ...a school with strict discipline.* ◆ **strictly** ADV *In those days we were raised very strictly by our parents.*
2 ADJ A **strict** rule or order must be obeyed absolutely. *Strict instructions were issued... The*

Opposition demanded stricter control of prices. ◆ **strictly** ADV *The curfew was strictly enforced.*
3 ADJ ATTRIB The **strict** sense of something is its precise meaning. *He may not be lying in the strict sense of the word, but he has not told the whole truth.* ◆ **strictly** SUBMOD *That's not strictly true.*
4 ADJ ATTRIB You use **strict** to describe someone who never does things that are against their beliefs, or to describe beliefs whose principles and conventions are carefully followed. *The majority of the islanders are strict Presbyterians. ...a return to strict Marxist-Leninism.*
strictly /strɪktli/
1 ADV+for If something is **strictly** for a particular thing or person, it is to be used or done only by them. *The discussion was strictly for members.*
2 SUBMOD **Strictly** is also used before adjectives to emphasize that something or someone is of one particular type rather than any other. *He insisted that this was a strictly humanitarian visit... 'I'm strictly apolitical.'... The British government takes a strictly non-interventionist stand on most commercial matters.*
3 ADV SEN You say **strictly speaking** to correct a statement or add more precise information. *Paul's a friend of mine. Well, strictly speaking my sister's friend.*
stricture /strɪktʃə/ **strictures**
N C or N U A **stricture** is a severe criticism or disapproval of something; a formal word. *Throughout history the strictures of society have weighed more heavily upon women than upon men... His administration of the company was even more deserving of stricture than it appeared.*
stridden /strɪdn/
Stridden is the past participle of **stride**.
stride /straɪd/ **strides, striding, strode, stridden**
1 VA If you **stride** somewhere, you walk there with quick, long steps. *Louisa watched him striding across the lawn... He was striding out of the entrance.*
2 NC A **stride** is a long step which you take when you are walking or running. *...the length of each stride.*
3 N SING A **stride** is also a way of walking with long steps. *She walked ahead with her purposeful stride.*
4 NC If you make **strides** in something that you are doing, you make rapid progress in it. *On the question of pay, giant strides have been made.*
5 If you **take** a difficult situation **in** your **stride**, you deal with it calmly and easily. *She takes examinations in her stride.*
stridency /straɪdnsi/
NU **Stridency** is the quality of stating your opinions and feelings very strongly; used showing disapproval. *...a writer who shocked the bourgeoisie with his sexual naughtiness and political stridency. ...the stridency of its campaign.*
strident /straɪdnt/
1 ADJ A **strident** sound is loud and unpleasant. *His voice was strident and triumphant.*
2 ADJ If someone is **strident**, they state their feelings or opinions very strongly; used showing disapproval. *...strident Marxists. ...a strident demand for rearmament.* ◆ **stridently** ADV *He stridently pledged to continue the struggle... The language is much less stridently Marxist.*
strife /straɪf/
NU **Strife** is strong disagreement or fighting; a formal word. *The prime duty of the state was to protect its citizens from internal strife and external attack. ...family strife.*
strike /straɪk/ **strikes, striking, struck**
1 NC When there is a **strike**, workers stop working for a period of time, to try to get better pay or conditions. *...the miners' strike... University students in Niger have ended their three-week strike... Workers will begin strike action on Monday... A national strike ballot was a possibility.*
2 V If workers **strike**, they stop working for a period of time, to try to get better pay or conditions. *Airline pilots are threatening to strike.* ◆ **striking** ADJ ATTRIB *The demonstrators shouted slogans in support of the striking workers.*
3 VO If you **strike** someone or something, you

deliberately hit them. *He struck the ball beautifully.*
4 V Oor V A If something **strikes** something else or **strikes** against it, it hits the other thing. *The house was struck by lightning... The trawler struck against the jetty.*
5 V Oor V If an illness or disaster **strikes**, it suddenly happens. *...the earthquake that struck Japan last Tuesday... When disaster strikes, you need sympathy and practical advice.*
6 V To **strike** means to attack someone or something quickly and violently. *Raising herself slightly, the snake strikes.* ▶ Also N C *The Air Force carried out air strikes as a result of the information received.*
7 V Oor V O-REPORT If an idea or thought **strikes** you, it comes into your mind suddenly. *What struck him most was the scale of the programme... It struck him how foolish his behaviour had been.*
8 V O If something **strikes** you in a particular way, it gives you a particular impression. *Gertie strikes me as a very silly girl... How did London strike you?*
9 V-PASS If you **are struck** by something, you are very impressed by it. *He had been struck by what he saw... American officials are nevertheless struck by the cautious nature of the Soviet response.*
10 V Oor V When a clock **strikes**, its bells make a sound to indicate what the time is. *The church clock struck eleven... The college clock strikes twelve times at noon.*
11 V O If you **strike** a deal or a bargain with someone, you come to an agreement with them. *He was released by the kidnappers amid rumours that they had struck a deal with the Bonn government... The council hoped to strike a deal that would give it more power.*
12 V O If you **strike** a match, you make it produce a flame. *He struck a match and put it to his pipe.*
13 V O If someone **strikes** oil or gold, they discover it in the ground as a result of mining or drilling. *Oil industry sources say that Marathon Oil Company has struck oil in Syria.*
14 See also **striking**. See also **hunger strike**. See also **rent strike**.
● **Strike** is used in these phrases. ● Workers who are **on strike** are refusing to work. *I would never go on strike for more money.* ● To **strike a balance** means to do something that is halfway between two extremes. *He was able to strike a balance between competing loyalties... The right balance has been struck between individual rights and the interests of the state.* ● If something **strikes fear** or **strikes terror** into people, it causes them to be suddenly very frightened. *The tanks struck terror into the hearts of the peasants.*
● If you **are struck dumb** or **are struck blind**, you suddenly become unable to speak or see. *I was struck dumb with amazement... Members of the committee were said to have been struck dumb by the news.* ● to **strike a note**: see note.

strike back PHRASAL VERB If you **strike back**, you attempt to harm someone who has hurt you. *The farmers, who had been under siege for months, now struck back.*

strike down PHRASAL VERB To **strike** someone **down** means to kill or severely harm them. *Kennedy was struck down by an assassin's bullet.*

strike off PHRASAL VERB 1 If a doctor or lawyer is **struck off**, their name is removed from the official register and they are not allowed to practise their profession, usually because they have done something wrong. *This could result in the two surgeons being struck off.* 2 If something or someone is **struck off** a list, they are removed from that list, usually because they are no longer considered appropriate to a particular purpose. *The issue was struck off the agenda... He's been struck off the list of MPs.*

strike out PHRASAL VERB 1 If you **strike out** somewhere, you set out in a particular direction. *He struck out for the village of Tracy.* 2 To **strike out** also means to begin to do something different on your own. *He decided to strike out on his own.*

strike up PHRASAL VERB 1 When you **strike up** a conversation or friendship with someone, you begin it. *Alice and I struck up a friendship immediately... Over*

the years he has struck up a relationship of respect and liking with Mr Wu. 2 When musicians **strike up**, they begin to play. *A military band struck up... The band had just struck up Ellington's 'Satin Doll'.*

strikebound /straɪkbaʊnd/
ADJ If a place is **strikebound**, people are unable to work or move around freely there because other people are on strike. *...the strikebound Lenin shipyard... They are likely to be strikebound for some time.*

strike-breaker, strike-breakers
N C A **strike-breaker** is a person who continues to work during a strike, or someone who replaces a worker who is on strike. *...mobile squads of strike-breakers.*

strike-breaking
N U **Strike-breaking** is the activity of working at a place when other people are on strike, or of replacing workers who are on strike. *Job seekers should know that strike-breaking is not a smart career move. ...strike-breaking replacement crews on board the company's ferries.*

strike pay
N U **Strike pay** is money which is paid by a trade union to workers who are on strike. *The unions have been paying out more than half a million pounds a week in strike pay.*

striker /straɪkə/ **strikers**
1 N C **Strikers** are people who are on strike. *The strikers didn't seek negotiations with the management. ...a clash between strikers and police.*
2 N C In football, a **striker** is a player whose main function is to attack and score goals, rather than defend. *...the Brazilian striker scoring in the last minute.*

striking /straɪkɪŋ/
1 ADJ Something that is **striking** is very noticeable or unusual. *The most striking thing about Piccadilly Circus is the statue of Eros in the centre.* ◆ **strikingly** SUBMOD *The two women appeared strikingly different.*
2 ADJ A **striking** person is very attractive. *...a striking redhead.* ◆ **strikingly** SUBMOD *...a strikingly beautiful child.*
● **Striking** is used in these phrases. ● If you are **within striking distance** of something, you are very near it and are able to reach it easily. *The rebels claim to be within striking distance of the bunker. ...a location within striking distance of Israel.* ● You can also use **within striking distance** to say that someone is very close to achieving something. *Five teams are within striking distance of first place... President Bush is within striking distance of a superpower strategic arms treaty with the Soviet Union.*

string /strɪŋ/ **strings, stringing, strung**
1 N Uor N C **String** is thin rope made of twisted threads. *...a ball of string. ...a bunch of balloons on a string.*
2 N C A **string** of things is a number of them on the same piece of thread or wire. *...a string of beads round her neck.*
3 N C You can refer to a row or series of similar things as a **string**. *...a string of islands. ...the latest in a string of hotel disasters.*
4 N C The **strings** on a musical instrument are the tightly-stretched lengths of wire or nylon which vibrate to produce notes. *The instrument has six strings. ...violin strings.*
5 N PL The section of an orchestra which consists of stringed instruments is called the **strings**. *We'll hear the singer accompanied by strings.*
6 V Oor A If you **string** something somewhere, you hang or tie a long line of it high up in the air, especially between two or more objects. *Barbed wire was strung around the building. ...a taut cable strung across the quarry.*
● **String** is used in these phrases. ● If someone **pulls the strings** in a situation, they use their authority or power in order influence events, although they do not openly admit it. *He prefers to pull the strings behind the scenes... He is happier pulling the strings of government than leading it.* ● If something is offered to you with **strings attached**, it is offered to you with special conditions. *They said that the deal did not have any strings attached to it... The government's*

decision has strings attached. ● See also: **purse strings.**

string out PHRASAL VERB If things **are strung out** somewhere, they are spread out in a long line. *...small towns strung out along the dirt roads.*

string together PHRASAL VERB If you **string** things **together**, you make them into one thing by adding them to each other, one at a time. *I strung together some rhymes to amuse her.*

string up PHRASAL VERB 1 To **string** someone **up** means to kill them by hanging them; an informal expression. *...a little corpse, strung up as a warning.* 2 If you **string** something **up** somewhere, you hang or tie a long line of it high up in the air, especially between two or more objects. *During the course of the day, people were stringing up decorations on the fronts of their homes.*

string bean, string beans
NC A **string bean** is the same as a **runner bean**. *...a heaped bowl of buttered string beans.*

stringed instrument, stringed instruments.
NC A **stringed instrument** is a musical instrument which has strings, such as a violin or a guitar. *The Kanun is a stringed instrument that's found throughout the Muslim world.*

stringency /strɪndʒənsi/
1 NU **Stringency** is severity in the application of rules and laws. *Obviously medical applications require an additional degree of stringency from those appropriate for an industrial application.*
2 NU **Stringency** is also shortage of money, either for spending or investing; a technical use in economics. *...a time of domestic stringency in the Soviet Union. ...the United States' present financial stringency.*

stringent /strɪndʒənt/
1 ADJ **Stringent** laws, rules, or conditions are severe or are strictly controlled; a formal use. *The Community has adopted more stringent standards on pollution... These requirements are often very stringent.* ♦ **stringently** ADV *Other countries apply the rules less stringently. ...a less stringently regulated category.*
2 ADJ **Stringent** can also be used to describe financial conditions in which there is a shortage of money for credit or loans; a technical use in economics. *These countries are mostly applying stringent economic reforms agreed with the World Bank.*

stringer /strɪŋə/ **stringers**
NC A **stringer** is a journalist who is employed part-time by a newspaper or a news service in order to report on a particular area; a technical term. *In November last year, the BBC Dhākā stringer was arrested. ...our former stringer in Harare.*

string quartet, string quartets
1 NC A **string quartet** is a group of four musicians that play stringed instruments together. The instruments are two violins, a viola and a cello. *One song is sung against the backdrop of a string quartet.*
2 NC A **string quartet** is also a musical composition for two violins, a viola and a cello. *I wrote four or five string quartets. ...an extract from one of his string quartets.*

stringy /strɪŋi/
ADJ **Stringy** food is tough and difficult to chew. *...stringy pieces of vegetables.*

strip /strɪp/ **strips, stripping, stripped**
1 NC A **strip** of something is a long, narrow piece of it. *...a thin strip of paper... There was only a narrow strip of beach.*
2 V or VA If you **strip**, or if you **strip** naked, you take off your clothes. *Women residents stripped naked in protest.*
3 VO If someone **strips** you, they remove your clothes. *They were partially stripped and dragged to the edge of a nearby park... Before the ship sailed they were stripped and searched.*
4 VO To **strip** something means to remove everything that covers it. *The wind stripped the tree of all its leaves... The paint could easily be stripped off.*
5 VOA To **strip** someone of something means to take it away from that person. *She was stripped of all her property and possessions... The plan would effectively*

strip power from the company's director... He was stripped of his gold medal after failing a drugs test.
6 NC or N+N A comic **strip** or **strip** cartoon is a series of drawings which tell a story, often with the words spoken by the characters written on them. *I begin with the comic strips and then I turn to the editorial pages... Despite the paper's emphasis on news and serious subjects, there will be room for strip cartoons and pop features.*
7 If you **tear a strip off** someone or if you **tear** them **off a strip**, you scold them severely; an informal expression.

strip away PHRASAL VERB 1 If you **strip away** something that is attached to a surface, you remove it completely. *There were numerous places on the road where the tarmac had been stripped away.* 2 To **strip away** people's rights, beliefs, or attitudes means to take them away. *I've now stripped away the sentimentality of the conventional Christian faith... Liberal thinkers stripped away the mechanical picture of the individual.*

strip down PHRASAL VERB If you **strip down** a piece of equipment such as an engine, you take it to pieces, in order to clean or repair it. *The aircraft's engines are being stripped down at the headquarters near Paris.*

strip off PHRASAL VERB To **strip off** clothing means to remove it. *Casson stripped off his raincoat... As soon as we got there, we stripped off too, and went swimming.*

strip club, strip clubs
NC A **strip club** is a club which people go to in order to see striptease. *I got thrown out of a strip club.*

stripe /straɪp/ **stripes**
1 NC **Stripes** are long, thin lines, usually of different colours. *...a shirt with blue and white stripes.*
2 NC **Stripes** are also narrow bands of material sewn onto a uniform to indicate someone's rank. *...a red uniform with sergeant's stripes.*

striped /straɪpt/
ADJ If something is **striped**, it has stripes on it. *...striped trousers.*

strip lighting
NU **Strip lighting** is a method of lighting which uses long tubes rather than light bulbs.

stripling /strɪplɪŋ/ **striplings**
NC A **stripling** is a young man who is no longer a boy but is not yet really a man; often used humorously. *He was a stripling, a boy of nineteen.*

stripper /strɪpə/ **strippers**
NC A **stripper** is a person who earns money by doing striptease; an informal word. *He conceded that the strippers at the Kitty Kat Lounge may not be great artists.*

striptease /strɪptiːz/
NU **Striptease** is a form of entertainment in which someone takes off their clothes slowly and in a sexy way to music. *He lost his position after a scandal involving a striptease artist. ...striptease dancing.*

stripy /straɪpi/ **stripier, stripiest**
ADJ Something that is **stripy** is made up of a lot of stripes. *...a very French shirt all stripy like a sailor's.*

strive /straɪv/ **strives, striving, strove, striven, strived.** The past tense can be either **strove** or **strived, and the past participle can be either striven** or **strived.**
V+for or V+to-INF If you **strive** for something or **strive** to do something, you make a great effort to get or do it. *They have striven for freedom for many years... He was confident that the things which he has strived for will happen... They strove to give the impression that they were leaving.*

strobe /strəʊb/
NU **Strobe** or **strobe lighting** is very bright lighting which flashes on and off very quickly. *The police helicopter circled above flashing strobe lights.*

strode /strəʊd/
Strode is the past tense of **stride**.

stroke /strəʊk/ **strokes, stroking, stroked**
1 VO If you **stroke** someone or something, you move your hand slowly and gently over them. *She put out a hand and stroked the cat... He stroked her hair affectionately.*

2 NC If someone has a **stroke**, they have a sudden and severe illness which affects their brain, and which can often kill them or cause one side of their body to be paralysed. *She had a stroke and was unable to walk again.*
3 NC The **strokes** of a pen or brush are the movements or marks you make with it when you are writing or painting. *She began to paint with bold, defiant strokes.*
4 NC When you are swimming or rowing, your **strokes** are the repeated movements you make with your arms or the oars. *She swam with steady strokes.*
5 NC A swimming **stroke** is a particular style or method of swimming. *This has been found to be the fastest stroke. ...the first to cross the channel using the butterfly stroke.*
6 NC In sports such as tennis, cricket and golf, a **stroke** is the action of hitting the ball. *A final round of 71 gave him a total of 282, three strokes ahead of Ian Baker-Finch. ...demonstrating strokes in tennis. ...every stroke of the table tennis bat.*
7 NC The **strokes** of a clock are the sounds that indicate each hour. *At the twelfth stroke, we welcomed in the New Year.*
8 N SING+*of* A **stroke** of luck is something lucky that suddenly happens. A **stroke** of genius is a sudden idea or inspiration. *Then it came, my stroke of great good fortune... Her idea was a stroke of genius.*
● **Stroke** is used in these phrases. ● If something happens **at a stroke** or **in one stroke**, it happens suddenly and completely because of one single action. *He was determined at a stroke to remove those distinctions.* ● Someone who **does not do a stroke** of work is very lazy; an informal expression. *He took up no profession and never did a stroke of work.*
stroll /strəʊl/ **strolls, strolling, strolled**
V A If you **stroll** somewhere, you walk in a slow, relaxed way. *They strolled along the beach.* ▶ Also NC *She decided to take a stroll in the garden.*
stroller /ˈstrəʊlə/ **strollers**
NC A **stroller** is a baby's pushchair; used in American English. *...a young couple with a baby in a stroller.*
strong /strɒŋ/ **stronger, strongest**
1 ADJ A **strong** person has powerful muscles. *His strong arms were around me, pinning me down.*
2 ADJ **Strong** also means very confident and not easily influenced or worried by other people. *I felt very strong in the knowledge of my own innocence. ...a strong personality.*
3 ADJ **Strong** objects are not easily damaged or broken. *...steel cylinders strong enough to survive even a nuclear catastrophe.*
4 ADJ **Strong** also means great in degree or intensity. *The strong possibility is that he will be told tomorrow... Mrs Thatcher has launched a strong attack on the European Community... They still spoke with a strong German accent. ...the strong wind.*
♦ **strongly** ADV *His mother will strongly influence his choice of a wife... I feel very strongly about drugs... The Irish Prime Minister also strongly condemned the killings.* ● See also **strongly-**.
5 ADJ **Strong** action is firm and severe. *They introduced a strong anti-inflation programme... They have taken strong measures to combat pollution.*
6 ADJ **Strong** arguments for something are supported by a lot of evidence. *There is a strong case for an Act of Parliament.*
7 ADJ A **strong** group is large or powerful. *It was essential to build a strong organization.*
8 ADJ after N You use **strong** to say how many people there are in a group. For example, a group that is twenty **strong** has twenty people in it. *By this time, the demonstrators were thirty or forty strong.*
9 ADJ ATTRIB Your **strong** points are the things you are good at or which are likely to make you successful. *Maths was always his strong subject... In fact, exports may be the economy's only strong point over the next six months.*
10 ADJ ATTRIB A **strong** competitor or candidate is likely to do well. *He is not the strongest candidate the party could put up.*
11 ADJ A **strong** relationship is close and likely to last. *...a much stronger relationship than existed 15*

years ago... Links with the trade unions were strong.
12 ADJ **Strong** industries, economies, or currencies are financially successful. *The report quotes a Cabinet Minister as saying that more people are going to benefit every month from a stronger economy.*
13 ADJ **Strong** drinks, chemicals, or drugs are very effective or contain a lot of a particular substance in proportion to the amount of water or other substances in them. *She made him a cup of tea so strong that he could not drink it. ...a strong household bleach.*
14 If someone or something is still **going strong**, they are still living or working well after a long time. *He's still going strong at the age of 82... The fire is still going strong.*
strong-arm
ADJ ATTRIB **Strong-arm** people or tactics rely on threats or force in order to persuade other people to behave in a particular way. *He brought along two strong-arm men from his private guard... They began by offering protection against the gang's strong-arm tactics.*
stronghold /ˈstrɒŋhəʊld/ **strongholds**
1 NC A **stronghold** is a place that is held and defended by an army or military organization. *The government had claimed major successes against the rebels in the mountain stronghold north-west of the city. ...a Lebanese Force's stronghold.*
2 NC+SUPP If a place is a **stronghold** of an attitude or belief, many people there have this attitude or belief. *It is a solid Labour stronghold. ...the old Communist stronghold of Albania.*
strongly- /ˈstrɒŋli-/
PREFIX **Strongly-** is used with past participles to form adjectives that describe the intensity of something. *The President issued a strongly-worded statement attacking apartheid in South Africa. ...strongly-held views. ...a strongly-rooted tradition.*
strong-minded
ADJ Someone who is **strong-minded** has their own attitudes and opinions and is not easily influenced by other people. *...a strong-minded local girl named Katharine.*
strong-willed
ADJ Someone who is **strong-willed** always tries to do what they want, even though other people may advise them to do something different. *Under this soft appearance there is a strong-willed man.*
stroppy /ˈstrɒpi/
ADJ Someone who is **stroppy** is bad-tempered and obstinate; an informal word. *She threatened to get stroppy.*
strove /strəʊv/
Strove is the past tense of **strive**.
struck /strʌk/
Struck is the past tense and past participle of **strike**. *The islands were struck by Hurricane Hugo.*
structural /ˈstrʌktʃərəl/
ADJ **Structural** is used to describe an aspect of the structure of something. *...structural faults in the walls... Gales with a potential to cause structural damage are heading for Britain.* ♦ **structurally** ADV *The government says that nearly one-fourth of the bridges in the United States are structurally deficient... Molecules can come together structurally in very curious ways.*
structuralism /ˈstrʌktʃərəlɪzəm/
N U **Structuralism** is the theory or method of analysing subjects such as literature, language, or society in a way that considers each aspect in terms of its relationship to underlying patterns or principles of organization. These underlying patterns or principles form an important basic structure for the subject. *Colin McCabe, who's a leading authority on structuralism, begins by talking about its uses in linguistics.*
structuralist /ˈstrʌktʃərəlɪst/ **structuralists**
1 NC A **structuralist** is someone whose work is based on structuralism. *Structuralists, by trying to discover the systems common to all cultures, reject the whole idea of superiority.*
2 ADJ ATTRIB **Structuralist** is used to refer to people and things that are connected with structuralism.

...Lévi-Strauss, the great French structuralist anthropologist... New theories about language and writing have supplanted the structuralist movement of the 1950s.

structure /strʌktʃə/ **structures, structuring, structured**
1 N U or N C The **structure** of something is the way in which it is made, built, or organized. *She analysed the structure of its skull in great detail... The whole structure of the film was rather simplistic... The class structures of England and America are quite different.*
2 N C or N U A **structure** is something that has been formed or arranged in a particular way; used especially in discussing chemistry, physics, or geometry. *I look at isolated carbohydrates and try to determine their 3-dimensional structures... The atomic structure of a crystal surface is fundamental in the design of complex silicon chips.*
3 N C A **structure** is also something that has been built or constructed. *We visited the Children's Palace, a great sprawling structure.*
4 N U A system or activity that has **structure** is well organized and efficient. *She loved the sense of structure, organization and enthusiasm.*
5 V O If you **structure** something, you arrange it in an organized pattern or system. *They structure their communication to meet the needs of the client.*

struggle /strʌgl/ **struggles, struggling, struggled**
1 V If you **struggle** to do something, you try hard to do it, even though other people or things may be making it difficult for you to succeed. *They struggle to build a more democratic society. ...a nationalist movement that has had to struggle for independence.* ▶ Also N C *...the day-to-day struggle for survival.*
2 V If you **struggle** when you are being held, you try hard to get free. *She struggled in his embrace.*
3 V-RECIP If two people **struggle**, they fight each other. *We struggled for the gun... I had to struggle with men I could not even see.* ▶ Also N C *There was a moment's struggle and the gun fell to the ground.*
4 N C or N U A **struggle** is also an attempt to obtain something or to defeat someone who is denying you something such as your freedom. *...the struggles of a modern woman in a repressive society. ...a shared struggle against racial oppression.*
5 V If a person or organization is **struggling**, they are likely to fail in what they are doing, even though they might be trying very hard. *There are signs that a number of government figures may be struggling to hang on to their seats in Parliament... Even his own brother's business was struggling.* ◆ **struggling** ADJ ATTRIB *The struggling English first division club Sheffield Wednesday have sacked their manager.*
6 V+to-INF or V A If you **struggle** to move yourself, you manage to do it with great difficulty. *He struggled to his feet... He struggled forward for about half a mile.*
7 N SING An activity that is a **struggle** is difficult and takes a lot of effort. *Reading was a struggle for him.*
struggle on PHRASAL VERB If you **struggle on**, you manage to continue doing something but with great difficulty. *Some struggled on, but those who couldn't were left behind.*

strum /strʌm/ **strums, strumming, strummed**
V O or V If you **strum** a guitar, you play it by moving your thumb or fingers or a small piece of plastic up and down across the strings. *It can be plucked or strummed... The guitar player started strumming softly.*

strung /strʌŋ/
Strung is the past tense and past participle of **string**.

strut /strʌt/ **struts, strutting, strutted**
1 V Someone who **struts** walks in a proud way, with their head high and their chest out. *Eddie turned around and strutted back to them. ...a peacock strutting on the lawn.*
2 N C A **strut** is a piece of wood or metal which strengthens or supports a building or structure. *Steel struts lie in wraps across a building site... Teams of men scamper across the seven-storey frame, glueing glass sheets over the struts.*
3 N C On an aeroplane, a **strut** is part of the framework; used especially to refer to the wing or

engine supports. *I want to find out about a main strut on the wing. ...engine struts and landing gear.*

strychnine /strɪkniːn/
N U **Strychnine** is a very poisonous drug which is sometimes used in very small amounts as a medicine. *Gaolers administered a poison to them that is believed to have been strychnine.*

stub /stʌb/ **stubs, stubbing, stubbed**
1 N C+SUPP The **stub** of a cigarette or a pencil is the short piece which remains when the rest has been used. *...an ashtray full of old cigarette stubs.*
2 N C The **stub** of a cheque is the part that you keep as a record of what you have paid for something. *I would make the cheque out for $15,000, but on the cheque stub I would show $20,000 dollars being paid to a given factory.*
3 N C The **stub** of a ticket for a theatre or cinema performance is the part which you keep when you have gone in to watch the performance. *The ticket stubs of the Remains Theatre say 'No refunds, no exchanges'.*
4 V O If you **stub** your toe, you hurt it by accidentally kicking something. *I stubbed my toe against a stone.*
stub out PHRASAL VERB When someone **stubs out** a cigarette, they put it out by pressing it against something hard.

stubble /stʌbl/
1 N U **Stubble** is the short stalks which remain after corn or wheat has been harvested. *The stubble was burning on the harvested fields.*
2 N U **Stubble** is also the very short hairs on a man's face when he has not shaved recently. *He had not shaved for two days, and a light stubble covered his chin.*

stubborn /stʌbən/
1 ADJ A **stubborn** person is determined to do what they want and refuses to change their mind. *Our son is stubborn and rebellious. ...his stubborn determination.* ◆ **stubbornly** ADV *'It was an accident,' he said stubbornly, 'and that's that.'* ◆ **stubbornness** N U *The area of most concern at this point is the mayor's stubbornness.*
2 ADJ A **stubborn** stain is difficult to remove. *Remove stubborn marks on tiles with a wire brush.*

stubby /stʌbi/
ADJ A **stubby** object is short and thick. *His stubby fingers were strong and mobile.*

stucco /stʌkəʊ/
N U **Stucco** is a type of plaster used for covering walls, decorating ceilings, and making ornaments. *The house was red brick without a covering of stucco. ...a grey stucco house.*

stuck /stʌk/
1 **Stuck** is the past tense and past participle of **stick**.
2 ADJ PRED If something is **stuck** in a particular position, it is fixed there and cannot move. *The lift seems to be stuck between the second and third floors.*
3 ADJ PRED If you are **stuck** when you are trying to do something, you cannot continue because it is too difficult. *Ask for help the minute you're stuck.*
4 ADJ PRED If you are **stuck** in a place or unpleasant situation, you cannot get away from it. *The boss rang to explain that he was stuck in Milan.*
5 ADJ PRED If you are **stuck** with something you do not want, you cannot get rid of it. *Blaise Campaore still finds himself stuck with the reputation of being the man who killed a legend... They've failed to solve this problem and they're stuck with it.*

stuck-up
ADJ Someone who is **stuck-up** has too high an opinion of their own importance and is very proud and unfriendly; an informal word. *He had never been a stuck-up celebrity.*

stud /stʌd/ **studs**
1 N C A **stud** is a small piece of metal attached to a surface. *...black leather with gold studs.*
2 N U Male horses or other animals that are kept for **stud** are kept for breeding. *I'm not going to race him, I'm going to put him to stud.*

studded /stʌdɪd/
ADJ Something that is **studded** is decorated with studs or things that look like studs. *...enamel bracelets*

studded with precious stones.

student /stjuːdnt/ students
1 NC A **student** is a person who is studying at a university or college. *...a part-time student at King's College, London.* ● See also **mature student**.
2 NC The **students** of a school are the children who go to it; used in American English. *Rufus King High School is sending a majority of its students to college now.*
3 NC+*of* A **student** of a particular subject is trying to learn about it. *It is our treatment of old people which most shocks students of our culture.*

studied /stʌdid/
1 ADJ ATTRIB A **studied** action has been carefully planned and is not spontaneous or natural. *With studied casualness he mentioned his departure to Hilary.*
2 See also **study**.

studio /stjuːdiəʊ/ studios
1 NC A **studio** is a room where a painter or photographer works. *At 13, I had set up my studio in the basement of the house, and I was an artist.*
2 NC A **studio** is also a room or building where radio or television programmes, films, or records are made. *There is usually no time to edit the programme in the studio... She soon won a contract with a Hollywood studio... The hits were largely the work of studio producer Trevor Horn.*
3 NC A **studio**, **studio apartment**, or **studio flat** is a small flat, usually with one room for living and sleeping in and a small kitchen and bathroom.

studio audience, studio audiences
N COLL A **studio audience** is a group of people who are in a television or radio studio and who are watching while a programme is being made. Their clapping and laughter and the things they say are recorded as part of the programme. *...the weekly programme Question Time, in which four public figures answer questions from a studio audience.*

studious /stjuːdiəs/
ADJ A **studious** person spends a lot of time reading and studying. *He comes across as a very serious, very studious, very conscientious man.*

studiously /stjuːdiəsli/
ADV If you do something **studiously**, you do it carefully and deliberately. *The Colonel studiously examined his folders... He studiously avoided the subject of internal Irish politics... The part played by Moscow in these events has been studiously ignored.*

study /stʌdi/ studies, studying, studied
1 V0or V If you **study** a subject, you spend time learning about it. *He studied chemistry at university... They are both studying for A levels... He studied at various universities before gaining a doctorate in 1964.*
2 NU **Study** is the activity of studying a subject. *There are no rooms specifically set aside for quiet study.*
3 N PL **Studies** are educational subjects or courses. *...the School of European Studies... Indian studies became part of the school curriculum.*
4 V0 If you study something, you look at it or watch it carefully. *I studied a map... He looked at her hard, studying her face.*
5 V0 To **study** something also means to consider it or observe it carefully in order to be able to understand it fully. *The various proposals need to be studied in depth... Although the illness has been studied for centuries, no clear single cause has emerged.*
6 NC A **study** of a subject is a piece of research on it. *She has made a close study of drinking habits... He has received a grant to pursue his studies into the way child stammerers respond to treatment.*
7 NC A **study** by an artist is a drawing done in preparation for a larger picture.
8 NC A **study** in a house is a room used for reading, writing, and studying. *...a scholar skimming through his books in his study.*

stuff /stʌf/ stuffs, stuffing, stuffed
1 NU **Stuff** is used to refer to things such as a substance, a collection of things, or the contents of something in a general way without mentioning the

thing itself by name. *What's that stuff in the bucket?... Quite a lot of stuff had been stolen... She was reading the travel stuff in the colour supplement.*
2 V0A If you **stuff** something somewhere, you push it there quickly and roughly. *Willie gathered up the bills and stuffed them carelessly into his pocket.*
3 V0 If a place or container **is stuffed** with things, it is full of them. *The cupboard was stuffed with old fishing tackle.* ◆ **stuffed** ADJ *He'd got a big rucksack, stuffed with notes, on his back.*
4 V-REFLor V0 If you **stuff** yourself, you eat a lot of food; an informal use. *Karin was stuffing herself with eggs and toast... I was stuffing my face with ice-cream.*
5 V0 If you **stuff** a bird or a vegetable, you put a mixture of food inside it before cooking it.
6 V0 If a dead animal **is stuffed**, it is filled with material so that it can be preserved and displayed. *The letter offers to have our beloved dog stuffed and exhibited in a museum.* ◆ **stuffed** ADJ *...a stuffed parrot.*
7 N SING+SUPP If one thing is the **stuff** of another, the first thing is a very important feature or characteristic of the second thing; a formal use. *Boycotts and marches were the stuff of the civil rights movement.*
8 If you say that someone **knows** their **stuff**, you mean that they are good at doing something because they are experienced and know a lot about it. *They've got a very professional agricultural department—the people that took me around certainly knew their stuff.*

stuffed shirt, stuffed shirts
NC If you describe someone as a **stuffed shirt**, you mean that they are extremely formal, old-fashioned, and pompous; an informal expression. *...all those stuffed shirts at the Ministry.*

stuffed-up
ADJ If you are **stuffed-up**, you have the passages of your nose blocked with mucus so that you cannot breathe properly through it. *I'm all stuffed-up today.*

stuffing /stʌfɪŋ/
1 NU **Stuffing** is a mixture of food that is put inside a bird or a vegetable before it is cooked. *We had chicken with stuffing and new potatoes.*
2 NU **Stuffing** is also material that is put inside pillows, cushions, or toys, to fill them and make them firm. *The plant produces propane oxide, which is used in the manufacture of stuffing for furniture.*

stuffy /stʌfi/
1 ADJ **Stuffy** people or institutions are formal and old-fashioned; an informal use. *...stern-faced workers carrying stuffy party slogans.*
2 ADJ If a place is **stuffy**, it is unpleasantly warm and there is not enough fresh air. *They find the museum hot, stuffy and generally unpleasant.*

stultify /stʌltɪfaɪ/ stultifies, stultifying, stultified
V0 If something **stultifies** you, it is so boring that it dulls your mind or destroys your interest; a formal word. *The regular use of calculators can stultify a child's capacity to do mental arithmetic.* ◆ **stultifying** ADJ *...the stultifying rituals of court procedure.*

stumble /stʌmbl/ stumbles, stumbling, stumbled
1 V If you **stumble**, you nearly fall while walking or running. *The man was drunk and he stumbled on the bottom step.*
2 V If you **stumble** while speaking, you make a mistake, and have to pause and say it again. *She stumbled over the foreign words.*
stumble across PHRASAL VERB If you **stumble across** something or **stumble on** it, you discover it unexpectedly. *In the course of their search they may stumble across something quite different... Sir Alexander Fleming stumbled on his great discovery of penicillin by accident.*

stumbling block, stumbling blocks
NC A **stumbling block** is a problem which stops you from achieving something. *Perhaps the biggest stumbling block to disarmament is the deterrent theory.*

stump /stʌmp/ stumps, stumping, stumped
1 NC A **stump** is a small part of something that remains when the rest of it has been broken off or removed. *Its tail is reduced to a tiny stump... We left*

him sitting on the stump of an old oak tree.
2 NC In cricket, the **stumps** are the three upright wooden sticks that form the wicket. *Basit dragged a delivery by McDermott onto his stumps with the score on 75.*
3 VO If a question or problem **stumps** you, you cannot think of a solution to it. *...the question that has stumped philosophers since the beginning of time.*
4 VA If you **stump** somewhere, you walk there angrily with heavy steps. *She stumped back into the house.*
5 If politicians are **on the stump**, they are campaigning for an election; used in American English. *They're out on the stump talking to people... But it turned out that he is, as he has always been, terrific on the stump.*
6 V If politicians **stump** for a candidate during an election campaign, they travel around making speeches in support of him or her as part of the campaign; used in American English. *The President was out stumping today for fellow Republicans.*
stump up PHRASAL VERB If you **stump up** a sum of money, you pay the money that is required for something, often reluctantly; an informal expression. *The government is being asked to stump up the balance.*

stumpy /stʌmpi/
ADJ **Stumpy** things are short and thick. *...a short stumpy tail.*

stun /stʌn/ **stuns, stunning, stunned**
1 VO If you **are stunned**, you are very shocked by something. *We were all stunned by the news.* ◆ **stunned** ADJ *I sat in stunned silence.*
2 VO If a blow on the head **stuns** you, it makes you unconscious or confused and unsteady. *He was stunned by a blow from the rifle.*
3 ADJ ATTRIB A **stun** gun or bomb is designed to stop someone by knocking them out rather than seriously injuring or killing them. *Stun guns have been tested by police forces in the United States to help in the arrest of violent suspects. ...stun bombs which could immobilize the terrorists.*
4 See also **stunning**.

stung /stʌŋ/
Stung is the past tense and past participle of **sting**.

stunk /stʌŋk/
Stunk is the past participle of **stink**.

stunner /stʌnə/ **stunners**
NC A **stunner** is an extremely attractive woman; an informal word. *Your sister is such a stunner.*

stunning /stʌnɪŋ/
1 ADJ Something that is **stunning** is very beautiful, attractive, or impressive. *The film is visually stunning... Her dress was simply stunning.*
2 ADJ Something that is **stunning** is also so unusual or unexpected that people are astonished by it. *...a stunning victory in the general election.*

stunt /stʌnt/ **stunts, stunting, stunted**
1 NC A **stunt** is something that someone does to get publicity. *Climbing up the church tower was a fine publicity stunt.*
2 NC A **stunt** is also a dangerous and exciting action that someone does in a film. *Steve McQueen did most of his own stunts.*
3 VO To **stunt** the growth or development of something means to prevent it from growing or developing as it should. *These insecticides can stunt plant growth.*

stunted /stʌntɪd/
ADJ Something that is **stunted** has been prevented from growing to its full height. *...old, stunted thorn trees.*

stunt man, stunt men
NC A **stunt man** is a man whose job is to do dangerous things in films instead of the actors so that they will not get hurt. *He first appeared on screen as an extra and was a stunt man in the silent era.*

stupefied /stjuːpɪfaɪd/
1 ADJ If you are **stupefied**, you feel so tired or bored that you are unable to think clearly. *I felt stupefied by the heavy meal.*
2 ADJ If you are **stupefied**, you are extremely surprised by something. *He was too stupefied to answer her.*

stupendous /stjuːpɛndəs/
ADJ Something that is **stupendous** is extremely large or impressive. *The roar of the explosion was stupendous... Hamish and I would cook stupendous suppers together.*

stupid /stjuːpɪd/ **stupider, stupidest**
1 ADJ A **stupid** person shows a lack of good judgement or intelligence and is not at all sensible. *I have been extremely stupid. ...a stupid question.* ◆ **stupidly** ADV *I once stupidly asked him why he smiled so often.*
2 ADJ You say that something is **stupid** to indicate that you do not like it or that it annoys you; an informal use. *I hate these stupid black shoes.*

stupidity /stjuːpɪdəti/ **stupidities**
1 NCorNU **Stupidity** is behaviour that is not at all sensible. *I used to find her occasional stupidities amusing... He is paying a big price for his stupidity.*
2 NU **Stupidity** is the quality of being stupid. *...the stupidity of their error.*

stupor /stjuːpə/ **stupors**
NC Someone who is in a **stupor** is almost unconscious, especially as a result of taking drugs, or drinking too much, or because of an illness. *He collapsed in a drunken stupor.*

sturdy /stɜːdi/ **sturdier, sturdiest**
ADJ Someone or something that is **sturdy** is strong and unlikely to be hurt or easily damaged. *...sturdy oak tables... A disaster had been averted by the sturdy nature of the building... The Soviet President is made of sturdy stuff.* ◆ **sturdily** ADV *...a sturdily built little boy.*

stutter /stʌtə/ **stutters, stuttering, stuttered**
1 VorV-QUOTE If you **stutter**, you have difficulty speaking, because you keep repeating certain sounds. *The man stuttered terribly when he spoke... 'I...I want to do it,' she stuttered.*
2 NC Someone who has a **stutter** tends to stutter when they speak. *He says it often takes someone with a stutter several minutes to send a phone message that could normally be sent in a few seconds.*

sty /staɪ/ **sties**
NC A **sty** is a pigsty. *Pigs were by no means confined to the filthy straw of their sty.*

stye /staɪ/ **styes**
NC A **stye** is an infection of the skin at the bottom of an eyelash, which makes the eyelid red and swollen. *Keep a child from rubbing the eyelid at the time a stye is coming to a head.*

style /staɪl/ **styles, styling, styled**
1 NC+SUPP The **style** of something is the general way in which it is done or presented, which often shows the attitudes of the people involved. *Some people find our leisurely style of decision-making rather frustrating. ...western styles of education.*
2 NC+SUPPorNU+SUPP Someone's **style** is all their general attitudes and usual ways of behaving. *...the Prime Minister's style of leadership... It's not his style to go out and canvas... In characteristic style, the President has since insinuated that they were involved in an anti-government plot.*
3 NU Someone or something that has **style** is smart and elegant. *Both were rather short and plump, but they had style... Here you can eat in style.*
4 NUorNC The **style** of a product is its design. *These pants come in several styles... The clothes I wore weren't different in style or appearance from those of the other children.*
5 NU Someone's **style** of writing is their choice of words and the way in which they structure sentences and paragraphs. *Like his other books, it is written in a direct colloquial style.*
6 VO If you **style** clothing or someone's hair, you design the clothing or do their hair. *Her hair was styled in a short cropped pony tail.* ● **to cramp** someone's style: see **cramp**. ● See also **hairstyle**.

stylised /staɪlaɪzd/. See **stylized**.

stylish /staɪlɪʃ/
ADJ Someone or something that is **stylish** is smart, elegant, and fashionable. *...the stylish Swiss resort of Gstaad.*

stylist /staɪlɪst/ **stylists**
1 NC A **stylist** is a hairdresser. *It's a very small salon*

with only one stylist.
2 NC A **stylist** is also someone who pays a lot of attention to the way they write, say, or do something, so that it is attractive and elegant. *Henry James was a great stylist.*

stylistic /staɪˈlɪstɪk/
ADJ ATTRIB **Stylistic** describes things relating to the methods and techniques used in creating a piece of writing, music, or art. *Such work lacks any development of stylistic features.*

stylized /ˈstaɪlaɪzd/; also spelt **stylised**.
ADJ Something that is **stylized** uses various artistic or literary conventions in order to create an effect, instead of being natural, spontaneous, or true to life. *...a stylised picture of a Japanese garden... In the past, acting performances were usually highly stylized.*

stylus /ˈstaɪləs/ **styluses** or **styli**
NC A **stylus** is the small pointed instrument on a record player that picks up the sound signals on the records. *The stylus was placed on a rotating disc coated in soft wax, thus scratching the wax.*

stymie /ˈstaɪmi/ **stymies, stymieing, stymied**
VO If something **stymies** you, it makes it difficult or impossible for you to take action or to do what you want to do; an informal word. *President Zia did attempt to rejoin the Commonwealth but his bid for re-entry was stymied by opposition from India.*

Styrofoam /ˈstaɪrəfəʊm/
NU In American English, **Styrofoam** is the same as **polystyrene**; **Styrofoam** is a trademark. *...Styrofoam cups.*

suave /swɑːv/
ADJ Someone who is **suave** is charming and polite. *...a smooth, suave television host.*

sub /sʌb/ **subs**; an informal word.
1 NC A **sub** is a fixed amount of money that you pay regularly in order to belong to a club or society. *...union leaders who squandered their members' subs.*
2 NC A **sub** is also the same as a **submarine**. *One of the tasks for such subs would be to patrol Arctic waters.*

sub- /sʌb-, səb-/
1 PREFIX **Sub-** combines with nouns to form other nouns. Nouns formed in this way refer to things which are part of a larger thing. *...subsection 1(b) of the report. ...the sub-groups of society.*
2 PREFIX **Sub-** is also used to form words that refer to or describe things that are beneath or lower down than something else. For example, a 'subterranean' river flows underground. *...subterranean water sources... The submarine had surfaced after its training run.*
3 PREFIX **Sub-** is also used to form nouns and adjectives that refer to or describe people or things as inferior, smaller, or less powerful than someone or something else. For example, if a plane flies at a 'subsonic' speed, it does not travel as fast as the speed of sound. *Lockheed has put forward many designs for both subsonic and supersonic planes... Workers are kept in what are described as sub-human conditions in camps on the plantations.*

subaltern /ˈsʌbltən/ **subalterns**
NC A **subaltern** is any commissioned officer in the army below the rank of a captain.

subcommittee /ˈsʌbkəmɪti/ **subcommittees**
N COLL A **subcommittee** is a small committee made up of members from a larger committee. The task of a subcommittee is to consider a particular subject in detail and then report what they find to their main committee. *...the security and terrorism subcommittee of the Senate judiciary committee.*

subconscious /sʌbˈkɒnʃəs/
1 N SING Your **subconscious** is the part of your mind that can influence you even though you are not aware of it. *The knowledge was there somewhere in the depths of his subconscious.*
2 ADJ Something that is **subconscious** happens or exists in your subconscious. *...a subconscious desire to punish himself.* ◆ **subconsciously** ADV *...a fictional character with whom millions could subconsciously identify.*

subcontinent /sʌbˈkɒntɪnənt/ **subcontinents**
NC A **subcontinent** is part of a larger continent, made up of a number of countries that form one large mass of land. 'The subcontinent' is often used to refer to the area that contains India, Pakistan, and Bangladesh. *...immigrants from the Indian subcontinent.*

subcontract /sʌbkənˈtrækt/ **subcontracts, subcontracting, subcontracted**
VO If one firm **subcontracts** a part of its work to another firm, it pays the second firm to do that part. *They had subcontracted some of the work to an electrician.*

subcontractor /sʌbkənˈtræktə/ **subcontractors**
NC A **subcontractor** is a person or firm that has a contract to do part of a job which another firm is responsible for. *The Corporation was a publicly-owned company and a subcontractor for private industry.*

subculture /ˈsʌbkʌltʃə/ **subcultures**
NC A **subculture** is the ideas, art, and way of life of a particular group within a society. *...the posters and poetry of the hippie subculture.*

subdivide /sʌbdɪˈvaɪd/ **subdivides, subdividing, subdivided**
VO If something is **subdivided**, it is made into several smaller areas, parts, or sections. *Our office was subdivided into departments.*

subdivision /ˈsʌbdɪvɪʒn/ **subdivisions**
NC A **subdivision** is an area or section which is a part of a larger area or section. *Each of these problems has several subdivisions... Unless the new parties can operate as independent bodies, they could become little more than subdivisions of the Communist Party.*

subdue /səbˈdjuː/ **subdues, subduing, subdued**
1 VO If soldiers or the police **subdue** a group of people, they bring them under control using force. *Troops were sent to subdue the rebels... He was subdued by four policemen and dragged from the court.*
2 VO If something **subdues** your feelings, it makes them less strong. *This thought subdued my delight at the news.*

subdued /səbˈdjuːd/
1 ADJ Someone who is **subdued** is quiet, often because they are sad or worried about something. *The General appeared more subdued than in previous appearances... The assembly murmured in subdued agreement... Only some fifty thousand joined the march and the atmosphere appeared subdued compared with earlier protests.*
2 ADJ **Subdued** sounds are quiet and difficult to hear. *I heard a subdued, delicate wailing.*
3 ADJ **Subdued** lights or colours are not very bright. *...subdued lights and soft music.*

sub-editor, sub-editors
NC A **sub-editor** is a person whose job is to check and correct articles in newspapers or magazines before they are printed. *He followed his father, a BBC newsroom sub-editor, into journalism.*

subgroup /ˈsʌbɡruːp/ **subgroups**
NC A **subgroup** is a group that is part of another, larger group. *They are members of a small subgroup, an elite.*

subheading /ˈsʌbhedɪŋ/ **subheadings**
NC A **subheading** is a heading to a piece of writing, which is less important than the main heading, and which divides the writing into shorter sections. *You can make 'PROBLEMS' your third subheading.*

subhuman /sʌbˈhjuːmən/
ADJ If you describe someone as **subhuman**, you mean that their behaviour is disgusting. *They were seen as, quote, 'something subhuman and repulsive, the way some people feel about cockroaches'.*

subject, subjects, subjecting, subjected; pronounced /ˈsʌbdʒɪkt/ for the meanings in paragraphs 1 to 7, and /səbˈdʒekt/ for the meaning in paragraph 8.
1 NC The **subject** of a conversation, letter, or book is the thing that is being discussed or written about. *I don't have any strong views on the subject... However much you try to change the subject, the conversation invariably returns to politics.*
2 NC In grammar, the **subject** of a clause is the noun group which refers to the person or thing that does the

action expressed by the verb.

3 NC A **subject** is also a field of knowledge such as chemistry, history, or English that is studied in schools, colleges, and universities. *Maths was my best subject at school.*

4 NC The **subjects** of a country are the people who have the right to live there. *...British subjects.*

5 ADJ ATTRIB **Subject** people are controlled by a government or ruler. **Subject** countries are controlled by another country. *...freedom for the subject peoples of the world.*

6 ADJ PRED+to If you are **subject** to something, you are affected, or likely to be affected, by it. *Your profit will be subject to tax... He is highly strung and, therefore, subject to heart attacks.*

7 PREP If one thing will happen **subject to** another, it will happen only if the other thing happens. *The property will be sold subject to the following conditions.*

8 VO+to If you **subject** someone to something unpleasant, you make them experience it. *He was subjected to the harshest possible punishment.*

subjective /səbdʒektɪv/
ADJ Something that is **subjective** is influenced by personal opinions and feelings. *He knew his arguments were subjective, based on intuition.*

subject matter
NU The **subject matter** of a conversation, book, or film, is the thing, person, or idea that is being discussed, written about, or shown. *These artists were blasted for their lack of skill and their subject matter... The songs are all rooted in the subject matter of everyday life.*

sub judice /sʌb dʒuːdɪsɪ/
ADJ PRED When something is **sub judice**, people are not allowed to comment about it in newspapers, on television, or on the radio, because it is the subject of a trial in a court of law; a legal expression. *Since the advocate-general has applied to the High Court of Justice for a decision, the spokesman said the matter was sub judice.*

subjugate /sʌbdʒʊgeɪt/ **subjugates, subjugating, subjugated**; a formal word.
1 VO If someone **subjugates** a group of people, they take complete control of them, especially by defeating them in a war. *They wondered where Hitler would turn when he had subjugated Europe.* ♦ **subjugation** /sʌbdʒʊgeɪʃn/ NU *These people are resisting attempted subjugation by armed minorities. ...Iraq's subjugation of Kuwait.*
2 VO If your wishes **are subjugated** to something, they are treated as less important than that thing. *She has subjugated her own desires to those of her husband.*

subjunctive /səbdʒʌŋktɪv/
N SING The **subjunctive** or **subjunctive mood** is one of the moods that a verb can take in some languages such as French and Latin. In contrast with the indicative and imperative moods, the subjunctive is usually used to express attitudes such as wishing, hoping, and doubting.

sublet /sʌblet/ **sublets, subletting**. The form **sublet** is used in the present tense and is also the past tense and past participle.
VOorV If you **sublet** a building or part of a building that you are renting, you allow someone to use it and you take rent from them, although you are not the owner. *They've sublet the flat to the countess.*

sub-lieutenant, sub-lieutenants
NC A **sub-lieutenant** is a naval officer of the lowest rank. *...two lieutenants and a sub-lieutenant from the elite US-trained battalion.*

sublimate /sʌblɪmeɪt/ **sublimates, sublimating, sublimated**
VO If you **sublimate** a strong desire or feeling, you express it in a way that is socially acceptable; a technical term in psychology. *She had been conditioned to sublimate her own desires in nurturing others.* ♦ **sublimation** /sʌblɪmeɪʃn/ NU *...the sublimation of sexuality.*

sublime /səblaɪm/
1 ADJ Something that is **sublime** has a wonderful quality that affects you deeply; a literary use. *This is*

the most poignant and sublime moment in the poet's long career.

2 You describe something as going **from the sublime to the ridiculous** when it changes from being of high quality to being silly or trivial. *The film goes from the sublime to the ridiculous.*

subliminal /səblɪmɪnl/
ADJ Something that is **subliminal** affects your mind without your being aware of it. *...subliminal advertising.* ♦ **subliminally** ADV *We've lost the ability to detect these smells consciously, but we detect them subliminally.*

sub-machine gun, sub-machine guns
NC A **sub-machine gun** is a light, portable machine gun. *Wearing flak jackets and armed with sub-machine guns and rocket-propelled grenades, the troops moved into the suburbs.*

submarine /sʌbməriːn/ **submarines**
NC A **submarine** is a naval vessel that can travel below the surface of the sea. *A Defence Ministry spokesman said the submarine was in international waters. ...a nuclear-powered submarine.*

submerge /səbmɜːdʒ/ **submerges, submerging, submerged**
1 V-ERG If something **submerges** or if you **submerge** it, it goes below the surface of some water. *The alligator showed its snout before submerging... The animals were submerged experimentally.*
2 VO If something **is submerged**, water rises so that it is below the surface of the water. *The floods rose swiftly, submerging highways and railway lines.* ♦ **submerged** ADJ *...a line of submerged rocks.*
3 V-REFL+in If you **submerge** yourself in an activity, you give all your attention to it. *He submerged himself in company reports.*

submission /səbmɪʃn/
1 NU **Submission** is a state in which people are not free to do as they want because they are under the control of someone else. *The trade unions were brought into submission.*
2 NU The **submission** of a proposal or application is the act of sending it to someone, so they can decide whether to accept it; a formal use. *...the submission of these plans to the local authority.*

submissive /səbmɪsɪv/
ADJ If you are **submissive**, you are quiet and obedient. *Is the relationship one between a strong patron and a submissive client eager to do his master's bidding?*

submit /səbmɪt/ **submits, submitting, submitted**; a formal word.
1 V If you **submit** to something, you accept it, because you are not powerful enough to resist it. *They were forced to submit to military discipline.*
2 VO If you **submit** something such as a proposal or application to someone, you send it to them so they can decide on what action to take. *I submitted my resignation... Three-quarters of all charities haven't submitted annual accounts for the last five years.*

subnormal /sʌbnɔːml/
ADJ If someone is **subnormal**, they have less ability or intelligence than a normal person of their age. *He has been sending his severely subnormal son to the centre for the past five years.*

subordinate, subordinates, subordinating, subordinated; pronounced /səbɔːdɪnət/ when it is a noun or an adjective, and /səbɔːdɪneɪt/ when it is a verb.
1 NC+POSS If someone is your **subordinate**, they have a less important position than you in the organization that you both work for. *He humiliated his senior staff before their subordinates.*
2 ADJ If one thing is **subordinate** to another, it is less important than the other thing; a formal use. *All other questions are subordinate to this one.*
3 VO+to If you **subordinate** one thing to another, you treat it as less important than the other thing; a formal use. *To keep his job, he subordinated his own interests to the objectives of the company.*

subordinate clause, subordinate clauses
NC A **subordinate clause** is a clause which begins with a subordinating conjunction such as 'while' or with a

relative pronoun, and which must be used with a main clause.

subpoena /səpiːnə/ subpoenas, subpoenaing, subpoenaed
1 NC A **subpoena** is a legal document telling someone that they must attend a court of law and give evidence as a witness. *A House committee tried to serve a subpoena on Harry Truman.*
2 VO To **subpoena** someone means to issue them with a subpoena telling them that they must attend a court of law and give evidence as a witness. *Our head of personnel was subpoenaed as a witness.*

subscribe /səbskraɪb/ subscribes, subscribing, subscribed
1 V If you **subscribe** to an opinion or belief, you have this opinion or belief. *The rest of us do not subscribe to this theory.*
2 V If you **subscribe** to a magazine or a newspaper, you pay to receive copies of it regularly. *I started subscribing to a morning newspaper.*
3 VAorVOA If you **subscribe** money to a charity or a campaign, you send money to it regularly. *They subscribed to local charities... Can we afford to subscribe 5,000 pounds a year to such an institution.*

subscriber /səbskraɪbə/ subscribers
1 NC The **subscribers** of a magazine, newspaper, or a television channel are the people who pay to receive that publication or that channel regularly. *Some quarterly journals go out to subscribers around the world... There are now 50 to 60 million cable subscribers who get CNN in this country.*
2 NC **Subscribers** to a service are the people who pay to receive the service. *...telephone subscribers.*
3 NC The **subscribers** to a charity or campaign are the people who support it by sending money regularly to it.

subscription /səbskrɪpʃn/ subscriptions
NC A **subscription** is a fixed amount of money that you pay regularly in order to belong to a club or society, or in order to receive copies of a magazine or newspaper. *...my first year's subscription to the National Union of Agricultural Workers. ...magazine subscriptions.*

subsection /sʌbsekʃn/ subsections
NC A **subsection** of a text or a document such as a law is one of the smaller parts into which its main parts are divided. *...under subsection 2 of section 13 of the Act.*

subsequent /sʌbsɪkwənt/
ADJ ATTRIB **Subsequent** describes something that happens or exists at a later time than something else. *Subsequent research has produced even better results.* ♦ **subsequently** ADV *Brooke was arrested and subsequently sentenced to five years' imprisonment.*

subservience /səbsɜːviəns/
NU **Subservience** is a state in which you do whatever someone else wants you to. *They accuse Mr Botha of trying to coerce the media into subservience. ...their often slavish subservience to the party line.*

subservient /səbsɜːviənt/
1 ADJ If you are **subservient**, you do whatever someone wants you to do. *She was subservient and eager to please... The public now sees the government as corrupt and subservient to big business.*
2 ADJ PRED+to If you treat one thing as **subservient** to another, you treat it as less important than the other thing. *Economic systems became subservient to social objectives... However beautiful the music, it must be subservient to the words and never obscure their clarity.*

subside /səbsaɪd/ subsides, subsiding, subsided
1 V If a feeling or sound **subsides**, it becomes less intense or quieter. *Tension in the town has subsided... She stopped and waited until the pain subsided... His voice subsided to a mutter.*
2 V If fighting **subsides**, it becomes less intense or widespread. *The rioting subsided when the government cancelled price rises... The violence in Delhi subsided but further trouble was reported from the neighbouring state of Haryana.*
3 V If water **subsides** or if the ground **subsides**, it sinks to a lower level. *The flooded river was subsiding*

rapidly... *The earth subsided under the foundations and the buildings began to crack.*

subsidence /səbsaɪdns, sʌbsɪdns/
NU When there is **subsidence**, the ground sinks to a lower level. *They have been moved out of their homes because of the risk of subsidence... The holes have been caused by subsidence in the old chalk workings under the city.*

subsidiary /səbsɪdiəri/ subsidiaries
1 ADJ If something is **subsidiary**, it is less important than something else with which it is connected. *The Department offers a course in Opera Studies as a subsidiary subject... I tried to discuss this and some subsidiary questions.*
2 NC A **subsidiary** is a company which is part of a larger company. *The British company is a subsidiary of Racal Electronics.*

subsidize /sʌbsɪdaɪz/ subsidizes, subsidizing, subsidized; also spelt **subsidise**.
VO If a government **subsidizes** a public service or an industry, they pay part of its costs. *In this country the State subsidizes education.* ♦ **subsidized** ADJ *...subsidized housing.*

subsidy /sʌbsədi/ subsidies
NCorNU A **subsidy** is money paid by a government to help a company or to pay for a public service. *The result of the negotiations has to be the removal of most farm subsidies... The Royal Opera gave more performances on less subsidy than any other opera house.*

subsist /səbsɪst/ subsists, subsisting, subsisted
V If you **subsist**, you only have just enough food to stay alive. *In some places, the settlers were subsisting on potato peelings.*

subsistence /səbsɪstəns/
NU **Subsistence** is the condition of only having just enough food to stay alive. *They do not have access to sufficient land for subsistence. ...living at subsistence level.*

subsonic /sʌbsɒnɪk/
ADJ ATTRIB **Subsonic** speeds are very fast but slower than the speed of sound. *They had flown at a high subsonic speed. ...the first generation of subsonic jets.*

subspecies /sʌbspiːʃiːz/; subspecies is both the singular and the plural form.
NC A **subspecies** of a particular type of plant or animal is a subdivision of that species. *...one of nine subspecies or races of seaside sparrow.*

substance /sʌbstəns/ substances
1 NC A **substance** is a solid, powder, liquid, or gas with particular properties. *The discovery of this marvellous substance made Fleming an international celebrity... We try to remove the harmful substances from cigarettes.*
2 NU You use **substance** to refer to something that you can touch, rather than something that you can only see, hear, or imagine. *They had no more substance than shadows.*
3 N SING The **substance** of what someone says is the main thing that they are trying to say. *The substance of their talk is condensed into a paragraph.*
4 NU **Substance** is also the quality of being important or significant. *There isn't anything of real substance in her book... He needs the help of Western economic aid and know-how to give those reforms some substance.*

substandard /sʌbstændəd/
ADJ Something that is **substandard** is of an unacceptably low standard. *He says the ships built so far are substandard. ...substandard housing.*

substantial /səbstænʃl/
1 ADJ **Substantial** means very large in amount or degree. *She will receive a substantial amount of money... Many factories suffered substantial damage... Preliminary results indicated a substantial majority for the incumbent president.*
2 ADJ A **substantial** building is large and strongly built. *I came to Tallinn in 1947, and then there were hardly any substantial buildings here.*

substantially /səbstænʃəli/
1 ADV If something increases or decreases **substantially**, it increases or decreases by a large

amount. *The price may go up quite substantially.*
2 SUBMOD If something is **substantially** true, it is
generally or mostly true. *Steed always maintained
that the story was substantially true.*
substantiate /səbstænʃieɪt/ **substantiates,
substantiating, substantiated**
VO To **substantiate** a statement or a story means to
supply evidence proving that it is true; a formal
word. *Your report might be difficult to substantiate.*
substantive /səbstæntɪv/
ADJ **Substantive** means concerned with real issues or
real effects; a formal word. *Hattersley argued that
more substantive measures were needed... He
promised that there would be substantive arms control
talks... Conflicts may not always be over substantive
issues.*
substitute /sʌbstɪtjuːt/ **substitutes, substituting,
substituted**
1 VO If you **substitute** one thing for another, you use it
instead of the other thing. *Force was substituted for
argument.* ◆ **substitution** /sʌbstɪtjuːʃn/ **substitutions**
NUorNC *...the substitution of local goods for those
previously imported.*
2 NC A **substitute** is something that you have or use
instead of something else that you had previously or
instead of something you would like to have. *Their
dog was a substitute for the children they never had.
...the development of a ceramic ivory substitute.*
3 If you say that one thing is **no substitute** for another,
you mean that it does not have certain desirable
features that the other thing has, and is therefore less
satisfactory. *They appreciated offers of food aid, but
it was no substitute for help in developing the
country's infrastructure.*
4 NC In football, a **substitute** is a player who is
brought onto the field to replace another who has been
withdrawn for some reason. *Substitute Marco Van
Basten made sure of AC's victory with a third goal...
He replaces Wolverhampton Wanderers striker Robbie
Dennison, who is named as one of the substitutes.*
substructure /sʌbstrʌktʃə/ **substructures**
NC A **substructure** is a structure that forms part of
another, larger structure. *...the organization and its
substructures.*
subsume /səbsjuːm/ **subsumes, subsuming, subsumed**
VO If something is **subsumed** within a larger group, it
is included within it, rather than being considered as
something separate; a formal word. *...an opportunity
to subsume their national identities within the larger
Islamic one... These amendments are expected to be
subsumed in a completely new constitution.*
subterfuge /sʌbtəfjuːdʒ/ **subterfuges**
NCorNU A **subterfuge** is a trick or a dishonest way of
getting what you want. *Rising food prices have
prompted people on fixed government incomes to use
various subterfuges to feed their families... Resistance
will be possible only through cheating, subterfuge and
sabotage... Evidence at the trial showed Barry had
used subterfuge to avoid being caught.*
subterranean /sʌbtəreɪniən/
ADJ ATTRIB A **subterranean** river or tunnel is
underground; a formal word. *...winding subterranean
passages.*
subtitles /sʌbtaɪtlz/
N PL **Subtitles** are the printed words which appear at
the bottom of a television or cinema screen, either for
the benefit of deaf people, or as a translation from a
foreign language. *...with subtitles for the hard of
hearing. ...an Italian film with English subtitles.*
subtle /sʌtl/ **subtler, subtlest**
1 ADJ Something that is **subtle** is not immediately
obvious or noticeable, and is therefore a little difficult
to explain or describe. *His whole attitude had
undergone a subtle change.* ◆ **subtly** ADV *The tastes
are subtly different.*
2 ADJ Someone who is **subtle** uses indirect and clever
methods to achieve something. *You must be more
subtle... My plan was subtler.* ◆ **subtly** ADV *He subtly
criticized me.*
subtlety /sʌtlti/ **subtleties**
1 NC A **subtlety** is a very small detail or difference
which is difficult to notice. *...the subtleties of English*

stress and intonation.
2 NU **Subtlety** is the quality of not being immediately
obvious or noticeable, and therefore a little difficult to
explain or describe. *In your cooking remember that
subtlety is everything.*
3 NU **Subtlety** is also the ability to use indirect and
clever methods to achieve something. *...their subtlety
of mind.*
subtract /səbtrækt/ **subtracts, subtracting,
subtracted**
VO If you **subtract** one number from another, you take
the first number away from the second. For example,
if you subtract 3 from 5, you get 2. *They look at the
value of the milk output and from that they subtract
the cost of the feed input and the difference is the
profitability.* ◆ **subtraction** /səbtrækʃn/ **subtractions**
NUorNC *...simple techniques for handling subtraction.
...simple additions and subtractions.*
sub-tropical
ADJ ATTRIB **Sub-tropical** describes things relating to the
areas of the world that lie between the tropical and
temperate regions. *...sub-tropical forests.*
suburb /sʌbɜːb/ **suburbs**
NC A **suburb** or the **suburbs** of a city is an area of it
which is away from the centre and where people live.
...people who live in the suburbs.
suburban /səbɜːbən/
1 ADJ ATTRIB **Suburban** means relating to a suburb.
...suburban areas of Rio.
2 ADJ If you describe something as **suburban**, you
mean that it is dull, conventional, and not exciting at
all. *...a suburban lifestyle.*
suburbia /səbɜːbiə/
NU **Suburbia** refers to suburbs considered as a whole.
*We stop at a convenience store, a kind found on every
street corner in suburbia.*
subversion /səbvɜːʃn/
NU **Subversion** is a secret or subtle attempt to weaken
or destroy a political system or government; a formal
word. *Those who signed the First Manifesto had
charges of subversion against them dropped.
...espionage, terrorism and subversion.*
subversive /səbvɜːsɪv/ **subversives**; a formal word.
1 ADJ Something that is **subversive** is intended to
weaken or destroy a political system or government.
*...subversive and seditious material... The régime
regarded teaching as subversive.*
2 NC **Subversives** are people who attempt to weaken
or destroy a political system or government. *The
strikers were described as anti-socialists, counter-
revolutionaries and subversives.*
subvert /səbvɜːt/ **subverts, subverting, subverted**
VO To **subvert** something means to destroy its power
and influence; a formal word. *Conflict and division
subvert the foundations of society.*
subway /sʌbweɪ/ **subways**
1 NC A **subway** is a passage for pedestrians
underneath a busy road. *There is graffiti in subways,
trains and buses.*
2 NC In the United States, a **subway** is an
underground railway. *Take the subway to 57th Street
or Soho.*
succeed /səksiːd/ **succeeds, succeeding, succeeded**
1 V If you **succeed** in doing something, you manage to
do it. *I succeeded in getting the job... I think he is
sincere and I hope he will succeed.*
2 V If something **succeeds**, it has the result that is
intended or works in a satisfactory way. *Nobody
expected that strike to succeed.*
3 V Someone who **succeeds** gains a high position in
what they do, for example in business. *She is eager to
succeed.*
4 VOorV If you **succeed** another person, you are the
next person to have their job or position. *Somebody's
got to succeed Murray as editor... Elizabeth succeeded
to the throne in 1952.*
5 VO If one thing **succeeds** another, it comes after it in
time. *The first demand would be succeeded by others.*
◆ **succeeding** ADJ ATTRIB *In the succeeding months,
little was heard about him.*
success /səksɛs/ **successes**
1 NU **Success** is the achievement of something that

you have been trying to do. *His attempt to shoot the president came very close to success... The success rate of this technique is still low.*
2 N U or N C Someone or something that has achieved **success** has reached an important position or made a lot of money. *Confidence is the key to success... His next film—'Jaws'—was a tremendous success.*
successful /səksɛsfl/
1 ADJ Something that is **successful** achieves what it was intended to achieve. *...a successful attempt to land on the moon.* ♦ **successfully** ADV *The operation had been completed successfully.*
2 ADJ You also say that something is **successful** if it is popular or makes a lot of money. *...a very successful film.*
3 ADJ Someone who is **successful** in their job or career achieves a high position, or makes a lot of money. *...a successful writer.*
succession /səksɛʃn/ **successions**
1 N C+*of* A **succession** of things is a number of them occurring one after the other. *My life is a succession of failures.*
2 NU **Succession** is the act or right of being the next person to have a particular job or position. *...his succession to the peerage.*
3 If something happens for a number of weeks, months, or years **in succession**, it happens in each of those weeks, months, or years, without a break. *Vita went to Florence for the third year in succession.*
successive /səksɛsɪv/
ADJ ATTRIB **Successive** means happening or existing one after another, without a break. *It was the third successive night of street protests in Nanking... The paper says successive Burmese governments have failed to accommodate such groups.*
successor /səksɛsə/ **successors**
N C Someone's **successor** is the person who takes their job after they have left. *Who will be Brearley's successor?... Mr Giray has been mentioned as a possible successor to the previous Foreign Minister.*
success story, success stories
N C Someone or something that is a **success story** is very successful, often unexpectedly or in spite of unfavourable conditions. *One of the greatest success stories in rapid industrialization was Singapore.*
succinct /səksɪŋkt/
ADJ Something that is **succinct** expresses facts or ideas clearly and in few words. *...an accurate and succinct account of their policies.* ♦ **succinctly** ADV *She puts the case very succinctly.*
succour /sʌkə/; spelt **succor** in American English.
NU **Succour** is help that is given to someone who is suffering or in difficulties; a formal word. *They were busy providing succour to the injured.*
succulence /sʌkjʊləns/
NU If you refer to the **succulence** of food, you are referring to the fact that it is juicy and delicious.
succulent /sʌkjʊlənt/
ADJ **Succulent** food is juicy and delicious. *...a succulent mango.*
succumb /səkʌm/ **succumbs, succumbing, succumbed**
1 V If you **succumb** to something such as persuasion or desire, you are unable to stop yourself being influenced by it. *He finally succumbed to the temptation to have another drink.*
2 V+*to*-INF If you **succumb** to a disease, you are made ill by it. *Indians in the Amazon forests have succumbed to diseases brought in from outside.*
such /sʌtʃ/
1 PREDET, DET, or PRON You use **such** to refer to the person or thing you have just mentioned or to something similar. *They lasted for hundreds of thousands of years. On a human time scale, such a period seems an eternity... The nobility held tournaments, but peasants had no time to spare for such frivolity... I don't believe in magic, there is no such thing... We have been asked to consider alternatives. Many such have been proposed in the last few years.*
2 PREDET or DET You also use **such** to emphasize the degree or extent of something. *It was such a lovely*

day... It was strange that such elegant creatures made such ugly sounds.
● **Such** is used in these phrases. ● You use **such** as or **such...as** to introduce one or more examples of something. *...a game of chance such as roulette. ...such things as pork pies, sausage rolls, and plum cake.* ● You use **such...that** or **such...as** when saying what the result or consequence of something is. *They have to charge in such a way that they don't make a loss... She got such a shock that she dropped the milk-can.* ● You use **such as it is** to indicate that something is not very good, important, or useful. *Dinner's on the table, such as it is.* ● You use **as such** to indicate that you are considering something by itself without considering related things or issues. *He is not terribly interested in politics as such.*
such and such
PREDET or PRON You use **such and such** to refer to something when you do not want to be precise or specific. *He'd like to give a course of lectures on such and such a topic... John will always tell me that I have not taken such and such into account.*
suchlike /sʌtʃlaɪk/
DET or PRON You use **suchlike** to refer to other things like the ones already mentioned. *...artichokes, smoked fish, and suchlike delicacies. ...mills, threshing machines and suchlike.*
suck /sʌk/ **sucks, sucking, sucked**
1 V O or V A If you **suck** something, you hold it in your mouth and pull at it with your cheeks and tongue, usually in order to get liquid out of it. *The baby went on sucking the bottle... The government has announced plans to ban tobacco products which are sucked inside the mouth... Ken was sucking on an orange.*
2 V O A If something **sucks** an object or liquid somewhere, it draws it there with a powerful force. *The water is sucked upwards through the roots.*
3 V O A If you **are sucked** into a situation, you are unable to prevent yourself from becoming involved in it. *In the late 1960's, the country was gradually sucked into the war raging in neighbouring Vietnam.*
suck up PHRASAL VERB If you **suck up** to someone in authority, you try to please them by flattering them or doing things for them; an informal expression, used showing disapproval. *He's been sucking up like mad to the boss.*
sucker /sʌkə/ **suckers**
1 N C If you call someone a **sucker**, you mean that it is easy to cheat or fool them because they believe anything they are told; an informal use. *He'd believe anything—he's such a sucker!*
2 N C A **sucker** is a device made from rubber that is used to attach things to the surface of something. *The shiny surface is the solar panel and the suckers enable you to stick the item onto a window.*
3 N C **Suckers** are pads on the bodies of some animals and insects which they use to stick to a surface.
suckle /sʌkl/ **suckles, suckling, suckled**
V-ERG When a mother **suckles** her baby or when a baby **suckles**, the mother feeds it by letting it suck milk from her breasts. *You don't suckle the child frequently enough... If the child doesn't suckle enough at the breast, milk production will be low.*
Sucre /suːkreɪ/
Sucre is the judicial capital of Bolivia and its sixth largest city. Population: 96,000 (1988).
suction /sʌkʃn/
1 NU **Suction** is the force involved when liquids, gases, or other substances are drawn from one space to another. *The draining process was assisted by suction... They use huge suction pumps to scoop up hundreds of tons of sand and gravel from the estuary.*
2 NU **Suction** is also the process by which two surfaces stick together when the air between them is removed. *Stick it to the surface by suction. ...stuck on to the bath by suction pads.*
Sudan /suːdɑːn/
The **Republic of Sudan** is a country in north-east Africa. It was ruled by Britain and Egypt from 1899 until independence in 1956. Ethnic conflict followed, with the Christian and animist south seeking secession from the Muslim, more developed north. The Sudanese

People's Liberation Army (SPLA), led by Colonel John Garang, is the main guerrilla force in the south. Lieutenant-General Omar Hassan Ahmad al-Bashir became Chairman of the Revolutionary Council and Prime Minister in a coup in 1989. Political parties were abolished in 1989. Sudan is a member of the Arab League and the Organization of African Unity. Large foreign debts and high inflation are major economic problems. Recurring famine and influxes of refugees from Chad and Ethiopia are additional problems. Sudan exports cotton, livestock, and gum arabic.
♦ **Sudanese** /suːdənˈiːz/ N, N PL, ADJ
▪ *per capita GNP:* US$340 ▪ *religion:* Islam (mainly Sunni), animism, Christianity ▪ *language:* Arabic (official) ▪ *currency:* pound ▪ *capital:* Khartoum
▪ *population:* 24 million (1989) ▪ *size:* 2,505,813 square kilometres.

sudden /sʌdn/
1 ADJ Something that is **sudden** happens quickly and unexpectedly. *...a sudden drop in the temperature.*
♦ **suddenly** ADV or ADV SEN *Reports claim that primary school children have suddenly become worse at reading than they used to be... Suddenly, the door opened and in walked the boss.* ♦ **suddenness** NU *...surprised by the suddenness of the attack.*
2 If something happens **all of a sudden**, it happens so quickly and unexpectedly that you are surprised by it. *We sat in our bunkers, and all of a sudden tanks came out of nowhere... You know, you are lying in bed trying to get to sleep and all of a sudden you hear the door.*

sudden-death
N+N In sporting competitions, a **sudden-death** playoff is an extra game that is played between two people or two teams that have finished on an equal score. The first person or team that gains the lead is the winner. *After two holes of a sudden-death playoff, Deb Richard outputted Cindy Rerick and won the 1991 Kemper Open.*

suds /sʌdz/
N PL **Suds** are the bubbles produced when soap is mixed with water. *...elbow deep in the suds.*

sue /suː/ **sues, suing, sued**
V O or V If you **sue** someone, you start a legal case against them to claim money from them because they have harmed you in some way. *He couldn't sue them for wrongful arrest... He let it be known that he would sue.*

suede /sweɪd/
NU **Suede** is thin, soft leather with a slightly rough surface. *...boots of light brown suede. ...a suede jacket.*

suet /suːɪt/
NU **Suet** is hard animal fat that is used in cooking. *Haggis is a concoction of sheep heart, liver and lungs, spiced suet and oatmeal.*

suffer /sʌfə/ **suffers, suffering, suffered**
1 V O or V If someone **suffers** pain or an illness, they are badly affected by it. *Patients who have suffered a heart attack can add years to their lives by taking regular exercise... She was suffering violent abdominal pains... Seventy-five per cent of its population suffers from malnutrition.*
2 V O or V If you **suffer**, you are badly affected by an unfavourable event or situation. *We were warned to support the government or suffer the consequences... They would be the first to suffer if these proposals were ever carried out.*
3 V If something **suffers**, it becomes worse in quality or condition as a result of neglect or an unfavourable situation. *I'm not surprised that your studies are suffering.*

sufferance /sʌfərəns/
If you are allowed to do something **on sufferance**, you can do it, although you know that the person who gave you permission would prefer that you did not do it. *The civilian authorities are only there on sufferance of the military.*

sufferer /sʌfərə/ **sufferers**
NC+SUPP A **sufferer** is someone who is badly affected by pain or illness. *There are 100,000 sufferers from Parkinson's disease in the UK. ...the only hospice for*

sufferers of the disease AIDS.

suffering /sʌfərɪŋ/ **sufferings**
NU or NC **Suffering** is serious pain which someone feels in their body or their mind. *This would cause great hardship and suffering... This might alleviate their sufferings.*

suffice /səfaɪs/ **suffices, sufficing, sufficed**
1 V If something **suffices**, it is enough to achieve a purpose or to fulfil a need; a formal use. *She hoped sanctions would suffice to get Iraq out of Kuwait, but warned that force might eventually be necessary.*
2 **Suffice it to say** or **suffice to say** is used at the beginning of a statement to show that what you are saying is enough to explain your meaning or to prove your argument, although you could say much more. *Suffice it to say that for an hour, the House of Commons was reduced to bedlam... Suffice to say that this has been a very productive summit.*

sufficiency /səfɪʃnsi/
N SING If there is a **sufficiency** of something, there is enough of it; a formal word. *We had 600 jet fighters and a sufficiency of airfields to support them.*

sufficient /səfɪʃnt/
ADJ If something is **sufficient** for a particular purpose, there is as much of it as is necessary. *Japan had a reserve of oil sufficient for its needs.* ♦ **sufficiently** ADV *He had not insured the house sufficiently.*

suffix /sʌfɪks/ **suffixes**
NC A **suffix** is a letter or group of letters added to the end of a word in order to make a new word with different grammar or with a different meaning. For example, the suffix '-ist' can be added to 'sex' to form the word 'sexist'.

suffocate /sʌfəkeɪt/ **suffocates, suffocating, suffocated**
V-ERG If someone **suffocates** or if something **suffocates** them, they die because there is not enough oxygen for them to breathe. *Sir, we are suffocating. We must surrender... The smoke and fumes almost suffocated me.* ♦ **suffocation** /sʌfəkeɪʃn/ NU *Many slaves died of heat and suffocation.*

suffrage /sʌfrɪdʒ/
NU **Suffrage** is the right that people have to vote for a government or national leader; a formal word. *...universal adult suffrage.*

suffragette /sʌfrədʒet/ **suffragettes**
NC In Britain during the early twentieth century, a **suffragette** was a woman who was involved in the campaign for women to be given the right to vote. *The election was a great triumph for the suffragettes who campaigned tirelessly for equal political rights.*

suffuse /səfjuːz/ **suffuses, suffusing, suffused**
V O If something is **suffused** with light or colour, light or colour spreads gradually over or through it; a literary word. *It was dawn, and the room was already suffused with light.*

sugar /ʃʊgə/ **sugars**
N MASS **Sugar** is a sweet substance, often in the form of white crystals, that is used to sweeten food and drink. *I take my coffee black with no sugar... Sugar and tobacco are already rationed.*

sugar beet
NU **Sugar beet** is a plant that is cultivated for the sugar which is obtained from its root. *He blamed poor sugar beet harvests and illegal production of alcohol for the rise in the price of sugar.*

sugar cane
NU **Sugar cane** is a tall tropical plant with thick stems from which sugar is obtained. *Heavy showers damaged the rice crop and also affected sugar cane and cotton.*

sugar daddy, sugar daddies
NC A **sugar daddy** is a man who gives money and presents to a woman younger than himself, usually in return for her company, affection, and often sexual intercourse; an old-fashioned, informal expression.

sugared /ʃʊgəd/
ADJ If you describe what people say and how they say it as **sugared**, you mean that it is pleasant and attractive, but not always to be trusted. *The proposition was couched in sugared terms... She spoke in sugared tones.*

sugar lump, sugar lumps
NC A **sugar lump** is a small cube of sugar.
sugary /ʃʊgəri/
1 ADJ Something that is **sugary** contains a lot of
sugar. ...*sugary breakfast cereal.*
2 ADJ Language or behaviour that is **sugary** seems to
be very pleasant and attractive, but is probably
insincere. ...*a sugary phrase, that didn't manage to
conceal his dislike of her... She gave a sweet sugary
smile that made my blood run cold.*
suggest /sədʒest/ **suggests, suggesting, suggested**
1 VO, V-QUOTE, or V-REPORT If you **suggest** something,
you put forward a plan or idea for someone to
consider. *We have to suggest a list of possible topics
for next term's seminars... Can you suggest
somewhere for a short holiday?... I'm not suggesting
that the accident was your fault.*
2 V-REPORT If one thing **suggests** another, it implies it
or makes you think that it is the case. *His expression
suggested pleasure at the fact that I had come... The
forecasts suggest that there will be higher
unemployment.*
suggestible /sədʒestəbl/
ADJ Someone who is **suggestible** can be easily
influenced by what other people say. *He was a
strange man: shy, eager to please, and very
suggestible.*
suggestion /sədʒestʃən/ **suggestions**
1 NC A **suggestion** is an idea or plan that is put
forward for people to think about. *I made a few
suggestions about how we could spend the afternoon.*
2 N SING+of If there is a **suggestion** of something, there
is a slight sign of it. *He replied to her question with
the merest suggestion of a smile.*
3 NU **Suggestion** is the act or process of giving people
a particular idea by associating it with other ideas.
*Such is the power of suggestion that within two
minutes the patient is asleep.*
suggestive /sədʒestɪv/
1 ADJ PRED+of If one thing is **suggestive** of another, it
gives a hint of it or reminds you of it. *His behaviour
was suggestive of a cultured man.*
2 ADJ **Suggestive** remarks, movements, and so on
cause people to think about sex. *A school rule bans
clothing considered suggestive, vulgar, or provocative.
...suggestive pelvic motions.*
Suharto, General /suːhɑːtəʊ/
General Suharto became President of Indonesia in
1968. He was Minister of the Army in 1965, and Chief
of Army Staff from 1965 to 1968. He assumed
emergency executive powers and served as Deputy
Prime Minister for Defence and Security in 1966. He
was Acting President from 1967 to 1968. Born: 1921.
suicidal /suːɪsaɪdl/
1 ADJ People who are **suicidal** want to kill
themselves. *Many disturbed and suicidal patients
were left in cells for dangerously long periods of time.*
2 ADJ **Suicidal** behaviour is so dangerous that it is
likely to result in death. *Some of the Burmese died
making suicidal assaults on the camp which is
defended by the national army.*
3 ADJ You can also describe behaviour as **suicidal** if it
likely to destroy something such as your career,
wealth, or position. *The Director described the vote as
an ill-judged and suicidal action.*
suicide /suːɪsaɪd/ **suicides**
1 NU or NC People who commit **suicide** deliberately kill
themselves. *He committed suicide in 1774... The
suicides were motivated in part by a sense of despair.*
2 NU If someone deliberately does something that is
likely to ruin something such as their career, wealth,
or position, you can refer to their actions as **suicide.**
*People had told me it was suicide to admit my
mistake.*
suit /suːt/ **suits, suiting, suited**
1 NC A man's **suit** consists of a matching jacket,
trousers, and sometimes a waistcoat. *He arrived at
the office in a suit and tie.*
2 NC A woman's **suit** consists of a matching jacket
and skirt. *She wore a black suit and a tiny black hat.*
3 NC A **suit** can also be a piece of clothing worn for a
particular activity. *She was wearing a short robe over*

her bathing suit.
4 VO If a piece of clothing or a particular style or
colour **suits** you, it makes you look attractive. *That
coat really suits you.*
5 VO If you say that something **suits** you, you mean
that it is convenient, acceptable or appropriate for
you. *Would Monday suit you?... All this suits my
purpose very well... A job where I was indoors all day
wouldn't suit me.*
6 V-REFL If you **suit** yourself, you do something just
because you want to do it, without considering other
people. *They have been running their businesses to
suit themselves.*
7 NC In a court of law, a **suit** is a legal action taken
by one person against another. *They originally wanted
to deny him a visa, but relented after a threatened law
suit from a civil rights group... Launching a libel suit
in Britain is enormously expensive... The US
administration had filed a suit to freeze their assets.*
8 NC A **suit** is also one of the four types of card in a
set of playing cards. The four suits are hearts,
diamonds, clubs, and spades.
9 If people **follow suit**, they do what someone else has
just done. *He bowed his head. Mother and Jenny
followed suit... President Mitterrand has responded
favourably, but it remains to be seen if other Western
leaders will follow suit.*
suitable /suːtəbl/
ADJ Someone or something that is **suitable** for a
particular purpose or occasion is right or acceptable
for it. *These flats are not really suitable for families
with children. ...a list of names of suitable people.*
♦ **suitability** /suːtəbɪləti/ NU ...*the candidate's
intellectual ability and suitability for admission.*
♦ **suitably** ADV *See that you are suitably dressed for
the weather.*
suitcase /suːtkeɪs/ **suitcases**
NC A **suitcase** is a case for carrying clothes when you
are travelling. *They should have with them no more
than one suitcase per person plus hand baggage...
They have come across terrorist devices where the
explosive has been packed flat in the lining of a
suitcase.*
suite /swiːt/ **suites**
1 NC A **suite** is a set of rooms in a hotel. *They always
stayed in a suite at the Ritz.*
2 NC A **suite** is also a set of matching furniture for a
sitting-room or bathroom. ...*a three-piece suite for the
lounge.*
suited /suːtɪd/
1 ADJ PRED If something is **suited** to a particular
purpose or person, it is right or appropriate for them.
*They preferred to join clubs more suited to their
tastes... He considered himself ideally suited for the
job.*
2 ADJ PRED If a couple are well **suited,** they are likely
to have a successful relationship because they have
similar personalities and interests. ...*if the couple are
clearly well-suited.*
suitor /suːtə/ **suitors**
NC A woman's **suitor** is a man who wants to marry
her; an old-fashioned word. *She had many suitors.*
sulfur /sʌlfə/. See sulphur.
sulk /sʌlk/ **sulks, sulking, sulked**
V If you **sulk**, you are silent and bad-tempered for a
while because you are annoyed. *He sulked and
behaved badly for weeks after I refused.* ► Also NC *I
thought you were in one of your sulks.*
sulky /sʌlki/
ADJ A **sulky** person is bad-tempered and silent because
they are annoyed about something. *Sam glowered at
him in sulky silence.* ♦ **sulkily** ADV *'I don't want
anything,' the boy answered sulkily.*
sullen /sʌlən/
ADJ A **sullen** person is bad-tempered and does not
speak much. ...*a sullen look in Ned's eyes.* ♦ **sullenly**
ADV *'So what?' Thomas said sullenly.*
sully /sʌli/ **sullies, sullying, sullied**; a literary word.
1 VO If you **sully** something, you make it dirty. *He
could not admit that pure water with his sweat.*
2 VO To **sully** something also means to spoil it so that
it is no longer pure or of such high value. *Nothing had*

ever happened to sully her reputation.

sulphur /sʌlfə/; spelt **sulfur** in American English.
NU **Sulphur** is a yellow substance with a strong,
unpleasant smell. *One thing that volcanoes give out in
abundance is sulphur... Some coal contains the
element sulphur.*

sulphur dioxide; spelt **sulfur dioxide** in American
English.
NU **Sulphur dioxide** is a colourless, soluble gas with a
strong, unpleasant smell. It is produced by burning
sulphur. *Sulfur dioxide is one of the main causes of
acid rain... Britain is to reduce sulphur dioxide
emissions from two of her biggest power stations.*

sultan /sʌltən/ **sultans**
NCorTITLE A **sultan** is a ruler in some Muslim
countries. *He went straight into an audience with the
Sultan... Sultan Qaboos will be visiting Egypt this
summer.*

sultana /sʌltɑːnə/ **sultanas**
NC **Sultanas** are large, white grapes that have been
dried. *I really like sultanas in curry.*

sultanate /sʌltənət/ **sultanates**
NC A **sultanate** is a country that is governed by a
sultan. *He has now flown from Singapore to the oil-
rich sultanate of Brunei.*

sultry /sʌltri/
1 ADJ **Sultry** weather is unpleasantly hot and humid.
*She was walking along the street on an insufferably
sultry New York night.*
2 ADJ If you describe the way a person looks as **sultry**,
you mean that they are attractive in a way that
suggests hidden passion. *In the late 1950s his sultry
good looks were featured in magazine photographs and
a number of Italian films.*

sum /sʌm/ **sums, summing, summed**
1 NC A **sum** of money is an amount of it. *...the
staggering sum of 212,000 million pounds...
Manufacturers spend huge sums of money on
advertising their product... The previous highest sum
paid for a violin was just over £47,500.*
2 NC A **sum** is a simple calculation in arithmetic. *He
couldn't do his sums.*
3 N SING+of The **sum** of something is all of it, when you
are suggesting that there is not very much of it or that
it is not very good. *This seems to be the entire sum of
our achievement.*
4 See also **lump sum**.

sum up PHRASAL VERB 1 If you **sum up** or **sum**
something **up**, you briefly describe the main features
of something. *My mood could be summed up by the
single word 'boredom'... To sum up: within our society
there still exist rampant inequalities.* 2 If you **sum up**
a person or situation, you make an accurate
judgement of the person's character or the situation.
*There is only one way to sum up the man's style—he
was crude... It was a Canadian official who summed
up the situation.* 3 When a judge **sums up**, he or she
makes a speech to the jury at the end of a trial
reminding them of the evidence and the main
arguments of the case they have heard. *At the end, he
summed up, adding a few points.* ● See also **summing
up**.

summarize /sʌməraɪz/ **summarizes, summarizing,
summarized**; also spelt **summarise**.
VOorV If you **summarize** something, you give a brief
description of its main points. *The seven categories
can be briefly summarized as follows... To summarize,
she is intuitive and decisive.*

summary /sʌməⁱri/ **summaries**
1 NC A **summary** is a short account of something
giving the main points but not the details. *Here is a
summary of the plot.*
2 ADJ ATTRIB **Summary** actions are done without delay
when something else should have been done first or
done instead. *...mass arrests and summary
executions.* ◆ **summarily** ADV *He summarily
dismissed our problem as unimportant.*

summer /sʌmə/ **summers**
NCorNU **Summer** is the season between spring and
autumn, when the weather is usually warm or hot. *I
am going to Greece this summer... The temperature
there can go as high as forty degrees Centigrade in

summer. ...summer holidays.*

summer camp, summer camps
NCorNU A **summer camp** is a place where children go
on holiday together, often without their parents, and
take part in sporting activities; used in American
English. *She was at a Jewish summer camp in
upstate New York... Margie will be going to summer
camp this year... There's a kindergarten and a
summer camp for the workers' children.*

summer school, summer schools
NCorNU A **summer school** is an educational course on
a particular subject that is run during the summer.
*Could the reason that you have to go to summer school
be that you've neglected your studies just a bit?... He
is promoting a new summer school in Oxford and
Rome next year.*

summertime /sʌmətaɪm/
NU **Summertime** is the period of time during which
summer lasts. *The town is 80 miles north of the
Arctic Circle, and for six full weeks in the
summertime it never gets dark there.*

summer time
NU **Summer time** is a period of time in the summer in
some countries during which the clocks are put
forward, so that people can have extra daylight in the
evening. *...plans to introduce single summer time,
which would be Greenwich Mean Time plus one hour.*

summery /sʌməri/
ADJ Something that is **summery** is suitable for
summer or characteristic of summer. *...a summery
dress. ...a summery fragrance.*

summing up, summings up
NC In a court of law, the **summing up** is a summary of
all the evidence that has been presented at the trial.
*Mr Matthew Thorpe, Q.C. said in his summing up that
there had been errors of judgement and breaches of
official rules.*

summit /sʌmɪt/ **summits**
1 NC A **summit** is a meeting between the leaders of
different countries to discuss important matters.
*Western leaders are gathering for this week's Ottawa
summit... President Mitterrand of France has opened
the Franco-African summit meeting in Morocco.*
2 NC The **summit** of a mountain is the top of it. *The
tape recorder froze just before he reached the summit,
but his diary described the climb up Mount McKinley.*

summon /sʌmən/ **summons, summoning, summoned**
VO If you **summon** someone, you order them to come
to you. *He summoned his secretary... He was
summoned to report on the accident.*

summon up PHRASAL VERB If you **summon up** your
strength or courage, you make a great effort to be
strong or brave. *...if you can't summon up enough
energy to get up early... He eventually summoned up
the courage to ask them if Melanie was all right.*

summons /sʌmənz/ **summonses, summonsing,
summonsed**
1 NC A **summons** is an order to come and see
someone; a formal use. *I waited in my office for a
summons from the boss.*
2 NC A **summons** is also an official order to appear in
court. *The former Prime Minister has received
another summons to appear before a special tribunal
on charges of abusing power.*
3 VO If someone is **summonsed**, they are officially
ordered to appear in court. *Over half the population
of Liverpool are expected to be summonsed if they
don't pay their bills soon.*

sump /sʌmp/ **sumps**
NC The **sump** is the place under an engine which holds
the engine oil. *...costly bills for replacing the sump.*

sumptuous /sʌmptʃuəs/
ADJ Something that is **sumptuous** is luxurious or
magnificent, and obviously expensive. *...sumptuous
furnishings.*

sum total
N SING The **sum total** of a number of things is all the
things added or considered together. *Half of the sum
total of taxes paid by US citizens goes to the
Pentagon... He said he believed that that was the sum
total of American support to any one group in the
election.*

Sun.
Sun. is a written abbreviation for 'Sunday'. ...*Sun. 7 Feb.*

sun /sʌn/ suns, sunning, sunned
1 N SING The **sun** is the ball of fire in the sky that the Earth goes round, and that gives us heat and light. *The sun is shining here in London.*
2 NU or N SING You also refer to the light and heat that reach us from the sun as **sun**. *You need plenty of sun and fresh air... We all sat in the sun.*
3 V-REFL If you **sun** yourself, you sit or lie where the sun shines on you. *He spent Saturday sunning himself on the beach.*

sunbathe /sʌnbeɪθ/ sunbathes, sunbathing, sunbathed
V When people **sunbathe**, they sit or lie in a place where the sun shines on them, in order to get a suntan. *I spent my afternoons sunbathing.*

sunbeam /sʌnbiːm/ sunbeams
NC A **sunbeam** is a ray of light from the sun; a literary word. *Swift created the imaginary island of Laputa, where scientists worked to extract sunbeams from cucumbers.*

Sunbelt /sʌnbelt/
N PROP The southern states of the USA are sometimes referred to as the **Sunbelt**. *The numbers clearly show that Americans are moving to the Sunbelt and the Pacific Coast... Democrats managed to score important victories last year in Texas and Florida, dampening Republican sunbelt dreams.*

sunburn /sʌnbɜːn/
NU If someone has **sunburn**, their skin is red and sore because they have spent too much time in the sun. *A few have suffered sunburn in the unusually good weather the islands are enjoying at the moment.*

sunburnt /sʌnbɜːnt/; also spelt **sunburned**.
1 ADJ Someone who is **sunburnt** has sore red skin because they have spent too much time in the sun. *His neck was badly sunburnt.*
2 ADJ You can also describe someone as **sunburnt** when they have very brown skin because they have spent a lot of time in the sunshine. *Carlo was handsomely sunburned.*

sundae /sʌndeɪ/ sundaes
NC A **sundae** is a dish of ice cream with whipped cream, nuts, and fruit on top. *My mother would take me there for an ice cream sundae after a day of shopping.*

Sunday /sʌndeɪ, sʌndi/ Sundays
NU or NC **Sunday** is the day after Saturday and before Monday. *A meeting on Sunday will consider a new strategy... Some shops in Britain which are open every Sunday are actually operating illegally... There are the usual assortment of stories in the Sunday papers.*

Sunday School, Sunday Schools
NU or NC **Sunday School** is a class organized by a church that some children go to on Sundays in order to learn about Christianity. *He insisted that John go to Sunday School each week... She received the greatest number of stars at her Sunday School.*

sundial /sʌndaɪəl/ sundials
NC A **sundial** is a device used for telling the time. It consists of a pointer which casts a shadow on a flat base which is marked with the hours. *The difference between the time as shown by a sundial and by GMT can amount to a maximum of 16 minutes.*

sundown /sʌndaʊn/
NU **Sundown** is the same as sunset; used in American English. *It was about an hour before sundown.*

sun-drenched
ADJ **Sun-drenched** places have a lot of hot sunny weather. ...*the sun-drenched beaches in the south of France.*

sundry /sʌndri/
1 ADJ If you refer to **sundry** things or people, you mean several things or people of various sorts; a formal use. ...*stools, wicker mats, food bowls, and sundry other objects.*
2 **All and sundry** means everyone; an informal expression. *She was fondly known to all and sundry as 'Little Madge'.*

sunflower /sʌnflaʊə/ sunflowers
NC A **sunflower** is a tall plant with large yellow flowers. Sunflowers are usually grown for their seeds, which are a source of oil and can be eaten. *Cultivated sunflowers and wild sunflowers usually grow in close proximity.* ...*sunflower oil.*

sung /sʌŋ/
Sung is the past participle of sing.

sunglasses /sʌnglɑːsɪz/
N PL **Sunglasses** are spectacles with dark lenses to protect your eyes from bright sunlight. *His eyes are hidden by black sunglasses.*

sunhat /sʌnhæt/ sunhats
NC A **sunhat** is a hat that protects your head from the sun. ...*fifty tourists in shorts and sunhats.*

sunk /sʌŋk/
Sunk is the past participle of sink.

sunken /sʌŋkən/
1 ADJ ATTRIB **Sunken** is used to describe things that have sunk to the bottom of a large expanse of water. ...*the remains of a sunken battleship.*
2 ADJ ATTRIB A **sunken** object or area is built below the level of the surrounding area. ...*a sunken garden.*
3 ADJ **Sunken** cheeks or eyes or a **sunken** chest curve inwards and make a person look thin and unwell. *His cheeks are sunken and his eyes are fixed in a blank stare.*

sun lamp, sun lamps
NC A **sun lamp** is a lamp that produces rays which can make people's skin sun-tanned. *Patients have been lying under sun lamps and listening to the sound of waves.*

sunless /sʌnləs/
ADJ Days or places that are **sunless** have no sunshine. *The street was grim and sunless.*

sunlight /sʌnlaɪt/
NU **Sunlight** is the light that comes from the sun. *The sea sparkled in the brilliant sunlight.*

sunlit /sʌnlɪt/
ADJ **Sunlit** places are brightly lit by the sun. ...*the sunlit slopes of the valley.*

sun lounge, sun lounges
NC A **sun lounge** is a sitting-room with walls that are made mostly of glass, so that a lot of sunlight gets into the room. *A glass sun lounge had been built against the back of the house.*

sunny /sʌni/ sunnier, sunniest
1 ADJ When it is **sunny**, the sun is shining. *The hot sunny weather over much of Britain has brought thousands of people out onto roads to the coast.*
2 ADJ **Sunny** places are brightly lit by the sun. ...*a lovely sunny region of green hills and valleys.*

sun parlor, sun parlors
NC A **sun parlor** is the same as a sun lounge; used in American English.

sunrise /sʌnraɪz/ sunrises
1 NU **Sunrise** is the time in the morning when the sun first appears. *They left their camp at sunrise... The majority of the population get up well after sunrise.*
2 NC A **sunrise** is the colours and light that you see in the sky when the sun first appears. ...*the beautiful sunrise over the sea... She wondered if she would ever see another sunrise.*

sunroof /sʌnruːf/ sunroofs
NC A **sunroof** is a part of the roof in a car which you can open to let sunshine or air in. ...*a sunroof which tilts and slides electrically.*

sunscreen /sʌnskriːn/ sunscreens
N MASS **Sunscreen** is a cream or lotion that you rub into your skin in order to protect it from the harmful effects of the sun's ultraviolet rays. ...*bottles of sunscreen... These compounds essentially act in the way that sunscreens do.*

sunset /sʌnset/ sunsets
1 NU **Sunset** is the time in the evening when the sun disappears. *We'll leave just before sunset.*
2 NC A **sunset** is the colours and light that you see in the sky when the sun disappears in the evening. *You must see some beautiful sunsets here.*

sunshade /sʌnʃeɪd/ sunshades
NC A **sunshade** is a type of umbrella that you use to protect yourself from strong sunshine. *The green lining of Mrs Courtney's sunshade flooded her skin with leafy light.*

sunshine /sʌnʃaɪn/
NU **Sunshine** is the light and heat that comes from the sun. *Families were scattered along the beach enjoying the sunshine... They walked out into the warm sunshine.*

sunstroke /sʌnstrəʊk/
NU **Sunstroke** is an illness caused by spending too much time in the sunshine. *About one hundred people are reported to have died of sunstroke during a heatwave in northern and central India.*

suntan /sʌntæn/ **suntans**
1 NC If you have a **suntan**, the sun has turned your skin darker than usual. *...an almost irresistible temptation to waste hours basking on the lawn, in order to gain that much prized suntan.*
2 ADJ **Suntan** lotions, creams, oils, and so on are used to protect your skin from the sun, and to help you develop a suntan.

sun-tanned /sʌntænd/
ADJ If you are **sun-tanned**, the sun has turned your skin darker than usual. *You look sort of sun-tanned.*

suntrap /sʌntræp/ **suntraps**
NC A **suntrap** is a very sunny, sheltered place. *That corner of the garden is a real suntrap.*

sun-up
NU **Sun-up** is the time in the morning when the sun is rising; used in American English. *I worked sun-up to sundown and sometimes long after.*

sup /sʌp/ **sups, supping, supped**; an old-fashioned word.
1 VO If you **sup** something, you drink it, especially in fairly small sips. *She supped the hot tea Delia had brought her.*
2 V If you **sup**, you eat dinner in the evening. *You must sup with me tonight to celebrate your engagement.*

super /suːpə/
ADJ **Super** means very nice or good; an informal use. *I've got a super secretary.*

super- /suːpə-/
1 PREFIX **Super-** combines with adjectives to form new adjective which express the idea that the quality described is present in an unusually large degree. *The problem is that her fingers and toes are supersensitive to changes in temperature... I'm not super-fit at all.*
2 PREFIX **Super-** combines with nouns to form new nouns that refer to a bigger, more powerful, or more important version of a particular thing. *It means the blurring of national frontiers and the creation of something close to a giant pan-European superstate... It's made of a new super-plastic that is resistant to high temperatures... Supercomputers have been used to develop nuclear weapons and design aircraft.*

superabundant /suːpərəbʌndənt/
ADJ Something that is **superabundant** exists in very large quantities or amounts; a formal word. *This species is famous for its neat foliage and superabundant flowers and fruits.*

superannuated /suːpərænjueɪtɪd/
ADJ Something that is **superannuated** is old and no longer used for its original purpose; a formal word. *We found ourselves aboard a superannuated trawler.*

superannuation /suːpərænjueɪʃn/
NU **Superannuation** is money which people pay regularly into a special fund so that when they retire from their job they will receive a regular pension. *Are you paying superannuation at the moment?... Teachers now have to come under the State Superannuation Scheme.*

superb /suːpɜːb/
ADJ If something is **superb**, it is very good indeed. *The children's library is superb.* ◆ **superbly** ADV *...a small but superbly equipped workshop.*

Super Bowl
N SING In the United States, the **Super Bowl** is the main championship game in American football, which is held in January. *Don't ask me any more about how the Super Bowl is going to come out... He said he'd leave if he won another Super Bowl.*

supercilious /suːpəsɪliəs/
ADJ **Supercilious** people are scornful of other people and think that they are superior to them. *...a slow*

supercilious smile that crossed his face.

superconductivity /suːpəkɒndʌktɪvəti/
NU **Superconductivity** is the property of being a superconductor; a technical term in physics. *There have been reports of materials that showed signs of superconductivity at higher and higher temperatures.*

superconductor /suːpəkəndʌktə/ **superconductors**
NC A **superconductor** is a substance that has no electrical resistance when it is cooled to a very low temperature; a technical term in physics. *So far, superconductors have all needed to be cooled by expensive and rare liquefied helium gas.*

super-ego, super-egos
NC Your **super-ego** is the part of your mind which makes you aware of what is right and wrong, and which causes you to feel guilt when you have done something wrong; a technical term in psychology. *He challenged the idea of woman's lack of a super-ego, her dependence upon the approval of others.*

superficial /suːpəfɪʃl/
1 ADJ Something that is **superficial** involves only the most obvious or easily understood features or aspects of it, even though there may be other, more important aspects that are less obvious. *...a superficial knowledge of linguistics.* ◆ **superficially** ADV SEN or SUBMOD *Superficially it looks rather harmless.*
2 ADJ **Superficial** is also used to describe the first impression that something gives, especially when this does not reflect what it is really like. *The new scheme has superficial similarities with the old one.* ◆ **superficially** ADV SEN or SUBMOD *The British economy, they say, is superficially successful but not sustainable.*
3 ADJ **Superficial** people do not care very deeply about anything serious or important. *This guy is a superficial yuppie with no intellect whatsoever.*
4 ADJ **Superficial** wounds are not very deep or severe. *The injured women have superficial wounds to their legs and feet and are expected to leave hospital in a day or two.*
5 ADJ **Superficial** damage is not very serious or severe. *Buildings in the area had however sustained superficial damage only.*

superficiality /suːpəfɪʃiæləti/
NU **Superficiality** is concern for only the most obvious or general aspects of something. *He exaggerates the superficiality of their current affairs programmes.*

superfluity /suːpəfluːəti/
NU+of If there is a **superfluity** of something, there is more of it than is needed; a formal word. *Do not be misled by the superfluity of allegedly scientific advice.*

superfluous /suːpɜːfluəs/
ADJ Something that is **superfluous** is unnecessary or is no longer needed. *Certain parts of our religion have become superfluous... Maps were superfluous with Eddie around.*

supergrass /suːpəgraːs/ **supergrasses**
NC A **supergrass** is someone, especially a criminal, who gives the police a lot of information about the activities of terrorists or other criminals. *She rounded on Ferris. 'Is he a supergrass?'*

superhighway /suːpəhaɪweɪ/ **superhighways**
NC A **superhighway** is a long dual carriageway on which cars can travel very fast; used in American English. *Here, everything is on an American scale, and there are big superhighways going all over the place.*

superhuman /suːpəhjuːmən/
ADJ If you describe a quality that someone has as **superhuman**, you mean that it is greater than that of ordinary people. *You must have superhuman strength... I controlled myself with a superhuman effort.*

superimpose /suːpərɪmpəʊz/ **superimposes, superimposing, superimposed**
VO If one image is **superimposed** on another, the first one is on top of the second. *Three photos were superimposed one on top of the other.*

superintend /suːpərɪntend/ **superintends, superintending, superintended**
VO If you **superintend** something or someone, you are

responsible for particular items or equipment or for
ensuring that a person does something correctly; a
formal word. *The children were dressing in the lobby,
superintended by Mrs Moffatt.*

superintendent /suːpəʳrɪntendənt/ **superintendents**
1 N C or TITLE A **superintendent** in the police force is an
officer above the rank of inspector. *...a former police
superintendent... Superintendent Gordon Clarke of
Humberside police predicts there could be more
problems.*
2 N C A **superintendent** is a person who is officially
responsible for a particular thing or department.
*Bahrain's Superintendent of Archaeology said that
foreign digging teams were very welcome.*

superior /suːpɪərɪə/ **superiors**
1 ADJ To be **superior** to something or someone means
to be better than them. *I secretly feel superior to
him... The school prided itself upon its policy of
providing a superior education.*
2 ADJ A person in an organization who is **superior** to
someone else has more authority than them. *These
matters are better left to someone superior to you.*
▶ Also N C *He was called to the office of a superior to
be reprimanded.*
3 ADJ Someone who is **superior** behaves in a way
which shows that they believe they are better than
other people. *'You wouldn't understand,' Clarissa said
in a superior way.*
4 See also **mother superior**.

superiority /suːpɪərɪɒrəti/
1 NU+SUPP The **superiority** of someone or something is
the fact that they are better than other people or
things. *...the great superiority of Hoyland over
younger abstract painters... China's official media
have published editorials describing the two week
event as proof of the superiority of socialism.*
2 NU+SUPP If a country has military **superiority**, it has
more advanced weapons or more troops than other
countries. *The West says Moscow has for years lied
about its massive conventional superiority... For many
years NATO has claimed that the Warsaw Pact has a
huge superiority in both tanks and men.*

superlative /suːpɜːlətɪv/ **superlatives**
1 N C In grammar, a **superlative** is the form of an
adjective which indicates that the person or object
being described has more of a particular quality or
character than anyone or anything else. Superlatives
often end in '-est'. *The papers use many superlatives
in their tributes to Leonard Bernstein, following his
death in New York at the age of seventy-two.*
2 ADJ If someone describes a performance or
achievement as **superlative**, they mean that it is
absolutely excellent. *...the superlative form of Steffi
Graf—one of the most outstanding players to emerge
for some years.*

superman /suːpəmæn/ **supermen**
N C A **superman** is a man who has extraordinarily
great physical or mental powers. *To succeed in that
task you need to be a superman.*

supermarket /suːpəmaːkɪt/ **supermarkets**
N C A **supermarket** is a large shop selling all kinds of
food and household goods. You select the food and
goods yourself and pay for them before leaving.
*Supermarkets are running low on supplies of fruit and
vegetables... How do corner shops survive in the face
of competition from the large supermarket chains?*

supernatural /suːpənætʃəʳrəl/
1 ADJ **Supernatural** creatures, forces, and events are
believed by some people to exist or happen, although
they are impossible according to scientific laws.
*...witchcraft, the supernatural power to cure or
control.*
2 N SING Supernatural things and events are referred
to as the **supernatural**. *Do you believe in the
supernatural?*

supernova /suːpənəʊvə/ **supernovae** /suːpənəʊviː/ or
supernovas
N C A **supernova** is a star that has exploded because it
has used up its nuclear fuel, and which becomes up to
a hundred million times brighter than the sun for a
few days. *It is the first supernova seen with the naked
eye for nearly 400 years.*

superordinate /suːpərɔːdəʳnət/ **superordinates**
N C A **superordinate** is a word which is related in
meaning to another word, but has a more general
meaning. For example, the word 'person' is a
superordinate of the words 'man' and 'woman'.

superpower /suːpəpaʊə/ **superpowers**
N C A **superpower** is a very powerful and influential
country that usually has nuclear weapons and is
economically successful. *Japan's position as the
regional economic superpower is not under threat...
Europe does not appear to be ready to join the ranks
of the superpowers... After that we should know the
fate of next month's superpower summit in Moscow.*

supersede /suːpəsiːd/ **supersedes, superseding,
superseded**
V O If one thing **supersedes** another thing that is older,
it replaces it because it is better or more efficient.
*Steam locomotives were superseded by diesel... New
ways of thinking superseded older ones.*

supersonic /suːpəsɒnɪk/
ADJ **Supersonic** aircraft travel faster than the speed of
sound. *Mr Lawson flew in and out on the supersonic
jet Concorde.*

superstar /suːpəstaː/ **superstars**
N C A **superstar** is a very famous entertainer or sports
player; an informal word. *The press built me up into
a superstar.*

superstition /suːpəstɪʃn/ **superstitions**
N U or N C **Superstition** is belief in things that are not
real or possible, for example magic. *They were
peasants filled with ignorance and superstition. ...old
prejudices and superstitions.*

superstitious /suːpəstɪʃəs/
ADJ People who are **superstitious** believe in things that
are not real or possible, for example magic. *...a
superstitious man with an unnatural fear of the dark.*

superstructure /suːpəstrʌktʃə/ **superstructures**
1 N C The **superstructure** of a building is the part that
is above the floor or above the foundations. *...a
drastic redesign of the superstructure over the stage.*
2 N C The **superstructure** of a ship is the part that is
above the main deck. *It suffered cracks in the
superstructure after hitting a mine yesterday... She
had ice accumulation in her rigging and
superstructure.*

supertanker /suːpətæŋkə/ **supertankers**
N C A **supertanker** is an extremely large ship that is
used for transporting oil. *The oil slick was caused by
the supertanker breaking up during a severe storm.*

supervise /suːpəvaɪz/ **supervises, supervising,
supervised**
V O If you **supervise** a person or the activity they are
doing, you make sure that they do it properly or that
they behave properly. *One evening, when there were
no staff to supervise her, she walked out of the
hospital... Miss Young had three netball games to
supervise.*

supervision /suːpəvɪʒn/
N U **Supervision** is the act of supervising people,
activities, or places to make sure that things are done
properly. *She'll be working under the supervision of
qualified social workers... That would mean immediate
supervision of the withdrawal.*

supervisor /suːpəvaɪzə/ **supervisors**
N C A **supervisor** is a person who supervises workers
or students. *The maintenance supervisor dispatched a
crew to repair the damage.*

supervisory /suːpəvaɪzəri/
ADJ ATTRIB **Supervisory** means concerned with the
supervision of people, activities, or places.
*Supervisory control was carried out by officials.
...supervisory staff.*

supine /suːpaɪn/
1 ADJ or ADV If you are **supine**, you are lying flat on
your back; a literary use. *She was relaxing, supine,
on the beach... His supine body was dragged out... He
lay supine on the bunk, watching, while Sally
undressed.*
2 ADJ You also use **supine** to describe someone who
just lets events happen, because they are too lazy or
afraid to try to influence them; a formal use. *The
newspaper says that this will depend on the Cabinet*

itself playing a less supine role than it has up to now.

supper /sʌpə/ **suppers**

NUorNC **Supper** is a meal eaten in the early part of the evening or one eaten just before you go to bed at night. *He insisted on staying for supper. ...tea, talks and a working supper.*

supplant /səplɑːnt/ **supplants, supplanting, supplanted**

VO To **supplant** something or someone means to take their place; a formal word. *Electric cars may one day supplant petrol-driven ones... He began his campaign to supplant Gaitskell as party leader.*

supple /sʌpl/

1 ADJ A **supple** person moves and bends easily and gracefully. *She had once been slim and supple.*

2 ADJ If an object or material is **supple**, it is soft and bends easily without cracking or breaking. *The leather straps were supple with use.*

supplement /sʌplɪmənt/ **supplements, supplementing, supplemented**

1 VO If you **supplement** something, you add something to it, usually in order to make it adequate. *They had to get a job to supplement the family income... I supplemented my diet with vitamin pills.*

2 NC A **supplement** is something that you add to something else, usually in order improve it or make it adequate. *The system of Family Income Support, which added a weekly supplement to the earnings of families, is being renamed Family Credit... They will sometimes eat fish as a supplement to their natural diet. ...vitamin and mineral supplements.*

3 NC A newspaper **supplement** is a separate, additional magazine that is sold with the newspaper. *The 'Financial Times' carries a six-page supplement on Yugoslavia.*

supplemental /sʌplɪmentl/

ADJ ATTRIB **Supplemental** means the same as **supplementary**; used in American English. *Nutritional counseling and supplemental food for pregnant women help prevent health problems... A supplemental spending request will be sent to Congress later this year.*

supplementary /sʌplɪmentəºri/

ADJ ATTRIB **Supplementary** is used to describe something that is added to another thing, usually in order to improve it or make it adequate. *You can claim a supplementary pension... The commissioner promised supplementary proposals next month.*

supplementary benefit

NU In Britain, **supplementary benefit** was an amount of money that people with a very low income or no income at all used to be able to claim from the government. It was replaced by income support. *They asked if I was on supplementary benefit.*

supplicant /sʌplɪkənt/ **supplicants**

NC A **supplicant** is a person who humbly asks God or an important person to help them or to give them something that they want very much; a formal word. *I come as a supplicant begging a favour.*

supplier /səplaɪə/ **suppliers**

NC A **supplier** is a person, company, or country that provides you with goods or equipment. *China is now a major international arms supplier. ...textile suppliers.*

supply /səplaɪ/ **supplies, supplying, supplied**

1 VO If you **supply** someone with something, you provide them with it, by giving or selling it to them. *I can supply you with food and drink... Germany is supplying the steel for the new pipeline... Washington and Moscow have undertaken to stop supplying arms to either side.*

2 NU **Supply** of something is the act or process of providing someone with it. *The electricity supply was also disrupted... Soviet and Afghan forces have been trying to re-open the main supply route linking the Soviet Union to Kabul.*

3 NU **Supply** is also the amount of a commodity that can be produced and made available for people to buy. *Economic stability can only be reached if supply and demand are balanced.*

4 NC A **supply** of something is an amount of it which someone has or which is available for them to use. *Bill had his own supply of whisky... Most houses now have lavatories and a hot water supply... The government will maintain tight control over the money supply.*

5 N PL **Supplies** are food, equipment, and other things needed by a group of people, for example by an army or people going on an expedition. *The plane had been ferrying military supplies over the border... Residents are boarding up their homes and stocking up on emergency supplies.*

6 If something is **in short supply**, there is very little of it available. *Food and water are now in short supply.*

supply-side

ADJ ATTRIB **Supply-side** economics is the economic theory that if taxation is reduced, the money that people and businesses save will be reinvested into industry, rather than being spent on consumer goods and services. *The deficit currently is precisely the result of supply-side economics in the first place... More than half the benefit of this supply-side tax break would go to households with high incomes.*

supply teacher, supply teachers

NC A **supply teacher** is a teacher who takes the place of other teachers at different schools when they are absent. *She worked as a supply teacher after the birth of her son.*

support /səpɔːt/ **supports, supporting, supported**

1 VO If you **support** someone or their aims, you agree with them and try to help them to succeed. *A lot of building workers supported the campaign... His work colleagues refused to support him... They fully support any move to toughen the government's stance.* ● If you do something **in support of** something that someone is trying to achieve, you do it in order to help them achieve it. *...the Navy's capacity to act in support of their political objectives.*

2 NU If you give someone your **support**, you agree with them or with their aims and try to help them. *The party declared its support for the campaign... The King has been seeking support in Europe for his plan... The bill had widespread support from MPs of all parties.*

3 NU If you give **support** to someone during a difficult time, you are kind to them and help them. *They find it hard to give their children emotional support.*

4 VO If something **supports** an object, it is underneath it and is holding it up. *...the steel girders that supported the walkway.*

5 NC A **support** is an object that holds something else up. *Most large scale buildings now have steel supports.*

6 V-REFL If you **support** yourself, you prevent yourself from falling by holding onto something. *I clung to the outside edge of the door to support myself.* ▶ Also NU *She was standing behind the ladder and holding on to it for support.*

7 NU Financial **support** is money that is provided to enable a person to live, or a firm or organization to continue. *The Kuwaiti government has also pledged financial support... These industries were dependent on state support. ...students dependent on parental support.*

8 VO If you **support** someone, you provide them with money or the things that they need. *He has a wife and three children to support.*

9 VO If you **support** a sports team, you go regularly to their games and encourage them to win, for example by cheering them. *...an entreaty to 'support your team in their hour of need'.*

10 VO If a fact **supports** a statement or a theory, it helps to show that it is true or correct. *There was simply no visible evidence to support such a theory.* ▶ Also NU *Scholars have found little support for this interpretation.*

11 See also **income support**.

supporter /səpɔːtə/ **supporters**

NC+SUPP A **supporter** is someone who supports someone or something, for example, a political leader or party, or a sports team. *The Minister's supporters did not desert him in his hour of need... He is known as a staunch supporter of reform. ...an Everton supporter.*

supportive /səpɔ:tɪv/
1 ADJ If you are **supportive**, you are kind and helpful to someone at a difficult time. *She doesn't know how she would have handled things if her employer hadn't been as supportive.*
2 ADJ If you are **supportive** of someone or of their aims, you agree with them and try to help them. *They are in general much more supportive of President Arias and the peace plan... He said he would be supportive of a greater dialogue with the Soviet Union.*

suppose /səpəʊz/ **supposes, supposing, supposed**
1 V-REPORT or VO If you **suppose** that something is true, you think that it is likely to be true. *He supposed that MPs were unaware of the danger... They'd supposed it to be sabotage... The situation was even worse than was supposed.*
2 CONJ You use **suppose** or **supposing** when you are considering a possible situation or action and trying to think what effects it would have. *Suppose we don't say a word, and somebody else finds out about it?... Supposing something should go wrong, what would you do then?*
3 You say I **suppose** to show that you are not certain or enthusiastic about something. *I suppose he wasn't trying hard enough... I don't suppose you would be prepared to stay in Edinburgh?... 'So it was worth doing?'—'I suppose so.'*

supposed; pronounced /səpəʊzɪd/ for the meaning in paragraph 1 and /səpəʊst/ or /səpəʊzd/ for the meanings in paragraphs 2 to 4.
1 ADJ ATTRIB You use **supposed** to express doubt about a way of describing someone or something that is generally believed. *...his supposed ancestor, the pirate Henry Morgan. ...the supposed benefits of a progressive welfare state.* ◆ **supposedly** ADV *...a robot supposedly capable of understanding spoken commands.*
2 ADJ PRED+to-INF If something is **supposed** to be done, it should be done because of a rule, instruction, or custom. *You are supposed to report it to the police as soon as possible... I'm not supposed to talk to you about this.*
3 ADJ PRED+to-INF If something is **supposed** to happen, it is planned or intended to happen, but often does not. *I was supposed to go last summer... A machine at the entrance is supposed to check the tickets.*
4 ADJ PRED+to-INF If something is **supposed** to be true, people generally think that it is true. *They are supposed to be the best in London... The hill was supposed to be haunted by a ghost.*

supposition /sʌpəzɪʃn/ **suppositions**
NC A **supposition** is an idea or statement which is thought or assumed to be true; a formal word. *The supposition is that the infiltrators knew the raids were to take place.*

suppress /səpres/ **suppresses, suppressing, suppressed**
1 VO If an army or government **suppresses** an activity, they prevent it from continuing. *The army soon suppressed the revolt.* ◆ **suppression** /səpreʃn/ NU *...the suppression of freedom.*
2 VO If someone **suppresses** a piece of information, they prevent it from becoming known. *The committee's report has been suppressed.* ◆ **suppression** NU *...the deliberate suppression of information.*
3 VO If you **suppress** your feelings, you prevent yourself from expressing them. *Suppressing her annoyance, she smiled at him... She was struggling to suppress her sobs.* ◆ **suppression** NU *...the polite suppression of a yawn.*

supremacist /su:preməsɪst/ **supremacists**
N+N or NC **Supremacist** organizations and ideas promote the belief that one group of people should be more powerful and have more influence than other groups. *The Klu Klux Klan, the white supremacist organization, plans a demonstration here. ...the growing body of right-wing white supremacists.*

supremacy /su:preməsi/
NU If one group of people has **supremacy** over another group, they are more powerful than the second group. *Their political supremacy continued.*

supreme /su:pri:m/
1 ADJ ATTRIB **Supreme** is used in a title to indicate that a person or group is at the highest level of an organization. *The Supreme Commander ordered their release. ...the Supreme Court.*
2 ADJ You also use **supreme** to emphasize the greatness of something. *...one of this century's supreme achievements. ...tasks of supreme importance. ...an act of supreme heroism.* ◆ **supremely** SUBMOD *...a supremely important moment.*

supremo /su:pri:məʊ/ **supremos**
NC+SUPP A **supremo** is someone who is considered to have the most authority or skill in a particular organization, situation, or area of activity. *He accused the South African rugby supremo, Dr Darney Craven, of taking part. ...Ted Dexter, the cricketing supremo.*

Supt
Supt is a written abbreviation for 'superintendent' when it is part of someone's title in the police force. *...Chief Supt Walker of Scotland Yard.*

surcharge /sɜ:tʃɑ:dʒ/ **surcharges**
NC A **surcharge** is an extra amount of money in addition to the usual payment for something. It is imposed for a specific reason, for example by a company because costs have risen or by a government as a tax. *West Germany's Lufthansa has added surcharges starting at $41... The Government is imposing a 15% import surcharge.*

sure /ʃɔ:, ʃʊə/ **surer, surest**
1 ADJ PRED If you are **sure** that something is true, you are certain that it is true and have no doubts about it. *I'm sure she's right... I'm not quite sure but I think it's half past five... The only thing we're sure about is that it's a boy.*
2 ADJ PRED If you are **sure** about your feelings or wishes, you know exactly what you feel or what you want to do. *Are you sure you won't have another drink?... Jane wasn't sure how she felt about being married.*
3 ADJ PRED+of If you are **sure** of yourself, you are very confident about your abilities or opinions. *You normally get that with younger directors—ones that are not so sure of themselves.*
4 ADJ PRED+of If someone is **sure** of getting something, they are certain to get it. *We can be sure of success... You could not always be sure of winning.*
5 ADJ PRED+to-INF If something is **sure** to happen, it will certainly happen. *He was sure to see her again... We're sure to get a place.*
6 ADJ **Sure** is used to describe something such as a method or sign which is reliable or accurate. *All this is a sure way of increasing the cost of electricity... Wood dust beneath a piece of furniture is a sure sign of woodworm... She had a sure grasp of the subject.*
7 **Sure** is an informal way of saying 'yes'. *'Can I go with you?'—'Sure.'*
8 ADV You can also use **sure** to emphasize what you are saying; used in informal American English. *He sure is cute... You sure do have an interesting job.*
● **Sure** is used in these phrases. ● If you **make sure** about something, you check it or take action to see that it is done. *He glanced over his shoulder to make sure that nobody was listening... The enquiry was supposed to recommend actions to make sure such an accident did not happen again.* ● If you say that something is **for sure** or that you know it **for sure**, you mean that it is definitely true or will definitely happen; an informal expression. *One thing was for sure, there was nothing wrong with Allen's eyesight... He told me he knew for sure that a large sum of money had been handed over.* ● You say **sure enough** to confirm that something is really true. *'The baby's crying,' she said. Sure enough, a yelling noise was coming from upstairs.*

sure-fire
ADJ ATTRIB **Sure-fire** means certain to succeed or win; an informal word. *There are no sure-fire techniques for guaranteeing equal representation. ...sure-fire winners.*

sure-footed
ADJ A **sure-footed** person or animal can move easily

over steep or uneven ground without falling. *You had to be sure-footed and ready to make a fast getaway.*

surely /ʃɔːli, ʃuəli/
1 ADV SEN You use **surely** to emphasize that you think something is true, and often to express surprise that other people do not agree. *He surely knew the danger... She was surely one of the rarest women of our time... You don't mind that surely?*
2 In American English, you use **surely** when you are agreeing with what someone has said or suggested. *'It's only a matter of weeks.'—'Surely, yes, I agree entirely with that.'... 'I'd like you to read that if you could.'—'Surely.'*
3 If something is happening **slowly but surely**, it is happening gradually and cannot be stopped. *Slowly but surely we're becoming a computer-centred society.*

surety /ʃɔːrəti, ʃuərəti/ **sureties**
1 NCorNU A **surety** is a person who accepts responsibility for another person's debt or for their behaviour. *There are some parents who are not prepared to act as sureties for the future good behaviour of their children... He agreed to stand surety for Mr Scott.*
2 NCorNU A **surety** is also something valuable which you give to someone to show that you will do what you have promised. *He has been ordered by a court to pay a surety of nine hundred thousand dollars before he is granted bail... He gave me a gold watch as surety.*

surf /sɜːf/
NU The **surf** is the mass of white foam formed by waves as they fall on the shore. *We watched the children play in the surf.*

surface /sɜːfɪs/ **surfaces, surfacing, surfaced**
1 NC The **surface** of something is the top part of it or the outside of it. *A gentle breeze rippled the surface of the sea. ...holes in the road surface... Seventy per cent of the earth's surface is water.*
2 NC The **surface** of a situation is what can be seen easily rather than what is not immediately obvious. *His job was not as enviable as it appeared on the surface... This dispute first came to the surface in 1962... You don't have to look far to encounter the tensions beneath the surface.*
3 V If someone or something under water **surfaces**, they come up to the surface of the water. *Bobby surfaced twenty feet in front of the boat.*
4 V When a piece of news or information **surfaces**, it becomes known and people start talking about it. *A row is surfacing in the Soviet Union about who should control the Russian state bank... The issue has surfaced again this week.*
5 to **scratch the surface**: see **surface**.

surface-to-air
ADJ ATTRIB **Surface-to-air** missiles are fired from the ground or sea at aircraft or at other missiles, rather than at targets that are on the ground or in the sea. *They have said nothing about who may have fired the surface-to-air missile that brought down the plane.*

surface-to-surface
ADJ ATTRIB **Surface-to-surface** missiles are fired from the ground or sea at targets that are on the ground or in the sea. *...the proliferation of long-range surface-to-surface missiles.*

surfboard /sɜːfbɔːd/ **surfboards**
NC A **surfboard** is a long narrow board that is used in surfing. *The shark took a bite about twelve inches wide out of his surfboard and knocked him into the water.*

surfeit /sɜːfɪt/
N SING If there is a **surfeit** of something, there is too much of it; a formal word. *Recently there has been a surfeit of cricket on the television.*

surfing /sɜːfɪŋ/
NU **Surfing** is the sport or activity of riding on top of a big wave while standing or lying on a special board. *They want less pressure and a life of sunshine, surfing and barbecues all day.*

surge /sɜːdʒ/ **surges, surging, surged**
1 NC A **surge** in something is a sudden great increase in it. *...a surge in sales of Waugh's novels... A surge of activity spread through the party... Bank lending*

may well show another surge as companies borrow to pay their tax bills.
2 VA If people or vehicles **surge** somewhere, they move forward suddenly in a mass. *The crowd then surged forward and surrounded him... When the doors were flung open, a crowd surged in.* ◆ **surging** ADJ ATTRIB *...surging crowds of demonstrators.*
3 V If water **surges**, it moves forward suddenly and powerfully. *...the tides surging over the rocks.* ▶ Also NC+SUPP *A second surge of floodwater is expected later this week.*
4 V If prices, votes, or sales **surge**, they suddenly increase by a very large amount. *Share prices on the Tokyo stock exchange have surged to a new record... Japanese stock surged while the US dollar lost ground today in Tokyo trading... The Freedom Party's electoral support surged from just under 10 per cent to nearly 17 per cent.*
5 VA If a participant in a contest **surges** ahead, they quickly move into a leading position. *The home team surged ahead after 7 minutes with a goal by Dean Saunders... Lopez surged into the lead... Labour has surged ahead to a lead of nineteen points.*
6 VA If an emotion or sensation **surges** in you, you feel it suddenly and powerfully; a literary use. *Hope surged in Peter... Relief surged through him.* ▶ Also N SING+of *She felt a surge of affection for him. ...a surge of jealousy.*

surgeon /sɜːdʒən/ **surgeons**
NC A **surgeon** is a doctor who performs surgery. *...a brain surgeon.*

surgery /sɜːdʒəri/ **surgeries**
1 NU **Surgery** is medical treatment which involves cutting open a person's body in order to repair or remove a diseased or damaged part. *He has had major abdominal surgery... He has been undergoing surgery on a head wound.*
2 NC A **surgery** is the room or house where a doctor or dentist works. *I went to the surgery to let him tell me about a new tooth-filling material.*
3 NUorNC A doctor's **surgery** is also the period of time each day when he or she sees patients at the surgery. *I'll be in for morning surgery at ten... Waiting lists were transferred from hospitals to doctor's surgeries.*
4 See also **plastic surgery**.

surgical /sɜːdʒɪkl/
1 ADJ ATTRIB **Surgical** means relating to surgery. *...surgical instruments... Some people can have their vision restored by a surgical operation.* ◆ **surgically** ADV *The cataract can then be removed surgically.*
2 ADJ **Surgical** military actions are designed to attack or destroy a particular target, without harming other people or damaging other buildings nearby. *...quick, short, surgical strikes... I don't think there is such a thing as surgical bombing... Anyone pretending the military strikes were surgical had to admit now that civilian neighbourhoods were being destroyed.*

Suriname /suːrɪnɑːmə/
The **Republic of Suriname** is a country in northern South America. It was a Dutch colony, known as Dutch Guiana, from the 17th century until independence in 1975. Lieutenant-Colonel Désiré Bouterse came to power in a coup in 1980 and imposed martial law. He remains Commander-in-Chief of the armed forces. In 1991 Ronald Venetiaan, of the New Front for Democracy and Development (NF), was elected President. Since 1986 the Surinamese Liberation Army (SLA) and other guerrilla groups have fought the government, seriously disrupting the economy. Suriname is a member of the Organization of American States. It exports bauxite, aluminium, and rice. ◆ **Surinamese** /suərɪnəmiːz/ N, ADJ
▪ *per capita GNP:* US$3,020 ▪ *religion:* Christianity, Hinduism, Islam ▪ *language:* Dutch (official), Hindustani, Javanese, Sranang Tongo ▪ *currency:* gulden ▪ *capital:* Paramaribo ▪ *population:* 436,000 (1989) ▪ *size:* 163,265 square kilometres.

surly /sɜːli/
ADJ A **surly** person is rude and bad-tempered. *His voice was surly.*

surmise /səmaɪz/ **surmises, surmising, surmised**
V-REPORT or VO If you **surmise** that something is true,

you guess that it is true, although it may not be; a formal word. *They have surmised that Iranian forces in Fao had been substantially scaled down in the months preceding the attack... The last question, Turing surmised, was the key one... The reason for their hesitation can only be surmised.*

surmount /səˈmaʊnt/ **surmounts, surmounting, surmounted**
1 VO If you **surmount** a difficulty, you deal successfully with it. *She managed to surmount this obstacle.*
2 VO If something **is surmounted** by a particular thing, that thing is on top of it; a formal use. *The column is surmounted by a statue.*

surname /ˈsɜːneɪm/ **surnames**
NC Your **surname** is the name that you share with other members of your family. *'What's your surname?'—'Barker.'*

surpass /səˈpɑːs/ **surpasses, surpassing, surpassed**
1 VO To **surpass** someone or something means to be better than them or to have more of a particular quality than them; a formal word. *The women were able to equal or surpass the men who worked beside them... In my opinion the jewel is surpassed in beauty by the other ornaments.*
2 VO If something **surpasses** expectations or understanding, it goes beyond the limit of what could have been expected or what could have been understood. *His performance surpassed all expectations... Your behaviour surpasses all understanding.*

surplice /ˈsɜːplɪs/ **surplices**
NC A **surplice** is a loose white knee-length garment which is worn over a long robe by priests and members of the choir in some churches. *...the choirboy in a frilled surplice.*

surplus /ˈsɜːpləs/ **surpluses**
1 NCorNU If there is a **surplus** of something, there is more than is needed. *In this continent there is a vast surplus of workers... There is actually a food surplus in the north of Sudan. ...a time of overall labour surplus.*
2 ADJ **Surplus** is used to describe something which is extra or more than is needed. *They will have surplus meat and milk to sell... He has now succeeded in stopping surplus production.*
3 NC If a country has a trade **surplus**, its exports exceed its imports. *Japan announced today that its trade surplus grew by 24 per cent last month... The latest overall balance of payment figures show a surplus of more than two hundred and sixty million dollars.*
4 NC If a government has a budget **surplus**, it has spent less than it has received in revenues. *The government says the only reason for raising taxes is to cover a budget deficit, but at present there's a huge surplus.*

surprise /səˈpraɪz/ **surprises, surprising, surprised**
1 NC A **surprise** is an unexpected event. *This ruling came as a surprise to everyone... 'Why don't you tell me?'—'Because I want it to be a surprise.'... The decision came as no surprise to them.*
2 NU **Surprise** is the feeling that you have when something unexpected happens. *Boylan looked at her in surprise... To my surprise, he nodded and agreed... Officials have expressed surprise at the timing of the remarks.*
3 ADJ ATTRIB You use **surprise** to describe something that happens suddenly or unexpectedly. *The air force launched a surprise attack on the village... Correspondents say the surprise announcement could cause an uproar in the United States... British Golfer Derrick Cooper is the surprise winner of the Madrid Open.*
4 VO If something **surprises** you, you did not expect it. *I surprised everyone by gobbling an enormous lunch... It would not surprise me if he ends up in jail.*
5 VO If you **surprise** someone, you attack them or find them when they are not expecting it. *They were surprised by a unit of US marines during the night... She feared her parents would return and surprise them.*

surprised /səˈpraɪzd/
ADJ If you are **surprised** by something, you have a feeling of surprise, because it is unexpected or unusual. *The twins were very surprised to see Ralph... I was surprised at the number of bicycles.*

surprising /səˈpraɪzɪŋ/
ADJ Something that is **surprising** is unexpected or unusual and makes you feel surprised. *He leapt out of the car with surprising agility... It was surprising how much money she managed to earn.* ◆ **surprisingly** SUBMOD or ADV SEN *It was surprisingly cheap... Not surprisingly the proposal met with hostile reactions.*

surreal /səˈrɪəl/
ADJ If you describe a situation as **surreal**, you mean that events in it combine in a strange, dreamlike way. *The scenes were surreal: while riot police chased demonstrators through the square, thousands of Berliners continued to celebrate.*

surrealism /səˈrɪəlɪzəm/
NU **Surrealism** is a style in art and literature in which ideas, images, or objects are combined in a strange, dreamlike way. *His early work was influenced by the European surrealism of the 1930's.*

surrealist /səˈrɪəlɪst/ **surrealists**
1 ADJ ATTRIB **Surrealist** means related to or in the style of surrealism. *Dali was celebrated both for his surrealist works and his eccentric personality.*
2 NC A **surrealist** is an artist or writer whose work is based on the ideas of surrealism. *In his early days he was very heavily influenced by the Surrealists.*

surrealistic /səˈrɪəlɪstɪk/
1 ADJ **Surrealistic** means the same as **surreal**. *The search had a kind of mad, surrealistic quality.*
2 ADJ **Surrealistic** also means related to or in the style of surrealism. *'Cruel Garden' is a surrealistic vision of the life and work of Federico Garcia Lorca.*

surrender /səˈrendə/ **surrenders, surrendering, surrendered**
1 V If you **surrender**, you stop fighting or resisting someone and agree that you have been beaten. *All the British forces surrendered... The protesters surrendered to the police after about an hour.* ► Also NU *They tried to starve us into surrender... The only truce possible at this stage would be the unconditional surrender of the rebels.*
2 V If you **surrender** to a force, temptation, or feeling, you allow it to gain control over you. *...surrendering to a sense of apathy.*
3 VO If you **surrender** something, you let someone else have it. *The United States would never surrender this territory... He is a determined man who will not surrender power easily.* ► Also NU *...the surrender of liberties.*

surreptitious /ˌsʌrəpˈtɪʃəs/
ADJ A **surreptitious** action is done secretly. *He began paying surreptitious visits to betting shops.* ◆ **surreptitiously** ADV *Rudolph looked surreptitiously at his watch.*

surrogacy /ˈsʌrəgəsi/
NU **Surrogacy** is an arrangement by which a woman gives birth to a baby on behalf of a woman who cannot have babies herself because she is infertile. *Another area of debate is the question of surrogacy.*

surrogate /ˈsʌrəgət/ **surrogates**
ADJ ATTRIB You use **surrogate** to describe a person or thing that acts as a substitute for someone or something else; a formal word. *For many black candidates, he's been a surrogate speaker... Uncle Paul has become a surrogate father to me.* ► Also NC *The island is of great value as a surrogate for Soviet operations in Central America.*

surrogate mother, surrogate mothers
NC A **surrogate mother** is a woman who has agreed to give birth to a baby on behalf of another woman. *She was paid ten thousand dollars to act as a surrogate mother... His surrogate mother now wants custody.*

surround /səˈraʊnd/ **surrounds, surrounding, surrounded**
1 VO If one thing **surrounds** another, it is situated all round it. *Muscles surround blood vessels in the body... The house was surrounded by high walls... Each piece of stained glass is held together by lead.*

2 vo If people **surround** a person or place, they position themselves all the way round them. *In the main shopping centre officers surrounded a group of around three hundred youths... The troops landed by helicopter, but they were quickly surrounded... Troops have surrounded the embassies and cut off all their supplies.*
3 vo If problems or dangers **surround** something, there are problems or dangers associated with it. *...the dangers which surround us. ...the uncertainty surrounding the future of the railways.*
4 v-REFL+*with* If you **surround** yourself with things, you make sure that you have a lot of them near you all the time. *Get involved in social activities and surround yourself with friends.*

surrounding /sərau̯ndɪŋ/ **surroundings**
1 ADJ ATTRIB You use **surrounding** to describe the area which is all around a particular place. *Foxes started coming in from the surrounding countryside. ...the roofs of the surrounding buildings.*
2 N PL You can refer to the place where you live or where you are as your **surroundings**. *We used to live in nice surroundings.*

surtax /sɜːtæks/
NU **Surtax** is an additional tax on incomes higher than a particular level. *One demand during the debate was for a surtax on millionaires.*

surveillance /səveɪləns/
NU **Surveillance** is the careful watching of someone, especially by the police or army; a formal word. *Armed police officers maintained a round-the-clock surveillance of the yacht... They kept the chief under surveillance until February 25th this year. ...surveillance aircraft.*

survey, surveys, surveying, surveyed; pronounced /səveɪ/ when it is a verb and /sɜːveɪ/ when it is a noun.
1 vo If you **survey** something, you look carefully at the whole of it; a formal use. *She stepped back and surveyed her work... The news agency did not report Mr Bendjedid's reactions as he surveyed the damage... A group of astronomers were surveying the sky with a radio telescope.*
2 vo To **survey** a building or piece of land means to examine it carefully in order to make a report or a plan of its structure and features. *Professor Carver has been surveying and excavating the ancient cemetery... The border line was never properly surveyed at the time when the maps were drawn.*
3 vo To **survey** a group of people means to ask them for their opinions on a particular topic. *The majority of teenagers surveyed expected to see more political terrorism in Britain... The organization surveyed families in Suffolk County, New York, as part of a national study.*
4 NC A **survey** is a detailed investigation of something, for example people's behaviour or opinions. *...a national survey of eye diseases among children... These findings contrast with those in a survey carried out by the environmental group Greenpeace.*
5 NC A **survey** is also an examination of an area of land or a house by a qualified surveyor in order to report on its condition and features. *By doing a survey around the area, we see what different water masses there are... The house-buyer had to pay for a structural survey of his new home.*

surveyor /səveɪə/ **surveyors**
NC A **surveyor** is a person whose job is to survey houses or land. *The new owner, a land surveyor from Oxfordshire, has inherited the village from his great aunt. ...the Royal Institute of Chartered Surveyors.*

survival /səvaɪvl/ **survivals**
1 NU **Survival** is the fact of continuing to live or exist in spite of great danger or difficulty. *A posthumous medal was awarded to Mr Skippern who gave up his chance of survival to help others... The most basic human instinct, after survival, is the raising and nurturing of children... Over the years, Mr Kadar has perfected the art of political survival... Many East Germans are too concerned with economic survival to celebrate.*
2 NC+SUPP Something that is a **survival** from an earlier time has continued to exist from that time; a

formal use. *The royal house is full of survivals from many centuries... The rotary press was a survival of the industrial 19th century.*

survival kit, survival kits
NC A **survival kit** is a pack of objects that you need in order to stay alive if you get hurt or lost in a dangerous place out of doors. *There was a survival kit for dropping into disaster areas.*

survive /səvaɪv/ **survives, surviving, survived**
1 Vorvo If someone **survives**, they continue to live or exist in spite of great danger or difficulty. *Four of his brothers died: the fifth survived... Most people are surviving by eating roots and berries... Very few people survived the immediate effects of the explosion... The doctors studied the sleep patterns of a man who had survived a heart attack.*
2 vo If you **survive** someone, you continue to live after they have died. *She will probably survive me by many years... He is survived by his brother Maichito, the leader of the conservative faction.* ♦ **surviving** ADJ ATTRIB *His sole surviving cat, Blackie, is being cared for by one of his relatives... The country's oldest surviving aviator, Sir Thomas Sopwith, celebrates his one hundredth birthday today.*
3 Vorvo If something **survives**, it continues to exist even though it has been under attack. *I doubt whether the National Health Service will survive to the end of the century... Officials are confident that communism will survive as an ideology... The project survived three changes of government... He assured them that the Party had survived a difficult Congress, and had taken a major step forward.*
4 Vorvo If you **survive** a difficult experience, you manage to cope with it and do not let it affect you badly. *You have to make difficult decisions to survive in business... She survived the divorce pretty well... The new Malaysian Prime Minister has survived his first electoral test.*

survive on PHRASAL VERB If you **survive on** a certain amount of money or food, you earn just enough money to buy essential things to live, or you have just enough food to live. *My salary's only just enough to survive on... They store water to survive on during the drought.*

survivor /səvaɪvə/ **survivors**
1 NC A **survivor** of a disaster is someone who continues to live in spite of coming close to death. *The Prince has been meeting some of the survivors of the crash... A major rescue operation is continuing to try and find survivors.*
2 NC Someone who is a **survivor** is able to carry on with their life in spite of difficult experiences. *President Barre has been one of Africa's great survivors, as he faces yet more economic and political problems. ...one of life's survivors.*

susceptible /səseptəbl/
1 ADJ PRED+*to* If you are **susceptible** to something, you are likely to be influenced by it. *We are all susceptible to advertising... They have never been susceptible to diplomatic pressure.*
2 ADJ If you are **susceptible** to a disease or injury, you are likely to be affected by it. *Many people were lightly dressed and therefore susceptible to burns... This may explain why alcoholic women are more susceptible to liver failure... We are working on a breeding programme of highly resistant and highly susceptible test animals.* ♦ **susceptibility** /səseptəbɪləti/ NU *...his susceptibility to infection.*

suspect, suspects, suspecting, suspected; pronounced /səspekt/ when it is a verb and /sʌspekt/ when it is a noun or an adjective.
1 V-REPORT or VO If you **suspect** that something is the case, you think that it is likely to be true. *People suspected that a secret deal had been made... I suspect she is keeping the baby hidden away somewhere... I travelled down the Nile, marvelling at the existence of a civilisation whose existence I had barely suspected... The post office suspect arson; there have been a number of suspicious fires in the last month.*
2 vo If you **suspect** someone or something, you doubt if they can be trusted or are reliable. *Stalin's aim was*

to make everyone distrust and suspect each other... I had many reasons for suspecting this approach.
3 VO+of If you **suspect** someone of a crime, you think that they are guilty of it. *The two men are suspected of corruption... Many suspect army officers of the crime, but no proper investigation has been carried out... They were suspected of being behind the riots.*
4 NC A **suspect** is a person who is thought to be guilty of a crime. *Last week police finally had a suspect for the murder. ...a confidential document relating to IRA suspects... His officials deny torturing suspects.*
5 ADJ If something is **suspect**, it cannot be trusted or regarded as genuine. *My friendliness was viewed as suspect by some people... Four other men were released after their confessions were thought to be suspect... Later today, army officials will examine a suspect car which is parked under a railway bridge.*

suspected /səspɛktɪd/
ADJ ATTRIB You use **suspected** in front of nouns when you want to say that someone or something is thought to be the thing referred to by the noun. For example, a 'suspected terrorist' is someone who is thought to be a terrorist. *The federal prosecutor announced the arrest of another suspected East German spy. ...a list of suspected war criminals... He was taken to hospital with a suspected fractured skull.*

suspend /səspɛnd/ **suspends, suspending, suspended**
1 VOA If something is **suspended** from a high place, it is hanging from that place. *A model aeroplane was suspended above the stage... They suspended the sphere in a magnetic field, then monitored its rotation.*
2 VO If you **suspend** something, you delay or stop it from being in effect for a while. *The UN announced that it was suspending activities which required supervision by foreign staff... Under the emergency, all fundamental rights were suspended... Trading in the group's shares was suspended after they lost more than half their value.*
3 VO If the sentence someone receives as the punishment for a crime is **suspended**, they do not serve it unless they commit another crime within a specified period of time. *He was given a one year prison sentence, suspended for three years... Judge Gessel concluded that he would suspend the three-year prison sentence and put him on probation for two years.*
4 VO If someone is **suspended** from their job, they are told not to do it for a period of time, usually as a punishment. *The people involved in the incident have been suspended from their duties... The soldier had been acting against orders, and had been suspended along with his company commander... The authorities have ordered the Athletics Board to suspend her for a year.*

suspended animation
NU **Suspended animation** is a state in which the important body functions of an animal are slowed down for a period of time. This is done by freezing or because the animal hibernates. *Normally the stored cultures are kept in suspended animation at minus 196° Celsius.*

suspended sentence, suspended sentences
NC A **suspended sentence** is a sentence to go to prison, which a criminal does not serve unless he or she commits another crime within a specified period of time. *He got a two-year suspended sentence... Now he'll be free, but the suspended sentence means that he will lose his National Assembly seat.*

suspender /səspɛndə/ **suspenders**
1 NC **Suspenders** are fastenings which hang down from a belt and hold up a woman's stockings. *Jenny was clothed in bra and suspenders.*
2 N PL **Suspenders** are a pair of straps that men use instead of a belt to prevent their trousers from falling down; used in American English. *The dealers sat hunched over their computers in their white shirts and red suspenders.*

suspender belt, suspender belts
NC A **suspender belt** is a piece of underwear for women that is used for holding up stockings. *...a lace suspender belt.*

suspense /səspɛns/
1 NU **Suspense** is a state of excitement or anxiety caused by not knowing exactly what is going to happen very soon. *I try to add an element of suspense and mystery to my novels... There was little suspense or excitement in the latest of the primary elections.*
2 If you keep someone **in suspense**, you delay telling them something that they are eager to know about. *I did not leave him in suspense, but quickly informed him that he had passed.*

suspension /səspɛnʃn/ **suspensions**
1 NU The **suspension** of something is the act of delaying or stopping it for a while. *...the suspension of all social security payments... The suspension of classes was lifted after being in force for almost a year... A spokesman said this did not represent a suspension of aid to Burma.*
2 NUorNC Someone's **suspension** is their removal from a job for a period of time, usually as a punishment. *If he is found guilty, he could face suspension from duty... The Health Minister ordered his suspension, pending the outcome of the enquiry... He's serving a one-match suspension after being involved in the incident.*
3 NU A vehicle's **suspension** consists of the springs and other devices, which give a smooth ride over bumps in the road. *The 2CV has been admired for its smooth suspension and roomy interior.*

suspension bridge, suspension bridges
NC A **suspension bridge** is a bridge that is supported from above by cables. *The government announced that it would use public funds for the construction of a suspension bridge to the airport.*

suspicion /səspɪʃn/ **suspicions**
1 NUorNC **Suspicion** is the feeling that someone should not be trusted or that something is wrong. *Derek shared Lynn's suspicion of Michael... These officials also regarded the peasants with suspicion... I had aroused his suspicions last week.*
2 NC A **suspicion** is a feeling that something is probably true or is likely to happen. *Investigators have strong suspicions of a clandestine trade... There is a widespread suspicion among foreign observers that the disaster could have been averted.*
3 N SING+of A **suspicion** of a quality or feeling is a very small amount of it. *My dog barks at the slightest suspicion of danger.*
● **Suspicion** is used in these phrases ● If someone is **under suspicion**, they are suspected of being guilty of something such as a crime. *Philby himself came under suspicion and was even interrogated.* ● If someone is **on suspicion** of something, they are suspected of committing a specific crime, but the charge has not been proven in a court of law. *Fourteen people have been arrested on suspicion of smuggling heroin... Twelve firms are under investigation on suspicion of supplying Iraq with equipment that could be used to make chemical weapons.* ● If you say that someone is **above** or **beyond suspicion**, you mean that they could not possibly be guilty of something, because of their good character. *We understand that it's no longer enough to be innocent; we must be above suspicion... The Somali embassy says that the NSC is above suspicion in this regard.*

suspicious /səspɪʃəs/
1 ADJ If you are **suspicious** of someone, you do not trust them. *The consignment of weapons was uncovered when a customs official became suspicious... Nuclear disasters at Windscale and Three Mile Island have left people suspicious and disenchanted... Labour, once so suspicious of the European Community, is now an eager champion of the EEC... It's not only the Americans that are suspicious that this is truly a chemical weapon plant.*
◆ **suspiciously** ADV *'Why are you laughing?' Rachel asked suspiciously... Businessmen were likely to be asked suspiciously where their money came from.*
2 ADJ **Suspicious** things make you think that something is wrong with a situation. *The public have been told to be careful, and to look out for suspicious packages... It is believed the couple were overcome by*

gas fumes, and police say there are no suspicious circumstances... If you see anyone suspicious with a Northern accent, report them immediately... The police are treating the incident as suspicious. ◆ **suspiciously** SUBMOD *A number of calls were received by the police about two men acting suspiciously near the school... The lump was suspiciously big.*

suss /sʌs/ **susses, sussing, sussed;** an informal word.
suss out PHRASAL VERB 1 If you **suss** something **out**, you discover how it works or how to do it. *Time spent sussing out the demands of the exam system is time well spent.* 2 If you **suss** someone **out**, you discover what their true character is. *She had me sussed out in ten minutes.*

sustain /səsteɪn/ **sustains, sustaining, sustained**
1 VO If you **sustain** something, you continue it or maintain it for a period of time. *They do not have enough money to sustain a strike... The problem was how to sustain public interest.* ◆ **sustained** ADJ *The frigate came under a sustained attack by American aircraft and ships... The changes have provoked sustained criticism from both the opposition and welfare groups. ...sustained economic growth.*
2 VO If food, drink, or medical attention **sustains** you, it keeps you alive or gives you energy and strength; a formal use. *This baby's life was sustained by a heart-lung bypass operation... She was in a vegetative state, her life sustained by a feeding tube... They had nothing to sustain them all day except two cups of coffee.*
3 VO If something **sustains** you, it supports you by giving you help, strength, or encouragement. *It is his belief in God that sustains him... You say that the emotion that sustained you through all these insults was pity for the perpetrators?*
4 VO If you **sustain** something such as a defeat, loss, or injury, it happens to you; a formal use. *The man had sustained only slight injuries... A fifteen-year old boy died of bullet wounds sustained last month... The navy was stronger than before, despite having sustained some damages and casualties.*

sustainable /səsteɪnəbl/
1 ADJ If a plan, method, or system is **sustainable**, it can be continued at the same level of activity or pace without harming its efficiency and the people affected by it. *...the creation of a sustainable health programme... Imports were cut last year, but this strategy is not sustainable in the long-term... They will be relieved to return to what they regard as a more sustainable level of growth... Local shipping sources said that such a level of traffic was not sustainable.*
2 ADJ You use **sustainable** to describe the use of natural resources when this use is kept at a steady level and is not likely to damage the environment. *The farmers in Western Kenya have achieved marvels with sustainable agriculture. ...a three year plan for the sustainable exploitation of the forest... The pilot project for sustainable development in the Amazon has won wide praise.*

sustenance /sʌstɪnəns/
NU **Sustenance** is food and drink which helps to keep you strong and healthy; a formal word. *We derive our sustenance from the land... There may be some basic sustenance for those who have survived, but it's not a very attractive life.*

Suva /suːvə/
Suva, on the island of Viti Levu, is the capital of Fiji and its largest city. Population: 70,000 (1986).

Sv
Sv is a written abbreviation for 'sieverts'.

svelte /svɛlt/
ADJ Someone who is **svelte** is attractively slim, elegant, and stylish. *Maria Callas married, and changed her image from the matronly to the svelte.*

SW
SW is a written abbreviation for 'south-west'. *The two girls come from SW London.*

swab /swɒb/ **swabs**
NC A **swab** is a small piece of cotton wool used for cleaning a wound or for taking a sample of something such as skin, blood, or bodily fluids. *The swabs used*

by police for the blood tests were found to be unsuitable because they contained alcohol.

swagger /swægə/ **swaggers, swaggering, swaggered**
V If you **swagger**, you walk in a proud way, holding your body upright and swinging your hips; used showing disapproval. *She swaggered back to her place by the window... He swaggered around the stage in a black jumpsuit covered in sequins.* ▶ Also N SING *Bernard left the room with a swagger.*

swallow /swɒləʊ/ **swallows, swallowing, swallowed**
1 VO If you **swallow** something, you cause it to go from your mouth down into your stomach. *He succeeded in committing suicide by swallowing a cyanide capsule... He worked in the furnaces, often choking on the dust and coal gas he swallowed... The bacteria is absorbed in the intestine if infected water is swallowed.* ▶ Also NC *Breen took a swallow of brandy.*
2 V If you **swallow**, you make a movement in your throat as if you are swallowing something, often because you are nervous or frightened. *He swallowed and closed his eyes... Ellen swallowed and said, 'Hi. It's me.'*
3 VO If someone **swallows** a story or a statement, they believe it completely. *I sometimes think that crowds will swallow whole any political speech whatsoever... Many of them, and increasingly the American public, are finding this argument difficult to swallow.*
4 VO If you **swallow** an insult or unpleasant situation, you accept it and do not protest. *She swallowed the sarcasm and got on with her work... It's undoubtedly a bitter result for Mrs Bhutto to swallow... It's obviously very difficult for the US to swallow the idea of repatriating people to a country they fought so bitterly against.*
5 NC A **swallow** is also a small bird with pointed wings and a forked tail. *The arrival of flocks of swallows is a sure sign that summer is on its way.*
● **Swallow** is used in these phrases. ● If you say that something is **a bitter pill to swallow**, you mean that you find it hard to accept. *Endorsing Mitterrand may be a very bitter pill for PFC members to swallow... Having the troops in Managua was a bitter pill to swallow, after all the blood that had been spilt.* ● to **swallow your pride**: see **pride**.

swallow up PHRASAL VERB 1 If one thing is **swallowed up** by another, it becomes part of the first thing and no longer has a separate identity of its own. *He talked of not allowing smaller nations to be swallowed up by bigger ones... Farmland is being swallowed up by towns at an alarming rate... The company has pursued an aggressive policy of swallowing up smaller specialist companies in the electronics field.* 2 If something **swallows up** money or resources, it uses them entirely while hardly improving things in any way. *Modern weapon systems swallow up funds at an alarming rate... British tax payers' money is being swallowed up by defence contracts which over-run their budgets... Economic advances of the past few years have been swallowed up by population increases.*

swam /swæm/
Swam is the past tense of **swim**.

swamp /swɒmp/ **swamps, swamping, swamped**
1 NCorNU A **swamp** is an area of wet land with wild plants growing in it. *This area is full of small islands and swamps... It smelled like rotten swamp.*
2 VO If something **swamps** a place or object, it fills it with water. *Sudden heavy seas swamped the ship... Floodwaters have swamped over 750 villages in southern Iran.*
3 VO If you **are swamped** by things, you have more of them than you can deal with. *At a time of drugs, AIDS, and crime, many cities are swamped by demands for services... City bread stores were swamped as buyers lined up for extra loaves which will triple in price tomorrow.*

swampy /swɒmpi/
ADJ A **swampy** area of land consists mainly of swamps. *...miles of swampy marshes... The only access to the swampy terrain was by barge.*

swan /swɒn/ swans

NC A **swan** is a large, usually white bird with a long neck that lives on rivers and lakes. *Sixteen swans are being treated at a bird sanctuary.*

swank /swæŋk/ swanks, swanking, swanked; an informal word.

V If someone is **swanking**, they boast about themselves in order to try to impress other people. *Stop swanking!* ► Also NU *It's all a lot of swank.*

swanky /swæŋki/

ADJ People describe something as **swanky** or **swank** when it is smart, fashionable, and expensive. *...the swank Hotel Princess... She goes to a swanky private school.*

swan song

N SING+POSS Someone's **swan song** is the last time that they do something for which they are famous, for example the last time that an actor gives a performance in the theatre. *For her swan song, Dame Joan Sutherland chose the part of Queen Marguerite in 'Les Huguenots'... Mr Reagan's swan song will be emotional, personal, and pitched towards the future.*

swap /swɒp/ swaps, swapping, swapped; also spelt **swop**.

1 VO When you **swap** something with someone, you give it to them and receive something else in exchange. *Many of the refugees were so hungry that they tried to swap clothes and household goods for food or water... I'll swap your Kodak for my Hallicrafters short-wave set... He faces charges over a plan to swap American hostages in exchange for weapons sold to Iran.* ► Also NC *He spent several years in jail before being exchanged in an East-West spy swap.*

2 VO+for If you **swap** one thing for another, you remove the first thing and replace it with the second. *The Princess has swapped the blue silk dress she wore in church for a yellow and white linen outfit.*

3 VO When you **swap** stories or opinions with someone, you tell each other stories or give each other your opinions. *The country store served as a gathering place for folks to swap hunting and fishing tales... He's been trying to keep up a cheerful public image, swapping banter with journalists. ...a popular meeting place for merchants who used to swap trading news and information.*

4 If someone **swaps sides** in a war, argument, or other disagreement, they decide to support the people that they were previously arguing or fighting against. *It is remarkable how few Mujahedin commanders have been tempted to swap sides, despite the hardship of guerrilla warfare... He does not command enough seats to topple the government even if he does swap sides.*

swarm /swɔːm/ swarms, swarming, swarmed

1 NC A **swarm** of bees or other insects is a large group of them flying together. *Swarms of desert locusts have already caused devastation in the region. ...the first swarm of African bees was destroyed in October.*

2 V When bees or other insects **swarm**, they move or fly in a large group. *Reporters speak of black clouds of locusts swarming across Nouachott and destroying crops.*

3 VA When people **swarm** somewhere, they move there quickly in a large group. *Thousands of people swarmed into Sydney for the big day... Supporters swarmed across the pitch at the end of the match.*

4 NC A **swarm** of people is a large group of them moving about quickly. *She left amid a swarm of photographers.*

5 V+with If a place is **swarming** with people or animals, it is full of them, moving about in a busy way. *The White House garden was swarming with security men... Britain's sewers are said to be swarming with rats.*

swarthy /swɔːði/

ADJ A **swarthy** person has a dark complexion. *...the swarthy, dark-eyed, Mediterranean type.*

swat /swɒt/ swats, swatting, swatted

VO If you **swat** an insect, you hit it with a quick, swinging movement, usually in order to kill it.

Soldiers are passing the hours by catching scorpions and swatting flies.

swathe /sweɪð/ swathes; a literary word.

1 NC A **swathe** is a long strip of cloth, especially one that is wrapped round someone or something. *...balconies strewn with swathes of silk.*

2 NC A **swathe** of land is a long strip of land that is different from the land on either side of it. *...new roads cutting swathes through our countryside.*

swathed /sweɪðd/

ADJ PRED+in If someone is **swathed** in cloth, they are completely wrapped in it; a literary word. *She was swathed in bandages.*

sway /sweɪ/ sways, swaying, swayed

1 V When people or things **sway**, they lean or swing slowly from one side to the other. *She sang and swayed from side to side. ...trees swaying in the wind... Passengers described how the boat swayed, rolled and pitched.*

2 VO If you **are swayed** by something that you hear or read, it influences you. *Do not be swayed by glamorous advertisements... It remains to be seen whether his supporters can be so easily swayed... My fear is that the jury may have been swayed by what has been said in the newspapers.*

● **Sway** is used in these phrases. ● If you are **under the sway** of someone or something, they have great influence over you. *Laing was coming increasingly under the sway of new ideas... In the 19th century, Algeria fell under the sway of the Ottoman Empire.* ● If someone or something **holds sway**, they have great power or influence. *The Khmer Rouge held sway over Cambodia for three and a half years. ...in a world where the dollar and the yen hold sway.*

Swaziland /swɑːzilænd/

The **Kingdom of Swaziland** is a country in southern Africa. It was a British protectorate from 1903 until independence in 1968. King Mswati III succeeded in 1986. Obed Dlamini was appointed Prime Minister in 1989. There are no political parties. Swaziland is a member of the Commonwealth and the Organization of African Unity. It exports sugar and wood pulp. ◆ **Swazi** /swɑːzi/ N, ADJ

▪ *per capita GNP:* US$790 ▪ *religion:* Christianity, animism ▪ *language:* English and Siswati (official) ▪ *currency:* lilangeni ▪ *capital:* Mbabane (the legislature is transferring to Lobamba) ▪ *population:* 761,000 (1989) ▪ *size:* 17,363 square kilometres.

swear /sweə/ swears, swearing, swore, sworn

1 V If someone **swears**, they use rude or blasphemous language, often because they are angry. *Glenys leant out of the car window and swore at the other driver... They got drunk, and swore and shouted like young people everywhere.*

2 V-REPORT, VO, or V+to-INF If you **swear** to do something, you solemnly promise that you will do it. *Party members were asked to swear that they would not join another political party... I, Ronald Reagan, do solemnly swear that I will faithfully execute the duties of the President of the United States... Three of them were excluded for refusing to swear allegiance... The Israeli government has sworn vengeance, and today it came... He was present at the ceremony, and he swore to uphold the new constitution.*

3 V-REPORT or V+to If you **swear** that something is true or if you **swear** to it, you say very firmly that it is true. *I swear that he never consulted me... If you saw the plant in its desiccated state, you would swear that it was dead. ...thousands of experts who would swear to its impossibility.*

4 See also **sworn**.

swear by PHRASAL VERB If you **swear by** a particular thing, you believe that it is especially effective or reliable, often because you have used it a lot yourself; an informal expression. *He swears by my herbal tea to make him sleep.*

swear in PHRASAL VERB When someone is **sworn in**, they solemnly promise to fulfil the duties of a new job or appointment. *Flanked by almost the entire Cabinet, Mr Heunis was sworn in as acting President.*

swearing-in, swearings-in

NC The **swearing-in** at the beginning of a trial or

official appointment is the act of making solemn promises to fulfil the duties it involves. *The procession celebrates the swearing-in of a new Lord Mayor... He returned to Capitol Hill for the swearing-in ceremony.*

swear-word, swear-words
NC A **swear-word** is a word which is considered rude or blasphemous. *What some people still find shocking today is the book's sexual frankness and use of swear-words.*

sweat /swɛt/ **sweats, sweating, sweated**
1 NU **Sweat** is the salty, colourless liquid which comes through your skin when you are hot, ill, or afraid. *Jack paused, wiping the sweat from his face... Plastic keys become slippery because of the sweat from the pianist's fingers.*
2 V When you **sweat**, sweat comes through your skin. *I lay and sweated in bed... The victims looked dazed, they sweated and shook, or became hysterical... You lose a lot of fluid by sweating.*
● **Sweat** is used in these phrases. ● If someone is **in a sweat** or **in a cold sweat**, they are sweating a lot, especially because they are afraid or ill. *He awoke trembling and in a cold sweat... MPs are in a cold sweat about an election occurring before the recession bottoms out.* ● If someone **sweats it out**, they endure something unpleasant in the hope that when it ends the situation will have improved; an informal expression. *Our troops are going to have to sweat it out. It will be a war of nerves.*

sweatband /swɛtbænd/ **sweatbands**
NC A **sweatband** is a thin strip of absorbent material which is worn around the head to stop sweat running into the eyes. *The sweatband was black and greasy.*

sweater /swɛtə/ **sweaters**
NC A **sweater** is a warm knitted piece of clothing which covers the upper part of your body and your arms. *Daniella was wearing a yellow sweater and brown-framed glasses... I pulled my sweater over my head.*

sweat gland, sweat glands
NC Your **sweat glands** are the organs under your skin which produce sweat. *A deficiency of concern to the athlete is a blocking of the sweat glands.*

sweatshirt /swɛtʃɜːt/ **sweatshirts**
NC A **sweatshirt** is a piece of casual cotton clothing which covers the upper part of your body and your arms. *His training partner wore an identical sweatshirt stencilled with his own name.*

sweatshop /swɛtʃɒp/ **sweatshops**
NC A **sweatshop** is a small factory or workshop where many people work together in poor conditions for low pay. *...the horrifying conditions in the sweatshops of the nineteenth century.*

sweaty /swɛti/
1 ADJ A **sweaty** place or activity makes you sweat because it is hot or tiring. *...the sweaty march along the blazing beach.*
2 ADJ If your clothing or body is **sweaty**, it is soaked or covered with sweat. *...students in sweaty sports shirts... The men, shirtless and sweaty, are shovelling dirt from a ten-foot deep hole.*

swede /swiːd/ **swedes**
NC A **swede** is a round yellow root vegetable with a brown or purple skin. *...fodder crops like cabbage and swedes.*

Sweden /swiːdn/
The **Kingdom of Sweden** is a country in northern Europe. It is a neutral country. It was ruled by the Social Democratic Labour Party (SDAP) almost continuously from 1932 until 1976, becoming the world's most advanced welfare state. Olof Palme was the leader of the SDAP from 1969 until his murder in 1986. King Carl XVI Gustav succeeded in 1973. Carl Bildt, of the Moderate Party, was elected Prime Minister in 1991. Sweden exports machinery and transport equipment, timber, and paper. ◆ **Swede** /swiːd/ N **Swedish** /swiːdɪʃ/ ADJ
■ *per capita GNP:* US$19,150 ■ *religion:* Christianity (mainly Evangelical Lutheran) ■ *language:* Swedish ■ *currency:* krona ■ *capital:* Stockholm ■ *population:* 8 million (1989) ■ *size:* 410,928 square kilometres.

sweep /swiːp/ **sweeps, sweeping, swept**
1 VO If you **sweep** an area of ground, you push dirt or rubbish off it with a broom. *I must sweep the kitchen floor... He swept away the broken glass.*
2 VOA If you **sweep** things off a surface, you push them off with a quick, smooth movement of your arm. *He went into the study and swept some books and papers off the couch.*
3 VA To **sweep** also means to move quickly and forcefully in a smooth line or curve. *He stared out at the traffic sweeping along the road... Gales and heavy rain have been sweeping across southern Britain... The dog was flung aside by the panther's sweeping paw.*
▶ Also NC *With a great sweep of the arm he flung the whole handful high in the air.*
4 VOA If a strong force **sweeps** you along, it moves you quickly along. *She was swept out to sea by the currents... The torrential rains turned streets into raging rivers, sweeping away cars with people trapped inside them.*
5 VOorVA If ideas, beliefs, or statements **sweep** a place, they are very influential, and spread quickly through it. *...the camping craze that is currently sweeping America... Change sweeps through the highly industrialized countries.*
6 VOA To **sweep** something away means to remove it quickly and completely. *The matter was soon swept from his mind. ...sweeping away restrictions on publication.*
7 VO If your gaze or a light **sweeps** an area, it moves over it. *We began rushing around in the dark, sweeping the ground with our flashlights... There may be a factor of error, depending on how fast the beam sweeps across the chart.*
8 to **sweep** something **under the carpet**: see **carpet.**
9 See also **chimney sweep, clean sweep.**
sweep up PHRASAL VERB If you **sweep up** dirt or rubbish, you push it together with a brush and then remove it. *There's a picture of a man trying to light a stove, and another of a woman sweeping up... Shoppers say they get fed up of sweeping up the needles that fall off natural pine trees.*

sweeper /swiːpə/ **sweepers**
1 NC A **sweeper** is someone who is employed to sweep roads, factories, and so on. *...increases for local government employees such as road sweepers and school cleaners.*
2 NC In football, a **sweeper** is a player who supports the main defenders. *Swindon Town have signed up Argentina's sweeper Nestor Gabriel Lorenzo on loan.*
3 NC A **sweeper** is also the same as a **carpet sweeper.**

sweeping /swiːpɪŋ/
1 ADJ ATTRIB A **sweeping** curve is long, wide, and stretched out. *...a place where the stream made a sweeping curve... The film makes use of sweeping camera movements.*
2 ADJ A **sweeping** statement or generalization is a general one that is made without considering facts or details carefully; used showing disapproval. *It is too easy to make sweeping generalizations about someone else's problems.*
3 ADJ ATTRIB **Sweeping** is also used to describe amounts or actions that are very large or significant. *...sweeping public expenditure cuts... He has promised sweeping changes in the law to benefit the poor... The secret police have been given sweeping new powers under the new decree.*
4 ADJ ATTRIB If something has **sweeping** effects or consequences, the effects or consequences are great or serious. *...the most sweeping environmental law to be passed in a decade... He has promised a sweeping overhaul of the nation's financial system.*

sweepstake /swiːpsteɪk/ **sweepstakes**
NC A **sweepstake** is a method of gambling in which each person is given the name of a horse in a race and pays a small amount of money. The person who has the winning horse's name wins the money. *We had a sweepstake in the office on the Grand National.*

sweet /swiːt/ **sweeter, sweetest; sweets**
1 ADJ Food or drink that is **sweet** contains, or tastes as if it contains, a lot of sugar. *...a cup of sweet tea... It's sort of sweet and soft and chewy.*

2 NC **Sweets** are sweet things such as toffees, chocolates, or mints. *Most of the children were given sweets as a reward. ...boiled sweets.*
3 NC A **sweet** is a dessert served at the end of a main meal; a formal use. *We get soup and a main meal and a sweet.*
4 ADJ A feeling or experience that is **sweet** gives you great pleasure and satisfaction. *However sweet love is, when it goes there is always bitterness... What makes this announcement so sweet for the company is that the contract has been won in the face of strong competition... This must be what they mean when they say revenge is sweet.* ♦ **sweetness** NU *...the sweetness of freedom.*
5 ADJ A **sweet** smell is pleasant and fragrant. *...the sweet smell of ripe blackberry bushes.*
6 ADJ A **sweet** sound is pleasant and gentle. *Her voice has the softness of sweet song.* ♦ **sweetly** ADV *...a piper who played sweetly on his pipes.*
7 ADJ Someone who is **sweet** is pleasant, kind, and gentle towards other people. *My grandparents were very sweet to me... The commercials showed men in new roles, for example being vulnerable, sweet, and sympathetic.*
8 ADJ You can also describe someone or something as **sweet** when you think that they are attractive and delightful, especially in a rather sentimental way. *Oh! Look at that kitten! How sweet!* ♦ **sweetly** ADV *She remembered him sitting so sweetly on the cot, looking up at her.*
9 Someone with a **sweet tooth** likes sweet, sugary foods very much. *...children with a sweet tooth.*

sweet-and-sour
ADJ ATTRIB **Sweet-and-sour** is used to describe Chinese food that contains both a sweet flavour and something sharp or sour such as lemon or vinegar. *...sweet-and-sour pork with bamboo shoots.*

sweet corn
NU **Sweet corn** is the yellow seeds of the maize plant, which are eaten as a vegetable. *...tinned sweet corn.*

sweeten /swiːtn/ **sweetens, sweetening, sweetened**
1 VO If you **sweeten** food or drink, you add sugar, honey, or another sweet substance to it. *...drinking tea sweetened with honey.*
2 VO If you **sweeten** a difficult situation for someone, you offer them something to try and persuade them to accept it, although they do not really want to. *In a gesture to sweeten the deal today, he offered to release all the French hostages... Kenneth Clarke wants more money from the government to sweeten the Health Service reforms.*

sweetener /swiːtnə/ **sweeteners**
1 N MASS A **sweetener** is an artificial substance that can be used instead of sugar. *The typical piece of chewing gum consists of sweeteners, flavours, and colours. ...artificial sweeteners.*
2 NC A **sweetener** is also something that you give or offer to someone in order to persuade them to do something that they do not want to do. *Labour accused the government of offering cash sweeteners to encourage hospitals to opt out of the NHS... Previous sell-offs of state-owned industries have involved sweeteners or tax concessions... His release was seen as a sweetener to encourage London to soften its stand towards Iran and Syria.*

sweetheart /swiːthɑːt/ **sweethearts**
1 VOCATIVE You call someone **sweetheart** if you are very fond of them. *I'm sorry sweetheart, I couldn't make it.*
2 NC Your **sweetheart** is your boyfriend or girlfriend. *February the 14th is the day when traditionally lovers send greeting cards to their sweethearts.*

sweetie /swiːti/ **sweeties**; an informal word.
1 VOCATIVE You call someone **sweetie** if you are fond of them, especially if they are younger than you are. *'Daddy, don't ever die'—'Sweetie, everyone dies eventually.'*
2 NC If you say that someone is a **sweetie**, you mean that they are kind, pleasant, and lovable. *Isn't she a sweetie!*
3 NC Children or adults speaking to children sometimes call sweets **sweeties**.

sweet nothings
N PL If someone whispers **sweet nothings** in your ear, they quietly say nice, loving, and rather flattering things to you. *The curfew dampened the possibilities for lingering exchanges of sweet nothings.*

sweet pea, sweet peas
NC A **sweet pea** is a climbing plant with delicate, light-coloured, fragrant flowers.

sweet potato, sweet potatoes
NC A **sweet potato** is a root vegetable that looks like an ordinary potato but has a pink skin and yellow flesh. *On the menu today is turkey, gravy, sweet potatoes, and cranberry sauce.*

sweet shop, sweet shops
NC A **sweet shop** is a small shop that sells sweets and cigarettes. *...like a bewildered child in a sweet shop.*

swell /swel/ **swells, swelling, swelled, swollen**. The past participle of the verb can be either **swelled** or **swollen**.
1 V If something **swells**, it becomes larger and rounder than normal. *The insect inflates her lungs so that they swell into her abdomen... The infection causes fluid to build up and the limbs to swell.*
2 V-ERG If the amount or size of something **swells** or if something **swells** it, it becomes larger than it was before. *It took another twenty years for the population to swell to twice its size... The town has prospered during the decades in which America's defense budget swelled... The army had its ranks swollen by new recruits... The villages were hit by flooding as heavy rain swelled Assam's main rivers.*
3 V If feelings or sounds **swell**, they suddenly get stronger or louder; a literary use. *The murmur swelled and then died away... His guilt swelled, but he quashed it.*
4 NC A **swell** is the regular movement of waves up and down in the sea. *...the gentle swell of the ocean... I mean, we ran around in boats in four-foot swells.*
5 ADJ You can describe something as **swell** when you think it is very good; used in informal American English. *You must get invited to some swell parties... You're doing a swell job.*
6 See also **swollen**.

swell up PHRASAL VERB If something **swells up**, it becomes larger and rounder than normal. *A mosquito had bitten her and her arm had swollen up... I noticed that when I put them in curry, the sultanas started to swell up.*

swelling /swelɪŋ/ **swellings**
N COR NU A **swelling** is a raised, curved patch on your body which appears as a result of an injury or an illness. *He had a painful swelling on his neck... No, I'll be alright, the swelling is going down.*

swelter /sweltə/ **swelters, sweltering, sweltered**
V If you **swelter** or are **sweltering**, you are very uncomfortable because the weather is extremely hot. *On the deck everyone was sweltering in the still air.*

sweltering /sweltərɪŋ/
ADJ If the weather is **sweltering**, it is very hot. *...the long, sweltering summer of 1976... The weather's been sticky and sweltering through much of the northern United States.*

swept /swept/
Swept is the past tense and past participle of **sweep**.

swerve /swɜːv/ **swerves, swerving, swerved**
V If a vehicle or other moving thing **swerves**, it suddenly changes direction, often in order to avoid colliding with something else. *The car swerved off the road and into the river... I swerved to avoid a lorry.*

swift /swɪft/ **swifter, swiftest; swifts**
1 ADJ A **swift** process or event happens very quickly. *I made a swift and complete recovery... They are pressing for a swift and orderly return to democracy.* ♦ **swiftly** ADV *Events moved swiftly at this much awaited Congress.* ♦ **swiftness** NU *They were stunned by the swiftness of the assault.*
2 ADJ Something that is **swift** moves very quickly. *...a swift stream... She shot me a swift glance of utter contempt.* ♦ **swiftly** ADV *He walked swiftly down the dark street... The floods rose swiftly, submerging highways.* ♦ **swiftness** NU *He moved with remarkable swiftness to one side.*

3 NC A **swift** is a small bird with crescent-shaped wings. *Most swifts are back now, and feeding high in the sky.*

swig /swɪg/ **swigs, swigging, swigged**
VO If you **swig** a drink, you drink it from a bottle or cup quickly and in large amounts; an informal word. *When her back was turned I swigged two cupfuls from the tub.* ► Also NC *She took a swig of brandy.*

swill /swɪl/ **swills, swilling, swilled**
1 VO If you **swill** an alcoholic drink, you drink a lot of it; an informal use. *He sits there swilling his gin-and-tonics without a care in the world.*
2 VOA To **swill** something also means to clean it by pouring a large amount of water over it. *I'll just go and swill this out under the tap.*
3 NU **Swill** is a liquid mixture containing waste food such as vegetable peelings, that is given to pigs to eat. *He was on his way to the sty with a bucket of swill.*

swim /swɪm/ **swims, swimming, swam, swum**
1 VorVO When you **swim**, or **swim** a particular stretch of water, you move through water by making movements with your arms and legs. *The children are learning to swim... We managed to swim ashore... The challenge of swimming Lake Baikal is not distance, but the coldness of the water.* ► Also N SING *Let's go for a swim.*
2 V If objects seem to you to **swim**, they seem to be moving backwards and forwards, usually because you are ill. *The room swam and darkened before his eyes.*
3 V If your head is **swimming**, you feel dizzy. *All that dancing has made my head swim.*

swimmer /swɪmə/ **swimmers**
NC A **swimmer** is someone who can swim or who is swimming. *The Soviet swimmer Igor Polianski has set a new world record... The new scheme is designed to encourage beginners and more experienced swimmers alike.*

swimming /swɪmɪŋ/
NU **Swimming** is the activity of moving through water using your arms and legs. *Her father encouraged her to take up swimming again... She's aiming for a gold medal in swimming at the Seoul Olympics.*

swimming baths
N PL A **swimming baths** is a public swimming pool, especially an indoor one. *The local council decided to apply flexible pricing at the town's swimming baths.*

swimming costume, swimming costumes
NC A **swimming costume** is a tight-fitting piece of clothing that a woman wears when she goes swimming. *She looked slightly plump in her one-piece swimming costume.*

swimmingly /swɪmɪŋli/
If something **goes swimmingly**, it proceeds in a very satisfactory way, without any problems. *Secretary of State Baker got along swimmingly with Eduard Shevardnadze.*

swimming pool, swimming pools
NC A **swimming pool** is a place that has been built for people to swim in. It consists of a large hole that has been tiled and filled with water. *...an open-air swimming pool.*

swimming trunks
N PL **Swimming trunks** are shorts that a man wears when he goes swimming. *He made a false start in the 25-yard event, and lost his swimming trunks.*

swimsuit /swɪmsuːt/ **swimsuits**
NC A **swimsuit** is the same as a **swimming costume**. *She wore an old-fashioned swimsuit and swimming cap all in black.*

swindle /swɪndl/ **swindles, swindling, swindled**
VO If someone **swindles** you, or **swindles** money out of you, they deceive you in order to get money or something valuable from you. *Detectives were called when a man who had been swindled by his business partner went to the authorities... Criminals are turning away from armed robbery, and are instead conspiring with bank employees to swindle banks out of vast sums of money.* ► Also NC *I'm afraid we have been the victims of a monumental swindle. ...the complexities of unravelling this hugely complicated international swindle.*

swindler /swɪndlə/ **swindlers**
NC A **swindler** is someone who swindles people. *He was accused of being a swindler and a thief.*

swine /swaɪn/ **swines; swine** is both the singular and plural form for the meaning in paragraph 2.
1 NC If you call someone a **swine**, you mean that you think they are very cruel or unpleasant. *OK, you swine, have your say then.*
2 NC A **swine** is a pig; an old-fashioned use.
3 ADJ ATTRIB **Swine** is also used to describe things that relate to pigs; a technical use. *...an outbreak of swine fever.*

swing /swɪŋ/ **swings, swinging, swung**
1 V-ERG If something **swings** or if you **swing** it, it moves repeatedly backwards and forwards or from side to side, from a fixed point. *She walked, her arms swinging and her head held high... He sat there swinging his legs.* ► Also N SING *She walked with an exaggerated swing of the hips.*
2 V-ERG A If something **swings** in a particular direction or if you **swing** it, it moves in that direction with a smooth, curving movement. *I pushed the door and it swung open... A compass has a magnetic needle which swings on a pivot to indicate direction... Boylan swung the bag on to the back seat... Jupiter's gravity will swing the space probe round in a great arc.* ► Also NC *...a grand, impatient swing of his arm.*
3 V-ERG A If a person or a vehicle they are driving **swings** in a particular direction or if they **swing** it, they turn suddenly in that direction. *I swing quickly around... He swung away to avoid a collision... He swung his car out of the side road.*
4 V AorVOA If you **swing** at someone or something, you try to hit them. *I swung at him and hit him forcefully... Gripping the bat well as you swing at the ball does increase the speed of the bat through the air... The soldier swung a slow, heavy right hand at Tom.*
5 NC A **swing** is a seat hanging by two ropes or chains from a metal frame or tree. You can sit on it and move forwards and backwards through the air. *The moving parts of the swing were not oiled properly.*
6 NC+SUPP A **swing** in people's opinions or attitudes is a significant change in them. *There was a 16.2% swing to the Social Democrats... Import policies are subject to erratic political swings... Ecuador has seen a strong swing to the left in the local elections.*
7 V A If something such as public opinion or a balance of power **swings** in a particular direction, it changes. *The balance of power had swung decisively in favour of the moderates... The General Secretary, Mr Sam McCluskie, said that public opinion was now swinging behind the NUS.*
● **Swing** is used in these phrases. ● If something is **in full swing**, it is operating fully and is no longer in its early stages. *The economic recovery programme is now in full swing... A colourful street party went into full swing on the main thoroughfare.* ● If you **get into the swing** of something, you become involved in it and enjoy what you are doing. *Dr Stein had got into the swing of his speech and enthusiastically quoted authors.*

swing door, swing doors
NC A **swing door** is a door that swings on a hinge so that it opens both towards you and away from you. *He went down a short flight of steps and pushed through the swing door at the bottom of it.*

swingeing /swɪndʒɪŋ/
ADJ ATTRIB You use **swingeing** to describe things that are very severe, and so cause serious harm or hardship. *This would involve swingeing cuts in the Warsaw Pact forces. ...swingeing tax increases... He's one of a number of celebrities who have been awarded swingeing damages for the lies written about them... There have been swingeing attacks on the newspaper, which published details of the affair.*

swinger /swɪŋə/ **swingers**
NC A **swinger** is a person who is lively and fashionable; an old-fashioned word. *Forty years ago Feldstein was a swinger... I'm not really a swinger like most of the girls here.*

swinging /swɪŋɪŋ/
ADJ Something or someone that is **swinging** is lively
and fashionable; an old-fashioned, informal word.
...*swinging London*... *He fancied himself as a swinging
chic dresser.*

swing voter, swing voters
NC A **swing voter** is the same as a **floating voter**; used
in American English. *Texas Democrat Lloyd Bentsen,
thought to be a swing voter, has now aligned himself
with Senators like Sam Nunn and George Mitchell.*

swipe /swaɪp/ **swipes, swiping, swiped**
1 V+at If you **swipe** at something, you try to hit it,
making a swinging movement with your arm. *The
batsman swiped at the ball and missed it.* ► Also
N SING   *She took a casual swipe at the nettles.*
2 VO If someone **swipes** something, they steal it; an
informal use. *The books will be found in my room, if
they haven't already been swiped.*

swirl /swɜːl/ **swirls, swirling, swirled**
V-ERG If something **swirls** or if you **swirl** it, it moves
round and round quickly. *Torrents of muddy water
swirled around the rubble... He swirled his drink round
his glass.* ► Also NC   *...the slow swirl of the stream.*
♦ **swirling** ADJ *She complained of being blinded by
swirling snow.*

swish /swɪʃ/ **swishes, swishing, swished**
V-ERG If something **swishes** or if you **swish** it, it moves
quickly through the air, making a soft sound. *The
curtains swished open... The flies didn't give them a
minute's peace, and the horses swished their tails, and
stamped their feet.* ► Also N SING   *...the swish of a
torpedo.*

switch /swɪtʃ/ **switches, switching, switched**
1 NC A **switch** is a small control for an electrical
device which you use to operate the device. *...electric
light switches... When you flick the switch, the motor
turns and twirls up the spaghetti... You fasten the
clips to the copper switch, put on your headset and
listen in.*
2 VAorVO If you **switch** to something different, for
example to a different task or subject of conversation,
you change to it from what you were doing or saying
before. *I would like now to switch to quite a different
topic... In her singing, Amina switches back and forth,
mainly between French and Arabic... Switching from
caffeinated to decaffeinated coffee is not necessarily a
good thing... He switched his attention back to the
magazine.* ► Also NC   *...a switch in policy.*
3 VO If you **switch** two things, you replace one with
the other. *The plane switched loads and took off... The
ballot boxes had been switched, and the results
changed.*
switch off PHRASAL VERB 1 If you **switch off** a light
or other electrical device, you stop it working by
pressing a switch. *He switched the radio off... Once
the lights are switched off, the show is over.* 2 If you
switch off, you stop paying attention to something; an
informal use. *I just switched off after the first speech.*
switch on PHRASAL VERB If you **switch on** a light or
other electrical device, you make it start working by
pressing a switch. *The officers switched on their lights
and sirens just as we entered the hotel... He switched
on the TV.*

switchback /swɪtʃbæk/ **switchbacks**
NC A **switchback** is something, such as a mountain
road, which rises and falls sharply many times or
which has many sharp bends.

switchblade /swɪtʃbleɪd/ **switchblades**
NC A **switchblade** is the same as a **flick-knife**. *Guns
have replaced switchblades and baseball bats as
common weapons in street violence.*

switchboard /swɪtʃbɔːd/ **switchboards**
NC The **switchboard** in an organization is a central
place where all the telephone calls are received.
*Local radio and newspaper switchboards were
jammed with callers telling the authorities not to give
in. ...a switchboard operator.*

Switzerland /swɪtsələnd/
The **Swiss Confederation** is a country in central
Europe. It has been a neutral country since 1815. The
President for 1992 was René Felber of the Social
Democratic Party. Banking, insurance, and tourism

are important industries. Exports include machinery,
precision instruments (clocks and watches), chocolate,
textiles, chemicals, and pharmaceuticals. ♦ **Swiss** /swɪs/
N, N PL, ADJ
▪ *per capita GNP:* US$27,260 ▪ *religion:* Christianity
▪ *language:* German, French, Italian ▪ *currency:* franc
▪ *capital:* Bern (Berne) ▪ *largest city:* Zürich
▪ *population:* 7 million (1989) ▪ *size:* 41,293 square
kilometres.

swivel /swɪvl/ **swivels, swivelling, swivelled**
1 V-ERG If something **swivels** or if you **swivel** it, it
turns around a central point so that it is facing in a
different direction. *These chairs can swivel, but they
can't move up and down... The tank turrets swivelled
as the planes dropped explosive charges... Mellors
slowly swivelled his chair round.*
2 VA If you **swivel** in a particular direction, you turn
suddenly in that direction. *I swivelled back to face the
row of bottles on the bar... I swivelled right round in
my chair.*
3 ADJ ATTRIB A **swivel** chair or lamp is one that can be
turned around a central point so that it faces a
different direction without moving the legs of the chair
or the base of the lamp. *In his swivel chair,
surrounded by TV screens, he looks like the owner of a
pirate TV station.*

swollen /swəʊlən/
1 **Swollen** is a past participle of **swell**.
2 ADJ Something that is **swollen** has grown outwards
and is larger and rounder than normal. *Her fingers
were badly swollen with arthritis. ...children with
swollen stomachs.*

swollen-headed
ADJ Someone who is **swollen-headed** behaves as if they
think that they are very clever or important, often
because someone has praised them. *She was growing
ever more swollen-headed and arbitrary.*

swoon /swuːn/ **swoons, swooning, swooned**
V If you **swoon**, you almost faint as a result of strong
emotion or shock; a literary word. *She frequently
brought proceedings to a halt by swooning
dramatically in the court room.*

swoop /swuːp/ **swoops, swooping, swooped**
1 V When a bird or aeroplane **swoops**, it suddenly
moves downwards through the air in a smooth,
curving movement. *We saw a distant eagle swoop
down from the sky... The two jets could be seen
swooping and diving over areas in the north.* ► Also
NC   *The swallow made a dazzling swoop through the
air.*
2 VA If soldiers or police **swoop** on a place, they move
towards it suddenly and quickly in order to attack it or
to arrest someone. *British troops swooped down twice
in dawn raids... Acting on information, the police
swooped on houses and offices in a number of West
German cities.* ► Also NC   *The police made a swoop
on the headquarters... The fifty-odd men arrested in
the swoop had not been allowed to go home.*
3 If you achieve something in **one fell swoop**, you do it
on a single occasion or by a single action. *In one fell
swoop Singapore Airlines, Swiss Air and Delta Airlines
will marry their operations in 63 different countries...
The amnesty should at one fell swoop solve the
problem of prison congestion.*

swop /swɒp/. See **swap**.

sword /sɔːd/ **swords**
1 NC A **sword** is a weapon with a handle and a long
blade. *The sixteen men were beheaded by sword in
public... Each beautifully-decorated sword was broken
before being immersed in the water.*
2 If you **cross swords** with someone, you disagree and
argue about something. *Bukharin sometimes crossed
swords with Lenin, but he was never anti-Lenin... This
is not the first time the present government and the
broadcast media have crossed swords over terrorism.*

swordfish /sɔːdfɪʃ/ **swordfishes**. The plural form can
be either **swordfishes** or **swordfish**.
NC A **swordfish** is a large sea fish with a very long
upper jaw. *The catch of the day was grilled swordfish,
but we chose the fillet mignon.*

swordplay /sɔːdpleɪ/
NU **Swordplay** is the activity and skill of fighting with

swords. *I taught him all I know of marksmanship and swordplay.*

swore /swɔː/
Swore is the past tense of **swear**.

sworn /swɔːn/
1 **Sworn** is the past participle of **swear**.
2 ADJ ATTRIB If you make a **sworn** statement or declaration, you swear that everything that you have said in it is true. *The American made a sworn statement to the police.*

swot /swɒt/ **swots, swotting, swotted**; an informal word.
1 V If you **swot**, you study very hard, especially when you are preparing for an examination. *How do you find time to swot for exams?*
2 NC If you call someone a **swot**, you mean that they study extremely hard and are not interested in other things; used showing disapproval. *I'm looked on as a swot because I've heard of Kipling.*
swot up PHRASAL VERB If you **swot up** a subject or **swot up** on it, you read as much as you can about it, usually in preparation for a test. *She swotted up American history... I was swotting up on my transformational grammar.*

swum /swʌm/
Swum is the past participle of **swim**.

swung /swʌŋ/
Swung is the past tense and past participle of **swing**.

sycamore /sɪkəmɔː/ **sycamores**
NC A **sycamore** is a tree. Its leaves have five points and it has yellow flowers. *...broad leave trees, such as oak, sycamore, and ash.*

sycophant /sɪkəfænt/ **sycophants**
NC A **sycophant** is a person who behaves in a sycophantic way. *He's a coward, a traitor, and a sycophant.*

sycophantic /sɪkəfæntɪk/
ADJ If someone is **sycophantic**, they flatter people who are more important than they are in order to gain an advantage for themselves; used showing disapproval. *They would break into peals of sycophantic laughter... He is noted for his aggressive questioning of politicians, but he adopted an almost sycophantic tone for the Princess.*

Sydney /sɪdni/
Sydney is the largest city in Australia and capital city of New South Wales. Population: 3,431,000 (1987).

syllable /sɪləbl/ **syllables**
NC A **syllable** is a part of a word that contains a single vowel-sound and that is pronounced as a unit. For example, 'book' has one syllable, and 'reading' has two syllables. *Every syllable you utter will be converted into computer data before transmission. ...syllable boundaries.*

syllabus /sɪləbəs/ **syllabuses**
NC You can refer to the subjects studied in a particular course as the **syllabus**. *They've got to cover a very wide syllabus.*

symbiosis /sɪmbiˈəʊsɪs/
1 NU **Symbiosis** is a close relationship between two organisms of different kinds which benefits both organisms; a technical use. *...the bacteria that live in the soil, sometimes in symbiosis with higher plants... When we talk about symbiosis, we usually mean organisms of different types getting together.*
2 NU **Symbiosis** is also any relationship between different things, people, or groups that benefits all the things or people concerned. *The Communist Party apparatus is trying to enter into a comfortable and lucrative symbiosis with private capital... The first steps toward some form of man-machine symbiosis are already being taken.*

symbiotic /sɪmbiɒtɪk/
ADJ A **symbiotic** relationship is one in which organisms, people, or things exist together in a way that benefits them all. *...a symbiotic relationship between algae and fungi... In the modern state there is a deeply symbiotic relationship based on shared power... The party's symbiotic relationship with the ANC is already under fire.*

symbol /sɪmbl/ **symbols**
1 NC+SUPP A **symbol** of something is a shape, design, or other thing that is used to represent it. *Picasso painted a red circle as a symbol of the Revolution. ...a peace symbol.*
2 NC+SUPP Something that is a **symbol** of a society or aspect of life seems to represent it because it is typical of it. *Perhaps the most glittering symbol of the new Britain was London's Post Office Tower... A metaphor running through her poems is gambling as a symbol of democracy.* ● See also **status symbol.**
3 NC A **symbol** for an item, for example in a calculation or formula, is a number, letter, or shape that represents the item. *I use my own symbol for 'approximately'... To help the illiterate, each candidate had a symbol beside their name.*

symbolic /sɪmbɒlɪk/
1 ADJ A thing that is **symbolic** of someone or something is regarded as being a symbol which represents them. *The crescent moon is symbolic of Allah. ...gold, with its rich symbolic significance... Behind this children's story is a symbolic tale of how people define their world.* ◆ **symbolically** ADV *To put on someone else's clothes is symbolically to take on their personality... Last year, they were symbolically reburied, and hundreds of people visited the cemetery.*
2 ADJ **Symbolic** is also used to describe things involving or relating to symbols. *Each brought forward symbolic bread for young women entering the church... They have removed the symbolic red star from the top of the Socialist Party headquarters.*
3 ADJ If you describe an event, procedure, or action as **symbolic**, you mean that it happens because people expect and want it to happen, although it has very little practical effect. *I think his attendance at the talks would be primarily symbolic... Although Mr Hattersley's post is largely symbolic, the news that Mr Prescott is to challenge him will come as a blow... The company described the sailing as a symbolic gesture to prove they could enter Calais without the help of French dockers.* ◆ **symbolically** ADV *Symbolically, at least, the talks were a success... The priest in rural communities has been a key figure, both symbolically and practically.*

symbolise /sɪmbəlaɪz/. See **symbolize.**

symbolism /sɪmbəlɪzəm/
NU **Symbolism** is the use of symbols in order to represent something. *...messages conveyed by symbolism in the architecture... The play is a strange mixture of symbolism and reality.*

symbolize /sɪmbəlaɪz/ **symbolizes, symbolizing, symbolized**; also spelt **symbolise.**
VO If one thing **symbolizes** another, it is used or regarded as a symbol of it. *...a dancer in a flame-red robe symbolizing the sun... Birmingham's Bull Ring came to symbolize all that was bad about the building boom years of the 1960s.*

symmetrical /sɪmetrɪkl/
ADJ Something that is **symmetrical** has two halves which are exactly the same, except that one half is like a reflection of the other half. *...pleasingly symmetrical designs.* ◆ **symmetrically** ADV *Smaller rooms were arranged symmetrically to either side.*

symmetry /sɪmətri/
1 NU Something that has **symmetry** is symmetrical in shape or design. *...the symmetry of the Square.*
2 NU **Symmetry** in a relationship or agreement is the fact of both sides giving and receiving an equal amount. *They overcome this problem by trying to incorporate symmetry into the Geneva agreement. ...American demands for symmetry in military disarmament.*

sympathetic /sɪmpəθetɪk/
1 ADJ If you are **sympathetic** to someone who has had a misfortune, you are kind to them and show that you understand their feelings. *My boyfriend was very sympathetic and it did make me feel better... I was sympathetic to Albert's despairing monologues, but became impatient with his complaints... He was freed after a sympathetic judge exploited a legal loop-hole.* ◆ **sympathetically** ADV *She put a hand sympathetically on his arm.*
2 ADJ If you are **sympathetic** to a proposal, action, or cause, you approve of it and are willing to support it.

He is sympathetic to our cause... The Prime Minister is one of the few leaders who is known to be genuinely sympathetic to reforms... Soviet officials have been showing a more sympathetic attitude to the Church... We have generally been given a sympathetic hearing.
3 ADJ You describe someone as **sympathetic** when you like them and approve of the way that they behave. *I found him a very sympathetic character.*

sympathize /sɪmpəθaɪz/ **sympathizes, sympathizing, sympathized; also spelt sympathise.**
1 V If you **sympathize** with someone who has had a misfortune, you show that you are sorry for them. *I sympathized with her and tried to help... Trading standard officers sympathised with him, but the law was unable to change his situation.*
2 V+with If you **sympathize** with someone's feelings, you understand them and are not critical of them. *I can sympathize with your hesitations... Many of his countrymen sympathise with this viewpoint... The Prince's frustration is there for all to see, and many people sympathise with his predicament.*
3 V+with If you **sympathize** with a proposal or action, you approve of it and are willing to support it. *Everyone sympathised with the anti-colonial cause... Most, if not all, the top army officers sympathise with the aims of the rebels.*

sympathizer /sɪmpəθaɪzə/ **sympathizers; also spelt sympathiser.**
NC The **sympathizers** of an organization or cause are the people who support it. *White was an ardent Communist sympathiser... The money was raised abroad by sympathizers.*

sympathy /sɪmpəθi/ **sympathies**
1 NU If you have **sympathy** for someone who has had a misfortune, you are sorry for them, and show this in your behaviour. *People feel immediate sympathy for a man left alone with his children... Messages of sympathy and support have been sent by many world leaders... The nurses' action evoked considerable public sympathy... The poor don't need our sympathy and pity, they need our love and compassion.*
2 NU If you have **sympathy** with someone's ideas or opinions, you agree with them. *The voters turned to him not through any left-wing sympathy, but in the hope of a fresh approach... Some members of the judiciary have expressed sympathy with Mr Donaldson's views... On that point I'm in sympathy with Mr McCabe.*
3 N PL Your **sympathies** are your feelings of approval and support for a particular organization, action, or cause. *He knows I have strong left-wing sympathies... Unless there's a major change in electoral sympathies, we're going to face the same problem after the election.*
4 ADJ ATTRIB You can use **sympathy** to describe an action that someone takes in order to indicate their support for another person or group of people. *There have been pledges of sympathy action by teachers, firemen, and car workers... Local government workers and miners were staging sympathy strikes... Many of them do not believe the corruption charges, and she could get the sympathy vote.*
5 If you take some action **in sympathy** with someone, you do it to show that you support them. *They were carrying out a hunger strike in sympathy with mine... The Israeli Arabs have staged a one-day strike in sympathy.*

symphony /sɪmfəni/ **symphonies**
NC A **symphony** is a piece of music for an orchestra, usually in four parts called movements. *Here's the Trio from Schubert's Third Symphony.*

symphony orchestra, symphony orchestras
NC A **symphony orchestra** is a large orchestra that plays classical music. *...the City of Birmingham Symphony Orchestra.*

symposium /sɪmpəʊziəm/ **symposia** /sɪmpəʊziə/ or **symposiums**
1 NC A **symposium** is a conference in which experts or scholars discuss a particular subject. *He took part in a symposium on Arab-Jewish relations... They have held many symposia on animal-welfare issues.*
2 NC A **symposium** is also a collection of essays by

experts or scholars on a particular subject. *His views were included in a symposium published in 1974.*

symptom /sɪmptəm/ **symptoms**
1 NC A **symptom** of an illness is something wrong with your body that is a sign of the illness. *The first symptom of a cold is often a sore throat... What is leptospirosis, what are its symptoms, and how is it treated?*
2 NC A **symptom** of a bad situation is something that happens which is considered to be a sign of this situation. *Migration is a symptom of rural poverty... The disastrous war was a symptom of the loss of judgement amongst the high command... He says a military solution would only treat the symptoms, not the cause of political tensions in the area.*

symptomatic /sɪmptəmætɪk/
ADJ PRED If one thing is **symptomatic** of something bad, it is a sign of it; a formal word. *The irritation seems symptomatic of something deeper... The price dispute was merely symptomatic of other problems.*

synagogue /sɪnəgɒg/ **synagogues**
NC A **synagogue** is a building where Jewish people meet to worship or to study their religion. *The huge and derelict synagogue in East Berlin is to be restored.*

sync /sɪŋk/
If two things are **out of sync**, they are badly matched or do not work simultaneously as they should. If they are **in sync**, they are well-matched and work simultaneously; an informal expression. *Our watches are out of sync. ...a Christmas story that is a little out of sync with the general feeling of goodwill around this time of year... They're all in sync, and they're all rowing in the same direction... Up to this point, we were all in sync and in agreement on our policy.*

synchronize /sɪŋkrənaɪz/ **synchronizes, synchronizing, synchronized; also spelt synchronise.**
1 V-RECIP If two people **synchronize** something that they do, they do it at the same time and speed as each other. *They frequently synchronize their movements as they talk... The rhythm was not synchronized with the pictures... We want to synchronise the process of German unification with European progress.*
2 V-RECIP If you **synchronize** two watches or clocks, you adjust them so that they say exactly the same time. *His watch has been accurately synchronized with the church clock... The Greenwich Time Signal has been used to synchronise watches around the world since 1923.*

syncopated /sɪŋkəpeɪtɪd/
ADJ PRED If a piece of music is **syncopated**, the weak beats in the bar are stressed instead of the strong beats. *The dancers found the primitive, syncopated rhythms extremely difficult... Her eight beats to the bar isn't as syncopated as some blues music.*
◆ **syncopation** /sɪŋkəpeɪʃn/ **syncopations** NU or NC *Most of the dances don't have this grace, syncopation, and rhythm... It was jazz music he loved, its syncopations, and the way a note was held back for half a beat longer.*

syncope /sɪŋkəpi/
1 NU **Syncope** is a temporary loss of consciousness; a medical use. *Motionless standing is a classic physical cause of syncope.*
2 NU **Syncope** is also the omission of sounds or letters from the middle of a word, for example changing 'is not' to 'isn't'; a technical use in linguistics.

syndicate /sɪndɪkət/ **syndicates**
NC A **syndicate** is an association of people or organizations that is formed for business purposes or to carry out a project. *...a syndicate of German industrialists... Colombian criminal syndicates have made vast fortunes manufacturing cocaine in secret factories.*

syndicated /sɪndɪkeɪtɪd/
ADJ A **syndicated** newspaper article or television programme is sold to several different organizations, who then publish the article or broadcast the programme; used in American English. *It's relying on syndicated features, as opposed to maybe trying to stimulate your own local columnists. ...the oldest syndicated newspaper column in America...*

Armstrong's residence was featured on a weekly syndicated television show 'Lives of the Rich and Famous'.

syndrome /ˈsɪndrəʊm/ **syndromes**

1 NC+SUPP A **syndrome** is a medical condition that is characterized by a particular group of symptoms. *They plan to use the device to help patients suffering from acute respiratory distress syndrome. ...a new blood test for Down's Syndrome.*

2 NC+SUPP You also use **syndrome** to refer to an undesirable condition that is characterized by a particular type of activity or behaviour. *...the capitalist syndrome of growth, profits, competition.*

synod /ˈsɪnəd/ **synods**

NC A **synod** is a special council of members of a Church, which meets regularly to discuss religious issues. *...the General Synod of the Church of England.*

synonym /ˈsɪnənɪm/ **synonyms**

NC A **synonym** is a word or expression which means the same as another word or expression. *'Totalitarian' is not a synonym for 'communist'.*

synonymous /sɪˈnɒnɪməs/

1 ADJ **Synonymous** words or expressions have the same meaning as each other. *This was the first time he had used the word 'condemn', but he said the earlier phrases used were synonymous.*

2 ADJ PRED If one thing is **synonymous** with another, the two things are closely associated with each other so that the first suggests the second. *Socialism became to him synonymous with peace... To many people, the words Sheffield and steel are synonymous... The Cannes film festival has become synonymous with international glamour.*

synopsis /sɪˈnɒpsɪs/ **synopses** /sɪˈnɒpsiːz/

NC A **synopsis** is a summary of a longer piece of writing or work. *...a memo containing a synopsis of a dispatch from their office in Geneva.*

syntactic /sɪnˈtæktɪk/ or **syntactical** /sɪnˈtæktɪkl/

ADJ **Syntactic** or **syntactical** is used to describe something relating to syntax; technical terms in linguistics. *...a program capable of syntactic and semantic analysis. ...the syntactical relationships between words.*

syntax /ˈsɪntæks/

NU **Syntax** is the grammatical arrangement of words in a language or the grammatical rules in a language; a technical term in linguistics. *It did not teach them about nouns, pronouns, syntax and so on.*

synthesis /ˈsɪnθəsɪs/ **syntheses** /ˈsɪnθəsiːz/

1 NC A **synthesis** of different ideas or styles is a mixture or combination of these ideas or styles; a formal use. *...a synthesis of Jewish theology and Greek philosophy.*

2 NU The **synthesis** of a substance is the production of it by means of chemical or biological reactions; a technical use. *We need sunlight for the synthesis of vitamin D... The target chemical compound is built up by step-by step synthesis.*

synthesize /ˈsɪnθəsaɪz/ **synthesizes, synthesizing, synthesized**; also spelt **synthesise**.

1 VO If you **synthesize** a substance, you produce it by means of chemical or biological reactions; a technical use. *...proteins which the body is unable to synthesise for itself.*

2 VO If you **synthesize** different ideas, facts, or experiences, you combine them to develop a single idea or impression; a formal use. *They synthesise their experience into principles and theories. ...the task of somehow synthesizing this radical reform with more cautious ideas.*

synthesizer /ˈsɪnθəsaɪzə/ **synthesizers**; also spelt **synthesiser**.

NC A **synthesizer** is an electronic machine that produces music, speech, or other sounds by using its computer to combine individual sounds that have been previously recorded and stored. *Acid house is a blend of rap and hip-hop, with newer sounds produced by synthesizers. ...a voice synthesizer... OMD are one of the original synthesizer bands.*

synthetic /sɪnˈθetɪk/

ADJ **Synthetic** products are made from chemicals or artificial substances rather than from natural ones.

Fitting wool covers may help against fire in cases where existing upholstery cloth is synthetic... This is a natural product which will replace synthetic colourants in food... She thought the new synthetic surface would suit her game better.

syphilis /ˈsɪfəlɪs/

NU **Syphilis** is a type of venereal disease. *Doctors at the time were not able to distinguish syphilis from the other common sexually transmitted disease, gonorrhoea.*

syphon /ˈsaɪfn/. See siphon.

Syria /ˈsɪriə/

The **Syrian Arab Republic** is a country in the eastern Mediterranean. The modern state was founded in 1946 and the Arab Socialist Renaissance (Baath) Party came to power in 1963. Lieutenant-General Hafiz al-Assad became President in 1971. Syria intervened in Lebanon's civil war in 1976 and 1987, and has been deeply involved in Lebanon's politics. Syria produces oil. It is a member of the Arab League. Syria's enormous defence expenditure has caused major economic problems. ♦ **Syrian** /ˈsɪriən/ N, ADJ ▪ *per capita GNP:* US$1,670 ▪ *religion:* Islam (mainly Sunni) ▪ *language:* Arabic ▪ *currency:* pound ▪ *capital:* Damascus ▪ *population:* 12 million (1989) ▪ *size:* 184,050 square kilometres.

syringe /sɪˈrɪndʒ, sɪˈrɪndʒ/ **syringes**

NC A **syringe** is a small tube with a plunger which is used with a fine hollow needle to inject drugs into a person's body or to take blood samples from them. *A shortage of disposable syringes and blood transfusion systems remained a big problem... AIDS is commonly transmitted through shared syringes.*

syrup /ˈsɪrəp/ **syrups**

N MASS **Syrup** is a sweet liquid made with sugar and water, often with a flavouring. *...waffles with maple syrup.*

syrupy /ˈsɪrəpi/

1 ADJ A **syrupy** liquid is sweet or thick like syrup. *Kosher wine is thick, syrupy and sweet, and an essential part of Passover.*

2 ADJ You can describe behaviour as **syrupy** when it is sentimental in an irritating way. *She admired everything she saw in a tone of syrupy earnestness.*

system /ˈsɪstəm/ **systems**

1 NC A **system** is a way of organizing or doing something in which you follow a fixed plan or set of rules. *They have developed a remarkably efficient system for gathering food... He said the authorities were introducing a new system as soon as possible.*

2 NU If a situation or activity has some **system**, it has a sense of orderliness or good organization. *There's got to be some sort of system around here or we won't be able to function properly.*

3 NC A **system** is also a particular set of rules, especially one in mathematics or science which is used to count or measure things. *...Egyptian or Roman number systems. ...the binary system.*

4 NC+SUPP You use **system** to refer to a whole institution or aspect of society that is organized in a particular way. *There's a difference between the Scottish legal system and the English one. ...the need to modernise Britain's transport system.*

5 N SING People sometimes refer to the government or administration of a country as the **system**. *...the revolutionary overthrow of the system... They need the will to reform Albania's repressive political system.*

6 NC+SUPP You can use **system** to refer to a set of roads, railways, canals, and so on that are linked together. *There's a complex system of canals connecting the Texas ports. ...the need to modernize Britain's transport system.*

7 NC+SUPP A particular **system** is a set of equipment or parts, for example the set of pipes or wiring which supplies water, heat, or electricity to a building. *Have you thought of installing a central heating system?*

8 NC+SUPP You can also refer to an electronic device such as a computer or hi-fi as that particular kind of **system**. *They stole the stereo system and the television set... They tried to make games cartridges for the Nintendo system independently from the Japanese company.*

9 NC+SUPP A **system** in your body is a set of organs or other parts that together perform a particular function. *...a diagram of the digestive system. ...the nervous system.*

10 If you get something **out of your system**, you do something that you have a strong urge to do, for example express the feelings of anger or anxiety that you have about a situation, so that you feel better afterwards; an informal expression. *Getting it out of my system made me relax a bit.*

systematic /sɪstəmætɪk/

ADJ Activity or behaviour that is **systematic** follows a fixed plan, so that things are done in an organized way. *These skills are developed in a formal and systematic way... Amnesty International says torture is systematic and widespread. ...systematic house-to-house searches.* ◆ **systematically** ADV *I wish they'd organise themselves more systematically.*

systemic /sɪstiːmɪk/

1 ADJ A **systemic** drug or poison affects the whole of the body, rather than just one part of it. *Systemic fungicides and insecticides can be used.*

2 ADJ You can also use **systemic** to refer to something which has an important effect on every aspect or level of a particular organization or country; a technical use. *He said much was being done to overcome the systemic crisis in his country... This is what the social scientists call a systemic collapse.*

T t

T, t /tiː/ **T's, t's**
NC **T** is the twentieth letter of the English alphabet.

ta /tɑː/
Ta means thank you; used in informal speech. *He passed it over to Myra, who smiled at him and said 'Ta'.*

tab /tæb/ **tabs**
1 NC A **tab** is a small piece of cloth or paper attached to something. *It had the maker's name on a small cloth tab inside.*
2 If you **pick up the tab,** you pay a bill on behalf of a group of people, or provide money that is needed for something; an informal expression. *The taxpayer is picking up the tab... The company picks up the tab for the Christmas light pageantry.*
3 If you **keep tabs on** someone, you make sure that you always know where they are and what they are doing; an informal expression. *The new system will make it easier to keep tabs on offenders.*

Tabai, Ieremia /jerəmiːə tæbaɪ/
Ieremia Tabai became President of Kiribati in 1979. He was elected to the House of Assembly in 1974, and served as Chief Minister of the Gilbert Islands (now Kiribati) from 1978 to 1979. He is an independent. Born: 1950.

Tabasco /təbæskəʊ/
NU **Tabasco** is a hot spicy sauce made from peppers; **Tabasco** is a trademark. *...a cocktail of vodka, Worcester sauce, and tabasco with tomato juice.*

tabby /tæbi/ **tabbies**
NC A **tabby** is a cat whose fur has grey, brown, or orange stripes. *He was a magnificent tabby with a white blaze on his chest. ...a tabby cat.*

table /teɪbl/ **tables, tabling, tabled**
1 NC A **table** is a piece of furniture with a flat top that you put things on or sit at. *In the middle of the room there was a chair and a table... She placed his teacup on the table in front of him.*
2 NC A **table** is also a written set of facts or figures arranged in columns or rows. *We include a table of feed composition and a table of nutrient guidelines.*
3 If you **turn the tables on** someone who is causing you problems, you change the situation so that you cause problems for them instead. *The China Daily turned the tables on the British by accusing London of undermining confidence in Hong Kong.*
4 VO If you **table** a proposal, you say formally that you want it to be discussed at a meeting. *They've tabled a motion criticizing the Government for doing nothing about the problem.*
5 See also **bargaining table, negotiating table.**

tableau /tæbləʊ/ **tableaux** /tæbləʊ, tæbləʊz/ or **tableaus**
NC A **tableau** is a scene from history or a legend, represented by people standing on a stage wearing costumes or by a painting, sculpture, or photograph. *A tableau at the end of the play shows Ariel mending the magic rod which Prospero has broken... The Prince of Wales is opening an exhibition of paintings, artefacts, and tableaux representing the event.*

tablecloth /teɪblklɒθ/ **tablecloths**
NC A **tablecloth** is a cloth which is used to cover a table. *...a long table covered with a white tablecloth.*

table manners
N PL Your **table manners** are the way you behave when you are eating a meal. *He had to be careful about his table manners.*

tablespoon /teɪblspuːn/ **tablespoons**
1 NC A **tablespoon** is a large spoon used for serving food.
2 NC You can use **tablespoon** to refer to the amount that a tablespoon contains. *Use 1 tablespoon of vinegar to 1 pint of warm water.*

tablespoonful /teɪblspuːnful/ **tablespoonfuls** or **tablespoonsful**
NC A **tablespoonful** is the amount that a tablespoon contains. *...two level tablespoonfuls of sugar.*

tablet /tæblət/ **tablets**
1 NC A **tablet** is a small capsule or pill containing a dose of medicine, which you swallow. *Take three tablets after each meal.*
2 NC A **tablet** is also a flat piece of stone with words cut into it; a formal use. *There is a tablet in memory of those who died.*

table tennis
NU **Table tennis** is a game played by two or four people. They stand at each end of a long table which has a low net across its middle and hit a small, light ball to each other, using small bats. *For twenty years, table tennis was dominated by Asian athletes. ...the World Table Tennis Championships.*

tableware /teɪblweə/
NU **Tableware** consists of the objects such as plates, glasses, cutlery, and so on that are placed on a table at mealtimes. *...silver tableware.*

tabloid /tæblɔɪd/ **tabloids**
NC A **tabloid** is a newspaper that is printed on small paper measuring approximately 30 cm. by 40 cm. Tabloids have short articles, lots of photographs, and are generally considered to be less serious than other newspapers. See also **broadsheet.** *They felt that the popular tabloids gave too much attention to stories about sex... The Sunday Correspondent was launched in tabloid form two months ago.*

Tabone, Dr Vincent /vɪnsnt təbəʊneɪ/
Dr Vincent Tabone became President of Malta in 1989. He was elected to Parliament in 1966. He served as Minister of Labour, Employment, and Welfare from 1966 to 1971, and of Foreign Affairs from 1987 to 1989. He was Secretary General of the Nationalist Party (PN) from 1962 to 1972, First Deputy Leader from 1972 to 1977, and President from 1978 to 1985. Born: 1913.

taboo /təbuː/ **taboos**
1 NC A **taboo** is a social rule that some words, subjects, or actions must be avoided because they are embarrassing or offensive. *There has been a gradual lifting of the taboo on talking about the war.* ▶ Also ADJ *In 1958, even the mention of his name was taboo... Money is no longer a taboo subject.*
2 NC A **taboo** is also a religious rule forbidding people to do something. *Tribal taboos forbade the Mandinkas to eat monkeys and baboons.*

tabular /tæbjʊlə/
ADJ ATTRIB **Tabular** is used to describe an arrangement of information in lists and columns; a

formal word. *The results are given in tabular form in Appendix III.*

tabulate /tæbjʊleɪt/ **tabulates, tabulating, tabulated**
vo If you **tabulate** information, you arrange it in columns on a page. *It took twenty hours to tabulate the results.*

tacit /tæsɪt/
ADJ **Tacit** means understood or implied without actually being said; a formal word. *They had by tacit agreement not renewed the contract... Her silence is interpreted by many as tacit approval.* ♦ **tacitly** ADV *He also tacitly supports the Egyptian proposals.*

taciturn /tæsɪtɜːn/
ADJ Someone who is **taciturn** does not talk very much and so seems unfriendly or depressed; a literary word. *He is taciturn and withdrawn, shrinking from the public gaze.*

tack /tæk/ **tacks, tacking, tacked**
1 NC A **tack** is a short nail with a broad, flat head. *...multi-coloured tacks.*
2 VOA If you **tack** something to a surface, you nail it there with tacks. *Gretchen had tacked some travel posters on the wall.*
3 NU If you change **tack** or try a different **tack**, you try a different method or policy from the one you were using before. *The Labour Party changed tack on the issue a few years ago.*
4 See also **brass tacks**.

tack on PHRASAL VERB If you **tack** something **on** to something else, you add it in an unsatisfactory way, often because you did not think of it earlier. *They've tacked a couple of new clauses on to the end of the contract.*

tackle /tækl/ **tackles, tackling, tackled**
1 VO If you **tackle** a problem, you start dealing with it in a determined way. *They have published proposals designed to tackle London's housing problems... Firemen in Hull are tackling a fire that has destroyed the Royal Hotel.*
2 VO If you **tackle** someone in a game such as football, you try to take the ball away from them. *He was tackled before he had a chance to shoot.* ► Also NC *The tackle looked fair but a free kick was awarded.*
3 VO If you **tackle** someone about a matter, you talk to them frankly about it, usually in order to get something changed or done. *He tackled me about several editorials I had written.*
4 NU **Tackle** is the equipment that you need for an activity, especially fishing. *...fishing tackle.*

tacky /tæki/
ADJ Something that is **tacky** is badly made and unpleasant; an informal word. *...tacky jewellery. ...tacky clothes.*

tact /tækt/
NU If you behave with **tact**, you are careful to avoid upsetting or offending people. *He performed the task with his usual tact and charm.*

tactful /tæktfl/
ADJ If you are **tactful**, you are careful not to upset or offend people. *Mr Hammond will have to be tactful if he hopes to retain the support of the Engineering Union... The tactful thing would have been not to say anything.* ♦ **tactfully** ADV *The topic was tactfully dropped.*

tactic /tæktɪk/ **tactics**
1 NC **Tactics** are the methods that you use to achieve what you want. *The government's tactics appeared to be to wear down the strikers with a combination of bribes and intimidation... He claimed that Moscow was using delaying tactics at the Geneva talks... OPEC has tried the tactic of restricting production to raise oil prices before but with little success.*
2 NC Military **tactics** are the way troops and equipment are moved in order to win a battle. *President Bush is said to be leaving the details of strategy and tactics to the American military commanders. ...the classic tactic of trying to break down the walls of a castle and starve out the enemy.*

tactical /tæktɪkl/
1 ADJ A **tactical** action is something that you do in order to be successful in a particular situation or to

gain an advantage in the future, rather than immediately. *Tactical errors cost him the lead... This was simply a tactical move by De Gaulle.* ♦ **tactically** ADV or ADV SEN *They may vote tactically for the Free Democrats... Tactically, I think we can be faulted for not voting against the strike.*
2 ADJ ATTRIB **Tactical** weapons are used over fairly short distances. *They have called for the removal of all tactical nuclear weapons from the Balkan region.*
3 ADJ ATTRIB **Tactical** also means relating to military tactics. *Tactical command will be taken by the marines' General... The information would help allied forces make tactical decisions during a war.*
♦ **tactically** ADV *Saddam Hussein has clearly concluded that it would be tactically wise to accept the cease-fire.*

tactical voting
NU **Tactical voting** is the act of voting for a particular person or political party in order to prevent someone else from winning, rather than because you agree with that person or party. *Labour blamed tactical voting for its poor performance.*

tactician /tæktɪʃn/ **tacticians**
1 NC A **tactician** is an expert in military tactics. *He is a tactician unrivalled since Napoleon.*
2 NC A **tactician** is also someone who is very good at choosing the best methods in order to achieve what they want. *An airport manager needed to be a tactician as well as a versatile administrator.*

tactile /tæktaɪl/
ADJ **Tactile** means relating to the sense of touch; a formal word. *...the tactile qualities of the physical world.*

tactless /tæktləs/
ADJ If someone is **tactless**, they behave in a way that is likely to upset or offend people. *I suppose it was rather tactless of me to ask... The Ambassador denied that the comments were tactless.* ♦ **tactlessly** ADV *She behaved very tactlessly in reminding him of their love affair.*

Tadjikistan /tədʒɪkɪstɑːn/
Tadjikistan became independent of the USSR in 1991. It is located in the south-east of the former USSR, bordering China and Afghanistan. Rakhmon Nabiyev, of the Socialist Party of Tadjikistan (formerly the Tadjik Communist Party), became President in 1991. Tadjikistan produces minerals, oil, carpets, cotton, and other textiles. In 1991 it joined the Commonwealth of Independent States. ♦ **Tadjik** /tədʒɪk/ N, ADJ
▪ *per capita GNP:* US$2,340 ▪ *religion:* Islam (mainly Sunni) ▪ *language:* Tadjik, Persian, Kyrgyz ▪ *currency:* rouble ▪ *capital:* Dushanbe ▪ *population:* 5 million (1989) ▪ *size:* 143,100 square kilometres.

tadpole /tædpəʊl/ **tadpoles**
NC **Tadpoles** are small, black water creatures which grow into frogs or toads. *It feeds on creatures like tadpoles and earthworms.*

taffeta /tæfɪtə/
NU **Taffeta** is shiny stiff material made of silk or nylon that is used mainly for making women's clothes. *...a taffeta cocktail dress.*

tag /tæg/ **tags, tagging, tagged**
NC A **tag** is a label which is tied to an object. *...a price tag. ...an electronic tag fastened around the wrist.*

tag along PHRASAL VERB If you **tag along** with someone, you go with them, especially when they have not asked you to. *Our sisters always wanted to tag along.*

tail /teɪl/ **tails, tailing, tailed**
1 NC The **tail** of an animal, bird, or fish is the part extending beyond the end of its body. *The dog was wagging his tail.*
2 NC You can use **tail** to refer to the end or back of something, especially something long and thin. *...the stairway descending from the tail of the plane. ...the tail of the queue.*
3 N PL If a man is wearing **tails**, he is wearing a formal evening jacket which has two long pieces hanging down at the back. *The bride and groom stand stiffly erect, he is in tails, she is in flouncy white. ...white tie and tails.*

4 vo If you **tail** someone, you follow them in order to find out where they go and what they do; an informal use. *All day he was tailed by police cars.*
5 ADV If you toss a coin and it comes down **tails**, you can see the side of it that does not have a person's head on it. *At least the toss went to form, I called tails, it fell heads.*
6 to **make head nor tail** of something: see **head**.
tail off PHRASAL VERB If something **tails off**, it gradually becomes less in amount or value, often before it ends completely. *The rains tail off in September... The average figure has tailed off in the last few years.*

tailback /teɪlbæk/ **tailbacks**
NC A **tailback** is a long queue of traffic stretching back along a road, moving very slowly or not at all, for example because of road works or an accident. *...a two-mile tailback on the M6... There is a long tailback of vehicles at the port.*

-tailed /-teɪld/
SUFFIX **-tailed** combines with adjectives to form new adjectives which describe the type of tail that an animal has. *...long-tailed monkeys. ...white-tailed deer.*

tailgate /teɪlɡeɪt/ **tailgates**
NC A **tailgate** is the door at the back of a hatchback car or a truck, hinged at the top so that it opens upwards. *Paul slammed the tailgate of the Volvo... Larry and Ace sat on the tailgate of their pick-up truck.*

tail light, tail lights
NC The **tail lights** on a car or other vehicle are the two red lights at the back. *Rudolph watched the red tail lights speeding off. ...headlight and tail light bulbs.*

tail-off
N SING A **tail-off** in something is a gradual decrease in its amount or value. *There's been a slight tail-off in profits this month.*

tailor /teɪlə/ **tailors, tailoring, tailored**
1 NC A **tailor** is a person who makes clothes, especially for men. *It normally takes a week for a tailor to complete a suit.*
2 vo If you **tailor** something such as a plan or system, you change it so that it is suitable for a particular person or purpose. *The basic system can be tailored to individual requirements.*

tailored /teɪləd/
1 ADJ ATTRIB **Tailored** clothes are made to fit close to your body. *She looked relaxed and elegant in a bottle green tailored suit.*
2 ADJ If something is **tailored** for a particular purpose, it is specially designed for that purpose. *...factories and equipment tailored to meet the needs of the 20th century.*

tailor-made
1 ADJ Something that is **tailor-made** for a person or purpose is very suitable or was specially designed for them. *Those taking part will be offered a tailor-made training plan to suit their needs.*
2 ADJ **Tailor-made** clothes have been specially made by a tailor to fit a particular person. *He was wearing a tailor-made jacket.*

tailwind /teɪlwɪnd/ **tailwinds**
NC A **tailwind** is a wind that is blowing from behind a vehicle such as an aeroplane and that helps it to move forward more quickly. *It's faster coming back across the Atlantic because of tailwinds.*

taint /teɪnt/ **taints, tainting, tainted**; a formal word.
1 vo If you **taint** something, you spoil it by adding an undesirable substance or quality to it. *He feared that this would taint the scheme with some element of commercialism.*
2 N SING+SUPP A **taint** is an undesirable quality in something which spoils it. *His career was never free of the taint of corruption.*

tainted /teɪntɪd/
ADJ Something that is **tainted** is spoiled because it contains an undesirable quality. *The report was heavily tainted with racism.*

Taipei /taɪpeɪ/
Taipei is the capital of Taiwan and its largest city. Population: 2,703,000 (1989).

Taiwan /taɪwɑːn/
The **Republic of China**, more commonly known as Taiwan and formerly known as Formosa, is an island off the south-east coast of China. It was governed by China from the 17th century and was ceded to Japan following the Sino-Japanese War in 1895. At the end of the Second World War it reverted to China. When the Communists under Mao Zedong established the People's Republic of China in 1949, the Kuomintang (KMT) forces under Chiang Kai-shek fled from mainland China to Taiwan and established the Republic of China. The KMT, also called the Nationalist Party of China, claimed to be the legitimate rulers of mainland China. Until 1971, when the People's Republic of China was recognized, the Republic of China occupied the Chinese seat at the United Nations. The United States recognized the People's Republic of China as the legitimate government of mainland China in 1979. Chiang Kai-shek ruled until his death in 1975. Lee Teng-hui, of the KMT, became President in 1988. General Hau Pei-tsun, of the KMT, became Premier in 1990. Taiwan exports textiles, electrical products, and machinery. It is not a member of the United Nations. ♦ **Taiwanese** /taɪwəniːz/ N, N PL, ADJ
■ *per capita GNP:* US$7,512 ■ *religion:* Buddhism
■ *language:* Chinese (mainly Mandarin) ■ *currency:* new dollar ■ *capital:* Taipei ■ *population:* 20 million (1989) ■ *size:* 36,179 square kilometres.

take /teɪk/ **takes, taking, took, taken**
1 vo You can use **take** to say that someone performs an action. For example, if you say that someone **takes** a look at something, you mean that they look at it. *She took a shower... He formed the habit of taking long, solitary walks... Certain decisions had to be taken... I took a magnificent photo of him.*
2 vo If you **take** a particular attitude or view, you have it. *The public was beginning to take a positive interest in defence.*
3 V A or V O A If something **takes** a certain amount of time, you need that amount of time in order to do it. *How long will it take?... It may take them several weeks to get back.*
4 vo If an action **takes** a particular quality or thing, that quality or thing is required in order to perform the action. *It took a lot of courage to admit his mistake... It takes a great deal of money to fight a general election.*
5 vo If you **take** something, you put your hand round it and hold it, often in order to move it somewhere. *Let me take your coat... She took the menu from him.*
6 vo If you **take** something from one place to another, you carry it there. *She gave me some books to take home.*
7 vo If you **take** someone somewhere, you drive them or lead them there. *A police helicopter was used to take a man to hospital.*
8 vo If someone **takes** something that belongs to you, they steal it or go away with it without asking your permission. *A pickpocket took Barry's wallet.*
9 vo If soldiers or terrorists **take** people or places, they capture them. *They said the purpose of the raid was to take hostages... We took the village without a shot being fired.*
10 vo If someone **takes** office or **takes** power, they start being in control of something. *Mrs Thatcher took office as Prime Minister in 1979... He asked me to take charge.*
11 vo If you **take** something that is offered to you, you accept it. *She took a job in publishing.*
12 vo If you **take** the responsibility or blame for something, you accept responsibility or blame for it. *I would be very willing to take the consequences.*
13 vo If you are in a shop and you say that you will **take** something, you mean that you will buy it. *I'll take a dozen eggs.*
14 vo If you **take** someone's advice or orders, you do what they say you should do. *They have to take instructions from her.*
15 vo If you **take** pills, medicine, or drugs, you swallow them. *I took a couple of aspirins.*
16 vo If someone **takes** a person's temperature or

pulse, they find out what it is by measuring it. *Let me take your pulse.*

17 vo If you **take** a particular road or route, you travel along it. *He took the road southwards into the hills.*

18 vo If you **take** a particular form of transport such as a car or train, you use it to travel from one place to another. *She said she'd take a taxi... I think we ought to take the car.*

19 vo If you cannot **take** something unpleasant, you cannot bear it. *I can't take any more... Ordinary people find his arrogance hard to take.*

20 voA If you **take** an event or piece of news well or badly, you react to it well or badly. *President Menem took the defeat badly.*

21 voA If you **take** what someone says in a particular way, you interpret it in that way. *They took what I said as a kind of rebuke.*

22 vo If you **take** students for a subject, you give them lessons in it. *She took them for geography.*

23 vo If you **take** a subject or course at school or university, you study it. *She took Greek at university... I took a course in marine biology.*

24 vo If you **take** a test or examination, you sit in it in order to obtain a qualification. *She took her degree last year... She's not yet taken her driving test.*

25 vo If you **take** a particular size in shoes or clothes, you wear that size. *She asked what size shoes he took.*

26 vo You use **take** in the imperative to introduce an example that you want to be considered. *Some men change the world. Take Albert Einstein, for instance.*

27 You can say '**I take it**' to check that the person you are talking to knows or understands something. *I take it you know what a stethoscope is?*

28 give or take: see give. See also taken, taker.

take aback PHRASAL VERB If you **are taken aback**, you are surprised or shocked. *I was a bit taken aback by this sudden reversal.*

take after PHRASAL VERB If you **take after** someone in your family, you look or behave like them. *You don't take after your sister.*

take apart PHRASAL VERB If you **take** something **apart**, you separate it into its different parts. *One way to understand the heart better is to take it apart and look at its components in great detail.*

take away PHRASAL VERB **1** If you **take** something **away** from someone, you remove it from them, so that they do not have it any more. *...people from whom everything has been taken away... A maid came to take away the tray.* **2** If you **take away** one number or amount from another, you subtract it or deduct it. For example, if you take 3 away from 5, you get 2. **3** See also takeaway.

take back PHRASAL VERB **1** If you **take** something **back**, you return it to the place you borrowed or bought it from, either because you have finished with it or because it is broken in some way. *Don't forget to take your books back to the library.* **2** If you **take back** something that you said, you admit that it was wrong. *I'm going to have to take back all those things I said about you.*

take down PHRASAL VERB **1** When people **take down** a structure, they separate it into pieces and remove it. *The scaffolding won't be taken down until next year.* **2** If you **take down** what someone is saying, you write it down. *She began to take down the message.*

take in PHRASAL VERB **1** If someone is **taken in** by, they are deceived. *I wasn't going to be taken in by sentimentality.* **2** If you **take in** information, you understand it when you hear it or read it. *People never take in new facts very easily when they're unhappy.*

take off PHRASAL VERB **1** When an aeroplane **takes off**, it leaves the ground and starts flying. *The plane took off twenty-five minutes late.* ● See also takeoff. **2** If you **take off** something that you are wearing, you move it off your body. *He took off his glasses and blinked.* **3** If you **take** time **off**, you do not go to work. *She's taken the day off.* **4** If something such as a product or a sport **takes off**, it suddenly becomes very successful and popular. *I bought a computer a couple of years before computers really began to take off.*

take on PHRASAL VERB **1** If you **take on** a job or responsibility, you accept it. *She takes on more work than is good for her.* **2** If something **takes on** a new quality, it begins to have that quality. *His voice took on a new note of uncertainty.* **3** If you **take** someone **on**, you start employing them. *They took me on because I was a good mathematician.* **4** If you **take on** someone more powerful than you, you fight them or compete against them. *British Leyland plans to take on the competition at home and abroad.*

take out PHRASAL VERB **1** If you **take** someone **out**, you take them to an enjoyable place, and you pay for both of you. *He offered to take her out for a meal.* **2** If something **takes** a lot **out** of you, it makes you very tired, because it is a very difficult task. *Talking in a foreign language all day takes a lot out of you.*

take out on PHRASAL VERB If you **take** your unhappiness or anger **out on** someone, you behave in an unpleasant way towards them, even though it is not their fault that you feel upset. *She took out most of her unhappiness on her husband.*

take over PHRASAL VERB **1** To **take over** something such as a company or country means to gain control of it. *The agency tried to take over another company.* ● See also takeover. **2** If you **take over** a job or if you **take over**, you start doing the job after someone else has stopped doing it. *They want me to take over as editor when Harold leaves. ...policies adopted by Mikhail Gorbachev when he took over.*

take to PHRASAL VERB **1** If you **take to** someone or something, you like them immediately. *We asked him if the Russians would take to golf.* **2** If you **take to** doing something, you begin to do it regularly. *He took to wearing black leather jackets.*

take up PHRASAL VERB **1** If you **take up** an activity or job, you start doing it. *I thought I'd take up fishing... My assistant left to take up another post.* **2** If you **take up** an activity that was interrupted, you continue doing it from the point where it had stopped. *Sam took up the story.* **3** If you **take up** an idea or suggestion, you discuss it further. *The committee is expected to take up the question of government grants.* **4** If something **takes up** an amount of time, space, or effort, it uses that amount. *I won't take up any more of your time.*

take up on PHRASAL VERB If you **take** someone **up on** an offer that they have made, you accept their offer. *I didn't expect her to take me up on my invitation so soon.*

take upon PHRASAL VERB If you **take** it **upon** yourself to do something, you do it even though it is not your duty; a literary expression. *She took it upon herself to turn round and say 'Sh'.*

takeaway /teɪkəweɪ/ **takeaways**
1 NC A **takeaway** is a shop or restaurant which sells hot cooked food to be eaten elsewhere. *...the Chinese takeaway... People are eating more food from takeaway restaurants.* **2** NC A **takeaway** is also a hot cooked meal sold to be eaten elsewhere. *I fancy an Indian takeaway. ...takeaway pizzas.*

take-home pay
NU Your **take-home pay** is the amount of your wages or salary that is left after deductions such as income tax, pension contributions, and so on have been made. *His pension amounts to about 75% of his take-home pay before he retired.*

taken /teɪkn/
1 Taken is the past participle of take. **2** ADJ PRED+*with* If you are **taken with** something, you find it attractive and interesting. *Philip had been rather taken with the idea.*

takeoff /teɪkɒf/ **takeoffs**
NU or NC **Takeoff** is the beginning of a flight, when an aircraft leaves the ground. *Preparations have now been made for takeoff.*

takeover /teɪkəʊvə/ **takeovers**
1 NC A **takeover** occurs when someone buys enough shares in a company to gain control of it. *The trend towards takeovers has intensified. ...the proposed takeover of the Rover Group by British Aerospace.* **2** NC When someone takes control of a country by force, this is also described as a **takeover**. *He may be*

ousted by a military takeover... The coup attempt started with a takeover of the northwestern Chiriqui province.

takeover bid, takeover bids

NC A **takeover bid** is an attempt by a person or organization to take control of a company, usually by buying a lot of shares in the company. *...a small company which needed the money to finance its takeover bid for Manpower.*

taker /teɪkə/ **takers**

NC If there are no **takers** or few **takers** for an offer or challenge, hardly anyone is willing to accept it. *Recruiters are already trying to get volunteers. No takers so far.*

takings /teɪkɪŋz/

N PL The **takings** are the money that a shop, theatre, or cinema gets from selling its goods or tickets. *Already shop-keepers have seen their takings plummet.*

talc /tælk/

NU **Talc** is the same as **talcum powder**; an informal word. *I dusted myself with talc and began to dress.*

talcum powder /tælkəm paʊdə/

NU **Talcum powder** is a soft, perfumed powder which people put on their bodies after they have had a bath or a shower. *She smelled of soap and talcum powder.*

tale /teɪl/ **tales**

1 NC A **tale** is a story, especially one involving adventure or magic. *The first tale in the book is the story of Om Gad.*

2 NC You can refer to an account of an interesting real event as a **tale**. *Everyone had some tale to tell about the very cold winter.*

3 See also **old wives' tale**.

talent /tælənt/ **talents**

NU or NC **Talent** is the natural ability to do something well. *Your work shows a lot of talent... Rudolph had a talent for music.*

talented /tæləntɪd/

ADJ Someone who is **talented** has a natural ability to do something well. *He's a talented artist.*

talent scout, talent scouts

NC A **talent scout** is someone whose job is to go around looking for people who have talent as actors, dancers, footballers, comedians, and so on in order to offer them work. *A lot of the singers seem serious about their performance, as if a talent scout might be lurking in the audience taking notes.*

talisman /tælɪzmən/ **talismans**

NC A **talisman** is an object which you believe has magic powers to protect you or bring you good luck; a formal word. *Those icons are sacred talismans for him.*

talk /tɔːk/ **talks, talking, talked**

1 V When you **talk**, you say things to someone. *They talked about old times... He was the only one in the family she could talk to.* ▶ Also NC or NU *I must have a long talk with him... There was a lot of talk about his divorce.*

2 V When someone can **talk**, they have the ability to use spoken words to express their thoughts, ideas, or feelings. *Is your baby talking yet?... Nancy's throat was so sore that she could not talk.*

3 VO If you **talk** something such as politics or sport, you discuss it. *Let's talk a little business, shall we?*

4 V If you **talk** about or on something, you make an informal speech about it. *I talked yesterday about the history of the project.* ▶ Also NC *I used to give the staff a talk on psychology every week.*

5 N PL **Talks** are formal discussions, especially between two countries or two sides in a dispute. *After talks in Luxembourg, the ministers decided to meet again in a week's time... New peace talks in Nicaragua have run into trouble.*

6 You use **talking** of to introduce a new topic that is connected with something just mentioned. *Talking of girls, has anyone seen Sylvia Wicks recently?*

7 See also **small talk**.

talk down to PHRASAL VERB If someone **talks down to** you, they talk to you in a way that shows that they think they are cleverer or more important than you. *Many people object strongly to what they see as being*

talked down to by ministers.

talk into PHRASAL VERB If you **talk** someone **into** doing something, you persuade them to do it. *She talked me into taking a week's holiday.*

talk out of PHRASAL VERB If you **talk** someone **out of** doing something, you persuade them not to do it. *He tried to talk me out of buying such a big car.*

talk over PHRASAL VERB If you **talk** something **over**, you discuss it with someone. *I agreed to go home and talk things over with my father.*

talk up PHRASAL VERB When someone **talks up** a situation, they publicly refer to it in a way that makes it seem very important in order to make people believe or support their views. *The US has been talking up the effect of this operation... Clearly, campaigners for all three contenders are talking up support for their man.*

talkative /tɔːkətɪv/

ADJ Someone who is **talkative** talks a lot. *The Bishop is grey haired, short in stature, and extremely talkative.*

talkie /tɔːki/ **talkies**

NC A **talkie** is a cinema film made with sound as well as pictures; an old-fashioned word. *...in the days of the silent film and the early talkies.*

talking book, talking books

NC A **talking book** is a tape or cassette recording of a book, made especially for use by people who are blind.

talking point, talking points

NC A **talking point** is an interesting subject for discussion or argument. *The main talking point yesterday was the letter from President Gorbachev.*

talking-to

N SING If you give someone a **talking-to**, you tell them that you are angry about something that they have done. *My teacher gave me a real talking-to for not doing my homework... I got a hell of a talking-to when I got home.*

talk show, talk shows

NC A **talk show** is a television or radio show in which an interviewer and his or her guests talk in a friendly, informal way about different topics. *Recently he was a guest on a Johannesburg radio talk show.*

tall /tɔːl/ **taller, tallest**

1 ADJ Someone or something that is **tall** is above average height. *He was a tall, dark man. ...a tall cypress tree.*

2 ADJ or ADJ after N **Tall** is used in questions and statements about height. *How tall is he?... They were six-foot tall.*

3 If you say that a task is a **tall order**, you mean that it will be difficult to do. *It will be a tall order for the negotiators to conclude a treaty by that time.*

Tallinn /tælɪn/

Tallinn is the capital of Estonia and its largest city. Population: 503,000 (1989).

tall story, tall stories

NC A **tall story** is a story or statement that is difficult to believe, usually because it is so exaggerated or unlikely. *He was full of tall stories.*

tally /tæli/ **tallies, tallying, tallied**

1 NC A **tally** is an informal record of amounts which you keep adding to as an activity progresses. *Can you keep a tally of your own marks, please?*

2 V-RECIP If numbers or statements **tally**, they are exactly the same as each other or they give the same results or conclusions. *We've checked their stories and they don't quite tally... The amount she mentioned failed to tally with the figure shown in the records.*

Talmud /tælmʊd/

N PROP The **Talmud** is the collection of ancient Jewish laws which governs the religious and non-religious life of Orthodox Jews. *Much of the advice corresponds with that in the Jewish Talmud.*

talon /tælən/ **talons**

NC The **talons** of a bird of prey are its hooked claws. *The owl's formidable talons can carry birds up to the size of a chicken.*

tambourine /tæmbəriːn/ **tambourines**

NC A **tambourine** is a musical instrument which you shake or hit. It consists of a skin on a circular frame with pieces of metal around the edge which clash together. ...*people singing hymns and playing tambourines.*

tame /teɪm/ **tamer, tamest; tames, taming, tamed**
1 ADJ A **tame** animal or bird is not afraid of people and is not violent towards them. *He kept a tame bear in a tower above his room.* ◆ **tameness** NU *We were amazed at their tameness.*
2 ADJ **Tame** people do what they are told to do without questioning it; used showing disapproval. *...the spirit of defiance shown by their normally tame friends.* ◆ **tamely** ADV *These measures are unlikely to be accepted as tamely as the government hopes.*
3 ADJ You describe an activity as **tame** when you think that it is uninteresting because it does not involve anything exciting or shocking. *It sounded like a rather tame party.*
4 VO If you **tame** wild animals, you train them to be obedient and not to be afraid of people. *...the man who tamed deadly crocodiles... If they are comfortable, condors will breed and lay eggs, but if they are tamed, they will never get out of the zoo.*
5 VO If you **tame** people or things that are dangerous or likely to cause trouble, you bring them under control. *It has been a long, hard battle, and taming the rebels completely is still going to take time... Inflation has been tamed and Bolivia now has one of the lowest rates in Latin America.*

tam-o'shanter /tæməʃæntə/ **tam-o'shanters**
NC A **tam-o'shanter** is a soft woollen hat with a bobble in the centre, worn especially by Scots. *Lying back in the grass, she put her tam-o'shanter over her face and started to snore.*

tamp /tæmp/ **tamps, tamping, tamped**
tamp down PHRASAL VERB If you **tamp** something **down**, you press it down by tapping it several times so that it becomes more solid and compact. *One man shovelled tarmac into the hole, the other tamped it down.*

Tampax /tæmpæks/; **Tampax** is both the singular and the plural form.
NC A **Tampax** is a tampon; **Tampax** is a trademark.

tamper /tæmpə/ **tampers, tampering, tampered**
tamper with PHRASAL VERB If you **tamper with** something, you do something to it, and perhaps damage it, when you have no right to do so. *He claimed that his briefcase had been tampered with.*

tampon /tæmpɒn/ **tampons**
NC A **tampon** is a firm piece of cotton wool that a woman puts inside her vagina to absorb menstrual blood.

tan /tæn/
1 N SING If you have a **tan**, your skin has become darker than usual because you have been in the sun. *She had a beautiful golden tan.* ● See also **tanned**.
2 ADJ Something that is **tan** is pale brown or golden. *...tan shoes.*

tandem /tændəm/ **tandems**
1 NC A **tandem** is a bicycle designed for two riders. *We travelled round Cornwall on a tandem.*
2 If two people do something **in tandem**, they do it working together. If two things happen **in tandem**, they happen together. *...a new play we had written in tandem... A new European currency should exist only in tandem with national currencies.*

tandoori /tænduəri/
ADJ **Tandoori** dishes are Indian meat dishes which are cooked in a clay oven. *...tandoori chicken.* ▶ Also N SING *Prabhu came in with the tandoori.*

tang /tæŋ/
N SING A **tang** is a strong, sharp smell or taste. *...the tang of an expensive perfume... Smell the aromatic tang of the thyme.*

tangent /tændʒənt/ **tangents**
1 NC A **tangent** is a straight line that touches a curve at one point but does not cross it.
2 If you **go off at a tangent** or **go off on a tangent**, you start talking about something that is not directly connected with what you were talking about before. *The discussion goes off on a tangent, sometimes reverting to the original theme, but just as often not.*

tangential /tændʒenʃl/
ADJ A remark, method, or so on that is **tangential** has only a slight or indirect connection with something else; a formal word. *My remark was considered somewhat tangential.* ◆ **tangentially** ADV *You can either confront a problem directly or approach it tangentially.*

tangerine /tændʒəriːn/ **tangerines**
NC A **tangerine** is a small, sweet orange.

tangible /tændʒəbl/
ADJ Something that is **tangible** can be easily seen, felt, or noticed; a formal word. *So far, sanctions have had little tangible effect... He said that there was tangible evidence of his government's determination to restore peace.* ◆ **tangibly** ADV *The evidence tangibly supports his claim.*

tangle /tæŋgl/ **tangles, tangling, tangled**
1 NC A **tangle** is a mass of things such as string or hair twisted together untidily. *...an impenetrable tangle of creepers and trees.*
2 V-PASS Something that is **tangled** is twisted together untidily. *The wires got all tangled.*
3 V-PASS If you **are tangled** in something such as ropes or **are tangled** up in them, you are caught or trapped in them. *His leg got tangled in a harpoon line.*
tangle with PHRASAL VERB If you **tangle with** someone, you get involved in a fight or quarrel with them. *I'd certainly rather not tangle with some of these characters.*

tangled /tæŋgld/
1 ADJ ATTRIB If a story is **tangled**, it is very complicated. *Investigations are unveiling a tangled story of intrigue in high places.*
2 ADJ If something is **tangled**, it is twisted together in an untidy or complicated way so that it is difficult to unravel or smooth out. *She pushed the tangled hair back from her face... Debris was scattered around the tangled wreck of the truck.*

tango /tæŋgəʊ/ **tangos, tangoing, tangoed**
1 NC A **tango** is a South American dance for two people that has an unusual, very strong rhythm. *Can you do the tango?*
2 V When you **tango**, you dance the tango.

tangy /tæŋi/ **tangier, tangiest**
ADJ A **tangy** flavour or smell is one that is sharp, especially a flavour like lemon juice or a smell like that of sea air. *Outside families noisily devour rice and tangy aromatic dishes.*

tank /tæŋk/ **tanks**
1 NC A **tank** is a large container for holding liquid or gas. *...a petrol tank. ...the cold water tank. ...a tank of tropical fish.*
2 NC A **tank** is also a military vehicle covered with armour and equipped with guns or rockets. *...a special brigade armed with tanks and anti-aircraft weapons.*

tankard /tæŋkəd/ **tankards**
NC A **tankard** is a large metal beer mug. *...silver tankards. ...tankards of beer.*

tanked up
ADJ PRED Someone who is **tanked up** is very drunk; an informal expression. *They were pretty well tanked up before they even got to the party.*

tanker /tæŋkə/ **tankers**
NC A **tanker** is a ship or truck used for transporting large quantities of gas or liquid. *The tanker was loaded with almost 2,000 tonnes of oil.*

tanned /tænd/
ADJ If you are **tanned**, your skin is darker than usual because you have been in the sun. *He looked fit and tanned.*

tannery /tænəri/ **tanneries**
NC A **tannery** is a place where animal skins are made into leather. *The companies concerned were reportedly offering them forty dollars a ton to take waste from tanneries.*

tannin /tænɪn/
NU **Tannin** is a yellow or brown chemical found in plants such as tea, which is used in the process of making leather and in dyeing. *Eaten in sufficient quantities, tannin kills by fatally damaging the stomach and liver.*

Tannoy /tænɔɪ/
N SING The **Tannoy** is a system of loudspeakers used to

make public announcements, for example at a fete or at a sports stadium; **Tannoy** is a trademark. *Could you make an announcement over the Tannoy?*

tantalize /tǽntəlaɪz/ **tantalizes, tantalizing, tantalized;** also spelt **tantalise.**
VO If something or someone **tantalizes** you, they make you feel hopeful and excited, and then do not allow you to have what you want. *The possibility of still finding a peaceful settlement of the Gulf crisis has tantalised diplomats and politicians.*

tantalizing /tǽntəlaɪzɪŋ/; also spelt **tantalising.**
ADJ Something that is **tantalizing** makes you feel hopeful and excited, although you know that it is probably not possible to have it, do it, or so on. *This raises the tantalizing possibility that there may be life on other stars... That tantalizing prospect of a glimpse of Hardy's England was what first drew the landscape-painter to Dorset.* ◆ **tantalizingly** ADV *Sometimes a new idea may be tantalizingly close.*

tantamount /tǽntəmaʊnt/
ADJ PRED+to If you say that one thing is **tantamount** to another, you mean that it is almost the same as it; a formal word, used showing disapproval. *They regard the measures as tantamount to blackmail.*

tantrum /tǽntrəm/ **tantrums**
NC A **tantrum** is a noisy and childish outburst of bad temper. *Men are just as likely as women to have fits of temper or throw tantrums.*

Tanzania /tænzənííə/
The **United Republic of Tanzania** is a country in eastern Africa, consisting of the former country of Tanganyika and the islands of Zanzibar and Pemba. Tanganyika was a German colony from 1884 until the First World War, and was then administered by Britain until independence in 1961. Dr Julius Nyerere was President from 1962 until 1985. In 1964 Tanganyika and Zanzibar, a British protectorate from 1890 until 1963, merged to form Tanzania. It was a one-party state from 1965 until 1992, when the ruling Revolutionary Party of Tanzania (CMM) voted to legalize opposition parties. Ali Hassan Mwinyi became President of Tanzania at the retirement of Julius Nyerere in 1985. Tanzania is a member of the Commonwealth and the Organization of African Unity. It exports coffee and cotton. Zanzibar is the world's main producer of cloves. Large foreign debts and high inflation are major economic problems. ◆ **Tanzanian** /tænzəníːən/ N, ADJ
▪ *per capita GNP:* US$160 ▪ *religion:* Islam, Christianity ▪ *language:* Swahili and English (official) ▪ *currency:* shilling ▪ *capital:* Dar es Salaam (the administrative capital is transferring to Dodoma) ▪ *population:* 26 million (1989) ▪ *size:* 945,087 square kilometres.

Taoism /táʊɪzəm/
NU **Taoism** is a Chinese religious philosophy which believes that people should lead a simple, honest life and not interfere with the course of natural events.

tap /tǽp/ **taps, tapping, tapped**
1 NC A **tap** is a device that you turn in order to control the flow of a liquid or gas from a pipe or container. *They came out to get water from a nearby tap.*
2 VOorVA If you **tap** something or **tap** on it, you hit it lightly with your fingers or with something else such as a hammer. *It will come loose if you tap it with a hammer... She tapped on the glass partition.* ▸ Also NC *I heard a soft tap at the front door.*
3 VO If a phone is **tapped**, a device is secretly connected to it so that one person can listen to another person's calls without them knowing. *The new security service will have wide powers to search people and premises and tap telephones... They accused him of ordering the phones of senior politicians to be tapped.* ● See also **phone tapping.**
4 VO If you **tap** a resource or a situation, you make use of it by getting from it something that you need or want. *...a new way of tapping the sun's energy... Those who are in Taiwan are eager to try to tap what is potentially the world's biggest market.*

tap dancer, tap dancers
NC A **tap dancer** is a dancer who does tap dancing.

tap dancing
NU **Tap dancing** is a style of dancing in which the dancers wear special shoes with pieces of metal on the heels and toes. The shoes make clicking noises as the dancers move their feet.

tape /téɪp/ **tapes, taping, taped**
1 NU **Tape** is a narrow plastic strip covered with a magnetic substance. It is used to record sounds, pictures, and computer information. *...a conversation recorded on tape... Video tape is relatively cheap.*
2 NC A **tape** is a cassette or spool with magnetic tape wound round it. *His manager persuaded him to make a tape of the song.*
3 VO If you **tape** music, sounds, or television pictures, you record them using a tape recorder or a video recorder. *The talk has been taped.* ◆ **taped** ADJ ATTRIB *...a taped message from President Bush.*
4 NCorNU A **tape** is also a strip of cloth used to tie things together or to identify who a piece of clothing belongs to. *...name tapes. ...three metres of white tape.*
5 NU **Tape** is also a sticky strip of plastic used for sticking things together. *...a bit of adhesive tape.*
6 VOA If you **tape** one thing to another, you attach it using sticky tape. *Experts have made safe a grenade which was taped under a car.*
7 See also **red tape, videotape.**

tape deck, tape decks
NC On a hi-fi system, a **tape deck** is a machine on which you can play or record tapes. *We've got Cowboy Junkies in the tape deck.*

tape drive, tape drives
NC A **tape drive** is a machine which can be used to transfer information from a tape onto a computer, or to store information from a computer. *This is the world's first optical tape drive.*

tape measure, tape measures
NC A **tape measure** is a strip of plastic or cloth marked with centimetres or inches, which is used for measuring. *He took a tape measure to find out how thick the trunk was.*

taper /téɪpə/ **tapers, tapering, tapered**
V Something that **tapers** gradually becomes thinner at one end. *Eventually the gallery tapered to a long, narrow corridor.* ◆ **tapered** ADJ *The trousers should have tapered legs.* ◆ **tapering** ADJ *...long tapering fingers.*

taper off PHRASAL VERB If something **tapers off**, it gradually becomes much smaller in size or quantity. *They warned that economic growth will taper off next year.*

tape recorder, tape recorders
NC A **tape recorder** is a machine used for recording and playing tapes of music and other sounds. *The journalists carried tape recorders but no cameras.*

tape recording, tape recordings
NC A **tape recording** is a recording of sounds that has been made on tape. *Officials said a tape recording of the interview had been lost.*

tapestry /tǽpɪstri/ **tapestries**
1 NCorNU A **tapestry** is a piece of heavy cloth with a picture or pattern sewn on it. *The police recovered stolen goods including paintings, tapestries, and jewellery... They're experts in stretching and framing tapestry.*
2 NC+of You can refer to something as a **tapestry** when it is made up of many varied types of people or things; a literary use. *The only way to learn about the rich tapestry of life is to study plants, animals, and microbes in their natural environments.*

tapeworm /téɪpwɜːm/ **tapeworms**
NC A **tapeworm** is a long flat creature which lives in the stomach and intestines of animals or people. Tapeworms are parasites and get their food from the body of the animal or person they live in. *Now there is an effective vaccine which can protect sheep against tapeworms.*

tapioca /tæpiáʊkə/
NU **Tapioca** is a food consisting of white grains, rather like rice, which come from the cassava plant. *Thailand exports rice and tapioca to the Soviet Union.*

tar /tɑː/
1 NU **Tar** is a thick, black, sticky substance. It is used especially in making roads. *The fire started when workmen spilled hot tar on the roof... It looks like a lizard on the road, dry and stuck to the tar.*
2 NU **Tar** is also one of the poisonous substances present in tobacco. *Make cigarettes safer by reducing tar, nicotine and carbon monoxide levels.*

taramasalata /tærəməsəlɑːtə/
NU **Taramasalata** is a pink, creamy food made from the eggs of fish such as cod or mullet. It is usually eaten at the beginning of a meal.

tarantula /tərɛntjʊlə/ **tarantulas**
NC A **tarantula** is a large hairy spider which has a poisonous bite. *In Hawaii there's a marvellous spider, a kind of tarantula, which is in a group called the big-eyed spiders.*

tardy /tɑːdi/ **tardier, tardiest**; a literary word.
1 ADJ Something that is **tardy** happens or is done later than it should or than it was expected to. *I spent Monday morning writing tardy 'thank you' letters.*
♦ **tardily** ADV *He always replied rather tardily to my letters.* ♦ **tardiness** NU *I apologize for my tardiness in getting here.*
2 ADJ Something that is **tardy** moves or happens slowly. *We made tardy progress across the ice.*
♦ **tardiness** NU *...the tardiness of evolution.*

target /tɑːgɪt/ **targets, targeting, targeted**; also spelt **targetting, targetted**.
1 NC A **target** is a somewhere such as a building, town, or other place at which a missile or bomb has been aimed. *The target of the attack on Saturday was Larak oil terminal.*
2 NC A **target** is also an object at which you fire arrows, bullets, and so on when you are shooting for sport or practice. *My first two shots missed the target... We used it as a target for our Nerf balls and frisbees.*
3 NC You can refer to someone as a **target** when they have been attacked by another person or group using weapons. *The group was suspected of having a list of assassination targets.*
4 NC Someone or something that is being criticized can also be described as a **target**. *The aeroplane manufacturer has been the target of criticism about quality control standards.*
5 NC A **target** is also a result that you are trying to achieve. *It set a target for economic growth in excess of 4% a year... They have already passed their target of 100 gold medals.* ● If you are **on target**, you are making good progress and are likely to achieve the result you want. *The latest sales figures are on target.*
6 VO or VOA If someone **targets** a missile or some other weapon on something, they aim it at that thing. *B-52s continue to target Iraq's Republican Guard... A military spokesman said that three missiles were targeted on Teheran and two on the city of Qom.*
7 VO If you **target** a particular group of people or **target** something at them, you try to appeal to or affect those people. *The plan also targets additional countries, including Jordan... The scheme is targeted at salaried workers... Ministers maintain the new system is designed to target the poorest in society.*

tariff /tærɪf/ **tariffs**
1 NC A **tariff** is a tax on goods coming into a country. *European countries have agreed to cut tariffs and remove obstacles to the import of Third World goods.*
2 NC A **tariff** is also the rate at which you are charged for public services such as gas or electricity. *Check that you are on the correct tariff.*

Tarmac /tɑːmæk/
1 NU **Tarmac** is a material used for making road surfaces. It consists of crushed stones mixed with tar; **Tarmac** is a trademark. *He surveyed the expanse of tarmac, crisscrossed by traffic pounding down the Boulevard de Montparnasse.*
2 N SING You can refer to any area with a tarmac surface as the **tarmac**, especially the parts of an airport where planes stand before they take off or after they land. *A British Airways jumbo jet is now standing on the tarmac at Heathrow Airport waiting for clearance.*

tarnish /tɑːnɪʃ/ **tarnishes, tarnishing, tarnished**
1 V-ERG If metal **tarnishes** or if something **tarnishes** it, it becomes stained and loses its brightness. *Chrome doesn't tarnish easily... The damp atmosphere tends to tarnish the brass taps.* ♦ **tarnished** ADJ *...a photo in a tarnished silver frame.*
2 VO If something **tarnishes** your reputation, it damages it and causes people to lose their respect for you. *The killings tarnished the country's image.*
♦ **tarnished** ADJ *...an attempt to restore some of their tarnished popularity.*

tarot /tærəʊ/
N SING The **tarot** is a pack of cards with pictures on them that is used to predict what will happen to people in the future. *It is not known who invented the tarot... He sat cross-legged on the floor laying out tarot cards.*

tarpaulin /tɑːpɔːlɪn/ **tarpaulins**
NC A **tarpaulin** is a sheet of heavy, waterproof material that is used as a protective cover. *The portrait was later covered over with a tarpaulin.*

tarred /tɑːd/
1 ADJ A **tarred** road has a surface of tar. *He said there were 4.382 kilometres of tarred roads in Namibia.*
2 If you say that two or more people or things are **tarred with the same brush**, you mean that they are all considered to have the same faults. *She does seem to be tarred with the same brush as Bertrand as far as ruthlessness is concerned... Frequently all genetic engineering is tarred with the same brush.*

tarry, tarries, tarrying, tarried; pronounced /tæri/ when it is a verb and /tɑːri/ when it is an adjective.
1 V If you **tarry** somewhere, you stay there longer than you meant to and delay leaving; an old-fashioned use. *Some stayed overnight, but most tarried only a few hours before moving on.*
2 ADJ Something that is **tarry** is covered with tar or marked with tar. *...tarry stones from the garage roof.*

tart /tɑːt/ **tarts**
1 NC or NU A **tart** is a shallow pastry case with a sweet filling. *...jam tarts... Have another slice of tart.*
2 ADJ A **tart** remark is unpleasant and rather cruel; a literary use. *He made a tart reference to the Kuwait government, saying its leaders were leaving the running of the war up to the United States.* ♦ **tartly** ADV *She tartly pointed out that he owed her some money.*
3 NC If you refer to a woman or girl as a **tart**, you think that her behaviour is sexually immoral or that her appearance is obscene or vulgar in some way; an offensive use.

tartan /tɑːtn/
ADJ **Tartan** cloth, which mainly comes from Scotland, has different coloured stripes crossing each other. *He was wearing a traditional tartan kilt.*

tartar /tɑːtə/ **tartars**
1 NU **Tartar** is a hard yellowish substance that forms on your teeth.
2 NC A **tartar** is a fierce, bad-tempered person who is in a position of authority; an offensive use. *Their new boss is a bit of a tartar.*

tartar sauce; also spelt **tartare sauce**.
NU **Tartar sauce** is a thick cold sauce, usually eaten with fish, consisting of chopped onions and capers mixed with mayonnaise.

Tashkent /tæʃkɛnt/
Tashkent is the capital of Uzbekistan and its largest city. Population: 2,100,000 (1990).

task /tɑːsk/ **tasks**
NC A **task** is a piece of work that must be done. *Computers can be applied to a wide range of tasks... Tackling pollution on that scale is an awesome task.*

task force, task forces
1 NC A **task force** is a small section of an army, navy, or air force that is sent to a particular place to deal with a military crisis. *Australia has sent a naval task force to the troubled South Pacific islands of Vanuatu.*
2 NC A **task force** is also a group of people assembled in order to do a particular piece of work. *The authorities have set up a task force to try to resolve the problem of petrol shortages.*

taskmaster /tɑːskmɑːstə/ **taskmasters**

NC A **taskmaster** is a person who makes people work very hard. *I shall prove a very hard taskmaster, I warn you.*

tassel /tæsl/ **tassels**

NC A **tassel** is a bunch of threads attached to something as a decoration. *...the tassels on their cloaks.*

taste /teɪst/ **tastes, tasting, tasted**

1 NU Your sense of **taste** is your ability to recognize the flavour of things with your tongue. *Hangovers distort your sense of taste.*
2 N SING The **taste** of something is the flavour that it has, for example whether it is sweet or salty. *The soup was peppered and spiced to improve the taste.*
3 V AorV C If food or drink **tastes** of something, it has that particular flavour which you notice when you eat or drink it. *The tea tasted faintly of bitter almonds... The bananas were small and tasted like soap... Tinned tomatoes taste delicious.*
4 VO If you can **taste** something that you are eating or drinking, you are aware of its flavour. *Roger chewed and swallowed so fast that he hardly tasted the meat.*
5 VO If you **taste** food or drink, you try a small amount to see what its taste is like. *We tasted bread made from maize and cassava root.* ▶ Also N SING *I opened one of the bottles and had a taste of the contents.*
6 N SING If you have a **taste** for something, you enjoy it. *The children soon acquired a taste for Western food... He seems to have developed a taste for power.*
7 N SING If you have a **taste** of a state or activity, you experience it for a short time. *Many parts of England and Wales have been experiencing their first taste of severe winter weather.*
8 NU A person's **taste** is their liking for some things and dislike of others. *She has very good taste in clothes... It's a little too gory for my taste.*
9 If something is **in bad taste**, it is rather offensive. If it is **in good taste**, it is not offensive. *That remark was in rather poor taste.*

taste bud, taste buds

NC Your **taste buds** are the little points on the surface of your tongue which enable you to recognize the flavour of a food or drink. *...the mouth watering taste of seven different organic chemicals, all jostling to stimulate my taste buds.*

tasteful /teɪstfl/

ADJ Something that is **tasteful** is attractive and elegant. *The bedroom was simple but tasteful.*
◆ **tastefully** ADV *Their house was tastefully furnished.*

tasteless /teɪstləs/

1 ADJ Something that is **tasteless** is vulgar and unattractive. *...tasteless ornaments.*
2 ADJ A **tasteless** remark or joke is rather offensive. *Many people thought the question tasteless and unnecessary.*
3 ADJ **Tasteless** food has very little flavour and is therefore unpleasant. *A top French chef has criticized Britain's bread for being tasteless.*

taster /teɪstə/ **tasters**

1 NC A **taster** is someone whose job is to taste different wines, teas, or other foods or drinks, in order to test their quality. *It is the job of the wine taster to determine exactly the right stage in its development for a particular wine to be bottled.*
2 NC A **taster** of something is a small amount of it which is intended to make you interested in it, or to make you want more. *As a taster, Mr Grove showed me the potted snails in his freezer... Among the tasters he has offered so far is information regarding the Libyan chemicals plant at Rabta.*

tasty /teɪsti/ **tastier, tastiest**

ADJ **Tasty** food has a fairly strong, often savoury flavour which you find pleasant. *He found the chicken to be delicious and very tasty.*

ta-ta /tætɑː/

Ta-ta is a way of saying goodbye; used in informal speech. *'Ta-ta,' she said, 'Be seeing you.'*

tattered /tætəd/

1 ADJ **Tattered** material or paper is torn or crumpled. *...tattered banners in black and red.*

2 ADJ A **tattered** idea, hope, plan, or organization has been badly damaged or has failed completely. *The reported peace agreement now looks very tattered. ...the tattered ideology of single party unity.*

tatters /tætəz/

1 If something such as a plan, organization, or a person's state of mind is **in tatters**, it is weak and has suffered a lot of damage, and therefore is likely to fail completely. *The economy is in tatters following a series of natural disasters... His career is in tatters.*
2 Clothes that are **in tatters** are badly torn. *He was so poor that he lived in a cave and his single robe was in tatters.*

tattoo /tətuː/ **tattoos, tattooing, tattooed**

1 VO If someone **tattoos** you, they draw a design on your skin by pricking little holes and filling them with coloured dye. *He had tattooed the name 'Marlene' on his upper arm.* ◆ **tattooed** ADJ *...a tattooed sailor.*
2 NC A **tattoo** is a design tattooed on someone's body. *They have treated several volunteers from the Australian army who wished to have tattoos removed.*
3 NC If you beat a **tattoo**, you hit something quickly and repeatedly. *He beat a frantic tattoo with his hands on the door.*
4 NC A military **tattoo** is a public display of exercises and music given by members of the armed forces. *...bands from the Edinburgh military tattoo.*

tatty /tæti/

ADJ Something that is **tatty** is in bad condition; an informal word. *The house is very tatty.*

Taufa'ahau Tupou IV, King /taʊfə əhaʊ tuːpəʊ/

King Taufa'ahau Tupou IV succeeded to the throne of Tonga on the death of his mother, Queen Salote Tupou III, in 1965. He served as Minister of Education in 1943, and of Health from 1944 to 1949. He was Premier from 1949 to 1965. Born: 1918.

taught /tɔːt/

Taught is the past tense and past participle of **teach**.

taunt /tɔːnt/ **taunts, taunting, taunted**

VO If you **taunt** someone, you speak offensively to them about their weaknesses or failures in order to upset or annoy them. *The prisoners are now perched on the edge of the roof from where they have been taunting the prison officers below.* ▶ Also NC *The children had to put up with taunts like 'You haven't got a Dad.'*

taut /tɔːt/

1 ADJ Something that is **taut** is stretched very tight. *There will be a very taut wire running along the ground.*
2 ADJ Someone who is **taut** is very tense and worried. *You see children's faces absolutely frantic, taut with the concentration of whether they are going to get their daily bread ration.*
3 ADJ If a piece of writing or a film is **taut**, it is very concentrated and controlled, with no unnecessary or irrelevant details. *The taut melodies and rhythms of the Turkish band began to play their magic... Mann is clearly a master of taut construction, and the film easily outclasses the average thriller.*

tauten /tɔːtn/ **tautens, tautening, tautened**

V If something **tautens**, it becomes very tightly stretched. *The rope tautened... The sinews in his neck tautened.*

tautological /tɔːtəlɒdʒɪkl/

ADJ A **tautological** statement is one that uses different words to say the same thing twice. 'The money should be adequate enough' is an example of a tautological statement because 'adequate' and 'enough' mean the same thing.

tautology /tɔːtɒlədʒi/ **tautologies**

NCorNU A **tautology** is a statement which uses different words to say the same thing twice. *...a speech full of tautology... 'I have rambled. I hope I have not been talking in tautologies.'*

tavern /tævən/ **taverns**

NC A **tavern** is a pub; an old-fashioned word. *No one could visit a tavern on a Sunday.*

tawdry /tɔːdri/ **tawdrier, tawdriest**

1 ADJ Something that is **tawdry** is cheap and badly made. *He was looking at some rather tawdry hats in a shop window.*

2 ADJ A **tawdry** act is shameful. *He spoke of Iraqi brutality as a tawdry performance that was base, outrageous and despicable.*

tawny /ˈtɔːni/ **tawnier, tawniest**
ADJ Something, especially fur or skin, that is **tawny** in colour is yellowish-brown. *...tawny cats. ...a tawny sunset.*

tax /tæks/ **taxes, taxing, taxed**
1 NUorNC **Tax** is an amount of money that you have to pay to the government so that it can pay for public services. *...a decision to alter the rate of tax on wine and beer... We do not propose to increase income tax... He has attacked plans to levy a tax on tourists visiting the Lake District. ...a reduction in taxes... The Chancellor seemed to have plenty of financial room for tax cuts.*
2 VO If a sum of money is **taxed**, you have to pay some money to the government when you get it. *Their pay is taxed at a very high rate.*
3 VO When goods are **taxed**, a part of their price has to be paid to the government. *Crops were taxed very heavily.*
4 VO If a person or company is **taxed**, they have to pay a part of their income or profits to the government. *Married women are to be taxed independently for the first time.*
5 See also **poll tax, taxing, withholding tax.**

taxable /ˈtæksəbl/
ADJ If something is **taxable**, you have to pay tax on it. *Revenues might increase because people would be earning more taxable income.*

taxation /tækˈseɪʃn/
1 NU **Taxation** is the system by which a government collects money from people and spends it on such things as defence, education, and health care. *The total cost of the NHS has to be raised through taxation.*
2 NU **Taxation** is also the amount that people have to pay in taxes. *The government is hoping to reduce taxation.*

tax avoidance
NU **Tax avoidance** is the use of legal methods to pay the smallest possible amount of tax. *...a government crack-down on tax avoidance.*

tax-deductible /ˌtæksdɪdˈʌktəbl/
ADJ An expense that is **tax-deductible** can be deducted from your taxable income, so that the amount of tax that you have to pay is smaller. *Because I work at home, some of my heating and lighting bills are tax-deductible.*

tax disc, tax discs
NC In Britain, a **tax disc** is a small round piece of paper which is displayed on the windscreen of a car or in a special holder on a motorcycle, which proves that the owner has paid the annual road tax. *Drivers not displaying a tax disc merely received a warning from the police.*

tax evasion
NU **Tax evasion** is the crime of not paying the full amount of tax that you should. *He has served a year in prison for tax evasion.*

tax-free
ADJ If goods or services are **tax-free**, you do not have to pay tax on them. *They are upset about restrictions on their ability to bring tax-free goods into the country.*

tax haven, tax havens
NC A **tax haven** is a country or place which has a low rate of taxation, so that people choose to live there or register companies there in order to avoid paying higher tax in their own countries. *The Isle of Man is still a tax haven.*

taxi /ˈtæksi/ **taxis; taxies, taxiing, taxied**
1 NC A **taxi** is a car whose driver is paid by people to take them where they want to go. *The two men were rushed away by taxi. ...a taxi driver.*
2 V When an aircraft **taxies**, it moves slowly along the runway before taking off or after landing. *The Boeing taxied down the runway.*

taxicab /ˈtæksikæb/ **taxicabs**
NC A **taxicab** is the same as a **taxi**. *On the evening I first met Natasha, we shared a taxicab.*

taxidermy /ˈtæksidɜːmi/
NU **Taxidermy** is the craft of stuffing dead animals and birds so that they look lifelike and can be displayed. *In a busy life of exploration and taxidermy, he learnt how to stuff a toucan without losing the delicate natural colour of the beak.*

taxing /ˈtæksɪŋ/
ADJ A **taxing** task requires a lot of mental or physical effort. *Of being Archbishop of Canterbury he said 'it's a very taxing job indeed'.*

taxi rank, taxi ranks
NC A **taxi rank** is a place where taxis wait for passengers, for example at an airport or outside a station. *They were standing at a crowded taxi rank.*

taxonomy /tækˈsɒnəmi/ **taxonomies**
NUorNC **Taxonomy** is the classification and naming of things such as animals and plants in groups within a larger system, according to their similarities and differences; a technical term.

taxpayer /ˈtækspeɪə/ **taxpayers**
NC **Taxpayers** are people who pay a percentage of their income to the government as tax. *All taxpayers will receive the same basic allowance... These measures will cost the taxpayer almost twenty-million pounds.*

tax relief
NU **Tax relief** is a reduction in the amount of tax that a person or company has to pay, for example because of expenses associated with their business, work, or house. *It is also proposed to phase out tax relief on mortgages.*

tax year, tax years
NC A **tax year** is a particular period of twelve months which is used by the government as a basis for calculating taxes and for organizing its own finances and accounts. In Britain, the tax year begins on April 6th and ends on April 5th. *Many of these benefits will be lost when the new tax year starts in April.*

Taya, Maawiya Ould Sid'Ahmed
/ˈmaʊjə wɪld sɪdi ɑːxməd ˈtɑːjə/
Colonel **Maawiya Ould Sid'Ahmed Taya** became President of Mauritania in a coup in 1984. He served as Minister of Defence from 1978 to 1979, Commander of the National Gendarmarie from 1979 to 1980, and Army Chief of Staff from 1980 to 1981, and in 1984. He was Prime Minister from 1981 to 1984. In 1991 he founded and became the Chairman of the Democratic and Social Republican Party (PRDS). Born: 1943.

TB /ˌtiːˈbiː/
NU **TB** is an infectious disease which usually attacks the lungs. **TB** is an abbreviation for 'tuberculosis'. *There are effective drugs available to cure TB.*

Tbilisi /tɪbɪˈliːsi/
Tbilisi is the capital of Georgia and its largest city. Population: 1,264,000 (1989).

tbs.
tbs. is a written abbreviation for 'tablespoonful'; used especially in recipes.

tbsp., tbsps.
tbsp. is a written abbreviation for 'tablespoonful'; used especially in recipes.

tea /tiː/ **teas**
1 N MASS **Tea** is a drink made with hot water and the chopped, dried leaves of a particular bush. *She went into the kitchen to make a fresh pot of tea... Two teas, please.*
2 NU **Tea** is also the chopped, dried leaves that you use to make tea. *...a packet of tea.*
3 N MASS+SUPP Other drinks made with hot water and leaves or flowers are also called **tea**. *...mint tea.*
4 NUorNC **Tea** is also a light meal that is eaten in the afternoon, or in the early evening. *Mr Evans is coming to tea. ...delicious afternoon teas.*
5 If you say that something is **not your cup of tea**, you mean that you do not like it and would not choose to do it or have it. *Ballet isn't really my cup of tea.*

tea bag, tea bags
NC A **tea bag** is a small paper bag with tea leaves in it which is put into hot water to make tea. *You put your tea leaves or your tea bags into the brewing column and pour the water in.*

tea break, tea breaks
NC A **tea break** is a short time, usually in the morning and the afternoon, when you stop working and have a cup of tea or coffee. *She usually takes a fifteen-minute tea break at 3 o'clock.*

tea caddy, tea caddies
NC A **tea caddy** is a small tin in which you keep tea.

teacake /tiːkeɪk/ **teacakes**
NC A **teacake** is a round, flat cake with raisins in it. It is usually toasted and eaten with butter.

teach /tiːtʃ/ **teaches, teaching, taught**
1 VOO, VO-REPORT, VO+*to*-INF, or VOA If you **teach** someone something, you give them instructions so that they know about it or know how to do it. *The trainers also teach them entrepreneurial skills... Mother taught me how to read... Boylan had taught him to drive... Some people are very anxious to teach you about all the plants. ...a kit to teach dental hygiene to blind children.*
2 VOO, VO-REPORT, or VO+*to*-INF If you **teach** someone to think or behave in a particular way, you persuade them to think or behave in that way. *We are trying to teach women self-reliance... Boys are often taught that they mustn't show their feelings... We've been taught to believe in the wisdom of those who govern us.*
3 VO, VO+*to*, or V If you **teach**, your job is to help students to learn about something at a school, college, or university. *I taught history for many years... What's the best way to teach technology to children?... He taught for many years at the London School of Economics.*

teacher /tiːtʃə/ **teachers**
NC A **teacher** is someone who teaches, especially at a school. *They are doing their best to recruit more teachers. ...a French teacher.*

tea chest, tea chests
NC A **tea chest** is a large wooden box in which tea is packed when it is exported. Some people use tea chests for putting things in when they move from one house to another. *I filled two and a half tea chests with my books.*

teach-in, teach-ins
NC A **teach-in** is a meeting between students and teachers at which important and controversial subjects can be discussed. Teach-ins are not usually part of a formal academic course. Used in American English. *Teach-ins are planned at 500 college campuses today to protest at the possibility of war in the Persian Gulf.*

teaching /tiːtʃɪŋ/ **teachings**
1 NU **Teaching** is the work that a teacher does. *...the professions of medicine, dentistry, and teaching.*
2 NPL The **teachings** of a religious or political thinker are the ideas that he or she teaches to other people. *His teachings still exert a strong influence.*

teaching hospital, teaching hospitals
NC A **teaching hospital** is a hospital that is linked with a medical school, where medical students and newly qualified doctors receive practical training. *Nurses at three big teaching hospitals in London have voted to strike.*

teaching practice
NU **Teaching practice** is a period that a student teacher spends at a school doing practical teaching as part of his or her training.

teacloth /tiːklɒθ/ **teacloths**
NC A **teacloth** is a cloth which you use to dry dishes, cutlery, and so on, after they have been washed. *He rinsed the cups and wiped them on a decorated teacloth.*

tea cosy, tea cosies
NC A **tea cosy** is a soft cover of cloth or wool which you put over a teapot to keep the tea hot.

teacup /tiːkʌp/ **teacups**
1 NC A **teacup** is a cup that you drink tea from. *...a china teacup.*
2 If you describe a situation as a **storm in a teacup**, you mean that you think that a lot of fuss is being made about something which is not really important; an informal expression. *This week's incidents look like a storm in a teacup.*

teak /tiːk/
NU **Teak** is a very hard wood that comes from a kind

of tree that grows in South-East Asia. *...the harvest of valuable timber such as mahogany and teak.*

tea leaf, tea leaves
NC **Tea leaves** are the small pieces of dried leaves that are left in a teapot or a cup after you have drunk the tea.

team /tiːm/ **teams, teaming, teamed**
1 N COLL A **team** is a group of people who play together against another group in a sport or game. *The Turkish football team have been beaten by five goals to nil... The women's gymnastics team won their fifth consecutive title.*
2 N COLL You can refer to any group of people who work together as a **team**. *He and his team devised a new sales leaflet to promote the Electrodyne... Mr Brooke and his team of ministers spent nearly five hours in formal talks with an Irish delegation.*
team up PHRASAL VERB If you **team up** with someone, you join with them in order to work together for a particular purpose. *He teamed up with a friend and set up a business doing interior decorating.*

team-mate, team-mates
NC If people who play a sport or game are **team-mates**, they are members of the same team. *Their team-mate Mauro Baldi finished second.*

team spirit
NU **Team spirit** is the feeling of pride and loyalty that exists among the members of a team and that makes them want their team to do well or to be the best. *...the unquenchable team spirit of the Lions.*

teamwork /tiːmwɜːk/
NU **Teamwork** is action in which a group of people work together effectively. *Teamwork was even more important in the later stages of the project.*

tea party, tea parties
NC A **tea party** is a social event in the afternoon at which people have tea, sandwiches, and cakes. *They gave a tea party for Queen Elizabeth and the Queen Mother.*

teapot /tiːpɒt/ **teapots**
NC A **teapot** is a container with a lid, a handle, and a spout, used for making and serving tea. *He poured himself some more tea from the teapot on the table.*

tear, tears, tearing, tore, torn; pronounced /tɪə/ for the meaning in paragraph 1, and /teə/ for the meanings in paragraphs 2 to 6.
1 NC **Tears** are the drops of liquid that come out of your eyes when you cry. *Tears were streaming down her face.* ● If someone is **in tears**, they are crying. *She rushed out of the room, in tears... When Curzon heard the news, he burst into tears.*
2 V-ERG If you **tear** something made of cloth or paper, or if it **tears**, you pull it so that a hole appears in it, or you pull it to pieces. *He tore both letters into small pieces... I tugged at the sleeve to get it free; it tore.*
◆ **torn** ADJ *...my torn sweater.*
3 NC A **tear** in something made of cloth is a hole that has been made in it. *There was a triangular tear at the knee of his trousers.* ● See also **wear and tear.**
4 If you **tear** something **open**, you open it by tearing it. *He tore open the envelope.*
5 VOA If you **tear** a page or a piece of paper out of a book, you remove it by pulling it out sharply rather than cutting it out. *She tore several sheets out of the book.*
6 VOA If a powerful force **tears** something from somewhere, it removes it roughly and violently. *Boats were torn from their moorings by the storm.*
7 VA If you **tear** somewhere, you move there very quickly. *They tore down the street after the dog.*
8 V-PASS If you **are torn** between two or more things, you cannot decide which one to choose. *The Government is torn between the desire to free citizens held by kidnappers and the refusal to do deals with terrorists.*
9 See also **tearing.**
tear apart PHRASAL VERB 1 If you **tear** something **apart**, you pull it into pieces violently. *I tore the parcel apart.* 2 If something **tears** an organization or country **apart**, it causes great quarrels or disturbances. *...a crisis which threatens to tear society apart.*

tear at PHRASAL VERB If you **tear at** something, you violently try to pull pieces off it. *The boys tore at the meat like wolves.*

tear away PHRASAL VERB If you **tear** yourself **away** from a place, you come away very unwillingly. *Mourners often find it difficult to tear themselves away from the grave.*

tear down PHRASAL VERB If you **tear down** a building, you destroy it. *It is often cheaper to tear down the buildings than to modify them.*

tear off PHRASAL VERB If you **tear** your clothes **off**, you take them off quickly in a rough way. *Some of the policemen tore off their uniforms and joined the demonstration.*

tear up PHRASAL VERB If you **tear up** a piece of paper, you pull it into a lot of small pieces. *Some of the students tore up their examination papers.*

tearaway /ˈteərəweɪ/ **tearaways**
NC A **tearaway** is a young person who behaves in a wild and uncontrolled way. *The drunken tearaway teenager may well be the victim of his genes rather than corruption by his peers.*

teardrop /ˈtɪədrɒp/ **teardrops**
NC A **teardrop** is a large pear-shaped tear that comes from your eye when you are crying quietly. *A teardrop glistened on her cheek.*

tearful /ˈtɪəfl/
ADJ Someone who is **tearful** is crying or is about to cry. *A small, naked, tearful boy sat at her side... There were many tearful reunions.* ◆ **tearfully** ADV *'I don't love you anymore,' explained Belinda tearfully.*

tear gas /ˈtɪə gæs/
NU **Tear gas** is a gas that causes your eyes to sting and fill with tears. It is used by the police to control violent crowds. *They used tear gas to disperse the demonstrators.*

tearing /ˈteərɪŋ/
ADJ ATTRIB If you are in a **tearing** hurry, you are trying to go somewhere or do something as quickly as possible. *I'm in a tearing hurry this morning.*

tear-jerker /ˈtɪədʒɜːkə/ **tear-jerkers**
NC A **tear-jerker** is a play, film, or book that is very sad or sentimental; an informal word.

tea-room, tea-rooms
NC A **tea-room** is the same as a **tea shop**. *At the far end of the tea-room, cafeteria service is available.*

tease /tiːz/ **teases, teasing, teased**
VO,VOA,orV-QUOTE If you **tease** someone, you deliberately embarrass them or make fun of them, because this amuses you. *I started to tease the people that continued to smoke... She teased him about his girlfriends... 'Ah hah,' the old man teased, 'perhaps you already have a child?'*

teasel /ˈtiːzl/ **teasels**; also spelt **teazel** or **teazle**.
NC A **teasel** is a plant with dry prickly flower-heads and prickly leaves.

teaser /ˈtiːzə/ **teasers**
1 NC A **teaser** is a difficult question, especially one in a quiz or competition; an informal use. *Every so often a teaser is thrown up that leaves everyone wondering.*
2 NC A **teaser** is also someone who makes fun of people in a slightly cruel way.

tea service, tea services
NC A **tea service** is the same as a **tea set**.

tea set, tea sets
NC A **tea set** is a set of cups, saucers, and plates, with a milk jug, a sugar bowl, and a teapot, used when tea is served.

tea shop, tea shops
NC A **tea shop** is a small restaurant or café where tea, coffee, cakes, and light meals are served. *If you sit in the tea shops in Rangoon, you'll hear incredible stories about what's going on.*

Teasmaid /ˈtiːzmeɪd/ **Teasmaids**
NC A **Teasmaid** is a device which automatically makes tea at a pre-set time. People use Teasmaids in order to have a cup of tea ready when they wake up in the morning. Teasmaid is a trademark.

teaspoon /ˈtiːspuːn/ **teaspoons**
1 NC A **teaspoon** is a small spoon, often used to stir sugar in cups of tea or coffee.

2 NC A **teaspoon** of food or liquid is the amount that a teaspoon will hold. *...a teaspoon of salt.*

teaspoonful /ˈtiːspuːnfʊl/ **teaspoonfuls** or **teaspoonsful**
NC A **teaspoonful** is the amount that a teaspoon will hold. *...a quarter of a teaspoonful of salt.*

tea strainer, tea strainers
NC A **tea strainer** is a metal or plastic object with small holes in it, used to stop tea leaves going into the cup when you are pouring tea.

teat /tiːt/ **teats**
1 NC A **teat** is a nipple on the chest or stomach of a female animal from which its babies suck milk. *...tiny naked pink creatures clinging to the teats with their mouths.*
2 NC A **teat** is also a piece of rubber shaped like a teat and fitted to a baby's feeding bottle. *The baby grabbed the teat and began to suck.*

teatime /ˈtiːtaɪm/
NU **Teatime** is the time in the afternoon when some people have a light meal. *At teatime there was much excited chatter around the table.*

tea-towel, tea-towels
NC A **tea-towel** is a cloth used for drying dishes and cutlery.

teazel /ˈtiːzl/. See teasel.

teazle /ˈtiːzl/. See teasel.

tech /tek/ **techs**
NC A **tech** is the same as a **technical college**; used in informal speech.

technical /ˈteknɪkl/
1 ADJ ATTRIB **Technical** means involving machines, processes, and materials used in industry, transport, and communications. *He agreed to provide technical assistance.* ◆ **technically** SUBMOD *They were very highly industrialised and technically advanced.*
2 ADJ ATTRIB You also use **technical** to describe the practical skills and methods used to do an activity such as an art, a craft, or a sport. *...wood carving of remarkable technical skill.*
3 ADJ **Technical** language involves using special words to describe the details of a specialized activity. *None of them were able to provide the sort of information we wanted in technical terms... Most of the discussions have been very technical.*

technical college, technical colleges
NC A **technical college** is a college in Britain where you can study art and technical subjects, usually as part of the qualifications and training required for a particular job. *There are many more training courses on offer—at technical colleges and other centres.*

technicality /teknɪˈkæləti/ **technicalities**
1 NC The **technicalities** of a process or activity are the detailed methods used to do it. *ICC delegates discussed the legal technicalities in London this morning... The petition does not say how these endorsements should be collected, but that, presumably, is a technicality.*
2 NC A **technicality** is a point that is based on a strict interpretation of a law or a set of rules. *On a technicality, the judge dismissed the case.*

technically /ˈteknɪkəli/
1 ADV If something is **technically** true or possible, it is true or possible according to the facts, laws, or rules but may not be important or relevant in a particular situation. *The two governments have never recognised each other, in fact they're still technically at war... He was technically in breach of contract.*
2 ADV You use **technically** when discussing the practical skills and methods used to do an art, a craft, or a sport. *Pollock was certainly a skilful artist technically.*

technician /tekˈnɪʃn/ **technicians**
NC A **technician** is someone whose job involves skilled practical work with scientific equipment. *They do require a trained technician to run them properly. ...a dental technician.*

Technicolor /ˈteknɪkʌlə/
NU **Technicolor** is a system of colour photography used in making cinema films; **Technicolor** is a trademark. *...staged in Technicolor by Warner Brothers in 1938. ...the most beautiful Technicolor movie ever made.*

technique /tekniːk/ **techniques**
1 NC A **technique** is a particular method of doing something. *...the techniques of film-making. ...a new technique developed in Germany.*
2 NU or NC **Technique** is skill and ability in an artistic, sporting, or other practical activity that is developed through training and practice. *...Sinead O'Connor's startling vocal technique... She owed her technique entirely to his teaching.*

technocracy /teknɒkrəsi/ **technocracies**; a formal word.
1 N COLL A **technocracy** is a group of scientists, engineers, and other experts who have political power as well as technical knowledge. *...the cream of the military technocracy.*
2 NC You can refer to a country or society that is controlled by scientists, engineers, and other experts as a **technocracy**.

technocrat /teknəkræt/ **technocrats**
NC A **technocrat** is a scientist, engineer, or other expert who is one of a group of similar people who have political power as well as technical knowledge; a formal word. *Key economic positions continue to be held by technocrats... He would be on the whole content to leave economic policy to qualified technocrats.*

technological /teknəlɒdʒɪkl/
ADJ ATTRIB **Technological** means relating to technology. *...modern scientific and technological knowledge. ...technological and managerial skills.*
♦ **technologically** ADV *...the world's most technologically advanced nations.*

technology /teknɒlədʒi/ **technologies**
1 NU **Technology** is the activity or study of using scientific knowledge for practical purposes. *...advances in technology and science.* ♦ **technologist** /teknɒlədʒɪst/ **technologists** NC *...a small group of distinguished scientists and technologists.*
2 NC+SUPP or NU+SUPP A **technology** is the scientific equipment and methods used in a particular area of activity. *...computer technology... The plane's advanced technology makes it easier to fly.*

teddy /tedi/ **teddies**
NC A **teddy** or a **teddy bear** is a children's soft toy that looks like a friendly bear. *Her face lit up when she was given a teddy bear.*

Teddy boy, Teddy boys
NC A **Teddy boy** is a man who dresses in a style that became popular in the 1950's. Teddy boys were associated with early rock and roll music, and often regarded as bad or violent. *This was the era of Teddy boys and mods and rockers.*

tedious /tiːdiəs/
ADJ **Tedious** things are boring, often detailed, and seem to last for a long time. *The arguments were tedious and complicated. ...remarkably tedious work.*

tedium /tiːdiəm/
NU The **tedium** of a situation is its quality of being boring and seeming to last for a long time; a formal word. *...a cricket match of unspeakable tedium.*

tee /tiː/ **tees, teeing, teed**
1 NC In golf, a **tee** is a small piece of wood or plastic which is pushed into the ground and is used to support the golf ball before it is hit at the start of an attempt to get the ball into one of the holes.
2 NC A **tee** is also one of the small flat areas of ground on a golf course from which people start their attempts to get the ball into each of the holes. *Standing on the final tee he was three strokes clear.*
tee off PHRASAL VERB If you **tee off**, you hit a golf ball from a tee at the start of a hole. *...teeing off for his daily game.*
tee up PHRASAL VERB If you **tee up**, you place a golf ball on a tee so that it is ready for you to hit it.

teem /tiːm/ **teems, teeming, teemed**
V+*with* If a place is **teeming** with people, there are a lot of people moving around in it in an unorganized way. *...a large, busy capital teeming with people.*
♦ **teeming** ADJ ATTRIB *She walked home through the teeming streets.*

teen /tiːn/ **teens**
1 N PL Your **teens** are the period of your life when you

are between thirteen and nineteen years old. *She was young, maybe still in her teens.*
2 ADJ ATTRIB In American English, **teen** is used to refer to things and activities relating to people aged between thirteen and nineteen. *...her teen days... 'Flute Song Magic' is a teen fantasy about a nobleman.*
3 NC In American English, a **teen** is someone aged between thirteen and nineteen. *Any teen who wanted to get a summer job could get one.*

teenage /tiːneɪdʒ/
1 ADJ ATTRIB **Teenage** people are aged between thirteen and nineteen. *...a divorced woman with two teenage children... So vivid was my teenage imagination, I think I believed it myself.*
2 ADJ ATTRIB **Teenage** fashions and activities are typical of young people aged between thirteen and nineteen, or are suitable for them. *...the teenage culture of pop music.*

teenaged /tiːneɪdʒd/
ADJ ATTRIB **Teenaged** people are aged between thirteen and nineteen. *...a survey of smoking habits among 500 teenaged children.*

teenager /tiːneɪdʒə/ **teenagers**
NC A **teenager** is someone between thirteen and nineteen years of age. *For teenagers the problems are particularly severe... Many teenagers travel daily into the city.*

teeny /tiːni/ **teenier, teeniest**
ADJ ATTRIB **Teeny** means very small; an informal word. *I must admit to a teeny touch of envy.*

teeny-bopper /tiːnibɒpə/ **teeny-boppers**
NC A **teeny-bopper** is a teenager, usually a girl, who is very interested in pop music; an old-fashioned, informal word, often used humorously. *...American teeny-bopper turned pop star, Debbie Gibson.*

tee shirt. See T-shirt.

teeter /tiːtə/ **teeters, teetering, teetered**
1 V If someone or something **teeters**, they seem about to fall over. *I hovered and teetered on the edge of the cliff.*
2 V+*on* **Teeter** is also used in expressions like 'teeter on the brink' and 'teeter on the edge' to describe situations which are very close to becoming disastrous. *British theatre is teetering on the brink of ruin... The situation is teetering daily on the edge of crisis.*

teeth /tiːθ/
Teeth is the plural of **tooth.**

teethe /tiːð/ **teethes, teething, teethed**
V When babies are **teething**, their teeth are starting to appear, usually causing them pain. *He's teething at the moment, poor little thing.*

teething troubles
N PL **Teething troubles** or **teething problems** are difficulties which arise at the beginning of a project or when something is new. *I think they're having teething troubles... Most of the engine's teething problems have been dealt with.*

teetotal /tiːtəʊtl/
ADJ Someone who is **teetotal** never drinks alcohol. *18 percent of people here claim to be teetotal.*

teetotaller /tiːtəʊtələ/ **teetotallers**
NC A **teetotaller** is someone who never drinks alcohol. *A non-smoking teetotaller is celebrating his one hundred and seventh birthday.*

TEFL /tefl/
NU **TEFL** is the teaching of English to people whose first language is not English. TEFL is an abbreviation for 'teaching English as a foreign language'.

Teflon /teflɒn/
NU **Teflon** is a type of plastic which is often used to coat cooking pans. Teflon provides a surface which food does not stick to, so the pan can be cleaned more easily. Teflon is a trademark. *...a Teflon baking tray... You can get Teflon frying-pans.*

Tegucigalpa /tɪɡuːsɪɡælpə/
Tegucigalpa is the capital of Honduras and its largest city. Population: 608,000 (1989).

Tehrān /teərɑːn/
Tehrān is the capital of Iran and its largest city. Population: 6,022,000 (1986).

Tel Aviv /tel əviːv/
Tel Aviv is Israel's second largest city and former capital. Although Jerusalem became the capital in 1967, many foreign governments refuse to move their embassies from Tel Aviv. Population: 318,000 (1988).

telecommunications /tɛlikəmjuːnɪkeɪʃnz/
NU Telecommunications is the science and activity of sending signals and messages over long distances using electronic equipment. *Central government departments spend some two hundred and eighty million pounds a year on telecommunications... Telecommunications out of Monrovia have been cut for some twelve hours. ...telecommunications satellites.*

telegram /tɛligræm/ **telegrams**
NC A telegram is a message that is sent by telegraph and then printed and delivered. *I sent a telegram to my mother saying I had arrived safely.*

telegraph /tɛligrɑːf/ **telegraphs, telegraphing, telegraphed**
1 N SING The telegraph is a system of sending messages over long distances by means of electrical or radio signals. *Wireless telegraph saves lives at sea... Libya has meanwhile restored telephone and telegraph links with Egypt.*
2 VO If you telegraph someone, you send them a message by telegraph. *Harold telegraphed him in France.*

telegraphic /tɛligræfɪk/
1 ADJ ATTRIB Telegraphic methods or systems are involved in sending information by telegraph.
2 ADJ ATTRIB Telegraphic messages or statements are written or spoken in a very concise style, using the smallest possible number of words. *Daniel delivered his message with telegraphic brevity.* ◆ **telegraphically** ADV *There was also a telegraphically short letter from Claude.*

telepathic /tɛlipæθɪk/
ADJ If someone claims to be telepathic they say they can communicate directly with other people using only their minds. *...telepathic messages.*

telepathy /təlɛpəθi/
NU Telepathy is direct communication between people's minds. *We are particularly interested in phenomena such as telepathy.*

telephone /tɛlifəʊn/ **telephones, telephoning, telephoned**
1 NU or N SING The telephone is an electrical system used to talk to someone in another place by dialling a number on a piece of equipment and speaking into it. *The Prime Minister said she'd also spoken by telephone to Archbishop Desmond Tutu... They spoke on the telephone... The Embassy in London received an almost continual stream of telephone calls offering help.*
2 NC A telephone is the piece of equipment used to talk to someone by telephone. *Many people, especially those without telephones, are extremely worried about the safety of relatives.*
3 VO or V If you telephone someone, you dial their telephone number and speak to them by telephone; a formal use. *He had not heard of the government's decision until our reporter telephoned him... More than a thousand people telephoned in response to the programme.*

telephone book, telephone books
NC A telephone book is a book containing an alphabetical list of names, addresses, and telephone numbers of the people in a town or area. *You can find me in the telephone book.*

telephone booth, telephone booths
NC A telephone booth is a place in a public building where there is a telephone that can be used by the public.

telephone box, telephone boxes
NC A telephone box is a small shelter in the street in which there is a public telephone. *British Telecom says it has met its target in getting most of the country's public telephone boxes back in order.*

telephone directory, telephone directories
NC A telephone directory is the same as a telephone book. *His address was published in the telephone directory.*

telephone exchange, telephone exchanges
NC A telephone exchange is a building where the telephone lines are connected when someone in the area makes or receives a telephone call. *Among the government buildings burnt were a telephone exchange and a railway booking office. ...the digital telephone exchanges that now route the majority of calls.*

telephone number, telephone numbers
NC Your telephone number is the number that other people dial when they want to talk to you on the telephone. *He gave her his telephone number... They took all our particulars, our name, address and telephone number.*

telephonist /təlɛfənɪst/ **telephonists**
NC A telephonist is someone who works in a telephone exchange, or whose job is to answer the telephone for a business or other organization. *The message was passed to Anne Grocott, the telephonist at the Stock Exchange.*

telephoto lens /tɛlifəʊtəʊ lɛnz/ **telephoto lenses**
NC A telephoto lens is a lens which you can attach to a camera and which makes far away things larger and clearer in the photographs. *Binoculars and telephoto lenses were trained on the comings and goings around the plane.*

teleprinter /tɛliprɪntə/ **teleprinters**
NC or NU A teleprinter is an electronic printer which prints out messages that it receives from machines in other places. *They are connected with their London offices by teleprinters... Reports came in by telephone and teleprinter during the meeting.*

telescope /tɛliskəʊp/ **telescopes**
NC A telescope is a long instrument shaped like a tube which has lenses which make distant things appear larger and nearer. *They peered at the targets through the telescope... The telescope is designed to provide the first clear images of distant galaxies.*

telescopic /tɛliskɒpɪk/
1 ADJ ATTRIB Telescopic instruments and lenses make things seem larger and nearer. *...a 400 mm telescopic lens... The commandos have rifles fitted with telescopic sights.*
2 ADJ ATTRIB A telescopic device has sections that fit or slide into each other so that it can be made shorter when it is not in use. *I pulled out the telescopic aerial to its fullest extent.*

Teletype /tɛlitaɪp/ **Teletypes**
NC or NU A Teletype is a teleprinter; Teletype is a trademark. *...assorted electronic gear and automatic Teletypes... Simultaneously, all other branches were informed by Teletype.*

televise /tɛlivaɪz/ **televises, televising, televised**
VO If an event is televised, it is filmed and shown on television. *His message was televised to fifty countries... 21 countries now televise proceedings in their parliaments.* ◆ **televised** ADJ ATTRIB *In tomorrow's televised address Mr Mandela will say thank-you. ...a televised speech.*

television /tɛlivɪʒn/ **televisions**
1 NC A television or a television set is a piece of electrical equipment consisting of a box with a glass screen on which you can watch programmes with pictures and sounds. *I turned on the television to watch the news... Facing the sofa were three television sets, each tuned to a different station.*
2 NU Television is the system of sending pictures and sounds by electrical signals over a distance so that people can receive them on a television set. *...television pictures transmitted from a camera on the other side of the world... The question is raised whether charities like Oxfam should advertise on television.*
3 NU Television also refers to all the programmes that are broadcast and that you can watch on a television set. *The boys were watching television... Television, he said, influences people much more when it is realistic.*
4 NU The business or industry concerned with making and broadcasting programmes is also called television. *...the most exciting job in television.*

telex /ˈtɛlɛks/ **telexes, telexing, telexed**
1 NU **Telex** is an international system of sending
written messages. The message is typed on a machine
in one place and is immediately printed out by a
machine in another place. *The decision will be
communicated by telex to the Community's finance
minister.*
2 NC A **telex** is a machine that sends and receives
telex messages. *The house where he was staying had
a telex on the upper floor.*
3 NC You can refer to a message that is sent by telex
as a **telex**. *Officials have sent a telex with their
demands to the foreign minister.*
4 VO If you **telex** a message, you send it by a telex
machine. *The file on this man had been telexed to
Paris... The committee's Secretary General telexed all
member countries.*

tell /tɛl/ **tells, telling, told**
1 V O-REPORT, V O-QUOTE, or VO If someone **tells** you
something, they give you information, usually in
words. *Six Swedish hostages have been told they can
leave the country tonight... She told a crowd of ten
thousand, 'Let's have clean, peaceful and orderly
elections.'... John refused to tell me her name.*
2 VO If you **tell** someone to do something, you order,
instruct, or advise them to do it. *They told the pilot to
take the plane to Taiwan... Just do as you're told.*
3 V O-REPORT If something **tells** you something, it
reveals a fact to you or indicates what you should do.
*These elections have told us little we didn't know
already... Your dry throat will tell you you're
dehydrated.*
4 VO If you can **tell** what is happening or what is true,
you are able to judge correctly what is happening or
what is true. *One cannot therefore tell if the good
effect will be maintained... I couldn't tell what they
were thinking... Children can tell the difference
between fiction and reality.*
5 V If an unpleasant or tiring experience begins to
tell, it begins to have a serious effect. *The strain was
beginning to tell... All these late nights were beginning
to tell on my health.*
6 If you say '**Time will tell**', you mean that the truth
about something will not be known until some time in
the future. *Time will tell whether the English seaside
will shake off its crumbling Victorian image.*
7 See also **telling**.
tell apart PHRASAL VERB If you can **tell** similar people
or things **apart**, you are able to recognize the
differences between them. *Both parties appear to hold
similar manifestos and it is difficult to tell them apart.
...a way to tell apart enemy and friendly planes.*
tell off PHRASAL VERB If you **tell** someone **off**, you
speak to them angrily or seriously because they have
done something wrong. *We don't want to get told off,
do we?* ♦ **telling-off** N SING *When she got back she
would give him such a telling-off about that doll.*

teller /ˈtɛlə/ **tellers**
1 NC A **teller** is a person who has been appointed to
count votes, for example at an election or in
parliament. *There were thousands of tellers trying to
classify the four-part ballot papers... Tellers will
collect the ballot forms and the result will be known at
midnight.*
2 NC A **teller** is also a cashier in a bank. *Bank tellers
were not prepared for the transactions. ...automatic
teller machines.*

telling /ˈtɛlɪŋ/
ADJ Something that is **telling** is significant or has an
important effect, often because it shows or reveals
clearly the true nature of a situation. *The financial
problems building up through this long political crisis
are likely to have a telling effect. ...a telling piece of
political propaganda... His resignation may be read
as a telling indication of the government's withdrawal
from the peace process.*

telltale /ˈtɛlteɪl/
ADJ A **telltale** sign reveals information about
something that people might want to be secret. *They
had altered their passports by hand to disguise their
age, leaving telltale smudges. ...the telltale cropped
heads of soldiers from the French military base.*

telly /ˈtɛli/ **tellies**
N CorNU A **telly** is the same as a **television**; an
informal word. *Dad was half asleep in front of a
flickering telly... Did you see it on telly last night?*

temerity /təˈmɛrəti/
NU+SUPP If someone has the **temerity** to do something,
they do it even though they know it will upset or annoy
other people; a formal word. *He had the temerity to
suggest that a few of us should leave.*

temp /tɛmp/ **temps**
NC A **temp** is a secretary who is employed by an
agency to work for short periods of time in different
offices. *Members include stockbrokers, office temps,
doctors and housewives... The number of people
signing up with temp agencies has gone up.*

temper /ˈtɛmpə/ **tempers, tempering, tempered**
1 NCorNU Your **temper** is the tendency you have to
become angry or to stay calm. *He had a most violent
temper. ...an awkward, self-conscious woman with a
short temper. ...her less than sweet temper.*
2 NC+SUPPorNU+SUPP Your **temper** is also the way you
are feeling at a particular time, especially how
cheerful or angry you are. *She might come home in a
better temper.*
3 VO To **temper** something means to make it less
extreme or more acceptable; a formal use. *Our
delight was tempered by surprise... She tempered her
approach to each child.*
● **Temper** is used in the following phrases. ● If you
are **in a temper**, you are extremely angry and cannot
control yourself. *One day the man attacked me in a
temper.* ● If you **lose** your **temper**, you become very
angry. *She suddenly lost her temper and left the
room.*

temperament /ˈtɛmpərəmənt/ **temperaments**
NUorNC Your **temperament** is your character, which
you show in your usual way of behaving towards
people or reacting in situations. *They were gamblers
by temperament. ...his placid and cautious
temperament.*

temperamental /ˌtɛmpərəˈmɛntl/
1 ADJ A **temperamental** person has moods that change
often and suddenly. *...a temperamental Polish
actress.*
2 ADJ **Temperamental** features relate to the
temperament a person has. *Temperamental
differences exist between them.* ♦ **temperamentally**
ADV *My father wasn't temperamentally suited for
business.*

temperance /ˈtɛmpərəns/
NU **Temperance** is the habit of not drinking alcohol
because you believe that it is dangerous or morally
wrong. *She didn't need temperance lectures from me.*

temperate /ˈtɛmpərət/
ADJ A **temperate** place has weather that is never
extremely hot or extremely cold. *...the temperate
woodlands of Tasmania.*

temperature /ˈtɛmpərətʃə/ **temperatures**
1 NCorNU The **temperature** of something is how hot or
cold it is. *...a temperature of 10°C... They'll be
travelling in high midday temperatures... The cause is
the steady rise in temperature.*
2 NC Your **temperature** is the temperature of your
body. *To take the baby's temperature, I take this
plastic thermometer and I very gently place it against
the skin... I went to bed with a high temperature. ...his
body temperature.*
3 NC If you say that the **temperature** in a particular
situation is rising, you mean that people are becoming
angry or excited and may possibly become violent.
*The temperature is rising with the approach of the
presidential elections... After six months of relative
calm, the political temperature in the Soviet republic
of Georgia is again climbing rapidly towards boiling
point.*
● **Temperature** is used in the following phrases. ● If
someone **takes** your **temperature**, they use a
thermometer to measure your temperature. ● If you
have a temperature or **are running a temperature**,
your temperature is higher than it usually is and you
feel ill.

tempest /tɛmpɪst/ **tempests**
NC A **tempest** is a very violent storm; a literary word. *Fierce raged the tempest o'er the deep.*

tempestuous /tɛmpɛstjuəs/
ADJ Something or someone that is **tempestuous** is full of strong emotions. *...a tempestuous love affair.*

template /tɛmpleɪt/ **templates**
NC A **template** is a thin piece of metal or plastic cut into a particular shape in order to help you cut wood, metal, etc accurately, or to reproduce the same shape many times. *...a different template for each letter of the alphabet.*

temple /tɛmpl/ **temples**
1 NC A **temple** is a building used for the worship of a god in some religions. *...the historic grandeur of the Buddhist temples of the Grand Palace... There used to be over six thousand such temples in Tibet. ...Hindu temples.*
2 NC Your **temples** are the flat parts on each side of your forehead. *He was struck above the left temple.*

tempo /tɛmpəʊ/ **tempos**
1 N SING or NU The **tempo** of an event is the speed at which it happens; a formal use. *Events had been moving at an equally dramatic tempo. ...the tempo of everyday life.*
2 NU or NC The **tempo** of a piece of music is the speed at which it is played; a technical use. *Fluctuations of tempo are possible in a romantic piece. ...the light-footed tempos of the Magic Flute.*

temporal /tɛmpərəl/
1 ADJ If you describe processes or features as **temporal**, you are referring to how they change or endure over a period of time; a formal use. *...the temporal and historical process. ...the temporal character of human bonds.*
2 ADJ ATTRIB **Temporal** events or matters involve earthly existence and are limited by time; a literary use. *...human institutions and temporal events.*
3 ADJ ATTRIB **Temporal** powers or authorities are not controlled by a church and are not connected with the religious or spiritual lives of people; a literary use. *...the temporal power of the state.*
4 ADJ ATTRIB **Temporal** is also used to refer to the part of your brain that is near your temples; a technical use. *...the temporal cortex of the brain.*

temporary /tɛmpərəri/
ADJ Something that is **temporary** lasts for only a short time. *He stressed that the closure would be temporary... He is being allowed to stay on a temporary basis. ...temporary jobs.* ♦ **temporarily** ADV *She is temporarily in charge.*

temporize /tɛmpəraɪz/ **temporizes, temporizing, temporized;** also spelt **temporise.**
V-QUOTE If you **temporize**, you keep talking about or keep doing something unimportant, in order to delay making a decision or stating your real opinion; a formal word. *'Well,' I temporized, 'you'll have to ask your mother.'*

tempt /tɛmpt/ **tempts, tempting, tempted**
1 VO If you **tempt** someone, you try to persuade them to do a particular thing, by offering them something. *The building societies are offering higher rates of interest to tempt new savers.*
2 VO If something **tempts** you, it attracts you and makes you want to do or have something, although you know it might be wrong or harmful. *There are now more expensive, attractive and easily portable goods to tempt thieves.*

temptation /tɛmpteɪʃn/ **temptations**
1 NC A **temptation** is something that you want to do or have, although you know it might be wrong or harmful. *...the temptations to which he was continually exposed... Most people seem to be resisting the temptation to spend lots of money.*
2 NU **Temptation** is the feeling of wanting to do or have something, although you know it might be wrong or harmful. *Officials are vulnerable to temptation by lucrative contracts from Western countries... He had the strength to resist further temptation.*

tempting /tɛmptɪŋ/
ADJ If something, or an aspect of it, is **tempting**, you want to have it or do it even though you know it might

be silly or wrong. *The advertisement makes it sound tempting. ...an extremely tempting price... It is tempting to jump to a simple conclusion.*

ten /tɛn/ **tens**
Ten is the number 10. *His wealth included ten houses and a big collection of antiques. ...within ten miles of the coast.*

tenable /tɛnəbl/
1 ADJ An argument or point of view that is **tenable** is reasonable and can be successfully defended against criticism; a formal use. *It seemed a tenable proposition.*
2 ADJ A job or position that is **tenable** is intended to be held by someone for a particular length of time. *The position of Chairman is tenable for a maximum of three years.*

tenacious /tɪneɪʃəs/
ADJ A **tenacious** person is very determined and does not give up easily. *They kept a tenacious grip on their possessions.* ♦ **tenacity** /tɪnæsəti/ NU *We respect their tenacity and courage.* ♦ **tenaciously** ADV *He has tenaciously held onto power.*

tenancy /tɛnənsi/ **tenancies**
NU or NC **Tenancy** is the renting of land or buildings belonging to someone else. *Once they took up the tenancy they couldn't be evicted. ...a three-year tenancy.*

tenant /tɛnənt/ **tenants**
NC A **tenant** is someone who pays rent for the place they live in, or for land or buildings that they use. *Tenants looking for private rented accommodation are likely to have to pay more... Extra help is to be given to council tenants who want to buy their homes.*

tench /tɛntʃ/; **tench** is both the singular and the plural form.
NC A **tench** is a dark green European fish that lives in lakes and rivers.

tend /tɛnd/ **tends, tending, tended**
1 V+to-INF If something **tends** to happen, it usually happens or it often happens. *I tend to wake up early in the morning... The report says left-handed people tend to be more creative and inventive.*
2 VO If you **tend** someone or something, you look after them carefully; a formal use. *She'd tended four very sick men. ...a young man who tended his crops well.*

tendency /tɛndənsi/ **tendencies**
1 NC+SUPP If there is a **tendency** for something, it starts happening more often or increases in intensity. *There is a growing tendency for people to opt out. ...a permanent tendency towards inflation.*
2 NC+SUPP If you have a particular **tendency**, you are likely to behave in that way. *I have a tendency to tease... The girl might have murderous tendencies.*
3 NC+SUPP You can refer to a group of people who share similar but often unpopular political views as a particular **tendency**. *The Labour Party has announced it is to hold an inquiry into alleged infiltration by the far left group known as Militant Tendency. ...confrontations between the various tendencies within Algeria.*

tendentious /tɛndɛnʃəs/
ADJ Something that is **tendentious** expresses a particular opinion or point of view very strongly, especially one that many people disagree with; a formal word. *The foreign news pages remained as boring and tendentious as ever.*

tender /tɛndə/ **tenderest; tenders, tendering, tendered**
1 ADJ A **tender** person expresses gentle and caring feelings. *He gave her a tender smile. ...tender understanding.* ♦ **tenderly** ADV *She cradled the baby tenderly.* ♦ **tenderness** NU *I have a feeling of great tenderness for you.*
2 ADJ ATTRIB If someone is at a **tender** age, they are young and inexperienced. *She was still at the tender age of 19.*
3 ADJ **Tender** meat is soft and easy to cut or chew. *The tender meat is from the younger animals.*
4 ADJ If a part of your body is **tender**, it hurts when you touch it. *...the tender, swollen side of his jaw.*
5 NC or NU A **tender** is a formal offer to supply goods or do a job for a particular price. *Tenders are to be*

submitted on 15 December at 10 a.m... Another health board has said it will put domestic and catering services out to tender. ▶ Also V *...allowing private firms to tender for certain services.*
6 VO If you **tender** a suggestion, an apology, or your resignation, you formally make it or offer it; a formal use. *He tendered his resignation to the prime minister about half an hour ago.*

tender-hearted
ADJ If you are **tender-hearted**, you have a gentle and caring nature. *He is a more tender-hearted, caring person than she is.*

tenderize /tɛndəraɪz/ **tenderizes, tenderizing, tenderized**; also spelt **tenderise**.
VO If you **tenderize** food, you make it more tender by preparing it in a particular way. *The meat should be marinated overnight to tenderize and flavour it.*

tendon /tɛndən/ **tendons**
NC A **tendon** is a strong cord of tissue in your body joining a muscle to a bone. *She hasn't been playing her best since injuring her tendon early last year.*

tendril /tɛndrəl/ **tendrils**
NC **Tendrils** are short, thin stems which grow on some plants and attach themselves to walls or other plants. *The insect sucks the sap from the tendrils of the plant.*

tenement /tɛnəmənt/ **tenements**
NC A **tenement** is a large building divided into a lot of flats. *...the windows of the tenement buildings opposite... The play is set in a Dublin tenement during the civil war.*

tenet /tɛnɪt/ **tenets**
NC The **tenets** of a theory or belief are the principles on which it is based; a formal word. *...one of the central tenets of capitalism.*

tenner /tɛnə/ **tenners**
NC A **tenner** is ten pounds or a ten-pound note; an informal word. *He's earning a tenner an hour.*

tennis /tɛnɪs/
NU **Tennis** is a game played by two or four players on a rectangular court in which a ball is hit over a central net by players using rackets. *Michiko played tennis and spoke English. ...a tennis court.*

tenor /tɛnə/ **tenors**
1 N SING+SUPP The **tenor** of something is the general meaning or mood that it expresses; a formal use. *The tenor of the commentary is typical of the attitude of the leadership... The general tenor of the bishops' statement is well known.*
2 NC A **tenor** is a male singer with a fairly high voice. *...'Roses of Picardy' sung by an Irish tenor... Britten wrote with Pears's unusual tenor voice specifically in mind.*
3 N+N A **tenor** musical instrument has a range of notes of fairly low pitch. *Getz played the tenor saxophone.*

tenpin bowling /tɛnpɪn bəʊlɪŋ/
NU **Tenpin bowling** is an indoor game in which you try to knock down ten bottle-shaped objects, called tenpins, by rolling a heavy ball towards them.

tense /tɛns/ **tenser, tensest; tenses, tensing, tensed**
1 ADJ A **tense** situation or period of time is one that makes people anxious and unable to relax. *The situation remains calm, but tense. ...a long, tense silence.*
2 ADJ If you are **tense**, you are worried and nervous, and cannot relax. *They began to grow tense over the likelihood of a long delay.*
3 V-ERG or V If your muscles quickly become tight and stiff because of a shock or other feeling, you can say that you **tense** your muscles, that your muscles **tense**, or that you **tense**. *He tensed his jaw muscles in fear. ...all the muscles of his body tensed... The man on the terrace tensed slightly.* ▶ Also ADJ *Your neck is tense.*
4 NU or NC The **tense** of a verb is the form which shows whether you are referring to past, present, or future time. *References to Deng are often in the past tense... I wrote in the present tense. ...the future tense.*

tensed up
ADJ PRED If you are **tensed up**, you are nervous and unable to relax. *You've been so tensed up, you're ready to explode.*

tensile /tɛnsaɪl/
ADJ ATTRIB The **tensile** strength of something such as wire, rope, or concrete, is its ability not to break when a force is applied to it; a technical term. *...the tensile strength of steel.*

tension /tɛnʃn/ **tensions**
1 NU or N PL **Tension** is a feeling of fear or nervousness produced before a difficult, dangerous, or important event. *No formal agreement had been reached on ways of easing tension between the two sides... Social tensions are rising.*
2 NU The **tension** in a rope or wire is how tightly it is stretched. *The loss of tension in the cables is a problem.*

tent /tɛnt/ **tents**
NC A **tent** is a shelter made of canvas or nylon and held up by poles and ropes. You sleep in a tent when you are camping. *They have pitched four tents across the street from the embassy... Thousands camped in tents on makeshift beds.*

tentacle /tɛntəkl/ **tentacles**
1 NC The **tentacles** of an animal such as an octopus are the long, thin parts that it uses to feel and hold things, to catch food, and to move. *Female giant squid can have tentacles as long as ten, or even twelve metres.*
2 N PL The **tentacles** of a political, commercial, or social organization are the power and influence that it has in the outside community; used showing disapproval. *...the cocaine industry, whose tentacles reach out into virtually every corner of the world.*

tentative /tɛntətɪv/
1 ADJ **Tentative** theories or arrangements are still at an experimental or preparatory stage. *There is a very tentative link between the nuclear tests and two types of cancer... There's now tentative agreement on a number of points.*
2 ADJ If you are **tentative**, you act or speak slowly and carefully because you are uncertain or afraid. *The tentative and uncertain mood at the start of the week could not be completely dispelled. ...tentative approaches.* ◆ **tentatively** ADV *He smiled tentatively.*

tenterhooks /tɛntəhʊks/
If you are **on tenterhooks**, you are nervous and excited about something that is going to happen. *I was on tenterhooks to see who his passenger was... I will keep him on tenterhooks for just a little longer.*

tenth /tɛnθ/ **tenths**
1 ADJ The **tenth** item in a series is the one that you count as number ten. *...the tenth anniversary of the revolution... The election will be held on May the tenth.*
2 NC A **tenth** is one of ten equal parts of something. *Sales for the month were actually down by a tenth of a percent.*

tenuous /tɛnjuəs/
ADJ If an idea, connection, or reason is **tenuous**, it is so slight or weak that it may not really exist or may easily cease to exist. *...tenuous evidence... Their links with the school were tenuous.*

tenure /tɛnjə/
1 NU **Tenure** is the legal right to live in a place or to use land or buildings for a period of time. *They get tenure under the Rent Act.*
2 NU **Tenure** is also the period of time during which someone holds an important job. *...her short tenure as acting governor.*
3 NU If you have **tenure** in your job, you can hold it until you retire, without having to have a contract renewed. *The University's president refused to grant him tenure.*

tepee /tiːpiː/ **tepees**
NC A **tepee** is a tent made by North American Indians from animal skins. *...a hippy community who live in American Indian style wigwams or tepees.*

tepid /tɛpɪd/
1 ADJ A **tepid** liquid is slightly warm. *...drinking tepid coffee.*
2 ADJ A **tepid** feeling or reaction lacks enthusiasm. *Tepid applause greeted her efforts.*

tercentenary /tɜːsɛntiːnəri/ **tercentenaries**
NC A **tercentenary** is a day or a year which is exactly

three hundred years after an important event such as the birth of a famous person. *...the tercentenary of the birth of Handel.*

term /tɜːm/ **terms, terming, termed**

1 NC A **term** is a word or expression, often used in relation to a particular subject. *'Habeas corpus' is a legal term... He asked them what they understood by the term 'radical'.*

2 VOC If something **is termed** a particular thing, that is what it is called; a formal use. *The press termed the visit a triumph. ...recent breakthroughs in what might be termed 'birth technology'.*

3 NCorNU A **term** is one of the periods of time that each year is divided into at a school or college. *...the spring term... It was the first week of term.*

4 NC+SUPP The period of time during which someone does a particular job or activity is also called a **term**. *His fifth term in office was brief. ...a long prison term.*

5 N PL The **terms** of an agreement or arrangement are the conditions that have been accepted by the people involved in it. *The terms included a pay increase of just under thirty percent. ...under the terms of the law.*

● **Term** is used in the following phrases. ● If you talk about something **in particular terms** or **in terms of** a particular thing, you are specifying which aspect of it you are discussing. *Petrol prices were quite high in international terms... We know what the refugees need in terms of food, warmth and shelter.* ● If you say you are **thinking in terms of** doing something or **talking in terms of** doing it, you mean that you are considering it. *You should be thinking in terms of paying off your debts.* ● If you talk about 'the **long term**' or 'the **short term**', you are talking about what will happen over a long or short period of time. *In the longer term the government has some difficult decisions to take... There will be further cuts in interest rates in the short term.* ● If you **come to terms with** something difficult or unpleasant, you learn to accept it. *Residents are still coming to terms with the disaster.* ● If two people are treated **on the same terms** or **on equal terms**, they are treated in the same way. ● If two people are **on good terms** or **on friendly terms**, they are friendly towards each other. *They haven't always been on the best of terms.* ● **on speaking terms**: see **speak**.

● **contradiction in terms**: see **contradiction**.

terminal /tɜːmɪnl/ **terminals**

1 ADJ A **terminal** illness or disease causes death gradually and is incurable. *Her husband has terminal cancer.* ◆ **terminally** SUBMOD *...people who are terminally ill with cancer.*

2 NC A **terminal** is a place where vehicles, passengers, or goods begin or end a journey. *Only one train left the terminal during the day... A second passenger terminal has opened at Gatwick airport.*

3 NC A computer **terminal** is a piece of equipment consisting of a keyboard and a screen that is used for putting information into a computer or for getting information from it. *...terminals giving access to larger computers.*

terminate /tɜːmɪneɪt/ **terminates, terminating, terminated**; a formal word.

1 V-ERG When you **terminate** something or when it **terminates**, it ends completely. *I thought that he would terminate the discussion then and there... We are confident that the case will terminate with two words: 'Not guilty'.* ◆ **termination** /tɜːmɪneɪʃn/ NU *...the termination of the agreement. ...medical termination of pregnancy.*

2 V A When a train or bus **terminates** somewhere, it ends its journey there. *There's a train that terminates there at 08.55.*

3 VO If a worker **is terminated**, they lose their job; used in American English. *More people were terminated as part of the reorganization.* ◆ **termination** NU *More than 1,400 workers have accepted early retirement or voluntary termination offers.*

terminology /tɜːmɪnɒlədʒi/ **terminologies**

N MASS The **terminology** of a subject is the set of special words and expressions used in connection with it. *...conflicting terminologies. ...using Marxist terminology.*

terminus /tɜːmɪnəs/ **terminuses**

NC A **terminus** is a place where trains or buses begin or end their journeys. *He had waited near the terminus until the last bus had come in.*

termite /tɜːmaɪt/ **termites**

NC **Termites** are small white insects that eat wood. *They had trouble with termites... It's been hollowed out by termites.*

term paper, term paper

NC A **term paper** is a long essay or dissertation; used in American English. *She starts researching a term paper on how the town fathers resisted the Nazis.*

tern /tɜːn/ **terns**

NC A **tern** is a small black and white seabird with long wings and a forked tail. *One species, the Arctic Tern, is in danger of extinction in Shetland.*

Ter-Petrosian, Levon /levɒn təpetrɒsjæn/

Levon Ter-Petrosian became President of Armenia in 1990. He founded the Armenian National Movement (ANM) in 1989 and was a member of the Karabakh Committee, which campaigned for Armenian control of Nagorny-Karabakh. Born: 1945.

terrace /terəs/ **terraces**

1 NC A **terrace** is a row of similar houses joined together by their side walls. *...a house in a fashionable terrace.*

2 NC A **terrace** is also a flat area of stone or grass next to a building, where people can sit. *He wandered out onto the terrace.*

3 NC A flat area of ground built like steps on a hillside where crops are grown is also called a **terrace**. *...the landscape with its terraces of vines and olives.*

4 N PL The **terraces** at a football ground are wide steps where some spectators stand. *...on the terraces of football clubs.*

terraced /terəst/

1 ADJ A **terraced** house is one of a row of similar houses joined together by their side walls. *...the launderettes and terraced houses of an industrial city. ...Victorian terraced houses.*

2 ADJ A **terraced** hillside has flat areas of ground like steps built on it so that people can grow crops there. *...the forests and terraced vineyards... The land is usually terraced and they grow crops for their own use.*

terra cotta /terə kɒtə/

NU **Terra cotta** is a brownish-red clay that has been baked but not glazed and that is used for making things such as flower pots and small statues. *...the terra cotta Roman brickwork.*

terra firma /terə fɜːmə/

NU **Terra firma** is used to refer to the ground when you are contrasting it with the sea or air, especially because it seems safer; often used humorously. *He found himself on terra firma at last.*

terrain /təreɪn/

NU The **terrain** in an area is the type of land there. *The hilly terrain here is making the search difficult... The police say they face a difficult task with bad weather and rough terrain.*

terrapin /terəpɪn/ **terrapins**

NC A **terrapin** is a small turtle.

terrestrial /tərestriəl/

1 ADJ ATTRIB A **terrestrial** animal lives on land or on the ground rather than in the sea, in trees, or in the air; a technical use. *...both marine life and terrestrial life.*

2 ADJ ATTRIB **Terrestrial** means relating to the planet Earth rather than to some other part of the universe. *Scientists believe that probing the magnetosphere and its changing features will help towards a better understanding of its effect on terrestrial weather.*

terrible /terəbl/

1 ADJ A **terrible** experience or situation is very serious and unpleasant. *It has caused terrible suffering to animals. ...this terrible disaster.*

2 ADJ If you feel **terrible**, you feel ill or feel a very strong and unpleasant emotion. *...a terrible sense of guilt.*

3 ADJ If something is **terrible**, it is very bad or of very poor quality. *I've had a terrible day at the office... The economy is in a terrible mess.*

4 ADJ You can also use **terrible** to emphasize the great degree or extent of something. *I've been a terrible fool... It's a terrible waste of their talents.*

terribly /ˈtɛrəbli/
SUBMOD You use **terribly** to emphasize the extent or degree of something. *I'm terribly sorry... I think it's terribly important.*

terrier /ˈtɛriə/ **terriers**
NC A **terrier** is a breed of small dog. There are many different types of terrier. *The RSPCA would like a ban on the importation of Pit Bull Terriers into Britain. ...a Yorkshire Terrier.*

terrific /təˈrɪfɪk/
1 ADJ If you say that something is **terrific**, you mean that you are very pleased with it or that you like it a lot; an informal use. *Our new carpet looks terrific.*
2 ADJ ATTRIB **Terrific** also means very great in amount, degree, or intensity. *...a terrific thunderstorm. ...a terrific amount of money.*

terrify /ˈtɛrɪfaɪ/ **terrifies, terrifying, terrified**
VO If something **terrifies** you, it makes you feel extremely frightened. *Rats terrify me.* ◆ **terrifying** ADJ *The most terrifying aspect of nuclear bombing is radiation.* ◆ **terrified** ADJ *I was too terrified to cry.*

territorial /ˌtɛrɪˈtɔːriəl/
ADJ ATTRIB **Territorial** means concerned with the ownership of a particular area of land or water. *...a bitter territorial dispute.*

Territorial Army
N PROP The **Territorial Army** is a British armed force whose members are not professional soldiers but train as soldiers in their spare time. *I've done 27 years in the Territorial Army.*

territorial waters
N PL A country's **territorial waters** are the parts of the sea close to its coast which it considers to be under its control, especially with regard to fishing rights. *It will not hesitate to protect its territorial waters.*

territory /ˈtɛrɪtəᵒri/ **territories**
1 NU **Territory** is land which is controlled by a particular country or ruler. *...British territory... This meeting is to be held on neutral territory.*
2 NC A **territory** is a country or region that is controlled by another country or region. *...the French territories on the Eastern coast... The breakaway territories continue to demand their freedom.*
3 NC An animal's **territory** is the area which it regards as its own and which it tries to prevent other animals from entering. *They stop along the boundaries of their territory and refresh its markings with urine. ...an animal's impulse to fight for its territory.*
4 NU+SUPP **Territory** is land that has a particular character. *We were passing through mountainous territory.*
5 NU+SUPP You can use **territory** to refer to an area of knowledge or experience. *All this is familiar territory to readers of her recent novels.*

terror /ˈtɛrə/ **terrors**
1 NU **Terror** is very great fear. *She awakened in terror as the flaming roof came crashing down... The very mention of his name struck terror into many people's hearts.*
2 NU **Terror** is also violence or the threat of violence, especially when it is used for political reasons. *He has called the move a surrender to Arab terror. ...a renewed IRA terror campaign.*
3 NC A **terror** is something that makes you very frightened. *They suffered untold terrors in the dark.*

terrorise /ˈtɛrəraɪz/. See **terrorize.**

terrorism /ˈtɛrərɪzəm/
NU **Terrorism** is the use of violence for political reasons; used showing disapproval. *No such act of terrorism must be allowed to happen again.*

terrorist /ˈtɛrərɪst/ **terrorists**
NC A **terrorist** is someone who uses violence, especially murder, kidnapping, and bombing, in order to achieve political aims or to force a government to do something; used showing disapproval. *The terrorists had planted a powerful car bomb near the town centre... Most of them had served jail sentences for terrorist acts.*

terrorize /ˈtɛrəraɪz/ **terrorizes, terrorizing, terrorized;**
also spelt **terrorise.**
VO or V If someone **terrorizes** you, they frighten you by threatening you. *Soldiers burned villages and terrorised the population... They got away with two murders, and they are alive to terrorise again.*

terror-stricken
ADJ If you are **terror-stricken** or **terror-struck**, you are extremely frightened. *...terror-stricken women and children.*

terse /tɜːs/ **terser, tersest**
ADJ A **terse** comment or statement is brief and unfriendly. *They would not disclose details but some did make a few terse comments.* ◆ **tersely** ADV *...a tersely worded paragraph.*

tertiary /ˈtɜːʃəri/
1 ADJ **Tertiary** means third in order, third in importance, or at a third stage of development; a formal use. *A much smaller group, which comprises the Gulf States, Jordan and Syria, have got secondary and tertiary boycotts.*
2 ADJ ATTRIB **Tertiary** education is education at university or college level. *It will make commerce and industry dominant forces in tertiary education... In 1976 there were only 565,000 students in the tertiary sector.*

Terylene /ˈtɛrəliːn/
NU **Terylene** is a light and strong artificial cloth which is used especially for making clothes; **Terylene** is a trademark. *...a pair of drip-dry Terylene trousers.*

TESL /ˈtɛsl/
NU **TESL** is the teaching of English to people who live in an English speaking country, but whose first language is not English. **TESL** is an abbreviation for 'teaching English as a second language'.

test /tɛst/ **tests, testing, tested**
1 VO When you **test** something, you try using it in order to find out what it is, what condition it is in, or how well it works. *The BBC in Scotland wanted to test the range of their transmitters... A number of new techniques were tested.* ► Also NC *...an underground nuclear test.*
2 VO If you **test** someone, you ask them questions to find out how much they know about something. *I will test you on your knowledge of French.* ► Also NC *...a mathematics test.*
3 NC If an event or situation is a **test** of a person or thing, it reveals their qualities or effectiveness. *...local elections are being seen as the first major test of the President's policies.*
4 NC A medical **test** is an examination of a part of your body in order to check the state of your health. *...a blood test.*
5 NC When a car is taken for a **test** drive or when an aircraft is taken for a **test** flight, the machine is given a practical examination by an expert driver or pilot to see how it operates under extreme conditions. *The headlights reportedly caused problems on the car's first test drive... Soviet television showed a test flight of the experimental Tupolev-155.*
6 If you **put** something **to the test**, you try using it to see how useful or effective it is. *The idea is being put to the test in a theatre in Paris.*

testament /ˈtɛstəmənt/ **testaments**
1 NC If one thing is a **testament** to another thing, it shows that the other thing exists or is true; a formal use. *It's really a testament to their hard work in Holland and Belgium... The 'Daily Express' sees the world's response as a testament to the brighter side of human nature.*
2 See also **Old Testament, New Testament.**

test case, test cases
NC A **test case** is a legal case which becomes an example for deciding other, similar cases. *It was the first such trial in US history and it's been regarded as a test case for artistic freedom.*

testes /ˈtɛstiːz/
N PL A man's **testes** are the same as his **testicles**. *...hormones produced by the testes.*

testicle /ˈtɛstɪkl/ **testicles**
NC A man's **testicles** are the two sex glands between his legs that produce sperm. *Radiation at levels*

previously considered safe might have lodged in the man's testicles and affected his sperm.

testify /tɛstɪfaɪ/ **testifies, testifying, testified;** a formal word
1 V, V O, or V-REPORT When someone **testifies**, they make a formal statement in a court of law. *None of the victims would appear in court to testify against him... Witnesses testify to his attempts at rape... One man testified that he had seen me with Jonathan.*
2 V+*to* If something **testifies** to an idea, it shows that the idea is likely to be true. *All kinds of human experience testify to the close link between love and fear.*

testimonial /tɛstɪməʊniəl/ **testimonials**
1 NC A **testimonial** is a statement made by someone in authority saying how good someone or something is. *I sent them background details of my career and testimonials.*
2 NC or N+N A **testimonial** or a **testimonial** match is a sports match which is specially arranged so that part of the profit from the tickets sold can be given to a particular player, for example because he has been injured and cannot play, or is retiring. *They face Finland at Lansdowne Road in a game which is also a testimonial for West Ham's Liam Brady... Moran's ten years' service with United was rewarded with a testimonial match against Manchester City at the weekend.*

testimony /tɛstɪməni/ **testimonies**
1 NU or NC **Testimony** is a formal statement that someone makes in a court of law. *Philip gave testimony against his own brother... Three women backed up her testimony.*
2 NU+*to* If one thing is **testimony** to another, it shows that the second thing exists or is true; a formal use. *This is spectacular testimony to the computer's creative powers.*

testing /tɛstɪŋ/
ADJ **Testing** problems or situations are very difficult to deal with. *...a testing situation. ...the very testing questions which are hurled at you in an exam.*

Test match, Test matches
NC A **Test match** is a cricket or rugby match that is one of a series played between the same two countries. *...the second day of the final Test match between India and the West Indies.*

testosterone /tɛstɒstərəʊn/
NU **Testosterone** is a hormone mainly produced in the testes. It can be made synthetically or taken from animals, and is used to treat some medical conditions or to improve athletic performance. *...a synthetic version of the natural male hormone testosterone. ...high levels of testosterone.*

test pilot, test pilots
NC A **test pilot** is a pilot who flies aircraft of a new design in order to test their performance. *Anatoly Artsebarski is a lieutenant colonel who's a test pilot in the Soviet Air Force.*

test tube, test tubes
NC A **test tube** is a small glass container used in chemical experiments. *The drugs could be tried out on bacteria in a test tube. ...the familiar image of the chemist standing in their laboratory with a test tube.*

test-tube baby, test-tube babies
NC A **test-tube baby** is a baby that develops from an egg that is fertilized outside the mother's body and then replaced in her womb. *...techniques used for producing test-tube babies.*

testy /tɛsti/ **testier, testiest**
ADJ You can describe someone as **testy** when they are impatient and easily become angry. *...the testy impatience of the old General. ...testy comments about their leader.* ◆ **testily** ADV *I answered, perhaps a bit testily, that my wife was safe and sound.*

tetanus /tɛtənəs/
NU **Tetanus** is a serious and painful disease caused by germs getting into wounds. *Be safe, get a tetanus injection as soon as you can... They vaccinate against whooping cough and tetanus.*

tetchy /tɛtʃi/
ADJ A **tetchy** person is irritable and likely to get cross suddenly without an obvious reason. *She started to get*

distinctly tetchy. ...a tetchy state of mind.

tether /tɛðə/ **tethers, tethering, tethered**
1 VO If you **tether** an animal, you tie it to a post. *...very strong ropes, which could even be used to tether sheep.*
2 If you are **at the end of** your **tether**, you are so tired or unhappy that you cannot cope with your problems. *Workers are just about at the end of their tethers, he said.*

text /tɛkst/ **texts**
1 N SING The **text** of a book is the main written part of it, rather than the introduction, pictures, or index. *The excellent photographs in the book did a lot to amplify the text.*
2 NU or NC **Text** is any written material. *These machines have the capacity to 'read' printed text... The texts were translated from Polish.*
3 NC A **text** is a book or other piece of writing connected with an academic subject. *...a text on Oriental philosophy.*
4 NC+SUPP The **text** of a speech or broadcast is a full written record of it. *The country's major newspapers carried the full text of a speech by the party leader.*

textbook /tɛkstbʊk/ **textbooks**
NC A **textbook** is a book about a particular subject that is intended for students to use. *His name has been excluded from all history textbooks.*

textile /tɛkstaɪl/ **textiles**
1 NC A **textile** is a woven cloth or fabric. *...cheap textiles and crafts.*
2 N PL **Textiles** are the industries concerned with making cloth. *There are more people employed in textiles than in computers.*

textual /tɛkstʃuəl/
ADJ ATTRIB **Textual** means relating to the way a work of literature is written; a technical term. *...textual analysis. ...textual criticism.*

texture /tɛkstʃə/ **textures**
NU or NC The **texture** of something is the way that it feels when you touch it. *...the slightly rough texture of the cloth.*

-th /-θ/
SUFFIX **-th** is added to numbers written in figures and ending in 4, 5, 6, 7, 8, 9, 0, and to the numbers 11, 12 and 13, in order to form ordinal numbers. These numbers are pronounced as if they were written as words. For example, 7th is pronounced the same as 'seventh'. *...6th June 1982. ...48th street.*

Thai /taɪ/ **Thais**
1 ADJ **Thai** means belonging or relating to Thailand or to its people. *...a Thai cabinet minister.*
2 NU **Thai** is the main language spoken by the people who live in Thailand. *Legal documents from England had not been translated into Thai.*
3 NC A **Thai** is a person who comes from Thailand. *There has been no word on the incident from the Thais.*

Thailand /taɪlənd/
The **Kingdom of Thailand** is a country in south-east Asia. In 1939 it changed its name from Siam to Thailand. The military has been the main political power since the 1950s. Major-General Chatichai Choonhaven was overthrown in 1991 and in 1992 General Suchinda Khraprayūn, the Supreme Commander of the armed forces, became acting Prime Minister. King Bhumibol Adulyadej became head of state in 1946. Tourism is an important industry. Thailand is the second largest tungsten producer and the third largest tin producer in the world. It also exports rice and textiles. Opium and cannabis are illegally produced. It is a member of the Association of South East Asian Nations. ◆ **Thai** /taɪ/ N, ADJ
- *per capita GNP:* US$1,000 ▪ *religion:* Buddhism
- *language:* Thai ▪ *currency:* baht ▪ *capital:* Bangkok
- *population:* 55 million (1989) ▪ *size:* 513,115 square kilometres.

than /ðən, ðæn/
1 PREP or CONJ You use **than** to link two parts of a comparison. *You've got more money than me... We talked for more than an hour. ...temperatures lower*

than 25 degrees... She was fatter than when he last saw her.
2 PREP or CONJ You use **than** in order to state a preference or to link two parts of a contrast. *I would sooner read than watch television... He chose the stairs rather than the lift.*

Thani, Shaikh Khalifa bin Hamad al-
/xəliːfə bɪn həmæd əl θɑːni/
Shaikh Khalifa bin Hamad al-Thani became Amir and Prime Minister of Qatar in 1972, when he deposed his cousin. He served as Deputy Ruler from 1960 to 1972, as Minister of Education from 1960 to 1970, and as Minister of Finance from 1970 to 1972. Born: 1932.

thank /θæŋk/ **thanks, thanking, thanked**
1 You say **thanks** or **thank you** to express your gratitude when someone does something for you or gives you something. *Many thanks for your long and interesting letter... 'What'll you have, Castle? A whisky?'—'A small one, thank you.'*
2 VO When you **thank** someone, you express your gratitude to them for something. *He thanked me for bringing the books.*
3 N PL When you express your **thanks** to someone, you express your gratitude to them for something. *He sent a letter of thanks to Haldane.*
● **Thank** is used in the following phrases. ● You say **'thank God'**, **'thank goodness'**, or **'thank heavens'** when you are very relieved about something. *Thank goodness it only lasts an hour.* ● If one thing happens **thanks** to another thing or a person, that thing or person caused it to happen. *Thanks to him I began to learn to trust my feelings... Incidents of violence were relatively few, partly thanks to a massive police presence.* ● You say **'Thanks all the same'** when you are thanking someone for an offer that you are refusing. *'Do you want a lift?'—'No, but thanks all the same.'*

thankful /θæŋkfl/
ADJ PRED When you are **thankful**, you feel happy and relieved that something has happened. *We were thankful that it was all over.*

thankfully /θæŋkfəli/
1 ADV If you do something **thankfully**, you do it feeling happy and relieved that something is the case or that something has happened. *We sat down thankfully... 'It wasn't like that with Tony,' Alice said, thankfully.*
2 ADV SEN You also use **thankfully** to express approval and relief about a statement that you are making. *Thankfully, the memory of it soon faded.*

thankless /θæŋkləs/
ADJ ATTRIB A **thankless** job or task is one which is hard work and which is not appreciated by other people. *She used to take on thankless jobs like running school dances.*

Thanksgiving /θæŋksgɪvɪŋ/
NU **Thanksgiving** or **Thanksgiving Day** is a public holiday in the United States and Canada. Thanksgiving is in the autumn. *He and Caitlin will probably spend Thanksgiving with friends. ...a special Thanksgiving dinner.*

thankyou /θæŋkjuː/ **thankyous**
N Cor N+N A **thankyou** is something that you say or do as a way of thanking someone. *I wanted to do the play just as a sort of thankyou... She went home and wrote Brody a thankyou note.*

that, those /ðəʊz/. That is pronounced /ðæt/ for the meaning in paragraph 1 and /ðət/ or /ðæt/ for the meanings in paragraphs 3 and 4.
1 DET or PRON You use **that** or **those** to refer to things or people already mentioned or known about. *That old woman saved my life... Not all crimes are committed for those reasons... 'Did you see him?'—'No.'—'That's a pity.'*
2 PRON or DET You can use **those** to refer to people or things you are going to give details about. *I want to thank those of you who've offered to help... The scheme was set up to help those concerned with the teaching of reading.*
3 CONJ You use **that** after some verbs, nouns, and adjectives to introduce a clause. *She suggested that I telephoned you... He was motivated by the conviction that these tendencies would increase... It is important*

that you should know precisely what is needed.
4 PRON You also use **that** to introduce a relative clause. *...the gate that opened onto the lake... For dessert there was ice cream that Mum had made.*
5 SUBMOD You can use **that** after 'not' and before an adjective to show that something does not have as much of a quality as other people think. *It isn't quite that bad.*
● **That** is used in the following phrases. ● You use **that is** or **that is to say** to give further details about something. *It deals with matters of social policy; that is to say, everything from housing to education.* ● You use **that's that** to say there is nothing more you can do or say about a particular matter. *It was an accident, and that's that... The Ravenscrofts refused and that was that.* ● **this and that:** see **this.**

thatch /θætʃ/ **thatches, thatching, thatched**
1 V or VO To **thatch** a house or its roof means to make a roof with straw or reeds. *I can remember the first house I thatched on my own.*
2 NU **Thatch** is straw or reeds used to make a roof. *The best quality roofing thatch is required.*
3 NC A **thatch** is a roof made from straw or reeds. *...sheltering under the thatch.*
4 N SING You can refer to a large amount of thick, untidy hair on a person's head as a **thatch**. *He was ruggedly handsome, with a thatch of thick brown hair.*

thatched /θætʃt/
ADJ ATTRIB A **thatched** house has a roof made of straw or reeds. *...a three-hundred-year old thatched cottage.*

thatcher /θætʃə/ **thatchers**
NC A **thatcher** is a person whose job is thatching roofs.

Thatcher, Margaret /mɑːgərət θætʃə/
Margaret Thatcher was Prime Minister of the United Kingdom from 1979 to 1990. She was Secretary of State for Education and Science from 1970 to 1974 and leader of the Conservative Party from 1975 to 1990. Born: 1925.

Thatcherism /θætʃərɪzəm/
NU **Thatcherism** refers to the policies and beliefs of Margaret Thatcher, in particular those of privatization, monetarism, self-help, and reducing state intervention. *People were proclaiming the high point of Thatcherism, calling it a capitalist revolution... The workers are applying Thatcherism by demanding a bigger share of the profits.*

Thatcherite /θætʃəraɪt/ **Thatcherites**
NC A **Thatcherite** is someone, especially a politician, who believes in the ideas of Thatcherism. *He is one of the few fervent Thatcherites left in the cabinet... He will no doubt prove a loyal Thatcherite.* ► Also ADJ ATTRIB *...the growth of Thatcherite ideas.*

that's /ðæts, ðæts/
That's is a spoken form of 'that is'.

thaw /θɔː/ **thaws, thawing, thawed**
1 V-ERG When ice or snow **thaws** or when something **thaws** it, it melts. *The snow soon thawed and they all went out for a walk... The ice was thawed by the warm wind.*
2 NC A **thaw** is a period of warmer weather when the snow and ice melts. *A thaw had set in and the streets were slushy.*
3 V-ERG When you **thaw** frozen food, or when it **thaws**, you leave it in a place where it can reach room temperature so that it is ready for use. *Unwrap the pastry and then thaw it overnight... Frozen chickens take a long time to thaw.*
4 V-ERG When unfriendly people or unfriendly relationships **thaw**, they start to be more friendly. *The Vatican indicated that it might be thawing and accepting the critics' argument... A similar invitation thawed Jimmy Carter in 1979.* ► Also N SING *...a gradual thaw in relations between the two countries.*

the; usually pronounced /ðə/ before a consonant and /ði/ before a vowel, but pronounced /ðiː/ when you are emphasizing it.
1 DET You use **the** in front of a noun in order to indicate that you are referring to a person or thing that is known about or has just been mentioned, or when you are going to give more details about them. *The sea was really rough. ...Her Majesty the Queen...*

He said that she ought to see the doctor... They continued walking on the opposite pavement.
2 DET You can also use **the** in front of a singular noun to refer to all people or things of that type. *The koala is a medium-sized creature that lives in trees.*
3 DET You can use **the** in front of a plural form of a surname to refer to a couple or to a whole family who have that surname. *...some friends of hers called the Hochstadts.*
4 DET You use **the** in front of an adjective to make it a noun referring to someone or something described by this adjective. *...the British and the French... We have exiles here at home, the poor, the sick, the old.*
5 DET You can use **the** in front of numbers which refer to dates. *...Tuesday, May the thirteenth.*
6 DET You can also use **the** in front of numbers when they refer to decades. *...Stockholm during the thirties.*
7 DET You use **the** in front of two comparative adjectives or adverbs to describe how one amount or quality changes in relation to another. *The more I hear about him, the less I like him... The longer we look at it the more interesting we find it.*

theatre /θɪətə/ **theatres**; spelt **theater** in American English.
1 NC A **theatre** is a building with a stage on which plays and other entertainments are performed. *Her mother never went to the theatre.*
2 N SING or NU You can use the **theatre** to refer to work in the theatre such as acting or writing plays. *He has been involved in directing other people's work for the theatre... There was an audience for his kind of theatre.*
3 NC In a hospital, a **theatre** is the same as an **operating theatre**.
4 NC In a war, a **theatre** is an area in which fighting takes place. *The Jaffna peninsula seems destined once again to become the main theatre of war in the country... Other forces will probably be brought into the theatre to supplement the air campaign.*
5 NC In American English, a **theater** is also the same as a **cinema**. *We managed, finally, to get a third-rate theater in New York to play the film.*

theatregoer /θɪətəɡəʊə/ **theatregoers**; spelt **theatergoer** in American English.
NC A **theatregoer** is a person who regularly goes to the theatre to see plays. *Theatergoers stood in lines for their Broadway shows.*

theatrical /θɪætrɪkl/
1 ADJ ATTRIB **Theatrical** means related to the theatre in some way. *...Shakespeare's theatrical interpretation of a violent period of English History. ...her theatrical career.*
2 ADJ ATTRIB You can use **theatrical** to describe behaviour that is exaggerated, unnatural, and done deliberately for effect. *...Mr Mitterrand's theatrical declaration. ...his intensely theatrical style of conducting.*

thee /ðiː/
PRON **Thee** is an old-fashioned, poetic, or religious word for 'you' when you are talking to only one person. It is used as the object of a verb or preposition. See also **thou**. *If I should meet thee after long years, how should I greet thee?*

theft /θeft/ **thefts**
N C or N U **Theft** is the act or crime of stealing. *Police believe the thefts may be the work of one gang. ...car thefts. ...the drop in petty crime and theft.*

The Hague /ðə heɪɡ/
The Hague is the seat of government in the Netherlands (the capital is Amsterdam) and the Netherlands' third largest city. It is the headquarters of the International Court of Justice. Population: 444,000 (1989).

their /ðeə/
1 DET You use **their** to indicate that something belongs or relates to people or things that have just been mentioned or whose identity is known. *...the car companies and their workers... Don't hope to change anyone or their attitudes.*
2 DET You also use **their** to refer to people with titles. *Their Lordships were already late for dinner.*

theirs /ðeəz/
PRON You use **theirs** to indicate that something belongs or relates to people or things that have just been mentioned or whose identity is known. *It was his fault, not theirs... They were off to visit a friend of theirs.*

theism /θiːɪzəm/
N U **Theism** is the belief in the existence of a god or gods.

them /ðəm, ðem/. **Them** is used as the object of a verb or preposition.
1 PRON You use **them** to refer to people or things that have just been mentioned or whose identity is known. *I think some of them may attempt to take an overdose... He took off his glasses and put them in his pocket.*
2 PRON You can use **them** instead of 'him' or 'her' to refer to a person whose sex is not known or not stated. Some people consider this use to be incorrect. *If anyone phones, tell them I'm out. ...saying something to someone that you really want them to understand.*

thematic /θɪmætɪk/
ADJ Something that is **thematic** is concerned with particular subjects or topics; a formal word. *...thematic teaching. ...a thematic approach.*

theme /θiːm/ **themes**
1 NC A **theme** in a discussion or lecture is a main idea or subject in it. *The theme of the speech was responsibility to oneself and to society.*
2 NC A **theme** in an artist's or writer's work is an idea that is developed or repeated in it. *The main theme of the play was clear... The exploration of the universe is the theme of four new stamps issued today.*
3 NC In music, a **theme** is a short simple tune on which a piece of music is based. *...variations on a theme.*
4 NC A **theme** is also a tune that is played at the beginning and end of a television or radio programme.

themselves /ðəmselvz/
1 PRON REFL You use **themselves** as the object of a verb or preposition when it refers to the same people or things as the subject of the clause or a previous object in the clause. *They are trying to educate themselves... They had ceased to think of themselves as rebels.*
2 PRON REFL You also use **themselves** to emphasize the subject or object of a clause, and to make it clear who or what you are referring to. *Let's turn to the books themselves. ...a cultural preference on the part of the Chinese themselves.*
3 PRON REFL If people do something **themselves**, they do it without any help or interference from anyone else. *They must settle it themselves and get their own solutions.*

then /ðen/
1 ADV **Then** means at a particular time in the past or in the future. *I didn't have it then... The situation's changed since then... I'm going to see him at lunchtime. He's busy till then.*
2 ADV You use **then** to say that one thing happens or comes after another. *He went to the village school, then to the grammar school, and then to the university... You go right, then left.*
3 ADV SEN You use **then** in conversation to link your statement to what has just been said. *'Are you a student?'—'No, I'm not'—'What do you do then?'*
4 ADV SEN You also use **then** to introduce a summary or conclusion to what you have just said, or to end a conversation. *Democracy, then, is a form of government... If any questions do occur to you, then don't hesitate to write... Well, that's settled, then... Bye then.*
5 ADV SEN You also use **then** after words like 'now', 'well', and 'okay', to emphasize what you are about to say. *Now then, it's time you went to bed.*
6 ADV SEN You use **then** at the beginning of a sentence or after 'and' or 'but' to introduce an extra piece of information. *Then there could be a tax problem... Iron would do the job much better, but then you can't weld iron so easily.*
7 **now and then**: see **now**. **there and then**: see **there**.

thence /ðɛns/
ADV **Thence** means from the place that has just been mentioned; an old-fashioned word. *He hitched south towards Italy, and thence into France.*

thenceforth /ˌðɛnsˈfɔːθ/
ADV **Thenceforth** means from that time on; an old-fashioned word. *...the man who would thenceforth be his master.*

theocracy /θiˈɒkrəsi/ **theocracies**
NC A **theocracy** is a society which is ruled by priests who represent a god. *These people were content, living in a kind of theocracy.*

theodolite /θiˈɒdəlaɪt/ **theodolites**
NC A **theodolite** is an instrument used in surveying for measuring angles. *To ensure precise measurements, triangulation pillars have had to be erected to align theodolites and the lights used for siting.*

theologian /ˌθiːəˈləʊdʒən/ **theologians**
NC A **theologian** is someone who studies religion and ideas about God. *At the beginning of this month, a group of leading theologians put out a statement condemning violence.*

theology /θiˈɒlədʒi/
1 NU **Theology** is the study of religion and ideas about God. *...a diploma in theology.* ♦ **theological** /ˌθiːəˈlɒdʒɪkl/ ADJ *...a theological college.*
2 See also **liberation theology**.

theorem /ˈθɪərəm/ **theorems**
NC A **theorem** is a statement in mathematics that can be logically proved to be true. *...the theorem of Pythagoras. ...a book about the attempts to prove Fermat's last theorem.*

theoretical /ˌθɪəˈrɛtɪkl/
1 ADJ ATTRIB **Theoretical** means based on or concerning the ideas and abstract principles of a subject, rather than the practical aspects of it. *...theoretical biology. ...theoretical ideas which, in practice, may not work.*
2 ADJ A **theoretical** situation is supposed to exist, but in reality it may not. *The government and the central bank were in theoretical harmony.*

theoretically /ˌθɪəˈrɛtɪkəˈli/
ADV SEN You use **theoretically** to say that although something is supposed to happen or to be the case, it may not in fact happen or be the case. *Laws still theoretically controlled the availability of alcohol... It was theoretically possible to get permission from the council.*

theoretician /ˌθɪərətɪʃn/ **theoreticians**
NC A **theoretician** is the same as a **theorist**. *...Marxist theoreticians.*

theorist /ˈθɪərɪst/ **theorists**
NC A **theorist** is someone who develops an abstract idea or set of ideas about a particular subject in order to explain it. *...the economic theorist, Adam Smith... Theorists are trying to explain this structure.*

theorize /ˈθɪəraɪz/ **theorizes, theorizing, theorized**; also spelt **theorise**.
V or V-REPORT If you **theorize** about something, you develop ideas about it to try and explain it. *...reports that define, redefine and theorise about the role of NATO... Particle physicists theorise that there are more quarks.*

theory /ˈθɪəri/ **theories**
1 NC A **theory** is an idea or set of ideas intended to explain something. *...Darwin's theory of evolution.*
2 NU **Theory** is the set of rules, principles, or ideas that a practical method or skill is based on. *...Marxist economic theory. ...the theory and practice of inoculation.*
3 You use **in theory** to say that although something is supposed to happen or to be the case, it may not in fact happen or be the case. *In theory all British citizens are eligible for this.*

therapeutic /ˌθɛrəˈpjuːtɪk/
1 ADJ If something is **therapeutic**, it helps you to feel happier and more relaxed. *All that fresh air is very therapeutic.*
2 ADJ **Therapeutic** treatment is designed to treat a disease or to improve a person's health. *...the therapeutic effects of antibiotics.*

therapist /ˈθɛrəpɪst/ **therapists**
NC A **therapist** is a person skilled in a particular type of therapy. *...a speech therapist.*

therapy /ˈθɛrəpi/
NU **Therapy** is the treatment of mental or physical illness, often without the use of drugs or operations. *...a short course of heat therapy.*

there; pronounced /ðə/ or /ðɛə/ when it is a pronoun and /ðɛə/ when it is an adverb.
1 PRON You use **there** as the subject of the verb 'be' to say that something exists or does not exist, or to draw attention to it. *There was a new cushion on one of the settees... There must be a reason.*
2 PRON You use **there** in front of some intransitive verbs to emphasize the meaning. The subject of the verb is placed after the verb; a formal use. *Beside them there curls up a twist of blue smoke... There still remains the point about creativity.*
3 ADV If something is **there**, it exists or is available. *We talked about reality, about whether things are really there... The problem is still there... The play group is there for the children of staff and students.*
4 ADV You use **there** to refer to a place that has already been mentioned. *I must get home—Bill's there on his own.*
5 ADV You say **there** to indicate a place that you are pointing to or looking at. *'Over there,' she said and pointed to the door... Where's the ball? Oh, there it is.*
6 ADV You use **there** when speaking on the telephone to ask if someone is available to speak to you. *Is Veronica there, please?*
7 ADV You use **there** to refer to a point that someone has made in a conversation. *Could I interrupt you just there?... You're right there Howard.*
8 ADV You also use **there** to refer to a stage reached in an activity or process. *I'll write to the headmaster and then take the matter from there.*
● **There** is used in the following phrases. ● If you say that someone is **not all there**, you mean that you think they are stupid or not mentally alert; an informal expression. *He's a bit funny you know, I don't think he's all there.* ● If something happens **there and then** or **then and there**, it happens immediately. *He terminated the discussion then and there.* ● You say **'There you are'** or **'There you go'** when accepting an unsatisfactory situation. *It wasn't a very good reason for refusing, but there you are.* ● You also use **'There you are'** or **'There you go'** to emphasize that something proves you right. *There you are, Mabel! What did I tell you?* ● You also say **'There you are'** or **'There you go'** when you are giving something to someone. *'There you are', he said, handing the screws to me.* ● You can add **'so there'** to what you are saying to show that you will not change your mind about a decision you have made; an informal expression. *Well, I won't apologize, so there.*

thereabouts /ˌðɛərəˈbaʊts/
You can add **or thereabouts** after a number or date to indicate that it is approximate. *It repeats every 11 years or thereabouts... It was in 1982 or thereabouts.*

thereafter /ˌðɛərˈɑːftə/
ADV **Thereafter** means after the event or date mentioned; a formal word. *We first met in 1966 and I saw him quite often thereafter.*

thereby /ˌðɛəˈbaɪ/
ADV SEN **Thereby** means as an inevitable result of the event or action mentioned; a formal word. *They were flooding the market with unwanted oil and thereby depressing prices.*

therefore /ˈðɛəfɔː/
ADV SEN You use **therefore** to introduce a logical result or conclusion. *We have a growing population and therefore we need more food... The new car is smaller and therefore cheaper.*

therein /ˌðɛərˈɪn/; a formal word.
1 ADV **Therein** means in the place just mentioned. *...the lakes and the fish therein.*
2 If you say **therein lies** a situation or problem, you mean that the situation or problem exists because of something you have just mentioned. *He was not a snob, you see, and therein lay his downfall.*

thereof /ðeˈərɒv/
ADV **Thereof** is used to refer back to a situation or thing that has previously been mentioned and to relate the word just used to that situation or thing; a formal word. *All persons born or naturalized in the United States, and subject to the jurisdiction thereof, are citizens of the United States... EC Law entitles an individual to go before his own National Court and to claim the benefits thereof.*

thereupon /ðeˈərəppɒn/
ADV **Thereupon** means immediately after an event and usually as a result of it; a formal word. *I flung a few copies of the report in his lap, which thereupon fell to the floor.*

therm /θɜːm/ **therms**
NC A **therm** is a measurement of heat. *They had installed all the heating equipment and the school was paying them a certain amount per therm.*

thermal /θɜːml/
1 ADJ ATTRIB **Thermal** means relating to heat or caused by heat; a technical use. *...the thermal efficiency of an engine. ...thermal energy.*
2 ADJ ATTRIB **Thermal** clothes are specially designed to keep you warm. *...thermal underwear.*

thermodynamics /θɜːməʊdaɪnæmɪks/
NU **Thermodynamics** is the branch of physics that is concerned with the relationship between heat and other forms of energy. *...the second law of thermodynamics. ...the science of thermodynamics.*

thermometer /θəmɒmɪtə/ **thermometers**
NC A **thermometer** is an instrument for measuring the temperature of a room or of a person's body. *The thermometer reads 92 degrees.*

thermonuclear /θɜːməʊnjuːkliə/
ADJ ATTRIB A **thermonuclear** weapon or device is one which uses the high temperatures that are generated in nuclear fission to detonate it. *...some of the most powerful thermonuclear explosions ever conducted.*

thermoplastic /θɜːməʊplæstɪk/ **thermoplastics**
NC A **thermoplastic** is a plastic which becomes soft when it is heated and hard when it cools down.

Thermos /θɜːməs/ **Thermoses**
NC A **Thermos** or a **Thermos flask** is a container used to keep drinks at a constant temperature; **Thermos** is a trademark. *Some families arrived ready with Thermos flasks of tea.*

thermostat /θɜːməstæt/ **thermostats**
NC A **thermostat** is a device used to keep the temperature of something at a particular level. *...ensuring that houses are well insulated and that thermostats are set no higher than necessary.*

thesaurus /θɪsɔːrəs/ **thesauruses**
NC A **thesaurus** is a reference book in which words with similar meanings are grouped together. *They have retired with a thesaurus in order to find another word for 'eliminate'.*

these /ðiːz/; often pronounced /ðiːz/ when it is a determiner.
These is the plural of **this**.

thesis /θiːsɪs/ **theses** /θiːsiːz/
1 NC A **thesis** is an idea or theory expressed as a statement and discussed in a logical way. *It is my thesis that Australia underwent fundamental changes in the 1920s.*
2 NC A **thesis** is also a long piece of writing, based on original research, that is done as part of a university degree. *She is writing a thesis on Jane Austen.*

thespian /θespiən/ **thespians**; an old-fashioned word.
1 NC A **thespian** is an actor or actress.
2 ADJ **Thespian** means relating to drama and the theatre.

The Valley /ðə væli/
The Valley is the capital of Anguilla and its principal settlement. Population: 500 (1988).

they /ðeɪ/ **They** is used as the subject of a verb.
1 PRON You use **they** to refer to people or things that have just been mentioned or whose identity is known. *All universities have chancellors. They are always rather senior people... These steels are too strong. They cannot give. They just get fatigue and crack.*
2 PRON You also use **they** to refer to people in general, or to a group of people whose identity is not actually

stated. *Isn't that what they call love?*
3 PRON You can use **they** instead of 'he' or 'she' to refer to a person whose sex is not known or not stated. Some people consider this use to be incorrect. *Nearly everybody thinks they're middle class... I was going to stay with a friend, but they were ill.*

they'd /ðeɪd/
They'd is the usual spoken form of 'they had', especially when 'had' is an auxiliary verb. **They'd** is also a spoken form of 'they would'. *They said they'd read it all before... I wish they'd publish more books like this.*

they'll /ðeɪl/
They'll is the usual spoken form of 'they will'. *They'll probably sell it cheaper.*

they're /ðeə, ðeɪə/
They're is the usual spoken form of 'they are'. *They're not interested.*

they've /ðeɪv/
They've is the usual spoken form of 'they have', especially when 'have' is an auxiliary verb. *They've been studying very hard.*

Thiam, Habib /həbiːb tjæm/
Habib **Thiam** became Prime Minister of Senegal in 1991. He was Secretary of State for the Development Plan in 1963, Minister for Planning and Development from 1964 to 1967, and Minister of Rural Development from 1968 to 1973. He became a member of the National Assembly in 1973, and was President of the National Assembly from 1983 to 1984. He previously served as Prime Minister from 1981 to 1983. He is a member of the Socialist Party (PS). Born: 1933.

thick /θɪk/ **thicker, thickest**
1 ADJ or ADV If something is **thick**, there is a large distance between its two opposite surfaces. *We were separated by thick concrete walls... Last winter the snow lay thick on the ground.* ◆ **thickly** ADV *She buttered my bread thickly.*
2 ADJ If something that consists of several things is **thick**, the things in it are present in large quantities. *She had a lot of thick black hair... They were on the edge of the thick forest... She came out of the thickest part of the crowd.* ◆ **thickly** ADV *Plants and trees grew thickly on both sides of the river.*
3 ADJ PRED You use **thick** to say how wide or deep something is. *The tree was one foot thick at the base.* ◆ **thickness** NU *Insert a new wire of the same thickness and wind it round the screws.*
4 ADJ **Thick** liquids do not flow easily because they are nearly solid. *The chef has made the sauce too thick. ...thick cream.*
5 ADJ **Thick** smoke or fog is difficult to see through. *The fog seemed to be getting thicker.*
6 ADJ If someone's voice is **thick**, they are not speaking clearly, for example because they are ill, upset, or drunk. *His voice sounded blurred and thick.* ◆ **thickly** ADV *'Let's get out of here,' Tom said thickly.*
7 ADJ If you say that someone is **thick**, you mean that you think they are stupid; an informal use. *They were too thick to notice it.*
● **Thick** is used in the following phrases. ● If things happen **thick and fast**, they happen very quickly and in large numbers. *More discoveries followed thick and fast.* ● To be **thick with** something means to be full of it or be covered with it. *The air was thick with butterflies... The windows were thick with grime.* ● If you are **in the thick of** an activity or situation, you are very involved in it. *It won't be long before Amanda is in the thick of O levels.* ● If you do something **through thick and thin**, you do it even though the conditions or circumstances are very bad. *She stayed with her husband through thick and thin.*

thicken /θɪkən/ **thickens, thickening, thickened**
1 V If something **thickens**, it becomes more closely grouped together or denser than it was before. *Here the vegetation thickens into a jungle... By noon the cloud layer had thickened.*
2 V-ERG When you **thicken** a liquid or when it **thickens**, it becomes stiffer and more solid. *You can use flour to thicken sauces... After a while the mixture thickens.*

thickener /θɪkə^ənə/ **thickeners**
NCorNU A **thickener** is a substance that is added to a liquid in order to make it stiffer and more solid. *You can use cornflour as a thickener for sauces, soups and stews.*

thicket /θɪkɪt/ **thickets**
NC A **thicket** is a small group of trees or bushes growing closely together. *...thickets of thorn bushes.*

thickset /θɪksɛt/
ADJ A **thickset** person is broad and heavy. *...a big, thickset man with heavy shoulders.*

thick-skinned
ADJ A **thick-skinned** person is not easily hurt by what other people say to them. *'Aren't you afraid you'll get hurt?'—'No I think I'm thick-skinned.'*

thief /θiːf/ **thieves**
NC A **thief** is a person who steals something from another person, especially without using violence. *...jewel thieves.*

thieving /θiːvɪŋ/
ADJ ATTRIB **Thieving** means involved in stealing things. *...those thieving village kids.*

thigh /θaɪ/ **thighs**
NC Your **thighs** are the top parts of your legs, between your knees and your hips. *I walked the last six miles in water up to my thighs.*

thimble /θɪmbl/ **thimbles**
NC A **thimble** is a small metal or plastic object, used to protect your finger when you are sewing.

thimbleful /θɪmblful/ **thimblefuls**
NC A **thimbleful** is a very small amount of liquid. *'More sherry?'—'Just a thimbleful please.'*

Thimphu /tɪmpuː/
Thimphu is the capital of Bhutan and its largest city. Population: 15,000 (1987).

thin /θɪn/ **thinner, thinnest; thins, thinning, thinned**
1 ADJ Something that is **thin** is much narrower than usual. *...their tall, thin house... His nose was long and thin.*
2 ADJ Something such as paper or cloth that is **thin** has a very short distance between its two opposite surfaces. *...thin cotton cloth. ...a thin layer of soil and coarse grass.* ◆ **thinly** ADV *...fresh, thinly cut bread.*
3 ADJ A **thin** person or animal has very little fat on their body. *Angela was dreadfully thin.*
4 ADJ **Thin** liquids flow very easily and may contain a lot of water. *The liquid was thin and greyish brown.*
5 ADJ A crowd of people that is **thin** has very few people in it. *The crowd seemed suddenly thinner.* ◆ **thinly** ADV *...a thinly populated region.*
6 V If someone's hair is **thinning**, they are beginning to go bald. *His hair was thinning slightly.*
● **Thin** is used in these phrases. ● If your patience or temper is **wearing thin**, you are beginning to get impatient or angry. *He said his patience was already wearing thin with the Baltic republics.* ● If people or things are **thin on the ground**, there are not very many of them; an informal expression. *Good new plays are still rather thin on the ground.* ● to disappear **into thin air**: see **air**.

thin down PHRASAL VERB When you **thin** a liquid **down**, you add more water or other liquid to it. *The paint has been thinned down too much.*

thine /ðaɪn/
PRON **Thine** is an old-fashioned, poetic, or religious word for 'yours' when you are talking to only one person. See **thou**. *Thine is the kingdom, the power, and the glory... I am thine for ever.*

thing /θɪŋ/ **things**
1 NC+SUPP You use **thing** as a substitute for another word when you do not want to be more precise, when you are referring to something that has already been mentioned, or when you are going to give more details about it. *He needed a few things so we went to the store to purchase them... It's silly to train a group of people just to do one thing... The fourth drawer holds family things such as photographs and letters... A terrible thing happened to me on my way to work.*
2 NC A **thing** is a physical object, rather than a human being, animal, or plant. *He's only interested in things and not people.*
3 N PL+POSS Your **things** are your clothes or

possessions. *She changed into her bathing things... I like my own things around me: my photos and books.*
4 N PL **Things** refers to life in general and the way it affects you. *Things are going very well for us at the moment.*
5 NC+SUPP You can call a person or an animal a **thing** when you are expressing your feelings towards them. *She was very cold, poor thing.*
● **Thing** is used in the following phrases. ● You can say **'The thing is'** to introduce an explanation or opinion relating to something that has just been said; used in speech. *I can't come on Thursday; the thing is, I've already arranged to do something.* ● You say **for one thing** when you give only one reason for something, but want to indicate that there are other reasons. *I prefer badminton to squash. It's not so tiring for one thing.* ● If you say it is **just one of those things**, you mean that you cannot explain why something happens. ● If you **have a thing** about something or if you **make a thing** about it, you have very strong feelings about it, often because you disapprove of it; an informal expression. *I've got a thing about drinking... He made a big thing of not eating chilli.*

thingamabob /θɪŋəməbɒb/ **thingamabobs**
NC You can refer to something or someone as **thingamabob** or **thingummy** when you cannot remember or do not know the proper word or name for them; used in informal speech. *Her phone is out of order. She's getting a new thingamabob.*

thingummy /θɪŋəmi/ **thingummies**
NC See **thingamabob**.

thingy /θɪŋi/ **thingies**
NC **Thingy** is used to refer to an object or person whose name you have forgotten, or who you do not want to refer to directly; used in informal speech. *Oh, I saw thingy the other day.*

think /θɪŋk/ **thinks, thinking, thought**
1 V-REPORT, V+of, or V+about If you **think** that something is the case, you have the opinion that it is the case. *I think a woman has as much right to work as a man... She's cleverer than I thought... What does she think of this song?... She thought of Deirdre simply as an old chum... People are the prisoners of what others think about them.*
2 V+about When you **think** about something, you make a mental effort to consider it. *That ought to make us think about how we can make a safer product. ...the society in which most of us live without even thinking about it.*
3 V+of When you **think** of something, you remember it or it comes into your mind. *I can never think of her name... He can think of no reason for going.*
4 V+of You can also say that you **think** of something when you create it in your mind, using your intelligence and imagination. *...a method which had never been thought of before.*
5 V+of or about To **think** of someone also means to show consideration for them. *It was very kind of you to think of him... You never think about anybody but yourself!*
6 V A If you **think** a lot of someone or something, you admire them. *She thinks a lot of you... I didn't think much of his letter.*
7 V-REPORT When you **are thinking** something, you are concentrating your attention on it. *I lay there thinking how funny it was.*
8 V-QUOTE If you **think** something at a particular moment, you have words and ideas in your mind without saying them out loud. *'That's good', I thought. 'Then there's nothing to argue about.'*
9 V+of or about If you **think** of doing something, you are planning to do it. *Is he still thinking of going away to Italy for a month?... The team is already thinking about trying again for the year 2000.*
10 See also **thinking, thought**.
● **Think** is used in these phrases. ● You can say **'I think'** to sound less forceful or rude. *I think I ought to go... I think that you will find my figures are correct... Thank you, I don't think I will.* ● If you **think again** or **think twice** about doing something, you reconsider it and may decide to do it differently or not to do it at

all. *They urged her to think again about the reform plans... They'll really have to think twice about their actions... The difficulties may well make the government think twice before privatizing British Rail.* ● If you were intending to do something but **think better of it**, you decide not to do it. *She was on the point of waking Ben again, but then thought better of it.* ● If you say that someone would **think nothing of** doing something difficult or strange, you mean that they would do it and not think that it was difficult or strange at all. *We would think nothing of walking six miles just to post a letter.* ● If you say **anybody would think** that a particular thing was true, you are expressing your surprise or disapproval at someone's behaviour. *Anybody'd think you were our nanny... You would have thought they'd never seen a man before.* ● **come to think of it**: see come. ● **to think the world of** someone: see world.

think back PHRASAL VERB If you **think back**, you remember things that happened in the past. *I'm thinking back to my own experience as a teacher.*

think out PHRASAL VERB If you **think out** a plan or a piece of writing, you prepare it fully and consider all the details of it before doing it. *She needed time to think out a strategy to deal with Gareth... He's a great believer in thinking things out... Ministers had not fully thought out that concession.* ● See also **thought-out**.

think over PHRASAL VERB If you **think** something **over**, you consider it carefully before making a decision. *I wanted to think over one or two business problems.*

think through PHRASAL VERB If you **think** a problem or situation **through**, you consider it thoroughly. *I haven't really thought the whole business through... They sit down and really think the ideas through over a whole day.*

think up PHRASAL VERB If you **think up** something clever or unusual, you create it in your mind. *...a new financial agreement he had thought up... He then thought up moves to counter the plan.*

thinker /ˈθɪŋkə/ **thinkers**
NC+SUPP A **thinker** is someone who spends time thinking about ideas and important issues, often in order to express them in new ways or to produce new ideas. *Hobbes is the first really modern political thinker. ...a newspaper article by a right-wing thinker.*

thinking /ˈθɪŋkɪŋ/
1 NU **Thinking** is the activity of using your brain to consider a problem or to create an idea. *That requires a great deal of serious thinking.*
2 NU+SUPP The general ideas or opinions of a person or group can be referred to as their **thinking**. *There are gaps in government thinking on the subject of welfare... We are so alike in our thinking.*
3 See also **wishful thinking**.

think tank, think tanks
NC A **think tank** is a group of experts who have been appointed by the government or an organization in order to examine various problems and consider possible solutions to them. *The Prime Minister appointed a think tank of independent experts. ...last week's so-called secret 'think-tank' report.*

thinly /ˈθɪnli/
SUBMOD A **thinly** veiled or **thinly** disguised remark is one that does not say exactly or truthfully what a person means, but which people clearly understand in spite of this. *That was a thinly veiled reference to the Sandinista government. ...a thinly veiled attack on Mrs Thatcher. ...a thinly disguised demand for sovereignty.*

thinner /ˈθɪnə/ **thinners**
N MASS **Thinner** is a liquid which you add to another liquid such as paint, in order to make it less thick and easier to use. *Try turpentine as a thinner.*

third /θɜːd/ **thirds**
1 ADJ The **third** item in a series is the one that you count as number three. *This room was on the third floor... For the third consecutive day, there have been anti-government demonstrations in the capital.*
2 NC A **third** is one of three equal parts of something. *It covers a third of the world's surface.*

third-class
1 ADJ or ADV **Third-class** is the cheapest and least comfortable section of accommodation on a ship or train. *I saw her emerging from a third-class carriage of the train... I shall go third-class.*
2 ADJ ATTRIB A **third-class** degree is the lowest honours degree that can be obtained from a British university.

third degree
N SING If someone is given the **third degree**, they are questioned aggressively or treated violently in order to make them admit something or reveal information that they want to keep secret; an informal expression. *He was probably being put through the third degree down there... Surely they were supposed to read you your rights before they gave you the third degree?*

thirdly /ˈθɜːdli/
ADV SEN You use **thirdly** when you want to make a third point or give a third reason for something. *And thirdly, remember that they have supported you in the past.*

third party, third parties; spelt **third-party** for the meaning in paragraph 2.
1 NC A **third party** is someone who is not one of the two main people or groups involved in a dispute or a discussion, but who becomes involved in it in order to contribute to the settlement. *Discussions between the Arabs and Israel would have to be joined by a credible third party... A third party from outside the village was brought in as a witness.*
2 ADJ If you have **third-party** insurance and you cause an accident, your insurance company will pay money only to other people who are hurt or whose property is damaged, and not to you. *...third-party insurance payments.*

third person
N SING In grammar, a statement in the **third person** is a statement about another person or thing, and not directly about yourself or about the person you are talking to.

third-rate
ADJ Something that is **third-rate** is of an extremely poor quality or standard. *...the seedy world of third-rate theatricals.*

Third World
N PROP The poorer countries of Africa, Asia, and South America are sometimes referred to as the **Third World**. *I had seen a good deal of the Third World before I visited Calcutta... He said developed countries had a common responsibility for the problems of the Third World. ...Third World aid.*

thirst /θɜːst/ **thirsts, thirsting, thirsted**
1 N SING If you have a **thirst**, you feel a need to drink something. *She had a terrible thirst.*
2 NU **Thirst** is the condition of not having enough to drink. *She was dying of thirst. ...an excruciating death through thirst and hunger.*
3 N SING+for A **thirst** for something is a very strong desire for it. *State radio announced that the revolt was over, condemning a few officers for their thirst for power... They had ambition, an inner discipline, and a thirst for knowledge.*

thirst for PHRASAL VERB If you **thirst for** something, you want it very much; a literary expression. *They were thirsting for revenge.*

thirsty /ˈθɜːsti/
1 ADJ If you are **thirsty**, you feel the need to drink something. *Have you got any water? I'm thirsty.*
◆ **thirstily** ADV *Jane drank thirstily.*
2 ADJ ATTRIB **Thirsty** is used to describe activities that make you thirsty. *Gardening is really thirsty work.*

thirteen /ˌθɜːˈtiːn/
Thirteen is the number 13. *He hadn't appeared in a film for thirteen years.*

thirteenth /ˌθɜːˈtiːnθ/
ADJ The **thirteenth** item in a series is the one that you count as number thirteen. *The thirteenth round of meetings began in Athens today.*

thirtieth /ˈθɜːtiəθ/
ADJ The **thirtieth** item in a series is the one that you count as number thirty. *...the thirtieth anniversary of the Cuban revolution.*

thirty /ˈθɜːti/ **thirties**
Thirty is the number 30. *...thirty years of marriage.*
this /ðɪs/ **these**; often pronounced /ðɪs/ when it is a
determiner in paragraphs 1, 2 and 4.
1 DET or PRON You use **this** to refer to a person or thing
that has been mentioned, to someone or something
that is present, or to something that is happening. *So,
for all these reasons, my advice is to be very, very
careful... Get these kids out of here... This was a sad
end to her career... This is Desiree, my father's
second wife... 'My God,' I said. 'This is awful.'*
2 DET You use **this** to refer to the present time or the
place you are currently in. *Could I make an
appointment to see the doctor this morning please?
...the prime minister of this country.*
3 DET You can use **this** to refer to the next occurrence
in the future of a particular day, month, or season.
Let's fix a time. This Sunday. Four o'clock.
4 DET In informal speech, people use **this** to introduce
a person or thing into a story. *I stopped at a junction
and this bowler-hatted gent comes up.*
5 SUBMOD You can also use **this** when you are
indicating the size or shape of something with your
hands. *It was about this big.*
6 You can refer to a variety of things as **this and
that**. *'What have you been up to?'—'This and that.'*
thistle /ˈθɪsl/ **thistles**
NC A **thistle** is a wild plant with prickly leaves and
purple flowers. *...thistles, nettles and weeds.*
thistledown /ˈθɪsldaʊn/
NU **Thistledown** is the soft, white hairs that are
attached to the seeds of thistles. **Thistledown** allows
the seeds to be carried by the wind. *...hundreds of
parachutes, descending like thistledown.*
thither /ˈðɪðə/
ADV **Thither** means to the place that has already been
mentioned; an old-fashioned word. *I did love Wilton,
and I came thither every summer.* ● **hither and
thither**: see hither.
thong /θɒŋ/ **thongs**
NC A **thong** is a long, thin strip of leather, plastic, or
rubber. *Two women were reportedly beaten with
leather thongs.*
thoracic /θɔːˈræsɪk/
ADJ ATTRIB **Thoracic** means relating to or affecting
your thorax; a medical term. *...an eminent thoracic
surgeon. ...the thoracic cavity.*
thorax /ˈθɔːræks/ **thoraxes** or **thoraces** /ˈθɔːrəsiːz/
1 NC Your **thorax** is the part of your body between
your neck and your waist, including the organs that
are inside, for example your heart and lungs; a
medical use. *The blood moves into the thorax.*
2 NC An insect's **thorax** is the central part of its body,
between the head and the abdomen, to which the legs
and wings are attached; a technical term in biology.
*Researchers found the fossilized head and thorax of an
insect.*
thorn /θɔːn/ **thorns**
NC **Thorns** are the sharp points on some plants and
trees, for example on a rose bush. *He stepped on a
sharp thorn.*
thorny /ˈθɔːni/ **thornier, thorniest**
1 ADJ A **thorny** plant or tree is covered with thorns. *It
is a very thorny, densely growing bush, which
provides very good hedges.*
2 ADJ ATTRIB A **thorny** problem or question is difficult
to deal with. *The negotiating team have already
discussed the thorny question of defence... A much
thornier problem is the type of regime that would be
left... Human rights had been the thorniest issue of
this conference.*
thorough /ˈθʌrə/
1 ADJ A **thorough** action or thing is done very
carefully and completely. *...a thorough search... The
Austrian government has ordered a thorough
investigation... He said that the talks had not been
very thorough.* ● **thoroughly** ADV or SUBMOD *They had
not studied the language thoroughly. ...a thoroughly
prepared takeover of power.* ● **thoroughness** NU
...the thoroughness of the training programme.
2 ADJ PRED People who are **thorough** do things in a
careful and methodical way. *He is enormously*

thorough and full of inspiration. ● **thoroughness** NU
*The President was impressed by his speed and
thoroughness.*
3 ADJ ATTRIB You can use **thorough** for emphasis. *I'd
enjoy giving him a thorough beating.* ● **thoroughly**
ADV or SUBMOD *Yes, I thoroughly agree. ...a thoroughly
unreasonable person.*
thoroughbred /ˈθʌrəbred/ **thoroughbreds**
NC A **thoroughbred** is an animal that has parents that
are of the same high quality breed. *The
thoroughbreds that thrill us at the Derby are all young
animals... Thoroughbred horses have been bred
exclusively for racing in Britain.*
thoroughfare /ˈθʌrəfeə/ **thoroughfares**
NC A **thoroughfare** is a main road in a town or city; a
formal word. *We went back towards the main
thoroughfare.*
thoroughgoing /ˈθʌrəɡəʊɪŋ/
ADJ ATTRIB A **thoroughgoing** action or quality is
complete and full. *More thoroughgoing analysis was
needed. ...a society founded on a thoroughgoing
radicalism. ...thoroughgoing market reforms.*
those /ðəʊz/
Those is the plural of that.
thou /ðaʊ/
PRON **Thou** is an old-fashioned, poetic, or religious
word for 'you' when you are talking to only one
person. *Thou must be damned perpetually.*
though /ðəʊ/
1 CONJ or ADV SEN You use **though** to introduce a fact or
comment which contrasts with something else that is
being said, or makes it seem surprising. *Though he
hadn't stopped working all day, he wasn't tired... She
wore a fur coat, even though it was a very hot day...
'It's not very useful.'—'It's pretty, though, isn't it?'*
2 **as though**: see as.
thought /θɔːt/ **thoughts**
1 **Thought** is the past tense and past participle of
think.
2 NC A **thought** is an idea in your mind. *It's a very
tempting thought... The thought never crossed my
mind.*
3 NU **Thought** is the activity of thinking. *She frowned
as though deep in thought... After giving our
predicament some thought, he said he had a proposal.*
4 NU+SUPP You can refer to a set of ideas as a
particular type of **thought**. *...two schools of socialist
thought.*
5 N PL Your **thoughts** are the ideas in your mind when
you are thinking about something; a literary use.
*They walked back, each deep in his own private
thoughts... His mind was empty except for thoughts of
her.*
6 N PL Your **thoughts** on something are your opinions
on it. *Rothermere disclosed his thoughts on Britain.*
7 See also **second thoughts**.
thoughtful /ˈθɔːtfl/
1 ADJ PRED If you are **thoughtful**, you are quiet
because you are thinking about something. *He looked
thoughtful for a moment.* ● **thoughtfully** ADV *Tom
closed the book thoughtfully.*
2 ADJ A **thoughtful** person remembers what other
people want or need, and is kind and helpful. *...an
intelligent and thoughtful man with a keen sense of
responsibility... I thanked him for his thoughtful
gesture... That's very thoughtful of you.* ● **thoughtfully**
ADV *The book thoughtfully provides a clue on how to
do this.* ● **thoughtfulness** NU *...courtesy and
thoughtfulness for others... I was very touched by his
thoughtfulness.*
thoughtless /ˈθɔːtləs/
ADJ **Thoughtless** people forget or ignore what other
people want, need, or feel. *I had to scold Vita
severely for being so thoughtless.* ● **thoughtlessly** ADV
*Traditional sources of employment are thoughtlessly
destroyed.* ● **thoughtlessness** NU *Many of the
incidents happened because of thoughtlessness.*
thought-out
ADJ If a plan or idea is well **thought-out**, it has been
prepared carefully. If it is badly **thought-out**, it has not
been considered carefully during its preparation.
...the government's well thought-out programmes of

reforms... The latest proposals are insufficiently thought-out. ...a properly thought-out strategy... Democracy has to be built up through carefully thought-out legislation.

thought-provoking

ADJ If something such as a novel, play, or film is **thought-provoking**, it makes you think about a subject in a new and interesting way. *His article is very thought-provoking... This book provides a further, thought-provoking challenge.*

thousand /θaʊznd/ **thousands**

1 A **thousand** is the number 1,000. *...an annual income of twenty thousand dollars.*
2 QUANT You can use **thousands** to refer to a very large number. *I've told him thousands of times.*
3 a **thousand and one**: see **one**.

thousandth /θaʊznθ/ **thousandths**

1 ADJ The **thousandth** item in a series is the one that you count as number one thousand. *The uprising has just passed its thousandth day.*
2 NC A **thousandth** is one of a thousand equal parts of something. *...a thousandth of a second.*

thrall /θrɔːl/

If you are **in thrall** to someone, you are completely in their power or are greatly influenced by them; a literary expression. *The poet was in thrall to the sophisticated woman... The story-teller held us all in thrall.*

thrash /θræʃ/ **thrashes, thrashing, thrashed**

1 VO If someone **thrashes** you, they hit you hard several times. *We were thrashed a lot at school.* ♦ **thrashing, thrashings** NC *He got a thrashing from his father.*
2 VO If someone **thrashes** you in a game or contest, they defeat you completely; an informal use. *Indonesia thrashed Singapore 5-nil.* ♦ **thrashing** NC *...the thrashing our team got at Southampton.*

thrash around PHRASAL VERB If you **thrash around**, you twist and turn your body quickly and violently. *The boy was thrashing around, trying to get free.*

thrash out PHRASAL VERB When people **thrash out** something such as a policy, they discuss it until they agree on an acceptable form of it. *A new economic strategy was being thrashed out... The meeting was called to try to thrash out a ceasefire agreement.*

thread /θred/ **threads, threading, threaded**

1 NCorNU A **thread** is a long, thin piece of cotton, silk, nylon, or wool. Thread is used in sewing. *If you break one thread in the seam you can pull it apart... He stood dressed in a golden robe, embroidered with red and purple thread.*
2 NC The **thread** on something such as a screw or the top of a container is the raised spiral line around it. *On one end, there's a little thread that fits into the valve on the tyre.*
3 NC The **thread** in an argument or story is the idea or theme that connects the different parts together. *He had lost his thread and didn't know what to say next.*
4 VO If you **thread** a long piece of thread, ribbon, tape, and so on through a hole or space, you put it through the hole or space. *He carefully threaded the film through the projector.* ● **Thread** is used in these phrases. ● If you **thread your way** through a group of people or things, you go through the narrow gaps between them. *We turned and threaded our way through the fairground.* ● If you say that the survival or success of someone or something **hangs by a thread**, you mean that it is very likely that they will not survive or succeed. *His political career hung by a thread while Mrs Thatcher came under pressure to sack him... The leadership is hanging by a thread.*

threadbare /θredbeə/

1 ADJ **Threadbare** clothes, carpets, and so on are old and have become thin and nearly worn out. *O'Shea's suit was baggy and threadbare. ...a big, empty, slightly threadbare rehearsal room.*
2 ADJ If something such as an argument or method of doing things is **threadbare**, it no longer has much force or effect, and people are not convinced by it. *This claim is now increasingly threadbare, and many*

people do not believe them... That strategy now looks more than a little threadbare... The announcement that the homeless would be housed within three years looked threadbare.

threat /θret/ **threats**

1 NCorNU If someone makes a **threat**, they say that they will harm you, especially if you do not do what they want. *A threat had been made against an unspecified flight... All Red Cross staff were withdrawn because of death threats against them... Under threat of death, he confessed.*
2 N SING You can refer to anything that seems likely to harm you as a **threat**. *I was becoming a real threat to his plans. ...the threat of flooding. ...the threat posed by the growing power of the drug dealers... They posed a definite military threat.*

threaten /θretn/ **threatens, threatening, threatened**

1 V+to-INForVO If you **threaten** to do something that will harm someone or that will cause them problems, you warn them that you will do it. *They were threatened with imprisonment... He threatened to resign.*
2 VO If someone or something **threatens** people or things, they are likely to harm them or cause them problems. *He said that the war threatened the peace of the whole world... The whole country is threatened with starvation.* ♦ **threatened** ADJ *He felt threatened. ...a threatened boycott of the elections.*
3 V+to-INF If something **threatens** to do something unpleasant, it seems likely to do it. *The riots threatened to get out of hand.*

threatening /θretᵊnɪŋ/

1 ADJ Someone or something that is **threatening** seems likely to cause harm. *He became angry and threatening. ...a threatening environment.* ♦ **threateningly** ADV *He advanced threateningly on the boy.*
2 ADJ ATTRIB A **threatening** letter or phonecall is one that contains threats. *...a series of threatening letters sent to the authorities... She's received dozens of threatening telephone calls in the last few days.*

three /θriː/ **threes**

Three is the number 3. *They have two or three small patches of land in different parts of the village.*

three-dimensional

1 ADJ A **three-dimensional** object can be measured in three different directions, usually the height, depth, and width. *...a three-dimensional model of the theatre.*
2 ADJ A **three-dimensional** image, film, or picture looks as though it is deep or solid rather than flat. *They used three-dimensional videos to launch the product.*

three-legged /θriːlegɪd/ **three-legged**

1 ADJ ATTRIB A **three-legged** animal has lost one of its legs, for example in an accident. *A small branch lands in front of a three-legged cat, who pounces on it. ...a three-legged dog hobbling down the cobbled street.*
2 NC A **three-legged** race is a race in which pairs of people try to run with one leg tied to the other person's leg. *They were waiting in pairs, with their legs tied together, to run in the three-legged race.*

three-line whip. See **whip**.

three-ply

ADJ **Three-ply** wool or rope has three strands. **Three-ply** wood has three layers. *If you want three-ply wool, do the same thing, only using three bobbins.*

three-point turn, three-point turns

NC When someone who is driving a vehicle does a **three-point turn**, they turn the vehicle around by driving it forwards in a curve, then backwards in a curve, and then forwards in a curve. *I turned the jeep past a pothole and did a three-point turn towards the gate.*

three-quarter, three-quarters

QUANT **Three-quarters** of something is a half of it plus a quarter of it. *Three-quarters of the world's surface is covered by water. ...one and three-quarter hours.* ▶ Also ADV *The tank is three-quarters full.*

three Rs /θriː ɑːz/

N PL When talking about children's education, you can refer to the basic skills of reading, writing, and arithmetic as the **three Rs**. *...traditionalists who* *believe in what's known as the three Rs.*

threesome /ˈθriːsəm/ **threesomes**

NC A **threesome** is a group of three people. *Meanwhile, the visually exciting threesome will continue to use old Greek songs for ideas.*

thresh /θreʃ/ **threshes, threshing, threshed**

VO When people **thresh** corn, wheat, or rice, they beat it in order to separate the grains from the rest of it. *After you have threshed the grain, you must winnow it... Oat straw, whether threshed or not, is the best of all the straws for feeding.*

threshold /ˈθreʃhəʊld/ **thresholds**; also spelt **threshhold**.

1 NC The **threshold** of a building or room is the floor in the doorway, or the doorway itself. *Madame stood on the threshold... Morris had never crossed the threshold of a public house before.*

2 NC A **threshold** is an amount, level, or limit on a scale. When the **threshold** is reached, something else happens or changes. *Three political parties complained that a five per cent threshold for entering Parliament was unfair for them... For every pound of extra income you earn over the threshold, you could find yourself liable to tax.*

3 If you are **on the threshold of** something exciting or new, you are about to experience it. *He was on the threshold of public life... He told the congregation that black America was on the threshold of a dream.*

threw /θruː/

Threw is the past tense of **throw**.

thrice /θraɪs/; a formal word.

1 ADV Something that happens **thrice** or is done **thrice** happens or is done three times. *Joseph Chamberlain was thrice mayor of Birmingham... Power cuts were occurring thrice daily in many parts of Greece.*

2 PREDET If something is **thrice** the size of something else, it is three times bigger. *His vegetables were thrice the size of mine... Our products were seen by twice or thrice that number.*

thrift /θrɪft/

NU **Thrift** is the practice of being thrifty. *The economy would be altered to take account of market forces and to encourage thrift and enterprise.*

thrifty /ˈθrɪfti/

ADJ Someone who is **thrifty** saves money and does not waste things. *She was a thrifty housekeeper... Malays must learn how to manage and be thrifty.*

thrill /θrɪl/ **thrills, thrilling, thrilled**

1 NC If something gives you a **thrill**, it gives you a sudden feeling of excitement or pleasure. *The sound of the bell sent a thrill of anticipation through her... The thrill for me was finding the rare specimens.*

2 VO If something **thrills** you, it gives you a thrill. *It's a sight that never fails to thrill me.*

thrilled /θrɪld/

ADJ PRED If you are **thrilled** about something, you are pleased and excited about it. *I was thrilled to be sitting next to such a distinguished author.*

thriller /ˈθrɪlə/ **thrillers**

NC A **thriller** is a book, film, or play that tells an exciting story about dangerous, frightening, or mysterious events. *...a spy thriller.*

thrilling /ˈθrɪlɪŋ/

ADJ Something that is **thrilling** is very exciting and enjoyable. *...a thrilling adventure... She gave a thrilling performance... His late poetry is thrilling.*

thrive /θraɪv/ **thrives, thriving, thrived**

V When people or things **thrive**, they are healthy, happy, or successful. *Are you the type of person who thrives on activity?... My business was thriving.*
◆ **thriving** ADJ *There's a thriving black market for videos. ...a thriving community.*

throat /θrəʊt/ **throats**

1 NC Your **throat** is the back of your mouth and the top part of the tubes that go down into your stomach and your lungs. *His throat was so dry that he could hardly swallow.*

2 NC Your **throat** is also the front part of your neck. *He grabbed the man by the throat.*

● **Throat** is used in these phrases. ● If two people or groups are **at each other's throats**, they are quarrelling or fighting. *...the rivals who have been at*

each other's throats for so long. ● If you **throw** or **ram** something **down** someone's **throat**, you keep mentioning it in order to make them accept it or believe it. *American culture's been thrown down your throat all morning... They have this viewpoint rammed down their throats every day.* ● to **clear** your **throat**: see **clear**.

throaty /ˈθrəʊti/ **throatier, throatiest**

ADJ A **throaty** voice, whisper, or laugh is low and rather rough. *'Mr Dennis!' she cries, in a throaty, incredulous voice... Her voice is low and cool and throaty, not like Agnes's girlish voice.*

throb /θrɒb/ **throbs, throbbing, throbbed**

1 V If a part of your body **throbs**, you feel a series of strong, painful beats there. *His head was throbbing. ...a freezing dampness that makes your fingers throb in the winter.*

2 V You say that something **throbs** when it vibrates and makes a loud, rhythmic noise. *The drums seemed to throb in his ears.* ▶ Also NC *...the throb of the engine.*

throes /θrəʊz/

1 If you are busy doing something that is very complicated, you can say that you are **in the throes of** it; a formal expression. *The British Army was in the throes of reorganization. ...at a time when Hungary is in the throes of an economic crisis.*

2 See also **death throes**.

thrombosis /θrɒmˈbəʊsɪs/ **thromboses** /θrɒmˈbəʊsiːz/

NUorNC A **thrombosis** is the formation of a blood clot in a person's heart or in one of their blood vessels, which can cause death; a medical term. *There is an increased incidence of coronary thrombosis.*

throne /θrəʊn/ **thrones**

1 NC A **throne** is a special chair used by a king or queen on important occasions. *26 Bishops sit on benches which are to the right of the throne.*

2 N SING The position of being king or queen is sometimes referred to as the **throne**. *...when Queen Victoria was on the throne. ...the heir to the throne.*

throng /θrɒŋ/ **throngs, thronging, thronged**; a literary word.

1 NC A **throng** is a large crowd of people. *A patient throng was waiting in silence.*

2 VAorVO When people **throng** somewhere, they go there in great numbers. *Mourners thronged to the funeral... Thousands of Spaniards thronged the streets of Barcelona... The lane was thronged with shoppers.*

throttle /ˈθrɒtl/ **throttles, throttling, throttled**

1 VO To **throttle** someone means to kill them by holding them tightly by the throat so that they cannot breathe. *She was stabbed and throttled with a cord by an old priestess and her assistants... Having pneumonia feels rather like being throttled.*

2 VO You can also say that someone or something **throttles** a process, procedure, or event when they defeat or destroy it by stopping the thing that helps it to exist. *Precision-guided weapons on the crossing points helped to throttle the supply lines to the enemy... The Bulls' defence throttled Philadelphia, and some accurate shooting had them 20 points ahead... The UN embargo of oil may throttle African industries.*

3 NCorNU The **throttle** of a motor vehicle is the device that controls the vehicle's speed by regulating the flow of fuel entering the engine. *The throttle wide open, she shot down the hill. ...an engine on full throttle.*

4 If something is done **at full throttle**, it is done with great speed and eagerness. *New Zealand played the game at full throttle and put Ireland under extreme pressure.*

through; pronounced /θruː/ when it is a preposition and /θruː/ when it is an adverb or adjective.

1 PREPorADV To move **through** a hole or opening means to move directly from one side of it to the other. *Go straight through that door and then turn right... No one can get their hand through.*

2 PREPorADV If you cut **through** something solid, you make a cut in it from one side to the other, so that it is in two pieces. *The fish must have chewed right through it... It went through like a knife through butter.*

3 PREP or ADV If you move **through** a place or area, you move across it or in it. *We drove through London... We decided to drive straight through to Birmingham.*
4 PREP or ADV If something goes into an object and comes out of the other side, you can say that it passes **through** the object. *...a hat with a feather stuck through it.*
5 PREP If you can see, hear, or feel something **through** a particular thing, that thing is between you and the thing you can see, hear, or feel. *Lonnie gazed out through a side window... I can hear John snoring right through the partition... She could feel the gravel through the soles of her slippers.*
6 PREP or ADV If something happens **through** a period of time, it happens from the beginning until the end. *I wished that I could stay through the winter... We had no rain from March right through to October.*
7 PREP From one date or time **through** another means from the first date or time until the second one; used in American English. *That meeting will take place July 15th through 17th.*
8 PREP If you go **through** an experience or event, you experience it, and if you behave in a certain way **through** it, you behave in that way while it is happening. *He didn't want to go through all that divorce business again... He lived through the decline of the Liberal Party... The girl slept through everything... Through it all, the Prince kept his sense of humour.*
9 ADJ PRED If you are **through** with something, you no longer do it, use it, or want to be involved with it. *He was through with seminars and tutorials.*
10 PREP If something happens because of something else, you can say that it happens **through** it. *Many people have difficulty in walking, for example through age or frailty... They were opposed to change through violence.*
11 PREP If you go **through** or look **through** a lot of things, you deal with them one after another. *I wanted to read through as much information as possible... She was sorting through a pile of socks.*
● **Through** is used in these phrases. ● You use expressions such as **halfway through** and **all the way through** to indicate to what extent an action or task is completed. *Harris tried to stop the operation halfway through... I do not think she ever saw a play right through.* ● **Through and through** means thoroughly or completely. *Those boards are rotten through and through.*

throughout /θruːˈaʊt/
1 PREP or ADV If something happens **throughout** an event or period of time, it happens during the whole of it. *This dream recurred throughout her life... We co-operated throughout with trade unionists.*
2 PREP or ADV If something happens or exists **throughout** a place, it happens or exists in all parts of it. *The pictures can be transmitted by satellite throughout the world... The house was carpeted throughout.*

throughput /θruːˈpʊt/
N SING The **throughput** of an organization, company, or system is the amount of things it can do or deal with in a particular period of time. *...government plans to increase the throughput of students... Refineries in Kuwait have a daily throughput capacity of some 600,000 barrels.*

throve /θrəʊv/
Throve is a past tense of **thrive**.

throw /θrəʊ/ **throws, throwing, threw, thrown**
1 VO If you **throw** an object that you are holding, you move your hand quickly and let go of the object, so that it moves through the air. *Roger picked up a stone and threw it at Henry.* ► Also NC *That was a good throw.*
2 VOA To **throw** something into a place or position means to cause it to fall there. *Tom undressed in the dark, throwing his clothes carelessly over a chair... The train braked violently, throwing everyone to the floor.*
3 VOA or V-REFL A If you **throw** a part of your body somewhere, you move it there suddenly and with a lot of force. *She threw her arms around his neck... He*

threw himself on his bed.
4 VO If a horse **throws** its rider, it causes the rider to fall off, for example by rearing or galloping very fast. *A horse threw its rider and galloped through market day crowds.*
5 VOA To **throw** someone into an unpleasant situation means to suddenly cause them to be in that situation. *The thought of being late would throw her into a state of panic... The Depression had thrown almost everybody out of work.*
6 VOA If something **throws** light or shadow on something else, it causes that thing to have light or shadow on it. *A spotlight threw a pool of violet light onto the stage.*
7 V-REFL+*into* or VO+*into* If you **throw** yourself into an activity, you become involved in it actively and enthusiastically. *Mrs Kaul threw herself into her work heart and soul... Many women throw all of their energies into a career.*
8 VO If someone **throws** a fit or tantrum, they suddenly start to behave in an uncontrolled way. *She threw a fit of hysterics... Throw a tantrum and feel better!*
9 VO If something such as a remark or an experience **throws** you, it confuses you because it is unexpected; an informal use. *It was the fact that she was married that threw me.*
● **Throw** is used in these phrases. ● If you **throw open** something that was previously not available to people, you make it available to them. *The area was thrown open to tourists 15 years ago... The government feels that it cannot throw open its frontiers... The Archbishop had declared his willingness to throw open the Church's war-time archives.* ● **a stone's throw**: see **stone**. **to throw in the towel**: see **towel**. **to throw in your lot with**: see **lot**. **to throw light on** something: see **light**.

throw aside PHRASAL VERB If you **throw aside** an attitude, principle, or idea, you suddenly abandon it or reject it. *...its own path to socialism, throwing aside the Brezhnev doctrine.*
throw away PHRASAL VERB **1** If you **throw away** something you do not want, you get rid of it, for example, by putting it in a dustbin. *She likes to keep things, even old things, rather than throw them away.*
2 If you **throw away** something good that you have, you waste it. *They threw away their advantage... He has thrown away a golden opportunity to end the war.*
throw in PHRASAL VERB If the person who is selling you something **throws** in something else, they give you the extra thing and only ask you to pay for the first one. *We only had to pay £12 for bed and breakfast, with lunch thrown in.*
throw off PHRASAL VERB If you **throw off** something that is restricting you, you free yourself from it. *They will throw off their chains and join the life of freedom of other nations in Europe... They seek to throw off decades of Soviet oppression.*
throw out PHRASAL VERB **1** If you **throw** something **out**, you get rid of it. *The broken cooking pots were thrown out... They also threw out some rubbish bags.*
2 If you **throw** someone **out** of a place or a job, you force them to leave. *Her parents threw her out when they found she was pregnant... There is not much difference between this government and the one they threw out in 1986.* **3** If you **throw out** something such as a plan or a proposal, you reject it. *They threw out the policy agreement between the two leaders... The executive bureau threw out this idea.* **4** If a court of law **throws out** a case, it decides that there is not enough evidence for it to be judged. *Last week, a court threw out cases accusing five other opposition figures of violence.*
throw up PHRASAL VERB **1** To **throw up** means to vomit; an informal use. *He threw up into a basin.* **2** If a situation **throws up** something, it reveals an unexpected feature or characteristic. *The third round threw up more than its fair share of surprises.* **3** If you **throw up** a job, position, or activity, you suddenly or unexpectedly decide to stop doing it. *In the 1960s, he threw up his job as Minister for Industry.*

throwaway /ˈθrəʊəweɪ/
1 ADJ ATTRIB A **throwaway** product is intended to be used only for a short time, and then to be thrown away. ...*a throwaway toothbrush.*
2 ADJ ATTRIB A **throwaway** remark or gesture is made in a casual way although it is important, in order to have a humorous or emotional effect. ...*a throwaway remark which he later retracted.*

throwback /ˈθrəʊbæk/ **throwbacks**
NC If something is a **throwback**, it is like something that existed a long time ago. *His sentiments were a throwback to the old colonial days.*

throw-in, throw-ins
NC When there is a **throw-in** in a football or rugby match, the ball is thrown back onto the field after it has been kicked off it. *Wales tried to break up the English pattern with quick throw-ins and tapped penalties.* ...*a throw-in close to the goal line.*

thrown /θrəʊn/
Thrown is the past participle of **throw**.

thru /θruː, θrʊ/
ADV, ADJ or PREP **Thru** means the same as **through**; an informal word, used in American English.

thrush /θrʌʃ/ **thrushes**
1 NC A **thrush** is a small brown bird with a speckled chest. *The Chinese thrush is an ordinary looking bird, but it has a loud voice.*
2 NU **Thrush** is an infectious disease that most often occurs in the mouths of babies or in women's vaginas. *We treat lots of yeast infections in the mouth, such as thrush.*

thrust /θrʌst/ **thrusts, thrusting**. The form **thrust** is used in the present tense and is also the past tense and past participle of the verb.
1 VOA If you **thrust** something somewhere, you push or move it there quickly with a lot of force. *The captain thrust his hands into his pockets.*
2 NC A **thrust** is a sudden forceful movement. ...*repeated sword thrusts... With a hard, well-aimed thrust, Morris pushed him into the lift.*
3 NC+SUPP The **thrust** of an activity or of an idea is the main or essential thing it expresses. ...*the general thrust of President Reagan's policy.* ...*the main thrust of the paper's argument... The thrust of his approach seems to be the democratization of the country.*

thrust upon PHRASAL VERB If you **thrust** something **upon** someone, you force them to have or accept it. *If war is thrust upon us, our forces are fully prepared to meet any challenge... The new religion was thrust upon the population by force.*

thud /θʌd/ **thuds, thudding, thudded**
1 NC A **thud** is a dull sound, usually made by a solid, heavy object hitting something soft. *He fell on the floor with a thud.*
2 VA If something **thuds** somewhere, it makes a dull sound, usually by hitting something else. *The mail bags thudded onto the platform.*

thug /θʌɡ/ **thugs**
NC A **thug** is a very rough and violent person. ...*a gang of thugs.* ...*armed thugs.*

thuggery /ˈθʌɡəri/
NU **Thuggery** is rough and violent behaviour. *The occupation of the consulate was an act of thuggery.* ...*football-related thuggery.*

thuggish /ˈθʌɡɪʃ/
ADJ If a person or their behaviour is **thuggish**, they are rough and violent. *These thuggish groups are causing panic among the population.* ...*a movement best known for the thuggish behaviour of its members... The Labour spokeswoman on health accused Mr Clarke of being thuggish in dealing with the doctors.*

thumb /θʌm/ **thumbs, thumbing, thumbed**
1 NC Your **thumb** is the short, thick digit on the side of your hand next to your first finger. ...*a small girl sucking her thumb.*
2 VO If you **thumb** a lift, you stand next to a road and stick out your thumb to indicate to the drivers that you want a lift. *Only two cars passed him in two miles, and they didn't slow down, so he finally gave up trying to thumb a lift.*

● **Thumb** is used in these phrases. ● If you are **under** someone's **thumb**, you are under their control, or heavily influenced by them. *The East German school system was firmly under the thumb of the Communist Party.* ● A **rule of thumb** is a rule or principle that you follow which is not based on exact calculations but rather on experience. *There's a general rule of thumb that the cost of drilling and the cost of the plant are probably about equal.* ● to stick out **like a sore thumb**: see **sore**. ● to **twiddle your thumbs**: see **twiddle**.

thumb through PHRASAL VERB If you **thumb through** a book or magazine, you turn the pages quickly and glance at the contents rather than reading each page carefully. ...*thumbing through the first editions of Sunday's British newspapers.*

thumbnail /ˈθʌmneɪl/ **thumbnails**
1 NC Your **thumbnail** is the nail on your thumb. ...*a device as small as your thumbnail.*
2 ADJ ATTRIB A **thumbnail** sketch or account is a very brief one. ...*its thumbnail sketches of terrorist organizations around the world.*

thumbprint /ˈθʌmprɪnt/ **thumbprints**
NC A **thumbprint** is a mark made by a person's thumb which shows the lines on the skin. **Thumbprints** can be used to identify people. *The thumbprints would be checked by forensic experts... They want voters to sign or leave a thumbprint opposite their names.*

thumbscrew /ˈθʌmskruː/ **thumbscrews**
1 NC A **thumbscrew** is an object that was used in the past to torture people by crushing their thumbs.
2 NC When people talk about **thumbscrews**, they are referring to forceful methods of persuasion. *If they found out the papers weren't mine, Major Fellah would get the thumbscrews out.*

thumbs-down
N SING If you give a plan, idea, or suggestion the **thumbs-down**, you indicate that you do not approve of it and refuse to accept it; an informal expression. *The verdict of the voters has been a clear thumbs-down for the Conservatives.*

thumbs-up
1 N SING A **thumbs-up** or a **thumbs-up sign** is a sign that you make by holding up your thumb to show that you agree with someone, or that you are happy with an idea or situation. *The workers would applaud and give the thumbs-up sign of approval.*
2 N SING or NU If you give a plan, idea, or suggestion the **thumbs-up**, you indicate that you approve of it and are willing to accept it; an informal expression. *We've got the thumbs-up, so now we can get down to work... It's thumbs-up for the new project.*

thumbtack /ˈθʌmtæk/ **thumbtacks**
NC A **thumbtack** is the same as a **drawing pin**; used in American English.

thump /θʌmp/ **thumps, thumping, thumped**
1 VO If you **thump** someone or something, you hit them with your fist. *I'll thump you, if you don't get out... She thumped the table.* ► Also NC *Ralph pushed between them and got a thump on the chest.*
2 VA If something **thumps** somewhere, it makes a loud, dull sound by hitting something else. *Feet thumped up the stairs... Two rockets thumped into the ground.* ► Also NC *He sat down with a thump.*
3 V When your heart **thumps**, it beats strongly and quickly. *My heart was thumping with happiness.*

thunder /ˈθʌndə/ **thunders, thundering, thundered**
1 NU **Thunder** is the loud noise that you hear in the sky after a flash of lightning. ...*a clap of thunder... There was a lot of rain, and a lot of thunder, and some of the golfers were hiding in ditches.*
2 V When it **thunders**, you hear thunder in the sky. *It thundered for much of the time, but there was no rain.*
3 NU+of The **thunder** of something that is moving or making a sound is the loud, deep noise it makes. ...*the thunder of five hundred war drums... The rumble of automobiles competes with the roar of motorcycles and the thunder of jets.*
4 VA If something **thunders**, it makes a loud continuous noise. *The sound of anti-aircraft and mortar fire thundered across the steep hills... Above his head, a train thundered by.*

thunderbolt /ˈθʌndəbəʊlt/ **thunderbolts**
NC A **thunderbolt** is a flash of lightning, accompanied by thunder. *He is killed by a divine thunderbolt.*

thunderclap /ˈθʌndəklæp/ **thunderclaps**
NC A **thunderclap** is a short, loud bang that you hear from the sky just after a flash of lightning. *The sound echoed like a thunderclap.*

thundering /ˈθʌndə⁰rɪŋ/
ADJ ATTRIB You can use **thundering** to emphasize how strong or bad something is. *Thundering denunciations flew from Washington. ...the final thundering collapse of his corporate empire.*

thunderous /ˈθʌndə⁰rəs/
ADJ ATTRIB A **thunderous** noise is very loud and deep. *The tree fell with a thunderous crash. ...thunderous applause.*

thunderstorm /ˈθʌndəstɔːm/ **thunderstorms**
NC A **thunderstorm** is a storm in which there is thunder and lightning. *A violent thunderstorm disrupted play in Rome.*

thunderstruck /ˈθʌndəstrʌk/
ADJ PRED If you are **thunderstruck**, you are very surprised or shocked; a literary word. *Kunta and the others were thunderstruck. There was clearly no limit to what their captors might order them to do.*

thundery /ˈθʌndə⁰ri/
ADJ When the weather is **thundery**, there is a lot of thunder, or there are heavy clouds which make you think that there will be thunder soon. *The night had been warm and thundery.*

Thur. or **Thurs.**
Thur. or **Thurs.** is a written abbreviation for 'Thursday'.

Thursday /ˈθɜːzdeɪ, ˈθɜːzdi/ **Thursdays**
N U or N C **Thursday** is the day after Wednesday and before Friday. *He is due in Israel on Thursday.*

thus /ðʌs/; a formal word.
1 ADV SEN You use **thus** to introduce the consequence or conclusion of something that you have just said. *They are down to their last £2,000 and thus qualify for social security benefits.*
2 ADV If you say that something is **thus** or happens **thus**, you mean that it is or happens in the way you are describing. *She lay down. Her eyelids closed. It was thus that Robert saw her... Thus encouraged, Lexington walked through the gate.*

thwack /θwæk/ **thwacks, thwacking, thwacked**
NC A **thwack** is a hard and noisy blow; an informal word. *Davis raised his walking stick and with a tremendous thwack broke the man's nose.* ► Also VO *He thwacked his cane idly against his thigh.*

thwart /θwɔːt/ **thwarts, thwarting, thwarted**
VO If you **thwart** someone or **thwart** their plans, you prevent them from doing or getting what they want; a formal word. *She had never tried to thwart him in any way... His hopes were thwarted by Taylor.*

thy /ðaɪ/
DET **Thy** is an old-fashioned, poetic, or religious word for 'your' when you are talking to only one person. See also **thou**. *Do not covet thy neighbour's one goods.*

thyme /taɪm/
N U **Thyme** is a type of herb used in cooking. *What is it? Is it the herb, thyme?*

thyroid /ˈθaɪrɔɪd/ **thyroids**
NC Your **thyroid** or your **thyroid gland** is a gland in your neck that produces chemicals which control the way your body grows and functions. *...the secreting glands of the body such as the thyroid. ...a particular type of antibody that attacks the thyroid gland.*

tiara /tiˈɑːrə/ **tiaras**
NC A **tiara** is a small crown worn by a woman of high social rank on formal occasions. *There are alternatives to the old-fashioned tiara.*

Tibetan /tɪˈbɛtn/ **Tibetans**
1 ADJ A **Tibetan** person or thing comes from, belongs to, or relates to Tibet. *...the exiled Tibetan spiritual leader. ...Tibetan religious and cultural customs.*
2 NC A **Tibetan** is a person who comes from Tibet. *Thousands of Tibetans took to the streets calling for political freedom.*

tibia /ˈtɪbiə/ **tibias**
NC Your **tibia** is one of the bones in your leg between

your knee and your ankle. *...a compound fracture of the tibia.*

tic /tɪk/ **tics**
NC If someone has a **tic**, a part of their face or body keeps moving suddenly and they cannot control it. *She developed a tic in her neck.*

tick /tɪk/ **ticks, ticking, ticked**
1 NC A **tick** is the written mark √. You use it to show that something is correct or has been dealt with. *There was a red tick in the margin.*
2 VO If you **tick** something that is written on a piece of paper, you put a tick next to it. *The Chief Whip might just tick the bills coming up in Parliament which they are going to object to.*
3 V When a clock or watch **ticks**, it makes a regular series of short sounds as it works. *A clock was ticking in the emptiness.* ◆ **ticking** NU *She could hear a faint ticking.*
4 NC The **tick** of a clock or watch is the series of short sounds it makes when it is working. *The clock in the kitchen had a noisy tick.*
5 V If you talk about what makes someone **tick**, you are talking about the reasons for their character and behaviour; an informal use. *What makes Patrick tick?*
6 NC A **tick** is a small creature like a flea which lives on the bodies of people or animals and sucks their blood as food. *The biggest stress on cattle in Africa is ticks. ...the control of ticks and the diseases they carry.*

tick away or **tick by** PHRASAL VERB If you say that the seconds, minutes, or hours **are ticking away** or **are ticking by**, you are emphasizing the fact that time is passing. *The seconds ticked by and still they heard no explosion.*

tick off PHRASAL VERB 1 If you **tick off** an item on a list, you put a tick by it to show that it has been dealt with. *It was items on the West's agenda that were being ticked off.* 2 If you **tick** someone **off**, you speak to them angrily because they have done something wrong; an informal use. *David had ticked her off for being careless.* 3 See also **ticking off**.

tick over PHRASAL VERB A system or process that is **ticking over** is working or operating steadily but not as hard or as well as it can do. *...enough to keep the essential processes ticking over for a few months.*

ticker tape
N U **Ticker tape** is long narrow strips of paper on which information such as stock exchange prices is printed. In the United States, people sometimes throw ticker tape from windows in high buildings to welcome a famous person driving in a procession through their city. *The marchers in the parade were showered with 200 miles of ticker tape... The city gave the royal couple a ticker-tape welcome.*

ticket /ˈtɪkɪt/ **tickets**
1 NC A **ticket** is an official piece of paper or card which shows that you have paid for a journey or have paid to enter a place of entertainment. *...bus tickets... I'd like a return ticket to Vienna, please... She bought two tickets for the opera.* ◆ See also **season ticket**.
2 NC A **ticket** is also a piece of paper or card that shows that you are entitled to receive or use something. *...library tickets... The customers all clutched ration tickets.*

ticking off, tickings off
NC If you give someone a **ticking off**, you speak rather angrily to them because they have done something wrong; an informal expression. *Then Lally confessed and got a ticking off.*

tickle /ˈtɪkl/ **tickles, tickling, tickled**
1 VO When you **tickle** someone, you move your fingers lightly over a part of their body, often in order to make them laugh. *Babies want to be tickled and hugged... He's tickling me and I just can't take a swing at him.*
2 V or VO If something **tickles**, it causes an irritating feeling by lightly touching a part of your body. *She ran a finger on to the hairs on my wrist and it tickled... He flicked away a strand of hair that was tickling Ellen's nose.*
3 VO If a fact or a situation **tickles** you, it amuses you

or gives you pleasure. *The Poles have been tickled by the Gorbachev credo of giving the workers more room to act and think.*

ticklish /tɪkəlɪʃ/
1 ADJ A **ticklish** problem or situation is awkward and embarrassing and needs to be dealt with carefully. *This will present ticklish problems for the West... It was a ticklish moment in the discussion.*
2 ADJ If someone is **ticklish**, you can make them laugh easily by tickling them. *She was extremely ticklish, particularly over the region of the ribs.*

tidal /taɪdl/
ADJ ATTRIB **Tidal** means relating to or produced by the tide. *...tidal estuaries.*

tidal wave, tidal waves
1 NC A **tidal wave** is a very large wave, often caused by an earthquake, that flows over the land and destroys things. *The cyclone caused a huge tidal wave which flooded large areas of the coast. ...a new satellite-based system for warning about tidal waves.*
2 NC You can also refer to a very large number of people or things which all come at the same time as a **tidal wave**. *If the plan was not modified, he claimed that emigration from Hong Kong could become a tidal wave... All the main roads have special lanes along which sweeps relentlessly a tidal wave of bicycles, rickshaws, and carts.*

tidbit /tɪdbɪt/ **tidbits**
NC A **tidbit** is the same as a **titbit**; used in American English.

tiddly /tɪdəli/ **tiddlier, tiddliest**; an informal word.
1 ADJ Someone who is **tiddly** is rather drunk. *She sings 'Knees up Mother Brown' and gets tiddly on Guinness.*
2 ADJ Something that is **tiddly** is very small. *They gave us tiddly little cups of coffee.*

tiddlywink /tɪdəliwɪŋk/ **tiddlywinks**
1 NU **Tiddlywinks** is a game in which the players try to make small round pieces of plastic jump into a container, by pressing the edge of them with a larger piece of plastic. *Everybody has to have something that they're good at, even if it's tiddlywinks.*
2 NC A **tiddlywink** is a small round piece of plastic used in the game of tiddlywinks.

tide /taɪd/ **tides, tiding, tided**
1 N SING The **tide** is the regular change in the level of the sea on the shore. When it is at its highest level, you say that the tide is in. When it is at its lowest level, you say that the tide is out. *The tide was coming in.* ● See also **high tide, low tide**.
2 N SING+of The **tide** of opinion or fashion is what the majority of people think or do at a particular time. *He's always gone against the tide of fashion... The results indicate that in Russia the tide of opinion is turning against the old system.*
3 N SING+SUPP You can also use **tide** to refer to a significant increase in something unpleasant. *...the rising tide of terrorist activity in Europe... There is a growing tide of anger and anguish in the city.*
tide over PHRASAL VERB If something will **tide** you **over**, it will help you through a difficult time. *I only want to borrow enough to tide me over till Monday.*

tideline /taɪdlaɪn/ **tidelines**
N SING The **tideline** is the highest or lowest point that the tide reaches on a shore. *The wind rustled the dead seaweed on the tideline.*

tidemark /taɪdmɑːk/ **tidemarks**
1 N SING The **tidemark** is the same as the **tideline**.
2 NC A **tidemark** is also a line of dirt left around the inside of a bath when the water is emptied out.

tidily /taɪdɪli/
ADV If you do something **tidily**, you do it in a neat, orderly, and organized way. *Printed on the label, not very tidily, were the words 'Contributions Please'.*

tidings /taɪdɪŋz/
N PL+SUPP **Tidings** are the same as **news**; an old-fashioned word. *He told her the good tidings.*

tidy /taɪdi/ **tidier, tidiest; tidies, tidying, tidied**
1 ADJ Something that is **tidy** is neat and arranged in an orderly way. *It is difficult to keep a house tidy. ...a tidy desk.* ◆ **tidiness** NU *...his parents' concern with tidiness.*

2 ADJ **Tidy** people keep their things tidy. *I wish you were a little bit tidier!*
3 VO When you **tidy** a place, you make it neat by putting things in their proper places. *You can't tidy a bedroom until you've made the beds.*
4 ADJ ATTRIB A **tidy** amount of money is a fairly large amount of it; an informal use. *He managed to make quite a tidy income every year.*
tidy away PHRASAL VERB When you **tidy** something **away**, you put it in a cupboard or drawer so that it is not in the way. *Someone had tidied my papers away.*
tidy up PHRASAL VERB When you **tidy up** or **tidy** a place **up**, you put things back in their proper places so that everything is neat. *I made the beds and tidied up... About three years ago we started tidying up the base.*

tie /taɪ/ **ties, tying, tied**
1 VOA If you **tie** one thing to another, you fasten it to the other thing using string or rope. *...one of those labels you tie onto the handle of your suitcase... Can you tie these ladders to the rope?*
2 VOA If you **tie** a piece of string round something or **tie** something with string, you put string round it and fasten the ends together in a knot or bow. *...a little dog which had a ribbon tied round its neck. ...a parcel tied with string... The children spent the morning tying the straw into bundles.*
3 VO When you **tie** your shoelaces, you fasten the ends together in a bow. *He was still tying his laces.*
4 NC A **tie** is a long, narrow piece of cloth worn under someone's shirt collar and tied in a knot at the front. *He took off his jacket and loosened his tie.* ● See also **bow tie**.
5 NC A **tie** is also a long, narrow piece of cloth, plastic, or wire that is used to attach one thing to another, or to close or fasten something. *Tuck the ends under the string tie.*
6 V-PASS+to Something that is **tied** to something else is closely linked to it. *The course I chose wasn't tied to a particular academic discipline.*
7 N PL+SUPP **Ties** are the connections you have with people or a place. *Family ties are often very strong... They want to loosen their ties with Britain... The visit would strengthen cultural ties between the two countries.*
8 V-RECIP If you **tie** with someone in a competition or a game, you have the same number of points or the same degree of success. *Bill tied with Margaret for first place... Two actresses tied for the Best Actress award.* ▶ Also NC *In the event of a tie, the winner will be the contestant who took the shortest time.*
9 NC In sport, a **tie** is a match that is played as part of a competition. The losers of the match are eliminated and the winners continue into the next round. *Dundee United managed only a one-one draw in the Cup Winners Cup tie against Dinamo Bucharest.*
tie down PHRASAL VERB A person or thing that **ties** you **down** restricts your freedom, for example by making you live, behave, or act in a particular way. *She doesn't want children because she says they tie you down.*
tie in with PHRASAL VERB An idea or fact that **ties in with** something else fits in with it or agrees with it. *His beliefs didn't seem to tie in at all with reality.*
tie up PHRASAL VERB 1 When you **tie** something **up**, you fasten string or rope round it so that it is secure. *Clarissa came in, carrying some canvases tied up in brown paper.* 2 If you **tie up** an animal, you fasten it to a fixed object with a piece of rope so that it cannot run away. *Is tethering just a question of tying a goat up by a bit of rope under a tree and letting it stand there?* 3 When you **tie up** your shoelaces, you fasten them in a bow. *He saw the man bending down and tying up his shoelace.* 4 If someone **ties** you **up**, they fasten ropes around you so that you cannot escape. *His wife and son were tied up and locked in a room.* 5 Something that is **tied up** with something else is closely linked with it. *It's all tied up with the attempt to build a new spire for the cathedral.* 6 To tie something **up** also means to use it in some way, with the result that it is not available for other people or other purposes. *The big companies were tying up*

supplies of minerals in long-term contracts... People don't want their money tied up for long periods.

tie-break, tie-breaks
NC A **tie-break** is a special extra game which is played in a tennis match when the score in a set is 6-6. The player who wins the tie-break wins the set. *He won the tie-break in the second set.*

tie-breaker, tie-breakers
1 NC In tennis, a **tie-breaker** is the same as a **tie-break**. *She had to survive a second set tie-breaker before taking the match.*
2 NC A **tie-breaker** is an extra question or round that decides the winner of a competition or game when two or more people have the same score at the end. *The solutions and the winning tie-breaker are printed on the left-hand page.*

tied /taɪd/
ADJ A **tied** cottage or house belongs to a farmer or other employer and is rented to someone who works for him or her. *Forty-three thousand farm workers live in tied cottages and currently pay no rent or rates.*

tied up
ADJ PRED If you are **tied up**, you are busy; an informal expression. *I'm tied up right now, can you call me back later?*

tie-in, tie-ins
NC A **tie-in** is a connection between two events or activities, which happens by chance or has been deliberately created. *Well, first of all there's no tie-in between any action that I took and the current campaign... Many business tie-ins would be severely curtailed if the boycott goes ahead.*

tie-pin, tie-pins
NC A **tie-pin** is a narrow brooch used to pin a person's tie to their shirt. *...a pearl tie-pin.*

tier /tɪə/ **tiers**
NC A **tier** is one of a series of layers or levels that form part of a structure. *The theatre had semicircular tiers of seats.*

tie-up, tie-ups
NC If two companies decide on a **tie-up**, they decide to join together in order to do something. *...a tie-up between these two vastly different industrial groups. ... a series of tie-ups, acquisitions and foreign investments.*

tiff /tɪf/ **tiffs**
NC A **tiff** is a small, unimportant quarrel, especially between two close friends or between a husband and wife. *...more speculation about the chances of a new tiff between the feuding ladies.*

tiger /taɪgə/ **tigers**
1 NC A **tiger** is a large, fierce animal belonging to the cat family. Tigers are orange with black stripes. *...an operation launched to save tigers from extinction... Tiger conservation projects have been set up in Bangladesh.*
2 See also **paper tiger**.

tight /taɪt/ **tighter, tightest; tights**
1 ADJ **Tight** clothes or shoes fit closely to your body or feet. *He was wearing tight cream-coloured trousers... The skirt was so tight in front that it was hard to walk.* ◆ **tightly** ADV *...a tightly fitting suit.*
2 ADV If you hold something or someone **tight**, you hold them firmly. *Ann was clutching the letter tight in her hand... Put your shoulders up to your ears and hold them there tight, and then let them down.* ◆ **tightly** ADV *They clung together very tightly.*
3 ADJ Something that is **tight** is firmly fastened, and difficult to move. *...a tight knot.* ◆ **tightly** ADV *He screwed the caps tightly onto the bottles.*
4 ADV Something that is shut **tight** is shut very firmly. *The windows were shut tight against the rain... He closed his eyes tight.*
5 ADJ Skin, cloth, or string that is stretched **tight** is stretched or pulled so that it is smooth or straight. *The skin was stretched tight over her smooth facial bones.* ◆ **tightly** ADV *The skin on his face was drawn back tightly like stretched leather.*
6 ADJ You use **tight** to describe things that are very close together. *They stood in a tight group.* ◆ **tightly** ADV *...houses tightly packed together.*

7 ADJ If your chest or stomach feels **tight**, it feels hard or painful, because you are ill or anxious. *My chest felt unpleasantly tight.* ◆ **tightness** NU *I went to the interview with the familiar tightness in my stomach.*
8 ADJ A **tight** schedule or budget allows very little time or money for any unexpected events or expenses. *The Soviet leader was a busy man with a tight schedule... A new low-cost system that will be especially valuable for hospitals on tight budgets.*
9 ADJ **Tight** controls or rules are very strict and restrict people quite a lot. *...calls for tighter controls on estate agents... Security has become visibly tighter over the last year... The villa in which he lives is under tight surveillance.* ◆ **tightly** ADV *...a society which is very tightly controlled.*
10 ADJ If a competition or sports match is **tight**, none of the competitors has a clear advantage or looks likely win, so it is difficult to say who the winner will be. *He and Jelen won a desperately tight match to give Germany a 2-1 lead... The men's race was always going to be tight, especially after the magnificent opening swim by Lane.*
11 N PL **Tights** are a piece of clothing made of thin material such as nylon that covers a woman's hips, and each of her legs and feet separately. *She discovered how difficult it was to find matching tights for her dress.*
12 to **keep a tight rein on** someone: see **rein**. to **sit tight**: see **sit**.

tighten /taɪtn/ **tightens, tightening, tightened**
1 V-ERG If you **tighten** your hold on something or if your hold **tightens**, you hold the thing more firmly. *He tightened his grip on the spear... His fingers tightened around his rifle.*
2 V-ERG If you **tighten** a rope, chain, strap, and so on or if it **tightens**, you stretch or pull it until it is straight. *The chain tightened and the pig's leg was pulled back... They were given gas masks, with adjustable straps to be tightened around their faces... She bent down to tighten the strap of her roller skate.*
3 VO To **tighten** controls or rules means to make them stricter or more efficient. *They approved plans to tighten control on exports of nuclear and chemical material... The authorities tightened security around the embassy.*

tighten up PHRASAL VERB 1 When you **tighten up** a fastening, you move it so that it is more firmly in place or holds something more firmly. *Tighten up the axle nut.* 2 To **tighten up** a rule or system means to make it stricter or more efficient. *Regulations on the testing of drugs have been tightened up... The Germans tried to tighten up their export controls.* ● See also **belt-tightening**. ● to **tighten the screws on** someone: see **screw**.

tight-fisted /taɪtfɪstɪd/
ADJ Someone who is **tight-fisted** is unwilling to spend money; an informal word, used showing disapproval. *He was unable to squeeze the extra cash out of his tight-fisted employers.*

tight-lipped /taɪtlɪpt/
1 ADJ Someone who is **tight-lipped** is unwilling to give any information about something. *The government has been very tight-lipped about it... Ministers have been tight-lipped on the subject in public.*
2 ADJ You also say that someone is **tight-lipped** when they have their lips pressed tightly together, especially because they are angry. *Her face was paler, more tight-lipped and furious than ever. ...a tight-lipped, taciturn woman.*

tightly- /taɪtli-/
PREFIX **Tightly-** is used with past participles to form adjectives that describe how closely or how firmly something is done. *...the heat and crush of the tightly-packed crowds. ...a tightly-guarded border. ...the tightly-knit community... The talks are being held behind tightly-closed doors. ...a tightly-controlled exchange rate.*

tightrope /taɪtrəʊp/ **tightropes**
1 NC A **tightrope** is a piece of rope which is stretched between two poles and on which an acrobat balances and performs tricks. *It's like watching a guy on a*

tightrope—you want to close your eyes because you know at some moment he may fall.
2 NC If you say that someone is walking a **tightrope**, you mean that they are in a very difficult or delicate situation and that they have to be very careful about what they say or do. *He will have to walk a political tightrope between the two opposite poles of Yugoslav politics... The government is walking a tightrope in trying to keep in balance all the various economic factors.*

tigress /ˈtaɪgrəs/ **tigresses**
NC A **tigress** is a female tiger. *...the tigress who defends her cubs.*

tilde /ˈtɪldə/ **tildes**
NC A **tilde** is a symbol that is written over the letter 'n' in Spanish (ñ) and the letters 'o' (õ) and 'a' (ã) in Portuguese to indicate the way in which they should be pronounced.

tile /taɪl/ **tiles**
NC **Tiles** are flat, square, thin objects that are used to cover floors, walls, or roofs. *...polystyrene ceiling tiles. ...brick houses roofed in reddish-brown tiles.*

tiled /taɪld/
ADJ A **tiled** surface is covered with tiles. *...footsteps on the tiled floor. ...red tiled roofs.*

till /tɪl/ **tills**
1 PREP or CONJ **Till** means the same as **until**. *He wrote from morning till night... Wait till I come back.*
2 NC A **till** is a drawer or box where money is kept in a shop. *...an unemployed citizen who robs a till.*

tiller /ˈtɪlə/ **tillers**
NC The **tiller** of a boat is a handle that is fixed to the rudder and is used to turn the rudder and steer the boat. *Many cruising and racing yachts are steered by a tiller.*

tilt /tɪlt/ **tilts, tilting, tilted**
1 V-ERG If you tilt an object or if it **tilts**, you change its position so that one end or side is higher than the other. *He tilted the flask and two or three drops trickled out... Let your head gently tilt forwards.*
▶ Also NC *He indicated, with a tilt of his head, a girl nearby.*
2 VA If someone's opinion or position **tilts** in a particular way, it changes slightly from what it was before and becomes more in agreement with another opinion or position. *Opinion has now tilted too dramatically towards Iraq... Yugoslavia has now tilted in favour of the Serbian leader.* ▶ Also N SING+*towards* *...a political or ideological tilt towards the Soviet position... The changes also give the government a tilt towards Europe.*
3 If something is moving or happening **at full tilt**, it is moving or happening with as much speed, energy, or force as possible. *He'd forget the lead was on, and wagging his tail would take off at full tilt for the woods... Adams was running full tilt and dived forward to take the ball... He's been on TV, and the cult of personality is still going at full tilt.*

Timakata, Fred /frɛd tɪməkɑːtə/
Fred Timakata became President of Vanuatu in 1989. He was Speaker of Parliament from 1985 to 1988, and Minister of Health from 1988 to 1989. He is a member of the Vanua'aku Party (VP). Born: 1936.

timber /ˈtɪmbə/
NU **Timber** is wood that is used for making houses and furniture. *Most of the region's timber is imported from the south.*

timbered /ˈtɪmbəd/
ADJ ATTRIB A **timbered** building has a wooden frame or wooden beams showing on the outside. *...an old timbered lodge.*

timbre /ˈtæmbə/
NU The **timbre** of a particular voice or musical instrument is the quality of sound that it has. *The voice had an ugly timbre to it.*

time /taɪm/ **times, timing, timed**
1 NU **Time** is what we measure in hours, days, and years. *...a period of time... Time passed, and finally he fell asleep again.*
2 NC You use **time** to refer to a specific point in time, which can be stated in hours and minutes and is shown on clocks. *What's the time?... Ask the times of planes from Rome to Vienna. ...at 6 in the evening, local time.*
3 NU or N SING You also use **time** to refer to the period of time that someone spends doing something. *How do you find time to write these books?... She spends most of her time sunbathing... It would take a long time to discuss.*
4 NC You use **time** to refer to an individual point in time, when you are describing what is happening then. *He blushed each time she spoke to him... Ask for something different next time... There were times when I didn't know what to do.*
5 NU+SUPP or N SING+SUPP If you say it is **time** for an action or it is **time** to do something, you mean that it ought to happen or be done immediately. *It was time for tea... It is time we realized that we were wrong... The time has come to change things.*
6 NC You use **time** after numbers to say how often something happens. *Ray and I play squash three times a week... The telephone rang a second time.*
7 NC+SUPP or NU+SUPP You also use **time** to refer to a stage in someone's life, or to a period of time in history. *...during my time in Toronto. ...the time of the Roman Empire. ...the history of modern times. ...one of the great unsolved mysteries of our time.*
8 N SING If something happens for a **time**, it happens for a fairly long period of time. *It's nice to be in London for a time... It became clear after a time that he was very ill.*
9 N PL You use **times** after numbers when you are saying how much bigger, smaller, better, or worse one thing is compared to another. *It would cost me ten times as much... It has become three times as difficult as it used to be.*
10 You use **times** in arithmetic to link numbers or amounts that are multiplied together. *5 times 50—that's 250.*
11 VO If an event or action **is timed** for a particular time, it has been planned that it should happen at that time. *They timed the attack for 6.00 pm... The proposal was timed to coincide with the President's departure.*
12 VO If you **time** something well or badly, you judge well or badly the moment at which to do it. *Keegan had timed the ball brilliantly.* ◆ **timed** ADJ PRED after ADV *His remarks were badly timed... You realize how perfectly timed a good comedian is.*
13 VO If you **time** an action or activity, you measure how long it lasts. *This was repeated at intervals which he timed on his watch.*
14 See also **timing**.
● **Time** is used in these phrases. ● If you are **in time** for something or to do something, you are not late. *We're just in time for a late supper... He returned to the stadium in time to watch another startling finish.* ● If you are **in good time**, you are earlier than necessary. *We got there in good time.* ● If something happens **on time**, it happens at the correct time. *Civil servants are still being paid on time and in full.* ● If a situation existed **at one time**, it existed in the past. *At one time, Burma had been known as the rice bowl of Asia.* ● If something happens **at times**, it happens occasionally. *She's really rude at times.* ● You use **at a time** after an amount to say how many things or people there are together in a particular sequence, group, or action. *He used to abandon his work for many months at a time... There was only room for one person at a time.* ● You use **at the same time** to introduce a statement that contrasts with the previous statement. *It made us cautious but at the same time it made us willing to take a risk.* ● If you say it is **about time** that something was done, you are saying firmly that it should be done. *It's about time that Parliament concentrated on unemployment.* ● If someone is **ahead of their time**, they have an idea long before other people start thinking in the same way. *Diaghilev was brilliantly ahead of his time.* ● Someone or something that is **behind the times** is old-fashioned. *The law is behind the times on a number of important issues.* ● If something exists or is true **for the time being**, it is true now but will not necessarily exist or be true in the future. *The security forces, for the time*

being, at least, seem to have restored order. ● If you do something **from time to time**, you do it occasionally, but not very often. *The authorities are forced to cut water supplies from time to time.* ● If something will happen **in time**, it will happen eventually. *No doubt in time the arguments will straighten themselves out.* ● If something will happen **in a week's time** or **in a month's time**, it will happen after one week or one month. *The race starts in under half an hour's time.* ● When you talk about how well a watch or clock **keeps time**, you are talking about how accurately it measures time. *This has kept perfect time since I got it back.* ● If you **have no time for** someone or something, you do not like them or approve of them. *I haven't got a lot of time for politicians.* ● If you **make good time** on a journey, you complete the journey more quickly than you expected. *We made pretty good time on the journey up here.* ● If you do something to **pass the time**, you do it because you are bored or are waiting for something, and not because you really want to. *They read every page with no other purpose than just to pass the time.* ● If something **takes time**, it happens or will be achieved slowly. *It will take time to adapt some of the equipment... The Americans want to be sure the others are severe, and that could take time.* ● If you **take** your **time** doing something, you do it slowly, without hurrying. *Oh, take your time, I'm in no hurry.* ● If something happens **time after time** or **time and again**, it happens often. *She had threatened time after time to leave him... Time and again, promised action has been postponed.*

time bomb, time bombs
1 NC A **time bomb** is a bomb with a mechanism that causes it to explode at a particular time. *The explosion was caused by time bombs planted by two agents.*
2 NC A **time bomb** is also something that will have a major effect on a situation or person at a later date, for example by causing a lot of damage. *Such a shortsighted policy is a time bomb that will one day explode in America's face.*

time-consuming
ADJ Something that is **time-consuming** takes a great deal of time to do. *...a difficult and time-consuming job.*

time frame, time frames
NC A **time frame** is a period of time that has been decided on for the completion of an action. *...agreement on the time frame for the withdrawal of Soviet troops. ...the time frame that they are looking at now.*

time-honoured
ADJ ATTRIB A **time-honoured** way of doing something has been used for a very long time. *...a time-honoured practice.*

timekeeper /ˈtaɪmkiːpə/ **timekeepers**
1 NC A **timekeeper** is a person or an instrument that records or keeps time. *He checked with the timekeeper before allowing Douglas to continue fighting... The Naval Observatory here in Washington is the official standard for the nation's timekeepers.*
2 NC+SUPP If you say that someone is a good **timekeeper**, or a poor **timekeeper**, you are saying how good or bad they are at arriving at work at the correct time. *Joanna? She's not a good timekeeper, I'm afraid, as we soon discovered after she started working for us.*

time lag, time lags
NC A **time lag** is an interval of time between one event and another related event that happens after it. *There is always a considerable time lag between the exam and results.*

timeless /ˈtaɪmləs/
ADJ Something which is **timeless** is so good or beautiful that it cannot be affected by changes in society or fashion; a formal word. *His art has something universal, something timeless about it.*

time limit, time limits
NC A **time limit** is a period of time during which a particular task must be completed. *I had set myself a time limit of two years... He failed to claim the*

reward within the prescribed time limit.

timely /ˈtaɪmli/
ADJ Something that is **timely** happens at just the right time. *...the timely arrival of reinforcements. ...a timely reminder of human concerns and ideas.*

time out
NU If you take **time out** to do something, you stop your normal activities for a while in order to do it. *He took time out to chair a meeting of local officials.*

timepiece /ˈtaɪmpiːs/ **timepieces**
NC A **timepiece** is a clock, watch, or other device that measures and shows time; an old-fashioned word. *...over 200 handmade timepieces, created by the 17th century Swiss watchmaker, Breguet.*

timer /ˈtaɪmə/ **timers**
NC A **timer** is a device that measures time, especially one that is part of a machine. *The timer on the stove started ringing.* ● See also **egg-timer**.

time scale, time scales
NC The **time scale** of an event is the length of time during which it happens. *...the time scale of technological development.*

time-share, time-shares
NC A **time-share** is the right to use holiday accommodation for a specific amount of time each year in a time-sharing system. *Winners will receive prizes ranging from hotel and shopping discounts to a time-share at a Scottish castle. ...companies in the holiday time-share business.*

time sharing
1 NU **Time sharing** is an arrangement in which different people each buy a share in a cottage or flat. Each person has the right to use that accommodation for a specific amount of time each year for their holidays. *What can I do for you? I can get you in on a nice little time sharing deal?*
2 NU **Time sharing** is also a system by which many different people can use the same computer at the same time.

time signature, time signatures
NC The **time signature** of a piece of music consists of two numbers written at the beginning that show how many beats in each bar there are. *His voice is so melodic, and his tunes use different time signatures and things like that.*

time switch, time switches
NC A **time switch** is a device that causes a machine to start or stop working at specific times. *Check whether or not you need a time switch for an electric blanket.*

timetable /ˈtaɪmteɪbl/ **timetables, timetabling, timetabled**
1 NC A **timetable** is a schedule of the times when activities or jobs should be done. *...the timetable agreed for the withdrawal of their troops... No timetable has been set for these changes. ...the timetable of a second year pupil at a comprehensive school... The authorities would draw up a proposed timetable.*
2 NC A **timetable** is also a list of the times when trains, boats, buses, or aeroplanes arrive and depart. *Passengers are not being given enough information about routes and timetables... Nearly half the population cannot read a railway timetable properly.*
3 VO If you **timetable** an event such as a meeting, you decide when it should happen, and write a timetable showing the order in which things will happen. *The impossibility of timetabling such proposals is clear.*

timeworn /ˈtaɪmwɔːn/
ADJ Something that is **timeworn** is old or has been used a lot over a long period of time, and so is no longer interesting or in good condition. *...a timeworn phrase.*

time zone, time zones
NC A **time zone** is one of the areas into which the world is divided, where the time is calculated as being a particular number of hours behind or ahead of Greenwich Mean Time. *The body will take 24 hours to readjust back to normal for every time zone you cross.*

timid /ˈtɪmɪd/
ADJ **Timid** people or animals are shy, nervous, and have no courage or self-confidence. *...a timid young girl. ...a timid smile.* ◆ **timidly** ADV *I left the car and*

timidly rang the doorbell. ◆ **timidity** /tɪmɪdəti/ NU *He had a terrible time in overcoming his timidity.*

timing /taɪmɪŋ/
1 NU Someone's **timing** is their skill in judging the right moment at which to do something. *She displayed perfect timing and control.*
2 NU When people decide about the **timing** of an event, they decide when it will happen. *They met to consider the timing of elections.*

timing device, timing devices
NC A **timing device** is a mechanism that is attached to a bomb or a missile in order to make it explode at a particular time. *The bomb was activated by a timing device... The rockets were all thought to have been set off by timing devices.*

timorous /tɪmᵊrəs/
ADJ A person who is **timorous** is frightened and nervous of other people or situations; a literary word. *The new occupants were too timorous to complain to the landlord about the high rent.*

timpani /tɪmpəni/; also spelt **tympani**.
N PL **Timpani** are the same as **kettledrums**; a formal word. *She plays marimba, timpani, xylophone, and many other percussion instruments.*

timpanist /tɪmpənɪst/ **timpanists**; also spelt **tympanist**.
NC A **timpanist** is someone who plays the timpani in an orchestra. *Earplugs are handy if you sit near the timpanist.*

tin /tɪn/ **tins**
1 NU **Tin** is a soft metal that is the same colour as silver. *World stocks of tin are still very high. ...Cornwall's disused tin mines.*
2 NC A **tin** is a metal container which is filled with food and sealed in order to preserve the food. *...baby food in tins and packets.*
3 NC A **tin** is also a small metal container with a lid. *...the biscuit tin.*
4 NC You can use **tin** to refer to a tin and its contents, or to the contents only. *Think twice before you open your next tin of soup... You've upset a tin of paint on the carpet.*

tincture /tɪŋktʃə/ **tinctures**
NC A **tincture** is a medicine consisting of alcohol and a small amount of a drug; an old-fashioned word. *Snip away the dead skin and apply tincture of iodine.*

tinder /tɪndə/
NU **Tinder** consists of small pieces of something dry, especially wood or grass, that burns easily and can be used for lighting a fire. *As the days passed, more and more pieces of tinder were added to the fire.*

tinder box, tinder boxes
1 NC A **tinder box** was a box that was used for holding tinder, especially one with a flint and steel to help light the tinder. *He carried the bundle into the garden, took out flint and tinder box, and set fire to it.*
2 N SING If you say that something is a **tinder box**, you mean that it can burn very easily. *The escalator where the fire broke out was a tinder box.*
3 N SING You can also use **tinder box** to describe a place or a situation in which people feel anxious because it is very tense and may become dangerous. *Officials have described the province as a tinder box. ...a tinder box of passions in the Middle East.*

tinfoil /tɪnfɔɪl/
NU **Tinfoil** consists of shiny metal in the form of a thin sheet which is used for wrapping food in. *...eggs wrapped in silver tinfoil.*

tinge /tɪndʒ/ **tinges**
NC+SUPP A **tinge** of a colour or a feeling is a small amount of it. *The sky had a greenish tinge. ...a tinge of envy.*

tinged /tɪndʒd/
ADJ PRED+*with* If something is **tinged** with a colour or a feeling, it has a small amount of that colour or feeling in it. *Her eyes were slightly tinged with red. ...joy tinged with bitterness.*

tingle /tɪŋgl/ **tingles, tingling, tingled**
1 V When a part of your body **tingles**, you feel a slight prickling feeling there. *The side of my face was still tingling from the blow she'd given me.* ◆ **tingling** NU *...a sharp tingling in her fingers.*
2 V If you **tingle** with excitement or shock, you feel it

very strongly. *Kunta felt himself tingle with that extra strength that fear brings.*

tinker /tɪŋkə/ **tinkers, tinkering, tinkered**
V If you **tinker** with something, you make some small adjustments to it in order to repair or improve it. *He's still tinkering with the motor.*

tinkle /tɪŋkl/ **tinkles, tinkling, tinkled**
V If something **tinkles**, it makes a sound like a small bell ringing. *He slammed the door so violently that the sherry glasses tinkled on their tray.* ▶ Also NC *The telephone gave a tinkle.*

tinned /tɪnd/
ADJ **Tinned** food has been preserved by being sealed in a tin. *They have been living off tinned fish and rice... Fresh vegetables can be sold, but not tinned ones.*

tinnitus /tɪnaɪtəs/
NU **Tinnitus** is a ringing, hissing, or booming sensation in your ear. It can be caused by an infection or by certain drugs; a medical term. *I'm suffering from tinnitus.*

tinny /tɪni/
ADJ A **tinny** sound has an unpleasant high-pitched quality. *...the tinny voice coming over the radio.*

tin-opener, tin-openers
NC A **tin-opener** is a tool used for opening tins of food. *Every time you pick up a tin-opener to open a can of soup you're about to consume processed food.*

tinsel /tɪnsl/
NU **Tinsel** consists of small strips of shiny paper attached to long pieces of thread. People use tinsel to decorate rooms at Christmas. *The Christmas tree has already been decorated with tiny multi-colored lights and lots of tinsel.*

tint /tɪnt/ **tints, tinted, tinting**
1 NC A **tint** is a small amount of a colour. *His eyes had a yellow tint.*
2 VO If you **tint** your hair, you change its colour slightly by adding a weak dye to it. *He acquired a preparation for tinting his hair chestnut brown.*

tinted /tɪntɪd/
ADJ **Tinted** glass is slightly coloured. *He glanced through the tinted rear window.*

tiny /taɪni/ **tinier, tiniest**
ADJ Something that is **tiny** is extremely small. *Only a tiny proportion of the cases involved Britons. ...a tiny little room.*

-tion /-ʃn/. See -ation.

tip /tɪp/ **tips, tipping, tipped**
1 NC The **tip** of something is the extreme end of it. *He was hanging by his finger tips from a window frame... It's a ninety-mile crossing from the Shetland Islands to the northern tip of Scotland. ...the tips of branches.*
2 VOA If you **tip** an object, you move it so that it is no longer horizontal or upright. *He tipped his soup bowl towards himself... He was sitting with his chair tipped back against the wall.*
3 VOA If you **tip** something somewhere, you pour it there quickly and carelessly. *He tipped the contents of the rucksack out on to the floor... A lorry driver accidentally tipped aluminium sulphate into a water treatment works.*
4 NC A **tip** is a place where rubbish is dumped. *The eggs will be dumped in local rubbish tips... Another company down the road continues to operate a disgusting tip, pouring all sorts of dangerous waste into it.*
5 NC If you give someone such as a waiter or a taxi driver a **tip**, you give them some money to thank them for their services. *The woman gave me a dollar tip.*
6 VO If you **tip** someone, you give them money as a tip. *I tipped the chauffeur.*
7 VO If someone is **tipped** for success or to do a particular job, people with knowledge of their area of activity say that they are likely to be successful or to get the job. *He been tipped for a bright political future... He is strongly tipped to become a cabinet minister.*
8 NC A **tip** is also a useful piece of advice or information. *He consulted books by well-known tennis players for tips on basic techniques... They have recently published a manual full of practical tips for*

anyone who wants to set up community services.
● **Tip** is used in these phrases. ● If you say that
something is **the tip of** the **iceberg**, you mean that it is
only a very small part of a much larger problem. *One
official calls the reports the tip of the iceberg and says
the unrest will grow once the casualty figures become
available... CFC's, dangerous as they may be, are only
the tip of an iceberg.* ● If you say that a word or
name is **on the tip of** your **tongue**, you mean that you
cannot remember it just at the moment, but you are
sure you will remember it very soon. *I'm just trying
to remember his name. It's on the tip of my tongue.*
tip off PHRASAL VERB If you **tip** someone **off**, you give
them information or a warning, often privately or
secretly. *The arrests were made after police were
tipped off about gun shots heard in a wood.*
tip over PHRASAL VERB If you **tip** something **over** or if
it **tips over**, it falls over or turns over. *She tipped the
pan over and a dozen fish flopped out.*
tip-off, tip-offs
NC A **tip-off** is a piece of information or a warning
that you give to someone, often privately or secretly.
The building was evacuated as the result of a tip-off.
tipped /tɪpt/
ADJ Something that is **tipped** with a substance has that
substance on its tip. *...arrows tipped with poison.*
tipple /tɪpl/ **tipples, tippling, tippled**; an old-fashioned,
informal word.
1 NC A person's **tipple** is the alcoholic drink that they
usually drink. *'What's your tipple?' said
Superintendent Garroway.*
2 V If you **tipple**, you drink alcoholic drinks quite often
but not in large quantities.
tipster /tɪpstə/ **tipsters**
NC A **tipster** is someone who tells you, usually in
exchange for money, which horses they think will win
particular races, so that you can bet money on the
horses.
tipsy /tɪpsi/
ADJ If you are **tipsy**, you are slightly drunk; an
informal word. *By the time the police were called in
they'd become slightly tipsy.*
tiptoe /tɪptəʊ/ **tiptoes, tiptoeing, tiptoed**
1 V If you **tiptoe** somewhere, you walk there very
quietly on your toes. *He knocked softly on the door
and tiptoed into the room.*
2 If you stand or walk **on tiptoe**, or **on tiptoes**, you
stand or walk on your toes. *He was very careful and
walked on tiptoe... When everyone is standing on
tiptoes, no one can see any better.*
tip-top
ADJ ATTRIB If you say that something is in **tip-top**
condition, you mean that it is in excellent condition;
an old-fashioned expression. *My car is in tip-top
condition at the moment... He kept his palace in tip-
top shape.*
tirade /taɪreɪd/ **tirades**
NC A **tirade** is a long, angry speech criticizing
someone or something; a formal word. *He has a
reputation for disturbing the poise of fashionable
London dinner parties with tirades about censorship
and nuclear disarmament.*
Tirana /tɪrɑːnə/
Tirana is the capital of Albania and its largest city.
Population: 226,000 (1987).
tire /taɪə/ **tires, tiring, tired**
1 V-ERG If something **tires** you, it makes you use a lot
of energy, so that you want to rest or sleep. *The run
did not seem to tire them at all... The other men
began to tire.* ◆ **tiring** ADJ *We should have an early
night after such a tiring day.*
2 V+of If you **tire** of something, you become bored with
it. *He tired of my questions.*
3 See also **tyre**.
tire out PHRASAL VERB If something **tires** you **out**, it
makes you exhausted.
tired /taɪəd/
1 ADJ If you are **tired**, you want to rest or sleep. *I'm
sure you must be tired after cycling all that distance...
I'm really tired, I'm not even fit to drive myself home.*
◆ **tiredness** NU *Tiredness overwhelmed me.*
2 ADJ PRED If you are **tired** of something, you are

bored with it. *Judy was tired of quarrelling with
him... East Germans, tired of buying second best,
want only Western goods.*
3 ADJ Something that is **tired** is no longer very
interesting because people have heard it or seen it
many times. *He said it was no longer enough to
repeat tired slogans.*
tireless /taɪələs/
ADJ Someone who is **tireless** has a lot of energy and
never seems to need a rest. *Both of them were
tireless workers.*
tiresome /taɪəsəm/
ADJ Someone or something that is **tiresome** makes you
feel irritated or bored. *...a tiresome problem.*
tissue /tɪʃuː, tɪsjuː/ **tissues**
1 N MASS In animals and plants, **tissue** consists of cells
that are similar in appearance and function. *...scar
tissue. ...living tissues.*
2 NU **Tissue** or **tissue paper** is thin paper used for
wrapping things that are easily damaged. *The next
year Mom wrapped all the presents in tissue paper so
delicate that they could not be unwrapped without
tearing.*
3 NC A **tissue** is a small, square piece of soft paper
that you use as a handkerchief. *Lynch sits on the sofa
with a box of tissues at her side.*
tit /tɪt/ **tits**
1 NC A **tit** is a small European bird that eats insects
and seeds. There are several kinds of tit. *...rare and
threatened species of birds such as the crested tit.*
2 NC If you refer to someone as a **tit**, you consider
them to be stupid; an informal, offensive use.
3 NC A woman's **tits** are her breasts; an informal
word which some people find offensive. *...a very nice
figure, rounded tits, a nice bum, blonde hair
preferably.*
titan /taɪtn/ **titans**
NC A **titan** is a person who is very big and strong or
very important; a literary word. *They stand up like
titans against their oppressors... He was a titan among
pygmies.*
titanic /taɪtænɪk/
ADJ Something that is **titanic** is very big or important.
He was a titanic force in the history of modernism.
titanium /taɪteɪniəm/
NU **Titanium** is a strong white metal used in making
lightweight alloys for machine parts. *...the Soviet
firm's ability to work the light but strong metal
titanium economically.*
titbit /tɪtbɪt/ **titbits**
1 NC A **titbit** is a small piece of gossip or scandal.
*Both the government and his supporters regularly
release titbits of information to the press.*
2 NC A **titbit** is a small, tasty piece of food. *...a dog
begging for titbits.*
titchy /tɪtʃi/ **titchier, titchiest**
ADJ A **titchy** thing is extremely small; an informal
word. *You're not dying. It's only a titchy little
scratch.*
tit-for-tat
ADJ ATTRIB **Tit-for-tat** measures are harsh measures
that you take against someone in response to similar
measures which they have taken against you. *Last
year, there was a series of tit-for-tat expulsions of
diplomats accused of spying.*
tithe /taɪð/ **tithes**
NC A **tithe** is a fixed amount of money or goods that
people give regularly in order to support a church, a
priest, or a charity. *Moderate parishioner Sue
Kaufman questions whether she wants her tithe to
support what she sees as a rigid fundamentalist
leadership.*
titillate /tɪtɪleɪt/ **titillates, titillating, titillated**
V OR V If something **titillates** someone, it pleases and
excites them, especially in a sexual way; used
showing disapproval. *...magazines and books with
lurid covers which have titillated the Chinese public
since an era of relative liberalism began at the end of
the 1970s. ...various other bits of scandal designed to
titillate.*
title /taɪtl/ **titles**
1 NC The **title** of a book, play, or piece of music is its

name. *The title of this book is somewhat misleading.*
2 NC Someone's **title** is a word such as 'Lord', 'Mrs',
or 'Doctor' that is used before their name to show
their status or profession. *There were a lot of*
gentlemen in tweed suits, some with titles and some
merely rich... The company's chairman has even been
honoured with the title of Chief in recognition of their
contribution to Ghana's growing timber industry.
3 NC Someone's **title** is also the name that describes
their job or status in an organization. *He played a*
role much greater than that suggested by his official
title as volunteer reservist.
4 NC A **title** in a sports competition is the position of
champion. *We had beaten Cornell and taken the*
title... He knocked out Buster Douglas in the third
round of their title fight last night in Las Vegas.

titled /ˈtaɪtld/
1 ADJ A **titled** person has a title such as 'Lord' or
'Lady' which shows their high social rank. *The House*
of Lords is made up of titled peers who have either
inherited their title or been awarded it as life peers.
2 ADJ PRED In American English, **titled** is also used
when mentioning the title of something such as a book,
film, or painting. *Her new book is titled 'Come Over,*
Come Over'.

title-holder, title-holders
NC The **title-holder** is the winner of a competition that
takes place regularly. They remain the title-holder
until someone else wins it. *Fadeev is the current*
title-holder and a former world champion.

title role, title roles
NC When an actor or singer plays the **title role**, he or
she plays the part of the character after whom the
play, film, or opera is named. *...an actor best known*
for the title role in 'The Eddie Cantor Story'... He was
invited to sing the title role in 'Otello'.

title track, title tracks
NC The **title track** on an album is the song or piece of
music after which the album is named. *This is the*
title track from the new album due out very soon.

titter /ˈtɪtə/ **titters, tittering, tittered**
V If you **titter**, you laugh quietly in a way that shows
that you are nervous or embarrassed. *The audience*
tittered. ▶ Also NC *A condescending titter went round*
the room.

tittle-tattle /ˈtɪtltætl/
NU **Tittle-tattle** is the gossip or unimportant things
that a group of people talk about. *...the tittle-tattle*
about publishing.

titular /ˈtɪtjʊlə/
ADJ ATTRIB A **titular** job or position has a name that
makes it seem important, although the person who has
it is not really important or powerful; a formal word.
...men who occupy the seats of titular power in these
countries. ...the titular head of state.

tizzy /ˈtɪzi/
If you **get in a tizzy** or **get into a tizzy**, you get
excited, worried, or nervous about something,
especially something that is not important; used in
informal English. *He got in a tizzy because the car*
wouldn't start... Don't get into a tizzy.

TM /tiː ˈem/
1 **TM** is a written abbreviation for 'trademark'.
2 **TM** is also a written abbreviation for 'transcendental
meditation'.

TNT /tiː en tiː/
NU **TNT** is a powerful explosive substance. *...a bomb,*
estimated at about three hundred pounds of TNT.

to; pronounced /tə/ or /tu:/ before a consonant and /tu/ or
/tu:/ before a vowel.
1 PREP You use **to** when indicating the place that
someone or something is moving towards or pointing
at. *I'm going with her to Australia... He thought he*
might go to a concert... He was pointing to an oil
tanker somewhere on the horizon.
2 PREP You use **to** when indicating what something is
touching or where it is tied or attached. *He clutched*
the parcel to his chest... I was planning to tie him to a
tree.
3 PREP You use **to** when indicating the position of
something. For example, if something is **to** your left, it
is nearer your left side than your right. *To one side,*

he could see the block of luxury flats... To the west lies
Gloucester.*
4 PREP You use **to** when indicating who or what an
action or a feeling is directed towards. *He showed the*
letter to Barbara... Write to me. Don't forget... They
were sympathetic to his ideas.
5 PREP You also use **to** to indicate the thing towards
which an action is directed or the thing which is
affected by an action. *We don't do repairs to farm*
machines... The bad weather resulted in severe frost
damage to Brazil's coffee plantations... What's
happened to poor old Andrew?
6 PREP You use **to** when indicating someone's reaction
to something. *To his surprise he was offered both*
jobs.
7 PREP You use **to** when indicating the person whose
opinion you are stating. *To me it didn't seem*
necessary.
8 PREP You use **to** when indicating what something or
someone is becoming, or the state or situation that
they are progressing towards. *It had turned to dust*
over the years. ...her rise to fame.
9 PREP You use **to** in expressions of time that state
the number of minutes before a particular hour. For
example, 'five to eight' means five minutes before
eight o'clock. *The bomb went off just before ten to*
nine.
10 PREP You use **to** in ratios and rates. *My car does*
35 miles to the gallon.
11 PREP You use **to** when indicating that something
happens at the same time as something else, perhaps
as a reaction. *To a chorus of laughter the President*
left the room.
12 ADV If you push a door **to**, you close it but do not
shut it completely.
13 You use **to** with an infinitive when indicating the
purpose of an action. *People would stroll down the*
path to admire the garden.
14 You also use **to** with an infinitive when commenting
on your attitude or intention in making a statement.
To be honest, we knew he was there... To sum up, the
law must be changed.
15 You also use **to** with an infinitive in various other
constructions when talking about an action or state.
...the first person to climb Everest... He was too proud
to apologize... They were lovely to watch... Some of us
have got work to do... She looked up to find Tony
standing there.
16 PREP You also use **to** with certain nouns or
adjectives showing that a following noun is related to
them. *She was an inspiration to all the world... The*
answer to your question is unexpectedly simple...
Governments came and went, none sympathetic to his
ideas.
● **To** is used in these phrases. ● You can say that
something happens **from** a certain time **to** another
time to show when something starts and finishes.
Breakfast was from 9 to 10... The job will take
anything from two to five weeks. ● If someone moves
to and fro, they move repeatedly from one place to
another and back again. *All day, he rushed to and fro*
between his living quarters and his place of work.

toad /təʊd/ **toads**
NC A **toad** is an animal like a frog, but with a drier
skin. *A female toad may lay 20,000 eggs each season.*

toad-in-the-hole
NU **Toad-in-the-hole** is a cooked dish consisting of
sausages baked in a mixture of beaten egg, milk, and
flour. *In toad-in-the-hole, another traditional dish,*
meat and pudding are mixed up together.

toadstool /ˈtəʊdstuːl/ **toadstools**
NC A **toadstool** is a type of poisonous fungus. *I*
learned at an early age to distinguish toadstools from
mushrooms.

toast /təʊst/ **toasts, toasting, toasted**
1 NU **Toast** is slices of bread heated until they are
brown and crisp. *Lally was spreading marmalade on*
a piece of toast.
2 VO When you **toast** slices of bread, you heat them so
that they become brown and crisp. *You can toast*
sliced bread while its still frozen.
3 NC When you drink a **toast** to someone or something,

you take a drink, usually of wine or some other alcohol, as a symbolic gesture in order to show your appreciation of them or to wish them success. *Let's drink a toast to that... This evening the two men are attending a banquet in the Kremlin where both have been proposing toasts.*
4 VO When you **toast** someone or something, you drink a toast to them. *Slovenians raised their republic's flag and toasted it with brandy... The Daily Mail has a picture of a beaming Mrs Parish toasting her liberty with a cup of tea.*

toaster /təʊstə/ **toasters**
NC A **toaster** is a piece of electric equipment used to toast bread.

toastmaster /təʊstmɑːstə/ **toastmasters**
NC A **toastmaster** is the person who proposes toasts and who introduces the speakers at formal receptions and dinners.

toast rack, toast racks
NC A **toast rack** is an object that is designed to hold pieces of toast in an upright position and separate from each other ready for people to eat.

tobacco /təbækəʊ/
NU **Tobacco** is the dried leaves of a particular plant which people smoke in pipes, cigars, and cigarettes. *Is someone who doesn't smoke hurt by the tobacco smoke they inhale from people around them?*

tobacconist /təbækənɪst/ **tobacconists**
NC A **tobacconist** or **tobacconist's** is a shop where things such as tobacco, cigarettes, and cigars are sold. *Tobacconists are not allowed to sell cigarettes to children under the age of sixteen.*

toboggan /təbɒgən/ **toboggans**
NC A **toboggan** is a small vehicle for travelling on snow. It consists of a flat seat attached to two long narrow pieces of wood or metal that slide easily over the snow.

tod /tɒd/
If you are **on your tod**, you are alone; an informal expression. *I came here on my tod.*

today /tədeɪ/
1 ADVorNU **Today** means the day on which you are speaking or writing. *I had a letter today from my solicitor... Today is Thursday.*
2 ADVorNU You can refer to the present period of history as **today**. *Today we are threatened on all sides by financial crises. ...the America of today and the America of thirty years ago.*

toddle /tɒdl/ **toddles, toddling, toddled**
V When a small child **toddles**, it walks unsteadily with short, quick steps. *His grandson was toddling around in the garden.*

toddler /tɒdələ/ **toddlers**
NC A **toddler** is a small child who has just learned to walk. *With immense concentration, the 18-month-old toddler fits red and yellow and green pieces of plastic into a big white frame.*

toddy /tɒdi/ **toddies**
NCorNU A **toddy** is a drink that is made by adding hot water and sugar to whisky, rum, or brandy. *Are you and Lila going to have a little toddy to ring in the New Year?*

to-do /təduː/
N SING+SUPP When there is a **to-do**, people are very excited, confused, or angry about something; an informal word. *There was an awful to-do about the election result.*

toe /təʊ/ **toes, toeing, toed**
1 NC Your **toes** are the five movable parts at the end of each foot. *Aouita had been out of action for three months after suffering a fractured toe... I've got sand between my toes.*
2 NC The **toe** of a shoe or sock is the part that covers the end of your foot. *Maria's shoes had holes in the toes.*
3 If you **toe the line**, you behave in the way that people in authority expect you to. *Gorbachev did threaten tough action if rebellious republics didn't toe his line... Now is the time to toe the party line.*

toehold /təʊhəʊld/ **toeholds**
1 NC A **toehold** is a small place on a rock or mountain, where there is just enough room for you to

put the end of your foot when you are climbing.
2 NC A **toehold** is also a first uncertain position in a job or area of work which you hope will give you the opportunity to go on to better things. *Starting off as a secretary on a local paper may give you a toehold in journalism.*

toenail /təʊneɪl/ **toenails**
NC Your **toenails** are the hard coverings that grow on the ends of your toes. *Cut your toenails very short.*

toffee /tɒfi/ **toffees**
NCorNU A **toffee** is a sweet made by boiling sugar and butter together with water. *Half a pound of toffees, please. ...a chunk of toffee.*

toffee apple, toffee apples
NC A **toffee apple** is an apple covered with a thin, hard layer of toffee and mounted on a stick.

toffee-nosed
ADJ If you say that someone is **toffee-nosed**, you mean that they have a high opinion of themselves and a low opinion of other people; used in informal English.

tog /tɒg/ **togs**
1 NC A **tog** is an official measurement that shows how warm a blanket, sleeping bag, or quilt is. *Down quilts vary between ten and fifteen togs.*
2 N PL Your **togs** are your clothes; an old-fashioned, informal use. *I'll just get my swimming togs.*

toga /təʊgə/ **togas**
NC A **toga** is a piece of clothing which was worn by citizens in ancient Rome. *...the classical toga portrayed in Greek and Roman sculpture.*

together /təgeðə/
1 ADV If people do something **together**, they do it with each other. *They flew back to London together... You all work together as a team.*
2 ADV If two things happen **together**, they happen at the same time. *The reports will have to be seen and judged together before we decide.*
3 ADV If things are joined or fixed **together**, they are joined or fixed to each other. *Her hands were clasped tightly together.*
4 ADV If things or people are **together**, they are next to each other. *The fossils are packed densely together in display cases.*
5 ADV If people are **together** on an issue, they have the same attitude towards it. *The two superpowers had moved closer together on the Cambodian issue... They are a disparate alliance, held together by dislike of Miss Bhutto.*
6 ADV You use **together** when considering the total amount that two or more things spend, produce, or are worth. *The two companies together spend more on research than the whole of the rest of the industry.*
7 ADV If you say that things go **together**, you mean that they fit or suit each other or can both happen at the same time or in the same place without causing problems. *Nell feels that marriage and studying don't go together.*

togetherness /təgeðənəs/
NU **Togetherness** is a warm happy feeling of affection and closeness to other people, especially your friends and family. *Grandma and Grandpa share the joys of togetherness made possible by a lifetime of giving.*

together with
PREP **Together with** something means in addition to that thing. *Lee handed over the key to his room, together with some forms and leaflets.*

togged /tɒgd/
If you are **togged up** or **togged out**, you are dressed in the right clothing for a particular activity; used in informal English. *She's all togged up to go climbing.*

toggle /tɒgl/ **toggles**
NC A **toggle** is a small piece of wood or plastic which is sewn to something such as a coat, bag, or tent flap, and which is attached to a string and used as a fastener or switch.

Togo /təʊgəʊ/
The **Republic of Togo** is a country in western Africa. From 1894 until 1914 it was a German colony called Togoland. The League of Nations divided it into British Togoland, which became part of Ghana in 1957, and French Togoland, which became the independent country of Togo in 1960. General Gnassingbe Eyadéma

became President in a coup in 1967. In 1969 the Togolese People's Assembly (RPT) became the sole legal party. During a pro-democracy conference in 1991, the RPT was dissolved, Kokou Koffigoh was appointed Prime Minister, and President Eyadéma was forced to ratify the appointment. Togo exports calcium phosphates, cotton, cocoa, and coffee. Large foreign debts are a major economic problem. It is a member of the Organization of African Unity.
♦ **Togolese** /təʊgəliːz/ N, N PL, ADJ
▪ *per capita GNP:* US$370 ▪ *religion:* animism, Christianity, Islam ▪ *language:* French, Ewe, Kabiye ▪ *currency:* CFA franc ▪ *capital:* Lomé ▪ *population:* 4 million (1989) ▪ *size:* 56,785 square kilometres.

toil /tɔɪl/ **toils, toiling, toiled**
v When people **toil**, they work hard doing unpleasant or tiring tasks; a literary word. *...factories where men toiled all through the night.* ► Also NU *The wealth of industrial society could only come from the toil of the masses.*

toil away PHRASAL VERB If you **toil away**, you work hard over a continuous period of time at a task that is unpleasant, difficult, or tiring. *Our mothers toiled away in the kitchen most of their lives.*

toilet /tɔɪlət/ **toilets**
1 NC A **toilet** is a large bowl connected to the drains which you use when you want to get rid of urine or faeces from your body. *He asked to go to the toilet... Only schools and teachers' homes have flush toilets and running water.*
2 NC A **toilet** is also a small room containing a toilet. *The toilet is an outhouse fifty yards down the road.*

toilet bag, toilet bags
NC A **toilet bag** is a small bag in which you put things such as your soap, shaving kit, or make-up when you are travelling.

toilet paper
NU **Toilet paper** is paper that you use to clean yourself after getting rid of urine or faeces from your body. *Peking is short of matches, toilet paper and soap.*

toiletries /tɔɪlətriz/
N PL **Toiletries** are things that you use when cleaning or taking care of your body, such as soap and toothpaste. *They can buy items such as tobacco, sweets and toiletries.*

toilet roll, toilet rolls
NC A **toilet roll** is a long strip of toilet paper wound around a cardboard tube. *...household goods like toothpaste, bleach, toilet rolls.*

toilet soap, toilet soaps
N MASS **Toilet soap** is soap that you use for washing yourself. *The Sugar and Spice range includes perfume, hand and body lotion, toilet soap and gift sets. ...any mild toilet soap.*

toilet-train, toilet-trains, toilet-training, toilet-trained
vo When you **toilet-train** a child, you teach it to control itself so that it only passes urine or faeces when it is sitting on a potty or toilet. *Most of them were rigidly toilet-trained as babies.*

toilet water, toilet waters
N MASS **Toilet water** is fairly weak and inexpensive perfume. *She would sprinkle toilet water on her handkerchief.*

to-ing and fro-ing /tuːɪŋ ən frəʊɪŋ/
NU **To-ing and fro-ing** is a situation in which the same movement between two places is repeated many times. *There was a lot of to-ing and fro-ing between London and Glasgow.*

Tokelau /tɒkəlaʊ/
Tokelau is a territory of New Zealand in the Pacific, north of Western Samoa. It consists of three atolls: Atafu, Nukunonu, and Fakaofo. They became a British protectorate in 1877. Administration was transferred to New Zealand in 1925. Tokelau exports copra. The sale of stamps and currency is an important source of income. ♦ **Tokelauan** /tɒkəlaʊən/ N, ADJ
▪ *religion:* Christianity (mainly Congregational Christian Church of Samoa) ▪ *language:* Tokelauan ▪ *currency:* New Zealand dollar ▪ *capital:* each atoll has its own administration centre ▪ *population:* 1,700 (1986) ▪ *size:* 12 square kilometres.

token /təʊkən/ **tokens**
1 NC A **token** is a piece of paper or card which is bought as a present and can be exchanged for goods. *...a book token.*
2 NC **Tokens** are also round, flat pieces of metal that are sometimes used instead of money. *Each citizen inserted a bronze token. ...tokens for the telephone.*
3 NC If you give something to someone as a **token** of your feelings for them, you give it as a way of expressing those feelings; a formal use. *He gave her a gold brooch as a token of his esteem... Courting couples are meant to send each other a token of their mutual love.*
4 ADJ You use **token** of things or actions which show your intentions or feelings but are small or unimportant. *Other protests have been no more than token gestures, mainly small meetings on university campuses... The Iranians fought back at every point, some of it token resistance, some much more determined.*
5 N+N A **token** person of a certain kind is present somewhere only because of certain rules or for appearance's sake, and not because they are really wanted or needed; used showing disapproval. *She herself was at pains to stress that she is not just a token woman.*
6 You use **by the same token** to introduce a statement that you think is true for the same reasons that were given for a previous statement. *We make people mentally old by retiring them, and we may even by the same token make them physically old.*

tokenism /təʊkənɪzəm/
NU **Tokenism** is the practice of taking actions which seem to avoid discrimination against some groups of people, but which are taken only because of certain rules or for appearance's sake, and not because the people involved really want to take them. *You get a lot of tokenism, you get one black judge, one Indian judge... Appointments must be based on competence, not on a sort of tokenism for women.*

Tokyo /təʊkiəʊ/
Tokyo is the capital of Japan and its largest city. Population: 8,156,000 (1988).

told /təʊld/
Told is the past tense and past participle of **tell**.

tolerable /tɒlərəbl/
ADJ If something is **tolerable**, it is acceptable or bearable, but not pleasant or good. *I was given a tolerable meal... I picked up a tolerable working knowledge of the language.*

tolerance /tɒlərəns/ **tolerances**
1 NU **Tolerance** is the quality of letting other people say and do as they like, even if you do not agree or approve of it; used showing approval. *We must listen as well as speak to each other and so learn tolerance through understanding. ...the importance of religious tolerance in schools.*
2 NU **Tolerance** is the ability to bear something painful or unpleasant. *The stench was beyond tolerance, and the men began to choke and vomit.*
3 NU+SUPP or NC+SUPP If someone or something has **tolerance** to a substance, they are exposed to it so often that it does not have very much effect on them. *...to stimulate the body to increase its tolerance to lactic acid... Bacteria can develop a tolerance to such chemicals, so no single chemical can provide a long-term solution.*

tolerant /tɒlərənt/
ADJ If you are **tolerant**, you let other people say and do what they like, even if you do not agree with it or approve of it. *I think I've become more tolerant of other people's attitudes.*

tolerate /tɒləreɪt/ **tolerates, tolerating, tolerated**
1 vo If you **tolerate** things that you do not agree with or approve of, you allow them to exist or happen. *They happily tolerated the existence of opinions contrary to their own.* ♦ **toleration** /tɒləreɪʃn/ NU *...toleration of religious variety.*
2 vo If you can **tolerate** something unsatisfactory or unpleasant, you are able to accept it. *They couldn't tolerate the noise.*

toll /təʊl/ **tolls, tolling, tolled**

1 NC+SUPP The death **toll** in an accident, disaster, or war is the number of people who have died in it. *By Wednesday the death toll had risen to more than 40. ...the mounting civilian death toll... Casualties on all sides have been exceptionally high, adding to the toll of death and devastation.*

2 If something **takes a toll** or **takes its toll**, it has the effect of causing suffering or damage. *The war continues to take an appalling toll... The walking was beginning to take its toll on all of us.*

3 NC A **toll** is a sum of money that you have to pay in order to use a particular bridge or road. *The project would be financed by public sector capital and traffic using it would pay a toll.*

4 V-ERG When someone **tolls** a bell or when it **tolls**, they ring it slowly and repeatedly, often as a sign that someone has died. *Temple bells tolled and sirens wailed throughout the city. Many people wept openly on the roadside... He tolled the bell at funerals.*

toll call, toll calls

NC In the United States, a **toll call** is a telephone call to a place which is outside your local area, so that its cost is not covered by the standing charge which you pay for local calls. *Everywhere in Vermont, we discovered, was a toll call away.*

toll-free

ADJ or ADV A **toll-free** telephone number is one that you can call without paying; used in American English. *Car owners will be given a toll-free number they can call any time night or day when their vehicle registrations are about to expire... For reservations, call toll-free Grimm Chamber of Commerce.*

tollhouse /təʊlhaʊs/ **tollhouses**

NC A **tollhouse** is a small house by a bridge or gate where people used to stop to pay a sum of money in order to be allowed to cross the bridge or to use a stretch of road.

tom /tɒm/ **toms**

NC A **tom** is a male cat.

tomahawk /tɒməhɔːk/ **tomahawks**

NC A **tomahawk** is a small light axe that is used by North American Indians.

tomato /təmɑːtəʊ/ **tomatoes**

NC A **tomato** is a small, soft red fruit that is used in cooking or eaten raw. *It tastes like a slightly underripe tomato. ...tinned tomatoes. ...spaghetti in tomato sauce.*

tomb /tuːm/ **tombs**

NC A **tomb** is a stone structure containing the body of a dead person. *The cities of Najaf and Karbala contain the tombs of Ali and his sons, Hussein and Abbas... President Bush began the day by laying a wreath at the Tomb of the Unknowns in Arlington National Cemetery.*

tombola /tɒmbəʊlə/ **tombolas**

NCorNU **Tombola** is a game in which you buy a ticket with a number on it. Another ticket is pulled out of a drum, called a tombola, and if the two ticket have the same number you win a prize. *...drop in and draw the lucky number out of the tombola.*

tomboy /tɒmbɔɪ/ **tomboys**

NC A **tomboy** is a girl who likes playing rough or noisy games. *Angela was the stereotyped tomboy, with close-cropped hair and baggy trousers.*

tombstone /tuːmstəʊn/ **tombstones**

NC A **tombstone** is a large, flat piece of stone on someone's grave, with their name written on it. *It was a verse from one of the tombstones in the neighbouring churchyard... The tombstone is in need of attention because of a recent attack by vandals.*

tomcat /tɒmkæt/ **tomcats**

NC A **tomcat** is a male cat.

tome /təʊm/ **tomes**

NC A **tome** is a large, heavy book; a literary word, often used humorously. *I was attempting to read a weighty tome.*

tomfoolery /tɒmfuːləri/

NU **Tomfoolery** is playful behaviour, usually of a rather silly, noisy, or rough kind. *Right, that's enough of this tomfoolery, it's time you got on with some work.*

tomorrow /təmɒrəʊ/

1 ADVorNU **Tomorrow** means the day after today. *They're coming tomorrow... They're arriving in Israel tomorrow night... Tomorrow's concert has been cancelled.*

2 ADVorNU You can refer to the future, especially the near future, as **tomorrow**. *They live today as millions more will live tomorrow... One of the big tasks of today and tomorrow is the investigation of repressed sexual energy.*

ton /tʌn/ **tons**

1 NC A **ton** is a unit of weight equal to 2240 pounds in Britain and 2000 pounds in the United States. *...ten million tons of coal.*

2 NC A **ton** is also the same as a **tonne**. *The crop is forecast for 230 million metric tons.*

3 N PL **Tons** of something means a lot of it; an informal use. *I've got tons of paper to draw on.*

tonal /təʊnl/

ADJ ATTRIB **Tonal** means relating to the qualities or pitch of a sound or to the tonality of a piece of music. *Charlie Parker was able to exploit its full tonal range, producing mellow and rhapsodic music.*

tonality /təʊnæləti/

NU **Tonality** is the presence of a musical key in a piece of music; a technical term. *Ben Johnston's 'Amazing Grace' marked a return to tonality and the use of Southern hymns in the composer's work.*

tone /təʊn/ **tones, toning, toned**

1 NC+SUPP Someone's **tone** is a quality in their voice or general actions which shows what they are feeling or thinking. *'Very good,' he said in an encouraging tone... Her tone was defiant... Mr Reagan adopted a conciliatory tone towards the Soviet Union.*

2 NC A **tone** is one of the sounds that you hear when you are using a telephone, for example the sound that tells you that a number is engaged. *I'm getting the ringing tone, but there doesn't appear to be anyone at home.*

3 NU The **tone** of a musical instrument or a singer's voice is the kind of sound it has. *I wish I had a piano with a better tone... He was famous for the clear tone of his virtuoso playing.*

4 NC In music, a **tone** is a fixed interval between two notes on a scale.

5 NC In American English, a **tone** is a sound in music of a particular pitch and duration. *I'd always felt at a disadvantage in comparison to vocalists who could sustain tones, and, you know, do these very interesting things with longer tones.*

6 NU The **tone** of a speech or piece of writing is its style and the feelings expressed in it. *I was greatly offended by the tone of the article.*

7 NCorNU A **tone** is also one of several lighter, darker, or brighter shades of the same colour. *...the tones of the sky... You need a blue that is darker in tone.*

8 To **lower the tone** of a place or conversation means to make it less respectable. *He said the new people had lowered the tone of the neighbourhood.*

tone down PHRASAL VERB If you **tone down** something that you have written or said, you make it less forceful, severe, or offensive. *He advised me to tone down my letter... Representatives of the Bush administration continue to tone down any talk of war.*

tone in PHRASAL VERB If something **tones in** with something else, the two things blend together because they are similar in colour or texture. *The thick velvet toned in with her dress.*

tone-deaf

ADJ Someone who is **tone-deaf** cannot sing in tune or recognize different tunes.

toneless /təʊnləs/

ADJ A **toneless** voice is dull and does not express any feeling. *He replied in a toneless mechanical voice.*
♦ **tonelessly** ADV *'You're back,' she said tonelessly.*

Tonga /tɒŋə/

The **Kingdom of Tonga** is a country in the Pacific. It consists of about 175 islands, formerly known as the Friendly Islands. The main island is Tongatapu. Tonga was a protectorate of Britain from 1900 until independence in 1970. It is a member of the Commonwealth. King Taufa'ahau Tupou IV succeeded in 1965. There are no political parties. Tonga exports coconut, watermelons, and vanilla. Tourism is an important industry. ◆ **Tongan** /tɒŋən/ N, ADJ ▪ *per capita GNP:* US$800 ▪ *religion:* Christianity (mainly Wesleyan) ▪ *language:* Tongan and English (official) ▪ *currency:* pa'anga ▪ *capital:* Nuku'alofa ▪ *population:* 101,000 (1988) ▪ *size:* 748 square kilometres.

tongs /tɒŋz/
N PL **Tongs** consist of two long pieces of metal joined together at one end. You press the pieces together in order to pick up an object. *She was putting lumps of sugar into her tea with a pair of silver tongs.*

tongue /tʌŋ/ **tongues**
1 NC Your **tongue** is the soft movable part inside your mouth that you use for tasting, licking, and speaking. *If you put your tongue to the back of your mouth you'll actually feel it.*
2 NC You can refer to a language as a **tongue**; a literary use. *I answered her in her own tongue.* ● See also **mother tongue**.
3 NU **Tongue** is the cooked tongue of an ox. *Have plenty of cold foods prepared in advance: cooked gammon or tongue with Cumberland sauce, chicken liver or duck paté.*
● **Tongue** is used in these phrases. ● If you **hold your tongue**, you do not say anything. *The Duke harshly told him to hold his tongue.* ● A **slip of the tongue** is a small mistake that you make when you are speaking. *The context of Mrs Thatcher's remarks suggest that the words were little more than a slip of the tongue.*

tongue-in-cheek
ADJ or ADV A **tongue-in-cheek** remark is made as a joke, and is not serious or sincere. *I've heard all kinds of tongue-in-cheek comments about the whole issue... Another Labour MP suggested tongue-in-cheek that the Foreign Affairs Committee might look into Scottish issues.*

tongue-tied
ADJ If you are **tongue-tied**, you are unable to say anything because you feel shy or nervous. *Ginny agreed, suddenly as tongue-tied as a schoolgirl.*

tongue-twister, tongue-twisters
NC A **tongue-twister** is a sentence or expression which is very difficult to say properly, especially when you try to say it quickly. For example, 'She sells seashells on the seashore' is a tongue-twister.

tonic /tɒnɪk/ **tonics**
1 N MASS **Tonic** or **tonic water** is a colourless, fizzy drink that has a slightly bitter flavour and is often mixed with alcoholic drinks. *...a gin and tonic... We have got the usual fruit juices and tonic waters.*
2 N MASS A **tonic** is a medicine that makes you feel stronger, healthier, and less tired. *The pharmacy is complete with stocks of original medicines, mostly liniments, tonics and countless laxatives... Vitamin pills and a good dose of tonic will help you to pick up.*
3 NC You can refer to anything that makes you feel stronger or more cheerful as a **tonic**. *It was a tonic to talk to her... The presence of Mr. Mandela was a tonic that strengthened them all.*

tonight /tənaɪt/
ADV or NU **Tonight** means the evening or night that will come at the end of today. *I think I'll go to bed early tonight... In tonight's programme we shall be explaining its history.*

tonnage /tʌnɪdʒ/
1 NU The **tonnage** of a ship is its size or the amount of cargo that it can carry; a technical use. *...8000 registered merchant ships with a gross tonnage of 20 million.*
2 NU The **tonnage** of something is the amount of it that there is, measured in tons. *...the total tonnage of TNT used during the last war.*

tonne /tʌn/ **tonnes**
NC A **tonne** is a unit of weight equal to 1000 kilograms. *Each day a million tonnes of untreated sewage is dumped into the sea off Hong Kong.*

tonsil /tɒnsl/ **tonsils**
NC Your **tonsils** are the two small, soft lumps at the back of your mouth. *Treatment is relatively easy, involving removal of over-sized tonsils.*

tonsillitis /tɒnsəlaɪtɪs/
NU **Tonsillitis** is a painful swelling of your tonsils caused by an infection. *He went down with suspected tonsillitis.*

tonsure /tɒnʃə/ **tonsures**
NC If a man has a **tonsure**, he has shaved the top, but not the sides, of his head. Some monks have their heads shaved like this. *...a small round spot like a tonsure.*

too /tuː/
1 ADV SEN You use **too** after mentioning another person, thing, or aspect that a previous statement applies to or includes. *I'm on your side. Seibert is too... There were carrots too.*
2 SUBMOD You also use **too** to indicate that there is more of a thing or quality than is desirable, acceptable, or necessary. *Avoid using too much water... Don't leave it in too warm a place... They say the figure is far too high... It was too early to expect any concrete results.*
3 SUBMOD You can use **too** with a negative to make what you are saying sound less forceful or more polite or cautious. *He wasn't too keen on it... That's probably not too far from the truth.*
● **Too** is used in these phrases. ● You use **all too** or **only too** to emphasize that something happens to a greater degree than is pleasant or desirable. *I can remember only too well the disasters that followed... The suspicions had proved all too true.* ● If you describe a situation as **too little, too late**, you are blaming someone for not doing enough to prevent a problem and for taking action only after the problem had become very bad. *He criticized the Central Electricity Generating Board for doing too little, too late, about acid rain.* ● **too bad:** see **bad**. ● **none too:** see **none**.

took /tʊk/
Took is the past tense of **take**.

tool /tuːl/ **tools**
1 NC A **tool** is any instrument or simple piece of equipment, for example a hammer or a knife, that you hold in your hands and use to do a particular kind of work. *He'd never consider using anything but the traditional hand-held tools to sculpt the wood.*
2 NC+SUPP You can refer to anything that you use for a particular purpose as a particular type of **tool**. *This video is a bit unusual as marketing tools go... The gunman apparently planned to take some of his hostages to Beirut to use them as a bargaining tool... So you think that your technique will eventually become a clinical test for cervical cancer or will it remain more of a research tool?*
3 NC+SUPP You can refer to a person or thing as another person's **tool** when the first person or thing is in the power of the second person and is being used by them; used showing disapproval. *He is regarded by some Tibetan radicals as a tool of the Chinese... Mr Torr said he would not serve in a force which was a tool of apartheid.*

tool box, tool boxes
NC A **tool box** is a metal or plastic box which contains general tools that you need at home, for example for repairing your house or car. *Keep your tool box in your garage.*

tool kit, tool kits
NC A **tool kit** is a special set of tools that are kept together and that are often used for a particular purpose. *A standard tool kit comes with the bicycle.*

toot /tuːt/ **toots, tooting, tooted**
V-ERG If you **toot** your car horn or if it **toots**, you make it produce a short sound or series of sounds. *In the streets of East Berlin people drank champagne, set off fireworks and tooted their car horns... A car horn tooted.* ▶ Also NC *'Look,' she said and gave a toot on the horn.*

tooth /tuːθ/ **teeth**
1 NC Your **teeth** are the hard, white objects in your mouth that you use for biting and chewing. *...people who clean their teeth regularly with toothpaste containing fluoride, and don't eat sugar... Half of all people in Britain above the age of fifty have none of their own teeth left at all.*

2 NC The **teeth** of something like a comb, saw, or zip are the hard parts that stick out in a row. *Each of these cogs has ten teeth.*
3 N PL If an official group or a law has **teeth**, it has power and will be able to enforce its decisions. *The opposition argues that the new council will be unconstitutional and without teeth.*
4 If people fight **tooth and nail** for something, they fight in a very determined way. *She let it be known, through her Press office, that she intended to fight tooth and nail to stay in office.*
5 to **grit your teeth**: see **grit**. **by the skin of** your **teeth**: see **skin**.

toothache /tuːθeɪk/
NU **Toothache** is pain in one of your teeth. *He began to complain of toothache.*

toothbrush /tuːθbrʌʃ/ **toothbrushes**
NC A **toothbrush** is a small brush used for cleaning your teeth. *Bring soap, a toothbrush and other necessities in case you have to stay overnight.*

toothcomb /tuːθkəʊm/. See **fine-tooth comb**.

toothless /tuːθləs/
1 ADJ If someone is **toothless**, they have no teeth. *Twenty-one per cent of British men have no teeth— they're totally toothless.*
2 ADJ If an organization or official group is **toothless**, it has no real power. *The two Countryside Commissions are often referred to as 'toothless watchdogs'.*

toothpaste /tuːθpeɪst/ **toothpastes**
N MASS **Toothpaste** is a thick substance which you use to clean your teeth. *He uses a silver device specially designed to squeeze the last blob out of a tube of toothpaste... Fluoridated toothpastes help protect teeth in areas with no natural fluoride in water.*

toothpick /tuːθpɪk/ **toothpicks**
NC A **toothpick** is a small stick which you use to remove food from between your teeth. *He chews on a toothpick constantly.*

toothpowder /tuːθpaʊdə/ **toothpowders**
N MASS **Toothpowder** is a powder which you put on your toothbrush and use to clean your teeth. *I use smoker's toothpowder once a week.*

toothy /tuːθi/ **toothier, toothiest**
ADJ ATTRIB A **toothy** smile is one in which a person shows a lot of teeth. *...a toothy, comedian's grin.*

tootle /tuːtl/ **tootles, tootling, tootled**; an old-fashioned, informal word.
1 V A If you **tootle** somewhere, you go there in a calm and unhurried way. *I don't imagine myself winning some grand prix; I like to tootle along in comparative comfort and safety.*
2 V A If you **tootle** on a musical instrument such as a recorder or flute, you play it in a casual way.

top /tɒp/ **tops, topping, topped**
1 NC+SUPP The **top** of something is its highest point or part. *...at the top of the steps... He filled his glass to the top. ...radar stations on bleak mountain tops.*
2 NC+SUPP The **top** of something such as a box or a table is its flat upper surface. *...the rough wooden top of the table.*
3 ADJ ATTRIB The **top** thing of a series of things is the highest one. *...a room on the top floor.*
4 N SING The **top** of a street is one end of it. *...a new building at the top of Victoria Street.*
5 N SING The **top** of an organization is its highest or most important level. *...the crazed twin brothers who rose to the top of Britain's underworld in the 1960s... Officials at the top make the decisions... The orders came straight from the top.*
6 ADJ ATTRIB **Top** people are more important or successful than other people. *He is also one of the country's top economic planners. ...top executives... Most of the game's top players will be there.*
7 N SING The **top** of a scale of measurement is the highest point on it. *This group is already near the top of the UK income scale.*
8 ADJ ATTRIB You use **top** to describe things or people that come near the highest point on a scale of measurement. *The vehicle's top speed is about 100 mph... Golfers figured highly in the list of top earners for 1989.*

9 NC The **top** of a bottle, jar, or tube is its cap or lid. *He unscrewed the top and put the bottle to his mouth.*
10 NC A **top** is a piece of clothing worn on the upper half of a woman's body. *The top doesn't fit very well but the skirt's all right.*
11 NC A **top** is also a toy shaped like a cone that can spin on its pointed end.
12 V O If someone **tops** a poll or popularity chart, they do better than anyone else in it. *Prince Charles tops the list of favourite Royals.*
13 V O If something **tops** a particular amount, it becomes greater than that amount. *US investments topped fifty million dollars.*
14 See also **topped**.
● **Top** is used in these phrases. ● Something that is **on top of** something else is on its highest part. *...a tower with a little flag on top... Pile the hymn books on top of each other.* ● **On top of** other things means in addition to them. *You don't want to give the poor man ulcers on top of all the problems he's already got.* ● If you are **on top of** a task, you are dealing with it successfully. *I know Mr Ozal is very anxious to get on top of this complaint.* ● When something **gets on top of** you, it makes you feel depressed because you cannot cope with it. *You may find the housework is getting on top of you.* ● If something or someone is **over the top**, they are unacceptable because they are too extreme. *While it's accepted he went over the top, some Conservatives insist that Mr Ridley voiced widely held concerns.* ● **off the top of** your **head**: see **head**. ● **at the top of** your **voice**: see **voice**.

top off PHRASAL VERB If you **top** something **off**, you do something to complete it in a satisfactory way. *Naderi Seyed Mohammed topped off a good day for Iran with a silver medal.*

top up PHRASAL VERB If you **top up** a container, you fill it again when it has been partly emptied. *The radiator will have to be topped up because of evaporation.*

topaz /təʊpæz/ **topazes**
NC A **topaz** is a precious stone which is usually yellowish-brown. It is used in making jewellery. *...a topaz ring.*

top-class
ADJ If you describe someone or something as **top-class**, you mean that you think they are excellent or of the highest standard. *The Royal Shakespeare Company says it is adopting new measures to attract more top-class actors... They can no longer afford to continue in top-class athletics.*

top-down
ADJ If someone has a **top-down** approach to a problem, they try to solve it by allowing people in authority to make all the decisions rather than the people who are actually affected by the problem. *They are still institutionally obsessed with large-scale, top-down industrial projects, such as large dams. ...a top-down style of leadership.*

top hat, top hats
NC A **top hat** is a tall hat with a narrow brim that men wear on very formal occasions. *He's taken to dressing in top hat and tails when he visits car shows.*

top-heavy
ADJ Something that is **top-heavy** is larger or heavier at the top than at the bottom, and is therefore not stable. *...high-heeled shoes and hats top-heavy with feathers and flowers.*

topiary /təʊpiəri/
NU **Topiary** is the art of cutting hedges and bushes into different shapes, for example into the shape of a bird or animal; a technical term.

topic /tɒpɪk/ **topics**
NC A **topic** is a particular subject that you write about or discuss. *The main topic of conversation was food.*

topical /tɒpɪkl/
ADJ **Topical** means relating to events that are happening at the time when you are speaking or writing. *They used to discuss topical issues.*

top-knot, top-knots
NC A **top-knot** is a hairstyle, especially for women, in which a person's hair is arranged in a small neat pile on the top of their head, and is sometimes decorated

with things like ribbons or feathers.

topless /tɒpləs/
ADJ When a woman is **topless**, she has no clothing covering her breasts. ...*in these days of nude and topless bathing.* ...*the topless models to be found on the third page of some of Britain's popular newspapers.*

top-level
ADJ ATTRIB A **top-level** discussion or activity is one that involves the people with the greatest amount of power and authority in an organization, group, or country. ...*top-level negotiations between the two embassies... The leadership of the ruling Communist Party has ordered a top-level investigation into the unrest.*

topmost /tɒpməʊst/
ADJ ATTRIB The **topmost** thing in a group of things is the one that is highest or nearest the top. ...*the topmost branches of the lime trees.*

top-notch
ADJ ATTRIB If you describe a person or activity as **top-notch**, you mean that they are of a very high standard or quality; an old-fashioned, informal word. ...*a top-notch footballer.* ...*absolutely top-notch tennis.*

top-of-the-line
ADJ ATTRIB **Top-of-the-line** items are the most expensive and best developed of their kind. *Analysts say the new top-of-the-line IBM mainframe will run at more than twice the speed of current mainframes... The country's troubled economy certainly cannot provide the resources to buy top-of-the-line military supplies.*

topographical /tɒpəgræfɪkl/
ADJ A **topographical** survey or map relates to or shows the physical features of an area of land, for example its hills, valleys, and rivers. *Owls have this very accurate topographical map inside their heads.*

topography /təpɒgrəfi/
1 NU The **topography** of a particular area is its physical shape, including features such as hills, valleys, and rivers. *Its climate, topography and location make it an ideal site for growing coca.*
2 NU **Topography** is the study and description of the physical features of an area, for example its hills, valleys, and rivers. **Topography** is also used to describe the representation of these features on maps.

topped /tɒpt/
ADJ PRED If something is **topped** by or with another thing, the other thing is on top of it. ...*a heap of stones topped by a wooden cross.*

topper /tɒpə/ **toppers**
NC A **topper** is a top hat; an informal word. ...*a man in a ridiculous topper.*

topping /tɒpɪŋ/ **toppings**
N MASS A **topping** is food, such as cream or cheese, that is poured or put on top of other food in order to decorate it or to add to its flavour. ...*a topping of whipped cream.*

topple /tɒpl/ **topples, toppling, toppled**
1 V-ERG If something **topples** or if you **topple** it, it becomes unsteady and falls over. *Badly built concrete tower blocks simply toppled and collapsed on their inhabitants... You don't need a hurricane to topple a banana or plantain tree.*
2 VO To **topple** a government or leader means to cause them to lose power. *His regime was toppled in a coup... He maintained that those who pretended to be supporting multi-party politics only wanted to topple the government.*

topple over PHRASAL VERB If something **topples over**, it becomes unsteady and falls down. *She looked at the young tree nervously, as if expecting it to topple over.*

top-ranking
ADJ ATTRIB A **top-ranking** person is one of the most important or powerful people in a country or organization. ...*a top-ranking agent.*

top-secret
ADJ Something that is **top-secret** is intended to be kept completely secret. ...*a top-secret experiment.*

topsoil /tɒpsɔɪl/
NU **Topsoil** is the layer of soil nearest the surface of the ground. *The topsoil has been almost completely washed away over the last few years.*

topsy-turvy /tɒpsitɜːvi/
1 ADJ If a situation or an account of events is **topsy-turvy**, it is very confused or wrong, for example because unimportant parts of it are considered important. ...*that's rather a topsy-turvy way of looking at things... What a topsy-turvy world politics is!*
2 ADJ If something you are looking at is **topsy-turvy**, it is upside down, or many of its parts are in the wrong place. *The room was all topsy-turvy.*

top-up, top-ups
1 NC A **top-up** is another serving of a drink in the same glass that you have just used. *Anyone ready for a top-up?*
2 N+N A **top-up** loan or sum of money is an amount added to a sum of money in order to bring it up to a required level. *From September grants will be frozen at existing levels and top-up loans made available for all full-time students under the age of fifty.*

torch /tɔːtʃ/ **torches, torching, torched**
1 NC A **torch** is a small electric light which you carry in your hand. *The power went off, no-one was particularly worried, and they reached for their torches... He took the torch and disappeared into the dark.*
2 NC A **torch** is also a stick with burning material at the end. *Protesters gathered near the home of the Prime Minister, Mr Shamir, carrying torches and slogans... The Olympic torch which had been carried across Canada by thousands of volunteers was taken the last few yards by a twelve-year-old girl... He thrust a lighted torch into the funeral mound.*
3 NC+SUPP A particular kind of **torch** is a device that uses a hot flame for a particular task such as welding or cutting metal. *The blaze is reported to have resulted from sparks from a welding torch... How many senators here have taken a cutting torch and removed people from a small car after an accident?*
4 VO To **torch** a building means to set fire to it deliberately. *The militants say that the houses and shops were torched by the security forces.*
5 NC+SUPP If you say that someone is carrying the **torch** of a particular belief or philosophy, you mean that they are working hard to ensure that it continues and grows stronger. *Since his death in 1985 his widow, Nexhmije, has carried the torch of his Stalinist legacy... They claim to be able to reunite the divided party and carry on the torch of Thatcherism.*

torchlight /tɔːtʃlaɪt/
1 NU **Torchlight** is light that is produced by an electric torch. ...*the circle of torchlight.*
2 NU **Torchlight** is also light that is produced by burning torches. ...*a torchlight procession from the station.*

tore /tɔː/
Tore is the past tense of **tear**.

torment, torments, tormenting, tormented;
pronounced /tɔːment/ when it is a noun and /tɔːˈment/ when it is a verb.
1 NU **Torment** is extreme pain or unhappiness. ...*the scream of a man dying in torment.*
2 NC A **torment** is something that causes extreme pain or unhappiness. *The boredom became a worse torment than the cold.*
3 VO To **torment** someone means to make them very unhappy. *She is forever tormenting and teasing Tom... He was tormented by his desire to see her again.*

tormentor /tɔːmentə/ **tormentors**
NC Someone's **tormentor** is a person who deliberately causes them pain or unhappiness. *He could not pardon their tormentors.*

torn /tɔːn/
Torn is the past participle of **tear**.

tornado /tɔːneɪdəʊ/ **tornadoes** or **tornados**
NC A **tornado** is a violent storm with strong circular winds. *The tornado that devastated the small central Kansas town of Andover cut a path of destruction nearly 40 miles long.*

Toronto /tərɒntəʊ/
Toronto is the largest city in Canada. Population: 3,427,000 (1986).

torpedo /tɔːpiːdəʊ/ **torpedoes, torpedoing, torpedoed**
1 NC A **torpedo** is a bomb shaped like a tube that travels underwater. *They say that torpedoes driven by steam turbines are faster, quieter and can operate at greater depth.*
2 VO If a ship is **torpedoed**, it is hit, and usually sunk, by a torpedo. *It carried on taking commercial passengers across the Atlantic, but in 1915 was torpedoed by a German submarine and sank.*
3 VO To **torpedo** something such as a negotiating process means to do something to stop it from being successful; an informal use. *Today's statement would seem to torpedo any possibility of progress being made on this next round of talks.*

torpid /tɔːpɪd/
ADJ If you are **torpid**, you are mentally or physically inactive, especially because you are feeling lazy or sleepy; a formal word.

torpor /tɔːpə/
NU **Torpor** is the state of being torpid; a formal word. *He was sunk in a dismal torpor.*

torque /tɔːk/
NU **Torque** is a force that causes something to spin around a central point such as an axle; a technical term. *What is the magnitude of the torque required?*

torrent /tɒrənt/ **torrents**
1 NC When a lot of water is falling or flowing very rapidly, you can say that it is moving in **torrents**. *The rain suddenly burst upon us in torrents.*
2 NC+SUPP A **torrent** of speech is a lot of it directed continuously at someone. *He was answered with a torrent of oaths.*

torrential /tərenʃl/
ADJ **Torrential** rain pours down very rapidly in great quantities. *Torrential rains triggered landslides and flooded more than 23,000 homes... Barefoot women and children toiled uphill through the mud and through torrential sleet and hail.*

torrid /tɒrɪd/; a literary word.
1 ADJ **Torrid** weather is very hot and dry in an unpleasant way. *She was sitting on the rocks in the torrid sun.*
2 ADJ A **torrid** love affair is one in which people feel very strong emotions. *Alma married the architect and then began an equally torrid affair with a writer whom she also eventually married.*

Tórshavn /taʊʃaʊn, tɔːʃaʊn/
Tórshavn is the capital of the Faroe Islands and its largest town. It is on Streymoy, the largest island of the Faroes. Population: 16,000 (1989).

torso /tɔːsəʊ/ **torsos**
NC Your **torso** is the main part of your body, excluding your head, arms, and legs; a formal word. *The poster shows a woman's naked torso.*

tort /tɔːt/ **torts**
NCorNU A **tort** is something that you do or fail to do which harms someone else and for which you can be sued for damages; a legal term. *It was either a breach of contract or a tort... The second defendant was liable in tort to the plaintiff.*

tortilla /tɔːtiːə/ **tortillas**
NC A **tortilla** is a Mexican pancake made from corn and eggs. *He cooks his breakfast of rice and tortillas over an open campfire.*

tortoise /tɔːtəs/ **tortoises**
NC A **tortoise** is an animal with a shell into which it can pull its head and legs for protection. Tortoises move very slowly. *The lumbering tortoises can perish within a day if they have no bushes to protect them from the glare of the sun... Ministers have so far acted on this issue with the speed of a hibernating tortoise.*

tortoiseshell /tɔːtəsʃel/
NU **Tortoiseshell** is the hard brown and yellow shell from a sea turtle. It is often polished and used to make jewellery and ornaments.

tortuous /tɔːtʃʊəs/; a formal word.
1 ADJ A **tortuous** road or route is full of bends and twists. *He twice broke the qualifying lap record as he averaged over 146 kilometres an hour round the tortuous street circuit.*
2 ADJ A **tortuous** process or piece of writing is long and complicated. *There would inevitably be tortuous*

and difficult negotiations once the guns had stopped firing.

torture /tɔːtʃə/ **tortures, torturing, tortured**
1 VO To **torture** someone means to deliberately cause them great pain in order to punish them or get information from them. *Many of those executed had been tortured while in detention... The police tried to torture them into confessing that they'd taken part in anti-government activities.*
2 NUorNC **Torture** is the practice of torturing people. *...the constant threat of death and torture... The list of alleged torture victims includes a 13-year-old boy, whose cousins were accused of supporting the guerrillas... Floggings and tortures were carried out almost daily.*
3 VO If one person **tortures** another, they cause them to suffer mentally. *Why do we have to keep on torturing ourselves by talking about it?*

torturer /tɔːtʃərə/ **torturers**
NC A **torturer** is someone who tortures people. *She knelt in despair and begged her torturers to stop... Some of the worst interrogators and torturers are still alive.*

Tory /tɔːri/ **Tories**
NC A **Tory** is a member or supporter of the Conservative Party in Britain; an informal word. *The Tories were restored to power. ...the Tory MP for Hornchurch.*

toss /tɒs/ **tosses, tossing, tossed**
1 VO If you **toss** something somewhere, you throw it there lightly and carelessly. *He took the bag and tossed it into some nearby bushes.*
2 VOorV If you **toss** a coin, you decide something by throwing the coin into the air and guessing which side will be facing upwards after it falls. *We'll toss a coin to see who does the washing-up... They used the penny to toss for the first round of drinks.* ▸ Also NC *Business deals were clinched by the toss of a coin.*
3 VO If you **toss** your head, you move it suddenly backwards. *'No,' she said, tossing her head in disgust.* ▸ Also NC *She gave a toss of her head.*
4 V-ERG If something or someone **tosses** or if they are **tossed**, they move repeatedly from side to side. *I tossed and turned all night... Ships were tossed at sea.*
toss up PHRASAL VERB If you **toss up**, you decide about something by throwing a coin into the air and guessing which side of the coin will be on top when it falls. *We tossed up to decide who should pay the bill.*

toss-up
N SING If you refer to a situation as a **toss-up**, you mean that either of two results seems equally likely. *It was a toss-up who would get there first.*

tot /tɒt/ **tots, totting, totted**
1 NC A **tot** is a very young child; an informal use. *...tiny tots.*
2 NC A **tot** of whisky, rum, or brandy is a small amount of it in a glass. *...huddled in warm coats and fortified with a tot of brandy.*
tot up PHRASAL VERB If you **tot up** numbers, you add them together. *The machine totted up your score... I'll just tot up what you owe me.*

total /təʊtl/ **totals, totalling, totalled;** also spelt **totaling, totaled** in American English.
1 ADJ ATTRIB The **total** number or cost of something is the number or cost that you get when you add together all the parts of it. *...the total number of students on campus... The total cost of the project was £220 million.*
2 NC A **total** is the number that you get when you add several numbers together. *The factory employed a total of forty workers.*
3 If there are a number of things in **total**, there are that many of them altogether. *It amounted to 16.9 percent in total with extra cash for paramedics and local pay flexibility. ...a force containing in total over half a million men.*
4 VC If several numbers **total** a certain figure, that is the figure you get when all the numbers are added together. *Conoco's 1980 revenues totalled £18.3 billion... Yugoslavia has Europe's highest annual inflation rate and a foreign debt totalling $20,000,000,000.*

5 VO If you **total** a set of numbers or objects, you add them all together. *Votes cast for each candidate will be totalled to get a result.*
6 ADJ **Total** also means complete. *He called for a total ban on cigarette promotion... The review had been undertaken in total secrecy.* ◆ **totally**
SUBMOD or ADV *He became almost totally blind... I totally disagree.*
7 ADJ ATTRIB You also use **total** to say that you are referring to everything that is included in a situation. *The total effect is intensely joyful... A total policy is being devised for the care of all.*
8 grand total: see grand.

totalitarian /taʊtælɪteəriən/
ADJ A **totalitarian** political system is one in which one political party controls everything and does not allow any other parties to exist. *...the collapse of Eastern Europe's totalitarian regimes.*

totalitarianism /taʊtælɪteəriənɪzəm/
NU **Totalitarianism** is the ideas, principles, and practices of totalitarian political systems. *We are all opposed to apartheid and totalitarianism.*

totality /taʊtælətɪ/
NU The **totality** of something is the whole of it; a formal word. *...the totality of life.*

tote /taʊt/ **totes, toting, toted**
1 N SING The **tote** is a system of betting money on horses at a racetrack, in which all the money bet on a race is divided among the people who have bet on the winning horses. *He always bets on the tote at the week-end.*
2 VO Someone who **totes** something, for example a gun, carries it with them wherever they go; an old-fashioned use. *In some small towns they tote guns.*

tote bag, tote bags
NC A **tote bag** is a kind of large, sturdy bag. *She put on her shoes and picked up her tote bag.*

totem /taʊtəm/ **totems**
NC A **totem** is an object that is regarded as a symbol by a particular group of people who treat it with great respect.

totem pole, totem poles
NC A **totem pole** is a long wooden pole with symbols and pictures carved and painted on it. Totem poles are made by some North American Indians and placed outside their homes. *As a young woodsman, Carter watched the Indians carve elaborate totem poles and dugout canoes.*

totter /tɒtə/ **totters, tottering, tottered**
V When someone **totters**, they walk in an unsteady way. *I tottered back to my bed.*

toucan /tuːkən/ **toucans**
NC A **toucan** is a South American bird that eats fruit. It has a large brightly-coloured beak.

touch /tʌtʃ/ **touches, touching, touched**
1 VO If you **touch** something, you gently put your fingers or hand on it. *The metal is so hot I can't touch it... Put it down! Don't touch anything... The user selects the region, county and city of their choice by touching the relevant key on the keyboard.* ▶ Also
N SING *He remembered the touch of her hand.*
2 V-RECIP When two things **touch**, their surfaces are in contact with one another. *Make sure that the wires are not touching... My feet touched the ground.*
3 NU Your sense of **touch** is your ability to tell what something is like when you feel it with your hands. *I had to rely on my sense of smell and touch.*
4 V-PASS If you **are touched** by something, it makes you feel sad, sympathetic, or grateful. *I was touched by his thoughtfulness... The soldiers were touched and proud that the Prince had come to see them.*
5 NC+SUPP A **touch** is a detail which is added to something to improve it. *The final touches were put to their report... The grandiose special effects are remarkable, with lots of memorable touches... Mr de Klerk has been putting the finishing touches to a speech he will make in parliament this afternoon.*
6 N SING+SUPP A **touch** of something is a very small amount of it. *There was a touch of frost this morning... Richard's voice suddenly became important and even a touch official.*
● **Touch** is used in these phrases. ● If you get **in touch**

with someone, you contact them by writing to them, telephoning them, or visiting them. *He appealed to anyone who had seen people behaving suspiciously in the shopping area over the weekend to get in touch with the police.* ● If you keep **in touch** with someone, or if you are **in touch** with them, you write to, phone, or visit each other regularly. If you **lose touch** with them, you gradually stop writing to, phoning, or visiting each other. *Please drop in when you can. I'd like to keep in touch... The police are in close touch with local community leaders... Rita is trying to find her brother, who has lost touch with the family.* ● If you are **in touch** with a subject or situation, or if you keep **in touch** with it, you know the latest information about it. If you are **out of touch** with it, your knowledge of it is out of date. *Scientists must also be taught foreign languages so as to stay in touch with scientific developments... He kept in touch with African politics during this period... I'm a bit out of touch with new developments.* ● If you say that something is **touch and go**, you mean that you are uncertain whether it will happen or succeed. *For the next few weeks it will be touch and go whether this crisis is going to end with more shooting and more fighting or whether it can be solved peacefully.*

touch down PHRASAL VERB When an aircraft **touches down**, it lands. *Finally, the plane touched down at Larnaca airport.*

touch on or **touch upon** PHRASAL VERB If you **touch on** or **touch upon** something, you mention it briefly. *...the topic which I touched on at the beginning of this chapter... The question of Japanese aid to China was touched upon during the four-day visit.*

touchdown /tʌtʃdaʊn/ **touchdowns**
1 NC In rugby or in American football, a **touchdown** is when a team scores points by taking the ball over the opposition's goal line. *Wigan's young winger kicked ahead and dived for the touchdown.*
2 NU or NC **Touchdown** or a **touchdown** is the landing of an aircraft. *Failure of any mechanical system to function after touchdown could destroy human lives... Survivors of the crash said that they thought the actual touchdown was perfectly normal, and it was only after landing that they experienced jolts and explosions.*

touché /tuːʃeɪ, tuːʃeɪ/
You say **touché** when you want to admit that the other person in an argument has won a point, usually with a short and witty remark; an old-fashioned expression.

touched /tʌtʃt/
ADJ PRED If you say that someone is **touched**, you mean that they are slightly mad; an old-fashioned, informal word. *We thought she was a bit touched.*

touching /tʌtʃɪŋ/
ADJ Something that is **touching** makes you feel sad or sympathetic. *...their touching faith in the power of education.*

touch paper
N SING The **touch paper** on a firework is a small piece of dark blue paper on one end of it which you light in order to start it. *...light the blue touch paper on the fireworks.*

touchstone /tʌtʃstəʊn/ **touchstones**
NC If one thing is a **touchstone** of another, you use it to judge the second thing, or to decide what you think about it. *Many now see Afghanistan as a touchstone of Mr Gorbachev's intentions... For more than two decades the success of arms control has been seen as the touchstone of the superpower relationship.*

touch-type, touch-types, touch-typing, touch-typed
V When someone **touch-types**, they type without looking at the keyboard.

touchy /tʌtʃɪ/ **touchier, touchiest**
1 ADJ **Touchy** people are easily upset or irritated. *Thomas was far too touchy and jealous of his reputation... Don't be so touchy... Most young parents are touchy about criticism.*
2 ADJ A **touchy** subject is one that needs to be dealt with carefully, because it might upset or offend people. *Extradition is becoming an increasingly touchy subject. ...the touchy question of private ownership of land.*

tough /tʌf/ **tougher, toughest**
  1 ADJ A **tough** person has a strong character and is able to tolerate a lot of pain, hardship, or difficulties. *...a tough reporter... The Americans found him a tough, no-nonsense negotiator.* ♦ **toughness** NU *...a man with an image of toughness and a reputation for discipline and strict professionalism.*
  2 ADJ **Tough** policies or actions are strict and firm. *We are convinced that her tough economic policies will succeed... Domestic pressure is growing for the government to take a tougher line in the drugs war.*
  3 ADJ A **tough** way of life is full of hardship. *It was about life within a community when things were very, very tough and hard.*
  4 ADJ A **tough** task or problem is difficult to solve. *The toughest problem is theft... It was to be one of the toughest by-elections for a long time.*
  5 ADJ A **tough** substance is strong, and difficult to break or cut. *Some plastics are as tough as metal.*
  6 ADJ **Tough** meat is difficult to cut and chew. *The steak was smelly and a little tough.*

toughen /tʌfn/ **toughens, toughening, toughened**
  1 VO To **toughen** something means to make it stronger so that it will not break easily. *...a new technique that toughens metal at only 100°c.* ♦ **toughened** ADJ *...the use of toughened glass in windscreens.*
  2 VO If an experience **toughens** you, it makes you stronger and more independent in character. *She had been toughened by Guy's death.*

toupee /tuːpeɪ/ **toupees**
  NC A **toupee** is a small wig worn by a man to cover a bald patch on his head. *Federal prisons don't allow toupees because they can be used for disguises or to hide drugs.*

tour /tʊə, tɔː/ **tours, touring, toured**
  1 NC A **tour** is an organized trip that someone such as a politician or musician goes on to several different places, stopping, for example, in order to meet people, or to perform. *Mr Nelson Mandela, who yesterday completed a six-week tour of Europe and North America, is now in Uganda... The government has criticised a proposed rugby tour of South Africa by a world team.* ● When people are travelling on a tour, you can say that they are **on tour**. *The dancers were perpetually on tour, with no time or money to create new works.*
  2 V or VO When someone such as a musician or a politician **tours**, they go on a tour, for example in order to perform or to meet people. *The band are currently touring with Fleetwood Mac... An England side is to tour New Zealand next February... He also plans to tour one-of the emirate's burning oil fields.*
  3 NC A **tour** is also a short trip round a city or an interesting building. *...guided tours... They've been treated to non-stop film shows and tours of the town's Laurel and Hardy museum.* ● See also **conducted tour**.
  4 VO If you **tour** an area, you go round it visiting places. *He spent his vacation touring the highlands of Scotland.*
  5 NC A **tour** is also a holiday during which you visit several different places that interest you. *I went on a tour of the North of Scotland during my vacation.*

tour de force /tʊə də fɔːs/
  N SING A **tour de force** is a brilliant and skilful action or theatrical performance. *President Mubarak's May Day speech was something of a tour de force: informal, vehement, laced with humorous asides.*

Touré, Amadou Toumani /æmədu: tuːmæni tʊəreɪ/
  Lieutenant-Colonel Amadou Toumani Touré became interim President of Mali in 1991, following the overthrow of General Moussa Traoré. He was formerly commander of a paratroop unit, the Red Berets.

tourism /tʊərɪzəm, tɔːrɪzəm/
  NU **Tourism** consists of the activities of people visiting a place on holiday, and the providing of services for these people. *There are prospects, too, for tourism, with long beaches, clean sands and a tropical climate.*

tourist /tʊərɪst, tɔːrɪst/ **tourists**
  1 NC A **tourist** is a person who is visiting a place for pleasure and interest. *She showed a party of tourists round.*
  2 ADJ ATTRIB **Tourist** means relating to or connected

with tourism. *English pubs are still high among the country's tourist attractions... Kenya also has a very well developed tourist industry. ...the height of the tourist season.*

tournament /tɔːnəmənt/ **tournaments**
  NC A **tournament** is a sports competition in which the winners of each match play further matches, until just one person or team is left. *...a table tennis tournament... Boris Becker is through to the final of the Stockholm Open Tournament.*

tourniquet /tʊənɪkeɪ/ **tourniquets**
  NC A **tourniquet** is a strip of cloth that you tie tightly round an injured arm or leg in order to stop it bleeding. *He put a tourniquet on Mrs. Babcock's upper arm.*

tour operator, tour operators
  NC A **tour operator** is a company which organizes holidays and sells them, usually through a travel agent. *All travellers are still being urged to contact their tour operators before setting off.*

tousled /taʊzld/
  ADJ **Tousled** hair is untidy. *Their teacher was an old man with tousled hair.*

tout /taʊt/ **touts, touting, touted**; an informal word.
  1 VO If someone **touts** something, they try to sell it. *...an exporter touting a range of plastic toys.*
  2 V+for If someone **touts** for business or custom, they try to obtain it. *...porters touting for loads at a railway station.*
  3 NC A **tout** is someone who sells things such as tickets unofficially, usually at prices which are higher than the official ones. *The ticket touts are out in force in the roads and side-streets around the All England Club approaching fans on their way to the tennis, offering to buy and sell.*

tow /təʊ/ **tows, towing, towed**
  1 VO If one vehicle **tows** another, the first vehicle pulls the second along behind it. *...a lorry towing a trailer of hay.* ▶ Also N SING *If you can't get a tow, you'll have to walk.*
  2 If you have someone **in tow**, they are with you because you are looking after them; an informal expression. *He arrived with his children in tow.*

towards /təwɔːdz/ or **toward**
  1 PREP If you move, look, or point **towards** something or someone, you move, look, or point in their direction. *He saw his mother running towards him.*
  2 PREP If people move **towards** a particular situation, that situation becomes likely to happen. *He has met fierce criticism of his intentions to move towards a market economy... There is a tendency towards inflation... They have failed to make any progress towards resolving the crisis.*
  3 PREP If you have a particular attitude **towards** something or someone, you feel like that about them. *Mr Hurd had expressed concern about Yemen's attitude towards sanctions... He felt very friendly towards them... A spokesman said the decision contradicted officially-stated US policy towards China.*
  4 PREP If you give money **towards** something, you give it to help pay for that thing. *They may give you something towards your housing costs.*
  5 PREP **Towards** the end of a period of time means just before its end. *I went to London towards the end of 1977.*
  6 PREP **Towards** a part of a place means near to that part. *He was sitting towards the back of the room.*

towel /taʊəl/ **towels**
  1 NC A **towel** is a piece of thick, soft cloth that you use to dry yourself with. *He gave each man a bar of soap and a towel.*
  2 If you **throw in the towel**, you stop trying to do something because you realize that you cannot succeed; an informal expression. *At this point, they threw in the towel.*

towelling /taʊəlɪŋ/
  NU **Towelling** is thick, soft cloth that is used especially for making towels. *...a bit of old towelling... She was dressed in a towelling bathrobe.*

tower /taʊə/ **towers, towering, towered**
  1 NC A **tower** is a tall, narrow building, or a tall part of a building such as a castle or church. *During the*

afternoon three television transmission towers were put out of action by Yugoslav Air Force jets... The famous tower is 55 metres tall and one of Italy's greatest tourist attractions. ● See also **control tower, ivory tower.**

2 V A Someone or something that **towers** over other people or things is a lot taller than they are; a literary use. *Jane stood up, towering over him.*

3 V A If someone **towers** over other people, they are far superior to them, or much more successful than them; a literary use. *Olivier had an unshakeable reputation as a classical actor who towered over everyone else.*

tower block, tower blocks
NC A **tower block** is a tall building divided into flats or offices. *They will demolish many of the high-rise tower blocks that are frequently associated with vandalism and deprivation.*

towering /taʊərɪŋ/
1 ADJ ATTRIB A **towering** building, tree, or mountain is very tall and impressive; a literary word. *Standing beneath the towering deserted edifice, I can see bricks missing from the veneer of the upper floors.*
2 ADJ ATTRIB A **towering** person or achievement is far better than others of the same kind. *There is no doubt that President Havel's towering moral presence has played a big part. ...a towering performance.*

town /taʊn/ **towns**
1 NC A **town** is a place with a lot of streets and buildings where people live and work. *He runs a health centre in the small town of Alice Springs in central Australia... The police have sealed off the town centre.*
2 NU People sometimes refer to the town they live in as **town**. *We packed our stuff and left town.*
3 See also **new town, shanty town, small-town.**

town crier, town criers
NC A **town crier** was a man who used to walk through the streets of a town shouting out news and official announcements.

town hall, town halls
NC The **town hall** in a town is a large building owned and used by the town council, often as its headquarters. *More than five hundred members of a rival party locked themselves in the town hall where the ceremony was due to take place.*

town house, town houses
1 NC A **town house** is a house which is tall and narrow and which is built in a town, usually in a row of similar houses. *It is one of the last 18th century town houses in the city suitable for private occupation.*
2 NC The **town house** of a wealthy person or member of the aristocracy is the house that they own in a town or city, rather than another house that they own in the country. *Here, till 1874, stood the town house of the Dukes of Northumberland.*

townie /taʊni/ **townies**
NC A **townie** is someone who lives in a town or city; an informal word, used showing disapproval.

town planning
NU **Town planning** is the planning and design of all the new buildings, roads, parks, and so on in a place, in order to make them attractive and convenient for the people who live there. *We held an architectural exhibition on town planning in our headquarters. ...the Town Planning Committee.*

townsfolk /taʊnzfəʊk/
N PL The **townsfolk** of a town or city are the people who live there; an old-fashioned word. *That's led to still other protests in Duncan, not only by students, but by parents and townsfolk.*

township /taʊnʃɪp/ **townships**
NC A **township** is a town in South Africa where only black people or coloured people live. *New fighting in South African townships has taken 26 more lives... The ANC demanded Pretoria take strong action to curb township violence.*

townspeople /taʊnzpiːpl/
N PL The **townspeople** of a town or city are the people who live there; an old-fashioned word. *The townspeople refused to buy anything from his shop.*

towpath /taʊpɑːθ/ **towpaths**
NC A **towpath** is a path along the side of a canal or river. *Would you like a little stroll along the towpath?*

towrope /taʊrəʊp/ **towropes**
NC A **towrope** is a strong rope used for towing vehicles.

toxic /tɒksɪk/
ADJ A **toxic** substance is poisonous; a technical term. *In the last five years, the use of toxic chemicals has been greatly curbed. ...the transfer of more than two thousand barrels of highly toxic waste from Belgium into West Germany.* ◆ **toxicity** /tɒksɪsəti/ NU *Are you concerned about the toxicity of some of these chemicals?*

toxicology /tɒksɪkɒlədʒi/
NU **Toxicology** is the study of poisons; a technical term. *Toxicology test results are expected tomorrow.* ◆ **toxicologist, toxicologists** NC *Known as the 'silent killer' to toxicologists, lead has been linked to physical and mental retardation in children.* ◆ **toxicological** /tɒksɪkəlɒdʒɪkl/ ADJ *...the toxicological experts and their learned textbooks.*

toxin /tɒksɪn/ **toxins**
1 NCorNU A **toxin** is a poisonous substance that is produced by bacteria and is very harmful to plants, people, or other living creatures. *...toxins from anthrax, cholera and diphtheria. ...the antibodies produced in response to cholera toxin.*
2 NCorNU A **toxin** is also any poisonous substance produced by animals or plants. *The poison was later identified as a powerful natural toxin called ricin. ... scorpion toxin... Tests showed increased levels of toxin from a species of naturally-occurring algae.*

toy /tɔɪ/ **toys, toying, toyed**
NC A **toy** is an object for children to play with. *...a move away from expensive, sophisticated toys to simple, traditional toys like train sets, box games and teddy bears. ...a toy car.*

toy with PHRASAL VERB 1 If you **toy with** an idea, you consider it casually, without making any decisions about it. *Dave and Valerie Burton are toying with the idea of catering for this tourist trade, setting up a hotel, a restaurant or even just a shop.* 2 If you **toy with** an object, you keep moving it slightly with your fingers while thinking about something. *He withdrew the key from his pocket where he had been toying with it.*

trace /treɪs/ **traces, tracing, traced**
1 V O If you **trace** something, you find it after looking for it. *They were trying to trace her missing husband.*
2 V O If you **trace** the development of something, you find out or describe how it developed. *...attempting to trace the evolution of man.*
3 V O If you **trace** a drawing or map, you copy it by covering it with a piece of transparent paper and drawing over the lines underneath. *It's quicker and easier to trace a map than to draw it yourself.*
4 NC A **trace** is a sign which shows that someone or something has been in a place. *No trace was found of either the bag or its contents... There was no trace of bitterness as she spoke warmly about her successor.* ● If someone disappears **without trace**, there is no sign of where they have gone. *The military regime which came to power in 1976 imprisoned thousands of people, many of whom disappeared without trace.*
5 NC A **trace** of something is a very small amount of it. *...traces of the paint... The first traces of the blue-green algae were found last month in Rutland Water.*

tracer /treɪsə/ **tracers**
N+NorNC **Tracer** bullets or **tracers** are bullets that can be seen in flight because they contain a substance that burns brightly. *The biggest danger is probably the falling tracer bullets fired from anti-aircraft guns... Tracer fire arched low over rooftops... The sky was illuminated with tracers and the streets were littered with the bodies of soldiers.*

trachea /trəkiːə/. The plural can be **tracheae** /trəkiːiː/ or **tracheas.**
NC Your **trachea** is your windpipe; a medical term.

tracing /treɪsɪŋ/ **tracings**
NC A **tracing** is a copy that has been made by covering a drawing or map with a piece of transparent

paper and drawing over the lines underneath. ...*a tracing of a Union Jack.*

tracing paper
NU **Tracing paper** is transparent paper that you use to make tracings.

track /træk/ **tracks, tracking, tracked**
1 NC A **track** is a narrow road or path. ...*a dusty mountain track.*
2 NC A **track** is also a piece of ground which athletes, cyclists, cars, or horses race around. *The highlight of the fifth day of competition in the Asian Games was a world record on the cycle track... It was the second day in a row he'd ridden three winners at the track.*
3 NC A railway **track** consists of the rails that a train travels along. *When all the carriages have been taken away, engineers will begin to repair the track.*
4 N PL **Tracks** are footprints or other marks left on the ground by a person or animal. *The fox didn't leave any tracks.*
5 VO If you **track** animals or people, you follow their footprints or other signs that they have left behind them. *All day I'd follow him, tracking him in the snow until finally he got tired.*
6 VO To **track** someone or something also means to follow their movements by means of a special device. *They worked closely with American Navy ships to track vessels heading towards the Gulf... Such devices are even able to track shoals of fish.*
7 NC A **track** on a record or tape is one of the songs or pieces of music on it. *We leave you with a track from that album, 'Money for Nothing'... This is the third track to be released as a single.* ● See also **title track.**
● **Track** is used in these phrases. ● A place that is **off the beaten track** is in a quiet and isolated area. *The village where Elaine lives is a bit off the beaten track.*
● If you **keep track of** things or people, you pay attention to them so that you know where they are or what is happening. If you **lose track of** them, you no longer know where they are or what is happening. *We would never be able to keep track of the luggage on such a long journey... The authorities have been unable to keep track of births among the growing number of migrants to the cities... Drivers can lose track of where they are... Gwyneth had lost all track of time.* ● If you are **on the right track**, you are thinking in a way that is likely to give you the right answer to a question or problem. If you are **on the wrong track**, you are thinking in a way that is likely to give you the wrong answer. *I suspect that the gentleman who suggested the spark plug wires may have been on the right track... Maybe it will show that we are on the wrong track and the theorists have to go back to the drawing board and start again.* ● If someone or something is **on track**, they are acting or happening in a way that is likely to bring success. *He said the ANC will do everything in its power to ensure the peace process remained on track... I think we're on track for some sort of an upturn... Mr Major said the step would put the country on track to get inflation down and keep it low.*

track down PHRASAL VERB If you **track down** someone or something, you find them by searching for them. *A worldwide hunt has been launched to track down the bombers... They lost all hope of tracking down the submarine.*

tracker /trækə/ **trackers**
NC A **tracker** is someone who is skilled at finding people or animals by following their footprints or other signs that they have left behind. *Peter was a brilliant tracker.*

tracker dog, tracker dogs
NC **Tracker dogs** are dogs that have been specially trained to search for people who are missing or who have escaped. *Rescue teams using tracker dogs found one survivor, a women who was seriously injured... Police are searching the surrounding countryside using a helicopter and tracker dogs.*

tracking /trækɪŋ/
NU **Tracking** is the act or system of teaching pupils in different groups according to their ability; used in American English. *A 1988 report indicates 63 per cent*

of all teachers use tracking, even though there's evidence that the stigmas it creates are sometimes irreversible.

tracking station, tracking stations
NC A **tracking station** is a building from which the movement of things like spacecraft and satellites can be followed by means of radar or radio. ...*a guided missile tracking station.*

track meet, track meets
NC A **track meet** is an athletics competition; used in American English. *At San Francisco's all-city track meet last week, high school athletes competed in the biggest and perhaps the last event of this kind.*

track record, track records
NC+SUPP The **track record** of a person or company consists of their past achievements or failures. *Hanson has a proven track record in efficient management... Bukharin's track record as a political leader was not one of unadulterated democracy and openness.*

tracksuit /træksuːt/ **tracksuits**
NC A **tracksuit** is a loose, warm suit consisting of trousers and a top, designed to be worn when exercising. *I do go out to see clients so I have one or two smart outfits, otherwise I'm in a tracksuit and trainers.*

tract /trækt/ **tracts**
1 NC A **tract** of land is a large area of it; a formal use. ...*immense tracts of impenetrable jungle.*
2 NC A **tract** is a short article making a religious, moral, or political point. *I'm not out to write a feminist tract.*
3 NC A **tract** is also a system of organs or tubes in a person's or animal's body that has a particular function. *It induces complex injuries of the skin, of the gastro-intestinal tract and of the liver. ...the upper respiratory tract.*

tractable /træktəbl/
ADJ A **tractable** person or problem is easily controlled or dealt with; a formal word. *Be good and tractable and you will be looked after... Airfields presented a less tractable problem.*

traction /trækʃn/
1 NU **Traction** is a form of medical treatment given to an injured limb which involves pulling it gently for long periods of time using a system of weights and pulleys. *His leg is in traction.*
2 NU **Traction** is also a particular form of power that makes a vehicle move; a technical term. ...*the increased use of electric traction.*
3 NU A vehicle's **traction** is the grip that its wheels have on the ground; a technical term. *Four wheel drive gives greatly improved traction in rain, snow and ice.*

traction engine, traction engines
NC A **traction engine** is a large vehicle that was used in the past for pulling heavy loads.

tractor /træktə/ **tractors**
NC A **tractor** is a farm vehicle with large rear wheels that is used for pulling machinery. *Kular makes his living driving a tractor in a farm collective in Tuva.*

trade /treɪd/ **trades, trading, traded**
1 NU **Trade** is the activity of buying, selling, or exchanging goods or services. *France is heavily dependent on foreign trade. ...the lucrative trade in tea and porcelain... Czechoslovakia has formally signed a new industrial trade agreement with the European Community. ...an agreement on removing barriers to world trade.*
2 V When people, firms, or countries **trade**, they buy, sell, or exchange goods or services. *They specialized in trading with China.* ◆ **trading** NU *In the first fifteen minutes of trading, share prices recovered most of yesterday's sharp losses. ...the fight over Sunday trading.*
3 NC Someone's **trade** is the kind of work that they do, especially when it requires special training in practical skills. ...*the trade of blacksmith... His trade was welding.*

trade in PHRASAL VERB If you **trade in** something you own, such as your car or TV set, you give it to a dealer when you buy a new one so that you get a reduction on the price. *You might trade the car in for a smaller one.*

trade off PHRASAL VERB If you **trade** one thing **off** against another, you make a compromise between them, or you exchange all or part of one thing for another. *Sustainability has to be traded off against increased productivity... They have hinted they will trade off western hostages.*

trade on PHRASAL VERB If you **trade on** something such as another person's weakness, you make use of it to your own advantage; used showing disapproval. *...people who trade on the hopes of the desperately ill.*

trade fair, trade fairs
NC A **trade fair** is an exhibition where manufacturers show products that they want to sell to other people in industry, rather than to members of the public. *...visitors returning from the Canton Trade Fair.*

trade figures
N PL A country's **trade figures** are the value of its exports and imports over a period and the difference between them. *The latest trade figures showed a sharp worsening in the deficit.*

trade-in, trade-ins
NC A **trade-in** is a business deal in which someone buys something like a new car or washing machine at a reduced price by giving their old car or washing machine as well as money in payment. *What is the car's trade-in value?*

trademark /ˈtreɪdmɑːk/ **trademarks**
1 NC A **trademark** is a name or symbol that a company uses on its products and that cannot legally be used by another company. *The Chancellor said he would press for a common law on patents and trademarks.*
2 NC+POSS A person's or thing's **trademark** is a feature which is considered to be typical of them. *One trademark of Pinter's plays are the long pauses that exist within and between speeches... His trademark was the leather rucksack with which he travelled.*

trade name, trade names
NC A **trade name** is the name which manufacturers give to a product or to a range of products. *Some acrylic trade names are Courtelle, Acrilan, and Dralon... This drug is being marketed under one trade name only.*

trade-off, trade-offs
NC A **trade-off** between two opposing things is a compromise or balance between them. *He has to manage the trade-off between military security and long term economic prosperity.*

trader /ˈtreɪdə/ **traders**
1 NC A **trader** is a person who buys goods in one country and sells them in another. *Oil traders believe the cuts will not significantly reduce the world surplus... Gold traders in Zurich have noticed an increase in Soviet gold in the market.*
2 NC A **trader** is also a person who buys and sells stocks and shares. *Michael Milken was one of the wealthiest traders on Wall Street... London traders weren't impressed by John Major's plans to promote the ECU.*
3 NC A **trader** is also a shopkeeper or other person who sells goods or services. *Wholesalers and motor traders are both suffering sharp losses in business compared with a year ago... Shopkeepers began to roll down their shutters and market traders packed up their stalls.*

trade school, trade schools
NCorNU In the United States, a **trade school** is a secondary school where students are taught a trade. *Lutzow is the Principal of a trade school on Chicago's south side. ...students who have received government loans to attend trade school.*

trade secret, trade secrets
NC A **trade secret** is information that is known and used by only one firm, for example about the substances required to produce something or about a particular method of producing it. *Kate Wilkinson has been investigating why famous and not-so-famous chefs are busy revealing their trade secrets.*

tradesman /ˈtreɪdzmən/ **tradesmen** /ˈtreɪdzmən/
NC A **tradesman** is a person who sells goods or

services, especially one who owns and runs a shop. *He accused local tradesmen of raising prices for essential goods.*

tradespeople /ˈtreɪdzpiːpl/
N PL **Tradespeople** are people who sell goods or services as their job. *Several hundred tradespeople—plumbers, carpenters and electricians—are providing free help.*

trades union. See trade union.
Trades Union Congress. See TUC.
trade union, trade unions. The form **trades union** is also used.
NC A **trade union** is an organization of workers that tries to improve the pay and working conditions of its members. *Although there are talks going on with the trade unions at the moment, there is little room for compromise... Trade Union leaders representing workers in the public sector have said they will oppose attempts to limit pay rises to seven per cent. ...the great powers held by the Trades Unions.*

trade unionism
NU **Trade unionism** is the system, practices, and ideology of trade unions. *Mr Scargill described the result as a stunning victory for trade unionism.*

trade unionist, trade unionists
NC A **trade unionist** is an active member of a trade union. *He alleges that politicians, religious leaders, trade unionists and academics are kept under regular surveillance.*

trading estate, trading estates
NC A **trading estate** is the same as an **industrial estate**.

tradition /trəˈdɪʃn/ **traditions**
NCorNU A **tradition** is a custom or belief that has existed for a long time. *...Britain's long tradition of political independence... We must have respect for tradition.*

traditional /trəˈdɪʃənl/
1 ADJ **Traditional** customs or beliefs have existed for a long time without changing. *The bride is dressed in traditional costume... The changing role of women flies in the face of traditional values... Their activities have disrupted the traditional way of life of the Yanomami Indians.* ◆ **traditionally** ADV *The dry season was traditionally a time of inactivity.*
2 ADJ A **traditional** organization or person prefers older methods and ideas to modern ones. *We'll send you to a traditional school.*

traditionalism /trəˈdɪʃənəlɪzəm/
NU **Traditionalism** is behaviour and ideas that support old customs and beliefs rather than modern ones. *The Royal Shakespeare Company is a bastion of traditionalism. ...the ideals of architectural traditionalism and human scale that the Prince of Wales has sought to promote.*

traditionalist /trəˈdɪʃənəlɪst/ **traditionalists**
1 NC A **traditionalist** is a person who supports the established customs and beliefs of their society or group, and does not want to change them. *The fact that many mothers now work need not threaten the family, as so many traditionalists fear.*
2 ADJ A **traditionalist** idea or argument supports the established customs and beliefs of a society. *This argument is too traditionalist and too boring to go into again.*

traduce /trəˈdjuːs/ **traduces, traducing, traduced**
VO If you **traduce** someone, you deliberately say unpleasant things about them that are untrue; a formal word.

traffic /ˈtræfɪk/ **traffics, trafficking, trafficked**
1 NU **Traffic** refers to all the vehicles that are moving along a road. *A police spokesman said that traffic was at a standstill for almost 19 miles. ...rush-hour traffic.*
2 NU **Traffic** also refers to all the ships or aircraft that are moving through a place. *The port cannot cope with the volume of traffic. ...air traffic control.*
3 NU+SUPP **Traffic** in something such as drugs is an illegal trade in them. *...illicit cocaine traffic. ...illegal traffic in protected animals.*
4 V+in Someone who **traffics** in drugs or other goods buys and sells them illegally. *He has denied trafficking in arms or drugs.*

traffic circle, traffic circles

NC A **traffic circle** is a roundabout in the road; used in American English.

traffic jam, traffic jams

NC A **traffic jam** is a long line of vehicles that cannot move or that can only move very slowly, because the road is blocked. *The stoppage caused huge traffic jams as commuters drove to work... The traditional Bank Holiday traffic jams on the road have been even worse than usual.*

trafficker /trǽfɪkə/ **traffickers**

NC A **trafficker** in particular goods, for example drugs, is a person who buys or sells them illegally. *A court in Los Angeles has convicted a Honduran drug trafficker of racketeering and conspiracy... The news agency says traffickers are using China as a transit route for narcotics produced in the Golden Triangle.*

traffic light, traffic lights

NC **Traffic lights** are the coloured lights at road junctions which control the flow of traffic. *...a line of vehicles waiting for the traffic lights to change.*

traffic warden, traffic wardens

NC A **traffic warden** is a person whose job is to make sure that cars are parked legally. *Extra traffic wardens have been taken on by the city authorities and the number of parking fines issued each day has tripled.*

tragedy /trǽdʒədi/ **tragedies**

1 NCorNU A **tragedy** is an extremely sad event or situation. *The change of flight plans was the principal cause of the tragedy... The Soviet Prime Minister described the disaster as a tragedy for the whole of the Soviet Union... When tensions are so high, tragedy is inevitable.*

2 NUorNC **Tragedy** is a type of literature, especially drama, that is serious and sad and often ends with the death of the main character. *She acted brilliantly in Greek tragedy. ...an Elizabethan tragedy... It is a tragedy, but also a farce.*

tragic /trǽdʒɪk/

1 ADJ Something that is **tragic** is very sad. *...the tragic death of his elder brother Michael... The tragic consequences of some recent air crashes show people the risk involved in air travel.* ♦ **tragically** ADV *He was tragically killed in a car crash.*

2 ADJ ATTRIB **Tragic** is also used to describe tragedy as a form of literature. *...Scott Fitzgerald's tragic novel 'Tender is the Night'... He makes his Faust a totally tragic figure.*

tragicomedy /trǽdʒɪkɒmədi/ **tragicomedies**

NC A **tragicomedy** is a play or other written work that is both sad and amusing.

tragicomic /trædʒɪkɒmɪk/

ADJ Something that is **tragicomic** is both sad and amusing at the same time.

trail /treɪl/ **trails, trailing, trailed**

1 NC A **trail** is a rough path across open country or through forests. *They trudged along the seemingly endless trail.*

2 NC A **trail** is also a series of marks or other signs left by someone or something as they move along. *Eventually we lost the trail... She didn't want him to leave a trail of wet footprints all over the house.*

3 If you are **on the trail of** a person or animal, you are trying to find them. *Security forces were combing the island on the trail of a group of mercenaries.*

4 V-ERG If you **trail** something or if it **trails**, it moves along, hanging down loosely. *She trails the fingers of her right hand through the water... She went out with her dress trailing behind her on the floor.*

5 VA If someone **trails** along, they move slowly, without any energy or enthusiasm, often following someone else. *I used to trail around after him like a small child.*

6 VorVO In a contest or competition, if a person or team is **trailing**, they have a lower score than their rivals. *Real Madrid were trailing 3-nil well into the second half... By the interval, they were trailing by 240 runs... Labour was trailing the Conservatives by more than five per cent only a month ago.*

7 NC You can refer to the places that are visited by someone who is seeking election to public office as

their campaign **trail**. *Bush argued his case on the campaign trail in stops in Akron and Chicago... Six months after multi-party elections in Hungary politicians are once again on the campaign trail.*

trail away or **trail off** PHRASAL VERB If a speaker's voice **trails away** or **trails off**, it gradually becomes quieter or more hesitant until it stops completely. *'I have an appointment that's very...' His voice trailed off unconvincingly.*

trailer /treɪlə/ **trailers**

1 NC A **trailer** is a vehicle which is pulled by a car or van and which is used for transporting large or heavy items. *It was packed up in quite a small trailer behind the van.*

2 NC A **trailer** is also the long rear section of an articulated lorry, in which the goods are carried. *Another twelve people were injured when the trailer broke away from a lorry near the town of Kalisz.*

3 NC A **trailer** is also a long vehicle which people use as a home or office and which can be pulled behind a car; used in American English. *They camp out along the river or stay in duplex trailers just off Main Street. ...the residents of the trailer park.*

4 NC A **trailer** for a film or television programme is a set of short extracts which are shown or broadcast to advertise it. *The trailer was screened immediately before the main nightly news.*

train /treɪn/ **trains, training, trained**

1 NC A **train** is a number of carriages or trucks pulled by an engine along a railway line. *I caught a train to Oxford... We are going by train. ...the train journey to Leeds.*

2 VO If you **train** a person or animal to do something, you teach them how to do it. *The police are trained to keep calm... The company trained 22 scientists in West Germany.* ♦ **trained** ADJ *...a trained nurse.*

3 V If you **train** as something, you learn how to do a particular job. *She started to train as a nurse.*

4 V-ERG If you **train** for an activity such as a race or if someone **trains** you, you prepare for it by doing exercises and sometimes eating special foods. *He was training for the marathon... China trained a team especially for the Games... He once trained a bodybuilder who went on to win the US championship.*

5 VOA If you **train** something such as a gun or a camera on someone, you aim it at them and keep it pointed towards them. *It includes British aircraft of the period and one of the guns that were trained on their German opponents.*

6 See also **training**.

● **Train** is used in these phrases. ● A **train of thought** is a connected series of thoughts. *I felt annoyed with her for interrupting my train of thought.* ● If something is **in train**, it is happening or in the process of being done. *Until an effective peace process involving the PLO is in train, he cannot stop the uprising in the occupied territories... He said a Labour government would immediately set in train measures to control carbon dioxide emissions.*

trainee /treɪniː/ **trainees**

NC A **trainee** is someone who is being taught how to do a job. *The trainees are shown around each of the departments. ...a trainee chef.*

trainer /treɪnə/ **trainers**

1 NC A **trainer** is a person who trains people or animals in a particular skill or for a particular purpose. *The trainers have a programme to teach them vocational skills... He is a former trainer of the Davis Cup team... National Hunt jockey Peter Scudamore and trainer Martin Pipe have won another race.*

2 NC **Trainers** are special shoes that are worn for running. *Many young people walk around in their trainers with the laces untied... The trainers that are in fashion are Nike, Reebok and LA Gear.*

training /treɪnɪŋ/

1 NU **Training** for a particular job involves learning the skills needed for that job. *...giving people training in computer programming. ...employment training.*

2 NU **Training** also involves doing exercises and eating special foods in preparation for an activity such as a race. *Budd says she is now in good condition and will*

resume training for the trials. ● If you are in training, you are preparing yourself for a sporting event of some kind, by doing a lot of exercise and eating a special diet. *He had been in training with the White Sox ever since his last game in 1980.*

traipse /treɪps/ **traipses, traipsing, traipsed**
v A If you **traipse** around somewhere, you walk slowly and wearily; an informal word. *I've been traipsing round the shops all day looking for Christmas presents.*

trait /treɪt, treɪ/ **traits**
NC+SUPP A **trait** is a characteristic or tendency that someone or something has. *Certain personality traits had made her unpopular.*

traitor /treɪtə/ **traitors**
NC A **traitor** is someone who betrays their country or the group which they belong to. *He was denounced as a traitor to France.*

trajectory /trədʒɛktəᵊri/ **trajectories**
NC+SUPP The **trajectory** of an object moving through air is the curving path that it follows after it has been hit or thrown upwards and as it moves forwards and down again towards the ground; a formal word. *It had come down, as footballs do, and under the trajectory of its descent there happened to be Henry.*

tram /træm/ **trams**
NC A **tram** is an electric vehicle which travels on rails along a street. *...a strike by bus and tram drivers.*

tramline /træmlaɪn/ **tramlines**
1 NC A **tramline** is one of the rails laid in the surface of a road that trams travel along.
2 NC In tennis or badminton, **tramlines** are the space between the two parallel lines on each side of the court. These lines mark an area which is only used when you are playing doubles.

tramp /træmp/ **tramps, tramping, tramped**
1 NC A **tramp** is a person with no permanent home or job who gets money by doing occasional work or by begging. *...tramps in rags queuing for food at soup kitchens.*
2 V or VO If you **tramp** somewhere, you walk there with slow, heavy footsteps. *She tramped slowly up the beach. ...tramping the streets all day as a postman.*

trample /træmpl/ **tramples, trampling, trampled**
1 V or VO If you **trample** on something, you tread heavily on it and damage it. *...trampling through the undergrowth... They had trampled his lovely rose garden.*
2 V-PASS If someone is **trampled** underfoot, they are injured or killed by being trodden on by other people or by animals. *The crowd surged forward and many were crushed or trampled underfoot... The protester, a woman, was apparently trampled to death in a stampede of demonstrators trying to escape a volley of tear gas fired by riot police.*
3 V+on If you **trample** on someone or on their rights or feelings, you behave towards them in a cruel or unjust way. *Nervousness does not excuse you to the point of trampling on the feelings of others.*

trampoline /træmpəliːn/ **trampolines**
NC A **trampoline** is a piece of apparatus on which you do acrobatic jumps. It consists of a large piece of strong cloth held by springs in a frame. *...bouncing on a trampoline.*

trance /trɑːns/ **trances**
NC A **trance** is a mental state in which you appear to be asleep, but you can see and hear things and respond to commands. *She used to go into a trance and talk to the spirits.*

tranquil /træŋkwɪl/
ADJ **Tranquil** means calm and peaceful; a literary word. *It's a tranquil oasis of some charm in the centre of an otherwise drab city.* ◆ **tranquillity** /træŋkwɪləti/ NU *...a time of political tranquillity.*

tranquillize /træŋkwəlaɪz/ **tranquillizes, tranquillizing, tranquillized**; also spelt **tranquillise** and, in American English, **tranquilize**.
VO To **tranquillize** a person or animal means to give them a drug so that they become calm, sleepy, or unconscious. *This powerful drug is used to tranquillize patients undergoing surgery.*

tranquillizer /træŋkwəlaɪzə/ **tranquillizers**; also spelt **tranquilliser** and, in American English, **tranquilizer**.
NC A **tranquillizer** is a drug that makes people feel calmer or less anxious. Tranquillizers are sometimes also used to make people or animals become sleepy or unconscious. *Tranquillizers, anti-depressants and anti-convulsants have been used to prevent the onset of a migraine attack... When residents get agitated, they're often given powerful tranquillizers.*

trans- /træns-, trænz-/
PREFIX **Trans-** is used to form adjectives that describe something that goes or exists from one side of a place to the other. *...the Trans-Siberian Railway. ...trans-continental flights.*

transact /trænzækt/ **transacts, transacting, transacted**
VO If you **transact** an arrangement that involves discussion or exchange, for example a business deal, you start it and continue it until an agreement has been reached. *He told them not to transact any business without him.*

transaction /trænzækʃn/ **transactions**
NC A **transaction** is a business deal, usually involving buying and selling something. *An oil transaction requires both a buyer and a seller. ...financial transactions.*

transatlantic /trænzətlæntɪk/
1 ADJ ATTRIB **Transatlantic** journeys or communications involve travelling or communicating across the Atlantic Ocean. *...regular transatlantic crossings. ...a transatlantic phone call.*
2 ADJ ATTRIB **Transatlantic** is also used to describe things that happen or exist in a country or region on one side of the Atlantic Ocean, as opposed to things that happen or exist in a country or region on the other side. *His band showed what happened when traditional African styles met their transatlantic cousins... For a transatlantic view, I spoke to Robert Hunter at the Center for Strategic and International Studies in Washington.*

transcend /trænsɛnd/ **transcends, transcending, transcended**
VO If one thing **transcends** another, it is not limited by the other thing, and is often more important; a formal word. *I believe that art transcends politics. ...a vital national issue that transcended party loyalties.*

transcendence /trænsɛndəns/
NU **Transcendence** is the quality of existing outside normal limits, or of being more important than other things; a formal word. *...if love is a genuine transcendence of self. ...transcendence of time and death.*

transcendent /trænsɛndənt/
ADJ Something that is **transcendent** exists outside normal limits, or is more important than other things; a formal word. *They believe in the transcendent unity of religions.*

transcendental /trænsɛndɛntl/
ADJ A **transcendental** experience or idea is based on things that lie beyond normal experience, and cannot be discovered or understood by ordinary reasoning; a formal word. *...a transcendental world view... I think people have a desire for an experience which is transcendental, by which I mean spiritual or aesthetic.*

transcendental meditation
NU **Transcendental meditation** is a kind of meditation derived from Hinduism, in which people mentally relax by silently repeating over and over again a special formula of words.

transcribe /trænskraɪb/ **transcribes, transcribing, transcribed**
VO If you **transcribe** something that is spoken or written, you write it out in a different form from the one in which it exists. *They sent us some tapes and we gave them to some friends to transcribe for us phonetically.*

transcript /trænskrɪpt/ **transcripts**
NC A **transcript** of something that is spoken is a written copy of it. *The newspaper has obtained a copy of the transcript of the police interrogation of Alexandre Chagas.*

transcription /trænskrɪpʃn/ **transcriptions**
1 NC A **transcription** is a written text that has been made from speech, or from a piece of writing that was in a different form. *...phonetic transcriptions of dialect speakers. ...transcriptions of Columbus' diaries.*
2 NU **Transcription** of a text or of speech is the process of typing it or writing it down. *Caxton liberated them from manual transcription of the holy word.*

transept /trænsept/ **transepts**
NC The **transept** of a cathedral or church is a part which projects to the north or south of the main part of the building. *The fire destroyed the roof of the south transept... Many of the hundreds present could only find room in the aisles and the transepts.*

transfer, transfers, transferring, transferred;
pronounced /trænsfɜː/ when it is a verb and /trænsfɜː/ when it is a noun.
1 VO If you **transfer** something from one place to another, you move it there. *Ten thousand pounds has been transferred into your account... He transferred the trout to a plate.* ► Also NU or NC *...the electronic transfer of money.*
2 VO If something is **transferred** from one person or group to another, the second one then has it instead of the first. *Ravenscroft transferred his affections to his secretary... The only move he has made so far has been to transfer control of the ruling Colorado Party to a group of his own political allies.* ► Also NU or NC *Few expected the transfer of power to happen so comparatively quickly... One transfer of a disputed region could lead to others, fuelling discontent elsewhere.*
3 V-ERG If you **transfer** to a different job or if you are **transferred** there, you move to a different place or job within the same organization. *What branch did you say you would like to transfer to?... I suspect she's going to be transferred.* ► Also NC or NU *He had applied for a transfer to the north... He resisted his transfer to the political section.*
4 VO If a sports player is **transferred**, he or she is sold to a different team. *The Soviet International Igor Belanov has been transferred from Dynamo Kiev to the Italian first division club, Atlanta.* ► Also NC *His transfer was finalised for a fee of around £300,000.*
5 NC A **transfer** is also a piece of paper with a design on one side. The design can be ironed or pressed onto cloth, paper, or china.

transferable /trænsfɜːrəbl/
ADJ If something is **transferable**, it can be passed to another person or organization and used by them. *He can't transfer the Austrian bank's letters of credit because they're not transferable... Cash is, by its nature, universally transferable. ...transferable skills.*

transference /trænsfərəns/
NU **Transference** is the transferring of something to a different place, person, or group; a formal word. *There has been no genuine transference of authority.*

transfigure /trænsfɪgə/ **transfigures, transfiguring, transfigured**
VO If you **are transfigured**, your appearance changes completely, often because something has made you very happy; a literary word. *The memory had transfigured her.* ♦ **transfigured** ADJ *Their faces became transfigured with joy.*

transfixed /trænsfɪkst/
ADJ PRED If you are **transfixed** by something, you are so impressed, fascinated, or frightened by it that you cannot move; a literary word. *I stood transfixed with terror.*

transform /trænsfɔːm/ **transforms, transforming, transformed**
VO If something is **transformed**, it is changed completely. *An area of pasture land can be transformed into a barren landscape in two or three years... They claimed to be able to transform the lives of millions of people.* ♦ **transformation** /trænsfəmeɪʃn/ **transformations** NC or NU *After a few months, the creature undergoes a transformation. ...the social and political transformation of society.*

transformer /trænsfɔːmə/ **transformers**
NC A **transformer** is a piece of electrical equipment which changes the voltage of a current. *It is connected to a transformer because the element works on a 24 volt system.*

transfusion /trænsfjuːʒn/ **transfusions**
1 NC When someone is given a blood **transfusion**, blood is injected into their body. *It's possible that some cancers may be made worse by blood transfusions... Since his first massive haemorrhage, he's been kept alive by transfusions and an intravenous drip.*
2 NC+SUPP When a country or organization is given a **transfusion** of money, they are given financial aid. *They believe the health service needs a big transfusion of financial help.*

transgress /trænzgres/ **transgresses, transgressing, transgressed**
V or VO When someone **transgresses**, they break a moral law or rule of behaviour; a formal word. *I had transgressed and now I must be punished for it... He claimed that the Romanian side had once again transgressed international law.* ♦ **transgression** /trænzgreʃn/ **transgressions** NC or NU *Apologize at once for your transgressions... The primary responsibility of the government is to maintain law and order and restrain certain organizations from transgression against the law.*

transience /trænziəns/
NU **Transience** is the quality of not lasting for very long; a formal word. *...the transience of human ties.*

transient /trænziənt/ **transients**; a formal word.
1 ADJ Something that is **transient** does not last very long. *...his bored wife's transient affair with a poet.*
2 NC **Transients** are people who stay in a place for only a short time; used especially to refer to people who are employed doing temporary work. *The authorities have announced further measures to enforce controls for the city's large population of transients.* ► Also ADJ *Joe's parents belong to a plucky transient class who are always on the move.*

transistor /trænzɪstə/ **transistors**
1 NC A **transistor** is a small electronic device in something such as a television or a radio. It is used for amplification and switching. *Basically, in a transistor you're storing a packet of electrical charge. ...transistors and computer chips.*
2 NC A **transistor** or **transistor radio** is a small portable radio containing transistors. *I would listen to White Sox games on a transistor radio.*

transit /trænzɪt/
1 People or things that are in **transit** are travelling or being taken from one place to another. *The tablets had been lost in transit.*
2 ADJ ATTRIB A **transit** area or building is a place where people wait or where goods are kept between different stages of a journey. *...the transit lounge.*

transition /trænzɪʃn/ **transitions**
NC or NU A **transition** is a change from one form or state to another. *...a transition from misery to happiness... The area is now in a state of transition.*

transitional /trænzɪʃənəl/
1 ADJ A **transitional** period or stage is one during which something changes from one form or state to another. *After a transitional period in which these reforms are implemented, free elections should be held.*
2 ADJ **Transitional** is also used to describe something that exists or happens during a transitional period or stage. *Pakistan has been demanding that a transitional government should be set up in Kabul.*

transitive /trænzətɪv/
ADJ In grammar, a **transitive** verb has an object. For example, in the sentence 'She baked a cake', the verb 'bake' is transitive.

transitory /trænzətəri/
ADJ If something is **transitory**, it lasts for only a short time; a formal word. *Love is transitory, but art is eternal.*

translate /trænzleɪt/ **translates, translating, translated**
1 VO or V If you **translate** something that someone has said or written, you say it or write it in a different language. *I translated it from Hebrew into English...*

My books have been translated into many languages...
This phrase is hard to translate precisely... 'Who are
you?' she asked as Chang translated. ◆ **translated**
ADJ ATTRIB *They brought all those translated text*
books together and burnt them.
2 V-ERG+*into* If you **translate** one thing into another, for
example an idea into action, you do the second thing
as a result of the first thing. *The problem is how to*
translate this awareness into effective action... You
can learn techniques for translating ideas into clay or
paint... These meetings have not so far translated into
the formal exchange of diplomatic representatives.
translation /trænzleɪʃn/ **translations**
1 NC A **translation** is a piece of writing or speech that
has been translated from a different language. *...a*
new translation of the Bible.
2 NU **Translation** is the act or process of translating
writing or speech into a different language. *Eight*
hundred letters were in Persian and were awaiting
translation.
translator /trænzleɪtə/ **translators**
NC A **translator** is a person whose job involves
translating writing or speech from one language to
another. *Mr Gorbachov, speaking through a*
translator, said their previous meetings had been
helpful... He's a translator of Spanish literature.
translucent /trænzluːsnt/
ADJ If something is **translucent**, light passes through
it, so that it seems to glow. *The leaves of the beeches*
are translucent in the setting sun.
transmission /trænzmɪʃn/ **transmissions**
1 NU The **transmission** of something involves passing
it or sending it to a different place or person. *Wearing*
a condom during sex prevents the transmission of
AIDS. ...data transmission.
2 NU The **transmission** of television or radio
programmes is the broadcasting of them. *...a unique*
film record that was destroyed after transmission.
3 NC A **transmission** is a broadcast. *Millions would*
have heard that transmission.
4 NCorNU The **transmission** on a car or other vehicle
is the system of gears and shafts by which the power
from the engine reaches and turns the wheels. *It was*
billed as the world's most advanced transmission
because of its electronic controls.
transmit /trænzmɪt/ **transmits, transmitting,**
transmitted
1 VO When a message or electronic signal is
transmitted, it is sent by radio waves. *The material*
was transmitted by satellite throughout the world.
2 VO To **transmit** something to a different place or
person means to pass or send it to the place or
person; a formal use. *...a disease that is sometimes*
transmitted to humans.
transmitter /trænzmɪtə/ **transmitters**
NC A **transmitter** is a piece of equipment used for
sending radio signals or for broadcasting
programmes. *The service is delivered by satellite,*
using a transmitter mounted on a high television
tower. ...a radio transmitter.
transmute /trænzmjuːt/ **transmutes, transmuting,**
transmuted
VO If something is **transmuted** into something
different, it is changed into that thing; a formal word.
The drizzle had been transmuted into thin layers of
mist... The agony of her loss had been transmuted into
numb acceptance. ◆ **transmutation** /trænzmjuːteɪʃn/
NU *...the transmutation of matter.*
transparency /trænspærənsi/ **transparencies**
1 NC A **transparency** is a small piece of photographic
film which is mounted in a frame. You project light
through the transparency in order to display the
picture on a screen. *Kodachrome was very difficult to*
use, and produced only transparencies.
2 NU **Transparency** is the quality that an object or
substance has if you can see through it. *The crystal*
lost its transparency.
transparent /trænspærənt/
1 ADJ If an object or substance is **transparent**, you can
see through it. *...a transparent plastic lid.*
2 ADJ If something such as a feeling or situation is
transparent, it is easily understood or recognized. *We*

wanted our goals to be transparent... The whole
process of government becomes a little more
transparent than it has been in the past.
3 ADJ If something such as a dishonest statement or
action is **transparent**, people are not deceived by it. *A*
spokeswoman said that the story is a transparent
attempt to blame foreigners for the problem.
◆ **transparently** SUBMOD *...an attitude that was*
transparently false.
transpire /trænspaɪə/ **transpires, transpiring,**
transpired; a formal word.
1 V-REPORT When it **transpires** that something is the
case, people discover that it is the case. *It finally*
transpired that he was a special investigator for the
CIA.
2 V When something **transpires**, it happens. *Nobody*
knows what transpired at the meeting.
transplant, transplants, transplanting,
transplanted; pronounced /trænsplɑːnt/ when it is a
noun and /trænsplɑːnt/ when it is a verb.
1 NCorNU A **transplant** is a surgical operation in which
a part of a person's body is replaced because it is
diseased. *Doctors say they have been forced to cancel*
liver transplants and to turn away organ donors...
More living relatives may have to give their own
kidneys for transplant.
2 VO If doctors **transplant** an organ such as a heart or
kidney, they use it to replace a patient's diseased
organ. *The proportion of suitable donor organs that*
are successfully transplanted is higher now than ever.
3 VO When you **transplant** something, you move it to a
different place. *The founding fathers of Israel*
transplanted a European race to the Middle East.
...how an established technology can be transplanted
to another region.
transport, transports, transporting, transported;
pronounced /trænspɔːt/ when it is a noun and /trænspɔːt/
when it is a verb.
1 NU You refer to vehicles that you travel in, for
example buses, cars, and trains, as **transport**. *It is*
easier if you have your own transport... Why can't he
use public transport?
2 NU **Transport** involves moving goods or people from
one place to another. *The essential means of transport*
for heavy equipment remained the railway. ...high
transport costs.
3 VO When goods or people **are transported** from one
place to another, they are moved there. *The goods*
were transported to East Africa... A large amount of
flour is blocked there, unable to be transported
because of heavy snow.
transportation /trænspɔːteɪʃn/; used in American
English.
1 NU You refer to vehicles that you travel in, for
example buses, cars, and trains, as **transportation**. *It*
typically costs about $1 a day for somebody to take
public transportation to and from their job.
2 NU **Transportation** involves moving goods or people
from one place to another. *The food is ready for*
transportation... Transportation costs are also high.
transport café, transport cafés
NC A **transport café** is a café beside a main road that
is used mainly by lorry drivers and that provides
cheap food and drink.
transporter /trænspɔːtə/ **transporters**
NC A **transporter** is a large vehicle that is used for
carrying very large or heavy objects, for example
cars. *He swung the enormous transporter back on the*
road. ...tank transporters.
transpose /trænspəʊz/ **transposes, transposing,**
transposed; a formal word.
1 VOA If you **transpose** something to a different place
or position, you move it to that place or position. *He*
was unable to transpose himself to the cockpit.
2 VO To **transpose** something also means to alter it to
a different form, while keeping its essential features.
...a Jacobean drama transposed into modern dress.
transverse /trænzvɜːs/
ADJ ATTRIB **Transverse** is used to describe something
that is in a direction or position at right angles to
something else; a technical term. *...the transverse*
arches in the nave of the cathedral.

transvestism /trænzvɛstɪzəm/
NU **Transvestism** is the practice of wearing clothes that are normally worn by a person of the opposite sex, especially for sexual pleasure; a formal word.

transvestite /trænzvɛstaɪt/ **transvestites**
NC A **transvestite** is a person, usually a man, who enjoys wearing clothes normally worn by people of the opposite sex. *It's not a drag show, and these men are not transvestites.*

trap /træp/ **traps, trapping, trapped**
1 NC A **trap** is a device or hole that is intended to catch animals or birds. *...an otter trap... We had a raccoon in the trap.*
2 NC A **trap** is also a trick that is intended to catch or deceive someone. *The police said they laid a trap for the gang with an officer posing as a rich businessman.*
3 VO To **trap** animals means to catch them using traps. *My father doesn't like the idea of trapping otters.*
4 VO If you **trap** someone, you trick them so that they do or say something which they did not want to. *This wasn't the first time we had been trapped into a situation like this.*
5 VO If you **are trapped** somewhere, you cannot move or escape because something is blocking your way or is holding you down. *I can't get up, I'm trapped here... A small section of the bridge caved in, trapping a number of vehicles.*
6 VO If you **are trapped**, you are in an unpleasant situation which is difficult to escape from. *Many women are trapped in loveless marriages.*
7 NC+SUPP A **trap** is also an unpleasant situation that you cannot easily escape from. *To break out of the poverty trap they need help from the government.*
8 See also **booby-trap**.

trapdoor /træpdɔː/ **trapdoors**
NC A **trapdoor** is a small horizontal door in a floor, ceiling, or stage. *Pull the bolt and allow the trapdoor to drop.*

trapeze /trəpiːz/ **trapezes**
NC A **trapeze** is a bar of wood or metal hanging from two ropes on which acrobats and gymnasts swing and perform skilful movements. *He makes an appearance perched on a trapeze high above the stage. ...trapeze artists.*

trapper /træpə/ **trappers**
NC A **trapper** is a person who traps animals, especially for their fur. *...trappers and fishermen.*

trappings /træpɪŋz/
N PL The **trappings** of a particular rank, position, or state are the things that you acquire as a result of having it. *...the trappings of power that have surrounded him since he took office.*

trash /træʃ/ **trashes, trashing, trashed**
1 NU **Trash** consists of unwanted things or waste material such as used paper or tins; used in American English. *The yards were filled with trash.*
2 NU If you think a book or film is of very poor quality, you can refer to it as **trash**; an informal use. *I've told you not to read that trash.*
3 VO If a place is **trashed**, it is deliberately destroyed, often as the result of a burglary or riot. *The bank was trashed: furniture broken, computers stolen, pools of water stagnating on the floor... Stores have been looted and offices trashed.*
4 VO If you **trash** people or their ideas, you try to influence others against them by ridiculing their beliefs or their way of life; used in informal American English. *This is an old attitude from the days when the Communist press was always trashing the Solidarity people on television... We sure don't need the kind of jingoism that trashes Arab-Americans.*

trashcan /træʃkæn/ **trashcans**
NC A **trashcan** is the same as a **dustbin**; used in American English. *Get that bottle and put it in the trashcan.*

trashy /træʃi/ **trashier, trashiest**
ADJ Something such as a film or a book that is **trashy** is very poor in quality; an informal word. *...trashy novels.*

trauma /trɔːmə/ **traumas**
N C or N U A **trauma** is an extremely upsetting experience which causes great stress and which may cause long-term psychological damage. *...the trauma of having their parents arrested... This would impose unnecessary trauma and suffering.*

traumatic /trɔːmætɪk/
ADJ A **traumatic** experience is extremely upsetting and causes great stress, and may cause long-term psychological damage. *I think the most traumatic experience of all was the civil war.*

traumatize /trɔːmətaɪz/ **traumatizes, traumatizing, traumatized**; also spelt **traumatise**
VO If someone is **traumatized** by an event or situation, it is extremely upsetting and causes great stress, and may cause long-term psychological damage. *Depression also afflicted her father, who had been permanently traumatized by his experiences in the First World War.* ◆ **traumatized** ADJ *The nation remained traumatized by the memory.*

travel /trævl/ **travels, travelling, travelled**; spelt **traveling, traveled** in American English.
1 V A or V When you **travel** somewhere, you go there from another place. *I travelled to work by train... I travelled sixty miles to buy those books... Some human rights activists have received permission to travel.*
2 VO If you **travel** a country or region, you go to many places in that country or region. *A businessman was arrested as he travelled the country with a Vietnamese official... The Dalai Lama has travelled the world drawing attention to Tibetan grievances.*
3 NU **Travel** is the activity of travelling. *...air travel. ...a travel writer.*
4 N PL+POSS Someone's **travels** are the journeys they make to places a long way from their home. *...his extensive travels abroad.*
5 VA When something reaches one place from another, you say that it **travels** there. *Sound travels better in water... News travels fast.*

travel agency, travel agencies
NC A **travel agency** is a business which makes arrangements for people's holidays and journeys. *Many of the tours had been arranged through other travel agencies. ...the travel agencies which organized the charter trip.*

travel agent, travel agents
NC A **travel agent** is someone who runs or works in a travel agency. *The Ceylon Tourist Board has advised all travel agents and tour operators to review their tour programmes.*

travel bureau, travel bureaux
NC A **travel bureau** is the same as a **travel agency**.

traveller /trævələ/ **travellers**; spelt **traveler** in American English.
1 NC A **traveller** is a person who is making a journey or who travels a lot. *Regular travellers are paying an average of nine per cent more for their rail tickets. ...air travellers.*
2 NC A **traveller** is also someone who travels from place to place, often living in a van or other vehicle, rather than living in one place. *The police will be distributing leaflets to hippies and travellers still on the site.*

traveller's cheque, traveller's cheques; spelt **traveler's check** in American English.
NC **Traveller's cheques** are special cheques that you can exchange for local currency when you are abroad. *At the Bank of External Trade, visitors can exchange foreign currency and traveller's cheques.*

travelling expenses
N PL **Travelling expenses** are money that you claim back from your employer when you have spent that amount of money on travelling as part of your work. *They get travelling expenses and are also paid a fee.*

travelling salesman, travelling salesmen; spelt **traveling salesman** in American English.
NC A **travelling salesman** is a salesman who travels to different places and meets people in order to sell goods or take orders.

travelogue /trævəlɒg/ **travelogues**; also spelt **travelog** in American English.
N C or N U A **travelogue** is a film, book, or talk about travel to an interesting place or about a particular

person's travels. *In his first travelogue, Mark Hudson takes part in the dramas and rituals of village life... This book is more than travelogue: it confronts and demolishes the Western stereotype of Korea.*

travel-sick
ADJ If someone is **travel-sick**, they feel sick as a result of travelling in a vehicle. *My son always gets travel-sick on car journeys.* ◆ **travel-sickness** NU *Take one tablet before the start of your journey to prevent travel-sickness occurring.*

traverse /trəvɜːs/ **traverses, traversing, traversed**
VO If you **traverse** an area of land or water, you go across it; a formal use. *I traversed the rest of the slope at a run.*

travesty /trævəsti/ **travesties**
NC A **travesty** of something is a very bad representation of it. *His account of my essay was a travesty. ...the travesties of justice played out in their courts.*

trawl /trɔːl/ **trawls, trawling, trawled**
1 V or VO When fishermen **trawl**, they drag a wide net behind a ship in order to catch fish. *When trawling you may catch hermit crabs. ...the fishermen who trawl the offshore waters.*
2 NC A **trawl** or **trawl net** is the wide net that fishermen use in trawling.
3 VOA If you **trawl** for something, you search among a large number of similar things in order to find the best or most suitable one. *She trawled the play for suitable quotations.* ▶ Also NC *As a result of a nation-wide trawl thirty actors were enlisted. ...a concerted trawl for new enthusiasts.*

trawler /trɔːlə/ **trawlers**
NC A **trawler** is a fishing boat from which fish are caught in large nets. *The trawler ran aground in heavy seas off the south-west coast of Ireland.*

tray /treɪ/ **trays**
NC A **tray** is a flat object with raised edges which is used for carrying things such as food or drinks. *She picked up a fruit and cheese tray and dumped it into a garbage bag. ...trays of cupcakes.*

treacherous /tretʃərəs/
1 ADJ A **treacherous** person is likely to betray you. *...my treacherous fellow travellers.*
2 ADJ If the ground or the sea is **treacherous**, it is dangerous or unpredictable in nature or has been affected by severe weather conditions. *Many drivers are refusing to travel the treacherous route... Sea conditions off the south coast are still treacherous in the high winds.*

treachery /tretʃəri/
NU If someone betrays their country or betrays a person who trusts them, you describe their action as **treachery**. *He could not believe that Clemenza was guilty of treachery.*

treacle /triːkl/
NU **Treacle** is a bitter-sweet, dark, sticky liquid that is used in making some cakes and toffee.

tread /tred/ **treads, treading, trod, trodden**
1 VA If you **tread** on something, you step on it or press your foot on it. *Don't tread on the flowers.*
2 VOA If you **tread** something into the ground or into a carpet, you step on it and crush it in. *Damp chips had been trodden into the carpet.*
3 VA If you **tread** in a particular way, you walk in that way. *She trod heavily out of the room.*
4 N SING+SUPP Someone's **tread** is the sound they make with their feet as they walk. *They could hear his heavy limping tread.*
5 VA or VO If you **tread** carefully, you behave cautiously. *The government was treading warily... The President must realize that he is treading a delicate diplomatic and political path.*
6 NC The **tread** of a tyre or shoe is the pattern of ridges on it that stops it slipping. *The tread was all worn out, and it was only a year-old tyre.*

treadle /tredl/ **treadles**
NC The **treadle** on a machine, for example on a spinning wheel or sewing machine, is a lever that you operate with your foot in order to turn a wheel in the machine. *The treadle or pedal was pushed by the feet in the same way as a foot-controlled sewing machine.*

...a treadle sewing machine.

treadmill /tredmɪl/ **treadmills**
NC+SUPP You refer to a task or a job as a **treadmill** when you must keep doing it although it is unpleasant and exhausting. *No woman should waste her life on the treadmill of housework.*

treason /triːzn/
NU **Treason** is the crime of betraying your country, for example by helping its enemies or by trying to overthrow its government. *The death sentence has been restricted to apply to espionage and acts of treason... He was detained last week and charged with treason.*

treasonable /triːzənəbl/
ADJ **Treasonable** activities are criminal activities which are intended to help your country's enemies or to overthrow its government. *He had been engaged in treasonable activities since 1974, passing on secrets and taking other actions aimed at undermining the interests of the state.*

treasure /treʒə/ **treasures, treasuring, treasured**
1 NU **Treasure** is a collection of gold, silver, or jewels, especially one that has been hidden. *It may contain treasure worth many hundreds of millions of dollars. ...buried treasure.*
2 NC **Treasures** are valuable works of art. *...the sale of art treasures.*
3 VO If you **treasure** something that you have, you are very pleased that you have it and regard it as very valuable. *...one of the memories which they would treasure... He treasured his friendship with her.* ◆ **treasured** ADJ ATTRIB *...my most treasured possessions.*

treasurer /treʒərə/ **treasurers**
NC The **treasurer** of an organization is the person in charge of its finances and accounts. *...the club's former treasurer. ...the Treasurer of the ruling Jatiya Party.*

treasure trove
N SING You refer to a large amount of money or to a collection of valuable objects as a **treasure trove** when it has been found somewhere and nobody knows who it belongs to. *Workmen have uncovered a treasure trove of coins, pottery and prehistoric fossils.*

treasury /treʒəri/
N PROP The **Treasury** is the government department in Britain and in some other countries that deals with the country's finances. *The Treasury was opposed in principle to the proposals. ...a former Treasury official.*

treat /triːt/ **treats, treating, treated**
1 VOA If you **treat** someone or something in a particular way, you behave towards them or deal with them in that way. *Their parents continue to treat them as children... Electricity is potentially dangerous, so treat it with respect.*
2 VO When a doctor **treats** a patient or an illness, he or she tries to make the patient well again. *More people are being treated for asthma than ever before... A new vaccine for treating AIDS is now ready for human testing. ...a way to treat cancer.*
3 VO If something such as wood or cloth is **treated**, a special substance is put on it to protect it or give it special properties. *New timber should be treated with a preservative.*
4 V-REFL or VO If you **treat** yourself, you buy or arrange something special which you will enjoy. If you **treat** someone else, you buy or arrange something special which they will enjoy. *Treat yourself to a new pair of shoes... I was treated to lunch by the Vice-President.*
5 NC If you give someone a **treat**, you buy or arrange something special for them which they will enjoy. *Granny took us for tea as a special treat.*

treatise /triːtɪz/ **treatises**
NC A **treatise** is a long, formal piece of writing about a particular subject. *Malthus published his treatise on population. ...a technical scientific treatise.*

treatment /triːtmənt/ **treatments**
1 NU or NC Medical **treatment** consists of all the things done to make a sick person well again. *...free dental treatment... I tried every treatment the doctor suggested.*

2 NU Your **treatment** of someone is the way you behave towards them or deal with them. *Their treatment of women is unspeakable... I didn't want special treatment.*

treaty /triːti/ **treaties**
NC A **treaty** is a written agreement between countries. *The Government has signed a treaty with Moscow. ...the Strategic Arms Reduction Treaty.*

treble /trɛbl/ **trebles, trebling, trebled**
1 V-ERG If something **trebles** or if you **treble** it, it becomes three times greater in amount or size. *The population has nearly trebled since 1950. ...a proposal to treble the price of bread.*
2 PREDET If something is **treble** the amount or size of another thing, it is three times greater in amount or size. *It's claimed that some owners are charging treble the normal price for a single voyage... rents that were treble their normal levels.*

tree /triː/ **trees**
1 NC A **tree** is a tall plant with a hard trunk, branches, and leaves. *One of the biggest threats has been the cutting down of trees for firewood. ...an apple tree.* • See also **Christmas tree, family tree.**
2 If someone is **barking up the wrong tree,** they are trying to do something without any chance of success because they do not understand the situation properly. *Well, if people bet with the notion that they're going to get rich, they're barking up the wrong tree.*

tree-lined
ADJ **Tree-lined** streets or roads have trees on either side of them. *...a pleasant tree-lined avenue in Bristol.*

treetop /triːtɒp/ **treetops**
NC The **treetops** are the top part of trees, especially in a wood or forest. *Monkeys were bounding away through the treetops.*

tree trunk, tree trunks
NC A **tree trunk** is the large main stem of a tree, from which the branches grow. *...cutting up tree trunks to make timber.*

trek /trɛk/ **treks, trekking, trekked**
VA If you **trek** somewhere, you go on a long and difficult journey there, especially on foot. *They trekked for three days along the banks of the Zambezi.*
▶ Also NC *We set off on a four hour trek.*

trellis /trɛlɪs/ **trellises**
NC A **trellis** is a frame which supports climbing plants. *They would build bamboo trellises which the plants could grow up.*

tremble /trɛmbl/ **trembles, trembling, trembled**
1 V If you **tremble,** you shake slightly, because you are frightened or cold. *...trembling with fear... The demonstrators were visibly trembling even before the shooting started.*
2 V If something **trembles,** it shakes slightly. *The wind made the branches shake and tremble.*

tremendous /trəmɛndəs/
1 ADJ **Tremendous** means very great in quantity or intensity. *They cost a tremendous amount of money... The play became a tremendous hit.* ◆ **tremendously** ADV *She envied and admired Judy tremendously.*
2 ADJ You also describe something as **tremendous** when you think it is very good or impressive. *The holiday was tremendous.*

tremor /trɛmə/ **tremors**
1 NC A **tremor** is a shaking of your body or voice which you cannot control. *...a tremor of pleasure... Burton detected a tremor in her voice.*
2 NC A **tremor** is also a small earthquake. *The tremor measured five point one on the Richter scale... The avalanche appears to have been caused by an earth tremor.*

tremulous /trɛmjʊləs/
ADJ A **tremulous** voice or smile is unsteady; a literary word. *Jack's voice went on, tremulous yet determined.*

trench /trɛntʃ/ **trenches**
1 NC A **trench** is a long, narrow channel that is dug in the ground in order to lay pipes or to provide drainage. *Seal the joints, fill in the trench and pump the tunnel dry... Dredge a trench along the river bed.*
2 NC A **trench** is also a long narrow channel in the ground that is used by soldiers as a defensive

position. *...front line troops in their trenches. ...the trenches of World War 1.*

trenchant /trɛntʃənt/
ADJ **Trenchant** writing or comments make their point strongly and clearly, and are often very critical; a formal word. *When the START negotiations began in 1982, President Reagan was making some of his most trenchant anti-Soviet statements.*

trench coat, trench coats
NC A **trench coat** is a type of raincoat with pockets and a belt, especially one that is similar in design to military coats.

trench warfare
NU **Trench warfare** is a situation that develops in a military conflict, when soldiers on both sides shelter in trenches and launch weapons at each other from there. *...a reminder of the trench warfare of the First World War.*

trend /trɛnd/ **trends**
NC A **trend** is a change or development towards something new or different. *There is a trend towards equal opportunities for men and women. ...the trend away from institutional care for handicapped children.*

trend-setter /trɛndsɛtə/ **trend-setters**
NC A **trend-setter** is a person or institution that starts a new fashion or trend. *Filofaxes are now regarded by trend-setters as passé.*

trendy /trɛndi/ **trendier, trendiest**
ADJ **Trendy** things or people are very fashionable and modern; an informal word. *...one of London's most trendy dance clubs. ...trendy clothes. ...trendy intellectuals talking about life.*

trepidation /trɛpɪdeɪʃn/
NU **Trepidation** is fear or anxiety; a formal word. *We await the result of this summit with anticipation, and trepidation... Mrs Thatcher continues to view German unity with some trepidation.*

trespass /trɛspəs/ **trespasses, trespassing, trespassed**
V If you **trespass** on someone's land, you go onto it without their permission. *The Bureau of Land Management says they are trespassing and wants them off this land.*

trespasser /trɛspəsə/ **trespassers**
NC A **trespasser** is a person who goes on someone's land without the owner's permission. *Trespassers will be prosecuted.*

tress /trɛs/ **tresses**
NC A woman's **tresses** are her long flowing hair; a literary word.

trestle /trɛsl/ **trestles**
NC A **trestle** is a wooden or metal structure that is used, for example, as one of the supports for a table. It has two pairs of sloping legs which are joined by a flat piece across the top. *Fix the frame to the cutter whilst it's supported on a special trestle.*

trestle table, trestle tables
NC A **trestle table** is a table made of a long board that is supported on trestles.

triad /traɪæd/ **triads**
NC A **triad** is a group of three similar things; a formal word. *Each of this sonorous triad of pleas was meant to be taken as of equal weight.*

trial /traɪəl/ **trials**
1 NCorNU A **trial** is the legal process in which a judge and jury listen to evidence and decide whether a person is guilty of a crime. *She won't get a fair trial... Huey was awaiting trial for murder.* • See also **show trial.**
2 NC A **trial** is also an experiment in which you test something by using it or doing it for a period of time to see how well it works. *We've completed a number of fairly successful trials with laboratory animals... Full clinical trials are beginning this month of a new way of treating certain brain cancers... The Egyptians wanted a further trial period.*
3 N SING A **trial** is also a test of whether someone is suitable for a particular job by letting them do it for a short period of time. *If you want the job I'm prepared to give you a trial.*
4 NC+SUPP Someone's **trials** are the unpleasant things that they experience. *...the trials of pregnancy.*
• **Trial** is used in these phrases. • If someone is **on**

trial, they are being tried in a court of law. *He is still on trial for his alleged involvement in the 1975 coup attempt.* ● If something or someone is **on trial**, they are being tested or closely examined. *The Parliamentary system is on trial... It's a principle that will be on trial in the elections... The selectors put him on trial.* ● If you do something by **trial and error**, you try different ways of doing it until you find a good one. *The best solution can only be found by a process of trial and error.* ● to **stand trial**: see **stand**.

trial run, trial runs
NC A **trial run** is a first attempt at doing something, to make sure that you can do it properly. *The electronic note book has had a successful trial run.*

triangle /ˈtraɪæŋgl/ **triangles**
NC A **triangle** is a shape with three straight sides.

triangular /traɪˈæŋgjʊlə/
ADJ Something that is **triangular** is in the shape of a triangle. *I punched two triangular holes in the tin.*

tribal /ˈtraɪbl/
ADJ ATTRIB **Tribal** describes things relating or belonging to tribes. *The tribal leader of the Zulus, Chief Buthelezi, has made a strong attack on anti-apartheid campaigners. ...the Pakistani tribal territory of Bajaur.*

tribalism /ˈtraɪbəlɪzəm/
1 NU **Tribalism** is the state of existing as a tribe. *...feudalism, tribalism, or slavery.*
2 NU **Tribalism** is also the behaviour and attitudes shown by the members of a particular group in society, especially with regard to the loyalty they feel for each other, and their hostility to other groups. *...a nationalist movement opposed to tribalism and devoted to national consolidation.*

tribe /traɪb/ **tribes**
NC A **tribe** is a group of people of the same race who share the same language and customs, especially a group that lives in a developing country. *Mr Otunnu is a member of the Acholi tribe.*

tribesman /ˈtraɪbzmən/ **tribesmen** /ˈtraɪbzmən/
NC A **tribesman** is a man who belongs to a tribe. *...Afghan hill tribesmen.*

tribulation /ˌtrɪbjʊˈleɪʃn/ **tribulations**
NU or N PL **Tribulation** is trouble or suffering; a formal word. *Life is uncertain and full of tribulation. ...after many trials and tribulations during the war.*

tribunal /traɪˈbjuːnl/ **tribunals**
N COLL A **tribunal** is a special court or committee that is appointed to deal with particular problems. *An industrial tribunal was hearing cases of unfair dismissal.*

tributary /ˈtrɪbjʊtəⁿri/ **tributaries**
NC The **tributaries** of a large river are the smaller rivers that flow into it. *...the Neander River, a tributary of the Rhine.*

tribute /ˈtrɪbjuːt/ **tributes**
1 NC or NU A **tribute** is something that you say or do to show your admiration and respect for someone. *She accepted the tribute graciously... Asquith paid tribute to his personal qualities.*
2 N SING If one thing is a **tribute** to another, it is the result of the other thing and shows how good it is. *The fact that I survived is a tribute to the indestructibility of the human body.*

triceps /ˈtraɪseps/; **triceps** is both the singular and the plural form.
NC Your **triceps** is the muscle in the back part of your upper arm. *It sends a ripple up your forearm, to your triceps.*

trick /trɪk/ **tricks, tricking, tricked**
1 VO If someone **tricks** you, they deceive you, often in order to make you do something. *He realized that the visitors had tricked him... She felt she had been tricked into marriage.*
2 NC A **trick** is an action that is intended to deceive someone. *They played a dirty trick on us.*
3 NC A **trick** is also a clever way of doing something. *An old campers' trick is to use three thin blankets instead of one thick one... What is the trick to get it to start?*
4 NC A **trick** is also a clever or skilful action that someone does in order to entertain people. *He*

sometimes did card tricks.
5 ADJ ATTRIB **Trick** devices and methods are intended to deceive people for entertainment. *...trick photography.*
6 If something **does the trick**, it achieves what you wanted; an informal expression. *Try putting copper sulphate on the thatch and seeing if that does the trick... There might be a slight change in tactics that could do the trick.*
7 See also **confidence trick, conjuring trick**.

trickery /ˈtrɪkəri/
NU **Trickery** is the use of dishonest tricks in order to achieve something. *He said Serbia tried to subvert the constitution through trickery... That result has not been achieved by any underhand trickery.*

trickle /ˈtrɪkl/ **trickles, trickling, trickled**
1 V If a liquid **trickles** somewhere, it flows slowly in a thin stream. *The tears were beginning to trickle down her cheeks.* ► Also NC *...a thin trickle of blood.*
2 VA If people or things **trickle** somewhere, they move there slowly in small groups or amounts. *The coach parties began trickling back to the car park.* ► Also NC *A small trickle have begun to return to their homes in Afghanistan... The trickle of Jews allowed to leave the Soviet Union turned into a steady stream earlier this year.*

trick question, trick questions
NC A **trick question** is one where the obvious answer is in fact wrong.

tricky /ˈtrɪki/ **trickier, trickiest**
1 ADJ A **tricky** task or problem is difficult to deal with. *Finding a site for a toxic waste dump can be a tricky and controversial business. ...the tricky question of deciding who is a genuine refugee fleeing persecution.*
2 ADJ A **tricky** person is likely to deceive you or cheat you. *These rustlers can be tricky.*

tricolour /ˈtrɪkələ/ **tricolours**
NC A **tricolour** is a flag that is made up of blocks of three different colours. *The tricolour flies triumphantly over the White House, the building of the Russian Federation's Parliament... All over Dunkirk the Union Jack is flying alongside the French Tricolour.*

tricycle /ˈtraɪsɪkl/ **tricycles**
NC A **tricycle** is a vehicle similar to a bicycle but which has three wheels, two wheels at the back and one at the front.

tried /traɪd/
Tried is the past tense and past participle of **try**.

trier /ˈtraɪə/ **triers**
NC You describe someone as a **trier** when they try very hard at things that they do. *Jack was always a trier... The others are tremendous triers.*

trifle /ˈtraɪfl/ **trifles, trifling, trifled**
1 A **trifle** means to a small extent or degree. *She was a trifle breathless.*
2 NC **Trifles** are things that are not considered important or valuable. *They worry over trifles.*
3 NC or NU A **trifle** is a cold pudding made of layers of sponge cake with either jam or jelly, fruit, custard, and cream.

trifle with PHRASAL VERB If you **trifle with** someone or something, you treat them in a frivolous or disrespectful way. *He said it would mean trifling with the interests of Yugoslavia... Mitchell was not someone to be trifled with.*

trifling /ˈtraɪflɪŋ/
ADJ A **trifling** matter is small and unimportant. *They will raise the fines imposed for illegal forest fires from the present trifling twenty-one pounds to a sum up to fifty times higher.*

trigger /ˈtrɪgə/ **triggers, triggering, triggered**
1 NC The **trigger** of a gun is the small lever which you pull to fire it. *...the trigger of his Colt 45 revolver.*
2 VO If something **triggers** an event, it causes it to happen. *The figures were not bad enough to trigger a rise in interest rates... The explosion was triggered by a collapse of the core of the star.*

trigger off PHRASAL VERB If something **triggers off** an event or process, it causes it to begin to happen or take place. *Serious economic problems triggered off a* *wave of strikes... During this time HIV is latent, and then something or other triggers it off and it becomes active.*

trigger-happy
ADJ Someone who is **trigger-happy** is too ready to use violence and weapons, especially guns; an informal word. *The national guard have been very trigger-happy lately... There are a number of trigger-happy soldiers in the area.*

trigonometry /trɪgənɒmətri/
NU **Trigonometry** is the branch of mathematics that is concerned with calculating the angles of triangles or the lengths of their sides. *I didn't do much trigonometry at school. ...a trigonometry problem.*

trilby /trɪlbi/ **trilbies**
NC A **trilby** or **trilby hat** is a man's hat made of felt with a dent along the top from front to back. *He crammed his trilby on his head... He was wearing a brown trilby hat.*

trill /trɪl/ **trills, trilling, trilled**
1 NC A **trill** is the playing of two musical notes repeatedly one after the other very quickly; a technical use in music. *...the famous orchestra trill at the end of the first act.*
2 V If a bird **trills**, it sings with short, high-pitched repeated notes. *I could hear a wren trilling in the garden.* ► Also NC *...the canary's high trills.*
3 V-QUOTE,VO,or V If a person, especially a woman, **trills**, they talk or laugh in a high-pitched voice that sounds rather musical. *'It's only us,' trilled the girls... Why do actresses always trill words so?*

trillion /trɪljən/ **trillions**
A **trillion** is a million million. *President Reagan has submitted a budget of more than one trillion dollars.*

trilogy /trɪlədʒi/ **trilogies**
NC A **trilogy** is a series of three books, plays, or films with the same characters or subject. *He is currently working on the third and final part of his trilogy on Third World dictators.*

trim /trɪm/ **trimmer, trimmest; trims, trimming, trimmed**
1 ADJ Something that is **trim** is neat, tidy, and attractive. *...the trim lawns and trees of suburbia.*
2 ADJ If someone has a **trim** figure, they are slim. *...a trim, balding man in his early sixties.*
3 VO If you **trim** something, you cut off small amounts of it to make it look neater. *After the crops have been planted the hedgerows are trimmed and the prunings are laid on the ground... The grass needed trimming.* ► Also N SING *My hair needs a trim.*
4 VO If a government or other organization **trims** something such as a plan, policy, or amount, they change it so that it is smaller in extent or size. *The French government has trimmed its defence budget recently... There is no suggestion that he has trimmed his highly radical long-term goals... The government is drastically trimming staff or shutting down factories which were inefficient.*

trim away or **trim off** PHRASAL VERB If you **trim away** parts of something or **trim** them **off**, you cut them off because they are not needed. *Press round the edges to seal and trim away excess pastry... Most of the fat should be trimmed off the meat.*

trimaran /traɪməræn/ **trimarans**
NC A **trimaran** is a fast sailing boat like a catamaran but with three hulls instead of two. *They set out from San Francisco in a 60-foot trimaran.*

trimmed /trɪmd/
ADJ PRED+*with* If a dress is **trimmed** with a particular material or ornament, the material or ornament has been added to it in order to make it look more attractive. *...red robes trimmed with white ermine fur. ...a hat trimmed with ribbons.*

trimming /trɪmɪŋ/ **trimmings**
1 NC The **trimmings** on a garment are extra parts that are added for decoration. *...a pink nightdress with nylon lace trimmings.*
2 N PL **Trimmings** are also nice things that can be added to something or included in something. *Tonight it was turkey with all the trimmings... Other luxury trimmings are leather handles and walnut door pulls.*

Trinidad and Tobago /trɪnɪdæd ənd təbeɪgəʊ/
The **Republic of Trinidad and Tobago** is a country in the Caribbean. Trinidad became a British colony in 1802 and Tobago in 1814. The two were joined for administration in 1888. They became independent from Britain in 1962. Noor Mohammed Hassanali, of the National Alliance for Reconstruction (NAR), became President in 1987. Patrick Manning, of the People's National Movement (PNM), became Prime Minister in 1991. Trinidad and Tobago is a member of the Commonwealth and the Organization of American States. It exports oil. Tourism is an important industry. ◆ **Trinidadian, Tobagoan** /trɪnɪdædiən, təbeɪgəʊən/ N, ADJ
▪ *per capita GNP:* US$3,350 ▪ *religion:* Christianity, Hinduism ▪ *language:* English (official) ▪ *currency:* dollar ▪ *capital:* Port of Spain ▪ *population:* 1 million (1989) ▪ *size:* 5,128 square kilometres.

trinity /trɪnəti/
1 N PROP In the Christian religion, the **Trinity** or the **Holy Trinity** is the union of Father, Son, and Holy Spirit in one God. *He explained the theological mystery of the Holy Trinity using the symbol of the shamrock, with its three leaves on one stem.*
2 N SING A **trinity** is a group of three things or people; a literary use. *...the evil trinity of imperialism, capitalism and fascism. ...a trinity of quality, mind, and matter.*

trinket /trɪŋkɪt/ **trinkets**
NC A **trinket** is a cheap ornament or piece of jewellery. *The goods they sell are the kind of trinkets that might appeal to tourists.*

trio /triːəʊ/ **trios**
NC A **trio** is a group of three people, especially musicians or singers. *...the Pump Room Trio. ...a trio of journalists.*

trip /trɪp/ **trips, tripping, tripped**
1 NC A **trip** is a journey that you make to a place and back again. *Morris decided to take a trip to London. ...executives on business trips abroad.*
2 V If you **trip** when you are walking, you knock your foot against something and fall or nearly fall. *He tripped and fell... She tripped over a stone.*
3 VO If you **trip** someone who is walking, you put your foot or something else in front of them so that they knock their own foot against it and fall or nearly fall. *Somebody thrust out a foot and tripped him.*
4 NC A **trip** is also an unreal experience caused by taking drugs; an informal use.
5 See also **round trip**.

trip up PHRASAL VERB 1 If you **trip up** someone who is walking, you put your foot or something else in front of them so that they knock their own foot against it and fall or nearly fall. *She tripped up the steward as he passed.* 2 To **trip** someone **up** also means to cause them to make a mistake or become confused. *The judge's questions tripped me up completely.*

tripartite /traɪpɑːtaɪt/
ADJ ATTRIB **Tripartite** means having three parts or involving three groups of people; a formal word. *...the tripartite system of education... The unions called for tripartite talks.*

tripe /traɪp/
1 NU **Tripe** is the stomach of a pig, cow, or ox, which is eaten as food. *Some foods, especially offal, liver, kidneys and tripe, are liable to cause gout in susceptible people.*
2 NU If you refer to something that someone has said or written as **tripe**, you think what they have said is worthless or silly; an informal use. *Chris Patten dismissed as tripe reports that only non-Tory councils would be capped. ...what nonsense, what tripe.*

triple /trɪpl/ **triples, tripling, tripled**
1 ADJ ATTRIB **Triple** means consisting of three things or parts. *...a triple alliance. ...a breath-taking triple somersault.*
2 V-ERG If you **triple** something or if it **triples**, it becomes three times greater in amount or size. *In three years the company had tripled its sales... Drug crimes here have tripled since 1987.*
3 PREDET If something is **triple** the amount or size of another thing, it is three times greater in amount or

size. *The government is worried about what consumers will do when shop clerks demand double or triple the old prices for everything.*

triple jump
N SING The **triple jump** is an athletic event in which competitors have to jump as far as they can, and are allowed to touch the ground once with each foot in the course of the jump. *Conley was the 1984 Olympic silver medalist in the men's triple jump.*

triplet /trɪplət/ **triplets**
NC **Triplets** are three children born at the same time to the same mother. *...eight-month-old triplets.*

triplicate /trɪplɪkət/
If you have a document in **triplicate**, you have three identical copies of it. *I had filled in the forms in triplicate.*

tripod /traɪpɒd/ **tripods**
NC A **tripod** is a stand with three legs that is used to support something such as a camera or telescope. *...a camera and tripod. ...a low powered laser mounted on a tripod.*

Tripoli /trɪpəli/
Tripoli is the capital of Libya and its largest city. Population: 859,000 (1981).

tripper /trɪpə/ **trippers**
NC A **tripper** is a person who is on a trip or on holiday; an old-fashioned word. *We were paddling in the sea, like elderly trippers at Southend.*

tripwire /trɪpwaɪə/ **tripwires**
NC A **tripwire** is a wire stretched just above the ground, which triggers a trap or an explosion if someone touches it.

trite /traɪt/
ADJ **Trite** ideas, remarks, and stories are dull because they have been heard too many times before. *There is a virtue in pop music which doesn't just pump out clichés about love or other trite sentiments.*

triumph /traɪəmf, traɪʌmf/ **triumphs, triumphing, triumphed**
1 NC A **triumph** is a great success or achievement, often one that has been gained by great skill or effort. *The election result was a personal triumph for the party leader... This machine is a triumph of advanced technology.*
2 NU **Triumph** is a feeling of great satisfaction when you win or achieve something. *I saw a gleam of triumph in his eye.*
3 V If you **triumph**, you win a victory or succeed in overcoming something. *She learned to triumph over her disabilities... Mrs Thatcher said that terrorists must never be allowed to triumph.*

triumphal /traɪʌmfl/
ADJ ATTRIB **Triumphal** is used to describe things that are done or made to celebrate a victory or great success. *...a triumphal arch. ...his triumphal return to Peking.*

triumphant /traɪʌmfənt/
ADJ If you are **triumphant**, you feel very happy because you have won a victory or achieved something. *In the Australian Open, John McEnroe made a triumphant return after an absence of three years. ...triumphant soldiers.* ◆ **triumphantly** ADV *Robert was looking at me triumphantly.*

triumvirate /traɪʌmvərət/ **triumvirates.**
N COLL A **triumvirate** is a group of three people who together are in charge of something; a formal word. *...the artistic triumvirate of playwright, actor, and director.*

trivia /trɪviə/
NU If you refer to things as **trivia**, you mean that they are unimportant. *She takes a childish delight in remembering trivia.*

trivial /trɪviəl/
ADJ **Trivial** things are unimportant. *All those little details of organization seemed trivial.*

triviality /trɪviæləti/ **trivialities**
1 N PL **Trivialities** are unimportant things. *...the daily trivialities which seem so important to men.*
2 NU The **triviality** of something is the fact that it is unimportant. *...conversations of unbelievable triviality.*

trivialize /trɪviəlaɪz/ **trivializes, trivializing, trivialized**; also spelt **trivialise.**
VO If you **trivialize** something, you make it seem unimportant, although it is actually important. *Their political role is often trivialized.*

trod /trɒd/
Trod is the past tense of **tread**.

trodden /trɒdn/
Trodden is the past participle of **tread**.

troll /trɒl, trəʊl/ **trolls**
NC A **troll** is an imaginary creature in Scandinavian mythology. Trolls look like very ugly people, live in caves or mountains, and turn to stone at daybreak.

trolley /trɒli/ **trolleys**
1 NC A **trolley** is a small cart that you use to carry things, for example shopping or luggage. *...supermarket trolleys. ...a middle-aged man pulling a luggage trolley.*
2 NC A **trolley** is also a small table on wheels on which food and drinks can be carried. *The room-service boy wheeled the trolley in.*
3 NC In American English, a **trolley** is the same as a **tram**. *A trolley unloading passengers in Boston was hit by another trolley this morning.*

trolley bus, trolley buses
NC A **trolley bus** is an electric bus that is driven by electric power taken from cables above the street. *If you don't live on an underground line then the network of buses and trolley buses is the alternative.*

trombone /trɒmbəʊn/ **trombones**
NC A **trombone** is a brass musical instrument which you play by blowing into it and sliding part of it backwards and forwards. *The sound is made by buzzing your lips as you would do to play a trombone or a tuba.*

trombonist /trɒmbəʊnɪst/ **trombonists**
NC A **trombonist** is a person who plays a trombone. *Roland Klemen is a trombonist with the local radio symphony orchestra.*

troop /truːp/ **troops, trooping, trooped.** For the meaning in paragraph 1, the form **troop** is used as a noun modifier.
1 N PL **Troops** are soldiers, especially when they are in a large controlled group. *They have more than 11,000 troops in Northern Ireland. ...reports on troop movements.*
2 NC A **troop** is a group of soldiers within a cavalry or armoured division. *There is no indication that the heavy pounding on Iraq's elite troop has broken their will to fight.*
3 NC A **troop** of people or animals is a group of them. *...a troop of monkeys.*
4 V A If people **troop** somewhere, they walk there in a group. *The twelve men trooped downstairs.*
5 When soldiers **troop the colour**, they take part in a regimental ceremony, especially a parade of some kind. *...the horse which carried the Queen to eighteen Trooping the Colour ceremonies.*

trooper /truːpə/ **troopers**
1 NCor TITLE A **trooper** is a soldier of low rank in an armoured regiment in the army. *He became a trooper in the Royal Tank Regiment... I spoke to Trooper Paul Duncan, from Sussex.*
2 NCor TITLE In the United States, a **trooper** is also a policeman in a state police force. *...a job as a trooper with the Ohio State Highway Patrol... State troopers evacuated more than 200 people after the fire moved dangerously close to campsites. ...Trooper Bill Polazi.*
3 If someone **swears like a trooper**, they swear a lot; an informal expression, used showing disapproval. *Thieves snatched a parrot which imitates police sirens, swears like a trooper and blows raspberries when Mrs Thatcher is on television.*

trophy /trəʊfi/ **trophies**
NC A **trophy** is a prize, for example a cup or shield, which is given to the winner of a competition. *He triumphantly showed off the men's singles trophy to the crowd. ...the first round of the John Player Trophy.*

tropical /trɒpɪkl/
ADJ ATTRIB **Tropical** means relating to or typical of the tropics. *...experts in tropical medicine. ...tropical rainforests. ...the sticky tropical heat of Panama.*

tropics /trɒpɪks/

N PL The **tropics** are the hottest parts of the world, near the equator. *The tropics are very lush and there's a great deal of life there... The big bamboos of the monsoon tropics can grow up to 40 metres in height.*

trot /trɒt/ **trots, trotting, trotted**

1 V When an animal such as a horse **trots**, it moves fairly fast, lifting its feet quite high off the ground. *He made the beast turn aside and trot away.* ▸ Also N SING *She urged her pony into an energetic trot.*

2 V A If you **trot** somewhere, you move fairly fast, taking small quick steps. *We trotted along behind him.*

3 If several things happen **on the trot**, they happen one after the other, without a break; an informal expression. *Try not to miss two lessons on the trot.*

trot out PHRASAL VERB If you **trot out** old ideas or pieces of information, you repeat them in a boring way. *They trot out all the old reasons for their failure.*

trotter /trɒtə/ **trotters**

N C **Trotters** are pigs' feet which you can cook and eat.

troubadour /truːbədɔː/ **troubadours**

N C A **troubadour** is a poet and singer. *Troubadours used to travel around and perform to noble families in Italy and Southern France in the twelfth and thirteenth centuries. Troubadours sang of ladies fair.*

trouble /trʌbl/ **troubles, troubling, troubled**

1 NU If you have **trouble** doing something, you have difficulties or problems doing it. *You shouldn't have any trouble locating them... This would save everyone a lot of trouble.*

2 N SING If you say that one aspect of a situation is the **trouble**, you mean that it is the aspect which is causing problems or making the situation unsatisfactory. *It's getting a bit expensive now, that's the trouble... The trouble with you is that you've forgotten what it's like to be young.*

3 N PL Your **troubles** are your personal problems. *She thought that all her troubles were over.*

4 N PL You can refer to a long and sustained period of civil unrest or fighting in a place as the **troubles**. *Since the troubles began again in 1969 over 2500 people have been murdered in Northern Ireland... We didn't deport people to Romania during the troubles there.*

5 NU+SUPP You use **trouble** to say that you have something wrong with a part of your body. *She had no medical history of heart trouble... He hasn't played for the team since 1986 and is currently suffering from ankle trouble.*

6 NU If there is **trouble**, people are quarrelling or fighting. *He's the sort of person who always makes trouble... He is believed to have disappeared during the trouble following the July 14th demonstrations.*

7 NU If you say that it is no **trouble** to do something for someone, you mean that you do not mind doing it. *'It wouldn't be any trouble.'—'That's very kind of you.'*

8 V O If something **troubles** you, it makes you feel worried or uneasy. *What's troubling you?* ◆ **troubling** ADJ *It was a new and troubling thought.*

9 V O If you say that you are sorry to **trouble** someone, you are apologizing for disturbing them. *I'm sorry to trouble you, but I wondered if we could have a word some time.*

● **Trouble** is used in these phrases. ● You can say that someone is **in trouble** when they have a serious problem such as a lack of money or when they have broken a rule or law and are likely to be punished. *Frank was still in deep financial trouble. ...if a child is in trouble with the police... I don't want to get you into trouble.* ● If you **take the trouble** to do something, you do it although it requires some time or effort. *At least they took the trouble to build railways, steelworks and refineries and added to America's wealth... Sir Geoffrey Howe took the trouble to pay the Professor a visit at his home in Islamabad.*

troubled /trʌbld/

1 ADJ Someone who is **troubled** is worried because they have problems. *...a troubled young man with a fascination for knives... She seemed to lapse into a troubled sleep.*

2 ADJ A **troubled** place, organization, or time has many problems or conflicts. *The Prime Minister has decided not to hold elections in the troubled Punjab state. ...the proposed takeover bid for the troubled British electronics company Ferranti.*

trouble-free

ADJ Something that is **trouble-free** does not cause any problems or difficulties. *Each submarine reported a trouble-free launch.*

troublemaker /trʌblmeɪkə/ **troublemakers**

N C A **troublemaker** is someone who causes unpleasantness, quarrels, ill feeling, or rebellion. *He was a troublemaker who has already been in court for burning down a school building.*

troublemaking /trʌblmeɪkɪŋ/

1 NU **Troublemaking** refers to activities which cause unpleasantness, quarrels, ill feeling, or rebellion. *Organs of public security, he said, should be fully prepared to deal with any kind of troublemaking.*

2 ADJ **Troublemaking** people cause unpleasantness, quarrels, ill feeling, or rebellion. *...a quarrelsome, troublemaking wife. ...troublemaking influences.*

troubleshooter /trʌblʃuːtə/ **troubleshooters**

N C A **troubleshooter** is a person whose job is to solve major problems or difficulties that occur in a company or government or in an aspect of the company or government's work. *The fire defied the efforts of Texan oil troubleshooter, Red Adair... The Kremlin troubleshooters have met representatives of the demonstrators and appealed for calm.*

troublesome /trʌblsəm/

1 ADJ Someone or something that is **troublesome** causes problems. *...troublesome tenants. ...a troublesome injury.*

2 ADJ A situation that is **troublesome** is full of difficulties which cannot easily be solved. *The Gulf crisis has provided only a temporary diversion from troublesome domestic problems. ...the troublesome issues of economic, monetary and political union.*

trouble spot, trouble spots

N C A **trouble spot** is a country or an area of a country where there is repeated fighting between two or more groups of people. *General Yazov said the worst trouble spots were on the edge of the disputed area of Nagorno Karabakh.*

trough /trɒf/ **troughs**

1 N C A **trough** is a long container from which farm animals drink or eat. *Of course, the poultry know their feeding and water troughs.*

2 N C A **trough** is also the low point in a pattern that has regular high and low points, for example in a series of waves or in a pattern of events that comes in cycles. *The heart has a sort of wave form of pressure, peak and trough, peak and trough... The light waves emerge with all the crests and troughs of the wave frequency aligned... The trade figures could mark the beginning of a climb out of an economic trough.*

trounce /traʊns/ **trounces, trouncing, trounced**

V O If you **trounce** someone, you defeat them heavily and completely; an informal word. *The Front trounced the FLN in local elections. ...the game in which the Boston Red Sox trounced the St Louis Browns by the score of 29-2.*

troupe /truːp/ **troupes**

N COLL A **troupe** is a group of actors, singers, or dancers who work together. *...a programme of visits by dance and music troupes.*

trousers /traʊzəz/. The form **trouser** is used as a noun modifier.

N PL **Trousers** are a piece of clothing that you wear over your body from the waist downwards. Trousers cover each leg separately. *...a pair of black trousers... He slid it gently into his trouser pocket.*

trouser suit, trouser suits

N C A **trouser suit** is a suit consisting of a pair of trousers and a jacket which is worn by women. *Sue wears a blue trouser suit and a neat scarf.*

trousseau /truːsəʊ/ **trousseaux** /truːsəʊ/ or **trousseaus**.

N C A **trousseau** is the clothes, linen, and other possessions that a bride collects for her marriage; an old-fashioned word.

trout /traʊt/; trout is both the singular and the plural form.
NUorNC A **trout** is a kind of fish that lives in rivers and freshwater lakes. Trouts can be cooked and eaten. *Wildlife such as frogs and trout are under threat... The coelacanth does not have a swim bladder like a trout or a sunfish.*

trove /trəʊv/. See **treasure trove**.

Trovoada, Miguel /miːɡel trʊvwɑːðə/
Miguel Trovoada became the President of São Tomé and Príncipe in 1991. He was Prime Minister from 1975 to 1979, and was in exile from 1981 to 1990. He is an independent, but is supported by the Democratic Convergence Party - Reflexion Group (PDC-GR). Born: 1937.

trowel /traʊəl/ **trowels**
1 NC A **trowel** is a small garden tool with a curved, pointed blade used for weeding and planting.
2 NC A **trowel** is also a small tool with a flat blade that is used for spreading cement. *Use your trowel to make it nice and flat.*

truancy /truːənsi/
NU When children stay away from school without permission, you describe their behaviour as **truancy**. *The longer the period of truancy, the harder it becomes to return to school.*

truant /truːənt/ **truants**
NC A **truant** is a child who stays away from school without permission. *His elder brother had been a habitual truant.* ● If children **play truant**, they stay away from school without permission. *In my last year I played truant a lot.*

truce /truːs/ **truces**
NC A **truce** is an agreement between two people or groups to stop fighting or arguing for a short time. *They have declared a unilateral 15-day truce... Despite efforts to restore the truce, violent clashes went on through the night... The summit has resulted in an uneasy truce between the US on one hand and the European nations on the other.*

truck /trʌk/ **trucks, trucking, trucked**
1 NC A **truck** is the same as a **lorry**. *The fire spread rapidly after a truck carrying chemicals exploded... The restaurant was full of truck drivers.*
2 NC A **truck** is also an open vehicle used for carrying goods on a railway. *They were herded into the square before being loaded onto railway trucks for the journey.*
3 VOA To **truck** something somewhere means to transport it there in a truck. *They are trucking food in from London, a three-day drive away... The wall sections are trucked away to be recycled.*
4 If you say that you will have **no truck with** someone, you mean that you will refuse to be involved with them or do business with them. *A Northern Ireland bishop has called on Roman Catholics to have no truck with the evil of the IRA... The government reaffirmed its policy of no truck with terrorists.*

trucker /trʌkə/ **truckers**
NC A **trucker** is someone who drives a lorry as their job; used in American English. *The trucker pulled over and asked police officers for directions.*

truckload /trʌkləʊd/ **truckloads**
NC A **truckload** of goods or people is the amount of them that a truck can carry. *One witness saw three truckloads of soldiers dressed in civilian clothes driving away from the port.*

truculence /trʌkjʊləns/
NU **Truculence** is the quality or state of being bad-tempered and aggressive; an old-fashioned word. *Sandy's brief moment of truculence had vanished.*

truculent /trʌkjʊlənt/
ADJ A **truculent** person is bad-tempered and aggressive. *He was a truculent and quarrelsome man.*

trudge /trʌdʒ/ **trudges, trudging, trudged**
VA If you **trudge** somewhere, you walk there with slow, heavy steps. *Michael trudged up the hill.* ► Also N SING *They set off for the long trudge home.*

true /truː/ **truer, truest**
1 ADJ A **true** story or statement is based on facts and is not invented or imagined. *The story about the murder is true... Unfortunately it was true about*

Sylvie... She gave a true account of what had happened.
2 ADJ ATTRIB **True** is used to describe people or things that have all the typical characteristics of a particular thing. *He's a true American, in every respect. ...true equality among the republics. ...true democracy.*
3 ADJ ATTRIB **True** feelings are sincere and genuine. *Fear was stopping people from expressing their true feelings... She smiled with true amusement.*
4 ADJ PRED+to If you are **true** to someone, you are faithful, loyal, and honest towards them; a formal use. *As a judge he will remain true to his commitments... He has remained true to the party.*
5 ADV SEN You can say **true** when you want to admit that a fact or opinion is real or valid, but that it is not important or that it does not have any consequences in the circumstances. *True, Mr Gorbachev has assigned to himself extensive powers. But they have proved largely theoretical... His room for manoeuvre was, it is true, limited by the hardliners in the party and military.*
● **True** is used in these phrases. ● If a dream, wish, or prediction **comes true**, it actually happens. *Helmut Kohl described unification as a dream come true.* ● If you are **true to your word**, you do what you had promised to do. *True to their word, the militia stood down as the troops advanced on foot through the shattered streets.*

true-blue
ADJ A **true-blue** person is conventional in their ideas, opinions, and behaviour, especially in a way that is associated with the Conservative Party in Britain. *He soon became a reliable true-blue country club conservative.*

true north
NU **True north** is the direction that is north according to the earth's geographical poles, rather than according to magnetic poles. *So we don't really know whether the innate direction of migration is referenced to true north?*

truffle /trʌfl/ **truffles**
1 NC A **truffle** is a soft round sweet flavoured with chocolate or rum.
2 NC A **truffle** is also a round mushroom-like fungus which grows underground and is considered very good to eat. *Your personal chef will prepare whatever you like, from salmon to caviare and truffles.*

truism /truːɪzəm/ **truisms**
NC A **truism** is a statement that is so clearly true and repeated so often that it is boring. *It is a trite and obvious truism that people act in accordance with their motives.*

truly /truːli/
1 ADV **Truly** means completely and genuinely. *He was now truly American. ...many of the new Soviet politicians who want to create a truly democratic society.*
2 ADV If you feel something **truly**, you feel it in a sincere way. *He knew he had behaved badly and he seemed truly sorry... I'm truly very proud, and it's a great honour to receive such an award.*
3 ADV SEN You can use **truly** to emphasize that what you are saying is true. *And truly, coming home was the nicest part of the trip.*
4 SUBMOD **Truly** also means to a very great degree; a formal use. *He possessed a truly remarkable talent... A Labour spokesman said the figures were truly dreadful.*
5 You can write **yours truly** before your signature at the end of a formal letter. *Yours truly, Desmond Burton-Cox.*
6 **well and truly**: see **well**.

Truman, Harry S /hæri es truːmən/
Harry S Truman was President of the United States from 1945 to 1953. He was born in 1884. He was a Democrat and served in the Senate from 1934 to 1944. From 1944 to 1945 he was Vice President, becoming President at the death of Franklin Roosevelt. He ordered the first use of nuclear weapons against Japan in 1945, was responsible for the Marshall Plan which provided economic aid for the reconstruction of post-war Europe, and sent US troops into Korea in 1950. He

died in 1972.

trump /trʌmp/ **trumps**

1 N PL In a game of cards, **trumps** is the suit with the highest value.

2 Your **trump card** is the most powerful thing that you can use or do to gain an advantage. *Spain has at last produced her trump card and sent on the field of battle her most deadly weapon... The military historian holds the trump card—a telegram incriminating the accused as a war criminal.*

trumped-up /trʌmpt ʌp/

ADJ **Trumped-up** charges are untrue, and made up in order to punish someone unfairly. *He was hauled into a military court on trumped-up charges of selling secrets... Anyone who dared challenge them was arrested on trumped-up charges.*

trumpet /trʌmpɪt/ **trumpets, trumpeting, trumpeted**

1 NC A **trumpet** is a brass wind instrument with three buttons that you press to get different notes. *The material used to make a trumpet may affect its tone. ...a fanfare of trumpets.*

2 VO If you **trumpet** something that you are proud of or that you think is important, you announce it widely so that many people get to hear about it. *Newspapers have been trumpeting reports of Ali Shah's imminent resignation for weeks... The government was not inclined to trumpet the policies of the past four decades.*

3 If you **blow your own trumpet**, you boast about yourself; an informal expression. *I'm not blowing my own trumpet, but I do all the top jobs.*

trumpeter /trʌmpɪtə/ **trumpeters**

NC A **trumpeter** is someone who plays a trumpet. *...Don Cherry, the American jazz trumpeter.*

truncate /trʌŋkeɪt/ **truncates, truncating, truncated**

VO If something is **truncated**, it is made shorter; an informal word. *The lines were truncated... The truncated corpse was stuffed into a bag.*

truncheon /trʌntʃən/ **truncheons**

NC A **truncheon** is a short, thick stick used by British policemen as a weapon. *Eye-witnesses talked of police using truncheons, dogs, and water cannon to disperse the crowd.*

trundle /trʌndl/ **trundles, trundling, trundled**

1 VA If a vehicle **trundles** somewhere, it moves there slowly. *17 convoys of supplies, each with 200 vehicles, have trundled off into the town... We watched the combine harvesters trundle through the field.*

2 VOA If you **trundle** something somewhere, you move or roll it along slowly. *She saw him trundling the push chair along in the nearby park.*

trunk /trʌŋk/ **trunks**

1 NC The **trunk** of a tree is the large main stem from which the branches grow. *The ideal Christmas tree has a straight trunk, conical shape and upward-pointing branches.*

2 NC Your **trunk** is the central part of your body; a formal use. *This exercise is helpful where you want trunk, arm, and shoulder movements to be made better.*

3 NC An elephant's **trunk** is its long nose. *He wore a pair of tusks fixed to the side of his head, and a large trunk made from a long sock.*

4 NC A **trunk** is also a large, strong case or box used for storing things or for taking on a journey. *He rummaged through his wife's trunk, taking the money hidden in it.*

5 NC The **trunk** of a car is a covered space at the back or front that is used for luggage; used in American English. *Police say they have found the bodies of five young men in the trunk of a car parked at a public housing project.*

trunk call, trunk calls

NC A **trunk call** is a telephone call to a different town from the one you are in; an old-fashioned expression. *When a trunk call fails, an alternative path is created in the network.*

trunk road, trunk roads

NC A **trunk road** is a main road, especially one that is suitable for heavy vehicles. *A hundred and sixty-four million pounds is to be spent on bringing Britain's trunk roads up to date.*

truss /trʌs/ **trusses, trussing, trussed**

1 VO If you **truss** a bird, you prepare it for cooking by tying its legs and wings. *I plucked and trussed the chicken.*

2 NC A **truss** is a device that a man wears to support a hernia and prevent it from getting worse.

truss up PHRASAL VERB If you **truss** someone **up**, you tie them up with ropes very tightly so that they cannot move; an old-fashioned expression. *The bank robbers trussed up the manager and his staff and locked them in the vault.*

trust /trʌst/ **trusts, trusting, trusted**

1 VO If you **trust** someone, you believe that they are honest and will not deliberately do anything to harm you. *Everybody liked and trusted him... You're the only one I can trust, because you're the only one without a vested interest.* ► Also NU *Adam could feel his father's trust in him.*

2 VO+to-INF If you **trust** someone to do something, you believe that they will do it. *She didn't trust anyone to look after her child properly... He doesn't trust the government to keep from tapping his phone.*

3 VO+with If you **trust** someone with something, you allow them to look after it or deal with it. *Next year I hope the company will trust me with a bigger budget.*

4 VO If you do not **trust** something, you feel that it is not safe or reliable. *I don't trust fancy gimmicks in cars... He wanted to get up and walk, but he didn't trust his legs.*

5 VO If you **trust** someone's judgement or advice, you believe that it is good or right. *Trust your own instincts... She seems to trust his advice... You should never trust an economist's predictions.*

6 V-REPORT If you **trust** that something is true, you hope or expect that it is true; an old-fashioned use. *They will give you a good pension, I trust?... We trust that you, Mr President, will do everything in your power to facilitate their speedy release.*

7 NU **Trust** is also responsibility that you are given to deal with important, valuable, or secret things. *The judge took the view that to betray a position of trust in such a manner was disgraceful. ...plain old American values: honesty, trust, responsibility, commitment.*

8 NC A **trust** is a financial arrangement in which an organization keeps and invests money for someone. *...a lifetime interest trust.*

9 NC A **trust** is also a group of people or an organization that has control of an amount of money and invests it on behalf of other people or as a charity. *...charitable trusts.*

10 NC A group of companies that join together in order to control the market for the particular thing that they produce is also called a **trust**. Trusts are illegal in the United States. *...anti-trust laws.*

● **Trust** is used in these phrases. ● If money is kept **in trust**, it is held and invested for someone by a group of people or an organization. *It's up to us to leave more resources in trust for our descendants.* ● If you **take** something that someone tells you **on trust**, you believe it completely without checking it. *It would be most unwise to take anything on trust from him.*

trustee /trʌstiː/ **trustees**

NC A **trustee** is someone with legal control of money or property that is kept or invested for another person. *Her request for money was turned down by the trustees.*

trustful /trʌstfl/

ADJ Someone who is **trustful** trusts other people easily; an old-fashioned word. *The meeting had been held in an open and trustful atmosphere.*

trust fund, trust funds

NC A **trust fund** is an amount of money or property that someone owns, usually by inheriting it, but which is kept and invested for them. *My money is all tied up in trust funds... She inherited part of a trust fund.*

trusting /trʌstɪŋ/

ADJ A **trusting** person believes that people are honest and sincere and do not intend to harm them. *Judy had an open and trusting nature... The officials targeted a particularly vulnerable and trusting group, such as old people with savings.*

trustworthy /trʌstwɜːðɪ/
ADJ A **trustworthy** person is reliable and responsible. *He was an experienced and trustworthy travelling companion... A Boy Scout is trustworthy, loyal, helpful, friendly, and brave.*

trusty /trʌstɪ/
ADJ ATTRIB **Trusty** things and animals are considered to be reliable because they have always worked well in the past; often used humorously. *I put on my trusty overcoat... We managed to find the place, but not without a trusty guide.*

truth /truːθ/ **truths**
1 N SING The **truth** is all the facts about something, rather than things that are imagined or invented. *He learned the truth about Sam... He's probably telling the truth... The people must learn the truth, the full truth.*
2 NU If you say that there is **truth** in a statement or story, you mean that it is true, or partly true. *There is an element of truth in this... I could not deny the truth of this statement.*
3 NC A **truth** is an idea or principle that is generally accepted to be true. *It's a book that contains important truths. ...a universal truth.*

truthful /truːθfl/
1 ADJ A **truthful** person is honest and tells the truth. *Many patients are more truthful when they talk to the computer than when they talk to the doctor... Most people consider the radio to be the most truthful source of information.* ♦ **truthfully** ADV *If I ask him a question he will answer it as truthfully as he can.*
2 ADJ A **truthful** statement or account is true rather than invented. *Iraq had already given a truthful list of its nuclear capabilities... Journalists and opposition leaders stormed his office demanding truthful coverage of the conflict.*

try /traɪ/ **tries, trying, tried**
1 V+to-INF If you **try** to do something, you want to do it, and you take actions which you hope will help you to do it. *I tried hard not to think about it... Mr Haughey said he had tried without success to achieve progress in dealings with Britain... Violence broke out when the police tried to arrest a priest... Several earlier administrations tried and failed to depose Mr Hernandez.* ► Also NC *After a few tries they gave up.*
2 V+for If you **try** for something, you make an effort to get it or achieve it. *The school advised Mr Denby to let his son try for university.*
3 V OorV+ING If you **try** something, you use it or do it in order to find out how useful, effective, or enjoyable it is. *I know it works, because I've tried it myself... I tried a different approach to the problem... He tried his wine... Farmers have tried burning down the thickets, but they just sprout up again.* ► Also NC *We can give it a try and see how it looks.*
4 VO If you **try** a particular place or person, you go to that place or person because you think they may be able to provide you with what you want. *We tried two or three hotels, but they were full.*
5 VO+for When a person is **tried**, he or she appears in a law court and is found innocent or guilty after the judge and jury have heard the evidence. *He is to be tried for possessing and supplying drugs... A youth was tried in the criminal courts for stealing.*
6 NC A **try** is also the action in a game of rugby when a player puts the ball down behind the goal line of the opposing team, and scores three or four points. *They ran in nine tries to beat the Soviet Union by 53 points to nil.*
7 to **try** your **hand** at something: see **hand**. to **try** your luck at something: see **luck**.

try on PHRASAL VERB If you **try on** a piece of clothing, you put it on to see if it suits or fits you. *She tried on her new dress... Just try it on for size.*

try out PHRASAL VERB If you **try** something **out**, you test it in order to find out how useful or effective it is. *Oxford is trying out an idea to help working parents... They completed a four-hour space walk while construction techniques were being tried out.*

try out for PHRASAL VERB If you **try out for** membership of a team or organization, you compete in order to gain membership of it; used in American

English. *He tried out for the basketball team, but after watching a few games, chose football instead... In 1965, Malpass tried out for the Mississippi All-State Concert Band.*

trying /traɪɪŋ/
ADJ Something or someone that is **trying** is difficult to deal with and makes you feel impatient or annoyed. *It had been a most trying experience for them.*

try-out, try-outs
NC If you give something a **try-out**, you try it or test it so that you can find out how useful or effective it is. *A neighbour had given the machine a good try-out.*

tryst /trɪst/ **trysts**
NC A **tryst** is a meeting between lovers in a quiet secret place; a literary word.

tsar /zɑː/ **tsars**; also spelt **czar** or **tzar**.
NCor TITLE A **tsar** was the male ruler of Russia in former times. *...Tsar Nicholas II of Russia.*

tsarina /zɑːriːnə/ **tsarinas**; also spelt **czarina** or **tzarina**.
NCor TITLE A **tsarina** was the female ruler of Russia or the wife of the tsar in former times. *His wife Tsarina Alexandra was the grand-daughter of Queen Victoria.*

tsarist /zɑːrɪst/; also spelt **czarist** or **tzarist**.
ADJ ATTRIB **Tsarist** means belonging to or believing in the system of government by a tsar, especially in Russia before 1917. *...tsarist dreams of empire.*

tsetse fly /tsetsɪ flaɪ/ **tsetse flies**; also spelt **tzetze fly**.
NCor NU A **tsetse fly** is an African fly that feeds on blood and can transmit serious diseases, such as sleeping sickness. *Mosquitoes and tsetse flies plagued us... The disease is carried by the tsetse fly, and is also transmitted to cattle.*

T-shirt /tiːʃɜːt/ **T-shirts**
NC A **T-shirt** is a cotton shirt with short sleeves and no collar or buttons. *They wear a distinctive uniform of red berets and white T-shirts.*

tsp., tsps.
Tsp. is a written abbreviation for 'teaspoon'.

tub /tʌb/ **tubs**
1 NC A **tub** is a wide, circular container. *...a tub big enough to hold eighteen gallons... The bonfire over there is being used to heat a tub of water.*
2 NC A **tub** is also the same as a **bath**; used in American English. *Maybe I'll go and sit in a hot tub for a while.*

tuba /tjuːbə/ **tubas**
NC A **tuba** is a very large brass musical instrument that can produce very low notes. *He's considering a career as a jazz player because it offers more challenges than playing the tuba.*

tubby /tʌbɪ/
ADJ A **tubby** person is rather fat; an informal word. *Sixty-six year old Shaliza, short and tubby, was decked out in his usual western-style necktie and shirt.*

tube /tjuːb/ **tubes**
1 NC A **tube** is a long, hollow object, especially one through which air or a liquid passes. *...a rubber tube fixed to the tap. ...breathing tubes.*
2 NC A **tube** of paste is a long, thin container which you squeeze in order to force the paste out. *...a tube of toothpaste... Epoxy resin comes in two tubes, a glue and a hardener, which you mix together.*
3 N SING The **Tube** is the underground railway system in London. *When I come by Tube it takes about an hour. ...a tube train.*
4 N SING You can refer to television as the **tube**; used in American English. *Every Saturday, when they turned on the tube, they saw that 75 per cent of the NBA players were black... By giving them revenue, the government hoped to foster creativity and diversity on the tube.*

tuber /tjuːbə/ **tubers**
NC A **tuber** is the swollen underground stem of particular types of plants. *Because it's a tuber, it has its own storage resources. ...tuber crops.*

tubercular /tjuːbɜːkjʊlə/
ADJ **Tubercular** means relating to, causing, or suffering from tuberculosis. *...a sanatorium for tubercular patients.*

tuberculosis /tjuːbɜːkjʊˈləʊsɪs/
N U **Tuberculosis** is a serious infectious disease that affects the lungs. *His medical speciality was tuberculosis... Many of the refugees have malaria, tuberculosis, and skin diseases such as scabies.*

tubing /ˈtjuːbɪŋ/
N U **Tubing** is a material such as plastic or rubber made into tubes. *The cooling system runs through 300 feet of copper tubing.*

tubular /ˈtjuːbjʊlə/
ADJ Something that is **tubular** is long, round, and hollow in shape, like a tube. *The whole thing fits into a tubular compartment for storage and carrying.*

TUC /ˌtiːjuːˈsiː/
N PROP The **TUC** is a British association of trade unions. **TUC** is an abbreviation for 'Trades Union Congress'. *The Labour Party has joined the TUC in opposing the Government's plans to sell off the nuclear industry. ...the TUC Congress in Blackpool.*

tuck /tʌk/ **tucks, tucking, tucked**
V O A If you **tuck** something somewhere, you put it there so that it is safe or comfortable. *He tucked the shell under his arm. ...small American flags just like the one he had tucked in his top pocket.*
tuck away PHRASAL VERB 1 If you **tuck** something **away**, you store it in a safe place. *She had a bit of money tucked away.* 2 If something is **tucked away**, it is in a place where it cannot easily be found. *The parish church is tucked away behind the cathedral... The article was tucked away in a provincial newspaper.*
tuck in PHRASAL VERB 1 If you **tuck** a child or other person **in**, you make them comfortable in bed by arranging the blankets and pushing the loose ends under the mattress. *He was asleep before I tucked him in.* 2 If you **tuck** your clothes **in**, you put the loose ends, for example of a shirt, inside your trousers or skirt. *Straighten your cap and tuck your shirt in... Older men wore the Arab headdress and a long robe with the bottom pulled up and tucked in at the waist. ...wearing blue jeans tucked into army boots.*
tuck into PHRASAL VERB If you **tuck into** food, you eat it with a lot of pleasure; an informal use. *She was happily tucking into whatever dishes were put in front of her... He was discovered at a roadside cafe tucking into a plate of fried food.*
tuck up PHRASAL VERB If you **tuck** a child or other person **up**, you make them comfortable in bed by arranging the blankets and pushing the loose ends under the mattress. *The children could look forward to being tucked up in warm beds by their mothers.*

Tudjman, Dr Franjo /ˈfrænjəʊ ˈtuːdʒmæn/
Dr Franjo **Tudjman** became President of Croatia in 1990. He is the leader of the Croatian Democratic Union (HDZ).

Tue. or Tues.
Tue. or Tues. is a written abbreviation for 'Tuesday'. *The report was published yesterday (Tue.).*

Tuesday /ˈtjuːzdeɪ, ˈtjuːzdi/ **Tuesdays**
N U or N C **Tuesday** is the day after Monday and before Wednesday. *She will appear in court on Tuesday.*

tuft /tʌft/ **tufts**
N C A **tuft** of hair or grass is a small bunch of it growing closely together. *Her tiny head was covered with tufts of fair hair.*

tug /tʌg/ **tugs, tugging, tugged**
1 V O or V+at If you **tug** something or **tug** at it, you give it a quick pull. *He tugged at the handle, and it came off in his hand.* ▶ Also N C *Tom felt a tug at his sleeve.*
2 N C A **tug** or a **tug boat** is a small, powerful boat used to pull large ships. *The captain was forcibly removed from the bridge and put on a tugboat.*

tug-of-love
ADJ ATTRIB **Tug-of-love** is used to describe a situation in which the parents of a child are divorced and the parent without custody tries to get the child, for example by kidnapping. *...tug-of-love children.*

tug-of-war
1 N SING or N U A **tug-of-war** is a sport in which two teams test their strength by pulling against each other on opposite ends of a rope. *The tug-of-war was the last event of the afternoon... The sailors won at tug-of-war.*
2 N SING or N U A **tug-of-war** is also a situation in which two people, or two groups of people, both want the same thing and are fairly equally matched in their struggle to get it. *Birmingham personality Rustie Lee is caught in a tug-of-war between Central and TV-am, who each want to sign her up. ...the ongoing tug-of-war over the budget.*

tuition /tjuˈɪʃn/
N U **Tuition** is the teaching of a subject, especially to one person or to a small group. *...private tuition.*

tulip /ˈtjuːlɪp/ **tulips**
N C A **tulip** is a flower that grows in the spring, and has a lot of oval or pointed petals packed closely together. *...paintings of tulips and African landscapes.*

tulle /tjuːl/
N U **Tulle** is a soft nylon or silk cloth that is rather like net, and is used for making evening dresses and veils.

tumble /ˈtʌmbl/ **tumbles, tumbling, tumbled**
1 V A or V If you **tumble** somewhere, you fall with a rolling or bouncing movement. *She pushed him and sent him tumbling downstairs.* ▶ Also N C *She suffered a tumble running after her kite.*
2 V A or V If water **tumbles** somewhere, it flows quickly over an uneven surface so that it splashes a lot. *He could hear the water tumbling over the rocks.*
tumble to PHRASAL VERB If you **tumble to** something, you suddenly understand it or realize what is happening; an informal expression. *What if he tumbles to what's going on?*

tumbledown /ˈtʌmbldaʊn/
ADJ A **tumbledown** building is in very bad condition and is partly falling down. *...a deserted, tumbledown building.*

tumble dryer, tumble dryers; also spelt **tumble drier.**
N C A **tumble dryer** is an electric machine that dries washing quickly. You put the wet clothes inside it and it turns them over slowly while blowing hot air onto them. *We have big tumble dryers which are heated via steam pipes.*

tumbler /ˈtʌmblə/ **tumblers**
N C A **tumbler** is a drinking glass with straight sides. *...a tumbler of whisky.*

tumescent /tjuˈmesənt/
ADJ Something that is **tumescent** is swelling so that it is becoming larger; a formal word.

tummy /ˈtʌmi/ **tummies**
N C Your **tummy** is your stomach; an informal word. *Not being used to the food there, she's suffering from a bit of an upset tummy.*

tumour /ˈtjuːmə/ **tumours;** spelt **tumor** in American English.
N C A **tumour** is a mass of diseased or abnormal cells that has grown in a person's or animal's body. *He was suffering from a brain tumour. ...heavy bleeding caused by an abdominal tumour. ...the genetic constitution of the tumour cell.*

tumult /ˈtjuːmʌlt/
N SING A **tumult** is a lot of noise caused by a crowd of people; a literary word. *A tumult of shots and yells could be heard... Presently the tumult died down.*

tumultuous /tjuːˈmʌltjuəs/
ADJ ATTRIB A **tumultuous** event is very noisy, because people are happy or excited; a literary word. *He was given a tumultuous welcome at an open air rally in Sydney... When the war was over, there was a tumultuous parade in London.*

tuna /ˈtjuːnə/; **tuna** is both the singular and the plural form.
N U or N C **Tuna** or **tuna fish** are large fish that live in warm seas and are caught for food. *...grilled tuna... Fishermen prefer the larger tuna that swim with dolphins... Food supplies are said to be adequate, although they consist mainly of tuna fish.*

tundra /ˈtʌndrə/ **tundras**
N U or N C **Tundra** is one of the large flat areas of land in the north of Europe, Asia, and America. The ground below the top layer of soil is always frozen and no trees grow there. *...the vast tundra of Canada's Northwest Territories... Canada's tundras could*

become rich forests.

tune /tjuːn/ **tunes, tuning, tuned**

1 NC A **tune** is a series of musical notes that is pleasing or memorable. A tune sometimes occurs repeatedly in a piece of music. *The orchestra was playing a selection of tunes from The Merry Widow.*
2 NC You can also refer to a song or a short musical piece as a **tune**. *She'll be playing some of your favourite pop tunes.*
3 VO When someone **tunes** a musical instrument, they adjust it so that it produces the right notes. *It's tuned like a regular cello, but it's double strung.*
4 VO When someone **tunes** an engine or machine, they adjust it so that it works well. *I told her the car needed tuning.*
5 VOor V+to If your radio or television is **tuned** to a particular broadcasting station, it has been adjusted so that you can listen to or watch the programmes on that station. *Stay tuned to Radio Desland for a further announcement... He just told me keep tuned to the news for the day.*
● **Tune** is used in these phrases. ● If you say that a particular person is the one who **calls the tune**, you mean that this person has authority and says what is to be done. *...a gesture to show it's not always the President who calls the tune.* ● If you play or sing **in tune**, you are playing or singing exactly the right notes. If you play or sing **out of tune**, you are playing or singing notes that are not quite right. *They suggest that what we think of as being in tune or out of tune may simply be a matter of what music we were exposed to as babies... Because this guitar is electronically tuned, it never goes out of tune.* ● If you are **in tune** with someone or something, you are in agreement with them or understand them well. *His ideas are in tune with the spirit of his age... Grey is perfectly in tune with his subject, witty yet sympathetic, and a prose writer of exceptional elegance.* ● If you **change** your **tune**, you say or do something different from what you previously said or did. *He soon changed his tune and started working as hard as the others.* ● **To the tune of** a particular amount means to the extent of that amount; a formal expression. *The university subsidises its students to the tune of £100,000 a year.*

tune in PHRASAL VERB If you **tune in** to a radio station, you adjust your radio so that you can listen to it. *He turned the dial and tuned in to Radio Paris.*
tune out PHRASAL VERB 1 To **tune out** a radio or television broadcast means to stop listening to the broadcast by changing or cutting out the radio signals. *He proposed a boycott, calling on people to tune the networks out.* 2 If you **tune** someone or something **out**, you stop listening to them or paying attention to them. *With the Superbowl just two days away, players are trying to tune out the normal distractions, such as endless interviews, autograph sessions, and celebrity appearances.*
tune up PHRASAL VERB When a group of musicians **tune up**, they adjust their instruments so that they produce the right notes exactly. *The orchestra was tuning up for its regular Sunday afternoon broadcast.*

tuned in

ADJ PRED+to If someone is **tuned in** to something, they are aware of it and understand it. *...as people become more tuned in to what computers can do... Possibly predatory fish are tuned in to surface disturbance indicating a shoal of small fish.*

tuneful /tjuːnfl/

ADJ A **tuneful** piece of music contains pleasant and memorable tunes. *Babies like more tuneful lullabies at bed-time.*

tuneless /tjuːnləs/

ADJ **Tuneless** music or singing has no pleasant or memorable tune. *Suddenly, you would have this curious, tuneless humming.*

tuner /tjuːnə/ **tuners**

1 NC+SUPP A piano **tuner** is a person whose job consists of tuning pianos. *Ms. Horn agreed to play, even though the piano tuner hadn't been.*
2 NC The **tuner** in a radio or television set is the part which you adjust to receive the radio signals or

television signals at the right wavelength.

tungsten /tʌŋstən/

NU **Tungsten** is a greyish-white metal. *The typical bullet materials we use are tantalum and tungsten. ...a tungsten halogen lamp.*

tunic /tjuːnɪk/ **tunics**

NC A **tunic** is a sleeveless garment covering the top part of your body. *They were dressed in their traditional red silk tunics and high black boots.*

tuning fork, tuning forks

NC A **tuning fork** is a small steel instrument which is used to tune instruments by striking it against something to produce a note of fixed musical pitch. *Ask your interviewee to sound a tuning fork so that it records on both machines.*

Tunis /tjuːnɪs/

Tunis is the capital of Tunisia and its largest city. Population: 597,000 (1984).

Tunisia /tjuːnɪziə/

The **Republic of Tunisia** is a country in northern Africa. It was a French colony from 1883 until 1957, when it became independent. The first President, Habib Bourguiba, ruled from 1957 to 1987. From 1963 until 1981 Tunisia was a one-party state. General Zine al-Abidine ben Ali, of the Democratic Constitutional Assembly (RCD), became President in 1987. Hamed Karoui (RCD) became Prime Minister in 1989. Tunisia is a member of the Arab League and the Organization of African Unity. It exports oil, textiles, and fertilizers. Tourism is an important industry. ◆ **Tunisian** /tjuːnɪziən/ N, ADJ
▪ *per capita GNP:* US\$1,230 ▪ *religion:* Islam (mainly Sunni) ▪ *language:* Arabic (official), Berber, French ▪ *currency:* dinar ▪ *capital:* Tunis ▪ *population:* 8 million (1989) ▪ *size:* 164,150 square kilometres.

tunnel /tʌnl/ **tunnels, tunnelling, tunnelled;** spelt **tunneling, tunneled** in American English.

1 NC A **tunnel** is a long underground or covered passage. *Suddenly the train roared into a tunnel and everything was black... Work on boring the tunnel would not resume until its inspectors had looked into the causes of the accident.* ● See also **Channel Tunnel**.
2 VA If someone or something **tunnels** somewhere, they make a tunnel. *One person suggested tunnelling under the walls... US agents tunnelled from West to East Berlin.*

tunnel vision

1 NU **Tunnel vision** is the inability to see things that are not straight in front of you. *This leads to tunnel vision, and eventually to blindness.*
2 NU If someone has **tunnel vision**, they concentrate on only one aspect of a subject, rather than considering every aspect of it; used showing disapproval. *The military mind looks at things only through tunnel vision.*

tuppenny /tʌpəⁿni/

ADJ ATTRIB A **tuppenny** item cost two old pence.

turban /tɜːbən/ **turbans**

NC A **turban** is a head-covering worn by a Hindu, Muslim, or Sikh man. It consists of a long piece of cloth wound round and round his head. *Many of the demonstrators wore saffron-coloured turbans, indicating their support for Khalistan.*

turbid /tɜːbɪd/

ADJ **Turbid** water or air is full of mud or dirt, and is usually swirling about; a literary word. *He gazed down at the turbid waters of the Thames.*

turbine /tɜːbaɪn/ **turbines**

NC A **turbine** is a machine or engine which produces power using a stream of air, gas, or water to turn a wheel. *The gases that spin the turbine are red hot— about 1,4000 degrees Celsius... The fine dust from the desert is damaging the turbine blades on the aircraft.*

turbo /tɜːbəʊ/ **turbos**

NC A **turbo** is a fan in a car or plane engine that improves its performance by blowing the fuel vapour into the engine. *The research proved to have an application in the design of the turbo... The Lancia boss ordered the team to reduce the turbo pressure on their cars.*

turbocharged /tɜːbəʊtʃɑːdʒd/

ADJ A **turbocharged** engine or vehicle is fitted with a

turbo in order to improve its performance. ...*high performance cars with fuel-injected and turbocharged engines.*

turbot /tɜːbət/; turbot is both the singular and the plural form.

N U or N C A **turbot** is a flat fish that lives in European seas and is caught for food. *The catching of some species of fish, notably turbot, has been banned.*

turbulence /tɜːbjuləns/

1 N U **Turbulence** is a state of confusion and constant, disorganized change. ...*periods of social turbulence... Political turbulence in India has spread to Gujarat and Rajasthan.*

2 N SING or N U **Turbulence** is also violent and uneven movement within an area of air or water. *The turbulence caused the plane to turn over... The region has a long history of seismic turbulence.*

turbulent /tɜːbjulənt/

1 ADJ A **turbulent** period of time is one in which there is a lot of change and confusion. ...*a period of fierce and turbulent struggle... The Tokyo stock exchange has had another turbulent session, with prices falling at one point to their lowest level for four years.*

2 ADJ **Turbulent** water or air contains strong currents which change direction suddenly. ...*in the midst of turbulent seas and clashing rocks.*

turd /tɜːd/ **turds**

N C A **turd** is a lump of faeces; an offensive word.

tureen /tjʊəriːn/ **tureens**

N C A **tureen** is a large bowl with a lid from which you can serve soup or vegetables. ...*a tureen decorated with shells and nautical themes was estimated at 7,000 pounds.*

turf /tɜːf/ **turfs, turfing, turfed**

N U **Turf** is short, thick, even grass. *He was busy levelling the ground and laying turf.*

turf out PHRASAL VERB If you **turf** someone **out**, you force them to leave; an informal expression. *She was turfed out of her flat.*

turf accountant, turf accountants

N C A **turf accountant** is the same as a **bookmaker**; a formal expression.

turgid /tɜːdʒɪd/; a literary word.

1 ADJ A **turgid** mass, especially of water or mud, is thick and rather unpleasant to look at. *The pool was full to the brim with some very brown, turgid water.*

2 ADJ A **turgid** piece of writing, play, or film is difficult to understand and very boring. ...*turgid religious verse... She described the current consent form used by hospitals as legalistic, turgid, and out of date.*

turkey /tɜːki/ **turkeys**

1 N C A **turkey** is a large bird that is kept on a farm for its meat. *The laughing stopped when the turkeys started damaging the lawn.*

2 N U **Turkey** is the meat of a turkey. *On the menu today; turkey, gravy, sweet potatoes, and cranberry sauce... President Bush says he will join American troops for Thanksgiving, enjoying a traditional turkey dinner with all the trimmings.*

Turkey /tɜːki/

The **Republic of Turkey** is a country in south-eastern Europe and western Asia. Turkey was the centre of the Ottoman Empire until 1922, when the last sultan was deposed. The Turkish Republic was declared in 1923, with Mustapha Kemal Atatürk as its first president. Turkey invaded and occupied northern Cyprus in 1974. It is a member of NATO and applied for membership of the European Community in 1987. Turgut Özal, of the Motherland Party (ANAP), became President in 1989. Mesut Yilmaz (ANAP) became Prime Minister in 1991. Tourism is an important industry, and Turkey also produces textiles, food, and chrome. High inflation and large foreign debts are major economic problems. ◆ **Turk** /tɜːk/ N **Turkish** /tɜːkɪʃ/ ADJ

■ *per capita GNP:* US$1,280 ■ *religion:* Islam
■ *language:* Turkish ■ *currency:* lira ■ *capital:* Ankara
■ *largest city:* Istanbul ■ *population:* 54 million (1988)
■ *size:* 779,452 square kilometres.

Turkish /tɜːkɪʃ/

1 ADJ **Turkish** means belonging or relating to Turkey.

A Turkish businessman was abducted in Geneva ten days ago.

2 N U **Turkish** is the language spoken by people who live in Turkey. *The Gagauz are Christians and speak a language similar to Turkish.*

Turkish bath, Turkish baths

N C A **Turkish bath** is a health treatment which involves sitting in a hot steamy room, then having a wash, massage, and cold shower.

Turkish delight

N MASS **Turkish delight** is a jelly-like sweet that is covered with powdered sugar or chocolate.

Turkmenistan /tʊəkmenɪstɑːn/

Turkmenistan became independent of the USSR in 1991. It is located in the south of the former USSR, bordering Iran and Afghanistan. The Kara-Kum desert occupies about four-fifths of its territory. Saparmurad Niyazov, of the Turkmen Communist Party, became President in 1990. Turkmenistan produces oil, chemicals, fish, cotton, and astrakhan furs. In 1991 it joined the Commonwealth of Independent States.

◆ **Turkmen** /tʊəkmen/ N, ADJ

■ *per capita GNP:* US$3,370 ■ *religion:* Islam (mainly Sunni) ■ *language:* Turkmen ■ *currency:* rouble
■ *capital:* Ashkhabad ■ *population:* 3,600,000 (1990)
■ *size:* 488,100 square kilometres.

Turks and Caicos Islands
/tɜːks ənd keɪkɒs aɪləndz/

The **Turks and Caicos Islands** are a territory of the United Kingdom in the Caribbean. South Caicos is the most populous of the thirty islands, and the capital is located on Grand Turk. They were settled by Britain from the late 17th century. From 1874 to 1959 they were a dependency of Jamaica. Fishing, tourism, and banking are important industries.

■ *per capita GNP:* US$4,600 ■ *religion:* Christianity (mainly Baptist) ■ *language:* English, Creole
■ *currency:* US dollar ■ *capital:* Cockburn Town
■ *population:* 13,000 (1989) ■ *size:* 430 square kilometres.

turmeric /tɜːmərɪk/

N U **Turmeric** is a yellow spice that is used to flavour hot food such as curry. *Turmeric worked particularly well on sweet potatoes, for example.*

turmoil /tɜːmɔɪl/

N U **Turmoil** is a state of confusion, disorder, or great anxiety. ...*his emotional turmoil... The city was in turmoil.*

turn /tɜːn/ **turns, turning, turned**

1 V or VO When you **turn** or **turn** part of your body, you move your body or part of your body so that you or it are facing in a different direction. *The shark turned and struck again, inflicting deep wounds on the boy's thigh... When the priest turned his head and saw the gun, he tried to escape... They turned their backs when the Queen arrived in the park.* ► Also N C *He made a smart military turn, clicking his heels.*

2 V-ERG When you **turn** something or when it **turns**, it moves and faces in a different direction, or keeps changing the direction it faces in. *I have turned the TV to the wall... The ship twisted and turned as it avoided the missiles.* ► Also N C ...*with an agile turn of the wrist.*

3 V-ERG When you **turn** something such as a knob, key, or switch, you hold it and twist your hand, for example in order to open, start, or adjust it. *He turned the handle and pushed open the door... The key turned easily in the lock.*

4 V A When you **turn** in a particular direction or **turn** a corner, you change the direction in which you are moving. *You come over a bridge and turn sharply to the right... When you travel in Rangoon, you're constantly amazed to turn a corner among the rice paddies and see a factory in front of you.* ► Also N C *The cars were waiting to make the turn into the campus.*

5 V+to If you **turn** to a particular page in a book, you find that page. *Turn to page 349 please.*

6 V-ERG+to If you **turn** your attention or thoughts to someone or something or if your attention or thoughts **turn** to them, you start thinking about them or discussing them. *I wonder if we can turn our attention*

to something you mentioned earlier... His thoughts turned to Calcutta.

7 V A If you **turn** to someone for help or advice, you ask them for it. Finally, they had turned to Cyprus which had earlier refused landing permission... As opposition against him grew, he turned increasingly for support to stalwarts such as Mr Romain.

8 V-ERG A When something **turns** into something else or when you **turn** it into something else, it becomes something different. If you apply more heat, the water turns into steam... Soon her glee turned to fear... Five Olympic medallists have turned professional.

9 V-ERG C You can use **turn** to say that a particular quality in something changes. For example, if something turns sour or if it is turned sour, it changes and becomes sour. My hair has turned completely grey... It will turn the water blue.

10 NC+SUPP A **turn** is also a change in the way that something is happening or being done. In that year things took a sharp turn for the worse... Employers are not happy about this turn of events.

11 NC If it is your **turn** to do something, you now have the right, chance, or duty to do it, after other people have done it. It is his turn to take the children to school. ...waiting his turn.

12 N SING If you refer to the **turn** of the century, you mean the period of time including the end of the previous century and the beginning of the century you are talking about. ...the problems facing the world in the years leading up to the turn of the century.

13 See also **turning** and **turned**.

● **Turn** is used in these phrases. ● A **good turn** is something that you do to help someone. It's strange, because on the surface it would appear that he was doing us a good turn. ● You use **in turn** to refer to people, things, or actions that are in a sequence one after the other. She went round the ward, talking to each woman in turn... It became in turn a stable, a chapel, and a theatre. ● If people **take turns** or **take it in turns**, they do something or share something one after the other. You can take turns paying... They took turns at the same typewriter. ● to **turn** your **back on** someone or something: see **back**. ● to **turn** the **tables on** someone: see **table**. ● to **turn sour**: see **sour**.

turn against PHRASAL VERB If someone **turns against** you, they start to dislike you or to become your enemy. They might at any time turn against their masters... Deng has already turned against his two appointed heirs.

turn around PHRASAL VERB See **turn round**.

turn away PHRASAL VERB If you **turn** someone **away**, you reject them or send them away. The college has been forced to turn away 300 prospective students... The ship was turned away from several European ports before docking at Livorno in Italy.

turn back PHRASAL VERB **1** If you **turn back** when travelling somewhere, you stop and begin going back to your starting place. The snow started to fall, so we turned back... Others turned back when they were fired on. **2** If you **turn** someone **back**, you stop them travelling any farther and make them return. A lot of the convoys had been turned back at the border... Women from the camps were being turned back by the soldiers.

turn down PHRASAL VERB **1** If you **turn down** a request or offer, you refuse or reject it. The British Foreign Office Minister has turned down an invitation to visit Romania... His appeal was turned down. **2** If you **turn down** something such as a radio or a heater, you reduce the amount of sound or heat being produced. If you are hot you can turn the heating down.

turn in PHRASAL VERB an informal expression. **1** When you **turn in**, you go to bed. Before turning in for the night he asked for an early morning call. **2** If you **turn in** someone who is suspected of a crime, you take them to the police. Some of them had turned in rebels, for whom the punishment would be the death penalty... Whinnery telephoned, saying he wanted to turn himself in.

turn off PHRASAL VERB **1** If you **turn off** a road, you

start going along a different road leading from it. They turned off the main road. ● See also **turn-off**. **2** If you **turn off** something such as a device or machine, you adjust the controls so that it stops working. We couldn't turn the heat off... She turned off the tap... The street lights are turned off at ten. **3** If something **turns** you **off**, it suddenly stops exciting you emotionally or sexually; an informal use. ● See also **turn-off**.

turn on PHRASAL VERB **1** If you **turn on** a machine or device, you adjust the controls so that it starts working. Shall I turn the fire on?... She turned on the shower. **2** To **turn** someone **on** means to attract them and make them sexually excited; an informal use. I don't really turn you on, do I? ● See also **turn-on**. **3** If someone **turns on** you, they suddenly attack you or speak angrily to you. She turned on the men. 'How can you treat your daughters like this!'... Many Australians in the crowd turned on the demonstrators and tore down their placards.

turn out PHRASAL VERB **1** If something **turns out** a particular way, it happens in that way. Nothing ever turned out right... The transaction turned out badly... She was evidently not pleased at the way things had turned out. **2** If something **turns out** to be a particular thing, it is discovered to be that thing. The Marvins' house turned out to be an old converted barn... The campaign is turning out to be the most bitterly contested election in the country's political history. **3** If you **turn out** a light or a gas fire, you adjust the controls so that it stops working. They turned out the lights every night at ten o'clock. **4** To **turn out** a particular product means to produce it in large quantities. Austin Rover has for months been turning out Japanese-designed cars under a special arrangement... His illness scared him into turning out paintings at the rate of one a day... Salford was turning out the type of graduate they wanted. **5** If you **turn** someone **out**, you force them to leave. ...a woman who had been turned out of the community 20 years before... They had turned out old people, children, and disabled people to make room for the wounded soldiers. **6** If you **turn out** your pockets or a container, you empty them. Come on everyone, turn out your pockets! **7** If people **turn out** for an event or activity, they go and take part in it or watch it. Voters turned out in extraordinary numbers for the election... People all over the Soviet Union have been turning out to give blood.

turn over PHRASAL VERB **1** If you **turn** something **over** in your mind, you think carefully about it. Going home that night, Dr Renshaw turned over the facts of the case. **2** If you **turn** something **over** to someone, you give it to them because they have a right to it. He had refused to turn over funds that belonged to Potter... The land will be turned over to state-run cooperatives. **3** See also **turnover**.

turn round PHRASAL VERB If you **turn** a sentence or idea **round** or **turn** it **around**, you change the way in which it is expressed. I can turn it round and make it sound funny... When you first asked me about this, I turned the whole question around.

turn up PHRASAL VERB **1** If someone or something **turns up**, they arrive, appear, or are discovered somewhere. He turned up at rehearsal the next day looking awful... You must be willing to take a job as soon as one turns up. **2** If you **turn up** a machine or device you adjust the controls so that it produces more heat, light, or sound. ...turning up the stereo to drown out the background noise.

turnabout /ˈtɜːnəbaʊt/ **turnabouts**

NC A **turnabout** is a complete change in opinion or attitude. The Prince's latest turnabout could produce sharp exchanges between him and the foreign minister.

turnaround /ˈtɜːnəraʊnd/ **turnarounds**. The form **turnround** is also used.

1 NC A **turnaround** or a **turnround** is a complete change in opinion or attitude. This was a complete turnaround from his stance on Thursday, when he insisted that the payments had been legal... There's no doubt among the delegates that they need a major *turnround in EEC attitudes.*

2 NC A sudden improvement, especially in the success of a business or a country's economy, can also be referred to as a **turnaround**. *Agricultural trade registered a growth, a remarkable turnaround from 1986 when it actually fell... The most optimistic report expects a turnaround in 1992.*

3 N SING The **turnaround** or the **turnaround** time of a task, for example the unloading of an aircraft or ship, is the amount of time that it takes. *How long was the turnaround on that last job?*

turncoat /ˈtɜːnkəʊt/ **turncoats**
NC A **turncoat** is a person who leaves one organization or political party and joins an opposing one; used showing disapproval. *It would be very difficult for us to sit down and negotiate with the people who have been traitors and turncoats.*

turned /tɜːnd/
If you say that someone is one thing **turned** another, you mean that they have changed from being the first sort of thing to being the second. *...the former top Yugoslavian politician turned dissident writer... It has become a fierce battle between him and his former Finance Minister turned arch-rival.*

turned out
ADJ You use **turned out** to describe how a person is dressed. *...attractive girls, well turned out and smart.*

turning /ˈtɜːnɪŋ/ **turnings**
NC A **turning** is a road leading away from another road. *It's the next turning on the left.*

turning point, turning points
NC A **turning point** is a time at which an event or change occurs which greatly affects the future of a person or thing. *The turning point for the business came in 1974 when I bought the computer.... It proved to be a turning point in his life... The declaration could mark a turning point in Korean history.*

turnip /ˈtɜːnɪp/ **turnips**
NCorNU A **turnip** is a round vegetable with a green and white skin. *...tuna lasagne with baby turnips... Haggis is served with mashed potatoes and turnip.*

turn-off, turn-offs
1 NC A **turn-off** is a road leading away from a major road or a motorway. *...the Newport-Pagnall turn-off.*
2 NC Something that is a **turn-off** causes you to lose interest or sexual excitement; an informal word. *I think effeminate voices are a complete turn-off.*

turn-on, turn-ons
NC Something or someone that is a **turn-on** makes you feel sexually excited; an informal word.

turnout /ˈtɜːnaʊt/ **turnouts**
1 NC The **turnout** at an event is the number of people who go to it. *There was a very large turnout at the trial. ...the biggest turnout for a religious event this decade.*
2 NC The **turnout** in an election is the number of people who vote in it. *Government officials estimate a seventy per cent turnout... The SPD has done marginally better, partly thanks to the low turnout.*

turnover /ˈtɜːnəʊvə/
1 NU The **turnover** of people in an organization is the rate at which people leave and are replaced. *The low wages may account for the extremely high turnover in the industry.*
2 NU The **turnover** of a company is the value of goods or services sold during a particular period of time. *Annual turnover is about £9,000 million.*

turnpike /ˈtɜːnpaɪk/ **turnpikes**
NC A **turnpike** is a motorway, usually one which you have to pay to drive on; used in American English. *...unforeseen traffic on the New Jersey turnpike.*

turnround /ˈtɜːnraʊnd/. See turnaround.

turnstile /ˈtɜːnstaɪl/ **turnstiles**
NC A **turnstile** is a mechanical barrier at the entrance to a zoo, football ground, etc, which has metal arms that you push round as you enter the area or building. *There will be no tickets for sale on the turnstile.*

turntable /ˈtɜːnteɪbl/ **turntables**
NC A **turntable** is the flat, round part of a record player on which the record is put. *The days of black vinyl records spinning around on turntables may be numbered.*

turn-up, turn-ups
1 NC The **turn-ups** of a pair of trousers are the ends of the trouser legs, which are folded upwards. *I invented a device to remove those little balls of fluff you get in trouser turn-ups.*
2 If you describe an event as a **turn-up for the books**, you mean that it is very surprising or unexpected; an informal expression. *There was another turn-up for the books at Brentford, where the third division side beat Manchester City.*

turpentine /ˈtɜːpəntaɪn/
NU **Turpentine** is a colourless liquid used for cleaning paint off brushes. *Leave them to soak in a jar of turpentine.*

turpitude /ˈtɜːpɪtjuːd/
NU **Turpitude** is wicked and unacceptable behaviour; a formal word. *She accused him of gross moral turpitude.*

turps /tɜːps/
NU **Turps** is turpentine; an informal word. *...an awful smell of turps and paint.*

turquoise /ˈtɜːkwɔɪz/ **turquoises**
1 ADJ Something that is **turquoise** is of a colour between light blue and green. *...the warm turquoise sea.*
2 NUorNC **Turquoise** is a semi-precious stone which is a colour between light blue and green. *...a veneered walnut throne, the back bearing a central turquoise set in gold.*

turret /ˈtʌrɪt/ **turrets**
NC A **turret** is a small, narrow tower on top of a larger tower or other building. *...the towers and turrets of King Arthur's Court of Camelot.*

turtle /ˈtɜːtl/ **turtles**
NC A **turtle** is a large reptile with a thick shell which lives in the sea. *I would question the ethics of keeping turtles and other reptiles as pets at all.*

turtledove /ˈtɜːtldʌv/ **turtledoves**
NC A **turtledove** is a light-brown wild bird that makes a soft cooing sound. *...the French habit of hunting the turtledove.*

turtleneck /ˈtɜːtlnek/ **turtlenecks**
NC A **turtleneck** or a **turtleneck** sweater is a sweater with a short, round collar that fits closely around your neck.

tusk /tʌsk/ **tusks**
NC The **tusks** of an elephant, wild boar, or walrus are its two very long, curved, pointed teeth. *According to the guidebook, the walrus tusks are more than 100 million years old.*

tussle /ˈtʌsl/ **tussles, tussling, tussled**
1 NC A **tussle** is a struggle or argument between two people. *He was still smarting from the tussle over the bottle. ...the tussle between dissidents and the authorities.*
2 V-RECIP If one person **tussles** with another or if they **tussle**, they struggle or argue with each other. *One hundred and twenty photographers tussled with security men when she visited a Crimean war museum to pay her respects. ...directors tussling about levels of authority.*

tussock /ˈtʌsək/ **tussocks**
NC A **tussock** is a small clump of long grass; a literary word. *Reed buntings usually build the nest in a tussock in a marshy field.*

tut /tʌt/
Tut is used in written English to represent a clicking sound you make with your tongue to indicate disapproval, annoyance, or sympathy.

tutelage /ˈtjuːtəlɪdʒ/
NU If people are under the **tutelage** of other people, the second group of people have authority over the first; a formal word. *He gained valuable experience and training under his father's tutelage... They began to aspire to throw off monarchical tutelage.*

tutor /ˈtjuːtə/ **tutors, tutoring, tutored**
1 NC A **tutor** is a teacher at a British university or college. *Dr John Durrant, a staff tutor in Biological Sciences at Oxford, is co-editor of a new book on the subject.*
2 NC A **tutor** is also someone who privately teaches one pupil or a very small group of pupils. *Akihito*

studied English with an American tutor.
3 V O or V If someone **tutors** a person or subject, they teach that person or subject. *In the past, they would have been tutored in near solitude by governesses... Perhaps you should spend a good part of the Christmas season being tutored by some good professors... Next year I want to tutor A level maths.*
◆ **tutoring** N U *With special tutoring, she is making progress.*

tutorial /tjuːtɔːriəl/ **tutorials**
N C A **tutorial** is a teaching session involving a tutor and a small group of students. *A Russian expert has been asked to give a series of tutorials.*

tutti frutti /tuːti fruːti/
N U **Tutti frutti** is ice cream containing little bits of preserved fruit.

tut-tut /tʌttʌt/ **tut-tuts, tut-tutting, tut-tutted**
1 **Tut-tut** is used in written English to represent a clicking sound you make with your tongue to indicate disapproval, annoyance, or sympathy.
2 V A If you **tut-tut** about something, you express your disapproval, annoyance, or sympathy. *...a solicitous porter who tut-tutted over his plastered foot... They spent the whole evening tut-tutting about the lack of discipline in young people.*

tutu /tuːtuː/ **tutus**
N C A **tutu** is a short, stiff dress made of many layers of material that is worn by female ballet dancers. *Most attractive are the girls' stiff, pleated tutus, like Japanese fans.*

Tuvalu /tuːvɑːluː/
Tuvalu, formerly known as the Ellice Islands, is a country in the Pacific. It consists of nine small atolls. It was administered by Britain from 1877 until independence in 1978. Bikenibeu Paeniu became Prime Minister in 1989. There are no political parties. Tuvalu is a member of the Commonwealth. It exports copra.
◆ **Tuvaluan** /tuːvɑːluːən/ N, ADJ
▪ *per capita GNP:* US$326 ▪ *religion:* Christianity (mainly Protestant) ▪ *language:* Tuvaluan, English ▪ *currency:* Australian or Tuvaluan dollar ▪ *capital:* Funafuti Atoll ▪ *population:* 8,000 (1985) ▪ *size:* 26 square kilometres.

tu-whit tu-whoo /təwɪt təwuː/
People write or say **tu-whit tu-whoo** in order to represent the sound made by an owl.

tuxedo /tʌksiːdəʊ/ **tuxedos**
N C A **tuxedo** is a black or white jacket worn by men for formal social events; used in American English. *Some bands grease their hair, and dress up in wing-tipped tuxedos.*

TV /tiːviː/ **TVs**
1 N U **TV** is television. *I've just been watching a film on TV. ...TV commercials.*
2 N C A **TV** is a television set. *Mr Brewington repairs video recorders and big-screen TVs.*

twaddle /twɒdl/
N U If something that someone says is **twaddle**, it is silly or untrue; an informal word. *Beata was talking a load of twaddle.*

twang /twæŋ/ **twangs, twanging, twanged**
1 N C A **twang** is a sound like the one made by pulling and then releasing a tight wire. *...the twang of tennis balls bouncing off tightly-strung rackets.*
2 V-ERG If you **twang** something such as a tight wire or string or if it **twangs**, it makes a repetitive vibrating sound because it has been pulled and then released. *He was sitting twanging a guitar... The bed springs twanged.*

tweak /twiːk/ **tweaks, tweaking, tweaked**
V O or V+*at* If you **tweak** something, you hold it between your finger and thumb and twist it or pull it. *He used to tweak the cat's tail.* ▶ Also N C *I'll just give the veil a tweak. That's better.*

twee /twiː/
ADJ Something that is **twee** is pretty, but seems too sentimental or in bad taste.

tweed /twiːd/
N U **Tweed** is a type of thick woollen cloth used for making suits. *She saw a man standing in a country garden dressed in a brown tweed suit.*

tweet /twiːt/ **tweets, tweeting, tweeted**
V When a small bird **tweets**, it makes short, high-pitched sounds.

tweezers /twiːzəz/
N PL **Tweezers** are a small tool consisting of two joined narrow strips of metal. Tweezers are used for pulling out hairs and picking up small objects. *We remove the membrane using sterilised tweezers.*

twelfth /twelfθ/
ADJ The **twelfth** item in a series is the one that you count as number twelve. *...the twelfth anniversary of the proclamation.*

twelve /twelv/
Twelve is the number 12. *Normally, we only have eleven or twelve members in all.*

twentieth /twentiəθ/
ADJ The **twentieth** item in a series is the one that you count as number twenty. *...the twentieth century. ...January the twentieth.*

twenty /twenti/ **twenties**
Twenty is the number 20. *More than twenty people have been injured.*

twerp /twɜːp/ **twerps**
N C A **twerp** is someone who is silly or stupid; an informal word.

twice /twaɪs/
1 ADV Something that happens **twice** happens two times. *I knocked on the door twice... His Foreign Minister has twice visited Iran.*
2 ADV or PREDET If one thing is **twice** as big or old as another thing, it is two times as big or old as the other thing. *This is twice as common in France as in England... He's twice my size.*
3 **once or twice:** see **once.**

twiddle /twɪdl/ **twiddles, twiddling, twiddled**
V O or V+*with* If you **twiddle** something or **twiddle** with it, you twist it or turn it using your fingers. *Ella sat twiddling her long, dark hair... Frank twiddled with the knobs of the radio.* ● If you say that someone is **twiddling** their **thumbs**, you mean that they do not have anything to do and are waiting for something to happen. *The Commission came into existence several years ago, but basically, they've sat around and twiddled their thumbs.*

twig /twɪg/ **twigs**
N C A **twig** is a very small, thin branch of a tree or bush. *...clusters of huts made of twigs and mud.*

twilight /twaɪlaɪt/
1 N U **Twilight** is the time after sunset when it is just getting dark. *We wandered around the temple until twilight.*
2 N SING+*of* The **twilight** of something is the final stages of it, when it is becoming less strong or important. *...the twilight of his political career.*

twilit /twaɪlɪt/
1 ADJ ATTRIB A **twilit** place or thing is seen by the dim light that there is just after sunset. *Huge clouds were growing, blotting out the twilit sky.*
2 ADJ ATTRIB A **twilit** state is one in which someone or something is between two other states, or in which someone is only just awake or aware of things. *...as she battled in a thorny twilit region of anguish and delirium.*

twin /twɪn/ **twins, twinned**
1 N C If two people are **twins**, they have the same mother and were born on the same day. *She's bringing up six children, including two sets of twins, on 170 US dollars a week... Incidents of one twin knowing that the other is in pain, despite being hundreds of miles apart, are quite common.* ▶ Also ADJ ATTRIB *They are twin brothers.* ● See also **identical twin.**
2 N+N You use **twin** to describe a pair of similar things that are close together or that happen together. *...the twin turrets of Tower Bridge. ...the twin evils of famine and war.*
3 V-PASS A town that is **twinned** with another town in a different country is linked by a special relationship with it. *Rather incongruously, this Somali front-line town is twinned with the sedate British town of Henley-on-Thames.*

twin bed, twin beds
NC **Twin beds** are two single beds in one bedroom.

twin-bedded /twɪnbedɪd/
ADJ ATTRIB A **twin-bedded** room, for example in a hotel, has twin beds.

twine /twaɪn/ **twines, twining, twined**
1 NU **Twine** is strong, smooth string. *...a ball of twine... The fibre is used for making binder twine.*
2 VOA If you **twine** one thing round another, you twist or wind the first thing around the second. *...twining the rope around his legs.*

twinge /twɪndʒ/ **twinges**
NC If you feel a **twinge** of an unpleasant emotion or pain, you feel this emotion or pain for a very short time. *...a twinge of fear... I feel a twinge in my back now and again.*

twinkle /twɪŋkl/ **twinkles, twinkling, twinkled**
1 V If a star or a light **twinkles**, it shines with an unsteady light. *He could see lights twinkling through the haze of rain. ...myriad stars twinkling silently on velvet-black heavens.*
2 V If your eyes **twinkle**, they show that you are amused or excited. *He is perfect for his role, with silver-hair and blue eyes twinkling behind horn-rimmed glasses.* ▸ Also N SING *She noticed a twinkle in his eye at the suggestion.*

twinkling /twɪŋklɪŋ/
If you do something **in the twinkling of an eye**, you do it very quickly. *The table was laid and the food set out ready in the twinkling of an eye.*

twin-set, twin-sets
NC A **twin-set** is a matching cardigan and sweater of the same colour, worn by women. *Her mother was wearing a pale blue twin-set and a tweed skirt.*

twin tub twin tubs
NC A **twin tub** is a washing machine that has one section for washing clothes and another for spinning them. *The houses were equipped with twin tubs at any rate.*

twirl /twɜːl/ **twirls, twirling, twirled**
1 V-ERG When you **twirl** something or if it **twirls**, it spins round and round. *She twirled her parasol... Around me, elm leaves twirled to the ground.*
2 V If you **twirl**, you spin round and round, for example when you are dancing. *He twirled round on his toes... Several hundred people twirl around the ballroom dance-floor, a kaleidoscope of color.*

twist /twɪst/ **twists, twisting, twisted**
1 V-ERG When you **twist** something or when it **twists**, you turn one end of it in one direction while holding the other end still or turning it in the opposite direction. *Never twist or wring woollen garments... Her fingers twisted the handle of her bag.* ▸ Also NC *He gave one short twist to its neck.*
2 V-ERG When something **twists** or when you **twist** it, it moves, bends, or turns into a strange, uncomfortable, or distorted shape or position, especially as a result of force, damage, or an unpleasant feeling. *Her features twisted into a stare of disgusted incredulity.* ◆ **twisted** ADJ *Hundreds of people were trapped under the twisted steel girders... He noticed the track ahead was twisted, and slowed the train.*
3 VOorVA If you **twist** part of your body such as your head or shoulders, you turn it while keeping the rest of your body still. *Swing your shoulders so that you twist from side to side... She twisted round on the couch to watch him.*
4 VO If you **twist** your ankle or wrist, you injure it by turning it too sharply or in an unusual direction. *Kuznetsov has twisted the ligaments in his knee, and won't be fit for the game on Saturday.*
5 VorVA If a road or river **twists**, it has a lot of sharp bends. *The road began to twist up past the lower slopes of a pine forest. ...one of the many tributary canals that came twisting inland.*
6 VO If you **twist** what someone has said, you repeat it in a way that changes its meaning; used showing disapproval. *You're twisting my words around... He had consistently lied and twisted the truth about his wartime activities... The facts about the situation can become twisted and distorted.*
7 NC A **twist** is also the shape of something that has

been twisted. *...a shell with a spiral twist... He used a tail rotor to counteract the twist in the helicopter lifting rotor blade.*
8 NC A **twist** in the aims, attitude, or nature of something is a significant or important change in it. *...every twist and turn in government economic policy... The microchip has added a new twist to the Las Vegas gambling scene.*
9 NC A **twist** in a story or film is an unexpected development. *There was an odd twist to the plot... From Sao Paulo, Robin Dilks reports on the latest twist in a long saga.*
● **Twist** is used in these phrases. ● If you **twist** someone's **arm**, you use strong methods to persuade them to do something; an informal expression. *All the potential Tory rebels are to be seen personally, to calm their fears or twist their arms.* ● If you can **twist** someone **round** your **little finger**, you can persuade them to do anything; an informal expression. *I don't think he'll be twisting the President round his little finger.*

twisted /twɪstɪd/
ADJ If someone's mind or behaviour is **twisted**, it is unpleasantly abnormal. *He has become bitter and twisted... He called the invasion the invention of a twisted mind.*

twister /twɪstə/ **twisters**
1 NC Someone who is a **twister** is dishonest and deliberately deceives people; an old-fashioned use. *...a wretched little twister like Harrington.*
2 NC A **twister** is a tornado; used in American English. *One of the twisters leveled several homes in Hutchinson in south central Kansas.*
3 See also **tongue-twister**.

twit /twɪt/ **twits**
NC A **twit** is someone who is silly or thoughtless; an informal word. *Don't be a twit!*

twitch /twɪtʃ/ **twitches, twitching, twitched**
1 V If you **twitch**, you make little jerky movements which you cannot control. *By providing a small electric shock, the patient's leg twitches and that helps to keep the blood flow moving... The whale was still twitching, and was obviously not quite dead.* ▸ Also NC *...twitches of the muscles.*
2 V-ERG If you **twitch** something or if it **twitches**, it moves slightly with a jerky motion. *She twitched the curtain into place... The rabbits don't show any signs of knowing the camera's there, not even twitching their noses.*

twitchy /twɪtʃi/
ADJ If you are **twitchy**, you are anxious or uneasy about something and so are behaving nervously; an informal word. *They are getting distinctly twitchy... Dartmoor, like the other prisons, was getting twitchy because of the trouble at Strangeways.*

twitter /twɪtə/ **twitters, twittering, twittered**
V When birds **twitter**, they make a lot of short, high-pitched sounds. *As we left the church, the birds were twittering and I felt a sense of release.*

two /tuː/ **twos**
1 **Two** is the number 2. *Co-operation between the two groups is crucial.*
2 If you **put two and two together**, you work out the meaning or the significance of something from the things that you see and hear, especially when other people do not want you to find out. *People put two and two together and they say, 'Something else must be going on'.*

two-bit
ADJ ATTRIB **Two-bit** means unimportant or of poor quality; an informal word. *All the parts they offered me were replays, or were elderly men falling about in two-bit parts... We're too great a country to be depending on some two-bit dictator over there.*

two-dimensional
1 ADJ Something that is **two-dimensional** is flat and in two dimensions only. *The theatre I'm dealing with is a two-dimensional space, seen from the side.*
2 ADJ If you say that something such as an idea, a character, or a work of art is **two-dimensional**, you mean that it is too simple and not realistic or interesting. *Many have seen it as an uncritical, and*

therefore two-dimensional portrait. ...rationalism, with its two-dimensional scheme of things.

two-edged
1 ADJ **Two-edged** blades have two cutting edges.
2 ADJ Things that are **two-edged** have two parts or meanings that are opposite to each other but that happen at the same time. *Their relationship is thus a two-edged one, at once intimate and distant.*
3 A **two-edged sword** is something that appears to be advantageous, but also has hidden difficulties and problems. *He must know that the present optimism is a two-edged sword.*

two-faced
ADJ A **two-faced** person criticizes someone when that person is not present but is pleasant to the same person when they are present; used showing disapproval. *He is a two-faced liar and an opportunist... How could she be so two-faced?*

twofold /tuːfəʊld/
ADJ You use **twofold** to introduce a topic that has two equally important parts. *Their targets were twofold: inflation and unemployment... The value of this procedure is twofold. In the first place... The strategy of the nationalist movements involved a twofold operation.*

two-ply
ADJ **Two-ply** material has two layers or strands. *...two-ply wool. ...two-ply tissues.*

twosome /tuːsəm/ **twosomes**
NC A **twosome** is a group of two people. *Even playing in twosomes, it took them four hours to complete the course.*

two-way
ADJ ATTRIB **Two-way** means moving or working in two opposite directions. *...a two-way channel of communication. ...two-way radio.*

tycoon /taɪkuːn/ **tycoons**
NC A **tycoon** is a person who is successful in business and so has become rich and powerful. *...a newspaper tycoon. ...provisions aimed at preventing the communications tycoon Silvio Berlusconi from exercising a television monopoly.*

type /taɪp/ **types, typing, typed**
1 NC+SUPP A **type** of something is a class of it whose members have particular features in common. *...several different types of accounts... They usually test your blood type during pregnancy... How much longer can you do this type of work? ...simple problems of this type.*
2 NC+SUPP A particular **type** of person has a particular appearance or quality. *He was good-looking, if you like the strong, dark type.*
3 VOorV If you **type** something, you use a typewriter or word processor to write it. *I typed the reply... When you hear that sound, you can start typing... Police say the packages contained a typed message.*
◆ **typing** NU *I had to do some typing for her.*
4 VO If you **type** information into a computer or word processor, you put it in by pressing the keys. *The letter was typed into a word processor... As messages are typed onto the pad, the signals are sent to the wristwatch which shows them in a liquid crystal display.*
5 NU **Type** is the size or style of printing that is used, for example, in a book or newspaper. *The declaration was proclaimed in type four inches deep on the front page.*
6 If you say that someone is **not** your **type**, you mean that they are not the sort of person who you find interesting or attractive; an informal expression. *He was bookish, bespectacled, non-athletic, and not her type.*

type up PHRASAL VERB If you **type up** a handwritten text, you produce a typed form of it. *After thinking about it, she typed it up, then we both read it.*

typecast /taɪpkɑːst/ **typecasts, typecasting.** The form **typecast** is used in the present tense and is also the past tense and past participle.
VO If actors **are typecast**, they play the same type of character in every play or film that they are in. *He's afraid if he does any more cover versions, he'll be typecast... He refused to be typecast as the loser.*

typeface /taɪpfeɪs/ **typefaces**
NC A **typeface** is the style and design of the individual letters that are printed in books, newspapers, magazines, and so on; a technical term. *The machine can be 'trained' to recognise a certain typeface.*

typescript /taɪpskrɪpt/ **typescripts**
NCorNU A **typescript** is a typed copy of an essay, article, or literary work. *...the typescript of his book. ...twenty-seven pages of typescript.*

typewriter /taɪpraɪtə/ **typewriters**
NC A **typewriter** is a machine with keys which are pressed in order to print letters, numbers, or other characters onto paper. *It looks a bit like an ultra-modern typewriter.*

typewritten /taɪprɪtn/
ADJ Something that is **typewritten** has been typed on a typewriter or word processor. *The camera is programmed to decipher the shape of a printed or typewritten word.*

typhoid /taɪfɔɪd/
NU **Typhoid** is an infectious disease that produces fever and diarrhoea and can cause death. It is spread by dirty water or food. *Cases of malaria and typhoid were on the increase. ...a typhoid scare.*

typhoon /taɪfuːn/ **typhoons**
NC A **typhoon** is a very violent tropical storm. *Hong Kong is prone to typhoons, forest fires, landslides, and oil pollution... The typhoon has left eight hundred and fifty people injured.*

typical /tɪpɪkl/
1 ADJ Something that is **typical** of a particular thing or way of behaving shows the most usual characteristics of that thing or behaviour. *It was typical tropical weather... Louisa is typical of many young women who attempt suicide.*
2 ADJ If you say that something is **typical** of a person, situation, or thing, you are criticizing or complaining about them, expressing the fact that they are as bad or as disappointing as you expected them to be. *It was typical of our luck that it happened to be raining.*

typically /tɪpɪkəˀli/
1 ADV SEN You use **typically** to say that something usually happens in the way that you are describing it. *She typically handles less than a dozen accounts at a time... He typically played down his own part in the rescue.*
2 SUBMOD You also use **typically** to say that something shows all the most usual characteristics of a particular type of thing. *...this group of typically American students... In the 1935 film 'Dangerous' she is involved in a typically bitchy onslaught.*
3 ADV SEN **Typically** can also be used to indicate that someone has behaved in the way that you expected them to. *Sheila was upset too, and said, typically, that she was going home.*

typify /tɪpɪfaɪ/ **typifies, typifying, typified**
VO To **typify** something means to be a typical example of it. *He typified the old Liberalism... The somewhat routine nature of this summit is likely to typify future meetings.*

typist /taɪpɪst/ **typists**
NC A **typist** is someone whose job is typing. *The initials at the end are those of the typist.*

typographical /taɪpəgræfɪkl/
ADJ ATTRIB **Typographical** is used to refer to the way in which printed material is presented. *...typographical layout. ...a few limited editions filled with typographical errors.*

typography /taɪpɒgrəfi/ **typographies**
NUorNC **Typography** is the way in which printed material is arranged and prepared. *The typography of dictionaries has deteriorated recently.*

tyrannical /tɪrænɪkl/
ADJ A **tyrannical** ruler, government, or organization acts cruelly and unjustly towards the people they control. *They are the victims of a long and tyrannical form of oppression... She was imprisoned as a supposed invalid by her tyrannical father.*

tyrannize /tɪrənaɪz/ **tyrannizes, tyrannizing, tyrannized**; also spelt **tyrannise.**
VO If someone **tyrannizes** you, they treat you cruelly and unjustly. *He used to tyrannize his younger*

brothers and sisters.

tyranny /tɪrəni/

1 NU **Tyranny** is cruel and unjust rule by a person or small group of people who have power over everyone else in their country or state. *They came here to escape political tyranny.*

2 NU **Tyranny** is a condition in which people are forced to live or work in a way that is very unpleasant or harsh. *Women should not have to submit to the tyranny of the assembly line.*

tyrant /taɪərənt/ **tyrants**

NC A **tyrant** is a ruler who uses his or her power cruelly and unjustly. *Only hypocrites grieve when a tyrant falls. ...a country ruled by a drug-smuggler and a tyrant.*

tyre /taɪə/ **tyres**; spelt **tire** in American English.

NC A **tyre** is a thick ring of rubber filled with air and fitted round the wheel of a vehicle. *In other places, people set up barricades and immobilized army trucks by letting down their tyres.*

tyro /taɪrəʊ/ **tyros**

A **tyro** is someone who is just beginning to learn something, or who is considered to be very inexperienced; an informal word. *Six eight-year old tyros arrived for their lesson, their new rackets neatly held in their hands.*

tzar /zɑː/. See tsar.

tzarina /zɑːriːnə/. See tsarina.

tzarist /zɑːrɪst/. See tsarist.

tzetze fly /tsetsi flaɪ/. See tsetse fly.

U u

U, u /juː/ U's, u's
NC U is the twenty-first letter of the English alphabet.

ubiquitous /juːˈbɪkwɪtəs/
ADJ Something that is **ubiquitous** is everywhere or seems to be everywhere; a formal word. *Aluminium is ubiquitous in the environment. ...ubiquitous opinion polls.*

ubiquity /juːˈbɪkwəti/
NU **Ubiquity** is the quality of existing in a lot of places at the same time. *...the success and ubiquity of the drugs business in Colombia.*

udder /ˈʌdə/ **udders**
NC A cow's **udder** is the organ that hangs below its body and produces milk. *The ointment is massaged into the udder... The cow's udder will change shape according to the stage of lactation.*

UFO /juːefˈəʊ, juːfəʊ/ **UFOs**
NC A **UFO** is a strange object usually seen in the sky which some people believe to be a spaceship from another planet. **UFO** is an abbreviation for 'unidentified flying object'. *UFOs are usually the subject of science-fiction films... Federal authorities expect a dramatic increase in reports of UFO sightings over the next few weeks.*

Uganda /juːˈgændə/
The **Republic of Uganda** is a country in eastern Africa. It was a British protectorate from the 19th century until independence in 1962. Idi Amin Dada came to power in a coup in 1971 and ruled until 1979. Yoweri Museveni opposed Milton Obote, who became President in 1980. As leader of the National Resistance Army (NRA), Museveni fought a guerrilla war from 1980 until 1986, when the NRA captured Kampala and Yoweri Museveni became President. The National Resistance Movement (NRM) became the governing party. Uganda is a member of the Commonwealth and the Organization of African Unity. It exports coffee. Large foreign debts and high inflation are major economic problems. ◆ **Ugandan** /juːˈgændən/ N, ADJ
▪ *per capita GNP:* US$280 ▪ *religion:* Christianity, animism ▪ *language:* English (official), Luganda ▪ *currency:* shilling ▪ *capital:* Kampala ▪ *population:* 16 million (1989) ▪ *size:* 241,139 square kilometres.

ugh
Ugh is used in writing to represent the sound that people make when they think that something is unpleasant, horrible, or disgusting. *Your clothes are filthy and your hair too—ugh, you're awful.*

ugly /ˈʌgli/ **uglier, ugliest**
1 ADJ Someone or something **ugly** is very unattractive in appearance. *She really was frightfully ugly... This is the ugliest dress I've ever worn.* ◆ **ugliness** NU *...the architectural ugliness of the place.*
2 ADJ An **ugly** situation is very unpleasant, and often involves violence. *A couple of ugly incidents occurred, and one man was killed... It was turning extremely ugly, and I was pushed to the floor by an officer.*

uh-huh
Uh-huh is used in writing to represent a sound that people make to show that they agree with you or understand what you are saying, or as a way of answering 'yes'; an informal word. *'Did you know he was rich?'—'Uh-huh. It said so in the paper.'*

UHT /juːeɪtʃˈtiː/
ADJ **UHT** is used to describe milk which has been treated at a very high temperature so that it will keep for a long time, if the container is not opened. **UHT** is an abbreviation for 'ultra-heat-treated'.

UK /juːˈkeɪ/
N PROP The **UK** consists of Great Britain and Northern Ireland. **UK** is an abbreviation for 'United Kingdom'. *They must explain why they have come to the UK. ...foreign interference in UK affairs.*

ukelele /juːkəˈleɪli/ **ukeleles**; also spelt **ukulele**.
NC A **ukelele** is a small guitar with four strings.

Ukraine /juːˈkreɪn/
Ukraine became independent of the USSR in 1991. It is located in the west of the former USSR, bordering Poland, Czechoslovakia, Hungary, and Romania. It was the second most populous republic of the USSR. Leonid Kravchuk became President in 1991. Ukraine produces coal, iron and steel, sugar, grain, and other agricultural products. In 1991 Ukraine joined the Commonwealth of Independent States. ◆ **Ukrainian** /juːˈkreɪniən/ N, ADJ
▪ *per capita GNP:* US$4,700 ▪ *religion:* Christianity ▪ *language:* Ukrainian ▪ *currency:* rouble (to be replaced by hrivna) ▪ *capital:* Kiev ▪ *population:* 52 million (1989) ▪ *size:* 603,700 square kilometres.

Ulaanbaatar /ʊlɑːnˈbɑːtɔː/
Ulaanbaatar is the capital of Mongolia and its largest city. It was formerly known as Urga and Niislel Khureheh. Population: 548,000 (1989).

ulcer /ˈʌlsə/ **ulcers**
NC An **ulcer** is a sore area on your skin or inside your body, which sometimes bleeds. *President Duarte is having urgent medical treatment for a stomach ulcer... It's thought he is suffering from a bleeding ulcer.*

ulcerated /ˈʌlsəreɪtɪd/
ADJ If a part of your body is **ulcerated**, ulcers have developed on it; a medical term. *He was admitted to hospital with an ulcerated leg.*

ulterior /ʌlˈtɪəriə/
ADJ ATTRIB If someone has an **ulterior** motive for doing something, they have a hidden reason for it. *I assure you there was no ulterior motive in my suggestion.*

ultimate /ˈʌltɪmət/
1 ADJ ATTRIB You use **ultimate** to describe the final result of a long series of events. *He knew this action was necessary for the ultimate success of the revolution... Independence is the ultimate goal.*
2 ADJ ATTRIB You also use **ultimate** to describe the most important or powerful thing of a particular kind. *Parliament retains the ultimate authority to dismiss the government... The ultimate waste is war. ...a call by some MPs for hanging to be brought back as the ultimate penalty in British law.*
3 **The ultimate** in something is the best or most advanced thing of its kind. *...the ultimate in luxury.*

ultimately /ˈʌltɪmətli/
1 ADV **Ultimately** means finally, after a long series of events. *Elections ultimately produced a Communist victory.*

2 ADV SEN You also use **ultimately** to emphasize that what you are saying is the most important point in a discussion. *Ultimately, the problems are not scientific but moral... Isn't it ultimately the fault of the universities?*

ultimatum /ˌʌltɪmeɪtəm/ **ultimatums** or **ultimata** /ˌʌltɪmeɪtə/
NC An **ultimatum** is a warning that unless someone acts in a particular way, you will take action against them; a formal word. *The workers issued an ultimatum to the government that they would go on strike unless their demands were met... Belgium rejected the ultimatum and war was declared. ...when the twenty-four hour ultimatum expired.*

ultra- /ˌʌltrə-/
PREFIX **Ultra-** is used to form adjectives that describe someone or something as having a quality to an extreme degree. *...ultra-sophisticated equipment. ...an ultra-modern building.*

ultramarine /ˌʌltrəməriːn/
ADJ Something that is **ultramarine** in colour is very bright blue; a literary word. *They don their resplendent vermilion, ultramarine, and gold robes.*

ultrasonic /ˌʌltrəsɒnɪk/
ADJ ATTRIB **Ultrasonic** sounds have very high frequencies, which human beings cannot hear. *Ultrasonic scans are used to inspect babies in the womb. ...an ultrasonic range finder that can calculate the dimensions of rooms.*

ultrasound /ˌʌltrəsaʊnd/
NU **Ultrasound** refers to sound waves that are at such high frequencies that human beings cannot hear them. *Ultrasound can have the same effects as heat and pressure without the dangers... An ultrasound examination of his heart showed no abnormalities.*

ultraviolet /ˌʌltrəvaɪələt/
ADJ ATTRIB **Ultraviolet** light or radiation is invisible, and is produced by the sun and by some artificial lamps. *...the ultraviolet rays of the sun. ...the ozone layer that protects us against potentially harmful ultraviolet radiation... He uses the very concentrated ultraviolet light from a laser.*

um
Um is used in writing to represent a sound that people make when they are hesitating, usually because they have not decided what to say next. *What can be done about it? Well, um, the first thing you can do is colour it.*

umber /ʌmbə/
ADJ Something that is **umber** in colour is yellowish or reddish brown; a literary word. *...the mellow umber bricks of Jo's house.*

umbilical cord /ʌmbɪlɪkl kɔːd/ **umbilical cords**
1 NC The **umbilical cord** is the tube connecting an unborn baby to its mother, through which it receives oxygen and nutrients. *Its food supply comes through the placenta and through the umbilical cord... Cut the umbilical cord and take the baby away from the mother immediately after the birth.*
2 NC You can refer to any system that supplies necessary things to a place or organization as an **umbilical cord**. *The fuel line serves as an umbilical cord between the shuttle and its external fuel tank. ...the new umbilical cord between East Berlin and Bonn. ...an umbilical cord between politics and economics in the communist system.* ● If you say that one person, organization, or country **cuts the umbilical cord** with another, you mean that they do something that makes them become more independent. *...the difficult task of cutting the umbilical cord with its powerful neighbour... They were eager to cut the umbilical cord tying them to the federation.*

umbrage /ʌmbrɪdʒ/
If you **take umbrage**, you feel upset or hurt by something that someone says or does to you; a formal expression. *It was clear that the Pope himself had taken great umbrage at the book.*

umbrella /ʌmbrelə/ **umbrellas**
1 NC An **umbrella** is an object which you use to protect yourself from the rain or hot sun. It consists of a long stick with a folding frame covered in cloth. *Put your umbrella up. It's going to rain.*

2 ADJ ATTRIB **Umbrella** describes a single organization or idea that includes a lot of different organizations or ideas. *...an umbrella organisation representing Indian tribes in Canada. ...an opposition umbrella group of right-wing political parties... Corn is an umbrella word for wheat, barley and oats.*
3 N SING+SUPP **Umbrella** is used to refer to a system or agreement which protects a country or a group of people from attack or war. *...under the protective umbrella of a full-scale international conference. ...a new European security umbrella. ...the American nuclear umbrella.*

umpire /ʌmpaɪə/ **umpires, umpiring, umpired**
1 NC In games such as cricket or tennis, the **umpire** is the person whose job is to make sure the game is played fairly and the rules are not broken. *The umpires declared that play should start.*
2 VO If you **umpire** a game, you are the umpire. *He has umpired World Series games in the United States.*
◆ **umpiring** NU *...the issues of pitch preparation and umpiring. ...criticising the standard of umpiring.*

umpteen /ʌmptiːn/
Umpteen means very many; an informal word. *They recounted umpteen tales of unfair treatment.*

umpteenth /ʌmptiːnθ/
ADJ If you do something for the **umpteenth** time, you do it again even though you have done it many times before; an informal word. *I went to the pictures and saw 'Hello Dolly' for the umpteenth time.*

un- /ʌn-/
PREFIX **un-** is added to words to form words which have the opposite meaning or refer to a reverse process. For example, if something is unavailable, it is not available. If you untie a knot, you reverse the process of tying it. *They either ignored the law or were unaware of it... She may unintentionally have caused suffering... He regretted his unkindness... He unlocked the door.*

UN /juː en/ See **United Nations**

unabashed /ʌnəbæʃt/
ADJ If you are **unabashed**, you are not ashamed, embarrassed, or discouraged by something that has been done or said. *...his unabashed declarations of support for the army... He remains unabashed by criticism of the way he reached office... He's unabashed about the school's pursuit of pure academic excellence.*

unabated /ʌnəbeɪtɪd/
ADV or ADJ If something continues **unabated**, it continues without any reduction in intensity or amount. *The war at sea continued unabated... They continued with unabated enthusiasm.*

unable /ʌneɪbl/
ADJ PRED+*to*-INF If you are **unable** to do something, you cannot do it, for example because you do not have the necessary skill. *Many people were unable to read or write... He was unable to sleep at night because of his anxiety.*

unabridged /ʌnəbrɪdʒd/
ADJ An **unabridged** piece of writing, for example a book or article, is complete and not shortened in any way. *This volume contains three unabridged novels. ...the unabridged version of 'War and Peace'.*

unacceptable /ʌnəkseptəbl/
ADJ If something is **unacceptable**, you strongly disapprove of it and feel you cannot allow it to continue. *That sort of behaviour was completely unacceptable... He said that the treaty was totally unacceptable. ...the unacceptable face of Mikhail Gorbachev's 'perestroika'.* ◆ **unacceptably** ADV *Their standard of performance has been unacceptably poor on several recent occasions... If this is the price of progress, then it is unacceptably high.*

unaccompanied /ʌnəkʌmpənid/
1 ADJ or ADV If someone is **unaccompanied**, they are alone. *I wouldn't leave him for a moment unaccompanied... It is estimated that every year 50 unaccompanied children arrive in Britain. ...a country where women don't feel afraid to walk unaccompanied, even late at night.*
2 ADJ ATTRIB **Unaccompanied** luggage or goods are being sent or transported separately from their

owner. ...*unaccompanied baggage.* ...*unaccompanied freight.*

3 ADJ or ADV An **unaccompanied** song is sung by a singer or choir alone, without musical instruments. ...*solemn, unaccompanied pieces*... *Don't you think those lovely carols sound much better unaccompanied?*... *They sing mostly unaccompanied and without microphones.*

4 ADJ PRED If a decision or action is **unaccompanied** by another, the other decision or action is not planned or included and therefore does not happen; used showing disapproval. *It would presumably be unaccompanied by provisions for inspection.* ...*a step which cannot be enough, unaccompanied as it is by any other reforms.*

unaccountable /ʌnəkaʊntəbl/; a formal word.

1 ADJ Something that is **unaccountable** does not seem to have any sensible explanation. *For some unaccountable reason, I put the letter in the wrong envelope.* ♦ **unaccountably** ADV or ADV SEN *Elaine felt unaccountably shy*... *She twice found herself, unaccountably, sharing a bed with him.*

2 ADJ PRED If you are **unaccountable**, you do not have to justify your actions to anyone. *Many of our important decision-makers are unaccountable to the public.*

unaccounted /ʌnəkaʊntɪd/

If people or things are **unaccounted for**, you do not know where they are or what has happened to them. ...*US servicemen still unaccounted for fifteen years after the Vietnam War*... *Fifty fishing vessels are still unaccounted for*... *More than a million pounds were unaccounted for.*

unaccustomed /ʌnəkʌstəmd/

1 ADJ PRED+to If you are **unaccustomed** to something, you are not used to it. *They were unaccustomed to wearing suits and ties.*

2 ADJ ATTRIB If someone's behaviour or experiences is **unaccustomed**, they do not usually behave like this or have experiences of this kind. *Judy cried with unaccustomed vehemence, 'Yes, I know!'* ...*his unaccustomed and unwelcome leisure time.*

unacknowledged /ʌnəknɒlɪdʒd/

1 ADJ If a fact or situation is **unacknowledged**, it is ignored by people or not accepted as being true or existing. *The true number of deaths remains unacknowledged*... *Its own ethnic problem remains unresolved and largely unacknowledged.* ...*a series of unacknowledged meetings between the leaders.*

2 ADJ If a person, their qualities, or their achievements are **unacknowledged**, they are not officially recognized as being important. ...*the unacknowledged inventor of cinematography*... *He died in 1555 with his discovery still unacknowledged.*

3 ADJ PRED If you are **unacknowledged** when you enter a room, the people who are already there do not show by their behaviour that they have seen and recognized you. *Unacknowledged, Ginny sat down on the sofa in silence.*

unacquainted /ʌnəkweɪntɪd/

ADJ PRED+with If you are **unacquainted** with something, you do not know about it or you have not had much experience of it. ...*people who are unacquainted with feminist ideas.* ...*if you're unacquainted with a place.*

unadorned /ʌnədɔːnd/

ADJ Something that is **unadorned** is plain, rather than having decorations or being artistically designed; a literary word. *They visited the unadorned graves of the murdered hostages*... *He is the master of unadorned dialogue.*

unadulterated /ʌnədʌltəreɪtɪd/

1 ADJ Something that is **unadulterated** is completely pure with nothing added to it. ...*unadulterated spring water.*

2 ADJ ATTRIB You can also use **unadulterated** to emphasize a quality, especially a bad quality. *It was going to be unadulterated misery from now on.*

unaffected /ʌnəfektɪd/

1 ADJ PRED Something that is **unaffected** by a particular thing is not changed in any way by it. *Jobs have been largely unaffected by automation*... *This acid is unaffected by heat.*

2 ADJ Someone who is **unaffected** behaves naturally rather than trying to impress people; used showing approval. *He was simple and unaffected.*

unaided /ʌneɪdɪd/

ADV or ADJ If you do something **unaided**, you do it without help. *The baby was sitting up unaided.* ...*men who have arrived at the top by their own unaided efforts.*

unalloyed /ʌnəlɔɪd/

ADJ Something that is **unalloyed** is not reduced in intensity or spoiled by being mixed with something else; a literary word. ...*unalloyed bliss*... *The report was received with almost unalloyed enthusiasm.*

unalterable /ʌnɔːltərəbl/

ADJ Something that is **unalterable** cannot be changed. ...*an unalterable decision.*

unaltered /ʌnɔːltəd/

ADJ Something that is **unaltered** has not been changed. *The Great Hall survives relatively unaltered.*

unambiguous /ʌnæmbɪgjuəs/

ADJ An **unambiguous** statement has only one meaning, which is very clear. *The conditions are stated in straightforward unambiguous terms*... *Palestinian sources say Mr Arafat's words in Geneva will be unambiguous and clear.* ♦ **unambiguously** ADV *Their demands have now been unambiguously formulated.*

unambitious /ʌnæmbɪʃəs/

1 ADJ **Unambitious** people do not particularly want to improve their way of life or to get a better job. *Guy's doctor was a pleasant unambitious GP.* ...*a mild-mannered, unambitious man in his sixties.*

2 ADJ An **unambitious** action or plan does not try to achieve very much. *The visit was relatively unambitious in its aims.* ...*to carry out a limited but not unambitious programme.*

un-American

ADJ If an American says or does anything against the United States, they are sometimes described by people from their own country as **un-American**; used in American English. *That kind of talk is downright un-American*... *Fearful of being branded un-American, politicians of all persuasions rallied to the cause.*

unanimity /juːnənɪməti/

NU When there is **unanimity** among a group of people, they all agree about something. *About this there is unanimity among the sociologists*... *There has not been unanimity within the US government over Angola*... *The Italians are worried about lack of unanimity over how best to negotiate with him.*

unanimous /juːnænɪməs/

ADJ When a group of people are **unanimous**, they all agree about something. *We reached unanimous agreement.* ...*a unanimous vote by all twelve member-states*... *Arab leaders were unanimous in condemning Israel.* ♦ **unanimously** ADV *The resolution was passed unanimously*... *The Council of Europe has unanimously approved its application for membership.*

unannounced /ʌnənaʊnst/

ADJ If an event is **unannounced**, it happens unexpectedly, without any warning. *Churchill arrived unannounced*... *The visit to Saudi Arabia was unannounced.*

unanswerable /ʌnɑːnsərəbl/

1 ADJ An **unanswerable** question cannot be answered, because it has no possible answer. *This topic is full of unanswerable questions.*

2 ADJ An **unanswerable** argument or criticism is so obviously correct that you cannot disagree with it. ...*a brilliant argument which seems to be unanswerable.* ...*the accusation that he intended to betray his country was unanswerable.*

unanswered /ʌnɑːnsəd/

ADJ Something that is **unanswered** has not been answered, often because you do not have the information to do so. ...*unanswered letters*... *There are still quite a number of unanswered questions*... *Other questions about the exact nature of his wartime work remain unanswered.*

unappealing /ʌnəpiːlɪŋ/

ADJ You describe people, places, or things as **unappealing** when you find them unpleasant. *He was*

forced to talk to his singularly unappealing hostess...
They have made the place as unappealing as possible.

unappetizing /ʌnˈæpɪtaɪzɪŋ/; also spelt **unappetising**.
ADJ You describe food as **unappetizing** when it is
unpleasant to eat, or when you think that it will be
unpleasant to eat because of its appearance. *If it is
overcooked, the flesh becomes rubbery and
unappetizing. ...an unappetizing hunk of dry cheese.
...an unappetising flavour.*

unapproachable /ʌnəˈprəʊtʃəbl/
ADJ An **unapproachable** person is difficult to talk to
and not very friendly. *He was becoming as
unapproachable and autocratic as his father.*

unarguable /ʌnˈɑːɡjuəbl/
ADJ If something is **unarguable**, you cannot disagree
with it, because it is obviously true or correct. *He
said something fairly unarguable. ...an action that
doesn't have complete and unarguable United Nations
authority.* ◆ **unarguably** SUBMOD or ADV SEN *This was
unarguably true... Games like chess are unarguably
intellectual pursuits.*

unarmed /ʌnˈɑːmd/
ADJ If you are **unarmed**, you are not carrying any
weapons. *They were shooting unarmed peasants... He
walked alone and unarmed.*

unarmed combat
NU Somebody who is trained in **unarmed combat** is
taught to fight in a skilful way without using any
weapons. *Girls were practising unarmed combat
together.*

unashamed /ʌnəˈʃeɪmd/
ADJ ATTRIB If someone behaves in an **unashamed** way,
they openly do things that other people find shocking.
*...their unashamed pursuit of money. ...an unashamed
admirer of Joseph Stalin.* ◆ **unashamedly** ADV *...his
view, held strongly and unashamedly, that the violence
should stop.*

unasked /ʌnˈɑːskt/
1 ADJ An **unasked** question has not been asked,
although it may be answered by someone as if it had
been asked. *...one of the great unasked questions of
our time... The question of what education is for is
usually unasked.*
2 ADV If you do something **unasked**, you do it without
being asked to do it. *...their readiness to proffer small
services, unasked, without wanting money.*

unassailable /ʌnəˈseɪləbl/
ADJ If something is **unassailable**, nothing can alter it
or destroy it; a formal word. *Their leaders are
usually in an unassailable position of authority until
they decide to go voluntarily... This argument is
logically unassailable. ...our client's integrity is
unassailable.*

unassuming /ʌnəˈsjuːmɪŋ/
ADJ ATTRIB An **unassuming** person is modest and quiet;
used showing approval. *They heard him described as
a gentle, kind, and unassuming man... He has a
reputation for unassuming honesty. ...her unassuming
manner.*

unattached /ʌnəˈtætʃt/
ADJ An **unattached** person is not married and is not
having a steady relationship. *A lot of unattached
women seem to be very happy.*

unattended /ʌnəˈtendɪd/
ADJ When people or things are **unattended**, they are
not being watched or looked after. *Most of the
casualties were lying unattended. ...unattended
baggage.*

unattractive /ʌnəˈtræktɪv/
1 ADJ **Unattractive** people and things are unpleasant
in their appearance or behaviour. *He was physically
unattractive. ...unattractive dwellings.*
2 ADJ If something such as an idea or proposal is
unattractive, people do not like it and do not want to
be involved with it. *Being unemployed is a most
unattractive prospect.*

unauthorized /ʌnˈɔːθəraɪzd/; also spelt **unauthorised**.
ADJ If an action or person is **unauthorized**, they do not
have official permission. *...a warning to people not to
get involved in unauthorized demonstrations. ...the
unauthorised disclosure of any official information.
...a simple device to stop unauthorized people from*

using your telephone.

unavailable /ʌnəˈveɪləbl/
ADJ When things or people are **unavailable**, you cannot
obtain them, meet them, or talk to them. *Basic food
products are frequently unavailable in the state shops.
...information which was unavailable to American
military personnel... Officials were unavailable for
comment.*

unavailing /ʌnəˈveɪlɪŋ/
ADJ If an attempt to do something is **unavailing**, it
does not succeed; a formal word. *Attempts to
persuade him to come down were unavailing... Tactics
which worked well enough last year have proved
unavailing.*

unavoidable /ʌnəˈvɔɪdəbl/
ADJ If something is **unavoidable**, it cannot be avoided
or prevented. *This delay was unavoidable... Is
pollution the unavoidable price of development?*

unaware /ʌnəˈweə/
1 ADJ PRED If you are **unaware** of something such as a
fact or difficulty, you do not know about it. *I was
unaware that he had any complaints.*
2 ADJ PRED If you are **unaware** of something that is
happening near you, you do not know about it because
you have not noticed it. *She seemed quite unaware of
the other people sitting around her.*

unawares /ʌnəˈweəz/
If something **catches** you **unawares** or **takes** you
unawares, it happens when you are not expecting it.
*The eruption of fighting last week caught many people
unawares... The news took the City of London
unawares.*

unbalance /ʌnˈbæləns/ **unbalances, unbalancing,
unbalanced**
VO If something **unbalances** a system, it disturbs or
upsets it so that it can no longer work properly. *A
half-century of western intrusion had seriously
unbalanced the traditional rural order... Russian
patriotism as a political force would unbalance the
whole structure of the Soviet Union.*

unbalanced /ʌnˈbælənst/
1 ADJ If someone is **unbalanced**, they are slightly
mad. *The strain of the past few days has made you
mentally unbalanced... The condition she's in now is
unbalanced, unstable and highly dangerous.*
2 ADJ An **unbalanced** account of something is unfair or
inaccurate because it emphasizes some things and
ignores others. *She complained that the magazine had
published an unbalanced report.*

unbearable /ʌnˈbeərəbl/
ADJ Something that is **unbearable** is so unpleasant,
painful, or upsetting that you feel unable to accept it
or cope with it. *I found it unbearable to be the centre
of attention. ...the unbearable heat and humidity of the
summer months.* ◆ **unbearably** SUBMOD *It was
unbearably painful.*

unbeatable /ʌnˈbiːtəbl/
1 ADJ Something that is **unbeatable** is considered the
best thing of its kind. *The food here is absolutely
unbeatable... Cuban salesmen go all over the world
selling their unbeatable Havana cigars.*
2 ADJ In a competition, if a person or team is
unbeatable, or is in an **unbeatable** position, they are
winning, succeeding, or performing so well that they
are unlikely to lose. *Mr Mitterrand has looked
unbeatable ever since the first round... With two more
days of competition to go, China is in an unbeatable
position.*

unbeaten /ʌnˈbiːtn/
1 ADJ A person or team that is **unbeaten** has not been
defeated. *...the unbeaten light-flyweight champion.
...the only unbeaten team in the league... France are
unbeaten in their last ten matches.*
2 ADJ An **unbeaten** run or record is one that does not
include any defeats, or one that is the best. *Liverpool
have stretched their unbeaten run to ten matches.
...Australia's nine-year unbeaten record.*

unbecoming /ʌnbɪˈkʌmɪŋ/; an old-fashioned word.
1 ADJ **Unbecoming** clothes or colours make you look
unattractive. *...ill-fitting, unbecoming garments.
...that dreadfully unbecoming shade of apricot they
wore.*

2 ADJ If you say that a person's remarks or behaviour are **unbecoming**, you mean that they are rather shocking and especially unsuitable for that person. *It's still considered unbecoming for a woman to mention marriage first... He behaved in a manner unbecoming a judge.*

unbeknown /ˌʌnbɪnˈəʊn/ or **unbeknownst** /ˌʌnbɪnˈəʊnst/
ADJ PRED If something is **unbeknown** or **unbeknownst** to you, you do not know about it; an old-fashioned word. *Meanwhile, unbeknown to Julie, Frank was coming down the hill... Unbeknownst to Peter, Mr Hopkins sent out invitations.*

unbelief /ˌʌnbɪˈliːf/
NU **Unbelief** is the attitude of not believing that something is true. *'You don't know?' Luciana exclaimed in a voice of unbelief... He says that the opposite of belief is not unbelief, but doubt.*

unbelievable /ˌʌnbɪˈliːvəbl/
1 ADJ You say that something is **unbelievable** when it is extremely good, large, or surprising. *They work with unbelievable speed... I went to her house in Henley: it was unbelievable.*
2 ADJ If an idea or theory is **unbelievable**, it is so unlikely or so illogical that you cannot believe it. *There are many unbelievable aspects to this theory.*

unbelievably /ˌʌnbɪˈliːvəbli/
1 ADV SEN You use **unbelievably** to indicate that the event or situation you are describing is very surprising. *Unbelievably, the door in the wall opened.*
2 SUBMOD You also use **unbelievably** to emphasize that something is extremely good, large, or surprising. *He has been unbelievably successful.*

unbeliever /ˌʌnbɪˈliːvə/ **unbelievers**
NC People are referred to as **unbelievers** when they do not believe in a particular religion. *...explaining the Christian concept of the Holy Trinity to an unbeliever. ...fighting a holy war for Islam against the unbelievers.*

unbelieving /ˌʌnbɪˈliːvɪŋ/
ADJ You describe people as **unbelieving** when they do not believe something that they have been told. *He looked unbelieving... Our son had died—we were stunned, shocked, unbelieving, all of those things.*

unbend /ˌʌnbˈend/ **unbends, unbending, unbent**
V If someone **unbends**, their attitude becomes less strict than it was. *The Palace unbent enough to say that the present generation of royal dogs are called Spark, Chipper and Harris.*

unbending /ˌʌnbˈendɪŋ/
ADJ When someone is **unbending**, they have very strict beliefs and attitudes, which they are unwilling to change. *The Minister was proving unbending on key issues. ...his unbending attitude toward what was right and wrong. ...strict, unbending theology.*

unbiased /ˌʌnbˈaɪəst/
ADJ Someone or something that is **unbiased** is fair and does not show prejudice or favouritism. *...an objective, unbiased view, free from all emotions and one-sided calculations. ...a fair and unbiased trial.*

unbidden /ˌʌnbˈɪdn/
ADV If something happens **unbidden**, it happens without you expecting or wanting it to happen; a literary word. *The sound of his voice came again, unbidden, into her mind... The words flowed unbidden from my pen.*

unbind /ˌʌnbˈaɪnd/ **unbinds, unbinding, unbound**
VO If you **unbind** someone or something, you untie a piece of string, rope, or cloth, which has been tied round them; a literary word. *Unbind him, let him go free... The youth unbound his sarong.*

unborn /ˌʌnbˈɔːn/
ADJ ATTRIB An **unborn** child has not yet been born and is still inside its mother's womb. *Pregnant women are likely to pass on the disease to their unborn children... One woman died, another lost her unborn baby.* ● If you refer to generations of people yet **unborn**, you are referring to people who will be born in future years. *...so as to affect the lives of people as yet unborn.*

unbound /ˌʌnbˈaʊnd/
1 **Unbound** is the past tense and past participle of **unbind**.
2 ADJ Something that is **unbound** is not tied or has just

been untied; a literary use. *...her unbound hair. ...armfuls of unbound wheat.*

unbounded /ˌʌnbˈaʊndɪd/
ADJ Something that is **unbounded** has, or seems to have, no limits. *Literacy brings to the young unbounded freedom... He has an almost unbounded admiration for his wife... My relief was unbounded.*

unbridled /ˌʌnbˈraɪdld/
ADJ You describe behaviour or feelings as **unbridled** when they are not controlled or limited in any way; a literary word, used showing disapproval. *...unbridled gluttony. ...the spectre of unbridled civil war. ...their unbridled search for profit.*

unbroken /ˌʌnbˈrəʊkən/
ADJ If something is **unbroken**, it is continuous or complete. *The silence continued, unbroken. ...two hours of unbroken sleep.*

unbuckle /ˌʌnbˈʌkl/ **unbuckles, unbuckling, unbuckled**
VO If you **unbuckle** something such as a belt or a shoe, you unfasten it by releasing the buckle on it. *She started to unbuckle her sandal.*

unburden /ˌʌnbˈɜːdn/ **unburdens, unburdening, unburdened**
V-REFL If you **unburden** yourself to someone, you tell them about something which you have been secretly worrying about. *Scylla unburdened herself to her guardian... Eventually Bartfuss meets someone he can unburden himself to.*

unburdened /ˌʌnbˈɜːdnd/
ADJ PRED If a person or system is **unburdened** by something, they are not limited or restricted by it. *Unburdened by the restraints of a state visit, the President and his wife plan to see as much as they can of the city. ...a generation unburdened with memories of partition. ...to let their national economies grow, unburdened by heavy taxes and needless regulations.*

unbutton /ˌʌnbˈʌtn/ **unbuttons, unbuttoning, unbuttoned**
VO When you **unbutton** something, you unfasten the buttons on it. *He unbuttoned his coat.*

uncalled-for /ˌʌnkˈɔːldfɔː/
ADJ An **uncalled-for** remark is unkind or unfair and should not have been made. *That last remark was uncalled-for.*

uncanny /ˌʌnkˈæni/
ADJ If something is **uncanny**, it is strange and hard to explain. *The owl strikes at its prey with uncanny accuracy... The actor, David Calder, bears an uncanny resemblance to Gorbachev... The silence was uncanny.*

uncapped /ˌʌnkˈæpt/
ADJ ATTRIB In sports, an **uncapped** player is one who has not played for a national team before. *They've named a team that includes five uncapped players... Into the squad comes the uncapped defender Luis Lopez Rekarte.*

uncared-for /ˌʌnkˈeədfɔː/
ADJ If people or animals are **uncared-for**, they have not been looked after properly and as a result are hungry, dirty, or ill. *Thousands of children were left uncared-for. ...uncared-for cats.*

uncaring /ˌʌnkˈeərɪŋ/
ADJ If you say that someone is **uncaring**, you mean that they have no feelings of sympathy for other people's suffering. *We now know how uncaring and selfish the landlords were... He is alleged to be uncaring about his children. ...an uncaring world.*

unceasing /ˌʌnsˈiːsɪŋ/
ADJ If something is **unceasing**, it continues without stopping. *The noise of the traffic was loud and unceasing... The operation was therefore part of its unceasing war against terrorism.*

uncensored /ˌʌnsˈensəd/
ADJ If a film, newspaper, or broadcast is **uncensored**, an official censor has not examined it or edited parts out of it before it is shown to the public. *In what Arnott said was an uncensored broadcast, he described the scene of the bombing.*

unceremonious /ˌʌnserɪmˈəʊniəs/
1 ADJ ATTRIB An **unceremonious** action is one that takes place suddenly and unexpectedly, and is often considered to be unfair or rude. *...despite her*

unceremonious sacking in August. ...an unceremonious end for the 83-year-old news agency.
♦ **unceremoniously** ADV *The door was unceremoniously pushed open... He was unceremoniously dumped the following year.*
2 ADJ You can use **unceremonious** to describe actions or people that are pleasant in a simple and informal way, without making a fuss. *She treated him with unceremonious friendliness.*

uncertain /ʌnsɜːtn/
1 ADJ If you are **uncertain** about something, you do not know what to do. *Investors were uncertain about the latest economic news... She hesitated, uncertain whether to continue.* ♦ **uncertainly** ADV *They looked at each other uncertainly.*
2 ADJ If something in the future is **uncertain**, nobody knows what will happen. *The outcome of his case was uncertain. ...refugees facing an uncertain future.*
3 ADJ If the cause of something is **uncertain**, nobody knows what caused it. *The cause of death remains uncertain.*
4 If you tell someone something **in no uncertain terms**, you say it so clearly or firmly that there can be no doubt about what you mean. *They rejected the complaints in no uncertain terms... He condemned the government in no uncertain terms.*

uncertainty /ʌnsɜːtnti/ **uncertainties**
1 NU When there is **uncertainty**, people do not know what will happen or what they should do. *...the continued uncertainty about the future of the aircraft industry. ...throwing the country into a period of political uncertainty.*
2 N PL **Uncertainties** are things, especially future events, which nobody is certain about. *The industry is still plagued by economic uncertainties. ...focused attention on the political uncertainties ahead.*

unchallenged /ʌntʃælɪndʒd/
ADJ When something is **unchallenged**, people accept it without questioning whether it is right or wrong. *His authority was secure and unchallenged... Her decisions on these matters went unchallenged... The coalition has ruled virtually unchallenged since independence.*

unchanged /ʌntʃeɪndʒd/
ADJ Something that is **unchanged** has stayed the same during a period of time. *The process remains unchanged... The driving test has remained virtually unchanged for fifty years.*

uncharacteristic /ʌnkærɪktərɪstɪk/
ADJ **Uncharacteristic** behaviour is not typical. *He jumped out of the car with uncharacteristic agility... He said that such an attack would be wholly uncharacteristic of a group such as Abu Nidal.*
♦ **uncharacteristically** ADV *For most of Britain it's been an uncharacteristically mild winter.*

uncharitable /ʌntʃærɪtəbl/
ADJ **Uncharitable** remarks, thoughts, or behaviour are unkind or unfair. *I hope I'm not being too uncharitable, but he really is very boring... They are known to have taken rather an uncharitable view of the comment.*

uncharted /ʌntʃɑːtɪd/
1 ADJ If an area of land or sea is **uncharted**, no maps have been made of it. *...an uncharted ocean.*
2 ADJ ATTRIB Unfamiliar situations are sometimes referred to as **uncharted** waters or **uncharted** territory. *Many executives are finding themselves in deep and uncharted waters... His career is about to enter uncharted territory.*

unchecked /ʌntʃekt/
ADJ or ADV If something undesirable is **unchecked**, it keeps growing without anyone trying to stop it. *...unchecked military expansion... Such horrors could not be allowed to continue unchecked.*

uncivil /ʌnsɪvl/
ADJ **Uncivil** behaviour is rude and impolite. *He was uncivil to other members of the household.* ♦ **uncivilly** ADV *'How long are you staying?' I asked him uncivilly.*

uncivilized /ʌnsɪvəlaɪzd/; also spelt **uncivilised**.
ADJ **Uncivilized** behaviour is unacceptable, for example because it is cruel or rude. *The conditions in which we keep them are uncivilized and inhumane.*

...their totally uncivilised and brutal behaviour.

unclaimed /ʌnkleɪmd/
ADJ If something is **unclaimed**, nobody has claimed it or said that it belongs to them. *After 14 years the reward remained unclaimed.*

unclasp /ʌnklɑːsp/ **unclasps, unclasping, unclasped**
VO If you **unclasp** your hands, you separate them again after holding them together. *He was clasping and unclasping his large freckled hands.*

unclassified /ʌnklæsɪfaɪd/
1 ADJ If something is **unclassified**, it has not been included in any of the classes into which a set of things has been divided. *They were simply labelled 'unclassified'. ...unclassified waste.*
2 ADJ **Unclassified** documents or information are not considered by a government to be secret or useful to an enemy. *...an unclassified document released by the State Department... It consisted only of already published, unclassified information.*

uncle /ʌnkl/ **uncles**
1 NC Your **uncle** is the brother of your mother or father, or the husband of your aunt. *...Uncle Harold.*
2 If you **cry uncle**, you give up and accept defeat; used in informal American English. *By last week, many Republicans in the House were ready to cry uncle... It's not likely that a man like that is going to cry uncle.*

unclean /ʌnkliːn/
1 ADJ Something that is **unclean** is dirty and likely to cause disease. *A major cause of illness in the Third World is unclean water.*
2 ADJ People sometimes use **unclean** to describe animals or practices which are unacceptable according to their religion. *Pigs are considered unclean and must not be eaten.*

unclear /ʌnklɪə/
ADJ If something is **unclear** or if you are **unclear** about it, it is not obvious or is so confusing that you cannot understand it properly. *Until this morning it was unclear whether the election would go ahead at all... It remains unclear how Mr Gonzales will use his new powers... Another Palestinian was shot dead in unclear circumstances in Jenin... I'm still very unclear about what he has actually done.*

Uncle Sam
N PROP People sometimes refer to the United States of America as **Uncle Sam**. In cartoons and statues, Uncle Sam is usually represented as a man wearing a top hat with stars on it, a tail-coat, and striped trousers. *Latin America's suspicions of Uncle Sam will not die down quickly... The demonstrators burned American flags and an effigy of Uncle Sam.*

unclothed /ʌnkləʊðd/
ADJ If you are **unclothed**, you are not wearing any clothes; a literary word. *...a large statue of an unclothed man.*

uncoil /ʌnkɔɪl/ **uncoils, uncoiling, uncoiled**
V-ERG If something **uncoils** or if you **uncoil** it, it becomes straight after it has been in a coil. *The second rope uncoiled and tumbled overboard... An enormous cobra had uncoiled itself at the foot of the rock... He uncoiled two wires connected to the battery.*

uncomfortable /ʌnkʌmftəbl/
1 ADJ If you are **uncomfortable**, you are not physically relaxed, and feel slight pain or discomfort. *I was cramped and uncomfortable in the back seat.*
♦ **uncomfortably** ADV *...sitting uncomfortably on the rock... My shirt was uncomfortably tight.*
2 ADJ **Uncomfortable** also means slightly worried or embarrassed and not relaxed. *Her presence made him uncomfortable. ...an uncomfortable reminder for the government.* ♦ **uncomfortably** ADV *She smiled across the room at him uncomfortably.*
3 ADJ An **uncomfortable** situation or fact causes problems and is difficult to accept. *It's an uncomfortable stand-off because both armies have heavy weapons pointed at the other side... That means admitting uncomfortable truths like the existence of homosexuality and prostitution.*
4 ADJ If a piece of furniture is **uncomfortable**, you do not feel comfortable when you are using it. *They were sitting on uncomfortable chairs.*

uncommitted /ʌŋkəmɪtɪd/
ADJ If you are **uncommitted**, you do not support either side in a dispute or have not yet decided which side you support. ...*their uncommitted position in the war.*

uncommon /ʌŋkɒmən/
1 ADJ If something is **uncommon**, it does not happen often, or it is not often seen. *Frost and snow are not uncommon during these months.* ...*uncommon birds.*
2 ADJ ATTRIB You also use **uncommon** to describe a quality that is unusually large in degree; a literary use. ...*a general of uncommon intelligence and subtlety.* ◆ **uncommonly** SUBMOD *Marcus was uncommonly gifted.*

uncommunicative /ʌŋkəmjuːnɪkətɪv/
ADJ An **uncommunicative** person is unwilling to talk to people, express opinions, or give information. *Roger, uncommunicative by nature, said nothing.*

uncomplaining /ʌŋkəmpleɪnɪŋ/
ADJ **Uncomplaining** people do difficult or unpleasant things without complaining about them; used showing approval. *They remained kind, generous, warm and uncomplaining.* ...*these courteous, uncomplaining young men.* ◆ **uncomplainingly** ADV *She was prepared to put up uncomplainingly with his wild temper.*

uncomplicated /ʌŋkɒmplɪkeɪtɪd/
ADJ **Uncomplicated** things are simple and straightforward. *The play had an uncomplicated plot.*

uncomprehending /ʌŋkɒmprɪhendɪŋ/
ADJ If someone is **uncomprehending**, they do not understand what is being said or done. *Bonasera turned to his uncomprehending wife and explained.*

uncompromising /ʌŋkɒmprəmaɪzɪŋ/
ADJ When people or their attitudes are **uncompromising** they are determined not to change their opinions or aims in any way. ...*an uncompromising opponent of the Great War... Addressing a crowded press conference , he was as uncompromising as ever... They have taken an uncompromising stand on terrorism.* ◆ **uncompromisingly** ADV *The President uncompromisingly rejected calls for his resignation.* ...*an uncompromisingly hostile attitude.*

unconcealed /ʌŋkənsiːld/
ADJ If something such as an emotion is **unconcealed**, you make no attempt to hide it. *Mary gazed with unconcealed curiosity.* ...*her unconcealed dislike for me.*

unconcern /ʌŋkənsɜːn/
NU **Unconcern** is behaviour which shows a surprising lack of interest or anxiety, even in a situation that would normally interest people or worry them. *He went his own way with unconcern for consequences that sometimes stunned people... Bernstein returned to his desk feigning unconcern.*

unconcerned /ʌŋkənsɜːnd/
ADJ If someone is **unconcerned** about something, they are not interested in it or worried about it. *You seem remarkably unconcerned... Opponents of the bill say it's been resurrected to brand President Bush as unconcerned about working families.*

unconditional /ʌŋkəndɪʃənəl/
ADJ Something that is **unconditional** has no conditions or limits associated with it. *Mr Beasley stressed that the offer was not unconditional... They offered unconditional support... The statement called for an unconditional withdrawal of Soviet troops.* ◆ **unconditionally** ADV *The laws had to be obeyed unconditionally... Half of those detained have been released unconditionally.*

unconfirmed /ʌŋkənfɜːmd/
ADJ If a report or rumour is **unconfirmed**, there is not yet any definite proof that it is true. *Unconfirmed reports say ten people were killed... There are suggestions, as yet unconfirmed, that the meeting may be cancelled.*

uncongenial /ʌŋkəndʒiːniəl/
ADJ If you find a place or an event **uncongenial**, you think that it is unfriendly and unpleasant; a literary word. ...*these uncongenial surroundings.*

unconnected /ʌŋkənektɪd/
ADJ If one thing is **unconnected** with another, the two

things are not related to each other in any way. *The two incidents were unconnected... A spokesman said the dispute was unconnected with the P&O strike.*

unconscious /ʌŋkɒnʃəs/
1 ADJ Someone who is **unconscious** is in a state similar to sleep, for example as a result of a shock or accident. *The blow knocked him unconscious... She lay unconscious on the table.* ◆ **unconsciousness** NU *He dropped back into unconsciousness.*
2 ADJ PRED+*of* If you are **unconscious** of something that has been said or done, you are not aware of it. *Dekker seemed totally unconscious of the insult.*
3 ADJ If feelings or attitudes are **unconscious**, you are not aware of them, but they show in the way that you behave. ...*unconscious feelings of envy.* ◆ **unconsciously** ADV *They can't help resenting the baby unconsciously.*
4 N SING Your **unconscious** is the part of your mind which contains feelings and ideas that you do not know about or cannot control. ...*images retrieved from the unconscious.*

unconstitutional /ʌŋkɒnstɪtjuːʃ°nəl/
ADJ Something that is **unconstitutional** breaks the rules of an organization or political system. ...*unconstitutional strikes... The extradition treaty with the United States was declared unconstitutional.*

uncontrollable /ʌŋkəntrəʊləbl/
ADJ If something such as an emotion is **uncontrollable**, you can do nothing to prevent it or control it. ...*the sudden uncontrollable note of fear in her voice.* ◆ **uncontrollably** ADV *He found himself giggling quite uncontrollably.*

uncontrolled /ʌŋkəntrəʊld/
1 ADJ If someone's behaviour is **uncontrolled**, they do not try to stop it or make it less extreme. *He was letting out loud uncontrolled shrieks.*
2 ADJ If a situation or activity is **uncontrolled**, nobody is responsible for controlling it and preventing it from becoming harmful. ...*uncontrolled building development.* ...*uncontrolled logging in rain forests.*

unconventional /ʌŋkənvenʃ°nəl/
1 ADJ If someone is **unconventional**, they do not behave in the same way as most other people in their society. *Pauling is an unconventional genius who ranks amongst the great scientists of history.* ...*her unconventional dress.*
2 ADJ If a method of doing something is **unconventional**, it is not the usual way of doing it, and may be rather surprising. *They are trying to evaluate whether unconventional treatments have a place in fighting cancer... Yeats had a rather unconventional education and he didn't go to university.*

unconvinced /ʌŋkənvɪnst/
ADJ PRED If you are **unconvinced** about something, you are not at all certain that it is true or right. *I remained unconvinced by what she had said... British opinion remains unconvinced of the virtues of the European Community. ...unconvinced that Ethiopia actually wants a political settlement... He appears unconvinced about any fundamental change in Soviet thinking.*

unconvincing /ʌŋkənvɪnsɪŋ/
ADJ If arguments or reasons are **unconvincing**, you do not believe that they are true or valid. ...*an unconvincing excuse.*

uncooked /ʌŋkʊkt/
ADJ **Uncooked** meat or other food has not yet been cooked. *There were three uncooked chops on the kitchen table.*

uncooperative /ʌŋkəʊɒpə°rətɪv/; also spelt **unco-operative**.
ADJ If someone is **uncooperative**, they make no effort at all to help other people. *He is deliberately being uncooperative... He was an uncooperative patient.*

unco-ordinated /ʌŋkəʊɔːdɪneɪtɪd/
1 ADJ If you are **unco-ordinated**, you do not have proper control over your movements and they are not graceful or smooth. *He's careless, clumsy, and unco-ordinated.* ...*unco-ordinated, jerky muscle movements.*
2 ADJ If an action or process is **unco-ordinated**, it has not been properly planned or organized, which usually results in a lack of success. *He describes the rescue*

effort as chaotic and unco-ordinated. ...an unco-ordinated revolt by junior army officers.

uncork /ʌnkɔːk/ **uncorks, uncorking, uncorked**
VO When you **uncork** a bottle, you open it by pulling the cork out of it. *The waiter brought a bottle of wine to the table and uncorked it.*

uncountable noun /ʌnkaʊntəbl naʊn/ **uncountable nouns**
NC An **uncountable noun** is the same as an **uncount noun**.

uncounted /ʌnkaʊntɪd/
ADJ ATTRIB If you refer to **uncounted** things or people, you mean that there is a large number of them. *And behind the bare figures lie uncounted stories of personal misery.*

uncount noun /ʌnkaʊnt naʊn/ **uncount nouns**
NC In grammar, an **uncount noun** is a noun which has only one form and refers to a general kind of thing rather than to an individual item. For example, 'food', 'courage', 'sleep', and 'fun' are normally used as uncount nouns.

uncouth /ʌnkuːθ/
ADJ Someone who is **uncouth** has bad manners and behaves in an unpleasant way. *...an uncouth soldier. ...her uncouth behaviour.*

uncover /ʌnkʌvə/ **uncovers, uncovering, uncovered**
1 VO If you **uncover** something secret or illegal, you find out about it. *Another plot to assassinate General de Gaulle was uncovered... German authorities uncovered a large arms cache... Investigators have uncovered evidence of widespread fraud.* ♦ **uncovering** NU *...the uncovering of an international agricultural fraud. ...the uncovering of new and substantial evidence.*
2 VO To **uncover** something also means to remove something that is covering it. *She uncovered her face.*

uncovered /ʌnkʌvəd/
ADJ Something that is **uncovered** does not have anything covering it. *...uncovered food... One of the youths said only his face was left uncovered.*

uncritical /ʌnkrɪtɪkl/
ADJ If you are **uncritical**, you accept or approve of something without being able or willing to judge whether it is good or bad; used showing disapproval. *...uncritical acceptance of traditional values. ...an uncritical audience.* ♦ **uncritically** ADV *She feels we have uncritically glorified the Gulf war.*

unctuous /ʌnktjuəs/
ADJ Someone who is **unctuous** pretends to be full of praise, kindness, or interest, but is obviously insincere; a literary word. *...his unctuous flirtatiousness.*

uncultured /ʌnkʌltʃəd/
ADJ If you describe someone as **uncultured**, you mean that they do not know much about art, literature, and other cultural topics; used showing disapproval. *He had a fear of being thought uncultured... She was regarded as an unintelligent, uninteresting and uncultured peasant.*

uncut /ʌnkʌt/
1 ADJ If a film, book, or play is **uncut**, it has not been shortened or censored. *The controversial film, the Last Temptation of Christ, is to be shown uncut to audiences over eighteen.*
2 ADJ **Uncut** diamonds or other precious stones have not been cut into a regular shape. *Reports say thieves have stolen more than a million dollars' worth of uncut diamonds.*

undaunted /ʌndɔːntɪd/
ADJ If you are **undaunted**, you are not discouraged by disappointing things that have happened. *Undaunted by his first setbacks, he decided to try once more... The undaunted reformers throughout the eastern bloc deserve all the help they can get.*

undecided /ʌndɪsaɪdɪd/
1 ADJ If you are **undecided** about something, you have not yet made a decision about it. *She was still undecided whether she would or would not return home... A lot of us came to the meeting undecided about taking strike action... A third of the voters were undecided.*
2 ADJ If a situation or competition is **undecided**, its

results are not yet known or have not yet happened. *The future of European security is still undecided... The power struggle within the party remains undecided... The tie between Yugoslavia and Switzerland is still undecided. ...to choose deputies for the remaining undecided forty-eight seats.*

undeclared /ʌndɪkleəd/
1 ADJ If you describe something as **undeclared**, you mean that it has not been officially stated or accepted, but seems to be true or likely. *...what it describes as an undeclared war against the country's minority black population... They claimed wide but undeclared support for their plans... While his candidacy is still undeclared, Mr Barre is ahead of Mr Chirac in the opinion polls. ...their chief, although undeclared goal.*
2 ADJ **Undeclared** money or goods have not been taxed, licensed, or approved by the authorities, and are therefore illegal. *According to the police, he was carrying $47,900 undeclared dollars in fees and prize money... Three planes landed in Brazil with undeclared cargos of arms.*

undemanding /ʌndɪmɑːndɪŋ/
1 ADJ An **undemanding** job is not difficult to do or does not involve any hard physical work. *The pay was adequate, the job undemanding.*
2 ADJ Someone who is **undemanding** is easy to be with and does not ask other people to do a lot for them. *...an undemanding husband.*

undemocratic /ʌndeməkrætɪk/
ADJ An **undemocratic** system, process, or decision is controlled by one person or a small number of people, rather than by all the people who are involved. *It attacked the use of undemocratic methods to strengthen the party... Mr Kinnock said the new tax was unfair and undemocratic... The government is seeking to use undemocratic powers.*

undemonstrative /ʌndɪmɒnstrətɪv/
ADJ Someone who is **undemonstrative** does not allow their feelings to show. *Usually undemonstrative, he couldn't resist a victory salute... The audiences are so politely British and undemonstrative... He was a rather unemotional, undemonstrative creature.*

undeniable /ʌndɪnaɪəbl/
ADJ Something that is **undeniable** is certainly true. *The evidence is undeniable.* ♦ **undeniably** SUBMOD *He was a tall, dark, and undeniably handsome man.*

under /ʌndə/
1 PREP If one thing is **under** another, it is directly below or beneath the other thing and may be covered or hidden by it. *There was a cask of beer under the bench... He had no shirt on under his thin jumper... We squeezed under the wire and into the garden.*
2 PREP If something happens **under** particular circumstances or conditions, it happens when those circumstances or conditions exist. *He travelled under difficult circumstances... The family cannot cope under stress.*
3 PREP If something happens **under** a law or system, it happens because that law or system says that it must happen or that it is allowed to happen. *Equal pay for men and women is guaranteed under English law.*
4 PREP If something happens **under** a particular person or government, it happens when that person or government is in power. *...China under Chairman Mao.*
5 PREP If you study or work **under** a particular person, that person is your teacher or boss. *He studied under Benton... He has a large number of executives under him.*
6 PREP If you do something **under** a name that is different to your usual one, you use the different name for that purpose. *He wrote an anti-war novel under an assumed name.*
7 PREP You use **under** to say what section of a list, book, or system of classification something is in. *You'll find it under O for Orwell.*
8 PREP If something is **under** an amount or number, it is less than that amount or number. *Expenditure this year should be just under 15 billion pounds... Tickets cost 50p for children under 16.*

under-/ˌʌndə-/
PREFIX **Under-** is used to form words that express the idea that there is not enough of something or that something has not been done or happened as much or as well as is needed. *Kids in Kentucky will remain among the most under-educated in the nation. ...an under-populated mountain area. ...the illness and under-nutrition which needlessly kills forty-thousand children every day.*

underage/ˌʌndəreɪdʒ/
1 ADJ If someone is **underage**, the law says they are too young to take part in a particular activity. *The law is designed to stop unscrupulous licensees deliberately serving drinks to underage customers... They must have known that I was underage. ...underage smokers.*
2 ADJ ATTRIB **Underage** activities such as drinking or smoking are carried out by people who are underage. *The revised licensing hours are coupled with measures to tighten the law on underage drinking... People who had experienced similar problems themselves, might be in a better position to help stop underage smoking.*

underarm/ˌʌndərɑːm/
1 ADJ ATTRIB You use **underarm** to refer to your armpits. *...underarm antiperspirant.*
2 ADV or ADJ You also use **underarm** to describe actions that you do, such as throwing a ball, in which you keep your arm below the level of your shoulder. *She would throw underarm. ...underarm shots.*

undercarriage/ˌʌndəkærɪdʒ/ **undercarriages**
NC The **undercarriage** of an aeroplane is the part, including the wheels, which supports the aeroplane when it is on the ground or in the process of landing or taking off. *The investigation showed that the pilots had not extended the undercarriage and wing flaps in preparation for landing. ...the door which covers the undercarriage when it is retracted.*

underclass/ˌʌndəklɑːs/
N SING A particular country's **underclass** is a number of its people who are extremely poor, and who have little chance of improving their situation. *She has created an underclass which has not shared in the benefits of the growth the rest of the country enjoys... That an underclass of dispossessed people now exists in Britain is generally accepted.*

underclothes/ˌʌndəkləʊðz/
N PL **Underclothes** are clothes such as a vest, bra, or pants that people wear next to their skin and under their other clothes. *Many of them stripped down to their underclothes because of the summer heat.*

undercover/ˌʌndəkʌvə/
ADJ ATTRIB or ADV **Undercover** work involves secretly obtaining information for the government or the police. *...police on undercover duty. ...undercover agents... He began working undercover for the Castro party.*

undercurrent/ˌʌndəkʌrənt/ **undercurrents**
NC An **undercurrent** is a feeling or opinion that you do not express or that you are hardly aware of but which influences the way that you think or behave. *There is already an undercurrent of unease among Palestinians in Tunis and Damascus. ...an undercurrent of dissatisfaction with the government.*

undercut/ˌʌndəkʌt/ **undercuts, undercutting.** The form **undercut** is used in the present tense and is also the past tense and past participle.
1 VO To **undercut** someone or **undercut** their prices means to sell a product more cheaply than they do. *The large-scale producer can usually undercut smaller competitors.*
2 VO If something **undercuts** your attempts to achieve something, it prevents them from being effective. *The delay would surely undercut efforts to force modernization.*

underdeveloped/ˌʌndədɪveləpt/
ADJ An **underdeveloped** region or country does not have modern industries and usually has a low standard of living. *They all contribute to a joint fund for investment in the underdeveloped areas... The Peace Corps is made up of young volunteers who help people in underdeveloped countries to improve their living standards.*

underdog/ˌʌndədɒg/ **underdogs**
NC The **underdog** in a competition or situation is the person who seems least likely to succeed or win. *The underdogs Australia beat New Zealand by 25 points to 12 in the World Cup final in Auckland... She was the underdog in the election.*

underdone/ˌʌndədʌn/
ADJ If food is **underdone**, it has been cooked for less time than usual. *The pastry crust was always underdone... Beef is nicest slightly underdone.*

underemployed/ˌʌndərɪmplɔɪd/
ADJ If someone is **underemployed**, they do not have enough work to do. *Many of those who do have a job are underemployed... Half the urban population is either unemployed, underemployed, or engaged in crime.*

underestimate/ˌʌndərestɪmeɪt/ **underestimates, underestimating, underestimated**
1 VO or V-REPORT If you **underestimate** something, you do not realize how large or great it is or will be. *The Americans underestimated the power of the explosion... It was easy to underestimate what she had endured.*
2 VO If you **underestimate** someone, you do not realize what they are capable of doing. *He had underestimated Muller... People underestimate Denis Healey at their peril—he can be as devastating an opponent as he can be charming to his friends.*

underfed/ˌʌndəfed/
ADJ People who are **underfed** do not get enough food to eat. *Underfed children are more likely to catch diseases.*

under-financed
ADJ **Under-financed** means the same as **under-funded**. *The hospitals were seriously under-financed. ...a small, under-financed school.*

underfoot/ˌʌndəfʊt/
1 ADJ after N, or ADV You describe something as **underfoot** when you are standing or walking on it. *The grass underfoot was short and springy... The ground was hardening underfoot.*
2 ADV If you trample or crush something **underfoot**, you spoil or destroy it by treading on it. *The banner was accidentally trampled underfoot.*

under-funded
ADJ An organization or institution that is **under-funded** does not have enough money spent on it, so that it cannot function properly. *Over the past few years the Health Service had been seriously under-funded... Many schools are under-funded and poorly equipped.*

undergarment/ˌʌndəgɑːmənt/ **undergarments**
NC An **undergarment** is a piece of clothing that people wear next to their skin and under their other clothes; a formal word. *...ladies' undergarments.*

undergo/ˌʌndəgəʊ/ **undergoes, undergoing, underwent, undergone**
VO If you **undergo** something necessary or unpleasant, it happens to you. *The United States will have to undergo radical changes... Her mother was about to undergo a major operation.*

undergraduate/ˌʌndəgrædʒuət/ **undergraduates**
NC An **undergraduate** is a student at a university or college who is studying for his or her first degree. *...a Cambridge undergraduate.* ▶ Also ADJ ATTRIB *...an undergraduate degree.*

underground; pronounced /ˌʌndəgraʊnd/ when it is an adjective or adverb and /ˈʌndəgraʊnd/ when it is a noun.
1 ADJ or ADV Something that is **underground** is below the surface of the ground. *...an underground car park... The larvae hatch and make their way underground.*
2 NU The **Underground** is a railway system in which electric trains travel underground in tunnels. *We went by Underground to Trafalgar Square.*
3 ADJ ATTRIB **Underground** activities take place secretly in a country where political opposition is not allowed, and are directed against the government. *...an underground newspaper.* ● If someone goes **underground**, they have to live or carry on their activities in secret because the government in their country does not allow them or disapproves of them.

A lot of people who were leading the protest movement here had to go underground... If the parties are outlawed, they will merely go underground. 4 N SING The **underground** in a country is an organized group of people who are engaged in illegal activities, often against the government in power. *Shabir Shah is currently the most influential leader of the underground. ...one of a band of underground fighters who risked their lives to defeat Nazism.*

undergrowth /ˈʌndəɡrəʊθ/
NU **Undergrowth** consists of bushes and plants growing close together under trees. *The body was found in dense undergrowth... We left the house and tiptoed through the undergrowth.*

underhand /ˌʌndəˈhænd/
ADJ **Underhand** actions are secret and dishonest. *Did they ever do anything which you regarded as underhand?*

underlay, underlays; pronounced /ˈʌndəleɪ/ for the meaning in paragraph 1 and /ˌʌndəˈleɪ/ for the meaning in paragraph 2.
1 N MASS **Underlay** is a thick material that you place between a carpet and the floor for extra warmth and in order to protect the carpet. *Clean, flexible, polyurethane foam could be sold to manufacturers of carpet underlay.*
2 **Underlay** is also the past tense of **underlie**.

underlie /ˌʌndəˈlaɪ/ **underlies, underlying, underlay, underlain**
VO If something **underlies** a situation, it is the cause or basis of it. *The social problems underlying these crises are unsolved.* ● See also **underlying**.

underline /ˌʌndəˈlaɪn/ **underlines, underlining, underlined**
1 VO If something **underlines** a feeling or problem, it emphasizes its importance. *It was a striking display of cordiality, underlining the new closeness of the relationship between the superpowers... An article in the Lancet underlined the same problem.*
2 VO If you **underline** a word or sentence, you draw a line underneath it. *He underlined his signature with a little flourish.*

underling /ˈʌndəlɪŋ/ **underlings**
NC You refer to someone as an **underling** when they are inferior in rank or status to someone else and take orders from them. *He expected his underlings to stand respectfully when he entered the room.*

underlip /ˈʌndəlɪp/ **underlips**
NC Your **underlip** is your lower lip. *She removed a fragment of cigarette paper from her underlip.*

underlying /ˌʌndəˈlaɪɪŋ/
ADJ ATTRIB **Underlying** features are important but not obvious. *The underlying cause of the economic crisis is the war... There are underlying similarities between all human beings... The underlying problem can only be resolved through a political settlement.*

undermanned /ˌʌndəˈmænd/
ADJ If an organization is **undermanned**, it does not have enough employees to function properly. *The industry is sadly undermanned... Poland's overworked and undermanned customs service is ill equipped to deal with the refugees.*

undermine /ˌʌndəˈmaɪn/ **undermines, undermining, undermined**
1 VO To **undermine** a feeling or a system means to make it less strong or less secure. *Public confidence in the company had now been completely undermined... They resented measures which undermined their authority.*
2 VO If you **undermine** a person, or **undermine** their position or authority, you make their authority or position less secure, often by indirect methods. *Mr Bush will be put in the awkward position of having to appease Mr Mandela while trying to avoid undermining President De Klerk... He has fatally undermined Mrs Thatcher's authority.*
3 VO If you **undermine** someone's efforts, or **undermine** their chances of achieving something, you do something which makes them less likely to succeed. *This will fatally undermine Gorbachev's efforts to bring the Baltics in to line... The unions feel that without the rail link, Britain's chances of*

prospering after 1992 would be seriously undermined.

underneath /ˌʌndəˈniːθ/
1 PREP or ADV If one thing is **underneath** another, it is directly below or beneath it. *The dog was underneath the table... There was a portrait with an inscription underneath.*
2 ADJ ATTRIB or ADV The **underneath** part of something is the part which normally touches or faces the ground. *The underneath part felt damp... I lifted the dog's foot and checked the soft pad underneath.* ▶ Also N SING *The underneath of the car was covered with rust.*
3 ADV or PREP You use **underneath** when talking about feelings and emotions that people do not show in their behaviour. *Underneath, most of us are shy... I seem confident, but underneath it all I'm terribly nervous.*

undernourished /ˌʌndəˈnʌrɪʃt/
ADJ An **undernourished** person is weak and unhealthy because they have not been eating enough food, or because the food they have been eating does not contain all the nutrients they need. *He said many of the refugees were undernourished and diseased.*

underpaid /ˌʌndəˈpeɪd/
ADJ People who are **underpaid** are not paid enough money for the job that they do. *...a great mass of underpaid workers.*

underpants /ˈʌndəpænts/
N PL **Underpants** are a piece of clothing worn by men and boys under their trousers, and next to their skin. *They stripped them down to their underpants.*

underpass /ˈʌndəpɑːs/ **underpasses**
NC An **underpass** is a road or footpath that goes underneath a railway or another road. *...a pedestrian underpass. ...the exit of a highway underpass. ...the underpass of the underground station.*

underpin /ˌʌndəˈpɪn/ **underpins, underpinning, underpinned**
VO If one thing **underpins** another, it helps the other thing to continue or succeed by supporting and strengthening it. *His determined move was underpinned by a formidable show of strength. ...the informal relationships that underpin any community... To underpin his view, he came up with a number of practical suggestions.* ◆ **underpinning, underpinnings** N U or NC *...the philosophic underpinning of science... We watched the imperial and commercial underpinnings of our society collapse.*

underplay /ˌʌndəˈpleɪ/ **underplays, underplaying, underplayed**
VO If you **underplay** something, you make it seem less important than it really is. *She underplays the fact that she's got the Corporation behind her... All attitudes and expressions of emotions are to be underplayed.*

underprivileged /ˌʌndəˈprɪvəlɪdʒd/
ADJ **Underprivileged** people have less money and fewer opportunities than other people. *...an underprivileged family.*

underrate /ˌʌndəˈreɪt/ **underrates, underrating, underrated**
VO If you **underrate** someone, you do not recognize how clever, important, or significant they are. *He soon discovered that he had underrated Lucy... Frank had underrated Sir James's knowledge of Africa... Cassava is often underrated as food.*

underscore /ˌʌndəˈskɔː/ **underscores, underscoring, underscored**
1 VO If one thing, for example an action or an event, **underscores** another, it draws attention to the other thing and emphasizes its importance. *The urgency of doing something was underscored by a wave of horror stories about rape and muggings... This very difference underscores our break with past traditions.*
2 VO If you **underscore** something such as a word or a sentence, you draw a line underneath it in order to make people notice it or to give it extra importance. *The words were heavily underscored by a ballpoint pen.*

undersea /ˈʌndəsiː/
ADJ ATTRIB **Undersea** means below the surface of the sea. *There are great rift systems in the ocean floor and undersea mountains to rival the Himalayas.*

...large, hidden resources of undersea oil and gas.
...the undersea world of the submarine.

under-secretary, under-secretaries
NC An **under-secretary** is a senior official with an important post in a government department. *Channon was made an under-secretary at the Department of the Environment. ...the Permanent Under-Secretary of State at the Foreign Office.*

undershirt /ˈʌndəʃɜːt/ **undershirts**
NC An **undershirt** is a garment worn for warmth on the top part of your body next to your skin and under your other clothes; used in American English.

underside /ˈʌndəsaɪd/ **undersides**
NC The **underside** of something is the part which normally faces towards the ground. *He turned the rifle over and examined the underside.*

undersized /ˈʌndəsaɪzd/
ADJ **Undersized** people or things are smaller than usual, or smaller than they should be. *...rows of undersized babies.*

understaffed /ˌʌndəstɑːft/
ADJ An **understaffed** organization does not have enough employees to do its work properly. *The prison hospital is grossly understaffed.*

understand /ˌʌndəstænd/ **understands, understanding, understood**
1 V Oor V-REPORT If you **understand** someone or **understand** what they are saying, you know what they mean. *His message was so short and indistinct that nobody could understand him... I don't understand what you mean... There are lots of words in it which they don't understand.*
2 V orVO To **understand** someone also means to know how they feel and why they behave in the way that they do. *They understand, because they went through the same experience... We want people to understand each other.*
3 V Oor V-REPORT You say that you **understand** something when you know why or how it happens. *There's still a lot we don't understand, and new discoveries have needed new theories to explain them. ...political forces that she does not even begin to understand... I don't understand why the engine isn't working.*
4 V-REPORT If you say that you **understand** that something is the case, you mean that you have been told that it is the case; a formal use. *I understand that a full debate will take place a week tomorrow... I understand she has several aunts... They will be working, I understand, at a new camp to be opened at Azra.*
5 VO If you **understand** a language, you know what someone is saying when they are speaking that language. *I don't understand English... They were speaking a language the settlers did not understand.*
6 If you **make** yourself **understood**, you get someone to understand what you are telling them. *They are having no difficulty at all in making themselves understood.*

understandable /ˌʌndəstændəbl/
ADJ If you say that someone's behaviour is **understandable**, you mean that they have reacted to a situation in a natural way. *His reaction was perfectly understandable.* ◆ **understandably** ADV SEN *Understandably, he was frightened.*

understanding /ˌʌndəstændɪŋ/ **understandings**
1 NU If you have an **understanding** of something, you know how it works or what it means. *It's hoped that this understanding of how the heart functions might be used to prevent heart disease... I doubt whether he had any real understanding of Shakespeare... The job requires an understanding of Spanish.*
2 ADJ If you are **understanding** towards someone, you are kind and forgiving. *I have always thought you were an understanding person.*
3 NU If there is **understanding** between people, they are friendly towards each other and trust each other. *What is needed is greater understanding between management and workers.*
4 NC An **understanding** is an informal agreement about something. *Tacit understandings had been reached.*

5 If you agree to do one thing **on the understanding** that another thing will be done, you do it because you have been told that the other thing will be done. *I signed the contract on the understanding that delivery would be this week.*

understate /ˌʌndəsteɪt/ **understates, understating, understated**
VO If you **understate** something, you suggest that it is less important than it really is. *They understate the magnitude of the problem.*

understatement /ˌʌndəsteɪtmənt/ **understatements**
NCorNU An **understatement** is a statement which does not fully express the extent to which something is true. *To say it's been good is quite an understatement... That sounds like typical British understatement.*

understood /ˌʌndəstʊd/
Understood is the past tense and past participle of **understand**.

understudy /ˈʌndəstʌdi/ **understudies**
NC An actor's or actress's **understudy** is a person who has learned their part in a play and can act the part if the actor or actress is ill. *He was an understudy to Charlie Chaplin on a tour of the USA.*

undertake /ˌʌndəteɪk/ **undertakes, undertaking, undertook, undertaken**; a formal word.
1 VO When you **undertake** a task or job, you start doing it and accept responsibility for it. *Reluctantly, he undertook the mission.*
2 V+to-INF If you **undertake** to do something, you promise that you will do it. *They have undertaken to accept the offer.*

undertaker /ˈʌndəteɪkə/ **undertakers**
NC An **undertaker** is a person whose job is to deal with the bodies of people who have died and to arrange funerals. *The undertaker who's handling the arrangements says he still hasn't been given any clear instructions.*

undertaking /ˌʌndəteɪkɪŋ/ **undertakings**; a formal word.
1 NC An **undertaking** is a task or job. *...a complex and expensive undertaking.*
2 NC If you give an **undertaking** to do something, you formally promise to do it. *Jenkins gave an undertaking not to stand again for election.*

undertone /ˈʌndətəʊn/ **undertones**
1 NC If you say something in an **undertone**, you say it very quietly. *Marcus said in an undertone, 'It doesn't matter, Lucas'.*
2 NC+SUPP If something has **undertones** of a particular kind, it suggests ideas or attitudes of this kind without expressing them directly. *The custom had religious undertones.*

undertook /ˌʌndətʊk/
Undertook is the past tense of **undertake**.

undervalue /ˌʌndəvæljuː/ **undervalues, undervaluing, undervalued**
VO If you **undervalue** something, you fail to recognize how valuable or important it is. *We tend to undervalue art... Teachers believe they are undervalued and underpaid.*

underwater /ˌʌndəwɔːtə/
ADV or ADJ ATTRIB **Underwater** means below the surface of the sea, a river, or a lake. *She swam underwater. ...underwater exploration.*

under way; also spelt **underway**.
ADJ PRED If an activity is **under way**, it has started. *... the current round of talks under way in Manila... A massive celebration is under way... An investigation is underway to try to determine the cause of the blaze.*

underwear /ˈʌndəweə/
NU **Underwear** is clothing such as a vest, bra, or pants that people wear next to their skin and under their other clothes. *They stripped down to their underwear... A number of women were found to be smuggling heroin into the United States in their underwear.*

underwent /ˌʌndəwɛnt/
Underwent is the past tense of **undergo**.

underworld /ˈʌndəwɜːld/
N SING The **underworld** is organized crime and the people involved in it. *The find was made after a tip-*

off to police from Bangkok's criminal underworld.
...professional thugs from the underworld...
Underworld gangs had moved in to demand protection
money.

underwrite /ˌʌndəraɪt/ **underwrites, underwriting,**
underwrote, underwritten
vo If you **underwrite** an activity or **underwrite** the
cost of it, you agree to provide any money that is
needed to cover losses or to buy special equipment; a
technical term. *2 million pounds was made available*
to underwrite the production of machine-tools...
Madrid will extend a £290 million export credit to
underwrite some of the cost.

underwriter /ˌʌndəraɪtə/ **underwriters**
NC An **underwriter** is someone whose job involves
agreeing to provide money for a particular activity or
paying for any losses that are made. *They hand the*
responsibility for risk handling over to a professional
underwriter... Christopher Rome is one of Lloyds top
underwriters, underwriting policies on behalf of a
number of syndicates... The underwriter may agree to
insure, say 2 percent of the risk.

undeserved /ˌʌndɪzɜːvd/
ADJ If you get something that is **undeserved**, you have
not earned it and should not really have it. *Their*
bitterness at Conway's undeserved promotion was
obvious... He wallows in the undeserved praise of his
colleagues... He thought all the rough treatment that I
underwent appeared undeserved.

undesirable /ˌʌndɪzaɪərəbl/
ADJ You describe people or things as **undesirable** when
you disapprove of them and think that they will have
harmful effects. *These cuts in education are very*
undesirable... The government has condemned these
practices as improper and undesirable.

undetected /ˌʌndɪtɛktɪd/
1 ADJ If you are **undetected**, people do not notice you
or recognize you. *It was important to my safety that I*
should remain undetected.
2 ADV If you do something **undetected**, people do not
notice you doing it. *I don't see any way I could get*
her out undetected.

undeveloped /ˌʌndɪvɛləpt/
ADJ **Undeveloped** countries or regions are not
industrialized and do not use modern methods of
farming. *Several poor and undeveloped republics are*
already in a state near disaster. ...the very remote
and undeveloped northern state of Amapa.

undid /ˌʌndɪd/
Undid is the past tense of **undo**.

undignified /ˌʌndɪgnɪfaɪd/
ADJ **Undignified** behaviour is foolish and
embarrassing. *It is by no means the first time that*
parliamentary debate has degenerated into undignified
brawling. ...an undignified pose.

undiluted /ˌʌndaɪluːtɪd/
1 ADJ An **undiluted** feeling or quality is very strong
and not mixed with any other feeling or quality. *The*
situation is not one of undiluted gloom. ...undying and
undiluted love. ...his undiluted Scottishness.
2 ADJ A liquid that is **undiluted** is concentrated and
has not had water added to make it weaker.
...undiluted orange squash.

undisciplined /ˌʌndɪsəplɪnd/
ADJ Someone who is **undisciplined** behaves badly, with
a lack of self-control. *People often complain that*
British children are undisciplined. ...undisciplined
behaviour and corruption.

undiscovered /ˌʌndɪskʌvəd/
ADJ If something is **undiscovered**, it has not been
discovered or noticed. *These authors were*
undiscovered geniuses... Old people who are ill often
lie undiscovered in their homes for days.

undisguised /ˌʌndɪsgaɪzd/
ADJ **Undisguised** feelings are shown openly, and are
not hidden. *He looked at her with undisguised*
admiration.

undismayed /ˌʌndɪsmeɪd/
ADJ PRED Someone who is **undismayed** by something
unpleasant or unexpected does not feel any fear,
worry, or sadness about it; a literary word. *She*
appeared quite undismayed and unrepentant over

Amelia's reproaches... The Freedom Association,
undismayed by its failure, is on the verge of
announcing fresh legal moves against the authorities.

undisputed /ˌʌndɪspjuːtɪd/
1 ADJ If something is **undisputed**, everyone accepts
that it exists or is true. *...her undisputed good looks...*
The facts are undisputed.
2 ADJ If someone is the **undisputed** leader of a group
of people, everyone accepts that they are the leader.
Mao became undisputed leader in China.

undistinguished /ˌʌndɪstɪŋgwɪʃt/
ADJ Something that is **undistinguished** has no
especially good qualities or features. *His political*
career had been undistinguished.

undisturbed /ˌʌndɪstɜːbd/
1 ADJ A place that is **undisturbed** is peaceful and has
not been affected by changes that have happened in
other places. *The village is still very undisturbed.*
2 ADJ PRED If you are **undisturbed** in something that
you are doing, you continue doing it and are not
affected by anything else that is happening. *The*
children pursued their studies undisturbed by the
many visitors.

undivided /ˌʌndɪvaɪdɪd/
ADJ ATTRIB If you give something your **undivided**
attention, you concentrate on it fully. *I was listening*
with undivided attention.

undo /ʌnduː/ **undoes, undoing, undid, undone**
1 vo If you **undo** something that is closed, tied, or
held together in some way, you open it or loosen it so
that its parts separate or so that you can remove what
is inside. *...undoing a newspaper parcel tied with*
string... He bent down and undid the laces of his
shoes.
2 vo If you **undo** something useful that has been done,
you prevent it from being effective. *He appeared to*
be undoing all their patient work.

undocumented /ʌndɒkjʊmentɪd/
ADJ An **undocumented** person is someone who has
gone to a particular country to live and work but who
is not officially allowed to do so; used in American
English. *As many as 30,000 illegal Irish or*
undocumented immigrants live in the greater Boston
area... This is a community that's poor, Spanish-
speaking, and largely undocumented. ▶ Also N PL *The*
undocumented must rely on charities that require no
proof of legal residency.

undoing /ʌnduːɪŋ/
NU If something is your **undoing**, it is the cause of
your failure; a formal word. *Stress can be the*
undoing of so many fine players.

undone /ʌndʌn/
ADJ PRED Something that is **undone** is no longer tied or
fastened. *His bow tie had come undone.*

undoubted /ʌndaʊtɪd/
ADJ You use **undoubted** to emphasize that something
exists or is true. *...her undoubted acting ability.*
♦ **undoubtedly** ADV SEN *A chauffeur is undoubtedly a*
status symbol.

undreamed of /ʌndriːmd ɒv/ or **undreamt of**
/ʌndremt ɒv/
ADJ Something that is **undreamed of** is much better,
worse, or more unusual than you thought was
possible. *The Kremlin was preaching conciliation and*
international co-operation on a scale hitherto
undreamed of.

undress /ʌndres/ **undresses, undressing, undressed**
1 v When you **undress**, you take off your clothes. *He*
had to completely undress.
2 vo If you **undress** someone, you take off their
clothes. *I used to dress and undress my brother and*
change his nappy... Patients are undressed the
moment they arrive.

undressed /ʌndrest/
ADJ PRED If you are **undressed**, you are wearing no
clothes or very few clothes. *He took ages getting*
undressed.

undue /ʌndjuː/
ADJ ATTRIB **Undue** means greater or more extreme
than is reasonable or desirable; a formal word. *She*
was reprimanded for putting undue pressure on her
clients... They have criticised the mass media for

paying undue attention to the Emperor's illness.

undulate /ˈʌndjʊleɪt/ **undulates, undulating, undulated**
v Something that **undulates** has gentle curves or slopes, or moves gently and slowly up and down; a literary word. *The road undulates through pleasant scenery.*

unduly /ʌnˈdjuːli/
ADV or SUBMOD You use **unduly** to say that something is done to an unnecessary or excessive extent. *This would not have surprised Morris unduly... This attitude seemed to me unduly fussy.*

undying /ʌnˈdaɪɪŋ/
ADJ If you describe a feeling or a belief as **undying**, you mean that it will last forever; a literary word. *To each and every one of those brave young men goes our heartfelt thanks and undying gratitude. ...Daniel's undying love for his wife.*

unearned /ʌnˈɜːnd/
ADJ **Unearned** income is money that you get from things such as property or investments rather than money that you earn from a job. *...a tax on unearned income.*

unearth /ʌnˈɜːθ/ **unearths, unearthing, unearthed**
VO If you **unearth** something that is hidden or secret, you discover it. *The dossier was unearthed along with many others.*

unearthly /ʌnˈɜːθli/
1 ADJ **Unearthly** means strange and unnatural. *The light was unearthly.*
2 ADJ ATTRIB If you do something at an **unearthly** hour, you do it very early in the morning or very late at night. *He began teaching at 9 o'clock in the morning—an unearthly hour for most students.*

unease /ʌnˈiːz/
NU If you have a feeling of **unease**, you feel that something is wrong and you are anxious about it. *'He'll be alright,' I said to myself, trying to quell a growing unease.*

uneasy /ʌnˈiːzi/
ADJ If you are **uneasy**, you feel anxious that something may be wrong or that there may be danger. *She had an uneasy feeling that they were following her... I felt increasingly uneasy about my answer.* ◆ **uneasily** ADV *Philip blushed and laughed uneasily.* ◆ **uneasiness** NU *Pat's uneasiness grew as each minute passed.*

uneatable /ʌnˈiːtəbl/
1 ADJ Food that is **uneatable** is so bad or tastes so unpleasant that you do not want to eat it. *She used to make that uneatable gingerbread.*
2 ADJ **Uneatable** also means unable to be eaten by people. *Everybody knows that uncooked rice is quite uneatable.*

uneconomic /ˌʌniːkəˈnɒmɪk, ˌʌnekəˈnɒmɪk/
ADJ Something that is **uneconomic** does not make a profit, or uses money in an inefficient way. *The line is up for sale because British Rail say it's uneconomic. ...uneconomic coal mines. ...a one-teacher school is uneconomic.*

uneconomical /ˌʌniːkəˈnɒmɪkl, ˌʌnekəˈnɒmɪkl/
ADJ Something that is **uneconomical** does not make a profit, or uses money in an inefficient way. *The company has now replied that such restrictions would make the service uneconomical. ...plans to begin closing the shipyard on the grounds that it's uneconomical. ...current sources of coal may become exhausted or uneconomical.*

uneducated /ʌnˈedjʊkeɪtɪd/
ADJ Someone who is **uneducated** has not received much education. *Many of them were uneducated farmers... In Afghanistan the majority of the population is uneducated.*

unemotional /ˌʌnɪˈməʊʃənəl/
ADJ Someone who is **unemotional** does not show any feelings. *He was cold and unemotional.*

unemployable /ˌʌnɪmˈplɔɪəbl/
ADJ Someone who is **unemployable** does not have a job and is unlikely to get a job, for example because of the way that they behave. *Many of them remain half-educated, virtually unemployable, and very resentful... Owing to their low intelligence, they were unemployable.*

unemployed /ˌʌnɪmˈplɔɪd/
1 ADJ Someone who is **unemployed** wants to work but cannot get a job. *The government ought to create more jobs for unemployed young people.*
2 N PL People who want to work but cannot get a job are often referred to as the **unemployed**. *...the problem of the unemployed.*

unemployment /ˌʌnɪmˈplɔɪmənt/
NU You say that there is **unemployment** in a place when many people there cannot get jobs. *The government is concerned about the level of unemployment in Scotland. ...its government has been concerned at the prospect of rising unemployment.*

unemployment benefit
NU **Unemployment benefit** is money that some people receive from the state when they are unemployed. *If you are unemployed you may be able to get unemployment benefit.*

unending /ʌnˈendɪŋ/
ADJ You say that something is **unending** when it has continued for a long time and seems as though it will never stop. *The unrest is taking place against a background of unending economic crisis. ...the unending debate about tobacco.*

unenviable /ʌnˈenviəbl/
ADJ ATTRIB An **unenviable** situation is one that you would not like to be in, because it is difficult or unpleasant. *The president may find himself in the unenviable position of having to curb insurgencies in both the North and South of the country. ...the unenviable task of phoning the parents of the dead child.*

unequal /ʌnˈiːkwəl/
1 ADJ An **unequal** system is unfair because it treats people in different ways. *...the unequal distribution of wealth.*
2 ADJ **Unequal** things are different in size or amount. *Her feet are of unequal sizes.*

unequalled /ʌnˈiːkwəld/
ADJ Something that is **unequalled** is greater, better, or more extreme than anything else of the same kind. *His experience of organizing warfare was unequalled... This was when architecture reached a point of extravagance unequalled in history.*

unequivocal /ˌʌnɪˈkwɪvəkl/
ADJ An **unequivocal** statement is clear and can only be understood in one way; a formal word. *The reply was unequivocal.* ◆ **unequivocally** ADV *They have stated unequivocally what they stand for.*

unerring /ʌnˈɜːrɪŋ/
ADJ If someone has an **unerring** ability to do something, they can always manage to do it. *Kohl has a reputation as a politician with an unerring instinct for what the grass roots of the electorate think and feel... Sheila's unerring sense of direction helped them... He described him as a politician of unerring judgement.*

unethical /ʌnˈeθɪkl/
ADJ **Unethical** behaviour is wrong and unacceptable according to a particular convention or system of beliefs; a formal word. *He was accused of unethical conduct... He still thinks the ruling was unethical.*

uneven /ʌnˈiːvn/
1 ADJ Something that is **uneven** does not have a flat, straight, smooth, or regular surface. *...uneven teeth... She stumbled on the uneven ground.*
2 ADJ You can describe something which is not consistent in quality or extent as **uneven**. *It was an uneven but inspired performance... There has been an uneven response to the strike call.*

uneventful /ʌnɪˈventfl/
ADJ If a period of time is **uneventful**, nothing interesting or important happens during it. *The day was quiet and uneventful.*

unexceptionable /ˌʌnɪkˈsepʃənəbl/
ADJ Something that is **unexceptionable** is not likely to be criticized, objected to, or disagreed with; a formal word. *Their conduct is rarely unexceptionable... His explanation, although unexceptionable, is scarcely illuminating.*

unexceptional /ˌʌnɪkˈsepʃənəl/
ADJ Something that is **unexceptional** is only of an

average quality, and not at all remarkable. *His academic career was unexceptional—by his own account, he was an average student. ...an unexceptional ivory chess set.*

unexciting /ʌnɪksaɪtɪŋ/

ADJ Something that is **unexciting** is slightly boring, and not likely to shock or surprise you in any way. *...wholesome but unexciting bread-and-butter pudding. ...Mr Bush's solid, respectable, if unexciting, virtues.*

unexpected /ʌnɪkspɛktɪd/

ADJ Something that is **unexpected** surprises you because you were not expecting it to happen. *His arrival here was completely unexpected... The new rules are not entirely unexpected... My hostess greeted me with unexpected warmth.* ◆ **unexpectedly** ADV *She died quite unexpectedly.*

unfailing /ʌnfeɪlɪŋ/

ADJ **Unfailing** qualities or attitudes stay the same and never get weaker; a formal word. *I could never have carried on without the unfailing support of the teaching staff.*

unfair /ʌnfeə/

ADJ Something that is **unfair** is not right or not just. *It would be quite unfair to expose him to publicity. ...reports of deaths in custody, unfair trials and many other human rights abuses... I knew I was being unfair to him.* ◆ **unfairly** ADV *Workers who have been unfairly dismissed may claim compensation.*

unfaithful /ʌnfeɪθfl/

ADJ If someone is **unfaithful** to their lover or to the person they are married to, they have a sexual relationship with someone else. *He said he had been unfaithful, but that his days of adultery were now over... You love her with all your soul, and are never tempted to be unfaithful to her.*

unfamiliar /ʌnfəmɪliə/

ADJ If something is **unfamiliar** to you or if you are **unfamiliar** with it, you have not seen, heard, or experienced it before. *This name may be unfamiliar to most of you. ...a person unfamiliar with the French railway system.*

unfashionable /ʌnfæʃəⁿəbl/

ADJ If something is **unfashionable**, it is not fashionable or popular. *His ideas were unfashionable among his colleagues... The place was quiet and unfashionable.*

unfasten /ʌnfɑːsn/ **unfastens, unfastening, unfastened**

VO If you **unfasten** a piece of clothing or something such as a seat belt, you undo its buttons, hooks, or straps. *He unfastened the buttons of his shirt.*

unfathomable /ʌnfæðəməbl/

ADJ If something is **unfathomable**, it is so strange or complicated that it cannot be understood or explained; a formal word. *A soul is irrational, unfathomable, mysterious. ...arbitrary and unfathomable regulations which need a whole branch of the legal profession to interpret them.*

unfavourable /ʌnfeɪvəⁿrəbl/; spelt **unfavorable** in American English.

1 ADJ **Unfavourable** conditions or circumstances cause problems and reduce the chance of success. *It's a universal problem, we think, because essentially it's caused by unfavourable geology. ...unfavourable weather conditions. ...unfavourable conditions for the development of British industry.*

2 ADJ If you have an **unfavourable** opinion of something, you do not like it. *He had formed an unfavourable opinion of my work... The reaction of the Romanian government has been very unfavourable.*

unfeeling /ʌnfiːlɪŋ/

ADJ Someone who is **unfeeling** is not sympathetic towards people who are suffering or unhappy. *That sounds terribly selfish and unfeeling, but it's part of what happens with this disease. ...unfeeling journalists... They described the new tax as being harsh and unfeeling.*

unfettered /ʌnfɛtəd/

ADJ **Unfettered** activities are not restricted in any way; a formal word. *...the right of free speech, unfettered by the party system.*

unfinished /ʌnfɪnɪʃt/

ADJ If something is **unfinished**, it has not been

completed. *The unfinished building grew rusty and dilapidated... He left a lot of business unfinished.*

unfit /ʌnfɪt/

1 ADJ If you are **unfit**, your body is not in good condition because you have not been taking regular exercise. *Lying down or sitting still for much of the day, they become so unfit that the slightest effort is painful.*

2 ADJ PRED If a sports player is **unfit**, he or she is unable to play or compete in a competition because of injury or illness. *The striker, Gianluca Vialli, who missed the world cup because of injury, is still unfit.*

3 ADJ PRED If someone or something is **unfit** for a particular purpose, they are not suitable for it, for example because they are not of a good enough quality. *Adams is clearly unfit to hold an administrative post... This meat is unfit for human consumption.*

unflagging /ʌnflægɪŋ/

ADJ Something that is **unflagging** is maintained without any reduction in effort, intensity, or enthusiasm. *She felt encouraged by his unflagging attention. ...a lifetime of unflagging scrutiny.*

unflappable /ʌnflæpəbl/

ADJ Someone who is **unflappable** is always calm and never panics or gets upset or angry. *Faithful to his unflappable image, he described the resignations as little local difficulties.*

unfocused /ʌnfəʊkəst/; also spelt **unfocussed**.

1 ADJ If someone's eyes are **unfocused**, they are open, but not looking at anything. *...his unfocused gaze resting on each peak in turn.*

2 ADJ If someone's desires, aims, or intentions are **unfocused**, they have not got a particular purpose in mind. *Voter interest seems low and unfocused. ...unfocused raw energy... The discussion so far is somewhat unfocused.*

unfold, unfolds, unfolding, unfolded; pronounced /ʌnfəʊld/ for the meanings in paragraphs 1 and 2 and /ʌnfəʊld/ for the meaning in paragraph 3.

1 V When a situation **unfolds**, it develops and becomes known or understood. *The great invasion plan was beginning to unfold... They were re-evaluating the situation as it unfolded... He wrote his story as it unfolded in letters to his father.*

2 VO If you **unfold** your plans or intentions, you tell someone about them. *She had soon unfolded her plans to him.*

3 V-ERG If you **unfold** something which has been folded, you open it so that it becomes flat. *She thrust a small piece of paper at me. I unfolded it... The older woman's hands unfolded.*

unforeseen /ʌnfɔːsiːn/

ADJ An **unforeseen** event happens unexpectedly. *This was an unforeseen complication... They had decided to postpone the visit due to what were described as unforeseen circumstances.*

unforgettable /ʌnfəgɛtəbl/

ADJ If something is **unforgettable**, it is so good or so bad that you are unlikely to forget it. *Many of those who were there found it an unforgettable experience... England put themselves on the threshold of a magnificent grand slam triumph with an unforgettable victory over Wales.*

unforgivable /ʌnfəgɪvəbl/

ADJ An **unforgivable** act is so bad or cruel that it can never be forgiven or justified. *...an unforgivable error in judgement.*

unforgiving /ʌnfəgɪvɪŋ/

ADJ If someone is **unforgiving**, they are unwilling to forgive other people for what they think are bad or mistaken actions. *He is unforgiving to his enemies... Lee has also been unforgiving towards domestic dissent.*

unformed /ʌnfɔːmd/

ADJ Something that is **unformed** is in an early stage of development and not yet fully formed. *...unformed ideas.*

unfortunate /ʌnfɔːtʃəⁿnət/

1 ADJ Someone who is **unfortunate** is unlucky. *We will do our utmost to help these unfortunate people.*

2 ADJ If you describe something that has happened as

unfortunate, you mean that you regret it because you think it is inappropriate or embarrassing. *It is rather unfortunate that the Prime Minister should have said this. ...one of those unfortunate conversations.*

unfortunately /ʌnfɔːtʃəˑnətli/
ADV SEN You use **unfortunately** to express regret about what you are saying. *'Will you be here in the morning?'—'No, unfortunately I won't.'*

unfounded /ʌnfaʊndɪd/
ADJ You say that a belief is **unfounded** when it is not based on facts or evidence. *Our worst fears have proved unfounded.*

unfriendly /ʌnfrendli/
1 ADJ Someone who is **unfriendly** does not behave in a friendly way. *He was being remarkably unfriendly. ...a cold, unfriendly stare.*
2 ADJ In warfare, a **unfriendly** country or armed force is one that is not likely to help you, but is likely to help your enemy. *They are surrounded by unfriendly nations... They were in what we consider to be unfriendly territory.*

unfrocked /ʌnfrɒkt/
ADJ An **unfrocked** priest has been forbidden by the Church to perform the duties of a priest, as a punishment for his bad behaviour.

unfruitful /ʌnfruːtfl/
ADJ Something that is **unfruitful** does not produce results or success. *Recent weeks have seen a series of attempts, as yet largely unfruitful, to form a new coalition... This line of questioning proved unfruitful.*

unfulfilled /ʌnfʊlfɪld/
ADJ An **unfulfilled** hope or promise is one that does not lead to the result that was hoped for or promised. *...the unfulfilled hopes that a second hostage would be freed. ...the many unfulfilled promises concerning political and economic reform... The treaty offers an opportunity to develop the Canadian economy, to realise much of its unfulfilled potential.*

unfurl /ʌnfɜːl/ **unfurls, unfurling, unfurled**
V-ERG If you **unfurl** something such as an umbrella, sail, or flag, or if it **unfurls**, you unroll or unfold it so that it is flat or spread out, and can be used or seen. *He began to unfurl a large scale map... The sails unfurled and filled in the breeze.*

unfurnished /ʌnfɜːnɪʃt/
ADJ If you rent an **unfurnished** flat or house, no furniture is provided by the owner. *We decided to try to rent an unfurnished cottage.*

ungainly /ʌngeɪnli/
ADJ **Ungainly** people move in an awkward or clumsy way. *...an ungainly, long-limbed lad... They walk in a rather peculiar and ungainly way.*

ungodly; pronounced /ʌŋgɒdli/ for the meaning in paragraph 1 and /ʌŋgɒdli/ for the meaning in paragraph 2.
1 ADJ ATTRIB If you describe something as **ungodly**, you mean that you think it is unreasonable or annoying; an informal use. *I had to get up at an ungodly hour... That thing made an ungodly racket.*
2 ADJ If you describe a person or their behaviour or language as **ungodly**, you mean that you think it is sinful or blasphemous. *Until recently, the Soviet Union was described in the Iranian press as a satanic, ungodly power.*

ungracious /ʌngreɪʃəs/
ADJ If you are **ungracious**, you are not polite or friendly in your speech or behaviour, especially when someone is apologizing to you or thanking you. *Don't be so ungracious. ...an ungracious reply.*

ungrateful /ʌngreɪtfl/
ADJ If someone is **ungrateful**, they do not show gratitude for something that has been given to them or done for them. *I hope I don't sound ungrateful... What an ungrateful lot they are!... He had worked hard for Bangladesh and the people were not ungrateful.*

unguarded /ʌngɑːdɪd/
1 ADJ If something is left **unguarded**, it is left without anyone to protect it or look after it. *They got out through an unguarded side door... The Treasury building was unguarded, but other key buildings still have troops outside.*
2 ADJ ATTRIB An **unguarded** moment is one when you

are careless in what you say or do, with the result that someone discovers something that you did not want them to know. *I told him, in an unguarded moment, what I planned to do... It was rather an unguarded statement.*

unhampered /ʌnhæmpəd/
ADJ PRED+by If you are **unhampered** by a particular problem or difficulty, you are free from it. *This would give black people the opportunity to live unhampered by racism... The new stock market is unhampered by tradition.*

unhappily /ʌnhæpɪli/
1 ADV If you do something **unhappily**, you are not happy or contented while you do it. *He trudged unhappily towards the house.*
2 ADV SEN You use **unhappily** to express regret about what you are saying. *Unhappily, George had died by the time Ralph got to America.*

unhappy /ʌnhæpi/ **unhappier, unhappiest**
1 ADJ If you are **unhappy**, you are sad and depressed. *She looked unhappy... I had an unhappy time at school.* ♦ **unhappiness** NU *The quarrel caused her intense unhappiness.*
2 ADJ PRED If you are **unhappy** about something, you are not pleased about it or not satisfied with it. *Farmers in the state are unhappy with many of the conservation plans... The residents of the area are unhappy about the noise... They are unhappy at what they regard as increasing anti-government bias.*
3 ADJ ATTRIB If you describe a situation as an **unhappy** one, you are expressing regret about it. *This unhappy state of affairs would not exist if Ministers acted in a responsible way.*

unharmed /ʌnhɑːmd/
ADJ If someone who has been attacked or involved in an accident is **unharmed**, they are not injured. *The four men managed to escape unharmed.*

unhealthy /ʌnhelθi/
1 ADJ Something that is **unhealthy** is likely to cause illness or poor health. *This is probably the most unhealthy place in the world... They have suffered from an image of producing unhealthy, high cholesterol food.*
2 ADJ **Unhealthy** people are not very fit or are often ill. *The insurance company was concerned about having to pay high health-care costs for an unhealthy child. ...a poorly dressed, unhealthy looking fellow with a poor complexion.*
3 ADJ **Unhealthy** is used to describe behaviour and attitudes that seem extreme or unnatural. *...an unhealthy interest in sex.*

unheard /ʌnhɜːd/
ADJ If something goes **unheard**, it is not listened to or taken into consideration. *The wishes of the minority go unheard... He wrote me off, unheard, long before my trial.*

unheard of; spelt **unheard-of** when used before a noun.
1 ADJ You say that an event or situation is **unheard of** when it never happens. *Contracts and written agreements are quite unheard of.*
2 ADJ You also say that an event is **unheard of** when it happens for the first time and is very surprising or shocking. *This is an unheard-of outrage.*

unheeded /ʌnhiːdɪd/
ADJ PRED If something goes **unheeded**, it is ignored. *Their appeals for help went unheeded.*

unhelpful /ʌnhelpfl/
ADJ An **unhelpful** person or action does nothing to help you, and often causes you problems. *The man she defeated was bitterly unhelpful to her... He came barging into the kitchen with unhelpful suggestions.*

unheralded /ʌnherəldɪd/
ADJ If something is **unheralded**, there is no indication beforehand that it is going to happen. *The Prince arrived unheralded in India. ...Tim's unheralded arrival at the party.*

unhesitating /ʌnhezɪteɪtɪŋ/
ADJ When you are **unhesitating**, you do or say something immediately, because you are confident that it is the right thing to do or say. *...her unhesitating readiness to help.* ♦ **unhesitatingly** ADV *He*

unhesitatingly pinned the blame for the party's weakness on Vadim Medvedev.

unhinge /ʌnhɪndʒ/ **unhinges, unhinging, unhinged**
VO If an experience **unhinges** someone, it affects them so deeply that they become mentally ill. *It seemed to me the accident had unhinged her.*

unhinged /ʌnhɪndʒd/
ADJ If someone is **unhinged**, they have become mentally ill because of an experience that has affected them deeply. *According to Morris, Gordon Masters is quite unhinged.*

unholy /ʌnhəʊli/
ADJ Something that is **unholy** is considered to be wicked or sinful. *I discovered the unholy pleasures of gossip and malice. ...unholy alliances between drug traffickers, death squads and elements of the armed forces.*

unhook /ʌnhʊk/ **unhooks, unhooking, unhooked**
1 VO If you **unhook** a piece of clothing such as a bra, you unfasten the hooks on it.
2 VO If you **unhook** something, you remove it from a hook. *She followed him into the hall, where he unhooked his hat and coat.*

unhurried /ʌnhʌrid/
ADJ **Unhurried** actions are done in a slow and relaxed way. *He proceeded up the stairs at his usual unhurried pace.* ♦ **unhurriedly** ADV *She walked unhurriedly out of the building.*

unhurt /ʌnhɜːt/
ADJ PRED If someone who has been attacked or involved in an accident is **unhurt**, they are not injured. *Two men crawled out unhurt.*

unhygienic /ʌnhaɪdʒiːnɪk/
ADJ Something that is **unhygienic** is dirty and likely to cause infection or disease. *The restaurant has been cleared of charges that the kitchen was unhygienic. ...unhygienic conditions. ...tiny unhygienic cages.*

unicorn /juːnɪkɔːn/ **unicorns**
NC In stories and legends, a **unicorn** is an imaginary animal that looks like a white horse and has a horn growing from its forehead. *Unicorns, mermaids, griffins, and dragons are just some of the imaginary creatures that make up the rich wealth of legends in cultures throughout the world.*

unidentifiable /ʌnaɪdentɪfaɪəbl/
ADJ If something is **unidentifiable**, you are not able to say exactly what it is. *He paused at a small unidentifiable sound from outside the room. ...unidentifiable fragments.*

unidentified /ʌnaɪdentɪfaɪd/
ADJ You can say that someone or something is **unidentified** when nobody knows who or what they are. *He was questioned by two unidentified Americans... He was shot dead by unidentified gunmen in broad daylight. ...the outbreak of an unidentified disease that is reported to have killed at least thirty people in the last few weeks.*

unification /juːnɪfɪkeɪʃn/
NU **Unification** is the process by which two or more countries join together and become one country. *An opinion poll published today claims a nine percent increase in support for the unification of Western Europe.*

uniform /juːnɪfɔːm/ **uniforms**
1 NCorNU A **uniform** is a special set of clothes which some people, for example soldiers or the police, wear at work, and which some children wear at school. *...a man in the uniform of a captain in the Air Force... She wasn't in uniform.*
2 ADJ A **uniform** policy, system, or action is consistent and is based on the same ideas or principles. *The officials will agree a uniform code of discipline for the 52 matches in the finals... The country is moving towards the introduction of a uniform national curriculum for pupils.* ♦ **uniformly** ADV *The report has been uniformly impartial in its criticism and praise... The budget cuts are uniformly imposed.*
3 ADJ If something is **uniform**, it does not vary, but is even and regular throughout. *...a structure of uniform width.* ♦ **uniformly** ADV *The weather throughout the region was uniformly good.*

uniformed /juːnɪfɔːmd/
ADJ ATTRIB **Uniformed** people are wearing uniforms. *...uniformed policemen.*

uniformity /juːnɪfɔːməti/
1 NU+SUPP If there is **uniformity** in something, it is consistent and is based on the same ideas or principles. *Throughout all those years Moscow demanded strict uniformity of policy from its allies... The EC has again insisted that it wants to have uniformity in indirect taxes by the time the single market is established.*
2 NU **Uniformity** is also a state in which every part of something is or appears to be the same. *...the dreary uniformity of the housing estate.*

unify /juːnɪfaɪ/ **unifies, unifying, unified**
VO If you **unify** a number of different things or people, you join or bring them together. *Smaller tribes are unified into larger societies... The liberation songs of South Africa have played an important role in unifying and politicizing disparate groups.* ♦ **unified** ADJ *An important factor is the unified European Market that comes into effect in 1992. ...a unified labour movement.* ♦ **unifying** ADJ *The coalition formed late last year has disintegrated—it lacked a unifying sense of purpose. ...the importance of Hinduism as a unifying cultural force.*

unilateral /juːnɪlætəºrəl/
ADJ ATTRIB A **unilateral** decision or action is made or done by only one of the groups involved in a particular situation, without the agreement of the other groups. *Mr Collins warned that any unilateral British action would have far-reaching consequences for European unity. ...Sunday's unilateral declaration of independence by the Soviet Republic of Lithuania. ...unilateral nuclear disarmament.* ♦ **unilaterally** ADV *The Contras responded by unilaterally postponing the talks for another week... Cuba and Yemen say that each country should decide unilaterally whether foodstuffs are needed.*

unilateralism /juːnɪlætəºrəlɪzəm/
NU **Unilateralism** is the belief that a country should get rid of its own nuclear weapons, without waiting for other countries to do the same. *The party had reversed its support of unilateralism.* ♦ **unilateralist** /juːnɪlætəºrəlɪst/ **unilateralists** NC *I am not a unilateralist.*

unimaginable /ʌnɪmædʒɪnəbl/
ADJ Something that is **unimaginable** is difficult to imagine or understand properly, because it is not part of people's normal experience. *...the unimaginable vastness of space. ...experiments carried out under unimaginable conditions.*

unimaginative /ʌnɪmædʒɪnətɪv/
ADJ You say that people are **unimaginative** when they do not use their imagination enough in what they do. *...unimaginative teachers. ...unimaginative projects.*

unimpeachable /ʌnɪmpiːtʃəbl/
ADJ If you describe someone as **unimpeachable**, you mean that they are completely honest and reliable and should not be doubted. *The woman was of unimpeachable character... She had been told by the most unimpeachable source: his mother.*

unimportant /ʌnɪmpɔːtnt/
ADJ If something is **unimportant**, it has very little significance or importance. *...a relatively unimportant feature of the system.*

unimpressed /ʌnɪmprest/
ADJ PRED If you are **unimpressed** by someone or something, you do not think they are very good, unusual, or worth your attention. *Thus far, Wall Street has been notably unimpressed. ...a frustrated and angry younger generation who are unimpressed by his conciliatory approach... It's hard to imagine anyone coming away unimpressed by Jodie Foster.*

unimpressive /ʌnɪmpresɪv/
ADJ You say that someone or something is **unimpressive** when they seem to have no good or interesting qualities. *Barney's wife was an unimpressive little woman.*

uninformed /ʌnɪnfɔːmd/
ADJ Someone who is **uninformed** does not have very much knowledge or information about a particular

subject. *This must have seemed quite plausible to the uninformed reader... Until recently, the Bulgarian public had been uninformed as to the scale of the disaster.*

uninhabitable /ʌnɪnhæbɪtəbl/
ADJ An **uninhabitable** place is one where it is impossible for people to live. *Worldwide pollution threatens to make the planet uninhabitable.*

uninhabited /ʌnɪnhæbɪtɪd/
ADJ An **uninhabited** place is one where nobody lives. *...an uninhabited island.*

uninhibited /ʌnɪnhɪbɪtɪd/
ADJ **Uninhibited** people behave freely and naturally and do not hide their feelings. *...a sound of uninhibited laughter.*

uninitiated /ʌnɪnɪʃieɪtɪd/
N PL You can refer to people who have no knowledge or experience of something as the **uninitiated**. *For the uninitiated, may I say that golf is one game that demands patience and concentration.*

uninspired /ʌnɪnspaɪəd/
ADJ Someone or something that is **uninspired** is dull and not lively or exciting, and fails to arouse interest or enthusiasm in other people. *The bureaucratic haggling has left most Europeans uninspired and just plain bored... The production was professional but uninspired.*

uninspiring /ʌnɪnspaɪərɪŋ/
ADJ Someone or something that is **uninspiring** is dull and not likely to cause interest or excitement. *The tone of her speech was cautious and some back-benchers described it as low-key—even uninspiring. ...a villa of uninspiring design.*

unintelligent /ʌnɪntelɪdʒənt/
ADJ Someone who is **unintelligent** is stupid. *She was regarded as an unintelligent, uninteresting and uncultured peasant... They were lazy and unintelligent.*

unintelligible /ʌnɪntelɪdʒəbl/
ADJ Something that is **unintelligible** is impossible to understand. *He answered in words unintelligible to her.*

unintended /ʌnɪntendɪd/
ADJ If something that happens is **unintended**, it is not planned. *...the unintended consequences of advertising.*

unintentional /ʌnɪntenʃəⁿnəl/
ADJ Something that is **unintentional** is not done deliberately, but happens by accident. *In passing sentence, the judge said that the killing had been unintentional.* ◆ **unintentionally** ADV *The television drama series set in a fictional South-East Asian country had unintentionally caused offence.*

uninterested /ʌnɪntrəstɪd/
ADJ If you are **uninterested** in something, you are not interested in it. *Lionel was uninterested in the house.*

uninteresting /ʌnɪntrəstɪŋ/
ADJ Something that is **uninteresting** is dull and boring. *He found her uninteresting as a person.*

uninterrupted /ʌnɪntərʌptɪd/
ADJ If something is **uninterrupted**, it continues without any breaks or interruptions. *Lynn did some uninterrupted reading.*

uninvited /ʌnɪnvaɪtɪd/
ADJ You use **uninvited** to describe a person who arrives somewhere or does something without being asked. *...uninvited guests... Henry sat down uninvited.*

union /juːnɪən/ **unions**
1 N C A **union** is a workers' organization that tries to improve such things as the pay and working conditions of its members. *The union has complained that the company isn't taking job security demands seriously. ...Mr Ray Buckton, leader of the train drivers' union... The teachers return to class today while their union continues negotiations towards a new contract.*
2 N U When the **union** of two or more things takes place, they are joined together and become one thing; a formal use. *We are working for the union of the two countries. ...the economic union of East and West Germany.*
3 N SING A **union** is also two or more things that have joined together to become one thing; used especially of countries or organizations that have been formed in

this way. *The campaign is a union of student, religious, labour, and human rights groups... For the previous 120 years there had been a union between Britain and Ireland.*

unionise /juːnɪənaɪz/. See **unionize**.

unionist /juːnɪənɪst/ **unionists**
1 N C A **unionist** is a member of a trade union or a supporter of a trade-union movement. *The unionists unanimously condemned what was described as the lack of investment in Britain's public transport system... Trade unionists across the country are beginning a day of action in support of the ambulancemen.*
2 N C A **unionist** is also a believer in a political union, for example the political union between Northern Ireland and the rest of the United Kingdom. *The Unionists want Northern Ireland to remain British, while the nationalists support much stronger ties with the Irish Republic... Unionist politicians in Northern Ireland are boycotting the meeting in protest at the Anglo-Irish Agreement.*

unionize /juːnɪənaɪz/ **unionizes, unionizing, unionized**; also spelt **unionise**.
V-ERG When a group of workers **unionize** or are **unionized**, they join or form a trade union in their place of work. *Clothing workers went on strike over the right to unionize. ...Belgium, where 71 per cent of employees are unionized.* ◆ **unionization** /juːnɪənaɪzeɪʃn/ N U *...the unionization of women office workers.*

Union Jack, Union Jacks
N C The **Union Jack** is the national flag of the United Kingdom of Great Britain and Northern Ireland. *One by one the French and American flags were lowered, then the Union Jack... The protests continued with some noisy groups of demonstrators waving banners and burning Union Jacks.*

Union of Soviet Socialist Republics
/juːnɪən əv səʊviət səʊʃəlɪst rɪpʌblɪks/
The **Union of Soviet Socialist Republics**, also called the Soviet Union, was formerly the largest country in the world. It occupied much of eastern Europe and stretched across the length of Asia. 104 nationalities and 114 languages were recognized. Mikhail Gorbachev became General Secretary of the Communist Party of the Soviet Union (KPSS) in 1985. His policies of perestroika (restructuring to revive the economy) and glasnost (openness in cultural and political areas) led to the end of the Cold War, but also to an increase in ethnic tensions and separatist movements within the Soviet Union. In 1991 the KPSS ceased to be the ruling party and virtually every constituent Soviet republic declared its independence. The three Baltic states of Lithuania, Latvia, and Estonia received international recognition. Eleven other former Soviet republics formed the Commonwealth of Independent States. ◆ **Soviet** /səʊviət/ N, ADJ
▪ *per capita GNP*: approximately US$8,700 ▪ *religion*: Christianity (mainly Russian Orthodox), Islam
▪ *language*: 114 languages were officially recognized (58% spoke Russian and 17% spoke other Slavic languages) ▪ *currency*: rouble ▪ *capital*: Moscow
▪ *population*: 289 million (1990) ▪ *size*: 22,402,200 square kilometres.

unique /juːniːk/
1 ADJ If something is **unique**, it is the only thing of its kind. *...a unique 13th century map of the world.* ◆ **uniqueness** NU *...the uniqueness of the individual.*
2 ADJ PRED+*to* If something is **unique** to one thing or person, it concerns or belongs only to that thing or person. *These problems are not unique to nuclear power. ...that unique human ability, speech.*
3 ADJ Some people use **unique** to mean very unusual and special. *It was a unique and exquisite performance. ...the National Gallery's unique collection of early Renaissance paintings.* ◆ **uniquely** SUBMOD *He had a fine singing voice, uniquely gentle and deep.*

unisex /juːnɪseks/
ADJ **Unisex** is used to describe things which are designed to be used by both men and women. *The*

women were dressed in nondescript unisex clothes.
unison /juːnɪsən/
1 If a group of people do something **in unison**, they all do it together at the same time. *'All of us,' they said in unison... Thousands of demonstrators waved in unison to bid him farewell.*
2 If people or organizations act **in unison**, they act in the same way because they agree with each other or because they want to achieve the same aims. *The main Communist Party newspaper, Pravda, quoted by the TASS news agency, accused the United States of acting in unison with Israel... And is the government now acting in unison over the rise of the pound?*
unit /juːnɪt/ **units**
1 NC If you consider something as a **unit**, you consider it as a single, complete thing. *...the decline of the family as a self-sufficient unit.*
2 NC When a small a part of a large organization or group of people has a particular, specialized purpose, the small part is often referred to as a **unit**. *The killings were carried out by an undercover army unit... The girl died in an intensive care unit in a hospital in Bristol... The unit will start work at the beginning of next month.*
3 NC A **unit** of measurement is a fixed, standard length, quantity, or weight. The metre, the litre, and the gram are all units. *It's a fitting tribute that a unit of sound—the decibel—was named after him... Each of us is exposed to about half a unit of radiation a year.*
unitary /juːnɪtəⁱri/
ADJ ATTRIB A **unitary** country or organization is one in which two or more areas or groups have joined together, have the same aims, and are controlled by a single government or group of people. *He reaffirmed his support for a unitary state embracing the whole island. ...the restoration of a unitary, centralist Yugoslavia... The party has all but ceased to exist as a unitary body.*
unite /juːnaɪt/ **unites, uniting, united**
V-ERG If a group of people or things **unite** or if something **unites** them, they join together and act as a group. *They must unite to combat the enemy... This measure would unite all the provinces into a single state.*
united /juːnaɪtɪd/
1 ADJ When people are **united** about something, they agree about it and act together. *They were united in their dislike of authority... The war has caused some groups, formerly united, to come apart... The coalition remains strong and united.*
2 ADJ **United** is used to describe a country which has been formed from two or more countries or states. *Some people want a united Ireland. ...the United States.*
United Arab Emirates /juːnaɪtɪd ærəb ɛmɪrəts/
The **United Arab Emirates** is a country in the Gulf. It consists of seven emirates: Abu Dhabi, Dubai, Sharjah, Fujairah, Ras al-Khaimah, Ajman, and Umm al-Qawain. The area became a British protectorate, known as Trucial Oman or the Trucial States, in the 19th century and became independent in 1971. There are no political parties. Shaikh Zaid bin Sultan al-Nahayan, the ruler of Abu Dhabi, became President in 1971. Shaikh Maktoum bin Rashid al-Maktoum, ruler of Dubai, became Prime Minister in 1990. The United Arab Emirates is a member of the Arab League, OPEC, and the Gulf Co-operation Council. Oil is exported. ◆ **Emirian** /ɪmɪərɪən/ N, ADJ
▪ *per capita GNP:* US$15,720 ▪ *religion:* Islam (mainly Sunni) ▪ *language:* Arabic (official) ▪ *currency:* dirham
▪ *capital:* Abu Dhabi ▪ *population:* 2 million (1989)
▪ *size:* 77,700 square kilometres.
United Kingdom /juːnaɪtɪd kɪŋdəm/
The **United Kingdom of Great Britain and Northern Ireland** is a country in western Europe, consisting of England, Scotland, Wales, and Northern Ireland. It is a member of the European Community, the Commonwealth, and NATO. In the post-war period over 30 colonies of Britain became independent countries, most of them becoming members of the Commonwealth. Queen Elizabeth II succeeded in 1952. Margaret Thatcher (Conservative Party) was Prime

Minister from 1979 to 1990. John Major (Conservative Party) became Prime Minister in 1990. Britain exports machinery, manufactured goods, chemicals, transport equipment, and oil and gas. Banking, insurance, and tourism are important industries. ◆ **Briton** /brɪtn/
N **British** /brɪtɪʃ/ ADJ, N PL
▪ *per capita GNP:* US$12,800 ▪ *religion:* Christianity
▪ *language:* English ▪ *currency:* pound sterling
▪ *capital:* London ▪ *population:* 56 million (1991) ▪ *size:* 244,103 square kilometres.
United Nations (UN) /juːnaɪtɪd neɪʃnz/
The **United Nations** was founded in 1945 as the successor to the League of Nations. Its aim is to maintain international peace and security. The Security Council of the United Nations has fifteen member states, of which five are permanent: China, France, Great Britain, the Russian Federation, and the United States. The Security Council is the UN's, and the world's, principal forum for resolving conflict between nations. The General Assembly of the United Nations deals with social, economic, and human rights problems. United Nations agencies include: United Nations High Commission for Refugees (UNHCR); United Nations Development Programme (UNDP); United Nations Children's Fund (UNICEF); and United Nations Educational, Scientific and Cultural Organization (UNESCO). Dr Boutros Boutros Ghali became Secretary General in 1992. The headquarters are in New York City. The only sovereign countries which are not members of the UN are: Andorra, Kiribati, Monaco, Nauru, Switzerland, Taiwan, Tonga, Tuvalu, and Vatican City.
United States of America
/juːnaɪtɪd steɪts əv əmɛrɪkə/
The **United States of America** is a country in North America. It is a member of NATO, ANZUS, and the Organization of American States. The United States emerged from the Second World War as a major world power. During the Cold War era the United States tried to prevent the USSR from extending its sphere of influence. Concern about the spread of Communism led to the involvement of the United States in the Korean War (1950-53) and the Vietnam War (1964-75). During the administrations of Reagan and Bush, the trade deficit and the federal budget deficit have become major economic problems. George Bush, of the Republican Party, became President in 1989. The United States exports machinery, cars, chemicals, agricultural products, drinks, and tobacco. ◆ **American** /əmɛrɪkən/ N, ADJ
▪ *per capita GNP:* US$19,780 ▪ *religion:* Christianity
▪ *language:* English ▪ *currency:* dollar ▪ *capital:* Washington, DC ▪ *largest city:* New York ▪ *population:* 248 million (1989) ▪ *size:* 9,372,614 square kilometres.
United States Virgin Islands See **Virgin Islands, United States**
unit trust, unit trusts
NC A **unit trust** is an organization which invests money in many different types of business and which offers units for sale to the public as an investment. *They've set up a stock market and unit trusts. ...unit trusts and other investments linked to stocks and shares.*
unity /juːnəti/
NU When there is **unity**, people are in agreement and act together for a particular purpose. *He failed to preserve his party's unity... Japan sees Britain as an ally in resisting greater European unity, and in maintaining free trade... They are discussing church unity.*
Univ.
Univ. is a written abbreviation for 'University'. *...Maths Dept, Univ. of Keele.*
universal /juːnɪvɜːsl/
1 ADJ Something that is **universal** relates to everyone in the world or to everyone in a particular group or society. *They touched on various topics of universal interest. ... the almost universal refusal on the part of the leaders.* ◆ **universally** ADV *This explanation is not yet universally accepted.*
2 ADJ You also say that something is **universal** when it relates to every part of the world or universe. *...the threat of universal extinction.*

universe /juːnɪvɜːs/
1 N SING The **universe** is the whole of space, including all the stars and planets. *They thought the earth was the centre of the universe.*
2 N SING The **universe** also refers to the world, or the part of it that we live in and have experience of. *It is the most wicked place in the universe... Each person is the centre of his own universe.*

university /juːnɪvɜːsəti/ **universities**
N or NU A **university** is an institution where students study for degrees and where academic research is done. *...Norwich University... Her one aim in life is to go to university.*

unjust /ʌndʒʌst/
ADJ An **unjust** action, system, or law is morally wrong because it treats a person or group badly in a way that they do not deserve. *...a thoroughly unjust society.* ◆ **unjustly** ADV *...schoolmates who had unjustly accused him of bullying.*

unjustifiable /ʌndʒʌstɪfaɪəbl/
ADJ You say that an action which harms someone is **unjustifiable** when there is no good reason for doing it. *What I had done was clearly unjustifiable. ...an unjustifiable and unpopular increase in licence fees.*

unjustified /ʌndʒʌstɪfaɪd/
ADJ You say that a belief or action is **unjustified** when there is no good reason for having it or doing it. *It was an unjustified attack. His pessimism was totally unjustified.*

unkempt /ʌŋkempt/
ADJ Something that is **unkempt** is untidy and not looked after carefully. *He had a shaggy, unkempt beard.*

unkind /ʌŋkaɪnd/ **unkinder, unkindest**
ADJ Someone who is **unkind** behaves towards you in an unpleasant or nasty way. *Why are you so unkind to me? ...a silly and unkind remark.*

unknowable /ʌnnəʊəbl/
ADJ If you describe something as **unknowable**, you mean that it is impossible for human beings to know anything about it; a literary word. *The future is unknowable... For him, God was wholly transcendent, unknowable.*

unknowing /ʌnnəʊɪŋ/
ADJ ATTRIB **Unknowing** is used to describe someone who is not aware of a particular fact or situation, or of what they are doing. *Up to one person in twenty five might be an unknowing carrier of the disease. ...an unknowing fool. ...an unknowing victim.*
◆ **unknowingly** ADV *William was unknowingly strengthening my trap.*

unknown /ʌnnəʊn/ **unknowns**
1 ADJ A fact that is **unknown** to you is one that you do not know about. *An unknown number of people have been injured... The prisoners were blindfolded and later removed to an unknown destination.* ► Also NC *The big unknown at present is the attitude of the president elect... This is of course all guesswork, as there are so many unknowns.*
2 ADJ An **unknown** person is someone whose name you do not know or whose character you do not know anything about. *She wouldn't be alone with an unknown male visitor... The gunman was unknown to the victim or her friends.*
3 ADJ You also use **unknown** to describe a person who is not famous or well-known. *Mao was replaced by an almost unknown party official.* ► Also NC *He cast the rest of the film with virtual unknowns.*
4 ADJ PRED If you say that a particular problem or situation is **unknown,** you mean that it never occurs. *Heart disease was almost unknown until recently.*
5 N SING You can refer to the things that people do not know about as the **unknown.** *...fear of the unknown.*

unlawful /ʌnlɔːfl/
ADJ Something that is **unlawful** is not legal; a formal word. *The court ruled that holding suspects for more than four days without charge was unlawful... The government, by taping the conversations, was engaged in unlawful activity.* ◆ **unlawfully** ADV *The Court of Appeal has ruled that Hammersmith and Fulham council acted unlawfully in trading on the money markets for profit.*

unleaded /ʌnledɪd/
ADJ ATTRIB **Unleaded** fuels contain a reduced amount of lead in order to reduce the pollution from cars. *The government says its campaign to persuade motorists to use unleaded petrol is beginning to pay off.*

unlearn /ʌnlɜːn/ **unlearns, unlearning, unlearned** or **unlearnt**
VO If you **unlearn** something that you have learned, you try to forget it or ignore it, often because you think it is wrong or having a bad influence on you. *It is learned behaviour, and, as such, can be unlearned... A lot of things had to be unlearned before you could learn anything at all.*

unleash /ʌnliːʃ/ **unleashes, unleashing, unleashed**
VO To **unleash** a powerful or violent force means to release it; a literary word. *Strong feelings had been unleashed in me by the news of the bomb.*

unleavened /ʌnlevnd/
ADJ **Unleavened** bread or dough is made without any yeast. *...dry unleavened bread.*

unless /ʌnles/
CONJ You use **unless** to introduce the only circumstances in which the event you are mentioning will not take place or in which the statement you are making is not true. *He phoned me to say that unless the paper stopped my articles he would withdraw his advertisements... I couldn't get a grant unless I had five years' teaching experience.*

unlicensed /ʌnlaɪsənst/
1 ADJ If a business or activity is **unlicensed**, no official permission has been given for it to exist or happen. *The police said that a number of large unlicensed parties had been held in the area recently and drugs had been found... The government is seeking more powers to curb the growth of unlicensed radio stations.*
2 ADJ An **unlicensed** building such as a restaurant, hotel, or club does not have a license for a particular activity, for example entertainment, or selling alcoholic drinks. *Children are playing truant to watch unsuitable video films in unlicensed premises. ...an unlicensed New York dance hall.*
3 ADJ If something that you use or own is **unlicensed**, you do not have official permission to use or own it. *The police have the power to arrest anyone in the possession of an unlicensed gun.*

unlike /ʌnlaɪk/
1 PREP If one thing is **unlike** another thing, the two things have different features from each other. *Rodin was unlike his predecessor in every way... He looked most unlike the energetic, business-like young men in suits who normally surround the President on such occasions.*
2 PREP You can use **unlike** to contrast two people, things, or situations, and to show how they are different. *Unlike Dickens or George Elliot, Hardy can claim greatness for his poetry as well as his novels.*
3 PREP If you describe something that someone has done as **unlike** them, you mean that it is not typical of their normal behaviour. *It was unlike her to mention it.*

unlikely /ʌnlaɪkli/
1 ADJ If something is **unlikely** to happen or **unlikely** to be true, it will probably not happen, or it is probably not true. *The dispute is unlikely to be settled for a long time... It is unlikely that you will get your own office... In the unlikely event that they give you any trouble, write to us.*
2 ADJ ATTRIB You also use **unlikely** to describe an actual situation or event that seems very strange because it is so unexpected. *Brody was startled by the unlikely sight of Hendricks in a bathing suit.*

unlimited /ʌnlɪmɪtɪd/
ADJ You say that something is **unlimited** when you can have as much of it as you want. *...unlimited travel... They were given unlimited amounts of food.*

unlit /ʌnlɪt/
1 ADJ An **unlit** fire or cigarette has not yet been lit. *He went back across to the unlit fire.*
2 ADJ An **unlit** street or building is dark because there are no lights switched on in it. *...a bankrupt city in a state of calamity with unlit streets full of holes, and blocked drains.*

unload /ʌnlˈəʊd/ **unloads, unloading, unloaded**
VO or V To **unload** goods from a vehicle means to remove them. *We began to unload the bricks from Philip's car... Dockers have returned to work, though no cargo has yet been unloaded... We had to wait for quite a long time before we could unload.*

unlock /ʌnlˈɒk/ **unlocks, unlocking, unlocked**
VO If you **unlock** something such as a door or a container, you open it using a key. *He unlocked the drawer and took out the money. The jailers refused to unlock the gates.*

unlocked /ʌnlˈɒkt/
ADJ An **unlocked** door has not been locked. *The door was always unlocked.*

unlooked-for /ʌnlˈʊktfɔː/
ADJ Something that is **unlooked-for** is not expected or is not wanted. *Once the play has reached dress-rehearsal, unlooked-for problems suddenly emerge. ...an unlooked-for change in the weather.*

unlovable /ʌnlˈʌvəbl/
ADJ **Unlovable** people are not likely to be loved by anyone, because they do not have any attractive qualities. *He perceives himself as being rejected and unlovable... They are selfish and unlovable.*

unloved /ʌnlˈʌvd/
ADJ Someone who is **unloved** is not loved by anyone. *She was feeling unloved and unwanted.*

unlovely /ʌnlˈʌvli/
ADJ Something that is **unlovely** is unattractive to look at. *The village hall was an unlovely corrugated iron building.*

unloving /ʌnlˈʌvɪŋ/
ADJ You say that people are **unloving** when they do not show love to other people, especially their own family. *...unloving parents.*

unlucky /ʌnlˈʌki/
1 ADJ If someone is **unlucky**, something bad happens to them which is not their fault. *Those unlucky enough not to have a ticket will be glued to their television sets... She had been unlucky in love.*
2 ADJ You can also say that a thing or person is **unlucky** when they seem to make bad things happen to other people in a way that cannot be explained. *13 is a very unlucky number.*

unmade /ʌnmˈeɪd/
ADJ An **unmade** bed has not had the bedclothes neatly arranged after it was last slept in. *Sometimes she did not even bother to get dressed but lay on her unmade bed all day.*

unman /ʌnmˈæn/ **unmans, unmanning, unmanned**
1 VO If something **unmans** you, it makes you lose courage or determination, or makes you unable to conceal your sadness; a literary use. *Their kindness quite unmanned Fanny, and she broke down and wept.*
2 See also **unmanned**.

unmanageable /ʌnmˈænɪdʒəbl/
ADJ If something is **unmanageable**, it is difficult to use, deal with, or control, often because it is too big. *The complete encyclopaedia is quite unmanageable. ...an almost unmanageable economic crisis.*

unmanly /ʌnmˈænli/
ADJ **Unmanly** behaviour is thought to be not suitable for a man. *...the attitude that it is unmanly to be domesticated.*

unmanned /ʌnmˈænd/
1 ADJ **Unmanned** aircraft or spacecraft do not carry people in them. *The technology of unmanned aircraft is as varied as their possible uses... The first Soviet shuttle flight will be unmanned.*
2 ADJ If a place or building is **unmanned**, it does not have anybody on duty there. *Their bus approached a level crossing that was unmanned but apparently well marked.*

unmarked /ʌnmˈɑːkt/
1 ADJ Something that is **unmarked** has no marks of damage or injury on it. *His face was unmarked.*
2 ADJ An **unmarked** object has no signs on it to identify it. *...plain clothes police in an unmarked car... His body was hurriedly buried in an unmarked grave.*

unmarried /ʌnmˈærɪd/
ADJ Someone who is **unmarried** is not married. *...an unmarried mother. ...a young unmarried couple with a baby son.*

unmask /ʌnmˈɑːsk/ **unmasks, unmasking, unmasked**
1 VO If you **unmask** someone or something bad, you show or make known their true nature or character, when they had previously been thought to be good. *My ineptitude had finally been unmasked.*
2 V or VO If someone **unmasks** or if you **unmask** them, the mask they are wearing is removed. *I recognized the face she had revealed when she unmasked herself to drink from her water bottle.*

unmatched /ʌnmˈætʃt/
ADJ Something that is **unmatched** is better or greater than all other things of the same kind. *We intend it to be unmatched in its quality... Mobility in the United States is probably unmatched anywhere in the world.*

unmentionable /ʌnmˈenʃənəbl/
ADJ Something that is **unmentionable** is too embarrassing or unpleasant to talk about. *He's had all kinds of unmentionable operations.*

unmercifully /ʌnmˈɜːsɪfəli/
ADV If you do something unpleasant to someone **unmercifully**, you do it a lot, showing no mercy or pity. *Pointing at Rick, we teased him unmercifully... A total stranger had been bullied unmercifully into driving her home.*

unmistakable /ʌnmɪstˈeɪkəbl/; also spelt **unmistakeable**.
ADJ If something is **unmistakable**, it is so obvious or noticeable that you cannot be wrong about it. *...the unmistakable stench of rotting eggs... The target of the attack was unmistakeable.* ♦ **unmistakably**
ADV or ADV SEN *He was unmistakably of Italian descent... Unmistakably, of course, this is Big Ben, the 13 ton bell in the tower of Britain's Houses of Parliament.*

unmitigated /ʌnmˈɪtɪɡeɪtɪd/
ADJ ATTRIB You use **unmitigated** to say that a bad situation or quality is totally bad; a formal word. *This kind of morality would be an unmitigated disaster. ...several days' unmitigated hell. ...his unmitigated selfishness.*

unmolested /ʌnməlˈestɪd/
ADV or ADJ If someone does something **unmolested**, they do it without being stopped or interfered with. *The tanks were allowed through unmolested. ...allowing people to enjoy themselves unmolested by drunken louts.*

unmoved /ʌnmˈuːvd/
ADJ PRED If you are **unmoved** by something, you are not emotionally affected by it. *No one can remain unmoved by this music... Some viewers were left completely unmoved by the story. ...a government seemingly unmoved by the difficulties of ordinary people.*

unnamed /ʌnnˈeɪmd/
ADJ PRED **Unnamed** people or things are talked about but their names are not mentioned. *Unnamed party activists were accused of corruption and abuse of power. ...unnamed security sources.*

unnatural /ʌnnˈætʃərəl/
1 ADJ If something is **unnatural**, it is strange and rather frightening, because it is different from what you normally expect. *...the house's unnatural silence. ...children who have an unnatural interest in death.* ♦ **unnaturally** ADV *Her arms felt unnaturally hot.*
2 ADJ **Unnatural** behaviour seems artificial and not typical. *Her voice was a little strained, a little unnatural.*

unnecessary /ʌnnˈesəsəri/
ADJ Something that is **unnecessary** is not needed or does not have to be done, and is undesirable. *The reason behind this is to avoid unnecessary expenses... The existing law is unfair and causes unnecessary bitterness.* ♦ **unnecessarily** ADV *Some parents worry unnecessarily about their children.*

unnerve /ʌnnˈɜːv/ **unnerves, unnerving, unnerved**
VO If something **unnerves** you, it frightens or startles you. *His touch unnerved her.* ♦ **unnerving** ADJ *This kind of experience can be quite unnerving.*

unnoticed /ʌnnˈəʊtɪst/
ADJ PRED If something happens or passes **unnoticed**, it is not seen or noticed by anyone. *We tried to get into the room unnoticed... He hoped his departure had passed unnoticed.*

unobserved /ʌnəbzˈɜːvd/
ADJ If you do something **unobserved**, you do it without being seen by anyone. *She was able to slip past the guard unobserved.*

unobtainable /ʌnəbtˈeɪnəbl/
ADJ If something is **unobtainable**, you cannot get it. *There is no baby food in the shops, no prams and no toys, and even cod liver oil has been unobtainable for the past two years. ...previously unobtainable information.*

unobtrusive /ʌnəbtrˈuːsɪv/
ADJ Something that is **unobtrusive** is not easily noticed or does not attract attention to itself; a formal word. *In the city centre the security forces were unobtrusive.* ◆ **unobtrusively** ADV *Unobtrusively, Ginny tried to close the drawer.*

unoccupied /ʌnˈɒkjupaɪd/
ADJ If a building is **unoccupied**, there is nobody in it. *The house was left unoccupied for fifteen years.*

unofficial /ʌnəfˈɪʃl/
ADJ An **unofficial** action is not authorized, approved, or organized by a person in authority. *It is the first time in twenty years that an unofficial gathering like this has not been banned... Unofficial reports say that seventy-eight people were killed.*

unopened /ʌnˈəʊpənd/
ADJ If something is **unopened**, it has not been opened yet. *Mr Hattersley said there were one hundred and fifty thousand unopened letters in the department. ...an unopened bottle of whisky.*

unopposed /ʌnəpˈəʊzd/
ADV or ADJ If a candidate in an election is **unopposed**, there are no other candidates. *Fifteen cabinet ministers are expected to be elected unopposed... The new senators were returned unopposed.*

unorthodox /ʌnˈɔːθədɒks/
1 ADJ **Unorthodox** behaviour, beliefs, or customs are very different from the generally accepted ones. *He launched ambitious and unorthodox economic programmes... Richard Branson is an unorthodox, flamboyant and apparently tireless man.*
2 ADJ **Unorthodox** ways of doing something may be considered wrong or may be illegal; used showing disapproval. *The press began publishing a number of highly critical reports on the unorthodox use of foreign funds. ...unorthodox share transactions.*

unpack /ʌnpˈæk/ **unpacks, unpacking, unpacked**
V or V When you **unpack** a suitcase, bag, or box, you take everything out of it. *He began to unpack his briefcase... The five new families begin to unpack their belongings... I'll leave you now so that you can unpack.*

unpaid /ʌnpˈeɪd/
1 ADJ If you are **unpaid**, you do a job without receiving any money for it. *Carol was Pat's unpaid teacher... More than two thousand unpaid dock workers went on indefinite strike.*
2 ADJ **Unpaid** work or leave is work or leave that you do not get paid for. *...unpaid overtime... Many others laid off staff or gave them unpaid leave as they struggled to keep going.*
3 ADJ If something such as rent or a bill is **unpaid**, it has not yet been paid. *He illegally obtained credit cards to run up unpaid bills of more than $45,000.*

unpalatable /ʌnpˈælətəbl/; a formal word.
1 ADJ **Unpalatable** food is so unpleasant that you can hardly eat it. *...an unpalatable breakfast.*
2 ADJ An **unpalatable** idea is one that you find unpleasant and difficult to accept. *It also makes them face up to some unpalatable truths... The alternative is almost equally unpalatable.*

unparalleled /ʌnpˈærəleld/
ADJ If something is **unparalleled**, it is bigger, better, more intense, or worse than anything else of its kind, or anything that has happened before. *Our specialist library is unparalleled... International trade has helped to bring unparalleled prosperity to the American*

people. ...an unparalleled bombing blitz. ...a time of unparalleled shortages of bread and flour.

unpardonable /ʌnpˈɑːdᵊnəbl/
ADJ **Unpardonable** behaviour is very wrong or rude, and completely unacceptable; a formal word. *Such attacks were utterly unpardonable. ...an unpardonable affront.*

unparliamentary /ʌnpɑːləmˈentᵊri/
ADJ **Unparliamentary** language or behaviour is not suitable for Parliament, usually because it is too rude or abusive. *He provoked uproar with a somewhat unparliamentary reference.*

unpick /ʌnpˈɪk/ **unpicks, unpicking, unpicked**
V O If you **unpick** a piece of sewing, you remove the stitches from it. *You'll have to unpick that seam.*

unplanned /ʌnplˈænd/
ADJ If an event is **unplanned**, it happens by accident or without preparation. *The most exciting discoveries in physics have been unplanned. ...the rapid rise in unplanned manufacturing output.*

unpleasant /ʌnplˈeznt/
1 ADJ If something is **unpleasant**, it gives you bad feelings, for example by making you feel upset or uncomfortable. *There have been some very unpleasant scenes... The drug has harmful and unpleasant side-effects.* ◆ **unpleasantly** ADV *The rain dripped unpleasantly.* ◆ **unpleasantness** NU *...the unpleasantness of being on the receiving end of negative campaigning.*
2 ADJ An **unpleasant** person is unfriendly and rude. *Their son is even more ill-tempered, difficult, and unpleasant.* ◆ **unpleasantly** ADV *He laughed unpleasantly.*

unpleasantness /ʌnplˈezntnəs/
NU **Unpleasantness** is disagreement, argument, or fighting. *Differences in customs sometimes made misunderstandings and even unpleasantness unavoidable. ...all the threats and unpleasantness which happened there.*

unplug /ʌnplˈʌg/ **unplugs, unplugging, unplugged**
V O If you **unplug** a piece of electrical equipment, you take its plug out of the socket. *It will retain its memory for at least five years when it is unplugged from the computer.*

unpopular /ʌnpˈɒpjʊlə/
ADJ Something or someone that is **unpopular** is disliked by most people. *The plan is unpopular with large sections of the public. ...unpopular measures like wage freezes.* ◆ **unpopularity** NU *Such pressure is likely to increase, despite its unpopularity.*

unprecedented /ʌnprˈesɪdentɪd/
ADJ If something is **unprecedented**, it has never happened before, or it is the best, largest, or worst of its kind so far. *The Vatican has taken the unprecedented step of publishing its annual accounts. ...unprecedented prosperity... The damage to wildlife is unprecedented.* ◆ **unprecedentedly** SUBMOD *...an unprecedentedly large number of results.*

unpredictable /ʌnprədˈɪktəbl/
ADJ If someone or something is **unpredictable**, you never know how they will behave or what effects they will have. *Parliamentary by-elections are notoriously unpredictable. ...the unpredictable price of oil.*

unprepared /ʌnprəpˈeəd/
ADJ If you are **unprepared** for something, you are not ready for it, and are therefore surprised or at a disadvantage when it happens. *They are psychologically unprepared for the reality of killing.*

unprepossessing /ʌnpriːpəzˈesɪŋ/
ADJ Someone or something that is **unprepossessing** is not very attractive or appealing in appearance; a formal word. *He was externally very unprepossessing... It is one of the most unprepossessing presidential headquarters in Africa.*

unprincipled /ʌnprˈɪnsəpld/
ADJ Someone who is **unprincipled** has no moral principles and does things which are wrong. *...a ruthless and unprincipled man.*

unprintable /ʌnprˈɪntəbl/
ADJ If you describe something that someone said or did as **unprintable**, you mean that it is so rude or shocking that you do not want to write or say exactly

what it was. *We continued yelling at each other, and she said unprintable things.*

unproductive /ˌʌnprədˈʌktɪv/
ADJ Something that is **unproductive** does not produce anything useful. *Their land is unproductive... The last round of meetings was unproductive.*

unprofessional /ˌʌnprəˈfeʃəⁿəl/
ADJ If someone is **unprofessional**, they do not behave according to the standards that are expected of a person in their profession. *He was also fined £150 for unprofessional conduct... I find your approach to this issue extremely unprofessional and opinionated.*

unprofitable /ˌʌnˈprɒfɪtəbl/
ADJ **Unprofitable** things do not make any profit or do not make enough profit. *Many of the banks are finding that it's just very unprofitable to make student loans. ...unprofitable business contracts.*

unprotected /ˌʌnprəˈtektɪd/
1 ADJ Someone or something that is **unprotected** is not protected in any way. *We were victims—unhelped and unprotected... Beware of the sun beating on unprotected fair skin.*
2 ADJ **Unprotected** sexual intercourse takes place when the man is not wearing a condom. *The AIDS virus is being spread around the world by unprotected sexual contact. ...the dangers of unprotected sex with strangers or prostitutes.*

unprovoked /ˌʌnprəˈvəʊkt/
ADJ If you make an **unprovoked** attack, you attack someone who has not tried to harm you in any way. *The attack was unprovoked and unlawful... They said the shooting had been unprovoked.*

unpublished /ˌʌnpʌbˈlɪʃt/
1 ADJ **Unpublished** books, manuscripts, or letters have never been published. *Daniel Quinn received the Turner Tomorrow Award for his unpublished novel, 'Ishmael'... In an unpublished report they recommended that there should be further prosecutions.*
2 ADJ An **unpublished** writer or poet is one whose work has not been published. *...previously unpublished writers.*

unpunished /ˌʌnˈpʌnɪʃt/
ADJ PRED If a crime or the person who has committed a crime goes **unpunished**, the guilty person is not punished. *Would he then forget the crime and let it go unpunished?... On this occasion the guilty should go unpunished.*

unputdownable /ˌʌnpʊtˈdaʊnəbl/
ADJ If you say that a book is **unputdownable**, you mean that it is so exciting or interesting that you cannot stop reading it; an informal word.

unqualified; pronounced /ˌʌnˈkwɒlɪfaɪd/ for the meaning in paragraph 1 and /ˌʌnkwɒlɪfaɪd/ for the meaning in paragraph 2.
1 ADJ If you are **unqualified**, you do not have any qualifications, or do not have the right qualifications for a particular job. *...an unqualified childminder... He was generally regarded as too inexperienced and unqualified.*
2 ADJ **Unqualified** also means total, unlimited, and complete. *Hadlee has won unqualified admiration and universal respect... He added that India's commitment to universal human rights was total and unqualified... These developments have not received an unqualified welcome in Austria.*

unquestionable /ˌʌŋkwestʃəⁿəbl/
ADJ Something that is **unquestionable** is so obviously true or real that nobody can doubt it. *His courage and commitment are unquestionable.* ◆ **unquestionably** ADV SEN *The visit to Greenland was unquestionably the highlight of the voyage.*

unquestioned /ˌʌŋkwestʃənd/
ADJ Something that is **unquestioned** is accepted by everyone, without anyone doubting or disagreeing. *...a system in which obedience and fortitude were unquestioned virtues.*

unquestioning /ˌʌŋkwestʃənɪŋ/
ADJ You use **unquestioning** to describe beliefs or attitudes that people have without thinking closely about them or doubting them in any way. *You were chosen because of your unquestioning obedience.*

unquote /ˌʌŋkwəʊt/
ADV SEN You use **unquote** to mark the end of a quotation which you have introduced with the word 'quote'. *Then he referred to the, quote, inequality of our circumstances, unquote.*

unravel /ˌʌnˈrævl/ **unravels, unravelling, unravelled**; spelt **unraveling, unraveled** in American English.
1 V-ERG If something that is knotted, woven, twisted, or knitted **unravels**, or if you **unravel** it, it becomes undone. *He would pull a knot and the rope would unravel and fall limply to the ground. ...the wool they had knit and unravelled a hundred times before.*
2 VO If you **unravel** a problem or mystery, you work out the answer to it. *Researchers are now beginning to unravel the causes of this common disease... Congress tried to unravel the mess in the government's finances.*
3 V If something such as a plan or system **unravels**, it breaks up or begins to fail very badly. *The economy itself has been unravelling very fast. ...the general concern that society is beginning to unravel... At the moment, it seems the deal has unravelled.*

unread /ˌʌnˈred/
ADJ If you describe a book or other piece of writing as **unread**, you mean that you or other people have not read it. *I returned the book unread. ...a pile of unread magazines.*

unreadable /ˌʌnˈriːdəbl/
1 ADJ An **unreadable** book or other piece of writing is very difficult or unpleasant to read, especially because it is dull or complicated. *I found the book virtually unreadable. ...unreadable computer data.*
2 ADJ Something that is **unreadable** is impossible to read because the letters are so unclear, especially because it has been damaged in some way. *The labels were blurred and unreadable.*

unreal /ˌʌnˈrɪəl/
ADJ If something is **unreal**, it is so strange that you find it difficult to believe that it is really happening or that it really happened. *This conversation is getting more and more unreal... Last night's events still feel unreal.* ◆ **unreality** NU *There is a slight air of unreality about the proceedings in Washington this week.*

unrealistic /ˌʌnrɪəˈlɪstɪk/
ADJ If you are **unrealistic** or have **unrealistic** ideas, you do not recognize, or are not prepared to recognize, the truth about a situation, so your actions may seem foolish or unreasonable. *Young people often come to London with unrealistic expectations... The target of holding the population to 1.2 billion by the year 2000 is now recognised as unrealistic... Official salaries are totally unrealistic.* ◆ **unrealistically** ADV *The original aims now seem unrealistically ambitious.*

unreasonable /ˌʌnˈriːzəⁿəbl/
1 ADJ People who are **unreasonable** are difficult to deal with because they behave in an unfair or illogical way. *We think he is being unreasonable. ...unreasonable behaviour.*
2 ADJ An **unreasonable** decision or action seems unfair and difficult to justify. *The request didn't seem unreasonable. ...accusations that they have made unreasonable increases in the price of petrol... It is not unreasonable to assume that even greater changes are possible.*

unreasoning /ˌʌnˈriːzəⁿnɪŋ/
ADJ ATTRIB **Unreasoning** feelings or beliefs are not logical, sensible, or controlled; a literary word. *His fear turned into unreasoning panic.*

unrecognizable /ˌʌnˈrekəgnaɪzəbl, ˌʌnrekəgˈnaɪzəbl/; also spelt **unrecognisable**.
ADJ Something that is **unrecognizable** is impossible to recognize or identify. *His voice was almost unrecognizable.*

unrecognized /ˌʌnˈrekəgnaɪzd/; also spelt **unrecognised**.
1 ADV If someone or something does something **unrecognized**, no-one recognizes them while they do it. *Unrecognized by any of the women, he entered the house.*
2 ADJ If something is **unrecognized**, people are not aware of it. *People are alone in their suffering because the illness is unrecognised... There was*

another consequence, at that time almost unrecognised.

3 ADJ If you or your achievements or qualities are **unrecognized**, you have not been properly appreciated or acknowledged by other people for what you have done. *It is a disgrace that such talent should go unrecognised.*

4 ADJ If a meeting, agreement, or political party is **unrecognized**, the authorities do not formally acknowledge that it exists or is legal. *Other churches, like the Ukrainian Catholics, are unlicenced and unrecognised.*

unreconstructed /ˌʌnriːkənstrʌktɪd/
ADJ If you describe systems, beliefs, policies, or people as **unreconstructed**, you mean that they have not changed at all, in spite of new ideas and circumstances; used showing disapproval. *The policies being pursued in Serbia are still purely Communist—unreconstructed and unreformed. ...bogged down in unreconstructed Marxist-Leninism. ...the Ukraine's long-time party leader, the unreconstructed hard-liner, Vladimir Shcherbitsky. ...unreconstructed Stalinists.*

unrefined /ˌʌnrɪfaɪnd/
1 ADJ An **unrefined** food or other substance is in its natural state and has not been processed. *...a variety of wholesome, unrefined foods. ...unrefined sugar. ...unrefined oil.*
2 ADJ **Unrefined** people have poor manners; used showing disapproval. *Refined girls are often drawn to unrefined men.*

unrehearsed /ˌʌnrɪhɜːst/
ADJ If something is **unrehearsed**, it has not been prepared, planned, or practised beforehand. *The highlight of the afternoon was an unrehearsed incident.*

unrelated /ˌʌnrɪleɪtɪd/
ADJ Things which are **unrelated** have no connection with each other. *...a series of unrelated incidents... New issues may arise, unrelated to the original ones.*

unrelenting /ˌʌnrɪlentɪŋ/
1 ADJ If your behaviour is **unrelenting**, you continue to do something in a determined way, often without caring whether you hurt or embarrass other people. *Their morale is sagging under unrelenting attacks from the opposition party. ...his unrelenting criticism of the current Prime Minister. ...the unrelenting pursuit of excellence. ...an unrelenting wave of violence.*
2 ADJ You can also describe something unpleasant as **unrelenting** when it continues without stopping and you have no relief or rest from it at all. *The pain is so great and so unrelenting that one begins to think of a way out. ...the choking dust and unrelenting sun. ...the general view that the region is in unrelenting decline.*

unreliable /ˌʌnrɪlaɪəbl/
ADJ If people, machines, or methods are **unreliable**, you cannot trust them or rely on them. *Godwin was a thoroughly unreliable man. ...an unreliable second-hand car.*

unrelieved /ˌʌnrɪliːvd/
ADJ **Unrelieved** is used of something unpleasant that is very severe and is never replaced by anything better, even for a short time. *...a prospect of almost unrelieved gloom. ...a life of unrelieved misery.*

unremarkable /ˌʌnrɪmɑːkəbl/
ADJ If you say that something is **unremarkable**, you mean that it is not beautiful, interesting, or exciting. *The view is unremarkable.*

unremarked /ˌʌnrɪmɑːkt/; a formal word.
1 ADJ If something goes or remains **unremarked**, nobody notices it. *His absence had gone unremarked... These qualities remained unremarked.*
2 ADV or ADJ PRED If you do something **unremarked**, nobody notices you doing it. *He was able to pass through the countryside unremarked.*

unremitting /ˌʌnrɪmɪtɪŋ/
ADJ Something that is **unremitting** continues without stopping; a formal word. *...their unremitting efforts to get him into college.*

unrepentant /ˌʌnrɪpentənt/
ADJ If you are **unrepentant**, you are not ashamed of your beliefs or actions. *...an unrepentant believer in free enterprise.*

unrepresentative /ˌʌnreprɪzentətɪv/
ADJ If you describe a group of people as **unrepresentative**, you mean that their views are not typical of the community or society to which they belong. *They see the community activists as unrepresentative minority groups.*

unrepresented /ˌʌnreprɪzentɪd/
ADJ If you are **unrepresented** in a parliament or law court, or at a meeting, there is nobody there speaking or acting for you. *Women have remained almost totally unrepresented in Japan's Parliament. ...groups who feel they've been officially unrecognized and unrepresented at international councils such as the United Nations... Some of the accused were technically unrepresented during a part of the hearing.*

unrequited /ˌʌnrɪkwaɪtɪd/
ADJ If your love for someone is **unrequited**, they do not love you; a literary word. *She committed suicide from unrequited love.*

unresolved /ˌʌnrɪzɒlvd/
ADJ If a problem or difficulty is **unresolved**, no satisfactory solution has been found to it; a formal word. *Several major technological problems remained unresolved. ...an unresolved dispute.*

unresponsive /ˌʌnrɪspɒnsɪv/
ADJ If you are **unresponsive** to something, you do not react to it or let it affect your behaviour. *The audience was unresponsive. ...a government that is unresponsive to our needs.*

unrest /ʌnrest/
NU If there is **unrest**, people are angry and dissatisfied, often to the extent of breaking the law or causing violence. *It's said to be the most serious unrest since similar clashes in May 1986. ...the country's growing civil unrest.*

unrestrained /ˌʌnrɪstreɪnd/
ADJ If something is **unrestrained**, it is not controlled or limited in any way. *...the dangers of unrestrained growth.*

unrestricted /ˌʌnrɪstrɪktɪd/
ADJ If something is **unrestricted**, it is not limited by any laws or rules. *...the unrestricted dumping of waste.*

unrewarding /ˌʌnrɪwɔːdɪŋ/
ADJ If a job or task is **unrewarding**, it does not give you any feelings of achievement or pleasure. *Learning a language often seems unrewarding at the time.*

unripe /ʌnraɪp/
ADJ **Unripe** fruit is not yet ripe. *We ate unripe apples from the garden.*

unrivalled /ʌnraɪvld/
ADJ If something is **unrivalled**, it is better than anything else of the same kind. *...an unrivalled collection of modern art.*

unroll /ʌnrəʊl/ **unrolls, unrolling, unrolled**
V-ERG If something such as a roll of paper or a roll of cloth **unrolls** or if you **unroll** it, you open it up so that it is flat. *Someone unrolled a map of America. ...with long streamers of cloth unrolling behind them.*

unruffled /ʌnrʌfld/
ADJ If you are **unruffled**, you are calm and not affected by surprising or frightening events. *She remained singularly unruffled when confronted with my discovery.*

unruly /ʌnruːli/
1 ADJ **Unruly** people are difficult to control or organize. *Unruly government troops are continuing to roam the city streets... More teachers are facing problems from unruly pupils.*
2 ADJ **Unruly** hair is difficult to keep tidy. *...a little girl with a huge head of unruly red hair.*

unsaddle /ʌnsædl/ **unsaddles, unsaddling, unsaddled**
V O When someone **unsaddles** something such as a horse or pony, they take the saddle off its back. *He orders his horse to be unsaddled... I unsaddled the camels and kept them close.*

unsafe /ʌnseɪf/
1 ADJ If something is **unsafe**, it is dangerous. *The*

house was declared unsafe for habitation... They wouldn't build and operate a power station that was unsafe.
2 ADJ PRED If you are **unsafe**, you are in danger of being harmed. *I feel very unsafe.*
3 ADJ PRED If a criminal conviction is **unsafe**, it was based on inadequate or false evidence. *He considered that the convictions were unsafe.*

unsaid /ʌnsɛd/
ADJ PRED If something is left **unsaid** or goes **unsaid** in a particular situation, it is not said, although you might have expected it to be said, and it may be understood by everyone present. *He left the rest unsaid... There was a lot that went unsaid.*

unsaleable /ʌnsɛɪləbl/; also spelt **unsalable** in American English.
ADJ If something is **unsaleable**, it cannot be sold, because nobody wants to buy it or it is of very poor quality. *Their calves make poor beef and are practically unsaleable. ...unsaleable items.*

unsatisfactory /ʌnsætɪsfæktə⁰ri/
ADJ Something that is **unsatisfactory** is not good enough to be acceptable. *I had an unsatisfactory discussion with him about my job. ...an unsatisfactory explanation.*

unsatisfied /ʌnsætɪsfaɪd/
ADJ If you are **unsatisfied**, you are disappointed because you have not got what you wanted. *He asked a lot of questions, and was unsatisfied with the answers.*

unsavoury /ʌnseɪvə⁰ri/; spelt **unsavory** in American English.
ADJ You describe people, places, and things as **unsavoury** when you find them unpleasant or morally wrong. *He has acquired his 40 million in a rather unsavoury way. ...unsavoury characters. ...his drugs and gun running and other unsavoury habits.*

unscathed /ʌnskeɪðd/
ADJ PRED If you are **unscathed** after a dangerous experience, you have not been injured or harmed by it. *We all escaped unscathed... Only a few of the business heroes of the 1980s have survived unscathed.*

unscheduled /ʌnʃedjuːld, ʌnskedjuːld/
ADJ An **unscheduled** event is not planned, but happens unexpectedly or because someone changes their plans. *Earlier, he made an unscheduled visit to Budapest to meet Hungarian leaders... This meeting is to be extended into an unscheduled fifth day.*

unscientific /ʌnsaɪəntɪfɪk/
ADJ If you say that something is **unscientific**, you mean that it is not based on facts or is not objective; used showing disapproval. *They argue that psychotherapy is unscientific.*

unscrew /ʌnskruː/ **unscrews, unscrewing, unscrewed**
VO If you **unscrew** something, you remove it by turning it, or by removing the screws that fasten it to something else. *He unscrewed the top and put the bottle to his mouth... The mirrors had been unscrewed and removed.*

unscripted /ʌnskrɪptɪd/
ADJ An **unscripted** talk or speech is spoken without a previously prepared script. *The President inserted one unscripted item in his speech.*

unscrupulous /ʌnskruːpjʊləs/
ADJ **Unscrupulous** people are prepared to act dishonestly and without consideration for other people in order to get what they want. *...unscrupulous money lenders. ...the unscrupulous ambitions of a few politicians.*

unseasonable /ʌnsiːzə⁰nəbl/
ADJ **Unseasonable** weather, clothing, or food is unusual or inappropriate for the time of year. *...an unseasonable heat-wave... He was sweating mightily in his unseasonable suit.* ◆ **unseasonably** SUBMOD *...an unseasonably cold and foggy night.*

unseat /ʌnsiːt/ **unseats, unseating, unseated**
1 VO When a person in an important post is **unseated**, they are removed from that post. *He looks strong enough to deal with any attempts to unseat him.*
2 VO To **unseat** someone also means to remove them from the place where they are sitting. *The donkey jibbed suddenly, almost unseating her.*

unseeded /ʌnsiːdɪd/
ADJ An **unseeded** tennis player has not got a good enough record to be given a special position in the early rounds of a tournament. *Martina Navratilova will play the unseeded American Terry Phelps... He was beaten 6-3, 4-6, 6-1 by another unseeded player, Carl Uwe Steeb.*

unseeing /ʌnsiːɪŋ/
ADJ You describe a person as **unseeing** or say that their eyes are **unseeing** when they are not looking at anything or noticing anything although their eyes are open; a literary word. *She stared ahead, unseeing... She was gazing with unseeing eyes at the harbour.*

unseemly /ʌnsiːmli/
ADJ **Unseemly** behaviour is not polite or not suitable for a particular occasion; an old-fashioned word. *...an unseemly public squabble.*

unseen /ʌnsiːn/
ADJ You use **unseen** to describe things that you cannot see. *A large unseen orchestra was playing jazzy rhythms.*

unselfish /ʌnselfɪʃ/
ADJ If you are **unselfish**, you think about other people's wishes and needs rather than your own; used showing approval. *He was a brave and unselfish man. ...her unselfish devotion to her children.*

unsentimental /ʌnsentɪmentl/
ADJ **Unsentimental** people do not allow gentle or affectionate feelings to interfere with their work or decisions. *He is astute, unsentimental and realistic... Antique dealers are an unsentimental lot.*

unsettle /ʌnsetl/ **unsettles, unsettling, unsettled**
VO If something **unsettles** you, it causes you to feel restless, dissatisfied, or rather worried. *It unsettled him not to know where he was... The unexpected airforce activity has unsettled the inhabitants.*

unsettled /ʌnsetld/
1 ADJ In an **unsettled** situation, there is a lot of uncertainty about what will happen. *...in the early days of 1968, when everything was unsettled... Stock markets have been very unsettled over the past few days. ...the process of resolving all the unsettled issues.*
2 ADJ PRED If you are **unsettled**, you cannot concentrate on anything, because you are worried. *I felt pretty unsettled all that week.*

unsettling /ʌnsetlɪŋ/
ADJ An **unsettling** experience causes you to feel nervous or worried. *Swift change is extremely uncomfortable and unsettling.*

unshaded /ʌnʃeɪdɪd/
ADJ ATTRIB An **unshaded** light or light bulb has no shade fitted to it. *A single unshaded light hung from a roof-beam.*

unshakable /ʌnʃeɪkəbl/; also spelt **unshakeable.**
ADJ **Unshakable** beliefs are so strong that they cannot be destroyed or altered. *...her unshakable faith in progress... She appears unshakeable in her belief that an identity card scheme is the best way forward.*

unshaken /ʌnʃeɪkən/
ADJ If your beliefs are **unshaken** or if you are **unshaken** in your beliefs, you still have these beliefs, although they have been attacked or challenged. *He emerged with his faith in the capitalist system unshaken... He was unshaken in his belief that history would prove him right.*

unshaven /ʌnʃeɪvn/
ADJ If a man is **unshaven**, he has not shaved recently and there are short hairs on his face and chin. *...his unshaven face.*

unsightly /ʌnsaɪtli/
ADJ If something is **unsightly**, it is unattractive to look at. *His skin was covered with unsightly blotches. ...a campaign to rid Britain's streets of unsightly litter.*

unskilled /ʌnskɪld/
1 ADJ People who are **unskilled** do not have any special training for a job. *...unskilled labourers. ...most of them women and most of them unskilled.*
2 ADJ **Unskilled** work does not require any special training. *They are all in low-paid, unskilled jobs.*

unsociable /ʌnsəʊʃəbl/
ADJ **Unsociable** people do not like talking to other

people and try to avoid meeting them; used showing disapproval. *She was an awkward and unsociable girl. ...unsociable behaviour.*

unsocial/ʌnsəʊʃl/
ADJ If you have to work **unsocial** hours, you work at times when most people do not, such as in the evenings or at weekends. *The nurses say they stand to lose up to forty pounds a week in payments for unsocial hours.*

unsolicited/ʌnsəlɪsɪtɪd/
ADJ Something that is **unsolicited** is given without being asked for, and may not be wanted; a formal word. *She was given much unsolicited advice. ...unsolicited mail.*

unsolved/ʌnsɒlvd/
ADJ An **unsolved** problem or mystery has never been solved. *Ninety percent of the murders in her district remain unsolved... This is one of the great unsolved mysteries of our time.*

unsophisticated/ʌnsəfɪstɪkeɪtɪd/
1 ADJ **Unsophisticated** people do not have wide experience or knowledge, and have simple tastes. *It is easy to write because the readers are relatively unsophisticated.*
2 ADJ An **unsophisticated** method or device is very simple and often not very effective. *In harvesting the methods are relatively unsophisticated and a great deal is left aside... These forecasts are based on rather unsophisticated economic analyses.*

unsound/ʌnsaʊnd/
1 ADJ If a conclusion or method is **unsound**, it is based on ideas that are wrong. *These procedures are economically unsound... They were released on the grounds that their convictions were unsound.*
2 ADJ If something such as a building or other structure is **unsound**, it is in poor condition and is likely to collapse or break. *...flaws in a component that make it unsound.*

unspeakable/ʌnspiːkəbl/
ADJ If something is **unspeakable**, it is extremely unpleasant. *Their treatment of women is unspeakable. ...unspeakable crimes.*

unspecified/ʌnspesɪfaɪd/
ADJ You say that something is **unspecified** when you are not told exactly what it is. *He was receiving medical treatment in prison for unspecified illnesses... Army and police personnel have been called in to rescue an unspecified number of people.*

unspoiled/ʌnspɔɪld, ʌnspɔɪlt/; also spelt **unspoilt**
ADJ If something is **unspoiled**, it has not been damaged or harmed. *...areas of unspoiled countryside... The wine's flavour was unspoiled.*

unspoken/ʌnspəʊkən/
1 ADJ If your thoughts, wishes, or feelings are **unspoken**, you do not tell other people about them. *I was full of unspoken fears. ...ancient unspoken grievances. ...their largely unspoken concerns... Her remarks hint at an unspoken British policy towards Hong Kong.*
2 ADJ When there is an **unspoken** agreement or understanding between people, their behaviour shows that they agree about something or understand it, even though they have never discussed it. *They have always had this unspoken understanding. ...the unspoken rules for international food aid. ...the unspoken assumption that it had been the work of the security forces... By unspoken agreement they all increased their pace.*

unsporting/ʌnspɔːtɪŋ/
ADJ If you are **unsporting** during a game, you behave in a selfish way that is unfair to your opponent; used showing disapproval. *The club's players were fined 16 thousand dollars for unsporting behaviour.*

unstable/ʌnsteɪbl/
1 ADJ You can describe something as **unstable** when it is likely to change suddenly, especially if this creates difficulties or danger in some way. *The pope warned that the world situation is still precarious and unstable. ...a sensitivity to the problems of unstable prices. ...a cargo of unstable chemical waste from Italy.*
2 ADJ **Unstable** objects are likely to move or fall.

...the unstable cliffs.
3 ADJ If people are **unstable**, their emotions and behaviour keep changing because their minds are disturbed or upset. *He was a neurotic and unstable man.*

unstated/ʌnsteɪtɪd/
ADJ You say that something is **unstated** when it has not been expressed in words. *Stephanie preferred things unstated and undiscussed. ...a judgement based on unstated assumptions.*

unsteady/ʌnstedi/
1 ADJ If you are **unsteady**, you have difficulty standing or walking. *She seemed unsteady on her feet.*
♦ **unsteadily** ADV *He rose unsteadily to his feet.*
2 ADJ If your hands are **unsteady**, you have difficulty controlling them. *Stephen poured two brandies with an unsteady hand.*
3 ADJ **Unsteady** objects are not held, fixed, or balanced securely. *She was balancing three boxes in an unsteady pile.*

unstinting/ʌnstɪntɪŋ/
ADJ **Unstinting** help, care, or praise is great in amount or degree and is given generously. *This incident did show the unstinting care that this firm takes of its clients... I cannot speak too highly of the unstinting help I received.*

unstoppable/ʌnstɒpəbl/
ADJ Something that is **unstoppable** cannot be prevented from continuing or developing. *This waste of resources is neither inevitable nor unstoppable... The advance of science is unstoppable. ...unstoppable industrial decline.*

unstructured/ʌnstrʌktʃəd/
ADJ If an activity is **unstructured**, it is not organized in a complete or detailed way. *...an unstructured but effective method of education.*

unstuck/ʌnstʌk/
1 If something **comes unstuck**, it becomes separated from the thing that it was attached to. *Some of the posters regularly came unstuck.*
2 If a plan or system **comes unstuck**, it fails; an informal expression. *Where economics comes unstuck is when it tries to become some mathematic formula.*
3 If someone **comes unstuck**, they fail badly with what they are trying to achieve; an informal expression. *I always knew he'd come unstuck somewhere.*

unsubstantiated/ʌnsəbstænʃieɪtɪd/
ADJ An **unsubstantiated** statement or story has not been proved true. *This follows a year of confused and unsubstantiated reports.*

unsuccessful/ʌnsəksesfl/
ADJ If you are **unsuccessful**, you do not succeed in what you are trying to do. *Tom tried to hypnotize me but he was unsuccessful. ...an unsuccessful attempt to kill him.* ♦ **unsuccessfully** ADV *I tried unsuccessfully to talk to him.*

unsuitable/ʌnsuːtəbl/
ADJ Someone or something that is **unsuitable** for a particular purpose or situation does not have the right qualities for it. *He was wholly unsuitable as chairman of such a body. ...areas that are entirely unsuitable for agriculture.* ♦ **unsuitably** ADV *She was most unsuitably dressed.*

unsuited/ʌnsuːtɪd/
ADJ Someone or something that is **unsuited** to a particular situation, place, or task, does not have the right qualities for it. *...vehicles that are clearly unsuited for use in the desert.*

unsullied/ʌnsʌlid/
ADJ Something that is **unsullied** has not been spoiled or made less pure by the addition of something unpleasant or unacceptable; a literary word. *...an unsullied reputation... She possessed an innocence unsullied by contact with the world.*

unsung/ʌnsʌŋ/
ADJ You use **unsung** to describe people who are not appreciated or praised, when you think they should be; a literary word. *...research by heroic but unsung volunteers.*

unsupported/ʌnsəpɔːtɪd/
1 ADJ A statement or theory that is **unsupported** is not supported by any evidence which proves that it is true

or correct. *They should not make unsupported
accusations. ...unsupported statements.*
2 ADJ Someone who is **unsupported** does not have
anyone such as a husband or wife to provide them
with money and the things they need. *The problems
are most intense for unsupported mothers.*
3 ADJ Someone or something that is **unsupported** is not
being physically supported or held up by anything.
They could not stand for long unsupported.

unsure /ʌnʃɔː, ʌnʃʊə/
1 ADJ If you are **unsure** of yourself, you lack
confidence. *His demands made the boy nervous and
unsure of himself.*
2 ADJ If you are **unsure** about something, you feel
uncertain about it. *She took a step back, unsure of his
reaction... Officials are unsure of Paul's whereabouts.*

unsurpassed /ʌnsɜːpɑːst/
ADJ Something that is **unsurpassed** is better or greater
than anything else of its kind. *...an economic analyst
of unsurpassed genius. ...a variety of trees,
unsurpassed anywhere in the world.*

unsuspected /ʌnsəspɛktɪd/
ADJ If something is **unsuspected**, people are not aware
of it. *As the project developed, unsuspected difficulties
came to light.*

unsuspecting /ʌnsəspɛktɪŋ/
ADJ Someone who is **unsuspecting** is not aware of what
is happening or going to happen. *The bomb would be
planted on an unsuspecting passenger. ...a scheme to
rob thousands of dollars from unsuspecting victims.*

unswerving /ʌnswɜːvɪŋ/
ADJ An **unswerving** attitude, feeling, or way of
behaving is strong and firm and does not weaken or
change. *...the consistent, unswerving loyalty of his
supporters... They all have the same unswerving aim.
...her unswerving devotion to Miss Crabbe.*

unsympathetic /ʌnsɪmpəθɛtɪk/
ADJ If you are **unsympathetic**, you are not kind or
helpful to a person in difficulties. *Posy had been
utterly unsympathetic. ...an unsympathetic reply.*

untangle /ʌntæŋgl/ **untangles, untangling, untangled**
1 VO If you **untangle** something such as string when it
is twisted together, you undo the knots in it and
straighten it. *He untangled the cable.*
2 VO If you **untangle** a complicated situation, you sort
out the different things involved in it so that it can be
understood better. *It was the only organisation which
could untangle the knots of world economic relations.*

untapped /ʌntæpt/
ADJ An **untapped** supply of something has not yet been
used. *...Britain's vast untapped reserves of coal. ...the
world's largest untapped advertising market.*

untenable /ʌntɛnəbl/
ADJ An **untenable** argument, theory, or position cannot
be defended successfully against criticism or attack; a
formal word. *Recent events now make this policy
untenable... Their leader put them in a totally
untenable position.*

untested /ʌntɛstɪd/
ADJ Something that is **untested** has not yet been
tested, so that you do not know what it is really like or
what will happen. *Our potential as a new party was
untested in national politics... Marriage is very much
like a flight in an untested airplane.*

unthinkable /ʌnθɪŋkəbl/
1 ADJ If something is **unthinkable**, it seems so strange
and different to the accepted way of doing things that
you cannot imagine it. *The opposing parties are so
entrenched that any compromise appears
unthinkable... The future is unthinkable without
nuclear energy... This would have been an unthinkable
concept even two months ago.* ► Also N SING *Two days
later the unthinkable happened and the Berlin Wall
fell.*
2 ADJ You can also call something **unthinkable** if it is
such a horrible possibility that you want to believe
that it cannot happen. *War was unthinkable. ...the
unthinkable horrors he'd seen in the South Pacific.*
► Also N SING *There was no experience of such a
disaster, and alarmingly little contingency planning
for how to deal with the unthinkable.*

unthinking /ʌnθɪŋkɪŋ/
ADJ Someone who is **unthinking** does not think
carefully about the effects of their behaviour. *Our
society seems to be rushing ahead, unthinking, into
ever greater mechanization... It is popular with the
unthinking crowd.*

untidy /ʌntaɪdi/ **untidier, untidiest**
1 ADJ Something that is **untidy** is messy and
disordered, and not neatly arranged. *The living-room
was untidier than usual. ...long, untidy hair.* ◆ **untidily**
ADV *It had been unwrapped and untidily tossed onto
the floor.*
2 ADJ An **untidy** person leaves things in an untidy
state. *She is so careless and untidy.*

untie /ʌntaɪ/ **unties, untying, untied**
VO If you **untie** someone or something, you remove the
string or rope that has been tied round them by
undoing the knots. *He quickly untied the captives...
She tried to untie the knot.*

untied /ʌntaɪd/
ADJ Something such as a tie, shoelace, or ribbon that
is **untied** has its ends loose rather than tied together in
a bow or knot. *Many young people walk around in
their trainers with the laces untied.*

until /əntɪl/
1 PREP or CONJ If something happens **until** a particular
time, it happens before that time and stops at that
time. *We went on duty at six in the evening and
worked until 2 a.m... You can get free prescriptions
until you are 16.*
2 PREP or CONJ If something does not happen **until** a
particular time, it does not happen before that time
and only happens after it. *They didn't find her until
the next day... Women did not gain the vote until after
the First World War.*

untimely /ʌntaɪmli/
1 ADJ An **untimely** event happens too soon or sooner
than expected. *It might spoil the atmosphere and
bring the meeting to an untimely end. ...her untimely
death.*
2 ADJ **Untimely** is used to describe something which is
not suitable for a particular time; a formal use. *The
resolution was rejected on the grounds that it was
untimely and unhelpful while diplomatic efforts were
going on elsewhere... But that is now an untimely
subject.*

unto /ʌntuː, ʌntə/
PREP **Unto** was sometimes used instead of the
preposition 'to'; an old-fashioned word. *Do unto others
as you would have them do unto you.*

untold /ʌntəʊld/
ADJ ATTRIB You use **untold** to emphasize how great in
degree or extent something is, especially something
unpleasant; a formal word. *The war brought untold
suffering upon the population.*

untouchable /ʌntʌtʃəbl/ **untouchables**
1 NC An **untouchable** is an Indian whose social status
is below that of the lowest caste. *At the very bottom
of the heap are the 'Scheduled Castes', sometimes
called the untouchables... They are landless labourers
from Bihar, of the untouchable caste.*
2 ADJ Someone who is **untouchable** cannot be affected
or punished in any way. *Their names are known but
they are untouchable because they have never
committed any known crime... I felt invincible,
untouchable.*

untouched /ʌntʌtʃt/
1 ADJ Something that is **untouched** has not been
changed, moved, or damaged in any way. *...an area
of the East End of London that has been untouched by
the planners for hundreds of years... Some silverware
was missing from a drawer but other valuables were
untouched.*
2 ADJ If a meal is **untouched**, none of it has been
eaten. *She sent back her breakfast tray untouched.*

untoward /ʌntəwɔːd/
ADJ You use **untoward** to describe something that
happens unexpectedly and causes difficulties; a formal
word. *Nothing untoward had happened.*

untrained /ʌntreɪnd/
1 ADJ Someone who is **untrained** has had no education
in the skills that they need for a particular job or

activity. *The leadership fears another coup d'état, so it has kept its troops undisciplined and untrained. ...untrained assistants.*

2 ADJ If you say that something appears a certain way to the **untrained** eye, or to the **untrained** ear, you mean that it appears that way to someone who is not an expert and might therefore be wrong about it. *To the untrained ear perhaps there isn't a great deal of difference... She's off the critical list, and yet to me, the untrained observer, she's pink and very vulnerable looking... Even to an untrained eye it was obvious that something peculiar had happened.*

untrammelled /ʌntræməld/; spelt **untrammeled** in American English.

ADJ Someone who is **untrammelled** is able to act freely, in the way they want to, rather than being restricted by rules and conventions; a literary word. *I felt free and untrammelled and I wanted to stay that way. ...its fight for the untrammelled self-expression of the individual.*

untreated /ʌntriːtɪd/

1 ADJ If an injury or illness is left **untreated**, it is not given medical treatment. *Paroskiv died of his untreated wounds. ...serious, untreated skin infections.*
2 ADJ Harmful materials, water, or chemicals that are **untreated** have not been made safe. *The untreated sewage is dumped into the Pacific Ocean right along the water's edge... A spokesman said people who drank untreated water could suffer stomach upsets.*

untried /ʌntraɪd/

ADJ Something that is **untried** has not yet been used, done, or tested. *It is still an untried policy.*

untroubled /ʌntrʌbld/

ADJ PRED If you are **untroubled** by something, you are not affected or worried by it. *Mr Lawson is untroubled by the balance of payments deficit.*

untrue /ʌntruː/

1 ADJ Something that is **untrue** is not true. *The growers say the report was untrue and caused them to lose millions of dollars. ...untrue and insulting articles.*
2 ADJ PRED If someone is **untrue** to their principles or to a friend, they betray them in some way; a literary use. *If we so much as discuss the matter we will be being untrue to our principles.*

untrustworthy /ʌntrʌstwɜːði/

ADJ Someone who is **untrustworthy** is unreliable and cannot be trusted. *He has proved himself completely untrustworthy.*

untruth /ʌntruːθ/ **untruths** /ʌntruːðz/

NC An **untruth** is a lie; a formal word. *I hesitated rather than tell a deliberate untruth.*

untruthful /ʌntruːθfl/

1 ADJ Someone who is **untruthful** is dishonest and says things that they know are not true; a formal word. *He was being untruthful when he claimed that he had never seen her before.*
2 ADJ If something that someone says or writes is **untruthful**, they know that it is not true. *Complaints about untruthful reporting in their own newspapers were justified.*

untutored /ʌntjuːtəd/

ADJ Someone who is **untutored** in a particular area of knowledge has not learnt about it from other people or from books; a formal word. *He was apparently untutored in the arts of polite social behaviour... To the untutored eye, the art of this region looks, if not uniform, then at least very similar.*

unusable /ʌnjuːzəbl/

ADJ Something that is **unusable** is not in a good enough state or condition to be used. *The living room was unusable.*

unused; pronounced /ʌnjuːzd/ for the meaning in paragraph 1 and /ʌnjuːst/ for the meaning in paragraph 2.

1 ADJ Something that is **unused** has not been used. *...a pile of unused fuel... Any unused material is simply recycled.*
2 ADJ PRED+to If you are **unused** to something, you have not often done it or experienced it. *She was unused to hardship.*

unusual /ʌnjuːʒuəl, ʌnjuːʒl/

ADJ If something is **unusual**, it does not often happen

or is not often found. *He had an unusual name... It was not unusual for me to come home at two or three in the morning.*

unusually /ʌnjuːʒuəli, ʌnjuːʒəli/

1 SUBMOD You use **unusually** to say that something is bigger than usual or has more of a quality than usual. *...a clump of weed that seemed unusually large... October has been unusually wet and cold.*
2 ADV SEN You also use **unusually** to say that something is not what normally happens. *The service charge, unusually, is 10 per cent.*

unutterable /ʌnʌtərəbl/

ADJ ATTRIB **Unutterable** is used to describe something that is very great in degree or intensity, especially a bad quality; a literary word. *...an expression of unutterable misery on the father's face... I tried to think how I could relieve my unutterable boredom.*
♦ **unutterably** SUBMOD *It tasted unutterably foul... I was busy and unutterably tired.*

unveil /ʌnveɪl/ **unveils**, **unveiling**, **unveiled**

1 VO When someone **unveils** something such as a new statue or painting, they draw back a curtain which is covering it, in a special ceremony. *The leaders unveiled a plaque at the organisation's headquarters... The window was unveiled by the Duke.*
2 VO If you **unveil** something that has been a secret, you make it known; a formal use. *British Rail has unveiled its plans for a new international rail terminal at Waterloo station... The United States has unveiled a new space programme.*

unwaged /ʌnweɪdʒd/

ADJ People who are **unwaged** do not have a paid job.

unwanted /ʌnwɒntɪd/

ADJ You say that something is **unwanted** when a particular person does not want it, or when nobody wants it. *...the appalling suffering caused by unwanted pregnancies... She was starting to feel unwanted.*

unwarranted /ʌnwɒrəntɪd/

ADJ Something that is **unwarranted** is not justified or deserved; a formal word. *It was a totally unwarranted waste of money.*

unwary /ʌnweəri/

ADJ Someone who is **unwary** is not cautious, and is likely to be harmed or deceived; a formal word. *...the shrieks of unwary animals taken by surprise.*

unwavering /ʌnweɪvərɪŋ/

ADJ An **unwavering** feeling or attitude is strong and firm and does not weaken. *Moscow and Washington are unwavering and united in their resolve. ...years of consistent and unwavering support. ...his unwavering commitment to achieving peace throughout the Middle East.*

unwelcome /ʌnwelkəm/

1 ADJ An **unwelcome** experience is one that you do not like and did not want. *...unwelcome publicity... The move from London was entirely unwelcome to her.*
2 ADJ If a visitor is **unwelcome**, you did not want them to come. *...an unwelcome guest.*

unwelcoming /ʌnwelkəmɪŋ/

1 ADJ Someone who is **unwelcoming** towards you is unfriendly or hostile when you visit or approach them. *He fixed her with an unwelcoming stare.*
2 ADJ A place that looks **unwelcoming** looks unattractive or difficult to live or work in. *...the island with its unwelcoming coastline... Westminster is still a very unwelcoming place for women.*

unwell /ʌnwel/

ADJ PRED If you are **unwell**, you are ill. *He complained of feeling unwell.*

unwholesome /ʌnhəʊlsəm/

1 ADJ Food or drink that is **unwholesome** is not healthy or good for you. *...plain, unwholesome food.*
2 ADJ If you describe someone's behaviour as **unwholesome**, you mean that you find it unpleasant or unnatural. *She disapproves of my unwholesome living.*

unwieldy /ʌnwiːldi/

1 ADJ An **unwieldy** object is difficult to move or carry because it is awkward and big or heavy. *...a space in an open hall, very crowded with a lot of rather unwieldy wooden furniture.*
2 ADJ An **unwieldy** system does not work well because

it is too large or is badly organized. *They found themselves dealing with an unwieldy bureaucracy, as well as language and legal problems. ...unwieldy and inefficient state-owned companies.*

unwilling /ʌnwɪlɪŋ/
ADJ If you are **unwilling** to do something, you do not want to do it. *She was unwilling to go out... Tens of thousands of unwilling patients were coerced into having the treatment... Many union members have been unwilling to remain on strike.* ◆ **unwillingly** ADV *He submitted unwillingly to his mother.* ◆ **unwillingness** NU *...their unwillingness to discuss common problems.*

unwind /ʌnwaɪnd/ **unwinds, unwinding, unwound**
1 V When you **unwind** after working hard, you relax. *It's hard to unwind after four months of 15 hour days.*
2 V-ERG or V If you **unwind** something that is wrapped up or wrapped round something else, you straighten it out. *Francis was unwinding his bandage... That allows the core fibres to slowly unwind again over time.*

unwise /ʌnwaɪz/
ADJ Something that is **unwise** is foolish. *It would be very unwise for the boy to marry her. ...an unwise choice.*

unwitting /ʌnwɪtɪŋ/
ADJ ATTRIB An **unwitting** person does something or becomes involved in something without realizing what is really happening; a formal word. *I became the unwitting instrument of that unscrupulous man.* ◆ **unwittingly** ADV *Sometimes we ourselves unwittingly invite trouble.*

unwonted /ʌnwəʊntɪd/
ADJ Something that is **unwonted** is unusual or has not often been experienced before; a literary word. *...things which were common and everyday to him, but unwonted luxuries to them. ...an unwonted sensation of buoyancy and freedom.*

unworkable /ʌnwɜːkəbl/
ADJ If an idea or plan is **unworkable**, it cannot succeed. *His proposals for reform of the Trades Unions are unworkable.*

unworldly /ʌnwɜːldli/
ADJ Someone who is **unworldly** is not interested in having a lot of money or possessions. *...the vision of a sensitive, unworldly and, frankly uncontroversial, poet.*

unworthy /ʌnwɜːði/
1 ADJ If someone is **unworthy** of something, they do not deserve it; a literary word. *I felt I was unworthy of her love. ...an unworthy partner.*
2 ADJ If you say that an action is **unworthy** of someone, you feel that they have a good reputation or a responsible position and so should behave better. *He says that Britain has displayed an arrogance unworthy of a democratic state. ...acts unworthy of a superpower.*

unwound /ʌnwaʊnd/
Unwound is the past tense and past participle of **unwind**.

unwrap /ʌnræp/ **unwraps, unwrapping, unwrapped**
V O When you **unwrap** something, you take off the paper or covering that is around it. *I started to unwrap my sandwiches.*

unwritten /ʌnrɪtn/
1 ADJ **Unwritten** things have not been printed or written down. *Thoughts of my unwritten novel nagged me... I have all this unwritten writing to do.*
2 ADJ Something such as a rule or law that is **unwritten** is known about, accepted, or understood by everyone without being officially written down. *That has been an unwritten understanding since 1985. ...unwritten laws... So far there has been an unwritten agreement between the various groups.*

unzip /ʌnzɪp/ **unzips, unzipping, unzipped**
V O When you **unzip** something which is fastened by a zip, you unfasten it. *I unzipped my anorak... I unzipped the tent door.*

up /ʌp/ **ups, upping, upped**; pronounced /ʌp/ when it is a preposition.
1 PREP or ADV **Up** means towards a higher place, or in a higher place. *I carried my suitcase up the stairs behind her... Bill put up his hand. ...comfortable houses up in the hills.*

2 ADV If someone stands **up**, they move so that they are standing. *She scrambled up from the floor... She helped Henry up from the bench.*
3 ADV A **Up** also means in the north or towards the north. *We're having brilliant sunshine up here.*
4 PREP or ADV If you go **up** a road, you go along it. *We walked up the road together... There's a cafe just a hundred yards further up.*
5 PREP If you go **up** a river, you go along it towards its source. *...a voyage up the Nile.*
6 ADV A You also use **up** to show that something is close to something else, or moves closer to it. *It's only when you get right up to them that you realise what they are... Ferdinand ran up to his father-in-law.*
7 ADJ PRED If you are **up**, you are not in bed. *They were up early.*
8 ADV If an amount goes **up**, it increases. *...when interest rates go up... The temperature was up in the nineties.*
9 ADJ PRED If a period of time is **up**, it has come to an end. *When the six weeks were up, everybody was sad that she had to leave.*
10 ADV or ADJ If someone or something comes **up** or is **up** for election, review, or examination, they are about to be considered, judged, or decided on. *One of my colleagues comes up for election next week... Complaints of vote-rigging have been filed in a third of the seats up for election.*
11 V O To **up** something means to increase it; used especially of money. *They stressed that there was no shortage of crude oil because the OPEC countries had upped production... Wages have been frozen since 1982, so upping income tax was ruled out.*
● **Up** is used in these phrases. ● If you move **up and down**, you move repeatedly in one direction and then in the opposite direction. *I was so happy I jumped up and down... He started pacing up and down the office.* ● If you have **ups and downs**, you experience a mixture of good things and bad things. *His political career has certainly had its ups and downs.* ● If you say that something **is up**, you mean that something is wrong or that something worrying is happening; an informal expression. *What's up, Myra? You look sad.* ● If you are **up against** something, or **up against it**, you have a difficult situation or problem to deal with. *The problem it will come up against is a radical difference of approach... If he ever finds out what you know, you will be up against it in a big way.* ● If you **up the ante** or **up the stakes**, when you are involved in a dispute with someone, you increase the intensity of the dispute in some way. *Northwest Airlines has upped the ante in the nation's air fare wars... The attack on Osijek has undoubtedly upped the stakes in the Yugoslav crisis.* ● You use **up to** to say how large something can be. *They might be up to a metre wide... Savings up to 65% are obtainable.* ● You also use **up to** to say what level something has reached. *The work isn't up to the standard I require.* ● If you say that something is **not up to much**, you mean that it is of poor quality; an informal expression. ● If you do not feel **up to** doing something, you do not feel well enough to do it; an informal expression. *Now past retirement, she says she is still up to doing some canvassing and leafleting.* ● If you say that someone is **up to** something, you mean that they are secretly doing something that they should not be; an informal expression. *The Drugs Enforcement Agency perused them for evidence that he was up to something from his jail cell... You can't fool me—I see what you are up to.* ● If you say that it is **up to** someone to do a particular thing, you mean that it is their responsibility to do it. *It is up to the teacher not to accept shoddy work.* ● If something happens **up to** or **up until** a particular time, it happens until that time. *Up until the early sixties there was no shortage.*

up-and-coming
ADJ **Up-and-coming** people are likely to be successful in the future. *...up-and-coming Third World exporters.*

upbeat /ʌpbiːt/
ADJ If people or their opinions are **upbeat**, they are cheerful and optimistic about a situation. *Mr Tambo was upbeat too about the country's prospects. ...an*

upbeat assessment of the improvement in relations last year... They took a more upbeat view of economic prospects.

upbraid /ʌpbreɪd/ **upbraids, upbraiding, upbraided**
VO If you **upbraid** someone, you tell them that they have done something wrong and criticize them for doing it; a formal word. *You mustn't upbraid Brian for comparing them.*

upbringing /ʌpbrɪŋɪŋ/
NU Your **upbringing** is the way your parents treat you and the things that they teach you when you are a child. *She herself had a very deprived upbringing in industrial North East England. ...a strict upbringing.*

upcoming /ʌpkʌmɪŋ/
ADJ ATTRIB **Upcoming** events will happen in the near future. *He could well be voted out of office in the upcoming elections for the presidency.*

update, updates, updating, updated; pronounced /ʌpdeɪt/ when it is a verb and /ʌpdeɪt/ when it is a noun.
1 VO If you **update** something, you make it more modern, usually by adding newer parts to it. *The information will need updating from time to time... Mrs Thatcher asked him to update his earlier report.*
♦ **updated** ADJ ATTRIB *This is only an updated version of an existing older missile.*
2 NC An **update** is a news item which has been rewritten so that it includes the very latest developments in a situation. *Here with this morning's update is Ian Gregory... During the programme there were further updates from Washington.*

upend /ʌpend/ **upends, upending, upended**
VO If something **is upended**, it is turned upside down. *The boys used to pretend to be upending the bottle and hiccup.*

up front; an informal expression.
1 ADJ If you are **up front** about something, you act openly or publicly so that people know what you are doing or what you believe. *We all get programmed anyhow—we may as well be up front about it.*
2 ADV If a payment is made **up front**, it is made in advance and openly, so that the person being paid knows they will receive the money. *All right, I'll do it but I want £500 up front... The owners used to pay a portion of their wages up front, and the remainder under the table in cash which is not declared.*

upgrade /ʌpgreɪd/ **upgrades, upgrading, upgraded**
VO To **upgrade** something means to change it so that it is more important or better. *Angola recently upgraded the status of its ambassador here in London... The motorway had been upgraded from six to eight lanes... Their weaponry and equipment was upgraded.* ♦ **upgrading** N SING *Japan has called for a major upgrading of relations.*

upheaval /ʌphiːvl/ **upheavals**
NCorNU An **upheaval** is a big change which causes a lot of trouble and confusion. *Great upheavals were taking place in the States... They have brought social upheaval and conflict into the country.*

upheld /ʌpheld/
Upheld is the past tense and past participle of **uphold**.

uphill /ʌphɪl/
1 ADV If you go **uphill**, you go up a slope. *She ran furiously uphill.* ▶ Also ADJ *Sean Kelly burst forward on the final uphill bend to win the tenth mountain stage.*
2 ADJ ATTRIB An **uphill** task requires a great deal of effort and determination. *The government faces an uphill struggle in its attempt to impose discipline on the armed forces... Real Madrid begin the uphill task of overcoming a 3-2 defeat.*

uphold /ʌphəʊld/ **upholds, upholding, upheld**
VO If you **uphold** a law, principle, or decision, you support and maintain it. *He had sworn to uphold the law... His conviction was upheld on appeal.*

upholder /ʌphəʊldə/ **upholders**
NC+SUPP The **upholder** of a particular tradition or system is someone who believes strongly in it and will support it when it is threatened. *He is regarded by many as the principal upholder of the traditional values of the Labour movement.*

upholstered /ʌphəʊlstəd/
ADJ **Upholstered** chairs and sofas have a soft covering that makes them comfortable to sit on. *...two chairs, upholstered in leather.*

upholstery /ʌphəʊlstəri/
NU **Upholstery** is the soft covering on chairs and sofas that makes them comfortable. *...the use of foam in the upholstery of household furniture. ...upholstery fabrics.*

upkeep /ʌpkiːp/
1 NU The **upkeep** of a system, building, or place is the continual process of keeping it in good condition. *...the organization responsible for the trail's upkeep and management. ...the upkeep of the Royal Yacht.*
2 NU The **upkeep** of a group of people or service is the act or the cost of providing them with the things that they need. *Often such fathers pay nothing towards the upkeep of their children... It is contributing financially to the upkeep of the Belgian force.*

upland /ʌplənd/ **uplands**
1 ADJ ATTRIB **Upland** places are situated on high hills or high land. *They move with their flocks to upland pastures.*
2 N PL **Uplands** are areas of high land. *...the chalk uplands of Wiltshire.*

uplift, uplifts, uplifting, uplifted; pronounced /ʌplɪft/ when it is a verb and /ʌplɪft/ when it is a noun.
VO If something **uplifts** people, it helps them to have a better life, for example by making them feel happy or by improving their social conditions; a literary word. *The whole reason for this development programme is that it is going to uplift people and make them richer.* ▶ Also NU *...a wide-ranging programme for social and economic uplift.*

uplifted /ʌplɪftɪd/
ADJ If people's faces or arms are **uplifted**, they are pointing them upwards or are holding them in a high position; a literary word. *We could just see him, a tiny silhouette with uplifted arms.*

uplifting /ʌplɪftɪŋ/
ADJ If something is **uplifting**, it makes you feel cheerful and happy. *They have a streak of idealism— they prefer songs with an uplifting social message... It's like a gospel tune, so hopefully it will be a little bit uplifting.*

upmarket /ʌpmɑːkɪt/
ADJ **Upmarket** places and goods are visited or bought by people who have sophisticated and expensive tastes; an informal word. *...a sunny, casual, upmarket and safe resort.*

upon /əpɒn/
1 PREP If one thing is **upon** another, it is on it; a formal use. *She was sitting with a cat upon her knee... He lay down upon the grass.*
2 PREP You use **upon** when mentioning an event that is followed immediately by another; a formal use. *Upon entering the cabin, she sat down.*
3 PREP You also use **upon** between two occurrences of the same noun in order to say that there are large numbers of the thing mentioned. *We drove through mile upon mile of brick villas. ...row upon row of red roofs.*
4 PREP If an event is **upon** you, it is just about to happen. *Suddenly the concert was upon us with me totally unprepared.*

upper /ʌpə/ **uppers**
1 ADJ ATTRIB You use **upper** to describe something that is above something else, usually the top one of a pair of things. *I pulled down a book from an upper shelf... To date, the upper atmosphere has been only briefly explored.*
2 ADJ ATTRIB The **upper** part of something is the higher part. *Dark glasses masked the upper half of his face.*
3 If you have **the upper hand** in a situation, you have more power than the other people involved and can make decisions about what happens. *The reformers are gaining the upper hand in the power struggle with the conservatives.*
4 NC The **upper** of a shoe is the top part of it, which is attached to the sole. *...the old-fashioned plimsoll or sneaker with its rubber sole and canvas uppers.*

upper case
NUorN+N **Upper case** letters are capital letters. *...an upper case M.*

upper class, upper classes
NC The **upper classes** are the people who belong to the social class above the middle class. They often own a lot of property and have special titles that they inherit. *The upper classes still send their children to Eton. ...upper-class families.*

upper crust
N COLL **Upper crust** means the same as **upper class**; an informal expression. *...the lifestyle of the privileged upper crust. ...an upper crust eccentric.*

uppercut /ˈʌpəkʌt/ **uppercuts**
NC An **uppercut** is a type of punch used in boxing. It is a hard upward blow to the opponent's chin. *Sot Chitalada of Thailand knocked out Jamaica's Richard Clarke with a series of uppercuts in the 11th round.*

Upper House, Upper Houses
1 NC The **Upper House** is the same as the **House of Lords**. *The Conservatives are the largest party in the Upper House.*
2 NC In other countries in which the government is divided into two debating chambers, the **Upper House** is one of these chambers, often called the Senate. *The Upper House, the Senate, has promised not to oppose the bill... There are to be elections for the Upper House of the Japanese parliament in the summer.*

upper lip, upper lips
NC Your **upper lip** is the part of your face between your mouth and your nose. *By the 1930s, his upper lip had become contorted by the exertions of so much playing. ...a quivering upper lip.* ● **a stiff upper lip**: see **stiff**.

uppermost /ˈʌpəməʊst/
1 ADJ You say that something is **uppermost** when it is higher than the rest of a particular thing, or when it is the highest thing in a group. *He was pointing with the whole of his hand, thumb uppermost... He gently examined the uppermost leaves.*
2 ADJ PRED If something is **uppermost** in a situation, it is the most important thing in that situation. *Political motives were uppermost... There were two thoughts uppermost in my mind.*

Upper Volta /ˌʌpə ˈvɒltə/ See **Burkina Faso**.

uppish /ˈʌpɪʃ/
ADJ **Uppish** means the same as **uppity**; an old-fashioned word. *They were being frightfully uppish and rude.*

uppity /ˈʌpəti/
ADJ If you say that someone is **uppity**, you mean that they are behaving as if they were very important and you do not think that they are; an old-fashioned word. *My boss felt I was getting slightly uppity... These uppity kids are all the same.*

upraised /ʌpˈreɪzd/
ADJ If your hand or arm is **upraised**, you are holding it up in the air. *The man just stood there with his arm upraised. ...her upraised hand.*

upright /ˈʌpraɪt/
1 ADV If you are sitting or standing **upright**, you are sitting or standing with your back straight. *I cannot stand upright any more... He sat bolt upright.*
2 ADJ An **upright** chair has a straight back and no arms. *I found him sitting on an upright metal office chair.*
3 ADJ **Upright** people are careful to behave in a way that is moral and socially acceptable. *They need to get references from their employers to prove that they are upright citizens.*

uprising /ˈʌpraɪzɪŋ/ **uprisings**
NC When there is an **uprising**, a group of people start fighting against the people who are in power in their country. *...the 1916 Easter uprising in Dublin against British rule... As news of the military uprising spread, thousands of people took to the streets.*

up-river; also spelt **upriver**.
1 ADV If something moves **up-river**, it moves along a river towards its source. *We paddled some 60 miles up-river to Bordeaux... He had advised that torpedo boats be brought upriver.*
2 ADJ PRED If something is **up-river** from a place, it is

on the same river but further towards the river's source. *...the village of Juffure, four days up-river.*

uproar /ˈʌprɔː/
1 N SING or NU If there is **uproar**, there is a lot of shouting and noise because people are angry or upset. *She could hear the uproar in the prisoners' coaches... Soon all was uproar.*
2 N SING or NU You can also refer to public debate and criticism about something as **uproar**. *The proposed law has set off an uproar in the computer industry... He said the decision to carry out the death sentences had caused international condemnation and uproar.*

uproarious /ʌpˈrɔːrɪəs/
ADJ **Uproarious** laughter is very noisy; a literary word. *...an uproarious burst of laughter.*
◆ **uproariously** ADV *He laughed uproariously.*

uproot /ʌpˈruːt/ **uproots, uprooting, uprooted**
1 V-REFL or VO If you **uproot** yourself or if you **are uprooted**, you leave or are made to leave a place where you have lived for a long time. *Protracted civil wars have caused large numbers of people to uproot themselves... People were uprooted and rehoused.*
2 VO To **uproot** a tree means to pull it out of the ground. *The stadium was hit by a violent hail storm which uprooted trees and telegraph poles.*

upset, upsets, upsetting: pronounced /ʌpˈset/ when it is an adjective, /ʌpˈset/ when it is a verb, and /ˈʌpset/ when it is a noun. The form **upset** is used in the present tense and is also the past tense and past participle of the verb.
1 ADJ PRED If you are **upset**, you are unhappy or disappointed because something unpleasant has happened. *I'm dreadfully upset about it all... They were upset by the poverty they saw.*
2 VO If something **upsets** you, it makes you feel worried or unhappy. *I didn't mean to upset you.*
◆ **upsetting** ADJ *It was a very upsetting experience.*
3 VO To **upset** something such as a procedure means to cause it to go wrong. *Davis's death has upset the routine.*
4 VO To **upset** something also means to turn it over accidentally. *He almost upset the canoe.*
5 NC An **upset** in a competition or election is the defeat of the person, team, or organization that was expected to win. *In the other semi-final, Jerome Potier continued his series of upsets beating Guy Forget 6-3, 7-6... Harvey Gantt is depending on the women's vote to pull off an upset against Jesse Helms. ...her upset victory over Republican Clayton Williams.* ► Also VO *Sabatini upset two-time defending champion Steffi Graf at the US Open Tennis Championship yesterday.*
6 NC A stomach **upset** is a slight illness in your stomach caused by an infection or by something that you have eaten. *He withdrew from their match because of a stomach upset.* ► Also ADJ *I've got an upset stomach.*

upshot /ˈʌpʃɒt/
N SING The **upshot** of a series of events or discussions is the final result. *The upshot of these events is that Father Lini remains in charge of the country... The upshot was that the entire agreement had to be re-negotiated.*

upside down /ˌʌpsaɪd ˈdaʊn/
1 ADJ PRED or ADV If something is **upside down**, it has been turned round so that the part that is usually lowest is above the part that is usually highest. *You are holding it upside down... They were hanging upside down.*
2 ADV If you turn a place **upside down**, you move everything around or make it untidy. *I've turned the house upside down, but I still can't find his watch.*
3 ADV If you turn something such as a system or organization **upside down**, you change it completely. *Schools in Britain have been turned upside down and inside out recently—what they need is stability... Our world and families have been turned upside down and our lives ruined... This could well turn our ideas about the Universe's origin upside down.*

upstage /ʌpˈsteɪdʒ/ **upstages, upstaging, upstaged**
VO If someone **upstages** you, they draw attention away from you by being more attractive or interesting. *He*

seems to be attempting to upstage the Prime Minister... The former Prime Minister's announcement upstaged the annual conference.

upstairs /ʌpˈsteəz/
1 ADV If you go **upstairs** in a building, you go up to a higher floor. *I ran back upstairs.*
2 ADV If something or someone is **upstairs** in a building, they are on an upper floor. *Upstairs, there were three little bedrooms.*
3 N SING The **upstairs** of a building is its upper floor or floors; an informal use. *They had to rent out the upstairs to make the mortgage payments.*
4 ADJ ATTRIB An **upstairs** room or object is situated on an upper floor of a building. *Neighbours watched from their upstairs windows.*

upstart /ʌpstɑːt/ **upstarts**
NC You refer to someone as an **upstart** when they behave as if they are important, but you think they are too new in a place or job to be treated as important. *...the upstarts whose families had only made money in, say, the nineteenth century... Manchester United put those upstarts from East London, Millwall, in their place.*

upstream /ʌpˈstriːm/
ADV Something that is moving **upstream** is moving along a river towards the source of the river. *He was making his way upstream.*

upsurge /ʌpsɜːdʒ/
N SING If there is an **upsurge** in something, there is a sudden, large increase in it; a formal word. *There has been an upsurge in local, national, and religious feeling in recent years. ...an upsurge in violence. ...a strong upsurge in share prices.*

upswing /ʌpswɪŋ/ **upswings**
N SING An **upswing** is a sudden increase or improvement in something that had previously been declining or had not been very good. *The second half of the 1960s brought an upswing in sales... Their fortunes took an upswing... He said he believed the country was at last moving into an economic upswing.*

uptake /ʌpteɪk/
If someone is **quick on the uptake**, they understand things quickly. If someone is **slow on the uptake**, they have difficulty understanding simple or obvious things; an informal expression. *She was not very quick on the uptake and needed time to take everything in... Her first instinct had been not to appear naive or slow on the uptake.*

uptight /ʌptaɪt/
ADJ Someone who is **uptight** is tense or annoyed about something but is not saying so directly; an informal word. *I really get uptight when people say that we pay extremely low wages.*

up-to-date
1 ADJ If something is **up-to-date**, it is the newest thing of its kind. *...a fleet of up-to-date lorries... It has up-to-date equipment for visitors to experiment on.*
2 ADJ If you are **up-to-date** about something, you have the latest information about it. *Governments concerned about the effects of AIDS can keep up-to-date with the situation.*

up-to-the-minute
ADJ **Up-to-the-minute** information is the latest information that you can get about something. *...up-to-the-minute news.*

uptown /ʌptaʊn/
ADV or ADJ If you go **uptown**, you go away from the centre of a city towards an outer part; used in American English. *He walked uptown. ...the penthouses of uptown Manhattan.*

upturn /ʌptɜːn/ **upturns**
N SING If there is an **upturn** in something such as a country's economy, it starts to improve. *A United Nations report says there are good prospects for an economic upturn in the world this year... There were signs of an upturn in business for Northwest Airlines today.*

upturned /ʌptɜːnd/
1 ADJ If something is **upturned**, it points upwards. *She had a small upturned nose.*
2 ADJ **Upturned** also means upside down. *She sat on an upturned bucket.*

upward /ʌpwəd/ **upwards**. Upwards is an adverb and **upward** is an adjective. In formal British English and in American English, **upward** is both an adjective and an adverb.
1 ADV If you move or look **upwards** or **upward**, you move or look towards a higher place. *He happened to look upwards.* ▶ Also ADJ ATTRIB *He would steal upward glances at the clock.*
2 ADV If an amount or rate moves **upwards** or **upward**, it increases. *The world urban population is rocketing upward at a rate of 6.5 per cent per year.*
3 PREP **Upwards of** or **upward of** a particular number means more than that number. *The cyclone killed upwards of 200,000 people.*

upwardly-mobile /ʌpwədli ˈməʊbaɪl/
ADJ An **upwardly-mobile** person or group of people is moving towards, or wants to move to, a higher social class, or to a position where they have more status or power. *As we have already suggested, many of the upwardly-mobile voters come from conservative homes. ...young upwardly-mobile professionals.*

upwind /ʌpwɪnd/
ADJ or ADV If something is **upwind**, it is in a place, position, or direction that the wind is blowing away from. *It suited me, because I was upwind of the smokers... The fallout stretched roughly 20 miles upwind of the island and 320 miles downwind.*

uranium /jʊˈreɪniəm/
NU **Uranium** is a naturally occurring radioactive metal that is used to produce nuclear energy and weapons. *The government needed uranium for atomic bombs.*

urban /ɜːbən/
ADJ ATTRIB **Urban** means belonging or relating to a town or city. *There have been huge traffic jams in urban areas. ...rural and urban development.*

urbane /ɜːbeɪn/
ADJ Someone who is **urbane** is well-mannered, relaxed, and appears comfortable in social situations; a formal word. *The professor was an urbane little man... On his trips abroad he acted as an urbane cultural ambassador for his country.*

urban guerrilla, **urban guerrillas**
NC An **urban guerrilla** is someone who carries out terrorist attacks and kidnappings with the aim of destabilizing the state. *Urban guerrillas are no longer considered a serious threat to democracy.*

urbanize /ɜːbənaɪz/ **urbanizes**, **urbanizing**, **urbanized**; also spelt **urbanise**.
VO If a country area **is urbanized**, it is made more like a town, with more buildings, industry, and business. *...the land which is likely to be urbanized between 1965 and 2000.* ◆ **urbanization** /ɜːbənaɪzeɪʃn/ NU *...the rapid urbanization of much of the Third World.*

urchin /ɜːtʃɪn/ **urchins**
NC You can refer to a young child who is dirty and poorly dressed as an **urchin**; an old-fashioned word. *...pictures like the two urchins cheerfully crossing the street in a Glasgow slum.*

Urdu /ʊədu:/
NU **Urdu** is one of the languages that is spoken by people who live in Pakistan, and by some people in India and Britain. *He is a British convert to Islam, who does not speak Urdu.*

urge /ɜːdʒ/ **urges**, **urging**, **urged**
1 NC If you have an **urge** to do or have something, you have a strong wish to do or have it. *They have a strong urge to communicate. ...our insane urge for greater and greater material wealth.*
2 VO, V-REPORT, or V-QUOTE If you **urge** someone to do something, you try hard to persuade them to do it. *Mr Reagan urged them not to lose heart... They urged that forthcoming elections should be open to international observers... 'At least stay for Christmas,' Pam urged.*
3 VO If you **urge** a course of action, you strongly advise that it should be taken; a formal use. *A judge involved in the case has urged a quick settlement... A review of security procedures has been urged by the Daily Express.*
urge on PHRASAL VERB If you **urge** someone **on**, you

encourage them to do something. *Urged on by cheering bystanders, the students surged through police lines and swept into the vast plaza... He is walking backwards, urging Alex on with smiles.*

urgency /ˈɜːdʒənsi/
1 NU **Urgency** is the need for something to be dealt with as soon as possible. *...matters of the greatest urgency.*
2 NU If you speak with **urgency**, you show that you are anxious for people to notice something or do something. *There was a note of urgency in his voice.*

urgent /ˈɜːdʒənt/
1 ADJ Something that is **urgent** needs to be dealt with as soon as possible. *Things could get worse unless urgent action is taken... Everyone agreed there was an urgent need for reform.* ◆ **urgently** ADV *Improved health and education are urgently needed.*
2 ADJ If you speak in an **urgent** way, you show that you are anxious for people to notice something or do something. *She spoke to him in a low and urgent voice.* ◆ **urgently** ADV *'Do you see it?' he demanded urgently.*

urinal /juˈraɪnl/ **urinals**
NC A **urinal** is a bowl or trough fixed to the wall of men's public lavatories for men to urinate in. *...the washbasins in a long row on the left hand side of the urinals.*

urinary /ˈjʊərɪnərⁱ/
ADJ ATTRIB **Urinary** means belonging to or related to the parts of a person's body through which urine flows; a formal word. *...a minor urinary complaint.*

urinate /ˈjʊərɪneɪt/ **urinates, urinating, urinated**
V When you **urinate**, you get rid of urine from your body; a formal word. *The substances form in the bladder and make it very painful to urinate.*

urine /ˈjʊərɪn/
NU **Urine** is the liquid that you get rid of from your body when you go to the toilet. *If an athlete has taken a banned substance, the urine will contain a specific chemical.*

urn /ɜːn/ **urns**
1 NC An **urn** is a decorated container that is used to hold the ashes of a person who has been cremated. *An Indian Air Force plane will take another urn to scatter over the Himalayas.*
2 NC A tea **urn** is a container used for making a large quantity of tea and for keeping it warm. *There was a long counter at one end with tea and coffee urns and racks of meat pies.*

Uruguay /ˈjʊərʊgwaɪ/
The **Eastern Republic of Uruguay** is a country in south-eastern South America. It became independent from Spain in 1825. In the late 1960s an urban guerrilla campaign by the Tupamaros led to increasing political suppression and to military control of the government in 1973. Democracy was restored in 1985. Luis Alberto Lacalle Herrera, of the National Party (PN), also called the Blanco Party, became President in 1990. Uruguay is a member of the Organization of American States. It exports textiles, beef and leather, wool, and fish. Tourism is an important industry. High inflation and large foreign debts are serious economic problems. ◆ **Uruguayan** /ˌjʊərʊgwaɪən/ N, ADJ
▪ *per capita GNP:* US$2,620 ▪ *religion:* Christianity (mainly Roman Catholic) ▪ *language:* Spanish ▪ *currency:* new peso ▪ *capital:* Montevideo ▪ *population:* 3 million (1990) ▪ *size:* 176,215 square kilometres.

US /juː ˈes/
N PROP **US** is an abbreviation for 'United States', used only about the United States of America. *...a brief visit to the US. ...the US army.*

us /ʌs, əs/
PRON **Us** is used as the object of a verb or preposition. A speaker or writer uses **us** to refer to a group of people which includes himself or herself. *Why didn't you tell us?... There wasn't room for us all.*

USA /ˌjuːesˈeɪ/
N PROP **USA** is an abbreviation for 'United States of America'. *The USA and Europe are cooperating with that project. ...Stanford University in the USA.*

usable /ˈjuːzəbl/
ADJ If something is **usable**, it is in a condition which makes it possible to use it. *He told me which wells were usable along the road... The runway was still usable and hundreds of flights have been landing there.*

U.S.A.F.
N PROP **U.S.A.F.** is an abbreviation for 'United States Air Force'. *...the USAF base at Bitburg.*

usage /ˈjuːsɪdʒ/ **usages**
1 NU **Usage** is the way in which words are actually used in particular contexts, especially with regard to their meanings. *...a guide to English usage... Students need to be told of differences between British and American usage... Today the word has virtually dropped out of usage.*
2 NC A **usage** is a meaning that a word has or a way in which it can be used. *It lists words in order of their first usage rather than their most familiar contemporary meaning.*
3 NU **Usage** is also the degree to which something is used or the way in which it is used. *...the environmental effects of energy usage... Residents of California's largest city will have to reduce their water usage by 10 percent on March 1st.*

use, uses, used; pronounced /juːz/ when it is a verb and /juːs/ when it is a noun.
1 VO If you **use** a particular thing, you do something with it in order to do a job or to achieve something. *The methods they use are quite simple... Many firms use consultants to recruit people... Wash this garment using a mild detergent.*
2 VO If you **use** a particular word or expression, you say or write it. *It's a phrase I once heard him use in a sermon.*
3 VO If you **use** people, you make them do things for you, without caring about them. *For the first time he felt used.*
4 NU The **use** of something is the act or fact of using it. *...the large-scale use of fertilizers and insecticides. ...a pamphlet for use in schools.*
5 N SING If you have the **use** of something, you have the ability or permission to use it. *He lost the use of his legs... I've got the use of the car this evening.*
6 NCorNU If something has a **use** or if you have a **use** for it, there is a purpose for which it can be used. *He might later have a use for it... Possibly I could find some use for these drawers.*
7 NC+SUPP A **use** of a word is a way of using it so that it has a particular meaning. *He brooded on her use of the word 'important'.*
● **Use** is used in these phrases. ● If you **make use of** something, you do something with it in order to do a job or to achieve something. *Industry is making increasing use of robots.* ● If a device, machine, or technique is **in use**, it is being used regularly by people. If it has gone **out of use**, it is no longer used regularly. *Drugs for this purpose have been in use for some time.* ● If something is **of use**, it is useful. If it is **no use**, it is not at all useful. *He said it was his duty to stay while his presence was of use... I don't know whether any of these things will be any use to you... He argued that dramatic diplomacy is of little use. 'What's needed', he said, 'is patience and understanding'.* ● You say it's **no use** doing something or **what's the use** of doing something as a way of saying that the action is pointless and will not achieve anything. *It is no use arguing with you... There's no use having regrets.*
use up PHRASAL VERB If you **use up** a supply of something, you finish it so that none of it is left. *He used up all the coins he had.*

used; pronounced /juːst/ for the meanings in paragraphs 1 and 2, and /juːzd/ for the meanings in paragraphs 3 and 4.
1 SEMI-MODAL If something **used to** be done or **used to** be the case, it was done regularly in the past or was the case in the past. *They used to send me a card at Christmas time... The situation is much better today than it used to be.*
2 If you **are used to** something, you are familiar with it because you have done or seen it often. If you **get used to** something, you become familiar with it. *San*

Diego was not used to such demonstrations... Sir Geoffrey said he was used to sitting opposite a woman Prime Minister... I've got used to it now, but it was quite daunting at first.
3 ADJ ATTRIB A **used** handkerchief, towel, or glass is dirty because it has been used. *There was a bottle of whisky and a used glass on the coffee table.*
4 ADJ ATTRIB A **used** car is not new but has already had an owner. *...more than three in five used cars being offered for sale.*

useful /juːsfl/
1 ADJ If something is **useful**, you can use it to do something or to help you. *It's a very useful study and points the way for the future. ...this useful bit of safety equipment... It's useful to have an agent who people can contact for technical information.* ◆ **usefulness** NU *...the usefulness of the computer.*
2 ADJ If you are being **useful**, you are doing things that help other people. *Make yourself useful and fry up some bacon.* ◆ **usefully** ADV *His time could be more usefully spent.*
3 If a possession or skill **comes in useful**, you are able to use it on a particular occasion; an informal expression. *This is where the parliamentary majority comes in useful.*

useless /juːsləs/
1 ADJ If something is **useless**, you cannot use it. *Land is useless without labour... Water in a car's brake fluid can make the brakes useless when they get hot.*
2 ADJ If a course of action is **useless**, it does not achieve anything. *I realized it was useless to pursue the subject.*
3 ADJ If someone is **useless** at something, they are no good at it; an informal use. *I was always useless at maths.*

user /juːzə/ **users**
NC+SUPP The **users** of a product, machine, service, or place are the people who use it. *...vehicle users. ...electricity users.*

user-friendly
ADJ **User-friendly** equipment is easy to understand and easy to use. *It's not about making the city more user-friendly for the motorists. ...user-friendly computers.*

usher /ʌʃə/ **ushers, ushering, ushered**
1 VOA If you **usher** someone somewhere, you show them where they should go, often by going with them. *The hostess ushered me into the room... She and her daughter were swiftly ushered out of the courtroom.*
2 NC An **usher** is a person who shows people where to sit, for example at a wedding or concert. *He started out at Carnegie Hall as an usher.*

usher in PHRASAL VERB 1 If someone or something **ushers in** an important change or development, they come before it and often help cause it to happen. *Gorbachev has ushered in a new era of detente. ...a design that experts say will usher in a new age of super-powerful personal computers... In January, they introduced economic reforms that have ushered in a free market.* 2 If you **usher in** a particular period of time or festival, you do something to celebrate it. *A tumultuous drunken celebration ushers in the new decade as fireworks light up the night... Pope John Paul the Second has ushered in Easter by leading a traditional Way of the Cross procession.*

usherette /ʌʃəret/ **usherettes**
NC An **usherette** is a woman who shows people where to sit in a cinema or theatre and who sells refreshments or programmes. *She got a job as an usherette at the Gaumont Cinema in Oxford Street.*

USSR /juːesesɑː/ See **Union of Soviet Socialist Republics**

usu.
Usu. is a written abbreviation for 'usual' or 'usually'.

usual /juːʒuəl/
1 ADJ **Usual** is used to describe what happens or what is done most often in a particular situation. *The capital is settling back into its usual routine... He performed the task with his usual tact and charm... The government's majority was much bigger than usual... The press is concentrating more than usual on international topics.*
2 You use **as usual** to indicate that you are describing something that normally happens or that is normally

the case. *Mr Schultz was, as usual, cautious... The centre of the city was crowded with people as usual.*

usually /juːʒuəli/
1 ADV SEN If something **usually** happens, it is the thing that most often happens in a particular situation. *She usually found it easy to go to sleep at night... There are usually no restrictions.*
2 SUBMOD You use **more than usually** to say that something shows even more of a particular quality than it normally does. *They had shown themselves to be more than usually gullible.*

usurp /juːzɜːp/ **usurps, usurping, usurped**
VO If you **usurp** someone's title or position, you take it from them when you have no right to; a formal word. *They are accused of an alleged attempt to usurp the authority of the state.*

usury /juːʒəri/
NU **Usury** is the practice of lending money at very high interest rates; used showing disapproval. *The party is also calling for an end to the interest rates system, which is regarded as usury under Islamic law.*

utensil /juːtensl/ **utensils**
NC **Utensils** are tools or other objects that you use when you are cooking or doing other tasks in your home; a formal word. *The kitchen had no cooker and no proper cooking utensils.*

uterus /juːtərəs/ **uteruses**
NC A woman's **uterus** is her womb; a medical term. *They normally carry eggs from the ovaries to the uterus. ...cancer of the uterus.*

utilise /juːtɪlaɪz/. See **utilize**.

utilitarian /juːtɪlɪteəriən/; a formal word.
1 ADJ Something that is **utilitarian** is intended to produce benefit for the greatest number of people possible. *This is a reference book and it should be utilitarian, I suppose.*
2 ADJ **Utilitarian** objects and buildings are designed to be useful rather than beautiful. *...a four storey utilitarian building.*

utility /juːtɪləti/ **utilities**
1 NU The **utility** of something is its usefulness. *...the utility and potential of computers.*
2 NC A **utility** is an important service such as water, electricity, or gas that is provided for everyone. *...the development of roads and public utilities in the area.*

utilize /juːtɪlaɪz/ **utilizes, utilizing, utilized**; also spelt **utilise**.
VO If you **utilize** something, you use it; a formal word. *Wildlife resources have not been utilized so that people can benefit... Solar energy is now being utilized to heat water in thousands of city homes.* ◆ **utilization** /juːtɪlaɪzeɪʃn/ NU *...the utilization of things like wind energy and wave-power.*

utmost /ʌtməʊst/
1 ADJ ATTRIB You use **utmost** to emphasize the quality that you are mentioning. *Learning is of the utmost importance... He had the utmost respect for his children.*
2 N SING If something is done to the **utmost**, it is done to the greatest extent possible. *We will do our utmost to help... Its facilities were stretched to the utmost.*

Utopia /juːtəʊpiə/ **Utopias**
NCorNU A **Utopia** is a perfect social system in which everyone is satisfied and happy. *Every so often someone invents a new Utopia. ...visions of Utopia.*

utopian /juːtəʊpiən/
ADJ You use **utopian** to refer to the idea of a perfect social system in which everyone is satisfied and happy. *...this utopian dream.*

utter /ʌtə/ **utters, uttering, uttered**
1 VO When you **utter** sounds or words, you say them. *Sam opened his mouth, then quickly shut it again without uttering a sound.*
2 ADJ ATTRIB You use **utter** to emphasize something such as a quality or state. *To my utter amazement I was made managing director... Judith is a complete and utter fool.* ◆ **utterly** SUBMOD or ADV *I am utterly convinced of your loyalty... She was trying to look like a young lady but failing utterly.*

utterance /ʌtərəns/ **utterances**
NC An **utterance** is something expressed in speech or writing, such as a word or a sentence; a formal word.

The children watched and copied every act and utterance of the older men.

uttermost /ˈʌtəməʊst/

Uttermost means the same as **utmost**; a literary word. *...uttermost hopelessness.*

U-turn /ˈjuːtɜːn/ **U-turns**

1 NC When a vehicle does a **U-turn**, it turns through a half circle and faces or moves in the opposite direction. *Four people died last September when a lorry driver attempted a U-turn on a busy section of the M4.*

2 NC When a government does a **U-turn**, it abandons a policy and does something completely different. *The government is about to do a U-turn over its plans to*

freeze child benefit.

Uzbekistan /ʊzbekɪˈstɑːn/

Uzbekistan became independent of the USSR in 1991. It is located in the south of the former USSR, bordering Afghanistan. Islam Karimov, of the People's Democratic Party of Uzbekistan, became President in 1990. Uzbekistan is the third largest producer of cotton in the world. It also produces wool, silk, and natural gas. In 1991 it joined the Commonwealth of Independent States. ◆ **Uzbek** /ˈʊzbek/ N, ADJ ▪ *per capita GNP:* US$2,750 ▪ *religion:* Islam ▪ *language:* Uzbek ▪ *currency:* rouble ▪ *capital:* Tashkent ▪ *population:* 20 million (1990) ▪ *size:* 447,400 square kilometres.

V v

V, v /viː/ **V's, v's**
1 NC **V** is the twenty-second letter of the English alphabet.
2 PREP **v** is used in writing to say that two people or two teams are competing against each other in a sporting event. **v** is an abbreviation for 'versus'. *...Arsenal v Liverpool.*

vac /væk/ **vacs**; an informal word.
1 NC A **vac** is the same as a **vacation**. *I can work all my vac. ...the Easter vac.*
2 NC A **vac** is also the same as a **vacuum cleaner**. *I'll just get the vac out.*

vacancy /veɪkənsi/ **vacancies**
1 NC A **vacancy** is a job or position which has not been filled. *...an unexpected vacancy in the Department... The unions say there are nearly 200 vacancies.*
2 NC If there are **vacancies** at a hotel or other building, some of the rooms are available for people to stay in or rent. *The hundreds of houseboats are all adorned with vacancy signs... 'Vacancy' signs hang from empty office buildings.*

vacant /veɪkənt/
1 ADJ If something is **vacant**, it is not being used by anyone. *I sat down in a vacant chair... The country has almost no vacant housing left.*
2 ADJ If a job or position is **vacant**, it has not yet been filled. *They keep a list of all vacant jobs in the area... René Jacquot captured the vacant European light-middleweight title last night.*
3 ADJ A **vacant** look suggests that someone does not understand or that they are not very intelligent. *She looked round with a rather vacant expression.* ◆ **vacantly** ADV *She stood idly, gazing vacantly through the bars of the iron grille.*

vacate /vəkeɪt, veɪkeɪt/ **vacates, vacating, vacated**
VO If you **vacate** a place or a job, you leave it and make it available for other people; a formal word. *He ordered her to vacate her apartment... I got the job Allister was vacating.*

vacation /vəkeɪʃn/ **vacations**
1 NC A **vacation** is a period of the year when universities or colleges are officially closed. *I've a lot of reading to do over the vacation. ...the summer vacation.*
2 NCorNU A **vacation** is also the same as a **holiday**; used in American English. *Harold used to take a vacation at that time... She plans to go on vacation for most of August.*

vaccinate /væksɪneɪt/ **vaccinates, vaccinating, vaccinated**
VO If you **are vaccinated** against a disease, you are given a vaccine, usually by injection, to prevent you from getting it. *Most of them were vaccinated against hepatitis... A huge operation is being mounted to vaccinate people against meningitis.* ◆ **vaccination** /væksɪneɪʃn/ **vaccinations** NUorNC *...vaccination against smallpox... Family doctors are being urged to carry out more vaccinations.*

vaccine /væksiːn/ **vaccines**
NCorNU A **vaccine** is a substance containing a harmless form of the germs that cause a disease

which is given to people to prevent them getting the disease. *...a new vaccine that can be given to even younger children... More than sixty-five thousand doses of vaccine had already been sent to the affected areas. ...the measles vaccine.*

vacillate /væsɪleɪt/ **vacillates, vacillating, vacillated**
V If you **vacillate** between two alternatives or choices, you keep changing your mind; a formal word. *He vacillated between periods of creative fever and nervous exhaustion.* ◆ **vacillation** /væsɪleɪʃn/ NU *The authorities have once again reverted to vacillation between attack and retreat. ...uncertainty and vacillation.*

vacuous /vækjuəs/; a formal word.
1 ADJ Something that is **vacuous** does not express any intelligent ideas. *Much abstract sculpture is more vacuous than its realistic counterpart... In practice, these are vacuous terms, and the solutions don't work.*
2 ADJ A **vacuous** expression or look is one that shows no sign of intelligence or understanding. *He has vacuous eyes... The men looked pale and vacuous, and presented a wretched and disgusting sight.*

vacuum /vækjuːm, vækjuəm/ **vacuums, vacuuming, vacuumed**
1 NC A **vacuum** is a space that contains no air or other gas. *The tunnel will be pumped almost entirely free of air to produce a very hard vacuum... A vacuum pump pulls up something like 10,000 gallons of water.*
2 NC If someone or something creates a **vacuum**, they leave a place or position which then needs to be filled by someone or something else. *Rival groups would seek to fill the power vacuum that the departing British would leave... Where once there was a notion of greater public purpose, there is now an intellectual and moral vacuum.*
3 VOorV If you **vacuum** something, you clean it using a vacuum cleaner. *He was supervising the young man who was vacuuming the hallway... Sometimes I clean the house—I vacuum, I help her cook.*

vacuum cleaner, vacuum cleaners
NC A **vacuum cleaner** is an electric machine which sucks up dust and dirt from carpets. *...a vacuum cleaner which will suck up and trap house dust mites... Ordinary vacuum cleaners get clogged with very fine dust.*

vacuum flask, vacuum flasks
NC A **vacuum flask** is a container which is used to keep hot drinks hot and cold drinks cold. A vacuum flask has two thin silvery glass walls with a vacuum between them. *With their next meal they asked for vacuum flasks full of coffee.*

vacuum-packed
ADJ Food that is **vacuum-packed** is packed in a container or packet from which most of the air has been removed, in order to keep the food fresh. *...three tons of vacuum-packed fish.*

Vaduz /vəduːts/
Vaduz is the capital of Liechtenstein and its largest town. Population: 4,200 (1988).

vagabond /vægəbɒnd/ **vagabonds**
NC A **vagabond** is someone who goes about from place

to place and has no real home or job; an old-fashioned word. *The refugees were labelled as 'vagabonds and escaped prisoners'.*

vagary /veɪgəri/ **vagaries**
NC **Vagaries** are unexpected and unpredictable changes in a situation or in someone's behaviour which you have no control over; a formal word. *...open to the vagaries of the weather. ...an astonishing vagary of fashion. ...the perplexing vagaries of politics.*

vagina /vədʒaɪnə/ **vaginas**
NC A woman's **vagina** is the passage connecting her outer sex organs to her womb. *...membranes such as those found in the vagina or anus. ...a weakening of the muscles round the vagina after childbirth.*

vaginal /vədʒaɪnl/
ADJ ATTRIB **Vaginal** means relating to or involving the vagina. *...a vaginal examination.*

vagrancy /veɪgrənsi/
NU **Vagrancy** is a way of life in which someone moves a lot from place to place because they have no permanent home or job, and have to beg or steal in order to live. *Police say the growth of vagrancy in London is largely a social problem.*

vagrant /veɪgrənt/ **vagrants**
NC A **vagrant** is a person who moves from place to place and has no regular home or job. *When he was fourteen he was abandoned by his mother, and found company among street vagrants.*

vague /veɪg/ **vaguer, vaguest**
1 ADJ If something is **vague**, it is not explained, expressed, or experienced clearly. *The terms of the agreement were left deliberately vague. ...vague instructions... I realized with a vague feeling of surprise that he had gone. ...a vague recollection.* ◆ **vaguely** ADV *I vaguely remember their house.*
2 ADJ PRED If you are **vague** about something, you avoid telling people about it, often deliberately. *They were vague and evasive about their backgrounds... Asked about allegations of supplying explosives to the IRA, the Ambassador remained vague.*
3 ADJ A **vague** shape or sound is not clear or easy to perceive. *It appeared in vague form at first and then in sharper outline... The gurgling and splashing sounds began again, vague and muffled... He discerned the large, vague figure in the distance.*

vain /veɪn/
1 If you do something **in vain**, you do not succeed in achieving what you intend. *We tried in vain to discover what had happened... Your son didn't die in vain.*
2 ADJ ATTRIB A **vain** attempt or action is not successful. *...the teacher's vain plea for silence... To all commentators it seems a vain hope.* ◆ **vainly** ADV *She vainly attempted to open the door.*
3 ADJ A **vain** person thinks a lot about their beauty, intelligence, or other good qualities and is extremely proud of them; used showing disapproval. *...a vain young aristocrat.*

vainglorious /veɪnglɔːriəs/
ADJ ATTRIB If you describe someone's behaviour as **vainglorious**, you mean that it is very boastful or proud, and that you find it ridiculous; a literary word. *...a vainglorious, strutting street-fighter. ...vainglorious posturing.*

valance /væləns/ **valances**; also spelt **valence**.
NC A **valance** is a decorative cover for the bottom part of a bed with a frill which hangs around the edge of the bed. *The mattress was concealed by the valance and its fringe.*

vale /veɪl/ **vales**
NC A **vale** is the same as a **valley**; a literary word. *Berkley Castle guards a rich, lush, vale of meadows and blossoms.*

valediction /vælɪdɪkʃn/ **valedictions**
NC A **valediction** is a speech made in order to say goodbye to someone, especially as part of a farewell ceremony; a formal word. *...an address that was not so much a summing up as a valediction.*

valedictorian /vælɪdɪktɔːriən/ **valedictorians**
NC In the United States, the **valedictorian** of a particular class or year-group at a school or college is

the student who graduates with the highest marks and who makes a speech at their graduation ceremony. *Anne Eisenstein was my high school class valedictorian... Thomas Algood and Jonathan Henderson were both named valedictorians of the class of 1991 at the Newton County High School.*

valedictory /vælɪdɪktəʳri/
ADJ ATTRIB A **valedictory** speech or letter is one in which you say goodbye to someone; a formal word. *Sir Robert's speech represents something of a valedictory message. ...the valedictory formulas for departing Politburo members.*

valence /veɪləns/ **valences**
1 NU **Valence** is the ability of atoms and chemical groups to form compounds; a technical term in chemistry.
2 NU **Valence** is the same as **valency**; used in American English.
3 See also **valance**.

valency /veɪlənsi/ **valencies**
NC The **valency** of an atom or chemical group is the number of atoms of hydrogen that it is able to combine with in forming compounds; a technical term in chemistry. *...a metal of higher valency such as germanium.*

valentine /væləntaɪn/ **valentines**
NC A **valentine** or a **valentine card** is a card that you send to someone you love on St Valentine's Day. *Most plumped for valentine cards with a bunch of flowers. ...a valentine from a male to a female telegraph operator.*

valet /væleɪ, vælɪt/ **valets, valeting, valeted**
1 NC A **valet** is a male servant who looks after his male employer by doing things such as caring for his clothes. *...various members of their entourage, including a priest, two personal bodyguards and a valet.*
2 VO If your car is **valeted**, the bodywork and fittings are cleaned and repaired, but no mechanical work is done.

valiant /væliənt/
ADJ ATTRIB A **valiant** action is very brave and determined, though it may lead to failure or defeat. *...a valiant attempt to rescue the struggling victim... Mr King said the IRA would be defeated by the valiant efforts of the security forces. ...the valiant struggle to rid the country of foreign occupation.*

valid /vælɪd/
1 ADJ Something that is **valid** is based on sound reasoning. *This is a valid argument against economic growth... This was the real reason, and it was a valid reason.* ◆ **validity** /vəlɪdəti/ NU *We should question the validity of those figures... The Financial Times says this argument has lost some of its validity.*
2 ADJ If a ticket or document is **valid**, it can be used and will be accepted by people in authority. *It's valid for six months from the date of issue.*
3 ADJ If something you do or say is **valid**, it is important enough or serious enough to make it worth saying or doing. *It was probably a more valid protest than picketing missile bases... Do you find his interpretation of Chopin entirely valid?*

validate /vælɪdeɪt/ **validates, validating, validated**
VO If something **validates** a statement or claim, it proves that it is true or correct. *Their remarkable achievement seems to validate Bomberg's claim... They are unlikely to believe the findings of the trials unless they are independently validated.*

valise /vəliːz/ **valises**
NC A **valise** is a small suitcase; an old-fashioned word. *I retrieved the black valise from the closet.*

Valium /væliəm/
NU **Valium** is a drug which is given to people to calm their nerves; **Valium** is a trademark. *One or two drugs might help such as sedatives, Valium or hormone treatments. ...hypnotics and relaxants such as Valium, Mogadon and Mandrax.*

Valletta /vəletə/
Valletta is the capital of Malta and its fourth largest town. Population: 9,200 (1988).

valley /væli/ **valleys**
NC A **valley** is a long, narrow area of land between

hills, often with a river flowing through it. *The valley, in the foothills of the Andes, is the world's largest single source of coca leaf. ...the flat land at the bottom of a valley... There was a fresh warning last night of more flooding along the Severn valley.*

valour /vælə/; spelt **valor** in American English.
NU **Valour** is great bravery, especially in battle; a literary word. *...an act of epic valour... In the past he was admired for the valour and verve with which he led the Pathans in the struggle for freedom.*

valuable /væljəbl, væljuəbl/ **valuables**
1 ADJ **Valuable** help or advice is very useful and can help someone a great deal. *They could also give valuable help. ...the valuable contribution of ambulancemen to patient care.*
2 ADJ **Valuable** objects such as paintings or jewellery are worth a lot of money. *She collected vintage cars and built up a valuable stamp collection.* ▶ Also N PL *They were robbed of money and valuables at gunpoint.*

valuation /væljueɪʃn/ **valuations**
1 NCorNU A **valuation** is a judgement about how much money something is worth. *The land's valuation was £6,000... The valuation of the pound has always been a subject of much discussion... She asked for a valuation on her house.*
2 NCorNU A **valuation** is also a judgement about how good or bad something is. *...his rather low valuation of the novel... This technique lends itself to scientific valuation.*

value /vælju/ **values, valuing, valued**
1 NU The **value** of something such as a quality or a method is its importance or usefulness. *Everyone realizes the value of sincerity.*
2 NUorNC The **value** of something you can own is the amount of money that it is worth. *Farmers are all the time being encouraged to diversify and add value to their present products... What will happen to the value of my property?*
3 N PL The **values** of a person or group are their moral principles and beliefs. *...the traditional values of civility and moderation... They have different values from the families they serve.*
4 VO If you **value** something, you think that it is important and you appreciate it. *Which do you value most—wealth or health?... For more than a century, France has valued women's fashion as a central part of its culture and economy.* ◆ **valued** ADJ *...one of our valued customers... The people of Oklahoma City have made graffiti a valued tradition.*
5 VO When experts **value** something, they decide how much money it is worth. *The table silver was valued at £20,000... The insurance company later hired a Miami appraiser who valued the property even higher... Any work valued at more than 20,000 dollars has to have an export licence.*
6 NU **Value** is used after another noun to say that something has a particular kind of importance or usefulness. For example, if something has propaganda **value**, it is useful as propaganda. *It should have novelty value, if nothing else... The fort has no strategic value, but is seen as a symbol of Sri Lankan sovereignty in Jaffna.*
● **Value** is used in these phrases. ● Something that is **good value** or **value for money** is worth the money it costs. *The set lunch is good value at £5.95... The Council could then assess which departments offered the best value for money, and allocate funds accordingly.* ● Something that is **of value** is useful or important. *Nothing of value can be said about this matter... Medical research has thrown up little of value for the treatment of this painful and depressing condition.* ● If you put **a high value** on something, you think that it is very important. *He places a high value on educating his children.* ● If you **take** a remark or action **at face value**, you accept it without thinking what its real meaning or purpose might be. *She took the praise at face value... The President could make up lost ground by taking the agreement between the two sides at face value... The claim by the government that the plant is used merely for training can hardly be taken at face value.*

value-added tax
Value-added tax is the same as **VAT**. *...the introduction of a value-added tax.*

value judgement, value judgements
NC A **value judgement** is an opinion about something that is based on a particular person's principles and beliefs and not on facts which can be checked or proved; used showing disapproval. *It is difficult to answer that question without making a value judgement. ...an argument based on value judgements... The fact that this disease was first identified among male homosexuals immediately cast a certain set of value judgements on it.*

valueless /væljuləs/
ADJ Something that is **valueless** is not effective, useful, or worth anything. *...involvement in valueless activities. ...the government's sudden decision to declare half the banknotes in the country valueless... Criticism was voiced that this would make the procedure valueless.*

valuer /væljuə/ **valuers**
NC A **valuer** is someone whose job is to decide how much money things are worth. *...the total worth of the industry, as estimated by the professional valuers commissioned by the government.*

valve /vælv/ **valves**
1 NC A **valve** is a part attached to a pipe or a tube which controls the flow of a gas or liquid. *...a radiator valve.*
2 NC A **valve** is also a small flap in your heart or in a vein, which controls the flow of blood and keeps it flowing in one direction only. *...a type of birth defect affecting the valves of the heart.*
3 See also **safety-valve**.

vampire /væmpaɪə/ **vampires**
NC In horror stories, **vampires** are people who come out of their graves at night and suck the blood of living people. *...old monster movies with werewolves and vampires coming out of the fog. ...the legendary home of Count Dracula and blood-sucking vampires.*

van /væn/ **vans**
NC A **van** is a vehicle like a large car or small lorry that is used for carrying goods. *A van standing outside was demolished and two cars badly damaged... Others are forced to make their living as delivery van drivers.*

vandal /vændl/ **vandals**
NC A **vandal** is someone who deliberately damages things, especially public property. *The phone box is attacked by vandals from time to time... We try to make it as vandal resistant as possible.*

vandalise /vændəlaɪz/. See **vandalize**.

vandalism /vændəlɪzəm/
NU **Vandalism** is the deliberate damaging of things, especially public property. *These housing estates suffer from widespread vandalism. ...unspecified acts of disorder and vandalism... Charles Slater described the decision to close the shipyards as 'an act of economic vandalism'.*

vandalize /vændəlaɪz/ **vandalizes, vandalizing, vandalized;** also spelt **vandalise.**
VO If someone **vandalizes** something, they damage it on purpose. *All our telephones were vandalized. ...youths going on the rampage, smashing windows and vandalizing cars.*

vane /veɪn/ **vanes**
NC A **vane** is a flat blade, for example on a propeller, which is part of the mechanism for using the energy of wind or water to drive a machine. *Until the 1960s, most centrifugal impellers were made of aluminium alloy, and had straight radial vanes.* ● See also **weather-vane.**

vanguard /vænɡɑːd/
N SING If someone is in the **vanguard** of something such as a revolution or an area of research, they are involved in the most advanced part of it. *They are in the vanguard of technological advance... That's where community radio might be in the vanguard of broadcasting... He called on the party to return to the role of political vanguard.*

vanilla /vənɪlə/
NU **Vanilla** is a flavouring used in ice cream and other

sweet food. ...*a double vanilla ice-cream with hot fudge. ...vanilla custard.*

vanish /vænɪʃ/ **vanishes, vanishing, vanished**
v If something **vanishes**, it disappears suddenly or ceases to exist altogether. *The car had vanished from sight... Madeleine vanished without trace. ...laws to protect vanishing American species.*

vanity /vænəti/
NU **Vanity** is a feeling of pride about your appearance or abilities; used showing disapproval. *He refused to wear glasses. It was sheer vanity.*

vanquish /væŋkwɪʃ/ **vanquishes, vanquishing, vanquished**
vO If you **are vanquished**, you are defeated completely in a battle or a competition; a literary word. *All their enemies were vanquished. ...the sort of thing that only a conqueror could do to a vanquished nation.*

vantage point /vɑːntɪdʒ pɔɪnt/ **vantage points**
NC A **vantage point** is a place from which you can see a lot of things. *From the vantage point on the hill, Port Philip shimmered beneath them... Scores of small boats jostled in the harbour for the best vantage point.*

Vanuatu /vænuːɑːtuː/
The **Republic of Vanuatu** is a country in the Pacific. It consists of 80 islands, including:Efaté, Espiritu Santo, Malekula, and Tanna. Known as the New Hebrides, they were jointly ruled by France and Britain from 1887 until independence in 1980. The Vanua'aku Party (VP) became the ruling party in 1980. Fred Timakata became President in 1989 and Maxime Carlot became Prime Minister in 1991. Vanuatu is a member of the Commonwealth. It exports copra, fish, and cocoa. Tourism is an important industry. ◆ **Vanuatuan** /vænuːɑːtuːən/ N, ADJ
▪ *per capita GNP:* US$820 ▪ *religion:* Christianity, animism ▪ *language:* Bislama, English, and French (all official) ▪ *currency:* vatu ▪ *capital:* Port Vila ▪ *population:* 143,000 (1989) ▪ *size:* 12,190 square kilometres.

vapid /væpɪd/
ADJ Something that is **vapid** is dull and uninteresting because it contains nothing stimulating or challenging; a formal word. *Their publications were vapid and amateurish... I'm not willing to waste two days arguing with a bunch of vapid schoolgirls.* ◆ **vapidity** /væpɪdəti/ NU *Her eyes rose to meet mine with a kind of adoring vapidity.*

vapor /veɪpə/. See **vapour.**

vaporize /veɪpəraɪz/ **vaporizes, vaporizing, vaporized**; also spelt **vaporise.**
V-ERG If a liquid or solid **vaporizes** or you **vaporize** it, it changes into vapour or gas. *...a fluid that vaporizes at a much lower temperature than water... These iron particles travel so fast they will vaporize or destroy targets a thousand times bigger than themselves.* ◆ **vaporization** /veɪpəraɪzeɪʃn/ NU *Vaporization occurs at body temperature.*

vapour /veɪpə/; spelt **vapor** in American English.
NU **Vapour** is a mass of tiny drops of water or other liquids in the air, which appear as a mist. *...water vapour. ...a little cloud of exhaust vapour.*

vapour trail, vapour trails
NC A **vapour trail** is a white trail of water vapour left in the sky, for example by a high-flying aeroplane. *An army helicopter pilot reported hearing a whooshing noise and seeing a vapour trail but no trace of the weapon.*

variability /veərɪəbɪləti/
NU The **variability** of something is the range of different forms that it can take. *...the enormous variability you get in speech sounds... We have to preserve as much genetic variability within a species as is possible.*

variable /veərɪəbl/ **variables**
1 ADJ Something that is **variable** changes quite often, and there usually seems to be no fixed pattern to these changes. *In the tropics, rainfall is notoriously variable... Sometimes I don't smoke at all, it's very variable. ...a variable price clause.*
2 NC A **variable** is a factor in a situation that can change. *How long your shoes will last depends on a lot of variables, such as how much you weigh, how far*

you walk, and so on... *The mean age of consumption and the mean age of income are the variables that are going to determine economic growth.*
3 NC In mathematics, a **variable** is an expression that can have any one of a set of values; a technical term. *...a technique that puts all the variables in simultaneously, whether it's by factor analysis or multiple regression.*

variance /veərɪəns/
If one thing is **at variance** with another, the two things seem to contradict each other; a formal expression. *Nothing in the story was at variance with what he understood to be true... Vasetskii argues that the politics of Trotsky were at variance with those of Lenin.*

variant /veərɪənt/ **variants**
NC A **variant** of something has a different form from the usual one. *This American bird is a variant of the English buzzard... The British variant, which is being built at Sizewell, is designed to meet demanding safety standards.* ▶ Also ADJ ATTRIB *...a variant form of the basic action.*

variation /veərɪeɪʃn/ **variations**
1 NC A **variation** on something is the same thing presented in a slightly different form. *...the same programme with only nightly variations... His books are all variations on a basic theme.*
2 NCorNU A **variation** is also a change or slight difference in a level, amount, or quantity. *The Boards have learned how to cope with a large variation in demand for electricity... Plants were observed for variation in flowering dates.*

varicose veins /værɪkəʊs veɪnz/
N PL **Varicose veins** are swollen and painful veins in a person's legs which sometimes need to be operated on. *...straightforward operations like hip replacements and varicose veins.*

varied /veərɪd/
1 **Varied** is the past tense and past participle of **vary.**
2 ADJ Something that is **varied** consists of things of different types, sizes, or qualities. *The work of a JP is very varied. ...a richer and more varied lifestyle.*

variegated /veərɪəgeɪtɪd/
ADJ A **variegated** plant or leaf has different coloured markings on it. *...a variegated holly.*

variety /vəraɪəti/ **varieties**
1 NU If something has **variety**, it consists of things which are different from each other. *Those are the holiday brochures that give you the most variety... It's a poem wonderfully rich in variety—sentimental, vulgar, comic, and philosophical.*
2 N SING A **variety** of things is a group of different kinds or examples of the same thing. *The college library had a wide variety of books... He served in a variety of Labour governments.*
3 NC A **variety** of something is a type of it. *...three varieties of whisky... It takes between ten and fifteen years to produce a new crop variety.*
4 NU **Variety** is a type of entertainment including many different kinds of acts in the same show. *...a high-quality variety show.*

various /veərɪəs/
1 ADJ ATTRIB If you say that there are **various** things, you mean there are several different things of the type mentioned. *There were various questions he wanted to ask. ...various bits of information... The birth had been delayed for various reasons.*
2 ADJ PRED If a number of things are described as **various**, they are very different from one another. *His excuses are many and various.*

variously /veərɪəsli/
ADV **Variously** is used to introduce a number of different ways in which something is described. *He married a Japanese lady who was variously described as a painter and a film maker.*

varnish /vɑːnɪʃ/ **varnishes, varnishing, varnished**
1 N MASS **Varnish** is an oily liquid which is painted onto wood to give it a hard, clear, shiny surface. *You want to put something on the wood to stop the varnish soaking into it.*
2 N SING The **varnish** on an object is the hard, clear, shiny surface that it has when it has been painted with

varnish. *The varnish was slightly chipped.*
3 VO If you **varnish** something, you paint it with
varnish. *He has varnished the table.*

vary /vɛəri/ **varies, varying, varied**
1 V If things **vary**, they change or are different in
size, amount, or degree. *The fees vary a lot... The
screens will vary in size depending upon what one
wants... The colour of the fruit varies with age...
Reactions to the bombing varied throughout the world.*
♦ **varying** ADJ ATTRIB *Its members have widely
varying views on foreign policy... The strike appeared
to have won varying degrees of support around the
country.*
2 VO If you **vary** something that you do, you keep
changing the way that you do it. *He took special care
to vary his daily routine.*
3 See also **varied**.

vascular /væskjʊlə/
ADJ ATTRIB **Vascular** is used to describe the channels,
veins, and so on through which fluids pass in the
bodies of animals and plants; a technical term in
biology. *...a stem with separate vascular bundles.*

vase /vɑːz/ **vases**
NC A **vase** is a jar, usually made of glass or pottery,
which is used for holding cut or dried flowers or as an
ornament. *...a crystal vase... She had to put the vase
of flowers down.*

vasectomy /vəsɛktəmi/ **vasectomies**
NCorNU A **vasectomy** is a surgical operation in which
the tube that carries sperm to a man's penis is cut in
order to sterilize him. *11% of men have had a
vasectomy... There's now a new kind of vasectomy
that sounds less worrying.*

Vaseline /væsəliːn/
NU **Vaseline** is a soft, clear jelly made from
petroleum, which is used as an ointment or as grease;
Vaseline is a trademark. *The car windscreen was
covered in Vaseline by a prankster.*

vassal /væsl/ **vassals**
1 NC In feudal society, a **vassal** was a man who was
protected by a lord, to whom he gave military service
and from whom he received lands to live on. *The
nobles became the vassals of the French king. ...the
relationship between lord and vassal.*
2 ADJ ATTRIB A **vassal** country or nation is one which
is dominated by another country or nation.
*Throughout history, it has had periods of unified rule,
but has more commonly survived as a vassal state...
The southern region was once a vassal state of
Thailand.*

Vassiliou, Georgios /jɔːjɒs væsɪliu:/
Georgios Vassiliou, an independent, became President
of Cyprus in 1988. Born: 1931.

vast /vɑːst/
ADJ Something that is **vast** is extremely large. *...a
vast organization. ...the roads that they're building at
vast expense... The territory in dispute between China
and India is vast.*

vastly /vɑːstli/
SUBMOD **Vastly** means very much or to a very large
extent. *Management of the factory could be vastly
improved.*

vat /væt/ **vats**
NC A **vat** is a large barrel or tank for storing liquids.
...a vat of water.

VAT /viːeɪtiː, væt/
NU **VAT** is a tax that is added to the price of goods or
services. **VAT** is an abbreviation for 'value added
tax'. *...discrepancies between VAT and the excise rate
in the community. ...exemption from VAT.*

Vatican City /vætɪkən sɪti/
The **State of the Vatican City**, also called the Holy See,
is the smallest state in the world, lying within the city
of Rome. It is the seat of the Papacy. The Papacy's
sovereignty over the Vatican was recognized by Italy
in the Lateran Treaty of 1929. Cardinal Karol Wojtyla
became Pope John Paul II in 1978.
▪ *religion:* Christianity (Roman Catholic) ▪ *language:*
Italian and Latin (official) ▪ *currency:* Italian lira
▪ *population:* 1000 (1985) ▪ *size:* 0.44 square kilometres.

vault /vɔːlt/ **vaults, vaulting, vaulted**
1 NC A **vault** is a secure room where money and other
valuable things can be kept safely. *The money was
deposited in the vaults of a firm of solicitors.*
2 NC The **vault** of a church or cemetery is the place
where people are buried. *A private ceremony took
place at the family vault this morning.*
3 NC A **vault** is also an arched roof or ceiling. *...the
vaults of a colonnaded temple.*
4 VOorVA If you **vault** something or **vault** over it, you
jump over it, putting one or both of your hands on it.
*One of Mrs Townsend's customers vaulted the back
fence and landed in the piggery... They vaulted
effortlessly over the wall.*

vaulted /vɔːltɪd/
ADJ A **vaulted** roof or ceiling, for example in a church,
is made of several arches joined together at the top.
*...a grid of cast iron columns and vaulted ceilings.
...adorned from flagstone floor to soaring vaulted roof
with magnificent coloured windows.*

vaunt /vɔːnt/ **vaunts, vaunting, vaunted**
VO If you **vaunt** something, you describe, praise, or
display your success or possessions in a boastful and
pompous way; a formal word. *They vaunt their
approach to life as if it were something unique.*
♦ **vaunted** ADJ ATTRIB *...a new and much vaunted
national cinema.*

VCR /viːsiːɑː/ **VCRs**
NC A **VCR** is a machine that can be used to record
television programmes or films onto video tapes, so
that people can play them back and watch them later
on a television set. **VCR** is an abbreviation for 'video
cassette recorder'. *...complete with a new colour TV
and a VCR... Over 70 percent of US households now
have a VCR.*

VD /viːdiː/
VD is an abbreviation for 'venereal disease'. *South
Korean prostitutes carry identity cards and have to
have weekly VD tests.*

VDU /viːdiːjuː/ **VDUs**
NC A **VDU** is a machine with a screen which is used
to display information from a computer. **VDU** is an
abbreviation for 'visual display unit'. *...VDU
operators and other keyboard workers.*

-'ve /-v/
SUFFIX **-'ve** is a short form of 'have', especially when
'have' is an auxiliary verb. It is used in spoken
English and informal written English. *I haven't seen
your mother since I've been back... I'd like to think
that Thorburn approves of what we've done for him.*

veal /viːl/
NU **Veal** is meat from a calf. *There was lobster and
veal on the menu.*

vector /vɛktə/ **vectors**; a technical term.
1 NC A **vector** is a variable quantity, such as force,
that has magnitude and direction. *...the nine possible
vectors of social action between an agent and a
respondent.*
2 NC A **vector** is also an animal or plant that carries a
disease-causing parasite from one place to another.
*They were left with trying to control the vector using
insecticides. ...the mosquito vectors for malaria.
...vector-borne diseases.*
3 NC You can also refer to the course or compass
direction that an aeroplane is following as a **vector**.
*...the vector triangles you have to draw up to make
sure that you point in the right direction.*

veer /vɪə/ **veers, veering, veered**
VA If something that is moving **veers** in a particular
direction, it suddenly starts moving in that direction.
*He veered away from a tree... The plane seemed to
veer off to one side... The wind was still veering in a
northerly direction.*

veg /vɛdʒ/
N PL **Veg** are the same as **vegetables**; an informal
word. *He sells fruit and veg... Every night there was
meat and two veg.*

vegan /viːgən/ **vegans**
NC A **vegan** is someone who does not eat meat or fish,
or anything that is produced from an animal, such as
cheese, butter, or milk. *Patients are advised to follow
a diet designed to make them feel better—basically a
wholefood vegan diet.*

vegetable /vɛdʒɪtəbl/ **vegetables**
1 NC **Vegetables** are plants such as cabbages, potatoes, and onions which you can cook and eat. *They have a much bigger intake of fruit and vegetables.*
2 NU **Vegetable** is used to refer to plants in general. *Pollution affects everything on the planet, animal, vegetable, or mineral. ...vegetable matter.*
3 NC A **vegetable** is someone whose brain has been damaged and who is unable to move or think. *He has been left a wheelchair-ridden vegetable after a cerebral accident... Nancy always said she didn't want to live as a vegetable.*

vegetarian /vɛdʒɪtɛərɪən/ **vegetarians**
NC A **vegetarian** is someone who does not eat meat or fish. *...a strict vegetarian... About 4 million people in Britain are vegetarians... There's a lot of variety in a vegetarian diet.*

vegetarianism /vɛdʒɪtɛərɪənɪzəm/
NU If you practise **vegetarianism**, you do not eat meat or fish. *My friends were talking about vegetarianism... That's why so many people are turning to vegetarianism.*

vegetate /vɛdʒɪteɪt/ **vegetates, vegetating, vegetated**
V If you **vegetate**, you have a very boring life with little to interest you. *Many elderly folk vegetate and die in loneliness.*

vegetation /vɛdʒɪteɪʃn/
NU **Vegetation** is plant life in general. *The forest floor is not rich in vegetation.*

vegetative /vɛdʒətətɪv/
1 ADJ **Vegetative** means relating to or involving plant life and growth. *Many places have lost their vegetative cover and forests... The vegetative material can be used for animal forage.*
2 ADJ You can say that someone is in a **vegetative** state when their brain has been damaged and they are unable to move or think. *The woman, who is brain-damaged, has been in a persistent vegetative state since 1987. ...permanent comas or vegetative states.*

vehemence /viːəməns/
NU **Vehemence** is intense and violent emotion, especially anger. *...the hate and vehemence in Hubert's eyes.*

vehement /viːəmənt/
ADJ Someone who is **vehement** has strong feelings or opinions and expresses them forcefully. *They are vehement in their praises of the new system... His speech was a tour de force—informal, vehement, laced with humorous asides... The government issued a fresh and vehement denial of the allegations.* ◆ **vehemently** ADV *They were arguing vehemently... The Cuban leader also vehemently denied charges made in the US Senate.*

vehicle /viːɪkl/ **vehicles**
1 NC A **vehicle** is a machine with an engine such as a car or bus that carries people or things from place to place. *We saw a vehicle travelling across the bridge.*
2 NC A **vehicle** is also something that is used to achieve a particular purpose; a formal use. *They saw education as a vehicle of liberation... They support the Labour Party as a vehicle for socialism.*

vehicular /vɪhɪkjʊlə/
ADJ ATTRIB **Vehicular** is used to describe something which relates to vehicles and traffic; a formal word. *Most of the roads were still impassable to vehicular movement.*

Veiga, Carlos /kɑːləʊs veɪgə/
Carlos Veiga became Prime Minister of Cape Verde in 1991. He was elected Chairman of the Movement for Democracy (MPD) in 1990. Born: 1949.

veil /veɪl/ **veils**
1 NC A **veil** is a piece of thin, soft cloth that women sometimes wear over their heads. *...close-up pictures of Princess Diana in a black hat and veil.*
2 N SING+*of* You can refer to something that conceals something else as a **veil**; a literary use. *Everything was wrapped in a veil of evening light... The research centre shrouded its communications with every possible veil of secrecy.*
3 If you **draw a veil** over something, you stop talking about it because it is too unpleasant or embarrassing

to talk about. *Let us draw a veil over the rest of the episode.*

veiled /veɪld/
ADJ ATTRIB A **veiled** comment is expressed in a disguised form rather than directly and openly *...thinly veiled criticism. ...veiled threats.*

vein /veɪn/ **veins**
1 NC Your **veins** are the tubes in your body through which your blood flows. *She then pushed a button causing a lethal dose of drugs to flow into her veins.* ● See also **varicose veins.**
2 NC The **veins** on a leaf are the thin lines on it.
3 NC+SUPP A **vein** of a metal or mineral is a layer of it in rock. *...the world's richest vein of copper.*
4 NU+SUPP Something that is written or spoken in a particular **vein** is written or spoken in that style or mood. *The letter continued in this vein for several pages... John Gielgud can be heard in a much lighter vein on Radio Four.*

veined /veɪnd/
ADJ **Veined** skin has a lot of veins showing on it. *...his veined nervous hand.*

vellum /vɛləm/
1 NU **Vellum** is fine parchment made from the skin of calves, lambs, or kids, which is used, for example to bind books or make lampshades, and was formerly used for writing on. *The map, which dates from about 1290, is on a huge single sheet of vellum and contains over 500 different pictures.*
2 NU **Vellum** also refers to strong, good quality paper for writing on. *The really expensive versions are printed on vellum.*

velocity /vəlɒsəti/ **velocities**
NU or NC **Velocity** is the speed at which something moves in a particular direction; a technical term. *...forcing it down the barrel at high velocity. ...the velocity of light.*

velour /vəlʊə/
NU **Velour** is a silk or cotton cloth similar to velvet. *...the plush velour interior of his new car.*

velvet /vɛlvɪt/
NU **Velvet** is soft material with a thick layer of short, cut threads on one side. *...a sumptuous gown of purple velvet. ...velvet curtains.*

velvety /vɛlvɪti/
ADJ Something that is **velvety** is soft to touch and has the appearance of velvet. *The spider has a velvety black body... I rubbed the velvety grooves inside the calf's ears.*

venal /viːnl/
ADJ Someone who is **venal** is prepared to do almost anything in return for money, even things which are dishonest or immoral. *Authoritarian rulers are typically venal and capricious... His impression of the General was that he was a venal man, involved in a lot of shady undertakings.*

vendetta /vɛndɛtə/ **vendettas**
NC A **vendetta** is a long-lasting, bitter quarrel between people in which they attempt to harm each other. *He conducted a vendetta against Haldane behind the scenes... I think you should realise that this is part of a vendetta against me.*

vending machine /vɛndɪŋ məʃiːn/ **vending machines**
NC A **vending machine** is a machine from which you can get things such as cigarettes, chocolate, or coffee by putting in money and pressing a button. *...a sort of scaled down vending machine.*

vendor /vɛndə/ **vendors**
1 NC A **vendor** is someone who sells things such as newspapers, cigarettes, or hamburgers from a small stall or cart. *...cigarette vendors.*
2 NC The **vendor** of a house or piece of land is the person who owns it and is selling it; a legal term. *The vendors should be under a legal duty to provide a detailed account of the condition of their house.*

veneer /vənɪə/
1 N SING Behaviour that hides someone's real feelings or character is called a **veneer.** *He hides his values beneath a veneer of scientific objectivity.*
2 NU **Veneer** is a thin layer of wood or plastic which is used to improve the appearance of something. *...a table whose veneer had come loose.*

venerable /ˈvenərəbl/
ADJ **Venerable** people are people who are entitled to respect because they are old and wise; a formal word. ...*the venerable head of the house.*

venerate /ˈvenəreɪt/ **venerates, venerating, venerated**
VO If you **venerate** someone or something, you value them or feel great respect for them; a formal word. *Lincoln was a lawyer and I always venerated him... Over the centuries, it has been venerated as the shroud in which Christ was lain to rest after the Crucifixion.* ◆ **veneration** /ˌvenəˈreɪʃn/ NU *The composer George Gershwin is no less worthy of the veneration accorded his classical counterparts... This statue is an object of religious veneration.*

venereal disease /vənˈɪəriəl dɪˈziːz/ **venereal diseases**
N Cor NU A **venereal disease** is a disease that is passed on by having sexual intercourse. *They have to have regular checks to see they are not infected with a venereal disease. ...the spread of prostitution and venereal disease.*

Venetiaan, Ronald /ˈraʊnəlt ˈveɪnetsjaːn/
Ronald Venetiaan was elected President of Suriname in 1991. He was Minister for Education from 1988 to 1990. He is a member of the Suriname National Party (NPS), which is part of the coalition, New Front for Democracy and Development (NF). Born: 1937.

Venetian blind /vənˈiːʃn blaɪnd/ **Venetian blinds**
NC A **Venetian blind** is a window blind made of thin horizontal strips which can be adjusted to let in more or less light. *The windows were shrouded in Venetian blinds.*

Venezuela /ˌvenəˈzweɪlə/
The Republic of Venezuela is a country in northern South America. It was a Spanish colony from the 15th century until 1830. In the 1920s oil was discovered and in 1985 Venezuela ranked as the eighth largest oil producer in the world. It is a member of OPEC and the Organization of American States. It also exports aluminium, and iron and steel. Cannabis and cocaine are illegally exported. Carlos Andrés Pérez Rodriguez, of the Democratic Action Party (AD), became President in 1989. High inflation and large foreign debts are major economic problems. ◆ **Venezuelan** /ˌvenəˈzweɪlən/ N, ADJ
▪ *per capita GNP:* US$3,170 ▪ *religion:* Christianity (mainly Roman Catholic) ▪ *language:* Spanish ▪ *currency:* bolívar ▪ *capital:* Caracas ▪ *population:* 19 million (1989) ▪ *size:* 912,050 square kilometres.

vengeance /ˈvendʒəns/
1 NU **Vengeance** is the act of killing, injuring, or harming someone because they have harmed you. *I want vengeance for the deaths of my parents and sisters.*
2 If something happens **with a vengeance**, it happens to a much greater extent than was expected. *He now broke the rules with a vengeance.*

vengeful /ˈvendʒfl/
ADJ A **vengeful** person feels a great desire for revenge; a literary word. *None of them turned out to be quite so vengeful and bloodthirsty as Stalin himself.*

venial /ˈviːniəl/
ADJ **Venial** is used to describe sin or wrongdoing that is not very serious and can therefore easily be forgiven or excused; a formal word. *'Women are subject to two defects, curiosity and vanity.'—'Venial sins,' said the monk.*

venison /ˈvenɪzn/
NU **Venison** is meat from a deer. *Some senior ministers are entitled to a hunk of venison from the Queen's deer herds.*

Venkataraman, Ramaswami /ˈrɑːməswɔːmi venˈkɑːtərɑːmən/
Ramaswami Venkataraman became President of India in 1987. He was a member of the Lok Sabha (lower house Parliament) from 1952 to 1957, and from 1977 to 1984. He was Minister of Finance and Industry from 1980 to 1982, and of Defence from 1982 to 1984. He was Vice President of India from 1984 to 1987. Born: 1910.

venom /ˈvenəm/
1 NU **Venom** is a feeling of great bitterness or anger towards someone. *'What a filthy trick,' she said with*
unexpected venom.
2 NU The **venom** of a snake, scorpion, or spider is the poison that it injects into you when it bites or stings you. *The only specific remedy for snake venom is the anti-venom.*

venomous /ˈvenəməs/
1 ADJ A **venomous** snake, scorpion, or spider uses poison to attack its enemy or prey. ...*a handful of venomous Gabon vipers.*
2 ADJ **Venomous** behaviour shows great bitterness or anger. ...*venomous glances... The Head of State cannot give way to calumnies, venomous demonstrations, and generalised condemnations.*

vent /vent/ **vents, venting, vented**
1 NC A **vent** is a hole in something through which air can come in and smoke, gas, or smells can go out. ...*the air vents of the bunkers.*
2 VO If you **vent** your feelings, you express them forcefully; a formal use. *He vented his rage on Bernard.*

ventilate /ˈventɪleɪt/ **ventilates, ventilating, ventilated**
VO To **ventilate** a room or building means to allow fresh air to get into it. *The air becomes thick if it is not ventilated by fans.* ◆ **ventilated** ADJ ...*badly ventilated houses.* ◆ **ventilation** /ˌventɪˈleɪʃn/ NU *The only ventilation was through a small door at the back of the hall.*

ventilator /ˈventɪleɪtə/ **ventilators**
1 NC A **ventilator** is a machine that helps people breathe when they cannot breathe naturally, for example because they are very ill or have been seriously injured. *He was rushed to Bradford Royal Infirmary and placed on a ventilator... He is now able to sit up in bed and breathe without the help of a ventilator.*
2 NC A **ventilator** is a device which lets fresh air into a room or building and lets stale air out. *Change the ventilator or alter the thermostat.*

ventricle /ˈventrɪkl/ **ventricles**; a medical term.
1 NC A **ventricle** is a chamber of the heart that pumps blood to the arteries. *They have been able to demonstrate defects in the ventricles and check blood flow through coronary bypasses.*
2 NC A **ventricle** is also one of the four main cavities of the brain. ...*a swelling of the ventricles which makes the head grow larger than normal.*

ventriloquism /venˈtrɪləkwɪzəm/
NU **Ventriloquism** is the ability to speak without moving your lips so that what you say seems to come from another person or from another part of the room. *The spirit voices were produced by clever ventriloquism and nothing more.*

ventriloquist /venˈtrɪləkwɪst/ **ventriloquists**
NC A **ventriloquist** is someone who can speak without moving their lips and who entertains people by making their words appear to be spoken by a puppet or a dummy. *The ventriloquist Shari Lewis is in Washington tonight for the Easter Egg Hunt.*

venture /ˈventʃə/ **ventures, venturing, ventured**
1 NC A **venture** is a project or activity which is new, exciting, and difficult but which involves the risk of failure. ...*an interesting scientific venture... The number of successful new business ventures is dwindling.*
2 VA If you **venture** into an activity, you do something that involves the risk of failure because it is new and different. *I might actually venture into advertising if I had enough money.*
3 V-QUOTE, VO, V-REPORT, or V+to-INF If you **venture** an opinion, you say it cautiously and hesitantly because you are afraid other people might think it is foolish or wrong. *'I'd make a good husband,' he ventured... President Aylwin has ventured the idea of a regional investment fund... One source ventured that they would be in the wrong if they totally dismissed it... No one has ventured to suggest why this should be.*
4 VA If you **venture** somewhere you go there, although it might be dangerous. *He wouldn't venture far from his mother's door.*

venturesome /ˈventʃəsəm/
ADJ Someone who is **venturesome** is willing to take risks and try out new things; a literary word. *There*

is a new venturesome spirit among today's young people.

venue /vɛnjuː/ **venues**
NC The **venue** for an event or activity is the place where it will happen. *The talks were postponed until Monday after an argument over the venue.*

veracious /vəreɪʃəs/
ADJ Someone who is **veracious** always tells the truth; a formal word.

veracity /vəræsəti/
NU **Veracity** is the quality of being true or the habit of telling the truth; a formal word. *There is no reason to doubt the veracity of the evidence... He'll have a hard time proving his veracity.*

veranda /vərændə/ **verandas**; also spelt **verandah.**
NC A **veranda** is a platform with a roof along the outside wall of a house. *I was on my veranda when they hit my house.*

verb /vɜːb/ **verbs**
NC In grammar, a **verb** is a word which you use with a subject to say what someone or something does, or what happens to them.

verbal /vɜːbl/
1 ADJ You use **verbal** to describe things connected with words and their use. *It was a contest in verbal skills... It makes you glad you can appreciate his verbal dexterity.*
2 ADJ **Verbal** refers to things that are spoken rather than written. *...a succession of verbal attacks on the chairman... Participants are instructed not to respond to verbal abuse. ...a verbal agreement.* ♦ **verbally** ADV *I will communicate your views verbally.*
3 ADJ **Verbal** also describes something that relates to verbs. *...the structure of verbal groups in English.*

verbalize /vɜːbəlaɪz/ **verbalizes, verbalizing, verbalized;** also spelt **verbalise.**
VOorV If you **verbalize** something, you use words to express your ideas, feelings and desires; a formal word. *She cannot verbalize her emotions... Children of his age group don't usually verbalize at this stage.*

verbatim /vɜːbeɪtɪm/
ADVorADJ If you repeat something **verbatim**, you use exactly the same words as were used originally; a formal word. *The rules for last year's contest were reprinted verbatim... It was almost a verbatim quotation of the article.*

verbiage /vɜːbiːɪdʒ/
NU **Verbiage** is the use of too many words, which makes something difficult to understand; a formal word. *a lot of meaningless verbiage.*

verbose /vɜːbəʊs/
ADJ A person or a piece of writing that is **verbose** uses more words than are necessary, and so makes you feel bored or annoyed. *Who was your verbose companion?* ♦ **verbosity** /vɜːbɒsəti/ NU *...empty rhetoric and verbosity.*

verdict /vɜːdɪkt/ **verdicts**
1 NC In a law court, a **verdict** is the decision that is given at the end of a trial by the jury as to whether a prisoner is guilty or not guilty, or whether the plaintiff or the defendant was right. *The jury gave a verdict of not guilty.*
2 NC Your **verdict** on something is your opinion of it, after thinking about it. *The critics hated the film, but the public verdict was favourable.*

verge /vɜːdʒ/ **verges, verging, verged**
1 If you are **on the verge** of something, you are about to do it or it is about to happen. *The unions are on the verge of settling their latest pay dispute. ...people living on the verge of starvation.*
2 NC The **verge** of a road is a narrow piece of grass at the side. *The car was abandoned later on the grass verge.*

verge on PHRASAL VERB If a particular quality **verges on** or **verges upon** another, it is very similar to it. *I had a feeling of distrust verging on panic. ...direct action verging on violence.*

verge upon PHRASAL VERB See **verge on.**

verifiable /vɛrɪfaɪəbl/
ADJ Something that is **verifiable** can be proved to be true. *...verifiable evidence.*

verification /vɛrɪfɪkeɪʃn/
1 NU **Verification** is the act of checking or confirming that something is true. *Any hypothesis must depend for its verification on observable evidence.*
2 NU **Verification** is also the practice of allowing each party in an arms control agreement to inspect each other's weapons and equipment to make sure that the agreement is being obeyed. *Other problems relate to troop verification... The verification commission goes next to El Salvador.*

verify /vɛrɪfaɪ/ **verifies, verifying, verified**
VO If you **verify** something, you check or confirm that it is true. *...evidence that could be tested and verified... I was asked to verify or deny this suggestion.*

verily /vɛrəli/
ADV SEN **Verily** means really or truly; an old-fashioned or literary word. *Verily, it is true... Verily, the righteous are upon us like fleas on a corpse.*

veritable /vɛrɪtəbl/
ADJ ATTRIB You use **veritable** when you are exaggerating, often humorously, in order to emphasize a feature that something has. *His toilet flushed like a veritable Niagara.*

verity /vɛrəti/ **verities**
NC The **verities** of something are all the general things that are believed to be true about it; a formal word. *He enunciated what, in my view, are some eternal verities. ...scientific verities.*

vermicelli /vɜːmɪtʃeli/
NU **Vermicelli** is very thin spaghetti. *...pineapple and vermicelli pudding.*

vermilion /vəmɪliən/
ADJ Something that is **vermilion** in colour is bright red. *...vermilion robes.*

vermin /vɜːmɪn/
N PL **Vermin** are small animals such as rats and mice, which can carry diseases. *Wild cats are treated as vermin, and are poisoned.*

vermouth /vɜːməθ/ **vermouths**
N MASS **Vermouth** is an alcoholic drink made from red or white wine flavoured with herbs. *He worked in the vermouth company that bore his name, Martini and Rossi.*

vernacular /vənækjʊlə/ **vernaculars**
NC The **vernacular** of a country or region is the language most widely spoken there, although it is not often used on formal occasions. *'Who is it?' asked Ash in the vernacular.*

verruca /vəruːkə/ **verrucas**
NC A **verruca** is a small, hard, infectious growth on the skin rather like a wart, which most commonly occurs on the sole of the foot. *...a 10 watt laser, suitable for the treatment of verrucas, for example.*

versatile /vɜːsətaɪl/
1 ADJ A **versatile** person has many different skills. *He's the most versatile of actors.*
2 ADJ A **versatile** tool, machine, or material can be used for many different purposes. *...this extremely versatile new kitchen machine.*

verse /vɜːs/ **verses**
1 NU **Verse** is writing arranged in lines which have a rhythm and which often rhyme at the end. *She used to write plays in verse.*
2 NC A **verse** is one of the parts into which a poem, a song, or a chapter of the Bible is divided. *...the first verse of the National Anthem. ...a verse of the psalm, 'The Lord's My Shepherd'.*

versed /vɜːst/
If you **are versed in** something, you know a lot about it; a formal expression. *She is well versed in French history.*

version /vɜːʃn/ **versions**
1 NC+SUPP A **version** of something is a form of it in which some details are different from earlier or later forms. *She asked a different version of the question. ...the 1939 film version of 'Wuthering Heights'.*
2 NC+SUPP Someone's **version** of an event is their description of what happened. *Each of the women had a different version of what actually happened.*

versus /vɜːsəs/
1 PREP You use **versus** to say that two ideas or things

are opposed. *...the problem of determinism versus freedom.*
2 PREP **Versus** is also used to say that two people or teams are competing against each other in a sporting event. *The big match tonight is England versus Spain.*

vertebra /vɜːtɪbrə/ **vertebrae** /vɜːtɪbreɪ/
NC Your **vertebrae** are the small bones in your spine. *Many of the injured suffered broken or sprained limbs or vertebrae. ...a complete skull, and pieces of cervical vertebrae.*

vertebrate /vɜːtɪbrət/ **vertebrates**
NC A **vertebrate** is a creature such as a mammal or bird which has a backbone; a technical term. *...land-living vertebrates.*

vertical /vɜːtɪkl/
ADJ Something that is **vertical** stands or points straight upwards. *The monument consists of a horizontal slab supported by two vertical pillars... A vertical line divides the page into two halves... The cliff plunged in a vertical drop to the bottom.*
♦ **vertically** ADV *The human brain is divided vertically down the middle into two hemispheres.*

vertigo /vɜːtɪgəʊ/
NU **Vertigo** is a feeling of dizziness, especially caused by looking down from a high place. *Looking out of the window gives him vertigo.*

verve /vɜːv/
NU **Verve** is lively and forceful enthusiasm; a literary word. *Rosa wrote with great verve.*

very /veri/
1 SUBMOD You use **very** in front of adverbs or adjectives in order to emphasize them. *...a very small child... Think very carefully... I liked it very much... She's a very, very good artist.*
2 ADJ ATTRIB You use **very** with nouns to emphasize a point in space or time, for example the top, bottom, or beginning of something. *I walked up to the very top... We were there from the very beginning... Yeah, it was my very first memory.*
3 ADJ ATTRIB You also use **very** with nouns to emphasize that something is exactly right or exactly the same as something else. *The very man I've been looking for!... Those are the very words he used.*
● **Very** is used in these phrases. ● You say **very much** so in answer to a question as an emphatic way of saying 'yes'. *'Did your father resist this?'—'Very much so.'... 'Does she put the town into her stories?'—'Oh yes, very much so.'* ● You can say **very well** when you agree to do something; a formal expression. *'Mr Brown wants to see you.'—'Very well. I'll be along in a moment.'* ● You use **not very** to say that something is the case only to a small degree. *There are a few people from working class areas, but not very many... His English is not very good... In that respect, her home is not very different from many others.* ● Something that is **of** your **very own** belongs only to you, and you do not have to share it with anyone. *The town has its very own bus service. ...the spiritual benefits that might accrue from owning my very own Buddha.* ● If you say that you **cannot very well** do something, you mean that it would not be the right thing to do. *I can't very well drag him out of the meeting, can I?* ● If something **could very well** be the case, it is almost certainly the case or is almost certain to happen. *It could very well be that these people who are opposed to the rebel groups could begin another campaign... 'Do you think the Chicago Bulls can get into the finals?'—'Yeah, I think it could very well be.'... Even if Yeltsin is removed from office this month, he could very well return as Russia's President.*

vessel /vesl/ **vessels**
1 NC A **vessel** is a ship or large boat. *...fishing vessels.*
2 NC A **vessel** is also a bowl or other container for keeping liquid in; a literary use. *...olive oil leaking from broken storage vessels. ...sacred vessels.*
3 See also **blood vessel**.

vest /vest/ **vests**
1 NC A **vest** is a piece of underwear which is worn to keep the top part of your body warm. *...wearing a vest and Y-fronts.*

2 NC A **vest** is also the same as a **waistcoat**; used in American English. *...black jeans, a leather vest and, of course, a cowboy hat.*

vested /vestɪd/
ADJ PRED+in Something that is **vested** in someone is given to them as a right or responsibility; a formal word. *...the authority vested in him by the State of Massachusetts.*

vested interest, vested interests
1 NC If you have a **vested interest** in something, you have a strong reason for acting in a particular way to protect your own money, power, or reputation. *They have vested interests in farming and forestry... They share a common vested interest in a strong modern army.*
2 N PL **Vested interests** are groups in society that are considered to have too much power or influence, and who are only concerned with getting what they want. *These establishment people, the vested interests, have been trying to resist change. ...political opposition from vested interests... The bill is being opposed by very powerful vested interests.*

vestibule /vestɪbjuːl/ **vestibules**
NC A **vestibule** is an enclosed area between the outside door of a building and an inner door; a formal word. *There were two services going on; one in the vestibule and one in the main body of the church.*

vestige /vestɪdʒ/ **vestiges**
NC If there is no **vestige** of something, there is not even a small part of it left; a formal word. *I would describe it as a country without any vestige of political freedom.*

vestigial /vestɪdʒɪəl/
ADJ **Vestigial** is used to describe the small amounts of something that still remain of a larger or more important thing; a formal word. *In Lorraine's mind there lurked some vestigial traces of conscience.*

vestments /vestmənts/
N PL **Vestments** are the special clothes worn by priests during church ceremonies. *One of the priests was also badly beaten, injuring him and ripping his vestments. ...elaborately woven vestments and carved altar pieces.*

vestry /vestri/ **vestries**
NC A **vestry** is a room in a church which a priest or minister uses as an office or to change into his official clothes for taking a church service. *The Register of Services book had been taken from the vestry.*

vet /vet/ **vets, vetting, vetted**
1 NC A **vet** is someone who is qualified to treat sick or injured animals. *Get your kitten checked by the vet.*
2 VO When someone or something is **vetted**, they are carefully checked to make sure that they are acceptable. *His speeches were vetted... He was thoroughly vetted... It is a chilling thought that thousands of its members are now vetting personnel.*
♦ **vetting** NU *He wanted to tighten the security vetting of civil servants.*
3 NC A **vet** is also the same as a **veteran**; used in American English. *He's a Vietnam vet who was a heroin addict, and when the novel opens, he's recovering. ...a World War Two vet, who became a lawyer in the Phillipines. ...a counselling group for vets.*

veteran /vetərən/ **veterans**
1 NC A **veteran** is someone who has served in the armed forces of their country, especially during a war. *...a World War Two veteran.*
2 NC A **veteran** is also someone who has been involved in a particular activity for a long time. *...a veteran of the civil rights movement.*

veterinarian /vetərɪneəriən/ **veterinarians**
NC A **veterinarian** is someone who is qualified to treat sick or injured animals; used in American English. *Once the contest begins the veterinarians regularly examine the horses to make sure the 150-mile race isn't hurting them.*

veterinary /vetərənəri/
ADJ ATTRIB **Veterinary** refers to the medical treatment of animals. *They had a veterinary practice in Perth.*

veterinary surgeon, veterinary surgeons
NC A **veterinary surgeon** is the same as a **vet**. *...using*

the professional expertise of veterinary surgeons to improve animal welfare.

veto /viːtəʊ/ **vetoes, vetoing, vetoed**
1 vo If someone in authority **vetoes** something, they forbid it, or stop it being put into action. *The government vetoed this proposal.* ▸ Also NC *The rest of the committee could not accept the veto... That has not been done with any of the President's previous 15 vetoes.*
2 NU **Veto** is the right that someone in authority has to forbid something. *...the Sovereign's power of veto.*

vex /veks/ **vexes, vexing, vexed**
vo If something **vexes** you, it makes you feel annoyed; a formal word. *It vexed her to be ignored like this.*

vexation /vekseɪʃn/ **vexations**
NCorNU A **vexation** is something which makes you feel annoyed and puzzled; a formal word. *It will be nothing but an annoyance and a vexation... She was crying with vexation and shock.*

vexed /vekst/
1 ADJ If you are **vexed**, you are annoyed and slightly puzzled. *Feeling vexed, I spoke up for myself.*
2 ADJ ATTRIB A **vexed** problem or question is very difficult and causes people a lot of trouble. *This leads to the vexed issue of priorities... Later Mr Moi raised the vexed question of refugees.*

VHF /viːeɪtʃef/
NU **VHF** is a range of very high radio frequencies. **VHF** is an abbreviation for 'very high frequency'. *The radio has been off the air for the last ten days, but the government makes sporadic broadcasts on a VHF transmitter.*

via /vaɪə, viːə/
1 PREP If you go to one place **via** another, you go through the second place to your destination. *...a ticket to Washington via Frankfurt and New York.*
2 PREP **Via** also means done or achieved using a particular thing or person. *...the transmission of television pictures via satellite... It was so kind of you to send that message via Toby.*

viable /vaɪəbl/
ADJ Something that is **viable** is capable of doing what it is intended to do. *It's important for farms to remain economically viable units. ...viable alternatives to petrol. ...a viable project.* ◆ **viability** /vaɪəbɪləti/ NU *...the commercial viability of the new product.*

viaduct /vaɪədʌkt/ **viaducts**
NC A **viaduct** is a long, high bridge that carries a road or railway across a valley. *...the line's spectacular twenty-four arch viaduct.*

vibes /vaɪbz/; an informal word.
1 N PL **Vibes** are the good or bad emotional reactions which you feel that a person has towards you or the good or bad atmosphere that you sense in a place. *There are bad vibes between us... The city held such hostile vibes that you felt you were being watched continually.*
2 N PL The **vibes** are the same as the **vibraphone**; an informal use. *The band got talking about a woman that played vibes and was getting a lot of work.*

vibrancy /vaɪbrənsi/
NU **Vibrancy** is a strong feeling of energy and enthusiasm. *...the tremendous vibrancy of the young people who were gathering there.*

vibrant /vaɪbrənt/
1 ADJ Something or someone that is **vibrant** is full of life, energy, and enthusiasm. *His vibrant talk fascinated and excited me. ...the vibrant tones of Richard Burton.*
2 ADJ **Vibrant** colours are very bright. *...a flower bed vibrant with red tulips.*

vibraphone /vaɪbrəfəʊn/ **vibraphones**
NC A **vibraphone** is an electronic musical instrument which conists of a set of metal bars in a frame. When you hit the bars, they produce vibrating notes that do not fade away immediately. *Bronka's latest composition has no guitar, but strings, vibraphone and piano.*

vibrate /vaɪbreɪt/ **vibrates, vibrating, vibrated**
v When something **vibrates**, it shakes with repeated small, quick movements. *The foundation of the city began to rumble and vibrate... The craft suddenly began to vibrate and a bang was heard.* ◆ **vibrating** ADJ ATTRIB *...special vibrating seats to keep drivers awake.* ◆ **vibration** /vaɪbreɪʃn/ **vibrations** NCorNU *...a series of sudden shakes and vibrations... The pilot reported severe engine vibration.*

vibrato /vɪbrɑːtəʊ/ **vibratos**
NCorNU A **vibrato** is a rapidly repeated slight variation in the pitch of a musical note, produced in order to add expressiveness to the music. *This enabled me to sing in a high-pitched vibrato.*

vibrator /vaɪbreɪtə/ **vibrators**
NC A **vibrator** is a device which vibrates and which is used in massage to give relief from pain or which is used to give sexual pleasure. *The cushions contain three sets of electrically-powered vibrators, which massage the driver's body.*

vicar /vɪkə/ **vicars**
NC In the Church of England, a **vicar** is a priest who is in charge of a parish. *...the vicar of the local parish.*

vicarage /vɪkərɪdʒ/ **vicarages**
NC A **vicarage** is a house in which a vicar lives. *He lived next door to the vicarage.*

vicarious /vɪkeəriəs/
ADJ ATTRIB A **vicarious** pleasure or feeling is one that you experience by watching, listening to, or reading about other people doing something, rather than by doing it yourself. *That provides a kind of vicarious pleasure for the reader. ...a vicarious sense of power and adventure.* ◆ **vicariously** ADV *This is a story that children enjoy because they vicariously get to wreck a house with no guilt and no consequences.*

vice /vaɪs/ **vices**; spelt **vise** in American English for the meaning in paragraph 3.
1 NC A **vice** is a moral fault in someone's character or behaviour. *...human vices such as greed and envy... Her one small vice was smoking.*
2 NU **Vice** refers to criminal activities, especially those connected with pornography or prostitution. *...impoverished ghettos rife with vice, drug abuse and social disintegration. ...a campaign against vice and violence. ...strict vice laws.*
3 NC A **vice** is also a tool that you use to hold an object tightly while you work on it. *I once caught my tie in the vice.*

vice- /vaɪs/
PREFIX **Vice-** is used before a rank or title to indicate that the person who holds that rank or title is next in importance to the person who holds the full rank or title. *The most resounding victory went to Kenya's Vice-President. ...the vice-chairman of the Welsh Arts Council. ...the vice-presidency.*

vice-chancellor, vice-chancellors
NC The **vice-chancellor** is the head of academic and administrative matters in a British University. *The Education Secretary told the conference of vice-chancellors that they had the means to expand higher education.*

viceroy /vaɪsrɔɪ/ **viceroys**
NC In former times, a **viceroy** was the person who ruled a colony on behalf of his king, queen, or government. *...the statue of the 19th century Croatian Viceroy.*

vice squad, vice squads
NC The **vice squad** is the section of a police force that deals with crime relating to pornography, prostitution, and gambling. *When members of the vice squad approached his car, King suddenly backed up.*

vice versa /vaɪsə vɜːsə/
Vice versa is used to indicate that the reverse of what you have said is also true. For example, 'Women may bring their husbands with them, and vice versa' means that men may also bring their wives with them. *What's OK today is bad tomorrow, or vice versa.*

vicinity /vɪsɪnəti/
N SING If something is in the **vicinity** of a place, it is in the nearby area. *The hotels in the vicinity of the campus were cheap and shabby... No television cameras will be allowed in the immediate vicinity.*

vicious /vɪʃəs/
ADJ Someone who is **vicious**, or who does something vicious, behaves in a cruel and violent way. ...*a vicious killer... The hijackers had carried out a particularly vicious act of terrorism.* ◆ **viciously** ADV *He twisted her wrist viciously.*

vicious circle
N SING A **vicious circle** is a problem or difficult situation that has the effect of creating new problems which in turn re-create the original problem. *Traffic problems in China's cities are caused by a vicious circle—the buses are so crowded and slow that people take to bicycles, which choke the roads and slow the buses down even further.*

vicissitudes /vɪsɪsɪtjuːdz/
N PL **Vicissitudes** are the changes in circumstances at different times in someone's life or in the development of something; a formal word. *The country's reputation has suffered many vicissitudes.*

victim /vɪktɪm/ **victims**
1 NC A **victim** is someone who has been hurt or killed by someone or something. *Most of the victims were shot in the back while trying to run away. ...a rape victim.*
2 NC A **victim** is also someone who has suffered as a result of someone else's actions or beliefs, or as a result of unpleasant circumstances. *The government insists that it is a victim of misunderstanding and exaggeration. ...the distribution of relief supplies to drought victims in Northern Ethiopia.*
3 If a person **falls victim to** someone or something, they are killed by them or they suffer as a result of them. *Policemen who have tried to combat such activities have themselves fallen victim to assassins. ...the courage of those who fell victim to Stalin's arbitrary rule.*

victimize /vɪktɪmaɪz/ **victimizes, victimizing, victimized**; also spelt **victimise**.
VO If someone is **victimized**, they are deliberately treated unfairly. *Management insisted that she was not being victimized... She accused the government of victimizing members of her family.* ◆ **victimization** /vɪktɪmaɪzeɪʃn/ NU *There must be no victimization of workers.*

victor /vɪktə/ **victors**
NC The **victor** in a battle or contest is the person who wins; a literary word. *...the victor of Waterloo... He emerged as the victor over Mulder.*

Victoria /vɪktɔːriə/
Victoria, on Mahé Island, is the capital of the Seychelles and its largest city. Population: 24,000 (1987).

Victoria Island /vɪktɔːriə aɪlənd/
Victoria Island is the capital of Hong Kong. Population: 591,000 (1981).

Victorian /vɪktɔːriən/
1 ADJ **Victorian** is used to describe things that existed or were made in the period of British history when Victoria was the Queen, between 1837 and 1901. *The bridge was one of the finest achievements of Victorian industry. ...a Victorian terraced house... Wilkie Collins was the Victorian writer who wrote the first real detective novel, 'The Moonstone'.*
2 ADJ You say that someone is **Victorian** when they believe in strict discipline and morals. *His parents were very Victorian and very domineering... The Prime Minister promised a return to Victorian values.*

Victoriana /vɪktɔːriɑːnə/
NU Objects made during the reign of Queen Victoria are sometimes referred to as **Victoriana**. *The clothes were later acquired by a collector of Victoriana.*

victorious /vɪktɔːriəs/
ADJ Someone who is **victorious** has won a victory, especially in a war. *...the four victorious powers of the Second World War... He said his people would emerge victorious... The victorious candidates called for dialogue with the army.*

victory /vɪktəri/ **victories**
N C or N U A **victory** is a success in a struggle, a war, or a competition. *They believe they've won an important strategic victory against the union... The election has resulted in a decisive victory for President Mitterrand*

over the Prime Minister, Mr Chirac... *Nobody believed she had any chance of victory.*

video /vɪdiəʊ/ **videos, videoing, videoed**
1 NU **Video** is the recording and showing of films and events, using a video camera, a video recorder, videotapes, and a television set. *I know that you use video for teaching these students.*
2 NC A **video** is a video recorder. *Turn off the video.*
3 NC A **video** is also a film or television programme recorded on videotape for people to watch on a television set. *I've seen this video before. ...a new video on the danger of AIDS... The film has earned more than $70 million in profits since it was released on video.*
4 VO If you **video** something, you record it on magnetic tape, either by using a video camera and recording the actual events, or by using a video to record a television programme as it is being transmitted, in order to watch it later. *They videoed what they were doing... I like the idea of videoing officials to make sure they keep their word.* ◆ **videoed** *The committee says it collected written and videoed statements from refugees.*

video camera, video cameras
NC A **video camera** is a camera that takes moving pictures and records them on videotape so that they can be played back on a video recorder. *A video camera filmed the proceedings from a window of the Embassy.*

video cassette, video cassettes
NC A **video cassette** is a cassette containing a video tape. *Video cassettes of the film are changing hands for two hundred pounds.*

video conference, video conferences
NC A **video conference** is a conference in which several people who are a long way from each other communicate using audio and video equipment. *...joining in the video conference halfway through. ...the latest video conference system.*

video game, video games
NC A **video game** is any of several games which are played by moving symbols on a visual display screen using an electronic control. *...the sound effects used in video games.*

video nasty, video nasties
NC A **video nasty** is a film which has been released on video and which is extremely violent or horrific. *There have been numerous reports of teenagers copying rape and violence after watching video nasties.*

video recorder, video recorders
NC A **video recorder** is a machine that can record and play videotapes on a television set. *If you have a video recorder, you can show the film in your flat.*

videotape /vɪdiəʊteɪp/ **videotapes, videotaping, videotaped**
1 NU or NC **Videotape** is magnetic tape that is used to record pictures or films which you can then play back and watch on a television set. *It's all down on videotape, you see... They saw the videotapes of Mr Frost's interviews.*
2 VO To **videotape** something means to **video** it. *We videotaped all the performances and all the audience's responses... Mr McGarry was videotaped transferring a briefcase to known Soviet agents.*

Videotex /vɪdiəʊteks/
NU **Videotex** is a system which can link you to a computer by telephone so that you can select the information you need from the computer; **Videotex** is a trademark. *Customers use a keyboard and personal computer or Videotex set to access their bank accounts.*

videotext /vɪdiəʊtekst/
NU **Videotext** is a system by which written or graphic forms of computerized information can be displayed on a screen.

vie /vaɪ/ **vies, vying, vied**
V-RECIP If you **vie** with someone, you try hard to get something before they do, or to do something sooner or better than they do; a formal word. *The country is in turmoil at the moment, with rival factions vying for power... Both countries are major oil producers, and*

*each has vied to inflict maximum damage to the
other's main source of income... Mr Tebbit and Mr
Heseltine were vying with each other for the
leadership of their party.*

Vieira, João Bernardo /ʒuˈænⁿʊ bənɔːˈduː vjɛɪrə/
Brigadier-General João Bernardo Vieira became
President of Guinea-Bissau in a coup in 1980. He was
State Commissioner for the Armed Forces from 1974
to 1984. From 1974 to 1979 he was President of the
People's National Assembly. Since 1973 he has been a
member of the Permanent Secretariat of the African
Party for the Independence of Guinea and Cape Verde
(PAIGC), the sole legal party until 1992, when
opposition parties were legalized. Born: 1939.

Vienna (Wien) /viˈenə/
Vienna is the capital of Austria and its largest city.
Population: 1,531,000 (1981).

Vientiane /vjɛntjɑːn/
Vientiane is the capital of Laos and its largest city.
Population: 377,000 (1985).

Vietnam /vietˈnæm/
The **Socialist Republic of Vietnam** is a country in
south-east Asia. It became a French colony in the
mid-19th century and was occupied by Japan from 1940
to 1945. The French withdrew in 1954 after the battle of
Dien Bien Phu and the conclusion of the Geneva
Agreements. The country was then divided into two,
the Communist North and the non-Communist South.
In 1965 the United States sent troops to the South to
help in the fight against invasion by the North. They
finally withdrew in 1973 after the Paris Agreements. In
1975, the regime in the South collapsed and the country
was reunited under Communist rule. Vietnam invaded
Cambodia in 1979 and was attacked by China. The
economy became dependent on Soviet aid. Private
industry and agriculture were gradually reintroduced
after 1986, and in 1989 Vietnam started to export rice.
Off-shore oil is being developed. Do Muoi became
Secretary General of the Communist Party of Vietnam
(CPV), the only party, in 1991. Vo Van Kiet became
Prime Minister in 1991. Vietnam has applied to join
the Association of South East Asian Nations.
◆ **Vietnamese** /vietnəmˈiːz/ N, N PL, ADJ
▪ *religion:* Buddhism ▪ *language:* Vietnamese
▪ *currency:* new dông ▪ *capital:* Hanoi ▪ *largest city:*
Ho Chi Minh City (formerly Saigon) ▪ *population:* 67
million (1989) ▪ *size:* 329,566 square kilometres.

view /vjuː/ **views, viewing, viewed**
1 NC Your **view** on a particular subject is what you
think about it. *I've changed my view on this issue...
He was sent to jail for his political views... Some of
the views expressed were highly critical.*
2 N SING Your **view** of a situation is the way you
understand and interpret it. *She has a view of life
which is deeply corrupt... He tends to take a wider,
more overall view of things... The Times takes a more
sombre view.*
3 VOA If you **view** something in a particular way, you
think of it in that way. *The Prime Minister is said to
be viewing the matter very seriously... Their missiles
are viewed as a defensive and deterrent force... His
request will nevertheless be viewed with astonishment
and outrage in many parts of the Arab world.*
4 NC The **view** from a particular place is everything
you can see from it. *From the top there is a fine view.*
5 N SING If you have a **view** of something, you can see
it. *Looking away from our galaxy, we can get quite a
good view of other parts of the universe... The driver
blocked his view.*
6 VO If you **view** something, you look at it; a formal
use. *...a drop of water from a pond, viewed through a
microscope.*
7 VO If you **view** a television programme, video, or
film, you watch it; a formal use. *The police are
hoping to arrest more people after viewing videotape
of the disturbances.*
8 See also **point of view.**
● **View** is used in these phrases. ● You use **in my view**
to emphasize that you are stating your opinion. *In my
view, we have a long way to go before we have a
United States of Europe.* ● If you **take the view that**
something is true, your opinion is that it is true. *We*

*take the view that international services should not
have subsidies.* ● You use **in view of** to specify the
main fact or event that causes you to do, say, or think
something. *In view of the fact that all the other
members of the group are going, I think you should go
too.* ● If you do something **with a view to** a particular
result, you do it to achieve that result. *We have
exchanged letters with a view to meeting to discuss
these problems.* ● If something is **in view**, you can see
it from where you are. *We crept around the cage to
keep the monkey in view... The bridge suddenly came
into view...* ● If something is **on view**, it is being
exhibited in public. *The Turner exhibition is on view
at the Tate Gallery.* ● **to take a dim view:** see **dim.**

Viewdata /vjuːdeɪtə/
NU **Viewdata** is the same as **Videotex; Viewdata** is a
trademark.

viewer /vjuːə/ **viewers**
NC **Viewers** are people who watch television, or who
are watching a particular programme on television.
*Some British television viewers will have a wider
viewing choice from this weekend... In the
programme, Prince Charles gave viewers a conducted
tour down the Thames by boat.*

viewfinder /vjuːfaɪndə/ **viewfinders**
NC A **viewfinder** is a small square of glass in a
camera that you look through in order to see what you
are going to photograph.

viewpoint /vjuːpɔɪnt/ **viewpoints**
1 NC+SUPP Someone's **viewpoint** is the way that they
think about things in general or about a particular
thing. *I cannot make sense of it from my particular
viewpoint as a Christian minister... The Daily Mail
looks at the OPEC negotiations from a purely British
viewpoint.*
2 NC A **viewpoint** is also a place from which you can
get a good view of something. *The polaroid prints
were shot from different viewpoints.*

vigil /ˈvɪdʒɪl/ **vigils**
NC A **vigil** is a period of time when you remain quietly
in a place, especially at night, for example because
you are praying or are making a political protest.
*...relatives of victims who maintained a silent vigil
outside the parliament buildings in The Hague... Last
weekend a nun on a hunger strike held a vigil at the
United Nations.*

vigilance /ˈvɪdʒɪləns/
NU **Vigilance** is careful attention that you give to a
situation, so that you notice any danger or trouble that
there might be; a formal word. *He underlined the
continuing need for extreme vigilance. ...their
vigilance against low-flying aircraft.*

vigilant /ˈvɪdʒɪlənt/
ADJ If you are **vigilant**, you are careful and try to
notice any danger or trouble that there might be; a
formal word. *He appealed to the public to remain
vigilant and alert the police to any suspicious
activity... This evening, I had to be especially vigilant.*

vigilante /ˌvɪdʒɪˈlænti/ **vigilantes**
NC **Vigilantes** are people who organize themselves into
an unofficial group to protect their community and to
catch and punish criminals. *The police believe the
presence of the vigilantes will lead to more violence.
...200 or more vigilante groups operating around the
country.*

vigilantism /ˌvɪdʒɪˈlæntɪzəm/
NU **Vigilantism** is the methods and attitudes of
vigilantes. *Successful development can block the
growth of vigilantism... Settler vigilantism could
worsen the violence in the occupied territories.*

vignette /vɪnˈjet/ **vignettes**
NC A **vignette** is a short piece of writing which
describes very clearly the typical characteristics of a
thing, place, or event. *...a fascinating vignette of
family life. ...composed as a collage of hundreds of
short vignettes.*

vigorous /ˈvɪgərəs/
1 ADJ A **vigorous** action or activity is done with a lot
of energy and enthusiasm. *Mary gave her skirt a
vigorous shake. ...the benefits of vigorous exercise...
The campaign for his release remains as vigorous as
ever... The Chancellor mounted a vigorous defence of*

his policies. ◆ **vigorously** ADV *Chomsky defended this view very vigorously... Officials in Tripoli have vigorously denied the charge.*
2 ADJ Someone who is **vigorous** is healthy and full of energy. *...an elderly but vigorous man.*

vigour /vɪgə/; spelt **vigor** in American English.
NU **Vigour** is energy and enthusiasm. *These problems were discussed with great vigour.*

Viking /vaɪkɪŋ/ **Vikings**
NC The **Vikings** were groups of seamen from Scandinavia who attacked villages in most parts of north-western Europe from the 8th to the 11th centuries. *The city was founded by the Vikings in 841 AD. ...the opening of a museum of Viking history.*

vile /vaɪl/ **viler, vilest**
ADJ If something is **vile**, it is very unpleasant or disgusting. *...England's vile weather. ...her vile language.*

vilify /vɪlɪfaɪ/ **vilifies, vilifying, vilified**
VO If you **vilify** someone, you say or write very unpleasant things about them, so that people will be influenced against them; a formal word. *He was vilified for making those broadcasts.* ◆ **vilification** /vɪlɪfɪkeɪʃn/ NU *...the vilification of the Spanish government.*

villa /vɪlə/ **villas**
NC A **villa** is a fairly large house, especially one that is used for holidays in Mediterranean countries. *...a flashy car and a villa by the sea.*

village /vɪlɪdʒ/ **villages**
NC A **village** consists of a group of houses, together with other buildings such as a church and school, in a country area. *She was born in a small Norfolk village. ...the village school.*

villager /vɪlɪdʒə/ **villagers**
NC **Villagers** are people who live in a village. *The villagers were suspicious of anything new... The guerrillas often have the support of local villagers.*

villain /vɪlən/ **villains**
1 NC A person who deliberately harms other people or breaks the law is sometimes referred to as a **villain**. *A villain named Thomson broke into the premises... The really clever villain will leave no traces.*
2 NC The **villain** in a particular situation is the person, group, or country that is held responsible for things going wrong. *France was seen as the main villain when the trade talks collapsed in Brussels.* ● The **villain of the piece** is the person, group, or country that is seen as being the cause of all the trouble in a situation; an old-fashioned expression. *The Polish marketing system is said to be the villain of the piece in creating current shortages.*
3 NC A **villain** in a play, film, or novel, is an important character who behaves badly and is responsible for many of the bad things that happen. *He was cast as the villain in the forthcoming production... He has starred as the main villain in two of the biggest box office hits of all time.*

villainous /vɪlənəs/
ADJ Someone who is **villainous** is very bad and willing to harm other people or break the law. *...villainous or wicked characters.*

villainy /vɪləni/
NU **Villainy** is very bad or criminal behaviour. *...the villainy of her landlord.*

Vilnius /vɪlnjuːs/
Vilnius is the capital of Lithuania and its largest city. Population: 582,000 (1989).

vinaigrette /vɪneɪgret/
NU **Vinaigrette** is a sauce made by mixing oil, vinegar, salt, pepper, and herbs, which is put on cold food, especially salads. *Use mayonnaise, not vinaigrette, for chicken salads.*

vindicate /vɪndɪkeɪt/ **vindicates, vindicating, vindicated**
VO When someone is **vindicated**, their ideas or actions are proved to be correct or worthwhile; a formal word. *Benn was decisively vindicated at the polls, receiving 23,275 votes to 10,231.* ◆ **vindication** /vɪndɪkeɪʃn/ **vindications** NCorNU *These changes to the law were widely regarded as a vindication of his long campaign... She took this as triumphant*

vindication of the effectiveness of the device.

vindictive /vɪndɪktɪv/
ADJ Someone who is **vindictive**, or who does something **vindictive**, intends deliberately to hurt someone, often because they think that person has done something to upset or annoy them. *...a vindictive and violent man... He said that the United Nations were conducting a vindictive vendetta against South Africa.* ◆ **vindictively** ADV *Her dress had been vindictively cut to shreds.* ◆ **vindictiveness** NU *The White House has accused him of vindictiveness and revenge.*

vine /vaɪn/ **vines**
NC A **vine** is a climbing or trailing plant, especially one which produces grapes. *A weekend cold snap has damaged vine buds in the French Bordeaux region... These pruners are only for use on vines.*

vinegar /vɪnɪgə/
NU **Vinegar** is a sharp-tasting liquid, usually made from sour wine or malt. *...onions and cabbage mixed together with vinegar. ...red wine vinegar.*

vinegary /vɪnɪgəri/
1 ADJ Something that is **vinegary** tastes or smells of vinegar. *...the vinegary smell of the cabbage.*
2 ADJ If you describe someone as **vinegary**, you mean that they are bad tempered; an old-fashioned use. *...a vinegary old woman.*

vineyard /vɪnjəd/ **vineyards**
NC A **vineyard** is an area of land where grape vines are grown to produce wine. *...the vineyards of Bordeaux.*

vintage /vɪntɪdʒ/ **vintages**
1 NC+SUPP The **vintage** of a good quality wine is the year and place that it was made in before being stored to improve it. *The oldest wine in the collection is a Spanish sherry of the 1775 vintage.*
2 ADJ ATTRIB **Vintage** wine is good quality wine that has been stored for several years to improve its quality. *...a 1928 vintage wine. ...vintage port.*
3 ADJ ATTRIB **Vintage** aeroplanes or cars are old but are admired because they are considered to be the best of their kind. *He runs a business repairing, buying and selling vintage aircraft.*
4 ADJ ATTRIB You can also use **vintage** to describe something that is the best of its kind. *Leconte produced some vintage attacking tennis to beat the 11th seeded Argentine.*

vintner /vɪntnə/ **vintners**
NC A **vintner** is someone whose job is to buy and sell wines; a formal word.

vinyl /vaɪnl/
1 NUorN+N **Vinyl** is a strong plastic used for making things such as furniture and floor coverings. *Linoleum, once found in almost every home in Britain, was gradually replaced by chemically-produced vinyl... Police also want to trace a red Ford Cortina car with a black vinyl roof which was parked outside the station.*
2 NU **Vinyl** is also used to refer to records, especially in contrast to cassettes or compact discs. *In the last 3 months of 1987, sales of CDs edged ahead of those on vinyl for the first time.*

viola /viəʊlə/ **violas**
NC A **viola** is a musical instrument which looks like a violin but is slightly larger. *...three beautiful concertos for viola, violin and cello. ...viola music by Hindemith.*

violate /vaɪəleɪt/ **violates, violating, violated**
1 VO If you **violate** an agreement, law, or promise, you break it. *He is violating his contract... They have accused the military government of violating human rights.* ◆ **violation** /vaɪəleɪʃn/ **violations** NUorNC *They blockaded the Suez Canal in violation of international agreements. ...alleged violations of the terms of the accord.*
2 VO If you **violate** someone's privacy or peace, you disturb it; a formal use. *The calm of the press lounge was suddenly violated.*
3 VO If an army or ship **violates** the territory of another country, they enter it without permission. *He accused them of violating Sudanese territory. ...a ship which had allegedly violated Kuwait's territorial waters.*

4 VO If someone **violates** a holy place, they damage it or treat it with disrespect. ...*a curse on those who violated the tomb of the king.* ◆ **violation** NU *The violation of the graves at Carpentras is not the first such incident.*

violator /vaɪəleɪtə/ **violators**
NC A **violator** of a rule or law is a person or country that violates it. ...*measures which allow the security forces to shoot on sight violators of the nightly curfews.*

violence /vaɪələns/
1 NU **Violence** is behaviour which is intended to hurt, injure, or kill people. *Large scale violence broke out... He condemned the continuing acts of violence both in Northern Ireland and elsewhere. ...threats of terrorist violence. ...robbery with violence.*
2 NU If you do something with **violence**, you use a lot of force and energy in doing it, often because you are angry. *He flung open the door with unnecessary violence.*

violent /vaɪələnt/
1 ADJ If someone is **violent**, or if they do something which is **violent**, they try to injure or kill people, for example by using physical force or weapons. *People in this society are prepared to be violent... Public frustration may boil over into violent demonstrations. ...the widespread violent protests against the plan. ...violent clashes with the police.* ◆ **violently** ADV *They have come into conflict, sometimes violently. ...protests which are said to have been violently suppressed.*
2 ADJ A **violent** event happens suddenly and with great force. ...*a violent explosion. ...the constant threat of violent death. ...the violent storms of summer.* ◆ **violently** ADV *The train braked violently.*
3 ADJ Something that is **violent** is said, done, or felt with great force and energy. *At times the argument grew violent... He had a violent urge to create.* ◆ **violently** ADV *They violently disagreed with their Commander-in-Chief... The Prime Minister is violently opposed to all aspects of the plan.*
4 ADJ ATTRIB **Violent** colours are unpleasantly bright. ...*a shirt of violent red.*

violet /vaɪələt/ **violets**
1 NC A **violet** is a small purple or white flower that blooms in the spring.
2 ADJ Something that is **violet** in colour is bluish-purple. *The sky darkened into a violet haze.*

violin /vaɪəlɪn/ **violins**
NC A **violin** is a musical instrument with four strings stretched over a shaped hollow box. You hold a violin under your chin and play it with a bow. *Grapelli invented a role for the jazz violin... The serenade is scored without violins.*

violinist /vaɪəlɪnɪst/ **violinists**
NC A **violinist** is someone who plays the violin. ...*principal violinist of the Medici Quartet.*

VIP /viːaɪpiː/ **VIPs**
NC A **VIP** is someone who is given better treatment than ordinary people because he or she is famous or important. **VIP** is an abbreviation for 'very important person'. ...*a private lounge for VIPs... They were allowed into the VIP section of the airport.*

viper /vaɪpə/ **vipers**
NC A **viper** is a small poisonous snake found mainly in Europe. ...*venomous vipers. ...a viper bite.*

viral /vaɪrəl/
ADJ **Viral** means caused by or related to a virus. ...*developing drugs to fight viral infections. ...a herbal remedy for viral hepatitis.*

virgin /vɜːdʒɪn/ **virgins**
1 NC A **virgin** is someone, especially a woman or girl, who has never had sex. *The girls they marry should be virgins.* ◆ **virginity** /vədʒɪnəti/ NU *His sister had lost her virginity many years before.*
2 ADJ Something that is **virgin** is fresh and clean, and its appearance shows that it has never been used. *There were piles and piles of books, all virgin, all untouched.*
3 ADJ ATTRIB **Virgin** land has not been explored, cultivated, or spoiled by people. ...*opening up virgin territory. ...virgin rain forest.*

virginal /vɜːdʒɪnl/
ADJ Someone who is **virginal** is young and innocent, and has had no experience of sex. *The men have decreed that their women must be pure, virginal, innocent.*

virgin birth, virgin births
1 N SING The **Virgin Birth** is the belief in the Christian religion that Mary conceived and gave birth to Jesus Christ through God's power and not as a result of sexual intercourse. ...*a literal belief in the Virgin Birth. ...traditional interpretations of the Virgin Birth.*
2 NU **Virgin birth** is also a type of reproduction in some animals and plants which does not require fertilization of the egg. ...*work to establish why virgin birth will occur in lower order creatures, such as frogs.*

Virgin Islands, British /brɪtɪʃ vɜːdʒɪn aɪləndz/
The **British Virgin Islands** are a territory of the United Kingdom in the Caribbean. Sixteen of the 60 islands are inhabited. The principal island, Tortola, was annexed by the British in 1672. Tourism and banking are important industries. ◆ **British Virgin Islander** /brɪtɪʃ vɜːdʒɪn aɪləndə/ N
▪ *religion:* Christianity (mainly Methodist) ▪ *language:* English (official) ▪ *currency:* US dollar ▪ *capital:* Road Town ▪ *population:* 13,000 (1989) ▪ *size:* 153 square kilometres.

Virgin Islands, United States /juːnaɪtɪd steɪts vɜːdʒɪn aɪləndz/
The **United States Virgin Islands** are a territory of the United States in the Caribbean. The principal islands are St Croix, St Thomas, and St John. They were originally settled by Denmark in the 17th century and were known as the Danish West Indies. In 1917 they were sold to the United States. Tourism is an important industry. ◆ **US Virgin Islander** /juː es vɜːdʒɪn aɪləndə/ N
▪ *per capita GNP:* US$8,717 ▪ *religion:* Christianity ▪ *language:* English (official), Spanish, Creole ▪ *currency:* US dollar ▪ *capital:* Charlotte Amalie ▪ *population:* 106,000 (1989) ▪ *size:* 355 square kilometres.

virile /vɪraɪl/
ADJ A **virile** man has the qualities that a man is traditionally expected to have, such as strength and sexuality. ...*virile young male actors.* ◆ **virility** /vɪrɪləti/ NU *The macho male wishes to prove his virility.*

virtual /vɜːtʃuəl/
1 ADJ ATTRIB **Virtual** means that something is so nearly true that for most purposes it can be regarded as true. ...*the twenty-four hour general strike which brought the province to a virtual standstill.* ◆ **virtually** /vɜːtʃuəli/ ADV *They are virtually impossible to detect... This opinion was held by virtually all the experts.*
2 ADJ ATTRIB **Virtual** also means that something has all the effects and consequences of a particular thing, but is not officially recognized as being that thing. *The peasants remain in a state of virtual slavery. ...a virtual revolution in organization.*

virtual reality
NU **Virtual reality** is an environment that has been created by a computer and that looks like reality to a person in it. *Charles Grimsdale explains to Keith Hart how virtual reality is created by computer. ...the launch of the first virtual reality computer in the UK.*

virtue /vɜːtʃuː/ **virtues**
1 NU **Virtue** is thinking and doing what is right, and avoiding what is wrong. *We accept certain principles of religion and traditional virtue.*
2 NC A **virtue** is a good quality or way of behaving. *Charity is the greatest of Christian virtues.*
3 NCorNU A **virtue** of something is an advantage that it has. ...*the virtues of female independence... There is no virtue in taking this action.*
4 You use **by virtue of** to explain why something happens or is true; a formal expression. *He was an object of interest simply by virtue of being British.*

virtuosity /vɜːtʃuɒsəti/
NU **Virtuosity** is great skill in performing something, such as playing an instrument, dancing, or acting.

...technical and artistic virtuosity. ...dancing his solos with brilliant virtuosity... Some of his plays call for great virtuosity on the part of the actors.

virtuoso /vɜːtʃuˈəʊzəʊ/ **virtuosos** or **virtuosi** /vɜːtʃuˈəʊzi/
NC A **virtuoso** is someone who is exceptionally good at playing a musical instrument. *He was a virtuoso of the jazz guitar... This was an extremely strong, virtuoso performance.*

virtuous /vɜːtʃuəs/
ADJ **Virtuous** behaviour is morally correct. *People who lead virtuous lives in this world are assured of paradise in the next.*

virulence /vɪrjʊləns/
1 NU **Virulence** is strong hostility that is directed against someone, usually in the form of an unpleasant verbal attack on them. *Observers were surprised by the rare virulence of Singapore's reaction to the American move.*
2 NU The **virulence** of a disease is its ability to spread quickly and to harm or kill people or animals. *As an indication of the virulence of the disease, the number of cases is expected to double in the following year.*
3 NU **Virulence** also refers to the ability that something, such as a belief, has to survive and to do harm. *The heresy flourished there with peculiar virulence.*

virulent /vɪrjʊlənt/
1 ADJ **Virulent** feelings or actions are extremely bitter and hostile. *They were the objects of special hatred and virulent attacks.* ◆ **virulently** ADV *Fighting broke out again much more virulently.*
2 ADJ A **virulent** disease spreads quickly and is extremely harmful. *...a virulent virus.*

virus /vaɪrəs/ **viruses**
1 NC A **virus** is a kind of germ that can cause disease. *She had a flu virus... A person can carry the virus without necessarily contracting the disease. ...a virus infection.*
2 NC In computer technology, a **virus** is a program that introduces itself into a system, altering or destroying the information stored in the system. *How then can computer operators protect their systems against viruses? ...a bad virus attack at a company depending exclusively on computers.*

visa /viːzə/ **visas**
NC A **visa** is an official document, or a stamp put in your passport, which allows you to enter or leave a particular country. *They did not have valid entry visas... The regime refused to grant exit visas. ...the abolition of British visa requirements for Czechoslovak citizens from October.*

visage /vɪzɪdʒ/ **visages**
NC Someone's **visage** is their face; a literary word. *A maudlin smile played across her normally grim visage.*

vis-à-vis /viːz æ viː/
PREP You use **vis-à-vis** when you are considering one thing in comparison with another; a formal word. *One solution would be for us to lower our exchange rate vis-à-vis other countries.*

viscount /vaɪkaʊnt/ **viscounts**
NC or TITLE A **viscount** is a British nobleman who is below an earl and above a baron in rank. *He was then made an hereditary viscount... When Viscount Whitelaw spoke, she was obliged to listen.*

viscountess /vaɪkaʊntes/ **viscountesses**
NC or TITLE A **viscountess** is either the wife of a viscount or a woman who holds the same rank as a viscount. *Among the guests were Viscountess Hambledon and two of her sons.*

viscous /vɪskəs/
ADJ A **viscous** liquid is thick and sticky. *...a viscous solution of sugar.*

vise /vaɪs/. See **vice**.

visibility /vɪzəbɪləti/
NU **Visibility** means how far or how clearly you can see in particular weather conditions. *Visibility was excellent that day.*

visible /vɪzəbl/
1 ADJ If an object is **visible**, it can be seen. *These tiny creatures are hardly visible to the naked eye... It*

was just visible from the beach.
2 ADJ **Visible** can also be used to describe something that can be noticed or recognized. *The results are visible... Homosexuals became an increasingly visible and militant minority.* ◆ **visibly** ADV *She was visibly nervous... He was visibly shocked by the dismal conditions he saw.*

vision /vɪʒn/ **visions**
1 NC If you have a **vision** of a possible situation, you have a mental picture of it, in which you imagine how things might be different from the way they are now. *...fighting for the vision of the new China... I had nightmarish visions of what could go wrong.*
2 NU **Vision** is the ability to see. *...children with poor vision... He said he was very weak and his vision was blurred.*
3 NU The **vision** on a television set is the picture that is shown on it. *We apologize for the temporary loss of vision.*

visionary /vɪʒənəri/ **visionaries**
NC A **visionary** is someone who has visions about how things might be different in the future, especially about how things might be improved. *...left-wing visionaries.* ▶ Also ADJ *...the visionary imagination.*

visit /vɪzɪt/ **visits, visiting, visited**
1 V or V If you **visit** someone, you go to see them and spend time with them. *She visited some of her relatives for a few days... You might need to visit a solicitor... My aunt and uncle did visit once.* ▶ Also NC *It would be nice if you paid me a visit... Mr Ibrahim's visit follows that of President Mubarak to Iraq last month.*
2 V or V If you **visit** a place, you go to see it. *This is the best museum we've visited... 'Do you live here?'— 'No, we're just visiting.'* ▶ Also NC *...a brief visit to the U.S.*

visitation /vɪzɪteɪʃn/ **visitations**
1 NC A **visitation** is an event which is thought to be a message from God, an angel, or some other divine force. *She thought her dream was a visitation from God.*
2 NC A **visitation** can also refer to an official visit; often used humorously. *...the visitation of the Council for National Academic Awards.*

visiting /vɪzɪtɪŋ/
ADJ ATTRIB A **visiting** speaker, head of state, etc, is attending an event as a guest in a country or organization other than their own. *Mr Mitterrand was the first visiting head of state to talk to a group of dissidents in person... The traditional wreath-laying at the grave of the unknown soldier, normally performed by every visiting dignitary, has been cancelled.*

visiting hours
N PL **Visiting hours** are the times during which visitors can go to see someone in a hospital, prison, or other institution. *The hunger strikers are calling for more visiting hours.*

visitor /vɪzɪtə/ **visitors**
NC A **visitor** is someone who is visiting a person or place. *Marsha was a frequent visitor to our house.*

visor /vaɪzə/ **visors**
NC A **visor** is a movable part of a helmet which can be pulled down to protect a person's eyes or face. *Many of them have taken to wearing visors to protect their eyes from the effects of sea spray.*

vista /vɪstə/ **vistas;** a literary word.
1 NC A **vista** is the view from a particular place, especially a beautiful view from a high place. *He could see through the tall windows a vista of green fields.*
2 NC+SUPP A **vista** also refers to a range of exciting or worrying new ideas and possibilities. *...a political vista. ...a whole new vista of troubles for me.*

visual /vɪʒuəl/ **visuals**
1 ADJ **Visual** means relating to sight, or to things you can see. *...a spot of light at a particular point in the visual field. ...visual jokes.* ◆ **visually** ADV SEN or ADV *Visually, it is a very exciting film... The island is visually stunning. ...visually handicapped people.*
2 NC A **visual** is a piece of display material, such as a photograph or film, that is used to illustrate or explain something. *In the past, many visuals for health and*

development have been far too dull.

visual aid, visual aids
NC **Visual aids** are things you can look at, such as films, maps, or slides, to help you understand something, or to remember information. *...the normal visual aids that you would use doing dental health education.*

visual arts
N PL The **visual arts** are the arts of painting, sculpture, cinema, etc., which are looked at rather than read or listened to. *Jamaica's music has so far been its most well-known art form, but its visual arts are just as rich and dynamic.*

visual display unit
A **visual display unit** is the same as a VDU.

visualize /vɪʒuəlaɪz/ **visualizes, visualizing, visualized**; also spelt **visualise**.
1 VO If you **visualize** something, you form a mental picture of it because you cannot see it at that time. *He found he could visualize her face quite clearly.*
2 VO If you **visualize** a situation that is assumed or invented, you imagine it. *It is difficult to visualize whether the President and Prime Minister have a coherent joint strategy... One could visualize a situation where construction workers would be able to work freely in the United States.*

vital /vaɪtl/
1 ADJ Something that is **vital** is necessary or very important. *It is vital to keep an accurate record of every transaction... Saudi Arabia is keen about protecting its territory and its vital interests. ...vital repair work.* ◆ **vitally** SUBMOD *The way we choose to bring up children is vitally important.*
2 ADJ People or organizations that are **vital** are energetic, exciting, and full of life. *The Chinese were trusting, open, and vital... We want to have a modern vital parliament.*

vitality /vaɪtælətɪ/
NU People who have **vitality** are energetic and lively. *...the vitality and eagerness of a normal toddler.*

vital statistics
N PL+POSS A woman's **vital statistics** are the measurements of her bust, waist, and hips; an old-fashioned expression. *You almost certainly know your vital statistics.*

vitamin /vɪtəmɪn/ **vitamins**
NC **Vitamins** are organic substances in food which you need in order to remain healthy. *She needs extra vitamins and protein... One tiny berry contained more vitamin C than an orange.*

vitiate /vɪʃɪeɪt/ **vitiates, vitiating, vitiated**
VO If someone or something **vitiates** a thing or a situation, they spoil or weaken it; a formal word. *...accusations that their opponents would engage in large scale electoral abuses which could vitiate the entire democratic process.*

vitreous /vɪtrɪəs/
ADJ Something that is **vitreous** is made of or resembles glass; a technical term. *...vitreous ice.*

vitriol /vɪtrɪɒl/
NU **Vitriol** is speech or writing that is full of hatred and bitterness and that is deliberately intended to cause distress or pain; a formal word. *Much later, after the divorce and the vitriol, I agreed to see him again.*

vitriolic /vɪtrɪɒlɪk/
ADJ ATTRIB **Vitriolic** language or behaviour is full of hatred and bitterness and is deliberately intended to cause distress and pain; a formal word. *He was subjected to the most vitriolic personal abuse.*

viva, vivas; pronounced /vaɪvə/ for the meaning in paragraph 1, and /viːvə/ for the meaning in paragraph 2.
1 NC A **viva** is an oral examination, especially in a university.
2 Viva is used as a way of showing that you approve of someone or something. *Viva Mandela!... Viva multi-party politics!*

vivacious /vɪveɪʃəs/
ADJ Someone who is **vivacious** is lively, exciting, and attractive. *She was young and vivacious.*

vivacity /vɪvæsətɪ/
NU **Vivacity** is the quality of being lively in an attractive and exciting way; a formal word. *...a man of great charm and vivacity.*

vivid /vɪvɪd/
1 ADJ Something that is **vivid** is very bright in colour. *...a vivid green lawn.* ◆ **vividly** ADV *...vividly coloured birds.*
2 ADJ **Vivid** memories or descriptions are very clear and detailed. *I have a vivid memory of an excursion with my grandmother... Her descriptions of the African countryside are vivid and evocative.* ◆ **vividly** ADV *'You remember Captain van Donck?'—'Oh, yes. Vividly.'* ◆ **vividness** NU *The descriptions of characters and locations possess an almost Dickensian vividness.*

vivisection /vɪvɪsekʃn/
NU **Vivisection** is the practice of using living animals for scientific experiments. *A book has been published claiming that vivisection serves no useful purpose at all.*

vixen /vɪksən/ **vixens**
1 NC A **vixen** is a female fox. *...the killing by game keepers of a vixen in the district recently.*
2 NC If you refer to a woman as a **vixen** you mean that she is unpleasant or bad-tempered; an old-fashioned use.

viz.
CONJ **viz.** is used in written English to introduce a list of specific items or examples. *These insects appear in warm wet weather, viz. early summer and early autumn.*

V-neck /viːnek/ **V-necks**
NC A **V-neck** is a neck on a pullover or on a dress that is in the shape of the letter V.

vocabulary /vəkæbjʊlərɪ/ **vocabularies**
1 NCorNU Your **vocabulary** is the total number of words you know in a particular language. *By the age of five, a child has a vocabulary of over 2,000 words. ...improvements in intelligence, vocabulary, and motivation.*
2 N SING The **vocabulary** of a language is all the words in it. *New words are constantly coming into use and then dropping out of the vocabulary.*
3 NU+SUPP The **vocabulary** of a particular subject is the group of words that are typically used when discussing it. *'Struggle' is a key word in the Marxist-Leninist vocabulary.*

vocal /vəʊkl/ **vocals**
1 ADJ You say that people are **vocal** when they speak loudly and forcefully about something. *The members had been quite vocal on issues of academic freedom. ...the emergence of a more vocal and radical right-wing lobby. ...increasingly vocal discontent in Yugoslavia.*
2 ADJ ATTRIB **Vocal** means involving the use of the human voice, especially in singing. *She amazed her audiences with her superb vocal range.*
3 N PL **Vocals** are the singing in a pop song, in contrast to the playing of instruments *The vocals have been rerecorded for the single... This time Becky Mitchell actually sings backing vocals.*

vocal cords; also spelt **vocal chords**.
N PL Your **vocal cords** are the part of your throat which can be made to vibrate when you breathe out, helping to make the sounds you use for speaking. *Doctors have now discovered several growths on her vocal chords.*

vocalist /vəʊkəlɪst/ **vocalists**
NC A **vocalist** is a singer who sings with a pop group. *She is a 26-year-old vocalist and multi-instrumentalist from New York.*

vocation /vəʊkeɪʃn/ **vocations**
NCorNU A **vocation** is a strong wish to do a particular job, especially one which involves serving other people. *Medicine is my vocation... By vocation I'm not a politician.*

vocational /vəʊkeɪʃ⁰nəl/
ADJ **Vocational** describes the skills needed for a particular job or profession. *...a college that does technical and vocational training.*

vocative /vɒkətɪv/ **vocatives**
1 NCor ADJ In some languages, for example Latin, the **vocative** or the **vocative** case is the form of a word, especially a name, that is used when you are speaking directly to someone or writing to them. *His use of the nominative case—Walesa—rather than the vocative— Waleso—sounded unnatural and perhaps unintentionally abrupt.*
2 NC In grammar, a **vocative** is a word that you use in the way that you would use a name when you are speaking directly to someone or writing to them. For example 'dad', 'darling', and 'madam' are vocatives.

vociferous /vəsɪfərəs/
ADJ Someone who is **vociferous** speaks with great energy and determination, because they want their views to be heard; a formal word. *They were supported by a vociferous group in the actors' union. ...the Archbishop's vociferous opposition to the government.*

vodka /vɒdkə/ **vodkas**
N MASS **Vodka** is a strong, clear alcoholic drink. *He had spent seven hours in a bar drinking vodka before boarding his ship.*

vogue /vəʊg/
1 N SING If something is the **vogue**, it is very popular and fashionable. *Flowery carpets became the vogue.*
2 Something that is **in vogue** is very popular and fashionable. *At that time aftershave was not in vogue in France.*

voice /vɔɪs/ **voices, voicing, voiced**
1 NC When someone speaks, you hear their **voice**. *He recognized me by my voice... 'I suppose we'd better go,' said John in a low voice... He had shouted so loud and for so long that he had no voice left.*
2 NC You use **voice** to refer to someone's opinion on a particular topic and what they say about it. *Numerous voices were raised against the idea... The only dissenting voice was Mr Foot's.*
3 N SING If you have a **voice** in something, you have the right to express an opinion on it. *Students should have a voice in determining the way universities develop.*
4 VO If you **voice** an opinion or an emotion, you say what you think or feel. *The African delegates voiced their anger... The Foreign Secretary voiced concern over the situation in Somalia. ...four days of street demonstrations voicing mass popular support for his rival.*
5 N SING In grammar, if a verb is in the active **voice**, the person who performs the action is the subject of the verb. If a verb is in the passive **voice**, the thing or person affected by the action is the subject of the verb.
● **Voice** is used in these phrases. ● If you **raise** your **voice**, you speak more loudly. If you **lower** your **voice**, you speak more quietly. *Raising his voice, he warned his opponents that he would not tolerate efforts to undermine national stability... She lowered her voice to a discreet whisper.* ● If someone tells you to **keep** your **voice down**, they want you to speak more quietly. *'Can't you keep your voice down?' Brody said in a hoarse whisper.* ● If someone **finds** their **voice**, they begin to express themselves despite fear or difficult circumstances. *The shock had helped her find her voice. ...support begins to gather and find its voice.* ● If you **give voice to** something, such as an opinion, you express it openly; a formal expression. *Delegates gave voice to traditional suspicions about the ruling National Party.* ● If you say something **at the top of** your **voice**, you say it as loudly as possible. *'I am drenched,' she declared at the top of her voice.*
● If a number of people say something **with one voice**, they all agree about it and wish to show their unity. *It is possible for the community to speak with one voice on quite substantive matters.*

voiced /vɔɪst/
ADJ A **voiced** speech sound is one that is produced with vibration of the vocal cords; a technical term in linguistics. *Vowels, and some consonants such as /v/ and /z/, are voiced sounds.*

voiceless /vɔɪsləs/
ADJ A **voiceless** speech sound is one that is produced

without vibration of the vocal cords; a technical term in linguistics. /f/ *and* /s/ *are voiceless consonants.*

voice-over, voice-overs
NC A **voice-over** is a commentary or explanation which is heard as part of a film or television programme which is spoken by someone who is not actually seen. *The narrative, the voice-over that accompanies much of the film, is all in the third person.*

void /vɔɪd/ **voids**
1 NC A **void** is a situation or state of affairs which seems empty because it has no interest, excitement, or value; a literary use. *Tending her mother had filled the void for a time. ...the need to fill the void of materialism with humane and spiritual values. ...an aching void in his heart.*
2 NC A **void** is also a big hole or space; a literary use. *He looked down into the gaping void at his feet.*
3 ADJ PRED Something that is **void** has no official value or authority; a technical use. *He is recommending that all results in New Caledonia should be declared void.* ● See also **null.**

vol.
vol. is the written abbreviation for **volume.**

volatile /vɒlətaɪl/
1 ADJ A situation that is **volatile** is liable to change suddenly and unexpectedly. *The situation in Lebanon was 'tense, dangerous and volatile'... The government is now anxious to defuse what was fast becoming a volatile situation.* ◆ **volatility** NU *...Latin America's political volatility.*
2 ADJ A person who is **volatile** is liable to change their mood or attitude quickly and frequently. *It was the same Judy, wild-eyed, dreamy, volatile as ever.*
3 ADJ A **volatile** liquid or solid is one which will quickly change into gas; a technical use. *The soil heats up and the volatile toxic substances evaporate.*

vol-au-vent /vɒləvɒnⁿ/ **vol-au-vents** /vɒləvɒnⁿz/
NC A **vol-au-vent** is a small, light pastry case that you can eat. Vol-au-vents are usually filled with a sauce made from ingredients such as chicken, ham, or mushrooms.

volcanic /vɒlkænɪk/
ADJ A place or region that is **volcanic** has a lot of volcanoes or was created by volcanoes. *The islands are volcanic.*

volcano /vɒlkeɪnəʊ/ **volcanoes**
NC A **volcano** is a mountain which hot melted rock, gas, steam, and ash sometimes burst out of, coming from inside the earth. *Six other volcanoes were still erupting. ...an active volcano deep under the sea.*

vole /vəʊl/ **voles**
NC A **vole** is a small animal that looks like a mouse but has very small ears and a short tail. Voles usually live in fields or near rivers.

volition /vəlɪʃn/
If you do something **of** your **own volition**, you do it because you have decided for yourself that you will do it; a formal expression. *She didn't go down there of her own volition.*

volley /vɒli/ **volleys, volleying, volleyed**
1 NC A **volley** of gunfire or stones is a lot of bullets or stones that travel through the air at the same time. *...a volley of automatic rifle fire... The demonstrators attacked police with volleys of stones outside the city's main hospital.*
2 NC In games such as tennis or football, a **volley** is a shot in which the player hits or kicks the ball before it touches the ground. *He resorted to the basics of serve and volley.* ▶ Also Vor VO *He volleyed home a cross from Villarroya.*

volleyball /vɒlibɔːl/
NU **Volleyball** is a game in which two teams hit a large ball with their hands, backwards and forwards over a high net. If you allow the ball to touch the ground, your team loses a point. *...the speed of movement demanded in modern volleyball.*

volt /vəʊlt/ **volts**
NC A **volt** is a unit used to measure the force of an electric current. *The unit itself operates from 12 or 24 volts.*

voltage /vəʊltɪdʒ/ **voltages**
NU or NC The **voltage** of an electrical current is its force measured in volts. *...any sort of normally available mains voltage. ...two high voltage power lines.*

volte-face /vɒltfæs/
N SING A **volte-face** is a complete change in someone's opinions about something, so that their opinion or their decision is the opposite of what it was before; a literary word. *His colleagues demanded an explanation of his extraordinary volte-face.*

voluble /vɒljʊbl/
ADJ Someone who is **voluble** talks a lot with great energy; a formal word. *He became very voluble and told her everything.*

volume /vɒljuːm/ **volumes**
1 NC A **volume** is one of a series of books or magazines. *It was published in three volumes.*
2 NC You can refer to a book, especially a large book, as a **volume**; a literary use. *She took from the shelf a large green volume.*
3 N SING The **volume** of something is the amount of space that it contains or occupies. *The gas expanded to nine times its original volume.*
4 N SING The **volume** of something is also the amount of it that there is. *The volume of work is incredible. ...the growing volume of imports. ...the sheer volume of their published works.*
5 NU The **volume** of a radio, TV, or record player is the loudness of the sound that it produces. *She turned up the volume... Black Flag play rock music at excruciatingly high volume.*
6 If you say that something **speaks volumes**, you mean that it gives you a lot of revealing information about a particular thing. *The fact that the first British astronaut will fly in a Russian craft rather than an American one, speaks volumes for the change in atmosphere brought about by Glasnost.*

voluminous /vəljuːmɪnəs/
ADJ **Voluminous** means very large in size or quantity; a formal word. *...a voluminous skirt... I took voluminous notes.*

voluntarism /vɒləntəʳrizəm/
NU **Voluntarism** is the practice of dealing with social problems on an individual and voluntary basis, rather than by the intervention of the state. *...voluntarism as a way of addressing dire social needs. ...to eliminate the drug problem from American life, essentially through voluntarism.*

voluntary /vɒləntəʳri/
1 ADJ **Voluntary** describes actions that you choose to do, rather than have been forced to do. *Attendance at the parade was voluntary... He went into voluntary exile... They are involved in arranging the voluntary repatriation of refugees.* ♦ **voluntarily** ADV *They were said to have left their land voluntarily.*
2 ADJ **Voluntary** work is done by people who are not paid for it. *I do voluntary home tuition some evenings. ...a voluntary organisation which patrols New York's subway train system... The group is run by voluntary helpers.*

volunteer /vɒləntɪəʳ/ **volunteers, volunteering, volunteered**
1 NC A **volunteer** is someone who does work for which they are not paid. *Teaching literacy to adults using volunteers began in 1963.* ► Also N+N *...volunteer work at the hospital.*
2 NC A **volunteer** is also someone who chooses to join the armed forces, especially in wartime, as opposed to someone who is forced to join by law. *Many Australians fought as volunteers on the Allied side.*
3 V+to-INF or V+for If you **volunteer** to do something, you offer to do it, rather than being forced to do it. *He volunteered to do whatever he could for them. ...an extra payment to those who volunteer for redundancy.*
4 V O or V-QUOTE If you **volunteer** information, you give it without being asked; a formal use. *I volunteered no explanation for our visit... 'It's all fascinating and intriguing,' Maria volunteered.*

voluptuous /vəlʌptʃuəs/; a literary word.
1 ADJ A **voluptuous** woman has large breasts and hips and is considered to be sexually desirable. *He is hired*

by a local gangster to tail a voluptuous and dangerous blonde.*
2 ADJ Something that is **voluptuous** gives you a great deal of pleasure because of the rich way it is experienced through your senses. *...voluptuous echoing violin strings.* ♦ **voluptuousness** NU *They tortured innocent people with voluptuousness and delight.*

vomit /vɒmɪt/ **vomits, vomiting, vomited**
1 V If you **vomit**, food and drink comes back up from your stomach and out through your mouth. *If they drink too much at once, they may vomit... Just the sight of a cigarette made me want to vomit.* ♦ **vomiting** NU *...typical symptoms including muscular spasms, vomiting, depression and headaches.*
2 NU **Vomit** is partly digested food and drink that has come back up from someone's stomach and out through their mouth. *Nothing can disguise the pervasive stench of diarrhoea and vomit.*

voodoo /vuːduː/
NU **Voodoo** is a form of religion involving witchcraft practised by some inhabitants of the West Indies, especially in Haiti. *...traditional voodoo practices. ...a voodoo priestess.*

voracious /vəreɪʃəs/
ADJ If you say that someone is **voracious** or that they have a **voracious** appetite for something, you mean that they want a lot of it; a literary word. *...the Duke's voracious capacity for food. ...voracious readers of detective stories.* ♦ **voraciously** ADV *Locusts eat voraciously.*

vortex /vɔːteks/ **vortexes** or **vortices** /vɔːtɪsiːz/; a formal word.
1 NC A **vortex** is a mass of wind or water which spins round so fast that it pulls objects into its empty centre. *...the polar vortex. ...the spiralling vortex air-flow that slows the plane.*
2 NC+SUPP You can refer to a situation as a **vortex** when you feel that you are being forced into it without being able to prevent it. *They found themselves sucked into the revolutionary vortex.*

vote /vəʊt/ **votes, voting, voted**
1 NC Your **vote** is your choice in an election or at a meeting where decisions are taken. *...an increase in votes for the Conservative Party... He will get my vote... The Prime Minister rejected allegations of vote rigging... The motion was defeated by 221 votes to 152.*
2 NC When a group of people have a **vote** or take a **vote**, they make a decision by allowing each person in the group to say what they would prefer. *The debate, and possibly a vote, will now take place at the end of next month... They took a vote and decided to join the scheme.*
3 N SING In an election, the **vote** is the total number of people who have indicated their choice. *They captured 13 per cent of the vote.*
4 V When you **vote**, you make your choice in an election or at a meeting, by writing on a piece of paper or by raising your hand. *Some 55% of the electorate voted.* ♦ **voting** NU *Another round of voting will take place tomorrow. ...a bill to lower the voting age from twenty-one to eighteen.*
5 V A, V+to-INF, or V O If you **vote** for a particular person, political party, or course of action, you show that you support that person, party, or course of action by making a choice at an election or meeting. *Some union leaders voted for the motion supporting Labour... 22 MPs have voted against the government decision... The House of Commons has voted overwhelmingly in favour of televising its proceedings... They voted to continue the strike... We've always voted Conservative.*
6 N SING People have the **vote** when they have the legal right to indicate in an election who they would like to represent them as their government. *Women have had the vote for over fifty years.*
7 If you **vote with** your feet, you show that you do not support something by leaving the place where it is happening or the organization that is supporting it. *Thousands of Romanians are already voting with their feet, and leaving the country in the hope of a better*

*life... Many party members have voted with their feet
and left an increasingly liberal Communist Party.*

vote down PHRASAL VERB If a proposal or demand **is
voted down**, it is rejected, especially as the result of a
formal vote. *They walked out of congress after being
voted down on demands for human rights.*

vote in PHRASAL VERB When people **vote in** a person
or political party, they give them enough votes in an
election for them to hold a position of power. *There
are already enough pensioners to vote a government
in.*

vote off PHRASAL VERB When people **vote** someone **off**
an elected committee, they do not give them enough
votes to continue to be a member of that committee.
*Boris Yeltsin was formally voted off the Praesidium of
the Supreme Soviet.*

vote out PHRASAL VERB When people **vote out** a person
or political party, they do not give them enough votes
in an election to allow them to continue holding a
position of power. *They voted Councillor Hitchcock
out of her seat.*

vote of confidence, votes of confidence
1 NC A **vote of confidence** is a vote in which members
of a group are asked to indicate that they still support
the person or group in power, usually the government.
*The government lost a vote of confidence and a
general election was called.*
2 NC A **vote of confidence** is also something that you
say or do which shows that you approve of or support
a person or a group such as a political party. *He
asked if this investment is a vote of confidence in
Hong Kong's future.*

vote of no confidence, votes of no confidence
NC A **vote of no confidence** is a vote in which
members of a group are asked to indicate that they do
not support the person or group in power, usually the
government. *The government survived two votes of no
confidence last night.*

vote of thanks, votes of thanks
NC A **vote of thanks** is an official speech in which the
speaker formally thanks a person for doing
something. *The chairman will be proposing the vote
of thanks.*

voter /vəʊtə/ **voters**
NC A **voter** is someone who has the legal right to vote
in an election. *Many of Britain's voters are looking
for new answers... Early unofficial estimates put
probable voter turnout as low as ten percent.*

vouch /vaʊtʃ/ **vouches, vouching, vouched**
vouch for PHRASAL VERB 1 If you say that you can or
will **vouch for** someone, you mean that you can
guarantee their good behaviour or support. *He said
that he could vouch for your discretion... I was
vouched for by the Tattaglia family.* 2 If you say that
you can **vouch for** something, you mean that you have
evidence from your own personal experience that it is
true or correct. *I can vouch for the accuracy of my
information.*

voucher /vaʊtʃə/ **vouchers**
NC A **voucher** is a piece of paper that can be used
instead of money to pay for something. *...meal
vouchers worth 15p each.*

vouchsafe /vaʊtʃseɪf/ **vouchsafes, vouchsafing,
vouchsafed;** a formal word.
1 VOorVOA If you **vouchsafe** something to someone,
you give or offer it to them and trust them with it. *I
have at least been vouchsafed a glimpse of what love
might be. ...facts which are vouchsafed to him.*
2 VO To **vouchsafe** something to someone also means
to offer an assurance that it is settled and safe. *...to
achieve economic arrangements that vouchsafe peace
and permanence.*

Vo Van Kiet /vəʊ vʌn kjɛt/
Vo Van Kiet became Prime Minister of Vietnam in
1991. In 1958 he became a member of the Central
Committee of the Communist Party of Vietnam, the
sole party. He was Vice Chairman of the Council of
Ministers from 1982 to 1991, and Chairman of the State
Planning Committee from 1982 to 1988. Born: 1922.

vow /vaʊ/ **vows, vowing, vowed**
1 V+to-INF, V-REPORT, V-QUOTE, or VO If you **vow** to do
something, you make a solemn promise to do it. *He*

*vowed never to let it happen again... He vowed that he
would ride at my side... The group vowed, 'We will
continue'... They vowed further reprisal strikes on
towns and cities.*
2 NC A **vow** is a solemn promise. *She made a vow to
give up smoking.*

vowel /vaʊəl/ **vowels**
NC A **vowel** is a sound such as the ones represented by
the letters 'a' or 'o', which you pronounce with your
mouth open. Most words are pronounced with a
combination of consonants and vowels. *The text
consists of the consonants alone, without the vowels.*

voyage /vɔɪɪdʒ/ **voyages**
NC A **voyage** is a long journey on a ship or in a
spacecraft. *...the long sea voyage from London to
Bombay.*

voyager /vɔɪɪdʒə/ **voyagers**
NC A **voyager** is someone who goes on a voyage,
especially a difficult or dangerous one; a literary
word. *...early ocean voyagers.*

voyeur /vwaɪɜː/ **voyeurs**
1 NC A **voyeur** is someone who gets pleasure from
secretly watching other people having sex or from
watching them undress.
2 NC You can refer to someone who enjoys watching
other people's sufferings or problems as a **voyeur**.
*Television tends to turn people into voyeurs of war... If
the voyeurs are lucky, the divorce case will end up in
the courts.*

voyeurism /vwaɪərɪzəm/
NU **Voyeurism** is the activity of obtaining pleasure
from watching other people having sex. *...his
obsessions with voyeurism and sexual desire.*

voyeuristic /vwaɪərɪstɪk/
ADJ If someone's behaviour is **voyeuristic**, they obtain
pleasure from watching other people having sex.
*...scenes in which men are voyeuristic. ...the
voyeuristic appeal of their bedroom.*

Vranitzky, Dr Franz /frænts vrænɪtski/
Dr Franz Vranitzky became Chancellor of Austria in
1986. He was Minister of Finance from 1984 to 1986. He
became Chairman of the Socialist Party of Austria
(SPO) in 1988. Born: 1937.

vs.
vs. is a written abbreviation for 'versus'. *The first
match is England vs. South America.*

V-sign /viːsaɪn/ **V-signs**
1 NC In Britain, a **V-sign** is a rude gesture which is
made by moving your hand quickly upwards with your
palm facing towards you, and with your first finger
and your middle finger pointing up and spread out like
a V. *If you try and stop them, all you get is V-signs
and a load of filthy language... I just gave him a V-
sign and ran.*
2 NC A **V-sign** can also mean 'victory' when you use a
similar gesture made with your palm facing away
from you. *If a defeated politician performs the victory
V-sign, it may reflect his fighting spirit.*

VSO /viːesəʊ/
N PROP **VSO** is a British organization that sends skilled
people to developing countries to work on projects that
help the local community. **VSO** is an abbreviation for
'Voluntary Service Overseas'. *We have agreed to
provide a volunteer from VSO.*

vulgar /vʌlgə/
1 ADJ Something that is **vulgar** is regarded as being in
bad taste or of poor artistic quality. *He wore vulgar
commercialized spectacles... Its critics said that Pop
Art was vulgar and unoriginal.* ♦ **vulgarity** /vʌlgærəti/
NU *The vulgarity of the decor made me wince.*
2 ADJ **Vulgar** pictures, gestures, or remarks are rude
because they refer to sex or other bodily functions.
*The cartoons show often rude and vulgar images.
...reports that he had made vulgar comments about
women.* ♦ **vulgarity** NU *Children who are freely
brought up about sex matters have an open mind
about so-called vulgarity.*
3 ADJ Someone who is **vulgar** lacks taste or behaves in
a way that is socially unacceptable. *She is so stupid
and vulgar... Don't be vulgar.* ♦ **vulgarity** NU
*Denise's mother had straightened him out and cured
him of his vulgarity.*

vulnerable /vʌlnəˀrəbl/
1 ADJ A **vulnerable** person is weak and without
protection, with the result that they are easily hurt
physically or emotionally. *Elderly people, living
alone, are especially vulnerable... Lack of employment
outside the home tends to make women vulnerable to
depression.* ◆ **vulnerability** NU ...*the particular
vulnerability of children.*
2 ADJ When a country or place is **vulnerable**, it is not
very well defended and is therefore an easy target to
attack. ...*Kuwait, a rich but small and vulnerable
state... Their embassy is in a less vulnerable position.*

◆ **vulnerability** /vʌlnəˀrəbɪləti/ NU ...*Britain's extreme
vulnerability to attack.*
vulture /vʌltʃə/ **vultures**
NC **Vultures** are large birds which live in hot countries
and eat the flesh of dead animals. *The bodies of the
victims had been eaten by vultures and hyenas and
other wild animals.*
vulva /vʌlvə/ **vulvas**
NC The **vulva** is the outer part of a woman's sexual
organs; a technical term. ...*the lips of the vulva.*
vying /vaɪɪŋ/
Vying is the present participle of **vie**.

W w

W, w /dʌblju:/ W's, w's
1 NC **W** is the twenty-third letter of the English alphabet.
2 **W** is a written abbreviation for 'west'.

wacky /wæki/, **wackier, wackiest**; also spelt **whacky**.
ADJ Something that is **wacky** is eccentric, funny, and exciting; an informal word. *Millions of people are wearing plastic noses and participating in wacky activities to raise money for the Comic Relief charity.*

wad /wɒd/ **wads**
NC A **wad** of something such as papers or banknotes is a thick bundle of them. *She handed over a wad of forms... Money-changers can be seen with wads of dollars, pounds and sacks of rials coaxing foreigners to change money.*

wadding /wɒdɪŋ/
NU **Wadding** is soft material which is put around things to protect them, for example in packing.

waddle /wɒdl/ **waddles, waddling, waddled**
V When fat people or ducks **waddle**, they walk with short, quick steps, swaying slightly from side to side.

wade /weɪd/ **wades, wading, waded**
V If you **wade** through water or thick vegetation, you walk through it. *The children waded out into the lake... I waded up to my knees through piles of dead leaves.*
wade through PHRASAL VERB To **wade through** a difficult book or document means to spend a lot of time and effort reading it. *Each evening, he had to wade through columns of Parliamentary reports.*

wader /weɪdə/ **waders**
1 NC A **wader** is a type of bird with long legs and a long neck, which lives near water and eats fish. *Threatened species include geese, ducks and many waders.*
2 N PL **Waders** are long waterproof rubber boots which cover all of your legs. People who are fishing sometimes wear waders. *He stood up and pulled on the waders.*

wadge /wɒdʒ/. See **wodge**.

wafer /weɪfə/ **wafers**
1 NC A **wafer** is a thin, crisp biscuit, often eaten with ice cream. *She handed them coffee and chocolate wafers.*
2 NC A **wafer** is also a circular piece of a special kind of bread which the priest gives people to eat in the Christian service of Holy Communion. *She opened her mouth to receive the papery-thin wafer.*

wafer-thin
ADJ **Wafer-thin** means extremely thin and flat. *...wafer-thin slices of bread.*

waffle /wɒfl/ **waffles, waffling, waffled**
1 V If you **waffle**, you talk or write a lot without saying anything clear or important. *He's still waffling away about economic recovery.* ▶ Also NU *I don't want waffle, I want the real figures.*
2 NC A **waffle** is a type of thick pancake. *I recklessly ordered orange juice, cornflakes, coffee, and waffles with bacon and maple syrup.*

waft /wɒft/ **wafts, wafting, wafted**
V-ERG A If a sound or scent **wafts** or **is wafted** through the air, it moves gently through the air. *A scent of lemon wafted up from the gardens below. ...the aromatic oils that are wafted upwards.*

wag /wæg/ **wags, wagging, wagged**
1 V-ERG When a dog **wags** its tail or when its tail **wags**, its tail moves repeatedly from side to side. *The dog waited, making happy little barks and wagging its tail... Bess joined the crowd in the lobby, her tail flicking drops as it wagged furiously.*
2 If you say that the **tail wags the dog**, you mean that something big and powerful, which you would expect to be in control, is not in fact in control, and an apparently smaller and weaker person or group is in control. *The Free Democrats have been called the tail that wags the dog.*
3 V-ERG If you **wag** your finger or head, or if it **wags**, you shake it repeatedly from side to side. *He wagged his finger at me through the dirty window... She never spoke to us, just hurried past with her head wagging.*

wage /weɪdʒ/ **wages, waging, aged**
1 N PL Someone's **wages** are the money they are paid each week for working, especially when they have a manual or unskilled job. *My wages had not increased for two years... Poorly paid workers are toiling long hours on low wages to produce fashion garments.*
2 VO To **wage** a campaign or war means to start it and carry it on over a period of time; a formal use. *Thailand is at present waging a legal war against the United States... Mr Mandela spoke of the struggle which had been waged by Kenya's freedom fighters.*

wage-packet, wage-packets
NC Someone's **wage-packet** is the envelope containing their wages that they are given at the end of every week. *When I opened my wage-packet, I found that I had more money than usual.*

wager /weɪdʒə/ **wagers, wagering, wagered**; an old-fashioned word.
1 NC A **wager** is a bet. *There have been several wagers on certain candidates since Dr Runcie announced his retirement.*
2 VO or V-REPORT If you **wager** on a future event, you make an agreement with someone which means that you receive money if you are right about what happens, and lose money if you are wrong. *Some thirty million pounds is expected to be wagered on the race... People who've known him for years say they would wager he hasn't lost a night's sleep through worry in his life.*

waggish /wægɪʃ/
ADJ A **waggish** person makes amusing jokes; an old-fashioned word. ◆ **waggishly** ADV *Miss Wells laughed at him waggishly.*

waggle /wægl/ **waggles, waggling, waggled**
V-ERG If you **waggle** something or if it **waggles**, it moves up and down or from side to side with short, quick movements. *He waggled his eyebrows.*

wagon /wægən/, **wagons**; also spelt **waggon**.
1 NC A **wagon** is a strong vehicle with four wheels which is used for carrying heavy loads, and which is usually pulled by a horse or tractor. *There will be shire horses pulling a wagon laden with beer barrels.*
2 NC **Wagons** are also large containers on wheels

pulled by a railway engine. *The cattle go by rail in wagons.*

wagtail /ˈwægteɪl/ **wagtails**
NC A **wagtail** is a type of small bird which moves its tail quickly up and down as it walks. *Pied wagtails are building ragged nests in holes in walls.*

waif /weɪf/ **waifs**
NC A **waif** is a young person, especially a child, who looks as if he or she is hungry and has nowhere to live. *There she sat, huddled up, like a waif.*

wail /weɪl/ **wails, wailing, wailed**
V or V-QUOTE To **wail** means to cry loudly when you are in pain or very unhappy. *One of the children began to wail... 'Come and help me, someone!' wailed Crabby.*
▶ Also NC *I could hear the wail of a baby next door.*

wainscot /ˈweɪnskət/ **wainscots**
NC A **wainscot** is a wooden covering on the lower half of the wall of a room, especially in old houses.

waist /weɪst/ **waists**
NC Your **waist** is the middle part of your body, above your hips. *She tied an apron around her waist... A man who is paralysed from the waist down has appeared in a court in Belfast in a wheelchair.*

waistband /ˈweɪstbænd/ **waistbands**
NC A **waistband** is a narrow piece of material sewn on to the waist of a skirt, pair of trousers, or other garment to strengthen it. *Fasten the clip onto my waistband.*

waistcoat /ˈweɪstkəʊt/ **waistcoats**
NC A **waistcoat** is a sleeveless piece of clothing with buttons, which people usually wear over a shirt. *They were wearing the traditional Irish costume with waistcoats decorated with elaborate embroidery.*

waistline /ˈweɪstlaɪn/ **waistlines**
NC Your **waistline** is your waist measurement. *You can eat all those rich and fatty pastries and puddings—and not so much as an extra inch around the waistline.*

wait /weɪt/ **waits, waiting, waited**
1 V If you **wait**, you spend some time, usually doing very little, before something happens. *He waited patiently for her... Wait until we sit down... The US navy task force is waiting to evacuate citizens who ask for assistance.* ◆ **waiting** ADJ ATTRIB *There was a waiting period of one month.*
2 NC A **wait** is a period of time in which you do very little, before something happens. *Passengers at Gatwick—the country's busiest holiday airport—face a wait of several hours... After a long wait they started to board the rescue ships.*
3 V If something is **waiting** for you, it is ready for you to use or do. *His bicycle waited for him at the station... I have a lot of work waiting.*
4 V If you say that something can **wait**, you mean that can be dealt with later. *The dishes can wait... It may be that the President believes that political reform can wait until the economy picks up.*
● **Wait** is used in these phrases. ● If you **can't wait** to do something, you are very excited about it and eager to do it. *He couldn't wait to tell Judy.* ● You say '**you wait**' to someone to threaten or warn them. *You wait! You'll find Robinson isn't as gentle as he seems.* ● If you **wait on** someone **hand and foot**, you are always doing things for them, even if they could do the things themselves.

wait around PHRASAL VERB If you **wait around** or **wait about**, you spend a lot of time, usually doing very little, before something happens. *She had waited around for nearly a whole year... Don't keep him waiting about in the hotel.*

wait on PHRASAL VERB If you **wait on** people in a restaurant, you serve them food. *The women were very eager to wait on his table.*

wait up PHRASAL VERB If you **wait up**, you do not go to bed, because you are expecting someone to return home late at night. *She said that you shouldn't bother to wait up for her.*

waiter /ˈweɪtə/ **waiters**
NC A **waiter** is a man who serves food and drink in a restaurant. *...hotel porters, waiters or cooks... He's had to give up his part-time job as a waiter in a Japanese restaurant in London.*

waiting game, waiting games
NC If you play a **waiting game**, you deal with a situation by deliberately not doing anything, because you gain an advantage by acting later. *Mr Baker has proved that he is willing to play a waiting game.*

waiting list, waiting lists
NC A **waiting list** is a list of people who have asked for something, for example medical treatment or a job, which is not immediately available but will be in the future. *He's on the waiting list for a council house... The latest official figures say that more than one million people are on hospital waiting lists.*

waiting-room, waiting-rooms
NC A **waiting-room** is a room in a place such as a railway station or a doctor's surgery, where people can sit down while they wait. *The official pushed the man away from the crowded waiting-room and into an office.*

waitress /ˈweɪtrəs/ **waitresses**
NC A **waitress** is a woman who serves food and drink in a restaurant. *...a waitress at the local cafe.*

waive /weɪv/ **waives, waiving, waived**
1 VO If someone **waives** a rule, they decide not to enforce it; a formal word. *Rules about proper dress may be waived.*
2 V If you **waive** your right to something, for example legal representation, you give up your right to receive it. *The Foreign Office has asked the ambassador to waive his diplomatic immunity.*
3 V If a government or bank **waives** a debt, they no longer seek repayment of it. *President Bush intends to ask Congress to waive Egypt's military debts.*

wake /weɪk/, **wakes, waking, woke, woken.** The form **waked** is also used for the past tense and past participle in American English.
1 V-ERG When you **wake** or when someone **wakes** you, you become conscious again after being asleep. *I sometimes wake at four in the morning... He woke me early.*
2 NC A **wake** is a gathering of people who have collected together to mourn someone's death. *A simple wake continued over the Emperor's body.*
● **Wake** is used in these phrases. ● If one thing follows **in the wake of** another, it happens after the other thing is over, often as a result of it. *Famine came in the wake of disastrous floods.* ● Your **waking hours** are the times when you are awake rather than asleep. *I spend most of my waking hours in the library.* ● If you leave something **in your wake**, you leave it behind you as you go. *They left trails of sweet papers in their wake.*

wake up PHRASAL VERB When you **wake up** or are **woken up**, you become conscious again after being asleep. *Ralph, wake up!... I woke them up again.*

wake up to PHRASAL VERB If you **wake up to** a dangerous situation, you become aware of it. *The West began to wake up to the danger it faced.*

wakeful /ˈweɪkfl/
1 ADJ Someone who is **wakeful** is constantly waking up and not sleeping very much. *Some babies are hungry and wakeful from birth.*
2 ADJ **Wakeful** also means awake and alert; a formal use. *This alarmed her and made her more wakeful.* ◆ **wakefulness** NU *The music shook me into wakefulness.*

waken /ˈweɪkən/ **wakens, wakening, wakened**
V-ERG When you **waken** or when someone **wakens** you, you wake up; a literary word. *They would not waken a sleeping girl... For children who might waken, it's important for the babysitter to be a person they know and like.*

Waldheim, Dr Kurt /kʊət ˈvælthaɪm/
Dr Kurt Waldheim became President of Austria in 1986. He served as Foreign Minister from 1968 to 1970. He was the Permanent Representative to the United Nations from 1964 to 1968, and from 1970 to 1971. He was Secretary General of the UN from 1971 to 1981. He is a member of the Austrian People's Party (ÖVP). Born: 1918.

Wales /weɪlz/
Wales, called **Cymru** in Welsh, is a country of the United Kingdom of Great Britain and Northern

Ireland. The population of Wales in 1983 was 3 million and it has an area of 20,768 square kilometres. It was joined to England in the Act of Union of 1536. The capital of Wales is Cardiff.

Waleşa, Lech /lɛx vauɛn⁰sə/
Lech Waleşa became President of Poland in 1990. He was a leader of the strike at the Lenin Shipyard in Gdańsk in 1980, which led to the founding of Solidarity. He was Chairman of Solidarity from 1980 to 1990. In 1983 he won the Nobel Peace Prize. Born: 1943.

walk /wɔːk/ **walks, walking, walked**
1 V or VO When you **walk**, you move forward by putting one foot in front of the other on the ground. *Most children learn to walk when they are about one... We walked along in silence... He could walk the streets and fear nothing... The two men walked through the night until they came to a village.*
2 N SING A **walk** is the action of walking rather than running. *He slowed down to a walk.*
3 NC A **walk** is also a journey or outing which you make by walking somewhere. *I'm looking forward to a walk in the green fields of Kent... Some African mothers can be seven days' walk away from the nearest health centre... The station is a three minute walk from the park.*
4 NC Your **walk** is the way you move when you walk. *He came in with his distinctive walk.*
5 VOA If you **walk** someone somewhere, you walk there with them as a way of being polite to them or to protect them. *I walked him to his car... He walked her home.*
6 VO If you **walk** your dog, you take it for a walk in order to keep it healthy. *Have you walked the dog yet?*
7 See also **walking**.

walk away with PHRASAL VERB If you **walk away with** something such as a prize, you win it; an informal expression. *She walked away with the title.*

walk in on PHRASAL VERB If you **walk in on** a person or an event, you go into a place and interrupt them without intending to, because you did not expect them to be there. *He walked in on me when I was having a bath.*

walk off PHRASAL VERB If you try to **walk off** a headache or other illness, you go for a walk in order to try to feel better.

walk off with PHRASAL VERB; an informal expression.
1 If someone **walks off with** something that does not belong to them, they take it without permission. *Who's walked off with my pen?... Police in Manchester are investigating how a man disguised as a postman walked off with cheques worth more than £750,000.* 2 If you **walk off with** something such as a prize, you win it very easily. *She'll walk off with a first class degree.*

walk out PHRASAL VERB 1 If you **walk out** of a meeting, performance, or unpleasant situation, you leave it suddenly, usually to show that you are angry or very bored. *Most of the audience walked out after the first half hour... He walked out of his job.* 2 If workers **walk out**, they go on strike. *If the men have walked out, it will prove vital for the strikers in Gdansk.* ● See also **walkout**.

walk out on PHRASAL VERB If you **walk out on** someone you have a close relationship with, you leave them suddenly. *His girlfriend walked out on him.*

walkabout /wɔːkəbaut/ **walkabouts**
NC When an important or famous person goes on a **walkabout**, they walk through crowds in a public place in order to meet people. *Mrs Thatcher went on a walkabout in the old city.*

walker /wɔːkə/ **walkers**
NC A **walker** is a person who walks, especially in the countryside for pleasure. *The woods are heavily visited by walkers.*

walkie-talkie /wɔːkitɔːki/ **walkie-talkies**
NC A **walkie-talkie** is a small portable radio which is used for sending and receiving messages. *There were hundreds of policemen around with walkie-talkies.*

walking /wɔːkɪŋ/
NU **Walking** is the activity of going for walks in the country. *Walking and mountaineering are very popular here. ...a walking holiday.*

walking stick, walking sticks
NC A **walking stick** is a long wooden stick which a person can lean on while walking.

Walkman /wɔːkmən/ **Walkmans**
NC A **Walkman** is a small cassette player with very light headphones, which people carry around so that they can listen to music while they are doing something; **Walkman** is a trademark. *He thought about you in the cafeteria reading and listening to your Walkman.*

walk of life, walks of life
NC The **walk of life** that you come from is the position that you have in society and the kind of job you have. *Members of this club come from many different walks of life.*

walk-on
ADJ ATTRIB A **walk-on** part in a play is a very small part which usually does not involve any speaking. *From drama school to walk-on parts, she chronicles the early years of a young, struggling actress.*

walkout /wɔːkaut/ **walkouts**
1 NC When people stage a **walkout** from a meeting, they leave the meeting in order to show their disapproval about an issue or a decision that has been made. *About sixty Scottish MPs staged a walkout from the Commons in protest over the government's decision.*
2 NC A **walkout** is a strike by workers. *The pay deal ended the 43-day-old walkout... The walkout brought rail traffic to a halt in the region.*

walkover /wɔːkəuvə/ **walkovers**
1 NC If someone who is playing in a competition or contest gets a **walkover**, they automatically win one stage of the competition or contest because the person who they should be playing against decides not to take part. *The world champion was given a walkover when Fiona Smith had to pull out because of influenza.*
2 NC If a competition or contest is a **walkover**, it is won very easily. *Carlos Salinas de Gortari is almost certain to win, but it will not be a walkover... It was wrong to suggest the war would be a walkover, and people had to be prepared for casualties.*

walk-up, walk-ups
NC In the United States, a **walk-up** is a tall block of flats which has no lift, or a flat in such a block. *I couldn't even afford the rent in my fifth-floor walk-up.*

walkway /wɔːkweɪ/ **walkways**
NC A **walkway** is an outdoor footpath that is raised above the ground. *...the concrete complex of walkways near London's Waterloo Station.*

wall /wɔːl/ **walls**
1 NC A **wall** is one of the vertical sides of a building or room. *There was a picture on the wall... We're tearing a wall down and making two rooms into one room.*
2 NC A **wall** is also a long narrow vertical structure made of stone or brick that surrounds or divides an area of land. *We crouched behind the wall and waited.*
3 NC+SUPP The **wall** of something that is hollow is its side. *We put in a mixture that caused the seals to wear against the cylinder walls... If the egg has been fertilized it implants in the wall of the womb and a pregnancy ensues.*
4 NC+SUPP A **wall** of things or people is a solid line of them forming a vertical barrier. *Survivors spoke of a wall of water up to twenty feet high smashing through the town... All roads were blocked by a solid wall of riot police standing four deep.*

wallaby /wɒləbi/ **wallabies**
NC A **wallaby** is an animal rather like a small kangaroo. Wallabies live in Australia and New Guinea.

walled /wɔːld/
ADJ A **walled** area of land is surrounded by a wall. *...the old walled city of Jerusalem.*

wallet /wɒlɪt/ **wallets**
1 NC A **wallet** is a small, flat case usually made of leather or plastic, in which you keep banknotes and other small things such as credit cards. *It's a plastic key for your car door and it goes into a sort of credit card in your wallet.*
2 NC You can talk about your **wallet** to refer to your

personal finances. *The new federal budget hits Americans in their wallets, by raising taxes for the first time in a decade.*

wallflower /wɔːlflauə/ **wallflowers**
1 NC A **wallflower** is a plant that is grown in gardens and has lots of yellow, red, orange, or purple flowers. *The children had brought bunches of cottage flowers, daffodils, polyanthus and wallflowers.*
2 NC If someone is a **wallflower**, they do not get involved in things that are taking place, usually because they are shy. *Curtis Strange is hardly a wallflower.*

Wallis and Futuna Islands
/wɒlɪs ənd fuːtuːnə aɪləndz/
The **Wallis and Futuna Islands** are a territory of France in the South Pacific. Wallis Island is also known as Uvea, and Futuna Island as Hooru. They became a French protectorate in 1842. Copra is exported. ◆ **Wallisean, Futunan** /wɒlɪsiən, fuːtuːnən/ N, ADJ
■ *religion:* Christianity (mainly Roman Catholic)
■ *language:* French, Wallisian ■ *currency:* Pacific franc
■ *capital:* Mata-Utu ■ *population:* 12,000 (1983) ■ *size:* 274 square kilometres.

wallop /wɒləp/ **wallops, walloping, walloped**
VO To **wallop** someone means to hit them very hard; an informal word. *His mother would have walloped him if she'd known.*

walloping /wɒləpɪŋ/ **wallopings**
NC If someone gives a child a **walloping**, they beat him or her severely, usually as a punishment; an informal word. *I got a terrific walloping from our father.*

wallow /wɒləu/ **wallows, wallowing, wallowed**
1 V+*in* If you **wallow** in an unpleasant situation or feeling, you allow it to continue longer than is reasonable or necessary because you lack the energy or will-power to change things. *At first I just wanted to wallow in misery... Her mother was wallowing in widowhood... Peru is now wallowing in an economic crisis.*
2 V When an animal **wallows** in mud or water, it lies or rolls about in it slowly. *Dogs love splashing in mud and hippos wallow in it.*

wallpaper /wɔːlpeɪpə/ **wallpapers**
N MASS **Wallpaper** is thick coloured or patterned paper that is used to decorate the walls of rooms. *Today's women are willing to strip off old wallpaper and paint woodwork... There were fifteen simple bedrooms, all hung with French wallpapers.*

Wall Street
N PROP **Wall Street** is a street in New York where the Stock Exchange and important banks are. **Wall Street** is often used to refer to the type of business carried out in the area and to the people who work there. *He started gambling on Wall Street... Wall Street welcomed this move as a sign of determination.*

wall-to-wall
ADJ A **wall-to-wall** carpet covers the floor of a room completely. *...three-bedroom houses with wall-to-wall carpets.*

wally /wɒli/ **wallies**
NC If you call someone a **wally**, you mean that they are stupid or foolish; an informal word. *He looked a right wally in that hat.*

walnut /wɔːlnʌt/ **walnuts**
1 NU A **walnut** is a tree. Its wood is light brown in colour and is also called **walnut**. *The exhibition has a veneered walnut throne inlaid with ebony.*
2 NC A **walnut** is also a nut with a wrinkled, hard brown shell that comes from a walnut tree. *There may be curbs on US dried fruits and walnuts.*

walrus /wɔːlrəs/ **walruses**. The plural can be either **walruses** or **walrus**.
NC A **walrus** is an animal which lives in the sea. It has long whiskers and two tusks pointing downwards. *The herds of walrus in the North Pacific are estimated to number about 240,000.*

waltz /wɔːls/ **waltzes, waltzing, waltzed**
1 NC A **waltz** is a type of dance which people do to music which has a rhythm of three beats in each bar. *Mr Shultz danced his last waltz with the Mayor of*

Vienna's wife.
2 V-RECIP When two people **waltz**, they dance a waltz together. *I dreamt of going to Hollywood to waltz with Ginger Rogers... Down by the lake, in the afternoon sunshine, couples waltz sedately at an open-air tea-dance.*
3 VA If you **waltz** into a place, you enter in a quick, confident way that makes other people notice you; an informal use. *She waltzed across to Helen and sat down beside her.*

wan /wɒn/
ADJ Someone who is **wan** looks pale and tired; a literary word. *...a wan smile.*

wand /wɒnd/ **wands**
1 NC A magic **wand** is a long, thin rod that magicians use when they perform magic tricks. *In fairy tales someone always waves a magic wand and makes good any problems.*
2 NU When political figures say they do not have a magic **wand**, they mean they cannot solve a difficult problem quickly and easily. *The state had no magic wand with which to resolve the country's many problems.*

wander /wɒndə/ **wanders, wandering, wandered**
1 V A or VO If you **wander** somewhere, you walk around in a casual or aimless way. *We wandered round the little harbour town... A man was found wandering in the hills... The children wandered the streets after school.*
2 V If something **wanders** away from its usual position, it changes direction, often for no apparent reason. *The Earth's atmosphere tends to make satellites wander off position and lose height.*
3 V If your mind **wanders** or your thoughts **wander**, you stop concentrating on something and start thinking about other things. *When she was alone, she would let her mind wander... My thoughts kept wandering back to that night.*

wandering /wɒndəᵒrɪŋ/ **wanderings**
1 ADJ ATTRIB **Wandering** people travel around rather than stay in one place for a long time. *...travelling with a wandering troupe of actors.*
2 N PL Someone's **wanderings** are journeys they make from place to place without staying anywhere for long. *I was tired of all our wanderings and never having a home for longer than a month.*

wane /weɪn/ **wanes, waning, waned**
1 V If a condition, attitude, or emotion **wanes**, it becomes weaker, often disappearing completely in the end. *Her enthusiasm for Harold was beginning to wane... The influence of this group waned considerably.* ● to **wax and wane**: see wax.
2 If a condition, attitude, or emotion is **on the wane**, it is becoming weaker. *They could claim that pollution for the first time was on the wane.*

wangle /wæŋgl/ **wangles, wangling, wangled**
VO If you **wangle** something that you want, you manage to get it by being clever or persuasive; an informal word. *He always managed to wangle the easy jobs.*

wank /wæŋk/ **wanks, wanking, wanked**
V If someone **wanks**, they masturbate; an offensive word.

wanker /wæŋkə/ **wankers**; an offensive word which you should avoid using.
1 NC Someone might refer to a person, usually a man, as a **wanker** when they think that he is very stupid or useless; an offensive use.
2 NC Some people might also use **wanker** to refer to someone, especially a man, who masturbates; an offensive use.

want /wɒnt/ **wants, wanting, wanted**
1 V O or V+*to*-INF If you **want** something, you feel a desire or a need for it. *Do you want a cup of coffee?... All they want is a holiday... I want to be an actress... I didn't want him to go.*
2 V+ING If something **wants** doing, it needs to be done. *We've got a couple of jobs that want doing in the garden.*
3 V+*to*-INF If you tell someone that they **want** to do a particular thing, you are advising them to do it. *You want to book your holiday early this year.*

4 vo If someone is **wanted**, the police are searching for them. *He is wanted for the crimes of murder and kidnapping.*

5 N SING+*of* A **want** of something is a lack of it; a formal use. *They had to confess their complete want of foresight.*

6 If you do something **for want of** something else, you do it because it is not possible to do the other thing; a formal expression. *For want of anything better to do, he continued to read.*

wanting /wɒntɪŋ/
ADJ PRED If you find something **wanting** or if it proves **wanting**, it is not as good as you think it should be; a formal word. *He judged the nation and found it wanting.*

wanton /wɒntən/
ADJ A **wanton** action deliberately causes unnecessary harm, damage, or waste; a formal word. *...senseless and wanton cruelty.*

war /wɔː/ **wars**
1 NCorNU A **war** is a period of armed conflict between countries. *They fought in the war against Britain... There are no winners in nuclear war... England and Germany were at war.*

2 NCorNU You also use **war** to refer to intense economic competition between countries or organizations. *A trade war between the European Community and the United States now looks inevitable.*

3 NU If you make **war** on someone or something that you are opposed to, you do things to stop them succeeding in what they are trying to do. *The Colombian government declared all-out war on the drugs barons.*

4 See also **civil war, cold war, war of words**: see **word**.
● **War** is used in these phrases. ● If a country **goes to war**, it starts fighting a war. *Under the terms of the treaty, we are obliged to go to war.* ● If someone **has been in the wars**, they have been injured, for example in a fight or accident; an old-fashioned, informal expression. *You look as though you've been in the wars.*

warble /wɔːbl/ **warbles, warbling, warbled**
v When a bird **warbles**, it sings pleasantly; a literary word.

ward /wɔːd/ **wards, warding, warded**
1 NC A **ward** is a hospital room which has beds for many people, often people who need similar treatment. *She stayed five days in the emergency ward for observation.*

2 NC A **ward** is a district which forms part of a political constituency or local council. *A by-election in a municipal ward has seen the right wing candidate soundly defeated.*

3 NC A **ward** or a **ward of court** is a child who is being looked after by an appointed guardian or by a court of law, either because their parents are dead or because they are considered to be in need of protection. *The boy was made a ward of court after his schoolteachers noticed suspicious injuries.*

ward off PHRASAL VERB To **ward off** a danger or illness means to prevent it from affecting you or harming you. *He wears a copper bracelet to ward off rheumatism.*

-ward /-wəd/
SUFFIX **-ward** and **-wards** are added to nouns referring to places or directions to form adverbs or adjectives which indicate the direction in which something is moving or facing. *He was gazing skyward... He led the group homewards... The westward drive of European settlers to the United States had come to an end.*

warden /wɔːdn/ **wardens**
1 NC+SUPP A **warden** is an official who makes sure that certain laws or regulations are being obeyed. *Measures to control dogs would include dog wardens with enhanced powers... A poacher was killed in an ambush by National Parks wardens.*

2 NC A **warden** is also a person in charge of a building or institution such as a youth hostel. *He is the warden of a youth hostel near Coniston. ...the warden of Green*

College, Oxford.

3 NC A **warden** is also somebody who works in a prison supervising the prisoners. *Prisoners at a high-security jail in Australia took advantage of a strike by wardens to order more than 300 pizzas from a nearby restaurant.*

4 NC In the United States, the **warden** of a prison is the person in charge of it. *The prison warden said inmates were given work according to the needs of the prison.*

warder /wɔːdə/ **warders**
NC A **warder** is a person who is in charge of prisoners in a jail. *He had his spine damaged in a beating received from a warder.*

wardrobe /wɔːdrəub/ **wardrobes**
1 NC A **wardrobe** is a tall cupboard in which you hang your clothes. *They were billeted in a sports hall decked out with beds and wardrobes.*

2 NC Someone's **wardrobe** is all of their clothes. *He was familiar with her entire wardrobe.*

wardrobe mistress, wardrobe mistresses
NC A **wardrobe mistress** is a woman who is in charge of the wardrobe in a theatre company.

-wards /-wədz/. See **-ward**.

ware /weə/
1 NU+SUPP **Ware** is used to refer to objects that are made of a particular substance, such as glass or china, or things that are used for a particular domestic purpose, such as cooking. *...glass ware. ...kitchen ware.*

2 N PL Someone's **wares** are the things that they sell, usually in the street or in a market; an old-fashioned use. *The market traders began to sell their wares at half-price.*

warehouse /weəhaus/ **warehouses**
NC A **warehouse** is a large building where raw materials or manufactured goods are stored. *A warehouse containing maize, beans, seed and sugar has been destroyed in a cyclone.*

warehouse club, warehouse clubs
NC A **warehouse club** is a shop which offers goods for sale at reduced prices to people who pay an annual subscription to be able to use the shop. *Costco, the third biggest chain of warehouse clubs in the US, plans to open up in Britain.*

warfare /wɔːfeə/
NU **Warfare** is the activity of fighting a war; a formal word. *They are anxious to prevent this conflict from erupting into open warfare.*

warhead /wɔːhed/ **warheads**
NC A **warhead** is the front end of a bomb or missile, where the explosives are carried. *Pakistan had fired a missile capable of carrying a nuclear warhead.*

war horse, war horses
NC You can refer to an old soldier or politician who is still active and aggressive as a **war horse**. *They are turning to a figure from the past, the war horse Leonel Brizola.*

warlike /wɔːlaɪk/
ADJ People who are **warlike** are aggressive and seem eager to start a war; a formal word. *As a warlike people, the Alawites were promoted as a tool to suppress the Arab Nationalist revolt.*

warm /wɔːm/ **warmer, warmest; warms, warming, warmed**
1 ADJ Something that is **warm** has some heat but not enough to be hot. *The fabric should then be sponged with warm water... All three countries offer a warm climate.*

2 VOorV-REFL If you **warm** a part of your body, you put it near a fire or heater to stop it feeling cold. *I warmed my hand on the radiator... Come and warm yourself in front of the fire.*

3 ADJ **Warm** clothes and blankets are made of a material such as wool which protects you from the cold. *Despite a lack of food, medicine and warm clothes, guerrilla morale remains high.* ◆ **warmly** ADV *I'll see that Chris dresses warmly.*

4 ADJ A **warm** person is friendly and affectionate. *She had a warm, generous heart... He was given a warm welcome.* ◆ **warmly** ADV *He shook Tony warmly by the hand.*

5 V+*to* If you **warm** to a person or an idea, you become fonder of the person or more interested in the idea. *This makes you warm to Meadows... He warmed to the prospect of a new job.*

warm up PHRASAL VERB **1** If you **warm** something up or if it **warms up**, it gets hotter. *Start warming up the soup now... When the weather warmed up mosquitoes began swarming.* **2** When athletes **warm up** for an sporting event, they prepare themselves by practising or by doing exercises just before it starts. *I always spend ten minutes warming up before a race. ...the stretches that you warmed up with.* ● See also **warm-up. 3** When a machine or engine **warms up**, it becomes ready for use a little while after being switched on or started. *I went across and switched on the TV and waited for it to warm up.*

warm-blooded
ADJ A **warm-blooded** animal, for example a bird or a mammal, has a relatively high body temperature which remains constant and is not affected by the surrounding temperature. *Scientists believe that the virus can affect all warm-blooded animals.*

warm front, warm fronts
NC A **warm front** is the weather condition that occurs when the front part of a mass of warm air pushes into a mass of cold air; a technical term.

warm-hearted
ADJ A **warm-hearted** person is friendly and affectionate. *She has two great qualities, warm-hearted affection, and loyalty to her friends.*

warmonger /wɔːmʌŋgə/ **warmongers**
NC A **warmonger** is someone, for example a politician, who encourages people to start a war or to prepare for one. *There was a shout of 'warmonger' when John Edmund gave his support on the Gulf issue.*

warmongering /wɔːmʌŋgəʰrɪŋ/
NU **Warmongering** is behaviour in which someone encourages people to start a war or to prepare for one. *The leader of the ruling Democratic Revolutionary Party has accused Washington of warmongering.*

warmth /wɔːmθ/
1 NU **Warmth** is friendly and affectionate behaviour. *He generates a great deal of personal warmth... There has been a new diplomatic warmth between the two countries... Mr Botha spoke of the warmth of the welcome he'd received in Yugoslavia and Czechoslovakia.* **2** NU **Warmth** is also a moderate amount of heat that something has, for example enough heat to make you feel comfortable. *We huddled together for warmth.*

warm-up, warm-ups
NC A **warm-up** is preparation that athletes do just before a sporting event such as a race, for example by exercising or practising. *The match is a warm-up for the first one-day international in Kingston.*

warn /wɔːn/ **warns, warning, warned**
1 V O, V, V-QUOTE, or V-REPORT If you **warn** someone about a possible danger or problem, you make them aware of it by telling them about it. *I did warn you of possible failure... United Nations officials warn of epidemics and famine... Manufacturers failed to warn doctors that their drugs should be used only in limited circumstances... 'Be careful with that,' he warned... Bankers warn that inflation will reach 50 or 60 percent this month alone.* **2** V O If you **warn** someone not to do something, you advise them not to do it so that they can avoid possible danger or punishment. *I warned him not to lose his temper with her... I'm warning you, if you do that again there'll be trouble.*

warn off PHRASAL VERB If you **warn** someone **off**, you tell them to go away or to stop doing something because of possible danger or punishment. *Intruders are warned off by the sound.*

warning /wɔːnɪŋ/ **warnings**
1 NC or NU A **warning** is something which is said or written to tell people of a possible danger, problem, or other unpleasant thing that might happen. *The hospital issued warnings about drugs to be avoided... Dad gave a warning to them not to look directly at the sun... Mary left her husband without any warning.*

2 ADJ ATTRIB **Warning** actions or signs give a warning. *Watch out for the warning signs of depression like insomnia... Police fired warning shots to bring the protestors under control.*

war of nerves
N SING A **war of nerves** is a conflict in which the opposing sides use psychological means to weaken each other, for example by making each other frightened or telling lies about each other. *It was a kind of war of nerves with the publishers.*

warp /wɔːp/ **warps, warping, warped**
1 V-ERG If a material such as wood **warps** or if something **warps** it, it becomes damaged by bending, often because of the effect of heat or water. *The cabinet doors began to warp soon after they were installed... The wooden balconies were warped and weatherbeaten.* ◆ **warped** ADJ *There was a thin gap between the wall and the warped wood of the service door.* **2** V O If something **warps** someone's character, it influences them and makes them abnormal or bad. *His whole character was warped by being bullied.* ◆ **warped** ADJ *...this sort of warped logic... He had a warped mind.* **3** N C A **warp** in time or space is an imaginary break or sudden change in the normal experience of time or space. *There's a kind of time warp in his education.* **4** N SING The **warp** in a piece of woven material is the threads which are held along a loom while other threads are passed across them; a technical use.

warpath /wɔːpɑːθ/
If someone is **on the warpath**, they are angry and are getting ready for a fight or an argument; an informal expression. *He scares me to death when he's on the warpath.*

warrant /wɒrənt/ **warrants, warranting, warranted**
1 V O If something **warrants** a particular action, it makes the action seem necessary; a formal use. *The case warrants further investigation.* **2** NC A **warrant** is an official document signed by a judge or magistrate, which gives the police special permission to do something such as arrest someone or search their house. *Grenoble has issued a warrant for the arrest of the former Mayor of Nice.* ● See also **arrest warrant, death warrant, extradition warrant, search warrant.**

warrant officer, warrant officers
NC A **warrant officer** is a person in the army, the air force, or the marines, who is above the rank of sergeant and below the rank of lieutenant. *A private will receive an allowance of 36 pence per day, whilst a warrant officer will earn £5.76.*

warranty /wɒrənti/ **warranties**
N U or NC A **warranty** is a written promise by a company that if their work has any faults it will be repaired or replaced free of charge. *The car was still under warranty.*

warren /wɒrən/ **warrens**
1 NC A **warren** is a group of holes in the ground connected by tunnels, which rabbits live in. *...a rabbit warren.* **2** NC+SUPP A **warren** is also a building or area of a city in which many people live in crowded conditions and there are many passages or narrow streets. *...the oldest part of the city, a warren of densely populated streets, crowded courtyards and bustling markets.*

warring /wɔːrɪŋ/
1 ADJ ATTRIB **Warring** nations or groups are people who are fighting against each other. *Soldiers and riot police kept the warring factions apart.* **2** ADJ ATTRIB You can also use **warring** to describe two groups of people when they disagree very strongly about something. *The warring factions in tennis may meet next month to discuss settling their differences.*

warrior /wɒriə/ **warriors**
NC **Warriors** are soldiers or experienced fighting men who act bravely; used especially of soldiers in ancient times. *The warriors knew that they were outnumbered and outgunned. ...stories of ancient kings, warriors and great battles.*

Warsaw /wɔːsɔː/
Warsaw is the capital of Poland and its largest city.

Population: 1,665,000 (1989).

warship /wɔːʃɪp/ **warships**

NC A **warship** is a ship with guns that is used for fighting in wars. *The warship tried to stop the vessel by firing across its bows.*

wart /wɔːt/ **warts**

NC A **wart** is a small, hard piece of skin which can grow on someone's face or hands. *...a large woman with a wart on her nose.*

warthog /wɔːthɒg/ **warthogs**

NC A **warthog** is a wild pig with two small tusks and several bumps on its face that look like warts. Warthogs live in Africa. *The bones included specimens from zebras, warthogs and baboons.*

wartime /wɔːtaɪm/

NU **Wartime** is a period of time when there is a war. *...the disruption of the environment in wartime. ...wartime memories.*

war widow, war widows

NC A **war widow** is a woman whose husband died while he was in the armed forces during a war. *The United States is to provide aid worth some five million dollars to Cambodian children and war widows.*

wary /weəri/

ADJ If you are **wary** of something, you are cautious about it, for example because it is a new experience or because there may be dangers or problems. *People are understandably wary of the new government.*

♦ **warily** ADV *She was watching Stuart warily.*

was /wəz, wɒz/

Was is the first and third person singular of the past tense of **be**.

wash /wɒʃ/ **washes, washing, washed**

1 VO If you **wash** something, you clean it using water and soap. *...the clatter of dishes being washed and put away... She washes and irons his clothes.* ► Also NC *Give it a good wash.*

2 N SING The **wash** is all the clothes that are washed together at one time. *...the average weekly wash.*

3 V or VO If you **wash** or if you **wash** part of your body, you clean your body using soap and water. *I'll have to wash... First wash your hands.* ► Also NC *He was having a wash.*

4 V A If a liquid **washes** somewhere, it flows there. *The surf washed over her ankles.*

5 V-ERG A If something **is washed** somewhere or if something **washes** it in a particular direction, it is carried there by a flow of liquid. *The body was washed ashore in Norway... Soil from the mountains washes down in the rivers.*

6 If you say that you **wash** your **hands of** something, you mean that you refuse to be involved with it any longer or to accept any further responsibility for it. *It was charged that Britain had washed its hands of Hong Kong.*

7 See also **washing**.

wash away PHRASAL VERB If floods **wash away** buildings, they destroy them and carry them away. *The water washed away a whole village.*

wash down PHRASAL VERB If you **wash down** food, you drink something after you have eaten or while you are eating it. *...a mash of overcooked rice, washed down with the local wine.*

wash out PHRASAL VERB 1 If you **wash** a stain **out** of something, you remove it using water and soap. *Wash out the remaining oil with some detergent.* 2 If you **wash out** a container, you wash the inside of it. *The vessel can be washed out and the whole process repeated.* 3 If a sporting event is **washed out**, bad weather has caused it to be cancelled. *Storms washed out the final days of the third Test match.*

wash up PHRASAL VERB 1 If you **wash up**, you wash the pans, plates, cups, and cutlery which have been used in cooking and eating a meal. *When the average woman gets home from work she still has to cook the evening meal and wash up the dishes... The burglar cooked a meal and then washed up his dirty dishes.* 2 To **wash up** also means to clean part of your body with soap and water, especially your hands and face; used in American English. *He asks permission before he washes up in the bathroom.* 3 If something is **washed up** on a piece of land, it is carried there by a

river or the sea. *His body was washed up under the bridge at Dakao.* 4 See also **washing-up**.

washable /wɒʃəbl/

ADJ **Washable** clothes or materials can be washed without being damaged. *Acrylic blankets are warm and washable... It is lightweight and fully machine washable.*

washbasin /wɒʃbeɪsn/ **washbasins**

NC A **washbasin** is a large basin for washing your hands and face, usually with taps for hot and cold water. *He walked across to the washbasin and looked in the mirror.*

washed-out

1 ADJ **Washed-out** colours are pale and dull. *...eyes of washed-out grey. ...a canopy of washed-out blue.*

2 ADJ If someone looks **washed-out**, they look very tired, usually because of illness or over-work. *He had lots of children and a washed-out wife.*

washed up

ADJ Someone who is **washed up** is at the end of their career with no prospects for the future; used in informal American English. *I was not going to be all washed up, an ex-sportsman with nothing to do at 30.*

washer /wɒʃə/ **washers**

NC A **washer** is a thin, flat ring of metal, plastic, or rubber, which is used to make a tight connection or seal between objects that are joined together with a nut and a bolt. *Take the thing apart and put in a new washer.*

washing /wɒʃɪŋ/

NU **Washing** is clothes, sheets, and towels that need to be washed, or have just been washed. *Her husband comes home at weekends, bringing his washing with him... There was nowhere to hang washing.*

washing machine, washing machines

NC A **washing machine** is a machine that washes clothes. *...a fully automatic washing machine.*

washing powder, washing powders

N MASS **Washing powder** is powdered detergent that you use to wash clothes. *In many other areas of the country, soap and washing powder are either totally unavailable or are rationed... Phosphates are added to washing powders to soften the water and increase the efficiency of the product.*

washing soda

NU **Washing soda** is a strong chemical detergent in the form of crystals which is used to clean very dirty things such as the drains in a house. *Clean the sink outlet by dissolving a handful of washing soda in warm water and pouring it down the sink and the outside drain.*

Washington, DC /wɒʃɪŋtən diːsiː/

Washington, DC is the capital of the United States. It is the headquarters of the Organization of American States. Population: 617,000 (1988).

washing-up

NU If you do the **washing-up**, you wash the pans, plates, cups, and cutlery which have been used in cooking and eating a meal. *Can I do the washing-up first?*

washing-up liquid, washing-up liquids

N MASS **Washing-up liquid** is thick, soapy liquid which you add to hot water to clean dirty dishes after a meal. *How many guys do you know that go in a supermarket with their wife and choose the washing-up liquid? ...washing-up liquids that are labelled 'phosphate-free'.*

washout /wɒʃaʊt/ **washouts**

NC If an event or project is a **washout**, it is a total failure; an informal word. *Thanks to you, today's been an appalling washout.*

washroom /wɒʃruːm, wɒʃrum/ **washrooms**

NC A **washroom** is a room with toilets and washing facilities in a large building such as a factory. *Clean out the washrooms.*

washstand /wɒʃstænd/ **washstands**

NC A **washstand** is a piece of old-fashioned furniture which was often kept in a bedroom and was designed to hold a washbasin and facilities for washing your face and hands. *...a washstand with a jug and basin on it.*

wasn't /wɒznt/
Wasn't is the usual spoken form of 'was not'. *I wasn't ready for it... He was first, wasn't he?*

wasp /wɒsp/ **wasps**
NC A **wasp** is a small insect which usually has yellow and black stripes across its body and a sting in its tail. *...a species of wasp which lays its eggs on caterpillars.*

waspish /wɒspɪʃ/
ADJ Someone who is **waspish** speaks or behaves in a sharp and bad-tempered way. *...victims of his waspish and chauvinist tongue.* ♦ **waspishness** NU *Despite his reputation for waspishness, he was positively angelic this time.*

wastage /weɪstɪdʒ/
NU **Wastage** of something is a waste of it; a formal word. *The Government is to blame for this serious wastage of talent.*

waste /weɪst/ **wastes, wasting, wasted**
1 VO If you **waste** time, money, or energy, you use it on something that is not important or necessary. *You're wasting your time... It's important not to waste time on potentially dangerous and useless traditional remedies... He accused Mr Bush of wanting to waste more money on unnecessary, hugely extravagant weapon systems.*
2 If you **waste no time** in doing something, you do that thing as quickly as possible, without delaying. *France should waste no time in getting back into this huge potential market... Norwegian authorities have wasted no time in expressing their displeasure to the Soviet Union.*
3 VO If you **waste** an opportunity, you do not take advantage of it. *They should not waste the opportunity for peace by committing acts which would lead to more bloodshed... Swinging round Venus just 16,000 km above the surface was too good an opportunity to waste for pictures and measurements.*
4 N SING An action or activity that is a **waste** of time, money, or energy involves using these resources when it is not important or necessary to do so. *It's probably a waste of time... After the hearing, Mr Whitty said the case had been politically motivated and a waste of police time... It's a waste of money hiring skis.*
5 NU **Waste** is the use of money or other resources on things that do not need it. *They thought that cutting out waste was going to solve all their problems... A committee was set up to avoid future waste of public money.*
6 NU **Waste** is also material which has been used and is no longer wanted, for example because the useful part has been removed. *The river was thick with industrial waste... Great Britain disposes of up to 2.5 billion tons of waste each year. ...waste paper.*
7 ADJ ATTRIB **Waste** land is an area of ground that is not used or looked after by anyone, and so is covered by wild plants and rubbish. *The car was found abandoned on waste ground near Leeds.*
8 N PL **Wastes** are large areas of land in which there are very few people, plants, or animals; a literary use. *...the endless wastes of the desert.*

waste away PHRASAL VERB If someone **wastes away**, they become thin and weak because they are ill or worried. *A hormone deficiency means that the diabetic wastes away and eventually dies.*

wastebasket /weɪstbɑːskɪt/ **wastebaskets**
NC A **wastebasket** is the same as a **wastepaper basket**; used in American English.

wasted /weɪstɪd/
ADJ A **wasted** action is one that achieves nothing. *It was a wasted journey... Voters are turning away from the smaller parties in the fear that a vote for them would be a wasted vote.*

wasteful /weɪstfl/
ADJ A **wasteful** action causes waste, because it uses resources in a careless or inefficient way. *...the wasteful use of scarce resources.*

wasteland /weɪstlænd/ **wastelands**
NCorNU A **wasteland** is an area of land which is of no use because it is infertile or has been misused. *The highways cross endless wastelands.*

wastepaper basket /weɪstpeɪpə bɑːskɪt/ **wastepaper baskets**
NC A **wastepaper basket** or **wastepaper bin** is a container where you put waste paper and other rubbish. *He crumpled the note and tossed it into the wastepaper basket.*

waster /weɪstə/ **wasters**
NC If you refer to someone as a **waster**, you mean that they are lazy and spend their time and money on foolish things; an informal word.

wasting /weɪstɪŋ/
ADJ ATTRIB A **wasting** disease is one which makes you gradually become thinner and weaker. *Muscular dystrophy is a distressing wasting disease.*

watch /wɒtʃ/ **watches, watching, watched**
1 NC A **watch** is a small clock which you wear on a strap on your wrist. *My watch has stopped... A reminder that British summertime has ended; all clocks and watches should be put back one hour. ...digital watches.*
2 VOorV If you **watch** someone or something, you look at them for a period of time, and pay attention to what is happening. *They have to read the newspapers and watch television. ...all these huge crowds going to watch professional football... A policeman stood watching.*
3 VO To **watch** someone also means to follow them secretly or spy on them. *He's going to be watched from now on... The British police watch the IRA like hawks, monitoring their every move.*
4 VOorV If you **watch** a person or situation, you pay attention to them in order to see what happens and what develops. *In the first Primary, Governor Michael Dukakis of Massachusetts, a Greek businessman, became the man to watch... Many companies have watched helplessly as their stock prices fell.*
5 VO If you **watch** someone or something, you take care that they do not get out of control or do something unpleasant. *I'm watching my weight... You ought to watch Barbara... Then he very much had to watch what he was saying about the military government.*
● **Watch** is used in these phrases. ● If someone **keeps watch** or **keeps a watch**, they keep a look-out for any potential danger or criminal activity. *A woman kept watch at the gate... A watch is being kept on ports and airports in case there's an attempt to take her out of the country.* ● You say 'watch it' to warn someone to be careful; an informal expression. *He's just a tin general and had better watch it.*

watch out PHRASAL VERB If you **watch out**, you are very careful because you feel that something unpleasant might happen to you. *If you don't watch out, he might stick a knife into you.*

watch out for PHRASAL VERB If you **watch out for** something, you look around all the time to try to see if it is near you, because it is something dangerous or something that you want. *Watch out for drifting snow on high ground... Fund managers believe it will be worthwhile to watch out for good bargains in the retailing and building sectors.*

watch over PHRASAL VERB If you **watch over** someone or something, you make sure that nothing bad happens to them. *The wives took turns to watch over the children.*

watchband /wɒtʃbænd/ **watchbands**
NC A **watchband** is the same as a **watchstrap**; used in American English.

watchdog /wɒtʃdɒg/ **watchdogs**
NC You use **watchdog** to refer to a person or committee whose job is to make sure that companies do not act illegally or irresponsibly. *They established the Atomic Energy Commission to act as a watchdog.*

watcher /wɒtʃə/ **watchers**
NC A **watcher** is someone who looks at something over a long period of time, often becoming an expert in the subject. *Professor Hertzberg is a close watcher of the Washington diplomatic scene.*

watchful /wɒtʃfl/
ADJ Someone who is **watchful** is careful to notice everything that is happening. *He spent his days under*

the watchful eyes of his grandmother.

watchman /wɒtʃmən/ **watchmen** /wɒtʃmən/
NC A **watchman** is a person whose job is to guard a
building, a ship, or property. *He is a watchman for an
agricultural company.* ● See also **night-watchman**.

watchstrap /wɒtʃstræp/ **watchstraps**
NC A **watchstrap** is a strip of leather, plastic, or metal
which is attached to a watch so that you can wear it
on your wrist.

watchtower /wɒtʃtaʊə/ **watchtowers**
NC A **watchtower** is a high building which gives a
sentry a good view of the area around a place that is
being guarded. *The security forces sit in their
watchtowers armed with rifles.*

watchword /wɒtʃwɜːd/ **watchwords**
NC A **watchword** is a word or phrase that sums up the
way that a particular group of people think or behave.
Today the watchword is 'Learn through playing'.

water /wɔːtə/ **waters, watering, watered**
1 NU **Water** is a clear, colourless liquid that has no
taste or smell and that is necessary for the survival of
all plant and animal life. *...a drink of water... The
essential services are safe: water, basic sanitation and
health care.*
2 NU or N PL You use **water** or **waters** to refer to a
large amount or area of water, for example a lake or
sea. *The children played at the water's edge. ...the
black waters of the Thames.*
3 N PL+SUPP A country's **waters** consist of the area of
sea near it which is regarded as belonging to it. *The
ship was in British waters.*
4 VO If you **water** plants, you pour water into the soil
to help them to grow. *I've been watering the garden...
The pitch hadn't been watered for a long time.*
5 V If your eyes **water**, you have tears in them
because they are hurting. *The onions made his eyes
water.*
6 V If your mouth **waters**, it produces more saliva,
usually because you can smell or see some appetizing
food. *This should make your mouth water.*
7 See also **water cannon. uncharted waters:** see
uncharted.
● **Water** is used in these phrases. ● If you are **in deep
water,** you are in a difficult situation which you cannot
get out of. ● When you **pass water,** you urinate. *Do
you have difficulty passing water?* ● If you say that an
event is **water under the bridge,** you mean that it has
happened and cannot now be changed, so there is no
point in worrying about it. *Mr Bruce said that he was
relieved it was over and that he regarded his time in
jail as water under the bridge.* ● If you say that **a lot
of water has passed under the bridge** since a
particular time or event, you mean that a lot of things
have happened since then and the situation is not the
same as it was. *Mr Gorbachev also said that at one
time, the question about how they got on had been a
difficult one, but a lot of water had passed under the
bridge.*

water down PHRASAL VERB 1 If you **water down** food
or drink, you add water to it to make it weaker. *The
milk had been watered down.* 2 If a speech or plan is
watered down, it is made less forceful. *The whole
article had been watered down.* ● See also **watered-
down.**

waterbed /wɔːtəbed/ **waterbeds**
NC A **waterbed** is a waterproof mattress filled with
water.

water biscuit, water biscuits
NC A **water biscuit** is a thin, crisp, unsweetened
biscuit which is usually eaten with butter or cheese.

water-borne
ADJ Something that is **water-borne** is carried or passed
on by water. *...water-borne diseases... Guinea-worm
is a water-borne parasite.*

water butt, water butts
NC A **water butt** is a large barrel for collecting rain as
it flows off a roof.

water cannon, water cannons. The plural form can
be either **water cannons** or **water cannon.**
NC A **water cannon** is a machine which shoots out a
powerful jet of water. It is used by police to break up
crowds of people who are demonstrating. *Police used*

water cannon and teargas to disperse the crowds.

water chestnut, water chestnuts
NC A **water chestnut** is the thick bottom part of the
stem of a plant which grows in China. Water chestnuts
have a mild taste and are used in Chinese cooking. *I
sat at a table alone, eating shredded beef and peppers,
water chestnuts and mushrooms.*

water closet. See **WC.**

watercolour /wɔːtəkʌlə/ **watercolours;** spelt
watercolor in American English.
1 N PL **Watercolours** are coloured paints which you
mix with water to use.
2 NC A **watercolour** is a picture which has been
painted using watercolours. *Among the most recent
items are two gentle watercolours by Prince Charles
of landscapes in Scotland. ...an exhibition of
watercolours.*

watercress /wɔːtəkres/
NU **Watercress** is a small plant with white flowers
which grows in streams and pools. Its leaves taste hot
and are eaten raw in salads. *Sprinkle with a little
paprika, garnish with watercress and serve with thin
slices of brown bread and margarine.*

watered-down; also spelt **watered down.**
ADJ If something such as a plan or demand has been
watered-down, it has been made less forceful. *...a
watered-down pay claim... The Equal Pay Act is so
watered down as to be useless.* ● See also **water down.**

waterfall /wɔːtəfɔːl/ **waterfalls**
NC A **waterfall** is a stream of water that flows rapidly
over the edge of a steep cliff and falls to the ground
below. *...waterfalls cascading down the one thousand
foot high cliffs.*

waterfowl /wɔːtəfaʊl/; **waterfowl** is both the singular
and the plural form.
NC **Waterfowl** are birds that swim in water, especially
ducks, geese, and swans. *Keep pigs separate from
waterfowl.*

waterfront /wɔːtəfrʌnt/ **waterfronts**
NC An area of **waterfront** is a street or piece of land
which is next to water, for example a river or the
sea. *...a warehouse on the waterfront.*

waterhole /wɔːtəhəʊl/ **waterholes**
NC A **waterhole** is a pool in a desert or other dry area
where animals can find water to drink. *So many of
the savanna's waterholes had dried into mud that the
game had moved into deep forest.*

water-ice, water-ices
N MASS A **water-ice** is a type of ice cream made of
frozen fruit juice, sugar, and water. *...a mouthful of
water-ice. ...an apricot water-ice.*

watering can, watering cans
NC A **watering can** is a container with a long spout
which is used to water plants. *Watering cans are
essential for any gardener whether for outdoor or
indoor plants.*

watering hole, watering holes
NC A **watering hole** is a place, especially a café or
pub, where people go to drink and meet; often used
humorously. *The restaurant was once a cosmopolitan
watering hole for actors and writers.*

waterlily /wɔːtəlɪli/ **waterlilies**
NC A **waterlily** is a plant with large flat leaves and
colourful flowers which floats on the surface of lakes
and rivers. *A frog sits in front of him on a waterlily
leaf.*

waterlogged /wɔːtəlɒgd/
ADJ **Waterlogged** ground is so wet that it cannot soak
up any more water and a layer of water remains on
the surface. *The wet summer and autumn had left the
ground waterlogged... For much of the match, the
waterlogged pitch and constant rain made the game a
slow battle of stamina.*

water main, water mains
NC A **water main** is a very large underground pipe
used for supplying water to houses and factories. *A
water main had broken and water was gushing out.*

watermark /wɔːtəmɑːk/ **watermarks**
1 NC A **watermark** is a design which is put onto paper
such as banknotes by the people who make it, and
which you can only see if you hold the paper up to the
light. *We can, of course, put watermarks, security*

*threads and various other types of security features
into this paper.*

2 NC A **watermark** is also a mark which shows the
highest or the lowest level reached by a river or the
sea. *The tide is almost at the high watermark.*

watermelon /wɔːtəmelən/ **watermelons**
NC A **watermelon** is a large, round fruit with green
skin, pink flesh, and black seeds. *Despite the rains,
the watermelons are getting ripe.*

water pistol, water pistols
NC A **water pistol** is a small toy gun which shoots out
water.

water power
NU **Water power** is the power obtained from flowing
water which is used to drive machines or to make
electricity. *These renewable energy sources include
solar energy, wind, wave and water power.*

waterproof /wɔːtəpruːf/ **waterproofs, waterproofing,
waterproofed**
1 ADJ Something that is **waterproof** does not let water
pass through it. *...a pair of waterproof trousers... The
new gear is completed by boots that are more
waterproof than the old type.*

2 NC A **waterproof** is a coat or other piece of clothing
which does not let water in. *He will also need a warm
anorak and waterproofs.*

3 VO If you **waterproof** something, you make it
waterproof. *It is similar to the material used to
waterproof the roofs of buildings.*

water rate, water rates
N PL In Britain, **water rates** are the charges made for
the use of water from the public water supply.
Claimants now have to pay water rates.

watershed /wɔːtəʃed/ **watersheds**
NC A **watershed** is an event or time which marks the
beginning of a new stage in something. *The Vietnam
war was one of the great watersheds of modern
history.*

waterside /wɔːtəsaɪd/
N SING The **waterside** is an area of land near a river,
canal, or lake. *I drove down to the waterside... I had
dinner at my favorite waterside restaurant.*

water-ski, water-skis, water-skiing, water-skied
V If you **water-ski**, you ski on water while being pulled
along by a boat. ◆ **water-skiing** NU *...excellent
facilities for sailing, water-skiing, and skin-diving.*

water softener, water softeners
NC A **water softener** is a device or substance which
you can add to water in order to remove minerals
such as calcium, so that soap mixes more easily and
makes a lather.

water-soluble
ADJ Something that is **water-soluble** is able to dissolve
in water. *Felt pen ink is water-soluble.*

waterspout /wɔːtəspaʊt/ **waterspouts**
NC A **waterspout** is a whirlwind over the sea which
causes a tall column of water to be formed, or the
column of water itself. *Once, he had seen a
waterspout moving across the face of the Caribbean.*

water supply, water supplies
NC The **water supply** in an area is the water which is
collected and passed through pipes to buildings for
people to use. *...the purification of the water supply.*

water table, water tables
NC The **water table** is the level below the surface of
the ground where water can be found. *It was
necessary to bore deep wells through to the water
table.*

watertight /wɔːtətaɪt/
1 ADJ A **watertight** container or door does not allow
water to get into it or past it because it is tightly
sealed. *The ferry is built in two sections with
watertight doors.*

2 ADJ If something such as a guarantee or plan is
watertight, it has been put together very carefully, so
that it deals with everything which it should deal with,
and nobody can criticize it or argue about it. *He still
hasn't gone far enough towards a watertight
guarantee... The police say that he gave his personal
approval to the watertight security arrangements now
in force.*

water tower, water towers
NC A **water tower** is a large tank of water which is
placed on a high metal structure so that water can be
supplied at a steady pressure to surrounding
buildings. *Health officials are disinfecting water
towers in Bolton.*

waterway /wɔːtəweɪ/ **waterways**
NC A **waterway** is a canal, river, or narrow channel of
sea which boats can sail along. *Since 1903, the US has
owned the Panama canal, the strategic waterway that
links the Atlantic Ocean with the Pacific.*

waterworks /wɔːtəwɜːks/; **waterworks** is both the
singular and the plural form.
NC A **waterworks** is a building where a supply of
water is stored and cleaned before being distributed to
the public. *Authorities declared the city a disaster
area after the waterworks ran dry.*

watery /wɔːtəri/
1 ADJ Something that is **watery** is weak or pale. *...a
watery smile. ...a watery April sun.*

2 ADJ Food or drink that is **watery** contains a lot of
water. *...watery cabbage... Take plenty of watery,
non-alcoholic liquids such as fruit drinks, milk or
water.*

3 ADJ **Watery** is also used to describe something which
contains, resembles, or consists of water. *It's caused
by a build-up of the watery fluid in the eyeball... The
magic sword was thrown into a lake where a woman's
arm emerged to draw it down into the watery depths.*

watt /wɒt/ **watts**
NC A **watt** is a unit of measurement of electrical
power. *The computer only consumes 150 watts of
power. ...a 60 watt bulb.*

wattage /wɒtɪdʒ/
NU The **wattage** of a piece of electrical equipment is
the amount of electrical power, expressed in watts,
which it uses or generates. *What wattage does it
give?... A low wattage bulb provided meagre light.*

wattle and daub /wɒtl ən dɔːb/
NU **Wattle and daub** is a building material made from
a mixture of wooden rods and clay. *...houses of wattle
and daub.*

wave /weɪv/ **waves, waving, waved**
1 V or VO If you **wave** or **wave** your hand, you move
your hand from side to side in the air, usually in order
to say hello or goodbye or in order to get someone's
attention. *His mother waved to him... The Espresso
Gratia steamed through the harbour entrance, its
decks full of Albanians waving their arms and
chanting 'Italia, Italia'.* ▶ Also NC *Jack gave his
usual cheery wave.*

2 VOA If you **wave** someone away or **wave** them on,
you make a movement with your hand to tell them
where to go. *I was waved through... He waves on the
traffic.*

3 VO If you **wave** something, you hold it up and move
it rapidly from side to side. *All along the route,
people applauded and waved flags at them.*

4 NC A **wave** is a raised mass of water on the sea or a
lake, caused by the wind or the tide. *...the line of
white foam where the waves broke on the beach.*

5 NC If someone's hair has **waves**, it curves slightly
instead of being straight.

6 NC+SUPP **Wave** is used to refer to the way in which
things such as sound, light, and radio signals travel, or
the way in which the force of an explosion or
earthquake spreads. *Radar employs radio waves
whereas sonar uses sound waves. ...the shock wave
from a one megaton bomb.*

7 NU+SUPP **Wave** is used in the expressions 'long
wave', 'medium wave', and 'short wave' to refer to a
range of radio waves used for broadcasting. *The BBC
World Service can be heard on 464m or 648kHz
medium wave in Northern Europe.*

8 NC+SUPP A **wave** of sympathy, alarm, or panic is a
steady increase in that feeling which spreads through
a person or group of people. *In the general wave of
panic, nobody thought of phoning for an ambulance.*

9 NC+SUPP You also use **wave** to refer to a sudden
increase in a particular activity or type of behaviour.
*In Paris in May 1968 there was a massive wave of
student riots... The cabinet resigned last month after a*

new wave of strikes. ...a crime wave.

10 If you say that someone is **on the crest of a wave**, you mean that they have reached a very successful part of their career. *Now members of the group are confident they are on the crest of a wave... Since his return from his tour, it's not surprising that some are saying he's on the crest of a wave with a new sense of direction and mission.*

11 See also **new wave, tidal wave**.

wave aside PHRASAL VERB If you **wave aside** an idea or comment, you decide that it is not important enough to be used or considered. *The Chief waved his objection aside.*

wave down PHRASAL VERB If you **wave down** a vehicle, you wave your hand as a signal to the driver to stop the vehicle. *A car with West German plates was waved down by border guards doing routine checks.*

waveband /weɪvbænd/ **wavebands**
NC A **waveband** is a group of radio waves of similar length which are used for radio transmission. *Two frequencies will be reassigned from the BBC: they could be the medium wavebands at present used on Radios One and Three.*

wavelength /weɪvlɛŋθ/ **wavelengths**
1 NC A **wavelength** is the distance between the same point on consecutive cycles of a wave of energy such as light or sound. *They used a series of filters to catch the light at different wavelengths. ...infra-red wavelengths.*
2 NC A **wavelength** is the size of radio wave which a particular radio station uses to broadcast its programmes. *Local broadcasting on medium wave is centred on wavelengths of about 300m.*
3 If two people are **on the same wavelength**, they share the same attitudes and get on well with each other. *The President said the two sides were on the same wavelength over the interaction of British and American forces in Saudi Arabia.*

waver /weɪvə/ **wavers, wavering, wavered**
1 V If you **waver** or if your confidence or faith **wavers**, your beliefs or intentions become less firm and your actions become less decisive. *Meehan has never wavered in his assertions of innocence... He felt his determination waver.* ◆ **wavering** ADJ ATTRIB *He must convince millions of wavering voters that Labour is fit to govern.*
2 V If something **wavers**, it moves or changes slightly. *I looked into his eyes. They didn't waver.*
◆ **wavering** ADJ *...his wavering falsetto voice.*

wavy /weɪvi/
ADJ Something that is **wavy** has curves in it. *He had wavy grey hair.*

wax /wæks/ **waxes, waxing, waxed**
1 NU **Wax** is a solid, slightly shiny substance made of fat or oil which is used to make candles and polish. It goes soft and melts when it is heated. *The sun's rays melted the wax... By the 1920s many families were replacing wax candles with battery-powered electric lights.*
2 VO If you **wax** something, you put a thin layer of wax onto it, usually in order to polish it or in order to make it waterproof. *I wash and wax the van and I do errands.* ◆ **waxed** ADJ ATTRIB *... a waxed green jacket that keeps out the worst of the weather.*
3 VO If you **wax** your legs or another part of your body, you use a special kind of wax to remove the hair from that part of your body. The wax is applied to the skin, and when it is removed it pulls the hairs out.
● **Wax** is used in these phrases. ● If you **wax lyrical** or **wax eloquent** about something, you talk or write about it in a way that shows your great admiration for it. *...the gorges about which Chinese poets have waxed lyrical for thousands of years.* ● If something **waxes and wanes**, it first increases and then decreases over a period of time; a literary expression. *The popularity of the film stars waxed and waned.*

waxen /wæksn/
ADJ A **waxen** face is very pale and unhealthy looking. *She had pink-rimmed eyes and a waxen complexion.*

wax paper
NU **Wax paper** or **waxed paper** is paper that has been covered in a thin layer of wax in order to make it waterproof. *...a bundle of bright red flowers wrapped in wax paper.*

waxwork /wækswɜːk/ **waxworks**
1 NC A **waxwork** is a model of a famous person, made out of wax.
2 NC A **waxworks** or **waxwork museum** is a place where waxwork models are on display for the public to look at. *Madame Tussaud's famous waxworks attracts a vast number of foreign visitors.*

waxy /wæksi/
ADJ Something that is **waxy** looks or feels like wax, or contains a lot of wax. *Pine needles have a waxy surface layer which acts as a protection.*

way /weɪ/ **ways**
1 NC+SUPP A **way** of doing something is a thing or series of things that you do in order to achieve a particular result. *...different ways of cooking fish... The only way to stop an accident is to remove the risk... We have no way of knowing.*
2 N SING+SUPP You can refer to the **way** that an action is done to indicate the quality that it has. *He smiles in a superior way... He hated the way she talked.*
3 N PL+SUPP The **ways** of a particular person or group of people are their customs or their usual behaviour. *...the difficulty of changing one's ways... He believed the President had changed his ways and become more democratic.*
4 NC+SUPP You say that something is the case in the **way** stated when you are referring to an aspect of something or the effect that something has. *Breast feeding is valuable in a number of ways... The job was changing me in a way that I had not expected.*
5 N SING+SUPP The **way** you feel about something is your attitude to it or your opinion about it. *I'm just wondering why you feel this way... Do you still feel the same way?... Darwin's impressions on this voyage changed his way of thinking.*
6 N SING+SUPP When you mention the **way** that something happens, you are mentioning the fact that it happens. *Do you remember the way the boat leaked?*
7 N SING+*with* If you have a **way** with people or things of a particular type, you are very skilful at dealing with them. *...a village boy who had a way with horses.*
8 N SING The **way** to a particular place is the route that you must take in order to get there. *A man asked me the way to Tower Bridge... They couldn't even find their way back to Haworth, where they were staying.*
9 N SING+SUPP If you go or look a particular **way**, you go or look in that direction. *Will you come this way, please?... I waved but she was looking the other way.*
10 N SING+SUPP You can use **way** in expressions such as 'the right way up' and 'the wrong way round' to refer to the position or arrangement that something has. *Have I got this the right way up?... I feel as if my limbs have been taken off and put on the wrong way round.*
11 N SING If someone or something is in the **way**, they prevent you from moving freely or from seeing clearly. *The tree was in the way... Judy barred Jim's way... Get out of my way.*
12 N SING+POSS You use **way** in expressions such as 'push your way somewhere' or 'work your way somewhere' which refer to movement or progress that is difficult or slow. *You can't force your way into somebody's house... He started to work his way through the back copies of The Times.*
13 N SING You use **way** in expressions such as 'a long way' and 'a little way' to say how far away something is in distance or time. *We're a long way away from Cuba... We still only have a little way to go before we see the retail price index turn down.*
14 N SING You use **way** in expressions such as 'all the way' and 'most of the way' which refer to a particular amount of a journey or distance. *They drove all the way back without a word.*
15 ADV A You use **way** with adjuncts to emphasize that something is a great distance away, or is very much below or above a particular level or amount; an informal use. *They're way ahead of us... You're way below the standard required.*

16 See also **one-way, out-of-the-way, part way, right of way, two-way, under way**; ● **Way** is used in these phrases. ● If you **lose your way**, you get lost and do not know which direction to follow in order to get to your destination. *The two pilots had lost their way and made an emergency landing... He lost his way in bad weather.* ● When you **make** your **way** somewhere, you walk or travel there. *I made my way back to my seat.* ● If one person or thing **makes way** for another, the other person or thing takes their place. *Slums have been cleared to make way for new high-rise apartments.* ● If you say that something **goes a long way** towards doing a particular thing, you mean that it helps a great deal to achieve that thing. *Goodwill and cooperation can go a long way towards smoothing your way to the top.* ● **On the way** or **on** your **way** means in the course of your journey. *Lynn was on her way home.* ● If you **go out of** your **way** to do something, you make a special effort to do it. *He didn't really go out of his way to help me... The nurses went out of their way to shampoo my hair and make me feel comfortable.* ● If you **keep out of** someone's **way**, you avoid them. *The latest advice is for them to keep out of the way, and wait for further directions from London.* ● When something **is out of the way**, it is over or you have dealt with it. *We'll be all right once this meeting is out of the way.* ● If you **get** or **have** your **way**, or if you **have everything your own way**, what you want to happen happens. *If Baker has his way, the money will be paid to you... Mr Todd's remarks suggest that the party leadership may not get everything their own way.* ● If you say that someone **wants to have it both ways**, you mean that they do not want to choose between two things that cannot both be done or had. *Saddam Hussein wants to have it both ways; he wants to portray himself as a champion of the Palestinians without running the military risks involved.* ● You use **the other way round** or **around** to refer to the opposite of what you have just said. *An interesting aspect of the Grameen Bank is that the bankers actually travel to the villagers, not the other way round. Here, the people are expected to go to the banks themselves.* ● You say **'No way'** in order to emphasize that you do not want to agree to something, or that you do not think something will happen; an informal expression. *'Shall I call you Countess?'—'No way. In the United States, we don't use titles.'* ● If you say that someone or something **has a way** of doing a particular thing, you mean that they commonly do it. *Ex-wives have a way of reappearing.* ● If someone is **set in** their **ways**, their habits and ideas are not likely to change. *Its population tends to be elderly, staid, set in its ways.* ● You say **by the way** when you add something to what you or another person has just said, especially something that you have just thought of. *By the way, this visit of Muller's is strictly secret.* ● If you do something **by way of** a particular thing, you do it as that thing; a formal expression. *I'm going to sketch in a bit of the background by way of introduction.* ● You use **in a way** to indicate that your statement is true to some extent or in one respect. *In a way, these officers were prisoners themselves.* ● You use **in a big way** and **in a small way** to suggest the scale or importance of an activity. *They are going into the arms business in a big way.* ● You use **in the way of** to specify exactly what you are talking about. *He received very little in the way of wages.*

wayfarer /ˈweɪfeərə/ **wayfarers**
NC A **wayfarer** is a traveller who walks from place to place; an old-fashioned word.

way in
N SING The **way in** is the door or gate through which you can enter a public building or area.

waylay /weɪˈleɪ/ **waylays, waylaying, waylaid**; an old-fashioned word.
1 VO If you **waylay** someone, you stop them when they are going somewhere, in order to talk to them. *She waylaid the film's director and demanded that she be allowed to play Barbie Bachelor.*
2 VO To **waylay** someone also means to stop them and attack them or steal something from them. *He killed*

a fifteen year old schoolgirl after waylaying her near a railway line.

way of life, ways of life
NC Someone's **way of life** consists of their habits and daily activities. *...the British way of life... Prospectors have disrupted the traditional way of life of the Yanomami Indians.*

way out
N SING The **way out** is the door or gate through which you can leave a public building or area.

way-out
ADJ Someone or something that is **way-out** is unusual or different from other things or people, especially by being very modern or fashionable; an old-fashioned word. *It was written about ten years ago as a piece of way-out black comedy.*

wayside /ˈweɪsaɪd/
1 N SING The **wayside** is the side of the road; an old-fashioned use. *Broken-down buses may frequently be seen by the wayside. ...travellers who buy food from wayside stalls.*
2 If someone or something **falls by the wayside**, they do not have the strength, ability, or desire to continue in something that they have started, and so they fail or stop. *Many of the political parties that fell by the wayside were unable to afford the election registration fee or were not in earnest about contesting elections.*
3 If something such as an idea or plan **falls by the wayside**, it is forgotten or ignored. *The pledge to hand over power after four years might just be another promise that has fallen by the wayside.*

wayward /ˈweɪwəd/
ADJ Someone who is **wayward** does not behave sensibly and is difficult to control; a literary word. *...wayward children... His wayward habits, his drinking and gambling, kept the family in poverty.*

WC, WCs; also written **wc**.
NC A **WC** is a toilet. **WC** is a written abbreviation for 'water closet'.

we /wi, wiː/
PRON **We** is used as the subject of a verb. A speaker or writer uses **we** to refer to a group of people which includes himself or herself. *We could hear the birds singing.*

weak /wiːk/ **weaker, weakest**
1 ADJ Someone who feels **weak** does not have very much strength or energy. *He was weak from hunger... He's over 90, and he looked weak.* ◆ **weakly** ADV *She sat down, rather weakly.* ◆ **weakness** NU *...his worsening pain and physical weakness.*
2 ADJ Something that is **weak** is not strong or good, and is likely to break or fail. *A fuse is a deliberately weak link in an electrical system... There are a number of other companies that are doing well despite the weak economy. ...a weak excuse.* ◆ **weakness, weaknesses** NU or NC *...the weakness of their economy... This would exploit a known weakness on the enemy's Eastern Front.*
3 ADJ If a person, organization, or country is **weak**, they do not have very much influence or power, and are easily defeated or exploited. *Many Africans have criticized these films for portraying them as weak and subservient... The democrats are weak and poorly organized. ...incompetent and weak leadership.* ◆ **weakness** NU or NC *...his apparent weakness under pressure... He added that the organisation would not exploit the weaknesses in Eastern Europe.*
4 ADJ A **weak** response to something is made without enthusiasm or emphasis. *He managed a weak smile.* ◆ **weakly** ADV *I argued weakly against these conclusions.*
5 ADJ Someone or something that is **weak** on a particular subject does not have much ability or information relating to it. *The book was weak on fact and documentation.*
6 ADJ **Weak** drinks are made using a lot of water and therefore do not have a strong taste. *...weak tea.*
7 ADJ **Weak** sounds or lights are very faint. *A weak signal from the plane's transmitter was picked up by satellite after radio contact was lost.*
8 N PL The **weak** are people who have very little influence or power in society, and who cannot defend

themselves against more powerful people. ...*a world where the strong respect the rights of the weak.*
9 See also **weakness**.

weaken /wi:kən/ **weakens, weakening, weakened**
1 V-ERG If you **weaken** something or if it **weakens**, it becomes less strong or less powerful. *Her armed forces had been weakened by the restriction on equipment supplies... The civil war of January 1986 weakened the regime and forced them to consider less centralized policies... Officials have warned that although the hurricane is weakening, it could still cause considerable damage... The British government faces the prospect of serious economic problems with the pound weakening on international exchanges.*
2 V If someone **weakens**, they become less certain about a decision they have made. *Do you think she's beginning to weaken?*
3 VO If something **weakens** you, it causes you to lose some of your physical strength. *I was weakened by my exertions.*

weak-kneed
ADJ Someone who is **weak-kneed** is not able or willing to make their own decisions or to stand up for their rights; an informal word. *I feared she'd think me very weak-kneed for giving in to him... The best policy now is neither the Democratic proposal, nor the weak-kneed Republican compromise.*

weakling /wi:klɪŋ/ **weaklings**; used showing disapproval.
1 NC A **weakling** is someone who is physically weak.
2 NC You can also refer to someone that you think is weak in character as a **weakling**. *Bush is showing that he is not afraid of Congress, that he is not the weakling that his critics made him out to be during the campaign.*

weakness /wi:knəs/ **weaknesses**
NC If you have a **weakness** for something, you like it very much, although this is perhaps surprising or undesirable. *He had a weakness for sweets.* ● See also **weak**.

weal /wi:l/ **weals**
NC A **weal** is a mark made on someone's skin by a blow, especially from something sharp or thin such as a sword or whip. *Mr Isaac showed reporters weals on his back which he said were the result of torture.*

wealth /welθ/
1 NU **Wealth** is a large amount of money or property that someone possesses, or the fact that they possess it. *He'll have to explain the source of his wealth... She was a woman of considerable wealth.*
2 NU A country's **wealth** is the large amount of financial and other resources that it has, especially when this leads to a high standard of living for a large number of its population; also used to refer to the fact that a country has this wealth. *The Spanish colonial authorities began to realize some of the potential wealth of the territory... The present debt is a modest sum for a developing country of South Africa's size and wealth... It was a period of wealth and prosperity.*
3 N SING+of A **wealth** of something means a very large amount of it; a formal use. *...ordinary people, who have a tremendous wealth of experience.*

wealthy /welθi/ **wealthier, wealthiest**
1 ADJ Someone who is **wealthy** has a large amount of money or property. *Sheikh Rashid was immensely wealthy, with a private fortune recently estimated at $4000 million.*
2 N PL The **wealthy** are people who own a large amount of money or property. *The Democrats had demanded higher taxes on the wealthy.*
3 ADJ A **wealthy** area has a lot of rich people living in it. *The arrests took place in a wealthy New York suburb.*
4 ADJ A **wealthy** country has a large amount of financial and other resources, which usually lead to a high standard of living for a large number of its population. *...the United Arab Emirates and other wealthy Gulf nations.*

wean /wi:n/ **weans, weaning, weaned**
1 VO When a mother **weans** her baby, she stops feeding it with milk from her breast and starts giving it other food. *...a mother who was having difficulty*

weaning her 16-month-old baby from the breast.
2 VOA If you **wean** someone off something, especially something that is bad for them, you gradually make them stop doing it or using it. *People can be weaned off cigarettes with nicotine chewing gum... The president was candid about the difficulty of weaning the nation from its dependence on foreign oil.*

weapon /wepən/ **weapons**
NC A **weapon** is an object which is used to·kill or hurt people in a fight or war. *Police say that large quantities of weapons and explosives were seized. ...nuclear weapons. ...chemical weapons.*

weaponry /wepənri/
NU **Weaponry** is all the weapons that a country has or that are available to it. *Their aim is to reduce the huge arsenals of non-nuclear weaponry... US troops had far superior technology and weaponry.*

wear /weə/ **wears, wearing, wore, worn**
1 VO The clothes that you **are wearing** are the clothes on your body. *She was wearing a T-shirt and jeans. ...a girl who wore spectacles.*
2 VOA If you **wear** your hair in a particular way, it is cut or arranged in that way. *His face was framed by his curly hair, which he wore too long.*
3 NU+SUPP You can refer to clothes that are suitable for a particular time or occasion as a particular kind of **wear**. *...evening wear. ...running shoes, track suits, and assorted sports wear.*
4 V If something **wears**, it becomes thinner or weaker from constant use. *Move the carpet up or down as it starts to wear.*
5 NU **Wear** is the use that clothes or other things have over a period of time, which causes damage to them. *...when your sheets are showing signs of wear.*
6 to **wear thin**: see **thin**. See also **wearing, worn**.
wear away PHRASAL VERB If something **wears away** or is **worn away**, it becomes thin and eventually disappears because it is touched a lot. *The grass was worn away where the children used to play.*
wear down PHRASAL VERB If you **wear** people **down**, you weaken them by repeatedly doing something or asking them to do something. *We tried to wear them down gradually and make them agree.*
wear off PHRASAL VERB If a feeling such as pain **wears off**, it slowly disappears. *By the next afternoon the shock had worn off.*
wear on PHRASAL VERB If time **wears on**, it seems to pass very slowly; a literary expression. *So the day wore on and still they sat, drinking, smoking, talking.*
wear out PHRASAL VERB When something **wears out** or is **worn out**, it is used so much that it becomes thin or weak and cannot be used any more. *His shoes keep wearing out.* ● See also **worn-out**.

wear and tear
NU **Wear and tear** is the damage which is caused to something as it is used. *These baseball mitts are subject to all the wear and tear that eventually ruins most articles of clothing... There's also the problem of wear and tear on the equipment in the harsh desert conditions.*

wearing /weərɪŋ/
ADJ An activity that is **wearing** makes you feel very tired. *...a very wearing and demanding job.*

wearisome /wɪərɪsəm/
ADJ Something that is **wearisome** is very tiring, boring, or frustrating; a formal word. *...a wearisome meeting. ...a wearisome re-run of an old film.*

weary /wɪəri/ **wearies, wearying, wearied**; a literary word.
1 ADJ If you are **weary**, you are very tired. *...a weary sigh.* ◆ **wearily** ADV *The farmers trudged wearily to the nearest stream.* ◆ **weariness** NU *There were lines of weariness around her eyes.*
2 ADJ PRED+of If you are **weary** of something, you wish that you were no longer doing it or that you were no longer involved in it. *Angolans are weary of the war.*
3 V+of If you **weary** of something, you wish that you were no longer doing it or that you were no longer involved in it. *He is beginning to weary of sitting still.*

weasel /wi:zl/ **weasels**
NC A **weasel** is a small wild animal with a long thin body, a tail, four short legs, and reddish-brown fur

which may turn white in winter.

weather /wɛðə/ **weathers, weathering, weathered**
1 N SING or NU The **weather** is the condition of the atmosphere in an area at a particular time, for example, whether it is raining, hot, or windy. *The weather was good for the time of year... The tractors couldn't be used in wet weather.*
2 V-ERG If something such as skin, rock, or wood **weathers**, it changes colour or shape as a result of the effects of wind, sun, rain, or frost. *The rocks weathered and turned to clay and mud... Geologists were already aware of the way in which mountains and coasts are gradually weathered and eroded away.*
♦ **weathered** ADJ *...a man with the weathered skin of a seafarer.*
3 VO If you **weather** a difficult time, you survive it. *Anyone who weathers the first four years seems to be all right... Not every school has weathered the last nine years of austere budgets so well.*
● **Weather** is used in these phrases. ● If someone is **making heavy weather** of a task, they are doing it in an inefficient way and making it seem more difficult than it really is. *Manchester United also made heavy weather of beating Rotherham 1-0.* ● If you feel **under the weather**, you feel slightly ill.

weatherbeaten /wɛðəbiːtn/
ADJ If your face is **weatherbeaten**, it is rough, wrinkled, and brown because you have spent a lot of time outside in all weather conditions.

weathercock /wɛðəkɒk/ **weathercocks**
NC A **weathercock** is a metal object in the shape of a rooster which is fixed to the roof of a building. It turns round in the wind and shows which way the wind is blowing.

weather forecast, weather forecasts
NC A **weather forecast** is a statement saying what the weather will be like the following day or for the next few days. *The weather forecast is for cooler air moving across the south of the country.*

weather forecaster, weather forecasters
NC A **weather forecaster** is someone who studies weather conditions and make reports predicting what the weather will be like for the next few days. *Weather forecasters say the rains are expected to continue for at least another two days.*

weatherman /wɛðəmæn/ **weathermen**
NC A **weatherman** is a man whose job involves making weather forecasts on the television or radio; an informal word. *The day proved to be as bright as the weatherman had predicted.*

weatherproof /wɛðəpruːf/
ADJ Something that is **weatherproof** is made of material which protects it from the weather, or which keeps out wind and rain. *The battery is mounted on the gatepost together with a weatherproof electronics box which operates the gate... Miraculously, the new skylight seems weatherproof.*

weather station, weather stations
NC A **weather station** is a building that is used for studying and recording facts about the weather, so that weather forecasts can be made. *One method of monitoring the earth's climate has been to take measurements from weather stations.*

weather-vane, weather-vanes
NC A **weather-vane** is a metal object on the roof of a building which turns round in the wind and shows which way the wind is blowing. *...an ancient weather-vane on the spire of the parish church.*

weave /wiːv/ **weaves, weaving, wove, woven**
1 VO or V If you **weave** cloth or a carpet, you make it by crossing threads over and under each other using a machine called a loom. *If you want to learn to weave, you must get somebody to teach you... They started weaving rugs and cloths.*
2 NC+SUPP The **weave** of a cloth or carpet is the way in which the threads are arranged. *...a tight, firm weave.*
3 VO or V If you **weave** something such as a basket, you make it by crossing long plant stems or fibres over and under each other. *The patients learn how to weave mats and baskets.*
4 VO A or V A If you **weave** your way somewhere, you

move between and around things as you go there. *He weaves his way through the crowd... She wove through the guests, smiling brightly.*

weaver /wiːvə/ **weavers**
NC A **weaver** is a person who weaves cloth, carpets, or baskets. *He had worked as a silk weaver. ...carpet weavers.*

web /wɛb/ **webs**
1 NC A **web** is a fine net that a spider makes from a sticky substance produced in its body. *The spider wraps up a fly in its web and bites its head off.*
2 NC+SUPP You can use **web** to refer to a complicated pattern, structure, or set of things; a literary use. *He may have been caught up in a complex web of international business intrigue. ...a web of corruption.*

webbed /wɛbd/
ADJ Water birds that have **webbed** feet have skin connecting their toes.

webbing /wɛbɪŋ/
NU **Webbing** is strong material which is woven in strips and used to make belts or straps, or used in seats to support the springs. *...a belt of green webbing. ...canvas webbing.*

wed /wɛd/ **weds, wedding, wedded.** The form **wed** is used in the present tense and is the usual form of the past tense and past participle.
V-RECIP When a man and woman **wed**, they get married; an old-fashioned word. *We were both nineteen when we wed... Maradona then rounded off an eventful week by hiring a jumbo jet to fly him back to Argentina to wed his childhood sweetheart.* ● To **get wed** means to get married; an old-fashioned expression. *He always gave them a shilling extra when they got wed.* ● See also **newlyweds, wedded, wedding.**

Wed.
Wed. is a written abbreviation for 'Wednesday'.

we'd /wid, wiːd/
We'd is the usual spoken form of 'we had', especially when 'had' is an auxiliary verb. **We'd** is also a spoken form of 'we would'. *We'd done a good job... We'd be looking at Britain's role in the world.*

wedded /wɛdɪd/
ADJ PRED+to If you are **wedded** to an idea or system, you support it strongly and refuse to change your views; a formal word. *They've also shown that they are firmly wedded to the idea of cleaning up the environment. ...a party wedded to unrestricted free enterprise.*

wedding /wɛdɪŋ/ **weddings**
NC A **wedding** is a marriage ceremony. *They had videotaped the church wedding.*

wedding ring, wedding rings
NC A **wedding ring** is a plain ring that you wear to show that you are married.

wedge /wɛdʒ/ **wedges, wedging, wedged**
1 VO If you **wedge** something such as a door or window, you keep it firmly in position by forcing something between it and the surface next to it. *Open the door wide and wedge it with a wad of newspaper.*
2 VO A If you **wedge** something somewhere, you put it there so that it fits tightly. *Captain Imrie wedged himself more deeply into his chair.*
3 NC A **wedge** is an object with one pointed edge and one thick edge, for example one that you put under a door to keep it firmly in position. *We slip a plastic wedge into the heel to alter the angle of the horse's foot.*
● **Wedge** is used in these phrases. ● If you **drive a wedge** between people or groups, you cause bad feelings between them in order to weaken their relationship. *They are accused of offering bribes to tribal leaders in an effort to drive a wedge between them and King Hussein.* ● If you describe something as **the thin end of the wedge**, you mean that it appears to be unimportant, but is actually the beginning of a harmful development. *Some Falkland Islanders see concessions over fishing as the thin end of the wedge leading to concessions on the vital principle of sovereignty.*

wedlock /wɛdlɒk/; an old-fashioned word.
1 NU **Wedlock** is the state of being married.

2 If someone is born **out of wedlock**, they are born at a time when their parents are not married. *Figures show that one in five babies born last year were born out of wedlock.*

Wednesday /wɛnzdeɪ, wɛnzdi/ **Wednesdays**
N U or N C **Wednesday** is the day after Tuesday and before Thursday. *The incident on Wednesday was more serious... The rail strike has been restricted to Wednesdays.*

Weds.
Weds. is a written abbreviation for 'Wednesday'.

wee /wiː/ **wees, weeing, weed**
1 ADJ ATTRIB **Wee** means small or little; used in Scottish English. *Can I ask you just one wee question?* **2** V When someone **wees**, they urinate; an informal use. ▶ Also N SING *I want a wee.*

weed /wiːd/ **weeds, weeding, weeded**
1 NC A **weed** is a wild plant growing where it is not wanted, for example in a garden. *Digging out the weeds without damaging your prized plants can often be difficult.* **2** V Oor V If you **weed** a place, you remove the weeds from it. *I had weeded the garden... Go and ask that man who's weeding there.* **3** NC If you call someone a **weed**, you mean that they are thin and physically weak, and that they have a weak character; an informal use. *He's such a weed.*
weed out PHRASAL VERB If you **weed out** things that are not wanted in a group, you get rid of them. *The government must weed out criminal elements from within the security forces... Natural selection had weeded out the weakest.*

weedy /wiːdi/
1 ADJ A place that is **weedy** is full of weeds. *...the long weedy path.* **2** ADJ If you describe someone as **weedy**, you mean that they are thin and physically weak; used in informal English, showing disapproval.

week /wiːk/ **weeks**
1 NCor NU A **week** is a period of seven days, especially one beginning on a Sunday or Monday. *He died in an explosion a few weeks ago... I bought them last week.* **2** NC+SUPP Your working **week** is the hours that you spend at work during a week. *I work a thirty-five hour week.* **3** N SING The **week** means the days in a week apart from Saturday and Sunday. *She never goes out during the week.* **4** You use **week** in expressions such as 'a week on Monday', 'a week next Tuesday', and 'tomorrow week' to mean exactly one week after the day that you mention. *'When is it to open?'—'Monday week.'... It's due a week tomorrow.* **5** You use **week** in expressions such as 'a week last Monday' and 'a week ago this Tuesday' to mean exactly one week before the day that you mention. *She died a week last Thursday.*

weekday /wiːkdeɪ/ **weekdays**
NC A **weekday** is any day of the week except Saturday and Sunday. *As usual on weekday mornings, the market was crowded with shop-keepers buying vegetables.*

weekend /wiːkɛnd/ **weekends**
NC The **weekend** is Saturday and Sunday. *I spent the weekend at home... Safety checks normally carried out at weekends did not get done until this morning.*

Wee Kim Wee /wiː kɪm wiː/
Wee Kim Wee became President of Singapore in 1985. He was the High Commissioner to Malaysia from 1973 to 1980, and Ambassador to Japan and South Korea from 1980 to 1984. He is a member of the People's Action Party (PAP). Born: 1915.

weekly /wiːkli/ **weeklies**
1 ADJ ATTRIB or ADV **Weekly** is used to describe something that happens or appears once a week. *...a weekly payment of seven shillings... Government ministers will meet representatives on a weekly basis to discuss humanitarian issues... Several groups meet weekly.* **2** NC A **weekly** is a newspaper or magazine that is published once a week. *...the Soviet weekly newspaper, Moscow News. ...the Weekly Mail.*

weeny /wiːni/ **weenier, weeniest**
ADJ ATTRIB **Weeny** is used to describe something that is extremely small; an informal word. *Take just a weeny bit more.*

weep /wiːp/ **weeps, weeping, wept**
V When someone **weeps**, they produce tears from their eyes because they are unhappy or hurt; a literary word. *The girl was weeping as she kissed him goodbye.* ▶ Also N SING *They had a little weep together.*

weeping willow, weeping willows
NC A **weeping willow** is a type of willow tree. It has long, thin branches that hang down to the ground. *It drooped like a weeping willow.*

weepy /wiːpi/
ADJ Someone who is **weepy** is sad and likely to cry easily. *She came in very weepy and said, 'Dad's leaving home'.*

weevil /wiːvɪl/ **weevils**
NC A **weevil** is a small beetle which feeds on grain and seeds and destroys crops. *The larvae of the weevil tunnel into the potato tubers, spoiling them for market. ...the grain weevil.*

weft /wɛft/
N SING The **weft** of a piece of woven material is the threads which are passed sideways in and out of the threads held in the loom; a technical term.

weigh /weɪ/ **weighs, weighing, weighed**
1 VC If something **weighs** a particular amount, that is how heavy it is. *It's made of steel and weighs ten tons.* **2** V O If you **weigh** something, you measure how heavy it is, using scales. *She was weighing a parcel.* **3** If you **weigh** your words, you think carefully before speaking. *He weighed his words carefully before commenting on the decision to destroy part of the nuclear arsenal.*
weigh down PHRASAL VERB **1** If you **are weighed down** by something, you are carrying a lot of it and it is very heavy. *He was weighed down with weapons and equipment.* **2** If you **are weighed down** by a difficulty, it is making you very worried. *Mr Gorbachov is weighed down with the burden of a worsening economic crisis.*
weigh on or **weigh upon** PHRASAL VERB If a problem **weighs on** you or **weighs upon** you, it makes you worry. *Worries about the Middle East weighed on the Tokyo stock exchange where the Nikkei average plunged more than 860 points... Her absence began to weigh upon me.*
weigh out PHRASAL VERB If you **weigh** something **out**, you measure a certain weight of it in order to make sure that you have the correct amount. *He weighed out a pound of tomatoes.*
weigh up PHRASAL VERB **1** If you **weigh up** a situation, you carefully consider the different factors involved before making a decision about what to do. *You have to weigh up in your mind whether to punish him or not.* **2** If you **weigh** someone or something **up**, you consider them and form an opinion of them. *The financial markets will also be weighing up the weekend's political speeches and interviews.*

weigh-in, weigh-ins
NC A **weigh-in** at a boxing match or a horse race is the occasion shortly before the event begins when each competitor is weighed. *Larry Holmes was ten pounds heavier than the champion at the weigh-in for their world title fight.*

weight /weɪt/ **weights, weighting, weighted**
1 NCor NU The **weight** of something is how heavy it is, which you can measure in units such as kilos or pounds. *The weight of the load is too great... It was 25 metres long and 30 tons in weight.* **2** NC A **weight** is a metal object which weighs a known amount. Weights are used with some sets of scales to weigh things. *On the one side of the balance they have standard weights.* **3** NC **Weights** are also sports equipment which some people lift in order to make their body stronger. *I did push-ups and lifted weights.* **4** NC You can refer to a heavy object as a **weight**. *I'm not allowed to carry heavy weights any more.*

5 VO If you **weight** something, you add something heavy to it, often in order to prevent it moving easily. *The net is a huge nylon curtain, supported by floats and weighted to hang vertically in the water... His gun weighted him to one side.*
6 N SING+*of* The **weight** of something is its great amount or power, which makes it difficult to contradict or oppose. *They had the weight of official support behind them.*
7 N SING If you feel a **weight** of some kind on you, you have a worrying problem or responsibility. *Without a producer, the weight of responsibility fell upon me.*
8 See also **dead weight**.
● **Weight** is used in these phrases. ● If you **lose weight**, your body becomes lighter and you look thinner. If you **put on weight** or **gain weight**, your body becomes heavier and you look fatter. *If you want to lose weight and keep it off, the best strategy is to resist the temptation of snacks between meal-times... Nobody's really had a look at what happens when people put on weight in middle age.* ● If you **pull your weight**, you put the same amount of effort into a task or activity as the other people who are involved in it. *West Germany and Japan had come under criticism from Washington for not pulling their weight over sharing the military cost of the Gulf war... She believes women more than pulled their own weight.*
weight down PHRASAL VERB If you **weight** something **down**, you add something heavy to it, often in order to prevent it moving easily. *...a plastic sheet weighted down with straw bales.*

weighted /wɛɪtɪd/
ADJ PRED A system that is **weighted** in favour of a person or group is organized so that this person or group has an advantage. *The law is weighted in favour of landlords... Higher education there is weighted towards the arts.*

weightless /wɛɪtləs/
ADJ Something that is **weightless** has or seems to have very little weight or no weight at all. *These creatures may have been virtually weightless in water.*
◆ **weightlessness** NU *...experiencing the weightlessness of space travel.*

weightlifter /wɛɪtlɪftə/ **weightlifters**
NC A **weightlifter** is a person who does weightlifting. *Suleymanoglu became the first weightlifter to snatch two-and-a-half times his own body-weight when he lifted 150 kilograms.*

weightlifting /wɛɪtlɪftɪŋ/
NU **Weightlifting** is a sport in which the competitor who can lift the heaviest weight wins. *The sport of weightlifting could be suspended from future Olympic games... Xing Liwei took China's fourth weightlifting gold with a total lift of 190 kilos.*

weighty /wɛɪti/ **weightier, weightiest**
ADJ **Weighty** matters are serious or important. *Weightier things get dealt with immediately.*

weir /wɪə/ **weirs**
NC A **weir** is a low dam built across a river in order to control or direct the flow of water. *...civil engineers designing weirs, canals and bridges.*

weird /wɪəd/ **weirder, weirdest**
ADJ **Weird** means strange and peculiar. *...odd religions and weird cults.* ◆ **weirdly** ADV *...weirdly shaped trees.*

weirdo /wɪədəu/ **weirdos**
NC If you call someone a **weirdo**, you mean that they behave in a strange and peculiar way; an informal word. *When we started up, the locals thought we were weirdos.*

Weizsäcker, Dr Richard von /rɪxɑːt fɒn vaɪtszekə/
Dr Richard von Weizsäcker became President of West Germany in 1984, and of re-unified Germany in 1990. He was a member of the German Parliament from 1969 to 1981, and was Vice President of the Parliament from 1979 to 1981. From 1981 to 1984 he was Mayor of West Berlin. He is a member of the Christian Democratic Union (CDU). Born: 1920.

welcome /wɛlkəm/ **welcomes, welcoming, welcomed**
1 VO If you **welcome** someone, you greet them in a friendly way when they arrive at the place where you are. *He moved eagerly towards the door to welcome his visitor.* ▶ Also NC *I was given a warm welcome by the President.* ◆ **welcoming** ADJ *She gave him a welcoming smile... The Americans were greeted with the cheers of the welcoming crowd.*
2 You can say '**Welcome**' to someone who has just arrived. *Welcome to Peking... Welcome back.*
3 ADJ If someone is **welcome** in a place, people are pleased when they come there. *All members of the public are welcome.*
4 ADJ PRED+*to*-INF If you tell someone that they are **welcome** to do something which you are inviting them to do, you are encouraging them to do it. *You will always be welcome to come back.*
5 VO If you **welcome** something new, you approve of it and support it. *I warmly welcomed his proposal.*
6 ADJ If something that happens or occurs is **welcome**, you are pleased about it or approve of it. *This is a welcome development.*
● **Welcome** is used in these phrases. ● If you **make someone welcome**, you make them feel happy and accepted in a situation, especially when they arrive in a new place. *They've always made each of us very welcome... He said that any miners on their way to the city would be made welcome in Victory Square.* ● You can acknowledge someone's thanks by saying '**You're welcome**'. *'Thank you for the beautiful scarf.'—'You're welcome. I'm glad you like it.'*

weld /wɛld/ **welds, welding, welded**
1 VO If you **weld** two pieces of metal together, you join them by heating their edges and putting them together so that they cool and harden into one piece. *It hasn't been possible to weld it by the usual gas or arc welding techniques. ...four barrels welded together.*
2 NC A **weld** is a join where two pieces of metal have been welded together. *Other lower quality welding requires less skill, but produces rougher, poor quality welds.*
3 VOA If you **weld** people into a group, you join them together to form a united organization; a formal use. *The challenge of welding Britain to Europe cannot be obscured by short-sighted wrangles... The diverse ethnic groups had been welded together by the great anti-fascist cause.*

welder /wɛldə/ **welders**
1 NC A **welder** is a person whose job is welding metal. *John is one of the welders who built the production set.*
2 NC A **welder** is also a machine which welds metal.

welfare /wɛlfeə/
1 NU+POSS The **welfare** of a person or group is their health, comfort, and prosperity. *I would devote my life to the child's welfare.*
2 N+N **Welfare** services are provided to help with people's living conditions and financial problems. *...welfare workers.*
3 NU In the United States, **welfare** is money that is paid by the government to people who are poor, ill, or unemployed. *I'm on welfare and I don't have the money for a private doctor... Many make ends meet with food stamps or other types of welfare.*

welfare state
N SING The **welfare state** is a system in which the government uses money from taxes to provide free social services such as health care and education. *They equated socialism with the welfare state, educational opportunity and the fair distribution of income.*

well /wɛl/ **wells, welling, welled**. When it is an adverb, the comparative is **better** and the superlative is **best**: see the separate entries for these words.
1 You say '**Well**' when you are about to say something, especially when you are hesitating or trying to make your statement less strong, or when you are about to correct a statement. *'Is that right?'—'Well, I think so.'... I suppose you want to know if I've changed my mind. Well, I haven't... Well, thank you Jim for talking to us about your work... Well, thank God for that... It took me years, well months at least, to realise that he'd actually lied to me.*
2 ADV If you do something **well**, you do it to a high

standard. *She speaks French well... He handled it well.*

3 ADV **Well** also means thoroughly or to a very great extent. *You say you don't know this man very well?... They were on the brink of war, but they were well prepared.*

4 ADV **Well** is also used in questions and statements about the extent or standard of something. *I don't know how well Dennis knew him... I could see almost as well at night as I could in sunlight.*

5 ADV or SUBMOD You use **well** to give emphasis to some adjuncts and to a few adjectives. *They stood well back from the heat... Actors are well aware of this problem.*

6 ADV If you say that something may **well** happen or exist, you mean that it is likely to happen or exist. *Your eyesight may well improve... There might well be external influences.*

7 ADJ If you are **well**, you are healthy. *They told me you weren't well.*

8 NC A **well** is a hole in the ground from which a supply of water is extracted. *People no longer had rain water to drink, and the water in the wells became increasingly polluted.*

9 NC You can also refer to an oil well as a **well**. *The latest find involves a 500 million dollar investment programme and the drilling of another 53 wells.*
● **Well** is used in these phrases. ● If things **are going well** or if **all is well**, things are satisfactory. *Things went well for John until the First World War.* ● If someone is **well out of** a situation, it is a good thing that they are no longer involved in it. *I'm glad to be well out of it.* ● If you say that something that has happened **is just as well**, you mean that it is fortunate that it happened. *He didn't have to speak very often, which was just as well as he was a man who liked to keep words to himself... He gave the Parliamentary performance of his political career. Which is just as well, because his career was at stake.* ● If one thing is involved **as well as** another, both things are involved. *Women, as well as men, have a fundamental right to work... The Yugoslav army is insisting it has a political as well as a military role... His father took home movies as well as constant snapshots.* ● If one thing is involved and another thing is involved **as well**, the second thing is also involved. *He needs to develop his reading further, and his writing as well.* ● If you say that you **may as well** or **might as well** do something, you mean that you are going to do it, or that you think you should do it, even though it is not the thing that you would most like to do. *I may as well admit that I knew the answer all along... If there is no agreement we might as well all pack up and go home.* ● You use **well and truly** to emphasize that something is definitely the case; an informal expression. *So the Space Age had now well and truly begun... Events in congress seem to confirm the belief that the days of plenty for the Pentagon are well and truly over.* ● You say '**oh well**' to indicate that you accept that a situation cannot be changed, although you are not happy about it. *Oh well, you wouldn't understand... Oh well, it's fate.* ● **would do well** to do something: see **do**. ● **very well**: see **very**. ● See also **well done**.

well up PHRASAL VERB If tears **well up** in your eyes, they come to the surface. *Tears welled up in his eyes and he broke down and sobbed.*

we'll /wil, wiːl/
We'll is the usual spoken form of 'we shall' or 'we will'. *Come on, then, we'll have to hurry.*

well-advised
ADJ PRED If someone says that you would be **well-advised** to do something, they are advising you to do it. *She's leaving, and I think you'd be well-advised to do the same.*

well-appointed
ADJ A **well-appointed** room or building is equipped or furnished to a very high standard. *...an exceptionally well-appointed kitchen.*

well-balanced
1 ADJ Someone who is **well-balanced** is sensible and does not have emotional or psychological problems.

Their children are well-balanced and sincere human beings.

2 ADJ Something that is **well-balanced** is designed to be acceptable to people with different opinions or attitudes, because it is fair and sensible. *It's got a well-balanced economy... He called it a well-balanced compromise that would further neighbourly relations.*

well-behaved
ADJ **Well-behaved** people act in a way that is considered polite and correct. *We were, of course, well-behaved, middle-class children... The majority of the people at the game were well-behaved and trouble was caused by a hooligan element.*

well-being
NU Someone's **well-being** is their health and happiness. *This new physical fitness will produce a general feeling of well-being.*

well-bred
ADJ Someone who is **well-bred** has good manners. *...a well-bred, elderly chaperon watching over our revels.*

well-brought-up
ADJ People, especially children, who are **well-brought-up** are very polite because they have been taught good manners. *They're very well-brought-up children.*

well-built
ADJ Someone, especially a man, who is **well-built** is strong and muscular. *Photographs show a strikingly good-looking young man, dark, well-built, in theatrical costume.*

well-connected
ADJ Someone who is **well-connected** has important or influential relatives or friends. *Relatively few of them have been high-ranking or well-connected. ...pupils from similar well-connected backgrounds.*

well-disposed
ADJ PRED + *to* or *towards* If you are **well-disposed** to a person, plan, or activity, you are likely to be sympathetic or friendly towards that person or willing to take part in that plan or activity. *Our kids are very well-disposed to what we're doing... The Czechs in 1945, he suggests, were well-disposed towards Communism and the Soviet Union.*

well done
1 You say '**Well done**' to indicate that you are pleased that someone has got something right or done something good. *Well done. Nice going with this puzzle... She said to the workforce here, 'Well done, you've got the skills, you've got the ability; the future can be yours'.*

2 ADJ If something that you have cooked, especially meat, is **well done**, it has been cooked thoroughly. *Pork has to be very well done, or you can't eat it.*

well-dressed
ADJ Someone who is **well-dressed** is wearing smart or elegant clothes. *She was a well-dressed woman of about 50, her hair pulled back into a bun, her suit and high heels very stylish and smart.*

well-earned
ADJ If you describe something as **well-earned**, you mean that someone deserves it, for example because they have been working very hard. *Let us take a well-earned rest.*

well-established
ADJ If something is **well-established**, it has existed for a long time and is successful. *Senegal already has a well-established film industry... Neo-Nazi groups are well-established in Britain, France and West Germany.*

well-fed
ADJ Someone who is **well-fed** gets enough healthy food regularly. *The refugees could use a night's sleep, but by and large they appear well-fed and healthy.*

well-founded
ADJ If an idea, opinion, or feeling is **well-founded**, it is based on facts. *These warnings proved well-founded... He repeated his belief that Mr Mendis did not have a well-founded fear of persecution.*

well-groomed
ADJ Someone who is **well-groomed** is neat and tidy in appearance; an old-fashioned word. *The sales force is expected to be well-groomed, and that means business suits.*

well-grounded
ADJ **Well-grounded** means the same as **well-founded**. *People are entitled to asylum as political refugees in another country if they can show that they have a 'well-grounded fear of persecution'.*

well-heeled
ADJ If you say that someone is **well-heeled**, you mean that they are wealthy; an informal word. *Such hotels are expected to concentrate on riding and field sports to lure a well-heeled clientele.*

well-informed
ADJ Someone who is **well-informed** knows a lot about something, or about many different things. *Well-informed sources say several military officers have been arrested in connection with unrest at army bases... The voters interviewed here in Turim today were uniformly thoughtful and well-informed.*

wellington /wˈelɪŋtən/ **wellingtons**
NC **Wellingtons** or **wellington boots** are long rubber boots which you wear to keep your feet dry.

Wellington /wˈelɪŋtən/
Wellington is the capital of New Zealand and its second largest city. Population: 325,000 (1988).

well-intentioned
ADJ Someone or something that is **well-intentioned** means to be helpful or kind, but is unsuccessful or causes unfortunate results. *Although well-intentioned, he gradually alienated his colleagues by his high-handedness... None of these measures, however well-intentioned, has had the desired effect.*

well-kept
ADJ A **well-kept** building, room, or place is looked after carefully, so that it is always neat and tidy. *...the first thing you see as you enter the old but well-kept building. ...a mansion with a well-kept lawn.*

well-known
ADJ Something or someone that is **well-known** is famous or familiar. *...his two well-known books on modern art. ...a well-known Democratic congressman... He is well-known for his outspoken remarks.*

well-mannered
ADJ Someone who is **well-mannered** is polite and has good manners. *I try to be well-mannered in these things: I try to be courteous at all times. ...his placid and well-mannered demeanor.*

well-meaning
ADJ Someone who is **well-meaning** tries to be helpful or kind, but is unsuccessful or causes unfortunate results. *Some well-meaning parents are too fussy about food.*

well-meant
ADJ Something that is **well-meant** is intended to be helpful or kind, but is unsuccessful or has unfortunate results. *I don't want anyone else's opinion, however well-meant.*

well-nigh. See **nigh.**

well-off; an informal word.
1 ADJ Someone who is **well-off** is fairly rich. *Only well-off Sri Lankans can afford to send their children away in search of safety.*
2 If you say that someone **doesn't know when** they are **well off**, you are criticizing them for not appreciating how fortunate they are.

well-preserved
ADJ If you say that someone is **well-preserved**, you mean that they do not look as old as they really are. *...a well-preserved man in his late fifties.*

well-read
ADJ Someone who is **well-read** has read a lot of books and has learnt a lot from them. *He was active, intelligent and very well-read.*

well-spoken
ADJ Someone who is **well-spoken** speaks in a polite, correct way. *He made few friends locally though he was well-spoken and often polite.*

well-thought-of
ADJ Someone or something that is **well-thought-of** is admired and respected, and has a good reputation. *...the desire to be well-thought-of by your neighbours and contemporaries.*

well-thought-out
ADJ Something that is **well-thought-out** is very carefully planned. *...a well written, entertaining, and well thought-out novel.*

well-thumbed
ADJ A book or magazine that is **well-thumbed** is creased and marked because it has been read so often.

well-timed
ADJ An action or remark that is **well-timed** is said or done at the most suitable time. *...well-timed purchases of stock... The government's recent announcement of a new package of reforms was well-timed to lead into this budget.*

well-to-do
ADJ Someone who is **well-to-do** is rich; an old-fashioned word. *Both Serrano and Carpio are well-to-do businessmen.*

well-tried
ADJ Something that is **well-tried** has been used or done many times before and so is known to work well or to be successful. *A combination of two well-tried antibiotics may well help AIDS sufferers. ...a well-tried technique.*

well-versed
ADJ PRED+*in* Someone who is **well-versed** in a particular subject knows a lot about it. *They were relatively well-versed in the rhetoric of Black liberation.*

well-wisher, well-wishers
NC A **well-wisher** is someone who tells you that they hope you will be successful in what you are doing. *Hundreds of telegrams arrived from well-wishers.*

well-worn
1 ADJ A **well-worn** expression or remark has been used so often that it is boring. *...a well-worn joke.*
2 ADJ A **well-worn** object or piece of clothing has been used so much that it looks old and untidy. *...a well-worn hat tipped to shade his eyes from the glaring sun.*

welly /wˈeli/ **wellies**
NC A **welly** is the same as a **wellington**; an informal word. *I put on my wellies and we went off into the rain.*

Welsh /wˈelʃ/
1 ADJ **Welsh** means belonging or relating to Wales. *...the Welsh city of Cardiff. ... a Welsh choir.*
2 NU **Welsh** is a language spoken in Wales. *There is a television channel that broadcasts exclusively in Welsh.*
3 N PL The **Welsh** are the people who come from Wales. *The survey says the Welsh eat more potatoes than anyone else.*

Welshman /wˈelʃmən/ **Welshmen** /wˈelʃmən/
NC A **Welshman** is a man who comes from Wales. *Hopes are high for a British success with Nick Faldo of England and the Welshman Ian Woosnam showing top form.*

Welsh rarebit or **Welsh rabbit**
NU **Welsh rarebit** or **Welsh rabbit** is grilled cheese on toast.

Welshwoman /wˈelʃwʊmən/ **Welshwomen**
NC A **Welshwoman** is a woman who comes from Wales.

welt /wˈelt/ **welts**
NC A **welt** is a mark which is made on someone's skin, usually by a blow from something such as a whip or sword. *His face was covered with welts and bruises.*

welter /wˈeltə/
N SING A **welter** of things is a large number of them; a literary word. *...the daily welter of details and little problems.*

wench /wˈentʃ/ **wenches**
NC A **wench** is a girl or young woman, especially a servant or prostitute; an old-fashioned word. *...serving wenches.*

wend /wˈend/ **wends, wending, wended**
If you **wend** your way in a particular direction, you go there slowly; a literary expression. *Those troops are now wending their way home along the Salang highway.*

went /wˈent/
Went is the past tense of **go.**

wept /wɛpt/
Wept is the past tense and past participle of **weep**.

were /wə, wɜ:/
1 **Were** is the plural and the second person singular of the past tense of **be**.
2 **Were** is sometimes used instead of 'was' in conditional clauses or wishes; a formal use. *He wished he were taking a bath... He treated me as if I were crazy.* ● **as it were:** see **as**.

we're /wɪə/
We're is the usual spoken form of 'we are'. *We're all here.*

weren't /wɜ:nt/
Weren't is the usual spoken form of 'were not'.

werewolf /wɛəwʊlf/ **werewolves**
NC In horror stories and films, a **werewolf** is a person who changes into a wolf. *...werewolves and vampires growling and snarling with saliva dripping out of their mouths.*

west /wɛst/
1 N SING The **west** is the direction in which you look to see the sun set. *The next settlement is two hundred miles to the west.*
2 N SING The **west** of a place is the part which is towards the west. *...the west of Ireland.* ▶ Also ADJ ATTRIB *...West Africa.*
3 ADV **West** means towards the west, or to the west of a place or thing. *...an English friend who had never been West.*
4 ADJ ATTRIB A **west** wind blows from the west.
5 N SING The **West** is also used to refer to the United States, Canada, and Western and Southern Europe. *Secretary of State Baker has called for free trade between the West and former Eastern Bloc countries.*

westbound /wɛstbaʊnd/
ADJ **Westbound** roads or vehicles lead to or are travelling towards the west. *...the westbound passenger express... There is heavy traffic on the M4, westbound outside London.*

westerly /wɛstəli/
1 ADJ **Westerly** means towards the west. *The harbour has a westerly outlook.*
2 ADJ A **westerly** wind blows from the west. *Windsurfers were swept out to sea by a westerly gale.*

western /wɛstən/ **westerns**
1 ADJ ATTRIB **Western** means in or from the west of a region or country. *...Western Nigeria.*
2 ADJ ATTRIB **Western** also means coming from or associated with the United States, Canada, or Western or Southern Europe. *...the impact of western technology.*
3 NC A **western** is a film or book about life in the west of America in the nineteenth century. *...westerns like A Fistful of Dollars and The Good, The Bad and The Ugly.*

westerner /wɛstənə/ **westerners**
NC A **westerner** is a person who was born in or who lives in the United States, Canada, or Western or Southern Europe. *Three planes carrying hundreds of Westerners, including Americans, left Baghdad today.*

westernize /wɛstənaɪz/ **westernizes, westernizing, westernized;** also spelt **westernise.**
V O If a society or system is **westernized**, ideas and behaviour which are common in the United States, Canada, and Western and Southern Europe are introduced into it. *His cricket career in England had entirely westernized him.* ◆ **westernized** ADJ *The more westernized sectors of Algerian society are clearly worried about the Islamic Front's success.*

westernmost /wɛstənməʊst/
ADJ ATTRIB The **westernmost** part of an area or the **westernmost** thing in a line is the one that is farther towards the west than any other. *...the westernmost stretches of the desert.*

Western Sahara /wɛstən səhɑːrə/
Western Sahara is a disputed territory in north-western Africa. It became a colony of Spain, known as the Spanish Sahara, in 1886. Morocco and Mauritania claimed the area in the late 1950s. The Polisario Front was founded in 1973 to fight for independence for Western Sahara. In the Green March of 1975, 300,000 Moroccans entered and occupied the northern area of Western Sahara. Spain agreed to divide the territory between Morocco and Mauritania, and withdrew its forces in 1976. Polisario declared the Saharan Arab Democratic Republic (SADR) and war between Morocco, Mauritania, and Polisario started. Mauritania withdrew its claim to Western Sahara in 1979. Polisario became a member of the Organization of African Unity in 1984, causing Morocco to withdraw from the OAU in 1985. Polisario has been recognized by over 70 countries worldwide. War between Polisario and Morocco continued through the 1980s. Fishing and phosphate mining are important industries. The principal town is Al-Ayoun.
▪ *religion:* Islam ▪ *language:* Moroccan, Hassaniya Arabic ▪ *currency:* Moroccan dirham ▪ *population:* 186,040 (1989) ▪ *size:* 252,120 square kilometres.

Western Samoa. See Samoa, Western

West German, West Germans
1 ADJ **West German** means belonging or relating to the part of Germany that was known as the Federal Republic of Germany before the reunification of Germany in 1990. *It was built by a West German firm... The West German leaders are still divided among themselves.*
2 NC A **West German** is someone who comes from the part of Germany that was known as the Federal Republic of Germany before the reunification of Germany in 1990. *The man arrested—a West German of Arab origin—had denied any involvement.*

West Indian /wɛst ɪndiən/ **West Indians**
1 ADJ **West Indian** means belonging or relating to the West Indies. *...the West Indian community in Paddington.*
2 NC A **West Indian** is a person who comes from the West Indies. *Many West Indians were hoping their leaders would overcome the sense of Caribbean impotence in dealing with Haiti.*

West Island /wɛst aɪlənd/
West Island is the capital of the Cocos Islands. Population: 218 (1988).

Westminster /wɛstmɪnstə/
N PROP **Westminster** is the name of the area in London where the Houses of Parliament are. **Westminster** is often used to refer to the British parliament. *At Westminster, the Opposition will be pressing for a debate on the economy when MPs return today after their summer recess... He was heartened that Westminster now recognised the crisis of confidence in Hong Kong.*

westward /wɛstwəd/ or **westwards**
1 ADV **Westward** or **westwards** means towards the west. *The reef stretches westwards from the tip of Florida.*
2 ADJ ATTRIB **Westward** is used to describe things which are moving towards the west or which face towards the west. *...the westward expansion of the city.*

wet /wɛt/ **wetter, wettest; wets, wetting, wetted.** The past tense and past participle of the verb can be either **wetted** or **wet.**
1 ADJ If something is **wet**, it is covered in or has absorbed water or another liquid. *The grass is wet... His face was wet with perspiration... The ground was wet and slippery.*
2 ADJ If the weather is **wet**, it is raining. *Take a raincoat if it's wet.*
3 ADJ If something such as paint, ink, or cement is **wet**, it is not yet dry or solid. *Clemente adopted the Fresco technique, learning to paint on wet plaster.*
4 ADJ If you say that someone is **wet**, you mean that they lack confidence, energy, or enthusiasm; an informal use.
5 V O To **wet** something means to cause it to have water or another liquid on it. *Uncle Ted wet his lips... A column of spray wetted them.*
6 V O or V-REFL If people, especially children, **wet** their beds or clothes or **wet** themselves, they urinate in their beds or clothes because they cannot control their bladder. *These children have nightmares and wet the bed... To put it plainly, they wet themselves; it's called stress incontinence.*

wet blanket, wet blankets

NC If you call someone a **wet blanket,** you mean that they refuse to join in an activity with other people or that they behave in a way that stops other people enjoying themselves; an informal expression.

wet-nurse, wet-nurses

NC In former times, a **wet-nurse** was a woman who was paid to feed another woman's baby with her breast milk.

wet suit, wet suits

NC A **wet suit** is a close-fitting rubber suit which a diver or underwater swimmer wears in order to keep his or her body warm. *We wear life jackets and wetsuits.*

we've /wiv, wiːv/

We've is the usual spoken form of 'we have', especially when 'have' is an auxiliary verb. *We've had a very interesting discussion.*

whack /wæk/ **whacks, whacking, whacked**

1 VO If you **whack** someone or something, you hit them hard; an informal use. *You really have to whack the ball.*

2 If something is **out of whack,** it is not working properly, often because its natural balance has been upset; used in informal American English. *If a country gets too weak or too strong it can really throw things out of whack in the Middle East.*

whacked /wækt/

ADJ PRED If you are **whacked,** you are extremely tired; an informal word. *By 9 p.m. I was whacked. By 9.30 I was asleep in bed.*

whacking /wækɪŋ/ **whackings;** an old-fashioned word.

1 NC A **whacking** is a severe beating, especially one given to a child by a parent as a punishment. *He waited until his father had gone, to avoid another whacking.*

2 ADJ ATTRIB or SUBMOD If you use **whacking** to describe something, you mean that it is very large. *We had a whacking phone bill this month... They greeted me from work by plonking down a whacking great tea in front of the fire.*

whacky /wæki/. See wacky.

whale /weɪl/ **whales**

NC A **whale** is a very large sea mammal. *Forty-five whales remain grounded on the beach at Hyannisport, Massachusetts. ...the song of the humpback whale.*

whalebone /weɪlbəʊn/

NU **Whalebone** is a hard material taken from the mouth of a whale and used, especially in olden times, as a cloth stiffener, for example in corsets.

whaler /weɪlə/ **whalers**

1 NC A **whaler** is a ship which is used in hunting whales. *A Japanese whaler left for the Antarctic last month to begin a hunt for mink whales.*

2 NC A **whaler** is also someone who works on a ship which is used in hunting whales. *A large number of people had emigrated to the USA to work as whalers off the East Coast.*

whaling /weɪlɪŋ/

NU **Whaling** is the activity of hunting whales. *Whaling for scientific research is permitted under the commission's rules... Commercial whaling is prohibited for the moment.*

wham /wæm/

You use **wham** to indicate that something such as a punch, kick, or idea happens suddenly or forcefully; an informal word. *'Wham!' said Charlie, and hit him. ...tears on both sides, packing up a suitcase—and wham! You're alone for the first time in years.*

whammy /wæmi/

N SING A double **whammy** is two unpleasant or difficult situations or problems which occur at the same time, or which occur one after the other. A triple **whammy** is three unpleasant or difficult situations or problems which do this; used in informal American English. *The city is trying to recover from a double whammy. They never quite bounced back from the recession of the 1980s; now residents are coping with the current economic downturn... It's a budget which has taken a triple whammy of deficits, recession and military operations in the Persian Gulf.*

wharf /wɔːf/ **wharves or wharfs**

NC A **wharf** is a platform by a river or the sea, where ships can be tied up. *Someone had forgotten to untie the mooring cable from the wharf... The once derelict quays and wharfs have undergone extensive restoration.*

what /wɒt, wɒt/

1 PRON or DET You use **what** in questions when you are asking for information. *What is your name?... What time is it?*

2 PRON or DET You also use **what** to introduce reported questions and reported statements. *I asked her what had happened... I don't know what to do... We didn't know what bus to get.*

3 PRON You use **what** at the beginning of a relative clause which is used as a subject, object, or complement. *What once took a century now took only ten months... She began what will be her main job for the week... Instability is what they fear most.*

4 DET or PRON You use **what** to indicate that you are talking about the whole of an amount. *I've spent what money I had... It took what I could give.*

5 PREDET or DET You use **what** in exclamations to express your opinion of something. *What a pity... What rubbish!*

6 Some people say **'What?'** when they want you to repeat something because they did not hear it properly. 'What' is not as polite as 'pardon' or 'sorry'. *'Do you want another coffee?'—'What?'—'Do you want another coffee?'*

7 You can say **'What'** to express surprise or disbelief. *'Could I see you?'—'What, right this minute?'*

● **What** is used in these phrases. ● You use **what about** when you are making a suggestion or offer. *What about some lunch, Colonel?* ● You use **what if** at the beginning of a question about the consequences of something, especially something undesirable. *What if I miss the train?* ● You say **what with** to introduce the reasons for a situation, especially an undesirable one. *What with paying for lunch and the theatre tickets, I'm very short of cash.* ● You can refer to someone as **what's his name** or **what's her name** when you cannot remember their name; an informal expression. *You're like what's his name.* ● **what's more:** see more. ● **so what:** see so.

whatever /wɒtevə/

1 PRON or DET You use **whatever** to refer to anything or everything of a particular type. *They asked the Sheik to do whatever he could to help obtain the release of the hostages... Refugees said they'd picked up whatever belongings they could carry... Whatever deal is being discussed, the hijackers have not dropped their demands.*

2 PRON or DET You also use **whatever** to refer to things of a particular type when you cannot be specific about their precise nature. *Whatever their reasons, nine out of ten couples last year chose to marry in church... We'll pay the cost, whatever it may be.*

3 You say **or whatever** to refer generally to something of the same kind as the thing you have just mentioned; an informal use. *You plug it into a computer or whatever and it does the rest.*

4 CONJ You also use **whatever** to say that something is the case in all circumstances. *Whatever happens, the company says significant redundancies among the two-thousand employees are inevitable... People are important as people, whatever they do.*

5 ADV You also use **whatever** after a noun group to emphasize a negative statement. *There is no scientific evidence whatever to support such a view... He knew nothing whatever about it.*

6 PRON **Whatever** can be used as an emphatic form of 'what', usually when you are surprised about something. *Whatever is the matter?*

what's /wɒts, wɒts/

What's is the usual spoken form of 'what is' or 'what has', especially when 'has' is an auxiliary verb. *What's it designed to do?... I don't know what's going to happen... Roy Haynes looks at what's happened since the disaster.*

whatsoever /wɒtsəʊevə/

ADV You use **whatsoever** after a noun group in order

to emphasize a negative statement. *There is no reason whatsoever to resign... He refused to make any comment whatsoever.*

wheat /wiːt/
NU **Wheat** is a cereal plant which is ground into flour to make bread. *Stocks of wheat are running low.*

wheatgerm /wiːtdʒɜːm/
NU **Wheatgerm** is the middle part of a grain of wheat which is rich in vitamins and is often added to other food.

wheatmeal /wiːtmiːl/
NU **Wheatmeal** is a flour which is made from wheat grains but from which some part has been removed or to which something has been added.

wheedle /wiːdl/ **wheedles, wheedling, wheedled**
1 VO+*into* If you **wheedle** someone into doing something, you gently and cleverly persuade them to do it. *They tried to wheedle her into leaving the house.*
2 VOA If you **wheedle** something out of someone, you persuade them to give it you. *She wheedled money out of him.*

wheel /wiːl/ **wheels, wheeling, wheeled**
1 NC A **wheel** is a circular object which turns round on a rod attached to its centre. Wheels are fixed underneath vehicles so that they can move along. *The train started, its wheels squealing against the metal tracks. ...a full-sized steel-framed bicycle with small wheels.*
2 N SING The **wheel** is the steering wheel of a car. *...a police operation against drivers who spend too long at the wheel... Simon found himself trapped behind the wheel.*
3 VO If you **wheel** something such as a bicycle or cart, you push it along. *My father was wheeling his bicycle up the hill... The equipment had to be wheeled around on a large trolley.*
4 V If someone or something **wheels**, they move round in the shape of a circle or part of a circle. *The sky becomes filled with birds wheeling back and forth... The plane banked and wheeled... I wheeled around and shook her hand.*

wheelbarrow /wiːlbærəʊ/ **wheelbarrows**
NC A **wheelbarrow** is a small, open cart with one wheel and handles that is used for carrying things, for example in the garden. *So you're going to dump the soil in the wheelbarrow next?*

wheelbase /wiːlbeɪs/ **wheelbases**
NC The **wheelbase** of a car or other vehicle is the distance between its front and back wheels.

wheelchair /wiːltʃeə/ **wheelchairs**
NC A **wheelchair** is a chair with wheels that sick or disabled people use in order to move about. *He is confined to a wheelchair.*

wheeler-dealer /wiːlədiːlə/ **wheeler-dealers**
NC A **wheeler-dealer** is someone who does a lot of wheeling and dealing; used showing disapproval. *He was, even at that age, a wheeler-dealer.*

wheelhouse /wiːlhaʊs/ **wheelhouses**
NC A **wheelhouse** is a small room or shelter on a boat or old-fashioned ship, where the wheel used for steering the boat is situated. *The reflectors are usually positioned on the mast or power-boat wheelhouse.*

wheeling and dealing
NU **Wheeling and dealing** is the process of trying to get what you want, especially in business, often by dishonest or unfair methods. *...complex business deals and financial wheeling and dealing. ...wheeling and dealing on the stock-exchange.*

wheelwright /wiːlraɪt/ **wheelwrights**
NC A **wheelwright** is someone who makes and repairs wooden wheels and other wooden things such as carts, carriages, and gates.

wheeze /wiːz/ **wheezes, wheezing, wheezed**
V If you **wheeze**, you breathe with difficulty, making a hissing or whistling sound. *Coughing and wheezing, he climbed up the last few steps.* ▶ Also NC *All this was said very slowly, between wheezes.*

wheezy /wiːzi/ **wheezier, wheeziest**
ADJ **Wheezy** coughs or other sounds are made by people who have difficulty in breathing and so are

hissing or whistling. *Asthma is an odd condition in which, at a mild level, nothing worse than wheezy breathing is produced.*

whelk /welk/ **whelks**
NC A **whelk** is a creature like a snail that is found in the sea near the shore. Whelks have hard shells and very soft bodies which can be eaten.

when /wen, wen/
1 ADV You use **when** to ask questions about the time at which things happen. *'I have to go to Germany.'—'When?'—'Now.'... When did you arrive?... When are we going to get an answer to this problem?*
2 CONJ You also use **when** in reported questions and reported statements about the time at which something happens. *He did not know when an election could be held... Ask her when the trouble first started.*
3 CONJ or PRON **When** is also used to introduce a clause which specifies or refers to the time at which something happens. *Mr King received a noisy welcome when he arrived at the camp... When I asked them why they were there, they refused to answer... I remember when I first met him some fifteen years ago... When you become older, you will have some security of your own to fall back on.*
4 CONJ You also use **when** to introduce the reason for an opinion, comment, or question. *How can I get a job when I can't even read or write?*
5 CONJ You also use **when** at the beginning of a subordinate clause to make a statement that makes your previous statement seem surprising. *You describe this policy as rigid and inflexible, when in fact it has been extremely flexible.*

whence /wens/
ADV or CONJ **Whence** means from where; an old-fashioned word. *He returned hastily to the United States, whence he originally came.*

whenever /wenevə/
CONJ You use **whenever** to refer to any time or every time that something happens or is true. *Come and see me whenever you feel depressed... I avoided conflict whenever possible.*

where; /weə, weə/.
1 ADV You use **where** to ask questions about the place something is in, or is coming from or going to. *Where's it hidden?... Where are you going?*
2 CONJ You also use **where** to specify or refer to the place in which something is situated or happens. *I think I know where we are... How did you know where to find me?... She walked over to where Madeleine stood.*
3 CONJ, PRON, or ADV You also use **where** when you are referring to or asking about a situation, a stage in something, or an aspect of something. *Bryan wouldn't know where to start. ...a situation where unemployment is three million and rising fast... This is where I profoundly disagree with you... Where do you see this method going in the future?*
4 CONJ **Where** is used to introduce a clause which contrasts with what is said in the main clause. *Sometimes a teacher will be listened to, where a parent might not.*

whereabouts; pronounced /weərəbaʊts/ for the meaning in paragraph 1 and /weərəbaʊts/ for the meaning in paragraph 2.
1 N PL+POSS or NU+POSS If you refer to the **whereabouts** of a person or thing, you mean the place where that person or thing is. *The whereabouts of the three dissidents are unknown... We have discovered the whereabouts of one of the paintings... Their exact whereabouts is not clear.*
2 ADV You use **whereabouts** in questions when you are asking precisely where something is. *Whereabouts are you going in Yugoslavia?*

whereas /weəræz/
CONJ You use **whereas** to introduce a comment which contrasts with what is said in the main clause. *Mr Premadasa's main support is here, whereas Mrs Bandaranaike's main support is in the rural areas... The official rate of exchange is 9,200 dông to the dollar at the moment, whereas in January it was about 7,000.*

whereby /weəbaɪ/
PRON A system or action **whereby** something happens

is one that makes that thing happen; a formal word.
*Britain has a unique system whereby one letter in a
car's number plate indicates the year in which the car
was sold. ...part of a clandestine intelligence operation
whereby the Americans obtained latest versions of
Soviet-made weapons systems.*

wherefores /we͟əfɔːz/
The **whys and wherefores** of something are the reasons
for it; a formal expression. *Martin wanted to know all
the whys and wherefores.*

wherein /weəri͟n/; an old-fashioned word.
1 PRON **Wherein** means in which place. *...the box
wherein she kept her wool.*
2 ADV or CONJ **Wherein** also means in which part or in
which respect. *Wherein lay her greatness? ...a
programme wherein children raise seedlings in
schools.*

whereupon /we͟ərəpɒn/
CONJ You use **whereupon** to say that one thing happens
immediately after another thing and usually as a
result of it; a formal word. *His department was shut
down, whereupon he returned to Calcutta.*

wherever /weəre͟və/
1 CONJ You use **wherever** to say that something is true
or happens in any place or situation. *He's greeted by
large enthusiastic crowds wherever he goes... Farmers
now keep livestock inside wherever possible.*
2 CONJ You also use **wherever** to indicate that you do
not know where a place or person is. *'Where does she
live?'—'Alten, wherever that is.'*
3 ADV **Wherever** can be used as an emphatic form of
'where', usually when you are surprised about
something. *Wherever have you been?*

wherewithal /we͟əwɪðɔːl/
N SING If you have the **wherewithal** to do something,
you have enough money to do it; a formal word.
*Where did they get the wherewithal to finance all those
concerts?*

whet /we͟t/ **whets, whetting, whetted**
If you **whet** someone's **appetite** for something, you
increase their desire for it. *The tutor at the college
had whetted her appetite for more work.*

whether /we͟ðə/
1 CONJ You use **whether** to talk about a choice or
doubt between two or more alternatives. *I can't tell
whether she loves me or she hates me... We're not
sure whether it's solid or not at this stage... The
Supreme Court will then decide whether he should
stand trial.*
2 CONJ You also use **whether** to say that something is
true in any of the circumstances you mention.
*They've given him a guarantee that he won't lose out
whether he buys it or not.*

whew /fjuː/
Whew is used to represent a sound that you make
when you breathe out very quickly, for example when
you are very hot or when you are relieved. *Whew!
It's nice to have that over with.*

whey /we͟ɪ/
NU **Whey** is the watery liquid that is separated from
the curds in sour milk, for example when you are
making cheese. *...wastes such as milk whey.*

which /wɪ͟tʃ/, wɪtʃ/
1 DET or PRON You use **which** to ask questions when
there are two or more possible answers or
alternatives. *Which department do you want?... Which
is her room?*
2 DET or PRON You also use **which** to refer to a choice
between two or more possible answers or alternatives.
*I don't know which country he played for... The book
says one thing and you say another. I don't know
which to believe.*
3 PRON You also use **which** at the beginning of a
relative clause that specifies the thing you are talking
about or that gives more information about it. *...the
awful conditions which exist in British prisons... We
sat on the carpet, which was pale green.*
4 PRON or DET You also use **which** to refer back to what
has just been said. *It takes me an hour from door to
door, which is not bad... I enjoy these dinners, unless I
have to make a speech, in which case I worry
throughout the meal.*

whichever /wɪtʃe͟və/
1 DET or PRON You use **whichever** to indicate that it
does not matter which of the possible alternatives
happens or is chosen. *The United States would be safe
whichever side won... Then they have lunch, have a
chat, have a sleep, whichever they like, up in the
lounge.*
2 DET or PRON You also use **whichever** to specify which
of a number of possibilities is the right one or the one
you mean. *Use whichever soap powder is
recommended by the manufacturer... The penalty will
be ten pounds or the value of a single fare to the next
stop, whichever is greater.*

whiff /wɪ͟f/
1 N SING+*of* If there is a **whiff** of something, there is a
faint smell of it. *...a little whiff of perfume as she
passed.*
2 N SING+*of* A **whiff** of a particular feeling or type of
behaviour is a slight sign of it. *...a whiff of rebellion.
...the first whiff of danger.*

Whig /wɪ͟g/ **Whigs**
N C A **Whig** was a member of an English political
group which in the 19th century represented people
who were eager for political and social reforms. *The
Hanoverian Monarchs looked to the Whigs for their
administration.*

while /wa͟ɪl/, waɪl/ **whiles, whiling, whiled**
1 CONJ If one thing happens **while** another thing is
happening, the two things happen at the same time.
*He stayed with me while Dad talked with Dr Leon...
They wanted a place to stay while in Paris... He killed
someone in a road accident while drunk.*
2 CONJ You also use **while** to introduce a clause which
contrasts with the other part of the sentence. *Fred
gambled his money away while Julia spent hers all on
dresses... While I have some sympathy for these
fellows, I think they went too far.*
3 N SING A **while** is a period of time. *They talked for a
short while... After a while, my eyes became
accustomed to the darkness.*
4 **once in a while**: see **once**. to be **worth** your **while**:
see **worth**.

while away PHRASAL VERB If you **while away** the time
in a particular way, you spend time in that way
because you are waiting for something or because you
have nothing else to do. *How about whiling away the
time by telling me a story?*

whilst /wa͟ɪlst/, waɪlst/
CONJ **Whilst** means the same as **while**. *I didn't want to
live at home whilst I was at university... Whilst these
cars are economical at a steady 56 mph, they perform
badly in traffic.*

whim /wɪ͟m/ **whims**
N C or NU A **whim** is a sudden desire to do or have
something without any particular reason. *She might
go, or might not, as the whim took her. ...his tendency
to change his mind at whim.*

whimper /wɪ͟mpə/ **whimpers, whimpering,
whimpered**
1 V If children or animals **whimper**, they make little,
low, unhappy sounds. *You don't have to feed the baby
the minute she whimpers.* ▶ Also N C *I was listening
for a cry or a whimper from upstairs.*
2 V-QUOTE If someone **whimpers** something, they say it
in an unhappy or frightened way. *'I want to go home,'
she whimpered.*

whimsical /wɪ͟mzɪkl/
ADJ Something that is **whimsical** is unusual and
slightly playful, and often seems to be done for no
particular reason. *...a whimsical smile. ...whimsical
images of birds and beasts.*

whimsy /wɪ͟mzi/ **whimsies**; also spelt **whimsey**.
N U or N C **Whimsy** is behaviour which is unusual and
often slightly playful, and which often seems to have
no strong reason or purpose. *They have through
whimsy put these drums to use as stools. ...a spasm of
whimsy and malice.*

whine /wa͟ɪn/ **whines, whining, whined**
1 V To **whine** means to make a long, high-pitched
noise, especially one which sounds sad or unpleasant.
*His dog was whining in pain... The clattering and
whining elevator began to move slowly upwards.*

▶ Also NC ...*the whine of the police sirens.*
2 V+*about*, V, or V-QUOTE If someone **whines** about something, you complain about it in an annoying way. *My father never whined about his work... It's time to stop whining... 'I have no money left', McFee whined.*

whinge /wɪndʒ/ **whinges, whinging** or **whingeing, whinged**
V If someone **whinges** about something, they complain about it in a way that annoys you; an informal word. *I'm sick of hearing her whinge.*

whinny /wɪni/ **whinnies, whinnying, whinnied**
V When a horse **whinnies**, it neighs softly. *Bonnie was whinnying from her stall.*

whip /wɪp/ **whips, whipping, whipped**
1 NC A **whip** is a piece of leather or rope fastened to a handle which is used for hitting people or animals. *He was lashed with whips.*
2 VO If you **whip** a person or animal, you hit them with a whip. *I saw him whipping his mules.*
◆ **whipping, whippings** NC *He could not possibly have endured a whipping.*
3 VO If the wind **whips** something, it strikes it sharply. *The wind whipped my face.*
4 V A If someone or something **whips** somewhere, they go there quickly and suddenly. *I whipped in, got my coat, and whipped out, and got back in the car... Vicious winds whipped through the area.*
5 VO A If you **whip** something out or off, you take it out or remove it very quickly and suddenly. *As the candidate for the presidency approached, his assailant whipped out his gun and opened fire on him... Glenn whipped off the mask to reveal his identity.*
6 VO If you **whip** cream or eggs, you stir them very quickly to make them thick and frothy. ◆ **whipped** ADJ ...*fruit flan with whipped cream.*
7 NC A **Whip** is a member of a particular party in parliament, who is responsible for making sure that party members are present to vote on important issues. *The members are voting the way their Chief Whips tell them to vote.*
8 When a political party issues a **three-line whip**, the MPs in that party are ordered to attend parliament and vote in a particular debate. MPs can be disciplined if they disobey a three-line whip without good reason. *A group of Conservative MPs ignored a three-line Whip in the Commons last night.*

whip up PHRASAL VERB If you **whip up** a strong emotion, you deliberately make people feel that emotion. *The poll has whipped up a storm of protest amongst students... The interview whipped up the Americans into a frenzy of rage.*

whiplash /wɪplæʃ/ **whiplashes**
NC A **whiplash** is the long piece of leather or rope that is part of a whip. *The whiplash hit the man.*

whiplash injury, whiplash injuries
NC A **whiplash injury** is a neck injury caused by your head suddenly jerking forwards and then back again, for example in a car accident.

whippersnapper /wɪpəsnæpə/ **whippersnappers**
NC If you refer to a young person as a **whippersnapper**, you mean that they are behaving more confidently and boldly than you think they should; an old-fashioned, informal word. *Impatient young whippersnapper!*

whippet /wɪpɪt/ **whippets**
NC A **whippet** is a small thin dog which looks like a greyhound. Some whippets take part in races. *The runner-up at Crufts was a whippet.*

whipping cream
NU **Whipping cream** is cream that becomes stiff when it is stirred very fast.

whip-round , whip-rounds
NC When a group of people have a **whip-round**, money is collected from each person so that it can be used to buy something for all of them or for someone they all know; an informal word. *Supporters in Wales and families organised a whip-round for them.*

whir /wɜː/. See whirr.

whirl /wɜːl/ **whirls, whirling, whirled**
1 V-ERG or V-ERG A When something **whirls** or when you **whirl** it round, it turns round very fast. *The gas cloud eddies and whirls, thickens in some places and thins in others... You whirl the conker around on a piece of string.* ▶ Also N SING ...*a whirl of dust.* ◆ **whirling** ADJ ATTRIB ...*the whirling blades of a helicopter.*
2 NC+SUPP You can refer to a lot of intense activity as a **whirl** of activity. *We flung ourselves into the mad whirl of pleasure.*

whirlpool /wɜːlpuːl/ **whirlpools**
1 NC A **whirlpool** is a small area in a river or sea where the water is moving quickly round and round, so that objects floating near it are pulled into its centre. *One man who was rescued from the sea was reported as saying a big whirlpool tossed several boats into the air before they sank.*
2 NC You can also use **whirlpool** to describe a situation in which there is a lot of activity and from which it is difficult to escape. *Tom plunged further into the metropolitan whirlpool... Congress has certainly been caught in a whirlpool.*

whirlwind /wɜːlwɪnd/ **whirlwinds**
1 NC A **whirlwind** is a tall column of air which spins round and round very fast. *A whirlwind damaged the roofs of several houses.*
2 ADJ ATTRIB A **whirlwind** event happens much more quickly than normal. ...*a whirlwind romance... We've had a whirlwind tour of small farms.*

whirr /wɜː/ **whirrs, whirring, whirred**; also spelt **whir**.
V When something **whirrs**, it makes a series of low sounds so fast that they seem to be continuous. *Fans whirred on the ceiling. ...insects whirring and buzzing through the air.* ▶ Also NC ...*the whirr of an engine.*

whisk /wɪsk/ **whisks, whisking, whisked**
1 VOA If you **whisk** someone or something somewhere, you take them there quickly. *She was whisked off to her official residence... Colonel Gaddafi was whisked away by helicopter.*
2 VO If you **whisk** eggs or cream, you stir air into them very fast. *Whisk the egg whites until stiff.*
3 NC A **whisk** is a kitchen tool used for whisking eggs or cream.

whisker /wɪskə/ **whiskers**
1 NC The **whiskers** of an animal such as a cat or mouse are the long, stiff hairs growing near its mouth.
2 N PL You can refer to the hair on a man's face, especially on the sides of his face, as his **whiskers**. *He tugged at his side whiskers.*
3 NC **Whisker** is also used to mean a very small amount; an informal use. *The United Socialist Alliance came within a whisker of defeating the UNP... Disaster had been just a whisker away.*

whiskered /wɪskəd/
ADJ A **whiskered** animal or man has whiskers.

whiskery /wɪskəri/
ADJ **Whiskery** means the same as **whiskered**. ...*his whiskery face.*

whiskey /wɪski/ **whiskeys**
N MASS **Whiskey** is whisky that is made in Ireland or the United States. ...*a company making Irish whiskey.*

whisky /wɪski/ **whiskies**; spelt **whiskey** in American English and Irish English.
N MASS **Whisky** is a strong alcoholic drink made from barley or rye. *Britain also hopes to persuade Japan to lower existing import duties on whisky.*

whisper /wɪspə/ **whispers, whispering, whispered**
VO, VOA, V-QUOTE, or V When you **whisper** something, you say it very quietly, using only your breath and not your throat. ...*a game where children sit in a ring and whisper information from one to the other... He whispered the news to President Reagan... 'Follow me,' Claude whispered. 'And keep quiet.'... Why are you whispering?* ▶ Also NC *Hooper lowered his voice to a whisper... We spoke in whispers.*

whist /wɪst/
NU **Whist** is a card game in which one pair of players tries to win more tricks than another pair.

whistle /wɪsl/ **whistles, whistling, whistled**
1 V or VO When you **whistle**, you make a high sound by forcing your breath out between your lips. *He walked home whistling cheerfully... I was whistling little bits of the song.* ▶ Also NC *Sean let out a low whistle of surprise.*

2 v If something **whistles**, it makes a loud, high sound. *The bullets whistled past his head... The train whistled as it approached the tunnel.*
3 NC A **whistle** is a small metal tube which you blow to produce a loud sound and attract someone's attention. *The guard blew his whistle and waved his green flag.*
4 If you **blow the whistle** on someone or on something secret or illegal that they are doing, you tell someone, especially someone in authority, what they are doing. *A report says companies should protect employees who blow the whistle on dishonest workmates... There are a lot of theories on who blew the whistle.*

whistle-stop
ADJ ATTRIB A **whistle-stop** tour is one in which you stop for a short time in a lot of different places, often as part of a political campaign. *The Prime Minister is expected in Pakistan today after a whistle-stop tour of five Middle East and North African nations.*

whit /wɪt/
1 You say **not a whit** or **no whit** to emphasize that something is not the case at all; an old-fashioned expression. *Some of these places haven't changed a whit... He was no whit less friendly for all that.*
2 NU **Whit** means the same as **Whitsun**; an informal use. *...the difficulty of getting anything done at Whit weekend when everyone is away.*

white /waɪt/ **whiter, whitest; whites**
1 ADJ Something that is **white** is the colour of snow or milk. *There were little white clouds high in the blue sky. ...the traditional white sari of Hindu mourning.*
▶ Also NU *A woman dressed in white came up to me.*
2 ADJ Someone who is **white** has a pale skin and is of European origin. *They had never seen a white person before.* ▶ Also NC *The race riots had been caused by whites attacking blacks.*
3 ADJ PRED If someone goes **white**, their hair becomes white as they get older. *My grandfather went white at the age of fifty.*
4 ADJ PRED To go **white** also means to become very pale because you are afraid or shocked. *My sister went white with rage.*
5 ADJ **White** coffee contains milk or cream.
6 ADJ **White** wine is wine of a pale yellowish colour. *The menu was pasta, roast veal and a sweet followed by a glass of sparkling white wine.*
7 NC The **white** of an egg is the transparent liquid surrounding the yolk. *...no animal proteins except for one egg white and one cup of skimmed milk a day.*
8 NC The **white** of someone's eye is the white part of their eyeball.

whitebait /waɪtbeɪt/
N PL or NU **Whitebait** are very small, young herrings or sprats that are fried and eaten as food.

white Christmas, white Christmases
NC A **white Christmas** is a Christmas day when it snows.

white-collar
ADJ ATTRIB **White-collar** workers work in offices rather than doing manual work. *...the breakdown of talks between the management and white-collar workers.*

whited sepulchre, whited sepulchres
NC If you refer to someone or something as a **whited sepulchre**, you mean that they appear to be morally good but are in reality evil or bad; a literary expression.

white elephant, white elephants
NC If something is a **white elephant**, it is a waste of money because it is completely useless. *The new naval base has proved to be a white elephant... Too many large dams around the world have proved to be expensive white elephants.*

Whitehall /waɪthɔːl/
N PROP **Whitehall** is the name of a street in London near which there are many government offices. **Whitehall** is sometimes used to refer to the British Civil Service or to the British Government itself. *At a news conference in Whitehall, she announced that five of the country's most difficult areas will be targeted... Whitehall does not seem to care about this problem at all.*

white-hot
ADJ If something is **white-hot**, it is extremely hot. *...the white-hot centre of the bonfire.*

White House
N PROP The **White House** is the official home of the American President. People also refer to the President and the President's staff as the **White House**. *He told a news conference at the White House that the agreement would redraw the military map of the continent... The White House immediately denied the story.*

white lie, white lies
NC A **white lie** is a lie that is told to avoid hurting someone's feelings or to avoid trouble, and not for an evil purpose.

white meat
NU **White meat** is meat such as chicken and pork, which is pale in colour after it has been cooked. *The diet includes skimmed milk, seafood, and white meat from chicken and turkey.*

whiten /waɪtn/ **whitens, whitening, whitened**
V-ERG When something **whitens** or when you **whiten** it, it becomes whiter or paler in colour. *Use very mild bleach to whiten white nylon.*

whiteout /waɪtaʊt/ **whiteouts**
NC If there is a **whiteout**, it is snowing or has snowed so heavily that everything seems white and it is very difficult to see. *She lost the trail in a whiteout. ...in the midst of whiteout conditions.*

White Paper, White Papers
NC In Britain, Australia, Canada, and some other countries, a **White Paper** is an official report which gives the policy of the Government on a particular subject. *...a recently published White Paper on the future democratic process in Hong Kong.*

white spirit
NU **White spirit** is a colourless liquid that is made from petrol and is used, for example, to make paint thinner or to clean surfaces.

whitewash /waɪtwɒʃ/
1 NU **Whitewash** is a mixture of chalk and water used for painting walls white. *...a beautiful brewery with tile all over it and glossy whitewash.*
2 N SING or NU A **whitewash** is an attempt to hide the unpleasant facts about something. *The first report on Chile was dubbed a whitewash. ...the refusal to accept official whitewash in police enquiries.*

white wedding, white weddings
NC A **white wedding** is a wedding where the bride wears white and the ceremony takes place in a church. *Although a lot of people still marry in church, they marry for the white wedding, for the social display.*

whither /wɪðə/
ADV or CONJ **Whither** means to which place; a formal or old-fashioned word. *Whither will this monstrous city then extend? ...Traitor's Gate, whither so many came by water to their death.*

whiting /waɪtɪŋ/; **whiting** is both the singular and the plural form.
N C or NU A **whiting** is a kind of sea fish that can be cooked and eaten.

whitish /waɪtɪʃ/
ADJ **Whitish** means very pale and almost white in colour. *The sky was a pale whitish blue.*

Whitsun /wɪtsən/
NU **Whitsun** is the seventh Sunday after Easter, and the week which follows that Sunday. *It's the Whitsun bank holiday weekend, and as usual at this time of year many of Britain's roads have been jammed with traffic.*

whittle /wɪtl/ **whittles, whittling, whittled**
whittle away or **whittle down** PHRASAL VERB To **whittle** something **away** or to **whittle** it **down** means to make it smaller or less effective. *This may whittle away our liberties... Profits are whittled down by the ever-rising cost of energy.*

whizz /wɪz/ **whizzes, whizzing, whizzed**; also spelt **whiz**. An informal word.
1 V A If something **whizzes** somewhere, it moves there very fast. *We just stood there with the cars whizzing by.*

2 NC If you are a **whizz** at something, you are very good at it. *He might be a whizz at electronics.*

whizz-kid, **whizz-kids**; also spelt **whiz-kid**.
NC A **whizz-kid** is someone who is very good at their job and achieves success quickly early in their career; an informal word. *...a multi-millionaire insurance whizz-kid.*

WHO /dʌbljuːeɪtʃəʊ/
N PROP **WHO** is an abbreviation for 'World Health Organization'; an international agency which is part of the United Nations and which is concerned with improving health standards and services throughout the world.

who /huː, huː/ **Who** is used as the subject or object of a verb. See also **whom**, **whose**.
1 PRON You use **who** when asking questions about someone's name or identity. *Who are you?... Who are you going to invite?*
2 PRON You also use **who** in reported questions and reported statements about someone's name or identity. *She didn't know who I was.*
3 PRON You also use **who** at the beginning of a relative clause that specifies the person you are talking about. *If you can't do it, we'll find someone who can... Joe, who was always early, was there already.*

whoa /wəʊ/
1 **Whoa** is a command that you give to a horse to slow down or stop.
2 You can also say **whoa** to someone who is talking to you, if you think they are going too fast or making assumptions; an informal use.

who'd /huːd, huːd/
Who'd is the usual spoken form of 'who had', especially when 'had' is an auxiliary verb. **Who'd** is also a spoken form of 'who would'. *It was the little girl who'd come to play with her that afternoon... I don't think he's the sort of young man who'd be thinking of marriage.*

whodunit /huːdʌnɪt/ **whodunits**; also spelt **whodunnit**.
NC A **whodunit** is a book, film, or play which is about a murder and in which the identity of the murderer is kept a mystery until the end; an informal word. *...the detectives who spend the last few pages of every whodunit revealing who really committed the murder.*

whoever /huːevə/
1 PRON You use **whoever** to refer to someone when their identity does not matter or is not known. *Whoever did this will sooner or later be caught and will be punished... The people can choose whoever they really want to represent them.*
2 CONJ You also use **whoever** to indicate that the actual identity of the person who does something will not affect a situation. *Whoever wins the war, there will be little peace... Whoever you vote for, prices will go on rising.*
3 PRON **Whoever** can be used as an emphatic form of 'who', usually when you are surprised about something. *Whoever could that be at this time of night?*

whole /həʊl/
1 N SING+of If you refer to the **whole** of something, you mean all of it. *Statistics for the whole of Germany are not yet available... The whole of the city centre was packed with demonstrators.* ▶ Also ADJ ATTRIB *I think the whole world feels outraged by this... He's lived his whole life under different circumstances.*
2 N SING A **whole** is a single thing containing several different parts. *The earth's weather system is an integrated whole.*
3 ADJ PRED If something is **whole**, it is not broken or damaged; a formal use. *Fortunately, the plates were still whole.*
4 ADV **Whole** means in one piece. For example, if you swallow something **whole**, you do not bite it into smaller bits. *The snake can swallow a small rat whole.*
5 SUBMOD or ADJ You also use **whole** to emphasize what you are saying; an informal use. *...a whole new way of life... Charles was a whole lot nicer than I had expected. ...a whole bunch of things.*
● **Whole** is used in these phrases. ● If you refer to something **as a whole**, you are referring to it generally

and as a single unit. *...projects which are intended to benefit the Central American region as a whole.* ● You say **on the whole** to indicate that what you are saying is true in general, but not in every detail. *The US policy seems to have worked on the whole.*

wholefood /həʊlfuːd/ **wholefoods**
N PL or NU **Wholefoods** are foods which have not been refined and do not contain additives or artificial ingredients. *Wholefoods and fresh fruit are essential in your diet. ...a wholefood shop.*

wholehearted /həʊlhɑːtɪd/
ADJ If you support something in a **wholehearted** way, you support it enthusiastically and completely. *The strike has failed to attract the wholehearted support of all miners.* ◆ **wholeheartedly** ADV *Mrs Thatcher told him that she agrees wholeheartedly with such policies.*

wholemeal /həʊlmiːl/
ADJ ATTRIB **Wholemeal** flour or bread is made from the complete grain of the wheat plant, including the husk. *They avoided processed foods and ate wholemeal or brown bread where possible.*

wholeness /həʊlnəs/
NU **Wholeness** is the quality of being complete or a single unit and not divided into parts; a literary word. *...a sense of the wholeness of life.*

whole number, **whole numbers**
NC A **whole number** is an exact number such as 1, 7, 24, as opposed to a number with fractions or decimals. *The equation could be solved using whole numbers.*

wholesale /həʊlseɪl/
1 ADJ ATTRIB or ADV You use **wholesale** to refer to the activity of buying and selling goods cheaply in large quantities, especially the activity of selling goods to shopkeepers who then sell them to the general public. *There has also been a rise in the wholesale price of manufactured goods... Stein got the food for me wholesale.*
2 ADJ ATTRIB or ADV You also use **wholesale** to describe something you consider undesirable or unpleasant that you think is done to an excessive extent. *Wholesale slaughter was carried out in the name of progress... In the 1950's, China copied wholesale the system of central planning used in the Soviet Union.*

wholesaler, **wholesalers**
NC A **wholesaler** is someone whose business is buying large quantities of goods and selling them in smaller amounts, usually to shops. *There has been substantial buying of children's toys from wholesalers.*

wholesome /həʊlsəm/
1 ADJ Something that is **wholesome** is good and morally acceptable. *Young people enter marriage nowadays with a much more wholesome attitude.*
2 ADJ **Wholesome** food is good for you. *Can't people influence their own health by adopting healthy lifestyles—not smoking, eating wholesome food and taking exercise, for example?*

wholewheat /həʊlwiːt/
ADJ ATTRIB **Wholewheat** means the same as **wholemeal**. *Wholewheat spaghetti takes slightly longer to cook.*

who'll /huːl, huːl/
Who'll is a spoken form of 'who will' or 'who shall'. *Who'll believe him?*

wholly /həʊlli/
ADV **Wholly** means completely. *...people whom we could not wholly trust... The idea was not a wholly new one.*

whom /huːm, huːm/. **Whom** is used in formal or written English instead of 'who' when it is the object of a verb or preposition.
1 PRON You use **whom** in questions, indirect questions, and other structures to refer to someone whose name or identity is unknown. *'I'm a reporter.'—'Oh yes? For whom?'... Whom do you suggest I should ask?*
2 PRON You also use **whom** at the beginning of a relative clause in which you specify the person you are talking about or give more information about them. *She was engaged to a sailor named Raikes, whom she had met at Dartmouth.*

whoop /wuːp/ **whoops**, **whooping**, **whooped**
V If you **whoop**, you shout loudly in a very happy or

excited way; used in written English. *Eddie whooped with delight.* ► Also NC *There were whoops of approval by the bar customers.*

whoopee /wʊpiː/
People sometimes shout '**whoopee**' when they are very happy or excited. *Whoopee! We've hit the jackpot.*

whooping cough /huːpɪŋ kɒf/
NU **Whooping cough** is a serious infectious disease which causes people to cough and make a loud noise when they breathe in. *They want to persuade more parents to get their children immunised against illnesses like measles and whooping cough.*

whoosh /wʊʃ/ **whooshes, whooshing, whooshed**
V A If something **whooshes** somewhere, it moves there quickly or suddenly; an informal word. *Thousands of rockets whooshed over our heads.* ► Also N SING *The train came in with a whoosh of dust.*

whopper /wɒpə/ **whoppers**; an old-fashioned, informal word.
1 NC A **whopper** is a very big lie. *They swallow any whopper which they hear.*
2 NC A **whopper** is also an unusually large example of something. *What a whopper! That must be the biggest one we've seen this year.*

whopping /wɒpɪŋ/
ADJ ATTRIB **Whopping** means much larger than usual; an informal word. *Real growth was at a whopping six and a half per cent.*

who're /huːə/
Who're is a spoken form of 'who are'. *...married couples who're waiting to be housed.*

whore /hɔː/ **whores**
1 NC A **whore** is the same as a prostitute; an old-fashioned use.
2 NC If someone calls a woman a **whore**, they mean that they consider her sexual behaviour to be immoral or unacceptable; an offensive use.

whorl /wɜːl/ **whorls**
NC A **whorl** is a spiral shape, for example the pattern on the tips of your fingers; a literary word. *The smoke dispersed into threads and clouds and whorls.*

who's /huːz, huːz/
Who's is the usual spoken form of 'who is' or 'who has', especially when 'has' is an auxiliary verb. *'Edward drove me up.'—'Who's Edward?'* *...an American author who's settled in London.*

whose /huːz, huːz/
1 DET You use **whose** at the beginning of a relative clause to indicate that something belongs to or is associated with the person or thing mentioned in the previous clause. *...a couple whose son was killed in a motoring accident. ...the defence pact with America whose main outlines had been agreed.*
2 DET or PRON You also use **whose** in questions, reported questions, and other structures in which you ask about or refer to the person that something belongs to or is associated with. *Whose fault is that?... It's morally her responsibility, no matter whose it is in law.*

who've /huːv, huːv/
Who've is the usual spoken form of 'who have,' especially when 'have' is an auxiliary verb. *...people who've gone to universities.*

why /waɪ, waɪ/
1 ADV You use **why** when asking questions about the reason for something. *'I had to say no.'—'Why?'... Why are people behaving like this?*
2 CONJ You also use **why** at the beginning of a clause in which you talk about the reason for something. *He told me why he had voted for the Democrats... I don't know why that is... There are several reasons why Kurris has made the deal... That's why people thought it was useless to participate in the election.*
3 ADV You use **why** with 'not' to introduce a suggestion in the form of a question. *Why don't you do something before it's too late?*

wick /wɪk/ **wicks**
1 NC The **wick** of a candle is the piece of string in it which burns when it is lit.
2 NC The **wick** of a paraffin lamp or cigarette lighter is the part which supplies the fuel to the flame when it is lit. *It's very hard to turn the wick up and down.*

wicked /wɪkɪd/
1 ADJ Someone or something that is **wicked** is very bad in a way that is deliberately harmful to people. *...a wicked slave dealer... She described the shooting as a wicked act.* ♦ **wickedness** NU *...the wickedness of his crime.*
2 ADJ **Wicked** also means mischievous in a way that you find attractive or enjoyable. *He had a wicked grin. ...the wicked wit of the cartoonist.* ♦ **wickedly** ADV *She smiled wickedly.*

wicker /wɪkə/
NU A **wicker** object is made of wickerwork. *Nearly fifty thousand buildings, mainly small wicker huts are said to have been destroyed. ...wicker baskets.*

wickerwork /wɪkəwɜːk/
NU **Wickerwork** is a material made by weaving twigs, canes, or reeds together. Wickerwork is used to make items such as furniture, baskets, and mats. *...wickerwork armchairs.*

wicket /wɪkɪt/ **wickets**
1 NC In cricket, a **wicket** is a set of three upright sticks with small sticks on top of them at which the ball is bowled. You also use **wicket** to refer to the area of grass between two wickets on a cricket pitch. *Derbyshire's bowlers hit the wicket once... The England cricket captain, Mike Gatting, will have to wait before he can inspect the wicket at Lancaster Park.*
2 In cricket, when a bowler **takes a wicket**, the batsman is out. *...Marshall taking the wicket of Marsh when the score was just fourteen.*

wicket-keeper, wicket-keepers
NC A **wicket-keeper** is the player in a cricket team who stands behind the wicket in order to stop balls that the batsman misses or to catch balls that the batsman hits. *Wicket-keeper Salim Yousuf took a fine catch.*

wide /waɪd/ **wider, widest**
1 ADJ Something that is **wide** measures a large distance from one side to the other. *Wreckage was scattered over a wide area... We were traveling through wooded country broken from time to time by wide, flat river valleys... We've got a framework of thin poles, stretched and bent across wide arches and curves.*
2 ADJ **Wide** is used in questions and statements about the distance something measures from one side or edge to the other. *The hurricane is several hundred miles wide. ...a belt of trees twenty-five kilometres wide... How wide is the bed?*
3 ADV If you open or spread something **wide**, you open or spread it to its fullest extent. *Rudolph always opened the window wide at night... He left his office door wide open... I spread my arms wide.* ♦ **widely** ADV *'That's all right,' she said, smiling widely.*
4 ADJ If your eyes are **wide** or **wide open**, they are more open than usual, because you are surprised or frightened. *She sat looking up at me, her eyes wide with pleasure.*
5 ADJ A **wide** variety, range, or selection includes a lot of different things. *The agenda is expected to cover a wide range of topics... The college library had a wide variety of books.* ♦ **widely** ADV *The helicopter has been sold widely abroad.*
6 ADJ You also use **wide** when describing something which is believed or known by many people. *The case received wide publicity.* ♦ **widely** ADV *These achievements are widely known.*
7 ADJ A **wide** difference or gap between two things is a large one. *The gap between the poor and the rich is very wide indeed.* ♦ **widely** ADV *Customs vary widely from one area to another.*
8 ADJ **Wide** is used to describe something relating to the most important or general parts of a situation. *The editorial discusses the nurses' dispute in the wider context of working conditions in Britain today.*
9 ADJ PRED or ADV A **wide** shot or punch does not hit its target. *The first shot went wide, the second hit the engine room.*
10 **far and wide**: see **far**. **wide of the mark**: see **mark**.

-wide
1 SUFFIX **-wide** combines with nouns that refer to a

place, area, or organization in order to form adjectives or adverbs indicating that something exists or happens throughout the whole of that place area or organization. For example, a 'worldwide' problem affects everybody in the world. *The opposition intends to launch a countrywide campaign of public meetings. ...community-wide policies. ...the first step in developing a multi-cultural curriculum citywide to help minority children build self-esteem.*
2 SUFFIX -**wide** can also combine with any unit of distance to form adjectives that describe the width of something. *His men cut the wall into three-feet-wide sections. ...the 60-kilometre-wide no-man's land. ...a 30-mile-wide strip.*

wide-angle
ADJ A **wide-angle** lens is a camera lens which allows you to photograph a wider view than a normal lens. *Any lens can be fitted, whether it's a zoom or a wide-angle.*

wide-awake
ADJ ATTRIB A **wide-awake** person is alert and completely awake. *A remarkably wide-awake John Gummer came to the Commons after twenty-six hours of gruelling talks in Brussels.*

wide-eyed
1 ADJ If someone is **wide-eyed**, their eyes are more open than usual. *Her face seemed frozen in an expression of wide-eyed alarm.*
2 ADJ If you describe someone as **wide-eyed**, you mean that they seem inexperienced, and do not have much common sense. *Part of me was still a wide-eyed American.*

widen /waɪdn/ **widens, widening, widened**
1 V-ERG If something **widens** or if you **widen** it, it becomes bigger from one side or edge to the other. *It had been decided to widen the road at this particular spot to improve security... The original trail had been widened. ...two rapidly widening holes in the road.*
2 V-ERG You can also say that something **widens** when it becomes greater in range, size, or variety or affects a larger number of people or things. *The gap between the rich and poor regions widened... Labour had to widen its appeal if it was to win the election... They could widen their experience by going on a course.*

wide-ranging
ADJ If something is **wide-ranging**, it includes or deals with a great variety of different things. *...a wide-ranging interview... This attack carried wide-ranging implications for the police.*

widespread /waɪdspred/
ADJ If something is **widespread**, it exists or happens over a large area, or to a very great extent. *These housing estates suffer from widespread vandalism and neglect.*

widow /wɪdəʊ/ **widows**
NC A **widow** is a woman whose husband has died. *...the death of Mrs Roberts, a widow and a former school-teacher.*

widowed /wɪdəʊd/
ADJ If someone is **widowed**, their husband or wife has died. *Neighbours say he visited his widowed mother at every opportunity.*

widower /wɪdəʊə/ **widowers**
NC A **widower** is a man whose wife has died. *He was an impoverished widower.*

widowhood /wɪdəʊhʊd/
NU **Widowhood** is the state of being a widow or a widower. *The shock of widowhood weakens resistance to illness.*

width /wɪdθ/
NU The **width** of something is the distance that it measures from one side to the other. *The area was just over a thousand yards in width. ...the width of a man's hand.*

widthways /wɪdθweɪz/
ADV If something is measured or folded **widthways**, it is measured or folded along its width rather than along its length.

wield /wiːld/ **wields, wielding, wielded**; a literary word.
1 VO If you **wield** a weapon, you carry it and use it. *They surrounded the Embassy, wielding sticks.*

2 VO If someone **wields** power, they have it and are able to use it. *The former Prime Minister continued to wield considerable power.*

wife /waɪf/ **wives**
NC A man's **wife** is the woman that he is married to. *He has now arrived back in Geneva, where he's expected to be reunited with his wife and daughter.*
● See also **old wives' tale**.

wifely /waɪfli/
ADJ ATTRIB **Wifely** is used to describe things a woman does, has, or is expected to do because she is married; an old-fashioned word. *Where's your wifely loyalty? ...wifely duty.*

wig /wɪg/ **wigs**
NC A **wig** is a mass of false hair which is worn on your head. *He stuck on bushy eyebrows and wore a wig to change his appearance.*

wiggle /wɪgl/ **wiggles, wiggling, wiggled**
1 V-ERG If you **wiggle** something or if it **wiggles**, it moves around with small, quick movements. *They wiggle their hips to the sound of pop music... Can you wiggle your ears?... You could actually see the tip of the compass needle wiggle.* ▶ Also NC *Give the wire a quick wiggle.*
2 NC A **wiggle** is a line with a lot of little bumps or curves in it. *He drew the sea as a series of wiggles.*

wigwam /wɪgwæm/ **wigwams**
NC A **wigwam** is a kind of tent used by North American Indians. *...members of a hippy community who have lived in American-Indian style wigwams.*

Wijetunge, Dingiri Banda
/dɪŋgɪri bʌndə wiːdʒətʊŋgə/
Dingiri Banda Wijetunge became Prime Minister of Sri Lanka in 1989. He was Minister of Information from 1978 to 1979, of Power from 1979 to 1982, of Posts and Telecommunications from 1982 to 1987, of Agricultural Development and Research from 1987 to 1988, and Finance and Planning in 1989. He was Governor of North West Province in 1988. He is a member of the United National Party (UNP). Born: 1922.

wild /waɪld/ **wilder, wildest**; **wilds**
1 ADJ ATTRIB **Wild** animals and plants live or grow in natural surroundings and are not looked after by people. *Hundreds and thousands of wild birds have migrated form the area... He lived on berries and wild herbs... They have planted plots with grasses and wild flowers.*
2 ADJ **Wild** land is natural and not cultivated. *...the wilder parts of Scotland.*
3 N PL The **wilds** are remote areas, far away from towns. *...the wilds of Australia.*
4 ADJ **Wild** is used to describe the weather or the sea when it is very stormy. *...a wild night in February.*
5 ADJ **Wild** behaviour is uncontrolled, excited, or energetic. *The men were wild with excitement... The audience went wild.* ◆ **wildly** ADV *The spectators applauded wildly.*
6 ADJ A **wild** idea, plan, or guess is unusual and made without much thought. *Childhood is full of wild hopes and dreams.* ◆ **wildly** ADV or SUBMOD *I was guessing wildly. ...wildly impractical ideas.*
● **Wild** is used in these phrases. ● Animals living in the **wild** live in a free and natural state and are not looked after by people. *They couldn't survive in the wild.* ● If something runs **wild**, it behaves in a natural, free, or uncontrolled way. *Early in the morning, dogs run wild in the park.* ● If you are **not wild about** something, you do not like it very much; an informal use. *Not all her former fans are wild about her new image.* ● If something is **beyond your wildest dreams**, it is far better than you believed possible. *He's paying them a salary beyond their wildest dreams.*

wild card
1 N SING In a sports tournament or competition, a **wild card** is a player or team that the judges allow to take part although they have not not qualified. *Woodforde, a wild card, has already achieved two victories over the former world number one this year... Leconte showed good form after being given a wild card entry.*
2 N SING A **wild card** is also an unpredictable person, organization, or situation. *The Kurdish rebels could*

prove to be the wild card in this mission.

wildcat /waɪldkæt/ **wildcats**

1 NC A **wildcat** is a cat which looks like a large pet cat but is very fierce and lives especially in mountains and forests. *In their gangly adolescence the swans were no match for the wildcats.*

2 ADJ ATTRIB A **wildcat** strike happens suddenly, as a result of a decision by a group of workers, and is not officially approved by a trade union. *Frustration, anger and desperation have led to a series of wildcat strikes throughout East Germany over the past fortnight.*

3 ADJ ATTRIB A **wildcat** scheme, project, or business is risky and likely to fail, usually because there has not been enough planning.

wildebeest /wɪldɪbiːst/; **wildebeest** is both the singular and the plural form.

NC A **wildebeest** is a large African antelope which has a hairy tail, short curved horns, and hair under its neck that looks like a beard. Wildebeest usually live in large herds. *...grazing animals like giraffe and wildebeest which live in large herds on the grasslands.*

wilderness /wɪldənəs/ **wildernesses**

1 NC A **wilderness** is an area of natural land which is not cultivated. *...the arctic wilderness... The garden's turned into a wilderness.*

2 If a politician spends time **in the wilderness**, he or she is not in an influential position in politics for that time. *He is enjoying a revival after four years in the wilderness.*

wildfire /waɪldfaɪə/

If something **spreads like wildfire**, it spreads very quickly. *Rumours spread like wildfire... The infection spread like wildfire.*

wildfowl /waɪldfaʊl/

N PL **Wildfowl** are birds such as ducks, pheasants, and quails which are hunted and shot by some people. *Millions of migrant sea birds, waders and wildfowl are expected to arrive in Alaska over the next few weeks.*

wild-goose chase, wild-goose chases

NC If you are on a **wild-goose chase**, you waste a lot of time searching for something that you have little chance of finding; an informal expression. *He sent us on a wild-goose chase.*

wildlife /waɪldlaɪf/

NU You can refer to animals that live in the wild as **wildlife**. *These chemicals would destroy crops and all wildlife.*

Wild West

N SING The **Wild West** is used to refer to the western part of the United States during the time when Europeans were first settling there. Films and stories about this period are mainly about cowboys, gunfights, and American Indians.

wiles /waɪlz/

N PL **Wiles** are clever tricks used to persuade people to do something; a formal word. *You seem familiar with the wiles of children.*

wilful /wɪlfl/

1 ADJ ATTRIB **Wilful** actions or attitudes are done or expressed deliberately, especially with the intention of hurting someone. *The five all pleaded not guilty to causing wilful damage to the army base.* ◆ **wilfully** ADV *She had wilfully betrayed him to his father.*

2 ADJ A **wilful** person is obstinate and determined to get what they want. *She was a wilful child.*

will /wɪl/ **wills, willing, willed**; often pronounced /wɪl/ when it is a modal. The usual spoken form of 'will not' is 'won't' /wəʊnt/.

1 MODAL If you say that something **will** happen, you mean that it is going to happen in the future. *Inflation is rising and will continue to rise... Perhaps this time it won't rain... Perhaps when I am fifty I will have forgotten.*

2 MODAL If you say that you **will** do something, you mean that you intend to do it or that it is acceptable to you. *I will never betray you... People won't admit that they can't read... 'You still haven't told me anything.'—'I will.'*

3 MODAL You can use **will** when making offers, invitations, or requests. *Will you have a whisky?... Will you do me a favour?... Will you shut up!*

4 MODAL You can also use **will** to say that someone or something is able to do something. *This will cure anything... The car won't go.*

5 MODAL You also use **will** to say that you are assuming that something is true, because it is likely, or because it is normally the case. *You will probably already be a member of a union... You will already have gathered that I don't like her... The bonus will usually be paid automatically.*

6 NU or NC **Will** is the determination to do something. *He lacked will and ambition... She lost her will to live... Their marriage became a fierce battle of wills.*

● See also **free will**.

7 N SING+POSS If something is the **will** of a person or group of people with power or authority, they want it to happen. *I must abide by the will of the people... It is the will of Allah.*

8 VO+to-INF If you **will** something to happen, you try to make it happen using mental rather than physical effort. *I willed my trembling legs to walk straight.*

9 NC A **will** is a legal document stating what you want to happen to your money and property when you die. *Has Des made a will?*

● **Will** is used in these phrases. ● If you can do something **at will**, you can do it whenever you want. *Chang told us that we could wander around at will.*

● If something is done **against** your **will**, it is done even though you do not want it to be done. *He would not insist on keeping them against their will.*

Willemstad /wɪləmstɑːt/

Willemstad, on the island of Curaçao, is the capital of the Netherlands Antilles and its largest town. Population: 50,000 (1970).

willie. See **willy**.

willing /wɪlɪŋ/

1 ADJ PRED+to-INF If you are **willing** to do something, you will do it if someone wants you to. *I was still willing to marry her... She said she was willing to discuss a limited halt in the fighting if the guerrillas made a formal request.* ◆ **willingly** ADV *It's not clear if the statement was made willingly or under some kind of duress.* ◆ **willingness** NU *You need initiative and a willingness to work... It looks as though the willingness for a compromise is not as strong at the moment as individual interests.*

2 ADJ If you describe someone as **willing**, you mean that they are eager and enthusiastic in the things they do, rather than being forced to do them. *There will be no shortage of willing volunteers. ...a class of willing students.* ◆ **willingly** ADV *Everyone who joins the military does so willingly... Many liberties were given up quite willingly during the war.* ◆ **willingness** NU *They complied with his request with the greatest willingness and interest.*

willow /wɪləʊ/ **willows**

N C or NU A **willow** is a tree that has long, narrow leaves. Its wood is also called **willow**, and is sometimes used for making items of furniture such as chairs or baskets. *They gathered on a white sandy beach lined with willows... This had once been a fence made with willow stakes.*

willowy /wɪləʊi/

ADJ A person who is **willowy** is tall, thin, and graceful. *She was looking so much more slender and willowy than in her photos.*

will-power

NU **Will-power** is a very strong determination to do something. *It will require great will-power and self control by both sides just to sit down and talk... She stayed calm by sheer will-power.*

willy /wɪli/ **willies**; also spelt **willie**.

1 NC A boy's or man's **willy** is his penis; an informal word.

2 If someone or something **gives** you **the willies**, they make you feel nervous or frightened; an informal expression. *It's that part of the story that gives me the willies.*

willy-nilly /wɪlinɪli/

ADV If something happens to you **willy-nilly**, it happens whether you like it or not; an informal word. *All of them were taken willy-nilly on a guided tour of the town.*

Wilson, Harold /hærəld wɪlsn/
Harold Wilson was Prime Minister of the United
Kingdom from 1964 to 1970, and 1974 to 1976. He was a
Labour MP from 1945 to 1983, and was leader of the
Labour Party from 1963 to 1976. He was knighted in
1976, following his resignation as Prime Minister, and
in 1983 was created Baron Wilson of Rievaulx. Born:
1916.

wilt /wɪlt/ **wilts, wilting, wilted**
1 v If a plant **wilts**, it gradually bends downwards and
becomes weak, because it needs more water or is
dying. *Crops are wilting and water authorities are
planning emergency conservation measures.*
2 v If someone **wilts**, they become weak or tired, or
lose confidence. *Man and beast wilted under the
merciless sun... It would appear that Mr Gandhi wilted
under pressure from his own party and decided
against an early poll.*

wily /waɪli/ **wilier, wiliest**
ADJ **Wily** people are clever and cunning, especially in
ways that are intended to deceive people. *The wily old
general used to keep his opponents confused. ...a wily
diplomat.*

wimp /wɪmp/ **wimps**
NC If you describe someone as a **wimp**, you mean they
lack confidence or determination, or that they are
often afraid; an informal word. *I don't want to be a
wimp, and I owe it to my country to fight for what's
right... He has finally thrown off his image as a weak
and indecisive president—a 'wimp' in the jargon of US
commentators.*

wimpish /wɪmpɪʃ/
ADJ If you say that someone is **wimpish**, you mean
they lack confidence or determination, or that they are
often afraid; an informal word. *...her role as a free-
spirited person who brings love to a rather wimpish
William Hurt in the film 'The Accidental Tourist'.*

win /wɪn/ **wins, winning, won**
1 VorVO If you **win** a fight, game, or argument, you
defeat your opponent. *Their side was winning...
Belgium won 5 nil over Spain... Aren't you interested
in who's winning the war?* ▶ Also NC *Helena Sukova
of Czechoslovakia had an easy win over the American
Kathrin Keil.*
2 VOorV To **win** an election or competition means to
do better than anyone else involved. *He won July's
elections amid allegations of fraud... The American
Eddie Lawson has won the 500cc world championship
for the fourth time... The results showed that Labour
had not won.*
3 VO If you **win** a prize or medal, you get it because
you have been very successful at something. *The 26-
year-old Frenchman won a bronze medal at the 1984
Olympics... Mum has just won a microwave cooker in
a competition.*
4 VO If you **win** something, for example someone's
approval or support, or your freedom, you succeed in
getting it. *...the party's failure to win mass support
among the working class... He spent four years in a
Soviet labour camp, until an international campaign
won his release in 1978.*
5 See also **winning**.
win over or **win round** PHRASAL VERB If you **win**
someone **over** or **win** them **round**, you persuade them
to support you or agree with you. *His charisma has
won over many local Conservative groups... There is
still a large pool of undecided voters who can be won
over... They stayed away from the last meeting, but
the Prince feels he can win them round.*

wince /wɪns/ **winces, wincing, winced**
v When you **wince**, the muscles of your face tighten
suddenly because you are in pain or have experienced
something unpleasant or embarrassing. *The pressure
made her wince with pain.* ▶ Also NC *His smile
became a wince as pain stabbed through him.*

winch /wɪntʃ/ **winches, winching, winched**
1 NC A **winch** is a machine for lifting heavy objects. It
consists of a cylinder around which a rope or chain is
wound. *The wheel is carried across the bridge using a
motorized winch.*
2 VOA If you **winch** an object or person somewhere,
you lift or lower them using a winch. *A Navy*

*helicopter winched a medical team down onto the
burning ship... Many of the oil rig crew were winched
to safety by helicopters.*

wind, winds, winding, winded, wound. Wind is
pronounced /wɪnd/ for the meanings in paragraphs 1 to
4, and the past tense and past participle is **winded**.
For the meanings in paragraphs 5 to 7 and the phrasal
verbs, **wind** is pronounced /waɪnd/, and the past tense
and past participle is **wound** /waʊnd/.
1 NCor NU A **wind** is a current of air moving across the
earth's surface. *High winds and heavy snowfalls have
delayed the start of the women's World Cup Downhill
at Altenmarkt. ...poppies fluttering in the wind...
There was a fierce wind blowing.*
2 N SING+POSS Your **wind** is your ability to breathe
easily. *I had to stop and regain my wind.*
3 VO If something such as a punch **winds** you, air is
suddenly knocked out of your lungs so that you have
difficulty breathing. *Her press secretary was also
winded by a rifle butt in the stomach.*
4 If you **get wind of** something that someone did not
want you to know about, you hear about it; an
informal use. *He somehow got wind of the party and
managed to get himself invited.*
5 VA If a road or river **winds** somewhere, it goes there
with a lot of bends in it. *The river winds through the
town.* ◆ **winding** ADJ *...the winding road leading to the
Castle.*
6 VOA When you **wind** something round something
else, you wrap it round it several times. *Wind the
wire round the screws until it is tight... I wet the
cloths and wound them around my head.*
7 VO When you **wind** a clock or watch, you make it
operate by turning a knob, key, or handle. *She
realised the clock she had just wound wasn't ticking.*
wind back PHRASAL VERB When you **wind back** the
tape in a tape player or the film in a camera, you
make it move back towards its starting position. *Wind
it back till the counter's at 15T.*
wind down PHRASAL VERB 1 If an activity or an
organization **winds down**, or if someone **winds** it **down**,
the amount of activity or work done is gradually
reduced, often until it eventually stops completely. *...a
year in which five wars came to an end or significantly
wound down... The American Bankers' Association is
winding down its annual conference in Orlando...
Evidence has emerged that the Soviet Union is
winding down its big naval base in Vietnam.* 2 If you
wind down, you relax after doing something that has
made you feel tired or tense. *The successful career
woman sometimes turns to drink to wind down after a
hard day at the office.* 3 When you **wind down** the
window of a car, you open it by turning the handle or
pushing the control switch. *Advice to drivers is to
keep the car doors locked, wind the window down just
one inch, and ask to see a warrant.* 4 If a mechanical
device such as a clock **winds down**, it gradually works
more slowly before stopping completely.
wind forward PHRASAL VERB When you **wind forward**
the tape in a tape player, you make it move forward
to a new position.
wind up PHRASAL VERB 1 When an activity is **wound
up**, it is finished and over. *The historians' commission
has said it will wind up its work next week... Last
night the parties wound up the hectic month-long
campaign.* 2 When a business is **wound up**, it stops
trading and is closed down. *The Bank of England
seems determined to wind up the company because
the fraud was so widespread.* 3 If you **wind up** in a
particular place or situation, or **wind up** doing
something, you eventually come to be in that place or
situation or come to do that thing, even though you
may not have expected it or wanted it. *She wound up
in a debtors' prison, where she died... Do you think
you'll wind up doing this kind of thing for a living?...
If you don't learn to laugh, you'll wind up with ulcers.*
4 When you **wind up** the window of a car, you close it
by turning the handle or pushing the control switch.
*The windows do not wind up and down as they do in
normal cars.* 5 If you **wind up** a mechanical device
such as a clock, you turn a knob or key on it
repeatedly in order to make it work. *I wound up the*

watch, listened to it tick, and set it to the right time.

windbag /ˈwɪndbæg/ **windbags**

NC If you describe someone as a **windbag**, you mean that they talk a great deal in a boring way; an informal word. *On the few times I have met him he struck me as a windbag.*

windbreak /ˈwɪndbreɪk/ **windbreaks**

NC A **windbreak** is barrier such as a line of trees or a fence which gives protection against the wind. *The orchard serves as a windbreak... Ukraine has vast plains of arable land, with occasional windbreaks of poplar trees.*

windbreaker /ˈwɪndbreɪkə/ **windbreakers**

NC A **windbreaker** is a jacket that has a close fitting collar and cuffs to keep out the wind. *...a tan windbreaker.*

winded /ˈwɪndɪd/

ADJ If you are **winded**, you are out of breath, either because you have been doing hard exercise such as running fast, or because you have been hit in the stomach. *If you go too fast, you get winded... I fell with a crash, winded but not hurt.*

windfall /ˈwɪndfɔːl/ **windfalls**

NC A **windfall** is a sum of money that you receive unexpectedly. *He had a windfall from the football pools.*

Windhoek /ˈvɪnthʊk/

Windhoek is the capital of Namibia and its largest city. Population: 115,000 (1988).

wind instrument, wind instruments

NC A **wind instrument** is a musical instrument such as a trumpet or a clarinet that you blow into in order to produce sounds. *The lips are tightly pursed when blowing a wind instrument.*

windlass /ˈwɪndləs/ **windlasses**

NC A **windlass** is a machine for lifting heavy objects. It consists of a cylinder around which a rope or chain is wound. *...a bucket hauled up with a windlass.*

windmill /ˈwɪndmɪl/ **windmills**

NC A **windmill** is a tall building with large sails on the outside which turn as the wind blows. This produces electricity which can be stored or used to perform particular tasks such as crushing grain. *The pumps in his home country are worked by windmills. ...a new, more powerful version of a windmill for generating electricity.*

window /ˈwɪndəʊ/ **windows**

NC A **window** is a space in a wall or roof or in a vehicle, usually with glass in it. *The kitchen windows were wide open.*

window-box, window-boxes

NC A **window-box** is a long, narrow container on a window-sill in which plants are grown. *...window-boxes full of flowering plants on window-sills or balconies.*

window-dressing

1 NU **Window-dressing** is used to refer to things that are done in order to create a good impression and to prevent people from realizing the real or more unpleasant nature of someone's activities. *Those who are cynical say that the consultation exercise was mere window-dressing... Such political window-dressing is unlikely to convince the internal opposition that he's legitimate.*

2 NU **Window-dressing** is also the skill of arranging goods attractively in a shop window, or the way in which they are arranged.

window-frame, window-frames

NC A **window-frame** is a frame round the edges of a window, which glass is fixed into. *The twisted wreckage of office furniture, window-frames and shattered glass spilled onto the road.*

window-pane, window-panes

NC A **window-pane** is a piece of glass in the window of a building. *They watched the proceedings through window panes... Behind broken window-panes, dirty curtains are floating in the wind.*

window seat, window seats

1 NC A **window seat** is a seat which is fixed to the wall underneath a window in a room. *I sat on the window seat in the hall.*

2 NC A **window seat** is also a seat next to a window in a train, bus, or aeroplane. *I'd like a window seat, please.*

window-shopping

NU If you go **window-shopping**, you spend time looking at the things in the windows of shops without intending to buy anything. *When they come to London, people like to do a bit of window-shopping, and they like to go and visit a pub.*

window-sill, window-sills

NC A **window-sill** is a ledge along the bottom of a window, either inside or outside a building. *Pots of herbs stood on the window-sill.*

windpipe /ˈwɪndpaɪp/ **windpipes**

NC Your **windpipe** is the tube in your body that carries air into your lungs when you breathe. *Another strap holds the breast strap in place, otherwise it would ride up and choke the animal's windpipe.*

windscreen /ˈwɪndskriːn/ **windscreens**

NC The **windscreen** of a car or other vehicle is the glass window at the front which the driver looks through. *To drive with safety it's important to have clear all-round vision, especially through the windscreen.*

windscreen wiper, windscreen wipers

NC A **windscreen wiper** is a device which wipes rain from a vehicle's windscreen. *It contains sensors which tell the car what's happening to it, so that the windscreen wipers come on when it starts raining, for instance.*

windshield /ˈwɪndʃiːld/ **windshields**

NC A **windshield** is the same as a **windscreen**; used in American English. *You may have to stop every ten miles to clean your windshield.*

windsurfer /ˈwɪndsɜːfə/ **windsurfers**

1 NC A **windsurfer** is a long, narrow board with a sail attached to it. You stand on a windsurfer in the sea or on a lake and are blown along by the wind. *Dinghies and windsurfers may be hired on the main beach.*

2 NC A **windsurfer** is also a person who rides on a windsurfer. *Lifeboats were called out twice when windsurfers were blown out to sea by a westerly gale.*

windsurfing /ˈwɪndsɜːfɪŋ/

NU **Windsurfing** is the sport of riding on a windsurfer. *Many stores have diversified into other sports like cycling and windsurfing.*

windswept /ˈwɪndswept/

1 ADJ A **windswept** place is exposed to strong winds. *The refugees stand trapped on a wet windswept mountain top. ...England's bleak, windswept, north-western coast.*

2 ADJ Someone who looks **windswept** has untidy hair because they have been out in the wind. *His hair was windswept and his face streaked with dirt.*

wind tunnel, wind tunnels

NC A **wind tunnel** is a room or passage which is designed so that air can be made to flow through it at controlled speeds. Wind tunnels are used to test new or experimental equipment and machinery, especially cars or aeroplanes. *They were doing this under controlled conditions in a wind tunnel... The air flow and pressures on the space shuttle can't be measured in a wind tunnel.*

windward /ˈwɪndwəd/

ADJ ATTRIB **Windward** is used to refer to the side of something which is facing the wind. *He can sit himself out on the windward side and concentrate entirely on filling the sails and driving the boat.*

windy /ˈwɪndi/ **windier, windiest**

ADJ If it is **windy**, the wind is blowing a lot. *The winter was cold, wet, and windy.*

wine /waɪn/ **wines**

N MASS **Wine** is an alcoholic drink which is usually made from grapes. There are two main kinds called red wine and white wine. *Beer and wine will not be served inside the amusement park... We stopped and bought a bottle of cheap wine.*

wine bar, wine bars

NC A **wine bar** is a place where people can buy and drink wine. *He drinks wine rather than beer, in a wine bar rather than a pub. ...the people who go to wine bars and expensive restaurants.*

wing /wɪŋ/ wings, winging, winged
1 NC The **wings** of a bird or insect are the parts of its body that it uses for flying. *Birds are actually controlling their flight while they are soaring, even without flapping their wings. ...the fluttering of a butterfly's wing.*
2 NC The **wings** of an aeroplane are the long, flat parts at each side which support it while it is flying. *A Boeing 747 jumbo jet was forced to cut short a flight from Manila to Tokyo when a hole appeared in one of the wings.*
3 NC A **wing** of a building is a smaller part which sticks out from the main part or which has been added at a later date. *...the west wing of the museum... She had been planning to build a wing onto the house.*
4 NC+SUPP A **wing** of an organization is a group within it which has a particular function or beliefs. *...the political wing of the IRA... He's likely to have opposition from the right wing of the Republican Party.*
5 NC The **wings** of a car are the parts around the wheels. *The car hit the truck with its nearside wing.*
6 V or VO If something such as an aeroplane **wings** somewhere or **wings** its way somewhere, it flies to that place. *The first of the airliners winged westwards and home... The spacecraft swings around Venus and the Earth before winging its way to Jupiter.*
7 See also **fixed-wing**, **left-wing**, **right-wing**.

wing commander, wing commanders
N Cor TITLE A **wing commander** is a senior officer in the air force. *...Wing Commander Warburton.*

winged /wɪŋd/
ADJ ATTRIB **Winged** means having wings. *...winged creatures. ...a winged statue.*

winger /wɪŋə/ wingers
NC In a game such as football or hockey, a **winger** is an attacking player who plays mainly on the far left or far right of the pitch. *Australian Winger, David Campese, scored two tries to bring his international total to a world record of 29.*

wingspan /wɪŋspæn/ wingspans
NC The **wingspan** of a bird, insect, or aeroplane is the distance from the end of one wing to the end of the other wing. *...dragonflies with a wingspan of seven centimetres.*

wink /wɪŋk/ winks, winking, winked
1 V When you **wink**, you close one eye briefly, usually as a signal that something is a joke. *Uncle John winked at me across the table.* ► Also NC *'What a hostess!' said Clarissa with a big wink at George.*
2 If you **don't sleep a wink**, you stay awake and do not sleep at all; an informal expression. *He hadn't slept a wink, because Elsa had cried all night.*

winkle /wɪŋkl/ winkles, winkling, winkled
NC A **winkle** is a small sea-snail with a hard shell and a soft body which you can eat. *...freshly boiled winkles.*

winkle out PHRASAL VERB; an informal expression.
1 If you **winkle** information **out** of someone, you get it from them when they do not want to give it to you, often by tricking them. *They usually manage to winkle out of people what they want to know.* 2 If you **winkle** someone **out** of a place where they are hiding or which they do not want to leave, you make them come out of the place. *The officers sometimes have to winkle idlers out of cupboards and toilets.*

winner /wɪnə/ winners
1 NC The **winner** of a prize, race, or competition is the person who wins it. *He was a worthy winner of the Nobel Prize... Stephen Roche, the winner of the 1987 Tour de France, is out of this year's race.*
2 NC If you refer to something as a **winner**, you mean that it is popular and successful, or likely to be popular and successful; an informal use. *Her new film is a real winner... The pregnancy testing kit devised by Unipath Ltd is a winner.*
3 N SING In games such as football, if a player scores the **winner**, they score the goal that wins a particular match. *Sanchez scored the winner in the 35th minute... The holders were beaten by a late winner from the Austrian international, Polster.*

winning /wɪnɪŋ/ winnings
1 ADJ ATTRIB The **winning** competitor, team, or entry in a competition is the one that has won. *The winning team in the shooting event was West Germany. ...the judges' decision on the winning book.*
2 ADJ ATTRIB **Winning** is used to describe actions or qualities that please people and make them feel friendly towards you; a literary use. *His chief asset is his winning smile.*
3 N PL You refer to money that you win in a competition or by gambling as your **winnings**. *The win boosts Sampras' winnings for the year to nearly $3 million... She collected her lottery winnings of nearly $2.8 million.*

winsome /wɪnsəm/
ADJ Someone who is **winsome** is attractive and charming; a literary word. *She looked winsome and alluring... She gave him her most winsome smile.*

winter /wɪntə/ winters
NU or NC **Winter** is the season between autumn and spring. In winter the weather is colder than during the other seasons. *There are more than thirty thousand extra deaths among the elderly in winter... It was a terrible winter.*

winter sports
N PL **Winter sports** are sports that take place on ice or snow, for example skating, skiing or bobsleigh racing. *...Alpine winter sports... It's early in the winter sports season but the downhillers are already getting used to the disruptive weather.*

wintertime /wɪntətaɪm/
NU **Wintertime** is the period of time during which winter lasts. *The EC's hoping to send the food to Russia before the end of wintertime.*

wintry /wɪntri/
ADJ Something that is **wintry** has features that are typical of winter. *Weather centres say that conditions in some areas are expected to become increasingly wintry this afternoon.*

wipe /waɪp/ wipes, wiping, wiped
1 VO If you **wipe** something, you rub its surface to remove dirt or liquid from it. *He wiped his mouth with the back of his hand.* ► Also NC *Give the table a wipe.*
2 VOA If you **wipe** dirt or liquid from something, you remove it, for example by using a cloth or your hand. *She wiped the tears from her eyes.*

wipe out PHRASAL VERB To **wipe out** groups of people or places means to destroy them completely. *Epidemics wiped out the local population... Sources say hundreds of civilians were killed and entire villages wiped out.*

wipe up PHRASAL VERB If you **wipe up** dirt or liquid from something, you remove it by using a cloth. *He began to wipe up the mess.*

wiper /waɪpə/ wipers
NC A **wiper** is the same as a **windscreen wiper**. *...millions of Ford's cars equipped with intermittent wipers.*

wire /waɪə/ wires, wiring, wired
1 NC or NU A **wire** is a long, thin piece of metal that is used to fasten things. *You can mend it with a length of wire. ...copper wire.*
2 NC A **wire** is also a thin piece of metal that carries electric current inside a piece of electrical equipment or through a building. *He also intends to replace the wires that connect the key pad to the microprocessor.*
3 NC A **wire** is also the same as a **telegram**; used in American English. *I decided to send a wire ordering a room with twin beds for the next night.*
4 VO If you **wire** a person, you send them a telegram; used in American English. *I wired Renata yesterday and asked her to marry me.*
5 See also **barbed wire**.

wire up PHRASAL VERB If you **wire** something **up**, you connect it to something else with electrical wires so that electricity can pass between them. *...electrical fittings wired up to the mains.*

wired /waɪəd/
1 ADJ ATTRIB **Wired** clothing or material has wires sewn into it in order to keep it stiff. *...padded and wired bras. ...a little wired cap.*

2 ADJ PRED If a place is **wired**, it is connected by electrical wires to an alarm system, in order to discourage burglars from entering it. *All the windows were wired.*

3 ADJ PRED If someone or something is **wired**, hidden microphones have been placed on them or in it, so that conversations can be listened to by someone outside. *Their letters would be censored, their hotel rooms wired.*

wireless /waɪələs/ **wirelesses**
NC A **wireless** is a **radio**; an old-fashioned word. *We would have been treated to a dose of him on our wireless every night, courtesy of the BBC. ...a 1930s wireless set.*

wire service, wire services
NC A **wire service** is the same as a **news agency**; used in American English. *A wire service report this week quotes Dr Ibrahim Nouri as saying that milk and wheat flour are in short supply.*

wire-tap, wire-taps, wire-tapping, wire-tapped
VO If someone **wire-taps** your telephone, they make a secret connection to your telephone line so that they can listen to your telephone conversations without you knowing about it; used in American English. *He sent men out to wire-tap the opposition party... He wire-tapped conversations of Democratic Party officials.*

wire wool
NU **Wire wool** is very thin pieces of wire twisted together, often in the form of small pads. Wire wool is used to clean metal objects, especially saucepans and other kitchen equipment.

wiring /waɪərɪŋ/
NU The **wiring** in a building is the system of wires that supply electricity to the rooms. *Will the cottage need new wiring?*

wiry /waɪəri/
1 ADJ Someone who is **wiry** is thin but has strong muscles. *...a short, wiry man... He's small and wiry.*
2 ADJ Something that is **wiry** is stiff and rough to touch. *...her wiry black hair.*

wisdom /wɪzdəm/
1 NU **Wisdom** is the ability to use your experience and knowledge to make sensible decisions and judgements. *She spoke with authority as well as wisdom... Old people have wisdom and maturity.*
2 N SING+of If you talk about the **wisdom** of an action or decision, you are talking about how sensible it is. *Doubts were expressed about the wisdom of the visit.*

wisdom tooth, wisdom teeth
NC Your **wisdom teeth** are the four teeth at the back of your mouth which usually grow much later than your other teeth. *She had to have her wisdom teeth pulled out.*

wise /waɪz/ **wiser, wisest**
1 ADJ **Wise** people are able to use their experience and knowledge to make sensible decisions and judgements. *He's a very wise man... Hugh made the wisest decision of all... President Kennedy was wise in giving the Russians a way out of the Cuban missile crisis.* ◆ **wisely** ADV *You have chosen wisely.*
2 ADJ If you say that nobody is **any the wiser** after an event or an explanation, or that someone is **no wiser** or **none the wiser** after it, you mean they have failed to understand it, or are not fully aware of what happened. *No one outside would be any the wiser.*

-wise /-waɪz/
SUFFIX **-wise** is added to nouns to form adverbs indicating that someone behaves in the same way as the person or thing that is mentioned. *I edged my way crab-wise along the row to my seat.*

wisecrack /waɪzkræk/ **wisecracks**
NC A **wisecrack** is a clever remark that is intended to be amusing, but is often rather unkind; used showing disapproval. *A few years ago he would have heightened the joke with wisecracks. ...a torrent of appalling puns and insulting wisecracks.*

wish /wɪʃ/ **wishes, wishing, wished**
1 NC A **wish** is a desire for something. *She told me of her wish to leave the convent... The President reiterated his wish for peace... It is my fervent wish that voters will flock to the polls in large numbers... His last wish was to be buried in Jalalabad.*

2 V+to-INF If you **wish** to do something, you want to do it; a formal use. *They are in love and wish to marry... The rebels have insisted they did not wish to overthrow the constitutional order... The US announced that American citizens who wished to be airlifted from Saudi Arabia will be.*

3 V-REPORT If you **wish** that something were the case, you would like it to be the case, even though it is impossible or unlikely. *I often wish that I were really wealthy... I wish I didn't have to do that.*

4 V+for If you **wish** for something, you express a desire that it should happen, often silently as part of a traditional ritual. *She blew out the candles on her birthday cake and wished for a new doll.* ▶ Also NC *The genie then granted Sinbad three wishes.*

5 VOO If you **wish** someone something such as good luck, you tell them that you hope they will have it. *They wished each other luck before the exam. ...wishing him happy birthday.*

6 N PL When you send someone your good **wishes**, you are indicating that you hope they will be happy or successful. *He will be going home with little more than their good wishes. ...bags of sweets sent with the best wishes of American and British schoolchildren.*

7 N PL You use **wishes** in expressions such as 'best wishes' or 'with all good wishes' at the end of informal letters, before you sign your name.

wishbone /wɪʃbəʊn/ **wishbones**
NC A **wishbone** is a V-shaped bone in chickens, turkeys, and other birds. When the meat has been eaten, two people pull the ends of the bone until it breaks. The person with the longer piece of bone is allowed to make a wish. *We found out there was no tooth fairy and that breaking wishbones didn't really make wishes come true.*

wishful thinking
NU If a hope or desire is **wishful thinking**, it is unlikely to be fulfilled. *It is wishful thinking to assume that the generals will agree to this... Is that an educated optimism, or is it just wishful thinking?*

wishy-washy /wɪʃiwɒʃi/
ADJ If you describe a person or their ideas as **wishy-washy**, you mean that their ideas are not firm or clear; an informal word. *He's just a wishy-washy liberal. ...a wishy-washy concept.*

wisp /wɪsp/ **wisps**
1 NC A **wisp** of hair is a thin, untidy bunch of it. *A wisp of grey hair stuck out from under her hat.*
2 NC A **wisp** of something, for example smoke or cloud, is a long, thin amount of it. *...a wisp of wool fibre.*

wispy /wɪspi/
ADJ **Wispy** hair is thin and grows in small, untidy bunches. *He looks like a typical young artist with dishevelled hair and a wispy beard.*

wisteria /wɪstɪəriə/
NU **Wisteria** is a climbing plant with mauve or white flowers.

wistful /wɪstfl/
ADJ If someone is **wistful**, they are sad because they want something and know they cannot have it. *She had a last wistful look round the flat.* ◆ **wistfully** ADV *'Guy doesn't want to see me,' said Manfred wistfully.*

wit /wɪt/ **wits**
1 NU **Wit** is the ability to use words or ideas in an amusing and clever way. *The girl laughed at his wit. ...the wit of the cartoonist.*
2 N PL You can refer to someone's ability to think quickly in a difficult situation as their **wits**. *Her only chance was to use her wits to bluff the enemy.*
3 N SING+to-INF If someone has the **wit** to do something, they have the intelligence and understanding to make the right decision or to take the right course of action. *No one had had the wit to bring a bottle opener.*
● **Wit** is used in these phrases. ● If you **have** or **keep your wits about** you, you are alert and ready to act in a difficult situation. *In this part of the city you have to keep your wits about you all the time.* ● If something frightens you **out of** your **wits**, it frightens you very much indeed. *The kids were scared out of their wits.* ● If someone **lives by** or **on** their **wits**, they manage to live by using clever but sometimes

dishonest methods, rather than by having a regular job. *I knew a fellow who lived for years on his wits.*
● If you are at your **wits' end**, you have so many problems or difficulties that you do not know what to do next. *I am at my wit's end to know what to do with my son who has suddenly begun to steal things.*
● to **pit** your **wits against** someone: see **pit**.

witch /wɪtʃ/ **witches**
NC A **witch** is a woman who is believed to have magic powers, especially evil ones. *They say Hernandez actually died after a witch cast a spell on her. ...an ugly old witch.*

witchcraft /wɪtʃkrɑːft/
NU **Witchcraft** is the use of magic powers, especially evil ones. *Religious leaders there were investigating what they believed to be witchcraft and devil-worship in their community. ...witchcraft and evil spirits.*

witch doctor, witch doctors
NC A **witch doctor** is a person in some societies, especially in Africa, who is thought to have magic powers. *He wasn't sure how to react to the witch doctor's claimed powers... Another candidate is said to have resorted to the services of a witch doctor.*

witch hazel
NU **Witch hazel** is a liquid that you put on your skin when it is sore or bruised, in order to heal it.

witch-hunt, witch-hunts
NC A **witch-hunt** is an attempt to find and punish people whose opinions or actions are considered to be harmful to society. Often the victims of witch-hunts are innocent people; used showing disapproval. *They had served the country with great distinction and deserved more than the present witch-hunt being conducted against them... He said that there should be no witch-hunt of former communists.*

witch-hunting
NU **Witch-hunting** is the activity of finding and punishing people whose opinions or actions are thought to be harmful to society; used showing disapproval. *The organization is notorious for witch-hunting and stupidity... He maintained the commission was appointed as an instrument of witch-hunting against him.*

with /wɪð, wɪθ/
1 PREP If one thing or person is **with** another, they are together in one place. *I stayed with her until dusk... 'Isn't Mr Boon with you?' was his hostess's first question.*
2 PREP If you do something **with** someone else, you do it together. *Boys do not generally play with girls... I discussed it with Phil.*
3 PREP If you fight or argue **with** someone, you oppose them. *...a naval war with France... Judy was tired of quarrelling with Bal.*
4 PREP If you do something **with** a particular tool or object, you do it using that tool or object. *Clean mirrors with a mop... He brushed back his hair with his hand.*
5 PREP You use **with** when you mention a feature, characteristic, or possession that someone or something has. *...an old man with a beard. ...an old house with steep stairs and dark corridors.*
6 PREP Something that is filled or covered **with** things has those things in it or on it. *The floor was littered with ashtrays, plates, cups and glasses... The building is decorated with bright banners.*
7 PREP You use **with** to indicate the manner in which someone does something, or the feeling they have when they do it. *Their fossils were studied with great care... Jordache looked over at his son with genuine surprise... She gazed on me with a sudden fear and disgust.*
8 PREP You also use **with** to indicate the feeling that makes someone behave in a particular way. *This experience leaves him quaking with fear... The children were screaming with laughter.*
9 PREP You can use **with** to indicate the thing that your statement relates to. *Don't be inflexible with shopping... There was a particular problem with claims for maternity allowance.*
10 PREP You can also use **with** to say that something happens at the same time as something else or as a

result of something else. *He didn't have the courage to put his hat on with Perkins watching him... With advancing age, reactions become slower.*
11 PREP You use **with** to introduce a factor that affects something and so is relevant to what you are saying. *With all the traffic jams, it wouldn't be wise to drive... With unemployment in the country growing, numbers staying on at school are increasing.*
12 PREP Someone **with** a particular illness is suffering from that illness. *I was taken to hospital with fierce abdominal pains... He's in bed with flu.*

withdraw /wɪðdrɔː/ **withdraws, withdrawing, withdrew, withdrawn;** a formal word.
1 VO If you **withdraw** something from a place, you remove it or take it away. *She withdrew the key from the door... She touched his cheek tenderly and withdrew her hand only when he shook his head.*
2 V-ERG When troops **withdraw** or when someone **withdraws** them, they leave the place where they are fighting or where they are based. *We could see the forces withdrawing... After a six-hour clash, the troops withdrew to a location outside the camp... They are willing to withdraw some troops.*
3 VO If you **withdraw** money from a bank account, you take it out of that account. *You must present your cheque card when you withdraw any money.*
4 V If you **withdraw** to another room, you go there. *He withdrew to his office to count the money... We withdrew into the library.*
5 V If you **withdraw** from an activity, you stop taking part in it. *Marsha withdrew from the argument... Mr Hart originally withdrew from the presidential campaign, but started campaigning again at Christmas... His original opponent withdrew with a back injury.*
6 VO If you **withdraw** your support from someone or something, you decide that you no longer wish to support them. *In October 1982, the Free Democrats withdrew their support from the government... In a change of policy last week, the United States withdrew recognition of the resistance coalition.*
7 VO If you **withdraw** your application for something, you decide that you no longer wish to apply for it. *His rival, Mr Jailani Naro, withdrew his candidacy at the last minute.*
8 VO If you **withdraw** a remark or statement that you have made, you say that you want people to ignore it. *I want to withdraw a statement I made earlier on.*

withdrawal /wɪðdrɔːəl/ **withdrawals;** a formal word.
1 NCorNU The **withdrawal** of something is the act or process of removing it or taking it away. *They are trying to negotiate the withdrawal of 20,000 troops... The withdrawal appears to be orderly. ...the cost of withdrawal, housing and retraining.*
2 NU **Withdrawal** from an activity or organization is a refusal to continue taking part in it. *...withdrawal from the Common Market... The opposition union of democratic forces announced its withdrawal from Parliament.*
3 NU+of The **withdrawal** of a remark or statement is the act of saying formally that you wish to change or deny it. *The trouble followed the withdrawal of an earlier announcement naming the eldest son of the late Sultan as his successor. ...President Gorbachev's demand for a withdrawal of their declaration of independence.*
4 NU **Withdrawal** is behaviour in which someone shows that they do not want to communicate with other people. *...intermittent spells of sulking, withdrawal and vindictiveness.*
5 NC A **withdrawal** is an amount of money that you take from your bank account. *It is not the bank's policy to deduct interest on withdrawals.*

withdrawal symptoms
N PL **Withdrawal symptoms** are the unpleasant physical and mental effects that people experience when they stop taking a drug that they are addicted to. *Chewing the gum eases the withdrawal symptoms that most people face when they stop smoking. ...withdrawal symptoms such as anxiety, depression, and inability to concentrate.*

withdrawn /wɪðˈdrɔːn/
1 **Withdrawn** is the past participle of **withdraw**.
2 ADJ Someone who is **withdrawn** is very quiet and shy. *The isolated life made them withdrawn... He thought it was partly my fault that she had become more and more depressed and withdrawn.*

withdrew /wɪðˈdruː/
Withdrew is the past tense of **withdraw**.

wither /ˈwɪðə/ **withers, withering, withered**
1 V When something **withers**, it becomes weaker, often until it no longer exists. *Links with the outside community withered... He said that if aid were cut off, the rebels would soon begin to wither.*
2 V If a plant **withers**, it shrinks, dries up, and dies. *The leaves had withered and fallen.*
wither away PHRASAL VERB When something **withers away**, it becomes weaker until it no longer exists. *The deficit will wither away as income increases on the back of continued economic growth... Orange trees are withering away for lack of irrigation.*

withered /ˈwɪðəd/
1 ADJ A **withered** plant has shrunk, dried up, and died. *...a pot of withered roses... The crops in the field are withered and stunted.*
2 ADJ If you describe an old person as **withered**, you mean that their skin has become wrinkled and dry. *...a withered old lady. ...her withered fingers.*

withering /ˈwɪðəʳrɪŋ/
ADJ A **withering** look or remark is intended to make the person it is directed at feel ashamed or stupid. *Scylla gave him a withering glare... He came under withering cross-examination from some of the best trial lawyers in Washington.*

withhold /wɪðˈhəʊld/ **withholds, withholding, withheld**
V O If you **withhold** something that someone wants, you do not let them have it; a formal word. *His salary was withheld... He'd deliberately withheld vital evidence from the defence team... I decided to withhold the information till later.*

withholding tax, withholding taxes
N U or N C In the United States, **withholding tax** is a proportion of an employee's salary that their employer pays direct to the government as part of the employee's income tax. *...major medical insurance and withholding tax... Until recently, Hamilton Taft handled payroll and withholding taxes for about 250 companies nationwide.*

within /wɪˈðɪn/
1 PREP or ADV If something is **within** a place, area, or object, it is inside it or surrounded by it. *The prisoners demanded the freedom to congregate within the prison... There were sounds of protest within.*
2 PREP or ADV **Within** is also used to refer to something that exists or happens inside a society, organization, or system, or to something that is part of it. *We are told to work within the system. ...the role of women within the family... Membership is by nomination from within.*
3 PREP or ADV If you experience a particular feeling, you can say that it is **within** you; a literary use. *A mounting wave of dislike and anger rose within me. ...the hatred he felt within.*
4 PREP If something is **within** a particular limit, it does not go beyond that limit. *The decree allows wholesale prices to rise within set limits throughout the country from the beginning of next year... We must ask the schools to keep within their budget.*
5 PREP If you are **within** a particular distance of a place, you are less than that distance from it. *They were within fifty miles of Chicago.*
6 PREP **Within** a particular length of time means before that length of time has passed. *Within minutes I was called to his office... He was reported as saying the crime will be solved within thirty days.*
7 PREP If something is **within** sight, **within** earshot, or **within** reach, you can see it, hear it, or reach it. *They finally came within sight of the gates... If he disappoints us, we won't say so—not within earshot anyway... Matches should not be left within reach of small children.*

without /wɪˈðaʊt/
1 PREP If a person or thing is **without** something, they

do not have it. *...city slums without lights, roads or water... She was without an ambition in the world.*
2 CONJ or PREP If you do one thing **without** doing another, you do not do the second thing. *They drove into town without talking to each other... 'No,' she said, without explanation.*
3 PREP If you do something **without** a particular feeling, you do not have that feeling when you do it. *They greeted him without enthusiasm... We must face the future without fear.*
4 PREP If one thing happens **without** another thing happening, the other thing does not happen. *I knocked twice, without reply... He had been held without trial for almost two years... Moscow is willing to leave, with or without an agreement.*
5 PREP If you do something **without** someone, you are not in their company or you do not have their help when you do it. *You can go without me... Her husband felt he couldn't face life without her.*

withstand /wɪðˈstænd/ **withstands, withstanding, withstood** /wɪðˈstʊd/
V O To **withstand** a force or action means to survive it or not to let it defeat you; a formal word. *They have to make the walls strong enough to withstand high winds... He was in no condition to withstand any further punishment... How long Honduras will be able to withstand US pressure is unclear.*

witless /ˈwɪtləs/
1 ADJ A **witless** person is silly. *I felt an unreasonable hatred for that witless woman.*
2 If you say that something **scares** you **witless**, you mean that it scares you very much indeed.

witness /ˈwɪtnəs/ **witnesses, witnessing, witnessed**
1 N C A **witness** to an event is a person who saw it. *Witnesses to the murder told what they had seen.*
2 V O If you **witness** something, you see it happen. *At least fifteen people witnessed the attack... He scored the most fantastic goal I had ever witnessed.*
3 N C A **witness** is someone who appears in a court of law to say what they know about a crime or other event. *Other witnesses were called to give evidence.*
4 N C A **witness** is also someone who writes their name on a document that you have signed, to confirm that it really is your signature. *If the document has not been signed either by Mr Windsor or by the witnesses, then that's something that needs investigation.*
5 V O If someone **witnesses** your signature, they write their name after it, to confirm that it really is your signature. *Now everything is signed and witnessed.*
● **Witness** is used in these phrases. ● If you are **witness to** something, you see it happen; a formal expression. *This was the first time I was witness to one of his rages.* ● If one thing **bears witness to** another, the first thing shows that the second thing exists or happened; a formal expression. *This lack of action bears witness to a complacency which has survived two World Wars.* ● See also **eyewitness, Jehovah's Witness**.

witness box or **witness stand**
N SING In a court of law, the **witness box** or **witness stand** is the place where people stand or sit when they give evidence. *Mr Swanepoel has decided to call one of the survivors to the witness box tomorrow... Hamadei's younger brother took the witness stand but refused to testify.*

witter /ˈwɪtə/ **witters, wittering, wittered**
V If you say that someone is **wittering** about something, you mean that they are saying a lot of silly and boring things; an informal word. *He can get away with wittering on about peace, love and harmony.*

witticism /ˈwɪtɪsɪzəm/ **witticisms**
N C A **witticism** is a witty remark or joke. *Don smiled at this witticism.*

wittingly /ˈwɪtɪŋli/
ADV If you do something **wittingly**, you are fully aware of what you are doing and what its consequences will be; a formal word. *Wittingly or not, he had ruined the plan.*

witty /ˈwɪti/ **wittier, wittiest**
ADJ **Witty** means amusing in a clever way. *He found her charming and witty. ...a witty play.*

wives /waɪvz/
Wives is the plural of **wife**.

wizard /wɪzəd/ **wizards**
1 NC A **wizard** is a man in a fairy story who has magic powers. *Merlin was the wizard who worked magic for King Arthur.*
2 NC+SUPP You can describe someone who is very good at a particular thing as that type of **wizard**. *He's built up a reputation as something of a keyboard wizard... He tends to see himself as a wizard in the kitchen.*

wizardry /wɪzədri/
NU+SUPP You can refer to a very clever achievement or piece of work as **wizardry**, especially when you do not understand how it is done. *...a sophisticated piece of computing wizardry. ...her reputation for financial wizardry.*

wizened /wɪzənd/
ADJ A **wizened** person is old and has wrinkled skin; a literary word. *Mr Solomon was a wizened little man with frizzy grey hair.*

wobble /wɒbl/ **wobbles, wobbling, wobbled**
V If someone or something **wobbles**, it makes small movements from side to side, because it is loose or unsteady. *My legs were wobbling under me... They hope they have solved the computer problem that was making the craft wobble.*

wobbly /wɒbli/
ADJ If something is **wobbly**, it is unstable and likely to move from side to side; an informal word. *...a wobbly bed... My legs still feel weak and wobbly.*

wodge /wɒdʒ/ **wodges**
NC A **wodge** of something is a large amount of it or a large piece of it; an informal word. *Professor Marvin banged his wodge of files down hard on the desk... He helped himself to a great wodge of chocolate cake.*

woe /wəʊ/ **woes**; a literary word.
1 NU **Woe** is great unhappiness or sorrow. *...an exclamation of woe.*
2 N PL You can refer to someone's problems or misfortunes as their **woes**. *They listened sympathetically to his woes.*
3 If you say **woe betide** someone who does a particular thing, you mean that something unpleasant will happen to them if they do it; an old-fashioned expression, often used humorously. *Woe betide the player who scores an own goal!... Woe betide us if we're not ready on time.*

woebegone /wəʊbɪgɒn/
ADJ Someone who looks or feels **woebegone** looks or feels very sad; a literary word. *...a little woebegone face.*

woeful /wəʊfl/; a literary word.
1 ADJ **Woeful** means very sad. *...the lovers' long and woeful farewell.* ◆ **woefully** ADV *She announced woefully, 'I've lost my job'.*
2 ADJ You also use **woeful** to emphasize how bad something is. *His work displays a woeful lack of imagination.* ◆ **woefully** SUBMOD *The quantities were woefully inadequate.*

wok /wɒk/ **woks**
NC A **wok** is a large bowl-shaped pan which is used for Chinese-style cooking. *We now sell far more woks than we sell frying pans.*

woke /wəʊk/
Woke is the past tense of **wake**.

woken /wəʊkən/
Woken is the past participle of **wake**.

wolf /wʊlf/ **wolves; wolfs, wolfing, wolfed.** The form **wolves** is the plural of the noun. The form **wolfs** is the third person singular, present tense, of the verb.
1 NC A **wolf** is a wild animal that looks like a large dog and kills and eats other animals. *In some remote areas wolves have come down from the mountains to look for food.*
2 If someone **cries wolf**, they say that there is a problem when it is not true, with the result that people do not believe them when there really is a problem. *She had cried wolf so often that her claims for attention were ignored... We are not crying wolf, we are crying for help.*

wolf down PHRASAL VERB If you **wolf down** food, you eat it quickly and greedily; an informal expression. *Thomas didn't seem worried about anything as he wolfed down his food.*

wolfhound /wʊlfhaʊnd/ **wolfhounds**
NC A **wolfhound** is a type of very large dog. *He appeared leading a pair of Russian wolfhounds on a leash.*

wolf-whistle, wolf-whistles, wolf-whistling, wolf-whistled
NC A **wolf-whistle** is a whistle which has a short rising note and a longer falling note. Some men make this sound to show that they think a woman is attractive, especially a woman who is passing in the street. *I'm always getting wolf-whistles.* ▶ Also V *They stared after her, laughing and wolf-whistling.*

wolves /wʊlvz/
Wolves is the plural of **wolf**.

woman /wʊmən/ **women**
1 NC A **woman** is an adult female human being. *...an old woman... There were men and women working in the fields... We had one woman teacher.*
2 NU You can refer to women in general as **woman**. *...man's inhumanity to woman.*

womanhood /wʊmənhʊd/
NU **Womanhood** is the state of being a woman rather than a girl, or the period of a woman's adult life. *...the threshold of womanhood. ...the years of her womanhood.*

womanish /wʊmənɪʃ/
ADJ If someone describes a man as **womanish**, they mean he behaves in a weak or emotional manner, or looks rather like a woman; used showing disapproval. *He seemed to look down on Phaedrus with womanish peevishness. ...his low womanish round shoulders.*

womanizer /wʊmənaɪzə/ **womanizers**; also spelt **womaniser**.
NC A **womanizer** is a man who likes to spend a lot of time in the company of women, usually in order to have short sexual relationships with them; used showing disapproval. *He was known as a reckless drinker and insatiable womanizer.*

womanizing /wʊmənaɪzɪŋ/; also spelt **womanising**.
NU When a man likes to spend a lot of time in the company of women, usually in order to have short sexual relationships with them, this practice is known as **womanizing**; used showing disapproval. *They have been embarrassed on too many occasions by his drinking habits and womanizing.*

womankind /wʊmənkaɪnd/
NU You can refer to all women as **womankind** when considering them as a group; a formal word. *I spoke up on behalf of womankind.*

womanly /wʊmənli/
ADJ **Womanly** behaviour is typical of a woman rather than a man or a girl; used showing approval. *...the womanly virtues of gentleness and compassion.*

womb /wuːm/ **wombs**
NC A woman's **womb** is the part inside her body where a baby grows before it is born. *The placenta is the organ in the womb through which the baby receives food and oxygen from the mother.*

wombat /wɒmbæt/ **wombats**
NC A **wombat** is a furry Australian animal which has very short legs and eats plants.

women /wɪmɪn/
Women is the plural of **woman**.

womenfolk /wɪmɪnfəʊk/
N PL The **womenfolk** of a particular community are its women; an old-fashioned word. *They emigrated to the towns with their womenfolk.*

women's libber /wɪmɪnz lɪbə/ **women's libbers**
NC A **women's libber** is a woman who supports feminist ideas; an old-fashioned, informal expression. *Just before we get mountains of letters from women's libbers, let's have a quick look at the other side of the coin.*

Women's Liberation
NU **Women's Liberation** is the ideal that women should have the same social and economic rights and privileges as men; an old-fashioned expression. *I got interested in Women's Liberation. ...the local Women's Liberation Movement.*

women's movement

N SING The **women's movement** is a social and political movement which aims to achieve women's liberation by organizing groups and campaigns and by causing individual women and men to change their attitudes. *The crowds heard speeches from trade union and women's movement leaders.*

won /wʌn/

Won is the past tense and past participle of **win**.

wonder /wʌndə/ **wonders, wondering, wondered**

1 V+about or V-REPORT If you **wonder** about something, you think about it and try to guess or understand more about it. *I keep wondering and worrying about what you said... I wonder what she'll look like... I am beginning to wonder why we ever invited them.*

2 V You can introduce a request or question by saying 'I **wonder** if' or 'I **wonder** whether' when you are being polite. *I wonder if you'd mind closing the window... I wonder whether by any chance you would care to join me?*

3 V+at or V-REPORT If you **wonder** at something, you are surprised and amazed by it. *I wondered at her strength... I don't wonder that she didn't come—you didn't invite her.*

4 N SING If you say that it is a **wonder** that something happened, you mean it is very surprising. *It was a wonder that she managed to come.*

5 NU **Wonder** is a feeling of surprise and amazement. *...exclamations of wonder.*

6 NC A **wonder** is something remarkable that people admire. *...the wonders of modern technology.*
• **Wonder** is used in these phrases. • You say **no wonder**, **little wonder**, or **small wonder** to indicate that you are not surprised by something. *Little wonder that today we are in such a mess... 'Anyway, he didn't win.'—'No wonder.'... It is small wonder that the government's economic policies have caused widespread resentment.* • If someone or something **works wonders** or **does wonders**, they have a very good effect. *A whisky at the end of the day will sometimes work wonders... The doctors have done wonders for your leg.*

wonderful /wʌndəfl/

1 ADJ You describe an experience as **wonderful** when it makes you very happy and pleased. *It was wonderful to be able to walk again.*

2 ADJ You can show your admiration for something by saying that it is **wonderful**. *I think the heart transplant is a wonderful thing.*

wonderfully /wʌndəfəli/

SUBMOD You use **wonderfully** to emphasize how good something is. *Both plays are wonderfully funny... She was always wonderfully kind to me.*

wonderland /wʌndəlænd/ **wonderlands**

1 NU **Wonderland** is an imaginary world that exists in fairy tales. *...the Cheshire Cat, a character from the children's book 'Alice in Wonderland'.*

2 NU or NC You can refer to a place as **wonderland** or a **wonderland** when it seems very strange or unusually beautiful. *He went into the old lady's house and found himself in wonderland... She drew back the curtain and gazed at the winter wonderland before her.*

wonderment /wʌndəmənt/

NU **Wonderment** is a feeling of amazement and admiration; a literary word. *I stood shaking my head in wonderment.*

wondrous /wʌndrəs/

ADJ ATTRIB **Wondrous** means amazing and impressive; an old-fashioned word. *It was a wondrous victory. ...the wondrous inventions of the twentieth century.*

wonky /wɒŋki/

ADJ Something that is **wonky** is likely to shake or not work properly because it is unsteady or not in its proper position; an informal word. *The legs have gone a bit wonky.*

wont /wəʊnt/

ADJ PRED+to-INF If someone is **wont** to do something, they do it regularly as a habit; an old-fashioned word. *They were wont to take long walks in the evening... It is—as book reviewers are wont to say these days—definitely a good read.*

won't /wəʊnt/

Won't is the usual spoken form of 'will not'.

woo /wuː/ **woos, wooing, wooed**

1 VO If you **woo** people, you try to get them to help or support you. *She hoped to woo the working-class voters of Warrington... The Soviet Union's new wave global diplomacy has wooed China into accepting the holding of a Sino-Soviet summit.*

2 VO When a man **woos** a woman, he tries to make himself attractive to her, because he wants to marry her; an old-fashioned use. *She falls in love with a handsome inarticulate youth who woos her with Cyrano's poetry.*

wood /wʊd/ **woods**

1 N MASS **Wood** is the material which forms the trunks and branches of trees. *We gathered wood for the fire. ...planks of wood... I'd like to know more about mahogany and alternative woods.*

2 NC A **wood** is a large area of trees growing near each other. *...the big wood where the pheasants lived.*

3 N PL You can refer to a large wood as the **woods**. *They walked through the woods.*

woodcock /wʊdkɒk/; **woodcock** is both the singular and the plural form.

NC A **woodcock** is a small brown bird with a long beak. Woodcock are sometimes shot for sport or food.

wooded /wʊdɪd/

ADJ A **wooded** area is covered in trees. *...a narrow wooded valley.*

wooden /wʊdn/

ADJ A **wooden** object is made of wood. *...a wooden box.*

wooden-headed

ADJ If you describe someone as **wooden-headed**, you think they are stupid; an informal word. *...their wooden-headed supporters.*

wooden spoon, wooden spoons

1 NC A **wooden spoon** is a spoon made of wood that you can use when you are cooking. *With a wooden spoon, she puts in the flour for the sweet rolls.*

2 N SING You can say that the person or team that finishes a race or competition in last place gets the **wooden spoon**; an informal use. *West Ham prised itself off the bottom of the first division with a 2-1 win at Derby, leaving Newcastle United holding the wooden spoon.*

woodland /wʊdlənd/ **woodlands**

NU or NC **Woodland** is land covered with trees. *...a patch of woodland in Malaysia... The boundaries of many woodlands have not changed for hundreds of years.*

woodlouse /wʊdlaʊs/ **woodlice** /wʊdlaɪs/

NC A **woodlouse** is a very small grey creature that looks rather like an insect. It has fourteen legs and lives in damp places.

woodpecker /wʊdpekə/ **woodpeckers**

NC A **woodpecker** is a bird with a long sharp beak. Woodpeckers use their beaks to make holes in tree trunks. *On the farm are three species of British woodpecker.*

woodpile /wʊdpaɪl/ **woodpiles**

NC A **woodpile** is a pile of firewood.

wood pulp

NU **Wood pulp** is wood that has been cut up into small pieces and crushed. Wood pulp is used to make paper. *The Company guaranteed supplies of the wood pulp needed for the newsprint.*

woodshed /wʊdʃed/ **woodsheds**

NC A **woodshed** is a small building which is used for storing firewood. *I fixed a small leak in the roof of the woodshed.*

woodwind /wʊdwɪnd/

ADJ A **woodwind** instrument is a musical instrument such as a clarinet or flute that you play by blowing into it or across it. Many woodwind instruments are made of wood. *The music is played by the Almeida Ensemble, using largely woodwind and percussion instruments.*

woodwork /wʊdwɜːk/

1 N SING or NU You can refer to the doors and other wooden parts of a house as the **woodwork**. *The paint was peeling from the woodwork... The rich woodwork*

had been carved by the same craftsmen.
2 NU **Woodwork** is the activity or skill of making
things out of wood. *Everybody who has done
woodwork at school is perfectly familiar with the G-
clamp.*
3 N SING If you talk about someone or something being
in the **woodwork**, you are referring to the fact that
they do exist, although their presence in a situation
may not always be obvious. *There's a lot of strange
things in the woodwork of the Carlton Club... Every
once in a while a Senator Phil Gramm comes out of
the woodwork and says, 'You know, the deficit actually
is smaller than it was'.*

woodworm /wʊdwɜːm/; **woodworm** is both the singular
and the plural form.
1 NC **Woodworm** are the larvae of certain types of
beetle which make holes in wood by feeding on it.
2 NU **Woodworm** is also the damage caused to wood,
especially to the wooden parts of a house or to
furniture, by the larvae of certain types of beetle. *The
problems which the survey had failed to pick up were
staggering, including woodworm, dry rot and
subsidence.*

woody /wʊdi/
1 ADJ **Woody** plants have very hard stems. *Certain
types of lentil have a very thick woody stem.*
2 ADJ A **woody** area has a lot of trees in it. *...a farm
set amid woody valleys.*

woof /wʊf/ **woofs**
NC A **woof** is the sound that a dog makes when it
barks.

wool /wʊl/ **wools**
1 N MASS **Wool** is the hair that grows on sheep and on
some other animals. *They work together to grow
vegetables and raise sheep for wool... Some of the
finest wool in the world is said to come from the
Shetland Islands.*
2 N MASS **Wool** is also a material made from animals'
wool. It is used for making clothes, blankets, and
carpets. *...soft leather jackets lined with wool. ...a
ball of wool... The machine will knit different types of
yarn including mohair, cotton and thick wools.*
3 If you **pull the wool over** someone's **eyes,** you
deliberately deceive them in order to have an
advantage over them. *The separatists said the offer
was a charade designed only to pull the wool over the
eyes of the French public.*
4 See also **cotton wool.**

wool-gathering
If someone is **wool-gathering**, they are thinking
vaguely about something and not paying attention to
what other people are saying or doing; an informal
expression.

woollen /wʊlən/; spelt **woolen** in American English.
ADJ ATTRIB **Woollen** clothes are made from wool, or
from a mixture of wool and artificial fibres. *...a
woollen scarf. ...a young woman in a checked woolen
shirt.*

woolly /wʊli/ **woollier, woolliest; woollies;** spelt **wooly**
in American English.
1 ADJ Something that is **woolly** is made of wool or
looks like wool. *...a woolly cap.*
2 NC A **woolly** is a woollen piece of clothing, especially
a pullover; an informal use. *She wore a long woolly
with a belt.*
3 ADJ If you describe people or their thoughts as
woolly, you mean that their ideas are very unclear.
*They cannot afford to be vague and woolly with their
messages.*

woolly-minded
ADJ If you describe someone as **woolly-minded**, you
mean that their ideas are confused or vague. *...an
enthusiastic researcher into the subject of UFOs, a
woolly-minded lady at best.*

woozy /wuːzi/ **woozier, wooziest**
ADJ If you feel **woozy**, you feel rather weak and
unsteady and cannot think clearly; an informal word.
I smiled uncertainly, feeling woozy from the whisky.

word /wɜːd/ **words, wording, worded**
1 NC A **word** is a single unit of language in writing or
speech. In English, a word has a space on either side
of it when it is written. Some words have more than

one meaning. *He has a terrible verbal memory and
can immediately forget every word of a poem he's
written... 'Surrender' is a strange word to use because
he's not looking for a military victory... It was
sickening in every sense of the word.*
2 NC If you have a **word** or a few **words** with
someone, you have a short conversation with them;
used in speech. *May I have a word with you please?...
Prince Charles exchanged a few words with one of the
models.*
3 N SING A **word** of advice or warning is a short
statement that gives advice or a warning. *He has a
word of warning for anyone wanting to take up the
challenge—it's a full-time occupation and very hard
work... There was one word of caution he did not need
to stress: the economic and social dangers when a
country allowed its manufacturing industry to run
down.*
4 N SING If you cannot hear, understand, or believe a
word of what someone is saying, you cannot hear,
understand, or believe it at all. *I did not understand
one word of what she'd said... In its editorial, the
Guardian sees no sign that millions of Scottish voters
believe a word of Scottish Conservative strategy.*
5 N U or N SING You can use **word** to mean news. *The
young man brought them word of her visit... There's
been no official word on the content of their
discussions... The word got out that he was leaving.*
6 N SING+POSS If you give your **word**, you promise to
do something. *I give you my word, I won't ask him...
I apologized for having doubted his word.*
7 VO When you **word** something in a particular way,
you express it that way. *How would one word such an
announcement?* ◆ **worded** ADJ *He wrote a strongly
worded report to the Secretary of the Interior.*
● **Word** is used in these phrases. ● If you repeat
something **word for word**, you repeat it exactly as it
was originally said or written. *The government
pledged to make sweeping democratic reforms,
adopting the language of the rebels' key demands
virtually word for word.* ● **The last word** or the **final
word** in an argument or situation is a comment or
action which ends it, and which is often considered to
defeat your opponents. *It's the establishment who
have the last word on who lead Pakistan at this
crucial time... He said the vote was not the final word,
and he would have more to say in a few weeks.* ● If
someone is **as good as their word**, they do what they
have promised to do. *She told a news conference that
she expected the Soviet Union to be as good as its
word.* ● If someone suggests that you said or meant
something that you did not say or mean, you can say
that they **are putting words into** your **mouth** or **in** your
mouth. *The question remains why the President didn't
notice the made-up quotes attributed to him, and ask
his press secretary why he was putting words in his
mouth.* ● If you **put in a word** for someone or **put in a
good word** for them, you speak favourably about them,
often to a person who has influence. *I'll put in a good
word at the meeting if I get a chance... The King put
in a good word for her and she was released.* ● You
say **in a word** to indicate that you are summarizing
what you have just been saying. *The house is roomy,
cool in summer, and in a word comfortable.* ● If you
have words with someone, you have an argument with
them, or let them know that you are not pleased about
something that they have done. *He had firm words
with his hosts about the limited nature of the tour.* ● A
war of words is fierce and bitter debate between
people or groups of people. *It was the Prime
Minister's most aggressive statement so far in the
increasing war of words with Pakistan over Kashmir.*
● You say **in other words** when introducing a simpler
or clearer explanation of something that has just been
said. *Is there a cheaper solution? In other words, can
you make a cheaper device?* ● If you say something **in
your own words**, you say it in your own way, without
copying or repeating what someone else has said. *He
was asked to tell the story in his own words.* ● If you
say that something was not said **in so many words**,
you mean that it was said indirectly, but that you are
giving its real meaning. *This is what he claims, only*

he does not state it in so many words. ● **cannot get a word in edgeways**: see **edgeways**.

word-blind
ADJ Someone who is **word-blind** has difficulty with reading because of a slight disorder of their brain. ◆ **word-blindness** NU *We've heard a lot in recent years about dyslexia, which is sometimes described as word-blindness.*

word class, word classes
NC A **word class** is a particular grammatical class of word, such as noun, adjective, verb, and so on.

wording /wɜːdɪŋ/
NU The **wording** of a piece of writing or a speech is the way it is expressed. *For a full hour he argued over the wording of the editorial... The wording of the UN resolution itself is rather ambiguous.*

word of mouth
NU If news or information passes by **word of mouth**, people find out about it when others tell them about it directly, rather than by reading about it or by hearing about it on the radio or television. *Most of those who come to the clinic find out about it by word of mouth... Relying on word of mouth is no longer enough; the school has to be sold, just like any other service.*

word-perfect
ADJ If you are **word-perfect**, you are able to repeat from memory the exact words of something that you have learned. *Noel was always word-perfect at the first rehearsal and expected the whole company to be the same.*

word-play
NU **Word-play** involves making jokes by using the meanings of words in an amusing or clever way. *...a fondness for word-play.*

word processing
NU **Word processing** is the work of producing documents, letters, and other printed material using a word processor. *...a new and interesting development in the world of word processing.*

word processor, word processors
NC A **word processor** is an electronic machine which has a keyboard and a screen like a computer terminal, but which is used as a typewriter to produce documents, letters, and other printed material. *They used word processors to generate the often enormous amounts of paperwork involved.*

wordy /wɜːdi/
ADJ Something that is **wordy** uses too many words. *...this very wordy book on biology.*

wore /wɔː/
Wore is the past tense of **wear**.

work /wɜːk/ **works, working, worked**
1 V A or V People who **work** have a job which they are paid to do. *He was working in a bank... Some of my salesmen formerly worked for a rival firm... She was accused of setting fire to the house where she worked as a baby-sitter and a maid.*
2 NU People who have **work** or are in **work** have a job. *...people who can't find work... This made it almost impossible to sack employees who had been in work for more than three months. ...the numbers out of work.*
3 V O or V A When you **work**, you do the tasks which your job involves, or a task that needs to be done. *I used to work a ten-hour day... I watched the people working at the weaving looms... She works hard at keeping herself fit... He has been working all season on his game... Eight dissident groups have issued a press release saying they are to join forces to work for peace.*
4 NU **Work** is also the tasks which your job involves, or any tasks which need to be done. *I've got some work to do... I finish work at 3... A housewife's work can take ten or twelve hours a day.*
5 NU Something produced as a result of an activity, job, or area of research is also called **work**. *That's an absolutely fascinating piece of work... There has been considerable work done in America on this subject.*
6 V O If you **work** the land, you cultivate it. *...peasants working the land.*
7 V O If you **work** an area, you travel around that area in order to do the tasks there that are your job. *They*

have worked these areas for years without interference from the police.
8 V O If you **work** a machine or piece of equipment, you use it or control it. *From inside, came the sound of Coyne working a lathe. ...the boy who worked the milking machine.*
9 V If a machine or piece of equipment **works**, it operates and performs its function. *The traffic lights weren't working properly.*
10 V If an idea, method, or system **works**, it is successful. *That kind of democracy will never work... He said the present one-party system had not worked... Police confiscated bottles and cans as fans entered the ground, and it worked well.*
11 V If a drug or medicine **works**, it produces a particular physical effect. *We must remember that these drugs worked not all that differently than barbiturates... It also worked against venereal disease.*
12 V A If something **works** against you, it causes problems for you. If something **works** in your favour, it helps you. *I think his speech was so brutal and so totally unacceptable that it actually worked against him... The apathy of the opposition is working in his favour.*
13 V+on If you **work** on an assumption or idea, you make decisions based on it. *Police are working on the theory that the bomb was detonated by an underground pressure plate... The flight controllers are working on the basis that there will be a 24-hour postponement.*
14 V A or V C If something **works** into a particular position, it gradually moves into that position. *The ropes had worked loose.*
15 V O A If you **work** your way somewhere, you manage to get there with difficulty. *I worked my way slowly out of the marsh... He gradually worked his way up the hierarchy of the Communist Party.*
16 NC+SUPP A **work** is something such as a painting, book, or piece of music. *...a large volume containing all of Chopin's works. ...a previously unknown work by Van Gogh.*
17 NC A **works** is a place where something is made or produced by an industrial process. The form **works** is both the singular and the plural. *...the gas works.*
18 N PL+SUPP **Works** are activities such as digging the ground or building on a large scale, especially in order to install systems of pipes or wires, or to construct roads, bridges, or buildings. *He was in charge of planning the great plumbing and civil engineering works of the city.*
19 See also **working, social work**.
● **Work** is used in these phrases. ● If someone is **at work**, they are doing their job or are busy doing a particular activity. *I'll be at work tomorrow... He had been at work on a book.* ● If you **have** your **work cut out** to do something, it is very difficult for you to do it. *We'll have our work cut out to finish on time.* ● If workers **work to rule**, they stop doing extra work and just do the minimum that is required of them. *The delivery men are working to rule.* ● See also **work-to-rule**.

work into PHRASAL VERB If you **work** yourself **into** a state of being upset or angry, you make yourself become upset or angry. *She worked herself into a rage.*

work off PHRASAL VERB If you **work off** a feeling, you overcome it by doing something energetic or violent. *We should all be able to work off our stress physically.*

work out PHRASAL VERB 1 If you **work out** a solution to a problem or mystery, you find the solution or calculate it. *We are always hoping that a more peaceful solution can be worked out... Now you can work out the area of the triangle.* 2 If something **works out** at a particular amount, it is calculated to be that amount. *Petrol prices here work out at around £1.15 a gallon.* 3 If a situation **works out** in a particular way, it happens or progresses in that way. *It's funny how life worked out... Things worked out well with Marian.* 4 If you **work out**, you do physical exercises to make your body fit and strong. *She worked out in a ballet class three hours a week.* 5 See also **workout**.

work up PHRASAL VERB 1 If you **work** yourself **up**, you gradually make yourself very upset or angry about something. *She worked herself up into a frenzy.* 2 If you **work up** a feeling, you gradually start to have it. *I can hardly work up enough energy to go to the shops... She went for a run to work up an appetite.* 3 See also **worked up**.

work up to PHRASAL VERB If you **work up to** a particular amount or level, you gradually increase or improve what you are doing until you reach that amount or level. *Start slowly and work up to a faster time.*

workable /wɜːkəbl/
ADJ Something that is **workable** can operate efficiently or can be used for a particular purpose. *This doesn't seem to be a workable solution.*

workaday /wɜːkədeɪ/
ADJ ATTRIB **Workaday** means ordinary and not especially interesting or unusual. *...a quiet workaday man... Gloucester is now a sprawling, even ugly, workaday city.*

workaholic /wɔːkəhɒlɪk/ **workaholics**
N C A **workaholic** is someone who finds it difficult to stop working in order to do other things. *He has spent most of his forty years since then being a workaholic... His manner is rather cold, and he's considered to be something of a workaholic.*

work basket, work baskets
N C A **work basket** is a small box or container in which people keep needles, cotton, and other small articles for sewing.

workbench /wɜːkbentʃ/ **workbenches**
N C A **workbench** is a heavy wooden table which is used for making or repairing things. *The packing case can be transformed into a simple workbench when it arrives at its destination.*

workbook /wɜːkbʊk/ **workbooks**
N C A **workbook** is a textbook that has questions in it with spaces for the answers. *We've developed a video and workbook which would train youth workers and youth leaders to get the message across.*

workday /wɜːkdeɪ/ **workdays**
N C A **workday** is a day on which people go to work. *In York, Pennsylvania, the workday begins at 7.00 a.m. ...the highs and lows of the workday cycle.*

worked up
ADJ PRED If you are **worked up** about something, you are upset or angry about it. *Why are you so worked up over that editorial?*

worker /wɜːkə/ **workers**
1 N C A **worker** is a person employed in an industry or business who has no responsibility for managing it. *Many workers lost their jobs. The dispute affected relations between management and workers. ...worker absenteeism.*
2 N C+SUPP You can use **worker** to say how well or badly someone works. *My husband was a hard worker... His boss says he's a good worker.*
3 N C A **worker** is also someone who does a particular kind of job. *...American research workers. ...the daily wage of a manual worker.* • See also **social worker**.

workforce /wɜːkfɔːs/
N SING+SUPP The **workforce** is all the people who work in a particular place, industry, or organization. *Asia's workforce will expand by 60 per cent.*

workhorse /wɜːkhɔːs/ **workhorses**
N C You can use **workhorse** to refer to someone or something that does a large amount of dull or routine work. *RFA ships are the Navy's unsung workhorses, keeping the men fed, fuelled, and fighting fit... Scientists were studying a gene in that workhorse of modern biology, the common fruitfly.*

workhouse /wɜːkhaʊs/ **workhouses**
N C A **workhouse** was a place where, in the seventeenth to nineteenth centuries in Britain, very poor, homeless people did very unpleasant jobs in return for food and shelter. *They tramped from workhouse to workhouse... The ultimate dread was the workhouse.*

working /wɜːkɪŋ/ **workings**
1 ADJ ATTRIB **Working** people have jobs which they are paid to do. *...children with working mothers.*
2 ADJ ATTRIB Your **working** life is the period of your life in which you have a job, or are of a suitable age to have a job. *Most of these people spend their entire working lives at General Motors.*
3 ADJ ATTRIB **Working** is used to refer to periods of time during which people normally have to do their job. *The unions will demand a reduction in working hours... The economy was plunged into a 3-day working week because of power cuts... The villagers lose a complete working day just getting their produce to market.*
4 ADJ ATTRIB **Working** is also used to refer to things connected with your job. *We want to achieve better working conditions for all women... I didn't bring any working clothes.*
5 ADJ ATTRIB A **working** lunch or dinner is one which arranged to enable people to discuss work matters formally over the meal. *He accompanied the President to the Palace for a round of talks that extended through a working lunch... The session, described as a working breakfast, was chaired by the Industry Minister.*
6 ADJ ATTRIB A **working** knowledge of something such as a foreign language is a reasonable knowledge of it that enables you to use it effectively. *In the first week I picked up a tolerable working knowledge of Spanish.*
7 N PL+SUPP The **workings** of a piece of equipment, an organization, or a system are the ways in which it operates. *...the workings of the free market economy... We're looking at the workings of human memory... It's as incomprehensible to most people as the workings of a breeder reactor.*
8 **in working order**: see **order**.

working capital
N U **Working capital** is money which is available for use immediately, rather than money which is invested in land or equipment and which becomes available only after the land or equipment has been sold; a technical term. *...whether the government is prepared to advance cash as working capital... Grants and loans had gone to finance the Company's working capital requirements.*

working class, working classes
N C The **working class** or **working classes** are the people in a society who do not own much property and whose work involves physical and practical skills rather than intellectual ones. *He was a staunch supporter of the working class and opposed to capitalism. ...a document on labour and the condition of the working classes. ...a working class suburb of Dublin.*

working party, working parties
N COLL A **working party** is a committee which is established to investigate a particular situation or problem and to produce a report about what should be done. *...the 1957 working party on African land tenure... The working party's report was hardly controversial.*

working relationship, working relationships
N C A **working relationship** is a relationship that you have with someone at work or in the context of a particular activity that contributes to the successful completion of the job or activity. *The two men appear to have established a good working relationship. ...a working relationship with the British government.*

workload /wɜːkləʊd/ **workloads**
N C+SUPP Your **workload** is the amount of work that you have to do. *...a simple system to reduce air traffic controllers' workloads... Head teachers are already worried about the extra workload they will have to face... The latest report says the existing workload of consultants exceeds their capacity, and they often have to rely on junior staff.*

workman /wɜːkmən/ **workmen** /wɜːkmən/
N C A **workman** is a man whose job involves working with his hands, for example building houses or plumbing. *Workmen wearing special protective suits have been out gathering the debris... The workmen are putting the finishing touches to the exhibition.*

workmanlike /wɜːkmənlaɪk/
ADJ You can use **workmanlike** to describe something

that is done skilfully and efficiently. *He described the talks with Mrs Thatcher as a good, workmanlike meeting... He produced a determined, workmanlike performance to come out the winner.*

workmanship /wɜːkmənʃɪp/
NU **Workmanship** is the skill with which something is made. *...good materials and sound workmanship.*

workmate /wɜːkmeɪt/ **workmates**
NC A **workmate** is a friend who works with you; an informal word. *This happened in front of his friends, neighbours and workmates.*

work of art, works of art
1 NC A **work of art** is a painting or piece of sculpture of high quality. *Some of the world's greatest works of art are on display here.*
2 NC You can refer to something that has been skilfully produced as a **work of art**. *His own papers were works of art on which he laboured with loving care.*

workout /wɜːkaʊt/ **workouts**
NC A **workout** is a period of physical exercise or training. *She bruised her right finger in a full-scale workout.*

workplace /wɜːkpleɪs/ **workplaces**
NC Your **workplace** is the place where you work. *Their houses were workplaces as well as dwellings. ...legislation to curb smoking in the workplace... Workplace canteens are offering healthier food than ever before.*

workshop /wɜːkʃɒp/ **workshops**
1 NC A **workshop** is a room or building containing tools or machinery for making or repairing things. *...a small engineering workshop.*
2 NC A **workshop** on a particular subject is a period of discussion and practical work on that subject by a group of people. *...a theatre workshop. ...a workshop on child care.*

work-shy
ADJ A **work-shy** person is lazy and does not want a job. *As wages now depend on performance, there's no room for people who are work-shy.*

workstation /wɜːksteɪʃn/ **workstations**
NC A **workstation** is a part of a computerized office system consisting of a display screen and keyboard and is used to deal with electronic office work. *...a bid to bridge the gap between high performance workstations and lower priced personal computers.*

work surface, work surfaces
NC A **work surface** is the same as a **worktop**. *...a kitchen work surface.*

worktop /wɜːktɒp/ **worktops**
NC A **worktop** is a flat surface on top of a fridge or low cupboard, on which you can prepare food or place something. *The machine sits quite happily on an ordinary worktop.*

work-to-rule
N SING A **work-to-rule** is a protest in which workers stop doing extra work and just do the minimum that is required of them. *Staff in Liverpool will start an overtime ban and a work-to-rule as part of a campaign against new allowances.*

work week, work weeks
NC The **work week** is the period of time during which you are working in your job; used in American English. *The contract includes a 35-hour work week... They complained of seven-day work weeks, no time off, racial harassment.*

world /wɜːld/ **worlds**
1 N SING The **world** is the planet that we live on. *He attempted to sail round the world. ...the growth in world population.*
2 N SING The **world** is also all the people who live on this planet. *The world must deal with all the weapons of mass destruction on an equal footing... Hungary appealed to world opinion to protest at the planned demolitions... He described the war as a threat to world peace. ...a challenge to world leaders.*
3 N+N **World** is used to describe someone or something that is one of the best or most important of its kind. *This book is a world classic... She became a world figure.*
4 NC+SUPP Someone's **world** is their life, experiences,

and the relationships they have with other people. *Look, Howard, we're in different worlds now... They were letting me into their world.*
5 NC+SUPP A particular **world** is a field of activity, and the people involved in it. *They are well-known names in the film world. ...the world of art. ...in the topsy-turvy world of Soviet economics.*
6 NC+SUPP You can refer to a particular group of countries or a particular period in history as the Western **World**, the Arab **World**, the Ancient **World**, and so on. *...the leaders of the Islamic World. ...the unrest in the Arab and Muslim Worlds.* ● See also **Third World**.
7 N SING You can refer to the state of being alive as this **world** and to a state of existence after death as the next **world**. *He is heading for the next world, the way he drinks.*
8 NC+SUPP You can refer to a group of living things as the animal **world**, the plant **world**, or the insect **world**. *The petunia is the laboratory rat of the plant world, we always experiment on it first... The microscope has given us a window on the tiny world of cells and bacteria.*
9 NC You can refer to another planet as a **world**. *...an alien world.*
● **World** is used in these phrases. ● You can use **in the world** with superlatives to emphasize that the thing you are talking about is the most important, significant, or extreme of its kind. *...one of the richest treasures in the world... To them housework was the most important activity in the world. ...the simplest job in the world.* ● **The world over** means throughout the world. *She has delighted and entranced opera lovers the world over... This town is holy to Christians the world over.* ● If someone has or wants **the best of both worlds**, they have or want all the benefits from two different situations, without the disadvantages. *They seem to want the best of both worlds: the freedom to pursue an independent policy, and the ability to rely on us when they need aid... What we have, then, is the best of both worlds—a better understanding of the UN, and the freedom to express our opinions.* ● If you **think the world of** someone or something, you admire them very much. ● If something **does you the world of good**, it makes you feel better; an informal expression. *A bit of fresh air will do you the world of good.* ● If **there is a world of difference** between two things, they are very different from each other. *There's a world of difference between day-old bread and a two-hour-old hamburger.*

world-class
ADJ ATTRIB A **world-class** sports player or musician is one of the best in the world at what they do. *...a world-class cricketer. ...giving school children the chance to make music with a world-class orchestra.*

world-famous
ADJ Someone or something that is **world-famous** is known about by people all over the world. *...a world-famous physicist... Our programme became world-famous, and people were actually flying into the area to listen.*

worldly /wɜːldli/
1 ADJ **Worldly** refers to things relating to the ordinary activities of life, rather than to spiritual things. *Coleridge had experienced a conversion and put aside worldly things... He fell seriously into debt by indulging himself in worldly pleasures.*
2 ADJ ATTRIB You can refer to someone's possessions as their **worldly** goods or possessions; a literary use. *Some huddled in sleeping bags, all their worldly goods beside them in supermarket trolleys.*
3 ADJ Someone who is **worldly** is experienced and knowledgeable about the practical aspects of life rather than about spiritual things. *He's thought to be too worldly for what is essentially a religious position.*

worldly-wise
ADJ Someone who is **worldly-wise** is experienced and knowledgeable about life, and is not often shocked or impressed by anything; a literary word. *In the final song, a worldly-wise response meets the request for a place where love lasts forever... To the worldly-wise, there is nothing surprising in the idea of a payment to*

accompany the sale of a public company.

World Series

N PROP In the United States, the **World Series** is an annual series of games that is held between the winners of the two major baseball leagues to decide the overall champions. *The Reds took the lead in the 1990 World Series by shutting out the Oakland Athletics 7-0 in the series opener in Cincinnati.*

world war, world wars

NCorNU A **world war** is a war involving countries from all over the world. *...the First World War... I do worry about world war breaking out.*

world-weary

ADJ A **world-weary** person no longer feels excited or enthusiastic about anything. *'I fear, young man,' said one world-weary politician, 'that you are wasting your time.'*

worldwide /wɜːldwaɪd/

ADV or ADJ **Worldwide** means happening throughout the world. *This move made headlines worldwide last year. ...in 1930, during the worldwide economic depression.*

worm /wɜːm/ **worms, worming, wormed**

1 NC A **worm** is a small thin animal without bones or legs. *The soil is crawling with worms... The adult worm lives in a nodule beneath the skin.*
2 N PL If animals or people have **worms**, worms are living as parasites in their intestines. *...a drug used to eliminate worms in cattle.*
3 If you **worm** your way somewhere, you move there slowly and with difficulty. *He wormed his way forward.*
worm out PHRASAL VERB If you **worm** information **out** of someone, you gradually persuade them to give you it. *The truth had been wormed out of him by his lawyers.*

worm-eaten

ADJ Something that is **worm-eaten** has been damaged by insects which have made holes in it. *...an old, worm-eaten piece of furniture.*

wormwood /wɜːmwʊd/

1 NU **Wormwood** is a bitter-tasting plant that is used to make medicines and alcoholic drinks.
2 NU **Wormwood** is used to refer to an experience which causes extreme bitterness, resentment, or regret. *The performances at the National must be wormwood to disappointed members... All his posturing before his friends was wormwood now.*

wormy /wɜːmi/

ADJ Something that is **wormy** is covered with worms or full of worms, for example because of neglect or decay. *...the wormy floor of the shack... It's a big apple, but probably wormy.*

worn /wɔːn/

1 **Worn** is the past participle of **wear**.
2 ADJ **Worn** things are damaged or thin because they are old and have been used a lot. *...the worn carpet... Look out for anything on the car that's bent or worn.*
3 ADJ Someone who is **worn** looks old and tired. *He lay on his bed, looking pinched and worn.*

worn-out

1 ADJ **Worn-out** things are too old, damaged, or out-of-date to be used any more. *...a worn-out sofa. ...obsolete and worn-out theories and systems.*
2 ADJ If you are **worn-out**, you are extremely tired, and feel no enthusiasm for anything. *You look worn-out... He would walk past the sick, worn-out bodies slouched against the buildings near his office.*
3 ADJ You can use **worn-out** to refer to opinions or attitudes that are out of date, or which you have heard many times before. *They will no longer be able to fall back on the worn-out clichés of the past... He complained that the authorities had rehashed their worn-out allegations against Vietnam.*

worried /wʌrɪd/

ADJ If you are **worried**, you are unhappy because you keep thinking about a problem or something unpleasant that might happen. *People are becoming increasingly worried about pollution... I was worried that she'd say no.*

worrier /wʌrɪə/ **worriers**

NC A **worrier** is someone who spends too much time

thinking about problems or unpleasant things. *He was a worrier by nature.*

worry /wʌri/ **worries, worrying, worried**

1 V, V+*about*, or V-REPORT If you **worry**, you keep thinking about a problem or about something unpleasant that might happen. *Don't worry, Andrew, you can do it... People worry about the safety of nuclear energy... I worried that when I got back he wouldn't be there.*
2 VO If someone or something **worries** you, they cause you to worry. *Terry was worried by the challenge... It worried him to think that Sylvie was alone.*
3 VO If you **worry** someone with a problem, you disturb or upset them by telling them about it. *Why worry her when it's all over?*
4 NU **Worry** is the state or feeling of anxiety and unhappiness caused by a problem or by thinking about something unpleasant that might happen. *She would be free from all financial worry... Bad housing is their main source of worry.*
5 NC A **worry** is a problem that you keep thinking about and that makes you unhappy. *The cost of fuel is a major worry for old people... I don't have any worries.*

worrying /wʌriɪŋ/

ADJ Something that is **worrying** causes you a lot of worry. *...a very worrying situation... She asked me a worrying question.*

worse /wɜːs/

1 ADJ **Worse** is the comparative of **bad**. *I have even worse news for you... The noise is getting worse.*
2 ADV **Worse** is also the comparative of **badly**. *Some people ski worse than others.*
3 ADJ PRED If someone who is ill gets **worse**, they become more ill. *You'll get worse if you don't take this medicine.*
● **Worse** is used in these phrases. ● If someone or something is **none the worse** for something, they are not harmed by it. *The children had gone to bed very late but they were none the worse for it... They were looking none the worse for their night spent in jail.*
● If something happens **for the worse**, the situation becomes more unpleasant or difficult. *There were constant changes, usually for the worse.*

worsen /wɜːsn/ **worsens, worsening, worsened**

V-ERG If a situation **worsens** or if something **worsens** it, it becomes more difficult, unpleasant, or unacceptable. *The weather steadily worsened... Sanitary conditions in the camps have worsened considerably... He claimed that the release of the French hostages would only worsen the plight of the Britons still being held... Economic sanctions would only worsen the situation.* ◆ **worsening** ADJ ATTRIB *The government's popularity is not helped by the worsening economic situation... The proposal comes at a time of worsening relations between the two countries.*

worse off

1 ADJ PRED Someone who is **worse off** has less money than before or less than someone else. *This budget would leave taxpayers far worse off... There are lots of people worse off than us... The black underclass are, if anything, worse off than before.*
2 ADJ PRED To be **worse off** also means to be in a more unpleasant situation than before or than someone else. *You believe the world to be worse off because of Kennedy's death.*

worship /wɜːʃɪp/ **worships, worshipping, worshipped**; spelt **worshiping, worshiped** in American English.

1 V O or V If you **worship** a god, you show your respect to the god, for example by saying prayers. *I knelt down and worshipped the Lord... In Bangladesh, the New Year is marked by worshipping the great river Ganges... The riot spilled over to the Western Wall, where thousands of Jews were worshipping.* ► Also NU *...freedom of worship. ...devil worship.*
2 VO If you **worship** someone or something, you love them or admire them very much. *Mrs Thatcher is revered, some would say worshipped, by the Conservative faithful. ...young teenagers who worshipped their screen idol.* ► Also NU *He has become a figure of hero worship here.*
3 TITLE **Your Worship** and **His Worship** are respectful

ways of addressing or referring to a magistrate or a mayor.

worshipper /wɜːʃɪpə/ **worshippers**; spelt **worshiper** in American English.

NC A **worshipper** is someone who believes in and worships a god. ...*shoes left by worshippers who had gone into the mosque... He is alleged to have urged worshippers to demonstrate against the government.*

worst /wɜːst/

1 ADJ **Worst** is the superlative of **bad.** ...*the worst thing which ever happened to me.*

2 ADV **Worst** is also the superlative of **badly.** *This University was the worst hit by Government spending cuts.*

3 N SING If you talk about a particular situation as the **worst**, you mean that it is the most unpleasant or the most unsatisfactory that you can imagine. *The worst is over.*

● **Worst** is used in these phrases. ● You use **at worst** when considering a situation in the most unfavourable or most pessimistic way. *At worst they are looked upon as an irritation... He was described as forceful at best, ruthless at worst.* ● If you say that something might happen **if the worst comes to the worst**, you mean that it might happen if the situation develops in the most unfavourable way. *If the worst comes to the worst I'll have to sell the house.*

worst- /wɜːst-/

PREFIX **Worst-** is used with a past participle to say that a person, place, or thing in an unpleasant or dangerous situation is the one that is most seriously or badly affected by it. *It is mostly livestock that have been dying in the worst-hit areas... He was refused permission to visit the worst-affected areas... Some districts in the city are undoubtedly among the poorest, worst-housed, most deprived places in Europe.*

worst-case

ADJ ATTRIB **Worst-case** is used to describe the likely outcome of situation if it is considered in the most unfavourable, pessimistic way; used in American English. *Well, the worst-case scenario is that the President could face political problems at home... The cost of bailing out the loan companies is likely to exceed Bush's worst-case estimation... The predictions were based on worst-case possibilities, such as the destruction of Saudi oilfields.*

worsted /wʊstɪd/

NU **Worsted** is a kind of thick woollen cloth which is used to make clothes. ...*his favourite dark blue worsted suit.*

worst-ever

ADJ ATTRIB **Worst-ever** is used to say that a situation is the most unpleasant, unfavourable, or harmful of its kind that there has ever been. ...*Britain's worst-ever air disaster... In October, the worst-ever trade figures were recorded... It was his worst-ever performance in front of a home crowd.*

worth /wɜːθ/

1 PREP If something is **worth** an amount of money, it can be sold for that amount or has that value. ...*a two-bedroom house worth 50,000 pounds... The contract was worth 2.5 billion dollars.*

2 NU You use **worth** to indicate that the value of something is equal to a particular amount of money. For example, fifty dollars' **worth** of equipment can be bought for fifty dollars. *Chile has proposed 700 million dollars' worth of reductions in every area of government spending.*

3 NU Someone's **worth** is their value, usefulness, or importance; a formal use. *This job has robbed me of all worth.* ► Also ADJ PRED *No man can say what another man is worth.*

4 NU You can use **worth** to say how long something will last. For example, a week's **worth** of food is the amount of food that will last you for a week. *They traded in their ration cards for a small amount of cash and a month's worth of wheat rations.*

5 PREP You use **worth** to say that something is so enjoyable or useful that it is a good thing to do or have. *The building is well worth a visit... They're expensive, but they're worth it... This film's really*

worth seeing... The risk is worth taking.

6 If an action or activity is **worth** your **while**, it will be helpful or useful to you. *It will be well worth your while to track down these treasures.*

worthless /wɜːθləs/

ADJ Something or someone that is **worthless** is of no real use or value. *The goods are often worthless by the time they arrive... This made the treaty worthless... His brother is a worthless fool.*

worthwhile /wɜːθwaɪl/

ADJ If something is **worthwhile**, it is enjoyable or useful, and worth the time, money, or effort spent on it. *A visit to Dorset will always be worthwhile.*

worthy /wɜːði/ **worthier, worthiest**

ADJ Someone or something that is **worthy** of respect, support, or admiration deserves it because of their qualities or abilities; a literary word. *Their cause is worthy of our continued support... He was a worthy winner.*

would /wəd, wʊd/. **Would** is sometimes considered to be the past form of **will**, but in this dictionary the two words are dealt with separately.

1 MODAL If someone said or thought that something **would** happen, they said or thought that it was going to happen. *She said a similar invitation would be extended to Nelson Mandela... I felt confident that everything would be all right... He made me promise that I would never break the law.*

2 MODAL You use **would** when you are referring to the result or effect of a possible situation. *If you can help me I would be very grateful... Many junior doctors could be suffering sleep deprivation, which would affect their ability to make decisions... The cost for each helicopter would drop if more were ordered.*

3 MODAL You use **would** to talk about the possible effects of an imaginary situation. *A flying bumblebee as big as a man would need 120 chocolate bars an hour... He's obviously been under appalling strain, as any of us would be.*

4 MODAL If you say that you **would** do something, you mean you are willing to do it. *He confirmed there had been an attack but would give no details... Though we were as rude as possible, she wouldn't go.*

5 MODAL If you **would** like to do or have something, you want to do it or have it. *Posy said she'd love to stay... Would you like a drink?*

6 MODAL You use **would** in polite questions and requests. *Would you tell her that Adrian phoned?... Put the light on, Bryan, would you?*

7 MODAL You say that someone **would** do something when it is typical of them and you are critical of it. *'Of course you would say that,' says Mrs Callendar... 'He's backed out of it.'—'He would.'*

8 MODAL If you say that someone or something **would** do something or **would** be in a particular state, you mean that they often used to do that thing or used to be in that state. *I used to meet her and she would say 'Can't stop. I must get home.'... Sometimes they'd wave at us.*

9 MODAL You use **would** think or **would have** thought to express your opinion in a polite and tentative way. *I would think that in our climate we might have a few problems... I would have thought that his chief asset was his enthusiasm... I would also imagine that it's going to be a long process.*

10 MODAL If you talk about what **would have** happened if a possible event had occurred, you are talking about the result or effect of that event. *If the bosses had known that he voted Liberal, he would have got the sack... They believed their lives would have been in danger if they had continued... Some of them would have liked a full coalition government.*

11 MODAL If you say that someone **would have** liked or preferred something, you mean that they wanted to do it or have it but were unable to. *I would have liked a year more... He would have liked Solidarity to be just a trade union, he said.*

would-be /wʊdbiː/

ADJ ATTRIB You use **would-be** to describe what someone wants to do or become. For example, if someone is a **would-be** writer, they want to become a writer. ...*the expulsion of dissidents and would-be* *emigrants... He ordered his crew to overcome the would-be hijacker.*

wouldn't /wʊdnt/
Wouldn't is the usual spoken form of 'would not'. *It wouldn't be safe.*

would've /wʊdəv/
Would've is a spoken form of 'would have', especially when 'have' is an auxiliary verb. *It would've meant leaving home.*

wound, wounds, wounding, wounded; pronounced /wuːnd/ for the meanings in paragraphs 1 to 3, and /waʊnd/ for the meaning in paragraph 4.
1 NC A **wound** is a cut in part your body, especially one caused by a weapon or a sharp instrument. *The most important thing is to clean the wound quickly... The wound on his face was burning... He was suffering from a leg wound.*
2 VO If someone **wounds** you, they damage your body using a weapon. *A large car bomb has killed at least fifteen people and wounded as many as forty-five... Their soldiers shot one man dead and wounded several other people.*
3 VO If you **are wounded** by what someone says or does, you feel hurt and upset; a literary use. *She had been grievously wounded by his words.*
4 **Wound** is also the past tense and past participle of most senses of the verb **wind**.

wounded /wuːndɪd/
1 ADJ A **wounded** person has been injured in some part of their body in a fight or an accident. *One wounded man was arrested, but the two others ran off... The gunman walked towards the wounded policeman.*
2 N PL The **wounded** are people who have been injured in an accident or battle. *...her tireless and unselfish dedication in nursing the wounded during the Crimean war. ...helping the wounded and dying.*

wound up /waʊnd ʌp/
ADJ If someone is **wound up**, they are very tense and nervous, often because they have been under too much pressure. *You get aggravated, and you get wound up.*

wove /wəʊv/
Wove is the past tense of **weave**.

woven /wəʊvn/
Woven is the past participle of **weave**.

wow /waʊ/ **wows, wowing, wowed;** an informal word.
1 You say '**wow**' when you are impressed or pleased by something. *Wow! What a view!... When a technical innovation is introduced, the farmer doesn't just sit down and say, 'Wow, that's good'.*
2 VO If something **wows** people, it impresses them because it is so good. *She's still wowing the audiences on her world tour with her controversial stage antics... Mike was wowed by the enormous statue of Abe Simon.*

WPC /dʌblju:pi:si:/ **WPCs**
TITLE In Britain, **WPC** is used in front of the name of a female police officer of the lowest rank. **WPC** is an abbreviation for 'woman police constable'. *...WPC Williams.*

wpm
wpm is a written abbreviation for 'words per minute'; used after a number to indicate the speed at which a person can type or take shorthand. *A typing speed of 40 wpm is required for both posts.*

wrack /ræk/. See **rack**.

wraith /reɪθ/ **wraiths**
NC A **wraith** is a ghost; a literary word. *She moved through the soft light like a wraith.*

wrangle /ræŋgl/ **wrangles, wrangling, wrangled**
1 V-RECIP If you **wrangle** with someone, you argue with them angrily, often about something unimportant. *For years, opposition politicians have been wrangling and squabbling... Congress continued to wrangle over crime legislation... Senior ministers trooped in, to wrangle with the Chief Treasurer about spending plans.* ◆ **wrangling** NU *The wrangling continues tomorrow, mediated by Mr Cordovez... Political wrangling has replaced personal feuds.*
2 NC A **wrangle** is an argument that is not very important, but is difficult to settle. *The two papers are involved in a legal wrangle over the published*

memoirs. ...unseemly wrangles over pay and conditions.

wrap /ræp/ **wraps, wrapping, wrapped**
1 VO If you **wrap** something, you fold paper or cloth tightly round it to cover it completely, for example in order to protect it or so that you can give it to someone as a present. *I wrapped the ring in my handkerchief... The book was wrapped in brown paper.*
2 VOA When you **wrap** something such as a piece of paper or cloth round another thing, you put it round it. *A handkerchief was wrapped around his left hand.*
3 VOA If you **wrap** your arms or fingers around something, you put them tightly around it. *He wrapped his arms around me.*
4 If you **keep** something **under wraps**, you keep it secret, often until you are ready to announce it at some time in the future. *They confirmed the Minister's resignation, but the reasons are being kept under wraps... So far details of this speech have been kept under tight wraps.*
5 See also **wrapping**.

wrap up PHRASAL VERB 1 If you **wrap** something **up**, you fold paper or cloth tightly around it to cover it. *Could you wrap the vase up?* 2 If you **wrap up**, you put warm clothes on. *Wrap up well; it's a cold night tonight.* 3 If you **wrap up** a job or an agreement, you complete it in a satisfactory way; an informal use. *There have been some reports that it could be wrapped up by the end of January.*

wrap-around
ADJ ATTRIB A **wrap-around** skirt is one that you put on by tying it round your body rather than by stepping into it.

wrapped up
ADJ PRED+*in* If you are **wrapped up** in a person or thing, you are giving them most of your attention; an informal expression. *All the household are completely wrapped up in the baby... He was always wrapped up in his work.*

wrapper /ræpə/ **wrappers**
NC A **wrapper** is a piece of paper, plastic, or foil which covers and protects something that you buy. *...the wrappers on their food packets. ...safety sealed anti-contamination wrappers.*

wrapping /ræpɪŋ/ **wrappings**
NU or NC **Wrapping** is paper or plastic used to cover and protect something. *It will replace its foam sandwich boxes with paper wrapping. ...the wrappings of a cigarette packet.*

wrapping paper
NU **Wrapping paper** is special pretty paper used for wrapping presents.

wrath /rɒθ/
NU **Wrath** is great anger; a literary word. *...a man who attracted the wrath of the United States... If you touch the churches of God, you unleash the wrath of the nation.*

wreak /riːk/ **wreaks, wreaking, wreaked** or **wrought**. For the meaning in paragraph 3, **wrought** is the only form that is used. A literary word.
1 VO If something **wreaks** havoc or damage, it causes it. *These chemicals can wreak havoc on crops... The civil war has wreaked havoc on the economy. ...the devastation wrought by the earthquake.*
2 VO If you **wreak** revenge or vengeance on someone, you do something to harm them, because they have harmed you. *They are intent on wreaking vengeance on anybody who is a member of that community.*
3 VO If something has **wrought** changes on something, it has caused them. *It was unprepared for changes wrought in the 80s... The computer has, however, wrought a vast change.*

wreath /riːθ/ **wreaths**
NC A **wreath** is a ring of flowers and leaves which is put onto a grave as a sign of remembrance for the dead person. *He also laid a wreath at a memorial to Japanese POWs... On the following day, the King attended a wreath-laying ceremony at the grave of the unknown warrior.*

wreathe /riːð/ **wreathes, wreathing, wreathed;** a literary word.
1 VO If one thing is **wreathed** in another thing,

especially mist or smoke, it is surrounded by it. *The dawn sky was pale, the sun was wreathed in mist... Smoke wreathed the Colonel's head like a halo.*
2 VO If something **is wreathed** in flowers or leaves, it has a circle or chain of flowers or leaves put round it. *...hats wreathed in artificial flowers. ...a cross wreathed with roses.*
3 If you say that someone is **wreathed in smiles**, you mean that they are smiling a lot. *The photograph shows the Irish deputy Prime Minister, his face wreathed in smiles, despite being sacked by his close ally, the Prime Minister.*

wreck /rek/ **wrecks, wrecking, wrecked**
1 VO If someone **wrecks** something, they break it or spoil it in some way. *I wrecked a good stereo by not following the instructions properly... I'm sorry if I wrecked your weekend.* ♦ **wrecked** ADJ *Piles of wrecked cars took up most of the space.*
2 VO If a ship **is wrecked**, it is damaged so much that it sinks. *...Spanish vessels that had been wrecked off the North American coast.*
3 NC A **wreck** is a plane, car, or ship which has been destroyed in an accident. *All around were the wrecks of previous crashes... The seabed where the wreck lies is level and rocky.*
4 NC If someone is a **wreck**, they are very unhealthy or exhausted; an informal use. *If you work like this you'll end up a wreck.* ● See also **nervous wreck**.

wreckage /rekɪdʒ/
NU When a plane, car, or building has been destroyed, you can refer to what remains as the **wreckage**. *Experts arrived to examine the wreckage of a cargo plane... Traces of the high explosive Semtex have been found in the wreckage.*

wrecker /rekə/ **wreckers**
1 NC A **wrecker** is someone who destroys or spoils something. *His track record suggests he is a political wrecker.*
2 NC A **wrecker** is also a truck which can remove broken down vehicles or vehicles that are stuck somewhere. *A half-hour later the wrecker arrives.*

wren /ren/ **wrens**
NC A **wren** is a very small brown bird. There are several kinds of wren.

wrench /rentʃ/ **wrenches, wrenching, wrenched**
1 VOCorVOA If you **wrench** something that is fixed into a particular position, you pull or twist it violently. *He was trying to wrench my button off... I wrenched the door open.*
2 VO If you **wrench** a limb or one of your joints, you twist it and injure it. *She wrenched her arm badly.*
3 VOA If you **wrench** your eyes or mind away from something, you make a great effort to stop looking at it or thinking about it. *I tried to wrench my gaze away from the appalling sight.*
4 N SING If leaving someone or something is a **wrench**, you feel very sad about it. *He said his retirement from the trades union movement was obviously a wrench for him.*
5 NC A **wrench** is an adjustable metal tool used for tightening or loosening nuts and bolts. *If you have a large enough wrench, you could grab that big nut on the front of the crankshaft and turn that.*
6 NC A **wrench** is the same as a **spanner**; used in American English. *If you have a large enough wrench, you could grab that big nut on the front of the crankshaft.*
7 If you **throw a wrench in** something such as a deal or arrangement, you do something which seriously damages it; used in American English. *The federal government has thrown a wrench in the multi-billion dollar Japanese buy-out of an American company.*

wrenching /rentʃɪŋ/
ADJ If something you see or experience is **wrenching**, it makes you feel deep sadness and sometimes a sense of loss. *Singing a song like 'Deliver Me' in concert is sometimes very wrenching for me... It was so absolutely wrenching; it was impossible not to feel sympathy.*

wrest /rest/ **wrests, wresting, wrested**; a literary word.
1 VOA If you **wrest** something away from someone

who is holding it, you take it from them by pulling it violently or by twisting it. *He wrested the knife from her.*
2 VOAorVO If you **wrest** something such as power from someone else, you take it from them with an effort in order to use it instead of them. *He will try to wrest control of the Communist movement in Russia from the hardline clique... Each side attempts to wrest the political initiative.*

wrestle /resl/ **wrestles, wrestling, wrestled**
1 V-RECIP If you **wrestle** with someone, you fight them by forcing them into painful positions or throwing them to the ground, rather than by hitting them. Some people wrestle as a sport. *John wrestled with the intruder... The males wrestle and fight... They ran, jumped, threw the discus and javelin, and wrestled.*
2 V+with When you **wrestle** with a problem, you try to deal with it. *That's the philosophical problem with which the British are wrestling... Almost every country in the region has been wrestling with the problem of unpayable debt.*

wrestler /reslə/ **wrestlers**
NC A **wrestler** is someone who wrestles as a sport. *The average wrestler carries twice or sometimes three times the weight of you or I.*

wrestling /reslɪŋ/
NU **Wrestling** is a sport in which two people wrestle and try to throw each other to the ground. *They took four golds in the wrestling events.*

wretch /retʃ/ **wretches**
NC A **wretch** is someone who is wicked or unfortunate; a literary word. *...the wretch who shot the President... The poor wretch groaned.*

wretched /retʃɪd/
1 ADJ Someone who is **wretched** is very unhappy, ill, or unfortunate; a formal use. *She spent the day in her room lying down and feeling wretched.*
2 ADJ ATTRIB You use **wretched** to describe something or someone that you dislike or feel angry with; an informal use. *I had to drag the wretched animal all the way... I hate this wretched system.*

wriggle /rɪgl/ **wriggles, wriggling, wriggled**
1 VorVO If you **wriggle** a part of your body, you twist and turn it with quick movements. *The children were wriggling in anticipation... She wriggled her toes.*
2 VAorVOA If you **wriggle** somewhere, you move there by twisting and turning your body. *We had to wriggle under the fence.*

wriggle out of PHRASAL VERB If you **wriggle out of** doing something that you do not want to do, you manage to avoid doing it; an informal expression. *I can't wriggle out of accompanying my parents to Europe.*

wring /rɪŋ/ **wrings, wringing, wrung**
1 VO When you **wring** a wet cloth, you squeeze the water out of it by twisting it tightly. *Rinse thoroughly, wring, and dry away from direct heat or sunlight.*
2 VO When someone **wrings** their hands, they hold them together and twist and turn them because they are very upset but feel they can do nothing. *He looked dazed and wrung his hands.*
3 VO If someone **wrings** a bird's neck, they kill the bird by twisting its neck. If one person is angry with another, they sometimes threaten to **wring** their neck. *Earl said 'I'm going to catch him and wring that scrawny neck'.*

wring out PHRASAL VERB 1 When you **wring out** a wet cloth, you squeeze the water out of it by twisting it strongly. *He stripped off his heavy wet trousers, wrung them out and spread them to dry along the fire guard.* 2 If you **wring** something **out** of someone, you manage to make them give it to you even though they do not want to. *Meanwhile Helmut Kohl had wrung an important concession from Mikhail Gorbachev.*

wringing wet
ADJ If a piece of clothing is **wringing wet**, it is extremely wet.

wrinkle /rɪŋkl/ **wrinkles, wrinkling, wrinkled**
1 NC **Wrinkles** are lines which form on someone's face as they grow old. *His small eyes were surrounded by many wrinkles.*
2 V-ERG If something **wrinkles** or if you **wrinkle** it, it

gets folds or lines in it. *Clean the surface well or the paint might wrinkle and peel... He's always telling me that the sun will wrinkle my skin.*
3 VO When you **wrinkle** your nose or forehead, you tighten the muscles in your face so that the skin folds. *He wrinkled his nose. 'What an awful smell.'*

wrinkled /rɪŋkld/
1 ADJ If your skin is **wrinkled**, it has wrinkles as a result of old age. *...a very old woman with a wrinkled face.*
2 If something is **wrinkled**, it has uneven folds or lines in it. *She looked to make sure her dress wasn't wrinkled.*

wrist /rɪst/ **wrists**
NC Your **wrist** is the part of your body between your hand and arm which bends when you move your hand. *The team have lost their captain Bleddyn Bowen with a wrist injury... It is usually fastened around the wrist.*

wristwatch /rɪstwɒtʃ/ **wristwatches**
NC A **wristwatch** is a watch with a strap which you wear round your wrist. *...a cheap quartz wristwatch.*

writ /rɪt/ **writs**
NC A **writ** is a legal document that orders a person to do a particular thing. *A writ has been issued against the Secretary General... The Committee succeeded in serving a writ on the SWAPO leader Sam Nujoma.*

write /raɪt/ **writes, writing, wrote, written**
1 VO, V-QUOTE, or V When you **write** something, you use a pen or pencil to produce words, letters, or numbers on a surface. *Write the appropriate letter on the label... 'These people,' he wrote, 'gave a great service to the cause of peace.'... I'm learning to read and write.*
2 VO If you **write** something such as a book, a poem, or a piece of music, you create it and record it on paper. *I have been asked to write a biography of Dylan Thomas... She has just written a book on the subject.*
3 V Someone who **writes** creates books, stories, or articles, usually for publication. *She writes on anthropology.*
4 VO+to, V+to, VOO, or V When you **write** to someone or **write** them a letter, you give them information, ask them something, or express your feelings in a letter. *She wrote a note to the chief of police... In 1825 Beethoven wrote to the Royal Philharmonic Society in London promising the work... She wrote me a letter from Singapore... I've written to invite him here.*
5 VO or VOO When you **write** something such as a cheque or a receipt, or **write** it out, you put the necessary information on it and sign it. *I remember writing a cheque for £100... I went to write out the death certificate... I'll write you a prescription.*
6 See also **writing, written**.

write back PHRASAL VERB If you **write back** to someone who has sent you a letter, you write them a letter in reply. *He wrote back accepting our offer.*
write down PHRASAL VERB When you **write** something **down**, you record it on a piece of paper using a pen or pencil. *I wrote down what the boy said.*
write in PHRASAL VERB 1 If you **write in** to an organization, you send them a letter. *People have been phoning and writing in asking for advice.* 2 In the United States, if people want to vote for someone whose name is not printed on a ballot paper, they sometimes **write in** that person's name on the paper themselves. *They are urging voters to flock to the polls to write in the name of one person of note.*
write into PHRASAL VERB If a rule or detail is **written into** a contract or agreement, it is included in it when the contract or agreement is made. *The new arrangements have been written into the agreement.*
write off PHRASAL VERB 1 If you **write off** an amount of money you have lost, you accept that you will never get it back. *The bank agreed to write off its loan of 800 thousand dollars.* 2 If you **write off** to a company or organization, you send them a letter asking for something. *I was writing off to various places asking about work opportunities.* 3 If you **write off** a plan or project, you accept that it will not be successful and you do not continue to support it. *It was too early, he maintained, to write off a peaceful solution.* 4 If you

write someone **off**, you decide that they are unimportant or that they have failed. *You will be written off as a hysterical woman... Everybody, all the political experts, wrote us off.*
write out PHRASAL VERB If you **write out** something such as a report or a list, you write it on paper. *I always write out a shopping list.*
write up PHRASAL VERB If you **write up** something that has been done or said, you record it on paper in a neat and complete form. *These are notes that you are going to write up afterwards... The results were written up into a report.* ● See also **write-up**.

write-in, write-ins
ADJ ATTRIB In the United States, a **write-in** vote is a vote that is cast by writing the name of the candidate that you support on the ballot paper, because their name is not already printed there. *Write-in votes prevented him from winning a majority.*

write-off, write-offs
NC If a vehicle is a **write-off**, it is so badly damaged in an accident that it is not worth repairing. *Their car was a write-off.*

writer /raɪtə/ **writers**
1 NC A **writer** is a person whose job is writing books, stories, or articles. *...the writer and critic, Hilary Spurling.*
2 NC+SUPP The **writer** of a particular article, story, or other piece of writing is the person who wrote it. *I arranged an appointment with the writer of the letter.*

writer's cramp
NU **Writer's cramp** is a feeling of uncomfortable stiffness in your hand which you can get as a result of writing continuously for a long time.

write-up, write-ups
NC A **write-up** is an article in a newspaper or magazine, in which someone gives their opinion of a play or a new product. *They performed quite a bit in the East and got a big write-up in People magazine.*

writhe /raɪð/ **writhes, writhing, writhed**
V If you **writhe**, you twist and turn your body violently backwards and forwards, usually because you are in great pain. *He writhed in agony.*

writing /raɪtɪŋ/ **writings**
1 NU **Writing** is something that has been written or printed. *Put the papers face down so that the writing cannot be seen... You must get the offer in writing.*
2 NU You can refer to any piece of written work as **writing**, especially when you are considering the style of language used in it. *...some brilliant and very witty writing.*
3 NU **Writing** is also the activity of writing, especially writing books for money. *I hate writing and I'm not very good at it.*
4 NU Your **writing** is the way that you write with a pen or pencil, which can usually be recognized as belonging to you. *I can't read your writing. ...small, neat, forward sloping writing.*
5 N PL An author's **writings** are all the things that he or she has written. *His political writings remind me of those of Sartre.*

writing desk, writing desks
NC A **writing desk** is a piece of furniture with drawers and an area for keeping paper, pens and ink in, and a surface on which you can rest your paper while writing. *...a lady's writing desk with two chairs.*

writing materials
N PL **Writing materials** are pens, pencils, ink, paper, and other things which you use for writing.

writing paper
NU **Writing paper** is paper for writing letters on. It is usually of good, smooth quality. *To all intents and purposes, the paper is identical to ordinary printing or writing paper.*

written /rɪtn/
1 **Written** is the past participle of **write**.
2 ADJ A **written** test or piece of work is one which involves writing rather than doing an experiment or giving spoken answers. *The group proposed a mixture of written tests and assessment by teachers. ...written exams.*
3 ADJ ATTRIB A **written** agreement, rule, or law has been officially written down. *No written agreement*

currently existed... I will send written confirmation.
written word
N SING You use **the written word** to refer to language expressed in writing. *When nobler examples of the written word were not to hand he read comics. ...the power of the written word.*
wrong /rɒŋ/ **wrongs, wronging, wronged**
1 ADJ PRED If there is something **wrong**, there is something unsatisfactory about the situation or thing that you are talking about. *The front door was unlocked—something was wrong... I asked what was wrong... There was nothing wrong with his eyesight.*
2 ADJ or ADV **Wrong** means unsuitable or incorrect. *I'm afraid I'll make the wrong decision... Her name was spelt wrong.* ◆ **wrongly** ADV *Many of us choose wrongly.*
3 ADJ ATTRIB If you choose the **wrong** thing or person, you make a mistake when you choose them, and do not choose the thing or person that you really want. *You are talking to the wrong people... He insisted, as he's done from the start, that the court had tried the wrong man.*
4 ADJ PRED If you are **wrong** about something, what you say or think about it is not correct. *We had to admit the possibility that we might be wrong.*
◆ **wrongly** ADV *She supposed, wrongly, that the other two agreed with her.*
5 ADJ If something that you do is **wrong**, it is bad or immoral. *You were wrong to speak to the newspapers first... Mrs Thatcher said there was nothing wrong with creating wealth.*
6 N U **Wrong** is used to refer to actions that are bad or immoral. *Any good parent feels strongly about right and wrong.*
7 N C A **wrong** is an unjust action or situation. *The Pope said he opposed confrontation and violence as a way of righting wrongs in the system. ...the wrongs done to the Tamil people. ...the argument concerns the rights and wrongs of going on strike.*
8 V O If someone **wrongs** you, they treat you in an unfair or unjust way; a literary use. *Russians identify with him as someone who has been wronged by the system.*
9 ADJ ATTRIB The **wrong** side of a piece of cloth or paper is the side which is intended to face inwards or downwards and not be seen.
● **Wrong** is used in these phrases. ● If you **get** something **wrong**, you make a mistake. *I think she got his name wrong.* ● If you **go wrong**, you make a mistake. *Where did I go wrong?* ● If something **goes wrong**, it stops working or is no longer successful. *Computers do go wrong... Things could still go wrong.* ● If something dangerous or secret gets into the **wrong hands**, it is obtained by people who will use it for illegal or harmful purposes. *There is no danger of these weapons falling into the wrong hands.* ● If you **are in the wrong**, what you are doing is not right. *The*

United States knows it is in the wrong and now says it made a mistake.
wrongdoer /rɒŋduːə/ **wrongdoers**
N C A **wrongdoer** is a person who does things that are immoral or illegal; a formal word. *Wrongdoers should be made to pay for their actions.*
wrongdoing /rɒŋduːɪŋ/ **wrongdoings**
N U or N C **Wrongdoing** is behaviour that is illegal or immoral; a formal word. *The bank has denied any wrongdoing. ...allegations of criminal wrongdoing.*
wrong-foot, wrong-foots, wrong-footing, wrong-footed
1 V O If you **wrong-foot** your opponent in a sports game, you cause your opponent to be off-balance by playing your shot in an unexpected way. *He was wrong-footed by a beautiful passing backhand.*
2 V O If you **wrong-foot** someone, you surprise and upset them by putting them into an embarrassing situation, often by asking a question that they cannot answer. *I tried to wrong-foot them with another question... It has to some extent wrong-footed NATO.*
wrongful /rɒŋfl/
ADJ ATTRIB A **wrongful** act is one regarded as illegal, immoral, or unfair; a formal word. *It led to the wrongful conviction of four motorists on drink-driving offences. ...wrongful dismissal.* ◆ **wrongfully** ADV *The workers were wrongfully dismissed.*
wrong-headed
ADJ A **wrong-headed** action is based on poor judgement although it is carried out in a very determined way. *Neil Kinnock thinks that such a challenge would be wrong-headed... The message is both wrong-headed and dangerous.*
wrote /rəʊt/
Wrote is the past tense of **write**.
wrought /rɔːt/
1 **Wrought** is a past tense and past participle of **wreak**.
2 ADJ ATTRIB **Wrought** metal has been made into a particular shape, usually a decorative one. *...wrought silver.*
wrought iron
N U **Wrought iron** is a pure type of iron that is formed into decorative shapes. *...a wrought iron gate.*
wrung /rʌŋ/
Wrung is the past tense and past participle of **wring**.
wry /raɪ/
1 ADJ If someone has a **wry** expression, it shows that they find a bad or difficult situation slightly amusing or ironic. *He came out with a wry smile on his face... She said this with a wry glance at me.* ◆ **wryly** ADV *My friend smiled wryly when he saw me.*
2 ADJ A **wry** remark or piece of writing refers to a bad or difficult situation in an amusing or ironic way. *On receipt of his insurance claim, there were some wry comments. ...his direct style of writing and wry humour.*

X x   Y y   Z z

X, x /ɛks/ **X's, x's**
1 NC **X** is the twenty-fourth letter of the English alphabet.
2 NU **X** is used to represent the name of a person or place, when you want to keep it secret. *She was always referred to as Miss X during the trial... I was born in X, a town somewhere in the south.*
3 You can use **x** or **X** to refer to a number, amount, person, or thing, when their value or identity is not important or cannot be specified. *...a house that will cost less than x number of pounds... They require X amount of steel for a building that size.*
4 In algebra, **x** is used as a symbol to represent a number whose value is not known. $y=x^2$.
5 In mathematics and any written calculations, **x** is used as a symbol for multiplication. When speaking, you usually say the word 'times', for example 'two times fourteen'. $...19 \times 3 = 57. ...2 \times 14.$
6 When writing down the size of something, you can use **x** in between two measurements, for example in between the length and breadth. When speaking you usually say the word 'by', for example 'four metres by ten metres'. *They were given the measurements, 12 feet × 8 feet... It's an enormous 3 × 8 metre torpedo-shaped tank.*
7 In sports, **x** is used in between the number of people taking part in a relay race and the distance that each person has to cover. When speaking you usually say the word 'by', for example 'the four by four hundred metres relay'. *West Germany began today's 3 × 10 kilometre Cross-Country with a narrow lead over Austria. ...the successful British 4 × 400 metres relay team.*
8 People sometimes write **x** on a map to mark a precise position that they want to refer to. *'Here's the map Aunt Jane,' she said competently. 'The picnic place is marked with an X.'*
9 You can write **x** to represent a kiss at the end of a letter. *See you soon, all my love, Jenny ×××.*

X chromosome /ɛks krəʊməsəʊm/ **X chromosomes**
NC In biology, an **X chromosome** is one of an identical pair of chromosomes found in a woman's cells, or one of a non-identical pair found in a man's cells. X chromosomes are associated with female characteristics. See also **Y chromosome**. *These diseases affect males because they only have one X chromosome.*

xenophobia /zɛnəfəʊbiə/
NU **Xenophobia** is a strong dislike or fear of people from other countries; a formal word. *...a report on racism and xenophobia... His particular brand of anti-immigrant xenophobia attracted a startling 15 per cent of the vote... The xenophobia issue is important.*

xenophobic /zɛnəfəʊbɪk/
ADJ Someone who is **xenophobic** shows a strong dislike or fear of people from other countries; a formal word. *The guerrillas are as fanatical and xenophobic as ever... He adopted a curiously xenophobic attitude for an educated man. ...strongly nationalist—even xenophobic—policies.*

Xerox /zɪərɒks/ **Xeroxes, Xeroxing, Xeroxed**
1 NC A **Xerox** or a **Xerox machine** is a machine that can make copies of pieces of paper with writing or pictures on them; **Xerox** is a trademark. *...if you possess a Xerox machine or a personal computer with a printer... The rooms are crammed with humming Xerox machines.*
2 NC A **Xerox** is also a copy of what is written or printed on a piece of paper, made by using a Xerox machine. *I enclose a Xerox of the letter. ...Xerox copies of the letter.*
3 VO If you **Xerox** a document, you make a copy of it using a Xerox machine. *That morning, Bernstein had Xeroxed copies of notes from reporters at the scene.*

Xmas
NU **Xmas** is used in informal written English to represent the word **Christmas**. *Happy Xmas!*

X-rated /ɛksreɪtɪd/
ADJ ATTRIB **X-rated** is used to describe films that contain a lot of sex or violence, and to describe cinemas which specialize in showing such films. *Many theatres refused to show X-rated movies... There are no adult bookshops there, nor X-rated cinemas. ...X-rated videotapes for rent.*

X-ray /ɛksreɪ/ **X-rays, X-raying, X-rayed**
1 NC **X-rays** are a type of radiation which can pass through most solid materials. X-rays can be produced by some stars, but can also be artificially produced by machines. *...the X-ray emission from these galaxies. ...a star, spinning about once a second and emitting X-rays.*
2 NC An **X-ray** is a picture of the inside of your body, which is made by sending X-rays through it and is used by doctors to check the condition of your bones or organs. *The chest X-ray showed enlargement of the heart... He agreed to go for an X-ray to see if the bone was broken. ...X-ray pictures of the man's stomach.*
3 VO If a doctor **X-rays** you, he or she takes a picture of the inside of your body using an X-ray machine. If a security officer **X-rays** you or your belongings, he or she uses an X-ray machine to search for illegal goods such as bombs or drugs. *Select your patients intelligently, X-ray them carefully and use the best equipment available... Suspected smugglers can be X-rayed... Each piece of luggage will be X-rayed before being loaded on board the plane.*

xylophone /zaɪləfəʊn/ **xylophones**
NC A **xylophone** is a musical instrument consisting of a row of wooden bars of different lengths. You play a xylophone by hitting the bars with special hammers. *Glenny plays marimba, tympani, xylophone, and many other percussion instruments. ...a large wooden xylophone.*

Y, y /waɪ/ **Y's, y's**
1 NC **Y** is the twenty-fifth letter of the English alphabet.
2 In algebra, **y** is used as a symbol to represent a number whose value is not known. *So you get $2x + y = 10$.*
3 N SING Americans sometimes refer to a YMCA or YWCA hostel as the **Y**. *It was at a concert at the 92nd Street Y... I took him to the Y.*

-y /-i/
SUFFIX **-y** is added to nouns, especially nouns referring

to substances, to form adjectives which indicate that one thing has the same quality or appearance as another, different thing. ...*spongy bread.* ...*her inky, chalky hand.*

yacht /jɒt/ **yachts**
NC A **yacht** is a boat with sails or a motor, used for racing or for pleasure trips. *They were forced to remain on board the yacht.* ...*fur coats, fancy motor cars and private yachts.* ...*a yacht race between Spain and England.*

yachting /jɒtɪŋ/
NU **Yachting** is the sport or activity of sailing a yacht. ...*the fun of yachting.* ...*yachting holidays.* ...*the World Women's Yachting Championships.*

yachtsman /jɒtsmən/ **yachtsmen**
NC A **yachtsman** is a man who sails a yacht. *Air and sea rescue teams have been searching for a missing yachtsman...* *Finally we hear from round-the-world yachtsman, Chay Blyth.*

yachtswoman /jɒtswʊmən/ **yachtswomen**
NC A **yachtswoman** is a woman who sails a yacht. ...*Clare Francis, once famous as a yachtswoman and now a successful novelist.*

yak /jæk/ **yaks**
NC A **yak** is a type of ox that has long hair and long horns. Yaks live mainly in the Himalayan mountains in Tibet, and are used to provide meat and milk. ...*yaks grazing near the Chinese border.* ...*the herdsmen and yak breeders of the grasslands.*

Yakuza /jækuːzə/
N COLL The **Yakuza** are members of a secret criminal organization that was founded in Japan. ...*links between the police and gangsters or Yakuza.* ...*organised criminals including the Yakuza in Japan.* ...*signs of the Yakuza moving into international crime through gun smuggling and drugs.*

yam /jæm/ **yams**
NC A **yam** is a root vegetable which grows in tropical regions. It is similar to a potato in appearance and texture. *He agreed to give him some meat in exchange for the yams.* ...*yams that have been used in medicine.*

yammer /jæmə/ **yammers, yammering, yammered;**
an informal word.
1 V If someone **yammers**, they keep talking about something in a loud or annoying way. *The ugly little woman yammered about 'honour' and 'pleasure'...* *Stop that yammering, I don't want to listen to you.*
2 V If a dog **yammers**, it howls loudly. *A dog yammered excitedly in his pen.*

Yamoussoukro /jæmʊsuːkrəʊ/
Yamoussoukro became the capital of Côte d'Ivoire in 1983. It is the third largest city in Côte d'Ivoire. Population: 75,000 (1984).

Yangon /jæŋɡəʊn⁰, ræŋɡuːn/ See **Rangoon.**

Yang Shangkun /jɑːŋ ʃɑːŋkʊn/
Yang Shangkun became President of China in 1988. He is a veteran of the Long March of 1934 to 1935. He held many senior party posts before the Cultural Revolution, when he was imprisoned. He was rehabilitated in 1978. From 1981 to 1989 he was Secretary General of the Chinese Communist Party (CCP) Central Committee Military Commission. He became a member of the Politburo of the CCP, the sole legal party, in 1982. Born: 1907.

yank /jæŋk/ **yanks, yanking, yanked**
1 NC A **Yank** is the same as a **Yankee**; used showing disapproval.
2 V OR V If you **yank** something somewhere, you pull it there suddenly with a lot of force; an informal use. *Glenn yanked out the sore tooth...* *He was yanking the cork out of a bottle...* *Mom yanks me back by the collar.*

Yankee /jæŋki/ **Yankees;** used showing disapproval.
1 NC A **Yankee** is a person from the United States of America. ...*several hundred young anarchists chanting 'Yankee, go home'.* ...*bitter memories of Yankee imperialism.*
2 NC People from the southern states of the USA sometimes refer to people from the northern states as **Yankees.** ...*the reaction of Yankees to a Southerner coming North.* ...*a Yankee governor.*

Yaoundé /jəʊndeɪ/
Yaoundé is the capital of Cameroon and its second largest city. Population: 654,000 (1986).

yap /jæp/ **yaps, yapping, yapped**
V If a dog **yaps**, it barks a lot with a high-pitched sound. *When jackals find a leopard in the open, they yap.* ...*annoyed by yapping dogs near his motel.*

yard /jɑːd/ **yards**
1 NC A **yard** is a unit of length equal to 36 inches or approximately 91.4 centimetres. *He was only a few hundred yards away from the village.* ...*troops patrolling every few yards.* ...*ten yards from my door.*
2 NC A **yard** is also a flat area of concrete or stone that is next to a building and often has a wall around it. ...*a tiny cramped house without even a back yard...* *The dog prowled round the yard, wagging her tail.*
3 NC You can refer to a large area where a particular type of work is done as a **yard.** ...*a ship repair yard...* *The housing project is located behind the boat yard.*

Yardie /jɑːdi/ **Yardies**
NC The **Yardies** are members of a secret criminal organization which was founded in Jamaica. *Police hope to prevent Yardies from establishing themselves in this country.* ...*the rapid growth of Yardie gangs.*

yardstick /jɑːdstɪk/ **yardsticks**
NC If you use someone or something as a **yardstick**, you use them as a standard for comparison when you are judging other people or things. *She was a yardstick against which I could measure what I had achieved...* *The United Nations use the same yardstick and apply it fairly and equally...* *Their methods of doing so would seem improper by the yardsticks of other countries.*

yarn /jɑːn/ **yarns**
1 N MASS **Yarn** is thread that is used for knitting or making cloth. ...*trying to improve the quality of the yarn...* *It takes that long to dye the yarn.* ...*exports of synthetic yarn and knitted gloves.*
2 NC A **yarn** is a story that someone tells, often a true story with invented details which make it more interesting; an informal use. ...*yarns about rich and glamorous characters.* ...*when I heard Grandaddy's yarns.* ● If you say that someone **spins a yarn**, you mean that they tell a story that is not true, often in an interesting or inventive way. ...*wit and humour, and above all, the ability to spin a yarn... It was not possible to tell truth from untruth, so it is understandable than such yarns are spun.*

yashmak /jæʃmæk/ **yashmaks**
NC A **yashmak** is a veil that some Muslim women wear in order to cover their faces when they are in public. ...*and there were donkeys and camels and beautiful girls in yashmaks.*

yaw /jɔː/ **yaws, yawing, yawed**
V If an aircraft or a ship **yaws**, it turns to one side so that it changes the direction in which it is moving; a technical term. *The planes yaw and tilt as they enter the cloud.*

yawn /jɔːn/ **yawns, yawning, yawned**
1 V When you **yawn**, you open your mouth wide and breathe in more air than usual. You often yawn when you are tired or bored. *I yawned all through the concert.* ▶ Also NC *She stifled a yawn.*
2 V A gap or opening that **yawns** is large and wide, and often frightening; a literary use. *A great gap yawned between the rocks.* ◆ **yawning** ADJ ATTRIB ...*yawning craters.*

Y chromosome /waɪ krəʊməsəʊm/ **Y chromosomes.**
NC In biology, a **Y chromosome** is the single chromosome in a man's cells which will produce a male baby if it joins with an X chromosome during the reproductive process. See also **X chromosome.** *If a Y chromosome is present, the foetus becomes male... Maleness was conferred by a gene or genes, carried on the Y chromosome.*

yd, yds. The plural form can be either **yds** or **yd.**
NC **yd** is a written abbreviation for 'yard'. *The reel holds 400 yds of line.*

ye /jiː, ji/
1 PRON **Ye** is an old-fashioned, poetic, or religious word for 'you' when you are talking to more than one person. *Abandon all hope, ye who enter here.*

2 DET **Ye** is also sometimes used in imitation of an old written form of the word 'the'. *...Ye Olde Coffee Shoppe.*

yea /jeɪ/; an old-fashioned word.
1 Yea is used to indicate that you are accepting, confirming, or agreeing with something. *They are taught to say yea to all that is negative in life.*
2 The expression **yea or nay** is used instead of 'yes' and 'no' when talking about someone's possible answers to an offer or suggestion. *I'll send you an estimate and you can answer yea or nay.*
3 ADV SEN **Yea** is a biblical form for 'yes', used especially to emphasize or to introduce a statement. *Yea, unto lost sheep will I liken them.*

yeah /jeə/
Yeah means the same as **yes**; an informal word. *'It must make a pretty big bang?'—'Yeah it does.'... All the time, yeah... Yeah? Five of them now?*

year /jɪə/ **years**
1 NC A **year** is a period of 365 or 366 days, usually beginning on the first day of January and ending on the last day of December. *...at the end of next year. ...in the year 2000... 1992 is an election year.*
2 NC A **year** is also any period of twelve months. *...a hundred years ago... For seven years I was a designer... The Press Council receives 1000 complaints a year. ...two pounds per person per year.*
3 NC A school **year** is the period of time in each twelve months when the school is open and students are studying there. In Britain, the school year runs from September to July, and is divided into three terms. *...at the beginning of the school year... Some students boycotted the first day of the new school year.*
4 NC+SUPP A financial or business **year** is an exact period of twelve months which businesses or institutions use as a basis for organizing their finances. *...the final account at the end of each trading year... The financial year does not end till June... Congress cut aid by thirty million dollars in the current fiscal year.*
5 NC+SUPP You can talk about a good **year** or a bad **year** when you are referring to the incidents that happened during that year. *1987 was a good year for the tourist industry. ...the most successful year of her career. ...a difficult year ahead.*
6 N PL You can use **years** to emphasize that you are referring to a very long time. *They've known each other for years and years.*
7 If you do something **all year round** or **all the year round,** you do it all the time. *They grow crops all the year round.*
8 See also **leap year, New Year.**

yearbook /jɪəbʊk/ **yearbooks**
NC A **yearbook** is a book that is published once a year and contains information about the events and achievements of the previous year, usually concerning a particular place or organization. *...the yearbook for the class of 1953 at her school.*

year-end
ADJ ATTRIB **Year-end** is used to describe events or activities that take place in December, or at the end of the financial year. *...his year-end report... Workers agitated for higher year-end bonuses. ...year-end demands for dollars by Japanese companies.* ▸ Also N SING *50,000 troops would be gone before the year-end... The year-end is a good time to take a longer look.*

year-long
ADJ ATTRIB **Year-long** is used to describe something that lasts for a year. *...attending year-long courses to help them with reading. ...ending a year-long row over the air link. ...the year-long national strike.*

yearly /jɪəli/
1 ADJ ATTRIB or ADV You use **yearly** to describe something that happens once a year or every year. *...a yearly meeting... Interest is paid yearly.*
2 ADJ ATTRIB or ADV You also use **yearly** to describe something such as an amount that relates to a period of one year. *...the yearly income of workers. ...infections that hit thousands of babies yearly.*

yearn /jɜːn/ **yearns, yearning, yearned**
V+for or V+to-INF If you **yearn** for something that you

think you cannot have, you want it very much. *He passionately yearned for happiness... She yearned to go back to the south.*

yearning /jɜːnɪŋ/ **yearnings**
NCorNU A **yearning** is a strong desire for something. *...to satisfy the yearnings of the workers... Both sides were tense with yearning.*

-year-old, -year-olds
SUFFIX **-year-old** is added to numbers to form adjectives and nouns that indicate the age of people or things. *...a fifteen-year-old boy. ...a class of 4-year-olds.*

year-round
ADJ ATTRIB **Year-round** is used to describe something that happens, exists, or is done throughout the year. *Nothing dries easily in Guangdong's year-round steamy heat... The strain of year-round cricket is telling on many of the world's top cricketers.*

yeast /jiːst/ **yeasts**
N MASS **Yeast** is a fungus which is used to make bread rise, and to make alcoholic drinks. *The rest of the flour is added, then the yeast... You can buy dried baker's yeast at the supermarket. ...micro-organisms—bacteria, yeasts and so on.*

yeasty /jiːsti/
ADJ Something that is **yeasty** tastes or smells strongly of yeast. *...warm yeasty bread... There was a strong yeasty smell.*

yell /jel/ **yells, yelling, yelled**
1 V, V-QUOTE, V O, or V-REPORT If you **yell**, you shout loudly, usually because you are excited, angry, or in pain. *I yelled at Richard to hang on... 'Speed up!' he yelled to the driver. ...slogans yelled by crowd cheerleaders... I yelled to him that we should stop.*
2 NC A **yell** is a loud shout given by someone who is afraid or in pain. *I heard a yell from inside the house.*

yellow /jeləʊ/ **yellows, yellowing, yellowed**
1 ADJ Something that is **yellow** is the colour of lemons or egg yolks. *...a bright yellow hat.*
2 V-ERG When something **yellows** or is **yellowed,** it becomes yellow, often because it is old. *...a photograph of her, yellowed with age. ...when autumn yellows all the leaves.* ♦ **yellowing** ADJ *The walls are covered floor to ceiling with yellowing posters... We saw samples of the linen which shows the yellowing image of the front and back of a man.*

yellow fever
NU **Yellow fever** is a serious infectious disease that is found in tropical countries. *The city was ravaged by yellow fever and cholera. ...during the worst yellow fever epidemic.*

yellowish /jeləʊɪʃ/
ADJ Something that is **yellowish** is slightly yellow. *...a soft yellowish glow.*

Yellow Pages
N PL The **Yellow Pages** is a telephone directory, or part of a directory, in which companies and people are listed and grouped according to the kind of business they are involved in; **Yellow Pages** is a trademark. *Look in your Yellow Pages for your nearest frozen food supplier.*

yellowy /jeləʊi/
ADJ Something that is **yellowy** is slightly yellow. *On one branch there was a bunch of yellowy-green mistletoe growing.*

yelp /jelp/ **yelps, yelping, yelped**
V When people or animals **yelp**, they give a sudden short cry, often because of fear or pain. *He yelped in pain... His small granddaughter yelped at a bug running onto her hand.* ▸ Also NC *I gave a little yelp and fled upstairs.*

Yeltsin, Boris /bɒrɪs jeltsɪn/
Boris Yeltsin was elected President of Russia in 1991. He was Secretary of the Central Committee of the Communist Party from 1985 to 1986, and First Secretary of the Moscow City Party Committee from 1985 to 1987. He was elected to the Congress of People's Deputies of the USSR in 1989. He was a member of the USSR Supreme Soviet from 1989 to 1990 and Chairman of the Russian Supreme Soviet from 1990 to 1991. He resigned from the Communist Party in 1990. Born: 1931.

Yemen /jɛmən/
The Republic of Yemen is a country in the southern
Arabian peninsula. The area formerly known as North
Yemen, or the Yemen Arab Republic, with its capital
at San'aa, became independent from the Ottoman
Empire in 1918. The area formerly known as South
Yemen, or the People's Democratic Republic of
Yemen, with its capital at Aden, was a British
protectorate until 1967. The two countries united in
1990. Lieutenant-General Ali Abdullah Saleh, formerly
President of North Yemen, became President of the
Republic of Yemen in 1990. The former Prime Minister
of South Yemen, Haydar Abu Bakr al-Attas, became
Prime Minister in 1990. Yemen is a member of the
Arab League. It exports cotton, coffee, hides, and
skins. The oil industry is being developed. Large
foreign debts are a major economic problem.
◆ **Yemeni** /jɛməni/ N, ADJ
▪ *per capita GNP:* approximately US$500 ▪ *religion:*
Islam ▪ *language:* Arabic ▪ *currency:* the former North
Yemen rial and South Yemen dinar are both legal
currency ▪ *capital:* San'aa ▪ *population:* 11 million
(1989) ▪ *size:* 540,000 square kilometres.

yen /jɛn/; **yen** is both the singular and the plural form.
1 NC A **yen** is the unit of money that is used in Japan.
*The company was fined two million yen. ...the fall in
the value of the dollar against the yen.*
2 N SING If you have a **yen** to do something, you have
a strong desire to do it. *Nicholas has a yen to hike
through Canada.*

yeoman /jəʊmən/ **yeomen** /jəʊmən/
NC In former times, a **yeoman** was a man who was
free and not a servant, and who cultivated his own
land. *...yeomen who searched the same cellars in
1605... Robin Hood's father was a yeoman.*

Yerevan /jerəvɑːn/
Yerevan is the capital of Armenia and its largest city.
Population: 1,300,000 (1991).

yes /jɛs/
1 You use **yes** when answering a question to which the
answer could be either 'yes' or 'no'. *'Did you enjoy
it?'—'Yes.'... 'You'll be away next Friday won't
you?'—'yes'... 'Do you want some coffee?'—'Yes
please.'*
2 You can also use **yes** to indicate that you agree with
or accept what someone has just said. *'It was a
beautiful day.'—'It was nice, yes.'... 'You'll have to fill
in a form when you come'—'Oh yes, that'll be no
problem.'*
3 You can use **yes** in a conversation to encourage
someone to continue speaking. *'I miss the country
very much.'—'Yes?'—'And yet, I would hate to give up
my job here.'*
4 You can also use **yes** when contradicting something.
*'Nowadays you don't learn any basic principles in
maths.'—'Oh, yes you do.'*
5 You can use **yes** to introduce something that you had
forgotten to say and that you have just remembered.
What was I going to mention? Oh yes, accidents.

yes-man, yes-men
NC A **yes-man** is someone who always agrees with
people who have authority over them, in order to gain
favour; used showing disapproval. *The boss is
surrounded by yes-men fearful for their jobs.*

yesterday /jɛstədeɪ, jɛstədi/
1 ADV or NU **Yesterday** means the day before today. *It
was hot yesterday... Yesterday morning there were
more than 500 boats on the lake.*
2 NU **Yesterday** can also mean the past, especially the
recent past. *The worker of today is different from the
worker of yesterday.*

yesteryear /jɛstəjɪə/
NU **Yesteryear** is used to refer to the past, especially
a past era or a way of life that has disappeared; a
literary word. *He often mentioned the scandals of
yesteryear.*

yet /jɛt/
1 ADV If something has not happened **yet**, it has not
happened up to the present time. *I haven't made up
my mind yet... It isn't dark yet... Have you had your
lunch yet?*
2 ADV If something should not be done **yet**, it should

not be done now but at a later time. *Loosen nuts with
a spanner but don't take them off yet.*
3 ADV You also use **yet** to say that there is still a
possibility that something will happen. *The figures
may yet be revised again... There is hope for me yet.*
4 ADV+*to*-INF If you have **yet** to do something, you have
not done it but may do it in the future. If something is
yet to happen, it has not happened but may happen in
the future. *I have yet to meet a man I can trust... A
whole range of issues had yet to be resolved.*
5 ADV You use **yet** after an expression referring to a
period of time, when you want to say how much longer
a situation will continue. *He's going to be around for
a long while yet... It will not be dark for half an hour
yet.*
6 CONJ You also use **yet** to introduce a fact which
seems rather surprising in relation to the thing you
have just mentioned. *Everything around him was
blown to pieces, yet the minister escaped without a
scratch. ...a firm yet gentle hand.*
7 ADV You can also use **yet** to emphasize a
comparative or a word that refers to an increase or
repetition. *I am sorry to bring up the subject of
money yet again... The queues are likely to grow
longer yet.*

yeti /jɛti/ **yetis**
NC A **yeti** is a large animal like a very hairy ape
which is supposed to live in the Himalayas, but which
many people do not believe exists. *...the mysterious
footprints of the Abominable Snowman or Yeti... A
scientist has recently reported making contact with
the legendary yeti.*

yew /juː/ **yews**
NC A **yew** or a **yew tree** is an evergreen tree. It has
sharp leaves which are broad and flattened, and
red berries. The wood obtained from this tree is also
called **yew**. *...yew trees, hundreds of years old.
...a yew log.*

YHA /waɪeɪtʃeɪ/
N PROP **YHA** is an abbreviation for 'Youth Hostels
Association', an organization which runs hostels all
over the world which provide cheap accommodation
for young people while they are travelling around on
holiday. *You don't have to be a member of YHA to
use many of them. ...YHA membership.*

Yiddish /jɪdɪʃ/
NU **Yiddish** is a language which is spoken by many
Jewish people of European origin, and is derived
mainly from German. *Yiddish continued to be taught
in some state schools. ...a novel in Yiddish. ...a
Yiddish literary journal.*

yield /jiːld/ **yields, yielding, yielded**
1 V+*to* If you **yield** to someone or something, you stop
resisting them; a formal use. *He was yielding to
public pressure.*
2 VO If you **yield** something that you have control of
or responsibility for, you allow someone else to have
control or responsibility; a formal use. *He will not
yield even a limited measure of editorial control... The
Maxwell family will have to yield control of Oxford
United and Derby County.*
3 V If something **yields**, it breaks or moves because of
force or pressure on it. *Any lock will yield to brute
force.*
4 VO If something such as a discussion, meeting, or
investigation **yields** a particular result or information,
it produces it. *Talks between the two sides yielded no
results... Nor can his visit be expected to yield a
breakthrough on the dispute... Furthermore, the rocks
do not yield any evidence to suggest an extended
period of cold climatic conditions... The Times says
the election has yielded a reasonably fair outcome.*
5 VO If an area of land or a number of animals **yields**
a particular amount of food, this amount is produced
by the land or the animals. *0.23 acres yields only 200
pounds of rice... Professor Thorpe sees no reason why
the upgraded cows could not yield 2000 litres of milk
per year... The crop in Saudi Arabia looks like being a
good one, yielding over three million tonnes.*
6 NC A **yield** is an amount of food produced on an
area of land or by a number of animals. *They have a
far better yield than any farm round here. ...a one per*

cent reduction in the yield of soya beans.
7 VO If a tax or investment **yields** an amount of money or profit, you get this money or profit from it. *...yieek... The bonds would yield a return to the investor of about six per cent.*

yielding /jiːldɪŋ/
ADJ A material that is **yielding** is fairly soft, and bends or changes shape rather than staying stiff when you put pressure on it. *Foam is less yielding, more springy... The metal, almost certainly lead, was soft and yielding.*

yippee /jɪpiː/
Some people, especially children, shout '**Yippee!**' when they are very happy and excited about something. *Mrs Pollard's first reaction was to shout 'yippee!'*

YMCA /waɪemsiːeɪ/ **YMCAs**
1 N PROP The **YMCA** is an organization which encourages young men to have Christian moral values. **YMCA** is an abbreviation for 'Young Men's Christian Association'. *The award scheme is run by BBC Radio Four in conjunction with the YMCA and the National Westminster Bank.*
2 NC A **YMCA** is a hostel run by the YMCA organization where men can stay. *The group meets in the local YMCA.*

yob /jɒb/ **yobs**
NC If you call a boy or man a **yob**, you mean that he behaves in a noisy, bad-mannered way in public; an informal word. *...gangs of beer-swilling yobs... The Daily Mail's headline declares: 'Yobs on rampage again'.*

yobbo /jɒbəʊ/ **yobbos**
NC A **yobbo** is the same as a **yob**; an informal word. *I'd like to get those yobbos.*

yodel /jəʊdl/ **yodels**, **yodelling**, **yodelled**; spelt **yodeling**, **yodeled** in American English.
V When someone **yodels**, they sing in a special way, putting short, high notes in between normal notes. *We would sing along to Slim Dusty, yodelling away about love. ...a troupe of yodelling dancers.*

yoga /jəʊgə/
NU **Yoga** is a type of exercise in which you move your body into various positions in order to become more fit or flexible, to improve your breathing, and to relax your mind. *...local practitioners of yoga... She'd done some yoga exercises.*

yoghurt /jɒgət/ **yoghurts**; also spelt **yoghourt** or **yogurt**.
N MASS **Yoghurt** is a slightly sour, thick liquid that is made by adding bacteria to milk. *...countries where curd or yoghurt are part of the normal daily diet... Dozens of people lined up to buy yogurt and milk. ...French yoghurts, cheese, and frozen chickens.*

yogi /jəʊgi/ **yogis**
NC A **yogi** is a person who has spent many years practising yoga, and is considered to have reached an advanced state of spiritual awareness. *A yogi in India can consciously lower his blood pressure.*

yogurt /jɒgət/. See **yoghurt**.

yoke /jəʊk/ **yokes**
1 N SING+SUPP If you say that people are under the **yoke** of a bad thing or person, you mean they are forced to be in a difficult or unhappy state because of that thing or person; a literary use. *...where people are still suffering under the yoke of slavery. ...to liberate Muslims from the yoke of imperialist powers. ...when Bulgaria threw off the Ottoman yoke and won its independence.*
2 NC A **yoke** is a long piece of wood which is tied across the necks of two animals such as oxen, in order to make them walk close together when they are pulling a plough. *We have been working on harnesses and we have been working on yokes.*

yokel /jəʊkl/ **yokels**
NC If you refer to someone as a **yokel**, you mean that they live in the countryside and do not seem to be very intelligent; often used humorously. *Breslow said it would impress the country yokels... 'They thought we were a load of yokels,' said one resident.*

yolk /jəʊk/ **yolks**
N Cor NU The **yolk** of an egg is the yellow part in the

middle. *Boil eggs until both the yolk and the white are solid. ...a solution of egg yolk and glycerol.*

Yom Kippur /jɒm kɪpə/
NU **Yom Kippur** is an annual Jewish holiday which is a day of fasting and prayers of repentance. *...as Israelis prepare for tomorrow's Yom Kippur, the holiest day in the Jewish calendar. ...Yom Kippur, the Day of Atonement.*

yon /jɒn/
DET **Yon** is an old-fashioned word for 'that' or 'those'. *What's yon place in America, Coney Island?*

yonder /jɒndə/
ADV **Yonder** means over there; an old-fashioned word. *They came galloping over that hill yonder.*

Yon Hyong Muk /jʌn hjʌŋ muk/
Yon Hyong Muk became Premier of North Korea in 1988. He was Vice Premier from 1985 to 1986. He became a member of the Korean Workers' Party (KWP) Central Committee in 1970, and a member of the Politburo in 1973. Born: 1931.

yonks /jɒŋks/
NU You use **yonks** to say that something has been happening for a very long time; an informal word. *I kept spotting people I hadn't seen for yonks... Didn't you know? She's been pregnant for yonks!*

yore /jɔː/
The expression **of yore** is used to refer to a period of time long ago; an old-fashioned expression. *In days of yore I had shared with him all my secrets.*

Yorkshire pudding /jɔːkʃə pʊdɪŋ/ **Yorkshire puddings**
N Uor NC **Yorkshire pudding** is a food which is made by baking a thick mixture of flour, milk, and eggs. It is often eaten with roast beef. *It has become as traditional a part of the British weekend as roast beef and Yorkshire Pudding. ...enormous Yorkshire puddings.*

you /ju, juː/. **You** is used as the subject of a verb or as the object of a verb or preposition. It can refer to one or more people.
1 PRON A speaker or writer uses **you** to refer to the person or people that he or she is speaking to. *What do you think?... The same rule applies to you... You people don't smoke, do you?*
2 PRON **You** is also used to refer to people in general rather than to a particular person or group. *You can get freezers with security locks.*

you-all /jɔːl/
PRON People from the southern United States often say **you-all** to refer to a group of people. *We owe you a tremendous amount, because I know what you-all did to build this city. ...the animosity between them and you-all.*

you'd /jud, juːd/
You'd is the usual spoken form of 'you had', when 'had' is an auxiliary verb. **You'd** is also a spoken form of 'you would'. *If you'd asked me that ten years ago, I'd have said yes... You'd be surprised how easy it is, when you try.*

you'll /jul, juːl/
You'll is the usual spoken form of 'you will'. *You'll have to get a job.*

young /jʌŋ/ **younger** /jʌŋgə/ **youngest** /jʌŋgəst/
1 ADJ A **young** person, animal, or plant has not lived or existed for long and is not yet mature. *Julia has two young boys... She was three years younger than me... The young seedlings grow very rapidly.*
2 ADJ ATTRIB You also use **young** to describe the time when a person was young. *I was fond of dancing in my younger days.*
3 N PL The **young** of an animal are its babies. *When the young first hatch, they are naked.*

youngish /jʌŋɪʃ/
ADJ Someone who is **youngish** is fairly young in appearance, behaviour, or age. *...a youngish man with blond hair.*

young lady, young ladies
NC+POSS Some people refer to a man's girlfriend as his **young lady**; an old-fashioned expression. *You have a young lady, I understand.*

young man, young men
NC+POSS Some people refer to a girl's boyfriend as her

young man; an old-fashioned expression. *Is your young man coming for tea?*

youngster /jʌŋstə/ **youngsters**
NC A **youngster** is a young person or child. *I don't know what the youngsters of today think.*

your /jɔː, juə/
1 DET A speaker or writer uses **your** to indicate that something belongs or relates to the person or people that he or she is speaking to. *Where's your father? ...your books.*
2 DET **Your** is also used to indicate that something belongs or relates to people in general rather than to a particular person or group. *You can't use your own name in a novel.*
3 DET **Your** is also used in some titles when addressing people with that title. *...your Majesty.*

you're /jɔː, juə/
You're is the usual spoken form of 'you are' when 'are' is an auxiliary verb. *You're quite right.*

yours /jɔːz, juəz/
1 PRON A speaker or writer uses **yours** to refer to something that belongs or relates to the person or people that he or she is speaking to. *Our swimming pool isn't as deep as yours... A student of yours came to see me.*
2 People write **Yours, Yours sincerely,** or **Yours faithfully** at the end of a letter before they sign their name. *I'm looking forward to hearing from you soon, Yours sincerely, David Thomas.*

yourself /jəsɛlf, jɔːsɛlf/ **yourselves**
1 PRON REFL A speaker or writer uses **yourself** as the object of a verb or preposition in a clause where 'you' is the subject or a previous object, or in a clause which consists of a command. *Would you call yourself a Marxist?... Help yourselves to sandwiches... Tell me about yourself... Would you mind sending me a photograph of yourself?*
2 PRON REFL **Yourself** is also used to emphasize 'you' when it is the subject or object of a clause. *You yourself said it's only a routine check. ...given that you yourself were born in the late forties.*
3 PRON REFL If you do something **yourself**, you do it without any help or interference from anyone else. *Did you make these cakes yourself?... Get on and do it yourself.*

youth /juːθ/ **youths** /juːðz/
1 NU Someone's **youth** is the period of their life when they are a child, before they are a fully mature adult. *We change and learn from youth to old age... He had visited Calcutta in his youth.*
2 NU **Youth** is the quality or state of being young and perhaps immature or inexperienced. *...marvelling at his freshness and apparent youth.*
3 NC A **youth** is a boy or a young man, especially a teenager. *...two youths in leather jackets. ...helping youths to find employment... The youths, all in their late teens, apparently escaped.*
4 N PL The **youth** are young people considered as a group. *...unemployment among the youth of this country.*

youth club, youth clubs
NC A **youth club** is a club where young people can go to meet each other and take part in various leisure activities. Youth clubs are often run by a church or local authority. *There's a disco at the youth club tonight.*

youthful /juːθfl/
1 ADJ Someone who is **youthful** is young, lively, and full of energy. *...youthful dancers.*
2 ADJ **Youthful** also means having qualities or characteristics that are typical of young people. *Despite her age she still had a youthful body.*

youth hostel, youth hostels
NC A **youth hostel** is a place where young people can stay cheaply when they are travelling around. *...the youth hostel in Salzburg where they've been staying... They had failed to return to their youth hostel.*

you've /juv, juːv/
You've is the usual spoken form of 'you have' when 'have' is an auxiliary verb. *You've been very lucky.*

yowl /jaʊl/ **yowls, yowling, yowled**
V If a person or an animal **yowls**, they make a loud

wailing noise. *Mountain lions yowled like tomcats.*
► Also NC *...the incessant screech and yowl of emergency sirens.* ◆ **yowling** NU *...the high-pitched yowling of a rock singer... I can't stand that yowling outside.*

yo-yo /jəʊjəʊ/ **yo-yos**
NC A **yo-yo** is a toy made of a round piece of wood or plastic attached to a piece of string. You play with a yo-yo by making it rise and fall on the string. *He's bringing a large assortment of yo-yos to give away as gifts. ...playing with a yo-yo.*

yr, yrs. The plural form can be either yrs or yr.
NC **Yr** is a written abbreviation for 'year'. *...children aged 3-11 yrs.*

yuan /juːæn/; **yuan** is both the singular and the plural form.
NC A **yuan** is the unit of money that is used in the People's Republic of China. *They were fined fifty yuan each... Tickets cost one, two or three yuan, and the average wage is about two hundred yuan a month.*

Yugoslavia /juːgəʊslɑːviə/
The **Socialist Federal Republic of Yugoslavia** is a country in south-eastern Europe, which consisted of six federal republics: Serbia, Croatia, Slovenia, Montenegro, Bosnia-Herzegovina, and Macedonia. It now includes only two republics: Serbia and Montenegro. It was occupied by Germany from 1941 to 1945. Josip Broz Tito led the resistance to German occupation and established a Communist state in 1945. He ruled until his death in 1980. The League of Communists of Yugoslavia (LCY) stopped being the only party in 1990. Ethnic violence has in recent years threatened the unity of the country. Rivalry is particularly strong between the two dominant groups, the Serbs (36%) and the Croats (20%). Slovenia, Croatia, Bosnia-Herzegovina, and Macedonia all declared independence in 1991, beginning a war between its former constituent republics.. The independence of Croatia and Slovenia was recognized in 1992. Yugoslavia exports manufactured goods and agricultural products. Tourism is an important industry. High inflation is a major economic problem.
◆ **Yugoslav, Yugoslavian** /juːgəʊslɑːv, juːgəʊslɑːviən/ N, ADJ
▪ *per capita GNP:* US$2,680 ▪ *religion:* Christianity (Catholic and Orthodox), Islam ▪ *language:* Serbo-Croatian, Macedonian, Slovene ▪ *currency:* dinar ▪ *capital:* Belgrade (Beograde) ▪ *population:* 24 million (1989) ▪ *size:* 255,804 square kilometres.

yuk /jʌk/
Some people say **yuk** when they think something is very unpleasant or disgusting; an informal word. *Cornflakes, yuk!*

Yule /juːl/
NU **Yule** is the same as **Christmas**; an old-fashioned word. *The strong community spirit that exists ensures that Yule is more of a community affair than a family one.*

Yuletide /juːltaɪd/
NU **Yuletide** means the time of year around Christmas; an old-fashioned word. *...Yuletide festivities.*

yummy /jʌmi/
ADJ Some people use **yummy** to describe food that they think is delicious; an informal word. *Can I have some more of that yummy yoghurt?... The result should be just as yummy without the cream.*

yuppie /jʌpi/ **yuppies**
NC **Yuppies** are young middle class people who earn a lot of money and spend it on expensive possessions and activities. *...at night-time, when all the office workers and the yuppies have gone home to the suburbs... It describes accurately the popular image of the London yuppie.*

YWCA /waɪdʌbljuːsiːeɪ/ **YWCAs**
1 N PROP The **YWCA** is an organization which encourages young women to have Christian moral values. **YWCA** is an abbreviation for 'Young Women's Christian Association'. *...a YWCA worker.*
2 NC A **YWCA** is a hostel run by the YWCA organization where women can stay. *She had a new address. She had moved from the YWCA.*

Z, z /zɛd/ **Z's, z's**
NC Z is the twenty-sixth letter of the English alphabet.

Zagreb /zɑːgreb/
Zagreb is the capital of Croatia and its largest city. Population: 856,000 (1981).

Zaïre /zɑːiːə/
The **Republic of Zaïre** is a country in central Africa, formerly known as the Belgian Congo. It was a Belgian colony from the 19th century until independence in 1960. Civil war followed the secession of Katanga (now Shaba) province. In 1965 Marshal Mobutu Sese Seko, of the Popular Movement of the Revolution (MPR), became President. He changed the name of the country to Zaïre in 1971. Nguza Karl-I-Bond became Prime Minister in 1991, during a period of mounting civil unrest and calls for democratic reform. Zaïre exports diamonds, copper, oil, coffee, and cobalt. High inflation and large foreign debts are major economic problems. It is a member of the Organization of African Unity. ◆ **Zaïrean** /zaɪlərɪən/ N, ADJ
▪ *per capita GNP:* US$170 ▪ *religion:* Christianity ▪ *language:* French (official), Luba, Kongo ▪ *currency:* zaïre ▪ *capital:* Kinshasa (formerly Léopoldville) ▪ *population:* 34 million (1989) ▪ *size:* 2,344,885 square kilometres.

Zambia /zæmbiə/
The **Republic of Zambia** is a country in southern Africa. The area came under British control in the 19th century and was known as Northern Rhodesia from 1911 until independence in 1964. Dr Kenneth Kaunda was President from 1964 until 1991, when Frederick Chiluba, of the Movement for Multi-Party Democracy, was elected President. Zambia is a member of the Commonwealth and the Organization of African Unity. It exports copper, cobalt, and zinc. Large foreign debts and high inflation are major economic problems. ◆ **Zambian** /zæmbiən/ N, ADJ
▪ *per capita GNP:* US$290 ▪ *religion:* Christianity ▪ *language:* English, Tonga, Kaonde, Lunda, Luvale (all official), Bembe ▪ *currency:* kwacha ▪ *capital:* Lusaka ▪ *population:* 8 million ▪ *size:* 752,610 square kilometres.

zany /zeɪni/
ADJ Someone or something that is **zany** is strange and eccentric in an amusing way. *I thought I'll make Louise a zany scarf, to fit her zany personality... Wild and zany things could happen and still be plausible.*

zap /zæp/ **zaps, zapping, zapped**; an informal word.
1 VO If someone **zaps** someone else, they kill them, usually by shooting them. *That guy got zapped later on the same day... I joke with my friends, you think you're zapping aliens but really you're just pushing a button over and over again.*
2 VO If you **zap** something on a computer screen, you erase it. *'Why don't you just edit the file?'—'Because that would mean zapping forty-five percent of it.'*
3 V If you **zap** while watching television, you change channels. *I watched him sit on the couch and zap with the remote control... Once you've started zapping, you just want to move on to the next thing.*

zeal /ziːl/
N U **Zeal** is great enthusiasm, especially in connection with work, religion, or politics; a formal word. *He never faltered in his religious zeal... From that moment on, John Wesley became filled with evangelical zeal.*

zealot /zelət/ **zealots**
NC A **zealot** is a person who acts with extreme zeal, especially because of political or religious ideals; a formal word. *...a religious zealot. ...the young communist zealots.*

zealous /zeləs/
ADJ A **zealous** person spends a lot of time or energy in supporting something, especially a political or religious ideal; a formal word. *...people who are zealous in defence of their country and their faith. ...zealous economic reformers... They thought the committee could become too zealous.*

zebra /zebrə, ziːbrə/ **zebras**. The plural form can be either **zebras** or **zebra**.
NC A **zebra** is an African wild horse which has black and white stripes. *...a zebra who has just come to drink at the water hole. ...two zebras at Madrid Zoo.*

zebra crossing, zebra crossings
NC In Britain, a **zebra crossing** is a place where the road is marked with black and white stripes. Vehicles must stop there to let people cross the road. *...30 or 40 metres of road on either side of a zebra crossing.*

Zen /zɛn/
N U **Zen** or **Zen Buddhism** is a form of Buddhism that concentrates on meditation rather than on studying religious writings. *Zen too has its highly structured rituals. ...absorbing Zen practices into his everyday life. ...a feature of Zen Buddhism.*

zenith /zɛnɪθ/
N SING The **zenith** of something is the time when it is most successful or powerful; a literary word. *...Greek civilization at its zenith... American influence was at its zenith... Most commentators here believe it was the zenith of the chancellor's political career.*

zephyr /zɛfə/ **zephyrs**
NC A **zephyr** is a gentle wind; a literary word. *Leaves turned to shimmering silver as zephyrs played through them.*

zero /zɪərəʊ/ **zeros** or **zeroes, zeroing, zeroed**
1 **Zero** is the number 0. *This scale goes from zero to forty.*
2 NU **Zero** is also freezing point on the Centigrade scale. It is often written as 0°C. *It was fourteen below zero when they woke up.*
3 ADJ You can use **zero** to say that there is none at all of the thing mentioned. *Its running costs were zero... We drove in zero visibility.*
zero in on PHRASAL VERB 1 To **zero in on** a target means to aim at it or move towards it. *The missile zeroed in on the tank.* 2 If you **zero in on** a problem or subject, you give it your full attention. *Well, I'd like to zero in on the food shortages.*

zero hour
N U **Zero hour** is the time at which something such as a military operation is planned to begin. *...zero hour for the deployment of the troops.*

zero option, zero options
NC In nuclear arms negotiations, a **zero option** is an offer by one party in the negotiations to remove all short-range nuclear missiles if the other party or parties will do the same. *France has strongly opposed proposals by East Germany for a zero option covering battle-field nuclear weapons. ...plans to pave the way for further zero options in Europe.*

zest /zɛst/
1 NU **Zest** is a feeling of pleasure and enthusiasm. *The children were full of life and zest... He has a zest for life and a quick intellect... Grapelli's sheer zest and charismatic stage presence was winning him international audiences.*
2 NU **Zest** is also a quality in an activity or situation which you find exciting. *Some of the zest had gone out of his life... If doing these things takes the joy and zest out of your life, think again.*
3 NU The **zest** of a lemon, orange, or lime is the rind when it is grated to give flavour to something such as a cake or a drink. *We have a platter with lemon and orange zest all ready to go down to the kitchen.*

Zhelev, Zhelyu /ʒɛlju: ʒɛlef/
Zhelyu Zhelev became President of Bulgaria in 1990. He was President of the Union of Democratic Forces (UDF) from 1989 to 1990. He is now an independent. Born: 1935.

Zia, Khaleda /xəliːdə zɪə/
Begum Khaleda Zia became Prime Minister of Bangladesh in 1991. She is a member of the Bangladesh Nationalist Party (BNP). She is the widow of General Zia, who was President of Bangladesh from 1977 until his assassination in 1981.

zigzag /zɪgzæg/ **zigzags, zigzagging, zigzagged**
1 NC A **zigzag** is a line with a series of angles in it, like a continuous series of 'W's. *Suddenly there was a flash and a zigzag of forked lightning. ...French tanks in zigzag formation.*
2 VA To **zigzag** means to move forward by going at an angle first to one side and then to the other. *We zigzagged laboriously up the track.*

Zimbabwe /zɪmbɑːbweɪ/
The **Republic of Zimbabwe** is a country in southern Africa. It was formerly known as Rhodesia. It was governed by British Royal Charter from 1889 until 1923, when it became a self-governing colony. In 1965 the Prime Minister, Ian Smith, made a unilateral declaration of independence. He belonged to the conservative Rhodesian Front, which aimed to preserve the political power of the white minority (1%). In the 1960s and 1970s several political and guerrilla organizations fought to achieve power for the black majority. ZAPU (Zimbabwe African People's Union) was led by Joshua Nkomo. ZANU (Zimbabwe African National Union) was led by Reverend Ndabaningi Sithole and, after 1975, by Robert Mugabe. The ANC (African National Council) was led by Bishop Abel Muzorewa. In 1979 the Lancaster House Conference successfully negotiated Zimbabwe's transition to full independence and black majority rule in 1980. Robert Mugabe was Prime Minister from 1980 to 1987, and became President in 1987. The merger of ZANU and ZAPU in 1987 to form ZANU-PF (Zimbabwe African National Union - Patriotic Front) has created a virtual one-party state. Zimbabwe is a member of the Commonwealth and the Organization of African Unity. It exports tobacco and other agricultural products, gold and other minerals. ◆ **Zimbabwean** /zɪmbɑːbwiən/ N, ADJ
▪ *per capita GNP:* US$660 ▪ *religion:* Christianity, animism ▪ *language:* English (official), Shona, Ndebele ▪ *currency:* dollar ▪ *capital:* Harare (formerly Salisbury) ▪ *population:* 10 million (1989) ▪ *size:* 390,759 square kilometres.

zinc /zɪŋk/
NU **Zinc** is a grey metal which is used to make other metals such as brass or to cover other metals such as iron to stop them rusting. *They were mainly looking for copper, lead and zinc... Those steel sections are sprayed with zinc. ...zinc smelting plants.*

zing /zɪŋ/
NU **Zing** is a quality in something that makes it lively or interesting; an informal word. *Small enterprises may lose their zing... Add a little white wine to give an extra zing to a recipe.*

Zionism /zaɪənɪzəm/
NU **Zionism** is a movement which was originally concerned with establishing a political and religious state in Palestine for Jewish people, and is now concerned with the development of Israel. *...the democratic and humanistic principles of early Zionism.* ◆ **Zionist** /zaɪənɪst/ **Zionists** NC *...failing to distinguish between Jews, Israelis and Zionists.*

zip /zɪp/ **zips, zipping, zipped**
1 NC A **zip** is a device used to open and close parts of clothes and bags. It consists of two rows of small metal or plastic teeth which separate or fasten together as you pull a small tag along them. *...long zips on the trousers. ...a golf-bag covered in zips... The zip on the briefcase was the plastic type.*
2 VO When you **zip** something, you close it using a zip. *Then he puts the camera away in the bag and zips it shut.*
zip up PHRASAL VERB When you **zip up** something such as a piece of clothing, you fasten it using a zip. *She zipped up the dress with difficulty.*

zip code, zip codes
NC In the United States, a **zip code** is a combination of letters and numbers that are part of an address. *Our zip code is 20036. ...Moose Song, Illinois, zip code 61091.*

zipper /zɪpə/ **zippers**
NC A **zipper** is the same as a **zip**; used in American

English. **Zipper** is a trademark. *...the zipper on the back of the costume... He is a zipper salesman.*

zither /zɪðə/ **zithers**
NC A **zither** is a musical instrument which consists of a number of strings stretched over a box. You play a zither by plucking the strings. *...an orchestra of gongs, drums, and zithers. ...a Vietnamese zither player.*

zodiac /zəʊdiæk/
N SING The **zodiac** is a diagram used by astrologers to represent the positions of the planets and stars. It is divided into 12 sections, each with a special name and symbol. The zodiac is used by astrologers to help calculate the influence of the planets on people's lives. *...the twelve signs of the zodiac used by modern western astronomers. ...the Dragon, the most auspicious of the twelve signs of the Chinese zodiac.*

zombie /zɒmbi/ **zombies**
NC If you refer to someone as a **zombie**, you mean that they seem completely unaware of things around them, and seem to act without thinking about what they are doing. *The men began to act as if they were zombies.*

zone /zəʊn/ **zones**
NC+SUPP A **zone** is an area that has particular features or characteristics. *...the war zone. ...people living in earthquake zones... Long aeroplane journeys to other time zones can produce problems.*

zonked /zɒŋkt/
ADJ PRED If you are **zonked** or feel **zonked**, you are completely exhausted; an informal word.

zoo /zuː/ **zoos**
NC A **zoo** is a park where live animals are kept so that people can look at them and study their behaviour. *The Mexico zoo has been the most successful at breeding pandas. ...by observing the behaviour of apes in zoos.*

zoology /zuːɒlədʒi/
NU **Zoology** is the scientific study of animals. *His lifelong interest was zoology.* ◆ **zoologist** /zuːɒlədʒɪst/ **zoologists** NC *...university zoologists.* ◆ **zoological** /zuːəlɒdʒɪkl/ ADJ ATTRIB *...zoological specimens.*

zoom /zuːm/ **zooms, zooming, zoomed**; an informal word.
1 V If you **zoom** somewhere, you go there very quickly. *They zoomed down to Folkestone on their bikes... He's destroying alien space invaders as they zoom across the screen towards him.*
2 V If something such as prices or sales **zoom** to a high level, they reach that level very quickly. *Sales had zoomed to 33 million... The amiable Ulsterman has zoomed to No. 1 in the charts with his third solo single.*
zoom in PHRASAL VERB If a camera **zooms in** on the thing being photographed, it gives a close-up picture of it. *...when the camera finally zooms in... He zoomed in on them for a better look... Soviet television zoomed in on the banners.*

zoom lens, zoom lenses
NC A **zoom lens** is a lens that you can attach to a camera, which allows you to make the details larger or smaller while always keeping the picture clear. *...a camera with a zoom lens... That's the kind of shot a zoom lens is really good for.*

zucchini /zuːkiːni/; **zucchini** is both the singular and the plural form.
NC A **zucchini** is the same as a **courgette**. *...hundreds of cucumbers, squash and zucchini.*

Zürich /zjʊərɪk/
Zürich is the largest city in Switzerland. Population: 343,000 (1989).